DIRECTORY of Nursing Homes

1990-1991
4th Edition

DIRECTORY of Nursing Homes
1990-1991
4th Edition

Administrators ■ Medical Directors
Directors of Nursing ■ Licensure ■ Capacity
Certification ■ Chain Ownership ■ Affiliation
Admissions Requirements ■ Staff
Facilities ■ Activities

ORYX PRESS
1990

The rare Arabian Oryx is believed to have inspired the myth of the unicorn. This desert antelope became virtually extinct in the early 1960s. At that time several groups of international conservationists arranged to have 9 animals sent to the Phoenix Zoo to be the nucleus of a captive breeding herd. Today the Oryx population is nearly 800, and over 400 have been returned to reserves in the Middle East.

LC 88-645965
ISSN 0888-7624
ISBN 0-89774-614-7

TABLE OF CONTENTS

INTRODUCTION

The revised and expanded *Directory of Nursing Homes 1990–1991 Fourth Edition* lists detailed information for 18,000 licensed nursing facilities in the United States, Puerto Rico, and the Virgin Islands. Information was compiled between May 1989 and April 1990 by means of a questionnaire sent to all facilities. Those facilities that did not return a questionnaire were checked against state licensing directories to verify that the information listed is the most accurate and current information to date.

DIRECTORY ARRANGEMENT AND CONTENT OF ENTRIES

Arranged alphabetically by state, then by city, then by nursing facility, almost all entries contain core information including name, address, telephone, number of beds, level of care provided and Medicaid, Medicare, and/or Medi-Cal* certification. Additionally, entries may include any or all of the following: name of the facility administrator, medical director, and/or director of nursing; ownership type: corporate, private, nonprofit organization/foundation, public (names of multiple facility owners are listed in parentheses; users may refer to the listing of corporate headquarters for more information); languages spoken; full- and part-time staff counts; admissions requirements including age, gender restrictions, and referral requirements; religious or fraternal affiliation; and a detailed list of special facilities or activities at each facility.

The directory section is followed by an Affiliations Index which is arranged alphabetically by state, then sponsor. Following the Affiliations Index is an alphabetical listing of all facilities. The directory concludes with an alphabetical listing of corporate nursing home headquarters.

GUEST ARTICLES HIGHLIGHT LONG-TERM CARE INSURANCE ISSUES

Preceding the State-by-State Listing of Facilities are opinion articles written by respected, distinguished insurance experts, which present their concerns, opinions, and forecasts on topics of concern to the industry. In this edition, Oryx Press is pleased to present two articles that discuss the future of long-term care insurance. "Public-Private Solution to Protection Against the Cost of Long-Term Care," by Robert M. Ball, a former Social Security Administration Commissioner and presently a consultant on Social Security, welfare, and social policy, and "Private Long-Term Care Insurance: Part of the Solution," by Susan Van Gelder, associate director of the Health Insurance Association of America's Department of Policy Development and Research.

FACILITY VISITS, INFORMED DECISIONS ESSENTIAL

The editors caution all users to visit and compare facilities before either becoming a resident or placing a loved one in a long-term care facility. If conditions make a personal visit impossible, potential residents should consult a qualified professional who is familiar with the facility to determine whether the programs, services, and costs associated with a facility are compatible with the potential resident's needs and resources.

Users of the directory should bear in mind that all information has been supplied either by the facility or through public sources. The editors have assumed all information supplied by the facilities to be factual and accurate. Listings are not meant to be comparative in nature nor is a listing in this directory meant to be an endorsement of any facility by the editors of Oryx Press.

A directory of this size is impossible to compile and publish without the dedicated and enthusiastic participation of a great number of people. The significant contributions of Magon Kinzie, Kathy Lumpkin,

*Medi-Cal is the Medicaid program in California.

Linda Archer, Susan Cain, Sandi Bourelle, and Linda Vespa merit special mention.

Inquiries concerning the directory should be addressed to: The Editors, *Directory of Nursing Homes,* The Oryx Press, 4041 N. Central, Suite 700, Phoenix, AZ 85012.

Public-Private Solution to Protection Against the Cost of Long-Term Care

by Robert M. Ball

Sometime in the not too distant future we will get a major national program protecting families against the cost of long-term care. I expect it to come, not primarily because of the political power of the elderly—although this is important—but because of pressure from those of middle age, the sons and daughters of the elderly. They are the ones most at risk. They may be faced with spending $30,000 or more a year for the nursing home care of a seriously impaired parent or, alternatively, bringing that parent into their own home. Whatever the decision, it may come down to the poignant choice of spending time and money on their parents at the sacrifice of their own children. The middle-aged need help.

The pressure for federal action will grow as the population ages because the need for long-term care increases rapidly with age. For example, the chances of needing nursing home care, the most expensive part of long-term care, are slight at age 65; at age 85, however, one in five persons resides in a nursing home. And the number of men and women 85 years of age and older is projected to increase at a rapid rate. The 1940 census counted only 365,000 who had reached that mark. But by 1980 there were 2.2 million over 85, accounting for about 1% of the total population. Now this population is really starting to grow. In 1990 this group will increase to more than 3 million and by the year 2000 to more than 5 million.[1] Comparative growth rates are striking: in the past 25 years the population of the United States as a whole has increased by about a third, the elderly population has nearly doubled, and the oldest old population has tripled.[1]

These trends will continue, leading to an even more dramatic age redisbribution. The 65-and-up population is expected to double again within 40 years, and the 85-and-up population will have nearly tripled again by that time. By then, the huge baby-boom population born after World War II and now traversing middle age will arrive at the threshold of advanced old age. Its ranks will swell the 85 and older population to more than 16 million by the year 2050.[1]

THE NEED FOR RESEARCH

If the current incidence of the chronic diseases of the elderly is applied to these huge numbers, we get quite frightening results: perhaps 7 to 8 million persons with Alzheimer's disease or related dementias, and millions more disabled by osteoporosis, arthritis, parkinsonism, or incontinence.[2] We clearly need a plan not only for long-term care but also for increased investment in research into the causes and treatment of the chronic diseases that particularly affect elderly people. It is not unreasonable, for example, on the basis of present progress being made in the understanding of Alzheimer's disease, to expect that a sustained and major research effort on this and similar diseases could in 10, 15, or 20 years result in a substantial reduction in the incidence of these diseases. This objective may be the most important of all long-term care objectives.

I would propose that any federal financing of long-term care services include a dedicated portion of that financing to go year in and year out to basic and applied research on the causes and treatment of the common conditions leading to long-term disability of the elderly. If the plan, for example, were financed in a way similar to Social Security, a mere 0.05% of covered payrolls devoted to such research would amount to an average of $1.4 billion a year over the five years 1990–1994. This is about the amount that could be well spent in such research.

A PUBLIC-PRIVATE PARTNERSHIP

There is real hope for disease reduction, but, of course, no matter how successful the research effort is, there will continue to be a need for more long-term care among the very old and for those at younger ages who are AIDS victims or otherwise physically or mentally disabled. Fortunately, we have a good model for how to approach the provision of long-term care in the way we have approached retirement income. In the area of retirement income we have a well-functioning public–private arrangement. Social Security is a truly universal program, but it has never been (and never was intended to be) a total program providing all the retirement income that anyone would ever want or need. It provides a platform on which to build, and pension plans, both public and private, are built on the base that Social Security provides. There are good reasons to approach the long-term care problem the same way. Budgetary constraints alone practically guarantee that in drafting and enacting a federal plan it will be necessary to choose priorities, leaving some needs unmet. This will create an important and appropriate role for private insurance—a role that builds logically upon a platform of public insurance providing basic, affordable, long-term coverage for all.

What we need is a three-part approach similar in concept to the retirement income system that has evolved in the United States

Part I—social insurance providing basic protection for everyone;

Part II—a private insurance supplement, offering to cover what the public program does not; and

Part III—an improved Medicaid program to protect low-income people against costs not covered by the other parts of the system.

LIMITS OF PRIVATE INSURANCE

A public–private partnership is needed because private insurance can just not do this job alone. It can do a lot more than it has. One might say it has nowhere to go but up, given the fact that only about 0.8% of nursing home costs were covered by private insurance in 1986, even less than the 1.6% covered by Medicare.[3] Yet as minuscule as insurance coverage now is, insurance, both public and private, is the right approach. It is inefficient for each individual to try to save for this risk entirely on his or her own. The result of trying to meet the need through saving is that everyone has to save for the extreme situation that only a few will encounter. Thus, many end up leaving larger estates than they had intended to leave. With insurance, people save for the average risk, and most of the money otherwise saved for long-term care can be saved for something else or spent for better purposes.

But there are fundamental problems that prevent private insurance from being a complete solution. It is basically as simple as this: it is offered at a cost too high for those with average and below-average incomes to bear. And with private insurance each person is going to have to pay his or her own way. There is almost no chance for long-term care insurance to be added to many employer-paid-for group health insurance plans, although the Ford Motor Company and the United Auto Workers are conducting a limited demonstration of such a plan for some workers and certain recent retirees in the Louisville area. Employers generally are concerned about what they have already committed themselves to for retirees and current worker protection. They will strongly resist adding to these costs by paying for long-term care. And unions generally are not likely to press for this kind of coverage as against other priorities, such as higher wages or fringe benefits that are of more immediate concern to their membership than the protection of those who, in most cases, may have retired many years earlier. So we can start with the assumption that the so-called "group plans" sold through employers are going to continue to be largely paid for by the employee. There are major advantages in marketing this way compared to individual selling; administrative savings, savings in selling costs, some assurance of quality because the employer will not want to promote just any plan—but this is not really group insurance. These plans are paid for by a premium charged to each individual without the great advantage of group insurance, through which the employer can subsidize poor risks among his employees and can subsidize the insurance for those receiving relatively low wages.

Flat payment, regardless of one's income—the premium approach of individually paid-for private insurance—is the most regressive way of paying for anything, but it is the only way open to private insurance paid for by the individual. This is in great contrast both to what group insurance does when provided by employers and to what the government does. The hospital insurance part of Medicare, for example, is financed very progressively. In hospital insurance, Part A under Medicare, a worker making $40,000 a year pays four times as much as a worker making $10,000 a year for exacly the same benefits. But charging some groups more than others for the same protection is not a possibility in a system based on individual election. If the policy is priced higher than the fair actuarial value for a particular group in order to subsidize some other group, competing insurance companies would offer lower-priced insurance to those who are being overcharged and take them away from the original carrier. As there is no way to cross-subsidize within these voluntary plans, whether sold individually or through employer groups or associations, and as the employee is going to have to pay all, this insurance is just not going to be affordable for a lot of people.

Another very major problem that private insurance has is how to deal with the inflation that can be expected in long-term care costs. The policies offered are indemnity plans—so many dollars a day in a nursing home and, quite commonly, one-half that amount for home health care. Consider a $50-a-day policy purchased at age 65; when the benefit is most likely to be used 15 or 20 years later, the actual need is no longer for $50 a day but for much more than that, probably twice as much or more. The insurance companies have tried to deal with this problem in different ways but the process gets very expensive. for example, policies that provide a 5% increase in protection each year for a 10-year period typically cost 30% to 40% more than policies that do not increase in benefits year by year, and, of course, such inflation protection is inadequate.

Suppose, however, you could buy a policy at age 50 with the opportunity to adjust for inflation indefinitely. The initial premium for a policy that provided $50/day with a 100-day waiting period might be in the neighborhood of $355 a year if sold on an individual basis. But if we assume that long-term care costs increase at a rate of 5% a year and that the premium is adjusted accordingly—that is, to reflect both the increase in cost of services covered and the increasing risk of needing those services as you grow older—the premium will have risen within 10 years to about $552. At the age of 70, you will be paying about $1,383 a year, and $5,628 at age 80. All told, by the time the risk of needing nursing home care becomes very serious, at age 85, the 36 years of premium payments will have amounted to $91,800 and, counting foregone interest on alternative investments at an average rate of 7%, would amount to $178,000. If sold through a group, the premiums could be considerably less, and, of course, if the policy had a substantially shorter waiting period, premium costs would be higher.

Another possible approach to inflation protection is to pay a level premium from a young age for a policy that includes automatic benefit increases to provide inflation protection. The Prudential Insurance Company offered such a plan to members of the American Association of Retired Persons (AARP) in the fall of 1989. The benefit level would increase 5% a year, compounded, until the policyholder enters benefit status. The purchase at, say age 50, the youngest age of eligibility for AARP membership, would cost $672 a year ($972 at age 60). This policy excludes the first 90 days from nursing home coverage and the first 45 days of home care coverage and there are lifetime limits of three years for nursing home stays and 730 visits for home care.

A nonforfeiture feature was not included, with the result that an individual might contribute for many, many years and, if unable to continue pay-ments, would have nothing to show for past contributions. But adding nonforfeiture features equal to what the individual has been paying under a level premium plan to meet high costs later would raise the price by another 10 to 15%. The dilemma is clear. The more of the problem a policy tries to meet, the smaller the number of people who can pay the cost.

Inflation is a problem for public plans too, but not to the same extent, as the base to which social insurance contribution rates might apply—for example, payrolls, income subject to taxation generally, or estates—also rises with inflation. Thus, although other cost factors may cause contribution rates to increase under a public program, inflation does not do so unless the inflation rate outpaces the growth in incomes. Even if this does happen—for example, if long-term care cost increases exceed wage increases—the rate adjustment is smaller and less frequent than for a premium-financed benefit. A rising premium in private insurance based on the assumption that policyholders' incomes will ordinarily increase is also possible, but it requires the application of a general assumption to individual policyholders and thus in many cases will not be valid, whereas in social insurance the increase occurs in the individual case only if the base (say, wages or income) increases for that individual.

There are other problems with private insurance when viewed as a total solution to protection against the cost of long-term care and they are familiar—the problems of adverse selection, the problems of benefit administration, particularly in the case of home care, and so on. Private insurance can do an important part of the job, but it cannot do the whole job alone.

PUBLIC-PRIVATE ALTERNATIVES

I now think that social insurance should be only a base, with a large role left for private insurance and a considerable role for an improved Medicaid program. I did not start out thinking this way. I started out favoring a very comprehensive social insurance approach that would have covered just about all aspects of home care, respite care, and nursing home care. But the cost of such a comprehensive plan is very high, beginning at, say, 50 to 60 billion dollars a year and rising, of course, as the population ages.

There is a case for this approach, nevertheless, because most of the costs have to be met in one way or another anyway. To a very considerable extent, social insurance would transfer to a new government plan what people now pay individually and what Medicaid pays. But even the incremental costs are not trivial. It is not at all unlikely that you would increase overally nursing home expenditures by perhaps 20%, under a social insurance plan, and home care expenditures by much more,[4] principally because some people are not getting the nursing home care they should and even more are not getting the home care they need. (The study referenced assumes a 20% across-the-board increase in nursing home use and expenditures as a result of the availability of comprehensive, public, long-term care insurance, and a 50% increase in home care use and expenditures.)

The main policy and political problem, however, is putting the very large total costs on the government. The social insurance plan has to raise enough money to meet the total costs, not just the incremental costs, and it would have to do this in the face of many other important social needs, such as the need of 31 million people under 65 for basic health insurance, the fact that over 20% of America's children are growing up in poverty, the need to improve education, provide housing, repair roads and bridges, and greatly improve many other public services. And all this in addition to the need to reduce the budget deficit. If complete coverage of the risk by a new federal social insurance plan is unrealistic, it becomes important to decide what is most essential for social insurance to cover and what private insurance and the means-tested Medicaid program should cover. One way of reducing the cost of social insurance is to provide a comprehensive home care benefit, but to require a long waiting period before covering the cost of a nursing home stay. A social insurance program might, for example, begin covering nursing home costs only after a patient has been in a nursing home for two or more years.

The major defect of this plan is that it requires the patient and family to figure out how to cope with an extremely large deductible—that is, the full cost of care for the first two years. Based on current costs, that deductible could easily exceed $60,000 for someone going into a nursing home in 1989, say; and of course, it will be much greater in the future as nursing home costs continue to rise. Few people could possibly hope to cover an expense of this magnitude entirely on their own. Faced with a two-year wait before they could expect any help from social insurance, most people would exhaust their own resources and would then be forced to turn to Medicaid just as they are forced to do now—unless they have bought private insurance to fill the two-year gap.

That, of course, is the key to this approach. The theory behind it is that the public cost of long-term care can be greatly reduced by creating a greatly enhanced market for private insurance—and that the market will be enhanced both because there will be a strong demand for insurance to fill the two-year gap and because insurers will be able to offer much more broadly affordable policies if they know that the maximum risk exposure for any given policy will be no more than two years.

There is no doubt that this approach would stimulate the sale of private insurance—that is, to people who are relatively well off and able to pass insurers' health screening criteria. It might even stimulate the

market for private insurance enough to marginally lower the total public cost of long-term care. But it raises many problems.

To begin with, this approach leaves entirely unprotected the two groups with the most immediate need for protection: those who are already old and disabled and those whose health problems make insurers unwilling to accept them. Enhancing the market for private insurance does not help these groups, because even under the most optimistic assumptions these people can neither afford nor qualify for coverage. Moreover, very large numbers of lower- and moderate-income people would still have to rely entirely on Medicaid if forced into a nursing home by a long-term illness. Even if they had actively wanted to buy private insurance to fill the two-year coverage gap, in most cases they would have had to use any spare income to meet more immediate priorities. So, with this approach, they would have no more protection against the risk of being rapidly overwhelmed by nursing home costs than they have now.

At the same time, however, they would in most cases have been contributing from their earnings to help finance the public part of the program. This raises a fundamental question about the equity of the proposal. Social insurance programs in the United States have generally been designed to serve all income levels and to offer lower-income contributors more in relation to their contributions than higher-income contributors. This proposal turns that principle on its head. Large numbers of workers would have to contribute to a long-term care protection program that would not, in fact, protect them. (Some versions of this proposal would finance the public long-term care program primarily by eliminating the cap on earnings taxable for Social Security purposes [$48,000 in 1989]. In this case it can be argued that the program would be financed in large part by the 6% of earners who earn more than $48,000, and that it is thus incorrect to state that average workers would be contributing to a long-term care protection program that would not in fact protect them. Perhaps, but people do not, as a rule, make distinctions about where their Social Security contributions go; they do not think in terms of so many dollars going to OASDI, so many to HI, etc. Thus, there is little question that this approach would be perceived as highly inequitable: "Why am I paying to support a program that won't support me when I need help?" It seems probable that sooner or later public opposition would grow to the point where this approach would have to be considerably modified.)

Only those who could also afford private insurance or meet a two-year deductible on their own would be served by this approach. Its effectiveness, even as a device to protect relatively well-off people, depends on private insurers being able to market policies that guarantee adequate protection, getting the great majority of middle-income Americans to buy these policies, and not letting them lapse—a doubtful outcome. And even among those who buy and retain these policies, situations would inevitably develop in which some policyholders, after decades of faithfully paying premiums, would still find themselves facing major out-of-pocket expenses because of a greater than anticipated gap between benefit levels and nursing home costs—the gap having developed either because benefit levels were too low all along or because they had not kept pace with increases in nursing home costs.

This approach, if adopted, would be likely to create an unstable situation. The new home care benefit would be important but would not adequately protect those who, for whatever reason, have to go into a nursing home. The nursing home benefit, with its two-year waiting period, would be of no use to a majority of nursing home residents because they would need help long before two years had elapsed and would not have been able to afford private insurance. People who have been paying into a program called "long-term care insurance" would have good reason to wonder just what it was they had been paying for, and public pressure would build to reduce or eliminate the two-year waiting period.

At that point, the respective roles of public and private insurance would once again become the focus of legislative debate—creating anew exactly the kind of controversy and uncertainty insurers want to avoid when they are trying to develop a stable market for their products.

The Executive Panel of the Ford Foundation's Project on Social Welfare and the American Future has recommended federal long-term care insurance after a two- or three-year waiting period but with a federal subsidy to help lower-income households buy private insurance covering the deductible period.[3] The report does not give details about the sliding scale subsidy proposed, but it prices the subsidy at $7.2 billion a year. There are still several problems with the approach of a lengthy deductible period even with a subsidy to encourage lower-income families to buy private insurance to fill the gap. The three most serious problems are:

1. Despite the subsidy, many people will not be able to buy the private insurance they need under the plan and still others for whom the ability to buy is a close question will decide not to buy. The plan seems to be based on the idea that most older people can afford private, long-term care insurance without undue sacrifice and therefore that the subsidy can be held to a relatively small amount and still do the job. That notion ignores the distribution of income among the elderly: for every elderly household with more than $50,000 a year in income, there are seven with less than $15,000.[5] In fact, most (62%) retired people live

mainly on their Social Security benefits and have few, if any, other resources to call upon.[6]

2. The approach is unnecessarily expensive. Built into the cost of private insurance are costs that social insurance does not have or that are lower for social insurance: the costs of promotion, sales commissions and profit, plus a higher cost of administration.

3. There is also reason to be concerned about the fact that lower-income people would have to submit to a means test in order to qualify for the subsidy. Today, except under Medicaid, beneficiaries are not subjected to any kind of inquiry or scrutiny regarding their relative ability to pay premiums.

A THREE-PART PROPOSAL FOR LONG-TERM CARE

It seems to me that the first and most important role for the government in financing long-term care is to help those families that have taken on the responsibility of caring for a disabled person at home, so that we can avoid putting people in institutions unnecessarily. The first need, then, would be for home care services and respite care services for the family caretaker. Home care is what most of the elderly want, and, to the extent that it can be worked out without a complete disruption of their own lives it is what relatives usually want for them. But in many parts of the country these services are not well organized or even available.

Of course, home care is not appropriate in some instances. We should not be trying to keep everybody at home, but appropriate home care is still the biggest unmet need. To shift the emphasis from institutionalization to home care, the public plan should, I believe, take the major responsibility for home care services. In this area the social insurance program should be comprehensive and depend for supplementation on private or Medicaid supplementation only for people who do not meet the strict eligibility standards (for example, the inability to perform two or more of the activities of daily living [ADLs] without active human assistance or to need supervision because of mental impairment) that will be necessary, at least at first, to make a social insurance program work well.

Where I would cut back from a comprehensive program of social insurance is in nursing home coverage. It seems to be most important to protect the income and assets of people in nursing homes in two situations: (1) when there is a real possibility of residents returning to the community and living in their own homes or in a semiprivate residence where they will need their income and assets for their own use; or (2) where there is a spouse or other close relative living in the community and dependent on the nursing home resident.

For many nursing home residents the additional objective of preserving their assets for their children will be important. But in the light of other needs for government expenditures, the protection of the assets of permanent nursing home residents without spouses or other dependents in the community, although important, is more appropriate for private insurance than for government insurance.

A one-year nursing home benefit extended indefinitely for those who have a spouse or other dependent living in the community would meet the priority needs described. This conclusion is supported by unpublished discharge data from the 1985 Nursing Home Survey. In the year before this survey, there were 877,000 live discharges from nursing homes. Of the live discharges who had been in a nursing home more than six months (284,900) nearly 90% (249,200) were discharged to hospitals or other health facilities. It can be assumed with considerable confidence that those discharged to other health facilities after six months in a nursing home, who had the degree of severe disability required by the proposal and who did not have a spouse in the community, died rather quickly, lived out the rest of their lives in such health facilities, or returned to a nursing home. It is extremely unlikely that any substantial number of this group would ever return to a private or semiprivate residence.

Of the 35,700 discharged to private or semiprivate homes, 9,800 were married. The plan I have described would have kept these people eligible for benefits up to discharge. Of the remaining 25,900, only 10,600 were either incontinent or needed help with mobility, a rough proxy for the disability standards proposed. Thus, of the 877,000 live discharges, only 10,600 or about 1% would have been in a nursing home more than six months, been disabled severely enough to meet the plan's criteria, and would have returned to a private or semiprivate residence without having had their income and assets protected by such a plan even if the benefit were only six months long, extended of course if there were a spouse or other dependent in the community.

A one-year plan, rather than a six-month plan, is proposed both to provide a margin for error in the data and to reduce even further the number who might go unprotected by the plan and still not be permanent nursing home residents, and also to provide for the possibility that in the long run we may get better at rehabilitation.

A one-year plan leaves unprotected those who are going to remain in nursing homes for the rest of their lives and have no spouse or other dependent on the outside. In their case, the need is to protect their assets for their heirs, once a reasonable living allowance, say $100 a month, is provided.

The question becomes: Is it really unreasonable to ask those who will be in nursing homes the rest of their lives (where the only reason to preserve their assets is to leave them to their heirs) to use their income and assets for the cost of their care in the nursing home if they or their heirs have failed to buy private insurance? If they have no income or assets, or if their income and assets are used up, they would be protected by an improved Medicaid program.

The answer to this question depends largely on whether the residual Medicaid program can be made to provide reasonable quality care. It can be taken for granted that a continuation of social insurance for those who cannot or do not buy private insurance compared to a means-tested approach would provide a better guarantee of quality care and would support people's desire to "pay their own way." There is more to protection by social insurance than asset protection. However, given all the other demands on government and given the deficit, is there enough to this point to call for a social insurance program for nursing home care of unlimited duration? I think not. I think the solution here is for an improved Medicaid program and improved private insurance to supplement the social insurance plan.

In summary, this social insurance plan would include the following features:

1. Home care services would be available for those who met a test of two ADLs, or their equivalent, including the need for supervision because of a mental impairment. It would be available both immediately—or after a short waiting period—and indefinitely.
2. An improved respite care benefit would be provided for caretakers.
3. A one-year nursing home benefit that would be extended as long as there was a spouse or other dependent of a nursing home resident in the community would be provided.
4. All benefits would have a 15% copayment.

Such a plan could be financed on a level contribution rate of between 1% and 1.3% of earnings for an employee and a matching amount from the employer, or from the equivalent amount of money raised in other ways, such as through dedicating a rate increase in the income tax to this purpose. The contribution rates could be held down somewhat by a dedicated tax on estates and by applying the capital gains tax at death, both of which put part of the cost on the estates of older people without decreasing their current standard of living.

This plan has several advantages:

● The public cost of long-term care is substantially lower under this plan than under a plan with an unrestricted nursing home benefit because the income and assets of permanent nursing home residents without spouses or other dependents in the community are used to help cover the cost of care. This plan is estimated to cost at least a third less than a plan with an unlimited nursing home benefit.

- All those who contribute to financing the plan are eligible for benefits on an equitable basis, and without having initially to "spend down" or undergo a means test. The plan thus provides broad coverage in a manner consistent with the traditional principles of social insurance.
- The plan protects those who are already elderly and disabled and those who cannot meet the health screening criteria of private insurance.
- The plan is balanced, covering both home care and nursing home care in a way that encourages home care when feasible without creating barriers for the use of a nursing home when necessary.
- The plan creates a logical and appropriate role for private insurance. Families wanting to protect assets for heirs will have good reason to buy private insurance, but no one needing to preserve assets for their own use or for a spouse or other dependent will be forced to depend on private insurance.

With this approach, insurance companies should be able to develop a major market among those with sizable assets—perhaps with the cost of premiums shared by sons and daughters interested in preserving their parents' assets. But the extent of coverage achieved by private insurance will not be crucial to the success of the social insurance plan. Private insurance would be focused on protecting the estates of those who have significant assets and want to make sure they are passed on to their heirs. Social insurance would be focused on those who need their income and assets for themselves, their spouses, or other dependents.

This approach provides for a stable division of responsibility between public and private insurance. With everyone protected against the cost of home care, respite care, and nursing home stays as long as there is a personal need for the protection of income and assets, there would be no strong public pressure to extend social insurance coverage to the estates of permanent nursing home residents without spouses or dependents in the community. The insurance industry will thus be free to develop a market among families who will want such assets protected without having to worry unduly that Congress may change the rules.

Obviously, this approach to long-term care insurance works properly only if accompanied by improvements in Medicaid. Although the social insurance plan becomes the first payor of nursing home bills, Medicaid continues to have a major role in long-term care, and the risk remains that some Medicaid patients will be treated as second-class patients. It is thus imperative—as it is in any case—that Medicaid be further improved to insure that all those served by the program are properly protected.

The improvements needed in Medicaid include especially the need for a federal requirement that all states adopt eligibility criteria guaranteeing Medicaid assistance to anyone who cannot otherwise meet nursing home costs, coupled with more stringent enforcement of Medicaid nursing home quality-of-care standards.

CONCLUSION

On balance, if we are going to have something less than a comprehensive program, which by all odds is the most likely outcome, it seems to me the emphasis should be first on home care and then on providing an up-front, one-year nursing home benefit under the social insurance plan (extended indefinitely if the resident has dependents in the community), with private insurance building on top of that, rather than depending on private insurance to fill in a major gap at the beginning of the coverage period, which it will only be able to do in part.

Long-term care will continue to be a complex issue, and there is room for disagreement on how best to deal with it. But we should be beyond debating whether some federal action is needed. A public program is not an option; it is a necessity. The next challenge is to agree on a sensible plan—one that assigns logical roles to social insurance, private insurance, and Medicaid—and then to implement it.

REFERENCES

1. U.S. Bureau of the Census: Current Population Reports, Series P-23, No. 128: America in Transition: An Aging Society, Washington, D.C., 1983; and Current Population Reports Series P-25, forthcoming report.

2. U.S. Congress, Office of Technology Assessment: Losing a Million Minds: Confronting the Tragedy of Alzheimer's Disease and Other Dementias. Washington, D.C., 1987, p 22.

3. Ford Foundation, Project on Social Welfare and the American Future. The Common Good: Policy of Recommendations of the Executive Panel. New York, 1989, p 75.

4. Rivlin A.M., Wiener J.M.: Caring for the Disabled Elderly, Who Will Pay? The Brookings Institution, Washington, D.C., 1988, p 223.

5. Social Security Administration, Office of Research and Statistics: Income of the Population 55 or Older, 1986. Washington, D.C., June 1988, p 23.

6. Social Security Administration, Office of Research and Statistics: Facts and Figures about Social Security. August 1988, p 6.

xvi / DIRECTORY OF NURSING HOMES

ABOUT THE AUTHOR

Robert M. Ball is former Commissioner of Social Security (1962–1973). Currently he is a consultant on Social Security, health, and welfare policy.

Some of this material appeared first in *The Future of Health Care: Public Concerns and Policy Trends, A Transcript of the Seminar Series, May 6, May 20, June 24, 1988* presented by Massachusetts Health Data Consortium, Inc., in cooperation with The Challenge to Leadership Project, the *Boston Globe,* WNEV-TV, WBUR Radio, and some of the material appeared first in *Because We're All in This Together: The Case for a National Long-Term Care Insurance Policy,* a report to Families, U.S.A. Foundation (formerly the Villers Foundation) by the author of this article, with assistance from Thomas N. Bethell.

Address correspondence and reprint requests to Robert Ball, 505 Capitol Court NE, 300, Washington, DC 20002.

Private Long-Term Care Insurance: Part of the Solution

by Susan Van Gelder

The Health Insurance Association of America (HIAA) welcomes this opportunity to discuss the growing role that private long-term care insurance is playing in financing long-term care for our nation's elderly citizens. Readers of this directory are probably well aware of the problems many people face when paying for nursing home care and other long-term care services. Simply put, individuals are expected to pay for this care with their own resources or resort to Medicaid, a health care program for the poor. Private long-term care insurance offers people the opportunity to preserve their resources for themselves, their spouses, and their families. It also provides people greater financial independence and opportunities to select the care provider of their choice, which frequently is not the case when they must rely on Medicaid.

WHO NEEDS LONG-TERM CARE?

In just 10 short years, 13 percent of our population—almost 35 million people—will be 65 years old or older. About one-quarter of this group (9 million people) are expected to require long-term care. The greatest need lies with those 85 years of age or older. Although they will represent less than two percent of the general population in the year 2000, about one-half of those 85 years old and older will require personal care assistance such as help in bathing, dressing, and walking according to government studies. Such needs are a key predictor of requirements for long-term care.

The probability of needing long-term care, especially care in a nursing home, is a great deal higher than most of us realize or probably care to admit. A recent study by the U.S. Department of Health and Human Services estimates that currently, about 40 percent of all persons 65 years old and older will require nursing home care sometime before death.

The statistics are clearly different for each gender; women face a 45 percent risk of requiring admission to a nursing home, whereas men face only a 28 percent risk. When the data are adjusted for future life expectancies, the probabilities are even greater. The impact is multiplied when families are considered. According to the study, "Nine out of 10 married children with four parents turning 65 can expect to have at least one parent use a nursing home."

Although the risk of entering a nursing home is relatively high, many people will stay for only a brief period. Fully 50 percent of all admitted people stay six months or less; about one-third stay longer than a year. Usually, residents with short stays are discharged back to their homes for recovery or die shortly after admission.

The majority of disabled elderly do not live in nursing homes; three-fourths reside in the community where families and friends provide needed support. Only about one-quarter of these elderly receive any paid services, which are split nearly evenly between government programs and out-of-pocket expenditures.

FOOTING THE BILL

An estimated $56 billion was spent on all long-term care services in 1987. More than half of this amount ($30.6 billion) was paid by the government. Assuming no change in our current financing system, the Congressional Budget Office has estimated that this figure could increase between 50 and 200 percent in 10 years.

Long-term care financing has generated increasing interest among insurance companies, providers, federal and state governments, and consumer advocacy organizations. Many groups assume that only the public sector can foot the bill. The aging population is a varied one, however, with many different needs and resources to pay for them. Two recent surveys, conducted on behalf of elderly organizations, suggest that general impressions of senior citizens are based more on perceptions from the past than on realities of the present.

In a survey conducted for the National Council on Aging by Louis Harris and Associates, nonelderly respondents reported that the elderly suffered more than other age groups from inadequate income, ill health, loneliness, above-average rates of crime, and other social and economic problems. However, according to the Brookings Institution, the elderly are in fact no more prone to these troubles and, in a number of ways, they are better off than other age groups. A survey conducted for the American Association of Retired Persons found similar results.

Government surveys have shown that most elderly people are able to maintain independent living arrangements—a key measure of financial and physical well-being. More than 86 percent of persons 75 years old or older lived independently in 1984 compared to 58 percent in 1960. Moreover, more than three-fourths of the elderly owned their own homes in 1985; over 80 percent owned them outright. The mean net worth of households headed by persons 65 years of age and over was $116,800 in 1985. This wealth was evenly distributed between home equity and financial assets.

The vast majority of Americans prefer to arrange for their own economic needs and support services through savings and insurance. A Gallup Organization poll in July 1989 found 60 percent of respondents willing to foot the bill for long-term care insurance to finance their own needs.

A 1988 national survey conducted by the University of Maryland's Center on Aging found surprising willingness by the public to purchase a long-term care plan if it met their long-term nursing home and home health care needs. Overall, more than one-half of those surveyed indicated they would pay $100 a month for such a plan. In addition, two-thirds of full-time workers said they would be more willing to purchase a policy if it were offered by their employer, even if the employee paid all or some of the premium.

Existing federal proposals for long-term-care financing reform range from a universal public entitlement program for long-term care to incentives to stimulate growth in the private insurance market. With current fiscal realities and competing national priorities, the public sector is unlikely to endorse sweeping expansions in public financial responsibility. Instead, public policy must focus on finding effective ways to use private funds already applied to long-term care, thereby reducing future public expenditures for such care.

At the same time, the federal government should respond to those who face needs beyond their individual financial capacity. Private insurance products, including long-term care, are not designed to be purchased by people who are poor, quite old, or disabled. The public sector must improve its ability to support these segments of the American population.

Congressional debate over how to meet the nation's needs for long-term care highlights the fact that the problem is not confined to financing it. Long-term care delivery systems are fragmented—there is no one accepted model to manage care and control costs, and if there were, it may not work in all communities across the country. Data on long-term care service use are inadequate for fully understanding the current situation or for making accurate estimates about future utilization and costs, especially for community-based services.

Surfacing long-term care financing and delivery demands have created a health care conundrum without clear-cut solutions. What is needed now is manageable innovation and experimentation leading to greater understanding of how financing and delivery affect cost and access to care.

GROWING PRIVATE MARKET

Responding to a growing public awareness of need, a number of insurance companies are entering the long-term care insurance market with ever-improving products. The growth is phenomenal. In 1987, the congressionally mandated Task Force on Long-Term Health Care Policies identified 73 companies selling the type of insurance meeting the National Association of Insurance Commissioners' (NAIC) definition of a long-term care insurance policy.

A survey of companies selling long-term care insurance, conducted in December 1989 by HIAA, found a total of 118 companies in the marketplace. The total number of policies sold now stands at more than 1.5 million—up 400,000 from a year earlier. Just as there is exceptional growth in the numbers of policies sold, important changes are also taking place in the products themselves.

As part of the 1989 HIAA survey, individual policies available from the top sellers in 1989 were analyzed to determine the kinds of long-term care policies consumers bought. These companies had sold three-fourths of all policies bought as of the end of 1989.

All but one of the top-selling plans offered all levels of nursing home care and a home health benefit (one plan sold coverage only for nursing home care). Many of the plans also offered coverage for adult day care. For policyholders to qualify for benefits, most plans required a physician's certification of need. Only one plan required a prior stay in a nursing home, and two plans required that the individual need assistance in a specified number of activities of daily living, such as walking, bathing, and dressing.

Most plans offered a choice of benefit amounts to pay for nursing home care, ranging from $40 to $120 per day. In 1989, the national average daily rate for nursing home care was estimated at $75 a day. However, this can vary significantly by area of the country and for urban and rural areas. Payment rates for home health care were generally 50 percent of the daily nursing home benefit. The plans also offered a choice of deductible periods, expressed in terms of days, before benefits were paid. The deductible periods ranged from none to 100 days. The shorter the deductible period and the higher the daily benefit chosen, the higher the premium.

The majority of the plans had separate periods of coverage for nursing home care and for home health care. For nursing home care, most offered at least five years, if not an unlimited lifetime benefit period. For home health care, choices ranged from six months to five years of coverage. The minimum age at which a person could purchase a plan was generally age 50 years, and the maximum purchase age was usually between 80 and 84 years. These applied only to the ages at which one might purchase a policy; they did not apply to the ages at which one could receive benefits.

Most plans also offered an inflation adjustment feature that increased the daily benefit amount over time to help meet the higher cost of care expected in the future. Because the inflation features often differed substantially across plans, consumers should give special attention to this feature when comparing plans.

Premiums were level and based on the age of purchase. This means that, unless the premium is increased for everyone in a similar group and for reasons other than deteriorating health or increasing age, the premium will remain constant over the policyholder's lifetime. To ensure that the policy cannot be cancelled, consumers should make certain the policy is guaranteed renewable.

For example, at 50 years of age, a policyholder's average annual premium for a plan providing an $80-a-day nursing home benefit, a 20-day deductible period, and four years of nursing home coverage, without an inflation feature, was $485. At 65 years of age, the consumer's premium was $1,135 a year, and at 79 years old, it was about $3,800 a year. When the cost of the inflation feature was added to the premium, the average annual premium was $660 at 50 years of age, $1,400 at 65 years old, and $4,200 at 79 years of age.

Most of the policies were sold on an individual basis to older people; the average purchase age was 72 years. As with all individual health products, these plans are medically underwritten and applicants must provide information about their past medical history. By providing coverage to only those persons of average health and risk for their ages, the insurance companies help to guarantee that the premiums they have developed and collected will be adequate to pay the claims they receive in the future.

Other forms of long-term care insurance are developing rapidly. Since 1987, several employers have offered long-term care benefits to employees and their spouses and to retirees. In most cases, the parents of the employee and the parents of the spouse have also been offered coverage. The plans have been "employee-pay-all," meaning the employer does not help pay the premium. The average age of an employee electing this coverage has been 43 years. The average annual premium at this age is about $200 a year. This market holds great promise because the premiums are more affordable, little or no underwriting is required because the intended consumers are healthier, and more people can be reached through the workplace.

Another long-term care option is to purchase a rider to a life insurance policy. These plans advance a portion of the death benefit in the event the policyholder needs long-term care before his or her death. Consumers should understand, however, that this type of policy only pays benefits under one event or the other. If nursing home care is needed, little or no death benefit will be available for a surviving spouse or family members.

Finally, long-term care insurance also is offered to those elderly who become members of continuing care retirement communities (CCRCs). CCRC developments, which offer housing and support to persons in their later years, usually have a one-time entrance fee and monthly housing charges.

CONSUMER PROTECTION AND EDUCATION NEEDS

As with other forms of insurance, long-term care insurance is regulated at the state level by state insurance departments. Because long-term care insurance is a new product, states have had to move quickly to establish regulations to govern it. Since 1987, 40 states have adopted legislation or regulations based on model statutes developed by the National Association of Insurance Commissioners. The model statutes include minimum plan benefits and many consumer protection standards that a policy must contain to be sold in a state. If there is a question about whether a state has such standards and what the standards are, a consumer should contact the state insurance department. HIAA firmly supports state regulation of long-term care insurance and has been working actively throughout the states for passage of legislation governing this product.

HIAA also provides a free consumer guide on long-term care insurance and a list of companies selling such policies. Consumers can write to HIAA, P.O. Box 41455, Washington, D.C. 20018. The consumer guide provides a checklist that allows people to comxx / DIRECTORY OF NURSING HOMES

pare plans on several important features. HIAA also helps sponsor a toll-free consumer helpline to answer questions about all types of insurance, including long-term care insurance. The helpline number is 1-800-942-4242.

Consumers should carefully consider all policies before they buy. They should not purchase a policy from an agent they do not trust or one using high-pressure sales tactics. If they are uncomfortable about a particular agent, they should change agents or call the insurance company's home office or state insurance department. Ask for the outline of coverage summarizing the policy's features. Companies are required to present this information in a uniform format so that consumers can easily and quickly compare plans. Most plans offer a 30-day free-look period after the plan has been purchased. If a policyholder changes his or her mind about the policy, it can be returned to the company within 30 days and the premium will be refunded. Consumers should make sure the company is financially secure. Those with high A.M. Best Company ratings often include this information in their marketing materials. If uncertain, call the state insurance department or check the most recent Best's Insurance Report available in many libraries.

CONCLUSIONS

All indications are that the long-term care insurance market is growing and that long-term care insurance is becoming more widely available through mechanisms other than the individual market. For example, employer-sponsored coverage, life insurance riders, and coverage provided to members of CCRCs are newly available forms of coverage.

The public and private sectors must combine their efforts and knowledge to create a comprehensive national policy for long-term care that will benefit the most Americans both today and in the future. Such a policy will give full measure to the resources that individuals, families, employers, providers, and the state and federal governments can produce to address the aging populations growing need for long-term care.

ABOUT THE AUTHOR

Susan Van Gelder is associate director of the Health Insurance Association of America's Department of Policy Development and Research, where she researches the older population and long-term care issues. Ms. Van Gelder previously was with the U.S. General Accounting Office, where she conducted research evaluations on the Medicare and Medicaid programs.

LIST OF ABBREVIATIONS

Ave	Avenue	N	North
Blvd	Boulevard	NE	Northeast
Ct	Court	NW	Northwest
DO	Doctor of Osteopathy	Pkwy	Parkway
DON	Director of Nursing	PO	Post Office
Dr	Doctor, Drive	pt	part-time
E	East	QMRP	Qualified Mental Retardation Professional
Expy	Expressway	Rd	Road
Ext	Extension	Rehab	Rehabilitation
ft	full-time	RCF	Residential Care Facility
Fwy	Freeway	Rev	Reverend
Hwy	Highway	RN	Registered Nurse
ICF	Intermediate Care Facility	RR	Rural Route

ICF   Intermediate Care Facility
> A certified facility that meets federal standards and provides less extensive health related care and services. It has regular nursing service, but not around the clock. Most intermediate care facilities carry on rehabilitation programs, with an emphasis on personal care and social services. Mainly, these homes serve people who are not fully capable of living by themselves, yet are not necessarily ill enough to need 24-hour nursing care.

		Rte	Route
		S	South
		SE	Southeast
		SNF	Skilled Nursing Facility

ICF/MR   Intermediate Care Facility for Mentally Retarded

Jr	Junior	
Ln	Lane	
LPN	Licensed Practical Nurse	
MD	Medical Doctor	
Mt	Mount	

SNF   Skilled Nursing Facility
> A facility that has been certified as meeting federal standards within the meaning of the Social Security Act. It provides the level of care that comes closest to hospital care with 24-hour nursing services. Regular medical supervision and rehabilitation therapy are also provided. Generally, a skilled nursing facility cares for convalescent patients and those with long-term illnesses.

Sr	Sister, Senior
St	Saint, Street
SW	Southwest
W	West

STATE-BY-STATE
LISTING OF FACILITIES

ALABAMA

Abbeville

Henry County Nursing Home
112 Briarhill Rd, Abbeville, AL 36310
(205) 585-2241
Admin J Juanita Ham. *Dir of Nursing* Sarah
Walker. *Medical Dir* Richard V Meadows
DO.
Licensure Skilled care. *Beds* SNF 60. *Certified*
Medicaid; Medicare.
Owner Nonprofit organization/foundation.

Alabaster

Briarcliff Nursing Home
850 NW 9th St, Alabaster, AL 35007
(205) 663-3859
Admin Mary Frances Eddings.
Medical Dir Harry Phillips MD.
Licensure Skilled care; Intermediate care. *Beds*
SNF 226; ICF 38. *Certified* Medicaid;
Medicare.
Owner Nonprofit corp.
Admissions Requirements Minimum age 18;
Medical examination; Physician's request.
Staff RNs 4 (ft); LPNs 16 (ft), 9 (pt); Physical
therapists; Speech therapists; Activities
coordinators 2 (ft); Dietitians; Podiatrists.
Facilities Dining room; Activities room;
Crafts room; Laundry room; Barber/Beauty
shop; Library.
Activities Arts & crafts; Cards; Games;
Reading groups; Prayer groups; Movies;
Shopping trips; Dances/Social/Cultural
gatherings.

Albertville

Albertville Nursing Home Inc
PO Box 749, Hwy 75 N, Albertville, AL
35950
(205) 878-1398
Admin Audrey Cole. *Dir of Nursing* Becky
Brown RN. *Medical Dir* Dr A Lynn Luther.
Licensure Skilled care; Intermediate care. *Beds*
SNF 67; ICF 66. *Certified* Medicaid;
Medicare.
Owner Proprietary corp.
Admissions Requirements Medical
examination; Physician's request.
Staff RNs 2 (ft), 1 (pt); LPNs 9 (ft), 3 (pt);
Nurses' aides 39 (ft), 19 (pt); Activities
coordinators 3 (ft).
Facilities Dining room; Activities room;
Chapel; Laundry room; Barber/Beauty shop.
Activities Arts & crafts; Cards; Games;
Reading groups; Prayer groups; Movies;
Shopping trips; Dances/Social/Cultural
gatherings; Baby day; Bus rides; Pet shows.

Alexander City

Adams Nursing Home
PO Box 1149, 1423 Hillabee St, Alexander
City, AL 35010
(205) 329-0847
Admin R Frank Brown Jr. *Dir of Nursing*
Chris McGill RN. *Medical Dir* Edvin Larson
MD.
Licensure Skilled care; Intermediate care. *Beds*
SNF 44; ICF 44. *Certified* Medicaid;
Medicare.
Owner Proprietary corp.
Admissions Requirements Medical
examination; Physician's request.
Staff RNs 2 (ft); LPNs 9 (ft); Nurses' aides 24
(ft); Activities coordinators 1 (ft).
Facilities Dining room; Activities room;
Crafts room; Laundry room; Barber/Beauty
shop.
Activities Arts & crafts; Cards; Games;
Reading groups; Prayer groups; Movies.

Brown Nursing Home
PO Box 1056, 1451 Washington St, Alexander
City, AL 36866
(205) 329-9061
Admin Connie J Weldon. *Dir of Nursing*
Diane Johnson. *Medical Dir* James P
Temple MD.
Licensure Skilled care; Intermediate care. *Beds*
Swing beds SNF/ICF 48. *Private Pay*
Patients 10%. *Certified* Medicaid; Medicare.
Owner Proprietary corp (Crown Investments
Inc).
Admissions Requirements Minimum age 18;
Medical examination; Physician's request.
Staff Physicians 1 (pt); RNs 1 (ft), 2 (pt);
LPNs 4 (ft), 1 (pt); Nurses' aides 14 (ft), 6
(pt); Physical therapists 1 (pt); Occupational
therapists 1 (pt); Speech therapists 1 (pt);
Activities coordinators 1 (ft); Dietitians 1
(ft); Podiatrists 1 (pt).
Facilities Dining room; Activities room;
Laundry room; Barber/Beauty shop.
Activities Arts & crafts; Cards; Games;
Reading groups; Prayer groups; Movies;
Dances/Social/Cultural gatherings.

Chapman Nursing Home Inc
Rte 5 Box 283, Dadeville Hwy, Alexander
City, AL 35010
(205) 234-6366
Admin Margaret S Chapman.
Licensure Skilled care. *Beds* SNF 151.
Certified Medicaid; Medicare.
Owner Proprietary corp.

Aliceville

Aliceville Manor Nursing Home
17th St NW, Aliceville, AL 35442
(205) 373-6307
Admin Mary Ellen Wheat.
Licensure Skilled care; Intermediate care. *Beds*
SNF 59; ICF 21. *Certified* Medicaid;
Medicare.
Owner Proprietary corp.

Altoona

Altoona Health Care Center
PO Box 68, Walnut Grove Rd, Altoona, AL
35952
(205) 589-6395
Admin Lee Guyton.
Medical Dir M Bailey.
Licensure Skilled care; Intermediate care. *Beds*
SNF 50; ICF. *Certified* Medicaid; Medicare.
Owner Proprietary corp.
Admissions Requirements Medical
examination.
Staff RNs 1 (ft), 2 (pt); LPNs 4 (ft), 2 (pt);
Nurses' aides 20 (ft), 10 (pt); Activities
coordinators 1 (ft); Dietitians 1 (ft).
Facilities Dining room; Activities room;
Laundry room; Barber/Beauty shop.
Activities Arts & crafts; Cards; Games;
Reading groups; Prayer groups; Movies;
Shopping trips; Dances/Social/Cultural
gatherings.

Anniston

Anniston Nursing Home
PO Box 1825, 500 Leighton Ave, Anniston,
AL 36201
(205) 237-8053
Admin Carolyn H Beck.
Licensure Skilled care. *Beds* 85. *Certified*
Medicaid.
Owner Proprietary corp.

Beckwood Manor
500 Leighton Ave, Anniston, AL 36201
(205) 236-4949
Admin Carolyn H Beck.
Licensure Skilled care. *Beds* SNF 85.

Golden Springs Health Care Center
PO Box 1790, 2300 Coleman Rd, Anniston,
AL 36201
(205) 831-5730
Admin Rebecca R Helton.
Medical Dir Dr Robert Lokey.
Licensure Skilled care; Intermediate care. *Beds*
114. *Certified* Medicaid; Medicare.
Owner Proprietary corp (National Health
Corp).
Admissions Requirements Medical
examination; Physician's request.
Staff Physicians 1 (pt); RNs 3 (ft), 2 (pt);
LPNs 7 (ft), 9 (pt); Nurses' aides 24 (ft), 15
(pt); Physical therapists 1 (ft); Activities
coordinators 1 (ft); Dietitians 1 (ft).
Facilities Dining room; Physical therapy
room; Activities room; Laundry room;
Barber/Beauty shop; Library.
Activities Arts & crafts; Cards; Games;
Reading groups; Prayer groups; Movies;
Shopping trips; Dances/Social/Cultural
gatherings.

Arab

Nursing Home of Arab
209 2nd St SE, Arab, AL 35016
(205) 586-3111
Admin Suzanne Shelton.
Licensure Skilled care; Intermediate care. *Beds* SNF 40; ICF 27. *Certified* Medicaid; Medicare.
Owner Proprietary corp.
Facilities Dining room; Activities room; Chapel; Laundry room; Barber/Beauty shop.
Activities Arts & crafts; Cards; Games; Prayer groups; Movies; Dances/Social/Cultural gatherings.

Ashland

Clay County Hospital & Nursing Home
544 E 1st Ave, Ashland, AL 36251
(205) 354-2131
Admin Joe McCaig.
Licensure Skilled care; Intermediate care. *Beds* SNF 59; ICF 4. *Certified* Medicaid; Medicare.
Owner Publicly owned.

Ashville

Ashville Manor Nursing Home
PO Box 130, Ashville, AL 35953
(205) 594-5148
Admin Pam Penland. *Dir of Nursing* Helen Wade. *Medical Dir* Dr Lynn Luther.
Licensure Intermediate care. *Beds* ICF 43. *Private Pay Patients* 5%. *Certified* Medicaid.
Owner Privately owned.
Admissions Requirements Physician's request.
Staff Physicians; RNs; LPNs; Nurses' aides; Recreational therapists; Activities coordinators; Dietitians.
Facilities Dining room; Activities room; Laundry room; Barber/Beauty shop; Dayroom.
Activities Arts & crafts; Cards; Games; Reading groups; Prayer groups; Movies; Shopping trips; Dances/Social/Cultural gatherings; Intergenerational programs.

Athens

Athens Convalescent Center Inc
611 W Market St, Athens, AL 35611
(205) 232-1620
Admin John L Wallace.
Licensure Skilled care; Intermediate care. *Beds* SNF 64; ICF 28. *Certified* Medicaid; Medicare.
Owner Proprietary corp.

Limestone Health Facility
1600 W Hobbs St, Athens, AL 35611
(205) 232-3461
Admin Bill R Hunt. *Dir of Nursing* Nancy P Louell RN. *Medical Dir* Dr W K Shannon.
Licensure Skilled care; Intermediate care; Retirement. *Beds* SNF 86; ICF 50. *Certified* Medicaid; Medicare.
Owner Proprietary corp.
Staff RNs 4 (ft); LPNs 13 (ft), 7 (pt); Nurses' aides 32 (ft), 20 (pt); Physical therapists 1 (pt); Reality therapists 2 (ft); Recreational therapists 2 (ft); Activities coordinators 2 (ft); Dietitians 1 (ft).
Facilities Dining room; Activities room; Chapel; Crafts room; Laundry room; Barber/Beauty shop.
Activities Arts & crafts; Cards; Games; Reading groups; Prayer groups; Movies.

Atmore

Atmore Nursing Care Center
715 E Laurel St, Atmore, AL 36504
(205) 368-9121
Admin Deborah A Grant.

Medical Dir Harold Q Wilson MD.
Licensure Skilled care; Intermediate care. *Beds* 100. *Certified* Medicaid; Medicare.
Owner Proprietary corp (Unicare).
Admissions Requirements Medical examination; Physician's request.
Staff Physicians 8 (pt); RNs 5 (ft), 2 (pt); LPNs 18 (ft), 10 (pt); Nurses' aides 40 (ft), 20 (pt); Recreational therapists 1 (ft); Activities coordinators 1 (ft); Dietitians 2 (pt); Social workers 1 (ft).
Facilities Dining room; Activities room; Chapel; Crafts room; Laundry room; Barber/Beauty shop.
Activities Arts & crafts; Reading groups; Prayer groups; Movies; Shopping trips; Dances/Social/Cultural gatherings.

Attalla

Attalla Health Care Inc
Rte 2, PO Box 239, 900 Stewart Ave, Attalla, AL 35954
(205) 538-7852
Admin Ted H Cook.
Licensure Skilled care; Intermediate care. *Beds* SNF 106; ICF 59. *Certified* Medicaid; Medicare.
Owner Proprietary corp.

Auburn

Wesley Terrace Methodist Home for the Aging
1365 Gatewood Dr, Auburn, AL 36830
(205) 826-7200
Admin Steven B Francis.
Licensure Skilled care. *Beds* SNF 55.

Bessemer

Jones Valley Nursing Home
PO Box 297, Bessemer, AL 35020
(205) 425-4359
Admin Carrie Phillips.
Licensure Skilled care; Intermediate care. *Beds* SNF 34; ICF 12. *Certified* Medicaid; Medicare.
Owner Proprietary corp.

Livingston Nursing Home
4201 Bessemer Super Hwy, Bessemer, AL 35020
(205) 428-3249
Admin Ruth L Osborne.
Licensure Skilled care; Intermediate care. *Beds* SNF 63; ICF 6. *Certified* Medicaid; Medicare.
Owner Proprietary corp.

Meadowood Nursing Home
820 Golf Course Rd, Bessemer, AL 35023
(205) 425-5241
Admin Cathy S Gagliano.
Licensure Skilled care; Intermediate care. *Beds* SNF 90; ICF 90. *Certified* Medicaid; Medicare.
Owner Proprietary corp (Beverly Enterprises).

Southgate Village Inc
325 Selma Rd, Bessemer, AL 35020
(205) 428-9383
Admin Joyce H Campbell. *Dir of Nursing* Louise G Parker RN. *Medical Dir* Dr Jerry McLane.
Licensure Skilled care; Intermediate care. *Beds* SNF 63; ICF 18. *Certified* Medicaid; Medicare.
Owner Proprietary corp (American Health Care Inc).
Admissions Requirements Medical examination; Physician's request.
Staff RNs; LPNs; Nurses' aides; Activities coordinators; Dietitians.
Facilities Dining room; Activities room; Chapel; Laundry room.
Activities Arts & crafts; Games; Reading groups.

Birmingham

Altamont Nursing Center & Retirement Home
2831 Highland Ave, Birmingham, AL 35222
(205) 323-2724
Admin Jeffrey B Kirby.
Licensure Intermediate care. *Beds* ICF 56.

Baptist Medical Center & Skilled Nursing Unit—Montclair
800 Montclair Rd, Birmingham, AL 35213
(205) 592-1200
Admin Mitzi Roberts.
Licensure Skilled care. *Beds* SNF 51.

Beverly Health Care Center
733 Mary Vann Ln, Birmingham, AL 35215
(205) 854-1361
Admin Chuck Beech.
Licensure Skilled care; Intermediate care. *Beds* SNF 102; ICF 18.
Owner Proprietary corp (Beverly Enterprises).

Burgess Nursing Home
1532 Bankhead Hwy W, Birmingham, AL 35214
(205) 798-3871
Admin William H Burgess Jr.
Licensure Skilled care. *Beds* 53. *Certified* Medicaid; Medicare.
Owner Proprietary corp.

Chalkville Health Care Inc
2350 Sweeny Hollow Rd, Birmingham, AL 35215
(205) 853-2340
Admin James H Cole.
Licensure Skilled care. *Beds* SNF 56.

Civic Center Nursing Home
1201 N 22nd St, Birmingham, AL 35234
(205) 251-5271
Admin Annette Lee Malloy.
Licensure Skilled care; Intermediate care. *Beds* SNF 85; ICF 10. *Certified* Medicaid; Medicare.
Owner Nonprofit corp.

East Haven Health Care
7110 1st Ave N, Birmingham, AL 35206
(205) 836-5226
Admin Myra Collier.
Licensure Skilled care; Intermediate care. *Beds* SNF 31; ICF 31. *Certified* Medicaid; Medicare.
Owner Proprietary corp.

Estes Health Care Center—East
733 Mary Vann Ln, Birmingham, AL 35215
(205) 854-1361
Admin Michael Dray.
Licensure Skilled care; Intermediate care. *Beds* SNF 102; ICF 18. *Certified* Medicaid; Medicare.
Owner Proprietary corp.

Estes Health Care Center—Riverchase
2500 Riverhaven Dr, Birmingham, AL 35244
(205) 823-6760
Admin Dennis Lee.
Licensure Skilled care; Intermediate care. *Beds* SNF 102; ICF 18. *Certified* Medicaid; Medicare.
Owner Proprietary corp.

Estes Nursing Facility—Civic Center
1201 N 22nd St, Birmingham, AL 35234
(205) 251-5271
Admin Ross M Taylor Jr.
Licensure Skilled care; Intermediate care. *Beds* SNF 90; ICF 5.

Estes Nursing Facility—Northway
1424 N 25th St, Birmingham, AL 35234
(205) 328-5870
Admin Robert L Crooks.
Licensure Intermediate care. *Beds* ICF 113.

Estes Nursing Facility—Oak Knoll
824 6th Ave W, Birmingham, AL 35204
(205) 787-2619
Admin Jack D Barnes Jr.
Licensure Skilled care; Intermediate care. *Beds* SNF 72; ICF 28. *Certified* Medicaid; Medicare.
Owner Proprietary corp (Northport Health Services).
Staff Physicians; RNs; LPNs; Nurses' aides; Speech therapists; Activities coordinators.
Facilities Dining room; Physical therapy room; Activities room; Crafts room; Barber/ Beauty shop.

Estes Nursing Facility—South
1220 S 17th St, Birmingham, AL 35205
(205) 933-2180
Admin Mary R Hardisty.
Licensure Skilled care; Intermediate care. *Beds* SNF 42; ICF 41.

Fairview Nursing & Convalescent Home
1028 Bessemer Rd, Birmingham, AL 35228
(205) 923-1777, 923-7374 FAX
Admin William G Allen Jr. *Dir of Nursing* Cathy Huneycutt. *Medical Dir* Dr Cemal Goral.
Licensure Skilled care; Intermediate care; Alzheimer's care. *Beds* SNF 154; ICF 11. *Private Pay Patients* 25%. *Certified* Medicaid; Medicare.
Owner Proprietary corp (Vari-Care Inc).
Admissions Requirements Medical examination.
Staff RNs 5 (ft); LPNs 18 (ft), 1 (pt); Nurses' aides 60 (ft), 6 (pt); Activities coordinators 2 (ft); Other staff 43 (ft), 5 (pt).
Facilities Dining room; Physical therapy room; Activities room; Crafts room; Laundry room; Barber/Beauty shop.
Activities Arts & crafts; Cards; Games; Reading groups; Prayer groups; Movies; Shopping trips; Dances/Social/Cultural gatherings; Intergenerational programs; Pet therapy.

Forestdale Health Care
1000 Dugan Ave, Birmingham, AL 35214
(205) 798-8780, 798-9864 FAX
Admin Darryl L Berryhill. *Dir of Nursing* Jennifer Kilpatrick. *Medical Dir* Dr Johnny Stevens.
Licensure Skilled care; Intermediate care. *Beds* SNF 40; ICF 80. *Private Pay Patients* 25%. *Certified* Medicaid; Medicare.
Owner Proprietary corp (Beverly Enterprises).
Admissions Requirements Minimum age 18.
Staff Physicians 2 (ft); RNs 2 (ft), 3 (pt); LPNs 19 (ft); Nurses' aides 38 (ft), 14 (pt); Physical therapists; Activities coordinators 1 (ft); Dietitians 1 (ft).
Facilities Dining room; Physical therapy room; Activities room; Chapel; Crafts room; Laundry room; Barber/Beauty shop; Library.
Activities Arts & crafts; Cards; Games; Reading groups; Prayer groups; Movies; Dances/Social/Cultural gatherings; Intergenerational programs; Pet therapy.

A G Gaston Home for Senior Citizens
PO Box 697, 9225 Airport Rd, Birmingham, AL 35201-0697
(205) 849-2273
Admin Loretha Chappell.
Medical Dir Dr C R Hixon.
Licensure Skilled care; Intermediate care. *Beds* SNF 39; ICF 12. *Certified* Medicare.
Owner Proprietary corp.
Admissions Requirements Medical examination; Physician's request.
Staff Physicians 1 (ft); RNs 1 (ft), 3 (pt); LPNs 5 (ft), 3 (pt); Nurses' aides 9 (ft), 3 (pt); Activities coordinators 1 (ft); Dietitians 1 (pt); Dentists 1 (pt).

Facilities Dining room; Activities room; Laundry room.
Activities Arts & crafts; Games; Prayer groups; Shopping trips; Dances/Social/Cultural gatherings.

Hanover House Nursing Home
39 Hanover Circle, Birmingham, AL 35205
(205) 933-1828
Admin Carol Grubis.
Licensure Skilled care. *Beds* 80.
Owner Proprietary corp.

Hillhaven Convalescent Center & Nursing Home—Birmingham
2728 10th Ave S, Birmingham, AL 35205
(205) 933-7010
Admin Celia Shell.
Medical Dir Dr John Buckingham.
Licensure Skilled care; Intermediate care. *Beds* 114. *Certified* Medicaid; Medicare.
Owner Proprietary corp (Hillhaven Corp).
Admissions Requirements Medical examination; Physician's request.
Staff RNs 5 (ft); LPNs 8 (ft), 5 (pt); Nurses' aides 27 (ft), 13 (pt); Physical therapists 1 (ft); Activities coordinators 1 (ft); Dietitians 1 (ft).
Facilities Dining room; Physical therapy room; Activities room; Barber/Beauty shop.
Activities Arts & crafts; Cards; Games; Reading groups; Prayer groups; Movies; Shopping trips; Dances/Social/Cultural gatherings.

Jefferson County Home
200 N Pine Hill Rd, Birmingham, AL 35217
(205) 841-5533
Admin Patrick E Nicovich.
Licensure Skilled care; Intermediate care. *Beds* SNF 148; ICF 312. *Certified* Medicaid; Medicare.
Owner Publicly owned.

Kirkwood by the River
3605 Ratliff Rd, Birmingham, AL 35210
(205) 956-2184
Admin John Hicks.
Licensure Skilled care. *Beds* 51.
Owner Nonprofit corp.

Lakeview Nursing Home
8017 2nd Ave S, Birmingham, AL 35206
(205) 836-4231
Admin Mary Mann.
Medical Dir William Doggett Jr MD.
Licensure Skilled care. *Beds* SNF 54. *Certified* Medicare.
Owner Nonprofit corp (Eastern Health System Inc).
Admissions Requirements Medical examination.
Staff RNs 2 (ft), 1 (pt); LPNs 5 (ft), 4 (pt); Nurses' aides 13 (ft), 9 (pt); Activities coordinators 1 (ft).
Facilities Dining room; Activities room; Crafts room; Laundry room; Barber/Beauty shop; Library; Sitting room.
Activities Arts & crafts; Cards; Games; Reading groups; Prayer groups; Movies; Shopping trips; Dances/Social/Cultural gatherings.

Lakeview Nursing Home Inc
8017 2nd Ave S, Birmingham, AL 35206
(205) 836-4231
Admin Mary Mann.
Licensure Skilled care; Intermediate care. *Beds* SNF 54. *Certified* Medicare.
Owner Proprietary corp.

Mary Lewis Convalescent Center/UAB
2600 Highland Ave, Birmingham, AL 35205
(205) 252-4397
Admin Grendel G Gaines. *Dir of Nursing* Grendel G Gaines. *Medical Dir* Dr T Michael Harrington.

Licensure Skilled care; Intermediate care. *Beds* SNF 20; ICF 27. *Private Pay Patients* 28%. *Certified* Medicaid; Medicare.
Owner Proprietary corp.
Admissions Requirements Medical examination.
Staff RNs 2 (ft), 2 (pt); LPNs 8 (ft), 2 (pt); Nurses' aides 12 (ft), 3 (pt); Activities coordinators 1 (ft).
Facilities Dining room; Activities room; Laundry room; Barber/Beauty shop.
Activities Arts & crafts; Cards; Games; Reading groups; Prayer groups; Movies; Shopping trips; Dances/Social/Cultural gatherings; Intergenerational programs; Pet therapy.

Methodist Home for the Aging
1424 Montclair Rd, Birmingham, AL 35210
(205) 956-4150
Admin Henry R Roberts.
Licensure Skilled care; Intermediate care. *Beds* SNF 105; ICF 16. *Certified* Medicaid; Medicare.
Owner Nonprofit corp.
Affiliation Methodist.

Mt Royal Towers
300 Royal Tower Dr, Birmingham, AL 35209
(205) 870-5666
Admin Elizabeth A Fondren.
Licensure Skilled care. *Beds* SNF 36.

Northway Convalescent Center
1424 N 25 St, Birmingham, AL 35234
(205) 328-5870
Admin Karen Waldrop.
Licensure Skilled care; Intermediate care. *Beds* SNF 60; ICF 53. *Certified* Medicaid; Medicare.
Owner Proprietary corp.

Riverchase Health Care Center
2500 Riverhaven Dr, Birmingham, AL 35244
(205) 987-0901
Admin Greg C Waycaster.
Licensure Skilled care. *Beds* SNF 120.

Rose Manor Health Care
7755 4th Ave S, Birmingham, AL 35206
(205) 833-0146
Admin Patricia Childs, acting.
Medical Dir Henry L Darnell Jr MD.
Licensure Skilled care; Intermediate care. *Beds* SNF 100; ICF 12. *Certified* Medicaid; Medicare.
Owner Proprietary corp.
Admissions Requirements Medical examination; Physician's request.
Staff Physicians 1 (pt); RNs 2 (ft); LPNs 9 (ft), 3 (pt); Nurses' aides 30 (ft); Physical therapists 1 (pt); Reality therapists 1 (pt); Recreational therapists 1 (ft); Occupational therapists 1 (pt); Speech therapists 1 (pt); Activities coordinators 1 (ft); Dietitians 1 (ft); Ophthalmologists 1 (pt); Podiatrists 1 (pt); Audiologists 1 (pt); Dentists 1 (pt).
Facilities Dining room; Activities room; Chapel; Crafts room; Barber/Beauty shop.
Activities Arts & crafts; Cards; Games; Reading groups; Prayer groups; Movies; Shopping trips.

Ruby Hill Nursing Home
PO Box 110037, Birmingham, AL 35211
(205) 428-3292
Admin Frankie H Jones. *Dir of Nursing* Veronica Scarbrough. *Medical Dir* Dr Dodson Curry.
Licensure Skilled care; Intermediate care. *Beds* SNF 25; ICF 51. *Certified* Medicaid; Medicare.
Owner Privately owned.
Admissions Requirements Medical examination; Physician's request.
Staff RNs 1 (ft), 2 (pt); LPNs 5 (ft), 4 (pt); Nurses' aides 17 (ft), 12 (pt); Activities coordinators 1 (ft), 2 (pt).

Facilities Dining room; Activities room;
Crafts room; Laundry room.
Activities Arts & crafts; Cards; Games;
Reading groups; Prayer groups; Movies.

St Lukes Nursing Home
1220 S 17th St, Birmingham, AL 35205
(205) 933-2180
Admin Terry L Durham.
Licensure Skilled care; Intermediate care. *Beds*
SNF 42; ICF 41. *Certified* Medicaid;
Medicare.
Owner Proprietary corp.

St Martin's-in-the-Pines
4941 Montevallo Rd, Birmingham, AL 35210
(205) 956-1831, 956-9124 FAX
Admin Jack K Holloway. *Dir of Nursing*
Phyllis Jacquemin. *Medical Dir* Dr Charles
Colvin.
Licensure Skilled care; Retirement;
Alzheimer's care. *Beds* SNF 125; Retirement
104. *Private Pay Patients* 100%.
Owner Nonprofit organization/foundation.
Admissions Requirements Minimum age 65;
Medical examination.
Staff Physicians 1 (ft); RNs 6 (ft); LPNs 19
(ft); Nurses' aides 70 (ft); Physical therapists
2 (ft); Recreational therapists 3 (ft);
Activities coordinators 1 (ft); Dietitians 1
(ft); Ophthalmologists 1 (ft); Podiatrists 1
(ft).
Affiliation Episcopal.
Facilities Dining room; Physical therapy
room; Activities room; Chapel; Crafts room;
Laundry room; Barber/Beauty shop; Library.
Activities Arts & crafts; Cards; Games;
Reading groups; Prayer groups; Movies;
Shopping trips; Dances/Social/Cultural
gatherings; Intergenerational programs.

South Haven Nursing Home Inc
3141 Old Columbiana Rd, Birmingham, AL
35226
(205) 822-1580
Admin Rheta S Skelton.
Medical Dir Dr Harold Simon.
Licensure Skilled care; Intermediate care. *Beds*
SNF 111. *Certified* Medicaid; Medicare.
Owner Proprietary corp.
Admissions Requirements Minimum age 65;
Medical examination; Physician's request.
Staff Physicians; RNs 5 (ft); LPNs 11 (ft);
Nurses' aides 40 (ft), 10 (pt); Recreational
therapists; Speech therapists; Activities
coordinators 1 (ft); Dietitians 1 (pt);
Podiatrists 1 (pt); Dentists 1 (pt); Medical
records persons 1 (pt).
Facilities Dining room; Physical therapy
room; Activities room; Chapel; Crafts room;
Laundry room; Barber/Beauty shop; Library;
TV rooms.
Activities Arts & crafts; Cards; Games;
Reading groups; Prayer groups; Movies;
Shopping trips; Dances/Social/Cultural
gatherings; Ceramics.

Boaz

Nursing Home of Boaz
PO Box 368, Corley Ave, Boaz, AL 35957
(205) 593-8380
Admin Martha W Williams.
Licensure Skilled care; Intermediate care. *Beds*
SNF 47; ICF 33. *Certified* Medicaid;
Medicare.
Owner Proprietary corp.

Brewton

West Gate Village Inc
Pineview St & 3rd Ave, Box 49, Brewton, AL
36427
(205) 867-6077
Admin Linda Jean Carter.

Licensure Skilled care; Intermediate care. *Beds*
SNF 82; ICF 22. *Certified* Medicaid;
Medicare.
Owner Proprietary corp.

Camden

Camden Nursing Facility
PO Box 787, Camden, AL 36726
(205) 682-4231
Admin Mildred M Jobe. *Dir of Nursing*
Mildred Hammonds RN. *Medical Dir* Dr
Sumpter Blackan.
Licensure Skilled care 10B. *Beds* Swing beds
SNF/ICF 75. *Private Pay Patients* 20%.
Certified Medicaid; Medicare.
Owner Proprietary corp (Mildred M Jobe).
Admissions Requirements Medical
examination; Physician's request.
Staff Physicians 3 (pt); RNs 3 (ft), 2 (pt);
LPNs 5 (ft), 1 (pt); Nurses' aides 25 (ft), 5
(pt); Activities coordinators 1 (ft); Dietitians
1 (ft), 1 (pt); Podiatrists 1 (pt).
Facilities Dining room; Activities room;
Chapel; Crafts room; Laundry room; Barber/
Beauty shop; Library.
Activities Arts & crafts; Cards; Games;
Reading groups; Prayer groups; Movies;
Shopping trips; Dances/Social/Cultural
gatherings.

Carbon Hill

Carbon Hill Health Care Inc
PO Box 607, 516 E 4th Ave, Carbon Hill, AL
35549
(205) 924-4404
Admin Sandra Browning. *Dir of Nursing* Judy
Dickson. *Medical Dir* Dr Greg Sullivan.
Licensure Intermediate care. *Beds* ICF 49.
Private Pay Patients 31%. *Certified*
Medicaid.
Owner Proprietary corp.
Staff LPNs 4 (ft), 2 (pt); Nurses' aides 18 (ft),
5 (pt); Activities coordinators 1 (ft); CDMs 1
(ft).
Facilities Dining room; Activities room;
Barber/Beauty shop.
Activities Arts & crafts; Cards; Games;
Reading groups; Prayer groups; Movies;
Shopping trips; Dances/Social/Cultural
gatherings; Intergenerational programs.

Centre

Cherokee County Nursing Home
PO Box 199, Hospital Ave, Centre, AL 35960
(205) 927-5778
Admin Jerry L Culberson. *Dir of Nursing* Sue
Estes RN. *Medical Dir* Dr Clark Smeltzer Jr.
Licensure Skilled care; Intermediate care;
Domiciliary care. *Beds* Swing beds SNF/ICF
53; Domiciliary care 12. *Private Pay Patients*
20%. *Certified* Medicaid; Medicare.
Owner Publicly owned.
Admissions Requirements Medical
examination; Physician's request.
Staff Physicians 2 (pt); RNs 2 (ft), 1 (pt);
LPNs 9 (ft), 1 (pt); Nurses' aides 24 (ft), 1
(pt); Physical therapists (contracted); Reality
therapists (contracted); Recreational
therapists (contracted); Occupational
therapists (contracted); Speech therapists
(contracted); Activities coordinators 1 (ft);
Dietitians 1 (ft); Social service 1 (ft).
Facilities Dining room; Activities room;
Crafts room; Laundry room; Barber/Beauty
shop.
Activities Arts & crafts; Cards; Games;
Reading groups; Prayer groups; Movies;
Shopping trips; Dances/Social/Cultural
gatherings; Intergenerational programs; Pet
therapy.

Centreville

Bibb Medical Center Hospital & Nursing Home
164 Pierson Ave, Centreville, AL 35042
(205) 926-7251
Admin Terry J Smith.
Medical Dir William O Owings MD.
Licensure Skilled care; Intermediate care. *Beds*
SNF 62; ICF 41. *Certified* Medicaid;
Medicare.
Owner Publicly owned.
Staff Physicians 4 (pt); RNs 2 (ft); LPNs 10
(ft), 2 (pt); Nurses' aides 25 (ft), 7 (pt);
Physical therapists 1 (pt); Activities
coordinators 1 (ft); Dietitians 1 (ft);
Ophthalmologists 1 (pt); Dentists 1 (pt).
Facilities Dining room; Physical therapy
room; Chapel; Barber/Beauty shop.
Activities Cards; Games; Reading groups;
Prayer groups.

Chatom

Washington County Infirmary & Nursing Home
PO Box 597, Chatom, AL 36518
(205) 847-2223
Admin Michael D Marshall. *Dir of Nursing*
Marjorie McNeal. *Medical Dir* Paul Petcher.
Licensure Skilled care; Intermediate care. *Beds*
Swing beds SNF/ICF 73. *Private Pay*
Patients 20%. *Certified* Medicaid; Medicare.
Owner Nonprofit corp.
Staff Physicians 2 (ft); RNs 2 (ft), 1 (pt);
LPNs 7 (ft), 2 (pt); Nurses' aides 28 (ft), 5
(pt); Physical therapists 1 (pt); Speech
therapists 1 (pt); Activities coordinators 1
(ft); Dietitians 1 (pt).
Facilities Dining room; Physical therapy
room; Activities room; Chapel; Crafts room;
Laundry room; Barber/Beauty shop; Library.
Activities Arts & crafts; Games; Prayer groups;
Movies; Dances/Social/Cultural gatherings;
Intergenerational programs.

Citronelle

Citronelle Convalescent Center
PO Drawer 38, 108 N 4th St, Citronelle, AL
36522
(205) 866-5509
Admin June Keller. *Dir of Nursing* Marsha
Reid. *Medical Dir* John H Prine MD.
Licensure Skilled care; Intermediate care. *Beds*
SNF 56; ICF 13. *Certified* Medicaid;
Medicare.
Owner Proprietary corp.
Admissions Requirements Minimum age 21;
Medical examination; Physician's request.
Staff RNs 1 (ft), 1 (pt); LPNs 5 (ft), 1 (pt);
Nurses' aides 19 (ft), 5 (pt); Dietitians 1 (ft).
Facilities Dining room; Physical therapy
room; Activities room; Laundry room;
Barber/Beauty shop.
Activities Arts & crafts; Cards; Games;
Reading groups; Prayer groups; Movies.

Clanton

Clanton Health Care Center Inc
1705 Lay Dam Rd, Clanton, AL 35045
(205) 755-4384
Admin Billy R Hatley.
Medical Dir Dr Kent Johns.
Licensure Skilled care; Intermediate care. *Beds*
SNF 40; ICF 10. *Certified* Medicaid;
Medicare.
Owner Proprietary corp.
Staff RNs 1 (ft), 3 (pt); LPNs 2 (ft), 3 (pt);
Nurses' aides 10 (ft), 9 (pt); Activities
coordinators 1 (ft); Dietitians 1 (ft).

Facilities Dining room; Activities room; Crafts room; Barber/Beauty shop.
Activities Arts & crafts; Cards; Games; Reading groups; Prayer groups; Movies; Dances/Social/Cultural gatherings.

Hatley Health Care Inc
300 Medical Ctr Dr, Clanton, AL 35045
(205) 755-4960
Admin Bill R Hatley. *Dir of Nursing* Betty Creest. *Medical Dir* Kent Johns MD.
Licensure Skilled care; Intermediate care. *Beds* SNF 96; ICF 23. *Certified* Medicaid; Medicare.
Owner Privately owned.
Staff RNs; LPNs; Nurses' aides; Recreational therapists; Activities coordinators; Dietitians.
Facilities Dining room; Activities room; Crafts room; Barber/Beauty shop.
Activities Arts & crafts; Cards; Games; Reading groups; Prayer groups; Movies; Dances/Social/Cultural gatherings.

Collinsville

Collinsville Nursing Home Inc
Drawer G, US Hwy 11 N, Collinsville, AL 35961
(205) 524-2117
Admin James Coker.
Licensure Skilled care; Intermediate care. *Beds* SNF 139; ICF 26. *Certified* Medicaid; Medicare.
Owner Proprietary corp.

Cook Springs

Baptist Home for Senior Citizens Inc
PO Box 10, Off I-20, Cook Springs, AL 35052
(205) 338-2221
Admin Jerry W Moss. *Dir of Nursing* Susan L Moss RN. *Medical Dir* Dr E H Edwards.
Licensure Skilled care; Intermediate care; Retirement. *Beds* SNF 93; ICF 33. *Certified* Medicaid; Medicare; VA.
Owner Proprietary corp (Northport Health Services).
Admissions Requirements Minimum age 62; Medical examination; Physician's request.
Staff Physicians 1 (pt); RNs 2 (ft), 2 (pt); LPNs 16 (ft); Nurses' aides; Physical therapists 1 (pt); Speech therapists 1 (pt); Activities coordinators 1 (ft); Dietitians 1 (ft); Ophthalmologists 1 (pt).
Affiliation Baptist.
Facilities Dining room; Physical therapy room; Activities room; Chapel; Crafts room; Laundry room; Barber/Beauty shop.
Activities Arts & crafts; Cards; Games; Reading groups; Prayer groups; Movies; Dances/Social/Cultural gatherings.

Jack Cline Nursing Home
PO Box 136, Cook Springs, AL 35052
(205) 640-5212
Admin Billie Bischoff.
Licensure Intermediate care. *Beds* 49. *Certified* Medicaid.
Owner Proprietary corp.

St Clair Health Care Center
PO Box 136, Cook Springs, AL 35052
(205) 640-5212
Admin Doris Howard.
Licensure Skilled care. *Beds* SNF 49.

Cordova

Cordova Health Care Center
200 Highland St, Cordova, AL 35550
(205) 483-9282, 483-9285 FAX
Admin John Bolton. *Dir of Nursing* Kathy Smothers. *Medical Dir* George H Weaver MD.
Licensure Skilled care; Intermediate care. *Beds* SNF 94; ICF 10. *Private Pay Patients* 20%. *Certified* Medicaid; Medicare.

Owner Proprietary corp (Northport Health Services).
Admissions Requirements Medical examination; Physician's request.
Staff Physicians; RNs; LPNs; Nurses' aides; Physical therapists; Occupational therapists; Activities coordinators; Dietitians; Podiatrists.
Facilities Dining room; Activities room; Crafts room; Laundry room; Barber/Beauty shop; Library.
Activities Arts & crafts; Cards; Games; Reading groups; Prayer groups; Movies; Shopping trips; Dances/Social/Cultural gatherings; Intergenerational programs.

Crossville

Crossville Nursing Home Inc
PO Box 97, Hwy 227, Crossville, AL 35962
(205) 528-7844
Admin Gerald Bell. *Dir of Nursing* Mary Colley RN. *Medical Dir* Raymond C Ufford MD.
Licensure Skilled care; Intermediate care. *Beds* SNF 118. *Certified* Medicaid; Medicare.
Owner Proprietary corp.
Admissions Requirements Medical examination; Physician's request.
Staff Physicians 1 (ft), 2 (pt); RNs 3 (ft); LPNs 8 (ft), 1 (pt); Nurses' aides 45 (ft), 6 (pt); Activities coordinators 1 (ft), 1 (pt); Dietitians 1 (ft).
Facilities Dining room; Physical therapy room; Activities room; Chapel; Crafts room; Laundry room; Barber/Beauty shop.
Activities Arts & crafts; Cards; Games; Reading groups; Prayer groups; Movies; Shopping trips; Dances/Social/Cultural gatherings.

Cullman

Cullman Health Care Center
PO Box 190, 1607 Main Ave NE, Cullman, AL 35055
(205) 734-8745
Admin Edith R Sinyard. *Dir of Nursing* Robin Self RN. *Medical Dir* Dr George Lyrene.
Licensure Skilled care; Intermediate care; Alzheimer's care. *Beds* SNF 44; ICF 121. *Certified* Medicaid; Medicare.
Owner Proprietary corp.
Admissions Requirements Medical examination; Physician's request.
Staff RNs 4 (ft); LPNs 18 (ft), 2 (pt); Physical therapists 1 (ft); Activities coordinators 2 (ft); Dietitians 12 (ft).
Facilities Dining room; Physical therapy room; Activities room; Chapel; Crafts room; Laundry room; Barber/Beauty shop; Library.
Activities Arts & crafts; Cards; Games; Reading groups; Prayer groups; Movies; Shopping trips; Dances/Social/Cultural gatherings; Exercise.

Woodland Village Health Care Center
PO Box 190, Cullman, AL 35056
(205) 739-1430, 739-1431 FAX
Admin Linda Robertson. *Dir of Nursing* Mattie Banks. *Medical Dir* Dr Henry Beeler.
Licensure Skilled care; Intermediate care; Domiciliary care. *Beds* SNF 46; ICF 103; Domiciliary care 44. *Certified* Medicaid; Medicare.
Owner Privately owned.
Admissions Requirements Medical examination; Physician's request.
Staff RNs 3 (ft); LPNs 16 (ft), 11 (pt); Nurses' aides 44 (ft), 19 (pt); Physical therapists 1 (pt); Activities coordinators 1 (ft); Dietitians 1 (ft).
Facilities Dining room; Physical therapy room; Activities room; Crafts room; Laundry room; Barber/Beauty shop.

Dadeville

Dadeville Convalescent Home
237 Lafayette St, Dadeville, AL 36853
(205) 825-9244
Admin Peggy Steed.
Licensure Skilled care; Intermediate care. *Beds* SNF 71; ICF 40. *Certified* Medicaid; Medicare.
Owner Proprietary corp.

Dadeville Health Care
300 Columbus St, Dadeville, AL 36853
(205) 825-7883
Admin Emma M Swindall.
Medical Dir Dr Jerry Swindall.
Licensure Skilled care. *Beds* SNF 29. *Certified* Medicaid; Medicare.
Owner Proprietary corp.
Staff Physicians 1 (ft); RNs 1 (ft), 1 (pt); LPNs 2 (ft), 6 (pt); Nurses' aides 6 (ft), 3 (pt); Recreational therapists 1 (pt); Activities coordinators 1 (pt).
Facilities Dining room; Activities room; Crafts room; Laundry room.
Activities Arts & crafts; Cards; Games; Reading groups; Prayer groups; Shopping trips.

Wilder Nursing Home
PO Box 217, 307 Lafayette St, Dadeville, AL 36853
(205) 825-7881
Admin Mary Walace Wilson.
Licensure Skilled care; Intermediate care. *Beds* SNF 47; ICF 17. *Certified* Medicaid; Medicare.
Owner Proprietary corp.

Daphne

Mercy Medical
PO Box 1090, 101 Villa Dr, Daphne, AL 36526
(205) 626-2694
Admin Sr Mary Eileen Wilhelm. *Dir of Nursing* Betty Bentley. *Medical Dir* Dr Samuel Eichold.
Licensure Skilled care; Specialized hospital; Retirement; Alzheimer's care. *Beds* SNF; Specialized hospital 137. *Certified* Medicare.
Owner Nonprofit corp.
Admissions Requirements Physician's request.
Staff Physicians 1 (pt); RNs 21 (ft), 12 (pt); LPNs 18 (ft), 3 (pt); Nurses' aides 22 (ft), 5 (pt); Physical therapists 2 (ft); Recreational therapists 1 (ft); Occupational therapists 1 (ft); Speech therapists 1 (pt); Dietitians 1 (pt).
Affiliation Roman Catholic.
Facilities Dining room; Physical therapy room; Activities room; Chapel; Crafts room; Laundry room; Barber/Beauty shop.
Activities Arts & crafts; Cards; Games; Reading groups; Prayer groups; Movies; Shopping trips; Dances/Social/Cultural gatherings.

Decatur

Flint City Nursing Home Inc
Rte 4 Box 500, Hwy 31 S, Decatur, AL 35601
(205) 355-2418
Admin Berneal McKennie.
Licensure Skilled care; Intermediate care. *Beds* SNF 46; ICF 30. *Certified* Medicaid; Medicare.
Owner Proprietary corp.

Medical Park Convalescent Center
1350 14th Ave SE, Decatur, AL 35601
(205) 355-6911

Admin Robert Anderson.
Licensure Skilled care; Intermediate care. *Beds* SNF 75; ICF 108. *Certified* Medicaid; Medicare.
Owner Proprietary corp.

South Morgan Health Care Center
PO Box 1821, Hwy 31 S, Decatur, AL 35602
(205) 355-2418
Admin Mary Jo Letson.
Licensure Skilled care; Intermediate care. *Beds* SNF 33; ICF 43.

Lurleen B Wallace Developmental Center
PO Box 2224, Decatur, AL 35609-2224
(205) 355-6810
Admin James L Vail Jr.
Licensure Intermediate care. *Beds* ICF 105.

West Morgan Health Care
PO Box 1215, Rte 1, Joe Wheeler Hwy, Decatur, AL 35601
(205) 353-5567, 353-5584 FAX
Admin Barry Bell. *Dir of Nursing* Deborah Allen. *Medical Dir* Dr Wiley.
Licensure Skilled care; Intermediate care. *Beds* SNF 20; ICF 23. *Private Pay Patients* 10%. *Certified* Medicaid; Medicare.
Owner Proprietary corp (Age Inc).
Admissions Requirements Medical examination; Physician's request.
Staff Physicians 1 (ft); RNs 1 (ft), 1 (pt); LPNs 6 (ft); Nurses' aides 18 (ft), 1 (pt); Physical therapists 1 (pt); Activities coordinators 1 (ft); Dietitians 1 (pt).
Facilities Dining room; Activities room; Crafts room; Barber/Beauty shop.
Activities Arts & crafts; Cards; Games; Reading groups; Prayer groups; Movies; Shopping trips; Dances/Social/Cultural gatherings.

Demopolis

Woodhaven Manor
105 W Windsor St, Demopolis, AL 36732
(205) 289-2741
Admin Alice Boggs.
Licensure Skilled care; Intermediate care. *Beds* SNF 35; ICF 40. *Certified* Medicaid; Medicare.
Owner Proprietary corp.

Dothan

Extendicare Health Center
814 S Saint Andrews St, Dothan, AL 36301
(205) 793-1177
Admin Helen Dennis.
Licensure Skilled care; Intermediate care. *Beds* SNF 52; ICF 57. *Certified* Medicaid; Medicare.
Owner Proprietary corp.

Wesley Manor Methodist Home for the Aging
210 Honeysuckle Rd, Dothan, AL 36301
(205) 792-0921
Admin W J Mathis Jr.
Medical Dir Lewe West MD.
Licensure Skilled care; Intermediate care. *Beds* Swing beds SNF/ICF 116. *Certified* Medicaid; Medicare.
Owner Nonprofit corp (Methodist Homes for Aging).
Admissions Requirements Minimum age 62; Medical examination.
Affiliation Methodist.
Facilities Dining room; Physical therapy room; Activities room; Chapel; Crafts room; Laundry room; Barber/Beauty shop; Library.
Activities Arts & crafts; Cards; Games; Reading groups; Prayer groups; Shopping trips; Dances/Social/Cultural gatherings; Ceramics.

Double Springs

Hendrix Health Care Center
Rte 1 Box 872, Double Springs, AL 35553
(205) 489-2136, 489-3436 FAX
Admin Larry Estes. *Dir of Nursing* Faye Donaldson. *Medical Dir* Richard Homer.
Licensure Skilled care; Intermediate care. *Beds* SNF 50; ICF 50. *Private Pay Patients* 14%. *Certified* Medicaid; Medicare.
Owner Privately owned.
Admissions Requirements Medical examination; Physician's request.
Staff Physicians 1 (ft), 1 (pt); RNs 2 (ft), 1 (pt); LPNs 8 (ft), 6 (pt); Nurses' aides 34 (ft), 10 (pt); Physical therapists 1 (pt); Occupational therapists 1 (pt); Speech therapists 1 (pt); Activities coordinators 1 (ft); Dietitians 1 (ft).
Facilities Dining room; Activities room; Laundry room; Barber/Beauty shop; Library.
Activities Arts & crafts; Cards; Games; Prayer groups; Weekend entertainment; Bible study; Exercises.

Eight Mile

Autumn Breeze Health Care Center
4525 Saint Stephens Rd, Eight Mile, AL 36613
(205) 452-0996
Admin Nancy Stanford. *Dir of Nursing* Rosalie Steiner. *Medical Dir* Howard Rubenstein.
Licensure Skilled care; Intermediate care. *Beds* SNF 86; ICF 86. *Private Pay Patients* 20%. *Certified* Medicaid; Medicare.
Owner Proprietary corp (Beverly Enterprises).
Staff RNs 4 (ft), 2 (pt); LPNs 31 (ft); Nurses' aides 75 (ft), 6 (pt); Physical therapists 1 (ft); Recreational therapists 1 (ft); Occupational therapists 1 (ft); Speech therapists 1 (ft); Activities coordinators 2 (ft); Dietitians 2 (ft); Ophthalmologists 1 (ft); Podiatrists 1 (ft).
Facilities Dining room; Physical therapy room; Activities room; Laundry room; Barber/Beauty shop.
Activities Arts & crafts; Cards; Games; Reading groups; Prayer groups; Movies; Shopping trips; Dances/Social/Cultural gatherings; Intergenerational programs; Pet therapy.

Elba

Elba General Hospital & Nursing Home
987 Drayton St, Elba, AL 36323
(205) 897-2257
Admin Marcy Campbell.
Medical Dir John Mason Kimmey MD.
Licensure Skilled care. *Beds* SNF 79. *Certified* Medicaid; Medicare.
Owner Proprietary corp (National Healthcare).
Admissions Requirements Medical examination; Physician's request.
Staff Physicians 3 (pt); RNs 3 (ft); LPNs 8 (ft); Nurses' aides 19 (ft); Physical therapists 1 (pt); Activities coordinators 1 (ft); Dietitians 1 (pt).
Facilities Dining room; Physical therapy room; Activities room; Laundry room; Barber/Beauty shop.
Activities Arts & crafts; Games; Reading groups; Prayer groups; Movies; Shopping trips; Dances/Social/Cultural gatherings; Television.

Elmore

Merry Wood Lodge
PO Box 7, Mount Hebron Rd, Elmore, AL 36025
(205) 567-8484
Admin Janell Vest.
Licensure Skilled care. *Beds* SNF 124.

Enterprise

Enterprise Hospital & Nursing Home
PO Box 1220, Enterprise, AL 36331
(205) 347-9541, 393-6364 FAX
Admin J Alan Kent. *Dir of Nursing* Marie Lepore. *Medical Dir* David N Rhyne MD.
Licensure Skilled care; Intermediate care; Intermediate care for mentally retarded; Retirement. *Beds* ICF/MR 41; Swing beds SNF/ICF 110; Retirement apts 40. *Private Pay Patients* 33%. *Certified* Medicaid; Medicare.
Owner Publicly owned.
Admissions Requirements Medical examination; Physician's request.
Staff RNs 3 (ft), 1 (pt); LPNs 20 (ft); Activities coordinators 4 (ft); Dietitians 1 (pt); Physical therapy aides 1 (ft).
Facilities Dining room; Physical therapy room; Activities room; Crafts room; Barber/Beauty shop.
Activities Arts & crafts; Cards; Games; Reading groups; Prayer groups; Movies; Shopping trips; Dances/Social/Cultural gatherings; Pet therapy.

Eufaula

Eufaula Geriatric Center
430 Rivers Ave, Eufaula, AL 36027
(205) 687-6627
Admin Diane Sanders, acting. *Dir of Nursing* Laura Perry RN. *Medical Dir* Tim Shaw MD.
Licensure Skilled care; Intermediate care. *Beds* SNF 120; ICF 60. *Certified* Medicaid; Medicare.
Owner Proprietary corp (Beverly Enterprises).
Admissions Requirements Physician's request.
Staff Physicians 1 (pt); RNs 4 (ft), 1 (pt); LPNs 20 (ft), 3 (pt); Nurses' aides 50 (ft), 8 (pt); Activities coordinators 2 (ft); Dietitians 1 (pt); Social services 1 (ft).
Affiliation Baptist.
Facilities Dining room; Activities room; Crafts room; Laundry room; Barber/Beauty shop.
Activities Arts & crafts; Games; Reading groups; Prayer groups; Movies.

Eutaw

Greene County Hospital & Nursing Home
509 Wilson Ave, Eutaw, AL 35462
(205) 372-3388
Admin Robert J Coker, Jr.
Medical Dir Dr Rucker Staggers.
Licensure Skilled care; Intermediate care. *Beds* SNF 52. *Certified* Medicaid; Medicare.
Owner Publicly owned.
Admissions Requirements Physician's request.
Staff Physicians 5 (ft), 1 (pt); RNs 1 (ft), 1 (pt); LPNs 6 (ft), 1 (pt); Nurses' aides 14 (ft), 10 (pt); Physical therapists 1 (pt); Activities coordinators 1 (pt); Dietitians 1 (ft).
Facilities Dining room; Physical therapy room; Laundry room; Barber/Beauty shop.
Activities Arts & crafts; Cards; Games; Reading groups; Dances/Social/Cultural gatherings.

Evergreen

Evergreen Nursing Home
PO Box 391, Knoxville St, Evergreen, AL 36401
(205) 578-3783
Admin James A Ansley.
Licensure Skilled care; Intermediate care. *Beds* SNF 41; ICF 10. *Certified* Medicaid; Medicare.
Owner Proprietary corp.

Evergreen Nursing Home
PO Box 391, Knoxville St, Evergreen, AL
36401
(205) 578-3783
Admin James A Ansley.
Licensure Skilled care; Intermediate care. *Beds*
SNF 41; ICF 10.

Fairfield

Beverly Health Care Center—West
6825 Grasslli Rd, Fairfield, AL 35064
(205) 780-3920
Admin John Mack.
Licensure Skilled care. *Beds* SNF 190.
Owner Proprietary corp (Beverly Enterprises).

Fairfield Health Care Center
6825 Grasselli Rd, Fairfield, AL 35064
(205) 780-3920
Admin Lee O'Dell.
Medical Dir Jack C Whites MD.
Licensure Skilled care; Intermediate care. *Beds*
SNF 115; ICF 75. *Certified* Medicaid;
Medicare.
Owner Proprietary corp.
Admissions Requirements Minimum age 21;
Medical examination; Physician's request.
Staff Physicians 1 (pt); RNs 3 (ft); LPNs 25
(ft), 10 (pt); Nurses' aides 40 (ft), 20 (pt);
Physical therapists 1 (pt); Recreational
therapists 1 (pt); Occupational therapists 1
(pt); Speech therapists 1 (pt); Activities
coordinators 2 (ft); Dietitians 1 (ft);
Podiatrists 1 (pt); Audiologists 1 (pt);
Dentists 1 (pt).
Facilities Dining room; Physical therapy
room; Activities room; Chapel; Crafts room;
Laundry room; Barber/Beauty shop;
Treatment room.
Activities Arts & crafts; Cards; Games;
Reading groups; Prayer groups; Movies;
Shopping trips; Dances/Social/Cultural
gatherings.

Fairhope

Eastern Shore Health Care
PO Box 976, Fairhope, AL 36532
(205) 928-2153
Admin Ron Smith. *Dir of Nursing* Mindy
Browning. *Medical Dir* Dr Sam Eichold.
Licensure Skilled care. *Beds* SNF 131. *Private
Pay Patients* 20%. *Certified* Medicaid;
Medicare.
Owner Proprietary corp (Beverly Enterprises).
Staff Physicians; RNs 5 (ft), 1 (pt); LPNs 10
(ft), 1 (pt); Nurses' aides 30 (ft), 5 (pt);
Physical therapists (contracted);
Occupational therapists (contracted); Speech
therapists (contracted); Activities
coordinators 2 (ft); Dietitians 1 (ft).
Facilities Dining room; Physical therapy
room; Activities room; Crafts room; Laundry
room; Barber/Beauty shop.
Activities Arts & crafts; Cards; Games;
Reading groups; Prayer groups; Movies;
Shopping trips; Dances/Social/Cultural
gatherings; Intergenerational programs; Pet
therapy.

Montrose Bay Health Care Center
PO Box 256, Scenic Hwy 98, Fairhope, AL
36559
(205) 928-2177
Admin Roland R Garney. *Dir of Nursing* Pat
McArthur RN. *Medical Dir* Thomas Yancey
MD.
Licensure Skilled care; Intermediate care. *Beds*
SNF 71; ICF 12. *Certified* Medicaid;
Medicare; VA.
Owner Proprietary corp (Vari-care Inc).
Admissions Requirements Medical
examination; Physician's request.

Staff RNs 2 (ft), 1 (pt); LPNs 6 (ft), 1 (pt);
Nurses' aides 28 (ft), 4 (pt); Physical
therapists 1 (pt); Speech therapists 1 (pt);
Activities coordinators 1 (ft); Dietitians 1
(pt).
Facilities Dining room; Physical therapy
room; Activities room; Crafts room; Laundry
room; Barber/Beauty shop.
Activities Arts & crafts; Cards; Games; Prayer
groups; Movies; Shopping trips; Dances/
Social/Cultural gatherings.

Falkville

Falkville Health Care Center
PO Box 409, 3rd St, Falkville, AL 35622
(205) 784-5291
Admin Frank Brown. *Dir of Nursing* Tommie
Ponter. *Medical Dir* Dinesh Gandhi MD.
Licensure Skilled care; Intermediate care. *Beds*
SNF 42; ICF 63. *Certified* Medicaid;
Medicare.
Owner Proprietary corp (Age Inc).
Staff Physicians 1 (ft); RNs 3 (ft); LPNs 17
(ft); Nurses' aides 45 (ft); Physical therapists
1 (ft); Activities coordinators 1 (ft);
Dietitians 1 (ft).
Facilities Dining room; Physical therapy
room; Activities room; Chapel; Laundry
room; Barber/Beauty shop.
Activities Arts & crafts; Games; Prayer groups;
Movies; Dances/Social/Cultural gatherings;
Pet therapy.

Summerford Nursing Home Inc
Rte 2 Box 18, Hwy 31 North, Falkville, AL
35622
(205) 784-5275
Admin Robert O Summerford. *Dir of Nursing*
Barbara Pruett. *Medical Dir* John
Summerford MD.
Licensure Skilled care; Intermediate care. *Beds*
SNF 163; ICF 33. *Certified* Medicaid;
Medicare.
Owner Proprietary corp.
Staff Physicians 3 (pt); RNs 3 (ft), 1 (pt);
LPNs 19 (ft), 4 (pt); Nurses' aides 56 (ft), 6
(pt); Physical therapists 1 (pt); Occupational
therapists 1 (ft); Speech therapists 1 (pt);
Activities coordinators 5 (ft); Dietitians 1
(pt).
Facilities Dining room; Physical therapy
room; Activities room; Chapel; Crafts room;
Laundry room; Barber/Beauty shop.
Activities Arts & crafts; Cards; Games;
Reading groups; Prayer groups.

Fayette

Fayette County Hospital & Nursing Home
PO Box 878, 1653 Temple Ave N, Fayette,
AL 35555
(205) 932-5966
Admin Barbara Flynn. *Dir of Nursing* Barbara
Flynn. *Medical Dir* Henry Hodo.
Licensure Skilled care; Intermediate care;
Alzheimer's care. *Beds* Swing beds SNF/ICF
101. *Private Pay Patients* 25%. *Certified*
Medicaid; Medicare.
Owner Nonprofit organization/foundation.
Admissions Requirements Medical
examination; Physician's request.
Staff Physicians 5 (ft), 8 (pt); RNs 2 (ft), 3
(pt); LPNs 11 (ft), 2 (pt); Nurses' aides 15
(ft), 12 (pt); Physical therapists 1 (ft);
Occupational therapists 1 (pt); Speech
therapists 1 (pt); Activities coordinators 1
(ft); Dietitians 1 (pt); Dentists 1 (pt).
Facilities Dining room; Physical therapy
room; Activities room; Laundry room;
Barber/Beauty shop; Library; Park.
Activities Arts & crafts; Cards; Games;
Reading groups; Prayer groups; Movies;
Shopping trips; Community church support.

Florence

El Reposo Sanitarium
Box 530, Rte 5, Florence, AL 35630
(205) 757-2143
Admin R Wayne Hayward. *Dir of Nursing*
Ramona Clarke RN.
Licensure Intermediate care. *Beds* ICF 40.
Certified Medicaid.
Owner Nonprofit corp.
Admissions Requirements Medical
examination; Physician's request.
Staff RNs 1 (ft); LPNs 2 (ft), 2 (pt); Nurses'
aides 9 (ft), 7 (pt); Activities coordinators 1
(ft); Dietitians 1 (ft).
Facilities Dining room; Activities room;
Lounge.
Activities Games; Prayer groups; Movies; Bus
rides.

Glenwood Convalescent Center
210 Ana Dr, Florence, AL 35630
(205) 766-8963
Admin Timothy L Morrow.
Licensure Skilled care. *Beds* 114. *Certified*
Medicaid; Medicare.
Owner Proprietary corp.

**Mitchell-Hollingworth Annex to Eliza Coffee
Memorial Hospital**
PO Box 818, Flagg Circle, Florence, AL 35631
(205) 767-4002
Admin J Thomas Whetstone. *Dir of Nursing* J
L Shelton. *Medical Dir* L L Hibbett MD.
Licensure Skilled care; Intermediate care;
Retirement. *Beds* 202. *Certified* Medicaid;
Medicare.
Owner Nonprofit corp.
Admissions Requirements Medical
examination; Physician's request.
Staff RNs 7 (ft), 2 (pt); LPNs 25 (ft), 1 (pt);
Nurses' aides 60 (ft), 6 (pt); Physical
therapists 1 (ft), 1 (pt); Recreational
therapists 2 (pt); Activities coordinators 1
(ft); Dietitians 1 (ft); Dentists 1 (pt).
Facilities Dining room; Physical therapy
room; Activities room; Crafts room; Laundry
room; Barber/Beauty shop; Library.
Activities Arts & crafts; Cards; Games;
Dances/Social/Cultural gatherings; Exercise
class.

Rolling Acres Nursing Home
2107 Cloyd Blvd, Florence, AL 35630
(205) 766-5771
Admin Hiller Dickerson.
Licensure Skilled care; Intermediate care. *Beds*
SNF 118; ICF 16.

Foley

Foley Nursing Home
1701 N Alston St, Foley, AL 36535
(205) 943-2781
Admin Lynn Wells.
Licensure Skilled care; Intermediate care. *Beds*
SNF 74; ICF 80. *Certified* Medicaid;
Medicare.
Owner Proprietary corp (Beverly Enterprises).

Fort Payne

Mountain Manor Nursing Home Inc
403 13th St NW, Fort Payne, AL 35967
(205) 845-5990
Admin Robert Morrow.
Medical Dir Dr William Holtlin.
Licensure Skilled care; Intermediate care. *Beds*
SNF 95; ICF 28. *Certified* Medicaid;
Medicare.
Owner Proprietary corp.
Admissions Requirements Physician's request.
Staff Physicians 4 (pt); RNs 3 (ft), 1 (pt);
LPNs 9 (ft), 6 (pt); Nurses' aides 44 (ft), 4
(pt); Activities coordinators 1 (ft); Dietitians
1 (pt).

Facilities Dining room; Activities room; Laundry room; Barber/Beauty shop; Two living rooms.
Activities Arts & crafts; Games; Reading groups; Prayer groups; Movies; Shopping trips.

Gadsden

Gadsden Health Care Center Inc
1945 Davis Dr, Gadsden, AL 35999
(205) 547-4938
Admin W R Lester.
Medical Dir Dr John B Keeling.
Licensure Skilled care; Intermediate care. *Beds* 152. *Certified* Medicaid; Medicare.
Owner Proprietary corp.
Facilities Dining room; Physical therapy room; Activities room; Chapel; Crafts room; Laundry room; Barber/Beauty shop.
Activities Arts & crafts; Cards; Games; Reading groups; Prayer groups; Movies; Shopping trips; Dances/Social/Cultural gatherings.

McGuffey Health Care Center
2301 Rainbow Dr, Gadsden, AL 35999
(205) 543-3467
Admin Linda C Withers. *Dir of Nursing* Janet Jacobs RN. *Medical Dir* Dr Myron Hawkins.
Licensure Skilled care; Intermediate care. *Beds* SNF 146; ICF 62. *Private Pay Patients* 28%. *Certified* Medicaid; Medicare.
Owner Proprietary corp.
Admissions Requirements Medical examination.
Staff Physicians 1 (pt); RNs 7 (ft); LPNs 16 (ft), 5 (pt); Nurses' aides 85 (ft), 8 (pt); Physical therapists (consultant); Speech therapists (contracted); Activities coordinators 1 (ft); Dietitians (consultant).
Facilities Dining room; Physical therapy room; Activities room; Barber/Beauty shop; Library.
Activities Arts & crafts; Cards; Games; Reading groups; Prayer groups; Movies; Shopping trips; Dances/Social/Cultural gatherings; Intergenerational programs.

Wessex House of Gadsen
700 Hutchins St, Gadsden, AL 35901
(205) 543-7101
Admin Carroll A Crane.
Licensure Skilled care. *Beds* SNF 105. *Certified* Medicaid; Medicare.
Owner Proprietary corp.

Gardendale

Gardendale Nursing Home
420 Dean Lane, Gardendale, AL 35071
(205) 631-8700
Admin Faith M Hammock. *Dir of Nursing* Sue Gibson RN.
Licensure Skilled care. *Beds* 148. *Certified* Medicaid; Medicare.
Owner Proprietary corp.
Admissions Requirements Minimum age 18; Medical examination; Physician's request.
Staff RNs 3 (ft), 1 (pt); LPNs 13 (ft), 4 (pt); Nurses' aides 52 (ft), 17 (pt); Recreational therapists 1 (ft), 2 (pt); Activities coordinators 1 (ft).
Facilities Dining room; Physical therapy room; Activities room; Chapel; Laundry room; Barber/Beauty shop.
Activities Arts & crafts; Cards; Games; Prayer groups; Movies.

Geneva

Wiregrass Nursing Home
1200 W Maple Ave, Geneva, AL 36340
(205) 684-3655
Admin Sue Paschall. *Dir of Nursing* Sue Paschall. *Medical Dir* John C Miller MD.

Licensure Skilled care; Intermediate care. *Beds* Swing beds SNF/ICF 86. *Private Pay Patients* 21%. *Certified* Medicaid; Medicare.
Owner Publicly owned.
Admissions Requirements Physician's request.
Staff Physicians 1 (pt); RNs 5 (ft); LPNs 9 (ft); Nurses' aides 29 (ft), 1 (pt); Activities coordinators 2 (ft), 1 (pt); Dietitians 1 (pt); Housekeepers 5 (ft).
Facilities Dining room; Activities room; Crafts room; Laundry room; Barber/Beauty shop; Library.
Activities Arts & crafts; Cards; Games; Reading groups; Prayer groups; Movies; Shopping trips; Dances/Social/Cultural gatherings; Pet therapy.

Georgiana

Georgiana Nursing Facility
Rte 2 Box 1C, Georgiana, AL 36033
(205) 376-2267, 376-2134 FAX
Admin Alice Newton. *Dir of Nursing* Martha Pettit. *Medical Dir* Dr Jeffrey Voreis.
Licensure Skilled care; Intermediate care. *Beds* SNF 56; ICF 5. *Certified* Medicaid; Medicare.
Owner Nonprofit corp (Northport Health Services).
Staff Physicians 2 (ft); RNs 1 (ft), 2 (pt); LPNs 8 (ft); Nurses' aides 23 (ft); Activities coordinators 1 (ft); Dietitians 1 (ft).
Facilities Dining room; Activities room; Chapel; Crafts room; Laundry room; Barber/Beauty shop; Library.
Activities Arts & crafts; Cards; Games; Reading groups; Prayer groups; Movies; Shopping trips; Pet therapy.

Glencoe

Coosa Valley Healthcare Inc
426 Pineview Ave, Glencoe, AL 35905
(205) 492-5350
Admin Mark J Cook.
Licensure Skilled care; Intermediate care. *Beds* SNF 124. *Certified* Medicaid; Medicare.
Owner Proprietary corp.

Goodwater

Goodwater Nursing Home
100 Mountain St, Goodwater, AL 35072
(205) 839-6711
Admin John R Chapman Jr. *Dir of Nursing* Janey Cox RN. *Medical Dir* Dr John James.
Licensure Skilled care; Intermediate care. *Beds* SNF 42; ICF. *Certified* Medicaid; Medicare.
Owner Proprietary corp.
Staff Physicians 1 (ft); RNs 1 (ft), 2 (pt); LPNs 3 (ft), 3 (pt); Nurses' aides 14 (ft), 1 (pt); Activities coordinators 1 (ft), 1 (pt); Dietitians 3 (ft), 4 (pt).
Facilities Dining room; Activities room; Chapel; Crafts room; Laundry room; Barber/Beauty shop; Library.
Activities Arts & crafts; Cards; Games; Reading groups; Prayer groups; Movies; Shopping trips; Dances/Social/Cultural gatherings.

Grand Bay

Grand Bay Convalescent Home
PO Box 328, Hwy 90 W, Grand Bay, AL 36541
(205) 865-6443
Admin Marlene H Hart.
Licensure Intermediate care. *Beds* 53. *Certified* Medicaid.
Owner Proprietary corp.

Greensboro

Greensboro Health Care Inc
616 Armory St, Greensboro, AL 36744
(205) 624-3054
Admin Margaret Kynart. *Dir of Nursing* Rebekah Bonds. *Medical Dir* Chester Singleton MD.
Licensure Skilled care. *Beds* 102. *Certified* Medicaid; Medicare.
Owner Proprietary corp.
Admissions Requirements Medical examination; Physician's request.
Staff RNs; LPNs; Nurses' aides; Physical therapists; Speech therapists; Activities coordinators; Dietitians.
Facilities Dining room; Activities room; Crafts room; Laundry room; Barber/Beauty shop.
Activities Arts & crafts; Cards; Games; Reading groups; Prayer groups; Movies; Dances/Social/Cultural gatherings.

Greenville

Greenville Nursing Home
408 Country Club Dr, Greenville, AL 36037
(205) 382-2693
Admin June P Joyner.
Licensure Skilled care; Intermediate care. *Beds* SNF 66; ICF 52. *Certified* Medicaid; Medicare.
Owner Proprietary corp.

Guin

Marion Sunset Manor
PO Box 159, Guin, AL 35563
(205) 468-3331
Admin R Stanley Junkin.
Medical Dir Dianna B Junkin.
Licensure Skilled care; Intermediate care; Alzheimer's care. *Beds* SNF 33; ICF 18. *Certified* Medicaid; Medicare.
Owner Proprietary corp.
Admissions Requirements Medical examination.
Staff Physicians 1 (pt); RNs 1 (ft), 1 (pt); LPNs 3 (ft), 3 (pt); Nurses' aides 11 (ft), 10 (pt); Activities coordinators 1 (ft); Dietitians 1 (ft).
Facilities Dining room; Crafts room; Laundry room; Barber/Beauty shop.
Activities Arts & crafts; Games; Prayer groups; Movies; Fishing trips; Picnics.

Guntersville

Barfield Health Care Inc
Star Rte 62 Box 167, Guntersville, AL 35976
(205) 582-3112
Admin E B Barfield Jr. *Dir of Nursing* Lorraine Hall RN. *Medical Dir* Dr Dalton Diamond.
Licensure Skilled care; Intermediate care. *Beds* SNF 38; ICF 65. *Private Pay Patients* 30%. *Certified* Medicaid; Medicare.
Owner Privately owned.
Admissions Requirements Medical examination.
Staff Physicians 2 (ft); RNs 3 (ft); LPNs 7 (ft); Nurses' aides 34 (ft), 1 (pt); Recreational therapists 1 (ft); Activities coordinators 1 (ft); Dietitians 1 (ft); Chaplains 1 (ft); Cosmetologists 1 (ft).
Languages Hungarian.
Facilities Dining room; Activities room; Chapel; Crafts room; Laundry room; Barber/Beauty shop; Covered patio; 2 Sun rooms; Front porches; Living room; TV lounges; Gazebo.
Activities Arts & crafts; Cards; Games; Reading groups; Prayer groups; Movies; Shopping trips; Dances/Social/Cultural

gatherings; Intergenerational programs; Pet therapy; Ceramics classes; Bible study; Religious services; Yearly revival.

Marshall Manor
3120 North St, Guntersville, AL 35976
(205) 582-6561
Admin Patti L Farley.
Licensure Skilled care. *Beds* SNF 91.

Haleyville

Haleyville Health Care Center
PO Box 160, 2201 11th Ave, Haleyville, AL 35565
(205) 486-9478
Admin Iris Schumann.
Licensure Skilled care; Intermediate care. *Beds* SNF 34; ICF 63. *Certified* Medicaid; Medicare.
Owner Proprietary corp.
Staff RNs 2 (ft), 2 (pt); LPNs 13 (ft), 2 (pt); Nurses' aides 50 (ft), 5 (pt); Activities coordinators 1 (ft); Dietitians 1 (ft), 1 (pt).
Facilities Dining room; Activities room; Crafts room; Laundry room; Barber/Beauty shop; Library.
Activities Arts & crafts; Cards; Games; Reading groups; Prayer groups; Movies; Shopping trips; Dances/Social/Cultural gatherings.

Hamilton

Marion County General Hospital & Nursing Home
1315 Military St South, Hamilton, AL 35570
(205) 921-7861
Admin Tom Cronemeyer, acting. *Dir of Nursing* Geri Gilliland RN. *Medical Dir* Charles Pyle MD.
Licensure Skilled care; Intermediate care. *Beds* 69. *Certified* Medicaid; Medicare.
Owner Proprietary corp.
Admissions Requirements Physician's request.
Staff RNs 2 (ft); LPNs 5 (ft), 5 (pt); Nurses' aides 13 (ft), 11 (pt); Physical therapists 1 (pt); Recreational therapists 1 (ft); Activities coordinators 1 (ft).

Hanceville

Hanceville Nursing Home
PO Box 409, US Hwy 31 N, Hanceville, AL 35077
(205) 352-6481
Admin James D Moody. *Dir of Nursing* Linda Looney. *Medical Dir* Henry Beeler MD.
Licensure Skilled care; Intermediate care. *Beds* SNF 136; ICF 20. *Certified* Medicaid; Medicare.
Owner Proprietary corp.
Staff RNs; LPNs; Nurses' aides; Activities coordinators; Dietitians.

Heflin

Cleburne Community Hospital & Nursing Home
PO Box 398, 411 Ross St, Heflin, AL 36264
(205) 463-2121
Admin James M Jumper.
Medical Dir Dr David Justice.
Licensure Skilled care. *Beds* 40. *Certified* Medicare.
Owner Proprietary corp (Healthcare Management).
Staff Physicians 3 (ft), 1 (pt); RNs 6 (ft), 4 (pt); LPNs 12 (ft), 4 (pt); Nurses' aides 13 (ft), 5 (pt); Activities coordinators 1 (ft).
Facilities Dining room; Activities room; Chapel; Laundry room; Barber/Beauty shop; Library.

Hueytown

Hueytown Nursing Home
190 Brooklane Dr, Hueytown, AL 35023
(205) 491-2905
Admin Charlotte Hooton. *Dir of Nursing* Judy Mink RN. *Medical Dir* Dr David Barthold.
Licensure Skilled care. *Beds* SNF 16. *Private Pay Patients* 20%. *Certified* Medicaid; Medicare.
Owner Proprietary corp (Vantage Healthcare).
Staff RNs; LPNs; Nurses' aides; Activities coordinators; Dietitians; Podiatrists.
Facilities Dining room; Activities room; Chapel; Laundry room; Barber/Beauty shop.
Activities Arts & crafts; Games; Reading groups; Movies; Shopping trips; Dances/Social/Cultural gatherings; Pet therapy.

Self Nursing Home Inc
131 Crest Rd, Hueytown, AL 35020
(205) 491-2411
Admin J A Self Jr.
Licensure Skilled care; Intermediate care. *Beds* SNF 75; ICF 56. *Certified* Medicaid; Medicare.
Owner Proprietary corp.

Huntsville

Big Spring Manor
500 Saint Clair Ave, Huntsville, AL 35801
(205) 539-5111
Admin Jerri C Dickerson. *Dir of Nursing* Jimmy Jones. *Medical Dir* John Piersma.
Licensure Skilled care; Intermediate care; Alzheimer's care. *Beds* SNF 102; ICF 30. *Private Pay Patients* 80%. *Certified* Medicaid; Medicare.
Owner Proprietary corp.
Admissions Requirements Medical examination; Physician's request.
Staff Physicians 40 (pt); RNs 5 (ft); LPNs 10 (pt); Nurses' aides 60 (ft); Physical therapists 1 (pt); Speech therapists 1 (pt); Activities coordinators 1 (ft); Dietitians 1 (ft); Ophthalmologists 1 (pt); Podiatrists 1 (pt).
Languages German.
Activities Arts & crafts; Cards; Games; Reading groups; Prayer groups; Movies; Shopping trips; Dances/Social/Cultural gatherings; Intergenerational programs; Pet therapy.

Huntsville Nursing Home Inc
4320 Judith Ln, Huntsville, AL 35805
(205) 837-1730
Admin Phillip Rollins. *Dir of Nursing* Lee Hardison.
Licensure Skilled care; Intermediate care. *Beds* SNF 19; ICF 110. *Certified* Medicaid; Medicare.
Owner Proprietary corp (Wessex Corp).
Admissions Requirements Medical examination; Physician's request.
Staff Physicians 1 (pt); RNs 2 (ft), 1 (pt); LPNs 15 (ft); Nurses' aides 50 (ft); Physical therapists 1 (ft); Speech therapists 1 (ft); Activities coordinators 1 (ft); Dietitians 1 (pt).
Facilities Dining room; Physical therapy room; Activities room; Crafts room; Barber/Beauty shop.
Activities Arts & crafts; Cards; Games; Reading groups; Prayer groups; Movies; Dances/Social/Cultural gatherings.

Volunteers of America ICF/MR No 20
1000 Church St, Huntsville, AL 35805
(205) 534-9921
Admin Victor H Tucker.
Licensure Intermediate care. *Beds* ICF 15.

Wessex House of Huntsville
4411 McAllister Dr SE, Huntsville, AL 35805
(205) 837-8585
Admin Phillip R Rollins.

Licensure Skilled care. *Beds* SNF 46; Unskilled 42.

Whitesburg Manor Health Care Center
105 Teakwood Dr, Huntsville, AL 35801
(205) 881-5000
Admin William H Birmingham Jr. *Dir of Nursing* Leslie Enright RN. *Medical Dir* Michael McCarthy MD.
Licensure Skilled care; Intermediate care; Alzheimer's care. *Beds* SNF 80; ICF 79. *Certified* Medicaid; Medicare.
Owner Proprietary corp (Hillhaven Corp).
Staff Physicians; RNs; LPNs; Nurses' aides; Physical therapists; Occupational therapists; Speech therapists; Activities coordinators; Dietitians; Ophthalmologists.
Languages German, Spanish.
Facilities Dining room; Physical therapy room; Activities room; Chapel; Laundry room; Barber/Beauty shop; Library; Sewing room.
Activities Arts & crafts; Cards; Games; Reading groups; Prayer groups; Movies; Shopping trips; Dances/Social/Cultural gatherings; Bingo; Garden club; Sittercise.

Jackson

Jackson Health Care Facility
2616 N College Ave, Jackson, AL 36545-0247
(205) 246-2476
Admin Bonnie Johnson.
Licensure Skilled care; Intermediate care. *Beds* SNF 70; ICF 21. *Certified* Medicaid; Medicare.
Owner Proprietary corp.

Jacksonville

Wessex of Jacksonville
410 Wilson Dr SW, Jacksonville, AL 36265
(205) 435-7704, 435-6917 FAX
Admin Gertie Lowe. *Dir of Nursing* Glenda Fells RN. *Medical Dir* Dr Russell Ulrich; Dr James Yates.
Licensure Skilled care; Intermediate care. *Beds* SNF 49; ICF 118. *Private Pay Patients* 33%. *Certified* Medicaid; Medicare.
Owner Privately owned (H Max Huie).
Admissions Requirements Minimum age 21; Medical examination; Physician's request.
Staff Physicians (consultant); RNs 5 (ft); LPNs 22 (ft); Nurses' aides 56 (ft); Physical therapists (consultant); Recreational therapists 1 (ft); Speech therapists (consultant); Activities coordinators 1 (ft); Dietitians (consultant).
Facilities Dining room; Physical therapy room; Activities room; Laundry room; Barber/Beauty shop.
Activities Arts & crafts; Cards; Games; Reading groups; Prayer groups; Movies; Shopping trips; Dances/Social/Cultural gatherings; Pet therapy.

Jasper

Ridgeview Health Care Center Inc
907 11th St NE, Jasper, AL 35501
(205) 221-9111
Admin Joe W Kelley Jr.
Licensure Skilled care; Intermediate care. *Beds* SNF 93; ICF 55. *Certified* Medicaid; Medicare.
Owner Proprietary corp.

Ridgewood Health Care Center Inc
201 4th Ave N, Jasper, AL 35501
(205) 221-4862
Admin J Frank Caldwell.
Licensure Skilled care. *Beds* 98. *Certified* Medicaid; Medicare.
Owner Proprietary corp.

Shadescrest Health Care Center
PO Box 1012, 2600 Old Parrish Hwy, Jasper,
AL 35501
(205) 384-9086
Admin Lynda D Ensor.
Licensure Skilled care; Intermediate care. *Beds*
SNF 77; ICF 30. *Certified* Medicaid;
Medicare.
Owner Proprietary corp.

Killen

Lauderdale Christian Nursing Home
PO Box 189, Rte 2, Killen, AL 35645
(205) 757-2103
Admin Louis E Cottrell Jr.
Licensure Skilled care; Intermediate care. *Beds*
SNF 38; ICF 20. *Certified* Medicaid;
Medicare.
Owner Nonprofit corp.

Lafayette

Lafayette Extended Care
805 Hospital St, Lafayette, AL 36862
(205) 864-8854
Admin Alice England. *Dir of Nursing* Bonnie
Mcvay RN. *Medical Dir* Emma M Swindall
MD.
Licensure Skilled care; Intermediate care. *Beds*
SNF 47. *Certified* Medicaid; Medicare.
Owner Proprietary corp.
Admissions Requirements Medical
examination.
Staff Physicians 1 (ft); RNs 1 (ft), 1 (pt);
LPNs 1 (ft), 8 (pt); Nurses' aides 11 (ft), 8
(pt); Activities coordinators 1 (ft).
Facilities Dining room; Activities room;
Laundry room; Barber/Beauty shop; Library.
Activities Arts & crafts; Cards; Games;
Reading groups; Prayer groups; Movies;
Shopping trips; Dances/Social/Cultural
gatherings.

LaFayette Nursing Home Inc
PO Box 109, 555 B St SW, Lafayette, AL
36862
(205) 864-9371
Admin Tommy F Pike. *Dir of Nursing* Kathy
Lamb LPN. *Medical Dir* J M D Holmes
MD.
Licensure Intermediate care. *Beds* ICF 45.
Private Pay Patients 99%. *Certified*
Medicaid.
Owner Privately owned.
Staff Physicians 1 (ft); RNs 1 (pt); LPNs 7
(ft); Nurses' aides 13 (ft); Activities
coordinators 1 (ft); Other staff 13 (ft).
Facilities Dining room; Laundry room.
Activities Arts & crafts; Cards; Games; Prayer
groups; Dances/Social/Cultural gatherings.

Lanett

Lanett Geriatric Center Inc
702 S 13th St, Lanett, AL 36863
(205) 644-1111
Admin Betty J Groover.
Licensure Skilled care; Intermediate care. *Beds*
SNF 44; ICF 21. *Certified* Medicaid;
Medicare.
Owner Proprietary corp.

Linden

Marengo Nursing Home
608 N Main St, Linden, AL 36748
(205) 295-8631
Admin J H Beckham.
Licensure Skilled care; Intermediate care. *Beds*
SNF 34; ICF 26. *Certified* Medicaid;
Medicare.
Owner Proprietary / corp.

Lineville

Lineville Nursing Facility
PO Box 545, Hwy 9 W, Lineville, AL 36266
(205) 396-2104
Admin Alexander E Baker. *Dir of Nursing*
Judy Isbell RN. *Medical Dir* George Smith
Sr MD.
Licensure Skilled care; Intermediate care. *Beds*
SNF 65; ICF 16. *Private Pay Patients* 22%.
Certified Medicaid; Medicare.
Owner Proprietary corp (Northport Health
Services).
Admissions Requirements Physician's request.
Staff RNs 1 (ft), 2 (pt); LPNs 9 (ft), 4 (pt);
Nurses' aides; Activities coordinators 1 (ft);
Dietitians 1 (ft).
Facilities Dining room; Activities room;
Chapel; Crafts room; Laundry room; Barber/
Beauty shop.
Activities Arts & crafts; Cards; Games; Prayer
groups; Movies; GED preparatory classes.

Luverne

Luverne Nursing Facility
310 W 3rd St, Luverne, AL 36049
(205) 335-5331
Admin Barbara K Ward. *Dir of Nursing*
Aneke Shirley. *Medical Dir* Dr S P Walker;
Dr Jean Senecal.
Licensure Skilled care. *Beds* SNF 137.
Certified Medicaid; Medicare.
Owner Proprietary corp.
Admissions Requirements Medical
examination; Physician's request.
Staff Physicians 4 (pt); RNs 2 (ft); LPNs 12
(ft), 6 (pt); Nurses' aides 50 (ft), 15 (pt);
Recreational therapists 1 (ft); Activities
coordinators 1 (ft); Dietitians 1 (ft); Dentists
1 (pt).
Facilities Dining room; Activities room;
Crafts room; Laundry room; Barber/Beauty
shop.
Activities Arts & crafts; Cards; Games;
Reading groups; Prayer groups; Movies;
Shopping trips; Dances/Social/Cultural
gatherings.

Madison

Madison Manor Nursing Home
3891 Sullivan St, Madison, AL 35758
(205) 772-9243
Admin Valeria Gamble.
Licensure Skilled care; Intermediate care. *Beds*
SNF 49; ICF 31. *Certified* Medicaid;
Medicare.
Owner Proprietary corp.

Marbury

Resurrection Catholic Nursing Home
PO Box 89, White City Rd, Marbury, AL
36051-0089
(205) 755-1139
Admin Farley Rudolph Jr. *Dir of Nursing*
Mary Coburn. *Medical Dir* Keith
Funderburk MD.
Licensure Intermediate care. *Beds* ICF 20.
Private Pay Patients 1%. *Certified* Medicaid.
Owner Nonprofit corp.
Admissions Requirements Females only;
Medical examination; Physician's request.
Staff LPNs 5 (ft); Nurses' aides 9 (ft);
Activities coordinators 1 (ft); Dietitians 1
(ft).
Affiliation Roman Catholic.
Facilities Dining room; Activities room;
Crafts room; Laundry room; Library.
Activities Arts & crafts; Games; Reading
groups; Prayer groups; Movies; Shopping
trips; Intergenerational programs.

Marion

Perry Community Hospital & Nursing Home
E Lafayette St, Marion, AL 36756
(205) 683-6111
Admin Marshall L Nero. *Dir of Nursing* Betty
Franklin RN. *Medical Dir* Sterling Haynes
MD.
Licensure Skilled care; Intermediate care. *Beds*
SNF 25; ICF 6. *Certified* Medicaid;
Medicare.
Owner Proprietary corp (Healthcare
Management).
Admissions Requirements Medical
examination; Physician's request.
Staff RNs 1 (ft), 1 (pt); LPNs 3 (ft), 3 (pt);
Nurses' aides 6 (ft), 6 (pt); Physical
therapists 1 (ft); Activities coordinators 1
(ft); Dietitians 1 (pt).
Facilities Dining room; Physical therapy
room; Activities room; Chapel; Crafts room;
Laundry room; Barber/Beauty shop.
Activities Arts & crafts; Cards; Games;
Reading groups; Prayer groups; Movies.

Southland Nursing Home
500 Shivers Terr, Marion, AL 36756
(205) 683-6141
Admin Cathy Swanson.
Licensure Skilled care; Intermediate care. *Beds*
SNF 54; ICF 17. *Certified* Medicaid;
Medicare.
Owner Proprietary corp (Vari-Care Inc).

McCalla

Plantation Manor
PO Box 97, McCalla, AL 35111
(205) 477-6161
Admin Cecil L Lee.
Medical Dir Cemal Goral MD.
Licensure Skilled care; Intermediate care. *Beds*
SNF 57; ICF 46. *Certified* Medicaid;
Medicare.
Owner Proprietary corp.
Admissions Requirements Medical
examination; Physician's request.
Staff Physicians 1 (pt); RNs 1 (ft), 1 (pt);
LPNs 9 (ft), 2 (pt); Nurses' aides 15 (ft), 5
(pt); Physical therapists 1 (pt); Recreational
therapists 1 (ft); Activities coordinators 1
(ft); Dietitians 1 (pt); Dentists 1 (pt).

Mobile

Allen Memorial Home
735 S Washington Ave, Mobile, AL 36603
(205) 433-2642
Admin Sr Marilyn Moore.
Licensure Skilled care; Intermediate care. *Beds*
SNF 80; ICF 14. *Certified* Medicaid;
Medicare.
Owner Proprietary corp.

Bay Manor Health Care Center
7020 Bruns Dr, Mobile, AL 36609
(205) 343-5588
Admin William A Hudson. *Dir of Nursing*
Posey Look. *Medical Dir* David McRae MD.
Licensure Skilled care. *Beds* SNF 120.
Certified Medicaid; Medicare.
Owner Proprietary corp (Beverly Enterprises).
Staff RNs 3 (ft), 3 (pt); LPNs 10 (ft), 8 (pt);
Nurses' aides 25 (ft), 12 (pt); Activities
coordinators 1 (ft); Social worker 1 (ft).
Facilities Dining room; Activities room;
Laundry room; Barber/Beauty shop.
Activities Arts & crafts; Cards; Games;
Reading groups; Prayer groups; Movies;
Shopping trips; Dances/Social/Cultural
gatherings.

Albert P Brewer Developmental Center
PO Box 8467, Shillinger Rd, Mobile, AL
36608
(205) 633-0400
Admin L W Pucket.

Licensure Intermediate care. *Beds* ICF 217.

Cogburn Health Center Inc
148 Tuscaloosa St, Mobile, AL 36607
(205) 471-5431
Admin Suzanne R Hughes.
Licensure Skilled care; Intermediate care. *Beds*
SNF 142; ICF 8. *Certified* Medicaid;
Medicare.
Owner Proprietary corp.

**Columbia Regional Medical Center & Nursing
Home**
PO Box 2394, Mobile, AL 36652
(205) 222-4141
Admin Jack Parsons. *Dir of Nursing* Merle
Neese RN.
Licensure Skilled care. *Beds* SNF 48. *Certified*
Medicaid; Medicare.
Owner Proprietary corp (Healthcare
Management).
Admissions Requirements Medical
examination; Physician's request.
Staff Physicians 1 (ft), 5 (pt); RNs 1 (ft), 4
(pt); LPNs 5 (ft), 2 (pt); Nurses' aides 18
(ft); Activities coordinators 2 (ft).
Facilities Dining room; Activities room;
Chapel; Crafts room; Laundry room; Barber/
Beauty shop.
Activities Arts & crafts; Cards; Games; Prayer
groups; Movies; Shopping trips; Dances/
Social/Cultural gatherings.

Dauphin Health Care Facility
3717 Dauphin St, Mobile, AL 36608
(205) 343-0909
Admin Nanette Mordachini. *Dir of Nursing*
Barbara Crummey RN. *Medical Dir* Dr
Liston Jones.
Licensure Skilled care; Intermediate care. *Beds*
SNF 36; ICF 115. *Certified* Medicaid;
Medicare.
Owner Proprietary corp (Diversicare Corp of
America).
Admissions Requirements Physician's request.
Staff Physicians 6 (pt); RNs 4 (ft); LPNs 13
(ft), 3 (pt); Nurses' aides 50 (ft), 10 (pt);
Physical therapists 1 (ft), 1 (pt); Speech
therapists 1 (pt); Activities coordinators 1
(ft), 1 (pt); Dietitians 1 (ft); Podiatrists 1
(pt).
Languages Spanish.
Facilities Dining room; Physical therapy
room; Activities room; Crafts room; Laundry
room; Barber/Beauty shop; Lobby.
Activities Arts & crafts; Cards; Games;
Reading groups; Prayer groups; Shopping
trips; Dances/Social/Cultural gatherings;
Intergenerational programs; Pet therapy.

Heritage Nursing & Convalescent Center
954 Navco Rd, Mobile, AL 36690
(205) 473-8684
Admin Virginia Dillon.
Medical Dir L D McLaughlin MD.
Licensure Skilled care. *Beds* 174. *Certified*
Medicaid; Medicare.
Owner Proprietary corp.
Staff Physicians 1 (pt); RNs 9 (ft); LPNs 25
(ft); Nurses' aides 45 (ft); Physical therapists
2 (pt); Recreational therapists 2 (ft); Speech
therapists 1 (pt); Dietitians 1 (pt).
Facilities Dining room; Physical therapy
room; Activities room; Chapel; Crafts room;
Laundry room; Barber/Beauty shop.
Activities Arts & crafts; Cards; Games;
Reading groups; Prayer groups; Movies;
Dances/Social/Cultural gatherings.

**Hillhaven Convalescent Center & Nursing
Home—Mobile**
1758 Springhill Ave, Mobile, AL 36607
(205) 479-0551
Admin Betty Thornburg.
Licensure Skilled care. *Beds* 174. *Certified*
Medicaid; Medicare.
Owner Proprietary corp (Hillhaven Corp).

Ideal Rest Home Inc
1203 Government St, Mobile, AL 36604
(205) 438-4566
Admin Mary G Turk.
Licensure Intermediate care. *Beds* 49.
Certified Medicaid.
Owner Proprietary corp.

Lynwood Nursing Home Inc
4164 Halls Mill Rd, Mobile, AL 36609
(205) 661-5404
Admin Towana Sue DuBose.
Licensure Skilled care; Intermediate care. *Beds*
SNF 20; ICF 107. *Certified* Medicaid;
Medicare.
Owner Proprietary corp (Wessex Corp).

Spring Hill Manor Nursing Home
PO Box 8395, 3900 Old Shell Rd, Mobile, AL
36608
(205) 342-5623
Admin Gerald B Hart. *Dir of Nursing* Sybile L
Bradley. *Medical Dir* James E Hassell.
Licensure Intermediate care for mentally
retarded; Alzheimer's care. *Beds* ICF 34.
Certified Medicaid.
Owner Proprietary corp.
Admissions Requirements Medical
examination.
Staff Physicians 1 (pt); RNs 1 (pt); LPNs 5
(pt); Nurses' aides 8 (ft), 6 (pt); Recreational
therapists 1 (ft); Occupational therapists 1
(ft); Activities coordinators 1 (ft); Dietitians
1 (pt).
Facilities Dining room; Activities room;
Crafts room; Laundry room.
Activities Arts & crafts; Cards; Games;
Reading groups; Prayer groups; Movies.

Twin Oaks Nursing Home
857 Crawford Ln, Mobile, AL 36617
(205) 476-3420
Admin Boyte Presnell. *Dir of Nursing* Vanessa
Perine RN. *Medical Dir* Herbert Stone MD.
Licensure Skilled care; Intermediate care;
Alzheimer's care. *Beds* SNF 62; ICF 48.
Certified Medicaid; Medicare.
Owner Privately owned.
Admissions Requirements Medical
examination; Physician's request.
Staff Physicians 4 (pt); RNs 4 (ft), 3 (pt);
LPNs 8 (ft), 6 (pt); Nurses' aides 26 (ft), 21
(pt); Physical therapists 1 (pt); Recreational
therapists 1 (ft); Speech therapists 1 (pt);
Activities coordinators 1 (ft); Dietitians 1
(pt); Ophthalmologists 1 (pt); Podiatrists 1
(pt).
Facilities Dining room; Physical therapy
room; Activities room; Laundry room;
Barber/Beauty shop.
Activities Arts & crafts; Cards; Games;
Reading groups; Prayer groups; Movies;
Shopping trips; Dances/Social/Cultural
gatherings; Intergenerational programs.

Monroeville

Englewood Health Care Center
Rte 2 Box 800, Monroeville, AL 36460
(205) 575-3285
Admin Patricia Jones.
Medical Dir Jack Whetstone MD.
Licensure Skilled care; Intermediate care. *Beds*
SNF 24; ICF 51. *Certified* Medicaid;
Medicare.
Owner Proprietary corp.
Admissions Requirements Medical
examination; Physician's request.
Staff RNs 2 (ft); LPNs 7 (ft), 1 (pt); Nurses'
aides 21 (ft), 3 (pt); Physical therapists 1
(pt); Activities coordinators 1 (ft); Dietitians
1 (pt).
Facilities Dining room; Activities room;
Barber/Beauty shop.

Monroe Manor Nursing Home
236 W Claiborne St, Monroeville, AL 36460
(205) 575-2648

Admin Debra C Rawls. *Dir of Nursing* Wanda
G Lett. *Medical Dir* Dr Tim Jones.
Licensure Intermediate care. *Beds* SNF 35;
ICF 19. *Certified* Medicaid.
Owner Privately owned.
Admissions Requirements Medical
examination; Physician's request.
Staff Physicians 1 (pt); RNs 1 (ft); LPNs 5
(ft), 2 (pt); Nurses' aides 13 (ft), 5 (pt);
Activities coordinators 1 (ft); Dietitians 1
(ft).
Facilities Dining room; Activities room;
Laundry room; Barber/Beauty shop.
Activities Arts & crafts; Games; Prayer groups;
Movies; Dances/Social/Cultural gatherings.

Montgomery

**Cambridge Health Care Facility of
Montgomery Inc**
100 Perry Hill Rd, Montgomery, AL 36193
(205) 272-0171, 272-0997
Admin David Slaten. *Dir of Nursing* Jerita
Braun. *Medical Dir* Gary McCulloch MD.
Licensure Skilled care; Intermediate care. *Beds*
SNF 40; ICF 90. *Private Pay Patients* 15%.
Certified Medicaid; Medicare.
Owner Proprietary corp (Cambridge Health
Care).
Admissions Requirements Medical
examination; Physician's request.
Staff Physicians 3 (pt); RNs 3 (ft), 1 (pt);
LPNs 18 (ft), 3 (pt); Nurses' aides 58 (ft), 2
(pt); Physical therapists 1 (pt); Recreational
therapists 1 (ft); Occupational therapists 1
(pt); Speech therapists 1 (pt); Activities
coordinators 1 (ft); Dietitians 1 (pt);
Ophthalmologists 1 (pt); Podiatrists 1 (pt);
Audiologists 1 (pt).
Facilities Dining room; Physical therapy
room; Activities room; Crafts room; Laundry
room; Barber/Beauty shop; Library.
Activities Arts & crafts; Cards; Games;
Reading groups; Prayer groups; Movies;
Shopping trips; Dances/Social/Cultural
gatherings; Intergenerational programs; Pet
therapy; Outside sun and recreational areas.

Capitol Hill Healthcare Center
520 S Hull St, Montgomery, AL 36104
(205) 834-2920
Admin Patti W Tureane. *Dir of Nursing*
Evelyn Johnson RN. *Medical Dir* Kynard
Adams MD.
Licensure Skilled care; Intermediate care;
Alzheimer's care. *Beds* Swing beds SNF/ICF
284. *Certified* Medicaid; Medicare.
Owner Privately owned.
Admissions Requirements Medical
examination.
Staff RNs 4 (ft), 3 (pt); LPNs 50 (ft), 10 (pt);
Nurses' aides 120 (ft), 6 (pt); Physical
therapists 1 (ft); Recreational therapists 1
(ft); Occupational therapists 1 (ft); Speech
therapists 1 (pt); Activities coordinators 5
(ft); Dietitians 2 (ft); Podiatrists 1 (pt);
Audiologists 1 (pt); Social workers 3 (ft).
Facilities Dining room; Physical therapy
room; Activities room; Crafts room; Barber/
Beauty shop.
Activities Arts & crafts; Cards; Games;
Reading groups; Prayer groups; Movies;
Shopping trips; Dances/Social/Cultural
gatherings; Intergenerational programs; Pet
therapy.

Cedar Crest
4490 Virginia Loop Rd, Montgomery, AL
36116
(205) 281-6826
Admin Kevin J Metz. *Dir of Nursing* Sue
Corley. *Medical Dir* Dr Michael Reeves.
Licensure Skilled care; Retirement;
Alzheimer's care. *Beds* 110. *Certified*
Medicaid; Medicare.
Owner Proprietary corp (Vari-Care Inc).

Admissions Requirements Minimum age 16;
Medical examination; Physician's request.
Staff Physicians 10 (pt); RNs 4 (ft), 1 (pt);
LPNs 7 (ft), 3 (pt); Nurses' aides 30 (ft), 9
(pt); Physical therapists 1 (pt); Speech
therapists 1 (pt); Activities coordinators 1
(ft); Dietitians 1 (ft), 1 (pt);
Ophthalmologists 1 (pt).
Facilities Dining room; Physical therapy
room; Activities room; Crafts room; Laundry
room; Barber/Beauty shop; Library; Resident
sitting areas.
Activities Arts & crafts; Cards; Games;
Reading groups; Prayer groups; Movies;
Shopping trips; Dances/Social/Cultural
gatherings; Special events; Van rides.

**Father Purcell Memorial Exceptional
Children's Center**
2048 W Fairview Ave, Montgomery, AL
36108
(205) 834-5590
Admin Frank J May Jr. *Dir of Nursing*
Carolyn Diehl. *Medical Dir* David Morrison
MD.
Licensure Skilled care. *Beds* SNF 58. *Private
Pay Patients* 5%. *Certified* Medicaid.
Owner Nonprofit organization/foundation.
Admissions Requirements Medical
examination; Physician's request; Age range
is birth to 14.
Staff Physicians 1 (pt); RNs 4 (ft), 1 (pt);
LPNs 12 (ft), 1 (pt); Nurses' aides 18 (ft), 16
(pt); Physical therapists 1 (pt); Occupational
therapists 1 (pt); Activities coordinators 1
(ft); Dietitians 1 (pt).
Affiliation Roman Catholic.
Facilities Dining room; Activities room;
Homebound special education classroom.
Activities Sensory; Developmental.

Father Walter Memorial Child Care Center
2815 Forbes Dr, Montgomery, AL 36199
(205) 262-6421
Admin Audrey Wright.
Licensure Skilled care. *Beds* 44. *Certified*
Medicaid.
Owner Nonprofit corp.
Admissions Requirements Medical
examination; Physician's request.
Staff RNs 2 (ft), 1 (pt); LPNs 5 (ft); Nurses'
aides 20 (ft); Physical therapists 1 (pt);
Recreational therapists 1 (pt); Dietitians 1
(pt); Dentists 1 (pt).
Affiliation Roman Catholic.
Facilities Dining room; Activities room;
Laundry room.
Activities Movies.

John Knox Manor Inc II
4401 Narrow Ln Rd, Montgomery, AL 36116
(205) 281-6336
Admin Sherry Rountree.
Medical Dir Dr Donald Marshall.
Licensure Skilled care; Intermediate care. *Beds*
SNF 98. *Certified* Medicaid; Medicare.
Owner Nonprofit corp.
Admissions Requirements Minimum age 21;
Medical examination; Physician's request.
Staff RNs 3 (ft), 1 (pt); LPNs 10 (ft), 3 (pt);
Nurses' aides 30 (ft), 5 (pt); Physical
therapists 1 (pt); Activities coordinators 2
(ft); Dietitians 1 (pt).
Affiliation Presbyterian.
Facilities Dining room; Physical therapy
room; Activities room; Chapel; Crafts room;
Laundry room; Barber/Beauty shop.
Activities Arts & crafts; Cards; Games;
Reading groups; Prayer groups; Movies;
Shopping trips; Dances/Social/Cultural
gatherings.

Magnolia Manor
1837 Upper Wetumpka Rd, Montgomery, AL
36199
(205) 264-8416
Admin Jimmy D Prince.
Medical Dir Malcolm Brown; Angela Self.

Licensure Skilled care; Intermediate care;
Pediatric long-term care; Alzheimer's care.
Beds SNF 50; ICF 135. *Certified* Medicaid;
Medicare; VA Contract.
Owner Proprietary corp.
Admissions Requirements Medical
examination; Physician's request.
Staff Physicians; RNs; LPNs; Nurses' aides;
Physical therapists; Reality therapists;
Recreational therapists; Speech therapists;
Activities coordinators; Dietitians;
Ophthalmologists.
Facilities Dining room; Physical therapy
room; Activities room; Chapel; Crafts room;
Laundry room; Barber/Beauty shop; Library;
Developed courtyards & playgrounds;
Special childrens unit.
Activities Arts & crafts; Cards; Games;
Reading groups; Prayer groups; Movies;
Shopping trips; Dances/Social/Cultural
gatherings.

South Haven Manor Nursing Home
1300 E South Blvd, Montgomery, AL 36116
(205) 288-0122
Admin Brunese O Seaborn.
Licensure Skilled care. *Beds* 86. *Certified*
Medicaid; Medicare.
Owner Proprietary corp (Vari-Care Inc).

Tyson Manor Health Facility
2020 N Country Club Dr, Montgomery, AL
36106
(205) 263-1643
Admin Suzanne Sherlock.
Licensure Skilled care; Intermediate care. *Beds*
SNF 125. *Certified* Medicaid; Medicare.
Owner Proprietary corp.

Woodley Manor Nursing Home Inc
3312 Woodley Rd, Montgomery, AL 36111
(205) 288-2780
Admin Juanita C Busby.
Medical Dir Dr Mont Highley.
Licensure Skilled care; Intermediate care. *Beds*
SNF 92; ICF 3. *Certified* Medicaid;
Medicare.
Owner Proprietary corp (Vari-Care Inc).
Admissions Requirements Minimum age 21;
Medical examination; Physician's request.
Staff Physicians 1 (pt); RNs 3 (ft); LPNs 7
(ft), 1 (pt); Nurses' aides 35 (ft), 3 (pt);
Physical therapists 1 (pt); Recreational
therapists 1 (ft); Speech therapists 1 (pt);
Activities coordinators 1 (ft); Dietitians 1
(ft); Ophthalmologists 1 (pt); Podiatrists 1
(pt); Social service workers.
Facilities Dining room; Physical therapy
room; Activities room; Chapel; Crafts room;
Laundry room; Barber/Beauty shop; Library.
Activities Arts & crafts; Cards; Games;
Reading groups; Prayer groups; Movies;
Shopping trips; Dances/Social/Cultural
gatherings.

Moulton

Moulton Health Care Center
PO Box 336, 300 Hospital St, Moulton, AL
35650
(205) 974-1146
Admin Karen C Free. *Dir of Nursing* Wanda
Hare RN. *Medical Dir* Robert Rhyne MD.
Licensure Skilled care; Intermediate care. *Beds*
SNF 71; ICF 65. *Certified* Medicaid;
Medicare.
Owner Proprietary corp (National Health
Corp).
Admissions Requirements Medical
examination; Physician's request.
Staff Physicians 3 (pt); RNs 5 (ft), 1 (pt);
LPNs 9 (ft), 3 (pt); Nurses' aides 65 (ft), 5
(pt); Physical therapists 1 (ft), 1 (pt); Speech
therapists 1 (pt); Activities coordinators 2
(ft); Dietitians 1 (ft).

Facilities Dining room; Physical therapy
room; Activities room; Crafts room; Laundry
room; Barber/Beauty shop; Speech therapy;
3 outdoor patios.
Activities Arts & crafts; Cards; Games;
Reading groups; Prayer groups; Movies;
Dances/Social/Cultural gatherings; Activities
for room-bound patients; Church services.

Moundville

Moundville Nursing Facility
PO Box 607, 4th St, Moundville, AL 35474
(205) 371-2252
Admin Bertha L Madison. *Dir of Nursing*
Kathy Fox. *Medical Dir* Dr Larry Shelton.
Licensure Skilled care; Intermediate care. *Beds*
SNF 52; ICF 6. *Certified* Medicaid;
Medicare.
Owner Proprietary corp.
Staff RNs 1 (ft), 3 (pt); LPNs 4 (ft), 3 (pt);
Nurses' aides 14 (ft), 4 (pt); Activities
coordinators 1 (ft); Dietitians 1 (ft).
Facilities Dining room; Activities room;
Chapel; Crafts room; Laundry room; Barber/
Beauty shop.
Activities Arts & crafts; Cards; Games;
Reading groups; Prayer groups; Shopping
trips.

Muscle Shoals

Muscle Shoals Nursing Home
200 Alabama Ave, Muscle Shoals, AL 35661
(205) 381-4330, 381-4331 FAX
Admin Carol C Rollins. *Dir of Nursing*
Connie Ledlow. *Medical Dir* James
Ashmore.
Licensure Skilled care; Intermediate care;
Alzheimer's care. *Beds* SNF 32; ICF 58.
Private Pay Patients 24%. *Certified*
Medicaid; Medicare.
Owner Proprietary corp (Medical Income
Properties 2A).
Staff Physicians; RNs 2 (ft), 1 (pt); LPNs 10
(ft), 6 (pt); Nurses' aides 31 (ft), 9 (pt);
Physical therapists 1 (ft); Occupational
therapists 1 (ft); Speech therapists 1 (ft);
Activities coordinators 1 (ft); Dietitians 1
(ft).
Facilities Dining room; Physical therapy
room; Activities room; Laundry room;
Barber/Beauty shop; 2 Living rooms.
Activities Arts & crafts; Cards; Games;
Reading groups; Prayer groups; Dances/
Social/Cultural gatherings; Pet therapy.

Northport

S D Allen Intermediate Care Facility
6901 5th St, Old Columbus Hwy, Northport,
AL 35476
(205) 339-0700
Admin Thomas H Allen.
Licensure Intermediate care. *Beds* ICF 138.

Estes Health Care Center—Glen Haven
2201 32nd St, Northport, AL 35476
(205) 339-5700
Admin Jim Turnipseed.
Licensure Skilled care; Intermediate care. *Beds*
SNF 99; ICF 66. *Certified* Medicaid;
Medicare.
Owner Proprietary corp (Northport Health
Services).

Estes Health Care Center—North
2201 32nd St, Northport, AL 35476
(205) 339-5700
Admin Jeanna Trapp.
Beds 165.

Estes Health Care Center—Park Manor
2201 Hwy 82 By-Pass, Northport, AL 35476
(205) 339-5300
Admin Kenneth Hoffman. *Dir of Nursing*
Jody Hurst. *Medical Dir* Gene Alldredge.

Licensure Skilled care; Intermediate care. *Beds* SNF 136; ICF 16. *Private Pay Patients* 15%. *Certified* Medicaid; Medicare.
Owner Proprietary corp (Northport Health Services Inc).
Admissions Requirements Medical examination; Physician's request.
Staff RNs 2 (ft), 2 (pt); LPNs 13 (ft), 5 (pt); Nurses' aides 48 (ft), 29 (pt); Activities coordinators 1 (ft).
Facilities Dining room; Activities room; Laundry room; Barber/Beauty shop; Library.
Activities Arts & crafts; Cards; Games; Reading groups; Prayer groups; Movies; Intergenerational programs.

Estes Health Care—North
600 34th St, Northport, AL 35476
(205) 339-5900
Admin David A Estes.
Medical Dir Dr Hayes Boyd.
Licensure Skilled care. *Beds* SNF 40; ICF 28. *Certified* Medicaid; Medicare.
Owner Proprietary corp (Northport Health Services).
Staff RNs 1 (ft), 1 (pt); LPNs 5 (ft), 4 (pt); Nurses' aides 15 (ft), 7 (pt); Activities coordinators 1 (ft); Dietitians 1 (ft).
Facilities Dining room; Activities room; Chapel; Barber/Beauty shop.
Activities Arts & crafts; Cards; Games; Reading groups; Prayer groups; Picnics.

Forest Manor Inc
2215 32nd St, Northport, AL 35476
(205) 339-5400
Admin Donald W Peak. *Dir of Nursing* Virginia O'Neal. *Medical Dir* J C Guin.
Licensure Skilled care; Intermediate care. *Beds* SNF 75; ICF 75. *Certified* Medicaid; Medicare.
Owner Proprietary corp.
Admissions Requirements Medical examination; Physician's request.
Staff Physicians 1 (pt); RNs 2 (ft), 1 (pt); LPNs 20 (ft), 3 (pt); Nurses' aides 50 (ft), 12 (pt); Activities coordinators 1 (ft); Dietitians 1 (pt).
Facilities Dining room; Physical therapy room; Activities room; Chapel; Crafts room; Laundry room; Barber/Beauty shop.
Activities Arts & crafts; Cards; Games; Reading groups; Prayer groups.

Oneonta

Oneonta Manor Nursing Home
210 Shirley St, Oneonta, AL 35121
(205) 274-2365
Admin Laurel Massey.
Licensure Skilled care; Intermediate care. *Beds* SNF 52; ICF 50. *Certified* Medicaid; Medicare.
Owner Proprietary corp.

Opelika

Opelika Health Care
1908 1/2 Pepperell Pkwy, Opelika, AL 36801
(205) 749-1471
Admin Linda P Hoffman. *Dir of Nursing* Carleen White RN; Mavis Brewer RN Asst Dir. *Medical Dir* Dr A Z Carter.
Licensure Skilled care; Intermediate care; Alzheimer's care. *Beds* Swing beds SNF/ICF 225. *Private Pay Patients* 30%. *Certified* Medicaid; Medicare.
Owner Proprietary corp (Southern Health Enterprises).
Admissions Requirements Medical examination; Physician's request.
Staff Activities coordinators 3 (ft), 1 (pt); Dietitians 1 (ft).
Facilities Dining room; Physical therapy room; Activities room; Chapel; Crafts room; Laundry room; Barber/Beauty shop; Library.

Activities Arts & crafts; Games; Reading groups; Prayer groups; Movies; Shopping trips; Dances/Social/Cultural gatherings; Pet therapy.

Opp

Covington Manor Inc
W Covington Ave, Opp, AL 36467
(205) 493-3096
Admin Barbara K Ward.
Medical Dir Dr J G Dunn.
Licensure Skilled care; Intermediate care. *Beds* SNF 73; ICF 16. *Certified* Medicaid; Medicare.
Owner Proprietary corp.
Admissions Requirements Medical examination; Physician's request.
Staff RNs 1 (ft), 2 (pt); LPNs 8 (ft), 1 (pt); Nurses' aides 21 (ft), 6 (pt); Activities coordinators 1 (ft); Dietitians 1 (ft).
Facilities Dining room; Activities room; Laundry room; Barber/Beauty shop.
Activities Arts & crafts; Cards; Games; Reading groups; Prayer groups.

OPP Nursing Facility
PO Box 638, Paulk Ave, Opp, AL 36467
(205) 493-4558
Admin Eula W McCord.
Licensure Skilled care; Intermediate care. *Beds* SNF 118; ICF 61. *Certified* Medicaid; Medicare.
Owner Proprietary corp.

Oxford

Colonial Pines Health Care Center
1130 Hale St, Oxford, AL 36203
(205) 831-0481
Admin Katie A Johnston. *Dir of Nursing* Betty Weathington. *Medical Dir* Dr Paul Siehl.
Licensure Skilled care; Intermediate care. *Beds* SNF 110; ICF 63. *Certified* Medicaid; Medicare.
Owner Proprietary corp (Beverly Enterprises).
Admissions Requirements Medical examination; Physician's request.
Staff RNs; LPNs; Nurses' aides; Speech therapists; Activities coordinators; Dietitians.
Facilities Dining room; Activities room; Chapel; Crafts room; Laundry room; Barber/Beauty shop.
Activities Arts & crafts; Cards; Games; Reading groups; Prayer groups; Movies; Shopping trips; Dances/Social/Cultural gatherings.

Ozark

Oak View Manor
Mixon Street Rd, Ozark, AL 36360
(205) 774-2631
Admin Shelia Cobb.
Licensure Skilled care; Intermediate care. *Beds* SNF 114. *Certified* Medicaid; Medicare.
Owner Proprietary corp.

Ozark Nursing Facility
201 Bryan Dr, Ozark, AL 36360
(205) 774-2561
Admin E M Beverly.
Licensure Skilled care. *Beds* 123. *Certified* Medicaid.
Owner Proprietary corp (Northport Health Services).

Pell City

Ingram Manor Nursing Home
510 Wolf Creek Rd N, Pell City, AL 35125
(205) 338-3329
Admin Katherine Ponder.

Licensure Skilled care; Intermediate care. *Beds* SNF 32; ICF 42. *Certified* Medicaid; Medicare.
Owner Proprietary corp.

Phenix City

Parkwood Health Care Facility
3301 Stadium Dr, Phenix City, AL 36867
(205) 297-0237
Admin Gloria Dunn.
Licensure Skilled care; Intermediate care. *Beds* SNF 39; ICF 35. *Certified* Medicaid; Medicare.
Owner Proprietary corp.

Phenix City Nursing Home
3900 Lakewood Dr, Phenix City, AL 36867
(205) 298-8247
Admin David H Godwin. *Dir of Nursing* Margaret Hutchins RN. *Medical Dir* William S Warr MD.
Licensure Skilled care; Intermediate care. *Beds* SNF 66; ICF 10. *Private Pay Patients* 21%. *Certified* Medicaid; Medicare; VA.
Owner Proprietary corp (Vari-Care Inc).
Admissions Requirements Medical examination; Physician's request.
Staff RNs 2 (ft); LPNs 9 (ft), 2 (pt); Nurses' aides 24 (ft), 5 (pt); Physical therapists 1 (pt); Recreational therapists 1 (pt); Activities coordinators 1 (ft); Dietitians 1 (ft).
Facilities Dining room; Physical therapy room; Activities room; Chapel; Crafts room; Laundry room; Barber/Beauty shop; Library.
Activities Arts & crafts; Cards; Games; Prayer groups; Movies; Shopping trips; Intergenerational programs; Pet therapy.

Piedmont

Piedmont Hospital & Nursing Home
Calhoun St, PO Box 330, Piedmont, AL 36272
(205) 447-6041
Admin Bill Jones.
Medical Dir Dr Russell Ulrich.
Licensure Skilled care; Intermediate care. *Beds* 31. *Certified* Medicaid; Medicare.
Owner Proprietary corp (Healthcare Management).
Staff Physicians 1 (pt); RNs 1 (ft), 1 (pt); LPNs 5 (ft), 2 (pt); Nurses' aides 8 (ft), 3 (pt); Activities coordinators 1 (ft); Dietitians 1 (pt).

Pleasant Grove

Cottage Hill Health Care Center
700 1st Ave, Pleasant Grove, AL 35127
(205) 744-8330
Admin William A Thomas. *Dir of Nursing* Joyce Raney. *Medical Dir* Chivers Woodruff MD.
Licensure Skilled care; Intermediate care. *Beds* SNF 20; ICF 44. *Certified* Medicaid; Medicare.
Owner Proprietary corp (Health Investments Inc).

Cottage Hill Nursing Home
700 1st Ave, Pleasant Grove, AL 35127
(205) 744-8330
Admin William G Allen Jr.
Licensure Skilled care; Intermediate care. *Beds* SNF 44; ICF 20. *Certified* Medicaid; Medicare.
Owner Proprietary corp.

Pleasant Grove Health Care Center
30 7th St, Pleasant Grove, AL 35127
(205) 744-8226
Admin Ruby Baker. *Dir of Nursing* Bonnie Hull. *Medical Dir* Dr Hugh Hood.
Licensure Skilled care. *Beds* SNF 198. *Certified* Medicaid; Medicare.
Owner Proprietary corp (Beverly Enterprises).

Staff Physicians 3 (pt); RNs 3 (ft), 1 (pt); LPNs 21 (ft), 4 (pt); Nurses' aides 54 (ft), 18 (pt); Physical therapists 1 (pt); Recreational therapists 2 (ft); Occupational therapists 1 (pt); Speech therapists 1 (pt); Dietitians 2 (ft); Ophthalmologists 1 (pt); Podiatrists 1 (pt).
Facilities Dining room; Physical therapy room; Activities room; Crafts room; Laundry room; Barber/Beauty shop; Library.
Activities Arts & crafts; Cards; Games; Reading groups; Prayer groups; Movies; Shopping trips; Dances/Social/Cultural gatherings; Intergenerational programs; Pet therapy.

Prattville

Autauga Health Care Center
750 Wetumpka St, Prattville, AL 36067
(205) 365-2241
Admin J Gordon Faulk; Carroll MacPherson, Bus Mrkt Mgr. *Dir of Nursing* Charlotte Goltry. *Medical Dir* Dr Danny Ingram.
Licensure Skilled care; Intermediate care. *Beds* SNF 58; ICF 14. *Private Pay Patients* 33%. *Certified* Medicaid; Medicare.
Owner Proprietary corp.
Admissions Requirements Medical examination; Physician's request.
Staff Physicians 7 (ft); RNs 3 (ft), 4 (pt); LPNs 7 (ft), 5 (pt); Nurses' aides 27 (ft), 10 (pt); Physical therapists (contracted); Reality therapists (contracted); Recreational therapists (contracted); Occupational therapists (contracted); Activities coordinators 1 (ft), 1 (pt); Dietitians 1 (ft); Podiatrists 1 (pt); Dentists 1 (pt).
Facilities Dining room; Laundry room; Barber/Beauty shop.
Activities Arts & crafts; Cards; Games; Reading groups; Prayer groups; Movies; Shopping trips; Dances/Social/Cultural gatherings; Alzheimer's support group.

Red Bay

Red Bay Nursing Home
106 10th Ave N, Red Bay, AL 35582
(205) 356-4982
Admin Christine T Crutchfield. *Dir of Nursing* Maxine Timbes RN. *Medical Dir* Walker Dempsey.
Licensure Skilled care; Intermediate care. *Beds* SNF 52; ICF 28. *Certified* Medicaid; Medicare.
Owner Proprietary corp.
Admissions Requirements Physician's request.
Staff RNs 3 (ft); LPNs 10 (ft); Nurses' aides 21 (ft), 3 (pt); Activities coordinators 1 (ft); Dietitians 1 (ft).
Facilities Dining room; Activities room; Laundry room; Barber/Beauty shop.
Activities Arts & crafts; Cards; Games; Reading groups; Prayer groups; Movies; Dances/Social/Cultural gatherings.

Reform

Fountain Nursing Home
PO Box 400, 2nd Ave NW, Reform, AL 35481
(205) 375-6379
Admin Ellen W Meyer.
Licensure Skilled care; Intermediate care. *Beds* SNF 58; ICF 27. *Certified* Medicaid; Medicare.
Owner Proprietary corp.

Pickens County Health Care Inc
PO Box 400, 512 W Columbus Ave, Reform, AL 35481
(205) 375-6379
Admin Ellen Chappell.
Licensure Skilled care; Intermediate care. *Beds* SNF 58; ICF 27.

Roanoke

Rosser Nursing Home
PO Box 667, Seymore St, Roanoke, AL 36274
(205) 863-4512
Admin Susie Rosser Minnifield.
Licensure Intermediate care. *Beds* ICF 50. *Certified* Medicaid.
Owner Proprietary corp.

Traylor Nursing Home Inc
402 Yancey St, Roanoke, AL 36274
(205) 863-6131
Admin Ronald L Traylor. *Dir of Nursing* Sarah Clemons. *Medical Dir* G W Everett MD.
Licensure Skilled care; Intermediate care; Retirement. *Beds* SNF 52; ICF 50; Retirement 12. *Private Pay Patients* 23%. *Certified* Medicaid; Medicare.
Owner Proprietary corp.
Admissions Requirements Medical examination; Physician's request.
Staff RNs 2 (ft), 3 (pt); LPNs 8 (ft), 1 (pt); Nurses' aides 23 (ft), 5 (pt); Activities coordinators 1 (ft), 1 (pt); Dietitians 2 (ft).
Facilities Dining room; Activities room; Chapel; Laundry room; Barber/Beauty shop.
Activities Arts & crafts; Cards; Games; Reading groups; Prayer groups; Movies.

Russellville

Burns Nursing Home Inc
701 Monroe St, Russellville, AL 35653
(205) 332-4111
Admin Larry M DeArman.
Licensure Skilled care; Intermediate care. *Beds* 47. *Certified* Medicaid; Medicare.
Owner Proprietary corp.
Admissions Requirements Physician's request.
Facilities Dining room; Activities room; Laundry room; Barber/Beauty shop.
Activities Arts & crafts; Games; Reading groups; Prayer groups; Shopping trips; Dances/Social/Cultural gatherings.

North Alabama Nursing Home
PO Box 608, 705 Gandy St, Russellville, AL 35653
(205) 332-3773
Admin Floree Thurman. *Dir of Nursing* Rebecca Livingston RN. *Medical Dir* W P Hyatt MD.
Licensure Skilled care; Intermediate care. *Beds* SNF 50; ICF. *Certified* Medicaid; Medicare.
Owner Privately owned.
Staff RNs 2 (ft); LPNs 5 (ft); Nurses' aides 18 (ft); Activities coordinators 1 (ft); Dietitians 5 (ft).
Facilities Dining room; Activities room; Crafts room; Laundry room; Barber/Beauty shop.
Activities Arts & crafts; Cards; Games; Reading groups; Prayer groups; Movies; Shopping trips.

Terrace Manor Nursing Home Inc
Box 12, Rte 1, Underwood Rd, Russellville, AL 35653
(205) 332-3826
Admin Roland Wade.
Medical Dir Wayne P Hyatt MD.
Licensure Skilled care; Intermediate care. *Beds* SNF 43; ICF. *Certified* Medicaid; Medicare.
Owner Proprietary corp.
Admissions Requirements Medical examination.
Staff RNs 1 (ft), 1 (pt); LPNs 4 (ft), 1 (pt); Nurses' aides 16 (ft), 5 (pt); Recreational therapists 1 (ft); Activities coordinators 1 (ft); Dietitians 1 (pt).
Facilities Dining room; Activities room; Chapel; Crafts room; Laundry room; Barber/Beauty shop.

Activities Arts & crafts; Cards; Games; Reading groups; Prayer groups; Dances/Social/Cultural gatherings.

Scottsboro

Jackson County Hospital & Nursing Home
PO Box 1050, Woods Cove Rd, Scottsboro, AL 35768
(205) 259-4444
Admin James K Mason. *Dir of Nursing* Merbil Reeves. *Medical Dir* Dr Larry Bolton.
Licensure Skilled care. *Beds* SNF 50. *Private Pay Patients* 20%. *Certified* Medicaid; Medicare.
Owner Publicly owned.
Admissions Requirements Physician's request.
Staff RNs 1 (ft), 3 (pt); LPNs 5 (ft), 3 (pt); Nurses' aides 16 (ft), 4 (pt); Physical therapists 1 (pt); Activities coordinators 1 (ft); Dietitians 1 (pt).
Facilities Dining room; Activities room; Chapel; Crafts room; Barber/Beauty shop.
Activities Arts & crafts; Cards; Games; Reading groups; Prayer groups; Movies; Shopping trips; Dances/Social/Cultural gatherings.

Scottsboro Nursing Home
412 Cloverdale Rd, Scottsboro, AL 35768
(205) 259-1505
Admin Judy B Haymon. *Dir of Nursing* Mary Colley. *Medical Dir* Larry Bolton.
Licensure Skilled care; Intermediate care. *Beds* Swing beds SNF/ICF 95. *Private Pay Patients* 19%. *Certified* Medicaid; Medicare.
Owner Proprietary corp.
Admissions Requirements Medical examination; Physician's request.
Staff Physicians 9 (pt); RNs 4 (ft); LPNs 9 (ft), 4 (pt); Nurses' aides 25 (ft), 16 (pt); Activities coordinators 1 (ft); Dietitians 1 (pt); Podiatrists 1 (pt).
Facilities Dining room; Activities room; Chapel; Laundry room; Barber/Beauty shop; Library; Conference room; Examination room; Sun rooms; Sun patio.
Activities Arts & crafts; Games; Reading groups; Prayer groups; Movies; Dances/Social/Cultural gatherings; Pet therapy.

Selma

Dunn Nursing Home
515 Mabry St, Selma, AL 36701
(205) 872-3471
Admin Sheryl McElhaney, acting.
Medical Dir Dr William E Ehlert.
Licensure Skilled care; Intermediate care. *Beds* SNF 87; ICF 6. *Certified* Medicaid; Medicare.
Owner Proprietary corp (Vari-Care).
Admissions Requirements Minimum age 21; Medical examination; Physician's request.
Staff Physicians 1 (ft), 10 (pt); RNs 3 (ft), 2 (pt); Nurses' aides 26 (ft), 6 (pt); Physical therapists 1 (pt); Activities coordinators 1 (ft); Dietitians 3 (ft), 1 (pt); Dentists 1 (pt).
Facilities Dining room; Activities room; Laundry room; Barber/Beauty shop.
Activities Arts & crafts; Cards; Games; Reading groups; Prayer groups; Movies; Shopping trips.

Lighthouse Convalescent Home
PO Box 993, 2911 Range Line Rd, Selma, AL 36701
(205) 875-1868
Admin John Crear.
Medical Dir C L Lett MD.
Licensure Intermediate care. *Beds* ICF 48. *Certified* Medicaid.
Owner Proprietary corp.
Staff RNs 1 (ft); LPNs 4 (ft), 2 (pt); Nurses' aides 3 (ft), 8 (pt); Activities coordinators 1 (ft); Dietitians 2 (ft), 4 (pt).

Facilities Dining room; Activities room; Chapel; Crafts room.
Activities Arts & crafts; Cards; Games; Prayer groups; Movies; Dances/Social/Cultural gatherings.

Warren Manor Nursing Home
11 Bell Rd, Selma, AL 36701
(205) 874-7425
Admin Harold Hicken.
Medical Dir Dr Freeman Singleton.
Licensure Skilled care; Intermediate care. *Beds* SNF 112; ICF 16. *Certified* Medicaid; Medicare.
Owner Proprietary corp (Vari-Care).
Admissions Requirements Minimum age 21; Medical examination; Physician's request.
Staff Physicians 1 (pt); RNs 2 (ft), 1 (pt); LPNs 9 (ft), 7 (pt); Nurses' aides 26 (ft), 18 (pt); Physical therapists 1 (pt); Activities coordinators 1 (ft); Dietitians 1 (ft).
Facilities Dining room; Physical therapy room; Activities room; Crafts room; Laundry room; Barber/Beauty shop; Library.
Activities Arts & crafts; Cards; Games; Reading groups; Prayer groups; Movies; Shopping trips; Dances/Social/Cultural gatherings.

Sylacauga

Coosa Valley Medical Center & Coosa Valley Nursing Home
W Hickory St, Sylacauga, AL 35150
(205) 249-4921
Admin Steven M Johnson.
Medical Dir Dr James G Wright.
Licensure Skilled care; Intermediate care. *Beds* 52. *Certified* Medicaid; Medicare.
Owner Publicly owned.
Staff RNs 1 (ft), 2 (pt); LPNs 6 (ft), 2 (pt); Nurses' aides 17 (ft), 8 (pt); Physical therapists 1 (ft); Activities coordinators 1 (ft); Dietitians 1 (ft).
Facilities Dining room; Physical therapy room; Activities room; Chapel; Crafts room; Laundry room; Barber/Beauty shop; Library.
Activities Arts & crafts; Games; Prayer groups; Dances/Social/Cultural gatherings.

Sylacauga Health Care Center Inc
PO Box 1123, Fayetteville Rd, Sylacauga, AL 35150
(205) 245-7402
Admin Charles Wilbanks.
Licensure Skilled care; Intermediate care. *Beds* SNF 71; ICF 52. *Certified* Medicaid; Medicare.
Owner Proprietary corp.

Talladega

Talladega Nursing Home
616 Chaffee St, Talladega, AL 35160
(205) 362-4197
Admin William P Patterson. *Dir of Nursing* Linda Skinner. *Medical Dir* Dr J W Davis.
Licensure Skilled care; Intermediate care. *Beds* SNF 73; ICF 128. *Private Pay Patients* 17%. *Certified* Medicaid; Medicare.
Owner Proprietary corp.
Admissions Requirements Medical examination; Physician's request.
Staff Physicians; RNs 3 (ft); LPNs 13 (ft); Nurses' aides 82 (ft); Recreational therapists 3 (ft); Activities coordinators 2 (ft); Dietitians 2 (ft).
Languages Chinese.
Facilities Dining room; Physical therapy room; Activities room; Chapel; Crafts room; Laundry room; Barber/Beauty shop.
Activities Arts & crafts; Cards; Games; Reading groups; Prayer groups; Movies; Shopping trips; Dances/Social/Cultural gatherings; Bird watching & feeding; Volunteers from community.

Tallassee

Nursing Home of Tallassee Inc
PO Box 516, Rte 2, Wetumpka Hwy, Tallassee, AL 36078
(205) 283-3975
Admin Mellie Jones.
Licensure Skilled care; Intermediate care. *Beds* SNF 59; ICF 22. *Certified* Medicaid; Medicare.
Owner Proprietary corp.

Tarrant

Glenn Ireland II Development Center
91 Black Creek Rd, Tarrant, AL 35217
(205) 849-0654
Admin Rita A Wright.
Licensure Intermediate care. *Beds* ICF 200.

Thomasville

Thomasville Nursing Home
1440 Hwy 43 N, Thomasville, AL 36784
(205) 636-4431
Admin Terry Caldwell.
Medical Dir Dr J L Dozier.
Licensure Skilled care. *Beds* 50. *Certified* Medicare.
Owner Publicly owned.
Staff RNs 2 (ft); LPNs 5 (ft), 2 (pt); Nurses' aides 14 (ft), 4 (pt); Activities coordinators 1 (ft).
Facilities Dining room; Chapel; Barber/Beauty shop; Library.
Activities Arts & crafts; Games; Prayer groups; Movies; Shopping trips.

Troy

Pike Manor Health Care Center
PO Drawer 787, Elba Hwy, Troy, AL 36081
(205) 566-0880
Admin Ralph N Railey. *Dir of Nursing* Robin Self RN. *Medical Dir* J D Colley Jr MD.
Licensure Skilled care; Intermediate care. *Beds* SNF 68; ICF 96. *Certified* Medicaid; Medicare.
Owner Proprietary corp.
Admissions Requirements Physician's request.
Staff RNs 3 (ft); LPNs 16 (ft), 3 (pt); Nurses' aides 47 (ft), 10 (pt); Activities coordinators 1 (ft); Dietitians 2 (ft).
Facilities Dining room; Activities room; Crafts room; Barber/Beauty shop; Library.
Activities Arts & crafts; Cards; Games; Reading groups; Prayer groups.

Trussville

Trussville Health Care Center
PO Box 65, 147 N Chalkville Rd, Trussville, AL 35173
(205) 655-3226, 655-3175 FAX
Admin Mary Alice Edmonds. *Dir of Nursing* Debbie Cantrell RN. *Medical Dir* James Hall MD.
Licensure Skilled care. *Beds* SNF 125. *Private Pay Patients* 25%. *Certified* Medicaid; Medicare.
Owner Proprietary corp (Beverly Enterprises).
Admissions Requirements Minimum age 18; Medical examination; Physician's request.
Staff RNs 3 (ft), 3 (pt); LPNs 14 (ft), 3 (pt); Nurses' aides 40 (ft), 10 (pt); Physical therapists (contracted); Activities coordinators 1 (ft); Dietitians 1 (ft).
Facilities Dining room; Physical therapy room; Activities room; Chapel; Crafts room; Laundry room; Barber/Beauty shop.
Activities Arts & crafts; Cards; Games; Reading groups; Prayer groups; Movies; Shopping trips; Dances/Social/Cultural gatherings; Intergenerational programs; Community supports.

Tuscaloosa

Heritage Health Care Center
1101 Snows Mill Ave, Tuscaloosa, AL 35406
(205) 759-5179
Admin Rev George L Jackson. *Dir of Nursing* Delores Sargent RN. *Medical Dir* Dr Henry Savery.
Licensure Skilled care; Intermediate care; Retirement. *Beds* SNF 114; ICF 38; Retirement 100. *Private Pay Patients* 48%. *Certified* Medicaid; Medicare.
Owner Privately owned.
Admissions Requirements Medical examination; Physician's request.
Staff Physicians; RNs; LPNs; Nurses' aides; Physical therapists; Reality therapists; Recreational therapists; Occupational therapists; Speech therapists; Activities coordinators; Dietitians; Ophthalmologists; Podiatrists; Audiologists.
Facilities Dining room; Physical therapy room; Activities room; Chapel; Crafts room; Laundry room; Barber/Beauty shop; Library.
Activities Arts & crafts; Cards; Games; Reading groups; Prayer groups; Movies; Dances/Social/Cultural gatherings; Intergenerational programs; Pet therapy.

La Rocca Nursing Home
403 34th Ave E, Tuscaloosa, AL 35401
(205) 553-1341
Admin Lyman H Hardy.
Medical Dir Evelyn W Hardy.
Licensure Skilled care. *Beds* SNF 75.
Owner Privately owned.
Admissions Requirements Medical examination; Physician's request.
Staff Physicians; RNs; LPNs; Nurses' aides; Activities coordinators; Dietitians.
Facilities Dining room; Physical therapy room; Activities room; Chapel; Crafts room; Laundry room; Barber/Beauty shop; Library.
Activities Cards; Games; Reading groups; Prayer groups.

Partlow Developmental Center
PO Box 1730, University Blvd E, Tuscaloosa, AL 35403-1730
(205) 553-4550
Admin James L Vail Jr, Dir. *Dir of Nursing* Mildred Darling RN. *Medical Dir* Louis Tyler MD.
Licensure Intermediate care for mentally retarded. *Beds* ICF/MR 360. *Certified* Medicaid.
Owner Publicly owned.

Tuscumbia

Great Hall-Riverbend Center for Mental Health
901 Keller Ln, Apt F-5, Tuscumbia, AL 35674
(205) 381-8006
Admin Thomas J Pirkle. *Dir of Nursing* Debra Craig LPN. *Medical Dir* Joseph Glaister.
Licensure Intermediate care for mentally retarded. *Beds* ICF/MR 8. *Certified* Medicaid.
Owner Nonprofit corp.
Admissions Requirements Minimum age 18; Medical examination; Physician's request.
Staff LPNs; Nurses' aides; Physical therapists (consultant); Recreational therapists; Speech therapists; Dietitians (consultant).
Facilities Dining room; Activities room; Crafts room; Laundry room.
Activities Arts & crafts; Cards; Games; Movies; Shopping trips; Dances/Social/Cultural gatherings; Supervised living program.

Oak Crest Nursing Home Inc
PO Box 647, 813 Keller Ln, Tuscumbia, AL 35674
(205) 383-1535

Admin Nancy Brewer. *Dir of Nursing* Cheryl Bullard. *Medical Dir* James Ashmore MD.
Licensure Skilled care; Alzheimer's care. *Beds* SNF 90; ICF 19. *Certified* Medicaid; Medicare.
Owner Proprietary corp.
Admissions Requirements Medical examination; Physician's request.
Staff Physicians 1 (ft); RNs 2 (ft); LPNs 14 (ft); Recreational therapists 2 (ft); Activities coordinators 1 (ft); Dietitians 10 (ft); Dentists 1 (pt).
Languages Sign.
Facilities Dining room; Activities room; Chapel; Crafts room; Laundry room; Barber/Beauty shop; Library.
Activities Arts & crafts; Cards; Games; Reading groups; Prayer groups; Movies; Dances/Social/Cultural gatherings.

Shoals Nursing Home
PO Box 516, 500 Hazelton St, Tuscumbia, AL 35674
(205) 383-4541
Admin Steven D Johnson. *Dir of Nursing* Judy Grissom RN. *Medical Dir* James D Ashmore MD.
Licensure Skilled care; Intermediate care. *Beds* SNF 52; ICF 51. *Private Pay Patients* 40%. *Certified* Medicaid; Medicare.
Owner Proprietary corp (Atrium Living Centers Inc).
Admissions Requirements Medical examination; Physician's request.
Staff RNs 2 (ft); LPNs 14 (ft); Nurses' aides 39 (ft); Physical therapists (contracted); Activities coordinators 1 (ft); Dietitians 1 (ft).
Facilities Dining room; Activities room; Laundry room; Barber/Beauty shop; Living room.
Activities Arts & crafts; Cards; Games; Reading groups; Prayer groups; Dances/Social/Cultural gatherings; Pet therapy.

Tuskegee

Magnolia Haven Nursing Home
603 Wright St, Tuskegee, AL 36083
(205) 727-4960, 727-4961 FAX
Admin Reginald L Eldridge. *Dir of Nursing* Fran Norfleet. *Medical Dir* Dr Calvin Dowe.
Licensure Skilled care; Intermediate care. *Beds* SNF 57; ICF 10. *Private Pay Patients* 25%. *Certified* Medicaid; Medicare; VA.
Owner Proprietary corp (Vari-Care Inc).
Admissions Requirements Medical examination; Physician's request.
Staff Physicians 1 (ft); RNs 1 (ft), 4 (pt); LPNs 7 (ft), 8 (pt); Nurses' aides 16 (ft), 20 (pt); Physical therapists 1 (pt); Occupational therapists 1 (pt); Activities coordinators 1 (ft); Dietitians 1 (ft).
Facilities Dining room; Physical therapy room; Activities room; Crafts room; Laundry room; Barber/Beauty shop.
Activities Arts & crafts; Cards; Games; Reading groups; Prayer groups; Movies; Shopping trips; Dances/Social/Cultural gatherings.

Tuskegee Health Care Facility Inc
502 Gautier St, Tuskegee, AL 36083
(205) 727-1945

Admin Margaret K Phillips. *Dir of Nursing* Dianne Sallas. *Medical Dir* Robert Story MD.
Licensure Skilled care; Intermediate care. *Beds* SNF 40; ICF 102. *Certified* Medicaid; Medicare.
Owner Proprietary corp (Wessex Corp).
Staff RNs 3 (ft), 2 (pt); LPNs 14 (ft), 4 (pt); Nurses' aides 35 (ft), 10 (pt); Activities coordinators 2 (ft).

Union Springs

Bullock County Nursing Home
102 W Conecuh Ave, Union Springs, AL 36089
(205) 738-2140
Admin Catherine Ellis. *Dir of Nursing* Doris Reynolds.
Licensure Skilled care; Intermediate care. *Beds* SNF 32; ICF 32. *Private Pay Patients* 33%. *Certified* Medicaid; Medicare.
Owner Publicly owned.

Valley

George H Lanier Memorial Nursing Home
4800 48th St, Valley, AL 36854
(205) 756-1424
Admin Robert Letson. *Dir of Nursing* Fay Hamm RN. *Medical Dir* Dr Arvind Kamath.
Licensure Skilled care; Intermediate care. *Beds* Swing beds SNF/ICF 75. *Private Pay Patients* 49%. *Certified* Medicaid; Medicare.
Owner Nonprofit corp.
Admissions Requirements Minimum age 18; Medical examination; Physician's request.
Staff Physicians 10 (ft); RNs 3 (ft); LPNs 13 (ft), 5 (pt); Nurses' aides 31 (ft), 4 (pt); Speech therapists (consultant); Activities coordinators 1 (ft); Dietitians 2 (ft); Ophthalmologists (consultant); Podiatrists (consultant).
Facilities Dining room; Activities room; Crafts room; Barber/Beauty shop.
Activities Arts & crafts; Cards; Games; Reading groups; Prayer groups; Dances/Social/Cultural gatherings.

Vernon

Lamar Convalescent Center
Rte 1 Box 70, Vernon, AL 35592
(205) 695-9313
Admin Kaye Steadman. *Dir of Nursing* Mary Jo Kelly. *Medical Dir* Dr R W Davis.
Licensure Skilled care. *Beds* SNF 144. *Certified* Medicaid; Medicare.
Owner Proprietary corp.
Admissions Requirements Medical examination; Physician's request.
Staff Physicians 3 (pt); RNs 4 (ft), 1 (pt); LPNs 20 (ft), 4 (pt); Nurses' aides 40 (ft), 10 (pt); Activities coordinators 1 (ft), 2 (pt); Dietitians 1 (pt).
Facilities Dining room; Physical therapy room; Activities room; Laundry room; Barber/Beauty shop.
Activities Arts & crafts; Cards; Games; Reading groups; Prayer groups; Shopping trips; Dances/Social/Cultural gatherings; Intergenerational programs.

Lamar County Hospital & Nursing Home
507 5th St SW, Vernon, AL 35592
(205) 695-7111
Admin Robert E Morrow.
Licensure Skilled care; Intermediate care. *Beds* SNF 61; ICF 10. *Certified* Medicaid; Medicare.
Owner Publicly owned.

Wetumpka

J S Tarwater Developmental Center
US 231, N Hwy 9, Wetumpka, AL 36092
(205) 567-8471
Admin Catherine Maddox.
Licensure Intermediate care. *Beds* ICF 208.

Wetumpka Nursing Facility
208 Marshall St, Wetumpka, AL 36092
(205) 567-5131
Admin Mary Ann Howard. *Dir of Nursing* Judy Waters. *Medical Dir* Dr Dunn Jr.
Licensure Skilled care; Intermediate care. *Beds* SNF 57; ICF 23. *Certified* Medicaid; Medicare.
Owner Proprietary corp.
Admissions Requirements Medical examination; Physician's request.
Staff Physicians 6 (pt); RNs 1 (ft), 1 (pt); LPNs 9 (ft), 2 (pt); Nurses' aides 25 (ft), 10 (pt); Activities coordinators 1 (ft); Dietitians 1 (ft).
Facilities Dining room; Activities room; Crafts room; Laundry room; Barber/Beauty shop.
Activities Arts & crafts; Games; Movies; Shopping trips; Pet therapy.

Winfield

Pineview Health Care
Rte 4 Box 34A, Winfield, AL 35594
(205) 487-4211, 487-4214 FAX
Admin Cynthia Moore. *Dir of Nursing* Lolita Hubbert RN. *Medical Dir* Dr Aubrey Sewell.
Licensure Skilled care. *Beds* SNF 123. *Private Pay Patients* 5%. *Certified* Medicaid; Medicare.
Owner Proprietary corp (Beverly Enterprises).
Admissions Requirements Minimum age 17; Medical examination.
Staff RNs 3 (ft), 1 (pt); LPNs 12 (ft), 4 (pt); Nurses' aides 26 (ft), 37 (pt); Physical therapists 1 (ft), 1 (pt); Occupational therapists 1 (ft); Speech therapists 1 (ft); Activities coordinators 1 (ft); Dietitians 1 (pt).
Facilities Dining room; Physical therapy room; Activities room; Laundry room; Barber/Beauty shop; Occupational therapy room; Speech therapy room.
Activities Arts & crafts; Reading groups; Prayer groups; Movies; Dances/Social/Cultural gatherings; Intergenerational programs; Pet therapy.

York

Sumter Nursing Home
Rte 1 Box 415A, York, AL 36925
(205) 392-5281
Admin Lowry Rush III.
Licensure Skilled care; Intermediate care. *Beds* SNF 100. *Certified* Medicaid; Medicare.
Owner Publicly owned.

ALASKA

Anchorage

Anchorage Pioneers Home
923 11th Ave, Anchorage, AK 99517
(907) 276-3414
Admin Stan Soth.
Beds 92.

Hope Park Cottage
2805 Bering St, Anchorage, AK 99503
(907) 561-5335
Admin Stephen P Lesko.
Licensure Intermediate care for mentally retarded. *Beds* 10.
Owner Publicly owned.

Mary Conrad Center
9100 Centennial, Anchorage, AK 99504
(907) 333-8100
Admin Robert G Ogden.
Beds 60.

Our Lady of Compassion Care Center
4900 Eagle Street, Anchorage, AK 99503
(907) 562-2281
Admin Tom Boling.
Medical Dir Dr Mark Agnew.
Licensure Skilled care; Intermediate care. *Beds* Swing beds SNF/ICF 224. *Certified* Medicaid; Medicare.
Owner Nonprofit organization/foundation.
Admissions Requirements Medical examination; Physician's request.
Staff Physical therapists 3 (ft); Recreational therapists 1 (ft); Occupational therapists 2 (ft); Speech therapists 1 (ft); Dietitians 1 (ft).
Languages Native Alaskan.
Affiliation Roman Catholic.
Facilities Dining room; Physical therapy room; Activities room; Chapel; Crafts room; Laundry room; Barber/Beauty shop; Library; Gift shop.
Activities Reading groups; Prayer groups; Recreation; Bus Trips.

Cordova

Cordova Community Hospital
PO Box 160, Cordova, AK 99574
(907) 424-8000, 424-8116 FAX
Admin Edward Zeine. *Dir of Nursing* Helen Kelley. *Medical Dir* Larry Ermold MD.
Licensure Skilled care; Intermediate care. *Beds* SNF 11; ICF 10. *Certified* Medicaid; Medicare.
Owner Publicly owned.
Staff Physicians 3 (ft); RNs 8 (ft), 6 (pt); LPNs 1 (ft); Nurses' aides 5 (ft), 2 (pt); Activities coordinators 1 (ft).
Facilities Dining room; Physical therapy room; Activities room; Crafts room; Laundry room; Library.
Activities Arts & crafts; Cards; Games; Reading groups; Prayer groups; Movies; Dances/Social/Cultural gatherings; Musical programs; Fishing trips.

Fairbanks

Denali Center
1949 Gillam Way, Fairbanks, AK 99701
(907) 452-1921
Admin Ronald J Oltnoff.
Licensure Skilled care; Intermediate care. *Beds* 101. *Certified* Medicaid; Medicare.

Fairbanks Pioneers Home
2221 Eagan, Fairbanks, AK 99701
(907) 456-4372
Beds 54.

Homer

South Peninsula Hospital
PO Box 275, 4300 Bartlett, Homer, AK 99603
(907) 235-8101
Admin Michael Herring.
Licensure Skilled care; Intermediate care. *Beds* SNF 16; ICF 2. *Certified* Medicaid.
Owner Nonprofit corp.
Admissions Requirements Physician's request.
Staff RNs 3 (ft); LPNs 2 (ft); Nurses' aides 4 (ft); Physical therapists 1 (pt); Occupational therapists 1 (pt); Speech therapists 1 (pt); Activities coordinators 1 (pt); Dietitians 1 (pt); Ophthalmologists 1 (pt); Podiatrists 1 (pt); Dentists 1 (pt).
Activities Arts & crafts; Cards; Games; Movies; Shopping trips; Dances/Social/Cultural gatherings.

Juneau

Juneau Pioneers Home
4675 Glacier Hwy, Juneau, AK 99801
(907) 780-6422
Admin Dan Meddleton.
Beds 32.

Sainte Ann's Nursing Home
415 6th St, Juneau, AK 99801
(907) 586-3883, 586-9822 FAX
Admin Grant B Asay. *Dir of Nursing* Susan Strand. *Medical Dir* Paul V Rocereto.
Licensure Skilled care. *Beds* SNF 45. *Private Pay Patients* 10%. *Certified* Medicaid.
Owner Nonprofit corp.
Admissions Requirements Medical examination; Physician's request.
Staff Physicians 2 (pt); RNs 6 (ft), 3 (pt); LPNs 1 (ft), 1 (pt); Nurses' aides 27 (ft), 4 (pt); Physical therapists 1 (pt); Recreational therapists 1 (ft), 1 (pt); Occupational therapists 1 (pt); Speech therapists 1 (pt); Activities coordinators 1 (ft); Dietitians 1 (pt).
Languages Native Alaskan.
Facilities Dining room; Physical therapy room; Activities room; Chapel; Crafts room; Laundry room; Barber/Beauty shop; Library.

Activities Arts & crafts; Cards; Games; Reading groups; Prayer groups; Movies; Shopping trips; Dances/Social/Cultural gatherings; Intergenerational programs; Pet therapy; Sight-seeing excursions.

Ketchikan

Island View Manor
3100 Tongass, Ketchikan, AK 99901
(907) 225-5171
Admin Ed Mahn. *Dir of Nursing* Kathy Lockhart RN. *Medical Dir* Dr Tom Conley.
Licensure Skilled care; Day care. *Beds* SNF 29. *Private Pay Patients* 3%. *Certified* Medicaid; Medicare.
Owner Nonprofit organization/foundation.
Staff RNs 2 (ft), 1 (pt); LPNs 7 (ft); Nurses' aides 16 (ft); Physical therapists 1 (ft); Recreational therapists 2 (ft); Occupational therapists (contracted); Speech therapists (contracted); Dietitians 1 (pt).
Facilities Dining room; Physical therapy room; Activities room; Barber/Beauty shop.
Activities Arts & crafts; Cards; Games; Reading groups; Prayer groups; Movies; Shopping trips; Dances/Social/Cultural gatherings; Intergenerational programs; Pet therapy; Inter-agency activities.

Ketchikan Pioneers Home
141 Bryant, Ketchikan, AK 99901
(907) 225-4111, 225-4115 FAX
Admin Roslyn Reeder. *Dir of Nursing* Patricia Cooper. *Medical Dir* James A Wilson MD.
Licensure Skilled care; Residential care. *Beds* SNF 28; Residential care 19. *Private Pay Patients* 100%.
Owner Publicly owned.
Admissions Requirements Minimum age 65; Physician's request; Resident of Alaska for 15 consecutive years or 30 years.
Staff Physicians 1 (pt); RNs 6 (ft), 2 (pt); LPNs 2 (ft); Nurses' aides 9 (ft), 4 (pt); Physical therapists (contracted); Dietitians; Podiatrists (visiting); Recreational therapists; Activities coordinators 1 (ft).
Languages Filipino, Tlingit, Haida, Vietnamese.
Facilities Dining room; Physical therapy room; Activities room; Crafts room; Laundry room; Barber/Beauty shop; Library.
Activities Arts & crafts; Cards; Games; Reading groups; Prayer groups; Movies; Shopping trips; Dances/Social/Cultural gatherings; Intergenerational programs; Pet therapy; Adventure club; Recon club.

Kodiak

Kodiak Island Hospital
1915 E Rezanof Dr, Kodiak, AK 99615
(907) 486-3050
Admin Donald We. *Dir of Nursing* Kate Fitzgerald.
Licensure Intermediate care. *Beds* ICF 19. *Certified* Medicaid.

Owner Nonprofit corp.
Admissions Requirements Physician's request.
Staff Physicians 12 (ft); RNs 1 (ft), 1 (pt);
LPNs 3 (ft), 2 (pt); Nurses' aides 5 (ft), 4
(pt); Physical therapists 1 (ft); Activities
coordinators 1 (ft); Dietitians 1 (pt).
Affiliation Lutheran.
Facilities Dining room; Physical therapy
room; Activities room; Crafts room; Laundry
room.
Activities Arts & crafts; Cards; Games;
Reading groups; Prayer groups; Movies;
Shopping trips; Dances/Social/Cultural
gatherings; Cooking events; Barbeques; Van.

Nome

Quyaana Care Center
PO Box 966, 50 & Bering, Nome, AK 99762
(907) 443-3311
Admin Wallace Boyd.
Medical Dir Dr Dennis Ohlragge.
Licensure Intermediate care. *Beds* 15.
Certified Medicaid.
Admissions Requirements Medical
examination.
Staff Physicians 4 (ft); RNs 11 (ft); Nurses'
aides 4 (ft); Activities coordinators 1 (ft);
Dietitians 1 (ft); Audiologists 1 (ft); Dentists
2 (ft); Physical Therapy assistants 1 (ft);
Optometrists 1 (ft).
Facilities Dining room; Physical therapy
room; Activities room.
Activities Arts & crafts; Games; Shopping
trips.

Palmer

Palmer Pioneer Home
250 E Fireweed, Palmer, AK 99645
(907) 745-4241
Admin Nancy Hardies.
Beds 55.

Valley Hospital
PO Box 1687, 515 E Dahlia St, Palmer, AK
99645
(907) 745-4813
Admin James G Walsh.
Licensure Acute care. *Beds* 36. *Certified*
Medicaid; Medicare.

Petersburg

Petersburg General Hospital
PO Box 589, Petersburg, AK 99833
(907) 772-4291, 772-9271 FAX
Admin Gary W Grandy. *Dir of Nursing* Joy
Janssen RN. *Medical Dir* T H Wood.

Licensure Skilled care; Intermediate care. *Beds*
Swing beds SNF/ICF 14; Acute swing beds
SNF/ICF 11. *Private Pay Patients* 12%.
Certified Medicaid; Medicare.
Owner Publicly owned.
Staff Physicians 2 (ft), 9 (pt); RNs 5 (ft), 11
(pt); Nurses' aides 6 (ft), 3 (pt); Physical
therapists 1 (pt); Recreational therapists 1
(pt); Speech therapists 1 (pt); Activities
coordinators 1 (pt); Dietitians 1 (pt);
Ophthalmologists 1 (pt); Podiatrists 1 (pt);
Dentists 2 (pt).
Facilities Dining room; Physical therapy
room; Activities room; Crafts room; Barber/
Beauty shop.
Activities Arts & crafts; Cards; Games;
Reading groups; Prayer groups; Movies;
Dances/Social/Cultural gatherings;
Intergenerational programs; Pet therapy.

Seward

Wesleyan Nursing Home Inc
PO Box 430, 431 1st Ave, Seward, AK 99664
(907) 224-5241, 224-5250 FAX
Admin Richard W Jones NHA MBA. *Dir of
Nursing* Joan Clemens RN. *Medical Dir*
Tim Pollard MD.
Licensure Skilled care; Intermediate care. *Beds*
Swing beds SNF/ICF 66. *Certified* Medicaid.
Owner Nonprofit corp.
Admissions Requirements Medical
examination; Physician's request.
Staff Physicians; RNs; LPNs; Nurses' aides;
Physical therapists; Reality therapists;
Recreational therapists; Occupational
therapists; Speech therapists; Activities
coordinators; Dietitians; Ophthalmologists
(consultant); Podiatrists (consultant);
Audiologists (consultant).
Facilities Dining room; Physical therapy
room; Activities room; Chapel; Crafts room;
Laundry room; Barber/Beauty shop; Library.
Activities Arts & crafts; Cards; Games;
Reading groups; Prayer groups; Movies;
Shopping trips; Dances/Social/Cultural
gatherings; Intergenerational programs; Pet
therapy.

Sitka

Sitka Pioneers Home
PO Box 198, 120 Katlian St, Sitka, AK 99835
(907) 747-3213
Admin Gary Sheridan.
Beds 45.

Soldotna

Heritage Place
232 Rockwell, Soldotna, AK 99669
(907) 262-2545

Admin Dennis Murray. *Dir of Nursing* Nora
Morrisett. *Medical Dir* Dr Elmer Gaete.
Licensure Skilled care; Intermediate care. *Beds*
Swing beds SNF/ICF 45. *Private Pay
Patients* 3%. *Certified* Medicaid; Medicare.
Owner Nonprofit corp (Lutheran Health
Systems).
Admissions Requirements Medical
examination; Physician's request.
Staff RNs 5 (ft); LPNs; Nurses' aides 16 (ft);
Physical therapists; Occupational therapists;
Speech therapists; Activities coordinators 1
(ft); Dietitians.
Affiliation Lutheran.
Facilities Dining room; Physical therapy
room; Activities room; Laundry room;
Barber/Beauty shop; Library.
Activities Arts & crafts; Cards; Games;
Reading groups; Prayer groups; Movies;
Shopping trips; Intergenerational programs;
Pet therapy.

Valdez

Sourdough Place
PO Box 487, Valdez, AK 99686
(907) 835-4344
Admin Patrick J Londo.
Medical Dir Bernard Gerard MD.
Licensure Intermediate care; Intermediate care
for mentally retarded; Alzheimer's care. *Beds*
ICF 16; ICF/MR 64. *Certified* Medicaid;
Medicare.
Owner Publicly owned.
Staff Physicians 3 (pt); RNs 9 (ft), 4 (pt);
LPNs 1 (ft); Nurses' aides 76 (ft), 6 (pt);
Physical therapists 1 (pt); Recreational
therapists 3 (ft); Occupational therapists 1
(ft); Dietitians 1 (pt); Podiatrists 1 (pt);;
Dentists 1 (pt); QMRPs 4 (ft).
Languages Yurak.
Facilities Dining room; Physical therapy
room; Activities room; Crafts room; Laundry
room; Barber/Beauty shop; Library.
Activities Arts & crafts; Games; Movies;
Shopping trips; Dances/Social/Cultural
gatherings.

Wrangell

Wrangell General Hospital—LTC Facility
PO Box 80, Wrangell, AK 99929
(907) 874-3356
Admin John Vowell.
Licensure Skilled care; Intermediate care. *Beds*
Swing beds SNF/ICF 14. *Certified* Medicaid;
Medicare.

ARIZONA

Apache Junction

Apache Junction Health Center
2012 W Southern Ave, Apache Junction, AZ 85220
(602) 983-0700
Admin Deborah Parziale.
Beds 120.

Avondale

Careage of Avondale
350 E La Canada, Avondale, AZ 85323
(602) 932-2282, 932-4036 FAX
Admin Kay Hardin. *Dir of Nursing* Lisa Thomas. *Medical Dir* Dr John Hopkins.
Licensure Skilled care; Intermediate care; Alzheimer's care. *Beds* SNF 78; ICF 42; Alzheimer's unit 20. *Private Pay Patients* 30%. *Certified* Medicaid; Medicare.
Owner Proprietary corp (Western Health Care).
Admissions Requirements Medical examination; Physician's request.
Staff RNs 5 (ft), 4 (pt).
Languages Spanish.
Facilities Dining room; Physical therapy room; Activities room; Chapel; Crafts room; Barber/Beauty shop; Library; Patio; TV lounges; Popcorn lounge; 20-bed Alzheimer's unit; Patio.
Activities Arts & crafts; Cards; Games; Reading groups; Prayer groups; Movies; Shopping trips; Dances/Social/Cultural gatherings; Intergenerational programs; Pet therapy; Exercise; Grooming.

Benson

Quiburi Mission Samaritan Center
PO Box 2260, 850 S Hwy 80, Benson, AZ 85602
(602) 586-2372
Admin Jeris M Tangen.
Beds 60.

Bisbee

Copper Queen Community Hospital
Cole Ave & Bisbee Rd, Bisbee, AZ 85603
(602) 432-5383
Admin Phil Mears.
Licensure Intermediate care. *Beds* 21.
Owner Nonprofit corp.

Bullhead City

Silver Ridge Village
2812 Silver Creek Rd, Bullhead City, AZ 86442
(602) 763-1404
Admin James Stahl. *Dir of Nursing* Mary Fickel RN. *Medical Dir* Dr T Dallman.
Licensure Skilled care. *Beds* SNF 120. *Private Pay Patients* 40%. *Certified* Medicaid; Medicare.

Owner Nonprofit organization/foundation (Life Core Inc).
Staff RNs 5 (ft), 1 (pt); LPNs 5 (ft), 1 (pt); Nurses' aides 40 (ft), 3 (pt); Recreational therapists 1 (ft); 49 (ft), 2 (pt).
Languages Spanish.
Facilities Dining room; Physical therapy room; Activities room; Laundry room; Barber/Beauty shop.
Activities Arts & crafts; Cards; Games; Reading groups; Prayer groups; Movies; Shopping trips; Dances/Social/Cultural gatherings; Intergenerational programs.

Camp Verde

Arbors Health Care Center
PO Box 550, General Crook Hwy & Salt Mine Rd, Camp Verde, AZ 86322
(602) 567-5253, 567-3794 FAX
Admin Reid E Halpern. *Dir of Nursing* Christene Walker RN. *Medical Dir* Mark Westerveld MD.
Licensure Skilled care; Intermediate care; Personal care; Supervisory care. *Beds* SNF 60; ICF 42; Personal and supervisory care 18. *Private Pay Patients* 60%. *Certified* Medicaid; Medicare.
Owner Proprietary corp.
Admissions Requirements Minimum age 16; Medical examination; Physician's request.
Staff RNs 3 (ft), 3 (pt); LPNs 5 (ft), 3 (pt); Nurses' aides 25 (ft), 10 (pt); Physical therapists 1 (pt); Occupational therapists 1 (pt); Speech therapists 1 (pt); Activities coordinators 1 (ft), 1 (pt); Dietitians 1 (ft); Ophthalmologists 1 (pt); Podiatrists 1 (pt); Audiologists 1 (pt).
Facilities Dining room; Physical therapy room; Activities room; Chapel; Crafts room; Laundry room; Barber/Beauty shop; Library.
Activities Arts & crafts; Cards; Games; Reading groups; Prayer groups; Movies; Shopping trips; Dances/Social/Cultural gatherings; Intergenerational programs; Pet therapy.

Casa Grande

Desert Valley Care Center
950 N Arizola Rd, Casa Grande, AZ 85222
(602) 836-0863
Admin Sheri Lewis MBA. *Dir of Nursing* Dale Allison RN. *Medical Dir* James Barsz MD.
Licensure Skilled care; Alzheimer's care. *Beds* SNF 128. *Private Pay Patients* 22%. *Certified* Medicaid; Medicare.
Owner Nonprofit organization/foundation.
Admissions Requirements Minimum age 18; Medical examination; Physician's request.
Staff RNs; LPNs; Nurses' aides; Recreational therapists; Activities coordinators.
Facilities Dining room; Physical therapy room; Activities room; Crafts room; Laundry room; Barber/Beauty shop; Gift shop.

Activities Arts & crafts; Cards; Games; Reading groups; Prayer groups; Movies; Shopping trips; Dances/Social/Cultural gatherings; Intergenerational programs; Pet therapy.

Hoemako Long-Term Care
1101 E Florence Blvd, Casa Grande, AZ 85222
(602) 836-7401
Admin Robert Benjamin.
Licensure Skilled care. *Beds* 29.
Owner Nonprofit corp.

Chandler

Chandler Healthcare Center
416 S Dobson Rd, Chandler, AZ 85224
(602) 899-6717
Admin Cathy A Williams. *Dir of Nursing* Kathleen Carrasco. *Medical Dir* H J Wiens MD.
Licensure Skilled care; Alzheimer's care. *Beds* SNF 120. *Certified* Medicare.
Owner Proprietary corp (Beverly Enterprises).
Admissions Requirements Minimum age 18; Medical examination; Physician's request.
Staff RNs; LPNs; Nurses' aides.
Facilities Dining room; Physical therapy room; Activities room; Chapel; Barber/Beauty shop.
Activities Arts & crafts; Cards; Games; Reading groups; Prayer groups; Movies; Shopping trips; Dances/Social/Cultural gatherings.

Desert Cove Nursing Center
1750 W Frye Rd, Chandler, AZ 85224
(602) 899-0641
Admin Mary Anne Stanford.
Beds 120.

Pecos Nursing & Rehabilitation Center
1980 W Pecos, Chandler, AZ 85224
(602) 821-1268
Admin Kathleen Gustafson. *Dir of Nursing* Mary Jane Falk. *Medical Dir* Dr Grace Busch.
Licensure Skilled care; Intermediate care. *Beds* SNF 60; ICF 60. *Private Pay Patients* 50%. *Certified* Medicaid; Medicare.
Owner Proprietary corp.
Admissions Requirements Minimum age 21; Medical examination; Physician's request.
Staff RNs 5 (ft), 3 (pt); LPNs 8 (ft), 8 (pt); Nurses' aides 40 (ft), 20 (pt); Activities coordinators 2 (ft); Dietitians 1 (ft); Podiatrists 1 (ft); Audiologists 1 (ft).
Facilities Dining room; Physical therapy room; Activities room; Laundry room; Barber/Beauty shop; Ventilator program; Peritoneal dialysis program.
Activities Arts & crafts; Cards; Games; Reading groups; Prayer groups; Movies; Shopping trips; Dances/Social/Cultural gatherings; Pet therapy.

Chinle

Chinle Nursing Home
PO Box 910, Chinle, AZ 86503
(602) 674-5216
Admin Verna Tsosie.
Licensure Skilled care. *Beds* 79. *Certified*
Medicare.
Owner Nonprofit corp.

Cottonwood

Rio Verde Healthcare Center
197 S Willard, Cottonwood, AZ 86326
(602) 634-5548
Admin Gary R Olson. *Dir of Nursing* Winnie
Bartling RN. *Medical Dir* Dr Welley.
Licensure Skilled care; Intermediate care;
Retirement. *Beds* SNF; ICF 80. *Certified*
Medicare.
Owner Proprietary corp.
Admissions Requirements Minimum age 18;
Medical examination.
Staff RNs; LPNs; Nurses' aides; Physical
therapists 1 (pt); Recreational therapists 1
(ft), 1 (pt); Occupational therapists 1 (pt);
Speech therapists 1 (pt); Activities
coordinators 1 (ft), 1 (pt); Dietitians 1 (pt).
Facilities Dining room; Physical therapy
room; Activities room; Crafts room; Laundry
room; Barber/Beauty shop.
Activities Arts & crafts; Cards; Games;
Reading groups; Prayer groups; Movies;
Shopping trips; Dances/Social/Cultural
gatherings.

Douglas

Douglas Manor Care Center
1400 N San Antonio, Douglas, AZ 85607
(602) 364-7937
Admin Maria J Montion.
Beds 64.

Southeast Arizona Medical Center
RR1 Box 30, Douglas, AZ 85607
(602) 364-7931
Admin Robert Benjamin. *Dir of Nursing* Ruth
Kish RN.
Licensure Skilled care; Intermediate care. *Beds*
Swing beds, SNF/ICF. *Certified* Medicare.
Owner Nonprofit corp.
Admissions Requirements Physician's request.
Staff Physicians 7 (pt); RNs 2 (ft), 2 (pt);
LPNs 3 (ft), 2 (pt); Nurses' aides 9 (ft), 5
(pt); Physical therapists 2 (ft); Activities
coordinators 1 (ft), 1 (pt); Dietitians 1 (pt);
Social workers 1 (ft); 1 (pt); Physician
assistants 1 (pt).
Languages Spanish.
Facilities Dining room; Physical therapy
room; Activities room; Chapel; Crafts room;
Barber/Beauty shop; Enclosed patio.
Activities Arts & crafts; Cards; Games;
Reading groups; Prayer groups; Movies.

Flagstaff

Los Arcos Health Care Center
800 W University Ave, Flagstaff, AZ 86002
(602) 779-6931
Admin Johnie Bradshaw-Durham. *Dir of
Nursing* L Martin RN. *Medical Dir* Dr
Seeby.
Licensure Skilled care; Intermediate care. *Beds*
SNF 60; ICF 10. *Certified* Medicare.
Owner Proprietary corp (US Care Corp).
Admissions Requirements Minimum age 18;
Medical examination; Physician's request.
Staff Physicians 1 (pt); RNs 8 (ft), 2 (pt);
LPNs 3 (ft), 1 (pt); Nurses' aides 12 (ft), 4
(pt); Physical therapists 1 (pt); Recreational
therapists 1 (ft); Occupational therapists 1
(pt); Speech therapists 1 (pt); Activities
coordinators 1 (ft); Dietitians 1 (pt);
Ophthalmologists 1 (pt).

Languages Spanish, Navajo.
Facilities Dining room; Physical therapy
room; Activities room; Chapel; Laundry
room; Barber/Beauty shop.
Activities Arts & crafts; Cards; Games;
Reading groups; Prayer groups; Movies;
Shopping trips; Dances/Social/Cultural
gatherings.

**Skilled Nursing Facility of Flagstaff Medical
Center**
1200 N Beaver St, Flagstaff, AZ 86001
(602) 779-3366, ext 4260
Admin Becky Nelson. *Dir of Nursing* Phyllis
Moore RN. *Medical Dir* B A Finney.
Licensure Skilled care. *Beds* SNF 18. *Certified*
Medicaid; Medicare.
Owner Nonprofit organization/foundation.
Admissions Requirements Medical
examination; Physician's request.
Staff Physicians 1 (pt); RNs 5 (ft); LPNs 2
(ft), 1 (pt); Nurses' aides 3 (ft), 5 (pt);
Physical therapists 1 (pt); Occupational
therapists 1 (pt); Speech therapists
(contracted); Activities coordinators 1 (pt);
Dietitians (contracted).
Languages Navajo.
Facilities Dining room; Physical therapy
room; Activities room; Crafts room.
Activities Arts & crafts; Cards; Games;
Reading groups; Prayer groups; Movies;
Shopping trips; Intergenerational programs;
Pet therapy; Mobility skills; Activities of
daily living.

Florence

Pinal County Nursing Center
400 S Central Ave, Florence, AZ 85232
(602) 868-5854
Admin Charles R Stevens P D FACHCA. *Dir
of Nursing* Pamela S Marquez RN. *Medical
Dir* O V Moreno MD.
Licensure Skilled care; Intermediate care;
Supervisory. *Beds* SNF 53; Supervisory 55.
Owner Nonprofit organization/foundation.
Admissions Requirements Medical
examination; Physician's request.
Staff RNs 4 (ft), 1 (pt); LPNs; Nurses' aides;
Physical therapists; Reality therapists;
Recreational therapists 4 (ft), 1 (pt); Speech
therapists; Activities coordinators 1 (ft);
Dietitians 1 (ft); Ophthalmologists 1 (pt);
Podiatrists 1 (pt); Dentists 1 (ft).
Languages Spanish.
Facilities Dining room; Activities room;
Crafts room; Laundry room; Barber/Beauty
shop; Library.
Activities Arts & crafts; Cards; Games;
Reading groups; Prayer groups; Movies;
Shopping trips; Dances/Social/Cultural
gatherings; College courses.

Pinal General Hospital
PO Box 789, Adamsville Rd, Florence, AZ
85232
(602) 868-5841
Admin Mary A Fields.
Licensure Intermediate care. *Beds* 21.
Certified Medicare.
Owner Publicly owned.

Glendale

Colter Village
5125 N 58th Ave, Glendale, AZ 85301
(602) 931-5800
Admin Carolyn Kindler. *Dir of Nursing* Kay
Hardin RN.
Licensure Skilled care; Intermediate care;
Independent retirement; Assisted retirement;
Personal care. *Beds* SNF 186; ICF;
Retirement apts 105.
Owner Proprietary corp (Basic America
Retirement Communities).
Staff Physicians.

Glen Ridge Manor
5910 W Northern Ave, Glendale, AZ 85302
(602) 937-2779
Admin Maureen R Groves. *Dir of Nursing*
Charlene Wagner. *Medical Dir* Jame Beech
MD.
Licensure Skilled care. *Beds* SNF 135.
Owner Proprietary corp.
Admissions Requirements Medical
examination; Physician's request.
Staff Physicians 1 (pt); RNs 9 (ft); LPNs 14
(ft), 2 (pt); Nurses' aides 1 (ft), 1 (pt);
Physical therapists 1 (pt); Occupational
therapists 1 (pt); Speech therapists 1 (pt);
Activities coordinators 1 (ft); Dietitians 1
(ft); Ophthalmologists 1 (pt); Dentists 1 (pt).
Languages Spanish.
Facilities Dining room; Physical therapy
room; Laundry room; Barber/Beauty shop.
Activities Arts & crafts; Cards; Games;
Reading groups; Prayer groups; Movies;
Shopping trips; Dances/Social/Cultural
gatherings.

Glencroft Care Center
8641 N 67th Ave, Glendale, AZ 85302
(602) 939-9475
Admin Norm Klassen. *Dir of Nursing* Linda
Byler RN. *Medical Dir* Dr R Vito.
Licensure Skilled care; Intermediate care;
Personal care. *Beds* SNF 161; ICF 40;
Personal 24.
Owner Nonprofit corp.
Staff Physicians; RNs; LPNs; Nurses' aides;
Physical therapists; Recreational therapists;
Occupational therapists; Speech therapists;
Activities coordinators; Dietitians;
Ophthalmologists; Podiatrists; Dentists.

Glendale Care Center
4704 W Diana Ave, Glendale, AZ 85302
(602) 247-3949
Admin Michael J Coretti.
Licensure Skilled care; Intermediate care;
Personal care. *Beds* SNF 98; ICF 63;
Personal 31.
Owner Nonprofit corp (Volunteers of America
Care).

Glendale Nursing Home
7022 N 48th Ave, Glendale, AZ 85301
(602) 934-7265
Admin Peggy C Wilson.
Medical Dir Honor L Jereb.
Licensure Skilled care. *Beds* SNF 61.
Owner Proprietary corp.
Admissions Requirements Medical
examination; Physician's request.
Staff RNs 3 (ft), 1 (pt); LPNs 8 (ft); Nurses'
aides 27 (ft); Activities coordinators 1 (ft).
Languages Spanish, Hindi, German.
Facilities Dining room; Activities room;
Crafts room; Laundry room.
Activities Arts & crafts; Cards; Games;
Reading groups; Prayer groups; Movies;
Shopping trips; Dances/Social/Cultural
gatherings; Parties.

Life Care Center of North Glendale
13620 N 55th Ave, Glendale, AZ 85304
(602) 843-8433
Admin Phillip Rollins.
Beds 192.

Globe

Gila County Care Center
1100 Monroe St, Globe, AZ 85501
(602) 425-5721
Admin Linda Palmer, RN. *Dir of Nursing*
Larry McGee. *Medical Dir* Efrain Pineres
MD.
Licensure Skilled care. *Beds* SNF 69.
Owner Nonprofit organization/foundation.
Admissions Requirements Physician's request.

Staff Physicians 1 (ft); RNs 4 (ft), 1 (pt); LPNs 4 (ft); Nurses' aides 20 (ft), 3 (pt); Physical therapists 1 (ft); Activities coordinators 1 (ft); Dietitians 1 (ft).
Languages Spanish, Italian.
Facilities Dining room; Physical therapy room; Activities room; Chapel; Crafts room; Barber/Beauty shop.
Activities Arts & crafts; Games; Reading groups; Prayer groups; Movies; Dances/Social/Cultural gatherings.

Heritage Health Care Center
1300 South St, Globe, AZ 85501
(602) 425-3118
Admin Norm Smith. *Dir of Nursing* Barbara Foree. *Medical Dir* Wilbur Haak MD.
Licensure Skilled care; Intermediate care. *Beds* Swing beds SNF/ICF 100. *Private Pay Patients* 20%. *Certified* Medicaid; Medicare.
Owner Proprietary corp.
Admissions Requirements Medical examination; Physician's request.
Staff RNs; LPNs; Nurses' aides; Activities coordinators.
Facilities Dining room; Physical therapy room; Activities room; Laundry room; Barber/Beauty shop.
Activities Arts & crafts; Cards; Games; Reading groups; Movies; Dances/Social/Cultural gatherings; Intergenerational programs; Pet therapy.

Green Valley

Park Centre Healthcare at La Posada
21341 S Heather Ridge Cir, Green Valley, AZ 85614
(602) 648-8381
Admin Lisa H Israel. *Dir of Nursing* Carol J Krause. *Medical Dir* Michael Amadei.
Licensure Skilled care; Independent living. *Beds* SNF 60; Independent living apartments 174. *Private Pay Patients* 91%. *Certified* Medicare.
Owner Nonprofit organization/foundation.
Admissions Requirements Physician's request.
Staff RNs 6 (ft), 2 (pt); LPNs 2 (ft), 1 (pt); Nurses' aides 22 (ft), 1 (pt); Physical therapists 1 (ft); Recreational therapists 1 (ft); Occupational therapists 1 (pt); Speech therapists 1 (pt); Dietitians.
Languages Spanish.
Facilities Dining room; Physical therapy room; Laundry room; Barber/Beauty shop; Library; Activities/craft room.
Activities Arts & crafts; Cards; Games; Reading groups; Prayer groups; Movies; Shopping trips; Dances/Social/Cultural gatherings; Intergenerational programs; Pet therapy.

Santa Rita Health Care Center
150 N La Canada Dr, Green Valley, AZ 85614
(602) 625-2500
Admin Margaret Y Mitchell. *Dir of Nursing* Audrey Perry. *Medical Dir* Dr Alex McGlamery.
Licensure Skilled care; Personal care. *Beds* SNF 98; Personal 19. *Certified* Medicare.
Owner Proprietary corp.
Admissions Requirements Minimum age 16; Medical examination; Physician's request.
Staff Physicians 7 (pt); RNs 6 (ft), 6 (pt); LPNs 3 (ft), 3 (pt); Nurses' aides 31 (ft), 17 (pt); Recreational therapists 1 (ft); Occupational therapists 1 (pt); Speech therapists 1 (pt); Activities coordinators 1 (ft); Dietitians 1 (pt); Ophthalmologists 1 (pt); Dentists 1 (pt).
Languages Spanish.
Facilities Dining room; Activities room; Chapel; Barber/Beauty shop; Library.
Activities Arts & crafts; Cards; Games; Reading groups; Prayer groups; Movies; Shopping trips.

Kingman

Kingman Health Care Center
1081 Kathleen Ave, Kingman, AZ 86401
(602) 753-5574
Admin Patsy A Hawtin.
Licensure Skilled care; Personal care. *Beds* SNF 80; Personal 40.
Owner Proprietary corp.

Lake Havasu

Havasu Nursing Center
3576 Kearsage, Lake Havasu, AZ 86403
(602) 453-1500, 453-6675 FAX
Admin Nancy Miller RN. *Dir of Nursing* Dolores Givens RN. *Medical Dir* Dr Thomas Wrona.
Licensure Skilled care. *Beds* SNF 120. *Private Pay Patients* 50%. *Certified* Medicaid; Medicare.
Owner Proprietary corp (Health Facilities Management Corp).
Admissions Requirements Medical examination; Physician's request.
Staff Physicians 10 (ft); RNs 5 (ft), 4 (pt); LPNs 8 (ft), 4 (pt); Nurses' aides 40 (ft), 20 (pt); Physical therapists 1 (ft); Recreational therapists 1 (ft); Occupational therapists 1 (ft); Activities coordinators 1 (ft); Dietitians 1 (ft); Ophthalmologists 1 (ft); Podiatrists 1 (ft).
Languages Spanish, German, Navajo.
Facilities Dining room; Physical therapy room; Activities room; Chapel; Crafts room; Laundry room; Barber/Beauty shop.
Activities Arts & crafts; Cards; Games; Reading groups; Prayer groups; Movies; Shopping trips; Dances/Social/Cultural gatherings; Intergenerational programs; Pet therapy.

Laveen

American Indian Nursing Home
8201 W Baseline, PO Box 9, Laveen, AZ 85339
(602) 237-3813
Admin Victor E Vallet.
Licensure Skilled care; Personal care. *Beds* 80.
Owner Nonprofit corp.
Admissions Requirements Physician's request.
Staff RNs 5 (ft); LPNs 7 (ft); Physical therapists 2 (ft); Reality therapists 2 (ft); Recreational therapists 2 (ft); Activities coordinators 1 (ft); Dietitians 1 (ft).
Facilities Dining room; Physical therapy room; Activities room; Laundry room.
Activities Arts & crafts; Cards; Games; Reading groups; Prayer groups; Movies; Shopping trips; Dances/Social/Cultural gatherings.

Mesa

Chula Vista Nursing Home
60 S 58th St, Mesa, AZ 85206
(602) 832-3903
Admin Jane Wagner.
Licensure Skilled care; Intermediate care. *Beds* SNF 55; ICF 45.
Owner Proprietary corp.

Citadel Care Center
5121 E Broadway, Mesa, AZ 85206
(602) 832-5555
Admin Robertta R Holka.
Beds 128.

Cosada Villa Nursing Center
420 W 10th Pl, Mesa, AZ 85201
(602) 833-4226
Admin Karen L Cooper, RN. *Dir of Nursing* Estelita Foley RN. *Medical Dir* Dr R L Smith.

Licensure Skilled care; Intermediate care. *Beds* 174. *Certified* Medicare; County.
Owner Proprietary corp.
Admissions Requirements Minimum age 18.
Staff Physicians; RNs; LPNs; Nurses' aides; Physical therapists; Recreational therapists; Occupational therapists; Speech therapists; Activities coordinators; Dietitians; Ophthalmologists.
Facilities Dining room; Physical therapy room; Activities room; Crafts room; Barber/Beauty shop.
Activities Arts & crafts; Cards; Games; Reading groups; Prayer groups; Movies; Shopping trips; Dances/Social/Cultural gatherings.

Desert SunQuest Care Center
2145 W Southern Ave, Mesa, AZ 85202
(602) 890-4800
Admin Kaye L Giese.
Beds 180.

East Mesa Care Center
51 S 48th St, Mesa, AZ 85206
(602) 832-8333
Admin Emmie Lester. *Dir of Nursing* Lois Charette. *Medical Dir* Dr Richard Adamson.
Licensure Skilled care; Intermediate care; Alzheimer's care. *Beds* SNF 136; ICF 48. *Private Pay Patients* 25%. *Certified* Medicaid; Medicare.
Owner Proprietary corp.
Admissions Requirements Minimum age over 18; Medical examination; Physician's request.
Staff RNs 7 (ft), 3 (pt); LPNs 23 (ft), 5 (pt); Nurses' aides 43 (ft), 8 (pt); Physical therapists 1 (ft); Activities coordinators 4 (ft), 2 (pt); Dietitians 1 (ft); Other staff 20 (ft).
Languages Spanish, Polish.
Facilities Dining room; Physical therapy room; Activities room; Chapel; Crafts room; Laundry room; Barber/Beauty shop; Library; Behavioral health unit.
Activities Arts & crafts; Cards; Games; Reading groups; Prayer groups; Movies; Shopping trips; Dances/Social/Cultural gatherings; Intergenerational programs; Pet therapy.

Golden Mesa Nursing Home
715 N Country Club, Mesa, AZ 85201
(602) 969-1305
Admin William Constable.
Licensure Skilled care. *Beds* 109.
Owner Proprietary corp.
Admissions Requirements Minimum age 21; Medical examination; Physician's request.
Staff RNs 4 (ft); LPNs 4 (ft), 2 (pt); Nurses' aides 29 (ft); Activities coordinators 2 (ft).
Facilities Dining room; Physical therapy room; Activities room; Laundry room; Barber/Beauty shop; Library.
Activities Arts & crafts; Cards; Games; Reading groups; Prayer groups; Movies; Shopping trips; Dances/Social/Cultural gatherings.

Good Shepherd Villa
5848 E University Dr, Mesa, AZ 85205
(602) 981-0098
Admin Luann Foos. *Dir of Nursing* Carla H Dolinka.
Licensure Skilled care; Retirement; Alzheimer's care. *Beds* SNF 80; Retirement apts 100. *Private Pay Patients* 70%. *Certified* Medicaid; Medicare.
Owner Nonprofit corp.
Facilities Dining room; Physical therapy room; Activities room; Chapel; Crafts room; Laundry room; Barber/Beauty shop.
Activities Arts & crafts; Cards; Games; Reading groups; Prayer groups; Movies; Shopping trips; Dances/Social/Cultural gatherings; Intergenerational programs; Pet therapy.

Hearthstone of Mesa
215 S Power Rd, Mesa, AZ 85206
(602) 985-6992
Admin Harald W Ackermann. *Dir of Nursing*
Susan Pyle. *Medical Dir* Dr Robert Tully.
Licensure Skilled care; Intermediate care. *Beds*
Swing beds SNF/ICF 120. *Private Pay
Patients* 85-95%. *Certified* Medicare.
Owner Proprietary corp (ARA Living
Centers).
Admissions Requirements Physician's request.
Activities Arts & crafts; Cards; Games;
Reading groups; Prayer groups; Movies;
Shopping trips; Dances/Social/Cultural
gatherings; Intergenerational programs.

Las Flores Nursing Center
6458 E Broadway, Mesa, AZ 85206
(602) 832-5160
Admin Kathleen M Bauer. *Dir of Nursing*
Darlene Raszler. *Medical Dir* Joseph
Chatham MD.
Licensure Skilled care; Alzheimer's care. *Beds*
SNF 100. *Certified* Medicare.
Owner Proprietary corp (Vari-Care Inc).
Admissions Requirements Minimum age 16;
Medical examination; Physician's request.
Staff Physicians 3 (pt); RNs 7 (ft), 6 (pt);
LPNs 7 (ft), 1 (pt); Nurses' aides 41 (ft), 3
(pt); Physical therapists 1 (ft); Occupational
therapists 1 (pt); Speech therapists 1 (pt);
Activities coordinators 1 (ft), 1 (pt);
Dietitians 1 (ft); Podiatrists 1 (pt); Social
workers 1 (ft), 1 (pt); Dentists 1 (pt).
Facilities Dining room; Physical therapy
room; Activities room; Crafts room; Laundry
room; Barber/Beauty shop; Library.
Activities Arts & crafts; Cards; Games;
Reading groups; Prayer groups; Movies;
Dances/Social/Cultural gatherings.

Mesa Christian Home
255 W Brown Rd, Mesa, AZ 85201
(602) 833-3988
Admin Sally W Worthington.
Licensure Skilled care; Intermediate care;
Personal care; Alzheimer's care. *Beds* SNF
112; Personal 45.
Owner Nonprofit corp (Luth Hosp & Homes
Socty).
Staff RNs 14 (ft), 5 (pt); LPNs 10 (ft), 5 (pt);
Nurses' aides 61 (ft), 20 (pt); Recreational
therapists 1 (ft); Activities coordinators 3
(ft), 1 (pt).
Facilities Dining room; Physical therapy
room; Activities room; Crafts room; Laundry
room; Barber/Beauty shop; Library;
Resident's kitchen.
Activities Arts & crafts; Games; Reading
groups; Movies; Shopping trips; Dances/
Social/Cultural gatherings; Swimming.

Mesa Extended Care
715 N Country Club Dr, Mesa, AZ 85201
(602) 969-1305
Admin Jacqueline Anderson.
Beds 109.

Mesa Lutheran Hospital
525 W Brown Rd, Mesa, AZ 85201
(602) 834-1211
Admin Betty Capes.
Beds 20.

Mi Casa Nursing Center
330 S Pinnule Cir, Mesa, AZ 85206
(602) 981-0687
Admin Rosemary Anderson. *Dir of Nursing*
Alice Manchester RN. *Medical Dir* Dr
Warren Koutnik.

Licensure Skilled care; Intermediate care;
Intermediate care for mentally retarded;
Alzheimer's care. *Beds* SNF 120; ICF 40;
ICF/MR 20. *Private Pay Patients* 43%.
Certified Medicaid; Medicare.
Owner Proprietary corp (Life Care Centers of
America).
Admissions Requirements Physician's request.
Staff Physicians; RNs; LPNs; Nurses' aides;
Physical therapists; Occupational therapists;
Speech therapists; Activities coordinators;
Dietitians.
Languages Spanish.
Facilities Dining room; Physical therapy
room; Activities room; Laundry room;
Barber/Beauty shop.
Activities Arts & crafts; Cards; Games;
Reading groups; Prayer groups; Movies;
Shopping trips; Dances/Social/Cultural
gatherings; Intergenerational programs; Pet
therapy.

Royal Nursing Home
108 E 2nd Ave, Mesa, AZ 85202
(602) 834-1490
Admin Bruce Grambley.
Licensure Skilled care. *Beds* 46.
Owner Proprietary corp.

Nogales

**Carondelet Holy Cross Hospital & Geriatric
Center**
1230 Target Range Rd, Nogales, AZ 85621
(602) 287-2771, 287-7314 FAX
Admin C Ray Honaker. *Dir of Nursing* Kay
Harding. *Medical Dir* Karl Meyer MD.
Licensure Skilled care; Intermediate care;
Alzheimer's care. *Beds* Swing beds SNF/ICF
49. *Certified* Medicaid; Medicare.
Owner Nonprofit corp (Carondelet Health
Care Corp).
Languages Spanish.
Affiliation Roman Catholic.
Activities Arts & crafts; Cards; Games;
Reading groups; Prayer groups; Movies;
Shopping trips; Dances/Social/Cultural
gatherings; Intergenerational programs; Pet
therapy.

Payson

Manzanita Manor
807 W Longhorn Rd, Payson, AZ 85541
(602) 474-1120
Admin Jeanne Cohill.
Beds 64.

Payson Care Center
107 E Lone Pine Dr, Payson, AZ 85541
(602) 474-6896
Admin Michael Denney. *Dir of Nursing*
JoAnne Dudley RN. *Medical Dir* W
Romberger MD.
Licensure Skilled care; Intermediate care;
Personal care. *Beds* SNF 41; ICF 19;
Personal care 33. *Certified* Medicare.
Owner Proprietary corp (Life Care Centers of
America).
Facilities Dining room; Physical therapy
room; Activities room; Chapel; Crafts room;
Barber/Beauty shop.
Activities Arts & crafts; Cards; Games;
Reading groups; Prayer groups; Movies;
Dances/Social/Cultural gatherings.

Peoria

Camelot Manor
11311 N 99th Ave, Peoria, AZ 85345
(602) 977-8373
Admin Sharon Kempton.
Licensure Personal care. *Beds* 48.
Owner Proprietary corp.

Good Shepherd Retirement Center
10323 W Olive Ave, Peoria, AZ 85345
(602) 974-2555
Admin Katheryn Pipho. *Dir of Nursing*
Loretta Reardanz RN. *Medical Dir* Peter
Chan MD.
Licensure Skilled care; Intermediate care;
Personal care. *Beds* SNF 116; ICF 77;
Personal 20. *Certified* Medicaid.
Owner Nonprofit corp (Evangelical Lutheran/
Good Samaritan Society).
Admissions Requirements Minimum age 18;
Medical examination; Physician's request.
Staff RNs 5 (ft), 6 (pt); LPNs 10 (ft), 8 (pt);
Nurses' aides 48 (ft), 11 (pt); Activities
coordinators 3 (ft); Dietitians 1 (ft).
Languages Spanish.
Affiliation Lutheran.
Facilities Dining room; Physical therapy
room; Activities room; Chapel; Crafts room;
Barber/Beauty shop; Library.
Activities Arts & crafts; Cards; Games;
Reading groups; Prayer groups; Movies;
Shopping trips; Dances/Social/Cultural
gatherings.

Plaza del Rio Care Center
13215 N 94th Dr, Peoria, AZ 85381
(602) 933-7722, (800) 243-5556 FAX
Admin Gail A Chase. *Dir of Nursing* Donna
Swicklik RN. *Medical Dir* Edward H
Kowaleski MD.
Licensure Skilled care; Intermediate care;
Personal care; Alzheimer's care. *Beds* SNF
86; ICF 34; Personal care 8. *Private Pay
Patients* 87%. *Certified* Medicaid; Medicare.
Owner Privately owned.
Admissions Requirements Medical
examination; Physician's request.
Staff RNs 7 (ft), 7 (pt); LPNs 9 (ft), 4 (pt);
Nurses' aides 62 (ft), 10 (pt); Recreational
therapists 1 (ft); Activities coordinators 1
(ft); Dietitians 1 (ft).
Languages Spanish.
Facilities Dining room; Physical therapy
room; Activities room; Chapel; Crafts room;
Laundry room; Barber/Beauty shop.
Activities Arts & crafts; Cards; Games;
Reading groups; Prayer groups; Movies;
Shopping trips; Dances/Social/Cultural
gatherings; Intergenerational programs; Pet
therapy; Cooking; Baking; Homemaking
exercises.

Sun Grove Care Center
20625 N Lake Pleasant Dr, Peoria, AZ 85345
(602) 247-5179
Admin Margaret M Mullan.
Beds 128.

Phoenix

Arizona Eastern Star Home
4602 N 24th St, Phoenix, AZ 85016
(602) 954-9178
Admin Dean Sloniger.
Licensure Skilled care. *Beds* SNF 36.
Owner Nonprofit corp.
Admissions Requirements Minimum age 18;
Medical examination.
Staff RNs 4 (ft), 4 (pt); LPNs 1 (ft), 1 (pt);
Nurses' aides 18 (ft), 4 (pt); Activities
coordinators; Dietitians.
Affiliation Order of Eastern Star.
Facilities Dining room; Activities room;
Chapel; Crafts room; Laundry room; Barber/
Beauty shop; Library.
Activities Arts & crafts; Cards; Games;
Reading groups; Prayer groups; Movies;
Shopping trips; Dances/Social/Cultural
gatherings.

Beatitudes Campus of Care
1616 W Glendale Ave, Phoenix, AZ 85021
(602) 995-2611
Admin Rev Kenneth H Buckwald, DD.

Licensure Skilled care; Personal care. *Beds* SNF 156; Personal 120.
Owner Nonprofit corp.

Bel Isle Nursing Home
PO Box 9576, Phoenix, AZ 85068-9576
(602) 266-4122
Admin Daniel J Belisle.
Licensure Skilled care. *Beds* 61.
Owner Proprietary corp.

Bells Lodge
4202 N 20th Ave, Phoenix, AZ 85015
(602) 264-3824
Admin Melanie S Seamans. *Dir of Nursing* Patricia Phillips. *Medical Dir* Dr William Morrissey.
Licensure Skilled care. *Beds* SNF 100. *Certified* Medicaid; Medicare.
Owner Proprietary corp (Hillhaven Corp).
Admissions Requirements Minimum age 18; Medical examination; Physician's request.
Staff RNs 8 (ft), 2 (pt); LPNs 12 (ft), 3 (pt); Nurses' aides 35 (ft), 8 (pt); Activities coordinators 1 (ft), 1 (pt).
Languages Spanish.
Facilities Dining room; Physical therapy room; Activities room; Laundry room; Barber/Beauty shop; Library; Lobby; Lounges; Enclosed patio.
Activities Arts & crafts; Cards; Games; Reading groups; Prayer groups; Shopping trips; Movies; Dances/Social/Cultural gatherings.

Bryans Memorial Extended Care Center
9155 N 3rd St, Phoenix, AZ 85020
(602) 944-1666
Admin Judy K Clements. *Dir of Nursing* Barbara Perry RN.
Licensure Skilled care. *Beds* SNF 170. *Certified* Medicaid; Medicare.
Owner Nonprofit organization/foundation.
Staff RNs; LPNs; Nurses' aides; Physical therapists; Recreational therapists; Occupational therapists; Speech therapists; Activities coordinators; Dietitians.
Facilities Dining room; Physical therapy room; Activities room; Crafts room; Laundry room; Barber/Beauty shop; Library; Ventilator unit.
Activities Arts & crafts; Cards; Games; Reading groups; Prayer groups; Movies; Shopping trips; Dances/Social/Cultural gatherings; Intergenerational programs; Pet therapy; Religious services.

Capri Nursing Home
1501 E Orangewood Ave, Phoenix, AZ 85020
(602) 944-1574
Admin William E Fay.
Licensure Skilled care. *Beds* 133.
Owner Proprietary corp.

Chris Ridge Village Health Center
6246 N 19th Ave, Bldg 1, Phoenix, AZ 85015
(602) 433-6300
Admin Lynn Dennis.
Beds 150.

Christian Care Nursing Center
11812 N 19th Ave, Phoenix, AZ 85029
(602) 861-3241
Admin Alba de Alcala.
Medical Dir Linda L Nelson.
Licensure Skilled care; Intermediate care. *Beds* 60.
Owner Nonprofit corp.
Admissions Requirements Medical examination; Physician's request.
Staff RNs 4 (ft), 1 (pt); LPNs 3 (ft), 2 (pt); Nurses' aides 26 (ft); Activities coordinators 1 (ft); Physical therapy aides 1 (ft).
Facilities Dining room; Physical therapy room; Activities room; Barber/Beauty shop.
Activities Arts & crafts; Games; Prayer groups; Singing; Exercises.

Crestview Convalescent Lodge
2101 E Maryland, Phoenix, AZ 85016
(602) 264-6427
Admin Michael L Fahey. *Dir of Nursing* Mary Jeffery RN. *Medical Dir* William Dunn MD.
Licensure Skilled care; Retirement. *Beds* SNF 66. *Private Pay Patients* 100%.
Owner Nonprofit corp.
Admissions Requirements Minimum age 62; Medical examination; Physician's request.
Staff RNs 8 (ft); LPNs 4 (ft), 2 (pt); Nurses' aides 25 (ft); Activities coordinators 1 (ft), 1 (pt).
Affiliation Roman Catholic.
Facilities Dining room; Activities room; Crafts room; Barber/Beauty shop; Library; Social services.
Activities Arts & crafts; Cards; Games; Reading groups; Prayer groups; Movies.

Desert Haven Nursing Center
2645 E Thomas Rd, Phoenix, AZ 85016
(602) 956-8000
Admin Michael K Fitz. *Dir of Nursing* Sharon Owen. *Medical Dir* Dr Mark Wyse.
Licensure Skilled care; Intermediate care. *Beds* Swing beds SNF/ICF 115. *Private Pay Patients* 17%. *Certified* Medicaid; Medicare.
Owner Proprietary corp (Vari-Care Inc).
Admissions Requirements Medical examination; Physician's request.
Staff RNs 4 (ft); LPNs 13 (ft); Nurses' aides 70 (ft); Activities coordinators 2 (ft).
Languages Spanish.
Facilities Dining room; Physical therapy room; Activities room; Barber/Beauty shop.
Activities Arts & crafts; Cards; Games; Prayer groups; Movies; Intergenerational programs; Pet therapy.

Desert Terrace Nursing Center
2509 N 24th St, Phoenix, AZ 85008
(602) 273-1347
Admin Ray McKisson. *Dir of Nursing* Susan Caswell RN. *Medical Dir* Joseph Freund MD.
Licensure Skilled care. *Beds* SNF 108. *Certified* Medicare.
Owner Proprietary corp (Vari-Care Inc).
Admissions Requirements Medical examination; Physician's request.
Staff Physicians 10 (pt); RNs 8 (ft), 3 (pt); LPNs 7 (ft), 3 (pt); Nurses' aides 40 (ft), 6 (pt); Physical therapists 2 (ft); Occupational therapists 1 (pt); Speech therapists 1 (pt); Activities coordinators 2 (ft); Dietitians 1 (pt); Ophthalmologists 1 (pt); Podiatrists 1 (pt); Dentists 1 (pt).
Languages Spanish.
Facilities Dining room; Physical therapy room; Activities room; Crafts room; Laundry room; Barber/Beauty shop; Library.
Activities Arts & crafts; Cards; Games; Reading groups; Prayer groups; Movies; Shopping trips; Dances/Social/Cultural gatherings.

Desert Valley Rehabilitation Medical Center
16640 N 38th St, Phoenix, AZ 85032
(602) 482-6671
Admin Adrian C Gambrill BSG. *Dir of Nursing* Martha M Schwegler RN. *Medical Dir* James Burks MD.
Licensure Skilled care; Intermediate care; Sub-acute care; Retirement. *Beds* SNF 150; ICF 50. *Private Pay Patients* 10%. *Certified* Medicaid; Medicare.
Owner Proprietary corp.
Admissions Requirements Minimum age 16; Medical examination; Physician's request.
Staff Physicians 6 (pt); RNs 4 (pt); LPNs 25 (ft), 5 (pt); Nurses' aides 65 (ft); Physical therapists 1 (pt); Reality therapists 1 (ft), 1 (pt); Recreational therapists 1 (pt); Occupational therapists 1 (pt); Speech therapists 1 (pt); Activities coordinators 3 (ft), 1 (pt); Dietitians 1 (pt);

Ophthalmologists 1 (pt); Podiatrists 1 (pt); Audiologists 1 (ft); Restorative nursing assistants 5 (ft), 1 (pt).
Languages Spanish.
Facilities Dining room; Physical therapy room; Activities room; Chapel; Crafts room; Laundry room; Barber/Beauty shop; Library; 24 private rooms; 88 semi-private rooms; Enclosed courtyards; Activity area.
Activities Arts & crafts; Cards; Games; Reading groups; Prayer groups; Movies; Shopping trips; Dances/Social/Cultural gatherings; Intergenerational programs; Pet therapy.

Good Samaritan Care Center
901 E Willetta, Phoenix, AZ 85006
(602) 223-3000
Admin Susan K White.
Beds 128.

Hacienda de los Angeles
1402 E South Mountain Ave, Phoenix, AZ 85040
(602) 243-4231
Admin William J Timmons. *Dir of Nursing* Lois Sloan. *Medical Dir* Dr David Hirsch, contracted.
Licensure Skilled care. *Beds* SNF 62. *Private Pay Patients* 10%.
Owner Nonprofit organization/foundation.
Admissions Requirements Medical examination.
Staff Physicians 1 (ft); RNs 6 (ft); LPNs 8 (ft); Nurses' aides 35 (ft); Physical therapists 1 (ft); Occupational therapists 1 (ft); Speech therapists 1 (ft); Activities coordinators 1 (ft); Dietitians 1 (ft).
Languages Spanish.
Facilities Dining room; Physical therapy room; Laundry room.
Activities Arts & crafts; Games; Reading groups; Movies; Shopping trips; Dances/Social/Cultural gatherings.

Highland Manor
4635 N 14th St, Phoenix, AZ 85014
(602) 264-9039
Admin Rhonda Buck. *Dir of Nursing* Doris Donithan. *Medical Dir* Walter Neiri MD.
Licensure Skilled care. *Beds* SNF 107. *Private Pay Patients* 15%. *Certified* Medicaid; Medicare.
Owner Proprietary corp (Vari-Care Inc).
Admissions Requirements Physician's request.
Staff RNs 6 (ft), 3 (pt); LPNs 9 (ft), 3 (pt); Nurses' aides 49 (ft); Activities coordinators 2 (ft).
Facilities Dining room; Physical therapy room; Activities room; Laundry room; Barber/Beauty shop.
Activities Arts & crafts; Cards; Games; Reading groups; Prayer groups; Movies; Shopping trips; Dances/Social/Cultural gatherings; Intergenerational programs; Pet therapy.

Hillhaven Health Care Center
531 W Thomas Rd, Phoenix, AZ 85013
(602) 264-9651
Admin David K Niess.
Medical Dir William Semmens MD.
Licensure Skilled care. *Beds* SNF 120; ICF 60; Medicare Certified 60. *Certified* Medicare.
Owner Proprietary corp (Hillhaven Corp).
Admissions Requirements Minimum age 16; Physician's request.
Staff Physicians 1 (pt); RNs 15 (ft), 5 (pt); LPNs 35 (ft), 5 (pt); Nurses' aides 60 (ft), 10 (pt); Physical therapists 2 (ft), 1 (pt); Recreational therapists 4 (ft); Occupational therapists 1 (pt); Speech therapists 1 (pt); Activities coordinators 1 (pt); Dietitians 1 (pt); Podiatrists 1 (pt); Dentists 1 (pt).
Facilities Dining room; Physical therapy room; Activities room; Crafts room; Laundry room; Barber/Beauty shop.

Activities Arts & crafts; Cards; Games; Prayer groups; Movies; Shopping trips.

Homestead Rest Home
343 W Lynwood Ave, Phoenix, AZ 85003
(602) 256-6772
Admin Lena Inman.
Licensure Personal care. *Beds* 13.
Owner Proprietary corp.

Kivel Care Center
3020 N 36th St, Phoenix, AZ 85018
(602) 956-3110
Admin Matthew Luger MPA. *Dir of Nursing* Peg Bratton RN. *Medical Dir* Jerome J Kastrul MD.
Licensure Skilled care; Intermediate care; Sub-acute care unit for Alzheimer's disease & related disorders; Retirement. *Beds* 191.
Owner Nonprofit corp.
Admissions Requirements Minimum age 18; Medical examination; Physician's request.
Staff RNs 10 (ft), 6 (pt); LPNs 15 (ft), 7 (pt); Nurses' aides 64 (ft), 4 (pt); Recreational therapists 1 (ft); Activities coordinators 4 (ft), 1 (pt); Occupational therapists 1 (pt).
Affiliation Jewish.
Facilities Dining room; Physical therapy room; Activities room; Chapel; Crafts room; Barber/Beauty shop; Library; Kiln for ceramics.
Activities Arts & crafts; Cards; Games; Reading groups; Prayer groups; Movies; Shopping trips; Dances/Social/Cultural gatherings; Cooking classes; Ceramics.

Life Care Center of Paradise Valley
4065 E Bell, Phoenix, AZ 85032
(602) 867-0212
Admin Michael Oliver.
Beds 180.

Maryland Gardens
31 W Maryland, Phoenix, AZ 85013
(602) 265-7484
Admin Paula Beebe Bakke.
Medical Dir Noreen Readel.
Beds 60.
Owner Proprietary corp.
Admissions Requirements Medical examination.
Staff RNs 2 (ft); LPNs 4 (ft); Nurses' aides 13 (ft), 6 (pt); Reality therapists 1 (ft); Recreational therapists 2 (ft); Activities coordinators 1 (ft); Dietitians 1 (ft).
Facilities Dining room; Activities room; Crafts room; Laundry room; Library.
Activities Arts & crafts; Cards; Games; Reading groups; Prayer groups; Movies; Shopping trips; Dances/Social/Cultural gatherings.

Orangewood Health Facility—American Baptist Estates
7550 N 16th St, Phoenix, AZ 85020
(602) 944-4455
Admin Robert O Stuewig.
Medical Dir Fernando Compos MD.
Licensure Skilled care; Intermediate care. *Beds* SNF 40; ICF 24. *Certified* Medicare.
Owner Nonprofit corp.
Admissions Requirements Minimum age 65.
Staff Physicians; RNs 6 (ft), 2 (pt); LPNs 2 (ft), 1 (pt); Nurses' aides 23 (ft), 1 (pt); Activities coordinators 1 (ft), 1 (pt).
Affiliation Baptist.
Facilities Dining room; Physical therapy room; Activities room; Chapel; Crafts room; Laundry room; Barber/Beauty shop; Library; Shop.
Activities Arts & crafts; Cards; Games; Reading groups; Prayer groups; Movies; Shopping trips.

Phoenix Jewish Care Center
11411 N 19th Ave, Phoenix, AZ 85029
(602) 256-7500
Admin Kenneth K Lancaster. *Dir of Nursing* Nancy Simms.

Licensure Skilled care; Alzheimer's care. *Beds* SNF 127. *Certified* Medicare.
Owner Privately owned.
Staff RNs 10 (ft); LPNs 9 (ft); Nurses' aides 52 (ft); Physical therapists 3 (ft); Activities coordinators 2 (ft); Dietitians 1 (ft).
Languages Yiddish, Hebrew, Italian.
Affiliation Jewish.
Activities Arts & crafts; Cards; Games; Reading groups; Prayer groups; Movies; Shopping trips; Dances/Social/Cultural gatherings.

Phoenix Mountain Nursing Center
13232 N Tatum Blvd, Phoenix, AZ 85032
(602) 996-5200
Admin Arlene Ringey. *Dir of Nursing* Elizabeth Griffin RN.
Licensure Skilled care; Retirement. *Beds* SNF 127. *Certified* Medicare.
Owner Proprietary corp.
Admissions Requirements Minimum age 16.
Staff RNs 8 (ft), 9 (pt); LPNs 6 (ft), 5 (pt); Nurses' aides 44 (ft), 8 (pt); Physical therapists 1 (ft); Recreational therapists 1 (pt); Occupational therapists 1 (pt); Speech therapists 1 (pt); Activities coordinators 1 (ft); Dietitians 1 (pt); Ophthalmologists 1 (pt).
Facilities Dining room; Physical therapy room; Activities room; Crafts room; Laundry room; Barber/Beauty shop; Library.
Activities Arts & crafts; Cards; Games; Reading groups; Prayer groups; Movies; Dances/Social/Cultural gatherings.

St Joseph's Care Center
531 W Thomas Rd, Phoenix, AZ 85013
(602) 264-9651, 265-5092 FAX
Admin Sharon L Barger. *Dir of Nursing* Cindy Lessow. *Medical Dir* Robert Garcia MD.
Licensure Skilled care; Alzheimer's care. *Beds* SNF 236. *Private Pay Patients* 25%. *Certified* Medicaid; Medicare.
Owner Nonprofit corp.
Admissions Requirements Minimum age 16.
Staff Physicians (consultant); RNs 7 (ft), 3 (pt); LPNs 30 (ft), 1 (pt); Nurses' aides 58 (ft), 2 (pt); Physical therapists 1 (ft); Recreational therapists 1 (ft); Occupational therapists 1 (pt); Speech therapists 1 (pt); Activities coordinators 1 (ft); Dietitians (consultant).
Languages Spanish.
Affiliation Roman Catholic.
Facilities Dining room; Physical therapy room; Activities room; Crafts room; Laundry room; Barber/Beauty shop; Library; Garden patio.
Activities Arts & crafts; Cards; Games; Reading groups; Prayer groups; Movies; Shopping trips; Pet therapy; Scheduled outside entertainment.

St Luke's Skilled Nursing Facility
1800 E Van Buren, Phoenix, AZ 85006
(602) 251-8323
Admin David A Gardner.
Beds 39.

South Mountain Manor Inc
2211 E Southern Ave, Phoenix, AZ 85040
(602) 276-7358
Licensure Intermediate care. *Beds* 115.
Owner Proprietary corp.

Tanner Chapel Manor Nursing Home
2150 E Broadway, Phoenix, AZ 85040
(602) 243-1735
Admin Grace Evans. *Dir of Nursing* Helen O'Halloran RN. *Medical Dir* Dr Fred Miller.
Licensure Skilled care. *Beds* SNF 64. *Private Pay Patients* 10%. *Certified* Medicaid; Medicare.
Owner Nonprofit corp.
Admissions Requirements Minimum age 18; Medical examination; Physician's request.

Staff RNs 3 (ft); LPNs 4 (ft), 2 (pt); Physical therapists (contracted); Reality therapists (contracted); Recreational therapists (contracted); Occupational therapists (contracted); Speech therapists (contracted); Activities coordinators 1 (ft); Dietitians 1 (pt); Ophthalmologists (contracted); Podiatrists (contracted); Audiologists (contracted).
Languages Spanish.
Facilities Dining room; Physical therapy room; Activities room; Crafts room; Laundry room; Barber/Beauty shop.
Activities Arts & crafts; Cards; Games; Reading groups; Prayer groups; Movies; Shopping trips; Dances/Social/Cultural gatherings; Pet therapy.

Thunderbird Health Care Center
8825 S 7th St, Phoenix, AZ 85040
(602) 243-6121
Admin Donald Wagner.
Beds 160.

Vantage Convalescent Center
1856 E Thomas Rd, Phoenix, AZ 85016
(602) 274-3508
Admin Virginia McLaren RN. *Dir of Nursing* Clara Naylor RN. *Medical Dir* Frances Sierakowski MD.
Licensure Skilled care. *Beds* SNF 84.
Owner Proprietary corp (Vantage Healthcare).
Admissions Requirements Minimum age 18; Medical examination; Physician's request.
Staff RNs 5 (ft), 2 (pt); LPNs 9 (ft); Nurses' aides 30 (ft); Activities coordinators 1 (ft); Social workers 1 (ft).
Languages Spanish.
Facilities Dining room; Physical therapy room; Activities room; Crafts room; Laundry room; Barber/Beauty shop; Library.
Activities Arts & crafts; Cards; Games; Reading groups; Prayer groups; Movies; Shopping trips; Dances/Social/Cultural gatherings; Cooking classes.

Village Green Nursing Home
2932 N 14th St, Phoenix, AZ 85014
(602) 264-5274, 266-2413 FAX
Admin Karen Finnigan. *Dir of Nursing* Kathleen Beattie. *Medical Dir* Dr Noel Smith.
Licensure Skilled care. *Beds* SNF 127. *Certified* Medicaid; Medicare.
Owner Nonprofit corp (Samaritan Senior Services).
Admissions Requirements Medical examination; Physician's request.
Staff RNs; LPNs; Nurses' aides; Activities coordinators; Dietitians.
Languages Spanish.
Facilities Dining room; Physical therapy room; Activities room; Laundry room; Barber/Beauty shop.
Activities Arts & crafts; Cards; Games; Reading groups; Prayer groups; Movies; Shopping trips; Dances/Social/Cultural gatherings; Pet therapy.

Prescott

Arizona Pioneers' Home
300 S McCormick St, Prescott, AZ 86303
(602) 445-2181
Admin Doris Marlowe, Super. *Dir of Nursing* Jeanine Montgomery, Geriatrics.
Licensure Skilled care; Intermediate care; Personal care. *Beds* SNF 23; ICF 28; Personal care 116. *Private Pay Patients* 88%. *Certified* Medicare.
Owner Publicly owned.
Admissions Requirements Minimum age 65; Medical examination.
Staff Physicians 5 (ft); RNs 10 (ft), 12 (pt); LPNs 5 (ft), 1 (pt); Nurses' aides 39 (ft), 11 (pt); Physical therapists; Reality therapists; Recreational therapists; Occupational therapists; Speech therapists; Activities

coordinators 2 (ft); Dietitians 1 (ft);
Ophthalmologists; Podiatrists; Audiologists;
Psychiatrists.
Languages Spanish.
Facilities Dining room; Activities room;
Chapel; Laundry room; Barber/Beauty shop;
Library.
Activities Arts & crafts; Cards; Games; Prayer
groups; Movies; Shopping trips; Dances/
Social/Cultural gatherings; Pet therapy.

Las Fuentes Care Center
1045 Scott Dr, Prescott, AZ 86301
(602) 778-9603
Admin Fred Kilfoy.
Beds 128.

Meadow Park Care Center
864 Dougherty St, Prescott, AZ 86301
(602) 778-9666
Admin Bettie A Robbins MSW COS. *Dir of
Nursing* Barbara T Ballard RN BSN.
Medical Dir Dr David Duncan.
Licensure Skilled care; Intermediate care;
Retirement. *Beds* SNF 44; ICF 20. *Private
Pay Patients* 40%. *Certified* Medicaid;
Medicare.
Owner Proprietary corp (Southwestern
Medical Centers).
Admissions Requirements Medical
examination; Physician's request.
Staff RNs 4 (ft), 3 (pt); LPNs 5 (ft), 1 (pt);
Nurses' aides 23 (ft), 4 (pt); Physical
therapists; Activities coordinators 1 (ft);
Dietitians 1 (ft); Social service coordinators
1 (ft).
Languages Spanish.
Facilities Dining room; Physical therapy
room; Activities room; Laundry room;
Barber/Beauty shop.
Activities Arts & crafts; Cards; Games;
Reading groups; Movies; Pet therapy;
Activities with other nursing facilities.

Prescott Samaritan Village
1030 Scott Dr, Prescott, AZ 86301
(602) 778-2450
Admin Ted Becker.
Licensure Skilled care; Personal care. *Beds*
SNF 60; Personal 20.
Owner Nonprofit corp (Evangelical Lutheran/
Good Samaritan Society).
Admissions Requirements Medical
examination; Physician's request.
Staff Physicians 1 (pt); RNs 3 (ft), 4 (pt);
LPNs 5 (ft), 3 (pt); Nurses' aides 18 (ft), 10
(pt); Physical therapists 1 (pt); Activities
coordinators 1 (ft).
Affiliation Lutheran.
Facilities Dining room; Physical therapy
room; Activities room; Chapel; Crafts room;
Laundry room; Barber/Beauty shop; Library;
Solarium.
Activities Arts & crafts; Cards; Games;
Reading groups; Prayer groups; Movies;
Shopping trips; Dances/Social/Cultural
gatherings; Foster grandparent program.

Sandretto Hills Care Center
1045 Sandretto Dr, Prescott, AZ 86301
(602) 778-4837
Admin K Lou Odell.
Beds 120.

Safford

Safford Care Center
1933 Peppertree Dr, Safford, AZ 85546
(602) 428-4910
Admin Ada M Miller.
Beds 128.

Scottsdale

Casa Delmar
3333 N Civic Center, Scottsdale, AZ 85251
(602) 947-7333

Admin Andrew J Kellogg.
Medical Dir Theodore Rudberg.
Licensure Skilled care. *Beds* 130. *Certified*
Medicare.
Owner Proprietary corp.
Admissions Requirements Minimum age 16;
Medical examination; Physician's request.
Staff Physicians 2 (pt); RNs 9 (ft), 3 (pt);
LPNs 9 (ft), 2 (pt); Nurses' aides 27 (ft), 3
(pt); Physical therapists 1 (ft); Reality
therapists 1 (pt); Recreational therapists 1
(pt); Occupational therapists 1 (pt); Speech
therapists 1 (pt); Activities coordinators 1
(ft); Dietitians 1 (ft); Podiatrists 1 (pt).
Facilities Dining room; Activities room;
Crafts room; Laundry room; Barber/Beauty
shop.
Activities Arts & crafts; Cards; Games;
Reading groups; Prayer groups; Movies;
Shopping trips; Dances/Social/Cultural
gatherings.

Hayden Manor Care Center
2501 N Hayden Rd, Scottsdale, AZ 85257
(602) 949-1824
Admin Berde J Groff.
Medical Dir Helen Learmont.
Licensure Skilled care. *Beds* 39.
Owner Proprietary corp (Quality Health Care
Specialists Inc).
Admissions Requirements Medical
examination; Physician's request.
Staff RNs 3 (ft); LPNs 1 (ft); Nurses' aides 35
(ft); Activities coordinators 1 (ft); Dietitians
1 (pt); FSM Food service 1 (ft).
Facilities Dining room; Activities room;
Crafts room; Laundry room; Barber/Beauty
shop.
Activities Arts & crafts; Games; Reading
groups; Prayer groups; Movies; Shopping
trips; Dances/Social/Cultural gatherings.

Health Center at the Forum—Pueblo Norte
7100 E Mescal St, Scottsdale, AZ 85254
(602) 948-5800
Admin Sonya Bloom. *Dir of Nursing* Lois
Reabe RN. *Medical Dir* Ruth Eckert MD.
Licensure Skilled care; Alzheimer's care;
Retirement. *Beds* SNF 128. *Private Pay
Patients* 92%. *Certified* Medicare.
Owner Nonprofit corp (Forum Group).
Admissions Requirements Medical
examination; Physician's request.
Staff RNs 11 (ft), 7 (pt); LPNs 6 (ft), 1 (pt);
Nurses' aides 25 (ft), 1 (pt); Physical
therapists (contracted); Recreational
therapists 1 (ft); Occupational therapists
(contracted); Speech therapists (contracted);
Activities coordinators 1 (ft); Dietitians 1
(ft); Ophthalmologists (contracted);
Podiatrists (contracted); Audiologists
(contracted).
Facilities Dining room; Physical therapy
room; Activities room; Chapel; Crafts room;
Laundry room; Barber/Beauty shop; Library;
Wanderguard system.
Activities Arts & crafts; Cards; Games;
Reading groups; Prayer groups; Movies;
Shopping trips; Dances/Social/Cultural
gatherings; Intergenerational programs; Pet
therapy.

Idaho Falls Nursing Home
4903 E Pershing Ave, Scottsdale, AZ 85254-
3522
(208) 525-6600
Admin Kenneth K Lancaster. *Dir of Nursing*
Karen Williams RN. *Medical Dir* D O
Smith MD.
Licensure Skilled care. *Beds* 92. *Certified*
Medicaid; Medicare.
Owner Proprietary corp (Beverly Enterprises).
Admissions Requirements Minimum age 20.
Staff RNs; LPNs; Nurses' aides; Activities
coordinators.
Facilities Dining room; Physical therapy
room; Activities room; Chapel; Crafts room;
Laundry room; Barber/Beauty shop.

Activities Arts & crafts; Cards; Games;
Reading groups; Prayer groups; Movies;
Dances/Social/Cultural gatherings.

Life Care Center of Scottsdale
9494 E Becker Ln, Scottsdale, AZ 85260
(602) 860-6396
Admin Linda D Exner. *Dir of Nursing* Naomi
Markle. *Medical Dir* Dr Jay Friedman.
Licensure Skilled care; Intermediate care;
Personal care; Alzheimer's care. *Beds* SNF
80; ICF 40; Personal care 40. *Certified*
Medicare.
Owner Proprietary corp (Life Care Centers of
America).
Admissions Requirements Medical
examination; Physician's request.
Staff RNs 8 (ft), 2 (pt); LPNs 6 (ft), 4 (pt);
Nurses' aides 35 (ft), 8 (pt); Physical
therapists 1 (ft); Recreational therapists 2
(ft); Occupational therapists 1 (pt); Speech
therapists 1 (pt); Dietitians 1 (pt).
Facilities Dining room; Physical therapy
room; Activities room; Chapel; Crafts room;
Laundry room; Barber/Beauty shop; Library;
Ice cream parlor; Alzheimer's therapeutic
center.
Activities Arts & crafts; Cards; Games;
Reading groups; Prayer groups; Movies;
Shopping trips; Dances/Social/Cultural
gatherings; Intergenerational programs; Pet
therapy.

Monterey Nursing Center
7303 E Monterey Way, Scottsdale, AZ 85251
(602) 947-7443
Admin Cheri L Allen. *Dir of Nursing* Joan
Sprain RN. *Medical Dir* Dr Theodore
Rudberg.
Licensure Skilled care. *Beds* SNF 90. *Certified*
Medicaid; Medicare.
Owner Proprietary corp (Vari-Care Inc).
Admissions Requirements Minimum age 18.
Staff Physicians; RNs; LPNs; Nurses' aides;
Physical therapists; Reality therapists;
Recreational therapists; Occupational
therapists; Speech therapists; Activities
coordinators; Dietitians; Ophthalmologists;
Podiatrists; Audiologists.
Facilities Dining room; Physical therapy
room; Activities room; Crafts room; Laundry
room; Barber/Beauty shop; Outside patio.
Activities Arts & crafts; Cards; Games;
Reading groups; Prayer groups; Movies;
Shopping trips; Dances/Social/Cultural
gatherings; Intergenerational programs; Pet
therapy.

Mountain Shadow Health Care Center
11150 N 92nd St, Scottsdale, AZ 85260
(602) 860-1766
Admin Barbara Brown. *Dir of Nursing*
Christine Walker RN. *Medical Dir* Joseph
Sandor MD.
Licensure Skilled care; Retirement;
Alzheimer's care. *Beds* SNF 120. *Certified*
Medicare.
Owner Proprietary corp (Beverly Enterprises).
Admissions Requirements Medical
examination.
Staff Physicians; RNs; LPNs; Nurses' aides;
Physical therapists; Reality therapists;
Recreational therapists; Occupational
therapists; Speech therapists; Activities
coordinators; Dietitians; Ophthalmologists;
Dentists; Dermatologists; Respiratory
therapists; Social workers.
Languages Spanish.
Facilities Dining room; Physical therapy
room; Activities room; Chapel; Crafts room;
Laundry room; Barber/Beauty shop; Library;
Smoking lounges; Whirlpool rooms.
Activities Arts & crafts; Cards; Games;
Reading groups; Prayer groups; Movies;
Shopping trips; Dances/Social/Cultural
gatherings; Outings; Educational courses;
Resident council sessions; Cocktail hour.

Scottsdale Heritage Court
3339 N Civic Center Plaza, Scottsdale, AZ 85251
(602) 949-5400
Admin Mary G Hill. *Dir of Nursing* Cynthia Jordan RN. *Medical Dir* Dr Gerald Wolfey.
Licensure Skilled care; Intermediate care. *Beds* SNF 108; ICF. *Certified* Medicare.
Owner Proprietary corp.
Admissions Requirements Minimum age 18; Medical examination; Physician's request.
Staff RNs 5 (ft); LPNs 7 (ft), 1 (pt); Nurses' aides 29 (ft), 2 (pt); Activities coordinators 1 (ft), 1 (pt); Dietitians 1 (ft).
Facilities Dining room; Physical therapy room; Activities room; Crafts room; Laundry room; Barber/Beauty shop; Library.
Activities Arts & crafts; Cards; Games; Reading groups; Prayer groups; Movies; Dances/Social/Cultural gatherings.

Scottsdale Memorial Convalescent Plaza
1475 N Granite Reef Rd, Scottsdale, AZ 85257
(602) 990-1904
Admin Vicki Bunda. *Dir of Nursing* Connie DeVita. *Medical Dir* Richard Levinson MD.
Licensure Skilled care; Alzheimer's care. *Beds* SNF 178. *Certified* Medicare; VA.
Owner Nonprofit corp.
Admissions Requirements Medical examination; Physician's request.
Staff RNs 12 (ft); LPNs 16 (ft); Nurses' aides 46 (ft), 1 (pt); Physical therapists 1 (pt); Occupational therapists 1 (pt); Speech therapists 1 (pt); Activities coordinators 2 (ft); Dietitians 1 (pt).
Languages Spanish.
Facilities Dining room; Activities room; Barber/Beauty shop; Library; TV lounges.
Activities Arts & crafts; Cards; Games; Reading groups; Prayer groups; Movies; Shopping trips; Dances/Social/Cultural gatherings; Outside trips for meals; Fishing trips; Exercise groups.

Scottsdale Memorial Skilled Nursing Facility
7400 E Osborn Rd, Scottsdale, AZ 85281
(602) 481-4360
Admin Mary A Hays. *Dir of Nursing* Janet F Rupel. *Medical Dir* Dr Jacqueline A Chadwick.
Licensure Skilled care. *Beds* SNF 30. *Private Pay Patients* 20%. *Certified* Medicare.
Owner Nonprofit organization/foundation (Scottsdale Memorial Hospitals).
Admissions Requirements Minimum age 16; Medical examination; Physician's request.
Staff Physicians (contracted); RNs 6 (ft), 1 (pt) (& contracted); LPNs 4 (ft), 1 (pt); Nurses' aides 2 (ft), 5 (pt); Physical therapists (contracted); Reality therapists (contracted); Recreational therapists (contracted); Occupational therapists (contracted); Speech therapists (contracted); Activities coordinators (contracted); Dietitians (contracted); Ophthalmologists (contracted); Podiatrists (contracted); Audiologists (contracted).
Facilities Dining room; Physical therapy room; Activities room; Chapel; Crafts room; Laundry room; Barber/Beauty shop; Library.
Activities Arts & crafts; Cards; Games; Reading groups; Prayer groups; Movies; Intergenerational programs; Pet therapy.

Scottsdale Village Square
2620 N 68th St, Scottsdale, AZ 85257
(602) 946-6571, 946-0082 FAX
Admin Leah R Jones. *Dir of Nursing* Linda Hurbis. *Medical Dir* Theodore Rudberg MD.
Licensure Skilled care; Intermediate care; Personal care; Day care; Alzheimer's care. *Beds* SNF 58; ICF 48; Personal care 36. *Private Pay Patients* 100%.
Owner Privately owned.
Admissions Requirements Medical examination; Physician's request.

Staff RNs 7 (ft), 1 (pt); LPNs 9 (ft), 4 (pt); Nurses' aides 37 (ft), 17 (pt); Activities coordinators 3 (ft), 3 (pt).
Languages Spanish.
Facilities Dining room; Physical therapy room; Activities room; Crafts room; Laundry room; Barber/Beauty shop; Library.
Activities Arts & crafts; Cards; Games; Reading groups; Prayer groups; Movies; Shopping trips; Dances/Social/Cultural gatherings; Pet therapy; Fashion shows; Picnics.

Westminster Village Inc
12000 N 90th St, Scottsdale, AZ 85260
(602) 451-2000
Admin David Van Ness. *Dir of Nursing* Judith Sgrillio RN. *Medical Dir* Gerald J Jogerst MD.
Licensure Skilled care; Intermediate care. *Beds* Swing beds SNF/ICF 60. *Private Pay Patients* 50%.
Owner Nonprofit corp.
Staff Physicians 1 (pt); RNs 3 (ft), 3 (pt); LPNs 3 (ft), 3 (pt); Nurses' aides 12 (ft); Physical therapists 1 (pt); Recreational therapists 1 (ft); Occupational therapists 1 (pt); Speech therapists 1 (pt); Activities coordinators 1 (ft); Dietitians 1 (pt); Ophthalmologists 1 (pt); Podiatrists 1 (pt); Audiologists 1 (pt).

Sedona

Kachina Point Health Center
505 Jacks Canyon Rd, Sedona, AZ 86336
(602) 284-1000
Admin Fran Crockett RN. *Dir of Nursing* Caroline Nejedlo. *Medical Dir* Ferenc Nagy MD.
Licensure Skilled care; Intermediate care; SCU for Alzheimer's patients; Retirement. *Beds* SNF 76; ICF 30. *Certified* Medicaid; Medicare.
Owner Proprietary corp (Hillhaven Corp).
Admissions Requirements Medical examination; Physician's request.
Staff Physicians; RNs; LPNs; Nurses' aides; Physical therapists; Reality therapists; Recreational therapists; Occupational therapists; Speech therapists; Activities coordinators; Dietitians; Ophthalmologists; Podiatrists; Dentists.
Languages Spanish, Swedish, German, French.
Facilities Dining room; Physical therapy room; Activities room; Crafts room; Laundry room; Barber/Beauty shop; Library.
Activities Arts & crafts; Cards; Games; Reading groups; Prayer groups; Movies; Shopping trips; Dances/Social/Cultural gatherings; Van outings.

Show Low

Pueblo Norte Nursing Center
2401 E Hunt St, Show Low, AZ 85901
(602) 537-5333
Admin Ron Smith. *Dir of Nursing* Joyce Johnson RN. *Medical Dir* Mark Rens MD.
Licensure Skilled care; Intermediate care. *Beds* SNF 80; ICF 20. *Private Pay Patients* 25%. *Certified* Medicaid; Medicare.
Owner Nonprofit corp (Pacific Living Centers).
Admissions Requirements Medical examination; Physician's request.
Staff RNs; LPNs; Nurses' aides; Physical therapists; Occupational therapists; Speech therapists; Activities coordinators; Dietitians; Ophthalmologists; Podiatrists; Audiologists.
Languages Apache, Navajo, German.
Affiliation Seventh-Day Adventist.
Facilities Dining room; Physical therapy room; Activities room; Chapel; Laundry room; Barber/Beauty shop.

Activities Arts & crafts; Cards; Games; Movies; Shopping trips; Dances/Social/ Cultural gatherings; Pet therapy.

Sierra Vista

Life Care Center of Sierra Vista
2305 E Wilcox, Sierra Vista, AZ 85635
(602) 458-1050
Admin Jeffrey L Ruth. *Dir of Nursing* Marge Burns. *Medical Dir* Ralph Mayberry MD.
Licensure Skilled care; Intermediate care; Personal care. *Beds* SNF 74; ICF 53; Personal care 35. *Private Pay Patients* 20%. *Certified* Medicaid; Medicare.
Owner Proprietary corp (Life Care Centers of America).
Admissions Requirements Physician's request.
Staff RNs 5 (ft), 3 (pt); LPNs 9 (ft), 5 (pt); Nurses' aides 20 (ft), 9 (pt); Physical therapists (contracted); Occupational therapists (contracted); Speech therapists (contracted); Activities coordinators 1 (ft); Ophthalmologists (contracted); Podiatrists (contracted).
Languages German, Spanish.
Facilities Dining room; Physical therapy room; Activities room; Crafts room; Laundry room; Barber/Beauty shop.
Activities Arts & crafts; Cards; Games; Reading groups; Prayer groups; Movies; Shopping trips; Dances/Social/Cultural gatherings; Intergenerational programs; Pet therapy.

Sierra Vista Care Center
660 Coronado Rd, Sierra Vista, AZ 85635
(602) 459-4900
Admin Peggy L Dean.
Licensure Skilled care; Intermediate care. *Beds* SNF 56; ICF 44.
Owner Proprietary corp.

Springerville

Samaritan White Mountains Care Center
PO Box 1700, 118-B South Mountain Ave, Springerville, AZ 85938
(602) 333-4368
Admin Bonnie H Greer.
Beds 44.

Sun City

Arizona Rehabilitation Center—SNF
13200 N 103rd Ave, No 2, Sun City, AZ 85351-3025
(602) 972-1153
Admin N Michael Kudelko, MD. *Dir of Nursing* Jeannette Slack RN. *Medical Dir* D Kanefield MD.
Licensure Skilled care; Intermediate care. *Beds* 128. *Certified* Medicare.
Owner Proprietary corp (Beverly Enterprises).
Admissions Requirements Physician's request.
Staff RNs; LPNs; Nurses' aides; Activities coordinators; Dietitians.
Languages French, Spanish, German.
Facilities Dining room; Physical therapy room; Activities room; Crafts room; Laundry room; Barber/Beauty shop; Library.
Activities Arts & crafts; Cards; Games; Reading groups; Prayer groups; Movies; Shopping trips; Dances/Social/Cultural gatherings; Variety.

Camelot Care Center
PO Box E, 11301 N 99th Ave, Sun City, AZ 85372
(602) 977-8373
Admin Jerene Maierle.
Beds 242.

Hearthstone of Sun City
13818 N Thunderbird Blvd, Sun City, AZ 85351
(602) 977-1325

Admin Pam Fisher. *Dir of Nursing* Shirley Nelson RN. *Medical Dir* Alan L Miles MD.
Licensure Skilled care; Intermediate care; Secured Alzheimer's unit. *Beds* Swing beds SNF/ICF 120. *Certified* Medicare.
Owner Proprietary corp (ARA Living Centers).
Staff RNs 4 (ft), 1 (pt); LPNs 7 (ft), 8 (pt); Nurses' aides 31 (ft), 16 (pt); Physical therapists; Activities coordinators 3 (ft); Dietitians.
Facilities Dining room; Physical therapy room; Activities room; Chapel; Crafts room; Laundry room; Barber/Beauty shop; Library; Private dining.
Activities Arts & crafts; Cards; Games; Reading groups; Prayer groups; Movies; Shopping trips; Dances/Social/Cultural gatherings; Intergenerational programs; Pet therapy; Alzheimer's program.

Royal Oaks Life Care Facility
10015 Royal Oak Rd, Sun City, AZ 85351
(602) 933-2807
Admin Dorothy Lewis. *Dir of Nursing* Eunice Zunker RN. *Medical Dir* Oliver Harper MD.
Licensure Skilled care; Retirement living; Alzheimer's care. *Beds* SNF 92; Retirement living 450. *Certified* Medicare.
Owner Nonprofit organization/foundation.
Admissions Requirements Physician's request.
Staff RNs 6 (ft), 1 (pt); LPNs 14 (ft), 2 (pt); Nurses' aides 43 (ft), 2 (pt); Activities coordinators 1 (ft).
Facilities Dining room; Physical therapy room; Activities room; Barber/Beauty shop; Library.
Activities Arts & crafts; Cards; Games; Reading groups; Prayer groups; Movies; Dances/Social/Cultural gatherings.

Sun Health Care Center
10601 W Santa Fe Dr, Sun City, AZ 85351
(602) 974-7000, 972-6928 FAX
Admin Genny Rose. *Dir of Nursing* Betty Bailey RN. *Medical Dir* Edward Dubrow MD.
Licensure Skilled care. *Beds* SNF 128. *Private Pay Patients* 90%. *Certified* Medicare.
Owner Nonprofit corp (Sun Health Corp).
Admissions Requirements Medical examination; Physician's request.
Staff RNs 4 (ft), 1 (pt); LPNs 12 (ft), 3 (pt); Nurses' aides 35 (ft), 5 (pt); Physical therapists 1 (pt); Occupational therapists 1 (pt); Speech therapists 1 (pt); Activities coordinators 1 (ft); Dietitians 1 (pt).
Facilities Dining room; Physical therapy room; Activities room; Crafts room; Laundry room; Barber/Beauty shop; Library.
Activities Arts & crafts; Cards; Games; Reading groups; Prayer groups; Movies; Intergenerational programs; Pet therapy.

Sun Valley Lodge
12415 N 103rd Ave, Sun City, AZ 85351
(602) 933-0137
Admin James Hilty. *Dir of Nursing* Carol Burden. *Medical Dir* Dr Phillip Turner.
Licensure Skilled care; Personal care. *Beds* SNF 64; Personal 50.
Owner Nonprofit corp.
Facilities Dining room; Physical therapy room; Activities room; Chapel; Crafts room; Laundry room; Barber/Beauty shop; Library.
Activities Arts & crafts; Cards; Games; Reading groups; Prayer groups; Movies; Shopping trips; Dances/Social/Cultural gatherings.

Wooddale Health Centre
9940 W Union Hills Dr, Sun City, AZ 85373-1899
(602) 933-0022
Admin Sherman M Rorvig.
Medical Dir Jeanette Magnus.

Licensure Skilled care; Intermediate care; Personal care; Alzheimer's care. *Beds* SNF 60; ICF 30; Personal care 10.
Owner Nonprofit corp (Lutheran Brethren Homes Inc).
Admissions Requirements Medical examination.
Staff RNs 6 (ft); LPNs 7 (ft); Nurses' aides 35 (ft); Physical therapists 1 (pt); Activities coordinators 1 (ft); Dietitians 1 (ft).
Affiliation Lutheran.
Facilities Dining room; Physical therapy room; Activities room; Crafts room; Laundry room; Barber/Beauty shop.
Activities Arts & crafts; Cards; Games; Reading groups; Movies; Shopping trips; Dances/Social/Cultural gatherings; Bible study.

Sun City West

Sunwest Nursing Center
14002 Meeker Blvd, Sun City West, AZ 85375
(602) 584-6161
Admin Rosalie Young.
Beds 120.

Surprise

Kiva at Sun Ridge
12221 W Bell Rd, Surprise, AZ 85374
(602) 583-9800
Admin Fran Donnellan.
Beds 64.

Tempe

Friendship Village of Tempe
2645 E Southern, Tempe, AZ 85282
(602) 831-0880
Admin Madalen Meyers. *Dir of Nursing* Phyllis Beaudien. *Medical Dir* Roger Boylan MD.
Licensure Skilled care; Retirement. *Beds* 120. *Certified* Medicare.
Owner Nonprofit corp (Life Care Services Corp).
Admissions Requirements Minimum age 62; Medical examination; Physician's request.
Staff RNs 11 (ft), 1 (pt); LPNs 9 (ft), 2 (pt); Nurses' aides 45 (ft), 5 (pt); Activities coordinators 2 (ft); Dietitians 1 (ft).
Facilities Dining room; Physical therapy room; Activities room; Laundry room; Barber/Beauty shop; Library.
Activities Arts & crafts; Cards; Games; Reading groups; Prayer groups; Movies; Shopping trips; Dances/Social/Cultural gatherings.

Westchester Care Center
6100 S Rural Rd, Tempe, AZ 85283
(602) 831-8660
Admin Eliot C Higbee. *Dir of Nursing* Roberta Holka RN. *Medical Dir* Richard O Flynn MD.
Licensure Skilled care; Intermediate care. *Beds* SNF 49; ICF 51.
Owner Nonprofit corp (Volunteers of America Care).
Admissions Requirements Medical examination; Physician's request.
Staff RNs 6 (ft), 10 (pt); LPNs 5 (ft), 10 (pt); Nurses' aides 32 (ft), 17 (pt); Physical therapists 2 (pt); Occupational therapists 1 (pt); Speech therapists 1 (pt); Activities coordinators 1 (ft), 2 (pt); Dietitians 1 (ft); Podiatrists 1 (pt); Dentists 1 (pt).
Affiliation Volunteers of America.
Facilities Dining room; Physical therapy room; Activities room; Chapel; Crafts room; Laundry room; Barber/Beauty shop; Dayrooms; Resident lounge.

Activities Arts & crafts; Cards; Games; Reading groups; Prayer groups; Movies; Shopping trips; Dances/Social/Cultural gatherings.

Tucson

Arizona Elks Long-Term Care
1900 W Speedway Blvd, Tucson, AZ 85745
(602) 623-5562
Admin Siena Wald. *Dir of Nursing* Lisa Olson.
Licensure Skilled care. *Beds* SNF 46.
Owner Nonprofit corp.
Admissions Requirements Males only; Medical examination; Physician's request.
Facilities Dining room; Physical therapy room; Activities room; Crafts room; Laundry room; Library.
Activities Arts & crafts; Cards; Games; Reading groups; Prayer groups; Movies; Shopping trips; Dances/Social/Cultural gatherings; Intergenerational programs; Pet therapy.

Arizona William-Wesley Nursing Home
2611 N Warren, Tucson, AZ 85719
(602) 795-9574
Admin Yvonne Balionis.
Medical Dir William Farr MD.
Licensure Skilled care. *Beds* 102.
Owner Proprietary corp.
Admissions Requirements Medical examination; Physician's request.
Staff Physicians 1 (pt); RNs 4 (ft), 2 (pt); LPNs 3 (ft), 6 (pt); Nurses' aides 33 (ft), 11 (pt); Physical therapists 1 (pt); Recreational therapists 1 (ft); Occupational therapists 1 (pt); Speech therapists 1 (pt); Activities coordinators 2 (ft); Dietitians 1 (ft); Ophthalmologists 1 (pt); Podiatrists 1 (pt); Audiologists 1 (pt); Dentists 1 (pt).
Facilities Dining room; Physical therapy room; Activities room; Chapel; Crafts room; Laundry room; Barber/Beauty shop; Library.
Activities Arts & crafts; Cards; Games; Reading groups; Prayer groups; Movies; Shopping trips; Dances/Social/Cultural gatherings; Employees' musical group.

Balmoral Care Center
5830 E Pima St, Tucson, AZ 85712
(602) 722-5515
Admin Susan Jordan Snell.
Beds 60.

Bonnie Brae's
5838 E Pima St, Tucson, AZ 85712
(602) 296-7151
Admin Annie M Markel.
Licensure Skilled care. *Beds* 122.
Owner Proprietary corp.

Carondelet Holy Family Center
1802 W St Mary's Rd, Tucson, AZ 85745
(602) 628-1991
Admin C Ray Honaker.
Beds 120.

Desert Life Health Care Center
1919 W Orange Grove Rd, Tucson, AZ 85704
(602) 297-8311
Admin John D Black.
Medical Dir John Pifre MD.
Licensure Skilled care; Intermediate care; Personal care. *Beds* 240. *Certified* Medicare.
Owner Proprietary corp (Hillhaven Corp).
Admissions Requirements Medical examination; Physician's request.
Staff RNs 7 (ft), 7 (pt); LPNs 20 (ft), 9 (pt); Nurses' aides 64 (ft), 15 (pt); Physical therapists 2 (pt); Recreational therapists 1 (ft); Occupational therapists 1 (ft); Speech therapists 1 (ft); Activities coordinators 2 (ft), 2 (pt); Dietitians 1 (ft); Social workers 1 (ft); COTA 1 (pt); Physical therapy aides.

Facilities Dining room; Physical therapy
room; Activities room; Chapel; Crafts room;
Barber/Beauty shop; Library; TV lounge;
Private patios; Jacuzzi; Occupational therapy
room.
Activities Arts & crafts; Cards; Games;
Reading groups; Prayer groups; Movies;
Shopping trips; Dances/Social/Cultural
gatherings; Special Olympics; Resident
council; Music therapy; Reality orientation.

Devon Gables Health Care Center
6150 E Grant Rd, Tucson, AZ 85712
(602) 296-6181
Admin Kathryn G Coheen.
Medical Dir Dr Loes; Dr Clark.
Licensure Skilled care; Intermediate care;
Intermediate care for mentally retarded;
Retirement; Alzheimer's care. *Beds* 312.
Certified Medicare.
Owner Proprietary corp (Hillhaven Corp).
Staff Physicians 2 (pt); RNs 20 (ft); LPNs 25
(ft); Nurses' aides 80 (ft); Physical therapists
1 (ft); Reality therapists 1 (ft); Recreational
therapists 5 (ft); Occupational therapists 1
(ft); Speech therapists 1 (pt); Activities
coordinators 1 (ft); Dietitians 1 (pt).
Languages Spanish.
Facilities Dining room; Physical therapy
room; Activities room; Chapel; Crafts room;
Laundry room; Barber/Beauty shop; Library.
Activities Arts & crafts; Cards; Games;
Reading groups; Prayer groups; Movies;
Shopping trips; Dances/Social/Cultural
gatherings; Barbeques; Cocktail hour.

Flower Square Health Care Center
2502 N Dodge Blvd, Tucson, AZ 85716
(602) 323-3200
Admin Mayra Mollica. *Dir of Nursing* Judy
Konen RN. *Medical Dir* Dr John Pellerito.
Licensure Skilled care; Intermediate care;
Retirement; Alzheimer's care. *Beds* SNF
120; ICF 144.
Owner Privately owned.
Admissions Requirements Medical
examination; Physician's request.
Staff RNs; LPNs; Nurses' aides; Recreational
therapists; Activities coordinators; Dietitians.
Languages Spanish.
Facilities Dining room; Physical therapy
room; Activities room; Chapel; Crafts room;
Laundry room; Barber/Beauty shop; Library.
Activities Arts & crafts; Cards; Games;
Reading groups; Prayer groups; Movies;
Shopping trips; Dances/Social/Cultural
gatherings; Monthly newsletter.

Handmaker Jewish Geriatric Center
2221 N Rosemont Blvd, Tucson, AZ 85712-
2172
(602) 881-2323
Admin Jeffrey S Yankow.
Medical Dir Robert S Hirsch MD.
Licensure Skilled care; Intermediate care;
Retirement living; Alzheimer's care. *Beds*
Swing beds SNF/ICF 161; Retirement living
15. *Certified* Medicare.
Owner Nonprofit corp.
Admissions Requirements Minimum age 55;
Medical examination; Physician's request.
Staff Physicians 1 (pt); Physical therapists 2
(pt); Occupational therapists 1 (ft), 1 (pt);
Speech therapists 1 (pt); Activities
coordinators 4 (ft); Dietitians 1 (pt);
Ophthalmologists 1 (pt); Podiatrists 1 (pt);
Dentists 1 (pt).
Affiliation Jewish.
Facilities Dining room; Physical therapy
room; Activities room; Chapel; Crafts room;
Laundry room; Barber/Beauty shop.
Activities Arts & crafts; Cards; Games;
Reading groups; Prayer groups; Movies;
Shopping trips; Dances/Social/Cultural
gatherings.

La Canada Care Center
7970 N La Canada Dr, Tucson, AZ 85704
(602) 797-1191
Admin Maria J Montion RN. *Dir of Nursing*
Felica Navarrete RN. *Medical Dir* Dr
Melvin Hector.
Licensure Skilled care; Intermediate care;
Alzheimer's care. *Beds* SNF 94; ICF 34.
Private Pay Patients 60%. *Certified*
Medicaid; Medicare.
Owner Proprietary corp (Hostmasters).
Admissions Requirements Medical
examination; Physician's request.
Staff Physicians 1 (ft); RNs 6 (ft); LPNs 10
(ft), 3 (pt); Nurses' aides 20 (ft), 6 (pt);
Physical therapists (contracted); Reality
therapists (contracted); Recreational
therapists (contracted); Occupational
therapists (contracted); Speech therapists
(contracted); Activities coordinators 1 (ft);
Dietitians 1 (ft); Ophthalmologists
(contracted); Podiatrists (contracted);
Audiologists (contracted).
Languages Spanish, French.
Facilities Dining room; Physical therapy
room; Activities room; Crafts room; Laundry
room; Barber/Beauty shop; Library; Lounges
with large screen TVs; Patios; Ice cream
parlor; Gift shop.
Activities Arts & crafts; Cards; Games;
Reading groups; Prayer groups; Movies;
Shopping trips; Dances/Social/Cultural
gatherings; Intergenerational programs; Pet
therapy.

La Colina Healthcare
2900 E Ajo Way, Tucson, AZ 85713
(602) 294-0005
Admin Wayne Eaton. *Dir of Nursing* Cindy
Kari RN.
Licensure Skilled care; Alzheimer's care. *Beds*
SNF 240. *Certified* Medicare.
Owner Proprietary corp (Beverly Enterprises).
Admissions Requirements Physician's request.
Staff RNs 13 (ft); LPNs 15 (ft); Nurses' aides
48 (ft); Recreational therapists 3 (ft); Speech
therapists 1 (pt); Activities coordinators 1
(ft); Dietitians 9 (ft).
Languages Spanish.
Facilities Dining room; Physical therapy
room; Activities room; Crafts room; Laundry
room; Barber/Beauty shop.
Activities Arts & crafts; Cards; Games;
Reading groups; Prayer groups; Movies;
Shopping trips; Dances/Social/Cultural
gatherings.

La Hacienda Nursing Home
2001 N Park Ave, Tucson, AZ 85719
(602) 795-6504
Admin Janet Green. *Dir of Nursing* Earline
Perkins RN. *Medical Dir* James Belitson
MD.
Licensure Skilled care. *Beds* 64.
Owner Proprietary corp.
Admissions Requirements Medical
examination; Physician's request.
Staff RNs 4 (ft), 4 (pt); LPNs 4 (ft), 1 (pt);
Nurses' aides; Activities coordinators;
Dietitians.
Languages Spanish.
Facilities Dining room; Activities room;
Crafts room; Laundry room; Barber/Beauty
shop.
Activities Arts & crafts; Cards; Games;
Reading groups; Prayer groups; Movies;
Shopping trips; Dances/Social/Cultural
gatherings.

Leewood Nursing Home
1020 N Woodland Ave, Tucson, AZ 85711
(602) 795-9891
Admin Peggy Wilson.
Licensure Skilled care. *Beds* 86.
Owner Proprietary corp.

Life Care Center of Tucson
6211 N La Cholla Blvd, Tucson, AZ 85741
(602) 575-0900
Admin Ed Chris. *Dir of Nursing* Lola Thomas
RN. *Medical Dir* Dr Floyd Swenson.
Licensure Skilled care; Intermediate care;
Personal care. *Beds* SNF 136; ICF 34;
Personal 10. *Private Pay Patients* 70%.
Certified Medicaid; Medicare AHCCC.
Owner Proprietary corp (Life Care Centers of
America).
Admissions Requirements Medical
examination.
Staff RNs 7 (ft), 4 (pt); LPNs 19 (ft), 8 (pt);
Nurses' aides 58 (ft), 2 (pt); Physical
therapists 1 (ft); Recreational therapists 1
(ft), 1 (pt); Occupational therapists 1 (ft);
Speech therapists 1 (ft); Dietitians 1 (ft).
Facilities Dining room; Physical therapy
room; Activities room; Chapel; Crafts room;
Laundry room; Barber/Beauty shop; Library;
Mall area with gift shop & ice cream parlor.
Activities Arts & crafts; Cards; Games;
Reading groups; Prayer groups; Movies;
Shopping trips; Dances/Social/Cultural
gatherings; Intergenerational programs; Pet
therapy.

Manor Care Nursing Center
3705 N Swan Rd, Tucson, AZ 85718
(602) 299-7088
Admin Monica Graves.

Park Villa Convalescent Center
2001 N Park Ave, Tucson, AZ 85719-3599
(602) 624-8877
Admin Jan Green.
Medical Dir Judy Sue Donnelly.
Licensure Skilled care. *Beds* SNF 200.
Certified Medicaid; Medicare.
Owner Proprietary corp.
Admissions Requirements Minimum age 18;
Medical examination; Physician's request.
Staff Physicians 1 (pt); RNs 10 (ft); LPNs 15
(ft), 3 (pt); Nurses' aides 40 (ft), 7 (pt);
Physical therapists 1 (pt); Occupational
therapists 1 (pt); Speech therapists 1 (pt);
Activities coordinators 2 (ft); Dietitians 1
(pt).
Languages Spanish.
Facilities Dining room; Physical therapy
room; Activities room; Crafts room; Laundry
room; Barber/Beauty shop; Library.
Activities Arts & crafts; Cards; Games;
Reading groups; Prayer groups; Movies;
Shopping trips; Dances/Social/Cultural
gatherings.

Posada Del Sol
2250 N Craycroft, Tucson, AZ 85712
(602) 886-5481, 722-5651 FAX
Admin Linda Darnell RN. *Dir of Nursing*
Sharon Corey. *Medical Dir* Robert White
MD.
Licensure Skilled care; Alzheimer's care. *Beds*
SNF 156. *Certified* Medicaid; Medicare.
Owner Publicly owned.
Admissions Requirements Physician's request.
Staff Physicians 1 (ft); RNs 15 (ft), 3 (pt);
LPNs 15 (ft); Nurses' aides 78 (ft); Physical
therapists 1 (ft); Recreational therapists 2
(ft); Occupational therapists 1 (ft); Speech
therapists 1 (ft); Activities coordinators 1
(ft); Dietitians 1 (ft).
Languages Spanish.
Facilities Dining room; Physical therapy
room; Activities room; Chapel; Crafts room;
Laundry room; Barber/Beauty shop; Library;
Ventilator program; Behavioral management
program.
Activities Arts & crafts; Cards; Games;
Reading groups; Prayer groups; Movies;
Shopping trips; Dances/Social/Cultural
gatherings; Intergenerational programs; Pet
therapy.

Santa Rita Health Care Center
150 N La Canada Dr, Tucson, AZ 85622
(602) 625-2500
Admin Margaret Y Mitchell.
Beds 117.

Santa Rosa Convalescent Center
1650 N Santa Rosa Ave, Tucson, AZ 85712
(602) 795-1610
Admin William J Mitchell.
Licensure Skilled care. *Beds* 144. *Certified*
Medicare.
Owner Proprietary corp.

Su Casa Personal Care
720 W 41st St, Tucson, AZ 85713
(602) 624-0784
Admin Elizabeth L Stapleton. *Dir of Nursing*
Elizabeth L Stapleton RN.
Licensure Personal care; Alzheimer's care.
Beds 16. *Certified* Medicaid; Indian Health
Services.
Owner Proprietary corp.
Admissions Requirements Medical
examination; Physician's request.
Staff RNs 1 (ft); LPNs 3 (ft), 2 (pt); Nurses'
aides 1 (ft), 2 (pt); Activities coordinators 1
(ft); Dietitians 1 (pt).
Languages Spanish, Papago.
Facilities Dining room; Activities room;
Laundry room; Living room; Fenced yard
provides protection.
Activities Arts & crafts; Cards; Games;
Reading groups; Prayer groups; Shopping
trips; Dances/Social/Cultural gatherings.

Tucson Medical Center Sub-Acute Unit
5301 E Grant Rd, Tucson, AZ 85713
(602) 327-5461
Admin Mary Lou Barraza.
Beds 35.

Valley House Healthcare
5545 E Lee, Tucson, AZ 85712
(602) 296-2306
Admin Thomas A Hines. *Dir of Nursing*
Midge Krebs RN. *Medical Dir* Dr James
Belitsos.
Licensure Skilled care; Retirement. *Beds* SNF
147. *Certified* Medicare; VA.
Owner Proprietary corp (Hillhaven Corp).
Admissions Requirements Medical
examination; Physician's request.
Staff Physicians 3 (pt); RNs 9 (ft), 15 (pt);
LPNs 8 (ft), 9 (pt); Nurses' aides 47 (ft), 17
(pt); Physical therapists 1 (pt); Occupational
therapists 1 (pt); Speech therapists 1 (pt);
Activities coordinators 2 (ft), 1 (pt);
Dietitians 1 (ft); Dentists 1 (pt).
Facilities Dining room; Physical therapy
room; Activities room; Crafts room; Laundry
room; Barber/Beauty shop; Library.
Activities Arts & crafts; Cards; Games;
Reading groups; Prayer groups; Movies;
Shopping trips; Dances/Social/Cultural
gatherings; Exercises; Bell ringing; Current
events.

Villa Campana Health Center
6651 E Carondelet Dr, Tucson, AZ 85710
(602) 296-6100
Admin Loris Gielczyk. *Dir of Nursing* Judy
Black. *Medical Dir* James Belitsos.
Licensure Skilled care; Retirement. *Beds* SNF
120. *Certified* Medicare.
Owner Proprietary corp (Hillhaven Corp).
Admissions Requirements Minimum age 55
(apartments only).
Staff Physicians 3 (pt); RNs 5 (ft), 4 (pt);
LPNs 12 (ft), 6 (pt); Nurses' aides 27 (ft), 11
(pt); Physical therapists 2 (ft); Occupational
therapists 1 (ft); Speech therapists 1 (pt);
Activities coordinators 2 (ft), 1 (pt); Dietitians 1
(ft), 1 (pt); Dentists 1 (pt).
Facilities Dining room; Physical therapy
room; Activities room; Laundry room;
Barber/Beauty shop.

Activities Arts & crafts; Cards; Games;
Reading groups; Prayer groups; Movies;
Shopping trips; Dances/Social/Cultural
gatherings; Field trips.

Villa Maria
4310 E Grant Rd, Tucson, AZ 85712
(602) 323-9351
Admin Maggie J Harris, Exec Dir. *Dir of
Nursing* Pat Torrington RN. *Medical Dir*
James G Belitsos MD.
Licensure Skilled care; Intermediate care;
Assisted living; Independent living. *Beds*
Swing beds SNF/ICF 93; Assisted living 19;
Independent living 29. *Certified* Medicaid;
Medicare.
Owner Nonprofit corp.
Admissions Requirements Medical
examination; Physician's request.
Staff RNs 5 (ft), 7 (pt); LPNs 7 (ft), 5 (pt);
Nurses' aides 34 (ft), 4 (pt); Physical
therapists (contracted); Recreational
therapists 1 (ft); Activities coordinators 1
(ft); Dietitians 1 (ft).
Languages Spanish.
Affiliation Roman Catholic.
Facilities Dining room; Physical therapy
room; Activities room; Chapel; Crafts room;
Laundry room; Barber/Beauty shop; Library;
Transportation for doctor appointments &
shopping.
Activities Arts & crafts; Cards; Games;
Reading groups; Prayer groups; Movies;
Shopping trips; Dances/Social/Cultural
gatherings; Intergenerational programs; Pet
therapy.

Wickenburg

Wickenburg Nursing Home
PO Box 1388, 111 Rose Ln, Wickenburg, AZ
85358
(602) 684-5421
Admin Robert C Frechette.
Beds 43.

Willcox

**Northern Cochise Community Hospital &
Nursing Home**
901 W Rex Allen Dr, Willcox, AZ 85643
(602) 384-3541
Admin Nancy A Holloway.
Licensure Skilled care. *Beds* 24.
Owner Nonprofit corp.
Admissions Requirements Medical
examination; Physician's request.
Staff RNs 1 (ft), 1 (pt); LPNs 3 (ft), 2 (pt);
Nurses' aides 7 (ft), 5 (pt); Physical
therapists 1 (pt); Activities coordinators 1
(ft); Dietitians 1 (pt).
Languages Spanish.
Facilities Dining room; Activities room;
Laundry room.
Activities Arts & crafts; Cards; Games;
Reading groups; Prayer groups; Movies;
Dances/Social/Cultural gatherings.

Winslow

Winslow Convalescent Center
116 E Hillview, Winslow, AZ 86047
(602) 289-4678
Admin William Constable.
Licensure Skilled care. *Beds* 38.
Owner Proprietary corp.

Youngtown

Cook Health Care
11527 W Peoria Ave, Youngtown, AZ 85363
(602) 933-4683, 972-4993 FAX
Admin Sonja S Jones. *Dir of Nursing* Noreen
Luders RN. *Medical Dir* Reynoldo Vito
MD.

Licensure Skilled care; Intermediate care;
Personal care; Independent living. *Beds* SNF
86; ICF 34; Personal care 8; Independent
living 118. *Private Pay Patients* 84%.
Certified Medicaid; Medicare.
Owner Nonprofit corp.
Admissions Requirements Medical
examination.
Staff RNs 12 (ft), 3 (pt); LPNs 13 (ft), 2 (pt);
Nurses' aides 46 (ft), 6 (pt); Physical
therapists (contracted); Activities
coordinators 1 (ft); Gerontologists 1 (ft);
Chaplains 1 (ft).
Languages Spanish.
Facilities Dining room; Physical therapy
room; Activities room; Chapel; Crafts room;
Laundry room; Barber/Beauty shop; Library.
Activities Arts & crafts; Cards; Games;
Reading groups; Prayer groups; Movies;
Shopping trips; Dances/Social/Cultural
gatherings; Intergenerational programs; Pet
therapy.

Yuma

Hillhaven Healthcare
2222 Ave A, Yuma, AZ 85364
(602) 783-8831
Admin David Reynolds. *Dir of Nursing*
Margene Nutt RN. *Medical Dir* Roger Nutt
MD, Fred Lindberg MD.
Licensure Skilled care; Intermediate care;
Personal care; Alzheimer's care. *Beds* 143.
Certified Medicare.
Owner Proprietary corp (Hillhaven Corp).
Admissions Requirements Minimum age 18;
Medical examination; Physician's request.
Staff RNs 5 (ft), 4 (pt); LPNs 10 (ft), 5 (pt);
Nurses' aides 40 (ft), 10 (pt); Physical
therapists 1 (pt); Reality therapists 1 (pt);
Recreational therapists 1 (pt); Occupational
therapists 1 (pt); Speech therapists 1 (pt);
Activities coordinators 2 (ft); Dietitians 1
(pt); Ophthalmologists 1 (pt); Podiatrists 1
(pt); Dentists 1 (pt).
Languages Spanish.
Facilities Dining room; Physical therapy
room; Activities room; Chapel; Crafts room;
Laundry room; Barber/Beauty shop; Library;
Private dining rooms; Large family room/
lounge; Facility van for transportation.
Activities Arts & crafts; Cards; Games;
Reading groups; Prayer groups; Movies;
Shopping trips; Dances/Social/Cultural
gatherings; Pet visits; Church services; Bible
study.

La Mesa Care Center
2470 Arizona Ave, Yuma, AZ 85364
(602) 344-8541, 344-1178 FAX
Admin Bonnie H Greer RN MSN CNAA. *Dir
of Nursing* Doris Lawseth RN. *Medical Dir*
Terence Tuttle MD.
Licensure Skilled care; Intermediate care;
Personal care. *Beds* SNF 64; ICF 44;
Personal care 20. *Private Pay Patients* 75%.
Certified Medicaid; Medicare.
Owner Nonprofit corp (Samaritan Senior
Services).
Admissions Requirements Medical
examination; Physician's request.
Staff Physicians 12 (pt); RNs 5 (ft), 4 (pt);
LPNs 3 (ft), 2 (pt); Nurses' aides 13 (ft), 7
(pt); Physical therapists 2 (pt); Recreational
therapists 1 (pt); Occupational therapists 2
(pt); Speech therapists 1 (pt); Activities
coordinators 1 (ft); Dietitians 1 (pt);
Ophthalmologists 1 (pt); Podiatrists 1 (pt);
Audiologists 1 (pt).
Facilities Dining room; Physical therapy
room; Activities room; Laundry room;
Barber/Beauty shop; Library.
Activities Arts & crafts; Cards; Games;
Reading groups; Prayer groups; Movies;
Shopping trips; Dances/Social/Cultural
gatherings; Intergenerational programs; Pet
therapy.

Life Care Center of Yuma
2450 S 19th Ave, Yuma, AZ 85364
(602) 344-0425
Admin Tom Rislow.
Beds 128.

Yuma Nursing Center
1850 W 25th St, Yuma, AZ 85364
(602) 726-6700
Admin Edith L Snyder.
Beds 120.

ARKANSAS

Alexander

Alexander Human Development Center
PO Box 320, Alexander, AR 72002
(501) 847-3506
Admin Michael McCreight. *Dir of Nursing* De Etta Buckelew RN BSN. *Medical Dir* Robert Farrell MD.
Licensure Intermediate care for mentally retarded. *Beds* ICF/MR 150. *Certified* Medicaid; Medicare.
Owner Publicly owned.
Admissions Requirements Minimum age 18.
Staff Physicians (contracted); RNs 3 (ft); LPNs 10 (ft); Recreational therapists 6 (ft); Occupational therapists 1 (pt); Speech therapists 3 (ft); Activities coordinators 3 (ft); Dietitians 1 (ft); Audiologists 1 (ft); Occupational therapy aides 2 (ft).
Facilities Dining room; Activities room; Crafts room; Laundry room; Barber/Beauty shop; Recreation room.
Activities Arts & crafts; Games; Movies; Shopping trips; Dances/Social/Cultural gatherings; Intergenerational programs; Competitive employment; Workshops.

Arkadelphia

Arkadelphia Human Developmental Center
PO Box 70, Arkadelphia, AR 71923
(501) 246-8011
Admin Russ Burbank.
Licensure Intermediate care for mentally retarded. *Beds* 167. *Certified* Medicaid.

Riverwood Convalescent Home
102 Caddo St, Arkadelphia, AR 71923
(501) 246-5566
Admin Jean D Reeder.
Licensure Intermediate care. *Beds* 120. *Certified* Medicaid.
Owner Proprietary corp (Beverly Enterprises).

Twin Rivers Medical Center
Box 98, 1420 Pine St, Arkadelphia, AR 71923
(501) 246-9801
Admin D W Gathright.
Licensure Intermediate care. *Beds* 42. *Certified* Medicaid.

Ash Flat

Ash Flat Convalescent Center
Box 5A, Star Rte, Ash Flat, AR 72513
(501) 994-2341
Admin Rebecca Frazier. *Dir of Nursing* Wanda Davis. *Medical Dir* Annette Racaniello DO.
Licensure Skilled care; Alzheimer's care. *Beds* SNF 105. *Certified* Medicaid.
Owner Proprietary corp (Diversicare Corp).
Admissions Requirements Physician's request.
Staff Physicians 1 (ft); RNs 3 (ft); LPNs 8 (ft); Nurses' aides 60 (ft); Physical therapists 1 (ft); Speech therapists 1 (ft); Activities coordinators 1 (ft); Dietitians 1 (ft).

Facilities Dining room; Activities room; Chapel; Crafts room; Laundry room; Barber/Beauty shop.
Activities Arts & crafts; Cards; Games; Reading groups; Prayer groups; Movies; Shopping trips; Dances/Social/Cultural gatherings.

Ashdown

Little River Nursing Home
PO Box 69, 5th & Locke, Ashdown, AR 71822
(501) 898-5101
Admin Eva Jane Bowman; Judy Adams, Chief Admin. *Dir of Nursing* Rebecca Smithpeters RN. *Medical Dir* Joseph Shelton Jr MD.
Licensure Intermediate care. *Beds* ICF 76. *Private Pay Patients* 15%. *Certified* Medicaid.
Owner Publicly owned.
Admissions Requirements Physician's request.
Staff RNs 1 (ft); LPNs 5 (ft), 1 (pt); Nurses' aides 21 (ft), 10 (pt); Activities coordinators 1 (ft), 1 (pt); Dietitians 1 (ft).
Facilities Dining room; Activities room; Laundry room; Barber/Beauty shop; Living room.
Activities Arts & crafts; Games; Reading groups; Movies; Birthday parties.

Pleasant Manor Nursing Home Inc
750 S Locust St, Ashdown, AR 71822
(501) 898-5001
Admin Maxine Rhodes. *Dir of Nursing* Judy Pickett RN. *Medical Dir* Dr Wayne Reid.
Licensure Intermediate care. *Beds* ICF 54. *Certified* Medicaid.
Owner Proprietary corp.
Admissions Requirements Medical examination; Physician's request.
Staff Physicians 1 (ft), 4 (pt); RNs 1 (ft); LPNs 5 (ft), 2 (pt); Nurses' aides 16 (ft), 5 (pt); Recreational therapists 1 (ft); Activities coordinators 1 (ft).
Facilities Dining room; Physical therapy room; Activities room; Crafts room; Laundry room; Barber/Beauty shop; Library.
Activities Arts & crafts; Cards; Games; Reading groups; Prayer groups; Shopping trips; Dances/Social/Cultural gatherings.

Batesville

Intermed of Batesville
PO Box 2698, Batesville, AR 72501
(501) 698-1853
Admin Richard L Case.
Licensure Skilled care. *Beds* 140. *Certified* Medicaid.
Owner Proprietary corp (Beverly Enterprises).

Wood-Lawn Inc
2901 Neeley St, Batesville, AR 72501
(501) 793-7195
Admin Joyce Skinner.
Licensure Skilled care. *Beds* 121. *Certified* Medicaid.

Bella Vista

Concordia Care Center
7 Professional Dr, Bella Vista, AR 72714
(501) 855-3735
Admin Pat Boyer.
Medical Dir Albert E Martin MD.
Licensure Skilled care. *Beds* 82. *Certified* Medicaid; Medicare.
Staff RNs 1 (ft), 2 (pt); LPNs 7 (ft), 2 (pt); Nurses' aides 27 (ft), 4 (pt); Activities coordinators 1 (ft).
Facilities Dining room; Chapel; Crafts room; Laundry room; Barber/Beauty shop; Library.
Activities Arts & crafts; Cards; Games; Reading groups; Prayer groups; Movies; Shopping trips; Dances/Social/Cultural gatherings.

Benton

Benton Services Center Nursing Home
Services Center Branch, Benton, AR 72015
(501) 778-1111
Admin Charles L Smith.
Licensure Intermediate care. *Beds* SNF 290. *Certified* Medicaid.

Rose Care Center of Benton I
3300 Military, Benton, AR 72015
(501) 778-8282
Admin Kaye Keller. *Dir of Nursing* Marion Bird. *Medical Dir* Dr Paul Hogue.
Licensure Skilled care. *Beds* SNF 103. *Private Pay Patients* 15%. *Certified* Medicaid.
Owner Proprietary corp (Rose Care Inc).
Admissions Requirements Medical examination; Physician's request.
Staff RNs 1 (ft), 2 (pt); LPNs 9 (ft); Nurses' aides 50 (ft), 10 (pt); Activities coordinators 1 (ft); Dietitians 1 (ft).
Facilities Dining room; Activities room; Laundry room; Barber/Beauty shop.
Activities Arts & crafts; Cards; Games; Reading groups; Prayer groups; Movies; Shopping trips; Dances/Social/Cultural gatherings; Intergenerational programs; Pet therapy.

Rose Care Center of Benton II
PO Box 280, 809 Kenwood Rd, Benton, AR 72015
(501) 778-7417
Admin Paula Binns. *Dir of Nursing* Kathy Norwood RN. *Medical Dir* Samuel Taggart MD.
Licensure Intermediate care. *Beds* ICF 140. *Certified* Medicaid.
Owner Proprietary corp (Rose Care Inc).
Admissions Requirements Minimum age 21; Medical examination; Physician's request.
Staff Physicians 1 (ft); RNs 1 (ft), 1 (pt); LPNs 12 (ft), 1 (pt); Nurses' aides 38 (ft), 8 (pt); Physical therapists 1 (pt); Activities coordinators 1 (ft); Dietitians 1 (pt); Ophthalmologists 1 (pt); Home economists 1 (ft).
Languages Sign.

Facilities Dining room; Activities room; Crafts room; Laundry room; Barber/Beauty shop; TV/Living room; Visitation rooms.
Activities Arts & crafts; Cards; Games; Reading groups; Prayer groups; Movies; Shopping trips; Dances/Social/Cultural gatherings; Bus rides; Picnics; Beauty contests.

Bentonville

Bentonville Manor
224 S Main, Bentonville, AR 72712
(501) 273-3373
Admin Marilu A Monroe. *Dir of Nursing* Jane Kinney RN. *Medical Dir* W H Howard Jr MD.
Licensure Skilled care. *Beds* SNF 105. *Private Pay Patients* 30%. *Certified* Medicaid.
Owner Proprietary corp (Rose Care Inc).
Admissions Requirements Minimum age 18; Medical examination; Physician's request.
Staff RNs 2 (ft); LPNs 9 (ft); Nurses' aides 30 (ft); Activities coordinators 1 (pt); Dietitians 1 (ft).
Facilities Dining room; Activities room; Crafts room; Barber/Beauty shop.
Activities Arts & crafts; Cards; Games; Reading groups; Prayer groups; Movies; Shopping trips; Dances/Social/Cultural gatherings; Intergenerational programs; Pet therapy.

Berryville

Berryville Health Care Center
Simpson Ave, Berryville, AR 72616
(501) 423-6966
Admin Roger L Curtis.
Licensure Intermediate care. *Beds* 52. *Certified* Medicaid.

Blytheville

Blytheville Nursing Center Inc
1400 N Division, Blytheville, AR 72315
(501) 763-0240
Admin Rose Jackson. *Dir of Nursing* Sally Jones RN. *Medical Dir* Joe Jones MD.
Licensure Skilled care. *Beds* SNF 105. *Certified* Medicaid.
Owner Proprietary corp (Beverly Enterprises).
Admissions Requirements Medical examination; Physician's request.
Staff RNs 1 (ft), 2 (pt); LPNs 8 (ft), 4 (pt); Nurses' aides 25 (ft), 4 (pt); Activities coordinators 1 (ft), 1 (pt).
Facilities Dining room; Barber/Beauty shop; Whirlpool bath; Shower room.
Activities Arts & crafts; Cards; Games; Reading groups; Prayer groups; Movies; Shopping trips; Dances/Social/Cultural gatherings.

Keith Acres Nursing Home
PO Box 716, 112 W Clinton, Blytheville, AR 72315-716
(501) 763-9213
Admin Jean L Carmon. *Dir of Nursing* Alice D Karr. *Medical Dir* C R Cole MD.
Licensure Intermediate care. *Beds* ICF 44. *Certified* Medicaid.
Owner Proprietary corp.
Admissions Requirements Medical examination; Physician's request.
Staff Physicians 1 (ft), 1 (pt); RNs 1 (ft); LPNs 2 (ft), 4 (pt); Nurses' aides 11 (ft), 4 (pt); Activities coordinators 1 (ft); Dietitians 1 (pt).
Facilities Dining room; Laundry room.
Activities Arts & crafts; Games; Prayer groups; Dances/Social/Cultural gatherings.

Mississippi County Nursing Home
PO Box 108, 1501 N 10th, Blytheville, AR 72315
(501) 762-3220, 763-3534 FAX

Admin Sandra B Ray. *Dir of Nursing* Carol A Couch.
Licensure Intermediate care. *Beds* ICF 70. *Private Pay Patients* 25%. *Certified* Medicaid.
Owner Publicly owned.
Admissions Requirements Medical examination; Physician's request.
Staff RNs 1 (ft); LPNs 7 (ft), 1 (pt); Nurses' aides 27 (ft), 5 (pt); Activities coordinators 1 (ft); Dietitians 1 (ft).
Facilities Dining room; Activities room; Barber/Beauty shop.
Activities Arts & crafts; Cards; Games; Reading groups; Prayer groups; Movies; Shopping trips; Pet therapy.

Parkview Manor Nursing Home—Blytheville
PO Box 664, 710 N Ruddle, Blytheville, AR 72315
(501) 763-3654
Admin Arvell Pate. *Dir of Nursing* Tammy McCormick RN. *Medical Dir* Dr C R Cole.
Licensure Intermediate care. *Beds* ICF 46. *Certified* Medicaid.
Owner Proprietary corp.
Admissions Requirements Medical examination; Physician's request.
Staff Physicians; RNs; LPNs; Nurses' aides.
Facilities Dining room; Activities room; Chapel; Laundry room.
Activities Arts & crafts; Games; Prayer groups; Shopping trips; Dances/Social/Cultural gatherings.

Booneville

Oak Manor Nursing Center
PO Box 170, Booneville, AR 72927
(501) 675-3763
Admin Eileen P Macklin.
Licensure Skilled care. *Beds* 101. *Certified* Medicaid.

Brinkley

Cla-Clif Home for the Aged Inc
PO Box 671, Brinkley, AR 72021
(501) 734-3636
Admin Billy Clay.
Licensure Intermediate care. *Beds* 77. *Certified* Medicaid.

St Joseph Home
509 S New York, Brinkley, AR 72021
(501) 734-1818
Admin Sharon S Perry. *Dir of Nursing* Melinda Duggin RN. *Medical Dir* Dr William Gilli.
Licensure Intermediate care. *Beds* ICF 28. *Certified* Medicaid.
Owner Publicly owned.
Admissions Requirements Medical examination; Physician's request.
Staff RNs 1 (ft); LPNs 3 (ft), 1 (pt); Nurses' aides 7 (ft), 3 (pt); Activities coordinators 1 (ft); Dietitians 1 (pt).
Facilities Dining room; Activities room; Laundry room; Barber/Beauty shop.
Activities Arts & crafts; Games; Prayer groups; Movies; Shopping trips; Dances/Social/Cultural gatherings.

Cabot

Cabot Manor Nursing Center
615 W Main, Cabot, AR 72023
(501) 843-6181, 843-2645 FAX
Admin Sheila Martin RN. *Dir of Nursing* Marilyn McColgan RN. *Medical Dir* Jerry Chapman MD.
Licensure Skilled care. *Beds* SNF 75. *Certified* Medicaid.
Owner Proprietary corp (Catlett Corp).
Admissions Requirements Minimum age 18; Medical examination; Physician's request.

Staff RNs 1 (ft), 2 (pt); LPNs 8 (ft), 1 (pt); Nurses' aides 20 (ft), 7 (pt); Activities coordinators 1 (ft).
Facilities Dining room; Activities room; Laundry room.
Activities Arts & crafts; Cards; Games; Reading groups; Prayer groups; Movies; Shopping trips; Dances/Social/Cultural gatherings; Pet therapy; Resident council; Family council.

Calico Rock

White River Convalescent Home Inc
PO Box 408, Calico Rock, AR 72519
(501) 297-3719
Admin Dean Hudson.
Licensure Skilled care. *Beds* 91. *Certified* Medicaid.

Camden

Leisure Lodge Inc—Camden Bruce Street
515 Bruce St, Camden, AR 71701
(501) 836-6831
Admin Terri Platt Callicott.
Licensure Intermediate care. *Beds* 70. *Certified* Medicaid.
Owner Proprietary corp (Beverly Enterprises).

Leisure Lodge Inc—Camden Magnolia Road
900 Magnolia Rd, Camden, AR 71701
(501) 836-6833
Admin Les Wallace.
Licensure Skilled care. *Beds* 106. *Certified* Medicare.
Owner Proprietary corp (Beverly Enterprises).

Longmeadow Nursing Home—Camden
Rte 1 Box 843, Camden, AR 71701
(501) 836-9337
Admin Jimmie Dean Henson.
Licensure Intermediate care. *Beds* 69. *Certified* Medicaid.

Ouachita Convalescent Center
1411 Country Club Rd, Camden, AR 71701
(501) 836-4111
Admin Annie Jo Young.
Medical Dir James Guthrie.
Licensure Skilled care. *Beds* 142.
Staff RNs 2 (ft); LPNs 8 (ft), 3 (pt); Nurses' aides 29 (ft), 4 (pt); Activities coordinators 1 (ft); Dietitians 1 (ft).

Caraway

Lane's Rest Home Inc—Caraway
PO Box 519, Caraway, AR 72419
(501) 482-3711
Admin Flossie Lane.
Licensure Intermediate care. *Beds* 40. *Certified* Medicaid.

Carlisle

Chambers Nursing Home Inc
Rte 1 Box 234, Carlisle, AR 72024
(501) 552-7811
Admin Hazel J Glover.
Licensure Intermediate care. *Beds* 52. *Certified* Medicaid.

J W Comer Nursing Home
Box 231, Rte 1, Carlisle, AR 72024
(501) 552-3350
Admin Helen L Comer. *Dir of Nursing* Betty J O'Cain RN. *Medical Dir* Dr B E Holmes.
Licensure Intermediate care. *Beds* ICF 22. *Certified* Medicaid.
Owner Privately owned.
Admissions Requirements Males only; Medical examination; Physician's request.
Staff Physicians 1 (pt); RNs 1 (ft); LPNs 1 (ft), 1 (pt); Nurses' aides 5 (ft), 3 (pt); Activities coordinators 1 (ft); Dietitians 1 (ft), 1 (pt).

Facilities Dining room; Activities room;
Laundry room.
Activities Arts & crafts; Cards; Games;
Reading groups; Shopping trips; Dances/
Social/Cultural gatherings.

Zimmerman Nursing Home Inc
PO Box 14, Rte 1, Carlisle, AR 72024
(501) 552-7449
Admin John F Zimmerman. *Dir of Nursing*
Tanya Wilson. *Medical Dir* Dr Fred C
Inman.
Licensure Intermediate care; Alzheimer's care;
Retirement. *Beds* 41. *Certified* Medicaid;
Medicare.
Owner Privately owned.
Admissions Requirements Minimum age 55;
Medical examination.
Staff RNs 1 (ft); LPNs 3 (ft); Nurses' aides 10
(ft), 10 (pt); Activities coordinators 1 (ft).
Facilities Dining room; Activities room;
Chapel; Crafts room; Laundry room; Barber/
Beauty shop.
Activities Arts & crafts; Cards; Games;
Reading groups; Shopping trips; Dances/
Social/Cultural gatherings.

Carthage

Carthage Nursing Home
PO Box 35, Hwy 48 W, Carthage, AR 71725
(501) 254-2222
Admin Morgan Treadwell.
Medical Dir John Delamore.
Licensure Intermediate care. *Beds* 85.
Certified Medicaid.
Staff Physicians 3 (pt); RNs 1 (ft); LPNs 3
(ft), 2 (pt); Nurses' aides 42 (ft), 5 (pt);
Recreational therapists 1 (ft); Activities
coordinators 1 (ft); Dietitians 1 (ft);
Ophthalmologists 1 (pt); Dentists 1 (pt).
Facilities Dining room; Activities room;
Laundry room; Barber/Beauty shop.
Activities Cards; Games; Reading groups;
Prayer groups; Shopping trips; Dances/
Social/Cultural gatherings.

Charleston

Greenhurst Nursing Home
PO Box 458, Charleston, AR 72933
(501) 965-7373
Admin Erich Z Schaffer. *Dir of Nursing*
Martin C Schaffer RN.
Licensure Skilled care. *Beds* SNF 73. *Certified*
Medicaid.
Owner Proprietary corp.
Staff Physicians 4 (ft); RNs 3 (ft); LPNs 8 (ft);
Nurses' aides 30 (ft), 20 (pt); Physical
therapists 1 (pt); Activities coordinators 1
(ft); Dietitians 1 (pt).
Languages German, Italian, French.
Facilities Dining room; Activities room;
Laundry room; Barber/Beauty shop.
Activities Arts & crafts; Cards; Reading
groups; Prayer groups; Movies; Dances/
Social/Cultural gatherings.

Clarksville

Clarksville Convalescent Home Inc
400 Oak Court St, Clarksville, AR 72830
(501) 754-8611
Admin Ronnie F Johnson.
Licensure Intermediate care. *Beds* 105.
Certified Medicaid.

Mickel Nursing Home
PO Box 250, Hwy 64 E, Clarksville, AR
72830
(501) 754-2052
Admin Mary Ann Farris.
Licensure Skilled care; Intermediate care for
mentally retarded. *Beds* SNF 24; ICF/MR
53. *Certified* Medicaid.

Clinton

Van Buren County Nursing Home
PO Box 206, Clinton, AR 72031
(501) 745-2401
Admin Lillian B Varnell. *Dir of Nursing* Joyce
Thomas RN. *Medical Dir* John A Hall MD.
Licensure Skilled care. *Beds* SNF 104.
Certified Medicaid.
Owner Nonprofit corp.
Admissions Requirements Medical
examination; Physician's request.
Staff Physicians 5 (ft); RNs 1 (ft), 2 (pt);
LPNs 13 (ft); Nurses' aides 26 (ft), 4 (pt);
Activities coordinators 1 (ft); Dietitians 1
(ft).
Facilities Dining room; Activities room;
Crafts room; Laundry room; Barber/Beauty
shop.
Activities Arts & crafts; Cards; Games;
Reading groups; Movies; Shopping trips;
Dances/Social/Cultural gatherings.

College Station

Jean's Nursing Home Inc
PO Box 720, College Station, AR 72053-0720
(501) 490-1533
Admin Eunice Reed.
Licensure Skilled care. *Beds* 105. *Certified*
Medicaid.

Conway

Heritage Center Inc—Conway
619 Center St, Conway, AR 72032
(501) 327-7642
Admin Janis Young. *Dir of Nursing* Vivian
Flack. *Medical Dir* Dr Robert Rook.
Licensure Intermediate care; Retirement. *Beds*
ICF 55; Retirement 40. *Private Pay Patients*
40%. *Certified* Medicaid.
Owner Privately owned.
Admissions Requirements Medical
examination; Physician's request.
Staff RNs 1 (ft); LPNs 4 (ft), 2 (pt); Nurses'
aides 25 (ft), 4 (pt); Physical therapists 1
(pt); Activities coordinators 1 (ft); Dietitians
1 (ft).
Facilities Dining room; Activities room;
Crafts room; Laundry room; Barber/Beauty
shop.
Activities Arts & crafts; Cards; Games;
Reading groups; Prayer groups; Movies;
Shopping trips; Dances/Social/Cultural
gatherings; Intergenerational programs; Pet
therapy.

Johnson's Meadowlake Home Inc
PO Box 10567, Conway, AR 72032
(501) 329-9879
Admin Mark Johnson.
Licensure Intermediate care. *Beds* 70.
Certified Medicaid.
Admissions Requirements Medical
examination; Physician's request.
Staff RNs 1 (ft); LPNs 4 (ft), 2 (pt); Nurses'
aides 19 (ft), 1 (pt); Activities coordinators 1
(ft).
Facilities Dining room; Activities room;
Laundry room; Barber/Beauty shop.
Activities Arts & crafts; Cards; Games;
Reading groups; Prayer groups; Shopping
trips; Dances/Social/Cultural gatherings;
Outings.

Oak Grove Nursing Center
PO Box 10549, Conway, AR 72032
(501) 327-4421
Admin Victoria Massey.
Medical Dir Dr Bob Banister.
Licensure Intermediate care. *Beds* 117.
Certified Medicaid; Medicare.
Admissions Requirements Medical
examination.

Staff Physicians 1 (pt); RNs 2 (ft), 2 (pt);
LPNs 5 (ft), 1 (pt); Nurses' aides 50 (ft), 5
(pt); Activities coordinators 1 (ft); Dietitians
1 (pt).
Facilities Dining room; Activities room;
Chapel; Laundry room; Barber/Beauty shop.
Activities Arts & crafts; Cards; Games;
Reading groups; Prayer groups; Movies;
Dances/Social/Cultural gatherings.

Corning

Corning Nursing Home
100 W 5th & Walnut Sts, Corning, AR 72422
(501) 857-3100
Admin David Edwards. *Dir of Nursing* Virgie
Mulligan. *Medical Dir* Dr B C Page.
Licensure Intermediate care. *Beds* ICF 117.
Private Pay Patients 10%. *Certified*
Medicaid; Medicare.
Owner Proprietary corp.
Admissions Requirements Medical
examination.
Staff RNs 1 (ft); LPNs 13 (ft); Nurses' aides
65 (ft); Activities coordinators 1 (ft);
Dietitians 1 (ft).
Facilities Dining room; Activities room;
Crafts room; Laundry room; Barber/Beauty
shop.
Activities Arts & crafts; Games; Reading
groups; Prayer groups; Shopping trips;
Dances/Social/Cultural gatherings.

Crossett

Leisure Lodge Inc—Crossett
1101 Waterwell Rd, Crossett, AR 71635
(501) 364-5721
Admin Elaine Colvin. *Dir of Nursing* LaNell
Johnson. *Medical Dir* Dr D L Toon.
Licensure Skilled care. *Beds* SNF 79. *Certified*
Medicaid.
Owner Proprietary corp (Beverly Enterprises).
Admissions Requirements Physician's request.
Staff Physicians; RNs; LPNs; Nurses' aides;
Activities coordinators; Dietitians.
Facilities Dining room; Activities room;
Chapel; Crafts room; Laundry room; Barber/
Beauty shop.
Activities Arts & crafts; Games; Reading
groups; Prayer groups; Movies; Shopping
trips; Dances/Social/Cultural gatherings; Zoo
trips; Tours; Luncheons.

Danville

Mitchell's Nursing Home Inc
Box 10, Danville, AR 72833
(501) 495-2914
Admin Maurine Mitchell.
Medical Dir Dr Walter P Harris.
Licensure Intermediate care. *Beds* 92.
Certified Medicaid.
Admissions Requirements Minimum age 18.
Staff Physicians 7 (ft); RNs 2 (ft); LPNs 7 (ft);
Nurses' aides 52 (ft); Physical therapists 1
(pt); Reality therapists 1 (pt); Recreational
therapists 1 (pt); Occupational therapists 1
(pt); Activities coordinators 1 (pt); Dietitians
1 (pt).
Facilities Dining room; Activities room;
Crafts room; Laundry room; Barber/Beauty
shop.
Activities Arts & crafts; Cards; Games;
Reading groups; Prayer groups; Movies;
Shopping trips.

Dardanelle

Dardanelle Nursing Center Inc
510 W Green St, Dardanelle, AR 72834
(501) 229-4884
Admin Vickie Rainey.
Medical Dir Dr Gene D Ring.
Licensure Skilled care. *Beds* 90. *Certified*
Medicare.

Owner Proprietary corp (Beverly Enterprises).
Staff RNs 1 (ft), 1 (pt); LPNs 8 (ft), 1 (pt); Nurses' aides 22 (ft), 1 (pt); Activities coordinators 1 (ft).
Facilities Dining room; Laundry room; Barber/Beauty shop.
Activities Arts & crafts; Cards; Games; Movies; Shopping trips; Dances/Social/Cultural gatherings.

De Witt

DeWitt City Nursing Home
Box 428, DeWitt, AR 72042
(501) 946-4541
Admin Vivian A Meins.
Licensure Intermediate care. *Beds* 54. *Certified* Medicaid.

Leisure Lodge Inc—DeWitt
PO Box 254, De Witt, AR 72042
(501) 946-3569
Admin Betty Fischer.
Licensure Intermediate care. *Beds* 140. *Certified* Medicaid.
Owner Proprietary corp (Beverly Enterprises).

DeQueen

DeQueen Manor Nursing Center
PO Box 1040, 1020 N 13th St, DeQueen, AR 71832
(501) 642-3317
Admin Nancy C Dossey. *Dir of Nursing* Beverly Peugh RN. *Medical Dir* Charles N Jones MD.
Licensure Skilled care. *Beds* SNF 105. *Private Pay Patients* 25%. *Certified* Medicaid.
Owner Proprietary corp.
Admissions Requirements Medical examination; Physician's request.
Staff Physicians 1 (pt); RNs 1 (ft), 1 (pt); LPNs 7 (ft), 2 (pt); Nurses' aides 19 (ft), 17 (pt); Activities coordinators 1 (ft); Dietitians 1 (ft).
Facilities Dining room; Activities room; Laundry room; Barber/Beauty shop.
Activities Games; Prayer groups; Movies; Pet therapy; Musicals.

Ridgeview Lodge Nursing Center
Hwy 70 W, c/o Town N Shopping, DeQueen, AR 71832
(501) 642-3562
Admin Jim Pearce.
Licensure Intermediate care. *Beds* 105. *Certified* Medicaid.

Des Arc

Des Arc Convalescent Center
Rte 2 Box 143-B, Des Arc, AR 72040
(501) 256-4194
Admin Helen Mixon.
Licensure Skilled care. *Beds* 80. *Certified* Medicaid.

Dumas

Dumas Nursing Center
960 E Bowles, Dumas, AR 71639
(501) 382-6100
Admin Louis Jefferson. *Dir of Nursing* Howard Harris. *Medical Dir* Dr Guy Robinson.
Licensure Skilled care; Alzheimer's care. *Beds* SNF 80. *Certified* Medicaid.
Owner Proprietary corp (Britwell).
Admissions Requirements Minimum age 18; Medical examination; Physician's request.

Staff Physicians 4 (pt); RNs 1 (ft), 4 (pt); LPNs 8 (ft), 5 (pt); Nurses' aides 19 (ft), 1 (pt); Activities coordinators 1 (ft); Dietitians 1 (ft); Ophthalmologists 1 (ft); Podiatrists 1 (ft); Environmental supervisor 1 (ft).
Facilities Dining room; Physical therapy room; Activities room; Laundry room; Barber/Beauty shop.
Activities Arts & crafts; Cards; Games; Reading groups; Prayer groups; Movies; Shopping trips; Dances/Social/Cultural gatherings; Intergenerational programs.

El Dorado

East Manor Nursing Center
100 Hargett, El Dorado, AR 71630
(501) 862-6681
Admin Penny Callison. *Dir of Nursing* Sook Langston. *Medical Dir* G W Smith MD.
Licensure Skilled care. *Beds* SNF 84. *Certified* Medicaid.
Owner Proprietary corp (Beverly Enterprises).
Admissions Requirements Medical examination; Physician's request.
Staff RNs; LPNs; Nurses' aides; Activities coordinators; Social service.
Facilities Dining room; Activities room; Laundry room; Barber/Beauty shop.
Activities Arts & crafts; Cards; Games; Reading groups; Prayer groups; Movies; Shopping trips; Dances/Social/Cultural gatherings; Intergenerational programs; Pet therapy.

Hillsboro Manor Nursing Home
1700 E. Hillsboro, El Dorado, AR 71730
(501) 862-5124
Admin John Reynolds.
Licensure Skilled care. *Beds* 72. *Certified* Medicaid.

Hudson Memorial Nursing Home
700 N College, El Dorado, AR 71730
(501) 863-8131
Admin Mervin Mast. *Dir of Nursing* Alberta Smith RN. *Medical Dir* Dr George W Warren.
Licensure Skilled care. *Beds* SNF 108. *Private Pay Patients* 40%. *Certified* Medicaid.
Owner Publicly owned.
Admissions Requirements Minimum age 16; Medical examination; Physician's request.
Staff RNs 1 (ft), 3 (pt); LPNs 10 (ft), 1 (pt); Nurses' aides 38 (ft), 5 (pt); Activities coordinators 1 (ft); Social service 1 (ft).
Affiliation Mennonite.
Facilities Dining room; Activities room; Crafts room; Laundry room; Barber/Beauty shop; Library; Fenced yard with walkways.
Activities Arts & crafts; Games; Reading groups; Prayer groups; Movies; Shopping trips; Dances/Social/Cultural gatherings; Intergenerational programs; Remotivation groups.

Oak Ridge Nursing Home
Griffin & Leon Sts, El Dorado, AR 71730
(501) 862-5511
Admin Kleve R Bassford.
Licensure Skilled care. *Beds* 180. *Certified* Medicaid.

England

England Manor
PO Box 302, 516 NE 4th, England, AR 72046
(501) 842-2771
Admin Pattie Sue Cox; Danny C Cox. *Dir of Nursing* Brenda Rushig. *Medical Dir* Dr Thomas Braswell.
Licensure Intermediate care. *Beds* ICF 63. *Private Pay Patients* 20%. *Certified* Medicaid.
Owner Proprietary corp.
Admissions Requirements Minimum age 18; Medical examination; Physician's request.

Staff Physicians 2 (pt); RNs 2 (ft); LPNs 3 (ft); Nurses' aides 22 (ft); Physical therapists 1 (pt); Recreational therapists 1 (pt); Occupational therapists 1 (pt); Speech therapists 1 (pt); Activities coordinators 2 (ft); Dietitians 1 (pt); Ophthalmologists 1 (pt); Podiatrists 1 (pt); Audiologists 1 (pt).
Facilities Dining room; Activities room; Chapel; Barber/Beauty shop; Library; Family room.
Activities Arts & crafts; Cards; Games; Reading groups; Prayer groups; Movies; Shopping trips; Dances/Social/Cultural gatherings; Intergenerational programs; Pet therapy; Community participation.

England Nursing Center
PO Box 146, England, AR 72046
(501) 842-3971
Admin Nancy K Rollins.
Medical Dir Tommy Braswell MD.
Licensure Intermediate care; Retirement. *Beds* ICF 113. *Certified* Medicaid.
Owner Privately owned.
Admissions Requirements Physician's request.
Staff Physicians; RNs; LPNs; Nurses' aides; Activities coordinators; Dietitians.
Facilities Dining room; Activities room; Crafts room; Barber/Beauty shop.
Activities Arts & crafts; Cards; Games; Reading groups; Prayer groups; Movies; Shopping trips.

Eureka Springs

Eureka Springs Convalescent Center
Rte 1 Box 23, Eureka Springs, AR 72632
(501) 253-7038
Admin Debbie Johnson. *Dir of Nursing* Olga Burrey. *Medical Dir* Dr Jess D Green.
Licensure Skilled care. *Beds* SNF 100. *Certified* Medicaid.
Owner Proprietary corp (Diversicare Corp of America).
Staff RNs 1 (ft), 1 (pt); LPNs 5 (ft); Nurses' aides 26 (ft); Activities coordinators 1 (ft); Dietitians 1 (ft).
Languages German.
Facilities Dining room; Chapel; Laundry room; Barber/Beauty shop.
Activities Arts & crafts; Cards; Games; Reading groups; Prayer groups; Movies; Shopping trips; Dances/Social/Cultural gatherings; Intergenerational programs; Pet therapy.

Fayetteville

Apple Tree Inn
3100 Old Missouri Rd, Fayetteville, AR 72701
(501) 521-4353
Admin Ginger Bridges.
Medical Dir James Patrick.
Licensure Intermediate care. *Beds* 140. *Certified* Medicaid.
Admissions Requirements Medical examination; Physician's request.
Staff RNs 4 (ft); LPNs 15 (ft); Nurses' aides 45 (ft); Physical therapists; Speech therapists; Activities coordinators; Podiatrists; Dentists.
Facilities Dining room; Activities room; Laundry room; Barber/Beauty shop.
Activities Arts & crafts; Cards; Games; Reading groups; Prayer groups; Shopping trips; Dances/Social/Cultural gatherings.

Fayetteville City Hospital Geriatrics Center
PO Box 1743, Fayetteville, AR 72701
(501) 442-5100
Admin Steve Dyer.
Licensure Skilled care. *Beds* 104. *Certified* Medicaid.

Sunrise Manor Care Center
1001 Rochier St, Fayetteville, AR 72701
(501) 443-5211
Admin Mary Ann Nubbie.

Licensure Skilled care. *Beds* 147. *Certified* Medicaid.

Fordyce

Dallas County Nursing Home
201 Clifton, Fordyce, AR 71742
(501) 352-3155
Admin Ellen Harrington.
Licensure Skilled care. *Beds* 34. *Certified* Medicaid.
Owner Proprietary corp (National Healthcare).

Millcreek of Arkansas
PO Box 727, Hwy 79 Industrial Dr, Fordyce, AR 71742
(501) 352-8203
Admin Paulette Bailey.
Beds 61.

Southern Nursing Home
PO Box 472, Fordyce, AR 71742
(501) 352-2104, 352-5800
Admin Janice E Roark. *Dir of Nursing* Barbara Crowder. *Medical Dir* Paul Davis MD.
Licensure Skilled care; Alzheimer's care. *Beds* 105. *Certified* Medicaid.
Owner Privately owned.
Admissions Requirements Medical examination; Physician's request.
Staff Physicians 3 (ft); RNs 1 (ft), 1 (pt); LPNs 8 (ft); Nurses' aides 25 (ft); Activities coordinators 1 (ft); Dietitians 1 (ft); Social directors 1 (ft).
Facilities Dining room; Activities room; Crafts room; Laundry room; Barber/Beauty shop; Lobby.
Activities Arts & crafts; Cards; Games; Reading groups; Prayer groups; Movies; Shopping trips; Dances/Social/Cultural gatherings; Intergenerational programs.

Forrest City

Crestpark Inn of Forrest City
PO Box 1658, 503 Kittel Rd, Forrest City, AR 72335
(501) 633-7630
Admin Janice Heath.
Medical Dir H N Cogburn MD.
Licensure Skilled care. *Beds* 88. *Certified* Medicaid.
Admissions Requirements Medical examination; Physician's request.
Staff Physicians 10 (pt); RNs 1 (ft), 1 (pt); LPNs 4 (ft), 2 (pt); Nurses' aides 22 (ft), 1 (pt); Activities coordinators 1 (ft); Dietitians 1 (ft), 1 (pt); Ophthalmologists 1 (pt); Dentists 4 (pt).
Facilities Dining room; Activities room; Crafts room; Laundry room; Barber/Beauty shop.
Activities Arts & crafts; Cards; Games; Reading groups; Prayer groups; Movies; Shopping trips.

Geriatrics Nursing Center Inc—Forrest City
PO Box 1081, Forrest City, AR 72335
(501) 633-7500
Admin Gerald Kimbrough.
Licensure Skilled care. *Beds* 70. *Certified* Medicaid.
Owner Proprietary corp (Beverly Enterprises).

Fort Smith

Armour Heights Nursing Home Inc
3900 Armour Ave, Fort Smith, AR 72904
(501) 782-8956
Admin Betty L Kirby. *Dir of Nursing* Fredora Hulse RN. *Medical Dir* Richard Darden MD.
Licensure Skilled care. *Beds* SNF 75. *Certified* Medicaid.
Owner Proprietary corp.

Staff Physicians; RNs; LPNs; Nurses' aides; Activities coordinators; Dietitians; Ophthalmologists.
Facilities Dining room; Laundry room; Barber/Beauty shop; Library.
Activities Arts & crafts; Games; Reading groups; Prayer groups; Movies; Shopping trips; Trips.

Brownwood Life Care Center Inc
2121 Towson Ave, Fort Smith, AR 72901
(501) 785-2273
Admin Dave Broaddrick. *Dir of Nursing* Karen Parish.
Licensure Intermediate care for mentally retarded. *Beds* ICF/MR 50. *Certified* Medicaid.
Owner Proprietary corp.
Staff Physicians 1 (pt); RNs 5 (ft); LPNs 12 (ft); Nurses' aides 50 (ft); Physical therapists 1 (pt); Occupational therapists 1 (pt); Speech therapists 1 (pt); Activities coordinators 1 (ft); Dietitians 1 (ft).
Facilities Dining room; Physical therapy room; Activities room; Crafts room; Laundry room; Barber/Beauty shop; Library.
Activities Arts & crafts; Games.

Medi-Home Inc—Fort Smith
4623 Rogers Ave, Fort Smith, AR 72903
(501) 452-1541
Admin Nancy Stein.
Medical Dir Dr Mort Wilson.
Licensure Skilled care. *Beds* 157. *Certified* Medicaid.
Admissions Requirements Medical examination; Physician's request.
Staff RNs 3 (ft), 2 (pt); LPNs 12 (ft), 2 (pt); Nurses' aides 43 (ft), 7 (pt); Activities coordinators 1 (ft), 1 (pt); Dietitians 1 (pt).
Facilities Dining room; Activities room; Chapel; Crafts room; Laundry room.
Activities Arts & crafts; Cards; Games.

Methodist Nursing Home Inc
1915 S 74th St, Fort Smith, AR 72903-2899
(501) 452-1611
Admin Gina L Cowan.
Medical Dir Lottie Klyne.
Licensure Skilled care; Intermediate care; Retirement. *Beds* SNF 145; ICF. *Certified* Medicaid.
Owner Nonprofit organization/foundation.
Admissions Requirements Medical examination; Physician's request.
Staff RNs 3 (ft); LPNs 20 (ft) 40 (ft); Nurses' aides; Activities coordinators 1 (ft); Dietitians 15 (ft); Laundry 4 (ft); Housekeeping 16 (ft).
Languages German.
Affiliation Methodist.
Facilities Dining room; Activities room; Chapel; Crafts room; Laundry room; Barber/Beauty shop.
Activities Arts & crafts; Cards; Games; Reading groups; Prayer groups; Movies; Dances/Social/Cultural gatherings.

Oaks Lodge Rest Home Inc
3310 Waldron Rd, Fort Smith, AR 72904
(501) 783-3101, 3102
Admin Becky Birch.
Licensure Intermediate care. *Beds* 105. *Certified* Medicaid.

Parkview Nursing Home—Fort Smith
425 N 51st St, Fort Smith, AR 72903
(501) 452-0530
Admin Marcia Webb.
Licensure Intermediate care. *Beds* 70. *Certified* Medicaid.

Rose Care Center of Fort Smith
5301 Wheeler Ave, Fort Smith, AR 72901
(501) 646-3454
Admin James E Milford.
Licensure Skilled care. *Beds* 187. *Certified* Medicaid.

Gassville

Gassville Nursing Center
PO Box 190, 104 E Cotter Rd, Gassville, AR 72635
(501) 435-2588
Admin Kay Hall.
Beds 70.
Owner Proprietary corp (APEX of Arkansas Inc).

Glenwood

Glenwood Nursing Home Inc
Box 1390, Glenwood, AR 71943
(501) 356-3953
Admin Roger Tidwell.
Licensure Intermediate care. *Beds* 70. *Certified* Medicaid.

Gravette

Gravette Manor Nursing Home
PO Box 180, Gravette, AR 72736
(501) 787-5381
Admin Bobbi R Wilks. *Dir of Nursing* Kathy Mitchell RN. *Medical Dir* Dr Billy V Hall.
Licensure Intermediate care. *Beds* 83. *Certified* Medicaid.
Owner Privately owned.
Admissions Requirements Medical examination; Physician's request.
Staff RNs 1 (ft); LPNs 3 (ft), 2 (pt); Nurses' aides 26 (ft), 10 (pt); Activities coordinators 1 (ft), 1 (pt); Dietitians 1 (ft).
Facilities Dining room; Activities room; Crafts room; Laundry room; Barber/Beauty shop; Fenced yard with patio.
Activities Arts & crafts; Cards; Games; Reading groups; Prayer groups; Movies; Shopping trips; Dances/Social/Cultural gatherings; Fishing trips; Picnics; Trips to zoo.

Greenwood

Pink-Bud Home for the Golden Years
PO Box 592, Old Hwy 71 S, Greenwood, AR 72936
(501) 996-4125
Admin Roger M Corbin. *Dir of Nursing* Vincy Hannaman. *Medical Dir* Vincy Hannaman.
Licensure Intermediate care; Residential care; Alzheimer's care. *Beds* ICF 100; Residential care 42. *Private Pay Patients* 30%. *Certified* Medicaid.
Owner Proprietary corp.
Admissions Requirements Medical examination.
Staff Physicians 5 (pt); RNs 1 (ft); LPNs 9 (ft), 2 (pt); Nurses' aides 38 (ft), 2 (pt); Physical therapists 1 (pt); Activities coordinators 2 (ft), 1 (pt); Dietitians 1 (pt).
Facilities Dining room; Physical therapy room; Activities room; Crafts room; Laundry room; Barber/Beauty shop; Library.
Activities Arts & crafts; Cards; Games; Reading groups; Prayer groups; Movies; Shopping trips; Dances/Social/Cultural gatherings; Intergenerational programs; Pet therapy.

Gurdon

Pineview Nursing Home
PO Box 10, 904 Seahorn, Gurdon, AR 71743
(501) 353-2566
Admin Nelda Walsh. *Dir of Nursing* Brenda Walters RN. *Medical Dir* H Blake Crow MD.
Licensure Intermediate care. *Beds* ICF 60. *Certified* Medicaid.
Owner Proprietary corp (Pineview Homes Inc).
Admissions Requirements Medical examination; Physician's request.

Staff Physicians; RNs; LPNs; Nurses' aides;
Physical therapists (contracted); Dietitians.
Facilities Dining room; Activities room;
Chapel; Laundry room; Barber/Beauty shop.
Activities Arts & crafts; Cards; Games;
Reading groups; Prayer groups; Movies;
Shopping trips; Dances/Social/Cultural
gatherings; Intergenerational programs; Pet
therapy.

Hamburg

Leisure Lodge Inc—Hamburg
Rte 3 Box 300, Hamburg, AR 71646
(501) 853-8204
Admin Julie Herren.
Licensure Skilled care. *Beds* 105. *Certified*
Medicaid.
Owner Proprietary corp (Beverly Enterprises).

Hampton

Hampton Nursing Home
PO Box 538, Hampton, AR 71744-0538
(510) 798-4273
Admin Linda Stringfellow.
Medical Dir Tom L Dunn MD.
Licensure Skilled care. *Beds* 74. *Certified*
Medicaid.
Staff Physicians 3 (pt); RNs 1 (ft), 2 (pt);
LPNs 9 (ft); Nurses' aides 17 (ft), 9 (pt);
Physical therapists 1 (pt); Activities
coordinators 1 (ft); Dietitians 2 (ft); Dentists
1 (pt); Optometrists 1 (ft); Social workers 1
(ft), 1 (pt).
Facilities Dining room; Activities room;
Crafts room; Laundry room; Barber/Beauty
shop; Dayroom.
Activities Arts & crafts; Games; Reading
groups; Prayer groups; Movies; Shopping
trips; Dances/Social/Cultural gatherings;
Fishing trips; Picnics; Special outing each
summer; Fund raisers.

Harrison

Harrison Nursing Center
115 Orendorff Ave, Harrison, AR 72601
(501) 741-3438, 741-9117 FAX
Admin Debbie Taylor. *Dir of Nursing* JoEtta
Schnetzler. *Medical Dir* Dr R H (Bob)
Langston.
Licensure Skilled care. *Beds* SNF 102.
Certified Medicaid.
Owner Nonprofit organization/foundation.
Admissions Requirements Medical
examination; Physician's request.
Staff RNs 1 (ft); LPNs 8 (ft); Nurses' aides 25
(ft); Physical therapists 1 (ft); Activities
coordinators 1 (ft).
Facilities Dining room; Activities room;
Crafts room; Laundry room; Barber/Beauty
shop; Courtyard.
Activities Arts & crafts; Cards; Games;
Reading groups; Prayer groups; Movies;
Shopping trips; Intergenerational programs;
Pet therapy.

Hillcrest Home
1111 Maplewood Rd, Harrison, AR 72601
(501) 741-5001
Admin Omar Miller. *Dir of Nursing* Susan P
Steckley RN. *Medical Dir* James T Crider
MD.
Licensure Intermediate care. *Beds* ICF 67.
Private Pay Patients 42%. *Certified*
Medicaid.
Owner Publicly owned.
Admissions Requirements Minimum age 18;
Medical examination.
Staff RNs 3 (ft), 1 (pt); LPNs 1 (ft), 5 (pt);
Nurses' aides 15 (ft); Activities coordinators
1 (ft); Dietitians 1 (ft).
Affiliation Mennonite.

Facilities Dining room; Physical therapy
room; Activities room; Chapel; Crafts room;
Laundry room; Library.
Activities Arts & crafts; Games; Reading
groups; Movies; Pet therapy.

Hilltop Nursing Center
202 Tims Ave, Harrison, AR 72601
(501) 741-7667
Admin Norean Bailey.
Medical Dir H V Kirby MD.
Licensure Skilled care. *Beds* SNF 140.
Certified Medicaid.
Owner Proprietary corp (Beverly Enterprises).
Admissions Requirements Minimum age 65;
Medical examination; Physician's request.
Staff Physicians 1 (pt); RNs 2 (ft), 1 (pt);
LPNs 6 (ft), 3 (pt); Nurses' aides 31 (ft);
Physical therapists 1 (pt); Activities
coordinators 1 (ft); Dietitians 1 (ft);
Restorative aides 1 (ft); Social workers 1 (ft).
Facilities Dining room; Physical therapy
room; Laundry room; Barber/Beauty shop.
Activities Arts & crafts; Cards; Games;
Reading groups; Prayer groups; Movies;
Shopping trips; Dances/Social/Cultural
gatherings.

Heber Springs

Geriatrics Nursing Center Inc—Heber Springs
1040 Weddingford Rd, Heber Springs, AR
72543
(501) 362-8137
Admin Bill Enfield.
Licensure Skilled care; Alzheimer's care. *Beds*
SNF 140. *Certified* Medicaid; Medicare.
Owner Nonprofit corp (Pride House Care
Corp).
Staff RNs 3 (ft), 2 (pt); LPNs 10 (ft), 2 (pt);
Nurses' aides 30 (ft), 4 (pt); Physical
therapists 1 (pt); Reality therapists 1 (pt);
Recreational therapists 1 (pt); Speech
therapists 1 (pt); Activities coordinators 1
(ft); Dietitians 1 (ft).
Facilities Dining room; Physical therapy
room; Activities room; Chapel; Crafts room;
Laundry room; Barber/Beauty shop.
Activities Arts & crafts; Cards; Games;
Reading groups; Prayer groups; Movies;
Shopping trips; Dances/Social/Cultural
gatherings; Intergenerational programs.

Lakeland Lodge Nursing Home
600 S 11th St, Heber Springs, AR 72543
(501) 362-3185
Admin Ronnie Mize. *Dir of Nursing* Phyllis
Guthrie. *Medical Dir* David Lay MD.
Licensure Skilled care; Alzheimer's care. *Beds*
SNF 102. *Private Pay Patients* 9%. *Certified*
Medicaid.
Owner Proprietary corp (Beverly Enterprises).
Admissions Requirements Medical
examination; Physician's request.
Staff RNs; LPNs; Nurses' aides; Reality
therapists; Activities coordinators; Dietitians.
Facilities Dining room; Activities room;
Laundry room; Barber/Beauty shop.
Activities Arts & crafts; Cards; Games;
Reading groups; Prayer groups; Movies;
Shopping trips; Dances/Social/Cultural
gatherings; Intergenerational programs; Pet
therapy.

Helena

Crestpark Inn of Helena Skilled Nursing Facility
PO Box 310, Helena, AR 72342
(501) 338-9886
Admin Jeanne Crisp.
Licensure Skilled care. *Beds* 111. *Certified*
Medicaid.

Crestpark Retirement Inn
PO Box 310, Hospital Dr, Helena, AR 72342
(501) 338-3405

Admin Rita Fincher. *Dir of Nursing* Pam
Crawford RN. *Medical Dir* Mark Robirds
MD.
Licensure Intermediate care; Retirement. *Beds*
ICF 75; Retirement 36. *Private Pay Patients*
50%. *Certified* Medicaid.
Owner Proprietary corp (CAP Care Inc).
Staff RNs 2 (ft); LPNs 5 (ft), 4 (pt); Nurses'
aides 30 (ft), 15 (pt); Physical therapists 1
(pt); Dietitians 6 (ft).
Facilities Dining room; Physical therapy
room; Activities room; Chapel; Crafts room;
Laundry room; Barber/Beauty shop; Library.
Activities Arts & crafts; Cards; Games;
Reading groups; Prayer groups; Movies;
Dances/Social/Cultural gatherings.

Hope

Heather Manor Nursing Center
PO Box 961, Hope, AR 71801
(501) 777-4673
Admin Nora McRoy.
Medical Dir Dr J C Little.
Licensure Skilled care. *Beds* 105. *Certified*
Medicaid.
Admissions Requirements Medical
examination; Physician's request.
Staff Physicians 7 (pt); RNs 2 (ft); LPNs 9
(pt); Nurses' aides 40 (ft); Physical therapists
1 (pt); Reality therapists 1 (pt); Recreational
therapists 1 (pt); Speech therapists 1 (pt);
Activities coordinators 1 (ft); Dietitians 1
(ft); Dentists 1 (pt).
Facilities Dining room; Physical therapy
room; Activities room; Chapel; Crafts room;
Laundry room; Barber/Beauty shop.
Activities Arts & crafts; Cards; Games;
Reading groups; Prayer groups; Movies;
Shopping trips.

Pinehope Nursing Home
1900 S Walker St, Hope, AR 71801
(501) 777-8855
Admin Ray Woodard.
Licensure Intermediate care. *Beds* 105.
Certified Medicaid.

Horseshoe Bend

North Arkansas Life Care Center
1203 S Bend Dr, Horseshoe Bend, AR 72512
(501) 670-5134
Admin David Lipford.
Beds 78.

Hot Springs

Arkansas Health Care
909 Golf Links Rd, Hot Springs, AR 71901
(501) 624-7149, 624-1851 FAX
Admin Barbara Gilmore. *Dir of Nursing* Patty
Ray. *Medical Dir* Rheta Stecker.
Licensure Skilled care; Intermediate care;
Medicare. *Beds* SNF 45; ICF 79; Medicare
28. *Private Pay Patients* 10%. *Certified*
Medicaid; Medicare.
Owner Proprietary corp (Beverly Enterprises).
Admissions Requirements Minimum age 30;
Medical examination; Physician's request.
Staff Physicians 7 (ft); RNs 3 (ft); LPNs 15
(ft); Nurses' aides 45 (ft); Physical therapists
1 (ft); Occupational therapists 1 (ft); Speech
therapists 1 (ft); Activities coordinators 1
(ft); Dietitians 1 (ft); Ophthalmologists 1 (ft);
Podiatrists 1 (ft).
Languages German.
Facilities Dining room; Physical therapy
room; Activities room; Laundry room;
Barber/Beauty shop.
Activities Arts & crafts; Cards; Games;
Reading groups; Prayer groups; Movies;
Shopping trips; Dances/Social/Cultural
gatherings; Religious services.

Arkansas Healthcare Nursing Center
909 Golf Links Rd, Hot Springs, AR 71901
(501) 624-7149
Admin Barbara Gilmore. *Dir of Nursing* Jane Tadlock RN. *Medical Dir* Dr Rheeta Stecker.
Licensure Skilled care. *Beds* 152. *Certified* Medicaid; Medicare.
Owner Proprietary corp (Beverly Enterprises).
Staff RNs 2 (ft), 1 (pt).
Facilities Dining room; Physical therapy room; Barber/Beauty shop.
Activities Arts & crafts; Games; Prayer groups; Shopping trips; Dances/Social/Cultural gatherings.

Garland Convalescent Center
600 Carpenter Dam Rd, Hot Springs, AR 71901
(501) 262-2571
Admin Tommy Monk. *Dir of Nursing* Linda Stephenson.
Licensure Skilled care. *Beds* SNF 105. *Certified* Medicaid.
Owner Proprietary corp (Diversicare Corp of America).
Admissions Requirements Physician's request.
Staff RNs 1 (ft), 2 (pt); LPNs 6 (ft); Nurses' aides 60 (ft); Physical therapists 1 (pt); Activities coordinators 1 (ft).
Languages Spanish.
Facilities Dining room; Chapel; Laundry room; Barber/Beauty shop.
Activities Arts & crafts; Games; Prayer groups.

Hot Springs Nursing Home
1401 Park Ave, Hot Springs, AR 71901
(501) 623-3781
Admin Rex Ann Waymon. *Dir of Nursing* Martin Koehn. *Medical Dir* Dr John Simpson.
Licensure Skilled care. *Beds* SNF 140. *Certified* Medicaid; Medicare.
Owner Proprietary corp (Vantage Healthcare Corp).
Admissions Requirements Physician's request.
Staff Physicians 2 (ft); RNs 2 (ft), 1 (pt); LPNs 16 (ft), 5 (pt); Nurses' aides 41 (ft), 10 (pt); Activities coordinators 1 (ft); Dietitians 1 (ft).
Facilities Dining room; Physical therapy room; Activities room; Crafts room; Laundry room; Barber/Beauty shop.
Activities Arts & crafts; Games; Reading groups; Prayer groups; Shopping trips; Dances/Social/Cultural gatherings; Pet therapy.

Lakewood Convalescent Home
Rte 17 Box 661, Carpenter Dam Rd, Hot Springs, AR 71901
(501) 262-1920
Admin Dorothy Smith. *Dir of Nursing* Joan Krahn RN. *Medical Dir* Kenneth Seifert MD.
Licensure Intermediate care; Retirement. *Beds* ICF 50. *Certified* Medicaid.
Owner Nonprofit corp.
Admissions Requirements Minimum age 60; Physician's request.
Staff Physicians 4 (pt); RNs 1 (ft), 1 (pt); LPNs 4 (ft), 2 (pt); Nurses' aides 25 (ft); Physical therapists 1 (pt); Occupational therapists 1 (pt); Speech therapists 1 (pt); Activities coordinators 1 (ft), 1 (pt); Dietitians 1 (ft), 1 (pt); Podiatrists 1 (pt); Dentists 1 (pt).
Facilities Dining room; Crafts room; Laundry room; Barber/Beauty shop.
Activities Arts & crafts; Games; Prayer groups; Movies; Shopping trips; Dances/Social/Cultural gatherings.

NuCare Convalescent Center Inc
1316 Park Ave, Hot Springs, AR 71901
(501) 624-2516
Admin Gladys Owens. *Dir of Nursing* Abby Littlejohn. *Medical Dir* Dr Robert Lewis.

Licensure Skilled care; Alzheimer's care. *Beds* 100. *Certified* Medicaid.
Owner Proprietary corp (Southeastern Health Care).
Admissions Requirements Medical examination; Physician's request.
Staff Physicians 2 (ft); RNs 1 (ft), 2 (pt); LPNs 15 (ft), 2 (pt); Nurses' aides 50 (ft); Physical therapists 1 (pt); Reality therapists 1 (pt); Recreational therapists 1 (pt); Occupational therapists 1 (pt); Speech therapists 1 (pt); Activities coordinators 1 (ft); Dietitians 1 (ft); Ophthalmologists 1 (pt); Podiatrists 1 (pt); Dentists 1 (pt); Psychiatrists 1 (pt).
Facilities Dining room; Activities room; Chapel; Crafts room; Laundry room; Barber/Beauty shop; Library.
Activities Arts & crafts; Cards; Games; Reading groups; Prayer groups; Movies; Shopping trips; Dances/Social/Cultural gatherings.

Ouachita Valley Nursing Center
Rte 7 Box 574, Hot Springs, AR 71901-9804
(501) 624-3800
Admin Bobby Hargis.
Licensure Skilled care; Intermediate care. *Beds* SNF 71; ICF 142. *Certified* Medicaid.

Quality Care Nursing Center
351 Woodfin St, Hot Springs, AR 71901
(501) 624-5238
Admin Richard D Thomas. *Dir of Nursing* Donna Guthrie RN.
Licensure Skilled care; Retirement; Alzheimer's care. *Beds* 113. *Certified* Medicaid.
Owner Proprietary corp (Beverly Enterprises).
Admissions Requirements Physician's request.
Staff Physicians; RNs; LPNs; Nurses' aides; Recreational therapists; Occupational therapists; Activities coordinators; Dietitians; Ophthalmologists; Dentists.
Facilities Dining room; Activities room; Laundry room; Barber/Beauty shop; Library.
Activities Arts & crafts; Cards; Games; Reading groups; Prayer groups; Movies; Shopping trips; Dances/Social/Cultural gatherings.

Hot Springs Village

Good Samaritan Cedar Lodge
5 Cortez Rd, Hot Springs Village, AR 71909
(501) 922-2000
Admin Jonathan Conrad. *Dir of Nursing* JoAnna Langford RN. *Medical Dir* Dr Thomas Cofer.
Licensure Intermediate care; Retirement. *Beds* ICF 40; Retirement apts 82. *Private Pay Patients* 73%. *Certified* Medicaid.
Owner Nonprofit corp (Evangelical Lutheran/ Good Samaritan Society).
Admissions Requirements Medical examination; Physician's request.
Staff RNs 1 (ft); LPNs 3 (ft), 5 (pt); Nurses' aides 11 (ft), 3 (pt); Activities coordinators 1 (pt); Dietitians 1 (ft).
Affiliation Lutheran.
Facilities Dining room; Physical therapy room; Activities room; Chapel; Crafts room; Laundry room; Barber/Beauty shop; Library; Billiard room; Whirlpool spa; Wood shop; Fitness center; Den.
Activities Arts & crafts; Cards; Games; Reading groups; Prayer groups; Movies; Pet therapy; Sight-seeing trips; Picnics.

Huntsville

Meadowview Lodge
Drawer E, Huntsville, AR 72740
(501) 738-2021
Admin Freda Crumley. *Dir of Nursing* Mary Robertson RN. *Medical Dir* Robert B Wilson MD.

Licensure Skilled care. *Beds* SNF 70. *Private Pay Patients* 20%. *Certified* Medicaid.
Owner Nonprofit organization/foundation.
Admissions Requirements Physician's request.
Staff Physicians 3 (ft); RNs 2 (ft), 1 (pt); LPNs 4 (ft), 2 (pt); Nurses' aides 24 (ft); Activities coordinators 1 (ft); Dietitians 1 (ft).
Facilities Dining room; Laundry room; Barber/Beauty shop.
Activities Games; Reading groups; Prayer groups; Dances/Social/Cultural gatherings; Pet therapy.

Jacksonville

Jacksonville Nursing Center
1320 W Braden, Jacksonville, AR 72076
(501) 982-0521
Admin Pat Hunter. *Dir of Nursing* Lucille Thomey. *Medical Dir* Dr George McCrary; Dr Joe Shotts.
Licensure Skilled care. *Beds* SNF 245. *Private Pay Patients* 13%. *Certified* Medicaid; Medicare; VA.
Owner Proprietary corp (Pride House Care Corp).
Admissions Requirements Medical examination; Physician's request.
Staff RNs; LPNs; Nurses' aides; Physical therapists; Occupational therapists; Speech therapists; Activities coordinators; Dietitians; Podiatrists.
Facilities Dining room; Physical therapy room; Activities room; Crafts room; Laundry room; Barber/Beauty shop.
Activities Arts & crafts; Games; Reading groups; Prayer groups; Movies; Shopping trips; Dances/Social/Cultural gatherings; Pet therapy.

Rose Care Center of Jacksonville
1701 S Hwy 161, Jacksonville, AR 72076
(501) 982-5141
Admin Doris A Beard RN. *Dir of Nursing* Kay Kwok RN.
Licensure Intermediate care. *Beds* 58. *Certified* Medicaid.
Owner Proprietary corp (Rose Care Inc).
Admissions Requirements Minimum age 21; Medical examination; Physician's request.
Staff RNs 1 (ft); LPNs 4 (ft), 1 (pt); Nurses' aides 19 (ft), 2 (pt); Activities coordinators 1 (ft).
Facilities Dining room; Activities room.
Activities Arts & crafts; Cards; Games; Reading groups; Prayer groups.

Jasper

Newton County Nursing Home
PO Box 442, Jasper, AR 72641
(501) 446-2204 or 446-2333
Admin Rick E. Eddings.
Licensure Intermediate care. *Beds* 42. *Certified* Medicaid.

Jonesboro

Craighead Nursing Center
Rte 9 Box 32, Jonesboro, AR 72401
(901) 932-4535
Admin Nevin Beachy. *Dir of Nursing* Donna Young RN. *Medical Dir* J F Thomas MD.
Licensure Skilled care; Alzheimer's care. *Beds* SNF 70. *Private Pay Patients* 25%. *Certified* Medicaid.
Owner Publicly owned.
Admissions Requirements Minimum age 40; Medical examination; Physician's request.
Staff Physicians 4 (pt); RNs 1 (ft), 3 (pt); LPNs 5 (ft), 3 (pt); Nurses' aides 20 (ft), 3 (pt); Physical therapists 1 (pt); Speech therapists 1 (pt); Activities coordinators 1 (ft); Dietitians 1 (pt); Podiatrists 1 (pt).
Languages German.

Facilities Dining room; Activities room; Laundry room; Barber/Beauty shop; Library.
Activities Arts & crafts; Games; Reading groups; Prayer groups; Movies; Shopping trips.

Geriatrics Nursing Center
800 Southwest Dr, Jonesboro, AR 72401
(501) 935-7550
Admin Kathy Atchley. *Dir of Nursing* Donna Kingsland RN. *Medical Dir* Fred Thomas MD.
Licensure Skilled care; Retirement. *Beds* SNF 103; Retirement 16. *Private Pay Patients* 12%. *Certified* Medicaid; Medicare.
Owner Proprietary corp (Beverly Enterprises).
Admissions Requirements Medical examination; Physician's request.
Staff RNs 5 (ft); LPNs 9 (ft), 7 (pt); Nurses' aides 38 (ft), 13 (pt); Activities coordinators 1 (ft); Dietitians 1 (ft).
Facilities Dining room; Laundry room; Barber/Beauty shop.
Activities Arts & crafts; Cards; Games; Reading groups; Prayer groups; Movies; Shopping trips; Dances/Social/Cultural gatherings; Intergenerational programs.

Jonesboro Human Development Center
4701 Colony Dr, Jonesboro, AR 72401
(501) 932-4043
Admin Jerry W Cooper. *Dir of Nursing* Shirley Holbrook. *Medical Dir* Darrell Ragland, contracted.
Licensure Intermediate care for mentally retarded. *Beds* ICF/MR 128. *Certified* Medicaid.
Owner Publicly owned.
Admissions Requirements Minimum age 6; Medical examination; Must be developmentally disabled.
Facilities Dining room; Physical therapy room; Activities room; Chapel; Crafts room; Laundry room; Library; School.
Activities Arts & crafts; Games; Movies; Shopping trips; Dances/Social/Cultural gatherings; Active treatment.

Rose Care Center of Jonesboro
Rte 12 Box 404, Jonesboro, AR 72401
(501) 932-3271
Admin Judy K Glasco. *Dir of Nursing* Thelma Henson. *Medical Dir* E L Hogue.
Licensure Skilled care. *Beds* SNF 108. *Private Pay Patients* 10%. *Certified* Medicaid.
Owner Proprietary corp (Rose Care Inc).
Admissions Requirements Medical examination; Physician's request.
Staff RNs 2 (ft); LPNs 11 (ft), 1 (pt); Nurses' aides 34 (ft); Activities coordinators 1 (ft); Dietitians 1 (ft).
Facilities Dining room; Activities room; Laundry room; Barber/Beauty shop.
Activities Arts & crafts; Cards; Games; Reading groups; Prayer groups; Shopping trips; Dances/Social/Cultural gatherings; Intergenerational programs.

Rose Skill Care Nursing Center of Jonesboro
2911 Brown's Ln, Jonesboro, AR 72401
(501) 935-8330
Admin Betty L Metz.
Medical Dir G D Wisdom MD.
Licensure Skilled care. *Beds* 152. *Certified* Medicaid; Medicare.
Admissions Requirements Minimum age 21; Medical examination; Physician's request.
Staff Physicians 2 (pt); RNs 1 (ft), 2 (pt); LPNs 14 (ft), 5 (pt); Nurses' aides 38 (ft), 1 (pt); Speech therapists 1 (pt); Activities coordinators 1 (ft); Dietitians 1 (pt); Dentists 1 (pt).
Facilities Dining room; Physical therapy room; Laundry room; Barber/Beauty shop.
Activities Arts & crafts; Cards; Games; Prayer groups; Shopping trips; Dances/Social/Cultural gatherings.

Judsonia

Oakdale Nursing Home
PO Box 670, Judsonia, AR 72081
(501) 268-2288
Admin Leonard M Wiggins.
Licensure Skilled care. *Beds* 100. *Certified* Medicaid.

Junction City

Junction City Nursing Home
Rte 1 Box 2, Maple & First, Junction City, AR 71749
(501) 924-4522
Admin Lisa Barnette.
Medical Dir Dixie Taylor.
Licensure Skilled care. *Beds* SNF 84. *Certified* Medicaid.
Owner Proprietary corp (Beverly Enterprises).
Admissions Requirements Medical examination; Physician's request.
Staff RNs; LPNs; Nurses' aides; Activities coordinators; Dietitians.
Facilities Dining room; Activities room; Laundry room; Barber/Beauty shop.
Activities Arts & crafts; Games; Reading groups; Prayer groups.

Lake City

Lakeside Nursing Center
PO Box 578, Lake City, AR 72437
(501) 237-8035
Admin Caren Gammill. *Dir of Nursing* Kathy Gooch RN. *Medical Dir* Dr Robert A Robbins.
Licensure Skilled care; Residential care. *Beds* SNF 40; Residential care 16. *Private Pay Patients* 20%. *Certified* Medicaid.
Owner Proprietary corp (Extendi-Care Inc).
Admissions Requirements Medical examination; Physician's request.
Staff Physicians (consultant); RNs 1 (ft), 2 (pt); LPNs 4 (ft), 2 (pt); Nurses' aides 14 (ft), 2 (pt); Physical therapists 1 (pt); Reality therapists (consultant); Recreational therapists 1 (pt); Occupational therapists 1 (pt); Speech therapists 1 (pt); Activities coordinators 1 (ft); Dietitians (consultant); Ophthalmologists; Podiatrists 1 (pt); Audiologists 1 (pt).
Facilities Dining room; Activities room; Laundry room; Barber/Beauty shop.
Activities Arts & crafts; Games; Reading groups; Shopping trips.

Lake Village

Leisure Lodge Inc—Lake Village
Hwy 65 S, Lake Village, AR 71653
(501) 265-5337
Admin Marcia Lewis Green.
Medical Dir Danny Berry.
Licensure Intermediate care. *Beds* 85. *Certified* Medicaid.
Owner Proprietary corp (Beverly Enterprises).
Staff Physicians 1 (ft); RNs 1 (ft); LPNs 8 (ft); Nurses' aides 28 (ft); Activities coordinators 1 (ft); Dietitians 1 (ft); Dentists 1 (pt).
Facilities Dining room; Activities room; Laundry room; Barber/Beauty shop.
Activities Arts & crafts; Games; Prayer groups; Movies; Shopping trips; Dances/Social/Cultural gatherings.

Little Rock

Arkansas Easter Seal Residential Center
PO Box 251706, 2801 Lee Ave, Little Rock, AR 72225
(501) 663-8331
Admin Glenn E Ballard. *Dir of Nursing* Donna Kroskey RN. *Medical Dir* Diane R Edwards MD.

Licensure Intermediate care for mentally retarded. *Beds* ICF/MR 25. *Certified* Medicaid.
Owner Nonprofit organization/foundation.
Admissions Requirements Minimum age 2; Physician's request.
Staff Physicians 5 (pt); RNs 1 (ft), 1 (pt); LPNs 6 (ft), 1 (pt); Nurses' aides 12 (ft); Physical therapists 2 (ft); Recreational therapists 1 (ft), 3 (pt); Occupational therapists 2 (ft); Speech therapists 2 (ft); Activities coordinators 1 (ft); Dietitians 1 (ft).
Facilities Dining room; Physical therapy room; Activities room; Laundry room.
Activities Arts & crafts; Cards; Games; Reading groups; Movies; Shopping trips; Dances/Social/Cultural gatherings.

Fountainbleau Nursing Home
10905 W Markham St, Little Rock, AR 72211
(501) 225-6501
Admin James David Hightower.
Medical Dir Jerry D Malott MD.
Licensure Intermediate care. *Beds* 70. *Certified* Medicaid.
Admissions Requirements Medical examination; Physician's request.
Staff RNs 1 (ft); LPNs 3 (ft), 3 (pt); Nurses' aides 20 (ft), 5 (pt); Activities coordinators 1 (ft).
Facilities Dining room; Activities room; Laundry room; Barber/Beauty shop.
Activities Arts & crafts; Games; Reading groups; Prayer groups.

Hillhaven of Little Rock
5720 W Markham, Little Rock, AR 72205
(501) 664-6200
Admin James W Ives.
Licensure Skilled care. *Beds* 174. *Certified* Medicaid; Medicare.
Owner Proprietary corp (Hillhaven Corp).

Little Rock Nursing Center
1516 Cumberland St, Little Rock, AR 72202
(501) 374-7565
Admin Patricia Miller. *Dir of Nursing* Majorie Ince. *Medical Dir* John Wolverton MD.
Licensure Skilled care; Alzheimer's care. *Beds* SNF 204. *Certified* Medicaid.
Owner Proprietary corp (Rose Care Inc).
Admissions Requirements Minimum age 55; Physician's request.
Staff Physicians 1 (ft), 6 (pt); RNs 2 (ft), 2 (pt); LPNs 21 (ft); Nurses' aides 60 (ft); Physical therapists; Reality therapists; Recreational therapists; Occupational therapists; Speech therapists; Activities coordinators 2 (ft); Dietitians 2 (ft); Ophthalmologists 1 (pt); Dentists 1 (pt).
Facilities Dining room; Physical therapy room; Activities room; Laundry room; Barber/Beauty shop; Library.
Activities Arts & crafts; Cards; Games; Reading groups; Prayer groups; Movies; Shopping trips; Dances/Social/Cultural gatherings.

Presbyterian Village Health Care Center
500 N Brookside Dr, Little Rock, AR 72205
(501) 225-0114
Admin Nelson Reinhardt.
Medical Dir James Flack MD.
Licensure Skilled care; Intermediate care. *Beds* 78.
Admissions Requirements Medical examination; Physician's request.
Staff Physicians 1 (pt); RNs 5 (ft); LPNs 13 (ft); Nurses' aides 45 (ft); Physical therapists 1 (ft); Reality therapists 1 (pt); Occupational therapists 1 (pt); Speech therapists 1 (pt); Dietitians 1 (ft); Ophthalmologists 1 (pt); Dentists 1 (pt).
Affiliation Presbyterian.
Facilities Dining room; Physical therapy room; Activities room; Chapel; Crafts room; Laundry room; Barber/Beauty shop; Library.

Activities Arts & crafts; Cards; Games; Reading groups; Prayer groups; Movies; Shopping trips; Dances/Social/Cultural gatherings.

Riley's Oak Hill Manor South
8701 Riley Dr, Little Rock, AR 72205
(501) 224-2700
Admin Pamela Althoff. *Dir of Nursing* Karen Delavan. *Medical Dir* Dr Harold Hedges.
Licensure Skilled care; Assisted living; Alzheimer's care. *Beds* SNF 224. *Private Pay Patients* 100%.
Owner Privately owned.
Staff RNs 2 (ft), 1 (pt); LPNs 10 (ft), 3 (pt); Nurses' aides; Physical therapists 1 (pt); Recreational therapists 2 (ft); Speech therapists 1 (pt); Activities coordinators 1 (ft); Dietitians 1 (pt).
Facilities Dining room; Physical therapy room; Activities room; Chapel; Crafts room; Laundry room; Barber/Beauty shop; Library.
Activities Arts & crafts; Cards; Games; Reading groups; Prayer groups; Movies; Dances/Social/Cultural gatherings; Intergenerational programs; Pet therapy.

Rose Care Center of Little Rock
800 Brookside Dr, Little Rock, AR 72205
(501) 224-3940
Admin Billie Brarzseal.
Medical Dir Dr Michael Hendren.
Licensure Intermediate care. *Beds* 143. *Certified* Medicaid.
Staff Physicians 1 (ft); RNs 2 (ft), 2 (pt); LPNs 20 (ft), 2 (pt); Nurses' aides 55 (ft), 5 (pt); Physical therapists 1 (pt); Occupational therapists 1 (pt); Activities coordinators 1 (ft); Dietitians 1 (pt); Ophthalmologists 1 (pt); Podiatrists 1 (pt); Audiologists 1 (pt); Dentists 1 (pt); Social workers 1 (ft).
Facilities Dining room; Activities room; Crafts room; Laundry room; Barber/Beauty shop; Library; Courtyard.
Activities Arts & crafts; Cards; Games; Reading groups; Prayer groups; Shopping trips; Dances/Social/Cultural gatherings; Exercise classes; Outings.

Southwest Homes
3915 Dixon Rd, Little Rock, AR 72206
(501) 888-4257
Admin Gerald O Geddes.
Licensure Intermediate care. *Beds* 125. *Certified* Medicaid.

Trinity Court Nursing Home
2000 Main St, Little Rock, AR 72206
(501) 375-9062
Admin Earnest Johnson.
Licensure Skilled care. *Beds* 160. *Certified* Medicaid.

Vantage Convalescent Center
8500 Mize Rd, Little Rock, AR 72209
(501) 562-2964
Admin Stormy Smith.
Licensure Skilled care. *Beds* 150. *Certified* Medicaid.
Owner Proprietary corp (Vantage Healthcare).

Williamsburg Retirement Inn
6301 Lee Ave, Little Rock, AR 72205
(501) 663-9461
Admin Michael A Mahan.
Medical Dir Carla Brakop MD.
Licensure Skilled care. *Beds* 101. *Certified* Medicaid.
Owner Proprietary corp (Beverly Enterprises).
Admissions Requirements Medical examination; Physician's request.
Staff RNs 2 (ft); LPNs 11 (ft), 4 (pt); Nurses' aides 18 (ft), 18 (pt); Activities coordinators 1 (ft); Dietitians 1 (ft).

Facilities Dining room; Laundry room; Barber/Beauty shop.
Activities Arts & crafts; Cards; Prayer groups; Movies; Dances/Social/Cultural gatherings; Music groups.

Lonoke

Golden Years Manor
PO Box 244, 1010 Barnes, Lonoke, AR 72086
(501) 676-3103
Admin Judy Clyburn.
Licensure Skilled care. *Beds* 101. *Certified* Medicaid.

Lonoke Nursing Home Inc
PO Box 276, 420 E Academy St, Lonoke, AR 72086
(501) 676-2785
Admin Kay Cooper. *Dir of Nursing* Frances Carter RN.
Licensure Intermediate care. *Beds* ICF 53. *Certified* Medicaid.
Owner Proprietary corp.
Admissions Requirements Physician's request.
Staff RNs 1 (ft); LPNs 4 (ft), 1 (pt); Nurses' aides 12 (ft), 3 (pt); Activities coordinators 1 (ft).
Facilities Dining room; Laundry room.
Activities Arts & crafts; Games; Movies; Church groups visit.

Magnolia

Magnolia Manor Nursing Center
301 S Boundry, Magnolia, AR 71753
(501) 234-1361, 234-1362
Admin Dorthay Gay. *Dir of Nursing* Stephanie Snider. *Medical Dir* Rodney Griffin.
Licensure Skilled care; Alzheimer's care. *Beds* SNF 113. *Certified* Medicaid.
Owner Proprietary corp (Beverly Enterprises).
Admissions Requirements Medical examination; Physician's request.
Staff RNs 3 (ft), 1 (pt); LPNs 10 (ft), 1 (pt); Nurses' aides 58 (ft); Physical therapists 1 (ft); Activities coordinators 1 (ft); Dietitians 1 (ft); Ophthalmologists 1 (ft); Podiatrists 1 (ft).
Facilities Dining room; Activities room; Chapel; Crafts room; Laundry room; Barber/Beauty shop; Library; Picnic area; Connected park; Paved walking trail.
Activities Arts & crafts; Cards; Games; Reading groups; Prayer groups; Movies; Shopping trips; Dances/Social/Cultural gatherings; Intergenerational programs; Pet therapy.

Meadowbrook Lodge
600 Lelia St, Magnolia, AR 71753
(501) 234-7000
Admin Sandy Whittington.
Licensure Intermediate care. *Beds* 140. *Certified* Medicaid.
Owner Proprietary corp (Beverly Enterprises).

Malvern

Longmeadow Nursing Home of Malvern
PO Box 567, Malvern, AR 72104
(501) 332-6934
Admin Mark Mitchell.
Medical Dir Dr N B Kersh.
Licensure Intermediate care. *Beds* 69. *Certified* Medicaid.
Staff RNs 1 (ft); LPNs 2 (ft), 3 (pt); Nurses' aides 20 (ft), 2 (pt); Speech therapists 1 (pt); Activities coordinators 1 (ft); Dietitians 1 (pt).
Affiliation Baptist.

Facilities Dining room; Activities room; Laundry room; Barber/Beauty shop.
Activities Arts & crafts; Cards; Games; Reading groups; Prayer groups; Movies; Shopping trips; Dances/Social/Cultural gatherings.

Malvern Nursing Home
Rte 8 Box 176, Malvern, AR 72104
(501) 337-9581
Admin Jayne Howard West.
Medical Dir C F Peters MD.
Licensure Skilled care. *Beds* 95. *Certified* Medicaid.
Staff Activities coordinators 1 (ft).
Facilities Dining room; Laundry room; Barber/Beauty shop.
Activities Arts & crafts; Movies; Shopping trips.

Stillmeadow Convalescent Center
Rte 2 Box 11, Malvern, AR 72104
(501) 332-5251, 337-4976 FAX
Admin Marion Cunningham. *Dir of Nursing* Ava McClenahan RN. *Medical Dir* Dr C F Peters.
Licensure Skilled care. *Beds* SNF 104. *Private Pay Patients* 10%. *Certified* Medicaid.
Owner Proprietary corp (Diversicare Corp).
Admissions Requirements Physician's request.
Staff Physicians 1 (pt); RNs 1 (ft), 3 (pt); LPNs 7 (ft), 5 (pt); Nurses' aides 26 (ft), 12 (pt); Activities coordinators 1 (ft); Dietitians 1 (ft).
Facilities Dining room; Physical therapy room; Activities room; Chapel; Laundry room; Barber/Beauty shop.
Activities Arts & crafts; Cards; Games; Prayer groups; Movies; Bus rides; Special days.

Manila

Manila Nursing Home
PO Box 429, Manila, AR 72442
(501) 561-4492
Admin Gaylon Gammill.
Medical Dir Eugene Shaneyfelt.
Licensure Intermediate care. *Beds* 53. *Certified* Medicaid.
Staff RNs 1 (ft), 1 (pt); LPNs 2 (ft), 3 (pt); Nurses' aides 12 (ft); Activities coordinators 1 (ft); Dietitians 1 (ft), 1 (pt).
Facilities Dining room; Activities room; Laundry room.
Activities Arts & crafts; Games; Prayer groups; Shopping trips.

Marianna

Crestpark Retirement Inn
PO Box 386, Hwy 79 W, Marianna, AR 72360
(501) 295-3466
Admin Melisha Pickett. *Dir of Nursing* Barbara Spain. *Medical Dir* Doung Ngnoc Ly.
Licensure Intermediate care. *Beds* ICF 90. *Private Pay Patients* 2%. *Certified* Medicaid.
Owner Proprietary corp (CAP Care of Arkansas).
Admissions Requirements Physician's request.
Staff Physicians 3 (pt); RNs 2 (ft); LPNs 7 (ft); Nurses' aides 17 (ft); Activities coordinators 1 (ft).
Facilities Dining room; Activities room; Laundry room; Barber/Beauty shop; Patio; Large yard.
Activities Arts & crafts; Cards; Games; Reading groups; Prayer groups; Movies; Shopping trips; Intergenerational programs.

Marked Tree

Three Rivers Nursing Center
PO Box 519, Marked Tree, AR 72365
(501) 358-2432
Admin Dorothy Abbott Castro.

Licensure Intermediate care. *Beds* 112.
Certified Medicaid.

Marshall

Marshall Nursing Center
PO Box 541, South Cedar St, Marshall, AR
72650
(501) 448-3151
Admin Karen Elliott. *Dir of Nursing* Sandra
Weaver RN. *Medical Dir* James Zini DO.
Licensure Intermediate care. *Beds* ICF 77.
Private Pay Patients 20%. *Certified*
Medicaid.
Owner Privately owned.
Admissions Requirements Medical
examination; Physician's request.
Staff Physicians 3 (ft); RNs 2 (ft); LPNs 7 (ft);
Nurses' aides 25 (ft); Activities coordinators
1 (ft); Dietitians (consultant).
Facilities Dining room; Activities room;
Laundry room.
Activities Arts & crafts; Cards; Games; Prayer
groups; Movies; Dances/Social/Cultural
gatherings.

Marvell

Cedar Lodge Nursing Center
PO Box 928, Marvell, AR 72366
(501) 829-2501, 829-3110 FAX
Admin Lisa Yahnke. *Dir of Nursing* Marzee
Chancey RN. *Medical Dir* Robert Miller
MD.
Licensure Skilled care. *Beds* SNF 132. *Private
Pay Patients* 1%. *Certified* Medicaid.
Owner Proprietary corp (Catlett Corp).
Admissions Requirements Medical
examination.
Staff Physicians 1 (ft); RNs 3 (ft); LPNs 12
(ft); Nurses' aides 35 (ft); Activities
coordinators 2 (ft); Dietitians (consultant).
Facilities Dining room; Laundry room;
Barber/Beauty shop.
Activities Cards; Games; Prayer groups;
Shopping trips; Dances/Social/Cultural
gatherings.

McCrory

Woodruff County Nursing Home
PO Box 407, McCrory, AR 72101
(501) 731-2543
Admin Shelley Lee. *Dir of Nursing* Kitty
Smith RN. *Medical Dir* Fred Wilson MD.
Licensure Skilled care. *Beds* SNF 105.
Certified Medicaid.
Owner Publicly owned.
Admissions Requirements Medical
examination.
Staff Physicians 4 (ft); RNs 2 (ft), 1 (pt);
LPNs 5 (ft), 6 (pt); Nurses' aides 26 (ft), 5
(pt); Physical therapists 2 (ft); Speech
therapists 1 (pt); Activities coordinators 1
(ft); Dietitians 1 (ft).
Facilities Dining room; Physical therapy
room; Activities room; Chapel; Crafts room;
Laundry room; Barber/Beauty shop; Gift
shop.
Activities Arts & crafts; Cards; Games; Prayer
groups; Movies; Dances/Social/Cultural
gatherings; Live bands; Beauty contests.

McGehee

Leisure Lodge
700 Westwood Dr, McGehee, AR 71638
(501) 222-5450
Admin Julianne McRae RN. *Dir of Nursing*
Cathy Bilberry. *Medical Dir* Dr Robert
Scott.
Licensure Skilled care; Alzheimer's care. *Beds*
SNF 140. *Certified* Medicaid; Medicare.
Owner Proprietary corp (Britwell).
Admissions Requirements Physician's request.

Staff Physicians; RNs; LPNs; Nurses' aides;
Physical therapists; Recreational therapists;
Speech therapists; Activities coordinators;
Dietitians; Podiatrists.
Facilities Dining room; Physical therapy
room; Activities room; Crafts room; Laundry
room; Barber/Beauty shop.
Activities Arts & crafts; Cards; Games;
Reading groups; Prayer groups; Movies;
Shopping trips; Dances/Social/Cultural
gatherings; Intergenerational programs.

Melbourne

Pioneer Nursing Home Inc
PO Box 550, 517 N Dixon St, Melbourne, AR
72556
(501) 368-4377
Admin Nancy Pratt. *Dir of Nursing* Cindy
Mason. *Medical Dir* Dr H M Tatum.
Licensure Intermediate care. *Beds* ICF 64.
Private Pay Patients 7%. *Certified* Medicaid.
Owner Proprietary corp.
Staff RNs 1 (ft); LPNs 4 (ft), 1 (pt); Nurses'
aides 20 (ft); Activities coordinators 1 (ft);
Dietitians 1 (pt).
Facilities Dining room; Activities room;
Laundry room.
Activities Arts & crafts; Cards; Games;
Reading groups; Prayer groups.

Mena

Mena Manor
100 9th St, Mena, AR 71953
(501) 394-2617
Admin Murlene Williams Autry.
Medical Dir Dr Lon Sessler.
Licensure Intermediate care. *Beds* 69.
Certified Medicaid.
Admissions Requirements Medical
examination; Physician's request.
Staff RNs 1 (ft); Nurses' aides 48 (ft); Physical
therapists 1 (ft); Activities coordinators 1
(ft); Dietitians 1 (ft).
Facilities Dining room; Activities room;
Laundry room.
Activities Arts & crafts; Cards; Games; Prayer
groups; Dances/Social/Cultural gatherings.

Rich Mountain Manor
504 Hornbeck, Mena, AR 71953
(501) 394-3511
Admin Vesta Rhoades. *Dir of Nursing* Betty
Anderson. *Medical Dir* Calvin Austin MD.
Licensure Skilled care. *Beds* SNF 115.
Certified Medicaid.
Owner Proprietary corp (Diversicare Corp).
Admissions Requirements Medical
examination; Physician's request.
Staff RNs 2 (ft), 1 (pt); LPNs 7 (ft), 2 (pt);
Nurses' aides 30 (ft); Activities coordinators
1 (ft).
Facilities Dining room; Activities room;
Chapel; Laundry room; Barber/Beauty shop.
Activities Arts & crafts; Games; Prayer groups;
Movies; Shopping trips; Dances/Social/
Cultural gatherings.

Monette

Lane's Nursing Home—Monette
PO Box 469, Monette, AR 72447
(501) 486-5419
Admin James Cliff Lane.
Licensure Skilled care. *Beds* 86. *Certified*
Medicaid.

Monticello

Leisure Lodge
1194 Chester St, Monticello, AR 71655
(501) 367-6852, 367-3910 FAX
Admin Kent McRae. *Dir of Nursing* Joan Ellis
RN. *Medical Dir* Dr Paul Wallick.

Licensure Skilled care. *Beds* SNF 124.
Certified Medicaid; Medicare.
Owner Proprietary corp (Beverly Enterprises).
Admissions Requirements Medical
examination.
Staff Physicians 4 (pt); RNs 2 (ft), 3 (pt);
LPNs 8 (ft), 6 (pt); Nurses' aides 28 (ft), 3
(pt); Physical therapists 1 (pt); Occupational
therapists 1 (pt); Speech therapists 1 (pt);
Activities coordinators 1 (ft); Dietitians 1
(pt); Podiatrists 1 (pt).
Facilities Dining room; Physical therapy
room; Activities room; Crafts room; Laundry
room; Barber/Beauty shop; Library.
Activities Arts & crafts; Games; Reading
groups; Prayer groups; Shopping trips;
Dances/Social/Cultural gatherings.

Morrilton

Morrilton Manor Inc
1212 W Childress, Morrilton, AR 72110
(501) 354-4585
Admin Judith L Havlik. *Dir of Nursing* Joy
Tannes. *Medical Dir* T H Hickey.
Licensure Skilled care. *Beds* SNF 118. *Private
Pay Patients* 25%. *Certified* Medicaid;
Medicare; VA.
Owner Proprietary corp.
Admissions Requirements Medical
examination.
Staff Physicians 8 (pt); RNs 2 (ft), 3 (pt);
LPNs 10 (ft), 1 (pt); Nurses' aides 45 (ft);
Physical therapists 1 (pt); Activities
coordinators 2 (ft); Dietitians 1 (ft).
Facilities Dining room; Barber/Beauty shop.
Activities Arts & crafts; Games; Prayer groups;
Movies; Shopping trips.

Riverview Manor Inc
1209 S Bridge St, Morrilton, AR 72110
(501) 354-4647
Admin Brenda Bane.
Licensure Intermediate care. *Beds* 53.
Certified Medicaid.

Mount Ida

Montgomery Country Nursing Home
PO Box 885, Ray St, Mount Ida, AR 71957
9(409) 867-2156
Admin Audean Kennedy.
Medical Dir James Davis MD.
Licensure Intermediate care. *Beds* 56.
Certified Medicaid.
Admissions Requirements Medical
examination.
Staff Physicians 1 (ft); RNs 2 (ft); LPNs 6 (ft),
1 (pt); Nurses' aides 26 (ft); Activities
coordinators 1 (pt); Dietitians 1 (pt);
Dentists 1 (pt).
Facilities Dining room; Activities room;
Chapel; Crafts room; Laundry room; Barber/
Beauty shop; Library.
Activities Arts & crafts; Cards; Games;
Reading groups; Prayer groups; Movies;
Shopping trips; Dances/Social/Cultural
gatherings; Community gospel singing.

Mountain Home

Baxter Manor Nursing Home
620 Hospital Dr, Mountain Home, AR 72653
(501) 425-6203
Admin William P Flippo. *Dir of Nursing*
Hazel LaVerne Johnson RN. *Medical Dir* Dr
Daniel Chock.
Licensure Skilled care. *Beds* SNF 105.
Certified Medicaid.
Owner Nonprofit organization/foundation.
Admissions Requirements Physician's request.
Staff RNs 3 (ft); LPNs 12 (ft); Nurses' aides
37 (ft); Activities coordinators 1 (ft);
Dietitians 1 (ft).

Facilities Dining room; Activities room; Chapel; Laundry room; Barber/Beauty shop.
Activities Arts & crafts; Cards; Games; Reading groups; Prayer groups; Movies; Shopping trips.

Mountain Home Good Samaritan Village
3031 Turnage Dr, Mountain Home, AR 72653
(501) 425-2494
Admin Arthur Rosenkotter.
Licensure Intermediate care. *Beds* 70. *Certified* Medicaid; Medicare.
Owner Nonprofit corp (Evangelical Lutheran/Good Samaritan Society).

Mountain Home Nursing Center
PO Box 325, Hwy 5 N, Mountain Home, AR 72653
(501) 425-6931
Admin Tod Mahoney. *Dir of Nursing* Phyllis Baxter RN. *Medical Dir* John Guenthner MD.
Licensure Intermediate care; Retirement. *Beds* SNF 105. *Certified* Medicaid.
Owner Proprietary corp.
Admissions Requirements Medical examination; Physician's request.
Staff Physicians 1 (ft); RNs 3 (ft); LPNs 11 (ft); Physical therapists 1 (ft); Activities coordinators 1 (ft); Dietitians 1 (ft).
Facilities Dining room; Physical therapy room; Laundry room; Barber/Beauty shop.
Activities Arts & crafts; Cards; Games; Reading groups; Prayer groups; Movies; Shopping trips; Dances/Social/Cultural gatherings; Bingo; Outings to fish hatchery; Fishing.

Pine Lane Healthcare
1100 Pine Tree Ln, Mountain Home, AR 72653
(501) 425-6316
Admin Randy S Musick. *Dir of Nursing* Dawn Northup RN. *Medical Dir* Dr R Burnett.
Licensure Skilled care. *Beds* SNF 105. *Private Pay Patients* 45%. *Certified* Medicaid.
Owner Proprietary corp (Hillhaven Corp).
Admissions Requirements Minimum age 18; Physician's request.
Staff Physicians (contracted); RNs 2 (ft), 1 (pt); LPNs 8 (ft); Nurses' aides 25 (ft); Physical therapists (contracted); Speech therapists (contracted); Activities coordinators 1 (ft); Dietitians (contracted); Ophthalmologists (contracted); Podiatrists (contracted).
Facilities Dining room; Activities room; Chapel; Laundry room; Barber/Beauty shop; Patio and porch areas; Dayrooms; Private rooms.
Activities Arts & crafts; Cards; Games; Reading groups; Prayer groups; Movies; Shopping trips; Dances/Social/Cultural gatherings; Intergenerational programs; Pet therapy; Field trips.

Mountain View

Compton's Oak Grove Lodge
PO Box 930, Mountain View, AR 72560
(501) 269-3886, 354-9000 FAX
Admin Kari Sue Henderson. *Dir of Nursing* Luanne Thiel RN. *Medical Dir* H U Monroe MD.
Licensure Skilled care; Medicare certified; Residential care. *Beds* SNF 97; Medicare certified 8; Residential care 16. *Private Pay Patients* 10%. *Certified* Medicaid.
Owner Privately owned.
Admissions Requirements Physician's request.
Staff Physicians 1 (pt); RNs 2 (ft); LPNs 8 (ft); Nurses' aides 30 (ft); Physical therapists 1 (pt); Reality therapists 1 (pt); Recreational therapists 1 (pt); Occupational therapists 1 (pt); Speech therapists 1 (pt); Activities coordinators 1 (ft); Dietitians 1 (pt).

Facilities Dining room; Activities room; Crafts room; Laundry room; Barber/Beauty shop; Library.
Activities Arts & crafts; Cards; Games; Prayer groups; Shopping trips; Dances/Social/Cultural gatherings; Basketball; Horseshoes; Dominoes; Folk & gospel musicals weekly.

Murfreesboro

Idlehour Nursing Center Inc
PO Box 666, Murfreesboro, AR 71958
(501) 285-2186
Admin JoAnn Brown.
Licensure Intermediate care. *Beds* 75. *Certified* Medicaid.
Owner Proprietary corp (Beverly Enterprises).

Nashville

Benson's Nursing Home Inc
1315 Hutchinson St, Nashville, AR 71852
(501) 845-4933
Admin Willie Benson Jr. *Dir of Nursing* Gynder D Benson. *Medical Dir* Dr T J Humphreys.
Licensure Skilled care. *Beds* SNF 105. *Private Pay Patients* 1%. *Certified* Medicaid.
Owner Proprietary corp.
Admissions Requirements Medical examination; Physician's request.
Staff Physicians 1 (ft); RNs 1 (ft), 1 (pt); LPNs 5 (ft), 2 (pt); Physical therapists 1 (pt); Speech therapists 1 (pt); Activities coordinators 1 (pt); Dietitians 1 (pt).
Facilities Dining room; Activities room; Laundry room; Barber/Beauty shop.
Activities Arts & crafts; Cards; Games; Reading groups; Prayer groups; Movies; Shopping trips; Dances/Social/Cultural gatherings; Intergenerational programs; Volunteer program.

Colonial Nursing Home Inc
311 W Henderson St, Nashville, AR 71852
(501) 845-4128
Admin Vicki Keeney. *Dir of Nursing* Sarita Floyd RN.
Licensure Intermediate care. *Beds* ICF 50. *Certified* Medicaid.
Owner Proprietary corp.
Admissions Requirements Medical examination; Physician's request.
Staff RNs 1 (ft); LPNs 3 (ft), 3 (pt); Nurses' aides 8 (ft), 5 (pt); Recreational therapists 1 (ft); Activities coordinators 1 (ft); Dietitians 1 (pt); Ophthalmologists 1 (pt).
Facilities Dining room; Laundry room; Barber/Beauty shop.
Activities Arts & crafts; Cards; Games; Reading groups; Prayer groups; Dances/Social/Cultural gatherings; Taped music.

Guest House of Nashville
PO Box 1680, Nashville, AR 71852
(501) 845-3881
Admin Jean Keeder. *Dir of Nursing* Vida Hopkins RN. *Medical Dir* Dr Samuel Peebles.
Licensure Skilled care. *Beds* SNF 70. *Private Pay Patients* 5%. *Certified* Medicaid.
Owner Proprietary corp.
Staff Physicians 7 (ft); RNs 3 (ft); LPNs 7 (ft); Nurses' aides 20 (ft); Dietitians 2 (ft); Ophthalmologists 2 (ft).
Facilities Dining room; Laundry room; Barber/Beauty shop.
Activities Arts & crafts; Cards; Games; Reading groups; Prayer groups; Movies; Shopping trips; Dances/Social/Cultural gatherings.

Leisure Lodge Inc of Nashville
PO Box 812, Nashville, AR 71852
(501) 845-2021
Admin Kim Raulerson. *Dir of Nursing* Jan Boggs RN. *Medical Dir* Dr Joe King.

Licensure Skilled care. *Beds* SNF 78. *Certified* Medicaid.
Owner Proprietary corp (Beverly Enterprises).
Admissions Requirements Minimum age 16; Medical examination; Physician's request.
Staff Physicians 6 (pt); RNs 1 (ft), 1 (pt); LPNs 5 (ft), 3 (pt); Nurses' aides 28 (ft), 5 (pt); Activities coordinators 1 (ft); Dietitians 1 (ft).
Facilities Dining room; Activities room; Chapel; Crafts room; Laundry room; Barber/Beauty shop; Picnic area.
Activities Arts & crafts; Cards; Games; Reading groups; Prayer groups; Movies; Shopping trips; Dances/Social/Cultural gatherings.

Nashville Nursing Home
810 N 8th, Nashville, AR 71852
(501) 845-1616
Admin Frances Joan McCrary.
Licensure Intermediate care. *Beds* 50. *Certified* Medicaid; Medicare.
Staff RNs 1 (ft); LPNs 4 (ft), 1 (pt); Nurses' aides 12 (ft), 4 (pt); Activities coordinators 1 (ft); Dietitians 1 (pt).
Facilities Dining room; Activities room; Laundry room; Barber/Beauty shop.
Activities Arts & crafts; Games; Reading groups; Movies; Shopping trips.

Newport

Pinedale Nursing Home
1311 N Pecan St, Newport, AR 72112
(501) 523-5881
Admin Carolyn S Thompson.
Medical Dir Guilford Dudley.
Licensure Skilled care. *Beds* 125. *Certified* Medicaid.
Admissions Requirements Medical examination; Physician's request.
Staff Physicians 1 (pt); RNs 1 (ft), 2 (pt); LPNs 9 (ft), 1 (pt); Nurses' aides 30 (ft), 8 (pt); Physical therapists 1 (pt); Recreational therapists 2 (ft); Activities coordinators 2 (ft); Dietitians 1 (pt); Dentists 1 (pt).
Facilities Dining room; Physical therapy room; Activities room; Laundry room; Barber/Beauty shop; Library.
Activities Arts & crafts; Cards; Games; Reading groups; Prayer groups; Movies; Shopping trips; Dances/Social/Cultural gatherings.

Regional Healthcare Inc
PO Box J, 410 Calhoun St, Newport, AR 72112
(501) 523-6539
Admin Betty Webster. *Dir of Nursing* Helen Sharp. *Medical Dir* Dr Jerry M Frankum.
Licensure Skilled care; Alzheimer's care. *Beds* SNF 105. *Private Pay Patients* 2%. *Certified* Medicaid.
Owner Proprietary corp.
Admissions Requirements Physician's request.
Staff Physicians 12 (pt); RNs 1 (ft), 1 (pt); Speech therapists 1 (pt); Activities coordinators 1 (ft); Dietitians 1 (ft).
Facilities Dining room; Activities room; Laundry room; Barber/Beauty shop.
Activities Arts & crafts; Cards; Games; Reading groups; Prayer groups; Movies; Shopping trips; Pet therapy.

North Little Rock

Mercy Nursing Home Inc
6401 E 47th St, North Little Rock, AR 72117
(501) 945-2356
Admin Geraldine Robinson. *Dir of Nursing* Jo Ann Curry. *Medical Dir* Dr M J Elders.
Licensure Intermediate care. *Beds* 85. *Certified* Medicaid.
Owner Proprietary corp.

Staff Physicians 2 (pt); RNs 1 (ft); LPNs 4 (ft); Nurses' aides 30 (ft); Physical therapists 1 (pt); Occupational therapists 1 (pt); Activities coordinators 1 (pt); Dietitians 1 (pt); Dentists 1 (pt).
Facilities Dining room; Physical therapy room; Activities room; Chapel; Laundry room; Barber/Beauty shop.
Activities Cards; Games; Prayer groups; Shopping trips; Dances/Social/Cultural gatherings.

Riley's Oak Hill Manor Inc North
2501 John Ashley Dr, North Little Rock, AR 72114
(501) 758-3800
Admin Steve Gates.
Licensure Skilled care. *Beds* 224. *Certified* Medicaid.

Ola

Yell County Nursing Home
PO Box 249, Ola, AR 72853
(501) 489-5237
Admin Barry N Tippin. *Dir of Nursing* Marilyn Tippin.
Licensure Skilled care. *Beds* SNF 74. *Private Pay Patients* 20%. *Certified* Medicaid.
Owner Privately owned.
Admissions Requirements Medical examination; Physician's request.
Facilities Dining room; Activities room; Crafts room; Laundry room; Barber/Beauty shop; Library.
Activities Arts & crafts; Games; Prayer groups; Movies; Shopping trips.

Osceola

Osceola Nursing Home
PO Box 545, 406 S Broadway, Osceola, AR 72370
(501) 563-3201
Admin Debora A Thomas. *Dir of Nursing* Jan Laseter RN. *Medical Dir* George Pollock MD.
Licensure Skilled care. *Beds* SNF 96. *Private Pay Patients* 3%. *Certified* Medicaid.
Owner Proprietary corp (Health Care Management).
Admissions Requirements Medical examination; Physician's request.
Staff Physicians 5 (pt); RNs 4 (ft), 1 (pt); LPNs 5 (ft), 4 (pt); Nurses' aides 24 (ft), 5 (pt); Physical therapists 1 (pt); Activities coordinators 1 (ft), 1 (pt); Dietitians 1 (ft), 1 (pt).
Facilities Dining room; Activities room; Laundry room; Barber/Beauty shop.
Activities Arts & crafts; Cards; Games; Reading groups; Prayer groups; Movies; Shopping trips; Dances/Social/Cultural gatherings; Pet therapy.

Ozark

Ozark Nursing Home Inc
600 N 12th St, Ozark, AR 72949
(501) 667-4791
Admin Gus S Schaffer.
Licensure Intermediate care. *Beds* 118. *Certified* Medicaid.

Paragould

Greene Acres Nursing Home Inc
PO Box 1027, Paragould, AR 72451-1027
(501) 236-8771
Admin Larry McFadden.
Medical Dir Asa Crow MD.
Licensure Intermediate care. *Beds* 89. *Certified* Medicaid.
Owner Nonprofit corp.
Admissions Requirements Physician's request.

Staff Physicians 14 (pt); RNs 1 (ft); LPNs 7 (ft), 5 (pt); Nurses' aides 17 (ft), 6 (pt); Activities coordinators 1 (ft); Dietitians 1 (pt).
Facilities Dining room; Laundry room; Barber/Beauty shop.
Activities Arts & crafts; Games; Reading groups; Dances/Social/Cultural gatherings.

Paragould Nursing Center
Rte 3 Box 45A, Paragould, AR 72450
(501) 236-7104
Admin Diana Goodman. *Dir of Nursing* Lucille Jackson. *Medical Dir* Dr Bennie Mitchell.
Licensure Skilled care. *Beds* SNF 180. *Certified* Medicaid.
Owner Proprietary corp (Beverly Enterprises).
Admissions Requirements Physician's request.
Staff RNs 2 (ft), 2 (pt); LPNs 20 (ft), 1 (pt); Nurses' aides 54 (ft); Activities coordinators 2 (ft).
Facilities Dining room; Activities room; Laundry room; Barber/Beauty shop.
Activities Arts & crafts; Games; Reading groups; Prayer groups; Movies; Shopping trips; Dances/Social/Cultural gatherings.

Paris

Logan County Nursing Center
PO Box 431, Paris, AR 72855
(501) 963-6151
Admin Erma Garner.
Licensure Intermediate care. *Beds* 31. *Certified* Medicaid.

Paris Retirement Inn Inc
513 N Roseville, Paris, AR 72855
(501) 963-3096
Admin Nancy Davis.
Licensure Intermediate care. *Beds* 72. *Certified* Medicaid.
Owner Proprietary corp (Beverly Enterprises).

Perryville

Perry County Nursing Center
PO Box 270, Perryville, AR 72126
(501) 889-2400
Admin Judy Weiss.
Medical Dir Cindy Weiss.
Licensure Intermediate care. *Beds* ICF 70. *Certified* Medicaid.
Owner Privately owned.
Staff Physicians 1 (ft), 2 (pt); RNs 1 (ft), 2 (pt); LPNs 4 (ft), 3 (pt); Nurses' aides 30 (ft), 8 (pt); Activities coordinators 1 (ft); Dietitians 1 (ft); Dentists 1 (ft).
Facilities Dining room; Physical therapy room; Activities room; Laundry room; Barber/Beauty shop.
Activities Arts & crafts; Cards; Games; Reading groups; Prayer groups; Movies; Shopping trips; Dances/Social/Cultural gatherings.

Piggott

Piggott Nursing Center
PO Box 388, 450 S 9th St, Piggott, AR 72454
(501) 598-2291
Admin Gaye Wiley. *Dir of Nursing* JoAnn Hoots RN. *Medical Dir* Jerry L Muse MD.
Licensure Skilled care. *Beds* SNF 105. *Private Pay Patients* 5%. *Certified* Medicaid.
Owner Proprietary corp (Beverly Enterprises).
Admissions Requirements Medical examination; Physician's request.
Staff Physicians 5 (pt); RNs 1 (ft), 3 (pt); LPNs 8 (ft); Nurses' aides 28 (ft), 2 (pt); Physical therapists 1 (pt); Activities coordinators 1 (ft); Dietitians 1 (pt); Ophthalmologists 1 (pt).

Facilities Dining room; Physical therapy room; Activities room; Crafts room; Laundry room; Barber/Beauty shop; Miniature golf course.
Activities Arts & crafts; Cards; Games; Reading groups; Prayer groups; Movies; Shopping trips; Dances/Social/Cultural gatherings.

Pine Bluff

Arkansas Convalescent Center—Pine Bluff
6301 S Hazel, Pine Bluff, AR 71603
(501) 534-8153
Admin Richard L Guy. *Dir of Nursing* Connie Robertson. *Medical Dir* Thomas Duckworth.
Licensure Skilled care. *Beds* SNF 73. *Private Pay Patients* 30%. *Certified* Medicaid.
Owner Proprietary corp (Arkansas Convalescent Centers Inc).
Staff RNs 1 (ft), 2 (pt); LPNs 8 (ft), 4 (pt); Nurses' aides 23 (ft), 3 (pt); Activities coordinators 1 (ft); Dietitians 1 (ft).
Facilities Dining room; Activities room; Chapel; Laundry room; Barber/Beauty shop; Library.
Activities Arts & crafts; Cards; Games; Reading groups; Prayer groups; Movies; Shopping trips; Intergenerational programs; Pet therapy.

Davis Skilled Nursing Facility
1111 W 12th, Pine Bluff, AR 71601
(501) 541-7191
Admin Robert L Dolan. *Dir of Nursing* Sandra Kortenber. *Medical Dir* William Harper.
Licensure Skilled care. *Beds* SNF 100. *Private Pay Patients* 35-40%. *Certified* Medicaid.
Owner Nonprofit organization/foundation.
Staff Physicians 30 (ft); RNs 5 (ft), 1 (pt); LPNs 10 (ft); Nurses' aides 35 (ft); Physical therapists (consultant); Occupational therapists (consultant); Speech therapists (consultant); Dietitians (consultant); Dentists (consultant); Recreational therapists; Activities coordinators 1 (ft).
Activities Arts & crafts; Cards; Games; Reading groups; Prayer groups; Movies; Shopping trips; Dances/Social/Cultural gatherings; Intergenerational programs; Pet therapy; Hospital-based pastoral services.

Jefferson Convalescent Home Inc
PO Box 7223, 3406 W Seventh, Pine Bluff, AR 71611
(501) 534-5681
Admin Linda Manasco.
Medical Dir James Lindsey.
Licensure Intermediate care. *Beds* 50. *Certified* Medicaid.
Owner Nonprofit organization/foundation.
Admissions Requirements Medical examination; Physician's request.
Staff RNs 1 (ft); LPNs 5 (ft); Nurses' aides 18 (ft); Activities coordinators 1 (ft); Dietitians 1 (ft), 1 (pt).
Facilities Dining room; Activities room; Laundry room; Barber/Beauty shop.
Activities Arts & crafts; Cards; Games; Reading groups; Prayer groups.

Loma Linda Rest Home
PO Box 1329, Pine Bluff, AR 71613
(501) 535-8878
Admin Carolyn A Compton.
Licensure Intermediate care. *Beds* 205. *Certified* Medicaid.

Oak Park Nursing Home Inc
PO Box 8270, Pine Bluff, AR 71611
(501) 536-2972
Admin Nancy K Rollins.
Medical Dir Shafqat Hussain.
Licensure Intermediate care. *Beds* ICF 67. *Certified* Medicaid.
Owner Proprietary corp.
Admissions Requirements Physician's request.

Staff RNs 1 (ft); LPNs 4 (ft), 3 (pt); Nurses' aides 14 (ft), 4 (pt); Activities coordinators 1 (ft); Dietitians 1 (ft).
Facilities Dining room; Activities room; Laundry room; Barber/Beauty shop.
Activities Arts & crafts; Cards; Games; Reading groups; Prayer groups; Movies; Shopping trips; Dances/Social/Cultural gatherings.

Pine Bluff Nursing Home
PO Box 1310, 3701 S Main, Pine Bluff, AR 71613
(501) 534-6614
Admin Robert L Wells. *Dir of Nursing* Mary Huntley. *Medical Dir* Herbert Fendley.
Licensure Skilled care; Retirement. *Beds* 245. *Certified* Medicaid; Medicare.
Owner Proprietary corp.
Admissions Requirements Minimum age 40; Medical examination; Physician's request.
Staff RNs 4 (ft); LPNs 19 (ft); Nurses' aides 59 (ft); Physical therapists 1 (pt); Activities coordinators 2 (ft); Dietitians 1 (ft), 1 (pt).
Facilities Dining room; Physical therapy room; Activities room; Laundry room; Barber/Beauty shop.
Activities Arts & crafts; Cards; Games; Reading groups; Prayer groups; Movies; Shopping trips; Dances/Social/Cultural gatherings.

Pocahontas

Pocahontas Convalescent Center
Rte 6 Box 87, Pocahontas, AR 72455
(501) 892-2523
Admin Bill Stubblefield; Shelba Doan, Asst.
Beds 80.
Owner Proprietary corp (Diversicare Corp of America-Arkansas).

Randolph County Nursing Home
1405 Hospital Dr, Pocahontas, AR 72455
(501) 892-5214
Admin Dickie C Smith.
Licensure Skilled care. *Beds* 80. *Certified* Medicaid.

Prairie Grove

Medi-Home of Prairie Grove
PO Box 616, 621 S Mock St, Prairie Grove, AR 72753
(501) 846-2169
Admin Maxine Thompson. *Dir of Nursing* Ellen Hedegard RN. *Medical Dir* Bob G Mitchell MD.
Licensure Skilled care. *Beds* SNF 70. *Private Pay Patients* 40%. *Certified* Medicaid.
Owner Privately owned.
Staff RNs 1 (ft), 1 (pt); LPNs 6 (ft), 2 (pt); Nurses' aides 38 (ft), 6 (pt).
Facilities Dining room; Laundry room; Barber/Beauty shop.
Activities Arts & crafts; Cards; Games; Reading groups; Prayer groups; Movies; Shopping trips; Dances/Social/Cultural gatherings; Intergenerational programs; Pet therapy.

Prescott

Hillcrest Nursing Home
1421 W 2nd N, Prescott, AR 71857
(501) 887-3811
Admin Margie Pickett. *Dir of Nursing* Lisa Barham RN. *Medical Dir* H Blake Crow MD.
Licensure Intermediate care. *Beds* ICF 70. *Private Pay Patients* 30%. *Certified* Medicaid.
Owner Proprietary corp.
Staff RNs 1 (ft); LPNs 9 (pt); Nurses' aides 30 (pt); Activities coordinators 1 (ft); Dietitians 1 (ft).

Facilities Dining room; Activities room; Laundry room; Barber/Beauty shop.
Activities Arts & crafts; Cards; Games; Reading groups; Prayer groups; Movies; Shopping trips; Dances/Social/Cultural gatherings; Intergenerational programs; Pet therapy.

Prescott Nursing Center
Rte 6 Box 227, Prescott, AR 71857
(501) 887-6639
Admin Beverly Starr. *Dir of Nursing* Paulette Collier. *Medical Dir* Dr Michael Young.
Licensure Skilled care. *Beds* SNF 111. *Private Pay Patients* 10%. *Certified* Medicaid.
Owner Proprietary corp (Beverly Enterprises).
Admissions Requirements Medical examination; Physician's request.
Staff RNs 1 (ft), 2 (pt); LPNs 7 (ft), 4 (pt); Nurses' aides 25 (ft); Activities coordinators 1 (ft); Dietitians 1 (ft).
Facilities Dining room; Activities room; Laundry room; Barber/Beauty shop.
Activities Arts & crafts; Cards; Games; Reading groups; Prayer groups; Movies; Shopping trips; Dances/Social/Cultural gatherings; Intergenerational programs; Pet therapy; Senior Olympics; Festivals; Fairs; Museum trips; Concerts; Barbecues.

Rison

Cleveland County Nursing Home
PO Box 365, Rison, AR 71665
(501) 325-6202
Admin Marilyn Reed-Hoover. *Dir of Nursing* Phyllis Attwood RN. *Medical Dir* H Mark Attwood MD.
Licensure Skilled care; Alzheimer's care. *Beds* SNF 67. *Certified* Medicaid.
Owner Proprietary corp (Beverly Enterprises).
Staff Physicians 1 (ft); RNs 1 (ft), 2 (pt); LPNs 8 (ft), 1 (pt); Nurses' aides 14 (ft), 9 (pt); Physical therapists 1 (pt); Activities coordinators 1 (ft); Dietitians 1 (ft).
Languages German.
Facilities Dining room; Physical therapy room; Crafts room; Laundry room; Barber/Beauty shop; Library.
Activities Arts & crafts; Games; Reading groups; Prayer groups; Shopping trips; Dances/Social/Cultural gatherings.

Rogers

Medi-Home of Rogers Inc
1603 W Walnut St, Rogers, AR 72756
(501) 636-9334
Admin Linda L Neely. *Dir of Nursing* Cheryl McCullough. *Medical Dir* Dr Robert Hull.
Licensure Intermediate care. *Beds* ICF 70. *Private Pay Patients* 20%. *Certified* Medicaid.
Owner Proprietary corp.
Admissions Requirements Medical examination; Physician's request.
Staff RNs 1 (ft); LPNs 4 (ft); Nurses' aides 19 (ft); Physical therapists 1 (ft); Activities coordinators 1 (ft); Dietitians 1 (ft).
Facilities Dining room; Activities room; Crafts room; Laundry room; Barber/Beauty shop.
Activities Arts & crafts; Games; Reading groups; Prayer groups; Movies; Shopping trips; Pet therapy.

Rogers Nursing Center
1151 W New Hope Rd, Rogers, AR 72756
(501) 636-6290
Admin Gerald Kimbrough. *Dir of Nursing* Barbara Talik RN. *Medical Dir* William Jennings MD.
Licensure Skilled care; Retirement; Alzheimer's care. *Beds* SNF 140. *Certified* Medicaid; Medicare; VA.
Owner Proprietary corp (Beverly Enterprises).

Admissions Requirements Minimum age 18; Medical examination.
Staff RNs 3 (ft); LPNs 9 (ft), 5 (pt); Nurses' aides 40 (ft), 20 (pt); Physical therapists 1 (pt); Activities coordinators 1 (ft); Dietitians 1 (ft); Social service coordinators 1 (ft).
Facilities Dining room; Physical therapy room; Activities room; Crafts room; Laundry room; Barber/Beauty shop.
Activities Arts & crafts; Cards; Games; Reading groups; Prayer groups; Movies; Shopping trips; Dances/Social/Cultural gatherings; Fishing trips; Outings once a month.

Rose Care Center of Rogers
1513 S Dixieland Rd, Rogers, AR 72756
(501) 636-5841
Admin John W Krouse.
Medical Dir Dr Jennings.
Licensure Skilled care. *Beds* 140. *Certified* Medicaid.
Staff RNs 4 (ft), 2 (pt); LPNs 8 (ft), 1 (pt); Nurses' aides 26 (ft), 3 (pt); Physical therapists 1 (pt); Recreational therapists 1 (ft); Speech therapists 1 (ft); Activities coordinators 1 (ft); Dietitians 1 (ft); Dentists 1 (pt).
Facilities Dining room; Activities room; Crafts room; Laundry room; Barber/Beauty shop; Library.
Activities Arts & crafts; Cards; Games; Reading groups; Prayer groups; Movies; Shopping trips; Dances/Social/Cultural gatherings.

Russellville

Legacy Lodge Nursing Home
900 W 12th St, Russellville, AR 72801
(501) 968-5858
Admin Erby E Rowell.
Medical Dir Finley Turner.
Licensure Skilled care; Alzheimer's care. *Beds* 122. *Certified* Medicaid.
Owner Proprietary corp.
Admissions Requirements Physician's request.
Staff Physicians 1 (pt); RNs 3 (ft); LPNs 14 (ft); Nurses' aides 28 (ft); Physical therapists 1 (pt); Activities coordinators 1 (ft); Dietitians 1 (ft); Ophthalmologists 1 (pt); Dentists 1 (pt).
Facilities Dining room; Activities room; Crafts room; Laundry room; Barber/Beauty shop.
Activities Arts & crafts; Cards; Games; Reading groups; Prayer groups; Movies; Shopping trips; Dances/Social/Cultural gatherings.

Russellville Nursing Center Inc
1700 W "C" St, Russellville, AR 72801
(501) 968-5256
Admin Debra Sue Gray.
Medical Dir Dennis Berner MD.
Licensure Skilled care. *Beds* SNF 92. *Certified* Medicaid.
Owner Privately owned.
Admissions Requirements Medical examination; Physician's request.
Staff RNs 1 (ft), 1 (pt); LPNs 6 (ft), 4 (pt); Nurses' aides 23 (ft), 12 (pt); Activities coordinators 1 (ft); Dietitians 1 (pt).
Facilities Dining room; Laundry room; Barber/Beauty shop.
Activities Arts & crafts; Cards; Games; Reading groups; Prayer groups; Movies; Shopping trips; Dances/Social/Cultural gatherings.

Stella Manor Nursing Center
400 N Vancouver, Russellville, AR 72801
(501) 968-4141
Admin Barbara S McCoy. *Dir of Nursing* LaVerne Johnson. *Medical Dir* Dennis Berner.
Licensure Skilled care. *Beds* SNF 144. *Certified* Medicaid.

Owner Privately owned.
Staff RNs 3 (ft); LPNs 15 (ft), 1 (pt); Nurses' aides 50 (ft); Activities coordinators 2 (ft); Dietitians 1 (ft).
Facilities Dining room; Activities room; Laundry room; Barber/Beauty shop.
Activities Arts & crafts; Cards; Games; Reading groups; Prayer groups; Movies; Shopping trips; Dances/Social/Cultural gatherings.

Salem

Fulton County Nursing Center
Box 397, Salem, AR 72576
(501) 895-3817
Admin James B Cooper. *Dir of Nursing* George Scheper. *Medical Dir* Betty Price.
Licensure Skilled care. *Beds* SNF 125. *Private Pay Patients* 4%. *Certified* Medicaid.
Owner Proprietary corp.
Staff RNs; LPNs; Nurses' aides; Dietitians.
Facilities Dining room; Activities room; Chapel; Crafts room; Laundry room; Barber/ Beauty shop.
Activities Arts & crafts; Games; Reading groups; Prayer groups; Movies; Shopping trips; Dances/Social/Cultural gatherings.

Searcy

Byrd Haven Nursing Home
105 S College, Searcy, AR 72143
(501) 268-2324
Admin Ralph Byrd Jr. *Dir of Nursing* Cloie Ross RN. *Medical Dir* Eugene Joseph MD.
Licensure Intermediate care. *Beds* ICF 75. *Private Pay Patients* 30%. *Certified* Medicaid.
Owner Privately owned.
Admissions Requirements Physician's request.
Staff RNs 1 (ft); LPNs 7 (ft), 4 (pt); Nurses' aides 42 (ft), 3 (pt); Activities coordinators 1 (ft); Dietitians 1 (ft).
Facilities Dining room; Activities room; Crafts room; Laundry room; Barber/Beauty shop.
Activities Arts & crafts; Cards; Games; Reading groups; Prayer groups; Movies; Dances/Social/Cultural gatherings; Pet therapy.

Leisure Lodge Inc—Searcy
211 Skyline Dr, Searcy, AR 72143
(501) 268-6188
Admin Tommie Pemberton.
Licensure Skilled care. *Beds* 245. *Certified* Medicaid.
Owner Proprietary corp.

Sheridan

Grant County Nursing Home
PO Box 100 BB, Rte 2, Sheridan, AR 72150
(501) 942-2183, 942-2212
Admin Mary E Scott. *Dir of Nursing* Susan Damion. *Medical Dir* Dr Jack Irvin.
Licensure Skilled care; Intermediate care. *Beds* SNF 110; ICF. *Certified* Medicaid.
Owner Proprietary corp (Diversicare Corp).
Admissions Requirements Medical examination; Physician's request.
Staff Physicians 3 (ft); RNs 2 (ft), 1 (pt); LPNs 4 (ft), 6 (pt); Nurses' aides 35 (ft), 5 (pt); Activities coordinators 1 (ft); Dietitians 1 (ft).
Languages Spanish.
Facilities Dining room; Activities room; Crafts room; Laundry room; Barber/Beauty shop.
Activities Arts & crafts; Cards; Games; Reading groups; Prayer groups; Movies; Shopping trips; Dances/Social/Cultural gatherings.

Sidney

Sharp Nursing Home
Nursing Home Ct, Sidney, AR 72577
(501) 283-5897
Admin James R Hollandsworth. *Dir of Nursing* Marjorie Fowler. *Medical Dir* Dr J R Baker.
Licensure Intermediate care. *Beds* ICF 67. *Private Pay Patients* 12%. *Certified* Medicaid.
Owner Nonprofit organization/foundation.
Admissions Requirements Medical examination; Physician's request.
Staff Physicians 1 (pt); RNs 1 (ft); LPNs 9 (ft), 3 (pt); Nurses' aides 12 (ft), 8 (pt); Activities coordinators 1 (pt); Dietitians 1 (pt); Podiatrists 1 (pt).
Facilities Dining room; Activities room; Laundry room; Barber/Beauty shop.
Activities Arts & crafts; Cards; Games; Reading groups; Prayer groups; Movies.

Siloam Springs

Woodland Manor Inc
811 W Elgin, Siloam Springs, AR 72761
(501) 524-3128
Admin Montie Vest.
Licensure Skilled care. *Beds* 120. *Certified* Medicaid; Medicare.

Smackover

Smackover Nursing Home
PO Drawer J, 210 E 5th St, Smackover, AR 71762
(501) 725-3871
Admin Earnest E Allen. *Dir of Nursing* Sheila Rowland. *Medical Dir* Dr G W Warren.
Licensure Skilled care. *Beds* SNF 80. *Private Pay Patients* 15%. *Certified* Medicaid.
Owner Privately owned (AMI Inc).
Admissions Requirements Medical examination.
Staff RNs 2 (ft), 1 (pt); LPNs 8 (ft); Physical therapists; Activities coordinators 1 (ft); Dietitians 1 (pt).
Facilities Dining room; Activities room; Laundry room; Barber/Beauty shop; Library.
Activities Arts & crafts; Cards; Games; Reading groups; Prayer groups; Movies; Shopping trips; Dances/Social/Cultural gatherings; Intergenerational programs.

Springdale

Holland Nursing Center North
PO Box Drawer 685, Springdale, AR 72764-0685
(501) 756-9000
Admin Deanna Shackelford.
Licensure Intermediate care. *Beds* 56. *Certified* Medicaid.

Holland Nursing Center West Inc
PO Box T, Springdale, AR 72765
(501) 756-1600
Admin Tommy Holland.
Licensure Intermediate care. *Beds* 70. *Certified* Medicaid.

Pleasant Valley Nursing Center
102 N Gutensohn, Springdale, AR 72764
(501) 756-0330
Admin Paul B Keener RN.
Licensure Skilled care. *Beds* 140. *Certified* Medicaid.

Stamps

Homestead Manor Nursing Home
405 North St, Stamps, AR 71860
(501) 533-4444
Admin Mary Jane Allen.

Licensure Skilled care. *Beds* SNF 116. *Certified* Medicaid.
Owner Proprietary corp.
Admissions Requirements Medical examination; Physician's request.
Staff RNs 2 (ft); LPNs 8 (ft); Nurses' aides; Activities coordinators 1 (ft); Dietitians 1 (ft).
Facilities Dining room; Activities room; Crafts room; Laundry room; Barber/Beauty shop.
Activities Arts & crafts; Cards; Games; Reading groups; Prayer groups; Movies; Shopping trips; Dances/Social/Cultural gatherings.

Star City

Gardner Nursing Home of Star City Inc
N Drew St, Star City, AR 71667
(501) 628-4144
Admin Annabelle Smith.
Licensure Intermediate care. *Beds* 72. *Certified* Medicaid.

Star City Nursing Center
Ford & Victory Sts, Star City, AR 71667
(501) 628-4295
Admin Suzanne Loe.
Licensure Skilled care. *Beds* 87. *Certified* Medicaid.
Owner Proprietary corp (Beverly Enterprises).

Stuttgart

Crestpark Inn of Stuttgart Inc
PO Box 790, Stuttgart, AR 72160
(501) 673-1657
Admin Brenda Dunbar Hardin.
Licensure Intermediate care. *Beds* 74. *Certified* Medicaid.

Rose Care Center of Stuttgart
PO Box 426, Stuttgart, AR 72160
(501) 673-6981
Admin Lucille Harper. *Dir of Nursing* Sue Borcherding RN. *Medical Dir* Noble B Daniel MD.
Licensure Skilled care. *Beds* SNF 90. *Private Pay Patients* 20%. *Certified* Medicaid.
Owner Proprietary corp.
Admissions Requirements Physician's request.
Staff RNs 2 (ft), 1 (pt); LPNs 7 (ft), 2 (pt); Nurses' aides 30 (ft), 6 (pt); Dietitians 1 (ft).
Facilities Dining room; Activities room; Laundry room; Barber/Beauty shop.
Activities Arts & crafts; Cards; Games; Reading groups; Prayer groups; Movies; Shopping trips; Pet therapy.

Taylor

Taylor Nursing Home
Rte 2 Box 419, Taylor, AR 71861
(501) 694-3781
Admin Ruby Pyle.
Licensure Intermediate care. *Beds* 41. *Certified* Medicaid; Medicare.
Admissions Requirements Medical examination; Physician's request.
Staff Physicians 3 (pt); RNs 1 (ft); LPNs 1 (ft), 6 (pt); Nurses' aides 11 (ft); Activities coordinators 1 (ft); Dentists 1 (pt).
Facilities Dining room; Activities room; Crafts room; Laundry room; Barber/Beauty shop.
Activities Arts & crafts; Cards; Games.

Texarkana

Arkansas Convalescent Center
2107 Dudley St, Texarkana, AR 75502
(501) 772-1831 (office), 772-4427 (nurses station)
Admin Mary E Scott.
Beds 105.

Evergreen Place
1100 E 36th St, Texarkana, AR 75502
(501) 773-7515 or 773-7516
Admin Sue Ward. *Dir of Nursing* Linda Alford RN. *Medical Dir* Dr Russell Mayo.
Licensure Intermediate care; Retirement. *Beds* ICF 69. *Certified* Medicaid.
Owner Proprietary corp.
Admissions Requirements Medical examination; Physician's request.
Staff Physicians 1 (ft); RNs 1 (ft); LPNs 8 (ft), 1 (pt); Nurses' aides 21 (ft); Activities coordinators 1 (ft); Dietitians 1 (ft).
Facilities Dining room; Physical therapy room; Activities room; Chapel; Crafts room; Laundry room; Barber/Beauty shop.
Activities Arts & crafts; Cards; Games; Reading groups; Prayer groups; Movies; Shopping trips.

Medicalodge Inc of Texarkana
1621 E 42nd St, Texarkana, AR 75502
(501) 774-3581
Admin Leo Sutterfield.
Licensure Skilled care. *Beds* 105. *Certified* Medicaid; Medicare.
Owner Proprietary corp.

Oakwood Place
1100 E 36th St, Texarkana, AR 75502
(501) 773-2341
Admin Elanda Callahan Newberry.
Licensure Intermediate care. *Beds* 42. *Certified* Medicaid; Medicare.
Owner Proprietary corp.

Trumann

Rose Care Center of Trumann
333 Melody Dr, Trumann, AR 72472
(501) 483-7623
Admin Judy K Glasco. *Dir of Nursing* Sally Houston RN. *Medical Dir* Dr Floyd Smith.
Licensure Skilled care. *Beds* SNF 77. *Certified* Medicaid.
Owner Proprietary corp (Rose Care Inc).
Admissions Requirements Medical examination; Physician's request.
Staff RNs 2 (ft), 1 (pt); LPNs 7 (ft), 2 (pt); Nurses' aides 25 (ft), 1 (pt); Activities coordinators 1 (ft); Dietitians 1 (ft).
Facilities Dining room; Activities room; Laundry room; Barber/Beauty shop.
Activities Arts & crafts; Cards; Games; Reading groups; Prayer groups; Movies; Shopping trips; Dances/Social/Cultural gatherings; Picnics; Various parties.

Van Buren

Brownwood Manor Inc
1404 N 28th St, Van Buren, AR 72956
(501) 474-8021
Admin Patricia Harris.
Licensure Skilled care; Retirement. *Beds* 99. *Certified* Medicaid.
Owner Proprietary corp.
Admissions Requirements Minimum age 21; Medical examination; Physician's request.
Staff RNs 2 (ft); LPNs 8 (ft); Activities coordinators 1 (ft).
Facilities Dining room; Activities room; Crafts room; Laundry room; Barber/Beauty shop.
Activities Arts & crafts; Cards; Games; Reading groups; Prayer groups; Movies; Dances/Social/Cultural gatherings.

New Haven O'Rest Inc
2010 Alma Hwy, Van Buren, AR 72956
(501) 474-6885
Admin Gelene Hendershot.
Licensure Skilled care. *Beds* 168. *Certified* Medicaid.

Van Buren Nursing Center
PO Drawer A, Van Buren, AR 72956
(501) 474-5276
Admin Linda Short.
Licensure Skilled care. *Beds* 105. *Certified* Medicaid.
Owner Proprietary corp (Beverly Enterprises).

Waldron

Pinewood Nursing Home
Box Q, 11th & Washington Sts, Waldron, AR 72958
(501) 637-3171
Admin Sr Donald Mary Lynch RSM. *Dir of Nursing* Carolyn Pugh. *Medical Dir* W Russell Young MD.
Licensure Skilled care; Retirement. *Beds* SNF 89; Retirement 22. *Private Pay Patients* 15%. *Certified* Medicaid.
Owner Nonprofit organization/foundation.
Admissions Requirements Physician's request.
Staff RNs 2 (ft), 1 (pt); LPNs 5 (ft), 4 (pt); Nurses' aides 13 (ft), 19 (pt); Recreational therapists 1 (pt); Activities coordinators 1 (pt).
Languages Spanish.
Affiliation Roman Catholic.
Facilities Dining room; Activities room; Crafts room; Laundry room; Barber/Beauty shop; Library.
Activities Arts & crafts; Games; Reading groups; Prayer groups; Movies; Shopping trips; Dances/Social/Cultural gatherings; Intergenerational programs; Pet therapy.

Walnut Ridge

Lawrence Hall Nursing Home
1309 W Main St, Walnut Ridge, AR 72476
(501) 886-1295
Admin Terry DePriest; Judy Belcher, Asst. *Dir of Nursing* Dawn Smith RN. *Medical Dir* Ralph Joseph MD.
Licensure Skilled care. *Beds* SNF 122. *Private Pay Patients* 25%. *Certified* Medicaid; Medicare.
Owner Publicly owned.
Admissions Requirements Medical examination; Physician's request.
Staff Physicians 6 (ft); RNs 2 (ft), 4 (pt); LPNs 15 (ft); Nurses' aides 35 (ft); Physical therapists (contracted); Speech therapists (contracted); Activities coordinators 1 (ft); Dietitians 1 (ft).
Facilities Dining room; Physical therapy room; Activities room; Laundry room; Barber/Beauty shop; Library; 18 private rooms; Courtyard; 24-hour physician coverage.
Activities Arts & crafts; Cards; Games; Reading groups; Prayer groups; Movies; Shopping trips; Dances/Social/Cultural gatherings; Intergenerational programs; Pet therapy; Popcorn parties.

Sheltering Arms Nursing Home
311 NW 2nd St, Walnut Ridge, AR 72476
(501) 886-3770
Admin Claude Cook Jr.
Medical Dir Robert Quevillon MD.
Licensure Intermediate care. *Beds* 36. *Certified* Medicaid; Medicare.
Admissions Requirements Medical examination; Physician's request.
Staff Physicians 1 (pt); RNs 1 (ft); LPNs 3 (ft), 1 (pt); Nurses' aides 7 (ft), 3 (pt); Physical therapists 1 (pt); Activities coordinators 1 (ft); Dietitians 1 (pt); Dentists 1 (pt).
Facilities Dining room; Activities room; Laundry room; Library.
Activities Arts & crafts; Cards; Games; Reading groups; Prayer groups; Movies; Shopping trips; Dances/Social/Cultural gatherings.

Walnut Ridge Convalescent Center
1500 Hwy 25 W, Walnut Ridge, AR 72476
(501) 886-9022
Admin Pamela W Murphy.
Medical Dir Ralph Joseph MD.
Licensure Skilled care. *Beds* 105. *Certified* Medicaid.
Admissions Requirements Medical examination; Physician's request.
Staff Physicians 2 (pt); RNs 1 (ft), 1 (pt); LPNs 8 (ft), 1 (pt); Nurses' aides 33 (ft); Physical therapists 1 (pt); Activities coordinators 1 (ft); Dietitians 1 (pt); Ophthalmologists 1 (pt); Dentists 1 (pt).
Facilities Dining room; Chapel; Laundry room; Barber/Beauty shop.
Activities Arts & crafts; Cards; Games; Reading groups; Prayer groups; Movies; Dances/Social/Cultural gatherings.

Warren

Pine Lodge Nursing Home
730 E Church St, Warren, AR 71671
(501) 226-5843
Admin Brenda Mercer. *Dir of Nursing* Jamison Nelson RN. *Medical Dir* Dr Joe H Wharton.
Licensure Skilled care. *Beds* 99. *Certified* Medicaid.
Owner Proprietary corp (Beverly Enterprises).
Staff RNs; LPNs; Nurses' aides; Activities coordinators; Dietitians.
Facilities Dining room; Activities room; Laundry room; Barber/Beauty shop.
Activities Arts & crafts; Cards; Games; Reading groups; Prayer groups; Movies; Shopping trips; Dances/Social/Cultural gatherings; Auctions; Fair.

Wagnon Place Inc
PO Box 230, Warren, AR 71671
(501) 226-6766
Admin Sue Wagnon. *Dir of Nursing* Susan Reynolds. *Medical Dir* George F Wynne MD.
Licensure Skilled care. *Beds* SNF 105. *Certified* Medicaid.
Owner Proprietary corp.
Admissions Requirements Medical examination; Physician's request.
Staff Physicians 5 (ft); RNs 2 (ft), 1 (pt); LPNs 7 (ft), 2 (pt); Nurses' aides 30 (ft), 3 (pt); Activities coordinators 2 (ft).
Facilities Dining room; Activities room; Chapel; Laundry room; Barber/Beauty shop.
Activities Arts & crafts; Cards; Games; Reading groups; Prayer groups; Movies; Shopping trips; Dances/Social/Cultural gatherings.

West Memphis

Geriatrics Nursing Center of West Memphis
610 S Avalon St, West Memphis, AR 72301
(501) 735-4543
Admin Jeanne Crisp.
Licensure Skilled care. *Beds* 155. *Certified* Medicaid.
Owner Proprietary corp (Beverly Enterprises).

Leisure Lodge Inc—West Memphis
111 E Jackson Ave, West Memphis, AR 72301
(501) 735-5174
Admin Dorothy Person.
Licensure Intermediate care. *Beds* 84. *Certified* Medicaid.
Owner Proprietary corp (Beverly Enterprises).

West Siloam Springs

Quail Ridge Living Center
Stateline Rd & Jefferson, West Siloam Springs, AR 72761
(918) 422-5138
Admin John S Carlile.
Medical Dir Glenda Copeland.

Licensure Intermediate care; Alzheimer's care.
Beds ICF 100. *Certified* Medicaid;
Medicare.
Owner Proprietary corp.
Admissions Requirements Medical
examination; Physician's request.
Staff Physicians 1 (ft); RNs 1 (pt); LPNs 5
(ft); Nurses' aides 25 (ft), 4 (pt); Physical
therapists 1 (ft); Recreational therapists 1
(ft); Activities coordinators 1 (ft); Dietitians
1 (ft), 1 (pt).
Languages Cherokee.
Facilities Dining room; Activities room;
Crafts room; Laundry room; Barber/Beauty
shop.
Activities Arts & crafts; Cards; Games;
Reading groups; Prayer groups; Movies;
Shopping trips; Dances/Social/Cultural
gatherings.

Wilmot

Wilmot Nursing Home
PO Box 37, Wilmot, AR 71676-0037
(501) 473-5505
Admin Vealetta Kellebrew.
Licensure Intermediate care. *Beds* 32.
Certified Medicaid.

Wynne

Crestpark of Wynne Skilled Nursing Facility
PO Box 1127, Arkansas & Rowena Sts,
Wynne, AR 72396
(501) 238-7941
Admin Charlotte Baskins. *Dir of Nursing*
Connie Jones. *Medical Dir* Kenneth Beaton
MD.
Licensure Skilled care. *Beds* SNF 137. *Private
Pay Patients* 25%. *Certified* Medicaid.
Owner Proprietary corp (CAP Care of
Arkansas).
Admissions Requirements Medical
examination; Physician's request.
Staff RNs 2 (ft); LPNs 9 (ft); Nurses' aides 40
(ft); Activities coordinators 1 (ft); Dietitians
1 (ft).
Facilities Dining room; Activities room;
Chapel; Crafts room; Laundry room; Barber/
Beauty shop; Library.
Activities Arts & crafts; Cards; Games;
Reading groups; Prayer groups; Movies;
Shopping trips; Dances/Social/Cultural
gatherings; Pet therapy.

Village Creek Manor Inc
PO Box 367, Wynne, AR 72396
(501) 238-2378
Admin Nancy Johnson.
Beds 100.
Owner Proprietary corp (Village Creek Manor
Inc).

Yellville

Marion County Nursing Home
Box 309, Yellville, AR 72687
(501) 449-4201
Admin F Gaynell Case. *Dir of Nursing* Anna
Davenport. *Medical Dir* Dr Robert Ahrens.
Licensure Intermediate care. *Beds* ICF 105.
Private Pay Patients 32%. *Certified*
Medicaid.
Owner Publicly owned.
Admissions Requirements Physician's request.
Staff RNs 2 (ft); LPNs 10 (ft), 1 (pt); Nurses'
aides 21 (ft), 32 (pt).
Facilities Dining room; Activities room;
Laundry room; Barber/Beauty shop.

CALIFORNIA

Alameda

Hillhaven Alameda
516 Willow St, Alameda, CA 94501
(415) 521-5600
Dir of Nursing Marie Wilson RN.
Licensure Skilled care; Alzheimer's care. *Beds*
SNF 180. *Certified* Medicare; Medi-Cal.
Owner Proprietary corp (Hillhaven Inc).
Admissions Requirements Medical
examination; Physician's request.
Staff Physicians 1 (pt); RNs 18 (ft); LPNs 17
(ft); Nurses' aides 105 (ft); Physical
therapists 2 (ft); Recreational therapists 1
(ft); Occupational therapists 1 (ft); Speech
therapists 1 (ft); Activities coordinators 1
(ft); Dietitians 1 (ft); Podiatrists 1 (pt);
Dentists 1 (pt).
Languages Spanish, Japanese.
Facilities Dining room; Physical therapy
room; Activities room; Crafts room; Laundry
room; Barber/Beauty shop.
Activities Arts & crafts; Cards; Games;
Reading groups; Prayer groups; Movies;
Shopping trips; Dances/Social/Cultural
gatherings; Therapeutic recreation.

Marina Convalescent Center
3201 Fernside Blvd, Alameda, CA 94501
(415) 523-2363
Licensure Skilled care. *Beds* SNF 33. *Certified*
Medicare; Medi-Cal.
Owner Privately owned.

Prather Methodist Memorial Home
508 Westline Dr, Alameda, CA 94501
(415) 521-5765
Admin Dudley Thompson. *Dir of Nursing*
Sally Erny RN. *Medical Dir* Herbert Lints
MD.
Licensure Skilled care. *Beds* SNF 141. *Private
Pay Patients* 45%. *Certified* Medicare; Medi-
Cal.
Owner Nonprofit corp (California-Nevada
Methodist Homes).
Admissions Requirements Medical
examination.
Staff RNs 7 (ft), 8 (pt); LPNs 7 (ft), 2 (pt);
Nurses' aides 45 (ft), 4 (pt); Physical
therapists 2 (pt); Occupational therapists 1
(pt); Speech therapists 1 (pt); Activities
coordinators 2 (ft); Dietitians 1 (pt).
Affiliation United Methodist.
Facilities Dining room; Physical therapy
room; Activities room; Barber/Beauty shop.
Activities Arts & crafts; Cards; Games;
Reading groups; Prayer groups; Movies; Pet
therapy.

South Shore Convalescent Hospital
625 Willow St, Alameda, CA 94501
(415) 523-3772
Medical Dir Lester Johnson MD.
Licensure Skilled care. *Beds* SNF 26. *Certified*
Medicare; Medi-Cal.
Owner Proprietary corp.
Admissions Requirements Physician's request.

Staff RNs 1 (ft), 1 (pt); LPNs 4 (ft), 3 (pt);
Nurses' aides 14 (ft), 6 (pt); Recreational
therapists 1 (ft); Activities coordinators 1
(ft); Dietitians 1 (ft).
Facilities Dining room; Activities room;
Crafts room; Laundry room.
Activities Arts & crafts; Cards; Games;
Reading groups; Prayer groups; Movies.

Waters Edge
2401 Blanding Ave, Alameda, CA 94501
(415) 522-1084
Licensure Skilled care; Intermediate care. *Beds*
Swing beds SNF/ICF 120. *Certified* Medi-
Cal.
Owner Proprietary corp.

Alhambra

Alhambra Convalescent Home
415 S Garfield Ave, Alhambra, CA 91801
(818) 282-3151
Admin Conchita J Gasendo RN. *Dir of
Nursing* Amelia Armada RN. *Medical Dir*
Dr Julitta Phillips.
Licensure Skilled care. *Beds* SNF 97. *Certified*
Medicare; Medi-Cal.
Owner Proprietary corp (Casner
Consolidated).
Admissions Requirements Medical
examination; Physician's request.
Staff RNs 2 (ft), 2 (pt); LPNs 7 (ft), 6 (pt);
Nurses' aides 32 (ft), 5 (pt); Physical
therapists 1 (pt); Recreational therapists 1
(pt); Occupational therapists 1 (pt); Speech
therapists 1 (pt); Activities coordinators 1
(ft); Dietitians 1 (pt); Ophthalmologists 1
(pt); Podiatrists 1 (pt); Audiologists 1 (pt).
Languages Italian, German.
Facilities Dining room; Activities room;
Crafts room; Laundry room; Barber/Beauty
shop; Library; Patio; Family room; Skylights.
Activities Arts & crafts; Cards; Games;
Reading groups; Prayer groups; Movies;
Shopping trips; Dances/Social/Cultural
gatherings; Intergenerational programs; Pet
therapy; Picnics; Family council; Resident
council; Church services; Men's special
groups; Special holidays; Show & tell;
Cooking; Grooming session; Senior
olympics; Nature trips; Reminiscence
groups; Sensory awareness.

Brykirk Extended Care Hospital
2339 W Valley Blvd, Alhambra, CA 91803
(818) 289-7809
Admin Sheryl L Brykman.
Licensure Skilled care. *Beds* SNF 43. *Certified*
Medicare; Medi-Cal.
Owner Proprietary corp.

California P E O Home
700 N Stoneman Ave, Alhambra, CA 91801
(818) 300-0400
Admin Mary Dow.
Licensure Skilled care; Intermediate care. *Beds*
SNF 42; ICF 2. *Certified* Medi-Cal.
Owner Nonprofit corp.

**Home for the Aged of the Protestant Episcopal
Church**
1428 S Marengo Ave, Alhambra, CA 91803
(818) 576-1032
Admin George W Cummings. *Dir of Nursing*
John Fraklin. *Medical Dir* Russell Simpson
MD; Linda Price MD.
Licensure Skilled care; Intermediate care;
Retirement. *Beds* SNF 99; ICF 99. *Certified*
Medicare; Medi-Cal.
Owner Nonprofit corp.
Admissions Requirements Minimum age 62.
Staff Physicians 1 (ft), 3 (pt); RNs 18 (ft);
LPNs 6 (ft); Nurses' aides 64 (ft).
Languages Spanish, Chinese.
Affiliation Episcopal.
Facilities Dining room; Physical therapy
room; Activities room; Chapel; Crafts room;
Laundry room; Barber/Beauty shop; Library.
Activities Arts & crafts; Cards; Games;
Reading groups; Prayer groups; Movies;
Shopping trips; Dances/Social/Cultural
gatherings.

Lutheran Health Facility
2021 Carlos St, Alhambra, CA 91803
(818) 289-6211
Admin Thomas K Pembleton Jr.
Licensure Skilled care. *Beds* SNF 50. *Certified*
Medicare; Medi-Cal.
Owner Nonprofit corp (California Lutheran
Homes Inc).
Affiliation Lutheran.

**Sam B West Health Care Center of Atherton
Baptist Home**
214 S Atlantic, Alhambra, CA 91801
(818) 289-4178
Admin Leeroy Peterson.
Licensure Skilled care; Intermediate care. *Beds*
SNF 87; ICF 26. *Certified* Medicare; Medi-
Cal.
Owner Proprietary corp.

Alpine

Alpine Convalescent Center
2120 Alpine Blvd, Alpine, CA 92001
(619) 445-2644
Admin Ruby N Doyle.
Licensure Intermediate care for mentally
retarded. *Beds* ICF/MR 99. *Certified* Medi-
Cal.
Owner Privately owned.

Alta Loma

Alta Loma Convalescent Hospital
9333 La Mesa Dr, Alta Loma, CA 91701
(714) 987-2501
Admin Emil W Lenkey.
Licensure Skilled care. *Beds* SNF 59. *Certified*
Medicare; Medi-Cal.
Owner Privately owned.

Altadena

Scripps Home
2212 N El Molino, Altadena, CA 91001
(213) 798-0934
Admin James W Graunke.
Medical Dir Dr Carol Thrun.
Licensure Skilled care; Intermediate care. *Beds* SNF 29; ICF 20. *Certified* Medi-Cal.
Owner Nonprofit corp.
Admissions Requirements Minimum age 70; Medical examination.
Staff Physicians 1 (pt); RNs 5 (ft), 5 (pt); Nurses' aides 14 (ft), 14 (pt); Physical therapists 2 (pt); Activities coordinators 1 (ft); Podiatrists 2 (pt).
Facilities Dining room; Physical therapy room; Activities room; Laundry room; Barber/Beauty shop; Library.
Activities Arts & crafts; Games; Prayer groups; Movies; Shopping trips; Dances/Social/ Cultural gatherings; Current events, poetry, & drama groups.

Alturas

Care West—Warner Mountain Nursing Center
225 McDowell Ave, Alturas, CA 96101
(916) 233-3416
Admin Robert King.
Licensure Skilled care. *Beds* SNF 59. *Certified* Medicare; Medi-Cal.
Owner Proprietary corp (Care Enterprises).

Anaheim

Anaheim Convalescent Center
3067 Orange Ave, Anaheim, CA 92804
(714) 827-2440
Admin C Linda Stevens.
Medical Dir Franklin Hanauer MD.
Licensure Skilled care. *Beds* 83. *Certified* Medicare; Medi-Cal.
Owner Proprietary corp.
Staff RNs 2 (ft); LPNs 6 (ft), 4 (pt); Nurses' aides 20 (ft), 20 (pt); Activities coordinators 1 (ft).
Facilities Dining room; Physical therapy room; Activities room; Crafts room; Laundry room; Barber/Beauty shop.
Activities Arts & crafts; Cards; Games; Reading groups; Prayer groups; Movies; Dances/Social/Cultural gatherings.

Anaheim Terrace Care Center
141 S Knott Ave, Anaheim, CA 92804
(714) 821-7310
Admin Christine Davis. *Dir of Nursing* Diane Edwards RN. *Medical Dir* Stanley Friedman MD.
Licensure Skilled care. *Beds* SNF 99. *Certified* Medicare; Medi-Cal.
Owner Proprietary corp.
Facilities Dining room; Physical therapy room; Activities room; Laundry room; Barber/Beauty shop; Living room.
Activities Arts & crafts; Cards; Games; Reading groups; Prayer groups; Movies; Shopping trips; Dances/Social/Cultural gatherings.

Buena Vista Care Center
1440 S Euclid St, Anaheim, CA 92802
(714) 377-2462
Admin Ferri F Kidane. *Dir of Nursing* Anne McLaughlin. *Medical Dir* Rakish Bhola MD.
Licensure Skilled care; Residential care; Alzheimer's care. *Beds* SNF 99; Residential care 15. *Private Pay Patients* 90%. *Certified* Medicaid; Medicare; Medi-Cal.
Owner Proprietary corp (Hillhaven Corp).
Staff RNs 5 (ft); LPNs 11 (ft); Nurses' aides 48 (ft); Physical therapists 1 (pt); Recreational therapists 1 (ft); Occupational therapists 1 (pt); Speech therapists 1 (pt);
Activities coordinators 2 (ft); Dietitians 1 (pt); Ophthalmologists 1 (pt); Podiatrists 1 (pt); Audiologists 1 (pt).
Languages Spanish, Tagalog.
Facilities Dining room; Physical therapy room; Activities room; Laundry room; Barber/Beauty shop; 26-bed secured Alzheimer's unit; Outdoor patio.
Activities Arts & crafts; Cards; Games; Prayer groups; Movies; Shopping trips; Dances/ Social/Cultural gatherings; Intergenerational programs; Pet therapy.

Casa Grande Intermediate Care Facility
3615 W Ball Rd, Anaheim, CA 92804
(714) 826-4400
Admin Mary Bennett.
Medical Dir John Hayes.
Licensure Intermediate care for mentally retarded. *Beds* ICF/MR 91. *Certified* Medi-Cal.
Owner Proprietary corp (Care Enterprises).
Admissions Requirements Minimum age 18.
Staff Physicians 4 (pt); RNs 1 (ft), 2 (pt); LPNs 6 (ft), 5 (pt); Nurses' aides 50 (ft), 12 (pt); Physical therapists 1 (pt); Recreational therapists 1 (pt); Occupational therapists 1 (pt); Speech therapists 1 (pt); Activities coordinators 1 (ft); Dietitians 1 (pt); Ophthalmologists 1 (pt); Podiatrists 1 (pt); Dentists 1 (pt).
Facilities Dining room; Activities room; Crafts room.
Activities Arts & crafts; Cards; Games; Prayer groups; Movies; Shopping trips; Dances/ Social/Cultural gatherings.

Casa Pacifica
861 S Harbor Blvd, Anaheim, CA 92805
(714) 635-8131
Admin Betty Clester.
Medical Dir Sultan Shah MD.
Licensure Skilled care. *Beds* SNF 99. *Certified* Medicare; Medi-Cal.
Owner Proprietary corp.
Admissions Requirements Minimum age 55.
Staff Physicians 1 (pt); RNs 2 (ft), 2 (pt); LPNs 15 (ft); Nurses' aides 29 (ft), 5 (pt); Physical therapists 1 (pt); Occupational therapists 1 (pt); Speech therapists 1 (pt); Activities coordinators 1 (ft), 1 (pt); Dietitians 1 (pt); Ophthalmologists 1 (pt); Podiatrists 1 (pt); Dentists 1 (pt).
Languages Spanish, Korean, Tagalog, Hindi, German.
Facilities Dining room; Activities room; Laundry room; Barber/Beauty shop; Library.
Activities Arts & crafts; Cards; Games; Reading groups; Movies; Shopping trips; Dances/Social/Cultural gatherings.

Extended Care Hospital of Anaheim
501 S Beach Blvd, Anaheim, CA 92804
(714) 828-7730
Admin Marc Landry.
Licensure Skilled care; Intermediate care for mentally retarded. *Beds* SNF 198; ICF/MR 52. *Certified* Medicare; Medi-Cal.
Owner Privately owned.

Fountainbleau Nursing Centre
3415 W Ball Rd, Anaheim, CA 92804
(714) 826-8950
Admin Jaime Deutsch.
Licensure Skilled care. *Beds* SNF 154. *Certified* Medicare; Medi-Cal.
Owner Privately owned.

Grand Care Convalescent Hospital
2040 S Euclid, Anaheim, CA 92802
(714) 636-2800
Admin Robert M Moses.
Licensure Skilled care. *Beds* SNF 99. *Certified* Medicare; Medi-Cal.
Owner Privately owned.

Guidance Center Sanitarium
1135 Leisure Ct, Anaheim, CA 92801
(714) 772-1353

Admin William J Cloonan. *Dir of Nursing* Eunice Parker. *Medical Dir* H M Guirgis MD.
Licensure Skilled care; Intermediate care. *Beds* SNF 87; ICF 28. *Certified* Medi-Cal.
Owner Proprietary corp.
Admissions Requirements Minimum age 18; Medical examination.
Staff Physicians 6 (pt); RNs 8 (ft), 1 (pt); LPNs 7 (ft); Nurses' aides 41 (ft); Physical therapists 1 (pt); Reality therapists 1 (pt); Recreational therapists 3 (ft), 2 (pt); Occupational therapists 1 (pt); Speech therapists 1 (pt); Activities coordinators 1 (ft); Dietitians 1 (pt), 1 (pt); Ophthalmologists 1 (pt); Podiatrists 1 (pt); Audiologists 1 (pt).
Languages Spanish.
Facilities Dining room; Activities room; Crafts room; Laundry room; Barber/Beauty shop; Large patios and outdoor areas.
Activities Arts & crafts; Cards; Games; Reading groups; Prayer groups; Movies; Shopping trips; Dances/Social/Cultural gatherings; Intergenerational programs; Exercise; Music; Reality orientation; Behavior modification.

Hallmark Nursing Center—Anaheim
3435 W Ball Rd, Anaheim, CA 92804
(714) 827-5880
Admin Marianne J Schultz.
Licensure Skilled care. *Beds* SNF 115. *Certified* Medicare; Medi-Cal.
Owner Proprietary corp.

Hillhaven Convalescent Hospital
1440 S Euclid Ave, Anaheim, CA 92802
(714) 772-7480
Admin Anne Marie Bulter.
Medical Dir Seawright Anderson MD.
Licensure Skilled care. *Beds* SNF 65. *Certified* Medicare; Medi-Cal.
Owner Proprietary corp (Hillhaven Inc).
Admissions Requirements Medical examination; Physician's request.
Staff RNs 3 (pt); Nurses' aides 5 (ft), 20 (pt); Activities coordinators 1 (ft); Dietitians 1 (pt).
Facilities Dining room; Physical therapy room; Activities room; Laundry room; Barber/Beauty shop; Library.
Activities Arts & crafts; Cards; Games; Movies; Shopping trips; Dances/Social/ Cultural gatherings.

Lutheran Health Facility of Anaheim
891 S Walnut St, Anaheim, CA 92802
(714) 776-7150, 774-1234
Admin Marion L Hopkins.
Medical Dir Dr Stanley Kerkhoff.
Licensure Skilled care; Retirement. *Beds* SNF 33. *Certified* Medi-Cal.
Owner Nonprofit corp (California Lutheran Homes Inc).
Admissions Requirements Minimum age 65; Medical examination; Physician's request.
Staff Physicians 1 (pt); RNs 2 (ft), 1 (pt); LPNs 3 (ft), 3 (pt); Nurses' aides 12 (ft), 3 (pt); Physical therapists 1 (pt); Occupational therapists 1 (pt); Speech therapists 1 (pt); Activities coordinators 1 (pt); Dietitians 1 (pt).
Affiliation Lutheran.
Facilities Dining room.
Activities Arts & crafts; Games; Reading groups; Prayer groups; Movies; Limo trips; Walks.

Parkview Convalescent Hospital
1514 E Lincoln Ave, Anaheim, CA 92805
(714) 774-2222
Admin Richard B Christensen. *Dir of Nursing* Diana J Hughes. *Medical Dir* John Cowles MD.
Licensure Skilled care. *Beds* SNF 41. *Private Pay Patients* 50%. *Certified* Medicare; Medi-Cal.

Owner Privately owned.
Admissions Requirements Medical examination; Physician's request.
Staff RNs 2 (ft), 2 (pt); LPNs 2 (ft), 2 (pt); Nurses' aides 15 (ft), 8 (pt); Activities coordinators 1 (ft).
Languages Spanish.
Facilities Dining room; Activities room; Crafts room; Laundry room; Barber/Beauty shop; Library.
Activities Arts & crafts; Cards; Games; Reading groups; Prayer groups; Movies; Shopping trips; Dances/Social/Cultural gatherings; Intergenerational programs; Pet therapy.

Sun Mar Nursing Center
1720 W Orange Ave, Anaheim, CA 92804
(714) 776-1720
Admin Phyllis Debelak.
Licensure Skilled care. *Beds* SNF 69. *Certified* Medicare; Medi-Cal.
Owner Proprietary corp.

Anderson

Anderson Care Center
3300 Franklin St, Anderson, CA 96007
(916) 365-0025
Admin Robert W Roy.
Licensure Skilled care; Intermediate care. *Beds* SNF 85; ICF 58. *Certified* Medicare; Medi-Cal.
Owner Proprietary corp (Western Care Management Corp).

Hospitality House Nursing Home
1450 Happy Valley Rd, Anderson, CA 96007
(916) 241-2804
Admin Shirley J Jacobsen.
Licensure Skilled care. *Beds* 34. *Certified* Medi-Cal.
Admissions Requirements Minimum age Adult services; Physician's request.
Facilities Dining room; Activities room; Crafts room; Barber/Beauty shop.
Activities Arts & crafts; Cards; Games; Reading groups; Prayer groups; Movies; Shopping trips; Dances/Social/Cultural gatherings.

Angwin

Crestwood Geriatric Treatment Center
295 Pine Breeze Dr, Angwin, CA 94508
(707) 965-2461
Admin Patty Blum.
Licensure Skilled care. *Beds* SNF 59.
Owner Proprietary corp (Crestwood Hospitals Inc).

Antioch

Antioch Convalescent Hospital
1210 A St, Antioch, CA 94509
(415) 757-8787
Dir of Nursing Marita Pato. *Medical Dir* Raymond Stotler.
Licensure Skilled care. *Beds* SNF 99. *Certified* Medicare; Medi-Cal.
Owner Proprietary corp.
Admissions Requirements Physician's request.
Staff Physicians 1 (pt); RNs 1 (ft), 1 (pt); LPNs 7 (ft), 3 (pt); Nurses' aides 25 (ft), 15 (pt); Physical therapists 1 (pt); Occupational therapists 1 (pt); Speech therapists 1 (pt); Activities coordinators 1 (ft); Dietitians 1 (pt); Ophthalmologists 1 (pt).
Facilities Dining room; Physical therapy room; Activities room; Laundry room; Barber/Beauty shop.
Activities Arts & crafts; Cards; Games; Reading groups; Prayer groups; Movies; Shopping trips; Dances/Social/Cultural gatherings.

Cavallo Convalescent Hospital
1907 Cavallo Rd, Antioch, CA 94509
(415) 757-5442
Admin Rilda M Scarfo. *Dir of Nursing* Claire Keeney RN. *Medical Dir* Dileep Kumar MD.
Licensure Skilled care. *Beds* SNF 38. *Private Pay Patients* 45%. *Certified* Medicare; Medi-Cal.
Owner Privately owned.
Admissions Requirements Medical examination.
Staff Physicians 1 (pt); RNs 1 (ft), 3 (pt); LPNs 3 (ft), 3 (pt); Nurses' aides 12 (ft), 5 (pt); Physical therapists 1 (pt); Occupational therapists 1 (pt); Speech therapists 1 (pt); Activities coordinators 1 (ft); Dietitians 1 (pt); Ophthalmologists 1 (pt); Podiatrists 1 (pt).
Languages Spanish, Filipino.
Facilities Dining room; Activities room; Laundry room; Barber/Beauty shop.
Activities Arts & crafts; Cards; Games; Reading groups; Prayer groups; Movies; Shopping trips; Dances/Social/Cultural gatherings; Pet therapy; Barbecues; Resident council.

Lone Tree Convalescent Hospital
4001 Lone Tree Way, Antioch, CA 94509
(415) 754-0470
Medical Dir Abe Kaplan MD.
Licensure Skilled care. *Beds* SNF 99. *Certified* Medicare; Medi-Cal.
Owner Proprietary corp.
Staff Physicians 1 (pt); RNs 3 (ft), 1 (pt); LPNs 3 (ft), 6 (pt); Nurses' aides 24 (ft), 16 (pt); Physical therapists 1 (pt); Occupational therapists 1 (pt); Speech therapists 1 (pt); Activities coordinators 2 (pt); Dietitians 1 (pt); Podiatrists 1 (pt); Dentists 1 (pt).
Facilities Dining room; Physical therapy room; Activities room; Laundry room; Barber/Beauty shop.
Activities Arts & crafts; Cards; Games; Prayer groups; Movies; Shopping trips.

Arcadia

Arcadia Convalescent Hospital
1601 S Baldwin Ave, Arcadia, CA 91006
(818) 445-2170
Admin Orlando Clarizio. *Dir of Nursing* Mina Villegas RN. *Medical Dir* Dr Jack Baker.
Licensure Skilled care; Retirement; Alzheimer's care. *Beds* SNF 117. *Certified* Medicare; Medi-Cal.
Owner Proprietary corp.
Staff Physicians; RNs; Nurses' aides; Physical therapists; Recreational therapists; Occupational therapists; Speech therapists; Activities coordinators; Dietitians; Ophthalmologists; Podiatrists; Dentists; LVNs.
Facilities Dining room; Physical therapy room; Activities room; Crafts room; Laundry room; Barber/Beauty shop.
Activities Arts & crafts; Cards; Games; Reading groups; Prayer groups; Movies; Shopping trips; Dances/Social/Cultural gatherings.

Huntington Drive Skilled Nursing Center
400 W Huntington Dr, Arcadia, CA 91007
(818) 445-2421, 574-8302 FAX
Admin Scott Carlson. *Dir of Nursing* Corinne Bergmann RN MS. *Medical Dir* Clifford Winchell MD.
Licensure Skilled care. *Beds* SNF 99. *Private Pay Patients* 70%. *Certified* Medicare.
Owner Proprietary corp (Beverly Enterprises).
Admissions Requirements Medical examination; Physician's request.
Staff Physicians 40 (pt); RNs 4 (ft), 3 (pt); LPNs 10 (ft), 6 (pt); Nurses' aides 36 (ft), 8 (pt); Physical therapists 1 (ft), 1 (pt); Recreational therapists 1 (pt); Occupational

therapists 1 (ft), 1 (pt); Speech therapists 2 (ft); Activities coordinators 2 (ft); Dietitians 1 (pt).
Languages Spanish.
Facilities Dining room; Physical therapy room; Activities room; Crafts room; Laundry room; Barber/Beauty shop; Aviary.
Activities Arts & crafts; Cards; Games; Reading groups; Prayer groups; Movies; Shopping trips; Dances/Social/Cultural gatherings; Intergenerational programs; Pet therapy; Field trips in facility van.

Arlington

Alta Vista Healthcare
9020 Garfield Ave, Arlington, CA 92503
(714) 688-8200
Admin Franklin A Ross.
Licensure Skilled care. *Beds* SNF 99. *Certified* Medicare; Medi-Cal.
Owner Proprietary corp (Hillhaven Corp).

Arroyo Grande

South County Convalescent Center
1212 Farroll Ave, Arroyo Grande, CA 93420
(805) 489-8137
Admin Ron Dodgen.
Medical Dir Dale Rodseth.
Licensure Skilled care. *Beds* SNF 99. *Certified* Medi-Cal.
Owner Privately owned.
Staff RNs; LPNs; Nurses' aides; Activities coordinators; Dietitians.
Facilities Dining room; Activities room; Chapel; Crafts room; Laundry room; Barber/Beauty shop.
Activities Arts & crafts; Cards; Games; Reading groups; Prayer groups; Movies; Dances/Social/Cultural gatherings.

Artesia

Artesia Christian Home Inc
11614 E 183rd St, Artesia, CA 90701
(213) 865-5218
Admin Elroy Vander Ley.
Medical Dir Janet Doppenburg.
Licensure Skilled care; Retirement. *Beds* SNF 59. *Certified* Medicare; Medi-Cal.
Owner Nonprofit corp.
Admissions Requirements Minimum age 65; Medical examination.
Staff RNs 1 (ft), 4 (pt); LPNs 8 (ft), 2 (pt); Nurses' aides 19 (ft), 5 (pt); Physical therapists 1 (pt); Speech therapists 1 (pt); Activities coordinators 2 (pt); Dietitians 1 (pt).
Affiliation Christian Reformed.
Facilities Dining room; Activities room; Crafts room; Laundry room; Barber/Beauty shop.
Activities Arts & crafts; Cards; Games; Reading groups; Prayer groups; Movies; Shopping trips; Dances/Social/Cultural gatherings; Church program & outings to church luncheons; Bible classes.

Twin Palms Care Center
11900 E Artesia Blvd, Artesia, CA 90701
(213) 865-0271
Admin Catherine M Eichberg. *Dir of Nursing* Norma Navarro. *Medical Dir* James M Hilton MD.
Licensure Skilled care; Alzheimer's care. *Beds* SNF 296. *Private Pay Patients* 24%. *Certified* Medi-Cal.
Owner Proprietary corp (Meritcare).
Admissions Requirements Minimum age 45.
Staff RNs 10 (ft); LPNs 22 (ft); Nurses' aides 122 (ft); Activities coordinators 2 (ft).
Facilities Dining room; Activities room; Crafts room; Laundry room; Barber/Beauty shop; Large grounds with trees, flowers, picnic tables.

Activities Arts & crafts; Games; Reading
groups; Prayer groups; Movies; Shopping
trips; Dances/Social/Cultural gatherings;
Cooking classes.

Arvin

Pacific Regency—Arvin
323 Campus Dr, Arvin, CA 93203
(805) 854-4475
Admin Chris Sturgeon.
Licensure Skilled care. *Beds* SNF 81. *Certified*
Medicare; Medi-Cal.

Atascadero

Country Care Convalescent Hospital
14900 El Camino Real, Atascadero, CA 93422
(805) 466-0282
Admin John M Arrambide.
Licensure Skilled care. *Beds* SNF 40. *Certified*
Medi-Cal.
Owner Nonprofit corp.

Danish Convalescent Hospital
PO Box 1749, Atascadero, CA 93423
(805) 466-9254
Admin Bryan Roldan.
Licensure Skilled care. *Beds* SNF 64. *Certified*
Medi-Cal.
Owner Proprietary corp.

Atwater

Meadows Convalescent Hospital
1685 Shaffer Rd, Atwater, CA 95301
(209) 357-3420
Admin Avanell Miller.
Licensure Skilled care. *Beds* SNF 99. *Certified*
Medicare; Medi-Cal.
Owner Privately owned.

Auberry

Wish-I-Ah Care Center Inc
35680 N Wish-I-Ah Rd, Auberry, CA 93602
(209) 855-2211
Admin Janice M Harshman.
Licensure Skilled care. *Beds* SNF 135.
Certified Medi-Cal.
Owner Proprietary corp.

Auburn

Auburn Gardens Convalescent Hospital
260 Racetrack St, Auburn, CA 95603
(916) 885-7051
Admin Ruth Stevenson.
Licensure Skilled care. *Beds* SNF 84. *Certified*
Medicare; Medi-Cal.
Owner Proprietary corp.

Auburn Ravine Terrace
750 Auburn Ravine Terrace, Auburn, CA
95603
(916) 823-6131
Admin David L Ferguson.
Licensure Skilled care. *Beds* SNF 57. *Certified*
Medi-Cal.
Owner Nonprofit corp.

Foothill Oaks Care Center
3400 Bell Rd, Auburn, CA 95603
(916) 888-6257
Admin Leona Costello.
Licensure Skilled care. *Beds* SNF 99. *Certified*
Medicare; Medi-Cal.
Owner Proprietary corp.

Hilltop Manor Convalescent Hospital No 2
12225 Shale Ridge Ln, Auburn, CA 95603
(916) 885-7511
Admin David Hutchinson.
Licensure Skilled care. *Beds* SNF 230.
Certified Medicare; Medi-Cal.
Owner Proprietary corp.

Bakersfield

Bakersfield Convalescent Hospital
730 34th St, Bakersfield, CA 93301
(805) 327-7687
Admin Patricia Cappello. *Dir of Nursing* Ann
Gregory. *Medical Dir* T Larwood MD.
Licensure Skilled care; Alzheimer's care. *Beds*
SNF 150. *Certified* Medicare; Medi-Cal.
Owner Proprietary corp.
Admissions Requirements Minimum age 18;
Medical examination; Physician's request.
Staff RNs 8 (ft); LPNs 17 (ft), 3 (pt); Nurses'
aides 33 (ft), 7 (pt); Physical therapists 2
(pt); Occupational therapists 1 (pt); Speech
therapists 1 (pt); Activities coordinators 1
(ft); Dietitians 1 (pt); Ophthalmologists 1
(pt).
Languages Spanish.
Facilities Dining room; Physical therapy
room; Activities room; Crafts room; Laundry
room; Barber/Beauty shop; Library; Private
suites.
Activities Arts & crafts; Cards; Games;
Reading groups; Prayer groups; Movies;
Shopping trips; Dances/Social/Cultural
gatherings; Outings to theater & places of
interest.

Beverly Manor Convalescent Hospital
3601 San Dimas St, Bakersfield, CA 93301
(805) 323-2894
Admin Marilyn Fowler.
Licensure Skilled care. *Beds* SNF 104.
Certified Medicare; Medi-Cal.
Owner Proprietary corp (Beverly Enterprises).

Californian Care Center
2211 Mount Vernon Ave, Bakersfield, CA
93306
(805) 872-2121
Admin James Williams.
Licensure Skilled care. *Beds* SNF 160. *Private
Pay Patients* 40%. *Certified* Medicare; Medi-
Cal.
Owner Proprietary corp (Hillhaven Corp).
Admissions Requirements Minimum age 18;
Physician's request.
Facilities Dining room; Physical therapy
room; Activities room; Crafts room; Barber/
Beauty shop; Private dining room.
Activities Arts & crafts; Cards; Games;
Reading groups; Prayer groups; Movies;
Shopping trips; Dances/Social/Cultural
gatherings; Intergenerational programs; Pet
therapy.

Colonial Convalescent Hospital
1611 Height St, Bakersfield, CA 93305
(805) 872-0705
Admin Lisa M McCarty.
Licensure Skilled care. *Beds* SNF 120.
Certified Medicare; Medi-Cal.
Owner Proprietary corp (Care Enterprises).

Hilltop Convalescent Hospital
1601 Height St, Bakersfield, CA 93305
(805) 872-2324
Admin Betty Clester.
Licensure Skilled care. *Beds* SNF 117.
Certified Medicare; Medi-Cal.
Owner Proprietary corp (Care Enterprises).
Admissions Requirements Medical
examination; Physician's request.
Staff Physicians 1 (pt); RNs 5 (ft); LPNs 6
(ft); Nurses' aides 35 (ft), 3 (pt); Physical
therapists 1 (pt); Occupational therapists 1
(pt); Speech therapists 1 (pt); Activities
coordinators 2 (ft); Dietitians 2 (pt);
Ophthalmologists 1 (pt).
Languages Spanish.
Facilities Dining room; Physical therapy
room; Activities room; Crafts room; Laundry
room; Barber/Beauty shop; Recreation areas
outside.
Activities Arts & crafts; Cards; Games; Prayer
groups; Movies; Shopping trips; Dances/
Social/Cultural gatherings.

Manor Lodge Convalescent Hospital
2607 Mount Vernon Ave, Bakersfield, CA
93306
(805) 871-8733
Admin Lynn Gann.
Medical Dir Dr Frank Chang.
Licensure Skilled care; Retirement. *Beds* SNF
37. *Certified* Medi-Cal.
Owner Privately owned.
Admissions Requirements Medical
examination; Physician's request.
Staff RNs 1 (ft), 1 (pt); Nurses' aides 14 (ft), 3
(pt); Activities coordinators 1 (ft).
Facilities Dining room; Activities room;
Laundry room; Barber/Beauty shop.
Activities Arts & crafts; Games; Reading
groups; Prayer groups; Movies; Shopping
trips.

Mercy Hospital
2215 Truxtun Ave, Bakersfield, CA 93301
(805) 327-3371
Admin Janice Duffy.
Licensure Skilled care. *Certified* Medicare;
Medi-Cal.
Owner Proprietary corp.

Pacific Regency—Bakersfield
6212 Tudor Way, Bakersfield, CA 93306
(805) 871-3133, 871-2592 FAX
Admin Deana Shannon. *Dir of Nursing* Don
Roberson. *Medical Dir* T Bosonetto MD.
Licensure Skilled care; Alzheimer's care. *Beds*
SNF 99. *Private Pay Patients* 65-70%.
Certified Medicare; Medi-Cal.
Owner Privately owned.
Admissions Requirements Physician's request.
Staff Physicians 1 (pt); RNs 6 (ft), 1 (pt);
LPNs 6 (ft), 5 (pt); Nurses' aides 42 (ft), 5
(pt); Physical therapists 2 (pt); Occupational
therapists 1 (pt); Speech therapists 1 (pt);
Activities coordinators 2 (ft); Dietitians 1
(pt); Podiatrists 1 (pt).
Languages Spanish, Tagalog, German.
Facilities Dining room; Physical therapy
room; Activities room; Laundry room;
Barber/Beauty shop; Library.
Activities Arts & crafts; Cards; Games;
Reading groups; Prayer groups; Movies;
Shopping trips; Dances/Social/Cultural
gatherings; Intergenerational programs; Pet
therapy.

Parkview Julian Convalescent
1801 Julian Ave, Bakersfield, CA 93304
(805) 831-9150
Admin Frank L Denham.
Medical Dir Samuel Schreiber MD.
Licensure Skilled care. *Beds* SNF 99. *Certified*
Medicare; Medi-Cal.
Owner Proprietary corp.
Admissions Requirements Physician's request.
Staff RNs 2 (ft); LPNs 10 (ft); Nurses' aides
25 (ft).
Facilities Dining room; Physical therapy
room; Activities room; Barber/Beauty shop.
Activities Arts & crafts; Cards; Games;
Reading groups; Movies; Dances/Social/
Cultural gatherings; Outside entertainment.

Parkview Real Convalescent Hospital
329 N Real Rd, Bakersfield, CA 93309
(805) 327-7107
Admin Lynn Gann. *Dir of Nursing* Janice
Martin. *Medical Dir* Dr Keni.
Licensure Skilled care. *Beds* SNF 184.
Certified Medicare; Medi-Cal.
Owner Proprietary corp.
Admissions Requirements Physician's request.
Staff RNs; LPNs; Nurses' aides; Physical
therapists; Recreational therapists; Speech
therapists; Activities coordinators; Dietitians;
Podiatrists.
Facilities Dining room; Physical therapy
room; Activities room; Barber/Beauty shop.
Activities Arts & crafts; Cards; Games;
Reading groups; Prayer groups; Movies;
Shopping trips; Dances/Social/Cultural

gatherings; Intergenerational programs; Pet therapy; Exercise; Discussion groups; Outings; Adult education classes.

Riverside Cottage Rest Home
1131 S "H" St, Bakersfield, CA 93304
(805) 831-9126
Admin Roberta Mills.
Licensure Intermediate care. *Beds* 15. *Certified* Medi-Cal.
Owner Proprietary corp.

Rosewood Health Facility
1401 New Stine Rd, Bakersfield, CA 93309
(805) 834-0620
Admin Ted Ahlem; Ted Burgess, Asst. *Dir of Nursing* Elaine Allen RN. *Medical Dir* H C Freedman MD.
Licensure Skilled care; Retirement living; Alzheimer's care. *Beds* SNF 79; Retirement living 200. *Private Pay Patients* 80%. *Certified* Medicaid; Medicare; Medi-Cal.
Owner Nonprofit corp (American Baptist Homes of the West).
Admissions Requirements Minimum age 62; Medical examination; Physician's request.
Staff RNs; LPNs; Nurses' aides; Physical therapists; Recreational therapists; Occupational therapists; Speech therapists; Activities coordinators; Dietitians; Ophthalmologists; Podiatrists.
Languages Sign.
Affiliation Baptist.
Facilities Dining room; Physical therapy room; Activities room; Chapel; Crafts room; Laundry room; Barber/Beauty shop; Library; Covered patio; Rose gardens.
Activities Arts & crafts; Cards; Games; Reading groups; Prayer groups; Movies; Shopping trips; Dances/Social/Cultural gatherings; Intergenerational programs; Pet therapy; Dinner outings.

Valley Convalescent Hospital
1205 8th St, Bakersfield, CA 93304
(805) 324-9468
Admin Ronald D O'Haver.
Medical Dir Samuel Schrieber.
Licensure Skilled care. *Beds* SNF 87. *Certified* Medicare; Medi-Cal.
Owner Privately owned.
Staff Physicians 6 (ft); RNs 1 (ft), 2 (pt); Nurses' aides 27 (ft), 8 (pt); Physical therapists 1 (pt); Recreational therapists 1 (pt); Occupational therapists 1 (pt); Speech therapists 1 (pt); Activities coordinators 1 (ft); Dietitians 1 (ft); Ophthalmologists 1 (pt); Podiatrists 1 (pt); Audiologists 1 (pt); Dentists 1 (pt).
Facilities Dining room; Physical therapy room; Activities room; Crafts room; Laundry room; Barber/Beauty shop; Library.
Activities Arts & crafts; Cards; Games; Reading groups; Prayer groups; Movies; Shopping trips; Dances/Social/Cultural gatherings.

Baldwin Park

Coast Care Convalescent Center
14518 E Los Angeles, Baldwin Park, CA 91706
(818) 337-7229
Admin Ann M Whitefoot.
Licensure Skilled care. *Beds* SNF 48. *Certified* Medicare; Medi-Cal.
Owner Proprietary corp (Coast Care Inc).

Golden State Habilitation Convalescent Center
1758 Big Dalton Ave, Baldwin Park, CA 91706
(818) 962-3274
Licensure Skilled care; Intermediate care for mentally retarded. *Beds* 155. *Certified* Medi-Cal.
Owner Proprietary corp (Care Enterprises).

Staff Physicians 1 (pt); RNs 8 (ft); LPNs 12 (ft); Nurses' aides 40 (ft); Physical therapists 1 (pt); Occupational therapists 1 (pt); Speech therapists 1 (pt); Activities coordinators 1 (ft); Dietitians 1 (pt); Ophthalmologists 1 (pt); Podiatrists 1 (pt); Audiologists 1 (pt); Dentists 1 (pt).
Facilities Dining room; Physical therapy room; Activities room; Laundry room; Barber/Beauty shop.
Activities Arts & crafts; Cards; Games; Movies; Shopping trips; Dances/Social/Cultural gatherings.

Rose Convalescent Hospital
3541 Puente Ave, Baldwin Park, CA 91706
(818) 962-1043, 337-2142 FAX
Admin Clair Meske. *Dir of Nursing* Vera Allen. *Medical Dir* Dr Febe Adincula.
Licensure Skilled care. *Beds* SNF 45. *Private Pay Patients* 15%. *Certified* Medicaid; Medicare; Medi-Cal.
Owner Proprietary corp (Regency Health Services).
Admissions Requirements Physician's request.
Staff RNs 1 (ft), 2 (pt); LPNs 3 (ft), 3 (pt); Nurses' aides 12 (ft), 5 (pt); Physical therapists 1 (pt); Occupational therapists 1 (pt); Speech therapists 1 (pt); Activities coordinators 1 (pt); Dietitians 1 (pt).
Languages Spanish.
Facilities Dining room; Physical therapy room; Activities room; Laundry room.
Activities Arts & crafts; Cards; Games; Reading groups; Prayer groups; Movies; Dances/Social/Cultural gatherings; Intergenerational programs; Pet therapy.

Sierra View Care Center
14318 Ohio St, Baldwin Park, CA 91706
(818) 960-1971
Admin A Rzepnick.
Medical Dir Ron Atturi.
Licensure Skilled care. *Beds* SNF 98. *Certified* Medicare; Medi-Cal.
Owner Proprietary corp.
Admissions Requirements Physician's request.
Staff Physicians 4 (pt); RNs 1 (ft); LPNs 7 (ft); Nurses' aides 23 (ft); Physical therapists 1 (pt); Occupational therapists 1 (pt); Speech therapists 1 (pt); Activities coordinators 1 (ft); Dietitians 1 (ft); Ophthalmologists 1 (pt); Podiatrists 1 (pt); Audiologists 1 (pt); Dentists 1 (pt).
Facilities Dining room; Physical therapy room; Activities room; Chapel; Crafts room; Laundry room; Barber/Beauty shop; Library.
Activities Arts & crafts; Cards; Games; Reading groups; Prayer groups; Movies; Shopping trips; Adult education.

Banning

Care West—Banning Nursing Center
3476 W Wilson St, Banning, CA 92220
(714) 849-4723
Admin Larry Fulbright.
Medical Dir Ronald Rothe MD.
Licensure Skilled care. *Beds* SNF 64. *Certified* Medicare; Medi-Cal.
Owner Proprietary corp (Care Enterprises).
Staff RNs 1 (ft), 2 (pt); LPNs 4 (ft), 4 (pt); Nurses' aides 14 (ft), 12 (pt); Activities coordinators 1 (ft); Dietitians 1 (pt).
Facilities Dining room; Physical therapy room; Activities room; Laundry room; Barber/Beauty shop.
Activities Arts & crafts; Cards; Games; Reading groups; Prayer groups; Movies.

Careage of Banning
5800 W Wilson St, Banning, CA 92220
(714) 845-1600
Admin Rena K Papp.
Licensure Skilled care. *Beds* SNF 120. *Certified* Medicare; Medi-Cal.
Owner Proprietary corp.

Barstow

Rimrock Villa Convalescent Hospital
27555 Rimrock Rd, Barstow, CA 92311
(619) 252-2515
Admin Rosalee Mitchell.
Licensure Skilled care. *Beds* SNF 59. *Certified* Medicare; Medi-Cal.
Owner Privately owned.

Beaumont

Beaumont Convalescent Hospital
1441 N Michigan Ave, Beaumont, CA 92223
(714) 845-1166
Admin Barbara Bogner.
Medical Dir Robert Payton MD.
Licensure Skilled care. *Beds* SNF 87. *Certified* Medicare; Medi-Cal.
Owner Proprietary corp.
Admissions Requirements Medical examination; Physician's request.
Staff RNs 2 (ft), 1 (pt); LPNs 9 (ft), 2 (pt); Nurses' aides 36 (ft), 3 (pt); Physical therapists 1 (ft); Occupational therapists 1 (pt); Speech therapists 1 (pt); Activities coordinators 1 (ft); Dietitians 1 (pt); Dentists 1 (pt).
Facilities Dining room; Physical therapy room; Activities room; Laundry room; Barber/Beauty shop.
Activities Arts & crafts; Cards; Games; Prayer groups; Movies; Shopping trips.

Valley View
40901 E 8th, Beaumont, CA 92223
(714) 845-3125
Admin Ms Terry Parker.
Medical Dir Dr William Beard.
Licensure Intermediate care for mentally retarded. *Beds* ICF/MR 56. *Certified* Medi-Cal.
Owner Proprietary corp (Care Enterprises).
Admissions Requirements Medical examination; Physician's request.
Staff RNs; LPNs; Nurses' aides; Physical therapists 1 (pt); Recreational therapists 1 (pt); Occupational therapists 1 (pt); Speech therapists 1 (pt); Dietitians 1 (pt).
Languages Spanish.
Facilities Dining room; Activities room; Laundry room.
Activities Arts & crafts; Cards; Games; Movies; Shopping trips.

Bell

Bell Convalescent Hospital
4900 E Florence Ave, Bell, CA 90201
(213) 560-2045
Admin Irene G Mulsoff.
Licensure Skilled care. *Beds* SNF 99. *Certified* Medicare; Medi-Cal.
Owner Proprietary corp.

Bell Gardens

Bell Gardens Convalescent Center
5648 Gotham St, Bell Gardens, CA 90201
(213) 927-2641, 771-4448
Admin Rachel Slomovic. *Dir of Nursing* William Slomovic RN.
Licensure Skilled care. *Beds* SNF 135. *Certified* Medicare; Medi-Cal.
Owner Proprietary corp.
Admissions Requirements Minimum age 18; Medical examination; Physician's request.
Staff Physicians; RNs; Nurses' aides; Physical therapists; Recreational therapists; Occupational therapists; Speech therapists; Activities coordinators; Dietitians; Ophthalmologists; Podiatrists; Dentists; LVNs.
Languages Spanish.

Facilities Dining room; Physical therapy room; Activities room; Crafts room; Laundry room; Barber/Beauty shop.
Activities Arts & crafts; Cards; Games; Reading groups; Prayer groups; Movies; Shopping trips; Dances/Social/Cultural gatherings; Outings.

Del Rio Convalescent Center
7002 E Gage Ave, Bell Gardens, CA 90201
(213) 773-7881
Admin Mahomood N Moledina. *Dir of Nursing* Elizabeth Stearns RN. *Medical Dir* Michael Platt MD.
Licensure Skilled care; Alzheimer's care. *Beds* SNF 99. *Certified* Medi-Cal; VA.
Owner Proprietary corp (Del Rio Healthcare Inc).
Admissions Requirements Minimum age 40; Physician's request.
Staff RNs 1 (ft), 1 (pt); LPNs 7 (ft), 1 (pt); Nurses' aides 36 (ft), 5 (pt); Activities coordinators 2 (ft); Dietitians 1 (pt).
Languages Spanish.
Facilities Dining room; Physical therapy room; Activities room; Crafts room; Laundry room; Barber/Beauty shop; Library; 4 1/2 acres fenced grounds; Canteen.
Activities Arts & crafts; Cards; Games; Prayer groups; Movies; Shopping trips; Dances/Social/Cultural gatherings; Outings.

Del Rio Sanitarium
7004 E Gage Ave, Bell Gardens, CA 90201
(213) 773-7881
Admin Steven D Highland. *Dir of Nursing* Jerry D Maxwell. *Medical Dir* Dr Michael Platt.
Licensure Skilled care; Alzheimer's care. *Beds* SNF 84. *Certified* Medi-Cal.
Owner Proprietary corp (Del Rio Healthcare Inc).
Admissions Requirements Minimum age 40; Medical examination; Physician's request; Must be ambulatory.
Staff RNs 1 (ft), 1 (pt); LPNs 7 (ft), 1 (pt); Nurses' aides 32 (ft), 5 (pt); Activities coordinators 2 (ft); Dietitians 1 (pt).
Languages Spanish.
Facilities Dining room; Physical therapy room; Activities room; Crafts room; Laundry room; Barber/Beauty shop; Library; 4 1/2 acres of fenced grounds.
Activities Arts & crafts; Cards; Games; Reading groups; Prayer groups; Movies; Shopping trips; Dances/Social/Cultural gatherings; Outings to state fairs, Disneyland, beaches.

Bellflower

Bel Tooren Villa Convalescent Hospital
16910 Woodruff Ave, Bellflower, CA 90706
(213) 867-1761
Admin Shirley B Schouleman. *Dir of Nursing* Vicki L Miller RN. *Medical Dir* K P Wong MD.
Licensure Skilled care. *Beds* SNF 99. *Certified* Medicare; Medi-Cal.
Owner Proprietary corp (Columbia Corp).
Admissions Requirements Medical examination; Physician's request.
Staff Physicians; RNs; LPNs; Nurses' aides; Physical therapists; Reality therapists; Recreational therapists; Occupational therapists; Speech therapists; Activities coordinators; Dietitians; Ophthalmologists; Podiatrists; Dentists.
Languages Spanish.
Facilities Dining room; Physical therapy room; Activities room; Crafts room; Laundry room; Barber/Beauty shop; Library.
Activities Arts & crafts; Cards; Games; Reading groups; Prayer groups; Movies; Dances/Social/Cultural gatherings.

Bellflower Convalescent Hospital
9710 E Artesia Ave, Bellflower, CA 90706
(213) 925-2274
Admin Pompeyo A Rosales.
Licensure Skilled care. *Beds* SNF 59. *Certified* Medicare; Medi-Cal.
Owner Proprietary corp.

Rose Villa Care Center
9028 Rose St, Bellflower, CA 90706
(213) 925-4252, 920-9171 FAX
Admin Darlene DeBona. *Dir of Nursing* Robert Brown. *Medical Dir* K P Wong.
Licensure Skilled care. *Beds* SNF 53. *Private Pay Patients* 25%. *Certified* Medicare; Medi-Cal.
Owner Proprietary corp (Wallmark Health Services).
Admissions Requirements Minimum age 40.
Staff RNs 1 (ft), 2 (pt); LPNs 3 (ft), 1 (pt); Nurses' aides 17 (ft), 3 (pt); Physical therapists (contracted); Recreational therapists (contracted); Occupational therapists (contracted); Speech therapists (contracted); Activities coordinators 1 (ft), 1 (pt); Dietitians (contracted); Ophthalmologists (contracted); Podiatrists (contracted); Audiologists (contracted).
Languages Spanish, Asian languages.
Facilities Dining room; Physical therapy room; Activities room; Crafts room; Laundry room; Barber/Beauty shop.
Activities Arts & crafts; Cards; Games; Reading groups; Prayer groups; Movies; Dances/Social/Cultural gatherings; Pet therapy; Adult education.

Woodruff Convalescent Center
17836 S Woodruff Ave, Bellflower, CA 90706
(213) 925-8457
Admin Martin Simon.
Medical Dir Lawrence Wallington MD.
Licensure Skilled care. *Beds* SNF 140. *Certified* Medicare; Medi-Cal.
Owner Proprietary corp.
Admissions Requirements Minimum age 16; Medical examination; Physician's request.
Staff RNs 4 (ft), 5 (pt); LPNs 6 (ft), 1 (pt); Nurses' aides 52 (ft); Activities coordinators 2 (ft); Dietitians 1 (ft).
Facilities Dining room; Physical therapy room; Activities room; Crafts room; Barber/Beauty shop.
Activities Arts & crafts; Games; Prayer groups; Movies.

Belmont

Belmont Convalescent Hospital
1041 Hill St, Belmont, CA 94002
(415) 591-7181
Admin Mary Lou South.
Medical Dir Jonathan F Feinberg.
Licensure Skilled care. *Beds* SNF 33.
Owner Proprietary corp.
Admissions Requirements Medical examination.
Staff RNs 2 (ft), 2 (pt); LPNs 1 (ft), 1 (pt); Nurses' aides 8 (ft), 1 (pt); Physical therapists 1 (pt); Activities coordinators 1 (pt).
Facilities Dining room; Activities room; Laundry room; Barber/Beauty shop.
Activities Arts & crafts; Cards; Games; Reading groups; Prayer groups; Movies; Van rides.

Carlmont Convalescent Hospital
2140 Carlmont Dr, Belmont, CA 94002
(415) 591-9601
Admin George M Lamb Jr. *Dir of Nursing* Dawn F Reyes RN. *Medical Dir* Norman Morrison MD.
Licensure Skilled care. *Beds* SNF 59. *Private Pay Patients* 100%.
Owner Proprietary corp.
Admissions Requirements Medical examination; Physician's request.

Staff Physicians (contracted); RNs 4 (ft), 2 (pt); LPNs 3 (ft), 3 (pt); Nurses' aides 21 (ft), 6 (pt); Physical therapists (contracted); Occupational therapists (contracted); Speech therapists (contracted); Activities coordinators 1 (ft), 1 (pt); Dietitians (contracted); Ophthalmologists (contracted); Podiatrists (contracted); Food service managers 1 (ft); Restorative aides 1 (ft); Medical records (contracted); Dentists (contracted); X-ray technicians (contracted); Lab technicians (contracted); Pharmacists (contracted).
Languages Spanish, Filipino, Czech.
Facilities Dining room; Physical therapy room; Activities room; Crafts room; Laundry room; Barber/Beauty shop; Private and semi-private rooms.
Activities Arts & crafts; Cards; Games; Reading groups; Prayer groups; Movies; Dances/Social/Cultural gatherings; Intergenerational programs; Pet therapy.

Berkeley

Ashby Geriatric Hospital Inc
2270 Ashby Ave, Berkeley, CA 94705
(415) 841-9494
Admin Bradley M Besaw.
Licensure Skilled care. *Beds* SNF 31. *Certified* Medicare; Medi-Cal.
Owner Proprietary corp.

Berkeley Pines Skilled Nursing Facility
2223 Ashby Ave, Berkeley, CA 94705
(415) 843-1430
Admin Sheryl Clark Nadell. *Dir of Nursing* Jan Sloan RN. *Medical Dir* Dr Thomas Richmond.
Licensure Skilled care. *Beds* SNF 36. *Private Pay Patients* 66%. *Certified* Medicare; Medi-Cal.
Owner Nonprofit corp (Eskaton/Alta Bates Corp).
Staff Physicians 1 (pt); RNs 1 (ft), 4 (pt); LPNs 2 (ft), 9 (pt); Nurses' aides 9 (ft), 3 (pt); Activities coordinators 1 (ft), 2 (pt).
Facilities Dining room; Activities room; Crafts room; Laundry room; Barber/Beauty shop; Library.
Activities Arts & crafts; Games; Reading groups; Prayer groups; Movies; Shopping trips; Dances/Social/Cultural gatherings; Intergenerational programs.

Chaparral House
1309 Allston Way, Berkeley, CA 94702
(415) 848-8774
Admin James M Johnson. *Dir of Nursing* Frankie Allison RN. *Medical Dir* Dr Nicola Hanchock.
Licensure Intermediate care. *Beds* ICF 49. *Certified* Medi-Cal.
Owner Nonprofit organization/foundation.
Staff RNs 1 (ft), 2 (pt); LPNs 7 (ft), 2 (pt); Nurses' aides 10 (ft), 4 (pt); Activities coordinators 1 (ft); Chaplains 1 (ft).
Facilities Dining room; Activities room; Crafts room; Laundry room; Barber/Beauty shop.
Activities Arts & crafts; Cards; Games; Reading groups; Prayer groups; Movies; Shopping trips.

Claremont Convalescent Hospital
2500 Ashby Ave, Berkeley, CA 94705
(415) 841-5260
Admin Cheryl K Lien.
Licensure Skilled care. *Beds* SNF 36. *Certified* Medicare.
Owner Nonprofit corp (Guardian Foundation Inc).
Staff RNs 2 (ft); LPNs 4 (pt); Nurses' aides 20 (ft), 4 (pt); Activities coordinators 1 (ft).

Elmwood Convalescent Hospital
2829 Shattuck Ave, Berkeley, CA 94705
(415) 848-3760

Admin Elizabeth Schmidt.
Medical Dir Frank Lucido MD.
Licensure Skilled care. *Beds* SNF 81. *Certified* Medicare.
Owner Proprietary corp.
Admissions Requirements Geriatric patients only.
Staff Physicians 2 (pt); RNs 5 (ft), 1 (pt); LPNs 8 (ft); Physical therapists 1 (pt); Reality therapists 1 (pt); Recreational therapists 1 (pt); Occupational therapists 1 (pt); Speech therapists 1 (pt); Activities coordinators 1 (ft), 1 (pt); Ophthalmologists 1 (pt); Dentists 1 (pt).
Languages Spanish, Chinese, Tagalog, German.
Facilities Dining room; Physical therapy room; Activities room; Crafts room; Laundry room; Barber/Beauty shop; Library; Sitting room.
Activities Arts & crafts; Cards; Games; Reading groups; Prayer groups; Movies; Shopping trips; Dances/Social/Cultural gatherings; Small group activities.

Kyakameena Sanitorium
2131 Carleton St, Berkeley, CA 94704
(415) 843-2131
Admin Portia H Strause. *Dir of Nursing* Virginia Toby RN. *Medical Dir* Dr Robert D Tufft.
Licensure Skilled care. *Beds* SNF 59. *Certified* Medicare; Medi-Cal.
Owner Privately owned.
Admissions Requirements Medical examination; Physician's request.
Staff RNs 1 (ft), 2 (pt); LPNs 7 (ft), 1 (pt); Nurses' aides 25 (ft); Physical therapists 1 (pt); Occupational therapists 1 (pt); Speech therapists 1 (pt); Activities coordinators 1 (ft); Dietitians 1 (pt); Ophthalmologists 1 (pt); Dentists 1 (pt).
Facilities Dining room; Activities room; Laundry room; Barber/Beauty shop; Garden patio.
Activities Arts & crafts; Cards; Games; Reading groups; Prayer groups; Movies; Shopping trips; Dances/Social/Cultural gatherings; Music; Canine companion program.

Big Pine

Big Pine Convalescent Hospital
PO Box 306, County Rd, Big Pine, CA 93513
(619) 938-2411
Admin Dorothea L Carlin.
Licensure Skilled care. *Beds* SNF 45. *Certified* Medicare; Medi-Cal.
Owner Proprietary corp.

Blythe

Blythe Nursing Care Center
285 W Chanslor Way, Blythe, CA 92225
(619) 922-8176
Admin Jimmy T Clifford.
Medical Dir William Wiley MD.
Licensure Skilled care. *Beds* SNF 50. *Certified* Medicare; Medi-Cal.
Owner Proprietary corp.
Admissions Requirements Medical examination; Physician's request.
Staff Physicians 1 (pt); RNs 2 (ft); LPNs 3 (ft), 1 (pt); Nurses' aides 13 (ft), 5 (pt); Physical therapists 1 (pt); Reality therapists 1 (pt); Recreational therapists 1 (ft); Occupational therapists 1 (pt); Activities coordinators 1 (ft); Dietitians 1 (ft); Ophthalmologists 1 (pt); Podiatrists 1 (pt); Audiologists 1 (pt); Dentists 1 (pt).
Facilities Dining room; Activities room; Crafts room; Laundry room; Barber/Beauty shop.
Activities Arts & crafts; Cards; Games; Reading groups; Prayer groups; Shopping trips; Dances/Social/Cultural gatherings.

Brawley

Royal Convalescent Hospital
PO Box 1380, 320 W Cattle Call Dr, Brawley, CA 92227
(714) 344-5431
Admin Tobias Friedman.
Licensure Skilled care. *Beds* SNF 99. *Certified* Medicare; Medi-Cal.
Owner Proprietary corp.

Buena Park

Buena Park Nursing Center
8520 Western Ave, Buena Park, CA 90620
(714) 828-8222
Licensure Skilled care. *Beds* SNF 143. *Certified* Medicare; Medi-Cal.
Owner Proprietary corp.
Admissions Requirements Physician's request.
Staff RNs 4 (ft), 3 (pt); LPNs 9 (ft), 4 (pt); Nurses' aides 35 (ft), 20 (pt); Physical therapists 3 (pt); Recreational therapists 1 (pt); Occupational therapists 1 (pt); Speech therapists 1 (pt); Activities coordinators 2 (ft); Dietitians 1 (pt); Ophthalmologists 1 (pt); Podiatrists 1 (pt); Dentists 1 (pt).
Facilities Dining room; Physical therapy room; Activities room; Laundry room; Barber/Beauty shop.
Activities Arts & crafts; Games; Prayer groups; Movies; Shopping trips; Dances/Social/Cultural gatherings.

Orange West Convalescent Hospital
9021 Knott Ave, Buena Park, CA 90620
(714) 826-2330
Admin Jo Pledge. *Dir of Nursing* Ann Fredricks. *Medical Dir* G D Kohler MD.
Licensure Skilled care. *Beds* SNF 99. *Certified* Medicare; Medi-Cal.
Owner Privately owned.
Staff RNs 6 (ft), 3 (pt); LPNs 7 (ft), 4 (pt); Nurses' aides 25 (ft), 6 (pt); Activities coordinators 1 (ft), 1 (pt); Dietitians 1 (ft).
Languages Spanish, Korean.
Activities Arts & crafts; Cards; Games; Reading groups; Prayer groups; Movies; Shopping trips; Dances/Social/Cultural gatherings; Outings; Musical entertainment.

Burbank

Beverly Manor
925 W Alameda Ave, Burbank, CA 91506
(818) 847-1771
Admin Victor Marefka. *Dir of Nursing* Lois Wallerstein RN. *Medical Dir* Stuart Shipco MD.
Licensure Skilled care; Alzheimer's care. *Beds* SNF 89. *Certified* Medi-Cal.
Owner Proprietary corp (Beverly Enterprises).
Admissions Requirements Minimum age 65; Medical examination; Physician's request.
Staff Physicians; RNs; LPNs; Nurses' aides; Recreational therapists; Activities coordinators; Dietitians; Ophthalmologists; Podiatrists; Dentists.
Languages Spanish.
Facilities Dining room; Activities room; Crafts room; Laundry room; Library.
Activities Arts & crafts; Cards; Games; Reading groups; Prayer groups; Movies; Shopping trips; Dances/Social/Cultural gatherings.

Beverly Manor Convalescent Hospital
1041 S Main St, Burbank, CA 91506
(818) 843-2330
Admin Berna-Dean Darms.
Medical Dir Dr Valentine Birds.
Licensure Skilled care. *Beds* SNF 188. *Certified* Medicare; Medi-Cal.
Owner Proprietary corp (Beverly Enterprises).
Admissions Requirements Medical examination.

Staff Physicians 32 (pt); RNs 8 (ft), 6 (pt); LPNs 11 (ft), 6 (pt); Nurses' aides 67 (ft), 1 (pt); Physical therapists 2 (pt); Occupational therapists 1 (pt); Speech therapists 3 (pt); Activities coordinators 2 (ft); Dietitians 1 (pt); Ophthalmologists 2 (pt); Podiatrists 3 (pt); Audiologists 1 (pt); Dentists 1 (pt).
Facilities Dining room; Physical therapy room; Activities room; Crafts room; Laundry room; Barber/Beauty shop.
Activities Arts & crafts; Cards; Games; Reading groups; Prayer groups; Movies; Shopping trips; Dances/Social/Cultural gatherings; Grooming class; Reality class; Restorative exercise; Cooking classes; Patient council; Birthday parties; Adult education; Outings.

Burbank Convalescent Hospital
2710 W Olive Ave, Burbank, CA 91505
(818) 848-5581
Admin Orlando Clarizio Jr.
Medical Dir Dr George Papkin.
Licensure Skilled care; Retirement. *Beds* SNF 54. *Certified* Medicare; Medi-Cal.
Owner Proprietary corp.
Staff Physicians 3 (ft), 12 (pt); RNs 1 (ft), 1 (pt); LPNs 5 (ft), 1 (pt); Nurses' aides 22 (ft); Physical therapists 1 (pt); Reality therapists 1 (pt); Recreational therapists 1 (ft); Occupational therapists 1 (ft); Speech therapists 1 (ft); Activities coordinators 1 (ft); Dietitians 1 (ft); Ophthalmologists 1 (ft); Podiatrists 1 (ft); Dentists 1 (ft).
Languages Spanish, Tagalog.
Facilities Dining room; Physical therapy room; Activities room; Laundry room.
Activities Arts & crafts; Cards; Games; Reading groups; Prayer groups; Movies.

St Joseph Medical Center Pavilion
2727 W Alameda Ave, Burbank, CA 91505
(818) 843-7900
Admin Scott T Seamons. *Dir of Nursing* Julie Theiring RN. *Medical Dir* Alonzo Y Olsen Jr MD.
Licensure Skilled care; Alzheimer's care. *Beds* SNF 149. *Certified* Medicare; Medi-Cal.
Owner Nonprofit corp.
Admissions Requirements Medical examination; Physician's request.
Staff RNs 1 (ft); LPNs 1 (ft); Nurses' aides 1 (ft); Physical therapists 1 (ft); Recreational therapists 1 (ft); Occupational therapists 1 (ft); Speech therapists 1 (ft); Activities coordinators 1 (ft); Dietitians 1 (ft); Ophthalmologists 1 (ft); Podiatrists 1 (pt).
Affiliation Roman Catholic.
Facilities Dining room; Physical therapy room; Activities room; Chapel; Crafts room; Laundry room; Barber/Beauty shop; Library.
Activities Arts & crafts; Cards; Games; Reading groups; Prayer groups; Movies; Shopping trips; Dances/Social/Cultural gatherings; Field trips.

Burlingame

Care West—Burlingame Nursing & Rehabilitation Center
1100 Trousdale Dr, Burlingame, CA 94010
(415) 692-3758
Admin Jack McDowell.
Medical Dir Robert Minkowsky.
Licensure Skilled care. *Beds* SNF 281. *Certified* Medicare; Medi-Cal.
Owner Proprietary corp (Care Enterprises).
Admissions Requirements Physician's request.
Staff RNs 10 (ft), 10 (pt); LPNs 10 (ft), 13 (pt); Nurses' aides 68 (ft), 29 (pt); Physical therapists 2 (pt); Occupational therapists 1 (pt); Speech therapists 1 (pt); Activities coordinators 4 (ft); Dietitians 1 (ft); Ophthalmologists 1 (pt); Dentists 1 (pt).
Facilities Dining room; Physical therapy room; Activities room; Crafts room; Laundry room; Barber/Beauty shop; Library.

Activities Arts & crafts; Cards; Games; Reading groups; Prayer groups; Movies; Shopping trips; Dances/Social/Cultural gatherings.

Hillhaven Convalescent Hospital
1609 Trousdale Dr, Burlingame, CA 94010
(415) 697-1865
Admin Georgia Otterson. *Dir of Nursing* Cathy Madrid. *Medical Dir* Dr Michael Taradash.
Licensure Skilled care; Alzheimer's care. *Beds* SNF 85. *Certified* Medicare; Medi-Cal.
Owner Proprietary corp (Hillhaven Inc).
Staff Physical therapists 1 (ft); Occupational therapists 1 (ft); Speech therapists 1 (pt); Activities coordinators 1 (ft); Dietitians; Ophthalmologists; Podiatrists; Audiologists.
Facilities Dining room; Physical therapy room; Activities room; Laundry room; Barber/Beauty shop; 3 patios; Security system for wanderers.
Activities Arts & crafts; Games; Prayer groups; Movies; Shopping trips; Dances/Social/Cultural gatherings; Intergenerational programs; Pet therapy.

Calistoga

Care West—Calistoga Nursing & Rehabilitation Center
1715 Washington, Calistoga, CA 94515
(707) 942-6253
Admin Roberta Kellogg.
Medical Dir Dr D O'Neil.
Licensure Skilled care. *Beds* SNF 72. *Certified* Medicare; Medi-Cal.
Owner Proprietary corp (Care Enterprises).
Admissions Requirements Physician's request.
Facilities Dining room; Physical therapy room; Activities room; Crafts room; Laundry room; Barber/Beauty shop; Library.
Activities Arts & crafts; Games; Reading groups; Prayer groups; Movies; Dances/Social/Cultural gatherings.

Camarillo

Camarillo Convalescent Hospital
205 Granada St, Camarillo, CA 93010
(805) 482-9805
Admin Gary Devoir.
Medical Dir Leonard Ackland MD.
Licensure Skilled care. *Beds* SNF 114. *Certified* Medicare; Medi-Cal.
Owner Proprietary corp.
Admissions Requirements Physician's request.
Facilities Dining room; Activities room; Crafts room; Laundry room; Barber/Beauty shop.
Activities Arts & crafts; Games; Reading groups; Movies; Shopping trips.

Pleasant Valley Hospital Extended Care
2309 Antonio Ave, Camarillo, CA 93010
(805) 484-2831
Admin Cheryl A Wilson. *Dir of Nursing* Judy Wess. *Medical Dir* R Gonzales; H Judy.
Licensure Skilled care. *Beds* SNF 99. *Private Pay Patients* 15%. *Certified* Medicare; Medi-Cal.
Owner Publicly owned.
Admissions Requirements Medical examination; Physician's request.
Staff RNs 9 (ft); LPNs 21 (ft); Nurses' aides 64 (ft); Physical therapists 2 (ft); Occupational therapists 1 (ft); Activities coordinators 4 (ft); Dietitians 3 (ft); Ophthalmologists 1 (ft); Podiatrists 1 (ft).
Facilities Dining room; Physical therapy room; Activities room; Chapel; Crafts room; Barber/Beauty shop.
Activities Arts & crafts; Cards; Games; Reading groups; Prayer groups; Movies; Shopping trips; Dances/Social/Cultural gatherings; Pet therapy.

Campbell

Camden Convalescent Hospital
1331 Camden Ave, Campbell, CA 95008
(408) 377-4030
Admin Vern Thompson.
Licensure Skilled care. *Beds* SNF 59. *Certified* Medi-Cal.
Owner Proprietary corp.

Canoga Park

Beverly Manor Convalescent Hospital
7940 Topanga Canyon, Canoga Park, CA 91304
(818) 347-3800
Admin Frances Foy.
Medical Dir Robert Watson MD.
Licensure Skilled care. *Beds* SNF 149. *Certified* Medicare; Medi-Cal.
Owner Proprietary corp (Beverly Enterprises).
Admissions Requirements Medical examination; Physician's request.
Staff Physicians 3 (pt); RNs 7 (ft), 1 (pt); LPNs 15 (ft); Nurses' aides 42 (ft); Physical therapists 2 (ft), 3 (pt); Recreational therapists 1 (pt) Occupational therapists 1 (pt); Speech therapists 1 (pt); Activities coordinators 2 (ft); Dietitians 1 (pt); Ophthalmologists 1 (pt); Podiatrists 1 (pt); Dentists 1 (pt).
Facilities Dining room; Physical therapy room; Activities room; Chapel; Barber/Beauty shop; Music room.
Activities Arts & crafts; Cards; Games; Reading groups; Movies; Shopping trips; Dances/Social/Cultural gatherings; Dining out.

Canoga Care Center
22029 Saticoy St, Canoga Park, CA 91304
(818) 887-7050
Admin Alan L Lien. *Dir of Nursing* Tess Acejo RN.
Licensure Skilled care; Alzheimer's care. *Beds* SNF 200. *Certified* Medicare; Medi-Cal.
Owner Proprietary corp.
Admissions Requirements Minimum age 55; Medical examination; Physician's request.
Staff RNs 6 (ft), 4 (pt); LPNs 10 (ft), 4 (pt); Nurses' aides 60 (ft), 18 (pt); Physical therapists 1 (ft); Activities coordinators 2 (ft).
Languages Spanish, Korean, Tagalog, Indian.
Facilities Dining room; Physical therapy room; Activities room; Crafts room; Laundry room; Barber/Beauty shop; Library.
Activities Arts & crafts; Cards; Games; Reading groups; Prayer groups; Movies; Shopping trips; Dances/Social/Cultural gatherings.

Golden State West Valley Convalescent Hospital
7057 Shoup Ave, Canoga Park, CA 91304
(818) 348-8422
Admin Marie S Mills.
Licensure Skilled care. *Beds* SNF 99. *Certified* Medicare; Medi-Cal.
Owner Nonprofit corp.

Holiday Manor Nursitarium
20554 Roscoe Blvd, Canoga Park, CA 91306
(818) 341-9800
Admin Hilda Wirth. *Dir of Nursing* Rosemary Scislow RN. *Medical Dir* Paul Diehl MD.
Licensure Skilled Alzheimer's care. *Beds* SNF Alzheimer's care 94. *Certified* Medi-Cal.
Owner Proprietary corp.
Admissions Requirements Minimum age 50; Ambulatory.
Staff Physicians 1 (pt); RNs 3 (ft), 1 (pt); Activities coordinators 1 (ft); Dietitians (consultant); Ophthalmologists (consultant); Podiatrists (consultant); Audiologists (consultant); SSDs 1 (ft).

Languages German, Swiss, Vietnamese, Spanish.
Facilities Dining room; Activities room; Crafts room; Laundry room; Barber/Beauty shop; Library.
Activities Arts & crafts; Games; Reading groups; Prayer groups; Movies; Pet therapy; Bus trips.

Topanga Terrace Convalescent Center
22125 Roscoe Blvd, Canoga Park, CA 91304
(818) 883-7292
Admin Cary Buchman. *Dir of Nursing* Doris Komph RN. *Medical Dir* Edwin Marcus MD.
Licensure Skilled care. *Beds* SNF 112. *Certified* Medicare; Medi-Cal.
Owner Proprietary corp.
Admissions Requirements Minimum age 18; Physician's request.
Staff RNs 5 (ft), 4 (pt); LPNs 5 (ft), 2 (pt); Nurses' aides 17 (ft), 1 (pt); Physical therapists; Occupational therapists; Speech therapists; Activities coordinators 1 (ft), 1 (pt); Dietitians 1 (pt); Ophthalmologists; Podiatrists; Dentists.
Languages Spanish, German, Hungarian, Czech.
Facilities Dining room; Physical therapy room; Activities room; Chapel; Crafts room; Laundry room; Barber/Beauty shop.
Activities Arts & crafts; Cards; Games; Reading groups; Prayer groups; Movies.

Capistrano Beach

Beverly Manor Convalescent Hospital
35410 Del Rey, Capistrano Beach, CA 92624
(714) 496-5786
Admin Jane Kinard.
Medical Dir Dr B Bundy.
Licensure Skilled care. *Beds* SNF 127. *Certified* Medicare; Medi-Cal.
Owner Proprietary corp (Beverly Enterprises).
Admissions Requirements Minimum age 21.
Staff RNs 20 (ft); LPNs 20 (ft); Nurses' aides 90 (ft); Activities coordinators 1 (ft); Dietitians 1 (ft).
Facilities Dining room; Physical therapy room; Activities room; Crafts room; Laundry room; Barber/Beauty shop.
Activities Arts & crafts; Cards; Games; Reading groups; Prayer groups; Movies; Shopping trips.

Capitola

Golden Age Convalescent Hospital
523 Burlingame, Capitola, CA 95010
(408) 475-0722
Admin Mercedes P Cachola.
Medical Dir Paul Weiss MD.
Licensure Skilled care. *Beds* SNF 40. *Certified* Medi-Cal.
Owner Privately owned.
Admissions Requirements Minimum age 56; Physician's request.
Staff Physicians 2 (pt); RNs 1 (ft), 3 (pt); LPNs 4 (ft), 3 (pt); Nurses' aides 4 (ft), 9 (pt).
Facilities Dining room; Activities room; Laundry room; Barber/Beauty shop.
Activities Arts & crafts; Cards; Games; Reading groups; Prayer groups; Movies; Shopping trips; Dances/Social/Cultural gatherings.

Rosscare Convalescent Hospital
1935 Wharf Rd, Capitola, CA 95010
(408) 476-0770
Admin Ralph N Tisdial.
Licensure Skilled care. *Beds* SNF 99. *Certified* Medicare; Medi-Cal.
Owner Privately owned.

Carlsbad

Lutheran Health Facility of Carlsbad
201 Grand Ave, Carlsbad, CA 92008
(619) 729-2377, 729-9045 FAX
Admin Jeff Jones. *Dir of Nursing* Joan
McQuilken RN. *Medical Dir* Dr David
Jones.
Licensure Skilled care. *Beds* SNF 59. *Certified*
Medicare; Medi-Cal.
Owner Nonprofit corp (California Lutheran
Homes).
Admissions Requirements Physician's request.
Staff Physicians 1 (pt); RNs 4 (ft), 3 (pt);
LPNs 1 (ft), 1 (pt); Nurses' aides 20 (ft), 15
(pt); Physical therapists 1 (pt); Occupational
therapists 1 (pt); Speech therapists 1 (pt);
Activities coordinators 1 (ft); Dietitians 1
(pt).
Affiliation Lutheran.
Facilities Dining room; Physical therapy
room; Activities room; Barber/Beauty shop.
Activities Arts & crafts; Cards; Games;
Reading groups; Prayer groups; Movies;
Dances/Social/Cultural gatherings.

Carmel

Carmel Convalescent Hospital
Hwy 1 & Valley Way, Carmel, CA 93921
(408) 624-8296
Admin Floyd P Hardcastle.
Licensure Skilled care. *Beds* SNF 65. *Certified*
Medi-Cal.
Owner Proprietary corp.

Carmel Valley Manor
8545 Carmel Valley Rd, Carmel, CA 93923
(408) 624-1281
Admin Jack D Knighton.
Medical Dir David Thorngate MD.
Licensure Skilled care. *Beds* SNF 28. *Certified*
Medicare; Medi-Cal.
Owner Nonprofit corp.
Admissions Requirements Minimum age 65;
Medical examination; Physician's request.
Staff Physicians 2 (pt); RNs 3 (ft), 7 (pt);
LPNs 1 (ft); Nurses' aides 14 (ft), 4 (pt);
Physical therapists 1 (pt); Recreational
therapists 1 (pt); Occupational therapists 1
(pt); Activities coordinators 1 (pt); Dietitians
1 (pt); Podiatrists 1 (pt); Dentists 1 (pt).
Affiliation Congregational.
Facilities Dining room; Physical therapy
room; Activities room; Chapel; Crafts room;
Laundry room; Barber/Beauty shop; Library.
Activities Arts & crafts; Games; Reading
groups; Prayer groups; Movies; Shopping
trips; Dances/Social/Cultural gatherings;
Picnics; Barbeques; Scenic rides.

Carmichael

Carmichael Convalescent Hospital Inc
8336 Fair Oaks Blvd, Carmichael, CA 95608
(916) 944-3100
Admin Carole Henry. *Dir of Nursing* Jennifer
Worden RN. *Medical Dir* Otto Neubuerger
MD.
Licensure Skilled care. *Beds* SNF 126.
Certified Medicare; Medi-Cal.
Owner Proprietary corp.
Admissions Requirements Physician's request.
Staff RNs 8 (ft); LPNs 16 (ft); Nurses' aides
53 (ft); Physical therapists 1 (ft);
Recreational therapists 2 (ft); Occupational
therapists 1 (ft); Speech therapists 1 (ft);
Activities coordinators 1 (ft); Dietitians 1
(pt); Ophthalmologists 1 (pt); Podiatrists 1
(pt).
Languages German, Russian, Spanish,
Tagalog.
Facilities Dining room; Physical therapy
room; Activities room; Crafts room; Laundry
room; Barber/Beauty shop; Library.

Activities Arts & crafts; Cards; Games;
Reading groups; Prayer groups; Movies;
Dances/Social/Cultural gatherings.

El Camino Convalescent Hospital
2540 Carmichael Way, Carmichael, CA 95608
(916) 482-0465
Admin Kathy Spake.
Licensure Skilled care. *Beds* SNF 178.
Certified Medicare; Medi-Cal.
Owner Proprietary corp (Crestwood Hospitals
Inc).

Eskaton Manzanita Manor
5318 Manzanita Ave, Carmichael, CA 95608
(916) 331-8513
Admin Bob Kegley. *Dir of Nursing* Kathy
Smith RN. *Medical Dir* William Hicks MD.
Licensure Skilled care; Alzheimer's care. *Beds*
SNF 99. *Certified* Medicare; Medi-Cal.
Owner Nonprofit corp (Eskaton Health Corp).
Staff RNs 5 (ft), 1 (pt); LPNs 12 (ft), 2 (pt);
Nurses' aides 35 (ft), 15 (pt); Physical
therapists 1 (ft); Recreational therapists 1
(ft); Occupational therapists 1 (ft); Speech
therapists 1 (ft); Dietitians 1 (pt);
Ophthalmologists 1 (pt); Dentists 1 (pt).
Facilities Dining room; Physical therapy
room; Activities room; Chapel; Laundry
room; Barber/Beauty shop; Living room.
Activities Arts & crafts; Cards; Games;
Reading groups; Prayer groups; Movies;
Shopping trips; Dances/Social/Cultural
gatherings.

Hillhaven Fair Oaks
8845 Fair Oaks Blvd, Carmichael, CA 95608
(916) 944-4312
Admin Perry Farahmand. *Dir of Nursing*
Virginia Ortiz RN. *Medical Dir* Donald
ReVidle MD.
Licensure Skilled care; Alzheimer's care. *Beds*
SNF 106. *Private Pay Patients* 60%. *Certified*
Medicare; Medi-Cal.
Owner Proprietary corp (Hillhaven Inc).
Staff RNs 5 (ft), 2 (pt); LPNs 9 (ft), 3 (pt);
Nurses' aides 58 (ft), 12 (pt); Physical
therapists 2 (ft), 1 (pt); Reality therapists 1
(ft); Recreational therapists 2 (ft), 1 (pt);
Occupational therapists 1 (pt); Speech
therapists 1 (ft); Activities coordinators 1
(ft); Dietitians 1 (pt).
Languages Spanish, Japanese, Portuguese.
Facilities Dining room; Physical therapy
room; Activities room; Chapel; Crafts room;
Laundry room; Barber/Beauty shop; Library.
Activities Arts & crafts; Games; Reading
groups; Prayer groups; Movies; Shopping
trips; Dances/Social/Cultural gatherings;
Intergenerational programs; Pet therapy.

Mt Olivette Care Center
6041 Fair Oaks Blvd, Carmichael, CA 95608
(916) 483-8103
Dir of Nursing Sharon Day. *Medical Dir* Dr
Otto Neubuerger.
Licensure Skilled care. *Beds* SNF 112.
Certified Medicare; Medi-Cal.
Owner Nonprofit corp (Eskaton Health Corp).
Admissions Requirements Medical
examination; Physician's request.
Staff Physicians 35 (pt); RNs 5 (ft), 10 (pt);
LPNs 8 (ft), 3 (pt); Nurses' aides 32 (ft), 9
(pt); Physical therapists 1 (pt); Occupational
therapists 1 (pt); Speech therapists 1 (pt);
Activities coordinators 1 (ft); Dietitians 1
(pt); Ophthalmologists 1 (pt); Podiatrists 1
(pt); Dentists 2 (pt).
Languages Chinese, Tagalog, Spanish.
Facilities Dining room; Physical therapy
room; Activities room; Laundry room;
Barber/Beauty shop.
Activities Arts & crafts; Games; Movies;
Shopping trips; Pet therapy.

Mountain Manor
6101 Fair Oaks Blvd, Carmichael, CA 95608
(916) 488-7211

Admin Stuart Drake.
Licensure Intermediate care; Residential care.
Beds ICF 47; Residential 33. *Certified*
Medi-Cal.
Owner Proprietary corp.
Admissions Requirements Minimum age 62;
Physician's request.
Staff RNs 1 (ft), 2 (pt); LPNs 3 (ft), 2 (pt);
Nurses' aides 10 (ft); Activities coordinators
3 (ft).
Facilities Dining room; Physical therapy
room; Activities room; Crafts room; Laundry
room; Barber/Beauty shop.
Activities Arts & crafts; Cards; Games;
Reading groups; Prayer groups; Movies;
Shopping trips; Dances/Social/Cultural
gatherings; Bingo; Exercise; Ceramics.

Sutter Oaks Nursing Center—Carmichael
3630 Mission Ave, Carmichael, CA 95608
(916) 488-1580
Admin Larry F Krepelka.
Licensure Skilled care. *Beds* SNF 138.
Certified Medicare; Medi-Cal.
Owner Nonprofit corp.

Walnut Whitney Convalescent Hospital
3529 Walnut Ave, Carmichael, CA 95608
(916) 488-8601, 488-3053 FAX
Admin Sheree Crum. *Dir of Nursing* Steven
Madrick RN. *Medical Dir* William E Hedges
MD.
Licensure Skilled care. *Beds* SNF 126. *Private
Pay Patients* 24%. *Certified* Medicare; Medi-
Cal.
Owner Proprietary corp (Sierra Medical
Enterprises Inc).
Admissions Requirements Medical
examination; Physician's request.
Staff Physicians 35 (pt); RNs 6 (ft), 6 (pt);
LPNs 10 (ft), 5 (pt); Nurses' aides 40 (ft), 10
(pt); Physical therapists 1 (pt); Reality
therapists 1 (pt); Recreational therapists 1
(pt); Occupational therapists 1 (pt); Speech
therapists 1 (pt); Activities coordinators 2
(ft); Dietitians 1 (pt); Ophthalmologists 1
(pt); Podiatrists 1 (pt); Audiologists 1 (pt);
Dentists 1 (pt).
Facilities Dining room; Physical therapy
room; Laundry room; Barber/Beauty shop;
Patient lounge.
Activities Arts & crafts; Cards; Games;
Reading groups; Prayer groups; Movies;
Shopping trips; Dances/Social/Cultural
gatherings; Intergenerational programs; Pet
therapy.

Castro Valley

Apple Geriatric Care
20524 Wisteria St, Castro Valley, CA 94546
(415) 581-7645
Licensure Skilled care. *Beds* SNF 25. *Certified*
Medi-Cal.
Owner Proprietary corp.

Hillhaven Castro Valley
20259 Lake Chabot Rd, Castro Valley, CA
94546
(415) 351-3700
Licensure Skilled care. *Beds* SNF 95. *Certified*
Medicare; Medi-Cal.
Owner Proprietary corp (Hillhaven Inc).
Admissions Requirements Physician's request.
Staff Physicians; RNs; LPNs; Nurses' aides;
Physical therapists; Recreational therapists;
Occupational therapists; Speech therapists;
Activities coordinators; Dietitians;
Ophthalmologists; Podiatrists; Dentists.
Facilities Dining room; Physical therapy
room; Activities room; Crafts room; Laundry
room; Barber/Beauty shop.
Activities Arts & crafts; Cards; Games;
Reading groups; Prayer groups; Movies;
Shopping trips; Dances/Social/Cultural
gatherings.

Redwood Convalescent Hospital
22103 Redwood Rd, Castro Valley, CA 94546
(415) 537-8848
Admin Robert J Myers. *Dir of Nursing* Angie
Lin RN. *Medical Dir* Dr I Moncrief.
Licensure Skilled care. *Beds* SNF 70. *Certified*
Medicare; Medi-Cal.
Owner Proprietary corp.
Admissions Requirements Physician's request.
Staff Physicians 1 (pt); RNs 3 (ft), 2 (pt);
LPNs 7 (ft), 3 (pt); Nurses' aides 27 (ft), 2
(pt); Physical therapists 1 (pt); Activities
coordinators 1 (ft), 1 (pt); Dietitians 1 (pt).
Facilities Dining room; Physical therapy
room; Activities room; Chapel; Crafts room;
Laundry room; Barber/Beauty shop.
Activities Arts & crafts; Cards; Games;
Reading groups; Prayer groups; Movies;
Shopping trips; Dances/Social/Cultural
gatherings.

St Anne's Convalescent Hospital
22424 Charlene Way, Castro Valley, CA
94546
(415) 537-5944
Admin Roland Rapp.
Medical Dir Andrew May MD.
Licensure Skilled care. *Beds* SNF 48. *Certified*
Medi-Cal.
Owner Proprietary corp.
Admissions Requirements Medical
examination; Physician's request.
Staff Physicians 9 (ft); RNs 1 (ft), 1 (pt);
LPNs 3 (ft), 3 (pt); Nurses' aides 17 (ft), 4
(pt); Physical therapists 1 (pt); Reality
therapists 1 (pt); Recreational therapists 1
(pt); Occupational therapists 1 (pt); Speech
therapists 1 (pt); Activities coordinators 1
(ft), 1 (pt); Dietitians 1 (ft);
Ophthalmologists 1 (pt); Podiatrists 1 (pt);
Dentists 1 (pt).
Languages Spanish, Tagalog.
Facilities Dining room; Activities room;
Crafts room; Laundry room; Barber/Beauty
shop.
Activities Arts & crafts; Cards; Games;
Reading groups; Prayer groups; Movies;
Shopping trips; Dances/Social/Cultural
gatherings; Bingo; Cooking; Gardening; Pet
visits.

St John Kronstadt Convalescent Center
4432 James Ave, Castro Valley, CA 94546
(415) 889-7000
Admin Fred Sanciangco. *Dir of Nursing*
Rosemary Noonan RN. *Medical Dir* Andrew
May Jr MD.
Licensure Skilled care. *Beds* SNF 49. *Private
Pay Patients* 60-70%. *Certified* Medicaid;
Medicare; Medi-Cal.
Owner Nonprofit corp.
Admissions Requirements Minimum age 65;
Medical examination; Physician's request.
Staff Physicians 8 (pt); RNs 1 (ft), 1 (pt);
LPNs 7 (ft); Nurses' aides 17 (ft); Physical
therapists 1 (pt); Occupational therapists 1
(pt); Speech therapists 1 (pt); Activities
coordinators 3 (ft); Dietitians 1 (ft);
Podiatrists 1 (pt).
Affiliation Russian Orthodox.
Facilities Dining room; Activities room;
Chapel; Crafts room; Laundry room; Barber/
Beauty shop.
Activities Arts & crafts; Cards; Games;
Reading groups; Prayer groups; Movies;
Shopping trips; Dances/Social/Cultural
gatherings; Pet therapy.

St Joseph Convalescent Hospital Inc
18949 Redwood Rd, Castro Valley, CA 94546
(415) 886-1101
Dir of Nursing Geneva Robinson. *Medical Dir*
Andrew May Jr MD.
Licensure Skilled care; Intermediate care. *Beds*
Swing beds SNF/ICF 82. *Certified* Medicare;
Medi-Cal.
Owner Proprietary corp.

Staff Physicians 1 (pt); RNs 2 (pt); LPNs 4
(ft); Nurses' aides 6 (ft); Physical therapists 1
(pt); Occupational therapists 1 (pt); Speech
therapists 1 (pt); Activities coordinators 2
(ft); Dietitians 1 (pt); Ophthalmologists 1
(pt); Podiatrists 1 (pt).
Languages Spanish.
Facilities Dining room; Activities room;
Crafts room; Laundry room; Barber/Beauty
shop.
Activities Arts & crafts; Cards; Games;
Reading groups; Prayer groups; Movies;
Shopping trips; Dances/Social/Cultural
gatherings.

Stanton Hill Convalescent Hospital Inc
20090 Stanton Ave, Castro Valley, CA 94546
(415) 538-8464
Admin Joy Marie Susko.
Licensure Skilled care. *Beds* SNF 50. *Certified*
Medicare; Medi-Cal.
Owner Proprietary corp.

Ceres

Ha-le Aloha Convalescent Hospital
1711 Richland Ave, Ceres, CA 95307
(209) 537-4581
Admin Mary E Baker.
Medical Dir Amos Henry MD.
Licensure Skilled care. *Beds* SNF 46. *Certified*
Medicare; Medi-Cal.
Owner Proprietary corp (Mark One Corp).
Admissions Requirements Physician's request.
Staff RNs 1 (ft), 1 (pt); LPNs 2 (ft), 2 (pt);
Nurses' aides 10 (ft), 3 (pt); Activities
coordinators 1 (ft).
Facilities Dining room; Laundry room.
Activities Arts & crafts; Games; Dances/Social/
Cultural gatherings.

Chatsworth

Chatsworth Health & Rehabilitation Center
21820 Craggy View, Chatsworth, CA 91311
(818) 882-8233
Admin Emmanuel Ruiz. *Dir of Nursing*
Christine Redman. *Medical Dir* Richard
Weiss.
Licensure Skilled care. *Beds* SNF 132.
Certified Medicaid; Medi-Cal.
Owner Proprietary corp (Golden State Health
Centers).
Admissions Requirements Minimum age 18;
Physician's request.
Staff Physicians; RNs; LPNs; Nurses' aides;
Recreational therapists; Occupational
therapists; Speech therapists; Activities
coordinators; Dietitians; Podiatrists;
Audiologists.
Facilities Dining room; Physical therapy
room; Activities room; Crafts room; Laundry
room; Barber/Beauty shop; Library.
Activities Arts & crafts; Cards; Games;
Reading groups; Prayer groups; Movies;
Shopping trips; Dances/Social/Cultural
gatherings; Intergenerational programs.

Chatsworth Park Convalescent Hospital
10610 Owensmouth Ave, Chatsworth, CA
91311
(818) 882-3200
Admin Claire Menard. *Dir of Nursing*
Marolyn Zieglgansberger RN. *Medical Dir*
David Chernof MD.
Licensure Skilled care; Intermediate care. *Beds*
SNF 94; ICF 34. *Certified* Medicare; Medi-
Cal.
Owner Proprietary corp.
Admissions Requirements Minimum age 50;
Physician's request.
Staff Physicians 12 (pt); RNs 2 (ft); LPNs 11
(ft), 2 (pt); Nurses' aides 27 (ft), 3 (pt);
Physical therapists 1 (pt); Recreational
therapists 1 (pt); Occupational therapists 1
(pt); Speech therapists 1 (pt); Activities

coordinators 2 (ft); Dietitians 1 (pt);
Ophthalmologists 1 (pt); Podiatrists 1 (pt);
Dentists 1 (pt).
Languages Tagalog, Spanish, Yiddish,
Hebrew, Portuguese.
Facilities Dining room; Physical therapy
room; Activities room; Crafts room; Laundry
room; Barber/Beauty shop; Library.
Activities Arts & crafts; Cards; Games;
Reading groups; Prayer groups; Movies;
Dances/Social/Cultural gatherings.

Cherry Valley

Sunset Haven Health Center
9246 Avenida Miravilla, Cherry Valley, CA
92223
(714) 845-3194
Admin Fran Morris. *Dir of Nursing* Barbara
Sherman RN. *Medical Dir* R E Rothe MD.
Licensure Skilled care; Residential care. *Beds*
SNF 59; Residential care 120. *Private Pay
Patients* 20%. *Certified* Medicaid.
Owner Nonprofit corp.
Admissions Requirements Medical
examination; Physician's request.
Staff Physicians; RNs; LPNs; Nurses' aides;
Physical therapists; Occupational therapists;
Speech therapists; Activities coordinators;
Dietitians; Podiatrists.
Languages Spanish, German.
Affiliation Church of Christ.
Facilities Dining room; Physical therapy
room; Activities room; Crafts room; Laundry
room; Barber/Beauty shop.
Activities Arts & crafts; Cards; Games;
Reading groups; Prayer groups; Movies;
Shopping trips; Dances/Social/Cultural
gatherings.

Chico

Beverly Manor Convalescent Hospital
188 Cohasset Ln, Chico, CA 95926
(916) 343-6084
Admin Frank Garrison. *Dir of Nursing* Gladys
Devore. *Medical Dir* William H Coats MD.
Licensure Skilled care. *Beds* SNF 76. *Private
Pay Patients* 20%. *Certified* Medicare; Medi-
Cal.
Owner Proprietary corp (Beverly Enterprises).
Admissions Requirements Minimum age 18;
Medical examination; Physician's request.
Staff RNs; LPNs; Nurses' aides; Physical
therapists; Activities coordinators; Dietitians.
Facilities Dining room; Physical therapy
room; Activities room; Laundry room;
Barber/Beauty shop.
Activities Arts & crafts; Cards; Games; Prayer
groups; Movies; Shopping trips;
Intergenerational programs; Pet therapy.

Care West—North Valley Nursing Center
1645 The Esplanade, Chico, CA 95926
(916) 343-6045
Admin Charlotte Mallory.
Licensure Skilled care. *Beds* SNF 59. *Certified*
Medicare; Medi-Cal.
Owner Proprietary corp (Care Enterprises).

Careage of Chico
1200 Springfield Dr, Chico, CA 95928
(916) 342-4885
Admin Joe Miceli.
Licensure Skilled care. *Beds* SNF 144.
Certified Medicare; Medi-Cal.

Crestwood Convalescent Hospital
587 Rio Lindo Ave, Chico, CA 95926
(916) 345-1306
Admin Larry E Bradley.
Medical Dir Philip Morgans MD.
Licensure Skilled care. *Beds* SNF 184.
Certified Medicare; Medi-Cal.
Owner Proprietary corp (Crestwood Hospitals
Inc).

Admissions Requirements Medical examination; Physician's request.
Staff RNs 6 (ft), 4 (pt); LPNs 14 (ft), 3 (pt); Nurses' aides 59 (ft), 7 (pt); Physical therapists 3 (pt); Recreational therapists 1 (ft); Activities coordinators 1 (ft); Dietitians 1 (ft).
Facilities Dining room; Physical therapy room; Activities room; Laundry room; Barber/Beauty shop.
Activities Arts & crafts; Cards; Games; Reading groups; Prayer groups; Movies; Shopping trips; Dances/Social/Cultural gatherings.

Riverside Convalescent Hospital
375 Cohasset Rd, Chico, CA 95926
(916) 343-5595
Admin Mary Ann Selak. *Dir of Nursing* Alicia Erpino RN. *Medical Dir* Dr William Coats.
Licensure Skilled care. *Beds* SNF 70. *Certified* Medicare; Medi-Cal.
Owner Privately owned.
Admissions Requirements Medical examination; Physician's request.
Staff RNs; LPNs; Nurses' aides; Activities coordinators.
Facilities Dining room; Physical therapy room; Activities room; Crafts room; Laundry room; Barber/Beauty shop; Library.
Activities Arts & crafts; Cards; Games; Reading groups; Prayer groups; Movies; Shopping trips; Dances/Social/Cultural gatherings; Intergenerational programs; Pet therapy.

Chowchilla

Chowchilla Convalescent Hospital
1000 Ventura St, Chowchilla, CA 93610
(209) 665-4826
Admin Beverly P Brown.
Medical Dir Thomas F Way MD.
Licensure Skilled care. *Beds* SNF 65. *Certified* Medicare; Medi-Cal.
Owner Proprietary corp.
Admissions Requirements Minimum age 18; Medical examination; Physician's request.
Staff Physicians 4 (pt); RNs 1 (ft), 2 (pt); LPNs 6 (ft), 2 (pt); Nurses' aides 27 (ft); Physical therapists 1 (pt); Occupational therapists 1 (pt); Speech therapists 1 (pt); Activities coordinators 1 (ft); Dietitians 1 (pt); Ophthalmologists 1 (pt); Podiatrists 1 (pt); Audiologists 1 (pt); Dentists 1 (pt).
Facilities Dining room; Activities room; Crafts room; Laundry room; Barber/Beauty shop.
Activities Arts & crafts; Cards; Games; Reading groups; Prayer groups; Movies; Shopping trips; Dances/Social/Cultural gatherings.

Chula Vista

Collingwood Manor
553 F St, Chula Vista, CA 92010
(714) 426-8611
Admin Mary C Norwood.
Licensure Intermediate care. *Beds* 88. *Certified* Medi-Cal.
Owner Nonprofit corp.

Fredericka Convalescent Hospital
111 3rd Ave, Chula Vista, CA 92010
(619) 427-2777
Admin Vito J Genna MBA. *Dir of Nursing* Grace Roldan RN. *Medical Dir* Harry Brookler MD.
Licensure Skilled care; Alzheimer's care; Retirement. *Beds* SNF 174. *Certified* Medicare; Medi-Cal.
Owner Nonprofit corp (Pacific Homes).
Admissions Requirements Minimum age 65.
Staff Physicians 1 (pt); RNs 13 (ft), 4 (pt); LPNs 10 (ft), 2 (pt); Nurses' aides 48 (ft), 12 (pt); Physical therapists 1 (pt); Recreational

therapists 1 (pt); Occupational therapists 1 (pt); Speech therapists 1 (pt); Activities coordinators 2 (ft), 1 (pt); Dietitians 1 (ft); Ophthalmologists 1 (pt); Podiatrists 1 (pt); Social workers 1 (pt).
Languages Spanish, Tagalog.
Facilities Dining room; Physical therapy room; Activities room; Chapel; Crafts room; Barber/Beauty shop.
Activities Arts & crafts; Cards; Games; Reading groups; Prayer groups; Movies; Shopping trips.

Citrus Heights

Manor Care of Citrus Heights
7807 Uplands Way, Citrus Heights, CA 95610
(916) 967-2929
Admin Jeffrey A Grillo.
Licensure Skilled care. *Beds* SNF 117. *Certified* Medicare; Medi-Cal.
Owner Proprietary corp (Manor Healthcare Corp).

City of Industry

El Encanto Convalescent Hospital
555 El Encanto Dr, City of Industry, CA 91744
(818) 336-1274
Admin Buck L Perkins MPA. *Dir of Nursing* Shirley Broaddus RN. *Medical Dir* Bernard Shaw MD.
Licensure Skilled care; Intermediate care for mentally retarded. *Beds* SNF 104; ICF/MR 144. *Private Pay Patients* 20%. *Certified* Medi-Cal.
Owner Nonprofit organization/foundation.
Admissions Requirements Minimum age 18.
Staff Physicians 5 (pt); RNs 5 (ft); LPNs 24 (ft); Nurses' aides 99 (ft); Physical therapists 1 (ft); Recreational therapists 1 (ft); Occupational therapists 1 (pt); Speech therapists 1 (pt); Dietitians 1 (ft); Podiatrists.
Facilities Dining room; Physical therapy room; Activities room; Crafts room; Laundry room; Barber/Beauty shop.
Activities Arts & crafts; Cards; Games; Reading groups; Movies; Shopping trips; Dances/Social/Cultural gatherings.

Claremont

Claremont Convalescent Hospital
650 W Harrison Ave, Claremont, CA 91711
(714) 626-1227
Admin Celeste S Ripberger.
Medical Dir Rinard Hart.
Licensure Skilled care. *Beds* SNF 57. *Certified* Medicare; Medi-Cal.
Owner Nonprofit corp (Pacific Homes).
Staff RNs 4 (ft); LPNs 6 (ft); Nurses' aides 19 (ft); Activities coordinators 1 (ft).
Facilities Dining room; Activities room; Crafts room; Laundry room; Barber/Beauty shop; Library; Pool room; Sewing room; Meeting hall.
Activities Arts & crafts; Cards; Games; Reading groups; Prayer groups; Movies.

Hillhaven Convalescent Hospital
590 Indian Hill Blvd, Claremont, CA 91711
(714) 624-4511
Admin Darleen M Curley. *Dir of Nursing* Julie Kidder. *Medical Dir* Rinard Hart MD.
Licensure Skilled care. *Beds* SNF 99. *Certified* Medicare; Medi-Cal.
Owner Proprietary corp (Hillhaven Inc).
Admissions Requirements Minimum age 65; Physician's request.
Staff Physicians 24 (ft); RNs 2 (ft); LPNs 10 (ft), 4 (pt); Physical therapists 1 (pt); Recreational therapists 1 (pt); Occupational therapists 1 (pt); Speech therapists 1 (pt);

Activities coordinators 1 (ft); Dietitians 1 (ft); Ophthalmologists 1 (pt); Podiatrists 1 (pt); Dentists 1 (pt).
Facilities Dining room; Physical therapy room; Activities room; Crafts room; Laundry room; Barber/Beauty shop; Library.
Activities Arts & crafts; Cards; Games; Reading groups; Prayer groups; Movies; Shopping trips; Dances/Social/Cultural gatherings; Outings to lunch, brunch & holiday festivities.

Pilgrim Place Health Services Center
721 W Harrison Ave, Claremont, CA 91711
(714) 621-9581
Admin Richard L Middlemiss RN. *Dir of Nursing* Edith Richardson RN. *Medical Dir* Henery Gallager MD.
Licensure Skilled care; Retirement; Alzheimer's care. *Beds* SNF 68; Retirement 300. *Certified* Medicaid; Medicare; Medi-Cal.
Owner Nonprofit corp.
Admissions Requirements Minimum age 18; Physician's request.
Staff RNs 4 (ft), 2 (pt); LPNs 12 (ft), 3 (pt); Nurses' aides 26 (ft), 10 (pt); Physical therapists 1 (pt); Recreational therapists 1 (pt); Occupational therapists 1 (pt); Speech therapists 1 (pt); Activities coordinators 1 (ft), 1 (pt); Dietitians 1 (pt).
Facilities Dining room; Physical therapy room; Activities room; Chapel; Crafts room; Laundry room; Barber/Beauty shop; Library.
Activities Arts & crafts; Cards; Games; Reading groups; Prayer groups; Movies; Shopping trips; Dances/Social/Cultural gatherings; Pet therapy; Volunteer program.

Cloverdale

CareWest—Manzanita Nursing Center
300 Cherry Creek Rd, Cloverdale, CA 95425
(707) 894-5201
Admin James Brende. *Dir of Nursing* Sylvia Pollard RN. *Medical Dir* William Van Der Weken MD.
Licensure Skilled care. *Beds* SNF 72. *Private Pay Patients* 50%. *Certified* Medicare; Medi-Cal.
Owner Proprietary corp (Care Enterprises).
Admissions Requirements Physician's request.
Staff RNs 6 (ft); LPNs 5 (ft), 2 (pt); Nurses' aides 24 (ft), 5 (pt); Activities coordinators 1 (ft), 1 (pt).
Languages Spanish.
Facilities Physical therapy room; Laundry room; Barber/Beauty shop; Dining/Activities & crafts room.
Activities Arts & crafts; Cards; Games; Reading groups; Prayer groups; Movies; Shopping trips; Dances/Social/Cultural gatherings; Intergenerational programs; Pet therapy.

Clovis

Clovis Convalescent Hospital
111 Barstow Ave, Clovis, CA 93612
(209) 299-2591
Admin Marjory Norris.
Licensure Skilled care. *Beds* SNF 57. *Certified* Medicare; Medi-Cal.
Owner Proprietary corp (Beverly Enterprises).

Clovis Nursing Home
2604 Clovis Ave, Clovis, CA 93612
(209) 291-2173
Admin Karen Loesch.
Licensure Skilled care. *Beds* SNF 59. *Certified* Medicare; Medi-Cal.
Owner Proprietary corp.

Coalinga

Coalinga Convalescent Center
834 Maple Rd, Coalinga, CA 93210
(209) 935-1575
Admin Jerry A Patton. *Dir of Nursing* Vickey
Keller RN.
Licensure Skilled care. *Beds* SNF 58. *Certified*
Medicare; Medi-Cal.
Owner Privately owned.
Admissions Requirements Physician's request.
Staff RNs 1 (ft), 3 (pt); LPNs 3 (ft), 4 (pt);
Nurses' aides 23 (ft), 8 (pt); Physical
therapists 1 (pt); Occupational therapists 1
(pt); Speech therapists 1 (pt); Activities
coordinators 1 (ft); Dietitians 1 (pt).
Languages Spanish.
Facilities Dining room; Physical therapy
room; Laundry room; Barber/Beauty shop;
Library.
Activities Arts & crafts; Games; Prayer groups;
Dances/Social/Cultural gatherings; Park
activities.

Colton

Grand Terrace Convalescent Hospital
12000 Mount Vernon, Colton, CA 92324
(714) 825-5221
Admin Ted Holt.
Medical Dir Richard Neil.
Licensure Skilled care. *Beds* SNF 59. *Certified*
Medicare; Medi-Cal.
Owner Proprietary corp.
Staff Physicians 7 (pt); RNs 1 (ft), 4 (pt);
LPNs 3 (ft), 4 (pt); Nurses' aides 15 (ft), 10
(pt); Physical therapists 1 (pt); Occupational
therapists 1 (pt); Speech therapists 1 (pt);
Activities coordinators 1 (ft); Dietitians 1
(pt); Ophthalmologists 1 (pt); Podiatrists 1
(pt); Dentists 1 (pt).
Facilities Dining room; Physical therapy
room; Activities room; Laundry room;
Barber/Beauty shop; Library.
Activities Arts & crafts; Cards; Games;
Reading groups; Prayer groups; Movies;
Dances/Social/Cultural gatherings.

Olivewood Convalescent Hospital
1700 E Washington St, Colton, CA 92324
(714) 824-1530
Admin Mildred Marshall.
Medical Dir Bernard Tilton MD.
Licensure Skilled care. *Beds* SNF 109.
Certified Medicare; Medi-Cal.
Owner Proprietary corp (Heritage Health Care
Inc).
Admissions Requirements Minimum age 60;
Physician's request.
Facilities Dining room; Physical therapy
room; Activities room; Crafts room; Laundry
room; Barber/Beauty shop; Library.
Activities Arts & crafts; Cards; Games;
Reading groups; Prayer groups; Movies.

Compton

Compton Convalescent Hospital
2309 N Santa Fe Ave, Compton, CA 90222
(213) 639-8111
Admin Mark F Wilson. *Dir of Nursing* Dan E
Davis RN.
Licensure Skilled care. *Beds* SNF 99. *Certified*
Medicare; Medi-Cal.
Owner Nonprofit corp.
Admissions Requirements Minimum age 25;
Physician's request.
Staff RNs 2 (ft); LPNs 10 (ft); Nurses' aides
50 (ft); Physical therapists; Recreational
therapists; Occupational therapists; Speech
therapists; Activities coordinators; Dietitians;
Ophthalmologists; Podiatrists; Dentists.
Facilities Dining room; Physical therapy
room; Activities room; Laundry room;
Barber/Beauty shop.

Activities Arts & crafts; Cards; Games;
Reading groups; Prayer groups; Movies;
Shopping trips; Dances/Social/Cultural
gatherings.

Concord

Bayberry Convalescent Hospital
1800 Adobe St, Concord, CA 94520
(415) 825-1300
Admin Andrea Anderson.
Licensure Skilled care. *Beds* SNF 99. *Certified*
Medicare; Medi-Cal.
Owner Nonprofit corp.

Casa San Miguel
1050 San Miguel Rd, Concord, CA 94518
(415) 825-4280
Dir of Nursing Marilyn Eipperle RN. *Medical
Dir* Martin Stuart MD.
Licensure Skilled care; Alzheimer's care. *Beds*
SNF 200. *Certified* Medi-Cal.
Owner Proprietary corp.
Facilities Dining room; Physical therapy
room; Activities room; Chapel; Crafts room;
Laundry room; Barber/Beauty shop; Library.
Activities Arts & crafts; Cards; Games; Prayer
groups; Movies; Shopping trips; Dances/
Social/Cultural gatherings.

Hillhaven Willow Pass
3318 Willow Pass, Concord, CA 94520
(415) 689-9222
Medical Dir D K Fisher MD.
Licensure Skilled care. *Beds* 83. *Certified*
Medicare; Medi-Cal.
Owner Proprietary corp (Flagg Industries).
Admissions Requirements Minimum age 65;
Medical examination; Physician's request.
Staff RNs 3 (ft), 6 (pt); LPNs 5 (ft), 2 (pt);
Nurses' aides 30 (ft), 6 (pt); Physical
therapists 1 (pt); Occupational therapists 1
(pt); Speech therapists 1 (pt); Activities
coordinators 1 (ft); Podiatrists 1 (pt).
Facilities Dining room; Physical therapy
room; Activities room; Laundry room;
Barber/Beauty shop.
Activities Arts & crafts; Cards; Games;
Reading groups; Prayer groups.

Valley Manor Care Center
3806 Clayton Rd, Concord, CA 94521
(415) 689-2266
Medical Dir Eugene B Whitney.
Licensure Skilled care; Intermediate care. *Beds*
SNF 190; ICF 33. *Certified* Medicare; Medi-
Cal.
Owner Proprietary corp.
Admissions Requirements Medical
examination.
Staff RNs 9 (ft), 4 (pt); LPNs 15 (ft), 8 (pt);
Nurses' aides 72 (ft), 10 (pt); Physical
therapists 1 (ft); Speech therapists 1 (pt);
Activities coordinators 3 (ft); Dietitians 1
(ft); Ophthalmologists 1 (pt); Podiatrists 1
(pt); Audiologists 1 (pt); Dentists 1 (pt).
Facilities Dining room; Physical therapy
room; Activities room; Crafts room; Laundry
room; Barber/Beauty shop; Library.
Activities Arts & crafts; Cards; Games;
Reading groups; Prayer groups; Movies;
Shopping trips; Dances/Social/Cultural
gatherings.

Corona

Corona Community Care Center
2600 S Main St, Corona, CA 91720
(714) 736-6222
Admin Byron J Streifling.
Owner Proprietary corp.

**Corona Gables Retirement Home &
Convalescent Hospital**
1400 Circle City Dr, Corona, CA 91720
(714) 735-0252
Admin Mona L Fisk.

Licensure Skilled care. *Beds* SNF 80. *Certified*
Medicare; Medi-Cal.
Owner Proprietary corp.

Costa Mesa

Beverly Manor Convalescent Hospital
340 Victoria Ave, Costa Mesa, CA 92627
(714) 642-0387
Admin Jeanne Beach. *Dir of Nursing* Sheryl
Kennedy. *Medical Dir* Alan Greenberg MD.
Licensure Skilled care; Alzheimer's care. *Beds*
SNF 79. *Certified* Medicare; Medi-Cal.
Owner Proprietary corp (Beverly Enterprises).
Admissions Requirements Physician's request.
Staff Physicians 3 (pt); RNs 4 (ft), 2 (pt);
Nurses' aides 34 (ft), 5 (pt); Physical
therapists 1 (ft), 1 (pt); Occupational
therapists 1 (pt); Speech therapists 1 (pt);
Activities coordinators 1 (ft); Dietitians 1
(pt); Ophthalmologists 1 (pt); Podiatrists 1
(pt); Dentists 1 (pt); LVNs 4 (ft), 3 (pt);
Social workers 1 (ft).
Languages Spanish.
Facilities Dining room; Physical therapy
room; Activities room; Crafts room; Laundry
room; Barber/Beauty shop.
Activities Arts & crafts; Cards; Games;
Reading groups; Prayer groups; Movies.

Mesa Verde Convalescent Hospital
661 Center St, Costa Mesa, CA 92627
(714) 548-5585
Admin Barbara Wunsch. *Dir of Nursing*
Louise McGuire. *Medical Dir* Paul Kuhn
MD.
Licensure Skilled care; Retirement. *Beds* SNF
80. *Certified* Medicare.
Owner Proprietary corp.
Admissions Requirements Medical
examination.
Staff Physicians 4 (pt); RNs 9 (ft), 1 (pt);
LPNs 8 (ft), 4 (pt); Nurses' aides 30 (ft), 8
(pt); Physical therapists 2 (ft); Reality
therapists 1 (pt); Recreational therapists 1
(pt); Occupational therapists 1 (pt); Speech
therapists 1 (pt); Activities coordinators 2
(ft); Dietitians 1 (pt); Ophthalmologists 1
(pt); Podiatrists 1 (pt); Dentists 1 (pt); Social
workers 1 (ft).
Facilities Dining room; Physical therapy
room; Activities room; Chapel; Crafts room;
Laundry room; Barber/Beauty shop; Library;
Conference room.
Activities Arts & crafts; Cards; Games;
Reading groups; Prayer groups; Movies;
Shopping trips; Dances/Social/Cultural
gatherings.

Cotati

Maralie Convalescent Hospital
PO Box 179, Cotati, CA 94931
(707) 542-1510
Admin Donald H Bais.
Medical Dir William Hopper MD.
Licensure Skilled care. *Beds* SNF 52. *Certified*
Medicaid; Medicare; Medi-Cal.
Owner Proprietary corp.
Admissions Requirements Minimum age 18;
Physician's request.
Staff RNs 3 (ft), 2 (pt); LPNs 4 (ft), 2 (pt);
Nurses' aides 15 (ft), 4 (pt); Physical
therapists 1 (ft); Activities coordinators 1
(ft), 1 (pt).
Facilities Dining room; Physical therapy
room; Activities room; Crafts room; Barber/
Beauty shop.
Activities Arts & crafts; Games; Reading
groups; Prayer groups; Movies; Dances/
Social/Cultural gatherings.

Covina

Badillo Convalescent Hospital
519 W Badillo St, Covina, CA 91723
(818) 915-5621
Admin Duane Van Dyke.
Licensure Skilled care. *Beds* SNF 59. *Certified*
Medicare; Medi-Cal.
Owner Privately owned.

Covina Convalescent Center
261 W Badillo St, Covina, CA 91722
(818) 967-3874
Admin Terry Parker. *Dir of Nursing* Carol
Cook RN. *Medical Dir* Dr Advincula.
Licensure Skilled care. *Beds* SNF 99. *Certified*
Medicare; Medi-Cal.
Owner Proprietary corp.
Admissions Requirements Physician's request.
Staff RNs 2 (ft), 1 (pt); LPNs 12 (ft), 3 (pt);
Activities coordinators 1 (ft), 1 (pt);
Dietitians 1 (ft).
Languages Spanish.
Facilities Dining room; Physical therapy
room; Activities room; Laundry room;
Barber/Beauty shop.
Activities Arts & crafts; Cards; Games;
Reading groups; Prayer groups; Movies;
Shopping trips; Dances/Social/Cultural
gatherings.

Rowland
330 W Rowland Ave, Covina, CA 91723
(818) 967-2741
Admin Anthony Kalomas.
Medical Dir E Mason MD.
Licensure Skilled care. *Beds* SNF 126.
Certified Medicare; Medi-Cal.
Owner Proprietary corp.
Admissions Requirements Minimum age 65.
Staff RNs 4 (ft), 2 (pt); LPNs 7 (ft), 2 (pt);
Nurses' aides 47 (ft), 6 (pt); Physical
therapists 1 (ft); Recreational therapists 1
(pt); Speech therapists 1 (pt); Activities
coordinators 1 (ft), 1 (pt); Dietitians 1 (pt);
Podiatrists 1 (pt); Dentists 1 (pt).
Facilities Dining room; Physical therapy
room; Activities room; Chapel; Crafts room;
Laundry room; Barber/Beauty shop; Library.
Activities Arts & crafts; Cards; Games;
Reading groups; Prayer groups; Movies;
Shopping trips; Dances/Social/Cultural
gatherings.

Crescent City

Crescent City Convalescent
1280 Marshall St, Crescent City, CA 95531
(707) 464-6151
Admin Neil Fassinger.
Licensure Skilled care. *Beds* SNF 99. *Certified*
Medicare; Medi-Cal.
Owner Proprietary corp.

Culver City

Marina Care Center
5240 Sepulveda Ave, Culver City, CA 90230
(213) 391-7266
Admin Jane Anderson.
Medical Dir Dr Keating.
Licensure Skilled care. *Beds* SNF 116.
Certified Medicare; Medi-Cal.
Owner Proprietary corp.
Staff RNs 3 (ft), 4 (pt); LPNs 9 (ft), 2 (pt);
Nurses' aides 28 (ft), 5 (pt); Physical
therapists 1 (pt); Recreational therapists 1
(ft); Occupational therapists 1 (pt); Speech
therapists 1 (pt); Activities coordinators 1
(ft); Dietitians 1 (ft); Ophthalmologists 1
(pt); Podiatrists 1 (pt); Audiologists 1 (pt);
Dentists 1 (pt).
Facilities Dining room; Physical therapy
room; Activities room; Crafts room; Laundry
room; Barber/Beauty shop; Staff developer.
Activities Arts & crafts; Cards; Games;
Reading groups; Prayer groups; Movies.

Marycrest Manor
10664 Saint James Dr, Culver City, CA
90230-5498
(213) 838-2778
Admin Sr Margaret Mary FitzSimons RSC.
Dir of Nursing Ellen Allard RN. *Medical Dir*
Dr Douglas Tyler.
Licensure Skilled care. *Beds* SNF 57. *Private
Pay Patients* 75%. *Certified* Medicare; Medi-
Cal.
Owner Nonprofit organization/foundation.
Admissions Requirements Minimum age 70;
Females only; Medical examination;
Physician's request.
Staff Physicians 15 (pt); RNs 1 (ft), 5 (pt);
LPNs 5 (ft), 7 (pt); Nurses' aides 30 (ft), 8
(pt); Physical therapists (consultant);
Recreational therapists (consultant);
Occupational therapists (contultant);
Activities coordinators 1 (ft), 3 (pt);
Dietitians 1 (ft); Podiatrists (consultant);
Audiologists (consultant).
Languages Spanish, Arabic.
Affiliation Roman Catholic.
Facilities Dining room; Activities room;
Chapel; Laundry room; Barber/Beauty shop;
Library; Private rooms; Lounges; Dental
office.
Activities Arts & crafts; Cards; Games;
Reading groups; Prayer groups; Movies;
Dances/Social/Cultural gatherings; Pastoral
care.

Cupertino

Pleasant View Convalescent Hospital
22590 Voss Ave, Cupertino, CA 95014
(408) 253-9034
Admin Kenneth V Dunton. *Dir of Nursing*
Ingrid Tillmann. *Medical Dir* Fred W
Schwertley MD.
Licensure Skilled care. *Beds* SNF 170.
Certified Medicare; Medi-Cal.
Owner Privately owned.
Admissions Requirements Minimum age 16;
Medical examination.
Staff RNs 7 (ft), 2 (pt); LPNs 8 (ft), 5 (pt);
Nurses' aides 65 (ft); Physical therapists 1
(ft); Activities coordinators 2 (ft); Dietitians
1 (ft).
Languages Spanish, Chinese, Tagalog,
German, Arabic, Portuguese.
Facilities Dining room; Physical therapy
room; Activities room; Barber/Beauty shop.
Activities Arts & crafts; Cards; Games;
Reading groups; Prayer groups; Movies;
Shopping trips; Dances/Social/Cultural
gatherings; Educational programs;
Horticulture therapy; Music therapy.

Sunny View Manor
22445 Cupertino Rd, Cupertino, CA 95014
(408) 253-4300
Admin Jan Douglas Straker. *Dir of Nursing*
Anne Ham. *Medical Dir* F W Schwertley
MD.
Licensure Skilled care; Retirement. *Beds* SNF
45. *Certified* Medicare; Medi-Cal.
Owner Nonprofit corp.
Admissions Requirements Minimum age 62;
Medical examination.
Staff RNs 2 (ft), 8 (pt); LPNs 1 (ft); Nurses'
aides 14 (ft), 5 (pt); Activities coordinators 1
(ft).
Languages Tagalog, Spanish.
Affiliation Lutheran.
Facilities Dining room; Physical therapy
room; Activities room; Chapel; Crafts room;
Barber/Beauty shop; Library.
Activities Arts & crafts; Games; Prayer groups;
Movies; Shopping trips.

Daly City

St Francis Convalescent Pavilion Inc
99 Escuela Dr, Daly City, CA 94015
(415) 994-3200
Admin Glen Goddard.
Licensure Skilled care. *Beds* SNF 239.
Certified Medicare; Medi-Cal.
Owner Proprietary corp.

St Francis Heights Convalescent Hospital
35 Escuela Dr, Daly City, CA 94015
(415) 755-9515
Admin Evelyn M Goddard.
Licensure Skilled care. *Beds* SNF 102.
Certified Medicare; Medi-Cal.
Owner Proprietary corp.

Villa Convalescent Center
130 Vale St, Daly City, CA 94014
(415) 755-0421
Admin Joseph Sarto.
Licensure Skilled care. *Beds* SNF 96. *Certified*
Medicare; Medi-Cal.
Owner Proprietary corp.

Danville

Diablo Convalescent Hospital
336 Diablo Rd, Danville, CA 94526
(415) 837-5536
Admin Pauline Elders.
Licensure Skilled care. *Beds* SNF 54. *Certified*
Medicare.
Owner Proprietary corp.

Davis

Driftwood Convalescent Hospital
1850 E 8th St, Davis, CA 95616
(916) 756-1800
Admin Jonathan Freer.
Medical Dir S Schaffer MD.
Licensure Skilled care. *Beds* SNF 124.
Certified Medicare; Medi-Cal.
Owner Proprietary corp (ARA Living
Centers).
Staff Physicians 3 (pt); RNs 9 (ft), 4 (pt);
LPNs 4 (ft), 1 (pt); Nurses' aides 34 (ft), 18
(pt); Physical therapists 1 (pt); Recreational
therapists 1 (pt); Speech therapists 1 (pt);
Activities coordinators 1 (ft), 1 (pt);
Dietitians 1 (pt); Podiatrists 1 (pt);
Audiologists 1 (pt); Dentists 1 (pt).
Facilities Dining room; Physical therapy
room; Activities room; Laundry room;
Barber/Beauty shop.
Activities Arts & crafts; Cards; Games;
Reading groups; Prayer groups; Movies;
Shopping trips; Dances/Social/Cultural
gatherings.

Sierra Health Care Convalescent Hospital
715 Pole Line Rd, Davis, CA 95616
(916) 756-4900
Admin Edward J Garrison.
Licensure Skilled care. *Beds* SNF 132.
Certified Medicare; Medi-Cal.
Owner Proprietary corp.
Admissions Requirements Minimum age 18.
Staff RNs 4 (ft), 4 (pt); LPNs 7 (ft), 3 (pt);
Nurses' aides 45 (ft), 10 (pt); Activities
coordinators 2 (ft).
Languages Spanish, Vietnamese, Farsi,
Arabic, Ethiopic.
Facilities Dining room; Physical therapy
room; Activities room; Chapel; Crafts room;
Laundry room; Barber/Beauty shop; Library.
Activities Arts & crafts; Cards; Games;
Reading groups; Prayer groups; Movies;
Shopping trips; Dances/Social/Cultural
gatherings; Resident & family council.

Del Mar

Casa Palmera Care Center
14750 El Camino Real, Del Mar, CA 92014
(619) 481-4411
Admin Lee Johnson. *Dir of Nursing* Judy
Ring RN. *Medical Dir* Michael Lundberg
MD.

Licensure Skilled care. *Beds* SNF 99. *Certified* Medicare.
Owner Privately owned.
Staff RNs 6 (ft); LPNs 19 (ft); Nurses' aides 74 (ft).

Delano

Browning Manor Convalescent Hospital
PO Box 68, 729 Browning, Delano, CA 93215
(805) 725-2501, 725-1417 FAX
Admin Carolyn J Johnson. *Dir of Nursing* Beverly Donley RN. *Medical Dir* Ivor Shore MD.
Licensure Skilled care. *Beds* SNF 53. *Private Pay Patients* 5%. *Certified* Medicare; Medi-Cal.
Owner Proprietary corp.
Admissions Requirements Medical examination; Physician's request.
Staff RNs 1 (ft), 1 (pt); LPNs 4 (ft), 2 (pt); Nurses' aides 20 (ft), 10 (pt); Physical therapists 1 (pt); Occupational therapists 1 (pt); Activities coordinators 1 (ft); Dietitians 1 (pt); Podiatrists 1 (pt).
Languages Spanish, Tagalog.
Facilities Dining room; Activities room; Laundry room.
Activities Arts & crafts; Cards; Games; Reading groups; Prayer groups; Movies; Dances/Social/Cultural gatherings.

Delano Regional Medical Center
1401 Garces Hwy, Delano, CA 93215
(805) 725-4800
Admin Sean O'Neal.
Owner Proprietary corp.

Dinuba

Dinuba Convalescent Hospital
1730 S College, Dinuba, CA 93618
(209) 591-3300
Admin John Ralff.
Licensure Skilled care. *Beds* SNF 99. *Certified* Medicare; Medi-Cal.
Owner Proprietary corp.

Downey

Brookwood Care Center
9300 Telegraph Rd, Downey, CA 90240
(213) 869-2567
Admin Catherine Rodriguez.
Medical Dir Joel M Sandler MD.
Licensure Skilled care. *Beds* SNF 70. *Certified* Medicare; Medi-Cal.
Owner Proprietary corp.
Admissions Requirements Minimum age 18; Medical examination; Physician's request.
Staff RNs 1 (ft), 2 (pt); LPNs 8 (ft), 2 (pt); Nurses' aides 2 (pt); Physical therapists 1 (pt); Recreational therapists 1 (pt); Occupational therapists 1 (pt); Speech therapists 1 (pt); Activities coordinators 1 (ft); Dietitians 1 (pt); Ophthalmologists 1 (pt); Podiatrists 1 (pt); Dentists 1 (pt).
Facilities Dining room; Barber/Beauty shop.

Downey Care Center
13007 S Paramount, Downey, CA 90242
(213) 923-9301
Admin Adrienne Rzepnick. *Dir of Nursing* Marie Weiler. *Medical Dir* Robert Tsai MD.
Licensure Skilled care. *Beds* SNF 99. *Certified* Medicare; Medi-Cal.
Owner Proprietary corp.
Staff RNs 3 (ft); LPNs 9 (ft); Nurses' aides 25 (ft); Recreational therapists 1 (ft); Activities coordinators 1 (ft).
Languages Spanish.
Facilities Dining room; Activities room; Crafts room; Laundry room; Barber/Beauty shop.

Activities Arts & crafts; Cards; Games; Reading groups; Prayer groups; Movies; Shopping trips; Dances/Social/Cultural gatherings.

Downey Community Health Center
8425 Iowa St, Downey, CA 90241
(213) 862-6506
Admin Richard Coberly.
Licensure Skilled care. *Beds* SNF 198. *Certified* Medicare; Medi-Cal.
Owner Privately owned.

Lakewood Park Health Center
12023 S Lakewood Blvd, Downey, CA 90242
(213) 869-0978
Admin Daniel C Zilafro. *Dir of Nursing* Lucy Brimbulea. *Medical Dir* Dr Robert Eston.
Licensure Skilled care; Intermediate care. *Beds* SNF 207; ICF 24. *Certified* Medicare; Medi-Cal.
Owner Proprietary corp.
Admissions Requirements Minimum age 21; Physician's request.
Staff Physicians 8 (pt); RNs 6 (ft); LPNs 20 (ft); Nurses' aides 96 (ft); Physical therapists 1 (pt); Recreational therapists 1 (pt); Occupational therapists 1 (pt); Speech therapists 1 (pt); Activities coordinators 1 (ft); Dietitians 1 (pt); Ophthalmologists 1 (pt); Podiatrists 1 (pt); Audiologists 1 (pt).
Languages Spanish, Korean, Japanese, Thai.
Facilities Dining room; Physical therapy room; Activities room; Chapel; Barber/ Beauty shop; Library.
Activities Arts & crafts; Cards; Games; Reading groups; Prayer groups; Movies; Shopping trips; Dances/Social/Cultural gatherings; Pet therapy.

Duarte

Buena Vista Manor
802 Buena Vista Ave, Duarte, CA 91010
(818) 359-8141
Admin Stephen T Paterson.
Medical Dir William Beard MD.
Licensure Skilled care. *Beds* SNF 69. *Certified* Medicare; Medi-Cal.
Owner Nonprofit corp (Southern California Presbyterian Homes).
Staff Physicians 3 (pt); RNs 1 (ft), 1 (pt); LPNs 7 (ft), 2 (pt); Nurses' aides 22 (ft), 2 (pt); Recreational therapists 1 (ft); Occupational therapists 1 (pt); Activities coordinators 1 (pt); Dietitians 1 (ft).
Affiliation Presbyterian.
Facilities Dining room; Activities room; Crafts room; Laundry room; Barber/Beauty shop; Library.
Activities Arts & crafts; Cards; Games; Reading groups; Prayer groups; Movies; Shopping trips; Dances/Social/Cultural gatherings; Teas; Exercise; Brunches.

Community Care Center
2335 S Mountain Ave, Duarte, CA 91010
(818) 357-3207
Admin Serge Reiss.
Licensure Skilled care. *Beds* SNF 167. *Certified* Medi-Cal.
Owner Proprietary corp (Community Care Centers Inc).

Highland Convalescent Hospital
PO Box 297, 1340 S Highland Ave, Duarte, CA 91010
(818) 359-9171
Admin Bonnie A Garcia. *Dir of Nursing* N Gatchalian RN. *Medical Dir* G Ramos MD.
Licensure Skilled care. *Beds* SNF 58. *Private Pay Patients* 25%. *Certified* Medicare; Medi-Cal.
Owner Proprietary corp.
Staff Physicians 16 (pt); RNs 1 (ft), 2 (pt); LPNs 4 (ft), 3 (pt); Physical therapists 2 (pt); Reality therapists 1 (pt); Occupational therapists 1 (pt); Speech therapists 1 (pt);

Activities coordinators 1 (ft), 1 (pt); Dietitians 1 (ft); Ophthalmologists 1 (pt); Podiatrists 1 (pt); Audiologists 1 (pt).
Languages Filipino, Spanish, Danish, German, Hindi, Hungarian.
Facilities Dining room; Activities room; Laundry room; Barber/Beauty shop; Library.
Activities Arts & crafts; Cards; Games; Reading groups; Prayer groups; Movies; Shopping trips; Dances/Social/Cultural gatherings; Intergenerational programs; Pet therapy.

Monrovia Convalescent Hospital
PO Box 216, Duarte, CA 91009-0216
(818) 359-6618
Admin Sherman Davidson.
Licensure Skilled care. *Beds* SNF 72. *Certified* Medicare; Medi-Cal.
Owner Proprietary corp.

Westminster Gardens
1420 Santo Domingo Ave, Duarte, CA 91010
(818) 359-2571
Admin John D Rollins. *Dir of Nursing* Dorothy J Kaufmann RN. *Medical Dir* Marshall P Welles MD.
Licensure Skilled care. *Beds* SNF 64. *Private Pay Patients* 100%.
Owner Nonprofit organization/foundation.
Admissions Requirements Physician's request.
Staff Physicians 1 (pt); RNs 3 (pt); LPNs 3 (ft), 8 (pt); Nurses' aides 19 (ft), 8 (pt); Physical therapists (contracted); Speech therapists (contracted); Activities coordinators 1 (ft); Podiatrists (contracted); Food service supervisors 1 (ft); Dentists 1 (pt).
Languages Spanish.
Affiliation Presbyterian.
Facilities Dining room; Physical therapy room; Barber/Beauty shop; Library; Activities & crafts room; Meditation room; Wheelchair accessible grounds.
Activities Arts & crafts; Games; Reading groups; Prayer groups; Movies; Pet therapy; Bible study; Current events; Hymn singing; Picnics; Trips to mall & restaurants; Mountain drives.

El Cajon

Anza Convalescent Hospital
622 S Anza St, El Cajon, CA 92020
(619) 442-0544
Admin Jeannette Ohanneson.
Licensure Skilled care. *Beds* SNF 160. *Certified* Medicare; Medi-Cal.
Owner Proprietary corp (Care Enterprises).

Carroll's Intermediate Care
151 Claydelle Ave, El Cajon, CA 92020
(714) 442-0245
Admin Joann Prather.
Medical Dir Dr Palmer.
Licensure Intermediate care. *Beds* 65. *Certified* Medi-Cal.
Owner Proprietary corp.
Admissions Requirements Physician's request.
Staff LPNs 3 (ft); Nurses' aides 7 (ft); Activities coordinators 1 (ft); Dietitians 1 (pt).
Facilities Dining room; Activities room; Crafts room; Laundry room; Barber/Beauty shop.
Activities Arts & crafts; Games; Reading groups; Prayer groups; Movies.

Carroll's Intermediate Care—Anza
654 S Anza, El Cajon, CA 92020
(714) 440-5005
Admin Roger L Caddell.
Licensure Intermediate care. *Beds* 120. *Certified* Medi-Cal.
Owner Proprietary corp.

El Cajon Valley Convalescent Hospital
510 E Washington Ave, El Cajon, CA 92020
(619) 440-1211
Admin H A Bunn & D Bunn.
Licensure Skilled care. *Beds* SNF 256.
Certified Medicare; Medi-Cal.
Owner Proprietary corp.
Facilities Dining room; Physical therapy
room; Activities room; Crafts room; Laundry
room; Barber/Beauty shop; Library.
Activities Arts & crafts; Games.

Helix View Healthcare Center
1201 S Orange Ave, El Cajon, CA 92020
(619) 441-1988
Admin Cathy Kitchell.
Licensure Skilled care. *Beds* SNF 124.
Certified Medicare; Medi-Cal.
Owner Proprietary corp.

Lo-Har Lodge Inc
794 Dorothy St, El Cajon, CA 92020
(619) 444-8270
Admin Sigridur Weatherson.
Licensure Skilled care. *Beds* SNF 32.
Owner Proprietary corp.

Madison Convalescent Center
1391 Madison Ave, El Cajon, CA 92021
(619) 444-1107
Admin Vicki Herrmann. *Dir of Nursing* Doris
Shultz. *Medical Dir* Frank Flint MD.
Licensure Skilled care; Alzheimer's care. *Beds*
SNF 96. *Certified* Medicare; Medi-Cal.
Owner Proprietary corp (Care Enterprises).
Admissions Requirements Minimum age 18;
Physician's request.
Staff RNs 3 (ft), 1 (pt); LPNs 8 (ft), 1 (pt);
Nurses' aides 38 (ft); Physical therapists 1
(ft); Recreational therapists 1 (ft);
Occupational therapists (contracted); Speech
therapists (contracted); Activities
coordinators 1 (ft); Dietitians 1 (ft).
Languages Spanish, Tagalog.
Facilities Dining room; Physical therapy
room; Activities room; Laundry room;
Barber/Beauty shop.
Activities Arts & crafts; Cards; Games;
Reading groups; Prayer groups; Shopping
trips; Dances/Social/Cultural gatherings; Pet
therapy; Music.

Magnolia Special Care Center
635 S Magnolia, El Cajon, CA 92020
(619) 442-8826
Admin Marriet Haugen.
Licensure Skilled care. *Beds* SNF 99. *Certified*
Medicare; Medi-Cal.
Owner Proprietary corp.

Parkside Special Care Center
444 W Lexington, El Cajon, CA 92020
(619) 442-7744
Admin Stephen F Winner. *Dir of Nursing*
Suzie Gilpatrick RN. *Medical Dir* Dr Duane
Palmer.
Licensure Skilled care; Alzheimer's care. *Beds*
SNF 50. *Private Pay Patients* 80%. *Certified*
Medi-Cal.
Owner Privately owned.
Admissions Requirements Medical
examination; Alzheimer's disease.
Staff Physicians 1 (pt); RNs 2 (ft), 1 (pt);
LPNs 5 (ft); Nurses' aides 24 (ft), 6 (pt);
Recreational therapists 1 (ft); Activities
coordinators 2 (ft); Dietitians 1 (pt).
Languages Spanish.
Facilities Dining room; Activities room;
Laundry room; Barber/Beauty shop; 1 acre
park secured for wanderers.
Activities Arts & crafts; Cards; Games; Reading
groups; Prayer groups; Movies; Shopping
trips; Dances/Social/Cultural gatherings; Pet
therapy; Activities specialized for patients
with Alzheimer's disease.

Royal Home
12436 Royal Rd, El Cajon, CA 92021
(619) 443-3886

Admin James E Carter I. *Dir of Nursing* Tina
Rahowski. *Medical Dir* Frank Fint MD.
Licensure Skilled care. *Beds* SNF 19. *Certified*
Medi-Cal.
Owner Privately owned.
Admissions Requirements Physician's request.
Staff RNs 1 (ft), 1 (pt); LPNs 1 (ft), 3 (pt);
Nurses' aides 2 (ft), 4 (pt); Activities
coordinators 1 (ft), 1 (pt); Dietitians 1 (ft).
Facilities Dining room; Laundry room; Patio.
Activities Arts & crafts; Cards; Games;
Reading groups; Prayer groups; Shopping
trips; Dances/Social/Cultural gatherings.

T L C Convalescent Hospital
1340 E Madison Ave, El Cajon, CA 92021
(619) 442-8855
Admin Donald L Linfesty.
Licensure Skilled care. *Beds* SNF 99. *Certified*
Medicare; Medi-Cal.
Owner Proprietary corp.

Vista Del Cerro Convalescent Center
675 E Bradley Ave, El Cajon, CA 92021
(619) 448-6633
Admin Clyde Prince.
Medical Dir Charles Miller MD.
Licensure Skilled care. *Beds* SNF 56. *Certified*
Medicare; Medi-Cal.
Owner Proprietary corp.
Admissions Requirements Physician's request.
Staff RNs 4 (ft); LPNs 9 (ft); Nurses' aides 30
(ft); Physical therapists 1 (pt); Recreational
therapists 1 (pt); Activities coordinators 1
(ft); Podiatrists 1 (pt).
Facilities Dining room; Laundry room.
Activities Arts & crafts; Cards; Games;
Reading groups; Prayer groups; Shopping
trips.

El Centro

Valley Convalescent Hospital
1700 Imperial, El Centro, CA 92243
(619) 352-8471
Admin Melvin L Fuller. *Dir of Nursing*
Debbie Brown. *Medical Dir* Dr Weiss.
Licensure Skilled care. *Beds* SNF 123. *Private
Pay Patients* 95%. *Certified* Medicaid;
Medicare; Medi-Cal.
Owner Proprietary corp (National Heritage).
Admissions Requirements Medical
examination; Physician's request.
Staff Physicians; RNs; LPNs; Nurses' aides;
Physical therapists; Recreational therapists;
Activities coordinators; Dietitians;
Ophthalmologists (consultant); Podiatrists
(consultant); Audiologists (consultant).
Languages Spanish, Chinese.
Facilities Dining room; Physical therapy
room; Activities room; Crafts room; Laundry
room; Barber/Beauty shop.
Activities Arts & crafts; Cards; Reading
groups.

El Cerrito

Shields Nursing Center
3230 Carlson Blvd, El Cerrito, CA 94530
(415) 525-3212
Admin Willie Shields. *Dir of Nursing* Birdie
Stafford LVN. *Medical Dir* Otis Rounds
MD.
Licensure Skilled care; Intermediate care. *Beds*
SNF 21; ICF 24. *Certified* Medicare; Medi-
Cal.
Owner Proprietary corp.
Admissions Requirements Medical
examination; Physician's request.
Staff LPNs 3 (ft); Nurses' aides 12 (ft);
Activities coordinators 1 (ft).
Facilities Dining room; Activities room;
Crafts room; Laundry room.
Activities Arts & crafts; Cards; Games; Prayer
groups; Movies; Dances/Social/Cultural
gatherings.

El Monte

Georgia Atkison Convalescent Center
3825 N Durfee Ave, El Monte, CA 91732
(818) 444-2535
Admin Regina F Zilafro.
Licensure Skilled care; Intermediate care. *Beds*
SNF 135; ICF 4. *Certified* Medicare; Medi-
Cal.
Owner Proprietary corp.

Cedars—Glen Care Center
11900 Ramona Blvd, El Monte, CA 91732
(818) 442-5721
Admin Gertrude M Yerkes.
Licensure Skilled care. *Beds* SNF 148.
Certified Medicare; Medi-Cal.
Owner Proprietary corp.

Chandler Care Center—Ramona
12036 Ramona Blvd, El Monte, CA 91732
(213) 448-9851
Admin Danny J Amador.
Licensure Skilled care. *Beds* 99. *Certified*
Medicare; Medi-Cal.
Owner Proprietary corp.

Cherrylee Lodge Sanitarium
5053 N Peck Rd, El Monte, CA 91732
(818) 448-4248
Admin Marcella A Brown. *Dir of Nursing*
Lettie Valmores. *Medical Dir* Richard Weiss
MD.
Licensure Skilled care; Alzheimer's care. *Beds*
SNF 46. *Certified* Medicare; Medi-Cal.
Owner Proprietary corp.
Admissions Requirements Medical
examination; Physician's request.
Staff RNs 1 (ft), 3 (pt); Nurses' aides 16 (ft), 1
(pt); Activities coordinators 1 (ft), 1 (pt);
Dietitians 1 (ft); LVNs 3 (ft), 4 (pt).
Languages Spanish, Tagalog.
Facilities Dining room; Activities room;
Laundry room; Barber/Beauty shop.
Activities Arts & crafts; Cards; Games; Prayer
groups; Movies; Shopping trips; Dances/
Social/Cultural gatherings.

El Monte Care Center
5043 N Peck Rd, El Monte, CA 91732
(818) 579-1602
Admin Marcella A Brown. *Dir of Nursing*
Virginia Estorninos RN. *Medical Dir* Dr
Rafael Elul.
Licensure Skilled care; Alzheimer's care. *Beds*
SNF 59. *Private Pay Patients* 50%. *Certified*
Medicare; Medi-Cal.
Owner Proprietary corp.
Admissions Requirements Physician's request;
Must have Alzheimer's or related disorders.
Staff Physicians 12 (pt); RNs 1 (pt); LPNs 6
(ft); Nurses' aides 15 (ft); Physical therapists;
Recreational therapists; Activities
coordinators 2 (ft); Dietitians 1 (ft), 1 (pt);
Podiatrists 1 (pt); Audiologists 1 (pt).
Languages Spanish, Tagalag, French.
Facilities Dining room; Activities room;
Crafts room; Laundry room; Barber/Beauty
shop.
Activities Arts & crafts; Cards; Games;
Reading groups; Prayer groups; Movies;
Shopping trips; Dances/Social/Cultural
gatherings; Intergenerational programs; Pet
therapy.

El Monte Convalescent Hospital
4096 Easy St, El Monte, CA 91731
(818) 442-1500
Admin Jesse Telles. *Dir of Nursing* Catherine
Maddux RNC. *Medical Dir* Dr Zaw Min.
Licensure Skilled care. *Beds* SNF 99. *Certified*
Medicare; Medi-Cal.
Owner Proprietary corp.
Staff Physicians 12 (pt); RNs 3 (ft), 2 (pt);
LPNs 5 (ft), 4 (pt); Nurses' aides 35 (ft), 9
(pt); Physical therapists 1 (pt); Occupational
therapists 1 (pt); Speech therapists 1 (pt);

Activities coordinators 2 (ft); Dietitians 1 (pt); Podiatrists 1 (pt); Audiologists 1 (pt); Dentists 1 (pt).
Facilities Dining room; Physical therapy room; Activities room; Crafts room; Laundry room; Barber/Beauty shop; Library.
Activities Arts & crafts; Cards; Games; Reading groups; Prayer groups; Movies; Bingo; Lunch outings.

Elmcrest Convalescent Hospital
3111 Santa Anita Ave, El Monte, CA 91733
(818) 443-0218
Admin Frank Garcia. *Dir of Nursing* Pam Chacon. *Medical Dir* Douglas Copley.
Licensure Skilled care. *Beds* SNF 96. *Certified* Medicare; Medi-Cal.
Owner Proprietary corp (Care Enterprises).
Admissions Requirements Physician's request.
Languages Spanish.
Facilities Dining room; Physical therapy room; Activities room; Laundry room; Barber/Beauty shop.
Activities Arts & crafts; Cards; Games; Reading groups; Prayer groups; Movies; Shopping trips; Dances/Social/Cultural gatherings.

Idle Acre Sanitarium & Convalescent Hospital
5044 Buffington Rd, El Monte, CA 91732
(213) 443-1351
Admin Barry Silberberg.
Medical Dir Gary Schlecter MD.
Licensure Skilled care. *Beds* SNF 53. *Certified* Medi-Cal.
Owner Proprietary corp.
Staff Physicians; RNs; LPNs; Nurses' aides; Activities coordinators; Dietitians.
Languages Spanish.
Facilities Dining room; Activities room; Laundry room; Barber/Beauty shop.
Activities Arts & crafts; Games; Prayer groups.

Penn Mar Therapeutic Center
3938 Cogswell Rd, El Monte, CA 91732
(818) 401-1557, 579-5284 FAX
Admin Dolores T Dimla. *Dir of Nursing* Betty McKeown. *Medical Dir* Robert H Maurice MD.
Licensure Skilled care. *Beds* SNF/STP -Psych 45. *Private Pay Patients* 0%. *Certified* Medi-Cal.
Owner Proprietary corp (Mitchell A Kantor).
Admissions Requirements Minimum age 18.
Staff Physicians 3 (ft); RNs 9 (ft); LPNs 12 (ft); Recreational therapists 1 (ft); Dietitians 1 (ft); Mental health workers 9 (ft); Social workers 3 (ft); Psychologists 1 (ft).
Facilities Dining room; Activities room; Crafts room; Barber/Beauty shop.
Activities Arts & crafts; Cards; Games; Reading groups; Movies; Shopping trips; Dances/Social/Cultural gatherings; Intergenerational programs.

Sunset Manor Convalescent Hospital
2720 Nevada Ave, El Monte, CA 91733
(818) 443-9425
Admin Blaine E Hendrickson. *Dir of Nursing* Linda Blankenship RN. *Medical Dir* Richard Hart MD.
Licensure Skilled care. *Beds* SNF 81. *Certified* Medicare; Medi-Cal.
Owner Proprietary corp.
Admissions Requirements Minimum age 18; Physician's request.
Staff Physicians 13 (pt); RNs 2 (ft), 2 (pt); LPNs 7 (ft), 4 (pt); Nurses' aides 28 (ft), 8 (pt); Physical therapists 1 (pt); Occupational therapists 1 (pt); Speech therapists 1 (pt); Activities coordinators 1 (ft), 1 (pt); Dietitians 1 (pt); Ophthalmologists 1 (pt); Podiatrists 1 (pt); Dentists 1 (pt).
Languages Sign, Spanish, Tagalog.
Facilities Dining room; Physical therapy room; Activities room; Crafts room; Laundry room; Barber/Beauty shop.

Activities Arts & crafts; Cards; Games; Reading groups; Prayer groups; Movies; Senior citizen gatherings.

Wellesley
11210 Lower Azusa Rd, El Monte, CA 91732
(818) 442-6863
Admin Regina N Trent. *Dir of Nursing* Mrs C Brown. *Medical Dir* Dr J Shah.
Licensure Skilled care; Intermediate care; Alzheimer's care. *Beds* SNF 84; ICF 6. *Private Pay Patients* 20%. *Certified* Medicare; Medi-Cal.
Owner Proprietary corp (Medicrest).
Admissions Requirements Minimum age 65.
Staff Physicians (consultant); RNs; Nurses' aides; Physical therapists; Occupational therapists; Speech therapists; Activities coordinators; Dietitians; Ophthalmologists; Podiatrists; Audiologists.
Languages Spanish, Chinese.
Facilities Dining room; Physical therapy room; Activities room; Laundry room; Barber/Beauty shop.
Activities Arts & crafts; Cards; Games; Reading groups; Prayer groups; Movies; Shopping trips; Dances/Social/Cultural gatherings; Intergenerational programs; Pet therapy.

El Toro

Freedom Village Healthcare Center
23442 El Toro Rd, El Toro, CA 92630
(714) 472-4700
Admin Dawn Didion.
Licensure Skilled care. *Beds* SNF 52.
Owner Privately owned.

Lake Forest Nursing Center
25652 Old Trabuco Rd, El Toro, CA 92630
(714) 380-9380
Admin Ronald W Millett.
Licensure Skilled care; Intermediate care. *Beds* SNF 119; ICF 60. *Certified* Medicare.
Owner Proprietary corp (Shive Nursing Centers Inc).

Elk Grove

Elk Grove Convalescent Hospital
9461 Batey Ave, Elk Grove, CA 95624
(916) 685-9525
Admin Betty M Dever.
Licensure Skilled care. *Beds* SNF 136. *Certified* Medicare; Medi-Cal.
Owner Privately owned.

Encinitas

Rancho Encinitas
944 Regal Rd, Encinitas, CA 92024
(619) 944-0331
Admin Laura Baker. *Dir of Nursing* Ojik Megerdichian. *Medical Dir* Dr Richard Jimenez.
Licensure Skilled care; Assisted living for Alzheimer's. *Beds* SNF 59; Assisted living for Alzheimer's 48. *Certified* Medicare.
Owner Proprietary corp (Health Care Group).
Staff Physicians 1 (pt); RNs 1 (ft), 1 (pt); LPNs 6 (ft), 2 (pt); Nurses' aides 22 (ft); Physical therapists (contracted); Occupational therapists (contracted); Speech therapists 1 (pt); Activities coordinators 2 (ft), 2 (pt); Dietitians 1 (ft); Ophthalmologists (contracted); Podiatrists (contracted); Audiologists (contracted); Caregivers and ancillary staff 50 (ft), 10 (pt).

Scripps Memorial Hospital—Oceanview Convalescent Hospital
900 Santa Fe Rd, Encinitas, CA 92024
(619) 753-6423
Admin Charles Bloom.
Medical Dir Dr Arthur Edwards.

Licensure Skilled care. *Beds* SNF 99. *Certified* Medicare; Medi-Cal.
Owner Nonprofit corp.
Admissions Requirements Minimum age 18; Medical examination.
Staff RNs 5 (ft); LPNs 10 (ft); Nurses' aides 33 (ft), 10 (ft); Physical therapists 1 (ft); Recreational therapists 1 (ft); Occupational therapists 1 (ft); Speech therapists 1 (ft); Activities coordinators 2 (pt); Dietitians 1 (pt).
Facilities Dining room; Physical therapy room; Activities room; Crafts room; Laundry room; Barber/Beauty shop; Private ocean view rooms.
Activities Arts & crafts; Cards; Games; Reading groups; Prayer groups; Movies; Shopping trips; Dances/Social/Cultural gatherings.

Escondido

Beverly Manor Convalescent Hospital
421 E Mission Ave, Escondido, CA 92025
(619) 747-0430
Admin Kevin Rougeux.
Medical Dir Raymond Dann MD.
Licensure Skilled care. *Beds* SNF 180. *Certified* Medicare; Medi-Cal.
Owner Proprietary corp (Beverly Enterprises).
Facilities Dining room; Physical therapy room; Activities room; Crafts room; Laundry room; Barber/Beauty shop; Library; TV/ Living room.
Activities Arts & crafts; Cards; Games; Reading groups; Prayer groups; Movies.

Escondido Convalescent Center
201 N Fig St, Escondido, CA 92025
(619) 746-0303
Admin Frana K Priddy RN. *Dir of Nursing* Rena Shaphard RN. *Medical Dir* Dr Thomas E Rastle.
Licensure Skilled care. *Beds* SNF 74. *Certified* Medicare; Medi-Cal.
Owner Proprietary corp (Care Enterprises).
Admissions Requirements Physician's request.
Staff RNs 3 (ft), 1 (pt); LPNs 6 (ft), 4 (pt); Nurses' aides 24 (ft); Physical therapists 1 (ft); Occupational therapists 1 (ft); Speech therapists 1 (ft); Activities coordinators 1 (ft); Dietitians 1 (ft); Ophthalmologists 1 (ft); Podiatrists 1 (ft).
Languages Spanish, Tagalog.
Facilities Dining room; Physical therapy room; Laundry room; Barber/Beauty shop.
Activities Arts & crafts; Games; Reading groups; Prayer groups; Movies; Shopping trips; Dances/Social/Cultural gatherings.

Hilltop Convalescent Center
1260 E Ohio St, Escondido, CA 92025
(619) 746-1100
Admin Marie Kessler. *Dir of Nursing* Candace Meyer RN. *Medical Dir* Dr Britton.
Licensure Skilled care. *Beds* SNF 98. *Certified* Medicare; Medi-Cal.
Owner Proprietary corp (Care Enterprises).
Admissions Requirements Minimum age 18.
Staff RNs 2 (ft); LPNs 10 (ft), 3 (pt); Nurses' aides 34 (ft); Physical therapists 1 (ft); Occupational therapists 1 (ft), 1 (pt); Speech therapists 1 (pt); Activities coordinators 1 (ft); Dietitians 1 (ft).
Languages Spanish, Slavic.
Facilities Dining room; Physical therapy room; Activities room; Crafts room; Barber/ Beauty shop; Library.
Activities Arts & crafts; Cards; Games; Reading groups; Prayer groups; Movies; Shopping trips; Dances/Social/Cultural gatherings; Field trips.

Las Villas Del Norte Health Center
1335 N Nutmeg, Escondido, CA 92026
(619) 741-1046
Admin Donald Perry.

Licensure Skilled care. *Beds* SNF 99. *Certified* Medicare; Medi-Cal.
Owner Privately owned.

Palomar Convalescent Center
1817 Ave Del Diablo, Escondido, CA 92025
(619) 480-6222
Admin Robert J Harenski.
Licensure Skilled care. *Beds* SNF 96. *Certified* Medicare; Medi-Cal.
Owner Publicly owned.

Redwood Terrace
710 W 13th Ave, Escondido, CA 92025
(619) 747-4306
Admin Don Smith. *Dir of Nursing* June Vorie. *Medical Dir* Stephen D Smith MD.
Licensure Skilled care; Residential care; Alzheimer's care. *Beds* SNF 59; Residential care 138. *Private Pay Patients* 95%. *Certified* Medicare; Medi-Cal.
Owner Nonprofit organization/foundation.
Admissions Requirements Minimum age 62; Medical examination; Physician's request.
Staff Physicians 25 (pt); RNs 8 (ft), 1 (pt); LPNs 7 (ft); Nurses' aides 18 (ft); Physical therapists 3 (pt); Reality therapists 1 (pt); Recreational therapists 1 (pt); Occupational therapists 1 (pt); Speech therapists 1 (pt); Activities coordinators 1 (ft); Dietitians 2 (ft); Ophthalmologists 1 (pt); Podiatrists 1 (pt); Audiologists 1 (pt).
Languages Spanish.
Facilities Dining room; Physical therapy room; Activities room; Chapel; Crafts room; Laundry room; Barber/Beauty shop; Library; Private rooms and baths.
Activities Arts & crafts; Cards; Games; Reading groups; Prayer groups; Movies; Shopping trips; Dances/Social/Cultural gatherings; Intergenerational programs; Pet therapy.

Regency Nursing Center
1980 Felicita Rd, Escondido, CA 92025
(619) 741-6109
Admin William E Stover.
Licensure Skilled care; Intermediate care. *Beds* SNF 85; ICF 35. *Certified* Medicare; Medi-Cal.
Owner Proprietary corp.

Valle Vista Convalescent Hospital
1025 W 2nd St, Escondido, CA 92025
(619) 745-1288
Admin C Ralph Cook.
Licensure Skilled care. *Beds* SNF 59. *Certified* Medicare; Medi-Cal.
Owner Proprietary corp.

Eureka

Crestwood Manor
2370 Buhne, Eureka, CA 95501
(707) 442-5721
Admin Cleatus V Weller. *Dir of Nursing* Loleta Turner RN. *Medical Dir* Ken Stiver MD.
Licensure Skilled care. *Beds* SNF 85. *Certified* Medi-Cal.
Owner Proprietary corp (Crestwood Hospitals Inc).
Admissions Requirements Minimum age 18; Medical examination; Physician's request.
Staff RNs 4 (ft), 2 (pt); LPNs 7 (ft), 2 (pt); Nurses' aides 30 (ft), 10 (pt); Recreational therapists 6 (ft), 1 (pt); Activities coordinators 1 (ft); Dietitians 1 (ft).
Facilities Dining room; Activities room; Crafts room; Laundry room; Barber/Beauty shop.
Activities Arts & crafts; Cards; Games; Reading groups; Prayer groups; Movies; Shopping trips; Dances/Social/Cultural gatherings.

Granada Convalescent Hospital
2885 Harris St, Eureka, CA 95501
(707) 443-1627
Admin Tom E Sutton. *Dir of Nursing* Jessie Laurendeau. *Medical Dir* Ken Stiver MD.
Licensure Skilled care. *Beds* SNF 87. *Certified* Medicaid; Medicare; Medi-Cal.
Owner Proprietary corp (Coastal Care Centers Inc).
Admissions Requirements Minimum age 5; Physician's request.
Staff RNs 4 (ft), 1 (pt); LPNs 4 (ft), 2 (pt); Nurses' aides 28 (ft), 5 (pt); Physical therapists 1 (ft), 2 (pt); Recreational therapists 1 (pt); Occupational therapists 1 (pt); Speech therapists 1 (pt); Activities coordinators 1 (ft); Dietitians 1 (pt).
Facilities Dining room; Physical therapy room; Activities room; Crafts room; Laundry room; Barber/Beauty shop.
Activities Arts & crafts; Cards; Games; Reading groups; Prayer groups; Movies; Shopping trips; Dances/Social/Cultural gatherings.

Pacific Convalescent Hospital
2211 Harrison Ave, Eureka, CA 95501
(707) 443-9767
Admin Thomas E Sutton. *Dir of Nursing* Phyllis Bowser RN. *Medical Dir* Ken Stiver MD.
Licensure Skilled care. *Beds* SNF 59. *Certified* Medicare; Medi-Cal.
Owner Proprietary corp (Coastal Care Centers Inc).
Admissions Requirements Medical examination; Physician's request.
Staff RNs 4 (ft); LPNs 5 (ft), 2 (pt); Nurses' aides 25 (ft), 3 (pt); Physical therapists 1 (ft); Recreational therapists 1 (ft); Speech therapists 1 (ft); Activities coordinators 1 (ft); Dietitians 1 (ft).
Languages Spanish, Cambodian.
Facilities Dining room; Physical therapy room; Activities room; Crafts room; Laundry room; Barber/Beauty shop; Deck; Patio.
Activities Arts & crafts; Cards; Games; Reading groups; Prayer groups; Movies; Shopping trips; Dances/Social/Cultural gatherings; Barbeques; Outings; Contests.

Seaview Convalescent Hospital
8400 Purdue Dr, Eureka, CA 95501
(707) 443-5668
Admin Rebecca Campbell. *Dir of Nursing* Janice Mauney. *Medical Dir* Ken Stiver MD.
Licensure Skilled care. *Beds* SNF 99. *Certified* Medicare; Medi-Cal.
Owner Proprietary corp (Coastal Care Centers Inc).
Admissions Requirements Medical examination; Physician's request.
Staff RNs 5 (ft); LPNs 6 (ft), 1 (pt); Nurses' aides 20 (ft), 6 (pt); Activities coordinators 1 (ft).
Languages Finnish, Spanish, Portuguese.
Facilities Dining room; Physical therapy room; Activities room; Crafts room; Laundry room; Barber/Beauty shop.
Activities Arts & crafts; Cards; Games; Reading groups; Prayer groups; Movies; Shopping trips; Dances/Social/Cultural gatherings.

Sunset Skilled Nursing & Rehabilitation Center
2353 23rd St, Eureka, CA 95501
(707) 445-3261
Admin Tim Aust.
Medical Dir Dr Ken Stiver.
Licensure Skilled care. *Beds* SNF 99. *Certified* Medicare; Medi-Cal.
Owner Proprietary corp (Coastal Care Centers Inc).
Admissions Requirements Medical examination; Physician's request.

Facilities Dining room; Physical therapy room; Activities room; Crafts room; Laundry room; Barber/Beauty shop; Library; Speech therapy room.
Activities Arts & crafts; Cards; Games; Reading groups; Prayer groups; Movies; Shopping trips; Dances/Social/Cultural gatherings.

Fair Oaks

Homestead of Fair Oaks
11300 Fair Oaks Blvd, Fair Oaks, CA 95628
(916) 965-4663
Admin Alan Honer.
Licensure Skilled care. *Beds* SNF 147. *Certified* Medicare; Medi-Cal.
Owner Privately owned.

Fairfield

Care West—La Mariposa Nursing & Rehabilitation Center
1244 Travis Blvd, Fairfield, CA 94533
(707) 422-7750
Admin John Coogan. *Dir of Nursing* Martha O'Donnell. *Medical Dir* Dr V Douglas Jodoin.
Licensure Skilled care. *Beds* SNF 99. *Certified* Medicare; Medi-Cal.
Owner Proprietary corp (Care Enterprises).
Admissions Requirements Medical examination.
Staff Physicians 1 (pt); Physical therapists 1 (ft); Occupational therapists 1 (ft); Speech therapists 2 (pt); Activities coordinators 1 (ft), 1 (pt); Dietitians 1 (ft); Ophthalmologists 1 (pt); Podiatrists 1 (pt); Social services 1 (pt); Physical therapy aides 2 (pt).
Languages Spanish, Chinese, German, French, Italian.
Facilities Dining room; Physical therapy room; Activities room; Laundry room; Barber/Beauty shop; ST room; OT room; TV room/lounge; Patio-garden.
Activities Arts & crafts; Cards; Games; Movies; Shopping trips; Dances/Social/Cultural gatherings; Church services; Music parties & performances; Discussion groups.

Fairfield Convalescent Hospital
1255 Travis Blvd, Fairfield, CA 94533
(707) 425-0623
Admin Annette S Eugenis CFACHCA. *Dir of Nursing* Lynn Holbrook RN. *Medical Dir* Daniel Green MD.
Licensure Skilled care. *Beds* SNF 99. *Private Pay Patients* 35%.
Owner Proprietary corp (Regency Health Services).
Admissions Requirements Medical examination; Physician's request.
Staff RNs; LPNs; Nurses' aides; Physical therapists; Occupational therapists; Speech therapists; Activities coordinators; Dietitians (consultant); Ophthalmologists (consultant); Podiatrists (consultant); Audiologists (consultant); Social Worker; Ancillary support staff.
Languages Spanish, Tagalog.
Facilities Dining room; Physical therapy room; Activities room; Crafts room; Laundry room; Barber/Beauty shop; Courtyard with a fountain and aviary.
Activities Arts & crafts; Cards; Games; Reading groups; Prayer groups; Movies; Shopping trips; Dances/Social/Cultural gatherings; Intergenerational programs; Pet therapy; Exercise; Cookouts; Volunteer program.

Sunny Acres Convalescent Hospital
1260 Travis Blvd, Fairfield, CA 94538
(707) 425-0669
Admin Brigitte Coleman.
Medical Dir Dr Edward Lopez.

Licensure Skilled care. *Beds* SNF 90. *Certified* Medicare; Medi-Cal.
Owner Proprietary corp.
Admissions Requirements Medical examination.
Staff RNs 2 (ft), 4 (pt); LPNs 5 (ft), 5 (pt); Nurses' aides 29 (ft), 11 (pt); Activities coordinators 1 (ft).
Facilities Dining room; Activities room; Crafts room; Laundry room; Barber/Beauty shop.
Activities Arts & crafts; Cards; Games; Reading groups; Prayer groups; Movies; Shopping trips; Dances/Social/Cultural gatherings; Outside facility activities; Wine & cheese tasting; Nature walks; Picnics; Exercise; Residential council.

Fall River Mills

Mayers Memorial Hospital DP/SNF
PO Box 459, Fall River Mills, CA 96028-0459
(916) 336-5511
Licensure Skilled care. *Beds* SNF 48. *Certified* Medicare; Medi-Cal.
Owner Publicly owned.

Fallbrook

Fallbrook Convalescent Hospital
325 Potter St, Fallbrook, CA 92028
(619) 728-2330
Admin Robert Durbin. *Dir of Nursing* G Cimino. *Medical Dir* E B Shields MD.
Licensure Skilled care. *Beds* SNF 99. *Certified* Medicare; Medi-Cal.
Owner Privately owned.
Admissions Requirements Minimum age 65; Medical examination; Physician's request.
Activities Arts & crafts; Cards; Games; Reading groups; Prayer groups; Movies; Shopping trips; Dances/Social/Cultural gatherings.

Fillmore

Fillmore Convalescent Center
118 B St, Fillmore, CA 93015
(805) 524-0083
Admin Simeon Robins.
Medical Dir Dinko Rosic MD.
Licensure Skilled care. *Beds* SNF 92. *Certified* Medicare; Medi-Cal.
Owner Privately owned.
Admissions Requirements Medical examination; Physician's request.
Staff Physicians 13 (pt); RNs 1 (ft), 5 (pt); LPNs 6 (ft); Physical therapists 1 (pt); Occupational therapists 1 (pt); Speech therapists 1 (pt); Activities coordinators 1 (ft); Dietitians 1 (pt); Podiatrists 1 (pt); Dentists 1 (pt).
Facilities Dining room; Physical therapy room; Activities room; Crafts room; Laundry room; Barber/Beauty shop.
Activities Arts & crafts; Games; Reading groups; Prayer groups; Movies; Shopping trips; Dances/Social/Cultural gatherings; Resident council; Cooking; Sewing.

Folsom

Folsom Convalescent Hospital
510 Mill St, Folsom, CA 95630
(916) 985-3641
Admin D V Callaway. *Dir of Nursing* Linda Michael RN GNP. *Medical Dir* Dr Donald Gutman.
Licensure Skilled care. *Beds* SNF 99. *Private Pay Patients* 23%. *Certified* Medicare; Medi-Cal.
Owner Proprietary corp.
Staff RNs 3 (ft), 2 (pt); LPNs 7 (ft), 3 (pt); Nurses' aides 60 (ft), 20 (pt); Physical therapists 1 (pt); Reality therapists 1 (pt); Recreational therapists 1 (pt); Occupational

therapists 1 (pt); Speech therapists 1 (pt); Activities coordinators 1 (ft); Dietitians 1 (pt).
Facilities Dining room; Physical therapy room; Activities room; Crafts room; Laundry room; Barber/Beauty shop.
Activities Arts & crafts; Cards; Games; Reading groups; Prayer groups; Movies; Pet therapy.

Fontana

Care West—Citrus Nursing Center
9440 Citrus Ave, Fontana, CA 92335
(714) 823-3481
Admin Elaine Fickett. *Dir of Nursing* Charlotte Keefer RN. *Medical Dir* Richard Neil MD.
Licensure Skilled care; Retirement. *Beds* SNF 99. *Certified* Medicare; Medi-Cal.
Owner Proprietary corp (Care Enterprises).
Admissions Requirements Minimum age 21; Medical examination.
Staff RNs 2 (ft), 1 (pt); LPNs 11 (ft), 1 (pt); Nurses' aides 34 (ft), 2 (pt); Physical therapists 1 (pt); Occupational therapists; Speech therapists; Activities coordinators 1 (ft); Dietitians 1 (pt).
Languages Spanish.
Facilities Dining room; Physical therapy room; Activities room; Laundry room; Barber/Beauty shop.
Activities Arts & crafts; Cards; Games; Reading groups; Prayer groups; Movies; Shopping trips; Dances/Social/Cultural gatherings.

Casa Maria Convalescent Hospital
17933 San Bernardino, Fontana, CA 92335
(714) 877-1555
Admin Lois Easterday.
Medical Dir Robert Bom MD.
Licensure Skilled care; Retirement. *Beds* SNF 57. *Certified* Medicare; Medi-Cal.
Owner Proprietary corp.
Admissions Requirements Minimum age 65; Medical examination; Physician's request.
Staff Physicians 4 (ft); RNs 3 (ft); LPNs 7 (ft); Nurses' aides 15 (ft); Physical therapists 1 (ft); Recreational therapists 2 (ft); Occupational therapists 1 (ft); Speech therapists 1 (ft); Activities coordinators 1 (ft); Dietitians 1 (ft); Ophthalmologists 1 (ft).
Languages Spanish.
Facilities Dining room; Physical therapy room; Activities room; Crafts room; Laundry room; Barber/Beauty shop.
Activities Arts & crafts; Games; Prayer groups; Movies; Shopping trips; Dances/Social/Cultural gatherings.

Laurel Convalescent Hospital
7509 N Laurel Ave, Fontana, CA 92336
(714) 822-8066
Admin Peter D Bennett. *Dir of Nursing* Kathy Sexton. *Medical Dir* William Thompson.
Licensure Skilled care. *Beds* SNF 99. *Certified* Medicare; Medi-Cal.
Owner Proprietary corp.
Admissions Requirements Minimum age 60; Medical examination; Physician's request.
Staff Physicians 12 (pt); RNs 3 (ft); LPNs 10 (ft); Nurses' aides 22 (ft); Physical therapists 1 (pt); Occupational therapists 1 (pt); Speech therapists 1 (pt); Activities coordinators 1 (ft); Dietitians 1 (pt); Ophthalmologists 1 (pt); Podiatrists 1 (pt); Dentists 1 (pt); Social workers 1 (ft).
Languages Spanish.
Facilities Dining room; Physical therapy room; Activities room; Barber/Beauty shop; Library; Large outdoor grounds.
Activities Arts & crafts; Cards; Games; Reading groups; Prayer groups; Movies; Shopping trips; Dances/Social/Cultural gatherings; Patient oriented council; Family council.

Fort Bragg

Sherwood Oaks Health Center
130 Dana St, Fort Bragg, CA 95437
(707) 964-6333
Admin Rosemary M Brown. *Dir of Nursing* Kathy Havicus RN. *Medical Dir* Richard White MD.
Licensure Skilled care; Intermediate care. *Beds* SNF 75; ICF 4. *Private Pay Patients* 30%. *Certified* Medicare; Medi-Cal.
Owner Privately owned.
Admissions Requirements Medical examination; Physician's request.
Staff RNs 4 (ft); LPNs 7 (ft); Nurses' aides 35 (ft); Physical therapists 1 (pt); Recreational therapists 1 (pt); Occupational therapists 1 (pt); Speech therapists 1 (pt); Activities coordinators 1 (ft); Dietitians 1 (pt); Podiatrists 1 (pt).
Languages Spanish.
Facilities Dining room; Physical therapy room; Activities room; Chapel; Laundry room; Barber/Beauty shop.
Activities Arts & crafts; Reading groups; Movies; Pet therapy; Volunteer auxiliary; Community interaction.

Fortuna

St Luke Manor
2321 Newberg Rd, Fortuna, CA 95540
(707) 725-4467
Admin John Henkel. *Dir of Nursing* Joyce Osborn. *Medical Dir* Harold Averhan MD.
Licensure Skilled care. *Beds* SNF 110. *Certified* Medicare; Medi-Cal.
Owner Nonprofit corp.
Admissions Requirements Minimum age 18; Medical examination.
Staff RNs 6 (ft), 3 (pt); LPNs 4 (ft), 2 (pt); Nurses' aides 20 (ft), 26 (pt); Activities coordinators 1 (ft).
Affiliation Lutheran.
Facilities Dining room; Physical therapy room; Activities room; Chapel; Laundry room; Barber/Beauty shop.
Activities Arts & crafts; Cards; Games; Reading groups; Prayer groups; Movies; Shopping trips; Dances/Social/Cultural gatherings.

Fountain Valley

Fountain Valley Regional Care Center of FVRH
17100 Euclid St, Fountain Valley, CA 92708
(714) 979-1211
Admin George Rooth.

Manor Care Nursing Center of Fountain Valley
11680 Warner Ave, Fountain Valley, CA 92708
(714) 241-9800, 966-1654 FAX
Admin Brian A Rougeux. *Dir of Nursing* Adrienne Smith RN. *Medical Dir* Michael Fine MD.
Licensure Skilled care; Alzheimer's care. *Beds* SNF 151; Alzheimer's unit 30. *Private Pay Patients* 85%. *Certified* Medicare.
Owner Proprietary corp (Manor Care Inc).
Admissions Requirements Minimum age 18; Medical examination; Physician's request.
Staff RNs 20 (ft), 3 (pt); LPNs 30 (ft), 15 (pt); Nurses' aides 50 (ft), 20 (pt); Physical therapists 1 (ft), 1 (pt); Recreational therapists 2 (ft); Occupational therapists 1 (ft); Speech therapists 1 (ft); Activities coordinators 1 (ft); Dietitians 1 (ft); Ophthalmologists 1 (ft); Podiatrists 1 (ft); Audiologists 1 (ft).
Languages Spanish, Filipino, Tagalog.
Facilities Dining room; Physical therapy room; Activities room; Crafts room; Laundry room; Barber/Beauty shop; Lounges; Alzheimer's unit.

Activities Arts & crafts; Cards; Games; Reading groups; Prayer groups; Movies; Shopping trips; Dances/Social/Cultural gatherings; Intergenerational programs; Pet therapy.

Fowler

Fowler Convalescent Hospital
1306 E Sumner, Fowler, CA 93625
(209) 834-2542
Admin Kris Lovely.
Medical Dir Bob Landford MD.
Licensure Skilled care. *Beds* SNF 49. *Certified* Medicare; Medi-Cal.
Owner Proprietary corp (Beverly Enterprises).
Admissions Requirements Minimum age 18.
Staff Physicians; RNs; LPNs; Nurses' aides; Physical therapists; Reality therapists; Recreational therapists; Occupational therapists; Speech therapists; Activities coordinators; Dietitians; Ophthalmologists; Podiatrists; Dentists.
Facilities Dining room; Activities room; Crafts room; Laundry room; Barber/Beauty shop.
Activities Arts & crafts; Cards; Games; Reading groups; Prayer groups; Movies; Shopping trips; Dances/Social/Cultural gatherings.

Kings Vista Convalescent Hospital
8448 E Adams Ave, Fowler, CA 93625
(209) 834-2519
Admin Jewel M Williams.
Licensure Skilled care. *Beds* SNF 49. *Certified* Medi-Cal.
Owner Proprietary corp (Beverly Enterprises).

Fremont

Care West—Park Central Nursing Center
2100 Parkside Dr, Fremont, CA 94536
(415) 797-5300
Medical Dir Phillip M Loeb MD.
Licensure Skilled care. *Beds* SNF 99. *Certified* Medicare; Medi-Cal.
Owner Proprietary corp (Care Enterprises).
Staff RNs 3 (ft), 4 (pt); LPNs 4 (ft), 6 (pt); Nurses' aides 25 (ft), 4 (pt); Physical therapists 1 (ft); Speech therapists 1 (pt); Activities coordinators 1 (ft); Dietitians 1 (ft); Podiatrists 1 (pt); Audiologists 1 (pt); Dentists 1 (pt).

Crestwood Geriatric Treatment Center
2171 Mowry Ave, Fremont, CA 94536
(415) 793-8383
Admin John Collister.
Licensure Skilled care. *Beds* SNF 88. *Certified* Medicare; Medi-Cal.
Owner Proprietary corp (Crestwood Hospitals Inc).

Crestwood Rehabilitation & Convalescent Hospital
2500 Country Dr, Fremont, CA 94536
(415) 792-4242
Admin Tomas Curry.
Medical Dir Dr P Loeb.
Licensure Skilled care. *Beds* SNF 126. *Certified* Medicare.
Owner Proprietary corp (Crestwood Hospitals Inc).
Staff RNs 4 (ft), 2 (pt); LPNs 7 (ft), 5 (pt); Nurses' aides 55 (ft), 5 (pt); Physical therapists 1 (ft); Reality therapists 1 (pt); Recreational therapists 1 (pt); Occupational therapists 1 (pt); Speech therapists 1 (pt); Activities coordinators 2 (ft); Dietitians 1 (ft); Podiatrists 2 (pt); Dentists 1 (pt).
Facilities Dining room; Physical therapy room; Activities room; Laundry room; Barber/Beauty shop.

Activities Arts & crafts; Cards; Games; Reading groups; Prayer groups; Movies; Shopping trips; Dances/Social/Cultural gatherings.

Driftwood Convalescent Hospital
39022 Presidio Way, Fremont, CA 94538
(415) 792-3743
Admin Maxine Niel.
Medical Dir Ashwani Bindal MD.
Licensure Skilled care. *Beds* SNF 122. *Certified* Medicare; Medi-Cal.
Owner Proprietary corp (ARA Living Centers).
Admissions Requirements Physician's request.
Staff Physicians; RNs; LPNs; Nurses' aides; Physical therapists; Occupational therapists; Speech therapists; Activities coordinators; Dietitians; Ophthalmologists; Podiatrists.
Facilities Dining room; Physical therapy room; Activities room; Laundry room; Barber/Beauty shop; Lounges; Sun room.
Activities Arts & crafts; Cards; Games; Reading groups; Prayer groups; Movies; Shopping trips; Dances/Social/Cultural gatherings.

Mission Boulevard Convalescent Hospital
38650 Mission Blvd, Fremont, CA 94536
(415) 793-3000
Admin Dwayne Baird.
Licensure Skilled care. *Beds* SNF 73. *Certified* Medicare; Medi-Cal.
Owner Proprietary corp.

Parkmont Care Center
2400 Parkside Dr, Fremont, CA 94536
(415) 793-7222
Admin Imogene Ellwanger. *Dir of Nursing* Mary Ferrara RN. *Medical Dir* Anmol Mahal MD.
Licensure Skilled care. *Beds* SNF 85. *Certified* Medicare; Medi-Cal.
Owner Proprietary corp.
Admissions Requirements Medical examination; Physician's request.
Staff RNs 3 (ft), 1 (pt); LPNs 11 (ft), 3 (pt); Nurses' aides 47 (ft), 9 (pt); Recreational therapists 1 (ft); Activities coordinators 1 (ft); Dietitians 1 (ft).
Languages German, Portuguese, Spanish, Tagalog, Italian, Chinese.
Facilities Dining room; Activities room; Crafts room; Laundry room; Barber/Beauty shop; Library; TV room.
Activities Arts & crafts; Cards; Games; Reading groups; Prayer groups; Movies; Shopping trips; Dances/Social/Cultural gatherings; Picnics; Sing-alongs; Glamour girls; Fashion shows.

Westwood
4303 Stevenson Blvd, Fremont, CA 94538
(415) 657-6000
Admin A J Caferata.
Licensure Intermediate care for mentally retarded. *Beds* ICF/MR 126.
Owner Proprietary corp.

Fresno

Beverly Manor Convalescent Hospital
2715 Fresno St, Fresno, CA 93721
(209) 486-4433
Admin George Sigler.
Medical Dir Diane Anthony.
Licensure Skilled care. *Beds* SNF 232. *Certified* Medicare; Medi-Cal.
Owner Proprietary corp (Beverly Enterprises).
Staff RNs; LPNs; Nurses' aides; Recreational therapists; Activities coordinators; Dietitians.
Facilities Dining room; Physical therapy room; Activities room; Crafts room; Laundry room; Barber/Beauty shop.
Activities Arts & crafts; Cards; Games; Reading groups; Prayer groups; Movies; Shopping trips; Dances/Social/Cultural gatherings.

California Home for the Aged Inc
6720 E Kings Canyon, Fresno, CA 93727
(209) 251-8414
Admin Ljubica Radojkovich. *Dir of Nursing* Helen Zulewski. *Medical Dir* Joan Rubinstein.
Licensure Skilled care; Intermediate care; Community care. *Beds* SNF 84; ICF 25; Community care 37. *Private Pay Patients* 40%. *Certified* Medicare; Medi-Cal.
Owner Nonprofit corp.
Admissions Requirements Minimum age 62; Medical examination.
Staff RNs 5 (ft); LPNs 14 (ft); Nurses' aides 50 (ft); Activities coordinators 1 (ft).
Languages Armenian.
Facilities Dining room; Physical therapy room; Activities room; Chapel; Crafts room; Barber/Beauty shop; Library.
Activities Arts & crafts; Cards; Games; Reading groups; Prayer groups; Movies; Shopping trips; Dances/Social/Cultural gatherings.

Casa Metropolitan
2020 N Weber, Fresno, CA 93705
(209) 237-0883
Admin David Altenberg.
Medical Dir Dr Walter Rohlfing.
Licensure Skilled care; Intermediate care. *Beds* SNF 221; ICF 12. *Certified* Medicare; Medi-Cal.
Owner Proprietary corp.
Admissions Requirements Medical examination; Physician's request.
Staff RNs 10 (ft), 5 (pt); LPNs 13 (ft), 6 (pt); Nurses' aides 62 (ft), 28 (pt); Physical therapists 1 (ft); Occupational therapists 1 (ft); Activities coordinators 3 (ft).
Facilities Dining room; Physical therapy room; Activities room; Chapel; Crafts room; Laundry room; Barber/Beauty shop.
Activities Arts & crafts; Cards; Games; Prayer groups; Movies; Dances/Social/Cultural gatherings.

Country View Convalescent Hospital
925 N Cornelia, Fresno, CA 93706
(209) 275-4785
Admin Kurt Hodges.
Medical Dir Dr Alvin Chaffin.
Licensure Skilled care. *Beds* SNF 59. *Certified* Medicare; Medi-Cal.
Owner Proprietary corp (Beverly Enterprises).
Admissions Requirements Physician's request.
Staff Physicians 1 (pt); RNs 1 (ft), 2 (pt); LPNs 3 (ft), 3 (pt); Nurses' aides 11 (ft), 4 (pt); Physical therapists 1 (pt); Reality therapists 1 (ft); Recreational therapists 1 (ft); Occupational therapists 1 (pt); Speech therapists 1 (pt); Activities coordinators 1 (ft); Dietitians 1 (pt); Ophthalmologists 1 (pt); Podiatrists 1 (pt); Audiologists 1 (pt); Dentists 1 (pt).

Fresno Care & Guidance Center
1715 S Cedar, Fresno, CA 93702
(209) 237-8377
Admin U Edwin Johnson. *Dir of Nursing* Simin Phanucharas RN. *Medical Dir* Dr Ruff.
Licensure Skilled care. *Beds* SNF 99. *Private Pay Patients* 2%. *Certified* Medi-Cal.
Owner Proprietary corp (Beverly Enterprises).
Staff RNs 2 (ft); LPNs 7 (ft); Nurses' aides 42 (ft); Recreational therapists 1 (ft); Activities coordinators 1 (ft).
Languages Spanish.
Activities Arts & crafts; Cards; Games; Reading groups; Movies; Dances/Social/Cultural gatherings.

Fresno Convalescent Hospital
3003 N Mariposa St, Fresno, CA 93703
(209) 222-7416
Admin Jean Dresslar. *Dir of Nursing* Frances de la Torre RN. *Medical Dir* Graham Ruff MD.

Licensure Skilled care. *Beds* SNF 116.
Certified Medicare; Medi-Cal.
Owner Nonprofit corp.
Admissions Requirements Medical examination; Physician's request.
Staff RNs 5 (ft), 3 (pt); LPNs 5 (ft), 2 (pt); Nurses' aides 40 (ft), 20 (pt); Physical therapists 1 (pt); Speech therapists 1 (pt); Activities coordinators 1 (ft); Dietitians 1 (pt); Ophthalmologists 1 (pt).
Languages Spanish.
Facilities Dining room; Physical therapy room; Activities room; Crafts room; Laundry room; Barber/Beauty shop.
Activities Arts & crafts; Games; Prayer groups; Movies; Musical programs; Exercise programs; Excursions in facility van; Visits to parks; Visits to zoo; School.

Hillcrest Convalescent Hospital
3672 N 1st St, Fresno, CA 93726
(209) 227-5383
Admin Amelia Drew.
Medical Dir W A Rohlfing MD.
Licensure Skilled care. *Beds* SNF 65. *Certified* Medicare; Medi-Cal.
Owner Proprietary corp (Beverly Enterprises).
Facilities Dining room; Physical therapy room; Activities room; Crafts room; Laundry room; Barber/Beauty shop; Library.
Activities Arts & crafts; Cards; Games; Reading groups; Prayer groups; Movies; Shopping trips; Dances/Social/Cultural gatherings.

Hope Manor
1665 M St, Fresno, CA 93721
(209) 268-5361
Admin Eugenia M Einhart. *Dir of Nursing* Jane Gliman; Carol Perez. *Medical Dir* J Malcolm Masten MD.
Licensure Skilled care; Intermediate care. *Beds* SNF 85; ICF 70. *Certified* Medicare; Medi-Cal.
Owner Privately owned.
Admissions Requirements Medical examination; Physician's request.
Staff RNs 2 (ft), 5 (pt); LPNs 9 (ft); Nurses' aides 45 (ft); Physical therapists 1 (pt); Activities coordinators 1 (pt).
Facilities Dining room; Physical therapy room; Activities room; Chapel; Crafts room; Laundry room; Barber/Beauty shop; Library.
Activities Arts & crafts; Cards; Games; Reading groups; Prayer groups; Movies; Dances/Social/Cultural gatherings.

Hy-Lond Convalescent Hospital
3408 E Shields, Fresno, CA 93726
(209) 227-4063, 227-4085 FAX
Admin Laverle A Emmerson. *Dir of Nursing* Thelma Braly RN. *Medical Dir* E H Holvey MD.
Licensure Skilled care. *Beds* SNF 121. *Private Pay Patients* 30%. *Certified* Medicare; Medi-Cal.
Owner Proprietary corp (Beverly Enterprises).
Admissions Requirements Minimum age 21; Physician's request.
Staff RNs 6 (ft), 2 (pt); LPNs 10 (ft); Nurses' aides 48 (ft), 14 (pt); Physical therapists 1 (ft); Recreational therapists 1 (ft); Activities coordinators 1 (ft).
Languages Spanish.
Facilities Dining room; Physical therapy room; Activities room; Crafts room; Laundry room; Barber/Beauty shop.
Activities Arts & crafts; Cards; Games; Reading groups; Prayer groups; Movies; Shopping trips; Dances/Social/Cultural gatherings; Intergenerational programs; Pet therapy.

Hy-Pana House Convalescent Hospital
3510 E Shields Ave, Fresno, CA 93726
(209) 222-4807
Admin Marjory Norris.

Licensure Skilled care. *Beds* SNF 112.
Certified Medicare; Medi-Cal.
Owner Proprietary corp (Beverly Enterprises).

Manning Gardens Convalescent Hospital
2113 E Manning Ave, Fresno, CA 93725
(209) 834-2586
Admin Cary J Hanson.
Licensure Skilled care. *Beds* SNF 59. *Certified* Medicare; Medi-Cal.
Owner Proprietary corp.
Staff Physicians 5 (pt); RNs 1 (ft), 1 (pt); LPNs 5 (ft), 2 (pt); Nurses' aides 25 (ft), 5 (pt); Physical therapists 1 (pt); Speech therapists 1 (pt); Activities coordinators 1 (ft), 1 (pt); Dietitians 1 (pt); Podiatrists 1 (pt); Dentists 1 (pt).

Nazareth House
2121 N 1st St, Fresno, CA 93703
(209) 237-2257
Admin Sr J Fidelis.
Medical Dir Sr Margaret Brody.
Licensure Skilled care; Retirement. *Beds* SNF 39. *Certified* Medi-Cal.
Owner Nonprofit corp.
Admissions Requirements Minimum age 65; Medical examination; Physician's request.
Staff RNs 5 (ft), 2 (pt); LPNs 2 (ft); Nurses' aides 17 (ft); Activities coordinators 1 (ft); Dietitians 1 (ft), 1 (pt); Ophthalmologists 1 (pt); Dentists 1 (pt).
Languages Spanish, Italian.
Affiliation Roman Catholic.
Facilities Dining room; Physical therapy room; Activities room; Chapel; Crafts room; Laundry room; Barber/Beauty shop; Library; TV.
Activities Arts & crafts; Games; Reading groups; Prayer groups; Movies; Shopping trips; Dances/Social/Cultural gatherings.

Pacific Gardens Convalescent Hospital
577 S Peach St, Fresno, CA 93727
(209) 251-8463
Admin Lisa McQuone. *Dir of Nursing* Valentine DiCerto. *Medical Dir* Robb Smith Jr MD.
Licensure Skilled care. *Beds* SNF 180. *Certified* Medicare; Medi-Cal.
Owner Proprietary corp (American-Cal Medical Services Inc).
Admissions Requirements Medical examination.
Staff RNs 6 (ft), 3 (pt); LPNs 15 (ft), 7 (pt); Nurses' aides 70 (ft), 20 (pt); Physical therapists (contracted); Occupational therapists (contracted); Speech therapists 1 (ft); Activities coordinators 3 (ft); Dietitians 1 (ft); Ophthalmologists (contracted); Social workers 1 (ft).
Languages Spanish.
Facilities Dining room; Physical therapy room; Activities room; Laundry room; Barber/Beauty shop; Covered patio.
Activities Arts & crafts; Cards; Games; Reading groups; Prayer groups; Movies; Shopping trips; Dances/Social/Cultural gatherings; Exercise; Cooking groups; Music therapy.

Raintree Convalescent Hospital
5265 E Huntington, Fresno, CA 93727
(209) 251-8244
Admin Patrick Uribe. *Dir of Nursing* Jessica Acosta. *Medical Dir* Alex Sherriffs.
Licensure Skilled care. *Beds* SNF 49. *Private Pay Patients* 8%. *Certified* Medi-Cal.
Owner Proprietary corp (Beverly Enterprises).
Admissions Requirements Medical examination; Physician's request.
Languages Spanish.
Facilities Dining room; Activities room; Laundry room; Barber/Beauty shop.
Activities Arts & crafts; Cards; Games; Prayer groups; Movies; Shopping trips; Intergenerational programs.

Riley Nursing Home
2604 Clovis Ave, Fresno, CA 93612-3902
(209) 237-0261
Admin Angela Shoberg.
Licensure Skilled care. *Beds* 25. *Certified* Medicare; Medi-Cal.
Owner Proprietary corp.

San Joaquin Gardens Health Facility
5555 N Fresno St, Fresno, CA 93710
(209) 439-4770
Admin Leonard P Kelly.
Medical Dir Edwin G Wiens MD.
Licensure Skilled care; Intermediate care. *Beds* SNF 56; ICF 32. *Certified* Medicare; Medi-Cal.
Owner Nonprofit corp (American Baptist Homes of the West Inc).
Staff RNs 4 (ft), 3 (pt); LPNs 3 (ft), 5 (pt); Nurses' aides 15 (ft), 23 (pt); Reality therapists 1 (pt); Recreational therapists 2 (ft).
Facilities Dining room; Activities room; Chapel; Crafts room; Laundry room; Barber/Beauty shop; Library.
Activities Arts & crafts; Games; Reading groups; Movies; Shopping trips; Dances/Social/Cultural gatherings.

Sierra View Convalescent Hospital
668 E Bullard Ave, Fresno, CA 93710
(209) 439-4461
Admin Darlene Dille.
Licensure Skilled care. *Beds* SNF 99. *Certified* Medicare; Medi-Cal.
Owner Nonprofit organization/foundation.

Sunnyside Convalescent Hospital
2939 S Peach Ave, Fresno, CA 93725
(209) 233-6248
Admin Michael L Fellen.
Licensure Skilled care. *Beds* SNF 116. *Certified* Medicare; Medi-Cal.
Owner Proprietary corp.

Townhouse Convalescent
1233 A St, Fresno, CA 93706
(209) 268-6317
Admin Martha LoPresti. *Dir of Nursing* Maxine Terry RN. *Medical Dir* Dr Howard Kennett.
Licensure Skilled care. *Beds* SNF 80. *Private Pay Patients* 3%. *Certified* Medicare; Medi-Cal.
Owner Proprietary corp.
Admissions Requirements Minimum age 18.
Staff RNs 1 (ft), 1 (pt); LPNs 8 (ft), 2 (pt); Nurses' aides 50 (ft), 5 (pt); Physical therapists; Speech therapists; Activities coordinators; Dietitians; Podiatrists.
Languages Spanish.
Facilities Dining room; Activities room; Crafts room; Laundry room; Barber/Beauty shop.
Activities Arts & crafts; Cards; Games; Reading groups; Prayer groups; Movies; Shopping trips; Dances/Social/Cultural gatherings; Intergenerational programs; Pet therapy.

Twilight Haven
1717 S Winery Ave, Fresno, CA 93727
(209) 251-8417
Admin David J Viancourt.
Medical Dir Mrs Dadian.
Licensure Skilled care. *Beds* SNF 50. *Certified* Medicare; Medi-Cal.
Owner Nonprofit corp.
Admissions Requirements Minimum age 62.
Staff Physicians; RNs; LPNs; Nurses' aides; Activities coordinators; Dietitians.
Facilities Dining room; Activities room; Chapel; Laundry room; Barber/Beauty shop.
Activities Arts & crafts; Games; Prayer groups; Movies; Shopping trips; Dances/Social/Cultural gatherings.

Valley Care & Guidance Center
9919 S Elm Ave, Fresno, CA 93706
(209) 834-5351
Admin Carolyn Hankinson. *Dir of Nursing*
Dorothy Nishi. *Medical Dir* Dr Parayno.
Licensure Skilled care; Alzheimer's care. *Beds*
SNF 79. *Certified* Medi-Cal.
Owner Proprietary corp (Beverly Enterprises).
Admissions Requirements Minimum age 18.
Staff RNs 2 (ft); LPNs 5 (ft); Nurses' aides 63
(ft); Activities coordinators 1 (ft).
Languages Spanish, Japanese, Hindi.
Facilities Dining room; Activities room;
Chapel; Crafts room; Laundry room; Barber/
Beauty shop; Library.
Activities Arts & crafts; Cards; Games;
Reading groups; Prayer groups; Movies;
Shopping trips; Dances/Social/Cultural
gatherings.

Valley Convalescent Center
4840 E Tulare St, Fresno, CA 93727
(209) 251-7161
Admin Robert S Stauff. *Dir of Nursing* Angela
Shoberg RN. *Medical Dir* Graham Ruff
MD.
Licensure Skilled care. *Beds* SNF 99. *Certified*
Medicare; Medi-Cal.
Owner Proprietary corp (Summit Care).
Admissions Requirements Minimum age 18;
Medical examination; Physician's request.
Staff Physicians 28 (ft); RNs 3 (ft), 2 (pt);
LPNs 7 (ft), 6 (pt); Nurses' aides 35 (ft), 14
(pt); Physical therapists 1 (ft), 1 (pt);
Occupational therapists 1 (ft); Speech
therapists 1 (ft); Activities coordinators 1
(ft), 2 (pt); Dietitians 1 (ft), 1 (pt);
Ophthalmologists 1 (ft), 1 (pt).
Facilities Dining room; Physical therapy
room; Activities room; Crafts room; Laundry
room; Barber/Beauty shop; Library.
Activities Arts & crafts; Cards; Games;
Reading groups; Prayer groups; Movies;
Shopping trips; Dances/Social/Cultural
gatherings; Cultural outings.

Fullerton

CareWest—Fullerton Nursing Center
2222 N Harbor Blvd, Fullerton, CA 92635
(714) 992-5701, 526-4884 FAX
Admin Roy W Behnke CFACHCA. *Dir of
Nursing* Eugenia Chapman RN. *Medical Dir*
Bruce Mutter MD.
Licensure Skilled care. *Beds* SNF 300.
Certified Medicare; Medi-Cal.
Owner Proprietary corp (Care Enterprises).
Admissions Requirements Medical
examination; Physician's request.
Staff RNs 22 (ft); LPNs 24 (ft); Nurses' aides
14 (ft); Physical therapists; Occupational
therapists; Speech therapists; Activities
coordinators 5 (ft); Dietitians 2 (ft); CNAs
115 (ft).
Languages Spanish, Filipino.
Facilities Dining room; Physical therapy
room; Activities room; Chapel; Crafts room;
Laundry room; Barber/Beauty shop; Library.
Activities Arts & crafts; Cards; Games;
Reading groups; Prayer groups; Movies;
Shopping trips; Dances/Social/Cultural
gatherings; Intergenerational programs; Pet
therapy.

Carriage House Manor
245 E Wilshire Ave, Fullerton, CA 92632
(714) 871-6020
Admin Carol L Demarco RN MS. *Dir of
Nursing* Julie Agsaulio RN. *Medical Dir* Dr
John Cowles.
Licensure Skilled care. *Beds* SNF 99. *Certified*
Medicare; Medi-Cal.
Owner Proprietary corp (Meritcare).
Admissions Requirements Medical
examination; Physician's request.

Staff RNs 3 (ft), 2 (pt); LPNs 5 (ft), 3 (pt);
Nurses' aides 29 (ft), 4 (pt); Activities
coordinators 1 (ft), 2 (pt); Dietitians 1 (ft).
Languages Spanish, German, Filipino.
Facilities Dining room; Physical therapy
room; Activities room; Crafts room; Laundry
room; Barber/Beauty shop; Patio.
Activities Arts & crafts; Cards; Games;
Reading groups; Prayer groups; Movies;
Shopping trips; Dances/Social/Cultural
gatherings; Intergenerational programs; Pet
therapy; Candlelight dinners; Monthly "out
to lunch bunch".

Fairway Convalescent Center
2800 N Harbor Blvd, Fullerton, CA 92635
(714) 871-9202, (213) 691-2015
Admin Pam Burnham. *Dir of Nursing* Frances
Kreuger. *Medical Dir* Bruce Mutter MD.
Licensure Skilled care. *Beds* SNF 59. *Certified*
Medicare; Medi-Cal.
Owner Proprietary corp.
Staff RNs 1 (ft), 2 (pt); LPNs 5 (ft), 6 (pt);
Nurses' aides 26 (ft), 6 (pt); Physical
therapists 1 (pt); Recreational therapists 1
(pt); Occupational therapists 1 (pt); Speech
therapists 1 (pt); Activities coordinators 1
(ft), 1 (pt); Dietitians 1 (pt);
Ophthalmologists 1 (pt); Podiatrists 1 (pt);
Dentists 1 (pt).
Facilities Dining room; Physical therapy
room; Activities room; Crafts room; Laundry
room; Barber/Beauty shop; Speech therapy
room; Whirlpool room.
Activities Arts & crafts; Cards; Games;
Reading groups; Prayer groups; Movies;
Shopping trips; Dances/Social/Cultural
gatherings; Cooking classes; Music.

Gordon Lane Convalescent Hospital
1821 E Chapman Ave, Fullerton, CA 92631
(714) 879-7301
Admin Vada Dane.
Medical Dir Frank Amato MD.
Licensure Skilled care. *Beds* SNF 99. *Private
Pay Patients* 100%.
Owner Proprietary corp.
Admissions Requirements Physician's request.
Staff RNs; Nurses' aides; Physical therapists;
Reality therapists; Recreational therapists;
Occupational therapists; Speech therapists;
Activities coordinators; Dietitians;
Ophthalmologists; Podiatrists; Audiologists;
LVNs.
Facilities Dining room; Physical therapy
room; Activities room; Laundry room;
Barber/Beauty shop.
Activities Games; Movies.

Seaside Care Center
2800 N Harbor Blvd, Fullerton, CA 92635-
1727
(213) 591-8701
Admin Thomas Higgins.
Licensure Skilled care; Intermediate care for
mentally retarded. *Beds* 99. *Certified*
Medicare.
Owner Proprietary corp.

Sunhaven Convalescent Hospital
201 E Bastanchury, Fullerton, CA 92635
(714) 870-0060
Admin David W Segler.
Medical Dir J Soffice MD.
Licensure Skilled care. *Beds* SNF 59. *Certified*
Medicare; Medi-Cal.
Owner Privately owned.
Admissions Requirements Medical
examination; Physician's request.
Staff RNs 2 (ft); LPNs 6 (ft), 3 (pt); Nurses'
aides 10 (ft); Activities coordinators 1 (ft).
Facilities Dining room; Activities room;
Crafts room; Barber/Beauty shop.
Activities Arts & crafts; Cards; Games;
Reading groups; Prayer groups; Dances/
Social/Cultural gatherings.

Sunny Hills Convalescent Hospital
330 W Bastanchury, Fullerton, CA 92635
(714) 879-4511
Admin Steve McKinley.
Licensure Skilled care. *Beds* SNF 99. *Certified*
Medicare; Medi-Cal.
Owner Proprietary corp.

Galt

Royal Oaks Convalescent Hospital
144 F St, Galt, CA 95632
(209) 745-1537
Admin Margherita Fagan. *Dir of Nursing*
Janet Farrell RN. *Medical Dir* James
McFarland MD.
Licensure Skilled care; Alzheimer's care. *Beds*
SNF 99. *Certified* Medicare; Medi-Cal.
Owner Proprietary corp (Beverly Enterprises).
Admissions Requirements Minimum age 21;
Medical examination; Physician's request.
Staff RNs 4 (ft), 1 (pt); LPNs 9 (ft), 1 (pt);
Nurses' aides 42 (ft), 2 (pt); Activities
coordinators 1 (ft), 1 (pt); Dietitians 1 (ft);
Ophthalmologists 1 (pt); Social workers 1
(pt).
Languages Italian, Spanish, German, Chinese,
Tagalog, Portuguese.
Facilities Dining room; Physical therapy
room; Activities room; Crafts room; Barber/
Beauty shop.
Activities Arts & crafts; Cards; Games;
Reading groups; Prayer groups; Movies;
Shopping trips; Dances/Social/Cultural
gatherings.

Garden Grove

Care West—Haster Nursing Center
12681 Haster St, Garden Grove, CA 92640
(714) 971-2153
Admin Douglas Nelson.
Medical Dir John Cowles MD.
Licensure Skilled care. *Beds* SNF 132.
Certified Medicare; Medi-Cal.
Owner Proprietary corp (Care Enterprises).
Admissions Requirements Physician's request.
Staff RNs 4 (ft); LPNs 8 (ft); Activities
coordinators 2 (ft).
Facilities Dining room; Physical therapy
room; Activities room; Chapel; Crafts room;
Laundry room; Barber/Beauty shop; Library.
Activities Arts & crafts; Cards; Games;
Reading groups; Prayer groups; Movies;
Shopping trips; Dances/Social/Cultural
gatherings.

Chapman Harbor Skilled Nursing Center
12232 Chapman Ave, Garden Grove, CA
92640
(714) 971-5517
Admin Keith T Goodell.
Medical Dir Dr Marcolesco.
Licensure Skilled care. *Beds* SNF 78. *Certified*
Medicare; Medi-Cal.
Owner Proprietary corp.
Admissions Requirements Minimum age 40;
Medical examination; Physician's request.
Staff Physicians; RNs; Nurses' aides;
Recreational therapists; Occupational
therapists; Speech therapists; Activities
coordinators; Dietitians; Ophthalmologists;
Podiatrists; Dentists; LVNs.
Facilities Dining room; Physical therapy
room; Activities room; Chapel; Crafts room;
Laundry room; Barber/Beauty shop; Library.
Activities Arts & crafts; Cards; Games;
Reading groups; Prayer groups; Movies;
Shopping trips; Dances/Social/Cultural
gatherings.

Garden Grove Convalescent Hospital
12882 Shackleford Ln, Garden Grove, CA
92641
(714) 638-9470
Admin Emanuel Newman.

Licensure Skilled care. *Beds* SNF 99. *Certified* Medicare; Medi-Cal.
Owner Privately owned.

Hy-Lond Home
9861 W 11 St, Garden Grove, CA 92644
(714) 531-8741
Admin Duane Dahlinx.
Licensure Intermediate care for mentally retarded. *Beds* ICF/MR 147. *Certified* Medi-Cal.
Owner Proprietary corp (Beverly Enterprises).

Meadow View Park
13392 Taft Ave, Garden Grove, CA 92643
(714) 638-5450
Admin Kenneth Goldblatt.
Medical Dir Dr S Osburn.
Licensure Developmental disabled. *Beds* Developmental disabled 59. *Certified* Medicare; Medi-Cal.
Owner Proprietary corp.
Staff Physicians 3 (pt); RNs 1 (ft), 1 (pt); LPNs 5 (ft), 4 (pt); Physical therapists 1 (pt); Occupational therapists 1 (pt); Speech therapists 1 (pt); Activities coordinators 1 (ft); Dietitians 1 (pt); Ophthalmologists 1 (pt); Podiatrists 1 (pt); Dentists 1 (pt).
Languages Spanish.
Facilities Dining room; Physical therapy room; Activities room; Crafts room; Laundry room.
Activities Arts & crafts; Games; Reading groups; Movies; Shopping trips; Dances/Social/Cultural gatherings.

Orangegrove Rehabilitation Hospital
12332 Garden Grove Blvd, Garden Grove, CA 92643
(714) 534-1041, 537-3873 FAX
Admin Alan F Dill. *Dir of Nursing* Martha Jaramillo RN. *Medical Dir* Samuel Gendler MD.
Licensure Skilled care. *Beds* SNF 99. *Certified* Medicare; Medi-Cal.
Owner Proprietary corp (Life Care Centers of America).
Admissions Requirements Minimum age 12; Medical examination; Physician's request.
Staff Physicians 5 (pt); RNs 4 (ft), 1 (pt); LPNs 7 (ft); Nurses' aides 26 (ft), 3 (pt); Physical therapists 1 (ft); Occupational therapists 1 (ft); Speech therapists 1 (ft); Activities coordinators 2 (ft); Dietitians 1 (pt); Ophthalmologists 1 (pt); Podiatrists 1 (pt).
Languages Spanish, Korean, Indian, Armenian, German, Tagalog.
Facilities Dining room; Physical therapy room; Activities room; Crafts room; Barber/Beauty shop; Library; Occupational therapy department; Speech therapy department.
Activities Arts & crafts; Cards; Games; Reading groups; Prayer groups; Movies; Shopping trips; Dances/Social/Cultural gatherings; Intergenerational programs.

Pacific Haven Convalescent Home
12072 Trask Ave, Garden Grove, CA 92643
(714) 534-1942
Admin Ray W Presall. *Dir of Nursing* Juanita Bailey RN. *Medical Dir* J D Cowles MD.
Licensure Skilled care. *Beds* SNF 99. *Certified* Medicare; Medi-Cal.
Owner Nonprofit corp.
Admissions Requirements Medical examination; Physician's request.
Staff Physicians 28 (ft); RNs 3 (ft); LPNs 10 (ft); Nurses' aides 33 (ft); Activities coordinators 1 (ft); Dietitians 1 (ft).
Languages Spanish.
Affiliation Reorganized Church of Jesus Christ of Latter-Day Saints.
Facilities Dining room; Physical therapy room; Activities room; Chapel; Crafts room; Laundry room; Barber/Beauty shop; Library.

Activities Arts & crafts; Cards; Games; Reading groups; Prayer groups; Movies; Shopping trips; Dances/Social/Cultural gatherings; Cooking classes; Resident/family councils.

Palm Grove Convalescent Center
13075 Blackbird St, Garden Grove, CA 92640
(714) 530-6322
Admin Frances Hoogstad. *Dir of Nursing* Marilyn Cothron. *Medical Dir* John Cowles MD.
Licensure Skilled care. *Beds* SNF 129. *Certified* Medicare; Medi-Cal.
Owner Proprietary corp (Summit Care).
Admissions Requirements Minimum age Adult; Physician's request.
Staff Physicians 1 (pt); RNs 5 (ft), 2 (pt); LPNs 12 (ft), 2 (pt); Nurses' aides 44 (ft); Physical therapists 2 (pt); Occupational therapists 1 (pt); Speech therapists 1 (pt); Activities coordinators 2 (ft); Dietitians 1 (pt); Ophthalmologists 1 (pt); Podiatrists 1 (pt); Dentists 1 (pt); Social service coordinators 1 (pt).
Languages Spanish.
Facilities Dining room; Physical therapy room; Activities room; Crafts room; Laundry room; Barber/Beauty shop; Family/patient lounge; 4 Outdoor patios.
Activities Arts & crafts; Cards; Games; Reading groups; Prayer groups; Movies; Shopping trips; Dances/Social/Cultural gatherings.

Gardena

Ayer-Lar Sanitarium
16530 S Broadway, Gardena, CA 90248
(213) 329-7581
Admin Lee M Ayers. *Dir of Nursing* Sugimoto. *Medical Dir* George Lee MD.
Licensure Skilled care. *Beds* SNF 50. *Certified* Medi-Cal.
Owner Proprietary corp.
Admissions Requirements Minimum age 25.
Staff RNs 1 (ft), 2 (pt); LPNs 6 (ft), 2 (pt); Nurses' aides 35 (ft).
Facilities Activities room.
Activities Arts & crafts; Cards; Games; Prayer groups; Movies.

Care West—Alondra Nursing Center
1140 W Rosecrans, Gardena, CA 90247
(213) 323-3194
Admin Ted Stulz.
Licensure Skilled care. *Beds* SNF 99. *Certified* Medicare; Medi-Cal.
Owner Proprietary corp (Care Enterprises).

Clear View Convalescent Center
15823 S Western Ave, Gardena, CA 90247-3788
(213) 770-3131
Admin Ronald W O Wong. *Dir of Nursing* Candice Rowedder RN. *Medical Dir* Magdy Salib MD.
Licensure Skilled care; Alzheimer's care. *Beds* SNF 99. *Certified* Medi-Cal.
Owner Proprietary corp.
Admissions Requirements Minimum age 18; Physician's request.
Staff Physicians 2 (pt); RNs 3 (ft); LPNs 10 (ft); Nurses' aides 60 (ft); Physical therapists 1 (pt); Reality therapists 1 (pt); Recreational therapists 1 (pt); Occupational therapists 1 (pt); Speech therapists 1 (pt); Activities coordinators 2 (ft); Dietitians 1 (pt); Ophthalmologists 1 (pt); Podiatrists 1 (pt); Dentists 1 (pt).
Facilities Dining room; Physical therapy room; Activities room; Crafts room; Laundry room; Barber/Beauty shop; Secured facility for the confused/disoriented patient.
Activities Arts & crafts; Cards; Games; Reading groups; Prayer groups; Movies; Shopping trips; Dances/Social/Cultural

gatherings; Barbeques; Picnics; Candlelight dinners; Wine socials; AA meetings; VFW meetings; Veterans assistance.

Clear View Sanitarium
15823 S Western Ave, Gardena, CA 90247-3788
(213) 538-2323
Admin Ronald W O Wong. *Dir of Nursing* Margaret Reid RN. *Medical Dir* Magdy Salib MD.
Licensure Skilled care. *Beds* SNF 73. *Certified* Medi-Cal.
Owner Proprietary corp.
Admissions Requirements Minimum age 18; Physician's request.
Staff Physicians 1 (pt); RNs 2 (ft); LPNs 7 (ft); Nurses' aides 45 (ft); Physical therapists 1 (pt); Reality therapists 1 (pt); Recreational therapists 1 (pt); Occupational therapists 1 (pt); Speech therapists 1 (pt); Activities coordinators 1 (ft); Dietitians 1 (pt); Ophthalmologists 1 (pt); Podiatrists 1 (pt); Dentists 1 (pt).
Facilities Dining room; Physical therapy room; Activities room; Crafts room; Laundry room; Barber/Beauty shop; Spacious grounds.
Activities Arts & crafts; Cards; Games; Prayer groups; Movies; Shopping trips; Dances/Social/Cultural gatherings.

Gardena Convalescent Center
14819 S Vermont, Gardena, CA 90247
(213) 321-6571
Admin Dorothy Bryson.
Licensure Skilled care. *Beds* SNF 74. *Certified* Medicare; Medi-Cal.
Owner Proprietary corp.

Las Flores Convalescent Hospital
14165 Purche Ave, Gardena, CA 90249
(213) 323-4570
Admin Diana Fortune.
Medical Dir Burton H Goldman MD.
Licensure Skilled care. *Beds* SNF 99. *Certified* Medicare; Medi-Cal.
Owner Proprietary corp.
Admissions Requirements Minimum age 21; Medical examination; Physician's request.
Staff RNs 1 (ft), 1 (pt); LPNs 9 (ft), 2 (pt); Nurses' aides 47 (ft), 1 (pt); Physical therapists 1 (pt); Recreational therapists 1 (ft); Occupational therapists 1 (pt); Speech therapists 1 (pt); Dietitians 1 (ft), 1 (pt); Ophthalmologists 1 (pt); Podiatrists 1 (pt); Audiologists 1 (pt); Dentists 1 (pt).
Facilities Dining room; Physical therapy room; Activities room; Crafts room; Laundry room; Barber/Beauty shop.
Activities Arts & crafts; Cards; Games; Reading groups; Prayer groups; Movies; Shopping trips; Dances/Social/Cultural gatherings.

South Bay Keiro Nursing Home
15115 S Vermont, Gardena, CA 90247
(213) 532-0700
Admin Harry Matoba.
Licensure Skilled care. *Beds* SNF 98. *Certified* Medi-Cal.
Owner Nonprofit corp.

Gilroy

Driftwood Convalescent Hospital
8170 Murray Ave, Gilroy, CA 95020
(408) 842-9311
Admin Michael Dunn.
Licensure Skilled care. *Beds* SNF 132. *Certified* Medicare; Medi-Cal.
Owner Proprietary corp (Western Medical Enterprises Inc).

Glendale

Autumn Hills Convalescent Hospital
430 N Glendale Ave, Glendale, CA 91206
(818) 246-5677
Admin Jeri-Anne Ickstadt.
Medical Dir Dr Donald Doty.
Licensure Skilled care. *Beds* SNF 99. *Certified* Medicare; Medi-Cal.
Owner Proprietary corp (Western Medical Enterprises Inc).
Admissions Requirements Physician's request.
Staff Physicians 20 (pt); RNs 2 (ft), 1 (pt); Nurses' aides 30 (ft); Physical therapists 1 (pt); Reality therapists 1 (pt); Recreational therapists 1 (pt); Occupational therapists 1 (pt); Speech therapists 1 (pt); Activities coordinators 1 (ft); Dietitians 1 (pt); Ophthalmologists 1 (pt); Podiatrists 1 (pt); Audiologists 1 (pt); Dentists 1 (pt).
Facilities Dining room; Physical therapy room; Activities room; Crafts room; Laundry room; Barber/Beauty shop.
Activities Arts & crafts; Cards; Games; Reading groups; Prayer groups; Movies; Shopping trips; Dances/Social/Cultural gatherings; Variety.

Beverly Manor Convalescent Hospital of Glendale
630 W Broadway, Glendale, CA 91204
(818) 247-3395
Admin William Mathies.
Medical Dir Albert P Killian MD.
Licensure Skilled care. *Beds* 140. *Certified* Medicare; Medi-Cal.
Owner Proprietary corp (Beverly Enterprises).
Facilities Dining room; Physical therapy room; Activities room; Laundry room; Barber/Beauty shop; Library.
Activities Arts & crafts; Cards; Games; Reading groups; Prayer groups; Movies; Shopping trips; Dances/Social/Cultural gatherings; Wheelchair walks; Adopt-a-grandparent; Adopt-a-friend.

Broadway Manor Convalescent Hospital
605 W Broadway, Glendale, CA 91204
(818) 246-7174
Admin Ralph M Guarino. *Dir of Nursing* Marie Savage. *Medical Dir* Albert P Killian MD.
Licensure Skilled care. *Beds* SNF 78. *Certified* Medicare; Medi-Cal.
Owner Proprietary corp.
Staff Physicians 16 (pt); RNs 2 (ft), 2 (pt); LPNs 6 (ft), 6 (pt); Nurses' aides 14 (ft), 6 (pt); Physical therapists 2 (ft), 3 (pt); Occupational therapists 1 (pt); Speech therapists 1 (pt); Activities coordinators 1 (ft); Dietitians 1 (ft); Ophthalmologists 1 (pt); Podiatrists 1 (pt); Dentists 1 (pt).
Languages Spanish, Tagalog.
Facilities Dining room; Physical therapy room; Activities room; Laundry room; Barber/Beauty shop.
Activities Arts & crafts; Cards; Games; Reading groups; Prayer groups; Movies; Shopping trips; Dances/Social/Cultural gatherings.

Cal Haven Convalescent Hospital
445 W Broadway, Glendale, CA 91204
(818) 241-2157
Admin Elaine Levine.
Medical Dir Dr A P Killian.
Licensure Skilled care. *Beds* SNF 35. *Certified* Medicare; Medi-Cal.
Owner Proprietary corp.
Admissions Requirements Minimum age 40; Medical examination.
Staff Physicians 1 (pt); RNs 2 (ft), 2 (pt); LPNs 3 (ft), 4 (pt); Nurses' aides 9 (ft), 7 (pt); Physical therapists 1 (pt); Reality therapists 1 (pt); Recreational therapists 1 (pt); Occupational therapists 1 (pt); Speech therapists 1 (pt); Activities coordinators 1

(ft), 1 (pt); Dietitians 1 (pt); Ophthalmologists 1 (pt); Podiatrists 1 (pt); Audiologists 1 (pt); Dentists 1 (pt).
Facilities Dining room; Physical therapy room; Activities room; Crafts room; Laundry room; Barber/Beauty shop; Library; Patios.
Activities Arts & crafts; Cards; Games; Reading groups; Prayer groups; Movies; Shopping trips; Dances/Social/Cultural gatherings; Walks in area.

Casa Verdugo Convalescent Lodge
1208 S Central Ave, Glendale, CA 91204
(818) 246-5516
Admin John E Wareham. *Dir of Nursing* Ruth Hull RN. *Medical Dir* Ethel Hamilton MD.
Licensure Skilled care. *Beds* SNF 48.
Owner Nonprofit corp (Southern California Presbyterian Homes).
Admissions Requirements Medical examination; Physician's request.
Staff RNs 2 (ft), 1 (pt); LPNs 5 (ft); Nurses' aides 15 (ft), 10 (pt); Activities coordinators 1 (ft).
Affiliation Presbyterian.
Facilities Dining room; Activities room; Laundry room; Barber/Beauty shop.
Activities Arts & crafts; Games; Reading groups; Prayer groups; Movies; Shopping trips; Educational classes/Glendale College.

Chandler Convalescent Hospital
525 S Central Ave, Glendale, CA 91204
(818) 240-1610
Admin Henry Levine.
Licensure Skilled care. *Beds* SNF 106. *Certified* Medicare; Medi-Cal.
Owner Proprietary corp.

Colby Center
1505 Colby Dr, Glendale, CA 91205
(818) 247-4476
Admin Carroll Gillespie.
Licensure Skilled care. *Beds* SNF 94. *Certified* Medicare; Medi-Cal.
Owner Proprietary corp.
Staff RNs 1 (ft), 4 (pt); LPNs 13 (ft), 4 (pt); Nurses' aides 38 (ft), 6 (pt); Physical therapists 1 (pt); Recreational therapists 2 (ft); Occupational therapists 1 (pt); Speech therapists 1 (pt); Dietitians 1 (pt).
Facilities Dining room; Activities room; Crafts room; Barber/Beauty shop.
Activities Arts & crafts; Cards; Games; Prayer groups; Movies.

Dreier's Sanitarium
1400 W Glenoaks Blvd, Glendale, CA 91201
(818) 242-1183
Admin Dolores D Haedrich. *Dir of Nursing* J Nuala Lane RN. *Medical Dir* George Papkin MD.
Licensure Skilled care. *Beds* SNF 59. *Certified* Medicare; Medi-Cal.
Owner Proprietary corp.
Admissions Requirements Physician's request.
Staff Physicians 1 (pt); RNs 1 (ft), 3 (pt); LPNs 4 (ft), 4 (pt); Nurses' aides 22 (ft), 1 (pt); Physical therapists 1 (pt); Recreational therapists 1 (pt); Occupational therapists 1 (pt); Speech therapists 1 (pt); Activities coordinators 1 (pt); Dietitians 1 (pt); Podiatrists 1 (pt).
Languages Spanish, Filipino, Korean.
Facilities Dining room; Activities room; Crafts room; Laundry room; Barber/Beauty shop.
Activities Arts & crafts; Cards; Games; Reading groups; Prayer groups; Movies; Dances/Social/Cultural gatherings; Intergenerational programs; Pet therapy.

Elms Convalescent Hospital
212 W Chevy Chase, Glendale, CA 91204
(818) 240-6720
Admin William L Knell. *Dir of Nursing* Carmen Garcia RN.
Licensure Skilled care. *Beds* SNF 52.

Owner Proprietary corp.
Admissions Requirements Physician's request.
Staff RNs 1 (ft), 1 (pt); LPNs 4 (ft), 5 (pt); Nurses' aides 14 (ft), 11 (pt); Physical therapists 1 (pt); Occupational therapists 1 (pt); Speech therapists 1 (pt); Activities coordinators 1 (ft), 2 (pt).
Languages Spanish, Tagalog.
Facilities Dining room; Activities room; Laundry room; Barber/Beauty shop; Library.
Activities Arts & crafts; Games; Reading groups; Prayer groups; Movies; Picnic outings.

Glendale Memorial Hospital & Health Center Skilled Nursing Facility
1420 S Central Ave, Glendale, CA 91204
(213) 502-1900
Licensure Skilled care. *Certified* Medicare; Medi-Cal.

Glenoaks Convalescent Hospital
409 W Glenoaks Blvd, Glendale, CA 91202
(818) 240-4300
Admin Pamela Scurlock.
Medical Dir O W Janes MD.
Licensure Skilled care. *Beds* SNF 99. *Certified* Medicare; Medi-Cal.
Owner Privately owned.
Admissions Requirements Medical examination; Physician's request.
Staff RNs 3 (ft), 2 (pt); LPNs 7 (ft), 3 (pt); Nurses' aides 40 (ft), 2 (pt); Reality therapists 1 (ft); Recreational therapists 1 (ft); Activities coordinators 1 (ft); Dietitians 1 (ft).
Facilities Dining room; Physical therapy room; Activities room; Crafts room; Laundry room; Barber/Beauty shop; Library.
Activities Arts & crafts; Cards; Games; Reading groups; Prayer groups; Movies; Shopping trips; Dances/Social/Cultural gatherings.

Glenridge Center
611 S Central, Glendale, CA 91203
(213) 246-6591
Admin Rodney Meacham.
Medical Dir R Cabnenn MD.
Licensure Skilled care. *Beds* ICF 116. *Certified* Medicare.
Owner Proprietary corp (Beverly Enterprises).
Admissions Requirements Minimum age 3.
Staff Physicians 2 (pt); RNs 10 (ft), 5 (pt); LPNs 10 (ft), 5 (pt); Nurses' aides 35 (ft); Physical therapists 1 (ft); Recreational therapists 1 (ft); Occupational therapists 1 (pt); Speech therapists 1 (pt); Activities coordinators 1 (ft); Dietitians 1 (ft); Ophthalmologists 1 (pt); Podiatrists 1 (pt); Audiologists 1 (pt); Dentists 1 (pt).
Facilities Dining room; Physical therapy room; Activities room; Crafts room; Laundry room; Barber/Beauty shop.
Activities Arts & crafts; Games; Movies; Shopping trips; Dances/Social/Cultural gatherings.

Riverdale Convalescent Center
201 Allen Ave, Glendale, CA 91201
(213) 849-1969, (818) 842-5832 FAX
Admin Sedy Demesa. *Dir of Nursing* Shirley Horst RN. *Medical Dir* Dr Roberto Beaton.
Licensure Skilled care. *Beds* SNF 94. *Private Pay Patients* 10%. *Certified* Medicare; Medi-Cal.
Owner Proprietary corp (Mastercare Health Facilities Inc).
Staff RNs; LPNs; Nurses' aides; Physical therapists; Activities coordinators; Dietitians.

Royal Oaks Convalescent Hospital
250 N Verdugo, Glendale, CA 91206
(818) 244-1133
Admin Sol Barrientos. *Dir of Nursing* Eden Salceda.
Licensure Skilled care. *Beds* SNF 136. *Certified* Medicaid; Medicare; Medi-Cal.

Owner Proprietary corp (Hardy Enterprises).
Staff Physicians; RNs; LPNs; Nurses' aides;
  Physical therapists; Occupational therapists;
  Speech therapists; Activities coordinators;
  Dietitians; Ophthalmologists; Podiatrists.
Facilities Dining room; Physical therapy
  room; Activities room; Laundry room;
  Barber/Beauty shop.
Activities Arts & crafts; Cards; Games;
  Reading groups; Prayer groups; Movies;
  Shopping trips; Dances/Social/Cultural
  gatherings; Intergenerational programs.

Tropico Convalescent Hospital
130 W Los Feliz Rd, Glendale, CA 91204
(818) 246-7134
Admin Sarah Klanche.
Licensure Skilled care. *Beds* SNF 56. *Certified*
  Medicare; Medi-Cal.
Owner Proprietary corp (Western Medical
  Enterprises Inc).

Windsor Manor
1230 E Windsor Rd, Glendale, CA 91205
(818) 245-1623
Admin Steven T Patterson.
Licensure Skilled care. *Beds* SNF 28. *Certified*
  Medi-Cal.
Owner Nonprofit corp.

Glendora

Adventist Convalescent Hospital
435 E Gladstone, Glendora, CA 91740
(818) 963-5955
Admin Peter Peabody. *Dir of Nursing* Urmila
  Patel RN. *Medical Dir* Timothy Ferguson
  MD.
Licensure Skilled care. *Beds* SNF 118. *Private
  Pay Patients* 58%. *Certified* Medicaid;
  Medicare; Medi-Cal.
Owner Nonprofit organization/foundation.
Admissions Requirements Minimum age 18;
  Physician's request.
Staff RNs 4 (ft), 6 (pt); LPNs 5 (ft), 6 (pt);
  Nurses' aides 40 (ft), 4 (pt); Activities
  coordinators 1 (ft).
Languages Spanish.
Affiliation Seventh-Day Adventist.
Facilities Dining room; Physical therapy
  room; Activities room; Chapel; Crafts room;
  Laundry room; Barber/Beauty shop.
Activities Arts & crafts; Cards; Games;
  Reading groups; Prayer groups; Movies;
  Dances/Social/Cultural gatherings;
  Intergenerational programs; Pet therapy.

Arbor Glen Care Center
1033 E Arrow Hwy, Glendora, CA 91740
(818) 963-7531
Admin Vivian Whistler.
Licensure Skilled care. *Beds* SNF 98. *Certified*
  Medicare; Medi-Cal.
Owner Proprietary corp.

Community Convalescent Hospital of Glendora
638 Colorado Ave, Glendora, CA 91740
(818) 963-6091
Admin Georganne Slapper. *Dir of Nursing* R
  Wittenbraker RN. *Medical Dir* Onn T Chan
  MD.
Licensure Skilled care. *Beds* SNF 96. *Certified*
  Medicare; Medi-Cal.
Owner Privately owned.
Admissions Requirements Physician's request.
Staff Physicians 1 (pt); RNs 1 (ft), 2 (pt);
  LPNs 7 (ft), 6 (pt); Nurses' aides 26 (ft), 5
  (pt); Physical therapists 1 (pt); Speech
  therapists 1 (pt); Activities coordinators 1
  (ft); Dietitians 1 (ft); Ophthalmologists 1
  (pt); Podiatrists 1 (pt); Dentists 1 (pt).
Languages Spanish, Russian, German,
  Hungarian, Chinese.
Facilities Dining room; Physical therapy
  room; Activities room; Barber/Beauty shop.
Activities Arts & crafts; Cards; Games;
  Reading groups; Prayer groups; Movies;
  Shopping trips.

Oakview Convalescent Hospital
805 W Arrow Hwy, Glendora, CA 91740
(818) 331-0781, 339-2603 FAX
Admin Barbara Dubiel. *Dir of Nursing*
  Cynthia Perez RN. *Medical Dir* George
  Magallon MD.
Licensure Skilled care; Intermediate care. *Beds*
  SNF 292; ICF 50. *Certified* Medicare; Medi-
  Cal.
Owner Proprietary corp (Oakview Health Care
  Inc).
Admissions Requirements Medical
  examination; Physician's request.
Staff Physicians 15 (ft) (admitting); RNs 9
  (ft); LPNs 35 (ft), 4 (pt); Nurses' aides 120
  (ft); Physical therapists 2 (ft); Occupational
  therapists 1 (pt); Speech therapists 1 (pt);
  Activities coordinators 5 (pt); Dietitians 1
  (ft); Ophthalmologists 1 (pt); Podiatrists 1
  (pt); Audiologists 1 (pt); Respiratory
  therapists 1 (pt).
Languages Spanish, Tagalog.
Facilities Dining room; Physical therapy
  room; Activities room; Crafts room; Laundry
  room; Barber/Beauty shop.
Activities Arts & crafts; Cards; Games;
  Reading groups; Prayer groups; Movies;
  Shopping trips; Dances/Social/Cultural
  gatherings; Intergenerational programs; Pet
  therapy.

Granada Hills

Casitas Care Center
10626 Balboa Blvd, Granada Hills, CA 91344
(818) 368-2802
Admin Evelyn N Dold.
Medical Dir A Beckerman.
Licensure Skilled care. *Beds* SNF 99. *Certified*
  Medicare; Medi-Cal.
Owner Privately owned.
Admissions Requirements Minimum age 35.
Staff RNs 3 (ft), 2 (pt); LPNs 8 (ft), 2 (pt);
  Nurses' aides 30 (ft), 4 (pt); Reality
  therapists 1 (pt); Recreational therapists 1
  (ft), 1 (pt); Activities coordinators 1 (ft).
Languages Spanish, Russian, Polish, Hebrew,
  Yiddish, Tagalog, Korean.
Facilities Dining room; Physical therapy
  room; Activities room; Chapel; Crafts room;
  Laundry room; Barber/Beauty shop; Library.
Activities Arts & crafts; Cards; Games;
  Reading groups; Prayer groups; Movies;
  Shopping trips; Dances/Social/Cultural
  gatherings.

Granada Hills Convalescent Hospital
16123 Chatsworth Ave, Granada Hills, CA
91344
(818) 891-1745
Admin Abraham Birnbaum.
Licensure Skilled care. *Beds* SNF 48. *Certified*
  Medicare; Medi-Cal.
Owner Proprietary corp.

Magnolia Gardens Convalescent
17922 San Fernando Mission Blvd, Granada
  Hills, CA 91344
(818) 360-1864
Admin Betty Schaper. *Dir of Nursing*
  Elizabeth McCutcheon RN. *Medical Dir*
  Felcar Morada.
Licensure Skilled care. *Beds* SNF 99. *Private
  Pay Patients* 30%. *Certified* Medicare; Medi-
  Cal.
Owner Proprietary corp (Libby Care).
Admissions Requirements Minimum age 18;
  Medical examination; Physician's request.
Staff Physicians; RNs; LPNs; Nurses' aides;
  Physical therapists (contracted); Reality
  therapists (contracted); Recreational
  therapists (contracted); Occupational
  therapists (contracted); Speech therapists
  (contracted); Activities coordinators;
  Dietitians; Ophthalmologists (contracted);
  Podiatrists (contracted); Audiologists
  (contracted); Restorative nurses.

Languages Spanish, Tagalog.
Facilities Dining room; Physical therapy
  room; Activities room; Chapel; Crafts room;
  Laundry room; Barber/Beauty shop; Library;
  Outside patio; Walkways; Gardens.
Activities Arts & crafts; Cards; Games;
  Reading groups; Prayer groups; Movies;
  Shopping trips; Dances/Social/Cultural
  gatherings; Intergenerational programs; Pet
  therapy; Trivia; Cookouts; Country
  breakfast; Candlelight dinner.

Rinaldi Convalescent Hospital
16553 Rinaldi St, Granada Hills, CA 91344
(818) 360-1003
Admin David L Hibarger.
Licensure Skilled care. *Beds* SNF 101.
  Certified Medicare; Medi-Cal.
Owner Proprietary corp.

Grass Valley

Golden Empire Convalescent Hospital
121 Dorsey Dr, Grass Valley, CA 95945
(916) 273-1316
Admin Cleolue White RN MS.
Licensure Skilled care. *Beds* SNF 158.
  Certified Medicare; Medi-Cal.
Owner Proprietary corp.

Grass Valley Convalescent Hospital
107 Catherine Ln, Grass Valley, CA 95945
(916) 273-4447
Admin Larry Roberts.
Medical Dir Jerome Frey MD.
Licensure Skilled care. *Beds* SNF 59. *Certified*
  Medicare; Medi-Cal.
Owner Proprietary corp.
Admissions Requirements Physician's request.
Staff RNs 3 (ft); LPNs 3 (ft), 4 (pt); Nurses'
  aides 18 (ft), 7 (pt); Activities coordinators 1
  (ft); Dietitians 1 (ft).
Facilities Dining room; Activities room;
  Crafts room; Laundry room; Barber/Beauty
  shop; Library; TV room.
Activities Arts & crafts; Games; Reading
  groups; Prayer groups; Movies; Shopping
  trips; Dances/Social/Cultural gatherings.

Meadow View Manor
396 Dorsey Dr, Grass Valley, CA 95945
(916) 272-2272, 272-6085 FAX
Admin Larry Roberts. *Dir of Nursing* Leslee
  Johnson. *Medical Dir* G A Dawkins.
Licensure Skilled care. *Beds* SNF 99. *Certified*
  Medicare; Medi-Cal.
Owner Proprietary corp.
Admissions Requirements Medical
  examination; Physician's request.
Facilities Dining room; Physical therapy
  room; Activities room; Crafts room; Laundry
  room; Barber/Beauty shop.
Activities Arts & crafts; Cards; Games;
  Reading groups; Prayer groups; Movies;
  Shopping trips; Dances/Social/Cultural
  gatherings; Intergenerational programs; Pet
  therapy.

Oak Park Nursing Center Inc
10716 Cedar Ave, Grass Valley, CA 95945
(916) 273-2470
Admin Iva Jean Harmon.
Licensure Skilled care. *Beds* SNF 27. *Certified*
  Medi-Cal.
Owner Proprietary corp.

Spring Hill Manor Convalescent Hospital
355 Joerschke Dr, Grass Valley, CA 95945
(916) 273-7247
Admin Anne Peterson. *Dir of Nursing* Carleen
  Carlson RN. *Medical Dir* Jerome F Frey
  MD.
Licensure Skilled care. *Beds* SNF 49. *Certified*
  Medicare; Medi-Cal.
Owner Privately owned.
Admissions Requirements Physician's request.

Staff Physicians 1 (pt); RNs 1 (ft), 2 (pt); LPNs 2 (ft), 3 (pt); Nurses' aides 23 (ft), 4 (pt); Physical therapists (contracted); Occupational therapists 1 (pt); Activities coordinators 1 (ft); Dietitians 3 (ft), 2 (pt); Maintenance 1 (ft); Housekeeping 2 (ft), 4 (pt).
Facilities Dining room; Physical therapy room; Activities room; Laundry room; Barber/Beauty shop.
Activities Arts & crafts; Cards; Games; Reading groups; Prayer groups; Movies; Pet therapy.

Greenbrae

Greenbrae Convalescent Hospital
1220 S Eliseo Dr, Greenbrae, CA 94904
(415) 461-9700
Admin Teresa Saltzman. *Dir of Nursing* Catherine Kelly RN. *Medical Dir* Janet Bodle MD.
Licensure Skilled care. *Beds* SNF 72. *Certified* Medicare.
Owner Nonprofit organization/foundation (Guardian Foundation Inc).
Admissions Requirements Medical examination; Physician's request.
Staff RNs 5 (ft), 8 (pt); LPNs 1 (pt); Nurses' aides; Activities coordinators 1 (ft), 1 (pt).
Facilities Dining room; Physical therapy room; Activities room; Crafts room; Laundry room; Barber/Beauty shop.
Activities Arts & crafts; Cards; Games; Reading groups; Prayer groups; Movies; Shopping trips; Dances/Social/Cultural gatherings.

Greenville

Indian Valley Hospital DP/SNF
174 Hot Springs Rd, Greenville, CA 95947
(916) 284-7191
Admin La Veta Alexander.
Licensure Skilled care. *Beds* SNF 17. *Certified* Medicare; Medi-Cal.
Owner Publicly owned.

Gridley

Biggs-Gridley Memorial Hospital Hovlid Community Care Center
PO Box 97, 240 Spruce St, Gridley, CA 95948
(916) 846-5671
Admin Charles Norton. *Dir of Nursing* Reba Fahey RN. *Medical Dir* Dr Shieh.
Licensure Skilled care. *Beds* SNF 21. *Private Pay Patients* 25%. *Certified* Medicare; Medi-Cal.
Owner Nonprofit organization/foundation.
Admissions Requirements Medical examination; Physician's request.
Staff Physicians 7 (ft); RNs 1 (ft); LPNs 3 (ft), 4 (pt); Nurses' aides 5 (ft), 9 (pt); Physical therapists 1 (pt); Reality therapists 1 (pt); Recreational therapists 1 (pt); Occupational therapists 1 (pt); Speech therapists 1 (pt); Activities coordinators 1 (pt); Dietitians 1 (pt); Podiatrists 1 (pt).
Languages Spanish, Punjab.
Facilities Dining room; Physical therapy room; Activities room; Chapel; Crafts room; Laundry room; Barber/Beauty shop; Covered patio; Big screen TV; VCR.
Activities Arts & crafts; Cards; Games; Reading groups; Prayer groups; Movies; Shopping trips; Dances/Social/Cultural gatherings; Intergenerational programs; Pet therapy.

Lakeview Nursing Home Inc
PO Box 1226, Gridley, CA 95943
(916) 533-1874
Admin Nellie K Walker.
Medical Dir W R Olson MD.

Licensure Skilled care. *Beds* SNF 28. *Certified* Medi-Cal.
Owner Proprietary corp.
Admissions Requirements Physician's request.
Staff RNs 1 (ft); LPNs 3 (ft), 1 (pt); Nurses' aides 11 (ft); Physical therapists 1 (pt); Reality therapists 1 (pt); Recreational therapists 1 (ft); Occupational therapists 1 (pt); Speech therapists 1 (pt); Activities coordinators 1 (ft); Dietitians 1 (pt); Podiatrists 1 (pt); Dentists 1 (pt).
Facilities Dining room; Activities room; Laundry room.
Activities Arts & crafts; Cards; Games; Reading groups; Prayer groups; Movies; Dances/Social/Cultural gatherings.

Valley Oaks Health Care Center
246 Spruce St, Gridley, CA 95948
(916) 846-6266
Admin Cheryl Haury.
Licensure Skilled care. *Beds* SNF 82. *Certified* Medicare; Medi-Cal.
Owner Proprietary corp.

Hacienda Heights

Helen Evans Home for Retarded Children
15125 Gale Ave, Hacienda Heights, CA 91745
(213) 330-4048
Admin Thomas Evans.
Medical Dir Rolando Atiga MD.
Licensure Intermediate care for mentally retarded. *Beds* 59. *Certified* Medi-Cal.
Owner Proprietary corp.
Staff RNs 3 (ft), 7 (pt); Nurses' aides 27 (ft), 13 (pt); Activities coordinators 1 (ft).
Facilities Dining room; Activities room.
Activities Arts & crafts; Outings.

Hanford

Hacienda Health Care
361 E Grangeville Blvd, Hanford, CA 93230
(209) 582-9221
Admin Robert A Barker. *Dir of Nursing* Delores Wheeler RN. *Medical Dir* George Guerwsey MD.
Licensure Skilled care. *Beds* SNF 133. *Certified* Medicare; Medi-Cal.
Owner Proprietary corp.
Admissions Requirements Physician's request.
Languages Spanish, Portuguese.
Facilities Dining room; Physical therapy room; Activities room; Laundry room; Barber/Beauty shop.
Activities Arts & crafts; Cards; Games; Reading groups; Prayer groups; Movies; Shopping trips; Dances/Social/Cultural gatherings.

Kings Convalescent Center
851 Leslie Ln, Hanford, CA 93230
(209) 582-4414
Admin Sheila Ockey. *Dir of Nursing* Glenda Coulter RN. *Medical Dir* George G Guernsey MD.
Licensure Skilled care. *Beds* SNF 59. *Certified* Medi-Cal.
Owner Nonprofit corp (Wilshire Foundation Inc).
Admissions Requirements Physician's request.
Staff Physicians 22 (pt); RNs 1 (ft), 2 (pt); LPNs 5 (ft), 2 (pt); Nurses' aides 22 (ft), 2 (pt); Physical therapists 1 (pt); Recreational therapists 1 (pt); Speech therapists 1 (pt); Activities coordinators 1 (ft); Dietitians 1 (ft); Podiatrists 1 (pt).
Languages Spanish, Japanese, Portuguese, Tagalog.
Facilities Dining room; Activities room; Crafts room; Laundry room; Barber/Beauty shop.
Activities Arts & crafts; Cards; Games; Reading groups; Prayer groups; Movies; Shopping trips; Dances/Social/Cultural

---

gatherings; Intergenerational programs; Pet therapy; Homecoming; Baby pageant; Special outings.

Lacey Manor
1007 W Lacey Blvd, Hanford, CA 93230
(209) 582-2871, 582-5853 FAX
Admin Brad Kikuta. *Dir of Nursing* Vickey Keller.
Licensure Skilled care. *Beds* SNF 99. *Certified* Medicare; Medi-Cal.
Owner Proprietary corp.
Staff RNs; LPNs; Nurses' aides; Recreational therapists; Activities coordinators.
Facilities Dining room; Physical therapy room; Activities room; Crafts room; Laundry room; Barber/Beauty shop; Library.
Activities Arts & crafts; Cards; Games; Reading groups; Prayer groups; Movies; Shopping trips; Dances/Social/Cultural gatherings; Intergenerational programs; Pet therapy.

Hawthorne

Golden West Convalescent Hospital
11834 Inglewood Ave, Hawthorne, CA 90250
(213) 679-1461
Admin Lydia P Milligan. *Dir of Nursing* Pastora C Lagmay RN. *Medical Dir* Marvin H Stein MD.
Licensure Skilled care; Intermediate care. *Beds* SNF 97; ICF 2. *Private Pay Patients* 6%. *Certified* Medicare; Medi-Cal.
Owner Privately owned.
Admissions Requirements Minimum age 30.
Staff Physicians 15 (pt); RNs 3 (ft), 1 (pt); LPNs 12 (ft); Nurses' aides 34 (ft), 1 (pt); Physical therapists 1 (pt); Occupational therapists 1 (pt); Speech therapists 1 (pt); Activities coordinators 1 (ft); Dietitians 1 (pt); Ophthalmologists 1 (pt); Podiatrists 1 (pt); Audiologists 1 (pt).
Languages Spanish.
Facilities Dining room; Physical therapy room; Activities room; Crafts room; Laundry room; Barber/Beauty shop; Library; Closed patio.
Activities Arts & crafts; Cards; Games; Reading groups; Prayer groups; Movies; Shopping trips; Dances/Social/Cultural gatherings; Intergenerational programs.

Hawthorne Convalescent Center
11630 S Grevillea, Hawthorne, CA 90250
(213) 679-9732
Admin Esther Williams. *Dir of Nursing* Gary S Wolfe RN. *Medical Dir* Daryl Hutchinson MD.
Licensure Skilled care; Alzheimer's care. *Beds* SNF 88. *Private Pay Patients* 25%. *Certified* Medicare; Medi-Cal.
Owner Nonprofit corp (Wilshire Foundation Inc).
Admissions Requirements Physician's request.
Staff RNs 2 (ft); LPNs 8 (ft); Nurses' aides 34 (ft); Activities coordinators 1 (ft); Dietitians.
Facilities Dining room; Physical therapy room; Activities room; Crafts room; Laundry room; Barber/Beauty shop.
Activities Arts & crafts; Cards; Games; Reading groups; Prayer groups; Movies; Shopping trips; Dances/Social/Cultural gatherings; Pet therapy; Restaurant dining program.

South Bay Child Care Center
13812 Cordary Ave, Hawthorne, CA 90250
(213) 679-9223
Admin Ethel Holtzclaw.
Licensure Skilled care; Intermediate care for mentally retarded. *Beds* 90. *Certified* Medicare; Medi-Cal.
Owner Proprietary corp.

Southwest Convalescent Center
13922 Cerise Ave, Hawthorne, CA 90250
(213) 675-3304

Admin Judy Gonzalez.
Medical Dir Michael Platt MD.
Licensure Skilled care. *Beds* SNF 99. *Certified* Medicare; Medi-Cal.
Owner Nonprofit organization/foundation (Everhealth Foundation).
Staff RNs 2 (ft), 2 (pt); LPNs 6 (ft), 3 (pt); Nurses' aides 30 (ft), 15 (pt); Recreational therapists 1 (ft), 1 (pt); Dietitians 1 (pt).
Facilities Dining room; Physical therapy room; Activities room; Crafts room; Laundry room; Barber/Beauty shop; Classroom.
Activities Arts & crafts; Cards; Games; Reading groups; Prayer groups; Movies; Shopping trips.

Hayward

Barrett Convalescent Hospital
1625 Denton Ave, Hayward, CA 94545
(415) 782-2133, 783-3659 FAX
Admin Nicholas DeFina.
Medical Dir Dr H Lints.
Licensure Skilled care. *Beds* SNF 74. *Certified* Medicaid; Medicare; Medi-Cal.
Owner Proprietary corp.
Admissions Requirements Physician's request.
Staff Physicians 7 (pt); RNs 3 (ft); LPNs 7 (ft); Nurses' aides 44 (ft); Physical therapists 1 (pt); Recreational therapists 1 (ft); Speech therapists 1 (pt); Activities coordinators 1 (ft); Dietitians 1 (ft); Podiatrists 1 (pt); Dentists 1 (pt).
Facilities Dining room; Activities room; Crafts room; Laundry room; Barber/Beauty shop.
Activities Arts & crafts; Cards; Games; Reading groups; Prayer groups; Movies; Shopping trips; Dances/Social/Cultural gatherings; Intergenerational programs; Pet therapy.

Bassard Convalescent Hospital Inc
3269 D St, Hayward, CA 94541
(415) 537-6700
Admin Yvonne Bassard.
Medical Dir Fred Meltz MD.
Licensure Skilled care; Alzheimer's care. *Beds* SNF 71. *Certified* Medicare; Medi-Cal.
Owner Proprietary corp.
Admissions Requirements Minimum age 9.
Staff Physicians 6 (pt); RNs 3 (pt); LPNs 7 (ft), 8 (pt); Nurses' aides 20 (ft), 4 (pt); Physical therapists 1 (pt); Recreational therapists 1 (pt); Occupational therapists 1 (pt); Speech therapists 1 (pt); Activities coordinators 1 (ft); Dietitians 1 (pt); Ophthalmologists 1 (pt); Podiatrists 1 (pt).
Languages Spanish, Tagalo.
Facilities Dining room; Activities room; Chapel; Laundry room; Barber/Beauty shop; Library.
Activities Arts & crafts; Cards; Games; Reading groups; Prayer groups; Movies; Shopping trips; Dances/Social/Cultural gatherings; Intergenerational programs; Pet therapy; Cooking classes; Catholic mass; Protestant services.

Bethesda Home
22427 Montgomery St, Hayward, CA 94541
(415) 538-8300
Admin Donald G Williams.
Medical Dir William Arthur MD.
Licensure Skilled care. *Beds* SNF 40. *Certified* Medicare; Medi-Cal.
Owner Proprietary corp.
Staff RNs 1 (ft), 3 (pt); Nurses' aides 16 (ft); Physical therapists 1 (pt); Activities coordinators 1 (ft); Dietitians 1 (pt); Ophthalmologists 1 (pt); Dentists 1 (pt).
Facilities Dining room; Activities room; Chapel; Crafts room; Laundry room; Barber/Beauty shop.
Activities Prayer groups; Movies; Shopping trips.

CareWest—Gateway Nursing Center
26660 Patrick Ave, Hayward, CA 94544
(415) 782-1845
Admin Bruce Strayer. *Dir of Nursing* Helen Jones RN. *Medical Dir* Fred Meltz MD.
Licensure Skilled care. *Beds* SNF 99. *Certified* Medicare; Medi-Cal.
Owner Proprietary corp (Care Enterprises).
Admissions Requirements Medical examination; Physician's request.
Staff RNs 2 (ft), 2 (pt); LPNs 10 (ft), 2 (pt); Nurses' aides 35 (ft), 5 (pt); Physical therapists 1 (ft); Occupational therapists 1 (ft); Speech therapists 1 (ft); Activities coordinators 1 (ft); Dietitians 1 (ft), 15 (ft).
Languages Spanish.
Facilities Dining room; Physical therapy room; Activities room; Laundry room; Barber/Beauty shop; Library.
Activities Arts & crafts; Games; Reading groups; Prayer groups; Movies; Shopping trips; Dances/Social/Cultural gatherings; Cooking; Exercise.

Creekside Terrace Intermediate Care Facility Inc
629 Hampton Rd, Hayward, CA 94541
(415) 276-5403
Admin Bradley M Besaw. *Dir of Nursing* Kathryn Fujii LVN. *Medical Dir* Gary Miller MD.
Licensure Intermediate care; Alzheimer's care. *Beds* 25. *Certified* Medi-Cal.
Owner Proprietary corp.
Admissions Requirements Medical examination; Physician's request.
Staff Physicians 4 (pt); RNs 1 (pt); LPNs 1 (ft), 2 (pt); Nurses' aides 4 (ft), 1 (pt); Occupational therapists 1 (pt); Activities coordinators 2 (pt); Dietitians 1 (pt).
Languages Spanish.
Facilities Dining room; Laundry room.
Activities Arts & crafts; Cards; Games; Reading groups; Prayer groups; Movies; Shopping trips; Dances/Social/Cultural gatherings.

Driftwood Manor
19700 Hesperian Blvd, Hayward, CA 94541
(415) 785-2880
Licensure Skilled care. *Beds* 85. *Certified* Medicare; Medi-Cal.
Owner Proprietary corp (ARA Living Centers).

Eden West Convalescent Hospital
1805 West St, Hayward, CA 94545
(415) 783-4811
Admin Margaret A Westerfield. *Dir of Nursing* Gloria Scott RN. *Medical Dir* Dr Sharp.
Licensure Skilled care. *Beds* SNF 99. *Certified* Medicare; Medi-Cal.
Owner Privately owned.
Admissions Requirements Minimum age 18.
Staff RNs 2 (ft), 2 (pt); LPNs 12 (ft), 4 (pt); Nurses' aides 30 (ft), 6 (pt); Physical therapists 1 (ft); Recreational therapists 1 (ft); Occupational therapists 1 (pt); Speech therapists 1 (pt); Activities coordinators 1 (ft); Dietitians 1 (pt); Podiatrists 1 (pt).
Facilities Dining room; Physical therapy room; Activities room; Laundry room; Barber/Beauty shop; Library.
Activities Arts & crafts; Cards; Games; Reading groups; Prayer groups; Movies; Shopping trips; Dances/Social/Cultural gatherings.

Glen Ellen Convalescent Hospital
21568 Banyan St, Hayward, CA 94541
(415) 538-2348
Admin Oleta Dillard.
Licensure Intermediate care. *Beds* 26. *Certified* Medi-Cal.
Owner Proprietary corp.

Hayward Convalescent Hospital
1832 B St, Hayward, CA 94541
(415) 538-3866
Admin Mark Tornga. *Dir of Nursing* Myra Leeper. *Medical Dir* Fred Meltz MD.
Licensure Skilled care. *Beds* SNF 99. *Private Pay Patients* 33%. *Certified* Medicare; Medi-Cal.
Owner Proprietary corp.
Admissions Requirements Physician's request.
Staff RNs 5 (ft), 6 (pt); LPNs 8 (ft), 7 (pt); Nurses' aides 49 (ft), 5 (pt); Physical therapists 1 (pt); Recreational therapists 1 (ft); Occupational therapists 1 (pt); Speech therapists 1 (pt); Activities coordinators 1 (ft); Dietitians 1 (pt); Ophthalmologists 1 (pt); Social workers.
Languages Spanish, Portuguese, Tagalog.
Facilities Dining room; Physical therapy room; Activities room; Crafts room; Laundry room; Barber/Beauty shop; Library.
Activities Arts & crafts; Cards; Games; Reading groups; Prayer groups; Movies; Shopping trips; As baseball games; Picnics; Barbeques.

Hayward Hills Convalescent Hospital
1768 B St, Hayward, CA 94541
(415) 538-4424
Dir of Nursing Helen Gustauson RN. *Medical Dir* Ernest Williamson MD.
Licensure Skilled care. *Beds* SNF 72. *Certified* Medicare; Medi-Cal.
Owner Proprietary corp (ARA Living Centers).
Admissions Requirements Medical examination; Physician's request.
Staff Physicians 4 (pt); RNs 1 (ft), 2 (pt); LPNs 8 (ft); Physical therapists 1 (pt); Recreational therapists 1 (pt); Occupational therapists 1 (pt); Speech therapists 1 (pt); Activities coordinators 1 (ft); Dietitians 1 (pt); Ophthalmologists 1 (pt); Podiatrists 1 (pt); Dentists 1 (pt).
Facilities Dining room; Physical therapy room; Crafts room; Laundry room.
Activities Arts & crafts; Cards; Games; Reading groups; Prayer groups; Movies; Shopping trips; Dances/Social/Cultural gatherings.

Hillhaven Hayward
442 Sunset Blvd, Hayward, CA 94541
(415) 582-8311
Admin William Kruse.
Licensure Skilled care. *Beds* SNF 99. *Certified* Medicare; Medi-Cal.
Owner Proprietary corp (Hillhaven Inc).

Holly Tree Convalescent Hospital
553 Smalley Ave, Hayward, CA 94541
(415) 537-2755
Admin Shirley A Ernest RN. *Dir of Nursing* Mildred Pickett RN. *Medical Dir* William Arthur MD.
Licensure Skilled care; Retirement. *Beds* SNF 30; Retirement 20. *Private Pay Patients* 3%. *Certified* Medicare; Medi-Cal.
Owner Privately owned.
Admissions Requirements Medical examination.
Staff RNs 1 (ft), 2 (pt); LPNs 3 (ft); Nurses' aides 5 (ft), 2 (pt); Activities coordinators 1 (pt).
Facilities Dining room; Activities room; Laundry room; TV/Living room; Enclosed outside patio.
Activities Arts & crafts; Cards; Games; Reading groups; Prayer groups; Movies; Dances/Social/Cultural gatherings; Intergenerational programs; Pet therapy.

Majestic Pines Care Center
1628 B St, Hayward, CA 94541
(415) 582-4636
Medical Dir William Arthur.
Licensure Skilled care. *Beds* SNF 75. *Certified* Medicare; Medi-Cal.

Owner Proprietary corp.
Admissions Requirements Medical examination; Physician's request.
Staff RNs 3 (ft), 3 (pt); LPNs 7 (ft), 1 (pt); Nurses' aides 23 (ft), 6 (pt); Recreational therapists 1 (ft); Activities coordinators 1 (ft).
Facilities Dining room; Physical therapy room; Activities room; Crafts room; Laundry room; Barber/Beauty shop.
Activities Arts & crafts; Cards; Games; Reading groups; Prayer groups; Movies; Shopping trips; Dances/Social/Cultural gatherings.

Parkview Convalescent Hospital
27350 Tampa Ave, Hayward, CA 94544
(415) 783-8150
Admin Nancy Zant.
Medical Dir Geraldine Fulks.
Licensure Skilled care. *Beds* SNF 121. *Certified* Medicare; Medi-Cal.
Owner Proprietary corp (ARA Living Centers).
Staff RNs; LPNs; Nurses' aides; Physical therapists 1 (pt); Occupational therapists 1 (pt); Speech therapists 1 (pt); Activities coordinators 1 (ft), 1 (pt); Dietitians 1 (ft).
Facilities Dining room; Physical therapy room; Activities room; Chapel; Crafts room; Laundry room; Barber/Beauty shop; Library.
Activities Arts & crafts; Cards; Games; Reading groups; Prayer groups; Movies; Shopping trips; Dances/Social/Cultural gatherings.

St Christopher Convalescent Hospital
22822 Myrtle St, Hayward, CA 94541
(415) 537-4844
Dir of Nursing Doll Coleman. *Medical Dir* Andrew May MD.
Licensure Skilled care. *Beds* SNF 36. *Certified* Medi-Cal.
Owner Proprietary corp.
Admissions Requirements Physician's request.
Staff RNs 1 (ft), 2 (pt); LPNs 3 (ft), 3 (pt); Nurses' aides 10 (ft); Activities coordinators 1 (ft).
Languages Spanish, Tagalog.
Facilities Dining room; Activities room; Laundry room.
Activities Arts & crafts; Games; Movies; Shopping trips.

St Francis Extended Care Inc
718 Bartlett Ave, Hayward, CA 94541
(415) 785-3630
Licensure Skilled care. *Beds* SNF 59. *Certified* Medi-Cal.
Owner Proprietary corp.

St Michael Convalescent Hospital
25919 Gading Rd, Hayward, CA 94544
(415) 782-8424
Licensure Skilled care. *Beds* SNF 99. *Certified* Medi-Cal.
Owner Proprietary corp.

St Therese Convalescent Hospital Inc
21863 Vallejo St, Hayward, CA 94541
(415) 538-3811
Licensure Skilled care. *Beds* SNF 36. *Certified* Medi-Cal.
Owner Proprietary corp.

Stonehaven Convalescent Hospital Inc
1782 B St, Hayward, CA 94541
(415) 581-3766
Medical Dir Andrew May MD.
Licensure Skilled care. *Beds* SNF 25. *Certified* Medicare; Medi-Cal.
Owner Proprietary corp.
Admissions Requirements Physician's request.
Facilities Dining room; Activities room; Crafts room; Laundry room.
Activities Arts & crafts; Cards; Games; Reading groups; Prayer groups; Movies; Dances/Social/Cultural gatherings.

Sunset Boulevard Convalescent Hospital 1
458 Sunset Blvd, Hayward, CA 94541
(415) 582-8311
Admin Charles W Drake.
Licensure Intermediate care. *Beds* 26. *Certified* Medi-Cal.
Owner Proprietary corp.

Healdsburg

Healdsburg Convalescent Hospital
PO Box 366, Healdsburg, CA 95448-0366
(707) 433-4813
Admin Evan D Keeney. *Dir of Nursing* Elsie Keller. *Medical Dir* Dr Martin Rubinger.
Licensure Skilled care. *Beds* SNF 46. *Certified* Medicare; Medi-Cal.
Owner Proprietary corp.
Admissions Requirements Medical examination; Physician's request.
Staff Physicians 10 (pt); RNs 1 (ft), 1 (pt); LPNs 7 (ft), 2 (pt); Nurses' aides 22 (ft), 4 (pt); Physical therapists 3 (pt); Recreational therapists 1 (pt); Occupational therapists 1 (pt); Speech therapists 1 (pt); Activities coordinators 1 (ft); Dietitians 1 (pt); Ophthalmologists 1 (pt); Podiatrists 1 (pt); Dentists 1 (pt); Social services 1 (pt).
Languages Spanish.
Facilities Dining room; Activities room; Crafts room; Laundry room; Barber/Beauty shop; Library.
Activities Arts & crafts; Games; Reading groups; Prayer groups; Movies; Shopping trips; Dances/Social/Cultural gatherings.

Hemet

Cloverleaf Healthcare
275 N San Jacinto, Hemet, CA 92343
(714) 658-9441
Admin Linda F Williams.
Licensure Skilled care. *Beds* SNF 99. *Certified* Medicare; Medi-Cal.
Owner Proprietary corp (Cloverleaf Enterprises Inc).

Hemet Convalescent Center
40300 E Devonshire, Hemet, CA 92343
(714) 925-2571
Admin Joy Annette Brinnon. *Dir of Nursing* Penny Beverly RN. *Medical Dir* Joseph Karcher MD.
Licensure Skilled care. *Beds* SNF 99. *Private Pay Patients* 40%. *Certified* Medicare; Medi-Cal.
Owner Proprietary corp (Summit Health Ltd).
Admissions Requirements Physician's request.
Staff RNs 4 (ft), 3 (pt); LPNs 6 (ft), 3 (pt); Nurses' aides 38 (ft), 3 (pt); Physical therapists (contracted); Recreational therapists 1 (ft); Occupational therapists (contracted); Speech therapists (contracted); Activities coordinators 1 (ft), 1 (pt); Dietitians (contracted); Ophthalmologists (contracted); Podiatrists (contracted); Audiologists (contracted).
Languages Spanish.
Facilities Dining room; Physical therapy room; Activities room; Barber/Beauty shop; Library; TV room.
Activities Arts & crafts; Cards; Games; Reading groups; Prayer groups; Movies; Shopping trips; Dances/Social/Cultural gatherings; Intergenerational programs; Pet therapy.

Manor Care Nursing Center of Hemet
1717 W Stetson Ave, Hemet, CA 92343
(714) 925-9171
Admin Kevin Burkin.
Licensure Skilled care. *Beds* SNF 120. *Certified* Medicare.
Owner Proprietary corp.

Meadowbrook Convalescent Hospital
461 E Johnston, Hemet, CA 92343
(714) 658-2293
Admin Brigitta Braswell.
Medical Dir Dr D Michael Crile.
Licensure Skilled care. *Beds* SNF 64. *Certified* Medicare; Medi-Cal.
Owner Proprietary corp.
Staff RNs 1 (ft), 2 (pt); LPNs 3 (ft), 3 (pt); Nurses' aides 20 (ft), 15 (pt); Activities coordinators 1 (ft), 1 (pt).
Facilities Dining room; Activities room; Laundry room; Barber/Beauty shop.
Activities Arts & crafts; Games; Prayer groups; Movies; Shopping trips; Dances/Social/Cultural gatherings; Music entertainment.

Ramona Manor Convalescent Hospital
485 W Johnston Ave, Hemet, CA 92343
(714) 652-0011
Admin Grant Liske. *Dir of Nursing* Francine Grant. *Medical Dir* Michael Crile MD.
Licensure Skilled care. *Beds* SNF 104. *Certified* Medicare; Medi-Cal.
Owner Proprietary corp.
Admissions Requirements Medical examination; Physician's request.
Staff Physicians 1 (pt); RNs 6 (ft), 3 (pt); LPNs 5 (ft), 4 (pt); Nurses' aides 30 (ft), 6 (pt); Physical therapists 1 (pt); Occupational therapists 1 (pt); Speech therapists 1 (pt); Activities coordinators 1 (ft), 2 (pt); Dietitians 1 (ft); Ophthalmologists 1 (pt); Dentists 1 (pt).
Languages Spanish.
Facilities Dining room; Physical therapy room; Activities room; Laundry room; Barber/Beauty shop; Library; Speech therapy room.
Activities Arts & crafts; Cards; Games; Reading groups; Prayer groups; Movies; Shopping trips; Dances/Social/Cultural gatherings; Various parties & entertainment by community groups.

Highland

Hillhaven Highland House
7534 Palm Ave, Highland, CA 92346
(714) 862-0611
Admin Marc Argabright. *Dir of Nursing* Susan Zmudka. *Medical Dir* Richard Neil MD.
Licensure Skilled care. *Beds* SNF 99. *Private Pay Patients* 35%. *Certified* Medicare; Medi-Cal.
Owner Proprietary corp (Hillhaven Corp).
Staff Physicians; RNs; LPNs; Nurses' aides; Physical therapists; Occupational therapists; Speech therapists; Activities coordinators; Dietitians; Ophthalmologists; Podiatrists; Audiologists.
Languages Spanish.
Facilities Dining room; Physical therapy room; Activities room; Crafts room; Laundry room; Barber/Beauty shop.
Activities Arts & crafts; Cards; Games; Movies; Shopping trips; Intergenerational programs; Pet therapy.

Sierra Vista
3455 E Highland Ave, Highland, CA 92346
(714) 862-6454
Admin Janet L Clark-Seawell.
Licensure Intermediate care for mentally retarded. *Beds* ICF/MR 116. *Certified* Medi-Cal.
Owner Proprietary corp.

Hollister

CareWest-Hollister Nursing Center
900 Sunset Dr, Hollister, CA 95023
(408) 637-5771
Admin Linda Carrigan. *Dir of Nursing* Eleanor Whitehead. *Medical Dir* Robert D Quinn MD.

Licensure Skilled care. *Beds* SNF 70. *Private Pay Patients* 15%. *Certified* Medicare; Medi-Cal.
Owner Proprietary corp (Care Enterprises).
Staff RNs 2 (ft); LPNs 3 (ft); Nurses' aides 25 (ft); Physical therapists 1 (ft); Occupational therapists 1 (ft); Speech therapists 1 (ft); Activities coordinators 1 (ft).
Facilities Dining room; Physical therapy room; Activities room; Laundry room; Barber/Beauty shop; Social service department.
Activities Arts & crafts; Cards; Games; Reading groups; Prayer groups; Movies; Shopping trips; Dances/Social/Cultural gatherings; Group discussions with staff.

Hazel Hawkins Convalescent Hospital
3110 Southside Rd, Hollister, CA 95023
(408) 637-5353
Admin Thomas J Harm. *Dir of Nursing* Dixie DeMaggio RN. *Medical Dir* Dr R Quinn.
Licensure Skilled care. *Beds* SNF 52. *Private Pay Patients* 50%. *Certified* Medicare; Medi-Cal.
Owner Publicly owned.
Admissions Requirements Physician's request.
Staff RNs 2 (ft), 6 (pt); LPNs 2 (ft), 2 (pt); Nurses' aides 16 (ft), 14 (pt); Physical therapists 1 (ft); Activities coordinators 1 (ft); Dietitians 1 (ft).
Languages Spanish, Filipino, German.
Facilities Dining room; Activities room; Barber/Beauty shop; 2 inner courtyards; Covered patio.
Activities Arts & crafts; Games; Reading groups; Prayer groups; Movies; Dances/Social/Cultural gatherings; Intergenerational programs; Pet therapy.

Hollywood

Orchard Gables Convalescent Hospital
1277 N Wilcox Ave, Hollywood, CA 90038
(213) 469-7231
Admin Marc Chopp.
Licensure Skilled care. *Beds* SNF 59. *Certified* Medicare; Medi-Cal.
Owner Nonprofit corp.

Huntington Beach

Care West—Garfield Nursing Center
7781 Garfield Ave, Huntington Beach, CA 92648
(714) 847-9671, 847-4196 FAX
Admin Adella Bierbaum. *Dir of Nursing* Donna M Wilson. *Medical Dir* Martin Steinfeld.
Licensure Skilled care. *Beds* SNF 59. *Private Pay Patients* 54%. *Certified* Medicaid; Medicare.
Owner Proprietary corp (Care Enterprises).
Admissions Requirements Minimum age 60; Medical examination; Physician's request.
Staff RNs 1 (ft), 2 (pt); Nurses' aides 23 (ft), 3 (pt); Physical therapists (contracted); Occupational therapists (contracted); Speech therapists (contracted); Activities coordinators 1 (pt); Dietitians (consultant); Ophthalmologists (consultant); Podiatrists (consultant); Audiologists (consultant); LVNs 4 (ft), 2 (pt).
Languages Spanish, Filipino.
Facilities Dining room; Physical therapy room; Activities room; Laundry room; Barber/Beauty shop.
Activities Arts & crafts; Games; Reading groups; Prayer groups; Movies; Dances/Social/Cultural gatherings; Intergenerational programs; Pet therapy; Adult education; Monthly candlelight dinners; Resident group; Family council.

CareWest—Huntington Valley
8382 Newman Ave, Huntington Beach, CA 92647
(714) 842-5551
Admin Rachel Bennett. *Dir of Nursing* Kristine C Bell. *Medical Dir* Gary Anderson MD.
Licensure Skilled care. *Beds* SNF 144. *Private Pay Patients* 1%. *Certified* Medicare; Medi-Cal.
Owner Proprietary corp (Care Enterprises).
Admissions Requirements Minimum age 65.
Staff RNs; LPNs; Nurses' aides; Physical therapists; Occupational therapists; Speech therapists; Activities coordinators; Dietitians; Podiatrists.
Languages Spanish, Romanian, Filipino.
Facilities Dining room; Physical therapy room; Activities room; Laundry room; Barber/Beauty shop; Library.
Activities Arts & crafts; Cards; Games; Reading groups; Prayer groups; Movies; Shopping trips; Weekly family support group; Family outreach service.

Huntington Beach Convalescent Hospital
18811 Florida St, Huntington Beach, CA 92648-1997
(714) 847-3515
Admin Bruce Cameron.
Medical Dir Victor Siew MD.
Licensure Skilled care; Intermediate care. *Beds* SNF 123; ICF 59. *Certified* Medicare; Medi-Cal.
Owner Proprietary corp.
Admissions Requirements Minimum age 60.
Staff RNs 15 (ft), 6 (pt); LPNs 15 (ft), 8 (pt); Nurses' aides 35 (ft), 14 (pt); Physical therapists 1 (pt); Reality therapists 3 (ft); Recreational therapists 1 (pt); Occupational therapists 1 (pt); Speech therapists 1 (pt); Activities coordinators 1 (ft); Dietitians 1 (ft); Ophthalmologists 1 (pt); Podiatrists 1 (pt); Audiologists 1 (pt); Dentists 1 (pt).
Facilities Dining room; Physical therapy room; Activities room; Chapel; Crafts room; Laundry room; Barber/Beauty shop; Library.
Activities Arts & crafts; Cards; Games; Reading groups; Prayer groups; Movies; Shopping trips; Dances/Social/Cultural gatherings.

Huntington Park

Huntington Park Convalescent Center
6425 Miles Ave, Huntington Park, CA 90255
(213) 589-5941
Admin Steve Ramsdell.
Medical Dir Edward Panzer MD.
Licensure Skilled care. *Beds* SNF 99. *Certified* Medicare; Medi-Cal.
Owner Nonprofit organization/foundation (Everhealth Foundation).
Admissions Requirements Physician's request.
Facilities Dining room; Physical therapy room; Activities room; Chapel; Crafts room; Laundry room; Barber/Beauty shop; Library.
Activities Arts & crafts; Cards; Games; Reading groups; Prayer groups; Movies; Shopping trips.

Imperial

Imperial Manor
100 E 2nd St, Imperial, CA 92251
(619) 355-2858
Admin Barbara C Carter. *Dir of Nursing* Gwen Smith. *Medical Dir* Sol Reisin MD.
Licensure Skilled care; Alzheimer's care. *Beds* SNF 29. *Private Pay Patients* 5%. *Certified* Medi-Cal.
Owner Nonprofit corp (Volunteers of America).
Admissions Requirements Minimum age 21; Medical examination; Physician's request.

Staff RNs 1 (ft), 3 (pt); LPNs 2 (ft), 5 (pt); Nurses' aides 6 (ft), 3 (pt); Physical therapists (outpatient); Reality therapists (outpatient); Recreational therapists (consultant); Occupational therapists (outpatient); Speech therapists (outpatient); Activities coordinators 1 (ft); Dietitians (consultant); Ophthalmologists (outpatient); Podiatrists (outpatient); Audiologists (outpatient).
Languages Spanish.
Affiliation Volunteers of America.
Facilities Dining room; Activities room; Chapel; Crafts room; Laundry room.
Activities Arts & crafts; Cards; Games; Reading groups; Prayer groups; Movies; Shopping trips; Walks; Trips to library; Alzheimer's care; Trips to park.

Indio

Desert Palms Convalescent Hospital
82-262 Valencia St, Indio, CA 92201
(619) 347-7779
Admin John W Ryan. *Dir of Nursing* Joyce Walton. *Medical Dir* David Christensen.
Licensure Skilled care. *Beds* SNF 68. *Certified* Medicare; Medi-Cal.
Owner Nonprofit corp.

Mul-Care Convalescent Hospital
45-500 Aladdin St, Indio, CA 92201
(619) 347-0876
Admin David L Tripp.
Licensure Skilled care. *Beds* SNF 64. *Certified* Medicare; Medi-Cal.
Owner Proprietary corp.

Inglewood

Angelus Convalescent Center East
1001 S Osage Ave, Inglewood, CA 90301
(213) 674-3216
Admin Jerry Eisinger.
Medical Dir Alan Allen MD.
Licensure Skilled care; Retirement. *Beds* SNF 55. *Certified* Medicare; Medi-Cal.
Owner Proprietary corp.
Admissions Requirements Minimum age 21.
Staff LPNs 4 (ft), 3 (pt); Nurses' aides 20 (ft), 4 (pt); Physical therapists 1 (ft); Reality therapists 1 (ft); Recreational therapists 1 (ft); Occupational therapists 1 (ft); Speech therapists 1 (ft); Activities coordinators 1 (ft); Dietitians 1 (ft); Ophthalmologists 1 (ft); Podiatrists 1 (ft); Dentists 1 (ft).
Facilities Dining room; Activities room; Chapel; Crafts room; Laundry room; Barber/Beauty shop.
Activities Arts & crafts; Cards; Games; Reading groups; Prayer groups; Movies; Shopping trips; Dances/Social/Cultural gatherings.

Angelus Convalescent Center West
950 Flower Ave, Inglewood, CA 90301
(213) 674-3216
Admin Jerry Eisinger.
Licensure Skilled care. *Beds* SNF 59. *Certified* Medicare; Medi-Cal.
Owner Proprietary corp.

Care West—Palomar Nursing Center
301 N Centinela Ave, Inglewood, CA 90302
(213) 674-2660
Admin Margaret Kane.
Licensure Skilled care. *Beds* SNF 99. *Certified* Medicare; Medi-Cal.
Owner Proprietary corp (Care Enterprises).

Centinela Park Convalescent Hospital
515 Centinela Ave, Inglewood, CA 90302
(213) 674-4500
Admin Thomas Erdosi.
Medical Dir Richard Heath MD.
Licensure Skilled care. *Beds* SNF 69. *Certified* Medicare; Medi-Cal.

Owner Proprietary corp.
Staff RNs 1 (ft), 3 (pt); LPNs 6 (ft), 3 (pt); Nurses' aides 20 (ft), 14 (pt).
Facilities Dining room; Activities room; Laundry room; Barber/Beauty shop.
Activities Arts & crafts; Cards; Games; Reading groups; Prayer groups; Movies.

Inglewood Health Care Center
100 S Hillcrest Blvd, Inglewood, CA 90301
(213) 678-7414
Admin Jane W Harmon.
Licensure Skilled care. *Beds* SNF 99. *Certified* Medicare; Medi-Cal.
Owner Proprietary corp (American-Cal Medical Services Inc).

St Erne Sanitarium
527 W Regent St, Inglewood, CA 90301
(213) 674-7851
Admin John W Funk II. *Dir of Nursing* Claudia Streaty RN. *Medical Dir* Paul Friedman MD.
Licensure Skilled care. *Beds* SNF 276. *Private Pay Patients* 10%. *Certified* Medicare; Medi-Cal.
Owner Proprietary corp.
Admissions Requirements Minimum age 21.
Staff Physicians 12 (pt); RNs 15 (ft); LPNs 25 (ft); Nurses' aides 130 (ft); Physical therapists 1 (pt); Recreational therapists 8 (ft); Speech therapists 1 (pt); Activities coordinators 10 (ft); Dietitians 1 (pt); Ophthalmologists 1 (pt); Podiatrists 1 (pt); Audiologists 1 (pt).
Languages Spanish.
Facilities Dining room; Physical therapy room; Activities room; Crafts room; Barber/Beauty shop.
Activities Arts & crafts; Cards; Games; Movies; Shopping trips.

Irvine

Windcrest at Regents Point
19191 Harvard Ave, Irvine, CA 92715
(714) 854-9500
Admin David K Parret. *Dir of Nursing* Kit Williams. *Medical Dir* R Thomarson MD.
Licensure Skilled care; Retirement. *Beds* SNF 59; Retirement 370. *Private Pay Patients* 93%. *Certified* Medicare.
Owner Nonprofit corp (Southern California Presbyterian Homes).
Facilities Dining room; Physical therapy room; Activities room; Crafts room; Laundry room; Barber/Beauty shop; Library.
Activities Arts & crafts; Cards; Games; Reading groups; Prayer groups; Movies; Shopping trips; Dances/Social/Cultural gatherings; Intergenerational programs; Pet therapy.

Jackson

Amador Hospital D/P
810 Court St, Jackson, CA 95642
(209) 223-6600 *Certified* Medicare; Medi-Cal.

Kit Carson Convalescent Hospital
811 Court St, Jackson, CA 95642
(209) 223-2231
Admin Meredith J Miller.
Licensure Skilled care. *Beds* SNF 140. *Certified* Medicare; Medi-Cal.
Owner Privately owned.

Kentfield

Care West—Bayside Nursing & Rehabilitation Center
1251 S Eliseo Dr, Kentfield, CA 94904
(415) 461-1900
Admin Catherine J Mohline. *Dir of Nursing* Mary Kay Carroll.
Licensure Skilled care. *Beds* SNF 99. *Certified* Medicare; Medi-Cal.

Owner Proprietary corp (Care Enterprises).
Staff RNs; Nurses' aides; Physical therapists; Occupational therapists; Speech therapists; Activities coordinators; Dietitians; Podiatrists.
Facilities Dining room; Physical therapy room; Activities room; Crafts room; Laundry room; Barber/Beauty shop.
Activities Arts & crafts; Cards; Games; Reading groups; Prayer groups; Movies; Shopping trips; Dances/Social/Cultural gatherings.

Kingsburg

Care West—Kingsburg Nursing Center
1101 Stroud Ave, Kingsburg, CA 93631
(209) 897-5881
Admin Beverly Harper. *Dir of Nursing* Mary Rosenthal RN.
Licensure Skilled care. *Beds* SNF 86. *Certified* Medicare; Medi-Cal.
Owner Proprietary corp (Care Enterprises).
Admissions Requirements Physician's request.
Staff RNs 4 (ft); LPNs 8 (ft), 6 (pt); Nurses' aides 38 (ft), 12 (pt); Physical therapists 2 (ft); Reality therapists 1 (ft); Recreational therapists 1 (ft); Occupational therapists 1 (pt); Speech therapists 1 (pt); Activities coordinators 1 (ft); Dietitians 1 (ft); Ophthalmologists 1 (pt); Volunteer social workers; Social services 1 (ft); Community services representatives.
Languages Japanese, Spanish.
Facilities Dining room; Physical therapy room; Activities room; Crafts room; Laundry room; Barber/Beauty shop; Lounge.
Activities Arts & crafts; Cards; Games; Reading groups; Prayer groups; Movies; Shopping trips; Dances/Social/Cultural gatherings; Shuffleboard; Field trips.

La Crescenta

Verdugo Vista Convalescent Hospital
3050 Montrose Ave, La Crescenta, CA 91214
(818) 957-0850
Admin Frances Foy.
Licensure Skilled care. *Beds* SNF 92. *Certified* Medicare; Medi-Cal.
Owner Proprietary corp.

La Habra

La Habra Convalescent Hospital
1233 W La Habra Blvd, La Habra, CA 90631
(213) 691-0781
Admin Adrian Rezenpnik.
Medical Dir Jorge Soffici MD.
Licensure Skilled care. *Beds* SNF 86. *Certified* Medicare; Medi-Cal.
Owner Privately owned.
Admissions Requirements Minimum age 18; Medical examination; Physician's request.
Staff RNs 3 (ft); LPNs 8 (ft); Nurses' aides 25 (ft); Activities coordinators 1 (ft); Dietitians 1 (ft).
Languages Spanish, Tagalog.
Facilities Dining room; Physical therapy room; Activities room; Crafts room; Barber/Beauty shop; Library.
Activities Arts & crafts; Cards; Games; Reading groups; Prayer groups; Movies; Shopping trips; Dances/Social/Cultural gatherings; Visits outside.

La Jolla

Cloisters of La Jolla
7160 Fay Ave, La Jolla, CA 92037
(619) 459-4361
Admin Lois M Banta. *Dir of Nursing* Carol Meech RN. *Medical Dir* Arthur Edwards MD.
Licensure Skilled care. *Beds* SNF 59. *Private Pay Patients* 100%.

Owner Privately owned.
Admissions Requirements Medical examination; Physician's request.
Staff RNs 2 (ft), 3 (pt); LPNs 6 (ft), 5 (pt); Nurses' aides 18 (ft), 8 (pt); Activities coordinators 1 (ft), 1 (pt).
Languages Spanish, Tagalog, Parsi, German, Portuguese.
Facilities Dining room; Activities room; Laundry room; Barber/Beauty shop.
Activities Arts & crafts; Games; Reading groups; Prayer groups; Movies; Pet therapy; Outings; Musical groups.

La Jolla Convalescent Hospital
6211 La Jolla Hermosa, La Jolla, CA 92037
(619) 454-0739
Admin Ruth E Copher.
Medical Dir Dr Leonard H Lazarus.
Licensure Skilled care; Retirement. *Beds* SNF 41; Retirement 550. *Certified* Medicare.
Owner Nonprofit organization/foundation (Pacific Homes).
Admissions Requirements Physician's request.
Staff RNs 1 (ft), 3 (pt); LPNs 3 (ft), 4 (pt); Nurses' aides 10 (ft), 5 (pt); Activities coordinators 1 (ft), 1 (pt); Restorative aides 1 (ft), 1 (pt).
Facilities Dining room; Activities room; Laundry room; Barber/Beauty shop.
Activities Arts & crafts; Cards; Games; Reading groups; Prayer groups; Movies; Shopping trips; Dances/Social/Cultural gatherings; Intergenerational programs; Pet therapy; Van trips; Exercise; Music; Entertainment.

Torrey Pines Convalescent Hospital
2552 Torrey Pines Rd, La Jolla, CA 92037
(619) 453-5810
Admin Elena Gulla.
Licensure Skilled care. *Beds* SNF 161. *Certified* Medicare; Medi-Cal.
Owner Nonprofit corp.

White Sands of La Jolla
7450 Olivetas Ave, La Jolla, CA 92037
(619) 454-4201
Admin Gregory Bearce.
Medical Dir L J Schwartz MD.
Licensure Skilled care. *Beds* SNF 50.
Owner Nonprofit corp.
Admissions Requirements Minimum age 62; Medical examination; Physician's request.
Staff Physicians 4 (pt); RNs 2 (ft), 3 (pt); LPNs 2 (ft), 5 (pt); Nurses' aides 20 (ft), 4 (pt); Physical therapists 1 (pt); Occupational therapists 1 (pt); Speech therapists 1 (pt); Activities coordinators 1 (ft); Dietitians 1 (pt); Podiatrists 1 (pt); Audiologists 1 (pt); Dentists 1 (pt).
Affiliation Presbyterian.
Facilities Dining room; Physical therapy room; Activities room; Chapel; Crafts room; Laundry room; Barber/Beauty shop; Library.
Activities Arts & crafts; Cards; Games; Reading groups; Prayer groups; Movies; Shopping trips; Dances/Social/Cultural gatherings.

La Mesa

Beverly Manor Convalescent Hospital
5696 Lake Murray Blvd, La Mesa, CA 92041
(619) 460-7871
Admin Marjorie A Hauer. *Dir of Nursing* Barbara Kerstetter RN. *Medical Dir* Frank B Flint MD.
Licensure Skilled care. *Beds* SNF 99. *Certified* Medicare; Medi-Cal.
Owner Proprietary corp (Beverly Enterprises).
Admissions Requirements Minimum age 18; Medical examination; Physician's request.
Staff Physicians; RNs 5 (ft), 1 (pt); LPNs 9 (ft), 3 (pt); Nurses' aides 37 (ft), 4 (pt); Physical therapists 1 (pt); Recreational therapists 1 (ft), 2 (pt); Occupational therapists 1 (pt); Speech therapists 1 (pt);

Activities coordinators 1 (ft); Dietitians 1 (pt); Ophthalmologists 1 (pt); Podiatrists 1 (pt); Dentists 1 (pt).
Facilities Dining room; Physical therapy room; Activities room; Crafts room; Laundry room; Barber/Beauty shop; Spacious living room.
Activities Arts & crafts; Cards; Games; Reading groups; Prayer groups; Movies; Shopping trips; Dances/Social/Cultural gatherings; Barbeque's; Special outings.

California Special Care Center Inc
8787 Center Dr, La Mesa, CA 92041
(619) 460-4444
Admin Robert E Long.
Medical Dir Robert Pullman MD.
Licensure Skilled care. *Beds* SNF 90. *Certified* Medicare; Medi-Cal.
Owner Proprietary corp.
Staff Physicians 1 (pt); RNs 3 (ft); LPNs 20 (ft); Nurses' aides 35 (ft); Physical therapists 1 (ft), 1 (pt); Recreational therapists 1 (ft); Occupational therapists 1 (pt); Speech therapists 1 (pt); Activities coordinators 1 (pt); Dietitians 1 (pt); Podiatrists 1 (pt); Dentists 1 (pt); Psychologists 1 (ft).

Community Convalescent Hospital of La Mesa
8665 La Mesa Blvd, La Mesa, CA 92041
(619) 465-0702
Admin Kenneth A Steele.
Licensure Skilled care. *Beds* SNF 122. *Certified* Medicare; Medi-Cal.
Owner Proprietary corp.

Grossmont Gardens Health Care Center
5480 Marengo Ave, La Mesa, CA 92042
(619) 463-0281
Admin Don Perry.
Licensure Skilled care. *Beds* SNF 40.
Owner Privately owned.

Hacienda de la Mesa Convalescent Hospital
7760 Parkway Dr, La Mesa, CA 92041
(619) 469-0124
Admin Siegmund Diener.
Licensure Skilled care. *Beds* SNF 59. *Certified* Medicare; Medi-Cal.
Owner Proprietary corp.

Hilldale Convalescent Center
7979 La Mesa Blvd, La Mesa, CA 92041
(619) 465-8010
Admin Kathryn E Mumford.
Medical Dir Daria Gaynes.
Licensure Intermediate care for mentally retarded. *Beds* ICF 57. *Certified* Medi-Cal.
Owner Proprietary corp (Care Enterprises).
Staff RNs; Nurses' aides; Activities coordinators; Dietitians.
Languages Spanish.
Facilities Dining room; Activities room; Laundry room.
Activities Arts & crafts; Movies; Shopping trips.

San Diego Convalescent Hospital
3780 Massachusetts Ave, La Mesa, CA 92041
(619) 465-1313
Admin William E Stover. *Dir of Nursing* Jeanne Caron RN. *Medical Dir* Seymour Mallis MD.
Licensure Skilled care. *Beds* SNF 94. *Private Pay Patients* 35%. *Certified* Medicare; Medi-Cal.
Owner Proprietary corp.
Admissions Requirements Minimum age 18; Medical examination.
Staff Physicians 1 (pt); RNs 4 (ft); LPNs 9 (ft); Nurses' aides 33 (ft); Physical therapists 1 (pt); Occupational therapists 1 (pt); Speech therapists 1 (pt); Activities coordinators 1 (ft); Dietitians 1 (pt); Ophthalmologists 1 (pt); Podiatrists 1 (pt); Audiologists 1 (pt).
Facilities Dining room; Physical therapy room; Activities room; Crafts room; Barber/Beauty shop.

Activities Arts & crafts; Cards; Games; Reading groups; Prayer groups; Movies; Shopping trips; Pet therapy.

Stanford Court Nursing Center of La Mesa
7800 Parkway Dr, La Mesa, CA 92041
(619) 460-2330
Admin Heidi A Hunsberger.
Licensure Skilled care. *Beds* SNF 110. *Certified* Medicare; Medi-Cal.
Owner Privately owned.

La Mirada

Imperial Convalescent Hospital
11926 La Mirada Blvd, La Mirada, CA 90638
(213) 943-7156
Admin Gail A Pearce.
Medical Dir Marion Jalil MD.
Licensure Skilled care. *Beds* SNF 99. *Certified* Medicare; Medi-Cal.
Owner Proprietary corp (Columbia Corp).
Admissions Requirements Medical examination; Physician's request.
Staff RNs 3 (ft), 4 (pt); LPNs 5 (ft), 4 (pt); Nurses' aides 25 (ft), 7 (pt).
Languages Spanish, Korean, Indian, Tagalog.
Facilities Dining room; Activities room; Barber/Beauty shop.
Activities Arts & crafts; Cards; Games; Reading groups; Prayer groups; Movies; Shopping trips; Dances/Social/Cultural gatherings; Adult education classes.

Mirada Hills Rehabilitation & Convalescent Hospital
12200 S La Mirada Blvd, La Mirada, CA 90638
(213) 947-8691
Admin Jim Nix.
Medical Dir William Welsh DO.
Licensure Skilled care. *Beds* SNF 158. *Certified* Medicare; Medi-Cal.
Owner Nonprofit corp (Columbia Corp).
Admissions Requirements Medical examination; Physician's request.
Staff Physicians 2 (pt); RNs 6 (ft), 4 (pt); LPNs 13 (ft), 8 (pt); Nurses' aides 60 (ft), 15 (pt); Activities coordinators 3 (ft).
Facilities Dining room; Physical therapy room; Activities room; Crafts room; Laundry room; Barber/Beauty shop; Library; Occupational therapy room; Speech therapy room.
Activities Arts & crafts; Cards; Games; Reading groups; Prayer groups; Movies; Shopping trips; Dances/Social/Cultural gatherings.

La Verne

Woods Memorial Convalescent Hospital
2600 A St, La Verne, CA 91750
(714) 593-4917
Admin Deborah Holling.
Medical Dir Eugene St Clair MD.
Licensure Skilled care. *Beds* SNF 75. *Certified* Medicare; Medi-Cal.
Owner Nonprofit corp.
Admissions Requirements Minimum age 65.
Facilities Dining room; Activities room; Chapel; Crafts room; Laundry room; Barber/Beauty shop; Library.
Activities Arts & crafts; Cards; Games; Reading groups; Prayer groups; Movies; Shopping trips; Dances/Social/Cultural gatherings.

Lafayette

Lafayette Convalescent Hospital
1010 1st St, Lafayette, CA 94549
(415) 284-1420
Admin Rodger Hogan. *Dir of Nursing* Christina Culhane. *Medical Dir* Eugene Whitney.

Licensure Skilled care. *Beds* SNF 52. *Certified* Medicare.
Owner Proprietary corp (Paracelsus Convalescent Hospitals Inc).
Admissions Requirements Physician's request.
Staff RNs 6 (ft), 3 (pt); LPNs 1 (pt); Nurses' aides 16 (ft), 8 (pt); Physical therapists; Activities coordinators 1 (ft), 1 (pt); Dietitians.
Languages Dutch, German, Spanish, Flemish.
Facilities Dining room; Activities room; Crafts room; Laundry room; Barber/Beauty shop.
Activities Arts & crafts; Cards; Games; Reading groups; Prayer groups; Movies; Dances/Social/Cultural gatherings; Intergenerational programs; Pet therapy.

Woodland Lafayette
3721 Mt Diablo Blvd, Lafayette, CA 94549
(415) 284-5544
Medical Dir Dennis Stone MD.
Licensure Skilled care. *Beds* SNF 30. *Certified* Medicare.
Owner Privately owned.
Admissions Requirements Medical examination; Physician's request.
Staff RNs 3 (ft), 5 (pt); LPNs 2 (ft), 2 (pt); Nurses' aides 13 (ft), 4 (pt); Occupational therapists 1 (pt); Speech therapists 1 (pt); Activities coordinators 1 (ft), 2 (pt); Dietitians 1 (ft).
Facilities Dining room; Activities room; Laundry room.
Activities Arts & crafts; Cards; Games; Reading groups; Movies; Dances/Social/Cultural gatherings; Pets; Outside music.

Laguna Beach

Ahimsa Care Center
450 Glenneyre, Laguna Beach, CA 92651
(714) 494-8075
Admin Sharon J Lucas LCSW. *Dir of Nursing* Nancy Gross RN. *Medical Dir* Korey Jorgensen MD.
Licensure Skilled care. *Beds* SNF 47. *Private Pay Patients* 100%.
Owner Proprietary corp.
Admissions Requirements Minimum age 18; Physician's request.
Staff Physicians 3 (pt); RNs 5 (ft), 5 (pt); Nurses' aides 18 (ft); Physical therapists 1 (pt); Occupational therapists 1 (pt); Speech therapists 1 (pt); Activities coordinators 1 (ft); Dietitians 1 (ft); Ophthalmologists 1 (pt); Podiatrists 1 (pt); Audiologists 1 (pt); Social workers 1 (ft).
Languages Spanish.
Facilities Dining room; Activities room; Chapel; Crafts room; Laundry room; Barber/Beauty shop; Library.
Activities Arts & crafts; Cards; Games; Reading groups; Prayer groups; Movies; Shopping trips; Dances/Social/Cultural gatherings; Pet therapy; Guided imagery; Spiritual services.

Laguna Hills

Beverly Manor Convalescent Hospital
24452 Health Center Dr, Laguna Hills, CA 92653
(714) 837-8000
Admin Wayne Grigsby.
Licensure Skilled care. *Beds* SNF 218. *Certified* Medicare; Medi-Cal.
Owner Proprietary corp (Beverly Enterprises).

Palm Terrace Healthcare Center
24962 Calle Aragon, Laguna Hills, CA 92653
(714) 586-3393, 583-9137 FAX
Admin G Gerald Powers PhD. *Dir of Nursing* Carol Davis RN.
Licensure Skilled care; Retirement. *Beds* SNF 99; Retirement apartments 192. *Private Pay Patients* 60%. *Certified* Medicare.

Owner Proprietary corp (Beverly Enterprises).
Admissions Requirements Physician's request.
Staff RNs 11 (ft), 3 (pt); LPNs 10 (ft), 2 (pt);
Nurses' aides 40 (ft), 8 (pt); Physical
therapists 3 (ft), 1 (pt); Occupational
therapists 1 (ft), 1 (pt); Speech therapists 2
(ft), 1 (pt); Activities coordinators 1 (ft), 1
(pt); Dietitians 1 (ft).
Languages Spanish, Farsi.
Facilities Dining room; Physical therapy
room; Activities room; Chapel; Laundry
room; Barber/Beauty shop.
Activities Arts & crafts; Cards; Games;
Reading groups; Prayer groups; Movies;
Shopping trips; Dances/Social/Cultural
gatherings; Intergenerational programs; Pet
therapy.

Villa Valencia
24552 Paseo de Val, Laguna Hills, CA 92653
(714) 581-6111

Lake San Marcos

Chateau Lake San Marcos Health Center
1502 Circa Del Lago, Lake San Marcos, CA
92069
(619) 471-0083
Admin C David Goodin.
Licensure Skilled care. *Beds* SNF 20.
Owner Proprietary corp.

Lakeport

Lakeport Skilled Nursing Center Inc
625 16th St, Lakeport, CA 95453
(707) 263-6101
Admin Patricia A Treppa. *Dir of Nursing*
Gretchen Lyne RN. *Medical Dir* Donald L
Browning MD.
Licensure Skilled care. *Beds* SNF 90. *Private
Pay Patients* 20%. *Certified* Medicare; Medi-
Cal.
Owner Proprietary corp (Sierra Medical
Enterprises).
Admissions Requirements Medical
examination; Physician's request.
Staff Physicians; RNs; LPNs; Nurses' aides;
Physical therapists; Reality therapists;
Recreational therapists; Occupational
therapists; Speech therapists; Activities
coordinators; Dietitians; Ophthalmologists;
Podiatrists.
Facilities Dining room; Physical therapy
room; Activities room; Crafts room; Laundry
room; Barber/Beauty shop; Library.
Activities Arts & crafts; Cards; Games;
Reading groups; Prayer groups; Movies;
Shopping trips; Dances/Social/Cultural
gatherings.

Pacific Regency—Lakeport
1291 Craig Ave, Lakeport, CA 95453
(707) 263-6382
Admin Chris Sturgeon.
Licensure Skilled care. *Beds* SNF 99. *Certified*
Medicare; Medi-Cal.
Owner Privately owned.

Lakeside

Friendship Manor Lakeside
11962 Woodside Ave, Lakeside, CA 92040
(619) 561-1222
Admin J Edwin Cheneweth. *Dir of Nursing*
Del Julian RN. *Medical Dir* Dr Maloney.
Licensure Skilled care. *Beds* SNF 94. *Certified*
Medi-Cal.
Owner Proprietary corp.
Admissions Requirements Minimum age 60;
Medical examination; Physician's request.
Staff RNs 3 (ft); Activities coordinators 1 (ft),
1 (pt); Dietitians 1 (ft).
Languages Spanish, Tagalog.
Facilities Dining room; Activities room;
Chapel; Crafts room; Laundry room; Barber/
Beauty shop; Courtyards.

Activities Arts & crafts; Games; Reading
groups; Prayer groups; Movies; Shopping
trips; Dances/Social/Cultural gatherings;
Cooking classes.

Lakeview Terrace

Good Shepherd Convalescent Center
11505 Kagel Canyon St, Lakeview Terrace,
CA 91342
(818) 896-5391, 897-4349 FAX
Admin Nathaniel R Chivi. *Dir of Nursing*
Lilia Skelton. *Medical Dir* H M Cohen MD.
Licensure Skilled care. *Beds* SNF 126.
Certified Medicare; Medi-Cal.
Owner Proprietary corp.
Staff Physicians; RNs; LPNs; Nurses' aides;
Occupational therapists; Speech therapists;
Activities coordinators; Dietitians;
Podiatrists.
Facilities Dining room; Physical therapy
room; Activities room; Crafts room; Laundry
room.
Activities Arts & crafts; Cards; Games;
Reading groups; Prayer groups; Movies;
Shopping trips; Dances/Social/Cultural
gatherings; Outings.

Lancaster

**Antelope Valley Convalescent Hospital &
Nursing Home**
44445 N 15th St W, Lancaster, CA 93534
(805) 948-7501
Admin Maury Van Der Hope.
Licensure Skilled care. *Beds* SNF 299.
Certified Medicare; Medi-Cal.
Owner Privately owned.

Lancaster Convalescent Hospital
1642 W Ave J, Lancaster, CA 93534
(805) 942-8463
Admin Genevieve L Skidmore. *Dir of Nursing*
L M Fils RN. *Medical Dir* B K Sudhir MD.
Licensure Skilled care; Alzheimer's care. *Beds*
SNF 99. *Certified* Medicare; Medi-Cal.
Owner Proprietary corp (American-Cal
Medical Services Inc).
Admissions Requirements Minimum age 18;
Physician's request.
Staff Physicians 1 (ft); RNs 5 (ft), 1 (pt);
LPNs 14 (ft); Nurses' aides 51 (pt); Physical
therapists 1 (pt); Reality therapists 1 (pt);
Recreational therapists 2 (ft); Occupational
therapists 1 (pt); Speech therapists 1 (pt);
Activities coordinators 1 (ft); Dietitians 1
(ft); Ophthalmologists 1 (pt).
Languages Spanish, German, French.
Facilities Dining room; Physical therapy
room; Activities room; Crafts room; Barber/
Beauty shop; Library; Enclosed patio; Indoor
garden.
Activities Arts & crafts; Cards; Games;
Reading groups; Prayer groups; Movies;
Shopping trips; Dances/Social/Cultural
gatherings; Annual ice cream social.

Mayflower Gardens Convalescent Hospital
6705 W Ave M, Lancaster, CA 93536
(805) 943-3212
Admin Janice Delano. *Dir of Nursing* Janice
McArthur. *Medical Dir* C Pathmarajah MD.
Licensure Skilled care; Retirement. *Beds* SNF
48; Retirement apts 500. *Certified* Medicare;
Medi-Cal.
Owner Nonprofit organization/foundation.
Admissions Requirements Minimum age 65;
Physician's request.
Staff RNs 1 (ft), 2 (pt); LPNs 5 (ft), 1 (pt);
Nurses' aides 14 (ft), 2 (pt); Physical
therapists 1 (pt); Activities coordinators 1
(ft); Dietitians 1 (pt).
Facilities Dining room; Physical therapy
room; Activities room; Crafts room; Laundry
room; Barber/Beauty shop; Library.

Activities Arts & crafts; Cards; Games;
Reading groups; Prayer groups; Movies;
Shopping trips; Dances/Social/Cultural
gatherings; Intergenerational programs; Pet
therapy.

Lawndale

Park Imperial Convalescent Center
15100 S Prairie Blvd, Lawndale, CA 90260
(213) 679-3344
Admin Theresa M Ward. *Dir of Nursing*
Michele Eichelberger. *Medical Dir* Darryl
Hutchinson.
Licensure Skilled care. *Beds* SNF 59. *Certified*
Medicare; Medi-Cal.
Owner Nonprofit corp.
Admissions Requirements Physician's request.
Staff Physicians 12 (pt); RNs 1 (ft), 2 (pt);
LPNs 6 (ft); Nurses' aides 21 (ft), 4 (pt);
Physical therapists (contracted);
Occupational therapists (contracted); Speech
therapists (contracted); Activities
coordinators 1 (ft), 1 (pt); Dietitians 1 (pt);
Ophthalmologists (contracted); Podiatrists
(contracted); Audiologists (contracted).
Languages Spanish, Filipino.
Facilities Dining room; Activities room;
Laundry room; Barber/Beauty shop.
Activities Arts & crafts; Cards; Games;
Reading groups; Prayer groups; Movies;
Shopping trips; Intergenerational programs.

Lemon Grove

Cresta Loma Convalescent & Guest Home
7922 Palm St, Lemon Grove, CA 92045
(619) 464-3488
Admin Mary C Norwood.
Medical Dir Simon Brumbaugh.
Licensure Skilled care. *Beds* SNF 99. *Certified*
Medicare; Medi-Cal.
Owner Privately owned.
Admissions Requirements Medical
examination; Physician's request.
Staff RNs 3 (ft), 1 (pt); LPNs 7 (ft), 4 (pt);
Nurses' aides 30 (ft), 4 (pt); Physical
therapists 2 (pt); Activities coordinators 2
(pt); Dietitians 1 (pt).
Languages Spanish, Tagalog.
Facilities Dining room; Physical therapy
room; Activities room; Chapel; Crafts room;
Laundry room; Barber/Beauty shop; Patios.
Activities Arts & crafts; Cards; Games;
Reading groups; Prayer groups; Movies;
Shopping trips; Dances/Social/Cultural
gatherings; Music concerts.

Lemon Grove Convalescent Center
8351 Broadway, Lemon Grove, CA 92045
(619) 463-0294
Admin Alma E Howe.
Licensure Skilled care. *Beds* SNF 165.
Certified Medicare; Medi-Cal.
Owner Proprietary corp (Care Enterprises).

Monte Vista Lodge
2211 Massachusetts Ave, Lemon Grove, CA
92045
(619) 465-1331
Admin Violet M Hertzberg.
Medical Dir Eunice Simmons MD.
Licensure Skilled care. *Beds* SNF 21.
Owner Privately owned.
Facilities Dining room; Activities room;
Chapel; Crafts room; Laundry room; Barber/
Beauty shop; Library.
Activities Arts & crafts; Cards; Games; Prayer
groups; Shopping trips; Dances/Social/
Cultural gatherings.

Lincoln

Lincoln Care Center
1550 3rd St, Lincoln, CA 95648
(916) 645-7777
Admin Gordon Case.

Licensure Skilled care. *Beds* SNF 97. *Certified* Medicare; Medi-Cal.
Owner Proprietary corp.

Livermore

Hacienda Care Center
76 Fenton St, Livermore, CA 94550
(415) 443-1800
Admin Linda Williams.
Medical Dir Lionel Pfefer MD.
Licensure Skilled care. *Beds* SNF 83. *Certified* Medicare; Medi-Cal.
Owner Proprietary corp.
Admissions Requirements Physician's request.
Staff Physicians 1 (pt); RNs 4 (ft), 1 (pt); LPNs 4 (ft), 4 (pt); Physical therapists 1 (pt); Speech therapists 1 (pt); Activities coordinators 2 (pt); Dietitians 1 (ft), 1 (pt); Podiatrists 1 (pt); Dentists 1 (pt).
Facilities Dining room; Physical therapy room; Activities room; Barber/Beauty shop; Library.
Activities Arts & crafts; Cards; Games; Prayer groups; Shopping trips; Dances/Social/Cultural gatherings.

Livermore Manor Convalescent Hospital
788 Holmes St, Livermore, CA 94550
(415) 447-2280
Admin Sylvia Chaney. *Dir of Nursing* Diann DiFranco. *Medical Dir* L M Pfefer MD.
Licensure Skilled care. *Beds* SNF 37. *Certified* Medicaid; Medi-Cal.
Owner Privately owned.
Admissions Requirements Medical examination; Physician's request.
Staff Physicians 1 (pt); RNs 1 (ft), 1 (pt); LPNs 3 (ft), 2 (pt); Nurses' aides 12 (ft); Activities coordinators 1 (ft); Dietitians 1 (pt).
Languages Spanish.
Facilities Dining room; Activities room; Crafts room; Laundry room.
Activities Arts & crafts; Games; Reading groups; Prayer groups; Movies; Shopping trips; Intergenerational programs; Pet therapy.

Livingston

Grace Nursing Home Inc
13435 W Peach Ave, Livingston, CA 95334
(209) 394-2440
Admin Wilmont Koehn. *Dir of Nursing* Joy Nightengale RN. *Medical Dir* Donald F Harrington MD.
Licensure Skilled care. *Beds* SNF 33. *Certified* Medi-Cal.
Owner Nonprofit corp.
Admissions Requirements Medical examination; Physician's request.
Staff Physicians 9 (pt); RNs 2 (ft), 3 (pt); LPNs 1 (ft), 3 (pt); Physical therapists 8 (ft), 10 (pt); Activities coordinators 1 (ft); Dietitians 1 (pt); Ophthalmologists 1 (pt).
Languages Spanish, Dutch.
Affiliation Church of God.
Facilities Dining room; Activities room; Chapel; Crafts room; Laundry room.
Activities Arts & crafts; Games; Reading groups; Prayer groups; Bible study.

Lodi

Arbor Convalescent Hospital
900 N Church St, Lodi, CA 95240
(209) 333-1222
Admin Paul Medlin.
Licensure Skilled care. *Beds* SNF 152. *Certified* Medi-Cal.
Owner Proprietary corp.

Crescent Court Nursing Home
610 S Fairmont, Lodi, CA 95240
(209) 368-2467

Admin Ann V Garren. *Dir of Nursing* Darleen Winkler. *Medical Dir* Dr Shiu Kow Ming.
Licensure Skilled care; Alzheimer's care. *Beds* SNF 28. *Private Pay Patients* 33%. *Certified* Medicare; Medi-Cal.
Owner Proprietary corp.
Staff Physicians 1 (pt); RNs 1 (ft), 1 (pt); LPNs 2 (ft), 1 (pt); Nurses' aides 9 (ft), 2 (pt); Physical therapists 2 (pt); Reality therapists 1 (pt); Recreational therapists 1 (ft); Occupational therapists 1 (pt); Speech therapists 1 (pt); Activities coordinators 1 (ft); Dietitians 1 (pt); Ophthalmologists 1 (pt); Podiatrists 1 (pt); Audiologists 1 (pt).
Languages Spanish, Filipino.
Facilities Dining room; Physical therapy room; Activities room; Laundry room.
Activities Arts & crafts; Games; Reading groups; Prayer groups; Movies; Shopping trips; Dances/Social/Cultural gatherings; Intergenerational programs; Pet therapy.

Delta Convalescent Hospital
1334 S Ham Ln, Lodi, CA 95242
(209) 334-3825
Admin Albert C Cross. *Dir of Nursing* Cheryl Novak RN. *Medical Dir* Paul M Inae MD.
Licensure Skilled care. *Beds* SNF 74. *Certified* Medicare; Medi-Cal.
Owner Privately owned.
Admissions Requirements Physician's request.
Staff Physicians 1 (pt); RNs 3 (ft), 2 (pt); LPNs 5 (ft), 4 (pt); Nurses' aides 28 (ft), 10 (pt); Physical therapists 2 (pt); Activities coordinators 2 (ft); Dietitians 1 (pt).
Languages Tagalog, Spanish.
Facilities Dining room; Physical therapy room; Activities room; Crafts room; Laundry room; Barber/Beauty shop; Library.
Activities Arts & crafts; Games; Reading groups; Prayer groups; Movies; Shopping trips; Dances/Social/Cultural gatherings.

Fairmont Rehabilitation Hospital
950 S Fairmont, Lodi, CA 95240
(209) 368-0693
Admin Beverly Mannon.
Medical Dir Dr Williams.
Licensure Skilled care. *Beds* SNF 59. *Certified* Medicare; Medi-Cal.
Owner Proprietary corp (Beverly Enterprises).

Gross Convalescent Hospital
321 W Turner Rd, Lodi, CA 95240
(209) 334-3760
Admin Paul G Gross MA.
Medical Dir Dr Ming.
Licensure Skilled care; Retirement. *Beds* SNF 90. *Certified* Medicare; Medi-Cal.
Owner Proprietary corp.
Admissions Requirements Females only; Medical examination.
Staff RNs 3 (ft); LPNs 8 (ft); Nurses' aides 38 (ft).
Languages Spanish, German, Japanese, Tagalog.
Facilities Dining room; Physical therapy room; Activities room; Chapel; Crafts room; Laundry room; Barber/Beauty shop; Library.
Activities Arts & crafts; Cards; Games; Reading groups; Prayer groups; Movies; Shopping trips; Dances/Social/Cultural gatherings.

Vienna Convalescent Hospital
800 S Ham Ln, Lodi, CA 95240
(209) 368-7141
Admin Kenneth D Heffel.
Licensure Skilled care. *Beds* SNF 150. *Certified* Medicare; Medi-Cal.
Owner Proprietary corp.

Vista Ray Convalescent Hospital
1120 Sylvia Dr, Lodi, CA 95240
(209) 368-6641
Admin Alice Mills.

Licensure Skilled care. *Beds* SNF 155. *Certified* Medicare; Medi-Cal.
Owner Privately owned.

Vista Ray Convalescent Hospital 2
1108 Sylvia Dr, Lodi, CA 95240
(209) 368-0677
Admin Alfred Johnson.
Licensure Skilled care. *Beds* SNF 42. *Certified* Medicare; Medi-Cal.
Owner Proprietary corp.

Loma Linda

Heritage Gardens Health Care Center
25271 Barton Rd, Loma Linda, CA 92354
(714) 796-0216
Admin Peter Peabody. *Dir of Nursing* Urmila Patel. *Medical Dir* Roger Woodruff.
Licensure Skilled care; Retirement. *Beds* SNF 134; Retirement 64. *Private Pay Patients* 30%. *Certified* Medicare; Medi-Cal.
Owner Proprietary corp.
Admissions Requirements Minimum age 18; Medical examination; Physician's request.
Staff RNs 8 (ft); LPNs 11 (ft); Nurses' aides 30 (ft); Physical therapists 1 (ft); Activities coordinators 1 (ft), 1 (pt); Dietitians 1 (ft).
Facilities Dining room; Physical therapy room; Activities room; Crafts room; Laundry room; Barber/Beauty shop; Library.
Activities Arts & crafts; Games; Reading groups; Prayer groups; Movies; Shopping trips; Intergenerational programs; Pet therapy.

Linda Valley Convalescent Hospital
25383 Cole St, Loma Linda, CA 92354
(714) 796-0235
Admin R Clifford Dinning. *Dir of Nursing* Bonnie Holle RN. *Medical Dir* William Beckner MD.
Licensure Skilled care. *Beds* SNF 83. *Private Pay Patients* 55%. *Certified* Medicaid; Medicare; Medi-Cal.
Owner Privately owned.
Admissions Requirements Nonsmokers; Nondrinkers.
Staff RNs 2 (ft), 4 (pt); LPNs 6 (ft), 8 (pt); Nurses' aides 25 (ft), 8 (pt); Physical therapists; Activities coordinators 1 (ft); Dietitians.
Languages Spanish, Cambodian.
Facilities Dining room; Physical therapy room; Activities room; Laundry room; Barber/Beauty shop; Caffeine-free, vegetarian kitchen.
Activities Arts & crafts; Games; Prayer groups; Movies; Shopping trips; Dances/Social/Cultural gatherings; Pet therapy.

Mt View Child Care Center Inc
10132 Mount View Ave, Loma Linda, CA 92354
(714) 796-0030
Admin Gail Horrigan.
Medical Dir Dr Robert McCormick.
Licensure Intermediate care for mentally retarded. *Beds* 59. *Certified* Medi-Cal.
Owner Proprietary corp.
Staff Physicians; RNs; Nurses' aides; Physical therapists; Recreational therapists; Occupational therapists; Speech therapists; Activities coordinators; Dietitians; Ophthalmologists; Audiologists; Dentists.
Facilities Dining room; Activities room; Laundry room.
Activities Arts & crafts; Games; Movies; Shopping trips.

Lomita

Lomita Care Center
1955 W Lomita Blvd, Lomita, CA 90717
(213) 325-1970
Admin James M Lewis Jr.
Medical Dir Stephen Russell MD.

Licensure Skilled care. *Beds* SNF 71. *Certified* Medicare; Medi-Cal.
Owner Proprietary corp.

Peninsula Rehabilitation Center
26303 S Western Ave, Lomita, CA 90717
(213) 325-3202, 534-2782 FAX
Admin Robert E Arsenault. *Dir of Nursing* N Kenneth Turner CRRN. *Medical Dir* Dr Christopher Traughber.
Licensure Skilled care. *Beds* SNF 48. *Private Pay Patients* 60%. *Certified* Medicare.
Owner Nonprofit corp.
Admissions Requirements Minimum age 8.
Staff Physicians 4 (pt); RNs 7 (ft), 3 (pt); LPNs 4 (ft), 7 (pt); Nurses' aides 14 (ft), 6 (pt); Physical therapists 2 (ft); Recreational therapists 1 (ft); Occupational therapists 2 (ft); Speech therapists 2 (ft); Activities coordinators 1 (ft); Dietitians 1 (ft); Ophthalmologists 1 (pt); Podiatrists; Audiologists 1 (ft); RNAs 1 (ft), 1 (pt).
Languages Spanish, French, Tagalog.
Facilities Dining room; Physical therapy room; Activities room; Crafts room; Barber/Beauty shop; Occupational therapy room.
Activities Arts & crafts; Cards; Games; Reading groups; Prayer groups; Movies; Shopping trips; Dances/Social/Cultural gatherings; Intergenerational programs; Pet therapy.

Lompoc

Lompoc Hospital District Convalescent Care Center
3rd & Walnut Sts, Lompoc, CA 93436
(805) 735-3351
Admin William E Diebner.
Licensure Skilled care. *Beds* SNF 110. *Certified* Medicare; Medi-Cal.
Owner Publicly owned.

Lone Pine

Lone Pine Convalescent Hospital
103 Pangborn Ln, Lone Pine, CA 93545
(619) 876-5537
Admin Dorothea L Carlin.
Licensure Skilled care. *Beds* SNF 51. *Certified* Medicare; Medi-Cal.
Owner Proprietary corp.

Long Beach

Akin's Convalescent Hospital
2750 Atlantic Ave, Long Beach, CA 90806
(213) 424-8101, 490-7358 FAX
Admin Ronald M Akin. *Dir of Nursing* Peggy Hale. *Medical Dir* David Bockoff MD.
Licensure Skilled care. *Beds* SNF 109. *Private Pay Patients* 38%. *Certified* Medicare; Medi-Cal.
Owner Privately owned.
Staff Physicians; RNs 3 (ft), 3 (pt); LPNs 6 (ft), 2 (pt); Nurses' aides 44 (ft), 3 (pt); Activities coordinators 1 (ft), 2 (pt).
Languages Spanish, Tagalog, Samoan.
Facilities Dining room; Activities room; Laundry room; Barber/Beauty shop; Library.
Activities Arts & crafts; Cards; Games; Movies; Shopping trips; Intergenerational programs.

Alamitos Belmont Rehabilitation Hospital
3901 E 4th St, Long Beach, CA 90814
(213) 434-8421, 433-6732 FAX
Admin Alan H Anderson. *Dir of Nursing* Helen Scalera. *Medical Dir* Robert Pinder MD.
Licensure Skilled care; Short-term rehabilitation. *Beds* SNF 97. *Private Pay Patients* 82%. *Certified* Medicare; Medi-Cal.
Owner Proprietary corp.
Admissions Requirements Physician's request.

Staff Physicians 1 (pt); RNs 19 (ft), 6 (pt); LPNs 16 (ft), 8 (pt); Nurses' aides 43 (ft), 22 (pt); Physical therapists 10 (ft), 8 (pt); Recreational therapists 2 (ft); Occupational therapists 6 (ft), 1 (pt); Speech therapists 3 (ft), 1 (pt); Dietitians 1 (ft); Ophthalmologists 1 (pt); Podiatrists 1 (pt); Audiologists 1 (pt); Physical therapy technicians 11 (ft).
Facilities Dining room; Physical therapy room; Activities room; Crafts room; Laundry room; Barber/Beauty shop; Occupational therapy room; Conference rooms.
Activities Arts & crafts; Cards; Games; Reading groups; Prayer groups; Movies; Shopping trips; Dances/Social/Cultural gatherings; Special dinners & luncheons.

Bay Convalescent Hospital
5901 Downey Ave, Long Beach, CA 90805
(213) 634-4693
Admin Eli Berkovits. *Dir of Nursing* June Carnes RN. *Medical Dir* Andrew Sun MD.
Licensure Skilled care. *Beds* SNF 70. *Private Pay Patients* 52%. *Certified* Medicaid; Medicare; Medi-Cal.
Owner Proprietary corp.
Admissions Requirements Minimum age 18; Medical examination; Physician's request.
Staff RNs 1 (ft), 1 (pt); LPNs 5 (ft), 2 (pt); Nurses' aides 20 (ft), 7 (pt); Activities coordinators 1 (ft); Dietitians 1 (ft).
Languages Spanish.
Facilities Dining room; Physical therapy room; Activities room; Barber/Beauty shop.
Activities Arts & crafts; Cards; Games; Reading groups; Prayer groups; Movies; Intergenerational programs.

Bel Vista Convalescent Hospital
5001 E Anaheim St, Long Beach, CA 90804
(213) 439-0414
Admin Hilary Pomatto & Irene Pomatto.
Licensure Skilled care. *Beds* SNF 46.
Owner Proprietary corp.
Admissions Requirements Medical examination; Physician's request.
Staff RNs 3 (ft); LPNs 4 (ft); Nurses' aides 24 (ft); Physical therapists 1 (pt); Reality therapists 1 (pt); Recreational therapists 1 (pt); Activities coordinators 1 (ft).
Activities Arts & crafts; Games; Prayer groups.

Bixby Knolls Towers
3747 Atlantic, Long Beach, CA 90807
(213) 424-7578, 426-1506 FAX
Admin Iris Doiron. *Dir of Nursing* Vicki Miller RN. *Medical Dir* Timm Holt MD.
Licensure Skilled care; Retirement. *Beds* SNF 99; Retirement 239. *Private Pay Patients* 80%. *Certified* Medicare; Medi-Cal.
Owner Nonprofit corp (Retirement Housing Foundation Inc).
Admissions Requirements Minimum age 50; Physician's request.
Staff RNs 1 (ft), 4 (pt); LPNs 11 (ft); Nurses' aides 45 (ft); Physical therapists 3 (ft); Recreational therapists 2 (ft); Occupational therapists 2 (ft); Speech therapists 1 (ft); Activities coordinators 1 (ft); Dietitians 1 (ft); Podiatrists 1 (pt); Audiologists 1 (pt).
Languages Spanish.
Affiliation United Church of Christ.
Facilities Dining room; Physical therapy room; Activities room; Crafts room; Barber/Beauty shop; Library.
Activities Arts & crafts; Cards; Games; Reading groups; Prayer groups; Movies; Shopping trips; Dances/Social/Cultural gatherings; Intergenerational programs; Pet therapy.

Candlewood Care Center
260 E Market St, Long Beach, CA 90805
(213) 428-4681
Admin Alice Riddell.
Medical Dir Dr Platt.

Licensure Skilled care. *Beds* SNF 120. *Certified* Medicare; Medi-Cal.
Owner Proprietary corp.
Admissions Requirements Medical examination; Physician's request.
Staff RNs 5 (ft), 5 (pt); LPNs 8 (ft), 10 (pt); Nurses' aides 35 (ft), 3 (pt); Activities coordinators 1 (ft).

Catered Manor
4010 Virginia Rd, Long Beach, CA 90807
(213) 426-0394, 424-1529 FAX
Admin Donna Williams. *Dir of Nursing* Carol Aryton. *Medical Dir* Mary O'Brian.
Licensure Skilled care. *Beds* SNF 83. *Private Pay Patients* 25%. *Certified* Medicare; Medi-Cal.
Owner Proprietary corp (Beverly Enterprises).
Admissions Requirements Minimum age 18; Physician's request.
Staff RNs 1 (ft), 2 (pt); LPNs 7 (ft), 4 (pt); Nurses' aides 30 (ft), 5 (pt); Physical therapists 1 (pt); Occupational therapists 1 (pt); Speech therapists 1 (pt); Activities coordinators 1 (ft), 1 (pt); Dietitians 1 (ft); Ophthalmologists 1 (pt); Podiatrists 1 (pt); Audiologists 1 (pt).
Facilities Dining room; Activities room; Laundry room; Barber/Beauty shop.
Activities Arts & crafts; Cards; Games; Reading groups; Prayer groups; Movies; Shopping trips; Intergenerational programs; Pet therapy.

Centralia Convalescent Hospital
5401 E Centralia St, Long Beach, CA 90808-1111
(213) 421-4717
Admin Robert Moses.
Medical Dir Francis James MD.
Licensure Skilled care. *Beds* SNF 194. *Certified* Medicare; Medi-Cal.
Owner Proprietary corp (Health Care Management).
Staff RNs; LPNs; Nurses' aides; Physical therapists; Recreational therapists; Speech therapists; Activities coordinators; Dietitians; Ophthalmologists; Podiatrists; Audiologists; Dentists.
Facilities Dining room; Physical therapy room; Activities room; Crafts room; Laundry room; Barber/Beauty shop; Library.
Activities Arts & crafts; Cards; Games; Reading groups; Prayer groups; Movies; Shopping trips.

Colonial Manor Convalescent Hospital
1913 E 5th St, Long Beach, CA 90812
(213) 432-5751
Licensure Skilled care. *Beds* SNF 181. *Certified* Medicare; Medi-Cal.
Owner Privately owned.

Country Park Health Care Center
3232 E Artesia Blvd, Long Beach, CA 90805
(213) 422-9219, 428-0280 FAX
Admin W Joseph Ganzenhuber. *Dir of Nursing* Linda Bince RN. *Medical Dir* Dr K P Wong.
Licensure Skilled care; Intermediate care; Sub-acute care; Alzheimer's care. *Beds* SNF 210; ICF 15; Sub-acute care 15. *Private Pay Patients* 33%. *Certified* Medicare; Medi-Cal.
Owner Proprietary corp.
Admissions Requirements Minimum age 18; Physician's request.
Staff Physicians; RNs 7 (ft), 8 (pt); LPNs 15 (ft), 7 (pt); Nurses' aides 66 (ft), 6 (pt); Activities coordinators 3 (ft), 2 (pt); Dietitians 1 (ft), 1 (pt).
Languages Spanish, Tagalog, Korean, German.
Facilities Dining room; Physical therapy room; Laundry room; Barber/Beauty shop; Library; Secured Alzheimer's unit; Patio.

Activities Arts & crafts; Cards; Games; Reading groups; Prayer groups; Movies; Shopping trips; Dances/Social/Cultural gatherings; Intergenerational programs; Pet therapy.

Eastwood Convalescent Hospital
4029 E Anaheim St, Long Beach, CA 90804
(213) 494-4421 FAX
Admin Ronald M Akin. *Dir of Nursing* Anadaisy D Abanilla RN. *Medical Dir* Joseph P Au MD.
Licensure Skilled care. *Beds* SNF 75. *Private Pay Patients* 50%. *Certified* Medicare; Medi-Cal.
Owner Proprietary corp (Akin Investments).
Admissions Requirements Minimum age 18; Medical examination; Physician's request.
Staff RNs 5 (ft), 2 (pt); LPNs 4 (ft), 2 (pt); Nurses' aides 27 (ft), 3 (pt); Physical therapists 1 (ft); Occupational therapists 1 (ft); Speech therapists 1 (ft); Activities coordinators 1 (ft); Dietitians 1 (ft); Ophthalmologists 1 (ft); Podiatrists 1 (ft).
Languages Spanish.
Facilities Dining room; Activities room; Barber/Beauty shop.
Activities Arts & crafts; Cards; Games; Reading groups; Prayer groups; Movies; Shopping trips; Dances/Social/Cultural gatherings; Intergenerational programs; Pet therapy.

Edgewater Convalescent Hospital
2625 E 4th St, Long Beach, CA 90814
(213) 434-0974
Admin Debbie Ketland Kremel. *Dir of Nursing* Victoria Thompson. *Medical Dir* Dr Michael Platt.
Licensure Skilled care. *Beds* SNF 81. *Private Pay Patients* 90%. *Certified* Medicare; Medi-Cal.
Owner Proprietary corp.
Admissions Requirements Minimum age 55; Physician's request.
Facilities Dining room; Physical therapy room; Activities room; Crafts room; Laundry room; Barber/Beauty shop; Library.
Activities Arts & crafts; Cards; Games; Reading groups; Prayer groups; Movies; Shopping trips; Dances/Social/Cultural gatherings.

Empress Convalescent Center
1020 Termino Ave, Long Beach, CA 90804
(213) 433-6791
Admin Dorothy Pine RN BS.
Medical Dir Sidney Wasserman MD.
Licensure Skilled care; Alzheimer's care. *Beds* SNF 133. *Private Pay Patients* 80%. *Certified* Medicare; Medi-Cal.
Owner Proprietary corp.
Admissions Requirements Minimum age 18; Medical examination; Physician's request.
Languages Spanish.
Facilities Dining room; Physical therapy room; Activities room; Crafts room; Laundry room; Barber/Beauty shop; Patios.
Activities Arts & crafts; Cards; Games; Reading groups; Prayer groups; Movies; Shopping trips; Dances/Social/Cultural gatherings; Intergenerational programs; Pet therapy.

Ennoble Center of Long Beach
2666 Grand Ave, Long Beach, CA 90815
(213) 426-8187
Admin Tom Williams.
Licensure Intermediate care; Intermediate care for mentally retarded. *Beds* 99.
Owner Nonprofit corp.

Grand Avenue Convalescent Hospital
1730 Grand Ave, Long Beach, CA 90804
(213) 597-8817
Medical Dir Marvelle Harris Pruitt.
Licensure Skilled care. *Beds* SNF 117. *Certified* Medicare; Medi-Cal.

Owner Proprietary corp.
Admissions Requirements Medical examination; Physician's request.
Staff Physicians; RNs; LPNs; Nurses' aides; Physical therapists; Occupational therapists; Speech therapists; Activities coordinators; Dietitians; Ophthalmologists.
Facilities Dining room; Physical therapy room; Activities room; Crafts room; Laundry room; Barber/Beauty shop.
Activities Arts & crafts; Cards; Games; Reading groups; Prayer groups; Movies.

Hacienda Convalescent Hospital
2725 E Broadway, Long Beach, CA 90803
(213) 434-4494
Admin Iris J Doiron. *Dir of Nursing* Shirley McDougal RN. *Medical Dir* Edward R Woerz MD.
Licensure Skilled care. *Beds* SNF 98. *Certified* Medicare; Medi-Cal.
Owner Proprietary corp.
Admissions Requirements Physician's request.
Staff Physicians 3 (pt); RNs 3 (ft); LPNs 9 (ft), 3 (pt); Nurses' aides 30 (ft); Physical therapists 3 (pt); Recreational therapists 1 (pt); Occupational therapists 2 (pt); Speech therapists 1 (pt); Activities coordinators 1 (ft); Dietitians 1 (pt); Ophthalmologists 1 (pt); Podiatrists 1 (pt); Dentists 1 (pt).
Languages Spanish.
Facilities Dining room; Physical therapy room; Activities room; Barber/Beauty shop.
Activities Arts & crafts; Cards; Games; Reading groups; Prayer groups; Movies; Monthly outings.

Harbor View Center
490 W 14th St, Long Beach, CA 90813
(213) 591-8701
Admin Jonie Nordstrom.
Licensure Intermediate care. *Beds* ICF 99.
Owner Proprietary corp.

Hillcrest Convalescent Hospital
3401 Cedar Ave, Long Beach, CA 90807
(213) 426-4461
Admin Teresita Valdez. *Dir of Nursing* P Tana. *Medical Dir* Robert Clough MD.
Licensure Skilled care. *Beds* SNF 154. *Certified* Medicare; Medi-Cal.
Owner Proprietary corp.
Admissions Requirements Minimum age 18; Medical examination; Physician's request.
Staff RNs 4 (ft), 3 (pt); LPNs 12 (ft), 7 (pt); Nurses' aides 50 (ft), 3 (pt); Activities coordinators 1 (ft), 1 (pt).
Languages Spanish, Tagalog, Russian, Romanian, Hebrew, Yiddish, French, German, Thai.
Facilities Dining room; Physical therapy room; Activities room; Crafts room; Laundry room; Barber/Beauty shop; Educational room.
Activities Arts & crafts; Cards; Games; Reading groups; Prayer groups; Movies; Shopping trips; Dances/Social/Cultural gatherings; Reality orientation; Group sessions; Current events; Entertainment by special groups; Music; Rhythm band; Cartoon shows; Cocktails; Music.

Intercommunity Sanitarium
2626 Grand Ave, Long Beach, CA 90815
(213) 427-8915, 427-2348 FAX
Admin Russell Boydston. *Dir of Nursing* Jackie Hunter. *Medical Dir* Sidney Wasserman.
Licensure Skilled care; Alzheimer's care. *Beds* SNF 147. *Private Pay Patients* 30%. *Certified* Medicaid.
Owner Nonprofit corp.
Admissions Requirements Minimum age Geriatric; Physician's request.
Staff RNs 5 (ft); LPNs 7 (ft); Nurses' aides 38 (ft); Physical therapists; Activities coordinators 3 (ft); Dietitians 1 (ft).

Facilities Dining room; Activities room; Crafts room; Laundry room; Barber/Beauty shop; Library.
Activities Arts & crafts; Cards; Games; Reading groups; Prayer groups; Movies; Shopping trips; Dances/Social/Cultural gatherings; Intergenerational programs; Pet therapy.

Marlora Manor Convalescent Hospital
3801 E Anaheim St, Long Beach, CA 90804
(213) 494-3311
Admin Marilyn J Hauser.
Licensure Skilled care. *Beds* SNF 99. *Certified* Medicare; Medi-Cal.
Owner Privately owned.

Palmcrest Medallion Convalescent
3355 Pacific Pl, Long Beach, CA 90806
(213) 595-4336
Admin Mark S Wilson.
Medical Dir George Bryant MD.
Licensure Skilled care. *Beds* SNF 99. *Certified* Medicare; Medi-Cal.
Owner Privately owned.
Admissions Requirements Minimum age 55; Medical examination; Physician's request.
Staff Physicians 1 (pt); RNs 2 (ft), 1 (pt); LPNs 7 (ft), 1 (pt); Nurses' aides 35 (ft), 6 (pt); Physical therapists 1 (ft), 1 (pt); Reality therapists 1 (pt); Recreational therapists 1 (ft); Occupational therapists 1 (ft); Speech therapists 1 (pt); Dietitians 1 (pt); Podiatrists 1 (pt); Dentists 1 (pt).
Facilities Dining room; Physical therapy room; Activities room; Chapel; Laundry room; Barber/Beauty shop.
Activities Arts & crafts; Games; Reading groups; Prayer groups; Movies; Dances/Social/Cultural gatherings.

Palmcrest North
3501 Cedar Ave, Long Beach, CA 90807
(213) 595-1731
Admin Richard Feingold. *Dir of Nursing* Eleanor Johnson. *Medical Dir* Dr John Prosser.
Licensure Skilled care; Residential care; Day care; Alzheimer's care. *Beds* SNF 99; Residential care 262. *Certified* Medicare.
Owner Privately owned.
Admissions Requirements Minimum age 55; Medical examination; Physician's request.
Staff RNs 3 (ft); LPNs 10 (ft); Nurses' aides 55 (ft); Physical therapists; Recreational therapists 1 (ft); Activities coordinators 1 (ft); Dietitians 1 (ft); Podiatrists 1 (ft).
Languages Spanish, Filipino, Chinese, Thai.
Facilities Dining room; Physical therapy room; Activities room; Crafts room; Laundry room; Barber/Beauty shop; Library; Theater; Art gallery; Greenhouse.
Activities Arts & crafts; Cards; Games; Reading groups; Movies; Shopping trips; Dances/Social/Cultural gatherings.

Regency Oaks Skilled Nursing Care
3850 E Esther St, Long Beach, CA 90804
(213) 498-3368
Admin Rebecca U Martin.
Medical Dir Thomas Hendon MD.
Licensure Skilled care. *Beds* SNF 99. *Certified* Medicare; Medi-Cal.
Owner Proprietary corp.
Facilities Dining room; Barber/Beauty shop.
Activities Arts & crafts; Cards; Games; Reading groups; Prayer groups; Movies; Dances/Social/Cultural gatherings.

Royal Care Skilled Nursing Facility
2725 Pacific Ave, Long Beach, CA 90806
(213) 427-7493, 424-1833 FAX
Admin Alice Riddell. *Dir of Nursing* Freda Henderson. *Medical Dir* George Manos.
Licensure Skilled care. *Beds* SNF 98. *Private Pay Patients* 20%. *Certified* Medicare; Medi-Cal.

Owner Proprietary corp.
Staff RNs 2 (ft), 3 (pt); LPNs; Nurses' aides;
Activities coordinators 1 (ft), 1 (pt);
Dietitians 1 (ft).

Santa Fe Convalescent Hospital
3294 Santa Fe Ave, Long Beach, CA 90810
(213) 424-0757
Admin Michael Kremer.
Licensure Skilled care. *Beds* SNF 90. *Certified*
Medicare; Medi-Cal.
Owner Proprietary corp.

Villa Maria Care Center
723 E 9th St, Long Beach, CA 90813
(213) 437-2797
Admin David Culbreth.
Licensure Skilled care. *Beds* SNF 52. *Certified*
Medicare.
Owner Privately owned.

Willowlake Convalescent Hospital
2615 Grand Ave, Long Beach, CA 90815
(213) 426-6141
Admin Margaret F Emery.
Licensure Skilled care. *Beds* SNF 163.
Certified Medicare; Medi-Cal.
Owner Nonprofit corp.

Los Alamitos

Alamitos West Convalescent Hospital
3902 Ketella Ave, Los Alamitos, CA 90720
(213) 596-5561, (714) 821-8580, 430-8174
FAX
Admin Kathryn T Creeth. *Dir of Nursing*
Marvella Pruitt. *Medical Dir* John Cowles
MD.
Licensure Skilled care. *Beds* SNF 199. *Private
Pay Patients* 40%. *Certified* Medicare; Medi-
Cal.
Owner Privately owned (Sage Company).
Admissions Requirements Medical
examination; Physician's request.
Staff Physicians 50 (pt); RNs 9 (ft), 3 (pt);
LPNs 15 (ft), 8 (pt); Nurses' aides 66 (ft), 13
(pt); Physical therapists 3 (pt); Reality
therapists 1 (pt); Recreational therapists 1
(pt); Occupational therapists 2 (pt); Speech
therapists 1 (pt); Activities coordinators 3
(ft), 1 (pt); Dietitians 1 (pt);
Ophthalmologists 1 (pt); Podiatrists 1 (pt);
Audiologists 1 (pt).
Languages Spanish, Filipino, French, German.
Activities Arts & crafts; Cards; Games;
Reading groups; Prayer groups; Movies;
Shopping trips; Pet therapy.

**John Douglas French Center for Alzheimer's
Disease**
3951 Katella Ave, Los Alamitos, CA 90720
(213) 493-1555
Admin Thomas M Henry. *Dir of Nursing*
Rose Ann Peterson RN. *Medical Dir* Dr
Stephen Read.
Licensure Skilled care; Alzheimer's care. *Beds*
SNF 148. *Certified* Medicare.
Owner Proprietary corp (Hillhaven Corp).
Admissions Requirements Medical
examination; Physician's request.
Staff Physicians 1 (ft); RNs 7 (ft), 4 (pt);
LPNs 12 (ft), 6 (pt); Nurses' aides 60 (ft), 30
(pt); Physical therapists 1 (pt); Recreational
therapists 5 (ft), 3 (pt); Occupational
therapists 1 (pt); Speech therapists 1 (pt);
Activities coordinators 1 (ft); Dietitians 1
(ft); Podiatrists 1 (pt); Audiologists 1 (pt);
Patient care coordinators; GNPs 1 (ft);
Family counselors 1 (ft).
Facilities Dining room; Physical therapy
room; Activities room; Crafts room; Laundry
room; Barber/Beauty shop; Library.
Activities Arts & crafts; Games; Reading
groups; Movies; Shopping trips; Dances/
Social/Cultural gatherings; Intergenerational
programs; Pet therapy.

Los Altos

Beverly Manor Convalescent Hospital
809 Fremont Ave, Los Altos, CA 94022
(415) 941-5255
Admin Leona Costello.
Licensure Skilled care. *Beds* SNF 152.
Certified Medicare; Medi-Cal.
Owner Proprietary corp (Beverly Enterprises).

Pilgrim Haven Health Facility
373 Pine Ln, Los Altos, CA 94022
(415) 948-8291
Admin William Gordon Maxwell. *Dir of
Nursing* Edith Azevedo RN. *Medical Dir*
Harold Cramer MD.
Licensure Skilled care; Retirement. *Beds* SNF
66; Retirement 127. *Private Pay Patients*
80%. *Certified* Medicare; Medi-Cal.
Owner Nonprofit corp (American Baptist
Homes of the West).
Admissions Requirements Minimum age 62;
Medical examination.
Staff RNs 11 (pt); LPNs 1 (pt); Nurses' aides
18 (ft), 8 (pt); Activities coordinators 1 (ft),
1 (pt); Dietitians 1 (ft).
Affiliation Baptist.
Facilities Dining room; Activities room;
Chapel; Crafts room; Laundry room; Barber/
Beauty shop; Library.
Activities Arts & crafts; Cards; Games;
Movies; Shopping trips; Dances/Social/
Cultural gatherings.

Los Angeles

Alcott Rehabilitation Hospital
3551 W Olympic, Los Angeles, CA 90019
(213) 737-2000, 734-3234 FAX
Admin Irving Bauman. *Dir of Nursing* Aurora
Ramos. *Medical Dir* Dr Bussarakum.
Licensure Skilled care; Alzheimer's care. *Beds*
SNF 121. *Private Pay Patients* 50%. *Certified*
Medicaid; Medicare; Medi-Cal.
Owner Proprietary corp.
Admissions Requirements Physician's request.
Staff Physicians 1 (pt); RNs 8 (ft); LPNs 10
(ft); Nurses' aides 50 (ft); Physical therapists
5 (ft).
Languages Korean, Spanish, Yiddish, Tagalog.
Facilities Dining room; Physical therapy
room; Activities room; Crafts room; Laundry
room; Barber/Beauty shop; Library.
Activities Arts & crafts; Cards; Games;
Reading groups; Prayer groups; Movies;
Shopping trips; Dances/Social/Cultural
gatherings; Intergenerational programs; Pet
therapy.

Alden Terrace Convalescent Hospital
1241 S Lake St, Los Angeles, CA 90006
(213) 382-8461
Admin Charles Stern.
Medical Dir Dr F Evans Powell.
Licensure Skilled care. *Beds* SNF 210.
Certified Medicare; Medi-Cal.
Owner Proprietary corp.
Admissions Requirements Physician's request.
Facilities Dining room; Physical therapy
room; Activities room; Crafts room; Laundry
room; Barber/Beauty shop.
Activities Arts & crafts; Cards; Games;
Reading groups; Prayer groups; Movies.

Alexandria Convalescent Hospital
1515 N Alexandria, Los Angeles, CA 90027
(213) 660-1800
Admin Salamon Mandel.
Licensure Skilled care. *Beds* SNF 177.
Certified Medicare; Medi-Cal.
Owner Privately owned.

Amberwood Convalescent Hospital
6071 York Blvd, Los Angeles, CA 90042
(213) 254-3407
Admin Marilyn Spaun.
Medical Dir Julita Phillips MD.

Licensure Skilled care. *Beds* SNF 107.
Certified Medicare; Medi-Cal.
Owner Proprietary corp.
Admissions Requirements Minimum age 18.
Facilities Dining room; Physical therapy
room; Activities room; Laundry room;
Barber/Beauty shop.
Activities Arts & crafts; Cards; Games;
Reading groups; Prayer groups; Movies;
Dances/Social/Cultural gatherings.

Angels Nursing Center
415 S Union Ave, Los Angeles, CA 90017
(213) 484-0784
Admin Michele L Nichols. *Dir of Nursing*
Lois Young RN. *Medical Dir* M Salant MD.
Licensure Skilled care. *Beds* SNF 49. *Private
Pay Patients* 1%. *Certified* Medicare; Medi-
Cal.
Owner Privately owned.
Admissions Requirements Minimum age 30;
Physician's request.
Staff RNs 1 (ft), 3 (pt); Nurses' aides 10 (ft), 6
(pt); Activities coordinators 1 (ft); LVNs 3
(ft), 3 (pt).
Facilities Dining room; Activities room;
Laundry room.
Activities Arts & crafts; Cards; Games;
Reading groups; Prayer groups; Dances/
Social/Cultural gatherings; Pet therapy.

Ararat Convalescent Hospital
2373 Colorado Blvd, Los Angeles, CA 90041
(818) 256-8012
Admin Evieny H Janbazian. *Dir of Nursing* E
H Janbazian RN.
Licensure Skilled care. *Beds* SNF 42. *Certified*
Medicare; Medi-Cal.
Owner Nonprofit corp.
Admissions Requirements Minimum age 65;
Physician's request.
Staff Physicians 1 (pt); RNs 3 (ft); Nurses'
aides 13 (ft).
Languages Armenian, Arabic, Spanish,
Turkish, Farsi, Russian, Italian.
Facilities Dining room; Activities room.
Activities Arts & crafts; Cards; Games;
Reading groups; Movies; Dances/Social/
Cultural gatherings.

Beverly Manor Convalescent Hospital
3002 Rowena Ave, Los Angeles, CA 90039
(213) 666-1544
Admin Marilyn Granger. *Dir of Nursing*
Barbara Williams RN.
Licensure Skilled care. *Beds* SNF 131.
Certified Medicare; Medi-Cal.
Owner Proprietary corp (Beverly Enterprises).
Staff RNs 4 (ft), 2 (pt); LPNs 12 (ft), 4 (pt);
Nurses' aides; Recreational therapists;
Activities coordinators.

Beverly Palms Rehabilitation Hospital
8000 Beverly Blvd, Los Angeles, CA 90048
(213) 651-3200
Admin Salvador Atendido. *Dir of Nursing* Lita
Boter RN.
Licensure Skilled care; Short-term rehab only.
Beds SNF 41. *Certified* Medicare.
Owner Privately owned.
Staff RNs 4 (ft), 3 (pt); LPNs 8 (ft), 4 (pt);
Nurses' aides 15 (ft), 4 (pt); Physical
therapists 4 (ft); Occupational therapists 2
(ft); Speech therapists 2 (ft); Activities
coordinators 1 (ft); Dietitians 2 (ft);
Ophthalmologists 1 (ft); Physical therapy
aides 4 (ft); Restorative nurses 1 (ft).
Languages Spanish, Yiddish.
Affiliation Jewish.
Facilities Dining room; Physical therapy
room; Activities room; Crafts room; Library.
Activities Arts & crafts; Cards; Games;
Reading groups; Prayer groups; Movies;
Dances/Social/Cultural gatherings.

Bonnie Brae Convalescent Hospital
420 Bonnie Brae, Los Angeles, CA 90057
(213) 483-8144

Admin Hope Longeretta.
Licensure Skilled care. *Beds* SNF 59. *Certified* Medicare; Medi-Cal.
Owner Proprietary corp.

Brier Oak Terrace Care Center
5154 Sunset Blvd, Los Angeles, CA 90027
(213) 663-3951
Admin Diana Schilling.
Medical Dir Steven Jacobs MD.
Licensure Skilled care; Intermediate care. *Beds* SNF 147; ICF 12. *Certified* Medicare; Medi-Cal.
Owner Proprietary corp.
Staff Physicians 22 (pt); RNs 5 (ft); LPNs 10 (ft); Nurses' aides 22 (ft); Physical therapists 2 (pt); Reality therapists 1 (pt); Occupational therapists 1 (pt); Speech therapists 1 (pt); Activities coordinators 1 (ft); Dietitians 1 (pt); Ophthalmologists 1 (pt); Podiatrists 1 (pt); Audiologists 1 (pt); Dentists 1 (pt).
Facilities Dining room; Physical therapy room; Activities room; Crafts room; Laundry room; Barber/Beauty shop.
Activities Arts & crafts; Cards; Games; Reading groups; Prayer groups; Movies; Shopping trips; Dances/Social/Cultural gatherings.

Buena Ventura Convalescent Hospital
1016 S Record Ave, Los Angeles, CA 90023
(213) 268-0106, 268-2010 FAX
Admin Wayne H Beck. *Dir of Nursing* Haydee Javier. *Medical Dir* Louis T Bascoy MD.
Licensure Skilled care. *Beds* SNF 99. *Private Pay Patients* 2%. *Certified* Medicare; Medi-Cal.
Owner Proprietary corp.
Admissions Requirements Medical examination; Physician's request.
Staff Physicians 6 (pt); RNs 2 (ft), 6 (pt); Nurses' aides 25 (ft); Physical therapists 1 (pt); Recreational therapists 1 (pt); Occupational therapists 1 (pt); Speech therapists 1 (pt); Activities coordinators 1 (ft); Dietitians 1 (pt); Ophthalmologists 1 (pt); Podiatrists 1 (pt); LVNs 6 (ft), 6 (pt).
Languages Korean, Tagalog, Spanish.
Facilities Dining room; Physical therapy room; Activities room; Barber/Beauty shop.
Activities Arts & crafts; Cards; Games; Reading groups; Prayer groups; Movies; Shopping trips.

Burlington Convalescent Hospital
845 S Burlington, Los Angeles, CA 90048
(213) 381-5585
Admin Charles Stern.
Licensure Skilled care. *Beds* SNF 124. *Certified* Medicare; Medi-Cal.
Owner Proprietary corp.

California Convalescent Center 1
909 S Lake St, Los Angeles, CA 90006
(213) 385-7301
Admin Hope Longeretta.
Licensure Skilled care. *Beds* SNF 66. *Certified* Medicare; Medi-Cal.
Owner Proprietary corp.

California Convalescent Center 2
1154 S Alvarado St, Los Angeles, CA 90006
(213) 385-1715
Admin Lualhati Domingo. *Dir of Nursing* Annette F Ordonia. *Medical Dir* James L Meltzer MD.
Licensure Skilled care. *Beds* SNF 72. *Certified* Medicare; Medi-Cal.
Owner Proprietary corp.
Admissions Requirements Minimum age 20.
Staff RNs 2 (ft), 1 (pt); LPNs 6 (ft); Nurses' aides 19 (ft); Physical therapists 1 (pt); Recreational therapists 1 (pt); Occupational therapists 1 (pt); Speech therapists 1 (pt); Activities coordinators 1 (ft); Dietitians 1 (ft); Ophthalmologists 1 (pt); Podiatrists 1 (pt).
Languages Spanish, Tagalog.

Facilities Dining room; Physical therapy room; Activities room; Crafts room; Laundry room; Barber/Beauty shop.
Activities Arts & crafts; Cards; Games; Reading groups; Prayer groups; Movies; Shopping trips; Dances/Social/Cultural gatherings.

Cheviot Garden Convalescent Hospital
3533 Motor Ave, Los Angeles, CA 90034
(213) 836-8900
Admin David Hiatt.
Licensure Skilled care. *Beds* SNF 99. *Certified* Medicare; Medi-Cal.
Owner Privately owned.

College Vista Convalescent Hospital
4681 Eagle Rock Blvd, Los Angeles, CA 90041
(213) 257-8151
Admin Robert H Clark. *Dir of Nursing* Vivian Gold RN. *Medical Dir* Albert Killian MD.
Licensure Skilled care. *Beds* SNF 49. *Certified* Medicare; Medi-Cal.
Owner Proprietary corp.
Admissions Requirements Minimum age 35.
Staff Physicians 13 (ft), 2 (pt); RNs 3 (ft), 3 (pt); LPNs 2 (ft), 3 (pt); Nurses' aides 16 (ft), 3 (pt); Physical therapists 1 (ft); Reality therapists 1 (pt); Recreational therapists 1 (pt); Occupational therapists 1 (pt); Speech therapists 1 (pt); Activities coordinators 1 (ft); Dietitians 1 (pt); Ophthalmologists 1 (pt); Podiatrists 1 (pt); Audiologists 1 (pt).
Languages Spanish, German.
Facilities Dining room; Activities room; Laundry room; Barber/Beauty shop; TV room; Whirlpool tub.
Activities Arts & crafts; Cards; Games; Reading groups; Prayer groups; Movies; Shopping trips; Dances/Social/Cultural gatherings; Pet therapy; Holiday celebrations; Country breakfasts; Candlelight dinners; Bingo; Garden club; Musical entertainment; Church services.

Columbia Convalescent Home
157 N Formosa Ave, Los Angeles, CA 90038
(213) 426-2557
Admin Zoltan Schwartz. *Dir of Nursing* Mara Lyn Miller RN. *Medical Dir* David Bockoff.
Licensure Skilled care. *Beds* 48. *Certified* Medicaid; Medicare; Medi-Cal.
Owner Privately owned.
Admissions Requirements Minimum age 40; Medical examination; Physician's request.
Staff RNs 1 (ft), 1 (pt); Nurses' aides 15 (ft), 5 (pt); Activities coordinators 1 (ft); LVN 3 (ft), 2 (pt).
Languages Spanish, Tagalog.
Facilities Dining room; Activities room; Laundry room; Barber/Beauty shop.
Activities Arts & crafts; Cards; Games; Reading groups; Prayer groups; Movies; Dances/Social/Cultural gatherings.

Convalescent Care Center
230 E Adams Blvd, Los Angeles, CA 90011
(213) 748-0491
Admin John Torrey.
Medical Dir William Cottles MD.
Licensure Skilled care. *Beds* SNF 88. *Certified* Medicare; Medi-Cal.
Owner Proprietary corp.
Admissions Requirements Minimum age 18; Physician's request.
Staff RNs 1 (ft), 4 (pt); LPNs 7 (ft), 6 (pt); Nurses' aides 21 (ft), 4 (pt); Physical therapists 1 (pt); Activities coordinators 1 (ft); Dietitians 1 (ft).

Convalescent Hospital Casa Descanso
4515 Huntington Dr, Los Angeles, CA 90032
(213) 225-5991
Admin Georgianna Tucci. *Dir of Nursing* Margaret Vickerson. *Medical Dir* Dr Marvin Salant.
Licensure Skilled care. *Beds* SNF 99. *Certified* Medi-Cal.

Owner Proprietary corp.
Admissions Requirements Minimum age 55; Medical examination; Physician's request.
Staff Physicians 7 (pt); RNs 4 (ft); LPNs 6 (ft); Nurses' aides 33 (ft); Physical therapists 1 (pt); Reality therapists 1 (pt); Recreational therapists 1 (pt); Occupational therapists 1 (pt); Speech therapists 1 (pt); Activities coordinators 2 (ft); Dietitians 1 (ft), 1 (pt); Ophthalmologists 1 (pt); Podiatrists 1 (pt).
Languages Spanish.
Facilities Dining room; Activities room; Crafts room; Laundry room; Barber/Beauty shop.
Activities Arts & crafts; Cards; Games; Reading groups; Prayer groups; Movies; Shopping trips; Dances/Social/Cultural gatherings.

Country Villa North Convalescent Hospital
3233 W Pico Blvd, Los Angeles, CA 90019
(213) 734-9122
Admin Dena Francis.
Licensure Skilled care. *Beds* SNF 99. *Certified* Medicare; Medi-Cal.
Owner Proprietary corp.

Country Villa South Convalescent Center
3515 Overland Ave, Los Angeles, CA 90034
(213) 839-5201, 839-8217 FAX
Admin Christopher Monroe. *Dir of Nursing* Ellen Allard RN. *Medical Dir* Alan Greenberg MD.
Licensure Skilled care; Alzheimer's care; Respite care. *Beds* SNF 87. *Private Pay Patients* 15%. *Certified* Medicaid; Medicare; Medi-Cal.
Owner Proprietary corp (Country Villa Service Corp).
Admissions Requirements Minimum age 18; Medical examination; Physician's request.
Staff RNs 4 (ft); LPNs 8 (ft); Nurses' aides 45 (ft); Physical therapists 2 (ft); Recreational therapists 2 (ft); Occupational therapists 1 (ft); Speech therapists 1 (ft); Activities coordinators 1 (ft); Dietitians 1 (pt).
Languages Spanish, Tagalog.
Facilities Dining room; Physical therapy room; Activities room; Crafts room; Laundry room; Barber/Beauty shop; Library.
Activities Arts & crafts; Cards; Games; Reading groups; Prayer groups; Movies; Shopping trips; Dances/Social/Cultural gatherings; Intergenerational programs; Pet therapy.

Country Villa Westwood Center
12121 Santa Monica Blvd, Los Angeles, CA 90025
(213) 826-0821
Admin Jane E Corr. *Dir of Nursing* Linda Blades. *Medical Dir* Alan Greenberg MD.
Licensure Skilled care. *Beds* SNF 93. *Certified* Medicare; Medi-Cal.
Owner Proprietary corp.
Admissions Requirements Minimum age 18; Physician's request.
Staff RNs; LPNs; Nurses' aides; Physical therapists; Recreational therapists; Occupational therapists; Speech therapists; Activities coordinators; Dietitians; Podiatrists.
Languages Spanish, Filipino.
Facilities Dining room; Physical therapy room; Activities room; Crafts room; Barber/Beauty shop.
Activities Arts & crafts; Cards; Games; Reading groups; Prayer groups; Movies; Pet therapy.

Country Villa Wilshire Convalescent Center
855 N Fairfax Ave, Los Angeles, CA 90046
(213) 653-1521, 852-9002 FAX
Admin Stephen P Blend MHA. *Dir of Nursing* Josie1 V Rodriguez RN. *Medical Dir* Dr Meltzer.

Licensure Skilled care. *Beds* SNF 81. *Private Pay Patients* 40%. *Certified* Medicare; Medi-Cal.
Owner Privately owned.
Admissions Requirements Physician's request.
Staff RNs 2 (ft), 4 (pt); LPNs 10 (ft), 3 (pt); Nurses' aides 30 (ft), 6 (pt); Physical therapists 1 (pt); Occupational therapists 1 (pt); Speech therapists 1 (pt); Activities coordinators 1 (ft); Dietitians 1 (ft); Ophthalmologists 1 (pt); Podiatrists 1 (pt); Audiologists 1 (pt).
Languages Spanish, Yiddish.
Facilities Dining room; Physical therapy room; Activities room; Laundry room; Barber/Beauty shop.
Activities Arts & crafts; Cards; Games.

Culver West Convalescent Hospital
4035 Grandview Blvd, Los Angeles, CA 90066
(213) 390-9506
Admin Florence Patton. *Dir of Nursing* Eve Krohn BS RN. *Medical Dir* I Kowakami MD.
Licensure Skilled care. *Beds* SNF 91. *Private Pay Patients* 33%. *Certified* Medicare; Medi-Cal.
Owner Privately owned.
Admissions Requirements Physician's request.
Staff Physicians (contracted); RNs 10 (ft); LPNs 12 (ft); Nurses' aides 40 (ft); Physical therapists (contracted); Reality therapists (contracted); Occupational therapists 1 (pt); Speech therapists (contracted); Activities coordinators 2 (ft), 1 (pt); Dietitians 1 (pt); Ophthalmologists (contracted); Podiatrists 1 (pt); Audiologists (contracted); Nurse practitioners.
Languages Korean, Japanese, Chinese, Spanish.
Facilities Dining room; Physical therapy room; Activities room; Barber/Beauty shop; Library.
Activities Arts & crafts; Cards; Games; Reading groups; Prayer groups; Movies; Shopping trips; Dances/Social/Cultural gatherings; Intergenerational programs; Pet therapy.

Dunlap Sanitarium
6011 West Blvd, Los Angeles, CA 90043
(213) 292-0748
Admin Mary F Jackson. *Dir of Nursing* Melvin Blackwell. *Medical Dir* Ralph Cole MD.
Licensure Skilled care; Retirement. *Beds* SNF 40. *Certified* Medicare; Medi-Cal.
Owner Privately owned.
Admissions Requirements Minimum age 40; Physician's request.
Staff Physicians; RNs; LPNs; Nurses' aides; Physical therapists; Recreational therapists; Occupational therapists; Speech therapists; Activities coordinators; Dietitians; Ophthalmologists; Podiatrists.
Activities Arts & crafts; Cards; Games; Reading groups; Prayer groups; Movies; Shopping trips; Dances/Social/Cultural gatherings; Intergenerational programs.

East Los Angeles Convalescent Hospital
101 S Fickett St, Los Angeles, CA 90033
(213) 261-8108
Dir of Nursing Candida Cardones. *Medical Dir* Louis T Bascoy.
Licensure Skilled care. *Beds* SNF 99. *Certified* Medicare; Medi-Cal.
Owner Proprietary corp.
Admissions Requirements Physician's request.
Staff RNs 1 (ft); Nurses' aides 24 (ft); Activities coordinators 1 (ft); LVNs 6 (ft).
Languages Spanish.
Facilities Dining room; Activities room; Crafts room; Laundry room.
Activities Arts & crafts; Cards; Games; Prayer groups; Movies; Dances/Social/Cultural gatherings; Trips to park.

Eastern Star Home
11725 Sunset Blvd, Los Angeles, CA 90049
(213) 472-1251
Admin Mary Lou McElroy.
Licensure Skilled care. *Beds* SNF 39.
Owner Nonprofit corp.
Affiliation Order of Eastern Star.

Echo Park Skilled Nursing Facility Hospital Inc
1633 E Echo Park Ave, Los Angeles, CA 90026
(213) 628-4228
Admin Carolyn Madison.
Licensure Skilled care. *Beds* SNF 59. *Certified* Medicare; Medi-Cal.
Owner Proprietary corp.

Elizabeth Manor Skilled Nursing Facility
340 S Alvarado St, Los Angeles, CA 90057
(213) 484-9730
Admin Linda Lem.
Medical Dir Robert Palmer MD.
Licensure Skilled care. *Beds* SNF 180. *Certified* Medi-Cal.
Owner Nonprofit corp (Physicians Aid Association).
Admissions Requirements Minimum age 65.
Staff RNs; LPNs; Nurses' aides; Activities coordinators.
Facilities Dining room; Activities room; Laundry room; Barber/Beauty shop.
Activities Arts & crafts; Cards; Games; Reading groups; Prayer groups; Movies; Dances/Social/Cultural gatherings.

Flora Terrace Convalescent Hospital Inc
5916 W Pico Blvd, Los Angeles, CA 90035
(213) 939-3184
Admin Flora Rosman.
Licensure Skilled care. *Beds* SNF 66. *Certified* Medicare; Medi-Cal.
Owner Proprietary corp.

Flora Terrace West Convalescent Hospital Inc
6070 W Pico Blvd, Los Angeles, CA 90035
(213) 653-3980
Admin Flora Rosman.
Licensure Skilled care. *Beds* SNF 49. *Certified* Medicare; Medi-Cal.
Owner Proprietary corp.

Fountain Gardens Convalescent Hospital
2222 Santa Ana Blvd, Los Angeles, CA 90059
(213) 564-4461
Admin Jack Markovitz.
Licensure Skilled care. *Beds* SNF 149. *Certified* Medicare; Medi-Cal.
Owner Proprietary corp.

Fountain View Convalescent Hospital
5310 Fountain Ave, Los Angeles, CA 90029
(213) 461-9961
Admin Barbara Mascari.
Licensure Skilled care. *Beds* SNF 99. *Certified* Medicare; Medi-Cal.
Owner Proprietary corp.

Garden Crest Convalescent Hospital
909 N Lucile Ave, Los Angeles, CA 90026
(214) 663-8281
Admin Paul Barron.
Licensure Skilled care. *Beds* SNF 72. *Certified* Medicare.
Owner Proprietary corp.

Garden Plaza Convalescent Hospital
12029 S Avalon Blvd, Los Angeles, CA 90061
(213) 756-8191
Admin Eleanor V Julian.
Licensure Skilled care. *Beds* SNF 131. *Certified* Medicare; Medi-Cal.
Owner Proprietary corp.

Grand Park Convalescent Hospital
2312 W 8th St, Los Angeles, CA 90057
(213) 382-7315
Admin Jane E Kapsch.

Licensure Skilled care. *Beds* SNF 151. *Certified* Medicare; Medi-Cal.
Owner Proprietary corp.

Guardian Rehabilitation Hospital Inc
533 S Fairfax Ave, Los Angeles, CA 90036
(213) 931-1061
Admin Sigmund Gest. *Dir of Nursing* Virginia Tingzon RN. *Medical Dir* William J Zack MD.
Licensure Skilled care. *Beds* SNF 93. *Certified* Medicare; Medi-Cal.
Owner Proprietary corp.
Admissions Requirements Minimum age 50; Medical examination; Physician's request.
Staff RNs; LPNs; Nurses' aides; Physical therapists; Reality therapists; Recreational therapists; Occupational therapists; Speech therapists; Activities coordinators; Dietitians.
Languages Spanish, Tagalog, German.
Facilities Dining room; Physical therapy room; Activities room; Crafts room; Laundry room; Barber/Beauty shop.
Activities Arts & crafts; Cards; Games; Reading groups; Movies; Shopping trips; Dances/Social/Cultural gatherings.

Hancock Park Convalescent Hospital & Rehabilitation Center
505 N La Brea Ave, Los Angeles, CA 90036
(213) 937-4860
Admin Claire Padama. *Dir of Nursing* Cyril Lazado. *Medical Dir* William Wanamaker MD.
Licensure Skilled care. *Beds* SNF 141. *Certified* Medicare; Medi-Cal.
Owner Proprietary corp.
Admissions Requirements Medical examination; Physician's request.
Staff RNs 10 (ft); LPNs 16 (ft); Nurses' aides 54 (ft); Physical therapists 1 (ft); Occupational therapists 1 (ft); Speech therapists 1 (ft); Activities coordinators 2 (ft); Dietitians 1 (pt); Ophthalmologists 1 (pt); Podiatrists 1 (pt); Dentists 1 (pt); Physical therapist aides 1 (ft); Social workers 1 (ft).
Languages Spanish, Yiddish.
Facilities Dining room; Physical therapy room; Activities room; Laundry room; Barber/Beauty shop; Speech & occupational therapy room.
Activities Arts & crafts; Cards; Games; Movies; Field trips; Bingo; Birthday parties.

Hollenbeck Home for Aged Convalescent Unit
573 S Boyle Ave, Los Angeles, CA 90033
(213) 263-6195
Admin William A Heideman. *Dir of Nursing* Dora Peterson RN. *Medical Dir* John D Walters MD.
Licensure Skilled care; Intermediate care; Retirement. *Beds* SNF 84; ICF 28. *Certified* Medicare; Medi-Cal.
Owner Nonprofit organization/foundation.
Admissions Requirements Minimum age 65; Medical examination.
Staff Physicians 3 (pt); RNs 2 (ft), 2 (pt); LPNs 8 (ft), 2 (pt); Nurses' aides 37 (ft), 5 (pt); Physical therapists 1 (pt); Occupational therapists 1 (pt); Speech therapists 1 (pt); Activities coordinators 2 (ft); Dietitians 1 (pt); Ophthalmologists 1 (pt); Podiatrists 1 (pt); Dentists 1 (pt).
Facilities Dining room; Physical therapy room; Activities room; Chapel; Crafts room; Laundry room; Barber/Beauty shop; Library; Ice cream parlor; Whirlpool.
Activities Arts & crafts; Cards; Games; Reading groups; Prayer groups; Movies; Shopping trips; Dances/Social/Cultural gatherings.

Hyde Park Convalescent Hospital
6520 W Blvd, Los Angeles, CA 90043
(213) 753-1354
Admin Elaine M Wiesel. *Dir of Nursing* Janet Bramhall RN. *Medical Dir* Dr Earl M Wolf.

Licensure Skilled care. *Beds* SNF 72. *Certified* Medicare; Medi-Cal.
Owner Proprietary corp.
Admissions Requirements Minimum age 21; Medical examination; Physician's request.
Staff RNs 1 (ft), 1 (pt); LPNs 6 (ft), 3 (pt); Nurses' aides 29 (ft), 4 (pt); Activities coordinators 1 (ft).
Languages Spanish, Hungarian, German, Hebrew.
Facilities Dining room; Physical therapy room; Activities room; Crafts room; Laundry room; Barber/Beauty shop.
Activities Arts & crafts; Cards; Games; Reading groups; Prayer groups; Movies; Dances/Social/Cultural gatherings; Pet therapy.

Japanese Retirement Home—Intermediate Care Facility
325 S Boyle Ave, Los Angeles, CA 90033
(213) 263-9651
Admin Edwin C Hiroto. *Dir of Nursing* Sachiko Ward RN. *Medical Dir* Dr Sakaye Shigekawa.
Licensure Intermediate care; Residential care. *Beds* ICF 96; Residential 112. *Certified* Medi-Cal.
Owner Nonprofit corp.
Admissions Requirements Minimum age 60.
Staff RNs 1 (ft); LPNs 3 (ft), 3 (pt); Nurses' aides 19 (ft), 5 (pt); Activities coordinators 1 (ft), 1 (pt); Dietitians 1 (pt).
Languages Japanese, Chinese, Korean.
Facilities Dining room; Activities room; Crafts room; Laundry room; Barber/Beauty shop; Auditorium.
Activities Arts & crafts; Games; Prayer groups; Movies; Shopping trips; Dances/Social/ Cultural gatherings; Music group.

Keiro Nursing Home
2221 Lincoln Park Ave, Los Angeles, CA 90031
(213) 225-1393
Admin Margaret F Hiroto.
Licensure Skilled care. *Beds* SNF 87. *Certified* Medicare; Medi-Cal.
Owner Nonprofit corp.
Languages Japanese.

Kennedy Convalescent Hospital
619 N Fairfax Ave, Los Angeles, CA 90036
(213) 651-0043
Admin Solomon Gruer.
Licensure Skilled care. *Beds* SNF 97. *Certified* Medicare; Medi-Cal.
Owner Proprietary corp.

Kingsley Convalescent Hospital
1055 N Kingsley Dr, Los Angeles, CA 90029
(213) 661-1128
Admin Betty J Betance. *Dir of Nursing* Nora Ong. *Medical Dir* Dr Killian.
Licensure Skilled care; Retirement; Alzheimer's care. *Beds* SNF 51; Retirement 200. *Certified* Medicare; Medi-Cal.
Owner Nonprofit corp (Pacific Homes).
Admissions Requirements Physician's request.
Staff RNs; LPNs; Nurses' aides; Activities coordinators; Dietitians.
Facilities Dining room; Activities room; Chapel; Crafts room; Barber/Beauty shop; Library; Alzheimer's unit.
Activities Arts & crafts; Cards; Games; Reading groups; Prayer groups; Movies; Shopping trips; Dances/Social/Cultural gatherings.

Lakewood Manor North
831 S Lake St, Los Angeles, CA 90057
(213) 380-9175
Admin Kim Elliott.
Medical Dir Dr Marvin Salant.
Licensure Skilled care. *Beds* SNF 99. *Certified* Medicare; Medi-Cal.
Owner Proprietary corp.
Admissions Requirements Physician's request.

Staff Physicians 8 (pt); RNs 1 (ft), 3 (pt); LPNs 22 (ft), 6 (pt); Nurses' aides 30 (ft), 15 (pt); Physical therapists 4 (pt); Reality therapists 1 (pt); Recreational therapists 1 (pt); Occupational therapists 2 (pt); Speech therapists 2 (pt); Activities coordinators 2 (pt); Dietitians 3 (pt); Ophthalmologists 1 (pt); Podiatrists 1 (pt); Audiologists 1 (pt); Dentists 2 (pt).
Facilities Dining room; Physical therapy room; Activities room; Barber/Beauty shop.
Activities Arts & crafts; Cards; Games; Reading groups; Prayer groups; Movies; Dances/Social/Cultural gatherings.

Longwood Manor Sanitarium
4853 W Washington, Los Angeles, CA 90016
(213) 935-1157
Admin Rosa Ramirez. *Dir of Nursing* Nina Tan. *Medical Dir* Richard Wise.
Licensure Skilled care. *Beds* SNF 198. *Certified* Medicare; Medi-Cal.
Owner Privately owned.
Staff Physicians (contracted); RNs; Nurses' aides; Physical therapists (contracted); Recreational therapists (contracted); Occupational therapists (contracted); Speech therapists (contracted); Activities coordinators; Dietitians (contracted).
Languages Spanish.
Facilities Dining room; Physical therapy room; Activities room; Crafts room; Laundry room; Barber/Beauty shop.
Activities Arts & crafts; Cards; Games; Prayer groups; Movies; Shopping trips; Intergenerational programs.

Manchester Manor Convalescent Hospital
837 W Manchester Ave, Los Angeles, CA 90044
(213) 753-1789
Admin Mabel Crockett.
Licensure Skilled care. *Beds* SNF 49. *Certified* Medicare; Medi-Cal.
Owner Proprietary corp.

Maple Convalescent Hospital
2625 S Maple Ave, Los Angeles, CA 90011
(213) 747-6371
Admin Andre Pollak.
Medical Dir Dr Edward J Panzer.
Licensure Skilled care. *Beds* SNF 59. *Certified* Medicare; Medi-Cal.
Owner Privately owned.
Facilities Dining room; Activities room; Laundry room.
Activities Arts & crafts; Cards; Games; Prayer groups; Movies.

Mar Vista Sanitarium
3966 Marcasel Ave, Los Angeles, CA 90066
(213) 870-3716
Admin Ruth Von Buskirk.
Medical Dir Dr Daniel Weston.
Licensure Skilled care. *Beds* SNF 68.
Owner Privately owned.
Admissions Requirements Minimum age 50; Females only.
Staff RNs 2 (ft), 1 (pt); LPNs 3 (ft), 3 (pt); Nurses' aides 30 (ft), 15 (pt); Activities coordinators 1 (ft), 1 (pt); Dietitians 1 (ft).
Facilities Dining room; Activities room; Laundry room; Barber/Beauty shop.
Activities Arts & crafts; Cards; Games; Reading groups; Movies.

Meadowbrook Manor
3951 East Blvd, Los Angeles, CA 90066
(213) 391-8266
Admin J Krider.
Medical Dir Paul Berns MD.
Licensure Skilled care. *Beds* SNF 77. *Certified* Medi-Cal.
Owner Proprietary corp.
Admissions Requirements Minimum age 18; Medical examination; Physician's request.

Facilities Dining room; Activities room; Laundry room.
Activities Arts & crafts; Games; Reading groups; Prayer groups; Movies; Shopping trips; Dances/Social/Cultural gatherings.

Mid-Wilshire Convalescent Hospital
676 S Bonnie Brae, Los Angeles, CA 90057
(213) 483-9921
Admin William Kite. *Dir of Nursing* Ann Clark. *Medical Dir* Richard Weiss MD.
Licensure Skilled care. *Beds* SNF 80. *Certified* Medicare; Medi-Cal; VA.
Owner Proprietary corp (Medicrest of California).
Admissions Requirements Minimum age 18; Medical examination; Physician's request.
Staff Physicians 2 (pt); RNs 1 (ft), 1 (pt); LPNs 6 (ft), 3 (pt); Nurses' aides 20 (ft), 5 (pt); Activities coordinators 8 (ft).
Languages Thai, Spanish.
Facilities Dining room; Physical therapy room; Activities room; Crafts room; Laundry room; Barber/Beauty shop; Library.
Activities Arts & crafts; Cards; Games; Reading groups; Prayer groups; Movies; Shopping trips; Dances/Social/Cultural gatherings; Walks.

Minami Keiro Nursing Home
3619 N Mission Rd, Los Angeles, CA 90031
(213) 225-1559
Admin Margaret Hiroto.
Licensure Skilled care. *Beds* SNF 97. *Certified* Medicare; Medi-Cal.
Owner Nonprofit corp.
Languages Japanese.

Nazareth House
3333 Manning Ave, Los Angeles, CA 90064
(213) 839-2361
Admin Sr Malachy McSweeny. *Dir of Nursing* Sr Kathrine Perkins. *Medical Dir* Dr James Engelman.
Licensure Skilled care; Residential care. *Beds* SNF 22; Residential care 100. *Certified* Medi-Cal.
Owner Nonprofit corp.
Admissions Requirements Minimum age 65; Medical examination; Physician's request.
Staff RNs; LPNs; Nurses' aides; Activities coordinators; Chaplains.
Affiliation Roman Catholic.
Facilities Dining room; Activities room; Chapel; Crafts room; Laundry room; Barber/ Beauty shop.
Activities Arts & crafts; Cards; Games; Reading groups; Prayer groups; Movies; Shopping trips; Dances/Social/Cultural gatherings; Daily mass and other religious services.

Olympia Convalescent Hospital
1100 S Alvarado St, Los Angeles, CA 90006
(213) 487-3000
Admin Otto Schwartz. *Dir of Nursing* Zenaida Medina RN. *Medical Dir* Marvin Salant MD.
Licensure Skilled care. *Beds* SNF 135. *Certified* Medicare; Medi-Cal.
Owner Privately owned.
Staff Physicians; RNs; LPNs; Nurses' aides; Physical therapists; Reality therapists; Recreational therapists; Occupational therapists; Speech therapists; Activities coordinators; Dietitians; Ophthalmologists; Podiatrists; Dentists.
Languages Spanish, Tagalog, Hungarian, Korean, Yiddish, Hebrew.
Facilities Dining room; Physical therapy room; Activities room; Laundry room; Barber/Beauty shop; Library; TV room.
Activities Arts & crafts; Cards; Games; Reading groups; Prayer groups; Movies; Shopping trips; Dances/Social/Cultural gatherings.

Paradise Rehabilitation Convalescent
2415 S Western Ave, Los Angeles, CA 90018
(213) 734-1101
Admin Jerry Sinay.
Licensure Skilled care; Intermediate care. *Beds*
SNF 95; ICF 4. *Certified* Medicare; Medi-
Cal.
Owner Proprietary corp.

R G R Sanitarium
12001 Santa Monica Blvd, Los Angeles, CA
90025
(213) 478-0273
Admin Ida H Rios.
Medical Dir Harry J Silver MD.
Licensure Skilled care. *Beds* SNF 59. *Certified*
Medicare; Medi-Cal.
Owner Proprietary corp.
Facilities Dining room; Physical therapy
room; Activities room; Crafts room; Laundry
room; Barber/Beauty shop.
Activities Arts & crafts; Cards; Games;
Movies; Shopping trips.

Rancho de Vida Convalescent Hospital
5125 Monte Vista St, Los Angeles, CA 90042
(213) 254-6125
Admin Kathleen Reinke.
Licensure Skilled care. *Beds* SNF 59. *Certified*
Medicare; Medi-Cal.
Owner Proprietary corp (Medstar
Management Systems Inc).

**Rubin's Brierwood Terrace Convalescent
Hospital**
1480 S La Cienega Blvd, Los Angeles, CA
90035
(213) 652-3030
Admin Eva Ury. *Dir of Nursing* Veronica
Istenes. *Medical Dir* Jack Goldin MD.
Licensure Skilled care. *Beds* SNF 41. *Certified*
Medicaid; Medicare; Medi-Cal.
Owner Privately owned.
Admissions Requirements Minimum age 50;
Medical examination; Physician's request.
Staff RNs 1 (ft), 1 (pt); LPNs 3 (ft), 3 (pt);
Nurses' aides 40 (ft); Physical therapists 1
(pt); Reality therapists 1 (pt); Recreational
therapists 1 (ft); Occupational therapists 1
(pt); Speech therapists 1 (pt); Activities
coordinators 1 (pt); Dietitians 1 (ft);
Ophthalmologists 1 (pt); Podiatrists 1 (pt);
Audiologists 1 (pt).
Languages Hebrew, Yiddish, Spanish,
Russian.
Facilities Dining room; Activities room;
Crafts room; Laundry room.
Activities Arts & crafts; Cards; Games;
Reading groups; Prayer groups; Movies;
Dances/Social/Cultural gatherings;
Intergenerational programs.

St John of God Nursing Hospital
2035 W Adams Blvd, Los Angeles, CA 90018
(213) 731-0641
Admin Thomas Kruze. *Dir of Nursing* JoAnne
Deisinger RN. *Medical Dir* Harry J Silver
MD.
Licensure Skilled care; Intermediate care;
Retirement; Alzheimer's care. *Beds* SNF 78;
ICF 26; RCF 40; Independent living 5.
Certified Medicare; Medi-Cal.
Owner Nonprofit corp.
Admissions Requirements Minimum age 50;
Medical examination; Physician's request.
Staff RNs 5 (ft); LPNs 9 (ft), 6 (pt); Nurses'
aides 45 (ft), 5 (pt); Activities coordinators 2
(ft); 73 (ft).
Languages Spanish, Korean.
Affiliation Roman Catholic.
Facilities Dining room; Physical therapy
room; Activities room; Chapel; Crafts room;
Laundry room; Barber/Beauty shop; Library.
Activities Arts & crafts; Cards; Games;
Reading groups; Prayer groups; Movies;
Shopping trips; Dances/Social/Cultural
gatherings.

Serrano Convalescent Hospital—North
5401 Fountain Ave, Los Angeles, CA 90029
(213) 465-2106
Admin Lydia F Cruz. *Dir of Nursing* Audrey
Dunnigan. *Medical Dir* Felipi Chu MD.
Licensure Skilled care; Alzheimer's care. *Beds*
SNF 99. *Certified* Medicare; Medi-Cal.
Owner Proprietary corp.
Admissions Requirements Minimum age 65.
Staff Physicians 1 (pt); RNs 2 (ft); LPNs 5
(ft), 5 (pt); Nurses' aides 24 (ft);
Occupational therapists 1 (pt); Speech
therapists 1 (pt); Activities coordinators 1
(pt); Dietitians 1 (ft); Ophthalmologists 1
(pt); Podiatrists 1 (pt); Dentists 1 (pt).
Facilities Dining room; Physical therapy
room; Activities room; Laundry room;
Barber/Beauty shop.
Activities Arts & crafts; Cards; Games;
Reading groups; Prayer groups; Movies;
Dances/Social/Cultural gatherings; Field
trips.

Serrano Convalescent Hospital—South
5400 Fountain Ave, Los Angeles, CA 90029
(213) 461-4301
Admin Lyndia Cruz.
Licensure Skilled care; Intermediate care. *Beds*
SNF 92; ICF 7. *Certified* Medicare; Medi-
Cal.
Owner Proprietary corp.

Sharon Care Center
8167 W 3rd St, Los Angeles, CA 90048
(213) 655-2023
Admin Jean B Salkind. *Dir of Nursing* June
Meshulam RN. *Medical Dir* James Meltzer
MD.
Licensure Skilled care. *Beds* SNF 86. *Private
Pay Patients* 60%. *Certified* Medicare.
Owner Proprietary corp (Summit Care Inc).
Admissions Requirements Minimum age 65;
Physician's request.
Staff RNs 3 (ft); LPNs 10 (ft); Nurses' aides
35 (ft); Physical therapists 2 (ft);
Occupational therapists 1 (pt); Speech
therapists 1 (pt); Activities coordinators 1
(ft); Dietitians 1 (ft), 1 (pt).
Facilities Dining room; Physical therapy
room; Activities room; Laundry room;
Barber/Beauty shop.
Activities Arts & crafts; Cards; Games;
Reading groups; Prayer groups; Movies;
Shopping trips; Dances/Social/Cultural
gatherings; Intergenerational programs; Pet
therapy; Creative living.

Skyline Adolescent Services
3711 Baldwin St, Los Angeles, CA 90031
(415) 632-0132
Admin Ginger Sumner.
Licensure Skilled care. *Beds* SNF 53.
Owner Privately owned.

Skyline Convalescent Hospital
3032 Rowena Ave, Los Angeles, CA 90039
(213) 665-1185
Admin Christine Rosensteel. *Dir of Nursing*
Mrs Sheler. *Medical Dir* Dr Salant.
Licensure Skilled care. *Beds* SNF 99. *Certified*
Medicare; Medi-Cal.
Owner Proprietary corp (Western Medical
Enterprises Inc).
Admissions Requirements Medical
examination; Physician's request; Geriatrics.
Staff Physicians; RNs; LPNs; Nurses' aides;
Activities coordinators; Dietitians.
Facilities Dining room; Physical therapy
room; Activities room; Crafts room; Laundry
room; Barber/Beauty shop; Library; TV
room; Living room.
Activities Arts & crafts; Cards; Games; Prayer
groups; Movies; Shopping trips; Dances/
Social/Cultural gatherings; Field trips to Los
Angeles Zoo, Chinatown, Glendale Galleria,
Verdugo park picnics, beach, & Lake
Cascade.

Solheim Lutheran Home
2236 Merton Ave, Los Angeles, CA 90041
(213) 257-7518
Admin Elizabeth C Batchelder. *Dir of Nursing*
Mary Pauls RN. *Medical Dir* Dr Ralph
Boyd.
Licensure Skilled care; Residential care. *Beds*
SNF 76; Residential care 127. *Private Pay
Patients* 80%. *Certified* Medi-Cal.
Owner Nonprofit organization/foundation.
Admissions Requirements Minimum age 62;
Medical examination.
Staff RNs; LPNs; Nurses' aides; Recreational
therapists; Activities coordinators.
Languages Spanish, Tagalog, German.
Affiliation Lutheran.
Facilities Dining room; Activities room;
Chapel; Crafts room; Laundry room; Barber/
Beauty shop; Library.
Activities Arts & crafts; Cards; Games;
Reading groups; Prayer groups; Movies;
Shopping trips; Dances/Social/Cultural
gatherings; Intergenerational programs; Pet
therapy.

Sparr Convalescent Hospital
2367 W Pico Blvd, Los Angeles, CA 90006
(213) 388-1481
Admin Patricia L Garvey. *Dir of Nursing*
Juanita Price. *Medical Dir* F Evans Powell
MD.
Licensure Skilled care; Alzheimer's care. *Beds*
SNF 59. *Certified* Medicare; Medi-Cal.
Owner Privately owned.
Admissions Requirements Minimum age 20;
Medical examination; Physician's request.
Staff Physicians 13 (pt); RNs 5 (ft); LPNs 4
(ft), 3 (pt); Nurses' aides 21 (ft), 3 (pt);
Physical therapists 1 (pt); Recreational
therapists 1 (pt); Occupational therapists 1
(pt); Speech therapists 1 (pt); Activities
coordinators 1 (ft), 1 (pt); Dietitians 1 (pt);
Ophthalmologists 1 (pt); Podiatrists 1 (pt).
Languages Spanish.
Facilities Dining room; Activities room;
Crafts room; Laundry room; Barber/Beauty
shop; Library; 2 patios; Wander-guard for
Alzheimer's patients; Picnic area; Large
grounds.
Activities Arts & crafts; Cards; Games; Prayer
groups; Movies; Shopping trips; Dances/
Social/Cultural gatherings; Intergenerational
programs.

Sunnyview Convalescent Center
2000 W Washington Blvd, Los Angeles, CA
90018
(213) 735-5146
Admin Kenneth C Casey.
Licensure Skilled care. *Beds* SNF 93. *Certified*
Medicare; Medi-Cal.
Owner Proprietary corp.

Sunray East Convalescent Hospital
3210 W Pico Blvd, Los Angeles, CA 90019
(213) 734-2173
Admin Jack Silverman.
Licensure Skilled care. *Beds* SNF 99. *Certified*
Medicare; Medi-Cal.
Owner Proprietary corp.

Sunshine Terrace Convalescent Hospital Inc
7951 Beverly Blvd, Los Angeles, CA 90048
(213) 655-1500
Admin A Goldstein.
Licensure Skilled care. *Beds* 50.
Owner Proprietary corp.

Sycamore Park Convalescent Hospital
4585 N Figueroa St, Los Angeles, CA 90065
(213) 223-3441, 223-9568 FAX
Admin Martin G Axel. *Dir of Nursing* C
Cardones. *Medical Dir* F Morada.
Licensure Skilled care. *Beds* SNF 90. *Certified*
Medicare; Medi-Cal.
Owner Proprietary corp.

Staff Physicians 1 (pt); RNs 2 (ft); LPNs 11 (ft), 2 (pt); Nurses' aides 25 (ft); Physical therapists 1 (ft); Recreational therapists 1 (pt); Occupational therapists 1 (pt); Speech therapists 1 (pt); Activities coordinators 1 (ft); Dietitians 1 (pt); Ophthalmologists 1 (pt); Podiatrists 1 (pt); Dentists 1 (pt).
Languages Spanish, Tagalog, Thai.
Facilities Dining room; Activities room; Chapel; Crafts room; Laundry room; Barber/Beauty shop; TV room.
Activities Arts & crafts; Cards; Games; Reading groups; Prayer groups; Movies; Shopping trips; Dances/Social/Cultural gatherings; Exercise groups; Adopt-a-grandparent program; Trips to local attractions.

Temple Park Convalescent Hospital
2411 W Temple St, Los Angeles, CA 90026
(213) 380-3210
Admin Barry Kohn.
Medical Dir Marilyn Constantino.
Licensure Skilled care. *Beds* SNF 99. *Certified* Medicare; Medi-Cal.
Owner Proprietary corp.
Staff RNs; LPNs; Nurses' aides; Physical therapists; Recreational therapists; Occupational therapists; Speech therapists; Dietitians; Ophthalmologists.
Languages Spanish, Tai, Tagalog.
Facilities Dining room; Physical therapy room; Activities room; Laundry room; Barber/Beauty shop.
Activities Arts & crafts; Cards; Games; Reading groups; Prayer groups; Movies; Shopping trips; Dances/Social/Cultural gatherings.

Vermont Knolls Convalescent Hospital
11234 S Vermont Ave, Los Angeles, CA 90044
(213) 754-3173
Admin Victor Rodgers MD.
Licensure Skilled care. *Beds* SNF 99. *Certified* Medicare; Medi-Cal.
Owner Proprietary corp.

Vernon Convalescent Hospital
1037 W Vernon, Los Angeles, CA 90037
(213) 232-4895
Admin Edward Markovitz.
Licensure Skilled care. *Beds* SNF 99. *Certified* Medicare; Medi-Cal.
Owner Privately owned.

View Heights Convalescent Hospital
12619 S Avalon Blvd, Los Angeles, CA 90061
(213) 757-1881
Admin Monica A Fenton.
Licensure Skilled care. *Beds* SNF 163. *Certified* Medicare; Medi-Cal.
Owner Proprietary corp.

View Park Convalescent Center
3737 Don Felipe Dr, Los Angeles, CA 90008
(213) 295-7737
Admin Katherine Campbell.
Licensure Skilled care. *Beds* SNF 99. *Certified* Medicare; Medi-Cal.
Owner Proprietary corp.

Virgil Sanitarium & Convalescent Hospital
975 N Virgil Ave, Los Angeles, CA 90029
(213) 665-5793
Admin Nancy S Chow. *Dir of Nursing* Madeline Rulon RN. *Medical Dir* Max Davidson MD.
Licensure Skilled care. *Beds* SNF 124. *Certified* Medicare; Medi-Cal.
Owner Proprietary corp.
Admissions Requirements Minimum age 21.
Staff RNs 6 (ft), 4 (pt); LPNs 8 (ft), 4 (pt); Nurses' aides 29 (ft), 12 (pt); Activities coordinators 2 (ft), 1 (pt).
Languages Russian, Armenian, Chinese, French, Egyptian, Hebrew, Yiddish.

Facilities Dining room; Activities room; Laundry room; Outdoor patio.
Activities Arts & crafts; Cards; Games; Reading groups; Prayer groups; Movies; Shopping trips; Field trips.

Vista Del Sol Care Center
11620 Washington Blvd, Los Angeles, CA 90066
(213) 390-9045
Admin Terry M Henry. *Dir of Nursing* Stella Mora-Henry RN. *Medical Dir* Max Davidson MD.
Licensure Skilled care; Retirement; Alzheimer's care. *Beds* SNF 50; Board & care 25. *Certified* Medicare.
Owner Proprietary corp.
Admissions Requirements Minimum age 65; Physician's request.
Staff RNs; LPNs; Nurses' aides; Recreational therapists; Activities coordinators.
Languages Spanish.
Facilities Dining room; Physical therapy room; Activities room; Crafts room; Laundry room; Barber/Beauty shop.
Activities Arts & crafts; Cards; Games; Reading groups; Prayer groups; Movies; Shopping trips; Dances/Social/Cultural gatherings.

Walnut Convalescent Hospital
PO Box 77287, Los Angeles, CA 90007-0287
(213) 591-7621
Admin John Hryze. *Dir of Nursing* Linda Bince RN. *Medical Dir* Alan Greenburg MD.
Licensure Skilled care. *Beds* SNF 78. *Certified* Medicare; Medi-Cal.
Owner Proprietary corp.
Admissions Requirements Minimum age 40; Medical examination; Physician's request.
Staff RNs 2 (ft); LPNs 11 (ft); Nurses' aides 40 (ft); Activities coordinators 1 (ft); Dietitians 1 (ft).
Languages Spanish.
Facilities Dining room; Physical therapy room; Activities room; Crafts room; Laundry room; Barber/Beauty shop; Library.
Activities Arts & crafts; Cards; Games; Reading groups; Prayer groups; Shopping trips; Dances/Social/Cultural gatherings; Movie videos.

Washington Nursing & Convalescent
2300 W Washington, Los Angeles, CA 90018
(213) 731-0861
Admin Henry Pagkalinawan.
Medical Dir Leroy Ewell MD.
Licensure Skilled care. *Beds* SNF 59. *Certified* Medicare; Medi-Cal.
Owner Publicly owned.
Admissions Requirements Medical examination; Physician's request.
Staff Physicians 8 (pt); RNs 1 (ft), 2 (pt); LPNs 3 (ft), 3 (pt); Nurses' aides 16 (ft), 8 (pt); Physical therapists 1 (pt); Occupational therapists 1 (pt); Speech therapists 1 (pt); Activities coordinators 1 (ft); Dietitians 1 (pt); Ophthalmologists 1 (pt); Podiatrists 1 (pt); Dentists 1 (pt).
Facilities Dining room; Activities room; Crafts room; Laundry room; Barber/Beauty shop.
Activities Arts & crafts; Cards; Games; Reading groups; Prayer groups; Dances/Social/Cultural gatherings.

WCTU Home for Women
2235 Norwalk Ave, Los Angeles, CA 90041
(213) 255-7108
Admin Edna Young.
Licensure Residential care. *Beds* 140.
Owner Nonprofit organization/foundation.
Admissions Requirements Minimum age 62; Females only; Medical examination; Physician's request.

Staff Nurses' aides 5 (ft), 2 (pt); Recreational therapists 1 (ft); Activities coordinators 1 (ft); Dietitians 1 (pt); Ophthalmologists 1 (pt).
Facilities Dining room; Activities room; Chapel; Crafts room; Laundry room; Barber/Beauty shop; Library; Auditorium.
Activities Arts & crafts; Cards; Games; Reading groups; Prayer groups; Movies; Dances/Social/Cultural gatherings; Teas; Sales; Grandmothers program.

West Los Angeles Pavilion
1516 Sawtelle Blvd, Los Angeles, CA 90025
(213) 477-5501
Admin Bernard Rosenson.
Licensure Skilled care. *Beds* SNF 99. *Certified* Medicare; Medi-Cal.
Owner Proprietary corp (Beverly Enterprises).

Western Convalescent Hospital
2190 W Adams Blvd, Los Angeles, CA 90018
(213) 737-7778
Admin Emma B Camanag.
Licensure Skilled care. *Beds* SNF 129. *Certified* Medicare; Medi-Cal.
Owner Proprietary corp.

Westlake Convalescent Hospital
316 S Westlake Ave, Los Angeles, CA 90057
(213) 484-0510
Admin Neng F Chen. *Dir of Nursing* Estrella Cayabyab. *Medical Dir* Minquan Bussarakum.
Licensure Skilled care. *Beds* SNF 114. *Private Pay Patients* 10%. *Certified* Medicare; Medi-Cal.
Owner Proprietary corp (Golden State Health Centers Inc).
Admissions Requirements Minimum age 65; Physician's request.
Staff RNs 4 (ft), 3 (pt); LPNs 9 (ft), 7 (pt); Nurses' aides 33 (ft), 3 (pt); Physical therapists; Activities coordinators 1 (ft); Dietitians 1 (pt).
Languages Spanish, Hebrew, Yiddish, Tagalog, Chinese.
Facilities Dining room; Activities room; Crafts room; Laundry room; Barber/Beauty shop; Enclosed patios.
Activities Arts & crafts; Cards; Games; Reading groups; Movies; Shopping trips; Dances/Social/Cultural gatherings.

Westside Health Care
1020 S Fairfax Ave, Los Angeles, CA 90019
(213) 938-2451
Admin Trudi Weimer.
Licensure Skilled care. *Beds* SNF 120. *Certified* Medicare; Medi-Cal.
Owner Privately owned.

Wilshire Care Center
915 S Crenshaw Blvd, Los Angeles, CA 90019
(213) 937-5466
Admin Tresita Valdez.
Licensure Skilled care. *Beds* SNF 98. *Certified* Medicare; Medi-Cal.
Owner Proprietary corp (Medstar Wilshire Inc).

Los Banos

Los Banos Convalescent Hospital
931 Idaho Ave, Los Banos, CA 93635
(209) 826-0790
Admin Barry W Byers. *Dir of Nursing* Glenn Eslinger. *Medical Dir* Oscar Ansaldo MD.
Licensure Skilled care. *Beds* SNF 59. *Certified* Medicare; Medi-Cal.
Owner Privately owned.
Admissions Requirements Medical examination; Physician's request.
Staff Physicians 1 (pt); RNs 1 (ft), 1 (pt); LPNs 4 (ft), 1 (pt); Nurses' aides 26 (ft), 9 (pt); Physical therapists 1 (pt); Speech

therapists 1 (pt); Activities coordinators 1 (ft), 1 (pt); Dietitians 1 (pt); Ophthalmologists 1 (pt).
Languages Spanish, Portuguese.
Facilities Dining room; Activities room; Courtyard; Patio.
Activities Arts & crafts; Cards; Games; Prayer groups; Movies.

Los Gatos

Bethesda Convalescent Center
371 Los Gatos Blvd, Los Gatos, CA 95032
(408) 356-3116, 356-2024 FAX
Admin Robert A DeBene. *Dir of Nursing* Geraldine Humecke. *Medical Dir* Richard Westing.
Licensure Skilled care. *Beds* SNF 124. *Private Pay Patients* 15%. *Certified* Medicare; Medi-Cal.
Owner Nonprofit corp.
Admissions Requirements Physician's request.
Staff Physicians 1 (pt); RNs 5 (ft); LPNs 8 (ft), 6 (pt); Nurses' aides 30 (ft), 18 (pt); Physical therapists 1 (pt); Occupational therapists 1 (pt); Speech therapists 1 (pt); Activities coordinators 2 (ft); Dietitians 1 (pt); Podiatrists 1 (pt).
Languages Spanish.
Affiliation Disciples of Christ.
Facilities Dining room; Physical therapy room; Activities room; Chapel; Laundry room; Barber/Beauty shop.
Activities Arts & crafts; Cards; Games; Prayer groups; Movies; Intergenerational programs.

Lark Manor Convalescent Hospital
16605 Lark Ave, Los Gatos, CA 95030
(408) 356-9146
Admin Gerald O Breithaupt. *Dir of Nursing* Jean Lyonn.
Licensure Skilled care. *Beds* SNF 30. *Certified* Medicare; Medi-Cal.
Owner Proprietary corp.
Admissions Requirements Minimum age 25; Medical examination.
Staff Physicians 1 (pt); RNs 1 (ft); LPNs 2 (ft); Nurses' aides 7 (ft), 4 (pt); Activities coordinators 1 (ft); Dietitians 1 (pt).
Languages Spanish, German.
Facilities Dining room; Physical therapy room; Activities room.
Activities Cards; Games; Reading groups; Movies; Shopping trips.

Los Gatos Convalescent Hospital
16412 Los Gatos Blvd, Los Gatos, CA 95030
(408) 356-2191
Admin Karen Waldrop.
Medical Dir Donna Bruns.
Licensure Skilled care. *Beds* SNF 50. *Certified* Medicare; Medi-Cal.
Owner Privately owned.

Los Gatos Meadows Geriatric Hospital
110 Wood Rd, Los Gatos, CA 95030
(408) 354-0242, 354-1758 FAX
Admin James P Hempler. *Dir of Nursing* Mary Fischer RN. *Medical Dir* John Rashkis MD.
Licensure Skilled care. *Beds* SNF 39. *Private Pay Patients* 3%. *Certified* Medicare.
Owner Nonprofit organization/foundation.
Admissions Requirements Physician's request.
Staff Physicians (contracted); RNs 5 (ft), 1 (pt); LPNs 3 (ft), 2 (pt); Nurses' aides 11 (ft), 8 (pt); Physical therapists (contracted); Occupational therapists (contracted); Speech therapists (contracted); Activities coordinators 1 (ft); Dietitians 1 (pt); Podiatrists (contracted).
Languages Dutch, Spanish.
Affiliation Episcopal.
Facilities Dining room; Physical therapy room; Activities room; Chapel; Crafts room; Laundry room; Barber/Beauty shop; Library.

Activities Reading groups; Movies; Shopping trips; Dances/Social/Cultural gatherings; Cooking; Music.

Oak Meadows Convalescent Center
350 De Soto Dr, Los Gatos, CA 95030
(408) 356-9151
Admin Danny Mar. *Dir of Nursing* Nedy Papas. *Medical Dir* Dr Woods.
Licensure Skilled care. *Beds* SNF 73. *Private Pay Patients* 20%. *Certified* Medicare; Medi-Cal.
Owner Proprietary corp (Long Term Care Group).
Languages Spanish, Greek, Filipino, Vietnamese.
Activities Arts & crafts; Cards; Games; Prayer groups; Movies.

Terreno Gardens Convalescent Center
14966 Terreno De Flores Ln, Los Gatos, CA 95030
(408) 356-8136
Admin Dan Platt.
Medical Dir Dr Stephen Tilles.
Licensure Skilled care. *Beds* SNF 65. *Certified* Medicare; Medi-Cal.
Owner Proprietary corp.
Staff Physical therapists; Occupational therapists; Speech therapists; Activities coordinators 1 (ft); Dietitians; Ophthalmologists; Dentists.
Facilities Dining room; Activities room; Crafts room; Laundry room; Barber/Beauty shop; Large patio area.
Activities Arts & crafts; Cards; Games; Reading groups; Prayer groups; Movies; Shopping trips; Dances/Social/Cultural gatherings; Bingo.

Loyalton

Sierra Valley Community Hospital
PO Box 178, 309 W 3rd St, Loyalton, CA 96118
(916) 993-1225, 993-4761 FAX
Admin James Harding. *Dir of Nursing* Joyce Pitcher RN. *Medical Dir* Ted Hanf DO.
Licensure Skilled care; Acute care. *Beds* SNF 34; Acute care 6. *Private Pay Patients* 25%. *Certified* Medicaid; Medicare; Medi-Cal.
Owner Publicly owned.
Admissions Requirements Physician's request.
Staff Physicians 2 (ft); RNs 5 (ft), 6 (pt); LPNs 4 (ft), 4 (pt); Nurses' aides 10 (ft), 6 (pt); Physical therapists 1 (pt); Occupational therapists 1 (ft), 1 (pt); Speech therapists 1 (pt); Activities coordinators 1 (pt).
Facilities Dining room; Physical therapy room; Activities room.
Activities Arts & crafts; Cards; Games; Reading groups; Prayer groups; Shopping trips; Pet therapy.

Lynwood

Community Convalescent Hospital
3611 Imperial Hwy, Lynwood, CA 90262
(213) 537-2500
Admin Michelle A Brozowski.
Licensure Skilled care. *Beds* SNF 99. *Certified* Medicare; Medi-Cal.
Owner Proprietary corp (Beverly Enterprises).

Lynwood Care Center
3598 E Century Blvd, Lynwood, CA 90262
(213) 639-5220
Admin Ronald Morgan.
Medical Dir Ramon Cabrera MD.
Licensure Skilled care. *Beds* 128. *Certified* Medicare; Medi-Cal.
Owner Proprietary corp (Beverly Enterprises).
Admissions Requirements Minimum age 3; Medical examination; Physician's request.
Staff Physicians 1 (pt); RNs 4 (ft), 2 (pt); LPNs 6 (ft), 2 (pt); Nurses' aides 35 (ft), 6 (pt); Physical therapists 1 (pt); Occupational

therapists 1 (pt); Speech therapists 1 (pt); Activities coordinators 1 (ft); Dietitians 1 (pt); Ophthalmologists 1 (pt); Podiatrists 1 (pt); Audiologists 1 (pt); Dentists 1 (pt).
Facilities Dining room; Physical therapy room; Activities room; Crafts room; Laundry room; Barber/Beauty shop.
Activities Arts & crafts; Cards; Games; Movies; Shopping trips.

Majestic Convalescent Hospital
3565 E Imperial, Lynwood, CA 90262
(213) 638-9377
Admin Ralph J Bak. *Dir of Nursing* Carolyn Marry RN. *Medical Dir* Robert Tsai MD.
Licensure Skilled care. *Beds* SNF 98. *Certified* Medicare; Medi-Cal.
Owner Proprietary corp.
Admissions Requirements Minimum age 30; Medical examination; Physician's request.
Staff Physicians 6 (pt); RNs 2 (ft), 1 (pt); LPNs 8 (ft), 2 (pt); Nurses' aides 32 (ft), 4 (pt); Physical therapists 1 (pt); Recreational therapists 1 (pt); Occupational therapists 1 (pt); Speech therapists 1 (pt); Activities coordinators 2 (ft); Dietitians 1 (pt); Ophthalmologists 1 (pt); Podiatrists 1 (pt); Dentists 1 (pt); Medical records 1 (pt); Pharmacy 1 (pt); Dietary staff 6 (ft), 2 (pt); Housekeeping, Laundry, Maintenance 8 (ft).
Languages Spanish.
Facilities Dining room; Physical therapy room; Activities room; Crafts room; Laundry room; Barber/Beauty shop.
Activities Arts & crafts; Cards; Games; Reading groups; Prayer groups; Movies; Shopping trips; Dances/Social/Cultural gatherings.

Marlinda Nursing Home
3615 Imperial Hwy, Lynwood, CA 90262
(213) 639-4623
Admin Martha E Lang.
Medical Dir Dr Robert S Tsai.
Licensure Skilled care. *Beds* SNF 130. *Certified* Medicare; Medi-Cal.
Owner Proprietary corp.
Staff RNs 5 (ft), 4 (pt); LPNs 11 (ft); Nurses' aides 50 (ft); Physical therapists 1 (pt); Recreational therapists 1 (ft); Occupational therapists 1 (pt); Speech therapists 1 (pt); Activities coordinators 1 (ft); Dietitians 1 (ft); Ophthalmologists 1 (pt).
Facilities Dining room; Physical therapy room; Activities room; Crafts room; Laundry room; Barber/Beauty shop; Library.
Activities Arts & crafts; Cards; Games; Reading groups; Prayer groups; Movies; Sing-alongs.

Madera

Madera Rehabilitation & Convalescent Center
517 S "A" St, Madera, CA 93638
(209) 673-9228, 673-1245 FAX
Admin George H Eslinger. *Dir of Nursing* Paula Wilson RN.
Licensure Skilled care. *Beds* SNF 176. *Certified* Medicare; Medi-Cal.
Owner Proprietary corp.
Admissions Requirements Physician's request.
Staff RNs 6 (ft); LPNs 12 (ft); Nurses' aides 44 (ft); Physical therapists 2 (ft); Recreational therapists 1 (ft), 1 (pt); Occupational therapists 1 (ft); Speech therapists 1 (ft); Activities coordinators 1 (ft); Dietitians 1 (pt); Ophthalmologists 1 (pt); Podiatrists 1 (pt).
Languages Spanish.
Facilities Dining room; Physical therapy room; Activities room; Crafts room; Laundry room; Barber/Beauty shop; Library.
Activities Arts & crafts; Cards; Games; Prayer groups; Movies; Shopping trips; Men's club.

Westgate Manor Convalescent Hospital
1700 Howard Rd, Madera, CA 93637
(209) 673-9278

Admin Roy Wagner. *Dir of Nursing* Mary Hyde RN.
Licensure Skilled care. *Beds* SNF 64. *Certified* Medicare; Medi-Cal.
Owner Proprietary corp (Beverly Enterprises).

Manteca

Care West—Manteca
PO Box 766, 410 Eastwood Ave, Manteca, CA 95336
(209) 239-1222
Admin Belinda Guzman. *Dir of Nursing* John Hayes. *Medical Dir* Russell Carter MD.
Licensure Skilled care. *Beds* SNF 99. *Private Pay Patients* 25%. *Certified* Medicaid; Medicare; Medi-Cal.
Owner Proprietary corp (Care Enterprises).
Admissions Requirements Physician's request.
Staff RNs 6 (ft), 2 (pt); LPNs 7 (ft), 2 (pt); Nurses' aides 37 (ft), 3 (pt); Physical therapists 2 (ft); Activities coordinators 2 (ft), 1 (pt).
Facilities Dining room; Physical therapy room; Activities room; Crafts room; Laundry room; Barber/Beauty shop; IV therapy.
Activities Arts & crafts; Cards; Games; Reading groups; Prayer groups; Movies; Shopping trips; Dances/Social/Cultural gatherings; Intergenerational programs; Pet therapy.

Palm Haven Convalescent Hospital
469 E North St, Manteca, CA 95336
(209) 823-1788
Admin John C Sloterbeek.
Licensure Skilled care. *Beds* SNF 99. *Certified* Medicare; Medi-Cal.
Owner Proprietary corp.

Mariposa

Mariposa Manor
5201 Crystal Aire Dr, Mariposa, CA 95338
(209) 966-2244
Admin JoAnn J Weston. *Dir of Nursing* Kay Martella RN. *Medical Dir* Arthur Dahlem MD.
Licensure Skilled care. *Beds* SNF 23. *Certified* Medi-Cal.
Owner Proprietary corp.
Admissions Requirements Physician's request.
Staff Physicians; RNs; LPNs; Nurses' aides; Activities coordinators.
Facilities Dining room; Activities room; Laundry room.
Activities Arts & crafts; Cards; Games; Reading groups; Prayer groups; Movies.

Martinez

Alhambra Convalescent Hospital
331 Ilene St, Martinez, CA 94553
(415) 228-2020
Admin Bob Lauderdale. *Dir of Nursing* Joyce Light RN. *Medical Dir* Dennis Stone MD.
Licensure Skilled care. *Beds* SNF 42. *Private Pay Patients* 80%. *Certified* Medicare; Medi-Cal.
Owner Privately owned.
Admissions Requirements Minimum age 55; Physician's request.
Staff Physicians 1 (pt); RNs 3 (ft), 2 (pt); LPNs 2 (ft), 3 (pt); Nurses' aides 18 (ft), 5 (pt); Physical therapists 1 (pt); Occupational therapists 1 (pt); Speech therapists 1 (pt); Activities coordinators 1 (ft); Dietitians 1 (ft), 1 (pt).
Languages Spanish, Portuguese, German, Tagalog, Italian.
Facilities Dining room; Physical therapy room; Laundry room; Barber/Beauty shop.
Activities Arts & crafts; Cards; Games; Reading groups; Prayer groups; Movies; Pet therapy.

Community Convalescent Center
1790 Muir Rd, Martinez, CA 94553
(415) 228-8383
Admin Melinda L Hutchings.
Medical Dir Dr Carlos Anderson.
Licensure Skilled care. *Beds* SNF 99. *Certified* Medicare; Medi-Cal.
Owner Proprietary corp.
Staff Physicians 1 (pt); RNs 2 (ft), 2 (pt); Nurses' aides 18 (ft), 6 (pt); Physical therapists 1 (pt); Recreational therapists 1 (pt); Occupational therapists 1 (pt); Speech therapists 1 (pt); Activities coordinators 1 (ft), 1 (pt); Dietitians 1 (pt); Ophthalmologists 1 (pt); Podiatrists 1 (pt); Audiologists 1 (pt); Dentists 1 (pt); LVNs 5 (ft), 3 (pt).
Facilities Dining room; Physical therapy room; Activities room; Laundry room; Barber/Beauty shop; Living room; Lounge.
Activities Arts & crafts; Cards; Games; Reading groups; Prayer groups; Movies; Shopping trips; Dances/Social/Cultural gatherings; Sight-seeing tours; Visits to senior center; Adult education classes.

Martinez Convalescent Hospital
4110 Alhambra Way, Martinez, CA 94553
(415) 228-4260
Admin Michael W Hart.
Licensure Skilled care. *Beds* SNF 36. *Certified* Medi-Cal.
Owner Privately owned.

Marysville

Marysville Care Center
1617 Ramirez St, Marysville, CA 95901
(916) 742-7311, 742-2356 FAX
Admin Shirley E Delamere. *Dir of Nursing* E Sutton RN. *Medical Dir* W Hoffman MD.
Licensure Skilled care. *Beds* SNF 86. *Private Pay Patients* 25%. *Certified* Medicare; Medi-Cal.
Owner Proprietary corp (Touchtone Health System Inc).
Admissions Requirements Physician's request.
Staff RNs 1 (ft), 1 (pt); LPNs 7 (ft), 2 (pt); Nurses' aides 25 (ft), 8 (pt); Physical therapists 1 (pt); Activities coordinators 1 (ft), 1 (pt); Dietitians 1 (pt); Ophthalmologists 1 (pt); Podiatrists 1 (pt).
Languages Tagalog, Spanish, Russian.
Facilities Dining room; Activities room; Crafts room; Laundry room; Barber/Beauty shop.
Activities Arts & crafts; Cards; Games; Reading groups; Prayer groups; Movies; Dances/Social/Cultural gatherings; Pet therapy.

Rideout Memorial Hospital D/P
726 4th St, Marysville, CA 95901
(916) 742-7383
Admin Thomas P Hayes.
Licensure Skilled care. *Certified* Medicare; Medi-Cal.

Maywood

Pine Crest Convalescent Hospital
6025 Pine Ave, Maywood, CA 90270
(213) 581-8151
Admin Michael Morales.
Medical Dir Edward Panzer MD.
Licensure Skilled care. *Beds* SNF 133. *Certified* Medicare; Medi-Cal.
Owner Proprietary corp (Western Medical Enterprises Inc).
Staff RNs; LPNs; Nurses' aides; Physical therapists; Reality therapists; Recreational therapists; Occupational therapists; Speech therapists; Activities coordinators; Dietitians; Ophthalmologists; Podiatrists; Audiologists; Dentists.

Facilities Dining room; Physical therapy room; Activities room; Laundry room; Barber/Beauty shop.
Activities Arts & crafts; Cards; Games; Reading groups; Prayer groups; Movies; Shopping trips; Dances/Social/Cultural gatherings.

Menlo Park

College Park Convalescent Hospital
1275 Crane St, Menlo Park, CA 94024
(415) 322-7261
Admin Charles Feist.
Licensure Skilled care. *Beds* SNF 160. *Certified* Medicare; Medi-Cal.
Owner Proprietary corp (Western Medical Enterprises Inc).

Convalescent Hospital University Branch
2122 Santa Cruz Ave, Menlo Park, CA 94025
(415) 854-4020
Admin Basil A Hogan.
Licensure Skilled care. *Beds* SNF 80. *Certified* Medicare.
Owner Proprietary corp.

Hillhaven Convalescent Hospital
16 Coleman Pl, Menlo Park, CA 94025
(415) 326-0802
Admin Elizabeth D Stanton. *Dir of Nursing* Dottie Heaney. *Medical Dir* Leo Harkavy.
Licensure Skilled care. *Beds* SNF 53. *Certified* Medicare; Medi-Cal.
Owner Proprietary corp (Hillhaven Inc).
Admissions Requirements Medical examination; Physician's request.
Staff RNs 4 (ft), 3 (pt); LPNs 4 (ft), 3 (pt); Nurses' aides 14 (ft), 6 (pt); Recreational therapists 1 (ft); Dietitians 1 (ft).
Languages Spanish, Tagalog.
Facilities Dining room; Activities room; Laundry room; Barber/Beauty shop.
Activities Arts & crafts; Games; Reading groups; Prayer groups; Shopping trips; Dances/Social/Cultural gatherings.

Le Havre Convalescent Hospital
800 Roble Ave, Menlo Park, CA 94025
(415) 323-6189
Admin Suzanne Heisler.
Licensure Skilled care. *Beds* SNF 52. *Certified* Medicare; Medi-Cal.
Owner Proprietary corp.
Admissions Requirements Minimum age 68; Medical examination.
Staff RNs; LPNs; Nurses' aides; Physical therapists; Recreational therapists; Occupational therapists; Activities coordinators; Dietitians.
Languages French, Spanish.
Facilities Dining room; Physical therapy room; Activities room; Laundry room; Barber/Beauty shop; Library.
Activities Arts & crafts; Cards; Games; Reading groups; Movies; Shopping trips; Singing group "Le Havre Seniorettes".

Sharon Heights Convalescent Hospital
1185 Monte Rosa Dr, Menlo Park, CA 94025
(415) 854-4230, 854-4950 FAX
Admin Leslee J Fennell. *Dir of Nursing* Dr Sara Roat. *Medical Dir* Morris Gutterman MD.
Licensure Skilled care. *Beds* SNF 96. *Certified* Medicare.
Owner Proprietary corp.
Admissions Requirements Medical examination; Physician's request.
Staff Physicians 2 (ft); RNs 16 (ft); LPNs 8 (ft); Nurses' aides 40 (ft); Physical therapists 4 (ft); Recreational therapists 1 (ft); Occupational therapists 1 (ft); Speech therapists 1 (ft); Activities coordinators 3 (ft); Dietitians 1 (ft).
Languages Tagalog, Spanish, Italian, Hindu, German, Dutch, Yiddish, Hebrew.

Facilities Dining room; Physical therapy room; Activities room; Chapel; Crafts room; Laundry room; Barber/Beauty shop; Library.
Activities Arts & crafts; Cards; Games; Reading groups; Prayer groups; Movies; Shopping trips; Dances/Social/Cultural gatherings; Intergenerational programs; Pet therapy.

Mentone

Braswell's Ivy Retreat
2278 Nice St, Mentone, CA 92359
(714) 794-1189
Admin Caroline J Braswell. *Dir of Nursing* Joan Byard. *Medical Dir* H J Cozzolino.
Licensure Skilled care. *Beds* SNF 50. *Certified* Medicare; Medi-Cal.
Owner Proprietary corp.
Admissions Requirements Physician's request.
Staff RNs 1 (ft), 3 (pt); LPNs 3 (ft), 2 (pt); Nurses' aides 20 (ft), 1 (pt); Activities coordinators 1 (ft); Dietitians 1 (ft).
Languages Spanish, German.
Facilities Dining room; Activities room; Laundry room; Barber/Beauty shop.
Activities Arts & crafts; Cards; Games; Reading groups; Prayer groups; Movies; Dances/Social/Cultural gatherings.

Merced

Franciscan Convalescent Hospital
3169 M St, Merced, CA 95340
(209) 722-6231
Admin Carmella Williams.
Licensure Skilled care. *Beds* SNF 71. *Certified* Medicare; Medi-Cal.
Owner Proprietary corp (Beverly Enterprises).
Affiliation Roman Catholic.

Hy-Lond Convalescent Hospital
3170 M St, Merced, CA 95340
(209) 723-1056
Admin Laverle Emmerson. *Dir of Nursing* Joyce Russo.
Licensure Skilled care. *Beds* SNF 121. *Certified* Medicare; Medi-Cal.
Owner Proprietary corp (Beverly Enterprises).
Admissions Requirements Medical examination; Physician's request.
Staff RNs; LPNs; Nurses' aides; Physical therapists; Occupational therapists; Speech therapists; Activities coordinators.
Languages Spanish, Italian, Portuguese, Tagalog.
Facilities Dining room; Physical therapy room; Activities room; Crafts room; Laundry room; Barber/Beauty shop; Library.
Activities Arts & crafts; Cards; Games; Reading groups; Prayer groups; Movies; Shopping trips; Dances/Social/Cultural gatherings; Field trips; Cooking groups.

La Sierra Convalescent Hospital
2424 M St, Merced, CA 95340
(209) 723-4224
Admin Charles Roy Wagner.
Medical Dir Dr Arthur Dahlem.
Licensure Skilled care. *Beds* SNF 68. *Certified* Medicare; Medi-Cal.
Owner Proprietary corp.
Admissions Requirements Medical examination; Physician's request.
Staff Physicians 1 (pt); RNs 1 (ft), 1 (pt); LPNs 5 (ft), 1 (pt); Nurses' aides 38 (ft), 6 (pt); Physical therapists 1 (pt); Occupational therapists 1 (pt); Speech therapists 1 (pt); Activities coordinators 1 (ft); Dietitians 1 (pt); Podiatrists 1 (pt); Audiologists 1 (pt); Dentists 1 (pt).

Merced Convalescent Hospital
510 W 26th St, Merced, CA 95340
(209) 723-2911
Admin Cory Glad.
Medical Dir Dr Arthur Dahlem.

Licensure Skilled care. *Beds* SNF 79. *Certified* Medicare; Medi-Cal.
Owner Proprietary corp.
Admissions Requirements Medical examination; Physician's request.
Staff Physicians 1 (pt); RNs 1 (ft), 1 (pt); LPNs 5 (ft), 2 (pt); Nurses' aides 28 (ft), 12 (pt); Physical therapists 1 (pt); Occupational therapists 1 (pt); Speech therapists 1 (pt); Activities coordinators 1 (ft); Dietitians 1 (pt); Podiatrists 1 (pt); Audiologists 1 (pt); Dentists 1 (pt).

Merced Manor
1255 B St, Merced, CA 95340
(209) 723-8814
Admin Eric Williams. *Dir of Nursing* Ruth Bonath RN. *Medical Dir* Arthur Harris MD.
Licensure Skilled care. *Beds* SNF 96. *Certified* Medi-Cal.
Owner Proprietary corp.
Admissions Requirements Minimum age 18; Physician's request.
Staff RNs 2 (ft), 1 (pt); LPNs 8 (ft); Nurses' aides 25 (ft); Activities coordinators 1 (ft); Counselors 9 (ft), 4 (pt).
Facilities Dining room; Activities room; Laundry room; Barber/Beauty shop.
Activities Arts & crafts; Cards; Games; Reading groups; Movies; Shopping trips; Dances/Social/Cultural gatherings.

Mill Valley

Hillhaven Convalescent Center
505 Miller Ave, Mill Valley, CA 94941
(415) 388-0661
Admin Paul D Tunnell.
Licensure Skilled care. *Beds* SNF 120. *Certified* Medicare; Medi-Cal.
Owner Proprietary corp (Hillhaven Inc).

Redwoods
40 Camino Alto, Mill Valley, CA 94941
(415) 383-2741
Admin Melvin Matsumoto.
Licensure Skilled care. *Beds* SNF 58. *Certified* Medi-Cal.
Owner Nonprofit corp.

Millbrae

Millbrae Serra Convalescent Hospital
150 Serra Ave, Millbrae, CA 94030
(415) 697-8386
Admin Vincent A Muzzi. *Dir of Nursing* Mrs Shiek RN. *Medical Dir* Richard Avlwurm MD.
Licensure Skilled care. *Beds* SNF 125. *Certified* Medi-Cal.
Owner Proprietary corp.
Admissions Requirements Physician's request.
Staff Physicians 1 (pt); RNs 10 (ft), 1 (pt); LPNs 4 (ft); Nurses' aides 60 (ft); Recreational therapists 3 (ft); Dietitians 1 (pt).
Languages Italian, Spanish.
Facilities Dining room; Activities room; Laundry room.
Activities Arts & crafts; Cards; Games; Reading groups; Prayer groups; Movies; Dances/Social/Cultural gatherings; Outings.

Sheltering Pine Convalescent Hospital
33 Mateo Ave, Millbrae, CA 94030
(415) 583-8937
Admin Anne Christine Dillon. *Dir of Nursing* Virginia Xroglione RN. *Medical Dir* Irving Stern MD.
Licensure Skilled care; Community care; Retirement. *Beds* SNF 140; Community care 50. *Certified* Medicare; Medi-Cal.
Owner Proprietary corp (Golden State Health Centers Inc).
Admissions Requirements Physician's request.

Staff RNs 7 (ft), 7 (pt); Nurses' aides 55 (ft); Physical therapists 1 (pt); Occupational therapists 1 (pt); Speech therapists 1 (pt); Activities coordinators 5 (ft); Dietitians 1 (ft).
Languages Spanish, Samoan, Filipino, Italian.
Facilities Dining room; Physical therapy room; Activities room; Laundry room; Barber/Beauty shop; Library.
Activities Arts & crafts; Cards; Games; Reading groups; Prayer groups; Movies; Shopping trips; Dances/Social/Cultural gatherings; Pet therapy.

Milpitas

Rosscare Convalescent Hospital
120 Corning Ave, Milpitas, CA 95035
(408) 262-0217
Admin Laura Eisenhart. *Dir of Nursing* Julie Dajano RN. *Medical Dir* Norman Woods MD.
Licensure Skilled care. *Beds* SNF 35. *Private Pay Patients* 40%. *Certified* Medicaid; Medicare; Medi-Cal.
Owner Privately owned.
Admissions Requirements Minimum age 55.
Staff RNs; Nurses' aides.
Facilities Dining room; Activities room.
Activities Arts & crafts; Cards; Games; Reading groups; Prayer groups; Movies; Dances/Social/Cultural gatherings; Pet therapy.

Mission Hills

Coronado Sanitarium
PO Box 5536, Mission Hills, CA 91395-0536
(213) 380-3186
Admin Lilly Binbaum.
Medical Dir Dr Ferdinand Kunze.
Licensure Skilled care. *Beds* SNF 22. *Certified* Medi-Cal.
Owner Proprietary corp.
Admissions Requirements Physician's request.
Facilities Dining room; Activities room; Crafts room; Laundry room.
Activities Arts & crafts; Cards; Games; Reading groups; Prayer groups.

Modesto

Casa De Modesto
1745 Eldena Way, Modesto, CA 95350
(209) 529-4950
Admin Carolyn Myers Amaral.
Licensure Skilled care. *Beds* SNF 59. *Certified* Medi-Cal.
Owner Nonprofit corp.

Colony Park Care Center
159 E Orangeburg, Modesto, CA 95350
(209) 526-2811
Admin Debra Campbell.
Medical Dir Dr M Harris.
Licensure Skilled care. *Beds* SNF 99. *Certified* Medicare; Medi-Cal.
Owner Proprietary corp.
Admissions Requirements Physician's request.
Staff RNs 1 (ft), 3 (pt); LPNs 7 (ft), 3 (pt); Nurses' aides 35 (ft), 6 (pt); Physical therapists 2 (pt); Recreational therapists 1 (ft), 1 (pt); Occupational therapists 1 (pt); Activities coordinators 1 (pt); Activities coordinators 1 (ft); Dietitians 2 (pt); Ophthalmologists 1 (pt).
Languages Spanish, Cambodian, Hindi, Portuguese.
Facilities Dining room; Physical therapy room; Activities room; Crafts room; Laundry room; Barber/Beauty shop; Coffee shop; Family style dining.
Activities Arts & crafts; Cards; Games; Reading groups; Prayer groups; Movies; Shopping trips; Dances/Social/Cultural gatherings; Exercises; Coffee social.

Crestwood Manor
1400 Celeste Dr, Modesto, CA 95355
(209) 526-8050
Admin Michael Wiederstein.
Licensure Intermediate care for mentally retarded. *Beds* ICF/MR 192. *Certified* Medi-Cal.
Owner Proprietary corp (Crestwood Hospitals Inc).

Edson Convalescent Hospital
3604 Kona Oak Dr, Modesto, CA 95355
(209) 577-3200
Admin David G Howell.
Licensure Skilled care. *Beds* 25. *Certified* Medicare; Medi-Cal.
Owner Proprietary corp.

English Oaks Convalescent Hospital & Rehabilitation Center
2633 W Rumble Rd, Modesto, CA 95350
(209) 577-1001, 577-0366 FAX
Admin Terry L Mundy; Michael Wray RN, Asst. *Dir of Nursing* Karl Olson RN. *Medical Dir* Dr Marvin Montgomery.
Licensure Skilled care; Alzheimer's care. *Beds* SNF 182. *Private Pay Patients* 75%. *Certified* Medicare; Medi-Cal.
Owner Proprietary corp.
Admissions Requirements Minimum age 16; Medical examination; Physician's request.
Staff RNs 30 (ft), 10 (pt); LPNs 20 (ft), 5 (pt); Nurses' aides 75 (ft), 25 (pt); Physical therapists 1 (ft), 2 (pt); Occupational therapists 1 (pt); Speech therapists 1 (pt); Activities coordinators 2 (ft), 1 (pt).
Languages Spanish, Portuguese.
Facilities Dining room; Physical therapy room; Activities room; Chapel; Crafts room; Laundry room; Barber/Beauty shop; Library.
Activities Arts & crafts; Cards; Games; Reading groups; Prayer groups; Movies; Shopping trips; Dances/Social/Cultural gatherings; Intergenerational programs; Pet therapy.

Evergreen Convalescent Hospital Inc
2030 Evergreen Ave, Modesto, CA 95350
(209) 577-1055
Admin Daniel J Cipponeri.
Licensure Skilled care. *Beds* SNF 175. *Certified* Medicare; Medi-Cal.
Owner Proprietary corp.

Hillhaven Convalescent Center—Modesto
1310 W Granger, Modesto, CA 95350
(209) 524-4817
Admin John J Roberts.
Medical Dir Marvin Montgomery MD.
Licensure Skilled care. *Beds* SNF 104. *Certified* Medicare; Medi-Cal.
Owner Proprietary corp (Hillhaven Inc).
Staff RNs 7 (ft); LPNs 11 (ft); Nurses' aides 42 (ft); Physical therapists 1 (pt); Occupational therapists 1 (pt); Speech therapists 1 (pt); Activities coordinators 1 (ft), 1 (pt); Dietitians 1 (pt); Podiatrists 1 (pt).
Facilities Dining room; Physical therapy room; Activities room; Crafts room; Laundry room; Barber/Beauty shop.
Activities Arts & crafts; Cards; Games; Reading groups; Prayer groups; Movies; Shopping trips; Dances/Social/Cultural gatherings.

Hy-Lond Convalescent Hospital
1900 Coffee Rd, Modesto, CA 95350
(209) 526-1775
Admin Mark Paulsen.
Medical Dir Mattice Harris MD.
Licensure Skilled care. *Beds* SNF 120. *Certified* Medicare; Medi-Cal.
Owner Proprietary corp (Beverly Enterprises).
Admissions Requirements Medical examination.

Staff RNs 4 (ft), 2 (pt); LPNs 12 (ft), 3 (pt); Physical therapists 1 (ft); Reality therapists 1 (pt); Recreational therapists 1 (pt); Speech therapists 1 (pt); Activities coordinators 1 (ft), 1 (pt); Dietitians 1 (ft), 1 (pt); Ophthalmologists 1 (pt); Podiatrists 1 (pt); Audiologists 1 (pt); Dentists 1 (pt).
Facilities Dining room; Physical therapy room; Activities room; Crafts room; Laundry room; Barber/Beauty shop; Library.
Activities Arts & crafts; Cards; Games; Reading groups; Prayer groups; Movies; Shopping trips; Dances/Social/Cultural gatherings.

Modesto Convalescent Hospital
515 E Orangeburg Ave, Modesto, CA 95350
(209) 529-0516
Admin Janice Rayome.
Licensure Skilled care. *Beds* SNF 70. *Certified* Medicare; Medi-Cal.
Owner Proprietary corp (Beverly Enterprises).

Orangeburg Convalescent Hospital
823 E Orangeburg Ave, Modesto, CA 95350
(209) 524-4641
Admin David G Howell.
Licensure Skilled care. *Beds* SNF 40. *Certified* Medi-Cal.
Owner Proprietary corp.

Reno Convalescent Hospital
1028 Reno Ave, Modesto, CA 95351
(209) 524-1146
Admin David G Howell. *Dir of Nursing* Vera Jennings RN. *Medical Dir* Dr Grant Bare.
Licensure Skilled care. *Beds* SNF 25. *Certified* Medi-Cal.
Owner Proprietary corp (Jaecare Inc).
Admissions Requirements Minimum age 65; Medical examination; Physician's request.
Staff RNs 2 (ft), 1 (pt); LPNs 1 (ft), 2 (pt); Nurses' aides 9 (ft), 1 (pt); Activities coordinators 1 (ft).
Languages Spanish, Hindi, Chinese.
Facilities Dining room; Activities room; Crafts room; Laundry room.
Activities Arts & crafts; Cards; Games; Reading groups; Prayer groups; Movies; Shopping trips; Dances/Social/Cultural gatherings.

Scenic Circle Care Center
1611 Scenic Dr, Modesto, CA 95355
(209) 523-5667
Admin Donna K Etchison. *Dir of Nursing* Paul Langenbacker. *Medical Dir* Robert Chin MD.
Licensure Skilled care. *Beds* SNF 99. *Private Pay Patients* 4%. *Certified* Medicare; Medi-Cal.
Owner Proprietary corp.
Staff RNs 4 (ft), 1 (pt); LPNs 3 (ft), 1 (pt); Nurses' aides 24 (ft); Physical therapists 2 (pt); Occupational therapists 1 (pt); Speech therapists 1 (pt); Activities coordinators 1 (ft), 1 (pt); Dietitians 1 (pt); Podiatrists 1 (pt); Audiologists 1 (pt).
Facilities Dining room; Physical therapy room; Activities room; Laundry room; Barber/Beauty shop.
Activities Arts & crafts; Cards; Games; Reading groups; Prayer groups; Movies; Shopping trips; Dances/Social/Cultural gatherings; Pet therapy.

Vintage Faire Convalescent Hospital
3620 B Dale Rd, Modesto, CA 95356
(209) 521-2094, 521-4159 FAX
Admin C Lynne Collins. *Dir of Nursing* Kathleen England. *Medical Dir* Vance Roget MD.
Licensure Skilled care; Residential care. *Beds* SNF 99; Residential care 49. *Private Pay Patients* 40%. *Certified* Medicare; Medi-Cal.
Owner Privately owned.
Admissions Requirements Physician's request.

Staff Physicians (contracted); RNs; Nurses' aides; Physical therapists; Recreational therapists (contracted); Occupational therapists; Speech therapists; Activities coordinators; Dietitians; Ophthalmologists (contracted); Podiatrists (contracted); Audiologists (contracted); LVNs.
Languages Spanish, Dutch.
Facilities Dining room; Physical therapy room; Activities room; Crafts room; Laundry room; Barber/Beauty shop.
Activities Arts & crafts; Cards; Games; Reading groups; Prayer groups; Movies; Shopping trips; Dances/Social/Cultural gatherings; Intergenerational programs; Pet therapy.

Monrovia

Beverly Manor Convalescent Hospital
615 W Duarte Rd, Monrovia, CA 91016
(818) 358-4547
Admin Slyvia Colton.
Licensure Skilled care. *Beds* SNF 99. *Certified* Medicare; Medi-Cal.
Owner Proprietary corp (Beverly Enterprises).

Montclair

Community Convalescent Hospital of Montclair
9620 Fremont Ave, Montclair, CA 91763
(714) 621-4751
Admin Richard J Kapsch.
Medical Dir Herman Mirkin MD.
Licensure Skilled care. *Beds* SNF 140. *Certified* Medicare; Medi-Cal.
Owner Proprietary corp.
Staff RNs 5 (ft), 4 (pt); LPNs 9 (ft), 8 (pt); Nurses' aides 52 (ft), 10 (pt); Physical therapists 1 (pt); Reality therapists 1 (pt); Recreational therapists 1 (pt); Occupational therapists 1 (pt); Speech therapists 1 (pt); Activities coordinators 2 (ft); Dietitians 1 (pt); Ophthalmologists 1 (pt); Podiatrists 1 (pt); Dentists 1 (pt).
Facilities Dining room; Physical therapy room; Activities room; Crafts room; Laundry room; Barber/Beauty shop; Library; Coffee room.
Activities Arts & crafts; Cards; Games; Reading groups; Prayer groups; Movies; Dances/Social/Cultural gatherings; Parties.

Montclair Manor Convalescent Hospital
5119 Bandera St, Montclair, CA 91763
(714) 626-1294
Admin Margaret Brown. *Dir of Nursing* Mary Fletcher. *Medical Dir* Robert Bom MD.
Licensure Skilled care. *Beds* SNF 59. *Certified* Medicare; Medi-Cal.
Owner Proprietary corp (Medicrest of California).
Staff RNs; Nurses' aides; Physical therapists; Reality therapists; Occupational therapists; Speech therapists; Activities coordinators; Dietitians; Podiatrists; Audiologists; LVNs.
Facilities Dining room; Physical therapy room; Activities room; Crafts room; Laundry room; Barber/Beauty shop; Library.
Activities Arts & crafts; Cards; Games; Prayer groups; Movies; Shopping trips; Pet therapy.

Monte Vista Child Care Center
9140 Monte Vista, Montclair, CA 91763
(714) 624-2774
Admin Barbara Risinger.
Licensure Intermediate care for mentally retarded. *Beds* 58. *Certified* Medi-Cal.
Owner Proprietary corp.
Admissions Requirements Minimum age 8; Medical examination; Physician's request.
Staff RNs; LPNs; Nurses' aides; Activities coordinators.
Facilities Dining room; Crafts room; Laundry room; Program rooms.
Activities Arts & crafts; Movies; Shopping trips.

Montebello

Care West—Montebello Convalescent Hospital
1035 W Beverly Blvd, Montebello, CA 90640
(213) 724-1315
Admin Joye Tsuchiyama.
Licensure Skilled care. *Beds* SNF 99. *Certified* Medicare; Medi-Cal.
Owner Proprietary corp (Care Enterprises).

Care West Rio Hondo Nursing Center
273 E Beverly Blvd, Montebello, CA 90640
(213) 724-5100
Admin Mike Yaldezian.
Medical Dir Dr L Pollock.
Licensure Skilled care. *Beds* SNF 200. *Certified* Medicare; Medi-Cal.
Owner Proprietary corp (Care Enterprises).
Admissions Requirements Minimum age 18; Medical examination; Physician's request.
Staff Physicians 30 (ft); RNs 15 (ft); LPNs 20 (ft); Nurses' aides 80 (ft); Physical therapists 1 (ft); Occupational therapists; Speech therapists; Activities coordinators 3 (ft); Dietitians 1 (ft); Ophthalmologists; Podiatrists; Dentists; Physical therapy aides 1 (ft); Assistants 1 (ft); Restorative CNAs 3 (ft).
Facilities Dining room; Physical therapy room; Activities room; Crafts room; Laundry room; Barber/Beauty shop.
Activities Arts & crafts; Cards; Games; Reading groups; Prayer groups; Movies; Shopping trips.

Montecito

Casa Dorinda
300 Hot Springs Rd, Montecito, CA 93108
(805) 969-8026
Admin William Ducharme.
Medical Dir Dr Robert Hartzman.
Licensure Skilled care. *Beds* 47. *Certified* Medicare; Medi-Cal.
Owner Proprietary corp.
Admissions Requirements Medical examination.
Staff Physicians 1 (pt); RNs 8 (ft), 3 (pt); LPNs 4 (ft), 1 (pt); Nurses' aides 13 (ft); Physical therapists 2 (ft); Occupational therapists 1 (pt); Speech therapists 1 (pt); Activities coordinators 1 (ft), 1 (pt); Dietitians 1 (pt); Podiatrists 1 (pt); Dentists 1 (pt).
Facilities Dining room; Physical therapy room; Activities room; Crafts room; Laundry room; Barber/Beauty shop; Library.
Activities Arts & crafts; Cards; Games; Reading groups; Prayer groups; Movies; Shopping trips; Dances/Social/Cultural gatherings; Picnics; Rides; Barbeques.

Monterey

Ave Maria Convalescent Hospital
1249 Josselyn Canyon Rd, Monterey, CA 93940
(408) 373-1216
Admin Sr M C Petrucelli.
Medical Dir Olga Titus.
Licensure Skilled care; Alzheimer's care. *Beds* SNF 30.
Owner Publicly owned.
Admissions Requirements Physician's request.
Staff RNs 2 (ft); LPNs 3 (ft); Nurses' aides 18 (ft); Activities coordinators 2 (ft).
Affiliation Roman Catholic.
Facilities Dining room; Activities room; Chapel; Crafts room; Laundry room; Barber/ Beauty shop; Library; TV room.
Activities Arts & crafts; Cards; Games; Reading groups; Prayer groups; Movies; Shopping trips; Dances/Social/Cultural gatherings; Music; Trips to fairs, horse shows & seashore.

Beverly Manor Convalescent Hospital
23795 W R Holman Hwy, Monterey, CA 93940
(408) 624-1875
Admin Issac Verhage.
Medical Dir Donald M Dubrasich MD.
Licensure Skilled care. *Beds* SNF 99. *Certified* Medicare; Medi-Cal.
Owner Proprietary corp (Beverly Enterprises).
Admissions Requirements Physician's request.
Facilities Dining room; Physical therapy room; Activities room; Crafts room; Laundry room; Barber/Beauty shop; Library.
Activities Arts & crafts; Cards; Games; Reading groups; Prayer groups; Movies; Shopping trips; Dances/Social/Cultural gatherings.

Driftwood Convalescent Hospital
1575 Skyline Dr, Monterey, CA 93940
(408) 373-2731
Admin David Holtz.
Licensure Skilled care. *Beds* SNF 77. *Certified* Medicare; Medi-Cal.
Owner Proprietary corp (Western Medical Enterprises Inc).
Staff RNs 4 (ft), 2 (pt); LPNs 3 (ft), 3 (pt); Nurses' aides 20 (ft), 8 (pt); Activities coordinators 1 (ft); Dietitians 1 (ft).
Facilities Dining room; Physical therapy room; Laundry room; Barber/Beauty shop.
Activities Arts & crafts; Cards; Games; Reading groups; Prayer groups; Movies.

Hospice of the Central Coast
PO Box 2480, Monterey, CA 93942-2480
(408) 625-0441, 648-4205 FAX
Admin James Shelton.
Licensure Skilled care. *Beds* SNF 6. *Certified* Medicare; Medi-Cal.
Owner Nonprofit corp.
Staff RNs; LPNs; Nurses' aides.

Monterey Convalescent Hospital
735 Pacific St, Monterey, CA 93940
(408) 373-1323
Licensure Skilled care. *Beds* SNF 52. *Certified* Medicare; Medi-Cal.
Owner Proprietary corp.

Monterey Pines Skilled Nursing Facility
1501 Skyline Dr, Monterey, CA 93940
(408) 373-3716
Admin Linda Curtis.
Medical Dir Harry Nervino MD.
Licensure Skilled care. *Beds* SNF 99. *Certified* Medicare; Medi-Cal.
Owner Proprietary corp.
Admissions Requirements Medical examination; Physician's request.
Staff RNs 3 (ft), 1 (pt); Nurses' aides 33 (ft), 5 (pt); Physical therapists 1 (pt); Occupational therapists 1 (pt); Speech therapists 1 (pt); Activities coordinators 1 (ft); Dietitians 1 (pt); Ophthalmologists 1 (pt); Podiatrists 1 (pt); Dentists 1 (pt); LVNs 8 (ft), 5 (pt).
Languages Spanish, Russian, German, Tagalog, Korean, Japanese.
Facilities Dining room; Physical therapy room; Activities room; Crafts room; Laundry room; Barber/Beauty shop.
Activities Arts & crafts; Cards; Games; Reading groups; Prayer groups; Movies; Shopping trips; Dances/Social/Cultural gatherings.

Monterey Park

Hillhaven Health Care
610 N Garfield Ave, Monterey Park, CA 91754
(213) 573-3141
Admin Dixie Leyhe.
Medical Dir Sander Peck.
Licensure Skilled care. *Beds* SNF 99. *Certified* Medicare; Medi-Cal.
Owner Proprietary corp (Hillhaven Inc).

Staff RNs 3 (ft); LPNs 8 (ft); Nurses' aides 42 (ft); Physical therapists 1 (pt); Reality therapists 1 (pt); Recreational therapists 1 (ft); Occupational therapists 1 (pt); Speech therapists 1 (pt); Activities coordinators 1 (ft); Dietitians 1 (pt); Ophthalmologists 1 (pt); Podiatrists 1 (pt); Audiologists 1 (pt); Dentists 1 (pt).
Facilities Dining room; Physical therapy room; Activities room; Crafts room; Laundry room; Barber/Beauty shop.
Activities Arts & crafts; Cards; Games; Reading groups; Prayer groups; Movies; Shopping trips; Dances/Social/Cultural gatherings.

Monterey Park Convalescent Hospital
416 N Garfield Ave, Monterey Park, CA 91754
(213) 280-0280
Admin Jon A Boerger.
Licensure Skilled care. *Beds* SNF 89. *Certified* Medicare; Medi-Cal.
Owner Proprietary corp.

Montrose

Montrose Convalescent Hospital
2123 Verdugo Blvd, Montrose, CA 91020
(818) 249-3925, 249-8832 FAX
Admin Kerry Davis. *Dir of Nursing* Janet Spivack RN. *Medical Dir* Albert P Killian MD.
Licensure Skilled care. *Beds* SNF 59. *Certified* Medicare; Medi-Cal.
Owner Proprietary corp (Beverly Enterprises).
Admissions Requirements Minimum age 21; Medical examination; Physician's request.
Staff RNs 2 (ft), 3 (pt); LPNs 5 (ft), 3 (pt); Nurses' aides 15 (ft), 9 (pt).
Languages Spanish.
Facilities Dining room; Activities room; Barber/Beauty shop.
Activities Prayer groups; Dances/Social/ Cultural gatherings; Entertainment; Musicals; Exercise; Religious gatherings; Special dinner groups.

Verdugo Valley Convalescent Hospital
2635 Honolulu Ave, Montrose, CA 91020
(818) 248-6856
Admin Helen Tanner.
Licensure Skilled care. *Beds* SNF 108; Swing beds SNF/ICF 30. *Certified* Medicare; Medi-Cal.
Owner Proprietary corp.

Moraga

Rheem Valley Convalescent Hospital
348 Rheem Blvd, Moraga, CA 94556
(415) 376-5995
Licensure Skilled care. *Beds* SNF 49. *Certified* Medicare.
Owner Proprietary corp.

Morgan Hill

Hillview Convalescent Hospital
530 W Dunne & Laselva, Morgan Hill, CA 95037
(408) 779-3633
Admin James S Ross. *Dir of Nursing* Elena Dunton. *Medical Dir* Dr B Joyce.
Licensure Skilled care; Intermediate care. *Beds* SNF 40; ICF 12. *Certified* Medi-Cal.
Owner Privately owned.
Admissions Requirements Medical examination; Geriatrics only.
Staff RNs 1 (ft), 2 (pt); LPNs 3 (ft), 2 (pt); Nurses' aides 16 (ft), 5 (pt); Activities coordinators 1 (ft), 1 (pt).
Languages Spanish, Tagalog, French.

Facilities Dining room; Activities room; Laundry room.
Activities Arts & crafts; Cards; Games; Prayer groups; Movies; Dances/Social/Cultural gatherings.

Pleasant Acres Convalescent Hospital
17090 Peak Ave, Morgan Hill, CA 95037
(408) 779-2252
Admin Ralph N Tisdial.
Licensure Skilled care. *Beds* 29. *Certified* Medicare; Medi-Cal.
Owner Proprietary corp.

Rosscare Convalescent Hospital
370 Noble Ct, Morgan Hill, CA 95037
(408) 779-7346
Admin Michael Skaggs.
Licensure Skilled care. *Beds* SNF 99. *Certified* Medicare; Medi-Cal.
Owner Privately owned.

Morro Bay

Morro Bay Convalescent Center
Hwy 1 at S Bay Blvd, Morro Bay, CA 93442
(805) 772-2237
Admin Pauline I Elders.
Licensure Skilled care. *Beds* 74. *Certified* Medicare; Medi-Cal.
Owner Proprietary corp.

Pacific Care Center Inc
1405 Teresa Dr, Morro Bay, CA 93442
(805) 772-2237
Admin George P Sigler.
Licensure Skilled care. *Beds* SNF 145. *Certified* Medicare; Medi-Cal.
Owner Proprietary corp.

Mount Shasta

Mercy Medical Center Mt Shasta DP/SNF
914 Pine St, Mount Shasta, CA 96067
(916) 926-6111
Admin James R Hoss.

Mountain View

Grant Cuesta Convalescent Hospital
1949 Grant Rd, Mountain View, CA 94040
(415) 986-2990
Admin Betsy Dickinson.
Medical Dir Patricia Guilfoy.
Licensure Skilled care. *Beds* SNF 104. *Certified* Medicare; Medi-Cal.
Owner Proprietary corp.
Admissions Requirements Physician's request.
Staff Physicians 1 (pt); RNs 3 (ft), 4 (pt); LPNs 6 (ft), 4 (pt); Nurses' aides 32 (ft), 11 (pt); Physical therapists 4 (pt); Reality therapists 1 (ft), 1 (pt); Occupational therapists 1 (pt); Speech therapists 1 (pt); Activities coordinators 1 (ft), 1 (pt); Dietitians 1 (ft), 1 (pt); Ophthalmologists 1 (pt).
Facilities Dining room; Physical therapy room; Activities room; Crafts room; Laundry room; Barber/Beauty shop; Library services; Patio; BBQ.
Activities Arts & crafts; Games; Reading groups; Prayer groups; Movies; Musical entertainment; Animal visits.

Julia Convalescent Hospital
276 Sierra Vista Ave, Mountain View, CA 94043
(415) 967-5714
Admin Ron McKaigg.
Medical Dir Dr Inocencio.
Licensure Skilled care. *Beds* SNF 99. *Certified* Medicare; Medi-Cal.
Owner Proprietary corp (Beverly Enterprises).
Staff Physicians; RNs; LPNs; Nurses' aides; Physical therapists; Reality therapists; Recreational therapists; Occupational therapists; Speech therapists; Activities coordinators; Dietitians; Ophthalmologists; Dentists.
Facilities Dining room; Physical therapy room; Activities room; Crafts room; Barber/Beauty shop; TV rooms.
Activities Arts & crafts; Cards; Games; Prayer groups; Movies; Dances/Social/Cultural gatherings; Adult education classes.

Mountain View Convalescent Hospital
2530 Solace Pl, Mountain View, CA 94040
(415) 961-6161, 967-7878 FAX
Admin Jennifer E Okamoto. *Dir of Nursing* Sylvie Deschenes. *Medical Dir* Stephen Nichols.
Licensure Skilled care; Alzheimer's care. *Beds* SNF 138; Alzheimer's care 33. *Certified* Medicare; Medi-Cal.
Owner Proprietary corp.
Admissions Requirements Physician's request.
Staff RNs 10 (ft), 2 (pt); LPNs 8 (ft), 1 (pt); Nurses' aides 60 (ft), 10 (pt); Physical therapists; Activities coordinators 1 (ft); Dietitians; Geriatric nurse practitioners.
Languages French, Spanish, Tagalog, Haitian.
Facilities Dining room; Physical therapy room; Activities room; Crafts room; Laundry room; Barber/Beauty shop.
Activities Arts & crafts; Cards; Games; Reading groups; Prayer groups; Movies; Shopping trips; Dances/Social/Cultural gatherings; Intergenerational programs; Pet therapy.

Villa Siena
1855 Miramonte Ave, Mountain View, CA 94040
(415) 961-6484
Admin Carl Braginsky. *Dir of Nursing* Mary McCue.
Licensure Skilled care; Retirement. *Beds* SNF 20. *Certified* Medi-Cal.
Owner Nonprofit corp.
Admissions Requirements Minimum age 62; Medical examination.
Staff RNs 2 (ft); LPNs 6 (ft).
Languages Spanish.
Facilities Dining room; Activities room; Chapel; Barber/Beauty shop.
Activities Arts & crafts; Games; Prayer groups; Movies.

Murrieta

Golden Triangle Nursing Center
25500 Medical Center, Murrieta, CA 92363
(714) 677-8606
Admin Daryl S Crane.
Licensure Skilled care. *Beds* SNF 99. *Certified* Medicare; Medi-Cal.
Owner Proprietary corp.

Napa

Crystal Care Center
2300 Brown St, Napa, CA 94558
(707) 226-1821
Admin Ralph Holder.
Licensure Skilled care; Alzheimer's care. *Beds* SNF 84. *Private Pay Patients* 10%. *Certified* Medicaid; Medicare; Medi-Cal.
Owner Proprietary corp.
Admissions Requirements Medical examination; Physician's request.
Staff Physicians; RNs; LPNs; Nurses' aides; Physical therapists; Recreational therapists; Occupational therapists; Speech therapists; Activities coordinators; Dietitians; Ophthalmologists; Podiatrists; Audiologists.
Facilities Dining room; Physical therapy room; Activities room; Crafts room; Laundry room; Barber/Beauty shop.

Activities Arts & crafts; Cards; Games; Reading groups; Prayer groups; Movies; Shopping trips; Dances/Social/Cultural gatherings; Intergenerational programs; Pet therapy.

Napa Nursing Center
3275 Villa Ln, Napa, CA 94558
(707) 257-0931
Admin John Collister. *Dir of Nursing* Shirley Collins.
Licensure Skilled care; Intermediate care. *Beds* SNF 30; ICF 100. *Private Pay Patients* 35-40%. *Certified* Medicare; Medi-Cal.
Owner Proprietary corp (Sierra Medical Enterprises).
Admissions Requirements Medical examination; Physician's request.
Staff RNs 14 (ft); LPNs 12 (ft); Nurses' aides 30 (ft); Physical therapists 2 (pt); Recreational therapists 1 (pt); Occupational therapists 1 (pt); Speech therapists 1 (pt); Activities coordinators 2 (ft); Dietitians 1 (ft); Ophthalmologists 2 (pt).
Languages Spanish.
Facilities Dining room; Physical therapy room; Activities room; Chapel; Laundry room; Barber/Beauty shop; Library; Reading room; TV room; Private & semi-private rooms; Enclosed courtyards.
Activities Arts & crafts; Games; Movies; Pet therapy; Seniorcise (Exercise).

Piner's Nursing Home
1800 Pueblo Ave, Napa, CA 94558
(707) 224-7925
Admin Gary Piner.
Medical Dir Robert Gaither.
Licensure Skilled care; Retirement. *Beds* SNF 49. *Certified* Medicare; Medi-Cal.
Owner Proprietary corp.
Admissions Requirements Medical examination; Physician's request.
Staff RNs; LPNs; Nurses' aides; Physical therapists; Recreational therapists; Occupational therapists; Speech therapists; Activities coordinators; Dietitians.
Facilities Dining room; Activities room; Crafts room; Laundry room; Barber/Beauty shop.
Activities Arts & crafts; Cards; Games; Reading groups; Movies.

Redwood Christian Convalescent Hospital
2465 Redwood Rd, Napa, CA 94558
(707) 255-3012
Admin Whiffy Kleimer. *Dir of Nursing* Geraldine Furth. *Medical Dir* Dr Ronald Julis.
Licensure Skilled care; Alzheimer's care. *Beds* SNF 59. *Certified* Medicare; Medi-Cal.
Owner Privately owned.
Admissions Requirements Physician's request.
Staff RNs; LPNs; Nurses' aides; Activities coordinators; Dietitians.
Languages Spanish.
Facilities Dining room; Activities room; Barber/Beauty shop; Library.
Activities Arts & crafts; Games; Reading groups; Prayer groups; Movies; Shopping trips.

Roberts Nursing Home
3415 Browns Valley Rd, Napa, CA 94558
(707) 257-3515
Admin Edythe Cambra. *Dir of Nursing* Pamela Kinsey RN.
Licensure Skilled care. *Beds* SNF 35. *Certified* Medi-Cal.
Owner Privately owned.
Admissions Requirements Medical examination; Physician's request.
Staff RNs; Nurses' aides; Activities coordinators; LVNs.
Activities Arts & crafts; Games; Reading groups; Prayer groups; Movies.

Sierra Vista Care Center
705 Trancas St, Napa, CA 94558
(707) 255-6060, 255-6081 FAX
Admin Leanne Martinsen. *Dir of Nursing*
Judy Temple RN. *Medical Dir* Allan
Northam MD.
Licensure Skilled care. *Beds* SNF 120. *Private
Pay Patients* 20%. *Certified* Medicare; Medi-
Cal.
Owner Proprietary corp (Beverly Enterprises).
Admissions Requirements Medical
examination; Physician's request.
Staff RNs 9 (ft), 2 (pt); LPNs 5 (ft), 4 (pt);
Nurses' aides 27 (ft), 7 (pt); Physical
therapists 1 (ft); Activities coordinators 1
(ft), 1 (pt).
Facilities Dining room; Physical therapy
room; Activities room; Crafts room; Barber/
Beauty shop; Gardens; Room with fireplace;
Sitting rooms; Smokers sitting room.
Activities Arts & crafts; Cards; Games;
Reading groups; Prayer groups; Movies;
Shopping trips; Dances/Social/Cultural
gatherings; Intergenerational programs;
Educational activities; Therapeutic activities.

National City

Castle Manor Convalescent Center
541 "V" Ave, National City, CA 92050
(619) 267-8800
Admin Michael B Levin.
Licensure Skilled care. *Beds* SNF 99. *Certified*
Medicare; Medi-Cal.
Owner Proprietary corp.

Continana Convalescent Hospital
220 E 24th St, National City, CA 92050
(619) 474-6741
Admin Walter N Ross.
Licensure Skilled care. *Beds* SNF 98. *Certified*
Medicare; Medi-Cal.
Owner Privately owned.

Friendship Homes
2300 E 7th St, National City, CA 92050
(619) 267-8400
Admin Charles I Cheneweth.
Medical Dir Leon Kelley MD.
Licensure Skilled care; Intermediate care for
mentally retarded. *Beds* SNF 8; ICF/MR 91.
Certified Medi-Cal.
Owner Proprietary corp.
Admissions Requirements Minimum age 3
months.
Staff Physicians 1 (pt); RNs 6 (ft); LPNs 10
(ft), 1 (pt); Nurses' aides 63 (ft), 12 (pt);
Physical therapists 1 (pt); Recreational
therapists 1 (pt); Occupational therapists 1
(pt); Speech therapists 1 (pt); Activities
coordinators 1 (pt); Dietitians 1 (pt);
Podiatrists 1 (pt).
Facilities Dining room; Physical therapy
room; Activities room; Laundry room.

Friendship Manor Convalescent Center
902 Euclid Ave, National City, CA 92050
(619) 267-9220
Admin Michael B Levin.
Medical Dir C G Maloney MD.
Licensure Skilled care. *Beds* SNF 104.
Certified Medicare; Medi-Cal.
Owner Proprietary corp.
Admissions Requirements Medical
examination; Physician's request.
Staff RNs 7 (ft), 2 (pt); LPNs 5 (ft), 2 (pt);
Nurses' aides 40 (ft), 7 (pt); Physical
therapists 1 (ft); Recreational therapists 1
(ft); Activities coordinators 1 (ft).
Facilities Dining room; Physical therapy
room; Activities room; Laundry room;
Barber/Beauty shop; Conference room; TV
lounge.
Activities Arts & crafts; Cards; Games; Prayer
groups; Movies; Shopping trips; Dances/
Social/Cultural gatherings; Picnics; Outings.

Hillcrest Manor Sanitarium
1889 National City Blvd, National City, CA
92050
(619) 477-1176
Admin Jean C Marsh. *Dir of Nursing*
Veronica delRosario RN. *Medical Dir* Louis
H Gessay MD.
Licensure Skilled care; Alzheimer's care. *Beds*
SNF 85. *Private Pay Patients* 25%. *Certified*
Medicare; Medi-Cal.
Owner Proprietary corp.
Admissions Requirements Minimum age 50;
Conservatorship under Lanterman, Petris,
Short Act.
Staff RNs 3 (ft), 1 (pt); LPNs 6 (ft), 4 (pt);
Nurses' aides 32 (ft), 7 (pt); Physical
therapists (consultant); Activities
coordinators 2 (ft), 1 (pt); Dietitians
(consultant).
Languages Spanish, Tagalog.
Facilities Dining room; Activities room;
Laundry room; 2 patios.
Activities Arts & crafts; Cards; Games;
Movies; Dances/Social/Cultural gatherings.

Paradise Valley Health Care Center
2575 E 8th St, National City, CA 92050
(619) 470-6700
Admin Richard A Dahlberg. *Dir of Nursing*
Carmelita Sevidal RN. *Medical Dir* Robert
Bock MD.
Licensure Skilled care; Board and care. *Beds*
SNF 86; Board and care 76. *Certified*
Medicare; Medi-Cal.
Owner Proprietary corp (Heritage Health
Group Inc).
Admissions Requirements Physician's request.
Staff RNs 4 (ft), 2 (pt); LPNs 8 (ft), 2 (pt);
Nurses' aides 59 (ft), 14 (pt); Physical
therapists; Activities coordinators 1 (ft);
Dietitians.
Languages Spanish, Tagalog.
Affiliation Seventh-Day Adventist.
Facilities Dining room; Physical therapy
room; Activities room; Chapel; Crafts room;
Laundry room; Barber/Beauty shop; Library.
Activities Arts & crafts; Games; Reading
groups; Prayer groups; Movies; Shopping
trips; Dances/Social/Cultural gatherings;
Intergenerational programs.

Newbury Park

Mary Health of the Sick
2929 Theresa Dr, Newbury Park, CA 91320
(805) 498-3644
Admin Charles F Comley.
Licensure Skilled care. *Beds* SNF 61. *Certified*
Medicare; Medi-Cal.
Owner Nonprofit corp.

Ventura Estates Health Manor
915 Estates Dr, Newbury Park, CA 91320
(805) 498-3691, 498-9838 FAX
Admin Philip C Lang. *Dir of Nursing* Dolores
Sheler RN. *Medical Dir* Arthur C Fingerle
MD.
Licensure Skilled care; Intermediate care;
Apartment living. *Beds* SNF 48; ICF 18;
Apartment living 164. *Private Pay Patients*
30%. *Certified* Medicare; Medi-Cal.
Owner Nonprofit organization/foundation.
Admissions Requirements Minimum age 50;
Medical examination; Physician's request;
Nonsmoker; Nondrinker.
Staff RNs 6 (ft), 6 (pt); LPNs 2 (ft); Nurses'
aides 18 (ft), 12 (pt); Physical therapists 1
(pt); Occupational therapists 1 (pt); Speech
therapists 1 (pt); Activities coordinators 2
(ft), 1 (pt); Dietitians 1 (ft); Podiatrists 1
(pt); Audiologists 1 (pt).
Affiliation Seventh-Day Adventist.
Facilities Dining room; Physical therapy
room; Activities room; Chapel; Crafts room;
Laundry room; Barber/Beauty shop; Library;
Vegetarian kitchen.

Activities Arts & crafts; Games; Reading
groups; Prayer groups; Movies; Dances/
Social/Cultural gatherings; Intergenerational
programs; Pet therapy; Plant club.

Newhall

Santa Clarita Convalescent Hospital
23801 San Fernando Rd, Newhall, CA 91321
(805) 259-3660
Admin Jean A Priestman.
Licensure Skilled care. *Beds* SNF 99. *Certified*
Medicare; Medi-Cal.
Owner Proprietary corp.

Newman

San Luis Convalescent Hospital
709 N St, Newman, CA 95360
(209) 862-2862
Admin Issac Verhage.
Medical Dir Dr La Torre.
Licensure Skilled care. *Beds* SNF 71. *Certified*
Medicare; Medi-Cal.
Owner Proprietary corp (Beverly Enterprises).
Staff Nurses' aides 19 (ft).
Facilities Dining room; Activities room;
Laundry room; Barber/Beauty shop.
Activities Arts & crafts; Cards; Games;
Reading groups; Prayer groups; Movies.

Newport Beach

Flagship Healthcare Center
466 Flagship Rd, Newport Beach, CA 92663
(714) 642-8044, 642-0102 FAX
Admin Marshall N Horsman BS MBA. *Dir of
Nursing* Robert Murphy RN BA. *Medical
Dir* Korey S Jorgensen MD.
Licensure Skilled care; Retirement. *Beds* SNF
167; Retirement 200. *Private Pay Patients*
50%. *Certified* Medicare; Medi-Cal.
Owner Proprietary corp (American-Cal
Medical Services Inc).
Admissions Requirements Minimum age 21;
Medical examination; Physician's request.
Staff RNs 5 (ft); LPNs 15 (ft); Nurses' aides
60 (ft); Physical therapists 2 (ft);
Recreational therapists 1 (pt); Occupational
therapists 1 (ft); Speech therapists 1 (ft);
Activities coordinators 2 (ft); Dietitians 1
(pt); Podiatrists 1 (pt); Audiologists 1 (pt).
Facilities Dining room; Physical therapy
room; Activities room; Barber/Beauty shop;
Gift shop; Van.
Activities Arts & crafts; Cards; Games;
Reading groups; Prayer groups; Movies;
Shopping trips; Intergenerational programs;
Pet therapy.

Newport Convalescent Center
1555 Superior Ave, Newport Beach, CA 92660
(714) 646-7764
Admin Steven Ross.
Licensure Skilled care. *Beds* SNF 59. *Certified*
Medicare; Medi-Cal.
Owner Proprietary corp.

Park Superior Healthcare
1445 Superior Ave, Newport Beach, CA 92660
(714) 642-2410
Admin Patrice Acosta.
Licensure Skilled care. *Beds* SNF 96. *Certified*
Medicare; Medi-Cal.
Owner Privately owned.

North Hollywood

All Saints Convalescent Center
11810 Saticoy St, North Hollywood, CA
91605
(818) 982-4600
Admin Hale J Scott.
Licensure Skilled care. *Beds* SNF 128.
Certified Medicare; Medi-Cal.
Owner Proprietary corp.

Chandler Convalescent Hospital
12140 Chandler Blvd, North Hollywood, CA 91607
(818) 985-1814, 985-3128 FAX
Admin Arthur E Goldfarb. *Dir of Nursing* Emma Parka RN. *Medical Dir* Sandor Zuckerman MD.
Licensure Skilled care; Residential care. *Beds* SNF 201; Residential care 50. *Private Pay Patients* 15%. *Certified* Medicaid; Medicare; Medi-Cal.
Owner Proprietary corp.
Admissions Requirements Minimum age 45; Physician's request.
Staff RNs 5 (ft), 3 (pt); LPNs 14 (ft), 3 (pt); Nurses' aides 54 (ft); Physical therapists 2 (pt); Occupational therapists 1 (ft); Speech therapists 1 (ft); Activities coordinators 3 (ft); Dietitians 18 (ft); Ophthalmologists 1 (ft); Podiatrists 2 (ft).
Languages Spanish, Hebrew, Korean, Hungarian.
Facilities Dining room; Physical therapy room; Activities room; Chapel; Crafts room; Laundry room; Barber/Beauty shop; Library; 3 patios; Barbecues.
Activities Arts & crafts; Cards; Games; Prayer groups; Movies; Dances/Social/Cultural gatherings; Outside entertainment; Birthday parties; Holiday parties; Holy days prayers.

Golden State Colonial Convalescent Hospital
10830 Oxnard, North Hollywood, CA 91606
(818) 763-8247
Admin Bette Zimmer. *Dir of Nursing* Treva D'Orazio RN. *Medical Dir* Dr David Antrobus.
Licensure Skilled care; Retirement. *Beds* SNF 49; Retirement 14. *Private Pay Patients* 30%. *Certified* Medicare; Medi-Cal.
Owner Proprietary corp (Golden State Health Care Centers Inc).
Admissions Requirements Minimum age 60; Medical examination; Physician's request.
Staff Physicians 3 (pt); RNs 1 (ft), 1 (pt); Nurses' aides 25 (ft), 3 (pt); Physical therapists 1 (pt); Recreational therapists 1 (ft); Occupational therapists 1 (pt); Speech therapists 1 (pt); Activities coordinators 1 (ft), 1 (pt); Dietitians 1 (ft); Ophthalmologists 1 (pt); Podiatrists 1 (pt); Audiologists 1 (pt); LVNs 3 (ft), 2 (pt).
Languages Spanish, German, Yiddish.
Facilities Dining room; Activities room; Crafts room; Laundry room; Barber/Beauty shop; Library.
Activities Arts & crafts; Cards; Games; Reading groups; Prayer groups; Movies; Shopping trips; Dances/Social/Cultural gatherings; Intergenerational programs; Pet therapy.

Riverside Convalescent Center
12750 Riverside Dr, North Hollywood, CA 91607
(818) 766-6105
Admin Glen Bennet.
Medical Dir Saeed Humayun MD.
Licensure Skilled care. *Beds* SNF 108. *Certified* Medicare; Medi-Cal.
Owner Proprietary corp.
Admissions Requirements Minimum age 65; Medical examination; Physician's request.
Staff RNs; LPNs; Nurses' aides; Physical therapists; Occupational therapists; Speech therapists; Activities coordinators; Dietitians; Ophthalmologists; Podiatrists; Dentists.
Languages Spanish.
Facilities Dining room; Physical therapy room; Activities room; Laundry room; Barber/Beauty shop.
Activities Arts & crafts; Cards; Games; Reading groups; Prayer groups; Movies; Shopping trips; Dances/Social/Cultural gatherings; Resident & family candlelight dinners held monthly.

St Elizabeth Toluca Lake Convalescent Hospital
10425 Magnolia Blvd, North Hollywood, CA 91601
(818) 984-2918
Admin Lorraine M Thomas. *Dir of Nursing* Margaret Pollack RN. *Medical Dir* Lewis Trostler MD.
Licensure Skilled care. *Beds* SNF 52. *Private Pay Patients* 60%. *Certified* Medicare; Medi-Cal.
Owner Nonprofit organization/foundation.
Admissions Requirements Minimum age 60; Medical examination; Physician's request.
Staff RNs; LPNs; Nurses' aides; Physical therapists; Occupational therapists; Speech therapists; Activities coordinators; Dietitians; Ophthalmologists; Podiatrists.
Languages Spanish, German.
Affiliation Roman Catholic.
Facilities Dining room; Activities room; Laundry room; Barber/Beauty shop.
Activities Arts & crafts; Cards; Games; Reading groups; Prayer groups; Movies; Shopping trips; Intergenerational programs; Pet therapy.

Valley Manor Convalescent Hospital
6120 N Vineland Ave, North Hollywood, CA 91606
(818) 763-6275
Admin Gonzalo del Rosario Jr. *Dir of Nursing* Nel Pineda RN. *Medical Dir* Nathan Grover MD.
Licensure Skilled care; Board and care. *Beds* SNF 72; Board and care 58. *Private Pay Patients* 7%. *Certified* Medicare; Medi-Cal.
Owner Proprietary corp.
Staff RNs 1 (ft), 1 (pt); Nurses' aides 19 (ft), 3 (pt); Physical therapists (contracted); Reality therapists (contracted); Recreational therapists (contracted); Occupational therapists (contracted); Speech therapists (contracted); Activities coordinators 1 (ft); LVNs 5 (ft), 4 (pt).
Languages Spanish, Tagalog.
Affiliation Roman Catholic.
Activities Arts & crafts; Cards; Games; Reading groups; Prayer groups; Movies; Shopping trips; Dances/Social/Cultural gatherings; Intergenerational programs; Pet therapy.

Valley Palms Care Center
13400 Sherman Way, North Hollywood, CA 91605
(818) 983-0103
Admin Brenda Manke.
Medical Dir Luz Villena.
Licensure Skilled care. *Beds* SNF 99. *Certified* Medicare; Medi-Cal.
Owner Proprietary corp (Summit Care Inc).
Admissions Requirements Physician's request.
Staff RNs 3 (ft); LPNs 12 (ft); Nurses' aides 50 (ft); Activities coordinators 1 (ft); Dietitians 1 (ft).
Languages Spanish.
Facilities Dining room; Physical therapy room; Activities room; Crafts room; Barber/Beauty shop.
Activities Arts & crafts; Cards; Games; Reading groups; Prayer groups; Movies; Shopping trips; Dances/Social/Cultural gatherings.

Norwalk

Care West Intercommunity Nursing Center
12627 Studebaker Rd, Norwalk, CA 90650
(213) 868-4767
Admin Jeanie Barrett.
Licensure Skilled care. *Beds* SNF 86. *Certified* Medicare; Medi-Cal.
Owner Proprietary corp (Care Enterprises).

Glen Terrace Convalescent Center
11510 Imperial Hwy, Norwalk, CA 90650
(213) 868-6791

Admin Ann Walshe.
Medical Dir Dr Lawrence Pollock.
Licensure Skilled care. *Beds* SNF 99. *Certified* Medicare; Medi-Cal.
Owner Proprietary corp (Western Medical Enterprises).
Admissions Requirements Minimum age 65; Physician's request.
Staff RNs 2 (ft), 1 (pt); LPNs 8 (ft); Nurses' aides 46 (ft); Physical therapists 1 (pt); Recreational therapists 1 (pt); Occupational therapists 1 (pt); Speech therapists 1 (pt); Activities coordinators 1 (ft); Dietitians 1 (ft); Ophthalmologists 1 (pt); Podiatrists 1 (pt); Dentists 1 (pt).
Languages Tagalog, Spanish.
Facilities Dining room; Physical therapy room; Activities room; Laundry room; Barber/Beauty shop.
Activities Arts & crafts; Cards; Games; Prayer groups; Movies; Shopping trips; Dances/Social/Cultural gatherings; Reality orientation.

La Casa Mental Health Center
11400 Norwalk Blvd, Norwalk, CA 90650
(213) 860-1000
Admin Anthony Bambu.
Licensure Skilled care. *Beds* SNF 136. *Certified* Medi-Cal.
Owner Proprietary corp.

North Walk Villa Convalescent Hospital
12350 Rosecrans, Norwalk, CA 90650
(213) 921-6624
Admin Katy F Link.
Licensure Skilled care. *Beds* SNF 59. *Certified* Medicare; Medi-Cal.
Owner Proprietary corp.

Southland Geriatric Center
11701 Studebaker Rd, Norwalk, CA 90650
(213) 868-9761
Admin Marion L Hopkins. *Dir of Nursing* Elli Maas RN. *Medical Dir* James H Holman MD.
Licensure Skilled care; Intermediate care; Retirement; Alzheimer's care. *Beds* SNF 80; ICF 40; Retirement. *Certified* Medicare; Medi-Cal.
Owner Nonprofit corp.
Admissions Requirements Minimum age 55; Medical examination; Physician's request.
Staff RNs 3 (ft), 5 (pt); LPNs 8 (ft), 6 (pt); Nurses' aides 49 (ft), 14 (pt); Physical therapists 1 (pt); Occupational therapists 1 (pt); Speech therapists 2 (pt); Activities coordinators 1 (ft), 2 (pt); Dietitians 1 (pt); Ophthalmologists 1 (pt); Podiatrists 1 (pt).
Affiliation Lutheran.
Facilities Dining room; Physical therapy room; Activities room; Chapel; Crafts room; Laundry room; Barber/Beauty shop; Library; Classroom.
Activities Arts & crafts; Cards; Games; Reading groups; Prayer groups; Movies; Shopping trips; Dances/Social/Cultural gatherings; Intergenerational programs.

Villa Elena Convalescent Hospital
13226 Studebaker Rd, Norwalk, CA 90650
(213) 868-0591
Admin James A Hall. *Dir of Nursing* Dora Craft RN. *Medical Dir* James Jetton MD.
Licensure Skilled care. *Beds* SNF 98. *Private Pay Patients* 15%. *Certified* Medicaid; Medicare; Medi-Cal.
Owner Proprietary corp.
Admissions Requirements Medical examination; Physician's request.
Staff RNs 2 (ft), 2 (pt); LPNs 8 (ft), 2 (pt); Nurses' aides 25 (ft), 5 (pt); Physical therapists 2 (pt); Occupational therapists 1 (pt); Activities coordinators 1 (ft); Dietitians 1 (pt).
Languages Spanish.

Facilities Dining room; Physical therapy room; Activities room; Laundry room; Barber/Beauty shop; Library.
Activities Arts & crafts; Cards; Games; Reading groups; Prayer groups; Movies; Shopping trips; Pet therapy.

Novato

Canyon Manor
655 Canyon Rd, Novato, CA 94947
(415) 892-1628
Admin Richard Evatz. *Dir of Nursing* Tom Hall. *Medical Dir* Richard M Yarvis MD.
Licensure Skilled care. *Beds* SNF 89. *Private Pay Patients* 5%. *Certified* Medi-Cal.
Owner Proprietary corp.
Admissions Requirements Minimum age 18; Specialize in severly mentally disabled adults.
Staff Physicians 1 (ft); RNs 4 (ft); Nurses' aides 12 (ft), 6 (pt); Physical therapists (consultant); Occupational therapists 2 (ft); Activities coordinators 1 (ft); Dietitians (consultant); Ophthalmologists (consultant); Podiatrists (consultant); Audiologists (consultant); Psychiatrists.
Facilities Dining room; Activities room; Crafts room; Laundry room; Library.
Activities Arts & crafts; Cards; Games; Movies; Shopping trips; Dances/Social/Cultural gatherings; Pet therapy.

Novato Convalescent Hospital
1565 Hill Rd, Novato, CA 94947
(415) 897-6161
Admin Sylvia L Nelson. *Dir of Nursing* Ann Allen. *Medical Dir* Wayne Cooper MD.
Licensure Skilled care. *Beds* SNF 187. *Private Pay Patients* 30%. *Certified* Medicaid; Medicare.
Owner Proprietary corp (Beverly Enterprises).
Admissions Requirements Physician's request.
Staff RNs; LPNs; Nurses' aides; Physical therapists 1 (ft); Occupational therapists 1 (pt); Speech therapists 1 (pt); Activities coordinators 2 (ft); Dietitians 1 (ft), 1 (pt).
Facilities Dining room; Physical therapy room; Activities room; Crafts room; Laundry room; Barber/Beauty shop.
Activities Arts & crafts; Cards; Games; Reading groups; Prayer groups; Movies; Shopping trips; Pet therapy.

Oakdale

Oak Valley Care Center
275 S Oak Ave, Oakdale, CA 95361
(209) 847-0367
Admin Cheryl Koff.
Licensure Skilled care. *Beds* SNF 99. *Certified* Medicare; Medi-Cal.
Owner Publicly owned.

Oakhurst

Sierra Meadows Convalescent Hospital
40131 Hwy 49, Box 2349, Oakhurst, CA 93644
(209) 683-2244
Admin Jo Ann J Weston.
Medical Dir C Mitchell MD.
Licensure Skilled care. *Beds* SNF 64. *Certified* Medicare; Medi-Cal.
Owner Nonprofit organization/foundation.
Admissions Requirements Physician's request.
Staff RNs 1 (ft), 4 (pt); LPNs 2 (ft), 5 (pt); Nurses' aides 12 (ft), 16 (pt); Speech therapists 1 (pt); Activities coordinators 1 (ft).
Facilities Dining room; Laundry room; Barber/Beauty shop; Library; Adjacent emergency center; lab & x-ray.

Activities Arts & crafts; Cards; Games; Reading groups; Prayer groups; Movies; Shopping trips; Dances/Social/Cultural gatherings.

Oakland

Altenheim Inc
1720 MacArthur Blvd, Oakland, CA 94702
(415) 530-4013
Admin Anne Morgan. *Dir of Nursing* Patricia Knight RN. *Medical Dir* Mark Marama.
Licensure Skilled care; Personal care; Residential care. *Beds* SNF 16; Personal care 28; Residential care 155. *Private Pay Patients* 100%.
Owner Nonprofit corp.
Admissions Requirements Minimum age 62; Medical examination; Physician's request.
Staff RNs 1 (ft), 2 (pt); LPNs 1 (ft), 2 (pt); Nurses' aides 1 (ft), 6 (pt).
Languages German, Greek, French.
Facilities Dining room; Activities room; Crafts room; Laundry room; Barber/Beauty shop; Library; Gardens; Walking areas.
Activities Arts & crafts; Cards; Reading groups; Prayer groups; Movies; Shopping trips; Intergenerational programs; Pet therapy.

Clinton Village Convalescent Hospital
1833 10th Ave, Oakland, CA 94606
(415) 536-6512
Admin Tom C Duarte.
Medical Dir John Chokatos MD.
Licensure Skilled care. *Beds* SNF 99. *Certified* Medicare; Medi-Cal.
Owner Proprietary corp.
Admissions Requirements Minimum age 65; Medical examination; Physician's request.
Facilities Dining room; Physical therapy room; Activities room; Chapel; Crafts room; Laundry room; Barber/Beauty shop; Library.
Activities Arts & crafts; Cards; Games; Reading groups; Prayer groups; Movies; Shopping trips; Dances/Social/Cultural gatherings; Social work.

Coberly Green Intermediate Care Facility
2420 Fruitvale Ave, Oakland, CA 94601
(415) 532-5090
Admin Virgil Rentaria. *Dir of Nursing* Elizabeth Lapitan. *Medical Dir* Gary Miller MD.
Licensure Intermediate care; Alzheimer's care. *Beds* ICF 21. *Private Pay Patients* 2%. *Certified* Medi-Cal.
Owner Proprietary corp.
Admissions Requirements Medical examination; Physician's request.
Staff RNs 1 (pt); LPNs 1 (ft), 1 (pt); Nurses' aides 3 (ft), 3 (pt); Physical therapists 1 (pt); Activities coordinators 1 (ft); Dietitians 1 (pt); Podiatrists 1 (pt); Audiologists 1 (pt).
Facilities Dining room; Activities room; Crafts room; Laundry room.
Activities Arts & crafts; Cards; Games; Reading groups; Movies.

Dowling Convalescent Hospital
451 28th St, Oakland, CA 94609
(415) 893-4066
Admin Ponselle R Lane.
Licensure Skilled care. *Beds* SNF 30. *Certified* Medi-Cal.
Owner Privately owned.
Staff RNs; Nurses' aides; Activities coordinators.
Languages Spanish, Chinese.
Activities Arts & crafts; Games; Prayer groups.

Fruitvale Care Convalescent Hospital
3020 E 15th St, Oakland, CA 94601
(415) 261-5613
Admin Remedios B Tibayan. *Dir of Nursing* Veronica Lane. *Medical Dir* Dr Robert Tufft.

Licensure Skilled care. *Beds* SNF 140. *Certified* Medicare; Medi-Cal.
Owner Proprietary corp (Hostmasters Inc).
Admissions Requirements Medical examination; Physician's request.
Staff Physicians; RNs; LPNs; Nurses' aides; Physical therapists; Recreational therapists; Occupational therapists; Speech therapists; Activities coordinators; Dietitians; Ophthalmologists; Podiatrists; Audiologists.
Facilities Dining room; Physical therapy room; Activities room; Laundry room; Barber/Beauty shop.
Activities Arts & crafts; Cards; Games; Reading groups; Prayer groups; Movies; Shopping trips; Dances/Social/Cultural gatherings; Intergenerational programs; Pet therapy.

Garfield Geropsychiatric Hospital
1451 28th Ave, Oakland, CA 94601
(415) 532-0820
Admin Jeffrey P Lambkin. *Dir of Nursing* Patricia Goehner RN MS. *Medical Dir* Martin Held MD.
Licensure SNF for geriatric/psychiatric patients; Alzheimer's care. *Beds* SNF for geriatric/psychiatric patients 96. *Private Pay Patients* 10%. *Certified* Medi-Cal.
Owner Proprietary corp (Telecare Corp).
Admissions Requirements Minimum age 57.
Staff Physicians 1 (ft), 3 (pt); RNs 4 (ft); LPNs 9 (ft), 2 (pt); Nurses' aides 30 (ft); Physical therapists 3 (ft); Recreational therapists 3 (ft); Occupational therapists 1 (ft); Speech therapists 1 (pt); Activities coordinators 2 (ft); Dietitians 1 (pt); Ophthalmologists 1 (pt); Podiatrists 1 (pt); Audiologists 1 (pt).
Languages Spanish.
Facilities Dining room; Physical therapy room; Activities room; Crafts room; Laundry room; Barber/Beauty shop; Lounge.
Activities Arts & crafts; Cards; Games; Reading groups; Prayer groups; Movies; Shopping trips; Dances/Social/Cultural gatherings; Intergenerational programs; Pet therapy; Individual & group therapy.

High Street Convalescent Hospital
3145 High St, Oakland, CA 94619
(415) 533-9970
Admin L Cannon.
Medical Dir Dr Richmond.
Licensure Skilled care. *Beds* SNF 44. *Certified* Medicare; Medi-Cal.
Owner Proprietary corp (Guardian Foundation Inc).
Admissions Requirements Medical examination; Physician's request.
Staff RNs 2 (ft), 4 (pt); LPNs 2 (ft), 6 (pt); Nurses' aides 15 (ft), 11 (pt); Physical therapists 1 (pt); Occupational therapists 1 (pt); Speech therapists 1 (pt); Activities coordinators 1 (ft); Podiatrists 1 (pt); Dentists 1 (pt).
Facilities Dining room; Activities room; Barber/Beauty shop.
Activities Arts & crafts; Cards; Games; Reading groups; Prayer groups; Movies; Shopping trips; Dances/Social/Cultural gatherings; Animals visits.

Highview Convalescent Hospital
1301 E 31st, Oakland, CA 94602
(415) 534-2295
Licensure Skilled care. *Beds* SNF 81. *Certified* Medicare; Medi-Cal.
Owner Nonprofit corp (Guardian Foundation Inc).

Hillhaven—Oakland
3030 Webster St, Oakland, CA 94609
(415) 451-3856, 451-7174 FAX
Admin William Kruse. *Dir of Nursing* Sharon Bowers.
Licensure Skilled care. *Beds* SNF 94. *Certified* Medicare; Medi-Cal.

Owner Proprietary corp (Hillhaven Inc).
Staff Physicians; RNs; LPNs; Nurses' aides;
Physical therapists; Occupational therapists;
Speech therapists; Activities coordinators;
Dietitians.

Home for Jewish Parents
2780 26th Ave, Oakland, CA 94601
(415) 536-4604
Dir of Nursing Kelly Gaglione. *Medical Dir*
Herbert Lints.
Licensure Skilled care; Retirement. *Beds* SNF
57; Residential 58. *Certified* Medicare;
Medi-Cal.
Owner Nonprofit corp.
Admissions Requirements Minimum age 65;
Medical examination.
Staff RNs 6 (ft); LPNs 6 (ft); Nurses' aides 24
(ft); Physical therapists 3 (pt); Reality
therapists 1 (pt); Occupational therapists 1
(pt); Speech therapists 1 (pt); Activities
coordinators 1 (ft); Dietitians 1 (ft);
Ophthalmologists 1 (pt); Podiatrists 1 (pt);
Dentists 1 (pt).
Languages Yiddish.
Affiliation Jewish.
Facilities Dining room; Physical therapy
room; Activities room; Chapel; Crafts room;
Laundry room; Barber/Beauty shop; Library.
Activities Arts & crafts; Cards; Games;
Reading groups; Prayer groups; Movies;
Shopping trips; Dances/Social/Cultural
gatherings.

Lake Park Retirement Residence
1850 Alice St, Oakland, CA 94612
(415) 835-5511
Admin Dudley Thompson. *Dir of Nursing*
Shirley Graham. *Medical Dir* Dr Thomas
Richmond.
Licensure Skilled care; Alzheimer's care;
Retirement. *Beds* SNF 26. *Certified*
Medicare; Medi-Cal.
Owner Nonprofit corp.
Admissions Requirements Minimum age 62;
Medical examination; Physician's request.
Staff RNs 3 (ft); LPNs 5 (ft), 5 (pt); Nurses'
aides 8 (ft), 2 (pt); Recreational therapists 1
(ft); Activities coordinators 1 (pt).
Affiliation Methodist.
Facilities Dining room; Physical therapy
room; Activities room; Chapel; Crafts room;
Laundry room; Barber/Beauty shop; Library.
Activities Arts & crafts; Cards; Games;
Reading groups; Prayer groups; Movies;
Shopping trips; Dances/Social/Cultural
gatherings.

Lakeshore Convalescent
1901 3rd Ave, Oakland, CA 94606
(415) 834-9880
Admin Carol Wooster. *Dir of Nursing* Anita
M Brass RN. *Medical Dir* Robert W Tufft
MD.
Licensure Skilled care; Alzheimer's care. *Beds*
SNF 38. *Private Pay Patients* 50%. *Certified*
Medicare; Medi-Cal.
Owner Privately owned.
Admissions Requirements Minimum age 60;
Medical examination; Physician's request.
Staff RNs 1 (ft); LPNs 4 (ft); Nurses' aides 10
(ft); Physical therapists 1 (pt); Occupational
therapists 1 (pt); Speech therapists 1 (pt);
Activities coordinators 1 (ft); Dietitians 1
(pt); Podiatrists 1 (pt); Audiologists 1 (pt).
Languages Spanish.
Facilities Dining room; Activities room;
Crafts room; Laundry room; Semi-private
rooms; Alzheimer's.
Activities Arts & crafts; Cards; Games;
Reading groups; Prayer groups; Movies;
Shopping trips; Dances/Social/Cultural
gatherings; Intergenerational programs; Pet
therapy.

MacArthur Convalescent Hospital
309 MacArthur Blvd, Oakland, CA 94610
(415) 836-3777

Admin Robert O Ewing.
Licensure Skilled care. *Beds* SNF 53. *Certified*
Medicare; Medi-Cal.
Owner Nonprofit organization/foundation
(Guardian Foundation Inc).

McClure Convalescent Hospital
2910 McClure St, Oakland, CA 94609
(415) 836-3677
Medical Dir Dr F Bongiorno.
Licensure Skilled care. *Beds* SNF 59. *Certified*
Medicare; Medi-Cal.
Owner Proprietary corp.
Staff RNs 1 (ft), 3 (pt); LPNs 5 (ft), 4 (pt);
Nurses' aides 17 (ft), 10 (pt); Physical
therapists 1 (pt); Recreational therapists 1
(pt); Occupational therapists 1 (pt); Speech
therapists 1 (pt); Activities coordinators 1
(ft); Dietitians 1 (pt); Podiatrists 1 (pt);
Dentists 1 (pt).
Facilities Dining room; Activities room;
Chapel; Crafts room; Laundry room; Barber/
Beauty shop.
Activities Arts & crafts; Cards; Games;
Movies; Shopping trips; Dances/Social/
Cultural gatherings; Monthly outings.

Medical Hill Rehabilitation Center
475 29th St, Oakland, CA 94609
(415) 832-3222
Licensure Skilled care. *Beds* SNF 99. *Certified*
Medicare; Medi-Cal.
Owner Nonprofit organization/foundation
(Guardian Foundation Inc).

Mercy Manor
3431 Foothill Blvd, Oakland, CA 94601
(415) 534-5169
Admin Sue Huttlinger. *Dir of Nursing* Kitti
Gordon RN. *Medical Dir* Herbert Lints MD.
Licensure Skilled care. *Beds* SNF 122.
Certified Medicare; Medi-Cal.
Owner Nonprofit corp.
Admissions Requirements Medical
examination; Physician's request.
Staff RNs 3 (ft), 3 (pt); LPNs 15 (ft), 6 (pt);
Nurses' aides 25 (ft), 4 (pt); Recreational
therapists 1 (ft); Activities coordinators 1
(ft), 1 (pt); Chaplains.
Languages Spanish, Indonesian.
Facilities Dining room; Physical therapy
room; Activities room; Crafts room; Laundry
room; Barber/Beauty shop.
Activities Arts & crafts; Cards; Games;
Reading groups; Prayer groups; Dances/
Social/Cultural gatherings; Outside
community visits; Ballgames; Fisherman's
Wharf.

Oakridge Convalescent Hospital
2919 Fruitvale Ave, Oakland, CA 94602
(415) 261-8564
Dir of Nursing Annie Dela Cuesta RN.
Medical Dir Herbert Lints MD.
Licensure Skilled care. *Beds* SNF 99. *Certified*
Medicare; Medi-Cal.
Owner Proprietary corp (Hillhaven Corp).
Admissions Requirements Medical
examination; Physician's request.
Staff RNs 3 (ft), 2 (pt); LPNs 10 (ft), 5 (pt);
Nurses' aides 35 (ft), 20 (pt); Physical
therapists 1 (pt); Occupational therapists 1
(pt); Speech therapists 1 (pt); Activities
coordinators 4 (pt); Dietitians 1 (pt).
Languages Spanish, Tagalog, Chinese.
Facilities Dining room; Physical therapy
room; Activities room; Chapel; Crafts room;
Laundry room; Barber/Beauty shop; Library.
Activities Arts & crafts; Cards; Games;
Reading groups; Prayer groups; Movies;
Shopping trips; Dances/Social/Cultural
gatherings; Intergenerational program;
Adopt-a-resident; Art with elders.

Our Lady's Home
3431 Foothill Blvd, Oakland, CA 94601
(415) 532-7034
Admin S Patrick Curran.

Licensure Skilled care. *Beds* SNF 59. *Certified*
Medicare; Medi-Cal.
Owner Proprietary corp.

Pacific Care Convalescent Hospital
3025 High St, Oakland, CA 94619
(415) 261-5200
Admin Trudy Patton.
Licensure Skilled care. *Beds* SNF 99. *Certified*
Medicare; Medi-Cal.
Owner Privately owned.

Park Merritt Intermediate Care
525 E 18th St, Oakland, CA 94606
(415) 834-8491
Admin Helen L Arbogast.
Licensure Intermediate care. *Beds* 24.
Certified Medi-Cal.
Owner Proprietary corp.
Facilities Dining room; Activities room;
Laundry room.
Activities Arts & crafts; Cards; Games;
Reading groups; Prayer groups; Movies;
Shopping trips; Dances/Social/Cultural
gatherings.

Pavilion Care Center
1935 Seminary Ave, Oakland, CA 94621
(415) 562-6184
Admin Dr Norman Jackson PhD. *Dir of
Nursing* Mary Brady RN AAS. *Medical Dir*
Gary Miller MD.
Licensure Skilled care. *Beds* SNF 99. *Certified*
Medicare; Medi-Cal.
Owner Proprietary corp (Elder Circle/Good
Hope).
Admissions Requirements Minimum age 55;
Medical examination.
Staff RNs 2 (ft); Nurses' aides 15 (ft), 6 (pt);
Physical therapists 1 (pt); Reality therapists
1 (pt); Recreational therapists 1 (pt);
Occupational therapists 1 (pt); Speech
therapists 1 (pt); Activities coordinators 1
(ft), 1 (pt); Dietitians 1 (pt);
Ophthalmologists 1 (pt); Podiatrists 1 (pt);
Audiologists 1 (pt); LVNs 6 (ft).
Languages Spanish, Chinese.
Facilities Dining room; Physical therapy
room; Activities room; Laundry room;
Barber/Beauty shop.
Activities Arts & crafts; Games; Reading
groups; Prayer groups; Movies.

Piedmont Gardens Health Facility
110 41st St, Oakland, CA 94611
(415) 654-7172
Admin Linda L Garland. *Dir of Nursing* Ruth
Johnston. *Medical Dir* Dr William Weeden.
Licensure Skilled care; Retirement;
Alzheimer's care. *Beds* SNF 94; Retirement
325. *Private Pay Patients* 75%. *Certified*
Medicare; Medi-Cal.
Owner Nonprofit corp (American Baptist
Homes of the West).
Admissions Requirements Minimum age 62;
Staff RNs 3 (ft), 7 (pt); LPNs 6 (ft), 4 (pt);
Nurses' aides 21 (ft), 7 (pt); Physical
therapists 1 (pt); Recreational therapists 1
(ft); Occupational therapists 1 (pt); Speech
therapists 1 (pt); Activities coordinators 1
(ft), 2 (pt); Dietitians 1 (pt);
Ophthalmologists 1 (pt); Podiatrists 1 (pt).
Languages Spanish, German.
Affiliation Baptist.
Facilities Dining room; Physical therapy
room; Laundry room; Barber/Beauty shop;
Library; Family conference room;
Alzheimer's unit.
Activities Arts & crafts; Cards; Games;
Reading groups; Prayer groups; Movies;
Shopping trips; Dances/Social/Cultural
gatherings; Intergenerational programs; Pet
therapy; Van trips.

**Wayne Rounseville Memorial Convalescent
Hospital**
210 40th Street Way, Oakland, CA 94611
(415) 658-2041

Admin Irmke Schoebel. *Dir of Nursing* Teri Reed RN. *Medical Dir* Thomas Richmond MD.
Licensure Skilled care. *Beds* SNF 70. *Certified* Medicare.
Owner Proprietary corp.
Admissions Requirements Physician's request.
Staff RNs 6 (ft); LPNs 10 (ft); Nurses' aides 32 (ft); Physical therapists 1 (pt); Reality therapists 1 (pt); Recreational therapists 1 (pt); Occupational therapists 1 (pt); Speech therapists 1 (pt); Activities coordinators 1 (ft), 1 (pt); Dietitians 1 (pt).
Facilities Dining room; Physical therapy room; Activities room; Crafts room; Laundry room; Barber/Beauty shop.
Activities Arts & crafts; Cards; Games; Reading groups; Prayer groups; Movies; Shopping trips; Dances/Social/Cultural gatherings; Pet therapy.

St Paul's Towers
100 Bay Pl, Oakland, CA 94610
(415) 835-4700, 835-4814 FAX
Admin Dolores K Crist. *Dir of Nursing* Patricia St Denis-Solem RN. *Medical Dir* Thomas Richmond MD.
Licensure Skilled care; Retirement. *Beds* SNF 43; Retirement 320. *Private Pay Patients* 95%. *Certified* Medicare.
Owner Nonprofit organization/foundation (Episcopal Homes Foundation).
Admissions Requirements Medical examination; Physician's request.
Staff Physicians 5 (pt); RNs 5 (ft), 4 (pt); LPNs 2 (ft), 1 (pt); Nurses' aides 17 (ft), 4 (pt); Physical therapists 1 (pt); Recreational therapists 1 (pt); Occupational therapists 1 (pt); Speech therapists 1 (pt); Activities coordinators 1 (pt); Dietitians 1 (pt); Ophthalmologists 1 (pt); Podiatrists 1 (pt); Audiologists 1 (pt).
Affiliation Episcopal.
Facilities Dining room; Physical therapy room; Activities room; Chapel; Crafts room; Barber/Beauty shop.
Activities Arts & crafts; Cards; Games; Reading groups; Prayer groups; Movies; Dances/Social/Cultural gatherings; Intergenerational programs; Pet therapy.

Salem Lutheran Home Skilled Nursing Facility
3003 Fruitvale Ave, Oakland, CA 94602
(415) 534-3219
Medical Dir Robert W Tufft MD.
Licensure Skilled care. *Beds* SNF 35. *Certified* Medicare; Medi-Cal.
Owner Nonprofit corp.
Admissions Requirements Minimum age 62; Medical examination; Physician's request.
Staff RNs 5 (pt); LPNs 3 (pt); Nurses' aides 15 (pt); Activities coordinators 1 (ft); Dietitians 1 (ft).
Affiliation Lutheran.
Facilities Dining room; Activities room; Laundry room; Barber/Beauty shop.
Activities Cards; Games; Prayer groups; Movies; Shopping trips; Dances/Social/Cultural gatherings.

Willow Tree Convalescent Hospital Ltd
2124 57th Ave, Oakland, CA 94621
(415) 261-2628
Admin Luealisyrine Cannon.
Medical Dir Dr Karl Konstantin.
Licensure Skilled care. *Beds* SNF 82. *Certified* Medicare; Medi-Cal.
Owner Proprietary corp.
Staff Physicians 7 (ft); RNs 1 (ft), 3 (pt); LPNs 7 (ft); Nurses' aides 20 (ft); Physical therapists 1 (ft); Reality therapists 1 (ft); Occupational therapists 1 (pt); Speech therapists 1 (pt); Activities coordinators 1 (ft); Dietitians 1 (pt); Ophthalmologists 1 (pt); Podiatrists 1 (pt); Dentists 1 (pt).
Facilities Dining room; Physical therapy room; Activities room; Crafts room; Laundry room; Barber/Beauty shop; Library.

Activities Arts & crafts; Cards; Games; Reading groups; Prayer groups; Dances/Social/Cultural gatherings; Project Outreach.

Oceanside

Tri City Convalescent Center
3232 Thunder Dr, Oceanside, CA 92054
(619) 724-2193
Admin Barry Zarling. *Dir of Nursing* Terri Jucenas. *Medical Dir* Dr Robert Nelson.
Licensure Skilled care. *Beds* SNF 93. *Certified* Medicare; Medi-Cal.
Owner Proprietary corp (Care Enterprises).
Admissions Requirements Medical examination; Physician's request.
Staff RNs 4 (ft); LPNs 6 (ft); Nurses' aides 50 (ft), 15 (pt); Physical therapists 1 (ft); Occupational therapists 1 (ft); Speech therapists 1 (pt); Activities coordinators 1 (ft); Dietitians 1 (ft); Ophthalmologists 1 (pt).
Languages Spanish, French.
Facilities Dining room; Physical therapy room; Activities room; Laundry room; Barber/Beauty shop; Garden & patio area.
Activities Arts & crafts; Games; Prayer groups; Movies; Dances/Social/Cultural gatherings; Exercise groups; Family & resident council.

Ojai

Acacias Care Center Inc
PO Box M, Ojai, CA 93023
(805) 646-8124
Admin James W Evans Jr.
Medical Dir Dr King.
Licensure Skilled care. *Beds* SNF 50. *Certified* Medicare; Medi-Cal.
Owner Proprietary corp.
Admissions Requirements Minimum age 62.
Facilities Dining room; Activities room; Laundry room; Barber/Beauty shop; Library.
Activities Arts & crafts; Games; Reading groups; Prayer groups; Movies; Shopping trips; Dances/Social/Cultural gatherings.

Ojai Valley Community Hospital
1306 Maricopa Hwy, Ojai, CA 93023
(805) 646-1401
Admin Mary Zacharias. *Dir of Nursing* Mary Ann Welsh RN. *Medical Dir* James Halverson MD.
Licensure Skilled care. *Certified* Medicare; Medi-Cal.
Owner Proprietary corp.
Admissions Requirements Medical examination.
Staff Physicians 8 (pt); RNs 2 (ft), 2 (pt); LPNs 2 (ft), 4 (pt); Physical therapists 2 (pt); Occupational therapists 1 (pt); Activities coordinators 1 (ft); Dietitians 1 (pt); Ophthalmologists 1 (pt); CNAs 10 (ft), 11 (pt).
Facilities Dining room; Activities room; Crafts room; Laundry room; Barber/Beauty shop.
Activities Arts & crafts; Cards; Games; Reading groups; Prayer groups; Movies; Shopping trips; Dances/Social/Cultural gatherings; SNF adjustment group.

St Joseph's Convalescent Hospital
PO Box 760, Ojai, CA 93023
(805) 646-1466
Admin Brother Michael Bassemier OH. *Dir of Nursing* Sandy Mangan RN. *Medical Dir* Raymond Sims MD.
Licensure Skilled care; Retirement. *Beds* SNF 28; Retirement 20. *Private Pay Patients* 80%. *Certified* Medicare; Medi-Cal.
Owner Nonprofit corp.
Admissions Requirements Minimum age 16; Medical examination.
Staff RNs; Nurses' aides; Physical therapists; Activities coordinators; Dietitians.
Languages Spanish.

Affiliation Roman Catholic.
Facilities Dining room; Physical therapy room; Activities room; Chapel; Crafts room; Laundry room; Barber/Beauty shop; Library.
Activities Arts & crafts; Cards; Games; Reading groups; Prayer groups; Movies; Pet therapy.

Ontario

Bella Vista Convalescent Hospital
933 E Deodar St, Ontario, CA 91764
(714) 985-2731
Admin Diane L Conway. *Dir of Nursing* Perdeta Bilka. *Medical Dir* Joanna Lund MD.
Licensure Skilled care. *Beds* SNF 59. *Private Pay Patients* 50%. *Certified* Medicare; Medi-Cal.
Owner Privately owned.
Admissions Requirements Medical examination; Physician's request.
Staff RNs 1 (ft), 2 (pt); LPNs 4 (ft), 2 (pt); Nurses' aides 19 (ft), 6 (pt); Activities coordinators 1 (ft).
Languages Spanish.
Facilities Dining room; Activities room; Chapel; Crafts room; Laundry room; Barber/Beauty shop; Large gated center patio.
Activities Arts & crafts; Cards; Games; Reading groups; Prayer groups; Movies; Shopping trips; Dances/Social/Cultural gatherings; Intergenerational programs; Pet therapy; Professional music programs.

Home of Angels
540 W Maple St, Ontario, CA 91761
(714) 986-5668
Admin Mark Duff. *Dir of Nursing* Pamela Fitzjerrells. *Medical Dir* Bharati Ghosh MD.
Licensure Skilled care. *Beds* SNF 59. *Private Pay Patients* 0%. *Certified* Medicaid.
Owner Proprietary corp (CareTech Inc).
Admissions Requirements 0-21; Medical examination.
Staff Physicians 1 (pt); RNs 1 (ft), 2 (pt); LPNs 4 (ft), 2 (pt); Nurses' aides 16 (ft), 7 (pt); Occupational therapists 1 (pt); Activities coordinators 1 (ft); Dietitians 1 (pt).
Languages Spanish.
Facilities Activities room; Laundry room.
Activities Movies; Special education by Ontario-Montclair School District.

Inland Christian Home Inc
1950 S Mountain Ave, Ontario, CA 91762
(714) 983-0084, 983-0431 FAX
Admin Peter Edwin Hoekstra. *Dir of Nursing* Sheila Norris. *Medical Dir* Dr Ron Davis.
Licensure Skilled care; Retirement. *Beds* SNF 59; Retirement 34. *Certified* Medicare; Medi-Cal.
Owner Nonprofit corp.
Admissions Requirements Minimum age 65; Physician's request.
Staff RNs; LPNs; Nurses' aides; Activities coordinators; Dietitians.
Languages Dutch.
Affiliation Dutch Reformed.
Facilities Dining room; Physical therapy room; Activities room; Chapel; Laundry room; Barber/Beauty shop; Library.
Activities Arts & crafts; Games; Prayer groups; Movies; Intergenerational programs; Pet therapy.

Ontario Nursing Home
1661 S Euclid Ave, Ontario, CA 91761
(714) 984-6713
Admin Diane L Conway. *Dir of Nursing* Sharon McGuyer. *Medical Dir* Johanna Lund MD.
Licensure Skilled care. *Beds* SNF 59. *Private Pay Patients* 30%. *Certified* Medicare; Medi-Cal.
Owner Privately owned.

Admissions Requirements Medical
examination; Physician's request.
Staff RNs 1 (ft), 2 (pt); LPNs 4 (ft), 3 (pt);
Nurses' aides 19 (ft), 6 (pt); Activities
coordinators 1 (ft).
Facilities Dining room; Activities room;
Laundry room; Barber/Beauty shop.
Activities Arts & crafts; Cards; Games;
Reading groups; Prayer groups; Movies;
Shopping trips; Dances/Social/Cultural
gatherings; Intergenerational programs; Pet
therapy; Professional music programs.

Plott Nursing Home
800 E 5th St, Ontario, CA 91764
(714) 984-8629
Admin Tony Scarpelli. *Dir of Nursing* Marlene
Migaiolo. *Medical Dir* Dr Kwee.
Licensure Skilled care. *Beds* SNF 216.
Certified Medicare; Medi-Cal.
Owner Proprietary corp (Thomas Plott).
Admissions Requirements Physician's request.
Staff RNs; LPNs; Nurses' aides; Physical
therapists; Recreational therapists;
Occupational therapists; Speech therapists;
Activities coordinators; Dietitians;
Ophthalmologists; Podiatrists; Audiologists.
Facilities Dining room; Physical therapy
room; Activities room; Crafts room; Laundry
room; Barber/Beauty shop; Library.
Activities Arts & crafts; Cards; Games;
Reading groups; Prayer groups; Movies;
Shopping trips; Dances/Social/Cultural
gatherings; Intergenerational programs.

Orange

Fountain Care Center
1835 W La Veta Ave, Orange, CA 92668
(714) 978-6800
Admin Claire D Crocker.
Medical Dir Bruce Muttey MD.
Licensure Skilled care. *Beds* SNF 283.
Certified Medicare; Medi-Cal.
Owner Proprietary corp (Summit Care).
Admissions Requirements Minimum age 55;
Medical examination; Physician's request.
Staff Physicians 30 (pt); RNs 6 (ft); LPNs 20
(ft); Nurses' aides 50 (ft); Physical therapists
1 (ft); Occupational therapists 1 (pt); Speech
therapists 1 (pt); Activities coordinators 1
(ft); Dietitians 1 (pt); Ophthalmologists 1
(pt); Podiatrists 1 (pt); Dentists 1 (pt).
Languages Spanish.
Facilities Dining room; Physical therapy
room; Activities room; Crafts room; Laundry
room; Barber/Beauty shop; Library; Garden
patios.
Activities Arts & crafts; Cards; Games;
Reading groups; Prayer groups; Movies;
Shopping trips; Dances/Social/Cultural
gatherings; Ball games; Picnics.

Hillhaven Convalescent Hospital
920 W La Veta St, Orange, CA 92668
(714) 633-3568
Admin Bruce Janssen.
Licensure Skilled care. *Beds* SNF 112.
Certified Medicare; Medi-Cal.
Owner Proprietary corp (Hillhaven Inc).

Orange Park Convalescent Hospital
5017 E Chapman Ave, Orange, CA 92669
(714) 997-7090
Admin Granger Butler.
Licensure Skilled care. *Beds* SNF 145.
Certified Medicare.
Owner Proprietary corp.

Orangevale

Orangevale Convalescent Hospital
9260 Loma Ln, Orangevale, CA 95662
(916) 988-1935
Admin J E Carper.

Licensure Skilled care. *Beds* SNF 25. *Certified*
Medicare; Medi-Cal.
Owner Proprietary corp.

Orinda

Orinda Rehabilitation & Convalescent Hospital
11 Altarinda Rd, Orinda, CA 94563
(415) 254-6500
Medical Dir Richard Homrighausen MD.
Licensure Skilled care. *Beds* SNF 49. *Certified*
Medicare.
Owner Proprietary corp.
Admissions Requirements Medical
examination; Physician's request.
Staff RNs 3 (ft), 6 (pt); LPNs 1 (ft); Nurses'
aides 20 (ft), 7 (pt); Activities coordinators 1
(ft); Dietitians 1 (pt).
Facilities Dining room; Physical therapy
room; Activities room; Laundry room;
Barber/Beauty shop; Sundeck.
Activities Arts & crafts; Cards; Games;
Reading groups; Prayer groups; Movies.

Oroville

Olive Ridge Care Center
1000 Executive Pkwy, Oroville, CA 95966
(916) 533-7335
Admin Carol T Walker.
Licensure Skilled care. *Beds* SNF 116.
Certified Medicare; Medi-Cal.
Owner Proprietary corp.

Oroville Community Convalescent Hospital
1511 Robinson St, Oroville, CA 95965
(916) 534-5701
Admin A Perreras & P Beltran.
Licensure Skilled care. *Beds* 41.
Owner Proprietary corp.

Shadowbrook Convalescent Hospital
1 Gilmore Ln, Oroville, CA 95965
(916) 534-1353
Admin Dixie Anderson.
Medical Dir Dr Olson.
Licensure Skilled care. *Beds* SNF 50. *Certified*
Medicare; Medi-Cal.
Owner Proprietary corp.
Admissions Requirements Physician's request.
Staff Physicians 12 (ft); RNs 2 (ft), 2 (pt);
LPNs 4 (ft), 2 (pt); Nurses' aides 16 (ft), 3
(pt); Physical therapists 1 (ft); Reality
therapists 1 (pt); Recreational therapists 1
(ft); Occupational therapists 1 (pt); Speech
therapists 1 (pt); Activities coordinators 1
(ft); Dietitians 1 (pt); Ophthalmologists 1
(pt); Podiatrists 2 (pt); Dentists 1 (pt).
Facilities Dining room; Physical therapy
room; Activities room; Crafts room; Laundry
room; Barber/Beauty shop.
Activities Arts & crafts; Cards; Games;
Reading groups; Prayer groups; Movies;
Dances/Social/Cultural gatherings.

Oxnard

Glenwood Convalescent Hospital
1300 N "C" St, Oxnard, CA 93030
(805) 983-0305
Admin Jerry Wells. *Dir of Nursing* Maricela
Santana RN. *Medical Dir* E Falcon MD.
Licensure Skilled care. *Beds* SNF 99.
Owner Proprietary corp.
Admissions Requirements Minimum age 18;
Medical examination; Physician's request.
Staff RNs 4 (ft); LPNs 11 (ft); Nurses' aides
40 (ft); Physical therapists 1 (ft); Reality
therapists 1 (ft); Recreational therapists 1
(ft); Occupational therapists 1 (ft); Speech
therapists 1 (ft); Activities coordinators 1
(ft); Dietitians 1 (ft); Ophthalmologists 1 (ft);
Podiatrists 1 (ft); Dentists 1 (ft).
Languages Spanish, Japanese, Tagalog.
Facilities Dining room; Physical therapy
room; Activities room; Crafts room; Laundry
room; Barber/Beauty shop; Library.

Activities Arts & crafts; Cards; Games;
Reading groups; Prayer groups; Movies;
Shopping trips; Dances/Social/Cultural
gatherings.

Maywood Acres Healthcare
2641 S "C" St, Oxnard, CA 93033
(805) 487-7840
Admin William Mohr.
Licensure Skilled care. *Beds* SNF 98. *Certified*
Medicare; Medi-Cal.
Owner Proprietary corp (Hillhaven Inc).

Oxnard Manor Convalescent Hospital
1400 W Gonzales Rd, Oxnard, CA 91301
(805) 983-0324
Admin Leigh Gori. *Dir of Nursing* Laurie
Adams RN. *Medical Dir* Josephine Solis
MD.
Licensure Skilled care. *Beds* SNF 82. *Certified*
Medicaid; Medicare.
Owner Privately owned.
Admissions Requirements Minimum age 21;
Medical examination; Physician's request.
Staff Physicians 2 (pt); RNs 1 (ft), 1 (pt);
LPNs 7 (ft), 1 (pt); Nurses' aides 20 (ft);
Physical therapists 1 (pt); Recreational
therapists 1 (pt); Occupational therapists 1
(pt); Speech therapists 1 (pt); Activities
coordinators 1 (ft); Dietitians 1 (pt);
Ophthalmologists 1 (pt); Podiatrists 1 (pt);
Audiologists 1 (pt).
Languages Spanish, Portuguese, Tagalog.
Activities Arts & crafts; Cards; Games;
Reading groups; Prayer groups; Movies;
Shopping trips; Dances/Social/Cultural
gatherings; Intergenerational programs; Pet
therapy.

**Pleasant Valley Rehabilitation & Convalescent
Hospital**
5225 S "J" St, Oxnard, CA 93030
(805) 488-3696
Admin John P Devine.
Medical Dir Joseph McGuire MD.
Licensure Skilled care. *Beds* 193. *Certified*
Medicare; Medi-Cal.
Owner Proprietary corp.
Admissions Requirements Medical
examination; Physician's request.
Staff RNs 8 (ft), 6 (pt); LPNs 13 (ft), 3 (pt);
Nurses' aides 58 (ft), 16 (pt); Recreational
therapists 1 (ft); Activities coordinators 2
(ft).
Facilities Dining room; Activities room;
Laundry room; Barber/Beauty shop.
Activities Arts & crafts; Cards; Games;
Reading groups; Prayer groups; Movies;
Shopping trips; Dances/Social/Cultural
gatherings.

**Pleasant Valley Rehabilitation & Convalescent
Hospital**
5225 S "J" St, Oxnard, CA 93030
(805) 488-3696
Admin John P Devine.
Licensure Skilled care. *Beds* SNF 193.
Certified Medicare; Medi-Cal.
Owner Proprietary corp.

St John's Regional Medical Center
333 N "F" St, Oxnard, CA 93030
(805) 988-2500, 483-4572 FAX
Admin Daniel R Herlinger. *Dir of Nursing*
Ruth Lacasse, VP Nursing Svcs.
Licensure Skilled care. *Beds* SNF 12. *Certified*
Medicare; Medi-Cal.
Owner Nonprofit organization/foundation.

Pacific Grove

Canterbury Woods
651 Sinex Ave, Pacific Grove, CA 93950
(408) 373-3111, 373-2140 FAX
Admin Robert B Butterfield. *Dir of Nursing*
Constance Golden. *Medical Dir* Dr John
Lord.

Licensure Skilled care; Intermediate care; Independent living; Alzheimer's care. *Beds* SNF 24; Independent living apartments 153. *Certified* Medicare.
Owner Nonprofit organization/foundation (Episcopal Homes Foundation).
Admissions Requirements Minimum age 65; Medical examination.
Staff Physicians 1 (pt); RNs 3 (ft), 3 (pt); Physical therapists; Dietitians.
Affiliation Episcopal.
Facilities Dining room; Physical therapy room; Activities room; Chapel; Crafts room; Laundry room; Barber/Beauty shop; Library.
Activities Arts & crafts; Cards; Games; Reading groups; Prayer groups; Movies; Shopping trips; Dances/Social/Cultural gatherings; Intergenerational programs; Pet therapy.

Pacific Grove Convalescent Hospital
200 Lighthouse Ave, Pacific Grove, CA 93950
(408) 375-2695
Admin Laura R Krueger.
Medical Dir Dr John Lord.
Licensure Skilled care. *Beds* SNF 51. *Certified* Medicare; Medi-Cal.
Owner Nonprofit corp.
Admissions Requirements Medical examination; Physician's request.
Staff RNs; LPNs; Nurses' aides; Activities coordinators 1 (ft), 1 (pt).
Affiliation Methodist.
Facilities Dining room; Activities room; Crafts room; Laundry room; Barber/Beauty shop.
Activities Arts & crafts; Cards; Games; Reading groups; Prayer groups; Movies; Shopping trips; Dances/Social/Cultural gatherings; Special outings.

Pacifica

Greenery Rehabilitation Center
385 Esplanade, Pacifica, CA 94044
(415) 993-5576, 359-9388 FAX
Admin Sally Rouses. *Dir of Nursing* Miriam O Shiro. *Medical Dir* Thomas Bowstead.
Licensure Skilled care; Respite care. *Beds* SNF 68. *Private Pay Patients* 60%. *Certified* Medicare.
Owner Proprietary corp (Greenery Rehabilitation Group Inc).
Staff Physicians 5 (pt); RNs 17 (ft); LPNs 15 (ft); Nurses' aides 45 (ft); Physical therapists 5 (ft); Recreational therapists 2 (ft); Occupational therapists 5 (ft); Speech therapists 3 (ft); Activities coordinators (consultant); Dietitians (consultant); Ophthalmologists (consultant); Podiatrists (consultant); Audiologists (consultant); COTAs.
Languages Spanish, Sign.
Facilities Dining room; Physical therapy room; Activities room; Chapel; Crafts room; Laundry room; Barber/Beauty shop; Library; Head injury program; Ventilator support program; Respite program; Day treatment/outpatient program; Short-term general rehabilitation program.
Activities Arts & crafts; Cards; Games; Reading groups; Prayer groups; Movies; Shopping trips; Dances/Social/Cultural gatherings; Intergenerational programs; Pet therapy.

Linda-Mar Convalescent Hospital
751 San Pedro Rd, Pacifica, CA 94044
(415) 359-4800, 359-8346 FAX
Admin Rosalyn R Isaac. *Dir of Nursing* Martha D Wheat RN. *Medical Dir* Herbert Fisher MD.
Licensure Skilled care. *Beds* SNF 59. *Certified* Medicare; Medi-Cal.
Owner Proprietary corp (Regency Health Services).

Admissions Requirements Minimum age 18; Medical examination.
Staff Physicians; RNs 1 (ft); LPNs 4 (ft); Physical therapists; Recreational therapists; Occupational therapists; Speech therapists; Activities coordinators; Dietitians; Ophthalmologists; Podiatrists; Audiologists; Respiratory therapists.
Languages Spanish, Tagalog, Russian, Hindi, French.
Facilities Dining room; Physical therapy room; Activities room; Laundry room; Barber/Beauty shop; Library; Occupational therapy and speech therapy room.
Activities Arts & crafts; Cards; Games; Reading groups; Prayer groups; Movies; Shopping trips; Dances/Social/Cultural gatherings; Intergenerational programs; Pet therapy; Adopt-a-pet; Volunteer group; 4-H Garden club; Adopt-a-grandparent; Pioneer Scouts; Community service projects.

Palm Desert

Carlotta
41-505 Carlotta Dr, Palm Desert, CA 92260
(619) 346-5420
Admin Dean Mertz.
Licensure Skilled care; Intermediate care. *Beds* SNF 53; ICF 6. *Certified* Medicare; Medi-Cal.
Owner Nonprofit corp (Evangelical Lutheran Good Samaritan Society).

Hacienda de Monterey
44600 Monterey Ave, Palm Desert, CA 92260
(619) 341-0890
Admin Martha L McGaughy, Exec Dir. *Dir of Nursing* Margaret Snow RN MS. *Medical Dir* Dr Robert B Wattsber.
Licensure Skilled care; Intermediate care; Residential care; Assisted living. *Beds* SNF 53; ICF 46; Residential care 140; Assisted living 40. *Certified* Medicare.
Owner Proprietary corp.
Admissions Requirements Minimum age 62; Medical examination; Physician's request.
Staff Physicians; RNs 8 (ft); LPNs 2 (ft); Nurses' aides 16 (ft); Physical therapists; Occupational therapists; Speech therapists; Activities coordinators 1 (ft); Dietitians 1 (pt); Ophthalmologists; Podiatrists; Audiologists.
Languages Spanish.
Facilities Dining room; Physical therapy room; Activities room; Crafts room; Barber/Beauty shop; Library.
Activities Arts & crafts; Cards; Games; Reading groups; Movies; Shopping trips; Dances/Social/Cultural gatherings; Intergenerational programs; Pet therapy.

Manor Care Nursing Center
74-350 Country Club Dr, Palm Desert, CA 92260
(619) 341-0261
Admin Judith Cox. *Dir of Nursing* Helen Keck. *Medical Dir* Dr Murray Taylor.
Licensure Skilled care; Retirement; Respite care; Alzheimer's care. *Beds* SNF 178; Retirement 50. *Certified* Medicare.
Owner Proprietary corp (Manor Care Inc).
Admissions Requirements Medical examination; Physician's request.
Staff Physicians 1 (ft); RNs 7 (ft), 1 (pt); LPNs 9 (ft); Nurses' aides 46 (ft); Physical therapists 1 (ft); Occupational therapists 1 (ft); Speech therapists 1 (ft); Activities coordinators 2 (ft), 1 (pt); Dietitians 1 (ft); Ophthalmologists 1 (ft); Podiatrists 1 (ft); Audiologists 1 (ft).
Languages Yiddish, Gaelic, Spanish.
Facilities Dining room; Physical therapy room; Activities room; Chapel; Crafts room; Laundry room; Barber/Beauty shop; Library; Private and formal dining; IV therapy; Alzheimer's unit.

Activities Arts & crafts; Cards; Games; Reading groups; Movies; Shopping trips; Dances/Social/Cultural gatherings; Intergenerational programs; Pet therapy; Alzheimer's programing; Shabbat services; Transportation to temple services; Wine and cheese hour.

Palm Springs

California Nursing & Rehabilitation Center
2299 N Indian Ave, Palm Springs, CA 92262
(619) 325-2937, 322-7250 FAX
Admin Carol Van Horst. *Dir of Nursing* Fely Mabbayad RN. *Medical Dir* Charles Supple MD.
Licensure Skilled care; Alzheimer's care. *Beds* SNF 80. *Certified* Medicare.
Owner Privately owned (Kennon Shea).
Admissions Requirements Medical examination; Physician's request.
Staff Physicians 1 (pt); RNs 4 (ft), 2 (pt); LPNs 4 (ft), 5 (pt); Nurses' aides 20 (ft), 3 (pt); Physical therapists 1 (pt); Occupational therapists 1 (pt); Speech therapists 1 (pt); Activities coordinators 1 (ft); Dietitians 1 (pt); Ophthalmologists 1 (pt); Podiatrists 1 (pt); Dentists 1 (pt).
Facilities Dining room; Physical therapy room; Activities room; Crafts room; Laundry room; Barber/Beauty shop; Library; Pool; Landscaped patios; Kosher kitchen available; IV therapy.
Activities Arts & crafts; Cards; Games; Reading groups; Prayer groups; Movies; Shopping trips; Dances/Social/Cultural gatherings; Intergenerational programs; Pet therapy; Friday Shabbot services; All Jewish holidays observed.

Care West—Palm Springs Nursing Center
2990 E Ramon Rd, Palm Springs, CA 92262
(619) 323-2638
Admin Jane L Beaver.
Licensure Skilled care. *Beds* SNF 99. *Certified* Medicare; Medi-Cal.
Owner Proprietary corp (Care Enterprises).

Palm Springs Healthcare
277 S Sunrise Way, Palm Springs, CA 92262
(619) 327-8541
Admin Jacqueline Arcara. *Dir of Nursing* Debra Bona. *Medical Dir* Irving Hershleifer.
Licensure Skilled care. *Beds* SNF 99. *Certified* Medicare; Medi-Cal.
Owner Proprietary corp (American-Cal Medical Services Inc).
Admissions Requirements Medical examination; Physician's request.
Staff RNs 2 (ft), 1 (pt); LPNs 7 (ft), 2 (pt); Nurses' aides 30 (ft), 2 (pt); Physical therapists 1 (pt); Recreational therapists 1 (ft); Occupational therapists 1 (pt); Speech therapists 1 (pt); Activities coordinators 1 (ft); Dietitians 1 (pt); Ophthalmologists 1 (pt); Podiatrists 1 (pt); Dentists 1 (pt); Staff developers.
Languages Spanish, Tagalog.
Facilities Dining room; Physical therapy room; Activities room; Laundry room; Barber/Beauty shop.
Activities Arts & crafts; Cards; Games; Reading groups; Prayer groups; Movies; Shopping trips; Dances/Social/Cultural gatherings; Overnight camping; Desert drives.

Palo Alto

Casa Olga Intermediate Health Care Facility
180 Hamilton Ave, Palo Alto, CA 94301
(415) 325-7821
Admin Penny Maloney. *Dir of Nursing* Pamela DiLucchio.
Licensure Intermediate care. *Beds* ICF 144. *Private Pay Patients* 6%. *Certified* Medi-Cal.

Owner Proprietary corp.
Staff RNs; LPNs; Nurses' aides; Activities coordinators.

Channing House
850 Webster St, Palo Alto, CA 94301
(415) 327-0950
Admin Fred H Seal.
Medical Dir Karen Fry.
Licensure Skilled care. *Beds* SNF 14.
Owner Nonprofit corp.
Admissions Requirements Minimum age 62; Medical examination.
Staff RNs 5 (ft), 6 (pt); Nurses' aides 12 (ft), 6 (pt); Activities coordinators 1 (ft); Dietitians 1 (ft).
Facilities Dining room; Physical therapy room; Activities room; Laundry room; Barber/Beauty shop; Library.
Activities Arts & crafts; Cards; Games; Reading groups; Movies.

Lytton Gardens Health Care Center
437 Webster St, Palo Alto, CA 94301
(415) 328-3300
Admin David Graber. *Dir of Nursing* Linda Harrop RN. *Medical Dir* W Bortz MD.
Licensure Skilled care; Retirement. *Beds* SNF 128. *Certified* Medicare; Medi-Cal.
Owner Proprietary corp.
Admissions Requirements Physician's request.
Staff RNs 5 (ft), 7 (pt); LPNs 10 (ft), 5 (pt); Nurses' aides 24 (ft), 12 (pt); Physical therapists 2 (ft); Recreational therapists 1 (ft); Occupational therapists 1 (ft); Activities coordinators 1 (ft).
Languages Spanish, Tagalog.
Facilities Dining room; Physical therapy room; Activities room; Chapel; Crafts room; Laundry room; Barber/Beauty shop.
Activities Arts & crafts; Cards; Games; Reading groups; Prayer groups; Movies; Shopping trips; Dances/Social/Cultural gatherings.

Palo Alto Nursing Center
911 Bryant St, Palo Alto, CA 94301
(415) 327-0511
Admin Wendy Corr.
Licensure Skilled care. *Beds* SNF 66. *Certified* Medicare; Medi-Cal.
Owner Proprietary corp.

Panorama City

Beverly Manor Convalescent Hospital
9541 Van Nuys Blvd, Panorama City, CA 91402
(818) 893-6385
Admin Marcia S Weldon. *Dir of Nursing* Oma Lockridge RN. *Medical Dir* Melvin Kirschner MD.
Licensure Skilled care. *Beds* SNF 151. *Private Pay Patients* 10%. *Certified* Medicare; Medi-Cal.
Owner Proprietary corp.
Admissions Requirements Medical examination.
Staff RNs; LPNs; Nurses' aides; Recreational therapists; Activities coordinators; Dietitians.
Languages Spanish, Farsi.
Facilities Dining room; Physical therapy room; Activities room; Laundry room; Barber/Beauty shop.
Activities Arts & crafts; Cards; Games; Reading groups; Prayer groups; Movies; Shopping trips; Dances/Social/Cultural gatherings; Intergenerational programs; Pet therapy.

Sun Air Convalescent Hospital
14857 Roscoe Blvd, Panorama City, CA 91402
(818) 894-5707
Admin David Schleidt. *Dir of Nursing* Freda Fahid RN.
Licensure Skilled care; Alzheimer's care. *Beds* SNF 98. *Certified* Medicare; Medi-Cal.

Owner Proprietary corp.
Staff Physicians; RNs 2 (ft), 4 (pt); LPNs 4 (ft), 4 (pt); Nurses' aides 30 (ft), 3 (pt); Activities coordinators 1 (ft), 1 (pt); Dietitians 1 (pt).
Languages Spanish, Farsi, Tagalog.
Facilities Dining room; Physical therapy room; Activities room; Chapel; Crafts room; Laundry room; Barber/Beauty shop; Library.
Activities Arts & crafts; Cards; Games; Prayer groups; Movies; Shopping trips; Dances/Social/Cultural gatherings.

Paradise

Cypress Acres Convalescent Hospital
1633 Cypress Ln, Paradise, CA 95969
(916) 877-9316
Admin Jean K Filer. *Dir of Nursing* Linda Livesay RN. *Medical Dir* M Wesley Farr MD.
Licensure Skilled care; Alzheimer's care. *Beds* SNF 107. *Certified* Medicare; Medi-Cal.
Owner Proprietary corp.
Admissions Requirements Medical examination; Physician's request.
Staff RNs 8 (ft), 3 (pt); LPNs 6 (ft), 1 (pt); Nurses' aides 26 (ft), 21 (pt); Physical therapists 2 (ft); Recreational therapists 1 (pt); Occupational therapists 1 (pt); Speech therapists 1 (pt); Activities coordinators 1 (ft), 2 (pt); Dietitians 1 (ft); Ophthalmologists 1 (pt); Dentists 1 (pt).
Facilities Dining room; Physical therapy room; Activities room; Chapel; Crafts room; Laundry room; Barber/Beauty shop; Library.
Activities Arts & crafts; Cards; Games; Reading groups; Prayer groups; Movies; Shopping trips; Dances/Social/Cultural gatherings.

Cypress Acres Intermediate Care Facility
6900 Clark Rd, Paradise, CA 95969
(916) 872-4055
Admin Jean K Filer.
Medical Dir M Wesley Farr MD.
Licensure Intermediate care; Alzheimer's care. *Beds* ICF 29. *Certified* Medi-Cal.
Owner Proprietary corp.
Admissions Requirements Medical examination; Physician's request.
Staff RNs 2 (ft); LPNs 1 (ft); Nurses' aides 7 (ft); Physical therapists 1 (pt); Recreational therapists 1 (pt); Occupational therapists 1 (pt); Speech therapists 1 (pt); Activities coordinators 1 (ft); Dietitians 1 (pt); Ophthalmologists 1 (pt); Dentists 1 (pt); Social workers 1 (ft).
Facilities Dining room; Physical therapy room; Activities room; Crafts room; Laundry room; Library.
Activities Arts & crafts; Cards; Games; Reading groups; Prayer groups; Movies; Shopping trips; Dances/Social/Cultural gatherings.

Heritage Paradise
8777 Skyway, Paradise, CA 95969
(916) 872-3200
Admin Raymond H Marks.
Licensure Skilled care. *Beds* SNF 99. *Certified* Medicare.
Owner Privately owned.

Paradise Convalescent Hospital
7419 Skyway, Paradise, CA 95969
(916) 877-7676
Admin Dixie Anderson.
Licensure Skilled care. *Beds* SNF 44. *Certified* Medicare; Medi-Cal.
Owner Proprietary corp.

Paramount

La Paz Geropsychiatric Center
8835 Vans St, Paramount, CA 90723
(213) 633-5111, 630-4100 FAX

Admin Steve McKinley. *Dir of Nursing* Pat Simonson. *Medical Dir* Dr Mark Honig.
Licensure Skilled care; STP program. *Beds* SNF 130. *Private Pay Patients* 0%. *Certified* Medi-Cal.
Owner Proprietary corp (Telecare Corp).
Admissions Requirements Minimum age 55; Medical examination.
Staff Physicians; RNs; LPNs; Activities coordinators; Dietitians.
Languages Spanish.
Facilities Dining room; Activities room; Crafts room.
Activities Arts & crafts; Cards; Games; Reading groups; Prayer groups; Movies; Shopping trips; Dances/Social/Cultural gatherings; Intergenerational programs.

Paramount Chateau Convalescent Hospital
7039 Alondra Blvd, Paramount, CA 90723
(213) 531-0990
Admin Meredith Denzel.
Licensure Skilled care. *Beds* SNF 99. *Certified* Medicare; Medi-Cal.
Owner Proprietary corp.

Paramount Convalescent Hospital
8558 E Rosecrans Ave, Paramount, CA 90723
(213) 634-6877
Admin Henriette Witzak.
Licensure Skilled care. *Beds* SNF 59. *Certified* Medicare; Medi-Cal.
Owner Privately owned.

Pasadena

Californian—Pasadena Convalescent Hospital
120 Bellefontaine, Pasadena, CA 91105
(818) 793-5116
Admin A Rose Bower. *Dir of Nursing* Jean Snell RN.
Licensure Skilled care. *Beds* SNF 82. *Certified* Medicare.
Owner Proprietary corp.
Admissions Requirements Medical examination; Physician's request.
Staff RNs 6 (ft), 4 (pt); Physical therapists 1 (ft); Occupational therapists 1 (pt); Speech therapists 1 (pt); Activities coordinators 1 (ft); Dietitians 1 (pt); Ophthalmologists 1 (pt).
Facilities Dining room; Physical therapy room; Barber/Beauty shop.
Activities Arts & crafts; Cards; Games; Reading groups; Movies.

Congress Convalescent of Huntington Memorial Hospital
716 S Fair Oaks Ave, Pasadena, CA 91105
(818) 793-6127
Admin Jacqueline Bartholomew.
Licensure Skilled care. *Beds* SNF 75. *Certified* Medicare; Medi-Cal.
Owner Nonprofit corp.

Crestwood Convalescent Pasadena
1836 N Fair Oaks, Pasadena, CA 91103
(818) 798-9125
Admin William E Kite. *Dir of Nursing* Jim Parker RN. *Medical Dir* T Hee MD.
Licensure Skilled care; Alzheimer's care. *Beds* SNF 99. *Certified* Medicare; Medi-Cal.
Owner Proprietary corp (Crestwood Hospitals Inc).
Admissions Requirements Minimum age 30; Medical examination; Physician's request.
Staff RNs 2 (ft), 3 (pt); LPNs 9 (ft), 4 (pt); Nurses' aides 42 (ft), 4 (pt); Physical therapists; Occupational therapists; Speech therapists; Activities coordinators 1 (ft); Dietitians; Ophthalmologists; Podiatrists; Dentists; SS cord 1 (ft).
Languages Armenian, Spanish.

Facilities Dining room; Physical therapy room; Activities room; Barber/Beauty shop.
Activities Arts & crafts; Cards; Games; Reading groups; Prayer groups; Movies; Shopping trips; Dances/Social/Cultural gatherings; Candlelight dinner; Country breakfast; Special events every month.

Eisenhower Nursing & Convalescent Hospital
1470 N Fair Oaks, Pasadena, CA 91103
(213) 798-9133
Admin David H Berger. *Dir of Nursing* Virginia Estorninos RN. *Medical Dir* Stanley Cuba MD.
Licensure Skilled care; Alzheimer's care. *Beds* SNF 71. *Certified* Medicare; Medi-Cal.
Owner Proprietary corp.
Admissions Requirements Physician's request.
Staff RNs 1 (ft); LPNs 5 (ft); Nurses' aides 20 (ft); Activities coordinators 1 (ft); Dietitians 1 (ft).
Facilities Dining room; Activities room; Laundry room; Barber/Beauty shop.
Activities Arts & crafts; Cards; Games; Reading groups; Prayer groups; Movies; Shopping trips; Dances/Social/Cultural gatherings; Country breakfast; Candlelight dinner; Wine/cheese social.

Hillhaven Care Center
1920 N Fair Oaks, Pasadena, CA 91103
(213) 798-6777
Admin Dorothy Montgomery. *Dir of Nursing* Dorothy Montgomery RN. *Medical Dir* William Putnam MD.
Licensure Skilled care; Alzheimer's care. *Beds* SNF 80. *Certified* Medicare; Medi-Cal.
Owner Proprietary corp (Flagg Industries Inc).
Admissions Requirements Minimum age 20; Medical examination; Physician's request.
Staff Physicians 40 (pt); RNs 3 (ft), 3 (pt); LPNs 6 (ft), 5 (pt); Nurses' aides 22 (ft), 4 (pt); Physical therapists 2 (ft); Reality therapists 1 (ft); Occupational therapists 1 (pt); Speech therapists 1 (pt); Activities coordinators 1 (ft); Dietitians 1 (ft); Ophthalmologists 1 (pt); Podiatrists 1 (pt); Dentists 1 (pt).
Facilities Dining room; Physical therapy room; Activities room; Crafts room; Laundry room; Barber/Beauty shop; Sun room; Lounge.
Activities Arts & crafts; Cards; Games; Reading groups; Prayer groups; Movies; Shopping trips; Dances/Social/Cultural gatherings.

Kent Convalescent Hospital
1640 N Fair Oaks, Pasadena, CA 91103
(213) 798-1175
Admin Malvina C Preyer. *Dir of Nursing* Nadine Ford RN. *Medical Dir* Peter Dunn MD.
Licensure Skilled care; Intermediate care; Retirement. *Beds* SNF 88; ICF 11. *Certified* Medicare; Medi-Cal.
Owner Proprietary corp.
Admissions Requirements Minimum age 65; Medical examination; Physician's request.
Staff RNs 1 (ft); LPNs 9 (ft); Nurses' aides 32 (ft); Activities coordinators 1 (ft).
Languages Spanish.
Facilities Dining room; Physical therapy room; Activities room; Barber/Beauty shop.
Activities Arts & crafts; Cards; Games; Movies; Shopping trips.

Sophia Lyn Convalescent Hospital
1570 N Fair Oaks Ave, Pasadena, CA 91103
(818) 798-0558
Admin Robert Taylor.
Licensure Skilled care. *Beds* SNF 54. *Certified* Medicare; Medi-Cal.
Owner Proprietary corp.

Marlinda Convalescent Hospital at Pasadena
2637 E Washington, Pasadena, CA 91107
(818) 798-8991

Admin Marthann Demchuk. *Dir of Nursing* Mrs Rohde. *Medical Dir* Dr Moritz.
Licensure Skilled care. *Beds* SNF 50. *Certified* Medicare; Medi-Cal.
Owner Privately owned.
Admissions Requirements Physician's request.
Staff Physicians; RNs; LPNs; Nurses' aides; Physical therapists; Reality therapists; Recreational therapists; Occupational therapists; Speech therapists; Activities coordinators; Dietitians; Ophthalmologists; Podiatrists; Dentists.
Languages Spanish, Tagalog.
Facilities Dining room; Activities room; Chapel; Crafts room; Laundry room; Barber/Beauty shop; Library; Patio; TV room.
Activities Arts & crafts; Cards; Games; Reading groups; Prayer groups; Movies; Shopping trips.

Marlinda-Imperial Convalescent Hospital
150 Bellefontaine, Pasadena, CA 91101
(818) 796-1103
Admin Marthann Demchuk. *Dir of Nursing* Lorene Wohlgemuth RN. *Medical Dir* Ray George MD.
Licensure Skilled care. *Beds* SNF 130. *Certified* Medicare; Medi-Cal.
Owner Privately owned.
Admissions Requirements Medical examination; Physician's request.
Staff Physicians 1 (pt); RNs 5 (ft), 4 (pt); LPNs 7 (ft), 2 (pt); Nurses' aides 20 (ft), 5 (pt); Physical therapists 1 (ft); Occupational therapists 1 (ft); Speech therapists 1 (pt); Activities coordinators 2 (ft); Dietitians 1 (pt); Ophthalmologists 1 (pt); Podiatrists 1 (pt);; Dentists 1 (pt); Respiratory aides 1 (ft); Physical therapy aides 2 (ft), 1 (pt); Hairdressers 1 (ft).
Languages Spanish, Tagalog, Polish, Lebanese.
Facilities Dining room; Physical therapy room; Activities room; Crafts room; Laundry room; Barber/Beauty shop; Outside patios.
Activities Arts & crafts; Cards; Games; Reading groups; Prayer groups; Movies; Shopping trips; Dances/Social/Cultural gatherings; Birthday parties; Exercise class.

Monte Vista Grove
2889 San Pasqual Ave, Pasadena, CA 91011
(818) 792-2712
Admin Sandra K Atkins. *Dir of Nursing* Helen Baatz. *Medical Dir* Dr Craig Milhouse.
Licensure Skilled care; Retirement. *Beds* SNF 40. *Private Pay Patients* 100%.
Owner Nonprofit corp.
Admissions Requirements Minimum age 65; Medical examination; Physician's request.
Staff Physicians 1 (pt); RNs 1 (ft), 2 (pt); LPNs 3 (ft); Nurses' aides 20 (ft), 2 (pt); Physical therapists 1 (pt); Occupational therapists 1 (pt); Speech therapists 1 (pt); Activities coordinators 1 (ft); Dietitians 1 (ft); Podiatrists 1 (pt).
Languages Spanish.
Affiliation Presbyterian.
Facilities Dining room; Physical therapy room; Activities room; Chapel; Crafts room; Laundry room; Barber/Beauty shop; Library; Gardens.
Activities Arts & crafts; Cards; Games; Reading groups; Prayer groups; Movies; Shopping trips; Dances/Social/Cultural gatherings; Intergenerational programs; Pet therapy; Social teas; Parties; Volunteer program.

Oakwood Care Center
1450 N Fairoaks Ave, Pasadena, CA 91103
(818) 791-1948, 791-9282 FAX
Admin Edith Avanzado RD. *Dir of Nursing* Linda Budy. *Medical Dir* Dr Punzalan.
Licensure Skilled care; Intermediate care; Alzheimer's care. *Beds* SNF 84; ICF 12. *Private Pay Patients* 10%. *Certified* Medicare; Medi-Cal.
Owner Proprietary corp.

Admissions Requirements Minimum age 40; Medical examination; Physician's request.
Staff Physicians; RNs; LPNs; Nurses' aides; Physical therapists; Recreational therapists; Occupational therapists; Activities coordinators; Dietitians; Podiatrists; LVNs.
Languages Spanish, Chinese, Tagalog, Japanese.
Facilities Dining room; Physical therapy room; Activities room; Crafts room; Laundry room; Barber/Beauty shop; Library.
Activities Arts & crafts; Cards; Games; Reading groups; Prayer groups; Movies; Shopping trips; Dances/Social/Cultural gatherings; Intergenerational programs.

Park Marino Convalescent Center
2585 E Washington, Pasadena, CA 91107
(818) 798-6753
Admin Kitty Batho.
Licensure Skilled care. *Beds* SNF 99. *Certified* Medicare.
Owner Proprietary corp.

Rose Garden Convalescent Center
1899 N Raymond Ave, Pasadena, CA 91103
(818) 797-2120
Admin Pompeyo Rosales.
Licensure Skilled care. *Beds* SNF 99. *Certified* Medicare; Medi-Cal.
Owner Proprietary corp.

Sacred Heart Convalescent Hospital
1810 N Fair Oaks, Pasadena, CA 91103
(213) 935-1262
Admin Norma L Abenoja. *Dir of Nursing* Thelma Grafil. *Medical Dir* Dr Jose Mutia.
Licensure Skilled care. *Beds* SNF 78. *Certified* Medicare; Medi-Cal.
Owner Proprietary corp.
Staff Physicians; RNs; LPNs; Nurses' aides; Physical therapists; Recreational therapists; Occupational therapists; Speech therapists; Activities coordinators; Dietitians; Ophthalmologists; Podiatrists; Dentists.
Facilities Dining room; Activities room; Crafts room; Laundry room; Barber/Beauty shop; Library.
Activities Arts & crafts; Cards; Games; Reading groups; Prayer groups; Movies; Shopping trips; Dances/Social/Cultural gatherings.

Villa Gardens
842 E Villa St, Pasadena, CA 91101
(818) 796-8162
Admin Tim Dettman.
Medical Dir Nancy Gibbs MD.
Licensure Skilled care; Residential care. *Beds* SNF 54; Residential care 220. *Certified* Medicare.
Owner Nonprofit organization/foundation.
Admissions Requirements Minimum age 62; Medical examination; Physician's request.
Staff RNs; LPNs; Nurses' aides; Activities coordinators.
Languages Spanish.
Facilities Dining room; Physical therapy room; Activities room; Crafts room; Barber/Beauty shop; Library.

Villa Oaks Convalescent Hospital
1515 N Fair Oaks Ave, Pasadena, CA 91103
(818) 798-1111
Admin Robert Taylor. *Dir of Nursing* Z Malcom RN.
Licensure Skilled care. *Beds* SNF 49. *Certified* Medicare; Medi-Cal.
Owner Proprietary corp.
Admissions Requirements Minimum age 40; Physician's request.
Staff Physicians; RNs; LPNs; Nurses' aides; Physical therapists; Reality therapists; Occupational therapists; Speech therapists; Activities coordinators; Dietitians; Ophthalmologists; Podiatrists; Dentists.
Languages Spanish, Tagalog.

Facilities Dining room; Activities room; Laundry room; Barber/Beauty shop.
Activities Arts & crafts; Cards; Games; Reading groups; Prayer groups; Shopping trips; Dances/Social/Cultural gatherings.

Paso Robles

Paso Robles Convalescent Hospital
321 12th St, Paso Robles, CA 93446
(805) 238-4637
Admin Doug Las Wamsley. *Dir of Nursing* Carlene Powell. *Medical Dir* Dr Tom Harper.
Licensure Skilled care. *Beds* SNF 42. *Certified* Medi-Cal.
Owner Proprietary corp.
Admissions Requirements Physician's request.
Staff Physicians 7 (pt); RNs 1 (ft), 3 (pt); LPNs 3 (ft), 3 (pt); Nurses' aides 13 (ft), 4 (pt); Physical therapists 1 (pt); Reality therapists 1 (pt); Recreational therapists 1 (pt); Occupational therapists 1 (pt); Speech therapists 1 (pt); Activities coordinators 1 (ft), 1 (pt); Dietitians 1 (pt); Ophthalmologists 1 (pt); Podiatrists 1 (pt); Dentists 1 (pt).
Facilities Dining room; Activities room; Crafts room; Laundry room; Barber/Beauty shop.
Activities Arts & crafts; Cards; Games; Reading groups; Prayer groups; Movies; Shopping trips; Dances/Social/Cultural gatherings.

Perris

Medical Arts Convalescent Hospital
2225 N Perris Blvd, Perris, CA 92370
(714) 657-2135, 657-4028 FAX
Admin L M Swegles. *Dir of Nursing* Ada Doss RN. *Medical Dir* C Rex La Grange MD.
Licensure Skilled care. *Beds* SNF 109. *Certified* Medicare; Medi-Cal.
Owner Proprietary corp.
Admissions Requirements Physician's request.
Staff Physicians; RNs; Nurses' aides; Physical therapists; Recreational therapists; Occupational therapists; Speech therapists; Activities coordinators; Dietitians; Podiatrists; Audiologists.
Facilities Dining room; Physical therapy room; Activities room; Crafts room; Laundry room; Barber/Beauty shop; Library.
Activities Arts & crafts; Cards; Games; Prayer groups; Movies; Shopping trips; Dances/ Social/Cultural gatherings; Intergenerational programs; Pet therapy.

Petaluma

Beverly Manor of Petaluma
101 Monroe St, Petaluma, CA 94952
(707) 763-4109
Admin Joy Conklin. *Dir of Nursing* Wanda Elliott RN. *Medical Dir* Rex Harner MD.
Licensure Skilled care. *Beds* SNF 99. *Certified* Medicare; Medi-Cal.
Owner Proprietary corp (Beverly Enterprises).
Admissions Requirements Medical examination; Physician's request.
Staff RNs; LPNs; Nurses' aides; Physical therapists; Occupational therapists; Speech therapists; Activities coordinators; Dietitians; Ophthalmologists; Dentists.
Languages Spanish, French.
Facilities Dining room; Physical therapy room; Activities room; Barber/Beauty shop.
Activities Arts & crafts; Cards; Games; Reading groups; Prayer groups; Movies; Shopping trips; Dances/Social/Cultural gatherings.

CareWest—Petaluma
1115 B St, Petaluma, CA 94952
(707) 763-6871

Admin Carol Bowman-Jones. *Dir of Nursing* Mary K Carroll. *Medical Dir* Dr Patty Glatt.
Licensure Skilled care. *Beds* SNF 90. *Private Pay Patients* 40%. *Certified* Medicare; Medi-Cal.
Owner Proprietary corp (Care Enterprises).
Admissions Requirements Medical examination; Physician's request.
Staff Physicians; RNs; LPNs; Nurses' aides; Physical therapists; Occupational therapists; Speech therapists; Activities coordinators; Dietitians; Ophthalmologists; Podiatrists; Audiologists.
Languages Spanish.
Facilities Dining room; Physical therapy room; Activities room; Crafts room; Laundry room; Barber/Beauty shop.
Activities Arts & crafts; Games; Reading groups; Prayer groups; Movies; Shopping trips; Dances/Social/Cultural gatherings; Intergenerational programs; Pet therapy.

Crestview Convalescent Hospital
523 Hayes Ln, Petaluma, CA 94952
(707) 763-2457
Admin Robert Peacock.
Medical Dir Dean O'Neil MD.
Licensure Skilled care. *Beds* SNF 90. *Certified* Medicare; Medi-Cal.
Owner Proprietary corp.
Admissions Requirements Minimum age 60; Medical examination; Physician's request.
Staff RNs 4 (ft); LPNs 6 (ft); Nurses' aides 30 (ft); Physical therapists 1 (pt); Occupational therapists 1 (pt); Speech therapists 1 (pt); Activities coordinators 1 (ft); Dietitians 1 (pt); Ophthalmologists 1 (pt); Podiatrists 1 (pt); Audiologists 1 (pt); Dentists 1 (pt).
Facilities Dining room; Physical therapy room; Activities room; Barber/Beauty shop.
Activities Arts & crafts; Cards; Games; Movies.

Hacienda Care Center
300 Douglas St, Petaluma, CA 94952
(707) 763-6887
Admin Tom Owens.
Licensure Skilled care. *Beds* SNF 98. *Certified* Medicare; Medi-Cal.
Owner Proprietary corp (Flagg Industries).

Oaks
450 Hayes Ln, Petaluma, CA 94952
(707) 778-8686
Admin Philip B Abbott.
Medical Dir John Rodnick MD.
Licensure Skilled care. *Beds* SNF 59. *Certified* Medicare; Medi-Cal.
Owner Proprietary corp.
Staff Physicians 4 (pt); RNs 4 (ft), 3 (pt); LPNs 3 (ft), 4 (pt); Nurses' aides 34 (ft); Physical therapists 2 (pt); Recreational therapists 1 (pt); Occupational therapists 1 (pt); Speech therapists 1 (pt); Activities coordinators 1 (ft); Dietitians 1 (pt); Ophthalmologists 1 (pt); Podiatrists 1 (pt); Audiologists 1 (pt); Dentists 1 (pt).
Facilities Dining room; Physical therapy room; Activities room; Chapel; Crafts room; Laundry room; Barber/Beauty shop; Library.
Activities Arts & crafts; Cards; Games; Reading groups; Prayer groups; Movies; Shopping trips; Dances/Social/Cultural gatherings; Outside entertainment.

Pico Rivera

Colonial Gardens Nursing Home
7246 S Rosemead Blvd, Pico Rivera, CA 90660
(213) 949-2591
Admin David H Lewis. *Dir of Nursing* Christine Chung RN. *Medical Dir* Rolando Atiga MD.
Licensure Skilled care; Alzheimer's care. *Beds* SNF 99. *Certified* Medi-Cal.
Owner Proprietary corp.

Admissions Requirements Minimum age 45; Medical examination.
Staff Physicians; RNs; LPNs; Nurses' aides; Physical therapists; Reality therapists; Recreational therapists; Occupational therapists; Speech therapists; Activities coordinators; Dietitians; Ophthalmologists; Podiatrists; Dentists; Social workers.
Languages Spanish, Korean, Tagalog.
Facilities Dining room; Activities room; Crafts room; Laundry room; Barber/Beauty shop; Library.
Activities Arts & crafts; Cards; Games; Reading groups; Prayer groups; Movies; Shopping trips; Dances/Social/Cultural gatherings; Outside trips for meals.

El Rancho Vista Convalescent Center
8925 Mines Ave, Pico Rivera, CA 90660
(213) 692-0319
Admin Bill Belanger. *Dir of Nursing* Kathy Blanco.
Licensure Skilled care. *Beds* SNF 86. *Certified* Medicare; Medi-Cal.
Owner Proprietary corp (Western Medical Enterprises Inc).
Admissions Requirements Minimum age 62; Medical examination; Physician's request.
Staff RNs 1 (ft), 1 (pt); LPNs 5 (ft); Nurses' aides 17 (ft); Physical therapists 1 (pt); Recreational therapists 1 (pt); Occupational therapists 1 (pt); Speech therapists 1 (pt); Activities coordinators 1 (ft); Dietitians 1 (pt); Ophthalmologists 1 (pt); Podiatrists 1 (pt); Dentists 1 (pt).
Languages Spanish.
Facilities Dining room; Physical therapy room; Activities room; Crafts room; Laundry room; Barber/Beauty shop; Library.
Activities Arts & crafts; Cards; Games; Reading groups; Prayer groups; Movies; Shopping trips; Dances/Social/Cultural gatherings.

Riviera Nursing & Convalescent Hospital
8203 Telegraph Rd, Pico Rivera, CA 90660
(213) 806-2576
Admin Kam-Amirshahi. *Dir of Nursing* Tessie Estonactoc. *Medical Dir* Dr Lawrence Pollock.
Licensure Skilled care; Intermediate care. *Beds* SNF 146; ICF 8. *Private Pay Patients* 5%. *Certified* Medicare; Medi-Cal.
Owner Proprietary corp.
Staff Physicians; RNs; LPNs; Nurses' aides; Physical therapists; Reality therapists; Occupational therapists; Speech therapists; Activities coordinators; Dietitians; Ophthalmologists (consultant); Podiatrists; Audiologists (consultant); Dentists (consultant).
Facilities Dining room; Physical therapy room; Activities room; Crafts room; Laundry room; Barber/Beauty shop; Patios.
Activities Arts & crafts; Cards; Games; Reading groups; Prayer groups; Movies; Dances/Social/Cultural gatherings; Outings.

St Theresa Convalescent Hospital
9140 Verner Ave, Pico Rivera, CA 90660
(213) 948-1961, 949-5998 FAX
Admin Vince Hambright. *Dir of Nursing* Deborah Jackson RN. *Medical Dir* Ismael Guerrero MD.
Licensure Skilled care. *Beds* SNF 99. *Private Pay Patients* 10%. *Certified* Medicaid; Medicare; Medi-Cal.
Owner Proprietary corp (Braswell Enterprises).
Admissions Requirements Medical examination.
Staff RNs 2 (ft); LPNs 9 (ft); Nurses' aides 33 (ft); Physical therapists 1 (ft); Activities coordinators 1 (ft), 1 (pt); Dietitians 1 (ft).
Languages Spanish.
Affiliation Roman Catholic.
Facilities Dining room; Physical therapy room; Activities room; Laundry room; Barber/Beauty shop.

Activities Arts & crafts; Cards; Games; Reading groups; Prayer groups; Movies; Shopping trips; Dances/Social/Cultural gatherings; Intergenerational programs; Pet therapy.

Pimole

Fresno Westview Convalescent Hospital
PO Box 10, Pimole, CA 94564
(209) 485-3750
Admin Juanita R Basye.
Medical Dir E H Holvey MD.
Licensure Skilled care; Intermediate care. *Beds* SNF 120; ICF 79. *Certified* Medi-Cal.
Owner Proprietary corp.
Admissions Requirements Minimum age 5.
Staff Physicians 3 (pt); RNs 4 (ft), 5 (pt); LPNs 13 (ft), 5 (pt); Nurses' aides 54 (ft), 14 (pt); Physical therapists 1 (pt); Reality therapists 2 (ft); Recreational therapists 1 (ft); Occupational therapists 1 (ft); Speech therapists 1 (pt); Activities coordinators 4 (ft), 2 (pt); Dietitians 3 (pt); Ophthalmologists 4 (pt); Podiatrists 1 (pt); Audiologists 1 (pt); Dentists 1 (pt).
Facilities Dining room; Physical therapy room; Activities room; Crafts room; Laundry room; Barber/Beauty shop.
Activities Arts & crafts; Cards; Games; Reading groups; Prayer groups; Movies; Shopping trips; Dances/Social/Cultural gatherings; Camping; Fishing; County fair.

Pittsburg

Pittsburg Care Center
535 School St, Pittsburg, CA 94565
(415) 432-3831
Admin William J Connell.
Medical Dir Edwin Boysen.
Licensure Skilled care. *Beds* SNF 49. *Certified* Medicare; Medi-Cal.
Owner Nonprofit corp.
Admissions Requirements Physician's request.
Staff Physicians 6 (pt); RNs 3 (pt); LPNs 3 (ft), 3 (pt); Nurses' aides 10 (ft), 7 (pt); Physical therapists 1 (pt); Occupational therapists 1 (pt); Speech therapists 1 (pt); Activities coordinators 1 (pt); Dietitians 1 (pt); Ophthalmologists 1 (pt); Dentists 1 (pt).
Facilities Dining room; Physical therapy room; Activities room; Crafts room; Laundry room.
Activities Arts & crafts; Cards; Games; Reading groups; Movies.

Regency Hills Convalescent Hospital
2351 Loveridge Rd, Pittsburg, CA 94565
(415) 427-4444
Admin Ivan Howard.
Licensure Skilled care. *Beds* SNF 120. *Certified* Medicare; Medi-Cal.

Placerville

El Dorado Convalescent Hospital
3280 Washington St, Placerville, CA 95667
(916) 622-6842
Admin James Anderson. *Dir of Nursing* Vicki Fry RN. *Medical Dir* Ted Christy MD.
Licensure Skilled care. *Beds* SNF 99. *Certified* Medicare; Medi-Cal.
Owner Proprietary corp.
Staff RNs 3 (ft), 5 (pt); LPNs 2 (ft), 2 (pt); Nurses' aides 25 (ft), 5 (pt); Physical therapists; Occupational therapists; Speech therapists; Activities coordinators.
Facilities Dining room; Physical therapy room; Activities room; Crafts room; Laundry room; Barber/Beauty shop; Library.
Activities Arts & crafts; Cards; Games; Reading groups; Prayer groups; Movies; Shopping trips; Dances/Social/Cultural gatherings.

Gold Country Health Center
4301 Golden Center Dr, Placerville, CA 95667
(916) 621-1100
Admin Richard Rell.
Licensure Skilled care. *Beds* SNF 135. *Certified* Medicare; Medi-Cal.
Owner Proprietary corp.

Placerville Pines Convalescent Hospital
1040 Marshall Way, Placerville, CA 95667
(916) 622-3400
Admin Mickie Snively.
Licensure Skilled care. *Beds* SNF 99. *Certified* Medicare; Medi-Cal.
Owner Proprietary corp.
Facilities Dining room; Physical therapy room; Activities room; Chapel; Crafts room; Laundry room; Barber/Beauty shop; Library.
Activities Arts & crafts; Cards; Games; Reading groups; Prayer groups; Movies; Shopping trips.

Playa Del Rey

Care West—Playa Del Rey Nursing Center
7716 Manchester Ave, Playa Del Rey, CA 90293
(213) 823-4694
Admin Julie Booth.
Licensure Skilled care. *Beds* SNF 99. *Certified* Medicare; Medi-Cal.
Owner Proprietary corp (Care Enterprises).

Pleasant Hill

Baywood Convalescent Hospital
550 Patterson Blvd, Pleasant Hill, CA 94523
(415) 939-5400
Licensure Skilled care. *Beds* SNF 166. *Certified* Medicare; Medi-Cal.
Owner Proprietary corp (ARA Living Centers).

Oak Park Convalescent Hospital
1625 Oak Park Blvd, Pleasant Hill, CA 94523
(415) 935-5222
Admin John Gallick.
Licensure Skilled care. *Beds* SNF 51. *Certified* Medicare; Medi-Cal.
Owner Proprietary corp.

Rosewood Convalescent Hospital
1911 Oak Park Blvd, Pleasant Hill, CA 94523
(415) 935-6630
Admin Lisa E Churches. *Dir of Nursing* Phyllis O'Leary RN. *Medical Dir* Dr D K Fisher.
Licensure Skilled care; Intermediate care; Alzheimer's care. *Beds* SNF 52; ICF 65. *Certified* Medicare; Medi-Cal.
Owner Proprietary corp (ARA Living Centers).
Admissions Requirements Screen patients.
Staff Physicians 17 (pt); Nurses' aides 24 (ft), 2 (pt).
Languages Spanish, Arabic, Finnish, German, Italian, Yiddish, Russian, Chinese.
Facilities Dining room; Physical therapy room; Activities room; Laundry room; Barber/Beauty shop; Library.
Activities Arts & crafts; Cards; Games; Reading groups; Prayer groups; Movies; Shopping trips; Dances/Social/Cultural gatherings; Exercise.

Sun Valley Manor
540 Patterson Blvd, Pleasant Hill, CA 94523
(415) 932-3850
Dir of Nursing Barbara S Gagne RN.
Licensure Skilled care. *Beds* SNF 105. *Certified* Medicare; Medi-Cal.
Owner Proprietary corp (ARA Living Centers).

Staff RNs; LPNs; Nurses' aides; Physical therapists; Recreational therapists; Occupational therapists; Speech therapists; Activities coordinators; Dietitians; Ophthalmologists.
Facilities Dining room; Physical therapy room; Activities room; Barber/Beauty shop.
Activities Arts & crafts; Cards; Games; Reading groups; Movies.

Pleasanton

Pleasanton Convalescent Hospital
300 Neal St, Pleasanton, CA 94566
(415) 537-8848
Licensure Skilled care. *Beds* SNF 129. *Certified* Medicare; Medi-Cal.
Owner Privately owned.

Pomona

Care West—Claremont Nursing Center
219 E Foothill Blvd, Pomona, CA 91768
(714) 593-1391
Admin Sharon L Kurtz.
Licensure Skilled care. *Beds* SNF 99. *Certified* Medicare; Medi-Cal.
Owner Proprietary corp (Care Enterprises).

Care West—Pomona Vista Nursing Center
651 N Main St, Pomona, CA 91767
(714) 623-2481
Admin Richard Tovar.
Licensure Skilled care. *Beds* SNF 66. *Certified* Medicare; Medi-Cal.
Owner Proprietary corp (Care Enterprises).
Staff Physicians; RNs; LPNs; Nurses' aides; Physical therapists; Occupational therapists; Speech therapists; Activities coordinators; Dietitians; Ophthalmologists; Podiatrists; Dentists.
Facilities Dining room; Activities room; Barber/Beauty shop.
Activities Arts & crafts; Cards; Games; Reading groups; Prayer groups; Movies; Shopping trips.

Country House
1041 S White Ave, Pomona, CA 91766
(213) 623-0581
Admin Dorothy Broadway.
Licensure Skilled care; Intermediate care for mentally retarded. *Beds* 91. *Certified* Medi-Cal.
Owner Proprietary corp (Beverly Enterprises).

Landmark Medical Center
2030 N Garey Ave, Pomona, CA 91767
(714) 593-2585
Admin Cassandra Grant.
Medical Dir Indran Selvaratnum.
Licensure Skilled care. *Beds* SNF 95. *Certified* Medi-Cal.
Owner Proprietary corp.
Admissions Requirements Minimum age 18.
Staff Physicians 2 (pt); RNs 3 (ft), 2 (pt); Nurses' aides 23 (ft), 6 (pt); Activities coordinators 1 (ft); Dietitians 1 (pt); STPs 10 (ft); LPTs 5 (ft), 10 (pt).
Languages Spanish.
Facilities Dining room; Activities room; Crafts room; Laundry room; Barber/Beauty shop; Dayroom.
Activities Arts & crafts; Cards; Games; Movies; Shopping trips; Dances/Social/Cultural gatherings; Birthday & holiday parties.

Lanterman Developmental Center
3530 W Pomona Blvd, Pomona, CA 91768
(714) 595-1221
Admin Rowena J Taylor. *Dir of Nursing* Celia Rios. *Medical Dir* Dr Lorenda Vergara.
Licensure Intermediate care for mentally retarded; Skilled care for mentally retarded. *Beds* Swing beds ICF/MR SNF/MR 1286. *Certified* Medicaid; Medicare; Medi-Cal.

Owner Publicly owned.
Admissions Requirements Must have mental retardation diagnosis; Retardation diagnosed before age 18; Referrals accepted only from regional centers.
Staff Physicians 19 (ft), 3 (pt); RNs 73 (ft), 3 (pt); Physical therapists 2 (ft); Recreational therapists 18 (ft), 2 (pt); Occupational therapists 2 (ft); Speech therapists 8 (ft); Dietitians 6 (ft); Podiatrists 1 (ft); Audiologists 2 (ft); Psychiatric technicians 700 (ft), 14 (pt).
Languages All major languages available.
Facilities Dining room; Physical therapy room; Activities room; Chapel; Laundry room; Barber/Beauty shop; Library; Rustic camp; Swimming pool.
Activities Arts & crafts; Cards; Games; Prayer groups; Movies; Shopping trips; Dances/Social/Cultural gatherings; Pet therapy; Swimming; Camping.

Laurel Park—A School for Effective Living
1425 Laurel Ave, Pomona, CA 91768
(714) 622-1069
Admin Lynnae Braswell. *Dir of Nursing* Jackie Curtin RN. *Medical Dir* Randy Firling MD.
Licensure Skilled care. *Beds* SNF 43. *Private Pay Patients* 0%. *Certified* Medi-Cal.
Owner Proprietary corp (Braswell Enterprises Inc).
Admissions Requirements Psychiatric diagnosis; Stable for open environment.
Staff Physicians (consultant); RNs 1 (ft), 1 (pt); LPNs 3 (ft), 3 (pt); Nurses' aides 7 (ft), 2 (pt); Activities coordinators 1 (ft); Dietitians (consultant); Psychologists 1 (pt); Social service workers 1 (pt); Counselors 2 (ft), 2 (pt).
Facilities Dining room; Activities room; Laundry room; Group rooms; Grounds.
Activities Arts & crafts; Cards; Games; Reading groups; Prayer groups; Movies; Shopping trips; Dances/Social/Cultural gatherings; Vocational training; Psychosocial skills training.

Mt San Antonio Gardens
900 Harrison Ave, Pomona, CA 91767
(714) 624-5061, 621-3327 FAX
Admin David L Pearce. *Dir of Nursing* Agnes Kutyla RN. *Medical Dir* Stephen N Rathbun MD.
Licensure Skilled care; Retirement. *Beds* SNF 66; Retirement 400. *Private Pay Patients* 8%. *Certified* Medicare.
Owner Nonprofit organization/foundation.
Admissions Requirements Minimum age 60; Physician's request.
Staff Physicians 1 (pt); RNs 7 (ft), 5 (pt); LPNs 4 (pt); Nurses' aides 19 (ft), 11 (pt); Physical therapists 1 (ft); Occupational therapists 1 (pt); Speech therapists 1 (pt); Activities coordinators 1 (ft); Dietitians 1 (pt); Podiatrists 2 (pt).
Languages Spanish.
Affiliation Church of Christ.
Facilities Dining room; Physical therapy room; Activities room; Chapel; Crafts room; Laundry room; Barber/Beauty shop; Library.
Activities Arts & crafts; Cards; Games; Reading groups; Prayer groups; Movies; Shopping trips; Intergenerational programs; Pet therapy.

Olive Vista
2350 Culver Ct, Pomona, CA 91766
(714) 628-6024
Admin Kathleen Millett. *Dir of Nursing* Judith Arterburn; Jack Hauck, Prog Dir. *Medical Dir* Dr Rajendra Patel.
Licensure Psychiatric care. *Beds* Psychiatric care 120. *Private Pay Patients* 10%. *Certified* Medicare; Medi-Cal; VA.
Owner Proprietary corp (Braswell Corp).
Admissions Requirements Minimum age 18.

Staff Physicians 6 (ft); RNs 4 (ft), 2 (pt); Nurses' aides 17 (ft), 15 (pt); Recreational therapists 1 (ft); Occupational therapists 1 (ft); Activities coordinators 1 (ft); Dietitians 1 (ft); Podiatrists 1 (pt); LPNs & LPTs 7 (ft), 10 (pt); Psychologists 1 (pt); MHCs 1 (pt).
Languages Spanish.
Facilities Dining room; Activities room; Crafts room; Laundry room; Library.
Activities Arts & crafts; Cards; Games; Reading groups; Prayer groups; Movies; Shopping trips; Dances/Social/Cultural gatherings; Pet therapy.

Palomares Care Center
250 W Artesia, Pomona, CA 91768
(714) 623-3564, 623-1569 FAX
Admin Roberta T Nelson. *Dir of Nursing* Lorraine Magner RN. *Medical Dir* Steven Barag DO.
Licensure Skilled care; Intermediate care. *Beds* SNF 116; ICF 125. *Private Pay Patients* 30%. *Certified* Medicare; Medi-Cal.
Owner Proprietary corp (Braswell Enterprise Inc).
Admissions Requirements Minimum age 20; Medical examination; Physician's request.
Staff Physicians 1 (pt); RNs 5 (ft), 2 (pt); LPNs 13 (ft), 5 (pt); Nurses' aides 49 (ft), 19 (pt); Physical therapists 3 (ft), 2 (pt); Occupational therapists 2 (pt); Speech therapists 1 (pt); Activities coordinators 2 (ft); Dietitians 1 (pt); Ophthalmologists 1 (pt); Podiatrists 1 (pt).
Languages Spanish.
Facilities Dining room; Physical therapy room; Activities room; Laundry room; Barber/Beauty shop; Library; Occupational therapy room; Speech therapy room; Semi-private rooms.
Activities Arts & crafts; Cards; Games; Reading groups; Prayer groups; Movies; Shopping trips; Intergenerational programs.

Pearl Villa Convalescent Hospital
215 W Pearl St, Pomona, CA 91768
(714) 622-1067
Admin Margaret Brown.
Medical Dir Felimon Soria.
Licensure Skilled care. *Beds* SNF 81. *Certified* Medicare; Medi-Cal.
Owner Proprietary corp.
Staff RNs 1 (ft), 1 (pt); LPNs 8 (ft), 4 (pt); Nurses' aides 30 (ft), 6 (pt); Physical therapists 1 (pt); Reality therapists 1 (pt); Recreational therapists 1 (ft), 2 (pt); Occupational therapists 1 (pt); Speech therapists 1 (pt); Activities coordinators 1 (pt); Dietitians 1 (ft), 1 (pt); Ophthalmologists 1 (pt); Podiatrists 1 (pt); Audiologists 1 (pt); Dentists 1 (pt).
Facilities Dining room; Activities room; Laundry room; Barber/Beauty shop.
Activities Arts & crafts; Cards; Games; Reading groups; Prayer groups; Movies; Shopping trips; Dances/Social/Cultural gatherings.

Pomona Valley Nursing Center
1550 N Park Ave, Pomona, CA 91768
(714) 623-0791
Admin Stephen L Ramsdell.
Licensure Skilled care; Intermediate care. *Beds* SNF 165; ICF 66. *Certified* Medicare; Medi-Cal.
Owner Nonprofit organization/foundation.

Towne Avenue Convalescent Hospital
2351 S Towne Ave, Pomona, CA 91766
(714) 628-1245
Admin Glen A Crume.
Licensure Skilled care. *Beds* SNF 94. *Certified* Medicare; Medi-Cal.
Owner Proprietary corp.
Admissions Requirements Minimum age 18.

Staff Physicians; RNs; LPNs; Nurses' aides; Physical therapists; Occupational therapists; Speech therapists; Activities coordinators; Dietitians.
Languages Spanish.
Facilities Dining room; Physical therapy room; Activities room; Crafts room; Laundry room; Barber/Beauty shop.
Activities Arts & crafts; Cards; Games; Reading groups; Prayer groups; Movies; Dances/Social/Cultural gatherings.

Porterville

Hacienda Convalescent Hospital
301 W Putnam, Porterville, CA 93257
(209) 784-7375, 784-5760
Admin Hernando E Guzman. *Dir of Nursing* Beverly G Brandt RN. *Medical Dir* Robert A Dexter MD.
Licensure Skilled care; Retirement. *Beds* SNF 139. *Certified* Medicare; Medi-Cal.
Owner Proprietary corp.
Admissions Requirements Medical examination; Physician's request.
Staff RNs 4 (ft), 3 (pt); LPNs 9 (ft), 6 (pt); Nurses' aides 39 (ft), 13 (pt); Activities coordinators 2 (ft), 1 (pt).
Facilities Dining room; Physical therapy room; Activities room; Laundry room; Barber/Beauty shop; Family room; Outside patio.
Activities Arts & crafts; Cards; Games; Reading groups; Prayer groups; Movies; Shopping trips; Dances/Social/Cultural gatherings.

Valley Care Center
661 W Poplar Ave, Porterville, CA 93257
(209) 784-8371
Admin Donald D Smith. *Dir of Nursing* Douglas Smith RN. *Medical Dir* Robert Dexter MD.
Licensure Skilled care. *Beds* SNF 55. *Certified* Medicare; Medi-Cal.
Owner Proprietary corp.
Admissions Requirements Medical examination; Physician's request.
Staff Physicians 1 (pt); RNs 2 (ft); LPNs 6 (ft); Nurses' aides 20 (ft), 4 (pt); Physical therapists 1 (pt); Activities coordinators 1 (ft); Dietitians 1 (pt); Ophthalmologists 1 (pt); Dentists 1 (pt).
Languages Spanish.
Facilities Dining room; Activities room; Crafts room; Laundry room; Barber/Beauty shop.
Activities Arts & crafts; Cards; Games; Reading groups; Prayer groups; Movies; Shopping trips; Dances/Social/Cultural gatherings; Greenhouse gardening.

Villa Manor Care Center Inc
350 N Villa, Porterville, CA 93257
(209) 784-6644
Admin R Wesley Jordan.
Medical Dir Robert Dexter MD.
Licensure Skilled care. *Beds* SNF 99. *Certified* Medicare; Medi-Cal.
Owner Proprietary corp.
Staff Physicians 1 (pt); RNs 2 (ft), 2 (pt); LPNs 10 (ft), 3 (pt); Nurses' aides 35 (ft), 10 (pt); Physical therapists 1 (pt); Recreational therapists 1 (pt); Occupational therapists 1 (pt); Speech therapists 1 (pt); Activities coordinators 1 (ft); Dietitians 1 (pt); Podiatrists 1 (pt); Dentists 1 (pt).
Facilities Dining room; Activities room; Laundry room; Barber/Beauty shop.
Activities Arts & crafts; Cards; Games; Reading groups; Prayer groups; Movies; Shopping trips; Dances/Social/Cultural gatherings.

Portola Valley

Sequoias
501 Portola Rd, Portola Valley, CA 94028
(415) 851-1501
Admin Harvey H Ray.
Licensure Skilled care. *Beds* SNF 48. *Certified*
Medicare.
Owner Nonprofit corp.

Poway

National Health Care
12696 Monte Vista Rd, Poway, CA 92064
(619) 487-6242
Admin Jan Bannon. *Dir of Nursing* Josie
Perpetua RN. *Medical Dir* Donald Ottilie
MD.
Licensure Skilled care. *Beds* SNF 145. *Private
Pay Patients* 70%. *Certified* Medicare; Medi-
Cal.
Owner Proprietary corp (National Health
Corp).
Admissions Requirements Medical
examination; Physician's request.
Staff RNs 8 (ft), 2 (pt); LPNs 18 (ft), 7 (pt);
Nurses' aides 42 (ft), 11 (pt); Physical
therapists 1 (ft), 1 (pt); Recreational
therapists 1 (ft); Occupational therapists 1
(ft); Speech therapists 1 (pt); Activities
coordinators 3 (ft); Dietitians 1 (pt);
Audiologists 1 (pt).
Languages Spanish.
Facilities Dining room; Physical therapy
room; Activities room; Crafts room; Laundry
room; Barber/Beauty shop; Library.
Activities Arts & crafts; Cards; Games;
Reading groups; Prayer groups; Movies;
Shopping trips; Dances/Social/Cultural
gatherings; Intergenerational programs; Pet
therapy.

Rancho Bernardo Convalescent Hospital
15632 Pomerado Rd, Poway, CA 92064
(619) 578-8720, 485-7694 FAX
Admin David Culbreth. *Dir of Nursing* Cindy
Tarlton RN. *Medical Dir* Gerald Wolfe MD.
Licensure Skilled care. *Beds* SNF 99. *Private
Pay Patients* 60%. *Certified* Medicare; Medi-
Cal.
Owner Privately owned.
Staff RNs 3 (ft), 3 (pt); LPNs 8 (ft), 4 (pt);
Nurses' aides 25 (ft), 10 (pt); Physical
therapists 1 (ft); Recreational therapists 1
(ft); Occupational therapists 1 (ft); Speech
therapists 1 (ft); Activities coordinators 1
(ft); Dietitians 1 (ft); Ophthalmologists 1 (ft);
Podiatrists 1 (ft); Audiologists 1 (ft).

Quincy

Care West—Quincy Nursing Center
PO Box L, Quincy, CA 95971
(916) 283-2110
Admin John Garber.
Medical Dir Dr Price.
Licensure Skilled care. *Beds* SNF 57. *Certified*
Medicare; Medi-Cal.
Owner Proprietary corp (Care Enterprises).
Staff Physicians; RNs; LPNs; Nurses' aides;
Physical therapists; Recreational therapists;
Speech therapists; Activities coordinators;
Dietitians; Podiatrists; Audiologists;
Dentists.
Facilities Dining room; Physical therapy
room; Activities room; Laundry room;
Barber/Beauty shop; Library.
Activities Arts & crafts; Cards; Games;
Reading groups; Prayer groups; Movies;
Dances/Social/Cultural gatherings; Exercise
program at local college.

Rancho Cordova

Casa Coloma Health Care Center
10410 Coloma Rd, Rancho Cordova, CA
95670
(916) 363-4843
Admin Arden Millermon.
Licensure Skilled care; Intermediate care. *Beds*
SNF 99; ICF 39. *Certified* Medicare; Medi-
Cal.
Owner Privately owned.

Rancho Mirage

Rancho Mirage Healthcare Center
39950 Vista Del Sol, Rancho Mirage, CA
92270
(619) 340-0053
Admin Lydia Carrillo.
Licensure Skilled care. *Beds* SNF 99. *Certified*
Medicare.
Owner Proprietary corp (Beverly Enterprises).

Rancho Palos Verdes

Canterbury
5801 W Crestridge Rd, Rancho Palos Verdes,
CA 90274
(213) 541-2410
Admin Alvin P Lafon. *Dir of Nursing* Joan
Roth RN. *Medical Dir* Dr Christopher J
Traughber.
Licensure Skilled care; Retirement. *Beds* SNF
28; Retirement community apts 127.
Certified Medicare.
Owner Nonprofit corp.
Admissions Requirements Minimum age 62;
Medical examination for retirement
apartments; Physician's request for SNF.
Staff Physicians; RNs; LPNs; Nurses' aides;
Physical therapists; Recreational therapists;
Activities coordinators; Dietitians; Masseuse.
Affiliation Episcopal.
Facilities Dining room; Physical therapy
room; Activities room; Crafts room; Laundry
room; Barber/Beauty shop; Library.
Activities Arts & crafts; Cards; Games;
Reading groups; Prayer groups; Movies;
Shopping trips; Dances/Social/Cultural
gatherings.

Red Bluff

Brentwood Convalescent Hospital
1795 Walnut St, Red Bluff, CA 96080
(916) 527-2046
Admin Carolyn J Hurst.
Licensure Skilled care. *Beds* SNF 55. *Certified*
Medicare; Medi-Cal.
Owner Proprietary corp.

Care West—Cedars Nursing Center
555 Luther Rd, Red Bluff, CA 96080
(916) 527-6232
Admin Niel John M Crowley.
Licensure Skilled care. *Beds* SNF 58. *Certified*
Medicare; Medi-Cal.
Owner Proprietary corp (Care Enterprises).

Tehema County Health Center
1850 Walnut St, Red Bluff, CA 96080
(916) 527-0350
Admin Nora M Roberson.
Medical Dir Eva Jalkotzy.
Licensure Skilled care. *Beds* SNF 67. *Certified*
Medicare; Medi-Cal.
Owner Publicly owned.
Staff Physicians; RNs; LPNs; Nurses' aides;
Physical therapists; Reality therapists;
Recreational therapists; Occupational
therapists; Speech therapists; Activities
coordinators; Dietitians; Ophthalmologists;
Podiatrists; Audiologists; Dentists.
Facilities Dining room; Physical therapy
room; Activities room; Crafts room; Laundry
room.

Activities Arts & crafts; Cards; Games;
Reading groups; Prayer groups; Movies.

Redding

Applewood Inn
PO Box 494280, 201 Hartnell Ave, Redding,
CA 96049
(916) 222-2273, 222-5159 FAX
Admin Shirley J Popejoy. *Dir of Nursing* Iris
Manfre RN. *Medical Dir* Seldon Greer MD.
Licensure Skilled care; Intermediate care. *Beds*
SNF 66; ICF 54. *Certified* Medicare; Medi-
Cal.
Owner Proprietary corp (Western Care
Management Corp).
Admissions Requirements Medical
examination; Physician's request.
Staff RNs 2 (ft), 1 (pt); LPNs 7 (ft), 2 (pt);
Nurses' aides 25 (ft), 10 (pt); Physical
therapists 1 (pt); Recreational therapists 1
(ft), 1 (pt); Dietitians 1 (ft); Patient
representatives 1 (pt).
Facilities Dining room; Physical therapy
room; Activities room; Laundry room;
Barber/Beauty shop; Library.
Activities Arts & crafts; Cards; Games;
Reading groups; Prayer groups; Movies;
Shopping trips; Dances/Social/Cultural
gatherings; Pet therapy.

Beverly Manor Convalescent Hospital
1836 Gold St, Redding, CA 96001
(916) 241-6756
Admin Betty L Groton. *Dir of Nursing* E
Evans RN. *Medical Dir* Paul Freeman MD.
Licensure Skilled care. *Beds* SNF 89. *Certified*
Medicare; Medi-Cal.
Owner Proprietary corp (Beverly Enterprises).
Admissions Requirements Medical
examination; Physician's request.
Staff RNs 6 (ft), 3 (pt); LPNs 8 (ft) 44 (ft);
Activities coordinators 1 (ft); Social services
1 (ft).
Languages Spanish, Thai.
Facilities Dining room; Physical therapy
room; Activities room; Crafts room; Laundry
room; Barber/Beauty shop; Library.
Activities Arts & crafts; Cards; Games;
Reading groups; Prayer groups; Movies;
Shopping trips; Dances/Social/Cultural
gatherings; Exercise; Facility van.

Canyonwood Nursing Center
2120 Benton Dr, Redding, CA 96003
(916) 243-6317
Admin Susan McPherson.
Licensure Skilled care. *Beds* SNF 120.
Certified Medicare; Medi-Cal.
Owner Proprietary corp (Hillhaven Inc).

Crestwood Convalescent Hospital
2490 Court St, Redding, CA 96001
(916) 246-0600
Admin Janet M Ayres.
Licensure Skilled care. *Beds* SNF 113.
Certified Medicare; Medi-Cal.
Owner Proprietary corp (Crestwood Hospitals
Inc).

Crestwood Geriatric Treatment Center
3062 Churn Creek Rd, Redding, CA 96002
(916) 221-0976
Admin Nicoletta Groff.
Licensure Skilled care. *Beds* SNF 99. *Certified*
Medi-Cal.
Owner Proprietary corp.

Shasta Convalescent Hospital
3550 Churn Creek Rd, Redding, CA 96002
(916) 222-3630
Admin Harold Becker. *Dir of Nursing* Helen
Pfilf. *Medical Dir* Norman Arai MD.
Licensure Skilled care. *Beds* SNF 165.
Certified Medicare; Medi-Cal.
Owner Proprietary corp.

Staff Physicians; RNs; LPNs; Nurses' aides; Physical therapists; Recreational therapists; Occupational therapists; Speech therapists; Activities coordinators; Dietitians.
Facilities Dining room; Physical therapy room; Activities room; Chapel; Crafts room; Laundry room; Barber/Beauty shop.
Activities Arts & crafts; Cards; Games; Reading groups; Prayer groups; Movies; Shopping trips; Dances/Social/Cultural gatherings.

Redlands

Asistencia Villa Convalescent Center
1875 Barton Rd, Redlands, CA 92373
(714) 793-1382
Admin Thomas M Lee. *Dir of Nursing* Margaret Key RN. *Medical Dir* Jon Tveten MD.
Licensure Skilled care. *Beds* SNF 99. *Private Pay Patients* 60%. *Certified* Medicare; Medi-Cal.
Owner Privately owned.
Staff RNs 2 (ft); LPNs 10 (ft); Nurses' aides 20 (ft); Physical therapists 1 (ft); Occupational therapists 1 (pt); Speech therapists 1 (pt); Activities coordinators 1 (ft); Dietitians 1 (pt); Audiologists 1 (pt).
Languages Spanish, German.
Facilities Dining room; Physical therapy room; Activities room; Laundry room; Barber/Beauty shop; Dayroom; 4 Courtyards; IV therapy.
Activities Arts & crafts; Cards; Games; Reading groups; Prayer groups; Movies; Dances/Social/Cultural gatherings; Intergenerational programs; Pet therapy; Gardening; Golf.

Beverly Manor Convalescent Hospital
700 E Highland Ave, Redlands, CA 92373
(714) 793-2678
Admin Sandra Haskins. *Dir of Nursing* Lenore Acosta. *Medical Dir* Tim O'Neal MD.
Licensure Skilled care. *Beds* SNF 82. *Certified* Medicare; Medi-Cal.
Owner Proprietary corp (Beverly Enterprises).
Admissions Requirements Medical examination; Physician's request.
Staff RNs 2 (ft), 2 (pt); LPNs 8 (ft), 2 (pt); Nurses' aides 40 (ft), 10 (pt); Activities coordinators 1 (ft); Dietitians 1 (ft).
Facilities Dining room; Physical therapy room; Activities room; Laundry room; Barber/Beauty shop.
Activities Arts & crafts; Cards; Games; Reading groups; Prayer groups; Movies; Shopping trips.

Braswell's Colonial Care
1618 Laurel, Redlands, CA 92373
(714) 792-6050
Admin D A Braswell.
Medical Dir Dr Tveten.
Licensure Skilled care; Intermediate care; Residential care. *Beds* SNF 120; ICF 58; Residential care 58. *Certified* Medicare; Medi-Cal.
Owner Privately owned.
Staff RNs; LPNs; Nurses' aides; Physical therapists; Recreational therapists; Occupational therapists; Speech therapists; Activities coordinators.
Facilities Dining room; Physical therapy room; Activities room; Chapel; Crafts room; Laundry room; Barber/Beauty shop; Library.
Activities Arts & crafts; Cards; Games; Reading groups; Prayer groups; Movies; Shopping trips; Pet therapy.

CareWest—Redlands
105 Terracina Blvd, Redlands, CA 92373
(714) 793-2271
Admin Valerie Machain. *Dir of Nursing* Kris Woods. *Medical Dir* William Thompson MD.

Licensure Skilled care; Alzheimer's care. *Beds* SNF 97. *Private Pay Patients* 15%. *Certified* Medicare; Medi-Cal.
Owner Proprietary corp (Care Enterprises).
Staff Physicians; RNs; LPNs; Nurses' aides; Physical therapists; Occupational therapists; Speech therapists; Activities coordinators; Dietitians; Ophthalmologists; Podiatrists.
Facilities Dining room; Physical therapy room; Activities room; Laundry room; Barber/Beauty shop.
Activities Arts & crafts; Cards; Games; Reading groups; Prayer groups; Movies.

Plymouth Village
900 Salem Dr, Redlands, CA 92373
(714) 793-1233
Admin Robert L Balsley. *Dir of Nursing* Joan Cox RN. *Medical Dir* Dr Jon Tueten.
Licensure Skilled care; Retirement. *Beds* SNF 48; Retirement 350. *Certified* Medicare; Medi-Cal.
Owner Nonprofit corp (American Baptist Homes of the West).
Admissions Requirements Medical examination; Physician's request.
Staff RNs 5 (pt); LPNs 5 (ft); Nurses' aides 17 (ft), 10 (pt); Occupational therapists 1 (pt); Speech therapists 1 (pt); Activities coordinators 2 (ft); Dietitians 1 (pt).
Affiliation Baptist.
Facilities Dining room; Physical therapy room; Activities room; Chapel; Crafts room; Barber/Beauty shop.
Activities Arts & crafts; Games; Prayer groups; Movies; Shopping trips; Dances/Social/Cultural gatherings; Exercise classes; Physical activities.

Terracina Convalescent Hospital
1620 Fern Ave, Redlands, CA 92373
(714) 793-2609
Admin Ritchie Weatherwax.
Medical Dir Bernard E Telton MD.
Licensure Skilled care. *Beds* SNF 78. *Certified* Medicare; Medi-Cal.
Owner Proprietary corp (Beverly Enterprises).
Admissions Requirements Minimum age 18.
Staff Physicians 1 (pt); RNs 1 (ft), 2 (pt); LPNs 6 (ft), 5 (pt); Nurses' aides 24 (ft), 11 (pt); Physical therapists 1 (pt); Occupational therapists 1 (pt); Speech therapists 1 (pt); Activities coordinators 1 (ft); Dietitians 1 (pt); Ophthalmologists 1 (pt); Podiatrists 1 (pt); Audiologists 1 (pt); Dentists 1 (pt).
Facilities Dining room; Physical therapy room; Activities room; Laundry room; Barber/Beauty shop.
Activities Arts & crafts; Games; Reading groups; Prayer groups; Movies; Shopping trips; Dances/Social/Cultural gatherings.

Redwood City

Cordilleras Mental Health Center
200 Edmonds Rd, Redwood City, CA 94062
(415) 367-1890
Admin Cecilia Smith RN. *Dir of Nursing* Barbara Dabney.
Licensure Skilled care. *Beds* SNF 120. *Private Pay Patients* 0%. *Certified* Medi-Cal.
Owner Proprietary corp (Telecare Corp).
Admissions Requirements Minimum age 18.
Staff Physicians 1 (ft), 3 (pt); RNs 8 (ft), 3 (pt); LPNs 15 (ft); Nurses' aides 27 (ft), 3 (pt); Recreational therapists 4 (ft); Occupational therapists 1 (ft); Activities coordinators 4 (ft); Dietitians 1 (ft).
Languages Spanish, French, Hindi, Danish, Maltese, Tagalog, Cantonese.
Activities Arts & crafts; Cards; Games; Reading groups; Prayer groups; Movies; Shopping trips; Dances/Social/Cultural gatherings.

Devonshire Oaks
3635 Jefferson Ave, Redwood City, CA 94062
(415) 366-9503

Admin Pearl Farkas RN. *Dir of Nursing* Marta Melghem. *Medical Dir* Henry Mayer MD.
Licensure Skilled care. *Beds* SNF 39. *Private Pay Patients* 100%.
Owner Privately owned.
Staff RNs 3 (ft), 2 (pt); LPNs 1 (ft), 2 (pt); Nurses' aides 15 (ft), 2 (pt); Activities coordinators 1 (ft); Dietitians 1 (pt).
Languages German, Italian, Native American, Indian, Fijian.
Facilities Dining room; Activities room; Crafts room; Laundry room; Barber/Beauty shop; Library.
Activities Arts & crafts; Cards; Games; Reading groups; Prayer groups; Movies; Intergenerational programs; Pet therapy; Religious services.

Laurel Glen Convalescent Hospital
885 Woodside Rd, Redwood City, CA 94061
(415) 368-4174
Admin Daniel Sheehan.
Licensure Skilled care. *Beds* SNF 45. *Certified* Medi-Cal.
Owner Proprietary corp.

Reedley

Pleasant View Manor
856 S Reed Ave, Reedley, CA 93654
(209) 638-3615
Admin Howard Fast.
Medical Dir Dr John Hayward.
Licensure Skilled care; Retirement. *Beds* SNF 99. *Certified* Medicare; Medi-Cal.
Owner Nonprofit corp (Mennonite Brethren Homes Inc).
Admissions Requirements Medical examination; Physician's request.
Staff RNs 5 (ft), 5 (pt); LPNs 6 (ft), 3 (pt); Nurses' aides 39 (ft), 11 (pt); Activities coordinators 2 (ft); Dietitians 10 (ft), 5 (pt).
Languages German, Spanish.
Affiliation Mennonite.
Facilities Dining room; Activities room; Crafts room; Laundry room; Barber/Beauty shop; Library.
Activities Arts & crafts; Games; Prayer groups; Movies; Dances/Social/Cultural gatherings.

Reedley Convalescent Hospital
1090 E Dinuba Ave, Reedley, CA 93654
(209) 638-3578
Admin Bill Murray.
Licensure Skilled care. *Beds* SNF 56. *Certified* Medicare; Medi-Cal.
Owner Proprietary corp (Beverly Enterprises).

Sierra View Homes Inc
1155 E Springfield, Reedley, CA 93654
(209) 638-9226
Admin Clayton Auernheimer. *Dir of Nursing* Gloria Jones RN. *Medical Dir* Marden C Habegger MD.
Licensure Skilled care; Retirement. *Beds* SNF 59. *Certified* Medicare; Medi-Cal.
Owner Nonprofit corp.
Admissions Requirements Medical examination; Physician's request.
Staff Physicians 1 (ft); RNs 6 (ft); LPNs 1 (ft), 1 (pt); Nurses' aides 24 (ft), 3 (pt); Activities coordinators 1 (ft), 1 (pt).
Languages Spanish.
Affiliation Mennonite.
Facilities Dining room; Activities room; Laundry room; Barber/Beauty shop; Library.
Activities Arts & crafts; Cards; Games; Reading groups; Prayer groups; Movies; Dances/Social/Cultural gatherings; Guest entertainers & speakers.

Reseda

Care West—Northridge
7836 Reseda Blvd, Reseda, CA 91335
(818) 881-7414

Admin Diane Hinkle.
Licensure Skilled care. *Beds* SNF 97. *Certified* Medicare; Medi-Cal.
Owner Proprietary corp (Care Enterprises).

Convalescent Center of Reseda
6740 Wilbur Ave, Reseda, CA 91335
(818) 881-2302
Admin Ronald D O'Haver.
Licensure Skilled care. *Beds* SNF 99. *Certified* Medicare; Medi-Cal.
Owner Proprietary corp.
Languages Spanish, Polish.

Grancell Village of the Jewish Homes for the Aging
7150 Tampa Ave, Reseda, CA 91335
(818) 774-3200
Admin Marilyn Green.
Licensure Skilled care; Intermediate care. *Beds* SNF 120; ICF 35. *Certified* Medicare; Medi-Cal.
Owner Nonprofit corp.

Victory Village of the Jewish Home for the Aging
18855 Victory Blvd, Reseda, CA 91335
(818) 774-3200
Admin Jeffrey Sherman. *Dir of Nursing* Dorothy Reid RN BSN. *Medical Dir* Dr Joe Ouslander.
Licensure Skilled care; Intermediate care; Board & care; Alzheimer's care. *Beds* Swing beds SNF/ICF 248; Board & care 271. *Certified* Medicaid; Medicare; Medi-Cal.
Owner Nonprofit organization/foundation (Jewish Home for the Aging).
Admissions Requirements Minimum age 70; Medical examination.
Staff Physicians 2 (ft), 5 (pt); RNs 12 (ft); LPNs 38 (ft); Nurses' aides 121 (ft); Physical therapists 4 (ft); Recreational therapists 6 (ft), 4 (pt); Occupational therapists 1 (ft); Speech therapists 1 (pt); Activities coordinators 1 (ft); Dietitians 1 (ft); Ophthalmologists 4 (pt); Podiatrists 3 (pt); Audiologists 1 (pt); RNAs 2 (ft).
Languages Hebrew, Yiddish, Spanish, Latino.
Facilities Dining room; Physical therapy room; Activities room; Chapel; Crafts room; Laundry room; Barber/Beauty shop; Library; Occupational therapy room; Speech therapy room.
Activities Arts & crafts; Cards; Games; Reading groups; Prayer groups; Movies; Shopping trips; Dances/Social/Cultural gatherings; Intergenerational programs; Pet therapy; Special events.

Woodland Care Center
7120 Corbin Ave, Reseda, CA 91335
(818) 881-4540, 881-0039 FAX
Admin Frances Foy. *Dir of Nursing* Helen Moore. *Medical Dir* Edwin Seligson.
Licensure Skilled care. *Beds* SNF 157. *Certified* Medicare; Medi-Cal.
Owner Proprietary corp (Summit Health).
Admissions Requirements Minimum age 18.
Staff RNs 3 (ft), 4 (pt); LPNs 13 (ft), 1 (pt); Nurses' aides 57 (ft), 1 (pt); Physical therapists 1 (ft), 2 (pt); Occupational therapists 1 (ft), 1 (pt); Speech therapists 1 (ft); Activities coordinators 2 (ft), 1 (pt).
Languages Spanish.
Facilities Dining room; Physical therapy room; Laundry room; Barber/Beauty shop.
Activities Arts & crafts; Cards; Games; Prayer groups; Movies; Shopping trips; Dances/Social/Cultural gatherings; Intergenerational programs; Pet therapy.

Rheem

Rheem Valley Convalescent Hospital
332 Park St, Rheem, CA 94570
(415) 376-5995
Admin Elizabeth Schmidt.
Medical Dir Gary Miller DO.

Licensure Skilled care. *Beds* 49. *Certified* Medicare; Medi-Cal.
Owner Proprietary corp.
Admissions Requirements Minimum age 55; Medical examination; Physician's request.
Staff Physicians 4 (pt); RNs 3 (ft), 5 (pt); LPNs 2 (ft); Nurses' aides 10 (ft), 25 (pt); Physical therapists 1 (pt); Speech therapists 1 (pt); Activities coordinators 1 (pt); Dietitians 1 (pt); Podiatrists 1 (pt); Dentists 1 (pt).
Facilities Dining room; Physical therapy room; Activities room; Crafts room; Barber/Beauty shop; Sitting rooms.
Activities Arts & crafts; Games; Reading groups; Prayer groups; Movies; Dances/Social/Cultural gatherings; Groups and/or individual volunteers.

Rialto

Crestview Convalescent Hospital
1471 S Riverside Ave, Rialto, CA 92376
(714) 877-1361
Admin Leona Berglund. *Dir of Nursing* Perlita Garciano. *Medical Dir* Roy V Berglund MD.
Licensure Skilled care; Retirement. *Beds* SNF 201; Retirement 75. *Private Pay Patients* 20%. *Certified* Medicare; Medi-Cal.
Owner Privately owned.
Admissions Requirements Minimum age 16; Medical examination; Physician's request.
Staff RNs 5 (ft), 2 (pt); LPNs 20 (ft), 9 (pt); Nurses' aides 95 (ft), 8 (pt); Physical therapists (consultant); Activities coordinators 3 (ft); Dietitians (consultant).
Facilities Dining room; Physical therapy room; Activities room; Crafts room; Laundry room; Barber/Beauty shop; Library.
Activities Arts & crafts; Cards; Games; Prayer groups; Movies; Shopping trips; Dances/Social/Cultural gatherings.

Richmond

Ellen's Memorial Convalescent Hospital
2716 Ohio Ave, Richmond, CA 94804
(415) 233-6720
Admin Rita Stevens.
Licensure Skilled care. *Beds* SNF 43. *Certified* Medicare; Medi-Cal.
Owner Proprietary corp.

Hallmark Nursing Center—Richmond
1919 Cutting Blvd, Richmond, CA 94804
(415) 233-8513
Admin William M Shields.
Licensure Skilled care. *Beds* SNF 84. *Certified* Medicare; Medi-Cal.
Owner Proprietary corp.

Live Oak Living Center—Greenridge Heights
2150 Pyramid Dr, Richmond, CA 94803
(415) 222-1242
Admin Stephen W Hooker.
Licensure Skilled care. *Beds* SNF 59. *Certified* Medicare; Medi-Cal.
Owner Proprietary corp.

Walker Convalescent Hospital Inc
955 23rd St, Richmond, CA 94804
(415) 235-6550
Admin Johnnie M Walker.
Licensure Intermediate care. *Beds* 25. *Certified* Medicare.
Owner Proprietary corp.

Ridgecrest

Beverly Manor Healthcare Center
1131 N China Lake, Ridgecrest, CA 93555
(619) 446-3591
Admin Joan Williams.
Licensure Skilled care. *Beds* SNF 99. *Certified* Medicare; Medi-Cal.
Owner Proprietary corp (Beverly Enterprises).

Ripon

Bethany Home Society San Joaquin County
930 W Main St, Ripon, CA 95366
(209) 599-4221
Admin Bruce Nikkel. *Dir of Nursing* Mary Anna Love RN. *Medical Dir* Dr Daryl Dutter.
Licensure Skilled care; Residential care; Alzheimer's care; Adult day care. *Beds* SNF 74; Residential care 49. *Private Pay Patients* 50%. *Certified* Medicare; Medi-Cal.
Owner Nonprofit corp.
Admissions Requirements Minimum age 21; Medical examination; Physician's request.
Staff RNs 2 (ft), 4 (pt); LPNs 4 (ft), 6 (pt); Nurses' aides 20 (ft), 10 (pt); Physical therapists 2 (pt); Activities coordinators 1 (ft); Dietitians 1 (pt); Podiatrists 1 (pt); Alzheimer's aide.
Facilities Dining room; Physical therapy room; Activities room; Crafts room; Laundry room; Barber/Beauty shop; Library.
Activities Arts & crafts; Cards; Games; Prayer groups; Movies; Shopping trips.

Riverbank

River Bluff Convalescent Hospital
2649 W Topeka, Riverbank, CA 95367
(209) 869-2569
Admin Helayne D Hendrickson.
Licensure Skilled care. *Beds* SNF 99. *Certified* Medicare; Medi-Cal.
Owner Proprietary corp.

Valley View Care Center
2649 W Topeka St, Riverbank, CA 95367
(209) 869-2569
Admin Helayne Hendrickson. *Dir of Nursing* Nancy Mendez RN. *Medical Dir* Marvin Montgomery MD.
Licensure Skilled care. *Beds* SNF 99. *Private Pay Patients* 15%. *Certified* Medicare; Medi-Cal.
Owner Proprietary corp.
Staff RNs 2 (ft); LPNs 7 (ft); Nurses' aides 30 (ft); Physical therapists 2 (pt); Occupational therapists 1 (pt); Speech therapists 1 (pt); Activities coordinators 1 (ft), 1 (pt); Dietitians 1 (pt); Ophthalmologists 1 (pt); Podiatrists 1 (pt); Audiologists 1 (pt).
Languages Spanish.
Facilities Dining room; Physical therapy room; Activities room; Crafts room; Laundry room; Barber/Beauty shop.
Activities Arts & crafts; Cards; Games; Reading groups; Prayer groups; Movies; Shopping trips; Dances/Social/Cultural gatherings; Intergenerational programs; Pet therapy.

Riverside

Air Force Village West Health Care Center
17050 Arnold Dr, Riverside, CA 92508
(714) 697-2200
Admin Darleen M Curley. *Dir of Nursing* Cindie Feuerstein RN. *Medical Dir* Dr Burdette Nelson.
Licensure Skilled care; Retirement. *Beds* SNF 59; Retirement 400. *Certified* Medicare.
Owner Privately owned.
Admissions Requirements Medical examination.
Staff RNs 4 (ft), 2 (pt); Nurses' aides 8 (ft), 3 (pt); Physical therapists; Activities coordinators 1 (ft); LVNs 4 (ft), 3 (pt).
Facilities Dining room; Physical therapy room; Activities room; Chapel; Crafts room; Laundry room; Barber/Beauty shop; Library; Pool.
Activities Arts & crafts; Cards; Games; Reading groups; Movies; Shopping trips; Intergenerational programs; Pet therapy.

Arlington Gardens Convalescent Hospital
3766 Nye Ave, Riverside, CA 92505
(714) 689-2340
Admin Margaret Brown. *Dir of Nursing* Peggy R Fuller RN. *Medical Dir* Stanley Chartier MD.
Licensure Skilled care. *Beds* SNF 28. *Private Pay Patients* 18%. *Certified* Medicare; Medi-Cal.
Owner Proprietary corp (Medicrest of California Inc).
Admissions Requirements Physician's request.
Staff RNs 1 (ft), 2 (pt); LPNs 1 (ft), 4 (pt); Nurses' aides 6 (ft), 6 (pt); Physical therapists 1 (pt); Reality therapists 1 (pt); Occupational therapists 1 (pt); Speech therapists 1 (pt); Activities coordinators 1 (ft); Dietitians 1 (pt); Ophthalmologists 1 (pt); Podiatrists 1 (pt); Audiologists 1 (pt); Dentists 1 (pt).
Languages Spanish.
Facilities Dining room; Laundry room; Barber/Beauty shop.
Activities Arts & crafts; Cards; Games; Reading groups; Prayer groups; Movies; Shopping trips; Pet therapy.

Beverly Manor Convalescent Hospital
4768 Palm Ave, Riverside, CA 92501
(714) 686-9000, 682-4863 FAX
Admin J Gregory Bordenkircher. *Dir of Nursing* Susan Brierly. *Medical Dir* Dr Bhagwant Singh.
Licensure Skilled care. *Beds* SNF 51. *Private Pay Patients* 13%. *Certified* Medicare; Medi-Cal.
Owner Proprietary corp (Beverly Enterprises).
Admissions Requirements Medical examination; Physician's request.
Staff Physicians; RNs; LPNs; Nurses' aides; Physical therapists; Recreational therapists; Occupational therapists; Speech therapists; Activities coordinators; Dietitians; Ophthalmologists; Podiatrists; Audiologists.
Languages Spanish, German.
Facilities Dining room; Physical therapy room; Activities room; Laundry room; Barber/Beauty shop.
Activities Arts & crafts; Cards; Games; Reading groups; Prayer groups; Movies; Shopping trips; Dances/Social/Cultural gatherings; Intergenerational programs; Pet therapy.

Beverly Manor Sanitarium
4580 Palm Ave, Riverside, CA 92501
(714) 684-7701
Admin Gerald E Bogard.
Medical Dir Dr L Murad.
Licensure Intermediate care for mentally retarded. *Beds* ICF/MR 120. *Certified* Medi-Cal.
Owner Proprietary corp (Beverly Enterprises).
Admissions Requirements Minimum age 18; Medical examination; Physician's request.
Staff Physicians; RNs; LPNs; Nurses' aides; Occupational therapists; Speech therapists; Activities coordinators; Dietitians; Ophthalmologists; Podiatrists; Audiologists; Dentists.

Care West—Mission Nursing Center
8487 Magnolia Ave, Riverside, CA 92504
(714) 688-2222
Admin Ruth M Howell.
Licensure Skilled care. *Beds* SNF 40. *Certified* Medicare; Medi-Cal.
Owner Proprietary corp (Care Enterprises).

Chapman Convalescent Hospital
4301 Caroline Ct, Riverside, CA 92506
(714) 683-7111
Admin Betty Lou Beeman.
Licensure Skilled care. *Beds* SNF 59. *Certified* Medicare; Medi-Cal.
Owner Proprietary corp.

Community Convalescent Center
4070 Jurupa Ave, Riverside, CA 92506
(714) 682-2522
Admin Bruce W Bennett.
Medical Dir H H Stone MD.
Licensure Skilled care. *Beds* SNF 162. *Certified* Medicare; Medi-Cal.
Owner Proprietary corp.
Staff Physicians 1 (pt); RNs 7 (ft), 7 (pt); LPNs 10 (ft), 7 (pt); Nurses' aides 66 (ft), 28 (pt); Physical therapists 3 (ft); Reality therapists 1 (ft); Occupational therapists 1 (pt); Speech therapists 1 (pt); Activities coordinators 3 (ft); Dietitians 1 (pt); Podiatrists 1 (pt); Dentists 1 (pt).
Facilities Dining room; Physical therapy room; Activities room; Crafts room; Barber/Beauty shop; Library.
Activities Arts & crafts; Cards; Games; Reading groups; Prayer groups; Movies; Shopping trips; Dances/Social/Cultural gatherings.

Cypress Gardens Convalescent Hospital
9025 Colorado Ave, Riverside, CA 92503
(714) 688-3643
Admin Gretchen Reynolds. *Dir of Nursing* Mary Ann Crowley. *Medical Dir* Rodney Soholt MD.
Licensure Skilled care; Alzheimer's care. *Beds* SNF 120. *Certified* Medicare; Medi-Cal.
Owner Proprietary corp.
Admissions Requirements Minimum age 18; Medical examination; Physician's request.
Staff Physicians 1 (pt); RNs 6 (ft), 4 (pt); LPNs 8 (ft), 2 (pt); Nurses' aides 45 (ft), 4 (pt); Physical therapists 1 (pt); Recreational therapists 2 (ft); Occupational therapists 1 (pt); Speech therapists 1 (pt); Activities coordinators 2 (ft); Dietitians 1 (ft); Ophthalmologists 1 (pt); Podiatrists 1 (pt); Dentists 1 (pt).
Languages Spanish.
Facilities Dining room; Physical therapy room; Activities room; Crafts room; Laundry room; Barber/Beauty shop.
Activities Arts & crafts; Cards; Games; Reading groups; Prayer groups; Movies; Shopping trips; Dances/Social/Cultural gatherings; Outings.

Extended Care Hospital of Riverside
8171 Magnolia Ave, Riverside, CA 92504
(714) 687-3842
Admin Shirley Y Leedy.
Licensure Skilled care. *Beds* SNF 99. *Certified* Medicare; Medi-Cal.
Owner Proprietary corp.

Magnolia Convalescent Hospital
8133 Magnolia Ave, Riverside, CA 92504
(714) 688-4321
Admin Raymond N Beeman.
Licensure Skilled care. *Beds* SNF 94. *Certified* Medicare; Medi-Cal.
Owner Proprietary corp.

Miller's Progressive Care
8951 Granite Hill Dr, Riverside, CA 92509
(714) 685-7474
Admin Wilmer W Miller. *Dir of Nursing* Alida Arnold. *Medical Dir* B Tilton MD.
Licensure Skilled care. *Beds* SNF 70. *Certified* Medicare.
Owner Proprietary corp.
Staff Physicians; RNs; LPNs; Nurses' aides; Activities coordinators; Dietitians; Ophthalmologists; Podiatrists.
Facilities Dining room; Activities room; Crafts room; Laundry room; Barber/Beauty shop.
Activities Arts & crafts; Cards; Games; Reading groups; Prayer groups; Movies; Shopping trips; Dances/Social/Cultural gatherings; Adult education from local school district.

Orangetree Convalescent Hospital
4000 Harrison St, Riverside, CA 92503
(714) 785-6060
Admin Elizabeth R Plott.
Licensure Skilled care. *Beds* SNF 146. *Certified* Medicare; Medi-Cal.
Owner Proprietary corp.

Palm Terrace Convalescent Center
11162 Palm Terrace Ln, Riverside, CA 92505
(714) 687-7330
Admin Marilynn G Smith.
Licensure Skilled care. *Beds* SNF 75. *Certified* Medicare; Medi-Cal.
Owner Privately owned.

Plymouth Tower
3401 Lemon St, Riverside, CA 92501
(714) 686-8202
Admin W William Jann. *Dir of Nursing* Nancy Hitchcock. *Medical Dir* Herman Stone MD.
Licensure Skilled care; Independent and assisted living. *Beds* SNF 36; Independent and assisted living 110. *Private Pay Patients* 72%. *Certified* Medi-Cal.
Owner Nonprofit organization/foundation (Retirement Housing Foundation).
Admissions Requirements Physician's request.
Staff RNs; LPNs; Nurses' aides; Physical therapists (consultants); Activities coordinators; Dietitians (consultants); Social services (consultants).
Affiliation Church of Christ.
Facilities Dining room; Activities room; Laundry room; Barber/Beauty shop.
Activities Arts & crafts; Games; Reading groups; Prayer groups; Movies; Pet therapy.

Regency Oaks
8781 Lakeview Ave, Riverside, CA 92509
(714) 685-1531
Admin Charles E Sinclair.
Licensure Skilled care; Intermediate care for mentally retarded. *Beds* SNF 59; ICF/MR 129. *Certified* Medi-Cal.
Owner Proprietary corp.

Villa Convalescent Hospital
8965 Magnolia Ave, Riverside, CA 92503
(714) 689-5788
Dir of Nursing Kathleen McConnel RN.
Licensure Skilled care. *Beds* SNF 59. *Certified* Medicare; Medi-Cal.
Owner Proprietary corp.
Admissions Requirements Physician's request.
Facilities Dining room; Activities room; Laundry room; Barber/Beauty shop.
Activities Arts & crafts; Cards; Games; Reading groups; Prayer groups; Movies; Shopping trips; Dances/Social/Cultural gatherings.

Vista Pacifica Convalescent Home
3662 Pacific Ave, Riverside, CA 92509
(714) 686-4362
Admin Thomas A Prchal. *Dir of Nursing* Peggy Kane. *Medical Dir* Peter Paul MD.
Licensure Skilled care. *Beds* SNF 49. *Certified* Medicare; Medi-Cal.
Owner Proprietary corp.
Admissions Requirements Minimum age 18; Medical examination; Physician's request.
Staff Physicians 4 (ft); RNs 1 (ft), 1 (pt); LPNs 3 (ft), 2 (pt); Nurses' aides 15 (ft), 4 (pt); Physical therapists 1 (ft); Activities coordinators 1 (ft); Dietitians 1 (ft); Ophthalmologists 1 (ft).
Languages Spanish.
Facilities Dining room; Activities room; Chapel; Crafts room; Laundry room; Barber/Beauty shop; Library.
Activities Arts & crafts; Cards; Games; Reading groups; Prayer groups; Movies; Shopping trips; Dances/Social/Cultural gatherings.

Vista Pacificia Center
3674 Pacific Ave, Riverside, CA 92509
(714) 682-4833
Admin Cheryl Jumonville. *Dir of Nursing*
Mary Duron. *Medical Dir* Paul DeSilva MD.
Licensure Intermediate care for mentally
retarded. *Beds* ICF/MR 108. *Certified* Medi-
Cal.
Owner Proprietary corp.
Admissions Requirements Minimum age 18;
Medical examination; Physician's request.
Staff Physicians 6 (ft); RNs 3 (ft), 4 (pt);
LPNs 6 (ft), 2 (pt); Nurses' aides 19 (ft), 1
(pt); Reality therapists 1 (ft); Recreational
therapists 2 (ft); Activities coordinators 1
(ft), 1 (pt); Dietitians 1 (ft).
Languages Spanish.
Facilities Dining room; Activities room;
Chapel; Crafts room; Laundry room; Barber/
Beauty shop; Library; Classroom.
Activities Arts & crafts; Cards; Games;
Reading groups; Prayer groups; Movies;
Shopping trips; Dances/Social/Cultural
gatherings; Pet therapy; Monthly family day
picnics; Yearly talent show.

Rosemead

California Christian Home
8417 E Mission Dr, Rosemead, CA 91770
(818) 287-0438
Admin Diana Foster. *Dir of Nursing* Anne
Keogh. *Medical Dir* Dr Francesco Vetri.
Licensure Skilled care; Retirement. *Beds* SNF
59. *Certified* Medi-Cal.
Owner Proprietary corp.
Admissions Requirements Minimum age 62;
Medical examination.
Staff Physicians 10 (pt); RNs 2 (ft); LPNs 7
(ft); Nurses' aides 20 (ft); Activities
coordinators 1 (ft); Dietitians 1 (pt).
Affiliation Disciples of Christ.
Facilities Dining room; Activities room;
Barber/Beauty shop.
Activities Arts & crafts; Games; Reading
groups; Movies; Shopping trips; Dances/
Social/Cultural gatherings.

Del Mar Convalescent Hospital
3136 N Del Mar Ave, Rosemead, CA 91770
(818) 288-8353
Admin Blaine E Hendrickson.
Licensure Skilled care. *Beds* SNF 59. *Certified*
Medicare; Medi-Cal.
Owner Proprietary corp.

Green Acres Lodge
8101 E Hill Dr, Rosemead, CA 91770
(213) 280-5682
Admin Marolyn Stahl.
Licensure Skilled care. *Beds* SNF 85. *Certified*
Medicare; Medi-Cal.
Owner Proprietary corp (CV American).

Monterey Care Center
1267 San Gabriel Blvd, Rosemead, CA 91770
(213) 280-3220
Admin John Farnsworth. *Dir of Nursing* Lydia
Pamintuan. *Medical Dir* William Beard.
Licensure Skilled care. *Beds* SNF 103.
Certified Medi-Cal.
Owner Proprietary corp (Care Enterprises).
Admissions Requirements Minimum age 45;
Physician's request.
Staff Physicians; RNs 4 (ft); LPNs 4 (ft);
Nurses' aides 20 (ft); Physical therapists;
Recreational therapists; Occupational
therapists; Speech therapists; Activities
coordinators 1 (ft); Dietitians 1 (ft);
Ophthalmologists; Podiatrists; Dentists.
Languages Spanish, Tagalog.
Facilities Dining room; Activities room;
Crafts room; Laundry room; Barber/Beauty
shop.
Activities Arts & crafts; Cards; Games;
Reading groups; Prayer groups; Movies;
Shopping trips; Dances/Social/Cultural
gatherings.

San Gabriel Convalescent Center
8035 E Hill Dr, Rosemead, CA 91770
(213) 280-4820
Admin Jan R Stine. *Dir of Nursing* Mary
Savage RN. *Medical Dir* Samuel Zia MD.
Licensure Skilled care. *Beds* SNF 151.
Certified Medicare; Medi-Cal.
Owner Proprietary corp.
Admissions Requirements Minimum age 55;
Medical examination; Physician's request.
Staff RNs 3 (ft), 3 (pt); LPNs 6 (ft), 4 (pt);
Nurses' aides; Physical therapists;
Occupational therapists; Speech therapists;
Activities coordinators 1 (ft); Dietitians;
Ophthalmologists; Podiatrists; Dentists.
Languages Spanish, Chinese, Korean, Tagalog.
Facilities Dining room; Physical therapy
room; Activities room; Crafts room; Laundry
room; Barber/Beauty shop; Library.
Activities Arts & crafts; Cards; Games;
Reading groups; Prayer groups; Movies;
Shopping trips; Dances/Social/Cultural
gatherings.

Roseville

Care West—Sierra Nursing Center
310 Oak Ridge Dr, Roseville, CA 95678
(916) 782-3188
Admin Andrew S Wallace. *Dir of Nursing* Lois
Maguire RN. *Medical Dir* Isidro Cardeno
MD.
Licensure Skilled care. *Beds* SNF 67. *Certified*
Medicare; Medi-Cal.
Owner Proprietary corp (Care Enterprises).
Admissions Requirements Minimum age 45;
Medical examination; Physician's request.
Staff RNs 4 (ft), 1 (pt); LPNs 5 (ft), 4 (pt);
Nurses' aides 27 (ft), 16 (pt); Activities
coordinators 1 (ft); Dietitians 1 (ft).
Languages Spanish.
Facilities Dining room; Physical therapy
room; Activities room; Crafts room; Laundry
room; Barber/Beauty shop; Library.
Activities Arts & crafts; Cards; Games;
Reading groups; Prayer groups; Movies;
Shopping trips; Dances/Social/Cultural
gatherings; Barbeques; Outings.

Hillhaven Roseville Convalescent Hospital
600 Sunrise Ave, Roseville, CA 95678
(916) 782-3131
Admin Douglas van Hee. *Dir of Nursing*
Jennie Desvignes RN. *Medical Dir* Dr
Douglas Luke.
Licensure Skilled care. *Beds* SNF 98. *Certified*
Medicaid; Medicare; Medi-Cal.
Owner Proprietary corp (Hillhaven Corp).
Admissions Requirements Minimum age 35.
Languages French, Spanish.
Facilities Dining room; Physical therapy
room; Activities room; Crafts room; Laundry
room; Barber/Beauty shop; Enclosed patio.
Activities Arts & crafts; Cards; Games;
Reading groups; Prayer groups; Movies;
Shopping trips; Dances/Social/Cultural
gatherings; Intergenerational programs; Pet
therapy.

Roseville Convalescent Hospital
1161 Cirby St, Roseville, CA 95678
(916) 782-1238
Admin Sheila Waddell.
Medical Dir Richard Chun MD.
Licensure Skilled care. *Beds* SNF 210.
Certified Medicare; Medi-Cal.
Owner Proprietary corp.
Admissions Requirements Medical
examination; Physician's request.
Staff RNs 7 (ft), 4 (pt); LPNs 12 (ft), 5 (pt);
Nurses' aides 56 (ft), 24 (pt); Physical
therapists 1 (pt); Occupational therapists 1
(pt); Speech therapists 1 (pt); Activities
coordinators 2 (ft); Dietitians 1 (pt);
Ophthalmologists 1 (pt); Podiatrists 1 (pt);
Audiologists 1 (pt); Dentists 1 (pt).

Facilities Dining room; Physical therapy
room; Activities room; Chapel; Crafts room;
Laundry room; Barber/Beauty shop; Library.
Activities Arts & crafts; Cards; Games;
Reading groups; Prayer groups; Movies;
Shopping trips; Dances/Social/Cultural
gatherings.

Rubidoux

Mt Rubidoux Convalescent Hospital
6401 33rd St, Rubidoux, CA 92509
(714) 681-2200
Admin Thomas Plott.
Medical Dir Dr Robert Bom.
Licensure Skilled care. *Beds* SNF 143.
Certified Medicare; Medi-Cal.
Owner Proprietary corp.
Admissions Requirements Physician's request.
Staff RNs 2 (ft), 2 (pt); LPNs 7 (ft), 3 (pt);
Nurses' aides 26 (ft), 5 (pt); Physical
therapists 1 (pt); Activities coordinators 4
(ft).
Facilities Dining room; Activities room;
Laundry room; Barber/Beauty shop; TV
room; Enclosed outdoor patios.
Activities Arts & crafts; Cards; Games;
Reading groups; Prayer groups; Movies;
Shopping trips; Dances/Social/Cultural
gatherings; Cooking classes.

Sacramento

Asian Community Nursing Home
7801 Rush River Dr, Sacramento, CA 95831
(916) 393-9020
Admin Linda WahlBaker. *Dir of Nursing*
Susan Green RN. *Medical Dir* William Y
Fong MD.
Licensure Skilled care. *Beds* SNF 99. *Private
Pay Patients* 25%. *Certified* Medicare; Medi-
Cal.
Owner Proprietary corp.
Staff RNs; LPNs; Nurses' aides; Activities
coordinators; Dietitians.
Languages Japanese, Cantonese, Tagalog.
Facilities Dining room; Physical therapy
room; Activities room; Crafts room; Laundry
room; Barber/Beauty shop.
Activities Arts & crafts; Cards; Games; Prayer
groups; Movies; Shopping trips; Dances/
Social/Cultural gatherings; Intergenerational
programs; Pet therapy.

Bruceville Terrace (D/P of Methodist)
8151 Bruceville Rd, Sacramento, CA 95823
(916) 423-4200
Admin James Cook.

Center Skilled Nursing Facility
2257 Fair Oaks Blvd, Sacramento, CA 95825
(916) 927-4763
Admin Tina Futch. *Dir of Nursing* Marie
Dibble RN. *Medical Dir* William T Kelley
MD.
Licensure Skilled care. *Beds* SNF 139.
Certified Medicare; Medi-Cal.
Owner Proprietary corp.
Admissions Requirements Physician's request.
Staff RNs 8 (ft), 2 (pt); LPNs 9 (ft), 2 (pt);
Nurses' aides 45 (ft), 8 (pt); Activities
coordinators 2 (ft); Dietitians 1 (ft).
Facilities Dining room; Physical therapy
room; Activities room; Crafts room; Laundry
room; Barber/Beauty shop.
Activities Arts & crafts; Cards; Games;
Reading groups; Prayer groups; Movies;
Shopping trips; Dances/Social/Cultural
gatherings; Outside expeditions to railroad
museum, zoo, etc.

Eskaton Glenwood Manor
501 Jessie Ave, Sacramento, CA 95838-2697
(916) 922-8855
Admin Jeffrey T Mangum. *Dir of Nursing*
Donna Webb RN. *Medical Dir* Justin
English MD.

Licensure Intermediate care. *Beds* ICF 128. *Private Pay Patients* 10%. *Certified* Medi-Cal.
Owner Nonprofit corp (Eskaton Health Corp).
Admissions Requirements Medical examination; Physician's request; Dependent adult or elderly.
Staff RNs 2 (ft), 4 (pt); LPNs 4 (ft), 4 (pt); Nurses' aides 11 (ft), 13 (pt); Activities coordinators 2 (ft), 1 (pt).
Languages Spanish.
Facilities Dining room; Activities room; Crafts room; Laundry room; Barber/Beauty shop; Wanderguard system.
Activities Arts & crafts; Cards; Games; Reading groups; Prayer groups; Movies; Shopping trips; Dances/Social/Cultural gatherings.

Florin Convalescent Hospital
7400 24th St, Sacramento, CA 95822
(916) 422-4825
Admin David Hutchinson. *Dir of Nursing* Margaret Pintea RN.
Licensure Skilled care. *Beds* SNF 122. *Certified* Medicare; Medi-Cal.
Owner Proprietary corp (Western Medical Enterprises).
Admissions Requirements Physician's request.
Staff RNs; LPNs; Nurses' aides; Physical therapists; Recreational therapists; Occupational therapists; Speech therapists; Activities coordinators; Dietitians.
Facilities Dining room; Physical therapy room; Activities room; Crafts room; Laundry room; Barber/Beauty shop.
Activities Arts & crafts; Cards; Games; Reading groups; Prayer groups; Movies; Shopping trips; Dances/Social/Cultural gatherings.

Gardens Skilled Nursing Facility
2221 Fair Oaks Blvd, Sacramento, CA 95825
(916) 927-1802
Admin Cynthia Lattavo. *Dir of Nursing* Betty Lumbert RN. *Medical Dir* Kenneth Hodge MD.
Licensure Intermediate care for mentally retarded. *Beds* ICF/MR 56. *Certified* Medi-Cal.
Owner Proprietary corp.
Admissions Requirements Minimum age 16.
Staff Physicians 2 (ft); RNs 3 (ft); LPNs 4 (ft); Activities coordinators 1 (ft); Psychiatrists; Psychologists; Social workers.
Facilities Dining room; Physical therapy room; Activities room; Laundry room.
Activities Arts & crafts; Cards; Games; Reading groups; Prayer groups; Movies; Shopping trips; Dances/Social/Cultural gatherings.

Greenhaven Country Place
455 Florin Rd, Sacramento, CA 95831
(916) 393-2550
Admin Diane Lonsdale.
Licensure Skilled care; Intermediate care. *Beds* SNF 140; ICF 8. *Certified* Medicare.
Owner Publicly owned.

Heritage Convalescent Hospital
5255 Hemlock St, Sacramento, CA 95841
(916) 331-4590
Admin Sandra Shetler.
Medical Dir William Hedges MD.
Licensure Skilled care. *Beds* SNF 99. *Certified* Medicare; Medi-Cal.
Owner Proprietary corp.
Staff Physicians 1 (pt); RNs 3 (ft), 1 (pt); LPNs 12 (ft), 2 (pt); Nurses' aides 45 (ft), 6 (pt); Physical therapists 2 (pt); Reality therapists 1 (pt); Recreational therapists 2 (pt); Occupational therapists 1 (pt); Speech therapists 1 (pt); Activities coordinators 2 (ft); Dietitians 1 (pt); Ophthalmologists 1 (pt); Podiatrists 1 (pt); Audiologists 1 (pt); Dentists 1 (pt).

Facilities Dining room; Physical therapy room; Activities room; Crafts room; Laundry room; Barber/Beauty shop.
Activities Arts & crafts; Cards; Games; Reading groups; Prayer groups; Movies; Shopping trips; Dances/Social/Cultural gatherings.

Hillhaven—Sherwood Convalescent Hospital
4700 Elvas Ave, Sacramento, CA 95819
(916) 454-5752
Admin Mary Tommolilo.
Licensure Skilled care. *Beds* SNF 62. *Certified* Medicare; Medi-Cal.
Owner Proprietary corp (Hillhaven Corp).
Staff Physicians 1 (pt); RNs 1 (ft); LPNs 1 (ft); Nurses' aides 1 (ft); Physical therapists 1 (pt); Reality therapists 1 (pt); Recreational therapists 1 (pt); Occupational therapists 1 (pt); Speech therapists 1 (pt); Activities coordinators 1 (ft); Dietitians 1 (pt); Ophthalmologists 1 (pt); Podiatrists 1 (pt); Dentists 1 (pt).

Hy-Lond Convalescent Hospital
4635 College Oak Dr, Sacramento, CA 95841
(916) 481-7434
Admin Karen Spector.
Licensure Skilled care. *Beds* SNF 120. *Certified* Medicare; Medi-Cal.
Owner Proprietary corp (Beverly Enterprises).

Mercycare (Mercy Hospital of Sacramento DP/SNF)
862 39th St, Sacramento, CA 95816
(916) 455-3014
Admin David C Ormiston Jr.
Licensure Skilled care. *Beds* SNF 77. *Certified* Medicare; Medi-Cal.
Owner Proprietary corp.

Methodist Hospital (SNF D/P Bruceville Terrace)
8151 Bruceville Rd, Sacramento, CA 95823
(916) 423-4200
Admin James Cook.
Licensure Skilled care. *Certified* Medicare; Medi-Cal.

Mt Olivette Meadows Convalescent Hospital
2240 Northrop Ave, Sacramento, CA 95825
(916) 927-1337
Admin Michael C Evans.
Licensure Intermediate care. *Beds* ICF 58. *Certified* Medi-Cal.
Owner Proprietary corp.

Pioneer House
415 P St, Sacramento, CA 95814
(916) 442-4906
Admin Philip S Richardson. *Dir of Nursing* Pearl Lamont. *Medical Dir* J English MD.
Licensure Skilled care; Retirement. *Beds* SNF 50. *Certified* Medi-Cal.
Owner Nonprofit corp.
Admissions Requirements Minimum age 62; Medical examination.
Staff RNs 3 (ft); LPNs 8 (ft); Nurses' aides 15 (ft); Physical therapists 1 (pt); Reality therapists 1 (pt); Recreational therapists 1 (pt); Occupational therapists 1 (pt); Speech therapists 1 (pt); Activities coordinators 1 (ft); Dietitians 1 (pt); Ophthalmologists 1 (pt); Podiatrists 1 (pt); Dentists 1 (pt).
Languages Spanish, Thai, Chinese, Tagalog.
Facilities Dining room; Activities room; Crafts room; Laundry room; Barber/Beauty shop; Library.
Activities Arts & crafts; Cards; Games; Reading groups; Prayer groups; Movies; Shopping trips; Dances/Social/Cultural gatherings.

Quinlan Manor
919 8th Ave, Sacramento, CA 95813
(916) 922-7177
Admin Ann Pelzman.

Licensure Intermediate care. *Beds* 22. *Certified* Medi-Cal.
Owner Proprietary corp.

River Valley Nursing Center Inc
5000 Folsom Blvd, Sacramento, CA 95819
(916) 452-4191
Admin Ronald W Petersen.
Licensure Skilled care. *Beds* SNF 121. *Certified* Medicare; Medi-Cal.
Owner Proprietary corp.

Riverside Convalescent Hospital
1090 Rio Ln, Sacramento, CA 95822
(916) 446-2506
Admin Constance A Smith. *Dir of Nursing* Donna L Albertson. *Medical Dir* G W O'Brien.
Licensure Skilled care. *Beds* SNF 51. *Private Pay Patients* 75%. *Certified* Medicare; Medi-Cal.
Owner Proprietary corp (Riverside Health Care Inc).
Admissions Requirements Medical examination; Physician's request.
Staff RNs 1 (ft), 1 (pt); LPNs 3 (ft), 4 (pt); Nurses' aides 26 (ft); Physical therapists 2 (pt); Occupational therapists 1 (pt); Speech therapists 1 (pt); Activities coordinators 1 (ft); Dietitians 1 (pt); Ophthalmologists 1 (pt); Podiatrists 1 (pt).
Languages Japanese, Tongan, Portuguese.
Facilities Dining room; Activities room; Crafts room; Laundry room; Barber/Beauty shop.
Activities Arts & crafts; Games; Reading groups; Prayer groups; Movies; Sewing; Woodworking.

Royal Manor Convalescent Hospital Inc
5901 Lemon Hill Ave, Sacramento, CA 95824
(916) 383-2741
Admin Bryan Jennings. *Dir of Nursing* Hester Tober RN. *Medical Dir* Anna Vaughn MD.
Licensure Skilled care. *Beds* SNF 49. *Certified* Medicare; Medi-Cal.
Owner Proprietary corp.
Admissions Requirements Physician's request.
Staff RNs 2 (ft); LPNs 5 (ft), 2 (pt); Nurses' aides 21 (ft), 8 (pt).
Facilities Dining room; Physical therapy room; Activities room; Crafts room; Laundry room; Barber/Beauty shop.
Activities Arts & crafts; Cards; Games; Reading groups; Prayer groups; Movies; Shopping trips; Dances/Social/Cultural gatherings.

Sacramento Convalescent Hospital
3700 H St, Sacramento, CA 95816
(916) 452-3592
Admin Sue Montag-Newby. *Dir of Nursing* Claire Rabidou RN. *Medical Dir* Dr Craig Pearson.
Licensure Skilled care. *Beds* SNF 86. *Certified* Medicare; Medi-Cal.
Owner Proprietary corp (Medicrest of California Inc).
Admissions Requirements Medical examination; Physician's request.
Staff Physicians 1 (pt); RNs 2 (ft); LPNs 5 (ft); Nurses' aides 21 (ft); Physical therapists 1 (pt); Occupational therapists 1 (pt); Speech therapists 1 (pt); Activities coordinators 1 (ft); Dietitians 1 (pt); Ophthalmologists 1 (pt); Podiatrists 1 (pt); Dentists 1 (pt).
Facilities Dining room; Physical therapy room; Activities room; Crafts room; Laundry room; Barber/Beauty shop.
Activities Arts & crafts; Cards; Games; Reading groups; Prayer groups; Movies; Shopping trips; Dances/Social/Cultural gatherings.

St Claire's Nursing Center
6248 66th Ave, Sacramento, CA 95823
(916) 392-4440

Licensure Skilled care; Intermediate care. *Beds* SNF 75; ICF 24. *Certified* Medicare; Medi-Cal.
Owner Proprietary corp.

Saylor Lane Convalescent Hospital
3500 Folsom Blvd, Sacramento, CA 95816
(916) 457-6521
Admin Gary Weimers. *Dir of Nursing* Violet Underwood. *Medical Dir* Dr Friedlander.
Licensure Skilled care. *Beds* SNF 42. *Private Pay Patients* 96%. *Certified* Medicare; Medi-Cal.
Owner Proprietary corp (Hillhaven Corp).
Admissions Requirements Medical examination; Physician's request.
Staff RNs 2 (ft), 2 (pt); LPNs 4 (ft); Nurses' aides 17 (ft), 6 (pt); Activities coordinators 1 (ft).
Facilities Dining room; Physical therapy room; Activities room; Laundry room; Barber/Beauty shop; Library.
Activities Arts & crafts; Cards; Games; Reading groups; Prayer groups; Movies; Dances/Social/Cultural gatherings; Intergenerational programs; Pet therapy; Van trips.

Sutter Oaks Alzheimer Center—Sacramento
500 Jessie Ave, Sacramento, CA 95838
(916) 922-7177
Admin Diane Hoyt.
Licensure Skilled care. *Beds* SNF 162. *Certified* Medicare; Medi-Cal.
Owner Nonprofit corp.

Sutter Oaks Nursing Center—Arden
3400 Alta Arden Expwy, Sacramento, CA 95825
(916) 481-5500
Admin Dan Wood.
Medical Dir B G Wagner MD.
Licensure Skilled care. *Beds* SNF 190. *Certified* Medicare; Medi-Cal.
Owner Proprietary corp.
Staff RNs 6 (ft), 6 (pt); LPNs 11 (ft), 5 (pt); Nurses' aides 63 (ft), 13 (pt); Activities coordinators 1 (ft).
Facilities Dining room; Physical therapy room; Activities room; Crafts room; Laundry room; Barber/Beauty shop.
Activities Arts & crafts; Cards; Games; Reading groups; Prayer groups; Movies; Dances/Social/Cultural gatherings.

Sutter Oaks Nursing Center—Midtown
2600 L St, Sacramento, CA 95816
(916) 444-7290
Dir of Nursing Carol Loftin RN. *Medical Dir* Dr David Dachler.
Licensure Skilled care. *Beds* SNF 132. *Certified* Medicare; Medi-Cal.
Owner Nonprofit organization/foundation.
Admissions Requirements Physician's request.
Staff RNs 9 (ft), 3 (pt); LPNs 13 (ft), 4 (pt); Nurses' aides 63 (ft); Physical therapists 1 (ft); Occupational therapists 1 (ft); Speech therapists 1 (ft); Activities coordinators 3 (ft); Dietitians 1 (ft).
Languages Spanish.
Facilities Dining room; Physical therapy room; Activities room.
Activities Arts & crafts; Cards; Games; Prayer groups; Movies; Dances/Social/Cultural gatherings.

Trinity House
2701 Capitol Ave, Sacramento, CA 95816
(916) 446-4806
Admin Philip S Richardson.
Medical Dir Dr Justin English.
Licensure Skilled care. *Beds* SNF 29. *Certified* Medi-Cal.
Owner Nonprofit corp.
Admissions Requirements Minimum age 62; Medical examination.

Staff Physicians 1 (pt); RNs 1 (ft), 1 (pt); LPNs 4 (ft); Nurses' aides 8 (ft), 2 (pt); Physical therapists 1 (pt); Speech therapists 1 (pt); Activities coordinators 1 (ft); Dietitians 1 (pt); Ophthalmologists 1 (pt); Podiatrists 1 (pt); Dentists 1 (pt).
Facilities Dining room; Activities room; Laundry room; Barber/Beauty shop; Library.
Activities Arts & crafts; Games; Reading groups; Prayer groups; Movies; Shopping trips; Dances/Social/Cultural gatherings.

Valley Skilled Nursing Facility
2120 Stockton Blvd, Sacramento, CA 95817
(916) 452-6631, 739-0961 FAX
Admin Terri L Sutton. *Dir of Nursing* Lori Olvera. *Medical Dir* Dr Don Reville.
Licensure Skilled care. *Beds* SNF 59. *Private Pay Patients* 8%. *Certified* Medicare; Medi-Cal.
Owner Proprietary corp (Hostmasters).
Admissions Requirements Medical examination; Physician's request.
Staff RNs 3 (ft); LPNs 5 (ft); Nurses' aides 25 (ft); Physical therapists 1 (ft); Recreational therapists 1 (ft); Occupational therapists 1 (ft); Speech therapists 1 (ft); Activities coordinators 1 (ft); Dietitians 1 (ft); Podiatrists 1 (ft).
Facilities Dining room; Physical therapy room; Activities room; Laundry room; Barber/Beauty shop.
Activities Arts & crafts; Cards; Games; Prayer groups; Movies; Shopping trips; Dances/Social/Cultural gatherings; Pet therapy; Visiting library.

Saint Helena

Care West—Madrone Nursing Center
830 Pratt Ave, Saint Helena, CA 94574
(707) 963-2791
Admin Calvin Baker.
Licensure Skilled care. *Beds* SNF 70. *Certified* Medicare; Medi-Cal.
Owner Proprietary corp (Care Enterprises).

Salinas

Casa Serena Skilled Nursing & Rehabilitation Hospital
720 E Romie Ln, Salinas, CA 93901
(408) 424-8072
Admin Ronald L Walton. *Dir of Nursing* Jan Steele RN. *Medical Dir* Dr Engerhorn.
Licensure Skilled care. *Beds* SNF 116. *Private Pay Patients* 50%. *Certified* Medicare; Medi-Cal.
Owner Proprietary corp.
Staff RNs 4 (ft), 2 (pt); LPNs 7 (ft), 6 (pt); Nurses' aides 48 (ft), 12 (pt); Physical therapists 1 (ft); Occupational therapists 1 (pt); Speech therapists 1 (pt); Activities coordinators 1 (ft), 2 (pt); Dietitians 1 (ft); Audiologists 1 (pt).
Languages Spanish.
Facilities Dining room; Physical therapy room; Activities room; Crafts room; Laundry room; Barber/Beauty shop.
Activities Arts & crafts; Cards; Games; Reading groups; Prayer groups; Movies; Shopping trips; Dances/Social/Cultural gatherings; Intergenerational programs; Pet therapy.

Driftwood Convalescent Hospital
350 Iris Dr, Salinas, CA 93906
(408) 449-1515
Admin Rachyl Bruton. *Dir of Nursing* Michele Noriega RN. *Medical Dir* James Daly MD.
Licensure Skilled care. *Beds* SNF 99. *Private Pay Patients* 40%. *Certified* Medicare; Medi-Cal.
Owner Proprietary corp (Touchstone Health Care Systems).

Admissions Requirements Medical examination.
Staff Physicians 2 (pt); RNs 4 (ft), 3 (pt); LPNs 7 (ft), 4 (pt); Nurses' aides 45 (ft), 5 (pt); Physical therapists 1 (pt); Recreational therapists 1 (pt); Occupational therapists 1 (pt); Speech therapists 1 (pt); Activities coordinators 1 (ft), 1 (pt); Dietitians 1 (ft); Ophthalmologists 1 (pt); Podiatrists 1 (pt); Audiologists 1 (pt).
Languages Spanish, Tagalog, Japanese.
Facilities Dining room; Physical therapy room; Activities room; Laundry room; Barber/Beauty shop.
Activities Arts & crafts; Cards; Games; Reading groups; Prayer groups; Movies; Shopping trips.

Katherine Convalescent Hospital
315 Alameda St, Salinas, CA 93901
(408) 424-1878
Admin Sue Montag. *Dir of Nursing* Margaret Adams RN. *Medical Dir* A L Wessels MD.
Licensure Skilled care. *Beds* SNF 51. *Certified* Medicare; Medi-Cal.
Owner Proprietary corp.
Admissions Requirements Minimum age 21; Physician's request.
Staff RNs; LPNs; Nurses' aides; Activities coordinators.
Facilities Dining room; Physical therapy room; Activities room; Chapel; Crafts room; Laundry room; Barber/Beauty shop.
Activities Arts & crafts; Cards; Games; Movies; Shopping trips.

Salinas Care Center
637 E Romie Ln, Salinas, CA 93901
(408) 424-0687
Admin Ralph B Unterbrink. *Dir of Nursing* Nancy K Heitzman. *Medical Dir* James Daly.
Licensure Skilled care. *Beds* SNF 99. *Private Pay Patients* 20%. *Certified* Medicare; Medi-Cal.
Owner Proprietary corp (Meritcare Inc).
Admissions Requirements Medical examination.
Staff Physicians; RNs; LPNs; Nurses' aides; Physical therapists; Reality therapists; Recreational therapists; Occupational therapists; Speech therapists; Activities coordinators; Dietitians; Podiatrists; Dentists.
Facilities Dining room; Physical therapy room; Activities room; Crafts room; Laundry room; Barber/Beauty shop.
Activities Arts & crafts; Games; Reading groups; Movies; Shopping trips; Dances/Social/Cultural gatherings; Pet therapy.

Skyline Convalescent
348 Iris Dr, Salinas, CA 93906
(408) 449-5496
Admin Laurie Behrend. *Dir of Nursing* Dorothy Turnbull. *Medical Dir* James Daly.
Licensure Skilled care. *Beds* SNF 80. *Private Pay Patients* 15%. *Certified* Medicaid; Medicare; Medi-Cal.
Owner Proprietary corp (Touchstone Health Systems).
Staff RNs 5 (ft); LPNs 4 (ft), 3 (pt); Nurses' aides 30 (ft), 7 (pt); Physical therapists 1 (pt); Occupational therapists 1 (pt); Speech therapists 1 (pt); Activities coordinators 1 (ft); Dietitians 1 (pt); Ophthalmologists 1 (pt); Podiatrists 1 (pt); Audiologists 1 (pt).
Languages Filipino, Spanish.
Facilities Dining room; Physical therapy room; Activities room; Laundry room.
Activities Arts & crafts; Cards; Games; Reading groups; Prayer groups; Movies; Shopping trips; Dances/Social/Cultural gatherings; Intergenerational programs; Pet therapy.

San Andreas

Mark Twain Convalescent Hospital
900 Mountain Ranch, San Andreas, CA 95249
(209) 754-3823
Admin Joyce Bahnsen.
Licensure Skilled care. *Beds* SNF 99. *Certified*
Medicare; Medi-Cal.
Owner Proprietary corp (Beverly Enterprises).

San Andreas Convalescent Hospital No 679
556 Toyon Rd, San Andreas, CA 95249
(209) 754-4213
Admin Joyce Bahnsen.
Licensure Skilled care. *Beds* SNF 33. *Certified*
Medicare; Medi-Cal.
Owner Proprietary corp (Beverly Enterprises).

San Bernardino

Arrowhead Home
4343 Sierra Way, San Bernardino, CA 92404
(714) 886-4731
Admin Donald N Popovich.
Licensure Intermediate care. *Beds* 58.
Certified Medi-Cal.
Owner Proprietary corp.

Del Rosa Convalescent Hospital
1311 Date St, San Bernardino, CA 92404
(714) 882-3316
Admin Sarah McEvoy.
Medical Dir Dr Leslie Musad.
Licensure Skilled care. *Beds* SNF 99. *Certified*
Medicare; Medi-Cal.
Owner Proprietary corp (Hillhaven Corp).
Admissions Requirements Minimum age 16;
Medical examination; Physician's request.
Staff Physicians 46 (pt); RNs 4 (ft), 4 (pt);
LPNs 7 (ft), 4 (pt); Nurses' aides 33 (ft), 9
(pt); Physical therapists 1 (ft), 1 (pt);
Occupational therapists 1 (pt); Speech
therapists 1 (pt); Activities coordinators 1
(ft); Dietitians 1 (pt); Podiatrists 1 (pt);
Audiologists 1 (pt); Dentists 1 (pt).
Facilities Dining room; Physical therapy
room; Activities room; Barber/Beauty shop;
Library.
Activities Arts & crafts; Cards; Games;
Reading groups; Prayer groups; Movies;
Shopping trips; Dances/Social/Cultural
gatherings.

Del Rosa Villa
2018 N Del Rosa Ave, San Bernardino, CA
92404
(714) 885-3261
Admin Peggy Blum.
Licensure Skilled care; Intermediate care. *Beds*
SNF 99; ICF 5. *Certified* Medicare; Medi-
Cal.
Owner Proprietary corp.

Hillcrest Nursing Home
4280 Cypress Dr, San Bernardino, CA 92407
(714) 882-2965
Admin Arthur H Douglass.
Licensure Skilled care. *Beds* SNF 59. *Certified*
Medi-Cal.
Owner Proprietary corp.

Medical Center Convalescent Hospital
467 E Gilbert St, San Bernardino, CA 92404
(714) 884-4781
Admin Duane Dahlin.
Licensure Skilled care. *Beds* SNF 99. *Certified*
Medicare; Medi-Cal.
Owner Proprietary corp.

Pacific Park Convalescent Hospital
1676 Medical Center, San Bernardino, CA
92405
(714) 887-6481
Admin George Vickerman. *Dir of Nursing*
Lois Kirschner RN. *Medical Dir* Frank
Randolph MD.
Licensure Skilled care. *Beds* SNF 99. *Certified*
Medicare; Medi-Cal.

Owner Nonprofit corp.
Admissions Requirements Medical
examination; Physician's request.
Staff Physicians 1 (pt); RNs 2 (ft); LPNs 7
(ft); Nurses' aides 25 (ft); Physical therapists
4 (pt); Occupational therapists 1 (pt); Speech
therapists 1 (pt); Activities coordinators 1
(ft); Dietitians 1 (pt); Ophthalmologists 1
(pt); Podiatrists 1 (pt); Dentists 1 (pt).
Languages Spanish.
Facilities Dining room; Physical therapy
room; Activities room; Crafts room; Laundry
room; Barber/Beauty shop.
Activities Arts & crafts; Cards; Games;
Reading groups; Prayer groups; Movies;
Shopping trips; Dances/Social/Cultural
gatherings.

Shandin Hills Behavior Therapy Center
4164 N 4th Ave, San Bernardino, CA 92407
(714) 886-6786
Admin Peter Bennett.
Licensure Intermediate care for mentally
retarded. *Beds* ICF/MR 78. *Certified* Medi-
Cal.
Owner Proprietary corp.

Shandin Hills Convalescent Hospital
4160 4th Ave, San Bernardino, CA 92407
(714) 886-6786
Licensure Skilled care. *Beds* 29. *Certified*
Medi-Cal.
Owner Proprietary corp.

Shea Convalescent Hospital
1335 N Waterman Ave, San Bernardino, CA
92404
(714) 885-0268, 888-5982 FAX
Admin Jocey Hallman. *Dir of Nursing* Carol
Wagner. *Medical Dir* David Phillips MD.
Licensure Skilled care. *Beds* SNF 120. *Private
Pay Patients* 25%. *Certified* Medicare; Medi-
Cal.
Owner Proprietary corp.
Admissions Requirements Medical
examination; Physician's request.
Staff RNs 4 (ft); LPNs 16 (ft); Nurses' aides
58 (ft); Physical therapists 2 (pt); Reality
therapists 1 (ft); Recreational therapists 1
(ft); Occupational therapists 1 (pt); Speech
therapists 1 (pt); Activities coordinators 1
(ft); Dietitians 1 (ft); Audiologists 1 (pt).
Languages Spanish.
Facilities Dining room; Physical therapy
room; Activities room; Crafts room; Laundry
room; Barber/Beauty shop; TV.
Activities Arts & crafts; Games; Reading
groups; Prayer groups; Movies; Shopping
trips; Dances/Social/Cultural gatherings;
Intergenerational programs; Pet therapy;
Staff and patient "Walk and Talk" program.

Valley Convalescent Hospital
1680 N Waterman Ave, San Bernardino, CA
92404
(714) 886-5291
Admin Stanley R Smith. *Dir of Nursing* Lois
Freeman RN.
Licensure Skilled care. *Beds* SNF 122.
Certified Medicare; Medi-Cal.
Owner Proprietary corp.
Admissions Requirements Medical
examination; Physician's request.
Staff Physicians; RNs; LPNs; Nurses' aides;
Physical therapists; Recreational therapists;
Occupational therapists; Speech therapists;
Activities coordinators; Dietitians;
Ophthalmologists; Podiatrists; Dentists.
Languages Spanish.
Facilities Dining room; Physical therapy
room; Activities room; Chapel; Crafts room;
Laundry room; Barber/Beauty shop; Patient
lounge.
Activities Arts & crafts; Cards; Games;
Reading groups; Prayer groups; Movies;
Shopping trips.

Waterman Convalescent Hospital
1850 N Waterman Ave, San Bernardino, CA
92404
(714) 882-1215
Admin Carol Donegan.
Licensure Skilled care. *Beds* SNF 166.
Certified Medicare; Medi-Cal.
Owner Proprietary corp.

San Bruno

San Bruno Convalescent Hospital
890 El Camino Real, San Bruno, CA 94066
(415) 583-7768
Admin Daniel W Alger.
Licensure Skilled care. *Beds* SNF 45. *Certified*
Medicare; Medi-Cal.
Owner Proprietary corp.

San Diego

**Alvarado Convalescent & Rehabilitation
Hospital**
6599 Alvarado Rd, San Diego, CA 92120
(619) 286-7421, 583-5925 FAX
Admin Francis X Rodgers. *Dir of Nursing*
Lynn Baits. *Medical Dir* Rolf Ehlers.
Licensure Skilled care; Alzheimer's care. *Beds*
SNF 301. *Private Pay Patients* 93%. *Certified*
Medicare.
Owner Proprietary corp (Hillhaven Corp).
Admissions Requirements Medical
examination; Physician's request.
Staff RNs 8 (ft); LPNs 12 (ft); Nurses' aides
41 (ft), 2 (pt); Physical therapists 1 (ft);
Activities coordinators 1 (ft); Dietitians 1
(ft).
Facilities Dining room; Physical therapy
room; Activities room; Chapel; Crafts room;
Laundry room; Barber/Beauty shop; Library.
Activities Arts & crafts; Cards; Games;
Reading groups; Prayer groups; Movies;
Shopping trips; Dances/Social/Cultural
gatherings; Intergenerational programs; Pet
therapy; Alzheimer's programming.

Arroyo Vista Convalescent Center
3022 45th St, San Diego, CA 92105
(619) 283-5855
Admin Judy Morton.
Medical Dir Dr A K Williams.
Licensure Skilled care. *Beds* SNF 53. *Certified*
Medicare; Medi-Cal.
Owner Proprietary corp (Care Enterprises).
Staff RNs 4 (ft), 1 (pt); LPNs 3 (ft), 1 (pt);
Nurses' aides 15 (ft), 5 (pt); Physical
therapists 1 (ft); Recreational therapists 1
(ft); Occupational therapists 1 (pt); Speech
therapists 1 (pt); Activities coordinators 1
(ft); Dietitians 1 (ft); Dentists 1 (pt).
Facilities Dining room; Physical therapy
room; Activities room; Laundry room;
Barber/Beauty shop; Library.
Activities Arts & crafts; Cards; Games;
Reading groups; Movies; Dances/Social/
Cultural gatherings.

Care With Dignity Convalescent Hospital
8060 Frost St, San Diego, CA 92123
(619) 278-4750
Admin Gary D Devoir.
Medical Dir Arthur G Edwards.
Licensure Skilled care. *Beds* SNF 99. *Certified*
Medicare; Medi-Cal.
Owner Proprietary corp.
Facilities Dining room; Physical therapy
room; Barber/Beauty shop.
Activities Arts & crafts; Cards; Games;
Reading groups; Prayer groups.

Carmel Mountain Healthcare Center
11895 Ave of Industry, San Diego, CA 92128
(619) 673-0101, 673-8320 FAX
Admin Carolyn Spradlin. *Dir of Nursing*
Linda Hager. *Medical Dir* Raymond
LaChance MD.

Licensure Skilled care; Alzheimer's care. *Beds* SNF 98; Alzheimer's care 22. *Certified* Medicare; Medi-Cal.
Owner Proprietary corp (Hillhaven Corp).
Admissions Requirements Medical examination; Physician's request.
Languages Tagalog, Spanish, Persian, Japanese.
Facilities Dining room; Physical therapy room; Activities room; Barber/Beauty shop; Library; Private dining room; Family room.
Activities Arts & crafts; Cards; Games; Reading groups; Prayer groups; Movies; Shopping trips; Dances/Social/Cultural gatherings; Intergenerational programs; Pet therapy.

Casa de las Campanas
18685 W Bernardo Dr, San Diego, CA 92127
(619) 451-9152, 451-8660 FAX
Admin Debra L Kurth. *Dir of Nursing* Diane M Brooks. *Medical Dir* David V Rousseau MD.
Licensure Skilled care; Residential living. *Beds* SNF 99; Residential apts 426. *Certified* Medicare.
Owner Nonprofit corp.
Admissions Requirements Physician's request.
Staff Physicians (contracted); RNs; LPNs; Nurses' aides; Physical therapists (contracted); Reality therapists (contracted); Recreational therapists (contracted); Occupational therapists (contracted); Speech therapists (contracted); Activities coordinators; Dietitians (contracted); Podiatrists (contracted).
Facilities Dining room; Physical therapy room; Activities room; Crafts room; Laundry room; Barber/Beauty shop; Library; Semi-private rooms.
Activities Arts & crafts; Cards; Games; Reading groups; Prayer groups; Movies; Shopping trips; Dances/Social/Cultural gatherings; Intergenerational programs; Pet therapy.

Cloisters of Mission Hills Convalescent Hospital
3680 Reynard Way, San Diego, CA 92103
(619) 297-4484
Admin L M Gray.
Licensure Skilled care. *Beds* SNF 70. *Certified* Medicare; Medi-Cal.
Owner Proprietary corp.

Del Capri Terrace Convalescent
5602 University Ave, San Diego, CA 92105
(619) 583-1993
Admin Barry B Zarling. *Dir of Nursing* Constance Cadicamo RN. *Medical Dir* A K Williams MD.
Licensure Skilled care. *Beds* SNF 87. *Private Pay Patients* 29%. *Certified* Medicare; Medi-Cal.
Owner Proprietary corp (Care Enterprises).
Admissions Requirements Medical examination; Physician's request.
Staff RNs 2 (ft); LPNs 9 (ft), 5 (pt); Nurses' aides 22 (ft), 6 (pt); Physical therapists 1 (ft); Activities coordinators 1 (ft), 1 (pt); Dietitians 1 (ft).
Languages Spanish, Filipino.
Facilities Dining room; Physical therapy room; Activities room; Barber/Beauty shop.
Activities Arts & crafts; Games; Reading groups; Prayer groups; Movies; Shopping trips; Dances/Social/Cultural gatherings; Intergenerational programs; Pet therapy.

Euclid Convalescent Center
1350 N Euclid Ave, San Diego, CA 92105
(619) 263-2166
Admin Violet M Sylvia. *Dir of Nursing* Judy Ashton. *Medical Dir* John Berger.
Licensure Skilled care. *Beds* SNF 99. *Private Pay Patients* 10%. *Certified* Medicare; Medi-Cal.
Owner Privately owned (Coordinated Care).

Staff RNs 1 (ft), 1 (pt); LPNs 6 (ft), 2 (pt); Nurses' aides 60 (ft), 10 (pt); Physical therapists (contracted); Recreational therapists (contracted); Occupational therapists (contracted); Speech therapists (contracted); Activities coordinators 1 (ft); Dietitians (contracted); Ophthalmologists (contracted); Podiatrists (contracted); Audiologists (contracted).
Languages Spanish, Filipino.
Facilities Dining room; Physical therapy room; Activities room; Crafts room; Laundry room; Barber/Beauty shop.
Activities Arts & crafts; Cards; Games; Reading groups; Prayer groups; Movies; Shopping trips; Dances/Social/Cultural gatherings; Intergenerational programs; Pet therapy.

Fraser Intermediate Care Facility
726 Torrance St, San Diego, CA 92103
(619) 296-2175
Admin Barbara C Carter. *Dir of Nursing* Esperanza Olarte LVN. *Medical Dir* Dr Sam C Hsieh.
Licensure Intermediate care; Retirement. *Beds* ICF 36. *Certified* Medi-Cal.
Owner Privately owned.
Admissions Requirements Medical examination; Physician's request.
Staff Physicians; RNs; LPNs 4 (ft), 3 (pt); Nurses' aides 5 (ft), 3 (pt); Recreational therapists; Occupational therapists; Speech therapists; Activities coordinators 1 (pt); Dietitians; Ophthalmologists; Dentists.
Languages Spanish.
Facilities Dining room; Activities room; Chapel; Crafts room; Laundry room.
Activities Arts & crafts; Cards; Games; Movies; Shopping trips; Dances/Social/ Cultural gatherings; Baseball games.

Georgian Court Nursing & Rehabilitation Center
2828 Meadowlark Dr, San Diego, CA 92123
(619) 277-6460
Admin Diana Schilling MPA. *Dir of Nursing* Candace Meyer RN. *Medical Dir* Arvin J Klein MD.
Licensure Skilled care; Alzheimer's care. *Beds* SNF 305. *Private Pay Patients* 10%. *Certified* Medicare; Medi-Cal.
Owner Proprietary corp (Care Enterprises).
Admissions Requirements Physician's request.
Staff Physicians; RNs; LPNs; Nurses' aides; Physical therapists; Recreational therapists; Occupational therapists; Speech therapists; Activities coordinators; Dietitians.
Facilities Dining room; Physical therapy room; Activities room; Crafts room; Laundry room; Barber/Beauty shop; Occupational therapy & speech therapy rooms; Patio.
Activities Arts & crafts; Cards; Games; Reading groups; Prayer groups; Movies; Shopping trips; Dances/Social/Cultural gatherings; Outside trips.

Golden Hill Health Care Center
1201 34th St, San Diego, CA 92102
(619) 232-2946
Admin Laurie Manners. *Dir of Nursing* Alberta Caneda RN. *Medical Dir* A K Williams.
Licensure Skilled care; Alzheimer's care. *Beds* SNF 99. *Certified* Medicare; Medi-Cal.
Owner Proprietary corp (American-Cal Medical Services Inc).
Admissions Requirements Minimum age 40; Medical examination; Physician's request.
Staff RNs; LPNs; Nurses' aides; Physical therapists; Reality therapists; Recreational therapists; Occupational therapists; Speech therapists; Activities coordinators; Dietitians; Ophthalmologists; Podiatrists; Dentists.
Facilities Dining room; Physical therapy room; Activities room; Crafts room; Laundry room; Barber/Beauty shop; Library; Outside recreation area.

Activities Arts & crafts; Cards; Games; Reading groups; Prayer groups; Movies; Shopping trips; Dances/Social/Cultural gatherings.

Healthcare Center at the Remington Club
16915 Hierba Dr, San Diego, CA 92128
(619) 451-9025
Admin Cheryl Carter. *Dir of Nursing* Carol Higgins. *Medical Dir* David Spees MD.
Licensure Skilled care; Independent living apartments. *Beds* SNF 59; Independent living apts 146. *Private Pay Patients* 98%. *Certified* Medicare.
Owner Proprietary corp (Forum Group Inc).
Admissions Requirements Minimum age 18.
Staff Physicians; RNs; LPNs; Nurses' aides; Physical therapists; Reality therapists; Recreational therapists; Occupational therapists; Speech therapists; Activities coordinators; Dietitians.
Languages Spanish, Filipino.
Facilities Dining room; Physical therapy room; Activities room; Chapel; Crafts room; Laundry room; Barber/Beauty shop; Library.
Activities Arts & crafts; Cards; Games; Reading groups; Prayer groups; Movies; Shopping trips; Dances/Social/Cultural gatherings; Intergenerational programs; Pet therapy.

Kearny Mesa Convalescent & Nursing Home
7675 Family Circle Dr, San Diego, CA 92111
(619) 278-8121
Admin Richard J Hebbel.
Licensure Skilled care. *Beds* SNF 98. *Certified* Medicare; Medi-Cal.
Owner Proprietary corp.

Meadowlark Convalescent Hospital
8001 Birmingham Dr, San Diego, CA 92123
(619) 279-7701
Admin Mark Miller.
Medical Dir Renato Masilungan MD.
Licensure Skilled care. *Beds* SNF 92. *Certified* Medicare; Medi-Cal.
Owner Nonprofit corp.
Admissions Requirements Minimum age 18.
Staff RNs 4 (ft), 2 (pt); LPNs 6 (ft), 3 (pt); Physical therapists 1 (ft), 2 (pt); Activities coordinators 1 (ft).
Facilities Dining room; Physical therapy room; Activities room; Laundry room.
Activities Arts & crafts; Cards; Games; Reading groups; Prayer groups; Movies; Family dinners.

Mercy Rehabilitation & Care Center
3520 4th Ave, San Diego, CA 92103
(619) 291-5270
Admin C David Goodin. *Dir of Nursing* Judy Harrington RN. *Medical Dir* A K Williams MD.
Licensure Skilled care. *Beds* SNF 194. *Private Pay Patients* 25%. *Certified* Medicare; Medi-Cal.
Owner Nonprofit corp.
Admissions Requirements Physician's request.
Staff Physicians 1 (pt); RNs 10 (ft); LPNs 22 (ft); Nurses' aides 64 (ft); Physical therapists 2 (ft), 2 (pt); Recreational therapists 1 (ft); Occupational therapists 2 (ft), 2 (pt); Speech therapists 2 (ft), 2 (pt); Dietitians 1 (ft).
Languages Spanish, Tagalog.
Affiliation Roman Catholic.
Facilities Dining room; Physical therapy room; Activities room; Crafts room; Laundry room; Barber/Beauty shop; Library.
Activities Arts & crafts; Cards; Games; Reading groups; Prayer groups; Movies; Shopping trips; Dances/Social/Cultural gatherings; Intergenerational programs; Pet therapy.

Nazareth House
6333 Rancho Mission, San Diego, CA 92108
(619) 563-0480

Admin Margaret P Flynn. *Dir of Nursing* V McDonnell RN BSN. *Medical Dir* Dr M Kielty.
Licensure Skilled care; Intermediate care. *Beds* SNF 30; ICF 8; Residential 88. *Certified* Medi-Cal.
Owner Nonprofit corp.
Staff RNs 11 (ft), 2 (pt); LPNs 3 (ft), 1 (pt); Nurses' aides 22 (ft), 3 (pt); Activities coordinators 1 (ft); Dietitians 1 (ft).
Affiliation Roman Catholic.
Facilities Dining room; Activities room; Chapel; Crafts room; Laundry room; Barber/Beauty shop.
Activities Arts & crafts; Cards; Games; Reading groups; Prayer groups; Movies; Shopping trips.

Paradise Hills Convalescent Center
6061 Banbury St, San Diego, CA 92139
(619) 475-2211
Admin Roger L Caddell. *Dir of Nursing* Patricia Youmans. *Medical Dir* Max Nelson MD.
Licensure Skilled care. *Beds* SNF 162. *Certified* Medicare; Medi-Cal.
Owner Proprietary corp.
Admissions Requirements Minimum age 18.
Staff Physicians 1 (pt); RNs 15 (ft), 2 (pt); LPNs 17 (ft), 6 (pt); Nurses' aides 62 (ft), 10 (pt); Physical therapists 2 (ft); Occupational therapists 1 (ft); Speech therapists 1 (ft); Activities coordinators 3 (ft), 1 (pt); Dietitians 1 (ft), 1 (pt); Ophthalmologists 1 (pt); Podiatrists 1 (pt); Dentists 1 (pt).
Languages Spanish, Tagalog, French.
Facilities Dining room; Physical therapy room; Activities room; Crafts room; Laundry room; Barber/Beauty shop; Library.
Activities Arts & crafts; Cards; Games; Reading groups; Prayer groups; Movies; Shopping trips; Dances/Social/Cultural gatherings; Trips to restaurants; Olympiatrics.

Point Loma Convalescent Hospital
3202 Duke St, San Diego, CA 92110
(619) 224-4141
Admin Vivian E Herrmann.
Medical Dir Kenneth Taylor MD.
Licensure Skilled care. *Beds* SNF 133. *Certified* Medicare; Medi-Cal.
Owner Privately owned.
Admissions Requirements Minimum age 18; Medical examination; Physician's request.
Staff RNs 5 (ft), 3 (pt); LPNs 4 (ft), 3 (pt); Nurses' aides 29 (ft), 15 (pt); Physical therapists; Activities coordinators; Dietitians.
Facilities Dining room; Physical therapy room; Laundry room; Barber/Beauty shop; Living room.
Activities Arts & crafts; Cards; Games; Reading groups; Prayer groups; Movies; Shopping trips; Outside activities.

St Paul's Health Care Center
235 Nutmeg St, San Diego, CA 92103
(619) 239-2097
Admin Almus Larsen.
Medical Dir Mary Ellen Dellefield.
Licensure Skilled care; Retirement. *Beds* SNF 59. *Certified* Medicare; Medi-Cal.
Owner Nonprofit corp.
Admissions Requirements Minimum age 62; Physician's request.
Staff Physicians; RNs; Nurses' aides; Physical therapists; Recreational therapists; Occupational therapists; Speech therapists; Activities coordinators; Dietitians; CNAs; Social services director.
Languages Spanish.
Affiliation Episcopal.
Facilities Dining room; Physical therapy room; Activities room; Chapel; Crafts room; Laundry room; Barber/Beauty shop.

Activities Arts & crafts; Games; Reading groups; Prayer groups; Movies; Dances/Social/Cultural gatherings; Church services; Special events; Birthdays; Family parties.

San Diego Hebrew Home for the Aged
4075 54th St, San Diego, CA 92105
(619) 582-5168
Admin Michael J Ellentuck.
Licensure Skilled care. *Beds* SNF 72. *Certified* Medicare; Medi-Cal.
Owner Nonprofit corp.
Affiliation Jewish.

San Diego Intermediate Care Center
1119 28th St, San Diego, CA 92102
(619) 233-0505
Admin Marietta (Mary) Vaughn.
Medical Dir Joseph P DeLuca.
Licensure Intermediate care. *Beds* ICF 37. *Private Pay Patients* 15%. *Certified* Medi-Cal.
Owner Privately owned.
Admissions Requirements Minimum age 18; Medical examination.
Staff Physicians (consultant); RNs; LPNs; Nurses' aides; Physical therapists (consultant); Reality therapists (consultant); Recreational therapists (consultant); Speech therapists (consultant); Activities coordinators; Dietitians (consultant); Ophthalmologists (consultant); Podiatrists (consultant); Audiologists (consultant).
Facilities Dining room; Activities room; Laundry room; Library.
Activities Arts & crafts; Cards; Games; Reading groups; Prayer groups; Movies; Shopping trips; Dances/Social/Cultural gatherings; Intergenerational programs; Pet therapy; Art; Music; Adult education.

Sharp Knollwood
7944 Birmingham Dr, San Diego, CA 92123
(619) 278-8810
Admin Linda Pinney MHA. *Dir of Nursing* Janine Kruger BSN RN. *Medical Dir* Thomas Spethmann MD.
Licensure Skilled care. *Beds* SNF 166. *Certified* Medicare; Medi-Cal.
Owner Nonprofit corp.
Staff Physicians; RNs 15 (ft); LPNs 17 (ft); Nurses' aides 70 (ft); Physical therapists 1 (ft); Occupational therapists 1 (ft); Activities coordinators 1 (ft); Dietitians 1 (ft); Psychologist, Social worker.
Facilities Dining room; Physical therapy room; Activities room; Laundry room; Barber/Beauty shop.
Activities Arts & crafts; Cards; Games; Reading groups; Prayer groups; Movies; Shopping trips; Dances/Social/Cultural gatherings.

Stanford Court Nursing Center of Mission Hills
4033 6th Ave Extension, San Diego, CA 92103
(619) 297-4086
Admin Susan Fazio.
Licensure Skilled care. *Beds* SNF 97. *Certified* Medicare; Medi-Cal.
Owner Proprietary corp.

Villa Rancho Bernardo
15720 Bernardo Center, San Diego, CA 92127
(619) 672-3900
Admin Carol Ann Scanlon. *Dir of Nursing* Adele Siosin. *Medical Dir* A Kent Williams.
Licensure Skilled care. *Beds* SNF 303. *Private Pay Patients* 30%. *Certified* Medicaid; Medicare; Medi-Cal.
Owner Proprietary corp.
Admissions Requirements Physician's request.
Languages Tagalog.
Facilities Dining room; Physical therapy room; Activities room; Crafts room; Barber/Beauty shop.

Activities Arts & crafts; Cards; Games; Reading groups; Prayer groups; Movies; Shopping trips; Dances/Social/Cultural gatherings; Intergenerational programs; Pet therapy.

San Dimas

Casa Bonita Convalescent Hospital
535 E Bonita Ave, San Dimas, CA 91773
(714) 599-1248
Admin Jean McCoy. *Dir of Nursing* Kim Butrum RN. *Medical Dir* Dr George McGallon.
Licensure Skilled care. *Beds* SNF 106. *Certified* Medicare; Medi-Cal.
Owner Proprietary corp.
Admissions Requirements Physician's request.
Facilities Dining room; Physical therapy room; Activities room; Crafts room; Laundry room; Barber/Beauty shop.
Activities Arts & crafts; Cards; Games; Reading groups; Prayer groups; Movies; Shopping trips.

San Fernando

Country Manor Convalescent Hospital
11723 Fenton Ave, San Fernando, CA 91342
(818) 899-0251
Admin Vernon Monson.
Licensure Skilled care. *Beds* SNF 99. *Certified* Medicare; Medi-Cal.
Owner Proprietary corp.

Forester Haven
12249 N Lopez Canyon Rd, San Fernando, CA 91342
(818) 899-7422, 890-3859 FAX
Admin Ha Taek Kwon. *Dir of Nursing* Dyan M Anderson RN. *Medical Dir* Aryeh Edelist MD.
Licensure Skilled care; Intermediate care; Residential care; Alzheimer's care. *Beds* SNF 49; ICF 35; Residential care 84. *Private Pay Patients* 3%. *Certified* Medi-Cal.
Owner Nonprofit corp.
Admissions Requirements Minimum age 65; Medical examination.
Staff RNs 1 (ft), 2 (pt); LPNs 8 (ft), 2 (pt); Nurses' aides 20 (ft); Activities coordinators 1 (ft), 1 (pt).
Facilities Dining room; Physical therapy room; Activities room; Chapel; Crafts room; Laundry room; Barber/Beauty shop; Library.
Activities Arts & crafts; Cards; Games; Reading groups; Movies; Shopping trips; Dances/Social/Cultural gatherings; Intergenerational programs; Pet therapy.

San Francisco

Beverly Manor Convalescent Hospital
1477 Grove St, San Francisco, CA 94117
(415) 563-0565
Admin Lora Seeloff.
Licensure Skilled care. *Beds* SNF 168. *Certified* Medicare; Medi-Cal.
Owner Proprietary corp (Beverly Enterprises).

Bowman-Harrison Convalescent Hospital
1020 Haight St, San Francisco, CA 94117
(415) 552-3198
Admin Paul M Levesque.
Licensure Skilled care. *Beds* 21.
Owner Proprietary corp.

Broderick Convalescent Hospital
1421 Broderick St, San Francisco, CA 94115
(415) 922-3244
Admin Grant N Edelstone. *Dir of Nursing* Elsie Loh RN. *Medical Dir* Joseph Muscat MD.
Licensure Skilled care. *Beds* SNF 48. *Certified* Medicare; Medi-Cal.
Owner Privately owned.
Admissions Requirements Physician's request.

Staff RNs 2 (ft), 1 (pt); LPNs 4 (ft), 3 (pt); Nurses' aides 13 (ft), 13 (pt); Physical therapists; Occupational therapists; Speech therapists; Activities coordinators 1 (ft); Dietitians; Ophthalmologists; Podiatrists; Dentist; X-ray personnel.
Languages Mandarin, Cantonese, Tagalog, Burmese.
Facilities Dining room; Physical therapy room; Activities room; Chapel; Crafts room; Laundry room; Barber/Beauty shop; Library.
Activities Arts & crafts; Games; Reading groups; Prayer groups; Dances/Social/Cultural gatherings; Field trips; Bingo; Workshops; Spelling bee; Story hour.

California Convalescent Hospital
2704 California St, San Francisco, CA 94115
(415) 931-7846
Admin Mary Ellen Forrest.
Licensure Skilled care. *Beds* SNF 29.
Owner Proprietary corp.

Central Gardens
1355 Ellis St, San Francisco, CA 94115
(415) 567-2967
Medical Dir Arthur Z Cerf MD.
Licensure Skilled care. *Beds* SNF 92. *Certified* Medicare; Medi-Cal.
Owner Proprietary corp.
Staff RNs 3 (ft), 5 (pt); LPNs 7 (ft), 3 (pt); Nurses' aides 26 (ft), 13 (pt); Activities coordinators 1 (ft).
Facilities Dining room; Physical therapy room; Laundry room.
Activities Arts & crafts; Cards; Reading groups; Prayer groups; Movies; Shopping trips.

Convalescent Center Mission Street
5767 Mission St, San Francisco, CA 94112
(415) 584-3294
Admin Joy Marie Susko.
Licensure Skilled care. *Beds* SNF 53. *Certified* Medicare; Medi-Cal.
Owner Proprietary corp.

Hayes Convalescent Hospital
1250 Hayes St, San Francisco, CA 94117
(415) 931-8806
Admin Eli Chalich.
Licensure Skilled care. *Beds* SNF 34. *Certified* Medi-Cal.
Owner Proprietary corp.

Hebrew Home for Aged Disabled
302 Silver Ave, San Francisco, CA 94112
(415) 334-2500
Admin Sandra Epstein. *Dir of Nursing* Mary Bonnar. *Medical Dir* Dr Bernard Blumberg.
Licensure Skilled care; Alzheimer's care. *Beds* SNF 400. *Private Pay Patients* 30%. *Certified* Medicaid; Medicare; Medi-Cal.
Owner Nonprofit corp.
Admissions Requirements Minimum age 65; Medical examination.
Staff Physicians 7 (pt); RNs 40 (ft); LPNs 20 (ft); Nurses' aides 200 (ft); Physical therapists 2 (ft); Reality therapists 1 (ft); Recreational therapists 4 (ft); Occupational therapists 2 (ft); Speech therapists 1 (ft); Activities coordinators 8 (ft); Dietitians 2 (ft); Ophthalmologists 1 (pt); Podiatrists 2 (pt); Audiologists 1 (pt).
Affiliation Jewish.
Facilities Dining room; Physical therapy room; Activities room; Chapel; Crafts room; Laundry room; Barber/Beauty shop; Library; Clinics.
Activities Arts & crafts; Cards; Games; Reading groups; Prayer groups; Movies; Shopping trips; Dances/Social/Cultural gatherings; Intergenerational programs; Pet therapy.

Heritage
3400 Laguna St, San Francisco, CA 94123
(415) 567-6900
Admin Edward J Benedict. *Dir of Nursing* Roberta Helms RN. *Medical Dir* John Henderson MD.
Licensure Skilled care; Retirement. *Beds* SNF 32; Life care 98.
Owner Nonprofit corp.
Admissions Requirements Minimum age 65; Medical examination.
Staff Physicians 1 (pt); RNs 3 (ft), 1 (pt); LPNs 2 (ft), 2 (pt); Nurses' aides 9 (ft), 4 (pt); Dietitians 1 (pt).
Facilities Dining room; Activities room; Chapel; Crafts room; Laundry room; Barber/Beauty shop; Library.
Activities Arts & crafts; Cards; Games; Reading groups; Prayer groups; Movies; Shopping trips; Dances/Social/Cultural gatherings.

Hillhaven Convalescent Center
2043 19th Ave, San Francisco, CA 94116
(415) 661-8787
Admin Sally A Craven.
Licensure Skilled care. *Beds* SNF 140. *Certified* Medicare; Medi-Cal.
Owner Proprietary corp.

Hillhaven Lawton Convalescent Hospital
1575 7th Ave, San Francisco, CA 94122
(415) 566-1200
Admin Catherine Colling.
Licensure Skilled care. *Beds* SNF 75. *Certified* Medicare; Medi-Cal.
Owner Proprietary corp (Hillhaven Inc).

Hillhaven San Francisco
1359 Pine St, San Francisco, CA 94109-4884
(415) 673-8405
Admin Charles D Wilcox.
Medical Dir Dr Richard Lanzerlti.
Licensure Skilled care. *Beds* SNF 180. *Certified* Medicare; Medi-Cal.
Owner Proprietary corp (Hillhaven Inc).
Admissions Requirements Medical examination.
Staff RNs 7 (ft), 4 (pt); LPNs 20 (ft), 15 (pt); Nurses' aides 50 (ft), 20 (pt); Physical therapists 2 (ft), 1 (pt); Recreational therapists 1 (ft); Occupational therapists 1 (ft); Speech therapists 1 (ft); Activities coordinators 2 (ft); Dietitians 1 (pt); Podiatrists 1 (pt); Dentists 1 (pt).
Facilities Dining room; Physical therapy room; Activities room; Chapel; Crafts room; Laundry room; Barber/Beauty shop; Library; Parking garage.
Activities Arts & crafts; Cards; Games; Reading groups; Prayer groups; Movies; Shopping trips; Dances/Social/Cultural gatherings; Field trips.

Hillhaven Victorian
2121 Pine St, San Francisco, CA 94115
(415) 922-5085
Admin Carol M Montgomery.
Medical Dir Robert Minkowsky.
Licensure Skilled care. *Beds* SNF 90. *Certified* Medicare; Medi-Cal.
Owner Proprietary corp.
Staff Physicians 1 (pt); RNs 4 (ft); Physical therapists 1 (pt); Reality therapists 1 (pt); Occupational therapists 1 (pt); Speech therapists 1 (pt); Activities coordinators 1 (ft), 1 (pt); Dentists 1 (pt).
Facilities Dining room; Physical therapy room; Activities room; Laundry room; Barber/Beauty shop.
Activities Arts & crafts; Cards; Games; Reading groups; Prayer groups; Movies; Shopping trips; Dances/Social/Cultural gatherings.

Laurel Heights Convalescent Hospital
2740 California St, San Francisco, CA 94115
(415) 567-3133
Admin Jill Lee.
Licensure Skilled care. *Beds* SNF 32.
Owner Privately owned.

Mission Bay Convalescent Hospital
331 Pennsylvania, San Francisco, CA 94107
(415) 647-3587
Admin May Wang. *Dir of Nursing* Catalina Madrid RN.
Licensure Skilled care. *Beds* SNF 50. *Certified* Medicare; Medi-Cal.
Owner Privately owned.
Staff RNs; LPNs; Nurses' aides.
Languages Chinese, Tagalog, Spanish.
Facilities Dining room; Physical therapy room; Activities room; Laundry room; Outdoor patio.
Activities Arts & crafts; Cards; Games; Prayer groups; Movies; Shopping trips; Dances/Social/Cultural gatherings.

Mission Villa Convalescent Hospital
1420 Hampshire, San Francisco, CA 94110
(415) 285-7660
Admin Barbara L Springer. *Dir of Nursing* Rita B Brown RN. *Medical Dir* Richard Munter MD.
Licensure Skilled care. *Beds* SNF 51. *Certified* Medicare; Medi-Cal.
Owner Proprietary corp.
Admissions Requirements Medical examination.
Staff Physicians 1 (pt); RNs 3 (ft), 2 (pt); LPNs 4 (ft), 1 (pt); Nurses' aides 11 (ft), 3 (pt); Physical therapists 1 (pt); Recreational therapists 1 (pt); Occupational therapists 1 (pt); Speech therapists 1 (pt); Activities coordinators 1 (ft), 1 (pt); Dietitians 1 (pt); Ophthalmologists 1 (pt).
Languages Spanish, Mandarin, Tagalog.
Facilities Dining room; Activities room; Crafts room; Laundry room; Barber/Beauty shop.
Activities Arts & crafts; Cards; Games; Prayer groups; Movies; Dances/Social/Cultural gatherings; Monthly outings.

Pine Towers Convalescent Hospital
2707 Pine St, San Francisco, CA 94115
(415) 563-7600
Admin Laura Eisenhart.
Medical Dir Robert V Brody.
Licensure Skilled care. *Beds* SNF 120. *Certified* Medicare; Medi-Cal.
Owner Proprietary corp.
Admissions Requirements Physician's request.
Staff RNs 7 (ft), 2 (pt); LPNs 12 (ft), 3 (pt); Nurses' aides 33 (ft), 12 (pt); Physical therapists 1 (pt); Recreational therapists 1 (ft); Occupational therapists 1 (pt); Speech therapists 1 (pt); Activities coordinators 1 (ft); Dietitians 1 (pt); Dentists 1 (pt).
Facilities Dining room; Physical therapy room; Activities room; Laundry room; Barber/Beauty shop; 5 Dayrooms.
Activities Arts & crafts; Cards; Games; Reading groups; Prayer groups; Movies; Shopping trips; Dances/Social/Cultural gatherings; Social outings; Singing group trips.

St Annes Home
300 Lake St, San Francisco, CA 94118
(415) 751-6510
Admin Sr Marie Anne. *Dir of Nursing* Sr Clotilde Jardim. *Medical Dir* Dr Quock Fong.
Licensure Skilled care; Intermediate care. *Beds* SNF 48; ICF 48. *Certified* Medi-Cal.
Owner Nonprofit corp.
Admissions Requirements Minimum age 60; Medical examination.
Staff Physicians 3 (ft), 9 (pt); RNs 4 (ft); LPNs 6 (ft); Nurses' aides 20 (ft), 8 (pt); Physical therapists 1 (pt); Recreational therapists 2 (ft); Activities coordinators 1 (ft); Dietitians 6 (ft), 2 (pt); Podiatrists 2 (pt); Dentists 2 (pt).
Affiliation Roman Catholic.

Facilities Dining room; Physical therapy room; Activities room; Chapel; Crafts room; Laundry room; Barber/Beauty shop; Library; Ice cream shop; Country store.
Activities Arts & crafts; Cards; Games; Reading groups; Prayer groups; Movies; Shopping trips; Dances/Social/Cultural gatherings; Resident council.

San Francisco Community Convalescent Hospital
2655 Bush St, San Francisco, CA 94115
(415) 922-4141
Admin Sum M Seto.
Medical Dir Richard Lanzerotti MD.
Licensure Skilled care. *Beds* SNF 116. *Certified* Medicare; Medi-Cal.
Owner Privately owned.
Staff Physicians 3 (pt); RNs 13 (ft), 3 (pt); LPNs 10 (ft), 6 (pt); Nurses' aides 40 (ft), 20 (pt); Physical therapists 2 (ft); Recreational therapists 3 (ft); Occupational therapists 1 (pt); Speech therapists 1 (pt); Activities coordinators 1 (ft); Dietitians 1 (ft); Podiatrists 1 (pt); Dentists 1 (pt).
Facilities Dining room; Physical therapy room; Activities room; Crafts room; Laundry room; Barber/Beauty shop.
Activities Arts & crafts; Cards; Games; Reading groups; Prayer groups; Movies; Dances/Social/Cultural gatherings.

Sequoias San Francisco Convalescent Hospital
1400 Geary Blvd, San Francisco, CA 94109
(415) 922-9700
Admin Michael Dougherty. *Dir of Nursing* Mary Jenkins RN. *Medical Dir* Wade Aubry MD.
Licensure Skilled care; Retirement. *Beds* SNF 49. *Certified* Medicare; Medi-Cal.
Owner Proprietary corp.
Admissions Requirements Minimum age 62; Medical examination; Physician's request.
Staff Physicians 4 (pt); RNs 4 (ft), 5 (pt); LPNs 2 (ft), 2 (pt); Nurses' aides 16 (ft), 4 (pt); Physical therapists 2 (pt); Occupational therapists 1 (pt); Speech therapists 1 (pt); Activities coordinators 1 (ft), 2 (pt); Dietitians 1 (pt); Ophthalmologists 2 (pt); Podiatrists 1 (pt).
Facilities Dining room; Physical therapy room; Activities room; Barber/Beauty shop.
Activities Arts & crafts; Cards; Games; Reading groups; Movies; Dances/Social/Cultural gatherings; Intergenerational programs; Restaurant outings.

Sheffield Convalescent Hospital
1133 S Van Ness Ave, San Francisco, CA 94110
(415) 647-3117
Admin Mary Ellen Forrest.
Licensure Skilled care. *Beds* SNF 34. *Certified* Medicare.
Owner Proprietary corp.

San Gabriel

Alderwood Manor Convalescent Hospital
115 Bridge St, San Gabriel, CA 91775
(818) 289-4439
Admin Carolyn L Zera.
Licensure Skilled care. *Beds* SNF 98. *Certified* Medicare.
Owner Proprietary corp.

Broadway
112 E Broadway, San Gabriel, CA 91776
(818) 285-2165, 287-1922 FAX
Admin Shelley Phillips. *Dir of Nursing* Nadine Ford. *Medical Dir* Norman Shrifter.
Licensure Skilled care. *Beds* SNF 59. *Private Pay Patients* 12%. *Certified* Medicare; Medi-Cal.
Owner Proprietary corp (Beverly Enterprises).
Staff RNs 2 (ft), 1 (pt); LPNs 7 (ft), 2 (pt); Nurses' aides 22 (ft), 2 (pt); Physical therapists 1 (pt); Reality therapists 1 (pt);

Recreational therapists 1 (pt); Occupational therapists 1 (pt); Speech therapists 1 (pt); Activities coordinators 1 (ft); Dietitians 1 (pt); Ophthalmologists 1 (pt); Podiatrists 1 (pt); Audiologists 1 (pt).
Facilities Dining room; Physical therapy room; Activities room; Crafts room; Laundry room; Barber/Beauty shop; Library.
Activities Arts & crafts; Cards; Games; Reading groups; Prayer groups; Movies; Shopping trips; Dances/Social/Cultural gatherings; Adopt-a-grandparent program.

Community Convalescent Hospital of San Gabriel
537 W Live Oak, San Gabriel, CA 91776
(818) 289-3763
Admin Anthony Riggio.
Medical Dir James Femino MD.
Licensure Skilled care. *Beds* SNF 99. *Certified* Medicare; Medi-Cal.
Owner Nonprofit corp.
Admissions Requirements Physician's request.
Staff RNs 4 (ft), 1 (pt); LPNs 10 (ft), 2 (pt); Nurses' aides 35 (ft).
Facilities Dining room; Physical therapy room; Activities room; Laundry room; Barber/Beauty shop.
Activities Arts & crafts; Cards; Games; Reading groups; Prayer groups; Movies.

Fernview Convalescent Hospital
126 N San Gabriel, San Gabriel, CA 91775
(213) 285-3131
Admin Mary Terrell.
Licensure Skilled care. *Beds* SNF 75. *Certified* Medicare; Medi-Cal.
Owner Proprietary corp.

Mission Convalescent Hospital
909 W Santa Anita, San Gabriel, CA 91776
(818) 289-5365
Admin Trudy Strano.
Medical Dir Juanita Philipps MD.
Licensure Skilled care. *Beds* SNF 99. *Certified* Medicare; Medi-Cal.
Owner Proprietary corp.
Admissions Requirements Minimum age 18.
Staff RNs 1 (ft), 2 (pt); LPNs 6 (ft), 3 (pt); Activities coordinators 2 (ft).
Languages Spanish, Korean, Chinese, Tagalog, Italian, Sicilian, French.
Facilities Dining room; Physical therapy room; Activities room; Crafts room; Laundry room; Barber/Beauty shop.
Activities Arts & crafts; Cards; Games; Reading groups; Prayer groups; Movies.

Mission Lodge Sanitarium
824 S Gladys Ave, San Gabriel, CA 91776
(818) 287-0753
Admin Norman E Gagliardi. *Dir of Nursing* Linda Scott RN. *Medical Dir* Douglas Copley MD.
Licensure Skilled care; Alzheimer's care. *Beds* SNF 153.
Owner Proprietary corp.
Staff RNs 5 (ft), 5 (pt); LPNs 8 (ft), 3 (pt); Nurses' aides 63 (ft), 14 (pt); Activities coordinators 2 (ft).
Facilities Dining room; Activities room; Crafts room; Laundry room; Barber/Beauty shop.
Activities Arts & crafts; Cards; Games; Reading groups; Prayer groups; Movies; Shopping trips; Dances/Social/Cultural gatherings; Adult education; Special sports programs; Mini-socials.

San Marino Manor
6812 N Oak Ave, San Gabriel, CA 91775
(818) 446-5263
Admin Barry Silberberg.
Medical Dir Gary Schlecter MD.
Licensure Skilled care. *Beds* SNF 59. *Certified* Medi-Cal.
Owner Proprietary corp.
Admissions Requirements Minimum age 40.

Facilities Dining room; Activities room; Laundry room; Barber/Beauty shop.
Activities Arts & crafts; Prayer groups.

San Jacinto

Colonial Convalescent Hospital
980 W 7th St, San Jacinto, CA 92383
(714) 654-9347
Admin Jean E Reed. *Dir of Nursing* Joy Mason RN. *Medical Dir* H E Kicenski MD.
Licensure Skilled care. *Beds* SNF 44. *Certified* Medicare; Medi-Cal.
Owner Privately owned.
Staff RNs; LPNs; Nurses' aides; Activities coordinators; Dietitians.
Facilities Dining room; Activities room; Crafts room; Laundry room; Barber/Beauty shop.
Activities Arts & crafts; Cards; Games; Reading groups; Prayer groups; Movies; Dances/Social/Cultural gatherings.

San Jose

Bellerose Convalescent Hospital
100 Bellerose Dr, San Jose, CA 95128
(408) 286-4161
Admin Francisco Cerezo.
Medical Dir Dr Howard Michael.
Licensure Skilled care. *Beds* SNF 39. *Certified* Medi-Cal.
Owner Privately owned.
Staff RNs 1 (ft), 2 (pt); LPNs 3 (ft), 2 (pt); Nurses' aides 9 (ft), 3 (pt); Activities coordinators 1 (ft); Dietitians 1 (pt); Podiatrists 1 (pt).
Facilities Dining room; Activities room; Laundry room; Barber/Beauty shop.
Activities Arts & crafts; Cards; Games; Reading groups; Prayer groups; Movies; Dances/Social/Cultural gatherings; Outings.

Bethany Convalescent Hospital
180 N Jackson Ave, San Jose, CA 95116
(408) 259-8700
Admin Doug Pannabecker. *Dir of Nursing* Sharon Green. *Medical Dir* James Guetzkow MD.
Licensure Skilled care; Intermediate care. *Beds* SNF 157; ICF 42. *Certified* Medicare; Medi-Cal.
Owner Nonprofit corp (National Benevolent Association Health Service Corp).
Admissions Requirements Minimum age 18.
Staff RNs 10 (ft), 2 (pt); LPNs 18 (ft), 10 (pt); Nurses' aides 44 (ft), 26 (pt); Physical therapists 1 (pt); Occupational therapists 1 (pt); Activities coordinators 3 (ft); Dietitians 1 (pt); Ophthalmologists 1 (pt).
Languages Spanish, Tagalog.
Affiliation Disciples of Christ.
Facilities Dining room; Physical therapy room; Activities room; Chapel; Crafts room; Laundry room; Barber/Beauty shop; Library.
Activities Arts & crafts; Cards; Games; Reading groups; Prayer groups; Movies; Shopping trips.

California PEO Home—San Jose Unit
10 Kirk Ave, San Jose, CA 95127
(408) 729-2000
Admin Marilyn R Sund.
Licensure Skilled care. *Beds* SNF 22. *Certified* Medi-Cal.
Owner Nonprofit corp.

Casa Serena Skilled Nursing & Rehabilitation Hospital
1990 Fruitdale Ave, San Jose, CA 95128
(408) 998-8447
Admin Michael A Dunn.
Medical Dir Dr William Weller.
Licensure Skilled care. *Beds* SNF 153. *Certified* Medicare; Medi-Cal.
Owner Privately owned.

Admissions Requirements Medical examination; Physician's request.
Staff Physicians 1 (pt); RNs 10 (ft), 2 (pt); LPNs 13 (ft), 2 (pt); Nurses' aides 57 (ft), 6 (pt); Physical therapists 1 (ft); Activities coordinators 2 (ft); Dietitians 1 (ft).
Facilities Dining room; Physical therapy room; Activities room; Chapel; Crafts room; Laundry room; Barber/Beauty shop; Library.
Activities Arts & crafts; Cards; Games; Reading groups; Prayer groups; Movies; Shopping trips; Dances/Social/Cultural gatherings.

Crestwood Manor—San Jose
1425 Fruitdale Ave, San Jose, CA 95128
(408) 275-1010
Admin John Suggs.
Licensure Skilled care. Beds SNF 174. Certified Medi-Cal.
Owner Proprietary corp (Crestwood Hospitals Inc).

Driftwood Convalescent Hospital
2065 Los Gatos-Almaden, San Jose, CA 95124
(408) 377-9275
Admin Sally Canepa. Dir of Nursing Sandra Mueller RN. Medical Dir Robert Reid MD.
Licensure Skilled care; Alzheimer's care. Beds SNF 77. Certified Medicare; Medi-Cal.
Owner Proprietary corp (Western Medical Enterprises Inc).
Admissions Requirements Medical examination; Physician's request.
Staff RNs 2 (ft), 1 (pt); LPNs 8 (ft), 4 (pt); Nurses' aides 31 (ft), 5 (pt); Physical therapists 1 (pt); Occupational therapists 1 (pt); Speech therapists 1 (pt); Activities coordinators 1 (ft); Podiatrists 1 (pt).
Languages Spanish.
Facilities Dining room; Physical therapy room; Activities room; Chapel; Crafts room; Laundry room; Barber/Beauty shop; Library.
Activities Arts & crafts; Cards; Games; Reading groups; Prayer groups; Movies; Shopping trips; Dances/Social/Cultural gatherings.

East Valley Pavilion
101 Jose Figueres A, San Jose, CA 95116
(408) 299-8364
Admin Barbara Arons MD.
Licensure Skilled care. Beds SNF 99. Certified Medi-Cal.
Owner Publicly owned.

Empress Convalescent Hospital
1299 S Bascom Ave, San Jose, CA 95128
(408) 287-0616
Admin Senta M Lambrecht. Dir of Nursing M Anderson RN. Medical Dir William Garcia MD.
Licensure Skilled care. Beds SNF 67. Certified Medicare; Medi-Cal.
Owner Proprietary corp.
Admissions Requirements Physician's request.
Staff RNs; LPNs; Nurses' aides; Activities coordinators.
Facilities Dining room; Physical therapy room; Activities room; Barber/Beauty shop.
Activities Arts & crafts; Games; Reading groups; Prayer groups; Movies; Shopping trips.

Herman Sanitarium
2295 Plummer Ave, San Jose, CA 95125
(408) 269-0701
Admin Robert H Sollis.
Licensure Skilled care. Beds SNF 99. Certified Medi-Cal.
Owner Privately owned.

Homewood Convalescent Hospital Inc
75 N 13th St, San Jose, CA 95112
(408) 295-2665
Admin Gayle Artimisi.
Medical Dir Dr William Ness.
Licensure Skilled care. Beds SNF 58. Certified Medicare; Medi-Cal.

Owner Nonprofit corp (Guardian Foundation Inc).
Admissions Requirements Medical examination; Physician's request.
Facilities Dining room; Activities room; Laundry room; Barber/Beauty shop.
Activities Arts & crafts; Cards; Games; Movies.

Lincoln Glen Skilled Nursing
2671 Plummer Ave, San Jose, CA 95125
(408) 265-3222
Admin Dan Wiebe.
Licensure Skilled care; Intermediate care. Beds SNF 13; ICF 46. Certified Medi-Cal.
Owner Proprietary corp.

Marcus Manor Convalescent Hospital
264 N Morrison Ave, San Jose, CA 95126
(408) 297-4420
Admin Steve R Marcus.
Medical Dir Karin Goodman MD.
Licensure Skilled care. Beds SNF 32. Certified Medi-Cal.
Owner Privately owned.
Admissions Requirements Minimum age 18; Medical examination; Physician's request.
Staff RNs 1 (ft), 4 (pt); LPNs 2 (ft), 6 (pt); Nurses' aides 10 (ft), 5 (pt); Activities coordinators 1 (ft).
Facilities Dining room; Activities room; Laundry room.
Activities Arts & crafts; Cards; Games; Prayer groups; Movies.

Meadowbrook Convalescent Hospital
340 Northlake Dr, San Jose, CA 95117
(408) 249-5200
Admin Thomas P Coffey.
Licensure Skilled care. Beds SNF 79. Certified Medicare.
Owner Proprietary corp.

Mt Pleasant Convalescent Hospital
1355 Clayton Rd, San Jose, CA 95127
(408) 251-3070
Admin Judith Woodby.
Medical Dir Dr Albert Currlin.
Licensure Skilled care. Beds SNF 56. Certified Medi-Cal.
Owner Proprietary corp.
Staff RNs 1 (ft), 1 (pt); LPNs 2 (ft), 2 (pt); Nurses' aides 20 (ft), 2 (pt); Activities coordinators 1 (ft); Restorative aide 1 (ft).
Facilities Dining room; Physical therapy room; Activities room; Chapel; Barber/Beauty shop.
Activities Arts & crafts; Games; Reading groups; Movies.

Park View Nursing Center
120 Jose Figueres Ave, San Jose, CA 95116
(408) 272-1400
Admin Barbara Anderson.
Licensure Skilled care. Beds SNF 99. Certified Medicare; Medi-Cal.
Owner Proprietary corp.

Plum Tree Convalescent Hospital
2580 Samaritan Dr, San Jose, CA 95124
(408) 356-8181
Admin John J Williams.
Medical Dir David Morgan MD.
Licensure Skilled care. Beds SNF 76. Certified Medicare.
Owner Nonprofit corp (Guardian Foundation Inc).
Staff RNs 3 (ft), 7 (pt); LPNs 3 (ft); Nurses' aides 27 (ft), 3 (pt); Physical therapists; Reality therapists; Recreational therapists; Occupational therapists; Activities coordinators 1 (ft), 1 (pt); Dietitians; Ophthalmologists; Podiatrists; Audiologists; Dentists.
Facilities Dining room; Physical therapy room; Activities room; Crafts room; Laundry room; Barber/Beauty shop.

Activities Arts' & crafts; Cards; Games; Reading groups; Prayer groups; Movies; Shopping trips; Dances/Social/Cultural gatherings.

San Jose Care & Guidance Center
401 Ridge Vista Ave, San Jose, CA 95127
(408) 923-7232
Admin Enid Begay.
Medical Dir Dr Mayerle.
Licensure Skilled care. Beds SNF 116. Certified Medi-Cal.
Owner Proprietary corp (Beverly Enterprises).
Admissions Requirements Minimum age 21.
Staff Physicians 2 (ft); RNs 6 (ft), 2 (pt); LPNs 8 (ft), 4 (pt).
Facilities Dining room; Activities room; Crafts room.
Activities Arts & crafts; Cards; Games; Prayer groups; Movies; Shopping trips; Dances/Social/Cultural gatherings.

San Tomas Convalescent Hospital
3580 Payne Ave, San Jose, CA 95117
(408) 248-7100
Admin Julita Javier.
Licensure Skilled care. Beds SNF 70. Certified Medicare; Medi-Cal.
Owner Privately owned.

Skyline Convalescent Hospital
2065 Forest Ave, San Jose, CA 95128
(408) 298-3950
Admin Mary MacPherson.
Licensure Skilled care. Beds SNF 277. Certified Medicare; Medi-Cal.
Owner Proprietary corp (Western Medical Enterprises Inc).

Westgate Convalescent Center
1601 Petersen Ave, San Jose, CA 95129
(408) 253-7502
Admin Linda Rowley. Dir of Nursing Gracia Barerra RN. Medical Dir Steven Tilles MD.
Licensure Skilled care. Beds SNF 268. Certified Medicare; Medi-Cal.
Owner Proprietary corp (Beverly Enterprises).
Admissions Requirements Minimum age 18; Medical examination; Physician's request.
Staff Physicians 1 (pt); RNs 13 (ft), 7 (pt); LPNs 17 (ft), 7 (pt); Nurses' aides 66 (ft), 18 (pt); Physical therapists 1 (pt); Recreational therapists 1 (ft); Occupational therapists 1 (pt); Speech therapists 1 (pt); Dietitians 1 (ft); Ophthalmologists 1 (pt); Podiatrists 1 (pt); Dentists 1 (pt).
Languages Spanish, Russian, Polish.
Facilities Dining room; Physical therapy room; Activities room; Crafts room; Barber/Beauty shop; Library.
Activities Arts & crafts; Cards; Games; Reading groups; Prayer groups; Movies; Shopping trips; Dances/Social/Cultural gatherings.

Willow Glen Convalescent Hospital Rest Care Center
1267 Meridian Ave, San Jose, CA 95125
(408) 265-4211
Admin Alice K Mau.
Licensure Skilled care. Beds SNF 152. Certified Medicare; Medi-Cal.
Owner Proprietary corp.

Winchester Living Center
1250 S Winchester Blvd, San Jose, CA 95128
(408) 241-8666
Admin Fred Frank. Dir of Nursing Patricia Fitzgerald RN. Medical Dir Mark Campbell MD.
Licensure Skilled care. Beds SNF 166. Certified Medicare; Medi-Cal.
Owner Proprietary corp (Western Medical Enterprises Inc).
Staff Physicians 1 (pt); RNs 4 (ft), 6 (pt); LPNs 12 (ft); Nurses' aides 61 (ft); Physical therapists 1 (ft); Occupational therapists 1

(ft), 1 (pt); Speech therapists 1 (ft), 1 (pt); Activities coordinators 1 (ft); Dietitians 1 (pt); Ophthalmologists 1 (pt); Dentists 1 (pt).
Facilities Dining room; Physical therapy room; Activities room; Laundry room; Barber/Beauty shop; Protected patios.
Activities Arts & crafts; Cards; Games; Reading groups; Prayer groups; Movies; Shopping trips; Dances/Social/Cultural gatherings; Live Oak community & core groups; In-room activities; Barbeques.

San Leandro

Bancroft Convalescent Hospital
1475 Bancroft Ave, San Leandro, CA 94577
(415) 483-1680
Admin Edith E Parrott.
Licensure Skilled care. *Beds* SNF 39. *Certified* Medicare.
Owner Privately owned.

Care West—Washington Manor Nursing Center
14766 Washington Ave, San Leandro, CA 94578
(415) 352-2211
Licensure Skilled care. *Beds* SNF 99.
Owner Proprietary corp (Care Enterprises).

Hillhaven San Leandro
368 Juana Ave, San Leandro, CA 94577
(415) 357-4015
Admin Nina F Roberts.
Licensure Skilled care. *Beds* SNF 62. *Certified* Medicare; Medi-Cal.
Owner Proprietary corp (Hillhaven Inc).

Jones Convalescent Hospital
524 Callan Ave, San Leandro, CA 94577
(415) 483-6200
Admin C Charles Monedero. *Dir of Nursing* Jan Barnette RN. *Medical Dir* Steven Rosenthal MD.
Licensure Skilled care; Residential care. *Beds* SNF 25; Residential care 23. *Private Pay Patients* 100%.
Owner Proprietary corp.
Admissions Requirements Medical examination; Physician's request.
Staff Physicians 1 (pt); RNs 1 (ft), 3 (pt); LPNs 2 (ft), 3 (pt); Nurses' aides 13 (ft), 4 (pt); Physical therapists 1 (pt); Occupational therapists 1 (pt); Activities coordinators 1 (ft); Dietitians 1 (pt).
Languages Spanish, Portuguese, Tagalog.
Facilities Dining room; Activities room; Crafts room; Laundry room; Barber/Beauty shop.
Activities Arts & crafts; Cards; Games; Reading groups; Prayer groups; Movies; Dances/Social/Cultural gatherings; Musical programs; Exercise classes; Bingo.

Parkland Convalescent Hospital
1440 168th Ave, San Leandro, CA 94578
(415) 278-4323
Admin Sandra Lawson.
Medical Dir Esther LaPorte.
Licensure Skilled care. *Beds* SNF 176. *Certified* Medicare; Medi-Cal.
Owner Proprietary corp (ARA Living Centers).
Admissions Requirements Physician's request.
Staff RNs; LPNs; Nurses' aides; Activities coordinators.
Facilities Dining room; Physical therapy room; Activities room; Crafts room; Laundry room; Barber/Beauty shop.
Activities Arts & crafts; Cards; Games; Reading groups; Prayer groups; Movies; Shopping trips; Dances/Social/Cultural gatherings; Baseball game trips.

St Lukes Extended Care Center & Nursing Centre
1652 Mono Ave, San Leandro, CA 94578
(413) 357-5351

Admin Guy R Seaton. *Dir of Nursing* Jacqueline L Seaton. *Medical Dir* Andrew May MD.
Licensure Skilled care. *Beds* SNF 72. *Certified* Medicare; Medi-Cal.
Owner Proprietary corp.
Admissions Requirements Physician's request.
Staff Physicians 20 (pt); RNs 10 (ft), 10 (pt); LPNs 12 (ft), 10 (pt); Nurses' aides 40 (ft), 10 (pt); Physical therapists 1 (pt); Recreational therapists 2 (ft); Occupational therapists 1 (pt); Speech therapists 1 (pt); Activities coordinators 1 (ft); Dietitians 1 (ft); Ophthalmologists 1 (pt); Podiatrists 1 (pt); Dentists 1 (pt).
Facilities Dining room; Physical therapy room; Activities room; Laundry room; Library.
Activities Arts & crafts; Cards; Games; Reading groups; Prayer groups; Movies; Shopping trips; Dances/Social/Cultural gatherings.

Villa Fairmont Mental Health Center
15400 Foothill Blvd, San Leandro, CA 94578
(415) 536-8111
Licensure Skilled care. *Beds* SNF 99. *Certified* Medi-Cal.
Owner Proprietary corp.

Washington Convalescent Hospital
2274 Washington Ave, San Leandro, CA 94577
(415) 483-7671
Licensure Skilled care. *Beds* SNF 25. *Certified* Medi-Cal.
Owner Privately owned.

San Luis Obispo

Cabrillo Extended Care Hospital
3033 Augusta St, San Luis Obispo, CA 93401
(805) 544-5100
Admin Dustin Brown.
Licensure Skilled care. *Beds* SNF 162. *Certified* Medicare; Medi-Cal.
Owner Proprietary corp.

Casa De Vida
879 Meinecke St, San Luis Obispo, CA 93401
(805) 544-5332
Admin George Brudney. *Dir of Nursing* Barbara Wisehart.
Licensure Intermediate care for mentally retarded. *Beds* ICF/MR 99. *Certified* Medi-Cal.
Owner Proprietary corp.
Admissions Requirements Minimum age 18; Medical examination.
Staff Physicians 1 (pt); RNs 3 (ft); LPNs 5 (ft); Nurses' aides 30 (ft); Physical therapists 1 (pt); Recreational therapists 1 (ft); Occupational therapists 1 (pt); Speech therapists 1 (pt); Dietitians 1 (ft), 1 (pt).
Languages Spanish.
Facilities Dining room; Physical therapy room; Activities room; Crafts room; Laundry room; Barber/Beauty shop; Clothing-work shop; Garden.
Activities Arts & crafts; Games; Reading groups; Movies; Shopping trips; Dances/Social/Cultural gatherings; Camping; Swimming; Boating.

Hillhaven Care Center
1425 Woodside Dr, San Luis Obispo, CA 93401
(805) 543-0210
Admin Anne Marie Butler. *Dir of Nursing* Paul Smith RN. *Medical Dir* Roger Steele MD.
Licensure Skilled care. *Beds* SNF 162. *Private Pay Patients* 25%. *Certified* Medicare; Medi-Cal.
Owner Proprietary corp (Hillhaven Corp).
Admissions Requirements Medical examination; Physician's request.

Staff RNs 8 (ft); LPNs 5 (ft); Nurses' aides 40 (ft); Physical therapists 1 (ft); Recreational therapists 1 (ft); Occupational therapists 1 (pt); Speech therapists 1 (pt); Dietitians 1 (ft); Ophthalmologists 1 (pt); Podiatrists 1 (pt); Audiologists 1 (pt).
Facilities Dining room; Physical therapy room; Activities room; Laundry room; Barber/Beauty shop; Library.
Activities Arts & crafts; Cards; Games; Reading groups; Prayer groups; Movies; Shopping trips; Intergenerational programs; Pet therapy.

San Mateo

Brookside Convalescent Hospital
2620 Flores St, San Mateo, CA 94403
(415) 349-2161
Admin Valerie Capone RN. *Dir of Nursing* Dottie Heaney RN.
Licensure Skilled care. *Beds* SNF 100. *Private Pay Patients* 37%. *Certified* Medicare; Medi-Cal.
Owner Nonprofit corp.
Admissions Requirements Physician's request.
Staff RNs 8 (ft), 5 (pt); LPNs 3 (ft), 1 (pt); Nurses' aides 25 (ft), 8 (pt); Activities coordinators 2 (ft); Dietitians 1 (ft).
Languages German, Spanish, Russian, Polish, Tagalog, Slovene, French.
Facilities Dining room; Physical therapy room; Activities room; Barber/Beauty shop.
Activities Arts & crafts; Cards; Games; Reading groups; Prayer groups; Movies; Shopping trips; Dances/Social/Cultural gatherings; Intergenerational programs; Pet therapy; Music; Current events; Physical fitness; Religious services; Bedside activities; Birthday parties; Bingo; Reality orientation; Volunteer groups.

Crystal Springs Rehabilitation Center
35 Tower Rd, San Mateo, CA 94402
(415) 573-3551
Admin Ronald M Davis.
Licensure Skilled care; Acute rehabilitation care. *Beds* SNF 60; Acute rehabilitation care 64. *Certified* Medicare; Medi-Cal.
Owner Publicly owned.

Hillsdale Manor Convalescent Hospital
2883 S Norfolk St, San Mateo, CA 94403
(415) 378-3000
Medical Dir Dr Donald Jaffe.
Licensure Skilled care. *Beds* SNF 61. *Certified* Medicare; Medi-Cal.
Owner Proprietary corp.
Admissions Requirements Medical examination; Physician's request.
Staff Physicians 1 (pt); RNs 4 (ft), 1 (pt); LPNs 2 (ft), 3 (pt); Nurses' aides 17 (ft), 6 (pt); Physical therapists 1 (pt); Activities coordinators 1 (ft); Dietitians 1 (pt); Podiatrists 1 (pt); Dentists 1 (pt).
Facilities Dining room; Physical therapy room; Activities room; Crafts room; Laundry room; Barber/Beauty shop; Library; Enclosed patio.
Activities Arts & crafts; Cards; Games; Reading groups; Prayer groups; Movies; Shopping trips; Dances/Social/Cultural gatherings.

San Mateo Convalescent Hospital
453 N San Mateo Dr, San Mateo, CA 94401
(415) 342-6255
Admin Betty J Frint. *Dir of Nursing* Donna Clark RN. *Medical Dir* Robert George Spencer MD.
Licensure Skilled care; Alzheimer's care. *Beds* SNF 34. *Private Pay Patients* 98%. *Certified* Medicare.
Owner Privately owned.
Admissions Requirements Physician's request.

Staff RNs 3 (ft), 1 (pt); LPNs 1 (ft), 3 (pt); Physical therapists; Recreational therapists; Occupational therapists; Speech therapists; Activities coordinators; Dietitians.
Languages Swedish, Tygala, Togan, Spanish.
Facilities Multipurpose room.
Activities Arts & crafts; Cards; Games; Reading groups; Prayer groups; Movies; Pet therapy.

San Pablo

Church Lane Convalescent Hospital
1900 Church Ln, San Pablo, CA 94806
(415) 235-5514
Admin Sandra Long. *Dir of Nursing* Karenlouise Johnson RN. *Medical Dir* V T Archibald MD.
Licensure Skilled care. *Beds* SNF 80. *Certified* Medicare.
Owner Proprietary corp.
Admissions Requirements Medical examination; Physician's request.
Languages Spanish, Tagalog.
Facilities Dining room; Activities room; Crafts room; Laundry room; Barber/Beauty shop.
Activities Arts & crafts; Cards; Games; Reading groups; Movies; Shopping trips; Dances/Social/Cultural gatherings.

Greenvale Convalescent Hospital
2140 Vale Rd, San Pablo, CA 94806
(415) 235-1052
Admin Eric Mawson.
Licensure Skilled care. *Beds* 57. *Certified* Medicare; Medi-Cal.
Owner Proprietary corp.

Hillhaven—Brookvue Convalescent Hospital
13328 San Pablo Ave, San Pablo, CA 94806
(415) 235-3720
Medical Dir Marilyn White.
Licensure Skilled care. *Beds* SNF 108. *Certified* Medicare; Medi-Cal.
Owner Proprietary corp (Hillhaven Corp).
Staff Physicians 1 (pt); RNs 3 (ft), 3 (pt); LPNs 8 (ft), 5 (pt); Nurses' aides 24 (ft), 20 (pt); Physical therapists 1 (ft), 1 (pt); Reality therapists 1 (pt); Recreational therapists 1 (ft); Occupational therapists 1 (ft); Speech therapists 1 (ft); Activities coordinators 1 (ft); Dietitians 1 (pt); Ophthalmologists 1 (pt); Podiatrists 1 (pt); Dentists 1 (pt); Chaplains 1 (pt).
Languages Spanish, German.
Facilities Dining room; Physical therapy room; Activities room; Laundry room; Barber/Beauty shop; Library.
Activities Arts & crafts; Cards; Games; Reading groups; Prayer groups; Movies; Shopping trips; Dances/Social/Cultural gatherings.

Vale Care Center
13484 San Pablo Ave, San Pablo, CA 94806
(415) 232-5945, 235-3768 FAX
Admin Deline Marie Davis. *Dir of Nursing* Remy Fox. *Medical Dir* Brazell Carter.
Licensure Skilled care; Intermediate care. *Beds* Swing beds SNF/ICF 202. *Private Pay Patients* 15%. *Certified* Medicare; Medi-Cal.
Owner Proprietary corp.
Admissions Requirements Physician's request.
Staff Physicians (contracted); RNs; LPNs; Nurses' aides; Physical therapists (contracted); Occupational therapists (contracted); Speech therapists (contracted); Activities coordinators; Dietitians (contracted); Podiatrists (contracted); Audiologists (contracted).
Languages Indian, Filipino, Spanish, Chinese, Samoan.
Facilities Dining room; Physical therapy room; Activities room; Crafts room; Laundry room; Barber/Beauty shop.

Activities Arts & crafts; Cards; Games; Reading groups; Prayer groups; Movies; Shopping trips; Dances/Social/Cultural gatherings; Intergenerational programs; Pet therapy.

San Pedro

Harbor View House
921 S Beacon St, San Pedro, CA 90731
(213) 547-3341
Admin David Acuna. *Dir of Nursing* Helen Holmes LVN. *Medical Dir* Allan Larner MD.
Licensure Intermediate care; Residential care. *Beds* ICF 83; Residential care 204. *Private Pay Patients* 1%. *Certified* Medi-Cal.
Owner Nonprofit organization/foundation.
Admissions Requirements Minimum age 18; Mentally ill.
Staff Physicians 2 (pt); RNs 2 (ft); LPNs 8 (ft); Nurses' aides 13 (ft); Physical therapists 1 (pt); Recreational therapists 2 (ft); Speech therapists 1 (pt); Activities coordinators 2 (ft); Dietitians 1 (ft); Ophthalmologists 1 (pt); Podiatrists 1 (pt); Audiologists 1 (pt).
Languages Spanish, Yiddish.
Facilities Dining room; Activities room; Crafts room; Laundry room; Barber/Beauty shop; Library; Gymnasium; Handball court; Thrift shop; Laboratory.
Activities Arts & crafts; Cards; Games; Reading groups; Prayer groups; Movies; Shopping trips; Dances/Social/Cultural gatherings; Intergenerational programs; Cultural, educational, recreational trips; Sport groups; Overnight vacations; Resident work program; Psychosocial groups and activities; Holiday celebrations.

Little Sisters of the Poor
2100 S Western Ave, San Pedro, CA 90732
(213) 548-0625
Admin Sr Mary John Cain.
Medical Dir Asa Hubbard MD.
Licensure Skilled care; Intermediate care. *Beds* SNF 38; ICF 48. *Certified* Medi-Cal.
Owner Nonprofit corp.
Admissions Requirements Minimum age 60; Medical examination.
Affiliation Roman Catholic.
Facilities Dining room; Physical therapy room; Activities room; Chapel; Crafts room; Laundry room; Barber/Beauty shop; Library; Medical offices; Country store; Ice cream parlor.
Activities Arts & crafts; Cards; Games; Reading groups; Prayer groups; Movies; Shopping trips; Dances/Social/Cultural gatherings.

Los Palos Convalescent Hospital
1430 W 6th St, San Pedro, CA 90732
(213) 832-6431, 514-0291 FAX
Admin Jose S Valdomar. *Dir of Nursing* Danny Ang. *Medical Dir* Robert Lewis MD.
Licensure Skilled care. *Beds* SNF 99. *Private Pay Patients* 40%. *Certified* Medicare; Medi-Cal.
Owner Proprietary corp.
Admissions Requirements Medical examination; Physician's request.
Staff RNs 5 (ft); LPNs 6 (ft); Nurses' aides 35 (ft); Physical therapists 1 (ft); Recreational therapists 2 (ft); Occupational therapists 1 (ft); Speech therapists 1 (ft); Activities coordinators 1 (ft); Dietitians 1 (ft); Ophthalmologists 1 (ft).
Languages Spanish.
Facilities Dining room; Physical therapy room; Activities room; Laundry room; Barber/Beauty shop.
Activities Arts & crafts; Cards; Games; Reading groups; Prayer groups; Movies; Shopping trips.

San Pedro Peninsula Hospital Pavilion
1322 W 6th St, San Pedro, CA 90732
(213) 514-5270
Admin Rodney Aymond. *Dir of Nursing* Rose Forbish RN. *Medical Dir* Dr S Stock; Dr F Workman; Dr H Webb.
Licensure Skilled care; Sub-acute. *Beds* SNF 128. *Certified* Medicare; Medi-Cal.
Owner Nonprofit corp.
Staff Physicians 3 (pt); RNs 2 (ft), 1 (pt); LPNs 9 (ft); Nurses' aides 36 (ft); Physical therapists 1 (ft); Activities coordinators 2 (ft); Dietitians 1 (pt).
Facilities Dining room; Physical therapy room; Activities room; Laundry room; Barber/Beauty shop.
Activities Arts & crafts; Cards; Games; Reading groups; Movies; Shopping trips; Dances/Social/Cultural gatherings.

Seacrest Convalescent Hospital
1416 W 6th St, San Pedro, CA 90732
(213) 833-3526, 831-3053 FAX
Admin Jose S Valdomar. *Dir of Nursing* Josie Valdomar. *Medical Dir* James Schmidt.
Licensure Skilled care; Intermediate care. *Beds* SNF 66; ICF 14. *Private Pay Patients* 30%. *Certified* Medicare; Medi-Cal.
Owner Proprietary corp.
Admissions Requirements Medical examination; Physician's request.
Staff RNs; LPNs; Nurses' aides; Activities coordinators; Social workers.
Languages Spanish.
Facilities Dining room; Activities room; Laundry room; Barber/Beauty shop.
Activities Arts & crafts; Cards; Games; Reading groups; Prayer groups; Movies; Shopping trips.

San Rafael

Aldersly Inc—Danish Home Senior Citizens
326 Mission Ave, San Rafael, CA 94901
(415) 453-7425
Admin Stephanie Sutton. *Dir of Nursing* Charlene Sharp. *Medical Dir* Dr Fred Yates.
Licensure Skilled care. *Beds* SNF 13; Residential retirement 120.
Owner Nonprofit corp.
Admissions Requirements Minimum age 62.
Staff Physicians 1 (pt); RNs 1 (ft), 3 (pt); LPNs 2 (ft), 2 (pt); Nurses' aides 5 (ft), 2 (pt); Activities coordinators 2 (pt).
Languages Danish.
Facilities Dining room; Activities room; Chapel; Crafts room; Laundry room; Barber/Beauty shop; Library; Lounges; Kitchen; Clinic.
Activities Arts & crafts; Cards; Games; Reading groups; Movies; Shopping trips; Dances/Social/Cultural gatherings; Educational programs; Health lectures.

Fifth Avenue Convalescent Hospital
1601 5th Ave, San Rafael, CA 94901
(415) 456-7170
Admin Rocio Rubio. *Dir of Nursing* Ann Smyth. *Medical Dir* Dr Carol Numelstein.
Licensure Skilled care. *Beds* SNF 57. *Certified* Medicare; Medi-Cal.
Owner Proprietary corp.
Admissions Requirements Physician's request.
Staff RNs 1 (ft); LPNs 3 (ft); Nurses' aides 13 (ft); Physical therapists 1 (ft); Activities coordinators 1 (ft).
Languages Spanish, French.
Facilities Dining room; Physical therapy room; Activities room; Laundry room; Barber/Beauty shop.
Activities Arts & crafts; Cards; Games; Reading groups; Prayer groups; Movies; Shopping trips; Dances/Social/Cultural gatherings; Adopt-a-resident.

Hillside Manor Convalescent Hospital
81 Professional Center Pkwy, San Rafael, CA 94903
(415) 479-5161
Admin Steve Shipley.
Licensure Skilled care. *Beds* SNF 99. *Certified* Medicare; Medi-Cal.
Owner Proprietary corp.

Nazareth House
245 Nova Albion Way, San Rafael, CA 94903
(415) 479-8282
Admin Gertrude Clare.
Licensure Skilled care. *Beds* SNF 45. *Certified* Medi-Cal.
Owner Nonprofit corp.

Northgate Convalescent Hospital
40 Professional Center Pkwy, San Rafael, CA 94903
(415) 479-1230
Admin Ursula Sommer-Lanz.
Licensure Skilled care. *Beds* SNF 52. *Certified* Medicare; Medi-Cal.
Owner Proprietary corp.
Admissions Requirements Medical examination; Physician's request.
Staff Physicians 1 (pt); Speech therapists 1 (pt); Activities coordinators 1 (ft); Dietitians 1 (pt); Ophthalmologists 1 (pt).
Facilities Dining room; Physical therapy room; Activities room; Crafts room; Laundry room; Barber/Beauty shop; Library.
Activities Arts & crafts; Cards; Games; Reading groups; Prayer groups; Movies; Dances/Social/Cultural gatherings.

Pine Ridge Care Center
45 Professional Center Pkwy, San Rafael, CA 94903
(415) 479-3610
Admin Larie Pepper.
Licensure Skilled care. *Beds* SNF 99. *Certified* Medicare; Medi-Cal.
Owner Proprietary corp.

Rafael Convalescent Hospital
234 N San Pedro Rd, San Rafael, CA 94903
(415) 479-3450
Admin Timothy Egan.
Licensure Skilled care. *Beds* SNF 168. *Certified* Medicare; Medi-Cal.
Owner Proprietary corp.

Villa Marin Retirement Residences
100 Thorndale Dr, San Rafael, CA 94903
(415) 499-8711
Admin Meredith S Bentley.
Licensure Skilled care. *Beds* SNF 26. *Certified* Medicare.
Owner Proprietary corp.

Sanger

Maple Grove Intermediate Care Home
1808 5th St, Sanger, CA 93657
(209) 875-6110
Admin Donald J Botts Jr.
Licensure Intermediate care. *Beds* 18. *Certified* Medi-Cal.
Owner Proprietary corp.

Sanger Convalescent Hospital
2550 9th St, Sanger, CA 93657
(209) 875-6501
Admin Samuel A Macomber.
Licensure Skilled care. *Beds* SNF 99. *Certified* Medicare; Medi-Cal.
Owner Proprietary corp (Beverly Enterprises).
Staff RNs 3 (ft); LPNs 10 (ft); Nurses' aides 46 (ft); Recreational therapists 1 (ft).
Languages Spanish, Chinese.
Facilities Dining room; Crafts room; Laundry room; Barber/Beauty shop.
Activities Arts & crafts; Cards; Games; Reading groups; Prayer groups; Movies; Shopping trips; Dances/Social/Cultural gatherings.

Santa Ana

Carehouse Convalescent Hospital
1800 Old Tustin Ave, Santa Ana, CA 92701
(714) 835-4900
Admin Nora Sauliettis.
Medical Dir Gordon Glasgow MD.
Licensure Skilled care. *Beds* SNF 150. *Certified* Medicare; Medi-Cal.
Owner Proprietary corp (Summit Care).
Admissions Requirements Medical examination.
Staff RNs 8 (ft), 3 (pt); LPNs 8 (ft), 1 (pt); Nurses' aides 57 (ft), 4 (pt); Physical therapists 1 (pt); Activities coordinators 2 (ft); Dietitians 1 (ft).
Facilities Dining room; Physical therapy room; Activities room; Crafts room; Laundry room; Barber/Beauty shop; Library; Transportation van.
Activities Arts & crafts; Cards; Games; Prayer groups; Movies; Shopping trips; Dances/Social/Cultural gatherings; Swimming; Bowling; Tennis; Picnics; Outings; Adopt-a-grandparent.

Country Club Convalescent Hospital Inc
20362 SW Santa Ana Ave, Santa Ana, CA 92707
(714) 549-3061
Admin Isabel C Hernandez.
Licensure Skilled care; Intermediate care. *Beds* SNF 41; ICF 12.
Owner Proprietary corp.

Country Villa Plaza Convalescent Center
1209 Hemlock Way, Santa Ana, CA 92707
(714) 546-1966
Admin Vickie Vergersen.
Licensure Skilled care. *Beds* SNF 145. *Certified* Medicare; Medi-Cal.
Owner Privately owned.

Hallmark Nursing Center—Tustin
2210 E 1st St, Santa Ana, CA 92705
(714) 547-7091, 547-4516 FAX
Admin Stella Chan-Mulkern. *Dir of Nursing* Carol DeCosta RN. *Medical Dir* David Sadaro MD.
Licensure Skilled care. *Beds* SNF 99. *Private Pay Patients* 48%. *Certified* Medicare; Medi-Cal.
Owner Proprietary corp (Hallmark Health Services Inc).
Admissions Requirements Minimum age 18; Physician's request.
Staff RNs 3 (ft), 4 (pt); LPNs 6 (ft), 4 (pt); Nurses' aides 28 (ft), 3 (pt); Physical therapists; Occupational therapists 1 (ft); Speech therapists 1 (ft); Activities coordinators 1 (ft); Dietitians 1 (ft).
Facilities Dining room; Physical therapy room; Activities room; Crafts room; Laundry room; Barber/Beauty shop; Occupational therapy room.
Activities Arts & crafts; Games; Prayer groups; Movies; Shopping trips; Dances/Social/Cultural gatherings; Intergenerational programs; Pet therapy.

Royale Convalescent Hospital
1030 W Warner Ave, Santa Ana, CA 92707
(714) 546-6450
Admin Don Connelly Jr.
Medical Dir H M Sung MD.
Licensure Skilled care; Intermediate care for mentally retarded. *Beds* SNF 173; ICF/MR 88. *Certified* Medicare; Medi-Cal.
Owner Proprietary corp.
Admissions Requirements Minimum age 21; Medical examination; Physician's request.
Staff RNs 10 (ft); LPNs 20 (ft); Nurses' aides 60 (ft); Physical therapists 1 (pt); Recreational therapists 2 (pt); Occupational therapists 1 (pt); Speech therapists 1 (pt); Activities coordinators 1 (ft); Dietitians 1 (pt); Ophthalmologists 1 (pt); Podiatrists 1 (pt); Audiologists 1 (pt); Dentists 1 (pt).

Facilities Dining room; Physical therapy room; Activities room; Crafts room; Laundry room; Barber/Beauty shop; Library.
Activities Arts & crafts; Cards; Games; Reading groups; Prayer groups; Movies; Shopping trips; Dances/Social/Cultural gatherings; Music therapy; World affairs; Current events; Resident & family councils.

St Edna Convalescent Center
1929 N Fairview St, Santa Ana, CA 92706
(714) 554-9700
Admin Rita Byrne. *Dir of Nursing* Barbara Pirc. *Medical Dir* Gordon A Glasgow MD.
Licensure Skilled care. *Beds* SNF 144. *Certified* Medicare; Medi-Cal.
Owner Privately owned.
Admissions Requirements Medical examination; Physician's request.
Staff Physicians 3 (pt); RNs 9 (ft), 1 (pt); LPNs 10 (ft), 2 (pt); Nurses' aides 54 (ft), 4 (pt); Physical therapists 2 (pt); Recreational therapists 1 (pt); Occupational therapists 2 (pt); Speech therapists 2 (pt); Activities coordinators 2 (ft); Dietitians 1 (pt); Ophthalmologists 1 (pt); Podiatrists 1 (pt); Dentists 1 (pt); Social workers 1 (ft), 1 (pt).
Facilities Dining room; Physical therapy room; Activities room; Crafts room; Laundry room; Barber/Beauty shop.
Activities Arts & crafts; Cards; Games; Reading groups; Prayer groups; Movies; Shopping trips; Dances/Social/Cultural gatherings.

Town & Country Manor
555 E Memory Ln, Santa Ana, CA 92706
(714) 547-7581
Admin Gail A Conser.
Medical Dir S A Kerkhoff MD.
Licensure Skilled care; Intermediate care. *Beds* SNF 42; ICF 80. *Certified* Medicare; Medi-Cal.
Owner Nonprofit corp.
Admissions Requirements Physician's request.
Staff Physicians 1 (pt); RNs 3 (ft), 5 (pt); LPNs 5 (ft), 3 (pt); Nurses' aides 22 (ft), 6 (pt); Activities coordinators 2 (ft); Dietitians 1 (ft).
Facilities Dining room; Physical therapy room; Activities room; Chapel; Crafts room; Laundry room; Barber/Beauty shop; Library.
Activities Arts & crafts; Games; Reading groups; Prayer groups; Movies; Shopping trips.

Western Medical Center—Bartlett
600 E Washington Ave, Santa Ana, CA 92701
(714) 973-1656, 836-4349 FAX
Admin Dian E Herschberg CFACHCA. *Dir of Nursing* Carole Gunderman. *Medical Dir* Joe Wu.
Licensure Skilled care. *Beds* SNF 241. *Private Pay Patients* 30%. *Certified* Medicare; Medi-Cal.
Owner Proprietary corp.
Admissions Requirements Minimum age 18.
Staff Physicians; RNs; LPNs; Nurses' aides; Physical therapists; Occupational therapists; Speech therapists; Activities coordinators; Dietitians; Ophthalmologists; Podiatrists; Audiologists.
Facilities Dining room; Physical therapy room; Activities room; Crafts room; Laundry room; Barber/Beauty shop.
Activities Arts & crafts; Cards; Games; Reading groups; Prayer groups; Movies; Shopping trips; Dances/Social/Cultural gatherings; Intergenerational programs; Pet therapy.

Santa Barbara

Beverly La Cumbre Convalescent Hospital
3880 Via Lucero, Santa Barbara, CA 93110
(805) 687-6651
Admin Philip Coldwell.

Licensure Skilled care. *Beds* SNF 189. *Certified* Medicare; Medi-Cal.
Owner Proprietary corp (Beverly Enterprises).

Beverly Manor Convalescent Hospital
2225 de la Vina, Santa Barbara, CA 93105
(805) 682-7451, 682-8133 FAX
Admin Sam DeMarco. *Dir of Nursing* Gayle Monk. *Medical Dir* Dr Paul Aijan.
Licensure Skilled care. *Beds* SNF 68. *Private Pay Patients* 20%. *Certified* Medicare; Medi-Cal.
Owner Proprietary corp (Beverly Enterprises).
Languages French, Spanish, Italian.
Facilities Dining room; Activities room; Crafts room; Laundry room; Barber/Beauty shop; Patios.
Activities Arts & crafts; Cards; Games; Reading groups; Prayer groups; Movies; Shopping trips; Dances/Social/Cultural gatherings; Intergenerational programs; Pet therapy; Intramural sports.

Casa Dorinda
300 Hot Springs Rd, Santa Barbara, CA 93108
(805) 969-8011, 969-8686 FAX
Admin Edward Steinfeldt.
Medical Dir Dr Robert Hartzman.
Licensure Skilled care; Residential care. *Beds* SNF 46; Residential care 280. *Certified* Medicare.
Owner Privately owned.
Admissions Requirements Minimum age 62; Medical examination.
Staff RNs; LPNs; Nurses' aides; Physical therapists.
Facilities Dining room; Physical therapy room; Barber/Beauty shop.
Activities Arts & crafts; Games; Reading groups; Movies.

Hillside House Inc
1235 Veronica Springs Rd, Santa Barbara, CA 93105
(805) 687-0788
Admin Cecil C Cooprider.
Licensure Skilled care. *Beds* 59. *Certified* Medi-Cal.
Owner Nonprofit corp.

Mission Terrace Convalescent Hospital
623 W Junipero St, Santa Barbara, CA 93105
(805) 682-7443
Admin Melanie Farkas. *Dir of Nursing* Julie McManus. *Medical Dir* Paul Aijian.
Licensure Skilled care. *Beds* SNF 138. *Certified* Medicare; Medi-Cal.
Owner Publicly owned.
Staff RNs 9 (ft), 1 (pt); LPNs 5 (ft); Nurses' aides 47 (ft); Physical therapists 1 (ft); Occupational therapists 1 (ft); Speech therapists 2 (pt); Activities coordinators 1 (ft); Dietitians 1 (ft).
Languages Spanish.
Facilities Dining room; Physical therapy room; Activities room; Laundry room; Barber/Beauty shop.
Activities Arts & crafts; Reading groups; Movies.

Patterson Gardens Convalescent Center
160 S Patterson Ave, Santa Barbara, CA 93111
(805) 964-4871
Admin Elizabeth C Gori.
Medical Dir Paul Aijian MD.
Licensure Skilled care. *Beds* SNF 150. *Certified* Medicare; Medi-Cal.
Owner Proprietary corp (Medstar Management Systems Inc).
Admissions Requirements Medical examination; Physician's request.
Staff RNs 10 (ft), 1 (pt); LPNs 12 (ft); Nurses' aides 42 (ft); Physical therapists 1 (ft); Recreational therapists 2 (ft); Occupational therapists 1 (pt); Speech therapists 1 (pt);

Activities coordinators 1 (ft); Dietitians 1 (pt); Ophthalmologists 1 (pt); Podiatrists 1 (pt); Audiologists 1 (pt); Dentists 1 (pt).
Facilities Dining room; Physical therapy room; Activities room; Crafts room; Laundry room; Barber/Beauty shop.
Activities Arts & crafts; Cards; Games; Reading groups; Prayer groups; Movies; Shopping trips; Dances/Social/Cultural gatherings.

Samarkand Health Center
2566 Treasure Dr, Santa Barbara, CA 93105
(805) 687-0701
Admin Wendell Rempel. *Dir of Nursing* Mary Jane Hensley. *Medical Dir* Robert Hartzman MD.
Licensure Skilled care; Retirement. *Beds* SNF 59; Retirement 330. *Private Pay Patients* 95%. *Certified* Medicare; Medi-Cal.
Owner Nonprofit corp (Covenant Retirement Communities Inc).
Admissions Requirements Minimum age 62; Medical examination; Physician's request.
Staff RNs; LPNs; Nurses' aides; Activities coordinators 1 (ft); Dietitians 1 (ft).
Languages Spanish, Danish, German.
Affiliation Evangelical Covenant Church.
Facilities Dining room; Physical therapy room; Activities room; Chapel; Laundry room; Barber/Beauty shop.
Activities Arts & crafts; Games; Reading groups; Prayer groups; Movies; Dances/Social/Cultural gatherings; Intergenerational programs; Pet therapy.

Santa Barbara Convalescent Hospital
540 W Pueblo St, Santa Barbara, CA 93105
(805) 682-7174
Admin Kehar S Johl.
Licensure Skilled care. *Beds* SNF 62. *Certified* Medicare.
Owner Proprietary corp.

Valle Verde Health Facility
900 Calle De Los Amigos, Santa Barbara, CA 93105
(805) 687-1571
Admin Raymond Schneider.
Medical Dir Henry L Holderman MD.
Licensure Skilled care. *Beds* 80. *Certified* Medicare; Medi-Cal.
Owner Nonprofit corp (American Baptist Home of the West Inc).
Staff Physicians 4 (pt); RNs 6 (ft), 6 (pt); LPNs 3 (ft), 3 (pt); Nurses' aides 18 (ft), 8 (pt); Physical therapists 1 (pt); Activities coordinators 3 (pt); Dietitians 1 (pt); Podiatrists 1 (pt).
Affiliation Baptist.
Facilities Dining room; Physical therapy room; Activities room; Chapel; Crafts room; Laundry room; Barber/Beauty shop; Library; Dental clinic; Grocery & variety store.
Activities Arts & crafts; Cards; Games; Reading groups; Prayer groups; Movies; Shopping trips; Dances/Social/Cultural gatherings; Resident string quartet; Trips; Putting green.

Vista Del Monte
3775 Modoc Rd, Santa Barbara, CA 93105
(805) 687-0793
Admin Charles E Frazier. *Dir of Nursing* Evelyn Bertanyi RN. *Medical Dir* James N Fisher MD.
Licensure Skilled care; Intermediate care; Retirement. *Beds* SNF 25; ICF 20. *Certified* Medicare; Medi-Cal.
Owner Nonprofit organization/foundation.
Admissions Requirements Minimum age 62; Medical examination.
Staff Physicians 1 (pt); RNs 2 (ft), 6 (pt); LPNs 3 (ft), 4 (pt); Nurses' aides 8 (ft), 6 (pt); Activities coordinators 1 (pt); Podiatrists 1 (pt).

Facilities Dining room; Activities room; Barber/Beauty shop; Lounges for personal "get-togethers"; Large meeting room & main lounge adjacent to dining room.
Activities Arts & crafts; Cards; Games; Reading groups; Movies; Dances/Social/Cultural gatherings; Reminiscence groups; Exercise; Motoring; Adaptive education; Cooking & baking.

Santa Clara

Beverly Manor
991 Clyde Ave, Santa Clara, CA 95050
(408) 988-7666
Admin Terri Campbell.
Medical Dir Harry Wong MD.
Licensure Skilled care. *Beds* SNF 205. *Certified* Medicare; Medi-Cal.
Owner Proprietary corp (Transworld Corp).
Admissions Requirements Minimum age 18; Medical examination; Physician's request.
Staff RNs 9 (ft), 2 (pt); LPNs 14 (ft), 6 (pt); Nurses' aides 67 (ft), 8 (pt); Activities coordinators 2 (ft); Dietitians 1 (ft).
Facilities Dining room; Physical therapy room; Activities room; Crafts room; Barber/Beauty shop.
Activities Arts & crafts; Cards; Games; Reading groups; Prayer groups; Movies; Shopping trips; Dances/Social/Cultural gatherings.

Mission Skilled Nursing Facility
410 N Winchester Blvd, Santa Clara, CA 95050
(408) 248-3736
Admin Yvonne Wood.
Licensure Skilled care. *Beds* SNF 111. *Certified* Medicare; Medi-Cal.
Owner Proprietary corp.

Santa Clarita

Santa Clarita Convalescent Hospital
23801 San Fernando Rd, Santa Clarita, CA 91321
(818) 365-9138
Admin Jean Priestman. *Dir of Nursing* Karen Ansell RN.
Licensure Skilled care. *Beds* 99. *Certified* Medicare; Medi-Cal.
Owner Proprietary corp.
Admissions Requirements Physician's request.
Staff Physicians; RNs; LPNs; Nurses' aides; Physical therapists; Reality therapists; Recreational therapists; Occupational therapists; Speech therapists; Activities coordinators; Dietitians; Ophthalmologists; Podiatrists; Dentists; Social workers.
Languages Spanish, German, Czech.
Facilities Dining room; Physical therapy room; Activities room; Crafts room; Laundry room; Barber/Beauty shop.
Activities Arts & crafts; Cards; Games; Reading groups; Prayer groups; Movies; Shopping trips; Dances/Social/Cultural gatherings.

Santa Cruz

Batterson Convalescent Hospital
2555 Mattison Ln, Santa Cruz, CA 95062
(408) 475-4065
Admin Ruth B Findlay. *Dir of Nursing* Patricia Battels RN. *Medical Dir* Francis M Jacks MD.
Licensure Skilled care; Retirement. *Beds* SNF 40. *Private Pay Patients* 95%. *Certified* Medicare.
Owner Privately owned.
Admissions Requirements Minimum age 18; Physician's request.
Staff RNs 1 (ft), 3 (pt); LPNs 3 (pt); Nurses' aides 14 (ft), 5 (pt); Activities coordinators 1 (pt).

Languages Spanish.
Facilities Dining room; Activities room; Crafts room; Library; Wheelchair accessible gardens; Outside patio; Covered porch.
Activities Arts & crafts; Cards; Games; Reading groups; Movies; Weekly church services.

Brommer Manor
2000 Brommer St, Santa Cruz, CA 95060
(408) 476-5500
Admin Charles L Puhl.
Licensure Skilled care. *Beds* SNF 38. *Certified* Medicare; Medi-Cal.
Owner Proprietary corp.
Activities Arts & crafts; Cards; Games; Reading groups; Movies; Shopping trips; Dances/Social/Cultural gatherings.

Cresthaven Nursing Home
740 17th Ave, Santa Cruz, CA 95062
(408) 475-3812
Admin Romeo F Hernandez. *Dir of Nursing* Ruth Hernandez. *Medical Dir* Dr John Catlin.
Licensure Skilled care. *Beds* SNF 20. *Certified* Medi-Cal.
Owner Privately owned.
Admissions Requirements Minimum age 60; Medical examination.
Staff Physicians 1 (pt); RNs 2 (ft), 2 (pt); LPNs 2 (ft), 1 (pt); Nurses' aides 5 (ft), 2 (pt); Recreational therapists 1 (pt); Activities coordinators 1 (ft), 1 (pt); Dietitians 1 (ft), 1 (pt); Ophthalmologists 1 (pt); Podiatrists 1 (pt); Dentists 1 (pt).
Facilities Dining room; Activities room; Chapel; Crafts room; Laundry room; Barber/Beauty shop.
Activities Arts & crafts; Cards; Games; Reading groups; Prayer groups; Movies; Shopping trips; Dances/Social/Cultural gatherings.

Cypress Care Center
1098 38th Ave, Santa Cruz, CA 95060
(408) 475-6901
Admin Dan Platt.
Medical Dir Dr Martin.
Licensure Skilled care. *Beds* SNF 99. *Certified* Medicare; Medi-Cal.
Owner Proprietary corp.
Staff RNs 3 (ft), 3 (pt); LPNs 6 (ft), 4 (pt); Nurses' aides 35 (ft), 15 (pt); Recreational therapists 1 (ft), 1 (pt); Activities coordinators.
Facilities Dining room; Physical therapy room; Activities room; Crafts room; Laundry room; Barber/Beauty shop.
Activities Arts & crafts; Cards; Games; Reading groups; Prayer groups; Movies; Shopping trips.

Driftwood Convalescent Hospital
675 24th Ave, Santa Cruz, CA 95060
(408) 475-6323
Admin Elizabeth P Byrne.
Medical Dir Dr Allan Martin.
Licensure Skilled care. *Beds* SNF 92. *Certified* Medicare; Medi-Cal.
Owner Proprietary corp (Western Medical Enterprises Inc).
Admissions Requirements Minimum age 18.
Staff RNs 5 (ft); LPNs 4 (ft); Nurses' aides 35 (ft); Occupational therapists 1 (pt); Speech therapists 1 (pt); Activities coordinators 1 (ft); Dietitians 1 (ft); Ophthalmologists 1 (pt); Podiatrists 1 (pt); Audiologists 1 (pt); Dentists 1 (pt).
Facilities Dining room; Physical therapy room; Activities room; Crafts room; Laundry room; Barber/Beauty shop.
Activities Arts & crafts; Cards; Games; Reading groups; Prayer groups; Movies.

Garden Nursing Home & Convalescent Hospital
1410 Ocean St, Santa Cruz, CA 95062
(408) 423-6045
Admin Margaret Amos.
Licensure Skilled care. *Beds* SNF 55. *Certified* Medicare; Medi-Cal.
Owner Proprietary corp.

Harbor Hills
1171 7th Ave, Santa Cruz, CA 95062
(408) 476-1700
Admin Richard A Knowles.
Medical Dir Ron Krasner MD.
Licensure Skilled care. *Beds* SNF 99. *Certified* Medi-Cal.
Owner Nonprofit corp.
Admissions Requirements Minimum age 18; Physician's request.
Staff Physicians 5 (pt); RNs 3 (ft), 1 (pt); LPNs 5 (ft), 5 (pt); Nurses' aides 32 (ft), 12 (pt); Activities coordinators 1 (ft); Dietitians 1 (ft); Dentists 1 (pt).
Facilities Dining room; Activities room; Crafts room; Laundry room; Barber/Beauty shop; Library; TV room.
Activities Arts & crafts; Cards; Games; Movies; Shopping trips; Dances/Social/ Cultural gatherings.

Hillhaven Extended Care
1115 Capitola Rd, Santa Cruz, CA 95060
(408) 475-4055
Admin Marise G Goetzl. *Dir of Nursing* Candace Eiseman RN. *Medical Dir* Dr Anthony Tyler.
Licensure Skilled care. *Beds* SNF 149. *Certified* Medicare; Medi-Cal.
Owner Proprietary corp (Hillhaven Inc).
Admissions Requirements Medical examination; Physician's request.
Staff RNs 3 (ft); LPNs 6 (ft); Nurses' aides 32 (ft); Physical therapists 1 (ft); Occupational therapists 1 (ft); Speech therapists 1 (ft); Activities coordinators 2 (ft); Dietitians 1 (ft); Ophthalmologists 1 (ft); Podiatrists 1 (ft); Dentists 1 (ft).
Facilities Dining room; Physical therapy room; Activities room; Crafts room; Laundry room; Barber/Beauty shop; Library.
Activities Arts & crafts; Cards; Games; Reading groups; Prayer groups; Movies; Dances/Social/Cultural gatherings.

Live Oak Care Center
2990 Soquel Ave, Santa Cruz, CA 95062
(408) 475-8832
Admin Pauline Phillips. *Dir of Nursing* Linda Roloff. *Medical Dir* Allen Martin MD.
Licensure Skilled care; Intermediate care. *Beds* SNF 121; ICF 93. *Certified* Medicare; Medi-Cal.
Owner Proprietary corp.
Admissions Requirements Physician's request.
Staff RNs; Nurses' aides; Physical therapists; Speech therapists; Activities coordinators; Dietitians; Ophthalmologists.
Languages Spanish.
Facilities Dining room; Physical therapy room; Activities room; Crafts room; Laundry room; Barber/Beauty shop; Library; Large screen TV.
Activities Arts & crafts; Cards; Games; Reading groups; Prayer groups; Movies; Dances/Social/Cultural gatherings; Pet therapy.

Santa Maria

Kimberly Convalescent Hospital
820 W Cook St, Santa Maria, CA 93454
(805) 925-8877
Admin Carroll Silvera.
Licensure Skilled care. *Beds* SNF 55. *Certified* Medicare; Medi-Cal.
Owner Privately owned.

Marian Extended Care Center
1530 Cypress Way, Santa Maria, CA 93454
(805) 925-7747, 925-1497 FAX
Admin Charles J Cova. *Dir of Nursing* Mary Lou Boyle RN. *Medical Dir* Kenneth L Clay MD.
Licensure Skilled care. *Beds* SNF 95. *Certified* Medicare; Medi-Cal.
Owner Nonprofit organization/foundation.
Admissions Requirements Medical examination; Physician's request.
Affiliation Roman Catholic.
Facilities Dining room; Physical therapy room; Activities room; Chapel; Barber/ Beauty shop.
Activities Arts & crafts; Cards; Games; Reading groups; Prayer groups; Movies; Shopping trips; Dances/Social/Cultural gatherings; Intergenerational programs; Pet therapy.

Rosscare Convalescent Hospital
830 E Chapel, Santa Maria, CA 93454
(805) 922-6657
Admin Douglas L Epperson. *Dir of Nursing* Janet M Brim RN. *Medical Dir* Riveria Robinson.
Licensure Skilled care. *Beds* SNF 59. *Private Pay Patients* 40%. *Certified* Medicare; Medi-Cal.
Owner Privately owned (Rosscare).
Admissions Requirements Medical examination.
Staff Physicians 1 (pt); RNs 6 (ft); Nurses' aides 30 (ft), 4 (pt); Physical therapists 1 (pt); Speech therapists 1 (pt); Activities coordinators 1 (ft); Dietitians 1 (ft); Podiatrists 1 (pt); Dentists 1 (pt).
Facilities Dining room; Physical therapy room; Activities room; Crafts room; Laundry room; Barber/Beauty shop.
Activities Arts & crafts; Cards; Games; Reading groups; Prayer groups; Movies; Shopping trips; Dances/Social/Cultural gatherings; Intergenerational programs; Pet therapy.

Villa Maria Care Center
425 E Barcellus Ave, Santa Maria, CA 93454
(805) 922-3558
Admin Laurie Osborn-Smith.
Medical Dir Joseph Cohan MD.
Licensure Skilled care. *Beds* SNF 88. *Certified* Medicare; Medi-Cal.
Owner Proprietary corp (Summit Care).
Staff Physicians 1 (ft); RNs 7 (ft), 2 (pt); Nurses' aides 37 (ft); Physical therapists 1 (pt); Reality therapists 1 (pt); Recreational therapists 1 (pt); Occupational therapists 1 (pt); Speech therapists 1 (pt); Activities coordinators 1 (ft); Dietitians 1 (pt); Ophthalmologists 1 (pt); Podiatrists 1 (pt); Audiologists 1 (pt); Dentists 1 (pt); LVNs 6 (ft), 3 (pt).
Facilities Dining room; Physical therapy room; Activities room; Crafts room; Laundry room; Barber/Beauty shop; Library.
Activities Arts & crafts; Cards; Games; Reading groups; Prayer groups; Movies; Shopping trips; Dances/Social/Cultural gatherings; Monthly luncheons; Holiday programs.

Santa Monica

Bay Vista
1338 20th St, Santa Monica, CA 90404
(213) 829-4731, 829-4494 FAX
Admin Jan Frank. *Dir of Nursing* Carole Sharp RN. *Medical Dir* Douglas Tyler MD.
Licensure Skilled care. *Beds* SNF 154. *Certified* Medicare; Medi-Cal.
Owner Proprietary corp (ARA Living Centers).
Admissions Requirements Physician's request.

Staff RNs 3 (ft); LPNs 11 (ft); Physical
therapists 1 (ft); Occupational therapists
(contracted); Speech therapists (contracted);
Dietitians (contracted); Ophthalmologists
(contracted); Podiatrists (contracted);
Audiologists (contracted); Recreational
therapists; Activities coordinators 1 (ft).
Facilities Dining room; Physical therapy
room; Activities room; Laundry room;
Barber/Beauty shop; Library; Enclosed
outdoor patio; Rehabilitation program.
Activities Arts & crafts; Cards; Games;
Reading groups; Prayer groups; Movies;
Intergenerational programs; "Joint Efforts".

Berkley East Convalescent Hospital
2021 Arizona Ave, Santa Monica, CA 90404
(213) 829-5377
Admin Paul Bartolucci.
Licensure Skilled care. *Beds* SNF 235.
Certified Medicare; Medi-Cal.
Owner Proprietary corp.

Berkley West Convalescent Hospital
1623 Arizona Ave, Santa Monica, CA 90404
(213) 829-4565
Admin Steven Galper. *Dir of Nursing* Kathryn
J Ghavamian RN.
Licensure Skilled care. *Beds* SNF 54. *Certified*
Medicare; Medi-Cal.
Owner Proprietary corp.
Admissions Requirements Minimum age 21;
Physician's request.
Staff RNs 2 (ft); LPNs 4 (ft), 3 (pt); Nurses'
aides 25 (ft); Physical therapists 2 (pt);
Reality therapists 1 (pt); Recreational
therapists 11 (pt); Occupational therapists 1
(pt); Speech therapists 1 (pt); Activities
coordinators 1 (ft); Dietitians 1 (ft);
Ophthalmologists 1 (pt); Podiatrists 1 (pt).
Languages Spanish.
Facilities Dining room; Activities room;
Crafts room; Laundry room; Barber/Beauty
shop; Patio with fish pond.
Activities Arts & crafts; Cards; Games;
Reading groups; Prayer groups; Movies; Paid
entertainers; Birthday parties for patients &
staff.

Berkshire Sanitarium
2602 Broadway, Santa Monica, CA 90404
(213) 453-8816
Admin William K Kolodin.
Medical Dir James H Shumaker MD.
Licensure Skilled care. *Beds* SNF 33.
Owner Proprietary corp.
Admissions Requirements Minimum age 62.
Staff RNs 1 (ft), 2 (pt); LPNs 2 (ft), 2 (pt);
Nurses' aides 12 (ft), 3 (pt); Physical
therapists 1 (pt); Recreational therapists 1
(pt); Occupational therapists 1 (pt); Speech
therapists 1 (pt); Activities coordinators 1
(ft), 1 (pt); Dietitians 1 (pt);
Ophthalmologists 1 (pt); Podiatrists 1 (pt);
Dentists 1 (pt).
Facilities Dining room; Activities room;
Laundry room; Barber/Beauty shop.
Activities Arts & crafts; Cards; Games; Prayer
groups; Movies; Dances/Social/Cultural
gatherings; Barbeques; Emeritus college
classes.

Care West—Arizona Nursing Center
1330 17th St, Santa Monica, CA 90404
(213) 829-5411
Admin Gita D Wheelis. *Dir of Nursing* Laida
Provido RN. *Medical Dir* Jane Bishop MD.
Licensure Skilled care. *Beds* SNF 72. *Certified*
Medicaid; Medicare; Medi-Cal.
Owner Proprietary corp (Care Enterprises).
Admissions Requirements Minimum age 35.
Staff RNs 2 (ft); LPNs 10 (ft); Nurses' aides
20 (ft); Physical therapists; Recreational
therapists; Occupational therapists; Speech
therapists; Activities coordinators; Dietitians;
Podiatrists; Audiologists.

Facilities Dining room; Physical therapy
room; Laundry room; Barber/Beauty shop.
Activities Arts & crafts; Cards; Games;
Reading groups; Prayer groups; Movies;
Shopping trips; Dances/Social/Cultural
gatherings; Pet therapy.

Care West—Santa Monica Nursing Center
1321 Franklin, Santa Monica, CA 90403
(213) 828-5596
Admin David Lefitz.
Medical Dir Victor Wylie MD.
Licensure Skilled care. *Beds* SNF 59. *Certified*
Medicare; Medi-Cal.
Owner Proprietary corp (Care Enterprises).
Staff RNs 1 (ft), 4 (pt); Nurses' aides 9 (ft), 4
(pt); Physical therapists 1 (ft); Occupational
therapists 1 (pt); Speech therapists 1 (pt);
Activities coordinators 1 (ft); Podiatrists 1
(pt); Audiologists 1 (pt); Dentists 1 (pt).
Facilities Dining room; Physical therapy
room; Activities room; Barber/Beauty shop.
Activities Arts & crafts; Cards; Games; Prayer
groups; Movies.

Crescent Bay Convalescent Hospital
1437 14th St, Santa Monica, CA 90404
(213) 394-3726
Admin Sherman Miller.
Licensure Skilled care. *Beds* SNF 69. *Certified*
Medicare; Medi-Cal.
Owner Privately owned.

Fireside Convalescent Hospital
947 3rd St, Santa Monica, CA 90403
(213) 393-0475
Admin Ida H Rios.
Licensure Skilled care. *Beds* SNF 66. *Certified*
Medicare; Medi-Cal.
Owner Proprietary corp.

Good Shepherd Convalescent Hospital
1131 Arizona Ave, Santa Monica, CA 90404
(213) 451-4809
Admin Paul W Cosgrove.
Licensure Skilled care. *Beds* SNF 48. *Certified*
Medicare; Medi-Cal.
Owner Proprietary corp.

Oceanview Convalescent Hospital
1340 15th St, Santa Monica, CA 90404
(213) 451-9706
Admin Naomi J Root. *Dir of Nursing* Paula A
May. *Medical Dir* Dr R Hallis.
Licensure Skilled care. *Beds* SNF 227. *Private
Pay Patients* 80%. *Certified* Medicare; Medi-
Cal.
Owner Proprietary corp.
Admissions Requirements Physician's request.
Staff Physicians; RNs 4 (ft), 1 (pt); LPNs 14
(ft), 4 (pt); Nurses' aides 26 (ft), 4 (pt);
Physical therapists 1 (ft); Occupational
therapists (contracted); Speech therapists
(contracted); Activities coordinators 1 (ft);
Dietitians 1 (ft); Ophthalmologists
(contracted); Podiatrists (contracted);
Audiologists (contracted).
Facilities Dining room; Physical therapy
room; Activities room; Crafts room; Laundry
room; Barber/Beauty shop; Living rooms;
Community rooms.
Activities Arts & crafts; Cards; Games;
Reading groups; Prayer groups; Movies;
Shopping trips; Dances/Social/Cultural
gatherings; Intergenerational programs; Pet
therapy; Religious services.

Pacific Convalescent Center
1323 17th St, Santa Monica, CA 90404
(213) 453-5456
Admin Virginia Joy.
Licensure Skilled care. *Beds* SNF 49. *Certified*
Medicare.
Owner Privately owned.

Santa Monica Convalarium
1320 20th St, Santa Monica, CA 90404
(213) 829-4301

Admin Carol A Wagner MS. *Dir of Nursing*
Julanne Rias RN. *Medical Dir* Phillip
Rossman MD.
Licensure Skilled care; Alzheimer's care. *Beds*
SNF 59. *Certified* Medicare.
Owner Proprietary corp (American Medical
Services Inc).
Staff Physicians 50 (pt); RNs 4 (ft), 1 (pt);
LPNs 1 (ft), 3 (pt); Nurses' aides 20 (ft), 5
(pt); Physical therapists 2 (pt); Occupational
therapists 2 (pt); Speech therapists 1 (pt);
Activities coordinators 1 (ft), 1 (pt);
Dietitians 1 (pt); Ophthalmologists 1 (pt);
Podiatrists 1 (pt); Audiologists 1 (pt).
Languages Spanish, Tagalog.
Facilities Dining room; Activities room;
Crafts room; Barber/Beauty shop; Library;
Patio; Lobby sitting room; Garden.
Activities Arts & crafts; Cards; Games;
Reading groups; Movies; Shopping trips;
Dances/Social/Cultural gatherings;
Intergenerational programs; Pet therapy;
Religious services; Special holiday events;
Entertainment.

Santa Monica Convalescent Center II
2250 29th St, Santa Monica, CA 90405
(213) 450-7694
Admin Robert V Smith.
Medical Dir Paul A Berns MD.
Licensure Skilled care. *Beds* SNF 44. *Certified*
Medicare; Medi-Cal.
Owner Privately owned.
Admissions Requirements Physician's request.
Staff Physicians 17 (ft); RNs 1 (ft), 3 (pt);
LPNs 3 (ft), 5 (pt); Nurses' aides 12 (ft), 1
(pt); Physical therapists 1 (pt); Recreational
therapists 1 (pt); Speech therapists 1 (pt);
Activities coordinators 1 (pt); Dietitians 1
(pt); Ophthalmologists 1 (pt); Podiatrists 1
(pt); Dentists 1 (pt).
Facilities Dining room; Laundry room;
Barber/Beauty shop.
Activities Arts & crafts; Cards; Games;
Reading groups; Prayer groups; Movies;
Shopping trips; Dances/Social/Cultural
gatherings.

Santa Paula

Santa Paula Health Care
220 W Main St, Santa Paula, CA 93060
(805) 525-6621
Admin Marieta J Moore. *Dir of Nursing* G
Paja RN. *Medical Dir* Sam Edwards MD.
Licensure Skilled care. *Beds* SNF 49. *Certified*
Medi-Cal.
Owner Proprietary corp (Hillhaven Corp).
Admissions Requirements Medical
examination; Physician's request.
Staff RNs; LPNs; Nurses' aides; Activities
coordinators; Dietitians.
Languages Spanish.
Facilities Dining room; Activities room;
Barber/Beauty shop.
Activities Arts & crafts; Cards; Games;
Reading groups; Prayer groups; Movies;
Shopping trips; Dances/Social/Cultural
gatherings.

Twin Pines Health Care
250 March St, Santa Paula, CA 93060-2592
(805) 525-7134
Admin Marieta J Moore. *Dir of Nursing*
Shirley Ebert RN. *Medical Dir* Samuel
Edwards MD.
Licensure Skilled care. *Beds* SNF 99. *Private
Pay Patients* 50%. *Certified* Medicare; Medi-
Cal.
Owner Proprietary corp (Hillhaven Corp).
Admissions Requirements Medical
examination; Physician's request.
Staff RNs; LPNs; Nurses' aides; Activities
coordinators.
Facilities Dining room; Activities room;
Crafts room; Laundry room; Barber/Beauty
shop.

Activities Arts & crafts; Games; Reading groups; Prayer groups; Movies; Pet therapy.

Santa Rosa

Creekside Convalescent Hospital
850 Sonoma Ave, Santa Rosa, CA 95404
(707) 544-7750
Admin Robert W Bates. *Dir of Nursing* Jackie Englestadt. *Medical Dir* Dr DeVore.
Licensure Skilled care. *Beds* SNF 181. *Certified* Medicare; Medi-Cal.
Owner Proprietary corp.
Admissions Requirements Physician's request.
Staff RNs; LPNs; Nurses' aides; Recreational therapists; Activities coordinators.
Languages Korean, German, Spanish, Italian.
Facilities Dining room; Physical therapy room; Activities room; Crafts room; Laundry room; Barber/Beauty shop; Library.
Activities Arts & crafts; Cards; Games; Reading groups; Prayer groups; Movies; Dances/Social/Cultural gatherings.

Friends House
684 Benicia Dr, Santa Rosa, CA 95409
(707) 538-0152
Admin Elizabeth F Boardman.
Licensure Skilled care. *Beds* SNF 30. *Certified* Medicare; Medi-Cal.
Owner Proprietary corp.

London House Convalescent Hospital
4650 Hoen Ave, Santa Rosa, CA 95405
(707) 546-0471
Admin Walter Atkin Jr. *Dir of Nursing* Susan Sutton.
Licensure Skilled care. *Beds* SNF 99. *Certified* Medicare; Medi-Cal.
Owner Proprietary corp (Beverly Enterprises).
Admissions Requirements Medical examination; Physician's request.
Staff RNs 9 (ft); LPNs 6 (ft); Nurses' aides 65 (ft); Physical therapists 1 (ft); Recreational therapists 1 (ft); Occupational therapists 1 (pt); Speech therapists 1 (pt); Activities coordinators 1 (ft); Dietitians 1 (ft); Ophthalmologists 1 (pt); Podiatrists 1 (pt); Audiologists 1 (pt); Dentists 1 (pt).
Facilities Dining room; Physical therapy room; Activities room; Chapel; Crafts room; Laundry room; Barber/Beauty shop; Library; TV lounge.
Activities Arts & crafts; Cards; Games; Reading groups; Prayer groups; Movies; Shopping trips; Dances/Social/Cultural gatherings.

Montgomery Manor
3751 Montgomery Dr, Santa Rosa, CA 95405
(707) 525-1250
Admin Dorothy J Bennett.
Licensure Skilled care. *Beds* SNF 122. *Certified* Medicare; Medi-Cal.
Owner Proprietary corp.

Santa Rosa Convalescent Hospital
446 Arrowood Dr, Santa Rosa, CA 95401
(707) 528-2100
Admin Henry Weiland III.
Medical Dir Kent Beams MD.
Licensure Skilled care. *Beds* SNF 59. *Certified* Medicare; Medi-Cal.
Owner Privately owned.
Admissions Requirements Medical examination; Physician's request.
Staff Physicians; RNs; LPNs; Nurses' aides; Activities coordinators.
Languages Spanish.
Facilities Dining room; Physical therapy room; Activities room; Chapel; Laundry room.
Activities Arts & crafts; Cards; Games; Reading groups; Prayer groups; Movies; Dances/Social/Cultural gatherings.

Spring Lake Village
5555 Montgomery Dr, Santa Rosa, CA 95405
(707) 538-8400
Admin Erling G Anderson.
Licensure Skilled care. *Beds* SNF 50. *Certified* Medicare.
Owner Proprietary corp.

Summerfield Convalescent Hospital
1280 Summerfield Rd, Santa Rosa, CA 95405
(707) 539-1515
Admin Mary Roberts.
Medical Dir Michael MacLean MD.
Licensure Skilled care. *Beds* SNF 70. *Certified* Medicare; Medi-Cal.
Owner Proprietary corp.
Facilities Dining room; Activities room; Crafts room; Laundry room.
Activities Arts & crafts; Cards; Games; Reading groups; Prayer groups; Movies; Dances/Social/Cultural gatherings.

Santee

Edgemoor Geriatric Hospital
9065 Edgemoor Dr, Santee, CA 92071
(619) 258-3001
Admin Florence McCarthy.
Medical Dir William Bailey MD.
Licensure Skilled care. *Beds* SNF 342. *Certified* Medicare; Medi-Cal.
Owner Publicly owned.
Admissions Requirements Minimum age 18; Medical examination.
Staff Physicians 2 (ft), 2 (pt); RNs 21 (ft), 10 (pt); LPNs 8 (ft); Nurses' aides 90 (ft), 15 (pt); Physical therapists 3 (ft); Reality therapists 2 (ft); Recreational therapists 2 (ft); Occupational therapists 1 (ft), 1 (pt); Speech therapists 1 (pt); Activities coordinators 1 (ft); Dietitians 2 (ft); Ophthalmologists 1 (pt); Podiatrists 1 (pt); Dentists 1 (pt).
Facilities Dining room; Physical therapy room; Activities room; Chapel; Crafts room; Laundry room; Barber/Beauty shop; Library.
Activities Arts & crafts; Games; Reading groups; Prayer groups; Movies; Shopping trips; Field trips.

Stanford Court Nursing Center
8778 Cuyamaca St, Santee, CA 92071
(619) 449-5555, 466-9091 FAX
Admin Robin A Leland. *Dir of Nursing* Rena Shephard RN. *Medical Dir* John J Dapolito Jr MD.
Licensure Skilled care. *Beds* SNF 105. *Private Pay Patients* 85%. *Certified* Medicaid; Medicare; Medi-Cal.
Owner Proprietary corp (Leland Healthcare Services Inc).
Admissions Requirements Medical examination; Physician's request.
Staff RNs; LPNs; Nurses' aides; Physical therapists 1 (ft), 2 (pt); Recreational therapists; Occupational therapists 1 (pt); Speech therapists 1 (pt); Activities coordinators 2 (ft); Dietitians 1 (ft), 1 (pt); Podiatrists 1 (pt).
Languages Spanish, Tagalog.
Facilities Dining room; Physical therapy room; Activities room; Crafts room; Laundry room; Barber/Beauty shop; Library.
Activities Arts & crafts; Cards; Games; Reading groups; Prayer groups; Movies; Shopping trips; Dances/Social/Cultural gatherings; Intergenerational programs; Pet therapy.

Saratoga

Odd Fellows Home of California Infirmary
14500 Fruitvale Ave, Saratoga, CA 95070
(408) 867-3891
Admin Juilyn Burns Gibbs. *Dir of Nursing* Violet Segura. *Medical Dir* John Henion.
Licensure Skilled care; Intermediate care. *Beds* SNF 62; ICF 6; Residential 174. *Certified* Medicare; Medi-Cal.
Owner Proprietary corp.
Admissions Requirements Minimum age 65; Medical examination.
Staff Physicians 1 (pt); RNs 3 (ft); LPNs 4 (ft); Nurses' aides 25 (ft); Physical therapists 1 (pt); Reality therapists 1 (pt); Recreational therapists 1 (pt); Activities coordinators 2 (ft); Dietitians 1 (ft); Ophthalmologists 1 (pt).
Languages Spanish, Asian dialects.
Facilities Dining room; Physical therapy room; Activities room; Chapel; Laundry room; Barber/Beauty shop; Library.
Activities Arts & crafts; Cards; Games; Reading groups; Prayer groups; Movies; Shopping trips; Dances/Social/Cultural gatherings.

Our Lady of Fatima Villa
20400 Saratoga-Los Gatos Rd, Saratoga, CA 95070
(408) 741-5100, 741-4930 FAX
Admin Preston H Wisner PhD. *Dir of Nursing* Susan Jones RN. *Medical Dir* John Wortley MD.
Licensure Skilled care. *Beds* SNF 85. *Private Pay Patients* 75%. *Certified* Medicare; Medi-Cal.
Owner Nonprofit corp.
Admissions Requirements Medical examination; Physician's request.
Staff RNs 9 (ft), 5 (pt); Nurses' aides 37 (ft), 3 (pt); Physical therapists; Activities coordinators 3 (ft); Dietitians.
Affiliation Roman Catholic.
Facilities Dining room; Physical therapy room; Activities room; Chapel; Crafts room; Laundry room; Barber/Beauty shop; Courtyard.
Activities Arts & crafts; Cards; Games; Reading groups; Prayer groups; Movies; Pet therapy; Religious activities.

Saratoga Place Subacute Hospital
18611 Sousa Ln, Saratoga, CA 95070
(408) 378-8875
Dir of Nursing Rose Silver RN. *Medical Dir* John Rashkis MD.
Licensure Skilled care. *Beds* SNF 38. *Private Pay Patients* 2%. *Certified* Medicaid; Medicare; Medi-Cal.
Owner Proprietary corp.
Admissions Requirements Minimum age 3 mo.
Staff RNs 10 (ft), 4 (pt); LPNs 21 (ft), 14 (pt); Nurses' aides 22 (ft), 10 (pt); Physical therapists 2 (pt); Recreational therapists 1 (ft); Occupational therapists 1 (ft); Speech therapists 1 (pt); Activities coordinators 1 (ft); Dietitians 1 (pt); Podiatrists 1 (pt); Neuropsychologists 1 (pt); Respiratory therapists 1 (pt); Rehabilitation aides 1 (ft).
Languages Spanish, Chinese, Indian.
Facilities Dining room; Physical therapy room; Activities room; Laundry room; Landscaped backyard with gazebo and waterfall; 8-bed neurostimulation unit.
Activities Arts & crafts; Cards; Games; Movies; Shopping trips; Dances/Social/Cultural gatherings; Intergenerational programs; Pet therapy; Outdoor rehabilitation course; Overnight camping trips; Barbecues.

Seal Beach

Beverly Manor Convalescent Hospital
3000 Beverly Manor Rd, Seal Beach, CA 90740
(213) 598-2477
Admin Marilyn Ryan. *Dir of Nursing* Joyce Ritz RNC. *Medical Dir* Dr Alan Greenberg.
Licensure Skilled care. *Beds* SNF 198. *Certified* Medicare; Medi-Cal.
Owner Proprietary corp (Beverly Enterprises).

Admissions Requirements Medical examination; Physician's request.
Staff Physicians 1 (pt); RNs 10 (ft); LPNs 30 (ft); Nurses' aides 60 (ft); Activities coordinators 1 (ft).
Facilities Dining room; Physical therapy room; Activities room; Crafts room; Laundry room; Barber/Beauty shop; Library; Fireside room; TV room; Patios.
Activities Arts & crafts; Cards; Games; Reading groups; Prayer groups; Movies; Shopping trips; Dances/Social/Cultural gatherings; Bowling; Stroke group.

Sebastopol

Apple Valley Convalescent
1035 Gravenstein Ave, Sebastopol, CA 95472
(707) 823-7675
Admin Dwayne l Baughman.
Licensure Skilled care. *Beds* SNF 95. *Certified* Medicare; Medi-Cal.
Owner Proprietary corp.

Fircrest Convalescent Hospital
7025 Corline Ct, Sebastopol, CA 95472
(707) 823-7444
Admin Robert Bates. *Dir of Nursing* Jane Wallers RN. *Medical Dir* Dr Bolt.
Licensure Skilled care. *Beds* SNF 49. *Private Pay Patients* 50%. *Certified* Medicaid; Medicare; Medi-Cal.
Owner Proprietary corp (Hermitage Health).
Staff RNs; LPNs; Nurses' aides; Activities coordinators.
Facilities Dining room; Activities room; Laundry room; Barber/Beauty shop; Library.
Activities Arts & crafts; Cards; Games; Reading groups; Prayer groups; Movies; Shopping trips; Dances/Social/Cultural gatherings; Intergenerational programs; Pet therapy.

Sebastopol Convalescent Hospital
477 Petaluma Ave, Sebastopol, CA 95472
(707) 823-7855
Admin Carol J Grundstrom.
Licensure Skilled care. *Beds* SNF 35. *Certified* Medicare; Medi-Cal.
Owner Privately owned.

Selma

Bethel Lutheran Home Inc
2280 Dockery Ave, Selma, CA 93662
(209) 896-4900
Admin Ken Truckenbrod.
Licensure Skilled care; Intermediate care. *Beds* SNF 49; ICF 10. *Certified* Medi-Cal.
Owner Proprietary corp.

Bethel Lutheran Home Inc
2280 Dockery Ave, Selma, CA 93662
(209) 896-4900
Admin Ken Truckenbrod.
Licensure Skilled care. *Beds* 30. *Certified* Medi-Cal.
Owner Nonprofit corp.

Selma Convalescent Hospital
2108 Stillman St, Selma, CA 93662
(209) 896-4990
Admin Jerry Barkman.
Licensure Skilled care. *Beds* SNF 34. *Certified* Medi-Cal.
Owner Proprietary corp (Beverly Enterprises).

Sepulveda

Sheraton Convalescent Center
9655 Sepulveda Blvd, Sepulveda, CA 91343
(818) 892-8665
Admin Ted Greenberg. *Dir of Nursing* Romy Brubaker RN. *Medical Dir* Melvin Kirschner MD.
Licensure Skilled care; Retirement. *Beds* SNF 138. *Certified* Medicare; Medi-Cal.

Owner Nonprofit organization/foundation (Wilshire Foundation Inc).
Admissions Requirements Minimum age 35; Physician's request.
Staff Physicians; RNs; LPNs; Nurses' aides; Activities coordinators; Dietitians.
Facilities Dining room; Physical therapy room; Activities room; Crafts room; Laundry room; Barber/Beauty shop.
Activities Arts & crafts; Cards; Games; Reading groups; Prayer groups; Movies; Shopping trips; Dances/Social/Cultural gatherings; Entertainment provided.

Shafter

Shafter Convalescent Hospital
140 E Tulare Ave, Shafter, CA 93263
(805) 746-3912
Admin T Wayne Smith.
Licensure Skilled care. *Beds* SNF 99. *Certified* Medicare; Medi-Cal.
Owner Proprietary corp (Beverly Enterprises).

Sherman Oaks

Sherman Oaks Convalescent Hospital
14401 Huston St, Sherman Oaks, CA 91423
(818) 986-7242
Admin Christine Geyer. *Dir of Nursing* Catherine Barabas RN. *Medical Dir* Glenn Randall MD.
Licensure Skilled care. *Beds* SNF 120. *Certified* Medicare; Medi-Cal.
Owner Proprietary corp (Beverly Enterprises).
Staff RNs 3 (ft), 3 (pt); LPNs 7 (ft), 3 (pt); Nurses' aides 28 (ft), 6 (pt); Activities coordinators 1 (ft), 2 (pt).
Languages Spanish, Tagalog.
Facilities Dining room; Physical therapy room; Activities room; Chapel; Laundry room; Barber/Beauty shop; Library.
Activities Arts & crafts; Cards; Games; Reading groups; Prayer groups; Movies; Dances/Social/Cultural gatherings; Lunch outings; Scenic rides.

Sierra Madre

Sierra Madre Skilled Nursing Facility
225 W Sierra Madre, Sierra Madre, CA 91024
(213) 355-7181
Admin Denis S Sutton. *Dir of Nursing* Dorothy Lacour RN. *Medical Dir* Ivan Reeve MD.
Licensure Skilled care. *Beds* SNF 56. *Certified* Medicare; Medi-Cal.
Owner Nonprofit corp.
Staff RNs 5 (ft), 5 (pt); LPNs 2 (ft), 1 (pt); Nurses' aides 30 (ft), 6 (pt); Physical therapists 2 (pt); Occupational therapists 1 (pt); Speech therapists 1 (pt); Activities coordinators 1 (ft), 1 (pt); Dietitians 1 (pt).
Languages Spanish, German, Tagalog.
Facilities Dining room; Physical therapy room; Activities room; Barber/Beauty shop.
Activities Arts & crafts; Cards; Games; Prayer groups; Movies; Dances/Social/Cultural gatherings.

Signal Hill

Care West—South Bay Nursing Center
2901 E Pacific Coast, Signal Hill, CA 90804
(213) 434-4451
Admin Sara Thomas.
Licensure Skilled care. *Beds* SNF 192. *Certified* Medicare; Medi-Cal.
Owner Proprietary corp (Care Enterprises).

St Christopher Convalescent Hospital & Sanitarium
1880 Dawson St, Signal Hill, CA 90806
(213) 433-0408
Admin Bernard Hornung.

Licensure Skilled care. *Beds* SNF 59. *Certified* Medicare; Medi-Cal.
Owner Privately owned.

Simi

Simi Valley Adventist Hospital
2975 Sycamore Dr, Simi, CA 93065
(805) 527-2462
Admin Rosalie Tkachuk.

Simi Valley

Hallmark Nursing Center—Simi Valley
5270 Los Angeles Ave, Simi Valley, CA 93063
(805) 527-6204
Admin Janiece M Lackey.
Licensure Skilled care. *Beds* SNF 99. *Certified* Medicare; Medi-Cal.
Owner Proprietary corp.

Solvang

Santa Ynez Valley Recovery Residence
636 Atterdag Rd, Solvang, CA 93463
(805) 688-3263
Admin David M Reyes.
Licensure Skilled care. *Beds* SNF 50. *Certified* Medicare; Medi-Cal.
Owner Nonprofit corp.

Sonoma

Care West—Sonoma Nursing & Rehabilitation Center
1250 Broadway, Sonoma, CA 95476
(707) 938-8406
Admin Judy Johnson.
Licensure Skilled care; Intermediate care. *Beds* SNF 132; ICF 12. *Certified* Medicare; Medi-Cal.
Owner Proprietary corp (Care Enterprises).

London House Convalescent Hospital
678 2nd St W, Sonoma, CA 95476
(707) 938-1096
Admin Donald H Bais.
Medical Dir Richard F H Kirk MD.
Licensure Skilled care. *Beds* SNF 83. *Certified* Medicare; Medi-Cal.
Owner Proprietary corp (Beverly Enterprises).
Admissions Requirements Minimum age 20; Medical examination; Physician's request.
Staff Physicians 1 (pt); RNs 4 (ft); LPNs 5 (ft); Nurses' aides 60 (ft); Physical therapists 1 (pt); Reality therapists 1 (pt); Occupational therapists 1 (pt); Speech therapists 1 (pt); Activities coordinators 1 (ft); Dietitians 1 (ft); Ophthalmologists 1 (pt); Podiatrists 1 (pt); Audiologists 1 (pt); Dentists 1 (pt).
Facilities Dining room; Physical therapy room; Activities room; Crafts room; Laundry room; Barber/Beauty shop.
Activities Arts & crafts; Cards; Games; Reading groups; Prayer groups; Movies; Shopping trips.

Sonoma Acres
765 Donald Ave, Sonoma, CA 95476
(707) 996-2161
Admin Ralph Holder.
Licensure Skilled care. *Beds* SNF 32.
Owner Nonprofit corp.

Sonora

Sonora Convalescent Hospital Inc
538 Ponderosa Dr, Sonora, CA 95370
(209) 532-3668
Licensure Skilled care. *Beds* SNF 36. *Certified* Medicare; Medi-Cal.
Owner Proprietary corp.

Tuolumne General Hospital SNF
101 Hospital Rd, Sonora, CA 95370
(209) 532-3401

Admin J Baker. *Dir of Nursing* K Stanick.
   Medical Dir Dr Munger.
Licensure Skilled care. *Beds* SNF 32. *Certified*
   Medi-Cal.
Owner Nonprofit organization/foundation.
Staff RNs; LPNs; Nurses' aides; Activities
   coordinators; Dietitians.
Facilities Dining room; Activities room;
   Barber/Beauty shop.
Activities Arts & crafts; Cards; Games;
   Reading groups; Prayer groups; Movies; Pet
   therapy.

South Gate

State Convalescent Hospital
8455 State St, South Gate, CA 90280
(213) 564-7761
Admin Aleene Brown.
Medical Dir Yvonne Jones.
Licensure Skilled care. *Beds* SNF 99. *Certified*
   Medicare; Medi-Cal.
Owner Proprietary corp.
Staff RNs 1 (ft), 2 (pt); LPNs 8 (ft), 1 (pt);
   Nurses' aides 34 (ft); Activities coordinators
   1 (ft).
Languages Spanish.
Facilities Dining room; Physical therapy
   room; Activities room; Crafts room; Laundry
   room; Barber/Beauty shop.
Activities Arts & crafts; Cards; Games;
   Reading groups; Prayer groups; Movies.

South Pasadena

South Pasadena Convalescent Hospital
904 Mission St, South Pasadena, CA 91030
(818) 799-9571
Admin Michael Spence. *Dir of Nursing*
   Beverly Fineman RN. *Medical Dir* Dr Barry
   Blum.
Licensure Skilled care; Retirement. *Beds* SNF
   156. *Certified* Medicare; Medi-Cal.
Owner Privately owned.
Admissions Requirements Minimum age 55;
   Medical examination; Physician's request.
Staff Physicians; RNs; LPNs; Nurses' aides;
   Physical therapists; Reality therapists;
   Recreational therapists; Occupational
   therapists; Activities coordinators; Dietitians;
   Ophthalmologists; Podiatrists; Dentists.
Languages Spanish, Japanese, Hebrew,
   Yiddish, Romanian, Hungarian, German,
   French, Italian, Chinese.
Facilities Dining room; Physical therapy
   room; Activities room; Chapel; Crafts room;
   Laundry room; Barber/Beauty shop; Library.
Activities Arts & crafts; Cards; Games;
   Reading groups; Prayer groups; Movies;
   Shopping trips; Dances/Social/Cultural
   gatherings.

Spring Valley

Mt Miguel Covenant Village
325 Kempton St, Spring Valley, CA 92077
(619) 479-4790
Admin Ingrid Kleven. *Dir of Nursing*
   Margaret Olson. *Medical Dir* Andrew
   Alongi.
Licensure Skilled care; Retirement;
   Alzheimer's care. *Beds* SNF 99; Retirement
   260. *Private Pay Patients* 55%. *Certified*
   Medicare; Medi-Cal.
Owner Nonprofit corp (Covenant Retirement
   Communities).
Admissions Requirements Minimum age 62;
   Physician's request.
Staff Physicians 1 (pt); RNs 3 (ft), 4 (pt);
   LPNs 7 (ft), 6 (pt); Nurses' aides 25 (ft), 25
   (pt); Physical therapists 1 (pt); Occupational
   therapists 1 (pt); Speech therapists 1 (pt);
   Activities coordinators 1 (ft), 3 (pt);
   Dietitians 1 (pt); Ophthalmologists 1 (pt);
   Podiatrists 1 (pt); Dentists 1 (pt).
Affiliation Evangelical Covenant Church.

Facilities Dining room; Physical therapy
   room; Activities room; Chapel; Crafts room;
   Laundry room; Barber/Beauty shop; Library;
   Patios; Nature trails.
Activities Arts & crafts; Cards; Games;
   Reading groups; Prayer groups; Movies;
   Dances/Social/Cultural gatherings;
   Intergenerational programs; Pet therapy.

Spring Valley Convalescent Hospital
9009 Campo Rd, Spring Valley, CA 92077
(619) 460-2711
Admin Michael Williams. *Dir of Nursing*
   Dorothy Morse. *Medical Dir* Dr Berger.
Licensure Skilled care. *Beds* SNF 75. *Certified*
   Medicare; Medi-Cal.
Owner Privately owned.
Admissions Requirements Minimum age 38;
   Medical examination; Physician's request.
Staff RNs 2 (ft), 1 (pt); LPNs 8 (ft), 2 (pt);
   Nurses' aides 40 (ft), 4 (pt); Activities
   coordinators 1 (ft).
Facilities Dining room; Physical therapy
   room; Activities room; Crafts room; Laundry
   room; Barber/Beauty shop; Library.
Activities Arts & crafts; Games; Reading
   groups; Prayer groups; Movies; Shopping
   trips; Dances/Social/Cultural gatherings;
   Dining out; Barbeques; Adapt-a-grandparent.

Wilson Manor Convalescent Hospital
8625 La Mar St, Spring Valley, CA 92077
(619) 461-3222
Admin Pam Ferris. *Dir of Nursing* Ann
   Amalfitano. *Medical Dir* Dr Berger.
Licensure Skilled care; Alzheimer's care. *Beds*
   SNF 50. *Certified* Medicare; Medi-Cal.
Owner Proprietary corp.
Admissions Requirements Minimum age 34.
Staff RNs 2 (ft); LPNs 7 (ft), 1 (pt); Nurses'
   aides 20 (ft), 4 (pt); Activities coordinators 1
   (ft).
Facilities Dining room; Physical therapy
   room; Activities room; Crafts room; Laundry
   room; Barber/Beauty shop; Library.
Activities Arts & crafts; Cards; Games;
   Reading groups; Prayer groups; Movies;
   Shopping trips; Dances/Social/Cultural
   gatherings; Candelight dinners; Barbeques;
   Outside entertainment; Adopt-a-grandparent.

Stanton

Quaker Gardens
12151 Dale St, Stanton, CA 90680
(714) 530-9100
Admin Charles Hise. *Dir of Nursing* Bonnie
   Lanz RN. *Medical Dir* Dr Michael Fine.
Licensure Skilled care; Retirement. *Beds* SNF
   58.
Owner Nonprofit corp.
Admissions Requirements Minimum age 62;
   Physician's request.
Staff Physicians; RNs; LPNs; Nurses' aides.
Affiliation Society of Friends.
Facilities Dining room; Activities room;
   Chapel; Crafts room; Laundry room; Barber/
   Beauty shop; Library.
Activities Arts & crafts; Cards; Games;
   Reading groups; Prayer groups; Shopping
   trips; Dances/Social/Cultural gatherings.

Stockton

Beverly Manor of Stockton
2740 N California St, Stockton, CA 95204
(209) 466-3522
Admin Tyah Geer.
Medical Dir George Shilling.
Licensure Skilled care. *Beds* SNF 99. *Certified*
   Medicare; Medi-Cal.
Owner Proprietary corp (Beverly Enterprises).
Admissions Requirements Physician's request.
Staff RNs 10 (ft); LPNs 10 (ft); Nurses' aides
   50 (ft); Recreational therapists 1 (ft);
   Activities coordinators 1 (ft); Dietitians 1
   (ft).

Facilities Dining room; Physical therapy
   room; Activities room; Crafts room; Laundry
   room; Barber/Beauty shop; Library.
Activities Arts & crafts; Cards; Games;
   Reading groups; Prayer groups; Movies;
   Shopping trips; Dances/Social/Cultural
   gatherings.

Carrington Convalescent Hospital
5320 Carrington Ctr, Stockton, CA 95210
(209) 473-3004
Admin Dennis L Toy.
Licensure Skilled care. *Beds* SNF 99. *Certified*
   Medicare; Medi-Cal.
Owner Proprietary corp.

Chateau Convalescent Hospital
1221 Rose Marie Ln, Stockton, CA 95207
(209) 477-2664
Admin Beverly Cortner. *Dir of Nursing*
   Claudia Styles. *Medical Dir* George Schilling
   MD.
Licensure Skilled care; Alzheimer's care. *Beds*
   SNF 106. *Certified* Medicare; Medi-Cal.
Owner Proprietary corp (Beverly Enterprises).
Staff RNs 5 (ft), 8 (pt); LPNs 5 (ft), 3 (pt);
   Nurses' aides 36 (ft), 8 (pt); Dietitians 1 (pt);
   Social service 1 (ft).
Languages Spanish, Tagalog.
Facilities Dining room; Physical therapy
   room; Activities room; Crafts room; Laundry
   room; Barber/Beauty shop.
Activities Arts & crafts; Cards; Games;
   Reading groups; Prayer groups; Movies;
   Shopping trips; Dances/Social/Cultural
   gatherings.

Crestwood Manor
1130 Monaco Ct, Stockton, CA 95207
(209) 478-2060
Admin John L Blaufus. *Dir of Nursing* Candy
   Hayashi. *Medical Dir* John Larson MD.
Licensure Intermediate care for mentally
   retarded. *Beds* ICF/MR 190. *Certified*
   Medicare; Medi-Cal.
Owner Proprietary corp (Crestwood Hospital
   Inc).
Staff Physicians 1 (ft), 6 (pt); RNs 4 (ft), 7
   (pt); LPNs 13 (ft), 12 (pt); Nurses' aides 61
   (ft), 14 (pt); Recreational therapists 1 (ft);
   Activities coordinators 3 (ft), 1 (pt);
   Dietitians 1 (ft); Ophthalmologists 1 (pt);
   Dentists 1 (pt).
Facilities Dining room; Activities room;
   Crafts room; Barber/Beauty shop.
Activities Arts & crafts; Cards; Games;
   Reading groups; Prayer groups; Movies;
   Shopping trips; Dances/Social/Cultural
   gatherings.

Crestwood Manor—Bakersfield
PO Box 7343, Stockton, CA 95207
(805) 366-5757
Admin Jim Garrett.
Medical Dir Arthur Unger MD.
Licensure Skilled care. *Beds* SNF 109.
   Certified Medicare.
Owner Proprietary corp (Crestwood Hospital
   Inc).
Admissions Requirements Minimum age 18.
Facilities Dining room; Activities room;
   Crafts room; Laundry room; Barber/Beauty
   shop; Library.
Activities Arts & crafts; Cards; Games;
   Reading groups; Prayer groups; Movies;
   Shopping trips; Dances/Social/Cultural
   gatherings.

**Crestwood Rehabilitation & Convalescent
Hospital**
442 Hampton St, Stockton, CA 95204
(209) 466-0456
Admin Dawn Martin.
Licensure Skilled care. *Beds* SNF 120.
   Certified Medicare; Medi-Cal.
Owner Proprietary corp (Crestwood Hospital
   Inc).

Delta Valley Convalescent Hospital
1032 N Lincoln St, Stockton, CA 95203
(209) 466-5341
Admin Alfred S Johnson. *Dir of Nursing*
Elizabeth Wright RN. *Medical Dir* Dr
Morishirna.
Licensure Skilled care. *Beds* SNF 68. *Private
Pay Patients* 10-15%. *Certified* Medicare;
Medi-Cal.
Owner Privately owned.
Staff RNs; LPNs; Nurses' aides; Physical
therapists; Activities coordinators.
Facilities Dining room; Physical therapy
room; Activities room; Crafts room; Laundry
room; Barber/Beauty shop; Library.
Activities Arts & crafts; Cards; Games;
Reading groups; Movies; Shopping trips;
Dances/Social/Cultural gatherings; Church
groups.

Elmhaven Convalescent Hospital
6940 Pacific Ave, Stockton, CA 95207
(209) 477-4817
Admin Bernice Wahler.
Licensure Skilled care. *Beds* SNF 128.
Certified Medicare; Medi-Cal.
Owner Proprietary corp (Crestwood Hospital
Inc).

Good Samaritan Rehabilitation & Care Center
1630 N Edison St, Stockton, CA 95204-5674
(209) 948-8762, 465-2827 FAX
Admin Rene B Abas. *Dir of Nursing* Julie
Abrahamson RN. *Medical Dir* Dr
Popplewell.
Licensure Skilled care. *Beds* SNF 98. *Private
Pay Patients* 20%. *Certified* Medicare; Medi-
Cal.
Owner Proprietary corp (Stockton-Edison
Health Care).
Admissions Requirements Medical
examination; Physician's request.
Staff RNs 2 (ft), 2 (pt); LPNs 6 (ft), 4 (pt);
Nurses' aides 35 (ft), 6 (pt); Physical
therapists 1 (ft); Recreational therapists 1
(ft); Occupational therapists 1 (ft); Speech
therapists 1 (ft); Activities coordinators 1
(ft); Dietitians 1 (ft); Ophthalmologists 1
(pt); Podiatrists 1 (pt); Audiologists 1 (pt).
Languages Spanish, Tagalog.
Facilities Dining room; Physical therapy
room; Activities room; Laundry room.
Activities Arts & crafts; Cards; Reading
groups; Prayer groups; Movies; Shopping
trips; Dances/Social/Cultural gatherings;
Intergenerational programs.

Heritage of Stockton
9107 N Davis Rd, Stockton, CA 95209
(209) 952-8362
Admin Judi H Johnson.
Owner Proprietary corp.

Hy-Pana House Convalescent Hospital
4520 N El Dorado, Stockton, CA 95207
(209) 477-0271
Admin Erik Wolfe.
Licensure Skilled care. *Beds* SNF 119.
Certified Medicare; Medi-Cal.
Owner Proprietary corp (Beverly Enterprises).

**La Salette Rehabilitation & Convalescent
Hospital**
537 E Fulton St, Stockton, CA 95204
(209) 466-2066
Admin Norman Allred. *Dir of Nursing* Susan
Hillenberand RNC BSN PhN. *Medical Dir*
A Wu MD.
Licensure Skilled care; Out-patient physical
therapy. *Beds* SNF 122. *Certified* Medicare;
Medi-Cal.
Owner Proprietary corp.
Admissions Requirements Medical
examination; Physician's request.
Staff Physicians 1 (pt); RNs 5 (ft), 2 (pt);
LPNs 10 (ft); Nurses' aides 58 (ft), 20 (pt);
Physical therapists 1 (ft); Speech therapists 1

(pt); Activities coordinators 3 (ft); Dietitians
1 (ft); Ophthalmologists 1 (pt); Social service
1 (ft).
Facilities Dining room; Physical therapy
room; Activities room; Crafts room; Laundry
room; Barber/Beauty shop; Library.
Activities Arts & crafts; Cards; Games;
Reading groups; Prayer groups; Movies;
Shopping trips; Dances/Social/Cultural
gatherings; Animal shows; Adopt-a-
grandparent; Night-time activities.

Plymouth Square
1319 N Madison St, Stockton, CA 95242
(209) 466-4341
Admin Donald Williams. *Dir of Nursing*
Barbara Thomson. *Medical Dir* Yi-Po
Anthony Wu MD MPH.
Licensure Skilled care; Assisted living;
Independent living. *Beds* SNF 38; Assisted
living 21; Independent living 68. *Certified*
Medi-Cal.
Owner Nonprofit organization/foundation
(Retirement Housing Foundation).
Admissions Requirements Minimum age 62;
Medical examination; Physician's request.
Staff Physicians 1 (pt); RNs 2 (ft), 3 (pt);
LPNs 3 (ft), 7 (pt); Nurses' aides 21 (ft), 11
(pt); Physical therapists 1 (pt); Recreational
therapists 2 (ft); Occupational therapists 1
(pt); Speech therapists 1 (pt); Activities
coordinators 2 (ft); Dietitians 1 (pt);
Ophthalmologists 1 (pt); Podiatrists 1 (pt);
Audiologists 1 (pt).
Facilities Dining room; Physical therapy
room; Activities room; Chapel; Crafts room;
Laundry room; Barber/Beauty shop; Library.
Activities Arts & crafts; Cards; Games;
Reading groups; Prayer groups; Movies;
Shopping trips; Dances/Social/Cultural
gatherings; Pet therapy.

Valley Gardens Health Care Center
1517 Knickerbocker, Stockton, CA 95210
(209) 957-4539
Admin Joann Steinmetz.
Licensure Skilled care. *Beds* SNF 120.
Certified Medicare; Medi-Cal.
Owner Proprietary corp.

Wagner Heights Convalescent Hospital
9289 Branstetter Pl, Stockton, CA 95209
(209) 477-5252, 952-8022 FAX
Admin M K Kane. *Dir of Nursing* Angela
Martin RN. *Medical Dir* Dr George
Schilling.
Licensure Skilled care; Residential care 75;
Residential care. *Beds* SNF 152. *Private Pay
Patients* 40%. *Certified* Medicare; Medi-Cal.
Owner Privately owned.
Admissions Requirements Medical
examination.
Staff Physicians; RNs 9 (ft); LPNs 16 (ft);
Nurses' aides 56 (ft); Physical therapists 5
(ft); Reality therapists 2 (ft); Recreational
therapists 2 (ft), 1 (pt); Occupational
therapists 1 (ft); Speech therapists 1 (ft);
Activities coordinators 2 (ft), 1 (pt);
Dietitians 2 (ft); Ophthalmologists 1 (ft);
Podiatrists 1 (ft); Audiologists 1 (ft).
Languages Chinese, Japanese, Russian,
Spanish, French, Italian, Filipino.
Facilities Dining room; Physical therapy
room; Activities room; Chapel; Crafts room;
Laundry room; Barber/Beauty shop;
Enclosed courtyards; Rehabilitation feeding
program and area; Jacuzzi.
Activities Arts & crafts; Cards; Games;
Reading groups; Prayer groups; Movies;
Shopping trips; Dances/Social/Cultural
gatherings; Pet therapy.

Studio City

Imperial Convalescent Hospital
11441 Ventura Blvd, Studio City, CA 91604
(818) 980-8200
Admin Catherine Mason.

Licensure Skilled care. *Beds* SNF 130.
Certified Medi-Cal.
Owner Publicly owned.

Studio City Convalescent Hospital
11429 Ventura Blvd, Studio City, CA 91604
(818) 766-9551
Admin Cvia Rosen. *Dir of Nursing* Tuula
Kauppinen RN. *Medical Dir* Michael Pomo
MD.
Licensure Skilled care. *Beds* SNF 109. *Private
Pay Patients* 40%. *Certified* Medicaid;
Medicare; Medi-Cal.
Owner Proprietary corp.
Admissions Requirements Minimum age 70.
Staff Physicians 15 (pt); RNs 4 (ft); LPNs 6
(ft); Nurses' aides 40 (ft); Physical therapists
1 (pt); Recreational therapists 1 (ft);
Occupational therapists 1 (pt); Speech
therapists 1 (pt); Activities coordinators 1
(ft); Dietitians 1 (ft); Ophthalmologists 1
(pt); Podiatrists 1 (pt); Audiologists 1 (pt);
Dentists 1 (pt).
Languages Spanish, Hebrew, Czech, Finnish,
Rumanian, Tagalog, Other European.
Facilities Dining room; Activities room;
Crafts room; Laundry room; Barber/Beauty
shop; Library.
Activities Arts & crafts; Cards; Games;
Reading groups; Prayer groups; Movies;
Shopping trips; Dances/Social/Cultural
gatherings; Intergenerational programs; Pet
therapy.

Sun City

Sun City Convalescent Center
27600 Encanto Dr, Sun City, CA 92381
(714) 679-6858
Admin Gary P Dickerson.
Medical Dir Dr Rex LaGrange.
Licensure Skilled care. *Beds* SNF 99. *Certified*
Medicare; Medi-Cal.
Owner Privately owned.
Admissions Requirements Minimum age 50;
Physician's request.
Staff RNs 1 (ft), 2 (pt); LPNs 7 (ft), 5 (pt);
Nurses' aides 29 (ft), 7 (pt); Physical
therapists 1 (pt); Activities coordinators 1
(ft).
Facilities Dining room; Physical therapy
room; Activities room; Crafts room; Laundry
room; Barber/Beauty shop.
Activities Arts & crafts; Reading groups;
Prayer groups; Movies; Dances/Social/
Cultural gatherings.

Sunland

Diana Lynn Lodge
8647 Fenwick St, Sunland, CA 91040
(818) 352-1421
Admin Bernard Rosenson.
Licensure Skilled care. *Beds* SNF 120.
Certified Medicare; Medi-Cal.
Owner Proprietary corp.

High Valley Lodge
7912 Topley Ln, Sunland, CA 91040
(818) 352-3158
Admin William Kite. *Dir of Nursing* P Albert.
Medical Dir F Morada MD.
Licensure Skilled care; Intermediate care. *Beds*
Swing beds SNF/ICF 50. *Private Pay
Patients* 5%. *Certified* Medicaid; Medicare;
Medi-Cal.
Owner Proprietary corp.
Admissions Requirements Minimum age 18;
Physician's request.
Staff Physicians 6 (pt); RNs 2 (ft), 1 (pt);
LPNs 6 (ft), 2 (pt); Nurses' aides 30 (ft), 6
(pt); Physical therapists 2 (pt); Reality
therapists 1 (pt); Recreational therapists 1
(pt); Occupational therapists 1 (pt); Speech
therapists 1 (pt); Activities coordinators 1

(ft), 1 (pt); Dietitians 1 (pt);
Ophthalmologists 1 (pt); Podiatrists 1 (pt);
Audiologists 1 (pt).
Languages Spanish, Korean, Farsi.
Affiliation Roman Catholic.
Facilities Dining room; Physical therapy
room; Activities room; Crafts room; Laundry
room; Barber/Beauty shop; Library; Patio;
Semi-private rooms.
Activities Arts & crafts; Cards; Games;
Reading groups; Prayer groups; Movies;
Shopping trips; Dances/Social/Cultural
gatherings; Intergenerational programs; Pet
therapy; Barbecues.

Shadow Hill Convalescent Hospital
10158 Sunland Blvd, Sunland, CA 91040
(818) 353-7800
Admin Orlando Clarizio Jr.
Medical Dir Dr James Johnson.
Licensure Skilled care; Retirement. *Beds* SNF
67. *Certified* Medicare; Medi-Cal.
Owner Proprietary corp.
Staff Physicians 12 (pt); RNs 1 (ft), 1 (pt);
LPNs 6 (ft); Nurses' aides 22 (ft); Physical
therapists 1 (ft); Reality therapists 1 (ft);
Recreational therapists 1 (ft), 1 (pt);
Occupational therapists 1 (pt); Speech
therapists 1 (ft); Activities coordinators 1
(ft); Dietitians 1 (ft); Ophthalmologists 1
(pt); Podiatrists 1 (pt); Dentists 1 (pt).
Languages Spanish, Tagalog.
Facilities Dining room; Physical therapy
room; Activities room; Crafts room; Laundry
room; Barber/Beauty shop.
Activities Arts & crafts; Cards; Games;
Movies; Shopping trips; Dances/Social/
Cultural gatherings.

Sunnyvale

Hy-Lond Convalescent Hospital
797 E Fremont Ave, Sunnyvale, CA 94087
(408) 738-4880
Admin Jean McKerlick.
Licensure Skilled care. *Beds* 99. *Certified*
Medicare; Medi-Cal.
Owner Privately owned.

Idylwood Acres Convalescent Hospital
1002 Fremont Ave, Sunnyvale, CA 94087
(408) 739-2383
Admin Adriana T Baams.
Licensure Skilled care. *Beds* SNF 185.
Certified Medicare; Medi-Cal.
Owner Proprietary corp.

Sunnyvale Convalescent Hospital
1291 S Bernardo Ave, Sunnyvale, CA 94087
(408) 245-8070
Admin Tom Heath.
Licensure Skilled care. *Beds* SNF 99. *Certified*
Medicare; Medi-Cal.
Owner Proprietary corp.

Susanville

Care West—Susanville Nursing Center
2005 River St, Susanville, CA 96130
(916) 257-5341
Admin Gerald Hamilton.
Medical Dir Dr Kenneth Korver.
Licensure Skilled care. *Beds* SNF 96. *Certified*
Medicare; Medi-Cal.
Owner Proprietary corp (Care Enterprises).
Admissions Requirements Physician's request.
Staff RNs 4 (ft), 1 (pt); LPNs 10 (ft), 1 (pt);
Nurses' aides 46 (ft); Physical therapists 1
(pt); Speech therapists 1 (pt); Activities
coordinators 1 (ft); Dietitians 1 (pt);
Podiatrists 1 (pt); Audiologists 1 (pt);
Dentists 1 (pt).
Facilities Dining room; Physical therapy
room; Activities room; Laundry room;
Barber/Beauty shop; Library.
Activities Arts & crafts; Cards; Games;
Movies; Shopping trips.

Lassen Community Skilled Nursing Facility
560 Hospital Ln, Susanville, CA 96130
(916) 257-5325
Admin Frank Weston. *Dir of Nursing* Estella
Olson. *Medical Dir* Dorothy Hoskamer.
Licensure Skilled care. *Beds* SNF 31. *Private
Pay Patients* 10%. *Certified* Medicare; Medi-
Cal.
Owner Proprietary corp.
Admissions Requirements Physician's request.
Staff Physicians 1 (pt); RNs 1 (ft), 1 (pt);
LPNs 2 (ft), 4 (pt); Nurses' aides 8 (ft), 8
(pt); Physical therapists 1 (pt); Occupational
therapists 1 (pt); Speech therapists 1 (pt);
Activities coordinators 1 (ft); Dietitians 1
(pt); Podiatrists 1 (pt); Audiologists 1 (pt).
Affiliation Roman Catholic.
Facilities Dining room; Laundry room;
Barber/Beauty shop.
Activities Arts & crafts; Cards; Games;
Reading groups; Prayer groups; Movies;
Shopping trips; Dances/Social/Cultural
gatherings; Intergenerational programs; Pet
therapy.

Sylmar

Astoria Convalescent Hospital
14040 Astoria St, Sylmar, CA 91342
(818) 367-5881
Admin Raquel Haas. *Dir of Nursing* D Jeanne
Phinney. *Medical Dir* Gary Prophet.
Licensure Skilled care; Retirement;
Alzheimer's care. *Beds* SNF 218. *Certified*
Medicare; Medi-Cal.
Owner Proprietary corp.
Admissions Requirements Minimum age 65;
Medical examination; Physician's request.
Staff Physicians 40 (pt); RNs 6 (ft), 2 (pt);
LPNs 12 (ft), 4 (pt); Nurses' aides 60 (ft), 5
(pt); Physical therapists 3 (pt); Reality
therapists 1 (ft); Recreational therapists 1
(ft); Occupational therapists 2 (pt); Speech
therapists 1 (pt); Activities coordinators 2
(ft); Dietitians 1 (pt); Ophthalmologists 2
(pt); Podiatrists 2 (pt); Dentists 1 (pt).
Languages Spanish.
Facilities Dining room; Physical therapy
room; Activities room; Crafts room; Barber/
Beauty shop; Library.
Activities Arts & crafts; Cards; Games;
Reading groups; Prayer groups; Movies;
Shopping trips; Dances/Social/Cultural
gatherings; Theater group.

Crestwood Convalescent Hospital
14122 Hubbard St, Sylmar, CA 91342
(818) 361-0191
Admin Kent Berkey.
Medical Dir Harold Cohen MD.
Licensure Skilled care. *Beds* SNF 59. *Certified*
Medicare; Medi-Cal.
Owner Proprietary corp (Crestwood Hospitals
Inc).
Staff RNs 3 (ft); LPNs 8 (ft), 4 (pt); Nurses'
aides 16 (ft), 1 (pt); Activities coordinators 1
(ft); Dietitians 1 (pt).
Facilities Dining room; Physical therapy
room; Activities room; Laundry room;
Barber/Beauty shop; Library.
Activities Arts & crafts; Cards; Games;
Movies; Shopping trips; Dances/Social/
Cultural gatherings.

Foothill Health & Rehabilitation Center
12260 Foothill Blvd, Sylmar, CA 91342
(818) 899-9545
Admin Kenton Brenegan.
Medical Dir J Clarfield MD.
Licensure Skilled care. *Beds* SNF 204.
Certified Medi-Cal.
Owner Nonprofit corp.
Facilities Dining room; Activities room;
Crafts room; Laundry room; Barber/Beauty
shop; Library.

Activities Arts & crafts; Cards; Games;
Reading groups; Prayer groups; Movies;
Shopping trips; Dances/Social/Cultural
gatherings.

Mountain View Sanitarium
13333 Fenton Ave, Sylmar, CA 91342
(818) 367-1033
Admin Norman A Zecca. *Dir of Nursing* Ethel
Riggs RN. *Medical Dir* Robert Skelton MD.
Licensure Skilled care. *Beds* SNF 114.
Certified Medicare; Medi-Cal.
Owner Privately owned.
Admissions Requirements Minimum age 50;
Medical examination.
Staff Physicians 8 (pt); RNs 5 (ft), 3 (pt);
LPNs 5 (ft); Nurses' aides 40 (ft), 5 (pt);
Physical therapists 1 (pt); Recreational
therapists 1 (pt); Occupational therapists 1
(pt); Speech therapists 1 (pt); Activities
coordinators 2 (ft); Dietitians 1 (pt);
Ophthalmologists 1 (pt); Podiatrists 1 (pt);
Dentists 1 (pt).
Facilities Dining room; Physical therapy
room; Activities room; Barber/Beauty shop.
Activities Arts & crafts; Cards; Games;
Reading groups; Prayer groups; Movies;
Dances/Social/Cultural gatherings; Outings;
Trips to ocean and parks; Luncheons;
Picnics.

**United Cerebral Palsy/Spastic Children's
Foundation**
12831 Maclay St, Sylmar, CA 91342
(818) 365-8081
Admin A Mae Stephenson.
Medical Dir Charles Parker.
Licensure Skilled care; Intermediate care. *Beds*
141. *Certified* Medi-Cal.
Owner Nonprofit corp.
Admissions Requirements Minimum age 16.
Staff Physicians 4 (pt); RNs 7 (ft); LPNs 7
(ft); Nurses' aides 70 (ft); Physical therapists
1 (pt); Recreational therapists 1 (pt);
Occupational therapists 1 (pt); Speech
therapists 1 (pt); Activities coordinators 1
(ft); Dietitians 1 (pt); Ophthalmologists 2
(pt); Podiatrists 1 (pt); Dentists 2 (pt).
Facilities Dining room; Physical therapy
room; Activities room; Crafts room; Laundry
room; Barber/Beauty shop; Library;
Educational classrooms.
Activities Arts & crafts; Cards; Games;
Reading groups; Prayer groups; Movies;
Shopping trips; Non-verbal communication
training.

Taft

Pacific Regency/Taft
111 W Ash St, Taft, CA 93268
(805) 763-3333
Admin Vera Traffanstedt. *Dir of Nursing*
Mona Vekas RN. *Medical Dir* T Hasadsri
MD.
Licensure Skilled care. *Beds* SNF 34. *Certified*
Medicare; Medi-Cal.
Owner Privately owned.
Admissions Requirements Medical
examination; Physician's request.
Staff RNs 3 (ft); LPNs 3 (ft), 4 (pt); Nurses'
aides 15 (ft), 10 (pt); Activities coordinators
1 (ft).
Facilities Dining room; Laundry room;
Barber/Beauty shop.
Activities Arts & crafts; Cards; Games;
Reading groups; Prayer groups; Movies;
Shopping trips; Dances/Social/Cultural
gatherings.

Tarzana

Tarzana Health Care Center
5650 Reseda Blvd, Tarzana, CA 91356
(818) 881-4261, 343-7451 FAX

Admin Peter Stong. *Dir of Nursing* Mary
Ghamkhari. *Medical Dir* Edwin Seligson
MD.
Licensure Skilled care. *Beds* SNF 192. *Private
Pay Patients* 28%. *Certified* Medicare; Medi-
Cal.
Owner Proprietary corp (American Medical
Services Inc).
Admissions Requirements Minimum age 55;
Physician's request.
Staff RNs 8 (ft), 2 (pt); LPNs 18 (ft), 2 (pt);
Nurses' aides 68 (ft); Physical therapists 2
(pt); Occupational therapists 1 (pt); Speech
therapists 1 (pt); Activities coordinators 4
(ft); Dietitians 1 (pt).
Languages Spanish, Tagalog, Farsi.
Facilities Dining room; Physical therapy
room; Activities room; Crafts room; Laundry
room; Barber/Beauty shop; Library; Gift
shop; 2 indoor patios.
Activities Arts & crafts; Cards; Games;
Reading groups; Prayer groups; Movies;
Shopping trips; Dances/Social/Cultural
gatherings; Intergenerational programs.

Temple City

Evergreen Convalescent Center Inc
10786 Live Oak Ave, Temple City, CA 91780
(818) 447-5404
Admin Lawanda Olson. *Dir of Nursing* John
Hudson RN. *Medical Dir* Jack Baker MD.
Licensure Skilled care. *Beds* SNF 59. *Certified*
Medicare; Medi-Cal.
Owner Proprietary corp (American Health
Care Inc).
Admissions Requirements Minimum age 18;
Physician's request.
Staff Physicians 1 (pt); RNs 1 (ft), 1 (pt);
Physical therapists 1 (pt); Occupational
therapists 1 (pt); Speech therapists 1 (pt);
Activities coordinators 1 (ft); Dietitians 1
(pt); Ophthalmologists 1 (pt); Podiatrists 1
(pt); Dentists 1 (pt); LVNs 3 (ft), 3 (pt);
CNAs 21 (ft).
Languages Spanish, Tagalog, Chinese.
Facilities Dining room; Physical therapy
room; Activities room; Laundry room;
Barber/Beauty shop; Patio.
Activities Arts & crafts; Cards; Games;
Reading groups; Prayer groups; Movies;
Shopping trips; Dances/Social/Cultural
gatherings.

Santa Anita Convalescent Hospital
5522 Gracewood Ave, Temple City, CA 91780
(818) 579-0310
Admin Israel Bastomski. *Dir of Nursing* Gail
Azain RN. *Medical Dir* Dr Marianne
Scarborough.
Licensure Skilled care; Retirement;
Alzheimer's care. *Beds* SNF 391. *Certified*
Medicare; Medi-Cal.
Owner Proprietary corp.
Admissions Requirements Minimum age 18;
Medical examination; Physician's request.
Staff Physicians 1 (ft); RNs 6 (ft), 7 (pt);
LPNs 30 (ft), 10 (pt); Nurses' aides 101 (ft),
5 (pt); Physical therapists 1 (ft); Recreational
therapists 1 (ft), 1 (pt); Occupational
therapists 1 (pt); Speech therapists 1 (pt);
Activities coordinators 7 (ft); Dietitians 1
(pt); Ophthalmologists 1 (pt); Dentists 1 (pt).
Languages Italian, Spanish, French, Japanese,
Chinese.
Facilities Dining room; Physical therapy
room; Activities room; Chapel; Crafts room;
Laundry room; Barber/Beauty shop; Library.
Activities Arts & crafts; Cards; Games;
Reading groups; Prayer groups; Movies;
Shopping trips; Dances/Social/Cultural
gatherings.

Temple City Convalescent Hospital
5101 Tyler Ave, Temple City, CA 91780
(818) 443-3028
Admin Brian Elliott.

Licensure Skilled care. *Beds* SNF 59. *Certified*
Medicare; Medi-Cal.
Owner Proprietary corp.

Templeton

Twin Cities Convalescent Center
290 Heather Ct, Templeton, CA 93465
(805) 434-3035
Admin Gailan L Nichols.
Licensure Skilled care. *Beds* SNF 99. *Certified*
Medicare; Medi-Cal.
Owner Proprietary corp.

Thousand Oaks

Thousand Oaks Health Care Center
93 W Avenida de los Arboles, Thousand Oaks,
CA 91360
(818) 889-0286
Admin Jane Borlaug. *Dir of Nursing* Sharon
Fischer.
Licensure Skilled care. *Beds* SNF 124.
Certified Medicare; Medi-Cal.
Owner Proprietary corp (American-Cal
Medical Services Inc).
Admissions Requirements Physician's request.
Staff Physicians; RNs 10 (ft); LPNs 20 (ft);
Nurses' aides 30 (ft), 25 (ft); Physical
therapists 3 (pt); Reality therapists 1 (pt);
Recreational therapists 1 (pt); Occupational
therapists 1 (pt); Speech therapists 1 (pt);
Activities coordinators 1 (ft), 1 (pt);
Dietitians; Ophthalmologists.
Facilities Dining room; Physical therapy
room; Activities room; Laundry room;
Barber/Beauty shop.
Activities Arts & crafts; Cards; Games;
Reading groups; Prayer groups; Movies;
Shopping trips; Dances/Social/Cultural
gatherings; Barbeques; Cooking class; Pet
therapy.

Tiburon

Marin Convalescent & Rehabilitation Hospital
30 Hacienda Dr, Tiburon, CA 94920
(415) 435-4554
Admin Mary E Kelly. *Dir of Nursing* Claire
Nadeay. *Medical Dir* Dr Thomas Stone.
Licensure Skilled care; Alzheimer's care. *Beds*
SNF 56. *Private Pay Patients* 100%.
Owner Proprietary corp.
Admissions Requirements Physician's request.
Staff Physicians 1 (pt); RNs 4 (ft), 4 (pt);
LPNs 2 (ft), 1 (pt); Physical therapists 2 (pt);
Occupational therapists 1 (pt); Speech
therapists 1 (pt); Activities coordinators 2
(pt); Dietitians 1 (pt); Podiatrists 1 (pt).
Facilities Dining room; Physical therapy
room; Activities room; Crafts room; Laundry
room; Barber/Beauty shop; Library.
Activities Arts & crafts; Cards; Games;
Reading groups; Prayer groups; Movies;
Shopping trips; Pet therapy.

Torrance

Bay Crest Care Center
3750 Garnet St, Torrance, CA 90503
(213) 371-2431
Admin Michelle A Brozowski. *Dir of Nursing*
Linda Williams. *Medical Dir* Dr Harold C
Dorin.
Licensure Skilled care. *Beds* SNF 80. *Private
Pay Patients* 41%. *Certified* Medicare; Medi-
Cal.
Owner Proprietary corp (Summit Care).
Admissions Requirements Minimum age 40;
Medical examination.
Staff RNs 1 (ft), 1 (pt); LPNs 6 (ft), 4 (pt);
Physical therapists (contracted); Recreational
therapists (contracted); Occupational
therapists (contracted); Speech therapists
(contracted); Activities coordinators 1 (ft), 1
(pt); Dietitians (contracted).

Languages Spanish.
Facilities Dining room; Activities room;
Laundry room; Barber/Beauty shop.
Activities Arts & crafts; Cards; Games;
Reading groups; Prayer groups; Movies;
Shopping trips; Intergenerational programs.

Bay Harbor Rehabilitation Center
3620 Lomita Blvd, Torrance, CA 90505
(213) 378-8587, 375-6992 FAX
Admin Douglas Lehnhoff. *Dir of Nursing*
Marian J Williams RN. *Medical Dir* Dr
Louis Magdaleno.
Licensure Skilled care. *Beds* SNF 212. *Private
Pay Patients* 65%. *Certified* Medi-Cal.
Owner Nonprofit corp (Harbor Health
Systems Inc).
Staff Physicians 2 (ft); RNs 10 (ft); LPNs 23
(ft); Nurses' aides 75 (ft); Physical therapists
10 (ft); Recreational therapists 5 (ft);
Occupational therapists 6 (ft); Speech
therapists 2 (ft); Activities coordinators 1
(ft); Dietitians 1 (ft); Ophthalmologists 1 (ft);
Podiatrists 1 (ft); Social workers 3 (ft).
Languages Spanish.
Facilities Dining room; Physical therapy
room; Activities room; Crafts room; Laundry
room; Barber/Beauty shop.
Activities Arts & crafts; Cards; Games;
Reading groups; Prayer groups; Movies;
Shopping trips; Dances/Social/Cultural
gatherings; Intergenerational programs.

Best Care Convalescent Hospital
22035 S Vermont Ave, Torrance, CA 90502
(213) 775-6427
Admin Maurice L Playford.
Licensure Skilled care; Intermediate care. *Beds*
SNF 194; ICF 6. *Certified* Medicare; Medi-
Cal.
Owner Proprietary corp.

Del Amo Gardens Convalescent Hospital
22419 Kent Ave, Torrance, CA 90505
(213) 378-4233
Admin Carol Demarco.
Licensure Skilled care. *Beds* SNF 94. *Certified*
Medicare; Medi-Cal.
Owner Privately owned.

Driftwood Convalescent Center
4109 Emerald Ave, Torrance, CA 90503
(213) 371-4628
Admin Kamran Dideban. *Dir of Nursing* Betty
J Riker. *Medical Dir* Brice T Martin MD.
Licensure Skilled care. *Beds* SNF 99. *Certified*
Medicare; Medi-Cal.
Owner Proprietary corp (Western Medical
Enterprises Inc).
Admissions Requirements Minimum age 18.
Staff RNs 1 (ft), 1 (pt); LPNs 8 (ft), 2 (pt);
Nurses' aides 32 (ft); Recreational therapists
1 (ft); Dietitians 1 (pt).
Languages Spanish, Tagalog.
Facilities Dining room; Physical therapy
room; Activities room; Crafts room; Laundry
room; Barber/Beauty shop.
Activities Arts & crafts; Cards; Games;
Reading groups; Prayer groups; Movies;
Shopping trips; Dances/Social/Cultural
gatherings; Picnics; Olympiatrics; Barbeques;
Music & singing; Zoo animals.

Earlwood Care Center
20820 Earl St, Torrance, CA 90503
(213) 371-1228
Admin Margaret Dockter. *Dir of Nursing*
Mary Lou Snudden RN. *Medical Dir* Dale
Vandenbrink MD.
Licensure Skilled care; Retirement. *Beds* SNF
87; Retirement 49. *Private Pay Patients*
66%. *Certified* Medicare; Medi-Cal.
Owner Proprietary corp (Summit Care Inc).
Admissions Requirements Minimum age 18;
Medical examination; Physician's request.
Staff Physicians (contracted); RNs 3 (ft);
LPNs 9 (ft), 2 (pt); Nurses' aides 25 (ft), 2
(pt); Physical therapists (contracted); Reality

therapists (contracted); Recreational therapists (contracted); Occupational therapists (contracted); Speech therapists (contracted); Activities coordinators 1 (ft), 1 (pt); Dietitians (contracted); Ophthalmologists (contracted); Podiatrists (contracted); Audiologists (contracted).
Languages Spanish.
Facilities Dining room; Activities room; Laundry room; Barber/Beauty shop; Library; Living room with fireplace and large-screen TV; 2 Resident lobbies.
Activities Arts & crafts; Cards; Games; Reading groups; Prayer groups; Movies; Shopping trips; Dances/Social/Cultural gatherings; Intergenerational programs; Pet therapy; On-site programs by community churches; Special events.

Harbor Convalescent Hospital
21521 S Vermont Ave, Torrance, CA 90502
(213) 320-0961
Admin Angelica Villanueva.
Licensure Skilled care. *Beds* SNF 127. *Certified* Medicare; Medi-Cal.
Owner Proprietary corp.

Heritage Convalescent Center
21414 S Vermont Ave, Torrance, CA 90502
(213) 320-8714
Admin Samuel G Bergstrom. *Dir of Nursing* Angela Tang RN. *Medical Dir* Wing Mar MD.
Licensure Skilled care; Alzheimer's care. *Beds* SNF 166. *Certified* Medicare; Medi-Cal.
Owner Proprietary corp.
Admissions Requirements Minimum age 45.
Staff RNs 14 (ft), 3 (pt); LPNs 20 (ft); Nurses' aides 80 (ft), 10 (pt); Occupational therapists 1 (ft); Speech therapists 1 (ft); Activities coordinators 2 (ft); Dietitians 1 (ft); Ophthalmologists 1 (ft); Podiatrists 1 (ft).
Languages French, Chinese, Tagalog, Spanish.
Facilities Dining room; Physical therapy room; Activities room; Chapel; Crafts room; Laundry room; Barber/Beauty shop; Library; Coffee shop.
Activities Arts & crafts; Cards; Games; Reading groups; Prayer groups; Movies; Shopping trips; Dances/Social/Cultural gatherings.

Mira Costa Convalescent Hospital
4320 Miracopa St, Torrance, CA 90503
(213) 542-5555
Admin Warren R Bratland.
Licensure Skilled care. *Beds* 124. *Certified* Medi-Cal.
Owner Proprietary corp (Care Enterprises).

Royalwood Care Center
22520 Maple Ave, Torrance, CA 90505
(213) 326-9131
Admin Kellie Neuman.
Medical Dir Dr Harry Silver.
Licensure Skilled care. *Beds* SNF 110. *Certified* Medicare; Medi-Cal.
Owner Proprietary corp (Summit Care).
Staff Physicians 1 (pt); RNs 13 (ft); LPNs 21 (ft); Physical therapists 1 (pt); Reality therapists 1 (pt); Recreational therapists 1 (ft); Occupational therapists 1 (pt); Speech therapists 1 (pt); Activities coordinators 1 (ft); Dietitians 1 (ft); Ophthalmologists 1 (pt); Podiatrists 1 (pt); Audiologists 1 (pt); Dentists 1 (pt).
Facilities Dining room; Physical therapy room; Activities room; Crafts room; Laundry room; Barber/Beauty shop.
Activities Arts & crafts; Cards; Games; Reading groups; Prayer groups; Movies.

Sunnyside Nursing Center
22617 S Vermont Ave, Torrance, CA 90502
(213) 320-4130
Admin Harry L McNamara.
Medical Dir Dr Allan Greenberg.

Licensure Skilled care. *Beds* SNF 299. *Certified* Medicare; Medi-Cal.
Owner Proprietary corp.
Staff Physicians 15 (pt); RNs 7 (ft), 4 (pt); LPNs 18 (ft), 5 (pt); Nurses' aides 100 (ft), 25 (pt); Physical therapists 1 (ft), 3 (pt); Recreational therapists 6 (ft); Occupational therapists 1 (pt); Speech therapists 1 (pt); Dietitians 1 (pt); Ophthalmologists 1 (pt); Podiatrists 1 (pt); Dentists 1 (pt).
Facilities Dining room; Physical therapy room; Activities room; Crafts room; Laundry room; Barber/Beauty shop; Library.
Activities Arts & crafts; Cards; Games; Reading groups; Prayer groups; Movies; Dances/Social/Cultural gatherings; Outings.

Torrance
4315 Torrance Blvd, Torrance, CA 90503
(213) 772-5782
Admin Glenn Kishaba.
Medical Dir Dr George Csengeri.
Licensure Skilled care; Intermediate care. *Beds* SNF 95; ICF 4. *Certified* Medicare; Medi-Cal.
Owner Privately owned.
Admissions Requirements Minimum age 18; Physician's request.
Staff Physicians 1 (pt); RNs 3 (ft), 3 (pt); LPNs 7 (ft); Nurses' aides 25 (ft), 10 (pt); Physical therapists 2 (pt); Occupational therapists 1 (pt); Speech therapists 1 (pt); Activities coordinators 1 (ft); Dietitians 1 (pt); Ophthalmologists 1 (pt); Podiatrists 1 (pt); Dentists 1 (pt).
Facilities Dining room; Physical therapy room; Activities room; Chapel; Crafts room; Laundry room; Barber/Beauty shop; Library.
Activities Arts & crafts; Cards; Games; Reading groups; Prayer groups; Movies.

West Torrance Care Center
4333 Torrance Blvd, Torrance, CA 90503
(213) 370-4561
Admin Glenn Kishaba.
Licensure Skilled care. *Beds* SNF 96. *Certified* Medicare; Medi-Cal.
Owner Privately owned.

Tracy

Careage of Tracy
2586 Buthmann Rd, Tracy, CA 95376
(209) 832-2273
Admin Ruby Rakow.
Licensure Skilled care. *Beds* SNF 99. *Certified* Medicare; Medi-Cal.
Owner Proprietary corp.

Tracy Convalescent Hospital
545 W Beverly Pl, Tracy, CA 95376
(209) 835-6034
Admin George G Ramirez. *Dir of Nursing* Mary McReynalds. *Medical Dir* H L McClelland MD.
Licensure Skilled care. *Beds* SNF 59. *Certified* Medicare; Medi-Cal.
Owner Proprietary corp.
Admissions Requirements Medical examination; Physician's request.
Staff Physicians 1 (pt); RNs 2 (ft), 1 (pt); LPNs 3 (ft); Nurses' aides 18 (ft); Physical therapists; Recreational therapists; Occupational therapists; Speech therapists; Activities coordinators 1 (ft); Dietitians; Ophthalmologists; Podiatrists; Dentists.
Languages Spanish, Japanese, German, Portuguese.
Facilities Dining room; Physical therapy room; Activities room; Chapel; Crafts room; Laundry room; Barber/Beauty shop; Library.
Activities Arts & crafts; Cards; Games; Reading groups; Prayer groups; Movies; Shopping trips.

Truckee

Tahoe Forest Hospital D/P SNF
Box 759, Truckee, CA 95734
(916) 587-6011
Admin James W Maki.
Licensure Skilled care. *Certified* Medicare; Medi-Cal.

Tujunga

Bay Shore Sanitarium
10105 Commerce Ave, Tujunga, CA 91042-2312
(213) 372-2090
Admin James M Lewis Jr.
Licensure Skilled care. *Beds* SNF 49. *Certified* Medicare; Medi-Cal.
Owner Nonprofit corp.

Care West—Wyngate Nursing Center
7660 Wyngate St, Tujunga, CA 91042
(818) 352-1454
Admin C T McDonald.
Licensure Skilled care. *Beds* SNF 92. *Certified* Medicare; Medi-Cal.
Owner Proprietary corp (Care Enterprises).

Oakview Convalescent Hospital
9166 Tujunga Canyon, Tujunga, CA 91042
(818) 352-4426
Admin Margaret Paliwoda. *Dir of Nursing* Elaine Martin RN. *Medical Dir* Leland Watkins MD.
Licensure Skilled care. *Beds* SNF 49. *Certified* Medicare.
Owner Proprietary corp (Oakview Health Care Inc).
Admissions Requirements Medical examination.
Staff RNs 2 (ft), 1 (pt); LPNs 7 (ft); Nurses' aides 12 (ft); Physical therapists (consultant); Reality therapists (consultant); Recreational therapists (consultant); Occupational therapists (consultant); Speech therapists (consultant); Activities coordinators 1 (ft), 1 (pt); Dietitians 1 (ft); Ophthalmologists (consultant); Podiatrists (consultant); Audiologists (consultant).
Languages Spanish, Filipino.
Facilities Dining room; Physical therapy room; Activities room; Crafts room; Laundry room; Barber/Beauty shop; Library.
Activities Arts & crafts; Cards; Games; Reading groups; Prayer groups; Movies; Dances/Social/Cultural gatherings; Intergenerational programs; Pet therapy.

Tulare

Merritt Manor Convalescent Hospital
604 E Merritt, Tulare, CA 93274
(209) 686-1601
Admin D Marlene Luiz. *Dir of Nursing* Marlene Overbeck RN. *Medical Dir* I M Schor MD.
Licensure Skilled care; Intermediate care. *Beds* SNF 78; ICF 20. *Private Pay Patients* 15-18%. *Certified* Medicare; Medi-Cal.
Owner Proprietary corp.
Admissions Requirements Medical examination; Physician's request.
Staff RNs 1 (ft), 1 (pt); LPNs 9 (ft); Nurses' aides 40 (ft), 10 (pt); Physical therapists (contracted); Occupational therapists (contracted); Speech therapists (contracted); Activities coordinators 2 (ft); Dietitians (contracted); Ophthalmologists (contracted); Podiatrists (contracted); Audiologists (contracted).
Languages Spanish, Portuguese.
Facilities Dining room; Activities room; Crafts room; Laundry room; Barber/Beauty shop; TV room.

Activities Arts & crafts; Cards; Games; Reading groups; Prayer groups; Movies; Shopping trips; Dances/Social/Cultural gatherings; Intergenerational programs; Pet therapy.

Terrace Park Convalescent Hospital
680 E Merritt, Tulare, CA 93274
(209) 686-8581
Admin D Marlene Luiz. *Dir of Nursing* Jean DiSieno RN. *Medical Dir* I M Schor MD.
Licensure Skilled care; Intermediate care. *Beds* SNF 91; ICF 6. *Private Pay Patients* 15-18%. *Certified* Medicare; Medi-Cal.
Owner Proprietary corp.
Admissions Requirements Medical examination; Physician's request.
Staff Physicians (contracted); RNs 1 (ft), 3 (pt); LPNs 10 (ft), 4 (pt); Nurses' aides 40 (ft), 10 (pt); Physical therapists (contracted); Occupational therapists (contracted); Speech therapists (contracted); Activities coordinators 2 (ft); Dietitians (contracted); Ophthalmologists (contracted); Podiatrists (contracted); Audiologists (contracted).
Languages Spanish, Portuguese.
Facilities Dining room; Activities room; Crafts room; Laundry room; Barber/Beauty shop; TV room.
Activities Arts & crafts; Cards; Games; Reading groups; Prayer groups; Movies; Shopping trips; Dances/Social/Cultural gatherings; Intergenerational programs; Pet therapy.

Turlock

Bel-Air Lodge Convalescent Hospital
180 Starr Ave, Turlock, CA 95380
(209) 632-1075
Admin Mary E Baker.
Licensure Skilled care. *Beds* SNF 31. *Certified* Medi-Cal.
Owner Proprietary corp (Mark One Corp).

Brandel Manor
1801 N Olive Ave, Turlock, CA 95380
(209) 667-4200
Admin John Trussler.
Medical Dir Robert Clark MD. *Certified* Medicare; Medi-Cal.
Owner Nonprofit corp.
Admissions Requirements Medical examination; Physician's request.
Staff RNs 6 (ft), 6 (pt); LPNs 8 (ft), 4 (pt); Nurses' aides 31 (ft), 30 (pt).
Affiliation Evangelical Covenant Church.
Facilities Dining room; Physical therapy room; Activities room; Chapel; Crafts room; Barber/Beauty shop; Smoking room.
Activities Arts & crafts; Games; Reading groups; Prayer groups; Movies; Shopping trips; Dances/Social/Cultural gatherings.

Elness Convalescent Hospital
812 W Main St, Turlock, CA 95380
(209) 667-2828
Admin Mary E Baker.
Licensure Skilled care. *Beds* SNF 99. *Certified* Medicare; Medi-Cal.
Owner Proprietary corp (Mark One Corp).

Turlock Convalescent Hospital
1111 E Tuolumne Rd, Turlock, CA 95380
(209) 632-7577
Admin Craig A Haupt.
Licensure Skilled care. *Beds* SNF 144. *Certified* Medicare; Medi-Cal.
Owner Proprietary corp.

Tustin

Tustin Manor
1051 Bryan St, Tustin, CA 92680
(714) 832-6780
Admin Donald J Beld.

Licensure Intermediate care. *Beds* 99. *Certified* Medi-Cal.
Owner Proprietary corp.

Western Neuro Care Center
165 N Myrtle St, Tustin, CA 92680
(714) 832-9200
Admin Sharon J Lucas.
Licensure Skilled care. *Beds* SNF 59. *Certified* Medicare.
Owner Proprietary corp.

Ukiah

Emerald Hills Skilled Nursing
333 Laws Ave, Ukiah, CA 95482
(707) 463-2336
Admin Kimbereley Marie Morgan. *Dir of Nursing* Patricia DeHesus RN MA. *Medical Dir* Theron Chan MD.
Licensure Skilled care; Intermediate care. *Beds* SNF 64; ICF 8. *Certified* Medicaid; Medicare; Medi-Cal.
Owner Proprietary corp.
Languages Spanish.
Facilities 26-bed special care unit.
Activities Arts & crafts; Cards; Games; Reading groups; Prayer groups; Movies; Shopping trips; Dances/Social/Cultural gatherings; Intergenerational programs; Pet therapy.

Mendocino Skilled Nursing Facility
131 Whitmore Ln, Ukiah, CA 95482
(707) 462-6636
Admin Renate Fassbender.
Licensure Skilled care. *Beds* SNF 113. *Certified* Medicare; Medi-Cal.
Owner Proprietary corp.

Ukiah Convalescent Hospital
1349 S Dora St, Ukiah, CA 95482
(707) 462-8864
Admin Constance M Nugent.
Licensure Skilled care. *Beds* SNF 58. *Certified* Medicare; Medi-Cal.
Owner Proprietary corp.

Valley View Skilled Nursing Center
1162 S Dora St, Ukiah, CA 95482
(707) 462-1436
Admin Nancy Hopp. *Dir of Nursing* Lorraine Vanoven RN. *Medical Dir* Bernard Lemke MD.
Licensure Skilled care. *Beds* SNF 68. *Certified* Medicare; Medi-Cal.
Owner Proprietary corp.
Admissions Requirements Physician's request.
Staff Physicians; RNs; LPNs; Nurses' aides; Physical therapists; Occupational therapists; Speech therapists; Activities coordinators; Dietitians; Ophthalmologists; Dentists.
Facilities Dining room; Physical therapy room; Activities room; Crafts room; Laundry room; Barber/Beauty shop.
Activities Arts & crafts; Cards; Games; Reading groups; Prayer groups; Shopping trips.

Union City

Masonic Home
34400 Mission Blvd, Union City, CA 94587
(415) 471-3434
Licensure Skilled care. *Beds* SNF 167.
Owner Proprietary corp.

Upland

Palm Vista Care Center
1207 E 14th St, Upland, CA 91786
(818) 962-7095
Admin Malvina C Preyer. *Dir of Nursing* Arlene Bumgarner RN.
Licensure Skilled care; Intermediate care. *Beds* SNF 93; ICF 4. *Certified* Medicare; Medi-Cal.

Owner Proprietary corp.
Admissions Requirements Minimum age 40; Medical examination; Physician's request.
Staff RNs 1 (ft), 1 (pt); LPNs 7 (ft), 2 (pt); Nurses' aides 35 (ft), 10 (pt); Activities coordinators 1 (ft).
Languages Spanish.
Facilities Dining room; Physical therapy room; Activities room; Crafts room; Barber/Beauty shop.
Activities Arts & crafts; Cards; Games; Reading groups; Prayer groups; Movies; Dances/Social/Cultural gatherings.

Shea Convalescent Hospital
867 E 11th St, Upland, CA 91786
(714) 985-1981
Admin Leona M Porcelli.
Medical Dir Sue Corey.
Licensure Skilled care; Retirement. *Beds* SNF 99. *Certified* Medicare; Medi-Cal.
Owner Proprietary corp.
Admissions Requirements Minimum age 55.
Staff RNs; LPNs; Nurses' aides; Physical therapists; Recreational therapists; Occupational therapists; Speech therapists; Activities coordinators; Dietitians; Ophthalmologists.
Facilities Dining room; Physical therapy room; Activities room; Crafts room; Laundry room; Barber/Beauty shop.
Activities Arts & crafts; Cards; Games; Reading groups; Prayer groups; Movies.

Upland Convalescent Hospital
1221 E Arrow Hwy, Upland, CA 91786
(714) 985-1903
Admin James W Milton.
Medical Dir C Sanborn Jr MD.
Licensure Skilled care. *Beds* SNF 216. *Certified* Medicare; Medi-Cal.
Owner Proprietary corp.
Admissions Requirements Minimum age 18.
Staff Physicians; RNs; LPNs; Nurses' aides; Physical therapists; Recreational therapists; Occupational therapists; Speech therapists; Dietitians; Ophthalmologists; Podiatrists; Audiologists; Dentists; Gerontological nurse practitioners.
Facilities Dining room; Physical therapy room; Activities room; Laundry room; Barber/Beauty shop.
Activities Arts & crafts; Cards; Games; Reading groups; Prayer groups; Movies.

Vacaville

Creekside Care Convalescent Hospital
585 Nut Tree Court, Vacaville, CA 95687
(707) 449-8000
Admin Richard Schachten.
Licensure Skilled care; Intermediate care. *Beds* SNF 99; ICF 21. *Certified* Medicare; Medi-Cal.
Owner Proprietary corp.

Windsor House Convalescent Hospital
101 S Orchard St, Vacaville, CA 95688
(707) 448-6458
Admin Richard Schachten.
Licensure Skilled care. *Beds* SNF 87. *Certified* Medicare; Medi-Cal.
Owner Proprietary corp.

Vallejo

Crestwood Convalescent Hospital
2200 Tuolumne, Vallejo, CA 94590
(707) 644-7401
Admin Joan Bosworth.
Licensure Skilled care. *Beds* SNF 166. *Certified* Medicare; Medi-Cal.
Owner Proprietary corp (Crestwood Hospitals Inc).

Crestwood Manor—Vallejo
2201 Tuolumne, Vallejo, CA 94590
(707) 552-0215
Admin George Lytal.
Medical Dir Matthew Gibbons MD.
Licensure Intermediate care for mentally
retarded. *Beds* ICF/MR 102. *Certified* Medi-
Cal.
Owner Proprietary corp (Crestwood Hospitals
Inc).
Admissions Requirements Minimum age 18;
Medical examination; Physician's request.
Staff Physicians 2 (pt); RNs 6 (ft), 2 (pt);
LPNs 2 (ft); Nurses' aides 20 (ft);
Occupational therapists 1 (ft); Activities
coordinators 1 (ft); Dietitians 1 (pt);
Ophthalmologists 1 (pt); Podiatrists 1 (pt);
Dentists 1 (pt).
Facilities Dining room; Activities room;
Crafts room; Laundry room; Barber/Beauty
shop.
Activities Arts & crafts; Cards; Games;
Reading groups; Prayer groups; Movies;
Shopping trips; Dances/Social/Cultural
gatherings.

Heartwood Avenue Living Center
1044 Heartwood Ave, Vallejo, CA 94590
(707) 643-2793
Admin Bruce C Strayer.
Medical Dir Alan Plutchok MD.
Licensure Skilled care. *Beds* SNF 59. *Certified*
Medicare; Medi-Cal.
Owner Proprietary corp.
Admissions Requirements Minimum age;
Medical examination; Physician's request.
Staff Physicians 1 (pt); RNs 2 (ft), 3 (pt);
LPNs 3 (ft), 3 (pt); Nurses' aides 19 (ft), 5
(pt); Occupational therapists 1 (pt);
Activities coordinators 1 (ft); Dietitians 1
(pt); Podiatrists 1 (pt); Dentists 1 (pt).
Facilities Dining room; Activities room;
Crafts room; Barber/Beauty shop; Library.
Activities Arts & crafts; Cards; Games;
Reading groups; Prayer groups; Movies;
Shopping trips; Dances/Social/Cultural
gatherings.

Louisiana Living Center
1101 Louisiana St, Vallejo, CA 94590
(707) 643-2793
Admin Bruce C Strayer.
Medical Dir Alan Plutchok MD.
Licensure Skilled care. *Beds* SNF 37. *Certified*
Medicare; Medi-Cal.
Owner Proprietary corp.
Admissions Requirements Minimum age 18;
Medical examination; Physician's request.
Staff Physicians 1 (pt); RNs 3 (ft), 3 (pt);
LPNs 1 (ft), 2 (pt); Nurses' aides 10 (ft), 4
(pt); Occupational therapists 1 (pt);
Activities coordinators 1 (ft); Dietitians 1
(pt); Podiatrists 1 (pt); Dentists 1 (pt).
Facilities Dining room; Activities room;
Crafts room; Barber/Beauty shop; Library.
Activities Arts & crafts; Cards; Games;
Reading groups; Prayer groups; Movies;
Shopping trips; Dances/Social/Cultural
gatherings.

Springs Road Living Center
1527 Springs Rd, Vallejo, CA 94590
(707) 643-2795
Admin Bruce C Strayer.
Medical Dir Alan Plutchok MD.
Licensure Skilled care. *Beds* SNF 62. *Certified*
Medicare; Medi-Cal.
Owner Proprietary corp.
Admissions Requirements Minimum age 18;
Medical examination; Physician's request.
Staff RNs 1 (ft), 5 (pt); LPNs 4 (ft), 1 (pt);
Nurses' aides 20 (ft), 8 (pt); Occupational
therapists 1 (pt); Activities coordinators 1
(ft); Dietitians 1 (pt); Podiatrists 1 (pt);
Dentists 1 (pt).

Facilities Dining room; Activities room;
Crafts room; Barber/Beauty shop; Library.
Activities Arts & crafts; Cards; Games;
Reading groups; Prayer groups; Movies;
Shopping trips; Dances/Social/Cultural
gatherings.

Vallejo Convalescent Hospital
900 Sereno Dr, Vallejo, CA 94589
(707) 643-8453
Admin Shirley O Sassman. *Dir of Nursing*
Alice Bettencourt. *Medical Dir* Dr Rubin
Velasquez.
Licensure Skilled care. *Beds* SNF 99. *Private
Pay Patients* 30%. *Certified* Medicare; Medi-
Cal.
Owner Proprietary corp (Medicrest).
Admissions Requirements Physician's request.
Staff Physicians 10 (pt); RNs 6 (ft); LPNs 6
(ft); Nurses' aides 15 (ft), 50 (pt); Physical
therapists 1 (ft); Occupational therapists 1
(pt); Speech therapists 2 (pt); Activities
coordinators 2 (ft); Dietitians 1 (pt);
Podiatrists 1 (pt).
Languages Spanish, Tagalog.
Facilities Dining room; Physical therapy
room; Activities room; Laundry room;
Barber/Beauty shop.
Activities Arts & crafts; Cards; Games;
Reading groups; Prayer groups; Movies;
Shopping trips; Dances/Social/Cultural
gatherings; Intergenerational programs; Pet
therapy.

Van Nuys

Balowen Care Center
16955 Vanowen St, Van Nuys, CA 91406
(818) 343-0700, 996-8670 FAX
Admin Dava A Downey. *Dir of Nursing*
Virginia S Clores RN. *Medical Dir* Dr H
Caplan.
Licensure Skilled care; Alzheimer's care. *Beds*
SNF 50. *Private Pay Patients* 50%. *Certified*
Medicare; Medi-Cal.
Owner Proprietary corp.
Admissions Requirements Medical
examination; Physician's request.
Staff RNs; LPNs; Nurses' aides; Physical
therapists; Activities coordinators; Dietitians.
Languages Spanish, Tagalog.
Facilities Dining room; Activities room;
Laundry room; Barber/Beauty shop.
Activities Arts & crafts; Games; Reading
groups; Prayer groups; Movies; Pet therapy.

Beverly Manor Convalescent Hospital
6700 Sepulveda Blvd, Van Nuys, CA 91401
(818) 988-2501
Admin Donald C Phillips. *Dir of Nursing*
Margaret White RN. *Medical Dir* R
Panchanathan MD.
Licensure Skilled care. *Beds* SNF 201.
Certified Medicare; Medi-Cal.
Owner Proprietary corp (Beverly Enterprises).
Admissions Requirements Minimum age 18;
Medical examination; Physician's request.
Staff RNs; LPNs; Nurses' aides.
Facilities Dining room; Physical therapy
room; Activities room; Crafts room; Laundry
room; Barber/Beauty shop; Library.
Activities Arts & crafts; Cards; Games;
Reading groups; Prayer groups; Movies;
Shopping trips; Dances/Social/Cultural
gatherings.

Hillhaven Healthcare
6600 Sepulveda Blvd, Van Nuys, CA 91411
(818) 786-0020
Admin Barbara J Davis. *Dir of Nursing*
Marilyn Riddleberger. *Medical Dir* Dr S
Ong.
Licensure Skilled care. *Beds* SNF 125. *Private
Pay Patients* 65%. *Certified* Medicare; Medi-
Cal.
Owner Proprietary corp (Hillhaven Corp).
Admissions Requirements Medical
examination; Physician's request.

Staff Physicians; RNs; LPNs; Nurses' aides;
Physical therapists; Recreational therapists;
Occupational therapists; Speech therapists;
Activities coordinators; Dietitians.
Languages Spanish.
Facilities Dining room; Physical therapy
room; Activities room; Crafts room; Laundry
room; Barber/Beauty shop; Library;
Rehabilitation department.
Activities Arts & crafts; Cards; Games;
Reading groups; Prayer groups; Movies;
Shopping trips; Dances/Social/Cultural
gatherings; Intergenerational programs; Pet
therapy; Religious services.

Sepulveda Convalescent Hospital Inc
5510 Sepulveda Blvd, Van Nuys, CA 91411
(818) 782-6800
Admin Ray Wark.
Licensure Skilled care. *Beds* SNF 115.
Certified Medicare; Medi-Cal.
Owner Proprietary corp.
Admissions Requirements Physician's request.
Staff RNs 4 (ft), 3 (pt); LPNs 8 (ft), 4 (pt);
Nurses' aides 26 (ft), 7 (pt); Activities
coordinators 1 (ft), 1 (pt).
Languages Spanish, Tagalog, Greek, Turkish,
Chinese, Korean.
Facilities Dining room; Physical therapy
room; Activities room; Crafts room; Laundry
room; Barber/Beauty shop; Library.
Activities Arts & crafts; Cards; Games; Prayer
groups; Movies; Dances/Social/Cultural
gatherings.

Sherwood Convalescent Hospital
13524 Sherman Way, Van Nuys, CA 91402
(818) 786-3470
Admin Robert Ives. *Dir of Nursing* Laura
Rogenson RN. *Medical Dir* Dr Edwin
Marcus.
Licensure Skilled care; Retirement. *Beds* SNF
99. *Certified* Medicare; Medi-Cal.
Owner Proprietary corp.
Staff RNs 4 (ft); LPNs 13 (ft); Nurses' aides
28 (ft); Physical therapists 1 (ft);
Recreational therapists 1 (ft); Speech
therapists 1 (ft); Activities coordinators 1
(ft); Dietitians 1 (ft); Ophthalmologists 1 (ft);
Dentists 1 (ft).
Languages Spanish, Hebrew, Yiddish.
Facilities Dining room; Physical therapy
room; Activities room; Crafts room; Laundry
room; Barber/Beauty shop; Library.
Activities Arts & crafts; Cards; Games;
Reading groups; Prayer groups; Movies;
Shopping trips.

Sunair Home for Asthmatic Children
5817 Nagle Ave, Van Nuys, CA 91401-4026
(818) 352-1461
Admin Damon DeCrow.
Licensure Intermediate care. *Beds* 39.
Certified Medi-Cal.
Owner Nonprofit corp.
Admissions Requirements Minimum age 5;
Medical examination.
Staff Physicians 1 (pt); RNs 4 (ft), 1 (pt);
LPNs 2 (ft), 1 (pt); Recreational therapists 1
(pt); Speech therapists 1 (pt); Activities
coordinators 1 (pt); Dietitians 1 (pt).
Facilities Dining room; Activities room;
Crafts room; Laundry room; Library.
Activities Arts & crafts; Games; Reading
groups; Movies; Shopping trips; Dances/
Social/Cultural gatherings.

Van Nuys Health Care
6835 Hazeltine Ave, Van Nuys, CA 91405
(818) 997-1841
Admin Dorothy Woodruff.
Medical Dir S Humayun MD.
Licensure Skilled care; Alzheimer's care. *Beds*
SNF 58. *Private Pay Patients* 50%. *Certified*
Medi-Cal.
Owner Proprietary corp (American-Cal
Medical Services Inc).

Ventura

Community Memorial Hospital San Buenaventura
Loma Vista at Brent, Ventura, CA 93003
(805) 648-7811
Owner Proprietary corp.

Ventura Convalescent Hospital
4020 Loma Vista Rd, Ventura, CA 93003
(805) 642-4196
Admin Roger T Shea.
Licensure Skilled care. *Beds* SNF 71. *Certified* Medicare; Medi-Cal.
Owner Proprietary corp.

Venturan Convalescent Center
4904 Telegraph Rd, Ventura, CA 93003
(805) 642-4101
Admin Linda G Pickel.
Licensure Skilled care. *Beds* SNF 99. *Certified* Medicare; Medi-Cal.
Owner Proprietary corp.

Verdugo City

Rockhaven Sanitarium
2713 Honolulu Ave, Verdugo City, CA 91046
(818) 249-2838
Admin Patricia Traviss.
Licensure Skilled care. *Beds* SNF 80.
Owner Proprietary corp.

Victorville

Desert Knolls Convalescent Hospital
14973 Hesperia Rd, Victorville, CA 92392
(619) 245-1558
Admin Gary L Bechtold.
Licensure Skilled care. *Beds* SNF 126. *Certified* Medicare; Medi-Cal.
Owner Proprietary corp.

Knolls West Convalescent Hospital
16890 Green Tree Blvd, Victorville, CA 92392
(619) 245-5361
Admin Gary L Bechtold.
Licensure Skilled care. *Beds* SNF 58. *Certified* Medicare; Medi-Cal.
Owner Privately owned.

Visalia

Delta Convalescent Hospital
514 N Bridge St, Visalia, CA 93291
(209) 732-8614
Admin Mary L Marchbanks.
Licensure Skilled care. *Beds* SNF 39. *Certified* Medicare; Medi-Cal.
Owner Privately owned.

Kaweah Manor Convalescent Hospital
3710 W Tulare Ave, Visalia, CA 93277
(209) 732-2244
Admin John Barna.
Licensure Skilled care. *Beds* SNF 99. *Certified* Medicare; Medi-Cal.
Owner Proprietary corp.

Linwood Gardens Convalescent Center
4444 W Meadow Ln, Visalia, CA 93277
(209) 627-1241
Admin Mary L Marchbanks.
Medical Dir E P Brauner MD.
Licensure Skilled care. *Beds* SNF 98. *Certified* Medicare; Medi-Cal.
Owner Proprietary corp (Medicrest of California Inc).
Admissions Requirements Medical examination; Physician's request.
Staff RNs 1 (ft), 3 (pt); LPNs 8 (ft); Nurses' aides 45 (ft), 10 (pt); Physical therapists 1 (ft); Speech therapists 1 (pt); Activities coordinators 1 (ft); Dietitians 1 (ft), 1 (pt).
Facilities Dining room; Physical therapy room; Activities room; Crafts room; Laundry room; Barber/Beauty shop.
Activities Arts & crafts; Cards; Games; Reading groups; Prayer groups; Movies; Shopping trips; Dances/Social/Cultural gatherings.

Visalia Convalescent Hospital
1925 E Houston St, Visalia, CA 93277
(209) 732-6661
Admin Delores L Helberg. *Dir of Nursing* Wanda Madden. *Medical Dir* L D Farrelly MD.
Licensure Skilled care; Intermediate care. *Beds* SNF 151; ICF 24. *Certified* Medicare; Medi-Cal.
Owner Proprietary corp.
Admissions Requirements Physician's request.
Staff Physicians 40 (pt); RNs 4 (ft), 1 (pt); LPNs 13 (ft), 4 (pt); Nurses' aides 58 (ft), 16 (pt); Recreational therapists 1 (ft); Occupational therapists 1 (pt); Speech therapists 1 (pt); Activities coordinators 1 (ft); Dietitians 1 (ft); Ophthalmologists 1 (pt).
Languages Spanish.
Facilities Dining room; Physical therapy room; Activities room; Crafts room; Laundry room; Barber/Beauty shop; Covered patio.
Activities Arts & crafts; Cards; Games; Reading groups; Prayer groups; Movies; Shopping trips; Dances/Social/Cultural gatherings.

Westgate Gardens Convalescent Center
4525 W Tulare Ave, Visalia, CA 93277
(209) 733-0901
Admin Gerald Williamson.
Licensure Skilled care. *Beds* SNF 140. *Certified* Medicare; Medi-Cal.
Owner Proprietary corp.

Vista

Garden Terrace Healthcare Center
247 E Bobier Dr, Vista, CA 92083
(619) 945-3033
Admin Victor V Tose.
Licensure Skilled care. *Beds* SNF 187.
Owner Proprietary corp.

Rancho Vista Health Center
760 E Bobier Dr, Vista, CA 92083
(619) 941-1480
Admin Kayda Johnson.
Licensure Skilled care; Intermediate care. *Beds* SNF 41; ICF 18.
Owner Proprietary corp (National Heritage).

Vista Del Mar Care Center
304 N Melrose Dr, Vista, CA 92083
(619) 724-8222
Admin David W Denton.
Licensure Skilled care. *Beds* SNF 176. *Certified* Medicare; Medi-Cal.
Owner Proprietary corp.

Walnut Creek

Elm Manor Convalescent Center
1310 Creekside Dr, Walnut Creek, CA 94596
(415) 947-1611
Admin Christina M Rial. *Dir of Nursing* Noreen Gentsch. *Medical Dir* Dennis Stone MD.
Licensure Skilled care. *Beds* SNF 42. *Certified* Medicare; Medi-Cal.
Owner Privately owned.
Admissions Requirements Medical examination; Physician's request.
Staff RNs 1 (ft), 4 (pt); LPNs 4 (ft), 2 (pt); Nurses' aides 11 (ft), 2 (pt); Activities coordinators 1 (ft).
Languages Spanish.
Facilities Dining room; Activities room; Laundry room; Outside patio with each room.
Activities Arts & crafts; Cards; Games; Reading groups; Prayer groups; Movies; Shopping trips; Dances/Social/Cultural gatherings; Intergenerational programs; Pet therapy.

Rossmoor Manor
1224 Rossmoor Pkwy, Walnut Creek, CA 94595
(415) 937-7450
Admin Eva Hecker. *Dir of Nursing* Dorothy Almquist RN. *Medical Dir* Roland Schoen MD.
Licensure Skilled care. *Beds* SNF 180. *Certified* Medicare; Medi-Cal.
Owner Proprietary corp (Guardian Foundation Inc).
Admissions Requirements Physician's request.
Staff RNs 13 (ft), 3 (pt); Nurses' aides 75 (ft); Physical therapists 1 (ft); Activities coordinators 1 (ft); LVNs 11 (ft).
Languages German, Spanish, French, Tagalog.
Facilities Dining room; Physical therapy room; Activities room; Crafts room; Laundry room; Barber/Beauty shop; Library; Lounges; Sundeck.
Activities Arts & crafts; Cards; Games; Reading groups; Prayer groups; Movies; Dances/Social/Cultural gatherings; Live entertainment.

San Marco Convalescent Hospital
130 Tampico St, Walnut Creek, CA 94598
(415) 933-7970
Licensure Skilled care. *Beds* SNF 128. *Certified* Medicare; Medi-Cal.
Owner Proprietary corp.

Walnut Creek Convalescent Hospital Inc
2015 Mount Diablo Blvd, Walnut Creek, CA 94596
(415) 935-2222
Admin Anne Morgan. *Dir of Nursing* Jan Saale RN.
Licensure Skilled care. *Beds* SNF 93. *Certified* Medicare.
Owner Nonprofit organization/foundation (Guardian Foundation Inc).
Admissions Requirements Medical examination; Physician's request.
Staff RNs 2 (ft), 4 (pt); LPNs; Nurses' aides.
Facilities Dining room; Barber/Beauty shop.
Activities Arts & crafts; Cards; Games; Prayer groups; Movies; Shopping trips.

Ygnacio Convalescent Hospital
1449 Ygnacio Valley, Walnut Creek, CA 94598
(415) 939-5820
Admin Zona Kalustian.
Licensure Skilled care. *Beds* SNF 99. *Certified* Medicare.
Owner Nonprofit organization/foundation (Guardian Foundation Inc).

Watsonville

Valley Convalescent Hospital
919 Freedom Blvd, Watsonville, CA 95076
(408) 722-3581
Admin Richard Murphy.
Licensure Skilled care. *Beds* SNF 59. *Certified* Medicare; Medi-Cal.
Owner Proprietary corp.

Watsonville Care Center East
421 Arthur Rd, Watsonville, CA 95076
(408) 724-0671
Admin Dennis Cox. *Dir of Nursing* Mary Andrews. *Medical Dir* Dr Stephen Smith.
Licensure Skilled care. *Beds* SNF 87. *Private Pay Patients* 12%. *Certified* Medicare; Medi-Cal; VA.
Owner Proprietary corp (Care Enterprises).
Admissions Requirements Minimum age 18; Physician's request.

Staff RNs; LPNs; Nurses' aides; Physical therapists (contracted); Activities coordinators; Dietitians (contracted); Podiatrists (contracted); Audiologists (contracted).
Facilities Dining room; Physical therapy room; Activities room; Crafts room; Barber/Beauty shop.
Activities Arts & crafts; Cards; Games; Reading groups; Prayer groups; Movies; Shopping trips; Dances/Social/Cultural gatherings; Intergenerational programs; Pet therapy.

Watsonville Care Center West
425 Arthur Rd, Watsonville, CA 95076
(408) 724-7505
Admin Frankie Ingram.
Licensure Skilled care. *Beds* SNF 95. *Certified* Medicare; Medi-Cal.
Owner Proprietary corp (Care Enterprises).

Weed

Care West—Weed Nursing Center
445 Park St, Weed, CA 96094
(916) 938-4429
Admin Gary Ralston. *Dir of Nursing* Annemetta Olsen RN. *Medical Dir* W S Williams MD.
Licensure Skilled care. *Beds* SNF 59. *Certified* Medicare; Medi-Cal.
Owner Proprietary corp (Care Enterprises).
Admissions Requirements Physician's request.
Staff RNs 1 (ft), 1 (pt); LPNs 4 (ft), 2 (pt); Nurses' aides 10 (ft), 6 (pt); Recreational therapists 1 (ft).
Languages Italian.
Facilities Dining room; Physical therapy room; Activities room; Crafts room; Laundry room; Barber/Beauty shop.
Activities Arts & crafts; Cards; Games; Reading groups; Prayer groups; Movies; Shopping trips; Dances/Social/Cultural gatherings.

West Covina

Ambassador Convalescent Hospital
1495 W Cameron Ave, West Covina, CA 91790
(818) 962-4461, 338-2771 FAX
Admin Jim Scanlon. *Dir of Nursing* Janet Herrera. *Medical Dir* P F Lagross MD.
Licensure Skilled care. *Beds* SNF 99. *Certified* Medicare; Medi-Cal.
Owner Proprietary corp (ARA Living Centers).
Admissions Requirements Minimum age 50.
Staff RNs 4 (ft); LPNs 10 (ft); Nurses' aides 40 (ft); Physical therapists 2 (ft); Reality therapists 1 (ft); Recreational therapists 1 (ft); Occupational therapists 1 (ft); Speech therapists 1 (ft); Activities coordinators 1 (ft); Dietitians 1 (ft); Ophthalmologists 1 (pt); Podiatrists 1 (pt); Audiologists 1 (pt).
Languages Spanish.
Facilities Dining room; Physical therapy room; Activities room; Laundry room; Barber/Beauty shop.
Activities Arts & crafts; Games; Reading groups; Shopping trips; Pet therapy.

Beverly Manor Convalescent Hospital
850 S Sunkist Ave, West Covina, CA 91790
(818) 962-3368
Admin Dorothy Pratt. *Dir of Nursing* Lorraine Magner RN. *Medical Dir* Forrest Tennant MD.
Licensure Skilled care. *Beds* SNF 97. *Certified* Medicare; Medi-Cal.
Owner Proprietary corp (Beverly Enterprises).
Admissions Requirements Minimum age 40; Physician's request.
Staff RNs 2 (ft), 1 (pt); LPNs 5 (ft), 3 (pt); Nurses' aides 25 (ft), 10 (pt); Activities coordinators 1 (ft).

Languages Spanish.
Facilities Dining room; Physical therapy room; Activities room; Crafts room; Laundry room; Barber/Beauty shop.
Activities Arts & crafts; Cards; Games; Reading groups; Prayer groups; Movies; Shopping trips; Dances/Social/Cultural gatherings.

Colonial Manor Convalescent Hospital
919 N Sunset, West Covina, CA 91790
(818) 962-4489
Admin Barbara Risinger.
Licensure Skilled care. *Beds* SNF 54. *Certified* Medicare; Medi-Cal.
Owner Proprietary corp.

Hospice of the East San Gabriel Valley
820 N Phillips Ave, West Covina, CA 91791
(818) 331-2626
Licensure Skilled care. *Beds* SNF 10. *Certified* Medicare; Medi-Cal.
Owner Proprietary corp.

Lark Ellen Towers Skilled Nursing Facility
1350 San Bernardino Rd, West Covina, CA 91790
(818) 966-7558
Admin Samuel Mintz MD. *Dir of Nursing* Pat Jorgensen RN. *Medical Dir* S Dhand MD.
Licensure Skilled care; Retirement. *Beds* SNF 40; Retirement 110. *Certified* Medicare.
Owner Proprietary corp.
Admissions Requirements Minimum age 65; Medical examination.
Staff Physicians 1 (ft), 2 (pt); RNs 1 (ft), 2 (pt); LPNs 3 (ft), 3 (pt); Nurses' aides 10 (ft), 3 (pt).
Facilities Dining room; Activities room; Laundry room; Barber/Beauty shop; Library; Independence Hall for movies; Parties.
Activities Arts & crafts; Cards; Games; Reading groups; Movies; Shopping trips; Dances/Social/Cultural gatherings.

Stocker Home for Women—Clara Baldwin Stocker
527 S Valinda Ave, West Covina, CA 91790
(213) 962-7151
Admin Robert P Mullender. *Dir of Nursing* Lorraine Salter RN. *Medical Dir* Dr Bradley.
Licensure Skilled care. *Beds* SNF 48.
Owner Nonprofit corp.
Admissions Requirements Minimum age 60; Medical examination; Physician's request.
Staff Physicians 1 (pt); RNs 3 (ft), 3 (pt); LPNs 3 (ft); Nurses' aides 23 (ft), 9 (pt); Activities coordinators 2 (ft); Dietitians 1 (pt); Ophthalmologists 1 (pt).
Languages Spanish, Japanese, French.
Facilities Dining room; Physical therapy room; Activities room; Crafts room; Laundry room; Barber/Beauty shop; Library.
Activities Arts & crafts; Cards; Games; Reading groups; Prayer groups; Movies.

West Sacramento

Somerset Golden State Convalescent Hospital
2215 Oakmont Way, West Sacramento, CA 95691
(916) 371-1890
Admin Donald J Hunter. *Dir of Nursing* Elsebeth Bryant RN. *Medical Dir* Shu Chen MD.
Licensure Skilled care; Alzheimer's care. *Beds* SNF 99. *Certified* Medicare; Medi-Cal.
Owner Proprietary corp.
Staff Physicians 1 (pt); RNs 5 (ft), 4 (pt); LPNs 4 (ft), 2 (pt); Nurses' aides 40 (ft), 6 (pt); Activities coordinators 1 (ft), 1 (pt); Dietitians 1 (ft).
Facilities Dining room; Physical therapy room; Activities room; Crafts room; Laundry room; Barber/Beauty shop.

Activities Arts & crafts; Cards; Games; Reading groups; Prayer groups; Movies; Shopping trips; Dances/Social/Cultural gatherings; Outings; Special dinners; Music.

Westminster

FHP Westminster Skilled Nursing Facility
206 Hospital Circle, Westminster, CA 92683
(714) 891-2769
Licensure Skilled care. *Beds* SNF 99. *Certified* Medicare; Medi-Cal.
Owner Proprietary corp (Care Enterprises).

Hy-Lond Convalescent Hospital
240 Hospital Circle, Westminster, CA 92683
(714) 892-6686
Admin Steve Pritt. *Dir of Nursing* Beverly Heberden. *Medical Dir* Dr Rifat.
Licensure Skilled care; Alzheimer's care. *Beds* SNF 99. *Certified* Medicare; Medi-Cal.
Owner Proprietary corp (Beverly Enterprises).
Admissions Requirements Physician's request.
Staff RNs 5 (ft), 4 (pt); LPNs 7 (ft), 3 (pt); Nurses' aides 23 (ft), 19 (pt); Activities coordinators 1 (ft); Social Services 1 (pt).
Languages German, Swedish, Spanish.
Facilities Dining room; Physical therapy room; Activities room; Crafts room; Laundry room; Barber/Beauty shop.
Activities Arts & crafts; Cards; Games; Reading groups; Prayer groups; Movies; Shopping trips; Dances/Social/Cultural gatherings; Self help & improvement skills.

Stanley Convalescent Hospital
14102 Springdale St, Westminster, CA 92683
(714) 893-0026
Admin Greg Goings. *Dir of Nursing* Susanne Kellogg RN. *Medical Dir* John D Cowles MD.
Licensure Skilled care. *Beds* SNF 30. *Certified* Medicare.
Owner Privately owned.
Staff Physicians 3 (pt); RNs 5 (pt); LPNs 2 (pt); Nurses' aides 8 (ft); Activities coordinators 1 (ft).
Languages Spanish, Polish, Arabic, German.
Facilities Dining room; Activities room; Crafts room; Laundry room; Barber/Beauty shop.
Activities Arts & crafts; Games; Reading groups; Movies.

Whittier

Beemans Sanitarium
14015 E Telegraph Rd, Whittier, CA 90604
(213) 944-3292, 941-0116
Admin Ann Whitefoot.
Medical Dir Donn D Beeman MD.
Licensure Skilled care. *Beds* SNF 74. *Certified* Medi-Cal.
Owner Proprietary corp.
Admissions Requirements Minimum age 45.
Staff Physicians 1 (ft); RNs 1 (ft), 1 (pt); LPNs 8 (ft); Nurses' aides 30 (ft); Activities coordinators 1 (ft); Dietitians 1 (ft).
Facilities Dining room; Activities room; Chapel; Crafts room; Laundry room; Barber/Beauty shop.
Activities Arts & crafts; Cards; Games; Movies; Church services; Exercise program; Yoga; Birthday parties once monthly; Ice cream social once monthly; Money management for country store.

Berryman Health—East Whittier
10426 Bogardus Ave, Whittier, CA 90603
(213) 691-2291
Admin Julie Campbell. *Dir of Nursing* Sheryle Williams RN.
Licensure Skilled care. *Beds* SNF 160. *Certified* Medicare; Medi-Cal.
Owner Proprietary corp (Beverly Enterprises).
Admissions Requirements Medical examination.

Staff Physicians; RNs; LPNs; Nurses' aides; Physical therapists; Reality therapists; Recreational therapists; Occupational therapists; Speech therapists; Activities coordinators; Dietitians; Ophthalmologists; Podiatrists; Dentists.
Facilities Dining room; Physical therapy room; Activities room; Crafts room; Laundry room; Barber/Beauty shop; Library.
Activities Arts & crafts; Cards; Games; Reading groups; Prayer groups; Movies; Shopping trips; Dances/Social/Cultural gatherings.

Berryman Health—West Whittier
12385 E Washington, Whittier, CA 90606
(213) 693-6470
Admin Ann E Koeckritz. *Dir of Nursing* Renee Bedard RN. *Medical Dir* Randolf Holmes MD.
Licensure Skilled care. *Beds* SNF 162. *Certified* Medicare; Medi-Cal.
Owner Proprietary corp.
Admissions Requirements Medical examination; Physician's request.
Staff RNs 15 (ft); LPNs 5 (ft), 10 (pt); Nurses' aides 35 (ft), 15 (pt); Physical therapists 1 (pt); Occupational therapists 1 (pt); Speech therapists 1 (pt); Activities coordinators 2 (ft); Dietitians 1 (pt); Ophthalmologists 1 (pt); Podiatrists 1 (pt); Dentists 1 (pt); Social workers 1 (ft), 1 (pt).
Facilities Dining room; Physical therapy room; Activities room; Crafts room; Laundry room; Barber/Beauty shop; Library.
Activities Arts & crafts; Cards; Games; Reading groups; Prayer groups; Movies; Dances/Social/Cultural gatherings; Exercise; Outings; In-room activities.

Doctor's Convalescent Hospital
7926 S Painter Ave, Whittier, CA 90602
(213) 693-5618
Admin Lucille Boulenaz.
Medical Dir Lawrence Pollock.
Licensure Skilled care. *Beds* SNF 36. *Certified* Medi-Cal.
Owner Privately owned.
Admissions Requirements Minimum age 21; Medical examination; Physician's request.
Staff Physicians 1 (pt); RNs 1 (ft), 2 (pt); LPNs 2 (ft), 3 (pt); Nurses' aides 13 (ft), 1 (pt); Physical therapists 1 (pt); Recreational therapists 1 (pt); Occupational therapists 1 (pt); Speech therapists 1 (pt); Activities coordinators 1 (ft); Dietitians 1 (pt); Ophthalmologists 1 (pt); Podiatrists 2 (pt); Audiologists 1 (pt); Dentists 1 (pt).

Shea Convalescent Hospital
7716 S Pickering Ave, Whittier, CA 90602
(213) 693-9229
Admin Marolyn Stahl.
Licensure Skilled care. *Beds* SNF 54. *Certified* Medicare; Medi-Cal.
Owner Proprietary corp.

Sorenson Convalescent Hospital
7931 Sorenson Ave, Whittier, CA 90606
(213) 698-0451
Admin Doris M Ruff.
Licensure Skilled care. *Beds* SNF 59. *Certified* Medicare; Medi-Cal.
Owner Proprietary corp.

Williams

Valley West Convalescent Hospital
PO Box 1059, Williams, CA 95987
(916) 473-5321
Admin Deborah Murillo.
Medical Dir Charles McCarl MD.
Licensure Skilled care. *Beds* SNF 59. *Certified* Medicare; Medi-Cal.
Owner Proprietary corp.
Admissions Requirements Medical examination; Physician's request.

Staff Physicians 8 (ft); RNs 8 (ft); LPNs 7 (ft); Nurses' aides 20 (ft); Physical therapists 1 (ft); Speech therapists 1 (pt); Activities coordinators 1 (ft); Dietitians 1 (pt); Podiatrists 1 (pt); Dentists 1 (pt).
Facilities Dining room; Activities room; Crafts room; Laundry room; Barber/Beauty shop.
Activities Arts & crafts; Cards; Games; Reading groups; Prayer groups; Movies; Dances/Social/Cultural gatherings.

Willits

Care West Northbrook
64 Northbrook Way, Willits, CA 95490
(707) 459-5592
Admin Denise Huggins AIT. *Dir of Nursing* Robin Martin-Lund RN. *Medical Dir* John Glyer MD.
Licensure Skilled care. *Beds* SNF 70. *Certified* Medicare; Medi-Cal.
Owner Proprietary corp (Care Enterprises).
Admissions Requirements Medical examination; Physician's request.
Staff RNs 1 (ft), 3 (pt); LPNs 6 (ft), 7 (pt); Nurses' aides 21 (ft), 10 (pt); Physical therapists 1 (pt); Speech therapists 1 (pt); Activities coordinators 1 (ft); Dietitians 1 (ft).
Facilities Dining room; Physical therapy room; Activities room; Barber/Beauty shop.
Activities Arts & crafts; Cards; Games; Reading groups; Movies; Shopping trips; Dances/Social/Cultural gatherings.

Willows

Willowview Convalescent Hospital
320 N Crawford, Willows, CA 95988
(916) 934-2834
Admin Catherine Rush.
Medical Dir Joseph Duba MD.
Licensure Skilled care. *Beds* SNF 79. *Certified* Medicare; Medi-Cal.
Owner Proprietary corp.
Staff Physicians 5 (pt); RNs 2 (ft), 2 (pt); LPNs 6 (ft), 6 (pt); Nurses' aides 28 (ft), 2 (pt); Physical therapists 1 (pt); Recreational therapists 1 (ft); Occupational therapists 1 (pt); Speech therapists 1 (pt); Activities coordinators 1 (ft); Dietitians 1 (pt); Ophthalmologists 1 (pt); Podiatrists 1 (pt); Audiologists 1 (pt); Dentists 2 (pt).
Facilities Dining room; Physical therapy room; Activities room; Laundry room; Barber/Beauty shop.
Activities Arts & crafts; Cards; Games; Reading groups; Prayer groups; Movies; Shopping trips; Dances/Social/Cultural gatherings.

Woodland

Alderson Convalescent Hospital
124 Walnut St, Woodland, CA 95695
(916) 662-9161
Admin Santiago Miguel.
Licensure Skilled care; Intermediate care. *Beds* SNF 98; ICF 57. *Certified* Medicare; Medi-Cal.
Owner Proprietary corp (United Health Systems Inc).

Countryside Intermediate Care Facility
435 Aspen St, Woodland, CA 95695
(916) 662-3128
Admin Santi Miguel.
Licensure Intermediate care. *Beds* 30. *Certified* Medi-Cal.
Owner Proprietary corp.

Hillhaven Convalescent Hospital
625 Cottonwood St, Woodland, CA 95695
(916) 662-9193
Admin James Bursey.
Medical Dir J T Barrett MD.

Licensure Skilled care. *Beds* SNF 98. *Certified* Medicare; Medi-Cal.
Owner Proprietary corp (Flagg Industries).
Admissions Requirements Minimum age 18.
Staff RNs 4 (ft), 2 (pt); LPNs 6 (ft), 3 (pt); Physical therapists 1 (ft); Recreational therapists 1 (ft); Occupational therapists 1 (pt); Speech therapists 1 (pt); Activities coordinators 1 (ft); Dietitians 1 (pt).
Facilities Dining room; Physical therapy room; Activities room; Crafts room; Laundry room; Barber/Beauty shop.
Activities Arts & crafts; Cards; Games; Reading groups; Prayer groups; Dances/Social/Cultural gatherings.

Stollwood Convalescent Hospital
135 Woodland Ave, Woodland, CA 95695
(916) 662-1290
Admin Carol L Dahnke. *Dir of Nursing* Bernice Blickle. *Medical Dir* Dr Ronald Harper.
Licensure Skilled care; Retirement. *Beds* SNF 48. *Certified* Medicare; Medi-Cal.
Owner Nonprofit corp.
Admissions Requirements Minimum age 65; Physician's request.
Staff RNs 4 (ft), 2 (pt); LPNs 4 (ft), 4 (pt); Nurses' aides 20 (ft), 5 (pt); Activities coordinators 1 (ft); Dietitians 1 (ft).
Languages Spanish.
Facilities Dining room; Physical therapy room; Activities room; Chapel; Crafts room; Laundry room; Barber/Beauty shop; Library.
Activities Arts & crafts; Cards; Games; Reading groups; Prayer groups; Movies; Shopping trips; Dances/Social/Cultural gatherings.

Woodland Skilled Nursing Facility
678 3rd St, Woodland, CA 95695
(916) 662-9643
Admin David J Tarpin. *Dir of Nursing* Margie Stapleton. *Medical Dir* Dr Stansell.
Licensure Skilled care. *Beds* SNF 55; ICF 41. *Certified* Medicare; Medi-Cal.
Owner Proprietary corp.
Admissions Requirements Physician's request.
Staff RNs 2 (ft); LPNs 7 (ft); Nurses' aides 42 (ft), 6 (pt).
Facilities Dining room; Physical therapy room; Activities room; Laundry room; Barber/Beauty shop.
Activities Cards; Games; Reading groups; Movies; Dances/Social/Cultural gatherings.

Yolo General Hospital SNF D/P
170 W Beamer, Woodland, CA 95695
(916) 666-8301
Admin David Hendry.
Licensure Skilled care. *Certified* Medicare; Medi-Cal.
Owner Publicly owned.

Yreka

Beverly Manor Convalescent Hospital
1515 Oregon St, Yreka, CA 96097
(916) 842-4361
Admin Harold G Hoof. *Dir of Nursing* Nancy Smith.
Licensure Skilled care. *Beds* SNF 99. *Certified* Medicare; Medi-Cal.
Owner Proprietary corp (Beverly Enterprises).
Staff Physicians 12 (pt); RNs 5 (ft); LPNs 9 (ft); Nurses' aides 70 (ft); Physical therapists 1 (ft); Recreational therapists 1 (ft); Speech therapists 1 (ft); Activities coordinators 2 (ft); Dietitians 1 (ft).
Facilities Dining room; Physical therapy room; Activities room; Crafts room; Laundry room; Barber/Beauty shop; Library.
Activities Arts & crafts; Cards; Games; Reading groups; Prayer groups; Movies; Shopping trips; Dances/Social/Cultural gatherings.

Yuba City

Driftwood Care Center
1220 Plumas St, Yuba City, CA 95991
(916) 671-0550
Admin Henry S Delamere. *Dir of Nursing*
Marcia Milani. *Medical Dir* William
Hoffman MD.
Licensure Skilled care; Retirement;
Alzheimer's care. *Beds* SNF 59; Retirement
67. *Certified* Medicare; Medi-Cal.
Owner Proprietary corp (Touchstone Health
Systems).
Admissions Requirements Physician's request.
Staff Physicians; RNs; LPNs; Nurses' aides;
Physical therapists; Occupational therapists;
Speech therapists; Activities coordinators;
Dietitians; Ophthalmologists; Podiatrists;
Audiologists.
Languages Spanish, Chinese, Japanese,
Panjabi.
Facilities Dining room; Physical therapy
room; Activities room; Laundry room;
Barber/Beauty shop.
Activities Arts & crafts; Cards; Games; Prayer
groups; Movies; Shopping trips; Dances/
Social/Cultural gatherings; Pet therapy.

Yuba City Care Center
521 Lorel Way, Yuba City, CA 95991
(916) 674-9140
Admin Fred Mabra.
Medical Dir Charles Cotham MD.

Licensure Skilled care. *Beds* SNF 151.
Certified Medicare; Medi-Cal.
Owner Proprietary corp.
Facilities Dining room; Physical therapy
room; Activities room; Crafts room; Laundry
room; Barber/Beauty shop.
Activities Arts & crafts; Cards; Games;
Reading groups; Movies; Shopping trips;
Dances/Social/Cultural gatherings.

Yucaipa

Braswell's Community Convalescent Center
13542 2nd St, Yucaipa, CA 92399
(714) 795-2421
Admin Betty Bennett.
Licensure Skilled care. *Beds* SNF 82. *Certified*
Medicare; Medi-Cal.
Owner Privately owned.

**Braswell's Yucaipa Valley Convalescent
Hospital**
35253 Ave H, Yucaipa, CA 92399
(714) 795-2476
Admin James H Braswell. *Dir of Nursing*
Gladys Emmerson. *Medical Dir* H J
Cozzolino MD.
Licensure Skilled care; Retirement. *Beds* SNF
59. *Certified* Medicare; Medi-Cal.
Owner Privately owned.
Admissions Requirements Physician's request.
Staff RNs; LPNs; Nurses' aides; Physical
therapists; Activities coordinators.

Facilities Dining room; Physical therapy
room; Activities room; Laundry room;
Barber/Beauty shop.
Activities Arts & crafts; Cards; Games;
Reading groups; Prayer groups; Movies;
Shopping trips; Dances/Social/Cultural
gatherings; Bus rides.

Yucca Valley

Moyle Manor
8515 Cholla Ave, Yucca Valley, CA 92284
(619) 365-0717
Admin Patricia Haklitch.
Licensure Skilled care. *Beds* SNF 56. *Certified*
Medicare; Medi-Cal.
Owner Proprietary corp.

Moyle's Hi-Desert Convalescent Hospital
55475 Santa Fe Trail, Yucca Valley, CA
92284
(619) 365-7635
Admin Kensett J Moyle.
Licensure Skilled care. *Beds* SNF 99. *Certified*
Medicare; Medi-Cal.
Owner Proprietary corp.

Moyle's Sky Harbor Healthcare Center
57333 Joshua Ln, Yucca Valley, CA 92284
(619) 365-4870
Admin Kensett J Moyle III.
Licensure Skilled care. *Beds* SNF 99. *Certified*
Medicare; Medi-Cal.
Owner Privately owned.

COLORADO

Aguilar

Simpsons Foster Care
212 W Main, Aguilar, CO 81082
(719) 941-4169
Admin Dorothy Simpson.
Licensure Developmentally disabled. *Beds*
Developmentally disabled 4.
Owner Proprietary corp.

Akron

Washington County Public Hospital & Nursing Home
465 Main St, Akron, CO 80720
(303) 345-2211
Admin Terry L Hoffart (acting). *Dir of Nursing* Gary Peterson RN. *Medical Dir* Dr Clark Brittain.
Licensure Skilled care. *Beds* SNF 29. *Certified* Medicaid.
Owner Nonprofit corp (Lutheran Hospital & Homes Society).
Admissions Requirements Physician's request.
Staff Physicians 1 (ft), 7 (pt); RNs 4 (ft), 3 (pt); LPNs 4 (ft), 3 (pt); Nurses' aides 6 (ft), 7 (pt); Physical therapists 1 (pt); Speech therapists 1 (pt); Activities coordinators 1 (pt); Dietitians 1 (pt).
Languages Spanish.
Facilities Dining room; Physical therapy room; Activities room; Crafts room; Laundry room; Barber/Beauty shop; Library.
Activities Arts & crafts; Cards; Games; Reading groups; Prayer groups; Movies; Shopping trips; Dances/Social/Cultural gatherings.

Alamosa

Evergreen Nursing Home
PO Box 1149, 1991 Carroll Ave, Alamosa, CO 81101
(719) 589-4951, 589-5651 FAX
Admin Rebecca Darnall RN NHA. *Dir of Nursing* Leeann Smith RN. *Medical Dir* Michael Firth MD.
Licensure Skilled care; Alzheimer's care. *Beds* SNF 60. *Private Pay Patients* 12%. *Certified* Medicaid; Medicare.
Owner Proprietary corp (Advanced Capitol Management).
Admissions Requirements Physician's request.
Staff Physicians 2 (pt); RNs 3 (ft); Physical therapists 1 (pt); Occupational therapists 1 (pt); Speech therapists 1 (pt); Activities coordinators 1 (ft), 1 (pt); Dietitians 1 (pt); Physical therapy aides 1 (ft), 1 (pt).
Languages Spanish.
Facilities Dining room; Physical therapy room; Activities room; Crafts room; Laundry room; Barber/Beauty shop; Library.
Activities Arts & crafts; Cards; Games; Reading groups; Prayer groups; Movies; Shopping trips; Dances/Social/Cultural gatherings; Intergenerational programs; Pet therapy.

La Posada
2017 Lava Ln, Alamosa, CO 81101
(303) 589-3673
Admin Luis B Medina.
Licensure Intermediate care. *Beds* 5.
Owner Nonprofit corp.

San Luis Care Center
240 Craft Dr, Alamosa, CO 81101
(719) 589-9081
Admin Mary LaCroix.
Licensure Skilled care. *Beds* SNF 60.

Stephens House
78 Monterey, Alamosa, CO 81101
(303) 589-5135
Admin Elaine C Marrangoni.
Licensure Developmentally disabled. *Beds* 7.
Owner Nonprofit corp.

Arvada

Ames Way House
8130 Ames Way, Arvada, CO 80005
(303) 424-2713
Admin Mike Hannon.
Licensure Intermediate care for mentally retarded. *Beds* 8.
Owner Nonprofit corp.

Arvada Health Center
6121 W 60th Ave, Arvada, CO 80003
(303) 420-4550
Admin Cynthia L Bostic. *Dir of Nursing* Gail Dewolf RN. *Medical Dir* Dr F Burdick.
Licensure Skilled care; Intermediate care. *Beds* SNF 23; ICF 31. *Private Pay Patients* 28%. *Certified* Medicaid.
Owner Proprietary corp.
Admissions Requirements Medical examination.
Staff Physicians 1 (pt); RNs 10 (ft), 2 (pt); LPNs 10 (ft), 3 (pt); Nurses' aides 15 (ft), 10 (pt); Physical therapists 1 (pt); Occupational therapists 1 (pt); Activities coordinators 1 (ft), 1 (pt); Dietitians 1 (pt).
Languages Spanish.
Facilities Dining room; Laundry room.
Activities Arts & crafts; Cards; Games; Reading groups; Prayer groups; Movies; Shopping trips; Intergenerational programs; Pet therapy; Family support group; Fireside lounge; Monthly newsletter; Community involvement; Resident council.

Colorado Lutheran Health Care Center
7991 W 71 Ave, Arvada, CO 80004
(303) 422-5088
Admin Donald C Colander.
Licensure Skilled care. *Beds* SNF 120. *Certified* Medicaid.
Owner Nonprofit corp.

58th Avenue
10925 W 58th Ave, Arvada, CO 80005
(303) 424-6824
Admin Mike Hannon.

Licensure Residential MR care. *Beds* Residential MR care 8. *Certified* Medicaid.
Owner Nonprofit corp.

King Family Care Home
8640 Calvin Dr, Arvada, CO 80002
(303) 425-6141
Admin Jeanette King.
Licensure Intermediate care. *Beds* 2.
Owner Proprietary corp.

Lake View
11059 W 82nd Pl, Arvada, CO 80003
(303) 425-1327
Admin Ruth Stallings.
Licensure Intermediate care for mentally retarded. *Beds* 8.
Owner Proprietary corp.

Lee Street
6039 Lee St, Arvada, CO 80004
(303) 423-7158
Admin Mike Hannon.
Licensure Intermediate care for mentally retarded. *Beds* 7.
Owner Nonprofit corp.

Spring Valley
5900 Nelson Court, Arvada, CO 80005
(303) 423-7158
Admin Mike Hannon.
Licensure Residential MR care. *Beds* Residential MR care 8. *Certified* Medicaid.
Owner Nonprofit corp.

Aurora

Aurora Care Center
10201 E 3rd Ave, Aurora, CO 80010
(303) 364-3364
Admin Anne E Chapman. *Dir of Nursing* Donna McCormack. *Medical Dir* William Solomon MD.
Licensure Skilled care; Intermediate care; Alzheimer's care. *Beds* Swing beds SNF/ICF 118. *Private Pay Patients* 60%. *Certified* Medicaid; Medicare.
Owner Proprietary corp (Hillhaven Corp).
Admissions Requirements Minimum age 21.
Staff RNs 6 (ft), 10 (pt); LPNs 14 (ft), 9 (pt); Nurses' aides 46 (ft), 12 (pt); Physical therapists 1 (ft); Reality therapists 1 (ft), 1 (pt); Occupational therapists 1 (ft); Speech therapists 1 (pt); Activities coordinators 4 (ft); Dietitians 1 (ft); Ophthalmologists (contracted); Podiatrists (contracted); Audiologists (contracted).
Facilities Dining room; Physical therapy room; Activities room; Crafts room; Laundry room; Barber/Beauty shop; Secured Alzheimer's unit; Enclosed courtyards.
Activities Arts & crafts; Cards; Games; Reading groups; Prayer groups; Movies; Shopping trips; Dances/Social/Cultural gatherings; Intergenerational programs; Pet therapy.

Camellia Care Center
500 Geneva St, Aurora, CO 80010
(303) 364-9311
Admin Claudia Kaye Hunter. *Dir of Nursing*
Linda Burniston RN. *Medical Dir* Dr
Alexander Jacobs.
Licensure Skilled care; Intermediate care. *Beds*
SNF 120; ICF 60. *Certified* Medicaid;
Medicare.
Owner Proprietary corp (American Medical
Services Inc).
Admissions Requirements Minimum age 45;
Medical examination; Physician's request.
Staff RNs 8 (ft), 4 (pt); LPNs 20 (ft), 10 (pt);
Nurses' aides 45 (ft), 15 (pt); Physical
therapists 1 (pt); Recreational therapists 2
(ft), 1 (pt); Speech therapists 1 (ft);
Dietitians 1 (pt).
Languages German, Spanish, Tagalog.
Facilities Dining room; Physical therapy
room; Activities room; Crafts room; Laundry
room; Barber/Beauty shop; Library.
Activities Arts & crafts; Cards; Games;
Reading groups; Prayer groups; Shopping
trips; Dances/Social/Cultural gatherings.

Cherry Creek Nursing Center
14699 E Hampden Ave, Aurora, CO 80014
(303) 693-0111
Admin Bernard C Heese. *Dir of Nursing*
Marleen Carlson. *Medical Dir* Dr Thomas
McCloskey.
Licensure Skilled care; Alzheimer's care. *Beds*
SNF 180. *Certified* Medicare.
Owner Proprietary corp (Life Care Centers of
America).
Admissions Requirements Minimum age 50;
Physician's request.
Staff RNs 6 (ft), 11 (pt); LPNs 4 (ft), 2 (pt);
Nurses' aides 28 (ft), 7 (pt); Physical
therapists 2 (ft); Reality therapists 1 (ft), 1
(pt); Recreational therapists 2 (ft);
Occupational therapists; Speech therapists;
Activities coordinators 3 (ft), 2 (pt);
Dietitians 1 (pt); Ophthalmologists; Dentists;
Social services.
Facilities Dining room; Physical therapy
room; Activities room; Chapel; Crafts room;
Laundry room; Barber/Beauty shop; Library.
Activities Arts & crafts; Cards; Games;
Reading groups; Prayer groups; Movies;
Shopping trips; Dances/Social/Cultural
gatherings; Dog races; Horse races; Tours;
Mountain trips.

Delmar
10801 Delmar Pkwy, Aurora, CO 80010
(303) 696-7002
Admin Margaret Lowe.
Licensure Residential MR care. *Beds*
Residential MR care 8. *Certified* Medicaid.
Owner Nonprofit corp.
Admissions Requirements Minimum age 18;
Medical examination; Physician's request.
Staff RNs 1 (pt); Recreational therapists 1
(pt).
Facilities Dining room; Laundry room.
Activities Movies; Shopping trips; Dances/
Social/Cultural gatherings; Community
integration.

Mountain View House
1125 Dayton St, Aurora, CO 80010
(303) 341-2086
Admin John Meeker.
Licensure Intermediate care for mentally
retarded. *Beds* 8.
Owner Nonprofit corp.

Ponderosa
11204 E Colorado Dr, Aurora, CO 80012
(303) 752-1920
Admin Margaret Lowe.
Licensure Residential MR care. *Beds*
Residential MR care 8. *Certified* Medicaid.
Owner Nonprofit corp.

Sable Care Center Inc
656 Dillon Way, Aurora, CO 80011
(303) 344-0636
Admin Ann D Romoglia.
Medical Dir Frances Burdrik.
Licensure Skilled care. *Beds* SNF 120.
Certified Medicaid; Medicare.
Owner Proprietary corp.
Facilities Dining room; Physical therapy
room; Activities room; Barber/Beauty shop;
Library.
Activities Arts & crafts; Games; Reading
groups; Prayer groups; Movies; Shopping
trips; Dances/Social/Cultural gatherings.

Village East
1505 S Ironton, Aurora, CO 80012
(303) 696-7002
Admin Margaret Lowe.
Licensure Residential MR care. *Beds*
Residential MR care 8. *Certified* Medicaid.
Owner Nonprofit corp.

Bayfield

Valley View Residential Care Home
Rte 1, Bayfield, CO 81122
(303) 884-2200
Admin Arline M Beaver.
Licensure Intermediate care. *Beds* 8.
Owner Proprietary corp.

Berthoud

Grandview Manor
PO Box 70, 855 Franklin Ave, Berthoud, CO
80513
(303) 532-2683
Admin Martin F Kuhn. *Dir of Nursing* Mrs
Edwards. *Medical Dir* David McCarty MD.
Licensure Skilled care; Intermediate care. *Beds*
54. *Certified* Medicaid.
Owner Proprietary corp (ARA Living
Centers).
Admissions Requirements Minimum age 18;
Physician's request.
Staff RNs 4 (ft), 4 (pt); LPNs 1 (ft); Nurses'
aides 13 (ft), 6 (pt); Activities coordinators.
Languages Spanish, German.
Facilities Dining room; Activities room;
Laundry room; Barber/Beauty shop.
Activities Cards; Games; Reading groups;
Prayer groups; Movies; Dances/Social/
Cultural gatherings.

Boone

Boone Guest Home
526 Main St, Boone, CO 81025
(719) 947-3045
Admin Ed Jordan; Louise Jordan.
Licensure Developmentally disabled. *Beds*
Developmentally disabled 15.
Owner Proprietary corp.

Boulder

Boulder Good Samaritan Health Care Center
2525 Taft Dr, Boulder, CO 80302
(303) 449-6157
Admin Jim Mertz.
Medical Dir Darvin Smith MD.
Licensure Skilled care. *Beds* 60. *Certified*
Medicaid.
Owner Nonprofit corp (Evangelical Lutheran/
Good Samaritan Society).
Admissions Requirements Minimum age 55;
Medical examination; Physician's request.
Staff RNs 3 (ft), 8 (pt); LPNs 1 (pt); Nurses'
aides 14 (ft), 7 (pt); Physical therapists 1
(pt); Recreational therapists 1 (ft), 1 (pt);
Dietitians 1 (pt).
Affiliation Lutheran.

Facilities Dining room; Physical therapy
room; Activities room; Chapel; Crafts room;
Laundry room; Barber/Beauty shop; Library;
Indoor heated swimming pool.
Activities Arts & crafts; Cards; Games;
Reading groups; Prayer groups; Movies;
Shopping trips; Dances/Social/Cultural
gatherings.

Boulder Manor
4685 Baseline Rd, Boulder, CO 80303
(303) 494-0535
Admin Ken Cafferty. *Dir of Nursing* Jaydene
Mathis RN. *Medical Dir* William Blanchet
MD.
Licensure Skilled care; Intermediate care. *Beds*
SNF 112; ICF 60. *Certified* Medicaid;
Medicare.
Owner Proprietary corp (ARA Living
Centers).
Admissions Requirements Minimum age 40;
Medical examination; Physician's request.
Staff RNs 5 (ft), 3 (pt); LPNs 7 (ft), 6 (pt);
Nurses' aides 31 (ft), 17 (pt); Physical
therapists 1 (ft), 1 (pt); Recreational
therapists 2 (ft); Occupational therapists 1
(ft); Speech therapists 1 (pt); Dietitians 2
(ft).
Facilities Dining room; Physical therapy
room; Chapel; Barber/Beauty shop; 3
lounges.
Activities Arts & crafts; Cards; Games;
Reading groups; Prayer groups; Movies;
Shopping trips; Dances/Social/Cultural
gatherings; Adopt-a-grandparent; Oral
history; Exercise; Music therapy.

Carmel Ltd
1005 12th St, Boulder, CO 80302
(303) 444-0573
Admin James Graves.
Medical Dir Marvin Dunaway MD.
Licensure Intermediate care for mentally
retarded. *Beds* ICF/MR 82. *Certified*
Medicaid; Medicare.
Owner Proprietary corp.
Admissions Requirements Minimum age 18;
Medical examination.
Staff Physicians 5 (pt); RNs 1 (pt); LPNs 5
(ft); Nurses' aides 8 (ft); Physical therapists 1
(pt); Recreational therapists 1 (pt); Activities
coordinators 1 (pt); Dietitians 1 (pt);
Podiatrists 1 (pt).
Facilities Dining room; Activities room;
Crafts room; Laundry room; Library.
Activities Arts & crafts; Games; Movies;
Shopping trips; Dances/Social/Cultural
gatherings.

Chestor House
3786 Eldorado Springs Dr, Boulder, CO
80303
(303) 494-3385
Admin Daniel H Fairchild.
Licensure Residential MR care. *Beds*
Residential MR care 8. *Certified* Medicaid.
Owner Proprietary corp.

Frasier Meadows Manor Health Care Center
350 Ponca Pl, Boulder, CO 80303
(303) 499-8412
Admin Dolores Pancoast MA NHA. *Dir of
Nursing* Marlene Taylor RN. *Medical Dir*
James T Murphy MD.
Licensure Skilled care; Retirement;
Alzheimer's care. *Beds* SNF 60; Alzheimer's
unit 40; Retirement 175. *Private Pay
Patients* 80%. *Certified* Medicaid.
Owner Nonprofit corp.
Admissions Requirements Minimum age 60;
Medical examination; Physician's request.
Staff RNs 5 (ft), 3 (pt); LPNs 13 (ft), 14 (pt);
Nurses' aides 25 (ft), 16 (pt); Physical
therapists 2 (pt); Activities coordinators 2
(ft); Dietitians 1 (pt).
Languages Spanish.
Affiliation United Methodist.

Facilities Dining room; Physical therapy room; Activities room; Chapel; Crafts room; Laundry room; Barber/Beauty shop; Library; Alzheimer's unit.
Activities Arts & crafts; Cards; Games; Reading groups; Prayer groups; Shopping trips; Dances/Social/Cultural gatherings; Pet therapy.

Johnson House
1478 Meadowlark Dr, Boulder, CO 80303
(303) 494-6249
Admin Timothy O'Neill.
Licensure Residential MR care. *Beds* 8. *Certified* Medicaid.
Owner Nonprofit corp.

Terrace Heights Care Center
2121 Mesa Dr, Boulder, CO 80302
(303) 442-4037
Admin Russell S Landcaster.
Medical Dir Frank Bolles MD.
Licensure Skilled care; Intermediate care. *Beds* SNF 138; ICF 24. *Certified* Medicaid; Medicare.
Owner Proprietary corp (Waverly Group).
Admissions Requirements Medical examination; Physician's request.
Staff RNs 12 (ft), 2 (pt); LPNs 20 (ft), 2 (pt); Nurses' aides 30 (ft), 5 (pt); Physical therapists 1 (ft); Recreational therapists; Occupational therapists 1 (pt); Speech therapists 1 (pt); Activities coordinators 2 (ft); Dietitians 1 (pt); Ophthalmologists 1 (pt); Podiatrists 1 (pt); Dentists 1 (pt).
Languages Spanish.
Facilities Dining room; Physical therapy room; Activities room; Crafts room; Laundry room; Barber/Beauty shop; Library; Patio; Garden spaces.
Activities Arts & crafts; Cards; Games; Reading groups; Prayer groups; Movies; Shopping trips; Dances/Social/Cultural gatherings; Gardening; Horticultural therapy; Family barbeques.

Brighton

Brighton Care Center
2025 Egbert St, Brighton, CO 80601
(303) 659-4580
Admin Margaret A Weedman. *Dir of Nursing* Julieann Scott-Hughes RN BSN.
Licensure Skilled care. *Beds* 120. *Certified* Medicaid.
Owner Proprietary corp (Hillhaven Corp).

Cottonwood Care Center
2311 E Bridge St, Brighton, CO 80601
(303) 659-2253
Admin Darlene Inman.
Licensure Intermediate care. *Beds* ICF 112. *Certified* Medicaid.
Owner Proprietary corp.

7th Street
441 S 7th St, Brighton, CO 80609
(303) 429-9714
Admin Jo Vincelli.
Licensure Intermediate care for mentally retarded. *Beds* 9. *Certified* Medicaid.
Owner Nonprofit corp.

Wilson's Family Care Services
2620 E 165th Ave, Rte 2, Brighton, CO 80601
(303) 451-9105
Admin Eileen Wilson.
Licensure Developmentally disabled. *Beds* Developmentally disabled 5.
Owner Proprietary corp.

Brush

Eben Ezer Lutheran Care Center
122 Hospital Rd, Brush, CO 80723
(303) 842-2861

Admin Robert A Herrboldt. *Dir of Nursing* Florence Liittjohann. *Medical Dir* Dr Harold Chapel.
Licensure Skilled care; Retirement, Alzheimer's care. *Beds* SNF 137; Retirement apts 75. *Private Pay Patients* 55%. *Certified* VA.
Owner Nonprofit organization/foundation.
Admissions Requirements Physician's request.
Staff Physicians 9 (pt); RNs 5 (ft), 7 (pt); LPNs 13 (ft), 1 (pt); Nurses' aides 38 (ft), 24 (pt); Physical therapists 1 (pt); Recreational therapists 1 (ft), 3 (pt); Occupational therapists 1 (pt); Speech therapists 1 (pt); Activities coordinators 1 (ft); Dietitians 1 (ft), 2 (pt); Podiatrists 1 (pt).
Languages Danish, German, Spanish, Chinese.
Affiliation Lutheran.
Facilities Dining room; Physical therapy room; Activities room; Chapel; Crafts room; Laundry room; Barber/Beauty shop; Library.
Activities Arts & crafts; Cards; Games; Reading groups; Prayer groups; Movies; Shopping trips; Dances/Social/Cultural gatherings; Intergenerational programs; Pet therapy.

Sunset Manor
2200 Edison St, Brush, CO 80723
(303) 842-2825
Admin Barbara Bradshaw.
Licensure Skilled care; Intermediate care. *Beds* SNF 45; ICF 38. *Certified* Medicaid; Medicare.
Owner Proprietary corp (ARA Living Centers).

Burlington

Grace Manor Care Center
Rte 1, PO Box 29A, 465 5th St, Burlington, CO 80807
(719) 346-7512
Admin Lottie Whitmer. *Dir of Nursing* Gerrie K Evans. *Medical Dir* R C Beethe MD.
Licensure Skilled care; Intermediate care. *Beds* 49. *Certified* Medicaid.
Owner Proprietary corp.
Staff RNs; LPNs; Nurses' aides; Activities coordinators.
Facilities Dining room; Laundry room; Barber/Beauty shop.
Activities Arts & crafts; Cards; Games; Prayer groups; Movies; Shopping trips; Dances/Social/Cultural gatherings.

Martin House
1776 Martin, Burlington, CO 80807
(719) 346-8550
Medical Dir Ray Rhodes, Interim Dir.
Licensure Intermediate care for mentally retarded. *Beds* ICF/MR 8.
Owner Nonprofit corp.
Admissions Requirements Minimum age 16; Females only; Medical examination.
Facilities Dining room; Activities room; Crafts room; Laundry room.
Activities Arts & crafts; Cards; Games; Reading groups; Movies; Shopping trips; Dances/Social/Cultural gatherings.

Canon City

Barr House
1115 Barr, Canon, CO 81212
(719) 275-0017
Admin Roger Jensen.
Licensure Intermediate care for mentally retarded. *Beds* ICF/MR 8. *Certified* Medicaid.
Owner Nonprofit corp.

Bethesda Care Center
515 Fairview St, Canon City, CO 81212
(719) 275-0665
Admin Larry Lavelle. *Dir of Nursing* Audrey Slater. *Medical Dir* Jack Vincent MD.
Licensure Skilled care; Retirement. *Beds* SNF 110; Retirement 47. *Private Pay Patients* 24%. *Certified* Medicaid; Medicare.
Owner Nonprofit corp (Bethesda Care Centers).
Admissions Requirements Medical examination; Physician's request.
Staff Physicians 1 (pt); RNs 4 (ft), 5 (pt); LPNs 5 (ft), 6 (pt); Nurses' aides 20 (ft), 30 (pt); Physical therapists 1 (pt); Reality therapists 1 (pt); Recreational therapists 1 (pt); Activities coordinators 1 (pt); Dietitians 1 (pt).
Facilities Dining room; Physical therapy room; Activities room; Chapel; Crafts room; Laundry room; Barber/Beauty shop.
Activities Arts & crafts; Cards; Games; Reading groups; Prayer groups; Movies; Shopping trips; Dances/Social/Cultural gatherings.

Canon Lodge
905 Harding, Canon City, CO 81212
(719) 275-4106
Admin Fred Hebard. *Dir of Nursing* Rebecca Green. *Medical Dir* Dr J F Vincent.
Licensure Skilled care. *Beds* SNF 60. *Private Pay Patients* 40%. *Certified* Medicaid; Medicare.
Owner Privately owned.
Admissions Requirements Physician's request.
Staff RNs; LPNs; Nurses' aides; Physical therapists; Activities coordinators.
Facilities Dining room; Activities room; Barber/Beauty shop.
Activities Arts & crafts; Cards; Games; Reading groups; Prayer groups; Movies; Shopping trips.

Field House
PO Box 2080, Canon City, CO 81212-7080
(719) 275-0031
Admin Roger Jensen.
Licensure Intermediate care for mentally retarded. *Beds* ICF/MR 8. *Certified* Medicaid.
Owner Nonprofit corp.

Hildebrand Care Center
1401 Phay St, Canon City, CO 81212
(719) 275-8656
Admin Joyce L Stapleton.
Medical Dir Dr Jack Vincent.
Licensure Skilled care. *Beds* SNF 110. *Certified* Medicaid; Medicare.
Owner Proprietary corp.
Admissions Requirements Medical examination.
Staff RNs 9 (ft), 2 (pt); LPNs 10 (ft); Nurses' aides 35 (ft), 5 (pt); Reality therapists 1 (pt); Activities coordinators 1 (ft), 1 (pt); Dietitians 1 (pt).
Affiliation Independent Order of Odd Fellows & Rebekahs.
Facilities Dining room; Physical therapy room; Activities room; Chapel; Crafts room; Laundry room; Barber/Beauty shop; Library; Picnics; Fishing trips.
Activities Arts & crafts; Cards; Games; Reading groups; Prayer groups; Movies; Shopping trips; Dances/Social/Cultural gatherings.

St Thomas More Hospital & Progressive Care Center
1019 Sheridan, Canon City, CO 81212
(719) 275-3381
Admin Sr Jacqueline. *Dir of Nursing* Charlotte Herman RN. *Medical Dir* Gary Mohr MD.

Licensure Skilled care; General hospital; Rehabilitation center; Hospice. *Beds* SNF 129; General hospial 60; Rehabilitation center 11, Hospice 1. *Certified* Medicaid; Medicare.
Owner Nonprofit corp.
Admissions Requirements Physician's request.
Staff RNs 4 (ft), 3 (pt); LPNs 8 (ft), 4 (pt); Nurses' aides 10 (ft), 2 (pt); Physical therapists 3 (ft); Occupational therapists 2 (ft); Speech therapists 1 (pt); Activities coordinators 1 (ft); Dietitians 1 (ft).
Affiliation Roman Catholic.
Facilities Dining room; Physical therapy room; Activities room; Chapel; Crafts room; Laundry room; Barber/Beauty shop.
Activities Arts & crafts; Cards; Games; Reading groups; Prayer groups; Movies; Shopping trips.

Valley View Health Care Center
2120 N 10 St, Canon City, CO 81212
(719) 275-7569
Admin Shirley Smylie.
Licensure Skilled care. *Beds* SNF 60. *Certified* Medicaid.
Owner Privately owned.

Westridge Apartments
329 Rudd, Canon City, CO 80212
(719) 275-1539, 275-2577
Admin Roger G Jensen; Exec Dir.
Licensure Intermediate care for mentally retarded. *Beds* ICF/MR 8. *Certified* Medicaid.
Owner Nonprofit corp.

Carbondale

Heritage Park Care Center
1200 Village Rd, Carbondale, CO 81623
(303) 963-1500
Admin Judith P Cloyd. *Dir of Nursing* Sarah Oliver. *Medical Dir* Dr Gary Knaus.
Licensure Skilled care; Intermediate care; Retirement. *Beds* Swing beds SNF/ICF 60; Retirement 6. *Certified* Medicaid; Medicare.
Owner Proprietary corp.
Admissions Requirements Physician's request.
Staff RNs; LPNs; Nurses' aides; Activities coordinators.
Languages Spanish.
Facilities Dining room; Physical therapy room; Activities room; Chapel; Crafts room; Laundry room; Barber/Beauty shop; Library.
Activities Arts & crafts; Cards; Games; Reading groups; Prayer groups; Movies; Shopping trips; Dances/Social/Cultural gatherings; Intergenerational programs; Pet therapy.

Castle Rock

Castle Rock Care Center
4001 Home St, Castle Rock, CO 80104
(303) 688-3174
Admin Norma Horner. *Dir of Nursing* Pat Patrocky.
Licensure Skilled care; Intermediate care. *Beds* SNF 75; ICF 20. *Certified* Medicaid.
Owner Proprietary corp.
Admissions Requirements Physician's request.
Staff RNs; LPNs; Nurses' aides; Activities coordinators; Social services directors.
Facilities Dining room; Physical therapy room; Activities room; Chapel; Laundry room; Barber/Beauty shop; Solarium.
Activities Arts & crafts; Games; Reading groups; Prayer groups; Shopping trips; Dances/Social/Cultural gatherings; Pet therapy.

Cheyenne Wells

Cheyenne Manor
561 W 1st N, Cheyenne Wells, CO 80810
(719) 767-5602

Admin Wayne L Bute. *Dir of Nursing* Doris Gibbs. *Medical Dir* Dr Keefe.
Licensure Intermediate care; Alzheimer's care. *Beds* ICF 44. *Private Pay Patients* 50%. *Certified* Medicaid.
Owner Publicly owned.
Admissions Requirements Minimum age 21; Medical examination.
Staff RNs 2 (ft); LPNs 4 (ft); Nurses' aides 16 (ft); Recreational therapists 1 (ft); Activities coordinators 1 (ft); Dietitians 1 (ft).
Facilities Dining room; Activities room; Chapel; Laundry room; Barber/Beauty shop; Secured Alzheimer's unit.
Activities Arts & crafts; Cards; Games; Reading groups; Prayer groups; Movies; Shopping trips; Dances/Social/Cultural gatherings; Intergenerational programs; Pet therapy; Van outings.

Clifton

Laurel Lane
3301 Laural Ln, Clifton, CO 81520
(303) 243-3702
Admin Laura Schumacher.
Licensure Residential MR care. *Beds* Residential MR care 8. *Certified* Medicaid.
Owner Nonprofit corp.

Collbran

Plateau Valley Hospital District Nursing Home
Rte 1 Box 6, 5812 Hwy 330, Collbran, CO 81624
(303) 487-3565, 245-3981
Admin Sharon Hill. *Dir of Nursing* Marvin Ivy LPN; Marilyn Fullmer RN. *Medical Dir* Thomas A Moore Jr DO; Daniel P Thompson DO.
Licensure Intermediate care. *Beds* ICF 26. *Private Pay Patients* 16-20%. *Certified* Medicaid.
Owner Publicly owned.
Admissions Requirements Medical examination; Physician's request.
Staff Physicians 2 (pt); RNs 1 (ft), 2 (pt); LPNs 3 (ft), 1 (pt); Nurses' aides 6 (ft), 7 (pt); Physical therapists 1 (pt); Activities coordinators 1 (ft); Dietitians 1 (pt).
Languages Spanish.
Facilities Dining room; Activities room; Crafts room; Library.
Activities Arts & crafts; Cards; Games; Reading groups; Prayer groups; Movies; Dances/Social/Cultural gatherings; Intergenerational programs; Pet therapy; Music; Travelogues; Exercise.

Colorado Springs

Aspen Living Center
1795 Monterey Rd, Colorado Springs, CO 80910
(719) 471-7850
Admin Randy May.
Medical Dir Dr Lester Williams.
Licensure Skilled care; Intermediate care; Alzheimer's care. *Beds* SNF 60; ICF 60. *Certified* Medicaid; Medicare.
Owner Proprietary corp (ARA Living Centers).

Bethesda Care Center of Bassett
1465 Kelly Johnson Blvd No 200, Colorado Springs, CO 80920-3997
(402) 684-3388
Admin Gene Schaaf. *Dir of Nursing* Catherine S Clark RN.
Licensure Intermediate care. *Beds* ICF 27. *Certified* Medicaid.
Owner Nonprofit corp (MTC West Inc).
Admissions Requirements Medical examination; Physician's request.

Staff RNs 1 (ft), 1 (pt); LPNs 1 (ft), 1 (pt); Nurses' aides 8 (ft), 3 (pt); Activities coordinators 1 (ft).
Facilities Dining room; Activities room; Laundry room; Barber/Beauty shop.
Activities Arts & crafts; Cards; Games; Reading groups; Prayer groups; Movies; Shopping trips; Dances/Social/Cultural gatherings; Weekly van rides.

Bethesda Care Center of Colorado Springs
3625 Parkmoor Village Dr, Colorado Springs, CO 80917
(719) 550-0200
Admin J Roger Call. *Dir of Nursing* Penny Spika RN BSN.
Licensure Skilled care; Intermediate care; Retirement; Alzheimer's care. *Beds* SNF 60; ICF 90. *Certified* Medicaid.
Owner Nonprofit corp (Bethesda Foundation).
Admissions Requirements Minimum age 18; Medical examination.
Staff Physicians 1 (pt); RNs 4 (ft), 4 (pt); LPNs 6 (ft), 5 (pt); Nurses' aides 23 (ft), 7 (pt); Physical therapists 1 (ft); Occupational therapists 1 (pt); Activities coordinators 1 (ft), 1 (pt); Dietitians 1 (pt).
Languages Spanish, German.
Facilities Dining room; Physical therapy room; Activities room; Chapel; Crafts room; Laundry room; Barber/Beauty shop; Library; Physician exam room; Family dayrooms; Outdoor patio.
Activities Arts & crafts; Cards; Games; Reading groups; Prayer groups; Movies; Shopping trips; Dances/Social/Cultural gatherings; Oil painting; Cooking; Exercise class; Van rides; Green thumbs club; Sewing circle; Newsletter.

Bethesda Care Centers
1465 Kelly Johnson Blvd, Ste 200, Colorado Springs, CO 80918
(303) 548-0500
Admin David Burdine Pres.
Medical Dir Don A Morgan Operations Dir.
Licensure Skilled care; Intermediate care; Acute care facility; Special treatment; Independent living. *Beds* SNF 896; ICF 1672; Acute care facility 103; Special treatment 20; Independent living 114. *Certified* Medicaid.
Owner Nonprofit corp (Bethesda Foundation).
Staff RNs; LPNs; Nurses' aides; Physical therapists; Activities coordinators; Dietitians; Social services directors.
Facilities Dining room; Physical therapy room; Activities room; Chapel; Laundry room; Barber/Beauty shop; Lounges; Resident kitchens; Patios; Whirlpool baths.
Activities Arts & crafts; Cards; Games; Reading groups; Prayer groups; Movies; Shopping trips; Dances/Social/Cultural gatherings; Van rides for picnics; Fishing; Trips; Rodeos; Sewing; Cooking; Art classes; Tutoring children; Hosting community events.

Cedarwood Health Care Center Inc
924 W Kiowa St, Colorado Springs, CO 80905
(719) 636-5221
Admin Marilyn Bertagnolli. *Dir of Nursing* Barbara Azbill. *Medical Dir* Dr Lester Williams.
Licensure Skilled care; Intermediate care. *Beds* SNF 60; ICF 40. *Certified* Medicaid; Medicare.
Owner Proprietary corp (ARA Living Centers).
Admissions Requirements Physician's request.
Staff RNs 5 (ft), 3 (pt); LPNs 5 (ft), 3 (pt); Nurses' aides 16 (ft), 2 (pt); Physical therapists 1 (pt); Recreational therapists 1 (ft); Occupational therapists 1 (pt); Speech therapists 1 (pt); Activities coordinators 1 (ft); Dietitians 1 (pt).
Languages Spanish.

Facilities Dining room; Activities room; Crafts room; Laundry room; Barber/Beauty shop; Library.
Activities Arts & crafts; Cards; Games; Reading groups; Prayer groups; Movies; Shopping trips; Dances/Social/Cultural gatherings.

Cheyenne Mountain Nursing Center
835 Tenderfoot Hill Rd, Colorado Springs, CO 80906
(719) 576-8380
Admin Mary Estlow NHA. *Dir of Nursing* Cathleen Kelley RN. *Medical Dir* Evans MD.
Licensure Skilled care; Alzheimer's care. *Beds* SNF 180. *Private Pay Patients* 95%. *Certified* Medicare.
Owner Proprietary corp (Life Care Centers of America).
Admissions Requirements Physician's request.
Staff Physical therapists 2 (ft); Recreational therapists 1 (ft); Occupational therapists 2 (ft); Speech therapists 1 (ft); Activities coordinators 1 (ft); Dietitians 1 (ft).
Facilities Dining room; Physical therapy room; Activities room; Chapel; Crafts room; Laundry room; Barber/Beauty shop.
Activities Arts & crafts; Cards; Games; Reading groups; Prayer groups; Movies; Shopping trips; Dances/Social/Cultural gatherings; Intergenerational programs; Pet therapy; Outings; Horseback riding; "Out to Lunch Bunch".

Colonial Columns Nursing Center
1340 E Fillmore St, Colorado Springs, CO 80907
(719) 473-1105
Admin Karl Schmidt.
Licensure Skilled care; Intermediate care. *Beds* SNF 46; ICF 47. *Certified* Medicaid; Medicare.
Owner Proprietary corp (ARA Living Centers).
Admissions Requirements Medical examination; Physician's request.
Staff RNs; LPNs; Nurses' aides; Recreational therapists.
Languages Spanish.
Facilities Dining room; Physical therapy room; Laundry room; Barber/Beauty shop; Library.
Activities Arts & crafts; Cards; Games; Reading groups; Prayer groups; Movies; Shopping trips; Dances/Social/Cultural gatherings.

Garden of the Gods Care Center
PO Box 6129, 104 Lois Ln, Colorado Springs, CO 80934
(719) 635-2569
Admin Robert Turner. *Dir of Nursing* Charlene Stillmunks RN. *Medical Dir* Lester Williams MD.
Licensure Skilled care; Alzheimer's care. *Beds* SNF 52. *Certified* Medicaid; Medicare.
Owner Proprietary corp (LTC).
Admissions Requirements Minimum age 50; Physician's request.
Staff RNs 3 (ft), 4 (pt); LPNs 2 (ft), 2 (pt); Nurses' aides 10 (ft), 10 (pt); Activities coordinators 2 (pt).
Languages Japanese, Spanish, Greek.
Facilities Dining room; Laundry room.
Activities Arts & crafts; Cards; Games; Reading groups; Prayer groups; Movies; Shopping trips; Dances/Social/Cultural gatherings.

Hampton Drive
6736 Hampton Dr, Colorado Springs, CO 80918
(719) 531-0511
Admin Sandra S Volker.
Licensure Residential DD care. *Beds* Residential DD care 8.

Owner Nonprofit corp.
Affiliation Lutheran.

Laurel Manor Care Center
920 S Chelton Rd, Colorado Springs, CO 80910
(719) 473-7780
Admin Connie J Miller. *Dir of Nursing* Joyce Miller RN. *Medical Dir* Lester L Williams MD.
Licensure Skilled care. *Beds* SNF 120. *Private Pay Patients* 24%. *Certified* Medicaid; Medicare.
Owner Nonprofit corp (Volunteers of America Care).
Admissions Requirements Physician's request.
Staff RNs 6 (ft), 2 (pt); LPNs 12 (ft); Nurses' aides 30 (ft); Physical therapists 1 (ft); Recreational therapists 1 (ft); Occupational therapists 1 (ft); Speech therapists 1 (ft); Dietitians 1 (pt); Podiatrists 1 (pt).
Languages Spanish.
Facilities Dining room; Physical therapy room; Activities room; Laundry room; Barber/Beauty shop.
Activities Arts & crafts; Cards; Games; Reading groups; Prayer groups; Movies; Pet therapy.

Medalion Health Center
1719 E Bijou, Colorado Springs, CO 80909
(719) 471-4800
Admin Jacklyn Friedman.
Medical Dir Lyle Graham DO.
Licensure Skilled care. *Beds* SNF 32. *Certified* Medicare.
Owner Nonprofit corp.
Admissions Requirements Minimum age 14; Physician's request.
Staff RNs 6 (ft), 1 (pt); Nurses' aides 15 (ft), 2 (pt); Physical therapists 1 (pt); Activities coordinators 1 (ft); Dietitians 1 (pt); Podiatrists 1 (pt); Dentists 1 (pt).
Facilities Dining room; Chapel; Laundry room; Barber/Beauty shop; Library; Swimming pool & deck.
Activities Arts & crafts; Games; Reading groups; Prayer groups; Movies; Shopping trips; Dances/Social/Cultural gatherings.

Mountain View Care Center
2612 W Cucharras St, Colorado Springs, CO 80904
(719) 632-7474
Admin Jean Bauermeister. *Dir of Nursing* Dana Olson. *Medical Dir* Dr Williams.
Licensure Skilled care; Intermediate care; Personal care. *Beds* SNF 60; ICF 30; Personal care 22. *Certified* Medicaid; Medicare.
Owner Proprietary corp.
Admissions Requirements Females only; Medical examination.
Staff Physicians; RNs 6 (pt); LPNs 8 (pt); Nurses' aides 24 (pt); Physical therapists; Reality therapists; Recreational therapists; Occupational therapists; Speech therapists; Activities coordinators 1 (pt); Dietitians; Ophthalmologists; Podiatrists; Audiologists.
Facilities Dining room; Activities room; Crafts room; Laundry room; Barber/Beauty shop.
Activities Arts & crafts; Cards; Games; Reading groups; Prayer groups; Movies; Shopping trips; Dances/Social/Cultural gatherings; Intergenerational programs; Pet therapy.

Pikes Peak Manor
2719 N Union, Colorado Springs, CO 80909
(719) 636-1676
Admin Lois Cave. *Dir of Nursing* Rosanna Forrest. *Medical Dir* John McWilliams MD.
Licensure Skilled care; Intermediate care. *Beds* SNF 150; ICF 100. *Certified* Medicaid; Medicare.
Owner Proprietary corp (National Heritage).

Admissions Requirements Medical examination; Physician's request.
Staff RNs 15 (ft), 5 (pt); LPNs 10 (ft), 9 (pt); Nurses' aides 50 (ft), 10 (pt); Recreational therapists 3 (ft), 1 (pt).
Languages Spanish.
Facilities Dining room; Physical therapy room; Activities room; Chapel; Crafts room; Laundry room; Barber/Beauty shop.
Activities Arts & crafts; Cards; Games; Reading groups; Prayer groups; Movies; Shopping trips; Dances/Social/Cultural gatherings; Intergenerational programs; Pet therapy.

St Francis Nursing Center
7550 Assisi Heights, Colorado Springs, CO 80919
(719) 598-1336, 598-1578 FAX
Admin Tressa Mendoza. *Dir of Nursing* Elizabeth Donahue. *Medical Dir* Dr Robert Reeves.
Licensure Skilled care. *Beds* SNF 113. *Private Pay Patients* 76%. *Certified* Medicaid.
Owner Nonprofit organization/foundation (Sisters of Saint Francis).
Admissions Requirements Medical examination; Physician's request.
Staff RNs 7 (ft), 3 (pt); LPNs 1 (ft), 2 (pt); Nurses' aides 21 (ft), 5 (pt); Physical therapists; Activities coordinators 1 (ft); Dietitians 1 (ft).
Affiliation Roman Catholic.
Facilities Dining room; Physical therapy room; Activities room; Crafts room; Laundry room; Barber/Beauty shop; Private rooms; 2 chapels.
Activities Arts & crafts; Cards; Games; Reading groups; Prayer groups; Movies; Shopping trips; Dances/Social/Cultural gatherings; Intergenerational programs; Pet therapy; Religious services.

Springs Village Care Center
110 W Van Buren, Colorado Springs, CO 80907
(719) 475-8686
Admin Larry W Smith.
Licensure Skilled care; Intermediate care; Residential care. *Beds* SNF 58; ICF 58; Residential 17. *Certified* Medicaid; Medicare.
Owner Nonprofit corp (Bethesda Care Centers).

Myron Stratton Home
2525 Hwy 115 S, Colorado Springs, CO 80906
(719) 579-0930
Admin Jerry Huson.
Licensure Skilled care. *Beds* SNF 19.

Stroh Resident Homes
2335 Montebello Dr W, Colorado Springs, CO 80918
(719) 634-3301
Admin Wayne D Stroh; Marjorie M Stroh.
Licensure Intermediate care for mentally retarded. *Beds* ICF/MR 14. *Private Pay Patients* 0%. *Certified* Medicaid.
Owner Privately owned.
Admissions Requirements Minimum age 18; Females only.
Staff Activities coordinators; Direct care.
Facilities Dining room; Activities room.
Activities Games; Prayer groups; Movies; Shopping trips; Dances/Social/Cultural gatherings.

Sunnyrest Health Care Facility Inc
2400 E Cache La Poudre, Colorado Springs, CO 80909
(719) 471-8700
Admin Cynthia J Cordle RN. *Dir of Nursing* Cheri Cash RN. *Medical Dir* Dr James Edwards.
Licensure Skilled care; Retirement. *Beds* SNF 107; Retirement 51. *Private Pay Patients* 31%. *Certified* Medicaid; Medicare.

Owner Nonprofit corp.
Staff RNs 4 (ft), 4 (pt); LPNs 3 (ft), 7 (pt);
Nurses' aides 35 (ft), 16 (pt); Activities
coordinators 2 (ft); Dietitians 1 (ft).
Languages Spanish.
Facilities Dining room; Physical therapy
room; Activities room; Chapel; Crafts room;
Laundry room; Barber/Beauty shop; Library.
Activities Arts & crafts; Cards; Games;
Reading groups; Prayer groups; Movies;
Shopping trips; Dances/Social/Cultural
gatherings; Intergenerational programs; Pet
therapy.

Terrace Gardens Health Care Center
2438 Fountain Blvd, Colorado Springs, CO
80910
(719) 473-8000
Admin Delores L Heidenreich. *Dir of Nursing*
Helen Hedemark RN. *Medical Dir* Lester
Williams MD.
Licensure Skilled care; Intermediate care. *Beds*
SNF 60; ICF 60. *Certified* Medicaid;
Medicare; VA.
Owner Proprietary corp (ARA Living
Centers).
Admissions Requirements Physician's request.
Staff RNs; LPNs; Nurses' aides; Recreational
therapists; Activities coordinators; Dietitians.
Facilities Dining room; Activities room;
Laundry room; Barber/Beauty shop.
Activities Arts & crafts; Cards; Games;
Reading groups; Prayer groups; Movies;
Shopping trips; Dances/Social/Cultural
gatherings.

Union Printers Home & Hospital
101 S Union Blvd, Colorado Springs, CO
80901
(719) 634-3711
Admin Donald M Fifield.
Licensure Skilled care; Intermediate care;
General hospital. *Beds* SNF 65; ICF 32;
General hospital 11.
Owner Nonprofit corp.

Whoolery's Residential Care Facility
607 Lansing Dr, Colorado Springs, CO 80909
(303) 596-2621
Admin Angeline Whoolery.
Licensure Intermediate care for mentally
retarded. *Beds* 5.
Owner Proprietary corp.
Admissions Requirements Minimum age 18;
Females only; Medical examination.
Facilities Dining room; Laundry room.
Activities Arts & crafts; Cards; Games;
Reading groups; Prayer groups; Movies;
Shopping trips; Dances/Social/Cultural
gatherings.

Commerce City

Crocker Family Care Home
6050 Ivanhoe, Commerce City, CO 80022
(303) 287-7604
Admin Shirley Crocker.
Licensure Intermediate care. *Beds* 4.
Owner Proprietary corp.

Giles Family Care Home
6391 Quebec St, Commerce City, CO 80222
(303) 287-0673
Admin Mildred Giles.
Licensure Intermediate care. *Beds* 4.
Owner Proprietary corp.

Ruth Owen Family Care Home
6801 E 64th Ave, Commerce City, CO 80022
(303) 287-7984
Admin Ruth Owen.
Licensure Intermediate care. *Beds* 2.
Owner Proprietary corp.

Rose Hill Care Center Inc
5230 E 66th Way, Commerce City, CO 80022
(303) 289-1848

Admin Marjorie Eller. *Dir of Nursing* Ruby
Torkilson RN.
Licensure Skilled care; Intermediate care. *Beds*
SNF 60; ICF 46. *Certified* Medicaid.
Owner Proprietary corp.
Admissions Requirements Physician's request.
Staff RNs 5 (ft); LPNs 4 (ft), 2 (pt); Nurses'
aides 16 (ft); Activities coordinators 2 (ft);
Dietitians 1 (ft).
Languages Spanish.
Facilities Dining room; Physical therapy
room; Activities room; Laundry room;
Barber/Beauty shop; Library.
Activities Arts & crafts; Games; Reading
groups; Prayer groups; Movies; Shopping
trips; Dances/Social/Cultural gatherings.

Sunshine Health Care Center Inc
PO Box 269, Commerce City, CO 80022
(303) 289-7110
Admin Tressa Mendoza.
Licensure Skilled care; Intermediate care. *Beds*
SNF 83; ICF 17. *Certified* Medicaid;
Medicare.
Owner Proprietary corp.

Cortez

Vista Grande Nursing Home
1311 N Mildred Rd, Cortez, CO 81321
(303) 565-6666
Admin Tyler M Erickson.
Medical Dir Edward Merritt MD; Marti Bills
MD.
Licensure Skilled care; Intermediate care. *Beds*
76. *Certified* Medicaid; Medicare.
Owner Publicly owned.
Admissions Requirements Medical
examination; Physician's request.
Staff Physicians 18 (ft); RNs 4 (ft), 2 (pt);
LPNs 9 (ft), 3 (pt); Nurses' aides 31 (ft), 7
(pt); Physical therapists 1 (ft); Occupational
therapists 1 (ft); Speech therapists 1 (pt);
Activities coordinators 1 (ft); Dietitians 1
(ft).
Languages Spanish, Navajo.
Facilities Dining room; Physical therapy
room; Activities room; Chapel; Crafts room;
Laundry room; Barber/Beauty shop; Library.
Activities Arts & crafts; Cards; Games;
Reading groups; Prayer groups; Movies;
Shopping trips; Dances/Social/Cultural
gatherings; Picnics; Exercises.

Craig

Valley View Manor
943 W 8th Dr, Craig, CO 81625
(303) 824-4432
Admin John Filkoski.
Licensure Skilled care; Intermediate care. *Beds*
SNF 54; ICF 6. *Certified* Medicaid.
Owner Proprietary corp (ARA Living
Centers).

Cripple Creek

Hilltop Nursing Home & Community Clinic
PO Box 397, A St at Hettig Ave, Cripple
Creek, CO 80813
(719) 689-2931
Admin Gary Bergen.
Medical Dir Dr Mitchell.
Licensure Intermediate care. *Beds* ICF 60.
Certified Medicaid.
Owner Nonprofit organization/foundation.
Staff Physicians 1 (ft); RNs 2 (ft); LPNs 5 (ft);
Nurses' aides 15 (ft); Physical therapists 1
(pt); Occupational therapists 1 (pt); Speech
therapists 1 (pt); Activities coordinators 1
(ft); Dietitians 1 (pt); Ophthalmologists 1
(pt).
Affiliation Lutheran.

Facilities Dining room; Activities room;
Laundry room; Barber/Beauty shop.
Activities Arts & crafts; Cards; Games; Prayer
groups; Movies; Shopping trips; Dances/
Social/Cultural gatherings; Activities on
volunteer basis.

Del Norte

**St Joseph's Hospital & Nursing Home of Del
Norte Inc**
1280 Grande Ave, Del Norte, CO 81132
(719) 657-3311
Admin Hazel Colvin. *Dir of Nursing* Judy
Kuske. *Medical Dir* Norman Haug MD.
Licensure Skilled care. *Beds* SNF 33. *Certified*
Medicaid.
Owner Nonprofit corp (CSJ Health Systems).
Admissions Requirements Medical
examination.
Staff RNs 1 (ft), 3 (pt); LPNs 2 (ft), 2 (pt);
Nurses' aides 14 (ft), 2 (pt); Physical
therapists 1 (pt); Activities coordinators 1
(ft); Dietitians 1 (pt).
Languages Spanish.
Affiliation Roman Catholic.
Facilities Dining room; Physical therapy
room; Activities room; Chapel; Barber/
Beauty shop.
Activities Arts & crafts; Games; Reading
groups; Prayer groups; Movies; Dances/
Social/Cultural gatherings; Intergenerational
programs.

Delta

Bethesda Care Center
2050 S Main St, Delta, CO 81416
(303) 874-9773
Admin Bruce Odenthal.
Licensure Skilled care. *Beds* 90. *Certified*
Medicaid.
Owner Nonprofit corp (Bethesda Care
Centers).

Delta Care Center
1102 Grand Ave, Delta, CO 81416
(303) 874-5773
Admin Jack C Hamlett.
Licensure Intermediate care. *Beds* ICF 40.
Certified Medicaid.
Owner Proprietary corp.
Admissions Requirements Physician's request.
Staff RNs 1 (ft); LPNs 4 (ft), 2 (pt); Nurses'
aides 6 (ft), 4 (pt); Physical therapists 1 (pt);
Recreational therapists 1 (ft); Activities
coordinators 1 (ft); Dietitians 1 (pt);
Podiatrists 1 (pt); Dentists 1 (pt).
Facilities Dining room; Activities room;
Crafts room; Laundry room.
Activities Arts & crafts; Cards; Games;
Reading groups; Prayer groups; Movies;
Shopping trips; Dances/Social/Cultural
gatherings.

Denver

Argyle
4115 W 38th Ave, Denver, CO 80212
(303) 455-9513
Admin Ann R Brown.
Licensure Intermediate care; Assisted living.
Beds ICF 26; Assisted living 100.
Owner Nonprofit organization/foundation.
Admissions Requirements Minimum age 65.
Staff RNs 1 (ft); LPNs 7 (ft), 3 (pt); Nurses'
aides 12 (ft), 3 (pt); Recreational therapists 1
(ft); Activities coordinators 1 (ft); Dietitians
1 (pt).
Facilities Dining room; Physical therapy
room; Activities room; Crafts room; Laundry
room; Barber/Beauty shop; Library.
Activities Arts & crafts; Cards; Games; Prayer
groups; Movies; Shopping trips; General
entertainment.

Arkansas Manor Nursing Home Inc
3185 W Arkansas, Denver, CO 80219
(303) 922-1169
Admin Betty Carlson.
Medical Dir Frank I Dubin MD.
Licensure Skilled care; Intermediate care. *Beds*
SNF 110; ICF 10. *Certified* Medicaid.
Owner Proprietary corp.
Admissions Requirements Minimum age 65.
Facilities Dining room; Laundry room;
Barber/Beauty shop; Library.
Activities Arts & crafts; Games; Reading
groups; Prayer groups; Movies; Shopping
trips; Dances/Social/Cultural gatherings.

Asbury Circle Living Center
4660 E Asbury Cr, Denver, CO 80222
(303) 756-1546
Admin Cheryl Gaul. *Dir of Nursing* Pauline
Williams.
Licensure Skilled care; Intermediate care;
Alzheimer's care. *Beds* SNF 60; ICF 22.
Certified Medicaid.
Owner Nonprofit corp (Adventist Health Sys-
USA).
Affiliation Seventh-Day Adventist.
Facilities Dining room; Activities room;
Crafts room; Laundry room; Barber/Beauty
shop.
Activities Arts & crafts; Cards; Games;
Reading groups; Prayer groups; Movies;
Dances/Social/Cultural gatherings.

Aspen Siesta
5353 E Yale Ave, Denver, CO 80222
(303) 757-1209
Admin Ruth D Horsley. *Dir of Nursing* Nancy
Stabel RN.
Licensure Skilled care; Retirement. *Beds* SNF
70.
Owner Privately owned.
Admissions Requirements Physician's request.
Facilities Dining room; Physical therapy
room; Activities room; Crafts room; Laundry
room; Barber/Beauty shop; Library.
Activities Arts & crafts; Cards; Games;
Reading groups; Movies; Dances/Social/
Cultural gatherings.

Autumn Heights Health Care Center
3131 S Federal Blvd, Denver, CO 80236
(303) 761-0260
Admin Marvin Bishop. *Dir of Nursing* Pat
Minyard RN. *Medical Dir* William Hines
MD.
Licensure Skilled care; Intermediate care. *Beds*
SNF 89; ICF 89. *Private Pay Patients* 20%.
Certified Medicaid; Medicare.
Owner Proprietary corp (Waverly Group).
Admissions Requirements Minimum age 65;
Medical examination; Physician's request.
Staff RNs 5 (ft); LPNs 20 (ft); Nurses' aides
53 (ft); Physical therapists 1 (ft);
Recreational therapists 1 (ft); Occupational
therapists 1 (ft); Speech therapists 1 (ft);
Activities coordinators 1 (ft); Dietitians 1
(ft); Podiatrists 1 (ft).
Facilities Dining room; Physical therapy
room; Activities room; Chapel; Crafts room;
Laundry room; Barber/Beauty shop; Library.
Activities Arts & crafts; Cards; Games;
Reading groups; Prayer groups; Movies;
Shopping trips; Dances/Social/Cultural
gatherings; Intergenerational programs; Pet
therapy.

Bella Vita Towers Inc
4450 E Jewell, Denver, CO 80222
(303) 757-7438
Admin Carl T Zarlengo. *Dir of Nursing* Lori
Elliott. *Medical Dir* Francis Burdick MD.
Licensure Skilled care; Alzheimer's care. *Beds*
SNF 136. *Certified* Medicaid; Medicare.
Owner Proprietary corp.
Staff RNs 9 (ft); LPNs 9 (ft); Nurses' aides 36
(ft); Physical therapists (contracted); Reality
therapists 1 (ft); Recreational therapists 1

(ft); Occupational therapists (contracted);
Speech therapists (contracted); Activities
coordinators 1 (ft); Dietitians 1 (ft).
Facilities Dining room; Physical therapy
room; Activities room; Chapel; Crafts room;
Laundry room; Barber/Beauty shop.
Activities Arts & crafts; Cards; Games;
Reading groups; Prayer groups; Movies;
Shopping trips; Dances/Social/Cultural
gatherings.

Berkley Manor
735 S Locust, Denver, CO 80224
(303) 320-4377
Admin John Milewski NHA. *Dir of Nursing*
Marti Foley. *Medical Dir* Dr Hines.
Licensure Skilled care. *Beds* SNF 120. *Private
Pay Patients* 90%. *Certified* Medicaid;
Medicare.
Owner Privately owned.
Admissions Requirements Minimum age 30.
Staff RNs; LPNs; Nurses' aides; Physical
therapists; Reality therapists; Recreational
therapists; Occupational therapists; Speech
therapists; Activities coordinators; Dietitians;
Ophthalmologists; Podiatrists; Audiologists.
Facilities Dining room; Physical therapy
room; Activities room; Chapel; Crafts room;
Laundry room; Barber/Beauty shop.
Activities Arts & crafts; Cards; Games;
Reading groups; Prayer groups; Movies;
Shopping trips; Dances/Social/Cultural
gatherings; Intergenerational programs; Pet
therapy.

Beth Israel Health Care Center
1601 Lowell Blvd, Denver, CO 80204
(303) 825-2190
Admin Ann Holland, CEO/ECF.
Medical Dir Dr Sydney Foster.
Licensure Skilled care; Intermediate care. *Beds*
SNF 82; ICF 65. *Certified* Medicaid;
Medicare.
Owner Nonprofit corp.
Admissions Requirements Minimum age 15;
Physician's request.
Staff Physicians 1 (ft); RNs 5 (ft), 3 (pt);
LPNs 18 (ft); Nurses' aides 32 (ft), 2 (pt);
Physical therapists 1 (pt); Occupational
therapists 1 (pt); Speech therapists 1 (pt);
Activities coordinators 3 (ft); Dietitians 1
(pt); Podiatrists 1 (pt); Audiologists 1 (pt);
Dentists 1 (pt).
Affiliation Jewish.
Facilities Dining room; Activities room;
Chapel; Crafts room; Laundry room; Barber/
Beauty shop; Library.
Activities Arts & crafts; Cards; Games;
Reading groups; Movies; Shopping trips;
Dances/Social/Cultural gatherings.

Bragg Residential Care Home Inc
1461 Cook St, Denver, CO 80206
(303) 355-0035
Admin Ellen M Bragg.
Licensure Developmentally disabled. *Beds* 6.
Owner Proprietary corp.

Brentwood Care Center
1825 S Federal Blvd, Denver, CO 80219
(303) 935-4609
Admin Kurtis Keele.
Licensure Skilled care; Intermediate care. *Beds*
SNF 60. *Certified* Medicaid.
Owner Proprietary corp.

Briarwood Health Care Center
1440 Vine St, Denver, CO 80206
(303) 399-0350
Admin Terrylea Entsminger. *Dir of Nursing*
Bethany A Davis RN. *Medical Dir* Robert L
McKenna MD.
Licensure Skilled care; Intermediate care. *Beds*
SNF 118; ICF 119.
Owner Proprietary corp.
Admissions Requirements Minimum age 18.

Staff RNs 10 (ft); LPNs 9 (ft); Nurses' aides
45 (ft); Physical therapists 1 (pt);
Occupational therapists 1 (pt); Speech
therapists 1 (pt); Activities coordinators 1
(ft); Dietitians 1 (pt); Ophthalmologists 1
(pt); Podiatrists 1 (pt).
Facilities Dining room; Physical therapy
room; Activities room; Chapel; Crafts room;
Laundry room; Barber/Beauty shop; Library.
Activities Arts & crafts; Cards; Games;
Reading groups; Prayer groups; Movies;
Dances/Social/Cultural gatherings; Bingo;
Pool; Bowling.

Burton Family Care Home
3553 Hudson, Denver, CO 80207
(303) 321-3693
Admin Oleria P Burton.
Licensure Intermediate care for mentally
retarded. *Beds* 4.
Owner Proprietary corp.

Christian Living Campus—University Hills
2480 S Clermont, Denver, CO 80222
(303) 758-4528, 758-1787 FAX
Admin Kenneth E Webb. *Dir of Nursing* Mary
Grace Smiegel. *Medical Dir* William Hines
MD.
Licensure Skilled care; Intermediate care;
Assisted living/Independent living;
Alzheimer's care. *Beds* SNF 50; ICF 44;
Assisted living units 30; Independent living
apts 145. *Private Pay Patients* 80%. *Certified*
Medicaid.
Owner Nonprofit organization/foundation
(Christian Living Campus).
Admissions Requirements Minimum age 62;
Medical examination.
Staff Physicians 40 (pt); RNs 6 (ft); LPNs 8
(pt); Nurses' aides 60 (ft); Physical therapists
1 (pt); Occupational therapists 1 (pt); Speech
therapists 1 (pt); Activities coordinators 3
(ft); Dietitians 1 (pt); Podiatrists 1 (pt);
Audiologists 1 (pt).
Affiliation Reformed Church.
Facilities Dining room; Physical therapy
room; Activities room; Chapel; Crafts room;
Laundry room; Barber/Beauty shop; Library.
Activities Arts & crafts; Cards; Games;
Reading groups; Prayer groups; Movies;
Shopping trips; Dances/Social/Cultural
gatherings; Intergenerational programs; Pet
therapy.

Costigan Family Care Home
600 S Quitman, Denver, CO 80219
(303) 934-4906
Admin Arabella M Costigan.
Licensure Intermediate care. *Beds* 4.
Owner Proprietary corp.

Doctors Hospital
1920 High St, Denver, CO 80218
(303) 320-5871
Admin Christopher A Smith.
Licensure General hospital. *Beds* General
hospital 45. *Certified* Medicaid.
Owner Proprietary corp.

Frickell Family Care Home
4988 Stuart St, Denver, CO 80212
(303) 455-9398
Admin Mary Frickell.
Licensure Intermediate care. *Beds* 4.
Owner Proprietary corp.

Gottesfeld House
8160 E Linsvale Pl, Denver, CO 80210
(303) 733-4034
Admin Ellen Ward.
Licensure Residential MR care. *Beds*
Residential MR care 8.
Owner Nonprofit corp.

Hallmark Nursing Center
3701 W Radcliffe Ave, Denver, CO 80236
(303) 794-6484
Admin Delvin Brake.
Licensure Skilled care. *Beds* SNF 120.

Heritage Rehabilitation Center
1500 Hooker, Denver, CO 80204
(303) 534-5968
Admin Theresa Johnson.
Licensure Rehabilitation. *Beds* Rehabilitaiton
  96. *Certified* Medicaid; Medicare.
Owner Proprietary corp (Regency Health Care
  Centers).

Holly Heights Nursing Home Inc
6000 E Iliff, Denver, CO 80222
(303) 757-5441
Admin Janet L Snipes. *Dir of Nursing* Jeanne
  Hurlburt RN. *Medical Dir* Stanley Kerstein
  MD.
Licensure Skilled care; Intermediate care. *Beds*
  SNF 60; ICF 91. *Private Pay Patients* 50%.
  Certified Medicaid; Medicare.
Owner Proprietary corp.
Admissions Requirements Minimum age 65.
Staff RNs 12 (ft); LPNs 12 (ft); Nurses' aides
  30 (ft); Activities coordinators 2 (ft), 2 (pt);
  Dietitians 1 (pt); Ophthalmologists 1 (pt).
Facilities Dining room; Activities room;
  Laundry room; Barber/Beauty shop; Semi-
  private & private rooms.
Activities Arts & crafts; Cards; Games;
  Reading groups; Prayer groups; Movies;
  Shopping trips; Dances/Social/Cultural
  gatherings.

Iliff Care Center
6060 E Iliff Ave, Denver, CO 80222
(303) 759-4221
Admin Donna Rayer. *Dir of Nursing* Carolyn
  Straka. *Medical Dir* Dr Karl Shipman.
Licensure Skilled care. *Beds* SNF 160. *Private
  Pay Patients* 40%. *Certified* Medicaid;
  Medicare.
Owner Proprietary corp (Hillhaven Corp).
Admissions Requirements Physician's request.
Staff RNs 7 (ft); LPNs 20 (ft); Nurses' aides
  55 (ft); Physical therapists 1 (ft); Reality
  therapists 1 (pt); Occupational therapists 1
  (ft); Speech therapists 1 (pt); Activities
  coordinators 1 (ft); Dietitians 1 (ft);
  Podiatrists (contracted).
Languages Korean, Spanish.
Facilities Dining room; Physical therapy
  room; Activities room; Crafts room; Barber/
  Beauty shop; Library.
Activities Arts & crafts; Cards; Games;
  Reading groups; Prayer groups; Movies;
  Shopping trips; Dances/Social/Cultural
  gatherings; Pet therapy.

Ivy Nursing Center
2205 W 29th Ave, Denver, CO 80211
(303) 458-1112
Admin Tracy Newman.
Medical Dir Dr Jardine.
Licensure Skilled care; Intermediate care. *Beds*
  SNF 102; ICF 60. *Certified* Medicaid.
Owner Proprietary corp (Beverly Enterprises).
Admissions Requirements Minimum age 18.
Staff RNs 2 (ft); LPNs 12 (ft); Nurses' aides
  39 (ft), 1 (pt); Activities coordinators 1 (ft);
  Dietitians 1 (ft).
Languages Spanish, German.
Affiliation Roman Catholic.
Facilities Dining room; Physical therapy
  room; Activities room; Chapel; Crafts room;
  Laundry room; Barber/Beauty shop; Library;
  Kitchen.
Activities Arts & crafts; Cards; Games;
  Reading groups; Prayer groups; Movies;
  Shopping trips; Dances/Social/Cultural
  gatherings; AA group; Entertainment;
  Exercises.

Lena Crews Family Care Home
838 S Vallejo, Denver, CO 80223
(303) 936-1414
Admin Lena Crews.
Licensure Intermediate care. *Beds* 2.
Owner Proprietary corp.

Manor Care Nursing Home
290 S Monaco Pkwy, Denver, CO 80224
(303) 355-2525
Admin Ed Parades.
Licensure Skilled care. *Beds* SNF 120.

Martin Family Care Home
1996 S Newton, Denver, CO 80219
(303) 935-7528
Admin Mary E Martin.
Licensure Intermediate care. *Beds* 3.
Owner Proprietary corp.

Mazotti Family Care Home
2767 W 38th Ave, Denver, CO 80211
(303) 433-5933
Admin Jeannie Mazotti.
Licensure Intermediate care. *Beds* 4.
Owner Proprietary corp.

McCallum Family Care Center
2536 Downing, Denver, CO 80205
(303) 355-6524
Admin Willie H McCallum.
Licensure Intermediate care. *Beds* 4.
Owner Proprietary corp.

McCovy Golden Age Home Inc
2858 California St, Denver, CO 80205
(303) 259-2219
Admin Gertrude McCovy.
Licensure Intermediate care for mentally
  retarded. *Beds* ICF/MR 8.
Owner Nonprofit corp.

Mullen Home—Little Sisters of the Poor
3629 29th Ave, Denver, CO 80211
(303) 433-7221
Admin Sr Maureen Courtney. *Dir of Nursing*
  Sr Therese Marie Reichard.
Licensure Skilled care; Intermediate care. *Beds*
  SNF 22; ICF 68. *Certified* Medicaid;
  Medicare.
Owner Nonprofit corp.

Nikkel Family Care Home
5030 W Park Pl, Denver, CO 80219
(303) 936-6430
Admin Mildred I Nikkel.
Licensure Intermediate care. *Beds* 6.
Owner Proprietary corp.

Park Avenue Baptist Home
1535 Park Ave, Denver, CO 80218
(303) 832-9323
Admin Norma J Harrison.
Medical Dir Mary Grace Smigiel.
Licensure Skilled care; Intermediate care;
  Residential care. *Beds* SNF 49; ICF 56;
  Residential 10. *Certified* Medicaid;
  Medicare.
Owner Nonprofit corp (Baptist Home
  Associates).
Admissions Requirements Minimum age 50.
Staff RNs 7 (ft); LPNs 10 (ft); Nurses' aides
  25 (ft); Physical therapists 2 (ft);
  Recreational therapists 2 (ft); Activities
  coordinators 1 (ft); Dietitians 1 (pt).
Affiliation Baptist.
Facilities Dining room; Physical therapy
  room; Activities room; Chapel; Crafts room;
  Laundry room; Barber/Beauty shop; Library.
Activities Arts & crafts; Cards; Games;
  Reading groups; Prayer groups; Movies;
  Shopping trips; Dances/Social/Cultural
  gatherings.

Park Manor
1801 E 19th Ave, Denver, CO 80218
(303) 839-7777
Admin Sandra L Martini.
Licensure Intermediate care. *Beds* ICF 24.

Parkview Manor Nursing Home Inc
3105 W Arkansas Ave, Denver, CO 80219
(303) 936-3497
Admin Ruth E Thomann.

Licensure Skilled care; Intermediate care. *Beds*
  SNF 88; ICF 2. *Certified* Medicaid.
Owner Proprietary corp.

Presbyterian Denver Hospital
1719 E 19th Ave, Denver, CO 80218
(303) 839-6000
Admin J Rock Tonkel.
Licensure General hospital. *Beds* General
  hospital 438.
Owner Nonprofit corp.

Rocky Mountain Health Care Center
2201 Downing St, Denver, CO 80205
(303) 861-4825
Admin Linda Lovato. *Dir of Nursing* Shirley
  William. *Medical Dir* Werner Prenzlau MD.
Licensure Skilled care; Intermediate care. *Beds*
  SNF 60; ICF 60. *Certified* Medicaid.
Owner Proprietary corp (National Heritage).
Admissions Requirements Minimum age 18;
  Physician's request.
Staff Physicians 5 (ft); RNs 8 (ft), 2 (pt);
  LPNs 8 (ft), 2 (pt); Nurses' aides 25 (ft);
  Recreational therapists 1 (ft); Activities
  coordinators 1 (ft); Dietitians 1 (ft).
Facilities Dining room; Physical therapy
  room; Activities room; Crafts room; Laundry
  room.
Activities Arts & crafts; Cards; Games;
  Reading groups; Prayer groups; Movies;
  Shopping trips; Dances/Social/Cultural
  gatherings.

Rose Mary's Home
7939 Pecos St, Denver, CO 80221
(303) 429-1857
Admin Rose Mary Hoff.
Licensure Intermediate care. *Beds* 4.
Owner Proprietary corp.

St Paul Health Center
1667 Saint Paul St, Denver, CO 80206
(303) 399-2040
Admin Richard Whelan.
Licensure Skilled care; Intermediate care. *Beds*
  SNF 100; ICF 150. *Certified* Medicaid;
  Medicare.
Owner Proprietary corp.

Sherrelwood Residential Care Facility
1780 Sherrelwood Dr, Denver, CO 80221
(303) 429-6534
Admin Anita M Sherman.
Licensure Skilled care; Retirement. *Beds* SNF
  10. *Certified* Medicaid; Medicare.
Owner Privately owned.
Admissions Requirements Minimum age 65;
  Medical examination; Physician's request.
Staff RNs; Nurses' aides; Recreational
  therapists; Activities coordinators.
Languages Spanish, Sign.
Facilities Dining room; Activities room;
  Crafts room; Laundry room; Library; Patios.
Activities Arts & crafts; Cards; Games;
  Reading groups; Movies; Shopping trips;
  Dances/Social/Cultural gatherings;
  Barbeques; Picnics; Sing-alongs; Cooking
  classes.

South Monaco Care Center
895 S Monaco, Denver, CO 80222
(303) 321-3110
Admin Palma Chambers.
Licensure Skilled care; Intermediate care. *Beds*
  SNF 60; ICF 57.
Owner Proprietary corp (Convalescent
  Services).
Admissions Requirements Minimum age 65;
  Medical examination.
Staff RNs 6 (ft); LPNs 2 (ft); Nurses' aides 14
  (ft); Recreational therapists 1 (ft).
Facilities Dining room; Physical therapy
  room; Activities room; Laundry room;
  Barber/Beauty shop.
Activities Arts & crafts; Cards; Games;
  Reading groups.

Stovall Care Center
3345 Forest St, Denver, CO 80207
(303) 355-1666, 355-1667
Admin Viola B Garlington NHA. *Dir of Nursing* Marva L Shoates. *Medical Dir* Jitze de Jong MD.
Licensure Skilled care; Alzheimer's care. *Beds* SNF 60. *Private Pay Patients* 1%. *Certified* Medicaid; Medicare.
Owner Nonprofit corp.
Admissions Requirements Minimum age 27; Physician's request.
Staff RNs 4 (ft), 4 (pt); LPNs 3 (ft), 2 (pt); Nurses' aides 16 (ft), 5 (pt); Activities coordinators 1 (ft); Social workers 1 (pt).
Affiliation Baptist.
Facilities Dining room; Activities room; Crafts room; Library; Wheelchair accessible bus; Senior recreation center on campus.
Activities Arts & crafts; Games; Prayer groups; Movies; Dances/Social/Cultural gatherings; Intergenerational programs; Pet therapy.

Sunny Hill
3400 E 34th Ave, Denver, CO 80205
(303) 333-3439
Admin Lillian Duran.
Licensure Intermediate care for mentally retarded. *Beds* 10.
Owner Proprietary corp.

Transitional Care Unit—Extended Care Facility
1719 E 19th Ave, Denver, CO 80218
(303) 321-2651
Admin Sandra L Martini.
Licensure Extended care. *Beds* Extended care 32.

Valley Manor Health Care Center
4601 E Asbury Cir, Denver, CO 80222
(303) 757-1228, 759-3390 FAX
Admin Kay Hunter. *Dir of Nursing* Kathryn Murray. *Medical Dir* Larry Plunkett MD.
Licensure Skilled care; Intermediate care. *Beds* SNF 46; ICF 39. *Certified* Medicaid; Medicare.
Owner Proprietary corp (American Medical Services Inc).
Admissions Requirements Minimum age 45; Medical examination.
Staff Physicians 35 (pt); RNs 6 (ft), 3 (pt); LPNs 5 (ft), 3 (pt); Nurses' aides 25 (ft), 6 (pt); Physical therapists 1 (pt); Recreational therapists 1 (pt); Occupational therapists 1 (pt); Speech therapists 1 (pt); Activities coordinators 1 (ft); Dietitians 1 (pt); Podiatrists 1 (pt).
Facilities Dining room; Physical therapy room; Activities room; Crafts room; Barber/Beauty shop.
Activities Arts & crafts; Cards; Games; Reading groups; Prayer groups; Movies; Shopping trips; Dances/Social/Cultural gatherings; Intergenerational programs; Pet therapy.

Wheatridge Manor Nursing Home Inc
2920 Fenton St, Denver, CO 80214
(303) 238-0481
Admin Sylvia Sara Ruda. *Dir of Nursing* Darlene Gaskin. *Medical Dir* Paul Fishman MD.
Licensure Skilled care; Intermediate care; Alzheimer's care. *Beds* Swing beds SNF/ICF 84. *Certified* Medicaid.
Owner Proprietary corp.
Admissions Requirements Medical examination; Physician's request.
Staff Physicians (on call); RNs 10 (ft); LPNs 7 (ft); Nurses' aides 22 (ft); Physical therapists 1 (ft), 1 (pt); Reality therapists 1 (pt); Activities coordinators 1 (ft); Dietitians 1 (pt); Ophthalmologists 1 (pt); Podiatrists 1 (pt); Social services 1 (ft), 1 (pt).
Languages French, German, Polish, Spanish, Russian.

Facilities Dining room; Physical therapy room; Activities room; Chapel; Crafts room; Laundry room; Barber/Beauty shop; Library.
Activities Arts & crafts; Cards; Games; Reading groups; Prayer groups; Movies; Shopping trips; Dances/Social/Cultural gatherings; Intergenerational programs; Pet therapy.

Willow Brook Care Center
3315 Sheridan Blvd, Denver, CO 80210
(303) 237-9521
Admin Maggie Decker. *Dir of Nursing* Maureen Burns. *Medical Dir* Frank Dubin MD.
Licensure Skilled care. *Beds* SNF 56. *Private Pay Patients* 10%. *Certified* Medicaid; Medicare.
Owner Proprietary corp (Waverly Group).
Admissions Requirements Medical examination.
Staff RNs 5 (ft), 2 (pt); LPNs 4 (ft); Nurses' aides 13 (ft), 3 (pt); Physical therapists (contracted); Recreational therapists 1 (ft); Occupational therapists (contracted); Speech therapists (contracted); Activities coordinators 1 (ft); Dietitians (contracted); Ophthalmologists (contracted); Podiatrists (contracted); Audiologists (contracted).
Languages Spanish.
Facilities Dining room; Physical therapy room; Library.
Activities Arts & crafts; Games; Reading groups; Prayer groups; Movies; Shopping trips; Dances/Social/Cultural gatherings; Pet therapy; Dining out.

Durango

Browning House
205 W Park Ave, Durango, CO 81301
(303) 259-2887
Admin Alice Archibald, Exec Dir.
Licensure Intermediate care for mentally retarded. *Beds* 13.
Owner Nonprofit corp.

Four Corners Health Care Center
2911 Junction St, Durango, CO 81301
(303) 247-2215
Admin Elizabeth Lee.
Licensure Skilled care; Intermediate care. *Beds* SNF 86; ICF 32. *Certified* Medicaid.
Owner Proprietary corp (ARA Living Centers).

Mercy Medical Center of Durango Inc
375 E Park Ave, Durango, CO 81301
(303) 247-4311
Admin Michael J Lawler.
Licensure Skilled care; General hospital. *Beds* SNF 11; General hospital 94.

Eads

Weisbrod Memorial County Hospital & Nursing Home
PO Box 817, Eads, CO 81036-0817
(719) 438-5401
Admin Paul Masar. *Dir of Nursing* Diana Ortega. *Medical Dir* John Hadley DO.
Licensure Intermediate care. *Beds* ICF 34. *Private Pay Patients* 10%. *Certified* Medicaid.
Owner Publicly owned.
Admissions Requirements Medical examination.
Staff Physicians 1 (ft); RNs 5 (ft), 1 (pt); LPNs 2 (ft); Nurses' aides 10 (ft), 5 (pt); Activities coordinators 1 (ft); Dietitians 1 (ft); Pool nurses.
Facilities Dining room; Activities room; Crafts room; Laundry room; Barber/Beauty shop.

Activities Arts & crafts; Cards; Games; Reading groups; Prayer groups; Movies; Dances/Social/Cultural gatherings; Pet therapy.

Eckert

Horizons Health Care
1141 Hwy 65, Eckert, CO 81418-9643
(303) 835-3113
Admin A Lucille Beals. *Dir of Nursing* Mary E Simin. *Medical Dir* Charles T Frey MD.
Licensure Skilled care. *Beds* SNF 68. *Certified* Medicaid.
Owner Nonprofit corp (Volunteers of America).
Admissions Requirements Minimum age 16; Physician's request.
Staff RNs 4 (ft), 4 (pt); LPNs 4 (ft), 4 (pt); Nurses' aides 15 (ft), 4 (pt); Recreational therapists 1 (ft).
Facilities Dining room; Physical therapy room; Activities room; Chapel; Crafts room; Laundry room; Barber/Beauty shop; Library.
Activities Arts & crafts; Cards; Games; Reading groups; Prayer groups; Movies; Shopping trips; Dances/Social/Cultural gatherings; Church groups come in on Sunday.

Englewood

Cherry Hills Nursing Home
3575 S Washington St, Englewood, CO 80110
(303) 789-2265
Admin June Richard.
Medical Dir Dr Angela Heaton.
Licensure Skilled care; Intermediate care. *Beds* SNF 89; ICF 6. *Certified* Medicaid; Medicare.
Owner Proprietary corp (Hillhaven Corp).
Admissions Requirements Medical examination; Physician's request.
Staff RNs 5 (ft), 4 (pt); LPNs 3 (ft), 4 (pt); Nurses' aides 38 (ft), 10 (pt); Physical therapists 1 (pt); Recreational therapists 1 (pt); Occupational therapists 1 (pt); Speech therapists 1 (pt); Activities coordinators 1 (ft); Dietitians 1 (ft); Podiatrists 1 (pt); Dentists 1 (pt).
Facilities Dining room; Physical therapy room; Activities room; Laundry room; Barber/Beauty shop; Library.
Activities Arts & crafts; Cards; Games; Reading groups; Prayer groups; Movies; Shopping trips; Dances/Social/Cultural gatherings.

Cherry Park Health Care Facility
3636 S Pearl St, Englewood, CO 80110
(303) 761-1640
Admin Marcia House.
Licensure Skilled care; Intermediate care. *Beds* SNF 52; ICF 44. *Certified* Medicaid.
Owner Proprietary corp (ARA Living Centers).

Englewood House
5001 S Hooker, Englewood, CO 80110
(303) 696-7002
Admin Margaret Lowe.
Licensure Developmentally disabled. *Beds* 8.
Owner Nonprofit corp.

Julia Temple Center
3401 S Lafayette St, Englewood, CO 80110
(303) 761-0075
Admin Marcia Pilgrim. *Dir of Nursing* Mary Kramer RN. *Medical Dir* A Lee Anneberg MD.
Licensure Skilled care; Intermediate care; Residential care; Alzheimer's care. *Beds* SNF 59; ICF 77; Residential 44. *Certified* Medicaid.
Owner Proprietary corp.
Admissions Requirements Minimum age 50; Medical examination; Physician's request.

Staff RNs; LPNs; Nurses' aides; Recreational therapists; Activities coordinators; Dietitians.
Languages Spanish.
Facilities Dining room; Activities room; Crafts room; Laundry room; Barber/Beauty shop; Outside secured courtyard.
Activities Arts & crafts; Cards; Games; Prayer groups; Movies; Shopping trips; Dances/Social/Cultural gatherings.

Erie

Bland Residential Care Home
RR 1 Box 5050, Erie, CO 80516
(303) 447-9196
Admin Marie Bland.
Licensure Intermediate care. *Beds* 6.
Owner Proprietary corp.

Estes Park

Prospect Park Skilled Nursing Facility
PO Box 2740, 555 Prospect, Estes Park, CO 80517
(303) 586-8103
Admin Andrew Wills CEO. *Dir of Nursing* Margie Greenlee RN. *Medical Dir* Thomas Nichol MD.
Licensure Skilled care; Retirement. *Beds* SNF 60; Retirement 8. *Private Pay Patients* 45%. *Certified* Medicaid; Medicare.
Owner Publicly owned.
Admissions Requirements Minimum age 55; Medical examination; Physician's request.
Staff Physicians 4 (ft); RNs 4 (ft), 4 (pt); LPNs 5 (ft), 2 (pt); Nurses' aides 9 (ft), 6 (pt); Physical therapists 1 (ft), 1 (pt); Recreational therapists 1 (ft), 1 (pt); Occupational therapists 1 (pt); Speech therapists 1 (pt); Activities coordinators 1 (ft); Dietitians 1 (pt).
Facilities Dining room; Physical therapy room; Activities room; Chapel; Crafts room; Laundry room; Barber/Beauty shop; Library.
Activities Arts & crafts; Cards; Games; Reading groups; Prayer groups; Movies; Shopping trips; Dances/Social/Cultural gatherings; Intergenerational programs; Pet therapy; Scenic tours.

Florence

Colorado State Veterans Nursing Home
Moore Dr, Florence, CO 81226
(719) 784-6331, 784-6334 FAX
Admin Mary Jeanne Logan RN NHA. *Dir of Nursing* James Vigil RN. *Medical Dir* John Buglewicz MD.
Licensure Skilled care; Alzheimer's care. *Beds* SNF 120; Secured Alzheimer's 20; Non-secured Alzheimer's 33. *Private Pay Patients* 1%. *Certified* Medicaid.
Owner Publicly owned.
Admissions Requirements Medical examination; Physician's request.
Staff Physicians 3 (pt); RNs 10 (ft), 1 (pt); LPNs 9 (ft), 1 (pt); Nurses' aides 37 (ft); Physical therapists 1 (pt); Speech therapists 1 (pt); Activities coordinators 2 (ft); Dietitians 1 (pt); Ophthalmologists 1 (pt); Podiatrists 1 (pt); Audiologists 1 (pt); Geriatric nurse practitioners 1 (ft).
Languages Spanish.
Facilities Dining room; Physical therapy room; Activities room; Chapel; Crafts room; Laundry room; Barber/Beauty shop; Outdoor fenced courtyard with gazebo.
Activities Arts & crafts; Cards; Games; Reading groups; Prayer groups; Movies; Shopping trips; Dances/Social/Cultural gatherings; Pet therapy; Exercise; Music; Socialization; Family support groups; Individual counseling; Outings.

St Joseph Manor
600 W 3rd St, Florence, CO 81226
(719) 784-4891
Admin Barbara Carochi NHA. *Dir of Nursing* Gail Petracca RN. *Medical Dir* Peter J Gamache MD.
Licensure Skilled care. *Beds* SNF 43. *Private Pay Patients* 20%. *Certified* Medicaid.
Owner Nonprofit organization/foundation.
Admissions Requirements Medical examination; Physician's request.
Staff Physicians 4 (pt); RNs 1 (ft), 3 (pt); LPNs 4 (ft), 2 (pt); Nurses' aides 7 (ft), 13 (pt); Physical therapists 2 (pt); Recreational therapists 1 (pt); Occupational therapists 1 (pt); Speech therapists 1 (pt); Activities coordinators 1 (ft); Dietitians 1 (pt); Ophthalmologists 1 (pt).
Affiliation Roman Catholic.
Facilities Dining room; Physical therapy room; Activities room; Crafts room; Laundry room; Barber/Beautician services available.
Activities Arts & crafts; Cards; Games; Reading groups; Prayer groups; Movies; Shopping trips; Dances/Social/Cultural gatherings; Intergenerational programs; Pet therapy.

Fort Collins

Columbine Care Center
421 Parker St, Fort Collins, CO 80525
(303) 482-1584
Admin Sharon Pebley. *Dir of Nursing* Jody Geilenkirchen BSRN. *Medical Dir* L A Merkel MD.
Licensure Skilled care. *Beds* SNF 102. *Private Pay Patients* 30%. *Certified* Medicaid; Medicare.
Owner Privately owned.
Admissions Requirements Medical examination; Physician's request.
Staff RNs 5 (ft), 6 (pt); LPNs 8 (ft), 2 (pt); Nurses' aides 33 (ft), 17 (pt); Physical therapists 1 (pt); Occupational therapists 1 (pt); Speech therapists 1 (pt); Activities coordinators 1 (ft), 1 (pt); Dietitians 1 (pt); Podiatrists 1 (pt).
Languages Spanish.
Facilities Dining room; Physical therapy room; Activities room; Barber/Beauty shop; Enclosed courtyard with fountain.
Activities Arts & crafts; Cards; Games; Reading groups; Prayer groups; Movies; Shopping trips; Dances/Social/Cultural gatherings; Intergenerational programs; Pet therapy.

Columbine Care Center West
940 Worthington Cir, Fort Collins, CO 80526
(303) 221-2273
Admin Jean Niedringhaus.
Licensure Skilled care; Intermediate care. *Beds* SNF 60; ICF 60.

Fort Collins Good Samaritan Retirement Village
508 W Trilby Rd, Fort Collins, CO 80525
(303) 226-4909
Admin Rev Eugene N Fox.
Medical Dir Dr James Bush.
Licensure Skilled care; Retirement. *Beds* SNF 50. *Certified* Medicaid; Medicare.
Owner Nonprofit corp (Evangelical Lutheran/Good Samaritan Society).
Admissions Requirements Minimum age 60; Medical examination.
Staff RNs; LPNs; Nurses' aides; Activities coordinators.
Affiliation Lutheran.
Facilities Dining room; Activities room; Chapel; Crafts room; Barber/Beauty shop; Library.
Activities Arts & crafts; Games; Reading groups; Movies; Shopping trips; Dances/Social/Cultural gatherings; Exercise group; Daily devotions; Weekly Bible study; Monthly Communion; Monthly memorial service; Sunday school; Sunday worship.

Fort Collins Health Care Center
1000 Lemay Ave, Fort Collins, CO 80524
(303) 482-7925
Admin Richard Crowley.
Medical Dir Dr Harold Dupper.
Licensure Skilled care; Intermediate care. *Beds* SNF 50; ICF 50. *Certified* Medicaid; Medicare.
Owner Proprietary corp (ARA Living Centers).
Admissions Requirements Physician's request.
Staff RNs 2 (ft), 5 (pt); LPNs 2 (ft), 5 (pt); Nurses' aides 8 (ft), 27 (pt); Activities coordinators 1 (pt).
Facilities Dining room; Physical therapy room; Activities room; Crafts room; Laundry room; Barber/Beauty shop.
Activities Arts & crafts; Games; Movies; Shopping trips; Dances/Social/Cultural gatherings.

Four Seasons Health Care Center
1020 Patton St, Fort Collins, CO 80524
(303) 484-6133
Admin Kathryn L Butler. *Dir of Nursing* Marilyn Garrity RN. *Medical Dir* Steven Tippin MD.
Licensure Skilled care; Alzheimer's care. *Beds* SNF 106. *Certified* Medicaid; Medicare.
Owner Proprietary corp (ARA Living Centers).
Admissions Requirements Physician's request.
Staff RNs; LPNs; Nurses' aides; Activities coordinators; Dietitians.
Languages Spanish, German.
Facilities Dining room; Laundry room; Barber/Beauty shop; Library; Private courtyard.
Activities Arts & crafts; Cards; Games; Reading groups; Prayer groups; Movies; Shopping trips; Dances/Social/Cultural gatherings; Men's group; Exercise group; Reality orientation group.

Golden West Nursing Home Inc
1005 E Elizabeth St, Fort Collins, CO 80521
(303) 482-2525
Admin Donna Weimer.
Medical Dir Dr William Abbey.
Licensure Intermediate care; Residential care. *Beds* ICF 60; Residential 10.
Owner Proprietary corp (Hillhaven Corp).
Admissions Requirements Physician's request.
Staff RNs 3 (pt); LPNs 2 (ft), 4 (pt); Nurses' aides 5 (ft), 11 (pt); Activities coordinators 1 (ft); Dietitians 1 (pt).
Facilities Dining room; Activities room; Laundry room; Barber/Beauty shop; Library.
Activities Arts & crafts; Cards; Games; Reading groups; Prayer groups; Movies; Shopping trips.

Pioneer Home
811 E Myrtle St, Fort Collins, CO 80521
(303) 482-5035
Admin J Klein.
Licensure Intermediate care for mentally retarded. *Beds* 34. *Certified* Medicaid.
Owner Proprietary corp.

Spring Creek Health Care Center
1000 Stuart St, Fort Collins, CO 80525
(303) 482-5712
Admin Wayne Clements.
Medical Dir David K Allen MD.
Licensure Skilled care; Intermediate care; Residential care. *Beds* SNF 117; ICF 40; Residential 50. *Certified* Medicaid; Medicare.
Owner Proprietary corp (ARA Living Centers).
Admissions Requirements Minimum age 6 months; Medical examination; Physician's request.

Staff Physicians 30 (pt); RNs 8 (ft), 6 (pt); LPNs 15 (ft), 5 (pt); Nurses' aides 40 (ft), 10 (pt); Physical therapists 1 (pt); Reality therapists 1 (ft); Recreational therapists 1 (ft); Occupational therapists 1 (pt); Speech therapists 1 (pt); Activities coordinators 1 (ft); Dietitians 1 (pt); Ophthalmologists 1 (pt); Podiatrists 1 (pt); Audiologists 1 (pt); Dentists 1 (pt).
Facilities Dining room; Physical therapy room; Activities room; Crafts room; Laundry room; Barber/Beauty shop; Library.
Activities Arts & crafts; Cards; Games; Reading groups; Prayer groups; Movies; Shopping trips; Dances/Social/Cultural gatherings.

Fort Morgan

Gayle Street Residential Center
425 Gayle St, Fort Morgan, CO 80701
(303) 867-5365
Admin William E Duffield.
Licensure Developmentally disabled. *Beds* 9.
Owner Nonprofit corp.

Valley View Villa Nursing Home
815 Fremont, Fort Morgan, CO 80701
(303) 867-8261
Admin Bob L Fesler.
Licensure Skilled care. *Beds* SNF 120.
Certified Medicaid.
Owner Proprietary corp (Life Care Centers of America).

Fowler

Fowler Health Care Center
2nd & Florence St, Fowler, CO 81039
(719) 263-4234
Admin Harry N Harrison. *Dir of Nursing* Beverly Harrison. *Medical Dir* Mary Jean Berg MD.
Licensure Skilled care; Residential care; Alzheimer's care. *Beds* SNF 45; Residential 63. *Certified* Medicaid; Medicare.
Owner Proprietary corp.
Admissions Requirements Medical examination; Physician's request.
Staff RNs 5 (ft), 3 (pt); LPNs 2 (ft), 1 (pt); Nurses' aides 14 (ft), 5 (pt); Recreational therapists 1 (ft); Activities coordinators 1 (ft); Dietitians 1 (pt).
Languages Spanish.
Facilities Dining room; Activities room; Crafts room; Laundry room; Barber/Beauty shop.
Activities Arts & crafts; Cards; Games; Reading groups; Prayer groups; Movies; Shopping trips; Dances/Social/Cultural gatherings.

Fruita

Family Health West
228 N Cherry St, Fruita, CO 81521
(303) 858-9871
Admin Carroll E Rushold. *Dir of Nursing* Jean Rose RN.
Licensure Skilled care; Secure Alzheimer's unit; Low income elderly housing. *Beds* SNF 148; Housing 75. *Certified* Medicaid.
Owner Nonprofit corp.
Admissions Requirements Physician's request.
Staff RNs 10 (ft), 4 (pt); LPNs 8 (ft), 4 (pt); Physical therapists 2 (ft); Occupational therapists 1 (pt); Speech therapists 1 (pt); Activities coordinators 2 (ft), 1 (pt); Dietitians 1 (ft), 1 (pt).
Facilities Dining room; Physical therapy room; Activities room; Crafts room; Barber/Beauty shop; Library.
Activities Arts & crafts; Cards; Games; Reading groups; Prayer groups; Movies; Shopping trips; Dances/Social/Cultural gatherings.

Glenwood Springs

Aspen Care Center—West
817 Colorado Ave No 205, Glenwood Springs, CO 81601
(303) 428-7481
Admin Carolyn S Westin.
Medical Dir Dr Foster Cline.
Licensure Skilled care; Intermediate care. *Beds* SNF 163; ICF 31. *Certified* Medicaid; Medicare.
Owner Proprietary corp.
Admissions Requirements Medical examination.
Staff RNs 8 (ft), 3 (pt); LPNs 14 (ft), 3 (pt); Nurses' aides 50 (ft), 7 (pt); Activities coordinators 1 (ft).
Facilities Dining room; Activities room; Laundry room; Barber/Beauty shop; Library.
Activities Arts & crafts; Cards; Games; Reading groups; Prayer groups; Movies; Shopping trips; Dances/Social/Cultural gatherings.

Glen Valley Nursing Home
PO Box 1179, 2305 Blake Ave, Glenwood Springs, CO 81602
(303) 945-5476
Admin Alice Applegate Letang.
Licensure Skilled care. *Beds* SNF 60. *Certified* Medicaid.
Owner Proprietary corp.

Grand Junction

Bethesda Care Center
2961 Hermosa Ct, Grand Junction, CO 81506
(303) 243-9824
Admin Betty Stephenson. *Dir of Nursing* Eileen Gooch.
Licensure Intermediate care. *Beds* ICF 60. *Certified* Medicaid.
Owner Nonprofit corp (Bethesda Care Centers).
Admissions Requirements Medical examination; Physician's request.
Staff RNs 1 (ft); LPNs 4 (ft), 3 (pt); Nurses' aides 12 (ft), 9 (pt); Activities coordinators 1 (ft).
Facilities Dining room; Activities room; Chapel; Crafts room; Laundry room; Barber/Beauty shop; Library.
Activities Arts & crafts; Cards; Games; Reading groups; Prayer groups; Movies; Shopping trips; Dances/Social/Cultural gatherings; Community trips; Picnics.

Bethesda Care Center of Grand Junction
2825 Patterson Rd, Grand Junction, CO 81501
(303) 242-7356
Admin David Stephenson.
Licensure Intermediate care. *Beds* ICF 67.

Grand Junction Care Center
2425 Teller Ave, Grand Junction, CO 81501
(303) 243-3381
Admin M June McCoy. *Dir of Nursing* Melissa Gentry RN. *Medical Dir* Roy E Kearns DO.
Licensure Skilled care. *Beds* SNF 108. *Certified* Medicaid; Medicare.
Owner Proprietary corp (Beverly Enterprises).
Admissions Requirements Physician's request.
Staff Physicians; RNs; LPNs; Nurses' aides; Physical therapists; Reality therapists; Recreational therapists; Occupational therapists; Speech therapists; Activities coordinators; Dietitians; Podiatrists; Dentists.
Languages Spanish.
Facilities Dining room; Physical therapy room; Activities room; Laundry room; Barber/Beauty shop.

Activities Arts & crafts; Cards; Games; Reading groups; Prayer groups; Movies; Shopping trips; Dances/Social/Cultural gatherings.

Grand Junction Regional Center
2800 D Rd, Grand Junction, CO 81501
(303) 245-2100
Admin William H Jackson. *Dir of Nursing* Rosemary Watson; Della Ehlers. *Medical Dir* Bronwen Magraw MD.
Licensure Skilled care; Intermediate care for mentally retarded; Group homes. *Beds* SNF 12; ICF/MR 236; Group homes 80. *Certified* Medicaid.
Owner Publicly owned.
Staff Physicians 1 (ft), 2 (pt); RNs 15 (ft), 4 (pt); LPNs 1 (ft), 6 (pt); Physical therapists 1 (ft); Recreational therapists 4 (ft); Occupational therapists 6 (ft); Speech therapists 4 (ft); Dietitians 3 (ft); Audiologists 1 (ft).
Facilities Dining room; Physical therapy room; Laundry room.
Activities Games; Movies; Shopping trips; Pet therapy.

Hilltop Rehabilitation Hospital
1100 Patterson Rd, Grand Junction, CO 81506
(303) 242-8980
Admin Thomas Piper. *Dir of Nursing* Arleene LaBelle RN. *Medical Dir* Dr Marge Keely.
Licensure Skilled care. *Beds* SNF 16.
Owner Nonprofit corp.
Staff RNs 19 (ft), 10 (pt); LPNs 2 (ft), 2 (pt); Nurses' aides 15 (ft), 10 (pt); Physical therapists 10 (ft), 5 (pt); Recreational therapists 1 (ft); Occupational therapists 7 (ft), 3 (pt); Speech therapists 3 (ft), 4 (pt); Activities coordinators 1 (ft); Dietitians 1 (ft).

Lavilla Grande
2501 Little Bookcliff Dr, Grand Junction, CO 81501
(303) 245-1211
Admin Terry Stephenson.
Medical Dir Dr Douglas C Shenk.
Licensure Skilled care. *Beds* SNF 120. *Certified* Medicaid.
Owner Nonprofit corp (Bethesda Care Centers).
Admissions Requirements Medical examination.
Staff RNs 6 (ft), 3 (pt); LPNs 5 (ft), 2 (pt); Nurses' aides 26 (ft), 12 (pt); Physical therapists 1 (ft); Activities coordinators 1 (ft).
Facilities Dining room; Physical therapy room; Activities room; Chapel; Crafts room; Barber/Beauty shop; Kitchen.
Activities Arts & crafts; Cards; Games; Reading groups; Prayer groups; Movies; Shopping trips; Dances/Social/Cultural gatherings; Pet therapy.

Mesa Manor Nursing Center
2901 N 12th St, Grand Junction, CO 81506
(303) 243-7211
Admin Eugene H Knight. *Dir of Nursing* Vickie L Newman RN. *Medical Dir* Jacobo A Ruybac MD.
Licensure Skilled care. *Beds* SNF 108. *Certified* Medicaid; Medicare.
Owner Proprietary corp (National Heritage).
Admissions Requirements Medical examination; Physician's request.
Staff RNs; LPNs; Nurses' aides; Activities coordinators; Dietitians.
Languages Spanish.
Facilities Dining room; Activities room; Chapel; Crafts room; Laundry room; Barber/Beauty shop.
Activities Arts & crafts; Cards; Games; Reading groups; Prayer groups; Movies; Shopping trips; Dances/Social/Cultural gatherings.

Greeley

Bonell Good Samaritan Center
708 22nd St, Greeley, CO 80631
(303) 352-6082
Admin Gary Peterson.
Licensure Skilled care; Intermediate care. *Beds*
SNF 168; ICF 71. *Certified* Medicaid;
Medicare.
Owner Nonprofit corp (Evangelical Lutheran/
Good Samaritan Society).

Centennial Health Care Center
1637 29th Ave Pl, Greeley, CO 80631
(303) 356-8181
Admin Bill Gust. *Dir of Nursing* Dee Ann
Bell. *Medical Dir* T E Baldwin MD.
Licensure Skilled care; Intermediate care. *Beds*
SNF 60; ICF 60. *Certified* Medicaid;
Medicare; VA.
Owner Proprietary corp (ARA Living
Centers).
Admissions Requirements Physician's request.
Staff RNs 6 (ft), 6 (pt); LPNs 7 (ft), 3 (pt);
Nurses' aides 29 (ft), 10 (pt); Physical
therapists 1 (pt); Recreational therapists;
Occupational therapists 1 (pt); Speech
therapists 1 (pt); Activities coordinators 1
(ft); Dietitians 1 (ft).
Languages German, Spanish.
Facilities Dining room; Physical therapy
room; Activities room; Laundry room;
Barber/Beauty shop.
Activities Arts & crafts; Cards; Games;
Reading groups; Prayer groups; Movies;
Shopping trips; Dances/Social/Cultural
gatherings; Intergenerational programs; Pet
therapy.

Fairacres Manor Inc
1700 18th Ave, Greeley, CO 80631
(303) 353-3370
Admin LaVern Weber. *Dir of Nursing* Jane
Rumrill. *Medical Dir* Dr David Bagley.
Licensure Skilled care. *Beds* SNF 116. *Private
Pay Patients* 40%. *Certified* Medicaid;
Medicare.
Owner Privately owned.
Admissions Requirements Minimum age
Geriatric preferred; Medical examination;
Physician's request.
Staff Physical therapists 1 (ft), 1 (pt);
Activities coordinators 1 (ft); Dietitians 1
(ft).
Languages Spanish, German.
Facilities Dining room; Physical therapy
room; Activities room; Chapel; Barber/
Beauty shop; Library; Ice cream parlor.
Activities Arts & crafts; Cards; Games; Prayer
groups; Movies; Shopping trips; Dances/
Social/Cultural gatherings; Pet therapy;
College classes.

Kenton Manor
850 27th Ave, Greeley, CO 80631
(303) 353-1018
Admin Donna Harding.
Licensure Skilled care; Intermediate care;
Retirement. *Beds* SNF 60; ICF 60; Apts 11.
Certified Medicaid; Medicare.
Owner Proprietary corp (ARA Living
Centers).

Wareheime Residential Care
1429 12th Ave, Greeley, CO 80631
(303) 352-2949
Admin Zella Mae Wareheime.
Licensure Intermediate care for mentally
retarded. *Beds* 8.
Owner Proprietary corp.

Weld County Community Center Group Home
1618 11th Ave, Greeley, CO 80631
(303) 339-5360
Admin John H Wooster.
Licensure Intermediate care for mentally
retarded. *Beds* 6.
Owner Nonprofit corp.

Gunnison

Gunnison Health Care Center
1500 W Tomichi Ave, Gunnison, CO 81230
(303) 641-0704
Admin Norma Horner.
Medical Dir Dr Ron Meyer.
Licensure Skilled care; Intermediate care. *Beds*
SNF 51. *Certified* Medicaid; Medicare.
Owner Nonprofit corp.
Admissions Requirements Medical
examination; Physician's request.
Staff RNs 4 (ft), 3 (pt); LPNs 1 (ft), 2 (pt);
Nurses' aides 6 (ft), 18 (pt); Recreational
therapists 1 (ft); Activities coordinators 1
(ft).
Facilities Dining room; Physical therapy
room; Activities room; Crafts room; Barber/
Beauty shop.
Activities Arts & crafts; Cards; Games;
Reading groups; Prayer groups; Movies;
Shopping trips; Dances/Social/Cultural
gatherings.

Haxtun

Haxtun Hospital District
235 W Fletcher, Haxtun, CO 80731
(303) 774-6123
Admin Brian Rahman. *Dir of Nursing*
Caroline Newth RN. *Medical Dir* Dr James
Ley.
Licensure Skilled care; Intermediate care;
Independent apartment living; Alzheimer's
care. *Beds* ICF 7; Swing beds SNF/ICF 10;
Independent apartment living 14. *Private
Pay Patients* 35%. *Certified* Medicaid;
Medicare.
Owner Nonprofit organization/foundation.
Staff Physicians 2 (ft); RNs 7 (ft); LPNs 4 (ft);
Nurses' aides 23 (ft); Physical therapists 1
(pt); Activities coordinators 1 (ft); Dietitians
1 (pt).
Facilities Dining room; Chapel; Barber/Beauty
shop.
Activities Arts & crafts; Cards; Games;
Reading groups; Prayer groups; Shopping
trips; Dances/Social/Cultural gatherings; Pet
therapy; Bus trips.

Hayden

Victory Way House
PO Box 579, Hayden, CO 81639
(303) 276-4250
Admin Christine K Collins.
Licensure Residential MR care. *Beds* 8.
Owner Nonprofit corp.

Holly

Holly Nursing Care Center
320 N 8th, Holly, CO 81047
(719) 537-6555
Admin Cindy Willis.
Medical Dir R G Ward DO.
Licensure Intermediate care. *Beds* ICF 60.
Certified Medicaid.
Owner Proprietary corp.

Holyoke

Prairie Vista Care Center
816 S Interocean Ave, Holyoke, CO 80734
(303) 854-2251
Admin JoAnne Freeman. *Dir of Nursing*
Margaret Ford RN. *Medical Dir* Myrlen
Chesnut DO.
Licensure Intermediate care. *Beds* ICF 55.
Private Pay Patients 50%. *Certified*
Medicaid.
Owner Privately owned.
Admissions Requirements Minimum age;
Medical examination; Physician's request.
Staff RNs 2 (ft), 2 (pt); LPNs 6 (pt); Physical
therapists; Dietitians.
Facilities Dining room; Physical therapy
room; Activities room; Chapel; Crafts room;
Laundry room; Barber/Beauty shop; Library.
Activities Arts & crafts; Cards; Games;
Reading groups; Prayer groups; Movies;
Shopping trips; Dances/Social/Cultural
gatherings; Intergenerational programs; Pet
therapy; Family participation.

Hugo

Lincoln Community Hospital & Nursing Home
PO Box 248, 111 6th St, Hugo, CO 80821
(719) 743-2421
Admin Roger Salisbury. *Dir of Nursing* Lotte
Broberg. *Medical Dir* Kathy Richie.
Licensure Skilled care. *Beds* SNF 35. *Certified*
Medicaid; Medicare.
Owner Publicly owned.
Admissions Requirements Medical
examination; Physician's request.
Staff Physicians 3 (ft); RNs 10 (ft), 1 (pt);
LPNs 5 (ft); Nurses' aides 9 (ft), 13 (pt);
Physical therapists 1 (pt); Activities
coordinators 1 (ft); Dietitians 1 (pt).
Facilities Dining room; Physical therapy
room; Activities room; Chapel; Crafts room;
Laundry room; Library.
Activities Arts & crafts; Cards; Games;
Dances/Social/Cultural gatherings.

Julesburg

Al Mar Residence
823 W 9th St, Julesburg, CO 80737
(303) 522-7121
Admin William Duffield.
Licensure Intermediate care for mentally
retarded. *Beds* ICF/MR 8. *Certified*
Medicare.
Owner Nonprofit corp.

Sedgwick County Hospital & Nursing Home
900 Cedar St, Julesburg, CO 80737
(303) 474-3323
Admin Michael Bildner. *Dir of Nursing*
Patricia Farmer. *Medical Dir* Kevin Shafer
DO.
Licensure Intermediate care. *Beds* ICF 32.
Certified Medicaid.
Owner Publicly owned.
Admissions Requirements Physician's request.
Staff RNs 1 (ft); LPNs 6 (ft); Nurses' aides 3
(ft), 11 (pt); Physical therapists 1 (pt);
Activities coordinators 1 (pt); Dietitians 1
(pt).
Facilities Dining room; Physical therapy
room; Activities room; Chapel; Crafts room;
Laundry room; Barber/Beauty shop; Library;
Covered patio.
Activities Arts & crafts; Cards; Games;
Reading groups; Prayer groups; Shopping
trips.

Kremmling

Kremmling Memorial Hospital
PO Box 399, 212 S 4th, Kremmling, CO
80459
(303) 724-3442
Admin Marc Gibbs.
Licensure Intermediate care for mentally
retarded; General hospital. *Beds* ICF/MR 2;
General hospital 19.

La Jara

Conejos County Hospital
PO Box 69, La Jara, CO 81140
(719) 274-5121
Admin Donn Swartz (temporary).
Licensure Skilled care; General hospital. *Beds*
SNF 4; General hospital 15.

La Junta

Arkansas Valley Regional Medical Center Nursing Care Center
514 W 10th, La Junta, CO 81050
(719) 384-5412, 384-5412, ext 101 FAX
Admin Synthia Morris JD. *Dir of Nursing* Janice Wilson RN. *Medical Dir* C C Weber MD.
Licensure Skilled care; Intermediate care. *Beds* SNF 43; ICF 107. *Private Pay Patients* 33%. *Certified* Medicaid.
Owner Nonprofit organization/foundation.
Admissions Requirements Minimum age 15; Physician's request.
Staff RNs 8 (ft), 2 (pt); LPNs 10 (ft), 1 (pt); Nurses' aides 38 (ft), 10 (pt); Physical therapists 1 (ft), 1 (pt); Speech therapists 1 (pt); Activities coordinators 2 (ft); Dietitians 1 (ft); Audiologists 1 (ft).
Affiliation Mennonite.
Facilities Dining room; Physical therapy room; Activities room; Chapel; Crafts room; Laundry room; Barber/Beauty shop.
Activities Arts & crafts; Cards; Games; Reading groups; Prayer groups; Movies; Shopping trips; Dances/Social/Cultural gatherings; Intergenerational programs; Pet therapy.

Lovato Residential Care Facility
302 Carson, La Junta, CO 81050
(303) 384-7687
Admin Josie Lovato.
Licensure Intermediate care. *Beds* 10.
Owner Proprietary corp.

Lakewood

Allison Health Care Center
1660 Allison St, Lakewood, CO 80215
(303) 232-7177
Admin McNair Ezzard. *Dir of Nursing* Patricia Jenkins. *Medical Dir* F Burdick MD.
Licensure Skilled care; Intermediate care; Respite. *Beds* SNF 60; ICF 60. *Certified* Medicaid.
Owner Proprietary corp (National Heritage).
Admissions Requirements Medical examination.
Staff Physicians; RNs; LPNs; Nurses' aides; Physical therapists; Reality therapists; Recreational therapists; Occupational therapists; Speech therapists; Activities coordinators; Dietitians.
Facilities Dining room; Physical therapy room; Activities room; Chapel; Crafts room; Laundry room; Barber/Beauty shop.
Activities Arts & crafts; Cards; Games; Reading groups; Movies; Shopping trips; Dances/Social/Cultural gatherings; Current events; Men's club; Church.

AMC Cancer Research Center & Hospital
1600 Pierce St, Lakewood, CO 80214
(303) 233-6501
Admin Terri Bernstein.
Licensure Skilled care; General hospital. *Beds* SNF 20; General hospital 12.

Bethany Care Center
5301 W 1st Ave, Lakewood, CO 80226
(303) 238-8333
Admin Cynthia L Olson Bostic. *Dir of Nursing* Ann Romaglia. *Medical Dir* Frances Burdick.
Licensure Skilled care; Intermediate care. *Beds* SNF 120; ICF 80. *Certified* Medicaid.
Owner Nonprofit corp (Bethesda Care Centers).
Staff RNs 7 (ft), 2 (pt); LPNs 29 (ft), 3 (pt); Nurses' aides 50 (ft); Recreational therapists 2 (ft), 1 (pt); Chaplains 1 (pt).
Facilities Dining room; Physical therapy room; Activities room; Chapel; Crafts room; Barber/Beauty shop; Patio.

Activities Arts & crafts; Cards; Games; Reading groups; Prayer groups; Movies; Shopping trips; Dances/Social/Cultural gatherings; Outings; Fishing; Picnics; Special events; Ceramics; Cooking.

Briarwood Way
11503 W Briarwood Dr, Lakewood, CO 80226
(303) 988-7776
Admin SeaJaye Sillasen.
Licensure Intermediate care for mentally retarded. *Beds* ICF/MR 6. *Certified* Medicaid; Medicare.
Owner Privately owned.
Admissions Requirements Minimum age 18; Females only; Medical examination; Physician's request.
Facilities Dining room; Activities room; Crafts room; Laundry room.
Activities Arts & crafts; Cards; Games; Reading groups; Movies; Shopping trips; Dances/Social/Cultural gatherings.

Cambridge Health Care Center
1685 Eaton St, Lakewood, CO 80215
(303) 232-4405
Admin Linda Braund.
Medical Dir Werner Prenzlau MD.
Licensure Skilled care; Intermediate care. *Beds* SNF 70; ICF 60. *Certified* Medicaid; Medicare.
Owner Proprietary corp.
Admissions Requirements Minimum age 21.
Staff RNs; LPNs; Nurses' aides; Physical therapists; Recreational therapists; Speech therapists; Activities coordinators; Dietitians; Podiatrists; Dentists.
Facilities Dining room; Physical therapy room; Activities room; Crafts room; Laundry room; Barber/Beauty shop; Library.
Activities Arts & crafts; Cards; Games; Reading groups; Prayer groups; Movies; Shopping trips; Dances/Social/Cultural gatherings.

Cedars Health Care Center
1599 Ingalls, Lakewood, CO 80214
(303) 232-3551
Admin James Levstek. *Dir of Nursing* Paula Walker. *Medical Dir* Francis Burdick MD.
Licensure Skilled care; Intermediate care. *Beds* SNF 140; ICF 60. *Certified* Medicaid; Medicare.
Owner Proprietary corp (American Medical Services Inc).
Admissions Requirements Minimum age 55; Medical examination; Physician's request.
Staff Physicians 40 (pt); Activities coordinators 1 (ft), 2 (pt); Dietitians 1 (ft); Ophthalmologists 1 (pt); Dentists 1 (pt).
Languages Spanish.
Facilities Dining room; Physical therapy room; Activities room; Chapel; Laundry room; Barber/Beauty shop; Library.
Activities Arts & crafts; Cards; Games; Reading groups; Prayer groups; Movies; Shopping trips; Dances/Social/Cultural gatherings; Bus trips; Camping.

Desserich House
9150 Morrison Rd, Lakewood, CO 80227
(303) 987-4396
Admin Mike Hannon.
Licensure Developmentally disabled. *Beds* 7.
Owner Nonprofit corp.

Everett Court Community
1325 Everett Ct, Lakewood, CO 80215
(303) 238-0501
Admin Melanie Tem.
Licensure Intermediate care. *Beds* 74. *Certified* Medicaid.
Owner Proprietary corp.

Evergren Terrace Care Center
1625 Simms St, Lakewood, CO 80215
(303) 238-8161
Admin Gary R House.
Medical Dir Jitze DeJong MD.

Licensure Skilled care. *Beds* SNF 60. *Certified* Medicaid; Medicare.
Owner Proprietary corp.
Staff RNs 5 (ft), 2 (pt); LPNs 2 (ft), 2 (pt); Nurses' aides 12 (ft), 5 (pt); Recreational therapists 1 (ft); Occupational therapists 1 (ft).
Facilities Dining room; Activities room; Laundry room; Barber/Beauty shop.
Activities Arts & crafts; Cards; Games; Reading groups; Prayer groups; Movies; Shopping trips; Dances/Social/Cultural gatherings; Exercises.

Garden Manor Nursing Home Inc
115 Ingalls St, Lakewood, CO 80226
(303) 237-1325
Admin Katherine Marshall.
Medical Dir Dr Robert Starr.
Licensure Skilled care; Intermediate care. *Beds* SNF 60; ICF 60. *Certified* Medicaid; Medicare.
Owner Proprietary corp (Arvada Management).
Admissions Requirements Minimum age 65; Medical examination; Physician's request.
Staff RNs 5 (ft); LPNs 3 (ft); Nurses' aides 15 (ft), 8 (pt); Physical therapists 1 (pt); Reality therapists 2 (ft); Occupational therapists 1 (pt); Activities coordinators 1 (ft); Dietitians 1 (pt); Podiatrists 1 (pt); Dentists 1 (pt).
Languages Spanish.
Facilities Dining room; Physical therapy room; Activities room; Crafts room; Laundry room; Barber/Beauty shop.
Activities Arts & crafts; Cards; Games; Reading groups; Prayer groups; Movies; Shopping trips; Dances/Social/Cultural gatherings; Current events; Resident council; Remotivation cart; Reality orientation.

Glen Ayr Health Center
1655 Eaton St, Lakewood, CO 80214
(303) 238-5363
Admin Deborah Stelock.
Medical Dir Karen Schutt.
Licensure Skilled care; Intermediate care; Alzheimer's care. *Beds* SNF 59; ICF 60. *Certified* Medicaid; Medicare.
Owner Proprietary corp.
Admissions Requirements Minimum age 60.
Staff RNs 6 (ft), 2 (pt); LPNs 4 (ft), 3 (pt); Nurses' aides 10 (ft), 4 (pt); Speech therapists 1 (ft); Activities coordinators 1 (ft), 1 (pt); Dietitians 1 (ft); Podiatrists 1 (pt); Dentists 1 (pt).
Languages Spanish.
Facilities Dining room; Physical therapy room; Activities room; Laundry room; Barber/Beauty shop; Library.
Activities Arts & crafts; Cards; Games; Reading groups; Prayer groups; Movies; Shopping trips; Dances/Social/Cultural gatherings; Exercise groups.

Grand Place
10365 W Grand Pl, Lakewood, CO 80127
(303) 978-0951
Admin Mike Hannon.
Licensure Residential MR care. *Beds* Residential MR care 7. *Certified* Medicaid.
Owner Nonprofit corp.

Lakeridge Village Health Care Center
1650 Yarrow St, Lakewood, CO 80215
(303) 238-1275
Admin Beverly Stephens. *Dir of Nursing* Joey Wall. *Medical Dir* Dr Eccles.
Licensure Skilled care; Intermediate care; Alzheimer's care. *Beds* SNF 143; ICF 37. *Certified* Medicaid; Medicare.
Owner Proprietary corp (National Heritage).
Admissions Requirements Medical examination; Physician's request.
Staff RNs; LPNs; Nurses' aides; Recreational therapists 2 (ft).
Languages Spanish.

Facilities Dining room; Physical therapy room; Activities room; Crafts room; Laundry room; Barber/Beauty shop; Library.
Activities Arts & crafts; Cards; Games; Reading groups; Prayer groups; Movies; Shopping trips; Dances/Social/Cultural gatherings.

Lakewood Meridian Health Center
1805 S Balsam, Lakewood, CO 80226
(303) 980-5500
Admin Gary R Wetzel.
Licensure Skilled care. *Beds* SNF 59.

Lakewood Nursing Home
1432 Depew St, Lakewood, CO 80214
(303) 238-1376
Admin Riva Weissbrot. *Dir of Nursing* Karen Steele RN. *Medical Dir* Dr Leonard Levisohn.
Licensure Skilled care; Intermediate care; Alzheimer's care. *Beds* SNF 93; ICF 60. *Certified* Medicaid.
Owner Proprietary corp.
Admissions Requirements Medical examination; Physician's request.
Staff Physicians; RNs; LPNs; Nurses' aides; Physical therapists; Reality therapists; Recreational therapists; Occupational therapists; Speech therapists; Activities coordinators; Dietitians; Ophthalmologists; Podiatrists; Dentists.
Facilities Dining room; Activities room; Laundry room; Barber/Beauty shop; Library.
Activities Arts & crafts; Cards; Games; Prayer groups; Movies.

Villa Manor Nursing Home
7950 W Mississippi Ave, Lakewood, CO 80226
(303) 986-4511
Admin Sara Jones.
Licensure Skilled care; Intermediate care. *Beds* SNF 120; ICF 120. *Certified* Medicaid; Medicare.
Owner Proprietary corp (Life Care Centers of America).

Western Hills Health Care Center
1625 Carr St, Lakewood, CO 80215
(303) 238-6881
Admin Rev Peter Adgie. *Dir of Nursing* Jean Schwartz RN BSN.
Licensure Skilled care; Intermediate care. *Beds* SNF 140; ICF. *Certified* Medicaid; Medicare.
Owner Proprietary corp.
Admissions Requirements Medical examination.
Staff RNs; LPNs; Nurses' aides; Physical therapists; Occupational therapists; Speech therapists; Activities coordinators; Dietitians.
Languages Spanish.
Facilities Dining room; Physical therapy room; Activities room; Crafts room; Laundry room; Barber/Beauty shop; Library; Ice cream parlor; Outdoor patio; Private formal dining room; Gift shop; Popcorn shop.
Activities Arts & crafts; Cards; Games; Reading groups; Prayer groups; Movies; Shopping trips; Dances/Social/Cultural gatherings; Restaurant outings.

Westland Manor Nursing Home
1150 Oak St, Lakewood, CO 80215
(303) 238-7505
Admin Judith A Dimon. *Dir of Nursing* Maureen Christensen-Oster RN. *Medical Dir* Dr Robert Starr.
Licensure Skilled care; Alzheimer's care. *Beds* SNF 150. *Certified* Medicaid; Medicare.
Owner Proprietary corp (Arvada Management).
Admissions Requirements Minimum age 50; Medical examination.
Staff Physicians 3 (pt); RNs 3 (ft), 7 (pt); LPNs 4 (ft), 10 (pt); Nurses' aides 20 (ft), 5 (pt); Physical therapists 1 (pt); Occupational

therapists 1 (pt); Speech therapists 1 (pt); Activities coordinators 1 (ft), 1 (pt); Dietitians 1 (pt).
Languages Spanish.
Facilities Dining room; Physical therapy room; Activities room; Laundry room; Barber/Beauty shop.
Activities Arts & crafts; Cards; Games; Reading groups; Prayer groups; Movies; Shopping trips; Dances/Social/Cultural gatherings.

Lamar

Sandhaven
Box 191, Lamar, CO 81052
(719) 336-3434
Admin Karen Hoskins.
Medical Dir Eldonna Mosier.
Licensure Intermediate care. *Beds* ICF 60. *Certified* Medicaid.
Owner Proprietary corp.
Admissions Requirements Physician's request.
Staff RNs 2 (ft); LPNs 3 (ft), 1 (pt); Nurses' aides 20 (ft), 3 (pt); Activities coordinators 2 (ft); Dietitians 1 (ft).
Facilities Dining room; Activities room; Crafts room; Laundry room; Barber/Beauty shop.
Activities Arts & crafts; Cards; Games; Reading groups; Prayer groups; Movies; Shopping trips; Dances/Social/Cultural gatherings.

Las Animas

Bent County Memorial Nursing Home
810 3rd St, Las Animas, CO 81054
(719) 456-1340
Admin David C Haneke.
Medical Dir Dr W R Wight.
Licensure Skilled care. *Beds* SNF 64. *Private Pay Patients* 25%. *Certified* Medicaid.
Owner Publicly owned.
Admissions Requirements Physician's request.
Staff Physicians 2 (ft); RNs 6 (ft); LPNs 2 (ft); Nurses' aides 15 (ft), 4 (pt); Physical therapists 1 (pt); Speech therapists 1 (pt); Activities coordinators 1 (ft); Dietitians 1 (ft); Ophthalmologists 1 (pt); Podiatrists 1 (pt); Audiologists 1 (pt).
Languages Spanish.
Facilities Dining room; Physical therapy room; Activities room; Chapel; Crafts room; Barber/Beauty shop; Library.
Activities Arts & crafts; Cards; Games; Reading groups; Prayer groups; Movies; Shopping trips; Dances/Social/Cultural gatherings; Intergenerational programs; Pet therapy.

Bueno's Group Home
PO Box 385, 903 Vine, Las Animas, CO 81054
(303) 456-1125
Admin Elizabeth Bueno.
Licensure Developmentally disabled. *Beds* 8.
Owner Proprietary corp.

Lucero Residential Care Facility
920 Vine, Las Animas, CO 81054
(303) 456-0643
Admin Maria Lucero.
Licensure Intermediate care. *Beds* 10.
Owner Proprietary corp.

Limon

Prairie View Care Center
1720 Circle Ln, Limon, CO 80828
(719) 775-9717
Admin Jan Hendrick. *Dir of Nursing* Sherry Bartley. *Medical Dir* Dr Olsen.
Licensure Intermediate care; Board & care. *Beds* ICF 60; Board & care 25. *Private Pay Patients* 12%. *Certified* Medicaid.
Owner Proprietary corp (LTC Inc).

Staff Physicians 3 (pt); RNs 1 (ft), 1 (pt); LPNs 3 (ft); Nurses' aides 15 (ft); Physical therapists 2 (pt); Speech therapists 1 (pt); Dietitians 1 (ft); Recreational therapistsActivities coordinators 1 (ft); Directors of nursing 1 (ft).
Languages Korean.
Facilities Dining room; Physical therapy room; Laundry room; Barber/Beauty shop; Activities & crafts room/library.
Activities Arts & crafts; Cards; Games; Reading groups; Prayer groups; Movies; Shopping trips; Dances/Social/Cultural gatherings; Intergenerational programs; Pet therapy.

Littleton

Cherrelyn Manor Health Care Center
5555 S Elati St, Littleton, CO 80120
(303) 798-8686, 798-0145 FAX
Admin Lori S Moore. *Dir of Nursing* Judy Rall. *Medical Dir* Dr William Hines.
Licensure Skilled care; Intermediate care. *Beds* SNF 176; ICF 69. *Private Pay Patients* 30%. *Certified* Medicaid; Medicare.
Owner Proprietary corp (American Medical Services Inc).
Staff Physicians; RNs 7 (ft), 3 (pt); LPNs 24 (ft), 4 (pt); Nurses' aides 55 (ft), 6 (pt); Physical therapists (contracted); Recreational therapists 2 (ft), 2 (pt); Occupational therapists (contracted); Speech therapists (contracted); Activities coordinators; Dietitians 1 (ft), 1 (pt); Ophthalmologists (contracted); Podiatrists (contracted); Audiologists (contracted); Nursing 5 (ft).
Facilities Dining room; Physical therapy room; Activities room; Chapel; Crafts room; Laundry room; Barber/Beauty shop; Ice cream shop; Gift shop.
Activities Arts & crafts; Cards; Games; Reading groups; Prayer groups; Movies; Shopping trips; Dances/Social/Cultural gatherings; Intergenerational programs; Pet therapy; Religious services.

Christian Living Campus—Johnson Center
5000 E Arapahoe, Littleton, CO 80122
(303) 779-5000
Admin Ernest Angell. *Dir of Nursing* Bernie Ferrero.
Licensure Skilled care; Intermediate care; Assisted living; Alzheimer's care. *Beds* SNF 43; ICF 18; Assisted living 29; Alzheimer's unit 33.
Owner Nonprofit organization/foundation Christian Living Campus.
Admissions Requirements Minimum age 62; Medical examination.
Staff Physicians; RNs; LPNs; Nurses' aides; Occupational therapists; Speech therapists; Activities coordinators; Dietitians; Ophthalmologists; Podiatrists; Audiologists.
Facilities Physical therapy room; Activities room; Chapel; Crafts room; Laundry room; Barber/Beauty shop; Examination room; Gift shop; Ice cream parlor; General, private, and rehabilitation dining rooms; Wheelchair-accessible bus; Enclosed courtyards; Alzheimer's unit with private courtyard and activities and dining rooms.
Activities Arts & crafts; Cards; Games; Reading groups; Prayer groups; Movies; Shopping trips; Dances/Social/Cultural gatherings; Intergenerational programs; Pet therapy.

Good Shepard Lutheran Home of the West
445 West Berry Ave, Littleton, CO 80120
(303) 795-2061
Admin Cynthia K Warren.
Licensure Intermediate care for mentally retarded. *Beds* ICF/MR 40. *Certified* Medicaid.
Owner Nonprofit corp.
Admissions Requirements Minimum age 18.

Affiliation Lutheran.
Facilities Dining room; Physical therapy room; Activities room; Crafts room; Laundry room.
Activities Arts & crafts; Games; Prayer groups; Movies; Shopping trips; Dances/Social/Cultural gatherings.

Heritage Park Manor
6005 S Holly St, Littleton, CO 80121
(303) 773-1000
Admin Ernest Angell.
Licensure Skilled care. *Beds* SNF 120.

Littleton Manor Nursing Home
5822 S Lowell Way, Littleton, CO 80123
(303) 798-2497
Admin Margaret Norton. *Dir of Nursing* Margaret Fitzgerald. *Medical Dir* Dr Thomas Pulk.
Licensure Skilled care; Intermediate care; Alzheimer's care. *Beds* Swing beds SNF/ICF 45. *Private Pay Patients* 100%.
Owner Proprietary corp.
Admissions Requirements Physician's request.
Staff Physicians; RNs; LPNs; Nurses' aides; Physical therapists; Reality therapists; Recreational therapists; Occupational therapists; Speech therapists; Activities coordinators; Dietitians; Ophthalmologists; Podiatrists; Dentists.
Facilities Dining room; Physical therapy room; Activities room; Crafts room; Laundry room; Barber/Beauty shop; Library.
Activities Arts & crafts; Cards; Games; Reading groups; Prayer groups; Movies; Shopping trips; Dances/Social/Cultural gatherings; Intergenerational programs; Pet therapy.

Longmont

Applewood Living Center
1800 Stroh Pl, Longmont, CO 80501
(303) 776-6081
Admin Bonnie Sue Larson.
Medical Dir David McCarty Sr MD.
Licensure Skilled care. *Beds* SNF 120. *Certified* Medicaid.
Owner Proprietary corp (ARA Living Centers).
Admissions Requirements Medical examination; Physician's request.
Staff RNs 10 (ft); LPNs 4 (pt); Nurses' aides 40 (ft); Recreational therapists 1 (ft); Activities coordinators 1 (ft); Dietitians 1 (ft).
Facilities Dining room; Physical therapy room; Activities room; Chapel; Crafts room; Laundry room; Barber/Beauty shop.
Activities Arts & crafts; Cards; Games; Reading groups; Prayer groups; Movies; Dances/Social/Cultural gatherings.

Country View Care Center
5425 Weld County Road No 32, Longmont, CO 80501
(303) 535-4491
Admin Sr M Jean Tenhaeff.
Medical Dir Erin Bee, Prog Dir.
Licensure Intermediate care for mentally retarded. *Beds* ICF/MR 87. *Certified* Medicaid.
Owner Proprietary corp (ARA Living Centers).
Admissions Requirements Minimum age 18; Medical examination; Physician's request.
Staff RNs 1 (ft); LPNs 8 (ft); Nurses' aides 40 (ft); Physical therapists 1 (pt); Occupational therapists 1 (pt); Speech therapists 1 (pt); Activities coordinators 1 (ft); Dietitians 1 (pt); Psychologist 1 (ft); Recreation assistants 10 (ft).
Facilities Dining room; Physical therapy room; Activities room; Crafts room; Laundry room; Library.

Activities Arts & crafts; Cards; Games; Reading groups; Prayer groups; Movies; Shopping trips; Dances/Social/Cultural gatherings; Socialization, self-help, recreation, & vocational classes.

Foothills Care Center Inc
1440 Coffman St, Longmont, CO 80501
(303) 776-2814
Admin Fred Kilfoy. *Dir of Nursing* Jeanette Morrell BSN. *Medical Dir* Dr D W McCarty Sr.
Licensure Skilled care; Intermediate care; Alzheimer's care. *Beds* SNF 120; ICF 60. *Certified* Medicaid; Medicare.
Owner Proprietary corp.
Staff RNs 10 (ft), 1 (pt); LPNs 14 (ft); Nurses' aides 38 (ft), 7 (pt); Physical therapists 1 (pt); Recreational therapists 1 (ft); Occupational therapists 1 (pt); Speech therapists 1 (pt); Activities coordinators 1 (ft); Dietitians 1 (pt); Podiatrists 1 (pt).
Facilities Dining room; Physical therapy room; Activities room; Laundry room; Barber/Beauty shop.
Activities Arts & crafts; Cards; Games; Reading groups; Prayer groups; Movies; Shopping trips; Dances/Social/Cultural gatherings.

Loveland

Eden Valley Nursing Home
6263 N County Rd No 29, Loveland, CO 80537
(303) 667-6911
Admin Polly Kim. *Dir of Nursing* Minnie Bird. *Medical Dir* Dr R Grosboll.
Licensure Skilled care; Intermediate care. *Beds* SNF 16; ICF 6. *Certified* Medicaid.
Owner Nonprofit corp.
Admissions Requirements Medical examination; Physician's request.
Staff Physicians 1 (pt); RNs 5 (ft), 3 (pt); Nurses' aides 5 (ft), 2 (pt); Physical therapists 1 (pt); Reality therapists 1 (pt); Recreational therapists 1 (pt); Occupational therapists 1 (pt); Speech therapists 1 (pt); Activities coordinators 1 (pt); Dietitians 1 (pt); Ophthalmologists 1 (pt); Podiatrists 1 (pt); Dentists 1 (pt).
Languages Korean.
Affiliation Seventh-Day Adventist.
Facilities Dining room; Physical therapy room; Activities room; Chapel; Barber/Beauty shop; Library.
Activities Arts & crafts; Games; Reading groups; Prayer groups; Movies; Shopping trips; Dances/Social/Cultural gatherings.

Loveland Good Samaritan Village
2101 S Garfield, Loveland, CO 80538
(303) 669-3100
Admin Irene Rasmussen.
Licensure Skilled care. *Beds* SNF 60. *Certified* Medicaid; Medicare.
Owner Nonprofit corp (Evangelical Lutheran/Good Samaritan Society).
Admissions Requirements Medical examination; Physician's request.
Staff RNs; LPNs; Nurses' aides; Occupational therapists; Activities coordinators.
Affiliation Lutheran.
Facilities Dining room; Activities room; Chapel; Crafts room; Laundry room; Barber/Beauty shop; Library.
Activities Arts & crafts; Games; Reading groups; Shopping trips; Dances/Social/Cultural gatherings.

North Shore Manor Inc
1365 W 29th St, Loveland, CO 80538
(303) 667-6111
Admin Barry Fancher.
Licensure Skilled care; Intermediate care. *Beds* SNF 120; ICF 32. *Certified* Medicaid; Medicare.
Owner Proprietary corp.

Sierra Vista Nursing Home
821 Duffield Ct, Loveland, CO 80537
(303) 669-0345
Admin Barbara Demars. *Dir of Nursing* Audry Bopp RN BSN. *Medical Dir* Dr Thomas Kasenberg.
Licensure Skilled care; Intermediate care; Residential apts. *Beds* SNF 60; ICF 60; Residential apts 10. *Certified* Medicaid; Medicare; VA.
Owner Proprietary corp (ARA Living Centers).
Admissions Requirements Medical examination; Physician's request.
Staff RNs; LPNs; Nurses' aides; Physical therapists; Reality therapists; Recreational therapists; Occupational therapists; Speech therapists; Activities coordinators; Dietitians.
Facilities Dining room; Physical therapy room; Activities room; Laundry room; Barber/Beauty shop; Private visiting areas; Patio; Courtyard area.
Activities Arts & crafts; Cards; Games; Reading groups; Prayer groups; Movies; Shopping trips; Dances/Social/Cultural gatherings; Library cart; Bingo.

Manitou Springs

Cheyenne Village Inc
441 Manitou Ave, Manitou Springs, CO 80829
(303) 685-1801
Admin Linda Bloom.
Medical Dir Mary Gannon.
Licensure Intermediate care for mentally retarded; Retirement. *Beds* ICF/MR 40; Group homes 8. *Certified* Medicaid; Medicare.
Owner Nonprofit corp.
Admissions Requirements Minimum age 18.
Staff RNs 1 (ft); LPNs 1 (pt); Nurses' aides 35 (ft); Recreational therapists 1 (ft); Dietitians 1 (ft).
Activities Arts & crafts; Cards; Games; Reading groups; Prayer groups; Movies; Shopping trips; Dances/Social/Cultural gatherings.

Manzanola

Horne Home
521 N Canal, Manzanola, CO 81085
(303) 465-5795
Admin Rozanna R Horn.
Licensure Intermediate care. *Beds* 10.
Owner Proprietary corp.

Meeker

Walbridge Memorial Convalescent Wing
345 Cleveland, Meeker, CO 81641
(303) 878-5047
Admin Calvin Graber. *Dir of Nursing* Beka Anderson.
Licensure Skilled care. *Beds* SNF 25. *Certified* Medicaid.
Admissions Requirements Medical examination; Physician's request.
Staff RNs 11 (ft), 2 (pt); LPNs 2 (pt); Dietitians 1 (ft).
Languages Greek, German, Spanish.
Facilities Dining room; Activities room; Chapel; Crafts room; Laundry room; Barber/Beauty shop.
Activities Arts & crafts; Games; Reading groups; Prayer groups; Movies; Shopping trips; Dances/Social/Cultural gatherings.

Monte Vista

Mountain Meadows Nursing Center Inc
2277 E Drive, Monte Vista, CO 81144
(719) 852-5138

Admin Barbara Fransen. *Dir of Nursing* Becky Hardaway RN. *Medical Dir* Jack Jordan MD.
Licensure Intermediate care. *Beds* ICF 60. *Certified* Medicaid.
Owner Proprietary corp.
Admissions Requirements Minimum age 50; Medical examination.
Staff RNs 1 (ft), 1 (pt); LPNs 7 (ft); Nurses' aides 25 (ft); Physical therapists 1 (pt); Activities coordinators 1 (ft).
Languages Spanish.
Facilities Dining room; Activities room; Chapel; Laundry room; Barber/Beauty shop.
Activities Arts & crafts; Cards; Games; Reading groups; Movies; Shopping trips; Dances/Social/Cultural gatherings.

Montrose

Chipeta Drive
16357 Chipeta Dr, Montrose, CO 81401
(303) 249-1133
Admin Mary Kalina.
Licensure Intermediate care for mentally retarded; Retirement. *Beds* 8. *Certified* Medicaid; Medicare.
Owner Nonprofit corp.
Admissions Requirements Minimum age 18.
Staff RNs; LPNs; Dietitians.
Facilities Dining room; Laundry room; Living room; Private bedrooms; Resident cooking facilities; Private sitting room; Resident garden & yard.
Activities Arts & crafts; Cards; Games; Movies; Shopping trips; Bowling; Picnics; Walks; Camping; Individualized vacations; Gardening; Pets allowed.

Evergreen Care Center
300 N Cascade Ave, Montrose, CO 81401
(303) 249-7764
Admin Cathy Cooling. *Dir of Nursing* Mary Rossiter RN. *Medical Dir* Dr Reginald Guy.
Licensure Skilled care; Intermediate care. *Beds* SNF 20; ICF 40. *Certified* Medicaid; Medicare.
Owner Proprietary corp.
Admissions Requirements Minimum age 18; Physician's request.
Staff RNs 4 (ft); LPNs 2 (ft), 1 (pt); Nurses' aides 12 (ft); Recreational therapists 1 (pt); Activities coordinators 1 (pt); Dietitians 1 (pt); Social workers 1 (pt).
Languages Spanish.
Facilities Dining room; Physical therapy room; Activities room; Crafts room; Laundry room; Barber/Beauty shop.
Activities Arts & crafts; Cards; Games; Reading groups; Prayer groups; Movies; Shopping trips; Dances/Social/Cultural gatherings.

San Juan Living Center
1043 Ridge St, Montrose, CO 81401
(303) 249-9683
Admin Michele Johnston. *Dir of Nursing* Anna K Ruggles.
Licensure Skilled care; Intermediate care for mentally retarded; Alzheimer's care. *Beds* SNF 68; ICF/MR 44. *Certified* Medicaid; Medicare.
Owner Proprietary corp (ARA Living Centers).
Admissions Requirements Minimum age 21; Mentally retarded; Physician's request.
Staff RNs 4 (ft); LPNs 5 (ft); Nurses' aides 12 (ft), 4 (pt); Activities coordinators 2 (ft); Psychologists 1 (pt).
Languages Spanish.
Facilities Dining room; Physical therapy room; Activities room; Chapel; Crafts room; Laundry room; Barber/Beauty shop.
Activities Arts & crafts; Cards; Games; Movies; Shopping trips; Dances/Social/Cultural gatherings.

South 4th Street
447 S 4th St, Montrose, CO 81401
(303) 249-2972
Admin Charles Allison.
Licensure Intermediate care for mentally retarded. *Beds* ICF/MR 9. *Certified* Medicaid.
Owner Nonprofit corp.

Valley Manor Care Center
1401 S Cascade Ave, Montrose, CO 81401
(303) 249-9634, 249-6880 FAX
Admin John Fitzmaurice.
Medical Dir Dr Robert Van Gemert.
Licensure Skilled care. *Beds* SNF 120. *Certified* Medicaid; Medicare.
Owner Nonprofit corp (Volunteers of America Care).
Admissions Requirements Medical examination.
Staff RNs 6 (ft), 3 (pt); LPNs 4 (ft), 2 (pt); Nurses' aides 31 (ft), 30 (pt); Physical therapists 2 (pt); Recreational therapists 2 (pt); Activities coordinators 1 (ft); Dietitians 1 (pt); Dentists 1 (pt).
Facilities Dining room; Physical therapy room; Activities room; Chapel; Crafts room; Laundry room; Barber/Beauty shop.
Activities Arts & crafts; Cards; Games; Reading groups; Prayer groups; Movies; Shopping trips; Dances/Social/Cultural gatherings.

Morrison

Bear Creek Nursing Center
150 Spring St, Morrison, CO 80465
(303) 697-8181
Admin Margaret Stauder. *Dir of Nursing* Gisella Kagy RN. *Medical Dir* Dr Lee Anneberg.
Licensure Skilled care; Intermediate care; Alzheimer's care. *Beds* SNF 120; ICF 60. *Certified* Medicaid; Medicare.
Owner Proprietary corp (Hillhaven Corp).
Admissions Requirements Minimum age 50; Medical examination.
Staff RNs 15 (ft), 1 (pt); LPNs 14 (ft); Nurses' aides 71 (ft); Physical therapists 1 (ft); Activities coordinators 3 (ft), 1 (pt); Dietitians 1 (ft).
Languages Spanish.
Facilities Dining room; Physical therapy room; Activities room; Chapel; Crafts room; Laundry room; Barber/Beauty shop; Library; Special dining room for oriented, sociable residents.
Activities Arts & crafts; Cards; Games; Reading groups; Prayer groups; Movies; Shopping trips; Dances/Social/Cultural gatherings.

Northglenn

Castle Garden Nursing Home
401 Malley Dr, Northglenn, CO 80233
(303) 452-4700, 280-0488 FAX
Admin Gregory A Drapes. *Dir of Nursing* Deanna Carter. *Medical Dir* Dr Robert Jardine.
Licensure Skilled care; Retirement. *Beds* SNF 180. *Private Pay Patients* 31%. *Certified* Medicaid; Medicare.
Owner Proprietary corp (Hillhaven Corp).
Admissions Requirements Physician's request.
Staff Physicians; RNs; LPNs; Nurses' aides; Physical therapists 1 (ft), 1 (pt); Occupational therapists 2 (ft); Speech therapists 2 (ft); Activities coordinators 1 (ft), 2 (pt); Dietitians 1 (pt); Podiatrists 1 (pt); Audiologists 1 (pt); Social workers 1 (ft), 1 (pt); Staff development 1 (ft), 1 (pt).
Facilities Dining room; Physical therapy room; Activities room; Chapel; Crafts room; Laundry room; Barber/Beauty shop; Library.

Activities Arts & crafts; Cards; Games; Reading groups; Movies; Shopping trips; Dances/Social/Cultural gatherings; Intergenerational programs; Pet therapy.

Olathe

Colorow Care Center
PO Box 710, 750 8th St, Olathe, CO 81425
(303) 323-5504
Admin Mary Pfalzgraff.
Medical Dir Dr Simon.
Licensure Intermediate care. *Beds* ICF 60. *Certified* Medicaid.
Owner Proprietary corp.
Admissions Requirements Physician's request.
Staff RNs 2 (ft); LPNs 6 (ft), 2 (pt); Nurses' aides 18 (ft), 3 (pt); Physical therapists 1 (pt); Activities coordinators 1 (ft), 1 (pt); Dietitians 1 (ft), 1 (pt).
Facilities Dining room; Physical therapy room; Activities room; Crafts room; Laundry room; Barber/Beauty shop; Library.
Activities Arts & crafts; Cards; Games; Reading groups; Prayer groups; Movies; Shopping trips.

Harold Group Home
PO Box 508, Olathe, CO 81425
(303) 323-5831
Admin John Harold.
Licensure Residential MR care. *Beds* Residential MR care 18.
Owner Proprietary corp.

Ordway

Crowley County Nursing Center
PO Box 488, 401 Idaho, Ordway, CO 81063
(719) 267-3561
Admin A Habib Khaliqi.
Licensure Intermediate care. *Beds* ICF 59. *Certified* Medicaid; Medicare.
Owner Nonprofit corp.
Staff RNs 2 (ft); LPNs 4 (ft); Nurses' aides 15 (ft), 5 (pt); Physical therapists 1 (pt); Dietitians 1 (pt).
Facilities Dining room; Activities room; Chapel; Laundry room; Barber/Beauty shop.
Activities Cards; Games; Prayer groups; Movies; Shopping trips; Dances/Social/Cultural gatherings.

Palisade

Palisade Nursing Home
PO Box 190, 151 E 3rd St, Palisade, CO 81526
(303) 464-7500
Admin Nickie Allen. *Dir of Nursing* Michaelene Kent RN.
Licensure Skilled care; Intermediate care. *Beds* SNF 94; ICF 2. *Certified* Medicaid; Medicare.
Owner Proprietary corp.
Admissions Requirements Minimum age 16.
Staff RNs; LPNs; Nurses' aides; Activities coordinators.
Facilities Dining room; Activities room; Crafts room; Laundry room; Barber/Beauty shop; Rehabilitation room.
Activities Arts & crafts; Cards; Games; Reading groups; Prayer groups; Movies; Shopping trips; Dances/Social/Cultural gatherings; Van rides.

Paonia

Bethesda Care Center
1625 Meadowbrook Blvd, Paonia, CO 81428
(303) 527-4837
Admin Beatrice Reece. *Dir of Nursing* Mary Ellen Cranor. *Medical Dir* Dr Don Ridgway.
Licensure Skilled care. *Beds* SNF 56. *Certified* Medicaid.

Owner Nonprofit corp (Bethesda Care Centers).
Admissions Requirements Physician's request.
Staff RNs 1 (ft); LPNs 4 (ft); Nurses' aides 18 (ft); Activities coordinators 1 (ft); Dietitians 1 (ft).
Facilities Dining room; Physical therapy room; Activities room; Barber/Beauty shop.
Activities Arts & crafts; Reading groups; Prayer groups; Movies; Dances/Social/Cultural gatherings.

Pueblo

Belmont Lodge
1601 Constitution Rd, Pueblo, CO 81001
(719) 584-2400
Admin Sandra Turner RN. *Dir of Nursing* Kathleen Williams RN. *Medical Dir* Mark Osborn.
Licensure Skilled care; Alzheimer's care. *Beds* SNF 120. *Private Pay Patients* 27%. *Certified* Medicaid; Medicare.
Owner Proprietary corp (ARA Living Centers).
Admissions Requirements Medical examination; Physician's request.
Staff Physicians 2 (pt); RNs 4 (ft), 4 (pt); LPNs 4 (ft), 4 (pt); Nurses' aides 28 (ft), 20 (pt); Physical therapists 1 (ft); Activities coordinators 2 (ft); Dietitians 1 (ft); Podiatrists 1 (pt); Dentists 1 (ft).
Languages Spanish.
Facilities Dining room; Physical therapy room; Activities room; Chapel; Crafts room; Laundry room; Barber/Beauty shop; Library.
Activities Arts & crafts; Cards; Games; Reading groups; Prayer groups; Movies; Shopping trips; Dances/Social/Cultural gatherings; Intergenerational programs; Pet therapy; Silver Key program.

Citadel Health Care
431 Quincy, Pueblo, CO 81005
(719) 545-0112
Admin Paula J Cicerelli. *Dir of Nursing* Carol Pannunzio. *Medical Dir* L J Farabaugh MD.
Licensure Intermediate care; Residential care; Alzheimer's care. *Beds* ICF 34; Residential care 4. *Certified* Medicaid.
Owner Privately owned.
Admissions Requirements Physician's request.
Staff Physicians; RNs; LPNs; Nurses' aides; Activities coordinators; Dietitians.
Languages Spanish.
Facilities Dining room; Activities room; Chapel; Crafts room; Laundry room; Barber/Beauty shop; Library.
Activities Arts & crafts; Cards; Games; Reading groups; Prayer groups; Movies; Shopping trips; Dances/Social/Cultural gatherings.

Cordova Residential Care
2108 E 12th, Pueblo, CO 81001
(719) 546-1475
Admin Donna Cordova.
Licensure Intermediate care. *Beds* 8.
Owner Proprietary corp.

Four Seasons Nursing Center
2515 Pitman Pl, Pueblo, CO 81004
(719) 564-0550
Admin William Arnol Nance.
Licensure Skilled care. *Beds* SNF 110.

Highland Park Complex
1610 Scranton Ave, Pueblo, CO 81004
(719) 564-0550
Admin Terrie Nance.
Licensure Skilled care. *Beds* SNF 49.

J & C Residential Care Facility
328 Colorado, Pueblo, CO 81004
(719) 546-1875
Admin Lydia Jordan.
Licensure Intermediate care. *Beds* 10.
Owner Proprietary corp.

Jordan & Cole Residential Care Facility
184 Harvard Ave, Pueblo, CO 81004-1224
(303) 456-1764
Admin Mary E Cole.
Licensure Skilled care. *Beds* 10.
Owner Proprietary corp.

Jordan Residential Services Inc
2202 E 6th St, Pueblo, CO 81001
(719) 544-3258
Admin Mike Jordan.
Licensure Intermediate care for mentally retarded. *Beds* ICF/MR 8. *Certified* Medicaid.
Owner Privately owned.
Admissions Requirements Minimum age 16; Medical examination.
Staff Podiatrists; Psychiatric techs 4 (ft); MR techs 2 (ft).
Facilities Dining room; Activities room; Crafts room; Laundry room.
Activities Arts & crafts; Cards; Games; Reading groups; Movies; Shopping trips; Dances/Social/Cultural gatherings; Camping; Boating; Fishing.

Minnequa Medicenter Inc
2701 California St, Pueblo, CO 81004
(719) 561-1300
Admin Lori Akre.
Licensure Skilled care; Intermediate care. *Beds* SNF 60; ICF 60.

Prospect Lake Health Care Center
1420 E Fountain Blvd, Pueblo, CO 80910
(719) 632-7604
Admin Barbara G Strombeck. *Dir of Nursing* Elsie Keith. *Medical Dir* Lester Williams MD.
Licensure Skilled care; Alzheimer's care. *Beds* SNF 49. *Private Pay Patients* 2%. *Certified* Medicaid; Medicare.
Owner Proprietary corp (Tealwood Care Centers).
Admissions Requirements Medical examination; Physician's request.
Staff RNs 3 (ft), 4 (pt); Nurses' aides 10 (ft), 9 (pt); Activities coordinators 1 (ft); Social services coordinators 1 (ft).
Languages Spanish.
Facilities Dining room; Activities room; Chapel; Laundry room; Alarm-monitored exits.
Activities Arts & crafts; Cards; Games; Reading groups; Prayer groups; Movies; Shopping trips; Dances/Social/Cultural gatherings; Intergenerational programs; Pet therapy.

Pueblo Manor Nursing Home
2611 Jones Ave, Pueblo, CO 81004
(303) 564-1735
Admin Brooke L Groff. *Dir of Nursing* Pat Vigil RN. *Medical Dir* Harold Smith MD.
Licensure Skilled care; Intermediate care. *Beds* SNF 148; ICF 12. *Certified* Medicaid; Medicare.
Owner Proprietary corp (National Heritage).
Admissions Requirements Medical examination.
Staff RNs 8 (ft), 1 (pt); LPNs 12 (ft), 4 (pt); Nurses' aides 45 (ft), 20 (pt); Physical therapists 2 (pt); Reality therapists 1 (pt); Recreational therapists 1 (pt); Activities coordinators 1 (ft), 1 (pt); Dietitians 1 (ft).
Languages Spanish.
Facilities Dining room; Physical therapy room; Activities room; Chapel; Crafts room; Laundry room; Barber/Beauty shop; Library; Large patio areas.
Activities Arts & crafts; Cards; Games; Reading groups; Prayer groups; Movies; Shopping trips; Dances/Social/Cultural gatherings.

Sharmar Nursing Center
1201 W Abriendo Ave, Pueblo, CO 81005
(719) 544-1173

Admin Donald J Prose.
Medical Dir Harvey W Phelp.
Licensure Intermediate care. *Beds* ICF 51. *Certified* Medicaid.
Owner Proprietary corp.
Admissions Requirements Physician's request.
Staff RNs 2 (ft); LPNs 3 (ft); Nurses' aides 10 (ft); Physical therapists 1 (pt); Recreational therapists 2 (ft); Occupational therapists 1 (pt); Speech therapists 1 (pt); Activities coordinators 1 (pt); Dietitians 1 (pt); Ophthalmologists 1 (pt); Podiatrists 1 (pt); Audiologists 1 (pt); Dentists 1 (pt).
Facilities Dining room; Physical therapy room; Activities room; Chapel; Crafts room; Laundry room; Barber/Beauty shop; Library.
Activities Arts & crafts; Cards; Games; Reading groups; Prayer groups; Movies; Shopping trips; Dances/Social/Cultural gatherings.

South Side Manor Nursing Home
1611 Acero St, Pueblo, CO 81004
(719) 564-5161
Admin John Nance.
Licensure Skilled care. *Beds* SNF 50.

Spanish Peaks Mental Health Center
1304 Chinook Ln, Pueblo, CO 81001-1851
(719) 948-3346
Admin Gilbert A Sanchez.
Licensure Intermediate care. *Beds* 10.
Owner Nonprofit corp.

2201 East 10th Street Home
2201 E 10th St, Pueblo, CO 81003
(719) 534-1170
Admin Lawrence Velasco, Exec Dir.
Licensure Intermediate care for mentally retarded. *Beds* ICF/MR 8.
Owner Nonprofit corp.

University Park Care Center
945 Desert Flower Blvd, Pueblo, CO 81001
(719) 545-5321
Admin Craig Conkling.
Licensure Skilled care. *Beds* SNF 173.

Villa Pueblo Towers
1111 Bonforte Blvd, Pueblo, CO 81001
(719) 545-5911
Admin Ann Genova.
Medical Dir D Manolis MD.
Licensure Skilled care. *Beds* SNF 32. *Certified* Medicare.
Owner Nonprofit corp.
Admissions Requirements Minimum age 62; Medical examination.
Facilities Dining room; Activities room; Chapel; Laundry room; Library.
Activities Cards; Games; Prayer groups; Movies; Shopping trips; Dances/Social/Cultural gatherings.

Rifle

Colorado State Veterans Nursing Home
PO Box 1420, 851 E 5th St, Rifle, CO 81650
(303) 625-0842, 625-3706 FAX
Admin Marvin E Self NHA. *Dir of Nursing* Becky Green. *Medical Dir* Dr Victor Hoefner III.
Licensure Skilled care; Alzheimer's care. *Beds* SNF 100. *Private Pay Patients* 75%. *Certified* Medicaid.
Owner Publicly owned.
Admissions Requirements Medical examination.
Staff Physicians 5 (pt); RNs 10 (ft); LPNs 12 (ft); Nurses' aides 25 (ft); Physical therapists 1 (pt); Reality therapists 1 (pt); Recreational therapists 1 (pt); Occupational therapists 1 (pt); Speech therapists 1 (pt); Activities coordinators 1 (ft); Dietitians 1 (ft); Podiatrists 1 (pt); Audiologists 1 (pt).

Activities Arts & crafts; Cards; Games;
Reading groups; Prayer groups; Movies;
Shopping trips; Dances/Social/Cultural
gatherings; Intergenerational programs; Pet
therapy.

E Dene Moore Memorial Home
PO Box 912, 701 E 5th St, Rifle, CO 81650
(303) 625-1510
Admin Edwin A Gast.
Licensure Skilled care. *Beds* SNF 57. *Certified*
Medicaid.
Owner Publicly owned.
Admissions Requirements Medical
examination.
Staff RNs 4 (ft), 3 (pt); LPNs 3 (ft), 1 (pt);
Nurses' aides 11 (ft), 15 (pt); Physical
therapists 1 (pt); Occupational therapists 1
(pt); Speech therapists 1 (pt); Activities
coordinators 1 (ft); Dietitians 1 (ft);
Podiatrists 1 (pt); Dentists 1 (pt).
Facilities Dining room; Physical therapy
room; Crafts room; Barber/Beauty shop;
Library.
Activities Arts & crafts; Cards; Games; Prayer
groups; Movies; Shopping trips; Dances/
Social/Cultural gatherings.

Rocky Ford

Bauer Residential Care Facility
803 Maple Ave, Rocky Ford, CO 81067-1621
(303) 254-7638
Admin Clara M Bauer LPN. *Dir of Nursing*
Clara M Bauer LPN.
Licensure Intermediate care; Alzheimer's care.
Beds ICF 10. *Certified* Medicaid; Medicare.
Owner Privately owned.
Staff Physicians 1 (pt); LPNs 1 (pt); Nurses'
aides 1 (pt); Recreational therapists;
Dietitians; Ophthalmologists.
Languages Italian, Spanish.
Facilities Dining room; Activities room;
Laundry room; Barber/Beauty shop.
Activities Arts & crafts; Cards; Games;
Reading groups; TV; Religious services;
Parties.

Pioneer Health Care Center
900 S 12th, Rocky Ford, CO 81067
(719) 254-3314, 254-7007 FAX
Admin Cynthia J Haffner-Romero. *Dir of
Nursing* Priscilla Nielsen. *Medical Dir* Dr
Ted Martin.
Licensure Skilled care; Intermediate care;
Personal care; Alzheimer's care. *Beds* SNF
36; ICF 62; Personal care 3. *Private Pay
Patients* 20%. *Certified* Medicaid; Medicare.
Owner Nonprofit corp (Gericare Inc).
Admissions Requirements Minimum age 18;
Physician's request.
Staff RNs 5 (ft); LPNs 13 (ft); Nurses' aides
45 (ft), 6 (pt); Physical therapists 1 (ft), 1
(pt); Activities coordinators 1 (ft); Dietitians
1 (ft).
Languages Spanish.
Facilities Dining room; Physical therapy
room; Activities room; Chapel; Laundry
room; Barber/Beauty shop; Library;
Alzheimer's unit; Special care unit.
Activities Arts & crafts; Games; Reading
groups; Movies; Shopping trips; Dances/
Social/Cultural gatherings; Intergenerational
programs.

Salida

Columbine Manor
530 W 16th, Salida, CO 81201
(719) 539-6112
Admin David J Stang. *Dir of Nursing* Ginger
Gentry.
Licensure Skilled care; Alzheimer's care. *Beds*
SNF 112. *Private Pay Patients* 30%. *Certified*
Medicaid; Medicare.
Owner Proprietary corp (Life Care Centers of
America).

Admissions Requirements Physician's request.
Staff Physicians; RNs; LPNs; Nurses' aides;
Physical therapists; Speech therapists;
Activities coordinators; Dietitians.
Activities Arts & crafts; Cards; Games;
Reading groups; Prayer groups; Movies;
Shopping trips; Dances/Social/Cultural
gatherings; Intergenerational programs; Pet
therapy.

I Street House
1110 I St, Salida, CO 81201
(303) 539-2782
Admin Roger Jensen, Exec Dir.
Licensure Intermediate care for mentally
retarded. *Beds* ICF/MR 8.
Owner Proprietary corp.
Admissions Requirements Minimum age 18;
Medical examination.
Staff RNs 1 (pt); Physical therapists 1 (pt);
Occupational therapists 1 (pt); Speech
therapists 1 (pt); Activities coordinators 1
(ft).
Facilities Dining room; Activities room;
Laundry room.
Activities Arts & crafts; Cards; Games;
Movies; Shopping trips; Dances/Social/
Cultural gatherings.

Simla

Simla Good Samaritan Center
PO Box 38, 320 Pueblo Ave, Simla, CO
80835
(719) 541-2269
Admin Lisa M Melby. *Dir of Nursing*
Maureen Armstrong. *Medical Dir* Dr G
Hamstra.
Licensure Intermediate care. *Beds* ICF 32.
Private Pay Patients 53%. *Certified*
Medicaid.
Owner Nonprofit corp (Evangelical Lutheran/
Good Samaritan Society).
Admissions Requirements Medical
examination; Physician's request.
Staff RNs 2 (ft), 2 (pt); LPNs 2 (ft), 2 (pt);
Nurses' aides 3 (ft), 8 (pt); Activities
coordinators 1 (ft), 1 (pt).
Affiliation Lutheran.
Facilities Dining room; Activities room;
Laundry room; Barber/Beauty shop; Library.
Activities Arts & crafts; Cards; Games; Prayer
groups; Movies; Dances/Social/Cultural
gatherings; Intergenerational programs; Van
outings; Field trips.

Springfield

Southeast Colorado Hospital & LTC
373 E 10th Ave, Springfield, CO 81073
(719) 523-4501
Admin Robert L Shaffer RN. *Dir of Nursing*
Joyce Stapel RN. *Medical Dir* Antonio
Manalo MD.
Licensure Intermediate care; General hospital.
Beds ICF 40; General hospital 25. *Certified*
Medicaid; Medicare.
Owner Publicly owned.
Admissions Requirements Physician's request.
Staff Physicians 2 (ft); RNs 5 (ft), 3 (pt);
LPNs 3 (ft), 2 (pt); Nurses' aides 38 (ft), 5
(pt); Physical therapists 1 (pt); Activities
coordinators 1 (ft); Dietitians 1 (pt);
Ophthalmologists 1 (pt).
Facilities Dining room; Physical therapy
room; Activities room; Chapel; Crafts room;
Laundry room; Barber/Beauty shop.
Activities Arts & crafts; Cards; Games;
Reading groups; Prayer groups; Movies;
Shopping trips; Dances/Social/Cultural
gatherings.

Steamboat Springs

**Routt Memorial Hospital Extended Care
Center**
80 Park Ave, Steamboat Springs, CO 80487
(303) 879-1322, 879-6066 FAX
Admin Drew Hartman. *Dir of Nursing* Carol
Schaffer. *Medical Dir* Mark McCaulley MD.
Licensure Skilled care. *Beds* SNF 50. *Private
Pay Patients* 25-35%. *Certified* Medicaid.
Owner Nonprofit organization/foundation.
Staff RNs 11 (ft), 5 (pt); LPNs 2 (ft); Nurses'
aides 8 (ft), 3 (pt); Physical therapists 1 (ft);
Occupational therapists 1 (ft); Speech
therapists (consultant); Activities
coordinators 1 (ft), 2 (pt); Dietitians 1 (pt);
Ophthalmologists (consultant); Podiatrists
(consultant).
Facilities Dining room; Physical therapy
room; Activities room; Barber/Beauty shop.
Activities Arts & crafts; Cards; Games;
Reading groups; Prayer groups; Movies;
Shopping trips; Dances/Social/Cultural
gatherings; Intergenerational programs; Pet
therapy; Bus trips.

Sterling

Devonshire Acres Ltd
PO Box 392, Sterling, CO 80751
(303) 522-4888
Admin Gloria Kaiser. *Dir of Nursing*
Elizabeth Beer RN. *Medical Dir* Dr Robert
Fillion.
Licensure Skilled care; Intermediate care;
Retirement. *Beds* SNF 70; ICF 14;
Retirement 26. *Certified* Medicaid;
Medicare.
Owner Proprietary corp.
Admissions Requirements Medical
examination; Physician's request.
Staff RNs 5 (ft); LPNs 12 (ft); Nurses' aides
32 (ft); Physical therapists (contracted);
Activities coordinators 1 (ft), 1 (pt);
Dietitians (contracted).
Facilities Dining room; Physical therapy
room; Activities room; Chapel; Crafts room;
Laundry room; Barber/Beauty shop; Library.
Activities Arts & crafts; Cards; Games;
Reading groups; Prayer groups; Movies;
Shopping trips; Dances/Social/Cultural
gatherings; Pet therapy.

North Division Residential Center
223 N Division, Sterling, CO 80751
(303) 522-2430
Admin William E Duffield.
Licensure Intermediate care for mentally
retarded. *Beds* ICF/MR 8. *Certified*
Medicaid.
Owner Nonprofit corp.
Admissions Requirements Minimum age 16.
Activities Arts & crafts; Cards; Games;
Reading groups; Movies; Shopping trips;
Dances/Social/Cultural gatherings.

Rose Arbor Manor
1420 S 3rd Ave, Sterling, CO 80751
(303) 522-2933
Admin Kathleen J Kaufman. *Dir of Nursing*
Dawn Neville. *Medical Dir* H J Ollhoff DO.
Licensure Skilled care; Intermediate care;
Board & care. *Beds* SNF 60; ICF 38; Board
& care 20. *Private Pay Patients* 33%.
Certified Medicaid; Medicare.
Owner Proprietary corp (ARA Living
Centers).
Admissions Requirements Medical
examination; Physician's request.
Staff RNs; LPNs; Nurses' aides; Activities
coordinators.
Languages Spanish, German.
Facilities Dining room; Physical therapy
room; Laundry room; Barber/Beauty shop;
Private & semi-private rooms; Whirlpool-

action tub; Private visiting areas; Fenced
patios & yard area; Fire protection systems;
Handicapped parking.
Activities Arts & crafts; Cards; Prayer groups;
Movies; Shopping trips; Dances/Social/
Cultural gatherings; Intergenerational
programs; Pet therapy; Exercise groups
"Joint Efforts".

Sprawka Residential Care Facility
117 Clark St, Sterling, CO 80751
(303) 522-2656
Admin William Duffield.
Licensure Developmentally disabled. *Beds* 12.
Owner Nonprofit corp.

Thornton

Alpine Manor
501 Thornton Pkwy, Thornton, CO 80229
(303) 452-6101
Admin Susan Keohane Grant.
Medical Dir Robert Jardine MD.
Licensure Skilled care; Intermediate care. *Beds*
SNF 60; ICF 60. *Certified* Medicaid.
Owner Proprietary corp (ARA Living
Centers).
Admissions Requirements Medical
examination.
Staff RNs 9 (ft), 4 (pt); LPNs 6 (ft), 2 (pt);
Nurses' aides 33 (ft), 7 (pt); Activities
coordinators 1 (ft).

Elms Haven Care Center
12080 Bellaire Way, Thornton, CO 80241
(303) 450-2700
Admin Sondra M Eppard. *Dir of Nursing*
Billie Greene. *Medical Dir* Dr G Singleton.
Licensure Skilled care; Intermediate care;
Alzheimer's care. *Beds* SNF 120; ICF 60.
Private Pay Patients 30%. *Certified*
Medicaid; Medicare.
Owner Privately owned.
Admissions Requirements Medical
examination; Physician's request.
Staff RNs 10 (ft), 2 (pt); LPNs 25 (ft), 5 (pt);
Nurses' aides 30 (ft), 10 (pt); Recreational
therapists 2 (ft); Activities coordinators 1
(ft).
Languages Japanese, Spanish.
Facilities Dining room; Physical therapy
room; Activities room; Chapel; Crafts room;
Laundry room; Barber/Beauty shop; Library;
Protected Alzheimer's unit; Atrium.
Activities Arts & crafts; Cards; Games;
Reading groups; Prayer groups; Movies;
Shopping trips; Dances/Social/Cultural
gatherings; Pet therapy.

Sunny Acres Villa
2501 E 104th Ave, Thornton, CO 80233
(303) 452-4181
Admin Cheryl Long. *Dir of Nursing* Nancy
Hokanson. *Medical Dir* Dr Robert Jardine.
Licensure Skilled care; Intermediate care;
Assisted living; Apartment living. *Beds*
Swing beds SNF/ICF 118; Assisted living 32;
Apartment living 400. *Private Pay Patients*
80%. *Certified* Medicaid; Medicare.
Owner Nonprofit corp.
Admissions Requirements Minimum age 55;
Medical examination.
Staff RNs 7 (ft), 8 (pt); LPNs 8 (ft), 6 (pt);
Nurses' aides 28 (ft), 13 (pt); Physical
therapists 1 (ft); Occupational therapists 1
(ft); Speech therapists 1 (ft); Activities
coordinators 1 (ft), 2 (pt); Dietitians 1 (ft).
Facilities Dining room; Physical therapy
room; Activities room; Chapel; Crafts room;
Barber/Beauty shop; Library; Covered patio.
Activities Arts & crafts; Cards; Games;
Reading groups; Prayer groups; Movies;
Shopping trips; Dances/Social/Cultural
gatherings; Intergenerational programs; Pet
therapy.

Trinidad

Trinidad State Nursing Home
409 Benedicta, Trinidad, CO 81082
(719) 846-9291, 846-9291, ext 117 FAX
Admin Orlando Gonzales, Supt. *Dir of
Nursing* Daria Gyurman. *Medical Dir* G E
Jimenez MD.
Licensure Skilled care; Intermediate care. *Beds*
SNF 135; ICF 91. *Private Pay Patients* 21%.
Certified Medicaid.
Owner Publicly owned.
Admissions Requirements Medical
examination; Physician's request.
Staff RNs 9 (ft); LPNs 22 (ft), 1 (pt); Nurses'
aides 44 (ft), 1 (pt); Physical therapists
(consultant); Activities coordinators 2 (ft), 1
(pt); Dietitians 1 (ft).
Languages Spanish, Italian.
Facilities Dining room; Physical therapy
room; Activities room; Chapel; Crafts room;
Laundry room; Barber/Beauty shop; Library;
Outdoor patios; Park areas.
Activities Arts & crafts; Cards; Games;
Reading groups; Prayer groups; Movies;
Shopping trips; Dances/Social/Cultural
gatherings; Intergenerational programs; Pet
therapy.

Walsenburg

Walsenburg Care Center Inc
135 W 7th St, Walsenburg, CO 81089
(719) 738-2750
Admin Fern B Sandoval.
Medical Dir Arthur Vialpando MD.
Licensure Intermediate care. *Beds* ICF 50.
Certified Medicaid.
Owner Proprietary corp (LTC).
Admissions Requirements Physician's request.
Staff Physicians 1 (pt); RNs 3 (ft), 1 (pt);
LPNs 2 (ft), 1 (pt); Nurses' aides 15 (ft), 5
(pt); Physical therapists 1 (pt); Occupational
therapists 1 (pt); Speech therapists 1 (pt);
Activities coordinators 1 (ft); Dietitians 1
(pt); Podiatrists 1 (pt); Dentists 1 (pt).
Facilities Dining room; Activities room;
Crafts room; Laundry room; Barber/Beauty
shop; Library; Living room.
Activities Arts & crafts; Cards; Games;
Reading groups; Prayer groups; Movies;
Shopping trips; Dances/Social/Cultural
gatherings.

Walsh

Walsh Healthcare Center
PO Box 206, 150 Nevada, Walsh, CO 81090
(719) 324-5262
Admin Marlo Miller. *Dir of Nursing* Marianne
Mills. *Medical Dir* Dr Roger Troup.
Licensure Intermediate care. *Beds* ICF 25.
Owner Nonprofit organization/foundation.

Westminster

Adams House Group Home
7666 Stuart St, Westminster, CO 80030
(303) 427-2779
Admin Jo Vincelli, Res Dir.
Licensure Intermediate care for mentally
retarded. *Beds* ICF/MR 8. *Certified*
Medicaid.
Owner Nonprofit corp.

Clear Creek Care Center
7481 Knox Pl, Westminster, CO 80030
(303) 427-7101
Admin Barry L Tuteur. *Dir of Nursing* Donna
Huber RN BSN. *Medical Dir* Leonard
Hellman MD.
Licensure Skilled care; Intermediate care;
Alzheimer's care. *Beds* Swing beds SNF/ICF
120. *Private Pay Patients* 25%. *Certified*
Medicaid; Medicare.
Owner Proprietary corp.

Admissions Requirements Medical
examination; Physician's request.
Staff RNs 8 (ft), 3 (pt); LPNs 18 (ft), 4 (pt);
Nurses' aides 30 (ft), 10 (pt); Activities
coordinators 2 (pt); Other staff 20 (ft), 5
(pt).
Languages Spanish.
Facilities Dining room; Activities room;
Laundry room; Barber/Beauty shop; Library;
Solariums.
Activities Arts & crafts; Cards; Games;
Reading groups; Prayer groups; Movies;
Shopping trips; Dances/Social/Cultural
gatherings; Intergenerational programs.

Johnson Home
4354 Apex Ln, Westminster, CO 80030
(303) 427-2779
Admin Marlene J Johnson.
Licensure Intermediate care. *Beds* ICF 7.
Owner Proprietary corp.
Facilities Dining room; Activities room;
Laundry room.

Plaza Health Care Center Inc
7045 Stuart St, Westminster, CO 80030
(303) 427-7045
Admin Cheryl Thomas. *Dir of Nursing* Marti
Jewell. *Medical Dir* Larry Plunkett MD.
Licensure Intermediate care. *Beds* ICF 103.
Certified Medicaid.
Owner Proprietary corp.
Admissions Requirements Minimum age 21;
Medical examination; Physician's request.
Staff RNs 2 (ft); LPNs 5 (ft), 2 (pt); Nurses'
aides 14 (ft); Recreational therapists 1 (ft);
Activities coordinators 1 (ft).
Languages Spanish.
Facilities Dining room; Activities room;
Laundry room.
Activities Arts & crafts; Cards; Games;
Reading groups; Prayer groups; Movies;
Shopping trips; Dances/Social/Cultural
gatherings.

Wheat Ridge

Christopher House Nursing Home
6270 W 38th Ave, Wheat Ridge, CO 80033
(303) 421-2272
Admin Louis C Lilly.
Licensure Skilled care. *Beds* SNF 90.
Owner Proprietary corp.
Staff Physicians; RNs; LPNs; Nurses' aides;
Physical therapists; Recreational therapists;
Speech therapists; Activities coordinators;
Dietitians; Ophthalmologists.
Facilities Dining room; Physical therapy
room; Activities room; Crafts room; Laundry
room; Barber/Beauty shop.
Activities Arts & crafts; Cards; Games;
Reading groups; Prayer groups; Movies;
Shopping trips; Dances/Social/Cultural
gatherings.

Columbine Manor Inc
3835 Harlan St, Wheat Ridge, CO 80033
(303) 422-2338
Admin Jennifer D Golden.
Medical Dir Robert Starr MD.
Licensure Skilled care; Intermediate care. *Beds*
SNF 44; ICF 107. *Certified* Medicaid;
Medicare.
Owner Proprietary corp (Arvada
Management).
Admissions Requirements Minimum age 65;
Medical examination.
Staff Physicians 1 (pt); RNs 4 (ft), 9 (pt);
LPNs 5 (ft), 8 (pt); Nurses' aides 31 (ft), 16
(pt); Physical therapists 1 (pt); Occupational
therapists 1 (pt); Speech therapists 1 (pt);
Activities coordinators 2 (ft); Dietitians 1
(pt); Podiatrists 1 (pt); Dentists 1 (pt).
Facilities Dining room; Physical therapy
room; Activities room; Crafts room; Laundry
room; Barber/Beauty shop.

Activities Arts & crafts; Cards; Games;
Reading groups; Prayer groups; Movies;
Shopping trips; Dances/Social/Cultural
gatherings; Swimming; Overnight camping;
Culinary arts.

Independence House
3900 Independence Court, Wheat Ridge, CO
80030
(303) 433-2801
Admin Sandra Hilbert, Area Admin.
Licensure Intermediate care for mentally
retarded. *Beds* ICF/MR 8.
Owner Nonprofit corp.

Mountain Vista Nursing Home
4800 Tabor St, Wheat Ridge, CO 80033
(303) 421-4161
Admin L Maxine Wendt. *Dir of Nursing*
Pamela Reese RN. *Medical Dir* Charles
Davis MD.
Licensure Skilled care; Apartments. *Beds* SNF
90; Apts 41. *Private Pay Patients* 55%.
Certified Medicaid; Medicare.
Owner Nonprofit corp (Baptist Home
Association).
Admissions Requirements Minimum age 50.
Staff RNs 14 (ft); LPNs 4 (ft); Nurses' aides
25 (ft), 9 (pt); Activities coordinators 1 (ft).
Affiliation Baptist.
Facilities Dining room; Physical therapy
room; Activities room; Chapel; Crafts room;
Laundry room; Barber/Beauty shop; Library.
Activities Arts & crafts; Cards; Games;
Reading groups; Prayer groups; Movies;
Shopping trips; Dances/Social/Cultural
gatherings; Intergenerational programs; Pet
therapy; Ceramics; Writing groups.

Temenos House Inc
3113 Teller St, Wheat Ridge, CO 80215
(303) 233-2808
Admin Marian Gibson. *Dir of Nursing* Judy
Ohs.
Licensure Intermediate care. *Beds* ICF 8.
Owner Proprietary corp.
Admissions Requirements Minimum age 55.
Staff RNs; Nurses' aides; Activities
coordinators; Ophthalmologists.
Facilities Dining room; Activities room;
Chapel; Crafts room; Laundry room;
Library.
Activities Arts & crafts; Cards; Games;
Reading groups; Prayer groups; Movies;
Shopping trips; Dances/Social/Cultural
gatherings.

Wheat Ridge Regional Center
10285 Ridge Rd, Wheat Ridge, CO 80033
(303) 424-7791
Admin Vicky Jeanene Campbell.
Medical Dir Gabriel Bonnet MD.
Licensure Intermediate care for mentally
retarded; Skilled care for mentally retarded;
Residential care facility for mentally
retarded. *Beds* ICF/MR 292; Skilled care for
mentally retarded 64; Residential care for
mentally retarded 114. *Certified* Medicaid.
Owner Publicly owned.
Admissions Requirements Medical
examination; Physician's request.
Staff Physicians 2 (ft), 2 (pt); RNs 36 (ft);
Nurses' aides 381 (ft); Physical therapists 5
(ft); Recreational therapists 8 (ft), 1 (pt);

Occupational therapists 4 (ft); Speech
therapists 1 (ft), 2 (pt); Activities
coordinators 1 (ft); Dietitians 1 (ft).
Facilities Dining room; Physical therapy
room; Activities room; Chapel; Crafts room;
Barber/Beauty shop; Library.
Activities Arts & crafts; Games; Movies;
Shopping trips; Dances/Social/Cultural
gatherings.

Wide Horizons Inc
8900 W 38th Ave, Wheat Ridge, CO 80033
(303) 424-4445
Admin Joe Wechsler.
Licensure Skilled care. *Beds* SNF 30.
Owner Nonprofit corp.

Wheatridge

Johnstone Developmental Center
5361 W 26th Ave, Wheatridge, CO 80214
(303) 233-8518
Admin Vicky J Campbell NHA. *Dir of
Nursing* Kay S Hainlen LPN HSS. *Medical
Dir* Emerson Harvey MD.
Licensure Intermediate care for mentally
retarded. *Beds* ICF/MR 40. *Private Pay
Patients* 0%. *Certified* Medicaid.
Owner Nonprofit corp.
Admissions Requirements Minimum age 18;
Medical examination.
Staff LPNs 3 (ft), 3 (pt); Nurses' aides 15 (ft),
3 (pt); Speech therapists (contracted);
Dietitians (contracted); Ophthalmologists
(contracted); Podiatrists (contracted);
Audiologists (contracted); Physical therapy
aides 1 (ft); Recreational therapistsActivities
coordinators 1 (ft).
Languages Spanish.
Facilities Dining room; Activities room;
Crafts room; Laundry room; Beautician
comes in.
Activities Arts & crafts; Cards; Games;
Reading groups; Movies; Shopping trips;
Dances/Social/Cultural gatherings;
Intergenerational programs; Pet therapy;
Resident council; Holiday & birthday
celebrations.

Windsor

Windsor Health Care Center
PO Box 999, 710 3rd St, Windsor, CO 80550
(303) 686-7473
Admin Dennis H Ziefel. *Dir of Nursing* Fran
James. *Medical Dir* Robert Bradley MD.
Licensure Skilled care; Intermediate care;
Alzheimer's care. *Beds* SNF 114; ICF 6.
Private Pay Patients 25%. *Certified*
Medicaid.
Owner Proprietary corp (ARA Living
Centers).
Admissions Requirements Minimum age 18;
Medical examination.
Staff Physicians; RNs; LPNs; Nurses' aides;
Physical therapists; Recreational therapists;
Occupational therapists; Speech therapists;
Activities coordinators; Dietitians;
Ophthalmologists; Podiatrists; Audiologists.
Languages Spanish, German.
Facilities Dining room; Crafts room; Laundry
room; Barber/Beauty shop; 3 activity rooms;
Alzheimer's unit.

Activities Arts & crafts; Cards; Games;
Reading groups; Prayer groups; Movies;
Shopping trips; Dances/Social/Cultural
gatherings; Intergenerational programs; Pet
therapy.

Wray

Cedardale Health Care Facility
PO Box 97, 720 Clay St, Wray, CO 80758
(303) 332-5375
Admin Clair Morrison. *Dir of Nursing* Sue
Sprague.
Licensure Intermediate care. *Beds* ICF 33.
Private Pay Patients 38%. *Certified*
Medicaid.
Owner Privately owned.
Admissions Requirements Minimum age 60;
Medical examination; Physician's request.
Staff RNs 1 (ft), 1 (pt); LPNs 2 (ft), 1 (pt);
Nurses' aides 5 (ft), 2 (pt); Physical
therapists; Speech therapists; Activities
coordinators 1 (ft); Dietitians 1 (ft);
Ophthalmologists; Podiatrists; Audiologists.
Languages Spanish.
Facilities Dining room; Activities room;
Chapel; Crafts room; Laundry room; Barber/
Beauty shop; Bus with wheelchair lift.
Activities Arts & crafts; Cards; Games;
Reading groups; Prayer groups; Movies;
Shopping trips; Dances/Social/Cultural
gatherings; Intergenerational programs; Pet
therapy; Trips to area plays, circus, parades,
fairs.

Renotta Nursing Home
815 Franklin St, Wray, CO 80758
(303) 332-4856
Admin Stanley C Fisher.
Licensure Intermediate care. *Beds* ICF 38.
Certified Medicaid.
Owner Proprietary corp.
Staff Physicians 2 (pt); RNs 2 (ft); LPNs 1
(ft), 6 (pt); Nurses' aides 6 (ft), 15 (pt);
Activities coordinators 1 (pt); Dietitians 1
(ft).
Facilities Dining room; Activities room;
Crafts room; Laundry room; Barber/Beauty
shop.
Activities Arts & crafts; Cards; Games;
Movies; Shopping trips.

Yuma

Yuma Life Care Center
323 W 9th Ave, Yuma, CO 80759
(303) 848-2403
Admin Prudence Mitchell. *Dir of Nursing*
Barbara Sweet RN. *Medical Dir* Jack Pearse
MD.
Licensure Skilled care. *Beds* SNF 60. *Certified*
Medicaid.
Owner Proprietary corp (ARA Living
Centers).
Admissions Requirements Physician's request.
Staff RNs 1 (ft), 3 (pt); LPNs; Nurses' aides;
Activities coordinators 1 (pt).
Facilities Dining room; Laundry room;
Barber/Beauty shop.
Activities Arts & crafts; Games; Reading
groups; Prayer groups; Movies; Shopping
trips.

CONNECTICUT

Ashford

Evangelical Baptist Home
PO Box 131, RFD 1, Ashford, CT 06278
(203) 429-2743
Licensure Intermediate care. *Beds* 30.
Owner Nonprofit corp.
Languages Spanish, French, German, Russian, Polish.
Affiliation Baptist.

Attawaugan

Westview Convalescent Center Inc
Ware Rd, Attawaugan, CT 06241
(203) 774-8574
Admin Eileen Panteleakes.
Medical Dir Dr R Philip Goyette.
Licensure Skilled care. *Beds* SNF 90. *Certified* Medicaid; Medicare.
Owner Proprietary corp.
Admissions Requirements Minimum age 14; Medical examination.
Staff Physicians 2 (pt); RNs 8 (ft); LPNs 15 (ft); Nurses' aides 32 (ft); Physical therapists 1 (ft); Reality therapists 1 (pt); Recreational therapists 2 (ft); Speech therapists 1 (pt); Activities coordinators 1 (ft); Dietitians 1 (ft); Ophthalmologists 1 (pt); Podiatrists 1 (pt); Audiologists 1 (pt); Dentists 1 (pt).
Languages French, Polish, Swedish, Spanish, Finnish.
Facilities Dining room; Physical therapy room; Activities room; Crafts room; Laundry room; Barber/Beauty shop; Library.
Activities Arts & crafts; Cards; Games; Reading groups; Prayer groups; Movies; Shopping trips; Dances/Social/Cultural gatherings.

Avon

Avon Convalescent Home
652 W Avon Rd, Avon, CT 06001
(203) 673-2521
Admin Rhonda T Lewis. *Dir of Nursing* Marcia Lysak RN. *Medical Dir* Leslie Lindenberg MD.
Licensure Skilled care; Alzheimer's care. *Beds* SNF 120. *Private Pay Patients* 50%. *Certified* Medicaid; Medicare.
Owner Proprietary corp.
Admissions Requirements Minimum age 21; Medical examination.
Staff RNs 11 (ft), 6 (pt); LPNs 1 (ft), 12 (pt); Nurses' aides 35 (ft), 17 (pt); Physical therapists 1 (pt); Recreational therapists 2 (ft), 1 (pt); Occupational therapists; Speech therapists; Activities coordinators 1 (pt); Dietitians 1 (pt); Ophthalmologists; Podiatrists; Audiologists.
Languages Italian, Polish, Spanish.
Facilities Dining room; Physical therapy room; Activities room; Chapel; Crafts room; Laundry room; Barber/Beauty shop; Library; Gardens; Orchard; Child day care center.

Activities Arts & crafts; Cards; Games; Reading groups; Prayer groups; Movies; Shopping trips; Dances/Social/Cultural gatherings; Intergenerational programs; Pet therapy; Alzheimer's group.

Brightview Nursing & Retirement Center
220 Scoville Rd, Avon, CT 06001
(203) 673-3265
Admin Gregory J Hamley. *Dir of Nursing* Sally Smith. *Medical Dir* Dr Wm Williams.
Licensure Skilled care; Alzheimer's care. *Beds* SNF 56.
Owner Proprietary corp.
Admissions Requirements Physician's request.
Staff RNs 8 (ft); LPNs 1 (ft); Nurses' aides 23 (ft); Physical therapists 1 (ft); Recreational therapists 1 (ft); Activities coordinators 1 (ft); Dietitians 1 (pt).
Languages Polish, German, Hungarian, French.
Facilities Dining room; Physical therapy room; Activities room; Crafts room; Barber/Beauty shop; Library.
Activities Arts & crafts; Games; Prayer groups; Movies; Dances/Social/Cultural gatherings.

Bloomfield

Bloomfield Convalescent Home
355 Park Ave, Bloomfield, CT 06002
(203) 242-8595
Licensure Skilled care. *Beds* SNF 120. *Certified* Medicaid; Medicare.
Languages Portuguese.

Canterbury Villa of Bloomfield
160 Coventry St, Bloomfield, CT 06002
(203) 243-2995
Licensure Intermediate care. *Beds* 113. *Certified* Medicaid.
Owner Proprietary corp (Health Enter of America).
Staff RNs 3 (ft); LPNs 3 (ft); Nurses' aides 4 (ft); Dietitians.
Languages Spanish, Farsi, Malayasain, Tagalog.
Activities Arts & crafts; Shopping trips; Dances/Social/Cultural gatherings; Exercise groups.

Caleb Hitchcock Health Center at Duncaster
40 Loeffler Rd, Bloomfield, CT 06002
(203) 726-2000
Admin Mary Fiorello. *Dir of Nursing* Carolyn Wrubel. *Medical Dir* Dr Cox Chapman.
Licensure Skilled care; Intermediate care. *Beds* SNF 30; ICF 30.
Owner Nonprofit corp.
Staff Physicians 1 (ft); RNs 9 (ft); Nurses' aides 19 (ft); Physical therapists 2 (ft); Recreational therapists 2 (ft); Occupational therapists 1 (ft); Speech therapists 1 (ft); Dietitians 1 (ft).
Languages Spanish.

Oak Ridge Convalescent Center
55 Tunxis Ave, Bloomfield, CT 06002
(203) 242-0703
Medical Dir Dr Daniel Marshall.
Licensure Skilled care. *Beds* SNF 120. *Certified* Medicaid; Medicare.
Owner Proprietary corp.
Admissions Requirements Minimum age 14; Medical examination; Physician's request.
Staff RNs 6 (ft), 2 (pt); LPNs 4 (ft); Nurses' aides 38 (ft), 1 (pt); Physical therapists 1 (pt); Recreational therapists 2 (ft); Dietitians 1 (pt); Ophthalmologists 1 (pt); Podiatrists 1 (pt); Audiologists 1 (pt); Dentists 1 (pt).
Facilities Dining room; Physical therapy room; Activities room; Crafts room; Laundry room; Barber/Beauty shop.
Activities Arts & crafts; Cards; Games; Reading groups; Prayer groups; Movies; Shopping trips; Dances/Social/Cultural gatherings.

Wintonbury Continuing Care Center
140 Park Ave, Bloomfield, CT 06002
(203) 243-9591
Admin Ray Talamona. *Dir of Nursing* Pat Fiocchetta RN. *Medical Dir* Joseph O'Keefe MD.
Licensure Skilled care; Intermediate care. *Beds* SNF 120; ICF 30. *Certified* Medicaid; Medicare.
Owner Proprietary corp.
Admissions Requirements Minimum age 18.
Staff RNs 11 (ft), 13 (pt); LPNs 8 (ft), 4 (pt); Nurses' aides 42 (ft), 16 (pt); Physical therapists 1 (ft), 3 (pt); Recreational therapists 2 (ft), 1 (pt); Speech therapists 1 (pt); Dietitians 1 (pt); Resident needs coordinator.
Languages Italian, Spanish.
Facilities Dining room; Physical therapy room; Activities room; Chapel; Crafts room; Laundry room; Barber/Beauty shop; Library.
Activities Arts & crafts; Cards; Games; Reading groups; Prayer groups; Movies; Shopping trips; Dances/Social/Cultural gatherings; Ceramics; Gardening.

Branford

Branford Hills Health Care Center
189 Alps Rd, Branford, CT 06405
(203) 481-6221
Licensure Skilled care. *Beds* SNF 120. *Certified* Medicaid; Medicare.
Owner Proprietary corp.
Staff LPNs 28 (ft); Nurses' aides 72 (ft); Physical therapists 2 (ft); Activities coordinators 5 (ft); Dietitians; Social workers 2 (ft).
Languages Polish, Italian.
Activities Arts & crafts; Games; Dances/Social/Cultural gatherings; Cooking; Gardening; Resident newspaper & council; Exercises.

Bridgeport

Barnett Multi-Health Care Facility
2875 Main St, Bridgeport, CT 06606
(203) 336-0232
Licensure Skilled care; Intermediate care. *Beds*
SNF 46; ICF 74. *Certified* Medicaid;
Medicare.
Languages Spanish, Hebrew, Portuguese,
Italian.

Burroughs Home Inc
2470 Fairfield Ave, Bridgeport, CT 06605
(203) 334-0293
Admin Sr Rita DuBois DW.
Licensure Home for aged. *Beds* 25.
Owner Nonprofit organization/foundation.
Admissions Requirements Minimum age 60;
Females only.
Facilities Dining room; Activities room;
Laundry room.
Activities Cards; Movies; Shopping trips;
Dances/Social/Cultural gatherings; Bingo.

Dinan Memorial Center
600 Bond St, Bridgeport, CT 06610
(203) 384-6400
Admin Marie Squattrito. *Dir of Nursing*
Judith Marin RN. *Medical Dir* Joseph
Connally MD.
Licensure Skilled care; Intermediate care. *Beds*
SNF 480; ICF 30. *Certified* Medicaid;
Medicare.
Owner Publicly owned.
Admissions Requirements Minimum age 14;
Medical examination; Physician's request.
Staff RNs 50 (ft); LPNs 50 (ft); Nurses' aides
203 (ft), 1 (pt); Physical therapists 5 (ft);
Recreational therapists 12 (ft); Occupational
therapists 1 (ft); Speech therapists 1 (ft);
Activities coordinators 3 (ft); Dietitians 3
(ft); Occupational therapists Social workers 4
(ft).
Languages Portuguese, Spanish, Italian.
Facilities Dining room; Physical therapy
room; Activities room; Chapel; Crafts room;
Laundry room; Barber/Beauty shop; Library.
Activities Arts & crafts; Cards; Games;
Reading groups; Prayer groups; Movies;
Shopping trips; Dances/Social/Cultural
gatherings.

Golden Heights Health Care Center Inc
62 Coleman St, Bridgeport, CT 06604
(203) 367-8444
Licensure Skilled care; Intermediate care. *Beds*
SNF 136. *Certified* Medicaid; Medicare.
Owner Proprietary corp.
Staff RNs 11 (ft); LPNs 14 (ft); Nurses' aides
42 (ft); Activities coordinators 1 (ft).
Languages Italian, Portuguese, Spanish,
Polish.
Activities Arts & crafts; Prayer groups;
Movies; Shopping trips; Resident council.

Laurel Avenue Rest Home Inc
217 Laurel Ave, Bridgeport, CT 06605
(203) 367-0945
Licensure Intermediate care. *Beds* 12.
Owner Proprietary corp.

Park Avenue Health Care Center
725 Park Ave, Bridgeport, CT 06604
(203) 366-3653
Admin Michael Fidre. *Dir of Nursing* Mary
Alice Chestnut RN. *Medical Dir* Wayne S
Levin MD.
Licensure Skilled care. *Beds* SNF 132.
Certified Medicaid; Medicare.
Owner Proprietary corp.
Staff Physicians 5 (pt); RNs 10 (ft), 4 (pt);
LPNs 20 (ft), 6 (pt); Nurses' aides 58 (ft);
Physical therapists 1 (pt); Recreational
therapists 3 (ft); Occupational therapists 1
(pt); Speech therapists 1 (pt); Activities
coordinators 1 (ft); Dietitians 1 (pt);
Ophthalmologists 1 (pt); Podiatrists 1 (pt).
Languages Spanish.

Facilities Dining room; Physical therapy
room; Activities room; Crafts room; Laundry
room; Barber/Beauty shop.
Activities Arts & crafts; Cards; Games;
Reading groups; Prayer groups; Movies;
Shopping trips; Dances/Social/Cultural
gatherings; Intergenerational programs; Pet
therapy.

Roncalli Health Center Inc
425 Grant St, Bridgeport, CT 06610
(203) 366-5255
Licensure Skilled care; Intermediate care. *Beds*
SNF 120; ICF 60. *Certified* Medicaid;
Medicare.
Owner Nonprofit corp.
Staff RNs 9 (ft); LPNs 14 (ft); Nurses' aides
58 (ft); Physical therapists 1 (ft); Activities
coordinators 2 (ft).
Languages Russian, Italian, Spanish, Polish,
French, German.

Sterling Home of Bridgeport
354 Prospect St, Bridgeport, CT 06604
(203) 334-2310
Admin Marie C Franck DW.
Licensure Independent living. *Beds*
Independent living 25. *Private Pay Patients*
100%.
Owner Nonprofit organization/foundation.
Admissions Requirements Minimum age 65;
Females only; Medical examination;
Physician's request.
Staff Dietitians; Podiatrists.
Languages Italian, Spanish, French.
Facilities Dining room; Activities room;
Chapel; Crafts room; Laundry room; Barber/
Beauty shop; Library; Plant room; Sewing
room.
Activities Arts & crafts; Cards; Games; Prayer
groups; Movies; Shopping trips; Dances/
Social/Cultural gatherings; Parties.

Sylvan Manor Inc
1037 Sylvan Ave, Bridgeport, CT 06606
(203) 372-3508
Admin Kenneth S Kopchik. *Dir of Nursing*
Janice Caserta RN. *Medical Dir* Dr Robert
Yasner.
Licensure Skilled care. *Beds* SNF 40. *Certified*
Medicaid; Medicare.
Owner Proprietary corp.
Admissions Requirements Medical
examination; Physician's request.
Staff Physicians 3 (pt); RNs 2 (ft), 5 (pt);
LPNs 1 (pt); Nurses' aides 8 (ft), 9 (pt);
Physical therapists 1 (pt) 9; Recreational
therapists 1 (ft); Occupational therapists 1
(pt); Speech therapists 1 (pt); Dietitians 1
(pt); Ophthalmologists 1 (pt); Podiatrists 1
(pt); Dentists 1 (pt); Social workers 1 (pt).
Languages Slavic.
Facilities Dining room; Physical therapy
room; Activities room; Crafts room; Laundry
room; Barber/Beauty shop; Patio.
Activities Arts & crafts; Cards; Games;
Reading groups; Prayer groups; Movies;
Garden.

3030 Park Health Center
3030 Park Ave, Bridgeport, CT 06604
(203) 374-5611
Admin Linda T Murphy. *Dir of Nursing* Joyce
Donnelly RN. *Medical Dir* Warren Heller
MD.
Licensure Skilled care; Intermediate care;
Retirement; Alzheimer's care. *Beds* SNF 28;
ICF 72; Retirement 325. *Private Pay
Patients* 70%. *Certified* Medicaid; Medicare.
Owner Nonprofit organization/foundation.
Admissions Requirements Minimum age 14;
Medical examination; Physician's request.
Staff Physicians; Physical therapists 2 (ft);
Occupational therapists; Speech therapists;
Dietitians; Podiatrists; Recreational
therapistsActivities coordinators 2 (ft), 2
(pt).
Languages Spanish, Portuguese.

Facilities Dining room; Physical therapy
room; Activities room; Chapel; Crafts room;
Laundry room; Barber/Beauty shop; Library.
Activities Arts & crafts; Cards; Games;
Reading groups; Prayer groups; Movies;
Shopping trips; Dances/Social/Cultural
gatherings; Intergenerational programs; Pet
therapy; Alzheimer's programs.

Bristol

Countryside Manor
1660 Stafford Ave, Bristol, CT 06010
(203) 583-8483
Admin Dorothy Hultman.
Licensure Intermediate care. *Beds* 59.
Certified Medicaid.
Owner Proprietary corp.
Staff RNs 5 (ft); LPNs 4 (ft); Physical
therapists 1 (ft); Recreational therapists 1
(ft); Dietitians 1 (ft); Social workers 1 (ft).
Languages Polish, Italian, German, Swedish.
Activities Prayer groups; Arts & crafts;
Shopping trips; Bus trips; Special education.

Nursing Care Center of Bristol
61 Bellevue Ave, Bristol, CT 06010
(203) 589-1682
Licensure Skilled care. *Beds* SNF 132.
Certified Medicaid; Medicare.
Owner Proprietary corp.
Staff RNs 22 (ft); LPNs 20 (ft); Nurses' aides
68 (ft); Recreational therapists; Social
workers.
Languages French, Polish, Japanese.

Sheriden Woods Health Care Center
321 Stonecrest Dr, Bristol, CT 06010
(203) 583-1827
Medical Dir Dr Steven Isaacs.
Licensure Skilled care. *Beds* SNF 160.
Certified Medicaid; Medicare.
Owner Proprietary corp.
Admissions Requirements Minimum age 14;
Medical examination; Physician's request.
Staff Physicians 10 (pt); RNs 6 (ft), 4 (pt);
LPNs 14 (ft), 9 (ft); Nurses' aides 37 (ft), 26
(pt); Physical therapists 1 (ft); Recreational
therapists 3 (ft); Occupational therapists 1
(pt); Speech therapists 1 (pt); Dietitians 1
(pt); Ophthalmologists 1 (pt); Podiatrists 1
(pt); Dentists 1 (pt).
Languages Italian, French, Polish.
Facilities Dining room; Physical therapy
room; Activities room; Crafts room; Barber/
Beauty shop.
Activities Arts & crafts; Cards; Games;
Reading groups; Prayer groups; Movies;
Shopping trips; Dances/Social/Cultural
gatherings.

Brooklyn

Brooklyn Rest Home
8 Wolf Den Rd, Brooklyn, CT 06234
(203) 774-2260
Admin Thomas Reese.
Medical Dir Dr Howe.
Licensure Intermediate care. *Beds* 30.
Certified Medicaid.
Owner Proprietary corp.
Admissions Requirements Minimum age 14;
Medical examination.
Staff Physicians 1 (pt); RNs 4 (ft), 4 (pt);
Nurses' aides 7 (ft), 6 (pt); Physical
therapists 1 (pt); Recreational therapists 1
(ft), 1 (pt); Dietitians 1 (pt).
Languages French.
Facilities Activities room; Laundry room.
Activities Arts & crafts; Cards; Games;
Reading groups; Prayer groups; Movies;
Shopping trips; Dances/Social/Cultural
gatherings.

Norcliffe Rest Home
Canterbury Rd, Brooklyn, CT 06234
(203) 774-3296

Licensure Intermediate care. *Beds* 60.
  Certified Medicaid.
Owner Proprietary corp.
Staff RNs 7 (ft); Nurses' aides 8 (ft); Activities
  coordinators 1 (ft); Dietitians 1 (ft).
Languages French, Polish, Italian.

Pierce Memorial Baptist Home Inc
PO Box 326, Rte 169, Brooklyn, CT 06234
(203) 774-9050
Admin Rev John H Zendzian Jr.
Medical Dir Lavius Robinson.
Licensure Home for aged. *Beds* SNF 30; ICF
  15. *Certified* Medicaid; Medicare.
Owner Nonprofit corp.
Admissions Requirements Minimum age 65;
  Medical examination.
Staff Physicians 6 (pt); RNs 3 (ft), 8 (pt);
  LPNs 1 (ft), 7 (pt); Nurses' aides 19 (ft), 6
  (pt); Physical therapists 1 (pt); Recreational
  therapists 1 (ft), 1 (pt); Speech therapists 1
  (pt); Dietitians 1 (pt); Ophthalmologists 2
  (pt); Podiatrists 1 (pt); Dentists 1 (pt).
Languages German, Spanish, Finnish, French.
Affiliation Baptist.
Facilities Dining room; Physical therapy
  room; Activities room; Chapel; Crafts room;
  Laundry room; Library.
Activities Arts & crafts; Games; Reading
  groups; Prayer groups; Movies; Shopping
  trips; Dances/Social/Cultural gatherings;
  Swimming; Dining out.

Canaan

Geer Memorial Health Center
PO Box 819, 99 S Canaan Rd, Canaan, CT
  06018
(203) 824-5137, 824-1474 FAX
Admin Steven M Jackson. *Dir of Nursing*
  Elizabeth Tierney. *Medical Dir* Malcolm M
  Brown MD.
Licensure Skilled care; Alzheimer's care. *Beds*
  SNF 120. *Private Pay Patients* 50%. *Certified*
  Medicaid; Medicare.
Owner Nonprofit corp.
Staff RNs 13 (ft), 5 (pt); LPNs 3 (ft), 2 (pt);
  Nurses' aides 45 (ft), 6 (pt); Physical
  therapists 1 (ft); Recreational therapists 3
  (ft); Dietitians.
Facilities Dining room; Physical therapy
  room; Activities room; Chapel; Crafts room;
  Laundry room; Barber/Beauty shop; Library;
  Greenhouse.
Activities Arts & crafts; Cards; Games;
  Reading groups; Prayer groups; Movies;
  Dances/Social/Cultural gatherings;
  Intergenerational programs; Pet therapy;
  Horticulture program.

Cheshire

Cheshire Convalescent Center
745 Highland Ave, Cheshire, CT 06410
(203) 272-7285
Admin Mary P Fehr.
Medical Dir Edward Oxnard MD.
Licensure Skilled care; Intermediate care. *Beds*
  SNF 80; ICF 40. *Certified* Medicaid;
  Medicare.
Owner Proprietary corp (Mediplex).
Admissions Requirements Minimum age 15;
  Medical examination.
Staff Physicians 4 (pt); RNs 14 (ft), 6 (pt);
  LPNs 7 (ft), 2 (pt); Nurses' aides 32 (ft), 12
  (pt); Physical therapists 1 (ft); Recreational
  therapists 2 (ft), 1 (pt); Occupational
  therapists 1 (pt); Speech therapists 1 (pt);
  Dietitians 1 (pt); Ophthalmologists 1 (pt);
  Podiatrists 1 (pt); Dentists 1 (pt).
Languages Spanish, French.
Facilities Dining room; Physical therapy
  room; Activities room; Chapel; Laundry
  room; Barber/Beauty shop.

Activities Arts & crafts; Cards; Games;
  Reading groups; Prayer groups; Movies;
  Shopping trips; Dances/Social/Cultural
  gatherings.

Elim Park Baptist Home Inc
140 Cook Hill Rd, Cheshire, CT 06410
(203) 272-3547
Medical Dir Gerhard T Mack MD.
Licensure Skilled care; Intermediate care;
  Home for aged. *Beds* SNF 60; ICF 30.
  Certified Medicaid; Medicare.
Owner Nonprofit corp.
Admissions Requirements Minimum age 60;
  Medical examination.
Staff RNs 6 (ft), 13 (pt); LPNs 1 (ft), 4 (pt);
  Nurses' aides 17 (ft), 29 (pt); Activities
  coordinators 2 (ft).
Affiliation Baptist.
Facilities Dining room; Physical therapy
  room; Activities room; Chapel; Crafts room;
  Laundry room; Barber/Beauty shop; Library.
Activities Arts & crafts; Games; Reading
  groups; Prayer groups; Movies; Shopping
  trips; Dances/Social/Cultural gatherings.

New Lakeview Convalescent Home
50 Hazel Dr, Cheshire, CT 06410
(203) 272-7204
Licensure Skilled care; Intermediate care. *Beds*
  SNF 210. *Certified* Medicaid; Medicare.
Owner Proprietary corp (Greenery Rehab
  Grp).
Staff RNs 14 (ft); LPNs 20 (ft); Nurses' aides
  61 (ft); Activities coordinators 3 (ft), 1 (pt);
  Social workers 2 (ft).
Languages Italian, Spanish, Japanese, Korean,
  German, Portuguese.

Chester

Aaron Manor Health Care Facility
Rte 148, Chester, CT 06412
(203) 526-5316
Licensure Intermediate care. *Beds* 60.
  Certified Medicaid.
Owner Proprietary corp.
Staff LPNs 4 (ft), 1 (pt); Nurses' aides 8 (ft), 1
  (pt); Activities coordinators 1 (ft).
Activities Arts & crafts; Games; Movies;
  Dances/Social/Cultural gatherings.

Chesterfields Chronic & Convalescent Hospital
132 Main St, Chester, CT 06412
(203) 526-5363
Licensure Skilled care. *Beds* SNF 60. *Certified*
  Medicaid; Medicare.
Owner Proprietary corp.
Staff RNs 5 (ft), 1 (pt); LPNs 5 (ft), 1 (pt);
  Nurses' aides 25 (ft), 1 (pt).
Languages Greek, Italian.
Activities Arts & crafts; Games; Movies; Bus
  trips; Music.

Clinton

Clinton Health Care Center
5 Harbor Pkwy, Clinton, CT 06413
(203) 669-5717
Medical Dir Arnold C Winokur MD.
Licensure Intermediate care. *Beds* 40.
  Certified Medicaid.
Owner Proprietary corp.
Admissions Requirements Minimum age 16;
  Medical examination; Physician's request.
Staff Physicians 6 (pt); RNs 3 (ft), 2 (pt);
  LPNs 1 (ft), 2 (pt); Nurses' aides 6 (ft), 10
  (pt); Physical therapists 1 (pt); Reality
  therapists 1 (ft); Recreational therapists 1
  (ft); Occupational therapists 1 (pt); Speech
  therapists 2 (pt); Activities coordinators 1
  (pt); Dietitians 1 (pt); Ophthalmologists 1
  (pt); Podiatrists 1 (pt); Audiologists 1 (pt);
  Dentists 1 (pt).
Languages Spanish, German.

Cobalt

Cobalt Lodge Convalescent Home
Rte 151 Box 246, Cobalt, CT 06414
(203) 267-9034
Admin F P Zgorski. *Dir of Nursing* JoAnn
  Brown RN. *Medical Dir* David Boxwell MD.
Licensure Skilled care. *Beds* SNF 60. *Private
  Pay Patients* 50%. *Certified* Medicaid;
  Medicare.
Owner Proprietary corp.
Staff RNs 2 (ft), 6 (pt); LPNs 1 (ft), 3 (pt);
  Nurses' aides 12 (ft), 7 (pt); Recreational
  therapists 1 (ft); Speech therapists 1 (pt);
  Dietitians 1 (pt).
Languages German, Spanish.
Facilities Dining room; Physical therapy
  room; Activities room; Laundry room;
  Barber/Beauty shop; Library; Private and
  semi-private rooms.
Activities Arts & crafts; Cards; Games;
  Reading groups; Prayer groups; Movies;
  Intergenerational programs; Pet therapy.

Colchester

Colchester Health Care
59 Harrington Ct, Colchester, CT 06415
(203) 537-2339, 537-4747 FAX
Admin Elaine M Cole. *Dir of Nursing* Mary
  Jane Toomey RN. *Medical Dir* Malcolm
  Gourlie MD.
Licensure Skilled care; Intermediate care. *Beds*
  SNF 85; ICF 35. *Certified* Medicaid;
  Medicare.
Owner Proprietary corp (Multicare
  Management Inc).
Staff Physicians 7 (pt); RNs 3 (ft), 14 (pt);
  LPNs 5 (ft), 6 (pt); Nurses' aides 41 (ft);
  Physical therapists 1 (pt); Recreational
  therapists 2 (ft); Occupational therapists 1
  (pt); Speech therapists 1 (pt); Dietitians 1
  (pt); Ophthalmologists 1 (pt); Podiatrists 1
  (pt); Audiologists 1 (pt); Physical therapy
  asst 1 (pt).
Languages Spanish, some Polish.
Facilities Dining room; Physical therapy
  room; Activities room; Chapel; Crafts room;
  Laundry room; Barber/Beauty shop; Library;
  Courtyard.
Activities Arts & crafts; Cards; Games;
  Reading groups; Prayer groups; Movies;
  Dances/Social/Cultural gatherings;
  Intergenerational programs; Pet therapy;
  Summer picnics every 2 weeks.

Liberty Hall Nursing Center
36 Broadway, Colchester, CT 06415
(203) 537-5053
Admin Stuart T Fisher. *Dir of Nursing*
  Rosemarie Hanover RN. *Medical Dir* David
  Boxwell MD.
Licensure Skilled care; Intermediate care. *Beds*
  SNF 60; ICF 60. *Certified* Medicaid;
  Medicare.
Owner Privately owned.
Staff RNs; LPNs; Nurses' aides; Physical
  therapists; Recreational therapists.
Languages Polish, French.
Facilities Dining room; Physical therapy
  room; Activities room; Laundry room;
  Barber/Beauty shop; Library.
Activities Arts & crafts; Cards; Games;
  Reading groups; Prayer groups; Movies;
  Dances/Social/Cultural gatherings; Cooking;
  Sing-alongs; Picnics.

Cromwell

Cromwell Crest Convalescent Home
PO Box 208, 385 Main St, Cromwell, CT
  06416
(203) 635-5613, 635-6330 FAX
Admin Richard A DiMeola. *Dir of Nursing*
  Sandra Muller RN. *Medical Dir* C B
  Montano MD.

Licensure Skilled care; Intermediate care. *Beds*
SNF 90; ICF 90. *Private Pay Patients* 12%.
Certified Medicaid; Medicare.
Owner Proprietary corp (Roncalli Health Care
Management).
Admissions Requirements Medical
examination; Physician's request.
Staff RNs 13 (ft), 5 (pt); LPNs 7 (ft), 12 (pt);
Nurses' aides 44 (ft), 7 (pt); Physical
therapists 1 (pt); Recreational therapists 3
(ft), 1 (pt); Dietitians 1 (pt); Pastoral
counselor 1 (ft).
Languages Spanish, Italian, Polish.
Facilities Dining room; Physical therapy
room; Activities room; Chapel; Barber/
Beauty shop.
Activities Arts & crafts; Cards; Games;
Reading groups; Prayer groups; Movies;
Shopping trips; Dances/Social/Cultural
gatherings; Intergenerational programs; Pet
therapy.

Pilgrim Manor
PO Box 180, 52 Missionary Rd, Cromwell,
CT 06416
(203) 635-5511
Admin Robert Johnson.
Licensure Skilled care; Intermediate care;
Alzheimer's care. *Beds* SNF 30; ICF 30.
Certified Medicaid; Medicare.
Owner Nonprofit corp (Covenant Benevolent
Institute).
Admissions Requirements Minimum age 62;
Medical examination.
Staff Physicians; RNs; Nurses' aides;
Activities coordinators.
Languages Swedish.
Affiliation Evangelical Covenant Church.
Facilities Dining room; Physical therapy
room; Activities room; Crafts room; Laundry
room; Barber/Beauty shop; Library.
Activities Arts & crafts; Games; Reading
groups; Prayer groups; Movies; Shopping
trips; Dances/Social/Cultural gatherings.

Ridgeview Rest Home Inc
156 Berlin Rd, Cromwell, CT 06416
(203) 828-6381, 635-1010
Admin Mrs Adel Coccomo. *Dir of Nursing*
Barbara Baron. *Medical Dir* Dr Richard
Alberti.
Licensure Intermediate care; Retirement. *Beds*
ICF 60. *Certified* Medicaid.
Owner Proprietary corp.
Admissions Requirements Minimum age 55.
Staff RNs 3 (ft), 5 (pt); LPNs 1 (ft); Nurses'
aides 4 (ft), 5 (pt); Activities coordinators 1
(ft); Dietitians 1 (pt); Ophthalmologists 1
(pt).
Languages Italian, French, Polish.
Facilities Dining room; Activities room;
Crafts room; Laundry room; Barber/Beauty
shop.
Activities Arts & crafts; Cards; Games;
Reading groups; Prayer groups; Movies;
Shopping trips; Dances/Social/Cultural
gatherings.

Danbury

Danbury Pavilion Healthcare
22 Hospital Ave, Danbury, CT 06810
(203) 744-3700
Medical Dir Alan Shafto MD.
Licensure Skilled care. *Beds* SNF 150.
Certified Medicaid; Medicare.
Owner Proprietary corp (Beverly Enterprises).
Admissions Requirements Medical
examination.
Staff Physicians 4 (ft); RNs 18 (ft); LPNs 7
(ft); Nurses' aides 84 (ft); Physical therapists
2 (ft); Recreational therapists 2 (ft), 1 (pt);
Speech therapists 1 (pt); Dietitians 1 (pt);
Ophthalmologists 1 (pt); Podiatrists 2 (pt);
Dentists 1 (pt).
Languages Spanish.

Facilities Dining room; Physical therapy
room; Activities room; Chapel; Crafts room;
Laundry room; Barber/Beauty shop; Library;
Outdoor patio.
Activities Arts & crafts; Cards; Games;
Reading groups; Prayer groups; Movies;
Shopping trips; Dances/Social/Cultural
gatherings.

Filosa Convalescent Home Inc
13 Hakim St, Danbury, CT 06810
(203) 744-3366
Admin Sherri Freitas RN BS. *Dir of Nursing*
Holly McGran RN BS. *Medical Dir* Arvid
Sieber MD.
Licensure Skilled care. *Beds* SNF 60. *Private
Pay Patients* 40%. *Certified* Medicaid;
Medicare.
Owner Proprietary corp (Barbara Filosa).
Staff RNs 9 (ft); LPNs 6 (ft); Nurses' aides;
Physical therapists 1 (ft); Reality therapists
20 (ft); Recreational therapists 2 (ft);
Dietitians 1 (pt).
Languages Spanish, Portuguese, Hungarian,
German.
Facilities Dining room; Physical therapy
room; Activities room; Chapel; Crafts room;
Laundry room; Barber/Beauty shop; Library.
Activities Arts & crafts; Cards; Games;
Reading groups; Prayer groups; Movies;
Shopping trips; Dances/Social/Cultural
gatherings; Intergenerational programs; Pet
therapy.

Glen Hill Convalescent Center
Glen Hill Rd, Danbury, CT 06810
(203) 744-2840
Admin James K Malloy. *Dir of Nursing*
Patricia Roth RN. *Medical Dir* W Alan
Schafto MD.
Licensure Skilled care; Retirement. *Beds* SNF
90. *Certified* Medicaid; Medicare.
Owner Proprietary corp.
Staff Physicians 5 (pt); RNs 10 (ft), 15 (pt);
LPNs 6 (ft), 2 (pt); Nurses' aides 25 (ft), 21
(pt); Physical therapists 1 (ft); Recreational
therapists 2 (ft); Occupational therapists 1
(pt); Speech therapists 1 (pt); Dietitians 1
(ft); Ophthalmologists 1 (pt); Dentists 1 (pt).
Languages Spanish, French, Portuguese.
Facilities Dining room; Physical therapy
room; Activities room; Crafts room; Laundry
room; Barber/Beauty shop; Library.
Activities Arts & crafts; Cards; Games;
Reading groups; Prayer groups; Movies;
Shopping trips; Dances/Social/Cultural
gatherings.

Mediplex of Danbury
107 Osborne St, Danbury, CT 06810
(203) 792-8102
Licensure Skilled care; Intermediate care. *Beds*
SNF 120; ICF 60. *Certified* Medicaid;
Medicare.
Owner Proprietary corp (Mediplex).
Staff LPNs 28 (ft); Nurses' aides 52 (ft);
Physical therapists 2 (ft); Activities
coordinators 2 (ft), 1 (pt); Social workers 1
(ft).
Languages Spanish, Hungarian, German,
French.
Activities Arts & crafts; Games; Dances/Social/
Cultural gatherings; Outings; Music.

Pope John Paul II Center for Health Care
33 Lincoln Ave, Danbury, CT 06810
(203) 797-9300
Licensure Skilled care; Intermediate care. *Beds*
SNF 88; ICF 32. *Certified* Medicaid;
Medicare.
Languages Lao, Khymer, Chinese, Portuguese,
Spanish, Vietnamese, Tagalog.

Danielson

Westcott Care Center
65 Westcott Rd, Danielson, CT 06239
(203) 774-9540

Admin E Leo Attella Jr. *Dir of Nursing*
Patricia Weiss. *Medical Dir* R Phillip
Goyette MD.
Licensure Skilled care; Intermediate care;
Short-term rehabilitaiton; Alzheimer's care.
Beds SNF 90; ICF 90. *Private Pay Patients*
25%. *Certified* Medicaid; Medicare.
Owner Proprietary corp (Sunrise Health Care
Corp).
Admissions Requirements Physician's request.
Staff RNs 15 (ft), 4 (pt); LPNs 40 (ft), 20 (pt);
Nurses' aides 65 (ft), 65 (pt); Physical
therapists 2 (pt); Reality therapists 3 (ft);
Recreational therapists 3 (ft); Occupational
therapists 1 (ft), 3 (pt); Speech therapists 1
(pt); Activities coordinators 1 (ft); Dietitians
1 (ft), 1 (pt); Podiatrists 1 (pt); Audiologists
1 (pt); Rehabilitation technicians 3 (ft).
Languages Spanish, Italian, French, Polish,
Russian.
Facilities Dining room; Physical therapy
room; Activities room; Chapel; Crafts room;
Laundry room; Barber/Beauty shop; Library;
Occupational therapy room; Speech therapy
room; Doctor's examination room.
Activities Arts & crafts; Cards; Games;
Reading groups; Prayer groups; Movies;
Shopping trips; Dances/Social/Cultural
gatherings; Intergenerational programs.

Darien

Darien Convalescent Center
599 Boston Post Rd, Darien, CT 06820
(203) 655-7727
Licensure Skilled care; Intermediate care. *Beds*
SNF 90; ICF 30. *Certified* Medicare.
Owner Proprietary corp (New Medico Assoc).
Staff RNs 11 (ft), 1 (pt); LPNs 4 (ft), 1 (pt);
Nurses' aides 36 (ft), 1 (pt); Physical
therapists 1 (ft), 1 (pt); Activities
coordinators 5 (ft), 1 (pt); Social workers 2
(ft), 1 (pt).
Languages Spanish, Portuguese, French,
Yiddish.

Deep River

Deep River Convalescent Home Inc
PO Box 393, 59 Elm St, Deep River, CT
06417-0393
(203) 526-5902
Licensure Skilled care. *Beds* SNF 30. *Certified*
Medicaid.
Owner Proprietary corp.
Staff RNs 3 (ft); Nurses' aides 18 (ft);
Activities coordinators 1 (ft); Social workers
1 (ft).
Languages Greek, French, Russian.
Activities Outings; Therapeutic recreation.

Derby

Derby Nursing Center
210 Chatfield St, Derby, CT 06418
(203) 735-7401
Admin Albert E Saunders. *Dir of Nursing*
Nancy Gambone RN. *Medical Dir* Donald
Roach MD.
Licensure Skilled care; Retirement. *Beds* SNF
121. *Certified* Medicaid; Medicare.
Owner Proprietary corp (National Healthcare
Affilates).
Admissions Requirements Medical
examination; Physician's request.
Staff Physicians 1 (pt); RNs 6 (ft), 8 (pt);
LPNs 5 (ft), 6 (pt); Nurses' aides 30 (ft), 16
(pt); Physical therapists 1 (pt); Recreational
therapists 2 (ft); Speech therapists 1 (pt);
Dietitians 1 (pt); Ophthalmologists 1 (pt);
Dentists 1 (pt).
Languages Spanish.
Facilities Dining room; Physical therapy
room; Activities room; Crafts room; Laundry
room; Barber/Beauty shop; TV rooms.

Activities Arts & crafts; Games; Reading groups; Prayer groups; Movies; Dances/Social/Cultural gatherings.

Marshall Lane Manor
101 Marshall Ln, Derby, CT 06418
(203) 734-3393
Admin Anthony F Simonetti. *Dir of Nursing* Jeanne Sarasin RN. *Medical Dir* John J Narowski MD.
Licensure Intermediate care. *Beds* ICF 120. *Private Pay Patients* 15%. *Certified* Medicaid.
Owner Proprietary corp.
Admissions Requirements Minimum age 14; Medical examination; Physician's request.
Staff RNs 15 (ft), 2 (pt); LPNs 5 (ft), 3 (pt); Nurses' aides 20 (ft), 5 (pt); Recreational therapists 2 (ft); Dietitians 1 (ft).
Languages Italian, Polish, Spanish.
Facilities Dining room; Activities room; Chapel; Crafts room; Laundry room; Barber/Beauty shop.
Activities Arts & crafts; Cards; Games; Reading groups; Prayer groups; Movies; Shopping trips; Dances/Social/Cultural gatherings; Intergenerational programs; Pet therapy.

Durham

Dogwood Acres Intermediate Care Facility
65 Brick Ln, Durham, CT 06422
(203) 349-8000, 827-8786 FAX
Admin Thomas Reese. *Dir of Nursing* Mary Ann Tinker RN. *Medical Dir* Matthew Raider MD.
Licensure Intermediate care. *Beds* ICF 29. *Certified* Medicaid.
Owner Proprietary corp.
Admissions Requirements Minimum age 14; Physician's request.
Staff Physicians 1 (pt); RNs 2 (ft), 8 (pt); LPNs 1 (ft), 2 (pt); Nurses' aides 4 (ft), 7 (pt); Physical therapists 1 (pt); Recreational therapists 1 (pt); Dietitians 1 (pt); Podiatrists 1 (pt).
Facilities Dining room; Activities room; Laundry room.
Activities Arts & crafts; Cards; Games; Reading groups; Prayer groups; Movies; Shopping trips; Dances/Social/Cultural gatherings; Pet therapy.

Twin Maples Health Care Facility
PO Box 423, 809R New Haven Rd, Durham, CT 06422-2412
(203) 349-1041
Admin Joanne Lukasik. *Dir of Nursing* Joanne Grenier RN. *Medical Dir* Victor Sawicki MD.
Licensure Intermediate care; Alzheimer's care. *Beds* ICF 44. *Private Pay Patients* 20%. *Certified* Medicaid.
Owner Proprietary corp.
Staff RNs 5 (ft); LPNs 1 (pt); Nurses' aides 10 (ft), 10 (pt); Physical therapists (contracted); Recreational therapists 1 (ft); Occupational therapists (contracted); Speech therapists (contracted); Dietitians 1 (pt); Ophthalmologists (contracted); Podiatrists (contracted); Audiologists (contracted); Dentists (contracted).
Languages Spanish, Italian.
Facilities Dining room; Activities room; Laundry room; Barber/Beauty shop; Library; Smoking room; Wanderguard system.
Activities Arts & crafts; Cards; Games; Reading groups; Prayer groups; Movies; Shopping trips; Dances/Social/Cultural gatherings; Intergenerational programs; Pet therapy; Outings to theater, ice capades, library.

East Hampton

Lakeside Residential Care Facility
PO Box 279, 9 W High St, East Hampton, CT 06424
(203) 267-4401
Licensure Intermediate care. *Beds* 41.
Owner Proprietary corp.
Activities Arts & crafts; Games; Mental health programs.

East Hartford

Burnside Convalescent Home Inc
870 Burnside Ave, East Hartford, CT 06108
(203) 289-9571
Admin Jean O'Connor.
Medical Dir Rhea Palczynski.
Licensure Skilled care; Alzheimer's care. *Beds* SNF 90. *Certified* Medicaid; Medicare.
Owner Proprietary corp.
Admissions Requirements Minimum age 80; Medical examination; Physician's request.
Staff Physicians 4 (pt); RNs 10 (ft); LPNs 12 (ft); Nurses' aides 18 (ft); Physical therapists 1 (ft); Recreational therapists 2 (ft); Dietitians 1 (ft); Ophthalmologists 1 (pt); Podiatrists 1 (pt); Dentists 1 (pt).
Languages Polish, Spanish.
Facilities Dining room; Physical therapy room; Activities room; Chapel; Crafts room; Laundry room; Barber/Beauty shop; Library; TV rooms.
Activities Arts & crafts; Cards; Games; Reading groups; Prayer groups; Movies; Shopping trips; Dances/Social/Cultural gatherings; Bingo.

Riverside Health Care Center
745 Main St, East Hartford, CT 06108
(203) 289-2791
Licensure Skilled care; Intermediate care. *Beds* SNF 360. *Certified* Medicaid; Medicare.
Owner Proprietary corp.
Staff Physicians; RNs 219 (ft); Physical therapists; Activities coordinators 7 (ft); Dietitians; Social workers.
Languages Lithuanian, Estonian, Yiddish, Hebrew, Spanish, Portuguese, Italian, Polish, French.
Activities Arts & crafts; Games; Reading groups; Prayer groups; Movies; Shopping trips; Dances/Social/Cultural gatherings; AA group; Cooking.

St Elizabeth Health Center
51 Applegate Ln, East Hartford, CT 06118
(203) 568-7520
Admin Jonathan A Neagle. *Dir of Nursing* Kay B LaForge RN. *Medical Dir* Michael Jacuch MD.
Licensure Skilled care. *Beds* SNF 180. *Certified* Medicaid; Medicare.
Owner Nonprofit organization/foundation.
Admissions Requirements Minimum age 14; Medical examination; Physician's request.
Staff Physicians 5 (pt); RNs 5 (ft), 19 (pt); LPNs 7 (ft), 12 (pt); Nurses' aides 58 (ft), 14 (pt); Physical therapists 1 (pt); Recreational therapists 3 (pt).
Languages Spanish, Italian, French, German, Polish, Dutch, Ukranian, Russian.
Affiliation Roman Catholic.
Facilities Dining room; Physical therapy room; Activities room; Chapel; Crafts room; Laundry room; Barber/Beauty shop; Library; Lounges.
Activities Arts & crafts; Cards; Games; Prayer groups; Movies; Shopping trips; Dances/Social/Cultural gatherings.

East Haven

East Haven Rest Home
83 Main St, East Haven, CT 06512
(203) 467-5828
Licensure Intermediate care. *Beds* 20.

Staff RNs 4 (ft), 1 (pt); LPNs 1 (ft), 1 (pt).
Languages Italian.

Talmadge Park Health Care
Talmadge Ave, East Haven, CT 06512
(203) 469-2316
Admin Lorraine A Franco. *Dir of Nursing* Pearl Mattie. *Medical Dir* Dr E Leach.
Licensure Skilled care; Intermediate care. *Beds* SNF 30; ICF 30. *Certified* Medicaid; Medicare.
Owner Privately owned.
Staff Physicians 1 (pt); RNs 11 (ft); LPNs 4 (pt); Nurses' aides 26 (ft); Physical therapists 1 (pt); Speech therapists 1 (pt); Activities coordinators 2 (pt); Dietitians 1 (pt); Ophthalmologists 1 (pt); Podiatrists 1 (pt).
Languages Italian.
Activities Arts & crafts; Games; Movies; Dances/Social/Cultural gatherings; Picnics; Current events; Cooking; Exercises; Sensory intergration.

Teresa Rest Home Inc
PO Box 313, 57 Main St, East Haven, CT 06512
(203) 467-0836
Admin Josephine Santino.
Medical Dir Dr Edward Scherr.
Licensure Rest Home. *Beds* Rest home 21.
Owner Proprietary corp.
Admissions Requirements Minimum age 50; Medical examination.
Staff Nurses' aides; Recreational therapists; Activities coordinators; Ophthalmologists.

East Windsor

D'Amore Rest Haven Inc
171 Main St, East Windsor, CT 06088
(203) 623-3174
Licensure Intermediate care. *Beds* 90. *Certified* Medicaid.
Owner Proprietary corp.
Staff RNs 3 (ft).
Languages Polish, French, Spanish, Italian.

Prospect Hill Rehabilitation Center
96 Prospect Hill Rd, East Windsor, CT 06088
(203) 623-4555
Licensure Skilled care; Intermediate care. *Beds* SNF 120; ICF 60. *Certified* Medicaid.
Owner Proprietary corp.
Staff LPNs 39 (ft); Nurses' aides 75 (ft); Physical therapists 1 (ft); Activities coordinators 2 (ft); Social workers 1 (ft).
Languages French, Italian, Polish.
Activities Games; Movies; Dances/Social/Cultural gatherings; Music; Discussion groups; Resident council.

Enfield

Enfield Nursing Center
612 Hazard Ave, Enfield, CT 06082
(203) 749-8388
Licensure Skilled care; Intermediate care. *Beds* SNF 130. *Certified* Medicaid; Medicare.
Owner Proprietary corp (Unicare).
Staff RNs 3 (ft); LPNs 3 (ft); Social workers 1 (ft).
Languages Italian, Polish, French.
Activities Arts & crafts; Shopping trips; Dances/Social/Cultural gatherings; Church; Discussions; Resident council.

Parkway Pavilion Healthcare
1157 Enfield St, Enfield, CT 06082
(203) 745-1641
Medical Dir Dr George Donahue.
Licensure Skilled care. *Beds* SNF 140. *Certified* Medicaid; Medicare.
Owner Proprietary corp.
Admissions Requirements Minimum age 14; Medical examination; Physician's request.

Staff Physicians 8 (pt); RNs 4 (ft), 18 (pt);
LPNs 4 (ft), 12 (pt); Nurses' aides 15 (ft), 36
(pt); Physical therapists 1 (pt); Reality
therapists 1 (pt); Speech therapists 1 (pt);
Activities coordinators 2 (ft), 1 (pt);
Dietitians 1 (pt); Ophthalmologists 1 (pt);
Podiatrists 1 (pt); Dentists 1 (pt).
Languages Polish, Italian.
Facilities Dining room; Physical therapy
room; Activities room; Chapel; Crafts room;
Laundry room; Barber/Beauty shop; Library.
Activities Arts & crafts; Cards; Games;
Reading groups; Prayer groups; Movies;
Shopping trips; Dances/Social/Cultural
gatherings.

St Joseph's Residence
1365 Enfield St, Enfield, CT 06082
(203) 741-0791
Admin Sr Marie Edward Quinn. *Dir of
Nursing* Sr Margaret Mary Jerousek. *Medical
Dir* Younus Masih.
Licensure Skilled care; Intermediate care. *Beds*
SNF 42; ICF 42. *Certified* Medicaid;
Medicare.
Owner Nonprofit corp.
Admissions Requirements Minimum age 65.
Staff Physicians; RNs; LPNs; Nurses' aides;
Physical therapists; Recreational therapists;
Occupational therapists; Dietitians;
Podiatrists.
Affiliation Roman Catholic.
Facilities Dining room; Physical therapy
room; Activities room; Chapel; Crafts room;
Laundry room; Barber/Beauty shop.
Activities Arts & crafts; Cards; Games; Prayer
groups; Movies; Shopping trips.

Essex

Highland Hall Manor
16 Prospect St, Essex, CT 06426
(203) 767-8244
Admin Amelia Cart.
Medical Dir Dr John Stanford.
Licensure Boarding-Rest home. *Beds* 33.
Certified Medicaid.
Owner Proprietary corp.
Admissions Requirements Minimum age 21.
Languages Spanish, Italian.
Facilities Dining room; Activities room;
Laundry room.
Activities Arts & crafts; Cards; Games; Prayer
groups; Movies; Shopping trips; Day trips.

Pettipaug Manor
63 S Main St, Essex, CT 06426
(203) 767-8422
Admin Betty Jane Cosenza RN. *Dir of Nursing*
Ellen Wasilewski RN. *Medical Dir* Andrea
Schaffner MD.
Licensure Intermediate care. *Beds* ICF 49.
Certified Medicaid.
Owner Proprietary corp.
Admissions Requirements Minimum age 21;
Medical examination; Physician's request.
Staff RNs 5 (ft); LPNs 1 (ft); Nurses' aides 7
(ft); Physical therapists (contracted);
Recreational therapists 1 (pt); Occupational
therapists (contracted); Speech therapists
(contracted); Dietitians (consultant);
Ophthalmologists (contracted); Podiatrists
(contracted); Audiologists (contracted); Food
services 5 (ft); Maintenance & Housekeeping
2 (ft); Laundry 1 (ft); Administration 2 (ft).
Facilities Dining room; Activities room;
Library; 1 lounge for smokers; 1 lounge for
non-smokers; Swimming pool.
Activities Arts & crafts; Cards; Games;
Reading groups; Prayer groups; Movies;
Shopping trips; Dances/Social/Cultural
gatherings; Intergenerational programs; Pet
therapy; Swimming; Bingo; Religious
services; Parties; Barbecues; Picnics.

Fairfield

Carolton Chronic & Convalescent Hospital Inc
400 Mill Plain Rd, Fairfield, CT 06430
(203) 255-3573
Dir of Nursing Angara Lombard. *Medical Dir*
Dr Richard Van de Berghe.
Licensure Skilled care. *Beds* SNF 219.
Certified Medicaid; Medicare.
Owner Proprietary corp.
Staff RNs 31 (ft), 26 (pt); LPNs 9 (ft), 13 (pt);
Nurses' aides 120 (ft), 22 (pt); Physical
therapists 4 (ft); Recreational therapists 4
(ft); Occupational therapists 3 (pt); Speech
therapists 3 (pt); Dietitians 1 (ft).
Languages Spanish, Dutch, Italian, Russian,
Yiddish, Hebrew, French.
Facilities Dining room; Physical therapy
room; Activities room; Laundry room;
Barber/Beauty shop; Library; Physical
therapy swimming pool.
Activities Arts & crafts; Cards; Games;
Reading groups; Prayer groups; Movies.

**Jewish Home for the Elderly of Fairfield
County**
175 Jefferson St, Fairfield, CT 06432
(203) 374-9461, 374-8082 FAX
Admin Dennis J Magid. *Dir of Nursing*
Donna Joyce. *Medical Dir* Marvin Garrell
MD.
Licensure Skilled care; Intermediate care;
Alzheimer's care; Adult day care. *Beds* SNF
120; ICF 120. *Private Pay Patients* 24%.
Certified Medicaid.
Owner Nonprofit corp.
Admissions Requirements Minimum age 65;
Medical examination.
Staff Physicians; RNs; LPNs; Nurses' aides;
Physical therapists; Recreational therapists;
Occupational therapists; Activities
coordinators; Podiatrists.
Languages Russian, Polish, German,
Hungarian.
Affiliation Jewish.
Facilities Dining room; Physical therapy
room; Activities room; Chapel; Crafts room;
Laundry room; Barber/Beauty shop; Library;
Alzheimer's/Dementia special care unit.
Activities Arts & crafts; Cards; Games;
Reading groups; Movies; Dances/Social/
Cultural gatherings; Intergenerational
programs; Pet therapy; Sheltered workshop;
Internship program; Resident fashion show;
Arts & crafts fair.

North Fairfield Geriatric Center
118 Jefferson St, Fairfield, CT 06432
(203) 372-4501
Admin Lois E Perrini. *Dir of Nursing*
Florence Kavulish RN. *Medical Dir* John A
Simpson MD.
Licensure Skilled care. *Beds* SNF 112.
Certified Medicaid; Medicare.
Owner Proprietary corp.
Staff Physicians 1 (ft), 3 (pt); RNs 15 (ft);
LPNs 10 (ft); Nurses' aides 58 (ft); Physical
therapists 1 (ft), 1 (pt); Reality therapists 1
(pt); Recreational therapists 1 (pt);
Occupational therapists 1 (pt); Speech
therapists 1 (pt); Activities coordinators 2
(ft), 3 (pt); Dietitians 1 (ft);
Ophthalmologists 1 (pt); Podiatrists 1 (pt);
Dentists 1 (pt); Social workers 1 (ft).
Languages French, Polish, German, Italian,
Hebrew, Yiddish, Spanish, Portugese.
Facilities Dining room; Physical therapy
room; Activities room; Chapel; Crafts room;
Laundry room; Barber/Beauty shop.
Activities Arts & crafts; Cards; Games;
Reading groups; Prayer groups; Movies;
Shopping trips.

Farmington

Care Manor of Farmington
Scott Swamp Rd, Farmington, CT 06032
(203) 677-7707, 676-0778 FAX
Admin Scott E Parker. *Dir of Nursing* Sharon
Uresa. *Medical Dir* Dr Mohanraj.
Licensure Skilled care; Alzheimer's care. *Beds*
SNF 120. *Private Pay Patients* 45%. *Certified*
Medicaid; Medicare.
Owner Proprietary corp (Health Care &
Retirement Corp).
Admissions Requirements Minimum age 14.
Staff RNs 6 (ft), 8 (pt); LPNs 6 (ft), 8 (pt);
Nurses' aides 25 (ft), 20 (pt); Physical
therapists 1 (ft); Recreational therapists 2
(ft); Occupational therapists 1 (pt); Speech
therapists 1 (pt); Activities coordinators 1
(pt); Dietitians 1 (pt); Ophthalmologists 1
(pt); Podiatrists 1 (pt); Audiologists 1 (pt).
Languages Spanish, Polish, Italian.
Facilities Dining room; Physical therapy
room; Activities room; Crafts room; Laundry
room; Barber/Beauty shop.
Activities Arts & crafts; Cards; Games;
Reading groups; Prayer groups; Movies;
Shopping trips; Dances/Social/Cultural
gatherings; Pet therapy.

Farmington Convalescent Home
Rte 6, 416 Colt Hwy, Farmington, CT 06032
(203) 677-1671
Licensure Skilled care; Intermediate care. *Beds*
SNF 70; ICF 60. *Certified* Medicaid;
Medicare.
Owner Proprietary corp.
Staff RNs 6 (ft), 1 (pt); LPNs 5 (ft), 1 (pt);
Nurses' aides 25 (ft), 1 (pt); Dietitians;
Activities coordinators 1 (ft), 1 (pt).
Languages French, Polish, Italian.
Activities Arts & crafts; Games; Movies;
Dances/Social/Cultural gatherings; Reality
orientation; Holiday celebrations.

Forestville

New Forestville Health & Rehabilitation Center
23 Fair St, Forestville, CT 06010
(203) 589-2923
Medical Dir Dr Moschello.
Licensure Skilled care. *Beds* SNF 120.
Certified Medicaid; Medicare.
Owner Proprietary corp.
Admissions Requirements Minimum age 14;
Medical examination.
Staff Physicians 6 (pt); RNs 14 (ft), 3 (pt);
LPNs 7 (ft), 5 (pt); Nurses' aides 50 (ft), 22
(pt); Physical therapists 1 (ft), 2 (pt);
Recreational therapists 4 (ft), 1 (pt);
Occupational therapists 1 (ft); Speech
therapists 2 (ft); Activities coordinators 1
(ft); Dietitians 1 (pt).
Languages Spanish.
Facilities Dining room; Physical therapy
room; Activities room; Crafts room; Laundry
room; Barber/Beauty shop.
Activities Arts & crafts; Cards; Games;
Reading groups; Prayer groups; Movies;
Shopping trips; Dances/Social/Cultural
gatherings.

Glastonbury

Glastonbury Health Care Center
1175 Hebron Ave, Glastonbury, CT 06033
(203) 659-1905
Licensure Skilled care. *Beds* SNF 66. *Certified*
Medicaid; Medicare.
Languages German, French.

Salmon Brook Convalescent Home
PO Box 475, 72 Salmon Brook Dr,
Glastonbury, CT 06033
(203) 633-5244
Admin James E Wrinn. *Dir of Nursing*
Marilyn Lathrop. *Medical Dir* Dr William
Vacek.

Licensure Skilled care. *Beds* SNF 120.
  Certified Medicaid; Medicare.
Owner Proprietary corp.
Admissions Requirements Minimum age 14;
  Physician's request.
Staff RNs 13 (ft), 4 (pt); LPNs 5 (ft); Nurses'
  aides 38 (ft), 7 (pt); Physical therapists 1 (ft);
  Recreational therapists 2 (ft).
Languages Italian, Spanish, French, Swedish.
Facilities Dining room; Physical therapy
  room; Activities room; Chapel; Barber/
  Beauty shop.
Activities Arts & crafts; Cards; Reading
  groups; Prayer groups; Movies; Dances/
  Social/Cultural gatherings.

Greenwich

**Greenwich Laurelton Nursing & Convalescent
Home**
1188 King St, Greenwich, CT 06831
(203) 531-8300
Admin Louise Caputo. *Dir of Nursing* Jeanne
  Miller RN. *Medical Dir* James Orphanos
  MD.
Licensure Skilled care. *Beds* SNF 75. *Certified*
  Medicaid; Medicare.
Owner Proprietary corp.
Admissions Requirements Minimum age 14;
  Medical examination; Physician's request.
Staff Physicians 17 (pt); RNs 5 (ft), 15 (pt);
  LPNs 3 (ft), 3 (pt); Nurses' aides 29 (ft), 2
  (pt); Physical therapists 1 (pt); Recreational
  therapists 1 (ft), 1 (pt); Speech therapists 1
  (pt); Dietitians 1 (ft), 1 (pt);
  Ophthalmologists 1 (pt); Podiatrists 1 (pt);
  Audiologists 1 (pt).
Languages Italian, French, Spanish.
Facilities Dining room; Physical therapy
  room; Activities room; Crafts room; Laundry
  room; Barber/Beauty shop; Library; Central
  patio.
Activities Arts & crafts; Cards; Games;
  Reading groups; Prayer groups; Movies;
  Shopping trips; Dances/Social/Cultural
  gatherings; Intergenerational programs;
  Support groups; Stroke group; Parkinson's
  group; Resident council; Cookouts;
  Barbecues.

Greenwich Woods Health Care Center
PO Box 178, 1165 King St, Greenwich, CT
  06831-0178
(203) 531-1335
Licensure Skilled care; Intermediate care. *Beds*
  SNF 60; ICF 60. *Certified* Medicaid;
  Medicare.
Languages Spanish, French.

Nathaniel Witherell
PO Box 1679, 70 Parsonage Rd, Greenwich,
  CT 06836-1679
(203) 869-4130
Admin Peter J Engelmann. *Dir of Nursing*
  Stephanie Paulmeno. *Medical Dir* Michael
  Whitcomb MD.
Licensure Skilled care; Retirement;
  Alzheimer's care. *Beds* SNF 200. *Private Pay
  Patients* 40%. *Certified* Medicaid; Medicare.
Owner Publicly owned.
Admissions Requirements Minimum age 16;
  Medical examination; Physician's request.
Staff Physicians 6 (pt); RNs 24 (ft), 10 (pt);
  LPNs 10 (ft), 1 (pt); Nurses' aides 61 (ft), 40
  (pt); Physical therapists 1 (ft), 1 (pt);
  Recreational therapists 4 (ft), 1 (pt);
  Occupational therapists 1 (ft); Speech
  therapists 1 (pt); Activities coordinators 1
  (ft); Dietitians 1 (ft); Ophthalmologists 1
  (pt); Podiatrists 5 (pt); Audiologists 1 (pt);
  Horticulture therapists 1 (pt).
Languages Italian, Polish, Spanish.
Facilities Dining room; Physical therapy
  room; Activities room; Chapel; Crafts room;
  Laundry room; Barber/Beauty shop; Library;
  Greenhouse; 2 Courtyards.

Activities Arts & crafts; Cards; Games;
  Reading groups; Prayer groups; Movies;
  Shopping trips; Dances/Social/Cultural
  gatherings; Intergenerational programs; Pet
  therapy; Horticultural therapy; Volunteer
  program.

Groton

Fairview
PO Box 218, Starr Hill Rd, Groton, CT 06340
(203) 445-7478
Medical Dir Richard Brent.
Licensure Skilled care; Intermediate care. *Beds*
  SNF 60; ICF 60. *Certified* Medicaid;
  Medicare.
Owner Nonprofit corp.
Admissions Requirements Minimum age 14;
  Medical examination; Physician's request.
Staff Physicians 2 (pt); RNs 10 (ft), 7 (pt);
  LPNs 5 (pt); Nurses' aides 12 (ft), 24 (pt);
  Physical therapists 1 (ft); Recreational
  therapists 2 (ft); Speech therapists 1 (pt);
  Activities coordinators 1 (ft); Dietitians 1
  (pt); Dentists 1 (pt).
Languages Tagalog.
Affiliation Independent Order of Odd Fellows
  & Rebekahs.
Facilities Dining room; Physical therapy
  room; Activities room; Chapel; Crafts room;
  Laundry room; Barber/Beauty shop;
  Auditorium.
Activities Arts & crafts; Cards; Games;
  Reading groups; Prayer groups; Movies;
  Shopping trips; Dances/Social/Cultural
  gatherings; Outside scenic trips; Dine out
  club.

Groton Regency Retirement & Nursing Center
1145 Poquonnock Rd, Groton, CT 06340
(203) 446-9960
Admin Arthur P Panteleakos. *Dir of Nursing*
  Claire Brennan RN. *Medical Dir* Dr Richard
  Benton.
Licensure Skilled care; Intermediate care;
  Home for aged. *Beds* SNF 119; ICF 59.
  Certified Medicaid; Medicare.
Owner Proprietary corp.
Staff Physicians 3 (pt); RNs 15 (ft), 2 (pt);
  LPNs 11 (ft), 4 (pt); Nurses' aides 56 (ft), 16
  (pt); Physical therapists 1 (ft); Recreational
  therapists 5 (ft), 1 (pt); Speech therapists 1
  (pt); Dietitians 1 (ft); Ophthalmologists 1
  (pt).
Languages French, Greek, Italian.
Facilities Dining room; Physical therapy
  room; Activities room; Chapel; Crafts room;
  Laundry room; Barber/Beauty shop; Library.
Activities Arts & crafts; Cards; Games;
  Reading groups; Prayer groups; Movies;
  Shopping trips; Dances/Social/Cultural
  gatherings.

Guilford

Fowler Nursing Center Inc
10 Boston Post Rd, Guilford, CT 06437
(203) 453-3725
Medical Dir Martin E Fink.
Licensure Skilled care. *Beds* SNF 90. *Certified*
  Medicaid; Medicare.
Owner Proprietary corp.
Admissions Requirements Minimum age 14;
  Medical examination; Physician's request.
Staff Physicians 1 (pt); RNs 8 (ft), 12 (pt);
  LPNs 3 (ft), 1 (pt); Nurses' aides 20 (ft), 22
  (pt); Physical therapists 1 (pt); Recreational
  therapists 1 (ft), 1 (pt); Speech therapists 1
  (pt); Dietitians 4 (pt), 1 (pt).
Languages French, Spanish.
Facilities Dining room; Physical therapy
  room; Activities room; Crafts room; Laundry
  room; Barber/Beauty shop.
Activities Arts & crafts; Cards; Games;
  Reading groups; Prayer groups; Movies;
  Shopping trips; Dances/Social/Cultural
  gatherings.

West Lake Lodge Nursing Home
109 West Lake Ave, Guilford, CT 06437
(203) 488-9142
Admin Mary D Carpinella. *Dir of Nursing*
  Barbara Vigneau. *Medical Dir* Jeff Kopp
  MD.
Licensure Skilled care. *Beds* SNF 60. *Private
  Pay Patients* 22%. *Certified* Medicaid;
  Medicare.
Owner Proprietary corp.
Admissions Requirements Medical
  examination.
Staff RNs 8 (ft), 8 (pt); LPNs 2 (pt); Nurses'
  aides 8 (ft), 18 (pt); Recreational therapists 1
  (ft).
Languages Italian, Spanish.
Facilities Dining room; Physical therapy
  room; Activities room; Crafts room; Laundry
  room; Barber/Beauty shop; Outdoor patios.
Activities Arts & crafts; Cards; Games;
  Reading groups; Prayer groups; Movies;
  Dances/Social/Cultural gatherings; Pet
  therapy; Therapeutic recreation program;
  Church services.

Hamden

Arden House
850 Mix Ave, Hamden, CT 06514
(203) 281-3500, 287-9534 FAX
Admin Rick Wallace. *Dir of Nursing* Pam
  Engingro RN. *Medical Dir* Will Schreiber
  MD.
Licensure Skilled care; Alzheimer's care. *Beds*
  SNF 360; Alzheimer's care 120. *Certified*
  Medicaid; Medicare.
Owner Proprietary corp.
Admissions Requirements Medical
  examination; Physician's request.
Languages Italian, Spanish.
Facilities Dining room; Physical therapy
  room; Activities room; Chapel; Crafts room;
  Laundry room; Barber/Beauty shop; Library;
  Gift shop; Child day care.
Activities Arts & crafts; Cards; Games;
  Reading groups; Prayer groups; Movies;
  Shopping trips; Dances/Social/Cultural
  gatherings; Intergenerational programs;
  Religious services.

Hamden Health Care Facility
1270 Sherman Ln, Hamden, CT 06514
(203) 281-7555
Licensure Skilled care; Intermediate care. *Beds*
  SNF 90; ICF 30. *Certified* Medicaid.
Owner Privately owned.
Admissions Requirements Minimum age 18;
  Medical examination.
Staff Physicians 3 (ft); RNs 30 (ft); LPNs 10
  (ft); Nurses' aides 60 (ft); Physical therapists
  1 (ft); Recreational therapists 3 (ft);
  Occupational therapists 1 (ft); Speech
  therapists 1 (ft); Dietitians 1 (ft);
  Ophthalmologists 1 (ft); Podiatrists 1 (ft);
  Dentists 1 (ft); Art therapists 1 (ft).
Languages Spanish.
Facilities Dining room; Physical therapy
  room; Activities room; Chapel; Crafts room;
  Laundry room; Barber/Beauty shop; Library.
Activities Arts & crafts; Cards; Games;
  Reading groups; Prayer groups; Movies;
  Shopping trips; Dances/Social/Cultural
  gatherings; Intergenerational programs; Pet
  therapy; Family support group.

Whitney Center Medical Unit
200 Leeder Hill Dr, Hamden, CT 06517
(203) 281-6745
Admin Keith Johannessen. *Dir of Nursing*
  Rose Stockman. *Medical Dir* Albert
  Dolinsky MD.
Licensure Skilled care; Retirement. *Beds* SNF
  59. *Certified* Medicaid; Medicare.
Owner Nonprofit corp (Life Care Services
  Corp).
Admissions Requirements Medical
  examination; Physician's request.

Staff RNs 2 (ft), 7 (pt); LPNs 7 (pt); Nurses' aides 11 (ft), 19 (pt); Physical therapists 1 (pt); Recreational therapists 1 (ft), 1 (pt); Speech therapists 1 (pt); Dietitians 1 (pt).
Languages Italian, German.
Facilities Dining room; Physical therapy room; Activities room; Barber/Beauty shop.
Activities Arts & crafts; Games; Reading groups; Prayer groups; Movies; Dances/ Social/Cultural gatherings.

Whitney Manor Convalescent Center Inc
2800 Whitney Ave, Hamden, CT 06518
(203) 288-6230
Admin Lawrence Amkraut. Dir of Nursing Shirley M Lee RN. Medical Dir Ronald E Coe MD.
Licensure Skilled care. Beds SNF 150. Certified Medicaid; Medicare.
Owner Proprietary corp.
Admissions Requirements Minimum age 14; Medical examination; Physician's request.
Staff Physicians 15 (pt); RNs 15 (ft), 5 (pt); LPNs 7 (ft), 4 (pt); Nurses' aides 60 (ft), 20 (pt); Physical therapists 1 (pt); Recreational therapists 3 (ft), 1 (pt); Occupational therapists 1 (pt); Speech therapists 1 (pt); Activities coordinators 1 (ft); Dietitians 1 (pt); Ophthalmologists 1 (pt); Podiatrists 1 (pt); Dentists 2 (pt).
Languages Italian, Spanish.
Facilities Dining room; Physical therapy room; Activities room; Crafts room; Laundry room; Barber/Beauty shop.
Activities Arts & crafts; Cards; Games; Reading groups; Prayer groups; Movies; Shopping trips; Dances/Social/Cultural gatherings.

Hartford

Avery Nursing Home
705 New Britain Ave, Hartford, CT 06106
(203) 527-9126
Medical Dir Dr John T Beebe.
Licensure Skilled care. Beds SNF 90; ICF 57. Certified Medicaid; Medicare.
Owner Nonprofit corp.
Staff Physicians; Nurses' aides.
Languages Spanish, Polish, Russian, French.
Activities Prayer groups.

Buckley Convalescent Home
210 George St, Hartford, CT 06114
(203) 249-9166
Admin Walter L Talarski. Dir of Nursing Rita Bonesio RN. Medical Dir Zbigniew Woznica MD.
Licensure Skilled care. Beds SNF 120. Certified Medicaid; Medicare.
Owner Proprietary corp.
Admissions Requirements Minimum age 18; Medical examination; Physician's request.
Staff Physicians 31 (pt); RNs 9 (ft), 1 (pt); LPNs 4 (ft), 4 (pt); Nurses' aides 34 (ft), 2 (pt); Physical therapists 1 (ft); Recreational therapists 2 (ft); Speech therapists 1 (pt); Dietitians 1 (ft), 1 (pt); Ophthalmologists 1 (pt); Podiatrists 1 (pt).
Languages Polish, French, Italian, Spanish.
Facilities Dining room; Physical therapy room; Activities room; Crafts room; Laundry room; Barber/Beauty shop.
Activities Arts & crafts; Cards; Games; Reading groups; Prayer groups; Movies; Shopping trips; Dances/Social/Cultural gatherings.

Greenwood Health Center
5 Greenwood St, Hartford, CT 06106
(203) 236-2901
Admin Terri Golec. Dir of Nursing Mary Brazel. Medical Dir Dr Giarnella.
Licensure Skilled care. Beds SNF 240. Certified Medicaid; Medicare.
Owner Proprietary corp (Beverly Enterprises).
Admissions Requirements Minimum age 18; Medical examination.

Staff Physicians 3 (pt); RNs 19 (ft), 16 (pt); LPNs 17 (ft), 19 (pt); Nurses' aides 64 (ft), 46 (pt); Physical therapists 1 (ft); Recreational therapists 4 (ft), 1 (pt); Occupational therapists 1 (pt); Speech therapists 1 (ft); Dietitians 1 (ft); Ophthalmologists 1 (pt); Podiatrists 1 (pt); Dietary technicians 1 (ft); Dentists 1 (pt).
Languages Portuguese, French, Spanish, Polish.
Facilities Dining room; Physical therapy room; Activities room; Laundry room; Barber/Beauty shop; Patio; Courtyard; Wheelchair garden; TV room.
Activities Arts & crafts; Cards; Games; Reading groups; Prayer groups; Movies; Shopping trips; Dances/Social/Cultural gatherings; Discussion groups; Dinner club; Cooking groups; Exercise; Resident council; Sensory groups; Pet therapy; Newspapers.

Hebrew Home & Hospital
615 Tower Ave, Hartford, CT 06112
(203) 242-6207
Admin Irving Kronenberg. Dir of Nursing Dorothy Varholak RN. Medical Dir J L Brandt MD.
Licensure Skilled care; Intermediate care; Alzheimer's care. Beds SNF 262; ICF 8. Certified Medicaid; Medicare.
Owner Nonprofit corp.
Admissions Requirements Medical examination.
Staff Physicians 2 (ft), 4 (pt); RNs 26 (ft), 9 (pt); LPNs 19 (ft), 4 (pt); Nurses' aides 93 (ft), 29 (pt); Physical therapists 2 (ft); Recreational therapists 3 (ft); Occupational therapists 2 (ft); Speech therapists 1 (pt); Activities coordinators 1 (ft); Dietitians 3 (ft).
Languages Yiddish, Hebrew, French, Spanish, Polish.
Affiliation Jewish.
Facilities Dining room; Physical therapy room; Activities room; Chapel; Crafts room; Laundry room; Barber/Beauty shop; Library.
Activities Arts & crafts; Games; Reading groups; Prayer groups; Movies; Shopping trips; Dances/Social/Cultural gatherings; Dinner theater; Outings.

Hillside Manor Nursing Home
151 Hillside Ave, Hartford, CT 06106
(203) 951-1060
Licensure Skilled care. Beds SNF 180. Certified Medicaid; Medicare.
Owner Proprietary corp.
Staff RNs 10 (ft); LPNs 10 (ft); Nurses' aides 70 (ft); Physical therapists 2 (ft); Occupational therapists 1 (ft); Activities coordinators 3 (ft); COTA 2 (ft); Social workers 2 (ft).
Languages Spanish, Portuguese, French.
Activities Theraputic recreation.

Lorraine Manor
25 Lorraine St, Hartford, CT 06105
(203) 233-8241
Licensure Skilled care. Beds 270. Certified Medicaid.
Owner Proprietary corp.
Staff Physicians; RNs 1 (ft), 10 (pt); LPNs 14 (ft); Nurses' aides 95 (ft); Physical therapists 3 (ft); Occupational therapists 1 (ft); Activities coordinators 6 (ft); Social workers 2 (ft); Special educator 1 (ft).
Languages Spanish.
Activities Arts & crafts; Shopping trips; Dances/Social/Cultural gatherings; Pet therapy; Music therapy.

Noble Building
705 New Britain Ave, Hartford, CT 06106
(203) 527-9126
Licensure Intermediate care. Beds 57. Certified Medicaid.
Owner Nonprofit corp.

Staff LPNs 9 (ft), 1 (pt); Activities coordinators 1 (ft), 1 (pt); Social workers 1 (pt).
Languages Spanish, Polish, Russian, French.
Affiliation Congregational.

Jewett City

Summit Convalescent Home Inc
15 Preston Rd, Jewett City, CT 06351
(203) 376-4438
Licensure Skilled care. Beds SNF 90. Certified Medicaid; Medicare.
Owner Proprietary corp.
Staff Physicians; Dietitians; Nurses' aides.
Languages French, Polish.
Activities Prayer groups; Dances/Social/ Cultural gatherings.

Kensington

Ledgecrest Convalescent Home
PO Box 453, 154 Kensington Rd, Kensington, CT 06037
(203) 828-4946
Licensure Skilled care. Beds SNF 60. Certified Medicaid; Medicare.
Owner Proprietary corp.
Staff Physicians; RNs 14 (ft), 1 (pt); LPNs 6 (ft), 1 (pt); Nurses' aides 44 (ft), 1 (pt); Activities coordinators; Dietitians; Social workers 1 (ft).
Languages Polish, Italian, Spanish, French.
Activities Arts & crafts; Games; Movies; Dances/Social/Cultural gatherings; Church services.

Litchfield

Rose-Haven Ltd
PO Box 157, North St, Litchfield, CT 06759
(203) 567-9475
Licensure Skilled care. Beds SNF 25.
Owner Proprietary corp.
Staff RNs 3 (ft), 1 (pt); LPNs 2 (ft), 1 (pt); Nurses' aides 8 (ft), 1 (pt); Activities coordinators 1 (pt); Dietitians 1 (pt).

Madison

Watrous Nursing Home Inc
PO Box 668, 9 Neck Rd, Madison, CT 06443
(203) 245-9483
Admin Carol Ernandez. Dir of Nursing Barbara Vigneau RN. Medical Dir Arnold Winokur MD.
Licensure Skilled care. Beds SNF 45. Certified Medicaid.
Owner Proprietary corp.
Admissions Requirements Minimum age 15; Medical examination; Physician's request.
Staff Physicians 4 (pt); RNs 14 (pt); Nurses' aides 10 (ft), 20 (pt); Physical therapists 1 (pt); Recreational therapists 1 (ft), 1 (pt); Speech therapists 1 (pt); Dietitians 1 (pt); Ophthalmologists 1 (pt); Podiatrists 1 (pt); Dentists 1 (pt).
Languages Spanish.
Facilities Dining room; Physical therapy room; Activities room; Crafts room; Laundry room; Barber/Beauty shop.
Activities Arts & crafts; Cards; Games; Reading groups; Prayer groups; Movies; Shopping trips; Dances/Social/Cultural gatherings; Outdoor garden club.

Manchester

Crestfield Convalescent Home—Fenwood
565 Vernon St, Manchester, CT 06040
(203) 643-5151
Licensure Skilled care; Intermediate care. Beds SNF 95; ICF 60. Certified Medicaid; Medicare.
Owner Proprietary corp.

Staff Physicians; Dietitians; Nurses' aides.
Languages Polish, French, Spanish, Yiddish, Portugese.
Facilities Dining room; Physical therapy room; Activities room; Barber/Beauty shop.
Activities Arts & crafts; Cards; Games; Reading groups; Prayer groups; Movies; Shopping trips; Dances/Social/Cultural gatherings.

Fenwood Manor Inc
565 Vernon Rd, Manchester, CT 06040
(203) 643-5151
Licensure Intermediate care. *Beds* 60.
Owner Proprietary corp.
Staff Physicians; Dietitians; Nurses' aides.
Languages Polish, Italian, French, Spanish.
Facilities Dining room; Physical therapy room; Activities room; Barber/Beauty shop.
Activities Arts & crafts; Cards; Games; Reading groups; Prayer groups; Movies; Shopping trips; Dances/Social/Cultural gatherings.

Holiday House
29 Cottage St, Manchester, CT 06040
(203) 649-2358
Admin Katherine M Giblin.
Licensure Home for aged. *Beds* 27. *Certified* Medicaid; Medicare.
Owner Proprietary corp.
Staff RNs 2 (ft); LPNs 1 (ft), 1 (pt); Nurses' aides 4 (ft); Social workers.
Languages French, German, Polish, Italian.
Activities Sing-along; Picnics.

Laurel Living Center Inc
91 Chestnut St, Manchester, CT 06040
(203) 649-4519
Licensure Home for aged. *Beds* 43.
Owner Proprietary corp.
Languages Italian, Spanish, French.
Activities Arts & crafts; Games; Movies; Dances/Social/Cultural gatherings; Field trips.

Manchester Manor Inc
385 W Center St, Manchester, CT 06040
(203) 646-0129
Licensure Skilled care; Intermediate care. *Beds* SNF 45; ICF 71.
Owner Proprietary corp.
Staff RNs 8 (ft); Nurses' aides 20 (ft), 1 (pt); Activities coordinators 1 (ft); Dietitians 1 (ft); Social workers 1 (ft).
Languages French, Italian.
Activities Arts & crafts; Cards; Games; Reading groups; Movies.

Meadows Manor South
349 Bidwell St, Manchester, CT 06040
(203) 647-9191
Admin Donna M Deitch NHA. *Dir of Nursing* Susan Tyrol RN. *Medical Dir* Russel Tonkin MD.
Licensure Skilled care; Intermediate care. *Beds* SNF 150; ICF 90. *Private Pay Patients* 28%. *Certified* Medicaid; Medicare.
Owner Proprietary corp (Health Care & Retirement Corp).
Admissions Requirements Medical examination; Physician's request.
Staff RNs 12 (ft); LPNs 8 (ft); Nurses' aides 40 (ft); Physical therapists 1 (ft); Recreational therapists 4 (ft); Occupational therapists 1 (ft); Speech therapists 1 (ft); Dietitians 1 (ft); Ophthalmologists 1 (pt); Podiatrists 1 (pt); Audiologists 1 (pt).
Languages French, Spanish, German.
Facilities Dining room; Physical therapy room; Activities room; Chapel; Laundry room; Barber/Beauty shop.
Activities Arts & crafts; Cards; Games; Reading groups; Prayer groups; Movies; Shopping trips; Dances/Social/Cultural gatherings; Intergenerational programs; Pet therapy.

Meadows Manor—West
333 Bidwell St, Manchester, CT 06040
(203) 647-9191
Licensure Skilled care. *Beds* SNF 162. *Certified* Medicaid; Medicare.
Languages French, Italian, Spanish, German.

Victorian Heights Nursing Center
341 Bidwell St, Manchester, CT 06040
(203) 647-9191
Admin Ilene Frances Berkon. *Dir of Nursing* Barbara Rushia. *Medical Dir* Dr Zbignew Woznica.
Licensure Skilled care. *Beds* SNF 116. *Certified* Medicaid; Medicare.
Owner Proprietary corp (Health Care and Retirement Corp).
Admissions Requirements Minimum age 14; Medical examination; Physician's request.
Staff RNs 14 (ft); LPNs 19 (ft); Nurses' aides 43 (ft); Physical therapists 2 (ft); Recreational therapists 3 (ft); Occupational therapists 1 (ft); Speech therapists 1 (ft); Activities coordinators 3 (ft); Dietitians 1 (ft); Ophthalmologists 1 (ft); Podiatrists 1 (ft); Audiologists 1 (ft); Physical therapy aides 1 (pt).
Languages Italian, Spanish, German.
Facilities Dining room; Physical therapy room; Activities room; Chapel; Crafts room; Laundry room; Barber/Beauty shop.
Activities Arts & crafts; Cards; Games; Reading groups; Prayer groups; Movies; Shopping trips; Dances/Social/Cultural gatherings; Intergenerational programs; Pet therapy.

Marlborough

Marlborough Health Care Center Inc
85 Stage Harbor Rd, Marlborough, CT 06447
(203) 295-9531
Medical Dir Dr Donald Timmerman.
Licensure Intermediate care. *Beds* 120. *Certified* Medicaid.
Owner Proprietary corp.
Admissions Requirements Minimum age 16; Medical examination.
Staff RNs 7 (ft); LPNs 2 (ft); Nurses' aides 13 (ft); Recreational therapists 2 (ft).
Languages Polish, Italian, Dutch, German, French.
Facilities Dining room; Activities room; Chapel; Laundry room; Barber/Beauty shop; Library.
Activities Arts & crafts; Cards; Games; Reading groups; Prayer groups; Movies; Shopping trips; Dances/Social/Cultural gatherings.

Meriden

Bradley Home Infirmary
PO Box 886, 320 Colony St, Meriden, CT 06450
(203) 235-5716
Licensure Skilled care. *Beds* SNF 30.
Owner Nonprofit corp.
Staff RNs 7 (ft); Nurses' aides 14 (ft).
Languages Spanish, Polish, French.
Activities Arts & crafts; Games; Movies; Shopping trips; Dances/Social/Cultural gatherings; Cooking; Exercises; Picnics; Discussion groups; Resident council.

Thomas A Coccomo Memorial
33 Cone Ave, Meriden, CT 06450
(203) 238-1606
Admin Jane DeVries. *Dir of Nursing* Paula Strode. *Medical Dir* Dr Jay Kaplan.
Licensure Intermediate care. *Beds* ICF 90. *Private Pay Patients* 50%. *Certified* Medicaid.
Owner Proprietary corp (Health Care Associates).
Admissions Requirements Minimum age 62; Medical examination; Physician's request.

Staff Physicians 1 (pt); RNs 6 (ft), 8 (pt); LPNs 2 (ft), 1 (pt); Nurses' aides 12 (ft), 8 (pt); Physical therapists 1 (pt); Recreational therapists 2 (ft), 1 (pt); Dietitians 1 (pt).
Languages French, Italian.
Facilities Dining room; Activities room; Chapel; Crafts room; Laundry room; Barber/Beauty shop; Library.
Activities Arts & crafts; Cards; Games; Reading groups; Prayer groups; Movies; Shopping trips; Dances/Social/Cultural gatherings; Intergenerational programs; Pet therapy.

Corner House Nursing Inc
1 Griswold St, Meriden, CT 06450
(203) 237-2257
Licensure Intermediate care. *Beds* 30. *Certified* Medicaid.
Owner Proprietary corp.
Staff RNs 8 (ft); LPNs 2 (ft); Nurses' aides 7 (ft); Activities coordinators 1 (ft); Dietitians 2 (ft).
Languages French, Polish.
Activities Arts & crafts; Games; Dances/Social/ Cultural gatherings.

Curtis Home—St Elizabeth Center
380 Crown St, Meriden, CT 06450
(203) 237-4338
Admin Walter A Stroly. *Dir of Nursing* Patricia Bishop RN. *Medical Dir* Dr C Martell.
Licensure Skilled care; Intermediate care; Home for aging; Independent elderly housing; Adult day health care. *Beds* SNF 15; ICF 45; Home for Aging 35. *Certified* Medicaid; Medicare.
Owner Nonprofit corp.
Admissions Requirements Females only.
Staff Nurses' aides 8 (ft).
Languages Spanish.
Facilities Dining room; Physical therapy room; Activities room; Chapel; Crafts room; Laundry room; Barber/Beauty shop; Library.
Activities Arts & crafts; Cards; Games; Reading groups; Prayer groups; Movies; Shopping trips; Dances/Social/Cultural gatherings; Sing-alongs; Excursions.

Independence Manor
33 Roy St, Meriden, CT 06450
(203) 237-8457
Licensure Skilled care; Intermediate care. *Beds* SNF 120; ICF 59. *Certified* Medicaid; Medicare.
Owner Proprietary corp.
Staff RNs 3 (ft); LPNs 15 (ft).
Languages Spanish, Polish.
Activities Arts & crafts; Shopping trips; Dances/Social/Cultural gatherings; Workshops; Music; Current events.

Meriden Nursing Home
845 Paddock Ave, Meriden, CT 06450
(203) 238-2645
Admin Michele Carney.
Medical Dir Dr Zimerman.
Licensure Skilled care; Alzheimer's care. *Beds* SNF 120. *Certified* Medicaid; Medicare.
Owner Proprietary corp.
Staff Physicians; RNs 7 (ft), 2 (pt); LPNs 6 (ft); Nurses' aides 40 (ft), 2 (pt); Physical therapists 1 (ft); Recreational therapists 2 (ft); Activities coordinators; Dietitians.
Languages Spanish.
Facilities Dining room; Physical therapy room; Activities room; Chapel; Crafts room; Laundry room; Barber/Beauty shop.
Activities Arts & crafts; Cards; Games; Reading groups; Prayer groups; Movies; Shopping trips; Dances/Social/Cultural gatherings; Van; Pet therapy.

Miller Memorial Community—Edward Pavilion/Caroline Hall
360 Broad St, Meriden, CT 06450
(203) 237-8815, 603-3714 FAX

166 / CONNECTICUT / Meriden

Admin Sr Ann Noonan RSM. *Dir of Nursing* Dolores Gambino RNC. *Medical Dir* Dr Neil Scollan.
Licensure Skilled care; Intermediate care; Independent housing. *Beds* SNF 30; ICF 60; Independent housing 33. *Private Pay Patients* 36%. *Certified* Medicaid; Medicare.
Owner Nonprofit corp.
Admissions Requirements Minimum age 62; Medical examination.
Staff RNs 5 (ft), 8 (pt); LPNs 1 (ft), 7 (pt); Nurses' aides 12 (ft), 15 (pt); Physical therapists 1 (pt); Recreational therapists 2 (ft); Activities coordinators 1 (ft); Dietitians 1 (pt).
Languages Polish, Italian, Jamaican, Spanish, Iranian, French.
Affiliation Congregational.
Facilities Dining room; Physical therapy room; Activities room; Crafts room; Laundry room; Barber/Beauty shop; Library; Lounges; Snack nooks; Secure care wanderer system.
Activities Arts & crafts; Cards; Games; Reading groups; Prayer groups; Movies; Shopping trips; Dances/Social/Cultural gatherings; Intergenerational programs; Pet therapy.

Mills Manor
292 Thorpe Ave, Meriden, CT 06450
(203) 237-1206
Licensure Skilled care. *Beds* SNF 30. *Certified* Medicaid; Medicare.
Owner Proprietary corp.
Staff RNs 3 (ft), 1 (pt); LPNs 1 (ft); Nurses' aides 9 (ft), 1 (pt); Activities coordinators 1 (pt).
Languages German, Spanish.
Activities Arts & crafts; Games; Movies; Shopping trips; Dances/Social/Cultural gatherings; Music.

Westfield Manor Health Care Center Inc
65 Westfield Rd, Meriden, CT 06450
(203) 238-1201
Licensure Skilled care. *Beds* SNF 120. *Certified* Medicaid; Medicare.
Owner Proprietary corp.
Staff RNs 15 (ft); LPNs 10 (ft); Nurses' aides 45 (ft).
Languages Polish, Spanish.
Activities Arts & crafts; Games.

Middlebury

Middlebury Convalescent Home Inc
778 Middlebury Rd, Middlebury, CT 06762
(203) 758-2471
Admin Genevieve Buckmiller. *Dir of Nursing* Norma Rossiter RN. *Medical Dir* Dr William P Arnold Jr.
Licensure Skilled care. *Beds* SNF 58. *Certified* Medicaid; Medicare.
Owner Proprietary corp.
Staff Physicians 1 (pt); RNs 5 (ft), 10 (pt); LPNs 1 (ft); Nurses' aides 17 (ft), 8 (pt); Physical therapists 1 (ft); Recreational therapists 1 (ft); Dietitians 1 (pt).
Languages Italian, German, Lithuanian, Polish, Albanian.
Facilities Dining room; Physical therapy room; Activities room; Laundry room; Barber/Beauty shop.
Activities Arts & crafts; Cards; Games; Reading groups; Prayer groups; Movies.

Middletown

High View Health Care Center Inc
600 Highland Ave, PO Box 1056, Middletown, CT 06457
(203) 347-3315
Medical Dir Felix G Sheehan MD.
Licensure Skilled care. *Beds* SNF 90. *Certified* Medicaid; Medicare.
Owner Proprietary corp.

Admissions Requirements Minimum age 21; Medical examination.
Staff Physicians 4 (pt); RNs 6 (ft), 4 (pt); LPNs 3 (ft), 4 (pt); Nurses' aides 28 (ft), 13 (pt); Physical therapists 1 (pt); Recreational therapists 1 (ft), 1 (pt).
Languages Italian, French.
Facilities Dining room; Physical therapy room; Activities room; Chapel; Crafts room; Laundry room; Barber/Beauty shop; Library.
Activities Arts & crafts; Cards; Games; Reading groups; Prayer groups; Movies; Shopping trips; Entertainment.

Lutheran Home of Middletown Inc
Ridgewood Rd, Middletown, CT 06457
(203) 347-7479
Admin Arnold R Eggert. *Dir of Nursing* Caroline Guilty RN. *Medical Dir* Dr Matthew Raider.
Licensure Skilled care. *Beds* SNF 28. *Certified* Medicaid.
Owner Nonprofit corp.
Admissions Requirements Minimum age 65; Medical examination.
Staff Physicians 5 (pt); RNs 3 (ft), 4 (pt); Nurses' aides 6 (ft), 9 (pt); Physical therapists 1 (pt); Activities coordinators 1 (ft), 1 (pt); Dietitians 1 (pt); Ophthalmologists 1 (pt); Dentists 1 (pt).
Languages Spanish, German, Italian.
Affiliation Lutheran.
Facilities Dining room; Physical therapy room; Activities room; Crafts room; Laundry room; Barber/Beauty shop; Library; Solariums.
Activities Arts & crafts; Cards; Games; Reading groups; Prayer groups; Movies; Shopping trips; Dances/Social/Cultural gatherings; Bingo; Excursions.

Middlesex Convalescent Center Inc
100 Randolph Rd, Middletown, CT 06457
(203) 344-0353
Admin Robert M Shepard. *Dir of Nursing* Margaret M Smith RN. *Medical Dir* A Wazed Mahmud MD.
Licensure Skilled care; Intermediate care. *Beds* SNF 120; ICF 30. *Private Pay Patients* 25%. *Certified* Medicaid; Medicare.
Owner Proprietary corp.
Admissions Requirements Minimum age 18.
Staff RNs 10 (ft), 9 (pt); LPNs 11 (ft), 9 (pt); Nurses' aides 43 (ft), 28 (pt); Physical therapists 1 (pt); Recreational therapists 2 (ft); Occupational therapists 1 (pt); Speech therapists 1 (pt); Activities coordinators 1 (ft); Dietitians 1 (pt).
Languages Spanish, Italian, Japanese, Cambodian.
Facilities Dining room; Physical therapy room; Activities room; Chapel; Crafts room; Barber/Beauty shop.
Activities Arts & crafts; Cards; Games; Reading groups; Prayer groups; Movies; Shopping trips; Dances/Social/Cultural gatherings; Pet therapy.

Middletown Healthcare Center Inc
111 Church St, Middletown, CT 06457
(203) 347-7286
Licensure Intermediate care. *Beds* 180.
Owner Proprietary corp.
Staff RNs 12 (ft), 1 (pt); LPNs 15 (ft), 1 (pt); Nurses' aides 32 (ft); Activities coordinators 5 (ft), 1 (pt); Social workers 4 (ft).
Languages Italian, Polish, Spanish.

Wadsworth Glen Health Care Center
30 Boston Rd, Middletown, CT 06457
(203) 346-9299
Licensure Skilled care; Intermediate care. *Beds* SNF 45; ICF 45. *Certified* Medicaid; Medicare.
Languages Italian, Spanish.

Milford

Golden Hill Health Care Center
2028 Bridgeport Ave, Milford, CT 06460
(203) 877-0371
Admin Gail Paradee. *Dir of Nursing* Betti Smith RN. *Medical Dir* Thelma Batiancila MD.
Licensure Skilled care. *Beds* SNF 120. *Certified* Medicaid; Medicare.
Owner Proprietary corp.
Admissions Requirements Minimum age 18; Medical examination; Physician's request.
Staff Physicians (contracted); RNs 9 (ft), 14 (pt); LPNs 8 (ft), 6 (pt); Nurses' aides 42 (ft), 27 (pt); Physical therapists 3 (pt); Recreational therapists 3 (ft), 2 (pt); Occupational therapists 1 (ft); Speech therapists; Dietitians 1 (ft), 1 (pt); Ophthalmologists (contracted); Podiatrists (contracted); Audiologists (contracted).
Languages Italian, Portuguese, Korean, Spanish.
Facilities Dining room; Physical therapy room; Activities room; Crafts room; Barber/Beauty shop; Coma maintenance program; Acquired head injury community re-entry program.
Activities Arts & crafts; Cards; Games; Reading groups; Prayer groups; Movies; Shopping trips; Dances/Social/Cultural gatherings; Intergenerational programs; Pet therapy.

Milford Health Care Center Inc
195 Platt St, Milford, CT 06460
(203) 878-5958
Admin Donna C Stango. *Dir of Nursing* Mildred Locke RN.
Licensure Skilled care. *Beds* SNF 120. *Certified* Medicaid; Medicare.
Owner Proprietary corp.
Admissions Requirements Physician's request.
Staff RNs; LPNs 12 (ft); Nurses' aides 35 (ft); Physical therapists; Recreational therapists 3 (ft); Activities coordinators 2 (ft); Dietitians 1 (ft); Social workers 1 (ft).
Languages Polish, Spanish, Italian.
Facilities Dining room; Physical therapy room; Activities room; Laundry room; Barber/Beauty shop.
Activities Arts & crafts; Games; Reading groups; Prayer groups; Movies; Shopping trips; Dances/Social/Cultural gatherings; Outside entertainment; Excursions.

Pond Point Health Care Center Inc
60 Platt St, Milford, CT 06460
(203) 878-5786
Licensure Skilled care; Alzheimer's care. *Beds* SNF 142. *Certified* Medicaid; Medicare.
Owner Proprietary corp (Beverly Enterprises).
Staff RNs 24 (ft); LPNs 9 (ft); Nurses' aides 41 (ft); Activities coordinators 3 (ft); Dietitians 1 (ft).
Languages Polish, Italian, Spanish, Thai, Portugese.
Facilities Waterfront.

Moodus

Chestelm Convalescent Home
534 Town St, Moodus, CT 06469
(203) 873-1455
Medical Dir Dr Phillip Berwick.
Licensure Skilled care; Intermediate care. *Beds* SNF 53; ICF 13. *Certified* Medicaid.
Owner Proprietary corp.
Staff Physicians 5 (pt); RNs 7 (ft), 4 (pt); LPNs 3 (ft), 5 (pt); Nurses' aides 18 (ft), 9 (pt); Physical therapists 1 (pt); Recreational therapists 2 (ft); Occupational therapists 1 (pt); Speech therapists 1 (pt); Activities coordinators 1 (pt); Dietitians 1 (pt); Podiatrists 1 (pt); Audiologists 1 (pt); Dentists 1 (pt).
Languages Czech, German.

Facilities Dining room; Physical therapy room; Activities room; Crafts room; Laundry room; Library.
Activities Arts & crafts; Cards; Games; Reading groups; Movies; Shopping trips; Dances/Social/Cultural gatherings.

Mystic

Mary Elizabeth Nursing Center
28 Broadway, Mystic, CT 06355
(203) 536-9655
Admin Judith Hilburger. *Dir of Nursing* Sharon Kaylor. *Medical Dir* Dr Howard Brensilver.
Licensure Skilled care. *Beds* SNF 50. *Private Pay Patients* 50%. *Certified* Medicaid; Medicare.
Owner Proprietary corp (Health Care Associates).
Admissions Requirements Medical examination.
Staff Physicians 11 (ft); RNs 12 (ft); LPNs 3 (ft); Nurses' aides 23 (ft); Recreational therapists 1 (ft); Activities coordinators 1 (ft); Dietitians (consultant); Podiatrists (consultant).
Facilities Dining room; Physical therapy room; Activities room; Laundry room; Barber/Beauty shop.
Activities Arts & crafts; Cards; Games; Reading groups; Prayer groups; Movies; Dances/Social/Cultural gatherings; Intergenerational programs; Pet therapy.

Mystic Manor Inc
PO Box 40, 475 High St, Mystic, CT 06355
(203) 536-2167, 536-6070
Admin Barry J Wojtcuk. *Dir of Nursing* Mariann Piver RN. *Medical Dir* Edmund West MD.
Licensure Skilled care; Intermediate care. *Beds* SNF 60; ICF 40. *Certified* Medicaid; Medicare.
Owner Proprietary corp.
Admissions Requirements Minimum age 14.
Staff RNs 6 (ft), 16 (pt); LPNs 1 (ft), 10 (pt); Nurses' aides 22 (ft), 19 (pt); Physical therapists 1 (pt); Recreational therapists 2 (ft), 2 (pt); Speech therapists 1 (pt); Dietitians 1 (pt); Podiatrists 1 (pt).
Languages Korean.
Facilities Dining room; Physical therapy room; Activities room; Laundry room; Barber/Beauty shop; Physician's examination room.
Activities Arts & crafts; Cards; Games; Prayer groups; Movies; Dances/Social/Cultural gatherings; Pet therapy.

Rita's Rest Home
14 Godfrey St, Mystic, CT 06355
(203) 536-8854
Admin Frank Nocera.
Medical Dir Dr Weiss.
Licensure Boarding home. *Beds* 25. *Certified* Medicaid; Aid to disabled.
Owner Proprietary corp.
Admissions Requirements Minimum age 21.
Staff Nurses' aides 10 (ft), 4 (pt).
Facilities Dining room; Activities room; Laundry room.
Activities Arts & crafts; Cards; Games; Movies; Shopping trips; Dances/Social/Cultural gatherings; Day trips.

Naugatuck

Glendale Health Care Center Inc
4 Hazel Ave, Naugatuck, CT 06770
(203) 444-6350
Admin Frank Salvatore.
Licensure Skilled care. *Beds* SNF 120. *Certified* Medicaid; Medicare.
Owner Proprietary corp.

Staff RNs 16 (ft); LPNs 5 (ft); Nurses' aides 66 (ft); Physical therapists 1 (ft); Activities coordinators 2 (ft); Social workers 1 (ft).
Languages German, Italian, French, Swedish, Polish, Portugese.

New Britain

Andrew House Healthcare
66 Clinic Dr, New Britain, CT 06051
(203) 225-8608
Admin Doris H Leitgeb. *Dir of Nursing* Lorraine Stachelek. *Medical Dir* Dr Edward Martin.
Licensure Skilled care. *Beds* SNF 90. *Private Pay Patients* 10%. *Certified* Medicaid; Medicare.
Owner Proprietary corp (Hillhaven Corp).
Admissions Requirements Physician's request.
Staff RNs 1 (ft), 9 (pt); LPNs 4 (ft), 3 (pt); Nurses' aides 18 (ft), 16 (pt); Physical therapists 1 (ft); Recreational therapists 1 (ft), 1 (pt); Dietitians 1 (pt).
Languages Polish, Italian, Spanish.
Facilities Dining room; Physical therapy room; Activities room; Laundry room; Barber/Beauty shop.
Activities Arts & crafts; Cards; Games; Reading groups; Prayer groups; Movies; Shopping trips; Dances/Social/Cultural gatherings; Intergenerational programs; Pet therapy.

Brittany Farms Health Center
400 Brittany Farms Rd, New Britain, CT 06053
(203) 224-3111
Admin Thomas V Tolisano. *Dir of Nursing* Sylvia Keiffer RN. *Medical Dir* Dr D Balaz; Dr Giarnella.
Licensure Skilled care; Intermediate care. *Beds* SNF 120; ICF 180. *Private Pay Patients* 35%. *Certified* Medicaid; Medicare.
Owner Proprietary corp.
Admissions Requirements Minimum age 55; Medical examination; Physician's request.
Staff Physicians 10 (ft); RNs 49 (ft); LPNs 13 (ft); Nurses' aides 100 (ft); Physical therapists 4 (ft); Recreational therapists 6 (ft); Occupational therapists 1 (ft); Speech therapists 1 (ft); Activities coordinators 6 (ft); Dietitians 2 (ft); Ophthalmologists 1 (ft); Podiatrists 1 (ft); Audiologists 1 (ft).
Languages Polish, Italian, French.
Facilities Dining room; Physical therapy room; Activities room; Crafts room; Laundry room; Barber/Beauty shop; Library; Health spa.
Activities Arts & crafts; Cards; Games; Reading groups; Prayer groups; Movies; Shopping trips; Dances/Social/Cultural gatherings; Intergenerational programs; Pet therapy; Outings.

Jerome Home
975 Corbin Ave, New Britain, CT 06052
(203) 229-3707, 229-4785 FAX
Admin Joseph Santonocito. *Dir of Nursing* Mary Banak RN. *Medical Dir* Dr Earle J Sittambalam.
Licensure Intermediate care; Home for aged. *Beds* ICF 60; Home for aged 24. *Private Pay Patients* 60%. *Certified* Medicaid.
Owner Nonprofit organization/foundation.
Staff RNs 8 (ft); LPNs 6 (ft); Nurses' aides 11 (ft); Physical therapists; Recreational therapists 1 (ft); Dietitians.
Languages Spanish, Polish, Italian.
Facilities Dining room; Activities room; Crafts room; Barber/Beauty shop; Private rooms.
Activities Arts & crafts; Cards; Games; Reading groups; Prayer groups; Movies; Shopping trips; Dances/Social/Cultural gatherings; Intergenerational programs; Pet therapy; Morning stretch; Outings; Religious services.

Lexington House
32 Lexington St, New Britain, CT 06052
(203) 225-6397
Medical Dir Abraham Bernstein.
Licensure Skilled care. *Beds* SNF 65. *Certified* Medicaid; Medicare.
Owner Proprietary corp.
Admissions Requirements Minimum age 18; Medical examination; Physician's request.
Staff RNs 4 (ft), 1 (pt); LPNs 5 (ft); Nurses' aides 18 (ft), 9 (pt); Physical therapists 1 (pt); Reality therapists 1 (ft), 1 (pt); Recreational therapists 1 (ft), 1 (pt).
Languages French, Italian, Polish, Spanish.
Facilities Dining room; Physical therapy room; Activities room; Crafts room; Laundry room.
Activities Arts & crafts; Cards; Games; Reading groups; Prayer groups; Movies; Shopping trips; Entertainment; Pet therapy.

Monsignor Bojnowski Manor Inc
50 Pulaski St, New Britain, CT 06053-3565
(203) 229-0336
Admin Sr M Deborah. *Dir of Nursing* Emelia Kurnik. *Medical Dir* Stephen E Zebrowski MD.
Licensure Skilled care; Residential care. *Beds* SNF 48; Residential care 6. *Private Pay Patients* 8%. *Certified* Medicaid.
Owner Nonprofit corp.
Admissions Requirements Minimum age 14; Medical examination.
Staff Physicians 1 (pt); RNs 5 (ft), 4 (pt); LPNs 2 (ft), 4 (pt); Nurses' aides 25 (ft), 3 (pt); Physical therapists 1 (pt); Recreational therapists 1 (ft); Occupational therapists 1 (pt); Speech therapists 1 (pt); Dietitians 1 (pt); Ophthalmologists 1 (pt); Podiatrists 1 (pt).
Languages Polish, Spanish, French, Russian.
Facilities Dining room; Physical therapy room; Activities room; Chapel; Crafts room; Laundry room; Barber/Beauty shop; Library.
Activities Arts & crafts; Cards; Games; Reading groups; Prayer groups; Movies; Shopping trips; Pet therapy.

Walnut Hill Convalescent Home
55 Grand St, New Britain, CT 06052
(203) 223-3617
Admin Donald J Griggs. *Dir of Nursing* Rita Dishong RN. *Medical Dir* Gerald McAuliffe MD.
Licensure Skilled care. *Beds* SNF 192. *Private Pay Patients* 20%. *Certified* Medicaid; Medicare.
Owner Proprietary corp.
Admissions Requirements Minimum age 18; Physician's request.
Staff RNs 8 (ft); LPNs 15 (ft), 4 (pt); Nurses' aides 60 (ft); Physical therapists 1 (ft); Recreational therapists 2 (ft), 1 (pt); Activities coordinators 1 (ft); Dietitians 1 (pt).
Languages Polish, Spanish, Italian.
Facilities Dining room; Physical therapy room; Activities room; Chapel; Crafts room; Laundry room; Barber/Beauty shop.
Activities Arts & crafts; Cards; Games; Reading groups; Prayer groups; Movies; Shopping trips; Pet therapy.

New Canaan

Waveny Care Center
3 Farm Rd, New Canaan, CT 06840
(203) 966-8725
Admin Charles E Otto. *Dir of Nursing* Dorothy Perkins RN. *Medical Dir* Dr Basil Papaharis.
Licensure Skilled care. *Beds* SNF 67. *Certified* Medicaid.
Owner Nonprofit corp.
Admissions Requirements Minimum age 16.

Staff Physicians 1 (pt); RNs 12 (ft), 13 (pt); LPNs 2 (ft), 2 (pt); Nurses' aides 21 (ft), 11 (pt); Recreational therapists 3 (ft); Occupational therapists 1 (pt); Speech therapists 1 (pt); Dietitians 2 (pt).
Languages Spanish, French.
Facilities Dining room; Physical therapy room; Activities room; Crafts room; Laundry room; Barber/Beauty shop; Library.
Activities Arts & crafts; Cards; Games; Reading groups; Prayer groups; Movies; Shopping trips; Dances/Social/Cultural gatherings.

New Haven

Carewell Rest Home
260 Dwight St, New Haven, CT 06511
(203) 562-8596
Admin Ann Griggs. *Dir of Nursing* Josephine Vitolo RN. *Medical Dir* Anthony V Scialla MD.
Licensure Intermediate care; Intermediate care for mentally retarded. *Beds* ICF 39; ICF/MR 6. *Private Pay Patients* 10%. *Certified* Medicaid; Medicare.
Owner Proprietary corp (Convalescent Associates).
Admissions Requirements Minimum age 21; Medical examination; Physician's request.
Staff Physicians 5 (pt); RNs 2 (ft), 4 (pt); LPNs 2 (ft); Nurses' aides 7 (ft), 5 (pt); Physical therapists 1 (pt); Recreational therapists 1 (ft); Activities coordinators 1 (ft); Dietitians 1 (pt); Ophthalmologists 1 (pt); Podiatrists 1 (pt).
Languages Italian.
Facilities Dining room; Activities room; Crafts room; Laundry room; Library.
Activities Arts & crafts; Cards; Games; Reading groups; Prayer groups; Movies; Shopping trips; Dances/Social/Cultural gatherings; Intergenerational programs; Pet therapy; One-on-one; Current events group; Bible study groups; Spiritual services & events.

Cove Manor Convalescent Center Inc
36 Morris Cove Rd, New Haven, CT 06512
(203) 467-6357
Admin Anne D Ryder. *Dir of Nursing* Lois Forgione RN. *Medical Dir* Luca E Celentano MD.
Licensure Skilled care. *Beds* SNF 70. *Certified* Medicaid; Medicare.
Owner Proprietary corp.
Admissions Requirements Minimum age 21.
Staff RNs 4 (ft), 7 (pt); LPNs 5 (ft), 6 (pt); Nurses' aides 22 (ft), 8 (pt); Physical therapists 1 (ft); Recreational therapists 1 (ft), 2 (pt); Speech therapists 1 (pt); Dietitians 1 (pt).
Languages Italian, Polish, Russian, Spanish.
Facilities Dining room; Physical therapy room; Activities room; Crafts room; Laundry room; Barber/Beauty shop.
Activities Arts & crafts; Cards; Games; Reading groups; Prayer groups; Movies; Shopping trips; Dances/Social/Cultural gatherings.

Jewish Home for the Aged
169 Davenport Ave, New Haven, CT 06519
(203) 789-1650, 787-0071 FAX
Admin Bryan R Mesh. *Dir of Nursing* K Robison. *Medical Dir* Dr J Henchel.
Licensure Skilled care; Intermediate care; Alzheimer's care. *Beds* SNF 150; ICF 60. *Private Pay Patients* 10%. *Certified* Medicaid.
Owner Nonprofit corp.
Admissions Requirements Minimum age 65; Medical examination.

Staff Physicians 1 (ft), 1 (pt); Nurses' aides 100 (ft); Physical therapists 4 (ft); Recreational therapists 5 (ft), 2 (pt); Occupational therapists 1 (pt); Dietitians 1 (ft); RNs & LPNs 50 (ft).
Languages Yiddish.
Affiliation Jewish.
Facilities Dining room; Physical therapy room; Activities room; Chapel; Crafts room; Laundry room; Barber/Beauty shop.
Activities Arts & crafts; Reading groups; Prayer groups; Movies; Shopping trips; Dances/Social/Cultural gatherings; Intergenerational programs.

New Fairview Health Care
181 Clifton St, New Haven, CT 06513
(203) 467-1666, 469-7213 FAX
Admin Mary Helen Craig. *Dir of Nursing* Marjorie Sullivan RN. *Medical Dir* Anthony Mancini MD.
Licensure Skilled care. *Beds* SNF 195. *Certified* Medicaid; Medicare.
Owner Proprietary corp (New Medico Associates Inc).
Admissions Requirements Minimum age 25; Medical examination; Physician's request.
Staff Physicians 5 (pt); RNs 11 (ft), 5 (pt); LPNs 11 (ft), 6 (pt); Nurses' aides 76 (ft), 8 (pt); Physical therapists 2 (ft); Recreational therapists 4 (ft); Speech therapists 1 (pt); Dietitians 1 (pt); Ophthalmologists 1 (pt); Podiatrists 1 (pt).
Languages Italian, German, Polish, French, Spanish.
Facilities Dining room; Physical therapy room; Activities room; Crafts room; Laundry room; Barber/Beauty shop; Library.
Activities Arts & crafts; Cards; Games; Reading groups; Prayer groups; Movies; Shopping trips; Dances/Social/Cultural gatherings; Intergenerational programs.

New Haven Nursing Center
50 Mead St, New Haven, CT 06511
(203) 777-3491
Medical Dir Dr Michael Devbaty.
Licensure Skilled care. *Beds* SNF 89. *Certified* Medicaid; Medicare.
Owner Proprietary corp.
Staff RNs 11 (ft), 9 (pt); LPNs 3 (ft), 5 (pt); Nurses' aides 30 (ft), 17 (pt); Dietitians 1 (pt).
Languages Portugese, Farsi.
Facilities Dining room; Activities room; Crafts room; Barber/Beauty shop.
Activities Arts & crafts; Cards; Games; Reading groups; Prayer groups; Movies; Dances/Social/Cultural gatherings.

Parkview Medical Recovery Center Inc
915 Boulevard, New Haven, CT 06511
(203) 865-5155
Medical Dir Quiyam Merjtaba MD.
Licensure Skilled care. *Beds* SNF 120. *Certified* Medicaid; Medicare.
Owner Proprietary corp.
Admissions Requirements Minimum age 16; Medical examination; Physician's request.
Staff Physicians 4 (pt); RNs 7 (ft); LPNs 10 (ft); Nurses' aides 47 (ft); Physical therapists 1 (pt); Recreational therapists 2 (ft); Speech therapists 1 (pt); Dietitians 1 (pt); Ophthalmologists 1 (pt); Podiatrists 1 (pt); Dentists 1 (pt).
Languages Spanish, Italian.
Facilities Dining room; Physical therapy room; Activities room; Chapel; Crafts room; Laundry room; Barber/Beauty shop; Library.
Activities Arts & crafts; Cards; Games; Reading groups; Prayer groups; Movies; Shopping trips; Dances/Social/Cultural gatherings.

St Regis Health Center
1354 Chapel St, New Haven, CT 06511
(203) 865-0505

Licensure Skilled care. *Beds* SNF 125. *Certified* Medicaid; Medicare.
Owner Proprietary corp.
Staff LPNs 18 (ft); Nurses' aides 46 (ft); Physical therapists 1 (pt); Activities coordinators 2 (ft), 1 (pt); Social workers 1 (ft).
Languages Spanish, Italian.
Affiliation Roman Catholic.

West Rock Health Care
34 Level St, New Haven, CT 06515
(203) 389-9744
Admin Luisa Franco Russo. *Dir of Nursing* Joanna Panzo RN. *Medical Dir* Andrew Weinberg MD.
Licensure Intermediate care. *Beds* ICF 90. *Certified* Medicaid.
Owner Proprietary corp.
Admissions Requirements Minimum age 16; Medical examination; Physician's request.
Staff Physicians 3 (ft), 1 (pt); RNs 9 (ft), 2 (pt); LPNs 4 (ft), 1 (pt); Recreational therapists 2 (ft), 1 (pt); Dietitians 1 (pt); Ophthalmologists 1 (pt); Podiatrists 1 (pt); Dentists 1 (pt).
Languages Spanish.
Facilities Dining room; Activities room; Laundry room; Barber/Beauty shop; Library.
Activities Arts & crafts; Cards; Games; Reading groups; Prayer groups; Movies; Shopping trips; Dances/Social/Cultural gatherings.

Winthrop Health Care Center
240 Winthrop Ave, New Haven, CT 06511
(203) 789-0500, 789-1694 FAX
Admin J P Lyke. *Dir of Nursing* Gale Jacabacci. *Medical Dir* Brett Gerstenhaber MD.
Licensure Skilled care; Intermediate care. *Beds* SNF 180; ICF 60. *Private Pay Patients* 12%. *Certified* Medicaid; Medicare.
Owner Proprietary corp.
Admissions Requirements Minimum age 21.
Staff Physicians 6 (pt); RNs 10 (ft), 15 (pt); LPNs 25 (ft), 21 (pt); Nurses' aides 3 (ft); Physical therapists 1 (pt); Recreational therapists 3 (ft); Occupational therapists 1 (pt); Speech therapists 1 (ft); Activities coordinators 1 (ft); Dietitians 1 (ft); Ophthalmologists 1 (pt); Podiatrists 1 (pt); Audiologists 1 (ft); Respiratory therapists 5 (ft), 4 (pt).
Languages Spanish, Italian, Hebrew.
Facilities Dining room; Physical therapy room; Activities room; Crafts room; Laundry room; Barber/Beauty shop; 60-bed ventilator unit.
Activities Arts & crafts; Cards; Games; Reading groups; Movies; Shopping trips; Dances/Social/Cultural gatherings; Intergenerational programs; Pet therapy.

New London

Beechwood Manor Inc
31 Vauxhall St, New London, CT 06320
(203) 442-4363
Medical Dir Clemens E Prokesch MD.
Licensure Skilled care. *Beds* SNF 45. *Certified* Medicaid.
Owner Proprietary corp.
Staff RNs 6 (ft), 2 (pt); LPNs 2 (ft), 1 (pt); Nurses' aides 12 (ft), 7 (pt); Physical therapists 1 (pt); Recreational therapists 1 (ft); Dietitians 1 (pt); Podiatrists 1 (pt); Dentists 1 (pt).
Languages Spanish.
Facilities Dining room; Physical therapy room; Activities room; Laundry room; Barber/Beauty shop.
Activities Arts & crafts; Games; Reading groups; Prayer groups; Movies; Shopping trips.

Briarcliff Manor
179 Colman St, New London, CT 06320
(203) 443-5376
Admin Amelia W Cart.
Licensure Home for aged. *Beds* 25.
Owner Proprietary corp.
Admissions Requirements Minimum age 21.
Languages Italian, Spanish.
Facilities Dining room; Activities room; Laundry room.
Activities Arts & crafts; Cards; Games; Reading groups; Prayer groups; Movies; Shopping trips.

Camelot Nursing Home
89 Viets St Ext, New London, CT 06320
(203) 447-1471
Admin David J Friedler. *Dir of Nursing* Joal Patterson RN. *Medical Dir* Melvin A Yoselevsky MD.
Licensure Skilled care. *Beds* SNF 60. *Certified* Medicaid; Medicare.
Owner Proprietary corp.
Staff Physicians 18 (pt); RNs 2 (ft), 8 (pt); LPNs 3 (pt); Nurses' aides 9 (ft), 19 (pt); Physical therapists 1 (pt); Reality therapists 1 (ft); Recreational therapists 1 (ft); Speech therapists 1 (pt); Dietitians 1 (pt); Podiatrists 1 (pt); Audiologists 1 (pt); Dentists 1 (pt).
Languages Italian, German, French, Polish.
Facilities Dining room; Physical therapy room; Activities room; Crafts room; Laundry room; Barber/Beauty shop.
Activities Arts & crafts; Games; Reading groups; Prayer groups; Movies; Shopping trips.

Nutmeg Pavilion Healthcare
78 Viets St Extension, New London, CT 06320
(203) 447-1416
Licensure Skilled care. *Beds* SNF 140. *Certified* Medicaid; Medicare.
Owner Proprietary corp.
Staff RNs 18 (ft); Nurses' aides 25 (ft); Physical therapists 2 (ft); Social workers 1 (ft).
Languages Spanish.
Activities Arts & crafts; Games; Reading groups; Dances/Social/Cultural gatherings; Reality orientation; Music.

New Milford

Candlewood Valley Care Center
30 Park Ln E, New Milford, CT 06776
(203) 355-0971
Admin Elinor B Baird.
Medical Dir Robert L McDonald MD.
Licensure Skilled care; Intermediate care; Residential care; Day care. *Beds* SNF 60; ICF 44; Residential 44. *Certified* Medicaid; Medicare.
Owner Proprietary corp.
Admissions Requirements Minimum age 14.
Staff Physicians 12 (pt); RNs 14 (ft), 8 (pt); LPNs 10 (ft), 4 (pt); Nurses' aides 42 (ft), 22 (pt); Physical therapists 1 (ft); Reality therapists 1 (pt); Recreational therapists 4 (ft); Occupational therapists 1 (ft); Speech therapists 1 (pt); Activities coordinators 1 (ft); Dietitians 1 (ft); Ophthalmologists 2 (pt); Podiatrists 1 (pt); Dentists 2 (pt); Medical social workers 1 (ft); 21 (ft), 10 (pt).
Languages French, German, Polish, Portugese.
Facilities Dining room; Physical therapy room; Activities room; Crafts room; Laundry room; Barber/Beauty shop; Library.
Activities Arts & crafts; Cards; Games; Reading groups; Prayer groups; Movies; Shopping trips; Dances/Social/Cultural gatherings; Community projects.

New Milford Nursing Home
19 Poplar St, New Milford, CT 06776
(203) 354-9365

Licensure Skilled care. *Beds* SNF 99. *Certified* Medicaid; Medicare.
Owner Proprietary corp.
Staff RNs 15 (ft); LPNs 14 (ft); Nurses' aides 53 (ft); Physical therapists 1 (ft); Activities coordinators 1 (ft); Social workers 1 (ft).
Languages Polish, German, Italian.

Newington

Bel-Air Manor
256 New Britain Ave, Newington, CT 06111
(203) 666-5689
Admin Gene Yacovone. *Dir of Nursing* Phyllis I Condon RN. *Medical Dir* John E Pulaski.
Licensure Intermediate care. *Beds* ICF 71. *Certified* Medicaid.
Owner Proprietary corp.
Admissions Requirements Medical examination; Physician's request.
Staff Physicians 1 (ft), 4 (pt); RNs 3 (ft), 9 (pt); LPNs 2 (ft), 3 (pt); Nurses' aides 11 (ft), 6 (pt); Recreational therapists 1 (ft), 1 (pt).
Languages Polish, French, Italian.
Facilities Dining room; Activities room; Chapel; Crafts room; Laundry room; Barber/Beauty shop; Library.
Activities Arts & crafts; Cards; Games; Reading groups; Prayer groups; Movies; Shopping trips; Dances/Social/Cultural gatherings; Exercises; Baking; Lunches out.

Jefferson House
1 John H Stewart Dr, Newington, CT 06111
(203) 667-4453
Medical Dir Dr Arthur Wolf.
Licensure Skilled care; Intermediate care. *Beds* SNF 60; ICF 30. *Certified* Medicaid; Medicare.
Owner Nonprofit corp.
Staff RNs 13 (ft); LPNs 10 (ft); Nurses' aides 40 (ft); Physical therapists 5 (ft), 1 (pt); Recreational therapists 3 (ft), 1 (pt); Dietitians 2 (ft).
Languages Spanish, Polish.
Facilities Dining room; Physical therapy room; Activities room; Crafts room; Laundry room; Barber/Beauty shop; Library.
Activities Arts & crafts; Cards; Games; Reading groups; Prayer groups; Movies; Shopping trips; Dances/Social/Cultural gatherings.

Mediplex of Newington
240 Church St, Newington, CT 06111
(203) 667-2256
Licensure Skilled care; Intermediate care. *Beds* SNF 120; ICF 60. *Certified* Medicaid; Medicare.
Owner Proprietary corp.
Staff Physicians; RNs 8 (ft); LPNs 4 (ft); Nurses' aides 27 (ft); Physical therapists 2 (ft); Activities coordinators 2 (ft); Social workers 1 (ft).
Languages Spanish, Polish, Italian.
Activities Arts & crafts; Reading groups; Shopping trips; Dances/Social/Cultural gatherings; Music; Current events.

Newtown

Ashlar of Newtown, A Masonic Home
Toddy Hill Rd, Newtown, CT 06470
(203) 426-5847
Licensure Skilled care. *Beds* SNF 156. *Certified* Medicaid; Medicare.
Owner Proprietary corp.
Staff RNs 22 (ft), 1 (pt); LPNs 10 (ft), 1 (pt); Nurses' aides 64 (ft), 14 (pt); Physical therapists 1 (ft), 1 (pt); Activities coordinators 3 (ft), 1 (pt); Social workers 1 (ft), 1 (pt).
Languages Spanish, German, Chinese.
Affiliation Masons.

North Haven

Montowese Health Care Center
163 Quinnipiac Ave, North Haven, CT 06473
(203) 624-3303
Admin Eileen M Ichan RN. *Dir of Nursing* Gena Tannoia RN. *Medical Dir* Bjorn Ringstad MD.
Licensure Skilled care; Alzheimer's care. *Beds* SNF 60. *Certified* Medicaid; Medicare.
Owner Proprietary corp.
Admissions Requirements Physician's request.
Staff RNs 12 (ft); LPNs 6 (ft); Nurses' aides 27 (ft); Physical therapists; Recreational therapists; Occupational therapists; Speech therapists; Activities coordinators 2 (ft); Dietitians; Ophthalmologists; Dentists.
Languages Italian, Spanish, Polish, Hebrew.
Facilities Dining room; Physical therapy room; Activities room; Laundry room; Barber/Beauty shop.
Activities Arts & crafts; Cards; Games; Reading groups; Prayer groups; Movies; Dances/Social/Cultural gatherings.

Norwalk

Fairfield Manor Health Care Center
23 Prospect Ave, Norwalk, CT 06850
(203) 853-0010
Medical Dir Robert Yazmer MD.
Licensure Skilled care; Intermediate care. *Beds* SNF 180; ICF 60. *Certified* Medicaid; Medicare.
Owner Proprietary corp (Beverly Enterprises).
Admissions Requirements Minimum age 17.
Staff RNs 11 (ft), 11 (pt); LPNs 10 (ft), 10 (pt); Nurses' aides 65 (ft), 25 (pt); Physical therapists 1 (ft), 1 (pt); Recreational therapists 1 (ft); Occupational therapists 1 (ft), 1 (pt); Speech therapists 1 (ft); Activities coordinators 2 (ft); Dietitians 1 (ft), 1 (pt).
Languages French, Spanish, Italian, German.
Facilities Dining room; Physical therapy room; Activities room; Chapel; Crafts room; Laundry room; Barber/Beauty shop; Library.
Activities Arts & crafts; Cards; Games; Reading groups; Prayer groups; Movies; Shopping trips; Dances/Social/Cultural gatherings.

Lea Manor Health Care Center
73 Strawberry Hill Ave, Norwalk, CT 06851
(203) 852-8833
Admin Margaret A Kalsched. *Dir of Nursing* Gail S Favano. *Medical Dir* Dr A Joel Papowitz.
Licensure Skilled care; Intermediate care. *Beds* SNF 60; ICF 60. *Certified* Medicaid; Medicare.
Owner Proprietary corp (Multicare Management).
Admissions Requirements Minimum age 18; Medical examination; Physician's request.
Staff Physicians; Dietitians; Nurses' aides.
Languages French, Polish.
Facilities Dining room; Physical therapy room; Activities room; Chapel; Crafts room; Laundry room; Barber/Beauty shop; Library.
Activities Arts & crafts; Cards; Games; Reading groups; Prayer groups; Movies; Shopping trips; Dances/Social/Cultural gatherings.

Notre Dame Convalescent Home Inc
76 W Rocks Rd, Norwalk, CT 06851
(203) 847-5893
Medical Dir Dr James Griffith.
Licensure Skilled care. *Beds* SNF 60. *Certified* Medicaid.
Owner Nonprofit corp.
Admissions Requirements Minimum age 14; Medical examination; Physician's request.
Staff Physicians 12 (pt); RNs 4 (ft), 12 (pt); LPNs 3 (ft); Nurses' aides 26 (ft), 6 (pt); Physical therapists 1 (pt); Recreational therapists 1 (ft); Speech therapists 1 (pt);

Activities coordinators 1 (ft); Dietitians 1 (pt); Podiatrists 1 (pt); Audiologists 1 (pt); Dentists 1 (pt); Optometrists 1 (pt).
Languages French, German, Spanish.
Affiliation Roman Catholic.
Facilities Dining room; Physical therapy room; Activities room; Chapel; Laundry room; Barber/Beauty shop; Library; Lounge.
Activities Arts & crafts; Cards; Games; Reading groups; Prayer groups; Movies; Shopping trips.

Overlook Park Health Care Center
4 Elmcrest Terr, Norwalk, CT 06850
(203) 838-1100
Admin Eugene Leso MPH. *Dir of Nursing* Barbara H Phillips RN BS MSNEA. *Medical Dir* Murray Hamada.
Licensure Skilled care. *Beds* SNF 90. *Certified* Medicaid; Medicare.
Owner Proprietary corp.
Languages Italian, French, Spanish, Polish.
Facilities Dining room; Physical therapy room; Activities room; Crafts room; Laundry room; Barber/Beauty shop.
Activities Arts & crafts; Cards; Games; Reading groups; Prayer groups; Movies; Pet therapy.

Norwich

Convalescent Center of Norwich Inc
60 Crouch Ave, Norwich, CT 06360
(203) 889-2631
Admin Raymond J LeBlanc.
Medical Dir Dr Torres.
Licensure Skilled care. *Beds* SNF 119. *Certified* Medicaid; Medicare.
Owner Proprietary corp.
Admissions Requirements Minimum age 14; Medical examination; Physician's request.
Staff Physicians 6 (pt); RNs 8 (ft), 14 (pt); LPNs 6 (ft), 10 (pt); Nurses' aides 27 (ft), 41 (pt); Physical therapists 2 (pt); Reality therapists 1 (pt); Recreational therapists 2 (ft); Speech therapists 1 (pt); Activities coordinators 2 (pt); Dietitians 2 (pt); Ophthalmologists 1 (pt); Podiatrists 1 (pt); Dentists 1 (pt).
Languages Polish, French.
Facilities Dining room; Physical therapy room; Activities room; Chapel; Laundry room; Barber/Beauty shop; Library; TV lounges; Patio; Sun room.
Activities Arts & crafts; Cards; Games; Reading groups; Prayer groups; Movies; Shopping trips; Dances/Social/Cultural gatherings.

Fairlawn Convalescent Home Inc
5 Rockwell Terrace, Norwich, CT 06360
(203) 886-5135
Licensure Skilled care. *Beds* SNF 45. *Certified* Medicaid.
Owner Proprietary corp.
Staff RNs 9 (ft); LPNs 3 (ft); Nurses' aides 17 (ft); Activities coordinators 1 (ft).
Languages Polish, French, Italian.
Activities Therapeutic recreation.

Hamilton Pavilion Healthcare
50 Palmer St, Norwich, CT 06360
(203) 889-8358
Licensure Skilled care. *Beds* SNF 160. *Certified* Medicaid; Medicare.
Owner Proprietary corp.
Staff RNs 21 (ft); LPNs 11 (ft); Nurses' aides 38 (ft); Activities coordinators 4 (ft); Social workers 1 (ft).

Norwichtown Convalescent Home
93 W Town St, Norwich, CT 06360
(203) 889-2614
Admin Alan DeBlasio. *Dir of Nursing* Catherine McMahon. *Medical Dir* Dr David Rousseau.
Licensure Skilled care. *Beds* SNF 120. *Certified* Medicaid; Medicare.

Owner Proprietary corp.
Admissions Requirements Minimum age 14.
Staff Physicians 17 (pt); RNs 5 (ft), 9 (pt); LPNs 1 (ft), 13 (pt); Nurses' aides 14 (ft), 53 (pt); Physical therapists 1 (pt); Recreational therapists 2 (ft); Speech therapists 1 (pt); Dietitians 1 (pt); Ophthalmologists 1 (pt); Podiatrists 1 (pt); Dentists 1 (pt).
Languages Spanish, Italian.
Facilities Dining room; Physical therapy room; Activities room; Crafts room; Barber/Beauty shop.
Activities Arts & crafts; Cards; Games; Reading groups; Prayer groups; Movies; Shopping trips; Dances/Social/Cultural gatherings; Bus trips; Cocktail lounge; Dinner & theater; State park outings; Restaurant outings.

Old Saybrook

Ferry Point—SNCF
PO Box F, 175 Ferry Rd, Old Saybrook, CT 06475
(203) 388-4677
Licensure Skilled care. *Beds* 120. *Certified* Medicaid; Medicare.
Owner Proprietary corp.
Staff RNs 9 (ft); LPNs 10 (ft); Physical therapists 1 (ft); Activities coordinators 1 (ft); Social workers 1 (ft).
Languages Italian, French.

Gladeview Health Care Center
60 Boston Post Rd, Old Saybrook, CT 06475
(203) 388-6696
Licensure Skilled care; Intermediate care. *Beds* SNF 30; ICF 60. *Certified* Medicaid; Medicare.

Saybrook Convalescent Hospital
1775 Boston Post Rd, Old Saybrook, CT 06475
(203) 399-6216
Admin James H Sbrolla. *Dir of Nursing* Therese Firgelewski. *Medical Dir* Donald Cook MD.
Licensure Skilled care. *Beds* SNF 120. *Certified* Medicaid; Medicare.
Owner Proprietary corp.
Admissions Requirements Minimum age 21.
Staff RNs 22 (ft); LPNs 7 (ft); Nurses' aides 50 (ft); Physical therapists 2 (ft); Activities coordinators 2 (ft).
Languages Spanish, French.
Facilities Dining room; Physical therapy room; Activities room; Laundry room; Barber/Beauty shop.
Activities Arts & crafts; Cards; Games; Reading groups; Prayer groups; Movies; Shopping trips; Dances/Social/Cultural gatherings.

Orange

Lydian Corporation
PO Box 945, 324 Grassy Hill Rd, Orange, CT 06477
(203) 878-0613
Admin Jean M Mario. *Dir of Nursing* Mary D Nigro. *Medical Dir* Vincent E Kerr.
Licensure Intermediate care. *Beds* ICF 27. *Certified* Medicaid.
Owner Proprietary corp.
Admissions Requirements Minimum age 15.
Staff Physicians 2 (pt); RNs 2 (ft), 8 (pt); Nurses' aides 4 (ft), 4 (pt); Physical therapists 1 (pt); Recreational therapists 1 (ft); Activities coordinators 1 (ft); Dietitians 1 (pt); Ophthalmologists 1 (pt); Podiatrists 1 (pt); Dentists 1 (pt).
Languages Italian, Spanish.
Facilities Dining room; Activities room; Laundry room.
Activities Arts & crafts; Cards; Games; Reading groups; Prayer groups; Shopping trips; Dances/Social/Cultural gatherings.

Orange Health Care Center
225 Boston Post Rd, Orange, CT 06477
(203) 795-0835
Medical Dir Evan M Ginsberg MD.
Licensure Intermediate care. *Beds* ICF 60. *Certified* Medicaid.
Owner Proprietary corp.
Admissions Requirements Minimum age 14.
Staff Physicians 3 (pt); RNs 7 (ft), 5 (pt); LPNs 5 (pt); Nurses' aides 6 (ft), 15 (pt); Recreational therapists 1 (ft); Speech therapists 1 (pt); Dietitians 1 (pt); Ophthalmologists 3 (pt); Podiatrists 1 (pt); Dentists 1 (pt).
Languages Italian, German, Spanish.
Facilities Dining room; Physical therapy room; Activities room; Crafts room; Laundry room; Barber/Beauty shop.
Activities Arts & crafts; Cards; Games; Reading groups; Prayer groups; Movies; Shopping trips; Dances/Social/Cultural gatherings.

Plainfield

Villa Maria Convalescent Home Inc
20 Babcock Ave, Plainfield, CT 06374
(203) 564-3387
Admin Daniel E Disco & Natalie D Disco.
Medical Dir Philip Goyette.
Licensure Skilled care. *Beds* SNF 52. *Certified* Medicaid; Medicare.
Owner Proprietary corp.
Admissions Requirements Medical examination; Physician's request.
Staff Physicians 1 (pt); RNs 5 (ft), 5 (pt); LPNs 3 (ft), 3 (pt); Nurses' aides 17 (ft), 7 (pt); Physical therapists 1 (pt); Recreational therapists 1 (ft); Activities coordinators 1 (ft); Dietitians 1 (pt); Ophthalmologists 1 (pt); Podiatrists 1 (pt); Audiologists 1 (pt); Dentists 1 (pt).
Facilities Dining room; Physical therapy room; Activities room; Chapel; Crafts room; Laundry room; Barber/Beauty shop; Library.
Activities Arts & crafts; Cards; Games; Reading groups; Prayer groups; Movies; Shopping trips; Dances/Social/Cultural gatherings.

Village Manor Health Care Inc
16 Windsor Ave, Plainfield, CT 06374
(203) 564-4081
Licensure Skilled care; Intermediate care. *Beds* SNF 60; ICF 60. *Certified* Medicaid; Medicare.
Languages Chinese, Polish, French, Spanish, Russian, Italian, Scottish.

Plainville

Plainville Health Care Center
269 Farmington Ave, Plainville, CT 06062
(203) 747-5579
Admin Raymond E Hackley. *Dir of Nursing* Sandra P Young RN. *Medical Dir* John P Iannotti MD.
Licensure Skilled care 120; Intermediate care 60. *Beds* SNF 120; ICF 60. *Certified* Medicaid; Medicare.
Owner Proprietary corp.
Admissions Requirements Minimum age 14; Medical examination; Physician's request.
Staff RNs 31 (ft); LPNs 8 (ft); Nurses' aides 74 (ft); Recreational therapists 3 (ft).
Languages French, Italian, Polish, Vietnamese.
Facilities Dining room; Physical therapy room; Activities room; Crafts room; Laundry room; Barber/Beauty shop.
Activities Arts & crafts; Cards; Games; Reading groups; Prayer groups; Movies; Shopping trips; Dances/Social/Cultural gatherings.

Plantsville

Woodmere Health Care Center
261 Summit St, Plantsville, CT 06479
(203) 628-0364
Licensure Skilled care; Intermediate care. *Beds* SNF 120; ICF 30. *Certified* Medicare.
Owner Proprietary corp.
Staff RNs 11 (ft); LPNs 11 (ft); Physical therapists 1 (ft); Activities coordinators 4 (ft).
Activities Arts & crafts; Games; Prayer groups; Shopping trips; Dances/Social/Cultural gatherings; Discussion groups; Baking; Music; Newsletter.

Plymouth

Cook-Willow Convalescent Hospital Inc
41 Hillside Ave, Plymouth, CT 06782
(203) 283-8208
Admin Susan C Armstrong.
Licensure Skilled care. *Beds* SNF 30. *Certified* Medicaid.
Owner Proprietary corp.
Staff RNs 5 (ft); LPNs 1 (ft); Activities coordinators 1 (ft).
Activities Therapeutic recreation.

Portland

Portland Convalescent Center Inc
333 Main St, Portland, CT 06480
(203) 342-0370
Licensure Skilled care. *Beds* SNF 89. *Certified* Medicaid; Medicare.
Owner Proprietary corp.
Staff LPNs 13 (ft), 1 (pt); Nurses' aides 37 (ft), 1 (pt); Physical therapists 1 (pt); Activities coordinators 1 (ft), 1 (pt).
Languages Polish, French.
Activities Arts & crafts; Games; Movies; Dances/Social/Cultural gatherings; Newspaper.

Prospect

Country Manor Health Care Center
PO Box 7060, 64 Summit Rd, Prospect, CT 06712
(203) 758-4431
Licensure Skilled care; Intermediate care. *Beds* SNF 150. *Certified* Medicaid; Medicare.
Owner Proprietary corp (Beverly Enterprises).
Staff LPNs 27 (ft); Nurses' aides 55 (ft); Activities coordinators 2 (ft), 1 (pt).
Languages Italian, Spanish.
Activities Games; Prayer groups; Singing group.

Eastview Manor Inc
170 Scott Rd, Prospect, CT 06712
(203) 758-5491
Admin Loretta J D'Alessio. *Dir of Nursing* Marion Stevenson RN. *Medical Dir* Evan J Whalley MD.
Licensure Skilled care. *Beds* SNF 30. *Certified* Medicaid; Medicare.
Owner Proprietary corp.
Admissions Requirements Minimum age 18; Medical examination.
Staff Physicians 6 (pt); RNs 3 (ft), 4 (pt); Nurses' aides 5 (ft), 6 (pt); Physical therapists 1 (pt); Recreational therapists 1 (pt); Dietitians 1 (pt); Ophthalmologists 1 (pt); Dentists 1 (pt).
Languages French, Portuguese, Lithuanian, Spanish, Italian.
Facilities Dining room; Physical therapy room; Crafts room; Barber/Beauty shop.
Activities Arts & crafts; Cards; Games; Reading groups; Prayer groups; Movies; Shopping trips; Dances/Social/Cultural gatherings.

Putnam

Matulaitis Nursing Home
Thurber Rd, Putnam, CT 06260
(203) 928-7976
Licensure Skilled care; Intermediate care. *Beds* SNF 60; ICF 59. *Certified* Medicaid.
Owner Nonprofit corp.
Admissions Requirements Medical examination.
Staff Physicians 7 (pt); RNs 12 (ft), 2 (pt); LPNs 1 (ft), 2 (pt); Nurses' aides 36 (ft), 6 (pt); Physical therapists 1 (pt); Recreational therapists 2 (ft); Speech therapists 1 (pt); Dietitians 1 (ft); Ophthalmologists 1 (pt); Podiatrists 1 (pt); Audiologists 1 (pt); Dentists 1 (pt).
Languages Lithuanian, French, Polish, Swedish.
Affiliation Roman Catholic.
Facilities Dining room; Physical therapy room; Activities room; Chapel; Crafts room; Laundry room; Barber/Beauty shop; Library.
Activities Arts & crafts; Cards; Games; Reading groups; Prayer groups; Movies; Shopping trips; Dances/Social/Cultural gatherings.

Rockville

Rockville Memorial Nursing Home
22 South St, Rockville, CT 06066
(203) 875-0771
Licensure Skilled care. *Beds* SNF 150. *Certified* Medicaid; Medicare.
Owner Proprietary corp.
Staff RNs 22 (ft), 1 (pt); LPNs 44 (ft), 1 (pt); Nurses' aides 13 (ft), 1 (pt); Activities coordinators; Dietitians 2 (ft), 1 (pt).
Languages French, Polish, Spanish.

Rocky Hill

Elm Hill Nursing Center
45 Elm St, Rocky Hill, CT 06067
(203) 529-8661
Admin Melvin C Smith. *Dir of Nursing* Barbara McCarthy RN. *Medical Dir* Dr Jacque Mendelsohn.
Licensure Skilled care; Intermediate care; Alzheimer's care. *Beds* SNF 120; ICF 30. *Certified* Medicaid; Medicare.
Owner Proprietary corp.
Admissions Requirements Minimum age 14; Physician's request.
Staff Physicians 1 (pt); RNs 12 (ft); LPNs 16 (ft); Nurses' aides 20 (ft), 5 (pt); Physical therapists 1 (pt); Reality therapists 1 (pt); Recreational therapists 3 (ft), 2 (pt); Speech therapists 1 (pt); Dietitians 2 (pt); Ophthalmologists 1 (pt); Podiatrists 1 (pt); Dentists 1 (pt).
Languages Polish, Italian, Spanish, French, Indian, Chinese, Portugese, Taiwanese.
Facilities Dining room; Physical therapy room; Activities room; Chapel; Crafts room; Laundry room; Barber/Beauty shop; Library.
Activities Arts & crafts; Cards; Games; Reading groups; Prayer groups; Movies; Shopping trips; Dances/Social/Cultural gatherings; Musical events.

Maple View Manor Inc
856 Maple St, Rocky Hill, CT 06067
(203) 563-2861
Licensure Skilled care. *Beds* SNF 120. *Certified* Medicaid; Medicare.
Owner Nonprofit corp.
Staff RNs 8 (ft); LPNs 7 (ft); Nurses' aides 22 (ft); Activities coordinators 1 (ft); Dietitians 1 (ft).
Languages Spanish.

West Hill Convalescent Home
60 West St, Rocky Hill, CT 06067
(203) 529-2521
Admin Malcolm Glazer.
Licensure Skilled care. *Beds* SNF 120. *Certified* Medicaid; Medicare.
Owner Proprietary corp.
Staff RNs 11 (ft), 1 (pt); LPNs 7 (ft), 1 (pt); Nurses' aides 43 (ft), 1 (pt); Physical therapists 1 (ft), 1 (pt); Activities coordinators 2 (ft), 1 (pt); Dietitians 1 (ft), 1 (pt).
Languages French, Polish, German, Italian.
Activities Arts & crafts; Games; Shopping trips.

Salisbury

Whitridge Nursing Wing RIGA Residence of Noble Horizons
Lower Cobble Rd, Salisbury, CT 06068
(203) 435-9851
Licensure Skilled care; Intermediate care. *Beds* SNF 30; ICF 30. *Certified* Medicaid; Medicare.
Owner Proprietary corp.
Staff RNs 7 (ft), 1 (pt); Nurses' aides 12 (ft); Dietitians 1 (ft).
Languages Spanish, Italian, Chinese, German, French.
Activities Arts & crafts; Movies; Dances/Social/Cultural gatherings; Musical programs; Greenhouse.

Shelton

Gardner Heights Inc
172 Rocky Rest Rd, Shelton, CT 06484
(203) 929-1481
Admin Suzanne Bosek. *Dir of Nursing* Lucille Wdowiak RN. *Medical Dir* Joel Zaretsky MD.
Licensure Skilled care; Intermediate care. *Beds* SNF 89; ICF 90.
Owner Nonprofit corp.
Staff RNs; LPNs; Nurses' aides; Recreational therapists; Dietitians.
Languages Spanish, Polish, German.
Facilities Dining room; Physical therapy room; Activities room; Chapel; Barber/ Beauty shop; Library.
Activities Arts & crafts; Cards; Games; Reading groups; Prayer groups; Movies; Shopping trips; Dances/Social/Cultural gatherings; Intergenerational programs; Pet therapy.

Flora & Mary Hewitt Memorial Hospital Inc
230 Coram Ave, Shelton, CT 06484
(203) 735-4671
Medical Dir Murugesapillai Koneswaran MD SNF & Donald P Roach MD ICF.
Licensure Skilled care; Intermediate care. *Beds* SNF 150; ICF 60. *Certified* Medicaid; Medicare.
Owner Nonprofit corp.
Admissions Requirements Minimum age 16; Medical examination; Physician's request.
Staff RNs 8 (ft), 16 (pt); LPNs 11 (ft), 6 (pt); Nurses' aides 34 (ft), 62 (pt); Physical therapists 1 (ft), 2 (pt); Recreational therapists 3 (ft), 1 (pt); Speech therapists 1 (pt); Dietitians 1 (ft), 1 (pt); Podiatrists 4 (pt); Dentists 1 (pt).
Languages Italian, Polish, Spanish.
Facilities Dining room; Physical therapy room; Activities room; Chapel; Crafts room; Laundry room; Barber/Beauty shop; Library.
Activities Arts & crafts; Cards; Games; Reading groups; Prayer groups; Movies; Shopping trips; Dances/Social/Cultural gatherings.

Shelton Lakes Residence & Health Care Center Inc
5 Lake Rd, Shelton, CT 06484
(203) 736-2635
Licensure Skilled care. *Beds* SNF 59.
Owner Nonprofit corp.
Languages Polish Italian.

United Methodist Convalescent Homes of Connecticut Inc
584 Long Hill Ave, Shelton, CT 06484
(203) 929-5321
Admin Shapleigh M Drisko. *Dir of Nursing* Corrine Conroy RN. *Medical Dir* M Koneswaraw MD.
Licensure Skilled care; Retirement. *Beds* SNF 120. *Certified* Medicaid; Medicare.
Owner Nonprofit corp.
Admissions Requirements Minimum age 16; Medical examination; Physician's request.
Staff Physicians 2 (pt); RNs 12 (ft), 2 (pt); LPNs 4 (ft), 7 (pt); Nurses' aides 60 (ft), 2 (pt); Physical therapists 2 (pt); Recreational therapists 2 (ft); Dietitians 1 (ft), 1 (pt); Dentists 3 (pt).
Affiliation United Methodist.
Facilities Dining room; Physical therapy room; Activities room; Chapel; Laundry room; Barber/Beauty shop; Library.
Activities Arts & crafts; Cards; Games; Reading groups; Prayer groups; Movies; Shopping trips; Dances/Social/Cultural gatherings.

Simsbury

McLean Home
75 Great Pond Rd, Simsbury, CT 06070
(203) 658-2254
Licensure Skilled care; Intermediate care. *Beds* SNF 58; ICF 37. *Certified* Medicaid; Medicare.
Owner Nonprofit corp.
Staff Physicians 1 (pt); LPNs 36 (ft), 1 (pt); Physical therapists 1 (pt); Dietitians 1 (pt); Dentists 1 (pt); Social workers 1 (pt), 1 (pt).
Languages French, German, Spanish.

South Windsor

South Windsor Nursing Center
1060 Main St, South Windsor, CT 06074
(203) 289-7771
Licensure Skilled care. *Beds* SNF 120. *Certified* Medicaid; Medicare.
Owner Proprietary corp.
Staff RNs 12 (ft), 1 (pt); LPNs 4 (ft), 1 (pt); Nurses' aides 33 (ft); Physical therapists 1 (ft); Activities coordinators 2 (ft); Social workers 1 (ft).
Languages French, Polish, Spanish.
Activities Arts & crafts; Games; Movies; Shopping trips; Dances/Social/Cultural gatherings.

Southbury

Lutheran Home of Southbury
990 Main St N, Southbury, CT 06488
(203) 264-9135
Admin David D Boyd.
Medical Dir Daniel G Goodman MD.
Licensure Skilled care; Intermediate care; Home for aged. *Beds* SNF 60; ICF 60; Home for aged 31. *Certified* Medicaid.
Owner Nonprofit corp.
Admissions Requirements Minimum age 65; Medical examination; Physician's request.
Staff Physicians 7 (pt); RNs 3 (ft), 9 (pt); LPNs 4 (pt); Nurses' aides 11 (ft), 14 (pt); Physical therapists 1 (pt); Speech therapists 1 (pt); Activities coordinators 3 (ft); Dietitians 1 (pt); Ophthalmologists 1 (pt); Podiatrists 1 (pt); Dentists 1 (pt).
Affiliation Lutheran.
Facilities Dining room; Physical therapy room; Activities room; Chapel; Crafts room; Laundry room; Barber/Beauty shop; Library.
Activities Arts & crafts; Cards; Games; Reading groups; Prayer groups; Movies; Shopping trips; Dances/Social/Cultural gatherings.

Pomperaug Woods
80 Heritage Rd, Southbury, CT 06488
(203) 262-6557
Licensure Skilled care. *Beds* SNF 22. *Certified* Medicaid.
Languages Spanish, French, Italian.

River Glen Continuing Care Center
S Britain Rd, Southbury, CT 06488
(203) 264-9600
Licensure Skilled care; Intermediate care. *Beds* SNF 60; ICF 60. *Certified* Medicaid; Medicare.
Owner Proprietary corp (New Medico Assoc).
Staff LPNs 18 (ft); Nurses' aides 33 (ft); Physical therapists 1 (ft); Occupational therapists 1 (ft); Activities coordinators 1 (ft); Social workers 1 (ft).
Languages Spanish.
Activities Therapeutic recreation.

Southington

Ridgewood Health Care Facility Inc
582 Meriden Ave, Southington, CT 06489
(203) 628-0388
Licensure Skilled care. *Beds* SNF 38. *Certified* Medicaid.
Owner Proprietary corp.
Staff RNs 9 (ft); Nurses' aides 10 (ft), 1 (pt); Activities coordinators 1 (ft).
Languages Polish, Italian, German.
Activities Therapeutic recreation.

Southport

Southport Manor Convalescent Center
930 Mill Hill Terrace, Southport, CT 06490
(203) 259-7894, 259-4521 FAX
Admin Anne P Toth, Pres/Admin. *Dir of Nursing* Gail Saxon RN. *Medical Dir* Dr Kenneth Higgins.
Licensure Skilled care. *Beds* SNF 140. *Certified* Medicaid; Medicare.
Owner Privately owned.
Admissions Requirements Minimum age 18; Medical examination; Physician's request.
Staff RNs 28 (ft), 8 (pt); LPNs 8 (ft), 1 (pt); Nurses' aides 41 (ft), 4 (pt); Physical therapists 1 (ft); Recreational therapists 2 (ft); Dietitians 1 (ft).
Languages Spanish.
Facilities Dining room; Physical therapy room; Activities room; Chapel; Crafts room; Barber/Beauty shop; Library.
Activities Arts & crafts; Cards; Games; Reading groups; Prayer groups; Movies; Shopping trips; Dances/Social/Cultural gatherings; Intergenerational programs; Pet therapy.

Stamford

Courtland Gardens Health Center
59 Courtland Ave, Stamford, CT 06902
(203) 359-2000
Licensure Skilled care. *Beds* SNF 180. *Certified* Medicare.
Owner Proprietary corp.
Staff RNs 24 (ft); LPNs 22 (ft); Nurses' aides 110 (ft); Activities coordinators; Dietitians.
Languages French, Spanish, Italian.

Homestead Health Center
160 Glenbrook Rd, Stamford, CT 06902
(203) 359-2000
Licensure Skilled care. *Beds* SNF 87. *Certified* Medicaid; Medicare.
Owner Proprietary corp.
Staff RNs 15 (ft); LPNs 9 (ft); Nurses' aides 49 (ft); Activities coordinators 2 (ft).
Languages French, Spanish, Italian.

Smith House Skilled Nursing Facility
88 Rockrimmon Rd, Stamford, CT 06903
(203) 322-3428

Admin Margaret Joyce. *Dir of Nursing* Kathryn M Dolan RN. *Medical Dir* Bernard O Nemoitin MD.
Licensure Skilled care; Retirement. *Beds* SNF 128. *Certified* Medicaid; Medicare.
Owner Publicly owned.
Admissions Requirements Minimum age 14; Medical examination.
Staff RNs 8 (ft), 11 (pt); LPNs 7 (ft), 8 (pt); Nurses' aides 54 (ft), 16 (pt); Physical therapists 1 (ft); Recreational therapists 2 (ft), 1 (pt); Social workers 1 (ft), 2 (pt).
Languages Spanish, French, German, Hebrew, Yiddish, Polish.
Facilities Dining room; Physical therapy room; Activities room; Laundry room; Barber/Beauty shop.
Activities Arts & crafts; Cards; Games; Reading groups; Prayer groups; Movies; Dances/Social/Cultural gatherings; Trips; Theater; Beach; Pet shows.

William & Sally Tandet Center for Continuing Care
146 W Broad St, Stamford, CT 06902
(203) 964-8500
Licensure Skilled care; Intermediate care. *Beds* SNF 80; ICF 40. *Certified* Medicaid.

Stratford

Lord Chamberlain Skilled Nursing Facility
7003 Main St, Stratford, CT 06497
(203) 375-5894, 375-1199 FAX
Admin Martin Sbriglio RN. *Dir of Nursing* L Chmielewski RN. *Medical Dir* Saul Feldman MD; Robert Sbriglio MD, Asst.
Licensure Skilled care; Intermediate care. *Beds* SNF 180; ICF 60. *Private Pay Patients* 50%. *Certified* Medicaid; Medicare.
Owner Proprietary corp.
Admissions Requirements Physician's request.
Staff Physicians; RNs; LPNs; Nurses' aides; Physical therapists; Reality therapists; Recreational therapists; Occupational therapists; Speech therapists; Activities coordinators; Dietitians; Ophthalmologists; Podiatrists; Audiologists.
Languages Spanish, Polish, Hebrew, French, Italian, Greek, German.
Facilities Dining room; Physical therapy room; Activities room; Chapel; Crafts room; Laundry room; Barber/Beauty shop; Library; Greenhouse.
Activities Arts & crafts; Cards; Games; Reading groups; Prayer groups; Movies; Shopping trips; Dances/Social/Cultural gatherings; Picnics; Horticulture in greenhouse.

Torrington

Adams House Healthcare
80 Fern Dr, Torrington, CT 06790
(203) 482-7668
Medical Dir Dr Frank Vanoni.
Licensure Skilled care. *Beds* SNF 90. *Certified* Medicaid; Medicare.
Owner Proprietary corp.
Staff RNs 8 (ft), 5 (pt); LPNs 3 (ft), 4 (pt); Nurses' aides 14 (ft), 29 (pt); Physical therapists 1 (pt); Recreational therapists 1 (ft), 1 (pt).
Languages Polish, Italian, French, Hungarian, Slovak.
Facilities Dining room; Physical therapy room; Laundry room; Barber/Beauty shop.
Activities Arts & crafts; Cards; Games; Reading groups; Prayer groups; Movies; Shopping trips; Dances/Social/Cultural gatherings.

Litchfield Woods Health Care Center
255 Roberts St, Torrington, CT 06790
(203) 489-5801, 489-6201 FAX

Admin Donna C Stango. *Dir of Nursing* Lynn Richman RN BSN. *Medical Dir* Dr Robert Scalice.
Licensure Skilled care; Intermediate care. *Beds* SNF 60; ICF 60. *Certified* Medicaid; Medicare.
Owner Proprietary corp.
Admissions Requirements Medical examination.
Staff Physicians; RNs; LPNs; Nurses' aides; Recreational therapists; Dietitians.
Facilities Dining room; Physical therapy room; Activities room; Chapel; Crafts room; Laundry room; Barber/Beauty shop; Library.
Activities Arts & crafts; Cards; Games; Reading groups; Prayer groups; Movies; Shopping trips; Dances/Social/Cultural gatherings; Intergenerational programs; Pet therapy.

Torrington Extend-A-Care Center
225 Wyoming Ave, Torrington, CT 06790
(203) 482-8563
Admin Christopher S Smith. *Dir of Nursing* Linda Koski RNBS. *Medical Dir* David P Hebert MD.
Licensure Skilled care. *Beds* SNF 120. *Certified* Medicaid; Medicare.
Owner Proprietary corp (Beverly Enterprises).
Admissions Requirements Medical examination; Physician's request.
Staff Physicians 6 (pt); RNs 8 (ft), 7 (pt); LPNs 6 (ft), 2 (pt); Nurses' aides 33 (ft), 20 (pt); Physical therapists 1 (pt); Recreational therapists 2 (ft); Speech therapists 1 (pt); Activities coordinators 1 (ft), 1 (pt); Dietitians 1 (pt); Ophthalmologists 1 (pt).
Languages Spanish, Polish, French, German.
Facilities Dining room; Physical therapy room; Activities room; Chapel; Crafts room; Laundry room; Barber/Beauty shop; TV lounge.
Activities Arts & crafts; Cards; Games; Reading groups; Prayer groups; Movies; Dances/Social/Cultural gatherings.

Valerie Manor
1360 Torringford St, Torrington, CT 06790
(203) 489-1008
Licensure Skilled care; Intermediate care. *Beds* SNF 30; ICF 90. *Certified* Medicaid; Medicare.
Languages Italian.

Wolcott Hall Nursing Center Inc
215 Forest St, Torrington, CT 06790
(203) 482-8554
Admin Robert Guastella. *Dir of Nursing* Dorothea Mercier RN. *Medical Dir* Dr Alfred J Finn.
Licensure Skilled care. *Beds* SNF 90. *Private Pay Patients* 40%. *Certified* Medicaid; Medicare.
Owner Proprietary corp (Health Care Associates).
Admissions Requirements Minimum age 14.
Staff Physicians 25 (pt); RNs 8 (ft), 6 (pt); LPNs 7 (ft), 2 (pt); Nurses' aides 33 (ft), 7 (pt); Physical therapists 1 (ft), 1 (pt); Occupational therapists 1 (pt); Speech therapists 1 (pt); Dietitians 1 (pt); Podiatrists 3 (pt).
Languages Polish, Italian, French, Slovak.
Facilities Dining room; Physical therapy room; Activities room; Crafts room; Laundry room; Barber/Beauty shop.
Activities Arts & crafts; Cards; Games; Reading groups; Prayer groups; Movies; Shopping trips; Dances/Social/Cultural gatherings; Intergenerational programs; Pet therapy; Resident council; Cocktail parties; Community support services.

Trumbull

St Joseph's Manor
6448 Main St, Trumbull, CT 06611
(203) 268-6204

Admin Sr Mary Ann Davis. *Dir of Nursing* Kathleen Shrauger RN. *Medical Dir* Everitt P Dolan MD.
Licensure Skilled care; Intermediate care; Home for aged; Independent living; Adult day health care. *Beds* SNF 201; ICF 72; Home for aged 21; Independent living units 86. *Private Pay Patients* 25%. *Certified* Medicaid; Medicare.
Owner Nonprofit corp.
Admissions Requirements Minimum age 60; Medical examination; Physician's request.
Staff Physicians 7 (pt); RNs 7 (ft), 54 (pt); LPNs 8 (ft), 13 (pt); Nurses' aides 98 (ft), 45 (pt); Physical therapists 1 (ft); Recreational therapists 5 (ft); Occupational therapists 2 (ft); Speech therapists 1 (pt); Activities coordinators 1 (ft); Dietitians 1 (ft); Ophthalmologists 2 (pt); Podiatrists 2 (pt); Audiologists 1 (pt); Dental hygienists 1 (pt); Dentists 2 (pt).
Languages Hispanic, Lao, Hungarian, Cambodian, German, French, Portuguese, Italian, Polish, Slovene.
Affiliation Roman Catholic.
Facilities Dining room; Physical therapy room; Activities room; Chapel; Crafts room; Laundry room; Barber/Beauty shop; Library; Store; Coffee shop/Lounge; Gift shop; Clinic; Pharmacy.
Activities Arts & crafts; Cards; Games; Reading groups; Prayer groups; Movies; Shopping trips; Dances/Social/Cultural gatherings; Intergenerational programs; Pet therapy; Resident council; Therapeutic groups; Drama; Swimming.

Vernon

Vernon Manor Health Care Facility
180 Regan Rd, Vernon, CT 06066-2824
(203) 871-0385, 871-9098 FAX
Admin David F Graves. *Dir of Nursing* Dolores P Rady RN. *Medical Dir* Neil H Brooks MD.
Licensure Skilled care; Retirement. *Beds* SNF 120; Retirement units 114. *Private Pay Patients* 86%.
Owner Privately owned (Paul G & Helen C Liistro).
Admissions Requirements Medical examination; Physician's request.
Staff Physicians 20 (pt); RNs 10 (ft), 13 (pt); LPNs 8 (ft), 9 (pt); Nurses' aides 40 (ft), 35 (pt); Physical therapists 1 (pt); Reality therapists 1 (pt); Recreational therapists 2 (ft); Occupational therapists 1 (pt); Speech therapists 1 (pt); Activities coordinators 1 (ft); Dietitians 1 (pt); Ophthalmologists 1 (pt); Podiatrists 1 (pt); Audiologists 1 (pt).
Languages Italian, Polish, French, Spanish, German, Chinese.
Facilities Dining room; Physical therapy room; Activities room; Chapel; Crafts room; Laundry room; Barber/Beauty shop; Library; Dental examination room; Greenhouse.
Activities Arts & crafts; Cards; Games; Reading groups; Prayer groups; Movies; Dances/Social/Cultural gatherings; Intergenerational programs; Pet therapy; Gardening.

Wallingford

Brook Hollow Health Care Center
55 Kondracki Ln, Wallingford, CT 06492
(203) 265-6771
Admin J Kevin Prisco. *Dir of Nursing* Sharon Hermonat RN. *Medical Dir* Dr Richard Wein.
Licensure Skilled care. *Beds* SNF 180. *Certified* Medicaid; Medicare.
Owner Proprietary corp (New Medico Assoc).

Staff Physicians 6 (pt); RNs 10 (ft), 17 (pt); LPNs 6 (ft), 13 (pt); Nurses' aides 75 (ft), 25 (pt); Physical therapists 1 (ft), 1 (pt); Recreational therapists 4 (ft); Speech therapists 2 (ft); Dietitians 1 (ft).
Facilities Dining room; Physical therapy room; Activities room; Crafts room; Laundry room; Barber/Beauty shop; Large lobby/sitting area; 4 large lounges w/entertainment units.
Activities Arts & crafts; Cards; Games; Reading groups; Prayer groups; Movies; Shopping trips; Dances/Social/Cultural gatherings.

Masonic Home & Hospital
22 Masonic Ave, Wallingford, CT 06492
(203) 284-3900, 284-3917 FAX
Admin Edgar G Kilby, Pres. *Dir of Nursing* Joanne Prefontaine RN. *Medical Dir* Erlinda A Rauch MD.
Licensure Skilled care; Intermediate care; Home for aged; Chronic disease hospital; Alzheimer's care. *Beds* SNF 148; ICF 234; Home for aged 86; Chronic disease hospital 100. *Private Pay Patients* 27%. *Certified* Medicaid; Medicare.
Owner Nonprofit organization/foundation.
Staff Physicians 5 (ft); RNs 70 (ft); LPNs 49 (ft); Nurses' aides 226 (ft), 31 (pt); Physical therapists 4 (ft), 1 (pt); Recreational therapists 11 (ft); Occupational therapists 2 (ft); Speech therapists 1 (pt); Dietitians 2 (ft); Ophthalmologists 1 (pt); Podiatrists 1 (pt); Audiologists 1 (ft).
Affiliation Masons.
Facilities Dining room; Physical therapy room; Activities room; Chapel; Crafts room; Laundry room; Barber/Beauty shop; Library; Occupational therapy room.
Activities Arts & crafts; Cards; Games; Reading groups; Prayer groups; Movies; Shopping trips; Dances/Social/Cultural gatherings; Intergenerational programs; Pet therapy.

Skyview Convalescent Hospital Inc
Marc Dr, Wallingford, CT 06492
(202) 265-0981
Licensure Skilled care; Intermediate care. *Beds* SNF 60; ICF 30. *Certified* Medicaid; Medicare.
Owner Proprietary corp.
Staff LPNs 8 (ft), 1 (pt); Nurses' aides 24 (ft), 1 (pt); Activities coordinators 1 (ft); Social workers 1 (ft).
Languages Spanish.

Wallingford Convalescent Home Inc
181 E Main St, Wallingford, CT 06492
(203) 265-1661
Admin Michele Wills.
Medical Dir Dr Breck.
Licensure Skilled care. *Beds* SNF 130. *Certified* Medicaid; Medicare.
Owner Proprietary corp.
Admissions Requirements Medical examination; Physician's request.
Staff RNs 14 (ft); LPNs 17 (ft); Nurses' aides 63 (ft); Physical therapists 1 (pt); Recreational therapists 2 (ft), 1 (pt); Occupational therapists 1 (pt); Dietitians 1 (ft).
Languages Spanish.
Facilities Dining room; Physical therapy room; Activities room; Laundry room; Barber/Beauty shop.
Activities Arts & crafts; Cards; Games; Prayer groups; Movies.

Waterbury

Abbott Terrace Health Center
44 Abbott Terr, Waterbury, CT 06702
(203) 755-4870
Licensure Skilled care; Intermediate care; Adult day care/child day care. *Beds* SNF 90; ICF 60. *Certified* Medicaid; Medicare.

Languages Spanish, Italian.

Birchwood Cluter Manor Inc
140 Willow St, Waterbury, CT 06710
(203) 754-6536
Licensure Intermediate care. *Beds* 23.
   Certified Medicaid.
Owner Proprietary corp.
Staff RNs 4 (ft); LPNs 6 (ft); Nurses' aides 6
   (ft); Activities coordinators 1 (ft); Dietitians
   1 (ft).
Languages Lithuanian, Russian, Italian.

**Cedar Lane Rehabilitation & Health Care
Center**
128 Cedar Ave, Waterbury, CT 06705
(203) 757-9271
Admin Ira M Schoenberger.
Medical Dir Louis Olore MD.
Licensure Skilled care. *Beds* SNF 180.
   Certified Medicaid; Medicare.
Owner Proprietary corp.
Admissions Requirements Minimum age 14;
   Medical examination; Physician's request.
Staff RNs 15 (ft), 20 (pt); LPNs 20 (ft), 12
   (pt); Nurses' aides 60 (ft), 20 (pt); Physical
   therapists 2 (ft), 2 (pt); Recreational
   therapists 3 (ft), 1 (pt); Occupational
   therapists 2 (ft); Speech therapists; Activities
   coordinators; Dietitians 1 (pt).
Languages Italian, Spanish, French, Hebrew.
Facilities Dining room; Physical therapy
   room; Activities room; Chapel; Crafts room;
   Laundry room; Barber/Beauty shop; Library.
Activities Arts & crafts; Cards; Games;
   Reading groups; Prayer groups; Movies;
   Shopping trips; Dances/Social/Cultural
   gatherings.

East End Convalescent Home
3396 E Main St, Waterbury, CT 06705
(203) 754-2161
Admin Pauline DiChiara. *Dir of Nursing*
   Joann Calabro. *Medical Dir* Louis Olore
   MD.
Licensure Skilled care; Alzheimer's care. *Beds*
   SNF 60. *Private Pay Patients* 30%. *Certified*
   Medicaid.
Owner Proprietary corp.
Admissions Requirements Minimum age 14;
   Medical examination; Physician's request.
Staff Physicians 2 (pt); RNs 5 (ft); LPNs 5
   (ft), 2 (pt); Nurses' aides 10 (ft), 10 (pt);
   Physical therapists 1 (ft); Recreational
   therapists 1 (ft); Speech therapists 1 (pt);
   Activities coordinators 1 (ft); Dietitians 1
   (pt); Ophthalmologists 1 (pt); Podiatrists 1
   (pt); Audiologists 1 (pt).
Languages Italian, Spanish.
Facilities Dining room; Physical therapy
   room; Activities room; Chapel; Crafts room;
   Laundry room; Barber/Beauty shop.
Activities Arts & crafts; Cards; Games;
   Reading groups; Prayer groups; Movies;
   Shopping trips; Dances/Social/Cultural
   gatherings.

Fleetcrest Manor Inc
62 Fleet St, PO Box 4147, Waterbury, CT
   06704
(203) 755-3383
Licensure Intermediate care. *Beds* 18.
   Certified Medicaid.
Owner Proprietary corp.
Staff Physicians 1 (pt); RNs 3 (ft); Nurses'
   aides 5 (ft); Recreational therapists 1 (pt).
Languages Italian.
Facilities Dining room.
Activities Arts & crafts; Cards; Games; Prayer
   groups; Movies; Shopping trips; Dances/
   Social/Cultural gatherings.

Grove Manor Nursing Home Inc
145 Grove St, Waterbury, CT 06710
(203) 753-7205
Licensure Skilled care. *Beds* SNF 60. *Certified*
   Medicaid; Medicare.
Owner Proprietary corp.

Staff RNs 5 (ft), 1 (pt); LPNs 4 (ft), 1 (pt);
   Nurses' aides 17 (ft), 1 (pt); Activities
   coordinators 1 (pt); Dietitians 1 (ft); Social
   workers 1 (pt).
Languages Italian, French, Spanish, Filipino.

Hillside Manor Retirement Home
157 Hillside Ave, Waterbury, CT 06710
(203) 755-2216
Admin Idylle B Patz. *Dir of Nursing*
   Georgieanna Roy RN. *Medical Dir* Joseph
   DeMayo MD.
Licensure Intermediate care; Alzheimer's care.
   Beds ICF 23. *Private Pay Patients* 100%.
Owner Proprietary corp.
Admissions Requirements Minimum age 50;
   Medical examination.
Staff Physicians 2 (pt); RNs 1 (ft), 8 (pt);
   Nurses' aides 2 (ft), 12 (pt); Recreational
   therapists 2 (pt); Dietitians 1 (pt); Podiatrists
   1 (pt).
Languages Spanish, Italian, French.
Facilities Dining room; Activities room;
   Laundry room; Library.
Activities Arts & crafts; Cards; Games;
   Reading groups; Movies; Shopping trips;
   Dances/Social/Cultural gatherings.

Hope Hall Convalescent Home Inc
355 Piedmont St, Waterbury, CT 06706
(203) 756-3617
Licensure Skilled care. *Beds* SNF 34.
Owner Proprietary corp.
Staff RNs 2 (ft); LPNs 1 (ft); Nurses' aides 5
   (ft); Activities coordinators 1 (ft); Social
   worker 1 (ft).
Languages French, Polish, Lithuanian.
Activities Arts & crafts; Prayer groups;
   Exercise; Music.

Mattatuck Extended Care Inc
21 Cliff St, Waterbury, CT 06710
(203) 574-0334
Licensure Skilled care. *Beds* SNF 52. *Certified*
   Medicaid.
Owner Proprietary corp.
Staff RNs 5 (ft); LPNs 4 (ft); Social workers 1
   (ft).
Languages Spanish.

Mattatuck Health Care Facility Inc
9 Cliff St, Waterbury, CT 06710
(203) 573-9924
Medical Dir Joseph A Vincitonio MD.
Licensure Intermediate care. *Beds* 43.
   Certified Medicaid; Medicare.
Owner Proprietary corp.
Admissions Requirements Minimum age 14;
   Medical examination; Physician's request.
Staff Physicians 1 (pt); RNs 3 (ft), 2 (pt);
   LPNs 1 (pt); Nurses' aides 4 (ft), 3 (pt);
   Recreational therapists 1 (ft); Dietitians 1
   (pt); Podiatrists 1 (pt); Dentists 1 (pt).
Languages Italian.
Activities Prayer groups; Arts & crafts;
   Shopping trips.

Medicare Pavilion Corporation
1132 Meriden Rd, Waterbury, CT 06705
(203) 757-1228
Licensure Skilled care. *Beds* SNF 94. *Certified*
   Medicaid; Medicare.
Owner Proprietary corp.
Staff RNs 6 (ft); LPNs 10 (ft); Nurses' aides
   36 (ft); Physical therapists 1 (ft); Activities
   coordinators 2 (ft); Social workers 1 (ft).
Languages Italian, Lithuanian, Spanish,
   French, German.
Activities Arts & crafts; Games; Dances/Social/
   Cultural gatherings; Exercises; Current
   events; Sing-alongs.

Oakcliff Convalescent Home Inc
71 Plaza Ave, Waterbury, CT 06710
(203) 754-6015
Medical Dir Arthur Sullivan MD.
Licensure Skilled care. *Beds* SNF 75. *Certified*
   Medicaid; Medicare.
Owner Proprietary corp.

Admissions Requirements Minimum age 18;
   Medical examination.
Staff RNs 8 (ft), 1 (pt); LPNs 3 (ft), 3 (pt);
   Nurses' aides 21 (ft), 5 (pt); Physical
   therapists 1 (pt); Recreational therapists 1
   (ft), 1 (pt); Speech therapists 1 (pt);
   Activities coordinators 1 (ft); Dietitians 1
   (pt); Ophthalmologists 1 (pt); Dentists 1 (pt).
Languages French, Spanish, Italian, Sign.
Facilities Dining room; Physical therapy
   room; Activities room; Crafts room; Laundry
   room.
Activities Arts & crafts; Cards; Games;
   Reading groups; Prayer groups; Movies;
   Shopping trips; Dances/Social/Cultural
   gatherings.

Park Manor
1312 W Main St, Waterbury, CT 06708
(203) 757-9464
Medical Dir Arthur Sullivan MD.
Licensure Skilled care. *Beds* SNF 148.
   Certified Medicaid; Medicare.
Owner Proprietary corp (Health Care &
   Retirement Corp).
Staff RNs 3 (ft), 13 (pt); LPNs 6 (ft), 18 (pt);
   Nurses' aides 20 (ft), 42 (pt); Recreational
   therapists 2 (ft), 1 (pt); Dietitians 1 (ft).
Languages Spanish, Italian, Polish.
Facilities Dining room; Physical therapy
   room; Activities room; Crafts room; Laundry
   room; Barber/Beauty shop; TV lounges.
Activities Arts & crafts; Cards; Games;
   Reading groups; Prayer groups; Movies;
   Shopping trips; Dances/Social/Cultural
   gatherings.

Roncalli Woodland Inc
3584 E Main St, Waterbury, CT 06705
(203) 754-4181
Admin Michael L Santoro. *Dir of Nursing*
   Virginia Allen RN.
Licensure Intermediate care. *Beds* 90.
   Certified Medicaid.
Owner Proprietary corp.
Admissions Requirements Physician's request.
Staff Physicians 1 (ft), 2 (pt); RNs; LPNs;
   Nurses' aides; Recreational therapists 2 (ft);
   Dietitians 1 (pt).
Languages Portuguese, Italian, Spanish,
   French.
Facilities Dining room; Activities room;
   Crafts room; Laundry room; Barber/Beauty
   shop.
Activities Arts & crafts; Cards; Games;
   Reading groups; Prayer groups; Movies;
   Shopping trips; Dances/Social/Cultural
   gatherings.

Rose Manor
107 S View St, Waterbury, CT 06706
(203) 754-0786
Licensure Intermediate care. *Beds* 22.
   Certified Medicaid.
Owner Proprietary corp.
Staff RNs 5 (ft), 1 (pt); Nurses' aides 7 (ft), 1
   (pt).
Languages Italian, Greek, Spanish.
Affiliation Roman Catholic.
Activities Arts & crafts; Games; Shopping
   trips; Dances/Social/Cultural gatherings;
   Picnics.

Waterbury Convalescent Center Inc
PO Box 4039, 2817 N Main St, Waterbury,
   CT 06704
(203) 757-0731
Licensure Skilled care. *Beds* SNF 120.
   Certified Medicaid; Medicare.
Owner Proprietary corp.
Staff RNs 7 (ft), 1 (pt); LPNs 12 (ft); Nurses'
   aides 35 (ft); Activities coordinators 2 (ft);
   Social workers 1 (ft).
Languages Spanish.
Activities Arts & crafts; Cards; Games;
   Reading groups; Prayer groups; Movies;
   Shopping trips; Dances/Social/Cultural
   gatherings.

Waterbury Nursing Center
1243 W Main St, Waterbury, CT 06708
(203) 757-0561
Admin Terrence Brennan. *Dir of Nursing*
Arlene Grossman-Potpinka RN. *Medical Dir*
Joseph Vincitorio MD.
Licensure Skilled care; Intermediate care;
Alzheimer's care. *Beds* SNF 100; ICF 29.
Certified Medicaid; Medicare.
Owner Proprietary corp.
Staff Physicians 40 (pt); RNs 3 (ft), 18 (pt);
LPNs 6 (ft), 1 (pt); Nurses' aides 21 (ft), 25
(pt); Physical therapists 1 (pt); Recreational
therapists 1 (ft), 1 (pt); Speech therapists 1
(pt); Activities coordinators 1 (ft); Dietitians
1 (pt); Ophthalmologists 1 (pt); Dentists 1
(pt); Psychiatrist 1 (pt).
Languages Italian, Spanish.
Facilities Dining room; Physical therapy
room; Activities room; Crafts room; Laundry
room; Barber/Beauty shop; Library on
wheels; 3rd floor dining room is used for
religious purposes.
Activities Arts & crafts; Cards; Games;
Reading groups; Prayer groups; Movies;
Shopping trips; Dances/Social/Cultural
gatherings.

Whitewood Rehabilitation Center
177 Whitewood Rd, Waterbury, CT 06708
(203) 757-9491, 575-1714 FAX
Admin Barbara Brown; Michele Carney,
Assoc. *Dir of Nursing* Patricia Rzwenicki.
Medical Dir Dr Coshak.
Licensure Skilled care. *Beds* SNF 180. *Private
Pay Patients* 15%. *Certified* Medicare.
Owner Proprietary corp (New Medico
Associates).
Admissions Requirements Minimum age 14.
Staff RNs; LPNs; Nurses' aides; Physical
therapists; Recreational therapists;
Occupational therapists; Speech therapists;
Activities coordinators; Dietitians; Learning
center teachers; Mental health clinicians.
Languages Italian, French, Spanish,
Portuguese.
Facilities Dining room; Physical therapy
room; Activities room; Crafts room; Laundry
room; Barber/Beauty shop; Library.
Activities Arts & crafts; Cards; Games;
Reading groups; Prayer groups; Movies;
Shopping trips; Dances/Social/Cultural
gatherings; Intergenerational programs; Pet
therapy.

Willow Rest Home
94 Willow St, Waterbury, CT 06710
(203) 753-5442
Licensure Intermediate care. *Beds* 17.
Certified Medicaid.
Owner Proprietary corp.
Staff RNs 4 (ft); Nurses' aides 3 (ft); Activities
coordinators 1 (ft).
Languages French.
Activities Arts & crafts; Movies; Shopping
trips; Therapeutic recreation; Dining out.

Waterford

Greentree Manor Convalescent Home
4 Greentree Dr, Waterford, CT 06385
(203) 442-0647
Licensure Skilled care. *Beds* SNF 90. *Certified*
Medicaid; Medicare.
Owner Proprietary corp.
Staff RNs 14 (ft); LPNs 7 (ft); Nurses' aides
36 (ft); Activities coordinators 2 (ft); Social
workers 1 (ft).
Languages Spanish, German, Italian.
Activities Arts & crafts; Games; Reading
groups; Dances/Social/Cultural gatherings;
Music.

New London Convalescent Home
88 Clark Ln, Waterford, CT 06385
(203) 442-0471
Licensure Skilled care. *Beds* SNF 120.
Certified Medicaid; Medicare.

Owner Proprietary corp.
Staff RNs 14 (ft); LPNs 12 (ft); Nurses' aides
46 (ft); Physical therapists.
Languages French, Spanish, Vietnamese.
Activities Arts & crafts; Games; Prayer groups;
Movies; Dances/Social/Cultural gatherings.

Waterford Health & Rehabilitation Center
171 Rope Ferry Rd, Waterford, CT 06385
(203) 443-8357
Admin John Kolenda. *Dir of Nursing* Joyce
Adamcewicz. *Medical Dir* Dr George
Burton.
Licensure Skilled care; Alzheimer's care. *Beds*
SNF 148. *Private Pay Patients* 11%. *Certified*
Medicare.
Owner Proprietary corp.
Admissions Requirements Medical
examination; Physician's request.
Staff Physicians 6 (pt); RNs 4 (ft), 13 (pt);
LPNs 10 (ft), 10 (pt); Nurses' aides 45 (ft),
24 (pt); Physical therapists 1 (pt);
Recreational therapists 2 (ft), 1 (pt);
Occupational therapists 1 (ft); Speech
therapists 1 (ft); Dietitians 1 (ft);
Ophthalmologists 1 (pt); Podiatrists 1 (pt);
Audiologists 1 (pt).
Languages Spanish, Italian, Greek, French.
Facilities Dining room; Physical therapy
room; Activities room; Laundry room;
Barber/Beauty shop; Library.
Activities Arts & crafts; Cards; Games;
Reading groups; Prayer groups; Movies;
Shopping trips; Dances/Social/Cultural
gatherings; Intergenerational programs; Pet
therapy; Theme dinners with entertainment.

Watertown

Pleasant View Manor
225 Bunker Hill Rd, Watertown, CT 06795
(203) 756-3557
Admin Antoinette Toule.
Medical Dir Dr Caporado.
Licensure Home for aged. *Beds* 19. *Certified*
Medicaid; Medicare.
Owner Proprietary corp.
Admissions Requirements Minimum age 45.
Staff RNs 1 (ft); Nurses' aides 6 (ft);
Dietitians 1 (ft); Ophthalmologists 1 (ft).
Facilities Dining room; Activities room;
Crafts room; Laundry room.
Activities Arts & crafts; Cards; Games;
Reading groups; Prayer groups; Movies;
Shopping trips; Dances/Social/Cultural
gatherings.

Waterbury Extended Care Facility Inc
35 Bunker Hill Rd, Watertown, CT 06795
(203) 274-5428
Admin Timothy L Curran Jr. *Dir of Nursing*
Judith A Griesbach RN. *Medical Dir* Dr
William Bassford.
Licensure Skilled care. *Beds* SNF 60. *Certified*
Medicaid; Medicare.
Owner Proprietary corp.
Admissions Requirements Physician's request.
Staff Physicians; RNs; LPNs; Nurses' aides;
Physical therapists; Recreational therapists;
Speech therapists; Activities coordinators;
Dietitians; Ophthalmologists.
Languages Spanish.
Affiliation Roman Catholic.
Facilities Dining room; Physical therapy
room; Activities room; Laundry room;
Barber/Beauty shop; Television rooms;
Patio.
Activities Arts & crafts; Cards; Games;
Reading groups; Prayer groups; Movies;
Entertainment; Family functions; Garden
club.

Watertown Convalarium
560 Woodbury Rd, Watertown, CT 06795
(203) 274-6748
Licensure Skilled care. *Beds* SNF 36. *Certified*
Medicaid.
Owner Nonprofit corp.

Staff Physicians; Dietitians; Nurses' aides.
Languages Italian, French, Polish.
Activities Prayer groups; Arts & crafts;
Shopping trips.

West Hartford

Brookview
130 Loomis Dr, West Hartford, CT 06107
(203) 521-8700
Admin Patricia Fried.
Medical Dir Robert Safer MD.
Licensure Skilled care; Intermediate care. *Beds*
SNF 90; ICF 90. *Certified* Medicaid;
Medicare.
Owner Proprietary corp.
Admissions Requirements Medical
examination; Physician's request.
Staff RNs 10 (ft), 34 (pt); LPNs 2 (ft), 9 (pt);
Nurses' aides 14 (ft), 74 (pt); Physical
therapists 1 (pt); Recreational therapists 2
(ft), 1 (pt); Activities coordinators 1 (ft).
Languages French, Spanish, Russian.
Facilities Dining room; Physical therapy
room; Activities room; Crafts room; Laundry
room; Barber/Beauty shop.
Activities Arts & crafts; Cards; Games;
Reading groups; Prayer groups; Movies;
Shopping trips; Dances/Social/Cultural
gatherings; Garden club; Jewish community
group; Overnight trips; Family dinners;
Racquetball.

Gables Inc
22 Berwyn Rd, West Hartford, CT 06107
(203) 522-8209
Admin Collin M Tierney. *Dir of Nursing*
Judith Carboni RN MSN. *Medical Dir* Paul
West MD.
Licensure Skilled care; Intermediate care;
Alzheimer's care. *Beds* 73. *Certified*
Medicaid; Medicare.
Owner Proprietary corp.
Admissions Requirements Medical
examination; Physician's request.
Staff Physicians 3 (pt); RNs 5 (ft), 4 (pt);
LPNs 5 (ft), 2 (pt); Nurses' aides 25 (ft), 5
(pt); Physical therapists 1 (pt); Recreational
therapists 2 (ft), 1 (pt); Speech therapists 1
(pt); Activities coordinators 1 (ft); Dietitians
1 (ft); Ophthalmologists 1 (pt); Podiatrists 1
(pt); Dentists 1 (pt).
Languages Spanish, French.
Facilities Dining room; Physical therapy
room; Activities room; Barber/Beauty shop;
Library.
Activities Arts & crafts; Games; Prayer groups;
Music; Psychogeriatric group; Reality
orientation; Remotivation.

Hughes Convalescent Inc
29 Highland St, West Hartford, CT 06119
(203) 236-5623, 233-6437 FAX
Admin Burton J Mitchell RN. *Dir of Nursing*
Iris C Zaricor RN. *Medical Dir* Joseph J
Lucas MD.
Licensure Skilled care. *Beds* SNF 180. *Private
Pay Patients* 65%. *Certified* Medicaid;
Medicare.
Owner Proprietary corp.
Staff RNs 17 (ft); LPNs 14 (ft); Nurses' aides
70 (ft); Physical therapists 3 (ft);
Recreational therapists 3 (ft); Speech
therapists 1 (pt); Dietitians 1 (pt); Podiatrists
(consultant); Social service staff 1 (ft).
Languages Spanish, Portuguese, Italian,
French, Polish, Chinese.
Affiliation Salvation Army.
Facilities Physical therapy room; Activities
room; Chapel; Crafts room; Laundry room;
Barber/Beauty shop; Library.
Activities Arts & crafts; Cards; Games;
Reading groups; Prayer groups; Movies;
Dances/Social/Cultural gatherings;
Intergenerational programs.

Mercyknoll Inc
243 Steele Rd, West Hartford, CT 06117
(203) 236-3503
Admin Sr Irene Holowesko RSM. *Dir of Nursing* Sr Margaret Ann Mathis RN. *Medical Dir* Dr Robert J Molloy.
Licensure Skilled care; Retirement. *Beds* SNF 38; Retirement 48 Retirement 48. *Private Pay Patients* 100%.
Owner Nonprofit organization/foundation.
Admissions Requirements Females only; Medical examination.
Staff Physicians 1 (pt); RNs 5 (ft), 7 (pt); LPNs 2 (pt); Nurses' aides 14 (ft), 5 (pt); Physical therapists 2 (pt); Recreational therapists 1 (ft); Occupational therapists 1 (pt); Dietitians 1 (pt); Pastoral care dir 1 (ft).
Languages Spanish, German, French.
Affiliation Roman Catholic.
Facilities Dining room; Physical therapy room; Activities room; Chapel; Crafts room; Laundry room; Barber/Beauty shop; Library.
Activities Arts & crafts; Games; Prayer groups; Movies; Shopping trips; Dances/Social/Cultural gatherings; Music programs.

St Mary Home
291 Steele Rd, West Hartford, CT 06117
(203) 236-1924
Licensure Skilled care; Intermediate care; Home for aged. *Beds* SNF 175; ICF 40; Home for aged 127. *Certified* Medicaid.
Owner Nonprofit corp.
Staff Physicians 1 (pt); RNs 2 (ft), 1 (pt); LPNs 1 (pt); Nurses' aides 5 (ft), 1 (pt); Physical therapists; Occupational therapists; Speech therapists; Dietitians; Social workers 1 (ft).
Languages Spanish, French.
Affiliation Roman Catholic.
Activities Arts & crafts; Games; Prayer groups; Dances/Social/Cultural gatherings; Outings.

West Hartford Manor
2432 Albany Ave, West Hartford, CT 06117
(203) 236-3557
Licensure Skilled care. *Beds* SNF 120. *Certified* Medicaid; Medicare.
Owner Proprietary corp.
Staff RNs 12 (ft); LPNs 3 (ft); Nurses' aides 43 (ft); Physical therapists 1 (ft); Activities coordinators 2 (ft); Social workers 1 (ft).
Languages Spanish.
Activities Reading groups; Prayer groups; Dances/Social/Cultural gatherings; Current events.

West Haven

Arterburn Home Inc
267 Union Ave, West Haven, CT 06516
(203) 934-5256
Admin Michael J Mahoney. *Dir of Nursing* Donna Masto RN. *Medical Dir* Dominic B Schioppo MD.
Licensure Intermediate care. *Beds* ICF 40. *Private Pay Patients* 5%. *Certified* Medicaid.
Owner Proprietary corp.
Admissions Requirements Minimum age 18; Medical examination; Physician's request.
Staff RNs 3 (ft), 4 (pt); LPNs 2 (ft); Nurses' aides 9 (ft), 5 (pt); Activities coordinators 1 (ft); Dietitians 1 (pt).
Facilities Dining room; Activities room; Crafts room; Laundry room; Barber/Beauty shop.
Activities Arts & crafts; Cards; Games; Reading groups; Prayer groups; Movies; Shopping trips; Dances/Social/Cultural gatherings; Intergenerational programs; Pet therapy.

Bentley Gardens Health Care Center
310 Terrace Ave, West Haven, CT 06516
(203) 932-2247
Admin Carole Bergeron RN.
Medical Dir Dr John Milici.

Licensure Skilled care. *Beds* SNF 97. *Certified* Medicaid; Medicare.
Owner Proprietary corp (Beverly Enterprises).
Admissions Requirements Minimum age 21; Medical examination.
Staff RNs 9 (ft), 10 (pt); LPNs 5 (ft), 5 (pt); Nurses' aides 32 (ft), 21 (pt); Physical therapists 1 (ft); Recreational therapists 4 (ft); Occupational therapists 1 (pt); Speech therapists 1 (pt); Activities coordinators 1 (pt).
Languages Spanish, French.
Facilities Dining room; Physical therapy room; Activities room; Crafts room; Laundry room; Barber/Beauty shop; Library; Garden & patio.
Activities Arts & crafts; Cards; Games; Reading groups; Prayer groups; Movies; Shopping trips; Dances/Social/Cultural gatherings.

Harbor View Manor
308 Savin Ave, West Haven, CT 06516
(203) 932-6411
Licensure Intermediate care. *Beds* 120. *Certified* Medicaid.
Owner Proprietary corp.
Staff RNs 4 (ft), 1 (pt); LPNs 7 (ft); Nurses' aides 14 (ft); Activities coordinators 2 (ft), 1 (pt); Social workers 1 (ft).
Languages Spanish, French.
Activities Arts & crafts; Movies; Shopping trips; Dances/Social/Cultural gatherings; Picnics; Discussion groups.

Seacrest Nursing & Retirement Center
588 Ocean Ave, West Haven, CT 06516
(203) 934-2676
Medical Dir Dr John Milici.
Licensure Intermediate care. *Beds* 39. *Certified* Medicaid.
Owner Proprietary corp.
Admissions Requirements Minimum age 21; Medical examination; Physician's request.
Staff Physicians 2 (pt); RNs 3 (ft), 4 (pt); LPNs 1 (ft); Nurses' aides 6 (ft), 4 (pt); Physical therapists 1 (pt); Activities coordinators 1 (ft); Dietitians 1 (pt); Podiatrists 1 (pt); Audiologists 1 (pt); Dentists 1 (pt).
Languages German, Spanish.
Facilities Dining room; Activities room; Crafts room; Laundry room.
Activities Arts & crafts; Cards; Games; Reading groups; Prayer groups; Movies; Shopping trips; Dances/Social/Cultural gatherings.

Sound View Specialized Care Center
1 Care Ln, West Haven, CT 06516
(203) 934-7955
Admin Carole Hersey Bergeron. *Dir of Nursing* Cecilia Roberge. *Medical Dir* Leo Cooney MD.
Licensure Skilled care. *Beds* SNF 100. *Private Pay Patients* 40%. *Certified* Medicaid; Medicare.
Owner Proprietary corp.
Admissions Requirements Minimum age 14.
Staff Physicians 3 (pt); RNs 6 (ft), 9 (pt); LPNs 4 (ft), 7 (pt); Nurses' aides 18 (ft), 8 (pt); Physical therapists 1 (ft), 2 (pt); Reality therapists 1 (ft), 1 (pt); Recreational therapists 1 (ft), 2 (pt); Occupational therapists 1 (pt); Speech therapists 1 (pt); Dietitians 1 (pt); Ophthalmologists 1 (pt); Podiatrists 1 (pt); Audiologists 1 (pt).
Languages Spanish, French.
Facilities Dining room; Physical therapy room; Activities room; Crafts room; Barber/Beauty shop; Library.
Activities Arts & crafts; Cards; Games; Reading groups; Prayer groups; Movies; Dances/Social/Cultural gatherings.

West Haven Nursing Center
555 Saw Mill Rd, West Haven, CT 06516
(203) 934-8326, 932-1646 FAX

Admin Margaret Bucknall. *Dir of Nursing* Evelyn Glass RN. *Medical Dir* Dominic B Schioppo MD.
Licensure Skilled care. *Beds* SNF 120. *Private Pay Patients* 8%. *Certified* Medicaid; Medicare.
Owner Proprietary corp (Beverly Enterprises).
Admissions Requirements Medical examination; Physician's request.
Staff Physicians 5 (pt); RNs 12 (ft); LPNs 8 (ft), 2 (pt); Nurses' aides 45 (ft), 45 (pt); Physical therapists 1 (ft), 1 (pt); Recreational therapists 2 (ft); Occupational therapists 1 (pt); Speech therapists 1 (pt); Dietitians 1 (pt); Ophthalmologists 1 (pt); Podiatrists 1 (pt); Audiologists 1 (pt).
Languages Portuguese, Polish, Italian, Spanish.
Facilities Dining room; Physical therapy room; Activities room; Crafts room; Laundry room; Barber/Beauty shop; Lounges; Patio.
Activities Arts & crafts; Cards; Games; Reading groups; Prayer groups; Movies; Shopping trips; Dances/Social/Cultural gatherings; Intergenerational programs; Pet therapy.

Wethersfield

Mediplex of Wethersfield
341 Jordan Ln, Wethersfield, CT 06109
(203) 563-0101
Licensure Skilled care; Intermediate care. *Beds* SNF 180; ICF 60. *Certified* Medicaid; Medicare.
Owner Proprietary corp (Mediplex).
Staff Nurses' aides 5 (ft); Physical therapists 1 (ft), 10 (pt); Activities coordinators 1 (ft); Dietitians.
Languages Italian, Polish, German, Spanish, Ukranian.
Activities Arts & crafts; Games; Shopping trips; Dances/Social/Cultural gatherings.

Willimantic

Windham Hills Healthcare Center
595 Valley St, Willimantic, CT 06226
(203) 423-2597, 423-7906 FAX
Admin Michael Chiappinelli. *Dir of Nursing* Arlene Bell. *Medical Dir* Marjorie Petro.
Licensure Skilled care. *Beds* SNF 120. *Private Pay Patients* 30%. *Certified* Medicaid; Medicare.
Owner Proprietary corp (Sunrise Healthcare Corp).
Admissions Requirements Minimum age 14; Medical examination; Physician's request.
Staff RNs 4 (ft), 3 (pt); LPNs 9 (ft), 8 (pt); Nurses' aides 33 (ft), 16 (pt); Physical therapists 1 (ft); Recreational therapists 2 (ft); Occupational therapists 1 (pt); Speech therapists 1 (pt); Dietitians 1 (pt).
Languages Spanish.
Facilities Dining room; Physical therapy room; Activities room; Laundry room; Barber/Beauty shop.
Activities Arts & crafts; Cards; Games; Reading groups; Movies; Shopping trips; Dances/Social/Cultural gatherings; Intergenerational programs; Pet therapy; College courses; Sensory awareness groups.

Wilton

Wilton Meadows Health Care
439 Danbury Rd, Wilton, CT 06897
(203) 834-0199, 834-2646 FAX
Admin Mindy J Cavicchia. *Dir of Nursing* Claire A Zizzo. *Medical Dir* Dr Alan Radin.
Licensure Skilled care; Intermediate care; Respite care. *Beds* SNF 60; ICF 60. *Certified* Medicaid; Medicare.
Owner Privately owned.
Admissions Requirements Minimum age 14; Medical examination.

Staff RNs; LPNs; Nurses' aides; Physical therapists 1 (ft); Recreational therapists 3 (ft); Occupational therapists (consultant); Speech therapists (consultant); Dietitians (consultant); Ophthalmologists (consultant); Podiatrists (consultant); Audiologists (consultant).
Languages Spanish, Portuguese, French.
Facilities Dining room; Physical therapy room; Activities room; Chapel; Crafts room; Barber/Beauty shop; Library; Gift shop.
Activities Arts & crafts; Cards; Games; Reading groups; Prayer groups; Movies; Shopping trips; Dances/Social/Cultural gatherings; Intergenerational programs; Pet therapy; Newspaper staff.

Windham

Abbey Manor Inc
Rte 14, 103 North Rd, Windham, CT 06280
(203) 423-4636
Admin Michael S Lawless RN. *Dir of Nursing* Hannah H Douville RN. *Medical Dir* Peter D Jones MD.
Licensure Skilled care; Alzheimer's care. *Beds* SNF 60. *Private Pay Patients* 33%. *Certified* Medicaid; Medicare.
Owner Proprietary corp.
Admissions Requirements Physician's request.
Staff Physicians (attending); RNs 6 (ft), 2 (pt); LPNs 3 (ft), 1 (pt); Nurses' aides 23 (ft), 5 (pt); Physical therapists 1 (ft); Recreational therapists 2 (ft); Occupational therapists (consultant); Speech therapists (consultant); Dietitians (consultant); Podiatrists (consultant); Audiologists (consultant); Optometrists (consultant); Medical directors (consultant).
Facilities Physical therapy room; Activities room; Laundry room; Barber/Beauty shop.
Activities Arts & crafts; Games; Movies; Shopping trips.

Windsor

Kimberly Hall Nursing Home—North
1 Kimberly Dr, Windsor, CT 06095
(203) 688-6443
Admin Mary Ellen Gaudette.
Medical Dir Sally Ardolino MD.
Licensure Skilled care. *Beds* SNF 150. *Certified* Medicaid; Medicare.
Owner Proprietary corp (Genesis Health Ventures).
Admissions Requirements Minimum age 18; Medical examination; Physician's request.
Staff Physicians 1 (pt); RNs; LPNs; Nurses' aides; Physical therapists; Recreational therapists; Occupational therapists; Speech therapists; Activities coordinators; Dietitians; Ophthalmologists; Podiatrists; Dentists.
Languages Spanish, Portuguese.
Facilities Dining room; Physical therapy room; Activities room; Chapel; Crafts room; Laundry room; Barber/Beauty shop; Library; TV lounges; Inner courtyards.
Activities Arts & crafts; Cards; Games; Reading groups; Prayer groups; Movies; Dances/Social/Cultural gatherings; Oil painting; Intergenerational learning.

Kimberly Hall Nursing Home—South
1 Kimberly Dr, Windsor, CT 06095
(203) 688-6443
Licensure Skilled care. *Beds* SNF 180. *Certified* Medicaid; Medicare.
Owner Proprietary corp.
Staff RNs 16 (ft); LPNs 7 (ft); Nurses' aides 78 (ft); Activities coordinators 3 (ft).
Languages Spanish, Portuguese.

Mountain View Healthcare
581 Poquonock Ave, Windsor, CT 06095
(203) 688-7211
Medical Dir Joseph Misiak MD.
Licensure Skilled care. *Beds* SNF 120. *Certified* Medicaid; Medicare.
Owner Proprietary corp.
Admissions Requirements Medical examination; Physician's request.
Staff Physicians; RNs; LPNs; Nurses' aides; Physical therapists 1 (ft), 1 (pt); Recreational therapists 2 (ft); Speech therapists; Dietitians; Podiatrists; Dentists.
Languages Spanish.
Facilities Dining room; Physical therapy room; Laundry room; Library.
Activities Arts & crafts; Cards; Games; Reading groups; Reading groups; Prayer groups; Movies; Dances/Social/Cultural gatherings.

Windsor Hall Retirement Center
519 Palisado Ave, Windsor, CT 06095
(203) 688-4918
Admin E Leo Attella Jr. *Dir of Nursing* Lilla Bruyette RN. *Medical Dir* Dr George Donahue.
Licensure Intermediate care; Alzheimer's care; Retirement. *Beds* ICF 170. *Certified* Medicaid.
Owner Proprietary corp (Genesis Health Ventures).
Admissions Requirements Minimum age 14; Medical examination; Physician's request.
Staff RNs 10 (ft), 5 (pt); LPNs 10 (ft), 6 (pt); Nurses' aides 19 (ft), 13 (pt); Physical therapists 1 (pt); Reality therapists; Recreational therapists 3 (ft); Occupational therapists; Speech therapists 1 (pt); Activities coordinators; Dietitians 1 (ft), 1 (pt); Ophthalmologists 1 (pt); Podiatrists 1 (pt); Dentists 1 (pt).
Languages Polish, French, German, Sign Language.
Facilities Dining room; Physical therapy room; Activities room; Chapel; Crafts room; Laundry room; Barber/Beauty shop; Library.
Activities Arts & crafts; Cards; Games; Reading groups; Prayer groups; Movies; Shopping trips; Dances/Social/Cultural gatherings; Bowling; Fishing trips; Baseball games.

Windsor Locks

Bickford Convalescent Home
14 Main St, Windsor Locks, CT 06096
(203) 623-4351
Admin Robert Srulowitz. *Dir of Nursing* LaVerne M Shary RN. *Medical Dir* John J Kennedy Jr MD.

Licensure Skilled care; Intermediate care. *Beds* SNF 48; ICF 11. *Certified* Medicaid.
Owner Proprietary corp.
Admissions Requirements Minimum age 65; Medical examination; Physician's request.
Staff Physicians 7 (pt); RNs 5 (ft), 5 (pt); LPNs 1 (ft), 1 (pt); Nurses' aides 19 (ft), 9 (pt); Physical therapists; Activities coordinators 1 (ft), 1 (pt); Dietitians; Podiatrists 1 (pt).
Languages French, Spanish, Polish.
Facilities Dining room; Physical therapy room; Activities room; Crafts room; Laundry room; Barber/Beauty shop.
Activities Arts & crafts; Cards; Games; Reading groups; Prayer groups; Movies; Shopping trips; Dances/Social/Cultural gatherings; Pet therapy; Church services.

Winsted

Highland Acres Extend-A-Care Center
108 E Lake St, Winsted, CT 06098
(203) 379-8591
Medical Dir Dr David Hebert.
Licensure Skilled care; Intermediate care. *Beds* SNF 45; ICF 30. *Certified* Medicaid; Medicare.
Owner Proprietary corp.
Admissions Requirements Minimum age 14.
Staff RNs 5 (ft), 10 (pt); LPNs 1 (ft), 1 (pt); Nurses' aides 9 (ft), 15 (pt); Physical therapists 1 (pt); Recreational therapists 1 (ft), 1 (pt); Dietitians 1 (pt).
Languages Italian.
Facilities Dining room; Physical therapy room; Activities room; Chapel; Laundry room; Barber/Beauty shop; Library.
Activities Arts & crafts; Cards; Games; Reading groups; Prayer groups; Movies; Shopping trips; Dances/Social/Cultural gatherings.

Wolcott

Wolcott Rest Home
55 Beach Rd, Wolcott, CT 06716
(203) 879-0600
Licensure Intermediate care. *Beds* 20.
Owner Proprietary corp.
Languages French, Italian.

Wolcott View Manor
PO Box 6192, 50 Beach Rd, Wolcott, CT 06716
(203) 879-1479
Licensure Skilled care; Intermediate care. *Beds* SNF 60; ICF 59. *Certified* Medicaid.
Owner Proprietary corp.
Staff RNs 3 (ft); Nurses' aides 4 (ft); Activities coordinators 3 (ft); Dietitians 1 (ft); Social workers 1 (ft).
Languages Italian, Polish, Spanish.

DELAWARE

Bear

Delaware Elwyn Lauren Farms
116 Walls Way, Bear, DE 19701
(302) 836-1379
Admin Peter Dakunchak.
Licensure Intermediate care for mentally retarded. *Beds* ICF/MR 8.

Lums Pond Group Home
457 Howell School Rd, Bear, DE 19701
(302) 834-2912
Admin Rebecca Cassedy.
Licensure Intermediate care for mentally retarded. *Beds* ICF/MR 8.

Bridgeville

Bridgeville Group Home
506 S Main St, Bridgeville, DE 19933
(302) 337-8125
Admin Michael Paoli.
Licensure Intermediate care for mentally retarded. *Beds* ICF/MR 8.

Camden

Thompson Farm Group Home
Lot 17, RD 2, Box 250H, Camden, DE 19934
(302) 697-6295
Admin Rebecca Cassedy.
Licensure Intermediate care for mentally retarded. *Beds* ICF/MR 8.

Claymont

Rose Wood Rest Home Inc
PO Box 10, 3 Wistar St, Claymont, DE 19703
(302) 798-9620
Admin Nancy Olsen. *Dir of Nursing* Barbara McCann.
Licensure Intermediate care. *Beds* ICF 13. *Private Pay Patients* 100%.
Owner Proprietary corp.
Admissions Requirements Medical examination.
Staff RNs 1 (ft), 2 (pt); LPNs 3 (pt); Nurses' aides 1 (ft), 7 (pt).
Activities Games; Prayer groups.

Delaware City

Governor Bacon Health Center
Tilton Bldg, Delaware City, DE 19706
(302) 834-9201
Admin C Ronald McGinnis.
Licensure Intermediate care. *Beds* ICF 122. *Certified* Medicaid.

Delmar

Harrison House of Delmar
101 E Delaware Ave, Delmar, DE 19940
(302) 846-8077
Admin Richard Platter.

Licensure Skilled care; Intermediate care. *Beds* 124.

Dover

Courtland Manor Nursing & Convalescent Home
889 S Little Creek Rd, Dover, DE 19901
(302) 674-0566
Admin Irma M Schurman.
Licensure Skilled care; Intermediate care. *Beds* 101. *Certified* Medicaid; Medicare.

Crescent Farm Nursing & Convalescent Home
PO Box 635, Artis Dr, Dover, DE 19903
(302) 734-5953
Admin John P Kelly.
Licensure Intermediate care. *Beds* ICF 80. *Certified* Medicaid.

Palmer Home Inc
PO Box 1751, 115 American Ave, Dover, DE 19901-1751
(302) 734-5591
Admin Iva Arnold.
Licensure Residential care. *Beds* 4.

Silver Lake Nursing & Rehabilitation Center
1080 Silver Lake Blvd, Dover, DE 19901
(302) 734-5990
Admin John A Shuford.
Licensure Skilled care; Intermediate care. *Beds* SNF 60; ICF 60.
Owner Proprietary corp (Genesis Health Ventures).

Walker Road Group Home
1180 Walker Rd, Dover, DE 19806
(302) 734-1648
Admin Rebecca Cassedy.
Licensure Intermediate care for mentally retarded. *Beds* ICF/MR 8.

Westminster Village Health Center
1175 McKee Rd, Dover, DE 19901
(302) 674-8030
Admin Jeffrey Shireman. *Dir of Nursing* Cheryl Perry-Noble.
Licensure Skilled care. *Beds* SNF 99. *Certified* Medicaid; Medicare.
Owner Nonprofit corp (Presbyterian Homes Inc).
Affiliation Presbyterian.
Facilities Dining room; Physical therapy room; Activities room; Chapel; Barber/Beauty shop.
Activities Arts & crafts; Cards; Games; Reading groups; Prayer groups; Movies; Shopping trips; Dances/Social/Cultural gatherings; Intergenerational programs; Pet therapy.

Felton

Felton Convalescent Home
Church & High St, Felton, DE 19943
(302) 284-4667

Admin Floyd Dickey. *Dir of Nursing* Lillian C Dodd LPN.
Licensure Intermediate care. *Beds* ICF 12.
Owner Privately owned.
Admissions Requirements Medical examination.
Staff Physicians 1 (ft); RNs 1 (ft); LPNs 2 (ft); Nurses' aides 6 (ft); Pharmacist 1 (ft).
Facilities Dining room; Activities room; Laundry room.
Activities Prayer groups; TV.

Golden Years Manor
Church & Sewell Sts, Felton, DE 19943
(302) 284-4510, 284-3510
Admin Rosemary Sluter. *Dir of Nursing* Arlieen Gloscoch. *Medical Dir* F B Lane Haines MD.
Licensure Intermediate care; Retirement; Alzheimer's care. *Beds* ICF 12. *Certified* Medicaid.
Owner Privately owned.
Staff Physicians 1 (pt); RNs 1 (ft); LPNs 2 (pt); Nurses' aides 16 (ft), 4 (pt); Activities coordinators 1 (pt); Dietitians 1 (pt).
Facilities Dining room; Activities room; Laundry room; Barber/Beauty shop.
Activities Arts & crafts; Games; Reading groups; Prayer groups.

Georgetown

Harrison House of Georgetown
110 W North St, Georgetown, DE 19948
(302) 856-4574
Admin Doris Walls. *Dir of Nursing* Carolyn Hoffacker RN. *Medical Dir* Fred T Kahn MD.
Licensure Skilled care; Intermediate care. *Beds* 101. *Certified* Medicaid; Medicare.
Owner Proprietary corp.
Admissions Requirements Medical examination.
Staff Physicians 1 (pt); Physical therapists 2 (pt); Activities coordinators 1 (ft); Dietitians 1 (pt).
Facilities Dining room; Physical therapy room; Activities room; Laundry room; Barber/Beauty shop.
Activities Arts & crafts; Cards; Games; Reading groups; Movies; Dances/Social/Cultural gatherings.

Stockley Center
Rte 1 Box 1000, Georgetown, DE 19947
(302) 934-8031
Admin Steven Schumacher.
Licensure Intermediate care for mentally retarded. *Beds* ICF/MR 380.

Greenville

Stonegates
4031 Kennett Pike, Greenville, DE 19807
(302) 658-6200
Admin Irene Owens.
Licensure Skilled care. *Beds* SNF 39.

Greenwood

Country Rest Home
Rte 2 Box 25, Greenwood, DE 19950
(302) 349-4114
Admin Mark Yoder. *Dir of Nursing* Laura
Lennefass.
Licensure Intermediate care; Retirement. *Beds*
ICF 32; Retirement 3. *Private Pay Patients*
100%.
Owner Proprietary corp.
Staff Physicians 1 (pt); RNs 3 (pt); LPNs 2
(ft), 3 (pt); Nurses' aides 10 (ft), 15 (pt);
Physical therapists 1 (pt); Activities
coordinators 1 (pt); Dietitians 1 (pt).
Affiliation Mennonite.
Facilities Dining room; Crafts room.
Activities Arts & crafts; Games; Reading
groups; Movies; Shopping trips.

Mast Boarding Home
Rte 1 Box 201, Greenwood, DE 19950
(302) 349-4179
Admin Sally Mast.
Licensure Residential care. *Beds* 4.

Harrington

Haven Hill Residential Home
Rte 2 Box 215, Harrington, DE 19952
(302) 398-8854
Admin Mrs Norman Rust.
Licensure Residential care. *Beds* 6.

Hockessin

Cokesbury Village
Lancaster Pike & Loveville Rd, Hockessin, DE
19707
(302) 289-8371
Admin Dianne Moran. *Dir of Nursing* June
Valentine RN. *Medical Dir* William L Jaffee
MD.
Licensure Skilled care; Residential care. *Beds*
SNF 80; Residential 36. *Certified* Medicare.
Owner Nonprofit corp (PA United Meth
Homes).
Admissions Requirements Minimum age 60;
Medical examination.
Staff Physicians 2 (pt); RNs 7 (ft), 21 (pt);
LPNs 3 (ft), 4 (pt); Nurses' aides 32 (ft), 15
(pt); Physical therapists 2 (pt); Reality
therapists 3 (pt); Occupational therapists 1
(pt); Speech therapists 1 (pt); Activities
coordinators 1 (ft); Podiatrists 2 (pt).
Affiliation Methodist.
Facilities Dining room; Physical therapy
room; Activities room; Chapel; Crafts room;
Laundry room; Barber/Beauty shop; Library;
Store; Woodshop.
Activities Arts & crafts; Cards; Games;
Reading groups; Prayer groups; Movies;
Shopping trips; Dances/Social/Cultural
gatherings.

Episcopal Church Home
Rte 3 Box 233, Hockessin, DE 19707
(302) 998-0181
Admin Davie Anna Alleman.
Medical Dir Tae Sup Song.
Licensure Skilled care; Intermediate care. *Beds*
SNF 135; ICF 38. *Certified* Medicaid;
Medicare.
Admissions Requirements Minimum age 14;
Medical examination; Physician's request.
Staff RNs 8 (ft), 7 (pt); LPNs 8 (ft), 8 (pt);
Nurses' aides 35 (ft), 45 (pt); Physical
therapists 1 (pt); Activities coordinators 1
(ft); Dietitians 1 (pt).
Affiliation Episcopal.
Facilities Dining room; Physical therapy
room; Activities room; Chapel; Crafts room;
Laundry room; Barber/Beauty shop; Library.
Activities Arts & crafts; Cards; Games;
Reading groups; Prayer groups; Movies;
Shopping trips.

Lewes

Harbor Healthcare & Rehabilitation Center Inc
301 Oceanview Blvd, Lewes, DE 19958
(302) 645-4664
Admin Christine Evans.
Licensure Skilled care; Intermediate care. *Beds*
119.

Lewes Convalescent Center
440 Market St, Lewes, DE 19958
(302) 645-6606
Admin Irene Witoski. *Dir of Nursing* Rose
Bussard RN. *Medical Dir* David Birch DO.
Licensure Skilled care; Intermediate care. *Beds*
SNF 50; ICF 40. *Private Pay Patients* 30%.
Certified Medicaid; Medicare.
Owner Proprietary corp (Forum Group).
Admissions Requirements Medical
examination.
Staff RNs; LPNs; Nurses' aides; Physical
therapists; Recreational therapists; Speech
therapists; Activities coordinators; Dietitians.
Facilities Dining room; Physical therapy
room; Activities room; Laundry room;
Barber/Beauty shop; Library.
Activities Arts & crafts; Cards; Games; Prayer
groups; Movies; Shopping trips;
Intergenerational programs; Pet therapy.

Sea Spray Group Home
51 Ebbtide Dr, Sea Spray Village, Lewes, DE
19958
(302) 645-0417
Admin Michael Paoli.
Licensure Intermediate care for mentally
retarded. *Beds* ICF/MR 8.

Milford

Delaware Care Center
Rte 1 Box 119, Rehoboth Hwy, Milford, DE
19963
(302) 422-4351
Admin Floyd Dickey.
Licensure Intermediate care. *Beds* ICF 14.
Certified Medicare.

Delaware Care Center
PO Box 119, Rte 1, Milford, DE 19963
(302) 422-4351
Admin Mario Schreiber. *Dir of Nursing* Lois
Cooper RN. *Medical Dir* Dr W F Chen.
Licensure Intermediate care. *Beds* ICF 14.
Owner Privately owned.
Staff Physicians 1 (pt); RNs 1 (ft); Nurses'
aides 3 (ft), 3 (pt); Dietitians 1 (ft).
Facilities Dining room.
Activities Cards; Reading groups.

Milford Manor
700 Marvel Rd, Milford, DE 19963
(302) 422-3303
Admin Tracy Jarman.
Medical Dir Harvey Mast MD.
Licensure Skilled care; Intermediate care;
Residential care. *Beds* SNF 50; ICF 62;
Residential 14. *Certified* Medicaid;
Medicare.
Owner Proprietary corp (Forum Grp).
Admissions Requirements Minimum age 50;
Medical examination.
Staff RNs 2 (ft), 4 (pt); LPNs 8 (ft), 4 (pt);
Nurses' aides 24 (ft), 28 (pt); Physical
therapists 1 (pt); Activities coordinators 1
(ft), 1 (pt); Dietitians 1 (pt).
Facilities Dining room; Physical therapy
room; Activities room; Crafts room; Laundry
room; Barber/Beauty shop.
Activities Arts & crafts; Cards; Games;
Reading groups; Prayer groups; Movies;
Shopping trips; Dances/Social/Cultural
gatherings.

Millsboro

Millsboro Nursing Home
PO Box 909, 231 S Washington St, Millsboro,
DE 19966
(302) 934-7300, 934-9399 FAX
Admin Jeannine C Aydelotte. *Dir of Nursing*
Nora J Murray RN. *Medical Dir* Dr William
Zeit.
Licensure Skilled care; Intermediate care. *Beds*
SNF 51; ICF 88. *Private Pay Patients* 54%.
Certified Medicaid; Medicare.
Owner Proprietary corp.
Admissions Requirements Minimum age 14;
Medical examination.
Staff Physicians 3 (pt); RNs 5 (ft), 4 (pt);
LPNs 7 (ft), 4 (pt); Nurses' aides 29 (ft), 25
(pt); Physical therapists 1 (pt); Occupational
therapists 1 (pt); Speech therapists 1 (pt);
Activities coordinators 1 (ft), 2 (pt);
Dietitians 1 (pt); Podiatrists 1 (pt);
Audiologists 1 (pt).
Facilities Dining room; Physical therapy
room; Activities room; Crafts room; Barber/
Beauty shop.
Activities Arts & crafts; Games; Reading
groups; Movies; Dances/Social/Cultural
gatherings; Intergenerational programs; Pet
therapy.

Newark

Churchmans Village Inc
4949 Ogletown-Stanton Rd, Newark, DE
19713
(302) 998-6900
Admin Vivian Heinbaugh. *Dir of Nursing*
Naomi Pinkerton. *Medical Dir* Dr E C
Hewlett.
Licensure Skilled care; Intermediate care;
Retirement; Alzheimer's care. *Beds* SNF 50;
ICF 49. *Certified* Medicaid; Medicare.
Owner Proprietary corp (Beverly Enterprises).
Admissions Requirements Medical
examination.
Staff Physicians; RNs; LPNs; Nurses' aides;
Physical therapists; Recreational therapists;
Occupational therapists; Speech therapists;
Activities coordinators; Dietitians;
Ophthalmologists; Podiatrists; Dentists.
Facilities Dining room; Physical therapy
room; Activities room; Chapel; Crafts room;
Laundry room; Barber/Beauty shop.
Activities Arts & crafts; Cards; Games;
Reading groups; Prayer groups; Movies;
Shopping trips; Dances/Social/Cultural
gatherings.

Forest Lane Group Home
154 Forest Lane, Newark, DE 19711
(302) 453-9727
Admin Robin Vaughan.
Licensure Intermediate care for mentally
retarded. *Beds* ICF/MR 8.

Millcroft
255 Possum Park Rd, Newark, DE 19711
(302) 366-0160
Admin Richard L Weimann. *Dir of Nursing*
Martha Galbo. *Medical Dir* Dr Thomas
Maxwell.
Licensure Skilled care; Intermediate care;
Retirement. *Beds* SNF 52; ICF 47. *Certified*
Medicaid; Medicare.
Owner Proprietary corp (Forum Group).
Staff RNs; LPNs; Nurses' aides; Physical
therapists; Activities coordinators; Dietitians.
Facilities Dining room; Physical therapy
room; Activities room; Crafts room; Laundry
room; Barber/Beauty shop; Library; Living-
dayroom; Porches; Courtyards.
Activities Arts & crafts; Cards; Games;
Reading groups; Prayer groups; Movies;
Shopping trips; Dances/Social/Cultural
gatherings.

Newark Manor Nursing Home
254 W Main St, Newark, DE 19711
(302) 731-5576
Admin Bruce E Boyer. *Dir of Nursing* Martha
Galbo. *Medical Dir* Allen Warrenton.
Licensure Intermediate care. *Beds* ICF 65.
Private Pay Patients 100%.
Owner Proprietary corp.
Staff Physicians 1 (pt); RNs 2 (ft), 6 (pt);
LPNs 2 (ft), 4 (pt); Physical therapists 1 (pt);
Reality therapists 1 (pt); Recreational
therapists 1 (ft); Occupational therapists 1
(pt); Speech therapists 1 (pt); Activities
coordinators 1 (ft); Dietitians 1 (pt).
Facilities Dining room; Activities room;
Crafts room; Laundry room; Barber/Beauty
shop; Library.
Activities Arts & crafts; Cards; Games;
Reading groups; Prayer groups; Movies;
Shopping trips; Dances/Social/Cultural
gatherings; Intergenerational programs; Pet
therapy.

Saint Georges

Chesapeake Group Home
Box 245, 378 County Rd, Saint Georges, DE
19733
(302) 834-3365
Admin Rebecca Cassedy.
Licensure Intermediate care for mentally
retarded. *Beds* ICF/MR 8.

Seaford

Methodist Manor House
1001 Middleford Rd, Seaford, DE 19973
(302) 629-4593
Admin John A Schuford.
Licensure Skilled care. *Beds* SNF 78. *Certified*
Medicaid; Medicare.
Owner Nonprofit corp (PA United Meth
Homes).
Affiliation Methodist.

Seaford Retirement & Rehabilitation Center
1100 Norman Eskridge Hwy, Seaford, DE
19973
(302) 629-3575
Admin Dennis K Chappell.
Licensure Skilled care; Intermediate care;
Retirement living. *Beds* SNF 66; ICF 58;
Retirement living 23. *Private Pay Patients*
35%. *Certified* Medicaid; Medicare.
Owner Proprietary corp (Forum Group).
Admissions Requirements Medical
examination; Physician's request.
Staff RNs 2 (ft), 6 (pt); LPNs 5 (ft), 10 (pt);
Nurses' aides 29 (ft), 27 (pt); Physical
therapists 1 (pt); Occupational therapists 1
(pt); Speech therapists 1 (pt); Activities
coordinators 1 (ft); Dietitians 1 (pt);
Ophthalmologists 1 (pt); Podiatrists 1 (pt);
Dentists 1 (pt).
Facilities Dining room; Physical therapy
room; Activities room; Barber/Beauty shop;
Library.
Activities Arts & crafts; Cards; Games; Prayer
groups; Shopping trips; Pet therapy.

Smyrna

Delaware Hospital for the Chronically Ill
Sunnyside Rd, Smyrna, DE 19977
(302) 653-8556, 653-0506 FAX
Admin Arnold E Morris. *Dir of Nursing*
Barbara Blades. *Medical Dir* Mark Van
Kooy.
Licensure Skilled care; Intermediate care. *Beds*
SNF 59; ICF 460. *Private Pay Patients* 20%.
Certified Medicaid.
Owner Publicly owned.
Admissions Requirements Medical
examination.

Staff Physicians 4 (ft); RNs 56 (ft), 13 (pt);
LPNs 20 (ft), 3 (pt); Physical therapists 1
(ft), 1 (pt); Speech therapists 1 (pt);
Activities coordinators 1 (ft); Dietitians 1
(ft), 1 (pt); Attendants 288 (ft), 21 (pt).
Facilities Physical therapy room; Activities
room; Chapel; Crafts room; Barber/Beauty
shop; Library; Young adult unit.
Activities Arts & crafts; Cards; Games;
Reading groups; Prayer groups; Movies;
Shopping trips; Dances/Social/Cultural
gatherings; Pet therapy; Discussion groups.

Haven Manor
Box 239A, Walker School Rd, Smyrna, DE
19977
(302) 834-4811
Admin Leonard R Edge CMRP.
Licensure Intermediate care for mentally
retarded. *Beds* ICF/MR 8.

Kent Convalescent Center
1455 S DuPont Hwy, Smyrna, DE 19977
(302) 653-5085
Admin E Ray Quillen. *Dir of Nursing* Diane
Townsend RN. *Medical Dir* William Rogers
MD.
Licensure Skilled care; Intermediate care;
Retirement. *Beds* SNF 36; ICF 118.
Certified Medicaid; Medicare.
Owner Proprietary corp (Forum Grp).
Admissions Requirements Medical
examination; Physician's request.
Staff Physicians 1 (pt); RNs 2 (ft), 8 (pt);
LPNs 7 (ft), 16 (pt); Nurses' aides 35 (ft), 20
(pt); Activities coordinators 2 (ft), 1 (pt);
Dietitians 1 (pt).
Facilities Dining room; Physical therapy
room; Activities room; Crafts room; Laundry
room; Barber/Beauty shop.
Activities Arts & crafts; Cards; Games;
Reading groups; Prayer groups; Movies;
Shopping trips; Dances/Social/Cultural
gatherings; Ceramics; Gardening.

Scott Nursing Home
Main & Mount Vernon St, Smyrna, DE 19977
(302) 653-8554
Admin Maryjane Copes. *Dir of Nursing* Ann
Ackles. *Medical Dir* Dr Ciriaco G Bongalos
Jr.
Licensure Intermediate care. *Beds* ICF 33.
Private Pay Patients 80%. *Certified*
Medicaid.
Owner Privately owned.
Staff Physicians; RNs; LPNs; Nurses' aides;
Activities coordinators; Dietitians;
Ophthalmologists; Podiatrists.
Facilities Dining room; Activities room;
Chapel; Crafts room; Laundry room; Barber/
Beauty shop.
Activities Arts & crafts; Cards; Games;
Reading groups; Prayer groups; Movies; Pet
therapy.

Wilmington

Emily P Bissell Hospital
3000 Newport Gap Pike, Wilmington, DE
19808
(302) 995-8434
Admin Cheryl Moore.
Licensure Skilled care; Intermediate care;
Intermingled SNF/ICF. *Beds* SNF 41; ICF
113; Intermingled SNF/ICF 46.

Brandywine Convalescent Home
505 Greenbank Rd, Wilmington, DE 19808
(302) 998-0101
Admin Thomas F Weymouth.
Medical Dir James Harkness DO.
Licensure Skilled care; Intermediate care. *Beds*
106. *Certified* Medicaid; Medicare.
Staff Physicians 1 (ft); RNs 1 (ft), 11 (pt);
LPNs 3 (ft), 3 (pt); Nurses' aides 17 (ft), 22
(pt); Physical therapists 1 (ft); Speech

therapists 1 (ft); Activities coordinators 1
(ft); Dietitians 1 (ft); Podiatrists 1 (ft);
Dentists 1 (ft); Technicians 2 (ft), 4 (pt).
Facilities Dining room; Physical therapy
room; Activities room; Crafts room; Laundry
room; Barber/Beauty shop; Library.
Activities Arts & crafts; Cards; Games;
Reading groups; Prayer groups; Movies;
Dances/Social/Cultural gatherings.

Mary Campbell Center
4641 Weldin Rd, Wilmington, DE 19803
(302) 762-6025
Admin Jerrold P Spilecki MSEd. *Dir of
Nursing* Susan K France RN. *Medical Dir*
Edward J McConnell MD.
Licensure Intermediate care; Intermediate care
for mentally retarded. *Beds* ICF 9; ICF/MR
44. *Private Pay Patients* 15%. *Certified*
Medicaid.
Owner Nonprofit corp.
Staff Physicians 1 (pt); RNs 4 (ft), 3 (pt);
LPNs 1 (ft), 3 (pt); Nurses' aides 14 (ft), 9
(pt); Physical therapists 3 (pt); Recreational
therapists 1 (ft); Occupational therapists 1
(pt); Speech therapists 2 (pt); Activities
coordinators 1 (ft); Dietitians 1 (pt).
Languages Sign.
Facilities Dining room; Physical therapy
room; Activities room; Crafts room; Laundry
room; Barber/Beauty shop.
Activities Arts & crafts; Cards; Games;
Reading groups; Prayer groups; Movies;
Shopping trips; Dances/Social/Cultural
gatherings; Intergenerational programs; Pet
therapy; Horticulture; Woodworking.

Carvel Building—Delaware State Hospital
1901 N DuPont Hwy, Wilmington, DE 19720
(302) 421-6441
Admin Nash N Keel.
Licensure Intermediate care; IMD;
Alzheimer's care. *Beds* ICF 58; IMD 28.
Private Pay Patients 0%. *Certified* Medicaid.
Owner Publicly owned.
Admissions Requirements Minimum age 18.
Staff Physicians 4 (ft); RNs 12 (ft); LPNs 18
(ft); Nurses' aides 24 (ft); Physical therapists
1 (ft); Recreational therapists 2 (ft);
Occupational therapists 1 (ft); Activities
coordinators 1 (ft); Dietitians 2 (ft).
Facilities Dining room; Physical therapy
room; Activities room; Crafts room; Laundry
room; Barber/Beauty shop; Library.
Activities Arts & crafts; Cards; Games;
Reading groups; Prayer groups; Movies; Pet
therapy.

Chariot Nursing & Convalescent Home
2735 W 6th St, Wilmington, DE 19807
(302) 654-7616
Admin Paul A Paradise Jr.
Licensure Intermediate care. *Beds* 30.
Certified Medicaid.

Delaware Elwyn Hockessin
4223 Newport Gap Pike, Wilmington, DE
19707
(302) 239-3651
Admin Peter Dakunchak.
Licensure Intermediate care for mentally
retarded. *Beds* ICF/MR 7.

Forwood Manor
1912 Marsh Rd, Wilmington, DE 19810
(302) 529-1600, 529-1689 FAX
Admin Sharon D Ragsdale LNHA. *Dir of
Nursing* Agnes C Ross RN. *Medical Dir*
Roger Rodrigue MD.
Licensure Skilled care; Intermediate care;
Residential care. *Beds* Swing beds SNF/ICF
60; Residential care 30. *Private Pay Patients*
98%. *Certified* Medicare.
Owner Proprietary corp (Forum Group).
Admissions Requirements Minimum age 15;
Medical examination; Physician's request.

Staff RNs 12 (pt); LPNs 3 (ft), 9 (pt); Nurses' aides 19 (ft), 5 (pt); Physical therapists 1 (ft); Occupational therapists 1 (pt); Speech therapists (contracted); Activities coordinators 2 (pt); Dietitians (contracted); Ophthalmologists (contracted); Podiatrists (contracted); Dentists (contracted).
Facilities Dining room; Physical therapy room; Activities room; Crafts room; Laundry room; Barber/Beauty shop; Library; Country store.
Activities Arts & crafts; Cards; Games; Reading groups; Prayer groups; Movies; Shopping trips; Dances/Social/Cultural gatherings; Intergenerational programs; Pet therapy.

Foulk Manor North
1212 Foulk Rd, Wilmington, DE 19803
(302) 478-4296
Admin Arthur J Stone. Dir of Nursing Jacqueline M Doherty. Medical Dir Lawrence Markman MD.
Licensure Skilled care; Retirement. Beds SNF 46. Certified Medicare.
Owner Proprietary corp (Forum Group Inc).
Admissions Requirements Minimum age 65; Medical examination; Physician's request.
Staff Physicians 1 (pt); RNs 2 (ft), 8 (pt); LPNs 3 (ft), 2 (pt); Nurses' aides 12 (ft), 3 (pt); Physical therapists 1 (pt); Occupational therapists 1 (pt); Speech therapists 1 (pt); Activities coordinators 1 (ft), 2 (pt); Dietitians 1 (pt); Ophthalmologists 1 (pt); Podiatrists 1 (pt); Audiologists 1 (pt).
Facilities Dining room; Physical therapy room; Activities room; Crafts room; Laundry room; Barber/Beauty shop; Library.
Activities Arts & crafts; Cards; Games; Reading groups; Prayer groups; Movies; Dances/Social/Cultural gatherings; Pet therapy.

Foulk Manor South
407 Foulk Rd, Wilmington, DE 19803
(302) 655-6249
Admin Janet Neville.
Medical Dir Linda Davis.
Licensure Skilled care; Intermediate care; Residential. Beds SNF 25; ICF 17; Residential 65.
Owner Proprietary corp (Forum Grp).
Admissions Requirements Minimum age 18; Medical examination.
Staff RNs 4 (ft), 5 (pt); LPNs 2 (ft), 1 (pt); Nurses' aides 40 (ft), 10 (pt); Physical therapists 1 (pt); Speech therapists 1 (pt); Activities coordinators 1 (ft), 1 (pt); Dietitians 1 (pt); Ophthalmologists 1 (pt).
Facilities Dining room; Physical therapy room; Laundry room; Barber/Beauty shop; Living room.
Activities Cards; Games; Reading groups; Prayer groups; Movies; Shopping trips; Dances/Social/Cultural gatherings; Paid entertainment.

Gibbs Boarding Home
177 Bunche Blvd, Wilmington, DE 19801
(302) 658-4739
Admin Mary Gibbs.
Licensure Residential care. Beds 5.

Hillside House
810 S Broom St, Wilmington, DE 19805
(302) 652-1181
Admin Dolores Williams.
Medical Dir D W MacKelcan MD.
Licensure Skilled care; Intermediate care. Beds SNF 34; ICF 72. Certified Medicaid; Medicare.
Owner Proprietary corp (Forum Grp).
Admissions Requirements Medical examination.

Staff Physicians 1 (pt); RNs 4 (ft), 6 (pt); LPNs 6 (ft), 7 (pt); Nurses' aides 30 (ft), 17 (pt); Physical therapists 1 (pt); Occupational therapists; Speech therapists; Activities coordinators 1 (ft), 1 (pt); Dietitians.
Facilities Dining room; Physical therapy room; Activities room; Barber/Beauty shop.
Activities Arts & crafts; Games; Shopping trips; Dances/Social/Cultural gatherings; Sight-seeing trips.

Home for Aged Women—Minquadale
1109 Gilpin Ave, Wilmington, DE 19806
(302) 655-6411
Admin Linda Schwind.
Medical Dir Frederick A Bowdle MD.
Licensure Intermediate care; Residential care. Beds ICF 41; Residential 4. Certified Medicaid.
Admissions Requirements Minimum age 65; Medical examination.
Staff Physicians 1 (pt); RNs 2 (ft), 1 (pt); LPNs 3 (ft), 1 (pt); Nurses' aides 10 (ft), 3 (pt); Physical therapists 1 (pt); Activities coordinators 1 (ft), 2 (pt); Dietitians 1 (pt).
Facilities Dining room; Physical therapy room; Activities room; Crafts room; Laundry room; Barber/Beauty shop; Library.
Activities Arts & crafts; Cards; Games; Reading groups; Prayer groups; Movies; Shopping trips.

Kentmere
1700 Lovering Ave, Wilmington, DE 19806
(302) 652-3311
Admin Frieda E Enss.
Medical Dir Stephen Bartoshesky.
Licensure Skilled care; Intermediate care. Beds SNF 49; ICF 57. Certified Medicaid; Medicare.
Owner Nonprofit organization/foundation.
Admissions Requirements Minimum age 18; Medical examination.
Staff RNs; LPNs; Nurses' aides; Physical therapists 1 (pt); Activities coordinators 1 (ft), 2 (pt); Dietitians 1 (pt); Ophthalmologists 1 (pt); Podiatrists 1 (pt).
Facilities Dining room; Physical therapy room; Activities room; Chapel; Crafts room; Laundry room; Barber/Beauty shop; Gift shop; Volunteer office.
Activities Arts & crafts; Cards; Games; Reading groups; Prayer groups; Movies; Shopping trips; Dances/Social/Cultural gatherings; Poetry group; Current events club; Garden club; Armchair travel club; Residents council.

Milton & Hattie Kutz Home
704 River Rd, Wilmington, DE 19809
(302) 764-7000
Admin Daniel G Thurman. Dir of Nursing Doris Redmond RN. Medical Dir M Javed Gilani MD.
Licensure Skilled care; Intermediate care; Alzheimer's care. Beds Swing beds SNF/ICF 82. Private Pay Patients 30%. Certified Medicaid.
Owner Nonprofit corp.
Admissions Requirements Minimum age 65; Medical examination.
Staff Physicians; RNs; LPNs; Nurses' aides; Physical therapists; Reality therapists; Recreational therapists; Occupational therapists; Speech therapists; Activities coordinators; Dietitians; Podiatrists.
Affiliation Jewish.
Facilities Dining room; Physical therapy room; Activities room; Chapel; Crafts room; Barber/Beauty shop; Library.
Activities Arts & crafts; Cards; Games; Reading groups; Movies; Shopping trips; Dances/Social/Cultural gatherings; Intergenerational programs; Pet therapy.

Layton Home
300 E 8th St, Wilmington, DE 19801
(302) 656-6413

Admin James B Manley Jr, Exec Dir. Dir of Nursing Clara E Hollis RN. Medical Dir James A Thomas MD.
Licensure Skilled care; Intermediate care. Beds SNF 36; ICF 72. Private Pay Patients 2%. Certified Medicaid; Medicare.
Owner Nonprofit corp.
Admissions Requirements Medical examination; Physician's request.
Staff Physicians 2 (pt); RNs 1 (ft), 7 (pt); LPNs 8 (ft), 5 (pt); Nurses' aides 27 (ft), 2 (pt); Physical therapists 1 (pt); Recreational therapists 1 (pt); Occupational therapists 1 (pt); Speech therapists 1 (pt); Activities coordinators 1 (pt); Dietitians 1 (pt); Podiatrists 1 (pt).
Facilities Dining room; Physical therapy room; Activities room; Chapel; Crafts room; Laundry room; Barber/Beauty shop; Library.
Activities Arts & crafts; Cards; Games; Prayer groups; Movies; Shopping trips; Dances/ Social/Cultural gatherings; Intergenerational programs; Workshops; Private therapy & reality sessions for residents, family and staff; Volunteer program.

Leader Nursing & Rehabilitation—Pike Creek
5651 Limestone Rd, Wilmington, DE 19808
(302) 239-8583, 239-9250 FAX
Admin Shirley A Ressler. Dir of Nursing Myra Brown. Medical Dir David Scheid.
Licensure Skilled care; Intermediate care; Alzheimer's care. Beds SNF 70; ICF 34; Alzheimer's care 34. Private Pay Patients 75%. Certified Medicaid; Medicare.
Owner Proprietary corp (Manor Care).
Admissions Requirements Medical examination.
Staff Physicians 10 (pt); RNs 6 (ft), 8 (pt); LPNs 6 (ft), 6 (pt); Nurses' aides 21 (ft), 13 (pt); Physical therapists 1 (ft); Occupational therapists 1 (ft); Speech therapists 1 (ft); Activities coordinators 2 (ft), 2 (pt); Dietitians 1 (ft); Ophthalmologists 1 (ft); Podiatrists 1 (ft).
Facilities Dining room; Physical therapy room; Activities room; Crafts room; Barber/ Beauty shop.
Activities Arts & crafts; Games; Reading groups; Prayer groups; Movies; Dances/ Social/Cultural gatherings; Pet therapy.

Leader Nursing & Rehabilitation Center
700 Foulk Rd, Wilmington, DE 19803
(302) 764-0181
Admin Mary M Korcz.
Licensure Skilled care. Beds SNF 128.

Masonic Home
4800 Lancaster Pike, Wilmington, DE 19807
(302) 994-4434
Admin Claude Husted.
Medical Dir Dr LeRoy Kimble.
Licensure Intermediate care; Residential care. Beds ICF 26; Residential care 60.
Admissions Requirements Medical examination.
Staff Physicians 2 (pt); RNs 3 (ft), 2 (pt); LPNs 2 (ft); Nurses' aides 17 (ft); Dietitians 1 (pt).
Affiliation Masons.
Facilities Dining room; Activities room; Chapel; Crafts room; Laundry room; Barber/ Beauty shop; Library; Smoking lounge; TV room.
Activities Arts & crafts; Movies; Shopping trips; Dances/Social/Cultural gatherings.

Methodist Country House
4830 Kennett Pike, Wilmington, DE 19807
(302) 654-5101
Admin Leona Brown.
Licensure Skilled care; Intermediate care. Beds SNF 67; ICF 5. Certified Medicare.
Owner Nonprofit corp (PA United Meth Homes).
Affiliation Methodist.

Millcreek Group Home
2945 Newport Gap Pike, Wilmington, DE 19808
(302) 999-1375
Admin Robin Vaughan.
Licensure Intermediate care for mentally retarded. *Beds* ICF/MR 8.

Parkview Convalescent Center
2801 W 6th St, Wilmington, DE 19805
(302) 655-6135
Admin Christine Schaeffer.
Medical Dir L Kimble MD.
Licensure Skilled care; Intermediate care; Alzheimer's care. *Beds* SNF 150. *Certified* Medicaid; Medicare.
Owner Privately owned.
Facilities Dining room; Physical therapy room; Activities room; Chapel; Crafts room; Laundry room; Barber/Beauty shop; Library.
Activities Arts & crafts; Cards; Games; Reading groups; Prayer groups; Movies; Shopping trips; Dances/Social/Cultural gatherings.

Shipley Manor Health Center
2723 Shipley Rd, Wilmington, DE 19810
(302) 479-0111
Admin Katherine H Jameson. *Dir of Nursing* Virginia Marzoula RN.
Licensure Skilled care; Intermediate care; Retirement. *Beds* 80. *Certified* Medicaid; Medicare.
Owner Proprietary corp (Forum Group).
Admissions Requirements Medical examination.
Staff Physicians 22 (pt); RNs 5 (ft), 3 (pt); LPNs 5 (ft), 5 (pt); Nurses' aides 18 (ft), 12 (pt); Activities coordinators 1 (ft), 2 (pt); Dietitians 1 (pt); Ophthalmologists 1 (pt); Podiatrists 1 (pt).
Facilities Dining room; Physical therapy room; Activities room; Crafts room; Laundry room; Barber/Beauty shop; Outside patio; TV with VCR.
Activities Arts & crafts; Cards; Games; Reading groups; Prayer groups; Movies; Shopping trips; Dances/Social/Cultural gatherings; Picnics; Trips to park; Longwood gardens; Live musical entertainment.

Tilton Terrace
801 N Broom St, Wilmington, DE 19806
(302) 652-3861
Admin Ruth G Murphy; James F Moran Exec Dir. *Dir of Nursing* Rita L Archangelo. *Medical Dir* Marvin H Dorph MD.
Licensure Skilled care; Intermediate care. *Beds* Swing beds SNF/ICF 100. *Private Pay Patients* 80%. *Certified* Medicaid; Medicare.

Owner Proprietary corp.
Admissions Requirements Minimum age 18.
Staff Physicians 1 (ft), 1 (pt); RNs 7 (ft), 10 (pt); LPNs 4 (ft), 3 (pt); Nurses' aides 32 (ft), 16 (pt); Physical therapists 1 (pt); Reality therapists (consultant); Recreational therapists 1 (pt); Occupational therapists (consultant); Speech therapists (consultant); Activities coordinators 2 (ft), 1 (pt); Dietitians (consultant); Ophthalmologists (consultant); Podiatrists (consultant); Audiologists (consultant); Chaplain 1 (ft); Other staff 20 (ft), 20 (pt).
Languages Spanish, Italian.
Facilities Dining room; Physical therapy room; Activities room; Chapel; Crafts room; Laundry room; Barber/Beauty shop; Library.
Activities Arts & crafts; Cards; Games; Reading groups; Prayer groups; Movies; Shopping trips; Dances/Social/Cultural gatherings; Intergenerational programs; Pet therapy; Ceramics; Gardening; Summer picnics; Religious services.

Windybush Group Home
5 Wollaston Rd, Wilmington, DE 19810
(302) 475-1009
Admin Robin Vaughan.
Licensure Intermediate care for mentally retarded. *Beds* ICF/MR 7.

DISTRICT OF COLUMBIA

Washington

Capitol Health Care Center Inc
900 3rd St NE, Washington, DC 20005
(202) 546-4513
Admin Barbara Savory.
Licensure Intermediate care. *Certified*
Medicaid.

DC Village Nursing Home
2 DC Village Ln SW, Washington, DC 20032
(202) 767-7740, 767-8909 FAX
Admin Terry B Thomas NHA. *Dir of Nursing*
Doris Dandridge. *Medical Dir* Dr Robert W
Yancey Jr.
Licensure Skilled care; Intermediate care. *Beds*
SNF 51; ICF 479. *Private Pay Patients* 1%.
Owner Publicly owned.
Admissions Requirements Medical
examination.
Staff Physicians 7 (ft), 5 (pt); RNs 31 (ft), 6
(pt); LPNs 23 (ft); Nurses' aides 204 (ft);
Physical therapists 3 (ft), 2 (pt); Recreational
therapists 8 (ft); Speech therapists 1 (ft);
Dietitians 7 (ft); Ophthalmologists 1 (pt);
Podiatrists 2 (pt).
Facilities Dining room; Physical therapy
room; Activities room; Chapel; Crafts room;
Laundry room; Barber/Beauty shop; Library.
Activities Arts & crafts; Cards; Games;
Reading groups; Prayer groups; Movies;
Shopping trips; Dances/Social/Cultural
gatherings; Pet therapy.

Grant Park Care Center
5000 Nannie Helen Burroughs Ave NE,
Washington, DC 20019
(202) 399-7504, 399-0430 FAX
Admin Barbara Ann Nash. *Dir of Nursing*
Gwendolyn Baker. *Medical Dir* Martina P
Callum.
Licensure Skilled care; Intermediate care. *Beds*
SNF 74; ICF 222. *Private Pay Patients* 1%.
Certified Medicaid; Medicare.
Owner Privately owned.
Admissions Requirements Minimum age 21;
Medical examination.
Staff Physicians 5 (pt); RNs 16 (ft); LPNs 40
(ft); Nurses' aides 117 (ft); Physical
therapists 1 (pt); Recreational therapists 3
(ft); Occupational therapists 1 (pt); Speech
therapists 1 (pt); Activities coordinators 1
(ft); Dietitians 1 (pt); Podiatrists 2 (pt);
Activity aides.
Languages Spanish.
Facilities Dining room; Physical therapy
room; Activities room; Crafts room; Laundry
room; Barber/Beauty shop.
Activities Arts & crafts; Cards; Games;
Reading groups; Prayer groups; Movies;
Shopping trips; Dances/Social/Cultural
gatherings; Intergenerational programs; Pet
therapy.

Health Care Institute
1380 Southern Ave SE, Washington, DC
20032
(202) 563-8100

Admin Craig Lakin. *Dir of Nursing* Sheila
Warren. *Medical Dir* Dr Yvonne Treakle.
Licensure Skilled care; Intermediate care. *Beds*
180. *Certified* Medicaid; Medicare.
Owner Nonprofit corp.
Staff RNs 16 (ft), 4 (pt); LPNs 16 (ft), 4 (pt);
Nurses' aides 60 (ft), 5 (pt); Physical
therapists 1 (ft); Recreational therapists 1
(ft); Activities coordinators 1 (ft); Dietitians
1 (pt).
Languages Spanish.
Facilities Dining room; Physical therapy
room; Activities room; Crafts room; Laundry
room; Barber/Beauty shop; Library.
Activities Arts & crafts; Cards; Games;
Reading groups; Prayer groups; Movies;
Shopping trips; Dances/Social/Cultural
gatherings; Pet therapy; Support groups;
Young residents stroke club; Discharge
group.

J B Johnson Nursing Center
901 1st St NW, Washington, DC 20001
(202) 289-7715
Admin Eugene Ziebrat.
Licensure Intermediate care. *Beds* 244.
Certified Medicaid.

Knollwood
6200 Oregon Ave NW, Washington, DC
20015
(202) 541-0150
Admin Tom Jenkins Jr. *Dir of Nursing* Kay
Kaye RN. *Medical Dir* Dr Joel Mulhauser.
Licensure Skilled care; Intermediate care;
Alzheimer's care; Retirement. *Beds* SNF 12;
ICF 36. *Private Pay Patients* 100%.
Owner Nonprofit corp.
Admissions Requirements Minimum age 62;
Medical examination.
Staff RNs 5 (ft), 2 (pt); LPNs 2 (ft), 2 (pt);
Nurses' aides 18 (ft), 15 (pt).
Facilities Dining room; Physical therapy
room; Activities room; Chapel; Laundry
room; Barber/Beauty shop; Library.
Activities Arts & crafts; Cards; Games;
Reading groups; Prayer groups; Movies;
Shopping trips; Dances/Social/Cultural
gatherings; Pet therapy.

Lisner-Louise Home
5425 Western Ave NW, Washington, DC
20015
(202) 966-6667
Admin Ward Orem.
Medical Dir James Brodsky MD.
Licensure Intermediate care; Community
residential facility; Retirement. *Beds* ICF 25;
Community residential facility 56. *Certified*
Medicaid.
Owner Nonprofit corp.
Admissions Requirements Medical
examination.
Staff RNs; LPNs; Nurses' aides; Physical
therapists; Reality therapists; Recreational
therapists; Activities coordinators; Dietitians.
Facilities Dining room; Activities room;
Crafts room; Laundry room; Barber/Beauty
shop; Library.

Activities Arts & crafts; Cards; Games;
Reading groups; Prayer groups; Movies;
Dances/Social/Cultural gatherings.

Little Sisters of the Poor
4200 Harewood Rd NE, Washington, DC
20017
(202) 269-1831
Admin Mother Regis.
Licensure Skilled care; Intermediate care. *Beds*
SNF 25; ICF 75.
Owner Nonprofit corp (Little Sisters of the
Poor).

Medlantic Manor at Lamond—Riggs
6000 New Hampshire Ave NE, Washington,
DC 20011
(202) 882-9300
Admin Lauren Rock. *Dir of Nursing* Cathy
Shine RN. *Medical Dir* Dr J Kelman.
Licensure Intermediate care. *Beds* ICF 63;
CRF 17. *Certified* Medicaid.
Owner Nonprofit corp.
Staff RNs 7 (ft), 2 (pt); LPNs 4 (ft), 2 (pt);
Nurses' aides 20 (ft), 6 (pt); Physical
therapists 5 (pt); Occupational therapists;
Speech therapists; Activities coordinators 1
(ft); Dietitians 1 (pt).
Affiliation Masons.

Methodist Home of DC
4901 Connecticut Ave NW, Washington, DC
20008
(202) 966-7623
Admin Elsie D Lesko.
Licensure Intermediate care. *Beds* 97.
Certified Medicaid.
Affiliation Methodist.

Presbyterian Home of DC
3050 Military Rd NW, Washington, DC
20015
(202) 363-8310, 363-0950 FAX
Admin Robert E Bell. *Dir of Nursing* Joy
Blackwood RN. *Medical Dir* Dr William E
Hurwitz.
Licensure Intermediate care; Residential care.
Beds ICF 46; Residential care 155. *Private
Pay Patients* 80%.
Owner Nonprofit organization/foundation.
Admissions Requirements Minimum age 65.
Staff RNs; LPNs; Nurses' aides; Physical
therapists (consultant); Recreational
therapists.
Affiliation Presbyterian.
Facilities Dining room; Physical therapy
room; Activities room; Chapel; Laundry
room; Barber/Beauty shop; Library.
Activities Arts & crafts; Cards; Games;
Reading groups; Prayer groups; Movies;
Shopping trips; Dances/Social/Cultural
gatherings; Intergenerational programs; Pet
therapy; Music; Trips; Lunch out.

Rock Creek Manor
2131 O St NW, Washington, DC 20037
(202) 785-2577

Admin Elizabeth Muchnick. *Dir of Nursing*
Maureen Gallager RN. *Medical Dir* Valery
Portnoi MD.
Licensure Intermediate care. *Beds* ICF 180.
Certified Medicaid.
Owner Proprietary corp.
Admissions Requirements Minimum age 18;
Medical examination.
Staff Physicians 1 (pt); RNs 10 (ft), 3 (pt);
LPNs 11 (ft), 2 (pt); Nurses' aides 58 (ft), 8
(pt); Recreational therapists 3 (ft);
Occupational therapists 1 (pt); Speech
therapists 1 (pt); Activities coordinators 1
(ft); Dietitians 1 (ft); Ophthalmologists 1
(pt); Social workers 2 (ft).
Facilities Dining room; Physical therapy
room; Activities room; Barber/Beauty shop.
Activities Arts & crafts; Cards; Games;
Reading groups; Prayer groups; Movies;
Dances/Social/Cultural gatherings; Picnics;
Exercise; Cooking.

Thomas House
1330 Massachusettes Ave NW, Washington,
DC 20005
(202) 628-2092
Admin David Zwald.
Medical Dir Dr Barbara Carroll.
Licensure Intermediate care. *Beds* 53.
Certified Medicaid.
Admissions Requirements Minimum age 62;
Medical examination.
Affiliation Baptist.
Facilities Dining room; Physical therapy
room; Activities room; Chapel; Crafts room;
Laundry room; Barber/Beauty shop; Library.
Activities Arts & crafts; Cards; Games;
Reading groups; Prayer groups; Movies;
Shopping trips; Dances/Social/Cultural
gatherings.

Washington Center for Aging Services
2601 18th St NE, Washington, DC 20018
(202) 269-1530
Admin Solanges Vivens. *Dir of Nursing* Elenor
Bonner Mullen RN. *Medical Dir* Vinod
Mody MD.
Licensure Skilled care; Intermediate care. *Beds*
SNF 37; ICF 225. *Certified* Medicaid;
Medicare.
Owner Publicly owned.
Admissions Requirements Minimum age 60;
Medical examination.
Staff RNs 18 (ft), 10 (pt); LPNs 32 (ft), 7 (pt);
Nurses' aides 119 (ft), 27 (pt); Recreational
therapists 5 (ft), 1 (pt).
Facilities Physical therapy room; Activities
room; Chapel; Barber/Beauty shop; Library.
Activities Arts & crafts; Cards; Games;
Reading groups; Prayer groups; Movies;
Shopping trips; Dances/Social/Cultural
gatherings; Resident council; Bingo; Music
therapy; Current events groups; Chorus.

Washington Home
3720 Upton St NW, Washington, DC 20016
(202) 966-3720
Admin Jared I Falek PhD. *Dir of Nursing*
Linda Pulley. *Medical Dir* Rebecca Elon.
Licensure Skilled care; Intermediate care;
Hospice/Respite; Alzheimer's care. *Beds*
SNF 15; ICF 165; Hospice/Respite 9.
Certified Medicaid; Medicare.
Owner Nonprofit corp.
Admissions Requirements Minimum age 16.
Staff Physicians; RNs; LPNs; Nurses' aides;
Physical therapists (contracted); Recreational
therapists; Occupational therapists
(contracted); Speech therapists (contracted);
Activities coordinators; Dietitians;
Ophthalmologists (contracted); Podiatrists
(contracted).

Facilities Dining room; Physical therapy
room; Activities room; Chapel; Crafts room;
Laundry room; Barber/Beauty shop; Library.
Activities Arts & crafts; Cards; Games;
Reading groups; Prayer groups; Movies;
Shopping trips; Dances/Social/Cultural
gatherings; Intergenerational programs; Pet
therapy.

Washington Nursing Facility
2425 25th St SE, Washington, DC 20020
(202) 889-3600
Admin Gail Jernigan.
Licensure Skilled care. *Certified* Medicaid;
Medicare.

Wisconsin Avenue Nursing Home
3333 Wisconsin Ave NW, Washington, DC
20016
(202) 362-5500, 244-7110 FAX
Admin Sybil J Hunter MS. *Dir of Nursing*
Hattie Courtney RN. *Medical Dir* Jerry
Earle MD.
Licensure Skilled care; Intermediate care. *Beds*
SNF 100; ICF 255. *Private Pay Patients*
15%. *Certified* Medicaid; Medicare.
Owner Proprietary corp (Beverly Enterprises).
Admissions Requirements Minimum age 60;
Physician's request.
Staff RNs 27 (ft), 3 (pt); LPNs 33 (ft), 4 (pt);
Nurses' aides 164 (ft), 16 (pt); Physical
therapists 1 (ft); Recreational therapists 2
(ft); Activities coordinators 3 (ft); Dietitians
2 (ft).
Facilities Dining room; Physical therapy
room; Activities room; Crafts room; Laundry
room; Barber/Beauty shop; Rehabilitation
department.
Activities Arts & crafts; Cards; Games;
Reading groups; Prayer groups; Movies;
Shopping trips; Dances/Social/Cultural
gatherings; Intergenerational programs; Pet
therapy.

FLORIDA

Altamonte Springs

Life Care Center of Altamonte Springs
989 Orienta Ave, Altamonte Springs, FL
32701
(407) 831-3446
Admin David Job. *Dir of Nursing* Mary
Naglee. *Medical Dir* Charles A Morgan MD.
Licensure Skilled care. *Beds* SNF 240.
Certified Medicaid; Medicare.
Owner Proprietary corp (Life Care Centers of
America).
Admissions Requirements Medical
examination; Physician's request.
Staff Physicians 1 (pt); RNs 12 (ft); LPNs 23
(ft); Nurses' aides 73 (ft); Physical therapists
3 (ft); Occupational therapists 1 (pt); Speech
therapists 1 (pt); Activities coordinators 1
(ft), 4 (pt).
Facilities Dining room; Physical therapy
room; Activities room; Crafts room; Laundry
room; Barber/Beauty shop; Library.
Activities Arts & crafts; Cards; Games;
Reading groups; Movies; Shopping trips;
Dances/Social/Cultural gatherings;
Intergenerational programs; Pet therapy.

Altoona

**Lakeview Terrace Christian Retirement
Community**
PO Drawer 100, 331 Raintree Dr, Altoona,
FL 32702
(904) 669-2133
Admin Linda Rowe. *Dir of Nursing* Karen
Atwell RN. *Medical Dir* Glenn E Miles MD.
Licensure Skilled care; Intermediate care;
Adult congregate living facility; Alzheimer's
care. *Beds* SNF 20; Adult congregate living
400. *Certified* Medicaid.
Owner Privately owned.
Admissions Requirements Minimum age 65;
Medical examination.
Staff Physicians 1 (pt); RNs 4 (ft); LPNs 8
(ft), 2 (pt); Nurses' aides 21 (ft), 4 (pt);
Physical therapists 1 (pt); Occupational
therapists 1 (pt); Speech therapists 1 (pt);
Activities coordinators 2 (ft); Dietitians 1
(pt).
Facilities Dining room; Physical therapy
room; Activities room; Chapel; Crafts room;
Laundry room; Barber/Beauty shop; Library;
Lawn bowling; Swimming; Pool;
Shuffleboard; Transportation.
Activities Arts & crafts; Cards; Games;
Reading groups; Prayer groups; Movies;
Shopping trips; Dances/Social/Cultural
gatherings.

Lakeview Terrace Medical Care Facility
PO Drawer 100, Altoona, FL 32702
(904) 669-2133
Admin Linda Rowe.
Medical Dir Glenn Miles MD.
Licensure Skilled care. *Beds* 20.
Owner Proprietary corp.
Admissions Requirements Minimum age 65;
Medical examination; Physician's request.

Staff Physicians 1 (pt); RNs 4 (ft), 4 (pt);
LPNs 4 (ft), 5 (pt); Nurses' aides 16 (ft), 11
(pt); Activities coordinators 1 (ft); Dietitians
1 (pt); Gerontologists 1 (ft); Physician
assistants 1 (pt).
Facilities Dining room; Activities room;
Crafts room; Barber/Beauty shop; Library.
Activities Arts & crafts; Cards; Games; Prayer
groups; Movies; Shopping trips; Dances/
Social/Cultural gatherings.

Apalachicola

Apalachicola Health Care Center Inc
150 10th St, Apalachicola, FL 32320
(904) 653-8844
Admin James Blue Darby. *Dir of Nursing*
Faye Deskins RN. *Medical Dir* Dr Photis
Nichols.
Licensure Skilled care. *Beds* SNF 60. *Certified*
Medicaid.
Owner Proprietary corp.
Admissions Requirements Minimum age 16;
Medical examination; Physician's request.
Staff Physicians 3 (pt); RNs 2 (ft), 1 (pt);
LPNs 5 (ft), 4 (pt); Nurses' aides 17 (ft), 8
(pt); Physical therapists 1 (pt); Recreational
therapists 1 (pt); Speech therapists 1 (pt);
Activities coordinators 1 (ft); Dietitians 1
(ft), 1 (pt); Ophthalmologists 1 (pt).
Languages Spanish.
Facilities Dining room; Physical therapy
room; Activities room; Crafts room; Laundry
room; Barber/Beauty shop.
Activities Arts & crafts; Cards; Games;
Reading groups; Prayer groups; Movies;
Shopping trips; Dances/Social/Cultural
gatherings.

Apopka

Florida Living Nursing Center
3355 Semdran Blvd, Apopka, FL 32703-6062
(305) 862-6263
Medical Dir Michael Gebauer MD.
Licensure Skilled care. *Beds* 104. *Certified*
Medicaid; Medicare.
Owner Nonprofit corp (Adventist Health Sys-
USA).
Admissions Requirements Minimum age 16;
Medical examination; Physician's request.
Staff Physicians 1 (pt); RNs 3 (ft), 3 (pt);
LPNs 10 (ft), 7 (pt); Nurses' aides 33 (ft), 10
(pt); Physical therapists; Speech therapists;
Activities coordinators 2 (ft), 1 (pt);
Podiatrists.
Languages Spanish.
Affiliation Seventh-Day Adventist.
Facilities Dining room; Physical therapy
room; Activities room; Chapel; Crafts room;
Laundry room; Barber/Beauty shop; Library.
Activities Arts & crafts; Games; Reading
groups; Prayer groups; Movies; Shopping
trips; Dances/Social/Cultural gatherings.

Arcadia

DeSoto Manor Nursing Home
1002 N Brevard, Arcadia, FL 33821
(813) 494-5766
Admin Richard Kjelland.
Medical Dir R C Gammad MD.
Licensure Skilled care; Intermediate care. *Beds*
SNF; ICF 63. *Certified* Medicaid; Medicare.
Owner Proprietary corp (Diversicare Corp).
Admissions Requirements Minimum age 16.
Staff RNs 2 (ft), 1 (pt); LPNs 7 (ft), 2 (pt);
Nurses' aides 18 (ft), 3 (pt); Recreational
therapists 1 (pt); Activities coordinators 1
(ft); Dietitians 1 (ft).
Languages Spanish, Italian.
Facilities Dining room; Physical therapy
room; Activities room; Crafts room; Laundry
room; Barber/Beauty shop; Library.
Activities Arts & crafts; Cards; Games;
Reading groups; Prayer groups; Movies.

Auburndale

Central Park Lodge Nursing Center
919 Old Winter Haven Rd, Auburndale, FL
33823
(813) 967-4125, 967-4128 FAX
Admin David Jones. *Dir of Nursing* Kaye
Howell. *Medical Dir* Harold Mines MD.
Licensure Skilled care; Intermediate care. *Beds*
Swing beds SNF/ICF 120. *Private Pay
Patients* 33%. *Certified* Medicaid; Medicare.
Owner Proprietary corp (Central Park
Lodges).
Admissions Requirements Minimum age 21;
Medical examination; Physician's request.
Staff Physicians 12 (ft); RNs 3 (ft), 2 (pt);
LPNs 13 (ft), 2 (pt); Nurses' aides 40 (ft), 4
(pt); Physical therapists 1 (pt); Recreational
therapists 1 (pt); Occupational therapists 1
(pt); Speech therapists 1 (pt); Activities
coordinators 1 (ft); Dietitians 1 (pt);
Ophthalmologists 1 (pt); Podiatrists 1 (pt);
Audiologists 1 (pt).
Facilities Dining room; Physical therapy
room; Activities room; Crafts room; Laundry
room; Barber/Beauty shop; Landscaped
enclosed courtyard.
Activities Arts & crafts; Cards; Games;
Reading groups; Prayer groups; Movies;
Shopping trips; Dances/Social/Cultural
gatherings; Individualized recreational
therapy.

Avon Park

Hillcrest Nursing Home
1281 Stratford Rd, Avon Park, FL 33825
(813) 453-6674
Medical Dir Donald B Geldart MD.
Licensure Skilled care. *Beds* 90. *Certified*
Medicaid.
Owner Proprietary corp.
Staff Physicians 8 (pt); RNs 3 (ft), 4 (pt);
LPNs 7 (ft), 6 (pt); Nurses' aides 22 (ft);
Physical therapists 1 (pt); Speech therapists

1 (pt); Activities coordinators 1 (pt); Dietitians 1 (pt); Podiatrists 1 (pt); Dentists 1 (pt).
Languages French, Spanish, German, Walon, Kituba, Ishiluba.
Facilities Dining room; Physical therapy room; Activities room; Barber/Beauty shop; Library.
Activities Arts & crafts; Cards; Games; Reading groups; Prayer groups; Movies; Shopping trips; Dances/Social/Cultural gatherings.

Bartow

Bartow Convalescent Center
2055 E Georgia St, Bartow, FL 33830
(813) 533-0578
Admin Judy E Hensley. *Dir of Nursing* Robin Gussepi RN. *Medical Dir* Alex I Garriga MD.
Licensure Skilled care. *Beds* SNF 120. *Private Pay Patients* 25%. *Certified* Medicaid; Medicare.
Owner Privately owned.
Admissions Requirements Medical examination; Physician's request.
Staff RNs 4 (ft), 2 (pt); LPNs 9 (ft), 2 (pt); Nurses' aides 40 (ft); Physical therapists 1 (pt); Reality therapists 1 (pt); Recreational therapists 1 (pt); Occupational therapists 1 (pt); Speech therapists 1 (pt); Activities coordinators 1 (ft), 1 (pt); Dietitians 1 (ft); Ophthalmologists 1 (pt); Podiatrists 1 (pt); Audiologists 1 (pt).
Facilities Dining room; Physical therapy room; Activities room; Crafts room; Laundry room; Barber/Beauty shop; Library.
Activities Arts & crafts; Cards; Games; Reading groups; Prayer groups; Movies; Shopping trips; Dances/Social/Cultural gatherings; Intergenerational programs; Pet therapy.

Rohr Home
2010 E Georgia St, Bartow, FL 33830
(813) 533-1111, 533-1806
Admin Sr M Constance Pellicer. *Dir of Nursing* Louise Gravel RN. *Medical Dir* Robert McMillan MD.
Licensure Skilled care. *Beds* SNF 60. *Private Pay Patients* 8%. *Certified* Medicaid.
Owner Publicly owned.
Admissions Requirements Minimum age 21; Medical examination; Physician's request.
Staff Physicians 1 (ft); RNs 4 (ft), 1 (pt); LPNs 5 (ft), 1 (pt); Nurses' aides 25 (ft), 2 (pt); Physical therapists 1 (pt); Activities coordinators 1 (ft); Dietitians 1 (pt).
Languages Spanish.
Facilities Dining room; Activities room; Crafts room; Laundry room; Barber/Beauty shop; Library.
Activities Arts & crafts; Cards; Games; Reading groups; Prayer groups; Movies; Pet therapy.

Belle Glade

Sunset Heights Nursing Home
841 SW Ave B, Belle Glade, FL 33430
(305) 996-9176
Licensure Skilled care. *Beds* 25. *Certified* Medicaid.
Owner Nonprofit corp.
Staff Physicians; Dietitians; Nurses' aides.
Languages Spanish, Italian.
Activities Prayer groups; Arts & crafts; Shopping trips.

Blountstown

Apalachicola Valley Nursing Center
1510 Crozier St, Blountstown, FL 32424
(904) 674-5464

Admin Lin Brightly. *Dir of Nursing* Mozelle Gates. *Medical Dir* Dr White.
Licensure Skilled care. *Beds* SNF 150. *Private Pay Patients* 20%. *Certified* Medicaid; Medicare.
Owner Proprietary corp (Advocare Inc).
Admissions Requirements Physician's request.
Staff RNs; LPNs; Nurses' aides; Activities coordinators; Dietitians.
Facilities Dining room; Physical therapy room; Activities room; Crafts room; Laundry room; Barber/Beauty shop.
Activities Arts & crafts; Cards; Games; Reading groups; Prayer groups; Movies; Shopping trips; Dances/Social/Cultural gatherings; Intergenerational programs; Pet therapy; Bed bound programs; Community programs.

Boca Raton

Boca Raton Convalescent Center
755 Meadows Rd, Boca Raton, FL 33432
(305) 391-5200
Admin Tom Glass. *Dir of Nursing* Doreen DeRoberts. *Medical Dir* George Dullghan MD.
Licensure Skilled care. *Beds* SNF 120. *Certified* Medicaid; Medicare.
Owner Proprietary corp (Hillhaven Corp).
Admissions Requirements Medical examination.
Staff Physicians 1 (pt); RNs 7 (ft), 5 (pt); LPNs 9 (ft), 3 (pt); Nurses' aides 35 (ft), 6 (pt); Physical therapists 1 (pt); Reality therapists 1 (pt); Recreational therapists 1 (pt); Occupational therapists 1 (pt); Speech therapists 1 (pt); Activities coordinators 1 (ft); Dietitians 1 (pt); Ophthalmologists 1 (pt); Podiatrists 1 (pt); Dentists 1 (pt).
Languages Spanish.
Facilities Dining room; Physical therapy room; Activities room; Crafts room; Laundry room; Barber/Beauty shop; Library; Outdoor screened patio.
Activities Arts & crafts; Cards; Games; Reading groups; Prayer groups; Movies; Shopping trips; Dances/Social/Cultural gatherings; Happy hour.

Edgewater Pointe Estates Medical Facility
23305 Blue Water Cir, Boca Raton, FL 33433
(305) 366-5600
Beds 35.

Fountains Nursing Home
3800 N Federal Hwy, Boca Raton, FL 33431
(407) 395-7510
Admin Mary C Brooks NHA. *Dir of Nursing* Ruth Fairbanks RN. *Medical Dir* Dr Roderick Santa Maria.
Licensure Skilled care. *Beds* SNF 51. *Private Pay Patients* 60%. *Certified* Medicaid; Medicare.
Owner Proprietary corp (Vari-Care Inc).
Staff Physicians; RNs 5 (ft), 50 (pt); LPNs 2 (ft), 50 (pt); Nurses' aides 13 (ft), 50 (pt); Physical therapists 1 (ft); Recreational therapists 1 (ft); Occupational therapists 1 (ft); Speech therapists 1 (ft); Dietitians 1 (ft); Ophthalmologists 1 (ft); Podiatrists 1 (ft); Audiologists 1 (ft).
Facilities Dining room; Physical therapy room; Laundry room; Barber/Beauty shop.
Activities Arts & crafts; Cards; Games; Reading groups; Prayer groups; Movies; Shopping trips; Dances/Social/Cultural gatherings; Intergenerational programs; Pet therapy; Religious services.

Manor Care Nursing Center
375 NW 51st St, Boca Raton, FL 33487
(407) 997-8111, 997-5351 FAX
Admin Sally B Hahn. *Dir of Nursing* Debbie Lysik. *Medical Dir* George Dullaghan.
Licensure Skilled care; Intermediate care. *Beds* SNF 20; ICF 100. *Private Pay Patients* 66%. *Certified* Medicaid; Medicare.

Owner Proprietary corp (Manor Care Inc).
Admissions Requirements Minimum age 18; Medical examination.
Staff Physicians 1 (pt); RNs 5 (ft), 3 (pt); LPNs 8 (ft), 8 (pt); Nurses' aides 23 (ft), 22 (pt); Physical therapists 1 (ft); Occupational therapists 1 (pt); Speech therapists 1 (pt); Activities coordinators 2 (ft), 1 (pt); Dietitians 1 (ft), 1 (pt); Ophthalmologists 1 (pt); Podiatrists 1 (pt); Audiologists 1 (pt).
Facilities Dining room; Physical therapy room; Activities room; Barber/Beauty shop.
Activities Arts & crafts; Cards; Games; Reading groups; Prayer groups; Movies; Shopping trips; Dances/Social/Cultural gatherings; Intergenerational programs; Pet therapy.

Meadowbrook Manor of Boca Cove
1130 NW 15th St, Boca Raton, FL 33432
(305) 394-6262
Beds 59.

Regents Park
6363 Verde Trail, Boca Raton, FL 33433
(407) 483-9282
Admin Lorna Mamelson. *Dir of Nursing* Sherri Niergodski. *Medical Dir* Dr John Chrwtakis.
Licensure Skilled care; Intermediate care. *Beds* SNF 60; ICF 60. *Certified* Medicaid; Medicare.
Owner Privately owned.
Admissions Requirements Medical examination; Physician's request.
Staff RNs 8 (ft); LPNs 12 (ft); Nurses' aides 44 (ft); Physical therapists 1 (ft); Occupational therapists 1 (ft); Speech therapists 1 (ft); Activities coordinators 1 (ft); Dietitians 1 (ft).
Languages French, Spanish, Creole, Polish.
Facilities Dining room; Physical therapy room; Activities room; Crafts room; Laundry room; Barber/Beauty shop.
Activities Arts & crafts; Cards; Games; Prayer groups; Movies; Shopping trips; Dances/Social/Cultural gatherings; Intergenerational programs; Pet therapy.

St Andrews Estates Medical Center
6152 N Verde Trail, Boca Raton, FL 33433
(407) 487-5200, 488-7419 FAX
Admin Juanita M Antley RNC BS MS NHA. *Dir of Nursing* Louise Newbery RN. *Medical Dir* Dr George Dullaghan.
Licensure Skilled care; Intermediate care; Retirement. *Beds* SNF 60; ICF 60. *Private Pay Patients* 0%. *Certified* Medicaid; Medicare.
Owner Nonprofit corp (ACTS Inc).
Admissions Requirements Life care community resident.
Staff RNs 9 (ft), 1 (pt); LPNs 13 (ft), 2 (pt); Nurses' aides 39 (ft), 6 (pt); Physical therapists (consultant); Recreational therapists (consultant); Occupational therapists (consultant); Speech therapists (consultant); Activities coordinators 2 (ft); Dietitians 1 (ft); Ophthalmologists (consultant); Podiatrists (consultant); Audiologists (consultant); Rehabilitation aides 1 (ft).
Facilities Physical therapy room; Activities room; Crafts room; Laundry room; Barber/Beauty shop; Library; Courtyard; Enclosed patio; Outdoor tables with umbrellas; Conference room; Rehabilitation dining; Large-screen TV; VCR; Traveling store; 3 dining rooms; Treatment room.
Activities Arts & crafts; Cards; Games; Reading groups; Prayer groups; Movies; Shopping trips; Dances/Social/Cultural gatherings; Intergenerational programs; Pet therapy; Nature appreciaton; Adult education ; Talking books; Senior & junior volunteer program; Alzheimer's support group.

Whitehall Boca Raton
7300 Del Prado S, Boca Raton, FL 33433
(305) 392-3000
Beds 42.

Bonifay

Bonifay Nursing Home
306 W Brock Ave, Bonifay, FL 32425
(904) 547-2418
Medical Dir H E Brooks MD.
Licensure Skilled care. *Beds* 60. *Certified*
Medicaid.
Owner Proprietary corp.
Admissions Requirements Minimum age 16;
Medical examination.
Staff RNs 3 (ft), 2 (pt); LPNs 3 (ft), 3 (pt);
Nurses' aides 21 (ft), 3 (pt); Activities
coordinators 1 (ft), 1 (pt).
Facilities Dining room; Physical therapy
room; Activities room; Laundry room;
Barber/Beauty shop; Library.
Activities Arts & crafts; Cards; Games;
Reading groups; Prayer groups; Movies;
Dances/Social/Cultural gatherings.

Boynton Beach

Boulevard Manor Nursing Center
2839 S Seacrest Blvd, Boynton Beach, FL
33435
(305) 732-2464
Medical Dir Dr Nayer.
Licensure Skilled care. *Beds* 110. *Certified*
Medicaid; Medicare.
Owner Proprietary corp (Vari-Care Inc).
Admissions Requirements Minimum age 16;
Medical examination; Physician's request.
Staff Physicians 1 (ft); RNs 10 (ft); LPNs 7
(ft); Nurses' aides 37 (ft); Physical therapists
2 (ft); Reality therapists 1 (ft); Recreational
therapists 2 (ft); Occupational therapists 1
(ft), 1 (pt); Speech therapists 1 (pt);
Activities coordinators 1 (ft); Dietitians 1
(pt); Ophthalmologists 1 (pt); Podiatrists 1
(pt); Audiologists 1 (pt); Dentists 1 (pt).
Languages French, Spanish, Norwegian,
German.
Facilities Dining room; Physical therapy
room; Activities room; Crafts room; Laundry
room; Barber/Beauty shop; Library.
Activities Arts & crafts; Cards; Games;
Reading groups; Prayer groups; Movies;
Shopping trips; Dances/Social/Cultural
gatherings.

Manor Care of Boynton Beach
3001 S Congress Ave, Boynton Beach, FL
33435
(305) 737-5600
Beds 38.

Bradenton

Asbury Towers
1533 4th Ave W, Bradenton, FL 34205
(813) 747-1881
Admin Austin R Pickering. *Dir of Nursing* S
Liebe. *Medical Dir* T Ganey.
Licensure Skilled care; Retirement. *Beds* SNF
34; Retirement 156. *Private Pay Patients*
100%.
Owner Nonprofit corp.
Admissions Requirements Minimum age 65;
Medical examination.
Staff Physicians 2 (pt); RNs 3 (ft); LPNs 5
(ft), 2 (pt); Nurses' aides 7 (ft), 5 (pt);
Activities coordinators 1 (ft); Dietitians 1
(ft).
Affiliation United Methodist.
Facilities Dining room; Activities room;
Chapel; Crafts room; Laundry room; Barber/
Beauty shop; Library.

Activities Arts & crafts; Cards; Games;
Reading groups; Prayer groups; Movies;
Shopping trips; Dances/Social/Cultural
gatherings; Intergenerational programs; Pet
therapy.

Bradenton Convalescent Center
105 15th St E, Bradenton, FL 34208
(813) 747-8681, 746-1561 FAX
Admin Ben E Eberly. *Dir of Nursing* Denise
Almy RN. *Medical Dir* B Vereb MD.
Licensure Skilled care. *Beds* SNF 110. *Private
Pay Patients* 20%. *Certified* Medicaid;
Medicare.
Owner Proprietary corp (Hillhaven Corp).
Admissions Requirements Medical
examination; Physician's request.
Staff RNs; LPNs; Nurses' aides; Activities
coordinators.
Facilities Dining room; Physical therapy
room; Activities room; Laundry room;
Barber/Beauty shop.
Activities Arts & crafts; Games; Movies;
Shopping trips; Pet therapy.

Bradenton Manor
1700 21st Ave W, Bradenton, FL 33505
(813) 748-4161
Licensure Skilled care. *Beds* 59.
Owner Nonprofit corp.
Admissions Requirements Medical
examination; Physician's request.
Staff RNs 4 (ft), 3 (pt); LPNs 5 (ft), 5 (pt);
Nurses' aides 21 (ft), 4 (pt); Activities
coordinators 1 (ft); Dietitians 1 (pt).
Affiliation Presbyterian.

Center at Manatee Springs
5627 9th St E, Bradenton, FL 34203
(613) 753-8941
Beds 62.

Freedom Care Pavilion
1902 59th St W, Bradenton, FL 34209
(813) 792-1515
Licensure Skilled care. *Beds* SNF 240.
Certified Medicaid; Medicare.
Owner Proprietary corp.
Staff RNs 10 (ft); LPNs 26 (ft); Nurses' aides
43 (ft).

Greenbriar Nursing Center
210 21st Ave W, Bradenton, FL 34205
(813) 747-3786
Admin Joyce A Coleman. *Dir of Nursing*
Dolores Green RN. *Medical Dir* Dr Gawey
Jr.
Licensure Skilled care; Alzheimer's care. *Beds*
60. *Certified* Medicaid; Medicare; VA.
Owner Proprietary corp (Unicare).
Admissions Requirements Minimum age 16;
Physician's request.
Staff RNs 5 (ft); LPNs 2 (ft), 3 (pt); Nurses'
aides 13 (ft), 5 (pt); Physical therapists 2
(pt); Reality therapists 1 (pt); Recreational
therapists 1 (ft); Occupational therapists 1
(pt); Speech therapists 1 (pt); Activities
coordinators 1 (ft); Dietitians 2 (pt);
Ophthalmologists 1 (pt); Podiatrists 1 (pt);
Dentists 1 (pt).
Facilities Dining room; Physical therapy
room; Activities room; Laundry room;
Barber/Beauty shop; Covered patio; BBQ
area.
Activities Arts & crafts; Cards; Games;
Reading groups; Prayer groups; Movies;
Shopping trips; Dances/Social/Cultural
gatherings.

Heritage Park of Bradenton
2302 59th St W, Bradenton, FL 33529
(613) 792-8480
Beds 74.

Manatee Convalescent Center Inc
302 Manatee Ave E, Bradenton, FL 34208
(813) 746-6131
Admin Joanne Proffitt.

Licensure Skilled care. *Beds* 147. *Certified*
Medicaid; Medicare.
Owner Proprietary corp (Beverly Enterprises).
Admissions Requirements Medical
examination.
Staff RNs 6 (ft), 3 (pt); LPNs 11 (ft); Nurses'
aides 46 (ft), 10 (pt); Recreational therapists;
Occupational therapists; Speech therapists;
Activities coordinators 2 (ft); Dietitians;
Ophthalmologists; Podiatrists; Audiologists;
Dentists.
Languages Spanish.
Facilities Dining room; Physical therapy
room; Activities room; Chapel; Crafts room;
Laundry room; Barber/Beauty shop.
Activities Arts & crafts; Cards; Games;
Reading groups; Prayer groups; Movies;
Shopping trips; Dances/Social/Cultural
gatherings.

Shores Health Center
1700 3rd Ave W, Bradenton, FL 33505
(813) 748-1700
Admin Lucretia L Hess NHA.
Medical Dir Joseph Dimino MD.
Licensure Skilled care; Alzheimer's care;
Retirement. *Beds* SNF 21.
Owner Proprietary corp.
Admissions Requirements Minimum age 64;
Medical examination; Physician's request.
Staff RNs 2 (ft), 3 (pt); LPNs 3 (ft); Nurses'
aides 6 (ft), 1 (pt).
Facilities Dining room; Activities room;
Chapel; Crafts room; Laundry room; Barber/
Beauty shop; Library.
Activities Arts & crafts; Cards; Games;
Reading groups; Prayer groups; Movies;
Shopping trips; Dances/Social/Cultural
gatherings.

Suncoast Manor Nursing Center
2010 Manatee Ave E, Bradenton, FL 34208
(813) 747-3706, 747-8627 FAX
Admin Patrick S La Rose. *Dir of Nursing*
Linda Schiffmeyer RN. *Medical Dir* Dr
Steven Greenfield.
Licensure Skilled care; Intermediate care;
Alzheimer's care. *Beds* SNF 55; ICF 153.
Private Pay Patients 65%. *Certified*
Medicaid; Medicare.
Owner Proprietary corp (National Heritage).
Admissions Requirements Minimum age 16;
Medical examination.
Staff RNs 11 (ft); LPNs 20 (ft); Nurses' aides
70 (ft); Physical therapists 1 (ft);
Recreational therapists 1 (ft); Occupational
therapists 1 (ft); Speech therapists 1 (ft);
Activities coordinators 1 (ft); Dietitians 1
(ft); Podiatrists 2 (ft).
Facilities Dining room; Physical therapy
room; Activities room; Chapel; Crafts room;
Laundry room; Barber/Beauty shop; Library;
Courtyards.
Activities Arts & crafts; Cards; Games;
Reading groups; Prayer groups; Movies;
Shopping trips; Dances/Social/Cultural
gatherings; Intergenerational programs; Pet
therapy.

Brandon

Village at Brandon
701 Victoria St, Brandon, FL 33510
(813) 681-4220, 684-5319 FAX
Admin Loma L Overmyer. *Dir of Nursing*
Anne B Rutherford. *Medical Dir* David
Worthington MD.
Licensure Skilled care; Intermediate care. *Beds*
Swing beds SNF/ICF 120. *Private Pay
Patients* 51%. *Certified* Medicaid; Medicare.
Owner Proprietary corp (Arbor Health Care).
Admissions Requirements Minimum age 16;
Medical examination; Physician's request.
Staff Physicians 1 (ft); RNs 5 (ft), 3 (pt);
LPNs 6 (ft), 2 (pt); Nurses' aides 24 (ft), 12
(pt); Activities coordinators 1 (ft), 1 (pt);
Dietitians 1 (ft).

Languages Spanish, Italian.
Facilities Dining room; Physical therapy room; Activities room; Crafts room; Laundry room; Barber/Beauty shop; Patios.
Activities Arts & crafts; Cards; Games; Reading groups; Prayer groups; Movies; Shopping trips; Dances/Social/Cultural gatherings; Intergenerational programs; Pet therapy.

Bristol

Liberty Intermediate Care—Bristol
PO Box 66, Bristol, FL 32321
(904) 643-2256
Licensure Intermediate care for mentally retarded. *Beds* 80. *Certified* Medicaid; Medicare.
Owner Proprietary corp.
Staff RNs 2 (ft); LPNs 3 (ft); Nurses' aides 31 (ft).

Brooksville

Brooksville Nursing Manor
1114 Chatman Blvd, Brooksville, FL 33512
(904) 796-6701
Admin Karen L Cross. *Dir of Nursing* Kathryn Schneider RN. *Medical Dir* James M Marlowe MD.
Licensure Skilled care. *Beds* 180. *Certified* Medicaid; Medicare; VA.
Owner Nonprofit organization/foundation.
Admissions Requirements Minimum age 18.
Staff RNs 6 (ft), 5 (pt); LPNs 19 (ft), 2 (pt); Nurses' aides 69 (ft), 3 (pt); Activities coordinators 1 (ft), 3 (pt); Dietitians 1 (ft).
Facilities Dining room; Physical therapy room; Activities room; Chapel; Crafts room; Laundry room; Barber/Beauty shop.
Activities Arts & crafts; Cards; Games; Reading groups; Prayer groups; Movies; Shopping trips; Dances/Social/Cultural gatherings.

Eastbrooke Health Care Center
10295 N Howell Ave, Brooksville, FL 33512
(904) 799-1451
Admin Nancy E Hall. *Dir of Nursing* Susan Snyder RN. *Medical Dir* Richard Henry MD.
Licensure Skilled care. *Beds* 120. *Certified* Medicaid; Medicare.
Owner Proprietary corp.
Admissions Requirements Minimum age 16; Medical examination; Physician's request.
Staff RNs 4 (ft), 1 (pt); LPNs 7 (ft), 2 (pt); Nurses' aides 30 (ft), 15 (pt); Activities coordinators 1 (ft).
Facilities Dining room; Physical therapy room; Activities room; Chapel; Laundry room; Barber/Beauty shop.
Activities Arts & crafts; Cards; Games; Reading groups; Prayer groups; Movies; Shopping trips; Dances/Social/Cultural gatherings.

Bunnell

Meadowbrook Manor of Flagler
PO Box 1850, 300 S Lemon St, Bunnell, FL 32110
(904) 437-4168
Admin Jennifer Seall NHA. *Dir of Nursing* Margaret Dolan RN. *Medical Dir* Lawrence Burns MD.
Licensure Skilled care; Intermediate care. *Beds* Swing beds SNF/ICF 100. *Private Pay Patients* 20%. *Certified* Medicaid; Medicare.
Owner Nonprofit organization/foundation.
Admissions Requirements Medical examination.

Staff RNs; LPNs; Nurses' aides; Physical therapists; Recreational therapists; Occupational therapists; Speech therapists; Activities coordinators; Dietitians; Ophthalmologists; Podiatrists; Audiologists.
Facilities Dining room; Physical therapy room; Activities room; Chapel; Crafts room; Laundry room; Barber/Beauty shop; Living room.
Activities Arts & crafts; Cards; Games; Reading groups; Prayer groups; Movies; Shopping trips; Dances/Social/Cultural gatherings; Pet therapy.

Cape Coral

Cape Coral Nursing Pavilion
2629 Del Prado Blvd, Cape Coral, FL 33904
(813) 574-4434
Medical Dir Lawrence D Hughes.
Licensure Skilled care. *Beds* 120. *Certified* Medicaid; Medicare.
Owner Proprietary corp.
Admissions Requirements Minimum age 16; Medical examination; Physician's request.
Staff RNs 11 (ft); LPNs 12 (ft); Nurses' aides 40 (ft); Physical therapists 2 (ft); Occupational therapists 1 (ft); Speech therapists 1 (ft); Activities coordinators 1 (ft); Dietitians 1 (ft); Podiatrists 1 (pt).
Languages Spanish.
Facilities Dining room; Physical therapy room; Activities room; Chapel; Crafts room; Laundry room; Barber/Beauty shop; Library.
Activities Arts & crafts; Cards; Games; Reading groups; Prayer groups; Movies; Dances/Social/Cultural gatherings; Birthday parties; Sing-alongs; Wine & cheese parties.

Coral Trace Manor
216 Santa Barbara Blvd, Cape Coral, FL 33904
(613) 772-4600
Beds 66.

Chipley

Washington County Convalescent Center
805 Usery Rd, Chipley, FL 32428
(904) 638-4654
Beds 120.
Owner Proprietary corp.

Clearwater

Belleair East Health Care Center
1150 Ponce de Leon Blvd, Clearwater, FL 33516
(813) 585-5491
Admin Brian A Rougeux.
Medical Dir Jeffrey Sourbee.
Licensure Skilled care; Intermediate care; Retirement; Alzheimer's care. *Beds* 120. *Certified* Medicaid; Medicare.
Owner Proprietary corp.
Admissions Requirements Minimum age 18; Medical examination; Physician's request.
Staff Physicians 1 (pt); RNs 15 (ft), 11 (pt); LPNs 10 (ft), 9 (pt); Nurses' aides 52 (ft), 29 (pt); Physical therapists 2 (pt); Reality therapists 1 (pt); Recreational therapists 1 (ft); Occupational therapists 1 (pt); Speech therapists 1 (pt); Activities coordinators 2 (ft), 1 (pt); Dietitians 2 (ft); Ophthalmologists 1 (pt); Podiatrists 1 (pt).
Languages Spanish.
Facilities Dining room; Physical therapy room; Activities room; Laundry room; Barber/Beauty shop; Library.
Activities Arts & crafts; Cards; Games; Reading groups; Prayer groups; Movies; Shopping trips; Dances/Social/Cultural gatherings; Cooking class; Picnics; Painting class.

Bethamy Gardens
2055 Palmetto St, Clearwater, FL 33575
(613) 441-4944
Beds 62.

Bruce Manor
1100 Pine St, Clearwater, FL 33516
(813) 442-7106
Admin Norman Rosewarne. *Dir of Nursing* Maria Miller RN. *Medical Dir* Joseph Baird MD.
Licensure Skilled care. *Beds* SNF 76.
Owner Proprietary corp.
Admissions Requirements Medical examination; Physician's request.
Staff RNs 3 (ft), 3 (pt); LPNs 5 (ft), 2 (pt); Nurses' aides 15 (ft); Activities coordinators 1 (ft); Dietitians 1 (ft).
Facilities Dining room; Physical therapy room; Activities room; Crafts room; Barber/Beauty shop; Library.
Activities Arts & crafts; Cards; Games; Reading groups; Prayer groups; Movies; Shopping trips; Dances/Social/Cultural gatherings.

Clearwater Convalescent Center
1270 Turner St, Clearwater, FL 33516
(813) 443-7639
Licensure Skilled care. *Beds* 120. *Certified* Medicaid; Medicare.
Owner Proprietary corp.
Staff RNs 4 (ft); LPNs 7 (ft); Nurses' aides 26 (ft).

Country Place of Clearwater
905 S Highland Ave, Clearwater, FL 34616
(813) 442-9606, 443-4006 FAX
Admin Bill Porterfield. *Dir of Nursing* Cyndi Sullivan. *Medical Dir* Angel Rivera.
Licensure Skilled care; Alzheimer's care. *Beds* SNF 103. *Private Pay Patients* 25%. *Certified* Medicaid; Medicare.
Owner Privately owned (Phillips Healthcare).
Admissions Requirements Medical examination; Physician's request.
Staff RNs 5 (ft); LPNs 12 (ft); Nurses' aides 22 (ft); Physical therapists 1 (ft); Reality therapists 3 (ft); Recreational therapists 3 (ft); Occupational therapists 1 (ft); Speech therapists 1 (ft); Activities coordinators 1 (ft); Dietitians 1 (ft); Ophthalmologists 1 (ft); Podiatrists 1 (ft); Audiologists 1 (ft).
Languages Spanish.
Facilities Dining room; Physical therapy room; Activities room; Crafts room; Laundry room; Barber/Beauty shop.
Activities Arts & crafts; Cards; Games; Reading groups; Prayer groups; Movies; Shopping trips; Dances/Social/Cultural gatherings; Intergenerational programs; Pet therapy.

Drew Village Nursing Center
401 Fairwood Ave, Clearwater, FL 34619
(813) 797-6313
Admin Jerry Harden. *Dir of Nursing* Joanne Tallirico. *Medical Dir* Charles Becker MD.
Licensure Skilled care. *Beds* SNF 120. *Private Pay Patients* 40%. *Certified* Medicaid; Medicare.
Owner Proprietary corp (Renaissance Healthcare Corp).
Admissions Requirements Minimum age 16; Medical examination; Physician's request.
Staff RNs 12 (ft); LPNs 20 (ft); Nurses' aides 40 (ft).
Languages Spanish.
Facilities Dining room; Physical therapy room; Activities room; Barber/Beauty shop; Library.
Activities Arts & crafts; Cards; Games; Reading groups; Prayer groups; Movies; Intergenerational programs; Pet therapy.

Highland Pines Nursing Manor
1111 S Highland Ave, Clearwater, FL 33516
(813) 446-0581

Admin Don Poteet. *Dir of Nursing* Charlene Barsky RN. *Medical Dir* Mark S Franklin DO.
Licensure Skilled care; Retirement. *Beds* SNF 120; Retirement 65. *Private Pay Patients* 70%. *Certified* Medicaid.
Owner Proprietary corp (Southern Management Services Inc).
Admissions Requirements Minimum age 18; Medical examination; Physician's request.
Staff Physicians; RNs; LPNs; Nurses' aides; Physical therapists; Reality therapists; Recreational therapists; Occupational therapists; Speech therapists; Activities coordinators; Dietitians; Ophthalmologists; Podiatrists; Audiologists.
Languages Spanish, German.
Facilities Dining room; Physical therapy room; Activities room; Crafts room; Laundry room; Barber/Beauty shop; Library.
Activities Arts & crafts; Cards; Games; Reading groups; Prayer groups; Movies; Shopping trips; Dances/Social/Cultural gatherings; Intergenerational programs; Pet therapy.

Oak Bluffs Nursing Center
420 Bay Ave, Clearwater, FL 34616
(813) 445-4700, 462-9902 FAX
Admin Robert Delimon NHA. *Dir of Nursing* Martha Widner RN. *Medical Dir* Dr Charles Becker.
Licensure Skilled care; Intermediate care; Independent & assisted living; Alzheimer's care. *Beds* SNF 15; ICF 45; Independent & assisted living apts 212. *Certified* Medicare.
Owner Nonprofit corp (Advance Living Technology).
Admissions Requirements Minimum age 55; Medical examination; Physician's request.
Staff Physicians 9 (pt); RNs 4 (ft); LPNs 7 (ft); Nurses' aides 22 (ft); Physical therapists 1 (ft); Occupational therapists 1 (ft); Speech therapists 1 (ft); Activities coordinators 1 (ft); Dietitians 1 (ft); Podiatrists 3 (ft).
Languages Greek.
Facilities Dining room; Activities room; Chapel; Crafts room; Barber/Beauty shop; Library.
Activities Arts & crafts; Cards; Games; Reading groups; Prayer groups; Movies; Shopping trips; Dances/Social/Cultural gatherings; Intergenerational programs; Pet therapy; Lunch bunch outings to restaurants.

Oak Cove Health Center
210 S Osceola Ave, Clearwater, FL 33516
(813) 441-3763
Admin R Eugene Fleming.
Medical Dir Julie Jackson.
Licensure Skilled care; Apartment living; Alzheimer's care. *Beds* SNF 56; Apartment living 253. *Certified* Medicare.
Owner Nonprofit corp.
Admissions Requirements Medical examination.
Staff Physicians; RNs; LPNs; Nurses' aides; Physical therapists; Recreational therapists; Occupational therapists; Speech therapists; Activities coordinators; Dietitians; Ophthalmologists; Podiatrists; Social service directors.
Facilities Dining room; Activities room; Crafts room; Laundry room; Barber/Beauty shop; Library.
Activities Arts & crafts; Cards; Games; Reading groups; Prayer groups; Movies; Shopping trips; Dances/Social/Cultural gatherings; Exercise.

Osceola Inn
221 N Osceola, Clearwater, FL 33515
(813) 461-3321
Medical Dir Gaylord Church MD.
Licensure Skilled care. *Beds* 13.
Owner Nonprofit corp.
Admissions Requirements Minimum age 65; Medical examination.

Staff RNs 2 (ft), 3 (pt); LPNs 1 (ft), 3 (pt); Nurses' aides 6 (ft), 3 (pt); Activities coordinators 1 (pt); Dietitians 1 (pt).
Languages French.
Affiliation Presbyterian.
Facilities Dining room; Activities room; Chapel; Laundry room; Barber/Beauty shop; Library.
Activities Arts & crafts; Cards; Games; Reading groups; Prayer groups; Dances/Social/Cultural gatherings.

Palm Garden
3460 McMullen-Booth Rd, Clearwater, FL 33519
(613) 786-6697
Beds 62.

Morton F Plant Rehabilitation & Nursing Center
1250 S Fort Harrison Ave, Clearwater, FL 33516
(813) 462-7600, 461-8861 FAX
Admin H Sandra Hugg. *Dir of Nursing* Sharon Schaefer RN. *Medical Dir* James E Lett II MD.
Licensure Skilled care. *Beds* SNF 126. *Private Pay Patients* 60%. *Certified* Medicaid; Medicare.
Owner Nonprofit corp.
Admissions Requirements Minimum age 18; Medical examination.
Staff RNs 9 (ft), 2 (pt); LPNs 10 (ft), 4 (pt); Nurses' aides 44 (ft), 7 (pt); Physical therapists 2 (ft); Occupational therapists 2 (ft); Speech therapists 1 (ft); Dietitians (contracted); Podiatrists (contracted); RTAs 5 (ft); Recreational therapists; Activities coordinators 2 (ft).
Languages Spanish, German, French.
Facilities Dining room; Activities room; Laundry room; Barber/Beauty shop.
Activities Arts & crafts; Cards; Games; Reading groups; Prayer groups; Movies; Shopping trips; Dances/Social/Cultural gatherings; Intergenerational programs; Pet therapy; Restaurant outings; Baking.

Sunset Point Nursing Center
1980 Sunset Point Rd, Clearwater, FL 33575
(813) 443-1588
Medical Dir Dr Raymond Zimmerman.
Licensure Skilled care; Intermediate care. *Beds* SNF 72; ICF 48. *Certified* Medicaid; Medicare.
Owner Proprietary corp (Shive Nursing Centers).
Staff Physicians 1 (pt); RNs 4 (ft), 3 (pt); LPNs 8 (ft), 2 (pt); Physical therapists 1 (pt); Recreational therapists 1 (pt); Occupational therapists 1 (pt); Speech therapists 1 (pt); Activities coordinators 1 (ft); Dietitians 1 (pt); Ophthalmologists 1 (pt); Podiatrists 1 (pt); Audiologists 1 (pt); Dentists 1 (pt).
Facilities Dining room; Physical therapy room; Activities room; Crafts room; Barber/Beauty shop; Library.
Activities Arts & crafts; Cards; Games; Reading groups; Prayer groups; Movies; Shopping trips; Dances/Social/Cultural gatherings.

Clermont

Lake Highlands Retirement & Nursing Home
151 E Minnehaha Ave, Clermont, FL 32711
(904) 394-2188
Admin Herbert Rogers.
Medical Dir Melvin Thomas MD.
Licensure Skilled care; Intermediate care; Retirement; Alzheimer's care. *Beds* 142. *Certified* Medicaid; Medicare; VA.
Owner Privately owned.
Admissions Requirements Medical examination.
Staff Physicians 1 (pt); RNs 6 (ft); LPNs 21 (ft); Nurses' aides 63 (ft), 8 (pt); Activities coordinators 1 (ft); Dietitians 1 (pt).

Languages Spanish, French, Swedish.
Facilities Dining room; Physical therapy room; Activities room; Chapel; Crafts room; Laundry room; Barber/Beauty shop.
Activities Arts & crafts; Cards; Games; Reading groups; Prayer groups; Movies; Shopping trips; Dances/Social/Cultural gatherings.

Clewiston

Clewiston Health Care Center
301 S Gloria St, Clewiston, FL 33440
(813) 983-5123
Licensure Skilled care. *Beds* 120. *Certified* Medicaid.
Owner Proprietary corp (Beverly Enterprises).
Staff Nurses' aides 19 (ft).

Coca

Bon Air Nursing Home
4185 Vancouver Ave, Coca, FL 32926
(207) 783-0550
Admin Pauline Robertson.
Licensure Intermediate care. *Beds* 13. *Certified* Medicaid.

Coral Gables

New Riviera Health Resort
6901 Yumuri St, Coral Gables, FL 33146
(305) 661-0078
Admin Shirley H St Clair JD. *Dir of Nursing* Beryl Rogers. *Medical Dir* Norman Spitzer MD.
Licensure Skilled care. *Beds* 52. *Certified* Medicaid; Medicare.
Owner Proprietary corp.
Admissions Requirements Physician's request.
Staff RNs 3 (ft), 1 (pt); LPNs 3 (ft); Nurses' aides 20 (ft); Physical therapists 1 (pt); Dietitians 1 (pt).
Languages Spanish.
Facilities Dining room; Activities room; Laundry room; Barber/Beauty shop.
Activities Arts & crafts; Cards; Games; Reading groups; Prayer groups; Movies; Dances/Social/Cultural gatherings.

Coral Springs

Park Summit
8500 Royal Palm Blvd, Coral Springs, FL 33065
(305) 752-9500, 755-9559 FAX
Admin Mary Joslin RN NHA. *Dir of Nursing* Bonnie Parker RN MHA. *Medical Dir* Peter Ruy MD.
Licensure Skilled care; ACLF; Retirement. *Beds* SNF 35; ACLF 216 apts. *Private Pay Patients* 85%. *Certified* Medicaid; Medicare.
Owner Proprietary corp (Forum Group).
Admissions Requirements Minimum age 16; Medical examination; Physician's request.
Staff RNs 4 (ft), 4 (pt); LPNs 2 (pt); Nurses' aides 10 (ft), 5 (pt); Physical therapists 1 (pt); Occupational therapists 1 (pt); Speech therapists 1 (pt); Activities coordinators 1 (ft); Dietitians 1 (pt); Ophthalmologists 1 (pt); Podiatrists 1 (pt); Audiologists 1 (pt).
Languages French, Spanish, Italian.
Facilities Dining room; Physical therapy room; Activities room; Laundry room; Barber/Beauty shop.
Activities Arts & crafts; Cards; Games; Reading groups; Prayer groups; Movies; Shopping trips; Dances/Social/Cultural gatherings; Intergenerational programs; Pet therapy.

Crawfordville

Wakulla Manor
PO Box 549, Crawfordville, FL 32427
(904) 926-7181
Licensure Skilled care. *Beds* 120. *Certified*
Medicaid; Medicare.
Owner Proprietary corp.
Staff RNs 8 (ft); LPNs 8 (ft); Nurses' aides 25
(ft).

Crescent City

Lakeshore Nursing Home
100 Lake St, Crescent City, FL 32012
(904) 698-2222
Admin Martha Jean Brown. *Dir of Nursing*
Caroline Kellerman. *Medical Dir* Bernard
Prudencio.
Licensure Skilled care; Intermediate care;
Alzheimer's care. *Beds* SNF 92; ICF.
Certified Medicaid.
Owner Proprietary corp (Beverly Enterprises).
Admissions Requirements Physician's request.
Staff Physicians 1 (pt); RNs 7 (ft); LPNs 7
(ft); Nurses' aides 37 (ft); Physical therapists
1 (ft); Speech therapists 1 (ft); Activities
coordinators 2 (ft); Dietitians 1 (ft).
Facilities Dining room; Physical therapy
room; Activities room; Crafts room; Laundry
room; Barber/Beauty shop; Library.
Activities Arts & crafts; Cards; Games;
Reading groups; Prayer groups; Movies;
Shopping trips; Dances/Social/Cultural
gatherings.

Crestview

Crestview Nursing & Convalescent Home
1849 E 1st St, Crestview, FL 32536
(904) 682-5322
Admin Cynthia K Ledford. *Dir of Nursing*
Patricia M Dingess. *Medical Dir* Kenneth E
Carroll MD.
Licensure Skilled care. *Beds* SNF 180. *Private
Pay Patients* 20%. *Certified* Medicaid;
Medicare.
Owner Proprietary corp.
Admissions Requirements Medical
examination; Physician's request.
Staff Physicians 10 (pt); RNs 8 (ft); LPNs 18
(ft); Nurses' aides 60 (ft); Physical therapists
1 (ft); Speech therapists 1 (pt); Activities
coordinators 2 (ft); Podiatrists 1 (pt);
Audiologists 1 (pt).
Facilities Dining room; Physical therapy
room; Activities room; Crafts room; Barber/
Beauty shop.
Activities Arts & crafts; Cards; Games;
Reading groups; Prayer groups; Movies;
Shopping trips; Dances/Social/Cultural
gatherings; Intergenerational programs; Pet
therapy.

Crystal River

Crystal River Geriatric Center
136 NE 12th Ave, Crystal River, FL 32629
(904) 795-5044
Medical Dir Dr Carlos Gonzalez.
Licensure Skilled care; Intermediate care. *Beds*
150. *Certified* Medicaid; Medicare.
Owner Proprietary corp (Waverly Group).
Admissions Requirements Minimum age 16.
Staff Physical therapists 1 (pt); Occupational
therapists 1 (pt); Speech therapists 1 (pt);
Activities coordinators 1 (ft); Dietitians 1
(pt); Podiatrists 1 (pt); Dentists 1 (pt).
Languages Spanish, German.
Facilities Dining room; Physical therapy
room; Activities room; Laundry room;
Barber/Beauty shop.
Activities Arts & crafts; Cards; Games;
Reading groups; Prayer groups; Movies;
Dances/Social/Cultural gatherings.

Cypress Cove Care Center
700 SE 8th Ave, Crystal River, FL 32629
(904) 795-8832
Admin Ted Hagey NHA. *Dir of Nursing* Betty
Klein RNC. *Medical Dir* James Marlowe
MD.
Licensure Skilled care. *Beds* SNF 120.
Certified Medicaid; Medicare.
Owner Proprietary corp.
Admissions Requirements Minimum age 16;
Medical examination; Physician's request.
Staff Physicians 15 (pt); RNs 3 (ft), 4 (pt);
LPNs 13 (ft), 5 (pt); Nurses' aides 41 (ft), 3
(pt); Activities coordinators 1 (ft); Dietitians
1 (ft); Ophthalmologists 2 (pt).
Languages Swedish.
Facilities Dining room; Physical therapy
room; Activities room; Chapel; Laundry
room; Barber/Beauty shop.
Activities Arts & crafts; Cards; Games;
Reading groups; Prayer groups; Movies;
Shopping trips; Dances/Social/Cultural
gatherings.

Cutler Ridge

Healthsouth Regional Rehabilitation Center
20601 Old Cutler Rd, Cutler Ridge, FL 33169
(305) 235-1937
Beds 93.

Dade City

Dade City Geriatric Center
805 W Coleman Ave, Dade City, FL 33525
(904) 567-8615
Medical Dir Dr McBath.
Licensure Skilled care. *Beds* 120. *Certified*
Medicaid; Medicare.
Owner Proprietary corp (Beverly Enterprises).
Admissions Requirements Minimum age 16;
Medical examination; Physician's request.
Staff Physicians 12 (pt); RNs 5 (pt); LPNs 14
(pt); Nurses' aides 36 (pt); Physical
therapists 1 (pt); Recreational therapists 1
(pt); Occupational therapists 1 (pt); Speech
therapists 1 (pt); Activities coordinators 1
(pt); Dietitians 1 (pt); Podiatrists 1 (pt);
Audiologists 1 (pt); Dentists 1 (pt).
Languages Spanish.
Facilities Dining room; Physical therapy
room; Activities room; Laundry room;
Barber/Beauty shop.
Activities Arts & crafts; Cards; Games;
Reading groups; Prayer groups; Movies;
Shopping trips; Dances/Social/Cultural
gatherings.

Pasco Nursing Center
PO Box 1197, 447 N 5th St, Dade City, FL
33526-1197
(904) 567-1978
Admin Gerald Struckhoff. *Dir of Nursing*
Peggy Guedesse. *Medical Dir* Donald
McBath DO.
Licensure Skilled care; Intermediate care;
Alzheimer's care. *Beds* Swing beds SNF/ICF
40. *Private Pay Patients* 5%. *Certified*
Medicaid.
Owner Proprietary corp.
Admissions Requirements Minimum age 16;
Physician's request.
Staff Physicians 1 (pt); RNs 1 (ft); LPNs 3
(ft), 3 (pt); Nurses' aides 12 (ft), 3 (pt);
Recreational therapists 1 (ft); Activities
coordinators 1 (ft); Dietitians 1 (ft).
Languages Spanish, German.
Facilities Dining room; Activities room.
Activities Arts & crafts; Cards; Games;
Reading groups; Prayer groups; Movies;
Shopping trips; Dances/Social/Cultural
gatherings; Pet therapy.

Royal Oak Nursing Resort
700 Royal Oak Ln, Dade City, FL 33525
(904) 567-3122
Admin David W Cross.

Medical Dir James Marlowe; James D
Murphy.
Licensure Skilled care. *Beds* 120. *Certified*
Medicaid; Medicare; VA.
Owner Nonprofit corp.
Admissions Requirements Minimum age 18;
Medical examination; Physician's request.
Staff RNs 4 (ft); LPNs 10 (ft), 5 (pt); Nurses'
aides 55 (ft), 20 (pt); Recreational therapists
1 (ft); Activities coordinators 2 (pt).
Languages Spanish.
Facilities Dining room; Physical therapy
room; Activities room; Chapel; Crafts room;
Laundry room; Barber/Beauty shop; Park.
Activities Arts & crafts; Cards; Games;
Reading groups; Prayer groups; Movies;
Shopping trips; Dances/Social/Cultural
gatherings.

Dania

Dania Nursing Home
440 Phippen Rd, Dania, FL 33004
(305) 927-0508
Licensure Skilled care. *Beds* 88. *Certified*
Medicaid; Medicare.
Owner Proprietary corp.
Staff RNs 3 (ft); LPNs 10 (ft); Nurses' aides
30 (ft).
Languages French, Hebrew, Yiddish.

Davenport

William L Hargrave Health Center
206 W Orange St, Davenport, FL 33837
(813) 422-4961
Medical Dir Edward Jukes.
Licensure Skilled care. *Beds* 60. *Certified*
Medicaid.
Owner Nonprofit corp.
Admissions Requirements Minimum age 70;
Medical examination.
Staff Physicians 2 (ft); RNs 4 (ft), 1 (pt);
LPNs 7 (ft), 2 (pt); Nurses' aides 28 (ft), 1
(pt); Occupational therapists 1 (pt); Speech
therapists 1 (pt); Activities coordinators 3
(ft), 1 (pt); Dietitians 1 (ft);
Ophthalmologists 1 (pt); Podiatrists 1 (pt);
Dentists 3 (pt).
Affiliation Episcopal.
Facilities Dining room; Activities room;
Chapel; Crafts room; Laundry room; Barber/
Beauty shop; Library.
Activities Arts & crafts; Cards; Games;
Reading groups; Prayer groups; Movies;
Shopping trips; Dances/Social/Cultural
gatherings; Church activities.

Davie

BARC Housing Inc
2750 SW 75th Ave, Davie, FL 33314
(305) 474-5277
Admin Carol Eger.
Medical Dir Irving Bratt MD.
Licensure Intermediate care for mentally
retarded. *Beds* 36. *Certified* Medicaid.
Owner Nonprofit corp.
Admissions Requirements Minimum age 18;
Medical examination; ICF MR eligibility.
Staff Physicians 1 (pt); RNs 1 (pt); LPNs 4
(ft); Physical therapists 1 (pt); Recreational
therapists 1 (ft); Occupational therapists 1
(pt); Speech therapists 2 (pt); Dietitians 1
(pt); Ophthalmologists 1 (pt); Podiatrists 1
(pt); Social worker 1 (ft); Instructors 19 (ft),
18 (pt); Psychologists 1 (pt).
Facilities Dining room; Recreation area;
Living room; Family room; Kitchen;
Bedrooms.
Activities Arts & crafts; Cards; Games;
Movies; Shopping trips; Dances/Social/
Cultural gatherings; Wide variety of
normalized recreational & leisure activities.

Daytona

Halifax Convalescent Center Ltd
820 N Clyde Morris Blvd, Daytona, FL 32117
(904) 274-4575
Admin Freda Lane. *Dir of Nursing* Barbara Kellerman. *Medical Dir* Dr Hana Chaim.
Licensure Skilled care; Assisted community living. *Beds* SNF 84; Assisted community living 36. *Private Pay Patients* 10%. *Certified* Medicaid; Medicare.
Owner Privately owned.
Admissions Requirements Medical examination; Physician's request.
Facilities Dining room; Physical therapy room; Activities room; Laundry room; Barber/Beauty shop; Sub-acute unit (ventilator, trach/oxygen, comatose, head injury, and other serious illnesses).
Activities Arts & crafts; Cards; Games; Reading groups; Prayer groups; Movies; Shopping trips; Dances/Social/Cultural gatherings; Intergenerational programs; Pet therapy.

Daytona Beach

Clyatt Memorial Center
1001 S Beach St, Daytona Beach, FL 32014
(904) 258-3334
Licensure Skilled care. *Beds* 99. *Certified* Medicaid; Medicare.
Owner Nonprofit corp.
Staff RNs 3 (ft); LPNs 7 (ft); Nurses' aides 31 (ft).

Daytona Beach Geriatric Center
1055 3rd St, Daytona Beach, FL 32117
(904) 252-3686
Admin Patrice Pelletier. *Dir of Nursing* Alice Strauss RN. *Medical Dir* Dr Ronald Cabreza.
Licensure Skilled care. *Beds* SNF 180. *Certified* Medicaid; Medicare.
Owner Proprietary corp.
Admissions Requirements Minimum age 18; Medical examination; Physician's request.
Staff Physical therapists; Recreational therapists; Occupational therapists; Speech therapists; Activities coordinators 1 (ft); Dietitians 1 (ft).
Facilities Dining room; Physical therapy room; Activities room; Laundry room; Barber/Beauty shop; Conference room; Treatment room.
Activities Arts & crafts; Cards; Games; Reading groups; Prayer groups; Movies; Dances/Social/Cultural gatherings.

Daytona Beach Olds Hall Good Samaritan Nursing Center
325 S Segrave St, Daytona Beach, FL 32014
(904) 253-6791
Admin Bruce W Markkula. *Dir of Nursing* Fran Jones. *Medical Dir* Ernest Cook Jr MD.
Licensure Skilled care; Intermediate care. *Beds* 120; Apts 67. *Certified* Medicaid.
Owner Nonprofit corp (Evangelical Lutheran/ Good Samaritan Society).
Admissions Requirements Minimum age 16; Medical examination.
Staff RNs 5 (ft), 1 (pt); LPNs 15 (ft), 13 (pt); Nurses' aides 39 (ft), 18 (pt); Recreational therapists 5 (ft), 1 (pt); Activities coordinators 1 (ft); Dietitians 1 (pt); Ophthalmologists 1 (pt); Chaplain 1 (ft); Educator 1 (ft); Staff development 1 (ft); Dentists 1 (pt).
Affiliation Lutheran.
Facilities Dining room; Activities room; Chapel; Crafts room; Laundry room; Barber/ Beauty shop; Library.
Activities Arts & crafts; Cards; Games; Reading groups; Prayer groups; Movies; Shopping trips; Dances/Social/Cultural gatherings; Adopt-a-grandparent program; Farmer's market; Picnics at state park.

Fountains
1350 S Nova Rd, Daytona Beach, FL 32114
(904) 258-5544
Admin Homer Winans. *Dir of Nursing* Irene Barboza. *Medical Dir* George Powell DO.
Licensure Skilled care; Intermediate care; ACLF; ALC; Retirement; Alzheimer's care. *Beds* Swing beds SNF 55; ACLF 112; ALC 36. *Certified* Medicaid; Medicare.
Owner Proprietary corp (Horizon Health Care).
Admissions Requirements Physician's request.
Staff RNs; LPNs; Nurses' aides; Physical therapists; Reality therapists; Recreational therapists; Occupational therapists; Speech therapists; Activities coordinators; Dietitians; Podiatrists; Audiologists.
Facilities Dining room; Physical therapy room; Activities room; Chapel; Laundry room; Barber/Beauty shop; Library.
Activities Arts & crafts; Cards; Games; Prayer groups; Movies; Shopping trips; Dances/ Social/Cultural gatherings; Intergenerational programs; Pet therapy.

Golden Age Health Care
324 Wilder Blvd, Daytona Beach, FL 32014
(904) 252-0600
Admin James L Adkins. *Dir of Nursing* Adrianna Patterson. *Medical Dir* Dr James Carratt.
Licensure Skilled care. *Beds* SNF 192. *Certified* Medicaid; Medicare.
Owner Proprietary corp.
Admissions Requirements Minimum age 16; Medical examination; Physician's request.
Staff RNs 14 (ft); LPNs 14 (ft); Nurses' aides 60 (ft); Speech therapists 1 (ft); Activities coordinators 1 (ft); Dietitians 1 (ft).
Languages Dutch, Spanish, Russian.
Facilities Dining room; Physical therapy room; Laundry room; Barber/Beauty shop.
Activities Arts & crafts; Games; Movies; Dances/Social/Cultural gatherings.

Holiday Care Center
1031 S Beach St, Daytona Beach, FL 32114
(904) 255-2453, 258-2958 FAX
Admin Lynne L Fagan. *Dir of Nursing* Sue Davis RN. *Medical Dir* C M Crouch MD.
Licensure Skilled care; Intermediate care; Retirement; Alzheimer's care. *Beds* Swing beds SNF/ICF 48. *Private Pay Patients* 50%. *Certified* Medicaid.
Owner Privately owned.
Admissions Requirements Minimum age 18; Medical examination; Physician's request.
Staff Physicians; RNs 4 (ft); LPNs 4 (ft); Nurses' aides 25 (ft), 5 (pt); Physical therapists; Occupational therapists; Speech therapists; Activities coordinators 1 (ft); Dietitians 1 (ft); Podiatrists; Audiologists.
Facilities Dining room; Activities room; Crafts room; Laundry room; Barber/Beauty shop; Library; Living rooms; Shower room; Tub room.
Activities Arts & crafts; Cards; Games; Reading groups; Prayer groups; Movies; Shopping trips; Dances/Social/Cultural gatherings; Intergenerational programs; Pet therapy.

Huntington Square Convalarium
100 Broadway, Daytona Beach, FL 32016
(904) 255-6571
Beds 9.

Indigo Manor
595 Williamson Blvd, Daytona Beach, FL 32014
(904) 257-4400
Beds 62.

Olds Hall Good Samaritan Center
325 S Segrave St, Daytona Beach, FL 32114
(904) 238-6791
Admin Dorothy R Frederick. *Dir of Nursing* Francis Jones. *Medical Dir* Ernest C Cook Jr MD.
Licensure Skilled care; Intermediate care; Retirement; Alzheimer's care. *Beds* Swing beds SNF/ICF 120; Retirement 67. *Private Pay Patients* 35%. *Certified* Medicaid; Medicare.
Owner Nonprofit corp (Evangelical Lutheran/ Good Samaritan Society).
Admissions Requirements Minimum age 18; Medical examination; Physician's request.
Staff RNs 3 (ft), 3 (pt); LPNs 11 (ft); Nurses' aides 43 (ft); Activities coordinators 1 (ft).
Affiliation Lutheran.
Facilities Dining room; Physical therapy room; Activities room; Chapel; Crafts room; Laundry room; Barber/Beauty shop.
Activities Arts & crafts; Cards; Games; Reading groups; Prayer groups; Movies; Shopping trips; Dances/Social/Cultural gatherings; Intergenerational programs; Pet therapy; Music therapy; Horticultural therapy.

DeBary

DeBary Manor
60 N Hwy 17-92, DeBary, FL 32713
(407) 668-4426
Admin Patrick Lane. *Dir of Nursing* Eloise Hughley RN. *Medical Dir* Dr Miltenberger.
Licensure Skilled care; Intermediate care. *Beds* Swing beds SNF/ICF 93. *Private Pay Patients* 60%. *Certified* Medicaid; Medicare; VA.
Owner Privately owned.
Admissions Requirements Minimum age 21.
Staff RNs 5 (ft), 2 (pt); LPNs 9 (ft), 2 (pt); Nurses' aides 20 (ft), 5 (pt); Activities coordinators 1 (ft).
Languages Spanish.
Facilities Dining room; Laundry room; Barber/Beauty shop; Covered porches; Gazebo; Lake view.
Activities Arts & crafts; Cards; Games; Reading groups; Prayer groups; Movies; Shopping trips; Dances/Social/Cultural gatherings; Intergenerational programs; Pet therapy.

DeFuniak Springs

Walton County Convalescent Center
614 S 2nd St, DeFuniak Springs, FL 32433
(904) 892-2176
Licensure Skilled care. *Beds* 107. *Certified* Medicaid.
Owner Proprietary corp (Beverly Enterprises).
Staff RNs 4 (ft); LPNs 5 (ft); Nurses' aides 22 (ft).

Deland

Alliance Nursing Center
151 W Winnemissett Ave, Deland, FL 32720
(904) 734-6401
Licensure Skilled care. *Beds* 60. *Certified* Medicaid; Medicare.
Owner Nonprofit corp.
Staff RNs 4 (ft); LPNs 8 (ft); Nurses' aides 15 (ft).
Languages Spanish.
Affiliation Christian & Missionary Alliance Foundation.

Deland Convalescent Center
451 S Amelia Ave, Deland, FL 32724
(904) 734-8614
Admin Patricia S Lane.
Medical Dir Carol Price.
Licensure Skilled care; Intermediate care. *Beds* 122. *Certified* Medicaid; Medicare.

Owner Proprietary corp.
Admissions Requirements Minimum age 16; Medical examination.
Staff RNs 5 (ft), 4 (pt); LPNs 4 (ft), 3 (pt); Nurses' aides 32 (ft), 17 (pt); Activities coordinators 1 (ft).
Languages Spanish, German.
Facilities Dining room; Barber/Beauty shop.
Activities Arts & crafts; Cards; Games; Reading groups; Prayer groups; Movies; Shopping trips.

Ridgecrest Manor
PO Box 880, 1200 N Stone St, DeLand, FL 32720
(904) 734-6200
Admin David R Dowell. *Dir of Nursing* Karen Dickerson RNC. *Medical Dir* Curt N Rausch MD.
Licensure Skilled care. *Beds* SNF 134. *Private Pay Patients* 34%. *Certified* Medicaid.
Owner Proprietary corp.
Admissions Requirements Medical examination.
Staff RNs 5 (ft), 4 (pt); LPNs 5 (ft), 10 (pt); Nurses' aides 19 (ft), 31 (pt); Physical therapists; Activities coordinators 1 (ft), 1 (pt); Rehabilitation aides 2 (ft).
Languages Spanish, Filipino.
Facilities Dining room; Physical therapy room; Activities room; Laundry room; Barber/Beauty shop; Outdoor patio area.
Activities Arts & crafts; Cards; Games; Reading groups; Prayer groups; Shopping trips; Dances/Social/Cultural gatherings; Intergenerational programs; Pet therapy.

University Convalescent Center East Inc
991 E New York Ave, Deland, FL 32724
(904) 734-9083
Admin Carol J McGauvran. *Dir of Nursing* Leyon E Frierson RN. *Medical Dir* D S Rauschenberger MD.
Licensure Skilled care; Alzheimer's care. *Beds* SNF 60. *Certified* Medicaid; Medicare.
Owner Proprietary corp.
Admissions Requirements Physician's request.
Staff Physicians; RNs 6 (ft); LPNs 7 (ft); Nurses' aides 18 (ft); Physical therapists; Speech therapists; Activities coordinators; Dietitians; Ophthalmologists.
Languages Spanish.
Facilities Dining room; Activities room; Laundry room; Barber/Beauty shop.
Activities Arts & crafts; Cards; Games; Prayer groups; Movies; Shopping trips; Dances/ Social/Cultural gatherings.

University Convalescent Center West
545 W Euclid Ave, Deland, FL 32720
(904) 734-9085
Admin Barbara Hodges. *Dir of Nursing* Carol Mee RN. *Medical Dir* D Rauschenberger MD.
Licensure Skilled care; Intermediate care; Alzheimer's care. *Beds* 60. *Certified* Medicaid; Medicare; VA.
Owner Proprietary corp.
Admissions Requirements Minimum age 18; Medical examination; Physician's request.
Staff RNs 3 (ft), 1 (pt); Nurses' aides 17 (ft), 3 (pt).
Facilities Dining room; Activities room; Crafts room; Laundry room; Barber/Beauty shop; Library; Outside activities space.
Activities Arts & crafts; Cards; Games; Reading groups; Prayer groups; Movies; Shopping trips; Dances/Social/Cultural gatherings; Reality orientation; Mental health group sessions.

DeLeon Springs

Van Hook School of Florida Inc
PO Box 607, DeLeon Springs, FL 32028
(904) 985-5031
Admin Linda Burgess. *Dir of Nursing* JoAnn Brown. *Medical Dir* Andrew Randolph MD.

Licensure Residential habilitation center for mentally retarded. *Beds* 84.
Owner Proprietary corp.
Admissions Requirements Minimum age 6; Medical examination.
Staff Physicians 1 (pt); LPNs 3 (ft); Nurses' aides 45 (ft), 7 (pt); Activities coordinators 1 (ft); Dietitians 1 (pt); Behavior specialists 1 (ft).
Facilities Dining room; Activities room; Crafts room; Laundry room.
Activities Arts & crafts; Cards; Games; Reading groups; Movies; Shopping trips; Dances/Social/Cultural gatherings; Outdoor games; Special Olympics training; Competitive games.

Delray Beach

Harbour's Edge
401 E Linton Blvd, Delray Beach, FL 33444
Beds 30.

Health Care Center at Abbey Delray South
1717 Homewood Blvd, Delray Beach, FL 33445
(305) 272-9600
Beds 35.

Health Center at Abbey Delray
2105 Lowson Blvd, Delray Beach, FL 33445
(305) 278-3249
Admin Gary J Vasquez. *Dir of Nursing* Betty Ann Abe. *Medical Dir* Donald Bebout.
Licensure Skilled care; Retirement. *Beds* SNF 100. *Certified* Medicaid; Medicare.
Owner Nonprofit corp (Life Care Services Corp).
Admissions Requirements Medical examination; Physician's request.
Staff RNs; LPNs; Nurses' aides; Physical therapists; Recreational therapists; Occupational therapists; Speech therapists; Activities coordinators; Dietitians.
Facilities Dining room; Physical therapy room; Activities room; Chapel; Crafts room; Laundry room; Barber/Beauty shop; Library.
Activities Arts & crafts; Cards; Games; Reading groups; Prayer groups; Movies; Shopping trips; Dances/Social/Cultural gatherings; Patients' council; Monthly field trips.

Hillhaven Convalescent Center of Delray Beach
5430 Linton Blvd, Delray Beach, FL 33445
(407) 495-3188, 495-3190 FAX
Admin Scott Lipman NHA. *Dir of Nursing* Susan Miller RN. *Medical Dir* Dr George Dullaghan.
Licensure Skilled care. *Beds* SNF 120. *Private Pay Patients* 20%. *Certified* Medicaid; Medicare.
Owner Proprietary corp (Hillhaven Corp).
Staff RNs 7 (ft), 2 (pt); LPNs 8 (ft), 1 (pt); Nurses' aides 43 (ft), 6 (pt); Physical therapists 1 (ft); Recreational therapists 1 (pt); Occupational therapists 1 (pt); Speech therapists 1 (ft), 1 (pt); Activities coordinators 1 (ft).
Facilities Dining room; Physical therapy room; Activities room; Laundry room; Barber/Beauty shop; Library.
Activities Arts & crafts; Cards; Games; Prayer groups; Movies; Shopping trips; Dances/ Social/Cultural gatherings; Pet therapy.

Deltona

Deltona Health Care Center
1851 Elkcam Blvd, Deltona, FL 32725
(904) 789-3769
Admin Helen H Smith. *Dir of Nursing* Patricia Tuten. *Medical Dir* Dr Clyde Meade.
Licensure Intermediate care. *Beds* ICF 120. *Certified* Medicaid; Medicare.
Owner Proprietary corp (Beverly Enterprises).

Admissions Requirements Minimum age 16; Medical examination; Physician's request.
Languages Spanish.
Facilities Dining room; Physical therapy room; Activities room; Chapel; Crafts room; Laundry room; Barber/Beauty shop.
Activities Arts & crafts; Cards; Games; Reading groups; Prayer groups; Movies; Shopping trips; Dances/Social/Cultural gatherings.

Dunedin

Dunedin Care Center
Drawer 937, 1351 San Christopher Dr, Dunedin, FL 33528
(813) 736-1421
Admin Patricia McCormack. *Dir of Nursing* Joy Pike RN.
Licensure Skilled care; Alzheimer's care. *Beds* 104. *Certified* Medicaid; Medicare.
Owner Proprietary corp.
Admissions Requirements Medical examination; Physician's request.
Staff Physicians 1 (ft); RNs 4 (ft), 3 (pt); LPNs 4 (ft), 2 (pt); Nurses' aides 30 (ft); Activities coordinators 1 (ft); Dietitians 1 (pt); Social Services 1 (ft).
Languages German, French, Spanish, Swedish.
Facilities Dining room; Physical therapy room; Activities room; Crafts room; Laundry room; Barber/Beauty shop; Library; Patio.
Activities Arts & crafts; Cards; Games; Reading groups; Prayer groups; Movies; Shopping trips; Dances/Social/Cultural gatherings; Rehab groups for restorative therapies.

Manor Care of Dunedin
670 Patricia Ave, Dunedin, FL 33526
(613) 734-8861
Beds 64.

Spanish Gardens Nursing Center
1061 Virginia St, Dunedin, FL 34698
(813) 733-4189, 734-7651 FAX
Admin Richard P Ninis. *Dir of Nursing* Dianna Parady RN. *Medical Dir* Javier Bleichner MD.
Licensure Skilled care; Retirement; Alzheimer's care. *Beds* SNF 93; Retirement 16. *Private Pay Patients* 20%. *Certified* Medicaid; Medicare.
Owner Proprietary corp (Beverly Enterprises).
Admissions Requirements Minimum age 16; Medical examination.
Staff RNs 4 (ft); LPNs 10 (ft); Nurses' aides 42 (ft); Physical therapists; Activities coordinators 1 (ft); Dietitians 1 (ft).
Languages Spanish, German.
Facilities Dining room; Physical therapy room; Activities room; Laundry room; Barber/Beauty shop; Library; Covered patio.
Activities Arts & crafts; Cards; Games; Reading groups; Prayer groups; Movies; Shopping trips; Dances/Social/Cultural gatherings.

Englewood

Englewood Health Care Center
1111 Drury Ln, Englewood, FL 33533
(613) 474-9371
Beds 72.

Eustis

Eustis Manor Inc
2810 Ruleme St, Eustis, FL 32726
(904) 357-1990
Admin Danny K Prince.
Medical Dir Dr B W Price.
Licensure Skilled care. *Beds* 120. *Certified* Medicaid.
Owner Proprietary corp.

Admissions Requirements Medical examination.
Staff Physicians 13 (pt); RNs 6 (ft), 1 (pt); LPNs 8 (ft), 2 (pt); Nurses' aides 38 (ft); Physical therapists 3 (pt); Reality therapists 1 (pt); Speech therapists 2 (pt); Activities coordinators 1 (ft); Dietitians 1 (ft); Ophthalmologists; Podiatrists; Audiologists; Dentists.
Facilities Dining room; Laundry room; Barber/Beauty shop.
Activities Arts & crafts; Cards; Games; Reading groups; Prayer groups; Movies; Shopping trips; Dances/Social/Cultural gatherings.

Lake Eustis Care Center
411 W Woodward Ave, Eustis, FL 32726
(904) 357-3565
Licensure Skilled care. *Beds* SNF 60. *Certified* Medicaid; Medicare.
Owner Proprietary corp.
Staff RNs 3 (ft), 1 (pt); LPNs 6 (ft), 2 (pt); Nurses' aides 15 (ft), 4 (pt); Activities coordinators 1 (ft); Dietitians 1 (ft).
Facilities Dining room; Activities room; Chapel; Laundry room; Barber/Beauty shop; TV Room.
Activities Arts & crafts; Cards; Games; Reading groups; Prayer groups; Shopping trips; Dances/Social/Cultural gatherings; Church; Exercise classes; Music; Fishing; Bowling.

Oakwood Nursing Center
301 S Bay St, Eustis, FL 32726
(904) 357-8105, 589-1182 FAX
Admin James P Massey. *Dir of Nursing* Myra Carpenter. *Medical Dir* Dr Robert Crow.
Licensure Skilled care; Alzheimer's care. *Beds* SNF 120. *Private Pay Patients* 18%. *Certified* Medicaid; Medicare; VA.
Owner Proprietary corp (National Health Care Affiliates Inc).
Admissions Requirements Medical examination; Physician's request.
Staff RNs 5 (ft), 2 (pt); LPNs 10 (ft), 3 (pt); Nurses' aides 37 (ft), 5 (pt); Physical therapists 1 (ft), 1 (pt); Occupational therapists 1 (pt); Speech therapists 1 (pt); Activities coordinators 2 (ft); Dietitians 1 (pt); Ophthalmologists 1 (pt); Podiatrists 1 (pt).
Languages French, Sign.
Facilities Dining room; Physical therapy room; Activities room; Laundry room; Barber/Beauty shop; Park; Courtyard.
Activities Arts & crafts; Cards; Games; Reading groups; Prayer groups; Movies; Shopping trips; Dances/Social/Cultural gatherings; Intergenerational programs; Pet therapy.

Fernandina Beach

Amelia Island Care Center
2700 Atlantic Ave, Fernandina Beach, FL 32034
(904) 261-5518
Admin Thelma L Phillips. *Dir of Nursing* Demetris Smith RN. *Medical Dir* Dr Edward Tribuzio.
Licensure Intermediate care for mentally retarded. *Beds* ICF/MR 90. *Certified* Medicaid.
Owner Proprietary corp (Unicare).
Admissions Requirements Minimum age 18; Medical examination.
Staff Physicians 1 (ft); RNs 2 (ft); LPNs 6 (ft); Nurses' aides 58 (ft), 12 (pt); Physical therapists 1 (ft); Occupational therapists 1 (ft); Speech therapists 1 (ft); Activities coordinators 1 (ft); Dietitians 1 (ft); Resident living aides 45 (ft).
Languages Spanish.

Facilities Dining room; Physical therapy room; Activities room; Crafts room; Laundry room; Barber/Beauty shop.
Activities Arts & crafts; Cards; Games; Reading groups; Prayer groups; Movies; Shopping trips; Dances/Social/Cultural gatherings.

Quality Health of Fernandina Beach
1625 Lime St, Fernandina Beach, FL 32034
(904) 261-0771
Beds 66.

Fort Lauderdale

Broward Convalescent Home
1330 S Andrews Ave, Fort Lauderdale, FL 33316
(305) 524-5587
Admin Keith V Kroeger. *Dir of Nursing* Barbara Gill RN.
Licensure Skilled care. *Beds* SNF 198. *Certified* Medicaid; Medicare.
Owner Proprietary corp (HBA Management Inc).
Admissions Requirements Minimum age 16.
Staff RNs 15 (ft), 2 (pt); LPNs 14 (ft), 5 (pt); Nurses' aides 55 (ft), 20 (pt); Physical therapists 1 (pt); Speech therapists 1 (pt); Activities coordinators 2 (ft), 1 (pt); Dietitians 1 (pt).
Languages Spanish.
Facilities Dining room; Physical therapy room; Activities room; Chapel; Crafts room; Laundry room; Barber/Beauty shop.
Activities Arts & crafts; Cards; Games; Reading groups; Prayer groups; Movies; Shopping trips; Dances/Social/Cultural gatherings.

Daystar Inc
3800 Flamingo Rd, Fort Lauderdale, FL 33330
(305) 473-0167
Admin Neal Frank. *Dir of Nursing* Ruby O Morris.
Licensure Skilled care. *Beds* 44. *Certified* Medicare.
Owner Nonprofit corp.
Staff RNs 6 (ft); LPNs 8 (ft); Nurses' aides 2 (ft); Activities coordinators 1 (ft); Dietitians 1 (ft).
Languages Spanish, German, Japanese, Portuguese.
Affiliation Christian Science.
Activities Arts & crafts; Cards; Games; Reading groups; Prayer groups; Movies; Shopping trips; Dances/Social/Cultural gatherings.

Harbor Beach Convalescent Home
1615 S Miami Rd, Fort Lauderdale, FL 33316
(305) 523-5673, 523-5676 FAX
Admin Joseph L Gage NHA. *Dir of Nursing* Grace Achille RN. *Medical Dir* Guillermo Rodriquez MD.
Licensure Skilled care; Intermediate care. *Beds* SNF 22; ICF 37. *Private Pay Patients* 20%. *Certified* Medicaid; Medicare.
Owner Proprietary corp (Beverly Enterprises).
Admissions Requirements Minimum age 16; Physician's request.
Staff Physicians 1 (pt); RNs 2 (ft), 2 (pt); LPNs 5 (ft), 1 (pt); Nurses' aides 18 (ft), 5 (pt); Physical therapists 3 (pt); Recreational therapists 1 (ft); Occupational therapists 1 (pt); Speech therapists 1 (pt); Activities coordinators 1 (ft); Dietitians 1 (ft); Ophthalmologists 1 (pt); Podiatrists 1 (pt); Audiologists 1 (pt).
Languages Spanish, Creole.
Facilities Dining room; Physical therapy room; Activities room; Laundry room; Barber/Beauty shop; 3 outdoor patios.

Activities Arts & crafts; Cards; Games; Reading groups; Prayer groups; Movies; Dances/Social/Cultural gatherings; Intergenerational programs; Pet therapy; Educational, religious, & physical activities.

Manor Pines Convalescent Center
1701 NE 26th St, Fort Lauderdale, FL 33305
(305) 566-8353, 566-1416 FAX
Admin Timothy Kimes. *Dir of Nursing* Peggy Bennett. *Medical Dir* Dr Kurien Jacob.
Licensure Skilled care; Intermediate care; Retirement. *Beds* Swing beds SNF/ICF 190; Retirement 350. *Private Pay Patients* 80%. *Certified* Medicare.
Owner Proprietary corp.
Admissions Requirements Medical examination; Physician's request.
Staff RNs 15 (ft), 6 (pt); LPNs 14 (ft), 3 (pt); Nurses' aides 73 (ft), 10 (pt); Physical therapists 1 (pt); Occupational therapists 1 (pt); Speech therapists 1 (pt); Activities coordinators 2 (ft); Dietitians 1 (ft).
Languages Spanish.
Facilities Dining room; Physical therapy room; Activities room; Crafts room; Laundry room; Barber/Beauty shop.
Activities Arts & crafts; Cards; Games; Prayer groups; Movies; Dances/Social/Cultural gatherings; Intergenerational programs; Pet therapy; Adult education; Reminiscence.

Monticello Manor Nursing Home
1701 N Federal Hwy, Fort Lauderdale, FL 33305
(305) 564-3237
Licensure Skilled care. *Beds* 34.
Owner Proprietary corp.
Admissions Requirements Minimum age 16; Medical examination; Physician's request.
Staff RNs 4 (ft); LPNs 2 (ft); Nurses' aides 8 (ft), 1 (pt); Physical therapists 1 (pt); Reality therapists 1 (pt); Recreational therapists 1 (pt); Occupational therapists 1 (pt); Speech therapists 1 (pt); Activities coordinators 1 (pt); Dietitians 1 (pt); Podiatrists 1 (pt); Dentists 1 (pt).
Facilities Dining room; Physical therapy room; Activities room; Crafts room; Laundry room; Barber/Beauty shop.
Activities Arts & crafts; Cards; Games; Reading groups; Prayer groups; Movies.

Mt Vernon Manor
2331 NE 53rd St, Fort Lauderdale, FL 33308
(305) 771-0739
Licensure Skilled care. *Beds* 29.
Owner Proprietary corp.
Staff RNs 3 (ft); LPNs 2 (ft); Nurses' aides 11 (ft).
Languages Spanish, German.

National Health Care Center of Fort Lauderdale
2000 E Commercial Blvd, Fort Lauderdale, FL 33308
(305) 771-2300
Admin J W Dunwoody. *Dir of Nursing* Delores Thompson RN. *Medical Dir* Dr Lawrence Katzell.
Licensure Skilled care; Intermediate care; Alzheimer's care. *Beds* SNF 209; ICF 44. *Certified* Medicaid; Medicare.
Owner Proprietary corp.
Admissions Requirements Minimum age 16; Physician's request.
Staff Physicians 1 (pt); RNs 18 (ft); LPNs 26 (ft); Nurses' aides 87 (ft); Physical therapists 1 (ft); Recreational therapists 1 (ft); Occupational therapists 1 (pt); Speech therapists 1 (pt); Activities coordinators 3 (ft); Dietitians 1 (pt); Ophthalmologists 1 (pt); Social workers 1 (ft); Medical records administrators 1 (ft).
Languages German, Spanish, Italian, Yiddish.
Facilities Dining room; Physical therapy room; Activities room; Laundry room; Barber/Beauty shop; Library.

Activities Arts & crafts; Cards; Games; Reading groups; Prayer groups; Movies; Dances/Social/Cultural gatherings.

Palm Court Nursing & Rehabilitation Center
2675 N Andrews Ave, Fort Lauderdale, FL 33311
(305) 563-5711
Admin Bruce Atlas. *Dir of Nursing* Nancy Moore. *Medical Dir* Dr Mark Copen.
Licensure Skilled care; Alzheimer's care. *Beds* SNF 118. *Certified* Medicaid; Medicare.
Owner Proprietary corp (Unicare).
Admissions Requirements Medical examination; Physician's request.
Staff RNs 6 (ft), 3 (pt); LPNs 8 (ft), 8 (pt); Nurses' aides 27 (ft), 7 (pt); Physical therapists 3 (ft); Occupational therapists 1 (ft); Speech therapists 2 (ft); Activities coordinators 2 (ft); Dietitians 2 (ft); Social service directors 1 (ft); Admissions coordinators 1 (ft).
Languages Spanish.
Facilities Dining room; Physical therapy room; Activities room; Crafts room; Laundry room; Barber/Beauty shop; Library.
Activities Arts & crafts; Cards; Games; Reading groups; Prayer groups; Movies; Shopping trips; Dances/Social/Cultural gatherings; Exercise class; Continuing education; Reality orientation; Pet therapy; Resident council.

Ann Stock Center
1790 SW 43rd Way, Fort Lauderdale, FL 33317
(305) 584-8000
Admin Jim McGuire, Exec Dir. *Dir of Nursing* Jean Berrier RN. *Medical Dir* Kenneth Kromberg MD.
Licensure Intermediate care for mentally retarded. *Beds* ICF/MR 48. *Private Pay Patients* 0%. *Certified* Medicaid.
Owner Nonprofit organization/foundation.
Admissions Requirements Minimum age 6 mos; Medical examination; Specializes in mentally retarded, multiply physically handicapped.
Staff Physicians 1 (ft); RNs 3 (ft); LPNs 9 (ft); Nurses' aides 88 (ft); Physical therapists 1 (pt); Recreational therapists 1 (ft); Occupational therapists 1 (ft); Speech therapists 1 (ft); Activities coordinators 1 (ft); Dietitians 2 (ft).
Facilities Dining room; Physical therapy room; Activities room; Laundry room; Preschool.
Activities Arts & crafts; Games; Movies; Shopping trips; Dances/Social/Cultural gatherings; Pet therapy; Developmental training day program for adults.

Fort Myers

Beacon-Donegan Manor
8359 Beacon Blvd, Fort Myers, FL 33907
(813) 936-1300, 936-8754 FAX
Admin Khrys Kantarze NHA. *Dir of Nursing* Patricia Miller RN. *Medical Dir* Washington Baquero MD.
Licensure Skilled care; Intermediate care. *Beds* Swing beds SNF/ICF 150. *Private Pay Patients* 22%. *Certified* Medicaid; Medicare.
Owner Proprietary corp (Beverly Enterprises).
Admissions Requirements Medical examination; Physician's request.
Staff RNs 9 (ft), 5 (pt); LPNs 11 (ft), 1 (pt); Nurses' aides 44 (ft), 5 (pt); Activities coordinators 2 (ft).
Languages Spanish.
Facilities Dining room; Physical therapy room; Activities room; Barber/Beauty shop.
Activities Arts & crafts; Cards; Games; Reading groups; Prayer groups; Movies; Dances/Social/Cultural gatherings; Intergenerational programs; Pet therapy; Lunch outings; "Mind Your Moves".

Calusa Harbour
2525 E 1st St, Fort Myers, FL 33901
(613) 332-3333
Beds 14.

Cypress Manor
7173 Cypress Dr SW, Fort Myers, FL 33907
(813) 936-0203
Admin Dennis X Stress. *Dir of Nursing* Billie M Sorter RN. *Medical Dir* Edward Gonzales MD.
Licensure Skilled care. *Beds* SNF 120.
Owner Proprietary corp.
Staff Physicians 3 (ft); RNs 8 (ft), 1 (pt); LPNs 4 (ft), 5 (pt); Nurses' aides 54 (ft), 3 (pt); Physical therapists 1 (pt); Occupational therapists 1 (pt); Speech therapists 1 (pt); Activities coordinators 1 (ft), 1 (pt); Dietitians 1 (pt).

Fort Myers Care Center
13755 Golf Club Pkwy, Fort Myers, FL 33919
(813) 482-2848, 482-7331 FAX
Admin Nancy Zant. *Dir of Nursing* Pauline Margaritis RN. *Medical Dir* Dr Baquero.
Licensure Skilled care; Intermediate care; Medicare certified. *Beds* Swing beds SNF/ICF 107; Medicare certified 21. *Private Pay Patients* 50%. *Certified* Medicaid; Medicare.
Owner Proprietary corp (National Heritage).
Admissions Requirements Minimum age 21.
Staff RNs 9 (ft), 3 (pt); LPNs 12 (ft), 2 (pt); Nurses' aides 62 (ft), 7 (pt); Physical therapists 1 (ft), 1 (pt); Occupational therapists 1 (pt); Speech therapists 1 (pt); Activities coordinators 1 (ft), 1 (pt); Dietitians 1 (pt).
Facilities Dining room; Physical therapy room; Activities room; Crafts room; Laundry room; Barber/Beauty shop; Library.
Activities Arts & crafts; Cards; Games; Reading groups; Prayer groups; Movies; Shopping trips; Dances/Social/Cultural gatherings; Intergenerational programs; Pet therapy.

Gulf Coast Center/Sunland
RR 1, PO Box 506, Fort Myers, FL 33902
(813) 692-2151 *Certified* Medicaid.
Owner Publicly owned.

Lee Convalescent Center
2826 Cleveland Ave, Fort Myers, FL 33901
(813) 334-1091
Admin Michael Ellis. *Dir of Nursing* Linda Strommen RN. *Medical Dir* Rolando Jamilla MD.
Licensure Skilled care; Alzheimer's care. *Beds* SNF 146. *Certified* Medicaid; Medicare; VA.
Owner Proprietary corp (Beverly Enterprises).
Admissions Requirements Minimum age 16; Medical examination.
Staff Physicians 7 (pt); RNs 5 (ft), 3 (pt); LPNs 15 (ft), 3 (pt); Nurses' aides 52 (ft), 7 (pt); Physical therapists 1 (pt); Recreational therapists 1 (pt); Occupational therapists 1 (pt); Speech therapists 1 (pt); Activities coordinators 2 (ft); Dietitians 1 (pt); Ophthalmologists 1 (pt); Podiatrists 1 (pt); Dentists 1 (pt).
Languages German.
Activities Arts & crafts; Cards; Games; Reading groups; Prayer groups; Movies; Shopping trips; Dances/Social/Cultural gatherings; Community entertainment.

Pavilion at Shell Point Village
15000 Shell Point Blvd, Fort Myers, FL 33908
(813) 454-2274
Admin Mary Lou Coleman. *Dir of Nursing* Susan Deems RN. *Medical Dir* David Nesselroade MD.
Licensure Skilled care; Personal care; Alzheimer's care. *Beds* SNF 180; Personal care 150. *Private Pay Patients* 30%.
Owner Nonprofit organization/foundation (Christian Missionary Alliance Foundation).

Admissions Requirements Medical examination; Physician's request.
Staff Physicians 3 (ft); RNs 7 (ft), 7 (pt); LPNs 12 (ft), 5 (pt); Nurses' aides 49 (ft), 17 (pt); Physical therapists 1 (ft); Occupational therapists 1 (pt); Speech therapists 1 (pt); Activities coordinators 2 (ft); Dietitians 1 (ft); Podiatrists 1 (pt); Audiologists 1 (pt); Dentists 1 (pt).
Languages Spanish, Indian.
Affiliation Christian & Missionary Alliance Foundation.
Facilities Dining room; Physical therapy room; Activities room; Chapel; Crafts room; Laundry room; Barber/Beauty shop; Library; Waterfront picnic area; Garden; Lanai; Health club; Swimming pools.
Activities Arts & crafts; Cards; Games; Reading groups; Prayer groups; Movies; Shopping trips; Dances/Social/Cultural gatherings; Intergenerational programs; Pet therapy; Music; Exercise; Current events.

Shady Rest Nursing Home
2300 N Airport Rd, Fort Myers, FL 33905
(813) 936-2357
Admin Roger J Soricelli. *Dir of Nursing* Lanette Cummings.
Licensure Skilled care. *Beds* SNF 105. *Certified* Medicaid.
Owner Publicly owned.
Admissions Requirements Medical examination.
Staff RNs 8 (ft); LPNs 12 (ft); Nurses' aides 46 (ft); Activities coordinators 1 (ft); Dietitians 1 (ft).
Languages Spanish.
Facilities Dining room; Activities room; Chapel; Laundry room; Barber/Beauty shop.
Activities Arts & crafts; Cards; Games; Reading groups; Prayer groups; Movies; Dances/Social/Cultural gatherings.

Fort Pierce

Fort Pierce Care Center
703 S 29th St, Fort Pierce, FL 33450
(305) 466-3322
Medical Dir Carmen Ebalo MD.
Licensure Skilled care. *Beds* 102.
Owner Proprietary corp.
Admissions Requirements Minimum age 16; Medical examination.
Staff RNs 5 (ft), 6 (pt); LPNs 4 (ft), 7 (pt); Nurses' aides 30 (ft), 7 (pt); Activities coordinators 1 (ft); Dietitians 1 (ft).
Facilities Dining room; Physical therapy room; Activities room; Laundry room; Barber/Beauty shop.

Abbiejean Russell Care Center
700 S 29th St, Fort Pierce, FL 33456
(305) 465-7560
Admin R C Schriever.
Medical Dir Richard F Kaine MD.
Licensure Skilled care. *Beds* 79. *Certified* Medicaid.
Owner Nonprofit corp.
Admissions Requirements Minimum age 21; Medical examination; Physician's request.
Staff Physicians 3 (pt); RNs 3 (ft), 3 (pt); LPNs 8 (ft), 3 (pt); Nurses' aides 26 (ft), 1 (pt); Physical therapists 4 (pt); Occupational therapists 2 (pt); Speech therapists 2 (pt); Activities coordinators 1 (ft); Dietitians 1 (pt); Podiatrists 1 (pt); Audiologists 1 (pt); Dentists 1 (pt); Psychologists 1 (pt).
Languages Spanish, German, Polish.
Facilities Dining room; Physical therapy room; Activities room; Laundry room; Barber/Beauty shop; Library; Large screened patio; Large fenced yeard; Shuffleboard court; Outdoor barbecue.

Activities Arts & crafts; Cards; Games;
Reading groups; Prayer groups; Movies;
Shopping trips; Dances/Social/Cultural
gatherings; Morning fitness class; Weekly
cooking class.

Abbiejean Russell Care Center
PO Box 2079, 700 S 29th St, Fort Pierce, FL
34954
(407) 465-7560
Admin Carolyn A Hartley. *Dir of Nursing*
Carol Clause. *Medical Dir* Dr Josef Ilcus.
Licensure Skilled care; Intermediate care. *Beds*
Swing beds SNF/ICF 79. *Private Pay
Patients* 10%. *Certified* Medicaid.
Owner Nonprofit organization/foundation.
Staff RNs 3 (ft), 1 (pt); LPNs 11 (ft), 1 (pt);
Nurses' aides 31 (ft); Activities coordinators
1 (ft); Dietitians 1 (ft).
Languages Spanish.
Facilities Dining room; Physical therapy
room; Activities room; Chapel; Crafts room;
Laundry room; Barber/Beauty shop; Library.
Activities Arts & crafts; Cards; Games;
Reading groups; Prayer groups; Movies;
Shopping trips; Dances/Social/Cultural
gatherings; Intergenerational programs; Pet
therapy.

Sunrise Manor
611 S 13th St, Fort Pierce, FL 33450
(305) 464-5262
Licensure Skilled care. *Beds* 171. *Certified*
Medicaid; Medicare.
Owner Proprietary corp.
Staff RNs 8 (ft); LPNs 16 (ft); Nurses' aides
50 (ft).
Languages Spanish, French, Tagalog.

Fort Walton Beach

Fort Walton Developmental Center
113 Barks Dr, Fort Walton Beach, FL 32548
(904) 862-0108
Admin Robert Bowman PhD. *Dir of Nursing*
Mary Harper RN HSD.
Licensure Intermediate care for mentally
retarded. *Beds* 63.

Gulf Convalescent
114 3rd St, Fort Walton, FL 32548
(904) 243-6134
Admin H Louise McCosland. *Dir of Nursing*
Margaret Thompson. *Medical Dir* Dr A
D'Amore.
Licensure Skilled care; Intermediate care. *Beds*
SNF 32; ICF 88. *Private Pay Patients* 25%.
Certified Medicaid; Medicare.
Owner Proprietary corp.
Admissions Requirements Minimum age 21;
Physician's request.
Staff RNs 2 (ft), 1 (pt); LPNs 10 (ft), 3 (pt);
Nurses' aides 45 (ft), 28 (pt); Physical
therapists (contracted); Reality therapists
(contracted); Recreational therapists
(contracted); Occupational therapists
(contracted); Speech therapists (contracted);
Activities coordinators 1 (ft), 1 (pt);
Dietitians 1 (pt); Podiatrists 1 (pt).
Languages Spanish.
Facilities Dining room; Physical therapy
room; Laundry room; Barber/Beauty shop.
Activities Arts & crafts; Cards; Games;
Reading groups; Prayer groups; Movies;
Shopping trips; Dances/Social/Cultural
gatherings; Pet therapy.

Westwood Healthcare Center
1001 Marwalt Dr, Fort Walton Beach, FL
32548
(904) 863-5174
Beds 60. *Certified* Medicaid; Medicare.
Owner Proprietary corp.

Gainesville

Community Convalescent Center
1000 SW 16th Ave, Gainesville, FL 32601
(904) 376-2461
Licensure Skilled care. *Beds* 120. *Certified*
Medicaid; Medicare.
Owner Proprietary corp.
Staff RNs 8 (ft); LPNs 7 (ft); Nurses' aides 26
(ft).

Gainesville Nursing Center
4000 SW 20th Ave, Gainesville, FL 32608
(904) 377-1981
Admin R B Lockeby. *Dir of Nursing* Betty J
Owens RN. *Medical Dir* Dr David Black.
Licensure Skilled care. *Beds* 93. *Certified*
Medicaid; VA.
Owner Proprietary corp.
Admissions Requirements Minimum age 16;
Medical examination; Physician's request.
Staff Physicians 3 (pt); RNs 4 (ft), 1 (pt);
LPNs 6 (ft), 2 (pt); Nurses' aides 40 (ft), 10
(pt); Physical therapists 2 (pt); Reality
therapists 1 (ft); Recreational therapists 1
(ft); Speech therapists 1 (pt); Activities
coordinators 1 (ft), 1 (pt); Dietitians 1 (pt);
Podiatrists 1 (pt).
Languages Spanish, German,.
Facilities Dining room; Physical therapy
room; Activities room; Crafts room; Laundry
room; Barber/Beauty shop; Library.
Activities Arts & crafts; Cards; Games;
Reading groups; Prayer groups; Movies.

North Florida Special Care Center
6700 NW 10th Pl, Gainesville, FL 32605
(904) 372-3102
Beds 64.

Oaks Residential & Rehabilitation Center
3250 SW 41st Pl, Gainesville, FL 32608
(904) 378-1558, (414) 347-4414 FAX
Admin Todd Warnock. *Dir of Nursing* Charles
Lancaster. *Medical Dir* Dr B Mansheim.
Licensure Skilled care. *Beds* SNF 60; Other
beds 115. *Private Pay Patients* 5%.
Owner Proprietary corp (Unicare).
Staff Physicians; RNs; LPNs; Nurses' aides;
Physical therapists; Recreational therapists;
Occupational therapists; Speech therapists;
Activities coordinators; Dietitians;
Podiatrists; Audiologists.

Palm Garden
222 SW 62nd Blvd, Gainesville, FL 32607
(904) 332-0601
Beds 62.

Sunland Center—Gainesville Facility I
PO Box 1150, Gainesville, FL 32602
(904) 395-1454
Admin Fahmi Natour. *Dir of Nursing* Nancy
Sypert. *Medical Dir* Dr Robert Brown.
Licensure Intermediate care for mentally
retarded. *Beds* ICF/MR 120.
Owner Publicly owned.
Staff Physicians 1 (ft); RNs 9 (ft); LPNs 4 (ft);
Physical therapists 1 (ft); Recreational
therapists 9 (ft); Occupational therapists 2
(ft); Speech therapists 2 (ft); Activities
coordinators 3 (ft); Dietitians 1 (ft);
Audiologists 1 (ft).

Sunland Center—Gainesville Facility II
PO Box 1150, Gainesville, FL 32602
(904) 376-5381
Licensure Intermediate care for mentally
retarded. *Beds* 120.
Owner Publicly owned.

Sunland Center—Gainesville Facility III
PO Box 1150, Gainesville, FL 32602
(904) 376-5381
Licensure Intermediate care for mentally
retarded. *Beds* 60.
Owner Publicly owned.

University Nursing Care Center
1311 SW 16th St, Gainesville, FL 32608
(904) 376-8821
Admin Gary L Keach. *Dir of Nursing* T Volk.
Medical Dir Dr Jim Certa.
Licensure Skilled care; Intermediate care;
Alzheimer's care. *Beds* Swing beds SNF/ICF
180. *Private Pay Patients* 15%. *Certified*
Medicaid; Medicare; VA.
Owner Proprietary corp.
Admissions Requirements Minimum age 21;
Medical examination; Physician's request.
Staff RNs 9 (ft), 5 (pt); LPNs 8 (ft), 4 (pt);
Nurses' aides 40 (ft), 10 (pt); Physical
therapists 2 (pt); Recreational therapists 1
(pt); Occupational therapists 1 (pt); Speech
therapists 1 (pt); Activities coordinators 1
(ft); Dietitians 1 (pt); Podiatrists 1 (pt).
Languages Spanish.
Facilities Dining room; Physical therapy
room; Activities room; Crafts room; Laundry
room; Barber/Beauty shop; Library.
Activities Arts & crafts; Cards; Games;
Reading groups; Prayer groups; Movies;
Shopping trips; Dances/Social/Cultural
gatherings; Pet therapy.

Glenwood

Duvall Home
PO Box 36, 3395 Grand Ave, Glenwood, FL
32722
(904) 734-2874
Admin W Blake Davis. *Dir of Nursing*
Carolyn Righter RN.
Licensure Home for special services. *Beds*
Home for special services 250. *Private Pay
Patients* 67%.
Owner Nonprofit corp.
Staff RNs 1 (ft), 1 (pt); LPNs 11 (ft); Physical
therapists 1 (ft); Recreational therapists 5
(ft); Activities coordinators 1 (ft); Dietitians
1 (ft).
Languages Spanish.
Facilities Dining room; Physical therapy
room; Activities room; Chapel; Crafts room;
Laundry room; Barber/Beauty shop; Junior-
sized Olympic swimming pool.
Activities Arts & crafts; Cards; Games;
Movies; Shopping trips; Dances/Social/
Cultural gatherings; Boy Scouts; Choir.

Goulds

Lincoln Memorial Nursing Home
11295 SW 216th St, Goulds, FL 33170
(305) 235-7461
Medical Dir Manuel E Abella MD.
Licensure Skilled care. *Beds* 32. *Certified*
Medicaid; Medicare.
Owner Nonprofit corp.
Admissions Requirements Minimum age 16;
Medical examination; Physician's request.
Staff Physicians 2 (pt); RNs 1 (ft), 1 (pt);
LPNs 3 (ft), 4 (pt); Nurses' aides 9 (ft), 3
(pt); Physical therapists 1 (pt); Recreational
therapists 1 (pt); Occupational therapists 1
(pt); Speech therapists 1 (pt); Activities
coordinators 1 (ft); Dietitians 1 (pt); Dentists
1 (pt).
Languages Spanish, French.
Facilities Dining room; Activities room;
Crafts room; Laundry room.
Activities Arts & crafts; Cards; Games; Prayer
groups; Dances/Social/Cultural gatherings.

Sunrise Community—Miami
22300 SW 162 Ave, Goulds, FL 33170
(305) 245-6150
Admin Henry C Sterner DPA. *Dir of Nursing*
Eliza Perry RN.
Licensure Intermediate care for mentally
retarded. *Beds* ICF/MR 120. *Certified*
Medicaid.
Owner Proprietary corp.
Admissions Requirements Minimum age 3;
Medical examination.

Staff Physicians 1 (ft); RNs 9 (ft); LPNs 12 (ft), 5 (pt); Nurses' aides 4 (ft); Physical therapists 2 (ft); Recreational therapists 4 (ft); Occupational therapists 2 (ft); Speech therapists 2 (ft), 1 (pt); Activities coordinators 1 (pt); Dietitians 1 (ft).
Facilities Dining room; Physical therapy room; Activities room; Crafts room; Laundry room; Bedroom; Medical clinic; Auditorium; Transportation.
Activities Arts & crafts; Cards; Games; Prayer groups; Movies; Shopping trips; Dances/ Social/Cultural gatherings.

Sunrise Group Home 1—Goulds
1600 SW 216th St, Goulds, FL 33170
(305) 248-3701
Licensure Intermediate care for mentally retarded. *Beds* 15. *Certified* Medicaid.
Owner Proprietary corp.

Graceville

Jackson County Convalescent Center
1002 Sanders Ave, Graceville, FL 32440
(904) 263-4447
Licensure Skilled care. *Beds* 99. *Certified* Medicaid.
Owner Proprietary corp (Beverly Enterprises).

Green Cove Springs

Green Cove Springs Geriatric Center
803 Oak St, Green Cove Springs, FL 32043
(904) 284-5606
Licensure Skilled care. *Beds* 120. *Certified* Medicaid; Medicare.
Owner Proprietary corp (Beverly Enterprises).
Staff RNs 5 (ft); LPNs 12 (ft); Nurses' aides 37 (ft).
Languages Spanish, German.

Greenville

Pine Lake Nursing Home
PO Box 445, Hwy 90 E, Greenville, FL 32331
(904) 948-4601
Admin Wilson C Wingate NHA. *Dir of Nursing* B Hardee RNC. *Medical Dir* J M Durant MD.
Licensure Skilled care. *Beds* SNF 58. *Private Pay Patients* 7%. *Certified* Medicaid; Medicare.
Owner Proprietary corp (Arbor Living Centers).
Admissions Requirements Medical examination; Physician's request.
Staff Physicians 2 (pt); RNs 1 (ft), 2 (pt); LPNs 6 (ft), 5 (pt); Nurses' aides 19 (ft), 7 (pt); Physical therapists 1 (pt); Recreational therapists 1 (pt); Occupational therapists 1 (pt); Speech therapists 1 (pt); Activities coordinators 1 (ft); Dietitians 1 (pt); Ophthalmologists 1 (pt); Podiatrists 3 (pt).
Facilities Dining room; Activities room; Laundry room; Barber/Beauty shop.
Activities Arts & crafts; Cards; Games; Reading groups; Prayer groups; Movies; Shopping trips; Dances/Social/Cultural gatherings.

Gulf Breeze

Bay Breeze Nursing & Retirement Center
3375 Gulf Breeze Pkwy, Gulf Breeze, FL 32561
(904) 932-9257
Beds 68.

Gulfport

Gulfport Convalescent Center
1414 59th St S, Gulfport, FL 33707
(813) 344-4608
Medical Dir Robert Jenkins MD.

Licensure Skilled care. *Beds* 120. *Certified* Medicaid; Medicare.
Owner Proprietary corp.
Staff Physicians; RNs; LPNs; Nurses' aides; Physical therapists; Speech therapists; Activities coordinators; Dietitians; Dentists.
Languages Spanish.
Facilities Dining room; Activities room; Barber/Beauty shop; Library.
Activities Arts & crafts; Cards; Games; Prayer groups; Movies; Shopping trips; Dances/ Social/Cultural gatherings.

Haines City

Haines City Health Care
409 S 10th St, Haines City, FL 33644
(613) 422-8656
Beds 65.

Hallandale

Hallandale Rehabilitation Center
2400 E Hallandale Beach Blvd, Hallandale, FL 33009
(305) 457-9722
Licensure Skilled care. *Beds* 149. *Certified* Medicaid; Medicare.
Owner Proprietary corp.
Staff RNs 6 (ft); LPNs 19 (ft); Nurses' aides 55 (ft).
Languages Spanish.

Hialeah

Hialeah Convalescent Home
190 W 28th St, Hialeah, FL 33010
(305) 885-2437
Admin Kathryn Saretsky. *Dir of Nursing* Madeline Sawin RN. *Medical Dir* Manuel Abella MD.
Licensure Skilled care. *Beds* SNF 276. *Certified* Medicaid; Medicare.
Owner Proprietary corp (Angell Group).
Admissions Requirements Minimum age 16; Medical examination; Physician's request.
Staff Physicians 1 (pt); RNs 28 (ft); LPNs 5 (ft); Nurses' aides 98 (ft); Occupational therapists 1 (pt); Speech therapists 1 (pt); Activities coordinators 1 (ft); Dietitians 1 (pt); Ophthalmologists 1 (pt); Podiatrists 1 (pt); Dentists 1 (pt).
Languages Spanish.
Facilities Dining room; Physical therapy room; Activities room; Crafts room; Laundry room; Barber/Beauty shop.
Activities Arts & crafts; Cards; Games; Reading groups; Prayer groups; Movies; Shopping trips; Dances/Social/Cultural gatherings.

Palmetto Health Center
6750 W 22nd Ct, Hialeah, FL 33016
(305) 823-3119, 825-8255 FAX
Admin Andrew R McKillop CFACHCA. *Dir of Nursing* Sue Ellen Laurent RN BSN. *Medical Dir* Andrew G Frank MD.
Licensure Skilled care; Intermediate care. *Beds* SNF 44; ICF 46. *Private Pay Patients* 7%. *Certified* Medicaid; Medicare.
Owner Nonprofit corp.
Admissions Requirements Minimum age 16.
Staff Physicians; RNs 10 (ft); LPNs 8 (ft); Nurses' aides 26 (ft); Physical therapists 3 (ft); Occupational therapists 2 (ft); Speech therapists 2 (ft); Activities coordinators 2 (ft); Dietitians 1 (ft); Podiatrists 2 (pt); Audiologists 1 (pt).
Languages Spanish, French, German, Russian.
Facilities Dining room; Physical therapy room; Activities room; Crafts room; Laundry room; Barber/Beauty shop; Dayroom.
Activities Arts & crafts; Cards; Games; Reading groups; Prayer groups; Movies; Shopping trips; Dances/Social/Cultural

gatherings; Intergenerational programs; Pet therapy; Adult education; Walking team; Exercise groups; Chess.

Susanna Wesley Health Center Inc
5300 W 16th Ave, Hialeah, FL 33012
(305) 556-5654
Beds 66.

Hialeah Gardens

Waterford Convalescent Center
8333 W Okeechobee Rd, Hialeah Gardens, FL 33016
(305) 556-9900, 362-1548 FAX
Admin Mr Spinelli. *Dir of Nursing* Leah Rodriguez. *Medical Dir* Dr Jose C Alvarez.
Licensure Skilled care; Intermediate care. *Beds* Swing beds SNF/ICF 89. *Certified* Medicaid; Medicare.
Owner Proprietary corp (Brookwood Investments Ltd).
Staff Physicians; RNs; LPNs; Nurses' aides; Physical therapists; Reality therapists; Recreational therapists; Occupational therapists; Speech therapists; Activities coordinators; Dietitians.
Languages Spanish.
Facilities Dining room; Physical therapy room; Activities room; Chapel; Crafts room; Laundry room; Barber/Beauty shop.
Activities Arts & crafts; Cards; Games; Reading groups; Prayer groups; Movies; Shopping trips; Dances/Social/Cultural gatherings; Intergenerational programs.

Hobe Sound

Manors at Hobe Sound
9555 SE Federal Hwy, Hobe Sound, FL 33455
(407) 546-5800
Admin Gladys McCathern. *Dir of Nursing* Pamela Terlitz. *Medical Dir* Dr M Thanvi.
Licensure Skilled care; ACLF. *Beds* SNF 120; ACLF 48. *Certified* Medicaid; Medicare.
Owner Proprietary corp.
Admissions Requirements Medical examination.
Staff Physicians; RNs; LPNs; Nurses' aides; Physical therapists; Occupational therapists; Speech therapists; Activities coordinators; Dietitians.
Languages Spanish.
Facilities Dining room; Physical therapy room; Activities room; Chapel; Crafts room; Laundry room; Barber/Beauty shop; Lake; Fountain.
Activities Arts & crafts; Cards; Games; Reading groups; Prayer groups; Movies; Shopping trips; Dances/Social/Cultural gatherings; Intergenerational programs; Pet therapy.

Holly Hill

Bishop's Glen
900 11th St, Holly Hill, FL 32117
(904) 255-9000, 252-4168 FAX
Admin Rev C Philip Laucks. *Dir of Nursing* Ruth Ann Sanders RN. *Medical Dir* Gerald Ehringer MD.
Licensure Skilled care; Intermediate care; Independent apartment living; Assisted care apartments. *Beds* Swing beds SNF/ICF 60; Independent apartment living 250; Assisted care apts 34. *Private Pay Patients* 48-50%. *Certified* Medicaid; Medicare.
Owner Nonprofit organization/foundation (Retirement Housing Foundation Inc).
Admissions Requirements Minimum age 18; Medical examination; Physician's request.
Staff Physicians 3 (pt); RNs 5 (ft), 3 (pt); LPNs 4 (ft), 3 (pt); Nurses' aides 18 (ft), 8 (pt); Physical therapists 1 (ft); Occupational

therapists 1 (pt); Speech therapists 1 (pt); Activities coordinators 1 (ft); Dietitians 3 (pt); Podiatrists 1 (pt); Audiologists 1 (pt).
Facilities Dining room; Physical therapy room; Activities room; Crafts room; Barber/ Beauty shop.
Activities Arts & crafts; Games; Reading groups; Prayer groups; Movies; Shopping trips; Dances/Social/Cultural gatherings; Intergenerational programs; Pet therapy; Outdoor nature trips.

Hollywood

Golfcrest Nursing Home
600 N 17th Ave, Hollywood, FL 33020
(305) 927-2531
Admin Van K Isler. *Dir of Nursing* Colleen Sturgis. *Medical Dir* Samuel Colton MD.
Licensure Skilled care; Alzheimer's care. *Beds* 67. *Certified* Medicaid; Medicare.
Owner Proprietary corp (Americare Corp).
Admissions Requirements Minimum age 16; Medical examination; Physician's request.
Staff RNs 6 (ft), 3 (pt); LPNs 6 (ft), 3 (pt); Nurses' aides 30 (ft), 8 (pt); Physical therapists 1 (pt); Speech therapists 1 (pt); Activities coordinators 1 (ft); Dietitians 1 (ft); Ophthalmologists 1 (pt); Podiatrists 1 (pt).
Languages Spanish.
Facilities Dining room; Physical therapy room; Activities room; Laundry room; Barber/Beauty shop.
Activities Arts & crafts; Games; Reading groups; Movies; Dances/Social/Cultural gatherings.

Hollywood Hills Nursing Home
1200 N 35th Ave, Hollywood, FL 33021
(305) 981-5511
Admin Karen Kallen NHA. *Dir of Nursing* Betty Hewlett RN. *Medical Dir* Robert Finberg MD.
Licensure Skilled care. *Beds* SNF 152. *Private Pay Patients* 45%. *Certified* Medicaid; Medicare.
Owner Proprietary corp.
Admissions Requirements Medical examination.
Staff Physicians; RNs; LPNs; Nurses' aides; Physical therapists; Recreational therapists; Occupational therapists; Speech therapists; Activities coordinators; Dietitians; Ophthalmologists; Podiatrists; Audiologists.
Languages German, Spanish.
Facilities Dining room; Physical therapy room; Activities room; Crafts room; Laundry room; Barber/Beauty shop.
Activities Arts & crafts; Cards; Games; Reading groups; Prayer groups; Movies; Shopping trips; Dances/Social/Cultural gatherings; Intergenerational programs; Pet therapy.

Washington Manor Nursing & Rehabilitation Center
4200 Washington St, Hollywood, FL 33021
(305) 981-6300
Medical Dir Dr Richard Reines.
Licensure Skilled care; Alzheimer's care. *Beds* SNF 240. *Certified* Medicare.
Owner Proprietary corp (Beverly Enterprises).
Admissions Requirements Minimum age 18; Medical examination.
Staff RNs 6 (ft), 2 (pt); LPNs 17 (ft), 6 (pt); Nurses' aides 50 (ft), 15 (pt); Physical therapists 1 (ft), 1 (pt); Reality therapists 1 (pt); Recreational therapists 1 (pt); Occupational therapists 1 (pt); Speech therapists 1 (pt); Activities coordinators 3 (ft); Dietitians 1 (ft); Ophthalmologists 1 (pt); Social worker 1 (ft), 1 (pt).
Languages Spanish.

Facilities Dining room; Physical therapy room; Activities room; Chapel; Laundry room; Barber/Beauty shop; Library; 2 Outdoor garden patios.
Activities Arts & crafts; Cards; Games; Reading groups; Prayer groups; Movies; Shopping trips; Dances/Social/Cultural gatherings; Pet therapy; Barbeques.

Homestead

Brookwood Gardens Convalescent Center
1990 N Canal Dr, Homestead, FL 33035
(305) 246-1200
Beds 64.

Homestead Manor Nursing Home
1330 NW 1st Ave, Homestead, FL 33030
(305) 248-0271
Medical Dir Dr Bankett & Dr Crump.
Licensure Skilled care. *Beds* 54. *Certified* Medicaid; Medicare.
Owner Proprietary corp.
Staff Physicians; Dietitians; Nurses' aides.
Languages Spanish, Italian, German, French.
Facilities Dining room; Activities room; Crafts room; Laundry room; Barber/Beauty shop.
Activities Arts & crafts; Games; Movies; Shopping trips; Dances/Social/Cultural gatherings.

Hudson

Bear Creek Nursing Center Inc
8041 SR 52 E, Hudson, FL 33567
(813) 863-5488
Admin Van S McGlawn.
Medical Dir Louise Maben.
Licensure Skilled care; Intermediate care. *Beds* SNF 120; ICF. *Certified* Medicaid; Medicare.
Owner Proprietary corp (Health Facilities Management Inc).
Admissions Requirements Minimum age 16.
Staff RNs 6 (ft); LPNs 12 (ft); Nurses' aides 40 (ft); Activities coordinators 2 (ft).
Activities Arts & crafts; Cards; Games; Prayer groups; Movies; Shopping trips; Dances/ Social/Cultural gatherings.

National Healthcare Center
7210 Beacon Woods Dr, Hudson, FL 33567
(613) 863-1521
Beds 64.

Windsor Woods Convalescent Center
13719 Lakeshore Blvd, Hudson, FL 34667
(813) 862-6795
Admin Frank Eckert. *Dir of Nursing* Sue Gardner. *Medical Dir* Dr Donald Vierling.
Licensure Skilled care; ACLF; Retirement; Alzheimer's care. *Beds* SNF 60; ACLF 44. *Private Pay Patients* 61%. *Certified* Medicaid; Medicare.
Owner Proprietary corp (Hillhaven Inc).
Admissions Requirements Medical examination; Physician's request.
Staff RNs 3 (ft), 15 (pt); LPNs 8 (ft), 15 (pt); Nurses' aides 19 (ft), 9 (pt); Activities coordinators 2 (ft).
Facilities Dining room; Physical therapy room; Activities room; Barber/Beauty shop; Library; Alzheimer's unit.
Activities Arts & crafts; Cards; Games; Reading groups; Prayer groups; Movies; Pet therapy.

Inverness

Heritage Health Care Center
611 Turner Camp Rd, Inverness, FL 32651
(904) 637-1130
Admin Susan A Michael NHA. *Dir of Nursing* Gwendolyn D Strawitch RN. *Medical Dir* John Gelin MD.

Licensure Skilled care; Intermediate care; Adult congregate living; Alzheimer's care. *Beds* Swing beds SNF/ICF 60; Adult congregate living 56. *Private Pay Patients* 20%. *Certified* Medicaid.
Owner Proprietary corp.
Admissions Requirements Minimum age 18; Medical examination; Physician's request.
Staff Physicians 6 (pt); RNs 4 (ft); LPNs 6 (ft); Nurses' aides 23 (ft); Physical therapists 1 (pt); Reality therapists 1 (pt); Recreational therapists 1 (ft); Occupational therapists 1 (pt); Speech therapists 1 (pt); Activities coordinators 1 (ft); Dietitians 1 (pt); Ophthalmologists 1 (pt); Podiatrists 1 (pt); Audiologists 1 (pt).
Facilities Dining room; Physical therapy room; Activities room; Crafts room; Laundry room; Barber/Beauty shop; Library.
Activities Arts & crafts; Cards; Games; Reading groups; Prayer groups; Movies; Shopping trips; Dances/Social/Cultural gatherings; Intergenerational programs; Pet therapy.

Inverness Healthcare Center
304 S Citrus Ave, Inverness, FL 32652
(904) 726-3141, 637-0333 FAX
Admin Suzanne Johns. *Dir of Nursing* Susan Nadeau. *Medical Dir* William D Winelle.
Licensure Skilled care; Intermediate care; Sub-acute care; Alzheimer's respite/day care. *Beds* Swing beds SNF/ICF 104. *Private Pay Patients* 10%. *Certified* Medicaid; Medicare.
Owner Proprietary corp (Beverly Enterprises).
Admissions Requirements Minimum age 18; Medical examination; Physician's request.
Staff Physicians 20 (pt); RNs 4 (ft); LPNs 9 (ft), 4 (pt); Nurses' aides 31 (ft), 5 (pt); Physical therapists (contracted); Occupational therapists (contracted); Speech therapists (contracted); Activities coordinators 1 (ft); Dietitians (contracted); Ophthalmologists (contracted); Podiatrists (contracted); Audiologists (contracted).
Languages Korean, Spanish.
Facilities Dining room; Physical therapy room; Activities room; Crafts room; Laundry room; Barber/Beauty shop; Library.
Activities Arts & crafts; Cards; Games; Reading groups; Prayer groups; Movies; Shopping trips; Dances/Social/Cultural gatherings; Intergenerational programs; Pet therapy.

Jacksonville

Adams Plaza
33 W Adams St, Jacksonville, FL 32202
(904) 358-1832
Admin James Lundy. *Dir of Nursing* Patti Kink. *Medical Dir* Dr Groover.
Licensure Skilled care; Retirement. *Beds* SNF 35. *Certified* Medicaid.
Owner Privately owned.
Staff Physicians 1 (ft); RNs 1 (ft), 1 (pt); LPNs 3 (ft), 2 (pt); Physical therapists 21 (ft); Activities coordinators 1 (pt); Dietitians 1 (pt).
Facilities Dining room; Physical therapy room; Activities room; Crafts room; Barber/ Beauty shop.
Activities Arts & crafts; Cards; Games; Reading groups; Prayer groups; Movies.

All Saints Catholic Nursing Home
2040 Riverside Ave, Jacksonville, FL 32204
(904) 389-4671
Licensure Skilled care. *Beds* 57. *Certified* Medicaid.
Owner Nonprofit corp.
Staff RNs 2 (ft); LPNs 6 (ft); Nurses' aides 25 (ft).
Languages Spanish, French, Italian, Tagalog.
Affiliation Roman Catholic.

Americana Healthcare Center of Jacksonville
3648 University Blvd S, Jacksonville, FL 32216
(904) 733-7440
Admin Brian C Pollett.
Medical Dir Thomas E Michelsen DO.
Licensure Skilled care. *Beds* SNF 89. *Certified* Medicaid; Medicare.
Owner Proprietary corp.
Admissions Requirements Medical examination; Physician's request.
Staff RNs 3 (ft), 3 (pt); LPNs 7 (ft), 6 (pt); Nurses' aides 32 (ft), 10 (pt); Recreational therapists 1 (pt); Activities coordinators 1 (ft); Dietitians 1 (ft).
Languages Spanish, Tagalog.
Facilities Dining room; Physical therapy room; Activities room; Chapel; Crafts room; Laundry room; Barber/Beauty shop; Lounge; Outdoor patio.
Activities Arts & crafts; Cards; Games; Reading groups; Prayer groups; Movies; Shopping trips.

Arlington Manor Care Center
7723 Jasper Ave, Jacksonville, FL 32211
(904) 725-8044
Admin Deborah L Simmons. *Dir of Nursing* Jean Staley RN. *Medical Dir* Dr John C Hackenberg.
Licensure Skilled care; Intermediate care. *Beds* 100. *Certified* Medicaid; Medicare.
Owner Proprietary corp (Unicare).
Admissions Requirements Minimum age 21; Females only.
Staff Physicians 1 (pt); RNs 3 (ft); LPNs 7 (ft); Nurses' aides 22 (ft); Physical therapists 1 (pt); Speech therapists 1 (pt); Activities coordinators 1 (ft); Dietitians 1 (ft); Podiatrists 1 (pt).
Languages Spanish.
Facilities Dining room; Activities room; Laundry room.
Activities Arts & crafts; Cards; Games; Reading groups; Prayer groups; Movies; Shopping trips; Dances/Social/Cultural gatherings.

Beauclerc Manor
9355 San Jose Blvd, Jacksonville, FL 32217
(904) 739-0677
Beds 72.

Cathedral Convalescent Center
333 E Ashley St, Jacksonville, FL 32202
(904) 356-5507
Licensure Skilled care. *Beds* 32. *Certified* Medicaid; Medicare.
Owner Nonprofit corp.
Languages Spanish, Tagalog.
Activities Prayer groups.

Cedar Hills Nursing Center
2061 Hyde Park Rd, Jacksonville, FL 32210
(904) 786-7331
Admin Billy F Miles. *Dir of Nursing* Elaine H Drury RN. *Medical Dir* Thomas Thommi MD.
Licensure Skilled care. *Beds* SNF 180. *Certified* Medicaid; Medicare.
Owner Proprietary corp (Americare Corp).
Admissions Requirements Medical examination.
Staff Physicians 1 (ft); Physical therapists 4 (pt); Speech therapists 1 (pt); Activities coordinators 3 (ft); Dietitians 1 (ft), 1 (pt); Ophthalmologists 1 (pt); Podiatrists 1 (pt); Dentists 1 (pt).
Languages French, German, Spanish.
Facilities Dining room; Physical therapy room; Activities room; Chapel; Laundry room; Barber/Beauty shop.
Activities Arts & crafts; Cards; Games; Reading groups; Prayer groups; Movies; Shopping trips.

Eagle Crest Nursing Center
2802 Parental Home Rd, Jacksonville, FL 32216
(904) 721-0088
Admin Craig A Hoover. *Dir of Nursing* Barbara Torrible. *Medical Dir* Thomas Michelsen.
Licensure Skilled care; Intermediate care; Alzheimer's care. *Beds* SNF 60; ICF 180. *Certified* Medicaid; Medicare.
Owner Proprietary corp (National Health Care Affiliates Inc).
Admissions Requirements Medical examination.
Staff RNs; LPNs; Nurses' aides; Recreational therapists; Activities coordinators.
Facilities Dining room; Physical therapy room; Activities room; Laundry room; Barber/Beauty shop; Library; Alzheimer's unit.
Activities Arts & crafts; Games; Reading groups; Prayer groups; Movies; Shopping trips; Dances/Social/Cultural gatherings; Pet therapy.

Florida Christian Health Center
1827 Stockton St, Jacksonville, FL 32204
(904) 384-3457, 681-2075 FAX
Admin W C Wheatley Jr. *Dir of Nursing* June King. *Medical Dir* Joseph Boyd.
Licensure Skilled care; Intermediate care; Retirement. *Beds* Swing beds SNF/ICF 128; Retirement apartments 270. *Private Pay Patients* 50%. *Certified* Medicaid; Medicare.
Owner Nonprofit organization/foundation (National Benevolent Association of Christian Homes).
Admissions Requirements Minimum age 17; Medical examination; Physician's request.
Staff Physicians 1 (pt); RNs 3 (ft), 2 (pt); LPNs 14 (ft), 2 (pt); Nurses' aides 46 (ft), 3 (pt); Physical therapists 1 (pt); Activities coordinators 1 (pt); Dietitians (consultant); Podiatrists 1 (pt).
Languages Spanish.
Affiliation Disciples of Christ.
Facilities Dining room; Physical therapy room; Activities room; Crafts room; Barber/Beauty shop; Dock.
Activities Arts & crafts; Games; Reading groups; Shopping trips; Dances/Social/Cultural gatherings; Pet therapy; Fishing.

Hodges Boulevard Cluster Homes
3615 Hodges Blvd, RR 1, Jacksonville, FL 32224
(904) 241-4173
Licensure Intermediate care for mentally retarded. *Beds* 24.
Owner Publicly owned.

Jacksonville Convalescent Center
730 College St, Jacksonville, FL 32204
(904) 354-5589
Licensure Skilled care; Intermediate care; Alzheimer's care. *Beds* 104. *Certified* Medicaid.
Owner Proprietary corp (Beverly Enterprises).
Admissions Requirements Medical examination; Physician's request.
Staff Physicians; RNs; LPNs; Nurses' aides; Physical therapists; Recreational therapists; Occupational therapists; Speech therapists; Activities coordinators; Dietitians; Ophthalmologists.
Facilities Dining room; Physical therapy room; Activities room; Chapel; Laundry room; Barber/Beauty shop.
Activities Arts & crafts; Cards; Games; Prayer groups; Movies; Shopping trips; Dances/Social/Cultural gatherings.

Mandarin Manor
10680 Old Saint Augustine Rd, Jacksonville, FL 32257
(904) 268-4953

Admin W Joseph Ganzenhuber. *Dir of Nursing* Norma Williams. *Medical Dir* Jack E Giddings MD.
Licensure Skilled care; Intermediate care; Retirement; Alzheimer's care. *Beds* 120. *Certified* Medicaid; Medicare.
Owner Proprietary corp.
Admissions Requirements Medical examination; Physician's request.
Staff Physicians 4 (pt); RNs 4 (ft), 2 (pt); LPNs 12 (ft), 2 (pt); Nurses' aides 35 (ft), 2 (pt); Physical therapists 1 (pt); Activities coordinators 2 (ft); Dietitians 1 (ft); Ophthalmologists 1 (ft).
Facilities Dining room; Physical therapy room; Activities room; Crafts room; Barber/Beauty shop; Library.
Activities Arts & crafts; Cards; Games; Prayer groups; Movies; Shopping trips; Dances/Social/Cultural gatherings.

Regents Park of Jacksonville
7130 Southside Blvd, Jacksonville, FL 32216
(904) 642-7300
Beds 62.

River Garden Hebrew Home for the Aged
11401 Old Saint Augustine Rd, Jacksonville, FL 32258
(904) 389-3665
Admin Elliott Palevsky.
Medical Dir Lawrence E Geeslin MD.
Licensure Skilled care; Intermediate care. *Beds* SNF 182; ICF 10. *Certified* Medicaid; Medicare.
Owner Nonprofit corp.
Admissions Requirements Medical examination; Physician's request.
Staff Physicians 1 (ft), 2 (pt); RNs 10 (ft), 2 (pt); LPNs 24 (ft); Nurses' aides 87 (ft); Physical therapists 2 (ft), 2 (pt); Reality therapists 1 (ft); Recreational therapists 5 (ft); Occupational therapists 1 (ft); Speech therapists 2 (pt); Activities coordinators 1 (ft); Dietitians 1 (pt); Ophthalmologists 4 (pt); Audiologists 2 (pt); Dentists 6 (pt); Social workers 3 (ft).
Languages Spanish, German, Hebrew, Yiddish.
Affiliation Jewish.
Facilities Dining room; Physical therapy room; Activities room; Chapel; Crafts room; Laundry room; Barber/Beauty shop; Library; Landscaped river front garden with walks; Medical clinic.
Activities Arts & crafts; Cards; Games; Reading groups; Prayer groups; Movies; Shopping trips; Dances/Social/Cultural gatherings.

Rosewood Nursing Home
12740 Lanier Rd, Jacksonville, FL 32226-1704
(904) 757-0600
Admin Pat Scanlin.
Medical Dir Annie Reese.
Licensure Skilled care; Intermediate care. *Beds* SNF 5; ICF 50. *Certified* Medicaid; Medicare.
Owner Privately owned.
Admissions Requirements Physician's request.
Facilities Dining room; Activities room.
Activities Arts & crafts; Cards; Games; Prayer groups; Shopping trips.

St Catherine Laboure Manor
1717 Barrs St, Jacksonville, FL 32204
(904) 387-0587
Admin E Jack Huben. *Dir of Nursing* Emily Edmondson RN. *Medical Dir* Gerald Gillrato MD.
Licensure Skilled care; Intermediate care. *Beds* 232. *Certified* Medicaid; Medicare.
Owner Nonprofit corp.
Admissions Requirements Females only; Medical examination.

Staff RNs 10 (ft); LPNs 31 (ft); Nurses' aides 87 (ft); Recreational therapists 3 (ft); Activities coordinators 1 (ft).
Languages Spanish, Vietnamese, Farsi.
Affiliation Roman Catholic.
Facilities Dining room; Physical therapy room; Activities room; Chapel; Barber/ Beauty shop.
Activities Arts & crafts; Cards; Games; Reading groups; Prayer groups; Movies; Shopping trips; Dances/Social/Cultural gatherings; Fishing.

St Jude Manor Nursing Home
2802 Parental Home Rd, Jacksonville, FL 32216
(904) 721-0088
Licensure Skilled care. *Beds* 238. *Certified* Medicaid; Medicare.
Owner Proprietary corp (National Healthcare Affiliates).
Staff RNs 12 (ft); LPNs 17 (ft); Nurses' aides 48 (ft).
Affiliation Roman Catholic.

Southside Nursing Center Inc
40 Acme St, Jacksonville, FL 32211
(904) 724-5933
Admin Raymond R Savage.
Medical Dir Guy T Selander MD.
Licensure Skilled care. *Beds* 118.
Staff Physicians 2 (pt); RNs 4 (ft); LPNs 8 (ft), 4 (pt); Nurses' aides 28 (ft), 10 (pt); Activities coordinators 1 (ft); Dietitians 1 (pt); Ophthalmologists 1 (pt); Podiatrists 1 (pt); Dentists 1 (pt).
Facilities Dining room; Activities room; Laundry room; Barber/Beauty shop; Library.

Taylor Care Center
6535 Chester Ave, Jacksonville, FL 32217
(904) 731-6230
Beds 64.

Fannie E Taylor Home for the Aged
3937 Spring Park Rd, Jacksonville, FL 32207
(904) 737-6777
Licensure Intermediate care. *Beds* 24. *Certified* Medicaid.
Owner Nonprofit corp.
Staff Physicians; Dietitians; Nurses' aides.
Activities Arts & crafts; Shopping trips.

Turtle Creek Health Care Center
11565 Harts Rd, Jacksonville, FL 32218
(904) 751-1834
Admin Joseph DeBelder. *Dir of Nursing* Sandra Hudson RN. *Medical Dir* Dr Samara.
Licensure Skilled care. *Beds* 180. *Certified* Medicaid.
Owner Proprietary corp (Beverly Enterprises).
Admissions Requirements Minimum age 18; Medical examination.
Staff RNs 6 (ft); LPNs 24 (ft); Nurses' aides 60 (ft).
Facilities Dining room; Physical therapy room; Activities room; Laundry room; Barber/Beauty shop.
Activities Arts & crafts; Cards; Games; Reading groups; Prayer groups; Movies; Shopping trips.

Wesley Manor Retirement Village
State Rd 13 at Julington Creek Rd, Jacksonville, FL 32223
(904) 262-7300
Dir of Nursing Virginia Johnson RN.
Licensure Skilled care; Retirement; Alzheimer's care. *Beds* 57.
Owner Nonprofit corp.
Admissions Requirements Minimum age 62; Medical examination.
Staff Physicians 3 (pt); Physical therapists 1 (pt); Recreational therapists 1 (pt); Occupational therapists 1 (pt); Speech therapists 1 (pt); Activities coordinators 1 (ft); Dietitians 1 (ft); Podiatrists 1 (pt).
Languages Italian.

Affiliation Methodist.
Facilities Dining room; Physical therapy room; Activities room; Chapel; Crafts room; Laundry room; Barber/Beauty shop; Library.
Activities Arts & crafts; Cards; Games; Reading groups; Prayer groups; Movies; Shopping trips; Dances/Social/Cultural gatherings.

Eartha M M White Nursing Home
5377 Moncrief Rd, Jacksonville, FL 32209
(904) 768-1506
Admin S L Patterson.
Licensure Skilled care. *Beds* 120. *Certified* Medicaid; Medicare.
Owner Nonprofit corp.
Admissions Requirements Minimum age 18; Medical examination.
Staff Physicians 4 (pt); RNs 3 (ft), 4 (pt); LPNs 10 (ft), 7 (pt); Nurses' aides 40 (ft), 1 (pt); Physical therapists 1 (ft); Reality therapists 1 (pt); Recreational therapists 1 (pt); Occupational therapists 1 (pt); Speech therapists 1 (pt); Activities coordinators 1 (ft); Dietitians 1 (pt); Ophthalmologists 1 (pt); Podiatrists 1 (pt); Audiologists 1 (pt); Dentists 1 (pt).
Languages Tagalog.
Facilities Dining room; Physical therapy room; Activities room; Chapel; Crafts room; Laundry room; Barber/Beauty shop; Library.
Activities Arts & crafts; Cards; Games; Reading groups; Prayer groups; Movies; Shopping trips; Dances/Social/Cultural gatherings; Birthday parties.

Jacksonville Beach

Avante Villa at Jacksonville Beach
1504 Seabreeze Ave, Jacksonville Beach, FL 32250
(904) 249-7421, 249-8208 FAX
Admin Jeffrey H Tomack MHSA. *Dir of Nursing* Mary F Buzza RN BSN. *Medical Dir* John Tanner DO.
Licensure Skilled care. *Beds* SNF 120. *Certified* Medicaid; Medicare.
Owner Proprietary corp.
Staff RNs 5 (ft); LPNs 13 (ft); Nurses' aides 38 (ft), 3 (pt); Activities coordinators 1 (ft), 1 (pt).
Languages Spanish.
Facilities Dining room; Physical therapy room; Activities room; Chapel; Crafts room; Laundry room; Barber/Beauty shop; Library.
Activities Arts & crafts; Cards; Games; Reading groups; Prayer groups; Movies; Shopping trips; Dances/Social/Cultural gatherings; Intergenerational programs; Pet therapy.

Jasper

Suwannee Valley Nursing Center
PO Drawer 1058, Jasper, FL 32502
(904) 792-1868
Licensure Skilled care. *Beds* 60. *Certified* Medicaid.
Owner Proprietary corp.
Staff RNs 5 (ft), 5 (pt); LPNs 2 (ft), 3 (pt); Nurses' aides 10 (ft), 10 (pt); Activities coordinators 1 (ft); Dietitians 1 (ft).

Juno Beach

Waterford Health Center
601 S US Hwy 1, Juno Beach, FL 33408
(305) 627-3800
Admin Becky Brown. *Dir of Nursing* Cathy Hazen.
Licensure Skilled care; Retirement. *Beds* SNF 60. *Certified* Medicaid; Medicare.
Owner Nonprofit corp (Life Care Services Corp).
Admissions Requirements Medical examination.

Staff RNs 4 (ft), 1 (pt); LPNs 8 (ft), 1 (pt); Nurses' aides 18 (ft), 3 (pt); Physical therapists 1 (pt); Occupational therapists; Speech therapists; Activities coordinators 1 (ft); Dietitians 1 (ft).
Facilities Dining room; Physical therapy room; Activities room; Crafts room; Barber/Beauty shop; Library.
Activities Arts & crafts; Cards; Games; Reading groups; Prayer groups; Movies; Shopping trips; Dances/Social/Cultural gatherings.

Jupiter

Jupiter Care Center
17781 Yancy Ave, Jupiter, FL 33458
(407) 746-2998, 743-8607 FAX
Admin Brian Lee Allen. *Dir of Nursing* Susan Hanssel. *Medical Dir* Dr Raj Bansal; Dr Mistry.
Licensure Skilled care. *Beds* SNF 120. *Private Pay Patients* 23%. *Certified* Medicaid; Medicare.
Owner Proprietary corp (Beverly Enterprises).
Admissions Requirements Medical examination; Physician's request.
Staff Physicians 2 (pt); RNs 5 (ft), 1 (pt); LPNs 10 (ft), 1 (pt); Nurses' aides 30 (ft), 2 (pt); Physical therapists 1 (ft); Occupational therapists 1 (ft), 1 (pt); Speech therapists 1 (ft), 1 (pt); Activities coordinators 1 (ft); Dietitians 1 (pt); Ophthalmologists 1 (pt); Podiatrists 1 (pt); Audiologists 1 (pt).
Languages Spanish, German, Hebrew, Norwegian.
Facilities Dining room; Physical therapy room; Activities room; Chapel; Crafts room; Laundry room; Barber/Beauty shop; Library; Screened patio; Dayroom.
Activities Arts & crafts; Cards; Games; Reading groups; Prayer groups; Movies; Shopping trips; Dances/Social/Cultural gatherings; Intergenerational programs; Pet therapy.

Jupiter Convalescence Pavilion
1230 S Old Dixie Hwy, Jupiter, FL 33458
(305) 744-4444
Dir of Nursing Doris M Ferriol RN. *Medical Dir* Andres Svarez MD.
Licensure Skilled care; Alzheimer's care. *Beds* 120. *Certified* Medicaid; Medicare.
Owner Nonprofit corp.
Admissions Requirements Minimum age 21; Medical examination; Physician's request.
Staff Physicians 3 (pt); RNs 9 (ft), 6 (pt); LPNs 9 (ft), 3 (pt); Nurses' aides 45 (ft), 5 (pt); Physical therapists 1 (ft); Activities coordinators 1 (ft); Dietitians 1 (ft).
Facilities Dining room; Physical therapy room; Activities room; Chapel; Crafts room; Laundry room; Barber/Beauty shop; Library.
Activities Arts & crafts; Cards; Games; Reading groups; Prayer groups; Movies; Shopping trips; Dances/Social/Cultural gatherings.

Key West

Key West Convalescent Center
5860 W Jr College Rd, Key West, FL 33040
(305) 296-2459, 294-8604 FAX
Admin Douglas Brown NHA. *Dir of Nursing* Joan Slack RN. *Medical Dir* George Wright MD.
Licensure Skilled care; Intermediate care. *Beds* Swing beds SNF/ICF 120. *Certified* Medicaid; Medicare.
Owner Nonprofit corp.
Admissions Requirements Minimum age 18; Medical examination; Physician's request.
Staff Physicians 3 (ft), 3 (pt); RNs 9 (ft), 1 (pt); LPNs 10 (ft); Nurses' aides 31 (ft), 3 (pt); Physical therapists 1 (ft); Activities coordinators 2 (ft); Dietitians 2 (ft); Podiatrists 1 (ft).

Languages Spanish.
Facilities Dining room; Physical therapy room; Laundry room; Barber/Beauty shop; Library.
Activities Arts & crafts; Cards; Games; Reading groups; Prayer groups; Movies; Shopping trips; Dances/Social/Cultural gatherings; Intergenerational programs; Pet therapy.

Kissimmee

Kissimmee Good Samaritan Nursing Center
1500 Southgate Dr, Kissimmee, FL 32741
(305) 933-3200
Medical Dir Pedro Gonzales.
Licensure Skilled care; Intermediate care. *Beds* SNF 142; ICF 28. *Certified* Medicaid.
Owner Nonprofit corp (Evangelical Lutheran/Good Samaritan Society).
Admissions Requirements Minimum age 21; Medical examination; Physician's request.
Staff RNs 3 (ft), 6 (pt); LPNs 11 (ft), 3 (pt); Nurses' aides 66 (ft), 2 (pt); Activities coordinators 3 (ft).
Languages Spanish, French, German.
Affiliation Lutheran.
Facilities Dining room; Physical therapy room; Activities room; Crafts room; Laundry room.
Activities Arts & crafts; Cards; Games; Reading groups; Prayer groups; Movies; Shopping trips; Dances/Social/Cultural gatherings.

Kissimmee Health Care Center
320 N Mitchell St, Kissimmee, FL 32741
(305) 847-7200
Licensure Skilled care. *Beds* 59. *Certified* Medicare.
Owner Proprietary corp (US Care Corp).
Staff Nurses' aides 17 (ft).

John Milton Nursing Home
1120 W Donegan Ave, Kissimmee, FL 32741
(305) 847-2854
Licensure Skilled care. *Beds* 149. *Certified* Medicaid.
Owner Proprietary corp (Beverly Enterprises).
Staff RNs 4 (ft); LPNs 10 (ft).
Languages Spanish.

LaBelle

Meadowbrook Manor of LaBelle
250 Broward Ave, LaBelle, FL 33935
(813) 675-1440
Admin Robert W Shaw. *Dir of Nursing* Michelle Steinfeldt. *Medical Dir* K F Chow.
Licensure Skilled care; Intermediate care; ACLF; Retirement. *Beds* Swing beds SNF/ICF 60; ACLF 32. *Private Pay Patients* 10%. *Certified* Medicaid.
Owner Nonprofit corp (RHA-South Florida Operations Inc).
Admissions Requirements Medical examination.
Staff Physicians 2 (ft); RNs 2 (ft), 3 (pt); LPNs 4 (ft), 2 (pt); Nurses' aides 23 (ft), 2 (pt); Physical therapists (consultant); Reality therapists (consultant); Recreational therapists (consultant); Occupational therapists (consultant); Speech therapists (consultant); Activities coordinators 1 (ft); Dietitians (consultant); Ophthalmologists (consultant); Podiatrists (consultant); Audiologists (consultant); Ward clerks 1 (ft).
Languages Spanish, German.
Facilities Dining room; Physical therapy room; Activities room; Crafts room; Laundry room; Barber/Beauty shop.
Activities Arts & crafts; Cards; Games; Prayer groups; Movies; Shopping trips; Intergenerational programs; Pet therapy; Community support.

Lake Alfred

Lake Alfred Restorium
PO Box 1427, 350 W Haines Blvd, Lake Alfred, FL 33850
(813) 956-1700
Admin Lavon R Childers. *Dir of Nursing* Flora Connelly RN. *Medical Dir* Ernest DiLorenzo MD.
Licensure Skilled care; ACLF; Retirement. *Beds* SNF 31; ACLF 25. *Certified* Medicaid.
Owner Proprietary corp (Sunbelt Healthcare Center).
Admissions Requirements Minimum age 19; Medical examination; Physician's request.
Staff RNs 1 (ft), 1 (pt); LPNs 3 (ft), 3 (pt); Nurses' aides 17 (ft), 2 (pt); Activities coordinators 1 (ft), 1 (pt).
Languages Spanish.
Affiliation Seventh-Day Adventist.
Facilities Dining room; Activities room; Laundry room; Barber/Beauty shop.
Activities Arts & crafts; Cards; Games; Reading groups; Prayer groups; Movies; Shopping trips; Dances/Social/Cultural gatherings; Ceramics.

Lake City

Tanglewood Convalescent Center
2400 S 1st St, Lake City, FL 32055
(904) 752-7900
Admin Nancy L Pryor.
Medical Dir Sarian Vunk.
Licensure Skilled care; Intermediate care. *Beds* 95. *Certified* Medicaid; Medicare.
Owner Nonprofit corp.
Admissions Requirements Minimum age 18; Medical examination.
Staff Physicians 12 (pt); RNs 4 (ft), 2 (pt); LPNs 7 (ft), 4 (pt); Nurses' aides 31 (ft), 7 (pt); Physical therapists 1 (pt); Recreational therapists 1 (pt); Speech therapists 1 (pt); Activities coordinators 1 (ft), 1 (pt); Dietitians 1 (ft), 1 (pt); Ophthalmologists 1 (pt).
Languages German, Spanish, Polish.
Facilities Dining room; Physical therapy room; Activities room; Crafts room; Laundry room; Barber/Beauty shop; Library.
Activities Arts & crafts; Cards; Games; Reading groups; Prayer groups; Movies; Shopping trips; Dances/Social/Cultural gatherings; Garden club; Travel club; Sunshine club.

Lake Park

Helen Wilkes Residence
750 Bayberry Dr, Lake Park, FL 33403
(305) 844-4457
Admin Charlotte L Mooradian.
Medical Dir Dr Antonio Rivera.
Licensure Skilled care; Intermediate care. *Beds* SNF 17; ICF 19; VA & Private pay 49. *Certified* Medicaid; Medicare; VA.
Owner Nonprofit corp (Renaissance).
Admissions Requirements Minimum age 16; Medical examination; Physician's request.
Staff RNs 6 (ft); LPNs 6 (ft); Nurses' aides 30 (ft); Physical therapists 1 (pt); Recreational therapists 1 (ft); Occupational therapists 1 (pt); Speech therapists 1 (pt); Activities coordinators 1 (ft); Dietitians 1 (pt); Medical directors.
Facilities Dining room; Physical therapy room; Activities room; Laundry room; Barber/Beauty shop.
Activities Arts & crafts; Cards; Games; Prayer groups; Movies; Shopping trips; Dances/Social/Cultural gatherings; Intergenerational programs; Pet therapy.

Lake Placid

Lake Placid Health Care Center
125 Tomoka Blvd, Lake Placid, FL 33652
(613) 465-7200
Beds 40.

Lake Wales

Lake Wales Convalescent Center
730 W Scenic Hwy, Lake Wales, FL 33853
(813) 676-1512, 5751
Admin Stephen C Brown. *Dir of Nursing* Virginia Cranfill RN. *Medical Dir* Fredrick M Rawlings MD.
Licensure Skilled care; Intermediate care; Alzheimer's care. *Beds* SNF 100; ICF. *Certified* Medicaid.
Owner Proprietary corp (Sunbelt Healthcare Centers).
Admissions Requirements Minimum age 18; Medical examination; Physician's request.
Staff Physicians 9 (pt); RNs 6 (ft), 2 (pt); LPNs 5 (ft), 5 (pt); Nurses' aides 26 (ft), 8 (pt); Physical therapists 1 (pt); Recreational therapists 2 (ft); Occupational therapists 1 (pt); Speech therapists 1 (pt); Activities coordinators 2 (ft); Dietitians 1 (pt); Ophthalmologists 1 (pt).
Affiliation Seventh-Day Adventist.
Facilities Dining room; Activities room; Crafts room; Laundry room; Barber/Beauty shop; Library.
Activities Arts & crafts; Cards; Games; Reading groups; Prayer groups; Movies; Shopping trips; Dances/Social/Cultural gatherings.

Lake Wales Hospital Extended Care Facility
414 S 11th St, Lake Wales, FL 33653
(613) 676-3481
Beds 64.

Ridge Convalescent Center
512 S 11th St, Lake Wales, FL 33853
(813) 676-8502
Admin David A Crosby. *Dir of Nursing* Josephine Meeks. *Medical Dir* Dr Joseph A Wiltshire.
Licensure Skilled care. *Beds* 120. *Certified* Medicaid; Medicare.
Owner Proprietary corp.
Admissions Requirements Medical examination.
Staff Physicians 4 (ft), 3 (pt); RNs 3 (ft), 1 (pt); LPNs 10 (ft), 3 (pt); Nurses' aides 40 (ft); Physical therapists 1 (ft); Speech therapists 1 (ft); Activities coordinators 1 (ft); Dietitians 1 (pt); Ophthalmologists 1 (pt); Podiatrists 1 (pt); Dentists 2 (pt).
Facilities Dining room; Activities room; Crafts room; Laundry room; Barber/Beauty shop.
Activities Arts & crafts; Cards; Games; Reading groups; Prayer groups.

Lake Worth

American Finnish Nursing Home Finnish-American Rest Home Inc
1800 South Dr, Lake Worth, FL 33461
(305) 588-4333
Admin Sara B Reid.
Licensure Skilled care; ACLF. *Beds* 60; ACLF 198. *Certified* Medicaid.
Owner Nonprofit corp.
Admissions Requirements Minimum age 55; Medical examination; Physician's request.
Staff RNs 5 (ft), 1 (pt); LPNs 8 (ft); Nurses' aides 21 (ft), 3 (pt); Physical therapists 1 (ft); Recreational therapists 2 (ft); Speech therapists 1 (ft); Activities coordinators 2 (ft); Dietitians 1 (pt).
Languages Finnish, Swedish, Spanish.

Facilities Dining room; Physical therapy room; Activities room; Chapel; Crafts room; Laundry room; Barber/Beauty shop; Library; Recreation hall.
Activities Arts & crafts; Cards; Games; Reading groups; Prayer groups; Movies; Shopping trips; Dances/Social/Cultural gatherings; Spontaneous & planned parties.

Crest Manor Nursing Center
504 3rd Ave S, Lake Worth, FL 33460
(407) 585-4695
Admin Amy H Roberts. *Dir of Nursing* Elice Holden RN. *Medical Dir* David Kiner DO.
Licensure Skilled care; Intermediate care. *Beds* 71. *Private Pay Patients* 33%. *Certified* Medicaid; Medicare.
Owner Proprietary corp (Rotsell Baldwin Inc).
Admissions Requirements Minimum age 16.
Staff Physicians; RNs; LPNs; Nurses' aides; Physical therapists; Occupational therapists; Speech therapists; Activities coordinators; Dietitians; Ophthalmologists; Podiatrists; Audiologists.
Languages Spanish, German.
Facilities Dining room; Physical therapy room; Activities room; Crafts room.
Activities Arts & crafts; Cards; Games; Reading groups; Prayer groups; Movies; Shopping trips; Dances/Social/Cultural gatherings; Intergenerational programs; Pet therapy.

Eason Nursing Home
1711 6th Ave S, Lake Worth, FL 33460
(305) 582-1472
Admin T C Gervais.
Medical Dir Robert J Miquel MD.
Licensure Skilled care. *Beds* 99. *Certified* Medicaid; Medicare.
Owner Proprietary corp.
Admissions Requirements Minimum age 65; Medical examination; Physician's request.
Staff RNs 6 (ft), 1 (pt); LPNs 5 (ft), 1 (pt); Nurses' aides 30 (ft), 5 (pt); Activities coordinators 1 (ft), 1 (pt); Dietitians 1 (ft); Social workers 1 (ft).
Languages French, Spanish, Finnish.
Facilities Dining room; Activities room; Crafts room; Laundry room; Barber/Beauty shop.
Activities Arts & crafts; Cards; Games; Prayer groups; Movies; Shopping trips; Dances/Social/Cultural gatherings; Picnics; Park outings.

Lake Worth Health Care Center
2501 N "A" St, Lake Worth, FL 33460
(407) 585-9301, 788-4548 FAX
Admin Gerald J DiMinico. *Dir of Nursing* Paula Mann. *Medical Dir* Gregory Aslanian MD.
Licensure Skilled care; Alzheimer's care. *Beds* SNF 162. *Private Pay Patients* 22%. *Certified* Medicaid; Medicare.
Owner Proprietary corp (Beverly Enterprises).
Admissions Requirements Medical examination; Physician's request.
Staff Physicians (consultants); RNs 5 (ft), 1 (pt); LPNs 7 (ft), 3 (pt); Nurses' aides 40 (ft), 2 (pt); Physical therapists (consultant); Occupational therapists (consultant); Speech therapists (consultant); Activities coordinators 2 (ft); Dietitians 1 (pt); Ophthalmologists (consultant); Podiatrists (consultant); Audiologists (consultant).
Languages Spanish.
Facilities Dining room; Physical therapy room; Activities room; Crafts room; Laundry room; Barber/Beauty shop; Library; Private dining room.
Activities Arts & crafts; Cards; Games; Reading groups; Prayer groups; Movies; Shopping trips; Dances/Social/Cultural gatherings; Intergenerational programs; Pet therapy; Reality orientation.

Maclen Rehabilitation Center
1201 12th Ave S, Lake Worth, FL 33460
(305) 566-7404
Beds 62.

Medicana Nursing Center
1710 Lucerne Ave, Lake Worth, FL 33460
(305) 582-5331
Admin Jeanne Trudell. *Dir of Nursing* Ruth Fairbanks. *Medical Dir* Benedicto San Pedro MD.
Licensure Skilled care. *Beds* 117. *Certified* Medicaid; Medicare; VA.
Owner Proprietary corp (Vari-Care Inc).
Admissions Requirements Minimum age 16.
Staff RNs 3 (ft), 2 (pt); LPNs 17 (ft), 2 (pt); Nurses' aides 35 (ft), 10 (pt); Physical therapists 2 (ft); Recreational therapists 1 (ft); Occupational therapists 2 (ft); Speech therapists 2 (ft); Activities coordinators 1 (pt); Dietitians 1 (pt); Ophthalmologists 1 (pt); Podiatrists 1 (pt); Dentists 1 (pt).
Languages French, Creole, Spanish, Finnish.
Facilities Dining room; Physical therapy room; Activities room; Chapel; Crafts room; Laundry room; Barber/Beauty shop; Library; Resident vehicle; Patio; TV lounge.
Activities Arts & crafts; Cards; Games; Reading groups; Prayer groups; Movies; Shopping trips; Dances/Social/Cultural gatherings; Adopt-a-grandparent; Resident council; Music therapy.

Regency Health Care Center
3599 S Congress Ave, Lake Worth, FL 33461
(305) 965-8876
Admin Mrs Lois G Collins. *Dir of Nursing* Ester D Calalo. *Medical Dir* Dr Randolph Romano.
Licensure Skilled care; Intermediate care; Alzheimer's care. *Beds* SNF 108; ICF 58. *Certified* Medicaid.
Owner Proprietary corp (Regency Health Care Centers).
Staff RNs 6 (ft); LPNs 11 (ft); Nurses' aides 32 (ft); Activities coordinators.
Languages Spanish, Japanese.

Sutton Place Convalescent Center
4405 Lakewood Rd, Lake Worth, FL 33461
(305) 969-1400
Beds 62.

Lakeland

Imperial Village Care Center
5245 N Socrum Loop Rd N, Lakeland, FL 33809
(813) 859-1446
Admin Dennis D Campbell. *Dir of Nursing* Gelen Campbell. *Medical Dir* Sergio Valejo.
Licensure Skilled care; Alzheimer's care. *Beds* SNF 120. *Private Pay Patients* 50%. *Certified* Medicaid; Medicare.
Owner Proprietary corp (Village Properties).
Admissions Requirements Minimum age 16; Medical examination; Physician's request.
Staff Physicians 11 (ft); Physical therapists 1 (ft); Occupational therapists 1 (ft); Speech therapists 1 (ft); Activities coordinators 1 (ft), 1 (pt); Dietitians 1 (ft); Podiatrists 2 (ft); Dentists 1 (ft).
Languages German.
Facilities Dining room; Physical therapy room; Activities room; Crafts room; Laundry room; Barber/Beauty shop.
Activities Arts & crafts; Cards; Games; Reading groups; Prayer groups; Movies; Shopping trips; Dances/Social/Cultural gatherings; Intergenerational programs; Pet therapy.

Johnson Health Center
6 Lake Hunter Dr, Lakeland, FL 33803
(813) 688-5521
Admin Russell C Owens. *Dir of Nursing* Victoria A Anderegg. *Medical Dir* R Eissman.

Licensure Skilled care; Retirement. *Beds* SNF 30; Retirement 213. *Private Pay Patients* 100%.
Owner Nonprofit organization/foundation.
Admissions Requirements Minimum age 18; Medical examination; Physician's request.
Staff RNs 3 (ft), 5 (pt); LPNs 2 (ft), 1 (pt); Nurses' aides 13 (ft); Activities coordinators 1 (ft); Dietitians 1 (ft).
Affiliation Presbyterian.
Facilities Dining room; Activities room; Chapel; Barber/Beauty shop; Library.
Activities Arts & crafts; Cards; Games; Reading groups; Prayer groups; Movies; Dances/Social/Cultural gatherings; Pet therapy.

Lakeland Convalescent Center
610 E Bella Vista Dr, Lakeland, FL 33805
(813) 688-8591
Licensure Skilled care. *Beds* 120. *Certified* Medicaid; Medicare.
Owner Proprietary corp.
Staff RNs 6 (ft); LPNs 10 (ft); Nurses' aides 26 (ft).

Lakeland Health Care Center
1530 Kennedy Blvd, Lakeland, FL 33802
(813) 858-4402
Admin John Case. *Dir of Nursing* Ruth Williams. *Medical Dir* Dr Sergio Vallejo.
Licensure Skilled care; Intermediate care. *Beds* 300. *Certified* Medicaid; Medicare.
Owner Proprietary corp.
Staff RNs 12 (ft); LPNs 10 (ft); Nurses' aides 53 (ft).

Presbyterian Nursing Center
1919 Lakeland Hills Blvd, Lakeland, FL 33805
(813) 688-5612, 682-4173 FAX
Admin E Max Hauth; Sylvia E Brooks Asst Admin. *Dir of Nursing* Rebecca D Johnson RN. *Medical Dir* Sergio Vallejo MD.
Licensure Skilled care; Intermediate care. *Beds* Swing beds SNF/ICF 120. *Private Pay Patients* 60%. *Certified* Medicaid; Medicare.
Owner Nonprofit organization/foundation.
Admissions Requirements Minimum age 16; Medical examination; Physician's request.
Staff Physicians contracted; RNs 10 (ft); LPNs 11 (ft), 2 (pt); Nurses' aides 58 (ft); Physical therapists 1 (ft); Occupational therapists contracted; Speech therapists contracted; Activities coordinators 1 (ft); Dietitians 1 (ft); Podiatrists contracted; Audiologists contracted; Medical records.
Languages Indonesian, Spanish.
Affiliation Presbyterian.
Facilities Dining room; Physical therapy room; Activities room; Chapel; Crafts room; Laundry room; Barber/Beauty shop.
Activities Arts & crafts; Cards; Games; Reading groups; Prayer groups; Movies; Shopping trips; Dances/Social/Cultural gatherings; Intergenerational programs; Pet therapy.

Lantana

Atlantis Nursing Center
6026 Old Congress Rd, Lantana, FL 33462
(305) 964-4430
Admin Barry Cohen.
Medical Dir Richard Sulman DO.
Licensure Skilled care. *Beds* 120. *Certified* Medicaid; Medicare.
Owner Proprietary corp (National Healthcare Affiliates).
Admissions Requirements Minimum age 55; Medical examination; Physician's request.
Staff RNs 5 (ft); LPNs 20 (ft); Nurses' aides 36 (ft); Physical therapists 3 (ft); Speech therapists 1 (ft); Activities coordinators 2 (ft); Dietitians 1 (ft); Podiatrists 2 (ft); Audiologists 1 (ft); Dentists 1 (ft).
Languages Spanish, German, French.

Facilities Dining room; Physical therapy room; Activities room; Crafts room; Laundry room; Barber/Beauty shop; Library; Outdoor patios & enclosed patio; Pharmacy services.
Activities Arts & crafts; Cards; Games; Reading groups; Prayer groups; Movies; Shopping trips; Dances/Social/Cultural gatherings; Wheelchair exercises; Bingo; Music therapy; Reality orientation.

Ridge Terrace Health Care Center
2180 Hypoluxo Rd, Lantana, FL 33462
(407) 582-6711, 582-2675 FAX
Admin Steven B Ostreich. *Dir of Nursing* Lois Gackenheimer. *Medical Dir* Dr Edward White.
Licensure Skilled care; Intermediate care. *Beds* Swing beds SNF/ICF 120.
Owner Privately owned.
Staff RNs; LPNs; Nurses' aides; Physical therapists; Recreational therapists; Occupational therapists; Speech therapists; Activities coordinators; Dietitians; Ophthalmologists; Podiatrists.

Largo

Oak Manor Nursing Center Inc
3500 Oak Manor Ln, Largo, FL 34644
(813) 581-9427, 581-9420 FAX
Admin Cloyd A Petro. *Dir of Nursing* Lois Fisher RN. *Medical Dir* Paul Straub MD.
Licensure Skilled care; Retirement; ACLF; Alzheimer's care. *Beds* SNF 180; Retirement apts 172; ACLF 32. *Certified* Medicare.
Owner Proprietary corp.
Admissions Requirements Physician's request.
Staff RNs 7 (ft), 1 (pt); LPNs 9 (ft), 3 (pt); Nurses' aides 61 (ft), 4 (pt); Physical therapists (contracted); Occupational therapists (contracted); Speech therapists (contracted); Activities coordinators 2 (ft); Dietitians (contracted).
Languages German, Italian, Spanish.
Facilities Dining room; Physical therapy room; Activities room; Laundry room; Barber/Beauty shop; Library; Areas for walking and biking.
Activities Arts & crafts; Cards; Games; Prayer groups; Movies; Dances/Social/Cultural gatherings; Intergenerational programs; Pet therapy; Restaurant night for patients and their families; Field trips; Exercise class.

Tierra Pines Nursing Center
7625 Ulmerton Rd, Largo, FL 33541
(813) 535-9833
Admin John P Williams.
Licensure Skilled care. *Beds* 120. *Certified* Medicaid; Medicare.
Owner Proprietary corp.
Admissions Requirements Minimum age 16; Medical examination; Physician's request.
Staff Physicians 2 (pt); RNs 6 (ft); LPNs 12 (ft); Nurses' aides 43 (ft); Physical therapists; Reality therapists; Recreational therapists 2 (ft); Occupational therapists; Speech therapists; Activities coordinators 1 (ft); Dietitians; Ophthalmologists; Podiatrists; Audiologists; Dentists.
Facilities Dining room; Physical therapy room; Activities room; Crafts room; Laundry room; Barber/Beauty shop; Library.
Activities Arts & crafts; Cards; Games; Reading groups; Prayer groups; Movies; Dances/Social/Cultural gatherings.

Wright's Nursing Home
11300 110th Ave N, Largo, FL 34648
(813) 391-9986
Admin Pat Shoemaker. *Dir of Nursing* Priscilla Bishop RN. *Medical Dir* Frank Norton MD.
Licensure Skilled care; Intermediate care. *Beds* Swing beds SNF/ICF 60. *Private Pay Patients* 95%.
Owner Privately owned.
Admissions Requirements Minimum age 65.

Staff RNs 1 (ft), 4 (pt); LPNs 3 (ft); Nurses' aides 17 (ft), 4 (pt); Activities coordinators 1 (ft).
Languages Slovak.
Facilities Dining room.
Activities Arts & crafts; Games; Reading groups; Prayer groups; Movies; Pet therapy; Couples dinners.

Lauderdale Lakes

Aviva Manor
3370 NW 47th Terrace, Lauderdale Lakes, FL 33319
(305) 733-0655
Medical Dir Arturo Blanco MD.
Licensure Skilled care. *Beds* 120. *Certified* Medicare.
Owner Proprietary corp.
Staff Physicians 4 (pt); RNs 3 (ft), 5 (pt); LPNs 6 (ft), 6 (pt); Nurses' aides 43 (ft), 3 (pt); Reality therapists 1 (pt); Recreational therapists 2 (ft); Occupational therapists 1 (pt); Activities coordinators 1 (ft); Dietitians 1 (ft), 1 (pt); Podiatrists 1 (pt); Dentists 1 (pt).
Affiliation Jewish.
Facilities Dining room; Physical therapy room; Activities room; Chapel; Crafts room; Laundry room; Barber/Beauty shop; Library; TV lounge.
Activities Arts & crafts; Cards; Games; Reading groups; Prayer groups; Movies; Shopping trips; Dances/Social/Cultural gatherings; Bread baking; Yiddish classes.

St John's Health Care Center
3075 NW 35th Ave, Lauderdale Lakes, FL 33311
(305) 739-6233, 733-9579 FAX
Admin Diane A Dube. *Dir of Nursing* Cynthia Kara RN. *Medical Dir* Mark Reiner MD.
Licensure Skilled care; Rehabilitation hospital; Retirement. *Beds* SNF 160; Rehabilitation hospital 20. *Certified* Medicaid; Medicare.
Owner Nonprofit organization/foundation.
Admissions Requirements Minimum age 18.
Staff RNs; LPNs; Nurses' aides; Physical therapists; Recreational therapists; Occupational therapists; Speech therapists; Activities coordinators; Dietitians; Pastoral care 1 (ft).
Affiliation Roman Catholic.
Facilities Dining room; Physical therapy room; Activities room; Chapel; Crafts room; Laundry room; Barber/Beauty shop; Library.
Activities Arts & crafts; Cards; Games; Reading groups; Prayer groups; Movies; Shopping trips; Dances/Social/Cultural gatherings; Intergenerational programs; Pet therapy; Arthritic, amputee, and stroke support groups.

Lecanto

Health Care of Brentwood
2333 N Brentwood Cir, Lecanto, FL 32661
(904) 746-6611
Beds 36.

Key Pine Village
1275 N Rainbow Loop, Lecanto, FL 32661-9759
(904) 746-3262
Admin Chester V Cole.
Licensure Intermediate care for mentally retarded; Retirement. *Beds* ICF/MR 48. *Certified* Medicaid.
Owner Nonprofit corp.
Admissions Requirements Minimum age 18; Medical examination.
Staff RNs 1 (ft); LPNs 3 (ft), 1 (pt); Nurses' aides 1 (pt); Recreational therapists 1 (ft).

Facilities Dining room; Physical therapy room; Activities room; Laundry room.
Activities Arts & crafts; Games; Movies; Shopping trips; Dances/Social/Cultural gatherings.

Leesburg

Leesburg Healthcare Center
2000 Edgewood Ave, Leesburg, FL 32748
(904) 787-3545
Medical Dir Dr George Engelhard.
Licensure Skilled care. *Beds* 116. *Certified* Medicaid; Medicare.
Owner Proprietary corp (Beverly Enterprises).
Staff RNs; LPNs; Nurses' aides; Physical therapists; Recreational therapists; Speech therapists; Activities coordinators.
Facilities Dining room; Physical therapy room; Activities room; Laundry room; Barber/Beauty shop; Library.
Activities Arts & crafts; Cards; Games; Reading groups; Prayer groups; Movies; Dances/Social/Cultural gatherings.

Leesburg Nursing Center
715 E Dixie Ave, Leesburg, FL 34748
(904) 728-3020, 728-6071 FAX
Admin Thomas R Robeson. *Dir of Nursing* Sue Maschke. *Medical Dir* Larry Foster.
Licensure Skilled care. *Beds* SNF 120. *Private Pay Patients* 35%. *Certified* Medicaid; Medicare.
Owner Proprietary corp (Diversicare Corp of America).
Admissions Requirements Minimum age 18; Medical examination; Physician's request.
Staff Physicians 1 (pt); RNs 6 (ft); LPNs 12 (ft), 6 (pt); Nurses' aides 28 (ft), 25 (pt); Physical therapists 1 (pt); Occupational therapists 1 (pt); Speech therapists 1 (pt); Activities coordinators 1 (ft); Dietitians 1 (ft); Podiatrists 1 (pt).
Facilities Dining room; Physical therapy room; Activities room; Crafts room; Laundry room; Barber/Beauty shop; Cable TV.
Activities Arts & crafts; Cards; Games; Reading groups; Shopping trips; Dances/Social/Cultural gatherings; Intergenerational programs; Pet therapy.

Lehigh Acres

Cross Key Manor
1515 Lee Blvd, Lehigh Acres, FL 33936
(613) 369-2194
Beds 56.

Live Oak

Suwannee Health Care Center
PO Box 1360, 1620 E Helvenston St, Live Oak, FL 32060
(904) 362-7860
Admin James T Lutes. *Dir of Nursing* Kathleen Carter RN. *Medical Dir* Dr Andrew C Bass.
Licensure Skilled care. *Beds* SNF 120. *Certified* Medicaid.
Owner Proprietary corp (Beverly Enterprises).

Longwood

Longwood Health Care Center
1520 S Grant Ave, Longwood, FL 32750
(407) 339-9200
Admin R E Delgado NHA. *Dir of Nursing* Carolyn Gross RN. *Medical Dir* David Parsons MD.
Licensure Skilled care. *Beds* SNF 120. *Private Pay Patients* 20%. *Certified* Medicaid; Medicare.
Owner Proprietary corp (Beverly Enterprises).
Admissions Requirements Minimum age 18; Medical examination; Physician's request.

Staff Physicians 20 (pt); RNs 6 (ft); LPNs 9
(ft); Nurses' aides 35 (ft); Physical therapists
1 (pt); Occupational therapists 1 (pt); Speech
therapists 1 (pt); Activities coordinators 1
(ft), 1 (pt); Dietitians 1 (pt); Audiologists 1
(pt).
Languages German, Spanish.
Facilities Dining room; Physical therapy
room; Activities room; Chapel; Crafts room;
Laundry room; Barber/Beauty shop; Library.
Activities Arts & crafts; Cards; Games;
Reading groups; Prayer groups; Movies;
Shopping trips; Intergenerational programs;
Pet therapy.

Village on the Green
500 Village Pl, Longwood, FL 32779
(305) 662-0230
Beds 16.

MacClenny

W Frank Wells Nursing Home
PO Box 484, 159 N 3rd St, MacClenny, FL
32063
(904) 259-6168, 259-4574 FAX
Admin Melba J Beaty. *Dir of Nursing* Retha
Burnsed RN. *Medical Dir* Nancy Fouts MD.
Licensure Skilled care. *Beds* SNF 68. *Certified*
Medicaid; Medicare.
Owner Publicly owned.
Admissions Requirements Minimum age 18;
Physician's request.
Staff RNs 4 (ft), 2 (pt); LPNs 8 (ft), 3 (pt);
Nurses' aides 28 (ft), 10 (pt); Activities
coordinators 1 (ft); Dietitians 1 (pt).
Facilities Dining room; Activities room.
Activities Arts & crafts; Cards; Games; Prayer
groups; Movies; Shopping trips;
Intergenerational programs; Pet therapy.

Madison

Madison Nursing Center
PO Box 2310, Rte 3, Madison, FL 32340
(904) 973-4880
Admin Frank Eckert. *Dir of Nursing* Joyce
Harrison. *Medical Dir* Dr A Dulay.
Licensure Skilled care. *Beds* SNF 60. *Certified*
Medicaid.
Owner Privately owned.
Admissions Requirements Medical
examination.
Staff RNs 2 (ft); LPNs 7 (ft), 3 (pt); Nurses'
aides 22 (ft), 4 (pt); Activities coordinators 1
(ft); Dietitians 1 (pt).
Facilities Dining room; Physical therapy
room; Activities room; Barber/Beauty shop;
OT room.
Activities Arts & crafts; Games; Prayer groups;
Movies; Shopping trips.

Maitland

Park Lake Health Care Center
1700 Monroe Ave, Maitland, FL 32751
(305) 647-2092
Beds 96.

Marathon

Marathon Manor
Sombrero Beach Rd, Marathon, FL 33050
(305) 743-4466
Beds 65.

Margate

Beverly Manor of Margate
5951 Colonial Dr, Margate, FL 33063
(305) 979-6401, 975-2011 FAX
Admin Elsie S Jensen. *Dir of Nursing* Marilyn
Rohrer RN. *Medical Dir* Dr Peter Ruy.
Licensure Skilled care. *Beds* SNF 120. *Private
Pay Patients* 55%. *Certified* Medicaid;
Medicare.

Owner Proprietary corp (Beverly Enterprises).
Admissions Requirements Medical
examination; Physician's request.
Staff RNs; LPNs; Nurses' aides; Recreational
therapists; Activities coordinators.
Languages Spanish, Italian.
Facilities Dining room; Physical therapy
room; Activities room; Laundry room;
Barber/Beauty shop; Screened-in-porch and
patio/courtyard.
Activities Arts & crafts; Cards; Games;
Reading groups; Movies; Intergenerational
programs; Pet therapy.

Marianna

Marianna Convalescent Center
PO Drawer L, Marianna, FL 32446
(904) 482-8091
Admin Jonnie Cloud. *Dir of Nursing* Carol
Morris RN.
Licensure Skilled care; Intermediate care;
Veterans Administration. *Beds* 180. *Certified*
Medicaid.
Owner Publicly owned.
Admissions Requirements Minimum age 16
(unless prior approval from department);
Medical examination; Physician's request.
Staff RNs 4 (ft), 6 (pt); LPNs 16 (ft), 14 (pt);
Nurses' aides 50 (ft), 24 (pt); Activities
coordinators 1 (ft).
Facilities Dining room; Physical therapy
room; Activities room; Crafts room; Laundry
room; Barber/Beauty shop; Library; Family
room; Privacy room.
Activities Arts & crafts; Games; Prayer groups;
Movies; Shopping trips; Dances/Social/
Cultural gatherings.

Sunland—Marianna Facility II
PO Box 852, Marianna, FL 32446
(904) 526-2123
Licensure Intermediate care for mentally
retarded. *Beds* 60. *Certified* Medicaid.
Owner Publicly owned.
Staff RNs 3 (ft); LPNs 7 (ft); Nurses' aides 32
(ft).

Melbourne

Carnegie Gardens Nursing Center
1415 S Hickory St, Melbourne, FL 32901
(407) 723-1321
Admin Maureen Laverty. *Dir of Nursing* Mary
Ann Jones. *Medical Dir* John Potomski DO.
Licensure Skilled care. *Beds* SNF 138. *Private
Pay Patients* 22%. *Certified* Medicaid;
Medicare.
Owner Proprietary corp (Southeast Health
Care Management).
Admissions Requirements Minimum age 18;
Medical examination; Physician's request.
Staff RNs 5 (ft); LPNs 16 (ft); Nurses' aides
47 (ft); Activities coordinators 2 (ft);
Dietitians 1 (ft).
Languages Spanish, Hungarian.
Facilities Dining room; Physical therapy
room; Activities room; Chapel; Crafts room;
Barber/Beauty shop; Library.
Activities Arts & crafts; Cards; Games;
Reading groups; Prayer groups; Movies;
Shopping trips; Dances/Social/Cultural
gatherings; Intergenerational programs; Pet
therapy.

Holmes Regional Convalescent Home
516 E Sheridan Rd, Melbourne, FL 32901
(305) 727-0964
Beds 16.

Holmes Regional Nursing Center
606 E Sheridan Rd, Melbourne, FL 32901
(407) 727-0984
Admin John H Patrick Jr. *Dir of Nursing*
Louise R Peacock. *Medical Dir* John H
Potomski Jr MD.

Licensure Skilled care; Intermediate care. *Beds*
SNF 9; ICF 51. *Private Pay Patients* 50%.
Certified Medicaid; Medicare.
Owner Proprietary corp.
Admissions Requirements Minimum age 18;
Medical examination.
Staff Physicians 1 (pt); RNs 3 (ft), 2 (pt);
LPNs 3 (ft), 3 (pt); Nurses' aides 18 (ft), 7
(pt); Physical therapists 1 (pt); Occupational
therapists 1 (pt); Activities coordinators 1
(pt); Dietitians Consultant; Podiatrists 1 (pt).
Languages Spanish.
Facilities Dining room; Physical therapy
room; Activities room; Crafts room; Laundry
room; Barber/Beauty shop; Family parlor.
Activities Arts & crafts; Cards; Games;
Reading groups; Prayer groups; Movies; Pet
therapy.

Medic Home Health Center
1420 S Oak St, Melbourne, FL 32901
(305) 723-3215
Admin Patricia Collins. *Dir of Nursing*
Catherine Baldwin. *Medical Dir* W S
Lanford MD.
Licensure Skilled care; Intermediate care. *Beds*
SNF; ICF 110. *Certified* Medicaid.
Owner Proprietary corp (Beverly Enterprises).
Staff RNs; LPNs; Nurses' aides; Activities
coordinators; Dietitians.
Facilities Dining room; Activities room;
Crafts room; Laundry room; Barber/Beauty
shop.
Activities Arts & crafts; Cards; Games;
Reading groups; Prayer groups; Movies;
Shopping trips; Dances/Social/Cultural
gatherings.

Medic-Home Health Center of Melbourne
1420 S Oak St, Melbourne, FL 32901
(305) 723-3215
Beds 32.

Merritt Island

Courtenay Springs Nursing Home
1100 S Courtenay Pkwy, Merrit Island, FL
32952
(305) 452-1233
Beds 55.

Merritt Manor Nursing Home
125 Alma Blvd, Merritt Island, FL 32952
(305) 453-0202
Admin Ed Hawkins. *Dir of Nursing* Aileen
Mueller RN. *Medical Dir* Dr Jack Hatfield.
Licensure Skilled care. *Beds* 120. *Certified*
Medicaid; Medicare.
Owner Proprietary corp (Beverly Enterprises).
Admissions Requirements Medical
examination.
Staff RNs 4 (ft), 1 (pt); LPNs 11 (ft), 1 (pt);
Nurses' aides 42 (ft), 4 (pt); Physical
therapists 1 (ft); Occupational therapists 1
(ft); Speech therapists 1 (ft); Activities
coordinators 1 (ft); Dietitians 1 (ft).
Facilities Dining room; Physical therapy
room; Activities room; Laundry room;
Barber/Beauty shop.
Activities Arts & crafts; Cards; Games;
Reading groups; Prayer groups; Movies.

Miami

Anderson Health Center
8401 NW 27th Ave, Miami, FL 33147
(305) 691-6052
Beds 8.

Ashley Manor Care Center Inc
8785 NW 32nd Ave, Miami, FL 33147
(305) 691-5711
Admin E Renee1 Gibson.
Medical Dir Ramon Alvarez MD.

Licensure Skilled care. *Beds* 120. *Certified*
Medicaid.
Owner Proprietary corp.
Admissions Requirements Medical
examination.
Staff RNs 5 (ft); LPNs 5 (ft), 8 (pt); Nurses'
aides 39 (ft), 3 (pt); Physical therapists 1
(pt); Reality therapists 1 (pt); Recreational
therapists 1 (ft); Speech therapists 1 (pt);
Activities coordinators 1 (ft); Dietitians 1
(pt); Ophthalmologists 1 (pt); Podiatrists 1
(pt); Dentists 1 (pt).
Languages French, Yiddish, Hebrew, Spanish,
Creole.
Facilities Dining room; Activities room;
Crafts room; Laundry room; Barber/Beauty
shop.
Activities Arts & crafts; Cards; Games;
Reading groups; Prayer groups; Movies;
Shopping trips; Dances/Social/Cultural
gatherings.

Coral Gables Convalescent Center
7060 SW 8th St, Miami, FL 33167
(305) 261-1363, 267-0751 FAX
Admin Jon H Steinmeyer NHA MHA. *Dir of
Nursing* Virginia Carpenter RN. *Medical Dir*
Norman Spitzer MD.
Licensure Skilled care; Intermediate care. *Beds*
Swing beds SNF/ICF 87. *Private Pay
Patients* 55%. *Certified* Medicaid; Medicare.
Owner Proprietary corp.
Admissions Requirements Medical
examination; Physician's request.
Staff RNs 8 (ft); LPNs 22 (ft); Nurses' aides
40 (ft); Physical therapists 2 (pt);
Occupational therapists 1 (pt); Speech
therapists 1 (pt); Activities coordinators 1
(ft), 1 (pt); Dietitians 1 (pt);
Ophthalmologists 1 (pt); Podiatrists 1 (pt);
Audiologists 1 (pt).
Languages Spanish, French.
Facilities Dining room; Activities room;
Crafts room; Laundry room; Barber/Beauty
shop; Library; Atrium.
Activities Arts & crafts; Cards; Games;
Reading groups; Prayer groups; Movies;
Shopping trips; Dances/Social/Cultural
gatherings; Intergenerational programs;
Current events; Painting classes; Music
therapy.

East Ridge Retirement Village Inc
19301 SW 87th Ave, Miami, FL 33157
(305) 238-2623
Admin Cathy S Davis.
Medical Dir Chauncey Stone MD.
Licensure Skilled care; Retirement. *Beds* SNF
60; Retirement 20. *Private Pay Patients* 5%.
Certified Medicare.
Owner Nonprofit corp.
Admissions Requirements Medical
examination.
Staff Physicians 1 (ft); RNs 3 (ft), 3 (pt);
LPNs 7 (ft), 1 (pt); Nurses' aides 23 (ft), 1
(pt); Physical therapists 1 (ft); Recreational
therapists 1 (ft); Activities coordinators 1
(ft); Dietitians 1 (ft).
Languages Polish, Spanish.
Facilities Dining room; Physical therapy
room; Activities room; Chapel; Crafts room;
Laundry room; Barber/Beauty shop; Library.
Activities Arts & crafts; Cards; Games;
Reading groups; Prayer groups.

El Ponce De Leon Convalescent Center
335 SW 12th Ave, Miami, FL 33130
(305) 545-5417
Admin Gail Lasris. *Dir of Nursing* Pusa Bouza
RN. *Medical Dir* Dr Edward Gottler.
Licensure Skilled care; Intermediate care;
Alzheimer's care. *Beds* 147. *Certified*
Medicaid; Medicare.
Owner Proprietary corp.
Staff RNs 21 (ft), 3 (pt); LPNs 4 (ft); Nurses'
aides 74 (ft); Physical therapists 2 (ft);
Recreational therapists 2 (ft); Occupational

therapists 1 (ft); Speech therapists 1 (ft);
Activities coordinators 1 (ft); Dietitians 1
(ft); Ophthalmologists 1 (ft); Dentists 1 (ft).
Languages Spanish, French.
Facilities Dining room; Physical therapy
room; Activities room; Chapel; Crafts room;
Laundry room; Barber/Beauty shop; Library.
Activities Arts & crafts; Cards; Games;
Reading groups; Prayer groups; Movies;
Shopping trips; Dances/Social/Cultural
gatherings.

Florida Club Care Center
220 Sierra Dr, Miami, FL 33179
(305) 653-6427
Beds 96.

Floridean Nursing Home Inc
47 NW 32nd Pl, Miami, FL 33125
(305) 649-2911, 649-2912 FAX
Admin Julia Rice NHA. *Dir of Nursing* Zonia
Lorenzo RN. *Medical Dir* James J Hutson
MD.
Licensure Skilled care; Adult day health care.
Beds SNF 52; Adult day health care 5.
Private Pay Patients 66%. *Certified*
Medicaid.
Owner Proprietary corp.
Admissions Requirements Medical
examination.
Staff Physicians; RNs 3 (ft); LPNs 8 (ft);
Nurses' aides 22 (ft); Physical therapists
(consultant); Occupational therapists; Speech
therapists; Activities coordinators; Dietitians;
Ophthalmologists; Podiatrists; Audiologists.
Languages Spanish.
Facilities Dining room; Physical therapy
room; Activities room; Crafts room; Laundry
room; Barber/Beauty shop; 3 outdoor
porches; Garden.
Activities Arts & crafts; Cards; Games;
Reading groups; Prayer groups; Movies;
Shopping trips; Dances/Social/Cultural
gatherings; Intergenerational programs; Pet
therapy; Outings; Family programs.

Four Freedoms Manor
42 Collins Ave, Miami, FL 33139
(305) 672-1771
Beds 84.

Gramercy Park Nursing Center
17475 S Dixie Hwy, Miami, FL 33157
(305) 255-1045, 255-4530 FAX
Admin Katherine F Rondinelli. *Dir of Nursing*
Sandra Sievert. *Medical Dir* Dr David
Goldberg.
Licensure Skilled care. *Beds* SNF 180. *Private
Pay Patients* 10%. *Certified* Medicaid;
Medicare.
Owner Proprietary corp.
Admissions Requirements Minimum age 21;
Medical examination; Physician's request.
Staff RNs 11 (ft), 3 (pt); LPNs 19 (ft), 8 (pt);
Nurses' aides 59 (ft), 1 (pt); Physical
therapists 1 (ft); Recreational therapists 2
(ft), 1 (pt); Occupational therapists 1 (pt);
Speech therapists 1 (pt); Activities
coordinators 1 (ft); Dietitians 1 (pt);
Ophthalmologists 1 (pt); Podiatrists 1 (pt);
Audiologists 1 (pt); Social workers 2 (ft).
Languages French, Spanish.
Facilities Dining room; Physical therapy
room; Activities room; Crafts room; Laundry
room; Barber/Beauty shop.
Activities Arts & crafts; Cards; Games;
Reading groups; Prayer groups; Movies;
Shopping trips; Dances/Social/Cultural
gatherings.

Green Briar Nursing Center
9820 N Kendall Dr, Miami, FL 33176
(305) 271-6311
Licensure Skilled care. *Beds* 203. *Certified*
Medicare.
Owner Proprietary corp.
Staff Physicians; Dietitians; Nurses' aides.

Languages Spanish, French, Yiddish.
Activities Prayer groups; Arts & crafts;
Shopping trips.

Healthsouth Regional Rehabilitation Center
20601 Old Cutler Rd, Miami, FL 33189
(305) 251-3800, 251-7905 FAX
Admin Les S Alt. *Dir of Nursing* Sandra
Smith. *Medical Dir* Dr David Goldberg,
Nursing care; Dr Murray Rolnick,
Rehabilitation.
Licensure Skilled care; Comprehensive
rehabilitation; Alzheimer's care. *Beds* SNF
180. *Certified* Medicaid; Medicare.
Owner Proprietary corp.
Admissions Requirements Minimum age 16;
Medical examination; Physician's request.
Staff Physicians 1 (ft), 2 (pt); RNs 11 (ft);
LPNs 11 (ft); Nurses' aides 45 (ft); Physical
therapists 9 (ft); Recreational therapists 3
(ft); Occupational therapists 8 (ft); Speech
therapists 3 (ft); Activities coordinators 2
(ft); Dietitians 1 (ft); Podiatrists 1 (ft).
Languages Spanish.
Facilities Dining room; Physical therapy
room; Activities room; Chapel; Crafts room;
Laundry room; Barber/Beauty shop; Library;
Courtyards.
Activities Arts & crafts; Cards; Games;
Reading groups; Prayer groups; Movies;
Shopping trips; Dances/Social/Cultural
gatherings; Intergenerational programs; Pet
therapy.

Human Resources Health Center
2500 NW 22nd Ave, Miami, FL 33142
(305) 638-6661
Admin Lou DiDomenico. *Dir of Nursing*
Maxine Austin. *Medical Dir* John Cleveland.
Licensure Skilled care; Intermediate care. *Beds*
SNF 150; ICF. *Certified* Medicaid;
Medicare.
Owner Publicly owned.
Admissions Requirements Minimum age 18;
Medical examination; Physician's request.
Staff Physicians 3 (pt); RNs 11 (ft); LPNs 23
(ft); Nurses' aides 67 (ft); Physical therapists
1 (ft); Recreational therapists 1 (ft);
Occupational therapists 1 (pt); Speech
therapists 1 (pt); Activities coordinators 1
(ft); Dietitians 1 (ft), 1 (pt);
Ophthalmologists 1 (pt); Dentists 1 (pt).
Languages Spanish, French, Yiddish, Hebrew,
Creole.
Facilities Dining room; Physical therapy
room; Activities room; Chapel; Crafts room;
Laundry room; Barber/Beauty shop.
Activities Arts & crafts; Cards; Games;
Reading groups; Prayer groups; Movies;
Shopping trips; Dances/Social/Cultural
gatherings; Adopt-a-grandparent.

Jackson Heights Nursing Home
1404 NW 22nd St, Miami, FL 33142
(305) 325-1050
Admin James Owens. *Dir of Nursing* Eulalia
Perez. *Medical Dir* Jesus Gonzalez.
Licensure Skilled care. *Beds* SNF 298.
Certified Medicaid; Medicare.
Owner Proprietary corp (Unicare).
Admissions Requirements Minimum age 18.
Staff RNs 12 (ft); LPNs 39 (ft); Nurses' aides
92 (ft); Physical therapists 1 (ft);
Recreational therapists 1 (ft); Occupational
therapists 1 (ft); Speech therapists 1 (ft);
Activities coordinators 2 (ft); Dietitians 1
(ft).
Languages Spanish, French, Creole.
Facilities Dining room; Physical therapy
room; Activities room; Crafts room; Barber/
Beauty shop.
Activities Arts & crafts; Cards; Games;
Reading groups; Prayer groups; Movies;
Intergenerational programs; Pet therapy.

Jackson Manor Nursing Home Inc
1861 NW 8th Ave, Miami, FL 33136
(305) 324-0280

Admin Isaac Mizrahi. *Dir of Nursing* Beverly Pelersen. *Medical Dir* Ed H Cottler MD.
Licensure Skilled care; Alzheimer's care. *Beds* SNF 174. *Certified* Medicaid; Medicare.
Owner Proprietary corp.
Admissions Requirements Minimum age 16; Medical examination.
Staff RNs 5 (ft); LPNs 20 (ft), 3 (pt); Nurses' aides 60 (ft); Physical therapists 4 (pt); Recreational therapists 2 (ft); Occupational therapists 3 (pt); Speech therapists 3 (pt); Activities coordinators 1 (ft); Dietitians 1 (ft); Ophthalmologists 1 (pt); Dentists 1 (pt).
Languages Creole, Arabic, Russian, Spanish, French.
Facilities Dining room; Physical therapy room; Chapel; Barber/Beauty shop; Library.
Activities Arts & crafts; Cards; Games; Reading groups; Prayer groups; Movies; Shopping trips; Dances/Social/Cultural gatherings.

La Posada Convalescent Home
5271 SW 8th St, Miami, FL 33134
(305) 443-5423
Licensure Skilled care. *Beds* 54. *Certified* Medicaid.
Owner Proprietary corp.
Admissions Requirements Minimum age 65.
Staff Nurses' aides 8 (ft); Dietitians 4 (ft).
Languages Spanish.
Facilities Dining room; Activities room.
Activities Arts & crafts; Cards; Games; Reading groups; Prayer groups; Movies; Shopping trips; Dances/Social/Cultural gatherings.

MACtown Inc
127 NE 62nd St, Miami, FL 33138
(305) 758-4485
Admin Gordon B Scott Jr.
Medical Dir Dr Gilbert White.
Licensure Intermediate care for mentally retarded. *Beds* 56. *Certified* Medicaid.
Owner Nonprofit corp.
Admissions Requirements Minimum age 18; Medical examination; Physician's request.
Staff Physicians 1 (pt); RNs 1 (pt); LPNs 3 (ft), 1 (pt); Physical therapists 1 (pt); Recreational therapists 2 (ft), 1 (pt); Occupational therapists 1 (pt); Speech therapists 1 (ft); Dietitians 1 (ft); Ophthalmologists 1 (pt).
Facilities Dining room; Physical therapy room; Activities room; Laundry room; Workshop.
Activities Arts & crafts; Cards; Games; Movies; Shopping trips; Dances/Social/ Cultural gatherings; Special Olympics.

Miami Jewish Home for the Aged at Douglas Gardens
151 NE 52nd St, Miami, FL 33137
(305) 751-8626
Admin Marc Lichtman. *Dir of Nursing* Joan Bilingsley. *Medical Dir* Dr Charles Beber.
Licensure Skilled care; Intermediate care. *Beds* 454. *Certified* Medicaid; Medicare.
Owner Nonprofit corp.
Admissions Requirements Minimum age 65; Medical examination.
Staff Physicians 3 (ft); RNs 32 (ft); LPNs 52 (ft); Nurses' aides 237 (ft); Physical therapists 2 (ft); Recreational therapists 6 (ft); Occupational therapists 1 (pt); Speech therapists 1 (pt); Activities coordinators 1 (ft).
Languages Spanish, German, Yiddish, Russian, French, Polish.
Affiliation Jewish.
Facilities Dining room; Physical therapy room; Activities room; Chapel; Crafts room; Laundry room; Barber/Beauty shop; Library; Convenience store in lobby of congregate living facility.

Activities Arts & crafts; Cards; Games; Reading groups; Prayer groups; Movies; Shopping trips; Dances/Social/Cultural gatherings.

North Shore Nursing Home
9380 NW 7th Ave, Miami, FL 33150
(305) 759-8711
Medical Dir Stanley Roth MD.
Licensure Skilled care. *Beds* 101. *Certified* Medicare.
Owner Proprietary corp.
Staff RNs 2 (ft), 2 (pt); LPNs 12 (ft), 4 (pt); Nurses' aides 26 (ft); Recreational therapists 1 (ft); Activities coordinators 1 (ft); Social workers 1 (ft).
Languages Spanish.
Facilities Dining room; Physical therapy room; Barber/Beauty shop.
Activities Arts & crafts; Cards; Games; Reading groups; Prayer groups; Movies; Shopping trips; Dances/Social/Cultural gatherings; Picnics.

Palmetto Extended Care Facility
PO Box 522812, Miami, FL 33152
(305) 261-2525
Licensure Skilled care; Intermediate care. *Beds* 85. *Certified* Medicaid; Medicare.
Owner Proprietary corp.
Staff RNs 3 (ft); LPNs 8 (ft); Nurses' aides 21 (ft).
Languages Spanish, Tagalog, Italian, Japanese.

Palms Convalescent Home
14601 NE 16th Ave, Miami, FL 33161
(305) 945-7631
Licensure Skilled care. *Beds* 85. *Certified* Medicaid.
Owner Proprietary corp.
Staff RNs 3 (ft); LPNs 15 (ft); Nurses' aides 18 (ft).
Languages Spanish, Hungarian, German, Yiddish, Hebrew, Polish.

Perdue Medical Center
19590 Old Cutler Rd, Miami, FL 33157
(305) 233-8931
Licensure Skilled care. *Beds* 197. *Certified* Medicaid; Medicare.
Owner Publicly owned.
Staff RNs 12 (ft); LPNs 10 (ft); Nurses' aides 55 (ft).
Languages Spanish.

Pines Nursing Home
301 NE 141st St, Miami, FL 33161
(305) 893-1102
Medical Dir Dr Walter DeMaio.
Licensure Skilled care. *Beds* 46. *Certified* Medicaid; Medicare.
Owner Proprietary corp.
Staff Physicians 5 (pt); RNs 2 (ft); LPNs 5 (ft), 3 (pt); Nurses' aides 42 (ft), 4 (pt); Physical therapists 1 (pt); Recreational therapists 1 (pt); Occupational therapists 1 (pt); Speech therapists 1 (pt); Activities coordinators 1 (pt); Dietitians 1 (ft); Ophthalmologists 1 (pt); Podiatrists 1 (pt) Dentists 1 (pt).
Languages French, Haitian, Hungarian, German, Russian, Polish, Spanish, Yiddish, Hebrew.
Facilities Dining room; Activities room; Crafts room; Laundry room; Library.
Activities Arts & crafts; Cards; Games; Reading groups; Prayer groups; Movies.

Riverside Care Center
899 NW 4th St, Miami, FL 33128
(305) 326-1236
Medical Dir Water J Demaio MD.
Licensure Skilled care. *Beds* 80. *Certified* Medicaid; Medicare.
Owner Proprietary corp.
Admissions Requirements Minimum age 21.

Staff RNs 2 (ft); LPNs 6 (ft), 6 (pt); Recreational therapists 1 (ft), 1 (pt); Activities coordinators 1 (ft), 1 (pt); Dietitians 1 (pt); Podiatrists 1 (pt); Dentists 1 (pt).
Languages Spanish.
Facilities Dining room; Activities room; Crafts room; Laundry room; Barber/Beauty shop.
Activities Arts & crafts; Cards; Games; Reading groups; Prayer groups; Movies; Shopping trips; Dances/Social/Cultural gatherings; Special holiday dinners.

Snapper Creek Nursing Home Inc
9200 SW 87th Ave, Miami, FL 33176
(305) 271-1313
Admin Daniel Lasso NHA. *Dir of Nursing* Marvel Walters RN. *Medical Dir* Ed H Cottler MD.
Licensure Skilled care. *Beds* SNF 115. *Private Pay Patients* 55%. *Certified* Medicaid; Medicare.
Owner Proprietary corp (JASPE Nursing Homes).
Admissions Requirements Minimum age 16; Medical examination; Physician's request.
Staff RNs 7 (ft), 2 (pt); LPNs 10 (ft), 3 (pt); Nurses' aides 42 (ft); Physical therapists 1 (ft), 1 (pt); Recreational therapists 1 (ft); Occupational therapists 1 (ft); Speech therapists 1 (ft); Activities coordinators 1 (ft); Dietitians 1 (ft); Ophthalmologists 1 (pt); Podiatrists 1 (pt); Audiologists 1 (pt).
Languages Spanish, Creole, French.
Facilities Dining room; Physical therapy room; Activities room; Chapel; Crafts room; Laundry room; Barber/Beauty shop; Library; Enclosed patios.
Activities Arts & crafts; Cards; Games; Reading groups; Movies; Shopping trips; Dances/Social/Cultural gatherings; Pet therapy.

Southdade Catholic Nursing Home Inc
11650 Quail Roost Dr, Miami, FL 33177
(305) 235-4105
Beds 93.

Treasure Isle Convalescent Home
1735 N Treasure Dr, Miami, FL 33141
(305) 665-2383
Beds 13.

Miami Beach

Gem Care Center
550 9th St, Miami Beach, FL 33139
(305) 531-3321, 531-2429 FAX
Admin Josefina Lardizabal. *Dir of Nursing* Pilar Alarcon. *Medical Dir* Charles Beber.
Licensure Skilled care. *Beds* SNF 196. *Private Pay Patients* 15%. *Certified* Medicaid; Medicare.
Owner Proprietary corp.
Admissions Requirements Minimum age 18.
Staff RNs 5 (ft), 11 (pt); LPNs 11 (ft), 4 (pt); Nurses' aides 64 (ft), 10 (pt); Physical therapists 1 (pt); Recreational therapists 2 (ft); Occupational therapists 1 (pt); Speech therapists 1 (pt); Dietitians 1 (ft), 2 (pt); Ophthalmologists 2 (pt); Podiatrists 2 (pt).
Languages Spanish, Creole, Hebrew, Filipino.
Facilities Dining room; Physical therapy room; Activities room; Laundry room; Barber/Beauty shop; Library; Roof garden.
Activities Arts & crafts; Cards; Games; Reading groups; Prayer groups; Movies; Shopping trips; Dances/Social/Cultural gatherings; Intergenerational programs; Pet therapy; Adult education classes.

Miami Beach Hebrew Home for the Aged
320 Collins Ave, Miami Beach, FL 33139
(305) 672-6464
Licensure Skilled care. *Beds* 104. *Certified* Medicaid; Medicare.
Owner Nonprofit corp.

Staff RNs 8 (ft); LPNs 4 (ft); Nurses' aides 53 (ft).
Languages Yiddish, Hebrew, Spanish, French.
Affiliation Jewish.

Southpoint Manor
42 Collins Ave, Miami Beach, FL 33139
(305) 672-1771, 672-5940 FAX
Admin Jesse Dunwoody. *Dir of Nursing* Toni Bannamon. *Medical Dir* Charles R Beber MD.
Licensure Skilled care. *Beds* SNF 230. *Private Pay Patients* 10%. *Certified* Medicaid; Medicare.
Owner Proprietary corp.
Admissions Requirements Minimum age 16; Medical examination; Physician's request.
Staff RNs 7 (ft), 6 (pt); LPNs 26 (ft), 4 (pt); Nurses' aides 95 (ft); Physical therapists 1 (ft); Reality therapists 1 (pt); Recreational therapists 1 (pt); Occupational therapists 1 (ft); Speech therapists 1 (pt); Activities coordinators 4 (ft), 1 (pt); Dietitians 1 (ft); Ophthalmologists 2 (pt); Podiatrists 1 (pt); Audiologists 1 (pt).
Languages Spanish, French, Italian, Yiddish, Hebrew, Tagalog, Russian.
Facilities Dining room; Physical therapy room; Activities room; Chapel; Crafts room; Laundry room; Barber/Beauty shop; Secured outdoor patio.
Activities Arts & crafts; Cards; Games; Reading groups; Prayer groups; Movies; Shopping trips; Dances/Social/Cultural gatherings; Pet therapy.

Miami Springs

Fair Havens Center
201 Curtiss Pkwy, Miami Springs, FL 33166
(305) 887-1565, 887-5786 FAX
Admin William D Cole. *Dir of Nursing* Georgiana Rivera. *Medical Dir* James Hutson MD.
Licensure Skilled care; Intermediate care; ACLF; Retirement. *Beds* SNF 223; ICF 45; ACLF 45. *Private Pay Patients* 15%. *Certified* Medicaid; Medicare.
Owner Nonprofit organization/foundation.
Admissions Requirements Minimum age 18; Medical examination.
Staff Physicians 23 (pt); RNs 15 (ft); LPNs 30 (ft); Nurses' aides 109 (ft); Physical therapists 4 (pt); Recreational therapists 3 (pt); Occupational therapists 1 (pt); Speech therapists 1 (pt); Activities coordinators 4 (ft); Dietitians 1 (ft); Ophthalmologists 3 (pt).
Languages Spanish, German, French, Creole, Italian.
Affiliation Lutheran.
Facilities Dining room; Physical therapy room; Activities room; Chapel; Crafts room; Laundry room; Barber/Beauty shop; Library; Gardens.
Activities Arts & crafts; Cards; Games; Reading groups; Prayer groups; Movies; Shopping trips; Intergenerational programs; Pet therapy; Adult education classes.

Fair Havens Center
201 Curtiss Pkwy, Miami Springs, FL 33166-5291
(305) 887-1565
Admin William D Cole. *Dir of Nursing* Pilar Alarcon RN BS. *Medical Dir* James J Hutson MD.
Licensure Skilled care; Intermediate care; Respite care; Adult congregate living. *Beds* SNF 221; ICF 48; Respite care; Adult congregate living 60. *Private Pay Patients* 32%. *Certified* Medicaid; Medicare.
Owner Nonprofit corp.
Admissions Requirements Minimum age 18; Medical examination.

Staff RNs; LPNs; Nurses' aides; Physical therapists (contracted); Recreational therapists; Occupational therapists (contracted); Speech therapists (contracted); Dietitians 1 (ft); Ophthalmologists (contracted); CNAs.
Affiliation Evangelical Lutheran.
Facilities Dining room; Physical therapy room; Activities room; Chapel; Crafts room; Barber/Beauty shop; Library; Private and semi-private rooms available; Emergency call systems; Gift shop.
Activities Arts & crafts; Cards; Games; Reading groups; Prayer groups; Movies; Shopping trips; Dances/Social/Cultural gatherings; Intergenerational programs; Pet therapy; Sing-along; Parties; Current events discussion; Religious services.

Milton

Sandy Ridge Care Center
101 Glover Ln, Milton, FL 32570
(904) 626-9225
Admin Felicia Fortune Northcuit. *Dir of Nursing* Glynda Cupp. *Medical Dir* Rufus Thames MD.
Licensure Skilled care. *Beds* SNF 60. *Private Pay Patients* 5%. *Certified* Medicaid; Medicare.
Owner Privately owned.
Admissions Requirements Minimum age 16; Medical examination.
Staff RNs 3 (ft), 1 (pt); LPNs 8 (ft), 2 (pt); Nurses' aides 15 (ft), 10 (pt); Physical therapists 1 (pt); Occupational therapists 1 (pt); Speech therapists 1 (pt); Activities coordinators 1 (ft); Dietitians 1 (pt); Podiatrists 1 (pt).
Facilities Dining room; Physical therapy room; Activities room; Crafts room; Barber/Beauty shop; Library.
Activities Arts & crafts; Cards; Games; Reading groups; Prayer groups; Movies; Dances/Social/Cultural gatherings; Intergenerational programs; Pet therapy.

Santa Rosa Convalescent Center
500 Broad St, Milton, FL 32570
(904) 623-4661
Medical Dir Rufus Thames.
Licensure Skilled care. *Beds* 120. *Certified* Medicaid; Medicare.
Owner Proprietary corp.
Admissions Requirements Minimum age 50; Medical examination; Physician's request.
Staff Physicians 6 (pt); RNs 4 (ft), 1 (pt); LPNs 8 (ft), 5 (pt); Nurses' aides 36 (ft), 15 (pt); Physical therapists 1 (pt); Speech therapists 1 (pt); Activities coordinators 1 (ft); Dietitians 1 (pt); Podiatrists 1 (pt); Dentists 1 (pt).
Languages French.
Facilities Dining room; Physical therapy room; Activities room; Chapel; Laundry room; Barber/Beauty shop; Library.
Activities Arts & crafts; Games; Reading groups; Prayer groups; Dances/Social/Cultural gatherings.

Monticello

Jefferson Nursing Center
PO Box 477, Monticello, FL 32344
(904) 997-2313
Licensure Skilled care. *Beds* 60. *Certified* Medicaid.
Owner Proprietary corp.
Staff RNs 1 (ft), 1 (pt); LPNs 3 (ft), 2 (pt); Nurses' aides 15 (ft), 5 (pt); Recreational therapists 1 (ft), 1 (pt); Activities coordinators 1 (ft); Dietitians 1 (pt).
Facilities Dining room; Activities room; Crafts room; Laundry room; Barber/Beauty shop.

Activities Arts & crafts; Games; Reading groups; Prayer groups; Movies; Shopping trips.

Meadowbrook Manor of Monticello
Rte 1, Hwy 19 S, Monticello, FL 32344
Beds 19.

Mount Dora

Mt Dora Healthcare Center
PO Box 65, Mount Dora, FL 32757
(904) 383-4161
Admin Joseph A Borho NHA. *Dir of Nursing* Joyce Saladin RN. *Medical Dir* C Robert Crow MD.
Licensure Skilled care. *Beds* SNF 116. *Certified* Medicaid; Medicare.
Owner Proprietary corp (Beverly Enterprises).
Admissions Requirements Minimum age 16; Medical examination; Physician's request.
Staff RNs 4 (ft), 1 (pt); LPNs 14 (ft), 2 (pt); Nurses' aides 37 (ft); Physical therapists 1 (pt); Speech therapists 1 (pt); Activities coordinators 1 (ft); Ophthalmologists 1 (pt); Podiatrists 1 (pt); Social Svcs Coord 1 (ft).
Languages Spanish.
Facilities Dining room; Physical therapy room; Activities room; Chapel; Crafts room; Laundry room; Barber/Beauty shop; Library.
Activities Arts & crafts; Cards; Games; Reading groups; Prayer groups; Movies; Shopping trips; Dances/Social/Cultural gatherings; Picnics; Candlelight dinners.

Naples

Americana Health Care Center of Naples
3601 Lakewood Blvd, Naples, FL 33962
(813) 775-7757
Admin Cindy Mehalshick. *Dir of Nursing* Anna Moore RN. *Medical Dir* Terrance A Johnson MD.
Licensure Skilled care; Alzheimer's care. *Beds* 120. *Certified* Medicaid; Medicare.
Owner Proprietary corp (Manor Care).
Admissions Requirements Minimum age 18; Medical examination; Physician's request.
Staff Physicians; RNs 7 (ft); LPNs 7 (ft); Nurses' aides 20 (ft); Physical therapists 1 (pt); Occupational therapists 1 (pt); Speech therapists 1 (pt); Activities coordinators 4 (ft); Dietitians 1 (pt); Ophthalmologists 1 (pt).
Languages Spanish, Haitian.
Facilities Dining room; Physical therapy room; Activities room; Laundry room; Barber/Beauty shop.
Activities Arts & crafts; Cards; Games; Reading groups; Prayer groups; Movies; Shopping trips; Dances/Social/Cultural gatherings; Daily cocktail hour; Pet therapy; Holiday events.

Bentley Village Health Care Facility
561 Bentley Village Ct, Naples, FL 33963
(813) 598-3191, 598-3194 FAX
Admin Margaret A Martin. *Dir of Nursing* Roberta Harris. *Medical Dir* Robert L Gilbert MD.
Licensure Skilled care. *Beds* SNF 93. *Private Pay Patients* 100%.
Owner Proprietary corp.
Staff Physicians 5 (pt); LPNs 7 (ft); Nurses' aides 12 (ft); Physical therapists 2 (pt); Recreational therapists 1 (ft), 1 (pt); Occupational therapists 1 (pt); Speech therapists 1 (pt); Activities coordinators 1 (ft); Dietitians 1 (pt); Ophthalmologists 1 (pt); Podiatrists 1 (pt); Audiologists 1 (pt).

Heritage Healthcare Center
777 9th St N, Naples, FL 33940
(813) 261-8126, 261-8647 FAX
Admin Douglas E Webb. *Dir of Nursing* Elaine R Farley RN. *Medical Dir* Louis Moore MD.

Licensure Skilled care. *Beds* SNF 97. *Private Pay Patients* 45%. *Certified* Medicaid; Medicare.
Owner Proprietary corp (Beverly Enterprises).
Admissions Requirements Medical examination; Physician's request.
Staff Physicians 2 (pt); RNs 5 (ft), 1 (pt); LPNs 8 (ft), 11 (pt); Nurses' aides 26 (ft), 6 (pt); Physical therapists 1 (pt); Occupational therapists 1 (pt); Speech therapists 1 (pt); Activities coordinators 1 (ft); Dietitians 1 (pt); Ophthalmologists 1 (pt); Podiatrists 1 (pt).
Languages Spanish, French.
Facilities Dining room; Physical therapy room; Activities room; Laundry room; Barber/Beauty shop; Screened porches.
Activities Arts & crafts; Cards; Games; Reading groups; Prayer groups; Movies; Shopping trips; Dances/Social/Cultural gatherings; Pet therapy.

Heritage Healthcare Center
777 9th St N, Naples, FL 33940
(813) 261-8126, 261-8647 FAX
Admin Douglas E Webb. *Dir of Nursing* Elaine Farley. *Medical Dir* Louis S Moore MD.
Licensure Skilled care; Intermediate care. *Beds* Swing beds SNF/ICF 97. *Private Pay Patients* 45%. *Certified* Medicaid; Medicare.
Owner Proprietary corp (Beverly Enterprises).
Admissions Requirements Medical examination; Physician's request.
Staff RNs 5 (ft), 2 (pt); LPNs 12 (ft), 6 (pt); Nurses' aides 29 (ft), 2 (pt); Physical therapists 1 (pt); Occupational therapists 1 (pt); Speech therapists 1 (pt); Activities coordinators 1 (ft), 1 (pt); Dietitians 1 (pt); Ophthalmologists 1 (pt); Podiatrists 1 (pt); Audiologists 1 (pt).
Languages Spanish.
Facilities Dining room; Physical therapy room; Activities room; Crafts room; Laundry room; Barber/Beauty shop; Library; Patio; Screened porches.
Activities Arts & crafts; Cards; Games; Reading groups; Prayer groups; Movies; Shopping trips; Dances/Social/Cultural gatherings; Intergenerational programs; Pet therapy; Music programs.

Lakeside Plantation
2900 12th St N, Naples, FL 33940
(813) 261-2554, 261-4540 FAX
Admin Pamela M Cox. *Dir of Nursing* Leslie Nowe, Acting. *Medical Dir* Rasik Mehta MD.
Licensure Skilled care; Intermediate care. *Beds* Swing beds SNF/ICF 120. *Private Pay Patients* 50%. *Certified* Medicaid; Medicare.
Owner Proprietary corp (Harborside Healthcare).
Admissions Requirements Medical examination; Physician's request.
Staff Physicians 1 (pt); RNs 4 (ft), 6 (pt); LPNs 8 (ft), 4 (pt); Nurses' aides 32 (ft), 7 (pt); Physical therapists 1 (pt); Occupational therapists 1 (pt); Speech therapists 1 (pt); Activities coordinators 1 (ft); Dietitians 1 (pt); Ophthalmologists (consultant); Podiatrists (consultant); Rehabilitation aides 1 (ft).
Languages Spanish.
Facilities Dining room; Physical therapy room; Activities room; Laundry room; Barber/Beauty shop; Private and semi-private rooms; TV Lounges; Covered veranda on a 5-acre lake; Aviary; Courtyard.
Activities Arts & crafts; Cards; Games; Reading groups; Movies; Shopping trips; Dances/Social/Cultural gatherings; Pet therapy; Beach trips; Religious services.

Lely Palms of Naples Health Care Center
1000 Lely Palms Dr, Naples, FL 33962
(613) 775-7661
Beds 60.

Moorings Park
120 Moorings Park Dr, Naples, FL 33942
(813) 261-1616
Admin Jerry Jaques. *Dir of Nursing* Lily L'Esperance. *Medical Dir* Dr Rasik Mehta.
Licensure Skilled care; Retirement. *Beds* SNF 60. *Certified* Medicare.
Owner Nonprofit corp (Life Care Services Corp).
Admissions Requirements Physician's request.
Staff Physicians 10 (pt); RNs 3 (ft), 4 (pt); LPNs 5 (ft), 1 (pt); Nurses' aides 23 (ft), 2 (pt); Physical therapists 1 (pt); Recreational therapists 1 (pt); Occupational therapists 1 (pt); Speech therapists 1 (pt); Activities coordinators 1 (ft); Dietitians 2 (pt); Ophthalmologists 1 (pt); Podiatrists 1 (pt).
Languages Spanish, Tagalog.
Facilities Dining room; Physical therapy room; Activities room; Crafts room; Laundry room; Barber/Beauty shop.
Activities Arts & crafts; Cards; Games; Reading groups; Prayer groups; Movies; Shopping trips; Dances/Social/Cultural gatherings.

New Port Richey

Hacienda Home for Special Service
201 W Main St, New Port Richey, FL 33552
(613) 848-6780
Beds 19.

Heather Hill Nursing Home
1151 E Kentucky Ave, New Port Richey, FL 33653
(813) 849-6939
Licensure Skilled care. *Beds* 120. *Certified* Medicaid; Medicare.
Owner Proprietary corp.
Staff RNs 7 (ft); LPNs 11 (ft); Nurses' aides 36 (ft).
Languages German, Greek, Spanish.

Orchard Ridge Nursing Center
700 Trouble Creek Rd, New Port Richey, FL 33552
(613) 848-3578
Beds 56.

Park Lake Village Care Center
6417 Cr 54, New Port Richey, FL 33552
(613) 376-1585
Beds 66.

Richey Manor Nursing Home
505 Indiana Ave, New Port Richey, FL 33552
(813) 849-7555
Admin Edward E Alderson. *Dir of Nursing* Patricia Hoppert RN. *Medical Dir* Francis K S Oey MD.
Licensure Skilled care; Alzheimer's care. *Beds* SNF 119. *Certified* Medicaid; Medicare.
Owner Proprietary corp (Unicare).
Admissions Requirements Minimum age 16; Medical examination; Physician's request.
Staff RNs 3 (ft), 2 (pt); LPNs 12 (ft), 2 (pt); Nurses' aides 38 (ft), 1 (pt); Recreational therapists 1 (ft); Activities coordinators 1 (ft); Dietitians 1 (pt).
Facilities Dining room; Physical therapy room; Activities room; Laundry room; Barber/Beauty shop.
Activities Arts & crafts; Cards; Games; Reading groups; Prayer groups; Movies; Shopping trips; Dances/Social/Cultural gatherings.

Southern Pines Nursing Center
312 S Congress St, New Port Richey, FL 33552
(813) 842-8402
Admin Vern V Charbonneau. *Dir of Nursing* Lorraine Sedlock RN.
Licensure Skilled care. *Beds* SNF 120. *Certified* Medicaid; Medicare.
Owner Proprietary corp (Care Enterprises).

Admissions Requirements Minimum age 18; Medical examination.
Staff RNs 6 (ft); LPNs 10 (ft); Nurses' aides 30 (ft); Reality therapists 1 (ft); Activities coordinators 1 (ft); Dietitians 1 (ft).
Languages Spanish.
Facilities Dining room; Physical therapy room; Activities room; Crafts room; Barber/Beauty shop.
Activities Arts & crafts; Cards; Games; Reading groups; Prayer groups; Movies; Dances/Social/Cultural gatherings.

Whispering Pines Convalescent Center
8151 Treelet Ct, New Port Richey, FL 34652
(813) 849-7205
Beds 24.

New Smyrna Beach

Ocean-View Nursing Home
2810 S Atlantic Ave, New Smyrna Beach, FL 32069
(904) 428-6424
Admin Dennis W O'Leary NHA. *Dir of Nursing* Margaret Varano RN. *Medical Dir* Durrand Wallar MD.
Licensure Skilled care; Alzheimer's care. *Beds* SNF 179. *Certified* Medicaid; Medicare.
Owner Proprietary corp (HBA Management Inc).
Admissions Requirements Minimum age 21; Medical examination; Physician's request.
Staff Physicians 1 (pt); RNs 8 (ft), 4 (pt); LPNs 11 (ft), 4 (pt); Nurses' aides 75 (ft), 20 (pt); Physical therapists 1 (ft); Speech therapists 1 (pt); Activities coordinators 2 (ft); Dietitians 1 (ft); Ophthalmologists 1 (pt); Podiatrists 1 (pt).
Languages Spanish, Italian, German.
Facilities Dining room; Physical therapy room; Activities room; Crafts room; Laundry room; Barber/Beauty shop.
Activities Arts & crafts; Cards; Games; Reading groups; Prayer groups; Movies; Shopping trips; Dances/Social/Cultural gatherings; Cookouts; Picnics.

Niceville

Bay Heritage Nursing & Convalescent Center
115 Hart St, Niceville, FL 32576
(904) 696-6667
Beds 32.

North Bay Village

Treasure Isle Care Center
1735 N Treasure Dr, North Bay Village, FL 33141
(305) 865-2383
Admin Donald Policastro. *Dir of Nursing* Janet Moritt. *Medical Dir* Dr Richard Jacobs.
Licensure Skilled care; Intermediate care; Alzheimer's care. *Beds* 176. *Certified* Medicaid; Medicare.
Owner Proprietary corp (Unicare).
Admissions Requirements Minimum age 18.
Staff Physicians 7 (pt); RNs 8 (ft), 15 (pt); LPNs 8 (ft), 4 (pt); Nurses' aides 53 (ft), 13 (pt); Physical therapists 4 (pt); Reality therapists 2 (pt); Recreational therapists 1 (pt); Occupational therapists 1 (pt); Speech therapists 1 (ft); Activities coordinators 1 (ft); Dietitians 1 (ft); Ophthalmologists 1 (pt); Podiatrists 1 (pt); Dentists 1 (pt).
Languages Spanish, Creole, Tagalog.
Facilities Dining room; Physical therapy room; Activities room; Chapel; Crafts room; Laundry room; Barber/Beauty shop; Outside patio; Prayer area.
Activities Arts & crafts; Cards; Games; Reading groups; Prayer groups; Movies; Shopping trips; Dances/Social/Cultural gatherings; Language classes.

North Fort Myers

Pines Village Care Center
991 Pondella Rd, North Fort Myers, FL
33903
(813) 995-8809, 995-1253 FAX
Admin Joann Szeliga Cameron. *Dir of Nursing*
Martha Bartholomew RN. *Medical Dir*
Romulo A Bernal MD.
Licensure Skilled care; Alzheimer's care. *Beds*
SNF 120. *Private Pay Patients* 30%. *Certified*
Medicaid; Medicare.
Owner Privately owned.
Admissions Requirements Minimum age 21;
Medical examination; Physician's request.
Staff Physicians 1 (ft); RNs 5 (ft), 4 (pt);
LPNs 8 (ft), 4 (pt); Nurses' aides 30 (ft), 3
(pt); Physical therapists 1 (ft); Recreational
therapists; Occupational therapists 1 (ft);
Speech therapists 1 (ft); Activities
coordinators 1 (ft), 1 (pt); Dietitians 1 (ft);
Podiatrists 1 (pt); Audiologists.
Facilities Dining room; Physical therapy
room; Activities room; Laundry room;
Barber/Beauty shop; 2 screened patios;
Fenced yard; Fish pond; Shuffleboard.
Activities Arts & crafts; Cards; Games;
Reading groups; Prayer groups; Movies;
Shopping trips; Dances/Social/Cultural
gatherings; Intergenerational programs; Pet
therapy; Religious programs; Resident
council; Family council.

North Miami

Arch Creek Nursing Home
12505 NE 16th Ave, North Miami, FL 33161
(305) 891-1710
Licensure Skilled care; Intermediate care. *Beds*
118. *Certified* Medicaid; Medicare.
Owner Proprietary corp.
Staff RNs 5 (ft); LPNs 13 (ft); Nurses' aides
26 (ft).
Languages Spanish, Russian, Yiddish,
Hebrew, French.

**Bon Secours Hospital/Villa Maria Nursing
Center**
1050 NE 125th St, North Miami, FL 33161
(305) 891-8850
Medical Dir Dr Harold Weiner & Dr David
Lipkin.
Licensure Rehabilitation; Nursing Center.
Beds Rehabilitation 60; Nursing Center 212.
Certified Medicaid; Medicare.
Owner Proprietary corp.
Admissions Requirements Medical
examination; Physician's request.
Staff Physicians 2 (ft); RNs 17 (ft), 6 (pt);
LPNs 18 (ft), 7 (pt); Nurses' aides 78 (ft), 12
(pt); Physical therapists 13 (ft); Recreational
therapists 2 (ft); Occupational therapists 12
(ft); Speech therapists 2 (ft); Activities
coordinators 1 (ft); Dietitians 1 (ft).
Languages Spanish, Hebrew, Yiddish, French,
German, Greek, Polish, Tagalog, Yomba.
Affiliation Roman Catholic.
Facilities Dining room; Physical therapy
room; Activities room; Chapel; Crafts room;
Laundry room; Barber/Beauty shop; Library.
Activities Arts & crafts; Cards; Games;
Reading groups; Prayer groups; Movies;
Shopping trips; Dances/Social/Cultural
gatherings.

Claridge House
13900 NE 3rd Ct, North Miami, FL 33161
(305) 893-2288
Admin Larry Mankoff.
Medical Dir Janet Morrit.
Licensure Skilled care; Alzheimer unit. *Beds*
240. *Certified* Medicaid; Medicare.
Owner Proprietary corp (CHR Assoc).
Admissions Requirements Minimum age 16;
Medical examination.

Staff RNs 24 (ft); LPNs 18 (ft); Nurses' aides
60 (ft); Recreational therapists 2 (ft);
Dietitians 1 (pt).
Languages Spanish, Yiddish, Hebrew,
German, Polish.
Facilities Dining room; Physical therapy
room; Activities room; Chapel; Crafts room;
Barber/Beauty shop; Day lounges; Shaded
outdoor patio.
Activities Arts & crafts; Cards; Games;
Reading groups; Prayer groups; Movies;
Shopping trips; Dances/Social/Cultural
gatherings; Resident council; Newsletter.

Fountainhead Nursing & Convalescent Home
390 NE 135th St, North Miami, FL 33161
(305) 893-0660
Licensure Skilled care. *Beds* 146. *Certified*
Medicaid.
Owner Proprietary corp (Angell Group).
Staff RNs 6 (ft); LPNs 10 (ft); Nurses' aides
34 (ft).
Languages Spanish, French.

Fountainhead Nursing Center
390 NE 135th St, North Miami, FL 33161
(305) 893-0660
Admin Donald Policastro. *Dir of Nursing*
Nilda Flores. *Medical Dir* Jesus Gonzalez.
Licensure Skilled care. *Beds* SNF 146. *Private
Pay Patients* 10%. *Certified* Medicaid;
Medicare.
Owner Nonprofit corp (Angell Care Inc).
Admissions Requirements Medical
examination.
Staff Physicians 2 (ft); RNs 5 (ft), 7 (pt);
LPNs 12 (ft), 4 (pt); Nurses' aides 36 (ft), 14
(pt); Physical therapists 2 (ft); Reality
therapists 1 (ft); Recreational therapists 1
(ft); Occupational therapists 1 (ft); Speech
therapists 2 (ft); Activities coordinators 1
(ft); Dietitians 14 (ft); Ophthalmologists 1
(ft); Podiatrists 2 (ft); Audiologists 1 (ft).
Languages French, Spanish.
Facilities Dining room; Physical therapy
room; Activities room; Laundry room;
Barber/Beauty shop; Library.
Activities Arts & crafts; Cards; Games;
Reading groups; Prayer groups; Shopping
trips; Intergenerational programs; Pet
therapy.

Meadow Brook Manor of North Miami
1255 NE 135th St, North Miami, FL 33161
(305) 891-6850
Admin Jon H Steinmeyer. *Dir of Nursing*
Barbara Cowart RN. *Medical Dir* Dr
Stanford Cooke.
Licensure Skilled care; Alzheimer's care. *Beds*
SNF; ICF 245. *Certified* Medicaid;
Medicare.
Owner Proprietary corp (Angell Group).
Admissions Requirements Minimum age 18.
Staff Physicians 1 (pt); RNs 6 (ft), 2 (pt);
LPNs 17 (ft); Nurses' aides 80 (ft); Physical
therapists 2 (ft), 2 (pt); Recreational
therapists 2 (pt); Occupational therapists 1
(pt); Speech therapists 1 (pt); Activities
coordinators 1 (ft); Dietitians 1 (pt);
Ophthalmologists 1 (pt); Podiatrists 1 (pt);
Dentists 1 (pt).
Languages Spanish, French, Creole.
Facilities Dining room; Physical therapy
room; Activities room; Crafts room; Barber/
Beauty shop; Outdoor patio with patio
furniture.
Activities Arts & crafts; Cards; Games;
Reading groups; Prayer groups; Movies;
Shopping trips; Dances/Social/Cultural
gatherings; Hispanic cultural activities;
Parties & food.

Pinecrest Convalescent Home
13650 NE 3rd Ct, North Miami, FL 33161
(305) 893-1170
Admin James Reiss. *Dir of Nursing* Virginia
Carpenter. *Medical Dir* Joel Pershkow.

Licensure Skilled care; Alzheimer's care. *Beds*
SNF 100. *Certified* Medicaid; Medicare.
Owner Privately owned.
Admissions Requirements Minimum age 16.
Staff Physicians 2 (pt); RNs 4 (ft); LPNs 10
(ft); Nurses' aides 33 (ft); Physical therapists
2 (pt); Recreational therapists 2 (ft);
Occupational therapists 1 (pt); Speech
therapists 1 (pt); Activities coordinators 2
(ft); Dietitians 1 (pt); Ophthalmologists 1
(pt); Dentists 1 (pt).
Languages German, Spanish.
Facilities Dining room; Physical therapy
room; Activities room; Crafts room; Laundry
room; Barber/Beauty shop; Library.
Activities Arts & crafts; Cards; Games;
Reading groups; Prayer groups; Movies;
Shopping trips; Dances/Social/Cultural
gatherings.

**Villa Maria Nursing & Rehabilitation Center
Inc**
1050 NE 125th St, North Miami, FL 33161
(305) 891-8850, 899-9004 FAX
Admin James A Hotchkiss Jr. *Dir of Nursing*
Carol Stuchins. *Medical Dir* Anthony J
Dorto MD.
Licensure Skilled care; Intermediate care;
Alzheimer's care. *Beds* SNF 68; ICF 144.
Private Pay Patients 65%. *Certified*
Medicaid; Medicare.
Owner Nonprofit corp (Bon Secours Health
Systems Inc).
Admissions Requirements Minimum age 18;
Physician's request.
Staff Physicians 1 (ft); RNs 17 (ft), 1 (pt);
LPNs 23 (ft); Nurses' aides 70 (ft), 1 (pt);
Physical therapists 1 (ft); Recreational
therapists 1 (ft); Occupational therapists 2
(ft), 1 (pt); Speech therapists 5 (ft); Activities
coordinators 1 (ft); Dietitians 1 (ft); RDTs 1
(ft).
Languages Spanish, Hebrew, French, Creole.
Affiliation Roman Catholic.
Facilities Dining room; Physical therapy
room; Activities room; Chapel; Crafts room;
Laundry room; Barber/Beauty shop; Library;
Auditorium; Patio area.
Activities Arts & crafts; Cards; Games;
Reading groups; Movies; Shopping trips;
Dances/Social/Cultural gatherings;
Intergenerational programs; Pet therapy;
Music; Singing; Therapeutic recreation.

North Miami Beach

Bayshore Convalescent Center
16650 W Dixie Hwy, North Miami Beach, FL
33160
(305) 945-7447
Beds 63.

Greynolds Park Manor Inc
17400 W Dixie Hwy, North Miami Beach, FL
33160
(305) 944-2361
Beds 4.

Greynolds Park Manor Rehabilitation Center
17400 W Dixie Hwy, North Miami Beach, FL
33160
(305) 944-2361, 949-9464 FAX
Admin George N Leader; Martin E Casper
Exec Dir. *Dir of Nursing* Londa Ilhardt RN.
Medical Dir Sheldon Staller MD; Francis
Komara DO.
Licensure Skilled care; Alzheimer's care. *Beds*
SNF 324. *Private Pay Patients* 20%. *Certified*
Medicaid; Medicare.
Owner Proprietary corp.
Admissions Requirements Medical
examination.
Staff Physicians 2 (pt); RNs 28 (ft); LPNs 22
(ft); Nurses' aides 109 (ft); Physical
therapists 2 (ft); Occupational therapists 2
(ft); Speech therapists 1 (pt); Activities

coordinators 1 (ft), 3 (pt); Dietitians 1 (pt); Ophthalmologists 1 (pt); Podiatrists 1 (pt); Dentists 1 (pt).
Languages Spanish, French, Creole, Yiddish, Hebrew.
Facilities Dining room; Physical therapy room; Activities room; Chapel; Crafts room; Laundry room; Barber/Beauty shop; Library; Nearby park.
Activities Arts & crafts; Cards; Games; Reading groups; Prayer groups; Movies; Shopping trips; Dances/Social/Cultural gatherings; Intergenerational programs; Pet therapy; Picnics; Monthly candelight dinners with live band.

Hebrew Home for the Aged—North Dade
1800 NE 168th St, North Miami Beach, FL 33162
(305) 947-3445, 949-4575 FAX
Admin Stuart Siegel NHA MACHCA. *Dir of Nursing* Lee B Tiger RN. *Medical Dir* Salvatore I Certo MD.
Licensure Skilled care; Intermediate care; Retirement; Alzheimer's care. *Beds* SNF 75; ICF 25. *Private Pay Patients* 10%. *Certified* Medicaid; Medicare.
Owner Nonprofit organization/foundation.
Admissions Requirements Minimum age 18; Medical examination.
Staff Physicians 1 (ft); RNs 5 (ft), 2 (pt); LPNs 5 (ft), 3 (pt); Nurses' aides 58 (ft), 5 (pt); Physical therapists 2 (ft), 2 (pt); Occupational therapists 1 (pt); Speech therapists 1 (pt); Activities coordinators 1 (ft); Dietitians 1 (pt); Ophthalmologists 2 (pt); Podiatrists 1 (pt); Audiologists 1 (pt).
Languages Spanish, Yiddish.
Facilities Dining room; Laundry room; Alzheimer's unit.
Activities Arts & crafts; Cards; Games; Reading groups; Movies; Shopping trips; Dances/Social/Cultural gatherings; Intergenerational programs; Pet therapy.

Hebrew Home for the Aged—North Dade
1800 NE 168th St, North Miami Beach, FL 33162
(305) 947-3445
Medical Dir Dr Salvatore Certo.
Licensure Skilled care. *Beds* 50. *Certified* Medicaid; Medicare.
Owner Nonprofit corp.
Admissions Requirements Minimum age 40; Medical examination.
Staff Physicians 1 (pt); RNs 4 (ft); LPNs 3 (ft); Nurses' aides 38 (ft); Physical therapists 1 (pt); Recreational therapists 1 (pt); Occupational therapists 1 (pt); Speech therapists 1 (pt); Activities coordinators 1 (ft); Dietitians 1 (pt); Podiatrists 1 (pt); Audiologists 1 (pt); Dentists 1 (pt).
Languages Spanish, Yiddish, Hebrew.
Affiliation Jewish.
Facilities Dining room; Activities room; Laundry room.
Activities Arts & crafts; Cards; Games; Reading groups; Movies; Shopping trips.

Heritage Nursing & Rehabilitation Center
2201 NE 170th St, North Miami Beach, FL 33160
(305) 945-1401, 947-2512 FAX
Admin Debbie Simmons. *Dir of Nursing* Kimberly Thompson. *Medical Dir* Dr Ira Abramson.
Licensure Skilled care; Intermediate care; Alzheimer's care. *Beds* Swing beds SNF/ICF 98. *Private Pay Patients* 30%. *Certified* Medicaid; Medicare.
Owner Proprietary corp (Unicare).
Admissions Requirements Medical examination.
Staff Physicians; RNs; LPNs; Nurses' aides; Physical therapists; Occupational therapists 1 (pt); Speech therapists 1 (pt); Activities

coordinators 2 (ft); Dietitians 1 (ft); Ophthalmologists 1 (pt); Podiatrists 1 (pt); Audiologists 1 (pt); Psychiatrists 1 (pt).
Languages Spanish, Creole.
Facilities Dining room; Physical therapy room; Activities room; Crafts room; Barber/Beauty shop; Library.
Activities Arts & crafts; Cards; Games; Reading groups; Prayer groups; Movies; Shopping trips; Dances/Social/Cultural gatherings; Intergenerational programs; Pet therapy.

Heritage Nursing & Rehabilitation Center
2201 NE 170th St, North Miami Beach, FL 33160
(305) 945-1401
Admin Deborah L Simmons. *Dir of Nursing* Cora Rich RN. *Medical Dir* Dr Sheldon Staller.
Licensure Skilled care. *Beds* SNF 99. *Certified* Medicaid; Medicare.
Owner Proprietary corp (Unicare).
Admissions Requirements Medical examination; Physician's request.
Staff Physicians 3 (ft); RNs 5 (ft); LPNs 7 (ft), 4 (pt); Nurses' aides 31 (ft), 5 (pt); Physical therapists 1 (ft), 1 (pt); Recreational therapists 1 (ft); Occupational therapists 1 (ft); Speech therapists 1 (ft); Activities coordinators 1 (ft); Dietitians 1 (ft); Ophthalmologists 1 (ft); Podiatrists 1 (ft); Dentists 1 (ft).
Facilities Dining room; Physical therapy room; Activities room; Barber/Beauty shop; Outdoor patio.
Activities Arts & crafts; Cards; Games; Reading groups; Prayer groups; Movies; Shopping trips; Dances/Social/Cultural gatherings.

Kraver Institute
1800 NE 168th St, North Miami Beach, FL 33162
(305) 947-3445
Licensure Intermediate care for mentally retarded. *Beds* 20.
Owner Nonprofit corp.
Staff Physicians; Dietitians; Nurses' aides.
Languages Spanish.
Activities Arts & crafts; Shopping trips.

Royal Glades Convalescent Home
16650 W Dixie Hwy, North Miami Beach, FL 33160
(305) 945-7447
Licensure Skilled care. *Beds* 150. *Certified* Medicaid; Medicare.
Owner Proprietary corp.
Staff RNs 6 (ft); LPNs 14 (ft); Nurses' aides 36 (ft).
Languages Spanish, French, Hebrew, Yiddish.

Ocala

New Horizon Rehabilitation Center
635 SE 17th St, Ocala, FL 32670
(904) 629-7921
Licensure Skilled care; Intermediate care. *Beds* 89. *Certified* Medicaid; Medicare; VA.
Owner Proprietary corp (Unicare).
Staff RNs 6 (ft); LPNs 9 (ft); Nurses' aides 28 (ft).
Languages German, French, Greek, Polish, Spanish.
Facilities Dining room; Physical therapy room; Activities room; Crafts room; Laundry room; Barber/Beauty shop; Enclosed patio area.
Activities Arts & crafts; Cards; Games; Reading groups; Prayer groups; Movies; Shopping trips; Dances/Social/Cultural gatherings.

Oakhurst Manor Nursing Center
1501 SE 24th Rd, Ocala, FL 32671
(904) 629-8900

Admin Steve Watson. *Dir of Nursing* Joan Whittenham. *Medical Dir* Dr James McLaughlin.
Licensure Skilled care. *Beds* SNF 120. *Private Pay Patients* 40%. *Certified* Medicaid; Medicare.
Owner Proprietary corp (Shive Nursing Inc).
Admissions Requirements Medical examination.
Staff Physical therapists 1 (pt); Recreational therapists 1 (ft); Occupational therapists 1 (pt); Speech therapists 1 (pt); Activities coordinators 1 (ft); Dietitians 1 (pt); Podiatrists 1 (pt); Audiologists 1 (pt).
Languages Spanish.
Facilities Dining room; Physical therapy room; Activities room; Crafts room; Laundry room; Barber/Beauty shop; Library.
Activities Arts & crafts; Cards; Games; Reading groups; Prayer groups; Movies; Shopping trips; Dances/Social/Cultural gatherings; Intergenerational programs; Pet therapy.

Ocala Geriatric Center Inc
1201 SE 24th Rd, Ocala, FL 32671
(904) 732-2449
Admin William I Riddle. *Dir of Nursing* Ellen Cain RN. *Medical Dir* Carl S Lytle MD.
Licensure Skilled care; Intermediate care; Alzheimer's care. *Beds* 180. *Certified* Medicaid; Medicare.
Owner Proprietary corp (Waverly Group).
Admissions Requirements Minimum age 16; Medical examination; Physician's request.
Staff Physicians 1 (pt); RNs 12 (ft), 2 (pt); LPNs 10 (ft), 4 (pt); Nurses' aides 55 (ft), 20 (pt); Physical therapists 1 (pt); Reality therapists 1 (ft); Recreational therapists 1 (ft); Occupational therapists 1 (pt); Speech therapists 1 (pt); Activities coordinators 1 (ft); Dietitians 1 (pt); Ophthalmologists 1 (pt); Podiatrists 1 (pt).
Languages Spanish.
Facilities Dining room; Physical therapy room; Activities room; Chapel; Crafts room; Laundry room; Barber/Beauty shop; Library; Dayroom; picnic area.
Activities Arts & crafts; Cards; Games; Reading groups; Prayer groups; Movies; Shopping trips; Dances/Social/Cultural gatherings.

Ocala Health Care Center
2021 SW 1st Ave, Ocala, FL 32671
(904) 629-0063
Licensure Skilled care. *Beds* 133. *Certified* Medicaid; Medicare.
Owner Proprietary corp (Beverly Enterprises).
Staff RNs 9 (ft); LPNs 11 (ft); Nurses' aides 29 (ft).

Palm Garden
3400 SW 27th Ave, Ocala, FL 32674
(904) 854-6262, 237-5652
Admin Pete Prins. *Dir of Nursing* Jean Botelle RN. *Medical Dir* James McLaughlin MD.
Licensure Skilled care; Intermediate care. *Beds* SNF 15; ICF 45. *Private Pay Patients* 20%. *Certified* Medicaid; Medicare.
Owner Proprietary corp.
Admissions Requirements Minimum age 16 per FS.
Staff RNs 4 (ft), 1 (pt); LPNs 4 (ft), 4 (pt); Nurses' aides 20 (ft), 4 (pt); Physical therapists 1 (pt); Occupational therapists 1 (pt); Speech therapists 1 (pt); Activities coordinators 1 (ft); Dietitians 1 (ft).
Languages Spanish, Italian, German.
Facilities Dining room; Physical therapy room; Activities room; Laundry room; Barber/Beauty shop.
Activities Arts & crafts; Cards; Games; Reading groups; Prayer groups; Movies; Dances/Social/Cultural gatherings; Intergenerational programs; Pet therapy.

Okeechobee

Okeechobee Health Care Facility
1646 Hwy 441-N, Okeechobee, FL 33472
(613) 763-7340
Beds 11.

Oldsmar

West Bay Nursing Center
400 State Rd 584 W, Oldsmar, FL 33557
(813) 855-4661
Admin Staci Harrison. *Dir of Nursing*
Elizabeth Mould RN. *Medical Dir* Don
DeHaven MD.
Licensure Skilled care; Intermediate care. *Beds*
120. *Certified* Medicaid; Medicare.
Owner Proprietary corp.
Admissions Requirements Medical
examination; Physician's request.
Staff RNs 4 (ft), 3 (pt); LPNs 5 (ft); Nurses'
aides 31 (ft), 4 (pt); Physical therapists 1 (ft);
Occupational therapists 1 (pt); Speech
therapists 1 (pt); Activities coordinators 1
(ft); Dietitians 1 (pt); Ophthalmologists 1
(pt).
Languages Spanish.
Facilities Dining room; Physical therapy
room; Activities room; Laundry room;
Barber/Beauty shop.
Activities Arts & crafts; Cards; Games; Prayer
groups; Movies; Shopping trips; Dances/
Social/Cultural gatherings.

Opa Locka

Landmark Learning Center—Facility I
PO Box 1898, Opa Locka, FL 33055
(305) 624-9671
Licensure Intermediate care for mentally
retarded. *Beds* 120. *Certified* Medicaid.
Owner Publicly owned.
Staff RNs 4 (ft); LPNs 7 (ft); Nurses' aides 71
(ft).

Landmark Learning Center—Miami Facility II
PO Box 1898, Opa Locka, FL 33055
(305) 624-9671
Licensure Intermediate care for mentally
retarded. *Beds* 60.
Owner Publicly owned.

Sunland Center—Miami Facility III
PO Box 1898, Opa Locka, FL 33055
(305) 624-9671
Licensure Intermediate care for mentally
retarded. *Beds* 60.
Owner Publicly owned.

Orange City

John Knox Village of Central Florida Inc
101 Northlake Dr, Orange City, FL 32763
(904) 775-3840
Admin Judith I Osborn. *Dir of Nursing* Paula
Kline. *Medical Dir* Padeep Mathur.
Licensure Skilled care; Intermediate care;
ACLF; Retirement. *Beds* Swing beds SNF/
ICF 120; ACLF 18. *Private Pay Patients* 5%.
Certified Medicaid; Medicare.
Owner Nonprofit organization/foundation.
Admissions Requirements Minimum age 65;
Medical examination; Physician's request.
Staff RNs; LPNs; Nurses' aides; Physical
therapists fee-for-service; Occupational
therapists fee-for-service; Activities
coordinators; Dietitians; Speech therapists
fee-for-service; Ophthalmologists fee-for-
service; Podiatrists fee-for-service;
Audiologists fee-for-service; Dentists fee-for-
service.
Facilities Physical therapy room; Chapel;
Laundry room; Barber/Beauty shop; Library;
Dining/Activities room.

Activities Arts & crafts; Cards; Games;
Reading groups; Movies; Shopping trips; Pet
therapy.

Orange Park

Holly Point Manor
633 Kingsley Ave, Orange Park, FL 32703
(904) 269-2610
Beds 64.

Moosehaven Health Center
Hwy 17, PO Box 102, Orange Park, FL 32073
(904) 264-9551
Medical Dir H L Stephens MD.
Licensure Skilled care; Intermediate care. *Beds*
SNF 20; ICF 180.
Owner Nonprofit corp.
Admissions Requirements Minimum age 65.
Staff Physicians 1 (ft), 3 (pt); Physical
therapists 2 (ft); Activities coordinators 1
(ft); Dietitians 1 (ft); Podiatrists 1 (ft);
Audiologists 1 (ft); Dentists 1 (ft).
Languages Spanish, Tagalog.
Affiliation Royal Order of Moose.
Facilities Dining room; Physical therapy
room; Chapel; Crafts room; Laundry room;
Barber/Beauty shop; Library.
Activities Arts & crafts; Cards; Games; Prayer
groups; Shopping trips; Dances/Social/
Cultural gatherings; Aerobic exercises.

Orange Park Care Center
2029 Professional Center Dr, Orange Park, FL
32073
(904) 272-6194
Admin Robert E Green. *Dir of Nursing*
Christine Martin. *Medical Dir* George
Wilson MD.
Licensure Skilled care; Intermediate care. *Beds*
105. *Certified* Medicaid; Medicare.
Owner Proprietary corp.
Admissions Requirements Medical
examination; Physician's request.
Staff RNs 5 (ft), 2 (pt); LPNs 7 (ft); Nurses'
aides 35 (ft); Physical therapists 2 (pt);
Occupational therapists 2 (pt); Speech
therapists 2 (pt); Activities coordinators 1
(ft); Dietitians 2 (pt); Ophthalmologists 1
(pt); Podiatrists 1 (pt).
Facilities Dining room; Physical therapy
room; Activities room; Crafts room; Laundry
room; Barber/Beauty shop; Library.
Activities Arts & crafts; Cards; Games; Prayer
groups; Movies; Shopping trips; Dances/
Social/Cultural gatherings.

Orlando

Americana Health Care Center of Orlando
2414 Bedford Rd, Orlando, FL 32803
(305) 898-5051
Licensure Skilled care. *Beds* 102. *Certified*
Medicare.
Owner Proprietary corp.
Staff RNs 7 (ft); LPNs 10 (ft), 1 (pt); Nurses'
aides 23 (ft).
Languages German, Spanish, Italian.

Barrington Terrace Nursing Home
215 Annie St, Orlando, FL 32806
(407) 841-4371
Admin David H Phillips. *Dir of Nursing* M E
Cross RN. *Medical Dir* G Lehman MD.
Licensure Skilled care. *Beds* SNF 60. *Private
Pay Patients* 100%.
Owner Proprietary corp.
Admissions Requirements Medical
examination; Physician's request.
Staff RNs; LPNs; Nurses' aides; Physical
therapists (consultant); Activities
coordinators; Dietitians (consultant).
Languages Spanish, Italian.

Facilities Dining room; Activities room;
Laundry room; Barber/Beauty shop.
Activities Arts & crafts; Cards; Games; Prayer
groups; Movies; Shopping trips; Dances/
Social/Cultural gatherings; Pet therapy.

Central Park Village Health Care Center
9309 S Orange Blossom Trail, Orlando, FL
32821
(407) 859-7990, 857-7083 FAX
Admin Beverly Gelvin RN NHA, Exec Dir;
Jan Heidle, Asst. *Dir of Nursing* Kelly
Higgins RN. *Medical Dir* Ignacio Hidalgo
MD.
Licensure Skilled care; Retirement. *Beds* SNF
120; Retirement 150. *Private Pay Patients*
30%. *Certified* Medicaid; Medicare.
Owner Proprietary corp.
Admissions Requirements Medical
examination; Physician's request.
Staff Physicians 4 (ft); RNs 2 (ft), 1 (pt);
LPNs 7 (ft), 3 (pt); Nurses' aides 34 (ft), 2
(pt); Physical therapists (contracted);
Activities coordinators 1 (ft), 1 (pt);
Dietitians 1 (ft).
Languages Spanish.
Facilities Dining room; Physical therapy
room; Activities room; Laundry room;
Barber/Beauty shop.
Activities Arts & crafts; Cards; Games; Prayer
groups; Movies; Dances/Social/Cultural
gatherings; Intergenerational programs.

Florida Manor
830 W 29th St, Orlando, FL 32805
(407) 843-3230
Admin Arthur H Harris; Gary P Beaulieu Asst
Admin. *Dir of Nursing* Joyce L Niec RN.
Medical Dir John Royer MD.
Licensure Skilled care; Intermediate care;
Alzheimer's care. *Beds* SNF 300; ICF 120.
Private Pay Patients 25%. *Certified*
Medicaid.
Owner Nonprofit organization/foundation.
Admissions Requirements Minimum age 16;
Medical examination; Physician's request.
Staff Physicians 47 (pt); RNs 21 (ft), 4 (pt);
LPNs 28 (ft), 2 (pt); Nurses' aides 135 (ft), 2
(pt); Physical therapists 1 (ft); Recreational
therapists 2 (ft); Occupational therapists 1
(pt); Speech therapists 1 (pt); Activities
coordinators 1 (ft); Dietitians 2 (ft);
Pharmacists 1 (ft), 2 (pt).
Languages Spanish.
Affiliation Roman Catholic.
Facilities Dining room; Physical therapy
room; Activities room; Chapel; Crafts room;
Laundry room; Barber/Beauty shop; Library;
Dental clinic; Swimming pool; Clothing
boutique; Enclosed picnic areas; Gardens.
Activities Arts & crafts; Cards; Games;
Reading groups; Prayer groups; Movies;
Shopping trips; Dances/Social/Cultural
gatherings; Intergenerational programs; Pet
therapy; Picnics, Cocktail parties.

Guardian Care Inc
PO Box 555877, 2500 W Church St, Orlando,
FL 32855-5877
(407) 295-5371, 292-6994 FAX
Admin Noel W Bridgett. *Dir of Nursing* Mary
Rose Williams. *Medical Dir* A L Bookhardt
MD.
Licensure Skilled care. *Beds* SNF 120. *Private
Pay Patients* 2%. *Certified* Medicaid.
Owner Nonprofit corp.
Admissions Requirements Minimum age 16;
Medical examination; Physician's request.
Staff Physicians 3 (ft); Physical therapists 4
(pt); Occupational therapists 2 (pt); Speech
therapists 1 (pt); Activities coordinators 1
(ft); Dietitians 1 (pt); Ophthalmologists 1 (ft);
Podiatrists 1 (ft); Audiologists 1 (ft).
Languages Spanish, Arabic, French.
Facilities Dining room; Physical therapy
room; Activities room; Chapel; Laundry
room; Barber/Beauty shop.

Activities Arts & crafts; Cards; Games; Reading groups; Prayer groups; Movies; Shopping trips; Dances/Social/Cultural gatherings; Intergenerational programs; Pet therapy.

Loch Haven Lodge
2250 Bedford Rd, Orlando, FL 32803
(305) 898-4721
Licensure Skilled care. *Beds* 50. *Certified* Medicaid.
Owner Proprietary corp (Beverly Enterprises).
Staff RNs 3 (ft); LPNs 5 (ft); Nurses' aides 15 (ft).

Orlando Care Center
1900 Mercy Ave, Orlando, FL 32658
(305) 299-5404
Beds 63.

Orlando Health Care Center
2000 N Semoran Blvd, Orlando, FL 32807
(407) 671-5400, 671-7312 FAX
Admin Suyrea L Reynolds. *Dir of Nursing* Francine Coleman RN. *Medical Dir* Glenn Bigsby DO.
Licensure Skilled care; Intermediate care. *Beds* Swing beds SNF/ICF 118. *Private Pay Patients* 10%. *Certified* Medicaid; Medicare.
Owner Proprietary corp (Beverly Enterprises).
Admissions Requirements Minimum age 16; Medical examination.
Staff RNs 6 (ft); LPNs 15 (ft); Nurses' aides 35 (ft); Physical therapists 1 (ft); Recreational therapists 1 (ft), 1 (pt); Occupational therapists 1 (ft); Speech therapists 1 (ft); Activities coordinators 5 (pt); Dietitians 1 (ft), 2 (pt).
Languages Spanish, Italian.
Facilities Dining room; Physical therapy room; Activities room; Laundry room; Barber/Beauty shop; Library.
Activities Arts & crafts; Cards; Games; Reading groups; Prayer groups; Movies; Shopping trips; Dances/Social/Cultural gatherings; Intergenerational programs; Pet therapy.

Orlando Lutheran Towers
300 E Church St, Orlando, FL 32801
(407) 425-1033, 422-7759 FAX
Admin Benjamin R Decker. *Dir of Nursing* Gretchen Schitter RNC. *Medical Dir* Dr Gary J Lehman.
Licensure Skilled care; Intermediate care; Retirement. *Beds* SNF 60; ICF 30; Retirement 300. *Certified* Medicaid.
Owner Nonprofit corp.
Admissions Requirements Minimum age 65.
Staff RNs 4 (ft), 1 (pt); LPNs 3 (ft); Nurses' aides 12 (ft), 1 (pt); Physical therapists 1 (pt); Activities coordinators 1 (ft), 1 (pt); Dietitians 1 (pt).
Languages German.
Affiliation Lutheran.
Facilities Dining room; Physical therapy room; Activities room; Crafts room; Laundry room; Barber/Beauty shop; Library.
Activities Arts & crafts; Cards; Games; Reading groups; Prayer groups; Movies; Shopping trips; Dances/Social/Cultural gatherings.

Orlando Memorial Convalescent Center
1730 Lucerne Terr, Orlando, FL 32806
(407) 423-1612
Admin Jocelyn Barnes RN NHA. *Dir of Nursing* Carol Niemiec RN. *Medical Dir* Dr D Parsons.
Licensure Skilled care. *Beds* SNF 115. *Private Pay Patients* 55%. *Certified* Medicaid; Medicare.
Owner Proprietary corp (Hillhaven Corp).
Admissions Requirements Minimum age 21; Medical examination.
Staff Physicians 20 (pt); RNs 4 (ft), 1 (pt); LPNs 11 (ft), 1 (pt); Nurses' aides 35 (ft), 10 (pt); Physical therapists 1 (pt); Occupational

therapists 1 (pt); Speech therapists 1 (pt); Activities coordinators 1 (ft), 1 (pt); Dietitians 1 (ft); Ophthalmologists 1 (pt); Podiatrists 1 (pt); Audiologists 1 (pt).
Facilities Dining room; Physical therapy room; Activities room; Barber/Beauty shop; Courtyard.
Activities Arts & crafts; Cards; Games; Reading groups; Prayer groups; Movies; Dances/Social/Cultural gatherings; Intergenerational programs; Pet therapy; Adopt-a-resident.

Palm Garden
654 S Econlockhatchee Trail, Orlando, FL 32617
(305) 273-6156
Beds 31.

Pinar Terrace Manor
7950 Lake Underhill Rd, Orlando, FL 32622
(305) 656-2046
Beds 94.

Rosemont Health Care Center
3920 Rosewood Way, Orlando, FL 32808
(407) 298-9335
Admin Jeff Gerst NHA. *Dir of Nursing* Glenda Hendrickson RN. *Medical Dir* Dr David Parson.
Licensure Skilled care; Intermediate care. *Beds* Swing beds SNF/ICF 120. *Private Pay Patients* 15%. *Certified* Medicaid; Medicare.
Owner Proprietary corp (Beverly Enterprises).
Admissions Requirements Minimum age 20.
Staff RNs 5 (ft); LPNs 8 (ft), 3 (pt); Nurses' aides 32 (ft), 2 (pt); Activities coordinators 1 (ft), 1 (pt); Dietitians 1 (ft).
Languages Spanish.
Facilities Dining room; Physical therapy room; Activities room; Crafts room; Laundry room; Barber/Beauty shop.
Activities Arts & crafts; Cards; Games; Reading groups; Prayer groups; Movies; Shopping trips; Dances/Social/Cultural gatherings; Intergenerational programs; Pet therapy.

Westminster Towers
70 Lucerne Cir, Orlando, FL 32801
(407) 841-1310
Admin Blaine Henry.
Licensure Skilled care; Congregate living; Retirement home; Alzheimer's care. *Beds* SNF 120; Congregate living 49; Retirement home 248.
Owner Nonprofit corp.
Admissions Requirements Medical examination.
Staff RNs; LPNs; Nurses' aides; Physical therapists; Activities coordinators; Dietitians.
Affiliation Presbyterian.
Facilities Dining room; Physical therapy room; Activities room; Chapel; Crafts room; Laundry room; Barber/Beauty shop; Library.
Activities Arts & crafts; Cards; Games; Reading groups; Prayer groups; Movies; Dances/Social/Cultural gatherings.

Ormond Beach

Bowman's Nursing Center
350 S Ridgewood Ave, Ormond Beach, FL 32074
(904) 677-4545
Admin Robert E Green. *Dir of Nursing* Pauline Ouellette RN. *Medical Dir* James Shoemaker.
Licensure Skilled care. *Beds* SNF 140. *Certified* Medicaid; Medicare.
Owner Proprietary corp (National Healthcare Affiliates Inc).
Admissions Requirements Medical examination; Physician's request.
Staff Physicians 1 (ft); RNs 4 (ft), 1 (pt); LPNs 9 (ft), 1 (pt); Nurses' aides 33 (ft), 3 (pt); Physical therapists 1 (ft); Occupational

therapists 1 (pt); Speech therapists 1 (ft); Activities coordinators 1 (ft); Dietitians 1 (ft); Ophthalmologists 1 (ft).
Facilities Dining room; Physical therapy room; Activities room; Crafts room; Laundry room; Barber/Beauty shop; Library.
Activities Arts & crafts; Cards; Games; Reading groups; Prayer groups; Movies; Shopping trips; Dances/Social/Cultural gatherings.

Ormond Beach Health Care
170 N Kings Rd, Ormond Beach, FL 32174
(904) 677-7955, 676-2657 FAX
Admin William McKillop SCD. *Dir of Nursing* Marlene Thomson RN. *Medical Dir* Roman Hendrickson MD.
Licensure Skilled care; Intermediate care. *Beds* Swing beds SNF/ICF 133. *Private Pay Patients* 30%. *Certified* Medicaid; Medicare.
Owner Proprietary corp (Beverly Enterprises).
Admissions Requirements Minimum age 25; Physician's request.
Staff Physicians 30 (ft); RNs 10 (ft), 4 (pt); LPNs 7 (ft), 2 (pt); Nurses' aides 38 (ft), 9 (pt); Physical therapists 3 (ft); Recreational therapists 2 (ft); Activities coordinators 1 (ft); Dietitians 1 (ft); Ophthalmologists 1 (ft); Dentists 1 (ft); Social service 1 (ft).
Languages French, Spanish, German.
Facilities Dining room; Activities room; Chapel; Crafts room; Laundry room; Barber/Beauty shop.
Activities Arts & crafts; Cards; Games; Reading groups; Prayer groups; Movies; Shopping trips; Dances/Social/Cultural gatherings.

Ormond in the Pines
100 Clyde Morris Blvd, Ormond Beach, FL 32074
(904) 673-0450
Beds 38.

Oviedo

Lutheran Haven
2041 W State Rte 426, Oviedo, FL 32765
(407) 365-5676
Admin Lori Jowett. *Dir of Nursing* Ann Clifton. *Medical Dir* Dr John Allen.
Licensure Skilled care; Retirement. *Beds* SNF 42. *Private Pay Patients* 100%.
Owner Nonprofit organization/foundation.
Admissions Requirements Minimum age 65.
Staff RNs 1 (ft), 1 (pt); LPNs 3 (ft), 3 (pt); Nurses' aides 11 (ft), 3 (pt); Activities coordinators 1 (ft).
Affiliation Lutheran.
Facilities Dining room; Crafts room; Laundry room; Barber/Beauty shop; Library.
Activities Arts & crafts; Cards; Games; Prayer groups; Shopping trips; Dances/Social/Cultural gatherings.

Pahokee

Glades Health Care Center
230 S Barfield Hwy, Pahokee, FL 33476
(305) 924-5561
Admin June L Doherty. *Dir of Nursing* Darrold Gooley RN. *Medical Dir* Dr Richard Sulman.
Licensure Skilled care. *Beds* SNF 120. *Certified* Medicaid; Medicare.
Owner Proprietary corp.
Admissions Requirements Minimum age 18; Medical examination.
Staff Physicians 1 (pt); RNs 6 (ft); LPNs 12 (ft); Nurses' aides 45 (ft); Activities coordinators 1 (ft).
Languages Haitian, Spanish.
Facilities Dining room; Physical therapy room; Activities room; Crafts room; Laundry room; Barber/Beauty shop; Dining room for large group activities.

Activities Arts & crafts; Cards; Games;
Reading groups; Prayer groups; Movies;
Church services; Birthday parties; Family
night; Musicals.

Palatka

Putnam Nursing Home
501 S Palm Ave, Palatka, FL 32077
(904) 328-1472
Licensure Skilled care. *Beds* 65. *Certified*
Medicaid; Medicare.
Owner Proprietary corp (Beverly Enterprises).
Staff RNs 4 (ft); LPNs 11 (ft); Nurses' aides
14 (ft).

Palm Bay

Palm Bay Care Center
115 NE Port Malabar Blvd, Palm Bay, FL
32905
(305) 723-1235
Beds 63.

Palm Harbor

Baytree Nursing Center
2600 Highlands Blvd N, Palm Harbor, FL
33563
(813) 785-5671
Admin Mary F Byrne. *Dir of Nursing* Susan
Fuller RN. *Medical Dir* Arthur Polin MD.
Licensure Skilled care; Alzheimer's care. *Beds*
120. *Certified* Medicaid; Medicare.
Owner Proprietary corp (Shive Nursing
Centers).
Admissions Requirements Medical
examination; Physician's request.
Staff Physicians; RNs; LPNs; Nurses' aides;
Physical therapists; Occupational therapists;
Speech therapists; Activities coordinators;
Dietitians; Ophthalmologists; Podiatrists.
Languages Spanish, German.
Facilities Dining room; Physical therapy
room; Activities room; Crafts room; Laundry
room; Barber/Beauty shop.
Activities Arts & crafts; Cards; Games; Prayer
groups; Movies; Dances/Social/Cultural
gatherings.

St Mark Village Inc
2655 Nebraska Ave, Palm Harbor, FL 33563
(813) 785-2576
Admin Jackson Pierce. *Dir of Nursing* Rosalie
Earley RN. *Medical Dir* Dr James R Kinney
DO.
Licensure Skilled care; Retirement. *Beds* SNF
60. *Certified* Medicare.
Owner Nonprofit corp.
Admissions Requirements Medical
examination; Physician's request.
Staff RNs 3 (ft), 3 (pt); LPNs 1 (ft), 4 (pt);
Nurses' aides 17 (ft), 7 (pt); Physical
therapists 1 (pt); Recreational therapists 1
(ft); Occupational therapists 1 (pt); Speech
therapists 1 (pt); Activities coordinators 1
(ft); Dietitians 1 (pt); Ophthalmologists 1
(pt); Podiatrists 1 (pt).
Affiliation Lutheran.
Facilities Dining room; Physical therapy
room; Activities room; Chapel; Crafts room;
Barber/Beauty shop.
Activities Arts & crafts; Cards; Games;
Reading groups; Prayer groups; Movies;
Dances/Social/Cultural gatherings.

Palm Harbour

Countryside Health Care Center
3625 Countryside Blvd, Palm Harbour, FL
34664
(613) 784-2848
Beds 66.

Panama City

Bay Convalescent Center
1336 Saint Andrews Blvd, Panama City, FL
32405
(904) 763-3911
Licensure Skilled care; Intermediate care. *Beds*
160. *Certified* Medicaid; Medicare.
Owner Proprietary corp.
Staff RNs 3 (ft); LPNs 15 (ft); Nurses' aides
37 (ft).
Languages Spanish.

Gulf Coast Convalescent Center
1937 Jenks Ave, Panama City, FL 32405
(904) 769-7686, 769-7680 FAX
Admin Roger D Strickland. *Dir of Nursing*
Hazel Harmon RN. *Medical Dir* James Shu
MD.
Licensure Skilled care. *Beds* SNF 120. *Private
Pay Patients* 16%. *Certified* Medicaid;
Medicare.
Owner Proprietary corp (Beverly Enterprises).
Admissions Requirements Minimum age 14;
Physician's request.
Staff RNs 6 (ft), 4 (pt); LPNs 7 (ft), 3 (pt);
Nurses' aides 23 (ft), 10 (pt); Physical
therapists 2 (pt); Recreational therapists 1
(ft); Occupational therapists 1 (pt); Speech
therapists 1 (pt); Activities coordinators 1
(ft); Dietitians 1 (ft); Ophthalmologists
Contracted; Podiatrists Contracted.
Facilities Dining room; Physical therapy
room; Activities room; Crafts room; Laundry
room; Barber/Beauty shop.
Activities Arts & crafts; Cards; Games;
Reading groups; Prayer groups; Movies;
Shopping trips; Dances/Social/Cultural
gatherings; Pet therapy.

Lelah G Wagner Nursing Home
3409 W 19th St, Panama City, FL 32401
(904) 785-0239
Licensure Skilled care. *Beds* 66. *Certified*
Medicaid; Medicare.
Owner Proprietary corp.
Staff RNs 3 (ft); LPNs 7 (ft); Nurses' aides 23
(ft).
Languages Spanish.

National Healthcare Center of Panama City
2100 Jenks Ave, Panama City, FL 32406
(904) 763-0446
Beds 62.

Panama City Developmental Center
1407 Lincoln Dr, Panama City, FL 32401
(904) 769-7636, 763-3100 FAX
Admin Debra Allison QMRP. *Dir of Nursing*
Theresa Moore-Chivers. *Medical Dir* Fred
Williams FAFP.
Licensure Intermediate care for mentally
retarded. *Beds* ICF/MR 64. *Private Pay
Patients* 0%. *Certified* Medicaid.
Owner Nonprofit corp (Pensacola Care Inc).
Admissions Requirements Medical
examination; Physician's request.
Staff Physicians; RNs 2 (ft); LPNs 6 (ft), 2
(pt); Nurses' aides 54 (ft); Physical therapists
1 (pt); Recreational therapists 1 (ft);
Occupational therapists 1 (pt); Speech
therapists 1 (pt); Dietitians 1 (pt).
Facilities Dining room; Activities room;
Crafts room; Laundry room; Training
facility.
Activities Arts & crafts; Games; Reading
groups; Prayer groups; Movies; Shopping
trips; Dances/Social/Cultural gatherings; Pet
therapy; Active treatment; Daily living skills.

Panama City Nursing Center
924 W 13th St, Panama City, FL 32402
(904) 763-8563
Admin Joy Raponi. *Dir of Nursing* Charlotte
Spears RN. *Medical Dir* Thomas G Merrill
DO.
Licensure Skilled care; Alzheimer's care. *Beds*
SNF 120. *Certified* Medicaid; Medicare; VA.

Owner Proprietary corp.
Admissions Requirements Minimum age 18;
Medical examination; Physician's request.
Staff Physicians 18 (pt); RNs 5 (ft); LPNs 12
(ft); Nurses' aides 41 (ft); Physical therapists
2 (ft); Occupational therapists 1 (pt); Speech
therapists 1 (pt); Activities coordinators 2
(ft); Dietitians 1 (pt); Ophthalmologists 1
(pt); Podiatrists 1 (pt); Dentists 1 (pt).
Languages Chinese, German.
Facilities Dining room; Physical therapy
room; Activities room; Chapel; Crafts room;
Laundry room; Barber/Beauty shop; Library.
Activities Arts & crafts; Cards; Games;
Reading groups; Prayer groups; Shopping
trips; Dances/Social/Cultural gatherings.

Penny Farms

Mary M Olin Clinic
PO Box 555, Penny Farms, FL 32079
(904) 284-8578
Licensure Skilled care; Retirement. *Beds* SNF
40.
Owner Nonprofit corp.
Admissions Requirements Minimum age 60;
Females only; Medical examination.
Staff Physicians 3 (pt); RNs 1 (ft), 5 (pt);
LPNs 3 (ft); Nurses' aides 13 (ft), 7 (pt);
Activities coordinators; Dietitians 1 (pt);
Ophthalmologists 1 (pt); Podiatrists 1 (pt).
Facilities Physical therapy room; Activities
room; Chapel; Barber/Beauty shop.
Activities Arts & crafts; Games; Reading
groups; Prayer groups; Shopping trips;
Dances/Social/Cultural gatherings; Afternoon
tour bus.

Pensacola

Azalea Trace
10100 Hillview Rd, Pensacola, FL 32514
(904) 474-0880
Admin William J Nuelle. *Dir of Nursing* Ruth
Ann Haller RN. *Medical Dir* Dr Finley
Holmes.
Licensure Skilled care; Retirement. *Beds* 90.
Certified Medicare.
Owner Nonprofit corp.
Admissions Requirements Minimum age 17.
Staff Physicians 1 (pt); RNs 4 (ft), 5 (pt);
LPNs 9 (ft), 2 (pt); Nurses' aides 22 (ft), 8
(pt); Physical therapists 1 (pt); Occupational
therapists 1 (pt); Speech therapists 1 (pt);
Activities coordinators 1 (ft); Dietitians 1
(pt); Ophthalmologists 1 (pt); Dentists 1 (pt);
Social workers 1 (ft).
Languages Spanish, French.
Facilities Dining room; Physical therapy
room; Activities room; Chapel; Crafts room;
Barber/Beauty shop; Library; Store.
Activities Arts & crafts; Cards; Games;
Reading groups; Prayer groups; Movies;
Shopping trips; Dances/Social/Cultural
gatherings; Handbell choir; Tea parties.

Baptist Manor Inc
10095 Hillview Rd, Pensacola, FL 32514
(904) 479-4000
Beds 70.

Bluffs Nursing Home
4343 Langley Ave, Pensacola, FL 32504
(904) 477-4550
Licensure Skilled care. *Beds* 120. *Certified*
Medicaid; Medicare.
Owner Proprietary corp.
Staff RNs 3 (ft); LPNs 13 (ft); Nurses' aides
27 (ft).

Cross Creek Health Care Center
10040 Hillview Rd, Pensacola, FL 32514
(904) 474-0570
Beds 68.

Escambia County Nursing Home
3107 N "H" St, Pensacola, FL 32501-1199
(904) 436-9300
Admin Shirley L Hoggard. *Dir of Nursing*
Helen H White. *Medical Dir* Finley C
Holmes.
Licensure Skilled care. *Beds* SNF 155. *Private
Pay Patients* 1%. *Certified* Medicaid.
Owner Publicly owned.
Admissions Requirements Medical
examination; Physician's request.
Staff Physicians 2 (pt); RNs; LPNs 21 (ft), 8
(pt); Nurses' aides 57 (ft), 18 (pt); Physical
therapists 2 (pt); Occupational therapists 2
(pt); Speech therapists 1 (pt); Activities
coordinators 1 (ft); Dietitians 1 (ft);
Podiatrists 2 (pt); Audiologists 1 (pt).
Languages Spanish.
Facilities Dining room; Physical therapy
room; Activities room; Crafts room; Laundry
room; Barber/Beauty shop; Library.
Activities Arts & crafts; Cards; Games;
Reading groups; Prayer groups; Movies;
Shopping trips; Dances/Social/Cultural
gatherings; Intergenerational programs; Pet
therapy; Fishing trips; Picnics; Annual
circus.

Haven of Our Lady of Peace
5203 N 9th Ave, Pensacola, FL 32504
(904) 477-0531, 474-6125 FAX
Admin Olin D Tisdale. *Dir of Nursing* Mary
Alice Conti RN. *Medical Dir* Finley C
Holmes MD.
Licensure Skilled care; Intermediate care. *Beds*
SNF 47; ICF 42. *Private Pay Patients* 80%.
Certified Medicaid.
Owner Nonprofit organization/foundation.
Admissions Requirements Minimum age 16;
Medical examination; Physician's request.
Staff Physicians 1 (pt); RNs 2 (ft), 2 (pt);
LPNs 10 (ft), 6 (pt); Nurses' aides 29 (ft), 3
(pt); Activities coordinators 2 (pt).
Languages Spanish.
Affiliation Roman Catholic.
Facilities Dining room; Activities room;
Chapel; Laundry room; Barber/Beauty shop;
Library.
Activities Arts & crafts; Cards; Games; Prayer
groups; Movies; Shopping trips; Dances/
Social/Cultural gatherings; Daily religious
service.

Magnolias Nursing & Convalescent Center
600 W Gregory St, Pensacola, FL 32501
(904) 438-2000
Admin Douglas R Eitel.
Medical Dir William Balk MD.
Licensure Skilled care. *Beds* 210. *Certified*
Medicaid; Medicare.
Owner Proprietary corp.
Admissions Requirements Minimum age 16;
Medical examination; Physician's request.
Staff Physicians 12 (pt); RNs 7 (ft), 8 (pt);
LPNs 15 (ft), 14 (pt); Nurses' aides 59 (ft),
21 (pt); Physical therapists 1 (ft);
Recreational therapists 1 (ft); Speech
therapists 1 (pt); Activities coordinators 1
(ft); Dietitians 1 (pt); Dentists; Social
workers 1 (pt); Physical therapy assistants.
Facilities Dining room; Physical therapy
room; Activities room; Crafts room; Laundry
room; Barber/Beauty shop.
Activities Arts & crafts; Cards; Games;
Reading groups; Prayer groups; Movies;
Shopping trips; Dances/Social/Cultural
gatherings.

Northview
1050 Hillview Rd, Pensacola, FL 32517
(904) 474-0667
Admin Ruthie Andrews. *Dir of Nursing*
Delores Morgan. *Medical Dir* Dr Jongko; Dr
Atwell.
Licensure Intermediate care for mentally
retarded. *Beds* ICF/MR 30. *Private Pay
Patients* 0%. *Certified* Medicaid.
Owner Nonprofit organization/foundation.

Admissions Requirements Minimum age 0-21;
Physically disabled.
Staff Physicians 2 (pt); RNs 1 (ft), 2 (pt);
LPNs 3 (ft), 5 (pt); Nurses' aides 8 (ft), 3
(pt); Physical therapists 1 (pt); Recreational
therapists 1 (ft); Occupational therapists 1
(pt); Speech therapists 1 (pt); Dietitians 1
(pt).
Facilities Dining room; Activities room;
Laundry room.
Activities Arts & crafts; Games; Movies;
Shopping trips; Dances/Social/Cultural
gatherings; Intergenerational programs.

Palm Garden (Pensacola)
6475 University Pkwy, Pensacola, FL 32514
(904) 474-1252
Beds 62.

Pensacola Health Care Facility
1717 W Avery St, Pensacola, FL 32501
(904) 434-2355
Admin John F McCullen. *Dir of Nursing*
Linda Seeley RNC. *Medical Dir* Finley
Holmes MD.
Licensure Skilled care. *Beds* SNF 118. *Private
Pay Patients* 20%. *Certified* Medicaid;
Medicare; VA.
Owner Proprietary corp (Beverly Enterprises).
Admissions Requirements Medical
examination; Physician's request.
Staff Physicians 2 (ft); RNs 5 (ft); LPNs 12
(ft), 2 (pt); Nurses' aides 22 (ft), 3 (pt);
Physical therapists 1 (pt); Occupational
therapists 1 (pt); Speech therapists 1 (pt);
Activities coordinators 1 (ft); Dietitians 1
(pt); Ophthalmologists 1 (pt); Podiatrists 1
(pt); Audiologists 1 (pt).
Languages Spanish.
Facilities Dining room; Physical therapy
room; Activities room; Chapel; Laundry
room; Barber/Beauty shop; Library.
Activities Arts & crafts; Cards; Games;
Reading groups; Prayer groups; Movies;
Shopping trips; Dances/Social/Cultural
gatherings; Intergenerational programs; Pet
therapy.

Perry

Perry Health Facility
207 Forest Dr, Perry, FL 32347
(904) 584-6334
Admin Debra O Delgado.
Medical Dir Susan Lore.
Licensure Skilled care. *Beds* SNF 120.
Certified Medicaid.
Owner Proprietary corp.
Admissions Requirements Minimum age 18;
Medical examination.
Staff RNs 4 (ft); LPNs 20 (ft); Nurses' aides
40 (ft); Physical therapists 1 (pt);
Recreational therapists 1 (ft); Occupational
therapists 1 (pt); Speech therapists 1 (ft);
Dietitians 1 (ft); Ophthalmologists 1 (pt).
Facilities Dining room; Physical therapy
room; Activities room; Barber/Beauty shop;
Protected garden/gazebo area.
Activities Arts & crafts; Cards; Games;
Reading groups; Prayer groups; Movies;
Shopping trips; Dances/Social/Cultural
gatherings; Pet therapy.

Pinellas Park

Central Park Lodge Nursing Center
6701 49th St N, Pinellas Park, FL 33565
(613) 546-4661
Beds 66.

Parkway Nursing Home
7575 65th Way N, Pinellas Park, FL 33565
(813) 544-6673
Licensure Skilled care. *Beds* 55. *Certified*
Medicaid; Medicare.

Owner Proprietary corp.
Staff RNs 6 (ft); LPNs 7 (ft); Nurses' aides 23
(ft).

Sunshine Village Nursing Home
6600 US Hwy 19 N, Pinellas Park, FL 33565
(613) 541-7515
Beds 67.

Plant City

Community Convalescent Center
2202 W Oak Ave, Plant City, FL 33567
(813) 754-3761
Admin Ronald E Speener. *Dir of Nursing*
Lydia Thomas MSN. *Medical Dir* Rees
Morgan MD.
Licensure Skilled care; Intermediate care. *Beds*
Swing beds SNF/ICF 120. *Certified*
Medicaid; Medicare.
Owner Proprietary corp.
Admissions Requirements Minimum age 18;
Medical examination.
Staff RNs 4 (ft), 2 (pt); LPNs 11 (ft), 1 (pt);
Nurses' aides 41 (ft), 6 (pt); Activities
coordinators 1 (ft).
Facilities Dining room; Physical therapy
room; Activities room; Laundry room;
Barber/Beauty shop.
Activities Arts & crafts; Cards; Games; Prayer
groups; Movies; Dances/Social/Cultural
gatherings; Intergenerational programs.

Forest Park Nursing Center
1702 W Oak Ave, Plant City, FL 33566
(813) 752-4129
Admin Patricia C Jordan. *Dir of Nursing*
Kathy Schiavinato RN. *Medical Dir* Edgar
Sapp MD.
Licensure Skilled care. *Beds* 97. *Certified*
Medicaid; Medicare.
Owner Proprietary corp (Beverly Enterprises).
Admissions Requirements Medical
examination.
Staff Physicians 1 (pt); RNs 4 (ft); LPNs 7
(ft), 1 (pt); Physical therapists 1 (pt);
Recreational therapists 1 (pt); Speech
therapists 1 (pt); Activities coordinators 1
(ft); Dietitians 1 (pt); Ophthalmologists 1
(pt).
Facilities Dining room; Activities room;
Laundry room; Barber/Beauty shop.
Activities Arts & crafts; Cards; Games;
Reading groups; Prayer groups; Movies;
Shopping trips; Dances/Social/Cultural
gatherings.

Plant City Health Care
701 N Wilder Rd, Plant City, FL 33566
(813) 752-3611
Admin Wanda J Hinton. *Dir of Nursing* Nora
McClendon. *Medical Dir* Dr Baskin.
Licensure Skilled care; Intermediate care. *Beds*
SNF 24; ICF 96. *Certified* Medicaid;
Medicare.
Owner Privately owned.
Admissions Requirements Medical
examination; Physician's request.
Staff RNs 13 (ft), 2 (pt); LPNs 5 (ft), 1 (pt);
Nurses' aides 40 (ft), 10 (pt); Physical
therapists; Activities coordinators 2 (ft);
Dietitians 1 (ft).
Facilities Dining room; Physical therapy
room; Activities room; Chapel; Crafts room;
Laundry room; Barber/Beauty shop; Library.
Activities Arts & crafts; Cards; Games;
Reading groups; Prayer groups; Movies;
Shopping trips; Dances/Social/Cultural
gatherings; Intergenerational programs; Pet
therapy.

Plantation

Manor Care of Plantation
6931 W Sunrise Blvd, Plantation, FL 33313
(305) 583-6200

Admin Garland Cline. *Dir of Nursing* Robin Neville. *Medical Dir* Dr Greiff.
Licensure Skilled care; Alzheimer's care. *Beds* SNF 120. *Certified* Medicaid; Medicare.
Owner Proprietary corp (Manor Health Care Inc).
Admissions Requirements Minimum age 16; Medical examination.
Staff Physicians; RNs; LPNs; Physical therapists; Recreational therapists; Occupational therapists; Speech therapists; Activities coordinators; Dietitians.
Languages Spanish.
Facilities Dining room; Physical therapy room; Activities room; Crafts room; Laundry room; Barber/Beauty shop.
Activities Arts & crafts; Cards; Games; Reading groups; Prayer groups; Movies; Shopping trips; Dances/Social/Cultural gatherings.

Meridian Nursing Center
7751 W Broward Blvd, Plantation, FL 33324
(305) 473-8040
Admin Paul D Bach. *Dir of Nursing* Carol U Campbell RN. *Medical Dir* Michael C Cunningham MD.
Licensure Skilled care; Intermediate care; Alzheimer's care. *Beds* SNF 60; ICF 60. *Certified* Medicaid; Medicare.
Owner Proprietary corp (Meridian Healthcare).
Admissions Requirements Physician's request.
Staff Physicians 1 (pt); RNs 7 (ft), 3 (pt); LPNs 10 (ft), 5 (pt); Nurses' aides 38 (ft), 8 (pt); Activities coordinators 2 (ft).
Facilities Dining room; Physical therapy room; Activities room; Chapel; Crafts room; Laundry room; Barber/Beauty shop; Library.
Activities Arts & crafts; Cards; Games; Reading groups; Prayer groups; Movies; Shopping trips; Dances/Social/Cultural gatherings.

Plantation Nursing Home
4250 NW 5th St, Plantation, FL 33317
(305) 587-3296
Licensure Skilled care. *Beds* 152. *Certified* Medicaid; Medicare.
Owner Proprietary corp (HBA Management Inc).
Staff RNs 12 (ft); LPNs 14 (ft); Nurses' aides 33 (ft).
Languages Spanish.

Pompano Beach

Colonial Palms East Nursing Home
3670 NE 3rd St, Pompano Beach, FL 33064
(305) 941-4100
Medical Dir Mike Solnik MD.
Licensure Skilled care. *Beds* 120.
Owner Proprietary corp.
Admissions Requirements Minimum age 16; Medical examination.
Staff RNs 9 (ft); LPNs 13 (ft); Nurses' aides 44 (ft); Physical therapists; Occupational therapists; Speech therapists; Activities coordinators 7 (ft); Dietitians 1 (ft); Ophthalmologists; Podiatrists; Audiologists; Dentists.
Facilities Dining room; Physical therapy room; Activities room; Chapel; Crafts room; Laundry room; Barber/Beauty shop; Library.
Activities Arts & crafts; Cards; Games; Reading groups; Prayer groups; Movies; Shopping trips; Dances/Social/Cultural gatherings.

Colonial Palms—West
51 W Sample Rd, Pompano Beach, FL 33064
(305) 942-5530, 782-0319 FAX
Admin Cheryl Policastro. *Dir of Nursing* Lois Borgol RN. *Medical Dir* Arnold Aaron MD.
Licensure Skilled care. *Beds* SNF 127. *Private Pay Patients* 80%. *Certified* Medicare.
Owner Proprietary corp (Trinity Living Centers).

Admissions Requirements Minimum age 16; Medical examination; Physician's request.
Staff Physicians 8 (pt); RNs 5 (ft), 1 (pt); LPNs 12 (ft); Nurses' aides 36 (ft); Physical therapists (contracted); Recreational therapists 3 (ft); Occupational therapists 1 (pt); Speech therapists 1 (pt); Activities coordinators 1 (ft); Dietitians (contracted); Ophthalmologists 1 (pt); Podiatrists 1 (pt); Audiologists 1 (pt).
Facilities Dining room; Physical therapy room; Activities room; Crafts room; Laundry room; Barber/Beauty shop; Library; Pub; Ice cream parlor.
Activities Arts & crafts; Cards; Games; Reading groups; Prayer groups; Movies; Shopping trips; Dances/Social/Cultural gatherings; Intergenerational programs; Pet therapy.

John Knox Village Medical Center
631 SW 6th St, Pompano Beach, FL 33060
(305) 782-1300, 781-1453 FAX
Admin John J Guyer. *Dir of Nursing* Joan Berzner RN C. *Medical Dir* Jerome Froelich MD.
Licensure Skilled care; Retirement. *Beds* SNF 120; Retirement 30. *Certified* Medicaid; Medicare.
Owner Nonprofit corp.
Admissions Requirements Minimum age 65.
Staff Physicians 1 (ft); RNs 10 (ft), 6 (pt); LPNs 15 (ft); Nurses' aides 48 (ft); Physical therapists 2 (ft); Recreational therapists 3 (ft); Occupational therapists 1 (ft); Speech therapists 1 (ft); Dietitians 1 (ft).
Languages Spanish, French, Creole, German, Tagalog, Greek.
Facilities Dining room; Physical therapy room; Activities room; Chapel; Crafts room; Laundry room; Barber/Beauty shop; Library; Gardens & lakes with swans & ducks.
Activities Arts & crafts; Cards; Games; Reading groups; Prayer groups; Movies; Shopping trips; Dances/Social/Cultural gatherings; Intergenerational programs; Pet therapy.

Pinehurst Convalescent Center
2401 NE 2nd St, Pompano Beach, FL 33062
(305) 943-5100
Admin Fred Austin. *Dir of Nursing* Susan Yerkes RN. *Medical Dir* Jean-C E Bourgue MD.
Licensure Skilled care. *Beds* 83. *Certified* Medicaid; Medicare.
Owner Proprietary corp (Beverly Enterprises).
Admissions Requirements Medical examination; Physician's request.
Staff RNs 3 (ft), 2 (pt); LPNs 9 (ft), 1 (pt); Nurses' aides 32 (ft), 1 (pt); Speech therapists 1 (pt); Activities coordinators 1 (ft); Dietitians 1 (pt); Ophthalmologists 1 (pt); Podiatrists 1 (pt); Dentists 1 (pt).
Languages Spanish, Italian.
Facilities Dining room; Physical therapy room; Activities room; Laundry room; Barber/Beauty shop; Courtyard; Conference room.
Activities Arts & crafts; Cards; Games; Reading groups; Prayer groups; Movies; Shopping trips; Dances/Social/Cultural gatherings.

Port Charlotte

Palmview Healthcare Center
25325 Rampart Blvd, Port Charlotte, FL 33954
(613) 629-7466
Beds 62.

Port Charlotte Care Center
4033 Beaver Ln, Port Charlotte, FL 33952
(813) 625-3200
Admin Richard A Nathans. *Dir of Nursing* Helen Morasco RN. *Medical Dir* David Ballestas MD.

Licensure Skilled care; Sub-acute care. *Beds* SNF 164. *Private Pay Patients* 33%. *Certified* Medicaid; Medicare.
Owner Proprietary corp (National Heritage/Southmark).
Admissions Requirements Minimum age 21; Medical examination; Physician's request.
Staff RNs 6 (ft), 6 (pt); LPNs 10 (ft), 4 (pt); Nurses' aides 38 (ft), 16 (pt); Physical therapists; Activities coordinators 2 (ft); Dietitians (consultant).
Languages French, Spanish.
Facilities Dining room; Physical therapy room; Activities room; Barber/Beauty shop; IV therapy; Enternal feeding therapy; Courtyard/Pavilion.
Activities Arts & crafts; Cards; Games; Reading groups; Prayer groups; Movies; Shopping trips; Dances/Social/Cultural gatherings; Intergenerational programs; Pet therapy; Gardening.

St Joseph Life Enrichment Center Inc
2370 Harbor Blvd, Port Charlotte, FL 33592
(613) 627-2578
Beds 54.

South Port Nursing Center
23013 Westchester Blvd, Port Charlotte, FL 33980
(613) 625-1100
Beds 120.
Owner Privately owned.

Port Saint Joseph

Bay St Joseph Care Center
220 9th St, Port Saint Joseph, FL 32456
(904) 229-8244
Dir of Nursing Judith Howell. *Medical Dir* Dr Jorge San Pedro.
Licensure Skilled care; Intermediate care. *Beds* 120. *Certified* Medicaid; Medicare.
Owner Proprietary corp (Horizon Healthcare Corp).
Admissions Requirements Physician's request.
Staff Physical therapists 1 (pt); Speech therapists 1 (pt); Activities coordinators 1 (ft).
Facilities Dining room; Physical therapy room; Activities room; Chapel; Laundry room; Barber/Beauty shop.
Activities Arts & crafts; Cards; Games; Reading groups; Prayer groups; Movies; Shopping trips; Dances/Social/Cultural gatherings.

Port Saint Lucie

Port St Lucie Convalescent Center
7300 Oleander Ave, Port Saint Lucie, FL 33452
(305) 466-4100
Beds 60.
Owner Proprietary corp (Eden Park Management).

Savana Cay Manor
PO Box 7009, 1655 SE Walton Rd, Port Saint Lucie, FL 34985
(407) 337-1333, 878-6666, 337-9856 FAX
Admin Cheryl Luke. *Dir of Nursing* Janice Bey RN. *Medical Dir* M Nayyar MD.
Licensure Skilled care. *Beds* SNF 91. *Certified* Medicaid; Medicare.
Owner Proprietary corp (Beverly Enterprises).
Admissions Requirements Medical examination; Physician's request.
Staff Physicians; RNs; LPNs; Nurses' aides; Physical therapists; Recreational therapists; Occupational therapists; Speech therapists; Activities coordinators; Dietitians; Ophthalmologists; Podiatrists; Audiologists.
Languages Spanish.

Facilities Dining room; Physical therapy room; Activities room; Crafts room; Laundry room; Barber/Beauty shop; Outside contained patio/gazebo area; Large screen TV.
Activities Arts & crafts; Cards; Reading groups; Prayer groups; Movies; Shopping trips; Dances/Social/Cultural gatherings; Intergenerational programs; Pet therapy.

Port Salereno

Salerno Bay Manor
4601 Cove Rd, Port Salereno, FL 33492
Beds 70.

Punta Gorda

Life Care Center of Punta Gorda
630 W Charlotte Ave, Punta Gorda, FL 33950
(613) 639-8771
Beds 104.

Quincy

Gadsden Nursing Home
1621 Experiment Station Rd, Quincy, FL 32351
(904) 627-9276
Licensure Skilled care. *Beds* 60. *Certified* Medicaid.
Owner Nonprofit corp.
Staff RNs 5 (ft); LPNs 11 (ft); Nurses' aides 14 (ft).

Meadowbrook Manor of Quincy
Strong Rd, Rte 6 Box 1000, Quincy, FL 32351
(904) 875-3711
Beds 66.

Rockledge

Adare Medical Center
1175 Huntington Ln, Rockledge, FL 32955
(305) 632-7341
Licensure Skilled care. *Beds* SNF 100. *Certified* Medicaid; Medicare.
Owner Proprietary corp.
Admissions Requirements Minimum age 21; Medical examination.
Staff Physicians 54 (pt); RNs 7 (ft), 2 (pt); LPNs 9 (ft), 3 (pt); Nurses' aides 35 (ft), 3 (pt); Physical therapists 4 (pt); Speech therapists 1 (pt); Activities coordinators 1 (ft); Dietitians 1 (pt); Ophthalmologists 1 (pt); Dentists 1 (pt).
Languages Spanish.
Facilities Dining room; Physical therapy room; Activities room; Laundry room; Barber/Beauty shop; Library; Privacy room.
Activities Arts & crafts; Cards; Games; Reading groups; Prayer groups; Movies; Dances/Social/Cultural gatherings; Pet therapy; Garden club.

Sunnypines Convalescent Center
587 Barton Blvd, Rockledge, FL 32955
(305) 632-6300
Licensure Skilled care. *Beds* 75. *Certified* Medicaid; Medicare.
Owner Proprietary corp (Unicare).
Languages Spanish.

Royal Palm Beach

Royal Manor
100 Bob White Ct, Royal Palm Beach, FL 33411
(305) 796-3700
Beds 70.

Safety Harbor

Village at Countryside
1410 4th St N, Safety Harbor, FL 34695
(813) 726-1181, 726-7658 FAX
Admin Jane Knight. *Dir of Nursing* Sandra Summers. *Medical Dir* Dr Dayton; Dr Nutt.
Licensure Skilled care; Intermediate care. *Beds* Swing beds SNF/ICF 120. *Certified* Medicaid; Medicare.
Owner Proprietary corp (Arbor Health Care Co).
Admissions Requirements Minimum age 16; Medical examination; Physician's request.
Staff RNs 7 (ft); LPNs 14 (ft); Nurses' aides 35 (ft); Physical therapists (contracted); Recreational therapists 1 (ft), 1 (pt); Activities coordinators 1 (ft), 1 (pt); Dietitians 1 (ft).
Facilities Dining room; Physical therapy room; Activities room; Crafts room; Barber/Beauty shop.
Activities Arts & crafts; Cards; Games; Reading groups; Prayer groups; Movies; Shopping trips; Dances/Social/Cultural gatherings; Intergenerational programs; Pet therapy.

Saint Augustine

Buckingham-Smith Memorial Home
169 Martin Luther King Ave, Saint Augustine, FL 32084
(904) 824-3638
Admin Lillian Gatlin.
Medical Dir Dr Julietta Alcontara.
Licensure Skilled care. *Beds* 51. *Certified* Medicaid.
Owner Nonprofit corp.
Staff RNs 4 (ft), 2 (pt); LPNs 2 (ft), 4 (pt); Nurses' aides 15 (ft), 2 (pt); Recreational therapists 1 (ft); Activities coordinators.
Facilities Dining room; Activities room; Laundry room.
Activities Arts & crafts; Cards; Games; Prayer groups; Shopping trips.

Gilmer Nursing Home
189 San Marco Ave, Saint Augustine, FL 32081
(904) 824-3326
Admin Barbara M Hunter. *Dir of Nursing* Deborah Ferquson RN. *Medical Dir* Dr Tessler.
Licensure Skilled care. *Beds* 68. *Certified* Medicaid.
Owner Proprietary corp (Beverly Enterprises).
Admissions Requirements Minimum age 18; Medical examination; Physician's request.
Staff RNs 3 (ft); LPNs 7 (ft); Nurses' aides 20 (ft); Physical therapists 1 (ft); Recreational therapists 1 (ft); Occupational therapists 1 (ft); Speech therapists 1 (ft); Activities coordinators 1 (ft); Dietitians 1 (pt); Ophthalmologists 1 (pt); Podiatrists 1 (pt).
Facilities Dining room; Activities room; Laundry room; Barber/Beauty shop.
Activities Arts & crafts; Cards; Games; Reading groups; Prayer groups; Movies; Shopping trips; Dances/Social/Cultural gatherings.

Meridian Nursing Center—St Augustine
7976 Meridian Dr, Saint Augustine, FL 32066
(904) 797-7563
Beds 30.
Owner Proprietary corp (Meridian Healthcare).

Ponce de Leon Care Center
1999 Old Moultrie Rd, Saint Augustine, FL 32086
(904) 824-3311, 829-8018 FAX
Admin Jeannine Keberle. *Dir of Nursing* Connie Doane. *Medical Dir* Terry Hayes MD.

Licensure Skilled care. *Beds* SNF 120. *Certified* Medicaid; Medicare.
Owner Proprietary corp (Healthcare Properties Inc).
Admissions Requirements Medical examination; Physician's request.
Staff RNs 6 (ft), 3 (pt); LPNs 13 (ft), 2 (pt); Nurses' aides 40 (ft), 4 (pt); Activities coordinators 1 (ft); Dietitians 1 (ft).
Facilities Dining room; Physical therapy room; Activities room; Laundry room; Barber/Beauty shop.
Activities Arts & crafts; Cards; Games; Prayer groups; Movies; Shopping trips; Dances/Social/Cultural gatherings; Pet therapy.

St Augustine Geriatric Center
51 Sunrise Blvd, Saint Augustine, FL 32084
(904) 824-4479
Medical Dir Dr Micheal P Tessler.
Licensure Skilled care. *Beds* 120. *Certified* Medicaid; Medicare.
Owner Proprietary corp (Waverly Group).
Admissions Requirements Medical examination; Physician's request.
Staff Physicians 21 (ft); RNs 3 (ft), 1 (pt); LPNs 15 (ft), 3 (pt); Nurses' aides 48 (ft), 4 (pt); Physical therapists 2 (ft), 1 (pt); Speech therapists 1 (pt); Activities coordinators 1 (ft); Dietitians 1 (ft), 1 (pt); Ophthalmologists 1 (pt); Podiatrists 2 (pt); Audiologists 1 (pt); Dentists 1 (pt); Psychologists 1 (pt).
Facilities Dining room; Physical therapy room; Activities room; Crafts room; Laundry room; Barber/Beauty shop; 2 Covered, paved, fenced outdoor patios.
Activities Arts & crafts; Cards; Games; Reading groups; Prayer groups; Movies; Shopping trips; Dances/Social/Cultural gatherings; Sports events; Mass & Rosary; Pet therapy; Adopt-a-grandchild.

St Johns County Senior Citizens Home
169 Marine St, Saint Augustine, FL 32084
(904) 824-1755
Licensure Skilled care. *Beds* 51. *Certified* Medicaid.
Owner Publicly owned.
Staff RNs 8 (ft); LPNs 6 (ft); Nurses' aides 15 (ft).

Saint Cloud

St Cloud Health Care Center
1301 Kansas Ave, Saint Cloud, FL 32769
(305) 892-5121
Licensure Skilled care. *Beds* 131. *Certified* Medicaid.
Owner Proprietary corp (Beverly Enterprises).
Staff RNs 4 (ft); LPNs 11 (ft); Nurses' aides 26 (ft).
Languages Spanish, French, German.

Southern Oaks Health Care
2355 Kissimmee Park Rd, Saint Cloud, FL 34769
(407) 957-2280
Admin Robert W Bruso. *Dir of Nursing* Norma Tesch. *Medical Dir* Peter T Morrow.
Licensure Skilled care; Intermediate care. *Beds* Swing beds SNF/ICF 120. *Private Pay Patients* 18%. *Certified* Medicaid; Medicare; VA.
Owner Proprietary corp.
Admissions Requirements Minimum age 18; Medical examination; Physician's request.
Staff RNs 8 (ft), 2 (pt); LPNs 16 (ft), 4 (pt); Nurses' aides 32 (ft), 12 (pt); Physical therapists 1 (pt); Recreational therapists 1 (ft); Activities coordinators 1 (ft); Dietitians 1 (ft).
Facilities Dining room; Physical therapy room; Activities room; Laundry room; Barber/Beauty shop; Patio.

Activities Arts & crafts; Cards; Games; Reading groups; Prayer groups; Movies; Shopping trips; Dances/Social/Cultural gatherings; Intergenerational programs; Pet therapy.

Saint Petersburg

Abbey Nursing Home Inc
7101 9th St N, Saint Petersburg, FL 33702
(813) 527-7231
Medical Dir Dr Ernest Frierson.
Licensure Skilled care. *Beds* SNF 152.
Certified Medicaid.
Owner Proprietary corp.
Admissions Requirements Minimum age 21;
Medical examination; Physician's request.
Staff RNs 11 (ft), 3 (pt); LPNs 8 (ft), 3 (pt);
Nurses' aides 54 (ft), 9 (pt); Activities
coordinators 2 (ft); Dietitians 1 (ft).
Languages Italian, Hungarian, German,
Spanish.
Facilities Dining room; Activities room;
Crafts room; Laundry room; Barber/Beauty
shop.
Activities Arts & crafts; Cards; Games;
Reading groups; Movies.

Alhambra Nursing Home Inc
7501 38th Ave N, Saint Petersburg, FL 33710
(813) 345-9307
Admin Larry Growney. *Dir of Nursing* Carol
Baumann. *Medical Dir* Roger Laughlin MD.
Licensure Skilled care. *Beds* 60. *Certified*
Private pay.
Owner Proprietary corp.
Admissions Requirements Minimum age 20;
Medical examination; Physician's request.
Staff Physicians 10 (pt); RNs 3 (ft), 3 (pt);
LPNs 4 (ft), 3 (pt); Nurses' aides 28 (ft), 3
(pt); Physical therapists 2 (pt); Recreational
therapists 2 (pt); Occupational therapists 2
(pt); Speech therapists 1 (pt); Activities
coordinators 1 (ft), 1 (pt); Dietitians 1 (ft);
Ophthalmologists 1 (pt); Podiatrists 1 (pt).
Facilities Dining room; Activities room;
Crafts room; Laundry room; Barber/Beauty
shop.
Activities Arts & crafts; Cards; Games;
Reading groups; Prayer groups; Movies;
Shopping trips; Dances/Social/Cultural
gatherings.

Alpine Nursing Center
3456 21st Ave S, Saint Petersburg, FL 33711
(813) 327-1988
Admin Doris Maxwell. *Dir of Nursing* Marge
Washer. *Medical Dir* Dr Robert Jenkins.
Licensure Intermediate care. *Beds* ICF 57.
Private Pay Patients 12%. *Certified*
Medicaid.
Owner Proprietary corp (United Health
Facilities Inc).
Admissions Requirements Medical
examination; Physician's request.
Staff RNs 2 (ft), 1 (pt); LPNs 2 (ft), 2 (pt);
Nurses' aides 14 (ft), 4 (pt); Physical
therapists (consultant); Reality therapists
(consultant); Recreational therapists
(consultant); Occupational therapists
(consultant); Speech therapists (consultant);
Activities coordinators 1 (ft); Dietitians 1
(ft); Ophthalmologists (consultant);
Podiatrists (consultant); Audiologists
(consultant).
Facilities Dining room; Activities room;
Crafts room; Laundry room; Barber/Beauty
shop.
Activities Arts & crafts; Cards; Games;
Reading groups; Prayer groups; Movies;
Shopping trips; Dances/Social/Cultural
gatherings; Pet therapy; Church services.

Bay Pointe Nursing Pavilion
4201 31st St S, Saint Petersburg, FL 33712
(613) 867-1104
Beds 62.

Bayou Manor Health Care
435 42nd Ave S, Saint Petersburg, FL 33705
(813) 822-1871
Admin Mick Addy. *Dir of Nursing* E Davis.
Medical Dir Robert Dawson MD.
Licensure Skilled care. *Beds* SNF 159.
Certified Medicaid.
Owner Proprietary corp (National Health
Corp).
Admissions Requirements Medical
examination; Physician's request.
Staff RNs 6 (ft); LPNs 12 (ft); Nurses' aides
48 (ft); Activities coordinators 4 (ft);
Dietitians 1 (ft).
Languages Spanish, French.
Facilities Dining room; Physical therapy
room; Activities room; Crafts room; Laundry
room; Barber/Beauty shop; Library.
Activities Arts & crafts; Cards; Games;
Reading groups; Prayer groups; Movies;
Shopping trips; Dances/Social/Cultural
gatherings; Intergenerational programs; Pet
therapy.

Beach Convalescent Hotel
8008 Blind Pass Rd, Saint Petersburg, FL
33706
(613) 367-3635
Beds 17.

College Harbor Inc
4200 54th Ave S, Saint Petersburg, FL 33711
(613) 866-3124
Beds 31.

Colonial Care Center
6300 46th Ave N, Saint Petersburg, FL 33709
(813) 544-1444
Admin Carol Sweetland. *Dir of Nursing* Diane
Mackey. *Medical Dir* Dr George Camarinos.
Licensure Skilled care; Intermediate care;
Alzheimer's care. *Beds* 102. *Certified*
Medicaid; Medicare.
Owner Proprietary corp (Unicare).
Admissions Requirements Minimum age 16;
Medical examination; Physician's request.
Staff Physicians 7 (pt); RNs 4 (ft), 4 (pt);
LPNs 7 (ft), 6 (pt); Nurses' aides 32 (ft), 6
(pt); Occupational therapists 1 (pt); Speech
therapists 1 (pt); Activities coordinators 1
(ft), 1 (pt); Dietitians 1 (pt);
Ophthalmologists 1 (pt); Podiatrists 1 (pt).
Languages Italian, Spanish.
Facilities Dining room; Activities room;
Crafts room; Barber/Beauty shop.
Activities Arts & crafts; Cards; Games;
Reading groups; Prayer groups; Movies;
Shopping trips.

Concordia Manor
321 13th Ave N, Saint Petersburg, FL 33701
(813) 822-3030
Licensure Skilled care. *Beds* 39. *Certified*
Medicaid.
Owner Proprietary corp (Unicare).
Staff RNs 2 (ft); LPNs 4 (ft); Nurses' aides 9
(ft).

Convalescent Care Center
550 62nd St S, Saint Petersburg, FL 33707
(813) 347-6151, 347-5683 FAX
Admin Thomas Robbins. *Dir of Nursing*
Kathy Hewitt. *Medical Dir* Dr Robert
Jenkins.
Licensure Skilled care; Intermediate care. *Beds*
SNF 60; ICF 60. *Certified* Medicaid;
Medicare.
Owner Proprietary corp.
Admissions Requirements Medical
examination; Physician's request.
Staff RNs 8 (ft); LPNs 8 (ft); Nurses' aides 25
(ft); Activities coordinators 1 (ft), 1 (pt);
Dietitians 1 (ft).
Facilities Dining room; Physical therapy
room; Activities room; Crafts room; Laundry
room; Barber/Beauty shop.

Activities Arts & crafts; Cards; Games;
Reading groups; Prayer groups; Movies;
Shopping trips; Dances/Social/Cultural
gatherings; Pet therapy.

Golfview Nursing Home
3636 10th Ave N, Saint Petersburg, FL 33713
(813) 323-3611
Admin Joseph Keenan. *Dir of Nursing*
Patricia Burgett. *Medical Dir* Dr Nanda.
Licensure Skilled care. *Beds* SNF 56. *Certified*
Medicaid; Medicare.
Owner Proprietary corp.
Admissions Requirements Minimum age 18.
Staff Physicians 1 (pt); RNs 3 (ft); LPNs 10
(ft); Nurses' aides 20 (ft); Activities
coordinators 1 (ft).
Facilities Dining room; Activities room;
Laundry room; Barber/Beauty shop.
Activities Arts & crafts; Cards; Games;
Dances/Social/Cultural gatherings; Pet
therapy.

Good Samaritan Nursing Home
3127 57th Ave N, Saint Petersburg, FL 33714
(813) 527-2171
Licensure Skilled care. *Beds* 60. *Certified*
Medicaid; Medicare.
Owner Proprietary corp.
Staff RNs 5 (ft); LPNs 5 (ft); Nurses' aides 14
(ft).
Languages German.

Greenbrook Nursing Center
1000 24th St N, Saint Petersburg, FL 33713
(813) 323-4711
Admin Scott W Clark. *Dir of Nursing* Gayle
Jones. *Medical Dir* Dr Joel Prawer.
Licensure Skilled care. *Beds* SNF 120.
Certified Medicaid; Medicare.
Owner Proprietary corp (Unicare).
Admissions Requirements Minimum age 17.
Staff Physicians 1 (pt); RNs 5 (ft); LPNs 9
(ft), 4 (pt); Nurses' aides 26 (ft), 10 (pt);
Physical therapists 1 (pt); Reality therapists
1 (pt); Recreational therapists 1 (pt);
Activities coordinators 1 (ft); Dietitians 1
(pt); Ophthalmologists 1 (pt); Podiatrists 1
(pt).
Languages Spanish, French.
Facilities Dining room; Physical therapy
room; Activities room; Crafts room; Barber/
Beauty shop.
Activities Arts & crafts; Cards; Games;
Reading groups; Prayer groups; Movies;
Shopping trips; Dances/Social/Cultural
gatherings.

Heartland of St Petersburg
1001 9th Street North, Saint Petersburg, FL
33701
(813) 896-8619
Admin Tonja D Pittman. *Dir of Nursing*
Geraldine White. *Medical Dir* Malcolm
Fraser.
Licensure Skilled care. *Beds* 108. *Certified*
Medicaid; Medicare.
Owner Proprietary corp (Health Care &
Retirement Corp).
Admissions Requirements Minimum age 18;
Medical examination; Physician's request.
Staff RNs 5 (ft), 2 (pt); LPNs 8 (ft), 1 (pt);
Nurses' aides 25 (ft); Physical therapists 1
(pt); Occupational therapists 1 (pt); Speech
therapists 1 (pt); Activities coordinators 1
(ft), 1 (pt); Dietitians 1 (pt);
Ophthalmologists 1 (pt); Podiatrists 1 (pt);
Dentists 1 (pt).
Languages Spanish.
Facilities Dining room; Physical therapy
room; Activities room; Crafts room; Laundry
room; Barber/Beauty shop; Library; Family
dining room.
Activities Arts & crafts; Cards; Games;
Reading groups; Prayer groups; Movies;
Shopping trips; Dances/Social/Cultural
gatherings.

Huber Restorium
521 69th Ave N, Saint Petersburg, FL 33702
(813) 526-7000
Admin Walter M Huber. *Dir of Nursing* Betty Thompson RN. *Medical Dir* Henry E Newman MD.
Licensure Skilled care; Retirement. *Beds* SNF 96. *Certified* Medicare.
Owner Proprietary corp.
Admissions Requirements Minimum age 21; Medical examination; Physician's request.
Staff Physicians 45 (pt); RNs 10 (ft), 2 (pt); LPNs 7 (ft), 4 (pt); Nurses' aides 35 (ft), 35 (pt); Physical therapists 2 (pt); Reality therapists 1 (pt); Recreational therapists 1 (ft); Occupational therapists 1 (pt); Speech therapists 1 (pt); Activities coordinators 1 (ft); Dietitians 1 (pt); Ophthalmologists 1 (pt); Podiatrists 1 (pt); Dentists 1 (pt).
Languages German, Italian, Spanish, French.
Facilities Dining room; Physical therapy room; Activities room; Chapel; Crafts room; Laundry room; Barber/Beauty shop; Library.
Activities Arts & crafts; Cards; Games; Reading groups; Prayer groups; Movies; Shopping trips; Dances/Social/Cultural gatherings.

Jacaranda Manor
4250 66th St N, Saint Petersburg, FL 33709
(813) 546-2405
Licensure Skilled care. *Beds* 299. *Certified* Medicare.
Owner Proprietary corp (Health Care & Retirement Corp).
Staff RNs 9 (ft); LPNs 12 (ft); Nurses' aides 68 (ft).
Languages Hebrew, Yiddish, Spanish, French, Tagalog.

Jaylene Manor Nursing Home
896 73rd Ave N, Saint Petersburg, FL 33702
Licensure Skilled care. *Beds* 63. *Certified* Medicaid.
Owner Proprietary corp.
Staff RNs 4 (ft); LPNs 6 (ft); Nurses' aides 20 (ft).
Languages Italian, Spanish.

Laurels, A Rehabilitation Center
550 9th Ave S, Saint Petersburg, FL 33701
(813) 898-4105, 821-3079 FAX
Admin Laurel J Chadwick RN. *Dir of Nursing* Barbara Quehl RN. *Medical Dir* Robert Dawson MD.
Licensure Skilled care; Intermediate care. *Beds* SNF 262. *Private Pay Patients* 5%. *Certified* Medicaid; Medicare.
Owner Privately owned (Beverly Enterprises).
Staff RNs 8 (ft); LPNs 22 (ft); Physical therapists 59 (ft); Physical therapists 1 (ft); Recreational therapists 1 (ft); Occupational therapists 1 (pt); Speech therapists 1 (pt); Activities coordinators 1 (ft); Dietitians 1 (ft); Ophthalmologists 1 (pt); Podiatrists 1 (pt).
Languages Spanish, German.
Facilities Dining room; Physical therapy room; Chapel; Barber/Beauty shop.
Activities Arts & crafts; Cards; Games; Reading groups; Prayer groups; Movies; Shopping trips; Dances/Social/Cultural gatherings; Intergenerational programs.

Leisure Manor
336 4th Ave N, Saint Petersburg, FL 33701
(813) 896-4171
Admin Fred C Austin. *Dir of Nursing* Clydette Ackett RN. *Medical Dir* Marion Wells MD.
Licensure Skilled care; Apts; Retirement. *Beds* SNF 24; Apts 73. *Private Pay Patients* 100%.
Owner Nonprofit organization/foundation.
Admissions Requirements Minimum age 65; Medical examination.
Staff Physicians; RNs 1 (ft), 2 (pt); LPNs 3 (ft); Nurses' aides 18 (ft); Recreational therapists 1 (pt).
Affiliation Presbyterian.

Facilities Dining room; Barber/Beauty shop.
Activities Arts & crafts; Cards; Games; Shopping trips.

Majestic Towers Health Center
1255 Pasadena Ave S, Saint Petersburg, FL 33707
(813) 381-7301
Admin Joyce A Smith. *Dir of Nursing* Callie Lovett RN BSN. *Medical Dir* Joseph Dibble MD.
Licensure Skilled care; Intermediate care; Retirement. *Beds* Swing beds SNF/ICF 150. *Private Pay Patients* 20%. *Certified* Medicaid; Medicare.
Owner Privately owned.
Admissions Requirements Physician's request; H & P/Chest.
Staff Physicians (consultant); RNs 4 (ft), 7 (pt); LPNs 11 (ft), 11 (pt); Nurses' aides 30 (ft), 24 (pt); Physical therapists (consultant); Occupational therapists (consultant); Speech therapists (consultant); Activities coordinators 3 (ft); Dietitians (consultant); Ophthalmologists (consultant); Podiatrists (consultant); Audiologists (consultant); Dentists (consultant).
Facilities Dining room; Physical therapy room; Activities room; Crafts room; Barber/Beauty shop; Library; Bank; Day care.
Activities Arts & crafts; Cards; Games; Reading groups; Prayer groups; Movies; Dances/Social/Cultural gatherings; Intergenerational programs; Pet therapy.

Maria Manor Health Care
10300 4th St N, Saint Petersburg, FL 33702
(813) 576-1025
Admin Margaret R McDonald. *Dir of Nursing* P Liles RN. *Medical Dir* Julio Valdes MD.
Licensure Skilled care. *Beds* SNF 274. *Certified* Medicaid.
Owner Nonprofit organization/foundation.
Admissions Requirements Medical examination; Physician's request.
Staff Physicians 3 (pt); RNs 12 (ft); LPNs 22 (pt); Nurses' aides 68 (ft), 10 (pt); Physical therapists 2 (pt); Activities coordinators 1 (ft); Dietitians 1 (ft); Ophthalmologists 2 (pt); Social services 2 (ft).
Languages Spanish, Italian, Polish, Yugoslavian.
Affiliation Roman Catholic.
Facilities Dining room; Physical therapy room; Activities room; Chapel; Crafts room; Laundry room; Barber/Beauty shop; Library.
Activities Arts & crafts; Cards; Games; Reading groups; Prayer groups; Movies; Shopping trips; Dances/Social/Cultural gatherings.

Masonic Home of Florida
3201 1st St NE, Saint Petersburg, FL 33704
(813) 822-3499, 821-6775 FAX
Admin Oscar G Laurene MHA NHA. *Dir of Nursing* Dorothy Higgins RN. *Medical Dir* Elbert Young MD.
Licensure Skilled care; Hospice care; Retirement. *Beds* SNF 85; Retirement 102. *Private Pay Patients* 0%.
Owner Nonprofit organization/foundation.
Admissions Requirements Minimum age 21; Medical examination.
Staff Physicians 3 (pt); RNs 8 (ft), 6 (pt); LPNs 4 (ft), 3 (pt); Nurses' aides 28 (ft), 4 (pt); Physical therapists (consultant); Occupational therapists 1 (pt); Speech therapists 1 (pt); Activities coordinators 2 (ft); Dietitians (consultant); Podiatrists 1 (pt); Audiologists 1 (pt); Physical therapy aides 1 (ft); Dentists (consultant).
Languages Polish, Greek, Spanish, German.
Affiliation Masons.
Facilities Dining room; Physical therapy room; Activities room; Chapel; Crafts room; Laundry room; Barber/Beauty shop; Library; Snack bar; Conference rooms; Gift shop;

Bandshell; Enclosed courtyard; Open patios; Fishing pier; Tricycles; Quadricycle surrey; Nature trail.
Activities Arts & crafts; Cards; Games; Prayer groups; Movies; Shopping trips; Dances/Social/Cultural gatherings; Intergenerational programs; Pet therapy; Hobby shop.

Menorah Manor
255 59th St N, Saint Petersburg, FL 33710
(813) 345-2775, 345-3957 FAX
Admin Marshall Seiden, Exec Dir. *Dir of Nursing* Virginia Holmes RN. *Medical Dir* H James Brownlee Jr MD.
Licensure Skilled care; Intermediate care; Retirement; Alzheimer's care. *Beds* Swing beds SNF/ICF 120; Retirement units 197. *Private Pay Patients* 42%. *Certified* Medicaid; Medicare.
Owner Nonprofit corp.
Admissions Requirements Minimum age 65; Medical examination.
Staff Physicians 1 (ft), 2 (pt); RNs 6 (ft); LPNs 24 (ft); Nurses' aides 50 (ft); Physical therapists 1 (pt); Reality therapists 1 (ft); Recreational therapists 3 (ft); Occupational therapists 1 (ft); Speech therapists 1 (pt); Activities coordinators 1 (ft); Dietitians 1 (ft), 1 (pt); Ophthalmologists 1 (pt); Podiatrists 1 (pt); Audiologists 1 (pt).
Affiliation Jewish.
Facilities Dining room; Physical therapy room; Activities room; Chapel; Crafts room; Barber/Beauty shop; Library; Kosher kitchen; Eye clinic; Alzheimer's therapy room; Private rooms.
Activities Arts & crafts; Cards; Games; Reading groups; Prayer groups; Movies; Shopping trips; Dances/Social/Cultural gatherings; Intergenerational programs; Pet therapy; Religios programs.

North Horizon Health Care Center
1301 16th St N, Saint Petersburg, FL 33705
(813) 898-5119
Admin Patricia M Lycett. *Dir of Nursing* Laurie A Miller. *Medical Dir* Joel S Prauler MD.
Licensure Skilled care. *Beds* 49. *Certified* Medicaid; Medicare.
Owner Proprietary corp (Unicare).
Staff RNs; LPNs; Nurses' aides; Activities coordinators; Ophthalmologists.
Activities Arts & crafts; Cards; Games; Reading groups; Prayer groups; Movies; Shopping trips; Dances/Social/Cultural gatherings.

North Shore Center
939 Beach Dr NE, Saint Petersburg, FL 33701
(813) 823-1571
Admin Beverly J Baxter. *Dir of Nursing* Julia Price RN. *Medical Dir* Susan Betzer MD.
Licensure Skilled care; Intermediate care; Retirement. *Beds* 26.
Owner Proprietary corp.
Admissions Requirements Minimum age; Medical examination; Physician's request.
Staff RNs 2 (ft); LPNs 2 (ft), 1 (pt); Nurses' aides 10 (ft), 1 (pt); Activities coordinators 1 (ft); Food Services Director 1 (ft); Medical Records 1 (pt).
Languages Spanish.
Facilities Dining room; Activities room; Barber/Beauty shop; Library.
Activities Arts & crafts; Cards; Games; Prayer groups; Movies; Shopping trips; Dances/Social/Cultural gatherings; Circus; Ice show.

Palm Shores Retirement Center
830 N Shore Dr, Saint Petersburg, FL 33701
(813) 894-2102
Licensure Skilled care. *Beds* 42.
Owner Nonprofit corp.
Staff RNs 4 (ft); LPNs 3 (ft); Nurses' aides 8 (ft).
Languages Spanish.
Affiliation Baptist.

Parc Center Apartments
3190 75th St N, Saint Petersburg, FL 33710
(813) 384-0607
Licensure Intermediate care for mentally retarded. *Beds* 48.
Owner Nonprofit corp.

PARC Cottage
3100 75th St N, Saint Petersburg, FL 33710
(813) 345-4508
Admin Faith Young Bedford. *Dir of Nursing* Jane Ott RN.
Licensure Intermediate care for mentally retarded. *Beds* ICF/MR 16. *Certified* Medicaid.
Owner Nonprofit organization/foundation.
Admissions Requirements Minimum age 3.
Staff Physicians; RNs; LPNs; Physical therapists; Recreational therapists; Occupational therapists; Speech therapists; Activities coordinators; Dietitians; Dentists.
Facilities Dining room; Activities room; Laundry room.
Activities Arts & crafts; Games; Movies; Shopping trips.

Pasadena Manor
1430 Pasadena Ave S, Saint Petersburg, FL 33707
(613) 347-1257
Beds 63.

Rosedale Manor
3479 54th Ave N, Saint Petersburg, FL 33714
(813) 527-7315
Licensure Skilled care. *Beds* 192. *Certified* Medicaid.
Owner Proprietary corp (Health Care & Retirement Corp).
Staff RNs 8 (ft); LPNs 18 (ft); Nurses' aides 40 (ft).

St Petersburg Cluster
1101 102nd Ave N, Saint Petersburg, FL 33702
(813) 536-5911
Licensure Intermediate care for mentally retarded. *Beds* 8.

Shore Acres Nursing & Convalescent Home
4500 Indianapolis St NE, Saint Petersburg, FL 33703
(813) 527-5801
Admin Frank Leeds III. *Dir of Nursing* Donna Petersen RN. *Medical Dir* Clayton Hauser MD.
Licensure Skilled care. *Beds* SNF 109. *Certified* Medicaid; Medicare.
Owner Proprietary corp.
Admissions Requirements Minimum age 18; Medical examination; Physician's request.
Staff Physicians 1 (pt); RNs 3 (ft); LPNs 10 (ft), 2 (pt); Nurses' aides 38 (ft); Physical therapists 1 (pt); Recreational therapists 1 (pt); Occupational therapists 1 (pt); Speech therapists 1 (pt); Activities coordinators 1 (ft); Dietitians 1 (pt); Ophthalmologists 1 (pt).
Languages Spanish, German.
Facilities Dining room; Physical therapy room; Activities room; Crafts room; Laundry room; Barber/Beauty shop; Library.
Activities Arts & crafts; Cards; Games; Reading groups; Prayer groups; Movies; Shopping trips; Dances/Social/Cultural gatherings; Intergenerational programs; Pet therapy.

South Heritage Nursing Center
718 Lakeview Ave S, Saint Petersburg, FL 33705
(813) 894-5125
Medical Dir Dr Malcolm Fraser.
Licensure Skilled care. *Beds* 75. *Certified* Medicaid; Medicare.
Owner Proprietary corp (Unicare).
Staff Physicians 1 (pt); RNs 3 (ft); LPNs 12 (ft); Nurses' aides 27 (ft), 4 (pt); Physical therapists 1 (pt); Speech therapists 1 (pt);

Activities coordinators 1 (ft); Dietitians 1 (pt); Podiatrists 1 (pt); Audiologists 1 (pt); Dentists 1 (pt).
Facilities Dining room; Activities room; Barber/Beauty shop.
Activities Arts & crafts; Cards; Games; Reading groups; Prayer groups; Movies; Shopping trips; Dances/Social/Cultural gatherings.

Suncoast Manor
6909 9th St S, Saint Petersburg, FL 33705
(813) 867-1131
Admin Yvonne Smallidge. *Dir of Nursing* Joy Pike. *Medical Dir* Dr John Backe.
Licensure Skilled care; Retirement. *Beds* SNF 161; Retirement 400. *Private Pay Patients* 100%.
Owner Nonprofit corp.
Admissions Requirements Minimum age 62; Medical examination.
Staff Physicians 2 (pt); RNs 7 (ft), 3 (pt); LPNs 9 (ft), 4 (pt); Nurses' aides 45 (ft), 6 (pt); Physical therapists 2 (pt); Recreational therapists 1 (pt); Occupational therapists 1 (pt); Speech therapists 1 (pt); Activities coordinators 1 (pt); Dietitians 1 (pt); Podiatrists 1 (pt).
Affiliation Episcopal.
Facilities Dining room; Physical therapy room; Activities room; Chapel; Crafts room; Laundry room; Barber/Beauty shop; Library.
Activities Arts & crafts; Cards; Games; Reading groups; Prayer groups; Movies; Shopping trips; Dances/Social/Cultural gatherings; Pet therapy.

Suncoast Nursing Home
2000 17th Ave S, Saint Petersburg, FL 33712
(813) 823-3544
Licensure Skilled care. *Beds* 59. *Certified* Medicaid.
Owner Proprietary corp.
Staff RNs 2 (ft); LPNs 5 (ft); Nurses' aides 9 (ft).

Sunny Shores Health Center
125 56th Ave S, Saint Petersburg, FL 33705
(813) 867-2131, ext 548
Admin Sarah S McGlathery. *Dir of Nursing* Florence R Wilde RN. *Medical Dir* Charles L Rast MD.
Licensure Skilled care; Retirement. *Beds* SNF 120. *Private Pay Patients* 100%.
Owner Nonprofit organization/foundation.
Admissions Requirements Minimum age 65.
Staff Physicians 2 (pt); RNs 13 (ft); LPNs 11 (ft); Nurses' aides 54 (ft); Physical therapists 1 (pt); Reality therapists 1 (pt); Recreational therapists 1 (pt); Occupational therapists 1 (pt); Speech therapists 1 (pt); Activities coordinators 1 (ft); Dietitians 1 (pt); Ophthalmologists 1 (pt); Podiatrists 1 (pt); Audiologists 1 (pt); Dentists 1 (pt); Social workers 1 (ft).
Affiliation Methodist.
Facilities Dining room; Activities room; Chapel; Crafts room; Laundry room; Barber/Beauty shop; Library.
Activities Arts & crafts; Cards; Games; Reading groups; Prayer groups; Movies; Shopping trips; Dances/Social/Cultural gatherings; Intergenerational programs; Pet therapy.

Swanholm Nursing & Rehabilitation Center
6200 Central Ave, Saint Petersburg, FL 33707
(813) 347-5196
Admin Harold E Bahlow. *Dir of Nursing* Barbara Quehl RN. *Medical Dir* Robert L Dawson MD.
Licensure Skilled care. *Beds* SNF 273. *Certified* Medicaid; Medicare.
Owner Nonprofit corp.
Admissions Requirements Minimum age 17; Medical examination; Physician's request.

Staff RNs; LPNs; Nurses' aides; Physical therapists 2 (ft), Aides 5 (ft); Activities coordinators 1 (ft).
Languages Spanish, Polish, French, Italian, Sign.
Affiliation Lutheran.
Facilities Dining room; Physical therapy room; Activities room; Chapel; Crafts room; Laundry room; Barber/Beauty shop; Library.
Activities Arts & crafts; Cards; Games; Reading groups; Prayer groups; Movies; Shopping trips; Dances/Social/Cultural gatherings; Bowling; Reality orientation; Exercise groups; Music therapy; Bingo; Happy hour.

Tyrone Medical Inn
1100 66th St N, Saint Petersburg, FL 33710
(813) 345-9331
Medical Dir Douglas W Hood MD.
Licensure Skilled care. *Beds* 59. *Certified* Medicare.
Owner Proprietary corp.
Staff RNs 2 (ft); LPNs 7 (ft); Nurses' aides 22 (ft).
Facilities Dining room; Activities room; Barber/Beauty shop.
Activities Arts & crafts; Games; Movies.

Victoria Martin Nursing Home
555 31st St S, Saint Petersburg, FL 33712
(813) 327-0995
Medical Dir Dr Orion T Ayer.
Licensure Skilled care. *Beds* 38. *Certified* Medicaid.
Owner Proprietary corp.
Admissions Requirements Medical examination; Physician's request.
Staff RNs 3 (ft), 5 (pt); LPNs 4 (pt); Nurses' aides 12 (ft), 2 (pt); Physical therapists; Activities coordinators 1 (ft).
Facilities Dining room; Activities room; Laundry room.
Activities Arts & crafts; Cards; Games; Reading groups; Prayer groups; Movies; Dances/Social/Cultural gatherings.

Wedgewood Health Care
1735 9th St S, Saint Petersburg, FL 33705
(813) 821-8866
Licensure Skilled care; Intermediate care. *Beds* SNF 109; ICF 163. *Certified* Medicaid; Medicare.
Owner Proprietary corp.
Staff RNs 10 (ft); LPNs 21 (ft); Nurses' aides 56 (ft).
Languages French, German.

Whitehall Convalescent Home
5601 31st St S, Saint Petersburg, FL 33712
(813) 867-6955
Admin Sandra L Bollenback.
Medical Dir Betty Barbieri.
Licensure Skilled care; Retirement. *Beds* SNF 58.
Owner Privately owned.
Admissions Requirements Minimum age 21; Medical examination.
Staff RNs 4 (ft); LPNs 5 (ft); Nurses' aides 18 (ft).
Languages French, Hindi, Spanish, Arabic.
Facilities Dining room; Activities room; Chapel; Crafts room; Barber/Beauty shop.
Activities Arts & crafts; Cards; Games; Reading groups; Prayer groups; Movies; Shopping trips; Dances/Social/Cultural gatherings.

William & Mary Nursing Center
811 Jackson St N, Saint Petersburg, FL 33705
(813) 896-3651
Admin Willard Roth. *Dir of Nursing* Karen Sciacchitano. *Medical Dir* Malcolm Fraser MD.

Licensure Skilled care; Intermediate care; Retirement living; Alzheimer's care. *Beds* SNF 58; ICF 38; Retirement living 46. *Private Pay Patients* 50%. *Certified* Medicaid; Medicare; VA.
Owner Proprietary corp (Integrated Health Services Inc).
Admissions Requirements Minimum age 17; Medical examination; Physician's request.
Staff Physicians 20 (pt); RNs 6 (ft); LPNs 9 (ft); Nurses' aides 24 (ft); Physical therapists 1 (pt); Reality therapists 1 (pt); Recreational therapists 1 (pt); Occupational therapists 1 (pt); Speech therapists 1 (pt); Activities coordinators 1 (ft), 1 (pt); Dietitians 1 (ft), 1 (pt); Ophthalmologists 1 (pt); Podiatrists 1 (pt); Audiologists 1 (pt).
Languages Spanish.
Facilities Dining room; Physical therapy room; Activities room; Chapel; Crafts room; Laundry room; Barber/Beauty shop; Library.
Activities Arts & crafts; Cards; Games; Reading groups; Prayer groups; Movies; Shopping trips; Dances/Social/Cultural gatherings; Pet therapy.

Saint Petersburg Beach

Beach Convalescent Home
8008 Blind Pass Rd, Saint Petersburg Beach, FL 33706
(813) 367-7651, 367-3121 FAX
Admin Stacey McCauley. *Dir of Nursing* Kathy Maratta. *Medical Dir* Malcolm Fraser MD.
Licensure Intermediate care; ACLF; Alzheimer's care. *Beds* ICF 38; ACLF 16. *Private Pay Patients* 10%. *Certified* Medicaid.
Owner Proprietary corp (Vantage Healthcare).
Admissions Requirements Minimum age 21; Medical examination; Physician's request.
Staff Physicians 1 (ft); RNs 5 (pt); LPNs 3 (ft), 1 (pt); Nurses' aides 12 (ft), 2 (pt); Physical therapists (contracted); Occupational therapists (contracted); Speech therapists (contracted); Activities coordinators 1 (ft); Dietitians (consultant); Podiatrists (contracted); Audiologists (contracted); ACLF aides 3 (ft), 2 (pt).
Facilities Dining room; Laundry room; Barber/Beauty shop.
Activities Arts & crafts; Cards; Games; Reading groups; Prayer groups; Movies; Shopping trips; Dances/Social/Cultural gatherings; Intergenerational programs; Pet therapy.

Crown Nursing Home
5351 Gulf Blvd, Saint Petersburg Beach, FL 33706
(813) 360-5548, 367-6939 FAX
Admin Joan Bayley. *Dir of Nursing* Maria Zeiders. *Medical Dir* Dr Malcolm Fraser.
Licensure Skilled care; Intermediate care. *Beds* SNF 10; ICF 44.
Owner Proprietary corp (Vantage Healthcare Corp).
Staff Physicians 4 (pt); RNs 2 (ft), 1 (pt); LPNs 3 (ft), 2 (pt); Nurses' aides 13 (ft), 3 (pt); Physical therapists 1 (pt); Recreational therapists 1 (pt); Occupational therapists 1 (pt); Speech therapists 1 (pt); Activities coordinators 1 (pt); Dietitians 1 (pt); Podiatrists 1 (pt).

Crown Nursing Home
5351 Gulf Blvd, Saint Petersburg Beach, FL 33706
(813) 360-5548, 367-6939 FAX
Admin Joan Bayley. *Dir of Nursing* Maria Zeiders RN. *Medical Dir* Dr Malcolm Fraser.
Licensure Skilled care. *Beds* SNF 54. *Certified* Medicaid; Medicare.
Owner Proprietary corp (Vantage Healthcare Corp).

Admissions Requirements Minimum age 18.
Staff Physicians 4 (pt); RNs 3 (ft), 1 (pt); LPNs 3 (ft), 3 (pt); Nurses' aides 14 (ft), 2 (pt); Physical therapists (contracted); Reality therapists (contracted); Recreational therapists (contracted); Occupational therapists (contracted); Activities coordinators 1 (ft); Dietitians 1 (pt); Ophthalmologists 1 (pt); Podiatrists 1 (pt); Audiologists 1 (pt).
Languages Polish, German.
Facilities Dining room; Activities room; Laundry room; Barber/Beauty shop.
Activities Arts & crafts; Cards; Games; Reading groups; Prayer groups; Movies; Shopping trips; Dances/Social/Cultural gatherings; Pet therapy; Balloon volleyball; Woodworking; Cooking class; Cookouts; Fishing tournaments.

Sanford

Hillhaven Healthcare Center
950 Mellonville Ave, Sanford, FL 32771
(407) 322-8566
Admin O K Eimers CMACHCA. *Dir of Nursing* Marietta Fenton. *Medical Dir* Anup Lahairy MD.
Licensure Skilled care. *Beds* SNF 114. *Private Pay Patients* 18%. *Certified* Medicaid; Medicare.
Owner Proprietary corp (Hillhaven Corp).
Admissions Requirements Medical examination; Physician's request.
Staff Physicians 2 (pt); RNs 6 (ft); LPNs 5 (ft); Nurses' aides 24 (ft), 4 (pt); Physical therapists 1 (ft); Occupational therapists 1 (pt); Speech therapists 1 (pt); Activities coordinators 1 (ft), 1 (pt); Dietitians 1 (pt); Podiatrists 1 (pt); Audiologists 1 (pt).
Facilities Dining room; Physical therapy room; Activities room; Crafts room; Laundry room; Barber/Beauty shop; Atrium; Landscaped areas.
Activities Arts & crafts; Cards; Games; Reading groups; Prayer groups; Movies; Shopping trips; Dances/Social/Cultural gatherings; Pet therapy.

Lakeview Nursing Center
919 E 2nd St, Sanford, FL 32771
(305) 322-6707
Licensure Skilled care. *Beds* 105.
Owner Proprietary corp.
Staff RNs 3 (ft); LPNs 8 (ft); Nurses' aides 29 (ft).
Languages Spanish, German.

Sarasota

Bay Village of Sarasota
8400 Vamo Rd, Sarasota, FL 33581
(813) 966-5611
Licensure Skilled care; Retirement. *Beds* SNF 107.
Owner Nonprofit corp.
Admissions Requirements Minimum age 65; Medical examination.
Staff RNs 8 (ft), 14 (pt); LPNs 4 (ft), 1 (pt); Nurses' aides 39 (ft), 8 (pt); Physical therapists 1 (pt); Occupational therapists 1 (pt); Speech therapists 1 (pt); Dietitians 1 (ft); Ophthalmologists 1 (pt).
Affiliation Presbyterian.
Facilities Dining room; Physical therapy room; Activities room; Chapel; Crafts room; Laundry room; Barber/Beauty shop; Library.
Activities Arts & crafts; Cards; Games; Reading groups; Prayer groups; Movies; Dances/Social/Cultural gatherings.

Beneva Nursing Pavilion
741 S Beneva Rd, Sarasota, FL 34232
(813) 957-0310
Admin David E Wilson NHA. *Dir of Nursing* Roberta Alexander RN. *Medical Dir* Forest Chapman MD.

Licensure Skilled care; Retirement. *Beds* SNF 120. *Private Pay Patients* 85%. *Certified* Medicaid; Medicare.
Owner Proprietary corp (Central Park Lodges).
Admissions Requirements Minimum age 18; Medical examination; Physician's request.
Staff Physicians 1 (pt); RNs 5 (ft), 3 (pt); LPNs 10 (ft), 3 (pt); Nurses' aides 36 (ft), 14 (pt); Physical therapists 1 (pt); Recreational therapists 1 (pt); Occupational therapists 1 (pt); Speech therapists 1 (pt); Activities coordinators 1 (ft), 1 (pt); Dietitians 1 (pt); Ophthalmologists 1 (pt); Podiatrists 1 (pt); Audiologists 1 (pt).
Languages French, Spanish.
Facilities Dining room; Physical therapy room; Activities room; Crafts room; Laundry room; Barber/Beauty shop; Library; Nature paths and ponds; Electrically operated beds; Private baths.
Activities Arts & crafts; Cards; Games; Reading groups; Prayer groups; Movies; Shopping trips; Dances/Social/Cultural gatherings; Intergenerational programs; Pet therapy.

Burzenski Nursing Home
4450 8th St, Sarasota, FL 34232
(813) 371-6438
Admin M Marlene Johnson. *Dir of Nursing* Cathi Stolte. *Medical Dir* Dr Lourdes O'Bautista.
Licensure Skilled care. *Beds* SNF 60. *Private Pay Patients* 38%. *Certified* Medicaid; Medicare.
Owner Proprietary corp.
Admissions Requirements Medical examination.
Staff RNs 1 (ft), 2 (pt); LPNs 5 (ft), 5 (pt); Nurses' aides 13 (ft), 10 (pt); Activities coordinators 1 (ft), 1 (pt).
Languages Spanish.
Facilities Dining room; Physical therapy room; Activities room; Laundry room.
Activities Arts & crafts; Cards; Games; Pet therapy.

East Manor Medical Care Center
1524 East Ave S, Sarasota, FL 33579
(813) 365-2422
Admin Richard N Thrower. *Dir of Nursing* Leonore Ruggles RN. *Medical Dir* Randy Powell MD.
Licensure Skilled care. *Beds* SNF 169. *Certified* Medicaid; Medicare.
Owner Proprietary corp (Hillhaven Corp).
Admissions Requirements Medical examination; Physician's request.
Staff RNs 11 (ft); LPNs 13 (ft); Nurses' aides 49 (ft); Physical therapists 1 (pt); Occupational therapists 1 (pt); Speech therapists 1 (pt); Activities coordinators 2 (ft); Dietitians 1 (pt); Podiatrists 1 (pt).
Facilities Dining room; Physical therapy room; Activities room; Laundry room; Barber/Beauty shop.
Activities Arts & crafts; Cards; Games; Reading groups; Prayer groups; Movies; Shopping trips; Dances/Social/Cultural gatherings.

J H Floyd Sunshine Manor
1755 18th St, Sarasota, FL 33578
(813) 955-4915
Licensure Skilled care. *Beds* 70. *Certified* Medicaid.
Owner Nonprofit corp.
Staff RNs 4 (ft); LPNs 5 (ft); Nurses' aides 24 (ft).

Hillhaven Convalescent Center—Sarasota1
5640 Rand Blvd, Sarasota, FL 33583
(813) 922-8009
Licensure Skilled care. *Beds* 77. *Certified* Medicaid; Medicare.

Owner Proprietary corp.
Staff RNs 13 (ft); LPNs 6 (ft); Nurses' aides 17 (ft).

Kensington Manor
3250 12th St, Sarasota, FL 33577
(813) 365-4185
Admin Al J Robbins. *Dir of Nursing* Carol Davies RN. *Medical Dir* Dr John Steel.
Licensure Skilled care; Intermediate care. *Beds* 147. *Certified* Medicaid; Medicare.
Owner Proprietary corp.
Admissions Requirements Medical examination; Physician's request.
Staff Physicians 1 (ft); RNs 8 (ft), 2 (pt); LPNs 8 (ft), 3 (pt); Nurses' aides 45 (ft), 4 (pt); Physical therapists 2 (pt); Occupational therapists 1 (pt); Speech therapists 1 (pt); Activities coordinators 2 (ft); Dietitians 1 (pt); Ophthalmologists 1 (pt).
Languages Spanish, Italian.
Facilities Dining room; Activities room; Crafts room; Laundry room; Barber/Beauty shop; Library.
Activities Arts & crafts; Cards; Games; Reading groups; Prayer groups; Movies; Shopping trips.

Manor Care of Sarasota
5511 Swift Rd, Sarasota, FL 33561
(613) 921-7462
Beds 76.

Oak Pointe Manor
1507 S Tuttle Ave, Sarasota, FL 34239
(813) 365-2737, 951-2063 FAX
Admin Mark A Chmielewski. *Dir of Nursing* Gail Chase. *Medical Dir* Dr Charles Hollen.
Licensure Skilled care; Intermediate care. *Beds* Swing beds SNF/ICF 114. *Private Pay Patients* 27%. *Certified* Medicaid; Medicare.
Owner Proprietary corp (Beverly Enterprises).
Admissions Requirements Medical examination; Physician's request.
Staff RNs 2 (ft), 1 (pt); LPNs 8 (ft), 1 (pt); Nurses' aides 30 (ft), 5 (pt); Physical therapists 1 (ft); Recreational therapists 1 (ft); Occupational therapists 1 (ft); Speech therapists 1 (ft); Activities coordinators 1 (ft); Dietitians 1 (pt); Podiatrists 1 (pt).
Languages Spanish.
Facilities Dining room; Physical therapy room; Activities room; Crafts room; Laundry room; Barber/Beauty shop.
Activities Arts & crafts; Cards; Games; Reading groups; Prayer groups; Shopping trips; Intergenerational programs; Pet therapy.

Plymouth Harbor Inc
700 John Ringling Blvd, Sarasota, FL 34236
(813) 365-2600
Admin Dorothy M Barichak RN NHA. *Dir of Nursing* Lenora Anderson RN. *Medical Dir* Scott Elsbree MD.
Licensure Skilled care; Retirement. *Beds* SNF 60. *Private Pay Patients* 100%.
Owner Nonprofit organization/foundation.
Admissions Requirements Minimum age 65; Medical examination.
Staff Physicians 1 (pt); RNs 6 (ft), 1 (pt); LPNs 8 (ft), 2 (pt); Nurses' aides 28 (ft), 1 (pt); Physical therapists 1 (pt); Recreational therapists 1 (pt); Occupational therapists 1 (pt); Speech therapists 1 (pt); Activities coordinators 1 (ft); Dietitians 1 (ft); Podiatrists 1 (pt); 5 (ft).
Languages Spanish, German, Hungarian.
Affiliation Church of Christ.
Facilities Dining room; Physical therapy room; Activities room; Chapel; Crafts room; Laundry room; Barber/Beauty shop; Library.
Activities Arts & crafts; Cards; Games; Reading groups; Prayer groups; Movies; Shopping trips; Dances/Social/Cultural gatherings; Intergenerational programs; Pet therapy; Plant therapy, Flower arranging.

Regents Park of Sarasota
7678 Beneva Rd, Sarasota, FL 34238
(813) 923-5694
Admin Beverly Baxter. *Dir of Nursing* Donna Vliet RN. *Medical Dir* Don Furci DO.
Licensure Skilled care; Retirement. *Beds* SNF 113. *Certified* Medicaid; Medicare.
Owner Proprietary corp (Health Quest).
Admissions Requirements Minimum age 16; Medical examination; Physician's request.
Staff RNs 9 (ft), 1 (pt); LPNs 3 (ft); Nurses' aides 26 (ft), 1 (pt); Physical therapists 2 (ft); Recreational therapists 1 (ft); Occupational therapists 1 (pt); Speech therapists 1 (pt); Activities coordinators 1 (ft); Dietitians 1 (pt).
Facilities Dining room; Physical therapy room; Activities room; Chapel; Laundry room; Barber/Beauty shop; Lanai; Ice cream parlor.
Activities Arts & crafts; Cards; Games; Movies; Dances/Social/Cultural gatherings; Pet therapy.

Sarasota Nursing Pavilion
2600 Courtland St, Sarasota, FL 33577
(813) 365-2926
Admin Claire Fellema. *Dir of Nursing* Esther Gatto RN. *Medical Dir* Ernest W Chapman MD.
Licensure Skilled care. *Beds* 180. *Certified* Medicaid; Medicare.
Owner Proprietary corp.
Admissions Requirements Minimum age 16; Medical examination; Physician's request.
Staff RNs 25 (ft), 5 (pt); LPNs; Nurses' aides 35 (ft), 20 (pt); Physical therapists 2 (ft); Recreational therapists 1 (ft); Occupational therapists 2 (ft), 2 (pt); Speech therapists 1 (pt); Activities coordinators 1 (ft); Dietitians 1 (ft).
Languages Spanish.
Facilities Dining room; Physical therapy room; Activities room; Crafts room; Laundry room; Barber/Beauty shop; Library.
Activities Arts & crafts; Cards; Games; Reading groups; Prayer groups; Movies; Shopping trips; Dances/Social/Cultural gatherings.

Sarasota Welfare Home Inc
1501 N Orange Ave, Sarasota, FL 33577
(813) 365-0250
Licensure Skilled care; Intermediate care; ACLF. *Beds* SNF 73; ICF 131; ACLF 72. *Certified* Medicaid; Medicare.
Owner Nonprofit corp.
Admissions Requirements Minimum age 65; Medical examination; 5 year county residency.
Staff Physicians; Nurses' aides; Dietitians.
Languages Spanish.
Facilities Dining room; Activities room; Chapel; Crafts room; Laundry room; Barber/Beauty shop; Library.
Activities Arts & crafts; Cards; Games; Reading groups; Prayer groups; Movies; Shopping trips; Dances/Social/Cultural gatherings.

Springwood Nursing Center Ltd
4602 Northgate Court, Sarasota, FL 33580
(813) 355-2913
Beds 120.
Owner Proprietary corp.

Sunnyside Nursing Home
5201 Bahia Vista St, Sarasota, FL 34232
(813) 371-2729
Admin David Ray Miller. *Dir of Nursing* Ruth Mast. *Medical Dir* Dr Loren Zehr.
Licensure Skilled care; Retirement. *Beds* SNF 60. *Private Pay Patients* 67%. *Certified* Medicaid.
Owner Nonprofit organization/foundation.
Admissions Requirements Minimum age 16; Medical examination.

Staff RNs 3 (ft), 1 (pt); LPNs 5 (ft), 4 (pt); Nurses' aides 21 (ft), 6 (pt); Activities coordinators 1 (ft).
Languages German, Spanish.
Affiliation Mennonite.
Facilities Dining room; Physical therapy room; Activities room; Laundry room; Barber/Beauty shop.
Activities Arts & crafts; Cards; Games; Reading groups; Prayer groups; Movies; Dances/Social/Cultural gatherings; Intergenerational programs; Pet therapy.

Wilhelms Nursing Home
1507 S Tuttle Ave, Sarasota, FL 33580
(813) 365-2737
Licensure Skilled care. *Beds* 123. *Certified* Medicaid.
Owner Proprietary corp (Beverly Enterprises).
Staff RNs 5 (ft); LPNs 11 (ft); Nurses' aides 22 (ft).
Languages Spanish.

Sebring

Palms Health Care Center
725 S Pine St, Sebring, FL 33870
(813) 385-0161
Admin Benjamin A Brooks. *Dir of Nursing* Jean Fishburn RN. *Medical Dir* Vinod Thakker MD.
Licensure Skilled care; Retirement Community. *Beds* SNF 104. *Certified* Medicaid; Medicare.
Owner Nonprofit corp.
Admissions Requirements Minimum age 62; Females only; Medical examination.
Staff Physicians 1 (pt); RNs 4 (ft); LPNs 11 (ft); Nurses' aides 40 (ft); Physical therapists 1 (pt); Reality therapists 1 (pt); Recreational therapists 1 (pt); Occupational therapists 1 (pt); Speech therapists 1 (pt); Activities coordinators 1 (ft), 2 (pt); Dietitians 1 (ft); Ophthalmologists 1 (pt); Podiatrists 1 (pt).
Affiliation Church of the Brethren.
Facilities Dining room; Physical therapy room; Activities room; Chapel; Crafts room; Laundry room; Barber/Beauty shop; Library; Lobby; Social space.
Activities Arts & crafts; Cards; Games; Reading groups; Prayer groups; Movies; Shopping trips; Dances/Social/Cultural gatherings; Ceramics; Basket weaving.

Sebring Care Center
3011 Kenilworth Blvd, Sebring, FL 33870
(813) 382-2153
Admin Carolyn Jacobs RN. *Dir of Nursing* Margaret Wilke RN. *Medical Dir* Dr Hanford Brace.
Licensure Skilled care. *Beds* SNF 104. *Certified* Medicaid; Medicare.
Owner Proprietary corp.
Admissions Requirements Medical examination; Physician's request.
Staff Physicians 1 (pt); RNs 6 (ft); LPNs 8 (ft), 2 (pt); Nurses' aides 36 (ft); Physical therapists 2 (ft), 2 (pt); Occupational therapists 1 (ft), 1 (pt); Speech therapists 2 (ft), 2 (pt); Activities coordinators 1 (ft); Dietitians 1 (pt); Ophthalmologists 1 (pt); Podiatrists 1 (pt); Dentists 1 (pt).
Languages Spanish.
Facilities Dining room; Physical therapy room; Activities room; Laundry room; Barber/Beauty shop.
Activities Arts & crafts; Cards; Games; Reading groups; Prayer groups; Movies; Shopping trips; Dances/Social/Cultural gatherings.

Seminole

Seminole Nursing Pavilion
10800 Temple Terrace, Seminole, FL 33542
(813) 398-0123

Admin Jerry Harden. *Dir of Nursing* Patricia J Steffenhagen RN. *Medical Dir* Mark F Franklin DO.
Licensure Skilled care; Intermediate care; Retirement. *Beds* 120. *Certified* Medicaid; Medicare; VA.
Owner Proprietary corp.
Admissions Requirements Medical examination; Physician's request.
Staff Physicians 1 (ft), 15 (pt); RNs 8 (ft), 3 (pt); LPNs 13 (ft), 2 (pt); Nurses' aides 40 (ft), 4 (pt); Physical therapists 1 (ft), 3 (pt); Occupational therapists 1 (ft); Speech therapists 1 (ft); Activities coordinators 1 (ft), 2 (pt); Dietitians 1 (ft); Ophthalmologists 1 (pt); Podiatrists 1 (pt).
Facilities Dining room; Physical therapy room; Activities room; Crafts room; Laundry room; Barber/Beauty shop; Library.
Activities Arts & crafts; Games; Reading groups; Prayer groups; Movies; Shopping trips.

South Daytona

Daytona Manor Nursing Home
650 Reed Canal Rd, South Daytona, FL 32119
(904) 767-4831
Admin Robert E Green. *Dir of Nursing* Elizabeth Foreman. *Medical Dir* James Shoemaker.
Licensure Skilled care; Intermediate care. *Beds* Swing beds SNF/ICF 65. *Private Pay Patients* 6%. *Certified* Medicaid; Medicare.
Owner Proprietary corp (Vantage Healthcare).
Admissions Requirements Minimum age 16; Medical examination; Physician's request.
Staff Physicians (contracted); RNs; LPNs; Nurses' aides; Physical therapists (contracted); Recreational therapists; Occupational therapists (contracted); Speech therapists (contracted); Activities coordinators; Dietitians (contracted); Podiatrists (contracted); Audiologists (contracted).
Languages German, French, Spanish, Greek, Slavic.
Facilities Dining room; Barber/Beauty shop.
Activities Arts & crafts; Cards; Games; Reading groups; Prayer groups; Movies; Shopping trips; Dances/Social/Cultural gatherings; Intergenerational programs; Pet therapy; Community involvement.

South Pasadena

Deluxe Care Inn
1820 Shore Dr S, South Pasadena, FL 33707
(813) 384-9300
Licensure Skilled care. *Beds* 58. *Certified* Medicare.
Owner Proprietary corp.
Staff RNs 4 (ft); LPNs 9 (ft); Nurses' aides 13 (ft).
Languages Spanish.

Pasadena Manor
1430 Pasadena Ave S, South Pasadena, FL 33707
(813) 347-1257
Licensure Skilled care. *Beds* 126. *Certified* Medicaid; Medicare.
Owner Proprietary corp.
Staff RNs 6 (ft); LPNs 6 (ft); Nurses' aides 28 (ft).
Languages Spanish, Tagalog.

Spring Hill

Evergreen Woods
7030 Evergreen Woods Trail, Spring Hill, FL 33526
(904) 596-2055
Beds 60. *Certified* Medicaid; Medicare.
Owner Nonprofit corp.

Starke

Whispering Pines Care Center
808 S Colley Rd, Starke, FL 32091
(904) 964-6220
Admin Joseph W McCorkle. *Dir of Nursing* Jeneane Lentz. *Medical Dir* Carlos M Hernandez MD.
Licensure Skilled care; Intermediate care. *Beds* Swing beds SNF/ICF 120. *Private Pay Patients* 5%. *Certified* Medicaid; Medicare; VA.
Owner Privately owned.
Admissions Requirements Minimum age 18; Medical examination; Physician's request.
Staff Physicians (contracted); RNs 5 (ft), 1 (pt); LPNs 9 (ft), 10 (pt); Nurses' aides 47 (ft), 9 (pt); Physical therapists (contracted); Recreational therapists (contracted); Occupational therapists (contracted); Speech therapists (contracted); Activities coordinators 2 (ft), 1 (pt); Dietitians (contracted); Ophthalmologists (contracted); Podiatrists (contracted); Audiologists (contracted).
Facilities Dining room; Physical therapy room; Activities room; Crafts room; Laundry room; Barber/Beauty shop; 2 dayrooms; Screened front porch; Covered patio.
Activities Arts & crafts; Cards; Games; Reading groups; Prayer groups; Movies; Shopping trips; Dances/Social/Cultural gatherings; Intergenerational programs; Pet therapy; Outings to restaurants, county fair, parades; Quarterly family nights; Barbecues.

Stuart

Stuart Convalescent Center
1500 Palm Beach Rd, Stuart, FL 34994
(407) 283-5887
Admin W R Rogers. *Dir of Nursing* Marilyn Pelitera RN. *Medical Dir* Ronald Allison MD.
Licensure Skilled care; Intermediate care. *Beds* Swing beds SNF/ICF 182. *Certified* Medicaid; Medicare.
Owner Proprietary corp (Eden Park Management Inc).
Admissions Requirements Minimum age 18; Medical examination; Physician's request.
Staff Physicians 25 (pt); RNs 10 (ft), 4 (pt); LPNs 10 (ft), 1 (pt); Nurses' aides 59 (ft); Physical therapists 2 (pt); Recreational therapists 3 (ft); Occupational therapists 1 (pt); Speech therapists 1 (pt); Activities coordinators 1 (ft); Dietitians 1 (pt); Podiatrists 1 (pt); Audiologists 1 (pt).
Languages Spanish.
Facilities Dining room; Physical therapy room; Activities room; Chapel; Crafts room; Laundry room; Barber/Beauty shop; Rehabilitation feeding program; Rehabilitation program.
Activities Arts & crafts; Cards; Games; Reading groups; Prayer groups; Movies; Shopping trips; Dances/Social/Cultural gatherings; Intergenerational programs; Pet therapy.

Sun City Center

Lake Towers Health Center
101 Trinity Lakes Dr, Sun City Center, FL 33570
(813) 634-3347
Medical Dir Gaspar Salvador MD.
Licensure Skilled care. *Beds* 60. *Certified* Medicare.
Owner Proprietary corp.
Staff RNs 2 (ft), 3 (pt); LPNs 7 (ft), 11 (pt); Nurses' aides 13 (ft), 9 (pt); Activities coordinators 1 (ft).
Languages Spanish, French, Italian.

Facilities Dining room; Physical therapy room; Activities room; Crafts room; Barber/Beauty shop; Library.
Activities Arts & crafts; Cards; Games; Reading groups; Prayer groups; Movies; Shopping trips; Dances/Social/Cultural gatherings.

Sun Terrace Health Care Center
101 Trinity Lakes Dr, Sun City Center, FL 33570
(813) 634-3324
Admin Christine LaCourse.
Medical Dir Gaspar Salvador MD.
Licensure Skilled care; Intermediate care; Retirement. *Beds* 120. *Certified* Medicaid; Medicare.
Owner Proprietary corp.
Staff Physicians 3 (pt); RNs 4 (ft), 2 (pt); LPNs 8 (ft), 4 (pt); Nurses' aides 22 (ft); Activities coordinators 1 (ft).
Languages Spanish, French, Italian.
Facilities Dining room; Physical therapy room; Activities room; Crafts room; Barber/Beauty shop.
Activities Arts & crafts; Cards; Games; Reading groups; Prayer groups; Movies; Shopping trips; Dances/Social/Cultural gatherings.

Tallahassee

Capital Health Care Center
3333 Capital Medical Blvd, Tallahassee, FL 32308
(904) 877-4115
Admin Mary Evelyn Hoffhaus. *Dir of Nursing* Jane Esielionis. *Medical Dir* Chris Van Sickle.
Licensure Skilled care. *Beds* SNF 156. *Private Pay Patients* 48%. *Certified* Medicaid; Medicare.
Owner Proprietary corp (Vantage Healthcare).
Admissions Requirements Minimum age 16; Medical examination; Physician's request.
Staff Dietitians; Nurses' aides.
Facilities Dining room; Physical therapy room; Activities room; Crafts room; Laundry room; Barber/Beauty shop; Library.
Activities Arts & crafts; Cards; Games; Reading groups; Prayer groups; Movies; Shopping trips; Dances/Social/Cultural gatherings.

Centerville Care Center
2255 Centerville Rd, Tallahassee, FL 32317
(904) 366-4054
Beds 16.

Heritage Health Care Center
1815 Ginger Dr, Tallahassee, FL 32308
(904) 677-2177
Beds 67.

McCauley Cluster
1385 McCauley Rd, Tallahassee, FL 32308
(904) 487-1724
Licensure Intermediate care for mentally retarded. *Beds* 24.
Owner Proprietary corp.

Miracle Hill Nursing & Convalescent Home
1329 Abraham St, Tallahassee, FL 32304
(904) 224-8486
Medical Dir Dr Earl Britt & Dr Charlie Richardson.
Licensure Skilled care. *Beds* 60. *Certified* Medicaid.
Owner Nonprofit corp.
Admissions Requirements Minimum age 18; Medical examination.
Staff Physicians 3 (pt); RNs 2 (ft), 3 (pt); LPNs 5 (ft), 2 (pt); Nurses' aides 24 (ft), 4 (pt); Physical therapists 1 (pt); Reality therapists 1 (pt); Recreational therapists 1 (pt); Speech therapists 1 (pt); Activities coordinators 1 (ft); Dietitians 1 (pt); Podiatrists 1 (pt); Dentists 1 (pt).

Facilities Dining room; Activities room;
Crafts room; Laundry room; Barber/Beauty
shop.
Activities Arts & crafts; Games; Reading
groups; Prayer groups; Movies; Shopping
trips; Dances/Social/Cultural gatherings.

Tallahassee Convalescent Home
2510 Miccosukee Rd, Tallahassee, FL 32303
(904) 877-3131
Medical Dir William T Kepper MD.
Licensure Skilled care. Beds 72. Certified
Medicaid.
Owner Proprietary corp.
Admissions Requirements Medical
examination.
Staff Physicians 1 (pt); RNs 4 (ft), 3 (pt);
LPNs 4 (ft), 3 (pt); Nurses' aides 22 (ft), 5
(pt); Reality therapists; Recreational
therapists; Occupational therapists; Speech
therapists; Activities coordinators; Dietitians;
Podiatrists.
Languages French, Spanish.
Facilities Dining room; Laundry room;
Barber/Beauty shop; 2 Large TV rooms.
Activities Arts & crafts; Cards; Games;
Reading groups; Prayer groups; Movies;
Shopping trips; Dances/Social/Cultural
gatherings.

Tallahassee Developmental Center
455 Appleyard Dr, Tallahassee, FL 32304
(904) 575-0619
Admin Steven Taylor.
Medical Dir Javonna McEnchin.
Licensure Intermediate care for mentally
retarded. Beds ICF/MR 63. Certified
Medicaid.
Owner Nonprofit organization/foundation.
Staff RNs 2 (ft); LPNs 6 (ft); Nurses' aides 70
(ft), 10 (pt); Recreational therapists 2 (ft);
Dietitians 1 (ft).
Facilities Dining room.
Activities Arts & crafts; Cards; Games;
Movies; Shopping trips; Dances/Social/
Cultural gatherings.

Westminster Oaks Health Center
4449 Meandering Way, Tallahassee, FL 32308
(904) 878-1136
Admin Robert F Wernet Jr.
Medical Dir Leslie S Emhof.
Licensure Skilled care. Beds 60.
Owner Nonprofit corp.
Admissions Requirements Minimum age 62;
Medical examination; Physician's request.
Staff Physicians 1 (pt); RNs 5 (ft); LPNs 4
(ft); Nurses' aides 15 (ft); Physical therapists
1 (pt); Reality therapists 1 (pt); Recreational
therapists 1 (ft); Speech therapists 1 (pt);
Activities coordinators 1 (ft); Dietitians 1
(ft); Podiatrists 1 (pt); Audiologists 1 (pt);
Dentists 1 (pt).
Affiliation Presbyterian.
Facilities Dining room; Physical therapy
room; Activities room; Chapel; Crafts room;
Laundry room; Barber/Beauty shop; Library.
Activities Arts & crafts; Cards; Games;
Reading groups; Prayer groups; Movies;
Shopping trips; Dances/Social/Cultural
gatherings.

Tamarac

Tamarac Convalescent Center
7901 NW 88th Ave, Tamarac, FL 33321
(305) 722-9330
Admin Paul H Hladick.
Medical Dir Juan Lopez.
Licensure Skilled care; Intermediate care;
Alzheimer's care. Beds SNF 60; ICF 60; VA.
Certified Medicaid; Medicare.
Owner Proprietary corp (HBA Management
Inc).
Admissions Requirements Physician's request.
Staff Physicians 6 (pt); RNs 2 (ft), 9 (pt);
LPNs 7 (ft), 4 (pt); Nurses' aides 40 (ft);
Physical therapists 2 (ft); Reality therapists 1

(ft); Recreational therapists 1 (ft);
Occupational therapists 1 (pt); Speech
therapists 1 (pt); Activities coordinators 1
(ft); Dietitians 1 (pt); Ophthalmologists 1
(pt); Podiatrists 1 (pt); Dentists 1 (pt).
Languages German, Spanish, Italian, Hebrew,
Yiddish.
Facilities Dining room; Physical therapy
room; Activities room; Crafts room; Laundry
room; Barber/Beauty shop; Library.
Activities Arts & crafts; Cards; Games;
Reading groups; Prayer groups; Movies;
Shopping trips; Dances/Social/Cultural
gatherings; Musical entertainment.

Tampa

Ambrosia Home Inc
1709 Taliaferro Ave, Tampa, FL 33602
(813) 223-4623
Admin Bert Shepard. Dir of Nursing Alice
Miller RN BSN. Medical Dir Frederick
Taylor DO.
Licensure Skilled care; Alzheimer's care. Beds
SNF 80. Certified Medicaid.
Owner Proprietary corp.
Admissions Requirements Minimum age 16;
Medical examination; Physician's request.
Staff RNs 4 (ft); LPNs 8 (ft); Nurses' aides 20
(ft); Activities coordinators 2 (ft); Social
Services 1 (ft).
Languages Spanish.
Facilities Dining room; Activities room;
Laundry room; Barber/Beauty shop; Patios;
Porches.
Activities Arts & crafts; Cards; Games;
Reading groups; Prayer groups; Movies;
Shopping trips; Dances/Social/Cultural
gatherings; Intergenerational programs; Small
group programs.

Bay to Bay Nursing Center Inc
3401-3405 Bay to Bay Blvd, Tampa, FL
33629
(813) 839-5325
Licensure Skilled care. Beds 75. Certified
Medicaid.
Owner Proprietary corp.
Staff RNs 7 (ft); LPNs 6 (ft); Nurses' aides 18
(ft).

Cambridge Convalescent Center
9709 N Nebraska Ave, Tampa, FL 33612
(813) 935-2101
Admin James B Hereford. Dir of Nursing
Suzanne Litton RN. Medical Dir Henry
Gomez MD.
Licensure Skilled care. Beds SNF 70. Certified
Medicaid.
Owner Proprietary corp.
Admissions Requirements Minimum age 21;
Medical examination; Physician's request.
Staff Physicians 1 (ft); RNs 2 (ft), 1 (pt);
LPNs 4 (ft), 3 (pt); Nurses' aides 17 (ft), 6
(pt); Physical therapists 1 (pt); Reality
therapists 1 (pt); Speech therapists 1 (pt);
Activities coordinators 1 (ft); Dietitians 1
(pt); Ophthalmologists 1 (pt).
Languages Spanish.
Facilities Dining room; Physical therapy
room; Activities room; Crafts room; Laundry
room; Barber/Beauty shop; Library.
Activities Arts & crafts; Cards; Games;
Reading groups; Prayer groups; Movies;
Dances/Social/Cultural gatherings; Picnics.

Canterbury Towers
3501 Bayshore Blvd, Tampa, FL 33629
(813) 837-1083
Licensure Skilled care. Beds 40. Certified
Medicaid; Medicare.
Owner Nonprofit corp.
Staff RNs 4 (ft); LPNs 5 (ft); Nurses' aides 12
(ft).
Languages French, Spanish, German.

Home Association Inc
1203 22nd Ave, Tampa, FL 33605
(813) 229-6901
Admin Ralph G Clutton.
Medical Dir R Maurice Bonilla MD.
Licensure Skilled care; Intermediate care. Beds
SNF 41; ICF 56. Certified Medicaid.
Owner Nonprofit corp.
Admissions Requirements Minimum age 65;
Medical examination.
Staff Physicians 3 (pt); RNs 3 (ft); LPNs 9
(ft); Nurses' aides 33 (ft); Activities
coordinators 1 (ft); Dietitians 1 (ft);
Ophthalmologists 1 (ft).
Facilities Dining room; Activities room;
Chapel; Crafts room; Laundry room; Barber/
Beauty shop.
Activities Arts & crafts; Cards; Games; Prayer
groups; Shopping trips; Dances/Social/
Cultural gatherings; Dinner theater.

John Knox Village Medical Center
4100 E Fletcher Ave, Tampa, FL 33613
(813) 971-7038
Admin John T Holcombe. Dir of Nursing
Carolyn H Boylan RN. Medical Dir J R
Warren MD.
Licensure Skilled care; Alzheimer's care;
Retirement. Beds SNF 110. Certified
Medicare.
Owner Nonprofit corp.
Admissions Requirements Minimum age 16;
Medical examination; Physician's request.
Staff RNs 5 (ft), 1 (pt); LPNs 11 (ft), 1 (pt);
Nurses' aides 36 (ft); Physical therapists 1
(ft); Activities coordinators 2 (ft); Dietitians
1 (ft); Social service 1 (ft).
Languages Spanish.
Facilities Dining room; Physical therapy
room; Activities room; Crafts room; Laundry
room; Barber/Beauty shop; Library.
Activities Arts & crafts; Cards; Games;
Reading groups; Prayer groups; Movies;
Shopping trips; Dances/Social/Cultural
gatherings.

Lakeshore Villas Health Care Center
16002 Lakeshore Villas Dr, Tampa, FL 33613
(813) 968-5093, 264-0476 FAX
Admin Jack Freeman. Dir of Nursing Cary
Boylan. Medical Dir Dr Bruce Robinson.
Licensure Skilled care; Intermediate care;
Alzheimer's care; Retirement. Beds Swing
beds SNF/ICF 120. Private Pay Patients
52%. Certified Medicaid; Medicare.
Owner Privately owned.
Admissions Requirements Medical
examination; Physician's request.
Staff RNs 11 (ft), 2 (pt); LPNs 16 (ft), 5 (pt);
Nurses' aides 43 (ft); Recreational therapists
3 (ft); Activities coordinators 1 (ft);
Dietitians 1 (ft), 1 (pt).
Languages Spanish.
Facilities Dining room; Physical therapy
room; Activities room; Crafts room; Laundry
room; Barber/Beauty shop; Library;
Alzheimer's unit.
Activities Arts & crafts; Cards; Games;
Reading groups; Prayer groups; Movies;
Shopping trips; Dances/Social/Cultural
gatherings; Intergenerational programs; Pet
therapy.

Manhattan Convalescent Center
4610 S Manhattan Ave, Tampa, FL 33611
(813) 839-5311
Licensure Skilled care. Beds 179. Certified
Medicaid.
Owner Proprietary corp (Beverly Enterprises).
Staff RNs 7 (ft); LPNs 19 (ft); Nurses' aides
36 (ft).
Languages Spanish, French.

Medicenter of Tampa
4411 N Habana Ave, Tampa, FL 33614
(813) 872-2771
Admin Charles Hines. Dir of Nursing Chris
Cosgrove. Medical Dir Juan Valdez MD.

Licensure Skilled care; Intermediate care. Beds SNF 116; ICF 58. Certified Medicaid; Medicare.
Owner Proprietary corp (Hillhaven Corp).
Admissions Requirements Medical examination; Physician's request.
Staff RNs 12 (ft); LPNs 11 (ft); Nurses' aides; Physical therapists; Occupational therapists; Activities coordinators.
Languages Spanish.
Facilities Dining room; Physical therapy room; Activities room; Crafts room; Laundry room; Barber/Beauty shop.
Activities Arts & crafts; Cards; Games; Prayer groups; Movies; Dances/Social/Cultural gatherings.

Oakwood Park Su Casa
1514 E Chelsea, Tampa, FL 33610
(813) 238-6406
Admin Sandra Stewart. Dir of Nursing Diane Mackey. Medical Dir Dr Dunnsworth.
Licensure Skilled care; Intermediate care; Retirement. Beds SNF 41; ICF 187; Retirement 116. Private Pay Patients 5%. Certified Medicaid; Medicare.
Owner Nonprofit corp (Center for Independent Living).
Admissions Requirements Minimum age 16; Medical examination; Physician's request.
Staff RNs 9 (ft), 1 (pt); LPNs 11 (ft), 10 (pt); Nurses' aides 76 (ft), 8 (pt); Activities coordinators 2 (ft); Dietitians 1 (pt); Rehabilitation aides 4 (ft).
Languages Spanish.
Facilities Dining room; Activities room; Chapel; Crafts room; Laundry room; Barber/Beauty shop; Library; Gazebo; Garden; Patio.
Activities Arts & crafts; Cards; Games; Reading groups; Prayer groups; Movies; Shopping trips; Dances/Social/Cultural gatherings; Intergenerational programs; Pet therapy; Plays.

Padgett Nursing Home
5010 40th St, Tampa, FL 33610
(813) 626-7109
Admin Rubin E Padgett.
Licensure Skilled care; Intermediate care. Beds 100. Certified Medicaid; Medicare.
Owner Proprietary corp.
Staff Physicians 1 (ft); RNs 3 (ft); LPNs 8 (ft), 3 (pt); Nurses' aides 32 (ft), 1 (pt); Activities coordinators 2 (ft), 1 (pt); Dietitians 1 (pt); Podiatrists 1 (ft).
Languages Spanish.
Facilities Dining room; Physical therapy room; Activities room; Laundry room.
Activities Arts & crafts; Cards; Games; Reading groups; Prayer groups; Movies; Shopping trips; Dances/Social/Cultural gatherings.

Palm Garden—Tampa
3612 138th Ave, Tampa, FL 33612
(813) 972-8775, 972-8111 FAX
Admin Thomas J Bell. Dir of Nursing Betsy Miller RN. Medical Dir Robert Rosequist MD.
Licensure Skilled care; Intermediate care; Alzheimer's care. Beds SNF 15; ICF 88. Certified Medicaid; Medicare.
Owner Publicly owned (National Health Corp LTD).
Admissions Requirements Medical examination; Physician's request.
Staff Physicians (on call); Physical therapists 1 (ft), 2 (pt); Recreational therapists 2 (pt); Occupational therapists 1 (ft); Speech therapists 1 (pt); Activities coordinators 1 (ft); Dietitians 2 (ft); Ophthalmologists 2 (ft) (on call); Podiatrists 2 (ft) (on call); Audiologists 2 (ft) (on call).
Languages Spanish, French.
Facilities Dining room; Physical therapy room; Activities room; Chapel; Crafts room; Laundry room; Barber/Beauty shop; Speech

therapy department; Outdoor patio; Screened-in porches; Alarms on doors for Alzheimer's patients.
Activities Arts & crafts; Cards; Games; Reading groups; Prayer groups; Movies; Shopping trips; Dances/Social/Cultural gatherings; Pet therapy; Outings.

River Heights Nursing Home
2730 Ridgewood Ave, Tampa, FL 33602
(813) 223-1303
Medical Dir Dr Luis Crespo.
Licensure Skilled care. Beds 42. Certified Medicaid.
Owner Proprietary corp.
Admissions Requirements Minimum age 18; Medical examination; Physician's request.
Staff Physicians 1 (pt); RNs 4 (pt); LPNs 6 (pt); Nurses' aides 10 (pt); Activities coordinators 1 (pt); Dietitians 1 (pt).
Languages Italian, Spanish, Czech.
Facilities Dining room; Physical therapy room; Activities room; Crafts room; Laundry room; Barber/Beauty shop.
Activities Arts & crafts; Cards; Games; Reading groups; Prayer groups; Movies; Shopping trips; Dances/Social/Cultural gatherings.

St Francis Residence
301 E 7th Ave, Tampa, FL 33602
(613) 229-1978
Beds 17.

Tampa Health Care Center
2916 Habana Way, Tampa, FL 33614
(813) 876-5141
Admin Johnnie D Gonzalez. Dir of Nursing Cheryl Seronick RN. Medical Dir E A Perez MD.
Licensure Skilled care. Beds SNF 150; ICF/MR 30. Certified Medicaid; Medicare.
Owner Proprietary corp (Beverly Enterprises).
Admissions Requirements Physician's request.
Staff Physicians; RNs; LPNs; Nurses' aides; Physical therapists; Reality therapists; Recreational therapists; Occupational therapists; Speech therapists; Activities coordinators; Dietitians; Ophthalmologists; Podiatrists; Audiologists.
Languages Spanish, Italian.
Facilities Dining room; Physical therapy room; Activities room; Chapel; Crafts room; Laundry room; Barber/Beauty shop.
Activities Arts & crafts; Cards; Games; Reading groups; Prayer groups; Movies; Shopping trips; Dances/Social/Cultural gatherings; Intergenerational programs; Pet therapy.

Town & Country Convalescent Center
8720 Jackson Springs Rd, Tampa, FL 33615
(813) 885-6053, 886-7364 FAX
Admin Thomas Robbins. Dir of Nursing Irene Leeds. Medical Dir Dr Azan.
Licensure Skilled care; Intermediate care. Beds SNF 34; ICF 86. Private Pay Patients 25%. Certified Medicaid; Medicare.
Owner Proprietary corp (Hillhaven Corp).
Admissions Requirements Medical examination; Physician's request.
Staff Physicians 1 (ft); RNs 4 (ft); LPNs 12 (ft), 2 (pt); Nurses' aides 28 (ft), 8 (pt); Physical therapists 1 (ft); Occupational therapists 1 (ft); Speech therapists 1 (ft); Activities coordinators 1 (ft); Dietitians 1 (ft); Podiatrists 1 (ft).
Languages Spanish.
Facilities Dining room; Physical therapy room; Activities room; Crafts room; Laundry room; Barber/Beauty shop; Courtyard.
Activities Arts & crafts; Cards; Games; Reading groups; Prayer groups; Shopping trips; Dances/Social/Cultural gatherings; Intergenerational programs; Pet therapy.

University Park Convalescent Center
1818 E Fletcher Ave, Tampa, FL 33612
(813) 971-2383
Medical Dir Aldo J Almaguer MD.
Licensure Skilled care. Beds 266. Certified Medicaid; Medicare.
Owner Proprietary corp.
Admissions Requirements Minimum age 17; Medical examination; Physician's request.
Staff RNs 12 (ft), 3 (pt); LPNs 23 (ft), 2 (pt); Nurses' aides 95 (ft); Physical therapists 1 (pt); Occupational therapists 1 (pt); Speech therapists 1 (pt); Activities coordinators 2 (ft); Dietitians 1 (pt); Podiatrists 1 (pt); Audiologists 1 (pt); Dentists 1 (pt).
Facilities Dining room; Physical therapy room; Activities room; Chapel; Barber/Beauty shop; Library.
Activities Arts & crafts; Cards; Games; Reading groups; Prayer groups; Movies; Shopping trips; Dances/Social/Cultural gatherings.

Wellington Manor
10049 N Florida Ave, Tampa, FL 33612
(813) 935-3183
Licensure Skilled care. Beds 180. Certified Medicaid.
Owner Proprietary corp (Beverly Enterprises).
Staff RNs 4 (ft); LPNs 17 (ft); Nurses' aides 35 (ft).

Woodlands Nursing Center
13606 N 46th St, Tampa, FL 33613
(613) 977-4214
Beds 61.

Tarpon Springs

Central Park Lodge—Tarpon Springs
900 Beckett Way, Tarpon Springs, FL 34689
(813) 934-0876
Admin Dennis J Norton. Dir of Nursing June Masour. Medical Dir David Lindberg MD.
Licensure Skilled care; Intermediate care; Alzheimer's care. Beds Swing beds SNF/ICF 120. Private Pay Patients 50%. Certified Medicaid; Medicare.
Owner Proprietary corp (Central Park Lodges).
Admissions Requirements Minimum age 16.
Staff Physicians; RNs; LPNs; Nurses' aides.
Languages French, Spanish, Greek.
Facilities Dining room; Physical therapy room; Activities room; Crafts room; Laundry room; Barber/Beauty shop; Library; Enclosed courtyard.
Activities Arts & crafts; Cards; Games; Reading groups; Prayer groups; Movies; Shopping trips; Dances/Social/Cultural gatherings; Intergenerational programs; Pet therapy.

Tarpon Health Care Center
501 S Walton Ave, Tarpon Springs, FL 33589
(813) 938-2814
Licensure Skilled care. Beds 120. Certified Medicaid.
Owner Proprietary corp (Beverly Enterprises).
Staff RNs 2 (ft); LPNs 2 (ft); Nurses' aides 26 (ft).

Tarpon Springs Convalescent Center
515 Chesapeake Dr, Tarpon Springs, FL 33589
(813) 934-4629
Admin Barbara Johnson.
Medical Dir Dr Sanchez.
Licensure Skilled care; Alzheimer's care. Beds 120. Certified Medicaid; Medicare.
Owner Proprietary corp.
Admissions Requirements Minimum age 18; Medical examination; Physician's request.
Staff RNs 2 (ft), 4 (pt); LPNs 7 (ft), 5 (pt); Nurses' aides 40 (ft), 1 (pt); Physical therapists 1 (pt); Occupational therapists 1 (pt); Speech therapists 1 (pt); Activities

coordinators 1 (ft); Dietitians 1 (pt); Ophthalmologists 1 (pt); Podiatrists 1 (pt); Dentists 1 (pt).
Languages Greek.
Facilities Dining room; Physical therapy room; Activities room; Chapel; Crafts room; Laundry room; Barber/Beauty shop; Library.
Activities Arts & crafts; Cards; Games; Reading groups; Prayer groups; Movies; Shopping trips; Dances/Social/Cultural gatherings.

Tavernier

Plantation Key Convalescent Center
46 High Point Rd, Tavernier, FL 33070
(305) 652-3021
Beds 120.

Thonotosassa

Lowe's Nursing & Convalescent Home
PO Box 187, Rte 1, Thonotosassa, FL 33592
(813) 986-4848
Admin Ed Vail. *Dir of Nursing* M Haffner. *Medical Dir* E A Perez MD.
Licensure Skilled care; Intermediate care. *Beds* SNF; ICF 180. *Certified* Medicaid; Medicare.
Owner Proprietary corp.
Admissions Requirements Medical examination.
Staff RNs 8 (ft); LPNs 22 (ft); Nurses' aides 50 (ft); Activities coordinators 2 (ft); Dietitians 1 (pt).
Languages Spanish.
Facilities Dining room; Physical therapy room; Activities room; Laundry room; Barber/Beauty shop.
Activities Arts & crafts; Cards; Games; Reading groups; Prayer groups; Movies; Shopping trips; Dances/Social/Cultural gatherings.

Titusville

Titusville Nursing & Convalescent Center
1705 Jess Parrish Ct, Titusville, FL 32796
(305) 269-5720
Admin Diane Kendrick. *Dir of Nursing* Pearlie Jackson. *Medical Dir* Victor Boodhoo MD.
Licensure Skilled care. *Beds* SNF 157. *Certified* Medicaid; Medicare.
Owner Proprietary corp (Hillhaven Corp).
Admissions Requirements Minimum age 21; Medical examination.
Staff Physicians 11 (pt); RNs 2 (pt); LPNs 16 (pt); Nurses' aides 35 (pt); Physical therapists 1 (pt); Occupational therapists 1 (pt); Speech therapists 1 (pt); Activities coordinators 2 (pt); Dietitians 1 (pt); Ophthalmologists 2 (pt); Podiatrists 1 (pt).
Languages French, Spanish.
Facilities Dining room; Physical therapy room; Activities room; Chapel; Crafts room; Laundry room; Barber/Beauty shop.
Activities Arts & crafts; Cards; Games; Reading groups; Prayer groups; Movies; Shopping trips; Dances/Social/Cultural gatherings.

Vista Manor
1550 Jess Parish Ct, Titusville, FL 32796
(407) 269-2200
Admin Kay A Cline. *Dir of Nursing* Frances E Myers. *Medical Dir* Onfre P Carrillo.
Licensure Skilled care; Intermediate care. *Beds* Swing beds SNF/ICF 120. *Private Pay Patients* 10%. *Certified* Medicaid; Medicare.
Owner Proprietary corp (Beverly Enterprises).
Admissions Requirements Minimum age 16; Medical examination; Physician's request.
Staff Physicians 11 (pt); RNs 2 (ft), 1 (pt); LPNs 15 (ft), 3 (pt); Nurses' aides 51 (ft), 4 (pt); Physical therapists 1 (ft); Occupational

therapists 1 (pt); Speech therapists 1 (pt); Activities coordinators 1 (ft), 1 (pt); Dietitians 1 (pt); Ophthalmologists 1 (pt); Podiatrists 1 (pt); Audiologists 1 (pt).
Languages Spanish, German.
Facilities Dining room; Physical therapy room; Activities room; Crafts room; Laundry room; Barber/Beauty shop; Library.
Activities Arts & crafts; Cards; Games; Reading groups; Prayer groups; Movies; Shopping trips; Dances/Social/Cultural gatherings; Intergenerational programs; Pet therapy; Exercise/Walking programs.

Trenton

Medic-Ayers Nursing Center
606 NE 7th St, Trenton, FL 32693
(904) 463-7101
Beds 60.
Owner Proprietary corp.

Venice

Heritage Healthcare Center Venice
1026 Albee Farm Rd, Venice, FL 34292
(613) 484-0425
Beds 67.

Pinebrook Place Healthcare Center
1240 Pinebrook Rd, Venice, FL 33595
(813) 488-6733
Admin Joyce Coleman. *Dir of Nursing* Jimmie Coffey RN BSN. *Medical Dir* Dr Thomas McNaughton.
Licensure Skilled care; Intermediate care; Alzheimer's care. *Beds* SNF 20; ICF 100. *Certified* Medicaid; Medicare.
Owner Proprietary corp.
Admissions Requirements Medical examination; Physician's request.
Staff Physicians; RNs; LPNs; Nurses' aides; Physical therapists; Reality therapists; Recreational therapists; Occupational therapists; Speech therapists; Activities coordinators; Dietitians; Ophthalmologists; Podiatrists; Dentists.
Languages German, French, Polish.
Facilities Dining room; Physical therapy room; Activities room; Chapel; Crafts room; Laundry room; Barber/Beauty shop; Library; Private dining room; Family room; Enclosed courtyards.
Activities Arts & crafts; Cards; Games; Reading groups; Prayer groups; Movies; Shopping trips; Dances/Social/Cultural gatherings.

Southwest Florida Retirement Center
910 Tamiami Trail S, Venice, FL 34285
(613) 484-9753
Admin Joe Keenan. *Dir of Nursing* Rosemary V Lane RN.
Licensure Skilled care; Retirement. *Beds* SNF 60; Retirement 400. *Private Pay Patients* 75%. *Certified* Medicaid; Medicare.
Owner Nonprofit organization/foundation.
Admissions Requirements Medical examination; Physician's request.
Staff Physicians 1 (ft); RNs 5 (ft), 2 (pt); LPNs 4 (ft), 6 (pt); Nurses' aides 20 (ft), 1 (pt); Physical therapists 1 (pt); Reality therapists 1 (pt); Recreational therapists 1 (ft); Occupational therapists 1 (pt); Speech therapists 1 (pt); Activities coordinators 1 (ft); Dietitians 1 (ft); Ophthalmologists 1 (pt); Podiatrists 1 (pt); Audiologists 1 (pt).
Languages Mexican, Spanish, German, Yiddish.
Affiliation Lutheran.
Facilities Dining room; Physical therapy room; Activities room; Chapel; Crafts room; Laundry room; Barber/Beauty shop; Library; Enclosed courtyard; Screened-in porch; Separate feeding room.

Activities Arts & crafts; Cards; Games; Reading groups; Prayer groups; Movies; Shopping trips; Shopping trips; Intergenerational programs; Pet therapy.

Venice Nursing Pavilion—North
437 S Nokomis Ave, Venice, FL 34285
(813) 488-9696
Admin Jack C Rutenberg. *Dir of Nursing* Evelyn Sembrot RN. *Medical Dir* Samuel E Kaplan MD.
Licensure Skilled care; Alzheimer's care. *Beds* SNF 178. *Certified* Medicaid; Medicare.
Owner Proprietary corp (Central Park Lodges Inc).
Staff RNs 10 (ft), 2 (pt); LPNs 10 (ft), 6 (pt); Nurses' aides 34 (ft), 6 (pt); Activities coordinators 3 (ft); Dietitians 1 (ft).
Languages Italian, Spanish, Polish, French, German.
Facilities Employee child day care.
Activities Arts & crafts; Cards; Games; Reading groups; Prayer groups; Movies; Shopping trips; Dances/Social/Cultural gatherings; Wine & cheese; Ice cream socials; Talent shows.

Venice Nursing Pavilion—South
200 Field Ave E, Venice, FL 33595
(813) 484-2477
Admin Yolanda Brewer. *Dir of Nursing* Ruth Perelli. *Medical Dir* Dr Kaplan.
Licensure Skilled care. *Beds* SNF 120. *Certified* Medicaid; Medicare.
Owner Proprietary corp (Fl Life Care).
Staff RNs 12 (ft); LPNs 6 (ft); Nurses' aides 26 (ft).
Languages Spanish.

Vero Beach

Florida Baptist Retirement Center Nursing Facility
1006 33rd St, Vero Beach, FL 32960
(305) 567-5248
Admin William H Lord.
Medical Dir Carol Burdette.
Licensure Skilled care; ACLF 34; Retirement; Alzheimer's care. *Beds* SNF 24; ACLF 34.
Owner Nonprofit corp.
Staff RNs 5 (ft), 24 (pt); LPNs 2 (ft), 24 (pt); Nurses' aides 9 (ft), 24 (pt); Activities coordinators 1 (ft), 24 (pt).
Affiliation Baptist.
Facilities Dining room; Activities room; Crafts room; Laundry room; Barber/Beauty shop.
Activities Arts & crafts; Prayer groups; Movies; Dances/Social/Cultural gatherings; Tapes.

Indian River Village Care Center
1310 37th St, Vero Beach, FL 32960
(305) 569-5107
Beds 66.

Royal Palm Convalescent Center
2180 10th Ave, Vero Beach, FL 32960
(305) 567-5166
Medical Dir Dr Donald Gold.
Licensure Skilled care. *Beds* 72. *Certified* Medicare.
Owner Proprietary corp.
Admissions Requirements Minimum age 16.
Staff Nurses' aides 32 (ft); Dietitians 9 (ft).
Languages German.
Facilities Dining room; Physical therapy room; Activities room; Crafts room; Laundry room; Barber/Beauty shop; Library.
Activities Arts & crafts; Cards; Games; Reading groups; Prayer groups; Movies; Shopping trips; Dances/Social/Cultural gatherings.

Vero Beach Care Center Inc
3663 15th Ave, Vero Beach, FL 32960
(407) 567-2552

Admin Virginia Rivers. *Dir of Nursing* Lorraine Dove RN. *Medical Dir* William Panakos MD.
Licensure Skilled care. *Beds* SNF 110. *Private Pay Patients* 40%. *Certified* Medicaid; Medicare.
Owner Proprietary corp.
Admissions Requirements Medical examination; Physician's request.
Staff RNs; LPNs; Nurses' aides; Activities coordinators.
Languages Spanish.
Facilities Dining room; Physical therapy room; Activities room; Laundry room; Barber/Beauty shop.
Activities Arts & crafts; Cards; Games; Reading groups; Prayer groups; Movies; Shopping trips; Pet therapy; Current events.

Wachula

Hardee Manor Care Center
401 Orange Pl, Wachula, FL 33873
(813) 773-3231
Admin Ruth A Lewis.
Medical Dir Felix E Perez MD.
Licensure Skilled care. *Beds* 60. *Certified* Medicaid; Medicare.
Owner Proprietary corp.
Staff RNs 3 (ft); LPNs 6 (ft), 1 (pt); Nurses' aides 15 (ft), 6 (pt); Physical therapists; Speech therapists; Activities coordinators 1 (ft).
Languages Spanish.
Facilities Dining room; Physical therapy room; Activities room; Chapel; Laundry room; Barber/Beauty shop.
Activities Arts & crafts; Games; Prayer groups; Movies; Dances/Social/Cultural gatherings.

West Melbourne

West Melbourne Health Care Center
2125 W New Haven Ave, West Melbourne, FL 32904
(305) 725-7360
Admin Lynette Reichner. *Dir of Nursing* Susan Burch RN. *Medical Dir* Dr Hugo Dujovne.
Licensure Skilled care; Intermediate care; Alzheimer's care. *Beds* SNF 120; ICF. *Certified* Medicaid; Medicare.
Owner Proprietary corp (Waverly Group).
Admissions Requirements Minimum age 18; Medical examination; Physician's request.
Staff RNs 9 (ft), 1 (pt); LPNs 8 (ft), 3 (pt); Nurses' aides 57 (ft), 5 (pt); Activities coordinators 1 (ft), 1 (pt); Dietitians 1 (ft).
Facilities Dining room; Physical therapy room; Activities room; Laundry room; Barber/Beauty shop; Library.
Activities Arts & crafts; Cards; Games; Reading groups; Prayer groups; Movies; Shopping trips; Dances/Social/Cultural gatherings.

West Palm Beach

Convalescent Center of the Palm Beaches
300 15th St, West Palm Beach, FL 33401
(305) 832-6409
Medical Dir Dr Wm Adkins.
Licensure Skilled care. *Beds* 99. *Certified* Medicaid; Medicare; VA Contract.
Owner Proprietary corp (Hillhaven Corp).
Admissions Requirements Medical examination.
Staff RNs 4 (ft), 1 (pt); LPNs 11 (ft), 1 (pt); Nurses' aides 29 (ft), 6 (pt); Physical therapists 1 (ft); Occupational therapists 1 (pt); Speech therapists 1 (pt); Activities coordinators 1 (ft); Dietitians 1 (pt); Ophthalmologists 1 (pt); Podiatrists 1 (pt); Dentists 1 (pt).

Facilities Dining room; Physical therapy room; Activities room; Crafts room; Laundry room; Barber/Beauty shop.
Activities Arts & crafts; Cards; Games; Reading groups; Prayer groups; Movies.

Darcy Hall
2170 Palm Beach Lakes Blvd, West Palm Beach, FL 33409
(407) 683-3333, 683-5625 FAX
Admin Jean DePonte. *Dir of Nursing* Judy Hatch. *Medical Dir* Rozanne Wilson.
Licensure Skilled care; Alzheimer's care. *Beds* SNF 220. *Private Pay Patients* 42%. *Certified* Medicaid; Medicare.
Owner Proprietary corp.
Staff Physicians 1 (pt); RNs 8 (ft); LPNs 20 (ft); Nurses' aides 66 (ft); Physical therapists 1 (ft); Recreational therapists 1 (ft); Occupational therapists 1 (ft); Speech therapists 1 (ft); Activities coordinators 3 (ft); Dietitians 1 (ft).
Languages French, Spanish, German.
Activities Arts & crafts; Cards; Games; Reading groups; Prayer groups; Movies; Shopping trips; Dances/Social/Cultural gatherings; Intergenerational programs; Pet therapy; Resident council.

Haverhill Care Center
5065 Wallis Rd, West Palm Beach, FL 33415
(407) 689-1799
Admin Elizabeth Shugar RN C. *Dir of Nursing* Maureen Soon RN. *Medical Dir* Dr David Stern.
Licensure Skilled care; Intermediate care. *Beds* SNF 28; ICF 92. *Private Pay Patients* 20%. *Certified* Medicaid; Medicare.
Owner Proprietary corp (Beverly Enterprises).
Admissions Requirements Minimum age 21; Medical examination.
Staff Physicians 2 (ft), 3 (pt); RNs 5 (ft), 2 (pt); LPNs 8 (ft), 6 (pt); Nurses' aides 29 (ft), 6 (pt); Physical therapists 1 (ft); Recreational therapists 1 (ft); Occupational therapists 1 (ft); Speech therapists 1 (ft); Activities coordinators 1 (ft); Dietitians 2 (ft); Ophthalmologists 1 (ft); Podiatrists 1 (ft); Audiologists 1 (pt).
Languages Spanish, French.
Facilities Dining room; Physical therapy room; Activities room; Laundry room; Barber/Beauty shop; Rehabilitation/Dining room.
Activities Arts & crafts; Cards; Games; Reading groups; Prayer groups; Movies; Shopping trips; Dances/Social/Cultural gatherings; Intergenerational programs; Pet therapy.

King David Center at Palm Beach
1101 54th St, West Palm Beach, FL 33407
(305) 844-4343
Admin Eugene Kruger. *Dir of Nursing* Jocelyn Cameau RN. *Medical Dir* Steven L Kanner DO.
Licensure Skilled care. *Beds* 191. *Certified* Medicaid; Medicare.
Owner Proprietary corp.
Admissions Requirements Medical examination; Physician's request.
Staff RNs 9 (ft); LPNs 18 (ft); Nurses' aides 65 (ft); Physical therapists 1 (ft); Occupational therapists 1 (ft); Speech therapists 1 (ft); Activities coordinators 1 (ft), 2 (pt).
Languages Italian, Spanish.
Affiliation Jewish.
Facilities Dining room; Physical therapy room; Activities room; Laundry room; Barber/Beauty shop.
Activities Arts & crafts; Cards; Games; Reading groups; Prayer groups; Movies; Dances/Social/Cultural gatherings.

Lakeside Health Center
2501 Australian Ave, West Palm Beach, FL 33407
(407) 655-7780, 655-9894 FAX
Admin Kathleen M Morrissey. *Dir of Nursing* Norma Gordon. *Medical Dir* Dr Dandiya.
Licensure Skilled care. *Beds* SNF 97. *Private Pay Patients* 11%. *Certified* Medicaid; Medicare.
Owner Proprietary corp (National Heritage).
Staff RNs 3 (ft), 1 (pt); LPNs 6 (ft), 2 (pt); Nurses' aides 22 (ft), 5 (pt); Physical therapists 1 (ft); Occupational therapists 1 (ft); Speech therapists 1 (ft); Activities coordinators 2 (pt); Dietitians 1 (ft); Ophthalmologists 1 (ft); Podiatrists 1 (ft); Audiologists 1 (ft).
Facilities Dining room; Physical therapy room; Activities room; Laundry room; Barber/Beauty shop.
Activities Arts & crafts; Cards; Games; Reading groups; Prayer groups; Movies; Shopping trips; Dances/Social/Cultural gatherings; Pet therapy.

Lourdes-Noreen McKeen Residence for Geriatric Care Inc
315 S Flagler Dr, West Palm Beach, FL 33401
(407) 655-8544, 650-8944 FAX
Admin Sr M Fidelis. *Dir of Nursing* Janice Peck. *Medical Dir* Dr Thomas E Murphy.
Licensure Skilled care; Retirement. *Beds* SNF 120; Retirement 198. *Certified* Medicaid; Medicare.
Owner Nonprofit corp.
Admissions Requirements Minimum age 65; Physician's request.
Staff Physicians; RNs; LPNs; Nurses' aides; Physical therapists; Reality therapists; Recreational therapists; Occupational therapists; Speech therapists; Activities coordinators; Dietitians; Podiatrists; Audiologists.
Languages Spanish.
Affiliation Roman Catholic.
Facilities Dining room; Physical therapy room; Activities room; Chapel; Crafts room; Laundry room; Barber/Beauty shop; Library; Coffee shop; Outside walking areas.
Activities Arts & crafts; Cards; Games; Reading groups; Prayer groups; Movies; Shopping trips; Dances/Social/Cultural gatherings; Pet therapy; Bus rides; Picnics.

Joseph L Morse Geriatric Center
4847 Fred Gladstone Dr, West Palm Beach, FL 33417
(407) 471-5111, 640-9209 FAX
Admin E Drew Gackenheimer. *Dir of Nursing* Elise I Gropper MS RN CS. *Medical Dir* Jamiy Bensimon MD.
Licensure Skilled care; Rehabilitation SNF. *Beds* SNF 240; Rehabilitation SNF 40. *Certified* Medicaid.
Owner Nonprofit organization/foundation.
Admissions Requirements Minimum age 16.
Staff Physicians 1 (ft); RNs 18 (ft), 3 (pt); LPNs 22 (ft), 4 (pt); Nurses' aides 102 (ft), 18 (pt); Physical therapists 2 (ft), 1 (pt); Recreational therapists 4 (ft), 1 (pt); Occupational therapists 1 (pt); Speech therapists 1 (pt); Activities coordinators 1 (ft); Dietitians 1 (ft); Ophthalmologists 1 (pt); Podiatrists 2 (pt); Audiologists 1 (pt).
Facilities Dining room; Physical therapy room; Activities room; Chapel; Crafts room; Laundry room; Barber/Beauty shop; Library; Deli; Day care.
Activities Arts & crafts; Cards; Games; Movies; Shopping trips; Dances/Social/ Cultural gatherings; Pet therapy.

Palm Beach County Home & General Care Facility
1200 45th St, West Palm Beach, FL 33407
(407) 842-6111
Admin Doris L Orestis. *Dir of Nursing* Karen Wigren. *Medical Dir* Dr Adil Sokmensuer.

Licensure Skilled care; Intermediate care; AIDS unit; Alzheimer's care. *Beds* SNF 128; ICF 82; AIDS unit 30. *Private Pay Patients* 0%. *Certified* Medicaid; Medicare.
Owner Publicly owned.
Admissions Requirements Minimum age 16; Medical examination; Physician's request.
Staff Physicians 1 (ft), 1 (pt); RNs 27 (ft), 1 (pt); LPNs 16 (ft), 4 (pt); Nurses' aides 109 (ft), 4 (pt); Physical therapists 1 (pt); Recreational therapists 1 (ft); Occupational therapists 2 (ft), 1 (pt); Speech therapists 1 (pt); Activities coordinators 1 (ft); Dietitians 1 (pt).
Languages Spanish, French, Italian.
Facilities Dining room; Physical therapy room; Activities room; Crafts room; Laundry room; Barber/Beauty shop; Fitness trail; Alzheimer's unit.
Activities Arts & crafts; Cards; Games; Reading groups; Prayer groups; Movies; Shopping trips; Dances/Social/Cultural gatherings; Intergenerational programs; Pet therapy; Lunches; Swimming.

West Palm Beach Village Care Center
1626 Davis Rd, West Palm Beach, FL 33406
(407) 439-8897
Admin David Deuschle.
Medical Dir Robert Campetilli.
Licensure Skilled care. *Beds* SNF 120. *Certified* Medicaid; Medicare.
Owner Proprietary corp.
Admissions Requirements Medical examination.
Staff Physicians; RNs; LPNs; Nurses' aides; Physical therapists; Recreational therapists; Occupational therapists; Speech therapists; Activities coordinators; Dietitians; Ophthalmologists; Podiatrists; Audiologists.
Languages Spanish.
Facilities Dining room; Physical therapy room; Activities room; Crafts room; Laundry room; Barber/Beauty shop; Park.
Activities Arts & crafts; Cards; Games; Reading groups; Prayer groups; Movies; Dances/Social/Cultural gatherings; Intergenerational programs; Pet therapy.

West Vero Beach

Indian River Estates Medical Facility
2200 Indian River Creek Blvd, West Vero Beach, FL 32966
(305) 562-7400

Wildwood

WECARE Nursing Center
490 S Old Wire Rd, Wildwood, FL 32785
(904) 748-3327, 748-7609 FAX
Admin Cathy Bowlin. *Dir of Nursing* Cynthia Griffin. *Medical Dir* C R Wiley MD.
Licensure Skilled care; Alzheimer's care. *Beds* SNF 180. *Private Pay Patients* 30%. *Certified* Medicaid; Medicare.
Owner Proprietary corp.
Admissions Requirements Minimum age 18; Medical examination.
Staff RNs 6 (ft), 4 (pt); LPNs 19 (ft), 6 (pt); Nurses' aides 66 (ft), 4 (pt).
Languages Spanish.
Facilities Dining room; Physical therapy room; Activities room; Chapel; Crafts room; Laundry room; Barber/Beauty shop; Library.
Activities Arts & crafts; Cards; Games; Reading groups; Prayer groups; Movies; Shopping trips; Dances/Social/Cultural gatherings; Intergenerational programs; Pet therapy.

Williston

Oakview Regional Care Center
300 NW 1st Ave, Williston, FL 32696
(904) 528-3561, 528-3312 FAX

Admin L Chuck Wilcox. *Dir of Nursing* Donna Nussel. *Medical Dir* T M Cometa MD.
Licensure Skilled care; Intermediate care. *Beds* Swing beds SNF/ICF 180. *Private Pay Patients* 9%. *Certified* Medicaid; Medicare.
Owner Nonprofit corp (National Medical Associates Inc).
Admissions Requirements Minimum age 18; Medical examination.
Staff RNs 4 (ft); LPNs 20 (ft), 4 (pt); Nurses' aides 79 (ft); Physical therapists; Activities coordinators 1 (ft); Dietitians.
Languages Vietnamese.
Facilities Dining room; Physical therapy room; Activities room; Laundry room; Barber/Beauty shop; Library.
Activities Arts & crafts; Cards; Games; Reading groups; Prayer groups; Movies; Dances/Social/Cultural gatherings; Intergenerational programs; Pet therapy.

Winter Garden

Quality Health of Orange County Inc
941 E Hwy 50, Winter Garden, FL 34787
(407) 877-6636
Admin Tarry E Harbilas. *Dir of Nursing* Cynthia Piper. *Medical Dir* Dr Razia Malik.
Licensure Skilled care; Intermediate care. *Beds* Swing beds SNF/ICF 120. *Certified* Medicaid; Medicare.
Owner Proprietary corp.
Admissions Requirements Medical examination; Physician's request.
Staff Physicians 12 (pt); RNs 5 (ft), 2 (pt); LPNs 8 (ft), 2 (pt); Nurses' aides 35 (ft), 2 (pt); Physical therapists 4 (pt); Reality therapists 1 (pt); Recreational therapists 1 (pt); Occupational therapists 1 (pt); Speech therapists 1 (pt); Activities coordinators 1 (ft); Dietitians 1 (ft); Ophthalmologists 3 (pt); Podiatrists 1 (pt); Audiologists 2 (pt); Dentists 2 (pt).
Languages Spanish.
Facilities Dining room; Physical therapy room; Activities room; Crafts room; Laundry room; Barber/Beauty shop.
Activities Arts & crafts; Cards; Games; Reading groups; Prayer groups; Movies; Shopping trips; Dances/Social/Cultural gatherings.

West Orange Manor
122 E Division St, Winter Garden, FL 32787
(305) 656-3810
Licensure Skilled care. *Beds* 118. *Certified* Medicaid.
Owner Publicly owned.
Staff RNs 5 (ft); LPNs 10 (ft); Nurses' aides 37 (ft).

Winter Garden Health Care Center
1600 W Hwy 50, Winter Garden, FL 32787
(407) 877-2394
Admin Brian C Pollett. *Dir of Nursing* Mary Ann Daniels. *Medical Dir* Dr Ignacio Hidalgo.
Licensure Skilled care. *Beds* SNF 120. *Private Pay Patients* 8%. *Certified* Medicaid; Medicare.
Owner Proprietary corp (Beverly Enterprises).
Admissions Requirements Medical examination; Physician's request.
Facilities Dining room; Physical therapy room; Activities room; Crafts room; Laundry room; Barber/Beauty shop; Library.
Activities Arts & crafts; Cards; Games; Reading groups; Prayer groups; Movies; Pet therapy.

Winter Haven

Brandywyne Convalescent Center
1601 N Lake Miriam Dr, Winter Haven, FL 33680
(613) 293-1989
Beds 62.

Grovemont Nursing & Rehabilitation
202 Ave "O" NE, Winter Haven, FL 33881
(813) 293-3103
Admin Jerry Pyle. *Dir of Nursing* Patricia Andrews. *Medical Dir* Michael Carey MD.
Licensure Skilled care; Alzheimer's care. *Beds* SNF 144. *Certified* Medicaid; Medicare.
Owner Proprietary corp (Unicare).
Admissions Requirements Minimum age 18; Medical examination; Physician's request.
Staff RNs 4 (ft), 3 (pt); LPNs 11 (ft), 3 (pt); Nurses' aides 43 (ft), 2 (pt); Physical therapists 1 (ft); Occupational therapists 1 (pt); Speech therapists 1 (ft); Activities coordinators 2 (ft); Dietitians 1 (ft); Ophthalmologists 2 (pt); Podiatrists 1 (pt); Dentists 1 (pt).
Facilities Dining room; Physical therapy room; Activities room; Chapel; Crafts room; Laundry room; Barber/Beauty shop.
Activities Arts & crafts; Cards; Games; Reading groups; Prayer groups; Movies; Shopping trips; Dances/Social/Cultural gatherings.

Palm Garden of Winter Haven
1120 Cypress Garden Blvd, Winter Haven, FL 33884
(813) 293-3100, 299-6691 FAX
Admin Leslie D Fraher. *Dir of Nursing* Laverne Bryan RN. *Medical Dir* Dr Garrett Snipes.
Licensure Skilled care; Intermediate care. *Private Pay Patients* 33%. *Certified* Medicaid; Medicare.
Owner Proprietary corp (Florida Convalescent Centers).
Admissions Requirements Medical examination; Physician's request.
Staff RNs; LPNs; Nurses' aides; Activities coordinators.
Facilities Dining room; Physical therapy room; Activities room; Chapel; Laundry room; Barber/Beauty shop.
Activities Arts & crafts; Cards; Games; Reading groups; Prayer groups; Movies; Intergenerational programs; Pet therapy.

Winter Park

Americana Healthcare Center of Winter Park
2075 Loch Lomond Dr, Winter Park, FL 32792
(305) 628-5418
Admin Frank S Bellinger. *Dir of Nursing* Jill Miller RN. *Medical Dir* Dr E Forrester.
Licensure Skilled care. *Beds* SNF 135. *Certified* Medicaid; Medicare.
Owner Proprietary corp.
Admissions Requirements Minimum age 16; Medical examination; Physician's request.
Staff RNs 10 (ft), 2 (pt); LPNs 11 (ft), 2 (pt); Nurses' aides 41 (ft), 5 (pt); Physical therapists; Occupational therapists; Speech therapists; Activities coordinators; Dietitians.
Languages German, Spanish.
Facilities Dining room; Physical therapy room; Activities room; Laundry room; Barber/Beauty shop; Occupational therapy room.
Activities Arts & crafts; Cards; Games; Reading groups; Prayer groups; Movies; Shopping trips; Dances/Social/Cultural gatherings.

Mary Lee Depugh Nursing Home
550 W Morse Blvd, Winter Park, FL 32789
(305) 644-6634
Medical Dir Dr Kenneth Richards.

Licensure Skilled care. *Beds* 40. *Certified* Medicaid.
Owner Nonprofit corp.
Admissions Requirements Minimum age 18; Medical examination; Physician's request.
Staff RNs 2 (ft); LPNs 5 (ft), 1 (pt); Nurses' aides 12 (ft), 2 (pt); Activities coordinators 1 (ft); Dietitians 1 (pt).
Facilities Dining room; Activities room; Crafts room; Laundry room.
Activities Arts & crafts; Cards; Games; Prayer groups; Movies; Shopping trips.

Winter Park Care Center
2970 Scarlet Rd, Winter Park, FL 32792
(305) 671-8030
Admin Judith M Durdik. *Dir of Nursing* Sandra Mitchell. *Medical Dir* Glenn Johnston.
Licensure Skilled care; Intermediate care. *Beds* SNF 19; ICF 103. *Private Pay Patients* 70%. *Certified* Medicaid; Medicare.
Owner Proprietary corp (National Heritage).
Admissions Requirements Medical examination.

Staff Physicians; RNs; LPNs; Nurses' aides; Physical therapists; Recreational therapists; Occupational therapists; Speech therapists; Activities coordinators; Dietitians; Ophthalmologists; Podiatrists.
Languages Spanish.
Facilities Dining room; Physical therapy room; Activities room; Crafts room; Laundry room; Barber/Beauty shop; Library; Secured patio; Courtyard patio.
Activities Arts & crafts; Cards; Games; Reading groups; Prayer groups; Movies; Shopping trips; Dances/Social/Cultural gatherings; Pet therapy; Adopt-a-grandparent; Lunch bunch.

Winter Park Towers
1111 S Lakemont Ave, Winter Park, FL 32792
(305) 647-4083
Licensure Skilled care. *Beds* 106.
Owner Nonprofit corp.
Staff RNs 19 (ft); LPNs 2 (ft); Nurses' aides 30 (ft).
Languages Polish, German, Italian, Russian, Hebrew, Yiddish, Spanish, French.
Affiliation Presbyterian.

Zephyrhills

Zephyr Haven Nursing Home
38250 Ave A, Zephyrhills, FL 33541
(813) 782-5508, 783-1586 FAX
Admin Patricia E Whitfield NHA. *Dir of Nursing* Judy Regan RN. *Medical Dir* Dr W C Chandler.
Licensure Skilled care; Alzheimer's care. *Beds* SNF 60. *Private Pay Patients* 75%. *Certified* Medicaid; Medicare.
Owner Publicly owned.
Admissions Requirements Minimum age 16; Medical examination; Physician's request.
Staff RNs 4 (ft), 2 (pt); LPNs 8 (ft), 3 (pt); Nurses' aides 27 (ft), 4 (pt); Activities coordinators 2 (ft).
Languages Spanish.
Facilities Dining room; Physical therapy room; Activities room; Chapel; Crafts room; Laundry room; Barber/Beauty shop; Library; 60 bed Alzheimer's annex.
Activities Arts & crafts; Cards; Games; Reading groups; Prayer groups; Movies; Shopping trips; Dances/Social/Cultural gatherings; Intergenerational programs; Cooking; Learning Together programs.

GEORGIA

Abbeville

River Willows Nursing Center
PO Box 428, Hwy 280 E, Abbeville, GA
31001
(912) 467-2515
Admin Ava Keene. *Dir of Nursing* Bernice
Futch. *Medical Dir* William Hammond MD.
Licensure Skilled care; Intermediate care. *Beds*
Swing beds SNF/ICF 101. *Private Pay
Patients* 3%. *Certified* Medicaid.
Owner Privately owned.
Admissions Requirements Medical
examination; Physician's request.
Staff Physicians 2 (ft); RNs 2 (ft), 1 (pt);
LPNs 10 (ft); Nurses' aides 35 (ft), 3 (pt);
Physical therapists 1 (pt); Speech therapists
1 (pt); Activities coordinators 1 (ft), 1 (pt);
Dietitians 1 (ft), 1 (pt); Podiatrists 1 (pt);
Audiologists 1 (pt).
Facilities Dining room; Physical therapy
room; Activities room; Laundry room;
Barber/Beauty shop.
Activities Arts & crafts; Cards; Games;
Reading groups; Prayer groups; Movies;
Shopping trips; Dances/Social/Cultural
gatherings; Programs designed for confused
residents or those with psychosocial
problems.

Adel

Memorial Convalescent Center
PO Box 677, Adel, GA 31620
(912) 896-3182
Admin James E Cunningham.
Licensure Skilled care; Intermediate care. *Beds*
80. *Certified* Medicaid; Medicare.

Adrian

Johnson County Intermediate Care
PO Box 207, Adrian, GA 31002
(912) 668-3225
Admin Juanelle McEachin.
Licensure Intermediate care. *Beds* ICF 59.
Certified Medicaid.

Albany

Hospitality Care Center of Albany
PO Box 2545, Albany, GA 31701
(912) 435-0741
Admin Anita McDonald.
Medical Dir Luellen Tucker.
Licensure Skilled care; Intermediate care;
Alzheimer's care. *Beds* 168. *Certified*
Medicaid.
Owner Proprietary corp.
Admissions Requirements Medical
examination.
Facilities Dining room; Physical therapy
room; Activities room; Crafts room; Laundry
room; Barber/Beauty shop; Library.
Activities Arts & crafts; Games; Reading
groups; Prayer groups; Movies; Shopping
trips; Dances/Social/Cultural gatherings.

Palmyra Nursing Home
1904 Palmyra Rd, Albany, GA 31707
(912) 883-0500
Admin Davis W King. *Dir of Nursing* Edith
Williams. *Medical Dir* Dr Chapel Collins.
Licensure Skilled care; Intermediate care;
Retirement. *Beds* SNF 250; ICF. *Certified*
Medicaid.
Owner Proprietary corp.
Admissions Requirements Medical
examination; Physician's request.
Staff Physicians 90 (ft); RNs 8 (ft); LPNs 30
(ft); Nurses' aides 125 (ft); Physical
therapists 2 (ft); Recreational therapists 1
(ft); Occupational therapists 1 (ft); Speech
therapists 1 (ft); Activities coordinators 3
(ft); Dietitians 1 (ft).
Facilities Dining room; Physical therapy
room; Activities room; Chapel; Crafts room;
Laundry room; Barber/Beauty shop; Library.
Activities Arts & crafts; Cards; Games;
Reading groups; Prayer groups; Movies;
Shopping trips; Dances/Social/Cultural
gatherings.

Alma

Twin Oaks Convalescent Center
Worth St, Alma, GA 31510
(912) 632-7293
Admin Harold Brown Jr.
Licensure Skilled care; Intermediate care. *Beds*
SNF 88. *Certified* Medicaid.

Americus

Magnolia Manor Intermediate Care Facility
PO Box 346, Lee St, Americus, GA 31709
(912) 924-9352
Admin J Ray Edwards.
Licensure Intermediate care. *Beds* ICF 67.
Certified Medicaid.

Magnolia Manor Methodist Nursing Care
Box 346, S Lee St, Americus, GA 31709
(912) 924-9352
Admin John Sims.
Medical Dir John H Robinson III.
Licensure Skilled care; Intermediate care;
Retirement. *Beds* 238. *Certified* Medicaid;
Medicare.
Admissions Requirements Medical
examination.
Staff Physicians 2 (pt); RNs 13 (ft), 3 (pt);
LPNs 25 (ft); Nurses' aides 68 (ft), 5 (pt);
Physical therapists 1 (ft), 1 (pt); Speech
therapists 1 (pt); Activities coordinators 3
(ft); Dietitians 1 (pt); Dentists 2 (pt).
Affiliation Methodist.
Facilities Dining room; Physical therapy
room; Activities room; Chapel; Crafts room;
Laundry room; Barber/Beauty shop; Library.
Activities Arts & crafts; Cards; Games;
Reading groups; Prayer groups; Movies;
Shopping trips; Dances/Social/Cultural
gatherings.

Ashburn

Ashburn Health Care Inc
Industrial Blvd, Box 629, Ashburn, GA 31714
(912) 567-3473
Admin M Gayle Calhoun.
Medical Dir Woodrow Gass MD.
Licensure Skilled care. *Beds* 76. *Certified*
Medicaid.
Admissions Requirements Medical
examination; Physician's request.
Staff Physicians 2 (ft); RNs 2 (ft); LPNs 7 (ft);
Nurses' aides 30 (ft); Activities coordinators
1 (ft); Dietitians 1 (ft).
Facilities Dining room; Activities room;
Chapel; Crafts room; Laundry room; Barber/
Beauty shop.
Activities Arts & crafts; Games; Prayer groups;
Movies.

Athens

Athens Health Care Center Inc
139 Alps Rd, Athens, GA 30610
(404) 549-8020
Admin Toni Moore.
Licensure Skilled care; Intermediate care. *Beds*
120. *Certified* Medicaid; Medicare.

Athens Heritage Home Inc
960 Hawthorne Ave, Athens, GA 30610
(404) 549-1613
Admin Garnelle T Armour.
Licensure rest home. *Beds* Rest home 104.
Admissions Requirements Minimum age 50;
Medical examination; Physician's request.
Staff Physicians 8 (pt); RNs 2 (ft), 1 (pt);
LPNs 8 (ft), 2 (pt); Physical therapists 1 (ft),
1 (pt); Activities coordinators 2 (ft);
Dietitians 1 (pt); Dentists 1 (pt).
Facilities Dining room; Physical therapy
room; Activities room; Chapel; Laundry
room; Barber/Beauty shop; Library.
Activities Arts & crafts; Cards; Games;
Reading groups; Prayer groups; Movies;
Shopping trips; Dances/Social/Cultural
gatherings.

Georgia Retardation Center—Athens
850 College Station Rd, Athens, GA 30601
(404) 542-8970
Admin Dr Sally Carter.
Medical Dir Victor Payton MD.
Licensure Intermediate care for mentally
retarded. *Beds* ICF/MR 40.
Owner Publicly owned.
Admissions Requirements Minimum age 3-18.
Staff Physicians 1 (pt); RNs 3 (ft); LPNs 5
(ft); Nurses' aides 55 (ft); Physical therapists
1 (pt); Recreational therapists 2 (ft);
Occupational therapists 1 (pt); Speech
therapists 1 (ft); Dietitians 1 (ft).
Facilities Dining room; Physical therapy
room; Activities room; Crafts room; Laundry
room; Library.
Activities Arts & crafts; Games; Movies;
Shopping trips; Dances/Social/Cultural
gatherings.

Grandview Center Inc
165 Winston Dr, Athens, GA 30607
(404) 549-6013
Admin Dorella Wilson. *Dir of Nursing* Mrs
Pam Smith RN. *Medical Dir* Dr W Morris.
Licensure Skilled care; Intermediate care. *Beds*
SNF 100; ICF. *Certified* Medicaid.
Owner Proprietary corp.
Admissions Requirements Medical
examination; Physician's request.
Staff Physicians 1 (pt); RNs 1 (ft), 2 (pt);
LPNs 12 (ft), 2 (pt); Nurses' aides 30 (ft), 4
(pt); Reality therapists 1 (ft).
Facilities Dining room; Physical therapy
room; Activities room; Crafts room; Laundry
room; Barber/Beauty shop; Library; Sitting
rooms.
Activities Arts & crafts; Games; Reading
groups; Prayer groups; Shopping trips;
Dances/Social/Cultural gatherings; Picnics.

New Horizon Health Care
PO Box 7547, Athens, GA 30604
(404) 549-5382
Admin Nancy A Seagraves. *Dir of Nursing*
Labretta Farr. *Medical Dir* Dr A P Brooks.
Licensure Skilled care; Intermediate care. *Beds*
SNF 122. *Certified* Medicaid.
Owner Proprietary corp (Angell Group).
Admissions Requirements Medical
examination.
Staff Physicians 6 (pt); RNs 2 (ft), 1 (pt);
LPNs 10 (ft), 2 (pt); Nurses' aides 34 (ft), 5
(pt); Physical therapists 1 (pt); Recreational
therapists 1 (ft); Dietitians 1 (pt); Podiatrists
1 (pt); Dentists 1 (pt).
Facilities Dining room; Physical therapy
room; Activities room; Laundry room;
Barber/Beauty shop.
Activities Arts & crafts; Games; Reading
groups; Prayer groups; Movies; Shopping
trips; Dances/Social/Cultural gatherings.

Atlanta

Ansley Pavilion
560 St Charles Ave, Atlanta, GA 30308
(404) 874-2233
Admin Aaron Baranan.
Licensure Intermediate care. *Beds* ICF 90.
Certified Medicaid.

Ashton Woods Convalescent Center
3535 Ashton Woods Dr, Atlanta, GA 30319
(404) 451-0236
Admin Ken O Stuck NHA. *Dir of Nursing*
Donna Nederlk RN. *Medical Dir* Mark
Skillon MD.
Licensure Skilled care. *Beds* SNF 157.
Certified Medicare.
Owner Proprietary corp (National Heritage).
Staff Physicians 1 (pt); RNs 6 (ft); LPNs 14
(ft); Nurses' aides 50 (ft); Physical therapists
1 (ft); Occupational therapists 1 (ft); Speech
therapists 1 (ft); Activities coordinators 1
(ft); Dietitians 1 (ft); Ophthalmologists 1
(pt); Podiatrists 1 (pt); Audiologists 1 (pt);
Dentists 1 (pt); Dermatologists;
Psychologists.
Facilities Dining room; Physical therapy
room; Activities room; Crafts room; Laundry
room; Barber/Beauty shop; Library.
Activities Arts & crafts; Games; Reading
groups; Prayer groups; Pet therapy.

Briarcliff Haven
1000 Briarcliff Rd NE, Atlanta, GA 30306
(404) 875-6456
Admin James I Kaufmann. *Dir of Nursing*
Agnes Church RN.
Licensure Skilled care; Intermediate care. *Beds*
SNF 103; ICF 53. *Certified* Medicaid.
Owner Proprietary corp.
Admissions Requirements Physician's request.
Facilities Dining room; Physical therapy
room; Activities room; Chapel; Crafts room;
Laundry room; Barber/Beauty shop; Library.

Activities Arts & crafts; Cards; Games;
Reading groups; Prayer groups; Movies;
Shopping trips; Dances/Social/Cultural
gatherings.

Budd Terrace Intermediate Care Home
1833 Clifton Rd NE, Atlanta, GA 30029
(404) 325-2988
Admin John Carlson. *Dir of Nursing* Jean
Copeland RN. *Medical Dir* Herbert Karp
MD.
Licensure Intermediate care; Retirement;
Alzheimer's care. *Beds* ICF 270.
Owner Nonprofit corp.
Admissions Requirements Minimum age 62;
Medical examination; Physician's request.
Staff RNs 3 (ft), 8 (pt); LPNs 18 (ft), 10 (pt);
Nurses' aides 40 (ft); Physical therapists 5
(ft); Recreational therapists 3 (ft);
Occupational therapists; Speech therapists;
Activities coordinators 1 (ft); Dietitians 1
(ft).
Affiliation Methodist.
Facilities Dining room; Physical therapy
room; Activities room; Chapel; Crafts room;
Laundry room; Barber/Beauty shop; TV
lounges on each unit.
Activities Arts & crafts; Cards; Games;
Reading groups; Prayer groups; Movies;
Shopping trips; Dances/Social/Cultural
gatherings.

Camilla Street Intermediate Care Home
PO Box 92384, 1011 Camilla St SW, Atlanta,
GA 30314
(404) 753-8839
Admin Arthur E Simpson. *Dir of Nursing*
Lula Mae Jackson. *Medical Dir* J B Ellison
MD.
Licensure Intermediate care. *Beds* ICF 14.
Certified Medicaid.
Owner Proprietary corp.
Admissions Requirements Medical
examination; Physician's request.
Staff Physicians 1 (ft); RNs 1 (ft); LPNs 4 (ft),
2 (pt); Nurses' aides 6 (ft), 1 (pt); Physical
therapists 1 (pt); Recreational therapists 1
(ft); Speech therapists 1 (pt); Activities
coordinators 1 (pt); Dietitians 1 (pt);
Ophthalmologists 1 (pt); Podiatrists 1 (pt).
Facilities Dining room; Activities room;
Crafts room; Laundry room.
Activities Arts & crafts; Cards; Games;
Reading groups; Prayer groups; Movies;
Shopping trips; Dances/Social/Cultural
gatherings.

Canterbury Court Intermediate Care Unit
3750 Peachtree Rd NE, Atlanta, GA 30319
(404) 261-6611
Admin R A Lawrence.
Licensure Intermediate care. *Beds* ICF 16.

Chattahoochee Health Services
3700 Cascade-Palmetto Rd, Atlanta, GA
30331
(404) 964-6950
Admin Donna B Scowden. *Dir of Nursing*
Brenda Giles LPN. *Medical Dir* Joe Cruise
MD.
Licensure Intermediate care. *Beds* ICF 60.
Certified Medicaid.
Owner Proprietary corp.
Admissions Requirements Medical
examination; Physician's request.
Staff Physicians 2 (pt); RNs 1 (ft); LPNs 4
(ft), 2 (pt); Nurses' aides 12 (ft), 6 (pt);
Physical therapists 1 (pt); Recreational
therapists 1 (ft); Occupational therapists 1
(ft); Activities coordinators 1 (pt); Dietitians
1 (pt); Ophthalmologists 1 (pt).
Facilities Dining room; Physical therapy
room; Activities room; Crafts room; Laundry
room; Barber/Beauty shop.
Activities Arts & crafts; Cards; Games;
Reading groups; Prayer groups; Movies;
Shopping trips; Dances/Social/Cultural
gatherings.

Christian City Convalescent Center
7300 Lester Rd, Atlanta, GA 30349
(404) 964-3301
Admin Fred A Watson.
Medical Dir Robert Webster MD.
Licensure Skilled care; Intermediate care. *Beds*
Swing beds SNF/ICF 200. *Certified*
Medicaid.
Admissions Requirements Minimum age 16;
Medical examination.
Staff Physicians 5 (pt); RNs 13 (ft), 3 (pt);
LPNs 5 (ft), 1 (pt); Nurses' aides 80 (ft), 20
(pt); Physical therapists 1 (pt); Reality
therapists 1 (ft); Recreational therapists 1
(ft); Occupational therapists 1 (pt); Speech
therapists 1 (pt); Activities coordinators 1
(ft); Dietitians 1 (ft); Ophthalmologists 1
(pt); Podiatrists 1 (pt); Dentists 1 (pt).
Facilities Dining room; Physical therapy
room; Activities room; Chapel; Laundry
room; Barber/Beauty shop; Library.
Activities Arts & crafts; Cards; Games;
Reading groups; Prayer groups; Movies;
Shopping trips; Dances/Social/Cultural
gatherings.

Crestview Nursing Home
2800 Springdale Rd SW, Atlanta, GA 30315
(404) 767-7407
Admin Joseph R Hunt.
Medical Dir Dr Phillip Benton.
Licensure Skilled care; Intermediate care. *Beds*
SNF 235; ICF. *Certified* Medicaid;
Medicare.
Owner Proprietary corp.
Admissions Requirements Medical
examination; Physician's request.
Staff Physicians 7 (pt); RNs 4 (ft), 3 (pt);
LPNs 38 (ft), 11 (pt); Nurses' aides 96 (ft),
17 (pt); Physical therapists 1 (ft);
Recreational therapists 5 (ft); Speech
therapists 1 (pt); Activities coordinators 1
(ft); Dietitians 1 (ft); Ophthalmologists 1
(pt); Podiatrists 1 (pt); Dentists 1 (pt).
Facilities Dining room; Physical therapy
room; Activities room; Chapel; Crafts room;
Laundry room; Barber/Beauty shop.
Activities Arts & crafts; Cards; Games;
Reading groups; Prayer groups; Movies;
Shopping trips; Dances/Social/Cultural
gatherings.

Emory Nursing Center
1466 Oxford Rd NE, Atlanta, GA 30307
(404) 378-7339, 378-7106
Admin Mary Alta Goodspeed. *Dir of Nursing*
Emma White. *Medical Dir* Dr Charles
Spencer.
Licensure Skilled care. *Beds* SNF 41. *Private
Pay Patients* 20%. *Certified* Medicaid.
Owner Proprietary corp.
Admissions Requirements Medical
examination; Physician's request.
Staff Physicians 10 (pt); RNs 2 (ft), 2 (pt);
LPNs 2 (ft), 4 (pt); Nurses' aides 15 (ft), 5
(pt); Physical therapists 1 (pt); Recreational
therapists 1 (pt); Occupational therapists 1
(pt); Speech therapists 1 (pt); Activities
coordinators 1 (ft); Dietitians 1 (pt);
Podiatrists 1 (pt); Audiologists 1 (pt).
Languages Korean, translators available for
other languages.
Facilities Dining room; Laundry room.
Activities Arts & crafts; Cards; Games;
Reading groups; Prayer groups; Movies;
Shopping trips; Dances/Social/Cultural
gatherings; Intergenerational programs; Pet
therapy; Rhythm band.

Fountainview Convalescent Center
1400 Briarcliff Rd NE, Atlanta, GA 30306
(404) 378-2303
Admin Robert E Bruce. *Dir of Nursing* Rose
Phillips. *Medical Dir* Roy Wiggins MD.
Licensure Skilled care. *Beds* SNF 97. *Private
Pay Patients* 100%.
Owner Proprietary corp.

Admissions Requirements Medical
examination.
Staff RNs 3 (ft), 1 (pt); LPNs 9 (ft), 7 (pt);
Nurses' aides 34 (ft); Physical therapists 1
(pt); Occupational therapists 1 (pt); Speech
therapists 1 (pt); Activities coordinators 1
(ft); Dietitians 1 (pt); Podiatrists 1 (pt);
Audiologists 1 (pt).
Facilities Dining room; Physical therapy
room; Activities room; Barber/Beauty shop.
Activities Arts & crafts; Games; Reading
groups; Prayer groups; Movies; Dances/
Social/Cultural gatherings; Exercise.

Georgia Retardation Center
4770 N Peachtree Rd, Atlanta, GA 30338-
5899
(404) 551-7157, 551-7040 FAX
Admin Allen G Marchetti PhD. *Dir of Nursing*
Selene M Yarbrough RN. *Medical Dir*
William S Talley MD.
Licensure Skilled care; Intermediate care for
mentally retarded. *Beds* SNF 94; ICF/MR
290. *Certified* Medicaid.
Owner Publicly owned.
Admissions Requirements Medical
examination.
Staff Physicians 5 (ft), 7 (pt); RNs 37 (ft), 4
(pt); LPNs 23 (ft); Nurses' aides 345 (ft);
Physical therapists 3 (ft), 2 (pt); Recreational
therapists 10 (ft); Occupational therapists 4
(ft), 1 (pt); Speech therapists 7 (ft); Activities
coordinators 1 (ft); Dietitians 5 (ft);
Ophthalmologists 1 (pt); Podiatrists 1 (pt);
Audiologists 1 (ft).
Facilities Dining room; Physical therapy
room; Activities room; Chapel; Crafts room;
Laundry room; Barber/Beauty shop; Library;
Horticulture center; Swimming pool.
Activities Arts & crafts; Cards; Games;
Reading groups; Prayer groups; Movies;
Shopping trips; Dances/Social/Cultural
gatherings; Intergenerational programs; Pet
therapy; Horticulture program; Infant
stimulation program; Workshop program;
Support employment program.

Heritage Convalescent Center
54 Peachtree Park Dr, Atlanta, GA 30309
(404) 351-6041
Admin Coralee Long.
Medical Dir Dr Roy A Wiggins Jr.
Licensure Skilled care; Intermediate care. *Beds*
180. *Certified* Medicaid; Medicare.
Admissions Requirements Medical
examination; Physician's request.
Staff RNs 2 (ft), 2 (pt); LPNs 10 (ft); Nurses'
aides 53 (ft); Physical therapists 1 (pt);
Activities coordinators 1 (ft); Dietitians 1
(ft).
Facilities Dining room; Physical therapy
room; Activities room; Chapel; Crafts room;
Laundry room; Barber/Beauty shop; Library.
Activities Arts & crafts; Cards; Games;
Reading groups; Prayer groups; Movies;
Shopping trips; Dances/Social/Cultural
gatherings.

Imperial Health Care Inc
2645 Whiting St NW, Atlanta, GA 30318
(404) 799-9267, 799-9278
Admin Coy C Williamson Jr; Loretta Barnes,
Operations Admin. *Dir of Nursing* Beulah
Craig. *Medical Dir* Dr Woods, Dr Williams.
Licensure Skilled care; Intermediate care. *Beds*
Swing beds SNF/ICF 120. *Private Pay*
Patients 10%. *Certified* Medicaid.
Owner Privately owned (Coy C Williamson
Jr).
Admissions Requirements Minimum age;
Medical examination; Physician's request.
Staff Physicians 2 (pt); RNs 2 (ft), 2 (pt);
LPNs 16 (ft), 4 (pt); Nurses' aides 50 (ft);
Physical therapists (consultant); Recreational
therapists 2 (ft); Occupational therapists
(consultant); Speech therapists (consultant);
Dietitians (consultant); Ophthalmologists
(consultant); Podiatrists (consultant).

Facilities Dining room; Physical therapy
room; Activities room; Crafts room; Laundry
room; Barber/Beauty shop.
Activities Arts & crafts; Cards; Games;
Reading groups; Prayer groups; Movies;
Shopping trips; Dances/Social/Cultural
gatherings; Intergenerational programs.

Jewish Home
3150 Howell Mill Rd NW, Atlanta, GA 30327
(404) 351-8410
Admin Deborah Beards. *Dir of Nursing*
Patrick Shipley RN. *Medical Dir* Sanford
Shmerling MD.
Licensure Skilled care; Intermediate care;
Alzheimer's care. *Beds* 120. *Certified*
Medicaid; Medicare.
Owner Nonprofit corp.
Admissions Requirements Minimum age 62;
Females only.
Staff Physicians 1 (pt); RNs 7 (ft); LPNs 17
(ft); Nurses' aides 50 (ft); Physical therapists
1 (ft); Recreational therapists 2 (ft);
Occupational therapists 1 (pt); Dietitians 1
(pt).
Languages Yiddish, Hebrew.
Affiliation Jewish.
Facilities Dining room; Physical therapy
room; Activities room; Chapel; Crafts room;
Laundry room; Barber/Beauty shop; Library.
Activities Arts & crafts; Cards; Games;
Movies; Dances/Social/Cultural gatherings.

Lenbrook Square
3747 Peachtree Rd NE, Atlanta, GA 30319
(404) 233-3000
Admin Gen Gordon Duquemin.
Licensure Nursing home. *Beds* Nursing home
60.

Sadie G Mays Memorial Nursing Home
1821 W Anderson Ave, Atlanta, GA 30314
(404) 794-2477
Admin Charles Robinson Jr. *Dir of Nursing*
Eva Price RN. *Medical Dir* A M Davis MD.
Licensure Skilled care; Intermediate care. *Beds*
206. *Certified* Medicaid.
Owner Nonprofit corp.
Admissions Requirements Medical
examination; Physician's request.
Staff Physicians 2 (pt); RNs 4 (ft); LPNs 20
(ft), 5 (pt); Nurses' aides 55 (ft); Physical
therapists 1 (ft); Speech therapists 1 (pt);
Activities coordinators 1 (ft); Dietitians 1
(ft); Ophthalmologists 1 (pt); Dentists 1 (pt).
Facilities Dining room; Physical therapy
room; Activities room; Chapel; Laundry
room; Barber/Beauty shop.
Activities Arts & crafts; Cards; Games; Prayer
groups; Movies; Shopping trips; Dances/
Social/Cultural gatherings; Exercise.

Newtonhouse
320 Parkway Dr NE, Atlanta, GA 30312
(404) 525-4647
Admin Peggy Beckett.
Licensure Skilled care; Intermediate care. *Beds*
146. *Certified* Medicaid; Medicare.

Northside Convalescent Center
993-E Johnson Ferry Rd NE, Atlanta, GA
30342
(404) 256-5131
Admin Roger Mills, Jeanine Braaton.
Medical Dir John McCoy MD.
Licensure Skilled care; Intermediate care. *Beds*
SNF 18; ICF 202. *Certified* Medicare.
Owner Proprietary corp (Beverly Enterprises).
Admissions Requirements Medical
examination; Physician's request.
Staff Physicians 112 (pt); RNs 19 (ft), 4 (pt);
LPNs 16 (ft), 7 (pt); Nurses' aides 90 (ft), 10
(pt); Physical therapists 3 (ft), 1 (pt); Reality
therapists 4 (ft); Recreational therapists 2
(ft); Occupational therapists 1 (ft); Speech
therapists 1 (ft); Dietitians 1 (ft);

Ophthalmologists 1 (ft); Podiatrists 2 (ft);
Dentists 1 (ft); Respiratory therapists 3 (ft),
2 (pt).
Facilities Dining room; Physical therapy
room; Activities room; Crafts room; Laundry
room; Barber/Beauty shop; Library; Bus &
limo services.
Activities Arts & crafts; Cards; Games;
Reading groups; Prayer groups; Movies;
Shopping trips; Dances/Social/Cultural
gatherings; Happy hour.

Nursecare of Atlanta
2920 S Pharr Ct NW, Atlanta, GA 30363
(404) 261-9043, 231-5402 FAX
Admin LaVenia R Miller. *Dir of Nursing* Kit
Giles RN. *Medical Dir* Bruce Geer.
Licensure Skilled care; Intermediate care;
Alzheimer's care. *Beds* Swing beds SNF/ICF
220. *Certified* Medicaid; Medicare.
Owner Proprietary corp.
Admissions Requirements Minimum age 50;
Medical examination.
Staff Physicians 3 (ft), 10 (pt); RNs 6 (ft);
LPNs 20 (ft), 6 (pt); Nurses' aides 60 (ft), 16
(pt); Physical therapists 1 (ft); Reality
therapists 1 (ft); Recreational therapists 2
(ft); Occupational therapists 1 (pt); Activities
coordinators 1 (ft); Dietitians 1 (ft).
Languages Spanish.
Facilities Dining room; Physical therapy
room; Activities room; Chapel; Crafts room;
Barber/Beauty shop; Library; Living room;
Patio.
Activities Arts & crafts; Cards; Games;
Reading groups; Prayer groups; Movies;
Shopping trips; Dances/Social/Cultural
gatherings; Intergenerational programs; Pet
therapy; Wine & cheese party.

Our Lady of Perpetual Help
760 Washington St SW, Atlanta, GA 30315
(404) 688-9515
Admin Sr Mary Peter. *Dir of Nursing* Sr Mary
de Paul RN. *Medical Dir* Dr Thomas F
Lowry.
Licensure Rest home. *Beds* 54.
Owner Nonprofit corp.
Admissions Requirements Medical
examination; Physician's request.
Staff Physicians 1 (pt); RNs 2 (ft); LPNs 11
(ft); Nurses' aides 2 (ft), 1 (pt); Activities
coordinators 2 (pt); Dietitians 1 (pt);
Ophthalmologists 1 (pt).
Affiliation Roman Catholic.
Facilities Chapel; Crafts room; Laundry room;
Barber/Beauty shop; Library.
Activities Arts & crafts; Cards; Games; Prayer
groups; Movies.

Parkview Manor Nursing Home
460 Auburn Ave NE, Atlanta, GA 30312
(404) 523-1613
Admin Tama D Douglas NHA. *Dir of Nursing*
Valerie Hamilton RN. *Medical Dir* Joseph
Williams MD.
Licensure Skilled care; Intermediate care. *Beds*
Swing beds SNF/ICF 186. *Certified*
Medicaid; Medicare.
Owner Proprietary corp.
Admissions Requirements Medical
examination; Physician's request.
Staff Physicians 2 (pt); RNs 2 (ft), 5 (pt);
LPNs 13 (ft), 6 (pt); Physical therapists
(contracted); Recreational therapists 3 (ft);
Occupational therapists 1 (pt); Speech
therapists 1 (pt); Activities coordinators 1
(ft); Dietitians (contracted); Podiatrists 1
(pt); Social workers 2 (ft).
Facilities Dining room; Physical therapy
room; Activities room; Chapel; Crafts room;
Barber/Beauty shop.
Activities Arts & crafts; Games; Prayer groups;
Movies; Shopping trips; Dances/Social/
Cultural gatherings; Pet therapy.

Piedmont Hospital Extended Care Unit
1968 Peachtree Rd NW, Atlanta, GA 30309
(404) 350-2222
Admin Hulett D Sumlin. *Dir of Nursing*
JoAnn Akers RN. *Medical Dir* Dan
Ferguson MD.
Licensure Skilled care. *Beds* SNF 42. *Certified*
Medicare.
Owner Nonprofit organization/foundation.
Staff Physicians; RNs; LPNs; Nurses' aides;
Physical therapists; Occupational therapists 1
(pt); Activities coordinators 1 (pt); Dietitians
1 (ft).
Facilities Physical therapy room; Activities
room; Chapel; Barber/Beauty shop; Library.
Activities Arts & crafts; Cards.

A G Rhodes Home Inc
350 Boulevard SE, Atlanta, GA 30312
(404) 688-6731
Admin Pat McMurry.
Medical Dir Libby Herman.
Licensure Skilled care. *Beds* 128. *Certified*
Medicaid; Medicare.
Owner Nonprofit corp.
Admissions Requirements Minimum age 21.
Staff Physicians; RNs 6 (ft), 2 (pt); LPNs 15
(ft), 5 (pt); Nurses' aides 65 (ft), 10 (pt);
Physical therapists 1 (ft), 1 (pt); Activities
coordinators 1 (ft), 1 (pt); Dietitians 1 (pt);
Ophthalmologists 1 (pt).
Facilities Dining room; Physical therapy
room; Activities room; Chapel; Crafts room;
Laundry room; Barber/Beauty shop; Library.
Activities Arts & crafts; Cards; Games;
Reading groups; Movies; Shopping trips;
Dances/Social/Cultural gatherings.

Springdale Convalescent Center
2850 Springdale Rd SW, Atlanta, GA 30315
(404) 762-8672
Admin Cheri S Underwood. *Dir of Nursing*
Carolyn H Boyd. *Medical Dir* Dr Jimmie
Williams.
Licensure Skilled care; Intermediate care. *Beds*
109. *Certified* Medicaid.
Owner Proprietary corp.
Admissions Requirements Medical
examination; Physician's request.
Staff Physicians; RNs; LPNs; Nurses' aides;
Physical therapists; Recreational therapists;
Speech therapists; Activities coordinators;
Dietitians.
Facilities Dining room; Physical therapy
room; Activities room; Laundry room;
Barber/Beauty shop.
Activities Arts & crafts; Cards; Games;
Reading groups; Prayer groups; Movies;
Shopping trips; Dances/Social/Cultural
gatherings.

Wesley Woods Health Center
1841 Clifton Rd NE, Atlanta, GA 30329
(404) 728-6400, 728-6429 FAX
Admin Raymond O Colston Jr. *Dir of Nursing*
Jean Copeland. *Medical Dir* Dr Herbert
Karp.
Licensure Skilled care; Retirement. *Beds* SNF
171. *Certified* Medicaid; Medicare.
Owner Nonprofit corp (Wesley Homes).
Admissions Requirements Medical
examination.
Staff RNs 7 (ft), 2 (pt); LPNs 17 (ft), 2 (pt);
Nurses' aides 30 (ft), 4 (pt); Physical
therapists 1 (ft); Recreational therapists 1
(ft); Occupational therapists 1 (pt); Speech
therapists 1 (pt); Activities coordinators 1
(ft); Dietitians 1 (ft).
Languages Spanish.
Affiliation Methodist.
Facilities Physical therapy room; Activities
room; Chapel; Barber/Beauty shop.
Activities Arts & crafts; Games; Reading
groups; Prayer groups; Movies; Shopping
trips; Dances/Social/Cultural gatherings.

Augusta

Augusta Health Care
PO Box 5778, Augusta, GA 30906
(404) 793-1057
Admin Paul W Phillips.
Medical Dir Louis Scharff III MD.
Licensure Skilled care. *Beds* 213. *Certified*
Medicaid; Medicare.
Owner Proprietary corp (Wessex Corp).
Admissions Requirements Medical
examination; Physician's request.
Staff Physicians 5 (pt); RNs 2 (ft), 1 (pt);
LPNs 17 (ft), 7 (pt); Nurses' aides 62 (ft), 4
(pt); Physical therapists 1 (ft), 1 (pt);
Recreational therapists 2 (ft); Speech
therapists 1 (pt); Activities coordinators 1
(ft); Dietitians 1 (ft), 1 (pt).
Facilities Dining room; Physical therapy
room; Activities room; Chapel; Crafts room;
Laundry room; Barber/Beauty shop; Library.
Activities Arts & crafts; Cards; Games;
Reading groups; Prayer groups; Movies;
Shopping trips; Dances/Social/Cultural
gatherings.

Beverly Manor Convalescent Center
1600 Anthony Rd, Augusta, GA 30904
(404) 738-3301
Admin Julia Huffman.
Medical Dir Dr Nathan Reeves.
Licensure Skilled care; Intermediate care. *Beds*
99. *Certified* Medicaid; Medicare.
Owner Proprietary corp (Beverly Enterprises).
Admissions Requirements Medical
examination; Physician's request.
Staff RNs 5 (ft); LPNs 15 (ft), 10 (pt); Nurses'
aides 27 (ft), 15 (pt); Physical therapists 1
(pt); Occupational therapists 1 (pt); Speech
therapists 1 (pt); Activities coordinators 1
(ft); Dietitians 1 (ft); Podiatrists 1 (pt);
Dentists 1 (pt).
Facilities Dining room; Physical therapy
room; Activities room; Chapel; Crafts room;
Laundry room; Barber/Beauty shop.
Activities Arts & crafts; Games; Prayer groups;
Movies; Shopping trips.

Blair House
2541 Milledgeville Rd, Augusta, GA 30904
(404) 738-2581
Admin Frank Feltham. *Dir of Nursing* Marie
Rollins. *Medical Dir* Luther M Thomas Jr.
Licensure Skilled care; Intermediate care. *Beds*
100. *Certified* Medicaid; Medicare.
Owner Proprietary corp.
Staff Physicians 5 (pt); RNs 1 (ft), 2 (pt);
LPNs 6 (ft), 10 (pt); Nurses' aides 16 (ft), 22
(pt); Activities coordinators 1 (ft); Dietitians
1 (ft).
Facilities Dining room; Physical therapy
room; Activities room; Chapel; Laundry
room; Barber/Beauty shop.
Activities Arts & crafts; Games; Reading
groups; Prayer groups; Shopping trips;
Dances/Social/Cultural gatherings.

Georgia War Veterans Nursing Home
1101 15th St, Augusta, GA 30910
(404) 721-2531
Admin Charles Esposito. *Dir of Nursing* Linda
Carter. *Medical Dir* Arthur O Gelbart MD.
Licensure Skilled care. *Beds* SNF 192.
Owner Nonprofit organization/foundation.
Staff Physicians 1 (ft), 2 (pt); RNs 16 (ft), 4
(pt); LPNs 24 (ft); Nurses' aides 83 (ft);
Physical therapists 2 (ft); Recreational
therapists 1 (ft); Occupational therapists 2
(ft); Speech therapists 1 (pt); Activities
coordinators 2 (ft); Dietitians 1 (ft);
Ophthalmologists 1 (pt).
Facilities Dining room; Physical therapy
room; Activities room; Chapel; Crafts room;
Laundry room; Barber/Beauty shop; Library;
Dental room.
Activities Arts & crafts; Cards; Games;
Reading groups; Prayer groups; Movies;
Shopping trips; Birthday parties.

Heritage House Summerville
2122 Cumming Rd, Augusta, GA 30904-4334
(404) 737-8258
Admin Wanda J Hinton.
Beds 128.

Heritage Summerville Inc
837 Hickman Rd, Augusta, GA 30904
(404) 737-8258
Admin Nita Crump-Howard.
Licensure Skilled care; Intermediate care. *Beds*
128. *Certified* Medicaid; Medicare.

Jennings Health Care Inc
3235 Deans Bridge Rd, Augusta, GA 30906
(404) 798-1430
Admin Diane Ray.
Medical Dir O L Gray.
Licensure Skilled care; Intermediate care. *Beds*
76. *Certified* Medicaid; Medicare.
Admissions Requirements Medical
examination; Physician's request.
Facilities Dining room; Physical therapy
room; Activities room; Laundry room;
Barber/Beauty shop; Library.
Activities Arts & crafts; Cards; Games;
Reading groups; Prayer groups; Movies;
Shopping trips; Dances/Social/Cultural
gatherings.

Kentwood
1227 W Wheeler Pkwy, Augusta, GA 30909
(404) 863-1188
Admin Vicki Peel RN. *Dir of Nursing* Dianne
L Peeples RN. *Medical Dir* Joseph D Lee
MD.
Licensure Skilled care; Personal care. *Beds*
SNF 60; Personal care 20. *Certified*
Medicaid; Medicare.
Owner Publicly owned.
Admissions Requirements Physician's request.
Staff Physicians 1 (pt); RNs 5 (ft); LPNs 12
(ft); Nurses' aides 16 (ft); Physical therapists
(contracted); Occupational therapists
(contracted); Speech therapists (contracted);
Activities coordinators 1 (pt); Dietitians
(contracted); Social workers 1 (pt).
Facilities Dining room; Physical therapy
room; Activities room; Crafts room; Laundry
room; Barber/Beauty shop; Patio; Garden
area.
Activities Arts & crafts; Cards; Games; Prayer
groups; Movies; Shopping trips.

West Lake Manor Health Care Center
820 Stevens Creek Rd, Augusta, GA 30907
(404) 860-6622
Medical Dir Fay T Cupstid.
Licensure Skilled care; Intermediate care. *Beds*
100. *Certified* Medicaid; Medicare.
Staff RNs 4 (ft), 1 (pt); LPNs 7 (ft), 4 (pt);
Nurses' aides 27 (ft), 10 (pt); Physical
therapists 1 (pt); Recreational therapists 1
(ft); Speech therapists 1 (pt); Activities
coordinators 1 (ft); Dietitians 1 (ft); Social
workers 1 (ft).
Facilities Dining room; Physical therapy
room; Activities room; Chapel; Crafts room;
Laundry room; Barber/Beauty shop.
Activities Arts & crafts; Cards; Games;
Reading groups; Prayer groups; Movies;
Dances/Social/Cultural gatherings.

Windermere
3618 J Dewey Gray Circle, Augusta, GA
30909
(404) 860-7572
Admin June R Barrett.
Licensure Skilled care; Intermediate care. *Beds*
120. *Certified* Medicaid; Medicare.
Owner Proprietary corp (Beverly Enterprises).

Austell

Atlanta Health Care Center
1700 Mulkey Rd, Austell, GA 30001
(404) 941-5750
Admin Sylvia Dalton.

Licensure Skilled care; Intermediate care. *Beds* 124. *Certified* Medicaid; Medicare.
Owner Proprietary corp (Wessex Corp).

Brian Center of Nursing Care—Austell
2130 Anderson Mill Rd, Austell, GA 30001
(404) 941-8813
Admin Paul W Shirley. *Dir of Nursing* Diane Brown RN. *Medical Dir* Ellis Malone MD.
Licensure Skilled care; Intermediate care. *Beds* 170. *Certified* Medicaid; Medicare.
Owner Proprietary corp (Brian Center Management Corp).
Staff Physicians 12 (pt); RNs 4 (ft); LPNs 15 (ft), 4 (pt); Nurses' aides 50 (ft), 10 (pt); Physical therapists 1 (ft); Occupational therapists 1 (pt); Speech therapists 1 (pt); Activities coordinators 1 (ft); Dietitians 1 (pt); Ophthalmologists 1 (pt); Podiatrists 1 (pt); Dentists 1 (pt).
Facilities Dining room; Physical therapy room; Activities room; Crafts room; Laundry room; Barber/Beauty shop; Inner enclosed courtyard.
Activities Arts & crafts; Cards; Games; Reading groups; Prayer groups; Dances/ Social/Cultural gatherings.

Presbyterian Village
2000 East-West Connector, Austell, GA 30001
(404) 739-3300
Admin Frank H McElroy Jr.
Licensure Skilled care; Intermediate care. *Beds* SNF 107. *Certified* Medicaid.

Bainbridge

Bainbridge Health Care Inc
Rte 2, 115 W College St Box 20, Bainbridge, GA 31717
(912) 243-0931
Admin Doris Grant.
Licensure Skilled care; Intermediate care. *Beds* 100. *Certified* Medicaid; Medicare.
Owner Proprietary corp (Stuckey Health Care).

Memorial Manor Nursing Home
1500 E Shotwell St, Bainbridge, GA 31717
(912) 246-3500
Admin Raymond W Wright.
Licensure Skilled care; Intermediate care. *Beds* 107. *Certified* Medicaid; Medicare.

Southwestern Developmental Center
PO Box 935, Southwestern Hospital, Bainbridge, GA 31717
(912) 246-6750
Admin Carl E Rolland Supt.
Medical Dir Dr Martin Bailey.
Licensure Intermediate care for mentally retarded. *Beds* ICF/MR 216.
Staff Physicians 2 (ft), 1 (pt); RNs 12 (ft); LPNs 15 (ft); Physical therapists 2 (ft); Recreational therapists 6 (ft); Occupational therapists 2 (ft); Speech therapists 2 (ft); Activities coordinators 1 (ft); Dietitians 2 (ft); Dentists 1 (ft), 1 (pt).
Facilities Dining room; Physical therapy room; Activities room; Chapel; Crafts room; Laundry room; Barber/Beauty shop; Library.
Activities Arts & crafts; Cards; Games; Reading groups; Prayer groups; Movies; Shopping trips; Dances/Social/Cultural gatherings.

Baldwin

Scenic View Health Care Center
PO Box 288, Baldwin, GA 30511
(404) 778-8377
Admin Sallie Y Powell.
Licensure Skilled care; Intermediate care. *Beds* 112. *Certified* Medicaid.

Barnesville

Heritage Inn—Barnesville
148 Ft Valley Rd, Barnesville, GA 30204
(404) 358-2485
Admin Susan Chapman. *Dir of Nursing* Mary Lou Harris RN. *Medical Dir* George Henry MD.
Licensure Skilled care; Intermediate care. *Beds* 117. *Certified* Medicaid.
Owner Privately owned.
Staff Physicians 2 (ft); RNs 3 (ft), 1 (pt); LPNs 12 (ft), 3 (pt); Nurses' aides 60 (ft), 4 (pt); Physical therapists 1 (ft); Occupational therapists 1 (ft); Activities coordinators 1 (ft); Dietitians 1 (ft).
Facilities Dining room; Physical therapy room; Activities room; Crafts room; Laundry room; Barber/Beauty shop.
Activities Arts & crafts; Cards; Games; Reading groups; Movies; Shopping trips.

Baxley

Appling County Nursing Home
E Walnut St, Baxley, GA 31513
(912) 367-4645
Admin Stanley Crews.
Licensure Skilled care. *Beds* 31. *Certified* Medicaid; Medicare.

Baxley Manor Inc
PO Box 507, Donnie Ln, Baxley, GA 31513
(912) 367-4663
Admin Brenda White.
Medical Dir A E Suarez MD.
Licensure Skilled care; Intermediate care. *Beds* SNF 70. *Certified* Medicaid; Medicare.
Owner Proprietary corp (Stuckey Health Care).
Admissions Requirements Physician's request.
Staff RNs 1 (ft), 1 (pt); LPNs 6 (ft), 2 (pt); Nurses' aides 13 (ft); Physical therapists 1 (pt); Activities coordinators 1 (ft); Dietitians 1 (pt); Podiatrists 1 (pt); Pharmacists 1 (pt).
Facilities Dining room; Physical therapy room; Activities room; Chapel; Crafts room; Laundry room; Barber/Beauty shop; Solarium.
Activities Arts & crafts; Cards; Games; Reading groups; Prayer groups; Movies; Shopping trips; Dances/Social/Cultural gatherings.

Blackshear

Pierce County Nursing Home
PO Box 32, Blackshear, GA 31516
(912) 449-6631, 449-4037 FAX
Admin Warnell Ziwolkowski RN. *Dir of Nursing* Emily Aguirre. *Medical Dir* L C Durrence MD.
Licensure Skilled care; Intermediate care. *Beds* SNF 41; ICF 23. *Private Pay Patients* 3%. *Certified* Medicaid; Medicare.
Owner Nonprofit organization/foundation.
Admissions Requirements Medical examination; Physician's request.
Staff RNs 2 (ft), 2 (pt); LPNs 9 (ft); Nurses' aides 30 (ft), 3 (pt); Physical therapists 1 (ft); Activities coordinators 1 (ft); Dietitians.
Facilities Dining room; Physical therapy room; Activities room; Chapel; Crafts room; Laundry room; Barber/Beauty shop; Library.
Activities Arts & crafts; Games; Prayer groups; Movies; Shopping trips; Dances/Social/ Cultural gatherings; Pet therapy.

Blairsville

Union County Nursing Home
Rte 7 Box 7650, Blairsville, GA 30512
(404) 745-4948
Admin Rebecca T Dyer. *Dir of Nursing* Fidelis Thompson. *Medical Dir* Dr G David Gowder III.
Licensure Skilled care; Intermediate care. *Beds* SNF 29; ICF 71. *Private Pay Patients* 10%. *Certified* Medicaid.
Owner Nonprofit corp (Union County Hospital Authority).
Admissions Requirements Medical examination; Physician's request.
Staff RNs 2 (ft), 3 (pt); LPNs 12 (ft), 1 (pt); Nurses' aides 37 (ft), 7 (pt); Dietitians 1 (ft).
Facilities Dining room; Physical therapy room; Activities room; Chapel; Laundry room; Barber/Beauty shop; Library.
Activities Arts & crafts; Cards; Games; Reading groups; Prayer groups; Movies; Shopping trips; Dances/Social/Cultural gatherings.

Blakley

Early Memorial Nursing Home
630 Columbia Rd, Blakley, GA 31723
(912) 723-3794
Admin Robert E Tiner.
Licensure Skilled care; Intermediate care. *Beds* 127. *Certified* Medicaid; Medicare.

Blue Ridge

Fannin County Nursing Home
PO Box 1227, Blue Ridge, GA 30513
(404) 632-2271
Admin Fuller Marshall.
Medical Dir Jack B Roof MD.
Licensure Skilled care; Intermediate care. *Beds* 101. *Certified* Medicaid.
Admissions Requirements Minimum age 18; Medical examination; Physician's request.
Staff RNs 1 (ft), 1 (pt); LPNs 7 (ft), 1 (pt); Nurses' aides 16 (ft), 6 (pt); Physical therapists 1 (pt); Recreational therapists 1 (ft); Activities coordinators 1 (ft); Dietitians 1 (pt); Podiatrists 1 (pt).
Facilities Dining room; Physical therapy room; Activities room; Chapel; Crafts room; Laundry room; Barber/Beauty shop.
Activities Arts & crafts; Cards; Games; Reading groups; Prayer groups; Movies; Shopping trips; Dances/Social/Cultural gatherings.

Bremen

Haralson County Nursing Home
Box 724, 315 Field St, Bremen, GA 30110
(404) 537-4482
Admin Linda G Kimball.
Licensure Skilled care; Intermediate care. *Beds* 120. *Certified* Medicaid; Medicare.

Brunswick

Goodwill Intermediate Care Home
2708 Lee St, Brunswick, GA 31520
(912) 267-6771
Admin Rev F B McKenzie.
Medical Dir Dr Mark T Pierce.
Licensure Intermediate care. *Beds* ICF 60. *Certified* Medicaid.
Staff Physicians 1 (ft); RNs 2 (ft); LPNs 3 (ft), 1 (pt); Nurses' aides 9 (ft), 3 (pt); Physical therapists 1 (pt); Recreational therapists 1 (ft); Activities coordinators 1 (ft); Dietitians 1 (pt).
Facilities Dining room; Laundry room; Barber/Beauty shop.
Activities Arts & crafts; Games; Reading groups; Prayer groups; Movies; Dances/ Social/Cultural gatherings.

Medical Arts Center—Coastal Georgia
2611 Wildwood Dr, Brunswick, GA 31520
(912) 264-1434
Admin Thelma W Davis.
Licensure Skilled care; Intermediate care. *Beds* 208. *Certified* Medicaid; Medicare.

Sears Manor
3311 Lee St, Brunswick, GA 31530
(912) 264-1826
Admin Claude G Sears.
Licensure Skilled care; Intermediate care. *Beds* SNF 100. *Certified* Medicaid.

Buchanan

Countryside Health Center
PO Box 750, 233 Carrollton St, Buchanan, GA 30113
(404) 646-3861, 646-3601 FAX
Admin Mary Ann Wood. *Dir of Nursing* Annette Clarke. *Medical Dir* Dr I S Kim.
Licensure Intermediate care. *Beds* ICF 62. *Private Pay Patients* 3%. *Certified* Medicaid.
Owner Proprietary corp (Nursing Centers of America Inc).
Admissions Requirements Medical examination; Physician's request.
Staff RNs 1 (ft); LPNs 5 (ft), 1 (pt); Nurses' aides 15 (ft); Physical therapists; Recreational therapists 1 (ft); Activities coordinators 1 (ft); Dietitians 1 (ft).
Facilities Dining room; Physical therapy room; Activities room; Laundry room; Barber/Beauty shop.
Activities Arts & crafts; Cards; Games; Reading groups; Movies; Shopping trips; Dances/Social/Cultural gatherings; Intergenerational programs.

Resthaven Intermediate Care Home
PO Box 409, Buchanan, GA 30113
(404) 646-5512
Admin Mary E Tucker. *Dir of Nursing* Emily Briscoe. *Medical Dir* Dr P J Kim.
Licensure Intermediate care. *Beds* ICF 60. *Certified* Medicaid.
Owner Proprietary corp.
Admissions Requirements Medical examination; Physician's request.
Staff RNs 1 (ft); LPNs 4 (ft), 1 (pt); Nurses' aides 12 (ft), 3 (pt); Dietitians 4 (ft), 2 (pt).
Facilities Dining room; Activities room; Chapel; Crafts room; Laundry room; Barber/Beauty shop.
Activities Arts & crafts; Games; Reading groups; Prayer groups; Movies; Shopping trips; Dances/Social/Cultural gatherings.

Buena Vista

Marion Memorial Nursing Home
PO Box 197, Hwy 41 N, Buena Vista, GA 31803
(912) 649-7100
Admin Jack P Story Jr. *Dir of Nursing* Deborah Harbuck. *Medical Dir* James R Hagler MD.
Licensure Skilled care; Intermediate care. *Beds* Swing beds SNF/ICF 50. *Private Pay Patients* 20%. *Certified* Medicaid.
Owner Nonprofit corp.
Admissions Requirements Physician's request.
Staff Physicians 4 (ft); RNs 1 (ft), 2 (pt); LPNs 7 (ft); Nurses' aides 15 (ft); Physical therapists 1 (ft); Reality therapists; Recreational therapists; Activities coordinators 1 (ft); Dietitians 1 (ft); Ophthalmologists 1 (pt); Podiatrists 1 (pt).
Facilities Dining room; Physical therapy room; Activities room; Laundry room; Barber/Beauty shop.
Activities Arts & crafts; Cards; Games; Prayer groups; Movies; Shopping trips; Dances/Social/Cultural gatherings; Intergenerational programs; Community involvement; Volunteer program.

Buford

Buford Manor Nursing Home
2451 Peachtree Industrial Blvd, Buford, GA 30518
(404) 945-6778
Admin Dana Phillips.
Licensure Skilled care; Intermediate care. *Beds* 117. *Certified* Medicaid; Medicare.

Byromville

Pinehill Nursing Center
PO Box 24, Byromville, GA 31007
(912) 433-5711
Admin Nancy M Herndon.
Licensure Skilled care; Intermediate care. *Beds* SNF 102. *Certified* Medicaid.

Calhoun

Cherokee Nursing Home
PO Box 937, 1387 US Hwy 41 N, Calhoun, GA 30701
(404) 629-1289
Admin Joyce L Crawford.
Medical Dir G W Brown MD.
Licensure Skilled care. *Beds* 100. *Certified* Medicaid.
Admissions Requirements Medical examination; Physician's request.
Staff Physicians 1 (pt); RNs 2 (ft), 1 (pt); LPNs 7 (ft), 5 (pt); Nurses' aides 20 (ft), 10 (pt); Activities coordinators 1 (ft), 1 (pt); Dietitians 1 (pt).
Facilities Dining room; Physical therapy room; Activities room; Crafts room; Laundry room; Barber/Beauty shop.
Activities Arts & crafts; Cards; Games; Reading groups; Prayer groups; Movies; Shopping trips; Dances/Social/Cultural gatherings.

Gordon Health Care Inc
PO Box 789, Calhoun, GA 30701
(404) 625-0044
Admin Ben E Crawford.
Licensure Skilled care; Intermediate care. *Beds* 117. *Certified* Medicaid; Medicare.

Camilla

Mitchell Convalescent Center
37 S Ellis, Camilla, GA 31730
(912) 336-8377
Admin Patrick Carrier. *Dir of Nursing* Lisa Bulloch. *Medical Dir* Dr A A McNeil.
Licensure Skilled care; Intermediate care. *Beds* Swing beds SNF/ICF 35. *Private Pay Patients* 9%. *Certified* Medicaid; Medicare.
Owner Publicly owned.
Admissions Requirements Medical examination; Physician's request.
Staff Physicians 4 (pt); RNs 1 (ft), 4 (pt); LPNs 4 (ft), 2 (pt); Nurses' aides 6 (ft), 8 (pt); Physical therapists (contracted); Speech therapists 1 (pt); Activities coordinators 1 (ft); Dietitians 1 (pt); Ophthalmologists 1 (pt); Podiatrists 1 (pt); Audiologists 1 (pt).
Facilities Dining room; Physical therapy room; Chapel; Laundry room; Barber/Beauty shop; Courtyard.
Activities Arts & crafts; Cards; Games; Prayer groups; Movies; Shopping trips; Dances/Social/Cultural gatherings.

Canton

Canton Nursing Center
321 Hospital Rd, Canton, GA 30114
(404) 479-8791
Admin Betty Soriano.
Medical Dir Dr David Field.
Licensure Skilled care; Intermediate care; Alzheimer's care. *Beds* SNF 100; ICF. *Certified* Medicaid.

Owner Proprietary corp.
Admissions Requirements Medical examination; Physician's request.
Staff RNs 1 (pt); LPNs 4 (ft), 3 (pt); Nurses' aides 5 (ft), 4 (pt); Speech therapists 1 (pt); Activities coordinators 1 (ft); Dietitians 1 (pt); Dentists 1 (pt).
Facilities Dining room; Activities room; Crafts room; Laundry room; Barber/Beauty shop.
Activities Arts & crafts; Games; Reading groups; Prayer groups; Movies; Shopping trips; Dances/Social/Cultural gatherings.

Coker Intermediate Care Home
150 Hospital Circle, Canton, GA 30114
(404) 479-5649
Admin Barbara J Baxter.
Medical Dir William Early MD.
Licensure Intermediate care. *Beds* ICF 81. *Certified* Medicaid.
Admissions Requirements Medical examination.
Staff RNs 1 (ft); LPNs 3 (ft), 2 (pt); Nurses' aides 15 (ft), 4 (pt); Activities coordinators 1 (ft); Dietitians 6 (ft), 5 (pt).
Facilities Dining room; Activities room; Chapel; Crafts room; Laundry room; Barber/Beauty shop; Library.
Activities Arts & crafts; Cards; Games; Prayer groups; Movies; Shopping trips; Dances/Social/Cultural gatherings; Exercise groups; Adopt-a-grandparent program; Bible study groups; Sunday school; Rhythm band & music-related activities.

Carrollton

Bagwell Nursing Home
443 Bagwell Rd, Carrollton, GA 30117
(404) 834-3501
Admin Mrs Bill Bagwell.
Medical Dir Dr E C Bass Jr.
Licensure Skilled care; Intermediate care. *Beds* 42. *Certified* Medicaid.
Admissions Requirements Medical examination; Physician's request.
Staff Physicians 1 (pt); RNs 1 (ft), 1 (pt); LPNs 3 (ft), 1 (pt); Nurses' aides 10 (ft), 5 (pt); Activities coordinators 2 (ft); Dietitians 2 (ft), 4 (pt).
Facilities Dining room; Activities room; Laundry room; Barber/Beauty shop.
Activities Arts & crafts; Games; Reading groups; Prayer groups; Shopping trips.

Carroll Convalescent Center
2327 N Hwy 27, Carrollton, GA 30117
(404) 834-4404
Admin Edgar Gable Jr.
Medical Dir Dr Dean B Talley.
Licensure Skilled care; Intermediate care. *Beds* 159. *Certified* Medicaid.
Admissions Requirements Medical examination; Physician's request.
Staff RNs 3 (ft), 1 (pt); LPNs 18 (ft), 6 (pt); Nurses' aides 65 (ft), 15 (pt); Physical therapists 1 (ft), 1 (pt); Recreational therapists 1 (ft), 1 (pt); Speech therapists 1 (pt); Activities coordinators 1 (ft), 1 (pt).
Facilities Dining room; Physical therapy room; Activities room; Laundry room; Barber/Beauty shop; Library.
Activities Arts & crafts; Cards; Games; Reading groups; Prayer groups; Shopping trips.

Carrollton Manor
PO Box 1216, 2450 Oak Grove Church Rd, Carrollton, GA 30117
(404) 834-1737
Admin Evelyn Windom. *Dir of Nursing* Theresa Thompson. *Medical Dir* Dean Talley.

Licensure Skilled care; Intermediate care; Retirement; Alzheimer's care. *Beds* Swing beds SNF/ICF 100; Retirement 40. *Private Pay Patients* 15%. *Certified* Medicaid; Medicare.
Owner Proprietary corp.
Admissions Requirements Medical examination; Physician's request.
Staff RNs 2 (ft), 3 (pt); LPNs 15 (ft), 3 (pt); Nurses' aides 35 (ft), 7 (pt); Physical therapists 1 (ft); Activities coordinators 1 (ft); Dietitian aides 14 (ft).
Facilities Dining room; Physical therapy room; Activities room; Laundry room; Barber/Beauty shop; Library.
Activities Arts & crafts; Cards; Games; Reading groups; Prayer groups; Movies; Shopping trips; Dances/Social/Cultural gatherings; Intergenerational programs; Pet therapy.

Pine Knoll Nursing Home
PO Box 2009, Carrollton, GA 30117
(404) 832-8243
Admin Shirley Green.
Licensure Skilled care; Intermediate care. *Beds* 122. *Certified* Medicaid.

Cartersville

Springdale Convalescent Center
78 Opal St, Cartersville, GA 30120
(404) 382-6120
Admin Elizabeth Russell.
Licensure Skilled care; Intermediate care. *Beds* 118. *Certified* Medicaid.

Cedartown

Cedartown Health Care
148 Cason Rd, Cedartown, GA 30125
(404) 748-3622
Admin John K Dupont.
Medical Dir Marc Well.
Licensure Skilled care; Intermediate care; Alzheimer's care. *Beds* SNF 116. *Certified* Medicaid.
Owner Proprietary corp.
Admissions Requirements Medical examination; Physician's request.
Activities Arts & crafts; Cards; Games; Reading groups; Prayer groups; Movies; Shopping trips; Dances/Social/Cultural gatherings.

Polk County Nursing Home
225 Philpot St, Cedartown, GA 30125
(404) 748-4116
Admin Debra Benefield.
Licensure Skilled care; Intermediate care. *Beds* 100. *Certified* Medicaid.

Chatsworth

Chatsworth Health Care Center
PO Box 1126, Chatsworth, GA 30705
(404) 695-8313
Admin Patricia W Haynes.
Medical Dir Dr Glenn Boyd.
Licensure Skilled care; Intermediate care. *Beds* 120. *Certified* Medicaid; Medicare.
Admissions Requirements Medical examination; Physician's request.
Staff Physicians 9 (pt); RNs 3 (ft); LPNs 12 (ft), 4 (pt); Nurses' aides 36 (ft), 8 (pt); Physical therapists 1 (ft); Reality therapists 1 (pt); Speech therapists 1 (pt); Activities coordinators 1 (ft); Dietitians 1 (pt); Ophthalmologists 2 (pt); Podiatrists 1 (pt); Dentists 1 (pt).
Facilities Dining room; Physical therapy room; Activities room; Chapel; Crafts room; Laundry room; Barber/Beauty shop; Library.
Activities Arts & crafts; Cards; Games; Reading groups; Prayer groups; Movies; Shopping trips; Dances/Social/Cultural gatherings.

Claxton

Claxton Nursing Home
PO Box 712, Claxton, GA 30417
(912) 739-2245
Admin John P Cowart.
Licensure Skilled care; Intermediate care. *Beds* 87. *Certified* Medicaid; Medicare.

Clayton

Mountain View Convalescent Center
Box 865, Warwoman Rd, Clayton, GA 30525
(404) 782-4276
Admin Lisa Garrett McKay.
Medical Dir Gene Westmoreland.
Licensure Skilled care; Intermediate care. *Beds* 117. *Certified* Medicaid.
Staff RNs 2 (ft); LPNs 6 (ft), 2 (pt); Nurses' aides 30 (ft), 8 (pt); Physical therapists 1 (ft); Activities coordinators 1 (ft); Dietitians 1 (ft); Podiatrists 1 (pt); Dentists 1 (pt).
Facilities Dining room; Physical therapy room; Activities room; Chapel; Crafts room; Laundry room; Barber/Beauty shop.
Activities Arts & crafts; Cards; Games; Reading groups; Prayer groups; Movies; Shopping trips; Dances/Social/Cultural gatherings.

Cleveland

Cross Roads Intermediate Care Facility
PO Box 1290, Cleveland, GA 30528
(404) 865-3131
Admin Ed L Stephens.
Licensure Intermediate care. *Beds* ICF 60. *Certified* Medicaid.

Friendship Nursing Home Inc
Rte 2 Box 2006, Cleveland, GA 30528
(404) 865-3131
Admin Debbie J Glore.
Licensure Skilled care; Intermediate care. *Beds* SNF 89. *Certified* Medicaid.

Cochran

Bryant Nursing Center
PO Box 476, 6th St, Cochran, GA 31014
(912) 934-7330
Admin Melanie Latham.
Medical Dir Grace Smith.
Licensure Skilled care. *Beds* SNF 75. *Certified* Medicaid.
Owner Proprietary corp (Beverly Enterprises).
Admissions Requirements Medical examination; Physician's request.
Staff Physicians 5 (ft); RNs 3 (ft), 1 (pt); LPNs 8 (ft), 3 (pt); Nurses' aides 16 (ft), 8 (pt); Physical therapists 1 (pt); Speech therapists 1 (pt); Activities coordinators 1 (ft); Dietitians 1 (pt).
Facilities Dining room; Physical therapy room; Activities room; Chapel; Crafts room; Laundry room; Barber/Beauty shop.
Activities Arts & crafts; Cards; Games; Reading groups; Prayer groups; Movies; Shopping trips; Dances/Social/Cultural gatherings.

College Park

College Park Convalescent Home
1765 Temple Ave, College Park, GA 30337
(404) 767-8600
Admin JoAnne Floyd.
Medical Dir Dr Reginald Smith.
Licensure Intermediate care. *Beds* ICF 100. *Certified* Medicaid.
Admissions Requirements Medical examination; Physician's request.
Staff Physicians 1 (ft); RNs 1 (pt); LPNs 6 (ft); Nurses' aides 56 (ft); Physical therapists 1 (pt); Speech therapists 1 (pt); Activities

coordinators 1 (ft); Dietitians 1 (ft); Ophthalmologists 1 (pt); Podiatrists 1 (ft); Dentists 1 (ft).
Facilities Dining room; Physical therapy room; Activities room; Laundry room; Barber/Beauty shop.
Activities Arts & crafts; Cards; Games; Reading groups; Prayer groups; Movies; Shopping trips; Dances/Social/Cultural gatherings.

Oak Hill Intermediate Care Home
4550 Janice Dr, College Park, GA 30337
(404) 761-3817
Admin Annell Smith.
Licensure Intermediate care. *Beds* 20.

Colquitt

Miller Nursing Home
209 N Cuthbert St, Colquitt, GA 31737
(912) 758-2500
Admin Edward W Johnson.
Licensure Skilled care; Intermediate care. *Beds* 83. *Certified* Medicaid; Medicare.

Columbus

Columbus Health Care Center
5131 Warm Springs Rd, Columbus, GA 31904
(404) 561-1371
Admin William Levinsohn.
Licensure Skilled care; Intermediate care. *Beds* SNF 210. *Certified* Medicaid.

Hamilton House Health Care Facility
1911 Hamilton Rd, Columbus, GA 31904
(404) 324-5194
Admin Mark Van Arsdale.
Licensure Skilled care. *Beds* SNF 128. *Certified* Medicaid; Medicare.

Medical Arts Health Facility
910 Talbotton Rd, Columbus, GA 31995
(404) 323-9513
Admin Rachel W Camp. *Dir of Nursing* Faye Bentley RN. *Medical Dir* Lavon Thurman MD.
Licensure Skilled care; Intermediate care. *Beds* Swing beds SNF/ICF 110. *Private Pay Patients* 5%. *Certified* Medicaid; Medicare.
Owner Nonprofit corp (Pleasant Valley Health Services Corp).
Admissions Requirements Medical examination; Physician's request.
Staff RNs 1 (ft), 2 (pt); LPNs 11 (ft), 2 (pt); Nurses' aides 39 (ft), 3 (pt); Physical therapists; Activities coordinators 1 (ft); Dietitians 1 (pt).
Facilities Dining room; Physical therapy room; Activities room; Crafts room; Laundry room; Barber/Beauty shop.
Activities Arts & crafts; Cards; Games; Reading groups; Prayer groups; Movies; Shopping trips; Pet therapy.

Muscogee Manor
7150 Manor Rd, Columbus, GA 31907
(404) 561-3218
Admin Joseph F Cobis.
Medical Dir Walker Rivers MD.
Licensure Skilled care; Intermediate care. *Beds* 242. *Certified* Medicaid; Medicare.
Admissions Requirements Medical examination; Physician's request.
Staff Physicians 1 (pt); RNs 8 (ft); LPNs 15 (ft); Nurses' aides 135 (ft); Physical therapists 1 (pt); Reality therapists 1 (pt); Recreational therapists 3 (pt); Occupational therapists 1 (pt); Speech therapists 1 (pt); Activities coordinators 1 (ft); Dietitians 1 (pt); Ophthalmologists 1 (pt); Podiatrists 1 (pt); Dentists 1 (pt).
Facilities Dining room; Physical therapy room; Activities room; Chapel; Crafts room; Laundry room; Barber/Beauty shop; Library; Dental office.

Activities Arts & crafts; Cards; Games; Reading groups; Prayer groups; Movies; Shopping trips; Dances/Social/Cultural gatherings.

Oak Manor Extended Care Facility
2010 Warm Springs Rd, Columbus, GA 31904
(404) 324-0387
Admin Clara K Brown. *Dir of Nursing* Carol Nahley RN. *Medical Dir* Dr Jack W Hirsch.
Licensure Skilled care. *Beds* SNF 210. *Certified* Medicaid; Medicare.
Owner Proprietary corp.
Admissions Requirements Medical examination; Physician's request.
Staff RNs 4 (ft), 1 (pt); LPNs 17 (ft), 4 (pt); Nurses' aides 70 (ft), 11 (pt); Physical therapists 1 (ft), 2 (pt); Occupational therapists 1 (pt); Speech therapists 1 (pt); Activities coordinators 2 (ft), 1 (pt); Dietitians 1 (ft).
Languages German, Spanish.
Facilities Dining room; Physical therapy room; Activities room; Chapel; Barber/Beauty shop; Library.
Activities Arts & crafts; Games; Reading groups; Prayer groups; Movies.

Pine Manor Nursing Home Inc
2000 Warm Springs Rd, Columbus, GA 31904
(404) 324-2252
Admin Clara K Brown. *Dir of Nursing* Carol Nahley RN. *Medical Dir* Dr Jack W Hirsch.
Licensure Skilled care; Intermediate care. *Beds* SNF 166. *Certified* Medicaid; Medicare.
Owner Proprietary corp.
Admissions Requirements Medical examination; Physician's request.
Staff RNs 3 (ft), 2 (pt); LPNs 11 (ft), 2 (pt); Nurses' aides 60 (ft), 14 (pt); Physical therapists 1 (ft), 2 (pt); Occupational therapists 1 (pt); Speech therapists 1 (pt); Activities coordinators 2 (ft), 1 (pt); Dietitians 1 (ft).
Languages German, Spanish.
Facilities Dining room; Physical therapy room; Activities room; Chapel; Barber/Beauty shop; Library.
Activities Arts & crafts; Games; Reading groups; Prayer groups; Movies.

Comer

Cobb Health Care Center
200 Paoli Rd, Comer, GA 30629
(404) 783-5116
Admin Frances Osborne. *Dir of Nursing* Frances Barrett. *Medical Dir* W W Harris MD.
Licensure Skilled care. *Beds* SNF 100. *Private Pay Patients* 5%. *Certified* Medicaid; Medicare.
Owner Nonprofit corp (Cobb Memorial Hospital).
Admissions Requirements Physician's request.
Staff Physicians 10 (ft); RNs 2 (ft), 2 (pt); LPNs 6 (ft), 4 (pt); Nurses' aides 34 (ft), 8 (pt); Physical therapists; Activities coordinators 1 (ft), 1 (pt); Dietitians.
Facilities Dining room; Physical therapy room; Activities room; Crafts room; Laundry room; Barber/Beauty shop.
Activities Arts & crafts; Cards; Games; Reading groups; Prayer groups; Movies; Shopping trips; Dances/Social/Cultural gatherings; Intergenerational programs; Pet therapy.

Commerce

Banks-Jackson-Commerce Nursing Home
Bolton Rd, Commerce, GA 30539
(404) 335-3181
Admin James David Lawrence Jr. *Dir of Nursing* Sharon Hix RN. *Medical Dir* Dr Joe L Griffeth.

Licensure Skilled care; Intermediate care. *Beds* Intermingled 72. *Certified* Medicaid; Medicare.
Owner Nonprofit organization/foundation.
Admissions Requirements Medical examination; Physician's request.
Staff Physicians 5 (ft); RNs 2 (ft); LPNs 8 (ft); Nurses' aides 22 (ft), 6 (pt); Physical therapists 2 (ft); Activities coordinators 1 (ft); Dietitians 1 (ft); Professional social workers 1 (ft).
Affiliation Baptist.
Facilities Dining room; Physical therapy room; Activities room; Laundry room; Barber/Beauty shop; Library.
Activities Arts & crafts; Cards; Games; Reading groups; Prayer groups; Movies; Shopping trips; Dances/Social/Cultural gatherings; Cooking; Arranging flowers; Garden club.

Crystle Springs Nursing Home Inc
Ridgeway Rd, Commerce, GA 30529
(404) 335-5118, 335-2118 FAX
Admin Joy C Brown. *Dir of Nursing* Lynda Allen RN. *Medical Dir* Dr Joe Griffeth.
Licensure Skilled care. *Beds* SNF 50. *Private Pay Patients* 100%.
Owner Proprietary corp.
Admissions Requirements Medical examination; Physician's request.
Staff Physicians 5 (pt); RNs 1 (ft); LPNs 6 (ft); Nurses' aides 17 (ft), 8 (pt); Physical therapists 1 (pt); Occupational therapists 1 (pt); Speech therapists 1 (pt); Activities coordinators 1 (ft), 2 (pt); Dietitians 1 (pt); Podiatrists 1 (pt).
Facilities Dining room; Physical therapy room; Activities room; Crafts room; Laundry room; Barber/Beauty shop; Veranda.
Activities Arts & crafts; Games; Reading groups; Prayer groups; Movies; Shopping trips; Dances/Social/Cultural gatherings; Intergenerational programs; Family gatherings; Barbecues.

Conyers

Starcrest Home of Conyers
PO Box 438, Conyers, GA 30207
(404) 483-3902
Admin Judy W Smith.
Licensure Skilled care; Intermediate care. *Beds* SNF 196. *Certified* Medicaid.

Cordele

Cordele Royal Care Center
902 Blackshear Rd, Cordele, GA 31015
(912) 273-1481
Admin W B Crane.
Licensure Skilled care; Intermediate care. *Beds* SNF 143. *Certified* Medicaid.

Crisp County Medical Nursing Center
1106 N 4th St, Cordele, GA 31015
(912) 273-1227
Admin Carolyn Kidd. *Dir of Nursing* Carolyn Howard. *Medical Dir* Dr J T Christmas.
Licensure Intermingled. *Beds* 100. *Certified* Medicaid; VA.
Owner Proprietary corp (Beverly Enterprises).
Admissions Requirements Medical examination.
Staff RNs; LPNs; Nurses' aides; Activities coordinators.
Facilities Dining room; Physical therapy room; Activities room; Laundry room; Barber/Beauty shop.
Activities Arts & crafts; Games; Reading groups; Prayer groups; Movies; Shopping trips; Dances/Social/Cultural gatherings.

Covington

Covington Manor
4148 Carroll St, Ex-C, Covington, GA 30209
(404) 786-0427
Admin C L Johnson. *Dir of Nursing* Jane Hicks RN.
Licensure Skilled care; Intermediate care. *Beds* Swing beds SNF/ICF 71. *Certified* Medicaid.
Staff RNs 1 (ft), 1 (pt); LPNs 4 (ft), 3 (pt); Nurses' aides 28 (ft), 1 (pt); Dietitians 1 (ft).

Riverside Nursing Center of Covington
5100 West St, Covington, GA 30209
(404) 787-0211
Admin Cheryl Coleman. *Dir of Nursing* Jane Jones RN. *Medical Dir* Timmothy Park MD.
Licensure Skilled care; Intermediate care. *Beds* SNF 128; ICF. *Certified* Medicaid.
Owner Proprietary corp.
Admissions Requirements Medical examination.
Staff Physicians; RNs 2 (ft), 2 (pt); LPNs 10 (ft), 5 (pt); Nurses' aides 48 (ft), 18 (pt); Physical therapists 2 (ft), 1 (pt); Speech therapists 1 (pt); Activities coordinators 1 (ft); Dietitians 1 (ft), 1 (pt).
Facilities Dining room; Physical therapy room; Activities room; Chapel; Laundry room; Barber/Beauty shop; Library.
Activities Games; Movies; Shopping trips; Dances/Social/Cultural gatherings; Exercise; Sing-alongs; Worship services; Luncheons.

Crawford

Quiet Oaks Health Care
PO Box 613, Oglethorpe St, Crawford, GA 30330
(404) 743-5452
Admin Brenda Butler.
Licensure Skilled care; Intermediate care. *Beds* SNF 61. *Certified* Medicaid.

Cumming

Cumming Convalescent Home
PO Box 24, Cumming, GA 30130
(404) 887-2308
Admin Harold Winters.
Licensure Intermediate care. *Beds* ICF 50. *Certified* Medicaid.

Lanier Nursing Home
125 Samaritan Dr, Cumming, GA 30130
(404) 889-0120
Admin Barbara J Baxter.
Medical Dir Fred Boling MD.
Licensure Skilled care; Intermediate care. *Beds* SNF 150. *Certified* Medicaid.
Admissions Requirements Medical examination; Physician's request.
Staff RNs 3 (ft); LPNs 9 (ft), 1 (pt); Nurses' aides 40 (ft), 10 (pt); Physical therapists; Occupational therapists; Speech therapists; Activities coordinators 1 (ft); Dietitians; Podiatrists.
Facilities Dining room; Physical therapy room; Activities room; Laundry room; Barber/Beauty shop.
Activities Cards; Games; Prayer groups; Movies; Shopping trips; Dances/Social/Cultural gatherings.

Cuthbert

Joe Anne Burgin Nursing Home
203 Randolph St, Cuthbert, GA 31740
(912) 732-2181
Admin Patricia R Prescott. *Dir of Nursing* Christina Scribner RN. *Medical Dir* Carl E Sills MD.
Licensure Skilled care; Intermediate care. *Beds* 80. *Certified* Medicaid; Medicare.
Owner Publicly owned.
Admissions Requirements Physician's request.

Staff RNs 2 (ft), 2 (pt); LPNs 6 (ft), 3 (pt); Nurses' aides 20 (ft), 12 (pt); Physical therapists 1 (pt); Recreational therapists 1 (pt); Activities coordinators 1 (pt); Dietitians 1 (pt).
Facilities Dining room; Physical therapy room; Activities room; Chapel; Crafts room; Laundry room; Barber/Beauty shop.
Activities Arts & crafts; Cards; Games; Prayer groups; Movies; Shopping trips; Dances/Social/Cultural gatherings; Outings.

Dahlonega

Gold City Convalescent Center Inc
PO Box 96, Hwy 19, Dahlonega, GA 30533
(404) 864-3045
Admin Peter Arms. *Dir of Nursing* Chris Robinson. *Medical Dir* Eugene Westmoreland MD.
Licensure Skilled care; Retirement. *Beds* SNF 102; Retirement 40. *Private Pay Patients* 14%. *Certified* Medicaid; Medicare.
Owner Proprietary corp (Older American Care).
Admissions Requirements Medical examination; Physician's request.
Staff Physicians 1 (pt); RNs 1 (ft), 3 (pt); LPNs 12 (ft), 4 (pt); Nurses' aides 33 (ft), 8 (pt); Physical therapists 1 (pt); Occupational therapists 1 (pt); Speech therapists 1 (pt); Activities coordinators 1 (ft); Dietitians 1 (ft).
Facilities Dining room; Physical therapy room; Activities room; Chapel; Laundry room; Barber/Beauty shop.
Activities Arts & crafts; Cards; Games; Prayer groups; Dances/Social/Cultural gatherings.

Dallas

Paulding Memorial Medical Center Long Term Care Unit
600 W Memorial Dr, Dallas, GA 30132
(404) 445-4411
Admin Ray C Brees. *Dir of Nursing* Carol Goen. *Medical Dir* J Henry Duntec MD.
Licensure Skilled care; Intermediate care. *Beds* Swing beds SNF/ICF 136. *Private Pay Patients* 15%. *Certified* Medicaid; Medicare.
Owner Nonprofit organization/foundation.
Admissions Requirements Medical examination; Physician's request.
Staff Physicians; RNs 3 (ft), 4 (pt); LPNs 17 (ft), 5 (pt); Nurses' aides 40 (ft); Physical therapists 1 (ft); Occupational therapists 1 (pt); Speech therapists 1 (pt); Activities coordinators 1 (pt); Dietitians 1 (pt); Ophthalmologists.
Facilities Dining room; Physical therapy room; Activities room; Chapel; Crafts room; Laundry room; Barber/Beauty shop; Library.
Activities Arts & crafts; Cards; Games; Reading groups; Prayer groups; Movies; Shopping trips; Dances/Social/Cultural gatherings; Intergenerational programs; Pet therapy.

Dalton

Quinton Memorial Health Care Center
1114 Burleyson Dr, Dalton, GA 30720
(404) 226-4642
Admin Eugene Harrison.
Medical Dir Neil Boggess MD.
Licensure Skilled care; Intermediate care. *Beds* 120. *Certified* Medicaid.
Admissions Requirements Medical examination.
Staff RNs 3 (ft); LPNs 9 (ft), 4 (pt); Nurses' aides 34 (ft), 4 (pt); Physical therapists 1 (ft), 1 (pt); Activities coordinators 1 (ft); Dietitians 1 (pt).
Facilities Dining room; Physical therapy room; Activities room; Chapel; Crafts room; Laundry room; Barber/Beauty shop.

Activities Arts & crafts; Cards; Games; Prayer groups; Movies; Shopping trips; Birthday parties; Devotionals by multi-denominational leaders.

Ridgewood Manor
1110 Burleyson Dr, Dalton, GA 30720
(404) 226-1021
Admin David Geary. *Dir of Nursing* Karen Ismail. *Medical Dir* Dr Earl McGhee.
Licensure Skilled care; Intermediate care. *Beds* 102. *Certified* Medicaid; Medicare.
Owner Proprietary corp.
Admissions Requirements Medical examination; Physician's request.
Staff RNs 3 (ft); LPNs 10 (ft), 2 (pt); Nurses' aides 22 (ft), 10 (pt); Physical therapists 1 (pt); Activities coordinators 1 (ft); Dietitians 1 (pt).
Facilities Dining room; Physical therapy room; Activities room; Chapel; Laundry room; Barber/Beauty shop.
Activities Arts & crafts; Cards; Games; Prayer groups; Shopping trips; Dances/Social/Cultural gatherings.

Wood Dale Health Care Center
1102 Burleyson Dr, Dalton, GA 30720
(404) 226-1285
Admin Darrell Chisholm.
Medical Dir Robert L Raitz MD.
Licensure Skilled care; Intermediate care. *Beds* SNF 108. *Certified* Medicaid.
Admissions Requirements Medical examination; Physician's request.
Staff Physicians 15 (pt); RNs 2 (ft), 1 (pt); LPNs 13 (ft), 6 (pt); Nurses' aides 28 (ft), 12 (pt); Physical therapists 1 (pt); Speech therapists 1 (pt); Activities coordinators 1 (ft); Dietitians 1 (pt); Dentists 1 (pt).
Facilities Dining room; Physical therapy room; Activities room; Chapel; Crafts room; Laundry room; Barber/Beauty shop.
Activities Arts & crafts; Cards.

Dawson

Dawson Manor
Box 607, 507 E Georgia Ave, Dawson, GA 31742
(912) 995-5016
Admin Jimmy C Johns.
Licensure Skilled care; Intermediate care. *Beds* SNF 74. *Certified* Medicaid.

Decatur

Americana Health Care Center
2722 N Decatur Rd, Decatur, GA 30033
(404) 296-5440
Admin Pamela Koen.
Medical Dir Dr Philip Jardina.
Licensure Skilled care. *Beds* 141. *Certified* Medicare.
Owner Proprietary corp (Manor Care).
Admissions Requirements Minimum age 21; Medical examination.
Staff Physicians 3 (pt); RNs 7 (ft), 4 (pt); LPNs 10 (ft), 7 (pt); Nurses' aides 47 (ft), 4 (pt); Physical therapists 2 (ft), 1 (pt); Reality therapists 2 (ft); Recreational therapists 2 (ft); Occupational therapists 1 (pt); Speech therapists 1 (pt); Activities coordinators 1 (ft); Dietitians 1 (ft); Podiatrists 1 (pt); Audiologists 1 (pt); Dentists 1 (pt).
Facilities Dining room; Physical therapy room; Activities room; Barber/Beauty shop; Occupational therapy room.
Activities Arts & crafts; Cards; Games; Reading groups; Prayer groups; Movies; Shopping trips; Dances/Social/Cultural gatherings.

Atlantacare Convalescent Center Intermediate Care Unit
304 5th Ave, Decatur, GA 30030
(404) 373-6231

Admin George Hunt.
Licensure Skilled care; Intermediate care. *Beds* SNF 103. *Certified* Medicaid.

Beverly Manor Convalescent No 53
2787 N Decatur Rd, Decatur, GA 30030
(404) 292-0626
Admin Donna W Huffstutler. *Dir of Nursing* Regina Ford. *Medical Dir* Dr J Tabatabai.
Licensure Skilled care. *Beds* SNF 73. *Certified* Medicaid; Medicare.
Owner Proprietary corp (Beverly Enterprises).
Admissions Requirements Medical examination.
Staff Physicians; RNs; LPNs; Nurses' aides; Physical therapists; Occupational therapists; Speech therapists; Activities coordinators; Dietitians; Ophthalmologists.
Facilities Dining room; Physical therapy room; Activities room; Crafts room; Laundry room; Barber/Beauty shop.
Activities Arts & crafts; Cards; Games; Reading groups; Prayer groups; Movies; Shopping trips; Dances/Social/Cultural gatherings.

DeKalb General Nursing Unit
2701 N Decatur Rd, Decatur, GA 30033
(404) 292-4444
Admin Naomi Harman. *Dir of Nursing* Pamela Koen. *Medical Dir* John A Harrel MD.
Licensure Skilled care. *Beds* 50. *Certified* Medicaid; Medicare.
Owner Nonprofit organization/foundation.
Admissions Requirements Medical examination; Physician's request.
Staff RNs 7 (ft), 7 (pt); LPNs 1 (ft), 1 (pt); Nurses' aides 12 (ft), 11 (pt); Physical therapists 1 (ft); Recreational therapists 1 (ft); Occupational therapists 1 (ft); Speech therapists 1 (ft); Activities coordinators 1 (ft); Dietitians 1 (ft); Ophthalmologists 1 (pt); Podiatrists 1 (ft).
Facilities Dining room; Physical therapy room; Activities room; Chapel; Crafts room; Barber/Beauty shop.
Activities Arts & crafts; Cards; Games; Reading groups; Prayer groups; Movies; Shopping trips; Dances/Social/Cultural gatherings.

Georgia Regional Development Learning Center
PO Box 32407, Decatur, GA 30306
(404) 243-2160
Admin Stephen L Watson.
Medical Dir Tomas Naura MD.
Licensure Intermediate care for mentally retarded. *Beds* ICF/MR 67.
Admissions Requirements Minimum age 1-17; Medical examination; Physician's request.
Staff Physicians 1 (ft); RNs 3 (ft); LPNs 14 (ft); Physical therapists 1 (ft); Recreational therapists 1 (ft); Occupational therapists 1 (ft); Speech therapists 1 (ft); Activities coordinators 1 (ft); Dietitians 1 (ft); Dentists 1 (ft).
Facilities Dining room; Physical therapy room; Activities room; Chapel; Crafts room; Laundry room; Barber/Beauty shop; Library.
Activities Arts & crafts; Cards; Games; Reading groups; Movies; Shopping trips; Dances/Social/Cultural gatherings.

Glenwood Manor
4115 Glenwood Rd, Decatur, GA 30032
(404) 284-6414
Admin Michael Winget.
Licensure Skilled care; Intermediate care. *Beds* 225. *Certified* Medicaid.
Owner Proprietary corp (Beverly Enterprises).

Harvest Heights
3200 Panthersville Rd, Decatur, GA 30034
(404) 243-8460
Admin Roger Geach. *Dir of Nursing* Darlene Greenhill.

Licensure Skilled care; Intermediate care. *Beds* 146. *Certified* Medicaid; Medicare.
Owner Nonprofit corp (GA Bapt Med Center).
Admissions Requirements Minimum age 18; Medical examination.
Staff Physicians 10 (ft); RNs 5 (ft), 6 (pt); LPNs 7 (ft), 5 (pt); Nurses' aides 45 (ft), 12 (pt); Physical therapists 1 (pt); Reality therapists 1 (pt); Recreational therapists 1 (pt); Occupational therapists 1 (pt); Speech therapists 1 (pt); Activities coordinators 2 (ft); Dietitians 2 (ft); Ophthalmologists 1 (pt); Podiatrists 2 (pt); Dentists 2 (pt); Social workers 1 (ft).
Affiliation Baptist.
Facilities Dining room; Physical therapy room; Activities room; Chapel; Crafts room; Laundry room; Barber/Beauty shop; Library; Patios.
Activities Arts & crafts; Cards; Games; Prayer groups; Movies; Shopping trips; Dances/ Social/Cultural gatherings.

Demorest

Habersham Home
PO Box 37, Demorest, GA 30535
(404) 754-2134
Admin John H Bridges Sr.
Licensure Skilled care; Intermediate care. *Beds* 84. *Certified* Medicaid; Medicare.

Donalsonville

Seminole Manor
PO Box 1006, Donalsonville, GA 31745
(912) 524-2062
Admin Linda Abbott.
Medical Dir Dr Jacob Holley.
Licensure Skilled care; Intermediate care. *Beds* SNF 62. *Certified* Medicaid.
Admissions Requirements Medical examination; Physician's request.
Staff RNs 1 (ft); LPNs 5 (ft); Nurses' aides 12 (ft); Activities coordinators 1 (ft); Dietitians 1 (ft).
Facilities Dining room; Activities room; Laundry room; Barber/Beauty shop.
Activities Arts & crafts; Cards; Games; Reading groups; Prayer groups; Movies; Shopping trips; Dances/Social/Cultural gatherings.

Douglas

Shady Acres Convalescent Center
PO Box 1059, Douglas, GA 31533
(912) 384-7811
Admin Joyce S Suttler. *Dir of Nursing* Judy O Brigmood RN. *Medical Dir* Dr Calvin Meeks.
Licensure Skilled care; Intermediate care. *Beds* 148. *Certified* Medicaid.
Owner Privately owned.
Admissions Requirements Medical examination; Physician's request.
Facilities Dining room; Physical therapy room; Activities room; Crafts room; Laundry room; Barber/Beauty shop.
Activities Arts & crafts; Cards; Games; Reading groups; Prayer groups; Movies; Shopping trips; Dances/Social/Cultural gatherings.

Douglasville

Garden Terrace Nursing Center
4028 Hwy 5, Douglasville, GA 30135
(912) 942-7111
Admin Cynthia G Hendry.
Medical Dir George Artress.
Licensure Skilled care; Intermediate care. *Beds* 246. *Certified* Medicaid; Medicare.
Owner Proprietary corp (Beverly Enterprises).
Admissions Requirements Medical examination; Physician's request.

Staff Physicians 5 (pt); RNs 4 (ft), 3 (pt); LPNs 19 (ft), 6 (pt); Nurses' aides 64 (ft), 18 (pt); Physical therapists 1 (ft); Speech therapists 1 (pt); Activities coordinators 2 (ft); Dietitians 1 (ft); Ophthalmologists 1 (pt); Podiatrists 1 (pt); Dentists 1 (pt).
Facilities Dining room; Physical therapy room; Activities room; Chapel; Laundry room; Barber/Beauty shop; Library; County book mobile.
Activities Arts & crafts; Cards; Games; Reading groups; Prayer groups; Movies; Shopping trips.

Dublin

Dublinaire Nursing Home
Rte 4 Box 147, Dublin, GA 31021
(912) 272-7437
Admin Kaye Bracewell.
Licensure Skilled care; Intermediate care. *Beds* 149. *Certified* Medicaid; Medicare.

Laurens County Convalescent Center Inc
PO Box 549, Dublin, GA 31021
(912) 272-1666
Admin Wonnie Oliver.
Medical Dir John A Bell MD.
Licensure Skilled care; Intermediate care. *Beds* SNF 130. *Certified* Medicaid.
Admissions Requirements Physician's request.
Staff Physicians 1 (ft), 10 (pt); RNs 1 (ft), 1 (pt); LPNs 9 (ft), 4 (pt); Nurses' aides 19 (ft), 10 (pt); Physical therapists 1 (pt); Activities coordinators 1 (ft); Dietitians 1 (pt); Podiatrists 1 (pt); Dentists 1 (pt).
Facilities Dining room; Physical therapy room; Activities room; Crafts room; Laundry room; Barber/Beauty shop.
Activities Arts & crafts; Cards; Games; Reading groups; Prayer groups; Shopping trips; Dances/Social/Cultural gatherings.

Shamrock Health Care
1634 Telfair St, Dublin, GA 31021
(912) 272-3220
Admin J Ralph Hargraves. *Dir of Nursing* Clen Lanier RN. *Medical Dir* N W Chism MD.
Licensure Skilled care; Intermediate care. *Beds* Swing beds SNF/ICF 105. *Certified* Medicaid; Medicare.
Owner Nonprofit corp (Pleasant Valley Health Services).
Admissions Requirements Medical examination; Physician's request.
Staff Physicians; RNs 2 (ft), 2 (pt); LPNs 14 (ft), 2 (pt); Nurses' aides 35 (ft); Physical therapists 1 (ft), 1 (pt); Occupational therapists 1 (ft), 1 (pt); Speech therapists 1 (ft), 1 (pt); Dietitians 1 (ft), 1 (pt); Podiatrists 1 (pt).
Facilities Dining room; Physical therapy room; Activities room; Chapel; Laundry room; Barber/Beauty shop.
Activities Arts & crafts; Cards; Games; Reading groups; Prayer groups; Movies; Shopping trips; Dances/Social/Cultural gatherings.

East Point

Bonterra Nursing Center
2801 Felton Dr, East Point, GA 30344
(404) 767-7591, 765-0547 FAX
Admin Timothy N Johnson. *Dir of Nursing* Elizabeth T Lonsdale. *Medical Dir* Joe S Cruise MD.
Licensure Skilled care. *Beds* SNF 118. *Certified* Medicaid; Medicare.
Owner Proprietary corp (Southeastern Health Care Management).
Admissions Requirements Physician's request.
Staff RNs 3 (ft), 1 (pt); LPNs 13 (ft), 3 (pt); Nurses' aides 45 (ft), 2 (pt); Activities coordinators 2 (ft); Dietitians 1 (pt).

Facilities Dining room; Physical therapy room; Activities room; Laundry room; Barber/Beauty shop; Private dining room.
Activities Arts & crafts; Games; Reading groups; Prayer groups; Movies; Shopping trips.

South Fulton Hospital—Extended Care Facility
1170 Cleveland Ave, East Point, GA 30044
(404) 669-4000
Admin David F Marr.
Licensure Skilled care. *Beds* SNF 36. *Certified* Medicare.
Admissions Requirements Medical examination; Physician's request.
Staff RNs 5 (ft), 1 (pt); LPNs 3 (ft), 2 (pt); Nurses' aides 11 (ft), 1 (pt); Physical therapists 4 (ft); Speech therapists 1 (ft); Activities coordinators 1 (pt); Dietitians 3 (ft).
Facilities Dining room; Physical therapy room; Activities room; Chapel; Barber/ Beauty shop.
Activities Cards; Games; Birthday parties monthly; Parties special holidays.

Ware Avenue Personal Care Home
1662 Ware Ave, East Point, GA 30344
(404) 767-0906
Admin Everett L Smith. *Dir of Nursing* Debbie Bohan. *Medical Dir* Robert Webster MD.
Licensure Intermediate care; Personal care. *Beds* ICF 24.
Owner Privately owned (Everett L Smith).
Admissions Requirements Minimum age 30; Medical examination; Physician's request.
Staff Nurses' aides 8 (ft); Physical therapists 1 (ft); Dietitians 1 (ft).
Affiliation Eastern Star.
Facilities Dining room; Activities room; Crafts room; Laundry room.
Activities Arts & crafts; Cards; Games; Prayer groups.

Eastman

Heart of Georgia Nursing Home
PO Box 493, Eastman, GA 31023
(912) 374-5571
Admin Beverly M Barrentine. *Dir of Nursing* Julianne Dunn. *Medical Dir* Dr D H Conner.
Licensure Skilled care; Intermediate care. *Beds* 100. *Certified* Medicaid.
Owner Proprietary corp.
Admissions Requirements Medical examination; Physician's request.
Staff RNs 2 (ft), 2 (pt); LPNs 8 (ft), 4 (pt); Nurses' aides 26 (ft), 12 (pt); Activities coordinators 1 (ft); Dietitians 1 (ft).
Facilities Dining room; Physical therapy room; Activities room; Crafts room; Laundry room; Barber/Beauty shop.
Activities Arts & crafts; Games; Reading groups; Prayer groups; Movies; Shopping trips.

Middle Georgia Nursing Home
PO Box 159, Page St & Chester Rd, Eastman, GA 31023
(912) 374-4733
Admin Willene C Dykes. *Dir of Nursing* Mable Conner. *Medical Dir* Dr David H Conner.
Licensure Skilled care; Intermediate care. *Beds* Swing beds SNF/ICF 100. *Private Pay Patients* 5%. *Certified* Medicaid.
Owner Proprietary corp (Kem Care Inc).
Admissions Requirements Medical examination; Physician's request.
Staff Physicians 7 (ft); RNs 2 (ft), 3 (pt); LPNs 9 (ft), 3 (pt); Nurses' aides 28 (ft), 17 (pt); Physical therapists 1 (ft); Reality therapists 1 (ft); Recreational therapists 1 (ft); Occupational therapists 1 (ft), 1 (pt); Speech therapists 1 (pt); Activities

coordinators 1 (ft); Dietitians 1 (ft);
Ophthalmologists 1 (ft); Podiatrists 2 (ft);
Audiologists 1 (pt).
Facilities Dining room; Physical therapy
room; Activities room; Chapel; Crafts room;
Laundry room; Barber/Beauty shop; Library
Outdoor areas; Gazebo; Screened porch.
Activities Arts & crafts; Cards; Games;
Reading groups; Prayer groups; Movies;
Shopping trips; Dances/Social/Cultural
gatherings; Intergenerational programs; Pet
therapy Cookouts; Fishing trips.

Eatonton

Regency Health Care Center
PO Box 541, Eatonton, GA 31024
(404) 485-8573
Admin Robert Hudson.
Licensure Skilled care; Intermediate care. *Beds*
92. *Certified* Medicaid; Medicare.
Owner Proprietary corp (Regency Health Care
Centers).

Edison

Calhoun Nursing Home
PO Box 387, Edison, GA 31746
(912) 835-2251
Admin Newana C Williams.
Licensure Skilled care; Intermediate care. *Beds*
60. *Certified* Medicaid; Medicare.
Owner Publicly owned.
Admissions Requirements Medical
examination; Physician's request.
Facilities Dining room; Physical therapy
room; Activities room; Crafts room; Laundry
room; Barber/Beauty shop; Library.
Activities Arts & crafts; Cards; Games;
Reading groups; Prayer groups; Movies;
Shopping trips; Dances/Social/Cultural
gatherings.

Elberton

Nancy Hart Memorial Medical Center
PO Box 753, Elberton, GA 30635
(404) 283-3335
Admin Lynn H Blackmon. *Dir of Nursing*
Judy Albertson. *Medical Dir* J Daniel
McAvoy MD.
Licensure Intermediate care. *Beds* ICF 67.
Certified Medicaid.
Owner Proprietary corp.
Admissions Requirements Medical
examination; Physician's request.
Staff Physicians 1 (ft), 1 (pt); RNs 1 (pt);
LPNs 3 (ft), 3 (pt); Nurses' aides 9 (ft), 3
(pt); Physical therapists 1 (ft); Speech
therapists 1 (pt); Activities coordinators 1
(ft); Dietitians 5 (ft), 2 (pt);
Ophthalmologists 1 (pt); Social services
directors 1 (ft).
Facilities Dining room; Activities room;
Laundry room; Barber/Beauty shop.
Activities Arts & crafts; Games; Reading
groups; Prayer groups; Movies; Picnics;
Outings.

Heardmont Health Care Center
Route 6, Box 249, Elberton, GA 30635
(404) 283-5429
Admin Aubrey T Fleming.
Licensure Skilled care; Intermediate care. *Beds*
60. *Certified* Medicaid; Medicare.
Owner Proprietary corp (Stuckey Health
Care).

Spring Valley Health Care Center Inc
651 Rhodes Dr, Elberton, GA 30635
(404) 283-3880
Admin Wilma Castellaw. *Dir of Nursing*
LaVerne Bowdoin RN. *Medical Dir* Dr M H
Arnold.
Licensure Skilled care; Intermediate care. *Beds*
SNF 60; ICF. *Certified* Medicaid.
Owner Privately owned.

Admissions Requirements Medical
examination; Physician's request.
Staff Physicians 1 (pt); RNs 1 (ft), 1 (pt);
LPNs 4 (ft), 2 (pt); Nurses' aides 19 (ft), 5
(pt); Physical therapists 2 (pt); Activities
coordinators 1 (ft), 1 (pt); Dietitians 1 (pt);
Ophthalmologists 1 (pt).
Facilities Dining room; Physical therapy
room; Activities room; Laundry room;
Barber/Beauty shop.
Activities Arts & crafts; Reading groups;
Prayer groups; Movies; Shopping trips.

Ellijay

Gilmer Nursing Home
PO Box 346, Ellijay, GA 30540
(404) 635-4741
Admin John J Downs. *Dir of Nursing* Joanne
Ferguson RN. *Medical Dir* Robert K Bond
MD.
Licensure Skilled care. *Beds* SNF 84. *Certified*
Medicaid; Medicare.
Owner Nonprofit corp (GA Bapt Med Center).
Admissions Requirements Medical
examination; Physician's request.
Staff Physicians 4 (ft); RNs 1 (ft), 1 (pt);
LPNs 6 (ft), 5 (pt); Nurses' aides 12 (ft), 7
(pt); Physical therapists 1 (pt); Speech
therapists 1 (pt); Activities coordinators 1
(ft); Dietitians 1 (pt).
Languages Spanish (translation available).
Facilities Dining room; Physical therapy
room; Activities room; Chapel; Crafts room;
Laundry room; Barber/Beauty shop;
Solarium; Large veranda; Fenced 1/2 acre
lawn.
Activities Arts & crafts; Cards; Games;
Reading groups; Prayer groups; Movies;
Shopping trips; Dances/Social/Cultural
gatherings; Bingo; Aerobics; Gardening;
Music.

Evans

Evans Health Care
PO Box 338, N Belair Rd, Evans, GA 30809
(404) 863-7514
Admin Jackie Blackson.
Licensure Skilled care; Intermediate care. *Beds*
120. *Certified* Medicaid; Medicare.
Owner Proprietary corp (Stuckey Health
Care).

Fairburn

Fairburn Health Care Center
178 Campbellton St, Fairburn, GA 30213
(404) 964-1320
Admin Juanita Patton Doss. *Dir of Nursing*
Pamela Howell. *Medical Dir* Stanley
Gregoroff MD.
Licensure Skilled care; Intermediate care. *Beds*
SNF 120; ICF. *Certified* Medicaid;
Medicare.
Admissions Requirements Medical
examination; Physician's request.
Staff Physicians 3 (ft); RNs 3 (ft); LPNs 10
(ft), 2 (pt); Nurses' aides 40 (ft); Physical
therapists 1 (pt); Speech therapists 1 (pt);
Activities coordinators 1 (ft); Dietitians 1
(ft).
Facilities Dining room; Physical therapy
room; Activities room; Laundry room;
Barber/Beauty shop.
Activities Arts & crafts; Games; Reading
groups; Prayer groups; Movies.

Fitzgerald

Fitzgerald Nursing Home
Rte 1 Box 22, Fitzgerald, GA 31750
(912) 423-4361
Admin Michael A Norkus.
Licensure Skilled care; Intermediate care. *Beds*
78. *Certified* Medicaid; Medicare.

Life Care Center Inc
PO Box 1289, Fitzgerald, GA 31750
(912) 423-4353
Admin Edward M Coop.
Medical Dir Dr Roy Johnson.
Licensure Skilled care; Intermediate care. *Beds*
167. *Certified* Medicaid; Medicare.
Owner Proprietary corp (Stuckey Health
Care).
Staff RNs 1 (ft), 5 (pt); LPNs 20 (ft), 10 (pt);
Nurses' aides 40 (ft), 10 (pt); Physical
therapists 2 (pt); Occupational therapists 1
(pt); Speech therapists 1 (pt); Activities
coordinators 2 (ft); Dietitians 1 (ft);
Ophthalmologists 1 (pt); Podiatrists 1 (pt);
Dentists 1 (pt).
Facilities Dining room; Physical therapy
room; Activities room; Crafts room; Laundry
room; Barber/Beauty shop.
Activities Arts & crafts; Games; Reading
groups; Prayer groups; Movies; Shopping
trips; Dances/Social/Cultural gatherings.

Flowery Branch

Flowery Branch Nursing Center
PO Box 640, Flowery Branch, GA 30542
(404) 967-2070
Admin Mike Coultas.
Licensure Skilled care; Intermediate care. *Beds*
100. *Certified* Medicaid; Medicare.

Folkston

Mullis Manor II
401 N Okefenokee Dr, Folkston, GA 31537
(912) 496-7396, 496-2087 FAX
Admin Marylou Waldron. *Dir of Nursing*
Phyllis Hendley RN. *Medical Dir* Dr Joseph
Proctor.
Licensure Skilled care; Intermediate care. *Beds*
Swing beds SNF/ICF 92. *Private Pay*
Patients 7%. *Certified* Medicaid.
Owner Privately owned Mullis Health Care.
Admissions Requirements Physician's request.
Staff Physicians 1 (ft); RNs 1 (ft), 1 (pt);
LPNs 7 (ft), 3 (pt); Nurses' aides 33 (ft), 5
(pt); Physical therapists 1 (ft), 1 (pt);
Activities coordinators 1 (ft); Dietitians 1
(ft); Podiatrists 1 (pt).
Facilities Dining room; Physical therapy
room; Activities room; Laundry room;
Barber/Beauty shop.
Activities Arts & crafts; Cards; Games;
Reading groups; Prayer groups; Movies;
Shopping trips; Dances/Social/Cultural
gatherings; Pet therapy.

Forsyth

Forsyth Nursing Home
PO Box 1067, Forsyth, GA 31029
(912) 994-5671
Admin Kate Cotton.
Medical Dir Dr A W Bramblett.
Licensure Skilled care; Intermediate care. *Beds*
SNF 72. *Certified* Medicaid.
Admissions Requirements Medical
examination; Physician's request.
Staff Physicians 7 (pt); RNs 1 (ft), 1 (pt);
LPNs 6 (ft), 2 (pt); Nurses' aides 17 (ft), 3
(pt); Physical therapists 1 (ft), 1 (pt);
Recreational therapists 1 (ft); Activities
coordinators 1 (ft).
Facilities Dining room; Physical therapy
room; Activities room; Chapel; Crafts room;
Laundry room; Barber/Beauty shop; Library.
Activities Arts & crafts; Cards; Games;
Reading groups; Prayer groups; Movies;
Shopping trips; Dances/Social/Cultural
gatherings.

Hilltop Nursing Home
Rte 2 Box 69, Forsyth, GA 31029
(912) 994-5662

Admin Rosalyn M Harbuck. *Dir of Nursing* Rachel Garrison.
Licensure Skilled care; Intermediate care. *Beds* SNF 83; ICF. *Certified* Medicaid.
Owner Proprietary corp.
Admissions Requirements Medical examination; Physician's request.
Staff Physicians 6 (pt); RNs 1 (ft), 2 (pt); LPNs 6 (ft), 6 (pt); Nurses' aides 25 (ft), 2 (pt); Physical therapists 1 (pt); Activities coordinators 2 (ft); Dietitians 1 (pt); Ophthalmologists 1 (pt); Dentists 1 (pt).
Facilities Dining room; Physical therapy room; Activities room; Crafts room; Laundry room; Barber/Beauty shop.
Activities Arts & crafts; Cards; Games; Prayer groups; Movies; Shopping trips; Dances/Social/Cultural gatherings.

Fort Gaines

Fort Gaines Nursing Home
PO Box 160, Fort Gaines, GA 31751
(912) 768-2522
Admin William Sowell. *Dir of Nursing* Bob Espy RN. *Medical Dir* Homer P Wood MD.
Licensure Skilled care; Intermediate care. *Beds* SNF 21; ICF 28. *Certified* Medicaid; Medicare.
Owner Proprietary corp (Healthcare Management).
Admissions Requirements Minimum age 16; Medical examination; Physician's request.
Staff Physicians; RNs; LPNs; Nurses' aides; Physical therapists; Recreational therapists; Speech therapists; Activities coordinators; Dietitians; Ophthalmologists; Podiatrists; Dentists.
Facilities Dining room; Physical therapy room; Activities room; Barber/Beauty shop.
Activities Arts & crafts; Cards; Games; Reading groups; Prayer groups; Movies; Shopping trips; Dances/Social/Cultural gatherings.

Fort Oglethorpe

Fort Oglethorpe Nursing Center
528 Battlefield Pkwy, Fort Oglethorpe, GA 30742
(404) 861-5154
Admin Alan Hutchins. *Dir of Nursing* Susan Scoggins. *Medical Dir* Howard Derrick MD.
Licensure Skilled care. *Beds* SNF 120. *Private Pay Patients* 5%. *Certified* Medicaid; Medicare.
Owner Proprietary corp (Pruitt Corp).
Admissions Requirements Medical examination; Physician's request.
Staff RNs 2 (ft), 1 (pt); LPNs 10 (ft), 5 (pt); Nurses' aides 39 (ft), 8 (pt); Physical therapists (contracted); Activities coordinators 1 (ft); Dietitians.
Facilities Dining room; Physical therapy room; Activities room; Laundry room; Barber/Beauty shop.
Activities Arts & crafts; Cards; Games; Reading groups; Prayer groups; Movies; Dances/Social/Cultural gatherings; Intergenerational programs; Pet therapy.

Hutcheson Extended Care Unit
200 Gross Crescent, Fort Oglethorpe, GA 30742
(404) 866-2121
Admin Tom R McGuire.
Medical Dir Dr Leroy Serrill.
Licensure Skilled care. *Beds* SNF 25. *Certified* Medicaid; Medicare.
Admissions Requirements Medical examination; Physician's request.
Staff RNs 3 (ft); LPNs 4 (ft), 1 (pt); Nurses' aides 9 (ft); Physical therapists 1 (ft); Activities coordinators 1 (ft); Dietitians 1 (ft); Dentists 1 (ft).

Facilities Dining room; Physical therapy room; Activities room; Chapel; Crafts room.
Activities Arts & crafts; Cards; Games; Reading groups; Prayer groups.

National Health Care Center
1160 Battlefield Pkwy, Fort Oglethorpe, GA 30742
(404) 866-7700, 866-1471 FAX
Admin Jarrett W Eschenfelder. *Dir of Nursing* Dianna Sharp RN. *Medical Dir* James Rimer MD; William Meadows MD.
Licensure Skilled care; Intermediate care. *Beds* SNF 12; ICF 69. *Private Pay Patients* 10%. *Certified* Medicaid; Medicare.
Owner Proprietary corp (National Health Corp).
Staff Physicians 6 (pt); RNs 3 (ft), 3 (pt); LPNs 8 (ft), 9 (pt); Nurses' aides 24 (ft), 11 (pt); Physical therapists 1 (pt); Recreational therapists 1 (ft); Speech therapists 1 (pt); Dietitians 1 (pt); Podiatrists 1 (pt).

Fort Valley

Fort Valley Health Care Center
PO Box 1237, Fort Valley, GA 31030
(912) 825-2031
Admin Carolyn J Wilson. *Dir of Nursing* Martha Martin RN. *Medical Dir* Dr Daniel E Nathan.
Licensure Skilled care; Intermediate care. *Beds* SNF 75. *Certified* Medicaid.
Owner Proprietary corp (Stuckey Health Care).
Admissions Requirements Medical examination; Physician's request.
Staff RNs 2 (ft), 3 (pt); LPNs 7 (ft), 4 (pt); Nurses' aides 15 (ft), 9 (pt); Activities coordinators 1 (ft).
Facilities Dining room; Physical therapy room; Activities room; Laundry room; Barber/Beauty shop.
Activities Reading groups; Prayer groups; Movies; Entertainment groups; Religious programs.

Franklin

Franklin Health Care Center
PO Box 472, Franklin, GA 30217
(404) 675-6674
Admin Jeanette Hammond. *Dir of Nursing* Reita Pope RN. *Medical Dir* J L Robinson MD.
Licensure Skilled care; Intermediate care. *Beds* 78. *Certified* Medicaid.
Owner Proprietary corp.
Admissions Requirements Medical examination; Physician's request.
Staff Physicians 10 (pt); RNs 3 (ft), 1 (pt); LPNs 7 (ft), 5 (pt); Nurses' aides 22 (ft), 3 (pt); Physical therapists 1 (ft), 1 (pt); Occupational therapists 1 (ft); Speech therapists 1 (pt); Activities coordinators 2 (ft); Dietitians 1 (ft), 1 (pt); Ophthalmologists 1 (pt); Podiatrists 1 (pt); Dentists 1 (pt).
Facilities Dining room; Physical therapy room; Activities room; Laundry room; Barber/Beauty shop; Library.
Activities Arts & crafts; Cards; Games; Reading groups; Prayer groups; Movies; Shopping trips; Dances/Social/Cultural gatherings.

Gainesville

Bell-Minor Home Inc
447 Bradford St NW, Gainesville, GA 30505
(404) 532-2066
Admin Doris G Bell.
Licensure Skilled care; Intermediate care. *Beds* 92. *Certified* Medicaid; Medicare.

Camelot Care Intermediate Care Facility
Rte 6 Box 471, Gainesville, GA 30501
(404) 983-3771
Admin Jo Stephens.
Medical Dir David N Westfall MD.
Licensure Intermediate care. *Beds* ICF 60. *Certified* Medicaid.
Owner Privately owned.
Admissions Requirements Medical examination.
Staff Physicians 1 (pt); RNs 1 (ft); LPNs 3 (ft), 2 (pt); Nurses' aides 16 (ft); Activities coordinators 1 (ft); Dietitians 1 (pt).
Facilities Dining room; Activities room; Crafts room; Laundry room; Barber/Beauty shop.
Activities Arts & crafts; Games; Movies; Shopping trips.

Gainesville Health Care Center
Box JJ, Dawsonville Hwy, Gainesville, GA 30501
(404) 536-9835
Admin Mary Kay Long.
Medical Dir Terry Jones MD.
Licensure Intermediate care. *Beds* 100. *Certified* Medicaid.
Staff RNs 2 (ft), 1 (pt); LPNs 8 (ft), 1 (pt); Nurses' aides 36 (ft); Physical therapists 1 (ft); Recreational therapists 1 (pt); Activities coordinators 1 (ft); Dietitians 1 (ft).
Facilities Dining room; Physical therapy room; Activities room; Chapel; Crafts room; Laundry room; Barber/Beauty shop; Library.
Activities Arts & crafts; Cards; Games; Reading groups; Movies; Shopping trips; Dances/Social/Cultural gatherings; Church groups.

Lakeshore Heights Nursing Center
PO Box D, Gainesville, GA 30501
(404) 536-3391
Admin Esther Susan Beard.
Licensure Skilled care; Intermediate care; Alzheimer's care. *Beds* Swing beds SNF/ICF 104. *Certified* Medicaid.
Owner Proprietary corp.
Admissions Requirements Medical examination.
Staff Physicians 1 (pt); RNs 3 (ft); LPNs 11 (ft); Nurses' aides 34 (ft), 2 (pt); Activities coordinators 1 (ft).
Facilities Dining room; Physical therapy room; Activities room; Laundry room; Barber/Beauty shop.
Activities Games; Reading groups; Prayer groups.

Lanier North Nursing Home
PO Box 907158, 103 Clarks Branch Rd, Gainesville, GA 30501
(404) 534-3565
Admin Inantha Garrett.
Licensure Skilled care; Intermediate care. *Beds* SNF 46. *Certified* Medicaid.

Gibson

Gibson Rest & Convalescent Home
Beall Springs Rd, Gibson, GA 30810
(404) 598-3201
Admin Mrs Jimmie Stewart.
Licensure Skilled care; Intermediate care. *Beds* SNF 104. *Certified* Medicaid.

Glenville

Glenvue Nursing Home
721 N Main St, Glenville, GA 30427
(912) 654-2138
Admin Dale P Dutton. *Dir of Nursing* Betty Durrence RN. *Medical Dir* Charles H Drake MD.
Licensure Skilled care; Intermediate care. *Beds* 160. *Certified* Medicaid; Medicare.
Owner Proprietary corp.

Admissions Requirements Medical
examination; Physician's request.
Staff Physicians 1 (pt); RNs 3 (ft), 1 (pt);
LPNs 14 (ft), 3 (pt); Nurses' aides 28 (ft), 8
(pt); Physical therapists 1 (ft), 2 (pt); Reality
therapists 1 (pt); Activities coordinators 1
(ft); Dietitians 1 (ft), 1 (pt);
Ophthalmologists 1 (pt).
Facilities Dining room; Physical therapy
room; Activities room; Chapel; Laundry
room; Barber/Beauty shop; Library.
Activities Arts & crafts; Cards; Games;
Reading groups; Prayer groups; Movies;
Shopping trips; Dances/Social/Cultural
gatherings.

Glenwood

Conner Nursing Home
PO Box 128, Glenwood, GA 30428
(912) 523-5597
Admin Ralph Hargraves.
Licensure Skilled care; Intermediate care. *Beds*
62. *Certified* Medicaid; Medicare.

Gracewood

Gracewood Developmental Center
Gracewood State Hospital, Division B,
Gracewood, GA 30812
(404) 790-2254
Admin W Martin Peterson.
Beds 596.

Gracewood Nursing Home
Unit 9, Bldg 76, Ward 1-2, Gracewood, GA
30812
(404) 790-2392
Admin Joann Miklas.
Licensure Skilled care. *Beds* SNF 56. *Certified*
Medicaid.

Gracewood State School & Hospital
Gracewood, GA 30812-1299
(404) 790-2030, 790-2025 FAX
Admin Joanne P Miklas PhD. *Dir of Nursing*
Jean Lynch. *Medical Dir* Donald Dunagan
MD.
Licensure Skilled care; Intermediate care for
mentally retarded. *Beds* SNF 54; ICF/MR
700. *Private Pay Patients* 19%.
Owner Publicly owned.
Admissions Requirements Mentally retarded &
residents of east region of Georgia.
Staff Physicians 8 (ft); RNs 37 (ft); LPNs 73
(ft); Nurses' aides 602 (ft); Physical
therapists 1 (ft); Recreational therapists 18
(ft); Occupational therapists 5 (ft); Speech
therapists 9 (ft); Activities coordinators 23
(ft); Dietitians 7 (ft); Audiologists 1 (ft).
Facilities Dining room; Physical therapy
room; Activities room; Chapel; Crafts room;
Laundry room; Barber/Beauty shop; Library.
Activities Arts & crafts; Games; Movies;
Shopping trips; Dances/Social/Cultural
gatherings; Developmental training.

Gray

Gray Nursing Home
PO Box 175, Gray, GA 31032
(912) 986-3151
Admin Lucy M Rogers.
Medical Dir H B Jones Jr MD.
Licensure Skilled care; Intermediate care. *Beds*
58. *Certified* Medicaid.
Staff Physicians 2 (pt); RNs 1 (ft), 1 (pt);
LPNs 4 (ft), 1 (pt); Nurses' aides 12 (ft), 2
(pt); Physical therapists 1 (pt); Activities
coordinators 1 (ft); Dietitians 1 (ft);
Podiatrists 1 (pt); Dentists 1 (pt).
Facilities Dining room; Physical therapy
room; Activities room; Laundry room.
Activities Arts & crafts; Cards; Games;
Reading groups; Prayer groups; Movies;
Shopping trips; Dances/Social/Cultural
gatherings.

Lynn Haven Nursing Home
Rte 1 Box 50, Gray, GA 31032
(912) 986-3196
Admin William Repzynski.
Licensure Skilled care; Intermediate care. *Beds*
104. *Certified* Medicaid; Medicare.

Greenville

Alvista Care Home Inc
PO Box E, Greenville, GA 30222
(404) 672-4241
Admin Charles L Green. *Dir of Nursing* Laura
Edwards RN. *Medical Dir* James W Smith
Jr MD.
Licensure Intermediate care. *Beds* ICF 113.
Certified Medicaid.
Owner Privately owned.
Admissions Requirements Medical
examination; Physician's request.
Staff Physicians 1 (ft); RNs 2 (ft); LPNs 6 (ft),
1 (pt); Nurses' aides 21 (ft), 4 (pt); Activities
coordinators 1 (ft); Dietitians 1 (pt).
Facilities Dining room; Physical therapy
room; Activities room; Chapel; Crafts room;
Laundry room; Barber/Beauty shop.
Activities Arts & crafts; Cards; Games;
Reading groups; Prayer groups; Movies;
Shopping trips.

Griffin

Brightmoor Medical Care Home
Rte 3 Box 119M, Griffin, GA 30223
(404) 228-8599
Admin R H Monkus.
Licensure Skilled care; Intermediate care. *Beds*
133. *Certified* Medicaid; Medicare.

Living Center of Griffin
415 Airport Rd, Griffin, GA 30223
(404) 227-8636
Admin Larry W Lawrence.
Medical Dir Kenneth Reynolds MD.
Licensure Skilled care; Intermediate care. *Beds*
146. *Certified* Medicaid; Medicare.
Staff Physicians 1 (pt); RNs 2 (ft), 1 (pt);
LPNs 12 (ft), 2 (pt); Nurses' aides 43 (ft), 4
(pt); Physical therapists 1 (pt); Reality
therapists 1 (pt); Activities coordinators 1
(ft); Dietitians 1 (pt); Ophthalmologists 1
(pt); Podiatrists 1 (pt); Dentists 1 (pt).
Facilities Dining room; Physical therapy
room; Activities room; Chapel; Crafts room;
Laundry room; Barber/Beauty shop.
Activities Arts & crafts; Games; Reading
groups; Prayer groups; Movies; Shopping
trips.

Spalding Convalescent Center
619 Northside Dr, Griffin, GA 30223
(404) 228-4517
Admin Edward Bond. *Dir of Nursing* Marie
Cody RN. *Medical Dir* Dr C C Releford.
Licensure Skilled care; Intermediate care. *Beds*
SNF 69. *Certified* Medicaid.
Owner Proprietary corp.
Admissions Requirements Medical
examination.
Staff Physicians 1 (ft); RNs 2 (ft); LPNs 5 (ft),
2 (pt); Nurses' aides 26 (ft), 2 (pt); Physical
therapists 1 (pt); Activities coordinators 1
(ft); Dietitians 1 (pt).
Facilities Dining room; Physical therapy
room; Activities room; Laundry room;
Barber/Beauty shop.
Activities Arts & crafts; Games; Reading
groups; Prayer groups; Movies.

Hartwell

Hart Care Center
127 Fairview Ave, Hartwell, GA 30643
(404) 376-7121
Admin Frances Osburn. *Dir of Nursing* Susan
Sanders. *Medical Dir* L G Cacchioli.

Licensure Skilled care; Intermediate care. *Beds*
SNF 117. *Certified* Medicaid.
Owner Proprietary corp (Angell Care Inc).
Admissions Requirements Medical
examination; Physician's request.
Staff Physicians 1 (pt); RNs 2 (ft), 1 (pt);
LPNs 5 (ft), 3 (pt); Nurses' aides 30 (ft), 10
(pt); Physical therapists 1 (pt); Speech
therapists 1 (pt); Activities coordinators 1
(ft); Dietitians 1 (pt).
Facilities Dining room; Physical therapy
room; Activities room; Crafts room; Laundry
room; Barber/Beauty shop.
Activities Arts & crafts; Cards; Games;
Reading groups; Prayer groups; Movies;
Dances/Social/Cultural gatherings.

Heritage Inn of Hartwell
108 Cade St, Hartwell, GA 31787
(404) 376-3185
Admin Susan Walters.
Medical Dir L C Cauhioli.
Licensure Skilled care; Intermediate care. *Beds*
92. *Certified* Medicaid; Medicare.
Admissions Requirements Physician's request.
Staff Physicians 5 (pt); RNs 1 (ft), 2 (pt);
LPNs 8 (ft), 1 (pt); Nurses' aides 15 (ft), 12
(pt); Physical therapists 1 (pt); Activities
coordinators 1 (ft); Dietitians 1 (pt); Dentists
1 (pt).
Facilities Dining room; Activities room;
Crafts room; Laundry room; Barber/Beauty
shop.
Activities Arts & crafts; Cards; Games;
Movies; Shopping trips; Dances/Social/
Cultural gatherings.

Hawkinsville

Pinewood Manor Inc
PO Box 587, Hawkinsville, GA 31036
(912) 892-7171
Admin Ronald G Crump.
Licensure Skilled care; Intermediate care. *Beds*
102. *Certified* Medicaid.

Hazlehurst

Mullis Manor III
PO Box 754, Burkett's Ferry Rd, Hazlehurst,
GA 31539
(912) 375-3677, 375-4786 FAX
Admin Eugene Cook. *Dir of Nursing* Nancy
Futch. *Medical Dir* Dr David Turfler.
Licensure Skilled care; Intermediate care. *Beds*
Swing beds SNF/ICF 73. *Private Pay
Patients* 2%. *Certified* Medicaid.
Owner Privately owned (Mullis Health Care).
Staff Physicians; RNs; LPNs; Nurses' aides;
Physical therapists; Reality therapists;
Recreational therapists; Speech therapists;
Activities coordinators; Dietitians;
Podiatrists; Audiologists.
Facilities Dining room; Physical therapy
room; Activities room; Chapel; Laundry
room; Barber/Beauty shop.
Activities Arts & crafts; Games; Reading
groups; Prayer groups; Movies; Shopping
trips; Dances/Social/Cultural gatherings; Pet
therapy; Exercise.

Hiawassee

Towns County Nursing Home
PO Box 509, Main St, Hiawassee, GA 30546
(404) 896-2222
Admin Donald C Novak. *Dir of Nursing* Alice
Cunningham RN. *Medical Dir* Robert F
Stahlkuppe MD.
Licensure Skilled care; Intermediate care. *Beds*
Swing beds SNF/ICF 76. *Private Pay
Patients* 20%. *Certified* Medicaid; Medicare.
Owner Nonprofit corp.
Admissions Requirements Medical
examination; Physician's request.

Staff RNs 2 (ft), 3 (pt); LPNs 8 (ft), 6 (pt); Nurses' aides 26 (ft), 7 (pt); Physical therapists 2 (pt); Recreational therapists 1 (pt); Occupational therapists 1 (pt); Activities coordinators 2 (ft); Dietitians (consultant).
Facilities Dining room; Physical therapy room; Activities room; Barber/Beauty shop.
Activities Arts & crafts; Cards; Games; Reading groups; Prayer groups; Movies; Shopping trips.

High Shoals

Family Life Enrichment Center
Highshoals Rd, Box 37A, High Shoals, GA 30645
(404) 769-7738
Admin Magda D Bennett.
Licensure Skilled care. *Beds* SNF 100. *Certified* Medicaid; Medicare.

Homerville

Mullis Manor Inc
410 Sweat St, Homerville, GA 31634
(912) 487-5328
Admin Barbara Mullis.
Licensure Intermediate care. *Beds* 92. *Certified* Medicaid.

Ideal

Ideal Health Care Center
201 Popular St, Ideal, GA 31041
(912) 949-2270
Admin J M Crawford. *Dir of Nursing* Don Smith. *Medical Dir* Richard Chase DO.
Licensure Skilled care; Intermediate care. *Beds* Swing beds SNF/ICF 100. *Private Pay Patients* 8%. *Certified* Medicaid; Medicare.
Owner Proprietary corp (Blue Ridge Nursing Homes Inc).
Admissions Requirements Medical examination; Physician's request.
Staff Physicians 2 (pt); RNs 2 (ft), 1 (pt); LPNs 7 (ft), 4 (pt); Nurses' aides 34 (ft), 4 (pt); Physical therapists 1 (pt); Activities coordinators 1 (ft); Dietitians 1 (pt).
Facilities Dining room; Physical therapy room; Activities room; Crafts room; Laundry room; Barber/Beauty shop.
Activities Arts & crafts; Cards; Games; Reading groups; Prayer groups; Movies; Shopping trips.

Jasper

Grandview Health Care Center
PO Box G, 208 S Main St, Jasper, GA 30143
(404) 692-5123
Admin Patton W Childers.
Licensure Intermediate care. *Beds* ICF 45.

Pickens General Nursing Center
1319 Church St, Jasper, GA 30143
(404) 692-2441
Admin John M Fulop. *Dir of Nursing* Joyce Bacot RN. *Medical Dir* Dr G H Perrow.
Licensure Skilled care; Intermediate care. *Beds* SNF 25; ICF 35. *Private Pay Patients* 10%. *Certified* Medicaid; Medicare.
Owner Nonprofit organization/foundation.
Admissions Requirements Medical examination; Physician's request.
Staff Physicians 4 (ft); RNs 1 (ft), 1 (pt); LPNs 8 (ft), 2 (pt); Nurses' aides 26 (ft), 7 (pt); Physical therapists 1 (pt); Speech therapists 1 (pt); Activities coordinators 1 (ft); Dietitians 1 (pt); Ophthalmologists 1 (ft); Podiatrists 1 (pt).
Facilities Dining room; Physical therapy room; Chapel; Laundry room; Barber/Beauty shop.
Activities Games; Prayer groups; Movies; Dances/Social/Cultural gatherings.

Jeffersonville

Spring Valley Health Care Center
PO Box 308, Jeffersonville, GA 31044
(912) 945-3255
Admin Corrine Hancock.
Licensure Skilled care; Intermediate care. *Beds* SNF 131. *Certified* Medicaid.
Owner Proprietary corp (Brian Center Management Corp).

Jenkinsburg

Westbury Nursing Home
PO Box 38, Jenkinsburg, GA 30234
(404) 775-7832
Admin James R Westbury.
Licensure Skilled care; Intermediate care. *Beds* 197. *Certified* Medicaid.

Jesup

Altamaha Convalescent Center
PO Box 807, 1311 W Cherry St, Jesup, GA 31545
(912) 427-7792
Admin Bobbye Richardson. *Dir of Nursing* Helen Ivey. *Medical Dir* R E Miller.
Licensure Skilled care; Intermediate care. *Beds* Swing beds SNF/ICF 62. *Private Pay Patients* 18%. *Certified* Medicaid.
Owner Proprietary corp.
Admissions Requirements Medical examination; Physician's request.
Staff RNs 1 (ft), 2 (pt); LPNs 6 (ft); Nurses' aides 19 (ft); Physical therapists; Activities coordinators 1 (ft); Dietitians 1 (ft).
Facilities Dining room; Physical therapy room; Activities room; Crafts room; Laundry room; Barber/Beauty shop.
Activities Arts & crafts; Cards; Games; Reading groups; Prayer groups; Movies; Shopping trips; Dances/Social/Cultural gatherings.

Jesup Manor Nursing Center
PO Box 917, 1090 W Orange St, Jesup, GA 31545
(912) 427-6858
Admin Sabra J Harvey. *Dir of Nursing* Charlotte Heirs RN.
Licensure Skilled care; Intermediate care. *Beds* 90. *Certified* Medicaid.
Staff RNs 1 (ft), 2 (pt); LPNs 10 (ft), 3 (pt); Nurses' aides 22 (ft), 5 (pt); Physical therapists 1 (pt); Recreational therapists 1 (ft); Speech therapists 1 (pt); Activities coordinators 1 (ft); Dietitians 1 (ft).
Facilities Dining room; Physical therapy room; Activities room; Crafts room; Laundry room; Barber/Beauty shop.
Activities Arts & crafts; Cards; Games; Reading groups; Prayer groups; Movies; Shopping trips; Dances/Social/Cultural gatherings.

Jesup Rest-A-While Nursing Home
PO Box 827, Jesup, GA 31545
(912) 427-6873
Admin Madeline Houston.
Medical Dir Dr R A Pumpelly Jr.
Licensure Skilled care; Intermediate care. *Beds* 72. *Certified* Medicaid.
Admissions Requirements Medical examination.
Staff Physicians 1 (ft); RNs 1 (ft), 1 (pt); LPNs 8 (ft), 1 (pt); Nurses' aides 16 (ft), 4 (pt); Physical therapists 1 (ft); Activities coordinators 1 (ft); Dietitians 1 (pt); Dentists 1 (pt).
Facilities Dining room; Physical therapy room; Activities room; Crafts room; Laundry room; Barber/Beauty shop.
Activities Arts & crafts; Games; Reading groups; Prayer groups; Movies; Shopping trips.

Jonesboro

Arrowhead Nursing Center
239 Arrowhead Blvd, Jonesboro, GA 30236
(404) 478-3013
Admin Patricia K Bart. *Dir of Nursing* Rose Street RN. *Medical Dir* Robert M Webster MD.
Licensure Skilled care; Intermediate care. *Beds* Swing beds SNF/ICF 116. *Private Pay Patients* 50%. *Certified* Medicaid.
Owner Proprietary corp (Health Management Inc).
Admissions Requirements Medical examination; Physician's request.
Facilities Dining room; Physical therapy room; Activities room; Chapel; Laundry room; Barber/Beauty shop.
Activities Arts & crafts; Cards; Games; Reading groups; Prayer groups; Movies; Dances/Social/Cultural gatherings; Intergenerational programs; Pet therapy.

Styrons Arrowhead Nursing Center
239 Arrowhead Blvd, Jonesboro, GA 30236
(404) 478-3013
Admin Marian Styron.
Licensure Skilled care; Intermediate care. *Beds* 116. *Certified* Medicaid.

Kennesaw

Shady Grove Rest Home
Rte 4 Box 84, Kennesaw, GA 30144
(404) 427-7256
Admin James W Ross.
Medical Dir Robert Townsend.
Licensure Intermediate care. *Beds* ICF 32. *Certified* Medicaid.
Owner Proprietary corp.
Admissions Requirements Physician's request.
Staff LPNs; Nurses' aides; Activities coordinators; Dietitians.
Facilities Dining room; Activities room; Laundry room; Barber/Beauty shop.
Activities Arts & crafts; Cards; Games; Reading groups; Prayer groups; Movies.

Keysville

Keysville Convalescent & Nursing Center Inc
Rte 1 Box 128, Keysville, GA 30816
(404) 547-2591
Admin William C Harmon. *Dir of Nursing* Elvie J Harmon. *Medical Dir* Dr Richard N Moss.
Licensure Skilled care; Intermediate care. *Beds* 64. *Certified* Medicaid; Medicare.
Owner Proprietary corp.
Staff Physicians 2 (pt); RNs 2 (ft), 3 (pt); LPNs 4 (ft), 2 (pt); Nurses' aides 23 (ft), 2 (pt); Physical therapists 1 (pt); Activities coordinators 1 (ft); Dietitians 1 (pt); Ophthalmologists 1 (pt).

LaFayette

LaFayette Health Care Inc
Rte 4 Box 4, LaFayette, GA 30728
(404) 638-4662
Admin David Currie.
Medical Dir Paul Shaw; Annie R Ledlow.
Licensure Skilled care; Intermediate care. *Beds* 100. *Certified* Medicaid; Medicare.
Owner Proprietary corp (Stuckey Health Care).
Admissions Requirements Physician's request.
Staff RNs 2 (ft), 1 (pt); LPNs 7 (ft), 2 (pt); Nurses' aides 32 (ft), 7 (pt); Physical therapists 1 (pt); Occupational therapists 1 (pt); Speech therapists 1 (pt); Activities coordinators 1 (pt); Dietitians 1 (pt); Ophthalmologists 1 (pt).
Facilities Dining room; Physical therapy room; Activities room; Laundry room; Barber/Beauty shop.

Activities Arts & crafts; Games; Reading groups; Prayer groups; Movies; Shopping trips.

Shepherd Hills Health Care
PO Box 647, 800 Patterson Rd, LaFayette, GA 30728
(404) 638-4112
Admin Michelle Coker. *Dir of Nursing* Tyra Carlton. *Medical Dir* H C Derrick Jr MD.
Licensure Skilled care; Intermediate care. *Beds* Swing beds SNF/ICF 112. *Private Pay Patients* 10%. *Certified* Medicaid; Medicare.
Owner Proprietary corp (Pruitt Corp).
Admissions Requirements Medical examination; Physician's request.
Staff RNs 2 (ft); LPNs 10 (ft); Nurses' aides 30 (ft); Physical therapists 1 (pt); Speech therapists 1 (pt); Activities coordinators 1 (ft); Dietitians 1 (pt); Podiatrists 1 (pt).
Facilities Dining room; Physical therapy room; Activities room; Chapel; Crafts room; Laundry room; Barber/Beauty shop; Living room; Outside sitting areas.
Activities Arts & crafts; Cards; Games; Reading groups; Prayer groups; Movies; Shopping trips; Dances/Social/Cultural gatherings.

LaGrange

Brian Center Nursing Care of LaGrange
PO Box 280, LaGrange, GA 30241
(404) 882-1405
Admin Judy L Gay.
Licensure Skilled care; Intermediate care. *Beds* SNF 138. *Certified* Medicaid.

Florence Hand Home
200 Medical Dr, LaGrange, GA 30240
(404) 884-6131
Admin Charles L Foster Jr. *Dir of Nursing* Katie McAlister RN. *Medical Dir* Mark Adams MD.
Licensure Skilled care; Intermediate care. *Beds* SNF 150; ICF. *Certified* Medicaid; Medicare.
Owner Nonprofit corp.
Admissions Requirements Medical examination; Physician's request.
Staff RNs 7 (ft); LPNs 21 (ft); Nurses' aides 46 (ft); Physical therapists; Recreational therapists 1 (ft); Speech therapists 1 (pt); Activities coordinators 1 (ft); Dietitians; Ophthalmologists; Podiatrists 1 (pt); Dentists.
Facilities Dining room; Physical therapy room; Activities room; Chapel; Crafts room; Laundry room; Barber/Beauty shop; Library.
Activities Arts & crafts; Cards; Games; Reading groups; Movies; Shopping trips; Dances/Social/Cultural gatherings; Picnics; Patio luncheons.

Negro Old Folks Home Inc
609 Union St, LaGrange, GA 30240
(404) 884-9466
Admin Mina B Wood.
Licensure Intermediate care. *Beds* ICF 12. *Certified* Medicaid.

Royal Elaine Intermediate Care Facility
Box 1346, Hogansville Rd, LaGrange, GA 30241
(404) 882-0121
Admin Eleanor S Neely.
Licensure Intermediate care. *Beds* ICF 116. *Certified* Medicaid.

Lakeland

Lakeland Villa Convalescent Center
888 W Thigpen Ave, Lakeland, GA 31635
(912) 482-2229
Admin Howard Karst. *Dir of Nursing* Pam Robbins. *Medical Dir* Guy Mann MD.

Licensure Skilled care. *Beds* SNF 62. *Private Pay Patients* 6%. *Certified* Medicaid; Medicare.
Owner Nonprofit organization/foundation (Sunbelt Healthcare Centers).
Admissions Requirements Medical examination; Physician's request.
Staff Physicians 1 (ft), 4 (pt); RNs 2 (ft), 1 (pt); LPNs 4 (ft), 3 (pt); Nurses' aides 20 (ft), 8 (pt); Physical therapists; Activities coordinators 1 (ft), 1 (pt); Dietitians 1 (ft).
Affiliation Seventh-Day Adventist.
Facilities Dining room; Activities room; Crafts room; Laundry room; Barber/Beauty shop.
Activities Arts & crafts; Cards; Games; Reading groups; Prayer groups; Movies; Shopping trips; Dances/Social/Cultural gatherings; Intergenerational programs; Pet therapy.

Lawrenceville

Medical Arts Health Facility
213 Scenic Hwy, Lawrenceville, GA 30245
(404) 963-5275
Admin Pat Tanner.
Medical Dir Dr Michael Lipsitt.
Licensure Skilled care; Intermediate care. *Beds* 124. *Certified* Medicaid; Medicare.
Owner Proprietary corp (Beverly Enterprises).
Admissions Requirements Medical examination.
Staff Physicians 9 (pt); RNs 3 (ft), 4 (pt); LPNs 6 (ft), 2 (pt); Nurses' aides 29 (ft), 30 (pt); Speech therapists 1 (pt); Activities coordinators 1 (ft).
Facilities Dining room; Physical therapy room; Activities room; Chapel; Crafts room; Laundry room; Barber/Beauty shop.
Activities Arts & crafts; Cards; Games; Reading groups; Prayer groups; Movies; Shopping trips; Dances/Social/Cultural gatherings.

Safehaven of Gwinnett
147 Lester Rd, Lawrenceville, GA 30244
(404) 923-0005
Admin Joyce Byars.
Licensure Nursing home. *Beds* Nursing home 106.

Lilburn

Lilburn Health Care Center
PO Box 488, 788 Indian Trail, Lilburn, GA 30247
(404) 923-2020
Admin Janice Russell.
Licensure Skilled care; Intermediate care. *Beds* 152. *Certified* Medicaid; Medicare.

Lithonia

Starcrest of Lithonia
PO Box 855, Lithonia, GA 30058
(404) 482-2961
Admin Kay Smith.
Licensure Skilled care; Intermediate care. *Beds* 137. *Certified* Medicaid.

Louisville

Old Capital Inn Convalescent & Nursing Home
PO Box 32, Louisville, GA 30434
(912) 625-3741
Admin Ronald Warnock. *Dir of Nursing* Gail McNure. *Medical Dir* Dr J B Polhill IV.
Licensure Skilled care; Intermediate care. *Beds* Swing beds SNF/ICF 143. *Private Pay Patients* 5%. *Certified* Medicaid; Medicare.
Owner Proprietary corp (Health Properties III).
Admissions Requirements Minimum age 14.

Staff RNs 2 (ft); LPNs 11 (ft), 5 (pt); Nurses' aides 14 (pt); Physical therapists (contracted); Recreational therapists 1 (ft); Activities coordinators 2 (ft); Dietitians; Podiatrists (contracted); Physical therapy aides 1 (ft).
Facilities Dining room; Physical therapy room; Activities room; Chapel; Laundry room; Barber/Beauty shop.
Activities Arts & crafts; Cards; Games; Reading groups; Prayer groups; Movies; Shopping trips; Dances/Social/Cultural gatherings.

Lumber City

Brian Center Nursing Care of Lumber City
PO Box 336, Lumber City, GA 31549
(912) 363-4356
Admin Jim Crawford. *Dir of Nursing* Sarah Quinn. *Medical Dir* B Macalalad MD.
Licensure Skilled care; Intermediate care. *Beds* SNF 86. *Certified* Medicaid.
Owner Proprietary corp (Brian Center Management Corp).
Staff Physicians; RNs; LPNs; Nurses' aides; Physical therapists; Recreational therapists; Speech therapists; Activities coordinators; Dietitians; Ophthalmologists.
Facilities Dining room; Physical therapy room; Activities room; Crafts room; Laundry room; Barber/Beauty shop.
Activities Arts & crafts; Cards; Games; Reading groups; Prayer groups; Movies; Shopping trips; Dances/Social/Cultural gatherings.

Lyons

Toombs Nursing & Intermediate Care Home
100 Oxley Dr, Lyons, GA 30436
(912) 526-6336
Admin Peggy M Yarbrough.
Licensure Skilled care; Intermediate care. *Beds* SNF 144. *Certified* Medicaid.

Macon

Bel Arbor Medical Care
3468 Napier Ave, Macon, GA 31204
(912) 474-4464
Admin W Charles Hampton. *Dir of Nursing* Faye Ryle. *Medical Dir* John P Atkinson MD.
Licensure Skilled care; Intermediate care; Alzheimer's care. *Beds* 131. *Certified* Medicaid; Medicare.
Owner Proprietary corp.
Admissions Requirements Medical examination.
Staff Physicians 1 (ft), 1 (pt); RNs 2 (ft), 1 (pt); LPNs 9 (ft), 2 (pt); Nurses' aides 84 (ft), 6 (pt); Physical therapists 1 (ft); Activities coordinators 2 (ft); Dietitians 2 (ft); Ophthalmologists 1 (pt).
Facilities Dining room; Physical therapy room; Activities room; Crafts room; Laundry room; Barber/Beauty shop.
Activities Arts & crafts; Cards; Games; Reading groups; Prayer groups; Movies; Shopping trips; Dances/Social/Cultural gatherings.

Bloomfield Nursing Home Inc
3520 Kenneth Dr, Macon, GA 31206
(912) 781-9951
Admin Mildred Hollingshed. *Dir of Nursing* Diane Noble. *Medical Dir* Robert Nelson MD.
Licensure Intermediate care. *Beds* ICF 90. *Certified* Medicaid.
Owner Privately owned.
Admissions Requirements Medical examination.

Staff Physicians 2 (ft), 2 (pt); RNs 1 (ft), 1 (pt); LPNs 4 (ft), 2 (pt); Nurses' aides 17 (ft); Physical therapists 1 (ft), 1 (pt); Recreational therapists 2 (ft); Occupational therapists 2 (ft); Activities coordinators 1 (ft); Dietitians 1 (ft), 1 (pt); Ophthalmologists 1 (ft); Podiatrists 1 (ft); Psychologist 1 (pt); Dentists 1 (pt).
Facilities Dining room; Physical therapy room; Activities room; Crafts room; Laundry room; Barber/Beauty shop.
Activities Arts & crafts; Cards; Games; Reading groups; Prayer groups; Movies; Shopping trips; Dances/Social/Cultural gatherings.

Bolingreen Nursing Center
Rte 1, Bolingreen Dr, Macon, GA 31210
(912) 477-1720
Admin Walt Cross. *Dir of Nursing* Terri Nichols. *Medical Dir* Dr Fountain.
Licensure Skilled care; Intermediate care; Retirement. *Beds* Swing beds SNF/ICF 121; Retirement apts 6. *Private Pay Patients* 10%. *Certified* Medicaid; Medicare.
Owner Nonprofit organization/foundation.
Admissions Requirements Medical examination; Physician's request.
Staff Physicians 2 (pt); RNs 3 (ft); LPNs 13 (ft); Nurses' aides 40 (ft); Physical therapists 1 (ft), 1 (pt); Occupational therapists 1 (pt); Speech therapists 1 (pt); Activities coordinators 1 (ft); Dietitians 1 (ft), 1 (pt); Ophthalmologists 1 (pt); Podiatrists 1 (pt).
Facilities Dining room; Physical therapy room; Activities room; Crafts room; Laundry room; Barber/Beauty shop.
Activities Arts & crafts; Cards; Games; Reading groups; Prayer groups; Movies; Shopping trips; Dances/Social/Cultural gatherings; Pet therapy.

Clinton Cove Convalescent Center
1060 Old Clinton Rd, Macon, GA 31211
(912) 746-0266
Admin Sandra Holton.
Licensure Skilled care; Intermediate care. *Beds* 122. *Certified* Medicaid.

Eastview Nursing Home
3020 Jeffersonville Hwy, Macon, GA 31201
(912) 746-3547
Admin Beverly F Hardison. *Dir of Nursing* Ann Smith. *Medical Dir* Robert Buckley MD.
Licensure Skilled care; Intermediate care. *Beds* 92. *Certified* Medicaid.
Admissions Requirements Minimum age 18.
Staff Physicians 5 (pt); RNs 2 (ft), 2 (pt); LPNs 12 (ft), 4 (pt); Nurses' aides 40 (ft), 8 (pt); Physical therapists 2 (ft), 1 (pt); Recreational therapists 2 (ft); Occupational therapists 1 (pt); Speech therapists 1 (pt); Activities coordinators 1 (ft); Dietitians 1 (pt); Ophthalmologists 1 (pt); Podiatrists 1 (pt); Dentists 1 (pt).
Facilities Dining room; Physical therapy room; Activities room; Crafts room; Laundry room; Barber/Beauty shop.
Activities Arts & crafts; Cards; Games; Reading groups; Prayer groups; Movies; Shopping trips; Dances/Social/Cultural gatherings.

Goodwill Nursing Home
4373 Houston Ave, Macon, GA 31206
(912) 788-4010
Admin Linda G Peachey. *Dir of Nursing* Diana Harden. *Medical Dir* William Pound.
Licensure Intermingled. *Beds* 172. *Certified* Medicaid.
Owner Proprietary corp.
Admissions Requirements Medical examination; Physician's request.

Staff Physicians 1 (pt); RNs 4 (ft), 1 (pt); LPNs 19 (ft), 8 (pt); Nurses' aides 51 (ft), 8 (pt); Physical therapists 1 (ft); Activities coordinators 2 (ft); Dietitians 1 (ft); Ophthalmologists 1 (pt).
Facilities Dining room; Physical therapy room; Activities room; Chapel; Crafts room; Laundry room; Barber/Beauty shop.
Activities Arts & crafts; Cards; Games; Reading groups; Prayer groups; Movies; Shopping trips; Dances/Social/Cultural gatherings.

Hospitality Care Center of Macon
505 Coliseum Dr, Macon, GA 31201
(912) 743-8687
Admin Charles Aspinwall.
Licensure Skilled care; Intermediate care. *Beds* 100. *Certified* Medicaid; Medicare.

Macon Health Care Center
3051 Whiteside Rd, Macon, GA 31206
(912) 788-1421
Admin Michael R Little. *Dir of Nursing* Pat Hall Tucker. *Medical Dir* Dr William Brooks.
Licensure Skilled care; Intermediate care. *Beds* SNF 147. *Certified* Medicaid.
Owner Proprietary corp.
Staff RNs 3 (ft), 1 (pt); LPNs 13 (ft), 4 (pt); Nurses' aides 39 (ft), 5 (pt); Physical therapists 1 (ft); Activities coordinators 2 (ft); Dietitians 1 (ft).
Facilities Dining room; Physical therapy room; Activities room; Barber/Beauty shop; Outdoor recreation area.
Activities Arts & crafts; Cards; Games; Prayer groups; Shopping trips; Dances/Social/ Cultural gatherings; Fishing; Pet therapy; Morning exercise; Sing-alongs; Cooking groups.

Memorial Nursing Home
1509 Cedar Ave, Macon, GA 31204
(912) 743-4678
Admin Edwina Evans Williams.
Medical Dir Dr C W James.
Licensure Skilled care; Intermediate care. *Beds* SNF 68. *Certified* Medicaid.
Staff RNs 1 (pt); LPNs 4 (ft), 3 (pt); Nurses' aides 9 (ft), 9 (pt); Physical therapists 1 (pt); Reality therapists 1 (pt); Recreational therapists 1 (ft); Occupational therapists 1 (pt); Speech therapists 1 (pt); Activities coordinators 1 (ft); Dietitians 1 (pt).
Facilities Dining room; Physical therapy room; Activities room; Crafts room; Laundry room; Barber/Beauty shop.
Activities Arts & crafts; Cards; Games; Reading groups; Prayer groups; Shopping trips; Dances/Social/Cultural gatherings.

North Macon Health Care Facility
2255 Anthony Rd, Macon, GA 31204
(912) 743-9347
Admin Susan Doreen Hansard. *Dir of Nursing* Mary Dunwody. *Medical Dir* Clyatt W James.
Licensure Skilled care; Intermediate care. *Beds* SNF 228. *Certified* Medicaid; Medicare.
Owner Proprietary corp.
Admissions Requirements Physician's request.
Staff Physicians 1 (ft); RNs 4 (ft); LPNs 25 (ft), 2 (pt); Nurses' aides 100 (ft), 7 (pt); Physical therapists 1 (ft); Recreational therapists 3 (ft); Speech therapists 1 (ft); Dietitians 1 (ft); Ophthalmologists 1 (pt).
Languages Sign.
Facilities Dining room; Physical therapy room; Activities room; Chapel; Laundry room; Barber/Beauty shop.
Activities Arts & crafts; Cards; Games; Reading groups; Prayer groups; Movies; Shopping trips; Dances/Social/Cultural gatherings.

Oak Valley Nursing Home
2795 Finney Cir, Macon, GA 31201
(912) 745-4231
Admin Mary Lu Flory RN NHA. *Dir of Nursing* Donna Long. *Medical Dir* Dr James Livingston.
Licensure Skilled care; Intermediate care. *Beds* Swing beds SNF/ICF 130. *Certified* Medicaid; Medicare.
Owner Proprietary corp (Nursing Center of America Inc).
Staff Physicians; RNs; LPNs; Nurses' aides; Physical therapists; Recreational therapists; Occupational therapists; Speech therapists; Activities coordinators; Dietitians; Ophthalmologists; Podiatrists.
Facilities Dining room; Physical therapy room; Activities room; Laundry room; Barber/Beauty shop.
Activities Games; Prayer groups; Intergenerational programs; Pet therapy.

Riverside of Macon
Rte 1, Pate Rd, Macon, GA 31210
(912) 477-1720
Admin Joseph W Butler.
Medical Dir Dr J R Fountain.
Licensure Skilled care; Intermediate care. *Beds* 121. *Certified* Medicaid.
Owner Proprietary corp (Riverside Med Services).
Staff Physicians 2 (pt); RNs 1 (ft), 2 (pt); LPNs 6 (ft), 2 (pt); Nurses' aides 40 (ft), 6 (pt); Physical therapists 1 (pt); Activities coordinators 1 (ft); Dietitians 1 (ft), 1 (pt); Ophthalmologists 1 (pt); Podiatrists 1 (pt); Dentists 1 (pt).
Facilities Dining room; Physical therapy room; Activities room; Chapel; Laundry room; Barber/Beauty shop.
Activities Arts & crafts; Games; Prayer groups; Movies; Shopping trips.

Three Oaks Intermediate Care Home
PO Box 7531, Macon, GA 31204
(912) 986-6245
Admin Kenneth A Goings.
Licensure Intermediate care. *Beds* 34. *Certified* Medicaid.

Madison

Hospitality Care Center
PO Box 228, Hwy 278, Madison, GA 30650
(404) 342-3200
Admin Cheryl H Coleman. *Dir of Nursing* Carol Burt. *Medical Dir* L K Lewis.
Licensure Skilled care; Intermediate care; Alzheimer's care. *Beds* Swing beds SNF/ICF 67. *Private Pay Patients* 3%. *Certified* Medicaid; Medicare.
Owner Proprietary corp (Beverly Enterprises).
Admissions Requirements Medical examination.
Staff RNs 2 (ft), 3 (pt); LPNs 6 (ft), 2 (pt); Nurses' aides 20 (ft), 14 (pt); Physical therapists (consultant); Occupational therapists 1 (pt); Speech therapists 1 (ft); Activities coordinators 1 (ft); Dietitians 1 (ft).
Facilities Dining room; Physical therapy room; Activities room; Laundry room; Barber/Beauty shop.
Activities Arts & crafts; Cards; Games; Reading groups; Movies; Shopping trips.

Marietta

Americana Healthcare Center
4360 Johnson Ferry Pl, Marietta, GA 30068
(404) 971-5870, 971-5876 FAX
Admin Robert W Dougherty. *Dir of Nursing* Elaine Nichols RN. *Medical Dir* Joseph Hannan MD.
Licensure Skilled care; Alzheimer's care. *Beds* SNF 120. *Private Pay Patients* 75%. *Certified* Medicare.

Owner Proprietary corp (Manor Care).
Admissions Requirements Minimum age 16; Medical examination; Physician's request.
Staff Physicians; RNs; LPNs; Nurses' aides; Physical therapists; Recreational therapists; Occupational therapists; Speech therapists; Activities coordinators; Dietitians; Audiologists.
Languages Spanish.
Facilities Dining room; Physical therapy room; Activities room; Crafts room; Laundry room; Barber/Beauty shop.
Activities Arts & crafts; Cards; Games; Reading groups; Prayer groups; Movies; Shopping trips; Dances/Social/Cultural gatherings; Intergenerational programs; Pet therapy.

Autumn Breeze Nursing Home
1480 Sandtown, Box 310, Marietta, GA 30060
(404) 422-1755
Admin Patricia K Bart.
Medical Dir George Artress MD.
Licensure Skilled care; Intermediate care. *Beds* 127.
Admissions Requirements Medical examination; Physician's request.
Staff Physicians 13 (ft); RNs 4 (ft), 2 (pt); LPNs 8 (ft), 3 (pt); Nurses' aides 45 (ft), 3 (pt); Physical therapists 1 (ft); Recreational therapists 1 (ft); Speech therapists 1 (pt); Activities coordinators 1 (ft); Dietitians 1 (ft).
Facilities Dining room; Physical therapy room; Activities room; Crafts room; Laundry room; Barber/Beauty shop.
Activities Arts & crafts; Cards; Games; Reading groups; Prayer groups; Movies; Shopping trips; Dances/Social/Cultural gatherings.

Hillhaven Rehabilitation Convalescent Center
26 Tower Rd, Marietta, GA 30060
(404) 422-8913
Admin Linda S Brooks.
Licensure Skilled care. *Beds* 146. *Certified* Medicaid; Medicare.
Owner Proprietary corp (Hillhaven Corp).

Marietta Health Care Center
85 Saine Dr, Marietta, GA 30060
(404) 429-8600
Admin Grace Bradshaw. *Dir of Nursing* Donna Kaminski RN. *Medical Dir* Gary Cowan MD.
Licensure Skilled care. *Beds* SNF 119. *Private Pay Patients* 5%. *Certified* Medicaid; Medicare.
Owner Proprietary corp (Beverly Enterprises).
Staff Physicians 6 (pt); RNs 3 (ft), 2 (pt); LPNs 14 (ft), 5 (pt); Nurses' aides 42 (ft), 7 (pt); Physical therapists (contracted); Occupational therapists (contracted); Speech therapists (contracted); Activities coordinators 2 (ft); Dietitians 1 (ft); Ophthalmologists (contracted); Podiatrists (contracted); Audiologists (contracted); Pharmacists.
Activities Arts & crafts; Cards; Games; Reading groups; Prayer groups; Movies; Shopping trips; Dances/Social/Cultural gatherings; Intergenerational programs; Pet therapy.

Shoreham Convalescent Center
811 Kennesaw Ave, Marietta, GA 30060
(404) 422-2451
Admin Beulah Holmberg.
Licensure Skilled care; Intermediate care. *Beds* SNF 154. *Certified* Medicaid; Medicare.

Marshallville

Oaks Nursing Home
Rte 1, Marshallville, GA 31057
(912) 967-2398
Admin N Jule Windham.

Licensure Skilled care; Intermediate care. *Beds* 48.

Martinez

Forrest Lake Health Care
PO Box 11529, 409 Pleasant Home Rd, Martinez, GA 30917-1529
(404) 863-6030
Admin Fay T Cupstid. *Dir of Nursing* Neva Cawthon. *Medical Dir* Dr John Baxley.
Licensure Skilled care; Intermediate care. *Beds* Swing beds SNF/ICF 100. *Private Pay Patients* 40%. *Certified* Medicaid; Medicare.
Owner Proprietary corp (Allgood Health Care).

McDonough

Starcrest of McDonough
PO Box 796, McDonough, GA 30253
(404) 957-9081
Admin Ruth Thomas.
Licensure Skilled care; Intermediate care. *Beds* SNF 210. *Certified* Medicaid.

McRae

McRae Manor Inc
1104 S 1st Ave, McRae, GA 31055
(912) 868-6473
Admin Buford T Cook.
Licensure Skilled care; Intermediate care. *Beds* 133. *Certified* Medicaid; Medicare.

Metter

Metter Nursing Home
PO Box 356, Metter, GA 30439
(912) 685-5734
Admin Kaye Galloway. *Dir of Nursing* Ann Cliett RN. *Medical Dir* Dr Dorsey Smith.
Licensure Skilled care; Intermediate care. *Beds* Swing beds SNF/ICF 89. *Private Pay Patients* 18%. *Certified* Medicaid.
Owner Proprietary corp (Coastal Health Management).
Admissions Requirements Medical examination; Physician's request.
Staff RNs 2 (ft); LPNs 10 (ft); Nurses' aides 34 (ft), 2 (pt); Physical therapists 1 (pt); Activities coordinators 1 (ft); Dietitians 1 (pt).
Facilities Dining room; Physical therapy room; Activities room; Crafts room; Laundry room; Barber/Beauty shop.
Activities Arts & crafts; Games; Movies; Shopping trips; Dances/Social/Cultural gatherings.

Pleasant View Health Care Center
PO Box 713, 303 Anderson St, Metter, GA 30439
(912) 685-2168
Admin Elaine Knight. *Dir of Nursing* Donna Dawson RN. *Medical Dir* Dr J D Smith.
Licensure Skilled care; Intermediate care. *Beds* Swing beds SNF/ICF 120. *Private Pay Patients* 1%. *Certified* Medicaid; Medicare.
Owner Proprietary corp (American Medical Group).
Admissions Requirements Medical examination; Physician's request.
Staff Physicians 4 (ft); RNs 4 (ft), 1 (pt); LPNs 12 (ft), 3 (pt); Nurses' aides 30 (ft), 5 (pt); Physical therapists 1 (ft); Recreational therapists 1 (ft); Occupational therapists 1 (ft); Speech therapists 1 (ft); Activities coordinators 1 (ft); Dietitians 1 (ft); Ophthalmologists 2 (ft); Podiatrists 2 (ft); Audiologists 1 (ft).
Facilities Dining room; Physical therapy room; Activities room; Crafts room; Laundry room; Barber/Beauty shop.

Activities Arts & crafts; Cards; Games; Reading groups; Prayer groups; Movies; Shopping trips; Dances/Social/Cultural gatherings; Pet therapy; Community involvement.

Midway

Liberty Manor Inc
PO Box 270, Hwy 17, Midway, GA 31320
(912) 884-3361
Admin Larry Swicegood.
Medical Dir Whitman Fraser.
Licensure Skilled care; Intermediate care. *Beds* 169. *Certified* Medicaid.
Admissions Requirements Medical examination; Physician's request.
Staff Physicians 3 (ft), 2 (pt); RNs 3 (ft), 1 (pt); LPNs 11 (ft), 3 (pt); Nurses' aides 24 (ft), 4 (pt); Physical therapists 1 (ft); Recreational therapists 1 (ft); Activities coordinators 1 (ft); Dietitians 1 (ft); Ophthalmologists 1 (ft); Podiatrists 1 (ft); Dentists 1 (ft).
Facilities Dining room; Physical therapy room; Activities room; Crafts room; Laundry room; Barber/Beauty shop; Library; Mental retardation room for skills teaching.
Activities Arts & crafts; Games; Reading groups; Prayer groups; Movies; Shopping trips; Dances/Social/Cultural gatherings.

Milledgeville

Allen Hall
Central State Hospital, Milledgeville, GA 31062
(912) 453-4145
Admin Myers Kurtz, Supt.
Licensure Intermediate care for mentally retarded. *Beds* ICF/MR 270.

Central State Hospital
Milledgeville, GA 31062-9989
(912) 453-4128
Admin Jerry Dene Walker; Myers R Kurtz, Supt. *Dir of Nursing* Judy Hodnett MSN. *Medical Dir* James E Umberhandt.
Licensure Skilled care. *Beds* SNF 110. *Private Pay Patients* 0%.
Owner Publicly owned.
Admissions Requirements Veterans of a war and disabled by age or physical disabilities or a special physician certificate.
Staff Physicians 2 (ft); RNs 8 (ft); LPNs 12 (ft); Nurses' aides 51 (ft); Physical therapists 2 (ft); Recreational therapists 2 (ft); Occupational therapists 3 (ft); Speech therapists 1 (pt); Activities coordinators 1 (ft); Dietitians 1 (ft); Audiologists 1 (pt).
Facilities Dining room; Physical therapy room; Activities room; Chapel; Crafts room; Laundry room; Barber/Beauty shop; Library; Music; Vending machine room; Visiting room; Occupational therapy room.
Activities Arts & crafts; Cards; Games; Reading groups; Prayer groups; Movies; Shopping trips; Dances/Social/Cultural gatherings; Overnight trips; Birthday parties.

Central State Hospital
Milledgeville, GA 31062
(912) 453-4219
Admin Alice K Paschal.
Medical Dir James Umberhandt MD.
Licensure Skilled care. *Beds* 236.
Owner Publicly owned.
Admissions Requirements Applicants to this facility must be veterans of a war & disabled by age or physical disability as described on a special physician's certificate.
Staff Physicians 4 (ft); RNs 19 (ft), 2 (pt); LPNs 27 (ft); Nurses' aides 130 (ft).
Facilities Dining room; Activities room; Crafts room; Laundry room; Barber/Beauty shop; Library.

Activities Arts & crafts; Cards; Games; Reading groups; Prayer groups; Movies; Shopping trips; Dances/Social/Cultural gatherings.

Chaplinwood Nursing Home
Allen Memorial Dr, Milledgeville, GA 31061
(912) 452-4596
Admin Sara Nixon.
Licensure Skilled care; Intermediate care. *Beds* 100. *Certified* Medicaid; Medicare.

Green Acres Inc
313 Allen Memorial Dr SW, Milledgeville, GA 31061
(912) 453-9437
Admin Edward C Nelson.
Licensure Skilled care; Intermediate care. *Beds* SNF 92. *Certified* Medicaid.

Nursing Center
Central State Hospital, No 1 Boone Bldg, Milledgeville, GA 31062
(404) 453-4311
Admin Meyers Kurtz, Supt.
Licensure Skilled care. *Beds* SNF 89. *Certified* Medicaid.

Pecan Manor 1
Central State Hospital, Milledgeville, GA 31062
(912) 452-3511
Admin Byron O Merritt III.
Licensure Intermediate care for mentally retarded. *Beds* 30. *Certified* Medicare.

Pecan Manor 3
Central State Hospital, Milledgeville, GA 31061
(912) 452-5558
Admin Meyrs Kurtz, Supt.
Licensure Intermediate care for mentally retarded. *Beds* ICF/MR 134.

Piedmont Hall
Central State Hospital, Milledgeville, GA 31061
(912) 453-5776
Admin Meyers Kurtz.
Licensure Intermediate care for mentally retarded. *Beds* ICF/MR 149.

Riverside Nursing Center
Central State Hospital, Milledgeville, GA 31062
(912) 453-4455
Admin Meyers Kurtz, Supt.
Licensure Skilled care. *Beds* SNF 99. *Certified* Medicaid.

Richard B Russell Building (GWV)
PO Box 325, Milledgeville, GA 31061
(912) 453-4128
Admin Meyers Kurtz, Supt.
Licensure Nursing home. *Beds* Nursing home 132.

Millen

Bethany Home for Men
PO Box 600, Gray St Exten, Millen, GA 30442
(912) 982-2531
Admin Raymond Vaughn. *Dir of Nursing* Sarah B Brinson RN. *Medical Dir* M L Campo MD.
Licensure Skilled care; Intermediate care. *Beds* SNF 100; ICF. *Certified* Medicaid.
Owner Nonprofit corp.
Admissions Requirements Minimum age 16; Males only; Medical examination; Physician's request.
Staff Physicians 1 (ft); RNs 1 (ft), 1 (pt); LPNs 6 (ft); Nurses' aides 20 (ft), 3 (pt); Physical therapists 1 (ft), 1 (pt); Reality therapists 1 (ft); Recreational therapists 1 (ft); Occupational therapists 1 (pt); Speech

therapists 1 (pt); Activities coordinators 1 (ft); Dietitians 1 (ft); Ophthalmologists 1 (pt); Podiatrists 1 (pt); Dentists 1 (pt).
Affiliation Baptist.
Facilities Dining room; Physical therapy room; Activities room; Chapel; Crafts room; Laundry room; Barber/Beauty shop; Library.
Activities Arts & crafts; Cards; Games; Reading groups; Prayer groups; Movies; Shopping trips; Farm; Coffee groups; Fishing trips; Picnics.

Molena

Molena Intermediate Care Home
PO Box 397, Molena, GA 30258
(404) 495-5138
Admin Michael S Greene.
Medical Dir Isabelle Bradsher.
Licensure Intermediate care. *Beds* ICF 62. *Certified* Medicaid.
Owner Proprietary corp.
Admissions Requirements Medical examination.
Staff Physicians 1 (pt); RNs 1 (ft); LPNs 5 (ft); Nurses' aides 18 (ft); Physical therapists 1 (pt); Reality therapists 1 (pt); Recreational therapists 1 (pt); Occupational therapists 1 (pt); Speech therapists 1 (pt); Activities coordinators 1 (ft); Dietitians 1 (ft); Ophthalmologists 1 (pt).
Facilities Dining room; Physical therapy room; Laundry room; Barber/Beauty shop.
Activities Arts & crafts; Cards; Games; Reading groups; Prayer groups; Shopping trips; Dances/Social/Cultural gatherings; Van trips.

Monroe

Monroe Intermediate Care Facility
Rte 3, Monroe, GA 30655
(404) 267-7541
Admin E Kenneth Murray.
Medical Dir Dr Phillip Enslen.
Licensure Intermediate care. *Beds* SNF 106. *Certified* Medicaid.
Admissions Requirements Minimum age 21; Medical examination; Physician's request.
Staff Physicians 5 (pt); RNs 1 (pt); LPNs 7 (ft), 1 (pt); Physical therapists 1 (pt); Reality therapists 1 (pt); Recreational therapists 1 (ft), 1 (pt); Occupational therapists 1 (pt); Speech therapists 1 (pt); Activities coordinators 1 (ft); Dietitians 1 (ft), 1 (pt); Ophthalmologists 1 (pt); Podiatrists 1 (pt); Audiologists 1 (pt); Dentists 1 (pt).
Facilities Dining room; Physical therapy room; Activities room; Chapel; Crafts room; Laundry room.
Activities Arts & crafts; Cards; Games; Reading groups; Prayer groups; Shopping trips; Dances/Social/Cultural gatherings.

Walton County Hospital Convalescent Wing
330 Alcova St, Monroe, GA 30655
(404) 267-8461
Admin Johnni Canup. *Dir of Nursing* Rita Michael RN. *Medical Dir* C C Moreland MD.
Licensure Skilled care. *Beds* SNF 58. *Certified* Medicaid; Medicare.
Owner Nonprofit corp.
Admissions Requirements Medical examination; Physician's request.
Staff RNs 1 (ft), 1 (pt); LPNs 7 (ft), 1 (pt); Nurses' aides; Recreational therapists 1 (ft).
Facilities Dining room; Physical therapy room; Activities room; Crafts room; Barber/Beauty shop.
Activities Arts & crafts; Cards; Games; Reading groups; Prayer groups; Movies; Shopping trips; Dances/Social/Cultural gatherings; Outside programs by groups.

Montezuma

Montezuma Health Care Center
521 Sumter St, Box 639, Montezuma, GA 31063
(912) 472-8168
Admin Lillian M Baggett.
Licensure Skilled care; Intermediate care. *Beds* 100. *Certified* Medicaid; Medicare.

Monticello

Retreat Nursing Home
898 College St, Monticello, GA 31064
(404) 468-8826
Admin Kathy Thomason. *Dir of Nursing* Kay Huff RN. *Medical Dir* J Corbitt Kelly MD.
Licensure Skilled care; Intermediate care; Hospital; Ambulance service. *Beds* SNF 44; ICF; Hospital 16. *Certified* Medicaid.
Owner Publicly owned.
Admissions Requirements Medical examination; Physician's request.
Staff Physicians 2 (ft), 5 (pt); RNs 6 (ft), 3 (pt); LPNs 5 (ft), 2 (pt); Nurses' aides 20 (ft), 3 (pt); Physical therapists 1 (pt); Activities coordinators 1 (ft), 1 (pt); Dietitians 1 (pt).
Facilities Dining room; Activities room; Laundry room.
Activities Cards; Games; Prayer groups; Movies; Shopping trips; Dances/Social/Cultural gatherings.

Morrow

Lakecity Healthcare Center Nursing Home
2055 Rex Rd, Box 728, Morrow, GA 30252
(404) 361-5114
Admin Barbara Rhodes.
Medical Dir J Nam Lee MD.
Licensure Skilled care; Intermediate care. *Beds* 242. *Certified* Medicaid.
Admissions Requirements Medical examination; Physician's request.
Staff Physicians 3 (ft); RNs 1 (ft), 1 (pt); LPNs 7 (ft), 1 (pt); Nurses' aides 41 (ft); Physical therapists 2 (ft); Recreational therapists 1 (ft); Activities coordinators 1 (ft); Dietitians 1 (ft).
Facilities Dining room; Physical therapy room; Activities room; Crafts room; Laundry room; Barber/Beauty shop; Library.
Activities Arts & crafts; Cards; Games; Reading groups; Prayer groups; Movies; Shopping trips; Dances/Social/Cultural gatherings.

Moultrie

Brownwood Nursing Home
PO Box 2010, 233 Sunset Cr, Moultrie, GA 31768
(912) 985-3422
Admin Jeffrey Jursik.
Medical Dir Seth Berl; Gwen Bonner.
Licensure Skilled care; Intermediate care. *Beds* 100. *Certified* Medicaid; Medicare.
Owner Proprietary corp (National Heritage).
Admissions Requirements Medical examination; Physician's request.
Staff Physicians 10 (ft); RNs 2 (ft), 1 (pt); LPNs 8 (ft), 2 (pt); Nurses' aides 34 (ft), 4 (pt); Physical therapists 1 (ft), 1 (pt); Speech therapists 1 (pt); Activities coordinators 1 (ft), 1 (pt); Dietitians 1 (pt); Ophthalmologists 1 (pt).
Facilities Dining room; Physical therapy room; Activities room; Crafts room; Laundry room; Barber/Beauty shop.
Activities Arts & crafts; Games; Reading groups; Prayer groups; Movies; Shopping trips; Dances/Social/Cultural gatherings.

Moultrie Rest-A-While Nursing Home
PO Box 666, 2015 1st Ave, Moultrie, GA
31768
(912) 985-4319
Admin Joann Sloan.
Licensure Skilled care; Intermediate care. *Beds*
68. *Certified* Medicaid; Medicare.

Rest Awhile Nursing Home
422 5th St SE, Moultrie, GA 31768
(912) 985-7413
Admin Eugene E Reid Jr. *Dir of Nursing*
Georgia Simmons. *Medical Dir* John W
McLeod MD.
Licensure Skilled care; Intermediate care. *Beds*
SNF 17; ICF 42. *Certified* Medicaid.
Owner Proprietary corp.
Admissions Requirements Medical
examination; Physician's request.
Staff Physicians 9 (ft); RNs 1 (ft), 2 (pt);
LPNs 4 (ft), 3 (pt); Nurses' aides; Physical
therapists 1 (pt); Activities coordinators 1
(ft); Dietitians 1 (pt).
Facilities Dining room; Physical therapy
room; Activities room; Laundry room;
Barber/Beauty shop.
Activities Arts & crafts; Cards; Games;
Reading groups; Prayer groups; Movies;
Shopping trips; Dances/Social/Cultural
gatherings; Pet therapy; Picnics.

Sunrise Nursing Home of Georgia Inc
2709 S Main St, Moultrie, GA 31768
(912) 985-4772
Admin P Z Clark Sr. *Dir of Nursing* Lisa
Trimble RN.
Licensure Skilled care; Intermediate care. *Beds*
60. *Certified* Medicaid.
Owner Proprietary corp.
Admissions Requirements Medical
examination; Physician's request.
Staff RNs 2 (ft); LPNs 7 (ft); Nurses' aides 20
(ft); Activities coordinators 1 (ft); Dietitians
1 (pt).
Facilities Dining room; Physical therapy
room; Activities room; Chapel; Crafts room;
Laundry room; Barber/Beauty shop.
Activities Arts & crafts; Cards; Games;
Reading groups; Prayer groups; Movies;
Shopping trips; Dances/Social/Cultural
gatherings.

Nashville

Berrien Nursing Center Inc
704 N Davis St, Nashville, GA 31639
(912) 686-2034
Admin DeMaris P Hughes.
Medical Dir Dr James R Wilhoite.
Licensure Skilled care; Intermediate care. *Beds*
108. *Certified* Medicaid; Medicare.
Owner Proprietary corp (National Healthcare).
Admissions Requirements Medical
examination; Physician's request.
Staff Physicians 5 (pt); RNs 1 (ft), 2 (pt);
LPNs 4 (ft), 3 (pt); Nurses' aides 11 (ft), 5
(pt); Physical therapists 1 (pt); Activities
coordinators 1 (ft); Dietitians 1 (pt);
Podiatrists 1 (pt); Dentists 1 (pt).
Facilities Dining room; Activities room;
Crafts room; Laundry room; Barber/Beauty
shop.
Activities Arts & crafts; Cards; Games;
Reading groups; Prayer groups; Movies;
Shopping trips; Dances/Social/Cultural
gatherings.

Newnan

Beaulieu Convalescent Center Inc
Box 40, E Broad St, Newnan, GA 30264
(404) 253-7160
Admin Kathleen Adams.
Licensure Skilled care. *Beds* 137. *Certified*
Medicaid; Medicare.

Newnan Healthcare Center
120 Spring St, Newnan, GA 30263
(404) 253-1475
Admin Carolyn Stenger.
Medical Dir John Wells MD.
Licensure Intermediate care. *Beds* ICF 117.
Certified Medicaid.
Owner Proprietary corp.
Staff Physicians 10 (pt); RNs 2 (ft); LPNs 10
(ft); Nurses' aides 3 (ft); Physical therapists 1
(pt); Activities coordinators 1 (ft); Dietitians
1 (pt); Ophthalmologists 1 (ft); Dentists 1
(pt).

Ocilla

Osceola Nursing Home Inc
PO Box 505, Ocilla, GA 31774
(912) 468-9431
Admin George Christopher Cook.
Medical Dir Dr W C Sams.
Licensure Skilled care; Intermediate care. *Beds*
83. *Certified* Medicaid; Medicare.
Admissions Requirements Minimum age 35;
Medical examination; Physician's request.
Staff Physicians 3 (ft); RNs 1 (ft), 2 (pt);
LPNs 10 (ft), 4 (pt); Nurses' aides 14 (ft), 8
(pt); Physical therapists 1 (ft); Reality
therapists 1 (ft); Recreational therapists 1
(ft); Speech therapists 1 (pt); Activities
coordinators 1 (pt); Dietitians 1 (pt);
Ophthalmologists 1 (pt); Podiatrists 1 (pt);
Dentists 1 (pt).
Facilities Dining room; Physical therapy
room; Activities room; Crafts room; Laundry
room; Barber/Beauty shop.
Activities Arts & crafts; Cards; Games;
Reading groups; Prayer groups; Movies;
Shopping trips; Dances/Social/Cultural
gatherings.

Palemon Gaskins Nursing Home
201 W Dismuke Ave, Ocilla, GA 31774
(912) 468-7456
Admin Jo Glenn. *Dir of Nursing* Nellie Jo
Spicer. *Medical Dir* W C Sams MD.
Licensure Skilled care; Intermediate care. *Beds*
Swing beds SNF/ICF 30. *Certified* Medicaid.
Owner Publicly owned.
Admissions Requirements Physician's request.
Staff Physicians 3 (ft), 2 (pt); RNs 1 (ft), 4
(pt); LPNs 5 (ft), 2 (pt); Nurses' aides 7 (ft),
7 (pt); Physical therapists (contracted);
Speech therapists (contracted); Activities
coordinators 1 (ft); Dietitians (contracted);
Podiatrists (contracted); Audiologists
(contracted).
Facilities Dining room; Physical therapy
room; Chapel; Laundry room; Barber/Beauty
shop.
Activities Arts & crafts; Games; Reading
groups; Prayer groups; Movies; Dances/
Social/Cultural gatherings.

Oconee

Oconee Health Care Center
PO Box 130, Oconee, GA 31067
(912) 552-7381
Admin Laverne Bloodworth.
Licensure Skilled care; Intermediate care. *Beds*
SNF 52. *Certified* Medicaid.

Pelham

Pelham Parkway Nursing Home
601 Dogwood Dr, Pelham, GA 31779
(912) 294-8602
Admin Sue H Rumble.
Medical Dir W C Arwood Jr MD.
Licensure Skilled care; Intermediate care;
Alzheimer's care. *Beds* SNF 108; ICF.
Certified Medicaid; Medicare.
Owner Publicly owned.
Admissions Requirements Medical
examination; Physician's request.

Staff Physicians 4 (ft); RNs 2 (ft), 2 (pt);
LPNs 7 (ft), 2 (pt); Nurses' aides 18 (ft), 10
(pt); Physical therapists 1 (ft); Speech
therapists 1 (pt); Activities coordinators 1
(ft); Dietitians 1 (pt); Ophthalmologists 1
(pt); Dentists 1 (pt).
Languages Spanish.
Facilities Dining room; Physical therapy
room; Activities room; Laundry room;
Barber/Beauty shop; Library.
Activities Arts & crafts; Cards; Games;
Reading groups; Prayer groups; Movies;
Dances/Social/Cultural gatherings.

Perry

Church Home for the Aged
PO Box 1376, Perry, GA 31069
(912) 987-1239
Admin Mariola H Cosby. *Dir of Nursing*
Deborah Warner. *Medical Dir* Harold
Gregory MD.
Licensure Skilled care; Intermediate care. *Beds*
Swing beds SNF/ICF 49. *Private Pay
Patients* 35%. *Certified* Medicaid.
Owner Nonprofit organization/foundation.
Admissions Requirements Physician's request.
Staff Physicians 5 (pt); RNs 3 (ft); LPNs 1
(ft), 4 (pt); Physical therapists 1 (pt);
Dietitians.
Facilities Dining room; Physical therapy
room; Activities room; Crafts room; Laundry
room; Barber/Beauty shop; Whirlpool.
Activities Arts & crafts; Prayer groups;
Movies; Shopping trips; Dances/Social/
Cultural gatherings.

New Perry Nursing Home
PO Drawer P, Perry, GA 31068
(912) 987-3251
Admin William C Davis Jr.
Medical Dir Dr J L Gallemore.
Licensure Skilled care; Intermediate care. *Beds*
73. *Certified* Medicaid.
Staff Physicians 4 (pt); RNs 3 (ft); LPNs 3
(ft), 2 (pt); Nurses' aides 27 (ft); Physical
therapists 1 (pt); Recreational therapists 1
(ft); Activities coordinators 1 (ft); Dietitians
1 (pt); Podiatrists 1 (pt).
Facilities Dining room; Activities room;
Chapel; Crafts room; Laundry room; Barber/
Beauty shop; Library.
Activities Arts & crafts; Cards; Games;
Movies; Dances/Social/Cultural gatherings.

Pineview

Pineview Health Care Center Inc
PO Box 148, Bay St, Pineview, GA 31071
(912) 624-2432
Admin Jaye M Stewart Jr.
Medical Dir Elise Wells.
Licensure Skilled care; Intermediate care;
Retirement. *Beds* SNF 102. *Certified*
Medicaid.
Owner Proprietary corp.
Staff Physicians; RNs; LPNs; Nurses' aides;
Physical therapists; Reality therapists;
Recreational therapists; Speech therapists;
Activities coordinators; Dietitians;
Ophthalmologists; Dentists.
Facilities Dining room; Physical therapy
room; Activities room; Chapel; Crafts room;
Laundry room; Barber/Beauty shop; Library.
Activities Arts & crafts; Cards; Games;
Reading groups; Prayer groups; Movies;
Shopping trips; Dances/Social/Cultural
gatherings.

Plains

Plains Nursing Center
PO Box 366, 225 Hospital St, Plains, GA
31780
(912) 824-7796

Admin Glenn Godwin. *Dir of Nursing* Susie E Potter RN. *Medical Dir* H L Simpson Jr MD.
Licensure Skilled care; Intermediate care. *Beds* SNF 100. *Certified* Medicaid.
Owner Proprietary corp.
Admissions Requirements Medical examination; Physician's request.
Staff Physicians 2 (pt); RNs 4 (ft), 1 (pt); LPNs 8 (ft), 4 (pt); Nurses' aides 45 (ft), 8 (pt); Physical therapists 1 (ft), 2 (pt); Reality therapists 1 (ft); Recreational therapists 1 (ft); Speech therapists 1 (pt); Activities coordinators 1 (ft), 1 (pt); Dietitians 1 (ft), 1 (pt); Ophthalmologists 1 (pt).
Languages Spanish.
Facilities Dining room; Physical therapy room; Activities room; Laundry room; Barber/Beauty shop.
Activities Arts & crafts; Cards; Games; Reading groups; Prayer groups; Movies; Shopping trips.

Pooler

Moss Oaks Health Care
508 Rogers St, Pooler, GA 31322
(912) 748-6840
Admin Matthew C Dempsey. *Dir of Nursing* Pat Kobleur. *Medical Dir* Dr Meatart.
Licensure Skilled care. *Beds* SNF 122. *Private Pay Patients* 7%. *Certified* Medicaid; Medicare.
Owner Proprietary corp (Allgood Health Care).
Staff RNs 2 (ft); LPNs 9 (ft); Nurses' aides 38 (ft); Physical therapists (contracted); Occupational therapists (contracted); Speech therapists (contracted); Activities coordinators 1 (ft); Dietitians (contracted); Ophthalmologists (contracted); Podiatrists (contracted); Audiologists (contracted); Physical therapy aides 1 (ft).
Facilities Dining room; Physical therapy room; Activities room; Laundry room; Barber/Beauty shop.
Activities Arts & crafts; Cards; Games; Reading groups; Prayer groups; Dances/Social/Cultural gatherings.

Port Wentworth

Westview Medical Care Home
PO Box 4134, Port Wentworth, GA 31407
(912) 964-1515
Admin Cleveland J Fountain.
Licensure Skilled care; Intermediate care. *Beds* SNF 101. *Certified* Medicaid.

Pulaski

Pulaski Nursing Home
PO Box 118, Pulaski, GA 30451
(912) 685-5072
Admin Kay Hendricks.
Medical Dir Dorsey Smith MD.
Licensure Skilled care; Intermediate care. *Beds* SNF 89. *Certified* Medicaid.
Staff Physicians 4 (ft); RNs 1 (ft), 1 (pt); LPNs 7 (ft), 5 (pt); Nurses' aides 16 (ft), 6 (pt); Physical therapists 1 (pt); Activities coordinators 1 (ft); Dietitians 1 (pt); Podiatrists 1 (pt); Dentists 1 (pt).
Facilities Dining room; Physical therapy room; Activities room; Laundry room; Barber/Beauty shop.
Activities Arts & crafts; Cards; Games; Reading groups; Prayer groups; Movies; Shopping trips; Dances/Social/Cultural gatherings.

Quitman

Presbyterian Home Inc
PO Box 407, 1850 W Screven St, Quitman, GA 31643
(912) 263-8633
Admin Rev F H McElroy. *Dir of Nursing* Sara Webb RN. *Medical Dir* Robert T Cain MD.
Licensure Skilled care; Intermediate care; Personal care; Retirement living; Alzheimer's care. *Beds* SNF 188; ICF; Personal 31; Retirement living 50. *Certified* Medicaid.
Owner Nonprofit corp.
Admissions Requirements Medical examination; Physician's request.
Staff Physicians 3 (ft); RNs 5 (ft), 1 (pt); LPNs 21 (ft), 7 (pt); Nurses' aides 85 (ft), 10 (pt); Physical therapists 1 (ft); Occupational therapists 1 (pt); Speech therapists 1 (pt); Activities coordinators 1 (ft); Dietitians 1 (ft); Ophthalmologists 1 (pt).
Affiliation Presbyterian.
Facilities Dining room; Physical therapy room; Activities room; Chapel; Crafts room; Laundry room; Barber/Beauty shop; Library; Swimming pool; Lake.
Activities Arts & crafts; Cards; Games; Reading groups; Prayer groups; Movies; Shopping trips; Dances/Social/Cultural gatherings; Pond for fishing; Paddle boating; Miniature golf; Shuffle board; Swimming.

Reidsville

Tattnall Nursing Care
PO Box 860, Memorial Drive, Reidsville, GA 30453
(912) 557-4345
Admin Linda Ray. *Dir of Nursing* Jewel Clifton RN. *Medical Dir* H J Kim MD.
Licensure Skilled care; Intermediate care. *Beds* SNF 92; ICF. *Certified* Medicaid.
Owner Nonprofit corp.
Admissions Requirements Medical examination; Physician's request.
Staff Physicians 1 (ft); RNs 2 (ft); LPNs 5 (ft), 4 (pt); Nurses' aides 25 (ft), 8 (pt); Physical therapists 1 (ft), 1 (pt); Reality therapists 1 (ft); Recreational therapists 1 (ft); Activities coordinators 1 (ft); Dietitians 1 (ft); Ophthalmologists 1 (pt).
Facilities Dining room; Physical therapy room; Activities room; Laundry room; Barber/Beauty shop.
Activities Arts & crafts; Cards; Games; Reading groups; Prayer groups; Movies; Shopping trips; Dances/Social/Cultural gatherings; 4-H; Adopt-a-grandparent.

Riverdale

Tara Health Care Center
PO Box 917, Riverdale, GA 30274
(404) 991-2144
Admin Mary Kay Long.
Licensure Skilled care; Intermediate care. *Beds* 152. *Certified* Medicaid; Medicare.

Roberta

Roberta Nursing Home
PO Box 146, Roberta, GA 31078
(912) 836-3101
Admin Jack W Smoot.
Licensure Skilled care; Intermediate care. *Beds* SNF 100. *Certified* Medicaid.

Rockmart

Rockmart Intermediate Care Center
528 Hunter St, Rockmart, GA 30153
(404) 684-5491
Admin Ann Gober.
Medical Dir Umpon Sangmalee MD.
Licensure Intermediate care. *Beds* ICF 73. *Certified* Medicaid.

Admissions Requirements Medical examination; Physician's request.
Staff Physicians 1 (ft); RNs 1 (ft); LPNs 3 (ft), 2 (pt); Nurses' aides 20 (ft), 4 (pt); Physical therapists 1 (pt); Activities coordinators 1 (ft); Dietitians 1 (pt); Ophthalmologists 1 (pt).
Facilities Dining room; Physical therapy room; Activities room; Chapel; Crafts room; Laundry room; Barber/Beauty shop.
Activities Arts & crafts; Cards; Games; Reading groups; Prayer groups; Movies; Shopping trips; Dances/Social/Cultural gatherings.

Rome

Brentwood Park Nursing Home
PO Box 1441, Moran Lake Rd, Rome, GA 30161
(404) 291-8212
Admin Louise Houser. *Dir of Nursing* Sharon Vaughan RN. *Medical Dir* Dr R Cook.
Licensure Skilled care; Intermediate care. *Beds* 100. *Certified* Medicaid; Medicare.
Owner Proprietary corp.
Admissions Requirements Minimum age 12; Medical examination; Physician's request.
Staff RNs 3 (ft), 3 (pt); LPNs 6 (ft), 3 (pt); Nurses' aides 36 (ft), 4 (pt); Physical therapists 1 (ft); Recreational therapists 1 (pt); Speech therapists 1 (pt); Activities coordinators 1 (ft); Dietitians 1 (pt); Ophthalmologists 1 (pt).
Facilities Dining room; Physical therapy room; Activities room; Chapel; Crafts room; Laundry room; Barber/Beauty shop.
Activities Arts & crafts; Cards; Games; Prayer groups; Movies; Shopping trips; Dances/ Social/Cultural gatherings; Resident council; Community activities participation; Videos.

Creswell Convalescent Center
1345 Redmond Rd, Rome, GA 30161
(404) 234-8281
Admin Patsy Haislip.
Medical Dir Grant Lewis.
Licensure Skilled care; Intermediate care. *Beds* 100. *Certified* Medicaid; Medicare.
Admissions Requirements Physician's request.
Staff RNs 2 (ft); LPNs 15 (ft); Nurses' aides 40 (ft), 26 (pt); Physical therapists 1 (ft); Reality therapists 1 (ft); Recreational therapists 1 (ft); Occupational therapists 1 (pt); Speech therapists 1 (pt); Activities coordinators 1 (ft); Dietitians 1 (pt); Podiatrists 1 (pt); Dentists 1 (pt).
Facilities Dining room; Physical therapy room; Activities room; Crafts room; Laundry room; Barber/Beauty shop; Library; Gift shop.
Activities Arts & crafts; Cards; Games; Reading groups; Prayer groups; Movies; Shopping trips; Dances/Social/Cultural gatherings.

Fifth Avenue Health Care Center
505 N 5th Ave, Rome, GA 30161
(404) 291-0521
Admin Clark H Peek.
Medical Dir Dr Ingrid Sturgis.
Licensure Skilled care; Intermediate care. *Beds* SNF 100; ICF. *Certified* Medicaid; Medicare.
Owner Proprietary corp.
Admissions Requirements Medical examination; Physician's request.
Staff RNs 3 (ft); LPNs 6 (ft), 5 (pt); Nurses' aides 27 (ft), 9 (pt); Activities coordinators 1 (ft).
Facilities Dining room; Physical therapy room; Activities room; Laundry room; Barber/Beauty shop; Library.
Activities Arts & crafts; Cards; Games; Reading groups; Prayer groups; Movies; Dances/Social/Cultural gatherings.

Northwest Regional Intermediate Care Home
400 Redmond Rd, Rome, GA 30161
(404) 234-9481
Admin Robert Pullian. *Dir of Nursing*
Georgette Wright.
Licensure Intermediate care for mentally
retarded. *Beds* ICF/MR 98.
Owner Publicly owned.
Admissions Requirements Medical
examination.
Staff Physicians 1 (ft); RNs 11 (ft); LPNs 13
(ft); Recreational therapists 3 (ft); Activities
coordinators 1 (pt); Dietitians 1 (ft); Social
workers 4 (ft); Special education teacher 1
(ft); Behavioral staff 7 (ft); Psychologist 1
(ft); Health service technicians 55 (ft); Shift
Supv 6 (ft).
Activities Arts & crafts; Cards; Games;
Movies; Shopping trips; Dances/Social/
Cultural gatherings.

Riverview Nursing Home
809 S Broad St, Rome, GA 30161
(404) 235-1337
Admin James Ambrose.
Licensure Skilled care; Intermediate care. *Beds*
100. *Certified* Medicaid.
Owner Proprietary corp (Riverside Med
Services).

Sun Mountain Nursing Center
2 Three Mile Rd NE, Rome, GA 30161
(404) 291-4606
Admin Harrison C Neal II. *Dir of Nursing* Jan
King. *Medical Dir* T Llorente.
Licensure Skilled care; Intermediate care. *Beds*
SNF 8; ICF 100. *Private Pay Patients* 5%.
Certified Medicaid; Medicare.
Owner Proprietary corp (Nepenthe Group
Inc).
Admissions Requirements Medical
examination; Physician's request.
Staff Physicians 1 (pt); RNs 1 (ft), 2 (pt);
LPNs 11 (ft); Nurses' aides 39 (ft); Physical
therapists 1 (pt); Occupational therapists 1
(pt); Speech therapists 1 (pt); Activities
coordinators 1 (ft); Dietitians 1 (pt);
Ophthalmologists 1 (pt); Podiatrists 1 (pt).
Facilities Dining room; Physical therapy
room; Activities room; Crafts room; Laundry
room; Barber/Beauty shop; Sun porches;
Atrium.
Activities Arts & crafts; Cards; Games;
Reading groups; Prayer groups; Movies;
Shopping trips; Dances/Social/Cultural
gatherings; Intergenerational programs; Pet
therapy.

Valley View Health Care
1166 Chulio Rd, Rome, GA 30161
(404) 235-1132
Admin Andrew J Morris. *Dir of Nursing*
Mildred Petty RN. *Medical Dir* Rebecca
Madden MD.
Licensure Skilled care. *Beds* SNF 77. *Private
Pay Patients* 5%. *Certified* Medicaid;
Medicare.
Owner Proprietary corp (Moroni Health Care
Inc).
Admissions Requirements Medical
examination; Physician's request.
Staff Physicians 1 (pt); RNs 2 (ft), 1 (pt);
LPNs 7 (ft), 2 (pt); Nurses' aides 29 (ft), 6
(pt); Physical therapists (consultant);
Recreational therapists (consultant);
Occupational therapists (consultant); Speech
therapists (consultant); Activities
coordinators 1 (ft); Dietitians 1 (ft);
Ophthalmologists (consultant).
Facilities Dining room; Physical therapy
room; Activities room; Chapel; Crafts room;
Laundry room; Barber/Beauty shop.
Activities Arts & crafts; Cards; Games;
Reading groups; Prayer groups; Movies;
Shopping trips; Dances/Social/Cultural
gatherings.

Winthrop Manor Nursing Home
12 Chateau Dr, Rome, GA 30161
(404) 235-8121
Admin Bruce Behner.
Licensure Skilled care; Intermediate care. *Beds*
SNF 100. *Certified* Medicaid.

Rossville

Rossville Convalescent Center
1425 McFarland Ave, Rossville, GA 30741
(404) 861-0863
Admin Doug Anderson. *Dir of Nursing* Hattie
English RN. *Medical Dir* Dr Garland
Kinard.
Licensure Skilled care; Intermediate care. *Beds*
SNF 32; ICF 80. *Private Pay Patients* 25%.
Certified Medicare.
Owner Proprietary corp (National Health
Corp).
Admissions Requirements Minimum age 65;
Medical examination; Physician's request.
Staff Physicians 1 (pt); RNs 2 (ft), 1 (pt);
LPNs 11 (ft), 1 (pt); Nurses' aides 35 (ft), 5
(pt); Physical therapists 3 (ft); Speech
therapists 1 (pt); Activities coordinators 1
(ft); Dietitians 1 (ft); Podiatrists 1 (pt);
Audiologists 1 (pt).
Facilities Dining room; Physical therapy
room; Activities room; Crafts room; Laundry
room; Barber/Beauty shop.
Activities Arts & crafts; Cards; Games;
Reading groups; Prayer groups; Movies;
Shopping trips; Pet therapy; Bible study.

Roswell

Great Oaks Nursing Home
Box 1698, 1109 Green St, Roswell, GA 30077
(404) 998-1802
Admin Chuck Gorham.
Licensure Skilled care; Intermediate care. *Beds*
268. *Certified* Medicaid; Medicare.

Royston

Brown Memorial Convalescent Center
PO Box 8, Royston, GA 30662
(404) 745-7257
Admin Johnnie Strathern. *Dir of Nursing*
Frances Osborne RN. *Medical Dir* William
Ford MD.
Licensure Skilled care; Intermediate care;
Retirement. *Beds* SNF; ICF 144. *Certified*
Medicaid; Medicare.
Owner Nonprofit corp.
Admissions Requirements Medical
examination; Physician's request.
Staff RNs 2 (ft), 2 (pt); LPNs 10 (ft), 6 (pt);
Nurses' aides 37 (ft), 34 (pt); Physical
therapists 1 (pt); Activities coordinators 2
(ft); Dietitians 1 (pt); Social workers 1 (ft).
Facilities Dining room; Physical therapy
room; Activities room; Chapel; Crafts room;
Laundry room; Barber/Beauty shop; In-house
pharmacy.
Activities Arts & crafts; Games; Reading
groups; Prayer groups; Movies; Shopping
trips; Dances/Social/Cultural gatherings.

Saint Mary's

St Mary's Convalescent Center
805 Dilworth St, Saint Mary's, GA 31558
(912) 882-4281
Admin Elizabeth Turner.
Licensure Skilled care; Intermediate care. *Beds*
69. *Certified* Medicaid.

Saint Simons Island

Heritage Inn
PO Box 287, 2255 Frederica Rd, Saint Simons
Island, GA 31522
(912) 638-9988

Admin John Driggers. *Dir of Nursing* Bonnie
Zane. *Medical Dir* Dr Grubbs.
Licensure Skilled care; Intermediate care;
Retirement. *Beds* Swing beds SNF/ICF 125;
Retirement 46. *Private Pay Patients* 40%.
Certified Medicaid.
Owner Proprietary corp.
Admissions Requirements Medical
examination; Physician's request.
Staff RNs 3 (ft); LPNs 12 (ft); Nurses' aides
40 (ft); Physical therapists 1 (pt);
Occupational therapists 1 (pt); Speech
therapists 1 (pt); Activities coordinators 1
(ft); Dietitians 1 (pt); Ophthalmologists 1
(pt); Podiatrists 1 (pt); Audiologists 1 (pt).
Facilities Dining room; Physical therapy
room; Activities room; Chapel; Laundry
room; Barber/Beauty shop.
Activities Arts & crafts; Cards; Games;
Reading groups; Prayer groups; Movies;
Shopping trips; Dances/Social/Cultural
gatherings; Pet therapy.

Sandersville

Rawlings Nursing Home
111 Brookins St, Sandersville, GA 31082
(912) 552-3015
Admin Jean J Ginn. *Dir of Nursing* Nancy
Robinson RN. *Medical Dir* Dr Chandler
McDavid.
Licensure Skilled care; Intermediate care. *Beds*
56. *Certified* Medicaid.
Owner Proprietary corp.
Admissions Requirements Medical
examination; Physician's request.
Staff Physicians 7 (pt); RNs 1 (ft), 4 (pt);
LPNs 6 (ft), 5 (pt); Nurses' aides 20 (ft), 1
(pt); Physical therapists 1 (pt); Reality
therapists 1 (ft); Activities coordinators 1
(ft).
Facilities Dining room; Activities room;
Crafts room; Laundry room; Barber/Beauty
shop.
Activities Arts & crafts; Games; Prayer groups;
Movies.

Smith Medical Nursing Care Center
501 E McCarty St, Sandersville, GA 31082
(912) 552-5155
Admin Kate Harris Smith.
Medical Dir Dr William E Taylor.
Licensure Skilled care; Intermediate care. *Beds*
SNF 56.
Admissions Requirements Medical
examination; Physician's request.
Staff Physicians 1 (pt); RNs 1 (ft), 2 (pt);
LPNs 6 (ft), 1 (pt); Nurses' aides 8 (ft), 1
(pt); Physical therapists 1 (ft), 1 (pt);
Activities coordinators 1 (ft), 2 (pt);
Dietitians 1 (ft).
Facilities Dining room; Physical therapy
room; Activities room; Crafts room; Laundry
room; Barber/Beauty shop.
Activities Arts & crafts; Cards; Games;
Reading groups; Prayer groups; Movies;
Shopping trips; Dances/Social/Cultural
gatherings.

Washington County Extended Care Facility
PO Box 636, Sandersville, GA 31082
(912) 552-3901
Admin Larry W Anderson. *Dir of Nursing*
Wylene Lewis RN. *Medical Dir* Dr William
Helton.
Licensure Skilled care; Intermediate care. *Beds*
SNF 58. *Certified* Medicaid.
Owner Nonprofit organization/foundation.
Admissions Requirements Physician's request.
Staff Physicians 8 (pt); RNs 1 (ft), 1 (pt);
LPNs 8 (ft), 1 (pt); Nurses' aides 12 (ft), 4
(pt); Physical therapists 2 (pt); Speech
therapists 1 (pt); Activities coordinators 1
(ft); Dietitians 1 (pt); Podiatrists 1 (pt).
Facilities Dining room; Physical therapy
room; Activities room; Chapel; Barber/
Beauty shop.

Activities Arts & crafts; Games; Reading groups; Prayer groups; Movies; Shopping trips; Dances/Social/Cultural gatherings.

Savannah

Azalealand Nursing Home Inc
2040 Colonial Dr, Savannah, GA 31406
(912) 354-2752
Admin Charles L Von Waldner.
Medical Dir Jules Victor Jr.
Licensure Skilled care; Intermediate care. *Beds* 107.
Admissions Requirements Minimum age 65; Medical examination; Physician's request.
Staff RNs 3 (ft), 2 (pt); LPNs 7 (ft), 2 (pt); Nurses' aides 20 (ft), 8 (pt); Physical therapists 1 (pt); Reality therapists 2 (pt); Recreational therapists 1 (ft), 1 (pt); Activities coordinators 1 (ft).
Facilities Dining room; Physical therapy room; Activities room; Chapel; Laundry room; Barber/Beauty shop; Library.
Activities Cards; Games; Movies; Shopping trips.

Chatham Nursing Home I
6711 La Roche Ave, Savannah, GA 31406
(912) 354-8225
Admin Meta Wright.
Licensure Skilled care; Intermediate care. *Beds* 284. *Certified* Medicaid; Medicare.

Chatham Nursing Home II
6711 La Roche Ave, Savannah, GA 31406
(912) 354-8225
Admin Meta Wright.
Licensure Skilled care; Intermediate care. *Beds* 100. *Certified* Medicaid; Medicare.

Cohen's Retreat
PO Box 13189, 5715 Skidaway Rd, Savannah, GA 31416
(912) 355-2873
Admin Jewell S Clifton. *Dir of Nursing* Eleanor McHugh. *Medical Dir* Lawrence J Lynch Jr MD.
Licensure Skilled care; Intermediate care. *Beds* Swing beds SNF/ICF 31. *Private Pay Patients* 16%. *Certified* Medicaid; Medicare.
Owner Nonprofit corp.
Admissions Requirements Males only; Medical examination; Physician's request.
Staff Physicians 3 (pt); RNs 1 (ft), 1 (pt); LPNs 5 (ft), 5 (pt); Nurses' aides 9 (ft), 4 (pt); Physical therapists 1 (pt); Recreational therapists 1 (pt); Occupational therapists 1 (pt); Activities coordinators 1 (ft); Dietitians 1 (ft); Podiatrists 1 (pt).
Facilities Dining room; Activities room; Laundry room; Barber/Beauty shop; Library.
Activities Arts & crafts; Cards; Games; Reading groups; Prayer groups; Movies; Shopping trips; Dances/Social/Cultural gatherings; Intergenerational programs; Pet therapy.

Hillhaven Convalescent Center
11800 Abercorn St, Savannah, GA 31406
(912) 925-4402
Admin Betty J Hargrett.
Licensure Skilled care. *Beds* 104. *Certified* Medicaid; Medicare.
Owner Proprietary corp (Hillhaven Corp).

Savannah Convalescent Center
815 E 63rd St, Savannah, GA 31405
(912) 352-8015
Admin Mary Burroughs. *Dir of Nursing* Rose Robbins RN. *Medical Dir* John Fillingim MD.
Licensure Skilled care. *Beds* SNF 120. *Certified* Medicaid; Medicare.
Owner Proprietary corp.
Admissions Requirements Medical examination.

Staff Physicians 40 (ft); RNs 6 (ft), 2 (pt); LPNs 13 (ft), 6 (pt); Nurses' aides 40 (ft), 13 (pt); Physical therapists 1 (ft), 1 (pt); Reality therapists 1 (pt); Recreational therapists 1 (pt); Occupational therapists 1 (pt); Speech therapists 1 (pt); Activities coordinators 1 (ft); Dietitians 1 (pt); Ophthalmologists 1 (pt); Podiatrists 1 (pt); Dentists 1 (pt).
Facilities Dining room; Physical therapy room; Activities room; Crafts room; Laundry room; Barber/Beauty shop.
Activities Arts & crafts; Cards; Games; Prayer groups; Movies; Dances/Social/Cultural gatherings; Religious services.

Savannah Square Retirement Community Nursing Home
1 Savannah Sq, Savannah, GA 31406-4497
Admin Kenneth L Lowery.
Licensure Nursing home. *Beds* Nursing home 30.

White Bluff Manor
12825 White Bluff Rd, Savannah, GA 31406
(912) 927-9416
Admin T H Wilson.
Licensure Skilled care; Intermediate care. *Beds* 120. *Certified* Medicaid; Medicare.

Sayrna

King Springs Village
404 King Spring Village Pkwy, Sayrna, GA 30080
(404) 432-4444
Admin David H Morgan.
Licensure Skilled care; Intermediate care. *Beds* 120. *Certified* Medicaid; Medicare.

Snellville

Snellville Nursing & Rehabilitation Center
3000 Lenora Church Rd, Snellville, GA 30278
(404) 972-2040
Admin M E Hill III. *Dir of Nursing* Dolly DeProspero RN. *Medical Dir* Bill Martin MD.
Licensure Skilled care; Intermediate care; Retirement. *Beds* SNF 125; ICF. *Certified* Medicaid.
Owner Proprietary corp.
Admissions Requirements Medical examination; Physician's request.
Staff Physicians 1 (ft); RNs 4 (ft), 2 (pt); LPNs 11 (ft), 1 (pt); Nurses' aides 31 (ft), 12 (pt); Physical therapists 1 (pt); Speech therapists 1 (pt); Activities coordinators 1 (ft); Dietitians 1 (ft); Ophthalmologists 1 (pt); Dentists 1 (pt).
Facilities Dining room; Physical therapy room; Activities room; Crafts room; Laundry room; Barber/Beauty shop; Library.
Activities Arts & crafts; Cards; Games; Reading groups; Prayer groups; Movies; Shopping trips; Dances/Social/Cultural gatherings; Bowling.

Social Circle

Social Circle Intermediate Care Facility
671 N Cherokee Rd, Social Circle, GA 30279
(404) 464-2019
Admin Mary Ann Wood.
Licensure Intermediate care. *Beds* ICF 65. *Certified* Medicare.

Soperton

Treutlen County Nursing Home
PO Box 646, Soperton, GA 30457
(912) 529-4418
Admin Johnnie R Brooks.
Licensure Skilled care; Intermediate care. *Beds* SNF 50. *Certified* Medicaid.

Sparta

Providence Health Care
Box 86, Providence St, Sparta, GA 31087
(404) 444-5153
Admin Joy A Hill.
Licensure Skilled care; Intermediate care. *Beds* 71. *Certified* Medicaid.
Owner Proprietary corp (Vantage Healthcare).

Sparta Health Care Center
PO Box 237, Hwy 22, Sparta, GA 31087
(404) 444-6057
Admin Martha Rogers.
Licensure Skilled care; Intermediate care. *Beds* SNF 81. *Certified* Medicaid.

Springfield

Effingham County—ECF
PO Box 386, Springfield, GA 31329
(912) 754-6451, 754-9901 FAX
Admin Norma Jean Morgan. *Dir of Nursing* Beverly R Yowmans RN. *Medical Dir* Jack D Heneisen MD.
Licensure Skilled care; Intermediate care. *Beds* Swing beds SNF/ICF 56. *Private Pay Patients* 32%. *Certified* Medicaid; Medicare.
Owner Nonprofit organization/foundation.
Admissions Requirements Minimum age 18; Medical examination; Physician's request.
Staff Physicians 6 (ft); RNs 1 (ft), 2 (pt); LPNs 7 (ft), 4 (pt); Nurses' aides 14 (ft), 13 (pt); Physical therapists 1 (pt); Speech therapists 1 (pt); Activities coordinators 1 (ft), 2 (pt); Dietitians 1 (ft).
Facilities Dining room; Physical therapy room; Activities room; Chapel; Laundry room; Barber/Beauty shop.
Activities Arts & crafts; Cards; Games; Reading groups; Prayer groups; Movies; Shopping trips; Dances/Social/Cultural gatherings; Pink lady program.

Statesboro

Browns Nursing Home
226 S College St, Statesboro, GA 30458
(912) 764-9631
Admin Harold H Brown.
Licensure Skilled care; Intermediate care. *Beds* 63. *Certified* Medicaid; Medicare.

Georgia Grace Memorial Home Inc
PO Box 421, Statesboro, GA 30458
(912) 764-6903
Admin Beatrice Riggs.
Licensure Skilled care; Intermediate care. *Beds* 60. *Certified* Medicaid.

Nightingale Home
307 Jones Mill Rd, Statesboro, GA 30458
(912) 764-9011
Admin Martha A Firges. *Dir of Nursing* Pansy Bird RN. *Medical Dir* Dr R H Smith.
Licensure Skilled care; Intermediate care. *Beds* 92. *Certified* Medicaid.
Owner Privately owned.
Admissions Requirements Medical examination; Physician's request.
Staff Physicians 1 (pt); RNs 2 (ft), 2 (pt); LPNs 5 (ft), 7 (pt); Recreational therapists 1 (pt); Activities coordinators 1 (ft); Dietitians 1 (pt).
Facilities Dining room; Physical therapy room; Activities room; Laundry room; Barber/Beauty shop.
Activities Arts & crafts; Games; Reading groups; Prayer groups; Movies.

Pecan Manor Nursing Home
101 Stockyard Rd, Statesboro, GA 30458
(912) 764-6005
Admin Arthur E Simpson.
Licensure Skilled care. *Beds* SNF 60. *Certified* Medicaid.

Statesboro Nursing Home
PO Box 746, Statesboro, GA 30458
(912) 764-4575
Admin Shirley Wilkes.
Medical Dir Dr D Scarborough & Dr R
Smith.
Licensure Skilled care; Intermediate care. *Beds*
99. *Certified* Medicaid.
Admissions Requirements Medical
examination; Physician's request.
Staff Physicians 5 (pt); RNs 2 (ft), 1 (pt);
LPNs 9 (ft), 2 (pt); Nurses' aides 24 (ft), 6
(pt); Physical therapists 1 (pt); Speech
therapists 1 (pt); Activities coordinators 1
(ft); Dietitians 1 (pt); Podiatrists 1 (pt);
Dentists 1 (pt).
Facilities Dining room; Physical therapy
room; Activities room; Laundry room;
Barber/Beauty shop.
Activities Arts & crafts; Games; Movies;
Shopping trips; Dances/Social/Cultural
gatherings.

Summerville

Oak View Nursing Home
PO Box 449, Summerville, GA 30747
(404) 857-3419
Admin Bobby L Throneberry.
Licensure Skilled care; Intermediate care. *Beds*
90. *Certified* Medicaid; Medicare.

Swainsboro

Emanuel County Nursing Home
PO Box 7, Swainsboro, GA 30401
(912) 237-9911
Admin Leland E Farnell.
Licensure Skilled care. *Beds* 49. *Certified*
Medicaid; Medicare.

Swainsboro Nursing Home
PO Box 1758, Swainsboro, GA 30401
(912) 237-7022, 237-3024 FAX
Admin Barbara Slater. *Dir of Nursing* Sharon
H Pye RN. *Medical Dir* James L Ray MD.
Licensure Skilled care; Intermediate care. *Beds*
Swing beds SNF/ICF 103. *Private Pay
Patients* 2%. *Certified* Medicaid.
Owner Proprietary corp (Taylor & Bird Inc).
Staff RNs 3 (ft), 5 (pt); LPNs 11 (ft); Nurses'
aides 31 (ft); Physical therapists 1 (ft);
Activities coordinators 1 (ft); Dietitians 1
(ft).
Facilities Dining room; Physical therapy
room; Activities room; Chapel; Crafts room;
Laundry room; Barber/Beauty shop.
Activities Arts & crafts; Cards; Games;
Reading groups; Prayer groups; Movies;
Shopping trips; Dances/Social/Cultural
gatherings; Intergenerational programs.

Sylvania

Syl-View Health Care Center
Box 199, 411 Pine St, Sylvania, GA 30467
(912) 564-2015
Admin Karen Zeigler.
Licensure Skilled care; Intermediate care. *Beds*
128. *Certified* Medicaid.

Sylvester

Sylvester Health Care Inc
PO Box 406, Sylvester, GA 31791
(912) 776-5541
Admin Douglas L Moody.
Medical Dir Faye Davidson.
Licensure Skilled care; Intermediate care;
Alzheimer's care. *Beds* SNF 59; ICF.
Certified Medicaid.
Owner Proprietary corp.
Admissions Requirements Medical
examination.
Staff RNs; LPNs; Nurses' aides; Physical
therapists; Activities coordinators; Dietitians.

Facilities Dining room; Physical therapy
room; Activities room; Laundry room;
Barber/Beauty shop; Library.
Activities Cards; Games; Reading groups;
Prayer groups; Movies; Shopping trips.

Talking Rock

Wildwood Intermediate Care Home
Rte 2, Talking Rock, GA 30175
(404) 692-6014
Admin Dee F Wilbanks.
Licensure Intermediate care. *Beds* ICF 44.
Certified Medicaid.

Thomaston

Clearview Nursing Care
Box 1162, 310 Ave F, Thomaston, GA 30286
(404) 647-6676
Admin Betty Weaver.
Licensure Skilled care; Intermediate care. *Beds*
119. *Certified* Medicaid; Medicare.

Providence Health Care
Box 49, 1011 Green St, Thomaston, GA
30286
(404) 647-6693
Admin Ann C Connell.
Licensure Skilled care. *Beds* SNF 110.
Certified Medicaid.

Riverside Nursing Center of Thomaston
101 Old Talbotton Rd, Thomaston, GA 30286
(404) 647-8161, 647-8207 FAX
Admin Sue G Estes RN BSEd. *Dir of Nursing*
Pam O'Rourke RN BSN. *Medical Dir*
Herbert D Tyler MD.
Licensure Skilled care; Intermediate care;
Medicare. *Beds* Swing beds SNF/ICF 45;
Medicare 28. *Certified* Medicaid; Medicare.
Owner Proprietary corp (Care More Inc).
Admissions Requirements Medical
examination; Physician's request.
Staff Physicians; RNs; LPNs; Nurses' aides;
Physical therapists; Reality therapists;
Recreational therapists (available);
Occupational therapists (available); Speech
therapists (available); Activities coordinators;
Dietitians; Ophthalmologists; Podiatrists.
Facilities Dining room; Physical therapy
room; Activities room; Chapel; Crafts room;
Laundry room; Barber/Beauty shop.
Activities Arts & crafts; Cards; Games;
Reading groups; Prayer groups; Movies;
Shopping trips; Intergenerational programs;
Pet therapy.

Thomasville

Camellia Garden of Life Care
PO Box 1959, Thomasville, GA 31792
(912) 226-0076
Admin Barbara Kiser.
Medical Dir Dr J Rawlings.
Licensure Intermediate care. *Beds* ICF 83.
Certified Medicaid.
Owner Proprietary corp (Life Care Centers of
America).
Admissions Requirements Medical
examination; Physician's request.
Staff RNs 1 (ft), 1 (pt); LPNs 7 (ft), 8 (pt);
Nurses' aides 16 (ft), 13 (pt); Activities
coordinators 1 (ft); Dietitians 1 (ft).
Facilities Dining room; Activities room;
Crafts room; Laundry room; Barber/Beauty
shop.
Activities Arts & crafts; Cards; Games;
Reading groups; Prayer groups; Movies;
Shopping trips; Dances/Social/Cultural
gatherings.

HCE Glenn-Mor Home
Rte 1 Box 464, Thomasville, GA 31792
(912) 226-8942

Admin Fred E West PhD. *Dir of Nursing*
Sandra Dunbar MSN RN. *Medical Dir* John
Brinson Jr MD.
Licensure Skilled care; Intermediate care. *Beds*
SNF Swing beds SNF/ICF 64. *Private Pay
Patients* 10%. *Certified* Medicaid; Medicare.
Owner Proprietary corp.
Admissions Requirements Medical
examination; Physician's request.
Staff Physicians 7 (pt); RNs 1 (ft), 2 (pt);
LPNs 5 (ft), 5 (pt); Nurses' aides 16 (ft), 7
(pt); Physical therapists 1 (pt); Speech
therapists 1 (pt); Activities coordinators 1
(ft); Dietitians 1 (pt); Ophthalmologists 1
(pt); Podiatrists 1 (pt); Audiologists 1 (pt).
Facilities Dining room; Physical therapy
room; Activities room; Crafts room; Laundry
room; Barber/Beauty shop; Rehabilitation
programs.
Activities Arts & crafts; Cards; Games;
Movies; Dances/Social/Cultural gatherings;
Pet therapy.

Hospitality Care Center of Thomasville
930 S Broad St, Thomasville, GA 31792
(912) 226-9322
Admin Patricia Goldsberry.
Licensure Skilled care; Intermediate care. *Beds*
68. *Certified* Medicaid; Medicare.
Owner Proprietary corp (Vantage Healthcare).

**Rose Haven ICF/MR & Skilled Nursing
Facility**
PO Box 1378, Pinetree Blvd S, Thomasville,
GA 31799
(912) 228-2272, 228-2365 FAX
Admin Andre H Marria. *Dir of Nursing* Linda
D Pack RN. *Medical Dir* Antonio Santos
MD.
Licensure Skilled care; Intermediate care for
mentally retarded; Respite care. *Beds* SNF
21; ICF/MR 91. *Private Pay Patients* 7%.
Certified Medicaid.
Owner Publicly owned.
Admissions Requirements Medical
examination; Physician's request.
Staff Physicians 1 (ft); RNs 7 (ft), 1 (pt);
LPNs 28 (ft); Nurses' aides 77 (ft); Physical
therapists 1 (pt); Recreational therapists 1
(ft); Occupational therapists 2 (pt); Speech
therapists 2 (ft); Activities coordinators 6
(ft); Dietitians 1 (ft).
Facilities Dining room; Physical therapy
room; Activities room; Chapel; Crafts room;
Laundry room; Barber/Beauty shop.
Activities Arts & crafts; Games; Reading
groups; Prayer groups; Movies; Shopping
trips; Dances/Social/Cultural gatherings.

Thomasville Health Care Center
PO Box 1714, 4 Skyline Dr, Thomasville, GA
31792
(912) 226-4101
Admin Mickey Pickler.
Medical Dir Dr Joe Rawlings.
Licensure Skilled care; Intermediate care. *Beds*
52. *Certified* Medicaid.
Admissions Requirements Medical
examination.
Facilities Dining room; Physical therapy
room; Activities room; Laundry room;
Barber/Beauty shop.
Activities Arts & crafts; Cards; Games; Prayer
groups; Movies; Shopping trips; Dances/
Social/Cultural gatherings.

Thomson

Thomson Manor Nursing Home Inc
PO Drawer 1080, Thomson, GA 30824
(404) 595-5574
Admin Marsha Todd.
Licensure Skilled care; Intermediate care. *Beds*
150. *Certified* Medicaid.
Owner Proprietary corp (Stuckey Health
Care).

Tifton

Tift Health Care Inc
PO Box 1668, 215 20th St, Tifton, GA 31794
(912) 382-7342
Admin Frances D Moody.
Licensure Skilled care; Intermediate care. *Beds*
SNF 86; ICF 92. *Certified* Medicaid.

Tifton Nursing Home
1451 Newton Dr, Tifton, GA 31794
(912) 382-1665
Admin R Vernon Bankston.
Medical Dir Morris Davis MD.
Licensure Skilled care; Intermediate care. *Beds*
100. *Certified* Medicaid.
Admissions Requirements Medical
examination; Physician's request.
Staff Physicians 6 (pt); RNs 1 (ft), 1 (pt);
LPNs 6 (ft), 6 (pt); Nurses' aides 16 (ft), 16
(pt); Physical therapists 1 (ft); Activities
coordinators 1 (ft); Dietitians 1 (ft);
Ophthalmologists 1 (pt); Podiatrists 1 (pt);
Audiologists 1 (pt); Dentists 1 (pt).
Facilities Dining room; Physical therapy
room; Activities room; Crafts room; Laundry
room; Barber/Beauty shop; Library.
Activities Arts & crafts; Cards; Games;
Reading groups; Prayer groups; Shopping
trips; Dances/Social/Cultural gatherings.

Toccoa

Toccoa Nursing Center
PO Box 1129, Toccoa, GA 30577
(404) 886-8491
Admin Joy King.
Medical Dir Arthur Singer MD.
Licensure Skilled care; Intermediate care. *Beds*
SNF 181. *Certified* Medicaid.
Admissions Requirements Medical
examination.
Staff RNs 2 (ft), 3 (pt); LPNs 8 (ft), 8 (pt);
Nurses' aides 63 (ft), 19 (pt); Activities
coordinators 1 (ft), 1 (pt).
Facilities Dining room; Physical therapy
room; Laundry room; Barber/Beauty shop.
Activities Arts & crafts; Cards; Games;
Reading groups; Prayer groups; Movies;
Shopping trips; Dances/Social/Cultural
gatherings.

Trenton

Sandmont Gala Nursing Home
Rte 2 Box 45, Trenton, GA 30752
(404) 657-4171
Admin Kathy Fitzpatrick. *Dir of Nursing* Jill
Shrader RN. *Medical Dir* Dr Alan Mangan.
Licensure Skilled care; Intermediate care. *Beds*
65. *Certified* Medicaid.
Owner Privately owned.
Admissions Requirements Medical
examination; Physician's request.
Staff Physicians 1 (ft); RNs 3 (ft), 2 (pt);
LPNs 4 (ft), 1 (pt); Nurses' aides 30 (ft), 2
(pt); Physical therapists 1 (ft); Activities
coordinators 1 (ft); Dietitians 1 (pt).
Facilities Dining room; Physical therapy
room; Activities room; Crafts room; Laundry
room; Barber/Beauty shop.
Activities Arts & crafts; Games; Reading
groups; Prayer groups; Movies; Dances/
Social/Cultural gatherings.

Tucker

Briarwood Nursing Center Inc
3888 LaVista Rd, Tucker, GA 30084
(404) 938-5740
Admin Judith R Peters.
Licensure Skilled care. *Beds* 100.
Owner Proprietary corp (Beverly Enterprises).

Meadowbrook Nursing Home
4608 Lawrenceville Hwy, Tucker, GA 30084
(404) 491-9444
Admin Robert L Greene.
Medical Dir Debra Lanter.
Licensure Skilled care; Intermediate care. *Beds*
42. *Certified* Medicaid.
Owner Privately owned.
Admissions Requirements Females only;
Medical examination.
Staff Physicians 1 (ft); RNs 1 (ft), 3 (pt);
LPNs 3 (ft), 1 (pt); Nurses' aides 14 (ft), 3
(pt); Physical therapists 1 (pt); Activities
coordinators 1 (ft); Dietitians 4 (ft), 1 (pt).
Facilities Dining room; Physical therapy
room; Activities room; Laundry room;
Barber/Beauty shop.
Activities Arts & crafts; Games; Reading
groups; Prayer groups; Movies; Shopping
trips; Dances/Social/Cultural gatherings;
Cooking classes; Picnics; Outings.

Tucker Nursing Center
2165 Idlewood Rd, Tucker, GA 30084
(404) 934-3172
Admin Michelle DesCarpenter.
Medical Dir Michael Lipsitt MD.
Licensure Intermediate care; Rest home. *Beds*
ICF 116; Rest home 32.
Staff Physicians 3 (pt); RNs 6 (ft), 3 (pt);
LPNs 4 (ft), 5 (pt); Nurses' aides 28 (ft), 11
(pt); Physical therapists 1 (pt); Activities
coordinators 2 (ft).
Facilities Dining room; Activities room;
Crafts room; Laundry room; Barber/Beauty
shop; Library.
Activities Arts & crafts; Cards; Games;
Movies; Dances/Social/Cultural gatherings;
Atlanta Braves games; Bus trips.

Twin City

Twin View Nursing Home
Box 128, Twin City, GA 30471
(912) 763-2141
Admin Theo H Fountain.
Licensure Skilled care; Intermediate care. *Beds*
SNF 110. *Certified* Medicaid.

Tybee Island

Oceanside Nursing Home
77 Van Horn, Tybee Island, GA 31328
(912) 786-4511
Admin Teresa Jackson.
Medical Dir Carmen Gannon MD.
Licensure Skilled care; Intermediate care. *Beds*
85. *Certified* Medicaid; Medicare.
Admissions Requirements Medical
examination; Physician's request.
Staff Physicians 3 (pt); RNs 4 (ft), 1 (pt);
LPNs 8 (ft), 2 (pt); Nurses' aides 22 (ft);
Recreational therapists 1 (ft); Activities
coordinators 1 (ft); Dietitians 1 (pt);
Podiatrists 1 (pt).
Facilities Dining room; Physical therapy
room; Activities room; Crafts room; Laundry
room; Barber/Beauty shop.
Activities Arts & crafts; Cards; Games;
Reading groups; Prayer groups; Movies;
Shopping trips; Dances/Social/Cultural
gatherings.

Savannah Beach Nursing Home Inc
90 Van Horn St, Tybee Island, GA 31328
(912) 786-5711
Admin Teresa Jackson.
Medical Dir A P Phillips.
Licensure Skilled care; Intermediate care. *Beds*
50. *Certified* Medicaid.
Admissions Requirements Minimum age 18;
Medical examination; Physician's request.
Staff Physicians 3 (pt); RNs 2 (ft); LPNs 3
(ft), 1 (pt); Nurses' aides 17 (ft), 1 (pt);
Physical therapists 1 (pt); Activities
coordinators 1 (ft); Dietitians 1 (ft);
Podiatrists; Dentists; Music therapists 1 (pt).

Facilities Dining room; Physical therapy
room; Activities room; Chapel; Crafts room;
Laundry room; Barber/Beauty shop; Library.
Activities Arts & crafts; Cards; Games;
Reading groups; Prayer groups; Movies;
Shopping trips; Dances/Social/Cultural
gatherings; Ceramics.

Union Point

Greene Point Health Care
PO Box 312, Union Point, GA 30669
(404) 486-2167
Admin Dorothy Key.
Licensure Skilled care; Intermediate care. *Beds*
71. *Certified* Medicaid; Medicare.
Owner Proprietary corp (Beverly Enterprises).

Valdosta

Crestwood Nursing Home
PO Box 31602, Valdosta, GA 31602
(912) 242-6868
Admin Charles O Templeton Jr. *Dir of
Nursing* Nancy Harnage RN. *Medical Dir*
Dr Joe C Stubbs.
Licensure Skilled care. *Beds* SNF 79. *Certified*
Medicaid.
Owner Proprietary corp.
Staff RNs 2 (ft), 1 (pt); LPNs 8 (ft), 1 (pt);
Nurses' aides 30 (ft), 8 (pt); Physical
therapists 1 (pt); Speech therapists 1 (pt);
Activities coordinators 1 (ft); Dietitians 1
(pt); Ophthalmologists 1 (pt); Dentists 1 (pt).

Heritage House Nursing Home
2501 N Ashley St, Valdosta, GA 31602
(912) 244-7368
Admin Olleta T Baggett. *Dir of Nursing* Mary
Ann Clark RN. *Medical Dir* Joe C Stubbs
MD.
Licensure Skilled care; Intermediate care. *Beds*
Swing beds SNF/ICF 98. *Private Pay
Patients* 25%. *Certified* Medicaid; Medicare.
Owner Proprietary corp (Pruitt Corp).
Admissions Requirements Minimum age 21;
Medical examination; Physician's request;
Free from communicable disease.
Staff RNs 1 (ft), 1 (pt); LPNs 9 (ft), 2 (pt);
Nurses' aides 35 (ft), 4 (pt); Physical
therapists (contracted); Occupational
therapists 1 (pt); Speech therapists
(contracted); Activities coordinators 1 (ft);
Dietitians 1 (pt); Podiatrists (contracted);
Food service supervisors 1 (ft).
Facilities Dining room; Physical therapy
room; Activities room; Chapel; Crafts room;
Laundry room; Barber/Beauty shop; Library.
Activities Arts & crafts; Cards; Games;
Reading groups; Prayer groups; Movies;
Shopping trips; Dances/Social/Cultural
gatherings; Pet therapy.

Holly Hill Intermediate Care Facility
PO Box 2999, Valdosta, GA 31601
(912) 244-6968
Admin Charles O Templeton Jr. *Dir of
Nursing* Betty Council LPN. *Medical Dir* Dr
Joe C Stubbs.
Licensure Intermediate care. *Beds* ICF 100.
Certified Medicaid.
Owner Proprietary corp.
Staff RNs 1 (pt); LPNs 9 (ft), 1 (pt); Nurses'
aides 35 (ft), 4 (pt); Physical therapists 1
(pt); Speech therapists 1 (pt); Activities
coordinators 1 (ft); Dietitians 1 (pt);
Ophthalmologists 1 (pt).

Lakehaven Nursing Home
410 E Northside Dr, Valdosta, GA 31602
(912) 242-7368
Admin John H Eades. *Dir of Nursing* Mattie
Roundtree RN BSN. *Medical Dir* Joe C
Stubbs Jr MD.
Licensure Skilled care; Intermediate care. *Beds*
Swing beds SNF/ICF 90. *Private Pay
Patients* 2%. *Certified* Medicaid; Medicare.

Owner Proprietary corp (Pruitt Corp).
Admissions Requirements Minimum age
  Adults.
Staff RNs 2 (ft); LPNs 9 (ft), 1 (pt); Nurses'
  aides 28 (ft), 5 (pt); Physical therapists 1
  (pt); Occupational therapists 1 (pt); Speech
  therapists 1 (pt); Activities coordinators 1
  (ft); Dietitians 1 (pt).
Facilities Dining room; Physical therapy
  room; Activities room; Chapel; Crafts room;
  Laundry room; Barber/Beauty shop.
Activities Arts & crafts; Cards; Games;
  Reading groups; Prayer groups; Movies;
  Shopping trips; Dances/Social/Cultural
  gatherings.

**Parkwood Development Center Intermediate
Care Facility**
1501 N Lee St, Valdosta, GA 31601
(912) 242-6268
Admin Ruth T Adkins.
Medical Dir Joseph C Stubbs MD.
Licensure Intermediate care for mentally
  retarded. *Beds* ICF/MR 110.
Owner Proprietary corp.
Admissions Requirements Minimum age 6;
  Medical examination.
Staff Physicians 6 (ft); RNs 5 (ft); Nurses'
  aides 110 (ft); Physical therapists 1 (ft);
  Recreational therapists 1 (ft); Occupational
  therapists 1 (pt); Speech therapists 1 (ft);
  Activities coordinators 1 (ft); Dietitians 1
  (ft); Ophthalmologists 2 (pt); Podiatrists 1
  (pt); Audiologists 1 (pt); Dentists 3 (pt);
  Pharmacists 1 (ft); Psychologists 1 (ft);
  Psychiatrist 1 (ft); Social workers 1 (ft);
  Social work technicians 2 (ft); Teachers 4
  (ft); QMRPs 2 (ft); Programing specialists 4
  (ft).
Facilities Dining room; Physical therapy
  room; Chapel; Crafts room; Laundry room;
  Barber/Beauty shop; Library; Classrooms;
  Speech therapy; Activities center.
Activities Arts & crafts; Cards; Games;
  Reading groups; Prayer groups; Movies;
  Shopping trips; Dances/Social/Cultural
  gatherings.

Vidalia

Bethany Home for Ladies
PO Box 668, Vidalia, GA 30474
(912) 537-7922
Admin JoAnn Vaughn.
Licensure Skilled care; Intermediate care. *Beds*
  168. *Certified* Medicaid; Medicare.
Admissions Requirements Females only.

Meadows Nursing Center
PO Box 1048, 1703 Meadows Ln, Vidalia, GA
  30474
(912) 537-5814, 537-0912 FAX
Admin Wes Bergman. *Dir of Nursing* Dorcas
  Joyce. *Medical Dir* J E Barfield.
Licensure Skilled care. *Beds* SNF 35. *Private
  Pay Patients* 1%. *Certified* Medicaid;
  Medicare.
Owner Publicly owned.
Admissions Requirements Medical
  examination; Physician's request.
Staff Physicians 6 (pt); RNs 2 (ft); LPNs 8
  (ft); Nurses' aides 16 (ft); Physical therapists
  1 (pt); Reality therapists 1 (ft); Recreational
  therapists 1 (ft); Occupational therapists 1
  (pt); Speech therapists 1 (pt); Activities
  coordinators 1 (ft); Dietitians 1 (pt);
  Ophthalmologists 1 (pt); Podiatrists 1 (pt).
Facilities Dining room; Physical therapy
  room; Activities room; Crafts room; Laundry
  room; Barber/Beauty shop; Library; Sitting
  room.
Activities Arts & crafts; Cards; Games;
  Reading groups; Prayer groups; Movies;
  Shopping trips; Dances/Social/Cultural
  gatherings; Intergenerational programs;
  Weekly family time.

Wadley

Glendale Nursing Home Inc
PO Box 326, Wadley, GA 30477
(912) 252-5254
Admin George T Harrison.
Licensure Skilled care; Intermediate care. *Beds*
  98. *Certified* Medicaid.

Warm Springs

**Meriwether Memorial Hospital & Nursing
Home**
PO Box 8, Warm Springs, GA 31830
(404) 655-3331
Admin Ed Johnson. *Dir of Nursing* Betty
  Mailey RN.
Licensure Skilled care; Intermediate care. *Beds*
  58. *Certified* Medicaid.
Owner Nonprofit organization/foundation.
Staff RNs 1 (ft), 1 (pt); LPNs 6 (ft), 2 (pt);
  Nurses' aides 23 (ft), 3 (pt); Physical
  therapists 1 (pt); Activities coordinators 1
  (ft); Dietitians 1 (ft).
Facilities Dining room; Physical therapy
  room; Activities room; Crafts room; Laundry
  room; Barber/Beauty shop; Library.
Activities Arts & crafts; Games; Movies;
  Shopping trips; Dances/Social/Cultural
  gatherings; Family group activities; Fishing.

Warner Robins

Elberta Health Care
419 Elberta Rd, Warner Robins, GA 31093
(912) 923-3146
Admin Lynn L Davis. *Dir of Nursing* Sherry
  Oliver. *Medical Dir* Dr Perry Melvin.
Licensure Skilled care. *Beds* SNF 66. *Certified*
  Medicaid.
Owner Proprietary corp (R Wayne Lowe
  Corp).
Admissions Requirements Medical
  examination; Physician's request.
Staff Physicians 1 (ft); RNs 1 (ft), 2 (pt);
  LPNs 6 (ft), 2 (pt); Nurses' aides 25 (ft), 2
  (pt); Physical therapists 1 (pt); Occupational
  therapists 1 (pt); Speech therapists 1 (pt);
  Activities coordinators 2 (ft); Dietitians 1
  (ft), 1 (pt); Podiatrists 1 (pt).
Facilities Dining room; Physical therapy
  room; Activities room; Laundry room;
  Barber/Beauty shop.
Activities Arts & crafts; Games; Reading
  groups; Prayer groups; Movies; Shopping
  trips; Dances/Social/Cultural gatherings; Pet
  therapy.

Hallmark Nursing Home
1601 Elberta Rd, Warner Robins, GA 31093
(912) 922-2241
Admin Leah Swinford. *Dir of Nursing* June
  Walker RN. *Medical Dir* Dr C Crawford.
Licensure Skilled care; Intermediate care. *Beds*
  126. *Certified* Medicaid.
Owner Proprietary corp (Southeastern Health
  Care Inc).
Admissions Requirements Minimum age
  Adult; Medical examination; Physician's
  request.
Staff Physicians 1 (ft); RNs 2 (ft), 1 (pt);
  LPNs 7 (ft), 7 (pt); Nurses' aides 41 (ft), 3
  (pt); Physical therapists 1 (pt); Activities
  coordinators 1 (ft); Dietitians 1 (ft).
Facilities Dining room; Physical therapy
  room; Laundry room; Barber/Beauty shop.
Activities Games; Reading groups; Prayer
  groups; Dances/Social/Cultural gatherings.

Peachbelt Nursing Home
801 Elberta Rd, Warner Robins, GA 31056
(912) 923-3156
Admin Irene Reynolds. *Dir of Nursing* Susan
  Ables. *Medical Dir* Perry Melvin.
Licensure Skilled care; Intermediate care;
  Retirement; Alzheimer's care. *Beds* SNF
  106. *Certified* Medicaid.

Owner Privately owned.
Admissions Requirements Medical
  examination.
Staff Physicians; RNs; LPNs; Nurses' aides;
  Physical therapists; Recreational therapists;
  Activities coordinators; Dietitians.
Facilities Dining room; Physical therapy
  room; Activities room; Crafts room; Laundry
  room; Barber/Beauty shop.
Activities Arts & crafts; Cards; Games;
  Reading groups; Prayer groups; Movies;
  Shopping trips; Dances/Social/Cultural
  gatherings.

Warrenton

Providence Health Care
PO Box 69, Warrenton, GA 30828
(404) 465-3328
Admin Cereta E Lawrence.
Medical Dir Dr John Lemley.
Licensure Skilled care; Intermediate care. *Beds*
  110. *Certified* Medicaid; Medicare.
Owner Proprietary corp (Beverly Enterprises).
Admissions Requirements Medical
  examination; Physician's request.
Staff RNs 2 (ft), 1 (pt); LPNs 8 (ft), 3 (pt);
  Nurses' aides 30 (ft), 6 (pt); Physical
  therapists 1 (pt); Recreational therapists 1
  (pt); Activities coordinators 1 (ft); Dietitians
  1 (pt); Podiatrists 1 (pt); Dentists 1 (pt).
Facilities Dining room; Physical therapy
  room; Activities room; Chapel; Crafts room;
  Laundry room; Barber/Beauty shop.
Activities Arts & crafts; Cards; Games;
  Reading groups; Prayer groups; Movies;
  Shopping trips; Dances/Social/Cultural
  gatherings.

Washington

Wilkes Health Care
PO Box 578, 112 Hospital Dr, Washington,
  GA 30673
(404) 678-7804, 678-3675 FAX
Admin Joyce B Barden. *Dir of Nursing* Joan
  Wigton. *Medical Dir* C E Pollock.
Licensure Skilled care; Alzheimer's care. *Beds*
  SNF 47. *Private Pay Patients* 20%. *Certified*
  Medicare; Medicaid.
Owner Proprietary corp (National Heritage
  Management).
Admissions Requirements Medical
  examination; Physician's request.
Staff RNs 1 (ft); LPNs 3 (ft); Nurses' aides 12
  (ft); Activities coordinators 1 (ft); Dietitians
  1 (ft).
Facilities Dining room; Physical therapy
  room; Laundry room; Barber/Beauty shop;
  Alarm system on exit doors for wanderers.
Activities Arts & crafts; Games; Reading
  groups; Prayer groups; Movies; Shopping
  trips; Dances/Social/Cultural gatherings; Pet
  therapy.

Waverly Hall

Oakview Home Intermediate Care
PO Box 468, 2 Oak View St, Waverly Hall,
  GA 31831
(404) 582-2117
Admin Theodore C Bowen. *Dir of Nursing*
  Kathy Layfield. *Medical Dir* Dr Thomas
  Blake.
Licensure Intermediate care. *Beds* ICF 100.
  Certified Medicaid.
Owner Proprietary corp.
Admissions Requirements Medical
  examination.
Staff Physicians 1 (pt); RNs 1 (ft); LPNs 6
  (ft); Nurses' aides 11 (ft), 1 (pt); Physical
  therapists 1 (pt); Speech therapists 1 (pt);
  Activities coordinators 2 (ft); Dietitians 1
  (pt); Ophthalmologists 1 (pt); Social workers
  1 (ft).

Facilities Dining room; Physical therapy room; Activities room; Chapel; Crafts room; Laundry room; Barber/Beauty shop.
Activities Arts & crafts; Cards; Games; Reading groups; Prayer groups; Movies; Shopping trips; Dances/Social/Cultural gatherings.

Waycross

Baptist Village Inc
PO Drawer 179, Waycross, GA 31502
(912) 283-7050, ext 21
Admin J Olan Jones. *Dir of Nursing* Suzanne McNeely SNF; Kaye Thigpen ICF. *Medical Dir* W B Bates Jr MD.
Licensure Skilled care; Intermediate care; Retirement. *Beds* SNF 148; ICF 106; Retirement 84. *Private Pay Patients* 54%. *Certified* Medicaid.
Owner Nonprofit organization/foundation.
Admissions Requirements Minimum age 65; Medical examination; Physician's request.
Staff RNs 7 (ft), 4 (pt); LPNs 28 (ft), 4 (pt); Nurses' aides 94 (ft), 13 (pt); Physical therapists (contracted); Dietitians (contracted).
Affiliation Baptist.
Facilities Dining room; Physical therapy room; Activities room; Chapel; Crafts room; Laundry room; Barber/Beauty shop; Library.
Activities Arts & crafts; Games; Reading groups; Prayer groups; Movies; Shopping trips; Dances/Social/Cultural gatherings.

Riverside Nursing Home
1600 Riverside Ave, Waycross, GA 31501
(912) 283-1185, 283-1182
Admin Alpha W Davis. *Dir of Nursing* Rebecca A Hester. *Medical Dir* Dr D Richard Lynch.
Licensure Skilled care; Intermediate care. *Beds* SNF 96. *Certified* Medicaid; Medicare.
Owner Nonprofit corp.
Admissions Requirements Medical examination; Physician's request.
Staff RNs 3 (ft), 1 (pt); LPNs 14 (ft), 2 (pt); Nurses' aides 23 (ft), 4 (pt); Physical therapists 2 (pt); Recreational therapists 2 (pt); Occupational therapists 1 (pt); Speech therapists 1 (pt); Activities coordinators 1 (ft); Dietitians 1 (ft); Ophthalmologists 1 (pt); Podiatrists 1 (pt).
Facilities Dining room; Physical therapy room; Activities room; Crafts room; Laundry room; Barber/Beauty shop; Dayrooms.
Activities Cards; Games; Prayer groups; Movies; Dances/Social/Cultural gatherings.

Ware Manor Nursing Home
2210 Dorothy St, Waycross, GA 31501
(912) 285-4721
Admin Barbara Aldridge. *Dir of Nursing* Cynthia Greene RN BSN. *Medical Dir* Wiley B Lewis MD.

Licensure Skilled care; Intermediate care; Retirement. *Beds* SNF 92; ICF. *Certified* Medicaid.
Owner Proprietary corp.
Admissions Requirements Medical examination; Physician's request.
Staff Physicians 1 (ft); RNs 3 (ft), 2 (pt); LPNs 8 (ft), 2 (pt); Nurses' aides 30 (ft), 15 (pt); Physical therapists 1 (ft); Recreational therapists 1 (ft); Speech therapists 1 (ft); Activities coordinators 1 (ft); Dietitians 1 (ft).
Facilities Dining room; Physical therapy room; Activities room; Chapel; Crafts room; Laundry room; Barber/Beauty shop; Library.
Activities Arts & crafts; Cards; Games; Reading groups; Prayer groups; Movies; Shopping trips; Dances/Social/Cultural gatherings.

Waynesboro

Brentwood Terrace Health Center
PO Box 820, Waynesboro, GA 30830
(404) 554-4425
Admin Shelia N Weddon.
Medical Dir Dr Joseph L Jackson.
Licensure Skilled care; Intermediate care. *Beds* SNF 103; ICF. *Certified* Medicaid.
Owner Proprietary corp (Beverly Enterprises).
Admissions Requirements Minimum age 18; Medical examination; Physician's request.
Staff Physicians 8 (pt); RNs 5 (ft), 3 (pt); LPNs 8 (ft), 6 (pt); Nurses' aides 24 (ft), 4 (pt); Physical therapists 1 (pt); Recreational therapists 1 (pt); Speech therapists 1 (pt); Activities coordinators 1 (ft); Dietitians 1 (pt).
Languages Spanish (Interpreter available).
Facilities Dining room; Physical therapy room; Activities room; Chapel; Crafts room; Laundry room; Barber/Beauty shop; Library.
Activities Arts & crafts; Cards; Games; Reading groups; Prayer groups; Movies; Shopping trips; Dances/Social/Cultural gatherings.

Whigham

Heritage Inn of Whigham
PO Box 46, Whigham, GA 31787
(912) 762-4121
Admin Rebecca Pitts.
Medical Dir William J Morton MD.
Licensure Skilled care; Intermediate care. *Beds* 108. *Certified* Medicaid; Medicare.
Staff RNs 1 (ft), 2 (pt); LPNs 10 (ft), 3 (pt); Nurses' aides 25 (ft), 7 (pt); Physical therapists 1 (pt); Activities coordinators 1 (ft); Dietitians 1 (pt).
Facilities Dining room; Physical therapy room; Activities room; Crafts room; Laundry room; Barber/Beauty shop.

Activities Arts & crafts; Cards; Games; Reading groups; Prayer groups; Movies; Shopping trips; Dances/Social/Cultural gatherings.

Winder

Winder Nursing Inc
PO Box 588, Winder, GA 30680
(404) 867-2108
Admin Sue Lane. *Dir of Nursing* Jane McDaniel. *Medical Dir* John House MD.
Licensure Skilled care; Intermediate care. *Beds* Swing beds SNF/ICF 156. *Private Pay Patients* 6%. *Certified* Medicaid.
Owner Proprietary corp.
Admissions Requirements Medical examination; Physician's request.
Staff RNs 6 (ft); Physical therapists; Dietitians.
Facilities Dining room; Physical therapy room; Activities room; Chapel; Crafts room; Laundry room; Barber/Beauty shop.
Activities Arts & crafts; Games; Reading groups; Movies.

Woodstock

Boddy Nursing Center
105 Arnold Mill Rd, Woodstock, GA 30188
(404) 926-0016
Admin Doris A Jones.
Licensure Skilled care; Intermediate care. *Beds* 117. *Certified* Medicaid; Medicare.

Wrightsville

Wrightsville Manor Nursing Home
PO Box 209, 608 W Court St, Wrightsville, GA 31096
(912) 864-2286
Admin Freddie M Webb. *Dir of Nursing* Cheryl Scofield RN. *Medical Dir* William A Dodd MD.
Licensure Skilled care; Intermediate care. *Beds* Swing beds SNF/ICF 94. *Certified* Medicaid; Medicare.
Owner Privately owned (Pineleaf Investments).
Admissions Requirements Medical examination; Physician's request.
Staff Physicians 12 (pt); RNs 1 (ft), 2 (pt); LPNs 6 (ft), 3 (pt); Nurses' aides 27 (ft), 4 (pt); Physical therapists 1 (pt); Activities coordinators 1 (ft); Dietitians 1 (ft); Podiatrists 1 (pt).
Facilities Dining room; Physical therapy room; Activities room; Barber/Beauty shop.
Activities Arts & crafts; Cards; Games; Reading groups; Prayer groups; Movies; Shopping trips.

HAWAII

Haleiwa

Crawford's Convalescent Home
58-130 Kamehameha Hwy, Haleiwa, HI 96712
(808) 638-8514
Admin Alice Lew.
Licensure Intermediate care. *Beds* ICF 68.
Certified Medicaid.
Admissions Requirements Medical
examination.
Staff RNs 3 (ft), 2 (pt); LPNs 1 (ft); Nurses'
aides 28 (ft); Physical therapists 1 (pt);
Recreational therapists 1 (ft); Occupational
therapists 1 (pt); Activities coordinators 1
(ft); Dietitians 1 (pt).
Facilities Dining room; Physical therapy
room; Activities room; Crafts room; Laundry
room.
Activities Arts & crafts; Cards; Games; Prayer
groups; Movies; Shopping trips; Dances/
Social/Cultural gatherings.

Hilo

Hilo Hospital
1190 Waianuenue Ave, Hilo, HI 96720
(808) 969-4111
Admin Fred D Horwitz. *Dir of Nursing*
Phoebe Lambeth. *Medical Dir* Ronald Ah
Loy MD.
Licensure Skilled care; Intermediate care. *Beds*
SNF 32; ICF 76. *Certified* Medicaid;
Medicare.
Owner Publicly owned.
Admissions Requirements Medical
examination.
Staff Physicians 1 (pt); RNs 11 (ft); LPNs 26
(ft); Nurses' aides 33 (ft); Physical therapists
1 (pt); Occupational therapists 1 (pt); Speech
therapists 1 (pt); Dietitians 1 (pt).
Languages Japanese, Chinese, Filipino,
Portuguese, Ilokano, Visayan.
Facilities Dining room; Physical therapy
room; Activities room; Chapel; Crafts room;
Laundry room; Barber/Beauty shop; Library.
Activities Arts & crafts; Cards; Games;
Reading groups; Prayer groups; Shopping
trips; Dances/Social/Cultural gatherings.

Life Care Center of Hilo
944 W Kawailani St, Hilo, HI 96720
(808) 959-9151
Admin Marcus M Kaya.
Medical Dir Ernest Bape; Liz Holt.
Licensure Intermediate care; Alzheimer's care.
Beds ICF 220. *Certified* Medicaid.
Owner Proprietary corp (Life Care Centers of
America).
Admissions Requirements Medical
examination; Physician's request.
Staff RNs 3 (ft), 3 (pt); LPNs 8 (ft), 8 (pt);
Nurses' aides 45 (ft), 20 (pt); Activities
coordinators 1 (ft); Dietitians 1 (ft).
Languages Tagalog, Japanese.
Facilities Dining room; Activities room;
Crafts room; Laundry room; Barber/Beauty
shop; Library.

Activities Arts & crafts; Cards; Games;
Reading groups; Prayer groups; Movies;
Shopping trips; Dances/Social/Cultural
gatherings.

Honoka'a

Honoka'a Hospital
PO Box 237, Honoka'a, HI 96727
(808) 775-7211
Admin Yoshito Iwamoto.
Licensure Skilled care. *Beds* SNF 8. *Certified*
Medicaid; Medicare.

Honolulu

Arcadia
1434 Punahou St, Honolulu, HI 96822
(808) 941-0941
Admin Lelan Yagi (Temp). *Dir of Nursing*
Patricia Vierw.
Licensure Skilled care. *Beds* SNF 58. *Certified*
Medicare.
Owner Nonprofit corp.
Admissions Requirements Minimum age 60;
Medical examination; Physician's request.
Staff RNs; LPNs; Nurses' aides; Geriatric
nurse practitioner 1 (ft).
Affiliation Church of Christ.
Facilities Dining room; Physical therapy
room; Activities room; Chapel; Crafts room;
Laundry room; Barber/Beauty shop.
Activities Arts & crafts; Cards; Games;
Reading groups; Prayer groups; Movies;
Shopping trips; Dances/Social/Cultural
gatherings.

Beverly Manor Convalescent Center
1930 Kamehameha IV Rd, Honolulu, HI
96819
(808) 847-4834
Admin Virginia Heftle.
Licensure Skilled care; Intermediate care. *Beds*
108. *Certified* Medicaid; Medicare.
Owner Proprietary corp (Beverly Enterprises).

Convalescent Center of Honolulu
1900 Bachelot St, Honolulu, HI 96817
(808) 531-5302
Admin Abe Sakai. *Dir of Nursing* Sai
Chantary RN. *Medical Dir* Dr Walter W Y
Chang.
Licensure Skilled care; Intermediate care. *Beds*
182. *Certified* Medicaid; Medicare.
Admissions Requirements Medical
examination; Physician's request.
Staff Physicians 1 (pt); RNs 16 (pt); LPNs 13
(pt); Nurses' aides 80 (pt); Physical
therapists 1 (pt); Reality therapists 1 (pt);
Recreational therapists 2 (pt); Occupational
therapists 1 (ft); Activities coordinators 1
(ft); Dietitians 1 (ft).
Facilities Dining room; Physical therapy
room; Activities room; Laundry room;
Library.
Activities Arts & crafts; Cards; Games; Prayer
groups; Movies; Shopping trips; Dances/
Social/Cultural gatherings.

Hale Ho Aloha
2630 Pacific Heights Rd, Honolulu, HI 96813
(808) 524-1955
Admin Lorraine Manayan.
Licensure Intermediate care. *Beds* ICF 85.
Owner Proprietary corp.
Admissions Requirements Medical
examination.
Staff Physicians 3 (pt); RNs 3 (ft), 5 (pt);
LPNs 3 (ft), 3 (pt); Nurses' aides 42 (ft), 6
(pt); Physical therapists 1 (pt); Recreational
therapists 1 (ft); Occupational therapists 1
(pt); Activities coordinators 1 (ft); Dietitians
1 (pt).
Facilities Dining room; Physical therapy
room; Activities room; Crafts room; Laundry
room; Barber/Beauty shop.
Activities Arts & crafts; Cards; Games;
Reading groups; Prayer groups; Movies;
Dances/Social/Cultural gatherings.

Hale Malamalama
6163 Summer St, Honolulu, HI 96821
(808) 396-0537
Admin Santiago Q Billena. *Dir of Nursing*
Dorothy Yue RN. *Medical Dir* Dr George
Seberg.
Licensure Intermediate care. *Beds* ICF 31.
Private Pay Patients 16%. *Certified*
Medicaid.
Owner Proprietary corp.
Staff Physicians 1 (pt); RNs 2 (ft), 6 (pt);
Nurses' aides 11 (ft), 3 (pt); Physical
therapists; Occupational therapists 1 (pt);
Activities coordinators 1 (pt); Dietitians 1
(pt).
Languages Japanese, Filipino, Chinese,
Korean, Samoan, Tongan.
Activities Arts & crafts; Cards; Games;
Dances/Social/Cultural gatherings; Pet
therapy.

Hale Nani Health Center
1677 Pensacola St, Honolulu, HI 96822
(808) 537-3371
Admin Jarold C Minson.
Medical Dir Dr Gladys Fryer.
Licensure Skilled care; SNF/ICF swing beds.
Beds SNF 40; SNF/ICF swing beds 192.
Certified Medicaid; Medicare.
Admissions Requirements Medical
examination; Physician's request.
Staff Physicians 1 (pt); RNs 10 (ft), 5 (pt);
LPNs 10 (ft), 6 (pt); Physical therapists 1
(ft); Recreational therapists 2 (ft), 4 (pt);
Occupational therapists 1 (ft); Speech
therapists 1 (pt); Activities coordinators 1
(ft); Dietitians 2 (pt).
Facilities Dining room; Physical therapy
room; Activities room; Chapel; Crafts room;
Laundry room; Barber/Beauty shop; Library.
Activities Arts & crafts; Cards; Games;
Reading groups; Prayer groups; Movies.

Hawaii Select Care Inc
1814 Liliha St, Honolulu, HI 96817
(808) 523-5402

Admin Sandra P Tanahara. *Dir of Nursing* Conchita Leavy. *Medical Dir* Dr Gerald Soon.
Licensure Intermediate care. *Beds* ICF 92. *Private Pay Patients* 3%. *Certified* Medicaid.
Owner Proprietary corp.
Admissions Requirements Medical examination.
Staff RNs 2 (ft), 3 (pt); LPNs 6 (ft), 3 (pt); Nurses' aides 22 (ft), 15 (pt); Activities coordinators 1 (ft); Dietitians 1 (ft).
Languages Japanese, Filipino, Chinese.
Facilities Dining room; Activities room; Laundry room.
Activities Arts & crafts; Cards; Games; Movies; Shopping trips; Dances/Social/ Cultural gatherings; Pet therapy; Dining out; Religious groups; Holiday activities.

Island Nursing Home
1205 Alexander St, Honolulu, HI 96822
(808) 946-5027
Admin Leland Yagi. *Dir of Nursing* Jean Sudduth RN.
Licensure SNF/ICF Swing beds. *Beds* SNF/ICF Swing beds 42. *Certified* Medicaid; Medicare.
Owner Privately owned.
Admissions Requirements Physician's request.
Staff RNs 5 (ft), 3 (pt); LPNs 1 (ft); Nurses' aides 21 (ft), 6 (pt); Occupational therapists 1 (pt); Activities coordinators 1 (ft), 1 (pt).
Languages Japanese.
Facilities Dining room; Activities room.
Activities Arts & crafts; Cards; Games; Reading groups; Prayer groups; Movies; Shopping trips; Dances/Social/Cultural gatherings; Beach; Zoo; Restaurants.

Kuakini Geriatric Care Inc
347 N Kuakini St, Honolulu, HI 96817
(808) 547-9231, 547-9547 FAX
Admin Masaichi Tasaka. *Dir of Nursing* Cecelia McLane. *Medical Dir* Dr Melvyn Kaneshiro.
Licensure Skilled care; Intermediate care; Home care. *Beds* SNF 50; ICF 133; Home care 50. *Certified* Medicaid; Medicare.
Owner Nonprofit organization/foundation.
Admissions Requirements Medical examination; Physician's request.
Staff RNs 8 (ft), 5 (pt); LPNs 23 (ft), 8 (pt); Nurses' aides 71 (ft), 19 (pt); Physical therapists; Recreational therapists; Occupational therapists; Speech therapists; Activities coordinators; Dietitians.
Languages Japanese, Samoan, Korean, Filipino, and access to language bank.
Facilities Dining room; Activities room; Chapel; Crafts room; Laundry room; Barber/ Beauty shop; Library.
Activities Arts & crafts; Cards; Games; Reading groups; Prayer groups; Movies; Shopping trips; Dances/Social/Cultural gatherings; Pet therapy.

Leahi Hospital
3675 Kilauea Ave, Honolulu, HI 96816
(808) 734-0221
Admin Abraham L Choy. *Dir of Nursing* Ellen F Sherman. *Medical Dir* Verne C Waite MD.
Licensure Skilled care; Intermediate care. *Beds* SNF 98; ICF 81. *Certified* Medicaid; Medicare.
Owner Publicly owned.
Admissions Requirements Medical examination; Physician's request.
Staff Physicians 1 (ft); RNs 26 (ft); LPNs 32 (ft); Nurses' aides 56 (ft); Physical therapists 1 (ft); Recreational therapists 2 (ft); Occupational therapists 3 (ft); Dietitians 3 (ft).
Languages Japanese, Chinese, Tagalog.
Facilities Dining room; Physical therapy room; Activities room; Crafts room; Laundry room; Library.

Activities Arts & crafts; Games; Reading groups; Prayer groups; Movies; Dances/ Social/Cultural gatherings.

Maluhia
1027 Hala Dr, Honolulu, HI 96817
(808) 845-2951, 842-1564 FAX
Admin Gilbert A Gima. *Dir of Nursing* June Nakashima. *Medical Dir* Edward Yamada.
Licensure Skilled care; Intermediate care. *Beds* Swing beds SNF/ICF 158. *Private Pay Patients* 10%. *Certified* Medicaid; Medicare.
Owner Publicly owned.
Admissions Requirements Minimum age 18; Physician's request.
Staff Physicians 2 (pt); RNs 8 (ft); LPNs 6 (ft); Nurses' aides 70 (ft); Physical therapists 1 (ft); Occupational therapists 2 (ft); Speech therapists 1 (pt); Dietitians 2 (ft).
Languages Filipino, Japanese, Hawaiian, Samoan, Chinese, Korean.
Facilities Dining room; Physical therapy room; Activities room; Crafts room; Laundry room; Library; Day care.
Activities Arts & crafts; Cards; Games; Prayer groups; Movies; Shopping trips; Dances/ Social/Cultural gatherings; Intergenerational programs; Pet therapy.

Maunalani Nursing Center
5113 Maunalani Circle, Honolulu, HI 96816
(808) 732-0771
Admin Kenneth Halpenny.
Medical Dir Dr George Mills.
Licensure Skilled care; Intermediate care. *Beds* 101. *Certified* Medicaid; Medicare.
Staff Physicians 1 (ft); RNs 9 (ft); LPNs 8 (ft); Nurses' aides 43 (ft); Physical therapists 1 (ft); Recreational therapists 1 (ft); Occupational therapists 1 (ft); Speech therapists 1 (ft); Activities coordinators 1 (ft); Dietitians 1 (ft).
Facilities Dining room; Physical therapy room; Activities room; Crafts room; Laundry room.
Activities Arts & crafts; Cards; Games; Reading groups; Movies; Shopping trips.

Nuuanu Hale
2900 Pali Hwy, Honolulu, HI 96817
(808) 595-6311
Admin Sallie Y Miyawaki.
Medical Dir Dr Dennis S Murakami.
Licensure Skilled care; Intermediate care. *Beds* 75. *Certified* Medicaid; Medicare.
Admissions Requirements Medical examination; Physician's request.
Staff Physicians 1 (pt); RNs 6 (ft), 5 (pt); LPNs 6 (pt); Nurses' aides 32 (ft), 7 (pt); Physical therapists 1 (pt); Occupational therapists 1 (pt); Speech therapists 1 (pt); Activities coordinators 1 (pt); Dietitians 1 (pt); Ophthalmologists 1 (pt); Podiatrists 1 (pt); Audiologists 1 (pt); Dentists 1 (pt).
Facilities Dining room; Physical therapy room; Activities room; Crafts room.
Activities Arts & crafts; Cards; Games; Reading groups; Prayer groups; Movies; Shopping trips; Dances/Social/Cultural gatherings; Outings.

Oahu Care Facility
1808 S Beretania St, Honolulu, HI 96822
Admin Leland Yagi.
Licensure Intermediate care. *Beds* ICF 82. *Certified* Medicaid.

St Francis Hospital
2230 Liliha St, Honolulu, HI 96817
(808) 547-6011
Admin Michael Matsuura.
Medical Dir Robert Ballard MD.
Licensure Skilled care. *Beds* SNF 52. *Certified* Medicaid; Medicare.
Admissions Requirements Medical examination; Physician's request.

Staff RNs 3 (ft), 2 (pt); LPNs 10 (ft); Nurses' aides 19 (ft), 2 (pt); Physical therapists 1 (ft); Recreational therapists 1 (ft); Occupational therapists 1 (ft); Speech therapists 1 (pt); Activities coordinators 1 (ft), 1 (pt); Dietitians 1 (ft); Podiatrists 1 (ft); Dentists 3 (ft).
Affiliation Roman Catholic.
Facilities Dining room; Physical therapy room; Activities room; Chapel; Crafts room; Laundry room; Library; Occupational therapy room.
Activities Arts & crafts; Cards; Games; Prayer groups; Movies; Shopping trips; Dances/ Social/Cultural gatherings; Monthly luncheons.

Kahuku

Kahuku Hospital
Box 218, Kahuku, HI 96731
(808) 293-9221
Admin Rikio Tanji. *Dir of Nursing* Judith Correa.
Licensure Skilled care; Acute/SNF. *Beds* SNF 11; Acute/SNF 15. *Certified* Medicaid; Medicare.
Owner Nonprofit organization/foundation.
Admissions Requirements Physician's request.
Staff Physicians 7 (ft); RNs 16 (ft); LPNs 8 (ft); Nurses' aides 8 (ft), 1 (pt); Physical therapists 1 (ft); Dietitians 1 (pt).
Languages Tagalog.
Facilities Physical therapy room; Activities room.
Activities Games; Prayer groups.

Kahului

Hale Makua Kahului
472 Kaulana St, Kahului, HI 96732
(808) 877-2761, 871-9261 FAX
Admin Anthony J Krieg. *Dir of Nursing* Patinee Dunn, Acting. *Medical Dir* Rod G Bjordahl DO.
Licensure Skilled care; Intermediate care; Alzheimer's care. *Beds* Swing beds SNF/ICF 120. *Private Pay Patients* 10%. *Certified* Medicaid; Medicare.
Owner Nonprofit organization/foundation.
Admissions Requirements Medical examination; Physician's request.
Staff Physicians 1 (pt); RNs 12 (ft); LPNs 4 (ft); Nurses' aides 38 (ft); Physical therapists (consultant); Occupational therapists (consultant); Speech therapists (consultant); Activities coordinators 1 (ft); Dietitians (consultant); Podiatrists (consultant).
Languages Japanese, Ilogano.
Facilities Dining room; Physical therapy room; Activities room; Crafts room; Barber/ Beauty shop; Courtyards.
Activities Arts & crafts; Cards; Games; Prayer groups; Movies; Shopping trips; Intergenerational programs; Pet therapy; Residents council; Volunteer program; Programs presented by organizations.

Kaneohe

Aloha Health Care
45-545 Kam Hwy, Kaneohe, HI 96744
Admin Rick Henry.
Licensure Skilled care; Intermediate care. *Beds* 120. *Certified* Medicaid.

Ann Pearl
45-181 Waikalua Rd, Kaneohe, HI 96744
(808) 247-8558
Admin Clifford Miller Jr.
Licensure Skilled care. *Beds* SNF 86. *Certified* Medicaid.

Pohai Nani Care Center
45-090 Namoku St, Kaneohe, HI 96744
(808) 247-6211

Admin Gunter W Brunk. *Dir of Nursing*
Susan Sims. *Medical Dir* Glenn Stahl MD.
Licensure Skilled care; Intermediate care;
Retirement. *Beds* Swing beds SNF/ICF 42;
Retirement 209. *Private Pay Patients* 82%.
Certified Medicaid; Medicare.
Owner Nonprofit corp (Evangelical Lutheran/
Good Samaritan Society).
Admissions Requirements Medical
examination; Physician's request.
Staff Physicians 1 (pt); RNs 4 (ft), 4 (pt);
LPNs 1 (ft); Nurses' aides 10 (ft), 8 (pt);
Recreational therapists 1 (ft); Activities
coordinators 1 (ft); Dietitians 1 (ft).
Languages Hawaiian, Spanish.
Affiliation Lutheran.
Facilities Dining room; Physical therapy
room; Activities room; Chapel; Crafts room;
Laundry room; Barber/Beauty shop; Library;
Lanai & garden area.
Activities Arts & crafts; Cards; Games;
Reading groups; Prayer groups; Movies;
Shopping trips; Dances/Social/Cultural
gatherings; Intergenerational programs; Pet
therapy.

Kapa'a

Samuel Mahelona Memorial Hospital
4800 Kawaihau Rd, Kapa'a, HI 96746
(808) 822-4961
Admin John M English. *Dir of Nursing* Sheila
Ventura. *Medical Dir* Sasha E Myers MD.
Licensure Skilled care; Acute/ICF; SNF/ICF
swing beds. *Beds* 8; Acute/ICF 6; SNF/ICF
swing beds 61. *Certified* Medicaid;
Medicare.
Admissions Requirements Medical
examination; Physician's request.
Staff Physicians 1 (ft), 11 (pt); RNs 17 (ft);
LPNs 28 (ft); Nurses' aides 20 (ft); Physical
therapists 1 (ft); Occupational therapists 2
(ft); Activities coordinators 1 (ft); Dietitians
1 (ft); Social worker 2 (ft).
Facilities Dining room; Physical therapy
room; Activities room; Crafts room; Laundry
room; Barber/Beauty shop; Library.
Activities Arts & crafts; Cards; Games; Prayer
groups; Movies; Shopping trips; Dances/
Social/Cultural gatherings.

Kapaau

Kohala Hospital
PO Box 10, Kapaau, HI 96755
(808) 889-6211, 889-6978 FAX
Admin Jack O Halstead. *Dir of Nursing* Tom
Knott RN. *Medical Dir* Patrick Siu MD.
Licensure Skilled care; Intermediate care;
Acute care. *Beds* SNF 4; ICF 18; Acute care
4. *Certified* Medicaid; Medicare.
Owner Publicly owned.
Admissions Requirements Medical
examination; Physician's request.
Staff Physicians 5 (ft), 1 (pt); RNs 6 (ft);
LPNs 5 (ft); Nurses' aides 2 (ft);
Occupational therapists 1 (ft); Activities
coordinators 1 (ft); Dietitians 1 (pt).
Languages Japanese, Tagalog, Chinese,
Hawaiian.
Facilities Activities room; Laundry room.
Activities Arts & crafts; Games; Prayer groups;
Movies; Mystery excursions.

Kaunakakai

Molokai General Hospital
PO Box 408, Kaunakakai, HI 96748
(808) 553-3123, 553-3133 FAX
Admin Herbert K Yim. *Dir of Nursing* JoAnn
Ennis RN. *Medical Dir* Phillip Reyes MD.
Licensure Skilled care; Intermediate care; OB;
Med-Surg. *Beds* SNF 8; ICF 14; OB 4; Med-
Surg 4. *Certified* Medicaid; Medicare.
Owner Nonprofit corp.
Admissions Requirements Physician's request.

Staff Physicians 2 (ft); RNs 5 (ft), 1 (pt);
LPNs 5 (ft); Nurses' aides 9 (ft), 1 (pt);
Physical therapists (consultant); Activities
coordinators 1 (ft); Dietitians 2 (pt).
Facilities Dining room; Physical therapy
room; Activities room.
Activities Arts & crafts; Games; Movies;
Intergenerational programs.

Kealakekua

Kona Hospital
PO Box 69, Kealakekua, HI 96750
(808) 322-9311, 322-4488 FAX
Admin Jennie Wung, RN. *Dir of Nursing*
Roberta DeMello. *Medical Dir* Morton Berk
MD.
Licensure Skilled care; Intermediate care. *Beds*
SNF 9; Swing beds SNF/ICF 13. *Certified*
Medicaid; Medicare.
Owner Publicly owned.
Admissions Requirements Physician's request.
Staff RNs 5 (ft); LPNs 4 (ft); Nurses' aides 6
(ft); Physical therapists 1 (ft); Occupational
therapists 2 (ft); Dietitians 1 (ft).
Facilities Physical therapy room; Activities
room.
Activities Arts & crafts; Cards; Games.

Kula

Kula Hospital
204 Kula Hwy, Kula, HI 96790
(808) 878-1221
Admin Shirley K Takahashi RN. *Dir of
Nursing* Abraham A Wong RN. *Medical Dir*
Daniel G White MD.
Licensure Skilled care; Intermediate care;
Intermediate care for mentally retarded;
Acute care. *Beds* ICF/MR 8; Swing beds
SNF/ICF 95; Acute care 2. *Certified*
Medicaid; Medicare.
Owner Publicly owned.
Admissions Requirements Physician's request.
Staff Physicians 2 (ft); RNs 24 (ft); LPNs 12
(ft); Nurses' aides 47 (ft); Physical therapists
1 (ft); Occupational therapists 1 (ft);
Dietitians 1 (ft).
Languages Japanese, Hawaiian, Chinese.
Facilities Dining room; Physical therapy
room; Activities room; Chapel; Crafts room;
Laundry room; Barber/Beauty shop; Library.
Activities Arts & crafts; Cards; Games;
Reading groups; Shopping trips;
Intergenerational programs; Pet therapy.

Lanai City

Lanai Community Hospital
PO Box 797, Lanai City, HI 96763
(808) 565-6411
Admin Monica L Borges. *Dir of Nursing* D
Fabrao. *Medical Dir* Robert Cary MD.
Licensure SNF/ICF swing beds. *Beds* SNF/
ICF swing beds 8. *Certified* Medicaid;
Medicare.
Owner Publicly owned.
Admissions Requirements Physician's request.
Staff Physicians 1 (ft); RNs 6 (ft); Nurses'
aides 5 (ft); Physical therapists 1 (pt);
Occupational therapists 1 (pt); Dietitians 1
(pt); Ophthalmologists 1 (pt).
Facilities Dining room; Physical therapy
room; Activities room; Laundry room;
Library; Whirlpool.
Activities Arts & crafts; Cards; Games;
Shopping trips; Parties for birthdays; Senior
Citizen dining groups.

Lawai

Hale Omao Nursing Home
4297-C Omao Rd, Lawai, HI 96765
(808) 742-7591, 742-6563 FAX
Admin Ron Cettie NHA. *Dir of Nursing* Jan
Sevy BSN RN. *Medical Dir* Dr Eric Yee.

Licensure Skilled care. *Beds* SNF 36. *Private
Pay Patients* 15%. *Certified* Medicaid.
Owner Privately owned.
Staff RNs 5 (ft); LPNs 5 (ft); Nurses' aides 40
(ft); Physical therapists 1 (ft); Occupational
therapists 1 (ft); Speech therapists 1 (ft);
Activities coordinators 3 (ft); Dietitians 1
(ft); Ophthalmologists 1 (ft); Podiatrists 1
(ft).

Lihue

Wilcox Memorial Hospital
3420 Kuhio Hwy, Lihue, HI 96766
(808) 245-1343, 245-1171 FAX
Admin Lynne Joseph. *Dir of Nursing* Joyce
MacAvaney RN. *Medical Dir* William A
Renti Cruz MD.
Licensure Skilled care; Intermediate care;
Alzheimer's care. *Beds* Swing beds SNF/ICF
110. *Private Pay Patients* 5%. *Certified*
Medicaid; Medicare.
Owner Nonprofit corp.
Admissions Requirements Medical
examination; Physician's request.
Staff Physicians 1 (pt); RNs 7 (ft); LPNs 15
(ft); Nurses' aides 36 (ft); Physical therapists
1 (pt); Occupational therapists 1 (pt); Speech
therapists 1 (pt); Activities coordinators 1
(ft); Dietitians 1 (pt).
Languages Japanese, Filipino.
Facilities Dining room; Physical therapy
room; Activities room; Chapel; Laundry
room; Private and semi-private rooms with
HCP access baths; Nurse call/locator system;
Lanais.
Activities Arts & crafts; Cards; Games;
Reading groups; Prayer groups; Movies;
Dances/Social/Cultural gatherings;
Intergenerational programs; Pet therapy.

Pahala

Ka'u Hospital
PO Box 248, Pahala, HI 96777
(808) 928-8331
Admin Kenji Nagao.
Medical Dir Debra M Javar.
Licensure Skilled care. *Beds* SNF 10. *Certified*
Medicaid; Medicare.
Admissions Requirements Medical
examination; Physician's request.
Staff Physicians 2 (ft), 1 (pt); RNs 7 (ft);
LPNs 6 (ft); Nurses' aides 5 (ft); Physical
therapists 1 (pt); Occupational therapists 1
(pt); Activities coordinators 1 (ft); Dietitians
1 (pt).
Facilities Dining room; Physical therapy
room; Activities room.
Activities Arts & crafts; Cards; Games;
Reading groups; Prayer groups; Movies;
Shopping trips; Dances/Social/Cultural
gatherings.

Pearl City

Waimano Training School & Hospital
2201 Waimano Home Rd, Pearl City, HI
96782
(808) 456-6255, 455-1156 FAX
Admin Lois Suenishi. *Dir of Nursing* Betty
Nakaji. *Medical Dir* Dr Nancy Kuntz.
Licensure Skilled care; Intermediate care;
Intermediate care for mentally retarded.
Beds SNF 27; ICF 22; ICF/MR 156. *Private
Pay Patients* 9%. *Certified* Medicaid.
Owner Publicly owned.
Admissions Requirements Medical
examination; Physician's request.
Staff Physicians 2 (ft); RNs 43 (ft); LPNs 47
(ft); Nurses' aides 177 (ft); Physical
therapists 1 (ft); Recreational therapists 9
(ft); Occupational therapists 3 (ft); Speech
therapists 2 (ft); Dietitians 2 (ft);
Audiologists 1 (ft).

Facilities Dining room; Physical therapy room; Activities room; Crafts room; Laundry room.
Activities Arts & crafts; Games; Movies; Shopping trips; Dances/Social/Cultural gatherings.

Wahiawa

Wahiawa General Hospital
PO Box 580, 128 Lehua St, Wahiawa, HI 96786
(808) 621-8411, 621-8223 FAX
Admin Kenam Kim, Pres. *Dir of Nursing* Grace M Primiano RN, Nursing Svc V Pres. *Medical Dir* Robert Mookini Jr MD.
Licensure Skilled care; Intermediate care. *Beds* Swing beds SNF/ ICF 93. *Private Pay Patients* 5%. *Certified* Medicaid; Medicare.
Owner Nonprofit organization/foundation.
Admissions Requirements Medical examination; Physician's request.
Staff Physicians 1 (pt); RNs 3 (ft), 2 (pt); LPNs 11 (ft), 2 (pt); Nurses' aides 36 (ft), 11 (pt); Physical therapists (contracted); Occupational therapists 1 (ft); Dietitians 1 (ft); COTAs 1 (pt).
Languages Japanese, Korean, Filipino, Samoan, Spanish, Portuguese, Chinese.
Facilities Dining room; Physical therapy room; Activities room; Crafts room; Barber/Beauty shop.
Activities Arts & crafts; Cards; Games; Reading groups; Prayer groups; Movies; Dances/Social/Cultural gatherings; Pet therapy.

Waianae

Leeward Nursing Home
94-404 Jade St, Waianae, HI 96792
(808) 695-9508
Admin Joe DiPardo. *Dir of Nursing* Linda Carr RN.
Licensure Intermediate care. *Beds* ICF 50. *Certified* Medicaid.
Owner Proprietary corp.
Admissions Requirements Medical examination; Physician's request.

Staff RNs 3 (ft); LPNs 1 (ft), 1 (pt); Nurses' aides 17 (ft), 1 (pt); Activities coordinators 1 (pt); Dietitians 1 (pt).
Languages Tagalog, Japanese, Chinese.
Facilities Dining room; Activities room; Chapel; Crafts room; Library; Laundry room; Barber/Beauty shop.
Activities Arts & crafts; Cards; Games; Reading groups; Prayer groups; Movies; Shopping trips; Dances/Social/Cultural gatherings; Reality orientation; Music; Picnics; Beauty class; Exercise; Sunshine therapy; Gardening; Birthday parties.

Wailuku

Hale Makua—Wailuku
1540 E Main St, Wailuku, HI 96732
(808) 871-9222, 871-9262 FAX
Admin Lillian Higa. *Dir of Nursing* Lillian Higa. *Medical Dir* Rod G Bjordahl DO.
Licensure Intermediate care. *Beds* ICF 124. *Private Pay Patients* 10%. *Certified* Medicaid.
Owner Nonprofit organization/foundation.
Admissions Requirements Medical examination; Physician's request.
Staff Physicians 1 (pt); RNs 6 (ft); LPNs 8 (ft); Nurses' aides 36 (ft); Physical therapists (consultant); Occupational therapists (consultant); Speech therapists (consultant); Activities coordinators 1 (ft); Dietitians (consultant); Podiatrists (consultant).
Languages Japanese, Ilogano.
Facilities Dining room; Activities room; Laundry room; Barber/Beauty shop; Library; Garden, Courtyards.
Activities Arts & crafts; Cards; Games; Reading groups; Prayer groups; Movies; Shopping trips; Dances/Social/Cultural gatherings; Intergenerational programs; Pet therapy; Resident's council; Volunteer program; Programs presented by organizations.

Waimea

Kauai Care Center
PO Box 507, 9611 Waena St, Waimea, HI 96796
(808) 338-1681

Admin Jan Schmidt. *Dir of Nursing* Kathie Meskell. *Medical Dir* Harold Spear.
Licensure Intermediate care; Residential care; Retirement. *Beds* ICF 21; Residential care 7; Retirement apts 5. *Private Pay Patients* 15%. *Certified* Medicaid.
Owner Proprietary corp (Regency Care Centers Inc).
Admissions Requirements Medical examination; Physician's request.
Staff Physicians (consultant); RNs 2 (ft), 1 (pt); LPNs 5 (ft); Nurses' aides 6 (ft), 6 (pt); Physical therapists (consultant); Occupational therapists (consultant); Activities coordinators 1 (ft); Dietitians (consultant); Food service managers 1 (ft).
Languages Filipino, Japanese, Hawaiian.
Facilities Dining room; Activities room; Laundry room; Large outdoor areas.
Activities Arts & crafts; Cards; Games; Reading groups; Prayer groups; Movies; Shopping trips; Dances/Social/Cultural gatherings; Intergenerational programs; Pet therapy.

Kauai Veterans Memorial Hospital
PO Box 337, Waimea, HI 96796
(808) 338-9431, 338-9420 FAX
Admin Keith Horinouchi DHSc MPH. *Dir of Nursing* Ethel Oyama RN.
Licensure Skilled care; Intermediate care; Swing beds Acute/SNF; Swing beds SNF/ICF; Acute care. *Beds* Swing beds Acute/SNF 5; Swing beds SNF/ICF 15; Acute care 24. *Private Pay Patients* 5%. *Certified* Medicaid; Medicare.
Owner Publicly owned (Hawaii State Department of Health).
Admissions Requirements Medical examination; Physician's request.
Staff Physicians 1 (ft); RNs 1 (ft); LPNs 5 (ft); Nurses' aides 5 (ft); Physical therapists 1 (ft); Occupational therapists 1 (ft); Activities coordinators 1 (ft); Dietitians 1 (ft); Podiatrists 1 (ft).
Languages Tagalog, Japanese, Hawaiian.
Facilities Physical therapy room; Activities room; Crafts room; Library.
Activities Arts & crafts; Games; Movies; Shopping trips; Monthly & holiday parties.

IDAHO

American Falls

Power County Nursing Home
PO Box 420, Gifford at Roosevelt, American Falls, ID 83211-0420
(208) 226-2327
Admin Francis X McNamara. *Dir of Nursing* Susan Fletcher RN. *Medical Dir* Jerry Knouf MD.
Licensure Skilled care; Intermediate care. *Beds* 31. *Certified* Medicaid; Medicare.
Owner Publicly owned.
Admissions Requirements Medical examination; Physician's request.
Staff Activities coordinators 1 (pt); Dietitians 1 (pt); Ophthalmologists 1 (pt).
Facilities Dining room; Physical therapy room; Activities room; Chapel; Crafts room; Laundry room; Barber/Beauty shop; Library.
Activities Arts & crafts; Cards; Games; Reading groups; Prayer groups; Movies; Shopping trips; Dances/Social/Cultural gatherings; Bingo; Volleyball; Quilting.

Ammon

Idaho Falls Group Homes Inc No 2
4360 Wanda, Ammon, ID 83406
(208) 522-4614, 523-0053
Admin Rex Redden.
Licensure Intermediate care for mentally retarded. *Beds* ICF/MR 8. *Certified* Medicaid.

Arco

Lost Rivers Nursing Home
PO Box 145, 551 Highland Dr, Arco, ID 83213
(208) 527-8207
Admin Martha Danz. *Dir of Nursing* Jessie Bell RN. *Medical Dir* R F Barter MD.
Licensure Skilled care; Intermediate care; Alzheimer's care. *Beds* 8. *Certified* Medicaid; Medicare.
Owner Publicly owned.
Admissions Requirements Minimum age 21; Medical examination; Physician's request.
Staff Physicians 1 (ft); RNs 3 (ft), 4 (pt); LPNs 3 (ft), 2 (pt); Physical therapists 1 (pt); Activities coordinators 1 (pt); Dietitians 1 (pt).
Facilities Dining room; Physical therapy room; Activities room; Crafts room; Laundry room; Barber/Beauty shop.
Activities Arts & crafts; Cards; Games; Reading groups; Prayer groups; Movies; Shopping trips; Dances/Social/Cultural gatherings.

Ashton

Ashton Memorial
PO Box 838, 801 Main, Ashton, ID 83420
(208) 652-7461
Admin Sheila Kellogg. *Dir of Nursing* Gene Ciciliano. *Medical Dir* Stephen Cheyne MD.

Licensure Skilled care. *Beds* SNF 22. *Private Pay Patients* 10%. *Certified* Medicaid; Medicare.
Owner Nonprofit organization/foundation.
Admissions Requirements Physician's request.
Staff RNs 2 (ft), 3 (pt); LPNs 1 (ft), 4 (pt); Nurses' aides 5 (ft), 7 (pt); Activities coordinators 1 (pt).
Facilities Dining room; Activities room; Laundry room.
Activities Arts & crafts; Cards; Games; Prayer groups; Movies.

Blackfoot

Bingham County Nursing Home
98 Poplar St, Blackfoot, ID 83221
(208) 785-4100
Admin Carl Staley. *Dir of Nursing* Ada Mae Exeter RN. *Medical Dir* Brian Carrigan MD.
Licensure Skilled care; Intermediate care; Residential care. *Beds* Swing beds SNF/ICF 58; Residential care 16. *Certified* Medicaid; Medicare.
Owner Publicly owned.
Admissions Requirements Medical examination; Physician's request.
Staff Physicians 7 (pt); RNs 1 (ft), 1 (pt); LPNs 4 (ft), 1 (pt); Nurses' aides 30 (ft), 2 (pt); Physical therapists 1 (pt); Occupational therapists 1 (pt); Speech therapists 1 (pt); Activities coordinators 1 (ft); Dietitians 1 (pt); Ophthalmologists 1 (pt); Podiatrists 1 (pt); Dentists 1 (pt).
Languages Spanish.
Facilities Dining room; Activities room; Crafts room; Laundry room; Barber/Beauty shop.
Activities Arts & crafts; Cards; Games; Reading groups; Prayer groups; Movies; Shopping trips.

State Hospital South Geriatric—Intermediate Care Facility
Box 400, State Hospital South, Blackfoot, ID 83221
(208) 785-1200
Admin Ken Brown.
Licensure Intermediate care. *Beds* 45. *Certified* Medicaid.

Boise

Boise Group Home 1
1736 N Five Mile Rd, Boise, ID 83704
(208) 376-1861
Admin Richard Davis.
Licensure Intermediate care for mentally retarded. *Beds* ICF/MR 12. *Certified* Medicaid.

Boise Group Home 2
10528 Milclay St, Boise, ID 83704
(208) 376-1861
Admin Richard Davis.
Licensure Intermediate care for mentally retarded. *Beds* ICF/MR 6. *Certified* Medicaid.

Owner Nonprofit corp.
Admissions Requirements Minimum age 6; Medical examination.
Staff Physicians 1 (pt); RNs 1 (pt); LPNs 1 (pt); Physical therapists 1 (pt); Recreational therapists 1 (pt); Occupational therapists 1 (pt); Speech therapists 1 (pt); Dietitians 1 (pt); Podiatrists 1 (pt).
Facilities Home setting.

Boise Group Home 3
10349 Summerwind Dr, Boise, ID 83704
(208) 376-1861
Admin Richard Davis.
Licensure Intermediate care for mentally retarded. *Beds* ICF/MR 5. *Certified* Medicaid.

Boise Group Home 4
10448 Garverdale, Boise, ID 83704
(208) 376-1861
Licensure Intermediate care for mentally retarded. *Beds* ICF/MR 6. *Certified* Medicaid.

Boise Group Home 5
10244 Molly Ct, Boise, ID 83704
(208) 376-1861
Admin Richard Davis.
Licensure Intermediate care for mentally retarded. *Beds* ICF/MR 6. *Certified* Medicaid.

Boise Group Home 6
11577 W Freedom, Boise, ID 83704
(208) 376-1861
Admin Richard Davis.
Licensure Intermediate care for mentally retarded. *Beds* ICF/MR 4. *Certified* Medicaid.

Boise Samaritan Village
3115 Sycamore Dr, Boise, ID 83703-4199
(208) 343-7726
Admin Dwight Wuenschel. *Dir of Nursing* Audry Smith. *Medical Dir* Ward Dickey MD.
Licensure Skilled care; Intermediate care; Residential care; Alzheimer's care. *Beds* 194; Residential care 15. *Certified* Medicaid; Medicare.
Owner Nonprofit corp (Evangelical Lutheran/Good Samaritan Society).
Admissions Requirements Medical examination.
Staff Physicians; RNs; LPNs; Nurses' aides; Recreational therapists; Speech therapists; Activities coordinators; Dietitians; Podiatrists.
Languages Sign.
Affiliation Lutheran.
Facilities Dining room; Physical therapy room; Activities room; Chapel; Crafts room; Laundry room; Barber/Beauty shop; Library; Snack bar.
Activities Arts & crafts; Cards; Games; Reading groups; Prayer groups; Movies; Shopping trips; Dances/Social/Cultural gatherings.

Capital Care Center
8211 Ustick, Boise, ID 83704
(208) 375-3700
Admin Jeff Piper. *Dir of Nursing* Cynthia
Mintun RN. *Medical Dir* Ward E Dickey
MD.
Licensure Skilled care; Intermediate care;
Sheltered care. *Beds* Swing beds SNF/ICF
196; Sheltered care 22. *Private Pay Patients*
39%. *Certified* Medicaid; Medicare.
Owner Proprietary corp (National Heritage).
Admissions Requirements Medical
examination.
Staff Physicians 1 (ft); RNs 10 (ft), 2 (pt);
LPNs 16 (ft), 4 (pt); Nurses' aides 67 (ft), 10
(pt); Physical therapists (contracted);
Occupational therapists (contracted); Speech
therapists (contracted); Activities
coordinators 2 (ft); Dietitians 1 (ft).
Facilities Dining room; Physical therapy
room; Activities room; Chapel; Laundry
room; Barber/Beauty shop; Activity kitchen.
Activities Arts & crafts; Games; Reading
groups; Prayer groups; Movies; Shopping
trips; Dances/Social/Cultural gatherings; Pet
therapy; Singing; Exercise.

Communicare Inc No 4
4150 Leland Way, Boise, ID 83709
(208) 362-3003
Admin Tom Whittemore.
Licensure Intermediate care for mentally
retarded. *Beds* ICF/MR 8. *Certified*
Medicaid.
Admissions Requirements Minimum age;
Medical examination; Physician's request.
Staff Physicians 1 (pt); RNs 1 (pt); LPNs 1
(pt); Physical therapists 1 (pt); Recreational
therapists 1 (pt); Speech therapists 1 (pt);
Dietitians 1 (pt); Audiologists 1 (pt);
Dentists 1 (pt).
Facilities Dining room; Activities room.
Activities Arts & crafts; Games; Movies;
Shopping trips; Dances/Social/Cultural
gatherings.

Communicare Inc No 3
2650 S Pond, Boise, ID 83705
(208) 344-6683
Admin Tom Whittemore.
Licensure Intermediate care for mentally
retarded. *Beds* ICF/MR 8. *Certified*
Medicaid.
Admissions Requirements Minimum age 18.
Staff Physicians 2 (pt); RNs 1 (pt); LPNs 1
(pt); Physical therapists 1 (pt); Recreational
therapists 1 (pt); Speech therapists 1 (pt);
Activities coordinators 1 (pt); Dietitians 1
(pt); Ophthalmologists 1 (pt); Podiatrists 1
(pt); Dentists 1 (pt).
Facilities Dining room; Activities room;
Crafts room.
Activities Arts & crafts; Cards; Games;
Movies; Shopping trips; Dances/Social/
Cultural gatherings.

Grand Oaks Healthcare Center
316 W Washington, Boise, ID 83702
(208) 343-7755
Admin Joe Turmis.
Licensure Skilled care. *Beds* 88. *Certified*
Medicaid; Medicare.

Hillcrest Care Center
1001 S Hilton St, Boise, ID 83705
(208) 345-4464
Admin Almeta Ingram.
Medical Dir Dr David Weeks.
Licensure Skilled care. *Beds* 123. *Certified*
Medicaid; Medicare.
Owner Proprietary corp (Hillhaven Corp).
Admissions Requirements Minimum age 16.
Staff Physicians 1 (pt); RNs 6 (ft), 5 (pt);
LPNs 5 (ft), 4 (pt); Nurses' aides 27 (ft), 25
(pt); Physical therapists 1 (ft); Occupational
therapists 1 (pt); Speech therapists 1 (pt);
Activities coordinators 1 (ft); Dietitians 1
(pt).

Facilities Dining room; Physical therapy
room; Activities room; Crafts room; Barber/
Beauty shop; Greenhouse.
Activities Arts & crafts; Cards; Games;
Reading groups; Prayer groups; Movies;
Shopping trips; Dances/Social/Cultural
gatherings.

Idaho State Veterans Home—Boise
PO Box 7765, 320 Collins Rd, Boise, ID
83707
(208) 334-5000, 334-4753 FAX
Admin Gary Bermeosolo. *Dir of Nursing* Sally
Johnson. *Medical Dir* Dr James Branahl.
Licensure Skilled care; Intermediate care;
Domiciliary care; Alzheimer's care. *Beds*
SNF 96; ICF 10; Domiciliary care 38.
Private Pay Patients 0%.
Owner Publicly owned.
Admissions Requirements Medical
examination; Physician's request.
Staff Physicians 2 (pt); RNs 11 (ft), 3 (pt);
LPNs 7 (ft), 1 (pt); Nurses' aides 32 (ft), 19
(pt); Physical therapists 1 (pt); Recreational
therapists 2 (ft); Occupational therapists 1
(pt); Activities coordinators 1 (pt); Dietitians
1 (pt); Podiatrists 1 (pt).
Facilities Dining room; Physical therapy
room; Activities room; Chapel; Crafts room;
Laundry room; Barber/Beauty shop; Library.
Activities Arts & crafts; Cards; Games;
Reading groups; Prayer groups; Movies;
Shopping trips; Dances/Social/Cultural
gatherings; Intergenerational programs; Pet
therapy; Horseback riding; Swimming;
Bowling.

Life Care Center of Boise
808 N Curtis Rd, Boise, ID 83706
(208) 376-5273
Admin Carlene J Barlow. *Dir of Nursing* Pat
McClain. *Medical Dir* Edward Newcombe
MD.
Licensure Skilled care. *Beds* SNF 164.
Certified Medicaid; Medicare.
Owner Proprietary corp (Life Care Centers of
America).
Admissions Requirements Medical
examination; Physician's request.
Staff RNs; LPNs; Nurses' aides; Recreational
therapists.
Facilities Dining room; Physical therapy
room; Activities room; Laundry room;
Barber/Beauty shop.
Activities Arts & crafts; Games; Reading
groups; Prayer groups; Movies; Shopping
trips; Dances/Social/Cultural gatherings;
Intergenerational programs; Pet therapy.

Solstice—Brookhollow
4696 Overland Rd, Ste 510, Boise, ID 83705-
2864
(208) 342-8055, 345-8806 FAX
Admin Merrick Dodds. *Dir of Nursing* Ron
Anderson. *Medical Dir* Dr William Terry.
Licensure Intermediate care for mentally
retarded. *Beds* ICF/MR 23. *Certified*
Medicaid.
Owner Proprietary corp (Solstice Inc).
Admissions Requirements Medical
examination; Physician's request.
Staff Physicians 1 (pt); RNs 1 (ft); LPNs 2
(ft); Physical therapists 1 (pt); Recreational
therapists 1 (ft); Occupational therapists 1
(pt); Speech therapists 1 (pt);
Ophthalmologists 1 (pt); Podiatrists 1 (pt);
Audiologists 1 (pt).
Facilities Dining room; Laundry room.
Activities Arts & crafts; Cards; Games;
Reading groups; Movies; Shopping trips;
Active treatment.

Solstice Inc—Shenandoah
4696 Overland Rd No 510, Boise, ID 83705
(208) 342-8055, 345-8806 FAX
Admin Merrick Dodds. *Dir of Nursing* Ron
Anderson RN. *Medical Dir* William Terry
MD.

Licensure Intermediate care for mentally
retarded. *Beds* ICF/MR 24. *Private Pay
Patients* 0%. *Certified* Medicaid.
Owner Proprietary corp (Solstice Inc).
Admissions Requirements Physician's request.
Staff Physicians 1 (pt); RNs 1 (ft); LPNs 2
(ft); Nurses' aides 1 (pt); Physical therapists
1 (pt); Recreational therapists 1 (ft);
Occupational therapists 1 (pt); Speech
therapists 1 (pt); Activities coordinators 1
(ft); Dietitians 1 (pt); Ophthalmologists 1
(pt); Podiatrists 1 (pt); Audiologists 1 (pt).
Facilities Dining room; Physical therapy
room; Activities room; Laundry room.
Activities Arts & crafts; Cards; Games;
Reading groups; Prayer groups; Movies;
Shopping trips; Pet therapy; Active
treatment.

Solstice—Lakewood
4696 Overland Rd, Ste 510, Boise, ID 83705
(208) 342-8055, 345-8806 FAX
Admin Merrick Dodds. *Dir of Nursing* Ron
Anderson RN. *Medical Dir* Dr William
Terry.
Licensure Intermediate care for mentally
retarded. *Beds* ICF/MR 23. *Private Pay
Patients* 0%. *Certified* Medicaid.
Owner Proprietary corp (Solstice Inc).
Admissions Requirements Males only; Medical
examination; Physician's request.
Staff LPNs 2 (ft); Recreational therapists 1
(ft); Occupational therapists 1 (pt); Speech
therapists 1 (pt); Activities coordinators 1
(ft); Ophthalmologists 1 (pt).
Activities Arts & crafts; Cards; Games;
Reading groups; Movies; Shopping trips;
Dances/Social/Cultural gatherings; Active
treatment.

Treasure Valley Manor
909 Reserve St, Boise, ID 83702
(208) 343-7717
Admin Lee Stickland. *Dir of Nursing* Kleone
Aschenbrenner. *Medical Dir* Theodore
Walters MD.
Licensure Skilled care; Alzheimer's care. *Beds*
SNF 165. *Private Pay Patients* 30%. *Certified*
Medicaid; Medicare.
Owner Privately owned.
Admissions Requirements Medical
examination.
Staff Physicians 1 (ft); RNs 8 (ft); LPNs 10
(ft); Nurses' aides 50 (ft); Physical therapists
1 (ft); Occupational therapists 1 (ft); Speech
therapists 1 (ft); Activities coordinators 1
(ft); Dietitians 1 (ft); Audiologists 1 (ft).
Facilities Dining room; Physical therapy
room; Activities room; Barber/Beauty shop;
Library.
Activities Games.

Valley View Retirement Community
1130 N Allumbaugh St, Boise, ID 83704
(208) 322-0311
Admin Larry Sieler.
Licensure Skilled care; Intermediate care. *Beds*
59. *Certified* Medicaid; Medicare.

Bonners Ferry

Boundary County Nursing Home
Box 1449, 551 Kaniksu, Bonners Ferry, ID
83805
(208) 267-3141
Admin Charles J Bouis, CEO.
Licensure Skilled care; Intermediate care. *Beds*
35. *Certified* Medicaid; Medicare.
Admissions Requirements Medical
examination; Physician's request.
Staff Physicians 5 (ft), 1 (pt); RNs 2 (ft);
LPNs 3 (ft), 2 (pt); Nurses' aides 8 (ft), 6
(pt); Physical therapists 1 (pt); Activities
coordinators 1 (ft); Dietitians 1 (pt).
Facilities Dining room; Physical therapy
room; Activities room.
Activities Arts & crafts; Games; Reading
groups.

Buhl

Harral's Nursing Home
820 Sprague Ave, Buhl, ID 83316
(208) 543-6401
Admin Bill Scifres. *Dir of Nursing* Nancy Montgomery.
Licensure Skilled care; Intermediate care. *Beds* 64. *Certified* Medicaid; Medicare.
Owner Proprietary corp (Beverly Enterprises).
Admissions Requirements Medical examination; Physician's request.
Staff RNs 3 (ft), 2 (pt); LPNs 5 (ft), 2 (pt); Nurses' aides 20 (ft), 8 (pt); Activities coordinators 1 (ft).
Facilities Dining room; Activities room; Crafts room; Laundry room; Barber/Beauty shop.
Activities Arts & crafts; Cards; Games; Reading groups; Prayer groups; Movies; Dances/Social/Cultural gatherings.

Burley

Burley Care Center
1729 Miller St, Burley, ID 83318
(208) 678-9474
Admin Jody Craig-Trujillo, RN.
Medical Dir H W Crawford MD.
Licensure Skilled care; Intermediate care. *Beds* 68. *Certified* Medicaid; Medicare.
Admissions Requirements Minimum age 21; Medical examination; Physician's request.
Staff RNs 3 (ft); LPNs 4 (ft), 5 (pt); Nurses' aides 12 (ft); Physical therapists 1 (pt); Speech therapists 1 (pt); Activities coordinators 1 (ft); Dietitians 1 (pt).
Facilities Dining room; Activities room; Crafts room; Barber/Beauty shop.
Activities Arts & crafts; Games; Reading groups; Prayer groups; Movies; Shopping trips.

Cassia Memorial Hospital Long-Term Care Unit
2303 Park Ave, Burley, ID 83318
(208) 678-4444
Admin Richard Packer. *Dir of Nursing* Mary Ovitt RN. *Medical Dir* James Kircher MD.
Licensure Skilled care; Intermediate care. *Beds* Swing beds SNF/ICF 34. *Certified* Medicaid; Medicare.
Owner Nonprofit corp.
Admissions Requirements Medical examination; Physician's request.
Staff Physicians 19 (ft); RNs 3 (ft); LPNs 2 (ft), 2 (pt); Nurses' aides 12 (ft), 6 (pt); Physical therapists 2 (ft), 1 (pt); Reality therapists 1 (ft); Recreational therapists 1 (ft); Occupational therapists 1 (ft); Speech therapists 1 (ft); Activities coordinators 1 (ft); Dietitians 1 (ft); Ophthalmologists 1 (ft); Dentists 2 (ft).
Facilities Dining room; Physical therapy room; Activities room; Crafts room; Laundry room; Barber/Beauty shop.
Activities Arts & crafts; Cards; Games; Reading groups; Prayer groups; Movies; Shopping trips; Dances/Social/Cultural gatherings.

Caldwell

Caldwell Care Center
210 Cleveland, Caldwell, ID 83605
(208) 459-1522
Admin Debbie Flowers.
Licensure Skilled care; Intermediate care. *Beds* 75. *Certified* Medicaid; Medicare.
Owner Proprietary corp (Hillhaven Corp).

Cascade Care Center
2814 S Indiana Ave, Caldwell, ID 83605
(208) 459-0808
Admin Claire Roper. *Dir of Nursing* Ginger Meeker. *Medical Dir* Dr Joe E McCary.

Licensure Skilled care. *Beds* SNF 112.
Certified Medicaid; Medicare.
Owner Proprietary corp (Hillhaven Corp).

Coeur d'Alene

Idaho Healthcare Center—Coeur d'Alene
2200 Ironwood Pl, Coeur d'Alene, ID 83814
(208) 667-6486
Admin Bridget Robson, acting.
Licensure Skilled care. *Beds* 125. *Certified* Medicaid; Medicare.
Owner Proprietary corp (Unicare).

Pinewood Care Center
2514 N 7th St, Coeur d'Alene, ID 83814
(208) 664-8128
Admin Taylor "Vic" Wallner. *Dir of Nursing* Sarah Luster RN. *Medical Dir* William T Wood MD.
Licensure Skilled care. *Beds* SNF 117.
Certified Medicaid; Medicare.
Owner Proprietary corp (National Heritage).
Admissions Requirements Medical examination; Physician's request.
Staff RNs 3 (ft), 1 (pt); LPNs 6 (ft), 2 (pt); Nurses' aides 27 (ft), 6 (pt); Recreational therapists 1 (ft), 1 (pt); Social service 1 (pt).
Facilities Dining room; Physical therapy room; Activities room; Crafts room; Laundry room; Barber/Beauty shop.
Activities Arts & crafts; Cards; Games; Reading groups; Prayer groups; Movies; Shopping trips; Dances/Social/Cultural gatherings; Cooking.

Sunset Terrace Convalescent Center
210 LaCrosse St, Coeur d'Alene, ID 83814
(208) 664-2185
Admin Brian Morris.
Licensure Skilled care. *Beds* 125. *Certified* Medicaid; Medicare.

Sunset Terrace Extended Care Facility
2003 Lincoln Way, Coeur d'Alene, ID 83814-2677
(208) 667-6441
Admin Brian Morris.
Licensure Skilled care; Intermediate care. *Beds* 32. *Certified* Medicaid; Medicare.

Emmett

Emmett Care Center
714 N Butte, Emmett, ID 83617
(208) 365-4425
Admin Gary Obenauer. *Dir of Nursing* Alice Ennis RN. *Medical Dir* Harmon Holverson MD.
Licensure Skilled care. *Beds* SNF 95. *Certified* Medicaid; Medicare; VA.
Owner Proprietary corp (Hillhaven Corp).
Admissions Requirements Physician's request.
Staff RNs 6 (ft); LPNs 8 (ft); Nurses' aides 28 (ft); Physical therapists 1 (ft); Activities coordinators 1 (ft).
Languages Spanish, German.
Facilities Dining room; Physical therapy room; Activities room; Crafts room; Laundry room; Barber/Beauty shop; Library.
Activities Arts & crafts; Cards; Games; Reading groups; Prayer groups; Movies; Shopping trips; Dances/Social/Cultural gatherings.

Holly Hills Care Center
501 W Idaho Blvd, Emmett, ID 83617
(208) 365-3597
Admin Don Kinnaman.
Medical Dir Dr Harmon Holverson.
Licensure Intermediate care. *Beds* 39.
Certified Medicaid; Medicare.
Owner Proprietary corp (National Heritage).
Admissions Requirements Physician's request.
Staff RNs 1 (ft), 2 (pt); LPNs 2 (ft), 4 (pt); Nurses' aides 5 (ft), 3 (pt); Activities coordinators 1 (pt); Audiologists 1 (ft).

Facilities Dining room; Physical therapy room; Activities room; Crafts room; Laundry room; Barber/Beauty shop.
Activities Arts & crafts; Cards; Games; Reading groups; Prayer groups; Shopping trips.

Gooding

Green Acres Care Center
1220 Montana, Gooding, ID 83330
(208) 934-5601
Admin Julie J Conrad. *Dir of Nursing* Sandy Mahl. *Medical Dir* Dr Douglas Smith.
Licensure Skilled care; Intermediate care; Alzheimer's care. *Beds* SNF 76; ICF 28. *Certified* Medicaid; Medicare.
Owner Proprietary corp (Beverly Enterprises).
Admissions Requirements Medical examination.
Staff RNs 4 (ft), 1 (pt); LPNs; Nurses' aides; Physical therapists; Activities coordinators; Dietitians.
Languages Spanish.
Facilities Dining room; Physical therapy room; Activities room; Crafts room; Laundry room; Barber/Beauty shop.
Activities Arts & crafts; Cards; Games; Reading groups; Prayer groups; Movies; Dances/Social/Cultural gatherings.

Greenacres Care Center
1220 Montana, Gooding, ID 83330
(208) 934-5601
Admin Julie J Conrad. *Dir of Nursing* Sandra Mohl. *Medical Dir* Douglas Smith.
Licensure Skilled care; Intermediate care; Intermediate care for mentally retarded; Alzheimer's care. *Beds* ICF/MR 28; Swing beds SNF/ICF 76. *Private Pay Patients* 25%. *Certified* Medicaid; Medicare.
Owner Proprietary corp (Beverly Enterprises).
Admissions Requirements Medical examination.
Staff Physicians; RNs; LPNs; Nurses' aides; Physical therapists; Reality therapists; Recreational therapists; Occupational therapists; Speech therapists; Activities coordinators; Dietitians; Podiatrists; Audiologists.
Facilities Dining room; Physical therapy room; Activities room; Crafts room; Laundry room; Barber/Beauty shop; Alzheimer's unit.
Activities Arts & crafts; Cards; Games; Reading groups; Prayer groups; Movies; Shopping trips; Dances/Social/Cultural gatherings; Pet therapy.

Grangeville

Grangeville Convalescent Inc
PO Box 429, 410 E N 2nd St, Grangeville, ID 83530
(208) 983-1131
Admin Ron Deeney; Arden Higgs. *Dir of Nursing* Lorene Halsted RN. *Medical Dir* Dr William Greenwood.
Licensure Skilled care; Intermediate care; Shelter care; Retirement; Alzheimer's care. *Beds* 46; Shelter care 16. *Certified* Medicaid; Medicare.
Owner Proprietary corp.
Admissions Requirements Minimum age 18; Medical examination; Physician's request.
Staff RNs 4 (ft), 1 (pt); LPNs 2 (ft); Nurses' aides 21 (ft); Physical therapists 1 (pt); Recreational therapists 1 (pt); Occupational therapists; Speech therapists; Activities coordinators 1 (ft); Dietitians 1 (pt).
Facilities Dining room; Activities room; Chapel; Crafts room; Laundry room; Barber/Beauty shop.
Activities Arts & crafts; Cards; Games; Reading groups; Prayer groups; Movies; Shopping trips; Dances/Social/Cultural gatherings.

Idaho County Nursing Home
W 722 North St, Grangeville, ID 83530
(208) 983-1470
Admin Douglas A Winter. *Dir of Nursing*
Carol Hackney. *Medical Dir* D J Soltman
MD.
Licensure Skilled care; Intermediate care. *Beds*
35. *Certified* Medicaid; Medicare.
Owner Nonprofit organization/foundation.
Admissions Requirements Minimum age 18;
Medical examination; Physician's request.
Staff Physicians; RNs; LPNs; Nurses' aides;
Physical therapists; Speech therapists;
Activities coordinators; Dietitians; Dentists.
Facilities Dining room; Activities room;
Crafts room; Laundry room; Barber/Beauty
shop.
Activities Arts & crafts; Cards; Games;
Reading groups; Prayer groups; Movies;
Shopping trips; Dances/Social/Cultural
gatherings.

Hailey

Blaine Manor
Box 927, Hailey, ID 83333
(208) 788-2222
Admin Gail Goglia RN.
Licensure Skilled care; Intermediate care. *Beds*
25. *Certified* Medicaid; Medicare.

Homedale

Homedale Care Center
PO Box A, 108 W Owyhee, Homedale, ID
83628
(208) 337-3168
Admin Rodney Roe.
Licensure Skilled care. *Beds* 38. *Certified*
Medicaid; Medicare.

Idaho Falls

Good Samaritan Center
840 E Elva, Idaho Falls, ID 83401
(208) 523-4795
Admin John Langemo.
Licensure Skilled care; Intermediate care;
Shelter care. *Beds* 120; Shelter care 24.
Certified Medicaid; Medicare.
Owner Nonprofit corp (Evangelical Lutheran/
Good Samaritan Society).
Affiliation Lutheran.

Idaho Falls Care Center
3111 Channing Way, Idaho Falls, ID 83404
(208) 529-0067
Admin Pat Gooding.
Licensure Skilled care; Intermediate care. *Beds*
108. *Certified* Medicaid; Medicare.

Idaho Falls Group Homes Inc
PO Box 50442, Idaho Falls, ID 83405
(208) 523-0053
Admin Rex Redden. *Dir of Nursing* Afton
Bills.
Licensure Intermediate care for mentally
retarded. *Beds* ICF/MR 16. *Certified*
Medicaid.
Owner Nonprofit organization/foundation.
Staff Physicians; RNs; LPNs; Nurses' aides;
Physical therapists; Recreational therapists;
Occupational therapists; Speech therapists;
Dietitians.
Facilities Dining room; Activities room;
Crafts room; Laundry room.
Activities Arts & crafts; Games; Reading
groups; Prayer groups; Movies; Shopping
trips; Pet therapy; Developmental workshop.

Valley Care Center
2725 E 17th, Idaho Falls, ID 83406
(208) 529-4567
Admin Fred Aufderheide.
Medical Dir Coy Lou Stephens.

Licensure Skilled care; Intermediate care. *Beds*
SNF; ICF 110. *Certified* Medicaid;
Medicare.
Owner Proprietary corp (National Heritage).
Admissions Requirements Minimum age 16;
Medical examination; Physician's request.
Staff RNs; LPNs; Nurses' aides; Activities
coordinators.
Languages Spanish.
Facilities Dining room; Physical therapy
room; Activities room; Chapel; Barber/
Beauty shop.
Activities Arts & crafts; Cards; Games;
Reading groups; Movies; Dances/Social/
Cultural gatherings.

Yellowstone Care Center
2460 S Yellowstone, Idaho Falls, ID 83401
(208) 523-9839
Admin Ferran Weeks.
Licensure Intermediate care for mentally
retarded. *Beds* ICF/MR 30. *Certified*
Medicaid.

Jerome

St Benedict's Family Medical Center Inc
709 N Lincoln, Jerome, ID 83338
(208) 324-4301
Admin David Farnes.
Medical Dir James Sloat MD.
Licensure Skilled care. *Beds* 40. *Certified*
Medicaid; Medicare.
Admissions Requirements Medical
examination; Physician's request.
Staff RNs 2 (ft), 1 (pt); LPNs 3 (ft), 2 (pt);
Nurses' aides 17 (ft), 9 (pt); Physical
therapists 1 (ft); Occupational therapists 1
(pt); Speech therapists 1 (pt); Activities
coordinators 1 (ft); Dietitians 1 (pt).
Affiliation Roman Catholic.
Facilities Dining room; Physical therapy
room; Activities room; Chapel; Barber/
Beauty shop.
Activities Arts & crafts; Cards; Games;
Reading groups; Prayer groups; Movies;
Dances/Social/Cultural gatherings.

Kellogg

Shoshone Living Center
Box 689, 601 W Cameron, Kellogg, ID 83837
(208) 784-1283
Admin Patsy Walker. *Dir of Nursing* Rita
Armor. *Medical Dir* Frederick Haller MD.
Licensure Skilled care; Intermediate care. *Beds*
SNF 68; ICF. *Certified* Medicaid; Medicare.
Owner Proprietary corp (Hillhaven Corp).
Admissions Requirements Physician's request.
Staff RNs 3 (ft), 1 (pt); LPNs 6 (ft); Nurses'
aides 28 (ft); Physical therapists 1 (pt);
Occupational therapists 1 (pt); Activities
coordinators 1 (ft); Dietitians 1 (pt); Dentists
1 (pt).
Facilities Dining room; Physical therapy
room; Activities room; Chapel; Crafts room;
Laundry room; Barber/Beauty shop.
Activities Arts & crafts; Cards; Games;
Reading groups; Prayer groups; Movies;
Shopping trips; Dances/Social/Cultural
gatherings.

Shoshone Medical Center Extended Care Unit
Jacobs Gulch, Kellogg, ID 83837
(208) 784-1221
Admin Langford Palmer.
Licensure Skilled care; Intermediate care. *Beds*
20. *Certified* Medicaid; Medicare.

Kimberly

Mountain View Care Center
Rte 1 Box X, Polk St E, Kimberly, ID 83341
(208) 423-5591
Admin Julie Johnson.

Licensure Skilled care; Intermediate care. *Beds*
64. *Certified* Medicaid; Medicare.
Owner Proprietary corp (National Heritage).

Kuna

Communicare Inc No 5
750 Swan Falls Rd, Kuna, ID 83634
(208) 922-1169
Admin Tom Whittemore.
Licensure Intermediate care for mentally
retarded. *Beds* ICF/MR 8. *Certified*
Medicaid.

Lewiston

Lewiston Care Center
3315 8th St, Lewiston, ID 83501
(208) 743-9543
Admin Turid K Reichert. *Dir of Nursing*
Mary Bodden. *Medical Dir* Richard M
Alford MD.
Licensure Skilled care; Intermediate care. *Beds*
Swing beds SNF/ICF 96. *Private Pay
Patients* 25%. *Certified* Medicaid; Medicare.
Owner Proprietary corp (Hillhaven Corp).
Staff RNs; LPNs; Nurses' aides; Activities
coordinators.
Languages Norwegian, Swedish, Danish,
German.
Facilities Dining room; Physical therapy
room; Activities room; Crafts room; Laundry
room; Barber/Beauty shop; Library; Social
Service conference/meeting room.
Activities Arts & crafts; Cards; Games;
Reading groups; Prayer groups; Movies;
Dances/Social/Cultural gatherings; Pet
therapy.

Orchards Villa Nursing Center
1014 Burrell Ave, Lewiston, ID 83501
(208) 743-4558
Admin Joe O'Donnell.
Licensure Skilled care; Intermediate care. *Beds*
140. *Certified* Medicaid; Medicare.

Malad

Oneida County Nursing Home
PO Box 182, 150 N 200 W, Malad, ID 83252
(208) 766-2231, 766-4819 FAX
Admin Jim L Russell. *Dir of Nursing* Paula
Gilbert RN. *Medical Dir* Stephen C Johnson
DO.
Licensure Skilled care; Intermediate care;
Retirement. *Beds* Swing beds SNF/ICF 24;
Retirement 25. *Private Pay Patients* 25%.
Certified Medicaid; Medicare.
Owner Publicly owned.
Admissions Requirements Medical
examination; Physician's request.
Staff Physicians 1 (pt); RNs 3 (ft), 1 (pt);
LPNs 5 (ft), 2 (pt); Nurses' aides 9 (ft), 1
(pt); Physical therapists 1 (ft); Recreational
therapists 1 (pt); Activities coordinators 1
(pt); Dietitians 1 (pt).
Facilities Dining room; Physical therapy
room; Activities room.
Activities Arts & crafts; Cards; Games; Prayer
groups; Movies.

McCall

Payette Lakes Care Center
PO Box P, 201 Floyd St, McCall, ID 83638
(208) 634-2112
Admin Ronald D Nelson.
Licensure Skilled care; Intermediate care. *Beds*
64. *Certified* Medicaid; Medicare.
Owner Proprietary corp (Beverly Enterprises).

Meridian

Gem State Homes Inc 2
40 W Franklin, Unit F, Meridian, ID 83642
(208) 888-1155

Admin Martin Landholm. *Dir of Nursing*
Leslie Madsen RN.
Licensure Intermediate care for mentally
retarded. *Beds* 16. *Certified* Medicaid.
Admissions Requirements Minimum age 6;
Medical examination.
Staff Physicians 1 (pt); RNs 1 (pt); LPNs 1
(pt); Physical therapists 1 (pt); Recreational
therapists 1 (pt); Speech therapists 1 (pt);
Dietitians 1 (pt); Ophthalmologists 1 (pt);
Podiatrists 1 (pt); Audiologists 1 (pt);
Dentists 1 (pt).
Activities Arts & crafts; Games; Movies;
Shopping trips; Dances/Social/Cultural
gatherings.

Tomorrows Hope Inc
4782 Armga Rd, Meridian, ID 83642
(208) 322-6550 or 322-6570
Admin Thair Pond.
Licensure Intermediate care for mentally
retarded. *Beds* ICF/MR 8. *Certified*
Medicaid.
Owner Nonprofit corp.
Admissions Requirements Minimum age 5;
Medical examination; Physician's request.
Staff Physicians 1 (pt); RNs 1 (pt); Nurses'
aides 9 (ft), 1 (pt); Recreational therapists 1
(pt); Occupational therapists 1 (pt); Speech
therapists 1 (pt); Activities coordinators 1
(pt); Dietitians 1 (pt); Ophthalmologists 1
(pt); Podiatrists 1 (pt); Dentists 1 (pt).
Facilities Dining room; Activities room;
Crafts room; Laundry room.
Activities Arts & crafts; Cards; Games;
Movies; Shopping trips; Dances/Social/
Cultural gatherings; Concerts; Bowling;
Swimming; Library.

Montpelier

Bear Lake Memorial Nursing Home
164 S 5th, Montpelier, ID 83254
(208) 847-1630
Admin Rod Jacobson.
Medical Dir R V Bjarnason DO.
Licensure Skilled care. *Beds* 37. *Certified*
Medicaid; Medicare.
Admissions Requirements Medical
examination; Physician's request.
Staff Physicians 4 (ft); RNs 2 (ft), 1 (pt);
LPNs 2 (ft), 2 (pt); Nurses' aides 13 (ft), 2
(pt); Physical therapists 1 (ft); Activities
coordinators 1 (ft); Dietitians 1 (pt); Dentists
3 (pt).
Facilities Dining room; Physical therapy
room; Activities room; Crafts room; Laundry
room; Barber/Beauty shop.
Activities Arts & crafts; Cards; Games;
Reading groups; Movies.

Moscow

Good Samaritan Village
640 N Eisenhower, Moscow, ID 83843
(208) 882-6560
Admin Michael Hinson. *Dir of Nursing*
Michelle Smith RN. *Medical Dir* Dr William
Marineau.
Licensure Skilled care; Retirement; Sheltered
care; Hospice; Home health care. *Beds* SNF
60; Retirement apts & duplexes 97;
Sheltered care 12. *Private Pay Patients* 80%.
Certified Medicaid; Medicare; VA.
Owner Nonprofit corp (Evangelical Lutheran/
Good Samaritan Society).
Admissions Requirements Medical
examination; Physician's request.
Staff RNs 8 (ft), 1 (pt); LPNs 6 (ft), 1 (pt);
Nurses' aides 20 (ft), 16 (pt); Physical
therapists 1 (pt); Recreational therapists 2
(ft), 1 (pt); Occupational therapists 1 (pt);
Speech therapists 1 (pt); Activities
coordinators 1 (ft); Dietitians 1 (pt);
Podiatrists 1 (pt).
Languages Indian.
Affiliation Lutheran.

Facilities Dining room; Physical therapy
room; Activities room; Chapel; Crafts room;
Laundry room; Barber/Beauty shop; Library.
Activities Arts & crafts; Cards; Games;
Reading groups; Prayer groups; Movies;
Shopping trips; Dances/Social/Cultural
gatherings; Intergenerational programs; Pet
therapy.

Latah Care Center Inc
W 510 Palouse River Dr, Moscow, ID 83843
(208) 882-7586
Admin Verla Olson. *Dir of Nursing* Sandy
Cameron. *Medical Dir* Frances Spain MD.
Licensure Skilled care; Sheltered care;
Retirement. *Beds* SNF 76; Sheltered care 42.
Certified Medicaid; Medicare.
Owner Nonprofit corp.
Admissions Requirements Minimum age 18;
Medical examination; Physician's request.
Staff RNs 10 (ft); LPNs 3 (ft); Nurses' aides
40 (ft); Physical therapists 7 (ft);
Recreational therapists 2 (ft); Dietitians 1
(pt).
Facilities Dining room; Activities room;
Crafts room; Laundry room; Barber/Beauty
shop; Library.
Activities Arts & crafts; Cards; Games;
Reading groups; Movies; Shopping trips;
Dances/Social/Cultural gatherings.

Moscow Care Center
Box 9406, 420 Rowe St, Moscow, ID 83843
(208) 882-4576
Admin David Parkhill.
Licensure Skilled care; Intermediate care. *Beds*
94. *Certified* Medicaid; Medicare.

Mountain Home

Elmore Memorial Nursing Home
PO Drawer H, Mountain Home, ID 83647
(208) 587-8401
Admin Jan Cox.
Licensure Skilled care. *Beds* 55. *Certified*
Medicaid; Medicare.

Nampa

Communicare Inc No 2
1210 W Boone St, Nampa, ID 83651
(208) 467-1617
Admin Tom Whittemore.
Licensure Intermediate care for mentally
retarded. *Beds* ICF/MR 8. *Certified*
Medicaid.

Gem State Homes Inc 1
512 Gem St, Nampa, ID 83651
(208) 467-7589
Admin Martin Landholm.
Licensure Intermediate care for mentally
retarded. *Beds* 8. *Certified* Medicaid.

Holly Care Center
472 Caldwell Blvd, Nampa, ID 83651
(208) 467-5721
Admin Meg Neumann.
Licensure Skilled care. *Beds* 50. *Certified*
Medicaid; Medicare.
Owner Proprietary corp (National Heritage).

Idaho State School & Hospital
3100 11th Ave N, Nampa, ID 83651
(208) 466-9255
Admin Nancy Gravley.
Licensure Intermediate care for mentally
retarded. *Beds* ICF/MR 250. *Certified*
Medicaid.

Midland Care Center
436C Midland Blvd, Nampa, ID 83651
(208) 466-7803
Admin Kathi Sillox. *Dir of Nursing* Irene
Decker. *Medical Dir* Dr Harold Brown.
Licensure Skilled care. *Beds* SNF 112. *Private
Pay Patients* 18%. *Certified* Medicaid;
Medicare.

Owner Proprietary corp (National Heritage).
Admissions Requirements Physician's request.
Staff RNs 5 (ft), 4 (pt); LPNs 10 (ft), 3 (pt);
Nurses' aides 36 (ft), 8 (pt); Physical
therapists 1 (ft); Occupational therapists 1
(ft); Speech therapists 1 (ft); Activities
coordinators 2 (ft); Dietitians 1 (ft).
Facilities Dining room; Activities room;
Crafts room; Laundry room; Barber/Beauty
shop; Library; Patio areas; Large backyard
area.
Activities Arts & crafts; Cards; Games;
Reading groups; Prayer groups; Movies;
Shopping trips; Dances/Social/Cultural
gatherings; Parties for staffs' children; Coffee
hours.

Nampa Care Center
404 Horton, Nampa, ID 83651-6599
(208) 466-9292
Admin Donna Lant. *Dir of Nursing* Millie
Holmes. *Medical Dir* Dr Michael Crim.
Licensure Skilled care; Intermediate care;
Alzheimer's care. *Beds* 151. *Certified*
Medicaid; Medicare.
Owner Proprietary corp (Hillhaven Corp).
Admissions Requirements Females only;
Medical examination.
Staff Physicians; RNs; LPNs; Nurses' aides;
Physical therapists; Occupational therapists;
Activities coordinators.
Languages Spanish.
Facilities Dining room; Physical therapy
room; Activities room; Laundry room;
Barber/Beauty shop.
Activities Arts & crafts; Cards; Games; Prayer
groups; Movies.

Sunny Ridge Health Services Center
2609 Sunnybrook Dr, Nampa, ID 83686
(208) 467-7298
Admin Janis Peters. *Dir of Nursing* Linda
Vail.
Licensure Skilled care; Retirement. *Beds* SNF
30. *Certified* Medicaid; Medicare.
Owner Privately owned.
Admissions Requirements Minimum age 55.
Staff RNs 3 (ft); LPNs 4 (ft), 1 (pt); Nurses'
aides 19 (ft); Activities coordinators 1 (ft);
Dietitians 1 (pt).
Languages Spanish.
Facilities Dining room; Crafts room; Laundry
room; Barber/Beauty shop; Library.
Activities Arts & crafts; Games; Prayer groups;
Movies; Dances/Social/Cultural gatherings;
Exercise group.

Orofino

Orofino Care Center
1225 School Rd, Orofino, ID 83544
(208) 476-4568
Admin Nancy Spencer. *Dir of Nursing* Jean
Stanton RN. *Medical Dir* Maurice Masar.
Licensure Skilled care; Intermediate care. *Beds*
SNF 45; ICF 15. *Private Pay Patients* 25%.
Certified Medicaid; Medicare.
Owner Proprietary corp (National Heritage).
Staff RNs 5 (ft); LPNs 5 (ft), 1 (pt); Nurses'
aides 35 (ft); Physical therapists (consultant);
Activities coordinators 1 (ft); Dietitians
(consultant).
Facilities Dining room; Activities room;
Laundry room; Barber/Beauty shop; Large
yard with grazing deer.
Activities Arts & crafts; Cards; Games;
Reading groups; Prayer groups; Movies;
Shopping trips; Dances/Social/Cultural
gatherings; Intergenerational programs; Van
outings; Image therapy.

Payette

Casa Loma Convalescent Center
1019 3rd Ave S, Payette, ID 83661
(208) 642-4455, 642-9412 FAX

Admin Kenneth G Salerno. *Dir of Nursing* Colleen Dawson RN. *Medical Dir* Eugene Carroll MD.
Licensure Skilled care. *Beds* SNF 103. *Private Pay Patients* 10%. *Certified* Medicaid; Medicare.
Owner Privately owned.
Admissions Requirements Physician's request.
Staff RNs 7 (ft), 2 (pt); LPNs 7 (ft); Nurses' aides 40 (ft), 7 (pt); Physical therapists 1 (ft); Reality therapists (contracted); Recreational therapists (contracted); Occupational therapists (contracted); Speech therapists (contracted); Dietitians 1 (pt).
Facilities Dining room; Physical therapy room; Activities room; Barber/Beauty shop.
Activities Arts & crafts; Games; Reading groups; Prayer groups; Movies; Dances/Social/Cultural gatherings.

Pocatello

Bannock County Nursing Home
527 Memorial Dr, Pocatello, ID 83201
(208) 232-8956
Admin Evelyn Richmond, Assoc Admin. *Dir of Nursing* Evelyn Richmond.
Licensure Skilled care; Intermediate care. *Beds* 56. *Certified* Medicaid; Medicare.
Owner Publicly owned.
Admissions Requirements Physician's request.
Staff RNs 1 (ft), 3 (pt); LPNs 1 (ft), 6 (pt); Nurses' aides 8 (ft), 21 (pt); Activities coordinators 1 (ft); Dietitians 1 (pt).
Facilities Dining room; Physical therapy room; Activities room; Crafts room; Laundry room; Barber/Beauty shop.
Activities Arts & crafts; Cards; Games; Dances/Social/Cultural gatherings.

Hillcrest Haven Convalescent Center
1071 Renee Ave, Pocatello, ID 83201
(208) 233-1411
Admin Kevin P Ryan.
Licensure Skilled care. *Beds* 113. *Certified* Medicaid; Medicare.

Rulon House
2369 Rulon, Pocatello, ID 83201
(208) 237-5538
Admin Frances L Roberts.
Licensure Intermediate care for mentally retarded. *Beds* ICF/MR 8. *Certified* Medicaid.
Owner Nonprofit corp.
Admissions Requirements Minimum age 18.
Staff LPNs 1 (pt).
Languages Spanish.
Activities Arts & crafts; Cards; Games; Movies; Shopping trips.

Skyline Healthcare
2200 E Terry, Pocatello, ID 83201
(208) 232-2570, 232-2583 FAX
Admin Linda Sharp. *Dir of Nursing* Donita Christensen. *Medical Dir* Jean Bokelmann MD.
Licensure Skilled care; Intermediate care. *Beds* SNF 121; ICF 121. *Private Pay Patients* 30%. *Certified* Medicaid; Medicare.
Owner Proprietary corp (Beverly Enterprises).
Admissions Requirements Medical examination; Physician's request.
Staff RNs 5 (ft), 2 (pt); LPNs 8 (ft), 2 (pt); Nurses' aides 45 (ft), 5 (pt); Physical therapists 2 (pt); Occupational therapists 1 (pt); Speech therapists 1 (pt); Activities coordinators 1 (ft); Dietitians 1 (pt); Podiatrists 1 (pt).
Facilities Dining room; Physical therapy room; Activities room; Laundry room; Barber/Beauty shop; Library.
Activities Arts & crafts; Cards; Games; Reading groups; Prayer groups; Movies; Shopping trips; Dances/Social/Cultural gatherings; Intergenerational programs; Pet therapy.

South Park Inc
3625 Vaughn, Pocatello, ID 83204
(208) 233-6833
Admin Russell C McCoy. *Dir of Nursing* Christy Day.
Licensure Intermediate care for mentally retarded; Integrated living/Personal care. *Beds* ICF/MR 23; Integrated living/Personal care 5. *Private Pay Patients* 0%. *Certified* Medicaid.
Owner Nonprofit corp.
Admissions Requirements Minimum age 18.
Staff LPNs 2 (ft), 1 (pt); Physical therapists 1 (pt); Recreational therapists 1 (pt); Speech therapists 1 (pt); Activities coordinators 1 (ft); Dietitians 1 (pt).
Facilities Dining room; Physical therapy room; Activities room; Laundry room.
Activities Arts & crafts; Games; Reading groups; Movies; Shopping trips; Dances/Social/Cultural gatherings.

Post Falls

Alpha Health Services Inc No 1
201 Park Ave, Post Falls, ID 83854
(208) 773-1521
Admin Michael C Breault.
Licensure Intermediate care for mentally retarded. *Beds* 8. *Certified* Medicaid.

Alpha Health Services Inc No 2
233 Eastwood, Post Falls, ID 83854
(208) 773-1521
Admin Michael C Breault.
Licensure Intermediate care for mentally retarded. *Beds* 8. *Certified* Medicaid.

Alpha Health Services Inc No 3
2572 Pioneer Ridge, Post Falls, ID 83854
(208) 773-1521
Admin Michael C Breault.
Licensure Intermediate care for mentally retarded. *Beds* 8. *Certified* Medicaid.

Preston

Franklin County Nursing Home
44 N 1st St E, Preston, ID 83263
(208) 852-0137
Admin Michael G Andrus. *Dir of Nursing* Maurene Hodges RN. *Medical Dir* Rodney Grover DO.
Licensure Skilled care; Intermediate care. *Beds* 45. *Certified* Medicaid; Medicare.
Owner Publicly owned.
Admissions Requirements Medical examination; Physician's request.
Staff Physicians 3 (ft); RNs 1 (ft), 1 (pt); LPNs 5 (ft), 3 (pt); Nurses' aides 20 (ft), 11 (pt); Physical therapists 1 (pt); Activities coordinators 1 (ft); Dietitians 1 (pt); Social workers 1 (pt).
Facilities Dining room; Physical therapy room; Activities room; Crafts room; Laundry room; Barber/Beauty shop; Library.
Activities Arts & crafts; Games; Reading groups; Prayer groups; Movies; Dances/Social/Cultural gatherings.

Rexburg

Rexburg Nursing Center
660 S 2 W, Rexburg, ID 83440
(208) 356-0220
Admin Richard L Wheeler. *Dir of Nursing* Rosemary Brown. *Medical Dir* Dr Lester J Peterson.
Licensure Skilled care. *Beds* SNF 120. *Private Pay Patients* 40%. *Certified* Medicaid; Medicare.
Owner Privately owned.
Admissions Requirements Medical examination; Physician's request.
Staff RNs; LPNs; Nurses' aides; Physical therapists.

Facilities Dining room; Physical therapy room; Activities room; Laundry room; Barber/Beauty shop; Library.
Activities Arts & crafts; Cards; Games; Reading groups; Prayer groups; Movies; Shopping trips; Dances/Social/Cultural gatherings; Intergenerational programs; Pet therapy; Community interaction.

Rupert

Minidoka Memorial Hospital & Extended Care Facility
1224 8th St, Rupert, ID 83350
(208) 436-0481, 436-0500 FAX
Admin Ed Richardson. *Dir of Nursing* Mary Kamp RN CNA. *Medical Dir* Howard Crawford MD.
Licensure Skilled care; Intermediate care. *Beds* Swing beds SNF/ICF 78. *Certified* Medicaid; Medicare.
Owner Publicly owned.
Admissions Requirements Medical examination; Physician's request.
Staff Physicians 6 (pt); RNs 1 (ft), 6 (pt); LPNs 10 (ft), 4 (pt); Nurses' aides 17 (ft), 27 (pt); Physical therapists 1 (ft); Occupational therapists 1 (pt); Speech therapists 1 (pt); Activities coordinators 1 (ft); Dietitians 1 (pt).
Languages Spanish, Basque, French.
Facilities Dining room; Physical therapy room; Activities room; Crafts room; Laundry room; Barber/Beauty shop; Library; Solariums; TV room; Patios; Fireplace room.
Activities Arts & crafts; Cards; Games; Reading groups; Prayer groups; Movies; Shopping trips; Dances/Social/Cultural gatherings; Dinners for residents, staff, families, and guests.

Saint Maries

Bethesda Care Center
820 Elm St, Saint Maries, ID 83861
(208) 245-4576
Admin Scott Burpee. *Dir of Nursing* Shirley White. *Medical Dir* Dr Katovich.
Licensure Skilled care; Intermediate care. *Beds* SNF; ICF 59. *Certified* Medicaid; Medicare.
Owner Nonprofit corp (Bethesda Care Centers).
Admissions Requirements Medical examination; Physician's request.
Staff RNs 2 (ft), 2 (pt); LPNs 4 (ft), 3 (pt); Nurses' aides 18 (ft), 5 (pt); Activities coordinators 1 (ft), 1 (pt).
Facilities Dining room; Physical therapy room; Activities room; Chapel; Crafts room; Laundry room; Barber/Beauty shop.
Activities Arts & crafts; Cards; Games; Reading groups; Prayer groups; Movies; Shopping trips; Dances/Social/Cultural gatherings; Pet therapy program.

Valley Vista Care Center
820 Elm St, Saint Maries, ID 83861
(208) 245-4576
Admin Scott Burpee.
Licensure Skilled care; Intermediate care. *Beds* 60. *Certified* Medicaid; Medicare.

Salmon

Salmon Valley Care Center
PO Box 221, Rte 1, Airport Rd, Salmon, ID 83467
(208) 756-3543
Admin Steven Lish.
Licensure Intermediate care. *Beds* 40. *Certified* Medicaid; Medicare.
Admissions Requirements Physician's request.
Staff RNs 2 (ft), 1 (pt); LPNs 3 (ft); Nurses' aides 6 (ft), 2 (pt); Activities coordinators 1 (pt).

Facilities Dining room; Activities room; Chapel; Crafts room; Laundry room; Barber/Beauty shop; Library; Garden room.
Activities Arts & crafts; Cards; Games; Reading groups; Prayer groups; Movies; Shopping trips; Dances/Social/Cultural gatherings.

Sandpoint

Sandpoint Manor
220 S Division, Sandpoint, ID 83864
(208) 265-4514
Admin Craig A Johnson.
Medical Dir Dr H Leedy.
Licensure Skilled care; Intermediate care. *Beds* 89. *Certified* Medicaid; Medicare.
Staff RNs 5 (ft), 4 (pt); LPNs 2 (ft), 2 (pt); Nurses' aides 25 (ft), 18 (pt); Physical therapists 1 (ft), 1 (pt); Occupational therapists 1 (pt); Speech therapists 1 (pt); Activities coordinators 1 (ft); Dietitians 1 (ft); Dentists 1 (pt).
Facilities Dining room; Physical therapy room; Activities room; Chapel; Crafts room; Laundry room; Barber/Beauty shop.
Activities Arts & crafts; Cards; Games; Movies; Shopping trips; Dances/Social/Cultural gatherings.

Shoshone

Wood River Convalescent Center
511 E 4th St, Shoshone, ID 83352
(208) 886-2228
Admin Samantha D Lopez. *Dir of Nursing* Chris Arrate RN. *Medical Dir* Keith Davis MD.
Licensure Skilled care; Alzheimer's care. *Beds* SNF 40. *Certified* Medicaid; Medicare; VA.
Owner Publicly owned.
Admissions Requirements Medical examination; Physician's request.
Staff Physicians 1 (pt); RNs 2 (ft), 1 (pt); LPNs 2 (ft), 3 (pt); Nurses' aides 10 (ft), 3 (pt); Physical therapists 1 (pt); Activities coordinators 1 (pt); Restorative therapists 2 (ft).
Facilities Dining room; Activities room; Laundry room.
Activities Arts & crafts; Cards; Games; Reading groups; Prayer groups; Movies; Shopping trips.

Silverton

Silver Wood Good Samaritan
Box 358, Silverton, ID 83867
(208) 556-1147
Admin Gary Bokelman. *Dir of Nursing* Louise A West RN. *Medical Dir* Thomas F Prenger MD.

Licensure Skilled care; Intermediate care; Retirement. *Beds* Swing beds SNF/ICF 89; Retirement apartments 13. *Private Pay Patients* 30%. *Certified* Medicaid; Medicare.
Owner Nonprofit corp (Evangelical Lutheran/Good Samaritan Society).
Admissions Requirements Minimum age 16; Medical examination; Physician's request.
Staff RNs 1 (ft), 3 (pt); LPNs 4 (ft), 4 (pt); Nurses' aides 12 (ft), 20 (pt); Physical therapists 1 (pt); Recreational therapists 1 (ft); Activities coordinators 1 (ft); Dietitians 1 (pt).
Affiliation Lutheran.
Facilities Dining room; Physical therapy room; Activities room; Chapel; Crafts room; Laundry room; Barber/Beauty shop; Multi-purpose/public meeting room.
Activities Arts & crafts; Cards; Games; Reading groups; Prayer groups; Movies; Shopping trips; Dances/Social/Cultural gatherings; Intergenerational programs; Pet therapy; Volunteer program.

Soda Springs

Caribou Memorial Nursing Home
300 S Third W, Soda Springs, ID 83276
(208) 547-3341
Admin Dell Maughan.
Licensure Skilled care. *Beds* 37. *Certified* Medicaid; Medicare.

Twin Falls

Clearwater Care Center
162 Blake St N, Twin Falls, ID 83301
(208) 734-8973
Admin Mike Hutchings.
Licensure Intermediate care for mentally retarded. *Beds* ICF/MR 15. *Certified* Medicaid.

Twin Falls Care Center
674 Eastland, Twin Falls, ID 83301
(208) 734-4264
Admin Helen Shewmaker.
Licensure Skilled care; Intermediate care. *Beds* 60. *Certified* Medicaid; Medicare.

West Magic Care Center
640 Filer Ave W, Twin Falls, ID 83301
(208) 734-8645
Admin Joyce Ellis. *Dir of Nursing* Susan Wegener RN. *Medical Dir* A C Emery MD.
Licensure Skilled care. *Beds* SNF 184. *Private Pay Patients* 45%. *Certified* Medicaid; Medicare.
Owner Proprietary corp (Western Health Care).
Admissions Requirements Medical examination; Physician's request.
Staff Physicians 2 (pt); RNs 7 (ft), 4 (pt); LPNs 15 (ft), 6 (pt); Nurses' aides 80 (ft), 10 (pt); Physical therapists 1 (pt); Recreational

therapists 1 (ft); Occupational therapists 1 (pt); Speech therapists 1 (pt); Activities coordinators 1 (ft); Dietitians 1 (pt).
Languages Hispanic.
Facilities Dining room; Physical therapy room; Activities room; Crafts room; Laundry room; Barber/Beauty shop; Library.
Activities Arts & crafts; Cards; Games; Reading groups; Prayer groups; Movies; Shopping trips; Dances/Social/Cultural gatherings; Intergenerational programs; Pet therapy.

Weiser

Communicare Inc No 6
80 E Park St, Weiser, ID 83642
(208) 549-3317
Admin Tom Whittemore.
Licensure Intermediate care for mentally retarded. *Beds* ICF/MR 15. *Certified* Medicaid.

Weiser Care Center
331 E Park St, Weiser, ID 83672
(208) 549-2416
Admin Ruth Beams. *Dir of Nursing* Janice Allen RN. *Medical Dir* Dr Richard Giever.
Licensure Skilled care. *Beds* SNF 89. *Certified* Medicaid; Medicare.
Owner Proprietary corp (Hillhaven Corp).
Admissions Requirements Minimum age 18.
Staff RNs 4 (ft), 3 (pt); LPNs 5 (ft), 1 (pt); Nurses' aides 25 (ft), 9 (pt); Physical therapists 1 (ft); Activities coordinators 1 (ft), 1 (pt).
Facilities Dining room; Physical therapy room; Activities room; Laundry room; Barber/Beauty shop.
Activities Arts & crafts; Games; Reading groups; Prayer groups; Movies; Shopping trips.

Wendell

Magic Valley Manor
PO Box 306, N Idaho St, Wendell, ID 83355
(208) 536-6623
Admin Louise Hranac.
Medical Dir Mark Spencer MD.
Licensure Skilled care. *Beds* 40. *Certified* Medicaid; Medicare.
Owner Proprietary corp (Beverly Enterprises).
Staff Physicians 1 (pt); RNs 1 (ft), 2 (pt); LPNs 1 (ft), 2 (pt); Nurses' aides 6 (ft), 5 (pt); Physical therapists 1 (pt); Occupational therapists 1 (pt); Speech therapists 1 (pt); Activities coordinators 1 (ft); Dietitians 1 (pt); Dentists 1 (pt).
Facilities Dining room; Activities room; Laundry room.
Activities Arts & crafts; Cards; Games; Prayer groups; Movies; Shopping trips; Dances/Social/Cultural gatherings.

ILLINOIS

Abingdon

Care Center of Abingdon
2000 W Martin St, Abingdon, IL 61410
(309) 462-2356
Admin J Michael Bibo.
Licensure Skilled care. *Beds* 74. *Certified*
Medicaid.
Owner Proprietary corp.

Addison

Iona Glos Specialized Living Center
50 S Fairbank St, Addison, IL 60101
(708) 543-2440
Admin Laura Abernathy.
Medical Dir Gail Ing.
Licensure Intermediate care for mentally
retarded. *Beds* ICF/MR 100. *Certified*
Medicaid.
Owner Nonprofit organization/foundation.
Admissions Requirements Minimum age 18.
Staff RNs 1 (ft); LPNs 4 (ft), 1 (pt); Nurses'
aides 56 (ft), 48 (pt); Occupational therapists
1 (ft); Speech therapists 1 (ft); Activities
coordinators 1 (ft); Dietitians 1 (pt); Social
workers 1 (ft).
Facilities Dining room; Activities room;
Crafts room; Laundry room; 6 Individual
homes.
Activities Arts & crafts; Games; Reading
groups; Movies; Shopping trips; Dances/
Social/Cultural gatherings; Special Olympics;
Social clubs; Community outings.

Albion

Rest Haven Manor Inc
120 W Main, Albion, IL 62806
(618) 445-2815
Admin Jane A Harris.
Licensure Intermediate care. *Beds* 49.
Certified Medicaid.
Owner Proprietary corp.

Aledo

Aledo Health Care Center
3rd Ave at 12th St SW, Aledo, IL 61231
(309) 582-5376
Admin Becky L Rasmussen. *Dir of Nursing*
Diane Calderone. *Medical Dir* Dennis
Palmer.
Licensure Skilled care; Alzheimer's care. *Beds*
SNF 96; Alzheimer's care 10. *Private Pay*
Patients 26%. *Certified* Medicaid; Medicare.
Owner Proprietary corp (Convalescent
Management Association Inc).
Admissions Requirements Minimum age 18.
Staff Physicians 1 (pt); RNs 5 (ft); LPNs 6
(ft), 1 (pt); Nurses' aides 25 (ft), 20 (pt);
Physical therapists 1 (pt); Occupational
therapists 1 (pt); Activities coordinators 1
(ft), 1 (pt); Dietitians 1 (pt); Podiatrists 1
(pt).

Facilities Dining room; Physical therapy
room; Activities room; Laundry room;
Barber/Beauty shop.
Activities Arts & crafts; Cards; Reading
groups; Prayer groups; Movies; Shopping
trips; Dances/Social/Cultural gatherings;
Intergenerational programs; Pet therapy.

Mercer County Nursing Home
NW 9th Ave & NW 3rd St, Aledo, IL 61231
(309) 582-5361
Admin Frederick J Ehrenhart.
Licensure Intermediate care. *Beds* 95.
Certified Medicaid.
Owner Publicly owned.

Alhambra

Hampton Nursing Care Inc
PO Box 237, Main & Warsaw Sts, Alhambra,
IL 62001
(618) 488-3565
Admin Carolyn Gibbons.
Medical Dir Betty Zweck.
Licensure Intermediate care. *Beds* ICF 87.
Certified Medicaid.
Owner Proprietary corp.
Staff RNs 1 (ft); LPNs 6 (ft), 2 (pt); Nurses'
aides 23 (ft).
Facilities Dining room; Activities room;
Crafts room; Laundry room; Barber/Beauty
shop.
Activities Arts & crafts; Cards; Games;
Reading groups; Prayer groups; Movies;
Shopping trips; Dances/Social/Cultural
gatherings.

Hitz Memorial Home
PO Box 79, Belle St, Alhambra, IL 62001
(618) 488-2355
Admin Jon R Lyerla. *Dir of Nursing* Ida M
Nuernberger RN. *Medical Dir* Dr Edward
Hediger.
Licensure Intermediate care. *Beds* ICF 67.
Certified Medicaid.
Owner Nonprofit corp.
Admissions Requirements Minimum age 55;
Medical examination; Physician's request.
Staff RNs 2 (ft), 2 (pt); LPNs 4 (ft), 1 (pt);
Nurses' aides 18 (ft), 7 (pt); Physical
therapists 1 (pt); Speech therapists 1 (pt);
Activities coordinators 1 (ft), 1 (pt);
Dietitians 1 (pt); Podiatrists 1 (pt); Dentists
1 (pt).
Affiliation Church of Christ.
Facilities Dining room; Physical therapy
room; Activities room; Crafts room; Laundry
room; Barber/Beauty shop; Library.
Activities Arts & crafts; Cards; Games;
Movies; Shopping trips; Dances/Social/
Cultural gatherings.

Altamont

Lutheran Care Center
Hwy 40 W, Altamont, IL 62411
(618) 483-6136

Admin David Wendler. *Dir of Nursing* Karen
Hille RN. *Medical Dir* Dr Delbert G
Huelskoetter.
Licensure Skilled care. *Beds* SNF 96. *Private*
Pay Patients 65%. *Certified* Medicaid;
Medicare.
Owner Nonprofit corp.
Admissions Requirements Minimum age 20;
Medical examination.
Staff Physicians 1 (ft); RNs 5 (ft), 2 (pt);
LPNs 8 (ft), 2 (pt); Nurses' aides 45 (ft), 6
(pt); Physical therapists 1 (pt); Occupational
therapists 1 (pt); Speech therapists 1 (pt);
Activities coordinators 3 (ft); Dietitians 1
(ft).
Affiliation Lutheran.
Facilities Dining room; Physical therapy
room; Activities room; Chapel; Crafts room;
Laundry room; Barber/Beauty shop; Library.
Activities Arts & crafts; Cards; Games;
Reading groups; Prayer groups; Movies;
Shopping trips; Dances/Social/Cultural
gatherings; Intergenerational programs; Pet
therapy.

Alton

Burt Sheltered Care Home
1414 Milton Rd, Alton, IL 62002
(618) 465-1351
Admin Mary Jo Swengrosh.
Licensure Sheltered care. *Beds* 29.
Owner Nonprofit corp.

Eldercare of Alton
3523 Wickenhauser, Alton, IL 62002
(618) 465-8887
Admin Joyce A Wild.
Licensure Skilled care; Intermediate care. *Beds*
SNF 147; ICF 49. *Certified* Medicaid;
Medicare.
Owner Proprietary corp.

Lifecare Center of Alton Inc
2349 Virden St, Alton, IL 62002
(618) 466-5331, 466-1446 FAX
Admin Nancy L Pryor. *Dir of Nursing*
Jeanette Schuh. *Medical Dir* Dr Suntra.
Licensure Intermediate care. *Beds* ICF 43.
Private Pay Patients 20%. *Certified*
Medicaid.
Owner Proprietary corp (Community Lifecare
Enterprises).
Admissions Requirements Minimum age 18.
Staff Physicians 1 (pt); RNs 1 (pt); LPNs 5
(ft); Nurses' aides 8 (ft), 5 (pt); Physical
therapists 1 (pt); Recreational therapists 1
(pt); Activities coordinators 1 (ft); Dietitians
1 (ft); Ophthalmologists 1 (pt); Podiatrists 1
(pt); Audiologists 1 (pt).
Facilities Dining room; Activities room;
Laundry room; Barber/Beauty shop.
Activities Arts & crafts; Cards; Games;
Reading groups; Prayer groups; Movies;
Shopping trips; Dances/Social/Cultural
gatherings; Intergenerational programs; Pet
therapy.

Eunice C Smith
1251 College Ave, Alton, IL 62002
(618) 463-7330
Admin Starkey Sloan. *Dir of Nursing* Marcella Keene. *Medical Dir* Chris Green.
Licensure Skilled care. *Beds* SNF 64. *Private Pay Patients* 100%. *Certified* Medicare.
Owner Nonprofit organization/foundation.
Admissions Requirements Minimum age 18.
Staff RNs; LPNs; Nurses' aides; Recreational therapists; Occupational therapists; Speech therapists; Dietitians.
Facilities Dining room; Physical therapy room; Activities room; Barber/Beauty shop.
Activities Arts & crafts; Cards; Games; Reading groups; Prayer groups; Movies.

Amboy

Mapleside Manor
15 W Wasson Rd, Amboy, IL 61310
(815) 857-2550
Admin Morris F Forman. *Dir of Nursing* Margaret L Otto RN. *Medical Dir* Pervez A Khan MD.
Licensure Skilled care. *Beds* SNF 97. *Certified* Medicaid; Medicare.
Owner Proprietary corp.
Admissions Requirements Minimum age 18.
Staff RNs 2 (ft), 2 (pt); LPNs 3 (ft), 5 (pt); Nurses' aides 20 (ft), 15 (pt); Recreational therapists 3 (ft).
Facilities Dining room; Physical therapy room; Activities room; Crafts room; Laundry room; Barber/Beauty shop; Library.
Activities Arts & crafts; Cards; Games; Reading groups; Prayer groups; Movies; Shopping trips; Dances/Social/Cultural gatherings.

Anna

City Care Center
Rte 1, Brady Mill Rd, Anna, IL 62906
(618) 833-6343
Admin Patricia L Chamness. *Dir of Nursing* Margaret Ury.
Licensure Skilled care. *Beds* SNF 70. *Certified* Medicaid.
Owner Privately owned.
Staff RNs 2 (ft); LPNs 4 (ft); Nurses' aides 25 (ft), 3 (pt); Activities coordinators 1 (ft); Dietitians 1 (ft); Housekeeping 6 (ft); Laundry 2 (ft); Cooks 6 (ft).
Facilities Dining room; Activities room; Crafts room; Laundry room; Barber/Beauty shop; Family lounge.
Activities Arts & crafts; Cards; Games; Reading groups; Prayer groups; Movies; Shopping trips; Dances/Social/Cultural gatherings.

Holly Hill
203 Lafayette St, Anna, IL 62906
(618) 833-3322
Admin James A Keller. *Dir of Nursing* Diana Alley RN.
Licensure Intermediate care for mentally retarded. *Beds* ICF/MR 15. *Certified* Medicaid.
Owner Privately owned.
Admissions Requirements Minimum age 18; Physician's request.
Staff RNs 1 (pt); Nurses' aides 3 (ft), 1 (pt).
Facilities Dining room; Activities room; Crafts room; Laundry room.
Activities Arts & crafts; Cards; Games; Reading groups; Prayer groups; Movies; Shopping trips; Dances/Social/Cultural gatherings.

Mulberry Manor Inc
612 E Davie St, Box 88, Anna, IL 62906
(618) 833-6012
Admin Joann A Keller.
Medical Dir William H Whiting MD.

Licensure Intermediate care for mentally retarded. *Beds* ICF/MR 80. *Certified* Medicaid.
Owner Proprietary corp.
Admissions Requirements Minimum age 18; Medical examination; Physician's request.
Staff RNs; LPNs; Nurses' aides; Activities coordinators.
Facilities Dining room; Physical therapy room; Activities room; Laundry room; Barber/Beauty shop; Lounge; Living room.
Activities Arts & crafts; Cards; Games; Reading groups; Prayer groups; Movies; Shopping trips; Dances/Social/Cultural gatherings.

New Way Inc
Rte 1, Anna, IL 62906
(618) 833-2299
Admin Patricia A Lewis. *Dir of Nursing* Donna Swink RSD. *Medical Dir* Dr William Whiting.
Licensure Intermediate care for mentally retarded. *Beds* ICF/MR 15. *Certified* Medicaid.
Owner Proprietary corp.
Admissions Requirements Minimum age 18; Medical examination.
Staff Physicians; RNs; LPNs; Nurses' aides; Physical therapists (consultant); Recreational therapists; Occupational therapists; Speech therapists; Activities coordinators; Dietitians (consultant); Audiologists.
Facilities Dining room; Activities room; Crafts room; Laundry room; Swimming pool.
Activities Arts & crafts; Cards; Games; Movies; Shopping trips; Dances/Social/Cultural gatherings; Pet therapy; ADL Training; Community living skills.

Union County Skilled Nursing Home
517 N Main St, Anna, IL 62906
(618) 833-4511
Admin Eugene A Helfrich. *Dir of Nursing* Carol Goodman. *Medical Dir* Marvin Powers MD.
Licensure Skilled care. *Beds* SNF 60. *Certified* Medicaid; Medicare.
Owner Publicly owned.
Admissions Requirements Medical examination.
Staff Physicians 9 (pt); RNs 2 (ft), 4 (pt); LPNs 5 (ft), 3 (pt); Nurses' aides 15 (ft), 5 (pt); Physical therapists 1 (ft); Speech therapists 1 (pt); Activities coordinators 1 (ft); Dietitians 1 (pt).
Facilities Dining room; Physical therapy room; Activities room; Crafts room; Barber/Beauty shop.
Activities Arts & crafts; Cards; Games; Reading groups; Prayer groups; Shopping trips.

Arcola

Hope House
102-104 E 2nd South St, Arcola, IL 61910
(217) 268-3732
Admin Alan G Ryle.
Licensure Intermediate care for mentally retarded. *Beds* ICF/MR 15.

We Care Nursing Facility
422 E 4th, Arcola, IL 61910
(217) 268-3555
Admin Michael E Martin. *Dir of Nursing* Michelle Franklin. *Medical Dir* Aarun Bajaj MD.
Licensure Intermediate care. *Beds* ICF 109. *Private Pay Patients* 25%. *Certified* Medicaid.
Owner Privately owned.
Admissions Requirements Minimum age 18; Medical examination.

Staff RNs; LPNs; Nurses' aides; Physical therapists; Occupational therapists; Speech therapists; Activities coordinators; Dietitians; Podiatrists.
Languages Spanish.
Facilities Dining room; Physical therapy room; Activities room; Crafts room; Laundry room; Barber/Beauty shop; Library.
Activities Arts & crafts; Cards; Games; Reading groups; Prayer groups; Movies; Shopping trips; Dances/Social/Cultural gatherings; Intergenerational programs; Pet therapy.

Arlington Heights

Americana Healthcare Center of Arlington Heights
715 W Central Rd, Arlington Heights, IL 60005
(708) 392-2020
Admin Janice Podwika. *Dir of Nursing* Debra Wexler. *Medical Dir* Dr Cameron Thomson.
Licensure Skilled care. *Beds* SNF 151. *Private Pay Patients* 85%. *Certified* Medicare.
Owner Proprietary corp (Manor HealthCare).
Admissions Requirements Minimum age 22.
Staff RNs 20 (ft), 2 (pt); LPNs 3 (ft); Nurses' aides 37 (ft); Physical therapists 1 (ft); Reality therapists 3 (ft); Recreational therapists 5 (ft); Occupational therapists 1 (ft), 2 (pt); Speech therapists 1 (ft); Activities coordinators 1 (ft); Dietitians 1 (ft); Podiatrists 1 (pt).
Facilities Dining room; Physical therapy room; Activities room; Crafts room; Barber/Beauty shop.
Activities Arts & crafts; Cards; Games; Reading groups; Prayer groups; Movies; Shopping trips; Dances/Social/Cultural gatherings; Intergenerational programs; Pet therapy.

Church Creek—A Marriott Retirement Community & Health Care Center
1200 W Central Rd, Arlington Heights, IL 60005
(708) 506-3200, 506-2598 FAX
Admin J Michael Eden. *Dir of Nursing* Judy Schillace RN. *Medical Dir* Dr Frank Carter.
Licensure Skilled care; Intermediate care; Hospice; Assisted living. *Beds* SNF 100; ICF 50; Medicare 10. *Private Pay Patients* 100%. *Certified* Medicare.
Owner Proprietary corp (Marriott Senior Living Services).
Admissions Requirements Minimum age 62; Medical examination; Physician's request.
Staff Physicians 3 (pt); RNs 12 (ft), 4 (pt); LPNs 4 (ft), 2 (pt); Nurses' aides 15 (ft), 15 (pt); Physical therapists 2 (ft), 1 (pt); Recreational therapists 1 (ft); Occupational therapists 1 (pt); Speech therapists 1 (pt); Activities coordinators 1 (ft), 1 (pt); Dietitians 1 (pt); Podiatrists 1 (pt); Audiologists 1 (pt).
Facilities Dining room; Physical therapy room; Activities room; Barber/Beauty shop; Library.
Activities Arts & crafts; Cards; Games; Reading groups; Prayer groups; Movies; Shopping trips; Dances/Social/Cultural gatherings; Intergenerational programs; Pet therapy; Field trips.

Clearbrook House
420 S Walnut, Arlington Heights, IL 60005
(708) 259-6820
Admin Rosanna McLain.
Licensure Community living facility. *Beds* Community living facility 20.

Lutheran Home & Services for the Aged
800 W Oakton St, Arlington Heights, IL 60004
(708) 253-3710

Admin Roger W Paulsberg. *Dir of Nursing* Shirley Maurer. *Medical Dir* Theodore M Homa MD.
Licensure Skilled care; Intermediate care for mentally retarded; Sheltered care; Alzheimer's care; Retirement. *Beds* SNF 252; ICF/MR 60; Sheltered care 167. *Private Pay Patients* 55%. *Certified* Medicaid.
Owner Nonprofit corp.
Admissions Requirements Minimum age 60; Medical examination.
Staff Physicians 3 (pt); RNs 15 (ft), 16 (pt); LPNs 5 (ft), 9 (pt); Nurses' aides 52 (ft), 69 (pt); Physical therapists 1 (ft); Reality therapists 2 (ft); Recreational therapists 2 (ft); Occupational therapists 1 (pt); Speech therapists 1 (pt); Activities coordinators 2 (ft); Dietitians 2 (ft); Ophthalmologists 1 (pt); Podiatrists 1 (pt); Audiologists 1 (pt); Chaplains 1 (ft).
Affiliation Lutheran.
Facilities Dining room; Physical therapy room; Activities room; Chapel; Crafts room; Laundry room; Barber/Beauty shop; Library.
Activities Arts & crafts; Cards; Games; Reading groups; Prayer groups; Movies; Shopping trips; Dances/Social/Cultural gatherings; Intergenerational programs; Pet therapy.

Moorings Health Center
811 E Central Rd, Arlington Heights, IL 60005
(708) 437-6700
Admin Arleene H Wajda. *Dir of Nursing* Lily Corasco RN. *Medical Dir* Morris Binder MD.
Licensure Intermediate care; Sheltered care. *Beds* ICF 32; Sheltered care 89. *Private Pay Patients* 100%.
Owner Nonprofit corp.
Admissions Requirements Minimum age 62; Medical examination.
Staff Physicians 1 (pt); RNs 6 (ft), 6 (pt); LPNs 1 (ft), 3 (pt); Nurses' aides 24 (ft), 7 (pt); Activities coordinators 1 (ft), 2 (pt); Food service staff 24 (ft), 22 (pt); Other staff 46 (ft), 19 (pt).
Languages Polish.
Affiliation Lutheran.
Facilities Dining room; Activities room; Chapel; Crafts room; Barber/Beauty shop.
Activities Arts & crafts; Cards; Games; Reading groups; Prayer groups; Movies; Shopping trips; Dances/Social/Cultural gatherings; Intergenerational programs.

Northwest Community Continuing Care Center
901 W Kirchoff Rd, Arlington Heights, IL 60005
(708) 259-5850
Admin Celeste J Little. *Dir of Nursing* Carol Klein. *Medical Dir* Dr R Treanor.
Licensure Skilled care; Intermediate care; Alzheimer's unit. *Beds* SNF; ICF; Alzheimer's unit 200. *Certified* Medicare.
Owner Nonprofit organization/foundation (Central Health Care Fdtn).
Admissions Requirements Medical examination; Physician's request.
Staff Physicians 145 (ft); RNs; LPNs; Nurses' aides; Physical therapists; Occupational therapists; Speech therapists; Dietitians; Ophthalmologists; Dentists.
Facilities Dining room; Physical therapy room; Activities room; Chapel; Crafts room; Laundry room; Barber/Beauty shop.
Activities Arts & crafts; Cards; Games; Reading groups; Prayer groups; Movies; Shopping trips; Dances/Social/Cultural gatherings; Intergenerational programs; Pet therapy.

Aroma Park

Park View Manor
103 W 4th St, Aroma Park, IL 60910
(815) 932-4332
Admin Audrey Cook.
Medical Dir Marie Williams.
Licensure Sheltered care. *Beds* Sheltered care 27. *Certified* Medicaid.
Owner Privately owned.
Admissions Requirements Minimum age 18.
Staff RNs; LPNs; Nurses' aides; Activities coordinators.
Facilities Dining room; Activities room; Laundry room; 3 Living rooms.
Activities Arts & crafts; Cards; Games; Reading groups; Prayer groups; Movies; Shopping trips; Dances/Social/Cultural gatherings.

Arthur

Arthur Home
423 Eberhardt Dr, Arthur, IL 61911
(217) 543-2103
Admin Leona M Hughes.
Licensure Skilled care. *Beds* SNF 69. *Certified* Medicaid; Medicare.
Owner Nonprofit corp.

Ashmore

Ashmore Estates
RFD Box 400, Ashmore, IL 61912
(217) 349-8328
Admin Araceli M Henson.
Medical Dir Dr Carl Johnson.
Licensure Intermediate care for mentally retarded.
Admissions Requirements Minimum age 18.
Staff Physicians 2 (pt); RNs 1 (ft), 1 (pt); LPNs 3 (ft); Nurses' aides 15 (ft); Activities coordinators 1 (ft).
Facilities Dining room; Activities room; Crafts room; Laundry room; Lounges; Multipurpose & motor development building.
Activities Arts & crafts; Cards; Games; Movies; Shopping trips; Dances/Social/Cultural gatherings; Special Olympics; Family nights; Church services; Softball games; Pizza nights.

Astoria

Astoria Healthcare Center
1008 E Broadway, Astoria, IL 61501
(309) 329-2136
Admin Ellen Williams. *Dir of Nursing* Janet Danner RN. *Medical Dir* Dr Robert Cox.
Licensure Intermediate care. *Beds* ICF 69. *Private Pay Patients* 35%. *Certified* Medicaid.
Owner Proprietary corp.
Admissions Requirements Medical examination.
Staff RNs 1 (ft); LPNs 4 (ft), 2 (pt); Activities coordinators 1 (ft), 1 (pt).
Facilities Dining room; Activities room; Crafts room; Laundry room; Barber/Beauty shop.
Activities Arts & crafts; Games; Reading groups; Prayer groups; Movies; Shopping trips; Dances/Social/Cultural gatherings; Intergenerational programs; Pet therapy; Scenic drives; Museum trips; Birthday dinners in private dining room; Monthly theme days with special menus.

Atlanta

Bartmann Health Care Center
RR 1 Box 145, Atlanta, IL 61723
(217) 642-5231

Admin Joyce J Pinney LNHA. *Dir of Nursing* Barbara Rushing. *Medical Dir* Albert Maurer LNHA MD.
Licensure Intermediate care; Sheltered care. *Beds* ICF 68; Sheltered care 19. *Private Pay Patients* 56%. *Certified* Medicaid.
Owner Nonprofit corp (First Humanics Corp).
Admissions Requirements Medical examination.
Staff Physicians 1 (pt); RNs 1 (pt); LPNs 6 (ft), 6 (pt); Nurses' aides 22 (ft); Physical therapists 1 (pt); Recreational therapists 3 (ft); Dietitians 1 (pt); Ophthalmologists 3 (pt); Podiatrists 6 (pt).
Languages German.
Facilities Dining room; Physical therapy room; Activities room; Laundry room; Barber/Beauty shop.
Activities Arts & crafts; Cards; Games; Reading groups; Prayer groups; Movies; Shopping trips; Dances/Social/Cultural gatherings; Pet therapy; Sing-alongs; Special church services.

Auburn

Park's Memorial Home
304 Maple Ave, Auburn, IL 62615
(217) 438-6125
Admin Lisa Miller.
Medical Dir Kenneth Malmberg MD.
Licensure Skilled care. *Beds* SNF 70. *Certified* Medicaid; Medicare.
Owner Proprietary corp.
Staff RNs 2 (ft), 1 (pt); LPNs 6 (ft), 2 (pt); Nurses' aides 18 (ft), 6 (pt); Physical therapists 1 (ft); Recreational therapists 1 (ft); Occupational therapists 1 (pt); Speech therapists 1 (pt); Activities coordinators 1 (ft); Dietitians 1 (ft); Ophthalmologists 1 (pt); Podiatrists 1 (pt); Audiologists 1 (pt); Dentists 1 (pt).
Facilities Dining room; Physical therapy room; Activities room; Laundry room; Barber/Beauty shop.
Activities Arts & crafts; Cards; Games; Reading groups; Prayer groups; Movies.

Augusta

Hancock County Sheltered Care
W Main St, Augusta, IL 62311
(217) 392-2116
Admin Vicki S Carriger.
Medical Dir Olive Maizie Mecum.
Licensure Sheltered care. *Beds* Shelter care 45.
Owner Publicly owned.
Admissions Requirements Minimum age 18; Medical examination.
Staff RNs 1 (ft), 1 (pt); LPNs 2 (ft); Nurses' aides 8 (pt); Activities coordinators 1 (ft); Dietitians 1 (pt).
Facilities Dining room; Activities room; Laundry room; Barber.
Activities Arts & crafts; Cards; Games; Reading groups; Prayer groups; Movies; Shopping trips; Dances/Social/Cultural gatherings.

Aurora

Aurora Community Living Facility
2080 Best Pl, Aurora, IL 60506
(708) 896-5200
Admin Linda Didier.
Licensure MR training facility. *Beds* 20. *Private Pay Patients* 0%.
Owner Nonprofit corp.
Admissions Requirements Minimum age 18; Medical examination.
Staff RNs 1 (pt); Dietitians 1 (pt).

Facilities Activities room; Laundry room; Self-contained apartments.
Activities Arts & crafts; Games; Movies; Shopping trips; Dances/Social/Cultural gatherings; Intergenerational programs; Community activities; Independent living skills.

Aurora Manor
1601 N Farnsworth, Aurora, IL 60505
(708) 898-1180
Admin Diana E Kramer.
Licensure Skilled care; Intermediate care. *Beds* SNF 54; ICF 151. *Certified* Medicaid; Medicare.
Owner Proprietary corp.

Bethesda Lutheran Home—Montgomery
1205 S Spencer, Aurora, IL 60505
(708) 820-8588
Admin Lawrence Bussard.
Licensure Intermediate care for mentally retarded. *Beds* ICF/MR 15.

Countryside Healthcare Center
2330 W Galena Blvd, Aurora, IL 60506
(708) 896-4686
Admin Kim Kohls.
Medical Dir Marc Schlesinger MD.
Licensure Skilled care; Intermediate care. *Beds* SNF 107; ICF 100. *Certified* Medicaid; Medicare.
Owner Proprietary corp.
Admissions Requirements Medical examination.
Staff Physical therapists 1 (pt); Reality therapists 1 (pt); Recreational therapists 1 (pt); Occupational therapists 1 (pt); Speech therapists 1 (pt); Activities coordinators 1 (ft); Dietitians 1 (pt); Ophthalmologists 1 (pt); Podiatrists 1 (pt); Dentists 1 (pt).
Facilities Dining room; Physical therapy room; Activities room; Barber/Beauty shop.
Activities Arts & crafts; Cards; Games; Reading groups; Prayer groups; Movies; Shopping trips; Dances/Social/Cultural gatherings; Church services.

Elmwood Nursing Home
1017 W Galena Blvd, Aurora, IL 60506
(708) 897-3100
Admin Peggy Snow. *Dir of Nursing* Marilyn Smith RN. *Medical Dir* Patrick McNellis MD.
Licensure Skilled care. *Beds* SNF 64.
Owner Nonprofit corp (Adventist Living Centers).
Admissions Requirements Minimum age 18; Medical examination; Physician's request.
Staff RNs 4 (ft); LPNs 5 (ft); Nurses' aides 20 (ft); Activities coordinators; Dietitians.
Languages Greek, Spanish.
Affiliation Seventh-Day Adventist.
Facilities Dining room; Physical therapy room; Activities room; Chapel; Barber/Beauty shop.
Activities Arts & crafts; Cards; Games; Reading groups; Prayer groups; Movies; Shopping trips; Dances/Social/Cultural gatherings.

Jennings Terrace
275 S LaSalle, Aurora, IL 60505
(708) 897-6946
Admin Martin J Scarpetta.
Licensure Sheltered care. *Beds* SNF 8; ICF 52; Sheltered care 103.
Owner Nonprofit corp.

McAuley Manor
400 W Sullivan Rd, Aurora, IL 60506-1452
(708) 859-3700
Admin Sr Brenda Finnegan RSM. *Dir of Nursing* Karen Kemp MSN RN. *Medical Dir* Gary Bowman MD.
Licensure Skilled care. *Beds* SNF 88. *Private Pay Patients* 100%.
Owner Nonprofit organization/foundation.

Admissions Requirements Medical examination; Physician's request.
Staff RNs 5 (ft), 11 (pt); LPNs 2 (ft), 1 (pt); Nurses' aides 23 (ft), 28 (pt); Physical therapists (contracted); Occupational therapists (contracted); Speech therapists (contracted); Activities coordinators 2 (ft), 2 (pt); Dietitians 1 (ft); Podiatrists 1 (pt); Audiologists (contracted).
Affiliation Roman Catholic.
Facilities Dining room; Physical therapy room; Activities room; Chapel; Crafts room; Laundry room; Barber/Beauty shop; Library.
Activities Arts & crafts; Cards; Games; Movies; Shopping trips; Pet therapy; (Religious).

New York Manor Inc
400 E New York, Aurora, IL 60505
(708) 897-8714
Admin Lester M Edelson.
Medical Dir William Weigel MD.
Licensure Skilled care; Intermediate care. *Beds* ICF 121.
Owner Proprietary corp (Signature Corp).
Admissions Requirements Minimum age 22.
Staff Physicians 2 (pt); RNs 3 (ft), 2 (pt); LPNs 2 (ft), 3 (pt); Nurses' aides 17 (ft), 8 (pt); Physical therapists 1 (pt); Occupational therapists 1 (pt); Speech therapists 1 (pt); Activities coordinators 1 (pt); Dietitians 1 (pt); Ophthalmologists 1 (pt); Podiatrists 1 (pt); Dentists 1 (pt).
Facilities Dining room; Physical therapy room; Activities room; Chapel; Crafts room; Laundry room; Barber/Beauty shop; Library; Ice cream parlour/snack shop.
Activities Arts & crafts; Games; Reading groups; Movies; Dances/Social/Cultural gatherings; Baking.

Sunnymere Inc
925 6th Ave, Aurora, IL 60505
(708) 898-7844
Admin Edith W Anderson.
Licensure Sheltered care. *Beds* Sheltered care 49.
Owner Nonprofit corp.

Aviston

Aviston Countryside Manor
450 W 1st St, Aviston, IL 62216
(618) 228-7615
Admin Dolores J Krebs.
Licensure Skilled care; Intermediate care; Sheltered care. *Beds* SNF 14; ICF 42; Sheltered care 14.

Aviston Terrace
349 W 1st St, Aviston, IL 62216
(618) 228-7040
Admin Julia M Lee.
Licensure Intermediate care for mentally retarded. *Beds* ICF/MR 15.

Avon

Avon Nursing Home Inc
710 W Woods, Box S, Avon, IL 61415
(309) 465-3102
Admin Nancy Stenger RN. *Dir of Nursing* Margaret Morey RN. *Medical Dir* Dr Mehta.
Licensure Intermediate care; Retirement cottages. *Beds* ICF 48; Retirement cottages 2. *Private Pay Patients* 46%. *Certified* Medicaid.
Owner Proprietary corp.
Admissions Requirements Medical examination; Physician's request.
Staff RNs 1 (ft), 1 (pt); LPNs 4 (ft), 3 (pt); Nurses' aides 19 (ft), 6 (pt); Activities coordinators 1 (ft), 1 (pt); Dietitians 1 (ft).
Facilities Dining room; Physical therapy room; Activities room; Laundry room; Barber/Beauty shop.

Activities Arts & crafts; Cards; Games; Reading groups; Prayer groups; Movies; Shopping trips; Dances/Social/Cultural gatherings.

Barrington

Governors Park Nursing & Rehabilitation Center
1420 S Barrington Rd, Barrington, IL 60010
(708) 382-6664, 382-6693 FAX
Admin Richard Wilk. *Dir of Nursing* Anne Huang RN. *Medical Dir* Dr John Kolb.
Licensure Skilled care; Intermediate care; Sub-acute care; Alzheimer's care. *Beds* SNF 68; ICF 67. *Private Pay Patients* 75%. *Certified* Medicaid; Medicare.
Owner Proprietary corp (Integrated Health Services).
Admissions Requirements Minimum age 18; Medical examination.
Staff RNs 15 (ft), 6 (pt); LPNs 4 (ft), 3 (pt); Nurses' aides 38 (ft), 18 (pt); Physical therapists 1 (ft); Reality therapists 2 (ft), 1 (pt); Recreational therapists 1 (pt); Occupational therapists 1 (pt); Speech therapists 1 (pt); Activities coordinators 1 (ft); Dietitians 1 (pt); Ophthalmologists 1 (pt); Podiatrists 1 (pt); Audiologists 1 (pt).
Languages Spanish.
Facilities Dining room; Physical therapy room; Activities room; Crafts room; Laundry room; Barber/Beauty shop; Library; Private dining room; Rehabilitation room.
Activities Arts & crafts; Reading groups; Prayer groups; Movies; Shopping trips; Pet therapy.

Barry

Barry Community Care Center
1313 Pratt, Barry, IL 62312
(217) 335-2326
Admin Mark W Hubbard; Janet Moore RN. *Dir of Nursing* Lucy Strubinger. *Medical Dir* Dr B J Rodriguez.
Licensure Skilled care; Intermediate care; Custodial care. *Beds* Swing beds SNF/ICF 76. *Private Pay Patients* 75%. *Certified* Medicaid.
Owner Proprietary corp.
Staff RNs 8 (ft); LPNs 8 (ft); Nurses' aides 34 (ft), 4 (pt); Physical therapists (consultant); Activities coordinators 2 (ft); Dietitians 1 (ft).
Facilities Dining room; Physical therapy room; Activities room; Crafts room; Laundry room; Barber/Beauty shop.
Activities Arts & crafts; Games; Prayer groups; Movies; Shopping trips; Intergenerational programs.

Batavia

Covenant Health Care Center Inc
831 Batavia Ave, Batavia, IL 60510
(708) 879-4300
Admin Richard K Waltmire. *Dir of Nursing* Alice Voruz. *Medical Dir* Dr John O'Dwyer.
Licensure Skilled care; Sheltered care; Alzheimer's care; Retirement. *Beds* SNF 128; Sheltered care 49. *Certified* Medicaid; Medicare.
Owner Nonprofit corp (Covenant Benevolent Institute).
Admissions Requirements Minimum age 18; Medical examination; Physician's request.
Staff Physicians; RNs; LPNs; Nurses' aides; Physical therapists; Recreational therapists; Occupational therapists; Speech therapists; Activities coordinators; Dietitians.
Affiliation Evangelical Covenant Church.
Facilities Dining room; Physical therapy room; Activities room; Chapel; Crafts room; Laundry room; Barber/Beauty shop.

Activities Arts & crafts; Cards; Games;
Reading groups; Prayer groups; Movies;
Shopping trips; Dances/Social/Cultural
gatherings.

Covenant Home
700 Fabyan Pkwy, Batavia, IL 60610
(312) 878-8200, ext 5013
Admin Lana L Heinrich. *Dir of Nursing* Doris
Johnson. *Medical Dir* Philip D Anderson
MD.
Licensure Skilled care; Sheltered care. *Beds*
SNF 52; Sheltered care 105. *Certified*
Medicaid; Medicare.
Owner Nonprofit corp (Covenant Benevolent
Institute).
Admissions Requirements Minimum age 62;
Medical examination.
Staff RNs; LPNs; Nurses' aides; Activities
coordinators.
Affiliation Evangelical Covenant Church.
Facilities Dining room; Activities room;
Chapel; Crafts room; Laundry room; Barber/
Beauty shop; Library.
Activities Arts & crafts; Games; Reading
groups; Prayer groups; Movies; Shopping
trips; Dances/Social/Cultural gatherings.

Firwood Health Care Center
520 Fabyan Pkwy, Batavia, IL 60510
(708) 879-5266
Admin Robert E Coon. *Dir of Nursing* Hilda
Witte RN. *Medical Dir* Robert Reeder, MD.
Licensure Intermediate care. *Beds* ICF 63.
Private Pay Patients 40%. *Certified*
Medicaid.
Owner Proprietary corp (Springwood
Associates).
Admissions Requirements Minimum age 60;
Medical examination; Physician's request.
Staff RNs; LPNs; Nurses' aides; Activities
coordinators; Dietitians.
Facilities Dining room; Physical therapy
room; Activities room; Chapel; Crafts room;
Laundry room; Barber/Beauty shop.
Activities Arts & crafts; Cards; Games;
Reading groups; Prayer groups; Movies;
Shopping trips; Dances/Social/Cultural
gatherings; Intergenerational programs; Pet
therapy; Family potluck dinners.

Michealsen Health Center
831 N Batavia Ave, Batavia, IL 60510
(708) 879-4300, 879-1153 FAX
Admin Sara Forsman. *Dir of Nursing* Alice
Voruz. *Medical Dir* Dr John O'Doyer.
Licensure Skilled care. *Beds* SNF 128. *Private
Pay Patients* 75%. *Certified* Medicaid;
Medicare.
Owner Nonprofit organization/foundation.
Admissions Requirements Minimum age;
Medical examination; Physician's request.
Staff RNs; LPNs; Nurses' aides; Physical
therapists 1 (ft); Activities coordinators 3
(ft), 1 (pt); Dietitians 1 (ft).
Languages Spanish, Swedish.
Affiliation Evangelical Covenant Church.
Facilities Dining room; Physical therapy
room; Activities room; Chapel; Laundry
room; Barber/Beauty shop; Family visitation
rooms.
Activities Arts & crafts; Cards; Games;
Reading groups; Prayer groups; Movies;
Dances/Social/Cultural gatherings;
Intergenerational programs; Pet therapy.

Beardstown

Beardstown Health Care Complex
RR 3, Beardstown, IL 62618
(217) 323-2720
Admin Susan Treadway.
Licensure Skilled care; Personal care
pediatrics. *Beds* SNF 79; Personal care
pediatrics 50.

Heritage Manor Nursing & Convalescent Home
1300 Grand Ave, Beardstown, IL 62618
(217) 323-4055
Admin Bonnie L Doty.
Licensure Intermediate care. *Beds* ICF 49.
Certified Medicaid.
Owner Proprietary corp.

Myers Nursing Home
1501 Canal St, Beardstown, IL 62618
(217) 323-1900
Admin John W Myers.
Medical Dir H C Zingher MD.
Licensure Skilled care; Intermediate care. *Beds*
SNF 83. *Certified* Medicaid; Medicare.
Owner Proprietary corp.
Admissions Requirements Minimum age 18;
Medical examination; Physician's request.
Staff Physicians 1 (pt); RNs 2 (ft), 3 (pt);
LPNs 9 (ft), 1 (pt); Nurses' aides 19 (ft), 13
(pt); Physical therapists 2 (pt); Recreational
therapists 1 (pt); Speech therapists 1 (pt);
Activities coordinators 1 (ft); Dietitians 1
(pt); Podiatrists 1 (pt); Audiologists 1 (pt);
Dentists 1 (pt).
Facilities Dining room; Activities room;
Crafts room; Barber/Beauty shop.
Activities Arts & crafts; Cards; Games;
Reading groups; Prayer groups; Movies;
Shopping trips.

Beecher

Anchorage of Beecher
PO Box 1112, 1201 Dixie Hwy, Beecher, IL
60401
(708) 946-2600, 946-9245 FAX
Admin Laura Stone. *Dir of Nursing* Linda
Wells. *Medical Dir* Raja Gowda.
Licensure Skilled care; Intermediate care. *Beds*
SNF 32; ICF 64. *Private Pay Patients* 65%.
Certified Medicaid; Medicare.
Owner Nonprofit corp (Lifelink Corp).
Admissions Requirements Medical
examination.
Staff RNs 11 (ft), 3 (pt); LPNs 5 (pt); Nurses'
aides 18 (ft), 16 (pt); Activities coordinators
1 (ft).
Affiliation United Church of Christ.
Facilities Dining room; Physical therapy
room; Activities room; Barber/Beauty shop.
Activities Arts & crafts; Cards; Games;
Reading groups; Movies; Pet therapy.

Belleville

Birchwood Health Care Center
900 Royal Heights Rd, Belleville, IL 62223
(618) 235-6133
Admin Gregory P Yanta.
Medical Dir Dr Paul Biedenharn.
Licensure Skilled care. *Beds* SNF 234.
Certified Medicaid; Medicare.
Owner Proprietary corp (Springwood
Associates).
Admissions Requirements Medical
examination.
Staff RNs 3 (ft); LPNs 14 (ft); Nurses' aides
80 (ft), 20 (pt); Physical therapists 1 (pt);
Recreational therapists 1 (pt); Speech
therapists 1 (pt); Activities coordinators 1
(ft); Dietitians 1 (pt); Dentists 1 (pt).
Facilities Dining room; Physical therapy
room; Activities room; Crafts room; Laundry
room; Barber/Beauty shop.
Activities Arts & crafts; Cards; Games;
Reading groups; Prayer groups; Movies;
Shopping trips; Dances/Social/Cultural
gatherings.

Castlehaven Nursing Center
225 Castellano Dr, Belleville, IL 62221
(618) 235-1300
Admin Dianne Strutynski. *Dir of Nursing*
Barbara LePere. *Medical Dir* A J Garces
MD.

Licensure Skilled care; Intermediate care. *Beds*
SNF 104; ICF 137. *Private Pay Patients*
45%. *Certified* Medicaid; Medicare.
Owner Proprietary corp.
Admissions Requirements Minimum age 18.
Staff Physicians 1 (pt); RNs 7 (ft); LPNs 15
(ft); Nurses' aides 66 (ft); Physical therapists
1 (ft); Reality therapists 1 (ft); Occupational
therapists 1 (pt); Speech therapists 1 (pt);
Activities coordinators 4 (ft); Dietitians 1
(pt); Podiatrists 1 (pt); Dentists 1 (pt).
Facilities Dining room; Physical therapy
room; Activities room; Chapel; Crafts room;
Laundry room; Barber/Beauty shop; Library;
5 Living rooms.
Activities Arts & crafts; Cards; Games;
Reading groups; Prayer groups; Movies;
Shopping trips; Dances/Social/Cultural
gatherings; Pet therapy; Bingo; Festivals;
Sight-seeing; Zoo.

Dammert Geriatric Center
Rte 15, 9500 W Illinois, Belleville, IL 62223
(618) 397-6700
Admin D Robert McCardle.
Medical Dir Charlotte Perillo.
Licensure Skilled care; Retirement. *Beds* SNF
56; Retirement apartments 173.
Owner Nonprofit corp (Missionary Oblates of
Mary Immaculate).
Admissions Requirements Minimum age 62;
Medical examination; Physician's request.
Staff RNs 3 (ft), 4 (pt); LPNs 3 (ft), 3 (pt);
Nurses' aides 17 (ft), 8 (pt); Activities
coordinators 1 (ft).
Affiliation Roman Catholic.
Facilities Dining room; Physical therapy
room; Activities room; Chapel; Crafts room;
Laundry room; Barber/Beauty shop; Library.
Activities Arts & crafts; Cards; Games;
Reading groups; Prayer groups; Movies;
Shopping trips; Dances/Social/Cultural
gatherings.

Four Fountains Convalescent Center
101 S Belt West, Belleville, IL 62220
(618) 277-7700
Admin Steven D Brant.
Licensure Skilled care; Intermediate care. *Beds*
SNF 156. *Certified* Medicaid; Medicare.
Owner Privately owned.
Staff Physicians 1 (pt); RNs 12 (ft); LPNs 10
(ft); Nurses' aides 60 (ft), 10 (pt); Physical
therapists 3 (ft), 2 (pt); Occupational
therapists 1 (pt); Speech therapists 1 (pt);
Activities coordinators 2 (ft); Dietitians 2
(pt); Podiatrists 1 (pt); Dentists 1 (pt).
Facilities Dining room; Physical therapy
room; Activities room; Crafts room; Laundry
room; Barber/Beauty shop; Library.
Activities Arts & crafts; Cards; Games; Prayer
groups; Movies; Shopping trips; Dances/
Social/Cultural gatherings.

Calvin D Johnson Nursing Home
727 N 17th St, Belleville, IL 62223
(618) 234-3323
Admin Michael L Brady.
Medical Dir J Paul Newell MD.
Licensure Skilled care; Intermediate care. *Beds*
SNF 188; ICF 49. *Certified* Medicaid;
Medicare.
Owner Proprietary corp.
Admissions Requirements Medical
examination; Physician's request.
Staff Physicians 4 (pt); RNs 3 (ft), 3 (pt);
LPNs 13 (ft), 9 (pt); Nurses' aides 50 (ft), 16
(pt); Physical therapists 1 (ft); Recreational
therapists 4 (pt); Occupational therapists 1
(ft); Speech therapists 1 (pt); Activities
coordinators 1 (ft); Dietitians 1 (pt);
Ophthalmologists 1 (pt); Podiatrists 1 (pt);
Dentists 1 (pt).
Facilities Dining room; Physical therapy
room; Activities room; Chapel; Crafts room;
Laundry room; Barber/Beauty shop.

Activities Arts & crafts; Cards; Games; Reading groups; Prayer groups; Movies; Shopping trips; Dances/Social/Cultural gatherings; Elderbuggy bus.

Lincoln Home Inc
150 N 27th St, Belleville, IL 62223
(618) 235-6600
Admin Hugh L Canaday. *Dir of Nursing* Eleanor Havens RN. *Medical Dir* Dr Paul Biedenharn.
Licensure Skilled care; Intermediate care. *Beds* SNF 25; ICF 127. *Private Pay Patients* 85%. *Certified* Medicaid.
Owner Proprietary corp.
Admissions Requirements Medical examination; Physician's request.
Staff Physicians; RNs 1 (ft), 2 (pt); LPNs 6 (ft), 3 (pt); Nurses' aides 15 (ft), 17 (pt); Physical therapists (contracted); Reality therapists (contracted); Recreational therapists (contracted); Occupational therapists (contracted); Speech therapists (contracted); Activities coordinators 2 (ft); Dietitians (contracted).
Facilities Dining room; Physical therapy room; Activities room; Chapel; Crafts room; Laundry room; Barber/Beauty shop; Library.
Activities Arts & crafts; Cards; Games; Reading groups; Prayer groups; Movies; Shopping trips; Dances/Social/Cultural gatherings; Intergenerational programs; Pet therapy; Volunteer program.

Memorial Conv Center
4315 Memorial Dr, Belleville, IL 62223
(618) 233-7750
Admin Patricia Adams.
Medical Dir Mathew Erscle.
Licensure Skilled care. *Beds* SNF 108. *Certified* Medicaid; Medicare.
Owner Nonprofit corp.
Admissions Requirements Minimum age 18; Medical examination; Physician's request.
Staff Physicians 1 (pt); RNs 7 (ft), 11 (pt); LPNs 3 (ft), 2 (pt); Nurses' aides 26 (ft), 29 (pt); Physical therapists 1 (pt); Recreational therapists 2 (ft).
Facilities Dining room; Physical therapy room; Activities room; Chapel; Crafts room; Barber/Beauty shop; Library.
Activities Arts & crafts; Cards; Games; Reading groups; Prayer groups; Movies; Shopping trips; Dances/Social/Cultural gatherings.

Notre Dame Hills Living Center
6401 W Main St, Belleville, IL 62223
(618) 397-8400
Admin Geneva Combre. *Dir of Nursing* Dorothy Miller. *Medical Dir* William Lesko MD.
Licensure Skilled care; Intermediate care. *Beds* SNF 61; ICF 61. *Certified* Medicaid; Medicare.
Owner Nonprofit corp (Adventist Health Sys-USA).
Admissions Requirements Minimum age 21; Medical examination; Physician's request.
Staff RNs 3 (ft), 4 (pt); LPNs 4 (ft), 4 (pt); Nurses' aides 24 (ft), 18 (pt); Physical therapists 1 (pt); Recreational therapists 1 (ft), 2 (pt); Occupational therapists 1 (pt); Dietitians 1 (pt); Ophthalmologists 1 (pt); Dentists 1 (pt).
Affiliation Seventh-Day Adventist.
Facilities Dining room; Physical therapy room; Activities room; Laundry room; Barber/Beauty shop; TV rooms; Patio; 3 Lounge areas.
Activities Arts & crafts; Cards; Games; Reading groups; Prayer groups; Movies; Shopping trips; Dances/Social/Cultural gatherings; Restaurant outings; Cooking; Reality orientation classes; Pet therapy.

St Clair County Specialized Living Center
1450 Caseyville Ave, Belleville, IL 62220
(618) 277-7730
Admin Agnes Schloemann.
Licensure Intermediate care for mentally retarded. *Beds* ICF/MR 100.

St Pauls Home
1021 W "E" St, Belleville, IL 62220
(618) 233-2095
Admin Warren W Peters.
Licensure Intermediate care; Sheltered care. *Beds* ICF 113; Sheltered care 62. *Certified* Medicaid.
Owner Nonprofit corp.

Weier Retirement Nursing Home
5 Gundlach Pl, Belleville, IL 62221
(618) 233-6625
Admin Roger W Hotson.
Licensure Intermediate care. *Beds* ICF 94. *Certified* Medicaid.
Owner Proprietary corp.

Bellwood

Dale Johnson Center
2614 Saint Charles Rd, Bellwood, IL 60104
(312) 547-3596
Admin Cathie J Kniebe.
Licensure Long-term care. *Beds* Long-term care 20. *Certified* Medicaid; Medicare.
Owner Nonprofit corp (Proviso Association for Retarded Citizens).
Admissions Requirements Minimum age 21; Medical examination; Physician's request.
Staff Occupational therapists (consultant); Speech therapists (consultant); Activities coordinators 1 (ft); Dietitians (consultant).
Facilities Laundry room.
Activities Arts & crafts; Games; Movies; Shopping trips; Dances/Social/Cultural gatherings.

PARC Home
105 Eastern Ave, Bellwood, IL 60104
(708) 547-3580
Admin Elaine P Bernabe.
Medical Dir Raymond McDonald MD.
Licensure Intermediate care; ICF/ Developmentally disabled. *Beds* 95.
Owner Nonprofit corp.
Admissions Requirements Minimum age 18; Medical examination.
Staff Physicians 1 (pt); RNs 1 (pt); LPNs 4 (ft), 3 (pt); Nurses' aides 20 (ft), 20 (pt); Reality therapists 3 (ft); Recreational therapists 1 (ft); Occupational therapists 1 (ft), 1 (pt); Speech therapists 1 (ft); Activities coordinators 1 (ft); Dietitians 1 (pt); Ophthalmologists 1 (pt); Podiatrists 1 (pt); Audiologists 1 (pt); Dentists 1 (pt).
Facilities Dining room; Activities room; Laundry room; Barber/Beauty shop.
Activities Arts & crafts; Games; Prayer groups; Movies; Shopping trips; Dances/Social/ Cultural gatherings.

Belvidere

Fairview Manor
1701 5th St, Belvidere, IL 61008
(815) 547-5451
Admin Norman John Gross.
Medical Dir Kent Hess MD.
Licensure Intermediate care. *Beds* ICF 80. *Certified* Medicaid.
Owner Proprietary corp.
Admissions Requirements Medical examination; Physician's request.
Staff RNs 1 (ft); LPNs 4 (ft), 2 (pt); Nurses' aides 16 (ft), 4 (pt); Physical therapists 1 (pt); Activities coordinators 1 (ft), 1 (pt); Dietitians 1 (ft).
Facilities Dining room; Physical therapy room; Activities room; Laundry room; Barber/Beauty shop; Library.

Activities Arts & crafts; Cards; Games; Reading groups; Prayer groups; Movies; Shopping trips; Dances/Social/Cultural gatherings.

Maple Crest Boone County Nursing Home
4452 Squaw Prairie Rd, Belvidere, IL 61008
(815) 547-6377
Admin Gregory A Olson NHA. *Dir of Nursing* Dolores A Moss RN. *Medical Dir* Harry W Darland MD.
Licensure Skilled care. *Beds* SNF 78. *Private Pay Patients* 45%. *Certified* Medicaid.
Owner Publicly owned.
Admissions Requirements Minimum age 18; Medical examination; Physician's request.
Staff Physicians 2 (pt); RNs 7 (ft), 3 (pt); LPNs 6 (ft), 2 (pt); Nurses' aides 44 (ft), 12 (pt); Physical therapists 1 (pt); Recreational therapists 1 (ft); Occupational therapists 1 (ft); Speech therapists 1 (pt); Activities coordinators 3 (ft), 1 (pt); Dietitians 1 (pt); Ophthalmologists 1 (pt); Podiatrists 1 (ft); Audiologists 1 (ft).
Facilities Dining room; Physical therapy room; Activities room; Chapel; Crafts room; Laundry room; Barber/Beauty shop; Library.
Activities Arts & crafts; Cards; Games; Reading groups; Prayer groups; Movies; Dances/Social/Cultural gatherings; Intergenerational programs; Pet therapy.

Northwoods Healthcare Center
2250 S Pearl Street Rd, Belvidere, IL 61108
(815) 544-0358
Admin Susan Mead.
Licensure Skilled care. *Beds* SNF 120. *Certified* Medicaid; Medicare.
Owner Proprietary corp.

Bement

Bement Manor
601 N Morgan St, Bement, IL 61813
(217) 678-2191
Admin Billy G Morgan. *Dir of Nursing* Sherri White. *Medical Dir* Dr Rohidas Patil.
Licensure Skilled care. *Beds* SNF 63. *Private Pay Patients* 16%. *Certified* Medicaid; Medicare.
Owner Proprietary corp (Convalescent Management Association Inc).
Admissions Requirements Minimum age 18; Medical examination.
Staff RNs 3 (ft), 1 (pt); LPNs 3 (ft); Nurses' aides 12 (ft), 4 (pt); Physical therapists 1 (pt); Recreational therapists 1 (pt); Occupational therapists 1 (ft); Activities coordinators 1 (ft); Dietitians 1 (pt); Podiatrists 1 (pt).
Facilities Dining room; Physical therapy room; Activities room; Chapel; Crafts room; Laundry room; Barber/Beauty shop.
Activities Arts & crafts; Cards; Games; Reading groups; Prayer groups; Movies; Shopping trips; Dances/Social/Cultural gatherings; Intergenerational programs; Outings to local colleges and universities for special shows and plays; Psychosocial programs; Health and fitness programs; Volunteer program.

Bensenville

Anchorage
111 E Washington St, Bensenville, IL 60106
(708) 766-5800, 860-5130 FAX
Admin Jane M Muller. *Dir of Nursing* Ada Bowen. *Medical Dir* Dr P Kini.
Licensure Skilled care; Intermediate care. *Beds* SNF 90; ICF 142. *Private Pay Patients* 75%. *Certified* Medicaid; Medicare.
Owner Nonprofit corp.
Admissions Requirements Minimum age 60.
Staff Physicians 3 (ft); RNs 6 (ft), 22 (pt); LPNs 7 (ft), 8 (pt); Nurses' aides 44 (ft), 19 (pt); Physical therapists 1 (ft); Recreational

therapists 3 (ft), 1 (pt); Activities coordinators 2 (ft); Dietitians 1 (ft); Podiatrists 1 (ft); Optometrists 1 (pt).
Affiliation United Church of Christ.
Facilities Dining room; Physical therapy room; Activities room; Chapel; Crafts room; Laundry room; Barber/Beauty shop; Library.
Activities Arts & crafts; Cards; Games; Prayer groups; Movies; Shopping trips; Dances/Social/Cultural gatherings; Intergenerational programs; Pet therapy; Bus rides; Outings; Ceramics; Music therapy.

Benton

Lifecare Center of Benton
PO Box 847, 1409 N Main, Benton, IL 62812
(618) 435-2712
Admin Troy E Callahan RN ADM BSN. *Dir of Nursing* Karen Rose RN. *Medical Dir* Dr Saeed A Khan.
Licensure Intermediate care. *Beds* ICF 71. *Private Pay Patients* 50%. *Certified* Medicaid.
Owner Proprietary corp (Community Lifecare Enterprises).
Staff RNs 1 (ft); LPNs 5 (ft), 3 (pt); Nurses' aides 30 (ft), 15 (pt); Physical therapists 1 (pt); Activities coordinators 1 (ft); Dietitians 1 (ft).
Facilities Dining room; Physical therapy room; Activities room; Laundry room; Barber/Beauty shop; Enclosed courtyard.
Activities Arts & crafts; Cards; Games; Reading groups; Prayer groups; Movies; Shopping trips; Dances/Social/Cultural gatherings.

Severin Intermediate Care Home
902 S McLeansboro St, Benton, IL 62812
(618) 439-4501
Admin Paul D Leffler.
Licensure Intermediate care. *Beds* ICF 96. *Certified* Medicaid.
Owner Proprietary corp.

Berwyn

Fairfax Health Care Center
3601 S Harlem Ave, Berwyn, IL 60402
(708) 749-4160, 749-7696 FAX
Admin Frances W Schweig RN BSN NHA. *Dir of Nursing* Lynda Rutka RN. *Medical Dir* Dr Alberto Saltiel.
Licensure Skilled care; Alzheimer's care. *Beds* SNF 160. *Private Pay Patients* 45%. *Certified* Medicaid; Medicare.
Owner Proprietary corp.
Admissions Requirements Minimum age 19; Medical examination; Physician's request.
Staff Physicians 3 (pt); RNs 7 (ft), 11 (pt); LPNs 13 (ft), 2 (pt); Nurses' aides 51 (ft), 4 (pt); Physical therapists 1 (pt); Reality therapists 2 (ft); Recreational therapists 1 (ft), 1 (pt); Occupational therapists 1 (pt); Speech therapists 1 (pt); Activities coordinators 6 (ft); Dietitians 1 (ft), 2 (pt); Ophthalmologists 1 (pt); Podiatrists 1 (pt); Audiologists 1 (pt); Other staff 51 (ft).
Languages Bohemian, Lithuanian, Polish, Spanish, Filipino, Korean.
Facilities Dining room; Physical therapy room; Activities room; Laundry room; Barber/Beauty shop; Sun rooms; Ventilator unit.
Activities Arts & crafts; Cards; Games; Reading groups; Prayer groups; Movies; Shopping trips; Dances/Social/Cultural gatherings; Intergenerational programs; Pet therapy.

Seguin Services Home I
3309 S Harvey, Berwyn, IL 60402
(708) 484-3398
Admin Sharon Mares.
Licensure Intermediate care for mentally retarded. *Beds* ICF/MR 15.

Seguin Services Home III
1800 S Grove Ave, Berwyn, IL 60402
(708) 749-7267
Admin Eloise Gorel.
Licensure Intermediate care for mentally retarded. *Beds* ICF/MR 8.

Bethalto

Bethalto Care Center Inc
815 S Prairie St, Bethalto, IL 62010
(618) 377-2144
Admin Linda M Daniels.
Licensure Intermediate care. *Beds* ICF 98. *Certified* Medicaid.
Owner Proprietary corp.

Bloomingdale

Bloomingdale Pavilion
311 Edgewater Dr, Bloomingdale, IL 60108
(708) 894-7400
Admin Carol L Terrill.
Licensure Skilled care. *Beds* SNF 259. *Certified* Medicaid; Medicare.
Owner Proprietary corp.

Carington Living Center
275 Army Trail Rd, Bloomingdale, IL 60108
(708) 893-9616
Admin Jerry L Rhoads CPA. *Dir of Nursing* Cathie Jackson RN, Health Care Svcs Dir. *Medical Dir* Dr Penny Brock.
Licensure Skilled care; Intermediate care; Medicare certified; Alzheimer's care. *Beds* Swing beds SNF/ICF 137; Medicare certified 70. *Private Pay Patients* 16%. *Certified* Medicaid; Medicare.
Owner Nonprofit corp (Adventist Living Centers).
Admissions Requirements Minimum age 18; Medical examination; Physician's request.
Staff Physicians 1 (pt); RNs 4 (ft), 4 (pt); LPNs 7 (ft), 5 (pt); Nurses' aides 34 (ft), 13 (pt); Physical therapists 1 (ft); Reality therapists 2 (ft); Recreational therapists 4 (ft), 1 (pt); Occupational therapists (contracted); Speech therapists (contracted); Activities coordinators 1 (ft); Dietitians 1 (ft); Podiatrists 1 (pt); Dentists 1 (pt).
Affiliation Seventh-Day Adventist.
Facilities Dining room; Physical therapy room; Activities room; Crafts room; Laundry room; Barber/Beauty shop; Dentist office; Podiatry office.
Activities Arts & crafts; Cards; Games; Reading groups; Prayer groups; Movies; Shopping trips; Dances/Social/Cultural gatherings; Intergenerational programs.

Marklund Children's Home
164 S Prairie Ave, Bloomingdale, IL 60108
(708) 529-2871
Admin Patricia Pearce.
Medical Dir Val Moller.
Licensure Skilled care. *Beds* 98. *Certified* Medicaid; Medicare.
Owner Nonprofit corp.
Admissions Requirements Medical examination; Physician's request.
Staff Physicians 1 (ft); RNs 4 (ft), 10 (pt); LPNs 1 (ft), 3 (pt); Nurses' aides 30 (ft), 34 (pt); Physical therapists 1 (ft); Recreational therapists 1 (ft); Occupational therapists 1 (ft); Speech therapists 1 (ft); Activities coordinators 1 (pt); Dietitians 1 (pt); Dentists 2 (pt).
Facilities Dining room; Physical therapy room; Activities room; Crafts room; Laundry room; Library.
Activities Arts & crafts; Games; Prayer groups; Movies; Shopping trips.

Bloomington

Bloomington Nursing & Rehabilitation Center
1509 N Calhoun St, Bloomington, IL 61701
(309) 827-6046
Admin Robert W Burdick.
Medical Dir Dr Virgil Short.
Licensure Skilled care. *Beds* SNF 123.
Owner Proprietary corp.
Admissions Requirements Minimum age 50; Medical examination.
Staff RNs 4 (ft), 1 (pt); LPNs 6 (ft), 3 (pt); Nurses' aides 30 (ft), 10 (pt); Physical therapists 1 (pt); Recreational therapists 1 (ft), 2 (pt); Speech therapists 1 (pt); Activities coordinators 1 (ft); Dietitians 1 (pt); Ophthalmologists 1 (pt); Podiatrists 1 (pt); Audiologists 1 (pt); Dentists 1 (pt).
Facilities Dining room; Physical therapy room; Activities room; Crafts room; Laundry room; Barber/Beauty shop.
Activities Arts & crafts; Cards; Games; Reading groups; Prayer groups; Movies; Shopping trips; Dances/Social/Cultural gatherings.

Hage House
806 Four Seasons Rd, Bloomington, IL 61701
(309) 827-6272
Admin Diane Boeck.
Licensure Intermediate care for mentally retarded. *Beds* ICF/MR 15. *Certified* Medicaid; Medicare.
Owner Nonprofit organization/foundation.
Admissions Requirements Minimum age 18; Medical examination.
Staff RNs 1 (pt); Activities coordinators 1 (ft).
Facilities Dining room; Activities room; Laundry room.
Activities Arts & crafts; Cards; Games; Dances/Social/Cultural gatherings; SOAR.

Heritage Manor
700 E Walnut St, Bloomington, IL 61701
(309) 827-8004, 827-2284 FAX
Admin Jean Dulin. *Dir of Nursing* Donna Sieg. *Medical Dir* Seymour R Goldberg MD.
Licensure Skilled care. *Beds* SNF 106. *Private Pay Patients* 70%. *Certified* Medicaid; Medicare.
Owner Proprietary corp (Heritage Enterprises).
Admissions Requirements Medical examination; Physician's request.
Staff RNs 5 (ft), 3 (pt); LPNs 5 (ft), 8 (pt); Nurses' aides 35 (ft); Physical therapists 2 (pt); Recreational therapists 1 (pt); Occupational therapists 1 (pt); Speech therapists 1 (pt); Activities coordinators 1 (ft); Dietitians 1 (ft); Podiatrists 1 (pt).
Facilities Dining room; Physical therapy room; Activities room; Laundry room; Barber/Beauty shop; Library; 2 large dayrooms.
Activities Arts & crafts; Cards; Games; Reading groups; Prayer groups; Movies; Shopping trips; Dances/Social/Cultural gatherings; Intergenerational programs; Pet therapy.

Scothwood Health Care Center
1925 S Main, Bloomington, IL 61701
(309) 829-4348
Admin Mary Whiteford Leung.
Medical Dir Dr Ravi Kottoor.
Licensure Intermediate care. *Beds* SNF 19; ICF 58. *Certified* Medicaid.
Owner Proprietary corp (Springwood Associates).
Admissions Requirements Medical examination.
Staff RNs 1 (ft); LPNs 3 (ft), 3 (pt); Nurses' aides 6 (ft), 5 (pt); Physical therapists 1 (pt); Reality therapists 1 (ft), 1 (pt); Recreational therapists 1 (ft); Activities coordinators 1 (ft); Dietitians 1 (pt).
Facilities Dining room; Physical therapy room; Activities room; Crafts room; Laundry room; Barber/Beauty shop; Library.

Activities Arts & crafts; Cards; Games; Reading groups; Prayer groups; Movies; Shopping trips; Dances/Social/Cultural gatherings.

Westminster Village Inc
2025 E Lincoln St, Bloomington, IL 61701
(309) 663-6474
Admin Martha K Butler. *Dir of Nursing* Carol DeVore RN. *Medical Dir* James E Swanson MD.
Licensure Skilled care; Intermediate care; Retirement. *Beds* SNF 39; ICF 39. *Private Pay Patients* 100%. *Certified* Medicare.
Owner Nonprofit corp.
Admissions Requirements Minimum age 62.
Facilities Dining room; Physical therapy room; Activities room; Crafts room; Barber/Beauty shop.
Activities Arts & crafts; Cards; Games; Reading groups; Prayer groups; Movies; Shopping trips; Dances/Social/Cultural gatherings; Intergenerational programs; Pet therapy.

Blue Island

Blue Island Nursing Home
2427 W 127th St, Blue Island, IL 60406
(708) 389-7799
Admin John A Heuser.
Licensure Intermediate care. *Beds* ICF 30. *Certified* Medicaid.
Owner Proprietary corp.

Bourbonnais

Bourbonnais Terrace
133 Mohawk Dr, Bourbonnais, IL 60914
(815) 937-4790
Admin Jacquelin Delong.
Medical Dir Samuel DeGuzman.
Licensure Skilled care; Intermediate care. *Beds* SNF 100; ICF 97. *Certified* Medicaid.
Owner Proprietary corp.
Admissions Requirements Minimum age 21.
Staff RNs 6 (ft); LPNs 7 (ft).
Facilities Dining room; Physical therapy room; Activities room; Laundry room; Barber/Beauty shop.
Activities Games; Prayer groups; Movies; Dances/Social/Cultural gatherings; Community programs.

Chamness Square
340 Heritage Dr, Bourbonnais, IL 60914
(815) 932-2745
Admin Martin J Downs.
Licensure Intermediate care for mentally retarded. *Beds* ICF/MR 15.

Kankakee Terrace
100 Belle Aire, Bourbonnais, IL 60914
(815) 939-0910
Admin Carol A Hurst.
Medical Dir Dr Samuel DeGuzman.
Licensure Intermediate care. *Beds* ICF 126.
Owner Proprietary corp.
Staff RNs 4 (pt); LPNs 2 (ft), 2 (pt); Nurses' aides 13 (ft), 9 (pt); Activities coordinators 3 (ft), 1 (pt); Dietitians 1 (ft).
Facilities Dining room; Activities room; Laundry room; Barber/Beauty shop.
Activities Arts & crafts; Cards; Games; Movies; Shopping trips; Dances/Social/Cultural gatherings.

Our Lady of Victory
20 Briarcliff Ln, Bourbonnais, IL 60914
(815) 937-2022
Admin Henrietta Chamness. *Dir of Nursing* Kim Gartner. *Medical Dir* Dr J M Dave.
Licensure Skilled care; Intermediate care. *Beds* SNF 38; ICF 59. *Private Pay Patients* 20%. *Certified* Medicaid; Medicare.
Owner Nonprofit organization/foundation.

Admissions Requirements Minimum age 18; Medical examination.
Staff Physicians (Med dir on 24 hr call); RNs 4 (ft); LPNs 6 (ft); Nurses' aides 40 (ft); Occupational therapists 1 (ft); Activities coordinators 2 (ft); Dietitians (consultant); Ophthalmologists (consultant); Podiatrists (consultant); Audiologists (consultant); Pastoral care.
Affiliation Roman Catholic.
Facilities Dining room; Physical therapy room; Activities room; Chapel; Barber/Beauty shop.
Activities Arts & crafts; Cards; Games; Reading groups; Prayer groups; Movies; Shopping trips; Dances/Social/Cultural gatherings; Intergenerational programs; Pet therapy; Pastoral care; Religious services.

Bradley

Bradley Royale Inc
650 N Kinzie, Bradley, IL 60915
(815) 933-1666
Admin Penny L Vassiliou.
Licensure Skilled care; Intermediate care. *Beds* SNF 48; ICF 50.
Owner Proprietary corp.

Collins Square
145 S Crosswell Ave, Bradley, IL 60915
(815) 933-1718
Admin Martin J Downs.
Licensure Intermediate care for mentally retarded. *Beds* ICF/MR 15.

Gravlin Square
482 S Schuyler St, Bradley, IL 60915
(815) 933-1718
Admin Martin J Downs.
Licensure Intermediate care for mentally retarded. *Beds* ICF/MR 15.

Breese

Breese Nursing Home
1155 N 1st St, Breese, IL 62230
(618) 526-4521
Admin Darlene M Trickey. *Dir of Nursing* Ted Paskovich. *Medical Dir* Dr Venerio Santos.
Licensure Skilled care. *Beds* SNF 123. *Private Pay Patients* 40%. *Certified* Medicaid; Medicare.
Owner Proprietary corp (Canadian International).
Admissions Requirements Medical examination; Physician's request.
Staff Physicians 11 (pt); RNs 4 (ft), 2 (pt); LPNs 7 (ft), 2 (pt); Nurses' aides 25 (ft), 23 (pt); Physical therapists 1 (pt); Reality therapists 1 (pt); Recreational therapists 1 (pt); Speech therapists 1 (pt); Activities coordinators 2 (pt); Dietitians 1 (pt); Ophthalmologists 1 (pt); Podiatrists 1 (pt); Audiologists 1 (pt); Psychosocial 1 (pt).
Facilities Dining room; Physical therapy room; Activities room; Chapel; Crafts room; Laundry room; Barber/Beauty shop; Library.
Activities Arts & crafts; Cards; Games; Reading groups; Prayer groups; Movies; Shopping trips; Dances/Social/Cultural gatherings; Psychosocial programs; Health fitness programs.

Bridgeport

Bridgeport Terrace
900 E Corporation St, Bridgeport, IL 62417
(618) 945-2091
Admin Michael P Duffy. *Dir of Nursing* Patricia Huff. *Medical Dir* Dr Gary D Carr.
Licensure Intermediate care. *Beds* ICF 99. *Private Pay Patients* 15%. *Certified* Medicaid.
Owner Proprietary corp (EKS Management Inc).

Admissions Requirements Minimum age 21; Medical examination.
Staff Physicians 2 (pt); RNs 2 (pt); LPNs 3 (ft), 4 (pt); Nurses' aides 24 (ft), 2 (pt); Physical therapists 1 (ft), 1 (pt); Recreational therapists 1 (pt); Occupational therapists 1 (ft), 1 (pt); Activities coordinators 1 (ft); Dietitians 1 (pt); Ophthalmologists 1 (pt); Podiatrists 1 (pt).
Facilities Dining room; Physical therapy room; Activities room; Laundry room; Barber/Beauty shop; Library; Conference room.
Activities Arts & crafts; Cards; Games; Reading groups; Prayer groups; Movies; Shopping trips; Dances/Social/Cultural gatherings; Intergenerational programs; Pet therapy; Community outreach; Picnics.

Bridgeview

Bridgeview Convalescent Center
8100 S Harlem Ave, Bridgeview, IL 60455
(708) 594-5440
Admin Paul J Dudek.
Medical Dir Dr P Punjabi.
Licensure Skilled care; Intermediate care. *Beds* SNF 101; ICF 51. *Certified* Medicaid; Medicare.
Owner Proprietary corp.
Staff Physicians 6 (pt); RNs 8 (ft), 4 (pt); LPNs 6 (ft), 10 (pt); Nurses' aides 77 (ft); Physical therapists 2 (pt); Reality therapists 1 (pt); Recreational therapists 1 (pt); Occupational therapists 1 (pt); Speech therapists 1 (pt); Activities coordinators 1 (ft); Dietitians 1 (pt); Ophthalmologists 1 (pt); Podiatrists 1 (pt); Dentists 1 (pt).
Facilities Dining room; Physical therapy room; Activities room; Crafts room; Laundry room; Barber/Beauty shop.
Activities Arts & crafts; Cards; Games; Reading groups; Prayer groups; Movies; Shopping trips; Dances/Social/Cultural gatherings.

Metropolitan Nursing Center
8540 S Harlem Ave, Bridgeview, IL 60455
(708) 598-2605, 598-5671 FAX
Admin Barry R Taerbaum. *Dir of Nursing* E Enriquez RN. *Medical Dir* S Dayan MD.
Licensure Skilled care; Alzheimer's care. *Beds* SNF 404. *Certified* Medicaid.
Owner Proprietary corp.
Facilities Dining room; Physical therapy room; Activities room; Crafts room; Laundry room; Barber/Beauty shop; Library.
Activities Arts & crafts; Cards; Games; Reading groups; Prayer groups; Movies; Shopping trips; Dances/Social/Cultural gatherings; Intergenerational programs; Pet therapy.

Brighton

Robings Manor Nursing Home
502 N Main, Brighton, IL 62012
(618) 372-3232
Admin Catherine D Hale.
Licensure Skilled care. *Beds* SNF 25; ICF 43. *Certified* Medicare.
Owner Proprietary corp.

Brookfield

British Home
31st St & McCormick, Brookfield, IL 60513
(708) 485-0135
Admin Carol Wieczorek.
Medical Dir Dr Richard Dirkes.
Licensure Skilled care; Intermediate care; Sheltered care; Independent living. *Beds* SNF 46; ICF 26; Sheltered care 64; Independent living 66. *Private Pay Patients* 100%.
Owner Nonprofit organization/foundation.

Admissions Requirements Minimum age 70; Medical examination; Physician's request.
Staff Physicians; RNs; LPNs; Nurses' aides; Recreational therapists; Activities coordinators; Dietitians; Podiatrists.
Facilities Dining room; Activities room; Crafts room; Barber/Beauty shop; Library.
Activities Arts & crafts; Cards; Games; Reading groups; Prayer groups; Movies; Shopping trips; Dances/Social/Cultural gatherings; Intergenerational programs; Pet therapy.

Bunker Hill

South Lawn Shelter Care
512 S Franklin, Bunker Hill, IL 62014
(618) 585-4875
Admin Gary G Rull.
Licensure Sheltered care. *Beds* Sheltered care 50. *Certified* Medicaid.
Owner Privately owned.
Admissions Requirements Minimum age 18; Medical examination.
Staff LPNs; Nurses' aides; Activities coordinators.
Facilities Dining room; Laundry room; Barber/Beauty shop.
Activities Arts & crafts; Cards; Games; Reading groups; Prayer groups; Movies; Shopping trips; Dances/Social/Cultural gatherings.

Burbank

Brentwood Nursing & Rehabilitation Center
5400 W 87th St, Burbank, IL 60459
(708) 432-1200
Admin Patrick J Finn. *Dir of Nursing* Mary Beth Desmond RN. *Medical Dir* Timothy Knox MD.
Licensure Skilled care; Alzheimer's care. *Beds* SNF 165. *Certified* Medicare.
Owner Proprietary corp (Integrated Health Services Inc).
Admissions Requirements Medical examination.
Staff RNs; LPNs; Nurses' aides; Physical therapists; Recreational therapists; Occupational therapists; Speech therapists; Activities coordinators; Dietitians; Ophthalmologists; Podiatrists.
Languages Spanish.
Facilities Dining room; Physical therapy room; Activities room; Crafts room; Laundry room; Barber/Beauty shop.
Activities Arts & crafts; Cards; Games; Prayer groups; Movies.

Parkside Gardens
5701 W 79th St, Burbank, IL 60459
(708) 636-3850
Admin Frances E Merz. *Dir of Nursing* Dorothy Meng RN. *Medical Dir* Dr Jolan Fejes.
Licensure Intermediate care. *Beds* ICF 78. *Private Pay Patients* 48%. *Certified* Medicaid.
Owner Proprietary corp.
Admissions Requirements Medical examination.
Staff Physicians (consultant); Physical therapists (consultant); Reality therapists 1 (ft); Occupational therapists 1 (ft); Speech therapists 1 (pt); Activities coordinators 1 (ft); Dietitians (consultant); Ophthalmologists 1 (pt); Podiatrists 1 (pt).
Facilities Dining room; Activities room; Barber/Beauty shop.
Activities Reading groups; Prayer groups; Movies; Shopping trips; Pet therapy.

Burnham

Burnham Terrace Ltd
PO Box 585, 14500 S Manistee, Burnham, IL 60633
(708) 862-1260
Admin Herman W Frey.
Licensure Skilled care; Intermediate care. *Beds* SNF 103; ICF 206.

Burr Ridge

King-Bruwaert House
6101 S County Line Rd, Burr Ridge, IL 60521
(708) 323-2250
Admin Carl Baker. *Dir of Nursing* Verda E Blackburn-Tures. *Medical Dir* Dr Lawrence LaPalio.
Licensure Skilled care; Sheltered care; Retirement. *Beds* SNF 35; Sheltered care 83; Retirement homes 63. *Private Pay Patients* 50%.
Owner Nonprofit organization/foundation.
Admissions Requirements Minimum age 65; Medical examination.
Staff Physicians 1 (pt); RNs 9 (ft), 5 (pt); LPNs 4 (ft); Nurses' aides 20 (ft), 5 (pt); Activities coordinators 4 (ft), 1 (pt); Dietitians 1 (pt); Ophthalmologists 1 (pt); Podiatrists 1 (pt); Audiologists 1 (pt).
Facilities Dining room; Activities room; Crafts room; Laundry room; Barber/Beauty shop; Library; Billiards room; Ice cream parlor; Kitchenettes.
Activities Arts & crafts; Cards; Games; Reading groups; Prayer groups; Movies; Shopping trips; Dances/Social/Cultural gatherings; Pet therapy.

Byron

Neighbors
PO Box 585, Byron, IL 61010
(815) 234-2511
Admin Grant Bullock.
Medical Dir P John Seward MD.
Licensure Skilled care. *Beds* SNF 99. *Certified* Medicaid; Medicare.
Owner Proprietary corp.
Admissions Requirements Medical examination.
Staff RNs 5 (ft), 2 (pt); LPNs 3 (ft), 4 (pt); Nurses' aides 33 (ft), 6 (pt); Speech therapists 1 (pt); Activities coordinators 1 (ft), 1 (pt).
Facilities Dining room; Physical therapy room; Activities room; Laundry room; Barber/Beauty shop.
Activities Arts & crafts; Cards; Games; Reading groups; Prayer groups; Movies; Shopping trips; Dances/Social/Cultural gatherings.

Cahokia

Cahokia Health Care Center
2 Annable Ct, Cahokia, IL 62206
(618) 332-0114
Admin Melvin L Zimmerman.
Licensure Skilled care. *Beds* SNF 150.

River Bluffs of Cahokia
3354 Jerome Ln, Cahokia, IL 62206
(618) 337-9400
Admin Phyllis Evans. *Dir of Nursing* Sandra Kinnear. *Medical Dir* Theodore Bryan MD.
Licensure Skilled care; Intermediate care. *Beds* SNF 50; ICF 85. *Certified* Medicaid; Medicare.
Owner Proprietary corp.
Admissions Requirements Minimum age 22; Medical examination; Physician's request.
Staff Physicians 6 (ft); RNs 2 (ft); LPNs 11 (ft); Nurses' aides 41 (ft); Physical therapists 2 (ft); Reality therapists 1 (ft); Recreational therapists 1 (ft); Occupational therapists 1

(ft); Speech therapists 1 (ft); Activities coordinators 1 (ft); Dietitians 2 (ft); Ophthalmologists 2 (ft); Podiatrists 1 (ft); Physical therapy aides.
Facilities Dining room; Physical therapy room; Activities room; Crafts room; Barber/Beauty shop; Library.
Activities Arts & crafts; Cards; Games; Reading groups; Prayer groups; Movies; Shopping trips; Dances/Social/Cultural gatherings.

Cairo

Daystar Care Center
2001 Cedar St, Cairo, IL 62964
(618) 734-1700, 734-2611 FAX
Admin Barbara R Connell. *Dir of Nursing* Mary Jane Holman. *Medical Dir* Gemo Wong MD.
Licensure Skilled care. *Beds* SNF 82. *Certified* Medicaid.
Owner Nonprofit organization/foundation.
Admissions Requirements Minimum age 18; Medical examination.
Staff RNs 3 (ft), 2 (pt); LPNs 6 (ft), 2 (pt); Nurses' aides 20 (ft), 10 (pt); Recreational therapists 2 (ft); Speech therapists 1 (pt); Activities coordinators 1 (ft); Dietitians 1 (pt); Podiatrists 1 (pt).
Facilities Dining room; Physical therapy room; Activities room; Crafts room; Laundry room; Barber/Beauty shop.
Activities Arts & crafts; Cards; Games; Reading groups; Prayer groups; Movies; Shopping trips; Dances/Social/Cultural gatherings; Intergenerational programs; Pet therapy.

Pilot House
1111 Washington Ave, Cairo, IL 62914
(618) 734-3706
Admin James A Keller. *Dir of Nursing* Linda Palmer RN, contracted. *Medical Dir* Gemo Wong MD.
Licensure Intermediate care for mentally retarded. *Beds* ICF/MR 15. *Private Pay Patients* 0%. *Certified* Medicaid.
Owner Privately owned.
Admissions Requirements Minimum age 18.
Staff Nurses' aides 4 (ft), 2 (pt); Physical therapists (contracted); Activities coordinators 1 (ft), 1 (pt); Dietitians (contracted).
Facilities Dining room; Activities room; Crafts room.
Activities Arts & crafts; Cards; Games; Reading groups; Prayer groups; Movies; Shopping trips; Dances/Social/Cultural gatherings.

Camp Point

Grandview Manor Nursing Home
205 Spring St, Camp Point, IL 62320
(217) 593-7734
Admin Mary Buffington.
Medical Dir Dr Frank Chamberlin.
Licensure Skilled care; Intermediate care. *Beds* ICF 118. *Certified* Medicaid.
Owner Proprietary corp.
Admissions Requirements Minimum age 21; Medical examination; Physician's request.
Staff RNs 3 (ft); LPNs 4 (ft), 5 (pt); Nurses' aides 25 (ft), 4 (pt); Activities coordinators 2 (ft).
Facilities Dining room; Physical therapy room; Activities room; Laundry room; Barber/Beauty shop.
Activities Arts & crafts; Cards; Games; Reading groups; Prayer groups; Movies; Shopping trips.

Canton

Emerald Estates
1577 E Myrtle St, Canton, IL 61520
(309) 647-6604
Admin Annabel C Gray.
Medical Dir Peter Chang.
Licensure Intermediate care for mentally retarded. *Beds* ICF/MR 15. *Private Pay Patients* 0%. *Certified* Medicaid.
Owner Proprietary corp (Illinois Developmental Association).
Admissions Requirements Minimum age 18; Must be ambulatory and attend workshop.
Staff Physicians; LPNs; Physical therapists; Occupational therapists; Speech therapists; Activities coordinators; Dietitians.
Facilities Dining room; Activities room; Laundry room.
Activities Arts & crafts; Cards; Games; Reading groups; Prayer groups; Movies; Shopping trips; Dances/Social/Cultural gatherings; Intergenerational programs; Active treatment.

Heartland Health Care Center—Canton
2081 N Main St, Box 40, Canton, IL 61520
(309) 647-6135
Admin Arthalene Widger. *Dir of Nursing* Debra Grushkin. *Medical Dir* Carlos Almeida MD.
Licensure Skilled care; Assisted living; Alzheimer's care. *Beds* SNF 72; Assisted living 28. *Private Pay Patients* 90%. *Certified* Medicaid; Medicare.
Owner Proprietary corp (Health Care & Retirement Corp).
Admissions Requirements Minimum age 18; Medical examination; Physician's request.
Staff Physicians 2 (pt); RNs 6 (ft), 2 (pt); LPNs 6 (ft), 3 (pt); Nurses' aides 24 (ft), 6 (pt); Physical therapists 2 (pt); Occupational therapists 1 (pt); Speech therapists 1 (pt); Activities coordinators 1 (ft); Dietitians 1 (ft); Ophthalmologists 1 (pt); Podiatrists 1 (pt); Audiologists 1 (pt).
Facilities Dining room; Physical therapy room; Activities room; Chapel; Crafts room; Laundry room; Barber/Beauty shop; Smoking and nonsmoking lounge; Wanderguard system.
Activities Arts & crafts; Cards; Games; Reading groups; Prayer groups; Movies; Shopping trips; Dances/Social/Cultural gatherings; Intergenerational programs; Pet therapy; Baking classes.

Nursing Center of Canton
1675 E Ash St, Canton, IL 61520
(309) 647-5631
Admin Sandi Spyres, acting. *Dir of Nursing* Beverly Biswell. *Medical Dir* Dr Peter Chang.
Licensure Skilled care; Intermediate care; Skilled pediatric care. *Beds* Swing beds SNF/ICF 162; Skilled pediatric care 32. *Private Pay Patients* 3%. *Certified* Medicaid; Medicare.
Owner Proprietary corp (Signature Corp).
Admissions Requirements Medical examination; Physician's request.
Staff Physicians 2 (pt); RNs 5 (ft); LPNs 13 (ft); Nurses' aides 65 (ft), 10 (pt); Speech therapists 1 (pt); Activities coordinators 3 (ft); Dietitians 1 (pt); Ophthalmologists 1 (pt); Podiatrists 1 (pt); QMRPs 1 (pt), 1 (pt).
Facilities Dining room; Physical therapy room; Activities room; Chapel; Crafts room; Barber/Beauty shop; Library; Fitness trail.
Activities Arts & crafts; Cards; Games; Reading groups; Prayer groups; Movies; Shopping trips; Dances/Social/Cultural gatherings; Pet therapy; Psychosocial groups; Resident advisory council; Active treatment.

Sunset Manor of Canton
129 S First Ave, Canton, IL 61520
(309) 647-4327

Admin Deborah Huggins.
Medical Dir Dr Linda Forrestier.
Licensure Intermediate care. *Beds* ICF 98. *Certified* Medicaid.
Owner Proprietary corp (National Heritage).
Admissions Requirements Minimum age 18; Medical examination.
Staff RNs 3 (ft), 2 (pt); LPNs 5 (ft), 2 (pt); Nurses' aides 21 (ft), 15 (pt); Physical therapists 1 (ft), 1 (pt); Occupational therapists 1 (ft), 1 (pt); Activities coordinators 1 (ft), 1 (pt); Dietitians 5 (ft), 3 (pt).
Facilities Dining room; Physical therapy room; Activities room; Laundry room; Barber/Beauty shop.
Activities Arts & crafts; Cards; Games; Reading groups; Prayer groups; Movies; Shopping trips; Dances/Social/Cultural gatherings.

Carbondale

Carbondale Manor
500 Lewis Ln, Carbondale, IL 62901
(618) 529-5355
Admin Barbara Chasteen.
Licensure Intermediate care. *Beds* ICF 209.
Owner Proprietary corp (Angell Group).

Greenbriar Manor
c/o Jamestown Management, 1719 W Main St, Carbondale, IL 62901
(618) 734-1816
Admin Angela Oliver. *Dir of Nursing* Bea Becton RN. *Medical Dir* Gemo Wong MD.
Licensure Intermediate care. *Beds* ICF 64. *Certified* Medicare.
Owner Proprietary corp.
Admissions Requirements Minimum age 18; Medical examination.
Staff RNs 1 (ft); LPNs 5 (ft), 2 (pt); Nurses' aides 19 (ft); Physical therapists; Occupational therapists; Speech therapists; Activities coordinators 1 (ft); Dietitians; Medical Social workers 1 (ft).
Facilities Dining room; Physical therapy room; Activities room; Laundry room; Barber/Beauty shop.
Activities Arts & crafts; Cards; Games; Reading groups; Prayer groups; Movies; Shopping trips; Dances/Social/Cultural gatherings; Resident Council.

Styrest Nursing Home
120 N Tower Rd, Carbondale, IL 62901
(618) 549-3355
Admin Betty S Vick.
Licensure Skilled care; Sheltered care. *Beds* SNF 127; Sheltered care 108. *Certified* Medicaid; Medicare.
Owner Proprietary corp.

Carlinville

Carlinville Terrace Ltd
RR 3, Box 81C, Carlinville, IL 62626
(217) 854-4491
Admin Elaine M Ottersburg.
Licensure Intermediate care. *Beds* ICF 71. *Certified* Medicaid.
Owner Proprietary corp.
Admissions Requirements Minimum age 18; Medical examination.
Staff Physicians 2 (pt); RNs 1 (ft); LPNs 3 (ft), 3 (pt); Nurses' aides 11 (ft), 9 (pt); Physical therapists 1 (pt); Recreational therapists 1 (pt); Occupational therapists 1 (pt); Speech therapists 1 (pt); Activities coordinators 1 (pt); Dietitians 1 (pt); Podiatrists 1 (pt); Audiologists 1 (pt); Dentists 1 (pt).
Facilities Dining room; Physical therapy room; Activities room; Chapel; Crafts room; Laundry room; Barber/Beauty shop.

Activities Arts & crafts; Games; Reading groups; Prayer groups; Movies; Shopping trips; Dances/Social/Cultural gatherings; Orientation.

Country Care of Carlinville
1200 University Ave, Carlinville, IL 62626
(217) 854-4433
Admin Robinette A Dykstra.
Licensure Skilled care. *Beds* SNF 98.
Owner Proprietary corp.

Meadowbrook Manor
826 N High St, Carlinville, IL 62626
(217) 854-9606
Admin Carolyn L Loges.
Licensure Intermediate care. *Beds* 49. *Certified* Medicaid.
Owner Proprietary corp.

Sunshine Manor Nursing Center
751 N Oak St, Carlinville, IL 62626
(217) 854-2511
Admin Eunice Adcock. *Dir of Nursing* Mary Raffety.
Licensure Skilled care. *Beds* SNF 98. *Certified* Medicaid; Medicare.
Owner Nonprofit corp (First Humanics).
Admissions Requirements Minimum age 18; Medical examination.
Staff RNs; LPNs; Nurses' aides; Physical therapists; Recreational therapists; Occupational therapists; Activities coordinators.
Facilities Dining room; Physical therapy room; Activities room; Crafts room; Barber/Beauty shop; Library.
Activities Arts & crafts; Games; Reading groups; Prayer groups; Movies; Shopping trips; Dances/Social/Cultural gatherings.

Carlyle

Carlyle Healthcare Center Inc
501 Clinton St, Carlyle, IL 62231
(618) 594-3112
Admin Joann L Brave.
Licensure Intermediate care. *Beds* ICF 127. *Certified* Medicaid.
Owner Proprietary corp.

Carmi

Wabash Christian Retirement Center
College Blvd, Carmi, IL 62821
(618) 382-4644
Admin Troy Hart. *Dir of Nursing* Kay Warten.
Licensure Skilled care; Retirement. *Beds* SNF 160; Retirement 8. *Certified* Medicaid.
Owner Nonprofit corp (Christian Homes).
Staff RNs 8 (ft), 2 (pt); LPNs 10 (ft), 4 (pt); Nurses' aides 25 (ft), 15 (pt); Activities coordinators 2 (ft), 2 (pt).
Facilities Dining room; Physical therapy room; Activities room; Chapel; Crafts room; Laundry room; Barber/Beauty shop.
Activities Arts & crafts; Cards; Games; Reading groups; Prayer groups; Movies; Shopping trips; Dances/Social/Cultural gatherings.

White County Nursing Home
PO Box 339, Rte 3, Carmi, IL 62821
(618) 382-7116
Admin Faye Frashie R Driggers.
Licensure Intermediate care. *Beds* 72. *Certified* Medicaid.
Owner Publicly owned.

Carol Stream

Windsor Park Manor Medical Facility
110 Windsor Park Dr, Carol Stream, IL 60188
(312) 682-4491, 682-4609 FAX

Admin Richard Ludwigson. *Dir of Nursing*
Arlene Los-Meyer. *Medical Dir* Maurice
Birt.
Licensure Skilled care; Alzheimer's care;
Retirement. *Beds* SNF 60. *Private Pay
Patients* 75%. *Certified* Medicare.
Owner Proprietary corp (American Lifecare
Corp).
Admissions Requirements Minimum age 65.
Staff RNs 8 (ft), 7 (pt); LPNs 2 (ft); Nurses'
aides 16 (ft), 12 (pt); Physical therapists 2
(ft); Occupational therapists 1 (ft); Activities
coordinators 1 (ft); Dietitians 3 (ft).
Facilities Dining room; Physical therapy
room; Activities room; Crafts room; Laundry
room; Barber/Beauty shop.
Activities Arts & crafts; Cards; Games;
Reading groups; Prayer groups; Movies;
Shopping trips.

Carrier Mills

Carrier Mills Nursing Home Inc
US Rte 45 E, Carrier Mills, IL 62917
(618) 994-2232
Admin Alice A Stallings. *Dir of Nursing* Mary
Barler. *Medical Dir* Larry Jones MD.
Licensure Skilled care. *Beds* SNF 68. *Certified*
Medicaid; Medicare.
Owner Proprietary corp.
Admissions Requirements Minimum age 22;
Medical examination; Physician's request.
Staff Physicians 8 (pt); RNs 2 (ft), 1 (pt);
LPNs 7 (ft), 4 (pt); Nurses' aides 17 (ft), 4
(pt); Physical therapists 1 (ft), 2 (pt);
Recreational therapists 1 (pt); Occupational
therapists 1 (pt); Speech therapists 1 (pt);
Activities coordinators 2 (ft), 1 (pt);
Dietitians 1 (ft), 1 (pt); Ophthalmologists 1
(pt); Podiatrists 1 (pt); Dentists 1 (pt).
Facilities Dining room; Physical therapy
room; Activities room; Crafts room; Laundry
room; Barber/Beauty shop.
Activities Arts & crafts; Cards; Games;
Reading groups; Prayer groups; Movies;
Dances/Social/Cultural gatherings.

Carrollton

Mt Gilead Shelter Care Home
Rte 3 Box 53, Carrollton, IL 62016
(217) 942-5362
Admin Luann Roth.
Licensure Sheltered care. *Beds* Sheltered care
28.
Owner Proprietary corp.
Admissions Requirements Minimum age 19;
Medical examination; Physician's request.
Facilities Dining room; Activities room.
Activities Arts & crafts; Cards; Games; Prayer
groups; Movies; Shopping trips; Dances/
Social/Cultural gatherings.

Reisch Memorial Nursing Home
800 School St, Carrollton, IL 62016
(217) 942-6946
Admin Thomas J McKula.
Licensure Skilled care. *Beds* 40. *Certified*
Medicaid.
Owner Nonprofit corp.

Carthage

Hancock County Nursing Home
S Adams St, Carthage, IL 62321
(217) 357-3131
Admin Steven T Moburg.
Licensure Skilled care. *Beds* SNF 52. *Certified*
Medicaid.
Owner Nonprofit corp.
Admissions Requirements Physician's request.
Staff RNs 1 (ft), 2 (pt); LPNs 2 (ft), 2 (pt);
Nurses' aides 18 (ft), 4 (pt); Physical
therapists 1 (pt); Speech therapists 1 (pt);
Activities coordinators 1 (ft), 1 (pt);
Dietitians 1 (pt).

Facilities Dining room; Physical therapy
room; Activities room; Chapel; Crafts room;
Laundry room; Barber/Beauty shop.
Activities Arts & crafts; Cards; Games;
Reading groups; Prayer groups; Movies;
Dances/Social/Cultural gatherings.

Casey

Birchwood Nursing Home
100 NE 15th St, Casey, IL 62420
(217) 932-5217
Admin Patricia J Bellinger. *Dir of Nursing*
Nancy A Collins RN.
Licensure Intermediate care. *Beds* ICF 75.
Owner Proprietary corp (Health Equity
Resources).
Admissions Requirements Minimum age 65;
Medical examination.
Staff RNs 1 (ft), 2 (pt); LPNs 12 (pt); Nurses'
aides 18 (pt); Activities coordinators 1 (ft).
Facilities Dining room; Activities room;
Crafts room; Laundry room; Barber/Beauty
shop; Library; Privacy area.
Activities Arts & crafts; Cards; Games;
Reading groups; Prayer groups; Movies;
Shopping trips; Dances/Social/Cultural
gatherings; Intergenerational programs; Pet
therapy.

Heartland Manor Inc Nursing Center
410 NW 3rd, Casey, IL 62420
(217) 932-4081
Admin David J Sauer. *Dir of Nursing*
Therease Carlson. *Medical Dir* Dr Sjanna
Johnston.
Licensure Skilled care. *Beds* SNF 92. *Private
Pay Patients* 45%. *Certified* Medicaid;
Medicare.
Owner Nonprofit corp.
Admissions Requirements Minimum age 18.
Staff Physicians 3 (ft); RNs 6 (ft), 2 (pt);
LPNs 5 (ft), 2 (pt); Nurses' aides 25 (ft), 18
(pt); Physical therapists 1 (pt); Occupational
therapists 1 (pt); Speech therapists 1 (pt);
Activities coordinators 1 (ft); Dietitians 1
(pt); Podiatrists 1 (pt); Audiologists 1 (pt).
Facilities Dining room; Physical therapy
room; Activities room; Laundry room;
Barber/Beauty shop.
Activities Arts & crafts; Cards; Games;
Reading groups; Prayer groups; Movies;
Shopping trips; Pet therapy.

Caseyville

Caseyville Health Care Center
601 W Lincoln, Caseyville, IL 62232
(618) 345-3072
Admin Josephine Thompson.
Licensure Skilled care. *Beds* SNF 150.

Centralia

Brookside Manor Inc
2000 W Broadway, Centralia, IL 62801
(618) 532-2428
Admin Floyd Wreath.
Medical Dir Dr M A Junidi.
Licensure Intermediate care. *Beds* ICF 49.
Certified Medicaid.
Owner Proprietary corp (Community Lifecare
Enterprises).
Admissions Requirements Medical
examination.
Staff LPNs 4 (ft); Nurses' aides 18 (ft);
Activities coordinators 1 (ft); Dietitians 1
(pt).
Facilities Dining room; Physical therapy
room; Activities room; Crafts room; Laundry
room; Barber/Beauty shop.
Activities Arts & crafts; Cards; Games;
Reading groups; Prayer groups; Movies;
Shopping trips; Dances/Social/Cultural
gatherings.

Centralia Care Center
1411 E Frazier, Centralia, IL 62801
(618) 533-1369
Admin Barbra Conners. *Dir of Nursing* Vickie
Wayman RN. *Medical Dir* Dr J Bacallao.
Licensure Skilled care; Intermediate care;
Alzheimer's care. *Beds* SNF 16; ICF 43.
Certified Medicaid; Medicare.
Owner Proprietary corp (Community Lifecare
Enterprises).
Admissions Requirements Minimum age 18;
Medical examination.
Staff RNs 2 (ft); LPNs 5 (ft), 2 (pt); Nurses'
aides 25 (ft); Physical therapists 1 (ft), 1 (pt);
Speech therapists 1 (pt); Activities
coordinators 1 (ft), 2 (pt); Dietitians 1 (pt).
Facilities Dining room; Physical therapy
room; Activities room; Crafts room; Laundry
room; Barber/Beauty shop.
Activities Arts & crafts; Cards; Games;
Reading groups; Prayer groups; Movies;
Shopping trips; Dances/Social/Cultural
gatherings; Pet therapy.

Centralia Fireside House
1030 McCord St, Centralia, IL 62801
(618) 532-1833
Admin David C Elfert.
Licensure Skilled care; Intermediate care. *Beds*
SNF 51; ICF 47. *Certified* Medicaid.
Owner Proprietary corp.

Centralia Friendship House
PO Box 454, 1000 E McCord, Centralia, IL
62801
(618) 532-3642, 532-3326, 532-3853 FAX
Admin Kyle C Moore. *Dir of Nursing* Patricia
Lane. *Medical Dir* Dr Naeem Khan.
Licensure Intermediate care. *Beds* ICF 94.
Certified Medicaid.
Owner Proprietary corp (Community Lifecare
Enterprises Inc).
Admissions Requirements Minimum age 18;
Medical examination.
Staff RNs 3 (ft), 1 (pt); LPNs 5 (ft), 3 (pt);
Nurses' aides 18 (ft), 9 (pt); Physical
therapists 1 (pt); Activities coordinators 2
(ft); Dietitians 5 (ft), 3 (pt).
Facilities Dining room; Physical therapy
room; Activities room; Laundry room;
Barber/Beauty shop.
Activities Arts & crafts; Cards; Games;
Reading groups; Prayer groups; Movies; Pet
therapy.

Colonial Apartments
920 W 4th St, Centralia, IL 62801
(618) 533-1199
Admin James F Bowers.
Licensure Intermediate care for mentally
retarded. *Beds* ICF/MR 15.

Champaign

Americana Healthcare Center of Champaign
309 E Springfield Ave, Champaign, IL 61820
(217) 352-5135
Admin Sarah Peters.
Medical Dir Dr Robert Bosler.
Licensure Skilled care. *Beds* SNF 102.
Certified Medicaid; Medicare.
Owner Proprietary corp (Manor Care).
Admissions Requirements Medical
examination; Physician's request.
Staff RNs 8 (ft), 2 (pt); LPNs 9 (ft); Nurses'
aides 27 (ft), 4 (pt); Physical therapists 1 (ft);
Reality therapists 1 (pt); Recreational
therapists 1 (ft); Occupational therapists 1
(pt); Speech therapists 1 (pt); Activities
coordinators 1 (ft); Dietitians 1 (ft).
Facilities Dining room; Physical therapy
room; Activities room; Barber/Beauty shop;
Enclosed outdoor patio.
Activities Arts & crafts; Cards; Games;
Reading groups; Prayer groups; Movies;
Shopping trips; Dances/Social/Cultural
gatherings.

Champaign Children's Home
109 Kenwood Rd, Champaign, IL 61820
(217) 356-5164
Admin Debra L Cutler. *Dir of Nursing* Kathy Schmidt. *Medical Dir* William Farris MD.
Licensure Skilled care. *Beds* SNF 87. *Private Pay Patients* 1%. *Certified* Medicaid.
Owner Nonprofit corp (Hoosier Care Inc).
Admissions Requirements Minimum age 0-22.
Staff Physicians 2 (ft); RNs 7 (ft); LPNs 12 (ft); Nurses' aides 40 (ft); Physical therapists 1 (ft); Recreational therapists 2 (ft); Occupational therapists 1 (pt); Speech therapists 1 (pt); Activities coordinators 15 (ft), 4 (pt); Dietitians 1 (pt); Audiologists 1 (ft).
Facilities Physical therapy room; Activities room; Crafts room; Laundry room.
Activities Arts & crafts; Cards; Games; Reading groups; Prayer groups; Movies; Shopping trips; Dances/Social/Cultural gatherings; Intergenerational programs; Pet therapy.

Champaign Opportunity House
1315-A Curt Dr, Champaign, IL 61820
(217) 351-3590
Admin Lynda Hagler. *Dir of Nursing* B Hutcherson. *Medical Dir* Na Nagawa MD.
Licensure Intermediate care for mentally retarded. *Beds* 60. *Certified* Medicaid.
Owner Proprietary corp.
Admissions Requirements Minimum age 21; Medical examination; Physician's request.
Staff LPNs 5 (ft), 1 (pt); Nurses' aides 21 (ft), 4 (pt); Activities coordinators; Physical therapy aide; 1 (ft) Occupational therapy aide 1 (ft); Speech therapy aide 1 (ft); FSS 1 (ft); QMRP 2 (ft).
Facilities Dining room; Physical therapy room; Activities room; Crafts room; Laundry room.
Activities Arts & crafts; Cards; Games; Reading groups; Prayer groups; Movies; Shopping trips; Dances/Social/Cultural gatherings.

Garwood Home
1515 N Market St, Champaign, IL 61820
(217) 352-1412
Admin Carol Ann Edwards. *Dir of Nursing* Jean Bagaasen RN. *Medical Dir* Robert Atkins MD.
Licensure Sheltered care. *Beds* Sheltered care 34. *Private Pay Patients* 100%.
Owner Nonprofit corp.
Admissions Requirements Minimum age 60; Medical examination; Physician's request.
Staff RNs 1 (ft); LPNs 4 (pt); Nurses' aides 4 (pt); Activities coordinators 1 (ft).
Facilities Dining room; Activities room; Crafts room; Laundry room; Barber/Beauty shop; Private rooms.
Activities Arts & crafts; Cards; Games; Reading groups; Prayer groups; Movies; Shopping trips; Dances/Social/Cultural gatherings; Intergenerational programs; Pet therapy.

Greenbrier Nursing Center Inc
1915 S Mattis Ave, Champaign, IL 61820
(217) 352-0516
Admin John P Slevin. *Dir of Nursing* Nancy Richardson RN. *Medical Dir* Charles R Shepardson MD.
Licensure Skilled care. *Beds* SNF 118. *Certified* Medicaid; Medicare.
Owner Proprietary corp.
Admissions Requirements Minimum age 21; Medical examination; Physician's request.
Staff Physicians 2 (pt); RNs 3 (ft), 2 (pt); LPNs 6 (ft); Nurses' aides 28 (ft), 2 (pt); Reality therapists 1 (pt); Recreational therapists 1 (pt); Occupational therapists 1 (pt); Speech therapists 1 (pt); Activities coordinators 1 (ft), 1 (pt); Dietitians 1 (pt); Ophthalmologists 1 (pt).

Facilities Dining room; Activities room; Crafts room; Laundry room; Barber/Beauty shop; Library; Smoking room.
Activities Arts & crafts; Games; Reading groups; Prayer groups; Movies; Shopping trips; Dances/Social/Cultural gatherings; Church services.

Heritage House of Champaign
1315 Curt Dr, Champaign, IL 61820
(217) 352-5707
Admin Candy J Carroll. *Dir of Nursing* Natalie Alagna RN. *Medical Dir* Dr W Gonzalez.
Licensure Intermediate care. *Beds* ICF 60. *Certified* Medicaid.
Owner Proprietary corp (National Heritage).
Admissions Requirements Minimum age 18; Medical examination; Physician's request.
Staff RNs 2 (ft); LPNs 4 (ft), 2 (pt); Nurses' aides 9 (ft), 5 (pt); Physical therapists 1 (pt); Reality therapists 1 (pt); Recreational therapists 1 (pt); Occupational therapists 1 (pt); Speech therapists 1 (pt); Activities coordinators 1 (ft), 1 (pt); Dietitians 1 (pt); Ophthalmologists 1 (pt).
Facilities Dining room; Physical therapy room; Activities room; Laundry room; Barber/Beauty shop.
Activities Arts & crafts; Cards; Games; Reading groups; Prayer groups; Movies; Shopping trips; Dances/Social/Cultural gatherings; Pet therapy.

Charleston

Alpha Community House
1701 18th St, Charleston, IL 61920
(217) 345-4224
Admin Stephen K Hutton. *Dir of Nursing* Lois White. *Medical Dir* Dr Carl Johnson.
Licensure Intermediate care for mentally retarded. *Beds* ICF/MR 15. *Private Pay Patients* 0%. *Certified* Medicaid; Medicare.
Owner Proprietary corp (Developmental Foundations Inc).
Admissions Requirements Minimum age 18; Medical examination; Physician's request; Developmentally disabled.
Staff LPNs; Occupational therapists; Speech therapists; Activities coordinators; Dietitians.
Facilities Dining room; Laundry room.
Activities Arts & crafts; Cards; Games; Movies; Shopping trips; Dances/Social/ Cultural gatherings; Intergenerational programs; Pet therapy; Living skills training.

Cambridge Court Manor Inc
716 18th St, Charleston, IL 61920
(217) 345-7054
Admin Robert Mattox.
Licensure Skilled care; Intermediate care. *Beds* SNF 45; ICF 94. *Certified* Medicaid.
Owner Proprietary corp.

Charleston Manor
415 18th St, Charleston, IL 61920
(217) 345-7048
Admin Linda S Simmons.
Licensure Intermediate care. *Beds* ICF 62. *Certified* Medicaid.
Owner Proprietary corp.
Admissions Requirements Medical examination.
Staff Physicians 1 (pt); RNs 1 (pt); LPNs 7 (ft); Nurses' aides 16 (ft); Physical therapists 1 (pt); Dietitians 1 (pt).
Facilities Dining room; Activities room; Crafts room; Laundry room; Barber/Beauty shop.
Activities Arts & crafts; Cards; Games; Reading groups; Prayer groups; Movies; Shopping trips; Dances/Social/Cultural gatherings.

Heritage House of Charleston
738 18th St, Charleston, IL 61920
(217) 345-2220

Admin Robert K Zabka.
Licensure Intermediate care for mentally retarded. *Beds* ICF/MR 89. *Certified* Medicaid.
Owner Proprietary corp.
Admissions Requirements Minimum age 18.
Facilities Dining room; Physical therapy room; Activities room; Chapel; Crafts room; Laundry room.
Activities Arts & crafts; Cards; Games; Reading groups; Prayer groups; Movies; Shopping trips; Dances/Social/Cultural gatherings.

Hilltop Convalescent Center
910 W Polk, Charleston, IL 61920
(217) 345-7066
Admin Araceli M Henson. *Dir of Nursing* Roberta Kerz. *Medical Dir* Leland McNeill.
Licensure Intermediate care. *Beds* ICF 108. *Certified* Medicaid.
Owner Proprietary corp (Nursing Home Managers Inc).
Facilities Dining room; Physical therapy room; Activities room; Laundry room; Barber/Beauty shop.
Activities Arts & crafts; Cards; Games; Reading groups; Prayer groups; Movies; Shopping trips; Dances/Social/Cultural gatherings; Intergenerational programs; Pet therapy.

Omega House
910 17th St, Charleston, IL 61920
(217) 345-2922
Admin Stephen K Hutton.
Licensure Intermediate care for mentally retarded. *Beds* ICF/MR 15.

Chenoa

Meadows Mennonite Home
RR 1, Chenoa, IL 61726
(309) 747-2702
Admin Velma J Loewen. *Dir of Nursing* Hazel Yoder RN BSN. *Medical Dir* Paul E Hakes MD.
Licensure Intermediate care; Sheltered care; Retirement; Alzheimer's care. *Beds* ICF 109; Sheltered care 33; Retirement 80. *Private Pay Patients* 80%. *Certified* Medicaid.
Owner Nonprofit organization/foundation.
Admissions Requirements Minimum age 60; Medical examination.
Staff RNs; LPNs; Nurses' aides; Activities coordinators.
Affiliation Mennonite.
Facilities Dining room; Physical therapy room; Activities room; Chapel; Crafts room; Laundry room; Barber/Beauty shop; Library.
Activities Arts & crafts; Cards; Games; Reading groups; Prayer groups; Movies; Shopping trips; Dances/Social/Cultural gatherings; Intergenerational programs; Fitness program.

Chester

St Anns Healthcare Center Inc
770 State St, Chester, IL 62233
(618) 826-2314
Admin J Michael Greer. *Dir of Nursing* Sr Angela Heimann RN. *Medical Dir* John R Beck MD.
Licensure Skilled care; Intermediate care. *Beds* SNF 27; ICF 87. *Certified* Medicaid; Medicare; VA.
Owner Proprietary corp.
Admissions Requirements Minimum age 21; Medical examination.
Staff Physicians 1 (pt); RNs 2 (ft), 5 (pt); LPNs 1 (ft), 6 (pt); Nurses' aides 21 (ft), 12 (pt); Physical therapists 1 (pt); Reality therapists 1 (ft); Recreational therapists 1 (pt); Occupational therapists 1 (pt); Speech

therapists 1 (pt); Activities coordinators 1 (ft); Dietitians 1 (ft), 1 (pt); Ophthalmologists 1 (pt).
Facilities Dining room; Activities room; Chapel; Crafts room; Laundry room; Barber/ Beauty shop.
Activities Arts & crafts; Cards; Games; Reading groups; Prayer groups; Movies; Shopping trips; Dances/Social/Cultural gatherings.

Three Springs Lodge Nursing Home Inc
Rte 1 Box 324, Chester, IL 62233
(618) 826-3210
Admin Kenneth Rowold.
Licensure Skilled care; Intermediate care. *Beds* SNF 52; ICF 33. *Certified* Medicaid.
Owner Proprietary corp.

Chicago

Alden Nursing Center—Lakeland
820 W Lawrence Ave, Chicago, IL 60640
(312) 769-2570, 769-0607 FAX
Admin Ann Richards.
Medical Dir B K Shah MD.
Licensure Skilled care. *Beds* SNF 300. *Certified* Medicaid; Medicare.
Owner Proprietary corp (Alden Management Services Inc).
Admissions Requirements Minimum age 18.
Staff Physicians; RNs; LPNs; Nurses' aides; Physical therapists; Occupational therapists; Speech therapists; Activities coordinators; Dietitians; Ophthalmologists; Podiatrists; Audiologists.
Facilities Dining room; Physical therapy room; Activities room; Crafts room; Laundry room; Barber/Beauty shop.
Activities Arts & crafts; Cards; Games; Reading groups; Prayer groups; Movies; Shopping trips; Dances/Social/Cultural gatherings; Intergenerational programs; Pet therapy.

Alden Nursing Center—Morrow
5001 S Michigan, Chicago, IL 60615
(312) 924-9292, 924-1308 FAX
Admin Albert R Witkins MHA. *Dir of Nursing* Linda Houston RN. *Medical Dir* Abdolmajid Rezvan MD.
Licensure Skilled care; Intermediate care; Alzheimer's care. *Beds* SNF 24; ICF 168. *Certified* Medicaid; Medicare.
Owner Privately owned (Alden Management Services Inc).
Admissions Requirements Minimum age 18.
Staff Physicians; RNs; LPNs; Nurses' aides; Physical therapists; Reality therapists; Occupational therapists; Speech therapists; Activities coordinators; Dietitians; Ophthalmologists; Podiatrists; Audiologists.
Facilities Dining room; Physical therapy room; Activities room; Crafts room; Laundry room; Barber/Beauty shop; Library.
Activities Arts & crafts; Cards; Games; Reading groups; Prayer groups; Movies; Shopping trips; Dances/Social/Cultural gatherings; Pet therapy.

Alden Nursing Center—Princeton
255 W 69th St, Chicago, IL 60621
Licensure Skilled care; Intermediate care. *Beds* Swing beds SNF/ICF 225. *Certified* Medicaid; Medicare.
Owner Proprietary corp (Alden Management Services Inc).
Admissions Requirements Minimum age 18; Medical examination.
Staff Physicians; RNs; LPNs; Nurses' aides; Physical therapists; Occupational therapists; Speech therapists; Activities coordinators; Dietitians; Ophthalmologists; Podiatrists; Audiologists.
Facilities Dining room; Physical therapy room; Activities room; Crafts room; Laundry room; Barber/Beauty shop; Library; Ice cream parlor.

Activities Arts & crafts; Cards; Games; Reading groups; Prayer groups; Movies; Shopping trips; Dances/Social/Cultural gatherings; Intergenerational programs; Pet therapy.

Alden Nursing Center—Wentworth
201 W 69th St, Chicago, IL 60621
(312) 487-1200, 487-4782 FAX
Admin Rory Tokar. *Dir of Nursing* Lynn T Cobb RN. *Medical Dir* Pancho DeGano MD.
Licensure Skilled care; Intermediate care; Hospice. *Beds* SNF 238; ICF 62. *Private Pay Patients* 1%. *Certified* Medicaid; Medicare.
Owner Proprietary corp (Alden Management Services Inc).
Admissions Requirements Minimum age 18; Medical examination; Physician's request.
Staff Physicians; RNs; LPNs; Nurses' aides; Physical therapists; Occupational therapists; Speech therapists; Activities coordinators; Dietitians; Ophthalmologists; Podiatrists; Audiologists.
Facilities Dining room; Physical therapy room; Activities room; Crafts room; Laundry room; Barber/Beauty shop; Courtyard mall.
Activities Arts & crafts; Cards; Games; Reading groups; Prayer groups; Movies; Shopping trips; Dances/Social/Cultural gatherings; Intergenerational programs; Bingo; Outings to zoo; Ball games; Theater; Picnics; Quarterly minister breakfast meetings; Community involvement.

All American Nursing Home
5448 N Broadway St, Chicago, IL 60640
(312) 334-2244
Admin Sharon Hinkle.
Medical Dir Riccardo Benvenuto MD.
Licensure Skilled care; Intermediate care. *Beds* SNF 48; ICF 96. *Certified* Medicaid.
Owner Proprietary corp.
Admissions Requirements Minimum age 23.
Staff Physicians 4 (pt); RNs 5 (ft); LPNs 12 (ft); Nurses' aides 38 (ft); Physical therapists 1 (pt); Reality therapists 1 (pt); Recreational therapists 1 (pt); Occupational therapists 1 (pt); Speech therapists 1 (pt); Activities coordinators 1 (ft); Dietitians 1 (pt); Podiatrists 1 (pt); Dentists 1 (pt).
Facilities Physical therapy room; Activities room; Chapel; Crafts room; Laundry room; Barber/Beauty shop; Library.
Activities Arts & crafts; Cards; Games; Reading groups; Prayer groups; Movies; Shopping trips; Dances/Social/Cultural gatherings.

Alshore House
2840 W Foster Ave, Chicago, IL 60625
(312) 561-2040
Admin Pamela Solomon.
Licensure Intermediate care. *Beds* ICF 48. *Certified* Medicaid.
Owner Proprietary corp.

Ambassador Nursing Center
4900 N Bernard St, Chicago, IL 60625
(312) 583-7130, 583-3929 FAX
Admin Fred Cantz ACSW. *Dir of Nursing* Maureen Malone RN. *Medical Dir* Ali Riazi MD.
Licensure Skilled care. *Beds* SNF 190. *Private Pay Patients* 20%. *Certified* Medicaid; Medicare.
Owner Proprietary corp.
Admissions Requirements Minimum age 50.
Staff Physicians 5 (pt); RNs 13 (ft), 3 (pt); LPNs 3 (ft); Nurses' aides 40 (ft); Physical therapists 1 (pt); Reality therapists 1 (pt); Recreational therapists 5 (ft); Activities coordinators 1 (ft); Dietitians 1 (ft); Ophthalmologists 1 (pt); Podiatrists 1 (pt); Audiologists 1 (pt).
Languages Korean, Spanish, Russian, Polish, Yiddish, Hebrew, Lithuanian.

Facilities Dining room; Physical therapy room; Activities room; Chapel; Crafts room; Laundry room; Barber/Beauty shop; Library.
Activities Arts & crafts; Cards; Games; Reading groups; Prayer groups; Movies; Shopping trips; Dances/Social/Cultural gatherings; Intergenerational programs; Pet therapy.

Approved Home Inc
909 W Wilson Ave, Chicago, IL 60640
(312) 275-2422
Admin Richard L Soule.
Medical Dir Roberta Phillips.
Licensure Intermediate care for mentally retarded. *Beds* ICF/MR 151. *Certified* Medicaid.
Owner Proprietary corp.
Admissions Requirements Minimum age 18; Medical examination; Physician's request.
Staff Physicians; RNs; LPNs; Recreational therapists; Occupational therapists; Speech therapists; Activities coordinators; Dietitians; Ophthalmologists; Podiatrists; Dentists.
Facilities Dining room; Activities room; Crafts room; Laundry room.
Activities Arts & crafts; Cards; Games; Reading groups; Prayer groups; Movies; Shopping trips; Dances/Social/Cultural gatherings.

Arbour Health Care Center Ltd
1512 W Fargo, Chicago, IL 60626
(312) 465-7751
Admin Patricia McDiarmid. *Dir of Nursing* Joyce Mixon. *Medical Dir* Dr Aboul Sattar.
Licensure Skilled care; Intermediate care. *Beds* SNF 70; ICF 29. *Certified* Medicaid.
Owner Proprietary corp.
Admissions Requirements Minimum age 60; Medical examination; Physician's request.
Staff RNs; LPNs; Nurses' aides; Physical therapists; Reality therapists; Recreational therapists; Occupational therapists; Activities coordinators; Dietitians.
Facilities Dining room; Physical therapy room; Activities room; Crafts room; Barber/Beauty shop; Library.
Activities Arts & crafts; Cards; Games; Reading groups; Prayer groups; Movies; Shopping trips; Dances/Social/Cultural gatherings.

Atrium Health Care Center Ltd
1425 W Estes, Chicago, IL 60626
(312) 973-4780
Admin Ronald B Silver.
Licensure Skilled care; Intermediate care. *Beds* SNF 160. *Certified* Medicaid.
Owner Proprietary corp.
Staff Physicians 8 (pt); RNs 16 (pt); Nurses' aides 24 (pt); Physical therapists 2 (pt); Reality therapists 1 (pt); Recreational therapists 1 (pt); Occupational therapists 1 (pt); Speech therapists 1 (pt); Activities coordinators 1 (pt); Dietitians 1 (pt); Ophthalmologists 1 (pt); Podiatrists 1 (pt); Audiologists 1 (pt); Dentists 1 (pt).
Facilities Dining room; Physical therapy room; Activities room; Crafts room; Barber/Beauty shop.
Activities Arts & crafts; Cards; Games; Reading groups; Prayer groups; Movies; Shopping trips.

Auburn Park Club
7748 S Emerald, Chicago, IL 60640
(312) 874-0012
Admin Fred D Jones.
Licensure Intermediate care for mentally retarded; Community living facility. *Beds* Community living facility 32. *Certified* Medicaid; Medicare.
Owner Nonprofit organization/foundation.
Admissions Requirements Males only.
Staff Activities coordinators 1 (ft).

Facilities Dining room; Activities room; Crafts room; Laundry room.
Activities Arts & crafts; Cards; Games; Reading groups; Movies; Shopping trips; Dances/Social/Cultural gatherings.

Avenue Care Center Inc
4505 S Drexel, Chicago, IL 60653
(312) 285-0550, 285-5618 FAX
Admin Ely M Indich. *Dir of Nursing* Annie Garrett. *Medical Dir* Keith O Roper.
Licensure Skilled care. *Beds* SNF 155. *Certified* Medicaid.
Owner Proprietary corp.
Facilities Dining room; Physical therapy room; Activities room; Chapel; Crafts room; Laundry room; Barber/Beauty shop.
Activities Arts & crafts; Cards; Games; Reading groups; Prayer groups; Movies; Shopping trips; Dances/Social/Cultural gatherings; Intergenerational programs.

Baggott House
6300 N Ridge Ave, Chicago, IL 60660
(312) 973-6300
Admin Teri Petrisko.
Licensure Intermediate care for mentally retarded. *Beds* ICF/MR 12.

Balmoral Nursing Centre Inc
2055 W Balmoral Ave, Chicago, IL 60625
(312) 561-8661
Admin Herman Katz.
Licensure Skilled care. *Beds* SNF 213. *Certified* Medicaid.
Owner Proprietary corp.

Warren N Barr Pavilion/Illinois Masonic Medical Center
66 W Oak St, Chicago, IL 60610
(312) 337-5400, 337-6438 FAX
Admin Glen E Zilmer. *Dir of Nursing* Karen Kraker MSN. *Medical Dir* Annie John MD.
Licensure Skilled care. *Beds* SNF 330. *Private Pay Patients* 75%. *Certified* Medicaid; Medicare.
Owner Nonprofit organization/foundation.
Admissions Requirements Minimum age 18; Medical examination.
Staff Physicians 1 (ft), 3 (pt); RNs 23 (ft), 2 (pt); LPNs 27 (ft); Nurses' aides 115 (ft), 4 (pt); Physical therapists 2 (ft); Recreational therapists 6 (ft), 1 (pt); Occupational therapists 2 (ft); Speech therapists 1 (ft), 2 (pt); Activities coordinators 1 (ft); Dietitians 1 (ft); Ophthalmologists 1 (pt); Podiatrists 1 (pt); Audiologists 1 (pt).
Languages Polish, Spanish.
Affiliation Masons.
Facilities Dining room; Physical therapy room; Activities room; Chapel; Crafts room; Laundry room; Barber/Beauty shop; Library; Gift shop; Ice cream & soda fountain; Sunroof/patio/garden.
Activities Arts & crafts; Cards; Games; Reading groups; Prayer groups; Movies; Shopping trips; Dances/Social/Cultural gatherings; Intergenerational programs; Pet therapy; Gardening; Exercise; Movies; Weekly outings; Special diets and menu selection.

Belhaven Inc
11401 S Oakley Ave, Chicago, IL 60643
(312) 233-6311
Admin John Conatser.
Licensure Skilled care; Intermediate care. *Beds* SNF 154; ICF 76.

Belmont Nursing Home Inc
1936 W Belmont Ave, Chicago, IL 60657
(312) 525-7176
Admin Laurie Hertz.
Licensure Intermediate care. *Beds* ICF 61. *Certified* Medicaid.
Owner Proprietary corp.

Bethesda Home & Retirement Center
2833 N Nordica Ave, Chicago, IL 60634
(312) 622-6144
Admin Carol P Beecher, CEO. *Dir of Nursing* Carolyn Vogel. *Medical Dir* Robin Uchitelle MD.
Licensure Intermediate care; Assisted living; Retirement. *Beds* ICF 63; Assisted living 55; Retirement units 19. *Private Pay Patients* 75%. *Certified* Medicaid.
Owner Nonprofit organization/foundation.
Admissions Requirements Minimum age 62; Medical examination.
Staff Physicians (contracted); RNs 6 (ft), 2 (pt); LPNs 1 (ft), 4 (pt); Nurses' aides 2 (ft), 4 (pt); Recreational therapists 1 (ft); Occupational therapists (contracted); Speech therapists (contracted); Activities coordinators 1 (ft); Dietitians (contracted); Ophthalmologists (contracted).
Languages Spanish, Polish.
Affiliation Lutheran.
Activities Arts & crafts; Cards; Games; Prayer groups; Movies; Shopping trips; Dances/Social/Cultural gatherings; Pet therapy.

Bethune Plaza Inc
4537 S Drexel, Chicago, IL 60653
(312) 268-8950
Admin Rosa W Morgan.
Licensure Intermediate care. *Beds* ICF 276.
Owner Proprietary corp.

Beverly Towers Nursing Home
8001 S Western Ave, Chicago, IL 60620
(312) 436-6600
Admin Dorothy Klein.
Licensure Skilled care; Intermediate care. *Beds* SNF 220; ICF 108. *Certified* Medicaid.
Owner Proprietary corp.

Birchwood Plaza Nursing & Rehabilitation Center
1426 W Birchwood Ave, Chicago, IL 60626
(312) 274-4405, (312) 274-4763 FAX
Admin Abraham Schiffman. *Dir of Nursing* Patricia Kessl RN. *Medical Dir* Norman Guttman MD.
Licensure Skilled care; Intermediate care; Retirement; Sheltered care; Alzheimer's care. *Beds* Swing beds SNF/ICF 192; Retirement 110. *Certified* Medicaid; Medicare.
Owner Proprietary corp.
Admissions Requirements Medical examination; Geriatric.
Staff Physicians 35 (pt); RNs 7 (ft), 3 (pt); LPNs 6 (ft), 3 (pt); Nurses' aides 47 (ft); Activities coordinators 1 (ft).
Languages Yiddish; Hebrew; Russian; Polish; Spanish; Hungarian.
Facilities Dining room; Physical therapy room; Activities room; Crafts room; Laundry room; Barber/Beauty shop; Kosher kitchen.
Activities Arts & crafts; Cards; Games; Reading groups; Prayer groups; Movies; Dances/Social/Cultural gatherings.

Bohemian Home for the Aged
5061 N Pulaski Rd, Chicago, IL 60630
(312) 588-1220
Admin Z Peter Brandler.
Medical Dir Stephen Dubala MD.
Licensure Skilled care; Intermediate care. *Beds* SNF 30; ICF 188. *Certified* Medicaid.
Owner Nonprofit corp.
Admissions Requirements Minimum age 75; Medical examination.
Staff Physicians 1 (pt); RNs 14 (ft), 7 (pt); LPNs 11 (ft); Nurses' aides 50 (ft); Activities coordinators 1 (ft); Dietitians 1 (ft).
Languages Czech, Polish.
Facilities Dining room; Physical therapy room; Activities room; Crafts room; Laundry room; Barber/Beauty shop; Library.
Activities Arts & crafts; Games; Reading groups; Prayer groups; Movies; Shopping trips; Dances/Social/Cultural gatherings.

Boulevard Care Center Inc
3405 S Michigan Ave, Chicago, IL 60616
(312) 791-0035
Admin Sherwin I Ray.
Medical Dir Dr Sheldon Levine.
Licensure Skilled care. *Beds* SNF 155. *Certified* Medicaid.
Owner Proprietary corp.
Admissions Requirements Medical examination; Physician's request.
Staff Physicians 3 (pt); RNs 2 (ft), 2 (pt); LPNs 10 (ft), 4 (pt); Nurses' aides 30 (ft), 5 (pt); Physical therapists 1 (pt); Recreational therapists 2 (ft); Occupational therapists 1 (pt); Speech therapists 1 (pt); Activities coordinators 1 (ft); Dietitians 1 (pt); Ophthalmologists 1 (pt); Podiatrists 1 (pt); Dentists 1 (pt).
Facilities Dining room; Physical therapy room; Activities room; Chapel; Crafts room; Laundry room; Barber/Beauty shop.
Activities Arts & crafts; Cards; Games; Reading groups; Prayer groups; Dances/Social/Cultural gatherings.

Brightview Care Center Inc
4538 N Beacon, Chicago, IL 60640
(312) 275-7200, 275-7543 FAX
Admin James Marc Emerson. *Dir of Nursing* Carol Colson. *Medical Dir* Dr A Rezvan.
Licensure Skilled care. *Beds* SNF 143. *Private Pay Patients* 5%. *Certified* Medicaid.
Owner Proprietary corp.
Admissions Requirements Medical examination; Physician's request.
Staff RNs; LPNs; Nurses' aides; Recreational therapists; Activities coordinators.
Languages Spanish.
Facilities Dining room; Physical therapy room; Activities room; Crafts room; Laundry room; Barber/Beauty shop; Library; Family and resident privacy areas; Kosher kitchen; Outdoor patio.
Activities Arts & crafts; Cards; Games; Reading groups; Prayer groups; Movies; Shopping trips; Dances/Social/Cultural gatherings; Intergenerational programs; Pet therapy; Picnics; Sports events.

Buckingham Pavilion Nursing & Rehabilitation Center Inc
2625 W Touhy Ave, Chicago, IL 60645
(312) 764-6850
Admin Margaret Stern. *Dir of Nursing* Maria Zaylor RN. *Medical Dir* Harry Kurz MD.
Licensure Skilled care; Intermediate care; Retirement; Alzheimer's care. *Beds* Swing beds SNF/ICF 247; Retirement units 500. *Private Pay Patients* 65%. *Certified* Medicaid; Medicare.
Owner Privately owned.
Admissions Requirements Medical examination.
Staff Physicians 1 (ft), 25 (pt); RNs 12 (ft), 2 (pt); LPNs 8 (ft), 4 (pt); Nurses' aides 25 (ft), 10 (pt); Physical therapists 1 (ft); Reality therapists 1 (pt); Recreational therapists 1 (ft); Occupational therapists 1 (ft); Speech therapists 1 (pt); Activities coordinators 2 (ft), 2 (pt); Dietitians 1 (pt); Ophthalmologists 10 (pt) (contracted); Podiatrists 10 (pt) (contracted); Audiologists 6 (pt) (contracted).
Languages Yiddish.
Facilities Dining room; Physical therapy room; Activities room; Chapel; Crafts room; Laundry room; Barber/Beauty shop; Library; Ice cream shop; Gift shop; IV room; Cinema; Synagogue.
Activities Arts & crafts; Cards; Games; Reading groups; Prayer groups; Movies; Shopping trips; Dances/Social/Cultural gatherings; Intergenerational programs; Pet therapy; Outings; Kosher meals.

Burnham Terrace Care Center
14500 S Manistee, Chicago, IL 60633
(312) 862-1260

Admin Herman W Frey.
Licensure Skilled care; Intermediate care. *Beds* SNF 103; ICF 206.
Owner Proprietary corp.

California Gardens Nursing Center
2829 S California Blvd, Chicago, IL 60608
(312) 847-8061
Admin Barry Carr. *Dir of Nursing* Jacquiline Eicher. *Medical Dir* Dr Bulmash.
Licensure Skilled care. *Beds* SNF 306. *Private Pay Patients* 1%. *Certified* Medicaid; Medicare.
Owner Proprietary corp (Nu Care Management).
Admissions Requirements Minimum age 21.
Staff Physicians 10 (ft); RNs 4 (ft), 8 (pt); LPNs 24 (ft), 4 (pt); Nurses' aides 90 (ft), 5 (pt); Physical therapists 2 (pt); Reality therapists 1 (pt); Recreational therapists 1 (pt); Occupational therapists 2 (pt); Speech therapists 2 (pt); Activities coordinators 1 (ft), 1 (pt); Dietitians 1 (ft), 1 (pt); Ophthalmologists 1 (pt); Podiatrists 2 (pt); Audiologists 1 (pt).
Languages Spanish, Lithuanian.
Facilities Dining room; Physical therapy room; Activities room; Crafts room; Laundry room; Barber/Beauty shop; Library; Occupational therapy room; Classroom.
Activities Arts & crafts; Cards; Games; Reading groups; Prayer groups; Movies; Shopping trips; Dances/Social/Cultural gatherings; Intergenerational programs; Pet therapy.

Carci Hall
11321 S Wentworth, Chicago, IL 60612
(312) 995-1127
Admin Janet Conner.
Licensure Intermediate care for mentally retarded. *Beds* ICF/MR 35.
Owner Nonprofit corp.

Carlton House Nursing Center
725 W Montrose Ave, Chicago, IL 60613
(312) 929-1700
Admin Rose Marie Betz RN. *Dir of Nursing* Esther Jenkins RN. *Medical Dir* David Edelberg MD.
Licensure Skilled care. *Beds* SNF 244. *Certified* Medicaid.
Owner Proprietary corp.
Staff Physicians; RNs 40 (ft); LPNs 8 (ft); Nurses' aides 60 (ft); Physical therapists 1 (ft); Reality therapists 1 (ft); Recreational therapists 1 (ft); Occupational therapists 2 (ft); Speech therapists 1 (ft); Activities coordinators 1 (ft); Dietitians 1 (ft); Ophthalmologists 1 (ft); Podiatrists 1 (ft); Audiologists 1 (ft).
Facilities Dining room; Physical therapy room; Activities room; Crafts room; Laundry room; Barber/Beauty shop; Library; Van.
Activities Arts & crafts; Cards; Games; Reading groups; Prayer groups; Movies; Shopping trips; Dances/Social/Cultural gatherings; Intergenerational programs; Pet therapy.

Carmen Manor
1470 W Carmen, Chicago, IL 60640
(312) 878-7000, 878-8335 FAX
Admin Mary Walker. *Dir of Nursing* Michelle Epps. *Medical Dir* Dr F Ojea.
Licensure Intermediate care. *Beds* ICF 113. *Private Pay Patients* 5%. *Certified* Medicaid.
Owner Proprietary corp.
Admissions Requirements Medical examination; Physician's request.
Staff LPNs; Nurses' aides; Recreational therapists; Activities coordinators.

Facilities Dining room; Physical therapy room; Activities room; Crafts room.
Activities Arts & crafts; Cards; Games; Reading groups; Prayer groups; Movies; Shopping trips; Dances/Social/Cultural gatherings; Intergenerational programs; Pet therapy.

Casa Central Center
1401 N California Ave, Chicago, IL 60622
(312) 276-1902
Admin Bitia I Alfonso.
Licensure Skilled care; Intermediate care. *Beds* SNF 91; ICF 49. *Certified* Medicaid.
Owner Nonprofit corp.

Central Nursing
2450 N Central Ave, Chicago, IL 60639
(312) 889-1333
Admin Henry Mermelstein.
Licensure Skilled care. *Beds* SNF 245. *Certified* Medicaid.
Owner Proprietary corp.

Central Plaza Residential Home
321 N Central, Chicago, IL 60644
(312) 626-2300
Admin Gwendolyn Washington. *Dir of Nursing* Maxine Brown. *Medical Dir* Dr R Velasco.
Licensure Intermediate care for mentally ill. *Beds* Intermediate care for mentally ill 260. *Private Pay Patients* 1%. *Certified* Medicaid.
Owner Proprietary corp.
Admissions Requirements Minimum age 21; Medical examination.
Staff Physicians 6 (pt); RNs 2 (ft); LPNs 12 (ft), 1 (pt); Nurses' aides 45 (ft); Physical therapists 1 (pt); Recreational therapists 1 (pt); Occupational therapists 2 (ft); Speech therapists 1 (pt); Activities coordinators 1 (ft); Dietitians 1 (ft), 1 (pt); Ophthalmologists 1 (pt); Podiatrists 1 (pt); Audiologists 1 (pt).
Facilities Dining room; Physical therapy room; Activities room; Crafts room; Laundry room; Library.
Activities Arts & crafts; Cards; Games; Reading groups; Prayer groups; Movies; Shopping trips; Dances/Social/Cultural gatherings; Pet therapy; Community outings.

Chevy Chase Nursing Center
3400 S Indiana Ave, Chicago, IL 60616
(312) 842-5000, 842-3790 FAX
Admin Steven L Frank. *Dir of Nursing* Eva Vivian RN. *Medical Dir* Abolmajid Rezvan MD.
Licensure Skilled care. *Beds* SNF 322. *Private Pay Patients* 7%. *Certified* Medicaid; Medicare.
Owner Privately owned.
Admissions Requirements Medical examination.
Staff Physicians 7 (pt); RNs 4 (ft), 2 (pt); LPNs 28 (ft), 3 (pt); Nurses' aides 95 (ft), 10 (pt); Physical therapists 2 (pt); Recreational therapists 1 (pt); Occupational therapists 2 (pt); Speech therapists 2 (pt); Activities coordinators 1 (ft); Dietitians 1 (pt); Ophthalmologists 1 (pt); Podiatrists 1 (pt); Audiologists 1 (pt).
Facilities Dining room; Physical therapy room; Activities room; Chapel; Crafts room; Laundry room; Barber/Beauty shop.
Activities Arts & crafts; Cards; Games; Reading groups; Prayer groups; Movies; Shopping trips; Dances/Social/Cultural gatherings; Intergenerational programs.

Clark Manor Convalescent Center
7433 N Clark St, Chicago, IL 60626
(312) 338-8778
Admin Mark Schlichting. *Dir of Nursing* Melvina McClendon.
Licensure Skilled care. *Beds* SNF 273. *Certified* Medicaid; Medicare.
Owner Privately owned.

Admissions Requirements Minimum age 55.
Staff Physicians 14 (pt); RNs 20 (ft); LPNs 3 (pt); Nurses' aides 50 (ft); Physical therapists 1 (pt); Recreational therapists 1 (ft); Occupational therapists 1 (pt); Speech therapists 1 (pt); Activities coordinators 1 (ft); Dietitians 1 (ft); Ophthalmologists 1 (pt); Podiatrists 1 (pt); Dentists 1 (pt).
Facilities Dining room; Physical therapy room; Activities room; Crafts room; Laundry room; Barber/Beauty shop; Library.
Activities Arts & crafts; Cards; Games; Reading groups; Prayer groups; Movies; Shopping trips; Dances/Social/Cultural gatherings.

Clayton Residential Home
2026 N Clark St, Chicago, IL 60614
(312) 549-1840
Admin Robert B Baily.
Medical Dir Lester Baranov MD.
Licensure Intermediate care. *Beds* ICF 252. *Certified* Medicaid.
Owner Proprietary corp.
Admissions Requirements Minimum age 18; Medical examination.
Staff Physicians 3 (pt); LPNs 9 (ft); Nurses' aides 20 (ft); Physical therapists 1 (ft), 1 (pt); Reality therapists 2 (ft); Recreational therapists 1 (ft); Occupational therapists 1 (ft); Activities coordinators 1 (ft); Dietitians 1 (ft); Podiatrists 1 (pt).
Facilities Dining room; Physical therapy room; Activities room; Crafts room; Laundry room.
Activities Arts & crafts; Games; Reading groups; Movies; Shopping trips; Dances/Social/Cultural gatherings.

Cojeunaze Nursing Center
3311 S Michigan Ave, Chicago, IL 60616
(312) 326-5700
Admin Faye H Nazon.
Medical Dir Pancho Degand MD.
Licensure Skilled care; Intermediate care; Retirement. *Beds* SNF 74; ICF 126. *Certified* Medicaid.
Owner Proprietary corp.
Admissions Requirements Minimum age 60; Medical examination; Physician's request.
Staff Physicians 4 (pt); RNs 2 (ft), 5 (pt); LPNs 9 (ft), 4 (pt); Nurses' aides 45 (ft), 3 (pt); Physical therapists; Reality therapists; Recreational therapists 1 (pt); Occupational therapists 1 (pt); Activities coordinators 1 (ft), 2 (pt); Dietitians 1 (pt); Ophthalmologists 1 (pt); Dentists 1 (pt).
Languages French.
Facilities Dining room; Activities room; Crafts room; Laundry room; Barber/Beauty shop; Library.
Activities Arts & crafts; Cards; Games; Reading groups; Prayer groups; Movies; Shopping trips; Dances/Social/Cultural gatherings.

Columbus Manor Residential Care Home
5107 W Jackson Blvd, Chicago, IL 60644
(312) 378-5490
Admin Daniel J O'Brien, Patrick J O'Brien. *Dir of Nursing* Philomina Philip RN.
Licensure Intermediate care. *Beds* ICF 189. *Certified* Medicaid.
Owner Proprietary corp.
Admissions Requirements Minimum age 35; Medical examination.
Staff Physicians; RNs; LPNs; Nurses' aides; Recreational therapists; Activities coordinators; Dietitians.
Languages Spanish, Polish.
Facilities Dining room; Activities room; Crafts room; Laundry room; Library.
Activities Arts & crafts; Cards; Games; Reading groups; Prayer groups; Movies; Shopping trips; Dances/Social/Cultural gatherings; Field trips.

Commodore Inn Inc
5547 N Kenmore, Chicago, IL 60640
(312) 561-7040
Admin Dr Jay Einhorn, PhD.
Licensure Intermediate care. *Beds* ICF 174.
Certified Medicaid.
Owner Proprietary corp.

Community Care Center Inc
4314 S Wabash Ave, Chicago, IL 60653
(312) 538-8300
Admin Lois D Young. *Dir of Nursing* Cecelia
Glinsey. *Medical Dir* Dr Williamson.
Licensure Skilled care; Intermediate care. *Beds*
SNF 128; ICF 76. *Private Pay Patients* 3%.
Certified Medicaid.
Owner Proprietary corp.
Admissions Requirements Medical
examination; Physician's request.
Staff RNs; LPNs; Nurses' aides; Activities
coordinators; Dietitians.
Facilities Dining room; Physical therapy
room; Activities room; Chapel; Crafts room;
Laundry room; Barber/Beauty shop; Library;
Outdoor patio.
Activities Arts & crafts; Cards; Games;
Reading groups; Prayer groups; Movies;
Shopping trips; Dances/Social/Cultural
gatherings; Intergenerational programs; Pet
therapy.

Congress Care Center
901 S Austin, Chicago, IL 60644
(312) 287-5959, 287-7909 FAX
Admin Leo Feigenbaum. *Dir of Nursing*
Michelle Cook RN. *Medical Dir* Saloman
Dayan MD.
Licensure Skilled care; Intermediate care. *Beds*
SNF 70; ICF 70. *Private Pay Patients* 25%.
Certified Medicaid.
Owner Proprietary corp.
Admissions Requirements Medical
examination; Physician's request.
Staff RNs; LPNs; Nurses' aides; Occupational
therapists; Activities coordinators.
Facilities Dining room; Physical therapy
room; Activities room; Crafts room; Laundry
room; Barber/Beauty shop; Library; Patio.
Activities Arts & crafts; Cards; Games;
Reading groups; Prayer groups; Movies;
Shopping trips; Dances/Social/Cultural
gatherings; Intergenerational programs; Pet
therapy.

Continental Care Center
5336 N Western Ave, Chicago, IL 60625
(312) 271-5600
Admin E Joseph Steinfeld. *Dir of Nursing*
Michele Janota. *Medical Dir* Dr Abdul
Sattar.
Licensure Skilled care; Intermediate care. *Beds*
Swing beds SNF/ICF 208. *Private Pay
Patients* 25%. *Certified* Medicaid.
Owner Proprietary corp.
Admissions Requirements Minimum age 65.
Staff Physicians 38 (pt); RNs 6 (ft), 1 (pt);
LPNs 11 (ft), 2 (pt); Nurses' aides 66 (ft);
Activities coordinators 1 (ft).
Facilities Dining room; Physical therapy
room; Activities room; Crafts room; Barber/
Beauty shop; Library; Fitness trail; Sun
porches; Patio areas.
Activities Arts & crafts; Cards; Games;
Movies; Shopping trips; Dances/Social/
Cultural gatherings; Pet therapy; Church
services; Outings; Monthly birthday parties;
Bingo; Citywide retirement fair; Holiday
bazaar; Volunteer luncheon.

Covenant Home of Chicago
2725 W Foster Ave, Chicago, IL 60625
(312) 878-8200, ext 5012, 878-2617 FAX
Admin Lana L Heinrich. *Dir of Nursing* Doris
Johnson RN. *Medical Dir* Dr Linda
Johnson.
Licensure Skilled care; Sheltered care. *Beds*
SNF 52; Sheltered care 69. *Certified*
Medicaid; Medicare.

Owner Nonprofit organization/foundation
(The Evangelical Covenant Church).
Admissions Requirements Physician's request.
Staff RNs 4 (ft), 3 (pt); LPNs 1 (ft), 1 (pt);
Nurses' aides 21 (ft), 2 (pt); Activities
coordinators 1 (ft); Ward clerks 1 (ft).
Affiliation Evangelical Covenant Church.
Facilities Dining room; Activities room;
Laundry room; Barber/Beauty shop.
Activities Arts & crafts; Games; Reading
groups; Prayer groups; Movies; Shopping
trips; Dances/Social/Cultural gatherings;
Intergenerational programs; Pet therapy.

Danforth House
4540 S Michigan Ave, Chicago, IL 60653
(312) 373-1073
Admin Linda Darling.
Licensure Intermediate care for mentally
retarded. *Beds* ICF/MR 15.

Davis House
4237 S Indiana Ave, Chicago, IL 60653
(312) 373-1044
Admin Timothy I Monahan.
Licensure Intermediate care for mentally
retarded. *Beds* ICF/MR 15.

William L Dawson Nursing Home
3500 S Giles Ave, Chicago, IL 60653
(312) 326-2000
Admin Pamela M Orr.
Licensure Skilled care. *Beds* SNF 245.
Certified Medicaid.
Owner Proprietary corp.

Deauville Health Care Center
7445 N Sheridan Rd, Chicago, IL 60626
(312) 338-3300
Admin Daniel Shabat. *Dir of Nursing* Loida
Villareal. *Medical Dir* Dr Merrill Zahtz.
Licensure Skilled care; Intermediate care;
Medicare. *Beds* SNF 27; ICF 98; Medicare
24. *Private Pay Patients* 30%. *Certified*
Medicaid; Medicare.
Owner Proprietary corp.
Admissions Requirements Minimum age 65;
Medical examination.
Staff Physicians 31 (ft); RNs 6 (ft), 1 (pt);
LPNs 7 (ft), 1 (pt); Nurses' aides 52 (ft), 8
(pt); Physical therapists 1 (ft), 1 (pt); Reality
therapists 3 (ft); Recreational therapists 5
(ft); Occupational therapists 3 (ft); Speech
therapists 1 (ft); Activities coordinators 1
(ft); Dietitians 1 (ft); Ophthalmologists 1 (ft);
Podiatrists 1 (ft); Audiologists 1 (ft).
Languages Spanish, Yiddish.
Facilities Dining room; Physical therapy
room; Activities room; Chapel; Crafts room;
Laundry room; Barber/Beauty shop; Library.
Activities Arts & crafts; Cards; Games;
Reading groups; Prayer groups; Movies;
Shopping trips; Dances/Social/Cultural
gatherings; Intergenerational programs; Pet
therapy.

Deborah House
7428 N Rogers, Chicago, IL 60626
(312) 761-0395
Admin Rav'l Nadal Jr.
Licensure Intermediate care for mentally
retarded. *Beds* ICF/MR 18.
Owner Nonprofit.

Edgewater Nursing & Geriatric Center
5838 N Sheridan Rd, Chicago, IL 60660
(312) 769-2230
Admin Lorraine Compton. *Dir of Nursing*
Lorraine Compton RN. *Medical Dir*
Solomon Dayan MD.
Licensure Skilled care; Intermediate care. *Beds*
SNF 127; ICF 61. *Certified* Medicaid;
Medicare.
Owner Proprietary corp.
Admissions Requirements Minimum age 35;
Medical examination; Physician's request.

Staff RNs 14 (ft); LPNs 3 (ft); Nurses' aides
28 (ft); Reality therapists 3 (ft); Recreational
therapists 4 (ft); Activities coordinators 2
(ft).
Facilities Dining room; Physical therapy
room; Activities room; Crafts room; Laundry
room; Barber/Beauty shop.
Activities Arts & crafts; Cards; Games;
Reading groups; Prayer groups; Movies;
Shopping trips; Dances/Social/Cultural
gatherings.

Elston Nursing Center
4340 N Keystone, Chicago, IL 60641
(312) 545-8700
Admin Steven Schayer.
Medical Dir Dr Paul Vega.
Licensure Skilled care; Intermediate care. *Beds*
SNF 83; ICF 33. *Certified* Medicaid;
Medicare.
Owner Proprietary corp.
Admissions Requirements Minimum age 18;
Medical examination; Physician's request.
Staff Physicians 10 (ft); RNs 6 (ft), 2 (pt);
LPNs 7 (ft), 1 (pt); Nurses' aides 33 (ft), 3
(pt); Physical therapists 1 (ft); Reality
therapists 4 (ft); Recreational therapists 3
(ft); Occupational therapists 1 (ft); Activities
coordinators F 1 (ft); Dietitians 1 (ft);
Ophthalmologists 1 (ft); Dentists 1 (ft);
Occupational aides 1 (ft); Superintendents 1
(ft).
Languages Polish, German, Tagalog.
Facilities Dining room; Physical therapy
room; Activities room; Crafts room; Laundry
room; Barber/Beauty shop.
Activities Arts & crafts; Cards; Games;
Reading groups; Prayer groups; Movies;
Shopping trips; Intergenerational stamp
collecting.

Garden View Home
6450 N Ridge, Chicago, IL 60626
(312) 743-8700, 743-8407 FAX
Admin Howard D Geller. *Dir of Nursing* L
Montaclaro. *Medical Dir* A Sattar.
Licensure Skilled care; Intermediate care. *Beds*
SNF 110; ICF 26. *Certified* Medicaid.
Owner Proprietary corp.
Staff Physicians; RNs; LPNs; Nurses' aides;
Physical therapists; Reality therapists;
Recreational therapists; Occupational
therapists; Speech therapists; Activities
coordinators; Dietitians; Ophthalmologists;
Podiatrists; Audiologists; Dentists.
Facilities Dining room; Physical therapy
room; Activities room.
Activities Arts & crafts; Cards; Games;
Reading groups; Prayer groups; Movies;
Shopping trips; Dances/Social/Cultural
gatherings; Intergenerational programs; Pet
therapy.

Glencrest Nursing Rehabilitation Center Ltd
2451 W Touhy Ave, Chicago, IL 60645
(312) 338-6800
Admin Nancy Crutcher.
Medical Dir Dr Paul Vega.
Licensure Skilled care; Intermediate care;
Alzheimer's care. *Beds* SNF 154; ICF 158.
Certified Medicaid; Medicare; VA.
Owner Proprietary corp.
Admissions Requirements Minimum age 50.
Staff Physical therapists; Activities
coordinators; Dietitians; Speech therapists;
Occupational therapists; Respiratory
therapists; Social worker; Geriatric
therapists.
Facilities Dining room (Restaurant style);
Physical therapy room; Activities room;
Crafts room; Laundry room; Barber/Beauty
shop; Library; Private sitting rooms.
Activities Arts & crafts; Cards; Games;
Reading groups; Prayer groups; Movies;
Shopping trips; Dances/Social/Cultural
gatherings; Intergenerational programs;
Speakers; Resident educational programs;
Courtesy van.

Gracell Terrace
6410 S Kenwood, Chicago, IL 60637
(312) 752-8600, 752-8734
Admin Ida Smith. *Dir of Nursing* Dollie
Chase. *Medical Dir* Dr Phillip Skoczelas.
Licensure Sheltered care. *Beds* Sheltered care
150. *Private Pay Patients* 5%.
Owner Proprietary corp.
Admissions Requirements Medical
examination; Physician's request.
Staff LPNs; Nurses' aides; Activities
coordinators; Social workers.
Facilities Dining room; Activities room;
Crafts room; Laundry room.
Activities Arts & crafts; Cards; Games;
Reading groups; Prayer groups; Movies;
Shopping trips; Dances/Social/Cultural
gatherings; Intergenerational programs; Pet
therapy; Barbeques; Drug & alcohol
treatment program.

Grasmere Resident Home Inc
4621 N Sheridan Rd, Chicago, IL 60640
(312) 334-6601
Admin Susan Morse.
Medical Dir Dr David Edelberg.
Licensure Intermediate care. *Beds* ICF 216.
Certified Medicaid.
Owner Proprietary corp.
Admissions Requirements Minimum age 18.
Staff Physicians 6 (pt); RNs 1 (ft); LPNs 7
(ft), 3 (pt); Nurses' aides 37 (ft), 1 (pt);
Occupational therapists 1 (pt); Activities
coordinators 4 (ft), 2 (pt); Dietitians 1 (pt).
Facilities Dining room; Activities room;
Crafts room; Laundry room; Barber/Beauty
shop; Library; Gym; Park.
Activities Arts & crafts; Cards; Games;
Reading groups; Movies; Shopping trips;
Dances/Social/Cultural gatherings; Sensory
integration; Reality orientation; Yoga.

Halsted Terrace Nursing Center
10935 S Halsted St, Chicago, IL 60628
(312) 928-2000
Admin Annie R Sutton.
Medical Dir William London; Nira West.
Licensure Skilled care. *Beds* SNF 300.
Certified Medicaid.
Owner Proprietary corp.
Admissions Requirements Physician's request.
Staff Physicians 6 (pt); RNs 6 (ft), 2 (pt);
LPNs 20 (ft), 5 (pt); Nurses' aides 76 (ft), 3
(pt); Physical therapists 1 (pt); Occupational
therapists 1 (pt); Speech therapists 1 (pt);
Activities coordinators; Dietitians 1 (pt).
Facilities Dining room; Physical therapy
room; Activities room; Crafts room; Laundry
room; Barber/Beauty shop.
Activities Arts & crafts; Cards; Games;
Movies; Shopping trips; Dances/Social/
Cultural gatherings.

Heart of Mercy T-4
6300 N Ridge Ave, Chicago, IL 60660
(312) 973-6300
Admin Teri Petrisko Lavassu.
Licensure Intermediate care for mentally
retarded. *Beds* ICF/MR 8.

Heart of Mercy T-7
6300 N Ridge Ave, Chicago, IL 60660
(312) 973-8300
Admin Teri Petrisko Lavassu.
Licensure Intermediate care for mentally
retarded. *Beds* ICF/MR 8.

Heritage Healthcare Center
5888 N Ridge Ave, Chicago, IL 60660
(312) 769-2626, 769-1799 FAX
Admin Sylvia Y Mostello RN. *Dir of Nursing*
Ann O'Connor RN. *Medical Dir* Felizardo
Belga MD.
Licensure Skilled care; Intermediate care;
Alzheimer's care. *Beds* SNF 44; ICF 84.
Private Pay Patients 25%. *Certified*
Medicaid.
Owner Proprietary corp.

Admissions Requirements Minimum age 60;
Medical examination.
Staff Physicians 10 (ft); RNs 4 (ft), 2 (pt);
LPNs 3 (ft), 4 (pt); Nurses' aides 23 (ft), 6
(pt); Physical therapists 1 (ft), 1 (pt);
Recreational therapists 1 (ft); Occupational
therapists 1 (ft); Speech therapists 1 (pt);
Activities coordinators 4 (ft); Dietitians 1
(ft), 1 (pt); Ophthalmologists 1 (ft);
Podiatrists 1 (ft); Audiologists 1 (ft); Social
workers 1 (ft).
Facilities Dining room; Physical therapy
room; Activities room; Crafts room; Laundry
room; Barber/Beauty shop; Psychosocial
room.
Activities Arts & crafts; Cards; Games;
Reading groups; Prayer groups; Movies;
Shopping trips; Dances/Social/Cultural
gatherings; Pet therapy; Sports outings;
Massage therapy.

Imperial Convalescent & Geriatric Center Inc
1366 W Fullterton Ave, Chicago, IL 60614
(312) 935-7474
Admin David Tessler.
Licensure Skilled care. *Beds* SNF 198.

Jackson Square Nursing Center
5130 W Jackson Blvd, Chicago, IL 60644
(312) 921-8000
Admin Mark Freeland.
Licensure Skilled care. *Beds* SNF 234.

Jewish Home for the Blind
3525 W Foster Ave, Chicago, IL 60625
(312) 478-7040
Admin Robert Lieberman.
Medical Dir Dr Jerome Dalinka.
Licensure Sheltered care. *Beds* Sheltered care
53. *Private Pay Patients* 25%.
Owner Nonprofit organization/foundation.
Admissions Requirements Minimum age 18;
Medical examination; Physician's request.
Staff Physicians; RNs; LPNs; Nurses' aides;
Physical therapists; Recreational therapists;
Occupational therapists; Activities
coordinators; Dietitians; Ophthalmologists;
Podiatrists.
Languages Yiddish, Russian, Polish.
Affiliation Jewish.
Facilities Dining room; Physical therapy
room; Activities room; Chapel; Crafts room;
Laundry room; Barber/Beauty shop.
Activities Arts & crafts; Cards; Games;
Reading groups; Prayer groups; Movies;
Shopping trips; Dances/Social/Cultural
gatherings; Intergenerational programs; Pet
therapy.

Jewish Peoples Convalescent Home
6512 N California Ave, Chicago, IL 60645
(312) 743-8077
Admin Mike Applebaum.
Medical Dir Dr Dan Stockhammer.
Licensure Sheltered care. *Beds* Sheltered care
35.
Owner Nonprofit corp.
Admissions Requirements Minimum age 60;
Medical examination.
Staff Physicians 1 (pt); RNs 1 (pt); LPNs 2
(ft), 2 (pt); Nurses' aides 4 (ft), 3 (pt);
Recreational therapists 1 (pt); Occupational
therapists 1 (pt); Activities coordinators 1
(pt); Dietitians 1 (pt).
Affiliation Jewish.
Facilities Dining room; Activities room;
Crafts room; Barber/Beauty shop.
Activities Arts & crafts; Cards; Games.

Johnson Rehabilitation Nursing Home
3456 W Franklin Blvd, Chicago, IL 60624
(312) 533-3033
Admin Shirley H Sneed.
Medical Dir Dorval R Carter MD.
Licensure Skilled care. *Beds* SNF 76. *Certified*
Medicaid; Medicare.
Owner Proprietary corp.

Admissions Requirements Minimum age 18;
Medical examination; Physician's request.
Staff Physicians 4 (pt); RNs 2 (ft); LPNs 8
(ft); Nurses' aides 17 (ft); Physical therapists
1 (pt); Recreational therapists 1 (ft);
Dietitians 1 (pt); Podiatrists 1 (pt); Dentists
1 (pt).
Facilities Dining room; Physical therapy
room; Activities room; Laundry room.
Activities Arts & crafts; Cards; Games;
Reading groups; Prayer groups; Movies;
Shopping trips; Dances/Social/Cultural
gatherings.

Kenwood Healthcare Center Inc
6125 S Kenwood Ave, Chicago, IL 60637
(312) 752-6000
Admin Ronnie Klein.
Licensure Skilled care; Intermediate care. *Beds*
SNF 128; ICF 190. *Certified* Medicare.
Owner Proprietary corp.

Ada S McKinley Knight House
100 E 34th St, Chicago, IL 60616
(312) 842-4518, 842-4603
Admin Timothy I Monahan. *Dir of Nursing*
Charlotte Triplett MSN. *Medical Dir* Josetta
Trevil MD.
Licensure Intermediate care for mentally
retarded. *Beds* ICF/MR 75 in 5 facilities.
Private Pay Patients 0%. *Certified* Medicaid.
Owner Nonprofit organization/foundation
(Ada S McKinley Community Services).
Admissions Requirements Minimum age 18;
Medical examination.
Staff Physicians 1 (pt); RNs 1 (ft); LPNs 1
(ft); Nurses' aides 40 (ft); Recreational
therapists 1 (pt); Speech therapists 1 (pt);
Activities coordinators 5 (ft).
Languages Spanish, Sign.
Facilities Dining room; Activities room;
Crafts room; Laundry room.
Activities Arts & crafts; Games; Movies;
Shopping trips; Dances/Social/Cultural
gatherings; Active treatment.

Kraus Home Inc
1620 W Chase, Chicago, IL 60626
(312) 973-2100
Admin Moshe Lerner.
Licensure Sheltered care. *Beds* Sheltered care
60.
Owner Proprietary corp.
Admissions Requirements Medical
examination.
Staff Physicians 1 (pt); RNs 1 (ft); LPNs 5
(ft); Nurses' aides 5 (ft); Recreational
therapists 1 (ft); Occupational therapists 1
(ft); Activities coordinators 1 (ft); Dietitians
1 (pt).
Facilities Dining room; Activities room;
Crafts room; Laundry room; Barber/Beauty
shop; Library.
Activities Arts & crafts; Cards; Games;
Reading groups; Movies; Shopping trips;
Dances/Social/Cultural gatherings.

Lake Shore Nursing Centre
7200-30 N Sheridan Rd, Chicago, IL 60626
(312) 973-7200
Admin Isadore Goldberg. *Dir of Nursing* Janet
Q Hawkins. *Medical Dir* Lester Baranov
MD.
Licensure Skilled care. *Beds* SNF 328.
Certified Medicaid; Medicare.
Owner Proprietary corp.
Admissions Requirements Minimum age 21.
Staff RNs 36 (ft), 8 (pt); LPNs 2 (ft); Nurses'
aides 89 (ft), 12 (pt); Physical therapists 4
(pt); Reality therapists 1 (ft); Recreational
therapists 3 (ft); Occupational therapists 2
(ft), 1 (pt); Speech therapists 1 (pt);
Activities coordinators 1 (ft); Dietitians 1
(ft), 1 (pt); Ophthalmologists 1 (pt);
Podiatrists 1 (pt); Dentists 1 (pt).
Facilities Dining room; Physical therapy
room; Activities room; Crafts room; Laundry
room; Barber/Beauty shop; Library.

Activities Arts & crafts; Cards; Games; Reading groups; Prayer groups; Movies; Shopping trips; Dances/Social/Cultural gatherings.

Lakefront Health Care Center Incorporated
7618 N Sheridan Rd, Chicago, IL 60626
(312) 743-7711
Admin Malka Mermelstein. *Dir of Nursing* Fina Selko. *Medical Dir* Dr Merrill J Zahtz.
Licensure Skilled care; Intermediate care. *Beds* SNF 33; ICF 66. *Private Pay Patients* 30%.
Owner Proprietary corp.
Admissions Requirements Minimum age 40.
Staff Physicians 8 (ft); RNs 7 (ft), 2 (pt); LPNs 8 (ft), 3 (pt); Nurses' aides 40 (ft); Physical therapists 1 (ft); Reality therapists 1 (ft); Recreational therapists 1 (ft); Occupational therapists 1 (ft); Speech therapists 1 (pt); Activities coordinators 1 (ft); Dietitians 1 (ft); Ophthalmologists 2 (ft); Podiatrists 2 (ft); Audiologists 1 (pt).
Languages Polish, Italian, Filipino.
Facilities Dining room; Physical therapy room; Activities room; Crafts room; Laundry room; Barber/Beauty shop; Library; TV rooms on each floor.
Activities Arts & crafts; Cards; Games; Reading groups; Prayer groups; Movies; Shopping trips; Dances/Social/Cultural gatherings; Intergenerational programs; Pet therapy; Dramatics.

Lakeside Boarding Home
6330 N Sheridan Rd, Chicago, IL 60660
(312) 338-2811
Admin Dinesh Gandhi. *Dir of Nursing* Dorothy Matthews. *Medical Dir* Pareshkumar Jani MD.
Licensure Sheltered care. *Beds* Sheltered care 34. *Private Pay Patients* 10%. *Certified* Medicaid; Medicare.
Owner Proprietary corp.
Admissions Requirements Minimum age 21; Physician's request; Ambulatory.
Staff Physicians (consultant); RNs (consultant); LPNs 1 (ft), 1 (pt); Nurses' aides 5 (ft); Activities coordinators 1 (ft); Dietitians (consultant); Ophthalmologists (consultant); Podiatrists (consultant); Maintenance 2 (ft), 1 (pt).
Facilities Dining room; Activities room; Laundry room.
Activities Arts & crafts; Cards; Games; Reading groups; Prayer groups; Movies; Shopping trips; Dances/Social/Cultural gatherings.

Lakeview Living Center
7270 S Shore Dr, Chicago, IL 60649
(312) 721-7700, 721-9719 FAX
Admin William Bockstahler. *Dir of Nursing* Fannie Chambers RN. *Medical Dir* Dr Sheldon Levine.
Licensure Intermediate care for mentally retarded. *Beds* ICF/MR 145. *Private Pay Patients* 98%. *Certified* Medicaid.
Owner Nonprofit corp.
Admissions Requirements Minimum age 18; Medical examination.
Staff Physicians 2 (pt); RNs 1 (ft); LPNs 4 (ft), 4 (pt); Nurses' aides 60 (ft), 10 (pt); Physical therapists 1 (pt); Speech therapists 1 (pt); Activities coordinators 1 (ft); Dietitians 1 (ft); Ophthalmologists 1 (pt); Podiatrists 1 (pt).
Languages Spanish.
Facilities Dining room; Activities room; Barber/Beauty shop.
Activities Arts & crafts; Games; Reading groups; Prayer groups; Movies; Shopping trips; Dances/Social/Cultural gatherings.

Lakeview Nursing & Geriatric Center Inc
735 W Diversey Pkwy, Chicago, IL 60614
(312) 348-4055
Admin Michael Elkes. *Dir of Nursing* Rosalisa Sebastian. *Medical Dir* T E Kioutas MD.

Licensure Skilled care; Intermediate care; Alzheimer's care. *Beds* SNF 63; ICF 117. *Private Pay Patients* 25%. *Certified* Medicaid; Medicare.
Owner Proprietary corp.
Admissions Requirements Minimum age 60; Medical examination; Physician's request.
Staff Physicians; RNs 12 (ft); LPNs 8 (ft); Nurses' aides 52 (ft); Physical therapists 2 (ft); Reality therapists; Recreational therapists 3 (ft); Occupational therapists; Speech therapists; Activities coordinators 1 (ft); Dietitians; Ophthalmologists; Podiatrists; Audiologists; Dentists.
Languages Spanish, Filipino.
Facilities Dining room; Physical therapy room; Activities room; Crafts room; Laundry room; Barber/Beauty shop; Library.
Activities Arts & crafts; Cards; Games; Reading groups; Prayer groups; Movies; Shopping trips; Dances/Social/Cultural gatherings; Intergenerational programs; Pet therapy.

Lincoln Park Terrace Inc
2732 N Hampden Ct, Chicago, IL 60614
(312) 248-6000
Admin Dov Solomon.
Medical Dir Solomon Dayan.
Licensure Skilled care. *Beds* SNF 109.
Owner Proprietary corp.
Admissions Requirements Minimum age 21.
Staff Physicians 6 (pt); RNs 5 (ft), 4 (pt); LPNs 8 (ft), 3 (pt); Nurses' aides 25 (ft), 3 (pt); Physical therapists 1 (pt); Occupational therapists 1 (pt); Speech therapists 1 (pt); Activities coordinators 2 (ft); Dietitians 1 (pt); Ophthalmologists 1 (pt); Podiatrists 1 (pt); Audiologists 1 (pt); Dentists 1 (pt).
Facilities Dining room; Physical therapy room; Activities room; Crafts room; Laundry room; Barber/Beauty shop; Library.
Activities Arts & crafts; Cards; Games; Reading groups; Movies; Shopping trips; Dances/Social/Cultural gatherings.

Little Sisters of the Poor
2325 N Lakewood Ave, Chicago, IL 60614
(312) 935-9600
Admin Paul Magyar. *Dir of Nursing* Sr Loraine. *Medical Dir* Dr Dayan.
Licensure Skilled care; Intermediate care; Retirement. *Beds* SNF 25; ICF 77. *Certified* Medicaid.
Owner Nonprofit corp.
Admissions Requirements Minimum age 60.
Staff RNs 7 (ft), 5 (pt); LPNs 3 (ft), 3 (pt); Nurses' aides 18 (ft), 15 (pt); Physical therapists 1 (ft); Occupational therapists 1 (ft); Activities coordinators 1 (ft).
Affiliation Roman Catholic.
Facilities Dining room; Physical therapy room; Activities room; Chapel; Crafts room; Laundry room; Barber/Beauty shop; Library; Outdoor park.
Activities Arts & crafts; Cards; Games; Reading groups; Prayer groups; Movies; Shopping trips; Dances/Social/Cultural gatherings.

Maple Terrace Shelter Care Home
8145 S Merrill Ave, Chicago, IL 60617-1157
(312) 626-1439
Admin Pearl J Brooks.
Licensure Sheltered care. *Beds* 12.
Owner Proprietary corp.

Margaret Manor
1121 N Orleans, Chicago, IL 60610
(312) 943-4300
Admin Cynthia Halgard.
Licensure Intermediate care. *Beds* ICF 135. *Certified* Medicaid.
Owner Proprietary corp.
Admissions Requirements Medical examination.
Staff RNs 1 (ft); LPNs 4 (ft); Nurses' aides 16 (ft); Activities coordinators 1 (ft).

Languages Polish, Spanish.
Facilities Dining room; Activities room; Chapel; Crafts room; Laundry room.
Activities Arts & crafts; Cards; Games; Reading groups; Prayer groups; Movies; Shopping trips; Dances/Social/Cultural gatherings.

Margaret Manor North Branch
940 W Cullom Ave, Chicago, IL 60613
(312) 525-9000
Admin Felisa B Talavera. *Dir of Nursing* Adelina Lagadan. *Medical Dir* S Day MD.
Licensure Intermediate care. *Beds* ICF 99. *Certified* Medicaid.
Owner Proprietary corp.
Admissions Requirements Minimum age 21-60; Medical examination; Physician's request.
Staff Physicians 4 (pt); RNs 3 (ft), 3 (pt); LPNs 1 (pt); Nurses' aides 11 (ft), 4 (pt); Occupational therapists 1 (pt); Activities coordinators 1 (ft); Dietitians 1 (pt); Ophthalmologists 1 (pt); Laboratory technicians 1 (pt).
Languages Spanish, German.
Facilities Dining room; Physical therapy room; Activities room; Crafts room; Laundry room; Library.
Activities Arts & crafts; Cards; Games; Reading groups; Prayer groups; Movies; Shopping trips; Dances/Social/Cultural gatherings.

Marian Center for Adult Resident
6300 N Ridge Ave, Chicago, IL 60660
(312) 973-6300
Admin Denise K Detzner.
Licensure Intermediate care for mentally retarded. *Beds* ICF/MR 51.

Mayfield Care Center
5905 W Washington, Chicago, IL 60644
(312) 261-7074, 261-2116 FAX
Admin Daryl Justice. *Dir of Nursing* Edith Southerland. *Medical Dir* Dr Sal Dayan.
Licensure Skilled care; Intermediate care. *Beds* SNF 104; ICF 52. *Private Pay Patients* 8%. *Certified* Medicaid.
Owner Proprietary corp.
Admissions Requirements Medical examination; Physician's request.
Staff RNs; LPNs; Nurses' aides; Activities coordinators.
Facilities Dining room; Physical therapy room; Activities room; Crafts room; Laundry room; Barber/Beauty shop; Library; Outdoor patio.
Activities Arts & crafts; Cards; Games; Reading groups; Prayer groups; Movies; Shopping trips; Dances/Social/Cultural gatherings; Intergenerational programs; Pet therapy.

McAuley House
6300 N Ridge Ave, Chicago, IL 60660
(312) 973-6300
Admin Gregory J Bublitz.
Licensure Intermediate care for mentally retarded. *Beds* ICF/MR 8.

Methodist Home
1415 W Foster Ave, Chicago, IL 60640
(312) 769-5500
Admin Annie D Mark. *Dir of Nursing* Karen Brors RN MSN. *Medical Dir* Dr Noel De Backer.
Licensure Skilled care; Intermediate care; Sheltered care; Alzheimer's care. *Beds* SNF 23; ICF 83; Sheltered care 23. *Private Pay Patients* 57%. *Certified* Medicaid; Medicare.
Owner Nonprofit organization/foundation.
Admissions Requirements Minimum age 60.
Staff Physicians 2 (ft), 7 (pt); RNs 3 (ft), 1 (pt); LPNs 8 (ft); Nurses' aides 23 (ft), 5 (pt); Physical therapists 1 (pt) (consultant); Occupational therapists 1 (pt) (consultant); Speech therapists 1 (pt) (consultant);

Activities coordinators 1 (ft), 1 (pt);
Ophthalmologists 1 (pt); Podiatrists 1 (pt);
Audiologists 1 (pt); Dentists 8 (pt); Chaplain
1 (pt); Psychosocial therapist 1 (pt).
Languages Spanish, Greek, French, Italian,
Tagalog.
Affiliation Methodist.
Facilities Dining room; Physical therapy
room; Activities room; Chapel; Crafts room;
Laundry room; Barber/Beauty shop; Library;
Greenhouse; Patio gardens; Occupational
therapy room; Occupational rehabilitation
room; Physical rehabilitation room;
Meditation room; Alzheimer's unit.
Activities Arts & crafts; Cards; Games;
Reading groups; Prayer groups; Movies;
Dances/Social/Cultural gatherings;
Intergenerational programs; Pet therapy;
Nutrition class; Drama; Poetry; Exercise
class; Vision support group; Massage
therapy.

Mid-America Convalescent Centers Inc
4920 N Kenmore Ave, Chicago, IL 60640
(312) 769-2700, 769-3226 FAX
Admin Annie Mark. *Dir of Nursing* Nelia
Tinio RN. *Medical Dir* Solomon Dayan
MD.
Licensure Skilled care. *Beds* SNF 310. *Private
Pay Patients* 5%. *Certified* Medicaid;
Medicare.
Owner Proprietary corp.
Admissions Requirements Medical
examination; Physician's request.
Staff RNs; LPNs; Nurses' aides; Activities
coordinators.
Languages Spanish, Chinese, Vietnamese.
Facilities Dining room; Physical therapy
room; Activities room; Crafts room; Laundry
room; Barber/Beauty shop; Library; Enclosed
outdoor patio.
Activities Arts & crafts; Cards; Games;
Reading groups; Prayer groups; Movies;
Shopping trips; Dances/Social/Cultural
gatherings; Intergenerational programs; Pet
therapy.

Misericordia Home
2916 W 47th St, Chicago, IL 60632
(312) 254-9595
Admin Elizabeth Flynn RN.
Medical Dir Roseanne V Proteau MD.
Licensure Skilled care. *Beds* 119. *Certified*
Medicaid.
Owner Nonprofit corp.
Admissions Requirements Minimum age Birth;
Medical examination.
Staff Physicians 2 (ft); RNs 8 (ft), 6 (pt);
LPNs 5 (ft), 3 (pt); Nurses' aides 50 (ft), 30
(pt); Occupational therapists 1 (ft).
Affiliation Roman Catholic.
Facilities Dining room; Physical therapy
room; Activities room; Chapel; Crafts room;
Laundry room; Library.
Activities Arts & crafts; Reading groups;
Prayer groups; Movies; Shopping trips.

Monroe Pavilion Health Center Inc
1400 W Monroe St, Chicago, IL 60607
(312) 666-4090
Admin Wayne J Hanik. *Dir of Nursing* Tom
Carroll RN. *Medical Dir* A Rezvan MD.
Licensure Intermediate care; Alzheimer's care.
Beds ICF 136. *Certified* Medicaid.
Owner Proprietary corp.
Admissions Requirements Minimum age 18;
Medical examination; Physician's request.
Staff Physicians 3 (pt); RNs 1 (ft); LPNs 10
(ft), 1 (pt); Nurses' aides 23 (ft); Physical
therapists 1 (ft), 2 (pt); Reality therapists 1
(pt); Recreational therapists 1 (pt);
Occupational therapists 1 (pt); Speech
therapists 1 (pt); Activities coordinators 1
(ft); Dietitians 1 (ft); Ophthalmologists 1
(pt); Podiatrists 1 (pt); Dentists 1 (pt);
Psychiatrists 2 (pt).

Facilities Dining room; Physical therapy
room; Activities room; Crafts room; Laundry
room; Barber/Beauty shop; Library.
Activities Arts & crafts; Cards; Games;
Reading groups; Prayer groups; Movies;
Shopping trips; Dances/Social/Cultural
gatherings.

Norridge Nursing Centre Inc
7001 W Cullom, Chicago, IL 60634
(312) 457-0700
Admin Barbara I Lyons. *Dir of Nursing*
Evelyn Troike. *Medical Dir* Samuel Kruger
MD.
Licensure Skilled care; Intermediate care;
Alzheimer's care. *Beds* SNF 210; ICF 105.
Certified Medicaid; Medicare.
Owner Privately owned.
Admissions Requirements Minimum age 18;
Medical examination; Physician's request.
Staff Physicians 5 (pt); RNs 21 (ft), 5 (pt);
LPNs 35 (ft), 3 (pt); Nurses' aides 120 (ft);
Physical therapists 2 (pt); Recreational
therapists 1 (pt); Occupational therapists 1
(pt); Speech therapists 1 (pt); Activities
coordinators 2 (pt); Dietitians 1 (pt);
Ophthalmologists 1 (pt); Dentists 1 (pt).
Facilities Dining room; Physical therapy
room; Activities room; Crafts room; Laundry
room; Barber/Beauty shop; Library.
Activities Arts & crafts; Cards; Games;
Reading groups; Prayer groups; Movies;
Shopping trips; Dances/Social/Cultural
gatherings; Luncheon trips; Cooking;
Exercise classes.

Northwest Home for the Aged
6300 N California Ave, Chicago, IL 60659
(312) 973-1900
Admin Fred I Oskin ACSW. *Dir of Nursing*
Everlyn Liberson RN. *Medical Dir* Michael
Preodor MD.
Licensure Skilled care. *Beds* SNF 162.
Certified Medicaid; Medicare.
Owner Nonprofit corp.
Admissions Requirements Minimum age 65;
Medical examination.
Staff Physicians 2 (pt); RNs 15 (ft), 10 (pt);
LPNs 8 (ft); Nurses' aides 59 (ft), 1 (pt);
Physical therapists 1 (pt); Recreational
therapists 5 (ft); Occupational therapists 1
(pt); Speech therapists 1 (pt); Activities
coordinators 1 (ft); Dietitians 1 (pt);
Ophthalmologists 1 (pt); Podiatrists 1 (pt);
Dentists 1 (pt).
Languages Yiddish, Hebrew.
Facilities Dining room; Physical therapy
room; Activities room; Chapel; Crafts room;
Laundry room; Barber/Beauty shop; Library.
Activities Arts & crafts; Cards; Games;
Reading groups; Prayer groups; Movies;
Dances/Social/Cultural gatherings.

Norwood Park Home
6016 N Nina Ave, Chicago, IL 60631
(312) 631-4856
Admin James E Herbon. *Dir of Nursing*
Nancy Lucarini RN. *Medical Dir* Thomas
Pawlowski MD.
Licensure Intermediate care; Sheltered care;
Adult day care. *Beds* ICF 131; Sheltered
care 140. *Certified* Medicaid.
Owner Nonprofit corp.
Admissions Requirements Minimum age 65;
Medical examination.
Staff Physicians 1 (pt); RNs 3 (ft), 6 (pt);
LPNs 8 (ft), 2 (pt); Nurses' aides 35 (ft), 6
(pt); Recreational therapists 4 (ft), 2 (pt);
Activities coordinators 1 (ft); Dietitians 1
(pt); Podiatrists.
Facilities Dining room; Physical therapy
room; Activities room; Chapel; Crafts room;
Laundry room; Barber/Beauty shop; Library.
Activities Arts & crafts; Cards; Games;
Reading groups; Movies; Shopping trips;
Dances/Social/Cultural gatherings; Scrabble
tournaments.

O'Donnell House
6300 N Ridge Ave, Chicago, IL 60660
(312) 973-6300
Admin Teri Petrisko.
Licensure Intermediate care for mentally
retarded. *Beds* ICF/MR 8.

Old Peoples Home—City of Chicago
909 W Foster Ave, Chicago, IL 60640
(312) 561-2900
Admin Robert R Porter.
Licensure Intermediate care; Sheltered care.
Beds ICF 50; Sheltered care 85.

Park House Ltd
2320 S Lawndale, Chicago, IL 60623
(312) 522-0400, 522-1692 FAX
Admin Dr Jakob Bakst ACSW. *Dir of Nursing*
Pamela Major RN. *Medical Dir* Solomon
Dayan MD.
Licensure Intermediate care. *Beds* ICF 106.
Certified Medicaid.
Owner Proprietary corp.
Admissions Requirements Minimum age 18;
Medical examination.
Staff Physicians; RNs 1 (ft); LPNs 6 (ft);
Nurses' aides 24 (ft); Physical therapists;
Occupational therapists; Activities
coordinators 1 (ft); Dietitians;
Ophthalmologists; Podiatrists; Activities
aides 2 (ft).
Facilities Dining room; Physical therapy
room; Activities room; Crafts room; Laundry
room; Psychosocial, family privacy room.
Activities Arts & crafts; Cards; Games;
Reading groups; Prayer groups; Shopping
trips; Dances/Social/Cultural gatherings.

Peterson Park Health Care Center
6141 N Pulaski Rd, Chicago, IL 60646
(312) 478-2000
Admin Sheila Bogen. *Dir of Nursing* Eleanor
Bulatao RN. *Medical Dir* Dr Ali Riazi.
Licensure Skilled care; Intermediate care. *Beds*
SNF 93; ICF 95. *Private Pay Patients* 18%.
Certified Medicaid; VA.
Owner Privately owned.
Admissions Requirements Minimum age 45.
Staff Physicians 30 (pt); RNs 18 (ft); LPNs 9
(ft); Nurses' aides 49 (ft); Physical therapists
2 (ft); Reality therapists 8 (ft); Recreational
therapists 5 (ft); Occupational therapists 2
(ft); Speech therapists 1 (pt); Activities
coordinators 1 (ft); Dietitians 1 (pt);
Ophthalmologists 1 (pt); Podiatrists 1 (pt);
Audiologists 1 (pt).
Languages Korean, Tagalog, Polish, Spanish,
Yiddish, Farsi.
Facilities Dining room; Physical therapy
room; Activities room; Laundry room;
Barber/Beauty shop.
Activities Arts & crafts; Cards; Games;
Reading groups; Prayer groups; Movies;
Shopping trips; Dances/Social/Cultural
gatherings; Intergenerational programs; Pet
therapy; Outings to sports events.

Providence Center
4250 N McVicker St, Chicago, IL 60634
(312) 545-8300
Admin Linda M Willette.
Licensure Community living facility. *Beds*
Community living facility 18.

Rainbow Beach Nursing Center Inc
7325 S Exchange, Chicago, IL 60649
(312) 731-7300
Admin Rita Hochenbaum. *Dir of Nursing*
Idell Whitfield. *Medical Dir* Mohammad
Shafai.
Licensure Intermediate care. *Beds* ICF 111.
Private Pay Patients 10%. *Certified*
Medicaid.
Owner Proprietary corp.
Admissions Requirements Minimum age 18.
Staff LPNs 9 (pt); Nurses' aides 30 (ft);
Activities coordinators 1 (ft).

Facilities Dining room; Activities room.
Activities Arts & crafts; Cards; Games; Reading groups; Prayer groups; Movies; Shopping trips; Dances/Social/Cultural gatherings; Intergenerational programs; Pet therapy.

Renaissance House
6050 N California Ave, Chicago, IL 60659
(312) 761-4651
Admin Eric Johnson.
Licensure Intermediate care for mentally retarded. *Beds* ICF/MR 20.
Owner Nonprofit corp.

Rice House
6300 N Ridge Ave, Chicago, IL 60660
(312) 973-6300
Admin Teri Petrisko.
Licensure Intermediate care for mentally retarded. *Beds* ICF/MR 8.

Rose Marian Hall
4200 N Austin, Chicago, IL 60634
(312) 545-8300, 545-2984 FAX
Admin Sr Beth Ann Dillon MA. *Dir of Nursing* Sr Savina Lasowski Health Svcs Dir. *Medical Dir* Kirit Joshi MD.
Licensure Intermediate care for mentally retarded. *Beds* ICF/MR 48. *Private Pay Patients* 0%. *Certified* Medicaid.
Owner Nonprofit organization/foundation (Daughters of Saint Mary of Providence).
Admissions Requirements Minimum age 18; Females only; Medical examination; Physician's request.
Staff Physicians 1 (ft); RNs 2 (ft); LPNs 2 (pt); Physical therapists; Recreational therapists 1 (ft), 1 (pt); Occupational therapists 1 (ft); Speech therapists 1 (ft); Activities coordinators 1 (ft); Dietitians 1 (pt); Habilitation aides 13 (ft), 13 (pt).
Languages Italian.
Affiliation Roman Catholic.
Facilities Dining room; Activities room; Chapel; Crafts room; Laundry room; Library; Multi-purpose room; Gym.
Activities Arts & crafts; Cards; Games; Reading groups; Prayer groups; Movies; Shopping trips; Dances/Social/Cultural gatherings; Drama; Art therapy; Music therapy; Active treatment.

Rosewood-Damen Nursing Home Inc
6700-10 N Damen Ave, Chicago, IL 60645
(312) 465-5000
Admin W E Lamz.
Licensure Skilled care; Intermediate care. *Beds* SNF 51; ICF 76. *Certified* Medicaid.
Owner Proprietary corp.

Sacred Heart Home
1550 S Albany, Chicago, IL 60623
(312) 277-6868
Admin Dorothy E Williams.
Licensure Intermediate care. *Beds* ICF 172. *Certified* Medicaid.
Owner Proprietary corp.

St Agnes Health Care Center
60 E 18th St, Chicago, IL 60616
(312) 922-2777
Admin Eugene Caldwell.
Licensure Skilled care; Intermediate care. *Beds* SNF 129; ICF 68.
Owner Proprietary corp.

St Elizabeth's Hospital/Skilled Nursing Unit
1431 N Claremont, Chicago, IL 60622
(312) 278-2000
Admin Patricia Monnelly RN. *Dir of Nursing* Patricia Monnelly RN. *Medical Dir* Dr Zenaida Racho.
Licensure Skilled care. *Beds* SNF 34. *Certified* Medicare.
Admissions Requirements Minimum age 18; Physician's request; 3 day prior hospital stay.

Staff RNs; LPNs; Nurses' aides; Physical therapists; Occupational therapists; Speech therapists; Activities coordinators; Dietitians; Social workers; Pastoral care.
Languages Spanish, Polish.
Activities Arts & crafts; Cards; Games; Prayer groups; Movies.

St Joseph Home of Chicago Inc
2650 N Ridgeway Ave, Chicago, IL 60647-1199
(312) 235-8600
Admin William A Ladra. *Dir of Nursing* Joanne O'Donnell. *Medical Dir* Salomon J Dayan MD.
Licensure Skilled care. *Beds* SNF 173. *Private Pay Patients* 50%. *Certified* Medicaid; Medicare.
Owner Nonprofit corp.
Admissions Requirements Medical examination.
Staff Physicians 2 (pt); RNs 8 (ft); LPNs 12 (ft); Nurses' aides 54 (ft); Physical therapists (consultant); Occupational therapists (consultant); Speech therapists (consultant); Activities coordinators 6 (ft), 2 (ft); Dietitians; Ophthalmologists (consultant); Podiatrists (consultant); Audiologists (consultant); Dermatologists (consultant).
Languages Polish.
Affiliation Roman Catholic.
Facilities Dining room; Physical therapy room; Activities room; Chapel; Crafts room; Laundry room; Barber/Beauty shop; Library; Lounges; Porches; Large garden area.
Activities Arts & crafts; Cards; Games; Prayer groups; Movies; Shopping trips; Dances/ Social/Cultural gatherings; Intergenerational programs; Pet therapy.

St Martha Manor
4621 N Racine Ave, Chicago, IL 60640
(312) 784-2300
Admin Kathleen Stumpf.
Medical Dir Arsenio Agngarayngay.
Licensure Skilled care; Intermediate care. *Beds* SNF 57; ICF 75. *Certified* Medicaid.
Owner Nonprofit corp.
Admissions Requirements Minimum age 18.
Staff Physicians 5 (pt); RNs 17 (ft); LPNs 4 (ft); Nurses' aides 20 (ft); Physical therapists 3 (pt); Reality therapists 1 (ft); Recreational therapists 1 (ft); Occupational therapists 1 (ft); Speech therapists 1 (ft), 1 (pt); Activities coordinators 5 (ft); Dietitians 1 (pt); Podiatrists 1 (pt); Dentists 1 (pt).
Facilities Dining room; Physical therapy room; Activities room; Crafts room; Laundry room; Barber/Beauty shop.
Activities Arts & crafts; Cards; Games; Reading groups; Prayer groups; Movies; Shopping trips; Dances/Social/Cultural gatherings.

St Pauls House/Grace Convalescent Home
3831 N Mozart St, Chicago, IL 60618
(312) 478-4222
Admin Carol Zech. *Dir of Nursing* Virginia DeLeon. *Medical Dir* Dr G M Edvenson.
Licensure Skilled care; Intermediate care; Sheltered care; Retirement. *Beds* SNF 51; ICF 90; Sheltered care 74. *Private Pay Patients* 86%. *Certified* Medicaid.
Owner Nonprofit organization/foundation.
Admissions Requirements Minimum age 18; Medical examination; Physician's request.
Staff Physicians 1 (ft); RNs 14 (ft), 7 (pt); LPNs 7 (ft); Nurses' aides 30 (ft), 29 (pt); Speech therapists 1 (pt); Activities coordinators 5 (ft); Dietitians 1 (ft); Ophthalmologists 1 (pt); Podiatrists 2 (pt); Audiologists 1 (pt).
Affiliation United Church of Christ.
Facilities Dining room; Physical therapy room; Activities room; Chapel; Laundry room; Barber/Beauty shop; Library.

Activities Arts & crafts; Cards; Games; Prayer groups; Movies; Shopping trips; Dances/ Social/Cultural gatherings; Intergenerational programs; Pet therapy.

Selfhelp Home for the Aged
908 W Argyle St, Chicago, IL 60640
(312) 271-0300
Admin Grace G Hayes. *Dir of Nursing* Evelyn Dagovitz. *Medical Dir* Hyman Mackler MD.
Licensure Intermediate care; Sheltered care; Retirement. *Beds* ICF 25; Sheltered care 21. *Certified* Medicaid.
Owner Nonprofit corp.
Admissions Requirements Minimum age 65; Medical examination; Physician's request.
Staff RNs 1 (ft); LPNs 2 (ft), 5 (pt); Nurses' aides 17 (ft), 6 (pt); Physical therapists 1 (pt); Recreational therapists 1 (pt); Occupational therapists 1 (pt).
Languages German.
Affiliation Jewish.
Facilities Dining room; Physical therapy room; Activities room; Chapel; Crafts room; Laundry room; Barber/Beauty shop; Library.
Activities Arts & crafts; Cards; Games; Reading groups; Prayer groups; Movies; Dances/Social/Cultural gatherings; Parties.

Shannon House
6300 N Ridge Ave, Chicago, IL 60660
(312) 973-6300
Admin Teri Petrisko.
Licensure Intermediate care for mentally retarded. *Beds* ICF/MR 8.

Sherwin Manor Nursing Center
7350 N Sheridan Rd, Chicago, IL 60626
(312) 274-1000
Admin Joseph Osina.
Licensure Skilled care. *Beds* SNF 219. *Certified* Medicaid.
Owner Proprietary corp.

Washington & Jane Smith Home
2340 W 113th Pl, Chicago, IL 60643
(312) 238-8305
Admin Gary T Johanson.
Licensure Skilled care; Sheltered care. *Beds* SNF 44; Sheltered care 201.
Owner Nonprofit corp.

Society for Danish Old Peoples Home
5656 N Newcastle Ave, Chicago, IL 60631
(312) 775-7383
Admin Leif Nielsen. *Dir of Nursing* Lina Robinson. *Medical Dir* Dr Philip Anderson.
Licensure Intermediate care; Sheltered care; Retirement. *Beds* ICF 15; Sheltered care 57.
Owner Nonprofit organization/foundation.
Admissions Requirements Minimum age 62; Medical examination.
Languages Danish.
Facilities Dining room; Activities room; Laundry room; Barber/Beauty shop; Library.
Activities Arts & crafts; Cards; Games; Movies; Shopping trips; Dances/Social/ Cultural gatherings.

Somerset House
5009 N Sheridan, Chicago, IL 60640
(312) 561-0700, 275-4212 FAX
Admin Michael J Filippo. *Dir of Nursing* Robert Rowlands RN. *Medical Dir* Dr David Edelberg.
Licensure Intermediate care. *Beds* ICF 450. *Private Pay Patients* 3%. *Certified* Medicaid.
Owner Proprietary corp.
Admissions Requirements Minimum age 18.
Staff Physicians 9 (ft); RNs 3 (ft); LPNs 20 (ft), 2 (pt); Nurses' aides 56 (ft); Recreational therapists 1 (ft); Occupational therapists 1 (ft); Speech therapists 1 (ft); Activities coordinators 1 (ft); Dietitians 1 (ft); Ophthalmologists 1 (ft); Podiatrists 1 (ft); Audiologists 1 (ft).

Facilities Dining room; Physical therapy room; Activities room; Crafts room; Laundry room; Barber/Beauty shop; Library; Rooftop deck.
Activities Arts & crafts; Cards; Games; Reading groups; Prayer groups; Movies; Shopping trips; Dances/Social/Cultural gatherings; Intergenerational programs; Pet therapy.

Sovereign Home
6159 N Kenmore Ave, Chicago, IL 60660
(312) 761-9050
Admin David Stern.
Licensure Intermediate care. *Beds* ICF 55. *Certified* Medicaid.
Owner Proprietary corp.

Vista Laguna Aftercare Facility Inc
449 W Winnecona Pkwy, Chicago, IL 60620
(312) 224-3900
Admin Myrtle Martin.
Licensure Intermediate care. *Beds* 164. *Certified* Medicaid.
Owner Proprietary corp.

Waterfront Terrace Inc
7750 S Shore Dr, Chicago, IL 60649
(312) 731-4200
Admin Michael Lebowicz. *Dir of Nursing* Anna Wiszowaty. *Medical Dir* Dr Solomon Dayan.
Licensure Intermediate care; Alzheimer's care. *Beds* ICF 118. *Private Pay Patients* 6%. *Certified* Medicaid.
Owner Proprietary corp.
Admissions Requirements Minimum age 55; Medical examination; Physician's request.
Staff Physicians; RNs 2 (ft); LPNs 12 (ft); Nurses' aides 17 (ft); Physical therapists 1 (ft); Reality therapists 1 (ft); Recreational therapists 3 (ft); Occupational therapists 1 (ft); Activities coordinators 1 (ft); Dietitians 1 (ft); Ophthalmologists 1 (pt); Podiatrists 1 (pt); Audiologists 1 (pt).
Languages Italian.
Facilities Dining room; Physical therapy room; Activities room; Laundry room; Barber/Beauty shop.
Activities Arts & crafts; Cards; Games; Reading groups; Prayer groups; Movies; Shopping trips; Dances/Social/Cultural gatherings; Pet therapy; Bingo; Popcornfest.

Wellington Plaza Therapy & Nursing Center
504 W Wellington Ave, Chicago, IL 60657
(312) 281-6200
Admin Gloria Krieger.
Medical Dir Martin Ross MD.
Licensure Skilled care; Intermediate care; Alzheimer's care. *Beds* SNF 34; ICF 62. *Certified* Medicare.
Owner Proprietary corp.
Admissions Requirements Minimum age 50; Medical examination; Physician's request.
Staff Physicians 4 (pt); RNs 7 (ft), 14 (pt); LPNs 3 (ft), 4 (pt); Nurses' aides 30 (ft), 5 (pt); Physical therapists 1 (ft); Reality therapists 3 (ft); Recreational therapists 1 (ft); Occupational therapists 1 (ft); Speech therapists 1 (pt); Activities coordinators 1 (ft); Dietitians 1 (ft); Ophthalmologists 1 (pt); Podiatrists 1 (pt); Dentists 1 (pt); Social workers 1 (pt).
Languages Hebrew, Yiddish, Spanish, Tagalog, Portuguese, German, Estonian.
Facilities Dining room; Physical therapy room; Activities room; Chapel; Crafts room; Laundry room; Barber/Beauty shop; Library.
Activities Arts & crafts; Cards; Games; Reading groups; Prayer groups; Movies; Shopping trips; Dances/Social/Cultural gatherings; Visiting pets.

Westwood Manor Inc
2444 W Touhy Ave, Chicago, IL 60645
(312) 274-7705
Admin Chaya Liberman.

Medical Dir Dr Lawrence Mazur.
Licensure Skilled care; Intermediate care. *Beds* SNF 26; ICF 89. *Certified* Medicaid.
Owner Proprietary corp.
Admissions Requirements Minimum age 18.
Facilities Dining room; Physical therapy room; Activities room; Crafts room.
Activities Arts & crafts; Cards; Games; Prayer groups; Movies; Shopping trips; Dances/Social/Cultural gatherings.

Whitehall Convalescent & Nursing Home
1901 N Lincoln Park W, Chicago, IL 60614
(312) 943-2846
Admin Patricia J Gottschalk RN MSA. *Dir of Nursing* Diane Fabro RN. *Medical Dir* Raja Khuri MD.
Licensure Skilled care. *Beds* SNF 76. *Private Pay Patients* 100%.
Owner Proprietary corp.
Admissions Requirements Minimum age 60; Medical examination; Physician's request.
Staff Physicians 1 (ft), 2 (pt); RNs 5 (ft), 3 (pt); LPNs 7 (ft), 5 (pt); Nurses' aides 29 (ft), 11 (pt); Physical therapists 1 (pt); Reality therapists 1 (pt); Recreational therapists 1 (pt); Speech therapists 1 (pt); Activities coordinators 1 (ft); Dietitians 1 (pt); Audiologists 1 (pt).
Languages German, French.
Facilities Dining room; Physical therapy room; Activities room; Laundry room; Barber/Beauty shop; Soda shop.
Activities Arts & crafts; Cards; Games; Reading groups; Movies; Shopping trips; Dances/Social/Cultural gatherings; Intergenerational programs; Pet therapy; Religious activities; Mass.

Wincrest Nursing Center
6326 N Winthrop Avenue, Chicago, IL 60660
(312) 338-7800
Admin Mark S Segal. *Dir of Nursing* Ernestine Hopson. *Medical Dir* Dr Sydney Feldman.
Licensure Intermediate care; Retirement. *Beds* ICF 82. *Certified* Medicaid.
Owner Proprietary corp.
Admissions Requirements Minimum age 50; Medical examination; Physician's request.
Staff RNs 1 (ft); LPNs 5 (ft), 6 (pt); Nurses' aides 11 (ft), 6 (pt); Physical therapists 1 (ft); Recreational therapists 1 (ft); Occupational therapists 1 (ft).
Facilities Dining room; Activities room; Laundry room; Barber/Beauty shop.
Activities Arts & crafts; Cards; Games; Prayer groups; Movies; Shopping trips; Dances/Social/Cultural gatherings.

Winston Manor Convalescent & Nursing Home
2155 W Pierce Ave, Chicago, IL 60622
(312) 252-2066
Admin Vincenzina A Roche.
Licensure Intermediate care. *Beds* ICF 180. *Certified* Medicaid.
Owner Proprietary corp.

Woodbridge Nursing Pavilion
2242 N Kedzie Ave, Chicago, IL 60647
(312) 486-7700
Admin Maurice I Aaron. *Dir of Nursing* Virginia Kurz RN. *Medical Dir* A Rezvan MD.
Licensure Skilled care; Alzheimer's care. *Beds* SNF 222. *Certified* Medicaid.
Owner Proprietary corp.
Staff Physicians 8 (pt); RNs 9 (ft); LPNs 14 (ft); Nurses' aides 44 (ft); Physical therapists 2 (ft), 1 (pt); Reality therapists 1 (pt); Occupational therapists 1 (ft), 1 (pt); Speech therapists 1 (ft), 1 (pt); Activities coordinators 5 (pt); Dietitians 1 (pt); Ophthalmologists 1 (pt); Podiatrists 2 (pt); Dentists 1 (pt).
Languages Spanish.
Facilities Dining room; Physical therapy room; Activities room; Crafts room; Laundry room; Barber/Beauty shop.

Activities Arts & crafts; Cards; Games; Reading groups; Prayer groups; Movies; Shopping trips; Dances/Social/Cultural gatherings; Outings to zoos; Bingo.

Chicago Heights

Prairie Manor
345 Dixie Hwy, Chicago Heights, IL 60411
(708) 754-7601
Admin Linda Cecconi.
Licensure Skilled care; Intermediate care. *Beds* SNF 51; ICF 97.

Riviera Manor Inc
490 W 16th Pl, Chicago Heights, IL 60411
(708) 481-4444
Admin Gus G Potekin.
Licensure Skilled care; Intermediate care. *Beds* SNF 100; ICF 100. *Certified* Medicaid; Medicare.
Owner Proprietary corp.

Thornton Heights Terrace Ltd
160 W 10th St, Chicago Heights, IL 60411
(708) 754-2220
Admin Elvira L Cull.
Licensure Intermediate care. *Beds* ICF 222. *Certified* Medicaid.
Owner Proprietary corp.
Admissions Requirements Minimum age 18.
Facilities Dining room; Activities room; Crafts room; Laundry room; Barber/Beauty shop; Library.
Activities Arts & crafts; Cards; Games; Reading groups; Prayer groups; Movies; Shopping trips; Dances/Social/Cultural gatherings.

Chicago Ridge

Chicago Ridge Nursing Center
10602 Southwest Hwy, Chicago Ridge, IL 60415
(312) 448-1540
Admin Stephen G Brumer.
Medical Dir Solomon Payan.
Licensure Skilled care. *Beds* SNF 231. *Certified* Medicaid; Medicare.
Owner Proprietary corp.
Admissions Requirements Minimum age 21.
Staff Physicians 4 (pt); RNs 12 (ft); LPNs 11 (ft); Nurses' aides 43 (ft); Physical therapists 2 (pt); Reality therapists 4 (ft), 2 (pt); Recreational therapists 4 (ft), 2 (pt); Occupational therapists 1 (pt); Speech therapists 1 (pt); Activities coordinators 4 (ft), 2 (pt); Dietitians 1 (pt); Ophthalmologists 1 (pt); Podiatrists 1 (pt); Dentists 1 (pt).
Facilities Dining room; Physical therapy room; Activities room; Chapel; Crafts room; Laundry room; Barber/Beauty shop; Library.
Activities Arts & crafts; Cards; Games; Reading groups; Prayer groups; Movies; Shopping trips; Dances/Social/Cultural gatherings; Outings; Baseball games; Circus.

Chillicothe

Crabel Court Community Living Facility
1105 Crabel Court, Chillicothe, IL 61523
(309) 686-3354
Admin Gail M Leiby.
Licensure Community living facility. *Beds* Community living facility 12.

Parkhill Medical Complex
1028 Hillcrest Dr, Chillicothe, IL 61523
(309) 274-2194
Admin Kenneth E Anderson. *Dir of Nursing* Marilyn K Rennolett RN.
Licensure Skilled care. *Beds* SNF 113. *Certified* Medicaid; Medicare; VA.
Owner Nonprofit corp.
Admissions Requirements Medical examination.

Staff Physicians 1 (pt); RNs 3 (ft), 7 (pt); LPNs 5 (ft), 5 (pt); Nurses' aides 27 (ft), 7 (pt); Physical therapists 1 (pt); Recreational therapists 1 (pt); Speech therapists 1 (pt); Activities coordinators 1 (pt); Dietitians 1 (pt).
Facilities Dining room; Physical therapy room; Activities room; Laundry room; Barber/Beauty shop.
Activities Arts & crafts; Cards; Games; Reading groups; Prayer groups; Movies; Shopping trips; Dances/Social/Cultural gatherings; Exercise groups.

Chrisman

Pleasant Meadows Christian Village
PO Box 375, 400 W Washington, Chrisman, IL 61924
(217) 269-2396
Admin Robert Vincent.
Licensure Skilled care. *Beds* SNF 99. *Certified* Medicaid.
Owner Nonprofit corp (Christian Homes).

Cicero

Seguin Services Home IV
3259 S 61st St, Cicero, IL 60650
(708) 780-7151
Admin Betty Kodl.
Licensure Intermediate care for mentally retarded. *Beds* ICF/MR 8.

Westshire Retirement & Healthcare Center
5825 W Cermak Rd, Cicero, IL 60650
(708) 656-9120
Admin Mark L Shapiro.
Medical Dir Dr S Slodki.
Licensure Skilled care; Intermediate care. *Beds* SNF 76; ICF 409. *Certified* Medicaid.
Owner Proprietary corp.
Staff RNs 13 (ft), 3 (pt); LPNs 24 (ft), 1 (pt); Nurses' aides 82 (ft); Physical therapists; Recreational therapists 1 (ft); Occupational therapists; Speech therapists; Podiatrists 1 (pt); Dentists 1 (pt).
Facilities Dining room; Physical therapy room; Activities room; Crafts room; Laundry room; Barber/Beauty shop; Library.
Activities Arts & crafts; Cards; Games; Prayer groups; Shopping trips; Dances/Social/Cultural gatherings; Cooking; Gardening.

Cisne

Cisne Manor
PO Box 370, Watkins St, Cisne, IL 62823
(618) 673-2177
Admin Dava A Downey. *Dir of Nursing* Sharolene Knight RN. *Medical Dir* Dr Michael Blood.
Licensure Intermediate care; Alzheimer's care. *Beds* ICF 35. *Certified* Medicaid.
Owner Privately owned.
Admissions Requirements Minimum age 18.
Staff RNs 2 (ft); LPNs 2 (ft), 2 (pt); Nurses' aides 6 (ft), 4 (pt); Activities coordinators 1 (ft).
Facilities Dining room; Activities room; Laundry room; Barber/Beauty shop.
Activities Arts & crafts; Cards; Games; Reading groups; Prayer groups; Movies; Shopping trips.

Clifton

A Merkle C Knipprath Nursing Home
RR 1, Clifton, IL 60927
(815) 694-2306
Admin Stephen A Debraikeleer.
Licensure Intermediate care. *Beds* ICF 99.
Owner Nonprofit corp.
Admissions Requirements Medical examination; Physician's request.
Affiliation Roman Catholic.

Facilities Dining room; Physical therapy room; Activities room; Chapel; Crafts room; Laundry room; Barber/Beauty shop; Library.
Activities Arts & crafts; Cards; Games; Reading groups; Prayer groups; Movies; Shopping trips; Dances/Social/Cultural gatherings.

Clinton

Allen Court
1650 E Main St, Clinton, IL 61727
(217) 935-8830
Admin Cherrill Vanlandingham.
Licensure Intermediate care for mentally retarded. *Beds* ICF/MR 15.

Crestview Nursing Center
RR 3, US Hwy 51 N, Clinton, IL 61727
(217) 935-3826
Admin Wm A Johnston.
Medical Dir Robert Myers MD.
Licensure Intermediate care. *Beds* ICF 103. *Certified* Medicaid.
Owner Proprietary corp.
Admissions Requirements Minimum age 18; Medical examination.
Staff RNs 1 (pt); LPNs 6 (ft), 3 (pt); Nurses' aides 24 (ft), 9 (pt); Recreational therapists 1 (pt); Occupational therapists 1 (pt); Activities coordinators 2 (ft); Dietitians 1 (pt).
Facilities Dining room; Physical therapy room; Activities room; Chapel; Crafts room; Laundry room; Barber/Beauty shop; Library.
Activities Arts & crafts; Cards; Games; Reading groups; Prayer groups; Movies; Shopping trips; Dances/Social/Cultural gatherings.

Dewitt County Nursing Home
RFD 1, Box 336, Clinton, IL 61727
(217) 935-9418
Admin Jean M Boggs.
Medical Dir Selah Obasi MD.
Licensure Intermediate care; Sheltered care. *Beds* ICF 60; Sheltered care 25.
Owner Publicly owned.
Admissions Requirements Minimum age 18; Medical examination; Physician's request.
Staff Physicians 7 (ft); RNs 2 (ft); LPNs 6 (ft), 1 (pt); Nurses' aides 37 (ft); Physical therapists 1 (pt); Occupational therapists 1 (pt); Speech therapists 1 (pt); Activities coordinators 1 (ft); Dietitians 1 (pt); Dentists 1 (pt).
Facilities Dining room; Physical therapy room; Activities room; Crafts room; Laundry room; Barber/Beauty shop; Library.
Activities Arts & crafts; Games; Reading groups; Prayer groups; Movies; Shopping trips; Dances/Social/Cultural gatherings.

Coal Valley

Oak Glen Nursing Home
11210 95th St, Coal Valley, IL 61240
(309) 799-3161
Admin Carolyn Matson. *Dir of Nursing* Shirley J Otts RN. *Medical Dir* Alex J Pareigis MD.
Licensure Skilled care. *Beds* SNF 285. *Private Pay Patients* 30%. *Certified* Medicaid; Medicare.
Owner Publicly owned.
Admissions Requirements Minimum age 18; Medical examination; Physician's request.
Staff Physicians 1 (pt); RNs 10 (ft); LPNs 28 (ft), 9 (pt); Nurses' aides 73 (ft), 14 (pt); Physical therapists 1 (pt); Occupational therapists 1 (pt); Speech therapists 1 (pt); Activities coordinators 1 (ft), 1 (pt); Dietitians 1 (pt); Ophthalmologists 2 (pt); Podiatrists 1 (pt); Dentists 2 (pt).
Facilities Dining room; Physical therapy room; Activities room; Chapel; Crafts room; Laundry room; Barber/Beauty shop; Library.

Activities Arts & crafts; Cards; Games; Reading groups; Prayer groups; Movies; Shopping trips; Dances/Social/Cultural gatherings; Intergenerational programs; Pet therapy.

Cobden

Hillside Terrace
PO Box 22038, Cobden, IL 62920
(618) 893-4214
Admin Gloria G DeWitt.
Medical Dir Dr William H Whiting.
Licensure Skilled care; Intermediate care; Alzheimer's care. *Beds* SNF 16; ICF 58. *Certified* Medicaid.
Owner Proprietary corp.
Admissions Requirements Minimum age 18; Females only; Medical examination.
Staff Physicians 5 (pt); RNs 1 (ft), 3 (pt); LPNs 1 (ft), 6 (pt); Nurses' aides 19 (ft); Physical therapists 1 (pt); Recreational therapists 1 (ft); Speech therapists 1 (pt); Activities coordinators 1 (ft); Dietitians 1 (pt).
Facilities Dining room; Physical therapy room; Activities room; Crafts room; Laundry room; Barber/Beauty shop.
Activities Arts & crafts; Cards; Games; Reading groups; Prayer groups; Movies; Shopping trips; Dances/Social/Cultural gatherings.

Tripp Shelter Care Home
Box 336, Cobden, IL 62920
(618) 893-2291
Admin Larry L Tripp.
Licensure Sheltered care. *Beds* Sheltered care 28.
Owner Proprietary corp.

Village Sheltered Care Home
114 Ash St, Cobden, IL 62920
(618) 893-4222
Admin Henrietta Smith.
Licensure Sheltered care. *Beds* Sheltered care 22.
Owner Proprietary corp.

Colchester

Colchester Nursing Center
222 Hun St, Colchester, IL 62326
(309) 776-3236
Admin Lynn M Lotz. *Dir of Nursing* Ramona Reed LPN. *Medical Dir* Stephen Roth MD.
Licensure Intermediate care. *Beds* ICF 54. *Certified* Medicaid.
Owner Proprietary corp.
Admissions Requirements Minimum age Geriatric; Medical examination.
Staff LPNs 5 (ft), 1 (pt); Nurses' aides 10 (ft), 6 (pt); Physical therapists 1 (ft), 1 (pt); Reality therapists 1 (pt); Recreational therapists 1 (pt); Speech therapists 1 (pt); Activities coordinators 1 (ft), 1 (pt); Dietitians 1 (pt).
Facilities Dining room; Physical therapy room; Activities room; Laundry room; Barber/Beauty shop; Family room.
Activities Arts & crafts; Cards; Games; Reading groups; Prayer groups; Movies; Shopping trips; Dances/Social/Cultural gatherings; Gardening; Bingo.

Colfax

Octavia Manor Inc
402 S Harrison, Colfax, IL 61728
(309) 723-2591
Admin Shirley J Geske.
Medical Dir Dr Marcus Que.
Licensure Intermediate care. *Beds* ICF 60. *Certified* Medicaid.
Owner Proprietary corp.
Admissions Requirements Minimum age 60; Medical examination; Physician's request.

Staff Physicians 1 (pt); RNs 1 (ft), 1 (pt); LPNs 4 (ft), 4 (pt); Nurses' aides 20 (ft), 15 (pt); Activities coordinators 1 (ft); Dietitians 1 (pt).
Facilities Dining room; Physical therapy room; Activities room; Crafts room; Laundry room; Barber/Beauty shop.
Activities Arts & crafts; Cards; Games; Reading groups; Prayer groups; Movies; Shopping trips; Dances/Social/Cultural gatherings.

Collinsville

Pleasant Rest Nursing Home
614 N Summit Ave, Collinsville, IL 62234
(618) 344-8476
Admin Michael R Myler. *Dir of Nursing* Shirley Hunsinger RN.
Licensure Skilled care. *Beds* SNF 122. *Certified* Medicaid; Medicare.
Owner Proprietary corp.
Admissions Requirements Minimum age 21; Medical examination.
Staff Physicians; RNs; LPNs; Nurses' aides; Physical therapists; Speech therapists; Activities coordinators; Dietitians; Ophthalmologists; Dentists.
Facilities Dining room; Physical therapy room; Activities room; Crafts room; Laundry room; Barber/Beauty shop.
Activities Arts & crafts; Cards; Games; Reading groups; Prayer groups; Movies; Shopping trips; Dances/Social/Cultural gatherings.

Creal Springs

Creal Springs Nursing Home
S Line St, Creal Springs, IL 62922
(618) 996-2313
Admin James F Avery.
Medical Dir Dr A Z Goldstein.
Licensure Skilled care. *Beds* SNF 80. *Certified* Medicaid.
Owner Proprietary corp.
Admissions Requirements Minimum age 21; Medical examination; Physician's request.
Staff Physicians 3 (pt); RNs 1 (ft), 2 (pt); LPNs 7 (ft), 2 (pt); Nurses' aides 19 (ft); Physical therapists 1 (pt); Reality therapists 1 (pt); Recreational therapists 1 (pt); Occupational therapists 1 (pt); Speech therapists 1 (pt); Activities coordinators 1 (ft); Dietitians 1 (pt); Dentists 1 (pt).
Facilities Dining room; Physical therapy room; Activities room; Crafts room; Laundry room; Barber/Beauty shop.
Activities Arts & crafts; Cards; Games; Reading groups; Prayer groups; Movies; Shopping trips; Dances/Social/Cultural gatherings.

Crestwood

Crestwood Terrace
13301 S Central, Crestwood, IL 60445
(708) 597-5251
Admin Maureen M Skopick. *Dir of Nursing* Judy Majchrowicz RN. *Medical Dir* Antonio Noreiga MD.
Licensure Intermediate care. *Beds* ICF 126. *Private Pay Patients* 70%. *Certified* Medicaid.
Owner Proprietary corp.
Admissions Requirements Medical examination; Physician's request.
Staff Physicians 1 (ft), 10 (pt); RNs 3 (ft), 2 (pt); LPNs 3 (ft), 2 (pt); Nurses' aides 18 (ft), 10 (pt); Physical therapists 1 (pt); Reality therapists 1 (ft), 1 (pt); Recreational therapists 2 (ft); Occupational therapists 1 (ft), 1 (pt); Speech therapists 1 (pt); Activities coordinators 1 (ft); Dietitians 1 (pt); Ophthalmologists 1 (pt); Podiatrists 1 (pt); Dentists 1 (pt).

Languages Polish, Italian.
Facilities Dining room; Physical therapy room; Activities room; Crafts room; Laundry room; Barber/Beauty shop; Library; OT PT.
Activities Arts & crafts; Cards; Games; Reading groups; Prayer groups; Movies; Shopping trips; Dances/Social/Cultural gatherings; Intergenerational programs; Pet therapy.

Crete

St James Manor
1251 E Richton Rd, Crete, IL 60417
(708) 672-6700, 672-4939 FAX
Admin George L Belock. *Dir of Nursing* Margi Carlson. *Medical Dir* D Sreekanth.
Licensure Skilled care. *Beds* SNF 110. *Private Pay Patients* 66%.
Owner Nonprofit organization/foundation.
Staff Physicians 1 (ft); RNs 2 (ft), 1 (pt); LPNs 4 (ft), 3 (pt); Nurses' aides 8 (ft), 12 (pt); Speech therapists 1 (pt); Activities coordinators 1 (ft); Dietitians 1 (pt); Ophthalmologists 1 (pt); Podiatrists 1 (pt).

Crystal Lake

Crystal Pines Nursing Home
335 N Illinois Ave, Crystal Lake, IL 60014
(815) 459-7791
Admin Joan P Swekosky. *Dir of Nursing* Jan Lavin. *Medical Dir* Z Ted Lorenc.
Licensure Skilled care. *Beds* SNF 83. *Certified* Medicare.
Owner Nonprofit corp (First Humanics).
Admissions Requirements Physician's request.
Staff RNs; LPNs; Nurses' aides; Activities coordinators.
Facilities Dining room; Physical therapy room; Activities room; Laundry room; Barber/Beauty shop.
Activities Arts & crafts; Cards; Games; Prayer groups; Movies; Shopping trips; Dances/Social/Cultural gatherings.

Fair Oaks Health Care Center
471 Terra Cotta Ave, Crystal Lake, IL 60014
(815) 455-0550
Admin Susan A Cheek.
Licensure Skilled care. *Beds* SNF 46.
Owner Proprietary corp.

Cuba

Clayberg
E Monroe St, Cuba, IL 61427
(309) 785-5012
Admin Vicki Sue Hoke.
Medical Dir Dr Bruce Long.
Licensure Intermediate care. *Beds* 49. *Certified* Medicaid.
Owner Publicly owned.
Admissions Requirements Minimum age 62.
Facilities Dining room; Activities room; Crafts room; Laundry room; Barber/Beauty shop.
Activities Arts & crafts; Cards; Games; Reading groups; Prayer groups; Movies; Dances/Social/Cultural gatherings.

Danforth

Prairieview Lutheran Home
PO Box 4, Danforth, IL 60930
(815) 269-2970
Admin John E Taylor. *Dir of Nursing* Becky Warlow. *Medical Dir* Ted Devas MD.
Licensure Skilled care; Intermediate care; Retirement. *Beds* Swing beds SNF/ICF 60; Retirement units 21. *Private Pay Patients* 80%. *Certified* Medicaid.
Owner Nonprofit corp.
Admissions Requirements Minimum age 60.

Staff Physicians (consultant); RNs 3 (ft), 1 (pt); LPNs 4 (ft), 1 (pt); Nurses' aides 21 (ft), 1 (pt); Physical therapists (consultant); Reality therapists (consultant); Recreational therapists (consultant); Occupational therapists (consultant); Speech therapists (consultant); Activities coordinators 2 (ft); Dietitians (consultant); Ophthalmologists (consultant); Podiatrists (consultant).
Affiliation Lutheran.
Facilities Dining room; Physical therapy room; Activities room; Chapel; Crafts room; Laundry room; Barber/Beauty shop; Library; Telephone room; Patios; Campus setting; Private rooms.
Activities Arts & crafts; Cards; Games; Reading groups; Prayer groups; Movies; Shopping trips; Dances/Social/Cultural gatherings; Intergenerational programs; Pet therapy.

Danville

Americana Healthcare Center
801 Logan Ave, Danville, IL 61832
(217) 443-3106
Admin Linda L Morrison. *Dir of Nursing* Mary Nagle RN.
Licensure Skilled care. *Beds* SNF 108. *Certified* Medicaid; Medicare.
Owner Proprietary corp (Manor Care).
Admissions Requirements Minimum age 18; Medical examination.
Staff RNs; LPNs; Nurses' aides; Physical therapists; Occupational therapists; Speech therapists; Activities coordinators; Dietitians.
Facilities Dining room; Physical therapy room; Activities room; Barber/Beauty shop.
Activities Arts & crafts; Cards; Games; Prayer groups; Movies; Shopping trips; Dances/ Social/Cultural gatherings.

Colonial Manor Inc
PO Box 1098, 620 Warrington Ave, Danville, IL 61832
(217) 446-0660
Admin Richard W Black; Mark R Black. *Dir of Nursing* Sandra L Meade RN. *Medical Dir* Dr W F Hensold.
Licensure Skilled care; Intermediate care. *Beds* Swing beds SNF/ICF 76. *Private Pay Patients* 85%. *Certified* Medicaid; Medicare.
Owner Proprietary corp.
Admissions Requirements Medical examination; Physician's request.
Staff RNs; LPNs; Nurses' aides; Physical therapists (consultant); Activities coordinators; Dietitians (consultant).
Facilities Dining room; Activities room; Crafts room; Laundry room; Barber/Beauty shop.
Activities Arts & crafts; Cards; Games; Reading groups; Prayer groups; Movies; Dances/Social/Cultural gatherings; Intergenerational programs.

Danville Care Center Ltd
1701 N Bowman, Danville, IL 61832
(217) 443-2955
Admin Norma D Goble.
Licensure Skilled care; Intermediate care. *Beds* SNF 118; ICF 82. *Certified* Medicaid.
Owner Proprietary corp.

Danville Independent Living Center
1210 Holiday Dr, Danville, IL 61832
(217) 443-4622
Admin Setsu Marks.
Licensure Community living facility. *Beds* Community living facility 8.

Danville Manor
1215 Holiday Dr, Danville, IL 61832
(217) 443-4123
Admin Terry Ellis.
Medical Dir Marcia Landers.

Licensure Intermediate care; Intermediate care for mentally retarded. *Beds* ICF 40; ICF/MR 43. *Certified* Medicaid.
Owner Proprietary corp (Springwood Associates).
Admissions Requirements Minimum age 21; Medical examination; Physician's request.
Staff RNs 2 (pt); LPNs 6 (ft), 2 (pt); Nurses' aides 30 (ft), 2 (pt); Activities coordinators 1 (ft).
Facilities Dining room; Physical therapy room; Activities room; Crafts room; Laundry room.
Activities Arts & crafts; Cards; Games; Reading groups; Movies; Shopping trips; Dances/Social/Cultural gatherings.

International Nursing Home
207 S Buchanan, Danville, IL 61832
(217) 446-1433
Admin Roger D Eack. *Dir of Nursing* Clara Mitchell. *Medical Dir* Edmund E Andracki.
Licensure Intermediate care. *Beds* ICF 48. *Private Pay Patients* 47%. *Certified* Medicaid.
Owner Proprietary corp (Beverly Enterprises).
Admissions Requirements Minimum age 21; Medical examination.
Staff RNs (consultants); LPNs 3 (ft), 4 (pt); Nurses' aides 9 (ft), 7 (pt); Physical therapists (consultant); Activities coordinators 1 (pt); Dietitians 1 (ft); Podiatrists (consultant).
Facilities Dining room; Activities room; Laundry room; Chapel/Dayroom.
Activities Arts & crafts; Cards; Games; Reading groups; Prayer groups; Movies; Shopping trips; Pet therapy.

Vermillion Manor Nursing Home
RR 1, Box 13, Danville, IL 61832
(217) 443-6430
Admin Joseph A Aeschleman. *Dir of Nursing* Marsha Lock RN. *Medical Dir* Joseph Karinattu MD.
Licensure Intermediate care. *Beds* ICF 249. *Certified* Medicaid.
Owner Publicly owned.
Admissions Requirements Minimum age 18; Medical examination; Physician's request.
Staff Physicians 1 (pt); RNs 4 (ft), 2 (pt); LPNs 11 (ft), 4 (pt); Nurses' aides 100 (ft); Physical therapists aides 4 (ft), 1 (pt); Occupational therapists 1 (pt); Speech therapists 1 (pt); Activities coordinators 5 (ft), 1 (pt); Dietitians 1 (pt).
Languages Spanish, Sign.
Facilities Dining room; Physical therapy room; Activities room; Chapel; Crafts room; Laundry room; Barber/Beauty shop.
Activities Arts & crafts; Cards; Games; Reading groups; Prayer groups; Movies; Shopping trips; Dances/Social/Cultural gatherings.

De Kalb

Community Center
360 E Grand Ave, De Kalb, IL 62526
(217) 428-6350
Admin Daniel Keefe.
Licensure Intermediate care. *Beds* 58.
Owner Proprietary corp.

De Kalb County Nursing Home
2331 Sycamore Rd, De Kalb, IL 60115
(815) 758-2477
Admin Richard T Baer.
Licensure Skilled care. *Beds* SNF 194. *Certified* Medicaid; Medicare.
Owner Publicly owned.

Oak Crest
2944 Greenwood Acres Dr, De Kalb, IL 60115
(815) 756-8461
Admin Stephen P Cichy. *Dir of Nursing* Mary A Burnell RN.

Licensure Intermediate care; Sheltered care; Retirement. *Beds* ICF 30; Sheltered care 49.
Owner Nonprofit corp.
Admissions Requirements Minimum age 62; Medical examination.
Staff RNs 1 (ft), 8 (pt); Nurses' aides 13 (ft), 13 (pt); Recreational therapists 2 (ft); Activities coordinators 1 (ft).
Affiliation Methodist.
Facilities Dining room; Physical therapy room; Activities room; Chapel; Crafts room; Laundry room; Barber/Beauty shop; Library.
Activities Arts & crafts; Cards; Games; Reading groups; Prayer groups; Movies; Shopping trips; Dances/Social/Cultural gatherings.

Pine Acres Care Center
1212 S 2nd St, De Kalb, IL 60115
(815) 758-8151, 758-6832 FAX
Admin Norm Gross. *Dir of Nursing* Sharlene Baker. *Medical Dir* Stuart Olson MD.
Licensure Skilled care; Intermediate care; Alzheimer's care. *Beds* SNF 83; ICF 20; Alzheimer's care 16. *Private Pay Patients* 76%. *Certified* Medicaid; Medicare.
Owner Nonprofit organization/foundation (Evangelical Health Systems).
Admissions Requirements Medical examination.
Staff RNs 2 (ft), 12 (pt); LPNs 8 (ft), 4 (pt); Nurses' aides 20 (ft), 20 (pt); Physical therapists 1 (pt); Activities coordinators 1 (ft).
Affiliation United Church of Christ.
Facilities Dining room; Physical therapy room; Barber/Beauty shop.
Activities Arts & crafts; Cards; Games; Reading groups; Prayer groups; Movies; Dances/Social/Cultural gatherings; Intergenerational programs; Pet therapy; Reminiscing groups; Music therapy; Religious services; Exercise.

Decatur

Americana Healthcare Center of Decatur
444 W Harrison St, Decatur, IL 62526
(217) 877-7333
Admin Pamela S Rosenkranz.
Medical Dir Mary Roberts.
Licensure Skilled care; Alzheimer's care. *Beds* SNF 96. *Certified* Medicaid; Medicare.
Owner Proprietary corp (Manor Care).

Cedarwood Health Care Center
136 S Dipper Ln, Decatur, IL 62522
(217) 428-7767
Admin Sami S Siders. *Dir of Nursing* Elizabeth A Bennett. *Medical Dir* Dr Patel.
Licensure Intermediate care. *Beds* ICF 58. *Private Pay Patients* 32%. *Certified* Medicaid.
Owner Proprietary corp (Springwood Associates).
Admissions Requirements Physician's request.
Facilities Dining room; Activities room; Crafts room; Laundry room; Barber/Beauty shop; Solarium.
Activities Arts & crafts; Cards; Games; Reading groups; Prayer groups; Movies; Shopping trips; Dances/Social/Cultural gatherings; Intergenerational programs; Pet therapy.

Community Center
360 E Grand Ave, Decatur, IL 62521
(217) 428-6350
Admin Joseph Trainor.
Licensure Intermediate care for mentally retarded. *Beds* ICF/MR 85.

Fair Havens Christian Home
1790 S Fairview Ave, Decatur, IL 62521
(217) 429-2551
Admin Brian K Hodges.
Medical Dir Dr Dale Sunderland.

Licensure Skilled care; Retirement. *Beds* SNF 161. *Certified* Medicaid; Medicare.
Owner Nonprofit corp (Christian Homes).
Admissions Requirements Minimum age 18; Medical examination.
Staff RNs 5 (ft), 5 (pt); LPNs 9 (ft), 9 (pt); Nurses' aides 35 (ft), 35 (pt); Physical therapists 1 (pt); Activities coordinators 1 (ft); Ophthalmologists 1 (pt).
Affiliation Church of Christ.
Facilities Dining room; Physical therapy room; Activities room; Chapel; Crafts room; Laundry room; Barber/Beauty shop; Library; Large dayroom; 5 Duplex apts.
Activities Arts & crafts; Cards; Games; Reading groups; Prayer groups; Movies; Shopping trips; Dances/Social/Cultural gatherings.

Lincoln Manor Inc
2650 N Monroe St, Decatur, IL 62526
(217) 875-1973
Admin Sheila A McClung.
Licensure Intermediate care. *Beds* ICF 136. *Certified* Medicaid.
Owner Proprietary corp.

McKinley Court
500 W McKinley, Decatur, IL 62526
(217) 875-0020, 875-9434 FAX
Admin Candy J Carroll. *Dir of Nursing* Beverley Wingard. *Medical Dir* Dr Gaurang Patel.
Licensure Intermediate care. *Beds* ICF 150. *Private Pay Patients* 47%. *Certified* Medicaid.
Owner Nonprofit corp (Decatur Memorial Hospital).
Admissions Requirements Minimum age 18; Medical examination.
Staff Physicians 1 (pt); RNs 2 (ft); LPNs 10 (ft), 5 (pt); Nurses' aides 33 (ft), 10 (pt); Speech therapists 1 (pt); Activities coordinators 1 (ft); Dietitians 1 (pt); Podiatrists 1 (pt).
Facilities Dining room; Physical therapy room; Activities room; Barber/Beauty shop; Library; Gift shop.
Activities Arts & crafts; Cards; Games; Reading groups; Movies; Shopping trips; Dances/Social/Cultural gatherings; Pet therapy.

McKinley Terrace
2530 N Monroe St, Decatur, IL 62526
(217) 875-0920
Admin Steven E Evans.
Licensure Skilled care. *Beds* SNF 204.
Owner Proprietary corp.

Oak Manor Health Care Center
438 W North St, Decatur, IL 62522
(217) 429-7265
Admin Lula Robertson.
Medical Dir Marcy Butts.
Licensure Intermediate care; Sheltered care. *Beds* ICF 126; Sheltered 5. *Certified* Medicaid.
Owner Nonprofit corp (First Humanics).
Admissions Requirements Minimum age 65; Physician's request.
Staff RNs 1 (ft), 1 (pt); LPNs 11 (ft), 1 (pt); Nurses' aides 27 (ft); Physical therapists 1 (pt); Occupational therapists 1 (pt); Activities coordinators 1 (ft); Dietitians 1 (pt); Ophthalmologists 1 (pt); Social workers 1 (ft), 2 (pt).
Languages Spanish.
Facilities Dining room; Physical therapy room; Activities room; Crafts room; Laundry room; Barber/Beauty shop.
Activities Arts & crafts; Cards; Games; Reading groups; Prayer groups; Movies; Shopping trips; Dances/Social/Cultural gatherings; Cooking clubs; Men's groups.

Pershing Estates
1016 W Pershing Rd, Decatur, IL 62526
(217) 875-0833
Admin Sheila Herndon. *Dir of Nursing* Bonnie
Truxell. *Medical Dir* Dr Patil.
Licensure Intermediate care. *Beds* ICF 127.
Certified Medicaid.
Owner Proprietary corp.
Admissions Requirements Minimum age 18;
Medical examination; Physician's request.
Staff LPNs 6 (ft), 4 (pt); Nurses' aides 24 (ft),
7 (pt); Recreational therapists 1 (ft);
Occupational therapists 1 (ft); Activities
coordinators 1 (ft); Dietitians 1 (ft).
Facilities Dining room; Activities room;
Laundry room; Barber/Beauty shop.
Activities Arts & crafts; Cards; Games;
Reading groups; Prayer groups; Movies;
Shopping trips; Dances/Social/Cultural
gatherings.

James R Thompson House
805 E Johns St, Decatur, IL 62521
(217) 423-4450
Admin Judy K Busing.
Licensure Intermediate care for mentally
retarded. *Beds* ICF/MR 15.

Deerfield

Whitehall North
300 Waukegan Rd, Deerfield, IL 60015
(708) 945-4600
Admin Barbara K Harms. *Dir of Nursing* Judy
Hattendorf RN. *Medical Dir* Dr David
Littman.
Licensure Skilled care. *Beds* SNF 170.
Owner Privately owned.
Admissions Requirements Medical
examination.
Staff Physicians 2 (pt); RNs 40 (ft); LPNs 2
(ft); Nurses' aides 80 (ft); Physical therapists
1 (ft); Occupational therapists 1 (ft); Speech
therapists 1 (pt); Activities coordinators 2
(ft), 3 (pt); Dietitians 1 (ft);
Ophthalmologists 1 (pt); Rehabilitation
specialists 1 (ft).
Facilities Dining room; Physical therapy
room; Activities room; Chapel; Crafts room;
Laundry room; Barber/Beauty shop; Library;
Soda shop; Solariums; Dental suite; Patio.
Activities Arts & crafts; Cards; Games;
Reading groups; Prayer groups; Movies;
Dances/Social/Cultural gatherings.

Des Plaines

Ballard Nursing Center Inc
9300 Ballard Rd, Des Plaines, IL 60016
(708) 299-0182
Admin Eli Pick.
Medical Dir Dr Mazur.
Licensure Skilled care. *Beds* SNF 231.
Certified Medicaid; Medicare.
Owner Proprietary corp.
Admissions Requirements Minimum age 60;
Medical examination.
Staff RNs 12 (ft), 4 (pt); LPNs 6 (ft), 1 (pt);
Nurses' aides 39 (pt); Physical therapists 1
(ft); Reality therapists 1 (pt); Recreational
therapists 1 (pt); Occupational therapists 1
(pt); Speech therapists 1 (pt); Activities
coordinators 1 (ft); Dietitians 1 (pt);
Ophthalmologists 1 (pt); Podiatrists 1 (pt);
Audiologists 1 (pt); Dentists 1 (pt).
Facilities Dining room; Physical therapy
room; Activities room; Crafts room; Laundry
room; Barber/Beauty shop.
Activities Arts & crafts; Cards; Games;
Reading groups; Prayer groups; Movies;
Dances/Social/Cultural gatherings; Foster
grandparents program; Pet therapy program.

Holy Family Health Center
2380 Dempster St, Des Plaines, IL 60016
(708) 296-3335

Admin Sr M Elizabeth Trembczynski. *Dir of
Nursing* Christine Busse. *Medical Dir*
William Bagnuolo MD.
Licensure Skilled care; Intermediate care. *Beds*
SNF 102; ICF 260. *Certified* Medicaid;
Medicare.
Owner Nonprofit corp.
Admissions Requirements Minimum age 18;
Medical examination.
Staff Physicians 1 (pt); RNs 33 (ft), 21 (pt);
LPNs 5 (ft), 3 (pt); Nurses' aides 99 (ft), 18
(pt); Physical therapists 3 (ft); Recreational
therapists 3 (ft), 2 (pt); Activities
coordinators 3 (ft).
Affiliation Roman Catholic.
Facilities Dining room; Physical therapy
room; Activities room; Chapel; Crafts room;
Laundry room; Barber/Beauty shop; Library.
Activities Arts & crafts; Cards; Games;
Reading groups; Prayer groups; Movies;
Shopping trips; Dances/Social/Cultural
gatherings.

Lee Manor
1301 Lee St, Des Plaines, IL 60018
(708) 827-9450
Admin Donald G Plodzien. *Dir of Nursing*
Barbara Rex RN. *Medical Dir* Dr K
Beckman.
Licensure Skilled care. *Beds* SNF 282.
Certified Medicaid; Medicare.
Owner Proprietary corp.
Staff RNs; LPNs; Nurses' aides; Physical
therapists 1 (pt); Recreational therapists 1
(pt); Occupational therapists 1 (pt); Speech
therapists 1 (pt); Activities coordinators 1
(ft); Dietitians 1 (ft); Ophthalmologists 1
(pt); Dentists 1 (pt).

Nazarethville
300 N River Rd, Des Plaines, IL 60016
(708) 297-5900
Admin Sr Ancilla Sojka. *Dir of Nursing*
Marcia O'Connor. *Medical Dir* John
Meyenberg MD.
Licensure Intermediate care; Sheltered care.
Beds ICF 68; Sheltered care 15. *Private Pay
Patients* 94%. *Certified* Medicaid.
Owner Nonprofit corp.
Admissions Requirements Minimum age 60;
Medical examination.
Staff Physicians 2 (pt); RNs 7 (ft), 5 (pt);
LPNs 3 (pt); Nurses' aides 19 (ft), 12 (pt);
Activities coordinators 1 (ft); Dietitians 1
(ft); Ophthalmologists 1 (pt); Podiatrists 1
(pt).
Languages Polish.
Affiliation Roman Catholic.
Facilities Dining room; Physical therapy
room; Activities room; Chapel; Crafts room;
Laundry room; Barber/Beauty shop; Library.
Activities Arts & crafts; Cards; Games; Prayer
groups; Movies; Shopping trips; Dances/
Social/Cultural gatherings.

Oakton Pavilion Inc
1660 Oakton Pl, Des Plaines, IL 60018
(708) 299-5588, 298-6017 FAX
Admin Jay Lewkowitz ACSW. *Dir of Nursing*
Dancy Koruna RN. *Medical Dir* Ruven
Levitan MD.
Licensure Skilled care; Retirement;
Alzheimer's care. *Beds* SNF 294. *Private Pay
Patients* 65%. *Certified* Medicaid; Medicare.
Owner Proprietary corp.
Admissions Requirements Minimum age 18.
Staff Physicians 4 (ft), 35 (pt); RNs 37 (ft), 3
(pt); LPNs 6 (ft); Nurses' aides 145 (ft);
Physical therapists 12 (ft); Occupational
therapists 1 (pt); Speech therapists 1 (pt);
Activities coordinators 1 (ft); Dietitians 1 (ft);
Ophthalmologists 1 (pt); Podiatrists 1 (pt);
Audiologists 1 (pt).
Languages German, Polish.

Facilities Dining room; Physical therapy
room; Activities room; Crafts room;
Laundry room; Barber/Beauty shop; Library;
Patio.
Activities Arts & crafts; Cards; Games;
Reading groups; Prayer groups; Movies;
Shopping trips; Dances/Social/Cultural
gatherings; Intergenerational programs.

Dixon

Dixon Health Care Center
141 N Court St, Dixon, IL 61021
(815) 288-1477
Admin Sandra D Burger.
Medical Dir Dr Howard Edwards Jr.
Licensure Intermediate care. *Beds* ICF 110.
Certified Medicaid.
Owner Proprietary corp.
Admissions Requirements Minimum age 18;
Medical examination; Physician's request.
Staff Physicians 6 (pt); RNs 6 (ft), 3 (pt);
LPNs 2 (ft), 1 (pt); Nurses' aides 14 (ft), 7
(pt); Physical therapists 1 (ft); Reality
therapists 1 (pt); Recreational therapists 1
(pt); Occupational therapists 1 (pt); Speech
therapists 1 (pt); Activities coordinators 1
(ft); Dietitians 1 (ft); Podiatrists 1 (pt);
Dentists 1 (pt).
Facilities Dining room; Physical therapy
room; Activities room; Crafts room; Laundry
room; Barber/Beauty shop; Library.
Activities Arts & crafts; Cards; Games;
Reading groups; Prayer groups; Movies;
Shopping trips; Dances/Social/Cultural
gatherings.

Heritage Square Retirement Home
620 N Ottawa Ave, Dixon, IL 61021
(815) 288-2251
Admin Sylvia E Montavon. *Dir of Nursing*
Trudie Matznick RN. *Medical Dir* Joseph
Welty MD.
Licensure Skilled care; Sheltered care;
Retirement. *Beds* SNF 19; Sheltered care 94.
Private Pay Patients 90%. *Certified*
Medicaid.
Owner Nonprofit organization/foundation.
Admissions Requirements Minimum age 60;
Medical examination; Physician's request.
Facilities Dining room; Physical therapy
room; Activities room; Crafts room; Laundry
room; Barber/Beauty shop.
Activities Arts & crafts; Cards; Games;
Reading groups; Prayer groups; Movies;
Shopping trips; Dances/Social/Cultural
gatherings; Pet therapy; Seasonal events.

Lee County Nursing Home
800 Division St, Dixon, IL 61021
(815) 284-3393
Admin John M Edmunds. *Dir of Nursing* L
Jeanne O'Connor RN. *Medical Dir* Thomas
Welty MD.
Licensure Skilled care; Alzheimer's care. *Beds*
SNF 97.
Owner Publicly owned.
Admissions Requirements Minimum age 18;
Medical examination; Physician's request.
Staff RNs 4 (ft), 2 (pt); LPNs 6 (ft), 3 (pt);
Nurses' aides 33 (ft), 10 (pt); Activities
coordinators 3 (ft), 5 (pt); Dietitians 7 (ft), 7
(pt).
Facilities Dining room; Physical therapy
room; Activities room; Chapel; Crafts room;
Laundry room; Barber/Beauty shop; Library.
Activities Arts & crafts; Cards; Games;
Reading groups; Prayer groups; Movies;
Shopping trips; Dances/Social/Cultural
gatherings.

Pine Acres
922 Washington Ave, Dixon, IL 61021
(815) 288-4422
Admin Jack Richey.
Licensure Intermediate care for mentally
retarded. *Beds* ICF/MR 10.

Village Inn Nursing Home
135 N Court St, Dixon, IL 61021
(815) 284-2253
Admin Pamela K Johnson. *Dir of Nursing*
Sheila McCarty RN.
Licensure Intermediate care for mentally
retarded. *Beds* ICF/MR 134. *Certified*
Medicaid.
Owner Proprietary corp (National Heritage).
Admissions Requirements Minimum age 18;
Medical examination.
Staff Physicians 1 (pt); RNs 1 (ft); LPNs 5
(ft), 2 (pt); Nurses' aides 52 (ft); Physical
therapists 1 (pt); Occupational therapists 1
(pt); Activities coordinators 1 (ft); Dietitians
1 (pt); Ophthalmologists 1 (pt); Podiatrists 1
(pt); Dentists 1 (pt).
Facilities Dining room; Physical therapy
room; Activities room; Laundry room;
Library.
Activities Arts & crafts; Cards; Games;
Reading groups; Prayer groups; Movies;
Shopping trips; Dances/Social/Cultural
gatherings; Sheltered workshop.

Dolton

Countryside Plaza
1635 E 154th St, Dolton, IL 60419
(708) 841-9550
Admin Joann Nickols.
Licensure Skilled care; Intermediate care. *Beds*
SNF 100; ICF 97. *Certified* Medicaid.
Owner Proprietary corp.

Dolton Healthcare Center
14325 S Blackstone, Dolton, IL 60419
(708) 849-5000
Admin Roxane Goad.
Medical Dir Judith Lovato.
Licensure Skilled care; Intermediate care. *Beds*
SNF 25; ICF 42. *Certified* Medicaid.
Owner Proprietary corp.
Admissions Requirements Medical
examination.
Staff Physicians 8 (pt); RNs 3 (ft), 4 (pt);
LPNs 2 (ft), 1 (pt); Nurses' aides 12 (ft), 9
(pt); Physical therapists 1 (ft), 1 (pt); Reality
therapists 1 (ft), 1 (pt); Recreational
therapists 1 (ft), 1 (pt); Occupational
therapists 1 (ft), 1 (pt); Activities
coordinators 1 (ft), 1 (pt); Dietitians 1 (pt);
Ophthalmologists 1 (pt); Dentists 1 (pt).
Facilities Dining room; Physical therapy
room; Activities room; Laundry room;
Barber/Beauty shop.
Activities Arts & crafts; Cards; Games;
Reading groups; Prayer groups; Movies;
Shopping trips; Dances/Social/Cultural
gatherings.

Dongola

Henard-Keller Shelter Care
201 Cross St, Dongola, IL 62926
(618) 827-4402
Admin Deborah L Peeler.
Licensure Sheltered care. *Beds* Sheltered care
26.
Owner Proprietary corp.

Downers Grove

Fairview Baptist Home
7 S 241 Fairview Ave, Downers Grove, IL
60516
(708) 852-4350, 852-0761 FAX
Admin Barbara A Anderson. *Dir of Nursing*
Barbara G Coleman RN. *Medical Dir* Dr
Kristen D Gray.
Licensure Skilled care; Intermediate care;
Sheltered care; Respite care; Retirement.
Beds SNF 40; ICF 66; Sheltered care 107;
Retirement 250. *Private Pay Patients* 100%.
Owner Nonprofit organization/foundation.

Admissions Requirements Minimum age 60;
Medical examination.
Staff Physicians 33 (pt); RNs 10 (ft), 10 (pt);
LPNs 4 (ft), 2 (pt); Physical therapists 1 (ft),
1 (pt); Recreational therapists 2 (ft), 1 (pt);
Occupational therapists 1 (pt); Speech
therapists 1 (pt); Activities coordinators 1
(ft); Dietitians 1 (pt); Podiatrists 1 (pt);
Audiologists 1 (pt); Certified nurses aides 28
(ft), 9 (pt); Chaplains 1 (ft); Dentists 2 (pt);
Beauticians 3 (pt); Barbers 1 (pt); Hospice 3
(pt); Manicurists 1 (pt).
Affiliation Baptist.
Facilities Dining room; Physical therapy
room; Activities room; Chapel; Crafts room;
Laundry room; Barber/Beauty shop; Library.
Activities Arts & crafts; Cards; Games;
Reading groups; Prayer groups; Movies;
Shopping trips; Dances/Social/Cultural
gatherings; Intergenerational programs; Pet
therapy; Greenhouse; Choir; Project PEP
(Program to Extend Productivity);
Volunteerism.

Rest Haven West Skilled Nursing Facility
3450 Saratoga Ave, Downers Grove, IL 60515
(708) 969-2900
Admin Scott A Studebaker. *Dir of Nursing*
Karen Black. *Medical Dir* Dr G DeJong.
Licensure Skilled care; Intermediate care;
Retirement living; Alzheimer's care. *Beds*
Swing beds SNF/ICF 145; Retirement living
96. *Private Pay Patients* 60%. *Certified*
Medicaid; Medicare.
Owner Nonprofit corp.
Admissions Requirements Medical
examination.
Staff RNs; LPNs; Nurses' aides; Recreational
therapists; Occupational therapists; Speech
therapists; Activities coordinators; Dietitians;
Ophthalmologists; Podiatrists; Audiologists;
Dentists; Unit operational managers;
pediatrists.
Affiliation Christian Reformed.
Facilities Dining room; Physical therapy
room; Activities room; Crafts room; Laundry
room; Barber/Beauty shop; Library.
Activities Arts & crafts; Cards; Games;
Reading groups; Prayer groups; Movies;
Shopping trips; Dances/Social/Cultural
gatherings; Intergenerational programs; Pet
therapy.

Du Quoin

Fair Acres Nursing Home Inc
514 E Jackson, Du Quoin, IL 62832
(618) 542-4731
Admin Randee Slover.
Licensure Skilled care; Intermediate care. *Beds*
SNF 29; ICF 45. *Certified* Medicaid;
Medicare.
Owner Proprietary corp.

Fairview Nursing Center
602 E Jackson St, Du Quoin, IL 62832
(618) 542-3441
Admin Carol S Robinson.
Medical Dir Joann Eickelman.
Licensure Intermediate care. *Beds* ICF 77.
Certified Medicaid.
Owner Proprietary corp (Jamestown
Management).
Admissions Requirements Medical
examination; Physician's request.
Staff RNs; LPNs; Nurses' aides; Physical
therapists; Activities coordinators; Dietitians;
Physical therapists.
Facilities Dining room; Physical therapy
room; Activities room; Laundry room;
Barber/Beauty shop.
Activities Arts & crafts; Cards; Games;
Reading groups; Prayer groups; Movies;
Shopping trips; Dances/Social/Cultural
gatherings.

Five Star Industries Inc
701 Terrace Dr, Du Quoin, IL 62832
(618) 542-4580
Admin Kelly Stacey. *Dir of Nursing* Linda
Searby. *Medical Dir* Dr Furry.
Licensure Intermediate care for mentally
retarded; Community residential alternative
living; Supportive living arrangement;
Independent living. *Beds* ICF/MR 15;
Community residential alternative living 2-8;
Supportive living arrangement apts 2;
Independent living apts 20. *Private Pay
Patients* 0%. *Certified* Medicaid.
Owner Nonprofit corp.
Admissions Requirements Minimum age 18;
Medical examination.
Staff Physicians (consultant); RNs
(consultant); Physical therapists (consultant);
Occupational therapists (consultant); Speech
therapists (consultant); Activities
coordinators (consultant); Dietitians
(consultant); Audiologists (consultant).
Facilities Dining room; Laundry room.
Activities Arts & crafts; Cards; Games;
Movies; Shopping trips; Dances/Social/
Cultural gatherings.

Durand

Medina Nursing Center Inc
PO Box 538, 402 S Center St, Durand, IL
61024
(815) 248-2151
Admin Holgeir J Oksnevad. *Dir of Nursing*
Lou Hill. *Medical Dir* Dr John Hulton.
Licensure Skilled care; Retirement;
Alzheimer's care. *Beds* SNF 89; Retirement
22. *Private Pay Patients* 55%. *Certified*
Medicaid; Medicare.
Owner Proprietary corp.
Admissions Requirements Medical
examination; Physician's request.
Staff Physicians 8 (pt); RNs 4 (ft), 3 (pt);
LPNs 3 (ft), 3 (pt); Nurses' aides 20 (ft), 20
(pt); Physical therapists 1 (pt); Speech
therapists 1 (pt); Activities coordinators 1
(ft); Dietitians 1 (pt); Podiatrists 1 (pt).
Facilities Dining room; Activities room;
Laundry room; Barber/Beauty shop.
Activities Arts & crafts; Cards; Games;
Reading groups; Prayer groups; Movies;
Shopping trips; Dances/Social/Cultural
gatherings; Intergenerational programs;
Tours.

Dwight

Fernwood Health Care Center
300 E Mazon Ave, Dwight, IL 60420
(815) 584-1240
Admin Harland L Bicking.
Medical Dir Lynn Terry.
Licensure Skilled care. *Beds* SNF 92. *Certified*
Medicaid; Medicare.
Owner Proprietary corp (Springwood
Associates).
Admissions Requirements Medical
examination.
Staff RNs 2 (ft), 1 (pt); LPNs 6 (ft), 1 (pt);
Nurses' aides 15 (ft), 8 (pt); Physical
therapists 1 (pt); Occupational therapists 1
(pt); Activities coordinators 1 (ft).
Facilities Dining room; Physical therapy
room; Activities room; Chapel; Crafts room;
Laundry room; Barber/Beauty shop.
Activities Arts & crafts; Cards; Games;
Reading groups; Prayer groups; Movies;
Shopping trips; Dances/Social/Cultural
gatherings.

East Moline

East Moline Care Center
4747 11th St, East Moline, IL 61244
(309) 796-0922
Admin Melvin L Zimmerman.

Medical Dir John M Peterson MD.
Licensure Skilled care; Intermediate care; Intermediate care for mentally retarded. *Beds* SNF 24; ICF 89; ICF/MR 40. *Certified* Medicaid.
Owner Proprietary corp.
Admissions Requirements Minimum age 65; Medical examination; Physician's request.
Staff RNs 4 (ft); LPNs 6 (ft); Nurses' aides 35 (ft); Physical therapists 1 (pt); Recreational therapists 1 (pt); Occupational therapists 1 (pt); Speech therapists 1 (pt); Activities coordinators 1 (ft); Dietitians 1 (pt); Dentists 1 (pt).
Facilities Dining room; Physical therapy room; Activities room; Crafts room; Barber/Beauty shop.
Activities Arts & crafts; Cards; Games; Reading groups; Movies; Shopping trips; Dances/Social/Cultural gatherings.

East Moline Garden Plaza
430 30th Ave, East Moline, IL 61244
(309) 755-3466
Admin D A Konecki. *Dir of Nursing* Heidi Klaus. *Medical Dir* Robert Flowers.
Licensure Intermediate care; Alzheimer's care. *Beds* ICF 120. *Private Pay Patients* 15-20%. *Certified* Medicaid.
Owner Proprietary corp (The Plazas).
Admissions Requirements Minimum age 18; Medical examination.
Staff Physicians 1 (pt); RNs 1 (ft); LPNs 8 (ft), 1 (pt); Nurses' aides 36 (ft); Physical therapists 1 (pt); Recreational therapists 1 (pt); Occupational therapists 1 (pt); Activities coordinators 1 (ft); Dietitians 1 (pt); Ophthalmologists 1 (pt); Podiatrists 1 (pt).
Languages Spanish.
Facilities Dining room; Physical therapy room; Activities room; Crafts room; Laundry room; Barber/Beauty shop.
Activities Arts & crafts; Cards; Games; Reading groups; Prayer groups; Movies; Shopping trips; Dances/Social/Cultural gatherings; Intergenerational programs; Pet therapy.

East Peoria

Fondulac Woods Health Care Center
901 Illini Dr, East Peoria, IL 61611
(309) 694-6446
Admin Marsha Reardon. *Dir of Nursing* Diana Alvis. *Medical Dir* Dr Gene Sidler.
Licensure Skilled care; Alzheimer's care. *Beds* SNF 98. *Private Pay Patients* 45%. *Certified* Medicaid; Medicare.
Owner Proprietary corp (Springwood Associates).
Admissions Requirements Minimum age 21; Medical examination.
Staff RNs 5 (ft); LPNs 8 (ft); Physical therapists 2 (ft); Speech therapists 1 (ft); Activities coordinators 3 (ft); Dietitians 1 (ft).
Facilities Dining room; Physical therapy room; Activities room; Crafts room; Laundry room; Barber/Beauty shop; Library; Sun room; Family lounge.
Activities Arts & crafts; Cards; Games; Reading groups; Prayer groups; Movies; Shopping trips; Dances/Social/Cultural gatherings; Intergenerational programs; Pet therapy; Coupon club; Alzheimer's programs; Guest meals & parties.

Good Samaritan Nursing Home
1910 Springfield Rd, East Peoria, IL 61611
(309) 694-1435
Admin David L Ennis.
Medical Dir Linda Krueger.
Licensure Intermediate care. *Beds* ICF 120. *Certified* Medicaid.
Owner Proprietary corp (National Heritage).

Admissions Requirements Minimum age 50; Medical examination; Physician's request.
Staff RNs 1 (ft); LPNs 8 (ft); Nurses' aides 20 (ft), 10 (pt); Physical therapists 2 (ft); Occupational therapists 2 (ft); Activities coordinators 2 (ft); Dietitians 1 (ft); Ophthalmologists 1 (pt).
Facilities Dining room; Physical therapy room; Activities room; Laundry room; Barber/Beauty shop; Library.
Activities Arts & crafts; Cards; Games; Reading groups; Prayer groups; Movies; Shopping trips; Dances/Social/Cultural gatherings.

Riverview Retirement Center
500 Centennial Dr, East Peoria, IL 61611
(309) 694-0022
Admin Arthur Ott.
Licensure Skilled care; Sheltered care. *Beds* SNF 45; Sheltered care 14.

East Saint Louis

Virgil L Calvert Care Center
5100 Summit Ave, East Saint Louis, IL 62206
(314) 231-0222
Admin John B Angelle.
Licensure Intermediate care. *Beds* ICF 150.

Wilford Manor—Center for Independent Living
1500 Wilford, East Saint Louis, IL 62207
(618) 271-3355
Admin Delores S Ray.
Licensure Community living facility. *Beds* Community living facility 12.

Edwardsville

Anna-Henry Nursing Home
637 Hillsboro Ave, Edwardsville, IL 62025
(618) 656-1136
Admin Mary Joann Newell.
Licensure Skilled care; Intermediate care. *Beds* SNF 64; ICF 61. *Certified* Medicaid.
Owner Proprietary corp.

Eden Village Care Center
400 S Station Rd, Edwardsville, IL 62025
(618) 288-5016
Admin Wesley D Barber. *Dir of Nursing* Juline Lambert. *Medical Dir* Max Eakin MD.
Licensure Skilled care; Retirement. *Beds* SNF 120. *Certified* Medicaid; Medicare.
Owner Nonprofit corp.
Admissions Requirements Minimum age 18; Medical examination; Physician's request.
Staff RNs 7 (ft); LPNs 9 (ft), 2 (pt); Nurses' aides 40 (ft), 12 (pt); Physical therapists 1 (ft), 1 (pt); Occupational therapists 3 (pt); Activities coordinators 1 (ft); Dietitians.
Affiliation Church of Christ.
Facilities Dining room; Physical therapy room; Activities room; Crafts room; Laundry room; Barber/Beauty shop; Library.
Activities Arts & crafts; Cards; Games; Reading groups; Prayer groups; Movies.

Edwardsville Care Center
1095 University Dr, Edwardsville, IL 62025
(618) 656-1081
Admin Sandra L Clay.
Medical Dir Robert Ayres.
Licensure Skilled care; Intermediate care. *Beds* SNF 92; ICF 28. *Certified* Medicaid; Medicare.
Owner Proprietary corp.
Admissions Requirements Minimum age 21.
Staff RNs 3 (ft), 2 (pt); LPNs 8 (ft), 2 (pt); Nurses' aides 30 (ft), 3 (pt); Physical therapists 1 (ft); Recreational therapists 1 (ft); Occupational therapists 1 (ft); Speech therapists 1 (pt); Activities coordinators 1 (ft); Dietitians 1 (pt); Podiatrists 1 (pt); Audiologists 1 (pt); Dentists 1 (pt).

Facilities Dining room; Physical therapy room; Activities room; Crafts room; Laundry room; Barber/Beauty shop.
Activities Arts & crafts; Cards; Games; Reading groups; Prayer groups; Movies; Shopping trips; Dances/Social/Cultural gatherings.

Edwardsville Care Center East
Rte 143 at Cheryl-Lynn Estates, Edwardsville, IL 62025
(618) 692-1330
Licensure Skilled care; Intermediate care. *Beds* SNF 92; ICF 28.

Madison County Nursing Home
2121 Troy Rd, Edwardsville, IL 62025
(618) 692-1040
Admin Billy L Rainwater.
Licensure Intermediate care. *Beds* ICF 100. *Certified* Medicaid.
Owner Publicly owned.

Madison County Sheltered Care Home
PO Box 441, 333 S Main, Edwardsville, IL 62025
(618) 692-6003
Admin Donna R Marrone. *Dir of Nursing* Laura Blotevogel LPN. *Medical Dir* Patrick Zimmermann MD, Advisory Physician.
Licensure Sheltered care. *Beds* Sheltered care 65. *Private Pay Patients* 21%. *Certified* Public Aid.
Owner Publicly owned.
Admissions Requirements Minimum age 18; Medical examination; Physician's request.
Staff LPNs 1 (ft); Nurses' aides 9 (ft), 9 (pt); Activities coordinators 1 (ft), 1 (pt); Dietitians.
Facilities Dining room; Library; Greenhouse.
Activities Arts & crafts; Cards; Games; Reading groups; Prayer groups; Movies; Shopping trips; Dances/Social/Cultural gatherings.

Effingham

Country Care Manor Inc
1115 N Wenthe Ave, Effingham, IL 62401
(217) 347-7121
Admin David Wendler. *Dir of Nursing* Alma Byrd RN.
Licensure Skilled care; Alzheimer's care. *Beds* SNF 120. *Certified* Medicaid.
Owner Proprietary corp.
Admissions Requirements Minimum age 18; Medical examination; Physician's request.
Staff RNs 3 (ft), 2 (pt); LPNs 6 (ft), 1 (pt); Nurses' aides 24 (ft), 3 (pt); Speech therapists 1 (pt).
Facilities Dining room; Physical therapy room; Activities room; Laundry room; Barber/Beauty shop.
Activities Arts & crafts; Cards; Games; Reading groups; Prayer groups; Movies; Shopping trips; Dances/Social/Cultural gatherings; Van rides.

Effingham Terrace
1101 S 3rd St, Effingham, IL 62401
(217) 342-2171
Admin Marilyn Meyer.
Licensure Intermediate care for mentally retarded. *Beds* ICF/MR 15.

Effingham Terrace
1101 S 3rd St, Effingham, IL 62401
(217) 342-9313
Admin Marilyn Meyer.
Licensure Intermediate care for mentally retarded. *Beds* ICF/MR 15. *Private Pay Patients* 0%. *Certified* Medicaid.
Owner Nonprofit organization/foundation.
Admissions Requirements Minimum age 18.
Staff Habilitation aides 10 (ft).

Facilities Dining room; Activities room;
Crafts room; Laundry room.
Activities Arts & crafts; Cards; Games;
Reading groups; Prayer groups; Movies;
Shopping trips; Dances/Social/Cultural
gatherings; Pet therapy; Trips.

Lakeland Healthcare Center
800 W Temple St, Effingham, IL 62401
(217) 342-2171
Admin Karen Sue Wendt.
Licensure Skilled care; Intermediate care;
Alzheimer's care. *Beds* SNF 53; ICF 141.
Certified Medicaid; Medicare.
Owner Nonprofit corp (First Humanics).
Admissions Requirements Physician's request.
Facilities Dining room; Physical therapy
room; Activities room; Chapel; Crafts room;
Laundry room; Barber/Beauty shop.
Activities Arts & crafts; Cards; Games;
Reading groups; Prayer groups; Movies;
Shopping trips; Dances/Social/Cultural
gatherings.

Van Dyke Convalescent Center
1610 Lakewood Dr, Effingham, IL 62401
(217) 347-7470
Admin Janice I Webb. *Dir of Nursing* Karen
King RN. *Medical Dir* Dr N Arora.
Licensure Skilled care. *Beds* SNF 84. *Private
Pay Patients* 54%. *Certified* Medicaid;
Medicare.
Owner Proprietary corp (Convalescent
Management Association Inc).
Admissions Requirements Minimum age 55.
Facilities Dining room; Physical therapy
room; Activities room; Laundry room;
Barber/Beauty shop.
Activities Arts & crafts; Cards; Games;
Reading groups; Prayer groups; Movies;
Shopping trips; Dances/Social/Cultural
gatherings; Pet therapy.

Wetherell Place
1026 N Merchant St, Effingham, IL 62401
(217) 342-6621
Admin Marilyn E Meyer.
Licensure Intermediate care for mentally
retarded. *Beds* ICF/MR 15.

El Paso

El Paso Health Care
850 E 2nd, El Paso, IL 61738
(309) 527-2700
Admin Rebecca Hall. *Dir of Nursing* Kathy
Mayotte. *Medical Dir* M D Patel MD.
Licensure Skilled care; Intermediate care. *Beds*
Swing beds SNF/ICF 123. *Private Pay
Patients* 10%. *Certified* Medicaid; VA.
Owner Nonprofit corp (First Humanics Corp).
Admissions Requirements Minimum age 18;
Medical examination.
Staff Physicians 2 (pt); RNs 4 (ft), 1 (pt);
LPNs 6 (ft), 2 (pt); Nurses' aides 15 (ft), 12
(pt); Physical therapists 1 (pt); Reality
therapists 2 (ft); Recreational therapists 3
(ft); Occupational therapists 1 (pt); Speech
therapists 1 (pt); Activities coordinators 1
(ft); Dietitians 1 (ft); Ophthalmologists 1
(pt); Podiatrists 1 (pt); Audiologists 1 (pt);
Dentists 1 (pt).
Languages Spanish.
Facilities Dining room; Physical therapy
room; Activities room; Crafts room; Laundry
room; Barber/Beauty shop; Library.
Activities Arts & crafts; Cards; Games;
Reading groups; Prayer groups; Movies;
Shopping trips; Dances/Social/Cultural
gatherings; Intergenerational programs; Pet
therapy; MI, MR, DD programs.

Heritage Manor Nursing & Convalescent Home
555 E Clay St, El Paso, IL 61738
(309) 527-6240
Admin Mary McDaniel.

Licensure Skilled care. *Beds* SNF 49. *Certified*
Medicaid; Medicare.
Owner Proprietary corp.

Eldorado

Eldorado Nursing Home Inc
3rd & Railroad Sts, Eldorado, IL 62930
(618) 273-3318
Admin George W Baker.
Licensure Intermediate care. *Beds* ICF 74.
Certified Medicaid.
Owner Proprietary corp.

Fountainview Inc
Rte 45, S Jefferson, Eldorado, IL 62930
(618) 273-3353
Admin Billy L Jones. *Dir of Nursing* Sandra
Dixon.
Licensure Intermediate care. *Beds* ICF 135.
Certified Medicaid.
Owner Proprietary corp.
Admissions Requirements Minimum age 18;
Medical examination.
Staff RNs 1 (ft); LPNs 10 (ft), 2 (pt); Nurses'
aides; Physical therapists 1 (pt); Reality
therapists 1 (ft); Activities coordinators 1
(ft), 2 (pt); Dietitians 1 (pt).
Facilities Dining room; Physical therapy
room; Activities room; Crafts room; Laundry
room; Barber/Beauty shop.
Activities Arts & crafts; Cards; Games;
Reading groups; Prayer groups; Movies;
Shopping trips; Dances/Social/Cultural
gatherings.

Life Care Center of Eldorado
1700 Jaspes St, Eldorado, IL 62930
(618) 273-2161
Admin Keith Hufsey. *Dir of Nursing* Carmen
Cox.
Licensure Intermediate care; Alzheimer's care.
Beds ICF 79. *Private Pay Patients* 50-60%.
Certified Medicaid.
Owner Proprietary corp (Community Lifecare
Enterprises).
Admissions Requirements Medical
examination.
Staff Physicians 1 (ft); RNs 1 (ft); LPNs 7 (ft);
Nurses' aides 27 (ft); Physical therapists 1
(ft), 5 (pt); Activities coordinators 3 (ft);
Dietitians 2 (ft), 7 (pt).
Facilities Dining room; Physical therapy
room; Activities room; Chapel; Laundry
room; Barber/Beauty shop.
Activities Arts & crafts; Cards; Games;
Reading groups; Prayer groups; Movies;
Shopping trips; Dances/Social/Cultural
gatherings; Intergenerational programs; Pet
therapy.

Elgin

Americana Healthcare Center of Elgin
180 S State St, Elgin, IL 60123
(708) 742-3310
Admin Mary J Schalow.
Medical Dir Vikram Shah MD.
Licensure Skilled care; Intermediate care. *Beds*
SNF 43; ICF 30. *Certified* Medicare.
Owner Proprietary corp (Manor Care).
Admissions Requirements Minimum age 18;
Medical examination; Physician's request.
Staff Physicians 3 (pt); RNs 11 (ft); LPNs 2
(ft); Nurses' aides 20 (ft), 3 (pt); Physical
therapists 1 (ft); Occupational therapists 1
(pt); Speech therapists 1 (pt); Activities
coordinators 1 (ft); Dietitians 1 (ft);
Ophthalmologists 1 (pt); Podiatrists 1 (pt);
Dentists 1 (pt).
Facilities Dining room; Physical therapy
room; Activities room; Crafts room; Laundry
room; Barber/Beauty shop; Living rooms.
Activities Arts & crafts; Cards; Games;
Reading groups; Prayer groups; Movies;
Shopping trips; Dances/Social/Cultural
gatherings; Country store.

Apostolic Christian Resthaven
2750 W Highland Ave, Elgin, IL 60123
(708) 741-4543
Admin Rick Schmidgall. *Dir of Nursing* Jan
Mogler. *Medical Dir* Walter Gasser MD.
Licensure Skilled care; Retirement. *Beds* SNF
50. *Private Pay Patients* 85%. *Certified*
Medicaid.
Owner Nonprofit corp.
Admissions Requirements Minimum age 18;
Medical examination.
Staff RNs 6 (ft), 3 (pt); LPNs 1 (ft); Nurses'
aides 18 (ft), 8 (pt); Activities coordinators 1
(ft).
Languages Spanish.
Affiliation Apostolic Christian.
Facilities Dining room; Physical therapy
room; Activities room; Crafts room; Laundry
room; Barber/Beauty shop.
Activities Arts & crafts; Games; Reading
groups; Prayer groups; Movies; Shopping
trips; Intergenerational programs; Pet
therapy.

Countryside Manor
971 Bode Rd, Elgin, IL 60120
(708) 695-9600
Admin William Strackany. *Dir of Nursing*
Tina Giacchetti RN.
Licensure Sheltered care. *Beds* Sheltered care
39. *Private Pay Patients* 100%.
Owner Privately owned.
Admissions Requirements Minimum age 55;
Medical examination.
Staff RNs 1 (ft); Nurses' aides 2 (ft), 15 (pt);
Physical therapists (consultant); Reality
therapists 1 (ft); Recreational therapists 1
(ft); Activities coordinators 1 (ft); Dietitians
(consultant).
Facilities Dining room; Activities room;
Crafts room; Laundry room; Barber/Beauty
shop; Library.
Activities Arts & crafts; Cards; Games;
Reading groups; Prayer groups; Movies;
Shopping trips; Dances/Social/Cultural
gatherings; Intergenerational programs; Pet
therapy.

Elgin Community Living Facility
1640 Mark Ave, Elgin, IL 60123
(708) 741-9175
Admin Catherine C Krikau.
Licensure Intermediate care for mentally
retarded. *Beds* ICF/MR 20.
Owner Nonprofit corp.

Heritage Manor
Raymond & Watch Sts, Elgin, IL 60120
(708) 697-6636
Admin Patricia F Patrick. *Dir of Nursing*
Cindy Krincke RN. *Medical Dir* Dr D Shah.
Licensure Skilled care. *Beds* SNF 90. *Private
Pay Patients* 50%. *Certified* Medicaid;
Medicare.
Owner Proprietary corp (Heritage Enterprises).
Admissions Requirements Minimum age 21;
Medical examination.
Staff Physical therapists 1 (pt); Recreational
therapists 1 (pt); Occupational therapists 1
(pt); Speech therapists 1 (pt); Activities
coordinators 1 (ft), 1 (pt); Dietitians 1 (pt);
Ophthalmologists 1 (pt); Podiatrists 1 (pt);
Audiologists 1 (pt).
Languages Spanish.
Facilities Dining room; Physical therapy
room; Activities room; Chapel; Crafts room;
Barber/Beauty shop; Library; Personal
laundry service.
Activities Arts & crafts; Cards; Games;
Reading groups; Prayer groups; Movies;
Dances/Social/Cultural gatherings;
Intergenerational programs; Pet therapy.

Imperial Nursing Center of Elgin
50 N Jane Dr, Elgin, IL 60120
(708) 697-3750
Admin Robert Molitor.

Licensure Skilled care. *Beds* SNF 203.
Certified Medicaid; Medicare.
Owner Proprietary corp.

Oak Crest Residence
204 S State St, Elgin, IL 60123
(708) 742-2255
Admin Susan Cincinelli.
Licensure Sheltered care; Retirement;
Alzheimer's care. *Beds* Sheltered care 39.
Private Pay Patients 100%.
Owner Nonprofit organization/foundation.
Admissions Requirements Minimum age 60;
Medical examination.
Staff Nurses' aides 2 (ft), 6 (pt); Activities
coordinators 1 (ft).
Facilities Dining room; Barber/Beauty shop.
Activities Arts & crafts; Cards; Games;
Reading groups; Prayer groups; Movies;
Shopping trips; Dances/Social/Cultural
gatherings; Pet therapy.

Elizabeth

Elizabeth Nursing Home Inc
540 Pleasant St, Elizabeth, IL 61028
(815) 858-2275
Admin Nelson E Marks. *Dir of Nursing* Helen
Reid.
Licensure Intermediate care. *Beds* ICF 49.
Private Pay Patients 86%. *Certified*
Medicaid.
Owner Proprietary corp.
Admissions Requirements Minimum age 65;
Medical examination.
Staff RNs; LPNs; Nurses' aides; Physical
therapists; Reality therapists; Recreational
therapists; Occupational therapists; Activities
coordinators; Dietitians.
Facilities Dining room; Physical therapy
room; Activities room; Chapel; Crafts room;
Laundry room; Barber/Beauty shop; Private
and semi-private rooms.
Activities Arts & crafts; Cards; Games;
Reading groups; Prayer groups; Movies;
Shopping trips; Dances/Social/Cultural
gatherings; Intergenerational programs; Pet
therapy; Picnics; Nursing home auxiliary.

Elk Grove Village

**Americana Healthcare Center of Elk Grove
Village**
970 W Nerge Rd, Elk Grove Village, IL 60007
Licensure Skilled care; Intermediate care. *Beds*
SNF 60; ICF 60.
Owner Proprietary corp (Manor Care).
Staff Physicians; RNs; LPNs; Nurses' aides;
Physical therapists.

Elmhurst

Elmhurst Extended Care Center Inc
200 E Lake St, Elmhurst, IL 60126
(708) 834-4337
Admin John Massard.
Medical Dir Paul J Concepcion MD.
Licensure Skilled care; Alzheimer's care. *Beds*
SNF 112. *Certified* Medicare.
Owner Proprietary corp.
Admissions Requirements Minimum age 18.
Staff Physicians 4 (pt); RNs 9 (ft), 4 (pt);
LPNs 5 (ft), 4 (pt); Nurses' aides 28 (ft), 29
(pt); Physical therapists 1 (pt); Recreational
therapists 1 (ft); Occupational therapists 1
(pt); Speech therapists 1 (pt); Activities
coordinators 2 (pt); Dietitians 1 (pt);
Ophthalmologists 1 (pt); Podiatrists 1 (pt);
Dentists 1 (pt).
Facilities Dining room; Physical therapy
room; Activities room; Chapel; Crafts room;
Laundry room; Barber/Beauty shop; Library.
Activities Arts & crafts; Cards; Games;
Reading groups; Prayer groups; Movies;
Shopping trips; Dances/Social/Cultural
gatherings; Resident council.

York Convalescent Center
127 W Diversey, Elmhurst, IL 60126
(708) 530-5225
Admin Shirley Holt. *Dir of Nursing* Ginger
Kloskowski. *Medical Dir* Dr Norton
Fishman.
Licensure Skilled care; Intermediate care. *Beds*
SNF 125; ICF 63. *Certified* Medicaid;
Medicare.
Owner Privately owned.
Admissions Requirements Minimum age 25.
Staff RNs; LPNs; Nurses' aides; Physical
therapists 1 (pt); Reality therapists 1 (ft);
Recreational therapists 1 (ft); Activities
coordinators 1 (ft); Dietitians 1 (ft);
Ophthalmologists 1 (pt); Podiatrists 1 (pt);
Dentists 1 (pt).
Facilities Dining room; Physical therapy
room; Activities room; Laundry room;
Barber/Beauty shop; Library.
Activities Arts & crafts; Cards; Games;
Reading groups; Prayer groups; Movies;
Shopping trips.

Elmwood Park

Royal Elm Inc
7733 W Grand Ave, Elmwood Park, IL 60636
(708) 452-9200
Admin Barbara J Minardi.
Licensure Skilled care; Intermediate care. *Beds*
SNF 245. *Certified* Medicaid; Medicare.
Owner Proprietary corp.
Admissions Requirements Minimum age 65;
Medical examination.
Staff Physicians; LPNs; Dietitians.
Facilities Dining room; Physical therapy
room; Activities room; Crafts room; Laundry
room; Barber/Beauty shop; Library.
Activities Arts & crafts; Cards; Games;
Reading groups; Prayer groups; Movies;
Shopping trips; Dances/Social/Cultural
gatherings; Intergenerational programs; Pet
therapy.

Energy

Mattingly Health Care Center
207 E College St, Energy, IL 62933
(618) 942-7014
Admin Brenda J Loyd. *Dir of Nursing* Carol
Johns RN. *Medical Dir* Robert D Kane MD.
Licensure Intermediate care; Intermediate care
for mentally retarded. *Beds* ICF 86; ICF/MR
73. *Private Pay Patients* 11%. *Certified*
Medicaid.
Owner Proprietary corp.
Admissions Requirements Minimum age 18;
Medical examination; Physician's request.
Staff RNs 1 (ft); LPNs 10 (ft), 2 (pt); Nurses'
aides 46 (ft), 6 (pt); Physical therapists
(consultant); Occupational therapists
(consultant); Speech therapists (consultant);
Activities coordinators 3 (ft); Dietitians
(consultants).
Facilities Dining room; Physical therapy
room; Laundry room; Barber/Beauty shop;
Classroom.
Activities Arts & crafts; Cards; Games;
Reading groups; Prayer groups; Movies;
Shopping trips; Dances/Social/Cultural
gatherings.

Enfield

Life Care of Enfield
N Wilson St, Enfield, IL 62835
(618) 963-2370
Admin Obe Bond. *Dir of Nursing* Karen
Tullis. *Medical Dir* Dr Murragappan.
Licensure Intermediate care. *Beds* ICF 49.
Certified Medicaid.
Owner Proprietary corp (Life Care Enterprises
Inc).

Staff RNs 1 (ft); LPNs 3 (ft); Nurses' aides 20
(ft); Activities coordinators 1 (ft); Dietitians
1 (ft).
Facilities Dining room; Physical therapy
room; Activities room; Crafts room; Laundry
room; Barber/Beauty shop.
Activities Arts & crafts; Games; Reading
groups; Prayer groups; Movies; Shopping
trips; Dances/Social/Cultural gatherings;
Intergenerational programs; Pet therapy.

Eureka

Eureka Apostolic Christian Home
610 W Cruger Ave, Eureka, IL 61530
(309) 467-2311
Admin Joel E Banwart. *Dir of Nursing* Jane
Stoller RN. *Medical Dir* Gary Knepp DO.
Licensure Skilled care; Intermediate care;
Sheltered care; Retirement; Alzheimer's care.
Beds SNF 46; ICF 30; Sheltered care 24;
Retirement 97. *Private Pay Patients* 75%.
Certified Medicaid; Medicare.
Admissions Requirements Minimum age 65;
Medical examination; Physician's request.
Staff RNs 4 (ft), 5 (pt); LPNs 7 (ft), 5 (pt);
Nurses' aides 21 (ft), 37 (pt); Physical
therapists 1 (ft), 1 (pt); Recreational
therapists 1 (ft); Activities coordinators 1
(ft), 1 (pt).
Affiliation Apostolic Christian.
Facilities Dining room; Physical therapy
room; Activities room; Crafts room; Laundry
room; Barber/Beauty shop; Library.
Activities Arts & crafts; Cards; Games;
Reading groups; Prayer groups; Movies;
Shopping trips; Pet therapy.

Maple Lawn Health Center
700 N Main, Eureka, IL 61530
(309) 467-2337
Admin Mary J Dyck MSN RN C; Robert O
Bertsche CEO/Pres. *Dir of Nursing* Rachel B
Tuhy RN BSN. *Medical Dir* Ronald L
Meyer MD.
Licensure Skilled care; Sheltered care;
Retirement. *Beds* SNF 90; Sheltered care 29.
Certified Medicaid; Medicare.
Owner Nonprofit corp.
Admissions Requirements Minimum age 60;
Medical examination.
Affiliation Mennonite.
Facilities Dining room; Physical therapy
room; Activities room; Chapel; Crafts room;
Laundry room; Barber/Beauty shop; Library;
Meeting rooms.
Activities Arts & crafts; Cards; Games;
Reading groups; Prayer groups; Movies;
Shopping trips; Dances/Social/Cultural
gatherings; Intergenerational programs; Pet
therapy.

Evanston

Albany House
901 Maple Ave, Evanston, IL 60202
(708) 475-4000
Admin Susan Koplin.
Licensure Intermediate care. *Beds* ICF 437.
Certified Medicaid.
Owner Proprietary corp.
Activities Arts & crafts; Cards; Games;
Reading groups; Prayer groups; Movies;
Shopping trips; Dances/Social/Cultural
gatherings.

Dobson Plaza Inc
120 Dodge, Evanston, IL 60202
(312) 869-7744, 869-2931 FAX
Admin Charlotte Kohn. *Dir of Nursing* Edith
Pangandian RN. *Medical Dir* Dr Michael T
Grendon.
Licensure Skilled care; Intermediate care;
Retirement; Alzheimer's care. *Beds* Swing
beds SNF/ICF 93; Retirement 110. *Private
Pay Patients* 80%. *Certified* Medicaid;
Medicare.

Owner Proprietary corp.
Admissions Requirements Medical examination; Geriatric.
Staff Physicians 10 (pt); RNs 10 (ft), 8 (pt); LPNs 3 (ft), 2 (pt); Nurses' aides 46 (ft), 5 (pt); Activities coordinators 2 (ft).
Languages Yiddish; Russian; French; Spanish; Hungarian; Haitian; Hebrew.
Facilities Dining room; Physical therapy room; Activities room; Crafts room; Laundry room; Barber/Beauty shop; Library; Kosher kitchen; Sundeck & patio; Private dining room.
Activities Arts & crafts; Cards; Games; Reading groups; Prayer groups; Movies; Shopping trips; Dances/Social/Cultural gatherings; Intergenerational programs.

Georgian Home
422 Davis St, Evanston, IL 60201
(708) 475-4100
Admin Timothy F Wenberg.
Licensure Skilled care; Sheltered care. *Beds* SNF 22; Sheltered care 223.
Owner Nonprofit corp.

Homecrest Foundation
1430 Chicago Ave, Evanston, IL 60201
(708) 869-2162
Admin Evelyn Wray.
Licensure Sheltered care. *Beds* Sheltered care 37.

James C King Home
1555 Oak Ave, Evanston, IL 60201
(708) 864-5460
Admin David Benni. *Dir of Nursing* Mary Helen O'Conner. *Medical Dir* Monte Levinson.
Licensure Intermediate care; Retirement home. *Beds* ICF 20; Retirement home 90. *Private Pay Patients* 100%.
Owner Nonprofit corp.
Admissions Requirements Minimum age 60; Males only.
Staff Physicians 1 (pt); RNs 5 (ft), 2 (pt); LPNs 3 (ft), 2 (pt); Nurses' aides 6 (ft), 2 (pt); Physical therapists 1 (pt); Recreational therapists 1 (pt); Occupational therapists 1 (pt); Activities coordinators 1 (ft); Dietitians 1 (pt); Ophthalmologists 1 (pt); Podiatrists 1 (pt).
Facilities Dining room; Physical therapy room; Activities room; Crafts room; Barber/Beauty shop; Library.
Activities Arts & crafts; Games; Movies; Intergenerational programs.

Lake Crest Villa
2601 Central St, Evanston, IL 60201
(708) 328-8700
Admin Blanche H Dunbar.
Licensure Sheltered care. *Beds* Sheltered Care 25.
Owner Nonprofit corp.

Mather Home
1615 Hinman Ave, Evanston, IL 60201
(708) 328-3042
Admin Edward F Otto.
Licensure Skilled care; Sheltered care. *Beds* SNF 32; Sheltered care 166.

Oakwood Terrace, Inc
1300 Oak Ave, Evanston, IL 60201
(708) 869-1300, 869-1378 FAX
Admin Ross S Brown. *Dir of Nursing* Linda Richards RN. *Medical Dir* Peter Jaggard MD.
Licensure Skilled care; Intermediate care. *Beds* SNF 4; ICF 53. *Private Pay Patients* 100%.
Owner Proprietary corp.
Staff Physicians 2 (ft) (consultant); RNs 2 (ft), 8 (pt); LPNs 1 (ft); Nurses' aides 23 (ft), 8 (pt); Physical therapists 1 (pt) (consultant); Recreational therapists 1 (ft); Occupational therapists 1 (pt) (consultant); Speech therapists 1 (pt) (consultant); Activities

coordinators 1 (ft); Dietitians 1 (pt) (consultant); Podiatrists 1 (pt) (consultant); Audiologists 1 (pt) (consultant).
Facilities Dining room; Physical therapy room; Activities room; Crafts room; Laundry room; Barber/Beauty shop; Library.
Activities Arts & crafts; Games; Reading groups; Prayer groups; Movies; Shopping trips; Dances/Social/Cultural gatherings; Intergenerational programs; Pet therapy.

Presbyterian Home
3200 Grant St, Evanston, IL 60201
(708) 492-2900
Admin Peter S Mulvey Pres/CEO. *Dir of Nursing* Becky DeLarm. *Medical Dir* Dr Monte Levinson.
Licensure Skilled care; Intermediate care; Sheltered care; Retirement; Alzheimer's care. *Beds* SNF 111; ICF 81; Sheltered care 51; Retirement 350. *Certified* Medicare.
Owner Nonprofit corp.
Admissions Requirements Minimum age 65; Medical examination; Physician's request.
Staff Physicians 3 (pt); RNs 26 (ft), 13 (pt); LPNs 7 (ft), 4 (pt); Nurses' aides 67 (ft), 3 (pt); Physical therapists 1 (ft), 1 (pt); Recreational therapists 4 (ft), 2 (pt); Occupational therapists 1 (ft); Speech therapists 1 (pt); Activities coordinators 1 (ft); Dietitians 2 (ft); Ophthalmologists 1 (pt); Podiatrists 1 (pt); Dentists 1 (pt).
Languages Spanish.
Affiliation Presbyterian.
Facilities Dining room; Physical therapy room; Activities room; Chapel; Crafts room; Laundry room; Barber/Beauty shop; Library.
Activities Arts & crafts; Cards; Games; Reading groups; Prayer groups; Movies; Shopping trips; Dances/Social/Cultural gatherings; Intergenerational programs; Pet therapy.

Raintree Health Care Center
1406 Chicago Ave, Evanston, IL 60202
(708) 328-6503
Admin Burton W Behr.
Licensure Intermediate care. *Beds* ICF 145. *Certified* Medicaid.
Owner Proprietary corp.

Ridgeview Pavilion
820 Foster St, Evanston, IL 60201
(708) 869-0142
Admin Bryan G Barrish.
Licensure Skilled care. *Beds* 300. *Certified* Medicaid.
Owner Proprietary corp.

St Francis Extended Care Center
500 Asbury, Evanston, IL 60202
(708) 492-3320
Admin Mary H Brow. *Dir of Nursing* Margaret Healy RN. *Medical Dir* Julio C Mora MD.
Licensure Skilled care; Intermediate care. *Beds* SNF 78; ICF 46. *Private Pay Patients* 50%. *Certified* Medicaid; Medicare.
Owner Nonprofit corp.
Admissions Requirements Minimum age 18; Medical examination.
Staff Physicians (consultant); RNs 12 (ft), 2 (pt); LPNs 3 (ft), 1 (pt); Nurses' aides 41 (ft); Physical therapists 2 (ft); Reality therapists 1 (ft); Recreational therapists 2 (ft), 1 (pt); Occupational therapists (consultant); Speech therapists (consultant); Activities coordinators 1 (ft); Dietitians 1 (ft); Ophthalmologists (consultant); Podiatrists (consultant); Audiologists (consultant).
Languages Spanish.
Affiliation Roman Catholic.
Facilities Dining room; Physical therapy room; Activities room; Chapel; Crafts room; Barber/Beauty shop; Library.

Activities Arts & crafts; Cards; Games; Reading groups; Prayer groups; Movies; Dances/Social/Cultural gatherings; Intergenerational programs; Ceramics; Gardening.

Saratoga of Evanston
814-820 Foster St, Evanston, IL 60201
(708) 869-0142
Admin Mary L Grondin. *Dir of Nursing* Sally A Woods. *Medical Dir* Salomon Dayan.
Licensure Skilled care; Intermediate care. *Beds* SNF 130; ICF 170. *Certified* Medicaid.
Owner Proprietary corp.
Admissions Requirements Minimum age 22; Medical examination; Physician's request.
Facilities Dining room; Physical therapy room; Crafts room; Laundry room; Barber/Beauty shop.
Activities Arts & crafts; Cards; Games; Reading groups; Prayer groups; Movies; Shopping trips; Dances/Social/Cultural gatherings; Intergenerational programs; Pet therapy.

Shore Homes East
503 Michigan Ave, Evanston, IL 60202
(708) 328-3755
Admin Kathleen Jesko.
Licensure Intermediate care for mentally retarded. *Beds* ICF/MR 12.

Swedish Retirement Association
2320 Pioneer Pl, Evanston, IL 60201
(708) 328-8700
Admin Clare N Boehm.
Licensure Intermediate care; Sheltered care. *Beds* ICF 50; Sheltered care 99.
Owner Nonprofit corp.
Admissions Requirements Minimum age 60; Medical examination.
Staff Physicians; RNs; LPNs; Nurses' aides; Physical therapists; Recreational therapists; Occupational therapists; Activities coordinators; Dietitians; Ophthalmologists; Podiatrists; Dentists.
Facilities Dining room; Physical therapy room; Activities room; Chapel; Crafts room; Laundry room; Barber/Beauty shop; Library.
Activities Arts & crafts; Cards; Games; Reading groups; Prayer groups; Movies; Shopping trips.

Evansville

Ellner Terrace
Market & Columbia Sts, Evansville, IL 62242
(618) 853-4451
Admin Joan F Lagage.
Licensure Intermediate care for mentally retarded. *Beds* ICF/MR 15.

Evergreen Park

Mercy Hospital
10240 S Saint Louis Ave, Evergreen Park, IL 60642
(319) 337-0500
Admin Sr Mary Venarda Lance.
Licensure Skilled care. *Beds* SNF 12.

Park Lane Nursing Home
9125 S Pulaski, Evergreen Park, IL 60642
(708) 425-3400
Admin Mark Steinberg. *Dir of Nursing* Paula Malpeli RN. *Medical Dir* Thomas Klein MD.
Licensure Skilled care. *Beds* SNF 249. *Private Pay Patients* 25%. *Certified* Medicaid.
Owner Proprietary corp.
Admissions Requirements Minimum age 45.
Staff RNs 3 (ft); LPNs 17 (ft); Nurses' aides 80 (ft); Recreational therapists 6 (ft); Activities coordinators 1 (ft).

Facilities Dining room; Physical therapy
room; Activities room; Barber/Beauty shop.
Activities Arts & crafts; Cards; Games;
Reading groups; Prayer groups; Movies;
Shopping trips; Dances/Social/Cultural
gatherings; Intergenerational programs.

Peace Memorial Home
10124 S Kedzie Ave, Evergreen Park, IL
60642
(708) 636-9200
Admin Rev Harold M Schoup. *Dir of Nursing*
Nancy Adas RN. *Medical Dir* John O'Brien
MD.
Licensure Skilled care; Retirement. *Beds* SNF
242. *Private Pay Patients* 80%. *Certified*
Medicaid.
Owner Nonprofit organization/foundation.
Admissions Requirements Minimum age 18;
Medical examination; Physician's request.
Staff Physicians 1 (pt); RNs 15 (ft); LPNs 18
(ft); Nurses' aides 107 (ft); Physical
therapists 1 (pt); Reality therapists 1 (pt);
Recreational therapists 1 (pt); Occupational
therapists 1 (pt); Speech therapists 1 (pt);
Activities coordinators 1 (pt); Dietitians 1
(pt); Podiatrists 1 (pt); Dentists 1 (pt).
Affiliation United Church of Christ.
Facilities Dining room; Physical therapy
room; Activities room; Chapel; Barber/
Beauty shop.
Activities Arts & crafts; Cards; Games;
Reading groups; Prayer groups; Movies;
Dances/Social/Cultural gatherings.

Fairbury

Fairview Haven Inc
605-609 N 4th St, Fairbury, IL 61739
(815) 692-2572
Admin Wayne Drayer. *Dir of Nursing* Marilyn
Dennis. *Medical Dir* Dr Kothari; Dr
Oreshkov.
Licensure Skilled care; Retirement. *Beds* SNF
57. *Certified* Medicaid.
Owner Nonprofit corp.
Admissions Requirements Minimum age 60;
Medical examination.
Staff RNs 1 (pt); LPNs 4 (ft), 2 (pt); Nurses'
aides 16 (ft), 8 (pt); Activities coordinators 1
(ft), 1 (pt).
Affiliation Apostolic Christian.
Facilities Dining room; Activities room;
Chapel; Crafts room; Laundry room; Barber/
Beauty shop.
Activities Arts & crafts; Games; Reading
groups; Movies; Shopping trips; Dances/
Social/Cultural gatherings; Bible study.

Helen Lewis Smith Pavilion
519 S Fifth St, Fairbury, IL 61739
(815) 692-2346
Admin Dr John Tummons. *Dir of Nursing*
Sandra Schlager. *Medical Dir* Vesselin
Oreshkov MD.
Licensure Intermediate care; Alzheimer's care.
Beds ICF 49. *Certified* Medicaid; Medicare.
Owner Nonprofit organization/foundation.
Admissions Requirements Minimum age 21;
Medical examination.
Staff Physicians 7 (ft), 1 (pt); RNs 1 (ft), 2
(pt); LPNs 5 (ft), 4 (pt); Nurses' aides 17
(ft), 3 (pt); Physical therapists 1 (ft); Speech
therapists 1 (pt); Activities coordinators 2
(ft); Dietitians 1 (ft), 1 (pt).
Facilities Dining room; Physical therapy
room; Activities room; Chapel; Barber/
Beauty shop.
Activities Arts & crafts; Cards; Games;
Reading groups; Prayer groups; Movies;
Dances/Social/Cultural gatherings.

Fairfield

Dyball Sunshine Home
RR 3 Enterprise Rd, Fairfield, IL 62837
(618) 842-4833

Admin James F Bowers.
Licensure Intermediate care for mentally
retarded. *Beds* ICF/MR 15.

Way Fair Restorium
11th & Harding Sts, Fairfield, IL 62837
(618) 842-2723
Admin Chalmers F Kerchner.
Licensure Skilled care. *Beds* SNF 104.
Certified Medicaid; Medicare.
Owner Nonprofit corp.

Farmer City

Jackson Heights Nursing Home
10 Brookview Dr, Farmer City, IL 61842
(309) 928-2118
Admin Mary K Hirsbrunner. *Dir of Nursing*
Kayla Porter. *Medical Dir* D J Lash MD.
Licensure Intermediate care. *Beds* ICF 51.
Certified Medicaid.
Owner Nonprofit organization/foundation.
Admissions Requirements Minimum age 60.
Staff Physicians 6 (pt); RNs 1 (ft), 6 (pt);
LPNs 1 (ft), 1 (pt); Nurses' aides 14 (ft), 10
(pt); Physical therapists; Reality therapists;
Activities coordinators 1 (ft); Dietitians;
Ophthalmologists.
Facilities Dining room; Activities room;
Chapel; Crafts room; Laundry room; Barber/
Beauty shop.
Activities Arts & crafts; Cards; Games;
Reading groups; Prayer groups; Movies;
Shopping trips; Dances/Social/Cultural
gatherings.

Farmington

Farmington Nursing Home
Hwy 78 S, Farmington, IL 61531
(309) 245-2408
Admin Mary L Record.
Medical Dir Mary Lou Record.
Licensure Skilled care. *Beds* SNF 92. *Certified*
Medicaid; Medicare.
Owner Proprietary corp (American Health
Care Inc).
Admissions Requirements Medical
examination.
Staff Physicians 8 (pt); RNs 3 (ft), 3 (pt);
LPNs 5 (ft), 5 (pt); Nurses' aides 20 (ft), 15
(pt); Physical therapists 2 (pt); Reality
therapists 1 (pt); Recreational therapists 1
(pt); Occupational therapists 1 (pt); Speech
therapists 1 (pt); Activities coordinators 2
(ft); Dietitians 1 (ft).
Facilities Dining room; Physical therapy
room; Activities room; Crafts room; Laundry
room; Barber/Beauty shop; Courtyard; 3
Lounges.
Activities Arts & crafts; Cards; Games;
Reading groups; Prayer groups; Movies;
Shopping trips; Dances/Social/Cultural
gatherings.

Flanagan

Beulah Land Christian Home
Rte 116, Flanagan, IL 61740
(815) 796-2267
Admin Thomas A Novy. *Dir of Nursing*
Margaret Jackson.
Licensure Skilled care; Intermediate care;
Independent living. *Beds* SNF 15; ICF 28;
Shelter care 32. *Certified* Medicaid.
Owner Nonprofit corp (Christian Homes).
Admissions Requirements Minimum age 18;
Medical examination.
Affiliation Church of Christ.
Facilities Dining room; Physical therapy
room; Activities room; Chapel; Crafts room;
Laundry room; Barber/Beauty shop; Library.
Activities Arts & crafts; Cards; Games;
Reading groups; Prayer groups; Movies;
Shopping trips.

Good Samaritan Home of Flanagan
E Lincoln St, Flanagan, IL 61740
(815) 796-2288
Admin Mark Hovren. *Dir of Nursing* Carolyn
Ringenberg. *Medical Dir* Dr John Purnell.
Licensure Skilled care; Retirement. *Beds* SNF
60. *Certified* Medicaid.
Owner Nonprofit corp.
Admissions Requirements Minimum age 60;
Medical examination.
Staff RNs 2 (ft), 6 (pt); LPNs 2 (ft), 3 (pt);
Nurses' aides 14 (ft), 35 (pt); Recreational
therapists 2 (pt); Activities coordinators 1
(ft).
Affiliation Lutheran.
Facilities Dining room; Physical therapy
room; Activities room; Chapel; Laundry
room; Barber/Beauty shop; Library.
Activities Arts & crafts; Cards; Games; Prayer
groups; Shopping trips; Dances/Social/
Cultural gatherings.

Flora

Flora Care Center
Frontage Rd W, Flora, IL 62839
(618) 662-8381
Admin Norma J Venters.
Medical Dir Eugene Foss MD.
Licensure Skilled care; Intermediate care. *Beds*
SNF 66; ICF 33. *Certified* Medicaid.
Owner Proprietary corp.
Staff RNs 3 (ft), 5 (pt); LPNs 2 (ft), 3 (pt);
Nurses' aides 26 (ft), 4 (pt); Activities
coordinators 1 (ft), 1 (pt).
Facilities Dining room; Physical therapy
room; Activities room; Crafts room; Laundry
room; Barber/Beauty shop; Library.
Activities Arts & crafts; Cards; Games;
Reading groups; Prayer groups; Movies;
Shopping trips.

Flora Manor
E 12th St, Flora, IL 62839
(618) 622-8494
Admin Charlotte A Cohen.
Licensure Intermediate care for mentally
retarded. *Beds* ICF/MR 59.
Owner Nonprofit corp.

Flora Nursing Center
701 Shadwell, Flora, IL 62839
(618) 662-8361
Admin Georgianna Feagans. *Dir of Nursing*
Arlene Mattox. *Medical Dir* Dr Galen Lue
King.
Licensure Skilled care; Intermediate care. *Beds*
SNF 56; ICF 54. *Private Pay Patients* 30%.
Certified Medicaid; Medicare.
Owner Proprietary corp (Gershaw Bassman).
Admissions Requirements Minimum age 18;
Medical examination; Physician's request.
Staff RNs 8 (ft), 2 (pt); LPNs 1 (ft), 1 (pt);
Nurses' aides 25 (ft), 4 (pt); Physical
therapists 1 (pt); Speech therapists 1 (pt);
Activities coordinators 2 (ft); Dietitians 1
(pt); Podiatrists 1 (pt).
Facilities Dining room; Physical therapy
room; Activities room; Laundry room;
Barber/Beauty shop; Library.
Activities Arts & crafts; Cards; Games;
Reading groups; Movies; Shopping trips;
Dances/Social/Cultural gatherings; Pet
therapy.

Prairie Estates
403 N State St, Flora, IL 62839
(618) 662-9440
Admin Teresa J Harrell.
Licensure Intermediate care for mentally
retarded. *Beds* ICF/MR 15.

Forest Park

Altenheim
7824 Madison St, Forest Park, IL 60130
(708) 366-2206

Admin Thomas Gora. *Dir of Nursing* Lois McIntyre. *Medical Dir* Dr Robert Vacek.
Licensure Intermediate care; Sheltered care/ Assisted living; Retirement. *Beds* ICF 99; Sheltered care/Assisted living 50; Retirement apartments 36. *Private Pay Patients* 80%.
Owner Nonprofit corp.
Admissions Requirements Minimum age 65; Medical examination.
Staff Physicians 2 (ft); RNs 1 (ft), 2 (pt); LPNs 10 (ft), 4 (pt); Nurses' aides 41 (ft), 5 (pt); Physical therapists 2 (ft); Recreational therapists 2 (ft); Occupational therapists (contracted); Speech therapists (contracted); Activities coordinators 1 (ft); Dietitians (consultant); Ophthalmologists (consultant); Podiatrists (consultant); Audiologists (consultant); Dentists (consultant).
Languages German, Spanish.
Facilities Dining room; Physical therapy room; Activities room; Chapel; Crafts room; Barber/Beauty shop; Library; Dental clinic.
Activities Arts & crafts; Cards; Games; Reading groups; Prayer groups; Movies; Shopping trips; Dances/Social/Cultural gatherings; Intergenerational programs; Pet therapy.

Frankfort

Frankfort Terrace
PO Box 460, 40 N Smith, Frankfort, IL 60423
(815) 469-3156
Admin Sharon Wallenberg.
Licensure Intermediate care. *Beds* ICF 120. *Certified* Medicaid.
Owner Proprietary corp.

Franklin Grove

Franklin Grove Health Care Center
N State St, Franklin Grove, IL 61031
(815) 456-2374
Admin Stuart Y Keller. *Dir of Nursing* Grace Rumph RN. *Medical Dir* Dr Wm Johanson.
Licensure Skilled care; Intermediate care. *Beds* SNF 70; ICF 51. *Certified* Medicaid; Medicare.
Owner Nonprofit corp (First Humanics).
Staff Physicians 1 (pt); RNs 5 (ft); LPNs 10 (ft), 6 (pt); Nurses' aides 20 (ft), 20 (pt); Physical therapists 1 (pt); Occupational therapists 1 (pt); Speech therapists 1 (pt); Activities coordinators 2 (ft), 1 (pt); Dietitians 1 (pt); Ophthalmologists 1 (pt); Podiatrists 1 (pt).

Franklin Park

Westlake Pavilion
10500 W Grand Ave, Franklin Park, IL 60131
(708) 451-1520
Admin Joseph D McGee.
Medical Dir Dr Glenn Kushner.
Licensure Skilled care; Intermediate care; Alzheimer's Program; Respite care. *Beds* SNF 129; ICF 25. *Certified* Medicaid; Medicare.
Owner Nonprofit corp.
Staff Physicians; RNs; LPNs; Nurses' aides; Physical therapists; Recreational therapists; Occupational therapists; Speech therapists; Activities coordinators; Dietitians; Ophthalmologists; Dentists.

Freeburg

Freeburg Care Center
Rte 2 Box 180M, Hwy 15 E, Freeburg, IL 62243
(618) 539-5856
Admin Robin Bozsa. *Dir of Nursing* Judy Gavin. *Medical Dir* Richard Koesterer MD.
Licensure Skilled care; Intermediate care. *Beds* SNF 94; ICF 14. *Private Pay Patients* 46%. *Certified* Medicaid; Medicare.

Owner Proprietary corp.
Admissions Requirements Minimum age 18.
Staff Physicians 2 (pt); RNs 2 (ft); LPNs; Nurses' aides; Physical therapists; Recreational therapists; Speech therapists; Activities coordinators; Dietitians; Ophthalmologists; Podiatrists; Audiologists.
Facilities Dining room; Physical therapy room; Activities room; Crafts room; Laundry room; Barber/Beauty shop; Library.
Activities Arts & crafts; Cards; Games; Reading groups; Prayer groups; Movies; Shopping trips; Dances/Social/Cultural gatherings.

Freeport

Freeport Manor Nursing Center
900 S Kiwanis Dr, Freeport, IL 61032
(815) 235-6196
Admin Dolores Currier. *Dir of Nursing* Nancy Lassiter. *Medical Dir* Dr Frank Descourovez.
Licensure Skilled care. *Beds* SNF 116. *Private Pay Patients* 70%. *Certified* Medicaid; Medicare.
Owner Nonprofit corp (First Humanics Inc).
Admissions Requirements Minimum age 18; Physician's request.
Staff RNs 4 (ft), 1 (pt); LPNs 7 (ft); Nurses' aides 34 (ft), 10 (pt); Physical therapists 1 (ft); Activities coordinators; Dietitians 1 (ft).
Facilities Dining room; Physical therapy room; Activities room; Crafts room; Laundry room; Barber/Beauty shop.
Activities Arts & crafts; Cards; Games; Reading groups; Prayer groups; Movies; Shopping trips; Dances/Social/Cultural gatherings; Intergenerational programs; Pet therapy.

Freeport Terrace
2942 Highlandview Dr, Freeport, IL 61032
(815) 232-8713
Admin Cindy Mix.
Licensure Intermediate care for mentally retarded. *Beds* ICF/MR 15.

Parkview Home
1234 S Park Blvd, Freeport, IL 61032
(815) 232-8612
Admin Dr M Gerald Robey. *Dir of Nursing* Lois Wachlin RN. *Medical Dir* Allen W Workman MD.
Licensure Intermediate care; Sheltered care; Retirement. *Beds* ICF 16; Sheltered care 49.
Owner Nonprofit corp.
Admissions Requirements Minimum age 60; Medical examination.
Staff Physicians 1 (pt); RNs 5 (ft), 1 (pt); LPNs 3 (ft); Nurses' aides 12 (ft), 8 (pt); Physical therapists 1 (pt); Recreational therapists 1 (pt); Occupational therapists 1 (pt); Speech therapists 1 (pt); Activities coordinators 1 (ft), 2 (pt); Dietitians 1 (pt); Ophthalmologists 1 (pt); Podiatrists 1 (pt); Dentists 1 (pt).
Facilities Dining room; Physical therapy room; Activities room; Chapel; Crafts room; Laundry room; Barber/Beauty shop; Library; Multi-purpose room; Game room; Lounge areas.
Activities Arts & crafts; Cards; Games; Reading groups; Prayer groups; Movies; Shopping trips; Dances/Social/Cultural gatherings; Exercise groups; Bowling; Singing groups; Field trips & tours.

Ridge Terrace
2911 Highlandview Dr, Freeport, IL 61032
(815) 232-8729
Admin Donna Slater. *Dir of Nursing* Julie Brady.
Licensure Intermediate care for mentally retarded. *Beds* ICF/MR 15.
Owner Nonprofit organization/foundation.
Admissions Requirements Minimum age 18; Medical examination; Physician's request.

Facilities Dining room; Activities room; Laundry room; Med room.
Activities Arts & crafts; Cards; Games; Reading groups; Prayer groups; Movies; Shopping trips; Dances/Social/Cultural gatherings; Intergenerational programs.

St Joseph Home for the Aged
649 E Jefferson St, Freeport, IL 61032
(815) 232-6181
Admin Peter J Witynski. *Dir of Nursing* Belle Dose. *Medical Dir* Robert Geller MD.
Licensure Intermediate care. *Beds* ICF 109. *Certified* Medicaid.
Owner Nonprofit corp.
Admissions Requirements Medical examination.
Staff Physicians 1 (pt); RNs 4 (ft), 2 (pt); LPNs 4 (ft), 5 (pt); Nurses' aides 29 (ft), 16 (pt); Occupational therapists 1 (pt); Activities coordinators 1 (ft), 2 (pt); Dietitians 1 (pt); Dentists 1 (pt).
Facilities Dining room; Physical therapy room; Activities room; Chapel; Crafts room; Laundry room; Barber/Beauty shop; Library.
Activities Arts & crafts; Cards; Games; Reading groups; Prayer groups; Movies; Shopping trips; Dances/Social/Cultural gatherings.

St Mary Square Living Center Inc
239 S Cherry, Freeport, IL 61401
(309) 343-4101
Admin Bobby Dillard.
Licensure Intermediate care. *Beds* 257.
Owner Nonprofit corp.

St Vincent Community Living Facility
659 E Jefferson, Freeport, IL 61032
(815) 232-6181
Admin Alria J Cole.
Licensure Intermediate care for mentally retarded. *Beds* ICF/MR 20.
Owner Nonprofit corp.

Stephenson Nursing Center
2946 S Walnut Rd, Freeport, IL 61032
(815) 235-6173
Admin Sherry M Gravenstein.
Medical Dir Dr William Metcalf.
Licensure Skilled care; Intermediate care. *Beds* SNF 40; ICF 124. *Certified* Medicaid; Medicare.
Owner Publicly owned.
Admissions Requirements Minimum age 18; Medical examination; Physician's request.
Staff RNs 7 (ft), 15 (pt); LPNs 2 (ft), 10 (pt); Nurses' aides 30 (ft), 20 (pt); Activities coordinators 1 (ft).
Facilities Dining room; Physical therapy room; Activities room; Laundry room; Barber/Beauty shop.
Activities Arts & crafts; Cards; Games; Reading groups; Prayer groups; Movies; Shopping trips; Dances/Social/Cultural gatherings.

Fulton

Harbor Crest Home Inc
817 17th St, Fulton, IL 61252-1020
(815) 589-3411
Admin Robert J Gale.
Licensure Intermediate care. *Beds* ICF 84. *Certified* Medicaid.
Owner Nonprofit corp.

Galatia

Finnie Good Shepherd Nursing Home Inc
Maincross & Legion Sts, Galatia, IL 62935
(618) 268-4631
Admin Bobby Joe Finnie.
Licensure Intermediate care. *Beds* ICF 73. *Certified* Medicaid.
Owner Proprietary corp.

Galena

Galena Stauss Hospital & Nursing Care Facility
215 Summit St, Galena, IL 61036
(815) 777-1340
Admin Roger D Hervey.
Licensure Skilled care; Intermediate care. *Beds* 34. *Certified* Medicaid.
Owner Publicly owned.

Galesburg

Applegate East
1145 Frank St, Galesburg, IL 61401
(309) 342-3103
Admin Carol Neal McCrery. *Dir of Nursing* Kathleen Highee. *Medical Dir* Jerry Ramunis MD.
Licensure Intermediate care; Sheltered care. *Beds* ICF 89; Sheltered care 16. *Certified* Medicaid.
Owner Proprietary corp (Springwood Associates).
Admissions Requirements Minimum age 60; Medical examination.
Staff RNs 1 (ft); LPNs 9 (ft); Nurses' aides 37 (ft); Activities coordinators 2 (ft).
Facilities Dining room; Activities room; Laundry room; Barber/Beauty shop.
Activities Arts & crafts; Cards; Games; Reading groups; Prayer groups; Movies; Shopping trips; Dances/Social/Cultural gatherings.

Cottonwood Health Care Center
820 E 5th St, Galesburg, IL 61401
(309) 342-5135
Admin Carol J Steenbergen. *Dir of Nursing* Deanna Ralston. *Medical Dir* Dr Jerry Ramunis.
Licensure ICF/MI. *Beds* ICF/MI 101. *Private Pay Patients* 10%. *Certified* Medicaid.
Owner Privately owned (Springwood Associates).
Admissions Requirements Minimum age 18; Medical examination.
Staff RNs 1 (ft); LPNs 5 (ft), 4 (pt); Nurses' aides 16 (ft), 10 (pt); Activities coordinators 1 (ft); Dietitians 1 (ft).
Activities Arts & crafts; Cards; Games; Reading groups; Prayer groups; Movies; Shopping trips; Dances/Social/Cultural gatherings; Intergenerational programs; Pet therapy.

Galesburg Nursing & Rehabilitation Center
280 E Losey St, Galesburg, IL 61401
(309) 343-2166
Admin Karen L Utterback. *Dir of Nursing* Joyce E Simms. *Medical Dir* Jeffery Hill MD.
Licensure Skilled care. *Beds* SNF 69. *Certified* Medicaid; Medicare.
Owner Proprietary corp (Health Care & Retirement Corp).
Admissions Requirements Minimum age 18; Medical examination; Physician's request.
Staff Physicians; RNs; LPNs; Nurses' aides; Physical therapists; Occupational therapists; Speech therapists; Activities coordinators; Dietitians; Ophthalmologists.
Facilities Dining room; Physical therapy room; Laundry room; Barber/Beauty shop.
Activities Arts & crafts; Cards; Games; Reading groups; Prayer groups; Movies; Shopping trips; Dances/Social/Cultural gatherings.

Marigold Health Care Center
275 E Carl Sandburg Dr, Galesburg, IL 61401
(309) 344-1151
Admin Marilyn M Burke. *Dir of Nursing* Elaine Carr RN. *Medical Dir* Dr Robert Currie.
Licensure Skilled care; Alzheimer's care. *Beds* SNF 180. *Certified* Medicaid; Medicare.

Owner Nonprofit corp (First Humanics).
Staff RNs; LPNs; Nurses' aides; Activities coordinators.
Facilities Dining room; Physical therapy room; Activities room; Crafts room; Laundry room; Barber/Beauty shop; Library.
Activities Arts & crafts; Cards; Games; Reading groups; Prayer groups; Movies; Shopping trips; Dances/Social/Cultural gatherings.

St Mary's Square Living Center
239 S Cherry, Galesburg, IL 61401
(309) 343-4101
Admin Bobby D Dillard.
Licensure Intermediate care for mentally retarded. *Beds* ICF/MR 265.

Sandburg Care Center Inc
1250 W Carl Sandburg Dr, Galesburg, IL 61401
(309) 344-5400
Admin Sandra Kendrick.
Licensure Skilled care; Intermediate care; Sheltered care. *Beds* SNF 51; ICF 24; Sheltered care 27.

Seminary Manor
2345 N Seminary St, Galesburg, IL 61401
(309) 344-1300
Admin Theodore Debonis.
Licensure Skilled care. *Beds* SNF 80.

Stevens House
2182 Windish Dr, Galesburg, IL 61401
(309) 342-8893
Admin Tim Bledsoe. *Dir of Nursing* Karen Thomas. *Medical Dir* Dr Currie.
Licensure Intermediate care for mentally retarded. *Beds* ICF/MR 15. *Private Pay Patients* 0%.
Owner Nonprofit corp (Saint Marys Square Living Centers Inc).
Staff Physicians 1 (pt); RNs 1 (pt); Nurses' aides 8 (pt); Occupational therapists 1 (pt); Speech therapists 1 (pt); Activities coordinators 1 (pt); Dietitians 1 (pt); Ophthalmologists 1 (pt); Podiatrists 1 (pt); Audiologists 1 (pt).

Trulson House
260 S Michigan Ave, Galesburg, IL 61401
(309) 342-8985
Admin Nancy J Dillard.
Licensure Intermediate care for mentally retarded. *Beds* ICF/MR 15.

Walsh Terrace
2016 Windish Dr, Galesburg, IL 61401
(309) 344-2337
Admin Nancy J Dillard.
Licensure Intermediate care for mentally retarded. *Beds* ICF/MR 15.

Geneseo

Geneseo Good Samaritan
704 S Illinois St, Geneseo, IL 61254
(309) 944-6424
Admin Barbara Mask.
Medical Dir Marilyn Klundt.
Licensure Intermediate care. *Beds* ICF 72. *Certified* Medicaid.
Owner Nonprofit corp (Evangelical Lutheran/ Good Samaritan Society).
Admissions Requirements Minimum age 21; Medical examination.
Staff RNs 5 (pt); LPNs 2 (pt); Nurses' aides 15 (ft), 19 (pt); Activities coordinators 1 (ft), 1 (pt).
Facilities Dining room; Physical therapy room; Activities room; Chapel; Crafts room; Laundry room; Barber/Beauty shop.
Activities Arts & crafts; Cards; Games; Reading groups; Prayer groups; Movies.

Hillcrest Home
Rte 4, Geneseo, IL 61254
(309) 944-2147

Admin Robert J Ruskin.
Licensure Skilled care; Intermediate care. *Beds* SNF 106; ICF 88. *Certified* Medicaid.
Owner Publicly owned.

Geneva

Geneva Care Center
1101 E State St, Geneva, IL 60134
(708) 232-7544, 573-0152 FAX
Admin Lester E Okun. *Dir of Nursing* Diane Johnson. *Medical Dir* Robert Reeder MD.
Licensure Intermediate care; Retirement. *Beds* ICF 105. *Private Pay Patients* 100%.
Owner Nonprofit organization/foundation.
Admissions Requirements Minimum age 21; Medical examination.
Staff Physicians 6 (pt); RNs 6 (ft), 3 (pt); LPNs 5 (ft), 3 (pt); Nurses' aides 9 (ft), 4 (pt); Physical therapists 1 (pt); Reality therapists 1 (pt); Recreational therapists 1 (pt); Occupational therapists 1 (pt); Speech therapists 1 (pt); Activities coordinators 1 (ft); Dietitians 1 (pt); Ophthalmologists 1 (pt); Podiatrists 1 (pt); Audiologists 1 (pt).
Facilities Dining room; Activities room; Chapel; Crafts room; Laundry room; Barber/ Beauty shop; Library.
Activities Arts & crafts; Cards; Games; Reading groups; Prayer groups; Movies; Shopping trips; Dances/Social/Cultural gatherings; Intergenerational programs; Pet therapy.

Genoa

Genesis House
Hwy 23 S, Box 237, Genoa, IL 60135
(815) 784-5146
Admin Valerie A Orcutt. *Dir of Nursing* Ellen Taylor.
Licensure Intermediate care for mentally retarded. *Beds* ICF/MR 94. *Certified* Medicaid.
Owner Proprietary corp.
Admissions Requirements Minimum age 18; Medical examination.
Staff RNs; LPNs; Activities coordinators.
Facilities Dining room; Activities room; Laundry room.
Activities Arts & crafts; Cards; Games; Reading groups; Prayer groups; Movies; Shopping trips; Dances/Social/Cultural gatherings.

Gibson City

Gibson Community Hospital Annex
430 E 19th St, Gibson City, IL 60936
(217) 784-4251
Admin Terry Thompson. *Dir of Nursing* James Dick Cates RN. *Medical Dir* Ross N Hutchison MD.
Licensure Skilled care. *Beds* SNF 26.
Owner Nonprofit organization/foundation.
Admissions Requirements Medical examination; Physician's request.
Staff Physicians 7 (ft), 1 (pt); RNs 1 (ft), 3 (pt); LPNs 5 (ft), 3 (pt); Nurses' aides 16 (ft), 7 (pt); Physical therapists 1 (ft); Activities coordinators 3 (ft); Dietitians 1 (ft).
Facilities Dining room; Physical therapy room; Activities room; Chapel; Crafts room; Barber/Beauty shop.
Activities Arts & crafts; Cards; Games; Reading groups; Prayer groups; Movies; Shopping trips; Dances/Social/Cultural gatherings.

Gibson Manor
525 W Hazel Dr, Gibson City, IL 60936
(217) 784-4257
Admin Robert Burdick. *Dir of Nursing* Marsha Music. *Medical Dir* Gregory Delost.

Licensure Intermediate care. *Beds* ICF 71.
Certified Medicaid.
Owner Proprietary corp (Heritage Enterprises).
Admissions Requirements Minimum age 18.
Staff RNs 3 (ft); LPNs 5 (ft); Nurses' aides 24
(ft).
Facilities Dining room; Activities room;
Crafts room; Laundry room; Barber/Beauty
shop.
Activities Arts & crafts; Cards; Games;
Reading groups; Prayer groups; Movies.

Gifford

Country Health Inc
RR 1 Box 14, Gifford, IL 61847
(217) 568-7362
Admin Michael Adkins. *Dir of Nursing* Roxie
Sage RN. *Medical Dir* Dr Tamara Mitchell.
Licensure Skilled care; Intermediate care;
Retirement. *Beds* SNF 79; ICF 10;
Retirement apts 15. *Private Pay Patients*
50%. *Certified* Medicaid.
Owner Nonprofit corp (Evangelical Lutheran/
Good Samaritan Society).
Admissions Requirements Minimum age 55;
Medical examination.
Staff Physicians 6 (pt); RNs 4 (ft), 2 (pt);
LPNs 3 (ft), 3 (pt); Nurses' aides 40 (ft), 6
(pt); Physical therapists (consultant);
Activities coordinators 2 (ft), 1 (pt);
Dietitians 2 (ft).
Affiliation Lutheran.
Facilities Dining room; Physical therapy
room; Activities room; Chapel; Crafts room;
Laundry room; Barber/Beauty shop.
Activities Arts & crafts; Games; Reading
groups; Prayer groups; Movies; Shopping
trips; Dances/Social/Cultural gatherings; Pet
therapy.

Gillespie

Country Care Center
Rte 2 Box 3B, Gillespie, IL 62033
(217) 839-2171
Admin Kenneth R Newell. *Dir of Nursing*
Nina Hinsey. *Medical Dir* Rudolf Sommer
MD.
Licensure Skilled care; Retirement. *Beds* SNF
98; Retirement 12. *Private Pay Patients*
54%. *Certified* Medicaid; Medicare.
Owner Proprietary corp (Country Care
Center).
Admissions Requirements Minimum age 18;
Medical examination.
Staff RNs 3 (ft); LPNs 5 (ft), 3 (pt); Nurses'
aides 32 (ft), 6 (pt); Physical therapists 1
(pt); Recreational therapists 2 (ft); Speech
therapists 1 (pt); Dietitians 1 (pt);
Ophthalmologists 1 (pt); Podiatrists 1 (pt);
Audiologists 1 (pt).
Facilities Dining room; Physical therapy
room; Activities room; Chapel; Crafts room;
Barber/Beauty shop; Library.
Activities Arts & crafts; Cards; Games;
Reading groups; Prayer groups; Movies;
Shopping trips; Dances/Social/Cultural
gatherings; Pet therapy.

Gilman

Gilman Nursing Center
Box 307, Rte 45 S, Gilman, IL 60938
(217) 265-7207
Admin Judy Pree.
Medical Dir Dr Harry Barnett.
Licensure Skilled care. *Beds* SNF 51. *Certified*
Medicaid; Medicare.
Owner Proprietary corp.
Admissions Requirements Minimum age 19.
Staff RNs 3 (ft), 2 (pt); LPNs 1 (ft), 1 (pt);
Nurses' aides 12 (ft), 10 (pt); Physical
therapists 1 (pt); Recreational therapists 1
(ft); Occupational therapists 1 (pt); Speech

therapists 1 (pt); Dietitians 1 (pt);
Ophthalmologists 1 (pt); Podiatrists 1 (pt);
Audiologists 1 (pt); Dentists 1 (pt).

Girard

Pleasant Hill Village
1010 W North, Girard, IL 62640
(217) 627-2181, 627-3274 FAX
Admin Ronald D LeCount M Div MPA.
Medical Dir David Riesenberger MD.
Licensure Intermediate care. *Beds* ICF 98.
Certified Medicaid.
Owner Nonprofit corp.
Admissions Requirements Medical
examination.
Staff RNs; LPNs; Nurses' aides; Physical
therapists (consultant); Activities
coordinators; Dietitians.
Facilities Dining room; Physical therapy
room; Activities room; Crafts room; Laundry
room; Barber/Beauty shop.
Activities Arts & crafts; Cards; Games;
Reading groups; Prayer groups; Movies.

Glenview

Glenview Terrace Nursing Home
1511 Greenwood Rd, Glenview, IL 60025
(708) 729-9090
Admin Mark Hollander. *Dir of Nursing*
Mariamma Pillai. *Medical Dir* Dr Levy.
Licensure Skilled care. *Beds* SNF 293.
Certified Medicaid; Medicare.
Owner Proprietary corp.
Admissions Requirements Minimum age 18;
Medical examination.
Staff Physicians; RNs; LPNs; Nurses' aides;
Physical therapists; Recreational therapists;
Occupational therapists; Speech therapists;
Activities coordinators; Dietitians;
Ophthalmologists; Podiatrists; Dentists.
Languages Spanish, Polish, Indian, Tagalog.
Facilities Dining room; Physical therapy
room; Activities room; Chapel; Crafts room;
Laundry room; Barber/Beauty shop; Library.
Activities Arts & crafts; Games; Reading
groups; Prayer groups; Movies; Shopping
trips; Dances/Social/Cultural gatherings;
Intergenerational programs.

Maryhaven Inc
1700 E Lake Ave, Glenview, IL 60025
(708) 729-1300
Admin Dennis G Lackie.
Licensure Skilled care; Intermediate care. *Beds*
SNF 42; ICF 105. *Certified* Medicaid.
Owner Nonprofit corp.

Glenwood

Glenwood Terrace Ltd
19330 S Cottage Grove, Glenwood, IL 60425
(708) 758-6200
Admin Irene Glass.
Medical Dir Dr Kruger.
Licensure Skilled care; Intermediate care. *Beds*
SNF 92; ICF 92. *Certified* Medicaid.
Admissions Requirements Medical
examination.
Facilities Dining room; Physical therapy
room; Activities room; Crafts room; Laundry
room; Barber/Beauty shop.
Activities Arts & crafts; Cards; Games;
Reading groups; Prayer groups; Movies;
Shopping trips; Dances/Social/Cultural
gatherings.

Godfrey

Alby Residence
110 N Alby Ct, Godfrey, IL 62035
(618) 466-8848
Admin Earleen Cashill.

Licensure Intermediate care for mentally
retarded. *Beds* ICF/MR 15. *Certified*
Medicaid.
Owner Proprietary corp.
Admissions Requirements Minimum age 18;
Medical examination.
Staff Nurses' aides 9 (pt); Speech therapists 1
(pt); Activities coordinators 1 (ft).
Facilities Dining room; Activities room;
Laundry room.
Activities Arts & crafts; Games; Prayer groups;
Movies; Shopping trips; Dances/Social/
Cultural gatherings.

Beverly Farm Foundation
6301 Humbert Rd, Godfrey, IL 62035
(618) 466-0367
Admin Monte E Welker. *Dir of Nursing*
Elvera Davis.
Licensure Skilled care; Intermediate care;
Intermediate care for mentally retarded.
Beds 431. *Certified* Medicaid; Medicare.
Owner Nonprofit organization/foundation.
Admissions Requirements Minimum age 5;
Medical examination.
Staff Physicians 3 (pt); RNs 5 (ft); Nurses'
aides 230 (ft), 4 (pt); Physical therapists 1
(pt); Recreational therapists 1 (ft);
Occupational therapists 1 (ft); Speech
therapists 1 (ft); Activities coordinators 5
(ft); Dietitians 1 (ft), 1 (pt); Podiatrists 1 (ft).
Facilities Dining room; Physical therapy
room; Activities room; Chapel; Crafts room;
Laundry room; Barber/Beauty shop.
Activities Arts & crafts; Cards; Games;
Reading groups; Prayer groups; Movies;
Shopping trips; Dances/Social/Cultural
gatherings.

Blu-Fountain Manor
1623-29 W Delmar, Godfrey, IL 62035
(618) 466-0443
Admin Arbedella A Carrico.
Licensure Skilled care; Intermediate care. *Beds*
SNF 29; ICF 46. *Certified* Medicaid.
Owner Proprietary corp.
Admissions Requirements Minimum age 16;
Medical examination; Physician's request.
Facilities Dining room; Activities room;
Crafts room; Laundry room; Barber/Beauty
shop; Library.
Activities Arts & crafts; Cards; Games;
Reading groups; Prayer groups; Movies;
Shopping trips; Dances/Social/Cultural
gatherings.

D'Adrian Convalescent Center
1318 W Delmar, Godfrey, IL 62035
(618) 466-0153
Admin Alan A Schmieg. *Dir of Nursing*
Brenda Rulo RN. *Medical Dir* George
Dirkers.
Licensure Intermediate care. *Beds* ICF 119.
Private Pay Patients 20%. *Certified*
Medicaid.
Owner Proprietary corp (Nursing Home
Managers Inc).
Admissions Requirements Minimum age 18;
Medical examination; Physician's request.
Staff RNs 1 (ft), 1 (pt); LPNs 7 (ft), 3 (pt);
Nurses' aides 23 (ft), 4 (pt); Activities
coordinators 1 (ft).
Facilities Dining room; Physical therapy
room; Activities room; Crafts room; Laundry
room; Barber/Beauty shop; Library.
Activities Arts & crafts; Games; Reading
groups; Prayer groups; Movies; Shopping
trips; Dances/Social/Cultural gatherings.

Golconda

Pope County Care Center Inc
Rosalie St, Box 69, Golconda, IL 62938
(618) 683-7711
Admin Alan L Robbs.
Licensure Intermediate care. *Beds* ICF 65.
Certified Medicaid.
Owner Proprietary corp.

Golden

Golden Good Shepherd Home Inc
RR 1 Box 71B, Golden, IL 62339
(217) 696-4421
Admin Lois B Albers. *Dir of Nursing* Marlene Collins RN. *Medical Dir* Frank E Adrian MD.
Licensure Intermediate care. *Beds* ICF 42. *Private Pay Patients* 86%. *Certified* Medicaid.
Owner Nonprofit corp.
Admissions Requirements Minimum age 65; Medical examination.
Staff RNs 1 (ft), 2 (pt); LPNs 2 (ft), 3 (pt); Nurses' aides 2 (ft), 20 (pt); Physical therapists 1 (pt); Activities coordinators 1 (ft), 1 (pt); Dietitians 1 (pt).
Facilities Dining room; Physical therapy room; Activities room; Chapel; Crafts room; Barber/Beauty shop.
Activities Arts & crafts; Cards; Games; Prayer groups; Movies.

Granite City

Colonial Haven Nursing Home Inc
3900 Stearns Ave, Granite City, IL 62040
(618) 931-3900
Admin Robert McDonald. *Dir of Nursing* Carol Swiatek RN. *Medical Dir* Dr Timothy Pratt.
Licensure Intermediate care. *Beds* ICF 122. *Private Pay Patients* 33%. *Certified* Medicaid.
Owner Proprietary corp.
Admissions Requirements Minimum age 65; Medical examination; Physician's request.
Staff RNs 2 (ft); LPNs 8 (ft), 4 (pt); Nurses' aides 29 (ft), 9 (pt); Physical therapists 2 (pt); Recreational therapists 1 (pt); Activities coordinators 1 (ft), 3 (pt).
Facilities Dining room; Physical therapy room; Activities room; Laundry room; Barber/Beauty shop; 3 Lounges.
Activities Arts & crafts; Cards; Games; Prayer groups; Movies; Dances/Social/Cultural gatherings.

Colonnades
1 Colonial Dr, Granite City, IL 62040
(618) 877-2700
Admin Roger M Martin.
Licensure Intermediate care. *Beds* ICF 90. *Certified* Medicaid.
Owner Proprietary corp.

Grayville

Meadowood
2nd & Commerce, Grayville, IL 62844
(618) 375-2171
Admin Rebecca S Alcorn.
Licensure Skilled care. *Beds* SNF 104. *Certified* Medicaid.
Owner Proprietary corp.

Greenup

Cumberland Nursing Center
RR 1 Box 86, Greenup, IL 62428
(217) 923-3186
Admin Lee Markwell. *Dir of Nursing* Joan Ettelbrick. *Medical Dir* Dr Lasso Varju.
Licensure Intermediate care. *Beds* ICF 60. *Certified* Medicaid.
Owner Proprietary corp.
Staff RNs 1 (ft); LPNs 6 (ft), 2 (pt); Nurses' aides 21 (ft); Activities coordinators 1 (ft); Dietitians (consultant).
Facilities Dining room; Activities room; Chapel; Laundry room; Barber/Beauty shop.
Activities Arts & crafts; Cards; Games; Reading groups; Prayer groups; Movies.

Greenville

Fair Oaks
Health Care Dr, Greenville, IL 62246
(618) 664-1230
Admin Alan D Harnetiaux.
Licensure Skilled care. *Beds* SNF 144.

Hillview Retirement Center
S 4th St, Greenville, IL 62246
(618) 664-1622
Admin Loren E Kessinger. *Dir of Nursing* Debarah Deavare RN. *Medical Dir* James Goggin MD.
Licensure Skilled care; Intermediate care. *Beds* SNF 34; ICF 64. *Certified* Medicaid.
Owner Proprietary corp.
Admissions Requirements Minimum age 21; Medical examination; Physician's request.
Staff Physicians 1 (pt); RNs 1 (ft), 3 (pt); LPNs 4 (ft), 3 (pt); Nurses' aides 10 (ft), 10 (pt); Physical therapists 1 (pt); Occupational therapists 1 (pt); Speech therapists 1 (pt); Activities coordinators 2 (ft); Dietitians 1 (ft); Ophthalmologists 1 (pt); Podiatrists 1 (pt); Dentists 1 (pt).
Facilities Dining room; Physical therapy room; Activities room; Crafts room; Laundry room; Barber/Beauty shop; Library.
Activities Arts & crafts; Cards; Games; Movies; Shopping trips; Dances/Social/Cultural gatherings.

Hamilton

Montebello Nursing Home
16th St & Keokuk, Hamilton, IL 62341
(217) 847-3931
Admin Kristin Whitaker.
Medical Dir B C Kappmeyer MD.
Licensure Skilled care. *Beds* SNF 139. *Certified* Medicaid.
Owner Proprietary corp.
Admissions Requirements Minimum age 18; Medical examination.
Staff Physicians 7 (pt); RNs 2 (ft), 4 (pt); LPNs 2 (ft), 4 (pt); Nurses' aides 17 (ft), 22 (pt); Physical therapists 2 (ft), 2 (pt); Reality therapists 2 (pt); Activities coordinators 2 (ft); Dietitians 1 (ft); Podiatrists 1 (pt); Dentists 1 (pt).
Facilities Dining room; Physical therapy room; Activities room; Laundry room; Barber/Beauty shop.
Activities Arts & crafts; Cards; Games; Reading groups; Prayer groups; Movies; Shopping trips; Dances/Social/Cultural gatherings.

Hardin

Calhoun Care Center
908 S Park, Hardin, IL 62047
(618) 576-9031
Admin Karen J Porter. *Dir of Nursing* Vickie Longnecker RN. *Medical Dir* Bernard Baalman MD.
Licensure Skilled care. *Beds* SNF 90. *Certified* Medicaid; Medicare.
Owner Proprietary corp (Springwood Associates).
Admissions Requirements Minimum age 21.
Staff Physicians 3 (pt); RNs 3 (pt); LPNs 3 (ft), 2 (pt); Nurses' aides 15 (ft), 8 (pt); Activities coordinators 1 (ft), 1 (pt); Dietitians 1 (ft).
Facilities Dining room; Physical therapy room; Activities room; Crafts room; Laundry room; Barber/Beauty shop.
Activities Arts & crafts; Cards; Games; Reading groups; Prayer groups; Movies; Shopping trips; Dances/Social/Cultural gatherings.

Harrisburg

Bacon Nursing Home Inc
PO Box 296, N Land St, Harrisburg, IL 62946
(618) 252-6341
Admin Loretta W Turner.
Medical Dir Dr H Andrew Cserny.
Licensure Intermediate care; Intermediate care for mentally retarded. *Beds* ICF 20; ICF/MR 30. *Certified* Medicaid.
Owner Proprietary corp.
Admissions Requirements Minimum age 18; Medical examination; Physician's request.
Staff Physicians 1 (pt); RNs 1 (pt); LPNs 5 (ft), 1 (pt); Nurses' aides 23 (ft), 3 (pt); Reality therapists 1 (ft); Occupational therapists 1 (pt); Speech therapists 1 (pt); Activities coordinators 1 (ft); Dietitians 1 (pt); Ophthalmologists 1 (pt); Podiatrists 1 (pt); Audiologists 1 (pt); Dentists 1 (pt).
Facilities Dining room; Physical therapy room; Activities room; Crafts room; Laundry room; Barber/Beauty shop.
Activities Arts & crafts; Cards; Games; Reading groups; Prayer groups; Movies; Shopping trips; Dances/Social/Cultural gatherings.

Harrisburg Manor Inc
1000 W Sloan St, Harrisburg, IL 62946
(618) 253-7807
Admin Patsy J Colson.
Licensure Skilled care. *Beds* SNF 68. *Certified* Medicaid.
Owner Proprietary corp.

Little Egypt Manor
901 N Webster, Harrisburg, IL 62946
(618) 252-0576
Admin Juli E Moore.
Medical Dir Dr Carl Hauptmann.
Licensure Intermediate care. *Beds* ICF 48. *Certified* Medicaid.
Owner Proprietary corp.
Admissions Requirements Minimum age 18; Medical examination; Physician's request.
Staff RNs 1 (pt); LPNs 3 (ft), 2 (pt); Nurses' aides 9 (ft); Speech therapists 1 (pt); Activities coordinators 1 (ft); Dietitians 3 (ft), 3 (pt); Dentists 1 (pt).
Facilities Dining room; Activities room; Crafts room; Laundry room; Barber/Beauty shop.
Activities Arts & crafts; Cards; Games; Reading groups; Prayer groups; Movies; Shopping trips; Dances/Social/Cultural gatherings.

Saline Care Center
120 S Land St, Harrisburg, IL 62946
(618) 252-7405
Admin Roxann Keasler.
Licensure Intermediate care. *Beds* ICF 131. *Certified* Medicaid.
Owner Proprietary corp.

Shawnee House
PO Box 743, 309 Seright St, Harrisburg, IL 62946
(618) 252-0518
Admin Trena Briscoe. *Dir of Nursing* Jeri Talley RN. *Medical Dir* Dr Larry Jones.
Licensure Intermediate care for mentally retarded. *Beds* ICF/MR 15. *Private Pay Patients* 0%. *Certified* Medicaid; Medicare.
Admissions Requirements Minimum age 21; Medical examination.
Facilities Dining room; Activities room; Laundry room; Kitchen.
Activities Arts & crafts; Cards; Games; Reading groups; Prayer groups; Movies; Shopping trips; Dances/Social/Cultural gatherings; Intergenerational programs.

Harvey

Alden Nursing Center—Heather
15600 S Honore, Harvey, IL 60426
(708) 333-9550, 333-9554
Admin Mickie Stanley LNHR. *Dir of Nursing*
Zoe Ann Simon RN. *Medical Dir* Ram K
Gopi MD.
Licensure Skilled care; Alzheimer's care. *Beds*
SNF 173. *Certified* Medicaid; Medicare.
Owner Proprietary corp (Alden Management
Services Inc).
Admissions Requirements Minimum age 18.
Staff Physicians; RNs; LPNs; Nurses' aides;
Physical therapists; Occupational therapists;
Speech therapists; Activities coordinators;
Dietitians; Ophthalmologists; Podiatrists;
Psychosocial therapists.
Facilities Dining room; Physical therapy
room; Activities room; Chapel; Crafts room;
Laundry room; Barber/Beauty shop.
Activities Arts & crafts; Cards; Games;
Reading groups; Prayer groups; Movies;
Shopping trips; Dances/Social/Cultural
gatherings; Intergenerational programs; Pet
therapy; Field trips; Community
involvement.

Dixie Manor Sheltered Care
15535 Dixie Hwy, Harvey, IL 60426
(708) 339-6438
Admin Leona Thompson.
Licensure Sheltered care. *Beds* Sheltered care
23.
Owner Proprietary corp.

Halsted Manor
16044 Halsted St, Harvey, IL 60426
(708) 339-5311
Admin Vondell L Kennibrew.
Licensure Sheltered care. *Beds* Sheltered care
42.
Owner Proprietary corp.

Kenniebrew Home
14812 S Marshfield Ave, Harvey, IL 60426
(708) 339-9345
Admin Erma Gardner.
Licensure Sheltered care. *Beds* Sheltered care
21.
Owner Proprietary corp.

Starnes Nursing Home Inc
14434 S Hoyne, Harvey, IL 60426
(708) 389-2730
Admin Shirley Q White.
Licensure Intermediate care. *Beds* ICF 39.
Certified Medicaid.
Owner Proprietary corp.

Havana

Havana Healthcare Center
609 N Harpham St, Havana, IL 62644
(309) 543-6121
Admin Vincent M Marquess. *Dir of Nursing*
Sally Strode RN. *Medical Dir* Albert Maurer
MD.
Licensure Intermediate care. *Beds* ICF 98.
Certified Medicaid.
Owner Proprietary corp (H S Healthcare).
Admissions Requirements Minimum age 21;
Medical examination; Physician's request.
Staff Physicians 2 (pt); RNs 5 (ft), 1 (pt);
LPNs 4 (ft), 3 (pt); Nurses' aides 20 (ft), 6
(pt); Physical therapists 1 (pt); Recreational
therapists 1 (ft), 1 (pt); Activities
coordinators 1 (ft), 1 (pt); Dietitians 1 (ft);
Ophthalmologists 2 (pt).
Facilities Dining room; Physical therapy
room; Activities room; Chapel; Crafts room;
Laundry room; Barber/Beauty shop.
Activities Arts & crafts; Cards; Games;
Reading groups; Prayer groups; Movies;
Shopping trips; Dances/Social/Cultural
gatherings.

Hazel Crest

Imperial Nursing Center of Hazel Crest
3300 W 175th St, Hazel Crest, IL 60429
(708) 335-2400
Admin Pamella Willett.
Licensure Skilled care. *Beds* SNF 204.
Certified Medicaid; Medicare.
Owner Proprietary corp.
Admissions Requirements Medical
examination; Physician's request.
Staff Physicians 3 (ft); RNs 11 (ft), 4 (pt);
LPNs 5 (ft), 3 (pt); Nurses' aides 45 (ft), 10
(pt); Physical therapists 1 (ft); Recreational
therapists 1 (ft); Occupational therapists 1
(pt); Speech therapists 1 (pt); Activities
coordinators 1 (ft); Dietitians 1 (pt);
Ophthalmologists 1 (pt); Podiatrists 1 (pt);
Audiologists 1 (pt); Dentists 1 (pt).
Facilities Dining room; Physical therapy
room; Activities room; Crafts room; Laundry
room; Barber/Beauty shop.
Activities Arts & crafts; Cards; Games;
Reading groups; Prayer groups; Movies;
Shopping trips; Dances/Social/Cultural
gatherings.

Henry

Heartland Health Care Center—Henry
1650 Indian Town Rd, Henry, IL 61537
(309) 364-2092
Admin Barbara J Chasteen.
Licensure Skilled care; Sheltered care. *Beds*
SNF 75; Sheltered care 25.

Herrin

Friendship Care Center
1900 N Park St, Herrin, IL 62948
(618) 942-2525
Admin Pamela Garris.
Licensure Intermediate care. *Beds* ICF 49.
Certified Medicaid.
Owner Proprietary corp.

Independence Place
1705 S Park Ave, Box 2123, Herrin, IL 62948
(618) 942-7964
Admin James A Keller.
Licensure Intermediate care for mentally
retarded. *Beds* ICF/MR 15.

Park Avenue Health Care Home
PO Box 68, Herrin, IL 62948
(618) 942-3928
Admin Connie Dodson.
Licensure Intermediate care. *Beds* ICF 69.
Certified Medicaid.
Owner Proprietary corp.

Shawnee Christian Nursing Center
1900 13th St, Herrin, IL 62948
(618) 942-7391
Admin Scott Payne.
Licensure Skilled care. *Beds* SNF 159.
Certified Medicaid; Medicare.
Owner Nonprofit corp (Christian Homes).

Hickory Hills

Hickory Nursing Pavilion Inc
9246 S Roberts Rd, Hickory Hills, IL 60457
(708) 598-4040, 598-0365 FAX
Admin Howard L Wengrow. *Dir of Nursing*
Lourdene Johnson RN.
Licensure Intermediate care. *Beds* ICF 74.
Private Pay Patients 10%. *Certified*
Medicaid.
Owner Proprietary corp.
Staff RNs 2 (ft); LPNs 3 (ft), 3 (pt); Nurses'
aides 16 (ft).
Facilities Dining room; Physical therapy
room; Activities room; Laundry room;
Barber/Beauty shop.

Activities Arts & crafts; Cards; Games;
Reading groups; Prayer groups; Movies;
Shopping trips; Dances/Social/Cultural
gatherings.

Highland

Faith Countryside Homes
PO Box 220, 1216 27th St, Highland, IL
62249
(618) 654-2393
Admin Sandra Buckmiller. *Dir of Nursing*
Lelynna Langdoc RN. *Medical Dir* Donald
Chaney MD.
Licensure Intermediate care; Retirement. *Beds*
ICF 65. *Certified* Medicaid.
Owner Nonprofit corp.
Admissions Requirements Minimum age 55;
Medical examination.
Staff Physicians 1 (pt); RNs 1 (ft), 1 (pt);
LPNs 6 (ft), 2 (pt); Nurses' aides 14 (ft), 7
(pt); Activities coordinators 1 (ft), 1 (pt);
Dietitians 1 (pt); Ophthalmologists 1 (pt).
Affiliation Church of Christ.
Facilities Dining room; Physical therapy
room; Activities room; Barber/Beauty shop.
Activities Arts & crafts; Cards; Games;
Reading groups; Prayer groups; Movies;
Shopping trips; Dances/Social/Cultural
gatherings.

Hillhaven of Highland Inc
2510 Lemon Street Rd, Highland, IL 62249
(618) 654-2368
Admin Bob Coleman. *Dir of Nursing* Carol
Kantner. *Medical Dir* Norbert Belz MD.
Licensure Skilled care; Intermediate care. *Beds*
SNF 28; ICF 100. *Private Pay Patients* 40%.
Certified Medicaid; Medicare.
Owner Proprietary corp (Hillhaven Corp).
Staff RNs 7 (ft), 1 (pt); LPNs 14 (ft), 1 (pt);
Nurses' aides 34 (ft), 2 (pt); Physical
therapists 1 (ft); Speech therapists 1 (pt);
Activities coordinators 1 (ft); Dietitians 1
(ft).
Facilities Dining room; Physical therapy
room; Activities room; Chapel; Laundry
room; Barber/Beauty shop.
Activities Arts & crafts; Cards; Games;
Reading groups; Prayer groups; Movies;
Shopping trips; Dances/Social/Cultural
gatherings.

Highland Park

Abbott House
405 Central Ave, Highland Park, IL 60035
(708) 432-6080
Admin Joanne Minorini. *Dir of Nursing* Maria
Martinez RN. *Medical Dir* Sam Kruger MD.
Licensure Intermediate care. *Beds* ICF 106.
Certified Medicaid.
Owner Privately owned.
Admissions Requirements Minimum age 18;
Medical examination; Physician's request.
Staff Physicians; RNs 4 (ft), 2 (pt); LPNs 2
(ft), 2 (pt); Nurses' aides 20 (ft), 1 (pt);
Activities coordinators; Ophthalmologists;
FSS; Psychosocial coordinators; Activity
assistants; Social workers.
Facilities Dining room; Activities room;
Laundry room; Barber/Beauty shop;
Occupational therapy room.
Activities Arts & crafts; Cards; Games; Prayer
groups; Movies; Shopping trips; Dances/
Social/Cultural gatherings.

Moraine Community Living Facility
1954 Green Bay Rd, Highland Park, IL 60035
(708) 432-7200
Admin Lisa K Dworkin.
Licensure Community living facility. *Beds*
Community living facility 20.

Villa St Cyril—Home For Aged
1111 Saint Johns Ave, Highland Park, IL
60035
(708) 432-9104
Admin Rosemarie H O'Brien.
Medical Dir Jules H Last MD.
Licensure Intermediate care. *Beds* ICF 82.
Certified Medicaid.
Owner Nonprofit corp.
Admissions Requirements Minimum age 65;
Medical examination.
Staff Physicians 2 (pt); RNs 7 (ft), 2 (pt);
LPNs 1 (ft); Nurses' aides 12 (ft), 4 (pt);
Reality therapists 1 (ft); Recreational
therapists 3 (ft), 1 (pt); Occupational
therapists 1 (pt); Activities coordinators 1
(ft); Dietitians 1 (ft); Podiatrists 1 (pt);
Dentists 1 (pt).
Affiliation Roman Catholic.
Facilities Dining room; Activities room;
Chapel; Crafts room; Laundry room; Barber/
Beauty shop; Library.
Activities Arts & crafts; Cards; Games;
Reading groups; Prayer groups; Movies;
Shopping trips; Dances/Social/Cultural
gatherings; Luncheons; Concert outings;
Children's outreach program.

Highwood

Highland Park Health Care Center Inc
50 Pleasant Ave, Highwood, IL 60040
(708) 432-9142
Admin Patricia McDiarmid. *Dir of Nursing*
Emily Harwood. *Medical Dir* Dr Solomon
Dayan.
Licensure Skilled care; Intermediate care. *Beds*
SNF 82; ICF 13. *Certified* Medicaid.
Owner Proprietary corp.
Admissions Requirements Minimum age 21;
Medical examination.
Staff Physicians; RNs 5 (ft), 6 (pt); LPNs 1
(ft); Nurses' aides 20 (ft), 5 (pt); Reality
therapists; Recreational therapists;
Occupational therapists; Activities
coordinators 1 (ft); Ophthalmologists;
Podiatrists.
Facilities Dining room; Physical therapy
room; Activities room; Crafts room; Laundry
room; Barber/Beauty shop.
Activities Arts & crafts; Cards; Games;
Reading groups; Prayer groups; Movies;
Shopping trips; Dances/Social/Cultural
gatherings; Intergenerational programs.

Hillsboro

Hillsboro Healthcare Center
1300 E Tremont St, Hillsboro, IL 62049
(217) 532-6191
Admin Carl D Johnson. *Dir of Nursing*
Maureen Folkerts RN. *Medical Dir* Dr
Douglas Byers.
Licensure Skilled care. *Beds* SNF 121.
Certified Medicare.
Owner Nonprofit corp (First Humanics).
Admissions Requirements Minimum age 18;
Medical examination; Physician's request.
Staff Physicians; RNs 3 (ft), 2 (pt); LPNs 6
(ft), 2 (pt); Nurses' aides 35 (ft), 10 (pt);
Physical therapists; Recreational therapists 1
(ft), 1 (pt); Occupational therapists; Speech
therapists; Activities coordinators 1 (ft), 1
(pt); Dietitians; Ophthalmologists;
Podiatrists; Dentists; Social service
(consultants).
Facilities Dining room; Physical therapy
room; Activities room; Crafts room; Laundry
room; Barber/Beauty shop.
Activities Arts & crafts; Cards; Games;
Reading groups; Prayer groups; Movies;
Shopping trips; Dances/Social/Cultural
gatherings; Quilting class; Cooking class.

Hillsboro Nursing Home
PO Box 309, S Rte 127, Hillsboro, IL 62049
(217) 532-6126

Admin Lorcye F Hamrock. *Dir of Nursing*
Betsy Stockstill RN. *Medical Dir* Roger
McFarlin MD.
Licensure Skilled care; Intermediate care. *Beds*
SNF 21; ICF 99. *Private Pay Patients* 15%.
Certified Medicaid; Medicare.
Owner Proprietary corp (Springwood
Associates).
Admissions Requirements Minimum age 18;
Medical examination.
Staff RNs 2 (ft), 1 (pt); LPNs 6 (ft), 1 (pt);
Nurses' aides 14 (ft), 10 (pt); Physical
therapists (consultant); Activities
coordinators 1 (ft), 1 (pt); Dietitians
(consultant).
Facilities Dining room; Physical therapy
room; Crafts room; Barber/Beauty shop.
Activities Arts & crafts; Cards; Games;
Reading groups; Prayer groups; Movies;
Shopping trips.

Hillside

Oakridge Convalescent Home Inc
323 Oakridge Ave, Hillside, IL 60162
(708) 547-6595
Admin Lynn L Acerra.
Licensure Skilled care; Intermediate care. *Beds*
SNF 58; ICF 15.
Owner Proprietary corp.

Hinsdale

Monticello Convalescent Center of Hinsdale
600 W Ogden Ave, Hinsdale, IL 60521
(708) 325-9630
Admin Jeanne M Chiligiris. *Dir of Nursing*
Dorothy Pustelnikas RN. *Medical Dir* Dr
Gary A Moore.
Licensure Skilled care; Alzheimer's care. *Beds*
SNF 200. *Certified* Medicare.
Owner Proprietary corp (Manor Care).
Admissions Requirements Minimum age 18;
Medical examination.
Staff Physicians; RNs; LPNs; Nurses' aides;
Physical therapists; Occupational therapists 1
(ft); Activities coordinators; Dietitians 1 (ft);
Ophthalmologists 1 (pt).
Facilities Dining room; Physical therapy
room; Activities room; Crafts room; Laundry
room; Barber/Beauty shop; Library; Ice
cream parlor.
Activities Arts & crafts; Cards; Games;
Reading groups; Prayer groups; Movies;
Shopping trips; Dances/Social/Cultural
gatherings; Gardening; Baseball.

West Suburban Shelter Care Center
Rte 83 & 91st, Hinsdale, IL 60521
(708) 323-0198
Admin Evelyn Komara.
Licensure Sheltered care. *Beds* 48.
Owner Proprietary corp.

Hoffman Estates

Alden—Poplar Creek
1545 Barrington Rd, Hoffman Estates, IL
60194
(708) 884-0011, 884-0121 FAX
Admin Susan Longfield. *Dir of Nursing* Linda
Springer RN. *Medical Dir* Edward Kogan
MD.
Licensure Skilled care; Intermediate care;
Alzheimer's care; Hospice. *Beds* SNF 154;
ICF 63. *Private Pay Patients* 75%. *Certified*
Medicaid; Medicare.
Owner Proprietary corp (Alden Management
Services Inc).
Admissions Requirements Minimum age 18;
Medical examination.
Staff Physicians; RNs; LPNs; Nurses' aides;
Physical therapists; Recreational therapists;
Occupational therapists; Speech therapists;
Activities coordinators; Dietitians;
Ophthalmologists; Podiatrists; Audiologists.

Facilities Dining room; Physical therapy
room; Activities room; Chapel; Crafts room;
Laundry room; Barber/Beauty shop; Library;
Ice cream parlor; Gift shop; Lounges; Dental
facilities; Crystal dining room; Hemodialysis
unit.
Activities Arts & crafts; Cards; Games;
Reading groups; Prayer groups; Movies;
Shopping trips; Dances/Social/Cultural
gatherings; Intergenerational programs; Pet
therapy; Holiday parties; Birthday parties.

Homewood

Mercy Health Care Rehabilitation Center
19000 Halsted St, Homewood, IL 60430
(708) 957-9200
Admin Joanne T Jurkovic.
Licensure Skilled care. *Beds* SNF 256.
Certified Medicaid; Medicare.
Owner Nonprofit corp.

Hoopeston

Hoopeston Regional Nursing Home
701 E Orange St, Hoopeston, IL 60942
(217) 283-5531
Admin Bradley V Solberg. *Dir of Nursing*
Margaret Feller. *Medical Dir* Dr T C Lee.
Licensure Skilled care. *Beds* SNF 50. *Certified*
Medicaid; Medicare.
Owner Nonprofit corp.
Staff RNs 1 (ft); LPNs 2 (ft), 2 (pt); Nurses'
aides 12 (ft), 8 (pt); Physical therapists 1 (ft);
Activities coordinators 1 (ft), 1 (pt).
Affiliation Lutheran.
Facilities Dining room; Physical therapy
room; Activities room; Crafts room; Laundry
room; Barber/Beauty shop.
Activities Arts & crafts; Cards; Games;
Reading groups; Prayer groups; Dances/
Social/Cultural gatherings.

Hopedale

Hopedale House
Corner Grove & Railroad, Hopedale, IL
61747
(309) 449-3321
Admin Cynthia F Noreuil.
Licensure Sheltered care. *Beds* Sheltered care
50.
Owner Nonprofit corp.

Hopedale Nursing Home
2nd St, Hopedale, IL 61747
(309) 449-3321
Admin Barbara S Wirtjes.
Licensure Skilled care. *Beds* SNF 96. *Certified*
Medicaid; Medicare.
Owner Nonprofit corp.

Hutsonville

Heritage Sheltered Care Home
207 Wood Ln, Hutsonville, IL 62433
(618) 563-4806
Admin Rena A Smith.
Licensure Sheltered care. *Beds* Sheltered care
48.
Owner Proprietary corp.
Admissions Requirements Minimum age 18;
Medical examination.
Facilities Dining room; Activities room;
Crafts room; Laundry room; Barber/Beauty
shop.
Activities Arts & crafts; Cards; Games;
Shopping trips; Dances/Social/Cultural
gatherings; Vacations.

Indian Head Park

Briar Place Ltd
6800 W Joliet Rd, Indian Head Park, IL
60525
(708) 246-8500

Admin Jane McNally. *Dir of Nursing* Mary Meldazis. *Medical Dir* Dr Angelo Chirban.
Licensure Skilled care; Intermediate care. *Beds* SNF 88; ICF 157. *Private Pay Patients* 25-30%. *Certified* Medicaid.
Owner Proprietary corp.
Admissions Requirements Minimum age 21; Medical examination; Physician's request.
Staff RNs 5 (ft), 2 (pt); LPNs 10 (ft), 6 (pt); Nurses' aides 48 (ft), 9 (pt); Activities coordinators 1 (ft).
Languages Spanish.
Facilities Dining room; Physical therapy room; Activities room; Chapel; Crafts room; Laundry room; Barber/Beauty shop; Psychosocial room.
Activities Arts & crafts; Cards; Games; Reading groups; Prayer groups; Movies; Shopping trips; Dances/Social/Cultural gatherings; Intergenerational programs; Pet therapy; Plant hospital; Cooking; Money management.

Irvington

Gateway Terrace
PO Box 189, Rte 177 W, Irvington, IL 62848
(618) 249-6216
Admin Harold L Pratner.
Licensure Intermediate care for mentally retarded. *Beds* ICF/MR 67.
Owner Nonprofit corp.

Island Lake

Sheltering Oak
PO Box 367, Island Lake, IL 60042
(708) 526-3636
Admin Robert A Bundy.
Licensure Intermediate care. *Beds* ICF 70. *Certified* Medicaid.
Owner Proprietary corp.

Itasca

Arbor of Itasca
535 S Elm St, Itasca, IL 60143
(708) 773-9416
Admin John C Florina Jr. *Dir of Nursing* Jane Geske. *Medical Dir* Dr Mark Pappadopoli.
Licensure Intermediate care. *Beds* ICF 80.
Owner Proprietary corp.
Admissions Requirements Minimum age 18; Medical examination.
Staff Physicians; RNs; LPNs; Nurses' aides; Recreational therapists; Activities coordinators; Dietitians; Ophthalmologists.
Facilities Dining room; Activities room; Chapel; Crafts room; Laundry room; Barber/Beauty shop; Library.
Activities Arts & crafts; Cards; Games; Reading groups; Prayer groups; Movies; Shopping trips; Dances/Social/Cultural gatherings; Intergenerational programs; Pet therapy; Bowling; Library visits; Lunch outings.

Jacksonville

Barton W Stone Christian Home
873 Grove St, Jacksonville, IL 62650
(217) 243-3376
Admin Loren T Cline.
Licensure Skilled care; Intermediate care; Sheltered care. *Beds* SNF 34; ICF 118; Sheltered care 24. *Certified* Medicaid.
Owner Nonprofit corp.

Jacksonville Convalescent Center
1517 W Walnut St, Jacksonville, IL 62650
(217) 243-6451
Admin Wesley Trendle.
Licensure Skilled care; Intermediate care. *Beds* SNF 61; ICF 27. *Certified* Medicaid; Medicare.
Owner Proprietary corp.

Jacksonville Terrace Ltd
1316 Tendick, Jacksonville, IL 62650
(217) 243-6405
Admin Alvin W Lynn.
Licensure Intermediate care. *Beds* ICF 93. *Certified* Medicaid.
Owner Proprietary corp.

Meline Manor Inc
1024 W Walnut, Jacksonville, IL 62650
(217) 245-5175
Admin Lexie D Quigg. *Dir of Nursing* Barbara Zulauf. *Medical Dir* James Hinchen MD.
Licensure Skilled care; Intermediate care. *Beds* SNF 78; ICF 60. *Private Pay Patients* 30%. *Certified* Medicaid; Medicare.
Owner Proprietary corp (Signature Corp).
Admissions Requirements Minimum age 18; Medical examination.
Facilities Dining room; Physical therapy room; Activities room; Crafts room; Laundry room; Barber/Beauty shop.
Activities Arts & crafts; Cards; Games; Reading groups; Prayer groups; Movies; Shopping trips; Dances/Social/Cultural gatherings; Pet therapy.

Modern Care Convalescent & Nursing Home
1500 W Walnut St, Jacksonville, IL 62650
(217) 245-4183
Admin Marian E Chalcraft. *Dir of Nursing* Gerry Coyle RN. *Medical Dir* John Peterson MD.
Licensure Skilled care. *Beds* SNF 68. *Certified* Medicaid; Medicare.
Owner Proprietary corp.
Admissions Requirements Minimum age 18; Physician's request.
Staff RNs 3 (ft), 2 (pt); LPNs 6 (ft), 2 (pt); Nurses' aides 26 (ft), 1 (pt); Activities coordinators 1 (ft), 1 (pt); Dietitians 1 (pt).
Facilities Dining room; Physical therapy room; Activities room; Laundry room; Barber/Beauty shop.
Activities Arts & crafts; Cards; Games; Reading groups; Prayer groups; Movies; Shopping trips; Dances/Social/Cultural gatherings.

Skyview Nursing Home
1021 N Church St, Jacksonville, IL 62650
(217) 245-4174
Admin Ann Newingham. *Dir of Nursing* Jeanie Teaney. *Medical Dir* James A Bohan MD.
Licensure Intermediate care. *Beds* ICF 113. *Private Pay Patients* 32%. *Certified* Medicaid.
Owner Proprietary corp (National Heritage).
Admissions Requirements Minimum age 18; Medical examination; Physician's request.
Staff Physicians 1 (ft); RNs 1 (ft); LPNs 7 (ft); Nurses' aides 14 (ft), 2 (pt); Physical therapists 1 (ft); Recreational therapists 1 (ft), 2 (pt); Activities coordinators 1 (ft); Dietitians 1 (ft).
Facilities Dining room; Physical therapy room; Activities room; Chapel; Crafts room; Laundry room; Barber/Beauty shop; Library; Semi-private rooms.
Activities Arts & crafts; Cards; Games; Reading groups; Prayer groups; Movies; Shopping trips; Dances/Social/Cultural gatherings.

Jerseyville

Garnets Chateau
608 W Pearl St, Jerseyville, IL 62052
(618) 498-4312
Admin Monica L Watson.
Licensure Intermediate care. *Beds* ICF 48. *Certified* Medicaid.
Owner Proprietary corp.

Greenwood Manor Nursing Home
410 Fletcher, Jerseyville, IL 62052
(618) 498-6427

Admin Barbara Molloy.
Licensure Skilled care. *Beds* SNF 98. *Certified* Medicaid.
Owner Proprietary corp.

Jerseyville Care Center
923 S State St, Jerseyville, IL 62052
(618) 498-6496
Admin Earnest Williams. *Dir of Nursing* Betty Warte RN. *Medical Dir* Janeth Zota MD.
Licensure Skilled care. *Beds* SNF 105. *Certified* Medicaid; Medicare.
Owner Proprietary corp (Springwood Associates).
Admissions Requirements Minimum age 21.
Staff RNs; LPNs; Nurses' aides; Activities coordinators.
Facilities Dining room; Physical therapy room; Activities room; Laundry room; Barber/Beauty shop; TV room.
Activities Arts & crafts; Cards; Games; Movies; Shopping trips.

Vahle Terrace
301 Maple Summit Rd, Jerseyville, IL 62052
(618) 498-5242
Admin Joan F Lagage.
Licensure Intermediate care for mentally retarded. *Beds* ICF/MR 15.

Johnston City

Heartland Healthcare Center
205 E 3rd, Johnston City, IL 62951
(618) 983-5731
Admin Sherril Benge. *Dir of Nursing* Pat Wood. *Medical Dir* Dr Javed.
Licensure Sheltered care. *Beds* Sheltered care 23. *Certified* Medicaid; Medicare.
Owner Proprietary corp.
Admissions Requirements Minimum age 18; Medical examination; Physician's request.
Staff Physicians 1 (pt); RNs 1 (pt); Nurses' aides 3 (ft), 2 (pt); Activities coordinators 1 (ft); Dietitians 1 (pt); Dentists 1 (pt).
Facilities Dining room; Activities room; Crafts room; Laundry room.
Activities Arts & crafts; Cards; Games; Reading groups; Prayer groups; Movies; Shopping trips; Dances/Social/Cultural gatherings.

Joliet

Broadway Nursing Home
216 N Broadway, Joliet, IL 60436
(815) 727-7672
Admin Louise Coburn RN NHA. *Dir of Nursing* Judy Koerner LPN. *Medical Dir* Dr Bruce Corwin.
Licensure Intermediate care; Independent residential; Alzheimer's care. *Beds* ICF 60; Independent residential 8. *Private Pay Patients* 100%.
Owner Proprietary corp (Southern Health Resources).
Admissions Requirements Minimum age 35; Medical examination.
Staff Physicians 1 (ft), 2 (pt); LPNs 4 (ft), 2 (pt); Nurses' aides 6 (ft), 3 (pt); Physical therapists 2 (pt); Recreational therapists; Occupational therapists; Activities coordinators; Dietitians; Ophthalmologists; Podiatrists.
Facilities Dining room; Activities room; Crafts room; Laundry room; Barber/Beauty shop; Lounge; TV room; Patio.
Activities Arts & crafts; Cards; Games; Reading groups; Prayer groups; Movies; Dances/Social/Cultural gatherings; Intergenerational programs; Pet therapy; Concerts; Picnics; Recitals; Parties.

Cornerstone Services Inc
PO Box 279, 611 E Cass St, Joliet, IL 60434
(815) 723-3411
Admin Peggy A Peterson.

Licensure CLF; SLA; CRA; ILP; CILA. *Beds* CLF 58; SLA 8; CRA 8; ILP 10; CILA 20.
Owner Nonprofit corp.
Admissions Requirements Minimum age 18; Medical examination.
Staff RNs 1 (pt); Recreational therapists 1 (ft); Activities coordinators 1 (ft).
Facilities Dining room; Laundry room; Living rooms.
Activities Arts & crafts; Cards; Games; Movies; Shopping trips; Dances/Social/ Cultural gatherings; Intergenerational programs; Special Olympics.

Deerbrook Nursing Centre
306 N Larkin Ave, Joliet, IL 60435
(815) 744-5560
Admin Emanuel Binstock.
Licensure Skilled care. *Beds* SNF 224. *Certified* Medicaid; Medicare.
Owner Proprietary corp.

Draper Plaza
777 Draper Ave, Joliet, IL 60432
(815) 727-4794
Admin Peg Obert-Voitik. *Dir of Nursing* Carolyn Schwiesow. *Medical Dir* Dr Chirban.
Licensure Skilled care; Intermediate care; Alzheimer's care. *Beds* SNF 84; ICF 84. *Certified* Medicaid; Medicare.
Owner Privately owned.
Admissions Requirements Minimum age 18; Medical examination; Physician's request.
Staff Physicians 1 (ft); RNs 5 (ft); LPNs 12 (ft); Nurses' aides 60 (ft), 5 (pt); Physical therapists 1 (pt); Recreational therapists 1 (ft); Occupational therapists 1 (pt); Speech therapists 1 (pt); Activities coordinators 1 (ft); Dietitians 1 (pt); Podiatrists 1 (pt).
Languages Spanish.
Facilities Dining room; Physical therapy room; Chapel; Laundry room; Barber/Beauty shop; Library; Activities/Crafts room.
Activities Arts & crafts; Cards; Games; Reading groups; Prayer groups; Movies; Shopping trips; Dances/Social/Cultural gatherings; Intergenerational programs; Pet therapy.

Franciscan Nursing Home
210 N Springfield, Joliet, IL 60435
(815) 725-3400
Admin Diane M Mikes. *Dir of Nursing* Carole Parrish RN. *Medical Dir* Anthony Razma MD.
Licensure Skilled care; Alzheimer's care. *Beds* SNF 129. *Private Pay Patients* 75%. *Certified* Medicaid; Medicare.
Owner Nonprofit corp (Franciscan Sisters Health Care Corp).
Admissions Requirements Medical examination; Physician's request.
Staff RNs 6 (ft), 1 (pt); LPNs 12 (ft), 6 (pt); Nurses' aides 34 (ft), 8 (pt); Activities coordinators 2 (ft), 3 (pt).
Languages Spanish.
Affiliation Roman Catholic.
Facilities Dining room; Physical therapy room; Activities room; Chapel; Crafts room; Laundry room; Barber/Beauty shop.
Activities Arts & crafts; Cards; Games; Reading groups; Prayer groups; Movies; Shopping trips; Dances/Social/Cultural gatherings; Intergenerational programs; Pet therapy; Breakfast club & lunch bunch.

Imperial Nursing Center of Joliet
222 N Hammes, Joliet, IL 60435
(815) 725-0443
Admin Richard J Payne.
Medical Dir Louis Minella.
Licensure Skilled care. *Beds* SNF 203. *Certified* Medicaid; Medicare.
Owner Proprietary corp.
Staff Physicians 3 (pt); RNs 10 (ft), 7 (pt); LPNs 10 (ft), 12 (pt); Nurses' aides 20 (ft), 8 (pt); Physical therapists 1 (ft); Reality

therapists 3 (ft); Recreational therapists 4 (ft); Occupational therapists 2 (ft), 1 (pt); Speech therapists 1 (ft); Activities coordinators 1 (ft); Dietitians 1 (ft), 1 (pt); Ophthalmologists 2 (pt); Podiatrists 1 (pt); Audiologists 1 (pt); Dentists 3 (pt).

Joliet Terrace
2230 McDonough, Joliet, IL 60436
(815) 729-3801
Admin Marilyn Ferbend.
Licensure Intermediate care. *Beds* ICF 120. *Certified* Medicaid.
Owner Proprietary corp.

Our Lady of Angels Retirement Home
1201 Wyoming Ave, Joliet, IL 60435
(815) 725-6631
Admin Sr Phyllis Pitz OSF. *Dir of Nursing* Sr Peter Didier RN. *Medical Dir* John Bowden MD.
Licensure Intermediate care; Sheltered care. *Beds* ICF 50; Sheltered care 50. *Certified* Medicaid.
Owner Nonprofit corp.
Admissions Requirements Minimum age 65; Medical examination.
Staff RNs 1 (ft), 5 (pt); LPNs 2 (pt); Nurses' aides 21 (ft), 12 (pt); Physical therapists 1 (pt); Activities coordinators 1 (ft); Dietitians 1 (ft).
Affiliation Roman Catholic.
Facilities Dining room; Physical therapy room; Activities room; Chapel; Crafts room; Laundry room; Barber/Beauty shop; Library.
Activities Arts & crafts; Cards; Games; Reading groups; Prayer groups; Movies; Shopping trips; Dances/Social/Cultural gatherings.

St Patrick's Residence
22 E Clinton St, Joliet, IL 60431
(815) 727-5291
Admin Sr M Jacqueline Wagner. *Dir of Nursing* Sr M Josa RN. *Medical Dir* Roy Alcala MD.
Licensure Skilled care; Intermediate care; Sheltered care; Alzheimer's care; Retirement. *Beds* SNF 10; ICF 97; Sheltered care 90. *Certified* Medicaid.
Owner Nonprofit organization/foundation.
Admissions Requirements Minimum age 65; Females only.
Staff Physicians 1 (pt); RNs 7 (ft), 2 (pt); LPNs 7 (ft), 7 (pt); Nurses' aides 55 (ft); Occupational therapists; Activities coordinators 1 (ft); Dietitians 1 (ft).
Affiliation Roman Catholic.
Facilities Dining room; Physical therapy room; Activities room; Chapel; Crafts room; Laundry room; Barber/Beauty shop; Library; Coffee shop.
Activities Arts & crafts; Cards; Games; Reading groups; Prayer groups; Movies; Shopping trips; Dances/Social/Cultural gatherings.

Salem Village
1314 Rowell Ave, Joliet, IL 60433
(815) 727-5451
Admin John B Carter. *Dir of Nursing* Mary Naughton-Walsh. *Medical Dir* Bruce C Corwin MD.
Licensure Skilled care; Intermediate care; Sheltered care; Retirement; Alzheimer's care. *Beds* SNF 36; ICF 246; Sheltered care 59. *Certified* Medicaid.
Owner Nonprofit organization/foundation.
Admissions Requirements Minimum age 62; Medical examination.
Staff Physicians 1 (pt); RNs 6 (ft), 5 (pt); LPNs 20 (ft), 8 (pt); Nurses' aides 55 (ft), 39 (pt); Physical therapists 1 (pt); Reality therapists 1 (pt); Recreational therapists 1 (pt); Occupational therapists 1 (pt); Activities coordinators 1 (ft), 6 (pt); Dietitians 1 (ft).
Affiliation Lutheran.

Facilities Dining room; Physical therapy room; Activities room; Crafts room; Laundry room; Barber/Beauty shop; Library; Retirement apartments; Townhouses; Resale shop.
Activities Arts & crafts; Cards; Games; Reading groups; Prayer groups; Movies; Shopping trips; Dances/Social/Cultural gatherings; Resident journal; Physical fitness.

Sunny Hill Nursing Home
Doris & Neal Sts, Joliet, IL 60433
(815) 727-8710, 727-8637 FAX
Admin Vicki Lynn Tomer. *Dir of Nursing* Annette Etheridge RN. *Medical Dir* Dr Kishor Ajmere.
Licensure Skilled care; Intermediate care. *Beds* SNF 50; ICF 250. *Private Pay Patients* 80%. *Certified* Medicaid.
Owner Publicly owned.
Admissions Requirements Minimum age 18; Medical examination.
Staff RNs 8 (ft), 3 (pt); LPNs 25 (ft), 10 (pt); Nurses' aides 91 (ft), 13 (pt); Recreational therapists 6 (ft); Activities coordinators 1 (ft); Dietitians 1 (ft).
Facilities Dining room; Physical therapy room; Activities room; Chapel; Crafts room; Laundry room; Barber/Beauty shop; Library.
Activities Arts & crafts; Cards; Games; Reading groups; Prayer groups; Movies; Shopping trips; Dances/Social/Cultural gatherings; Pet therapy; Resident council; Reality orientation; Fitness trail; Exercises; Service projects; Resident newsletter.

Jonesboro

Gibbs-McRaven Sheltered Care Home
PO Box G, 204 S Pecon, Jonesboro, IL 62952
(618) 833-5740
Admin Howard H McRaven. *Dir of Nursing* Kathryn Robinson. *Medical Dir* Steve Beatty MD.
Licensure Sheltered care. *Beds* Sheltered care 25. *Private Pay Patients* 50%.
Owner Privately owned.
Admissions Requirements Minimum age 21; Medical examination.
Staff Physicians 1 (pt); RNs 1 (pt); Nurses' aides 5 (ft); Activities coordinators 1 (ft); Dietitians 1 (pt).
Facilities Dining room; Activities room; Crafts room; Laundry room; Barber/Beauty shop; Library.
Activities Arts & crafts; Cards; Games; Reading groups; Prayer groups; Movies; Shopping trips; Dances/Social/Cultural gatherings; Pet therapy 414K Services and transportation by area churches.

Henard Sheltered Care Home
204 S Main, Jonesboro, IL 62952
(618) 833-6134
Admin Joyce Harrington.
Licensure Sheltered care. *Beds* 16.
Owner Proprietary corp.

Lifecare Center of Jonesboro Inc
PO Box B, Rte 127 S, Jonesboro, IL 62952
(618) 833-7093
Admin Lonnie D Harvel.
Medical Dir Dr William H Whiting.
Licensure Intermediate care. *Beds* ICF 82. *Certified* Medicaid.
Owner Proprietary corp (Community Lifecare Enterprises).
Admissions Requirements Medical examination.
Staff RNs 1 (ft); LPNs 7 (ft); Nurses' aides 21 (ft); Physical therapists 1 (ft); Recreational therapists 2 (ft); Activities coordinators 2 (ft); Dietitians 1 (pt).
Facilities Dining room; Physical therapy room; Activities room; Crafts room; Laundry room; Barber/Beauty shop.

Activities Arts & crafts; Cards; Games; Reading groups; Prayer groups; Movies; Shopping trips; Dances/Social/Cultural gatherings.

Justice

Rosary Hill Home
9000 Rosary Hill Dr, Justice, IL 60458
(708) 458-3040
Admin Sr Catherine M Lasiewicki.
Medical Dir Frank J Wall Jr MD.
Licensure Intermediate care; Sheltered care. *Beds* ICF 18; Sheltered care 32.
Owner Nonprofit corp.
Admissions Requirements Minimum age 65; Females only.
Staff RNs 1 (ft); LPNs 1 (ft); Nurses' aides 8 (ft); Activities coordinators 1 (pt); Dietitians 1 (pt); Ophthalmologists 1 (pt).
Affiliation Roman Catholic.
Facilities Dining room; Activities room; Chapel; Laundry room; Barber/Beauty shop; Library.
Activities Arts & crafts; Cards; Games; Prayer groups; Movies.

Kankakee

Americana Healthcare Center
900 W River Pl, Kankakee, IL 60901
(815) 933-1711
Admin Scott B Frank. *Dir of Nursing* Sharon Leydens RN. *Medical Dir* Reinhold Schuller MD.
Licensure Skilled care. *Beds* SNF 97. *Certified* Medicaid; Medicare.
Owner Proprietary corp (Manor Care).
Staff RNs 5 (ft), 3 (pt); LPNs 6 (ft), 4 (pt); Nurses' aides 20 (ft), 10 (pt); Activities coordinators 1 (ft); Dietitians 1 (ft).
Facilities Dining room; Physical therapy room; Activities room; Crafts room; Laundry room; Barber/Beauty shop; 2 Resident lounges.
Activities Arts & crafts; Cards; Games; Reading groups; Prayer groups; Movies; Shopping trips; Dances/Social/Cultural gatherings.

Heritage House
901 N Entrance Ave, Kankakee, IL 60901
(815) 939-4506
Admin Carol D Kehoe BS. *Dir of Nursing* Judy Fasig RN.
Licensure Skilled care; Sheltered care. *Beds* SNF 41; Sheltered care 89. *Private Pay Patients* 100%.
Owner Nonprofit organization/foundation.
Admissions Requirements Minimum age 60; Medical examination.
Staff RNs 5 (ft), 2 (pt); LPNs 4 (pt); Nurses' aides 23 (ft), 5 (pt); Occupational therapists 1 (ft); Activities coordinators 2 (ft).
Facilities Dining room; Activities room; Chapel; Crafts room; Laundry room; Barber/Beauty shop; Library.
Activities Arts & crafts; Cards; Games; Reading groups; Prayer groups; Movies; Shopping trips; Dances/Social/Cultural gatherings; Intergenerational programs.

Kankakee Royale Inc
1050 W Jeffrey St, Kankakee, IL 60901
(815) 933-1660
Admin Dino Varnavas.
Licensure Skilled care; Intermediate care. *Beds* SNF 91; ICF 111. *Certified* Medicaid.
Owner Proprietary corp.

Knox Estates
611 N Greenwood Ave, Kankakee, IL 60901
(815) 672-7611
Admin Cynthia J Dear.
Licensure Intermediate care for mentally retarded. *Beds* ICF/MR 15. *Certified* Medicaid.

Owner Nonprofit corp.
Admissions Requirements Minimum age 18; Medical examination; Physician's request.
Staff Physicians 1 (pt); RNs 1 (pt); Recreational therapists 1 (pt); Speech therapists 1 (pt); Activities coordinators 1 (pt); Dietitians 1 (pt).
Facilities Dining room; Laundry room.
Activities Arts & crafts; Cards; Games; Movies; Shopping trips; Dances/Social/Cultural gatherings.

Kewanee

Kewanee Care Home
144 Junior Ave, Kewanee, IL 61443
(309) 853-4429
Admin Robert L Petersen. *Dir of Nursing* Helen L Park LPN. *Medical Dir* Glenn Miller MD.
Licensure Intermediate care. *Beds* ICF 65. *Certified* Medicaid.
Owner Proprietary corp.
Admissions Requirements Minimum age 18; Medical examination; Physician's request.
Staff Physicians 1 (ft); RNs 3 (pt); LPNs 4 (ft), 1 (pt); Nurses' aides 3 (ft), 18 (pt); Physical therapists 1 (ft); Recreational therapists 1 (ft); Activities coordinators 1 (pt); Dietitians 1 (pt); Ophthalmologists 1 (pt); Podiatrists 1 (pt); Dentists 1 (pt).
Facilities Dining room; Activities room; Laundry room; Barber/Beauty shop.
Activities Arts & crafts; Cards; Games; Reading groups; Prayer groups; Movies; Shopping trips.

Oakwood Health Care Center
605 E Church St, Kewanee, IL 61443
(309) 852-3389
Admin Vicky L Debord.
Medical Dir Glenn Miller; Debra Hurley.
Licensure Skilled care; Alzheimer's care. *Beds* SNF 200. *Certified* Medicaid; Medicare.
Owner Proprietary corp (Springwood Associates).
Admissions Requirements Medical examination; Physician's request.
Staff RNs 6 (ft), 2 (pt); LPNs 11 (ft), 4 (pt); Nurses' aides 49 (ft), 36 (pt); Physical therapists 1 (pt); Occupational therapists 1 (pt); Activities coordinators 2 (ft), 1 (pt).
Facilities Dining room; Physical therapy room; Activities room; Crafts room; Laundry room; Barber/Beauty shop.
Activities Arts & crafts; Cards; Games; Reading groups; Prayer groups; Movies; Shopping trips; Pet therapy; Church services; Intergenerational visits; Music appreciation.

Knoxville

Good Samaritan Nursing Home
407 N Hebard St, Knoxville, IL 61448
(309) 289-2614
Admin Anna Wang. *Dir of Nursing* Sharlene Morris LPN. *Medical Dir* Robert G Hickerson Jr MD.
Licensure Intermediate care. *Beds* ICF 49. *Certified* Medi-Cal.
Owner Nonprofit corp.
Admissions Requirements Minimum age 18; Medical examination; Physician's request.
Staff RNs 1 (ft), 1 (pt); LPNs 4 (ft), 1 (pt); Nurses' aides 26 (ft), 10 (pt); Physical therapists 1 (ft); Reality therapists 1 (ft); Recreational therapists 2 (ft), 1 (pt); Occupational therapists 1 (ft); Activities coordinators 1 (ft), 1 (pt); Dietitians 1 (ft).
Facilities Dining room; Physical therapy room; Activities room; Chapel; Crafts room; Laundry room; Library; Garden; Social hall.
Activities Arts & crafts; Cards; Games; Reading groups; Prayer groups; Movies; Shopping trips; Dances/Social/Cultural gatherings; Music band; Sunshine singers.

Knox County Nursing Home
N Market St, Knoxville, IL 61448
(309) 289-2338
Admin Karen Cheline-Cisco. *Dir of Nursing* Beverly Asbury.
Licensure Skilled care. *Beds* SNF 204. *Certified* Medicaid.
Owner Nonprofit organization/foundation.
Admissions Requirements Medical examination; Physician's request.
Staff RNs 7 (ft), 2 (pt); LPNs 10 (ft), 10 (pt); Nurses' aides 54 (ft), 37 (pt).
Facilities Dining room; Physical therapy room; Activities room; Chapel; Crafts room; Laundry room; Barber/Beauty shop; Library.
Activities Arts & crafts; Cards; Games; Prayer groups; Movies; Dances/Social/Cultural gatherings.

La Grange

Colonial Manor Living Center
339 S 9th Ave, La Grange, IL 60525
(708) 354-4660
Admin Leland R Schultz. *Dir of Nursing* Koren Hart RN. *Medical Dir* Russell Zitek MD.
Licensure Skilled care; Intermediate care; Alzheimer's care. *Beds* SNF 96; ICF 107. *Certified* Medicaid; Medicare.
Owner Nonprofit corp (Adventist Health Sys-USA).
Admissions Requirements Medical examination; Physician's request.
Staff Physicians; RNs; LPNs; Nurses' aides; Physical therapists; Reality therapists; Recreational therapists; Occupational therapists; Speech therapists; Activities coordinators; Dietitians.
Facilities Dining room; Physical therapy room; Activities room; Chapel; Crafts room; Laundry room; Barber/Beauty shop; Library.
Activities Arts & crafts; Cards; Games; Reading groups; Prayer groups; Movies; Shopping trips; Dances/Social/Cultural gatherings.

La Grange Park

Fairview Health Care Center
701 N La Grange Rd, La Grange Park, IL 60525
(708) 354-7300, 354-8928 FAX
Admin Phyllis Lavenau RN. *Dir of Nursing* Sue Bruzan RN. *Medical Dir* Alberto Saltiel MD.
Licensure Skilled care; Hospice care. *Beds* SNF 131. *Private Pay Patients* 80%. *Certified* Medicare.
Owner Privately owned.
Admissions Requirements Minimum age 19; Medical examination.
Staff Physicians (consultant); RNs 7 (ft), 9 (pt); LPNs 11 (ft), 1 (pt); Nurses' aides 45 (ft), 8 (pt); Physical therapists 1 (ft); Reality therapists 1 (ft); Recreational therapists 3 (ft), 2 (pt); Occupational therapists 1 (pt) (contracted); Speech therapists 1 (pt) (contracted); Activities coordinators 1 (ft); Dietitians 1 (pt) (consultant); Ophthalmologists 1 (pt) (consultant); Podiatrists 1 (pt) (consultant); Audiologists 1 (pt) (consultant).
Facilities Dining room; Physical therapy room; Activities room; Crafts room; Barber/Beauty shop; Library cart; Hospice program; Rehabilitation program.
Activities Arts & crafts; Cards; Games; Reading groups; Prayer groups; Movies; Shopping trips; Dances/Social/Cultural gatherings; Intergenerational programs; Pet therapy; Field trips; Picnics; Religious services.

Plymouth Place Inc
315 N La Grange Rd, La Grange Park, IL
60525
(708) 354-0340
Admin Donald E Clawson. *Dir of Nursing*
Anne Schultz. *Medical Dir* Dr Thomas J
Schnitzer.
Licensure Skilled care; Intermediate care;
Independent living; Sheltered care;
Alzheimer's care. *Beds* SNF 24; ICF 76;
Independent living 200; Sheltered care 134.
Private Pay Patients 100%.
Owner Nonprofit corp.
Admissions Requirements Minimum age 60;
Medical examination.
Staff Physicians 8 (pt); RNs 6 (ft), 5 (pt);
LPNs 7 (ft), 6 (pt); Nurses' aides 26 (ft), 4
(pt); Physical therapists (contracted);
Recreational therapists 2 (ft); Occupational
therapists (contracted); Speech therapists
(contracted); Activities coordinators 1 (ft);
Dietitians 1 (pt); Ophthalmologists (private);
Podiatrists (private); Audiologists
(contracted).
Affiliation Church of Christ.
Facilities Dining room; Physical therapy
room; Activities room; Chapel; Crafts room;
Laundry room; Barber/Beauty shop; Library.
Activities Arts & crafts; Cards; Games;
Reading groups; Prayer groups; Movies;
Shopping trips; Dances/Social/Cultural
gatherings; Intergenerational programs; Pet
therapy.

La Salle

Care Inn Convalescent Center
1445 Chartres St, La Salle, IL 61301
(815) 223-4700, 223-6630 FAX
Admin John G Koehler. *Dir of Nursing* Mary
Pelka RN. *Medical Dir* Maya Jagasia MD.
Licensure Skilled care; Intermediate care. *Beds*
SNF 50; ICF 51. *Private Pay Patients* 30%.
Certified Medicaid; Medicare.
Owner Proprietary corp (ARA Living
Centers).
Admissions Requirements Minimum age 21;
Medical examination; Physician's request.
Staff RNs 7 (ft), 2 (pt); LPNs 6 (ft), 2 (pt);
Nurses' aides 25 (ft), 20 (pt); Physical
therapists 1 (pt); Speech therapists 1 (pt);
Activities coordinators 1 (ft), 2 (pt);
Dietitians 1 (pt); Ophthalmologists 2 (pt);
Rehabilitation aides 2 (pt).
Facilities Dining room; Physical therapy
room; Laundry room; Barber/Beauty shop;
Library.
Activities Arts & crafts; Cards; Games;
Reading groups; Prayer groups; Movies;
Shopping trips; Dances/Social/Cultural
gatherings; Intergenerational programs; Pet
therapy; Joint Efforts exercise program for
arthritic patients; ADL rehabilitation
program.

Lacon

St Joseph Nursing Home
401 9th St, Lacon, IL 61540
(309) 246-2175
Admin Sr Catherine Platte.
Licensure Intermediate care. *Beds* ICF 103.
Certified Medicaid.
Owner Nonprofit corp.

Lake Bluff

Hill Top
502 Waukegan Rd, Lake Bluff, IL 60044
(708) 295-1550
Admin Barry J Rosen.
Licensure Skilled care. *Beds* SNF 24.
Owner Nonprofit corp.
Affiliation Christian Science.

Facilities Dining room; Activities room;
Chapel; Crafts room; Laundry room; Barber/
Beauty shop; Library.
Activities Arts & crafts; Reading groups;
Prayer groups; Movies.

Lake Bluff Health Care Center
700 Jenkisson Ave, Lake Bluff, IL 60044
(708) 295-3900
Admin Barbara Lyons. *Dir of Nursing* Pat
Miller RN. *Medical Dir* David Schimel MD.
Licensure Skilled care; Alzheimer's care. *Beds*
SNF 231. *Certified* Medicaid; Medicare.
Owner Proprietary corp.
Admissions Requirements Minimum age 21;
Medical examination; Physician's request.
Staff Physicians 8 (pt); RNs 19 (ft); LPNs 26
(ft); Nurses' aides 90 (ft); Physical therapists
1 (ft); Reality therapists 1 (ft); Recreational
therapists 1 (ft); Occupational therapists 1
(pt); Speech therapists 1 (pt); Activities
coordinators 1 (ft); Dietitians 1 (ft);
Ophthalmologists 1 (pt); Podiatrists 1 (pt);
Dentists 1 (pt).
Facilities Dining room; Physical therapy
room; Activities room; Crafts room; Laundry
room; Barber/Beauty shop; Library.
Activities Arts & crafts; Cards; Games;
Reading groups; Prayer groups; Movies;
Shopping trips; Dances/Social/Cultural
gatherings.

Lake Forest

Grove School Resident Center
40 E Old Mill Rd, Lake Forest, IL 60045
(708) 234-5540
Admin Robert E Matson.
Medical Dir Dr Shaku Chhabria.
Licensure Skilled care. *Beds* SNF 48. *Certified*
Medicaid.
Owner Nonprofit corp.
Admissions Requirements Minimum age 10;
Medical examination; Physician's request.
Staff Physicians 1 (ft), 3 (pt); RNs 3 (ft), 1
(pt); LPNs 1 (ft), 2 (pt); Nurses' aides 22
(ft); Physical therapists 1 (pt); Occupational
therapists 1 (pt); Speech therapists 1 (ft);
Activities coordinators 1 (ft); Dietitians 1
(pt).
Facilities Dining room; Physical therapy
room; Activities room; Crafts room; Laundry
room.
Activities Arts & crafts; Games; Movies;
Shopping trips.

Latham Estates
Box 6, Lake Forest, IL 62543
(217) 674-3738
Admin Donna M Britton.
Licensure Intermediate care. *Beds* 139.
Owner Proprietary corp.

Lake Zurich

Mt St Joseph
24955 N Hwy 12, Lake Zurich, IL 60047
(708) 438-5050
Admin Bernardine Kauffmann. *Dir of Nursing*
Sr Mary Walker. *Medical Dir* Dr Sanjoy
Majumdar.
Licensure Intermediate care for mentally
retarded. *Beds* ICF/MR 162. *Certified*
Medicaid.
Owner Nonprofit corp.
Admissions Requirements Minimum age 21;
Females only.
Staff Physicians 1 (pt); RNs 6 (ft); LPNs 3
(ft); Nurses' aides 40 (ft), 20 (pt);
Recreational therapists; Occupational
therapists; Speech therapists 2 (ft); Activities
coordinators 8 (ft); Dietitians 1 (pt);
Ophthalmologists 1 (pt); Dentists 1 (pt).
Affiliation Roman Catholic.
Facilities Dining room; Physical therapy
room; Activities room; Chapel; Crafts room;
Laundry room; Library.

Activities Arts & crafts; Cards; Games;
Reading groups; Prayer groups; Movies;
Shopping trips; Dances/Social/Cultural
gatherings; Music therapy; Recreational
therapy.

Lansing

Tri State Manor Nursing Home
2500 E 175th St, Lansing, IL 60438
(708) 474-7330
Admin Olive J Horeshimer.
Licensure Intermediate care. *Beds* ICF 56.
Owner Proprietary corp.

Latham

Countryview Living Center
PO Box 6, Main St & Rte 121, Latham, IL
62543
(217) 674-3392
Admin Gerald Owen.
Licensure Intermediate care for mentally
retarded. *Beds* ICF/MR 110.

Lawrenceville

United Methodist Village
1616 Cedar St, Lawrenceville, IL 62439
(618) 943-3347
Admin C Dale Swenson; Dowain McKiow
Exec Dir. *Dir of Nursing* Joyce Brunson RN.
Medical Dir Dr R T Kirkwood.
Licensure Skilled care; Intermediate care;
Sheltered care; Adult day care; Alzheimer's
care; Retirement. *Beds* SNF 162; ICF 49;
Sheltered care 80; Adult day care 12;
Alzheimer's care 28; Retirement 53. *Private
Pay Patients* 55%. *Certified* Medicaid;
Medicare.
Owner Nonprofit organization/foundation.
Admissions Requirements Minimum age 18.
Staff Physicians 6 (pt); RNs 6 (ft), 11 (pt);
LPNs 9 (ft), 7 (pt); Nurses' aides 50 (ft), 26
(pt); Physical therapists 1 (ft), 1 (pt);
Activities coordinators 1 (ft); Dietitians 1
(ft).
Affiliation Methodist.
Facilities Dining room; Physical therapy
room; Activities room; Chapel; Crafts room;
Laundry room; Barber/Beauty shop; Library;
Gift shop; Ceramics; Home care.
Activities Arts & crafts; Cards; Games;
Reading groups; Prayer groups; Movies;
Shopping trips; Dances/Social/Cultural
gatherings; Support groups; Walking groups.

Lebanon

Bohannon Nursing Home Inc
1201 N Alton, Lebanon, IL 62254
(618) 537-4401
Admin Mary Shain.
Licensure Intermediate care. *Beds* ICF 101.
Certified Medicaid.
Owner Proprietary corp.

Emerald Gardens Health Care
1 Perryman St, Lebanon, IL 62254
(618) 537-6165
Admin Aurelia Reilman.
Licensure Skilled care. *Beds* SNF 120.

Lebanon Manor
221 E 3rd, Lebanon, IL 62254
(618) 537-4404
Admin Earleen Cashill.
Licensure Intermediate care for mentally
retarded. *Beds* ICF/MR 15.

Lemont

Alvernia Manor
1598 Main St, Lemont, IL 60439
(708) 257-7721
Admin Sr M Kathleen Vugrinovich.

Medical Dir Sr M Josephine Tominac.
Licensure Sheltered care; Retirement. *Beds* Sheltered care 56.
Owner Privately owned.
Admissions Requirements Minimum age 65; Medical examination.
Staff RNs 2 (pt); LPNs 1 (ft), 1 (pt); Activities coordinators 1 (ft); Dietitians 1 (pt).
Languages Polish, Slavic, Spanish, German.
Affiliation Roman Catholic.
Facilities Dining room; Activities room; Chapel; Crafts room; Laundry room; Barber/Beauty shop; Library; Lounge; Auditorium; Solarium.
Activities Arts & crafts; Cards; Games; Reading groups; Prayer groups; Movies; Shopping trips; Dances/Social/Cultural gatherings.

Holy Family Villa
123rd St & Father Linkus Dr, Lemont, IL 60439
(708) 257-2291
Admin Sr Genevieve Kripas. *Dir of Nursing* Sr Stella Stanevich. *Medical Dir* Dr Stanley Palutsis.
Licensure Intermediate care. *Beds* ICF 99. *Certified* Medicaid.
Owner Nonprofit corp.
Admissions Requirements Minimum age 65; Medical examination.
Staff Physicians; RNs; LPNs; Nurses' aides; Physical therapists (consultant); Recreational therapists; Speech therapists (consultant); Activities coordinators; Dietitians (consultant); Ophthalmologists; Podiatrists; Audiologists (consultant).
Languages Lithuanian.
Affiliation Roman Catholic.
Facilities Dining room; Activities room; Chapel; Crafts room; Laundry room; Barber/Beauty shop; Library.
Activities Arts & crafts; Cards; Games; Reading groups; Prayer groups; Movies; Shopping trips; Dances/Social/Cultural gatherings; Intergenerational programs; Pet therapy.

Mother Theresa Home
1270 Franciscan Dr, Lemont, IL 60439
(708) 257-5801
Admin Charles Killion. *Dir of Nursing* Maureen Derkacz. *Medical Dir* Dr Bruce Corwin.
Licensure Skilled care; Intermediate care; Sheltered care; Retirement. *Beds* SNF 60; ICF 60; Sheltered care 30. *Private Pay Patients* 80%. *Certified* Medicaid.
Owner Nonprofit corp (Franciscan Sisters).
Admissions Requirements Minimum age 65; Medical examination; Physician's request.
Staff Physicians 1 (pt); RNs 6 (ft), 1 (pt); LPNs 3 (ft), 1 (pt); Nurses' aides 26 (ft), 4 (pt); Recreational therapists 1 (ft); Podiatrists 1 (pt).
Languages Polish.
Affiliation Franciscan Sisters of Chicago.
Facilities Dining room; Activities room; Chapel; Laundry room; Barber/Beauty shop; Library.
Activities Arts & crafts; Cards; Games; Reading groups; Prayer groups; Movies; Shopping trips; Dances/Social/Cultural gatherings; Intergenerational programs; Pet therapy.

Lena

Lena Continental Manor Nursing Home Inc
1010 S Logan, Lena, IL 61048
(815) 369-4561
Admin Lynn M Lyvers. *Dir of Nursing* Norma Streeb.
Licensure Intermediate care; Retirement. *Beds* ICF 92; Retirement 32. *Private Pay Patients* 71%. *Certified* Medicaid.
Owner Proprietary corp.

Admissions Requirements Minimum age Geriatric; Medical examination.
Staff RNs; LPNs; Nurses' aides; Physical therapists; Activities coordinators; Dietitians.
Facilities Dining room; Physical therapy room; Activities room; Crafts room; Laundry room; Barber/Beauty shop.
Activities Arts & crafts; Cards; Games; Reading groups; Prayer groups; Movies; Dances/Social/Cultural gatherings; Pet therapy.

Lewistown

Broadway Arms Community Living Center
1003 N Broadway, Lewistown, IL 61542
(309) 686-3310
Admin Gail Leiby.
Licensure Intermediate care for mentally retarded. *Beds* ICF/MR 12.
Owner Nonprofit corp.

Clarytona Manor
175 Sycamore Dr, Lewistown, IL 61542
(309) 547-2267
Admin Bonnie Anderson. *Dir of Nursing* Harriet. *Medical Dir* Dr Carlos Almeida.
Licensure Intermediate care; Alzheimer's care. *Beds* ICF 99. *Private Pay Patients* 10%. *Certified* Medicaid.
Owner Proprietary corp (Signature Corp).
Admissions Requirements Medical examination; Physician's request.
Staff RNs; LPNs; Nurses' aides; Physical therapists; Recreational therapists; Speech therapists; Activities coordinators; Dietitians; Podiatrists; Physical therapy aides.
Facilities Dining room; Physical therapy room; Activities room; Crafts room; Laundry room; Barber/Beauty shop.
Activities Arts & crafts; Cards; Games; Reading groups; Prayer groups; Movies; Shopping trips; Dances/Social/Cultural gatherings; Pet therapy; Community integration program.

Lexington

Lexington House
301 S Vine St, Lexington, IL 61753
(309) 365-2541
Admin Jean Dulin. *Dir of Nursing* Jacqueline French. *Medical Dir* M D Patel MD.
Licensure Intermediate care. *Beds* ICF 52. *Private Pay Patients* 6%. *Certified* Medicaid.
Owner Proprietary corp (National Heritage).
Admissions Requirements Medical examination; Physician's request.
Staff Physicians 1 (pt); RNs 1 (pt); LPNs 3 (ft), 3 (pt); Nurses' aides 9 (ft), 4 (pt); Physical therapists 1 (ft), 1 (pt); Occupational therapists 1 (ft), 1 (pt); Activities coordinators 1 (ft); Dietitians 1 (pt); Ophthalmologists 1 (pt); Podiatrists 1 (pt); Dentists 1 (pt).
Facilities Dining room; Activities room; Laundry room; Barber/Beauty shop.
Activities Arts & crafts; Games; Movies; Shopping trips.

Libertyville

Americana Healthcare Center of Libertyville
1500 S Milwaukee Ave, Libertyville, IL 60048
(708) 816-3200
Admin David K Carmichael. *Dir of Nursing* Donna Graves RN. *Medical Dir* Charles Colodny MD.
Licensure Skilled care; Sheltered care. *Beds* SNF 120; Sheltered care 30. *Certified* Medicaid; Medicare.
Owner Proprietary corp (Manor Care).
Admissions Requirements Medical examination; Physician's request.

Staff RNs; LPNs; Nurses' aides; Physical therapists; Recreational therapists; Occupational therapists; Speech therapists; Activities coordinators; Dietitians.
Facilities Dining room; Physical therapy room; Activities room; Laundry room; Barber/Beauty shop; Library.
Activities Arts & crafts; Cards; Games; Reading groups; Prayer groups; Movies; Shopping trips; Dances/Social/Cultural gatherings; Intergenerational programs.

Lambs Inc
PO Box 520, Libertyville, IL 60048
(708) 362-4636
Admin Jacqueline M Cohen.
Licensure Intermediate care for mentally retarded. *Beds* ICF/MR 40.
Owner Nonprofit corp.

Libertyville Manor Extended Care Facility
610 Peterson Rd, Libertyville, IL 60048
(708) 367-6100
Admin Slavko Stokovich. *Dir of Nursing* Brenda Dahl. *Medical Dir* Dr Antonio Chua Lee.
Licensure Skilled care; Intermediate care; Assisted living. *Beds* Swing beds SNF/ICF 174; Assisted living 60. *Certified* Medicaid; Medicare.
Owner Proprietary corp.
Admissions Requirements Medical examination.
Staff Physicians 6 (pt); RNs 8 (ft), 4 (pt); LPNs 1 (ft), 2 (pt); Nurses' aides 28 (ft), 8 (pt); Physical therapists 1 (pt); Recreational therapists 3 (ft); Occupational therapists 1 (pt); Speech therapists 1 (pt); Dietitians 1 (pt); Podiatrists 1 (pt); Dentists 1 (pt).
Facilities Dining room; Physical therapy room; Activities room; Crafts room; Laundry room; Barber/Beauty shop; Library.
Activities Arts & crafts; Cards; Games; Reading groups; Prayer groups; Movies; Shopping trips; Dances/Social/Cultural gatherings; Intergenerational programs; Pet therapy.

Winchester House
1125 N Milwaukee Ave, Libertyville, IL 60048
(708) 362-4340
Admin Robert H Roiland. *Dir of Nursing* Diane Schultz RN. *Medical Dir* Dr Louis Planas.
Licensure Skilled care; Intermediate care; Alzheimer's care. *Beds* SNF 359. *Private Pay Patients* 20%. *Certified* Medicaid; Medicare.
Owner Publicly owned.
Admissions Requirements Minimum age 18 (must be Lake County resident).
Staff RNs 30 (ft); LPNs 13 (ft); Nurses' aides 146 (ft); Physical therapists 1 (pt); Recreational therapists 1 (ft); Occupational therapists 1 (ft); Speech therapists 1 (pt); Activities coordinators 1 (ft); Dietitians 2 (ft).
Facilities Dining room; Physical therapy room; Activities room; Chapel; Crafts room; Laundry room; Barber/Beauty shop; Library.
Activities Arts & crafts; Cards; Games; Reading groups; Prayer groups; Movies; Shopping trips; Dances/Social/Cultural gatherings.

Lincoln

Christian Nursing Home Inc
1507 7th St, Lincoln, IL 62656
(217) 732-2189
Admin Timothy E Searby.
Licensure Skilled care. *Beds* SNF 99. *Certified* Medicaid.
Owner Nonprofit corp (Christian Homes).

Lawrence Place
715 S Washington St, Lincoln, IL 62656
(217) 732-3625

Admin J Michael Bibo.
Licensure Intermediate care for mentally retarded. Beds ICF/MR 15.

Lincoln House
510 S Kickapoo, Lincoln, IL 62656
(217) 732-1131
Admin Judy K Busing.
Licensure Intermediate care for mentally retarded. Beds ICF/MR 15.

Lincoln Land Nursing Home
2202 N Kickapoo St, Lincoln, IL 62656
(217) 735-1538
Admin Mabel M Myrick.
Licensure Skilled care; Intermediate care. Beds SNF 59; ICF 25. Certified Medicaid.
Owner Proprietary corp.

North Kickapoo
1903 N Kickapoo, Lincoln, IL 62656
(217) 735-5333
Admin Kim B Jacobus.
Licensure Intermediate care for mentally retarded. Beds ICF/MR 15.

Sainte Clara's Manor
200 5th, Lincoln, IL 62656
(217) 735-1507
Admin George E Davis. Dir of Nursing Mary Jane O'Donnell. Medical Dir Dean A Hauter.
Licensure Skilled care; Intermediate care. Beds SNF 70; ICF 70. Certified Medicaid.
Owner Nonprofit corp.
Admissions Requirements Minimum age 60; Physician's request.
Staff RNs 9 (ft); LPNs 12 (ft); Nurses' aides 50 (ft); Physical therapists 1 (pt); Recreational therapists 3 (ft); Speech therapists 1 (pt); Activities coordinators 3 (ft); Dietitians 1 (pt).
Facilities Dining room; Physical therapy room; Activities room; Chapel; Crafts room; Laundry room; Barber/Beauty shop.
Activities Arts & crafts; Cards; Games; Reading groups; Prayer groups; Movies; Shopping trips; Dances/Social/Cultural gatherings.

Sunshine Meadow Care Center
1800 5th St, Lincoln, IL 62656
(217) 735-5436
Admin Duane J Warren. Dir of Nursing Sharon Tumilty. Medical Dir Gilbert Ghearing.
Licensure Intermediate care. Beds ICF 61.
Private Pay Patients 25%. Certified Medicaid.
Owner Proprietary corp (National Heritage).
Admissions Requirements Physician's request.
Staff RNs 2 (ft); LPNs 6 (ft); Nurses' aides 16 (ft); Activities coordinators 1 (ft).
Facilities Dining room; Activities room; Crafts room; Laundry room; Barber/Beauty shop.
Activities Arts & crafts; Cards; Games; Reading groups; Movies; Shopping trips; Intergenerational programs.

Lincolnshire

Riverside Foundation
14588 W Hwy 22, Lincolnshire, IL 60069
(708) 634-3973, 634-0227 FAX
Admin Patricia T Weisser.
Licensure Intermediate care for mentally retarded. Beds ICF/MR 99. Certified Medicaid.
Owner Nonprofit corp.
Admissions Requirements Minimum age 18.
Staff Physicians 2 (pt); RNs 3 (ft), 3 (pt); LPNs 2 (ft), 8 (pt); Nurses' aides 45 (ft); Physical therapists 1 (pt); Recreational therapists 1 (ft); Occupational therapists 1 (pt); Speech therapists 2 (pt); Activities coordinators 1 (pt); Dietitians 1 (pt); Other staff 30 (ft).

Facilities Dining room; Physical therapy room; Activities room; Crafts room; Laundry room.
Activities Arts & crafts; Movies; Shopping trips; Active treatment, individual education programs for developmentally disabled adults.

Lindenhurst

Victory Lakes Convalescent Care Center
1055 E Grand Ave, Lindenhurst, IL 60046
(708) 356-5900
Admin Mary E Riggs.
Licensure Skilled care. Beds SNF 120.

Lisle

Snow Valley Living Center
5000 Lincoln, Lisle, IL 60517
(708) 852-5100
Admin Mary Anne Coburn. Dir of Nursing Kathy Ross. Medical Dir Dr Paul Bicek.
Licensure Skilled care; Intermediate care; Alzheimer's care. Beds SNF 51.
Owner Nonprofit corp.
Admissions Requirements Minimum age 18.
Staff RNs 10 (pt); LPNs 1 (ft); Nurses' aides 10 (ft), 9 (pt); Activities coordinators 1 (pt); Podiatrists 1 (pt).
Affiliation Seventh-Day Adventist.
Facilities Dining room; Activities room; Barber/Beauty shop.
Activities Arts & crafts; Cards; Games; Prayer groups; Movies; Dances/Social/Cultural gatherings; Pet therapy.

Litchfield

Care Inn Convalescent Center of Litchfield
1285 E Union St, Litchfield, IL 62056
(217) 324-3996
Admin Nicholas E Wineburner.
Medical Dir J J Epplin MD.
Licensure Skilled care; Intermediate care. Beds SNF 26; ICF 97. Certified Medicaid; Medicare.
Owner Proprietary corp (ARA Living Centers).
Admissions Requirements Minimum age 18; Physician's request.
Staff RNs 4 (ft); LPNs 8 (ft); Nurses' aides 31 (ft); Physical therapists 1 (ft); Recreational therapists 1 (ft); Occupational therapists 1 (ft); Speech therapists 1 (pt); Activities coordinators 1 (ft); Dietitians 1 (ft); Dentists 1 (pt).
Facilities Dining room; Physical therapy room; Activities room; Chapel; Crafts room; Laundry room; Barber/Beauty shop; Library.
Activities Arts & crafts; Cards; Games; Reading groups; Prayer groups; Movies; Shopping trips; Dances/Social/Cultural gatherings.

Country Care of Litchfield
628 S Illinois St, Litchfield, IL 62056
(217) 324-2153
Admin Margery A Oblinger.
Medical Dir Dr Rudolph Sommers.
Licensure Skilled care; Retirement. Beds SNF 102. Certified Medicaid; Medicare.
Owner Privately owned.
Admissions Requirements Medical examination.
Staff RNs; LPNs; Nurses' aides; Physical therapists; Recreational therapists; Occupational therapists; Speech therapists; Activities coordinators; Dietitians; Podiatrists.
Affiliation Baptist.
Facilities Dining room; Physical therapy room; Activities room; Chapel; Crafts room; Laundry room; Barber/Beauty shop; Library.

Activities Arts & crafts; Cards; Games; Reading groups; Prayer groups; Movies; Shopping trips; Dances/Social/Cultural gatherings.

Litchfield Terrace Ltd
1024 E Tyler, Litchfield, IL 62056
(217) 324-3842
Admin Judith Hickerson.
Medical Dir Dr R Somner.
Licensure Intermediate care. Beds ICF 65. Certified Medicaid.
Owner Proprietary corp.
Admissions Requirements Minimum age 18.
Staff RNs 1 (pt); LPNs 6 (ft); Nurses' aides 20 (ft), 2 (pt); Physical therapists 1 (ft); Reality therapists 1 (ft); Recreational therapists 1 (ft); Speech therapists 1 (pt); Activities coordinators 1 (ft); Dietitians 1 (pt); Ophthalmologists 1 (pt); Podiatrists 1 (pt); Audiologists 1 (pt); Dentists 1 (pt).
Facilities Dining room; Physical therapy room; Activities room; Chapel; Crafts room; Laundry room; Barber/Beauty shop.
Activities Arts & crafts; Cards; Games; Reading groups; Prayer groups; Movies; Shopping trips; Dances/Social/Cultural gatherings.

Lombard

Beacon Hill
2400 S Finley Rd, Lombard, IL 60148
(708) 620-5850
Admin Dale Lilburn.
Licensure Skilled care; Alzheimer's care; Retirement. Beds SNF 45. Certified Medicare.
Owner Nonprofit organization/foundation (Life Care Services Corp).
Admissions Requirements Physician's request.
Staff RNs 3 (ft), 2 (pt); LPNs 5 (ft), 2 (pt); Nurses' aides 14 (ft); Recreational therapists 1 (ft); Activities coordinators 1 (ft); Dietitians 1 (ft).
Facilities Dining room; Physical therapy room; Activities room; Crafts room; Barber/Beauty shop; Library.
Activities Arts & crafts; Cards; Games; Reading groups; Prayer groups; Movies; Shopping trips; Dances/Social/Cultural gatherings; Travelogs.

Lexington Health Care Center
2100 S Finley Rd, Lombard, IL 60148
(708) 495-4000
Admin James Samatas.
Licensure Skilled care; Intermediate care. Beds SNF 175; ICF 40.

Ray Graham Lombard Community Living Facility
143 E Grove, Lombard, IL 60148
(708) 543-2440
Admin Dennis Bonner.
Licensure Intermediate care for mentally retarded. Beds ICF/MR 18.
Owner Nonprofit corp.

Long Grove

Maple Hill Nursing Home Ltd
RFD, Box 2308, Hicks Rd, Long Grove, IL 60047
(708) 438-8275
Admin Lucille Devaux.
Medical Dir Bijan Farah MD.
Licensure Skilled care; Intermediate care. Beds SNF 61; ICF 93. Certified Medicaid.
Owner Proprietary corp.
Staff Physicians 8 (pt); RNs 7 (ft), 4 (pt); LPNs 1 (ft), 3 (pt); Nurses' aides 3 (ft); Physical therapists 1 (pt); Recreational therapists 4 (ft); Occupational therapists 1 (pt); Dietitians 1 (ft), 1 (pt); Podiatrists 1 (pt); Dentists 1 (pt).

Facilities Dining room; Physical therapy
room; Activities room; Chapel; Crafts room;
Laundry room; Barber/Beauty room; Library.
Activities Arts & crafts; Cards; Games;
Reading groups; Prayer groups; Movies;
Shopping trips; Dances/Social/Cultural
gatherings.

Louisville

Chestnut Corner Sheltered Care
905 W Chestnut St, Louisville, IL 62858
(618) 665-4085
Admin Linda Kincaid.
Licensure Sheltered care. *Beds* Sheltered care
60.
Owner Proprietary corp.

Country Manor
RR 4, Box 195, Louisville, IL 62858
(618) 686-4542
Admin Carolyn M Frazier.
Licensure Intermediate care for mentally
retarded. *Beds* ICF/MR 15.
Owner Proprietary corp.

Loves Park

Fountain Terrace
6131 Park Ridge Rd, Loves Park, IL 61111
(815) 633-6810
Admin Christopher D Alexander.
Licensure Intermediate care. *Beds* ICF 54.

Lovington

Moultrie County Community Center
PO Box 135, 240 E State, Lovington, IL
61937
(217) 873-5266
Admin H Douglas Henry.
Licensure Intermediate care for mentally
retarded. *Beds* ICF/MR 15. *Certified*
Medicaid.
Owner Proprietary corp.
Admissions Requirements Minimum age 18;
Physician's request.
Staff Physicians 1 (pt); RNs 1 (pt); Nurses'
aides 2 (ft), 10 (pt); Occupational therapists
1 (pt); Speech therapists 1 (pt); Podiatrists 1
(pt).
Facilities Dining room; Activities room;
Crafts room; Laundry room.
Activities Arts & crafts; Cards; Games; Prayer
groups; Movies; Shopping trips; Dances/
Social/Cultural gatherings; Family visits;
Exercise programs.

Macomb

Elms
1212 Madelyn Ave, Macomb, IL 61455
(309) 837-5482
Admin Cherles Kneedy. *Dir of Nursing* Jean
Huff RN. *Medical Dir* David Reem MD.
Licensure Skilled care. *Beds* SNF 98. *Certified*
Medicaid; Medicare.
Owner Publicly owned.
Admissions Requirements Minimum age 18;
Medical examination; Physician's request.
Facilities Dining room; Physical therapy
room; Activities room; Crafts room; Laundry
room; Barber/Beauty shop; Library.
Activities Arts & crafts; Cards; Games;
Reading groups; Prayer groups; Movies;
Dances/Social/Cultural gatherings.

Macomb Nursing & Rehabilitation Center
8 Doctor's Ln, Macomb, IL 61455
(309) 833-5555
Admin Marcia Moulden. *Dir of Nursing* Kay
McCance. *Medical Dir* Dr Rodger Lefler.
Licensure Skilled care. *Beds* SNF 58. *Certified*
Medicaid; Medicare.
Owner Proprietary corp (Healthcare &
Retirement Corp).

Admissions Requirements Medical
examination; Physician's request.
Staff RNs; LPNs; Nurses' aides; Physical
therapists; Recreational therapists;
Occupational therapists; Speech therapists;
Activities coordinators; Dietitians;
Podiatrists.
Facilities Dining room; Physical therapy
room; Activities room; Crafts room; Laundry
room; Barber/Beauty shop; Library.
Activities Arts & crafts; Cards; Games;
Reading groups; Prayer groups; Movies;
Shopping trips; Intergenerational programs;
Pet therapy.

Sprucewood Health Care Center
S Johnson & W Grant Sts, Macomb, IL 61455
(309) 837-2386
Admin Karen J Oaks.
Licensure Intermediate care. *Beds* ICF 65.
Certified Medicaid.
Owner Proprietary corp.

Wesley Village U M C Health Care Center
1200 E Grant St, Macomb, IL 61455
(309) 833-2123
Admin David Pease.
Licensure Intermediate care; Sheltered care.
Beds ICF 48; Sheltered care 10.
Owner Nonprofit corp.
Affiliation Methodist.

Macon

Eastern Star Home
PO Box 516, Macon, IL 62544
(217) 764-3348
Admin Mardell K Taft.
Medical Dir Dr Robert Atz.
Licensure Intermediate care; Sheltered care.
Beds ICF 52; Sheltered care 34.
Owner Nonprofit corp.
Admissions Requirements Minimum age 62;
Medical examination.
Staff Physicians 1 (pt); RNs 1 (ft); LPNs 6
(ft); Nurses' aides 22 (ft); Physical therapists
1 (pt); Reality therapists 1 (pt); Recreational
therapists 1 (pt); Occupational therapists 1
(pt); Activities coordinators 2 (ft); Dietitians
1 (pt).
Affiliation Order of Eastern Star.
Facilities Dining room; Physical therapy
room; Activities room; Chapel; Crafts room;
Laundry room; Barber/Beauty shop.
Activities Arts & crafts; Cards; Games;
Reading groups; Prayer groups; Movies;
Shopping trips; Dances/Social/Cultural
gatherings.

Marengo

Florence Nursing Home
546 E Grant Hwy, Marengo, IL 60152
(815) 568-8322
Admin Alice L Aumiller. *Dir of Nursing*
JoAnn Wilde RN. *Medical Dir* Charles J
Lockwood MD.
Licensure Intermediate care; Retirement. *Beds*
ICF 49. *Private Pay Patients* 100%.
Owner Privately owned.
Admissions Requirements Minimum age 22;
Medical examination.
Facilities Dining room; Activities room;
Crafts room; Laundry room; Barber/Beauty
shop.
Activities Arts & crafts; Cards; Games;
Reading groups; Prayer groups; Movies;
Shopping trips; Dances/Social/Cultural
gatherings; Intergenerational programs; Pet
therapy.

Marion

Fountains Nursing Home
1301 E DeYoung St, Marion, IL 62959
(618) 997-1365
Admin Joan W Baugher.

Medical Dir Elizabeth Brymer LPM.
Licensure Intermediate care. *Beds* ICF 68.
Certified Medicaid.
Owner Proprietary corp.
Admissions Requirements Medical
examination; Physician's request.
Staff Physicians 1 (pt); RNs 1 (pt); LPNs 4
(ft), 1 (pt); Nurses' aides 19 (ft), 2 (pt);
Recreational therapists 1 (pt); Occupational
therapists 1 (pt); Speech therapists 1 (pt);
Activities coordinators 1 (pt); Dietitians 1
(pt).
Facilities Dining room; Activities room;
Laundry room; Barber/Beauty shop.
Activities Arts & crafts; Cards; Games;
Reading groups; Prayer groups; Movies;
Shopping trips; Dances/Social/Cultural
gatherings.

Friendship Care Center
1101 N Madison St, Marion, IL 62959
(618) 993-8650
Admin Eileene C Norman.
Medical Dir Geneva Bloodworth.
Licensure Intermediate care. *Beds* ICF 57.
Certified Medicaid.
Owner Proprietary corp.
Admissions Requirements Medical
examination; Physician's request.
Staff Physicians; RNs; LPNs; Nurses' aides;
Physical therapists; Recreational therapists;
Speech therapists; Dietitians.
Facilities Dining room; Laundry room;
Barber/Beauty shop.
Activities Arts & crafts; Cards; Games;
Reading groups; Prayer groups; Movies;
Shopping trips.

Liberty House
1304 W 4th Ave, Marion, IL 62959
(618) 997-9336
Admin Stephen R Brown. *Dir of Nursing*
Mary Jane Jones. *Medical Dir* Douglas Sims
MD.
Licensure Intermediate care for mentally
retarded. *Beds* ICF/MR 15. *Private Pay
Patients* 0%. *Certified* Medicaid.
Owner Privately owned.
Admissions Requirements Minimum age 18;
Medical examination.
Staff Nurses' aides 5 (ft), 2 (pt); Recreational
therapists 1 (ft).
Facilities Dining room; Activities room.
Activities Arts & crafts; Cards; Games;
Reading groups; Prayer groups; Movies;
Shopping trips; Dances/Social/Cultural
gatherings.

Marseilles

Rivershores Living Center
578 Commercial St, Marseilles, IL 61351
(815) 795-5121
Admin Eric J Wrangell. *Dir of Nursing* Susan
N Norsen RN. *Medical Dir* Don E
Morehead MD.
Licensure Skilled care. *Beds* SNF 99. *Certified*
Medicaid; Medicare.
Owner Nonprofit corp (Adventist Health Sys-
USA).
Admissions Requirements Minimum age 18;
Medical examination; Physician's request.
Staff Physicians 2 (pt); RNs 5 (ft), 3 (pt);
LPNs 1 (ft), 4 (pt); Nurses' aides 24 (ft), 13
(pt); Physical therapists 1 (pt); Recreational
therapists 1 (pt); Occupational therapists 1
(pt); Speech therapists 1 (pt); Activities
coordinators 1 (ft); Dietitians 1 (pt);
Ophthalmologists 1 (pt).
Languages Sign.
Affiliation Seventh-Day Adventist.
Facilities Dining room; Physical therapy
room; Activities room; Chapel; Laundry
room; Barber/Beauty shop; Lift van; TV
room; Patient lounge.

Activities Arts & crafts; Cards; Games; Reading groups; Prayer groups; Movies; Shopping trips; Dances/Social/Cultural gatherings; Outside entertainers; Demonstrations; Music therapy; Sing-alongs; Guessing games.

Marshall

Burnsides Nursing Home
410 N 2nd St, Marshall, IL 62441
(217) 826-2358
Admin Jackie L Williams. *Dir of Nursing* Mary Turner. *Medical Dir* Steven Macke.
Licensure Skilled care; Retirement. *Beds* SNF 109; Retirement apts 8. *Private Pay Patients* 50%. *Certified* Medicaid; Medicare.
Owner Nonprofit organization/foundation.
Admissions Requirements Minimum age 18; Medical examination.
Staff RNs 5 (ft), 2 (pt); LPNs 14 (ft), 6 (pt); Nurses' aides 30 (ft), 7 (pt); Physical therapists (consultant); Recreational therapists 2 (ft), 3 (pt); Activities coordinators 1 (ft); Dietitians 1 (ft).
Facilities Dining room; Physical therapy room; Activities room; Chapel; Crafts room; Laundry room; Barber/Beauty shop.
Activities Arts & crafts; Cards; Games; Reading groups; Prayer groups; Movies; Shopping trips; Dances/Social/Cultural gatherings; Intergenerational programs.

Marysville

Elmwood Health Care Center
Rte 159, Interstate 70, Marysville, IL 62062
(708) 742-8822
Admin Nancy G Clark. *Dir of Nursing* Sandra Krug. *Medical Dir* Dr Biedenharn.
Licensure Intermediate care. *Beds* ICF 104. *Certified* Medicaid.
Owner Proprietary corp (Springwood Associates).
Admissions Requirements Minimum age 21; Medical examination; Physician's request.
Staff RNs 1 (ft); LPNs 7 (ft), 2 (pt); Nurses' aides 20 (ft), 2 (pt); Physical therapists 1 (pt); Occupational therapists 1 (pt); Speech therapists 1 (pt); Activities coordinators 1 (ft); Dietitians 1 (pt).
Facilities Dining room; Activities room; Chapel; Laundry room; Barber/Beauty shop.
Activities Arts & crafts; Cards; Games; Reading groups; Prayer groups; Movies; Shopping trips; Dances/Social/Cultural gatherings.

Mascoutah

Grange Nursing Home
901 N 10th St, Mascoutah, IL 62258
(618) 566-2183
Admin Alice A Langstraat.
Medical Dir Paul Biedenharn MD.
Licensure Intermediate care. *Beds* ICF 54. *Certified* Medicaid.
Owner Nonprofit corp.
Admissions Requirements Minimum age 18.
Staff RNs 1 (ft), 1 (pt); LPNs 3 (ft), 2 (pt); Nurses' aides 12 (ft), 3 (pt); Activities coordinators 1 (ft).
Facilities Dining room; Physical therapy room; Laundry room.
Activities Arts & crafts; Cards; Games; Movies; Dances/Social/Cultural gatherings.

Mar-Ka Nursing Home
201 S 10th St, Mascoutah, IL 62258
(618) 566-8000, 566-4631 FAX
Admin Julie Savage. *Dir of Nursing* Jenny Andres RN. *Medical Dir* Larry Leone MD.
Licensure Skilled care; Intermediate care. *Beds* SNF 23; ICF 53. *Private Pay Patients* 48%. *Certified* Medicaid; Medicare.

Owner Proprietary corp (Community Care Centers).
Admissions Requirements Minimum age 18.
Staff RNs 3 (ft); LPNs 4 (ft); Nurses' aides 26 (ft); Physical therapists (consultant); Reality therapists (consultant); Recreational therapists (consultant); Occupational therapists (consultant); Speech therapists (consultant); Activities coordinators 1 (ft); Dietitians 1 (ft).
Facilities Dining room; Physical therapy room; Activities room; Chapel; Crafts room; Laundry room; Barber/Beauty shop; Library.
Activities Arts & crafts; Cards; Games; Reading groups; Prayer groups; Movies; Shopping trips; Dances/Social/Cultural gatherings; Intergenerational programs.

West Main Nursing Home
1244 W Main St, Mascoutah, IL 62258
(618) 566-7327
Admin Mary Keenan. *Dir of Nursing* Theresa Poole. *Medical Dir* Galloway MD.
Licensure Intermediate care. *Beds* ICF 34. *Certified* Medicare.
Owner Proprietary corp (Community Care Centers).
Admissions Requirements Minimum age 18; Medical examination.
Staff Physicians 1 (pt); RNs 2 (ft); LPNs 4 (ft), 1 (pt); Nurses' aides 5 (ft), 2 (pt); Physical therapists 1 (pt); Recreational therapists 1 (ft), 1 (pt); Occupational therapists 1 (pt); Dietitians 1 (pt).
Facilities Dining room; Activities room; Crafts room; Laundry room; Barber/Beauty shop.
Activities Arts & crafts; Cards; Games; Reading groups; Prayer groups; Movies; Shopping trips; Dances/Social/Cultural gatherings.

Mason City

Mason City Area Nursing Home
520 N Price St, Mason City, IL 62664
(217) 482-5022
Admin Joyce Conrady. *Dir of Nursing* Marilyn Blakeley. *Medical Dir* Dr Jack Means; Dr Gilbert Ghearing.
Licensure Skilled care; Intermediate care; Sheltered care; Retirement. *Beds* SNF 17; ICF 49; Sheltered care 33; Retirement 17. *Private Pay Patients* 74%. *Certified* Medicaid; Medicare.
Owner Nonprofit organization/foundation.
Admissions Requirements Medical examination.
Facilities Dining room; Physical therapy room; Activities room; Chapel; Crafts room; Laundry room; Barber/Beauty shop; Library.
Activities Arts & crafts; Cards; Games; Movies; Dances/Social/Cultural gatherings; Intergenerational programs; Pet therapy.

Matteson

Applewood Living Center
21020 S Kostner Ave, Matteson, IL 60443
(708) 747-1300
Admin Steven Bakken. *Dir of Nursing* Louise Biltgen RN. *Medical Dir* E G Wygant MD.
Licensure Skilled care. *Beds* SNF 105.
Owner Nonprofit corp (Adventist Health Sys-USA).
Admissions Requirements Medical examination.
Staff RNs; LPNs; Nurses' aides; Activities coordinators.
Affiliation Seventh-Day Adventist.
Facilities Dining room; Physical therapy room; Activities room; Crafts room; Laundry room; Barber/Beauty shop.
Activities Arts & crafts; Cards; Games; Reading groups; Prayer groups; Movies; Shopping trips; Dances/Social/Cultural gatherings.

Mattoon

Convalescent Care Center of Mattoon
PO Box 209, 1000 Palm, Mattoon, IL 61938
(217) 234-7403, 258-6642 FAX
Admin Kathy M Baird. *Dir of Nursing* Carol Arnold. *Medical Dir* Wilfred Brunswick MD.
Licensure Skilled care; Intermediate care. *Beds* SNF 162; ICF 92. *Certified* Medicaid.
Owner Proprietary corp.
Staff RNs 4 (ft), 2 (pt); LPNs 14 (ft); Nurses' aides 34 (ft); Speech therapists (contracted); Activities coordinators 1 (ft); Dietitians (contracted); Physical therapy aides 1 (ft); Occupational therapy aides 1 (ft).
Facilities Dining room; Physical therapy room; Activities room; Chapel; Crafts room; Laundry room; Barber/Beauty shop; Library.
Activities Arts & crafts; Cards; Games; Reading groups; Prayer groups; Movies; Shopping trips; Dances/Social/Cultural gatherings.

Douglas Living Center
W Rte 121, Mattoon, IL 61938
(217) 234-6401
Admin Rick Harding. *Dir of Nursing* Roxanne Osborne RN. *Medical Dir* Wilfred Brunsloick MD.
Licensure Skilled care; Retirement. *Beds* SNF 75. *Certified* Medicaid; Medicare.
Owner Nonprofit corp (Adventist Health Sys-USA).
Admissions Requirements Minimum age 18; Medical examination; Physician's request.
Staff RNs 3 (ft); LPNs 4 (ft), 5 (pt); Nurses' aides 22 (ft), 4 (pt); Physical therapists 1 (ft); Activities coordinators 1 (ft); Dietitians 1 (ft).
Affiliation Seventh-Day Adventist.
Facilities Dining room; Physical therapy room; Activities room; Chapel; Crafts room; Laundry room; Barber/Beauty shop.
Activities Arts & crafts; Cards; Games; Reading groups; Prayer groups; Movies; Shopping trips.

Mattoon Health Care Center
2121 S 9th St, Mattoon, IL 61938
(217) 235-7138
Admin Carl D Taniges. *Dir of Nursing* Elizabeth Howard RN. *Medical Dir* L E McNiell MD.
Licensure Skilled care. *Beds* SNF 148. *Certified* Medicaid; Medicare.
Owner Proprietary corp.
Admissions Requirements Medical examination; Physician's request.
Staff RNs 3 (ft); LPNs 10 (ft), 3 (pt); Nurses' aides 30 (ft); Physical therapists 1 (pt); Occupational therapists 1 (pt); Speech therapists 1 (pt); Activities coordinators 2 (ft), 1 (pt); Dietitians 1 (pt); Ophthalmologists 1 (pt); Podiatrists 1 (pt); 1 (ft), 1 (pt).
Facilities Dining room; Physical therapy room; Activities room; Crafts room; Laundry room; Barber/Beauty shop.
Activities Arts & crafts; Cards; Games; Reading groups; Prayer groups; Movies; Shopping trips; Dances/Social/Cultural gatherings.

Odd Fellow-Rebekah Home
201 E Lafayette Ave, Mattoon, IL 61938
(217) 235-5449, 235-5936 FAX
Admin Lualyce C Brown. *Dir of Nursing* Mary Jane Taylor RN. *Medical Dir* Dr Robert F Swengel.
Licensure Skilled care; Intermediate care. *Beds* Swing beds SNF/ICF 120. *Certified* Medicaid.
Owner Nonprofit corp.
Admissions Requirements Minimum age 65; Medical examination; Physician's request.
Staff RNs 5 (ft), 2 (pt); LPNs 9 (ft), 2 (pt); Nurses' aides 40 (ft), 8 (pt); Physical therapists 1 (ft); Occupational therapists 1

(ft); Speech therapists 1 (pt); Activities coordinators 2 (ft), 1 (pt); Dietitians 1 (ft); Social services 2 (ft), 1 (pt); Physical therapy aides 3 (ft).
Affiliation Independent Order of Odd Fellows & Rebekahs.
Facilities Dining room; Physical therapy room; Activities room; Chapel; Crafts room; Laundry room; Barber/Beauty shop; Library.
Activities Arts & crafts; Cards; Games; Reading groups; Prayer groups; Movies; Shopping trips; Dances/Social/Cultural gatherings.

Maywood

Baptist Retirement Home
316 Randolph St, Maywood, IL 60153
(708) 344-1541
Admin Edith Young. *Dir of Nursing* Shirley Triphahn. *Medical Dir* Raymond J McDonald MD.
Licensure Intermediate care; Retirement. *Beds* ICF 69. *Private Pay Patients* 82%. *Certified* Medicaid.
Owner Nonprofit organization/foundation.
Admissions Requirements Medical examination.
Staff Physicians 2 (ft); RNs 3 (ft); LPNs 5 (ft); Nurses' aides 24 (ft); Physical therapists 1 (pt); Reality therapists 1 (pt); Recreational therapists 2 (ft); Occupational therapists 1 (pt); Speech therapists 1 (pt); Activities coordinators 2 (ft); Dietitians 1 (ft); Ophthalmologists 1 (pt); Podiatrists 1 (pt); Audiologists 1 (pt); Dentists 1 (pt).
Affiliation Baptist.
Facilities Dining room; Physical therapy room; Activities room; Chapel; Crafts room; Laundry room; Barber/Beauty shop; Library.
Activities Arts & crafts; Cards; Games; Reading groups; Prayer groups; Movies; Shopping trips; Dances/Social/Cultural gatherings; Intergenerational programs; Pet therapy.

McHenry

Pioneer Center Community Living Facility
4001 Dayton St, McHenry, IL 60050
(815) 338-5584
Admin C Meschine. *Dir of Nursing* Carol Neff RN.
Licensure Community living facility. *Beds* Community living facility 20.
Owner Nonprofit corp.
Admissions Requirements Minimum age 18; Medical examination.
Staff RNs 1 (pt); Activities coordinators 1 (pt); 1 (pt).
Facilities Dining room; Laundry room.
Activities Arts & crafts; Cards; Games; Reading groups; Movies; Shopping trips; Dances/Social/Cultural gatherings; Community & special recreational events/ activities.

Royal Terrace Health Care Center
803 Royal Dr, McHenry, IL 60050
(815) 344-2600, 344-8418 FAX
Admin Haim Perlstein. *Dir of Nursing* Ellen Boulnois. *Medical Dir* James Skopec MD.
Licensure Skilled care. *Beds* SNF 316. *Private Pay Patients* 25%. *Certified* Medicaid; Medicare.
Owner Privately owned.
Admissions Requirements Minimum age 18; Medical examination; Physician's request.
Staff RNs; LPNs; Nurses' aides; Physical therapists; Reality therapists; Recreational therapists; Occupational therapists; Speech therapists; Activities coordinators; Dietitians.
Languages Spanish, Polish.

Facilities Dining room; Physical therapy room; Activities room; Chapel; Crafts room; Laundry room; Barber/Beauty shop; Library; Greenhouse; Fitness trails both outside & inside.
Activities Arts & crafts; Cards; Games; Reading groups; Prayer groups; Movies; Shopping trips; Dances/Social/Cultural gatherings; Intergenerational programs; Pet therapy.

McLeansboro

Hamilton Memorial Nursing Center
S Marshall Ave, McLeansboro, IL 62859
(618) 643-2325
Admin Michael C Karcher. *Dir of Nursing* Mary Mauser RN.
Licensure Intermediate care. *Beds* ICF 60. *Private Pay Patients* 50%. *Certified* Medicaid.
Owner Publicly owned.
Facilities Dining room; Physical therapy room; Activities room; Laundry room; Barber/Beauty shop.
Activities Arts & crafts; Cards; Games; Reading groups; Prayer groups; Shopping trips.

Lifecare Center of McLeansboro Inc
PO Box 70, 405 W Carpenter, McLeansboro, IL 62859
(618) 643-3728
Admin Troy E Callahan. *Dir of Nursing* Vickie Hughes RN. *Medical Dir* I A Tomaneng MD.
Licensure Intermediate care. *Beds* ICF 43. *Private Pay Patients* 10%. *Certified* Medicaid.
Owner Proprietary corp (Community Lifecare Enterprises).
Admissions Requirements Medical examination.
Staff RNs 2 (ft); LPNs 5 (ft), 1 (pt); Nurses' aides 15 (ft), 5 (pt); Physical therapists 1 (pt); Dietitians 1 (pt).
Facilities Dining room; Physical therapy room; Activities room; Crafts room; Laundry room; Barber/Beauty shop.
Activities Arts & crafts; Cards; Games; Reading groups; Prayer groups; Movies; Shopping trips; Dances/Social/Cultural gatherings; Intergenerational programs; Pet therapy.

Meadowbrook Estates
319 N Locust, McLeansboro, IL 62859
(618) 643-2106, 643-3084 FAX
Admin James Bowers.
Licensure Intermediate care for mentally retarded. *Beds* ICF/MR 15. *Certified* Medicare.
Owner Proprietary corp (LaMatt Management).
Admissions Requirements Minimum age 18.
Staff Physical therapists; Occupational therapists; Speech therapists; Dietitians.
Activities Arts & crafts; Cards; Games; Dances/Social/Cultural gatherings; Intergenerational programs.

Mendon

North Adams Home Inc
Rte 2 Box 100, Mendon, IL 62351
(217) 936-2137
Admin John D Bainum. *Dir of Nursing* Donna R Smith RN.
Licensure Intermediate care; Retirement; Alzheimer's care. *Beds* SNF 99. *Certified* Medicaid.
Owner Nonprofit corp.
Admissions Requirements Minimum age Adult; Medical examination.
Staff RNs 1 (ft), 1 (pt); LPNs 5 (ft), 9 (pt); Nurses' aides 14 (ft), 22 (pt); Activities coordinators 1 (ft).

Facilities Dining room; Physical therapy room; Activities room; Chapel; Crafts room; Laundry room; Barber/Beauty shop; Library; Lounge.
Activities Arts & crafts; Cards; Games; Prayer groups; Movies; Dances/Social/Cultural gatherings.

Mendota

Heritage Manor Nursing Home
1201 1st Ave, Mendota, IL 61342
(815) 539-6745
Admin Marilee T Holzner RN. *Dir of Nursing* Marianne Etzbach RN. *Medical Dir* R H Musick MD.
Licensure Skilled care; Intermediate care. *Beds* SNF 50; ICF 49. *Certified* Medicaid; Medicare.
Owner Proprietary corp (Heritage Enterprises).
Admissions Requirements Minimum age 19; Medical examination.
Staff RNs 5 (ft), 4 (pt); LPNs 3 (ft), 2 (pt); Nurses' aides 20 (ft), 10 (pt); Physical therapists 1 (pt); Activities coordinators 1 (ft).
Facilities Dining room; Physical therapy room; Activities room; Crafts room; Laundry room; Barber/Beauty shop; Library.
Activities Arts & crafts; Cards; Games; Reading groups; Prayer groups; Movies; Shopping trips; Dances/Social/Cultural gatherings.

Mendota Lutheran Home
500 6th St, Mendota, IL 61342
(815) 539-7439
Admin Earnest L Serr.
Medical Dir William Schuler MD.
Licensure Intermediate care; Sheltered care. *Beds* ICF 80; Sheltered care 21.
Owner Nonprofit corp.
Admissions Requirements Minimum age 65.
Staff Physicians 1 (pt); RNs 2 (ft), 3 (pt); LPNs 3 (ft), 4 (pt); Nurses' aides 23 (ft), 19 (pt); Activities coordinators 1 (ft).
Affiliation Lutheran.
Facilities Dining room; Activities room; Chapel; Laundry room; Barber/Beauty shop; Library.
Activities Arts & crafts; Cards; Games; Reading groups; Prayer groups; Movies; Dances/Social/Cultural gatherings.

Metamora

Snyder Village Health Center
1200 E Partridge, Metamora, IL 61548
(309) 367-4300
Admin Keith Swartzentruber. *Dir of Nursing* Sherry Mullins RN. *Medical Dir* Dr Ronald Meyer.
Licensure Skilled care; Retirement. *Beds* SNF 60; Retirement 30. *Private Pay Patients* 90%. *Certified* Medicaid; Medicare.
Owner Nonprofit organization/foundation.
Admissions Requirements Medical examination; Physician's request.
Staff RNs 3 (ft), 7 (pt); LPNs 2 (ft), 1 (pt); Nurses' aides 15 (ft), 18 (pt); Physical therapists 1 (pt); Occupational therapists 1 (pt); Speech therapists 1 (pt); Activities coordinators 1 (ft); Dietitians 1 (pt).
Facilities Dining room; Physical therapy room; Activities room; Chapel; Laundry room; Barber/Beauty shop.
Activities Arts & crafts; Cards; Games; Reading groups; Prayer groups; Movies; Shopping trips; Dances/Social/Cultural gatherings; Intergenerational programs; Pet therapy.

Metropolis

Krypton House
PO Box 709, 502 W 8th, Metropolis, IL 62960
(618) 524-8996
Admin Don Pippin. *Dir of Nursing* Paula McIntosh RN QMRP RSO. *Medical Dir* Dr Enrique Yap.
Licensure DD/MR. *Beds* DD/MR 15. *Private Pay Patients* 0%. *Certified* Medicaid.
Owner Privately owned.
Admissions Requirements Minimum age Adult; Medical examination; Physician's request.
Staff Physicians 1 (pt); RNs 1 (ft); Nurses' aides 5 (ft), 1 (pt); Physical therapists (consultant); Speech therapists (consultant); Activities coordinators 1 (ft); Dietitians (consultant); Cooks 1 (ft), 1 (pt); Maintenance 1 (pt); QMRPs 1 (ft).
Facilities Dining room; Activities room; Laundry room; Van.
Activities Arts & crafts; Cards; Games; Reading groups; Movies; Shopping trips; Dances/Social/Cultural gatherings; Work at day program centers; Community activities.

Magnolia Manor Inc
2101 Metropolis St, Metropolis, IL 62960
(618) 524-5677
Admin Michelle Cavitt. *Dir of Nursing* Bernita Hubbard. *Medical Dir* Dr E T Yap.
Licensure Skilled care. *Beds* SNF 88. *Private Pay Patients* 20%. *Certified* Medicaid.
Owner Proprietary corp.
Admissions Requirements Minimum age 18.
Staff Physicians; RNs; LPNs; Nurses' aides; Physical therapists; Speech therapists; Activities coordinators; Dietitians; Podiatrists.
Facilities Dining room; Physical therapy room; Activities room; Laundry room; Barber/Beauty shop.
Activities Arts & crafts; Cards; Games; Reading groups; Prayer groups; Movies; Shopping trips; Dances/Social/Cultural gatherings.

Metropolis Good Samaritan Home
2299 Metropolis St, Metropolis, IL 62960
(618) 524-2634
Admin Ronald D Philips. *Dir of Nursing* Zena Wells. *Medical Dir* Dr Benito Bajuyo.
Licensure Skilled care. *Beds* SNF 85. *Certified* Medicaid.
Owner Nonprofit corp (Evangelical Lutheran/Good Samaritan Society).
Admissions Requirements Medical examination.
Staff RNs 2 (ft), 2 (pt); LPNs 6 (ft), 3 (pt); Nurses' aides 17 (ft), 5 (pt); Activities coordinators 1 (ft).
Affiliation Lutheran.
Facilities Dining room; Physical therapy room; Activities room; Laundry room; Barber/Beauty shop.
Activities Arts & crafts; Cards; Games; Reading groups; Prayer groups; Movies; Shopping trips; Dances/Social/Cultural gatherings.

Southgate Health Care
900 E 9th, Metropolis, IL 62960
(618) 524-2683
Admin Jane Parker. *Dir of Nursing* Pat Wetherington. *Medical Dir* Dr E T Yap.
Licensure Skilled care; Intermediate care; Alzheimer's care. *Beds* SNF 68; ICF 67. *Certified* Medicaid; Medicare; VA.
Owner Privately owned.
Admissions Requirements Minimum age 21.
Staff Physicians 7 (pt); RNs 4 (ft); LPNs 12 (ft); Nurses' aides 36 (ft); Physical therapists 4 (ft), 1 (pt); Activities coordinators 3 (ft), 1 (pt); Dietitians 8 (ft), 1 (pt); Podiatrists 1 (pt).

Facilities Dining room; Physical therapy room; Activities room; Crafts room; Laundry room; Barber/Beauty shop.
Activities Arts & crafts; Cards; Games; Reading groups; Prayer groups; Movies; Shopping trips; Dances/Social/Cultural gatherings; Pet therapy.

Midlothian

Bowman Nursing Home
3249 W 147th St, Midlothian, IL 60445
(708) 389-3141
Admin Earl S Ebers Jr. *Dir of Nursing* Francine J Petrarca RN. *Medical Dir* Sheldon Levine MD.
Licensure Intermediate care; Alzheimer's care. *Beds* ICF 92. *Private Pay Patients* 50%. *Certified* Medicaid.
Owner Privately owned.
Admissions Requirements Minimum age 18; Medical examination.
Staff Physicians; RNs 3 (ft), 2 (pt); LPNs 6 (ft), 6 (pt); Nurses' aides 18 (ft), 16 (pt); Recreational therapists 2 (ft); Speech therapists; Activities coordinators (consultant); Dietitians (consultant); Ophthalmologists; Podiatrists; Audiologists.
Languages Polish.
Facilities Dining room; Activities room; Crafts room; Laundry room; Barber/Beauty shop.
Activities Arts & crafts; Cards; Games; Reading groups; Prayer groups; Movies; Shopping trips; Dances/Social/Cultural gatherings; Intergenerational programs; Pet therapy.

Crestwood Heights Nursing Center
14255 S Cicero Ave, Midlothian, IL 60445
(708) 371-0400
Admin Jeanette Fox.
Licensure Skilled care; Intermediate care. *Beds* SNF 108; ICF 216.

Crestwood Terrace
13301 S Central Ave, Midlothian, IL 60445
(708) 597-5251
Admin Maureen M Skopick.
Medical Dir Dr A Noreiga.
Licensure Intermediate care. *Beds* ICF 126. *Private Pay Patients* 40%. *Certified* Medicaid.
Owner Proprietary corp.
Admissions Requirements Medical examination.
Staff Physicians 1 (ft), 10 (pt); RNs 2 (ft), 2 (pt); LPNs 3 (ft), 6 (pt); Nurses' aides 14 (ft), 10 (pt); Reality therapists 3 (ft); Recreational therapists 3 (ft); Occupational therapists 1 (pt); Speech therapists 1 (pt); Activities coordinators 1 (ft); Dietitians 1 (pt); Ophthalmologists 1 (pt); Podiatrists 1 (pt); Dentists 2 (pt).
Languages Polish, Italian.
Facilities Dining room; Physical therapy room; Activities room; Crafts room; Laundry room; Barber/Beauty shop; Library.
Activities Arts & crafts; Cards; Games; Reading groups; Prayer groups; Movies; Shopping trips; Dances/Social/Cultural gatherings; Pet therapy.

Milan

Comfort Harbor Home
114 W 2nd St, Milan, IL 61264
(309) 787-2066
Admin J Michael Lavery.
Licensure Sheltered care. *Beds* Sheltered care 38.
Owner Proprietary corp.

Millstadt

Mill Haven Care Center
415 Veterans Dr, Millstadt, IL 62260
(618) 476-3575
Admin Dorothy Davis.
Licensure Intermediate care. *Beds* ICF 101. *Certified* Medicaid.
Owner Proprietary corp.

Minonk

Lida Home Nursing Home
201 Locust, Minonk, IL 61760
(309) 432-2557
Admin John C Kirkton.
Licensure Intermediate care. *Beds* ICF 49. *Certified* Medicaid.
Owner Nonprofit corp.

Simater Memorial Home Inc
215 Locust St, Minonk, IL 61760
(309) 432-3087
Admin Mary J Kirkton.
Licensure Sheltered care. *Beds* Sheltered care 23.

Moline

Heritage Fifty-Three
4601 53rd St, Moline, IL 61265
(309) 764-4974
Admin Rick Carlson. *Dir of Nursing* Ruth Morrison.
Licensure Intermediate care for mentally retarded. *Beds* ICF/MR 64. *Certified* Medicaid; Medicare.
Owner Nonprofit corp.
Admissions Requirements Minimum age 18.

Moline Nursing & Rehabilitation Center
833 16th Ave, Moline, IL 61265
(309) 764-6744
Admin Mark L Leafgreen. *Dir of Nursing* Diana Van Wychen. *Medical Dir* Dr Bruce Vesole.
Licensure Skilled care. *Beds* SNF 115. *Private Pay Patients* 60%. *Certified* Medicaid; Medicare.
Owner Proprietary corp (Health Care & Retirement Corp).
Admissions Requirements Medical examination.
Staff Physicians 1 (pt); RNs 4 (ft), 3 (pt); LPNs 8 (ft), 4 (pt); Nurses' aides 30 (ft), 10 (pt); Physical therapists 1 (pt); Occupational therapists 1 (pt); Speech therapists 1 (pt); Activities coordinators 2 (ft), 1 (pt); Dietitians 1 (pt); Podiatrists 1 (pt); Audiologists 1 (pt).
Languages Spanish.
Facilities Dining room; Physical therapy room; Activities room; Barber/Beauty shop.
Activities Arts & crafts; Cards; Games; Reading groups; Prayer groups; Movies; Shopping trips; Dances/Social/Cultural gatherings; Intergenerational programs; Pet therapy.

Rose House
7301 34th Ave, Moline, IL 61265
(309) 796-2949
Admin Connie L Pleinis.
Licensure Intermediate care for mentally retarded. *Beds* ICF/MR 15.

Smith Square
7401 34th Ave, Moline, IL 61265
(309) 796-2676
Admin Connie L Pleinis.
Licensure Intermediate care for mentally retarded. *Beds* ICF/MR 15.

Momence

Momence Meadows Nursing Home
500 S Walnut, Momence, IL 60954
(815) 472-2423, 472-6212 FAX
Admin Kim Bacon. *Dir of Nursing* Leilani
Swick RN. *Medical Dir* Paul L Wolfe MD.
Licensure Skilled care. *Beds* SNF 128. *Private
Pay Patients* 30%. *Certified* Medicaid.
Owner Proprietary corp.
Admissions Requirements Minimum age 21;
Medical examination; Physician's request.
Staff Physicians 1 (ft); RNs 3 (ft); LPNs 9 (ft),
3 (pt); Nurses' aides 18 (ft), 16 (pt); Physical
therapists 1 (ft); Activities coordinators 3
(ft); Dietitians.
Facilities Dining room; Physical therapy
room; Activities room; Crafts room; Laundry
room; Barber/Beauty shop.
Activities Arts & crafts; Cards; Games;
Reading groups; Prayer groups; Movies;
Shopping trips; Dances/Social/Cultural
gatherings; Intergenerational programs; Pet
therapy.

Monmouth

Monmouth Nursing Home
117 S 'I' St, Monmouth, IL 61462
(309) 734-3811
Admin SuzAnn Pieper. *Dir of Nursing* Gwen
Gladfelter RN. *Medical Dir* Madhav
Ratnakar MD.
Licensure Intermediate care. *Beds* ICF 54.
Private Pay Patients 100%.
Owner Privately owned.
Admissions Requirements Medical
examination; Physician's request.
Staff Physicians 10 (pt); RNs 1 (ft); LPNs 3
(ft), 2 (pt); Nurses' aides 11 (ft), 5 (pt);
Physical therapists 1 (pt); Activities
coordinators 1 (ft); Dietitians 1 (ft).
Facilities Dining room; Laundry room;
Barber/Beauty shop.
Activities Arts & crafts; Games; Reading
groups; Prayer groups; Movies; Shopping
trips; Dances/Social/Cultural gatherings.

Pinewood Health Care Center
515 E Euclid Ave, Monmouth, IL 61462
(309) 734-5163
Admin Jovann Johnson.
Licensure Skilled care; Intermediate care;
Sheltered care. *Beds* SNF 30; ICF 58;
Sheltered care 30.
Owner Proprietary corp.

Monticello

Cornerstone Home
1009 S Irving, Monticello, IL 61856
(217) 762-5326
Admin Alan G Ryle.
Licensure Intermediate care for mentally
retarded. *Beds* ICF/MR 15.

Piatt County Nursing Home
PO Box 449, 1111 N State St, Monticello, IL
61856
(217) 762-2506
Admin Marilyn Benedino.
Licensure Skilled care. *Beds* SNF 99. *Certified*
Medicaid.
Owner Publicly owned.
Admissions Requirements Minimum age 55.
Facilities Dining room; Activities room;
Crafts room; Laundry room; Barber/Beauty
shop.
Activities Arts & crafts; Cards; Games;
Reading groups; Prayer groups; Movies;
Shopping trips; Dances/Social/Cultural
gatherings.

Morris

Grundy County Home
PO Box 669, Clay & Quarry Sts, Morris, IL
60450
(815) 942-3255
Admin Sue Morse. *Dir of Nursing* RoseMarie
Munch. *Medical Dir* Warren Breisch MD.
Licensure Intermediate care; Alzheimer's care.
Beds ICF 143. *Private Pay Patients* 65%.
Certified Medicaid.
Owner Publicly owned.
Admissions Requirements Minimum age 18;
Medical examination; Physician's request.
Facilities Dining room; Physical therapy
room; Activities room; Chapel; Crafts room;
Laundry room; Barber/Beauty shop.
Activities Arts & crafts; Cards; Games;
Reading groups; Prayer groups; Movies;
Shopping trips; Dances/Social/Cultural
gatherings; Intergenerational programs; Pet
therapy; Swimming parties.

Morris Lincoln Nursing Home
916 Fremont Ave, Morris, IL 60450
(815) 942-1202
Admin Marjorie D Johnson. *Dir of Nursing*
Pam Logan RN. *Medical Dir* Dr I B Kim.
Licensure Intermediate care; Sheltered care.
Beds ICF 47; Sheltered care 34. *Private Pay
Patients* 49%. *Certified* Medicaid.
Owner Proprietary corp.
Admissions Requirements Medical
examination.
Staff RNs 2 (ft), 2 (pt); LPNs 3 (ft), 1 (pt);
Nurses' aides 14 (ft), 4 (pt); Recreational
therapists 2 (ft); Physical therapy aides 1 (ft);
Dietitian supervisors 1 (ft).
Facilities Dining room; Laundry room;
Barber/Beauty shop; Large lawn.
Activities Arts & crafts; Cards; Games;
Reading groups; Movies; Shopping trips;
Dances/Social/Cultural gatherings; Pet
therapy.

Walnut Grove Village
Twilight Dr, Morris, IL 60450
Admin Rebecca L Togliatti.
Licensure Skilled care; Intermediate care;
Sheltered care. *Beds* SNF 50; ICF 17;
Sheltered care 30.

Morrison

**Morrison Community Hospital Skilled Nursing
Facility**
303 N Jackson, Morrison, IL 61270
(815) 772-4003, 772-7391 FAX
Admin Wayne A Sensor, Interim Admin. *Dir
of Nursing* Joyce Ginn RN. *Medical Dir*
Richard C Vandermyde MD.
Licensure Skilled care. *Beds* SNF 38. *Private
Pay Patients* 50-60%. *Certified* Medicare.
Owner Nonprofit organization/foundation.
Admissions Requirements Minimum age 18;
Physician's request.
Staff Physicians 4 (ft); RNs 4 (ft), 8 (pt);
LPNs 1 (ft); Nurses' aides 12 (ft), 3 (pt);
Physical therapists 1 (ft); Recreational
therapists 1 (ft); Occupational therapists 1
(ft); Speech therapists 1 (pt); Activities
coordinators 1 (pt); Dietitians 1 (pt).
Facilities Dining room; Physical therapy
room; Activities room; Chapel; Crafts room;
Laundry room; Barber/Beauty shop; Library.
Activities Arts & crafts; Cards; Games;
Reading groups; Prayer groups; Movies;
Shopping trips.

Pleasant View Home
N Jackson St, Morrison, IL 61270
(815) 772-7288
Admin Mary K McKnight.
Licensure Intermediate care. *Beds* ICF 74.
Certified Medicaid.
Owner Publicly owned.

Resthave Home of Whiteside County
408 Maple Ave, Morrison, IL 61270
(815) 772-4021
Admin James A Huber.
Medical Dir Dr R Londo.
Licensure Intermediate care; Sheltered care;
Retirement. *Beds* ICF 49; Sheltered care 27.
Certified Medicare.
Owner Nonprofit corp.
Admissions Requirements Medical
examination.
Staff RNs 2 (ft), 2 (pt); LPNs 1 (ft), 3 (pt);
Nurses' aides 15 (ft), 10 (pt); Activities
coordinators 1 (ft); Dietitians 1 (pt).
Facilities Dining room; Activities room;
Crafts room; Laundry room; Barber/Beauty
shop.
Activities Arts & crafts; Cards; Games;
Reading groups; Prayer groups; Movies.

Morton

Apostolic Christian Restmor Inc
935 E Jefferson, Morton, IL 61550
(309) 266-7141
Admin James L Metzger. *Dir of Nursing* Judy
Witzig RN. *Medical Dir* Dr James Early.
Licensure Skilled care; Sheltered care;
Alzheimer's care. *Beds* SNF 120; Sheltered
care 26. *Private Pay Patients* 75%. *Certified*
Medicaid; Medicare.
Owner Nonprofit organization/foundation.
Admissions Requirements Minimum age 18;
Medical examination.
Staff RNs 10 (ft); LPNs 8 (ft); Nurses' aides
43 (ft); Physical therapists 1 (pt);
Recreational therapists 1 (ft); Occupational
therapists 1 (pt); Speech therapists 1 (pt);
Activities coordinators 1 (ft); Dietitians 1
(ft).
Affiliation Apostolic Christian.
Facilities Dining room; Physical therapy
room; Activities room; Chapel; Crafts room;
Laundry room; Barber/Beauty shop; Library;
Ventilator dependent care; Closed head
injury care.
Activities Arts & crafts; Cards; Games;
Reading groups; Prayer groups; Movies;
Shopping trips; Dances/Social/Cultural
gatherings; Intergenerational programs; Pet
therapy.

Apostolic Morton
RR 3, Veterans Rd, Morton, IL 61550
(309) 266-9781
Admin Robert Knobloch. *Dir of Nursing*
Maureen Collette.
Licensure Intermediate care for
developmentally disabled. *Beds* ICF/DD
106. *Certified* Medicaid.
Owner Nonprofit organization/foundation.
Admissions Requirements Minimum age 18;
Medical examination.
Staff RNs; LPNs; Nurses' aides; Physical
therapists; Recreational therapists;
Occupational therapists; Activities
coordinators.
Affiliation Apostolic Christian.
Facilities Dining room; Physical therapy
room; Activities room; Chapel; Crafts room;
Laundry room; Barber/Beauty shop.
Activities Arts & crafts; Cards; Games;
Reading groups; Prayer groups; Movies;
Shopping trips; Dances/Social/Cultural
gatherings.

Morton Health Care Limited
190 E Queenwood Rd, Morton, IL 61550
(309) 266-9741
Admin Irene Johnson.
Medical Dir Dr Phillip A Immesoete.
Licensure Skilled care. *Beds* SNF 106.
Certified Medicaid; Medicare.
Owner Proprietary corp.
Admissions Requirements Minimum age 18.

Staff Physicians 1 (ft), 2 (pt); RNs 3 (ft), 2 (pt); LPNs 2 (ft), 3 (pt); Nurses' aides 22 (ft), 1 (pt); Physical therapists 1 (pt); Occupational therapists 1 (ft); Speech therapists 1 (pt); Activities coordinators 1 (pt); Dietitians 1 (pt); Ophthalmologists 1 (pt); Podiatrists 1 (pt); Dentists 1 (pt).
Facilities Dining room; Physical therapy room; Activities room; Crafts room; Laundry room; Barber/Beauty shop; Library.
Activities Arts & crafts; Cards; Games; Reading groups; Prayer groups; Movies; Dances/Social/Cultural gatherings.

Morton Terrace Ltd
191 E Queenwood, Morton, IL 61550
(309) 266-5331, 266-9885 FAX
Admin Patricia Chism. *Dir of Nursing* Judith Tidaboele. *Medical Dir* Norman Johnson.
Licensure Intermediate care. *Beds* ICF 144. *Private Pay Patients* 25%. *Certified* Medicaid.
Owner Proprietary corp (EKS Management).
Admissions Requirements Minimum age 18; Medical examination.
Staff RNs 3 (ft); LPNs 6 (ft); Nurses' aides 20 (ft); Physical therapists (consultant); Recreational therapists (consultant); Occupational therapists (consultant); Speech therapists (consultant); Activities coordinators 1 (ft); Dietitians (consultant); Podiatrists (consultant).
Facilities Dining room; Physical therapy room; Activities room; Crafts room; Barber/Beauty shop; Library.
Activities Arts & crafts; Cards; Games; Reading groups; Prayer groups; Movies; Shopping trips; Dances/Social/Cultural gatherings; Intergenerational programs; Psychosocial programs.

Oakwood Estate
2213 Veterans Rd, Morton, IL 61550
(309) 263-8484
Admin Ron Messner.
Licensure Intermediate care for mentally retarded. *Beds* ICF/MR 15.

Morton Grove

Bethany Terrace Retirement & Nursing Home
8425 Waukegan Rd, Morton Grove, IL 60053
(708) 965-8100
Admin Larry K Loecker. *Dir of Nursing* Trudee Gast RN. *Medical Dir* Paul Vega MD.
Licensure Skilled care; Intermediate care; Sheltered care. *Beds* SNF 103; ICF 160; Sheltered care 12. *Certified* Medicaid; Medicare.
Owner Nonprofit corp.
Admissions Requirements Minimum age 18; Medical examination; Physician's request.
Staff Physicians 3 (pt); RNs 15 (ft), 25 (pt); LPNs 8 (ft), 1 (pt); Nurses' aides 81 (ft), 26 (pt); Physical therapists 3 (ft); Reality therapists 4 (ft), 3 (pt); Occupational therapists 1 (pt); Activities coordinators 1 (ft); Dietitians 1 (ft).
Affiliation Methodist.
Facilities Dining room; Physical therapy room; Activities room; Chapel; Crafts room; Laundry room; Barber/Beauty shop; Library; Occupational Therapy room; Rehab room; Enclosed patios.
Activities Arts & crafts; Cards; Games; Reading groups; Prayer groups; Movies; Shopping trips; Dances/Social/Cultural gatherings; Luncheons; Baseball; Community activities; Church; Botanical gardens; Tropical fish; Parakeets; Rabbits; Baking; Resident council; Gardening; Mens' club; Parkinsons' group; Choral club; Community service projects.

Mounds

Meridian Manor
420 S Blanche, Mounds, IL 62964
(618) 745-6537
Admin Jane Connell Flournoy. *Dir of Nursing* Patricia Smith LPN. *Medical Dir* Genio Wong MD.
Licensure Intermediate care. *Beds* ICF 64. *Certified* Medicaid.
Owner Proprietary corp.
Admissions Requirements Minimum age 18; Medical examination.
Staff LPNs 4 (ft), 4 (pt); Nurses' aides 12 (ft), 6 (pt); Physical therapists 1 (pt); Activities coordinators 1 (ft), 1 (pt); Dietitians 1 (pt).
Facilities Dining room; Physical therapy room; Activities room; Laundry room; Barber/Beauty shop.
Activities Arts & crafts; Cards; Games; Reading groups; Prayer groups; Movies.

Mount Carmel

General Baptist Nursing Home
RR 4, 1320 W 9th St, Mount Carmel, IL 62863
(618) 263-4337
Admin Jack R Cole. *Dir of Nursing* Yvonne Pohl. *Medical Dir* R L Fuller MD.
Licensure Skilled care; Alzheimer's care. *Beds* SNF 160. *Private Pay Patients* 50%. *Certified* Medicaid; Medicare.
Owner Nonprofit corp.
Admissions Requirements Minimum age 18; Medical examination; Physician's request.
Staff RNs 2 (ft), 5 (pt); LPNs 9 (ft), 5 (pt); Nurses' aides 45 (ft); Physical therapists 1 (pt); Speech therapists 1 (pt); Activities coordinators 2 (ft), 1 (pt); Dietitians 10 (ft), 5 (pt); Ophthalmologists 2 (pt).
Affiliation Baptist.
Facilities Dining room; Physical therapy room; Activities room; Chapel; Crafts room; Laundry room; Barber/Beauty shop; Library; 2 Lobbies.
Activities Arts & crafts; Cards; Games; Reading groups; Prayer groups; Movies; Shopping trips; Dances/Social/Cultural gatherings; Intergenerational programs; Pet therapy.

River Oaks
PO Box 487, Mount Carmel, IL 62863
(618) 262-8614
Admin David M Roberts.
Licensure Intermediate care for mentally retarded. *Beds* ICF/MR 15.

Shurtleff Manor Residential
PO Box 577, Mount Carmel, IL 62863
(618) 263-3511
Admin Helen R Lewis.
Medical Dir Dr C L Johns.
Licensure Intermediate care. *Beds* ICF 84. *Certified* Medicaid.
Owner Proprietary corp.
Staff Physicians 7 (ft); RNs 1 (ft); LPNs 5 (ft); Nurses' aides 15 (ft); Physical therapists 1 (ft); Reality therapists 1 (ft); Recreational therapists 2 (ft); Speech therapists 1 (ft); Activities coordinators 2 (ft); Dietitians 1 (ft); Ophthalmologists 2 (ft); Podiatrists 1 (ft); Audiologists 1 (ft); Dentists 2 (ft).
Facilities Dining room; Activities room; Crafts room; Laundry room; Barber/Beauty shop; Smoking & drinking lounge.
Activities Arts & crafts; Cards; Games; Reading groups; Prayer groups; Movies; Shopping trips; Dances/Social/Cultural gatherings.

Mount Carroll

Carroll County Good Samaritan Center
PO Box 111, 1006 N Lowden Rd, Mount Carroll, IL 61053
(815) 244-7715
Admin Margaret D Charlton. *Dir of Nursing* Delores Iben RN. *Medical Dir* Dr L B Hussey.
Licensure Intermediate care. *Beds* ICF 68. *Private Pay Patients* 63%. *Certified* Medicaid.
Owner Nonprofit corp (Evangelical Lutheran/ Good Samaritan Society).
Admissions Requirements Minimum age 22; Medical examination; Physician's request.
Staff RNs 1 (ft), 4 (pt); LPNs 1 (ft), 2 (pt); Nurses' aides 16 (ft), 16 (pt); Physical therapists; Activities coordinators 2 (ft), 1 (pt); Dietitians.
Affiliation Lutheran.
Facilities Dining room; Physical therapy room; Activities room; Chapel; Crafts room; Laundry room; Barber/Beauty shop; Bus.
Activities Arts & crafts; Cards; Games; Reading groups; Prayer groups; Movies; Shopping trips; Dances/Social/Cultural gatherings; Intergenerational programs; Pet therapy; Outings; Volunteer program.

Mount Morris

Pinecrest Manor
414 S Wesley Ave, Mount Morris, IL 61054
(815) 734-4103, 737-4102 FAX
Admin Vernon C Showalter. *Dir of Nursing* Joyce Person. *Medical Dir* C Lowell Edwards MD.
Licensure Skilled care; Intermediate care; Retirement living; Alzheimer's care. *Beds* SNF 54; ICF 65; Retirement living 114. *Private Pay Patients* 60%. *Certified* Medicaid; Medicare.
Owner Nonprofit organization/foundation.
Admissions Requirements Minimum age 62.
Staff Physicians; RNs; LPNs; Nurses' aides; Physical therapists; Activities coordinators; Dietitians; Podiatrists.
Affiliation Church of the Brethren.
Facilities Dining room; Physical therapy room; Activities room; Chapel; Crafts room; Laundry room; Barber/Beauty shop; Library.
Activities Arts & crafts; Games; Reading groups; Prayer groups; Movies; Shopping trips; Dances/Social/Cultural gatherings; Pet therapy.

Mount Pulaski

Henry & Jane Vonderlieth Living Center Inc
Rte 121 & Elkhart Rd, Mount Pulaski, IL 62548
(217) 792-3218
Admin Mary L Brown. *Dir of Nursing* Elaine Sheaffer. *Medical Dir* James B Borgerson MD.
Licensure Skilled care; Retirement. *Beds* SNF 90; Retirement apts 18. *Private Pay Patients* 80%. *Certified* Medicaid.
Owner Nonprofit organization/foundation.
Admissions Requirements Minimum age 60; Medical examination; Physician's request.
Staff RNs 4 (ft), 3 (pt); LPNs 7 (ft), 3 (pt); Nurses' aides 32 (ft), 5 (pt); Physical therapists (consultant); Recreational therapists 1 (pt); Occupational therapists 1 (pt); Speech therapists 1 (pt); Activities coordinators 1 (ft), 2 (pt); Dietitians (consultant); Podiatrists 1 (pt).
Facilities Dining room; Physical therapy room; Activities room; Crafts room; Laundry room; Barber/Beauty shop; Library; Living room; Lounge area; Courtyards.

Activities Arts & crafts; Cards; Games; Prayer groups; Shopping trips; Dances/Social/ Cultural gatherings; Intergenerational programs; Family Support group.

Mount Sterling

Heritage Manor Nursing & Convalescent Home
Camden Rd, Mount Sterling, IL 62353
(217) 773-3377
Admin Francis Greer.
Medical Dir Russell R Dohner MD.
Licensure Skilled care. *Beds* SNF 87. *Certified* Medicaid; Medicare.
Owner Proprietary corp.
Admissions Requirements Medical examination.
Staff RNs 4 (ft); LPNs 4 (ft), 1 (pt); Nurses' aides 13 (ft), 16 (pt); Activities coordinators 1 (ft).
Facilities Dining room; Physical therapy room; Activities room; Chapel; Laundry room; Barber/Beauty shop.
Activities Arts & crafts; Cards; Games; Prayer groups; Movies; Shopping trips; Dances/ Social/Cultural gatherings.

Mount Vernon

Casey Care Center
5 Doctors' Park Rd, Mount Vernon, IL 62864
(618) 242-1064
Admin Cord Bear. *Dir of Nursing* Junetta Bullard RN. *Medical Dir* Dr Robert J Parks.
Licensure Intermediate care. *Beds* ICF 113. *Private Pay Patients* 15%. *Certified* Medicaid.
Owner Proprietary corp (Gary Towler).
Admissions Requirements Minimum age 18; Medical examination.
Staff RNs 1 (ft); LPNs 9 (ft); Nurses' aides 40 (ft); Physical therapists 1 (ft); Occupational therapists 1 (pt); Speech therapists 1 (pt); Activities coordinators 2 (ft); Dietitians 1 (ft); Ophthalmologists 1 (pt); Podiatrists 1 (pt).
Facilities Dining room; Physical therapy room; Activities room; Laundry room; Barber/Beauty shop; 2 Patios; Front lobby.
Activities Arts & crafts; Cards; Games; Reading groups; Movies; Shopping trips; Dances/Social/Cultural gatherings.

Jeffersonian Nursing Home
1700 White St, Mount Vernon, IL 62864
(618) 242-4075
Admin Bruce Flanigan. *Dir of Nursing* Ann Bargaresser RN. *Medical Dir* Goff Thompson.
Licensure Skilled care. *Beds* SNF 64. *Certified* Medicaid.
Owner Privately owned.
Admissions Requirements Minimum age 16; Medical examination; Physician's request.
Staff Physicians; RNs; LPNs; Nurses' aides; Physical therapists; Recreational therapists; Dietitians.
Facilities Dining room; Physical therapy room; Chapel; Laundry room; Barber/Beauty shop.
Activities Arts & crafts; Cards; Games; Reading groups; Prayer groups; Movies; Shopping trips; Dances/Social/Cultural gatherings.

Mt Vernon Care Center Inc
1717 Jefferson, Mount Vernon, IL 62864
(618) 244-2864
Admin Darleen E Dycus. *Dir of Nursing* Pat Wellen. *Medical Dir* Dr Feastherston.
Licensure Intermediate care; Alzheimer's care. *Beds* ICF 64. *Private Pay Patients* 1%. *Certified* Medicaid.
Owner Proprietary corp (G & T Resources).
Admissions Requirements Minimum age 21; Medical examination; Physician's request.

Staff RNs; LPNs; Nurses' aides; Physical therapists; Recreational therapists; Occupational therapists; Speech therapists; Activities coordinators; Dietitians; Ophthalmologists; Podiatrists.
Facilities Dining room; Physical therapy room; Activities room; Laundry room; Barber/Beauty shop.
Activities Arts & crafts; Games; Reading groups; Prayer groups; Movies; Shopping trips; Dances/Social/Cultural gatherings.

Nature Trail Home Inc
1001 S 34th St, Mount Vernon, IL 62864
(618) 242-5700
Admin Doris Brickey. *Dir of Nursing* Marge Frakes.
Licensure Intermediate care. *Beds* ICF 74. *Certified* Medicaid.
Owner Proprietary corp.
Admissions Requirements Minimum age 55; Medical examination.
Staff RNs 1 (ft), 1 (pt); LPNs 4 (ft), 1 (pt); Nurses' aides 17 (ft); Physical therapists 1 (pt); Activities coordinators 3 (ft).
Facilities Dining room; Physical therapy room; Activities room; Crafts room; Laundry room; Barber/Beauty shop.
Activities Arts & crafts; Cards; Games; Reading groups; Prayer groups; Movies; Shopping trips.

Oak Terrace
4219 Lincolnshire Dr, Mount Vernon, IL 62864
(618) 242-2117
Admin James F Bowers.
Licensure Intermediate care for mentally retarded. *Beds* ICF/MR 15.

Sutton House
4241 Lincolnshire Dr, Box 1447, Mount Vernon, IL 62864
(618) 242-0132
Admin Linda Horton.
Licensure Intermediate care for mentally retarded. *Beds* ICF/MR 15.

Mount Zion

Woodland Nursing Center
1225 Woodland Dr, Mount Zion, IL 62549
(217) 428-0909
Admin Judy Weger. *Dir of Nursing* Millie Gromoll RN. *Medical Dir* Dr Glen Dust.
Licensure Skilled care. *Beds* SNF 73. *Private Pay Patients* 45%. *Certified* Medicaid; Medicare.
Owner Proprietary corp (Lifecare Centers of Illinois).
Admissions Requirements Medical examination.
Staff Physicians 1 (ft); RNs 2 (ft), 2 (pt); LPNs 8 (ft), 6 (pt); Nurses' aides 23 (ft), 10 (pt); Physical therapists; Activities coordinators 1 (ft), 1 (pt); Dietitians 1 (pt).
Facilities Dining room; Physical therapy room; Activities room; Crafts room; Laundry room; Barber/Beauty shop.
Activities Arts & crafts; Cards; Games; Reading groups; Prayer groups; Movies; Dances/Social/Cultural gatherings; Pet therapy.

Mundelein

Glenkirk Circle
26719 N Owens Rd, Mundelein, IL 60060
(708) 526-1333
Admin Dayna M Novak.
Medical Dir Theresa Holmes.
Licensure Intermediate care for mentally retarded. *Beds* ICF/MR 15. *Certified* Medicaid.
Owner Nonprofit corp.
Admissions Requirements Minimum age 18; Medical examination.

Staff Physicians 1 (pt); RNs 1 (ft), 1 (pt); LPNs 2 (pt); Occupational therapists 1 (pt); Speech therapists 1 (pt); Activities coordinators 1 (pt).
Facilities Dining room; Activities room; Den.
Activities Arts & crafts; Movies; Shopping trips; Dances/Social/Cultural gatherings.

Murphysboro

Jackson County Nursing Home
1441 N 14th St, Murphysboro, IL 62966
(618) 684-2136
Admin Richard A Ligon. *Dir of Nursing* Marge Eisenhauer RN. *Medical Dir* Andrew R Esposito MD.
Licensure Skilled care. *Beds* SNF 260. *Certified* Medicaid; Medicare.
Owner Nonprofit organization/foundation.
Admissions Requirements Minimum age 18; Medical examination; Physician's request.
Staff Physicians; RNs; LPNs; Nurses' aides; Physical therapists; Recreational therapists; Occupational therapists; Speech therapists; Activities coordinators; Dietitians; Ophthalmologists.
Facilities Dining room; Physical therapy room; Activities room; Chapel; Crafts room; Barber/Beauty shop; Library.
Activities Arts & crafts; Cards; Games; Reading groups; Prayer groups; Movies; Shopping trips; Dances/Social/Cultural gatherings; Library study; Cooking class; Weekly bingo.

Our Place
301 N 13th St, Murphysboro, IL 62966
(618) 687-1415
Admin Trena Briscoe.
Licensure Intermediate care for mentally retarded. *Beds* ICF/MR 15.

Roosevelt Square
PO Box 707, 1501 Shomaker Dr, Murphysboro, IL 62966
(618) 684-2693
Admin Dorothy M Davis.
Licensure Intermediate care for mentally retarded. *Beds* ICF/MR 83.
Owner Proprietary corp.

Naperville

Alden Nursing Center—Naperville
1525 Oxford Ln, Naperville, IL 60565
(708) 983-0300, 983-9360 FAX
Admin Kathy Brockmann. *Dir of Nursing* Diane Ng. *Medical Dir* Lawrence LaPalio MD.
Licensure Skilled care; Alzheimer's care. *Beds* SNF 203; Alzheimer's unit 33. *Certified* Medicaid; Medicare.
Owner Proprietary corp (Alden Management Services Inc).
Admissions Requirements Minimum age 18.
Staff Physicians; RNs; LPNs; Nurses' aides; Physical therapists; Occupational therapists; Speech therapists; Activities coordinators; Dietitians; Ophthalmologists; Podiatrists; Audiologists.
Facilities Dining room; Physical therapy room; Activities room; Chapel; Crafts room; Laundry room; Barber/Beauty shop; Library; Occupational therapy room; Lounge; Patio; Ice cream parlor; General store; Cocktail club; Courtyard mall; Popcorn wagon.
Activities Arts & crafts; Cards; Games; Reading groups; Prayer groups; Movies; Shopping trips; Dances/Social/Cultural gatherings; Intergenerational programs; Pet therapy.

Americana Healthcare Center of Naperville
200 Martin Ave, Naperville, IL 60540
(708) 355-4111
Admin Linda J Morris. *Dir of Nursing* Marcia Fick RN. *Medical Dir* Dr Farouk Girgis.

Licensure Skilled care. *Beds* SNF 114. *Private Pay Patients* 75%. *Certified* Medicaid; Medicare.
Owner Proprietary corp (Manor Care).
Admissions Requirements Minimum age 25; Physician's request.
Staff Physicians 1 (ft); RNs 7 (ft); LPNs 3 (ft), 4 (pt); Nurses' aides 20 (ft), 12 (pt); Physical therapists 1 (ft); Recreational therapists 1 (ft); Occupational therapists 1 (ft); Speech therapists 1 (pt); Dietitians 1 (ft); Podiatrists 1 (pt).
Facilities Dining room; Physical therapy room; Activities room; Laundry room; Barber/Beauty shop.
Activities Arts & crafts; Cards; Games; Reading groups; Prayer groups; Movies; Intergenerational programs; Pet therapy; Monthly theme days.

Community Convalescent Center—Naperville
1136 N Mill St, Naperville, IL 60540
(708) 355-3300
Admin Richard Nolden.
Medical Dir Dr William Perkins.
Licensure Skilled care. *Beds* SNF 155. *Certified* Medicare.
Owner Proprietary corp.
Admissions Requirements Minimum age 18; Medical examination; Physician's request.
Staff Physicians 4 (pt); RNs 10 (ft), 10 (pt); LPNs 5 (ft), 5 (pt); Physical therapists 1 (ft); Occupational therapists 1 (pt); Speech therapists 1 (pt); Activities coordinators 1 (ft); Dietitians 1 (pt); Ophthalmologists 1 (pt); Podiatrists 1 (pt); Dentists 2 (pt).
Facilities Dining room; Physical therapy room; Activities room; Crafts room; Laundry room; Barber/Beauty shop; Library.
Activities Arts & crafts; Cards; Games; Reading groups; Prayer groups; Movies; Shopping trips; Dances/Social/Cultural gatherings.

Little Friends Inc
140 W Wright, Naperville, IL 60540
(708) 355-9858
Admin Deborah Darzinskis.
Licensure Community living facility. *Beds* Community living facility 40.

Nashville

Colonial Plaza
801 Goodner St, Nashville, IL 62263
(618) 327-3911
Admin Holly J Szopinski.
Licensure Intermediate care for mentally retarded. *Beds* ICF/MR 15.

Friendship Manor Nursing Home
305 Friendship Dr, Nashville, IL 62263
(618) 327-3041
Admin Judith A McGuire.
Licensure Skilled care; Intermediate care. *Beds* SNF 90; ICF 140. *Certified* Medicaid; Medicare.
Owner Proprietary corp.

New Athens

New Athens Home For the Aged
203 S Johnson St, New Athens, IL 62264
(618) 475-2550
Admin Richard Sutter.
Licensure Intermediate care. *Beds* ICF 64. *Certified* Medicaid.
Owner Nonprofit corp.

New Baden

Clinton Manor Living Center
111 E Illinois St, New Baden, IL 62265
(618) 588-4924
Admin Michael Brave. *Dir of Nursing* Jeanette Hart. *Medical Dir* Lery Leone.

Licensure Intermediate care; Intermediate care for mentally retarded; Alzheimer's care. *Beds* ICF 26; ICF/MR 43. *Private Pay Patients* 13%. *Certified* Medicaid.
Owner Proprietary corp.
Admissions Requirements Minimum age 18; Medical examination.
Staff RNs 1 (ft); LPNs 5 (ft); Nurses' aides 28 (ft); Activities coordinators 1 (ft); Dietitians 1 (ft).
Facilities Dining room; Activities room; Crafts room; Laundry room; Barber/Beauty shop.
Activities Arts & crafts; Cards; Games; Reading groups; Prayer groups; Movies; Shopping trips; Dances/Social/Cultural gatherings.

Royal Living Center
200 S 9th, New Baden, IL 62265
Admin Dolores Krebs.
Licensure Intermediate care for mentally retarded. *Beds* ICF/MR 15.

Newman

Boxwood Health Care Center
PO Box 335, Memorial Dr, Newman, IL 61942
(217) 837-2421
Admin Stacy J B Gordon. *Dir of Nursing* Carolyn Flowers. *Medical Dir* Reid Sutton MD.
Licensure Skilled care; Intermediate care. *Beds* Swing beds SNF/ICF 60. *Private Pay Patients* 30%. *Certified* Medicaid; Medicare.
Owner Proprietary corp (Springwood Associates).
Staff Physicians 1 (ft), 3 (pt); RNs 2 (pt); LPNs 3 (ft), 1 (pt); Nurses' aides 10 (ft), 10 (pt); Physical therapists 1 (pt); Reality therapists 1 (pt); Occupational therapists 1 (pt); Activities coordinators 1 (ft); Dietitians 1 (pt); Podiatrists 1 (pt).
Facilities Dining room; Physical therapy room; Activities room; Crafts room; Laundry room; Barber/Beauty shop.
Activities Arts & crafts; Cards; Games; Reading groups; Prayer groups; Shopping trips; Intergenerational programs; Pet therapy.

Newton

Newton Rest Haven Inc
PO Box 360, 300 S Scott St, Newton, IL 62448
(618) 783-2309
Admin Karen Eyman Kinder.
Medical Dir JoAnn Miller.
Licensure Skilled care. *Beds* SNF 92. *Certified* Medicaid.
Owner Proprietary corp.

Niles

Forest Villa Nursing Center
6840 W Touhy Ave, Niles, IL 60648
(708) 647-8994, 647-1539 FAX
Admin Michael Kaplan. *Dir of Nursing* Rani Rao. *Medical Dir* Todd Michael Grendon MD.
Licensure Skilled care; Intermediate care. *Beds* SNF 55; ICF 151. *Private Pay Patients* 50%. *Certified* Medicaid.
Owner Proprietary corp.
Admissions Requirements Minimum age 62; Medical examination.
Staff Physicians 4 (pt); RNs 7 (ft), 3 (pt); LPNs 8 (ft); Nurses' aides 34 (ft); Physical therapists 1 (pt); Recreational therapists 1 (pt); Occupational therapists 1 (pt); Activities coordinators 1 (ft); Dietitians 1 (pt); Ophthalmologists 1 (pt); Podiatrists 1 (pt); Dentists 1 (pt).
Languages Polish, Filipino.

Facilities Dining room; Physical therapy room; Activities room.
Activities Arts & crafts; Cards; Games; Reading groups; Prayer groups; Movies; Shopping trips; Dances/Social/Cultural gatherings; Intergenerational programs; Pet therapy; Nature walk.

Glen Bridge Nursing & Rehabilitation Center
8333 W Golf Rd, Niles, IL 60648
(708) 966-9190
Admin Nancy Crutcher RN; Holly Harris, Asst. *Dir of Nursing* Barbara Cunningham RN. *Medical Dir* Solomon Dayan MD.
Licensure Skilled care; Intermediate care; Alzheimer's care. *Beds* SNF 148; ICF 148. *Private Pay Patients* 15%. *Certified* Medicaid.
Owner Proprietary corp (Health and Home Management Inc).
Staff Physicians 7 (ft); RNs 14 (ft); LPNs 9 (ft); Nurses' aides 72 (ft); Physical therapists 1 (ft); Recreational therapists 6 (ft); Occupational therapists 2 (ft); Speech therapists 1 (ft); Activities coordinators 1 (ft); Dietitians 1 (pt); Ophthalmologists 1 (pt); Podiatrists 1 (pt); Audiologists 1 (pt).
Languages Polish, Spanish, Yiddish, German.
Facilities Dining room; Physical therapy room; Activities room; Chapel; Crafts room; Laundry room; Barber/Beauty shop; Resident operated gift shop; Family privacy rooms; Patio.
Activities Arts & crafts; Cards; Games; Reading groups; Prayer groups; Movies; Shopping trips; Dances/Social/Cultural gatherings; Intergenerational programs; Pet therapy.

George J Goldman Memorial Home for the Aged
6601 W Touhy Ave, Niles, IL 60648
(708) 647-9875
Admin Daniel E Novick. *Dir of Nursing* Evelyn Troike. *Medical Dir* Dr E Sutoris.
Licensure Skilled care; Intermediate care. *Beds* SNF 99. *Certified* Medicaid.
Owner Nonprofit organization/foundation.
Admissions Requirements Minimum age 65.
Languages Yiddish, Hebrew.
Facilities Dining room; Physical therapy room; Activities room; Chapel; Crafts room; Laundry room; Barber/Beauty shop; Library.
Activities Arts & crafts; Cards; Games; Reading groups; Prayer groups; Movies; Shopping trips; Dances/Social/Cultural gatherings; Intergenerational programs; Pet therapy.

Hampton Plaza
8555 Maynard Rd, Niles, IL 60648
(708) 967-7000
Admin Mary L Grondin. *Dir of Nursing* Rosita Samson. *Medical Dir* David Edelberg MD.
Licensure Skilled care; Intermediate care. *Beds* SNF 150; ICF 150. *Private Pay Patients* 10%. *Certified* Medicaid.
Owner Nonprofit organization/foundation (Caremor).
Admissions Requirements Minimum age 21; Medical examination; Physician's request.
Staff Physicians 30 (pt); RNs 10 (pt); LPNs 10 (pt); Nurses' aides 80 (pt); Physical therapists 1 (pt); Recreational therapists 1 (pt); Occupational therapists 1 (pt); Speech therapists 1 (pt); Activities coordinators 5 (pt); Dietitians 1 (pt); Ophthalmologists 1 (pt); Podiatrists 2 (pt); Audiologists 1 (pt).
Languages Spanish, Polish, Russian.
Facilities Dining room; Physical therapy room; Activities room; Crafts room; Laundry room; Barber/Beauty shop; Library.
Activities Arts & crafts; Cards; Games; Reading groups; Prayer groups; Movies; Shopping trips; Dances/Social/Cultural gatherings; Intergenerational programs; Pet therapy.

Regency Nursing Centre
6631 Milwaukee Ave, Niles, IL 60648
(708) 647-7444, (312) 647-6403 FAX
Admin Barbara Hecht. *Dir of Nursing* Danuta
Solik. *Medical Dir* A LaPorta MD.
Licensure Skilled care; Respite care;
Alzheimer's care. *Beds* SNF 300. *Certified*
Medicaid; Medicare.
Owner Privately owned.
Admissions Requirements Minimum age 60;
Medical examination.
Facilities Dining room; Physical therapy
room; Activities room; Laundry room;
Barber/Beauty shop; Library; Patio;
Transportation.
Activities Arts & crafts; Cards; Games; Prayer
groups; Movies; Shopping trips; Dances/
Social/Cultural gatherings; Intergenerational
programs; Pet therapy; Community and local
church involvement; Volunteer program;
Respite program; Alzheimer's and related
disorders support group (monthly); Outings.

St Benedict Home for Aged
6930 W Touhy Ave, Niles, IL 60648
(708) 774-1440
Admin Sr Irene I Sebo.
Medical Dir Donald Quinlan MD.
Licensure Intermediate care. *Beds* ICF 52.
Owner Nonprofit corp.
Admissions Requirements Minimum age 70;
Medical examination.
Staff Physicians; RNs; LPNs 3 (ft), 2 (pt);
Nurses' aides 3 (ft), 2 (pt); Reality therapists
1 (pt); Occupational therapists 1 (pt);
Dietitians 1 (ft); Ophthalmologists 1 (pt);
Dentists 1 (pt).
Affiliation Roman Catholic.
Facilities Dining room; Activities room;
Chapel; Laundry room; Barber/Beauty shop.
Activities Arts & crafts; Cards; Games;
Reading groups; Prayer groups; Movies;
Shopping trips; Dances/Social/Cultural
gatherings; Gardening; Trips.

Nokomis

Montgomery Terrace
215 N Walnut, Box 1584, Nokomis, IL 62075
(217) 563-7013
Admin Anna Brackenbush.
Licensure Intermediate care for mentally
retarded. *Beds* ICF/MR 15.

Nokomis Golden Manor
505 Stevens St, Nokomis, IL 62075
(217) 563-7513, 563-7022 FAX
Admin Joyce A Pauley. *Dir of Nursing*
Marilyn Holliday RN. *Medical Dir* Dr D
Quizon.
Licensure Skilled care. *Beds* SNF 94. *Private
Pay Patients* 58%. *Certified* Medicaid;
Medicare.
Owner Proprietary corp.
Admissions Requirements Minimum age 18;
Medical examination; Physician's request.
Staff RNs 2 (ft), 1 (pt); LPNs 3 (ft), 3 (pt);
Nurses' aides 20 (ft), 20 (pt); Physical
therapists 1 (pt); Recreational therapists 1
(pt); Occupational therapists 1 (pt); Speech
therapists 1 (pt); Activities coordinators 1
(ft); Dietitians 1 (pt); Ophthalmologists 1
(pt); Dentists 1 (pt).
Facilities Dining room; Physical therapy
room; Activities room; Chapel; Laundry
room; Barber/Beauty shop; Library.
Activities Arts & crafts; Games; Prayer groups;
Movies; Shopping trips; Dances/Social/
Cultural gatherings.

Normal

Americana Healthcare Center of Normal
510 Broadway, Normal, IL 61761
(309) 452-4406
Admin Linda L Staulcup.

Licensure Skilled care. *Beds* SNF 90. *Certified*
Medicaid; Medicare.
Owner Proprietary corp (Manor Care).

Heritage Manor of Normal
509 N Adelaide St, Normal, IL 61761
(309) 452-7468
Admin Rose M Stadel. *Dir of Nursing* Diane
Schraufnagel. *Medical Dir* Pramern Sriratana
MD.
Licensure Skilled care; Intermediate care;
Retirement. *Beds* SNF 44; ICF 130.
Certified Medicaid.
Owner Proprietary corp (Heritage Enterprises).
Admissions Requirements Medical
examination.
Staff RNs 3 (ft), 2 (pt); LPNs 11 (ft), 5 (pt);
Nurses' aides 27 (ft), 4 (pt); Activities
coordinators 1 (ft); Dietitians 1 (ft).
Facilities Dining room; Physical therapy
room; Activities room; Chapel; Crafts room;
Laundry room; Barber/Beauty shop; Library.
Activities Arts & crafts; Cards; Games;
Reading groups; Prayer groups; Movies;
Shopping trips; Dances/Social/Cultural
gatherings.

McLean County Nursing Home
901 N Main, Normal, IL 61761
(309) 452-8337
Admin Donald W Lee.
Licensure Skilled care. *Beds* SNF 150.
Certified Medicaid.
Owner Publicly owned.

Norridge

Central Baptist Home for the Aged
4750 N Orange Ave, Norridge, IL 60656
(708) 452-3700
Admin Alan Kegel.
Medical Dir Dorothy Rittmueller.
Licensure Intermediate care; Sheltered care;
Retirement. *Beds* ICF 118; Sheltered care
23. *Certified* Medicaid.
Owner Nonprofit corp.
Admissions Requirements Minimum age 62;
Medical examination.
Staff RNs; LPNs; Nurses' aides; Recreational
therapists 7 (ft); Activities coordinators 1
(ft); Dietitians 1 (ft).
Affiliation Baptist.
Facilities Dining room; Physical therapy
room; Activities room; Chapel; Crafts room;
Laundry room; Barber/Beauty shop; Library.
Activities Arts & crafts; Cards; Games;
Reading groups; Prayer groups; Movies;
Shopping trips; Dances/Social/Cultural
gatherings.

Norris City

Spencer Terrace
401 W 4th St, Norris City, IL 62869
Licensure Intermediate care for mentally
retarded. *Beds* ICF/MR 15.

North Aurora

Maplewood Health Care Center
PO Box E, 310 Banbury Rd, North Aurora, IL
60542
(708) 892-7627
Admin Lisa K Johnson.
Medical Dir H Kim MD.
Licensure Intermediate care. *Beds* ICF 129.
Certified Medicaid.
Owner Proprietary corp (Springwood
Associates).
Admissions Requirements Minimum age 55;
Medical examination; Physician's request.
Staff Physicians; RNs; LPNs; Nurses' aides;
Physical therapists; Occupational therapists;
Speech therapists; Activities coordinators;
Dietitians.

Facilities Dining room; Physical therapy
room; Activities room; Chapel; Barber/
Beauty shop; Solarium.
Activities Arts & crafts; Cards; Games;
Reading groups; Prayer groups; Movies;
Shopping trips; Dances/Social/Cultural
gatherings.

North Riverside

Scottish Home
28th St & Des Plaines Ave, North Riverside,
IL 60546
(708) 447-5092
Admin Wayne Rethford. *Dir of Nursing* Doris
Burt. *Medical Dir* Edwin Nebblett MD.
Licensure Intermediate care; Sheltered care;
Retirement. *Beds* ICF 14; Sheltered care 49.
Owner Nonprofit organization/foundation.
Admissions Requirements Minimum age 60;
Medical examination.
Staff Physicians 13 (pt); RNs 1 (ft), 2 (pt);
LPNs 4 (ft); Nurses' aides 9 (ft), 5 (pt);
Physical therapists 1 (pt); Activities
coordinators 2 (ft), 1 (pt); Dietitians 1 (ft);
Ophthalmologists 1 (pt); Podiatrists 1 (pt);
Dentists 1 (pt).
Facilities Dining room; Physical therapy
room; Activities room; Crafts room; Laundry
room; Barber/Beauty shop; Library; Living
room.
Activities Arts & crafts; Cards; Games;
Reading groups; Prayer groups; Movies;
Shopping trips; Dances/Social/Cultural
gatherings; Theatre trips; Musical
entertainment; Parties; Residents council;
Restaurant dining.

Northbrook

Covenant Health Care Center Inc
2155 Pfingsten Rd, Northbrook, IL 60062
(708) 480-6350, 205-9552 FAX
Admin Beverly Z Smith. *Dir of Nursing* Geri
Wessner. *Medical Dir* Dr Russell Elmer.
Licensure Skilled care; Intermediate care;
Sheltered care; Retirement. *Beds* SNF 102;
Sheltered care 76. *Certified* Medicaid;
Medicare.
Owner Nonprofit organization/foundation.
Admissions Requirements Minimum age 18;
Medical examination; Physician's request.
Staff Physicians; RNs; LPNs; Nurses' aides;
Physical therapists; Occupational therapists;
Speech therapists; Activities coordinators;
Dietitians; Ophthalmologists; Podiatrists.
Affiliation Evangelical Covenant Church.
Facilities Dining room; Physical therapy
room; Activities room; Chapel; Laundry
room; Barber/Beauty shop; Library.
Activities Arts & crafts; Cards; Games;
Reading groups; Prayer groups; Movies;
Shopping trips; Dances/Social/Cultural
gatherings.

G A F Lake Cook Terrace
222 Dennis Dr, Northbrook, IL 60062
(708) 564-0505
Admin Flavia Ambrogi. *Dir of Nursing* Marla
Yanes RN. *Medical Dir* Scott Braunlich
MD.
Licensure Skilled care; Intermediate care. *Beds*
SNF 90; ICF 50. *Certified* Medicaid.
Owner Proprietary corp.
Admissions Requirements Minimum age 50.
Staff Physicians 1 (ft), 3 (pt); RNs 6 (ft), 3
(pt); LPNs 4 (ft), 1 (pt); Nurses' aides 31
(ft), 3 (pt); Reality therapists 1 (pt);
Occupational therapists 2 (pt); Activities
coordinators 1 (ft); Dietitians 1 (pt).
Facilities Dining room; Physical therapy
room; Activities room; Crafts room; Laundry
room; Barber/Beauty shop; Library; Patio.

Activities Arts & crafts; Cards; Games; Reading groups; Prayer groups; Movies; Shopping trips; Dances/Social/Cultural gatherings; Writing groups; Breakfast club; Lunch groups; In-house luncheons.

Glen Oaks Nursing Home Inc
270 Skokie Hwy, Northbrook, IL 60062
(708) 498-9320
Admin Rita Steinback.
Medical Dir Dr Edward Sutoris.
Licensure Skilled care; Intermediate care. *Beds* SNF 164; ICF 130. *Certified* Medicaid; Medicare.
Owner Proprietary corp.
Staff Physicians 7 (pt); RNs 38 (ft); LPNs 14 (ft); Nurses' aides 64 (ft), 3 (pt); Physical therapists 5 (ft), 2 (pt); Reality therapists 2 (ft); Recreational therapists 7 (ft); Occupational therapists 1 (ft); Speech therapists 1 (pt); Activities coordinators 1 (ft); Dietitians 1 (pt); Ophthalmologists 1 (pt); Podiatrists 2 (pt); Dentists 1 (pt); Art therapists 1 (ft).
Facilities Dining room; Physical therapy room; Activities room; Crafts room; Laundry room; Barber/Beauty shop; Library.
Activities Arts & crafts; Cards; Games; Reading groups; Prayer groups; Movies; Shopping trips; Dances/Social/Cultural gatherings.

Northlake

Villa Scalabrini
480 N Wolf Rd, Northlake, IL 60164
(708) 562-0040
Admin Margaret A Becker. *Dir of Nursing* Lorraine Compton RN. *Medical Dir* Joseph D Gigante MD.
Licensure Skilled care; Intermediate care; Sheltered care; Alzheimer's care; Retirement. *Beds* SNF 120; ICF 82; Sheltered care 63. *Certified* Medicaid; Medicare.
Owner Nonprofit corp (Catholic Charities).
Admissions Requirements Minimum age 60.
Staff Physicians 4 (ft); RNs 20 (ft); LPNs 25 (ft); Nurses' aides 65 (ft); Physical therapists 1 (pt); Occupational therapists 1 (pt); Speech therapists 1 (pt); Activities coordinators 1 (ft); Dietitians 2 (ft); Ophthalmologists 1 (pt); Podiatrists 1 (pt); Audiologists 1 (pt).
Languages Italian.
Affiliation Roman Catholic.
Facilities Dining room; Physical therapy room; Activities room; Chapel; Crafts room; Laundry room; Barber/Beauty shop.
Activities Arts & crafts; Cards; Games; Reading groups; Prayer groups; Movies; Shopping trips; Dances/Social/Cultural gatherings; Intergenerational programs; Pet therapy.

Oak Forest

Kosary Home
6660 W 147th St, Box E, Oak Forest, IL 60452
(708) 687-4300
Admin Julius Kosary.
Licensure Sheltered care. *Beds* 66.
Owner Proprietary corp.

Oak Lawn

Americana Healthcare Center of Oak Lawn
9401 S Kostner Ave, Oak Lawn, IL 60453
(708) 423-7882, 423-5779 FAX
Admin John Ralosky. *Dir of Nursing* Diana Dean. *Medical Dir* Dr Martin Shobris.
Licensure Skilled care. *Beds* SNF 157. *Private Pay Patients* 66%. *Certified* Medicare.
Owner Proprietary corp (Manor Care Inc).
Admissions Requirements Minimum age 18.

Staff RNs 10 (ft); LPNs 18 (ft), 6 (pt); Nurses' aides 41 (ft), 20 (pt); Physical therapists 4 (ft), 3 (pt); Recreational therapists 3 (ft), 2 (pt); Occupational therapists 3 (ft), 2 (pt); Speech therapists 2 (ft).
Facilities Dining room; Physical therapy room; Activities room; Laundry room; Barber/Beauty shop; Speech therapy room; Occupational therapy room.
Activities Arts & crafts; Cards; Games; Reading groups; Prayer groups; Movies; Shopping trips; Dances/Social/Cultural gatherings; Pet therapy; "Green Thumb" plant club; Ceramics.

Americana—Monticello Convalescent Center
6300 W 95th St, Oak Lawn, IL 60453
(708) 735-5454
Admin Philip S Mendelson.
Medical Dir Dr Stanley Ruzich.
Licensure Skilled care; Intermediate care. *Beds* SNF 122; ICF 63. *Certified* Medicare.
Owner Proprietary corp (Manor Care).
Facilities Dining room; Physical therapy room; Activities room; Laundry room; Barber/Beauty shop.
Activities Arts & crafts; Cards; Games; Reading groups; Prayer groups; Movies; Shopping trips; Dances/Social/Cultural gatherings.

Concord Extended Care
9401 S Ridgeland Ave, Oak Lawn, IL 60453
(708) 599-6700
Admin Elsie Hoover. *Dir of Nursing* Christine Wayer. *Medical Dir* B G Shreenivas.
Licensure Skilled care; Alzheimer's care. *Beds* SNF 133. *Private Pay Patients* 75%. *Certified* Medicaid; Medicare.
Owner Proprietary corp.
Admissions Requirements Minimum age 45; Medical examination.
Staff Physicians 1 (pt); RNs 4 (ft), 2 (pt); LPNs 7 (ft), 5 (pt); Nurses' aides 30 (ft), 17 (pt); Physical therapists 1 (pt); Recreational therapists 2 (ft), 2 (pt); Occupational therapists 1 (pt); Speech therapists 1 (pt); Dietitians 1 (pt); Ophthalmologists 1 (pt); Podiatrists 1 (pt).
Languages Polish, Spanish.
Facilities Physical therapy room; Activities room; Chapel; Crafts room; Laundry room; Barber/Beauty shop; Sun porch; Patio; Yard; Living room; 2 atrium dining rooms.
Activities Arts & crafts; Cards; Games; Reading groups; Prayer groups; Movies; Shopping trips; Dances/Social/Cultural gatherings; Intergenerational programs; Pet therapy.

Oak Lawn Convalescent Home
9525 S Mayfield, Oak Lawn, IL 60453
(708) 636-7000
Admin William Krukar. *Dir of Nursing* Judith Oftedahl. *Medical Dir* Dr Richard Mon.
Licensure Skilled care; Intermediate care. *Beds* SNF 77; ICF 66. *Private Pay Patients* 30%. *Certified* Medicaid.
Owner Privately owned.
Admissions Requirements Minimum age 18; Medical examination; Physician's request.
Staff Physicians; RNs; LPNs; Nurses' aides; Physical therapists; Reality therapists; Occupational therapists; Activities coordinators; Dietitians; Ophthalmologists; Podiatrists; Audiologists.
Facilities Dining room; Physical therapy room; Activities room; Laundry room; Barber/Beauty shop.
Activities Arts & crafts; Cards; Games; Reading groups; Prayer groups; Movies; Shopping trips; Intergenerational programs; Pet therapy; Welcoming adjustment groups; Trips to concerts and dinner.

Oak Park

Arrise Group Home for Young Adults—Autism
702 S Maple, Oak Park, IL 60304
(708) 771-2945
Admin Andrea L Moline.
Licensure Intermediate care for mentally retarded. *Beds* ICF/MR 6.

Oak Park Convalescent & Geriatric Center
625 N Harlem Ave, Oak Park, IL 60302
(708) 848-5966
Admin Martha L Reid. *Dir of Nursing* Dorothy Sweet. *Medical Dir* Dr Wallace Turkland.
Licensure Skilled care; Intermediate care; Alzheimer's care. *Beds* SNF 176; ICF 28. *Certified* Medicaid; Medicare.
Owner Proprietary corp.
Admissions Requirements Medical examination.
Staff RNs; LPNs; Nurses' aides; Physical therapists; Occupational therapists; Speech therapists; Activities coordinators; Dietitians; Ophthalmologists; Podiatrists.
Facilities Dining room; Physical therapy room; Activities room; Crafts room; Laundry room; Barber/Beauty shop.
Activities Arts & crafts; Cards; Games; Reading groups; Prayer groups; Movies; Shopping trips.

Renaissance Manor
637 S Maple, Oak Park, IL 60304
(708) 848-4400
Admin Suzanne M Eberl. *Dir of Nursing* Dorothy Murray.
Licensure Sheltered care. *Beds* Sheltered care 26. *Private Pay Patients* 100%.
Owner Privately owned.
Admissions Requirements Medical examination.
Staff RNs 1 (pt); LPNs 1 (ft), 6 (pt); Nurses' aides 2 (ft), 4 (pt); Activities coordinators 1 (pt).
Facilities Dining room; Activities room; Crafts room; Barber/Beauty shop; Library.
Activities Arts & crafts; Cards; Games; Prayer groups; Movies; Dances/Social/Cultural gatherings; Intergenerational programs; Pet therapy.

Woodbine
6909 W North Ave, Oak Park, IL 60302
(312) 386-1112
Admin Helen Soyer Smith RN LNA. *Dir of Nursing* Mary Buckley RN. *Medical Dir* Fred Barber MD.
Licensure Skilled care. *Beds* SNF 66. *Private Pay Patients* 100%.
Owner Proprietary corp.
Admissions Requirements Minimum age 21; Medical examination; Physician's request.
Staff Physicians 3 (pt); RNs 7 (ft), 5 (pt); LPNs 2 (ft), 4 (pt); Nurses' aides 30 (ft); Physical therapists 2 (pt); Reality therapists 1 (pt); Recreational therapists 1 (pt); Occupational therapists 1 (pt); Speech therapists 1 (pt); Activities coordinators 1 (pt); Dietitians 1 (pt); Ophthalmologists 1 (pt); Podiatrists 1 (pt); Dentists 1 (pt).
Facilities Dining room; Physical therapy room; Activities room; Crafts room; Laundry room; Barber/Beauty shop; Library.
Activities Arts & crafts; Cards; Games; Reading groups; Prayer groups; Movies; Dances/Social/Cultural gatherings.

Oakbrook

Oakbrook Healthcare Centre Inc
2013 Midwest Rd, Oakbrook, IL 60521
(708) 495-0220
Admin Margaret A Becker. *Dir of Nursing* Sheila Nelson RN. *Medical Dir* Norton Fishman MD.

Licensure Skilled care; Intermediate care. *Beds*
SNF 110; ICF 28. *Certified* Medicaid;
Medicare.
Owner Proprietary corp.
Admissions Requirements Minimum age 65;
Medical examination.
Staff RNs 4 (ft), 4 (pt); LPNs 8 (ft), 5 (pt);
Nurses' aides 27 (ft), 10 (pt); Physical
therapists 1 (ft), 1 (pt); Recreational
therapists 1 (pt); Occupational therapists 2
(ft), 1 (pt); Speech therapists 1 (pt);
Activities coordinators 3 (ft); Dietitians 1
(pt); Ophthalmologists 1 (pt).
Facilities Dining room; Physical therapy
room; Activities room; Chapel; Crafts room;
Laundry room; Barber/Beauty shop; Gift
shop; Patio; TV room; Dayrooms.
Activities Arts & crafts; Cards; Games;
Reading groups; Prayer groups; Shopping
trips; Dances/Social/Cultural gatherings;
Bingo; Trips to parks; Zoo.

Oblong

Ridgeview Care Center
1 Ridgeview Ln, Oblong, IL 62449
(618) 592-4228
Admin Eileen W Cunningham.
Licensure Skilled care. *Beds* SNF 90. *Certified*
Medicaid.
Owner Proprietary corp.

Odin

Odin Care Center
Green St, Odin, IL 62870
(618) 775-6444
Admin Stacy M Des Jardins.
Medical Dir P T Durion MD.
Licensure Skilled care; Intermediate care. *Beds*
SNF 65; ICF 34. *Certified* Medicaid;
Medicare.
Owner Proprietary corp.
Admissions Requirements Minimum age 18;
Medical examination; Physician's request.
Staff Physicians 11 (pt); RNs 3 (ft); LPNs 6
(ft); Nurses' aides 30 (ft); Physical therapists
1 (pt); Occupational therapists 1 (ft); Speech
therapists 1 (pt); Activities coordinators 2
(ft); Dietitians 1 (pt); Ophthalmologists 1
(pt); Podiatrists 1 (pt); Audiologists 1 (pt);
Dentists 1 (pt).
Facilities Dining room; Physical therapy
room; Activities room; Crafts room; Laundry
room; Barber/Beauty shop; Library; Living
room; Patio.
Activities Arts & crafts; Cards; Games;
Reading groups; Prayer groups; Movies;
Shopping trips; Dances/Social/Cultural
gatherings; Remotivation group; Community
affairs; Bingo.

O'Fallon

Parkview Colonial Manor
300 Weber Dr, O'Fallon, IL 62269
(618) 632-3511
Admin Gerri Isenberg. *Dir of Nursing* Terri
Rumler. *Medical Dir* Dr Prosser.
Licensure Skilled care; Intermediate care. *Beds*
SNF 108; ICF 41. *Private Pay Patients* 10%.
Certified Medicaid; Medicare.
Owner Proprietary corp.
Admissions Requirements Minimum age 21;
Medical examination.
Staff Physicians 17 (pt); RNs 3 (ft), 2 (pt);
LPNs 5 (ft), 4 (pt); Nurses' aides 35 (ft), 25
(pt); Physical therapists 1 (pt); Recreational
therapists 1 (pt); Occupational therapists 1
(pt); Speech therapists 1 (pt); Activities
coordinators 1 (ft); Dietitians 1 (pt);
Ophthalmologists 1 (pt); Podiatrists 1 (pt);
Dentists 1 (pt).
Facilities Dining room; Physical therapy
room; Activities room; Laundry room;
Barber/Beauty shop.

Activities Arts & crafts; Cards; Games;
Reading groups; Prayer groups; Movies;
Shopping trips; Dances/Social/Cultural
gatherings.

Oglesby

Horizon South Living Center
Pool Dr & Lehigh Ave, Oglesby, IL 61348
(815) 883-3317
Admin Gerlyn J Koehler.
Medical Dir Dr W Y Kim.
Licensure Intermediate care for mentally
retarded. *Beds* ICF/MR 84.
Admissions Requirements Minimum age 18;
Medical examination; Physician's request.
Staff RNs 3 (ft); LPNs 3 (ft); Recreational
therapists 1 (ft); Activities coordinators 1
(ft); Training staff 15 (ft), 18 (pt).
Facilities Dining room; Activities room;
Crafts room; Laundry room.
Activities Arts & crafts; Cards; Games;
Reading groups; Prayer groups; Movies;
Shopping trips; Dances/Social/Cultural
gatherings.

Olney

Burgin Manor
900-928 E Scott St, Olney, IL 62450
(618) 393-2914
Admin Sue E Burgin RN. *Dir of Nursing*
Donna Brant RN. *Medical Dir* Dr Arcot
Suresh.
Licensure Skilled care. *Beds* SNF 151.
Certified Medicaid; Medicare.
Owner Proprietary corp.
Admissions Requirements Medical
examination.
Staff RNs 8 (ft), 2 (pt); LPNs 6 (ft), 2 (pt);
Nurses' aides 36 (ft), 24 (pt); Physical
therapists 1 (ft), 1 (pt); Reality therapists 1
(ft); Recreational therapists 2 (ft);
Occupational therapists 1 (ft), 1 (pt); Speech
therapists 1 (ft), 1 (pt); Activities
coordinators 1 (ft); Dietitians 1 (ft), 1 (pt).
Languages Japanese, Arabic.
Facilities Dining room; Physical therapy
room; Activities room; Chapel; Crafts room;
Laundry room; Barber/Beauty shop.
Activities Arts & crafts; Cards; Games;
Reading groups; Prayer groups; Movies;
Shopping trips; Dances/Social/Cultural
gatherings; Intergenerational programs; Bus
trips; Fishing; Gardening; ASPIRE program.

Marks Sunset Manor
1044 Whittle Ave, Olney, IL 62450
(618) 392-0846
Admin Glen E Marks.
Medical Dir Jane Shaw.
Licensure Sheltered care. *Beds* Sheltered care
49. *Certified* Medicaid.
Owner Proprietary corp.
Admissions Requirements Minimum age 18.
Staff Physicians 1 (pt); RNs 1 (pt); Reality
therapists 1 (ft); Activities coordinators 1
(ft); Dietitians 1 (pt).
Facilities Dining room; Activities room;
Crafts room; Laundry room; Library.
Activities Arts & crafts; Cards; Games;
Reading groups; Prayer groups; Movies;
Shopping trips; Dances/Social/Cultural
gatherings.

Olney Care Center
410 E Mack Ave, Olney, IL 62450
(618) 395-7421
Admin Linda M Wade.
Licensure Skilled care. *Beds* SNF 98. *Certified*
Medicaid; Medicare.
Owner Proprietary corp.

Richland Manor
1066 W Main, Olney, IL 62450
(618) 395-2437
Admin Rita Armbrust.

Licensure Intermediate care for mentally
retarded. *Beds* ICF/MR 15.

Oregon

Stouffer Terrace
910 S 5th St, Oregon, IL 61061
(815) 732-3178
Admin Kathleen A Demler.
Licensure Intermediate care for mentally
retarded. *Beds* ICF/MR 15.

White Pines Living Center
811 S 10th St, Oregon, IL 61061
(815) 732-7994, 732-3733 FAX
Admin Wally Hanson. *Dir of Nursing* Cathy
Flanagan. *Medical Dir* Dr Laxman Iyer.
Licensure Skilled care. *Beds* SNF 104. *Private
Pay Patients* 30%. *Certified* Medicaid;
Medicare.
Owner Nonprofit corp (Adventist Living
Centers).
Staff RNs 4 (ft), 2 (pt); LPNs 4 (ft); Nurses'
aides 15 (ft), 4 (pt); Physical therapists;
Activities coordinators 1 (ft); Dietitians.
Affiliation Seventh-Day Adventist.
Facilities Dining room; Physical therapy
room; Activities room; Chapel; Laundry
room; Barber/Beauty shop.
Activities Arts & crafts; Cards; Games; Prayer
groups; Movies; Shopping trips;
Intergenerational programs; Pet therapy;
Geriobics.

Oswego

Tillers
PO Box 950, Rte 71, Oswego, IL 60543
(708) 554-1001
Admin Robert M Saxon. *Dir of Nursing* Sue
Woods. *Medical Dir* Dr Kenneth Albrecht.
Licensure Skilled care; Intermediate care. *Beds*
SNF 90; ICF 9. *Private Pay Patients* 100%.
Owner Proprietary corp.
Admissions Requirements Minimum age 18.
Staff Physicians 1 (pt); RNs 6 (ft), 4 (pt);
LPNs 2 (pt); Nurses' aides 25 (ft), 15 (pt);
Physical therapists 2 (ft); Recreational
therapists 1 (ft); Occupational therapists 1
(pt); Speech therapists 1 (pt); Activities
coordinators 1 (ft); Dietitians 1 (pt);
Ophthalmologists 1 (pt); Podiatrists 1 (pt);
Audiologists 1 (pt).
Facilities Dining room; Physical therapy
room; Activities room; Chapel; Crafts room;
Laundry room; Barber/Beauty shop; Library.
Activities Arts & crafts; Cards; Games;
Reading groups; Prayer groups; Movies;
Shopping trips; Pet therapy.

Ottawa

LaSalle County Nursing Home
RR 1, Dee Bennett Rd, Ottawa, IL 61350
(815) 433-0476
Admin Richard A Cranford FACHE. *Dir of
Nursing* Linda Kidd RN. *Medical Dir* Brian
S Rosborough MD.
Licensure Intermediate care. *Beds* ICF 104.
Private Pay Patients 25%. *Certified*
Medicaid.
Owner Nonprofit organization/foundation.
Admissions Requirements Minimum age 18;
Medical examination; Physician's request.
Staff RNs 5 (ft), 1 (pt); LPNs 5 (ft), 2 (pt);
Nurses' aides 45 (ft), 10 (pt); Physical
therapists 1 (pt); Occupational therapists 1
(pt); Activities coordinators 1 (ft); Dietitians
1 (pt); Podiatrists 1 (pt).
Facilities Dining room; Activities room;
Chapel; Crafts room; Laundry room; Barber/
Beauty shop; Library.
Activities Arts & crafts; Cards; Games;
Reading groups; Prayer groups; Movies; Pet
therapy; Activities of daily living program;
Religious services; Volunteer program.

Ottawa Care Center
800 E Center St, Ottawa, IL 61350
(815) 434-7144
Admin Lois M Kallestad. *Dir of Nursing*
Cindy Myer RN. *Medical Dir* Dr G
Andrews.
Licensure Skilled care. *Beds* SNF 93. *Certified*
Medicaid; Medicare.
Owner Proprietary corp.
Admissions Requirements Medical
examination; Physician's request.
Staff Physicians 1 (pt); RNs 8 (ft); LPNs 4
(ft); Nurses' aides 35 (ft); Physical therapists
1 (pt); Occupational therapists 1 (pt); Speech
therapists 1 (pt); Activities coordinators 1
(ft); Dietitians 1 (pt); Ophthalmologists 1
(pt).
Facilities Dining room; Physical therapy
room; Activities room; Chapel; Crafts room;
Laundry room; Barber/Beauty shop; Library;
Hospice for family.
Activities Arts & crafts; Cards; Games;
Reading groups; Prayer groups; Movies;
Shopping trips; Dances/Social/Cultural
gatherings.

Pleasant View Luther Home
505 College Ave, Ottawa, IL 61350
(815) 434-1130, 434-3838 FAX
Admin Karl O Norem. *Dir of Nursing* Dora
Seth RN. *Medical Dir* Dr A G Giger.
Licensure Intermediate care; Retirement. *Beds*
ICF 235; Retirement 40. *Private Pay
Patients* 76%. *Certified* Medicaid.
Owner Nonprofit corp.
Admissions Requirements Minimum age 60.
Staff Physicians 1 (pt); RNs 9 (ft), 8 (pt);
LPNs 7 (ft), 6 (pt); Nurses' aides 39 (ft), 40
(pt); Physical therapists 1 (pt); Recreational
therapists 1 (pt); Occupational therapists 1
(pt); Speech therapists 1 (pt); Activities
coordinators 1 (ft); Dietitians 1 (pt);
Ophthalmologists 1 (pt); Podiatrists 1 (pt).
Affiliation Lutheran.
Facilities Dining room; Physical therapy
room; Activities room; Chapel; Crafts room;
Laundry room; Barber/Beauty shop; Library.
Activities Arts & crafts; Cards; Games;
Reading groups; Prayer groups; Movies;
Shopping trips; Dances/Social/Cultural
gatherings.

Sullivan House
600 E Grover, Ottawa, IL 61350
(815) 433-5858
Admin R S Gomes.
Licensure Intermediate care for mentally
retarded. *Beds* ICF/MR 15.

Palatine

Plum Grove Nursing Home
24 S Plum Grove Rd, Palatine, IL 60067
(708) 358-0311, 358-8875 FAX
Admin Susan Lippert. *Dir of Nursing* Karen A
Schneid RN. *Medical Dir* Dr Daniel
Schnuda.
Licensure Skilled care; Intermediate care;
Alzheimer's care. *Beds* SNF 35; ICF 34.
Private Pay Patients 90%. *Certified*
Medicare.
Owner Proprietary corp (Convalescent
Services Inc).
Admissions Requirements Minimum age 18;
Medical examination.
Staff RNs; LPNs; Nurses' aides; Physical
therapists; Reality therapists; Recreational
therapists; Occupational therapists; Speech
therapists; Activities coordinators; Dietitians;
Ophthalmologists; Podiatrists; Audiologists.
Languages Spanish, Polish.
Facilities Dining room; Physical therapy
room; Activities room; Crafts room; Laundry
room; Barber/Beauty shop.

Activities Arts & crafts; Cards; Games;
Reading groups; Prayer groups; Movies;
Shopping trips; Dances/Social/Cultural
gatherings; Intergenerational programs; Pet
therapy; Moms & tots club.

St Joseph's Home for the Elderly
80 W Northwest Hwy, Palatine, IL 60067
(708) 358-5700
Admin Sr Margaret Hogarty. *Dir of Nursing*
Sr Denise Lane. *Medical Dir* Dr Andres
Cornejo.
Licensure Skilled care; Intermediate care;
Sheltered care; Retirement. *Beds* SNF 18;
ICF 79; Sheltered care 35. *Certified*
Medicaid.
Owner Nonprofit corp.
Admissions Requirements Minimum age 65.
Staff Physicians 4 (pt); RNs 20 (ft); LPNs 2
(pt); Nurses' aides 40 (ft); Physical therapists
1 (pt); Occupational therapists 1 (pt);
Activities coordinators 1 (ft); Dietitians 1
(pt); Ophthalmologists 1 (pt); Podiatrists 2
(pt); Dentists 1 (pt).
Affiliation Roman Catholic.
Facilities Dining room; Physical therapy
room; Activities room; Chapel; Crafts room;
Laundry room; Barber/Beauty shop; Library.
Activities Arts & crafts; Cards; Games;
Reading groups; Prayer groups; Movies;
Shopping trips; Dances/Social/Cultural
gatherings.

Palos Heights

Americana Healthcare Center of Palos Heights
7850 W College Dr, Palos Heights, IL 60463
(708) 361-6990, 361-9512 FAX
Admin Susan A Lucas. *Dir of Nursing* Regina
Yeater RN. *Medical Dir* Dr William
Mikaitis.
Licensure Skilled care; Intermediate care;
Sheltered care; Alzheimer's care. *Beds* Swing
beds SNF/ICF 120; Sheltered care 30.
Private Pay Patients 75%. *Certified*
Medicaid; Medicare.
Owner Proprietary corp (Manor Healthcare).
Admissions Requirements Physician's request.
Staff RNs; LPNs; Nurses' aides; Physical
therapists; Activities coordinators; Dietitians.
Facilities Dining room; Physical therapy
room; Activities room; Laundry room;
Barber/Beauty shop; Library.
Activities Arts & crafts; Cards; Games;
Reading groups; Prayer groups; Movies;
Shopping trips; Dances/Social/Cultural
gatherings; Intergenerational programs; Pet
therapy.

Bethshan Association
12927 S Monitor, Palos Heights, IL 60463
(708) 371-0800
Admin Joseph Lanenga.
Licensure Intermediate care for mentally
retarded. *Beds* ICF/MR 45.

Bethshan Association II
12927 S Monitor, Palos Heights, IL 60463
(708) 388-1888
Admin Peggy Mollema.
Licensure Intermediate care for mentally
retarded. *Beds* ICF/MR 15.

Rest Haven Central Skilled Nursing Center
13259 S Central Ave, Palos Heights, IL 60463
(708) 597-1000, 597-8679 FAX
Admin Edwin T Mulder. *Dir of Nursing*
Marion Kickert. *Medical Dir* Marian
Kickert.
Licensure Skilled care; Intermediate care. *Beds*
SNF 96; ICF 97. *Private Pay Patients* 45%.
Certified Medicaid.
Owner Nonprofit organization/foundation.
Admissions Requirements Minimum age 60;
Medical examination.

Staff RNs; LPNs; Nurses' aides; Physical
therapists; Reality therapists; Recreational
therapists; Occupational therapists; Activities
coordinators; Dietitians; Podiatrists.
Facilities Dining room; Physical therapy
room; Activities room; Chapel; Crafts room;
Laundry room; Barber/Beauty shop; Library.
Activities Arts & crafts; Cards; Games; Prayer
groups; Movies; Shopping trips; Dances/
Social/Cultural gatherings; Intergenerational
programs; Pet therapy.

Ridgeland Living Center
12550 S Ridgeland Ave, Palos Heights, IL
60463
(708) 597-9300
Admin Wilma M Karst.
Licensure Skilled care. *Beds* SNF 92.

Palos Hills

**Windsor Manor Nursing & Rehabilitation
Center**
10426 S Roberts Rd, Palos Hills, IL 60465
(708) 598-3460, 598-2520 FAX
Admin Lawrence J Putz. *Dir of Nursing*
Monica Bessinger. *Medical Dir* Dr Kenneth
Ramsey.
Licensure Skilled care; Intermediate care. *Beds*
SNF 83; ICF 120. *Private Pay Patients* 20%.
Certified Medicaid; Medicare.
Owner Proprietary corp.
Admissions Requirements Minimum age 45;
Medical examination.
Staff Physicians 1 (ft), 6 (pt); RNs 4 (ft), 7
(pt); LPNs 6 (ft), 8 (pt); Nurses' aides 46
(ft), 16 (pt); Physical therapists 1 (pt);
Reality therapists 1 (pt); Recreational
therapists 1 (pt); Occupational therapists 1
(pt); Speech therapists 1 (pt); Activities
coordinators 4 (ft), 2 (pt); Dietitians 1 (ft);
Ophthalmologists 1 (pt); Podiatrists 1 (pt);
Audiologists 1 (pt).
Languages Polish, Spanish.
Facilities Dining room; Physical therapy
room; Activities room; Crafts room; Laundry
room; Barber/Beauty shop; Outdoor patio;
Van.
Activities Arts & crafts; Cards; Games; Prayer
groups; Movies; Shopping trips; Dances/
Social/Cultural gatherings; Pet therapy;
Men's workshop; Baking class; Weekly
outings; Recreational therapy.

Pana

Country Care of Pana
1000 E 6th Street Rd, Pana, IL 62557
(217) 562-2174
Admin Michael A Van Meter.
Licensure Skilled care. *Beds* SNF 160.
Certified Medicaid; Medicare.
Owner Proprietary corp.

Pana Health Care Center
900 S Chestnut St, Pana, IL 62557
(217) 562-3996
Admin Kathy Epley NHA. *Dir of Nursing*
Mary Schneider RN. *Medical Dir* Virgilio
Dycoco MD.
Licensure Skilled care. *Beds* SNF 121.
Certified Medicaid; Medicare.
Owner Nonprofit corp (First Humanics Inc).
Admissions Requirements Minimum age 18;
Medical examination.
Staff Physicians 3 (ft); RNs 2 (ft), 1 (pt);
LPNs 9 (ft), 1 (pt); Nurses' aides 19 (ft), 8
(pt); Physical therapists (by company);
Activities coordinators 2 (ft), 3 (pt);
Dietitians (by company).
Facilities Dining room; Physical therapy
room; Activities room; Crafts room; Laundry
room; Barber/Beauty shop; Kitchen; Quiet
room.

Activities Arts & crafts; Cards; Games; Reading groups; Prayer groups; Movies; Shopping trips; Dances/Social/Cultural gatherings; Intergenerational programs; Pet therapy; Psychosocial programs.

Paris

Heritage Convalescent Center
310 S Eads Ave, Paris, IL 61944
(217) 465-5395
Admin Patricia Revell. *Dir of Nursing* Linda Stanfield. *Medical Dir* Dr Reid Sutton.
Licensure Skilled care; Retirement. *Beds* SNF 62. *Certified* Medicaid.
Owner Proprietary corp.
Admissions Requirements Medical examination.
Staff Physicians; RNs 5 (ft); LPNs 3 (ft), 2 (pt); Nurses' aides 40 (ft); Physical therapists 1 (pt); Occupational therapists 1 (pt); Speech therapists 1 (pt); Activities coordinators 1 (ft); Dietitians 1 (pt); Ophthalmologists; Dentists.
Facilities Dining room; Laundry room; Barber/Beauty shop.
Activities Arts & crafts; Cards; Games; Reading groups; Prayer groups; Movies; Shopping trips; Dances/Social/Cultural gatherings; Van rides; Dining out; Groups; Exercise programs; Fitness trail.

Highview Terrace
409 N High St, Paris, IL 61944
(217) 463-1809
Admin Marilyn Meyer.
Licensure Skilled care. *Beds* SNF 15.

Paris Healthcare Center
1011 N Main St, Paris, IL 61944
(217) 465-5376
Admin Nancy D Davis.
Licensure Skilled care. *Beds* SNF 98. *Certified* Medicaid; Medicare.
Owner Proprietary corp.
Admissions Requirements Minimum age 18; Medical examination.
Staff RNs; LPNs; Nurses' aides; Physical therapists; Speech therapists; Activities coordinators; Dietitians.
Facilities Dining room; Physical therapy room; Activities room; Crafts room; Laundry room; Barber/Beauty shop; 3 Living rooms.
Activities Arts & crafts; Cards; Games; Reading groups; Prayer groups; Movies; Shopping trips; Dances/Social/Cultural gatherings; Birthday parties.

Park Ridge

Clifton House
100 N Clifton, Park Ridge, IL 60068
(708) 825-6498
Admin Robert Okazaki.
Licensure Community living facility. *Beds* Community living facility 20.

Park Ridge Healthcare Center
665 Busse Hwy, Park Ridge, IL 60068
(708) 825-5517
Admin Patricia F Patrick. *Dir of Nursing* Pat Mikes RN. *Medical Dir* Dr E Forkos.
Licensure Intermediate care. *Beds* ICF 49.
Owner Proprietary corp (H S Healthcare).
Admissions Requirements Minimum age 21; Medical examination.
Staff Physicians 8 (pt); RNs 1 (ft), 1 (pt); LPNs 3 (ft), 2 (pt); Nurses' aides 10 (ft), 5 (pt); Physical therapists 1 (pt); Recreational therapists 1 (ft); Occupational therapists 1 (pt); Speech therapists 1 (pt); Activities coordinators 1 (ft); Dietitians 1 (pt); Ophthalmologists 1 (pt); Social services 1 (pt).

Facilities Dining room; Activities room; Laundry room; Sun room; Outdoor terrace.
Activities Arts & crafts; Cards; Games; Reading groups; Prayer groups; Movies; Dances/Social/Cultural gatherings; Musical entertainment; Parties; Reality orientation; Picnics; Celebrations of all kinds.

Resurrection Nursing Pavilion
1001 N Greenwood Ave, Park Ridge, IL 60068
(708) 692-5600
Admin Paul Crevis.
Licensure Skilled care. *Beds* SNF 298. *Certified* Medicaid; Medicare.
Owner Nonprofit corp.

St Matthew Lutheran Home
1601 N Western Ave, Park Ridge, IL 60068
(708) 825-5531, 318-6659 FAX
Admin Will C Rasmussen. *Dir of Nursing* Karen Carter RN. *Medical Dir* Dr S Shastri.
Licensure Skilled care; Intermediate care; Alzheimer's care. *Beds* SNF 130; ICF 53. *Private Pay Patients* 66%. *Certified* Medicaid.
Owner Nonprofit corp (Lutheran Social Services).
Admissions Requirements Minimum age 65; Medical examination.
Staff Physicians 1 (pt); RNs 13 (ft), 5 (pt); LPNs 4 (ft), 2 (pt); Nurses' aides 46 (ft), 29 (pt); Activities coordinators 1 (ft); Dietitians 1 (pt).
Affiliation Lutheran.
Facilities Dining room; Physical therapy room; Activities room; Chapel; Crafts room; Laundry room; Barber/Beauty shop.
Activities Arts & crafts; Cards; Games; Reading groups; Prayer groups; Movies; Shopping trips; Dances/Social/Cultural gatherings; Intergenerational programs; Pet therapy.

Paxton

Ford County Nursing Home
RR 2 Box 120, Paxton, IL 60957-9545
(217) 379-4896
Admin Judith L Ondercho. *Dir of Nursing* Rebecca Hill. *Medical Dir* Dr Richard Foellner.
Licensure Skilled care. *Beds* SNF 69. *Certified* Medicaid.
Owner Publicly owned.
Admissions Requirements Minimum age 18; Medical examination; Physician's request.
Staff Physicians 4 (ft); RNs 4 (ft), 3 (pt); LPNs 5 (ft); Nurses' aides 25 (ft), 3 (pt); Recreational therapists 1 (ft), 1 (pt); Activities coordinators 1 (ft); Dietitians 1 (ft), 1 (pt).
Languages German, Spanish.
Facilities Dining room; Physical therapy room; Activities room; Crafts room; Laundry room; Barber/Beauty shop; Outside screened shelter; Horseshoe pit; Open front porch.
Activities Arts & crafts; Cards; Games; Reading groups; Prayer groups; Movies; Shopping trips; Dances/Social/Cultural gatherings; Intergenerational programs; Pet therapy; Community projects; Interhome outings; Special dinners; Baking/Cooking sessions.

Heartland Health Care Center—Paxton
1001 E Pells St, Paxton, IL 60957
(217) 379-2942
Admin Jay M Eyre.
Licensure Skilled care. *Beds* SNF 59.

Illinois Knights Templar Home for Aged
450 Fulton St, Paxton, IL 60957
(217) 379-2116
Admin John W Becker.
Medical Dir Robert C Basler MD.
Licensure Skilled care; Retirement. *Beds* SNF 56. *Certified* Medicaid; Medicare.

Owner Nonprofit corp.
Admissions Requirements Minimum age 60; Medical examination.
Staff RNs 5 (ft); LPNs 4 (ft); Nurses' aides 13 (ft), 10 (pt); Activities coordinators 1 (ft), 1 (pt); Dietitians 1 (ft); Social service 1 (ft).
Affiliation Masons.
Facilities Dining room; Physical therapy room; Activities room; Laundry room; Barber/Beauty shop; Library; Dayroom.
Activities Arts & crafts; Cards; Games; Reading groups; Prayer groups; Movies; Shopping trips; Dances/Social/Cultural gatherings; Monthly banquets.

Pekin

Beechwood Health Care Center
2220 State St, Pekin, IL 61554
(309) 347-1110
Admin Palma Nardozza.
Licensure Skilled care. *Beds* SNF 202. *Private Pay Patients* 20%. *Certified* Medicaid; Medicare.
Owner Proprietary corp.
Staff RNs 6 (ft); LPNs 13 (ft); Nurses' aides 49 (ft); Physical therapists 1 (ft); Recreational therapists 3 (ft); Occupational therapists 1 (ft); Speech therapists 1 (ft); Activities coordinators 3 (ft); Dietitians 2 (ft); Ophthalmologists 1 (ft); Podiatrists 1 (ft); Audiologists 1 (ft).

Davies Square
1817 Cresent Dr, Pekin, IL 61554
(309) 347-2609
Admin Cherrill Vanlandingham.
Licensure Intermediate care for mentally retarded. *Beds* ICF/MR 15.

Hallmark House
2501 Allentown Rd, Pekin, IL 61554
(309) 347-3121
Admin Harold Smith.
Licensure Skilled care. *Beds* SNF 71. *Certified* Medicaid.
Owner Proprietary corp.

Pekin Manor
1520 Camino Dr, Pekin, IL 61544
(309) 353-1099
Admin Cherrill Vanlandingham.
Licensure Skilled care. *Beds* SNF 100.

B J Perino Nursing Home Inc
601-603 Prince St, Pekin, IL 61554
(309) 346-1118
Admin Sharon S Fels. *Dir of Nursing* Bonita Lutz. *Medical Dir* Dr Norman Johnson.
Licensure Intermediate care. *Beds* ICF 84. *Certified* Medicaid.
Owner Proprietary corp.
Admissions Requirements Medical examination.
Staff Physicians; RNs; LPNs; Nurses' aides; Physical therapists; Activities coordinators; Dietitians; Podiatrists.
Facilities Dining room; Physical therapy room; Activities room; Crafts room; Laundry room; Barber/Beauty shop; Library.
Activities Arts & crafts; Cards; Games; Reading groups; Prayer groups; Movies; Shopping trips; Dances/Social/Cultural gatherings.

Twin Oaks Community Living Facility
2421 S 14th St, Pekin, IL 61554
(309) 686-3310
Admin Joseph Budde.
Licensure Intermediate care for mentally retarded. *Beds* ICF/MR 12.
Owner Nonprofit corp.

Peoria

Americana Healthcare Center of Peoria
5600 Glen Elm Dr, Peoria, IL 61614
(309) 688-8777

Admin Cathryn E Bradbury.
Licensure Skilled care. *Beds* SNF 114.
  Certified Medicaid; Medicare.
Owner Proprietary corp (Manor Care).

Apostolic Peoria
7023 NE Skyline Dr, Peoria, IL 61614
(309) 691-2816
Admin Roger D Herman.
Medical Dir Glenna M Coats.
Licensure Intermediate care; Sheltered care.
  Beds ICF 37; Sheltered care 32.
Owner Nonprofit corp.
Staff RNs 1 (ft); LPNs 5 (ft), 2 (pt); Nurses'
  aides 16 (ft), 14 (pt); Activities coordinators
  1 (ft).
Affiliation Apostolic Christian.

Bel-Wood Nursing Home
6701 W Plank Rd, Peoria, IL 61604
(309) 697-4541
Admin Stella Marie Lewis.
Medical Dir William R Nace MD.
Licensure Intermediate care. *Beds* ICF 300.
  Certified Medicaid.
Owner Publicly owned.
Admissions Requirements Minimum age 18;
  Medical examination.
Staff RNs 16 (ft); LPNs 15 (ft); Nurses' aides
  72 (ft); Activities coordinators 1 (ft);
  Dietitians 1 (ft); Podiatrists 1 (pt); Dentists
  1 (pt).
Facilities Dining room; Physical therapy
  room; Activities room; Chapel; Crafts room;
  Laundry room; Barber/Beauty shop; Library.
Activities Arts & crafts; Cards; Games;
  Reading groups; Prayer groups; Movies;
  Shopping trips; Swimming; Bowling.

Christian Buehler Memorial Home
3415 N Sheridan Rd, Peoria, IL 61604
(309) 685-6236
Admin Louis E Amberg, Jr.
Licensure Skilled care. *Beds* SNF 71.
Owner Nonprofit corp.

Galena Park Home
5533 N Galena Rd, Peoria, IL 61614
(309) 682-5428
Admin Julia K King.
Licensure Skilled care; Sheltered Home. *Beds*
  SNF 60; Sheltered care 4. *Certified*
  Medicaid.
Owner Nonprofit corp.

Hart House
905 NE Perry St, Peoria, IL 61603
(309) 673-2676
Admin Robert H Becker.
Licensure Intermediate care for mentally
  retarded. *Beds* ICF/MR 15.

Hartrick House
702 NE Madison St, Peoria, IL 61603
(309) 673-4645
Admin Robert M Becker.
Licensure Intermediate care for mentally
  retarded. *Beds* ICF/MR 15.

Hunter House
505 NE Perry St, Peoria, IL 61603
(309) 637-7920
Admin Robert H Becker.
Licensure Intermediate care for mentally
  retarded. *Beds* ICF/MR 15.

Lindenwood Health Care Center
2308 W Nebraska Ave, Peoria, IL 61604
(309) 673-8251
Admin Ramona Brooks. *Dir of Nursing* Sally
  Webster RN. *Medical Dir* Benito Camacho
  MD.
Licensure Skilled care. *Beds* SNF 105.
  Certified Medicaid; Medicare.
Owner Proprietary corp (Springwood
  Associates).
Admissions Requirements Minimum age 18;
  Medical examination.

Staff Physicians 1 (pt); RNs 3 (ft), 2 (pt);
  LPNs 9 (ft), 5 (pt); Nurses' aides 28 (ft), 11
  (pt); Physical therapists 1 (pt); Occupational
  therapists 1 (pt); Speech therapists 1 (pt);
  Activities coordinators 1 (ft); Dietitians 1
  (pt); Ophthalmologists 1 (pt).
Facilities Dining room; Physical therapy
  room; Activities room; Crafts room; Laundry
  room; Barber/Beauty shop; Library; 3
  Courtyards.
Activities Arts & crafts; Cards; Games;
  Reading groups; Prayer groups; Movies;
  Shopping trips; Dances/Social/Cultural
  gatherings.

Lutheran Home
7019 N Galena Rd, Peoria, IL 61614-2294
(309) 692-4494
Admin G H Vander Schaaf. *Dir of Nursing*
  Mary Helen Erdman. *Medical Dir* Dr Robert
  Brandes.
Licensure Skilled care; Intermediate care;
  Retirement center. *Beds* SNF 72; ICF 8;
  Retirement center 50. *Certified* Medicaid.
Owner Nonprofit corp.
Admissions Requirements Minimum age 62;
  Medical examination.
Staff RNs 9 (ft); LPNs 12 (ft); Nurses' aides
  39 (ft); Physical therapists 1 (pt);
  Recreational therapists 1 (pt); Occupational
  therapists 1 (pt); Speech therapists 1 (pt);
  Activities coordinators 1 (ft); Dietitians 1
  (pt); Ophthalmologists 1 (pt); Podiatrists 1
  (pt); Dentists 1 (pt).
Affiliation Lutheran.
Facilities Dining room; Physical therapy
  room; Activities room; Chapel; Crafts room;
  Laundry room; Barber/Beauty shop; Library.
Activities Arts & crafts; Cards; Games;
  Reading groups; Prayer groups; Movies;
  Shopping trips; Dances/Social/Cultural
  gatherings.

PARC Residential Care Facility
3000 W Rohmann, Peoria, IL 61604
(309) 674-4018
Admin Ann Coletta.
Licensure Intermediate care for mentally
  retarded. *Beds* ICF/MR 114.

John C Proctor Endowment Home
2724 W Reservior, Peoria, IL 61615
(309) 685-6580
Admin Andrew Cali III. *Dir of Nursing* Mary
  Clauser RN. *Medical Dir* Michael Gulley
  MD.
Licensure Skilled care; Retirement. *Beds* SNF
  59; Retirement 224. *Private Pay Patients*
  100%.
Owner Nonprofit organization/foundation.
Admissions Requirements Medical
  examination.
Activities Arts & crafts; Cards; Games;
  Reading groups; Prayer groups; Movies;
  Shopping trips; Dances/Social/Cultural
  gatherings.

Rochelle Community Living Facility
3505A N Rochelle, Peoria, IL 61604
Admin Joseph L Budde.
Licensure Community living facility. *Beds*
  Community living facility 12.

St Joseph's Home of Peoria
2223 W Heading, Peoria, IL 61604
(309) 673-7425
Admin Sr Mary Dries; Sr Mary Paul
  Mazzorana. *Dir of Nursing* Ann Steiner RN.
Licensure Intermediate care; Sheltered care;
  Retirement. *Beds* ICF 43; Sheltered care
  151. *Private Pay Patients* 75%. *Certified*
  Medicaid.
Owner Nonprofit organization/foundation
  (Sisters of Saint Francis of the Immaculate
  Conception).
Admissions Requirements Minimum age 65;
  Medical examination.

Staff RNs 1 (ft), 2 (pt); LPNs 10 (ft), 9 (pt);
  Nurses' aides 18 (ft), 8 (pt); Physical
  therapists (consultant); Activities
  coordinators 1 (ft), 4 (pt); Dietitians 1 (pt);
  Physical therapy aides 1 (ft).
Affiliation Roman Catholic.
Facilities Dining room; Physical therapy
  room; Activities room; Chapel; Crafts room;
  Laundry room; Barber/Beauty shop; Library;
  Snack bar & gift shop.
Activities Arts & crafts; Cards; Games;
  Reading groups; Prayer groups; Movies;
  Shopping trips; Dances/Social/Cultural
  gatherings; Intergenerational programs; Pet
  therapy.

Sharon Health Care Elms Inc
3611 N Rochelle, Peoria, IL 61604
(309) 688-4412
Admin Joanne Schuely. *Dir of Nursing* Joanne
  Schuely. *Medical Dir* Dr Phillip Immesoete.
Licensure Intermediate care; Alzheimer's care.
  Beds ICF 99. *Certified* Medicaid.
Owner Proprietary corp (Pavillion Care
  Centers).
Admissions Requirements Minimum age 50;
  Medical examination; Physician's request.
Staff Physicians; RNs; LPNs; Nurses' aides;
  Physical therapists; Recreational therapists;
  Occupational therapists; Speech therapists;
  Activities coordinators; Dietitians;
  Ophthalmologists; Podiatrists; Dentists.
Languages Sign.
Facilities Dining room; Physical therapy
  room; Activities room; Crafts room; Laundry
  room; Barber/Beauty shop; Library; Patio &
  park setting.
Activities Arts & crafts; Cards; Games;
  Reading groups; Prayer groups; Movies;
  Shopping trips; Dances/Social/Cultural
  gatherings.

Sharon Health Care Oaks Inc
3111 W Richwoods Blvd, Peoria, IL 61604
(309) 688-2457
Admin Thomas E Becher. *Dir of Nursing*
  Kimberly Henry.
Licensure Intermediate care. *Beds* ICF 120.
  Certified Medicaid.
Owner Proprietary corp.
Staff RNs 1 (ft); Dietitians (consultant).
Facilities Dining room; Physical therapy
  room; Activities room; Crafts room; Laundry
  room; Barber/Beauty shop.
Activities Arts & crafts; Cards; Games;
  Reading groups; Prayer groups; Movies;
  Shopping trips; Dances/Social/Cultural
  gatherings; Intergenerational programs; Pet
  therapy.

Sharon Health Care Pines Inc
3614 N Rochelle Ln, Peoria, IL 61604
(309) 688-0350
Admin Sandra Wood. *Dir of Nursing* Cherrill
  Vanlandingham. *Medical Dir* Phillip
  Immesoete MD.
Licensure Intermediate care. *Beds* ICF 120.
  Certified Medicaid.
Owner Proprietary corp.
Admissions Requirements Medical
  examination; Physician's request.
Staff RNs 1 (pt); LPNs 7 (ft), 3 (pt); Nurses'
  aides 20 (ft), 9 (pt); Physical therapists 1 (ft);
  Occupational therapists 2 (pt); Speech
  therapists 1 (pt); Activities coordinators 2
  (ft).
Facilities Dining room; Physical therapy
  room; Activities room; Barber/Beauty shop.
Activities Arts & crafts; Games; Shopping
  trips; Dances/Social/Cultural gatherings;
  Exercises.

Sharon Health Care Regency
3520 N Rochelle, Peoria, IL 61604
(309) 688-0451
Admin June George. *Dir of Nursing* Louise M
  Wilson. *Medical Dir* Dr Phillip Immesoete.

Licensure Skilled care. *Beds* SNF 99. *Certified* Medicaid; Medicare.
Owner Proprietary corp (Pavillion Health Care Centers).
Admissions Requirements Minimum age 18; Medical examination; Physician's request.
Staff Physicians 1 (ft); RNs 3 (ft), 2 (pt); LPNs 10 (ft), 4 (pt); Nurses' aides 30 (ft), 5 (pt); Physical therapists 1 (ft), 1 (pt); Reality therapists 1 (pt); Recreational therapists 1 (pt); Occupational therapists 1 (pt); Speech therapists 1 (ft); Activities coordinators 1 (ft); Dietitians 1 (pt); Ophthalmologists 1 (pt); Podiatrists 1 (pt); Dentists 1 (pt).
Facilities Dining room; Physical therapy room; Activities room; Chapel; Crafts room; Laundry room; Barber/Beauty shop; Library.
Activities Arts & crafts; Cards; Games; Reading groups; Prayer groups; Movies; Shopping trips; Dances/Social/Cultural gatherings.

Sharon Health Care Woods Inc
3301 W Richwoods Blvd, Peoria, IL 61604
(309) 685-5241, 686-8609 FAX
Admin Ben Perkins. *Dir of Nursing* Dorene Creasy. *Medical Dir* Dr Immesoete.
Licensure Intermediate care. *Beds* ICF 152. *Private Pay Patients* 5%. *Certified* Medicaid.
Owner Proprietary corp (Leon Schlefrock).
Admissions Requirements Physician's request.
Staff RNs 1 (ft); LPNs 6 (ft); Nurses' aides 15 (ft); Physical therapists 1 (ft); Occupational therapists 4 (ft); Activities coordinators 4 (ft); Dietitians.
Facilities Dining room; Physical therapy room; Crafts room; Laundry room; Barber/Beauty shop; Gymnasium/auditorium.
Activities Arts & crafts; Cards; Games; Prayer groups; Movies; Shopping trips; Dances/Social/Cultural gatherings.

Barbara P Smiley Living Center
6847 N Allen Rd, Peoria, IL 61614
(309) 692-0720
Admin Sharon A Mercer.
Licensure Intermediate care for mentally retarded. *Beds* ICF/MR 56.

Stuttle Community Living Facility
201 W Columbia Terr, Peoria, IL 61606
(309) 682-1575
Admin Gail Leiby. *Dir of Nursing* Judy Szaboas.
Licensure Intermediate care for mentally retarded. *Beds* ICF/MR 19. *Certified* Medicaid; Medicare.
Owner Nonprofit organization/foundation.
Admissions Requirements Minimum age 18; Medical examination.
Staff Physicians; RNs; Physical therapists (contracted); Recreational therapists; Activities coordinators; Dietitians; Ophthalmologists; Podiatrists; Audiologists.
Facilities Dining room; Activities room; Crafts room; Laundry room.
Activities Arts & crafts; Cards; Games; Reading groups; Prayer groups; Movies; Shopping trips; Dances/Social/Cultural gatherings.

Peoria Heights

Galena Park Nursing Home
5533 N Galena Rd, Peoria Heights, IL 61614
(309) 682-5428
Admin Jane S Foster. *Dir of Nursing* Patricia M Pritchard RN. *Medical Dir* John Coon MD.
Licensure Skilled care; Intermediate care; Sheltered care; Retirement. *Beds* SNF 60; ICF 34; Sheltered care 4. *Private Pay Patients* 60%. *Certified* Medicaid; Medicare.
Owner Nonprofit organization/foundation.
Admissions Requirements Minimum age 18; Medical examination; Physician's request.

Staff RNs 3 (ft), 3 (pt); LPNs 10 (ft), 5 (pt); Nurses' aides 30 (ft), 3 (pt); Physical therapists 2 (ft), 2 (pt); Occupational therapists 2 (ft); Speech therapists 1 (ft); Activities coordinators 1 (ft); Dietitians 1 (ft); Podiatrists (monthly); Dentists (monthly).
Facilities Dining room; Physical therapy room; Activities room; Chapel; Laundry room; Barber/Beauty shop; Library; Speech therapy room; Occupational therapy room; Courtyards; Van.
Activities Arts & crafts; Games; Reading groups; Movies; Shopping trips; Bible study; Bingo; Church services.

Peoria Healthcare Centre
1629 E Gardner Ln, Peoria Heights, IL 61614
(309) 688-8758
Admin Sandra Wood. *Dir of Nursing* Carol McGuire. *Medical Dir* Phillip Immesoete.
Licensure Skilled care; Intermediate care. *Beds* SNF 55; ICF 55. *Private Pay Patients* 1%. *Certified* Medicaid.
Owner Proprietary corp (Northern Illinois Management).
Admissions Requirements Minimum age 18; Medical examination; Physician's request.
Staff Physicians 1 (pt); RNs 3 (ft); LPNs 8 (ft); Nurses' aides 15 (ft); Physical therapists 1 (ft); Reality therapists 1 (ft); Recreational therapists 1 (ft); Occupational therapists 1 (ft); Speech therapists 1 (pt); Activities coordinators 1 (ft); Dietitians 1 (ft); Ophthalmologists 1 (pt); Podiatrists 1 (pt).
Facilities Dining room; Physical therapy room; Activities room; Crafts room; Laundry room; Barber/Beauty shop.
Activities Arts & crafts; Cards; Games; Reading groups; Prayer groups; Movies; Shopping trips; Dances/Social/Cultural gatherings; Intergenerational programs; Pet therapy.

Peotone

Peotone Bensenville Home
PO Box 669, 104 S West St, Peotone, IL 60468
(708) 258-6879
Admin Anita Bogart.
Licensure Sheltered care; Assisted living. *Beds* Sheltered care 34. *Private Pay Patients* 100%.
Owner Nonprofit corp.
Admissions Requirements Medical examination.
Staff RNs 2 (ft); LPNs 2 (ft), 2 (pt); Activities coordinators 1 (ft), 1 (pt); Dietitians 1 (ft), 5 (pt).
Affiliation Church of Christ.
Facilities Dining room; Activities room; Crafts room; Laundry room; Barber/Beauty shop.
Activities Arts & crafts; Games; Reading groups; Prayer groups; Movies.

Peru

Heritage Manor
22nd & Rock St, Peru, IL 61354
(815) 223-4901, 223-6912 FAX
Admin Rosemary Zimmer. *Dir of Nursing* Judy Wright RN. *Medical Dir* Dr Jerome F Sickley.
Licensure Skilled care. *Beds* SNF 129. *Certified* Medicaid; Medicare.
Owner Proprietary corp (Heritage Enterprises).
Admissions Requirements Minimum age 18; Medical examination.
Staff RNs 10 (ft), 2 (pt); LPNs 4 (ft), 1 (pt); Nurses' aides 27 (ft), 8 (pt); Physical therapists 1 (pt); Recreational therapists 2 (ft), 2 (pt); Activities coordinators 1 (ft).
Facilities Dining room; Physical therapy room; Activities room; Crafts room; Laundry room; Barber/Beauty shop.

Activities Arts & crafts; Cards; Games; Prayer groups; Movies; Shopping trips.

Petersburg

Menard Convalescent Center
120 Antle St, Petersburg, IL 62675
(217) 632-2249
Admin Larry Trigg.
Medical Dir Dr Barry Free.
Licensure Skilled care; Intermediate care. *Beds* SNF 59; ICF 27. *Certified* Medicaid; Medicare.
Owner Proprietary corp.
Staff Physicians 3 (pt); RNs 2 (ft), 1 (pt); LPNs 10 (ft); Nurses' aides 50 (ft); Physical therapists 1 (pt); Activities coordinators 1 (ft); Dietitians 1 (pt); Dentists 1 (pt).
Facilities Dining room; Physical therapy room; Barber/Beauty shop.
Activities Arts & crafts; Cards; Games; Prayer groups; Movies; Shopping trips.

Sunny Acres Nursing Home
RR 3, Petersburg, IL 62675
(217) 632-2334
Admin Dick R Warren.
Licensure Skilled care. *Beds* SNF 96. *Certified* Medicaid.
Owner Publicly owned.

Pinckneyville

Lifecare Center of Pinckneyville
PO Box 407, 708 Virginia Ct, Pinckneyville, IL 62274
(618) 357-2493
Admin Hildred Secrease.
Licensure Intermediate care. *Beds* ICF 60. *Certified* Medicaid.
Owner Proprietary corp (Community Lifecare Enterprises).
Admissions Requirements Medical examination.
Staff RNs 1 (ft); LPNs 3 (ft); Nurses' aides 23 (ft); Physical therapists 1 (pt); Activities coordinators 1 (ft); Dietitians 1 (pt).
Facilities Dining room; Physical therapy room; Activities room; Crafts room; Laundry room; Barber/Beauty shop.
Activities Arts & crafts; Cards; Games; Reading groups; Prayer groups; Movies; Shopping trips; Dances/Social/Cultural gatherings.

Piper City

Palmwood Health Care Center
600 S Maple, Piper City, IL 60959
(815) 686-2277
Admin Rita M Kelly.
Medical Dir Dr A G Baxter.
Licensure Intermediate care. *Beds* ICF 60. *Certified* Medicaid.
Owner Proprietary corp.
Admissions Requirements Minimum age 18.
Staff RNs 3 (ft), 1 (pt); LPNs 1 (ft), 3 (pt); Nurses' aides 17 (ft), 10 (pt); Physical therapists 1 (pt); Activities coordinators 1 (ft); Dietitians 1 (ft); Podiatrists 1 (pt).
Facilities Dining room; Physical therapy room; Activities room; Crafts room; Laundry room; Barber/Beauty shop.
Activities Arts & crafts; Cards; Games; Reading groups; Prayer groups; Movies; Shopping trips; Dances/Social/Cultural gatherings.

Pittsfield

Kepley House
408 E Washington, Pittsfield, IL 62363
(217) 285-4955
Admin Ann Ferguson.
Licensure Intermediate care for mentally retarded. *Beds* ICF/MR 15.

Pittsfield Nursing Center
RR 3 Box 24, Pittsfield, IL 62363
(217) 285-4491
Admin Mary Ellen Wade. *Dir of Nursing* Gina Graham. *Medical Dir* Dr Rodriguez.
Licensure Intermediate care. *Beds* ICF 99. *Private Pay Patients* 20%. *Certified* Medicare.
Owner Privately owned (Booth Nursing Center).
Admissions Requirements Minimum age 18; Medical examination.
Staff RNs 1 (pt); LPNs 8 (ft), 1 (pt); Nurses' aides 20 (ft), 9 (pt); Physical therapists 2 (pt); Recreational therapists 1 (pt); Activities coordinators 1 (ft), 1 (pt); Dietitians 1 (pt); Ophthalmologists 1 (pt); Podiatrists 1 (pt); Audiologists 1 (pt).
Facilities Dining room; Physical therapy room; Activities room; Crafts room; Laundry room; Barber/Beauty shop.
Activities Arts & crafts; Cards; Games; Reading groups; Prayer groups; Movies; Shopping trips; Dances/Social/Cultural gatherings; Intergenerational programs; Pet therapy.

Plainfield

Lakewood Nursing Home
1112 N Eastern Ave, Plainfield, IL 60544
(815) 436-3400
Admin Kevin R Erich. *Dir of Nursing* Bonnie McDavitt. *Medical Dir* Frank Bender MD.
Licensure Skilled care. *Beds* SNF 50.
Owner Nonprofit corp (Adventist Health Sys-USA).
Admissions Requirements Minimum age 18; Medical examination; Physician's request.
Staff Physicians 1 (pt); RNs 2 (ft), 10 (pt); LPNs 2 (pt); Nurses' aides 5 (ft), 21 (pt); Activities coordinators 1 (ft), 2 (pt); Dietitians 1 (pt).
Affiliation Seventh-Day Adventist.
Facilities Dining room; Activities room; Chapel; Crafts room; Barber/Beauty shop.
Activities Arts & crafts; Cards; Games; Reading groups; Prayer groups; Movies; Shopping trips; Dances/Social/Cultural gatherings.

Pleasant Hill

Pleasant Hill Nursing Center
204 S Bay, Pleasant Hill, IL 62366
(217) 734-9252
Admin Donna Holcomb. *Dir of Nursing* Debbie Grimsley. *Medical Dir* Dr Ronald Johnson.
Licensure Intermediate care. *Beds* ICF 31. *Private Pay Patients* 40%. *Certified* Medicaid.
Owner Proprietary corp.
Admissions Requirements Medical examination; Physician's request.
Staff Physicians 1 (ft); RNs 2 (ft); LPNs 4 (ft); Nurses' aides 5 (ft); Activities coordinators 1 (ft); Dietitians 1 (ft); Podiatrists 1 (ft).
Facilities Dining room; Activities room; Crafts room; Laundry room; Barber/Beauty shop.
Activities Arts & crafts; Games; Reading groups; Movies; Dances/Social/Cultural gatherings; Pet therapy.

Polo

Polo Continental Manor
703 E Buffalo, Polo, IL 61064
(815) 946-2203
Admin Dennis L Grobe.
Medical Dir Dr Franklin Swan.
Licensure Intermediate care. *Beds* ICF 81. *Certified* Medicaid; Medicare.
Owner Nonprofit corp (First Humanics).

Admissions Requirements Medical examination.
Staff RNs 3 (ft), 2 (pt); LPNs 3 (ft), 4 (pt); Nurses' aides 12 (ft), 6 (pt); Physical therapists 1 (pt); Activities coordinators 1 (ft), 2 (pt); Dietitians 1 (pt); Ophthalmologists 1 (pt); Dentists 1 (pt).

Pontiac

Evenglow Lodge
215 E Washington St, Pontiac, IL 61764
(815) 844-6131
Admin Tyler B Schoenherr. *Dir of Nursing* Nancy Stedman RN BSN. *Medical Dir* Narendra Garg MD.
Licensure Intermediate care; Sheltered care; Retirement. *Beds* ICF 73; Sheltered care 141. *Certified* Medicaid.
Owner Nonprofit corp.
Admissions Requirements Minimum age 65; Medical examination.
Staff RNs 4 (ft), 6 (pt); LPNs 7 (ft), 2 (pt); Nurses' aides 26 (ft), 4 (pt); Physical therapists (contracted); Activities coordinators 2 (ft), 2 (pt); Dietitians (contracted).
Affiliation Methodist.
Facilities Dining room; Physical therapy room; Activities room; Chapel; Crafts room; Laundry room; Barber/Beauty shop; Library.
Activities Arts & crafts; Cards; Games; Reading groups; Prayer groups; Movies; Shopping trips; Dances/Social/Cultural gatherings; Intergenerational programs; Pet therapy.

Humiston Haven
300 W Lowell Ave, Pontiac, IL 61764
(815) 842-1181
Admin Phylis A VerSteegh. *Dir of Nursing* Sharon Roberts LPN. *Medical Dir* John Purnell MD.
Licensure Intermediate care. *Beds* ICF 88. *Private Pay Patients* 28%. *Certified* Medicaid.
Owner Nonprofit corp.
Admissions Requirements Minimum age 21; Medical examination.
Staff RNs 3 (ft), 2 (pt); LPNs 6 (ft), 3 (pt); Nurses' aides 27 (ft), 12 (pt); Physical therapists (consultant); Activities coordinators 1 (ft), 2 (pt); Dietitians (consultant).
Facilities Dining room; Physical therapy room; Activities room; Chapel; Crafts room; Laundry room; Barber/Beauty shop; Library; Wheelchair equipped van.
Activities Arts & crafts; Cards; Games; Reading groups; Prayer groups; Movies; Shopping trips; Dances/Social/Cultural gatherings; Pet therapy; Outings.

Livingston Manor
RR 1, Pontiac, IL 61764
(815) 844-5121
Admin Ann L Klein RN. *Dir of Nursing* Kathy Duffy. *Medical Dir* Leslie S Lowenthal MD.
Licensure Intermediate care. *Beds* ICF 125. *Private Pay Patients* 26%. *Certified* Medicaid.
Owner Publicly owned.
Admissions Requirements Minimum age 50; Medical examination.
Staff Physicians 1 (pt); RNs 2 (ft); LPNs 11 (ft), 5 (pt); Nurses' aides 56 (ft), 10 (pt); Physical therapists 1 (pt); Recreational therapists 1 (ft); Occupational therapists 1 (pt); Activities coordinators 1 (ft); Dietitians 1 (pt); Podiatrists 1 (pt).
Facilities Dining room; Physical therapy room; Activities room; Chapel; Crafts room; Laundry room; Barber/Beauty shop.

Activities Arts & crafts; Cards; Games; Reading groups; Prayer groups; Movies; Shopping trips; Dances/Social/Cultural gatherings; Pet therapy; ADL program.

Martin Luther Homes Inc
223 1/2 N Mill, Pontiac, IL 61764
(815) 842-4166
Admin Maurice Grafton.
Licensure Intermediate care for mentally retarded. *Beds* ICF/MR 12.

Prairie City

Prairie City Nursing Center
Rte 41, Prairie City, IL 61470
(309) 775-3313
Admin Charles Ackers. *Dir of Nursing* Joan Sinnett. *Medical Dir* Dr John Arnold.
Licensure Intermediate care. *Beds* ICF 49. *Private Pay Patients* 50%. *Certified* Medicaid.
Owner Proprietary corp.
Admissions Requirements Minimum age 21; Medical examination; Physician's request.
Staff RNs 1 (pt); LPNs 6 (ft), 2 (pt); Nurses' aides 14 (ft), 10 (pt); Activities coordinators 1 (ft), 1 (pt).
Facilities Dining room; Activities room; Crafts room; Laundry room; Barber/Beauty shop; Library.
Activities Arts & crafts; Cards; Games; Reading groups; Prayer groups; Movies; Shopping trips; Dances/Social/Cultural gatherings.

Princeton

Basswood Health Care Center
1015 Park Ave E, Princeton, IL 61356
(815) 875-1144
Admin Diane R Baccheschi. *Dir of Nursing* Anna Jean Bell. *Medical Dir* Edwin L Johnson MD.
Licensure Intermediate care. *Beds* ICF 63. *Certified* Medicaid.
Owner Proprietary corp (Springwood Associates).
Admissions Requirements Minimum age 18; Medical examination; Physician's request.
Staff RNs 2 (ft); LPNs 5 (ft); Nurses' aides 20 (ft).
Facilities Dining room; Physical therapy room; Chapel; Laundry room; Barber/Beauty shop.
Activities Arts & crafts; Cards; Games; Reading groups; Prayer groups; Movies; Shopping trips; Dances/Social/Cultural gatherings.

Colonial Hall Nursing Home
515 S 6th St, Princeton, IL 61356
(815) 875-3347
Admin Mark A Seibold. *Dir of Nursing* Renee Denault.
Licensure Skilled care; Retirement. *Beds* SNF 72. *Certified* Medicaid; Medicare.
Owner Nonprofit corp (Adventist Health Sys-USA).
Admissions Requirements Minimum age 18; Medical examination.
Staff RNs 8 (ft); LPNs 4 (ft); Nurses' aides 14 (ft), 10 (pt); Physical therapists 1 (pt); Occupational therapists 1 (pt); Speech therapists 1 (pt); Activities coordinators 1 (ft); Dietitians 1 (pt); Ophthalmologists 1 (pt); Podiatrists 1 (pt); Dentists 1 (pt).
Affiliation Seventh-Day Adventist.
Facilities Dining room; Physical therapy room; Activities room; Chapel; Crafts room; Laundry room; Barber/Beauty shop.
Activities Arts & crafts; Cards; Games; Reading groups; Prayer groups; Movies; Shopping trips; Dances/Social/Cultural gatherings.

Greenfield
508 Park Ave E, Princeton, IL 61356
(815) 872-2261
Admin Betty L Redmond RN. *Dir of Nursing* Ruth Pierson RN. *Medical Dir* Dr Greg Davis.
Licensure Sheltered care; Retirement. *Beds* Sheltered care 49. *Private Pay Patients* 100%.
Owner Nonprofit organization/foundation.
Admissions Requirements Minimum age 55; Medical examination.
Staff RNs; LPNs; Nurses' aides; Activities coordinators; Dietitians.
Facilities Dining room; Activities room.
Activities Arts & crafts; Cards; Games; Reading groups; Prayer groups; Movies; Shopping trips; Dances/Social/Cultural gatherings; Intergenerational programs; Pet therapy; Community activities; Volunteer program.

Prairie View Home
RR 5, Princeton, IL 61356
(815) 875-1196
Admin George E Maupin. *Dir of Nursing* Lana Pogliano RN. *Medical Dir* Edwin Johnson MD.
Licensure Skilled care; Intermediate care; Sheltered care. *Beds* SNF 88; ICF 61; Sheltered care 11. *Private Pay Patients* 40%. *Certified* Medicaid.
Owner Publicly owned.
Admissions Requirements Minimum age 18; Medical examination; Physician's request.
Staff Physicians 1 (pt); RNs 10 (ft), 2 (pt); LPNs 4 (ft), 1 (pt); Nurses' aides 49 (ft), 7 (pt); Physical therapists (consultant); Recreational therapists 3 (ft); Occupational therapists 1 (pt); Activities coordinators 1 (pt); Dietitians (consultant); Ophthalmologists 1 (pt); Podiatrists 1 (pt).
Facilities Dining room; Physical therapy room; Activities room; Chapel; Crafts room; Laundry room; Barber/Beauty shop; Library.
Activities Arts & crafts; Cards; Games; Reading groups; Prayer groups; Movies; Shopping trips; Pet therapy.

Prophetstown

Prophets Riverview Good Samaritan Center
310 Mosher Dr, Prophetstown, IL 61277
(815) 537-5175
Admin Tim A Schneider. *Dir of Nursing* Kathy Smith. *Medical Dir* Dr Brad Meek.
Licensure Intermediate care; Sheltered care; Retirement. *Beds* ICF 68; Sheltered care 5; Retirement 4. *Private Pay Patients* 60%. *Certified* Medicaid.
Owner Nonprofit corp (Evangelical Lutheran/ Good Samaritan Society).
Admissions Requirements Medical examination; Physician's request.
Staff RNs 1 (ft), 4 (pt); LPNs 4 (ft), 3 (pt); Physical therapists; Dietitians.
Facilities Dining room; Physical therapy room; Activities room; Chapel; Laundry room; Barber/Beauty shop.
Activities Arts & crafts; Cards; Games; Reading groups; Prayer groups; Movies; Shopping trips; Dances/Social/Cultural gatherings; Intergenerational programs; Pet therapy.

Winning Wheels Inc
701 E 3rd St, Prophetstown, IL 61277
(815) 537-6168, 537-5268 FAX
Admin David B Conklin. *Dir of Nursing* Mary J Burgess RN. *Medical Dir* Bradley Meek DO.
Licensure Skilled care. *Beds* SNF 80. *Private Pay Patients* 20%. *Certified* Medicaid; Medicare.
Owner Nonprofit corp.

Admissions Requirements Minimum age 18; Medical examination; Physician's request; Physically challenged.
Staff Physicians 2 (pt); RNs 4 (ft), 1 (pt); LPNs 5 (ft), 3 (pt); Nurses' aides 30 (ft), 15 (pt); Physical therapists 1 (pt); Recreational therapists 3 (ft); Occupational therapists 1 (pt); Speech therapists 1 (pt); Dietitians 1 (pt); Ophthalmologists (contracted); Podiatrists (contracted); Audiologists (contracted).
Languages Spanish.
Facilities Dining room; Physical therapy room; Activities room; Chapel; Crafts room; Laundry room; Barber/Beauty shop; Library; Nature trail; Recreational therapy clinic; Computer lab.
Activities Arts & crafts; Cards; Games; Reading groups; Prayer groups; Movies; Shopping trips; Dances/Social/Cultural gatherings; Intergenerational programs; Pet therapy.

Quincy

Christian Shelticenter
1340 N 10th St, Quincy, IL 62301
(217) 222-0083
Admin Ruth A Lefoe.
Medical Dir Janis Brink.
Licensure Sheltered care. *Beds* 212. *Certified* Medicaid.
Owner Proprietary corp.
Admissions Requirements Minimum age 14; Physician's request.
Staff LPNs 6 (ft); Nurses' aides 7 (ft); Activities coordinators 1 (ft).
Facilities Dining room; Activities room; Chapel; Laundry room; Barber/Beauty shop.
Activities Arts & crafts; Cards; Games; Reading groups; Prayer groups; Movies; Shopping trips; Dances/Social/Cultural gatherings.

Good Samaritan Home of Quincy
2130 Harrison St, Quincy, IL 62301
(217) 223-8717
Admin Dr Larry M Watson.
Medical Dir Sally Lehner.
Licensure Skilled care; Intermediate care; Sheltered care; Retirement living; Alzheimer's care. *Beds* SNF 36; ICF 138; Sheltered care 101; Cottages 90. *Certified* Medicaid.
Owner Nonprofit corp.
Admissions Requirements Medical examination.
Staff RNs 4 (ft), 1 (pt); LPNs 20 (ft), 15 (pt); Nurses' aides 80 (ft), 20 (pt).
Affiliation Church of Christ.
Facilities Dining room; Physical therapy room; Activities room; Chapel; Crafts room; Laundry room; Barber/Beauty shop; Library.
Activities Arts & crafts; Cards; Games; Reading groups; Prayer groups; Movies; Shopping trips; Dances/Social/Cultural gatherings.

Lincoln Hill Nursing Center
1440 N 10th St, Quincy, IL 62301
(217) 224-3780
Admin Diane Peter. *Dir of Nursing* Joyce Oakley RN. *Medical Dir* Karl Laping MD.
Licensure Skilled care. *Beds* SNF 99. *Private Pay Patients* 10%. *Certified* Medicaid; Medicare.
Owner Proprietary corp (Canadian International Health Services).
Admissions Requirements Minimum age 18; Medical examination; Physician's request.
Staff RNs 2 (ft), 1 (pt); LPNs 6 (ft), 1 (pt); Nurses' aides 23 (ft), 6 (pt); Activities coordinators 1 (ft).
Facilities Dining room; Physical therapy room; Activities room; Chapel; Laundry room; Barber/Beauty shop.

Activities Arts & crafts; Cards; Games; Reading groups; Prayer groups; Movies; Dances/Social/Cultural gatherings; Intergenerational programs; Pet therapy.

Quinsippi LTC Facility Inc
720 Sycamore St, Quincy, IL 62301
(217) 222-1480
Admin Penny L Griffin. *Dir of Nursing* Joye Anderson RN. *Medical Dir* David Lockhart MD.
Licensure Skilled care; Intermediate care; Alzheimer's care. *Beds* SNF 94; ICF 120. *Certified* Medicaid; Medicare.
Owner Proprietary corp.
Admissions Requirements Minimum age 18.
Staff Physicians 2 (pt); RNs 5 (ft), 3 (pt); LPNs 13 (ft), 9 (pt); Nurses' aides 49 (ft), 16 (pt); Activities coordinators 3 (ft).
Facilities Dining room; Physical therapy room; Activities room; Chapel; Crafts room; Laundry room; Barber/Beauty shop; Alzheimers unit.
Activities Arts & crafts; Cards; Games; Reading groups; Prayer groups; Movies; Shopping trips; Dances/Social/Cultural gatherings.

Sunset Home of the United Methodist Church
418 Washington St, Quincy, IL 62301
(217) 223-2636
Admin Herbert A Crede. *Dir of Nursing* Cassie Rocke. *Medical Dir* Dr Debra Phillips.
Licensure Skilled care; Intermediate care; Sheltered care; Independent living. *Beds* SNF 19; ICF 138; Sheltered care 96; Independent living apts 12. *Certified* Medicaid.
Owner Nonprofit organization/foundation.
Admissions Requirements Minimum age 65; Medical examination.
Staff RNs 7 (ft); LPNs 24 (ft), 6 (pt); Nurses' aides 50 (ft), 14 (pt); Physical therapists 1 (pt); Occupational therapists 1 (pt); Speech therapists 1 (pt); Activities coordinators 1 (ft), 4 (pt); Dietitians 1 (pt).
Affiliation United Methodist.
Facilities Dining room; Physical therapy room; Activities room; Chapel; Crafts room; Laundry room; Barber/Beauty shop; Library; Lounges.
Activities Arts & crafts; Cards; Games; Reading groups; Movies; Shopping trips; Dances/Social/Cultural gatherings; Intergenerational programs; Pet therapy.

Red Bud

Maria Care
350 W South 1st St, Red Bud, IL 62278
(618) 282-3891
Admin Carl A Eilbes. *Dir of Nursing* Marilyn Ettling. *Medical Dir* David Walls.
Licensure Skilled care. *Beds* SNF 115. *Private Pay Patients* 45%. *Certified* Medicaid; Medicare.
Owner Nonprofit corp.
Admissions Requirements Minimum age 18.
Staff RNs 3 (ft), 1 (pt); LPNs 4 (ft), 2 (pt); Nurses' aides 12 (ft), 15 (pt); Activities coordinators 1 (ft).
Facilities Dining room; Physical therapy room; Activities room; Chapel; Crafts room; Barber/Beauty shop.
Activities Arts & crafts; Cards; Games; Reading groups; Prayer groups; Movies; Shopping trips; Dances/Social/Cultural gatherings; Intergenerational programs.

Richton Park

Richton Crossing Convalescent Center
PO Box B345, Imperial Dr & Cicero Ave, Richton Park, IL 60471
(708) 747-6120

Admin Roberta Magurany. *Dir of Nursing* Rita Piepenbrink. *Medical Dir* Dr Sheldon Levine.
Licensure Skilled care; Intermediate care. *Beds* SNF 142; ICF 152. *Certified* Medicaid; Medicare.
Owner Privately owned.
Admissions Requirements Medical examination.
Staff Physicians 16 (pt); RNs 9 (ft), 6 (pt); LPNs 14 (ft), 10 (pt); Nurses' aides 54 (ft), 13 (pt); Physical therapists 2 (ft), 1 (pt); Reality therapists 2 (ft); Recreational therapists 2 (ft); Occupational therapists 1 (pt); Speech therapists 1 (ft); Activities coordinators 8 (ft); Dietitians 1 (pt); Ophthalmologists 1 (pt); Podiatrists 1 (pt); Dentists 1 (pt).
Facilities Dining room; Physical therapy room; Activities room; Barber/Beauty shop; Library.
Activities Arts & crafts; Cards; Games; Reading groups; Movies; Shopping trips; Dances/Social/Cultural gatherings; In-house talent shows & entertainers.

Ridgway

Ridgway Manor Nursing Center
Rte 1 Box 181A, Ridgway, IL 62979
(618) 272-8831
Admin Gennia S Canimore.
Licensure Intermediate care. *Beds* ICF 71. *Certified* Medicaid.
Owner Proprietary corp.

Riverside

Scottish Home
28th & Des Plaines Ave, Riverside, IL 60546
(708) 447-5092
Admin Edward W Rethford.
Licensure Intermediate care; Sheltered care. *Beds* ICF 14; Sheltered care 49.

Riverwoods

Brentwood North Nursing & Rehabilitation Center
3705 Deerfield, Riverwoods, IL 60015
(708) 459-1200
Admin Sheldon M Novoselsky. *Dir of Nursing* Diane Sage RN. *Medical Dir* Rohit Shah MD.
Licensure Skilled care; Alzheimer's care. *Beds* SNF 248. *Certified* Medicare.
Owner Proprietary corp.
Admissions Requirements Minimum age 21; Medical examination; Physician's request.
Staff RNs 38 (ft), 27 (pt); LPNs 3 (ft), 3 (pt); Nurses' aides 44 (ft), 13 (pt); Physical therapists 5 (ft), 2 (pt); Occupational therapists 3 (ft), 1 (pt); Activities coordinators 1 (ft); Dietitians 2 (ft).
Facilities Dining room; Physical therapy room; Activities room; Chapel; Crafts room; Laundry room; Barber/Beauty shop; Library; Alzheimer's unit.
Activities Arts & crafts; Cards; Games; Reading groups; Prayer groups; Movies; Shopping trips; Dances/Social/Cultural gatherings; Intergenerational programs.

Roanoke

Apostolic Christian Home
1102 W Randolph, Roanoke, IL 61561
(309) 923-2071
Admin Richard D Isaia.
Medical Dir Marj Moritz.
Licensure Intermediate care; Alzheimer's care. *Beds* ICF 75. *Certified* Medicaid.
Owner Nonprofit corp.
Admissions Requirements Medical examination.
Affiliation Apostolic Christian.

Facilities Dining room; Physical therapy room; Activities room; Crafts room; Laundry room; Barber/Beauty shop.
Activities Arts & crafts; Cards; Games; Reading groups; Prayer groups; Movies; Dances/Social/Cultural gatherings.

Robbins

Lydia Healthcare Center
13901 S Lydia Ave, Robbins, IL 60472
(708) 385-8700
Admin Dolores Z Medwetz.
Licensure Intermediate care. *Beds* ICF 262. *Certified* Medicaid.
Owner Proprietary corp.
Admissions Requirements Minimum age 18; Medical examination.
Staff Physicians 1 (ft), 6 (pt); RNs 2 (ft), 2 (pt); LPNs 18 (ft); Nurses' aides 31 (ft); Physical therapists 1 (pt); Reality therapists 1 (pt); Recreational therapists 1 (ft); Occupational therapists 1 (pt); Activities coordinators 1 (ft); Dietitians 1 (ft); Ophthalmologists 1 (pt); Podiatrists 1 (pt); Dentists 1 (pt).
Facilities Dining room; Physical therapy room; Activities room; Chapel; Crafts room; Laundry room; Barber/Beauty shop; Library; Gift shop; Coffee shop; Boutique (free clothes); Pool hall.
Activities Arts & crafts; Cards; Games; Reading groups; Prayer groups; Movies; Shopping trips; Dances/Social/Cultural gatherings; Fashion shows; Private bus service.

Robinson

Cotillion Ridge Nursing Center
RR 3, Robinwood Dr, Robinson, IL 62454
(618) 544-3192
Admin JoAnn Miller RN. *Dir of Nursing* Susan Atteberry RN. *Medical Dir* Dean Pelley MD.
Licensure Intermediate care. *Beds* ICF 73. *Private Pay Patients* 50%. *Certified* Medicaid.
Owner Proprietary corp (Columbia Corp).
Admissions Requirements Minimum age 18; Medical examination; Physician's request.
Staff RNs 3 (ft); LPNs 3 (ft), 3 (pt); Nurses' aides 13 (ft), 9 (pt); Physical therapists (consultant); Recreational therapists 1 (pt); Activities coordinators 1 (ft), 1 (pt); Dietitians (consultant).
Facilities Dining room; Physical therapy room; Activities room; Chapel; Crafts room; Laundry room; Barber/Beauty shop; Fenced patio and shelter; Bus for outings.
Activities Arts & crafts; Cards; Games; Reading groups; Prayer groups; Movies; Shopping trips; Dances/Social/Cultural gatherings; Intergenerational programs; Pet therapy.

Crawford County Convalescent Center
902 W Mefford St, Robinson, IL 62454
(618) 546-5638
Admin Dwight L Miller. *Dir of Nursing* Barbara Hancock. *Medical Dir* D J Pelley MD.
Licensure Intermediate care. *Beds* ICF 54. *Certified* Medicaid.
Owner Proprietary corp.
Staff Physicians 5 (pt); RNs 4 (ft); LPNs 1 (ft); Nurses' aides 25 (ft); Physical therapists 1 (pt); Recreational therapists 1 (pt); Speech therapists 1 (pt); Activities coordinators 1 (ft); Dietitians 1 (pt); Ophthalmologists 1 (pt).
Facilities Dining room 21.
Activities Arts & crafts; Cards; Games; Reading groups; Prayer groups; Shopping trips; Dances/Social/Cultural gatherings.

Southhaven Home
500 S Reed, Robinson, IL 62454
(618) 546-1204, 544-2187 FAX
Admin Alan G Ryle. *Dir of Nursing* Lois White.
Licensure Intermediate care for mentally retarded. *Beds* ICF/MR 15. *Private Pay Patients* 0%. *Certified* Medicaid; Medicare.
Owner Privately owned (Residential Developers).
Admissions Requirements Medical examination.
Staff RNs 1 (pt); LPNs 1 (pt); Occupational therapists 1 (pt); Speech therapists 1 (pt); Activities coordinators 1 (ft); Dietitians 1 (pt); Habilitation aides 4 (ft), 7 (pt).
Facilities Dining room; Activities room; Laundry room; Living room.
Activities Arts & crafts; Cards; Games; Movies; Shopping trips; Dances/Social/Cultural gatherings; Pet therapy.

Rochelle

Rochelle Health Care Center West
900 N 3rd St, Rochelle, IL 61068
(815) 562-4111
Admin Carol J Wake.
Medical Dir L T Koritz MD.
Licensure Intermediate care. *Beds* ICF 53. *Certified* Medicaid; Medicare.
Owner Proprietary corp.
Admissions Requirements Minimum age 19.
Staff RNs 2 (ft), 4 (pt); LPNs 3 (pt); Nurses' aides 10 (ft), 10 (pt); Recreational therapists 1 (ft); Activities coordinators 1 (ft).
Facilities Dining room; Physical therapy room; Activities room; Laundry room; Barber/Beauty shop.
Activities Arts & crafts; Cards; Games; Reading groups; Prayer groups; Movies; Shopping trips; Dances/Social/Cultural gatherings.

Rochelle Healthcare East
1021 Caron Rd, Rochelle, IL 61068
(815) 562-4047
Admin Susan Fitzgerald. *Dir of Nursing* Linda Good. *Medical Dir* Donald Hinderliter.
Licensure Intermediate care. *Beds* ICF 74. *Private Pay Patients* 30%. *Certified* Medicaid.
Owner Proprietary corp (H S Healthcare).
Staff LPNs 5 (ft), 2 (pt); Nurses' aides 15 (ft), 10 (pt); Activities coordinators 1 (ft); Dietitians 1 (ft).
Facilities Dining room; Activities room; Crafts room; Laundry room; Barber/Beauty shop.
Activities Arts & crafts; Cards; Games; Reading groups; Prayer groups; Movies; Shopping trips; Dances/Social/Cultural gatherings; Intergenerational programs; Pet therapy.

Rock Falls

Colonial Acres Inc
1000 Dixon Ave, Rock Falls, IL 61071
(815) 625-8510
Admin Donna M Lattimer.
Licensure Skilled care. *Beds* SNF 55. *Certified* Medicaid; Medicare.
Owner Proprietary corp.

Willow Wood Health Care
430 Martin Rd, Rock Falls, IL 61071
(815) 626-4575
Admin Denise St Peters. *Dir of Nursing* Carolyn White. *Medical Dir* Dr Woo Kim.
Licensure Intermediate care; Retirement. *Beds* ICF 57; Retirement 21. *Certified* Medicaid.
Owner Proprietary corp (Springwood Associates).
Admissions Requirements Medical examination; Physician's request.

Staff LPNs; Nurses' aides; Physical therapists; Activities coordinators; Dietitians.
Languages French.
Facilities Dining room; Physical therapy room; Activities room; Crafts room; Laundry room; Barber/Beauty shop.
Activities Arts & crafts; Cards; Games; Reading groups; Prayer groups; Movies; Shopping trips; Dances/Social/Cultural gatherings; Intergenerational programs; Pet therapy; Community events.

Rock Island

Friendship Manor
1209 21st Ave, Rock Island, IL 61201
(309) 786-9667
Admin Marie Brobston. *Dir of Nursing* Patty Stetson. *Medical Dir* Dr Mark Valliere.
Licensure Skilled care; Sheltered care; Independent living. *Beds* SNF 63; Sheltered care 34; Independent living 234. *Private Pay Patients* 100%.
Owner Nonprofit organization/foundation.
Admissions Requirements Minimum age 62; Medical examination; Physician's request.
Staff Physicians 1 (pt); RNs 8 (ft); LPNs 8 (ft); Nurses' aides 30 (ft); Physical therapists (consultant); Reality therapists 1 (pt); Recreational therapists 1 (pt); Occupational therapists 1 (pt); Speech therapists 1 (pt); Activities coordinators 2 (ft); Dietitians (consultant); Ophthalmologists 1 (pt); Podiatrists 1 (pt); Audiologists 1 (pt).
Affiliation King's Daughters & Sons.
Facilities Dining room; Physical therapy room; Activities room; Chapel; Crafts room; Laundry room; Barber/Beauty shop; Library.
Activities Arts & crafts; Cards; Games; Reading groups; Prayer groups; Movies; Shopping trips; Dances/Social/Cultural gatherings; Intergenerational programs; Pet therapy.

Laurelwood Health Care Center
2545 24th St, Rock Island, IL 61201
(309) 788-0458
Admin Margaret L Trousil.
Licensure Skilled care. *Beds* SNF 177. *Certified* Medicaid; Medicare.
Owner Proprietary corp.

Rock Island County Health Care Center
2122 25th Ave, Rock Island, IL 61201
(309) 786-4429
Admin David Johansen. *Dir of Nursing* Kathleen Crawford RN. *Medical Dir* Mark J Valliere MD.
Licensure Skilled care; Alzheimer's care. *Beds* SNF 83. *Certified* Medicaid.
Owner Nonprofit organization/foundation.
Admissions Requirements Minimum age 21; Medical examination; Physician's request.
Staff Physicians 1 (pt); RNs 6 (ft), 3 (pt); LPNs 9 (ft), 3 (pt); Nurses' aides 24 (ft), 14 (pt); Physical therapists 1 (pt); Occupational therapists 1 (pt); Speech therapists 1 (pt); Dietitians 1 (pt); Ophthalmologists 1 (pt); Dentists 2 (pt); Social workers 1 (pt).
Languages Spanish, German.
Facilities Dining room; Physical therapy room; Activities room; Crafts room; Laundry room; Barber/Beauty shop.
Activities Arts & crafts; Cards; Games; Reading groups; Prayer groups; Movies; Shopping trips; Dances/Social/Cultural gatherings.

St Anthonys Continuing Care Center
767 30th St, Rock Island, IL 61201
(309) 788-7631
Admin Mother Mary Anthony OSF.
Licensure Skilled care. *Beds* SNF 183. *Certified* Medicaid; Medicare.
Owner Nonprofit corp.
Affiliation Roman Catholic.

Rockford

Alma Nelson Manor Inc
550 S Mulford Rd, Rockford, IL 61108
(815) 399-4914, 399-0054 FAX
Admin Judy K Larson. *Dir of Nursing* Karin Swanson RN. *Medical Dir* John Schoenwald MD.
Licensure Skilled care; Sheltered care. *Beds* SNF 174. *Private Pay Patients* 60-80%. *Certified* Medicaid; Medicare.
Owner Proprietary corp (Debes Corp).
Admissions Requirements Minimum age 18; Medical examination; Physician's request.
Staff Physicians (consultant); RNs; LPNs; Nurses' aides; Physical therapists; Recreational therapists; Occupational therapists; Speech therapists; Activities coordinators; Dietitians.
Facilities Dining room; Physical therapy room; Activities room; Crafts room; Laundry room; Barber/Beauty shop; Rehabilitation unit.
Activities Arts & crafts; Cards; Games; Reading groups; Prayer groups; Movies; Shopping trips; Dances/Social/Cultural gatherings; Intergenerational programs; Pet therapy.

Alpine Fireside Health Center
3650 N Alpine Rd, Rockford, IL 61111
(815) 877-7408
Admin Kenneth E Alberts.
Licensure Intermediate care; Sheltered care. *Beds* ICF 47; Sheltered care 80.
Owner Proprietary corp.

Deacon Home Ltd
611 N Court St, Rockford, IL 61103
(815) 964-0234
Admin Ivan Gibbs.
Licensure Sheltered care. *Beds* Sheltered care 16.
Owner Proprietary corp.

Fairhaven Christian Home
3470 N Alpine Rd, Rockford, IL 61111
(815) 877-1441
Admin Marvin E Johnson. *Dir of Nursing* Beth Faust RN. *Medical Dir* Michael Werckle MD.
Licensure Intermediate care; Sheltered care. *Beds* ICF 96; Sheltered care 158. *Private Pay Patients* 90%. *Certified* Medicaid.
Owner Nonprofit organization/foundation.
Admissions Requirements Minimum age 65; Medical examination; Physician's request.
Staff Physicians 2 (pt); RNs 10 (ft); LPNs 8 (ft); Nurses' aides 60 (ft); Physical therapists 1 (pt); Occupational therapists 3 (ft); Speech therapists 1 (pt); Activities coordinators 2 (ft); Dietitians 1 (pt); Podiatrists 1 (pt).
Affiliation Evangelical Free Church.
Facilities Dining room; Physical therapy room; Activities room; Chapel; Crafts room; Laundry room; Barber/Beauty shop; Library.
Activities Arts & crafts; Games; Reading groups; Prayer groups; Movies; Shopping trips.

Fairview Plaza Limited Partnership
321 Arnold, Rockford, IL 61108
(815) 397-5531
Admin Theresa Okun.
Licensure Skilled care. *Beds* SNF 213. *Certified* Medicaid; Medicare.
Owner Proprietary corp.

Fountain Terrace
6131 Park Ridge Rd, Rockford, IL 61111
(815) 633-6810
Admin Kathleen A Demler.
Licensure Skilled care. *Beds* 54.
Owner Proprietary corp.

Hallam Terrace
1108 Taylor St, Rockford, IL 61103
(815) 963-0570
Admin Kathleen A Demler.

Licensure Intermediate care for mentally retarded. *Beds* ICF/MR 15.

Highview Retirement Home Association
4149 Safford Rd, Rockford, IL 61103
(815) 964-3368
Admin Clifford D Redding. *Dir of Nursing* Helen Minnick RN.
Licensure Intermediate care; Sheltered care; Retirement. *Beds* ICF 16; Sheltered care 37.
Owner Nonprofit corp.
Admissions Requirements Medical examination.
Staff RNs; LPNs; Nurses' aides; Reality therapists; Recreational therapists; Occupational therapists; Activities coordinators; Dietitians.
Facilities Dining room; Activities room; Crafts room; Laundry room; Barber/Beauty shop; Library.
Activities Arts & crafts; Cards; Games; Reading groups; Prayer groups; Movies; Shopping trips; Dances/Social/Cultural gatherings.

Holt Manor Inc
707 W Riverside Blvd, Rockford, IL 61103
(815) 877-5752
Admin Jill A Meyer.
Medical Dir Dr Mrizek.
Licensure Skilled care. *Beds* SNF 135. *Certified* Medicaid; Medicare.
Owner Proprietary corp.
Facilities Dining room; Physical therapy room; Activities room; Chapel; Crafts room; Laundry room; Barber/Beauty shop; Lounge areas; Pool table.
Activities Arts & crafts; Cards; Games; Reading groups; Prayer groups; Movies; Shopping trips; Dances/Social/Cultural gatherings.

Walter J Lawson Memorial Home for Children
1820 Walter Lawson Dr, Rockford, IL 61111
(815) 633-6636
Admin Theo A Brandel.
Licensure Skilled care. *Beds* SNF 93.

Maria Linden
3330 Maria Linden Dr, Rockford, IL 61111
(815) 877-7416
Admin Patricia A Grady. *Dir of Nursing* Jean Johnson RN. *Medical Dir* Robin Spencer MD.
Licensure Intermediate care; Sheltered care; Retirement. *Beds* ICF 43; Sheltered care 65.
Owner Nonprofit corp (School Sisters of St Francis).
Admissions Requirements Females only.
Staff RNs 4 (ft); LPNs 2 (ft), 5 (pt); Nurses' aides 21 (ft), 5 (pt); Program directors 1 (ft).
Languages German.
Affiliation Roman Catholic.
Facilities Dining room; Physical therapy room; Activities room; Chapel; Crafts room; Laundry room; Barber/Beauty shop; Library; Reading lounges; TV & VCR viewing area.
Activities Arts & crafts; Cards; Games; Reading groups; Prayer groups; Movies; Shopping trips; Dances/Social/Cultural gatherings.

Milestone Inc
109 W State St, Rockford, IL 61101-1105
(815) 968-8962
Admin Robert Stephenson.
Licensure Community living facility. *Beds* Community living facility 20.

Milestone Inc—Elmwood East
2642 Elmwood Rd, Rockford, IL 61103
(815) 877-7001
Admin James Hamilton.
Licensure Intermediate care for mentally retarded. *Beds* ICF/MR 12.

Milestone Inc—Elmwood Heights
2662 Elmwood Rd, Rockford, IL 61103
(815) 877-7001

Admin Elaine E Hand.
Licensure Intermediate care for mentally
retarded. *Beds* ICF/MR 100.

North Rockford Convalescent Home
1920 N Main St, Rockford, IL 61103
(815) 964-6834
Admin Scott L Swanson. *Dir of Nursing*
Myrna Pullin RN. *Medical Dir* Dr Michael
Werckle.
Licensure Intermediate care. *Beds* ICF 97.
Certified Medicaid.
Owner Nonprofit corp.
Admissions Requirements Medical
examination.
Staff Physicians 1 (pt); RNs 7 (ft), 1 (pt);
LPNs 8 (ft); Nurses' aides 36 (ft), 3 (pt);
Physical therapists 1 (pt); Occupational
therapists 1 (pt); Speech therapists 1 (pt);
Activities coordinators 1 (ft); Dietitians 1
(ft); Ophthalmologists 1 (pt); Podiatrists 1
(pt); Dentists 1 (pt).
Affiliation Methodist.
Facilities Dining room; Physical therapy
room; Activities room; Crafts room; Laundry
room; Barber/Beauty shop.
Activities Arts & crafts; Cards; Games;
Reading groups; Prayer groups; Movies;
Shopping trips; Dances/Social/Cultural
gatherings.

Olson Terrace
3006 Alida St, Rockford, IL 61103
(815) 963-0355
Admin Kathleen A Demler.
Licensure Intermediate care for mentally
retarded. *Beds* ICF/MR 15.

Park Strathmoor
5668 Strathmoor Dr, Rockford, IL 61107
(815) 229-5200
Admin Joyce H Dale. *Dir of Nursing* Dixie
Costanza RN. *Medical Dir* Dr Ralph
Valezquez.
Licensure Skilled care; Alzheimer's care. *Beds*
SNF 189. *Certified* Medicaid; Medicare.
Owner Proprietary corp.
Admissions Requirements Minimum age 18.
Staff RNs 6 (ft), 5 (pt); LPNs 20 (ft), 6 (pt);
Nurses' aides 30 (ft), 18 (pt); Physical
therapists 1 (pt); Recreational therapists 1
(pt); Activities coordinators 1 (ft).
Facilities Dining room; Physical therapy
room; Activities room; Barber/Beauty shop.
Activities Arts & crafts; Cards; Games;
Reading groups; Prayer groups; Movies;
Shopping trips; Dances/Social/Cultural
gatherings.

P A Peterson Home for the Aging
1311 Parkview Ave, Rockford, IL 61107
(815) 399-8832
Admin Scott Swanson. *Dir of Nursing* Carol
Couper. *Medical Dir* William Gorski MD.
Licensure Intermediate care; Sheltered care;
Independent apartments. *Beds* ICF 101;
Sheltered care 77; Independent apts 13.
Private Pay Patients 80%. *Certified*
Medicaid.
Owner Nonprofit organization/foundation
(Lutheran Social Services of Illinois).
Admissions Requirements Minimum age 62;
Medical examination.
Staff RNs 6 (ft), 1 (pt); LPNs 7 (ft), 1 (pt);
Nurses' aides 35 (ft), 15 (pt); Activities
coordinators 1 (ft); Dietitians 1 (ft).
Affiliation Lutheran.
Facilities Dining room; Physical therapy
room; Activities room; Chapel; Crafts room;
Laundry room; Barber/Beauty shop; Library.
Activities Arts & crafts; Cards; Games;
Reading groups; Prayer groups; Movies;
Shopping trips; Dances/Social/Cultural
gatherings; Intergenerational programs; Pet
therapy; Woodworking shop.

Riverbluff Nursing Home
4401 N Main St, Rockford, IL 61103
(815) 877-8061
Admin John M Ross. *Dir of Nursing* Mary
Wilson RN. *Medical Dir* Warren C Lewis
MD.
Licensure Skilled care. *Beds* SNF 304.
Certified Medicaid.
Owner Publicly owned.
Admissions Requirements Minimum age 18;
Medical examination; Physician's request.
Staff Physicians 2 (pt); RNs 18 (ft), 2 (pt);
LPNs 18 (ft), 2 (pt); Nurses' aides 109 (ft),
47 (pt); Physical therapists 1 (pt); Activities
coordinators 1 (ft); Ophthalmologists 1 (pt);
Dentists 1 (pt).
Facilities Dining room; Physical therapy
room; Activities room; Chapel; Crafts room;
Laundry room; Barber/Beauty shop; X-ray;
Dental unit.
Activities Arts & crafts; Cards; Games;
Reading groups; Prayer groups; Movies;
Shopping trips; Dances/Social/Cultural
gatherings.

Rockford Health Care Center
310 Arnold Ave, Rockford, IL 61108
(815) 398-7954
Admin Margaret M Patton.
Medical Dir Merrikay Armour.
Licensure Intermediate care. *Beds* ICF 81.
Certified Medicaid.
Owner Proprietary corp (H S Healthcare).
Admissions Requirements Minimum age 55;
Medical examination; Physician's request.
Staff RNs 1 (pt); LPNs 4 (ft), 2 (pt); Nurses'
aides 7 (ft), 12 (pt); Physical therapists 1
(pt); Activities coordinators 2 (ft); Dietitians
1 (pt); Podiatrists 1 (pt); Dentists 1 (pt).
Facilities Dining room; Activities room;
Crafts room; Laundry room; Barber/Beauty
shop.
Activities Arts & crafts; Cards; Games;
Reading groups; Prayer groups; Movies;
Shopping trips; Dances/Social/Cultural
gatherings.

Locustwood Health Care Center
3520 School St, Rockford, IL 61103
(815) 963-4212
Admin Marilyn M Gibson. *Dir of Nursing*
Roberta Bonsall. *Medical Dir* Dr Warren
Lewis.
Licensure Intermediate care. *Beds* ICF 63.
Certified Medicaid.
Owner Proprietary corp (Springwood
Associates).
Admissions Requirements Medical
examination; Physician's request.
Staff RNs 1 (ft); LPNs 5 (ft); Nurses' aides 25
(ft), 5 (pt); Physical therapists 1 (pt);
Recreational therapists 1 (pt); Activities
coordinators 1 (pt); Dietitians 1 (pt);
Ophthalmologists 1 (pt); Podiatrists 1 (pt);
Dietary Supervisor 1 (ft).
Facilities Dining room; Physical therapy
room; Activities room; Crafts room; Laundry
room; Barber/Beauty shop; Library.
Activities Arts & crafts; Cards; Games;
Reading groups; Prayer groups; Movies;
Shopping trips; Dances/Social/Cultural
gatherings; Daily exercises; Intellectual
activities; Community involvement;
Remotivation therapy; Reality orientation;
Music therapy; Adopt-a-grandparent; Pets;
Contacts w/children.

St Anne Center
4405 Highcrest Rd, Rockford, IL 61107
(815) 229-1999, 229-9354 FAX
Admin Thomas Keller. *Dir of Nursing* Mary
Carlson. *Medical Dir* Dr John Roska.
Licensure Skilled care; Intermediate care;
Sheltered care. *Beds* SNF 60; ICF 59;
Sheltered care 1. *Private Pay Patients* 70%.
Certified Medicaid; Medicare.
Owner Nonprofit organization/foundation.
Admissions Requirements Minimum age 62.

Facilities Dining room; Physical therapy
room; Chapel; Laundry room; Barber/Beauty
shop.
Activities Arts & crafts; Cards; Games;
Reading groups; Prayer groups; Movies;
Shopping trips; Dances/Social/Cultural
gatherings; Intergenerational programs; Pet
therapy.

Searles Group Home
3310 Searles Ave, Rockford, IL 61103
(815) 965-3390
Admin James Hamilton.
Licensure Intermediate care for mentally
retarded. *Beds* ICF/MR 12.

Seborg Terrace
3024 Alida St, Rockford, IL 61103
(815) 963-0332
Admin Kathleen A Demler.
Licensure Intermediate care for mentally
retarded. *Beds* ICF/MR 15.

Willows Health Center
4141 N Rockton Ave, Rockford, IL 61103
(815) 654-2534, 654-8160 FAX
Admin John D Currier. *Dir of Nursing* Peggy
Richard. *Medical Dir* Dr Craig Rogers.
Licensure Skilled care; Sheltered care;
Independent living. *Beds* SNF 91; Sheltered
care 202. *Private Pay Patients* 90%. *Certified*
Medicaid.
Owner Nonprofit organization/foundation.
Admissions Requirements Minimum age 62;
Medical examination.
Staff Physicians 1 (pt); RNs 9 (ft); LPNs 11
(ft); Nurses' aides 40 (ft); Physical therapists
(consultant); Occupational therapists 1 (ft);
Speech therapists (consultant); Activities
coordinators 2 (ft); Dietitians 2 (ft);
Podiatrists (consultant); Audiologists 1 (pt)
(consultant).
Affiliation Methodist.
Facilities Dining room; Physical therapy
room; Activities room; Chapel; Crafts room;
Laundry room; Barber/Beauty shop; Library.
Activities Arts & crafts; Cards; Games;
Reading groups; Prayer groups; Movies;
Shopping trips; Dances/Social/Cultural
gatherings; Intergenerational programs; Pet
therapy.

Yorkdale Health Center Inc
2313 N Rockton Ave, Rockford, IL 61107
(815) 964-4611
Admin William M Bersted.
Medical Dir Harry Darland MD.
Licensure Skilled care. *Beds* SNF 160.
Certified Medicaid; Medicare.
Owner Privately owned.
Admissions Requirements Minimum age 21;
Medical examination; Physician's request.
Staff RNs 4 (ft), 1 (pt); LPNs 5 (ft), 2 (pt);
Nurses' aides 49 (ft), 11 (pt); Activities
coordinators 1 (ft); Dietitians 1 (ft).
Facilities Dining room; Physical therapy
room; Activities room; Laundry room;
Barber/Beauty shop; 2 Courtyards.
Activities Arts & crafts; Cards; Games;
Reading groups; Prayer groups; Movies;
Shopping trips; Dances/Social/Cultural
gatherings; Trips to zoo, Metro Centre.

Rolling Meadows

**Americana Healthcare Center of Rolling
Meadows**
4225 Kirchoff Rd, Rolling Meadows, IL 60008
(708) 397-2400
Admin Carolyn J Floyd.
Licensure Skilled care. *Beds* SNF 155.
Certified Medicaid; Medicare.
Owner Proprietary corp (Manor Care).
Admissions Requirements Medical
examination.
Staff Physicians 2 (pt); RNs; LPNs; Nurses'
aides; Physical therapists 1 (ft), 2 (pt);
Recreational therapists 1 (ft); Occupational

therapists 1 (pt); Speech therapists 1 (pt); Activities coordinators 1 (ft); Dietitians 1 (pt); Podiatrists 1 (pt); Dentists 1 (pt).
Facilities Dining room; Physical therapy room; Activities room; Crafts room; Laundry room; Barber/Beauty shop.
Activities Arts & crafts; Cards; Games; Reading groups; Prayer groups; Movies; Shopping trips; Dances/Social/Cultural gatherings.

Clearbrook Center
3201 W Campbell St, Rolling Meadows, IL 60008
(708) 255-0120
Admin Rosanna McLain.
Licensure Intermediate care for mentally retarded. *Beds* ICF/MR 92.

Clearbrook Center East
2800 W Central Rd, Rolling Meadows, IL 60008
Admin Rosanna McLain.
Licensure Intermediate care for mentally retarded. *Beds* ICF/MR 15.

Clearbrook Center West
3980 Fairfax, Rolling Meadows, IL 60008
Admin Rosanna McLain.
Licensure Intermediate care for mentally retarded. *Beds* ICF/MR 15.

Meadows
3250 S Plum Grove Rd, Rolling Meadows, IL 60008
(708) 397-0055
Admin Byrn T Witt.
Medical Dir Dr Petel.
Licensure Intermediate care for mentally retarded. *Beds* ICF/MR 98. *Certified* Medicaid.
Owner Proprietary corp.
Admissions Requirements Minimum age 18; Medical examination.
Staff Physicians 1 (pt); RNs 2 (ft), 2 (pt); LPNs 3 (ft), 4 (pt); Nurses' aides 5 (ft); Physical therapists 1 (pt); Recreational therapists 1 (pt); Occupational therapists 1 (pt); Speech therapists 1 (pt); Activities coordinators 1 (ft); Dietitians 1 (pt); Ophthalmologists 1 (pt); Podiatrists 1 (pt); Audiologists 1 (pt); Dentists 1 (pt); Acting aides 8 (ft); Rehabilitation aides 10 (ft).
Facilities Dining room; Physical therapy room; Activities room; Crafts room; Laundry room; Barber/Beauty shop.
Activities Arts & crafts; Games; Reading groups; Movies; Shopping trips; Dances/Social/Cultural gatherings.

Roselle

Abbington House
31 W Central, Roselle, IL 60172
(708) 894-5058
Admin Marvin M Struck. *Dir of Nursing* Phyllis Struck RN. *Medical Dir* Dr Robert Dick.
Licensure Intermediate care. *Beds* ICF 82. *Certified* Medicaid.
Owner Privately owned.
Admissions Requirements Minimum age 65; Medical examination.
Staff Physicians 5 (pt); RNs 3 (ft); LPNs 3 (pt); Nurses' aides 6 (ft), 5 (pt); Physical therapists 1 (pt); Activities coordinators 1 (ft); Dietitians 1 (pt); Ophthalmologists 1 (pt); Dentists 1 (pt).
Facilities Dining room; Activities room; Crafts room; Laundry room; Barber/Beauty shop; Library.
Activities Arts & crafts; Cards; Games; Reading groups; Prayer groups; Movies; Shopping trips; Dances/Social/Cultural gatherings.

Sunrise Courts
439 Lawrence, Roselle, IL 60172
(708) 543-2440
Admin Daniel Tallman.
Licensure Intermediate care for mentally retarded. *Beds* ICF/MR 20.
Owner Nonprofit corp.

Roseville

LaMoine Christian Nursing Home
PO Box 747, 145 S Chamberlain St, Roseville, IL 61473-0747
(309) 426-2134
Admin James M Oliver. *Dir of Nursing* Shirley Simmons RN. *Medical Dir* Ronald Leonard MD.
Licensure Skilled care; Intermediate care. *Beds* SNF 55; ICF 44. *Private Pay Patients* 60%. *Certified* Medicaid.
Owner Nonprofit organization/foundation (Christian Homes).
Admissions Requirements Minimum age 18; Physician's request.
Staff RNs 6 (ft), 4 (pt); LPNs 4 (ft), 3 (pt); Nurses' aides 26 (ft), 17 (pt); Physical therapists 1 (ft); Activities coordinators 2 (ft).
Facilities Dining room; Physical therapy room; Activities room; Chapel; Crafts room; Laundry room; Barber/Beauty shop; Library.
Activities Arts & crafts; Cards; Games; Reading groups; Prayer groups; Movies; Shopping trips; Dances/Social/Cultural gatherings; Intergenerational programs; Pet therapy.

Rosiclare

Fairview House
Rte 1 Box 56B, Fairview Rd, Rosiclare, IL 62982
(618) 285-6613
Admin Mark Stunson. *Dir of Nursing* Rhonda Belford. *Medical Dir* Marcos N Sunga MD.
Licensure Skilled care; Intermediate care. *Beds* Swing beds SNF/ICF 60. *Private Pay Patients* 15%. *Certified* Medicaid.
Owner Proprietary corp.
Admissions Requirements Medical examination.
Staff RNs 2 (ft), 1 (pt); LPNs 4 (ft); Nurses' aides 30 (ft); Physical therapists 1 (pt); Speech therapists 1 (pt); Activities coordinators 1 (ft), 1 (pt); Dietitians 1 (pt).
Facilities Dining room; Physical therapy room; Activities room; Chapel; Crafts room; Laundry room; Barber/Beauty shop; Library.
Activities Arts & crafts; Cards; Games; Reading groups; Prayer groups; Movies; Shopping trips; Dances/Social/Cultural gatherings.

Round Lake Beach

Hillcrest Retirement Village Ltd
1740 N Circuit Dr, Round Lake Beach, IL 60073
(708) 546-5301
Admin Ruth C Lange. *Dir of Nursing* Mary Ann Gedvilas RN. *Medical Dir* Mark J Round MD.
Licensure Intermediate care. *Beds* ICF 93. *Certified* Medicaid.
Owner Proprietary corp.
Admissions Requirements Minimum age 40; Medical examination; Physician's request.
Staff RNs; LPNs; Nurses' aides; Activities coordinators.
Facilities Dining room; Activities room; Chapel; Laundry room; Barber/Beauty shop; Library.
Activities Arts & crafts; Cards; Games; Reading groups; Prayer groups; Movies; Shopping trips; Dances/Social/Cultural gatherings.

Rushville

Snyder's Vaughn-Haven Inc
135 S Morgan St, Rushville, IL 62681
(217) 322-3420
Admin John R Snyder.
Medical Dir Dr Russel Dohner.
Licensure Skilled care; Intermediate care. *Beds* SNF 49; ICF 50. *Certified* Medicaid; Medicare.
Owner Proprietary corp.
Admissions Requirements Minimum age 18.
Staff RNs 4 (ft), 2 (pt); LPNs 8 (ft), 1 (pt); Nurses' aides 32 (ft); Recreational therapists 1 (ft); Activities coordinators 2 (ft); Dietitians 1 (ft).
Facilities Dining room; Physical therapy room; Activities room; Crafts room; Laundry room; Barber/Beauty shop.
Activities Arts & crafts; Cards; Games; Reading groups; Prayer groups; Movies; Shopping trips; Dances/Social/Cultural gatherings.

Saint Charles

Pine View Care Center
611 Allen Ln, Saint Charles, IL 60174
(708) 377-2211
Admin Wendell Studebaker.
Medical Dir Dr Robert Reeder.
Licensure Skilled care. *Beds* SNF 120. *Certified* Medicare.
Owner Nonprofit corp.
Admissions Requirements Minimum age 22; Medical examination.
Staff Physicians 3 (pt); RNs 8 (ft); LPNs 12 (ft); Nurses' aides 25 (ft); Physical therapists 4 (pt); Occupational therapists 1 (pt); Speech therapists 1 (pt); Activities coordinators 1 (ft); Dietitians 1 (pt); Ophthalmologists 1 (pt); Podiatrists 1 (pt); Dentists 1 (pt).
Languages Spanish.
Affiliation Church of Christ.
Facilities Dining room; Physical therapy room; Activities room; Crafts room; Barber/Beauty shop; Library; Library cart (use of all audio/visual & reading material from public library).
Activities Arts & crafts; Cards; Games; Reading groups; Prayer groups; Movies; Shopping trips; Dances/Social/Cultural gatherings; Lunch outings; Holiday & special events monthly.

Saint Elmo

Heritage Home Care Center
Rte 40 Box 126, Saint Elmo, IL 62458
(618) 829-5581
Admin Tammy B Woolsey. *Dir of Nursing* Karen Lee. *Medical Dir* Dr Lawrence G Oder.
Licensure Intermediate care. *Beds* ICF 68. *Private Pay Patients* 40%. *Certified* Medicaid.
Owner Proprietary corp (Community Lifecare Enterprises).
Admissions Requirements Minimum age 18.
Staff Physicians 1 (ft), 5 (pt); RNs 2 (ft); LPNs 3 (ft), 2 (pt); Nurses' aides 8 (ft), 12 (pt); Physical therapists 1 (pt); Activities coordinators 1 (ft); Dietitians 1 (pt); Ophthalmologists 1 (pt); Podiatrists 1 (pt).
Languages German.
Facilities Dining room; Physical therapy room; Activities room; Laundry room; Barber/Beauty shop; Family room.
Activities Arts & crafts; Cards; Games; Reading groups; Prayer groups; Movies; Shopping trips; Dances/Social/Cultural gatherings; Intergenerational programs; Outings; Family gatherings.

Saint Joseph

Champaign Terrace
PO Box 536, 808 N 3rd, Saint Joseph, IL 61873
(217) 469-8006, 469-2312 FAX
Admin Alan G Ryle. *Dir of Nursing* Lois White. *Medical Dir* Philip Johnson.
Licensure Intermediate care for mentally retarded. *Beds* ICF/MR 15. *Private Pay Patients* 0%. *Certified* Medicaid.
Owner Privately owned (Residential Developers).
Admissions Requirements Minimum age 18; Medical examination.
Staff Physicians 1 (pt); RNs 1 (pt); Speech therapists 1 (pt); Activities coordinators 1 (ft); Dietitians 1 (pt).
Facilities Dining room; Activities room; Laundry room.
Activities Arts & crafts; Cards; Games; Movies; Shopping trips; Dances/Social/Cultural gatherings.

Salem

Bryan Manor
PO Box 1205, Rte 37 N, Salem, IL 62881
(618) 548-4561
Admin Paula J Ross.
Licensure Intermediate care for mentally retarded. *Beds* ICF/MR 85.
Owner Nonprofit corp.

Doctors Nursing Home
1201 Hawthorn Rd, Salem, IL 62881
(618) 548-4884
Admin Catherine E Bailey. *Dir of Nursing* Virginia Milam RN.
Licensure Skilled care. *Beds* SNF 122. *Certified* Medicaid; Medicare.
Owner Proprietary corp (Columbia Corp).
Staff RNs; LPNs; Nurses' aides; Physical therapists; Occupational therapists; Speech therapists; Activities coordinators; Dietitians.

Twin Willow Nursing Center
Rte 37 N, Salem, IL 62881
(618) 548-0542
Admin Todd C Woodruff.
Licensure Intermediate care. *Beds* ICF 76. *Certified* Medicaid.
Owner Proprietary corp.

Sandwich

Dogwood Health Care Center
902 E Arnold Rd, Sandwich, IL 60548
(815) 786-8409
Admin Carol C Price. *Dir of Nursing* William Goss. *Medical Dir* Dr Marawha.
Licensure Intermediate care; Retirement. *Beds* ICF 63; Retirement apartments 20. *Private Pay Patients* 50%. *Certified* Medicaid.
Owner Proprietary corp (Springwood Associates).
Admissions Requirements Minimum age 55; Medical examination; Physician's request.
Staff RNs; LPNs; Nurses' aides; Activities coordinators.
Facilities Dining room; Activities room; Crafts room; Laundry room; Barber/Beauty shop.
Activities Arts & crafts; Cards; Games; Reading groups; Prayer groups; Movies; Shopping trips; Dances/Social/Cultural gatherings.

Open Door Community Living Facility
11 Fayette St, Sandwich, IL 60548
(815) 786-8468
Admin Marilyn Barman.
Licensure Community living facility.

Sandhaven Convalescent Center
515 N Main, Sandwich, IL 60548
(815) 786-8426

Admin Carole A Whalen.
Licensure Skilled care; Intermediate care. *Beds* SNF 58; ICF 58. *Certified* Medicaid; Medicare.
Owner Proprietary corp (Signature Corp).

Savanna

Big Meadows Inc
1000 Longmoor Ave, Savanna, IL 61074
(815) 273-2238
Admin Julienne Lund. *Dir of Nursing* K Carroll RN. *Medical Dir* Dr L B Hussey.
Licensure Intermediate care; Alzheimer's care. *Beds* ICF 122. *Certified* Medicaid.
Owner Proprietary corp.
Admissions Requirements Physician's request.
Staff Physicians 4 (pt); RNs 3 (ft), 2 (pt); LPNs 4 (ft), 1 (pt); Nurses' aides 31 (ft), 5 (pt); Activities coordinators 1 (pt); Dietitians 1 (ft); Social worker 1 (ft).
Facilities Dining room; Physical therapy room; Activities room; Chapel; Crafts room; Laundry room; Barber/Beauty shop; Library.
Activities Arts & crafts; Cards; Games; Reading groups; Prayer groups; Movies; Shopping trips; Dances/Social/Cultural gatherings.

Savoy

Carle Arbours
302 Burwash Ave, Savoy, IL 61874
(217) 337-3090, 337-3194 FAX
Admin Joy P Rathe. *Dir of Nursing* Nancy Richardson. *Medical Dir* Dr Boyd.
Licensure Skilled care; Adult day care; Alzheimer's units; Hospice; Respite care; Retirement. *Beds* SNF 240; Alzheimer's units 2; Retirement 138. *Private Pay Patients* 40%. *Certified* Medicaid; Medicare.
Owner Nonprofit organization/foundation.
Staff Physicians 1 (ft); RNs 3 (ft), 6 (pt); LPNs 16 (ft), 7 (pt); Nurses' aides 43 (ft), 28 (pt); Physical therapists 1 (ft); Activities coordinators 4 (ft); Dietitians 1 (ft); Podiatrists 1 (ft); Respiratory therapists.
Facilities Dining room; Physical therapy room; Activities room; Crafts room; Laundry room; Barber/Beauty shop; Library.
Activities Arts & crafts; Cards; Games; Reading groups; Prayer groups; Movies; Shopping trips; Dances/Social/Cultural gatherings; Intergenerational programs; Pet therapy; Alzheimer's support groups; Family support groups; Alzheimer's family forum.

Schaumburg

Friendship Village—Schaumburg
350 W Schaumburg, Schaumburg, IL 60194
(708) 884-5005, 843-4271 FAX
Admin Cary P Anastasio. *Dir of Nursing* Benicia Miguel BSN. *Medical Dir* Gregory Ostrom MD.
Licensure Skilled care; Retirement; Alzheimer's care. *Beds* SNF 180; Retirement 600. *Private Pay Patients* 90%. *Certified* Medicaid; Medicare.
Owner Nonprofit organization/foundation.
Admissions Requirements Minimum age 62; Medical examination; Physician's request.
Staff Physicians 3 (pt); RNs 16 (ft), 14 (pt); LPNs 4 (ft), 2 (pt); Nurses' aides 40 (ft), 36 (pt); Physical therapists 1 (pt); Occupational therapists 1 (pt); Speech therapists 1 (pt); Activities coordinators 2 (ft), 3 (pt); Dietitians 1 (pt); Ophthalmologists 1 (pt); Podiatrists 1 (pt).
Facilities Dining room; Physical therapy room; Activities room; Crafts room; Laundry room; Barber/Beauty shop; Library.

Activities Arts & crafts; Cards; Games; Reading groups; Prayer groups; Movies; Shopping trips; Dances/Social/Cultural gatherings; Intergenerational programs; Pet therapy; Exercises.

Shabbona

Shabbona HealthCare Center
Rte 30, Comanche St, Shabbona, IL 60550
(815) 824-2194, 824-2196 FAX
Admin Jackie Goken. *Dir of Nursing* Jill Lovett. *Medical Dir* Dr Robert Purdy.
Licensure Skilled care. *Beds* SNF 91. *Private Pay Patients* 45-50%. *Certified* Medicaid; Medicare.
Owner Proprietary corp.
Admissions Requirements Minimum age 50; Medical examination; Physician's request.
Staff Physicians 4 (pt); RNs 8 (ft), 2 (pt); LPNs 1 (ft), 1 (pt); Nurses' aides 25 (ft), 12 (pt); Physical therapists 1 (pt); Activities coordinators 2 (ft); Dietitians 1 (pt); Podiatrists 1 (pt).
Facilities Dining room; Activities room; Crafts room; Laundry room; Barber/Beauty shop.
Activities Arts & crafts; Cards; Games; Reading groups; Movies; Shopping trips; Dances/Social/Cultural gatherings; Intergenerational programs.

Shannon

Villas of Shannon Nursing Home
418 S Ridge St, Shannon, IL 61078
(815) 864-2425
Admin Blaine Fox.
Licensure Intermediate care. *Beds* ICF 73. *Certified* Medicaid.
Owner Proprietary corp.

Shawneetown

Loretta Nursing Home
Logan & Lincoln Sts, Shawneetown, IL 62984
(618) 269-3109
Admin Delbert H York.
Medical Dir Andrew Cserny MD.
Licensure Skilled care. *Beds* SNF 107. *Certified* Medicaid.
Owner Proprietary corp.
Admissions Requirements Minimum age 18; Medical examination; Physician's request.
Staff RNs 2 (ft), 2 (pt); LPNs 5 (ft), 4 (pt); Nurses' aides 27 (ft), 7 (pt); Activities coordinators 1 (ft); Dietitians 1 (pt).

Shelbyville

Olivewood Health Care Center
2116 W South 3rd & Darcey Dr, Shelbyville, IL 62565
(217) 774-2128
Admin Lula M Robertson.
Medical Dir Dr Edwin Sirov.
Licensure Intermediate care. *Beds* ICF 80. *Certified* Medicaid.
Owner Proprietary corp (Springwood Associates).
Admissions Requirements Minimum age 21; Medical examination.
Staff Physicians 6 (ft); RNs 1 (pt); LPNs 5 (ft), 1 (pt); Nurses' aides 9 (ft), 9 (pt); Occupational therapists 1 (pt); Activities coordinators 1 (ft), 1 (pt); Dietitians 1 (pt); Podiatrists 1 (pt); Dentists 1 (pt).
Facilities Dining room; Activities room; Crafts room; Laundry room; Barber/Beauty shop.
Activities Arts & crafts; Games; Reading groups; Prayer groups; Movies; Shopping trips; Dances/Social/Cultural gatherings.

Reservoir Manor
PO Box 467, 419 E Main St, Shelbyville, IL
62565
(217) 774-9545
Admin Charlotte Cohen. *Dir of Nursing* Karen
Forcum RN.
Licensure Intermediate care for mentally
retarded. *Beds* ICF/MR 15. *Certified*
Medicaid.
Owner Proprietary corp (Health Care
Management).
Admissions Requirements Minimum age 18;
Medical examination.
Staff RNs 1 (ft); Nurses' aides 5 (ft), 3 (pt);
Activities coordinators 1 (ft).
Facilities Dining room; Activities room;
Laundry room.
Activities Arts & crafts; Cards; Games;
Reading groups; Movies; Shopping trips;
Dances/Social/Cultural gatherings; Many
community activities.

Shelby Memorial Home
Rte 128 N, Shelbyville, IL 62565
(217) 774-2111
Admin Albert E Wimer.
Licensure Skilled care. *Beds* SNF 99. *Certified*
Medicaid.
Owner Proprietary corp.

Shelby Memorial Hospital Nursing Home
200 S Cedar St, Shelbyville, IL 62565
(217) 774-3961, 774-5713 FAX
Admin Daniel M Colby. *Dir of Nursing*
Lilliam Yates RN. *Medical Dir* Lillian Yates
RN.
Licensure Skilled care. *Beds* SNF 19. *Certified*
Medicare.
Owner Nonprofit corp.
Admissions Requirements Physician's request.
Staff LPNs 1 (ft), 2 (pt); Nurses' aides 10 (ft);
Physical therapists; Occupational therapists 1
(pt); Activities coordinators 1 (pt); Dietitians
1 (pt).
Facilities Dining room; Activities room;
Barber/Beauty shop.
Activities Arts & crafts; Games; Prayer groups;
Pet therapy.

Sheldon

Sheldon Healthcare Inc
PO Box 456, 170 W Concord St, Sheldon, IL
60966
(815) 429-3522
Admin Janice K Conrad. *Dir of Nursing*
Myrna Steiner RN. *Medical Dir* N D
Hungness MD.
Licensure Intermediate care; Retirement. *Beds*
ICF 31. *Certified* Medicaid.
Owner Proprietary corp.
Admissions Requirements Minimum age 70;
Medical examination; Physician's request.
Staff Physicians 9 (pt); RNs 2 (ft); LPNs 2
(ft), 5 (pt); Nurses' aides 10 (ft), 4 (pt);
Recreational therapists 1 (pt); Activities
coordinators 1 (ft), 1 (pt); Dietitians 2 (ft), 1
(pt).
Facilities Dining room; Activities room;
Crafts room; Laundry room; Barber/Beauty
shop.
Activities Arts & crafts; Cards; Games;
Reading groups; Prayer groups; Movies;
Dances/Social/Cultural gatherings.

Sherman

Villa Health Care Center
100 Stardust Dr, Sherman, IL 62684
(217) 744-9891
Admin Vicki S Schmidt.
Licensure Sheltered care. *Beds* Sheltered care
50.

Silvis

Aspenwood Health Care Center
1403 E 9th Ave, Silvis, IL 61282
(309) 786-8409
Admin Shirley J Schroeder.
Medical Dir Shirley J Schroeder.
Licensure Intermediate care. *Beds* ICF 63.
Certified Medicaid.
Owner Proprietary corp (Springwood
Associates).
Staff RNs; LPNs; Nurses' aides; Activities
coordinators; Dietitians.
Activities Arts & crafts; Cards; Games;
Reading groups; Prayer groups; Movies;
Shopping trips; Dances/Social/Cultural
gatherings.

Simpson

Shawnee Shelter Care
Rte 1, Simpson, IL 62985
(618) 695-3321
Admin Georgia L Brown.
Licensure Sheltered care. *Beds* 13.
Owner Proprietary corp.

Skokie

Lieberman Geriatric Health Centre
9700 Gross Point Rd, Skokie, IL 60076
(708) 674-7210, 674-6366 FAX
Admin Barbara Wexler. *Dir of Nursing* Gale
Vogler. *Medical Dir* Dr Herschel Weller,
Acting.
Licensure Skilled care; Retirement;
Alzheimer's care. *Beds* SNF 240; Retirement
53. *Private Pay Patients* 40%. *Certified*
Medicaid.
Owner Nonprofit organization/foundation.
Admissions Requirements Medical
examination.
Staff Physicians 1 (ft); RNs 31 (ft); LPNs 7
(ft); Nurses' aides 94 (ft); Physical therapists
(contracted); Recreational therapists 7 (ft);
Activities coordinators 1 (ft); Dietitians 2
(ft); MSWs 5 (ft).
Languages Yiddish, Hebrew, Russian.
Affiliation Jewish.
Facilities Dining room; Physical therapy
room; Activities room; Crafts room; Laundry
room; Barber/Beauty shop; Library;
Synagogue; Private rooms.
Activities Arts & crafts; Cards; Games;
Reading groups; Prayer groups; Movies;
Shopping trips; Dances/Social/Cultural
gatherings; Intergenerational programs; Pet
therapy; Jewish education; Art therapy;
Music therapy.

Old Orchard Manor
4660 Old Orchard Rd, Skokie, IL 60076
(708) 676-4800
Admin Jane Ionescu. *Dir of Nursing* Sharon
Eager. *Medical Dir* Arthur R Peterson MD.
Licensure Skilled care. *Beds* SNF 61. *Private
Pay Patients* 100%.
Owner Proprietary corp (432 Poplar Corp).
Admissions Requirements Minimum age 18;
Medical examination; Physician's request.
Staff RNs 8 (ft), 7 (pt); Nurses' aides 16 (ft);
Physical therapists 3 (pt); Recreational
therapists 1 (ft), 3 (pt); Occupational
therapists 1 (pt); Speech therapists 1 (pt);
Activities coordinators 1 (ft); Dietitians 1
(pt); Ophthalmologists 1 (pt); Podiatrists 1
(pt).
Facilities Dining room; Physical therapy
room; Activities room; Crafts room; Laundry
room; Barber/Beauty shop; Enclosed patio
with garden and dining area.
Activities Arts & crafts; Cards; Games;
Reading groups; Prayer groups; Movies;
Shopping trips; Dances/Social/Cultural
gatherings; Intergenerational programs; Pet
therapy; Friday cocktail party.

Orchard Village Intermediate Care Facility
7671 Marmora Manor, Skokie, IL 60077
(708) 967-1800
Admin Cheryl Smith.
Licensure Intermediate care for mentally
retarded. *Beds* ICF/MR 13. *Certified*
Medicaid.
Owner Nonprofit corp.
Admissions Requirements Minimum age 18;
Males only; Medical examination.
Staff Physicians (consultant); RNs
(consultant); Activities coordinators 1 (pt);
Dietitians (consultant); Rehabilitation aides
6 (ft), 4 (pt).
Languages Sign.
Facilities Dining room; Activities room;
Laundry room.
Activities Arts & crafts; Cards; Games;
Reading groups; Movies; Shopping trips;
Dances/Social/Cultural gatherings;
Intergenerational programs.

Shore Home West
8167-69 Lincoln Ave, Skokie, IL 60077
Admin Kathleen Jesko.
Licensure Community living facility. *Beds*
Community living facility 12.

Skokie Meadows Nursing Center No I
9615 N Knox Ave, Skokie, IL 60076
(708) 679-4161
Admin John Langland. *Dir of Nursing* Judith
Singson. *Medical Dir* Dr Boris Gurevich.
Licensure Skilled care. *Beds* SNF 113.
Certified Medicaid; Medicare.
Owner Proprietary corp.
Admissions Requirements Minimum age 20;
Medical examination.
Staff RNs; LPNs; Nurses' aides; Physical
therapists; Reality therapists; Recreational
therapists; Occupational therapists; Speech
therapists; Activities coordinators; Dietitians;
Ophthalmologists; Podiatrists; Audiologists;
Dentists.
Facilities Dining room; Physical therapy
room; Activities room; Crafts room; Laundry
room; Barber/Beauty shop; Library; Enclosed
patio.
Activities Arts & crafts; Cards; Games;
Reading groups; Prayer groups; Movies;
Shopping trips; Dances/Social/Cultural
gatherings; Intergenerational programs; Pet
therapy; Picnics; Geri-Olympics.

Skokie Meadows Nursing Center No II
4600 W Golf Rd, Skokie, IL 60076
(708) 679-1157
Admin Joan Willey.
Licensure Intermediate care. *Beds* ICF 111.
Certified Medicaid.
Owner Proprietary corp.

Village Nursing Home Inc
9000 La Vergne Ave, Skokie, IL 60077
(708) 679-2322
Admin Samuel Brandman.
Licensure Skilled care; Intermediate care. *Beds*
SNF 98; ICF 51. *Certified* Medicaid;
Medicare.
Owner Proprietary corp.

Smithton

Park Haven Care Center
107 S Lincoln, Smithton, IL 62285
(618) 235-4600
Admin Joyce Haege.
Licensure Intermediate care. *Beds* ICF 101.
Certified Medicaid.
Owner Proprietary corp.

South Beloit

Fair Oaks Nursing Home
1515 Blackhawk Blvd, South Beloit, IL 61080
(815) 389-3911

Admin Sandra Nienaber. *Dir of Nursing* Betty Thurner RN. *Medical Dir* T P Long MD.
Licensure Skilled care; Alzheimer's care. *Beds* SNF 42.
Owner Nonprofit corp.
Admissions Requirements Minimum age 19; Medical examination; Physician's request.
Staff RNs 2 (ft), 3 (pt); LPNs 4 (pt); Nurses' aides 10 (ft), 10 (pt); Activities coordinators 1 (ft), 1 (pt).
Facilities Dining room; Physical therapy room; Activities room; Laundry room; Barber/Beauty shop.
Activities Arts & crafts; Cards; Games; Reading groups; Prayer groups; Movies; Shopping trips; Dances/Social/Cultural gatherings.

South Chicago Heights

Woodside Manor
120 W 26th St, South Chicago Heights, IL 60411
(708) 756-5200
Admin Carolyn S Bessette.
Licensure Skilled care; Intermediate care. *Beds* SNF 64; ICF 48.
Owner Proprietary corp.

South Elgin

Alderwood Health Care Center
746 Spring St, South Elgin, IL 60177
(708) 697-0565
Admin Barbara L Freeman.
Licensure Intermediate care. *Beds* ICF 90. *Certified* Medicaid.
Owner Proprietary corp (Springwood Associates).

Fox Valley Nursing Center Inc
759 Kane St, South Elgin, IL 60177
(708) 697-3310
Admin Janet Lapidos.
Medical Dir Barbara Blust.
Licensure Skilled care; Intermediate care. *Beds* SNF 107; ICF 99. *Certified* Medicaid; Medicare.
Owner Privately owned.
Admissions Requirements Minimum age 18.
Staff RNs 10 (ft); LPNs 2 (ft); Nurses' aides 30 (ft); Physical therapists 1 (ft); Occupational therapists 1 (pt); Speech therapists 1 (pt); Activities coordinators 1 (ft).
Languages French, Italian, Polish.
Facilities Dining room; Physical therapy room; Activities room; Chapel; Crafts room; Laundry room; Barber/Beauty shop.
Activities Arts & crafts; Cards; Games; Reading groups; Prayer groups; Movies; Shopping trips; Dances/Social/Cultural gatherings.

South Holland

Americana Healthcare Center of South Holland
2145 E 170th St, South Holland, IL 60473
(708) 895-3255
Admin Karen Lauderback.
Licensure Skilled care; Intermediate care. *Beds* SNF 90; ICF 30.

Bethshan Association—Tibstra House
271 E 161st St, South Holland, IL 60473
(708) 596-4442
Licensure Intermediate care for mentally retarded. *Beds* ICF/MR 15.
Admissions Requirements Minimum age 21.

Holland Home for the Aged
16300 S Louis Ave, South Holland, IL 60473
(708) 596-3050
Admin Peter J Schuman.
Licensure Sheltered care. *Beds* Sheltered care 326. *Certified* Medicaid.
Owner Nonprofit corp.

Rest Haven South Skilled Nursing Center
16300 Wausau Ave, South Holland, IL 60473
(708) 596-5500, 596-6502 FAX
Admin Peter Schurman. *Dir of Nursing* Judith McDonald RN. *Medical Dir* G Gnade MD.
Licensure Skilled care; Intermediate care; Retirement; Alzheimer's care. *Beds* SNF 116; ICF 50; Retirement 326. *Private Pay Patients* 100%. *Certified* Medicare.
Owner Nonprofit organization/foundation (Rest Haven Christian Services).
Admissions Requirements Minimum age 65; Medical examination.
Staff Physicians 4 (pt); RNs 8 (ft), 12 (pt); LPNs 2 (ft), 4 (pt); Nurses' aides 25 (ft), 50 (pt).
Languages Dutch.
Affiliation Christian Reformed.
Facilities Dining room; Physical therapy room; Activities room; Chapel; Crafts room; Barber/Beauty shop; Library.
Activities Arts & crafts; Cards; Games; Reading groups; Prayer groups; Movies; Dances/Social/Cultural gatherings; Intergenerational programs; Pet therapy.

Windmill Nursing Pavilion LTD
16000 S Wabash Ave, South Holland, IL 60473
(708) 339-0600
Admin Evonne L Casson.
Medical Dir Dr S Levine.
Licensure Skilled care; Intermediate care; Alzheimer's care. *Beds* SNF 100; ICF 50. *Certified* Medicaid.
Owner Proprietary corp.
Admissions Requirements Minimum age 21; Physician's request.
Staff Physicians; RNs; LPNs; Nurses' aides; Physical therapists; Occupational therapists; Speech therapists; Activities coordinators; Dietitians; Ophthalmologists; Podiatrists; Dentists.
Facilities Dining room; Physical therapy room; Activities room; Chapel; Crafts room; Laundry room; Barber/Beauty shop; Library.
Activities Arts & crafts; Cards; Games; Reading groups; Prayer groups; Movies; Shopping trips; Dances/Social/Cultural gatherings; Outings.

Sparta

Randolph County Nursing Home
310 W Belmont, Sparta, IL 62286
(618) 443-4351
Admin Paulette A Buch. *Dir of Nursing* Edith Besher RN.
Licensure Skilled care; Intermediate care. *Beds* SNF 74; ICF 62. *Private Pay Patients* 50%. *Certified* Medicaid; Medicare.
Owner Nonprofit organization/foundation.
Admissions Requirements Minimum age 18; Medical examination.
Staff RNs 3 (ft), 1 (pt); LPNs 5 (ft), 7 (pt); Nurses' aides 30 (ft), 17 (pt); Physical therapists 1 (pt); Recreational therapists 1 (pt); Occupational therapists 1 (pt); Speech therapists 1 (pt); Activities coordinators 1 (ft); Dietitians 1 (pt); Audiologists 1 (pt).
Facilities Dining room; Physical therapy room; Activities room; Chapel; Crafts room; Laundry room; Barber/Beauty shop.
Activities Arts & crafts; Cards; Games; Reading groups; Prayer groups; Movies; Shopping trips; Dances/Social/Cultural gatherings; Intergenerational programs; Pet therapy.

Senior Manor Nursing Center Inc
223 E 4th St, Sparta, IL 62286
(618) 443-4411
Admin Ruth Jung. *Dir of Nursing* Lois McDaniel. *Medical Dir* Dr O Pflasterer.
Licensure Intermediate care. *Beds* ICF 59. *Private Pay Patients* 65%. *Certified* Medicaid.

Owner Proprietary corp.
Admissions Requirements Minimum age 21.
Staff RNs 1 (ft); LPNs 3 (ft), 4 (pt); Nurses' aides 10 (ft), 6 (pt); Activities coordinators 1 (ft), 1 (pt); Dietitians 1 (ft).
Facilities Dining room; Physical therapy room; Activities room; Chapel; Crafts room; Laundry room; Barber/Beauty shop; Library.
Activities Arts & crafts; Cards; Games; Reading groups; Prayer groups; Movies; Shopping trips; Dances/Social/Cultural gatherings; Intergenerational programs; Pet therapy.

Sparta Terrace
1501 Melmar Dr, Sparta, IL 62286
(618) 443-2122
Admin Patrick A Devine.
Licensure Intermediate care for mentally retarded. *Beds* ICF/MR 15.

Spring Valley

Spring Valley Nursing Center
1300 N Greenwood St, Spring Valley, IL 61362
(815) 664-4708
Admin Shirley M Michalski RN. *Dir of Nursing* Barbara J Lansing RN. *Medical Dir* Dr Donald Gallagher.
Licensure Skilled care; Medicare certified. *Beds* SNF 98; Medicare certified 9. *Private Pay Patients* 30%. *Certified* Medicaid; Medicare.
Owner Proprietary corp.
Admissions Requirements Minimum age 18; Medical examination; Physician's request.
Staff Physicians; RNs 2 (ft), 7 (pt); LPNs 2 (ft), 1 (pt); Nurses' aides 35 (ft), 6 (pt); Physical therapists (consultant); Recreational therapists 2 (ft), 2 (pt); Occupational therapists (consultant); Dietitians (consultant); Ophthalmologists (consultant); Podiatrists (consultant); Audiologists (consultant).
Facilities Dining room; Physical therapy room; Activities room; Laundry room; Barber/Beauty shop; Library.
Activities Arts & crafts; Games; Movies; Pet therapy.

Springfield

Argyle House
534 W Miller, Springfield, IL 62702
(217) 789-2564
Admin John D Walz.
Licensure Community living facility. *Beds* Community living facility 20.
Owner Nonprofit organization/foundation.

Bethesda Lutheran Home
1100 S Pasfield, Springfield, IL 62704
(217) 789-1960
Admin Bart D Quick.
Medical Dir Kenneth Malmberg MD.
Licensure Intermediate care for mentally retarded. *Beds* ICF/MR 15. *Certified* Medicaid; Medicare.
Owner Nonprofit organization/foundation (Bethesda Lutheran Home).
Admissions Requirements Minimum age 18; Medical examination.
Staff Physicians 1 (pt); RNs 1 (pt); Physical therapists 1 (pt); Occupational therapists (consultant); Speech therapists (consultant); Activities coordinators (consultant); Dietitians (consultant); Ophthalmologists (consultant); Podiatrists (consultant); Audiologists (consultant).
Affiliation Lutheran.
Facilities Dining room; Laundry room.
Activities Arts & crafts; Cards; Games; Prayer groups; Movies; Shopping trips; Dances/Social/Cultural gatherings.

Brother James Court
RR 1, Sangamon Ave Rd E, Springfield, IL
62707
(217) 544-4876
Admin James C Sarnecki. *Dir of Nursing*
Michael Groesch. *Medical Dir* H B Henkel
MD.
Licensure Intermediate care for mentally
retarded. *Beds* ICF/MR 96. *Certified*
Medicaid.
Owner Nonprofit corp.
Admissions Requirements Minimum age 18;
Males only; Medical examination;
Physician's request.
Staff RNs 2 (ft); LPNs 2 (ft), 2 (pt); Nurses'
aides 14 (ft), 2 (pt); Recreational therapists 5
(ft); Occupational therapists 1 (pt); Speech
therapists 1 (pt); Activities coordinators 1
(ft); Dietitians 1 (pt).
Affiliation Roman Catholic.
Facilities Dining room; Activities room;
Chapel; Crafts room; Laundry room;
Library.
Activities Arts & crafts; Games; Prayer groups;
Movies; Shopping trips; Dances/Social/
Cultural gatherings.

Mary Bryant Home for the Visually Impaired
2960 Stanton Ave, Springfield, IL 62703
(217) 529-1611
Admin Frances J Trees. *Dir of Nursing* Ann
Toenjes RN, consultant. *Medical Dir* Mark
E Hansen MD.
Licensure Sheltered care. *Beds* Sheltered care
46.
Owner Nonprofit corp.
Admissions Requirements Minimum age 18;
Medical examination; Visually impaired.
Staff RNs; Nurses' aides; Activities
coordinators.
Facilities Dining room; Activities room;
Crafts room; Laundry room; Barber/Beauty
shop; Library; Family room.
Activities Arts & crafts; Cards; Games;
Reading groups; Prayer groups; Movies;
Shopping trips; Dances/Social/Cultural
gatherings.

Clarkston Court
2301 W Monroe St, Springfield, IL 62704
(217) 546-0272
Admin Judy Weger.
Licensure Intermediate care. *Beds* ICF 194.
Certified Medicaid.
Owner Proprietary corp.

Dirksen House Healthcare
555 W Carpenter, Springfield, IL 62702
(217) 525-1880, 525-7762 FAX
Admin Michael Barth. *Dir of Nursing* Marilyn
Will RN. *Medical Dir* James Kufdakis MD.
Licensure Skilled care; Intermediate care;
Adult day care; Respite care; Alzheimer's
care. *Beds* SNF 67; ICF 192. *Certified*
Medicaid; Medicare.
Owner Proprietary corp (Hillhaven Corp).
Admissions Requirements Medical
examination; Physician's request.
Staff Physicians 1 (pt); RNs 4 (ft), 1 (pt);
LPNs 25 (ft), 2 (pt); Nurses' aides 55 (ft), 5
(pt); Physical therapists 1 (pt); Occupational
therapists 1 (ft); Speech therapists 1 (pt);
Activities coordinators 1 (ft); Dietitians 1
(ft).
Facilities Dining room; Physical therapy
room; Activities room; Crafts room; Laundry
room; Barber/Beauty shop; Lobby.
Activities Arts & crafts; Cards; Games;
Reading groups; Prayer groups; Movies;
Shopping trips; Dances/Social/Cultural
gatherings.

Gaines Mill Place
3310 Gaines Mill Rd, Springfield, IL 62704
Admin Terry Braidwood.
Licensure Intermediate care for mentally
retarded. *Beds* ICF/MR 15.

Glenwood Terrace
2724 Glenwood Ave, Springfield, IL 62704
Admin Patrick Finn.
Licensure Intermediate care for mentally
retarded. *Beds* ICF/MR 15.

Heritage Manor Nursing & Convalescent Home
900 N Rutledge, Springfield, IL 62702
(217) 789-0930, 789-0621 FAX
Admin Kathleen Peters-Cross. *Dir of Nursing*
Pat McNeal. *Medical Dir* Dr Craig Backs.
Licensure Skilled care; Intermediate care. *Beds*
SNF 126; ICF 30. *Private Pay Patients* 50%.
Certified Medicaid; Medicare.
Owner Proprietary corp (Heritage Enterprises).
Staff RNs; LPNs; Nurses' aides; Physical
therapists; Speech therapists 1 (pt); Activities
coordinators 1 (ft); Dietitians 1 (pt).
Facilities Dining room; Physical therapy
room; Activities room; Chapel; Laundry
room; Barber/Beauty shop; Library.
Activities Arts & crafts; Cards; Games;
Reading groups; Prayer groups; Movies;
Shopping trips; Dances/Social/Cultural
gatherings; Intergenerational programs.

Hope School
50 Hazel Ln, Springfield, IL 62703
(217) 786-3350
Admin Naomi Mueller.
Licensure Intermediate care for mentally
retarded. *Beds* ICF/MR 40.

Illinois Presbyterian Home
2005 W Lawrence, Springfield, IL 62704
(217) 546-5622
Admin Thomas P O'Fallon.
Licensure Intermediate care; Sheltered care.
Beds ICF 15; Sheltered care 68. *Certified*
Medicaid.
Owner Nonprofit corp.
Admissions Requirements Minimum age 65;
Medical examination.
Staff RNs 2 (ft), 2 (pt); LPNs 2 (ft), 3 (pt);
Nurses' aides 7 (ft), 3 (pt); Activities
coordinators 1 (ft); Dietitians 1 (pt).
Affiliation Presbyterian.
Facilities Dining room; Activities room;
Crafts room; Laundry room; Library.
Activities Arts & crafts; Cards; Games;
Reading groups; Prayer groups; Movies;
Shopping trips; Dances/Social/Cultural
gatherings.

Karlson Specialized Living Center
200 W Lake Dr, Springfield, IL 62703
(217) 786-2554
Admin Charles T Cook. *Dir of Nursing* Carole
Keiller. *Medical Dir* Kenneth Malmberg
MD.
Licensure Intermediate care for mentally
retarded. *Beds* ICF/MR 64. *Private Pay
Patients* 3%.
Owner Nonprofit organization/foundation.
Staff Physicians 2 (pt); RNs 1 (ft); LPNs 3
(ft), 3 (pt); Physical therapists 1 (pt);
Occupational therapists 1 (pt); Speech
therapists 1 (pt); Dietitians 1 (pt); Program
technicians 48 (ft); QMRPs 4 (ft).
Languages Sign.
Facilities Dining room; Activities room.
Activities Arts & crafts; Games; Movies;
Shopping trips; Dances/Social/Cultural
gatherings; "Zone" activities.

Lewis Memorial Christian Village
3400 W Washington, Springfield, IL 62707
(217) 787-9600, 787-9622 FAX
Admin Robert Florence. *Dir of Nursing* Arlene
Colclasure RN. *Medical Dir* John Meyer
MD.
Licensure Skilled care; Intermediate care;
Retirement. *Beds* SNF 76; ICF 79. *Private
Pay Patients* 70%. *Certified* Medicaid.
Owner Nonprofit organization/foundation
(Christian Homes).
Admissions Requirements Minimum age 18;
Medical examination; Physician's request.

Staff RNs 5 (ft); LPNs 15 (ft); Nurses' aides
50 (ft); Physical therapists; Activities
coordinators 1 (ft).
Affiliation Church of Christ.
Facilities Dining room; Physical therapy
room; Activities room; Chapel; Crafts room;
Laundry room; Barber/Beauty shop.
Activities Arts & crafts; Cards; Games;
Reading groups; Prayer groups; Movies;
Shopping trips; Dances/Social/Cultural
gatherings; Intergenerational programs.

Oak Terrace Healthcare Center
1750 W Washington, Springfield, IL 62704
(217) 787-6466
Admin Anasue L Haines.
Medical Dir Norman Scheibling.
Licensure Intermediate care; Sheltered care.
Beds ICF 68; Sheltered care 30.
Owner Proprietary corp.
Admissions Requirements Minimum age 18;
Medical examination.
Staff RNs 1 (ft), 2 (pt); LPNs 4 (ft), 2 (pt);
Nurses' aides 4 (ft), 10 (pt); Activities
coordinators 1 (ft), 1 (pt); Dietitians 1 (pt).
Facilities Dining room; Activities room;
Crafts room; Laundry room; Barber/Beauty
shop; Library.
Activities Arts & crafts; Cards; Games;
Reading groups; Prayer groups; Movies;
Shopping trips.

Regency
911 N Rutledge, Springfield, IL 62702
(217) 525-0200
Admin Harry J Sabath.
Licensure Intermediate care. *Beds* ICF 53.

Roosevelt Square Nursing Home
2120 W Washington Ave, Springfield, IL
62702
(217) 546-1325
Admin Johanna Coverstone.
Medical Dir Marge Thompson.
Licensure Intermediate care. *Beds* ICF 77.
Certified Medicaid.
Owner Proprietary corp.
Admissions Requirements Minimum age 18;
Medical examination.
Staff LPNs 4 (ft), 2 (pt); Nurses' aides 10 (ft),
8 (pt); Physical therapists 1 (ft); Recreational
therapists 2 (ft); Occupational therapists 2
(ft); Dietitians 1 (ft).
Facilities Dining room; Laundry room.
Activities Arts & crafts; Games; Reading
groups; Prayer groups; Movies; Shopping
trips; Dances/Social/Cultural gatherings.

Rutledge Manor Care Home Inc
913 N Rutledge St, Springfield, IL 62702
(217) 525-1722
Admin Betty Hickman.
Licensure Intermediate care; Sheltered care.
Beds ICF 155; Sheltered care 12.
Owner Proprietary corp.

St Joseph's Home of Springfield
3306 S 6th St Rd, Springfield, IL 62703
(217) 529-5596, 529-1573 FAX
Admin Sr Mary Barbara Buckley; Sr Judith
Morris. *Dir of Nursing* Judith Keller RN.
Medical Dir Dr Richard H Suhs.
Licensure Intermediate care; Sheltered care.
Beds ICF 73; Sheltered care 60. *Private Pay
Patients* 95%.
Owner Nonprofit corp.
Staff RNs 2 (ft); LPNs 15 (ft), 2 (pt); Nurses'
aides 27 (ft), 1 (pt); Activities coordinators 2
(ft), 1 (pt).
Affiliation Roman Catholic.
Activities Arts & crafts; Games; Shopping
trips; Pet therapy.

Springfield Terrace Ltd
525 S Martin Luther King Dr, Springfield, IL
62703
(217) 789-1680
Admin Jill Spurgeon.

Licensure Intermediate care. Beds 65. Certified Medicaid.
Owner Proprietary corp.
Admissions Requirements Minimum age 18; Medical examination.
Facilities Dining room; Physical therapy room; Activities room; Chapel; Crafts room; Laundry room; Barber/Beauty shop.
Activities Arts & crafts; Games; Reading groups; Prayer groups; Movies; Shopping trips; Dances/Social/Cultural gatherings; Orientation.

Taylor House
3021 Taylor Ave, Springfield, IL 62703
Admin Terry Braidwood.
Licensure Intermediate care for mentally retarded. Beds ICF/MR 15.

Staunton

Country Care of Staunton
215 W Pennsylvania Ave, Staunton, IL 62088
(618) 635-5577
Admin Judith Ann Ragland.
Licensure Skilled care. Beds SNF 99. Certified Medicaid; Medicare.
Owner Proprietary corp.

Sterling

Casa Willis
910 Woodburn, Sterling, IL 61081
(815) 625-4444
Admin Connie L Pleinis.
Licensure Intermediate care for mentally retarded. Beds ICF/MR 15.

Exceptional Care & Training Center
2601 Woodlawn Rd, Sterling, IL 61081
(815) 626-5820
Admin Jarolyn B Fyhrlund.
Licensure Skilled care. Beds SNF 64. Certified Medicaid.
Owner Proprietary corp.

Hammett House
1845 1st Ave, Sterling, IL 61081
(815) 626-9547
Admin Connie L Pleinis.
Licensure Intermediate care for mentally retarded. Beds ICF/MR 15.

Parkway Center
1801 Ave G, Sterling, IL 61081
(815) 626-1121
Admin Ronald L Garwick. Dir of Nursing Paula Chamley. Medical Dir Mark Styczynski MD.
Licensure Sheltered care; Assisted apartment living. Beds Sheltered care 29; Assisted apartment living 32.
Owner Proprietary corp.
Admissions Requirements Medical examination.
Staff RNs 2 (ft), 2 (pt); LPNs 4 (pt); Nurses' aides 3 (ft), 3 (pt); Activities coordinators 1 (ft); Dietitians 1 (pt).
Facilities Dining room; Physical therapy room; Activities room; Chapel; Crafts room; Laundry room; Barber/Beauty shop; Library.
Activities Arts & crafts; Cards; Games; Reading groups; Prayer groups; Movies; Shopping trips; Intergenerational gatherings; Pet therapy.

Sterling Care Center
105 E 23rd St, Sterling, IL 61081
(815) 626-4264
Admin Jeanne E Radunz.
Licensure Skilled care. Beds SNF 121. Certified Medicaid; Medicare.
Owner Proprietary corp.

Stern Square
1328 W 7th St, Sterling, IL 61081
(815) 625-1600, 626-8104 FAX

Admin Connie L Pleinis. Dir of Nursing Concha Sitter BSN. Medical Dir Dr Bondy.
Licensure Intermediate care for mentally retarded. Beds ICF/MR 15. Private Pay Patients 0%. Certified Medicaid.
Owner Nonprofit organization/foundation.
Admissions Requirements Minimum age 18; Medical examination.
Staff Physicians; RNs; Recreational therapists; Occupational therapists; Speech therapists; Activities coordinators; Dietitians; Podiatrists; Habilitation aides.
Facilities Dining room; Activities room; Laundry room.
Activities Arts & crafts; Cards; Games; Movies; Shopping trips; Dances/Social/Cultural gatherings; Intergenerational programs.

Tammerlane Inc
3601 16th Ave, Sterling, IL 61081
(815) 626-0233
Admin Nola L Duffy.
Licensure Intermediate care. Beds ICF 70.

Stickney

Pershing Convalescent Home Inc
3900 S Oak Park Ave, Stickney, IL 60402
(708) 484-7543, 484-7586 FAX
Admin Lucille R Engelsman. Dir of Nursing Theresa Dvorak. Medical Dir Dr I Desai.
Licensure Intermediate care. Beds ICF 51. Private Pay Patients 70%. Certified Medicaid.
Owner Proprietary corp.
Staff Physicians (consultant); RNs 3 (ft); LPNs 4 (pt); Nurses' aides 8 (ft), 3 (pt); Physical therapists (consultant); Speech therapists (consultant); Dietitians (consultant); Ophthalmologists (consultant); Podiatrists (consultant); Audiologists (consultant).
Affiliation Roman Catholic.
Facilities Dining room; Physical therapy room; Activities room; Laundry room.
Activities Arts & crafts; Cards; Games; Reading groups; Prayer groups; Movies; Shopping trips; Dances/Social/Cultural gatherings; Intergenerational programs; Pet therapy.

Stockton

Morgan Memorial Home
501 E Front Ave, Stockton, IL 61085
(815) 947-2215
Admin Kim M Heid.
Medical Dir Ruth Chumbler.
Licensure Intermediate care. Beds ICF 37. Certified Medicaid.
Owner Proprietary corp.
Admissions Requirements Minimum age 18; Medical examination.
Staff RNs 3 (ft); LPNs 6 (ft); Nurses' aides 6 (ft), 13 (pt); Activities coordinators 1 (ft); Dietitians 2 (ft); Social Consultant; Social service designer 2 (ft).
Facilities Dining room; Activities room; Crafts room; Laundry room; Barber/Beauty shop; Living room.
Activities Arts & crafts; Cards; Games; Reading groups; Prayer groups; Movies; Shopping trips; Dances/Social/Cultural gatherings; Pet show yearly; Flea market involving entire area; Bingo; Music.

Streator

Camelot Manor
516 W Frech St, Streator, IL 61364
(815) 672-9390
Admin R S Gomes.
Licensure Intermediate care. Beds ICF 100. Certified Medicaid.
Owner Proprietary corp.

Admissions Requirements Minimum age 18; Medical examination.
Staff RNs 1 (ft), 2 (pt); LPNs 3 (ft), 4 (pt); Nurses' aides 13 (ft), 3 (pt); Recreational therapists 1 (ft), 2 (pt); Activities coordinators 1 (ft); Podiatrists 1 (pt).
Facilities Dining room; Physical therapy room; Activities room; Laundry room; Barber/Beauty shop.
Activities Arts & crafts; Cards; Games; Reading groups; Prayer groups; Movies; Shopping trips; Dances/Social/Cultural gatherings; Bowling league.

Heritage Manor
1525 E Main St, Streator, IL 61364
(815) 672-4516
Admin Mary Colson. Dir of Nursing Vela Hogue. Medical Dir Dr Bacayo.
Licensure Skilled care; Alzheimer's care. Beds SNF 110. Private Pay Patients 40%. Certified Medicaid; Medicare; VA.
Owner Proprietary corp (Heritage Enterprises).
Admissions Requirements Physician's request.
Staff Physicians; RNs; LPNs; Nurses' aides; Physical therapists; Occupational therapists; Speech therapists; Activities coordinators; Dietitians.
Languages German.
Facilities Dining room; Physical therapy room; Activities room; Crafts room; Laundry room; Barber/Beauty shop.
Activities Arts & crafts; Cards; Games; Reading groups; Prayer groups; Movies; Shopping trips; Dances/Social/Cultural gatherings; Intergenerational programs; Pet therapy.

Sullivan

Illinois Masonic Home
Rte 121 E, Sullivan, IL 61951
(217) 728-4394
Admin James E Hart.
Licensure Intermediate care; Sheltered care. Beds ICF 242; Sheltered care 108.
Owner Nonprofit corp.
Affiliation Masons.

Sullivan Health Care Center
11 Hawthorne Ln, Sullivan, IL 61951
(217) 728-4327
Admin Duane J Warren. Dir of Nursing Dolores Ryherd RN. Medical Dir Dr Dean McLaughin.
Licensure Skilled care. Beds SNF 123. Certified Medicaid; Medicare.
Owner Nonprofit corp (First Humanics).
Staff RNs 3 (ft), 2 (pt); LPNs 6 (ft), 3 (pt); Nurses' aides 18 (ft), 10 (pt); Activities coordinators 2 (ft).
Facilities Dining room; Physical therapy room; Activities room; Crafts room; Laundry room; Barber/Beauty shop.
Activities Arts & crafts; Cards; Games; Reading groups; Prayer groups; Movies; Shopping trips; Dances/Social/Cultural gatherings.

Sullivan Living Center
E View Pl, Sullivan, IL 61951
(217) 728-7367
Admin John M Brinkoetter.
Licensure Intermediate care. Beds ICF 62. Certified Medicaid.
Owner Proprietary corp.
Staff Physicians 1 (pt); RNs 1 (pt); LPNs 4 (ft); Nurses' aides 17 (ft), 6 (pt); Physical therapists 1 (pt); Reality therapists 1 (pt); Recreational therapists 1 (pt); Occupational therapists 1 (pt); Speech therapists 1 (pt); Activities coordinators 1 (ft), 1 (pt); Dietitians 1 (pt); Ophthalmologists 1 (pt); Podiatrists 1 (pt); Audiologists 1 (pt); Dentists 1 (pt).
Facilities Dining room; Activities room; Chapel; Crafts room; Laundry room; Barber/Beauty shop; Library.

Activities Arts & crafts; Cards; Games; Reading groups; Prayer groups; Movies; Shopping trips; Dances/Social/Cultural gatherings.

Titus Memorial Presbyterian Home
513 N Worth St, Sullivan, IL 61951
(217) 728-4725
Admin Peggy Auten.
Licensure Sheltered care. *Beds* Shelterd care 14.
Owner Nonprofit corp.
Affiliation Presbyterian.

Summit

Helping Hand Intermediate Care Facility
7434 W 61st Pl, Summit, IL 60501
(708) 458-4035
Admin Edward Morman.
Licensure Intermediate care for mentally retarded. *Beds* ICF/MR 15.

Sumner

Hickory Estates Incorporated
Rte 250 W, Sumner, IL 62466
(618) 936-2004
Admin Donald M Tharp.
Licensure Intermediate care for mentally retarded. *Beds* ICF/MR 15.

Pine Lawn Manor Care Center
PO Box 166, Poplar & Maple Sts, Sumner, IL 62466
(618) 936-2703
Admin Peter B Narish.
Medical Dir Nancy Wells.
Licensure Intermediate care; Intermediate care for mentally retarded; Retirement. *Beds* ICF 48; ICF/MR 58. *Certified* Medicaid.
Owner Proprietary corp.
Staff Physicians 1 (pt); RNs 1 (pt); LPNs 7 (ft); Nurses' aides 20 (ft); Physical therapists 1 (pt); Reality therapists 4 (ft); Recreational therapists 4 (ft); Speech therapists 1 (pt); Activities coordinators 1 (ft); Dietitians 1 (pt).
Facilities Dining room; Physical therapy room; Activities room; Chapel; Crafts room; Laundry room; Barber/Beauty shop; Library.
Activities Arts & crafts; Cards; Games; Reading groups; Prayer groups; Movies; Shopping trips; Dances/Social/Cultural gatherings.

Red Hills Rest Haven Corporation
1 Poplar Dr, Sumner, IL 62466
(618) 936-2522
Admin Gwenda J Zellars. *Dir of Nursing* Edna Couch. *Medical Dir* Dr Gary Carr.
Licensure Skilled care; Alzheimer's care. *Beds* SNF 96. *Certified* Medicaid; Medicare; VA.
Owner Proprietary corp.
Admissions Requirements Minimum age 18.
Staff Physicians 7 (pt); RNs 4 (pt); LPNs 6 (pt); Nurses' aides 29 (pt); Physical therapists 2 (pt); Reality therapists 1 (pt); Speech therapists 1 (pt); Activities coordinators 2 (pt); Dietitians 1 (pt); Ophthalmologists 1 (pt); Podiatrists 1 (pt).
Facilities Dining room; Physical therapy room; Activities room; Crafts room; Laundry room; Barber/Beauty shop.
Activities Arts & crafts; Cards; Games; Reading groups; Prayer groups; Movies; Shopping trips; Dances/Social/Cultural gatherings; Van rides.

Swansea

Rosewood C Center Inc of Swansea
100 Rosewood Village Dr, Swansea, IL 62220
(618) 236-1391
Admin Valerie S Kempf.
Licensure Skilled care; Intermediate care. *Beds* SNF 56; ICF 56.

Sycamore

Opportunity House Inc
PO Box 301, 202 Lucas St, Sycamore, IL 60178
(815) 895-5108
Admin John Kroos.
Licensure Community living facility. *Beds* Community living facility 17.
Owner Nonprofit corp.

Tamms

H & S Care Center
PO Box 367, 3rd & Carpenter, Tamms, IL 62988
(618) 747-2613
Admin Carolyn L Harvel.
Licensure Sheltered care. *Beds* Sheltered care 26.
Owner Proprietary corp.
Admissions Requirements Minimum age 18; Medical examination; Physician's request.
Staff Physicians 1 (pt); RNs 1 (pt); Nurses' aides 3 (ft), 4 (pt); Activities coordinators 1 (pt).
Facilities Dining room; Activities room; Laundry room.
Activities Arts & crafts; Cards; Games; Reading groups; Prayer groups; Shopping trips.

Taylorville

Meadow Manor Inc
Rte 48 N, Taylorville, IL 62568
(217) 824-2277
Admin Shelby Warner.
Medical Dir I DelValle; Carol Harden.
Licensure Intermediate care. *Beds* ICF 150. *Certified* Medicaid; Medicare.
Owner Proprietary corp.
Admissions Requirements Minimum age 18.
Staff Physicians; RNs; LPNs; Nurses' aides; Physical therapists; Speech therapists; Activities coordinators; Dietitians; Ophthalmologists.
Facilities Dining room; Physical therapy room; Activities room; Laundry room; Barber/Beauty shop.
Activities Arts & crafts; Cards; Games; Reading groups; Prayer groups; Movies; Shopping trips; Dances/Social/Cultural gatherings.

Taylorville Care Center Inc
600 S Houston, Taylorville, IL 62568
(217) 824-9636
Admin Constance J Le Vault. *Dir of Nursing* J Griffith RN. *Medical Dir* Dr T E Brewer.
Licensure Skilled care. *Beds* SNF 98. *Certified* Medicaid; Medicare.
Owner Proprietary corp.
Admissions Requirements Medical examination; Physician's request.
Staff RNs 1 (ft), 2 (pt); LPNs 5 (ft), 5 (pt); Nurses' aides 20 (ft), 9 (pt).
Facilities Dining room; Physical therapy room; Activities room; Crafts room; Laundry room; Barber/Beauty shop.
Activities Arts & crafts; Games; Reading groups; Prayer groups; Movies; Shopping trips; Dances/Social/Cultural gatherings.

Victorian Manor
815 E Vine St, Taylorville, IL 62568
(217) 287-1484
Admin Judy K Busing.
Licensure Intermediate care for mentally retarded. *Beds* ICF/MR 15.

Tinley Park

Mc Allister Nursing Home Inc
18300 S LaVergne Ave, Tinley Park, IL 60477
(708) 798-2272

Admin Theresa M Russo.
Medical Dir Bakul K Pankya MD.
Licensure Skilled care; Intermediate care. *Beds* SNF 59; ICF 42. *Certified* Medicaid; Medicare.
Owner Proprietary corp.
Admissions Requirements Minimum age 18; Medical examination; Physician's request.
Staff Physicians 2 (pt); RNs 6 (ft), 2 (pt); LPNs 5 (ft), 2 (pt); Physical therapists 1 (ft), 1 (pt); Reality therapists 1 (pt); Recreational therapists 2 (ft); Occupational therapists 1 (ft), 1 (pt); Speech therapists 1 (pt); Activities coordinators 1 (pt); Dietitians 1 (ft), 1 (pt); Ophthalmologists 1 (pt); Audiologists 1 (pt); Dentists 1 (pt).
Facilities Dining room; Physical therapy room; Activities room; Chapel; Crafts room; Laundry room; Barber/Beauty shop; Library.
Activities Arts & crafts; Cards; Games; Reading groups; Prayer groups; Movies; Shopping trips; Dances/Social/Cultural gatherings.

Toluca

Monte Cassino Healthcare Center
101 E Via Ghiglieri, Toluca, IL 61369
(815) 452-2367
Admin Betty Adolphson.
Licensure Skilled care; Intermediate care. *Beds* SNF 71; ICF 33. *Certified* Medicaid.
Owner Proprietary corp.

Troy

Professional Care Inc
200 E Taylor, Troy, IL 62294
(618) 667-6691
Admin Neva B Wojcik.
Licensure Intermediate care for mentally retarded. *Beds* ICF/MR 149. *Certified* Medicaid; Medicare.
Owner Proprietary corp.
Admissions Requirements Minimum age 18; Medical examination; Physician's request.
Staff Physicians 11 (pt); RNs 1 (pt); LPNs 12 (ft); Nurses' aides 34 (ft); Physical therapists 2 (ft); Reality therapists 3 (ft); Recreational therapists 5 (ft); Occupational therapists 1 (pt); Speech therapists 1 (pt); Activities coordinators 1 (ft); Dietitians 1 (ft); Ophthalmologists 1 (pt); Podiatrists 1 (pt); Dentists 1 (pt).
Facilities Dining room; Physical therapy room; Activities room; Crafts room; Laundry room; Barber/Beauty shop; Library; Dayroom.
Activities Arts & crafts; Cards; Games; Reading groups; Prayer groups; Movies; Shopping trips; Dances/Social/Cultural gatherings; Dining trips; Trips to big league baseball games & museums.

Tuscola

Douglas Manor Nursing Complex
RR 2, Tuscola, IL 61953
(217) 253-2337
Admin George S Barnett.
Licensure Skilled care; Intermediate care. *Beds* SNF 30; ICF 123. *Certified* Medicaid.
Owner Proprietary corp.

Urbana

Americana Healthcare Center of Urbana
600 N Coler Ave, Urbana, IL 61801
(217) 367-1191
Admin Dorothy J Mikucki.
Medical Dir Dr Phillip Johnson.
Licensure Skilled care. *Beds* SNF 100. *Certified* Medicaid; Medicare.
Owner Proprietary corp (Manor Care).
Admissions Requirements Medical examination.

Staff Physicians; RNs; LPNs; Nurses' aides; Physical therapists; Reality therapists; Recreational therapists; Occupational therapists; Speech therapists; Activities coordinators; Dietitians; Ophthalmologists; Podiatrists; Audiologists; Dentists.
Facilities Dining room; Physical therapy room; Activities room; Crafts room; Laundry room; Barber/Beauty shop.
Activities Arts & crafts; Cards; Games; Reading groups; Prayer groups; Movies; Shopping trips; Dances/Social/Cultural gatherings.

Champaign County Nursing Home
1701 E Main, Urbana, IL 61801
(217) 384-3784
Admin Joyce Ettensohn. *Dir of Nursing* Marjorie Letot RN. *Medical Dir* Dr Kathleen O'Hare.
Licensure Skilled care; Intermediate care; Sheltered care; Adult day care; Alzheimer's care; Respite. *Beds* SNF 153; ICF 56; Sheltered care 79; Adult day care 30. *Certified* Medicaid; Medicare.
Owner Publicly owned.
Admissions Requirements Minimum age 45; Medical examination; Physician's request.
Staff RNs 16 (ft); LPNs 10 (ft); Nurses' aides 87 (ft); Recreational therapists 5 (ft), 1 (pt); Activities coordinators 1 (ft); Dietitians 1 (ft); COTAs 1 (ft); PTAs 1 (ft); PRAs 1 (ft); ORAs 1 (ft); Dental hygienists.
Facilities Dining room; Physical therapy room; Activities room; Chapel; Crafts room; Barber/Beauty shop; Library; Dental clinic.
Activities Arts & crafts; Cards; Games; Reading groups; Prayer groups; Movies; Shopping trips; Dances/Social/Cultural gatherings; Intergenerational programs; Pet therapy; Educational programs; Alzheimer's support group.

Clark-Lindsey Village
101 W Windsor Rd, Urbana, IL 61801
(217) 344-2144
Admin Clifford E Ingersoll. *Dir of Nursing* Margaret Hoffman.
Licensure Skilled care; Intermediate care; Sheltered care; Retirement. *Beds* SNF 44; ICF 12; Sheltered care 40; Retirement 260. *Private Pay Patients* 100%. *Certified* Medicare.
Owner Nonprofit corp.
Admissions Requirements Minimum age 62; Medical examination.
Staff RNs 2 (ft), 1 (pt); LPNs 9 (ft), 1 (pt); Nurses' aides 25 (ft), 1 (pt); Physical therapists 1 (ft); Reality therapists 1 (ft); Recreational therapists 1 (ft); Occupational therapists 1 (ft); Speech therapists 1 (ft); Activities coordinators 2 (ft); Dietitians 1 (ft).
Facilities Dining room; Physical therapy room; Activities room; Chapel; Crafts room; Laundry room; Barber/Beauty shop; Library.
Activities Arts & crafts; Cards; Games; Reading groups; Prayer groups; Movies; Shopping trips; Dances/Social/Cultural gatherings; Intergenerational programs; Pet therapy.

Royal Fontana Nursing Center Inc
907 Lincoln Ave, Urbana, IL 61801
(217) 367-8421
Admin Stephanie Smith.
Licensure Skilled care. *Beds* SNF 99. *Certified* Medicaid; Medicare.
Owner Proprietary corp.

Urbana Nursing Home
2006 S Philo Rd, Urbana, IL 61801
(217) 344-0777
Admin David D Dale. *Dir of Nursing* Roxie Sage.
Licensure Intermediate care. *Beds* ICF 48. *Certified* Medicaid.
Owner Proprietary corp.

Admissions Requirements Physician's request.
Staff RNs; LPNs; Nurses' aides; Physical therapists; Activities coordinators; Dietitians.
Facilities Dining room; Activities room; Laundry room; Barber/Beauty shop.
Activities Arts & crafts; Cards; Games; Reading groups; Prayer groups; Movies; Shopping trips; Dances/Social/Cultural gatherings.

Vandalia

Cherrywood Health Care Center
1500 W Saint Louis Ave, Vandalia, IL 62471
(618) 283-4262
Admin Sharrill A Rice.
Licensure Intermediate care. *Beds* ICF 116. *Certified* Medicaid.
Owner Proprietary corp (Springwood Associates).

Heritage House of Vandalia
1610 Hillsboro Rd, Vandalia, IL 62471
(618) 283-1434, 283-2174 FAX
Admin Charles Hutson. *Dir of Nursing* Marianne Schwarm RN. *Medical Dir* Hans Rollinger MD.
Licensure Intermediate care. *Beds* ICF 79. *Private Pay Patients* 15%. *Certified* Medicaid.
Owner Proprietary corp (National Heritage).
Admissions Requirements Minimum age 18; Medical examination.
Staff RNs; LPNs; Nurses' aides; Physical therapists; Activities coordinators; Dietitians.
Facilities Dining room; Physical therapy room; Activities room; Chapel; Crafts room; Laundry room; Barber/Beauty shop.
Activities Arts & crafts; Cards; Games; Reading groups; Prayer groups; Movies; Shopping trips; Dances/Social/Cultural gatherings; Intergenerational programs; Pet therapy.

Randolph House
403 S 1st St, Vandalia, IL 62471
(618) 283-0689
Admin Trena Briscoe.
Licensure Intermediate care for mentally retarded. *Beds* ICF/MR 15.

Vienna

Hillview Healthcare Center
11th St, Vienna, IL 62995
(618) 658-2951
Admin Janice F Miller.
Licensure Intermediate care. *Beds* ICF 71. *Certified* Medicaid.
Owner Proprietary corp.

Mt Shelter Care Home
PO Box 215, Vienna, IL 62995
(618) 695-2494
Admin Phyllis M Taylor.
Licensure Sheltered care. *Beds* Sheltered care 29.
Owner Proprietary corp.

Spanish Oaks Center
RR 3 Box 561, Vienna, IL 62995
(618) 833-8013
Admin Connie L Ury.
Licensure Sheltered care. *Beds* 49.
Owner Proprietary corp.

Virden

Sunrise Manor of Virden Inc
333 S Wrightman St, Virden, IL 62690
(217) 965-4821
Admin Patricia J Barnes.
Medical Dir Dr Kenneth Malmberg.
Licensure Intermediate care. *Beds* ICF 99. *Certified* Medicaid; Medicare.
Owner Proprietary corp.
Admissions Requirements Physician's request.

Staff RNs 2 (ft); LPNs 7 (ft), 5 (pt); Nurses' aides 20 (ft), 25 (pt); Activities coordinators 2 (ft).
Facilities Dining room; Physical therapy room; Activities room; Chapel; Crafts room; Laundry room; Barber/Beauty shop; TV room with fireplace.
Activities Arts & crafts; Cards; Games; Reading groups; Prayer groups; Movies; Shopping trips; Dances/Social/Cultural gatherings.

Virden Nursing Center
402 W Loud, Virden, IL 62690
(217) 965-4336
Admin Mary Ellen Wade.
Medical Dir Dr Malmberg.
Licensure Intermediate care. *Beds* ICF 51. *Certified* Medicaid.
Owner Privately owned.
Admissions Requirements Minimum age 18; Physician's request.
Staff LPNs 5 (ft); Nurses' aides 23 (ft), 23 (pt); Activities coordinators 1 (ft); Dietitians 1 (ft).
Facilities Dining room; Physical therapy room; Activities room; Laundry room; Barber/Beauty shop.
Activities Arts & crafts; Cards; Games; Reading groups; Prayer groups; Movies; Shopping trips; Dances/Social/Cultural gatherings.

Virginia

Walker Nursing Home Inc
530 E Beardstown St, Virginia, IL 62691
(217) 452-3218
Admin George W White.
Licensure Skilled care. *Beds* SNF 71. *Certified* Medicaid.
Owner Proprietary corp.

Walnut

Walnut Manor
308 S 2nd St, Walnut, IL 61376
(815) 379-2131
Admin Robert D Yearian. *Dir of Nursing* Nancy Christensen RN.
Licensure Intermediate care. *Beds* ICF 62. *Certified* Medicaid.
Owner Proprietary corp.
Staff RNs 1 (ft), 4 (pt); LPNs 1 (ft), 3 (pt); Nurses' aides 10 (ft), 20 (pt); Physical therapists 1 (pt); Activities coordinators 1 (ft), 2 (pt); Dietitians 1 (pt).

Washington

Toulon Health Care Center
RR 2, School St, Washington, IL 61571
(309) 286-2631
Admin Ella K Allbritton.
Medical Dir Josef Unhold MD.
Licensure Skilled care; Intermediate care. *Beds* SNF 82; ICF 54. *Certified* Medicaid; Medicare.
Owner Proprietary corp.
Admissions Requirements Medical examination; Physician's request.
Facilities Dining room; Physical therapy room; Activities room; Chapel; Crafts room; Laundry room; Barber/Beauty shop; Library; TV rooms; Greenhouse.
Activities Arts & crafts; Cards; Games; Reading groups; Prayer groups; Movies; Dances/Social/Cultural gatherings; Nail care; Cooking.

Washington Christian Village
1110 New Castle Rd, Washington, IL 61571
(309) 444-3161
Admin Andrew T Felix. *Dir of Nursing* Jaqueline Henderson RN. *Medical Dir* Dr Phillip Immesoete.

Licensure Skilled care; Retirement. *Beds* SNF 122; Retirement 30. *Private Pay Patients* 60%. *Certified* Medicaid; Medicare.
Owner Nonprofit organization/foundation (Christian Homes).
Admissions Requirements Minimum age 18.
Staff RNs 5 (ft), 5 (pt); LPNs 6 (ft), 5 (pt); Nurses' aides 30 (ft), 30 (pt); Physical therapists 2 (ft), 1 (pt); Activities coordinators 1 (ft).
Affiliation Church of Christ.
Facilities Dining room; Physical therapy room; Activities room; Chapel; Crafts room; Laundry room; Barber/Beauty shop.
Activities Arts & crafts; Cards; Games; Movies; Shopping trips; Volunteer program.

Waterloo

Bellefontaine Place
PO Box 225, 98 Debra Ln, Waterloo, IL 62298
(618) 939-3336
Admin Joan F Lagage.
Licensure Intermediate care for mentally retarded. *Beds* ICF/MR 15.

Canterbury Manor Nursing Center
718 N Market, Waterloo, IL 62298
(618) 939-8565
Admin Mary G Wood. *Dir of Nursing* Kathy Asselmeier. *Medical Dir* Dr Maglasang.
Licensure Intermediate care. *Beds* ICF 74. *Private Pay Patients* 75%. *Certified* Medicaid.
Owner Proprietary corp.
Admissions Requirements Minimum age 18.
Staff Physicians 6 (pt); RNs 1 (ft); LPNs 4 (ft), 3 (pt); Nurses' aides 25 (ft), 15 (pt); Physical therapists (consultant); Recreational therapists (consultant); Occupational therapists (consultant); Speech therapists (consultant); Activities coordinators 1 (ft), 1 (pt); Dietitians (consultant); Podiatrists (consultant); Audiologists (consultant).
Facilities Dining room; Physical therapy room; Activities room; Chapel; Crafts room; Laundry room; Barber/Beauty shop; Lounge.
Activities Arts & crafts; Cards; Games; Reading groups; Prayer groups; Movies; Shopping trips; Dances/Social/Cultural gatherings; Pet therapy.

Monroe County Nursing Home
500 Illinois Ave, Waterloo, IL 62298
(618) 939-3488
Admin Bruce L Vaca.
Medical Dir Russell W Jost MD.
Licensure Skilled care; Intermediate care. *Beds* SNF 142; ICF 83. *Certified* Medicaid; Medicare.
Owner Publicly owned.
Admissions Requirements Minimum age 16; Medical examination; Physician's request.
Staff Physicians 7 (pt); RNs 4 (ft), 8 (pt); LPNs 7 (ft), 11 (pt); Nurses' aides 47 (ft), 60 (pt); Physical therapists 1 (pt); Reality therapists 1 (pt); Recreational therapists 1 (pt); Activities coordinators 1 (ft); Dietitians 1 (pt); Podiatrists 1 (pt); Dentists 1 (pt).
Facilities Dining room; Physical therapy room; Activities room; Chapel; Crafts room; Laundry room; Barber/Beauty shop.
Activities Arts & crafts; Cards; Games; Reading groups; Prayer groups; Movies; Shopping trips; Dances/Social/Cultural gatherings.

Watseka

Iroquois Resident Home
200 Fairman, Watseka, IL 60970
(815) 432-5841
Admin Dallas K Larson. *Dir of Nursing* Donna Gossett. *Medical Dir* Dr Blandine.
Licensure Skilled care. *Beds* SNF 51. *Private Pay Patients* 100%.

Owner Nonprofit corp.
Admissions Requirements Minimum age 19; Medical examination; Physician's request.
Staff Physicians 16 (ft); RNs 3 (ft); LPNs 5 (ft), 3 (pt); Nurses' aides 17 (ft), 3 (pt); Physical therapists 1 (ft); Occupational therapists 1 (pt); Speech therapists 1 (pt); Activities coordinators 1 (ft); Dietitians 1 (ft).
Facilities Dining room; Physical therapy room; Activities room; Crafts room; Laundry room; Barber/Beauty shop.
Activities Arts & crafts; Games; Reading groups; Prayer groups; Movies; Shopping trips; Dances/Social/Cultural gatherings; Intergenerational programs.

Magnolia Wood Health Care Center
900 N Market St, Watseka, IL 60970
(815) 432-5261
Admin Donna Carlson. *Dir of Nursing* Janet Burton RN. *Medical Dir* Phillip Zumwalt MD.
Licensure Skilled care; Intermediate care. *Beds* SNF 13; ICF 62. *Private Pay Patients* 40%. *Certified* Medicaid; Medicare.
Owner Privately owned (Springwood Associates).
Admissions Requirements Minimum age 21; Medical examination.
Staff RNs 2 (ft), 1 (pt); LPNs 3 (ft), 2 (pt); Nurses' aides 30 (ft), 10 (pt); Activities coordinators 1 (ft), 1 (pt).
Facilities Dining room; Physical therapy room; Activities room; Crafts room; Laundry room; Barber/Beauty shop; Library.
Activities Arts & crafts; Cards; Games; Reading groups; Prayer groups; Movies; Shopping trips; Dances/Social/Cultural gatherings; Intergenerational programs; Pet therapy.

Watseka Health Care Center
715 E Raymond, Watseka, IL 60970
(815) 432-5476
Admin Janet Frizzel. *Dir of Nursing* Jeanne Kinder RN. *Medical Dir* Dean Hungness MD.
Licensure Skilled care. *Beds* SNF 123. *Certified* Medicaid; Medicare; VA.
Owner Nonprofit corp (First Humanics).
Admissions Requirements Minimum age 18; Physician's request.
Staff Physicians 8 (pt); RNs 5 (ft); LPNs 10 (ft), 2 (pt); Nurses' aides 40 (ft), 10 (pt); Physical therapists 1 (pt); Recreational therapists 1 (pt); Occupational therapists 1 (pt); Speech therapists 1 (pt); Activities coordinators 1 (ft); Dietitians 1 (pt); Ophthalmologists 1 (pt); Podiatrists 1 (pt); Dentists 1 (pt).
Facilities Dining room; Physical therapy room; Activities room; Crafts room; Laundry room; Barber/Beauty shop; Reality orientation room; Family social room.
Activities Arts & crafts; Cards; Games; Reading groups; Prayer groups; Movies; Shopping trips; Dances/Social/Cultural gatherings.

Wauconda

Town Hall Estates Nursing Center
176 Thomas Ct, Wauconda, IL 60084
(708) 526-5551
Admin Jerry Willis. *Dir of Nursing* Jeannette Bolger.
Licensure Intermediate care; Alzheimer's care. *Beds* ICF 98. *Private Pay Patients* 66%. *Certified* Medicaid.
Owner Nonprofit corp.
Admissions Requirements Minimum age 18; Medical examination.

Staff Physicians; RNs; LPNs; Nurses' aides; Physical therapists; Reality therapists; Recreational therapists; Occupational therapists; Speech therapists; Activities coordinators; Dietitians; Podiatrists.
Facilities Dining room; Activities room; Chapel; Crafts room; Laundry room; Barber/Beauty shop; Library; Two TV lounges.
Activities Arts & crafts; Cards; Games; Reading groups; Prayer groups; Movies; Dances/Social/Cultural gatherings; Intergenerational programs; Field trips.

Waukegan

Bayside Terrace
1100 S Lewis Ave, Waukegan, IL 60085
(708) 244-8196
Admin Betty A Satterfield.
Medical Dir Norberto J Martinez MD.
Licensure Intermediate care. *Beds* ICF 168. *Certified* Medicaid.
Owner Proprietary corp.
Admissions Requirements Minimum age 30; Medical examination; Physician's request.
Staff Physicians 2 (ft); RNs 3 (ft), 1 (pt); LPNs 4 (ft), 4 (pt); Nurses' aides 16 (ft); Reality therapists 1 (ft); Occupational therapists 1 (ft); Activities coordinators 3 (ft), 1 (pt); Dietitians 1 (pt); Ophthalmologists 1 (pt).
Facilities Dining room; Physical therapy room; Activities room; Crafts room; Laundry room; Barber/Beauty shop; Library; TV rooms; Smoking lounge.
Activities Arts & crafts; Cards; Games; Reading groups; Prayer groups; Movies; Shopping trips; Dances/Social/Cultural gatherings; Exercise.

Lake Park Center
919 Washington Park, Waukegan, IL 60085
(708) 623-9100
Admin Neal R Kjos.
Medical Dir Sam Krugez; Sandra Hernandez.
Licensure Skilled care; Intermediate care. *Beds* SNF 108; ICF 102. *Certified* Medicaid.
Owner Proprietary corp.
Admissions Requirements Minimum age 18.
Facilities Dining room; Physical therapy room; Activities room; Laundry room; Barber/Beauty shop.
Activities Arts & crafts; Cards; Games; Reading groups; Movies; Shopping trips; Dances/Social/Cultural gatherings.

North Shore Terrace
2222 W 14th St, Waukegan, IL 60085
(708) 249-2400, 249-8409 FAX
Admin Daniel Rexroth. *Dir of Nursing* Daisy Villalor. *Medical Dir* Sam Kruger MD.
Licensure Skilled care; Intermediate care. *Beds* SNF 125; ICF 146. *Private Pay Patients* 20%. *Certified* Medicaid.
Owner Proprietary corp (E K S Management).
Admissions Requirements Minimum age 30.
Staff Physicians 10 (pt); RNs 16 (ft); LPNs 8 (ft); Nurses' aides 70 (ft), 8 (pt); Physical therapists 1 (pt); Reality therapists 1 (pt); Recreational therapists 1 (pt); Occupational therapists 1 (pt); Speech therapists 1 (pt); Activities coordinators 1 (ft); Dietitians 1 (ft); Ophthalmologists 1 (pt); Podiatrists 1 (pt); Audiologists 1 (pt); Dentists 1 (pt).
Languages Polish, Spanish.
Facilities Dining room; Physical therapy room; Activities room; Chapel; Crafts room; Laundry room; Barber/Beauty shop; Library.
Activities Arts & crafts; Cards; Games; Reading groups; Prayer groups; Movies; Shopping trips; Dances/Social/Cultural gatherings; Intergenerational programs; Pet therapy.

Terrace Nursing Home Inc
1615 Sunset Ave, Waukegan, IL 60087
(708) 244-6700

Admin Patricia J Sheridan. *Dir of Nursing*
Shirley Hollech RN. *Medical Dir* Bruce
Frazer MD.
Licensure Skilled care. *Beds* SNF 112.
Certified Medicaid; Medicare; VA.
Owner Proprietary corp.
Admissions Requirements Minimum age 18;
Medical examination.
Staff Physicians 17 (pt); RNs 12 (ft), 2 (pt);
LPNs 4 (ft), 3 (pt); Nurses' aides 38 (ft), 7
(pt); Physical therapists 1 (pt); Reality
therapists 2 (ft); Recreational therapists 1
(ft); Occupational therapists 2 (pt); Speech
therapists 1 (pt); Activities coordinators 1
(ft); Dietitians 1 (pt); Ophthalmologists 1
(pt); Podiatrists 1 (pt); Dentists 1 (pt).
Languages Spanish.
Facilities Dining room; Physical therapy
room; Activities room; Crafts room; Laundry
room; Barber/Beauty shop; Library; Lounge;
Family group room.
Activities Arts & crafts; Cards; Games;
Reading groups; Prayer groups; Movies;
Shopping trips; Dances/Social/Cultural
gatherings; Cocktail party.

Waukegan Pavilion
2217 Washington St, Waukegan, IL 60085
(708) 244-4100
Admin James E Willcox.
Licensure Skilled care. *Beds* SNF 99. *Certified*
Medicaid.
Owner Proprietary corp.

West Chicago

Fox Crest Manor
30 W 300 North Ave, West Chicago, IL 60185
(708) 231-4050
Admin Judith J Swanstrom. *Dir of Nursing*
Marlene Liske. *Medical Dir* Dr Tom Klein.
Licensure Skilled care; Intermediate care;
Sheltered care. *Beds* SNF 45; ICF 262;
Sheltered care 20. *Private Pay Patients* 20%.
Certified Medicaid.
Owner Nonprofit corp.
Admissions Requirements Minimum age 65;
Medical examination.
Staff Physicians 6 (ft); RNs 6 (ft), 2 (pt);
LPNs 13 (ft), 4 (pt); Nurses' aides 40 (ft), 10
(pt); Physical therapists 2 (pt); Occupational
therapists 1 (pt); Speech therapists 1 (pt);
Activities coordinators 1 (pt); Dietitians 1
(pt); Ophthalmologists 1 (pt); Podiatrists 3
(pt); Audiologists 1 (pt); Psychiatrists 2 (pt).
Languages German, Italian, Polish.
Facilities Dining room; Physical therapy
room; Activities room; Chapel; Crafts room;
Laundry room; Barber/Beauty shop; Library.
Activities Arts & crafts; Cards; Games;
Reading groups; Prayer groups; Movies;
Shopping trips; Dances/Social/Cultural
gatherings; Intergenerational programs; Pet
therapy; Cubs games; Cookouts.

West Chicago Terrace
928 Joliet St, West Chicago, IL 60185
(312) 231-9292
Admin Christine Cherney. *Dir of Nursing*
Rene Gill. *Medical Dir* Thomas Klein.
Licensure Intermediate care. *Beds* ICF 120.
Private Pay Patients 10%. *Certified*
Medicaid.
Owner Privately owned.
Admissions Requirements Minimum age 60.
Staff RNs 2 (ft); LPNs 4 (ft), 1 (pt); Nurses'
aides 16 (ft), 4 (pt); Activities coordinators 1
(ft).
Facilities Dining room; Physical therapy
room; Activities room; Chapel; Laundry
room; Barber/Beauty shop; Library.
Activities Arts & crafts; Cards; Games; Prayer
groups; Movies; Shopping trips; Dances/
Social/Cultural gatherings; Pet therapy.

West Frankfort

American Beauty Nursing Home
6th St & Columbia, West Frankfort, IL 62896
(618) 932-2109
Admin Shirley A Earnheart. *Dir of Nursing* Jo
Schofield. *Medical Dir* Dr Y Norman Chiou.
Licensure Skilled care. *Beds* SNF 96. *Certified*
Medicaid.
Owner Privately owned.
Admissions Requirements Minimum age 18;
Medical examination; Physician's request.
Staff Physicians 6 (pt); RNs 1 (ft), 2 (pt);
LPNs 6 (ft), 2 (pt); Nurses' aides 25 (ft), 6
(pt); Physical therapists 1 (pt); Speech
therapists 1 (pt); Activities coordinators 1
(ft), 2 (pt); Dietitians 1 (pt).
Facilities Dining room; Activities room;
Laundry room; Barber/Beauty shop.
Activities Arts & crafts; Cards; Games;
Reading groups; Prayer groups; Shopping
trips; Dances/Social/Cultural gatherings.

Frankfort Heights Manor
2500 E Saint Louis St, West Frankfort, IL
62896
(618) 932-3236
Admin Rosalie Rounds. *Dir of Nursing*
Branda Bybee. *Medical Dir* Dr Y N Chiou.
Licensure Intermediate care. *Beds* ICF 57.
Private Pay Patients 55%. *Certified*
Medicaid.
Owner Proprietary corp (Leo Mattingly).
Staff RNs 1 (ft); LPNs 5 (ft); Nurses' aides 17
(ft); Occupational therapists 2 (ft); Activities
coordinators 1 (ft); Dietitians 1 (ft);
Podiatrists 1 (pt).

Parkview Nursing Home
301 E Garland St, West Frankfort, IL 62896
(618) 937-2428
Admin Jeanetta D Underwood. *Dir of Nursing*
Lois Eubanks.
Licensure Intermediate care. *Beds* ICF 59.
Certified Medicaid.
Owner Proprietary corp.
Admissions Requirements Minimum age 18.
Staff RNs 1 (pt); LPNs 4 (ft), 2 (pt); Nurses'
aides 20 (ft); Activities coordinators 1 (ft).
Facilities Dining room; Activities room;
Barber/Beauty shop.
Activities Arts & crafts; Cards; Games;
Reading groups; Prayer groups; Movies;
Shopping trips; Dances/Social/Cultural
gatherings.

West Salem

West Salem Manor
RR 1 Box 94, West Salem, IL 62476
(618) 456-8405
Admin Carol Bowen. *Dir of Nursing* Janet
Stewart. *Medical Dir* Janet Stewart.
Licensure Skilled care. *Beds* SNF 36. *Private
Pay Patients* 80%.
Owner Proprietary corp (A J Mason Corp).
Admissions Requirements Medical
examination.
Staff Physicians; RNs; Nurses' aides; Reality
therapists; Activities coordinators; Dietitians.
Facilities Dining room; Activities room;
Laundry room; Barber/Beauty shop.
Activities Arts & crafts; Cards; Games;
Reading groups; Prayer groups; Movies;
Shopping trips; Pet therapy; Vacation tours.

Westmont

Americana Healthcare Center of Westmont
512 E Ogden Ave, Westmont, IL 60559
(708) 323-4400
Admin Katherine K Keane.
Medical Dir Azizar Arain MD.
Licensure Skilled care. *Beds* SNF 155.
Certified Medicaid; Medicare.
Owner Proprietary corp (Manor Care).

Admissions Requirements Medical
examination; Physician's request.
Staff Physicians 16 (pt); RNs 12 (ft), 6 (pt);
LPNs 10 (ft), 8 (pt); Nurses' aides 50 (ft), 10
(pt); Physical therapists 1 (ft), 2 (pt);
Recreational therapists 1 (ft), 3 (pt);
Occupational therapists; Speech therapists;
Dietitians; Ophthalmologists; Podiatrists;
Dentists.
Facilities Dining room; Physical therapy
room; Activities room; Crafts room; Laundry
room; Barber/Beauty shop.
Activities Arts & crafts; Cards; Games;
Reading groups; Prayer groups; Movies;
Shopping trips; Dances/Social/Cultural
gatherings.

Burgess Square Healthcare Centre
5801 S Cass Ave, Westmont, IL 60559
(708) 971-2645
Admin Jo Anne Fisher. *Dir of Nursing* Irene
Kubina.
Licensure Skilled care; Intermediate care. *Beds*
SNF 106; ICF 105. *Certified* Medicaid;
Medicare.
Owner Proprietary corp.
Admissions Requirements Minimum age 50;
Medical examination; Physician's request.
Staff RNs 3 (ft); LPNs 9 (ft), 4 (pt); Nurses'
aides 37 (ft), 9 (pt); Activities coordinators 4
(ft), 2 (pt).
Languages Polish, Spanish, German.
Facilities Dining room; Physical therapy
room; Activities room; Crafts room; Laundry
room; Barber/Beauty shop.
Activities Arts & crafts; Cards; Games;
Reading groups; Prayer groups; Movies;
Shopping trips; Dances/Social/Cultural
gatherings.

Westmont Convalescent Center
6501 S Cass Ave, Westmont, IL 60559
(708) 960-2026
Admin Nancy Geraci.
Medical Dir Lawrence LaPalio.
Licensure Skilled care; Intermediate care;
Alzheimer's care. *Beds* SNF 108; ICF 107.
Certified Medicaid; Medicare.
Owner Proprietary corp.
Admissions Requirements Minimum age 60.
Staff Physicians; RNs; LPNs; Nurses' aides;
Physical therapists; Occupational therapists;
Speech therapists; Activities coordinators;
Dietitians; Ophthalmologists; Podiatrists;
Dentists.
Languages Polish, Spanish.
Facilities Dining room; Physical therapy
room; Activities room; Laundry room;
Barber/Beauty shop.
Activities Arts & crafts; Games; Reading
groups; Prayer groups; Movies; Shopping
trips; Dances/Social/Cultural gatherings.

Wheaton

Du Page Convalescent Center
PO Box 708, 400 N County Farm Rd,
Wheaton, IL 60187
(708) 665-6400
Admin Ronald R Reinecke. *Dir of Nursing*
Kathryn Wiggins. *Medical Dir* John B Pace
MD.
Licensure Skilled care. *Beds* SNF 408.
Certified Medicaid.
Owner Publicly owned.
Admissions Requirements Minimum age 18;
Staff Physicians; RNs; LPNs; Nurses' aides;
Physical therapists; Recreational therapists;
Occupational therapists; Speech therapists;
Activities coordinators; Dietitians;
Ophthalmologists; Podiatrists.
Facilities Dining room; Physical therapy
room; Activities room; Crafts room; Laundry
room; Barber/Beauty shop; Library.

Activities Arts & crafts; Cards; Games; Reading groups; Prayer groups; Movies; Shopping trips; Dances/Social/Cultural gatherings.

Parkway Terrace Nursing Home
219 E Parkway Dr, Wheaton, IL 60187
(708) 668-4635
Admin Mary Lynne Mount. Dir of Nursing Lynn Montes RN. Medical Dir Dr Joseph.
Licensure Skilled care; Intermediate care. Beds SNF 35; ICF 34. Private Pay Patients 90%. Certified Medicaid.
Owner Proprietary corp (HS Healthcare Inc).
Admissions Requirements Minimum age 55; Medical examination; Physician's request.
Staff Physicians 1 (ft); RNs 3 (ft), 3 (pt); LPNs 6 (ft), 3 (pt); Nurses' aides 18 (ft), 10 (pt); Physical therapists 1 (pt); Recreational therapists 1 (pt); Speech therapists 1 (pt); Activities coordinators 1 (pt); Dietitians 1 (pt); Podiatrists 1 (pt).
Affiliation Assembly of God.
Facilities Dining room; Physical therapy room; Activities room; Laundry room; Barber/Beauty shop; Library; Flower garden; Wheelchair accessible vegetable garden; Porch.
Activities Arts & crafts; Cards; Games; Reading groups; Prayer groups; Movies; Shopping trips; Dances/Social/Cultural gatherings; Intergenerational programs; Pet therapy.

Sandalwood Healthcare Centre
2180 W Manchester Rd, Wheaton, IL 60187
(708) 665-4330
Admin Nancy E Kasky Fox. Dir of Nursing Jena Villarreal RN. Medical Dir Lawrence Schouten MD.
Licensure Skilled care; Intermediate care; Alzheimer's care. Beds SNF 106; ICF 103. Certified Medicaid; Medicare.
Owner Proprietary corp.
Admissions Requirements Minimum age 55; Medical examination.
Staff Physicians 37 (ft); RNs 9 (ft), 3 (pt); LPNs 6 (ft), 3 (pt); Nurses' aides 39 (ft), 6 (pt).
Facilities Dining room; Physical therapy room; Activities room; Laundry room; Barber/Beauty shop.
Activities Arts & crafts; Cards; Games; Reading groups; Prayer groups; Movies; Shopping trips; Dances/Social/Cultural gatherings.

Wheeling

Addolorata Villa
555 McHenry Rd, Wheeling, IL 60090
(708) 537-2900
Admin Sr Mary Roberta Prince OSM. Dir of Nursing Sandra Michael. Medical Dir Irwin Smith MD.
Licensure Skilled care; Intermediate care; Sheltered care; Independent living; Alzheimer's care. Beds SNF 20; ICF 60; Sheltered care 45; Independent living units 100. Private Pay Patients 85%. Certified Medicaid.
Owner Nonprofit corp.
Admissions Requirements Minimum age 60; Medical examination.
Staff Physicians 4 (pt); RNs 5 (ft), 4 (pt); LPNs 3 (ft), 1 (pt); Nurses' aides 12 (ft), 3 (pt); Physical therapists 1 (pt); Activities coordinators 1 (ft); Dietitians 1 (ft), 1 (pt); Ophthalmologists 1 (pt); Podiatrists 1 (pt).
Languages Polish, Italian.
Affiliation Roman Catholic.
Facilities Dining room; Physical therapy room; Activities room; Chapel; Crafts room; Laundry room; Barber/Beauty shop; Library.

Activities Arts & crafts; Games; Reading groups; Prayer groups; Movies; Shopping trips; Dances/Social/Cultural gatherings; Intergenerational programs.

White Hall

North American Healthcare Center
620 W Bridgeport, White Hall, IL 62092
(217) 374-2144
Admin Stephen B Hopkins.
Licensure Skilled care. Beds SNF 126. Certified Medicaid.
Owner Proprietary corp.

Willowbrook

Chateau Village Living Center
7050 Madison St, Willowbrook, IL 60521
(708) 323-6380
Admin Gary D Hixon.
Licensure Skilled care; Intermediate care; Sheltered care. Beds SNF 100; ICF 43; Sheltered care 7.

Wilmette

Baha'i Home Inc
401 Greenleaf Ave, Wilmette, IL 60091
(708) 251-7000
Admin George T Walker.
Licensure Sheltered care. Beds Sheltered care 22.
Owner Nonprofit corp.
Admissions Requirements Minimum age 65; Medical examination.
Staff RNs 1 (pt); LPNs 1 (pt); Nurses' aides 3 (ft), 3 (pt); Recreational therapists 1 (ft); Occupational therapists 1 (pt); Activities coordinators 1 (ft); Dietitians 1 (pt); Ophthalmologists 1 (pt); Podiatrists 1 (pt).
Affiliation Baha'i Faith.
Facilities Dining room; Activities room; Crafts room; Laundry room; Barber/Beauty shop; Library; Large & small lounges.
Activities Arts & crafts; Cards; Games; Reading groups; Prayer groups; Movies; Dances/Social/Cultural gatherings; Discussion groups; Exercise groups; Sing-alongs; Field trips.

Normandy House
432 Poplar Dr, Wilmette, IL 60091
(708) 256-5000
Admin O E Lufkin. Dir of Nursing Missy Ware RN. Medical Dir A R Peterson MD.
Licensure Skilled care; Intermediate care; Retirement; Alzheimer's care. Beds SNF 28; ICF 52. Private Pay Patients 100%.
Owner Proprietary corp.
Admissions Requirements Minimum age 22; Medical examination; Physician's request.
Staff Physicians 34 (pt); RNs 12 (ft), 9 (pt); Nurses' aides 21 (ft), 6 (pt); Physical therapists 3 (pt); Speech therapists 1 (pt); Activities coordinators 1 (ft), 3 (pt); Dietitians 1 (pt); Podiatrists 3 (pt).
Facilities Dining room; Physical therapy room; Activities room; Crafts room; Barber/Beauty shop; Library.
Activities Arts & crafts; Cards; Games; Reading groups; Prayer groups; Movies; Dances/Social/Cultural gatherings.

Wilmington

Royal Willow Nursing Care Center
555 Kahler Rd, Wilmington, IL 60481
(815) 476-7931
Admin Barbara J Thomas MS. Dir of Nursing Rose Aschenbrener RN. Medical Dir Simon Migale MD.
Licensure Skilled care; Intermediate care. Beds SNF 98; ICF 98. Private Pay Patients 30%. Certified Medicaid; Medicare.
Owner Proprietary corp.

Admissions Requirements Medical examination.
Staff Physicians; RNs; LPNs; Nurses' aides; Physical therapists; Occupational therapists; Speech therapists; Activities coordinators; Dietitians; Ophthalmologists; Podiatrists.
Facilities Dining room; Physical therapy room; Activities room; Laundry room; Barber/Beauty shop; TV room.
Activities Arts & crafts; Cards; Games; Prayer groups; Movies; Shopping trips; Pet therapy.

Winchester

Scott County Nursing Center
RR 2 Box 173, Winchester, IL 62694
(217) 742-3101
Admin Inez M Holderman. Dir of Nursing Rhonda Dunn RN. Medical Dir James Bohan MD.
Licensure Intermediate care. Beds ICF 64. Private Pay Patients 47%. Certified Medicaid.
Owner Publicly owned.
Admissions Requirements Minimum age 18; Medical examination.
Staff Physicians (consultant); RNs 1 (ft), 1 (pt); LPNs 11 (ft); Nurses' aides 28 (ft), 2 (pt); Physical therapists (consultants); Recreational therapists 2 (pt); Speech therapists (consultant); Dietitians (consultant).
Facilities Dining room; Laundry room; Barber/Beauty shop.
Activities Arts & crafts; Cards; Games; Reading groups; Movies; Shopping trips.

Winfield

Liberty Hill Healthcare Center
28 W 141 Liberty Rd, Winfield, IL 60190
(708) 668-2928
Admin Mary R Kastner. Dir of Nursing Kenneth Haugen RN. Medical Dir G A Kushner MD.
Licensure Intermediate care; Retirement; Alzheimer's care. Beds ICF 115. Certified Medicaid.
Owner Proprietary corp.
Admissions Requirements Minimum age 55.
Staff Physicians 4 (ft); RNs 8 (ft); LPNs 9 (ft), 2 (pt); Nurses' aides 16 (ft); Physical therapists 2 (ft); Reality therapists 2 (ft); Recreational therapists 2 (ft); Occupational therapists 1 (ft); Activities coordinators 2 (ft); Dietitians 1 (pt); Ophthalmologists 1 (pt); Podiatrists 1 (pt); Dentists 1 (pt).
Languages Spanish, Polish.
Facilities Dining room; Physical therapy room; Activities room; Chapel; Crafts room; Laundry room; Barber/Beauty shop; Resident fitness.
Activities Arts & crafts; Cards; Games; Reading groups; Prayer groups; Movies; Shopping trips; Dances/Social/Cultural gatherings.

Wood River

Thelma Terrace
1450 Virginia Ave, Wood River, IL 62095
(618) 259-2777
Admin Joan F Lagage.
Licensure Intermediate care for mentally retarded. Beds ICF/MR 15.

VIP Manor
393 Edwardsville Rd, Wood River, IL 62095
(618) 259-4111
Admin Linda L McGaughey.
Licensure Skilled care; Intermediate care. Beds SNF 38; ICF 68. Certified Medicaid; Medicare.
Owner Proprietary corp.

Woodstock

Sunset Manor
920 N Seminary Ave, Woodstock, IL 60098
(815) 338-1749
Admin R Douglas McGrew. *Dir of Nursing*
Roberta Liebmann RN. *Medical Dir* Dr
Robin Purdy.
Licensure Skilled care; Intermediate care;
Sheltered care; Alzheimer's care; Retirement.
Beds SNF 29; ICF 46; Sheltered care 53.
Private Pay Patients 85%. *Certified*
Medicaid.
Owner Nonprofit corp.
Admissions Requirements Minimum age 62;
Medical examination; Physician's request.
Staff RNs 5 (ft), 8 (pt); LPNs 3 (ft), 3 (pt);
Nurses' aides 23 (ft), 10 (pt); Activities
coordinators 3 (ft), 1 (pt).
Affiliation Free Methodist.
Facilities Dining room; Physical therapy
room; Activities room; Chapel; Crafts room;
Laundry room; Barber/Beauty shop; Library.
Activities Arts & crafts; Cards; Games;
Reading groups; Prayer groups; Movies;
Shopping trips; Dances/Social/Cultural
gatherings; Intergenerational programs; Pet
therapy.

Valley Hi Nursing Home
2406 Hartland Rd, Woodstock, IL 60098
(815) 338-0312
Admin Virginia G Leavitt.
Medical Dir Dr Leo A Reyes.
Licensure Skilled care; Intermediate care. *Beds*
SNF 47; ICF 43. *Certified* Medicaid.
Owner Publicly owned.
Admissions Requirements Minimum age 18;
Medical examination; Physician's request.
Staff RNs 9 (ft), 5 (pt); LPNs 3 (ft); Nurses'
aides 28 (ft), 4 (pt); Activities coordinators 1
(ft).
Facilities Dining room; Physical therapy
room; Activities room; Chapel; Laundry
room; Barber/Beauty shop.
Activities Arts & crafts; Cards; Games;
Movies; Shopping trips.

Woodstock Residence
309 McHenry Ave, Woodstock, IL 60098
(815) 338-1700
Admin Sally Henslee.
Medical Dir John C Paul MD.
Licensure Skilled care. *Beds* SNF 114.
Certified Medicaid; Medicare.
Owner Proprietary corp.
Admissions Requirements Minimum age 21;
Medical examination; Physician's request.
Staff Physicians 1 (ft), 12 (pt); RNs 15 (ft);
LPNs 1 (ft); Nurses' aides 44 (ft), 4 (pt);
Physical therapists 3 (ft), 1 (pt); Reality
therapists 2 (ft), 1 (pt); Recreational
therapists 2 (ft), 1 (pt); Occupational
therapists 2 (ft); Speech therapists 1 (ft);
Activities coordinators 3 (ft); Dietitians 1
(ft); Ophthalmologists 1 (pt); Podiatrists 1
(pt); Dentists 1 (pt).
Facilities Dining room; Physical therapy
room; Activities room; Chapel; Crafts room;
Laundry room; Barber/Beauty shop; Library;
Covered patios; Gardens.
Activities Arts & crafts; Cards; Games; Prayer
groups; Movies; Shopping trips; Dances/
Social/Cultural gatherings.

Worth

Park Lawn Center
5831 W 115th St, Worth, IL 60482
(708) 396-1117
Admin Marjorie Chwastecki.
Medical Dir Noreen Payne.
Licensure Intermediate care for mentally
retarded. *Beds* ICF/MR 41. *Certified*
Medicaid.
Owner Nonprofit corp.
Staff RNs; LPNs; Physical therapists;
Recreational therapists; Occupational
therapists; Speech therapists; Activities
coordinators; Dietitians.
Facilities Dining room; Activities room;
Laundry room.
Activities Arts & crafts; Cards; Games;
Movies; Shopping trips; Dances/Social/
Cultural gatherings.

Yorkville

Hillside Living Center
Rte 34 & Game Farm Rd, Yorkville, IL 60560
(708) 553-5811
Admin Anita J Eversole. *Dir of Nursing*
Marama Leifheit. *Medical Dir* Daniel
Hatcher.
Licensure Skilled care. *Beds* SNF 79. *Private
Pay Patients* 75%. *Certified* Medicare.
Owner Nonprofit corp (Adventist Living
Centers).
Admissions Requirements Minimum age 18;
Medical examination.
Staff Physicians; RNs; LPNs; Nurses' aides;
Physical therapists; Reality therapists;
Recreational therapists; Occupational
therapists; Speech therapists; Activities
coordinators 1 (ft), 1 (pt); Dietitians 1 (pt);
Podiatrists 1 (pt).
Facilities Dining room; Activities room;
Crafts room; Laundry room; Barber/Beauty
shop; Living rooms; 12 Private rooms.
Activities Arts & crafts; Cards; Games;
Reading groups; Prayer groups; Movies;
Shopping trips; Dances/Social/Cultural
gatherings; Intergenerational programs; Pet
therapy.

Zeigler

Zeigler Colonial Manor Inc
300 Church St, Zeigler, IL 62999
(618) 596-6635
Admin Terra Potocki.
Licensure Intermediate care; Intermediate care
for mentally retarded. *Beds* ICF 27; ICF/MR
22. *Certified* Medicaid.
Owner Proprietary corp.
Admissions Requirements Minimum age 18;
Medical examination; Physician's request.
Staff RNs 1 (ft); LPNs 2 (ft), 3 (pt); Nurses'
aides 15 (ft); Activities coordinators 1 (ft).
Facilities Dining room; Activities room;
Crafts room; Laundry room; Barber/Beauty
shop.
Activities Arts & crafts; Cards; Games;
Reading groups; Prayer groups; Movies;
Shopping trips; Dances/Social/Cultural
gatherings.

Zion

Crown Manor Living Center
1805 27th St, Zion, IL 60099
(312) 746-3736

Admin Sylvia L Williams. *Dir of Nursing* June
Townsend.
Licensure Skilled care. *Beds* SNF 113. *Private
Pay Patients* 40%. *Certified* Medicaid;
Medicare.
Owner Nonprofit corp (Adventist Living
Centers).
Admissions Requirements Medical
examination.
Staff Physicians 20 (pt); RNs 4 (ft), 1 (pt);
LPNs 6 (ft); Nurses' aides 22 (ft), 18 (pt);
Physical therapists 1 (pt); Occupational
therapists 1 (pt); Speech therapists 1 (pt);
Activities coordinators 1 (ft); Dietitians 1
(pt); Ophthalmologists 1 (pt); Podiatrists 1
(pt).
Affiliation Seventh-Day Adventist.
Facilities Dining room; Physical therapy
room; Activities room; Chapel; Crafts room;
Laundry room; Barber/Beauty shop.
Activities Arts & crafts; Cards; Games;
Reading groups; Prayer groups; Movies;
Shopping trips; Dances/Social/Cultural
gatherings; Pet therapy.

Rolling Hills Manor
3615 16th St, Zion, IL 60099
(708) 746-8382
Admin Carolyn A Lofland. *Dir of Nursing*
Janet Knoll RN. *Medical Dir* C David
Engstrom MD.
Licensure Skilled care. *Beds* SNF 135. *Private
Pay Patients* 40%. *Certified* Medicaid;
Medicare.
Owner Nonprofit organization/foundation.
Admissions Requirements Minimum age 63;
Medical examination.
Staff RNs 3 (ft), 3 (pt); LPNs 8 (ft), 4 (pt);
Nurses' aides 33 (ft), 1 (pt); Physical
therapists 1 (pt); Reality therapists 1 (pt);
Recreational therapists 2 (ft); Occupational
therapists 1 (pt); Speech therapists 1 (pt);
Activities coordinators 1 (ft); Dietitians 1
(pt); Ophthalmologists 1 (pt); Podiatrists 1
(pt); Dentists 1 (pt).
Languages Slovak.
Affiliation Slovak American Charitable
Association.
Facilities Dining room; Physical therapy
room; Activities room; Crafts room; Laundry
room; Barber/Beauty shop.
Activities Arts & crafts; Cards; Games;
Reading groups; Prayer groups; Movies;
Shopping trips; Dances/Social/Cultural
gatherings; Intergenerational programs; Pet
therapy; Family involvement.

Sheridan Health Care Center
2534 Elim Ave, Zion, IL 60099
(312) 746-8435, 746-1744 FAX
Admin Nanjean Painter RN. *Dir of Nursing*
Patricia Davis RN. *Medical Dir* Abdul Aziz
MD.
Licensure Skilled care; Intermediate care. *Beds*
SNF 95; ICF 193. *Certified* Medicaid.
Owner Privately owned.
Admissions Requirements Minimum age 40;
Medical examination.
Staff Physicians; RNs; LPNs; Nurses' aides;
Physical therapists; Recreational therapists;
Occupational therapists; Speech therapists;
Activities coordinators; Dietitians;
Ophthalmologists.
Facilities Dining room; Physical therapy
room; Activities room; Laundry room;
Barber/Beauty shop; Library.
Activities Arts & crafts; Cards; Games;
Reading groups; Prayer groups; Movies;
Shopping trips; Dances/Social/Cultural
gatherings; Intergenerational programs.

INDIANA

Albany

Albany Nursing Care Inc
910 W Walnut, Albany, IN 47320
(317) 789-4423
Admin Nicholas E Lefevre. *Dir of Nursing*
Brenda Minix-Cox RN. *Medical Dir* Dr
Robert Reilly.
Licensure Intermediate care; Retirement. *Beds*
ICF 101; Retirement 7. *Private Pay Patients*
25%. *Certified* Medicaid.
Owner Proprietary corp.
Admissions Requirements Minimum age 21;
Medical examination.
Staff Physicians 1 (ft), 3 (pt); RNs 2 (ft), 1
(pt); LPNs 4 (ft), 1 (pt); Nurses' aides 35
(ft), 10 (pt); Physical therapists 1 (pt);
Activities coordinators 2 (ft); Dietitians 1
(pt); Podiatrists 1 (pt); Audiologists 1 (pt).
Facilities Dining room; Physical therapy
room; Activities room; Crafts room; Laundry
room; Barber/Beauty shop; Screened-in
porch.
Activities Arts & crafts; Cards; Games;
Reading groups; Prayer groups; Movies;
Shopping trips; Dances/Social/Cultural
gatherings; Intergenerational programs; Pet
therapy.

Alexandria

Alexandria Convalescent Center
PO Box 461, Hwy 9 S, Alexandria, IN 46001
(317) 724-4478
Admin Bruce Gooding. *Dir of Nursing*
Melinda Stout. *Medical Dir* Steven
Gatewood.
Licensure Intermediate care; Alzheimer's care.
Beds ICF 70. *Private Pay Patients* 33%.
Certified Medicaid.
Owner Privately owned.
Staff Physicians 4 (pt); RNs 1 (ft), 1 (pt);
LPNs 3 (ft), 3 (pt); Nurses' aides 15 (ft), 7
(pt); Physical therapists 1 (pt); Reality
therapists 1 (pt); Recreational therapists 1
(pt); Occupational therapists 1 (pt); Speech
therapists 1 (pt); Activities coordinators 1
(ft); Dietitians 1 (ft); Ophthalmologists 1
(pt); Podiatrists 1 (pt); Audiologists 1 (pt).
Facilities Dining room; Physical therapy
room; Activities room; Crafts room; Laundry
room; Barber/Beauty shop.
Activities Arts & crafts; Cards; Games;
Reading groups; Prayer groups; Shopping
trips; Dances/Social/Cultural gatherings; Pet
therapy.

Willows Nursing Home
RR 4, Box 220, Alexandria, IN 46001
(317) 724-4464
Admin Tanya A Dickey RN.
Licensure Intermediate care; Comprehensive
care. *Beds* 48; Comprehensive care 36.
Certified Medicaid.

Anderson

Americana-Family Tree Healthcare Center
1112 Monticello Dr, Anderson, IN 46011
(317) 649-0496
Admin Marjorie E Shell. *Dir of Nursing*
Rebecca Bergman RN. *Medical Dir* Ronald
Harmening MD.
Licensure Intermediate care; Alzheimer's care.
Beds ICF 110. *Certified* Medicaid.
Owner Proprietary corp (Manor Care).
Admissions Requirements Medical
examination; Physician's request.
Staff RNs; LPNs; Nurses' aides; Activities
coordinators.
Facilities Dining room; Activities room;
Crafts room; Barber/Beauty shop.
Activities Arts & crafts; Cards; Games;
Reading groups; Prayer groups; Movies;
Shopping trips; Dances/Social/Cultural
gatherings.

Americana Healthcare Center
1345 N Madison Ave, Anderson, IN 46011
(317) 644-2888
Admin Betty A Crum. *Dir of Nursing* Cheryl
Thrash RN. *Medical Dir* Stephen J Wright
MD.
Licensure Skilled care; Intermediate care. *Beds*
SNF 81; ICF 45. *Certified* Medicaid;
Medicare.
Owner Proprietary corp (Manor Care).
Admissions Requirements Minimum age 18;
Medical examination; Physician's request.
Staff Physicians 1 (pt); RNs 5 (ft), 3 (pt);
LPNs 11 (ft), 4 (pt); Nurses' aides 37 (ft), 12
(pt); Physical therapists 1 (ft); Occupational
therapists 1 (pt); Speech therapists 1 (pt);
Activities coordinators 1 (ft), 2 (pt);
Dietitians 1 (pt); Ophthalmologists 1 (pt);
Podiatrists 1 (pt).
Facilities Dining room; Physical therapy
room; Activities room; Chapel; Laundry
room; Barber/Beauty shop.
Activities Arts & crafts; Cards; Games;
Reading groups; Prayer groups; Movies;
Shopping trips; Dances/Social/Cultural
gatherings.

Anderson Healthcare Center
1809 N Madison Ave, Anderson, IN 46012
(317) 644-0903
Admin Loretta G Folsom.
Licensure Skilled care; Intermediate care. *Beds*
SNF 83; ICF 92. *Certified* Medicaid;
Medicare.
Owner Proprietary corp (ARA Living
Centers).

Community Care Center of Anderson
1235 W Cross St, Anderson, IN 46012
(317) 644-6230
Admin Brad Webber.
Licensure Skilled care; Intermediate care;
Comprehensive care. *Beds* SNF 39; ICF 40;
Comprehensive care 20.

Countryside Manor Healthcare Center
205 Marine Dr, Anderson, IN 46014
(317) 643-0939
Admin Timothy Yale.
Licensure Skilled care; Intermediate care;
Comprehensive care. *Beds* SNF 61; ICF 63;
Comprehensive care 1.

Hoover
1310 Bramble Way, Anderson, IN 46011-2827
(317) 642-8156
Admin Eva Hoover. *Dir of Nursing* Lynn
Henthorn RN. *Medical Dir* John Woodall
MD.
Licensure Intermediate care; Residential. *Beds*
ICF 30; Residential 10. *Certified* Medicaid.
Owner Proprietary corp (Buckeye Fam &
Nursing Hm).
Admissions Requirements Minimum age 21;
Medical examination; Physician's request.
Staff RNs 2 (ft); LPNs 2 (ft), 3 (pt); Nurses'
aides 6 (ft), 5 (pt); Activities coordinators 1
(ft); Dietitians 1 (pt).
Facilities Dining room; Activities room;
Barber/Beauty shop.
Activities Arts & crafts; Cards; Games;
Reading groups; Movies; Shopping trips;
Dances/Social/Cultural gatherings.

Rolling Hills Convalescent Center
1821 Lindberg Rd, Anderson, IN 46012
(317) 649-2532
Admin Mary Jo Powers.
Medical Dir Dr Linda Stropes.
Licensure Skilled care; Intermediate care. *Beds*
SNF 64; ICF 102. *Certified* Medicaid;
Medicare.
Owner Proprietary corp (Beverly Enterprises).
Admissions Requirements Medical
examination; Physician's request.
Staff RNs 5 (ft), 2 (pt); LPNs 15 (ft), 4 (pt);
Nurses' aides 58 (ft), 5 (pt); Physical
therapists 1 (ft); Occupational therapists 1
(ft); Speech therapists 1 (ft); Activities
coordinators 1 (ft); Dietitians 1 (ft).
Facilities Dining room; Physical therapy
room; Activities room; Crafts room; Laundry
room; Barber/Beauty shop.
Activities Arts & crafts; Cards; Games;
Reading groups; Prayer groups; Movies;
Shopping trips; Dances/Social/Cultural
gatherings; Family/New admission
adjustment workshops.

Angola

Angola Nursing Home
600 N Williams St, Angola, IN 46703
(219) 665-6313
Admin Laura Marie Winebrenner. *Dir of
Nursing* Maxine Martin. *Medical Dir* Dr
Thomas Miller.
Licensure Intermediate care. *Beds* ICF 40.
Private Pay Patients 0%. *Certified* Medicaid.
Owner Proprietary corp (Beverly Enterprises).
Admissions Requirements Minimum age 18;
Medical examination; Physician's request;
Prescreening, prior approval.

Staff Physicians 1 (pt); RNs 1 (pt); LPNs 3 (ft), 2 (pt); Nurses' aides 5 (ft), 5 (pt); Speech therapists 1 (pt); Activities coordinators 1 (ft); Dietitians 1 (pt); Podiatrists 1 (pt); Audiologists 1 (pt).
Facilities Dining room; Activities room; Crafts room; Laundry room; Dayroom.
Activities Arts & crafts; Cards; Games; Reading groups; Prayer groups; Movies; Shopping trips; Dances/Social/Cultural gatherings; Intergenerational programs.

Carlin Park Healthcare Center
516 N Williams St, Angola, IN 46703
(219) 665-9467
Admin John Klein.
Medical Dir George David MD.
Licensure Intermediate care. *Beds* ICF 99. *Certified* Medicaid.
Admissions Requirements Minimum age 18; Medical examination; Physician's request.
Staff Physicians 1 (pt); RNs 2 (ft), 1 (pt); LPNs 6 (ft), 2 (pt); Nurses' aides 35 (ft), 7 (pt); Physical therapists 1 (pt); Recreational therapists 1 (ft); Activities coordinators 1 (ft); Dietitians 1 (pt); Ophthalmologists 1 (pt); Dentists 1 (pt).
Facilities Dining room; Physical therapy room; Activities room; Chapel; Crafts room; Laundry room; Barber/Beauty shop.
Activities Arts & crafts; Cards; Games; Reading groups; Prayer groups; Movies; Shopping trips; Dances/Social/Cultural gatherings.

Lakeland Nursing Center
500 N Williams, Angola, IN 46703
(219) 665-2161, 665-1124 FAX
Admin Mary M Moore. *Dir of Nursing* Ann Armey RN. *Medical Dir* Dr Thomas Miller.
Licensure Intermediate care. *Beds* ICF 60. *Private Pay Patients* 47%. *Certified* Medicaid.
Owner Proprietary corp (Shive Nursing Centers Inc).
Admissions Requirements Medical examination.
Staff RNs 2 (pt); LPNs 4 (ft), 1 (pt); Nurses' aides 16 (ft), 14 (pt); Activities coordinators 1 (ft), 1 (pt).
Facilities Dining room; Activities room; Laundry room; Barber/Beauty shop.
Activities Arts & crafts; Cards; Games; Reading groups; Movies; Shopping trips; Pet therapy.

Arcadia

Arcadia Children's Home
303 Franklin Ave, Arcadia, IN 46030
(317) 984-9321
Admin Leonard A Hall.
Licensure Intermediate care for mentally retarded. *Beds* ICF/MR 60. *Certified* Medicaid.
Owner Privately owned.

Hamilton Heights Health Center
706 W Main St, Arcadia, IN 46030
(317) 984-3555
Admin Lester M Roland.
Medical Dir Dr Jerry Royer.
Licensure Intermediate care. *Beds* ICF 154. *Certified* Medicaid.
Owner Proprietary corp (Community Care Centers).
Admissions Requirements Minimum age 18; Medical examination; Physician's request.
Staff Physicians 3 (pt); RNs 3 (ft); LPNs 9 (ft), 2 (pt); Nurses' aides 35 (ft), 6 (pt); Physical therapists 1 (pt); Recreational therapists 1 (ft); Occupational therapists 1 (pt); Speech therapists 1 (pt); Activities coordinators 1 (ft); Dietitians 1 (pt); Podiatrists 1 (pt); Audiologists 1 (pt); Dentists 1 (pt).

Facilities Dining room; Physical therapy room; Activities room; Chapel; Crafts room; Laundry room; Barber/Beauty shop; Library.
Activities Arts & crafts; Cards; Games; Reading groups; Prayer groups; Movies; Shopping trips; Dances/Social/Cultural gatherings.

Attica

Woodland Manor Nursing Center
PO Box 166, State Rd 28 East, Attica, IN 47918
(317) 762-6133
Admin Linda Short RN. *Dir of Nursing* Peggy Evans RN. *Medical Dir* William A Ringer MD.
Licensure Intermediate care. *Beds* ICF 53. *Certified* Medicaid.
Owner Proprietary corp.
Admissions Requirements Minimum age 18; Medical examination; Physician's request.
Staff Physicians 3 (pt); RNs 2 (ft), 3 (pt); LPNs 2 (ft), 2 (pt); Nurses' aides 10 (ft), 16 (pt); Activities coordinators 1 (ft); Dietitians 1 (pt); Ophthalmologists 1 (pt); Dentists 1 (pt).
Facilities Dining room; Activities room; Chapel; Crafts room; Laundry room; Barber/Beauty shop; Library.
Activities Arts & crafts; Cards; Games; Prayer groups; Movies; Dances/Social/Cultural gatherings.

Auburn

Betz Nursing Home Inc
3009 C R 38, Auburn, IN 46706
(219) 925-3814
Admin Doris Betz Marshall LPN. *Dir of Nursing* V Carol Marks RN.
Licensure Intermediate care; Comprehensive care. *Beds* ICF 144; Comprehensive care 1. *Certified* Medicaid.
Owner Proprietary corp.
Admissions Requirements Medical examination; Physician's request.
Staff RNs 3 (ft), 1 (pt); LPNs 5 (ft); Nurses' aides 75 (ft); Activities coordinators 1 (ft), 4 (pt); Dietitians 1 (ft).
Facilities Dining room; Activities room; Crafts room; Laundry room; Barber/Beauty shop.
Activities Arts & crafts; Cards; Games; Reading groups; Prayer groups; Dances/Social/Cultural gatherings.

DeKalb Health Care Center
1751 Wesley Rd, Auburn, IN 46706
(219) 925-5494
Admin Rosemary Klemm. *Dir of Nursing* Linda Cook RN. *Medical Dir* William Goudy DO.
Licensure Intermediate care. *Beds* ICF 51. *Private Pay Patients* 50%. *Certified* Medicaid.
Owner Proprietary corp (Central Health Care Management Co).
Admissions Requirements Minimum age 18; Medical examination; Physician's request.
Staff RNs 1 (ft); LPNs 3 (ft); Nurses' aides 7 (ft), 3 (pt); Speech therapists 1 (pt); Activities coordinators 1 (ft); Dietitians 1 (pt).
Facilities Dining room; Laundry room; Barber/Beauty shop.
Activities Arts & crafts; Cards; Games; Reading groups; Prayer groups; Movies; Dances/Social/Cultural gatherings; Intergenerational programs; Pet therapy.

Oak Meadows Learning Center
1313 E 7th St, Auburn, IN 46706
(219) 925-1111, 925-1112 FAX
Admin Pamela S DeKoninck. *Dir of Nursing* Pamela Williams. *Medical Dir* Dr Philip Chase; Dr Paul Rexroth; Dr Gary Sheeler.

Licensure Intermediate care. *Beds* ICF 73. *Private Pay Patients* 0%. *Certified* Medicaid.
Owner Proprietary corp (Res-Care Inc).
Admissions Requirements Minimum age 18; Medical examination.
Staff RNs 2 (ft); LPNs 3 (ft), 1 (pt); Activities coordinators 1 (ft); Dietitians; Program trainers 15 (ft), 1 (pt).
Facilities Dining room; Activities room; Laundry room; Barber/Beauty shop.
Activities Arts & crafts; Cards; Games; Reading groups; Prayer groups; Movies; Shopping trips; Dances/Social/Cultural gatherings; Special Olympics.

Avilla

Sacred Heart Home
Rte 2 Box 2A, State Rd 3, Avilla, IN 46710-9602
(219) 897-2841, 897-3724 FAX
Admin Sr M Alexine Knotek OSF. *Dir of Nursing* Carla Frymier RN, Acting. *Medical Dir* Max E Sneary MD.
Licensure Intermediate care; Alzheimer's care. *Beds* ICF 133. *Certified* Medicaid.
Owner Nonprofit corp (Franciscan Sisters Health Care Corp).
Staff RNs 4 (ft), 2 (pt); LPNs 5 (ft), 4 (pt); Nurses' aides 29 (ft), 30 (pt); Physical therapists (contracted); Activities coordinators 2 (ft), 1 (pt); Dietitians 1 (ft).
Affiliation Roman Catholic.
Facilities Dining room; Physical therapy room; Activities room; Chapel; Laundry room; Barber/Beauty shop; Library.
Activities Arts & crafts; Cards; Games; Reading groups; Prayer groups; Movies; Shopping trips; Dances/Social/Cultural gatherings; Intergenerational programs; Group outings.

Batesville

Dreyerhaus
PO Box 310, Batesville, IN 47006
(812) 934-2436
Admin Marcella L Shaul RN. *Dir of Nursing* Bonnie Greathouse RN. *Medical Dir* Ivan Lindgren MD.
Licensure Skilled care; Intermediate care. *Beds* SNF 38; ICF 110. *Certified* Medicaid; Medicare.
Owner Proprietary corp.
Admissions Requirements Minimum age 18; Medical examination.
Staff Physicians 1 (pt); RNs 4 (ft); LPNs 9 (ft); Nurses' aides 40 (ft); Physical therapists 1 (ft); Activities coordinators 1 (ft); Dietitians 1 (pt).
Facilities Dining room; Physical therapy room; Activities room; Chapel; Crafts room; Laundry room; Barber/Beauty shop; Library.
Activities Arts & crafts; Cards; Games; Reading groups; Prayer groups; Movies; Shopping trips; Dances/Social/Cultural gatherings.

Bedford

Bedford Nursing Home
514 E 16th St, Bedford, IN 47421
(812) 279-4611
Admin Nellie M Camp. *Dir of Nursing* Hellie Diehl.
Licensure Intermediate care. *Beds* ICF 40. *Certified* Medicaid.
Owner Proprietary corp.
Admissions Requirements Minimum age 18.
Staff RNs 1 (pt); LPNs 4 (ft), 2 (pt); Nurses' aides 6 (ft), 5 (pt); Recreational therapists 1 (pt); Activities coordinators 1 (ft); Dietitians 1 (pt).

Facilities Dining room; Activities room;
Laundry room.
Activities Arts & crafts; Cards; Games;
Reading groups; Prayer groups; Movies;
Shopping trips; Dances/Social/Cultural
gatherings.

Hospitality House
2111 Norton Ln, Bedford, IN 47421
(812) 279-4437
Admin Steven Sanders.
Medical Dir Dr Lawrence Benham.
Licensure Skilled care; Intermediate care;
Comprehensive care. *Beds* SNF 70; ICF 136;
Comprehensive care 7. *Certified* Medicaid;
Medicare.
Owner Proprietary corp.
Admissions Requirements Medical
examination; Physician's request.
Staff Physicians 14 (pt); RNs 7 (ft); LPNs 17
(ft); Nurses' aides 40 (ft), 7 (pt); Physical
therapists 1 (pt); Occupational therapists 2
(pt); Speech therapists 1 (pt); Activities
coordinators 1 (ft); Dietitians 1 (ft).
Facilities Dining room; Physical therapy
room; Activities room; Laundry room;
Barber/Beauty shop; Speech therapy room.

Westview Manor Health Care Center
1510 Clinic Dr, Bedford, IN 47421
(812) 279-4494
Admin Marilyn Johnson. *Dir of Nursing* June
Styborski RN. *Medical Dir* Dr D J
Kaderabek.
Licensure Skilled care; Intermediate care. *Beds*
SNF 58; ICF 60. *Certified* Medicaid.
Owner Proprietary corp.
Admissions Requirements Minimum age 18;
Medical examination; Physician's request.
Staff Physicians 8 (pt); RNs 7 (ft), 1 (pt);
LPNs 11 (ft); Nurses' aides 43 (ft), 8 (pt);
Physical therapists 1 (ft); Activities
coordinators 2 (ft); Dietitians 1 (ft);
Ophthalmologists 1 (pt).
Facilities Dining room; Physical therapy
room; Activities room; Crafts room; Laundry
room; Barber/Beauty shop.
Activities Arts & crafts; Cards; Games;
Reading groups; Prayer groups; Movies;
Shopping trips; Dances/Social/Cultural
gatherings.

Beech Grove

Beech Grove Healthcare Center
2002 Albany Ave, Beech Grove, IN 46107
(317) 783-2911
Admin Joan Foley.
Medical Dir Dr Thomas Moran.
Licensure Skilled care; Intermediate care. *Beds*
SNF 77; ICF 122. *Certified* Medicaid;
Medicare.
Owner Proprietary corp (ARA Living Center).
Admissions Requirements Medical
examination; Physician's request.
Staff RNs 5 (ft), 2 (pt); LPNs 8 (ft), 3 (pt);
Nurses' aides 46 (ft), 12 (pt); Physical
therapists 2 (pt); Occupational therapists 2
(pt); Speech therapists 1 (pt); Activities
coordinators 2 (ft); Dietitians 1 (ft);
Podiatrists 1 (pt); Dentists 2 (pt).
Facilities Dining room; Physical therapy
room; Activities room; Chapel; Laundry
room; Barber/Beauty shop.
Activities Arts & crafts; Cards; Games;
Reading groups; Prayer groups; Movies;
Shopping trips; Dances/Social/Cultural
gatherings.

St Paul Hermitage
501 N 17th Ave, Beech Grove, IN 46107
(317) 786-2261
Admin Sr Patricia Dede OSB. *Dir of Nursing*
Sr Mary Frederic Turner OSB. *Medical Dir*
Frank Fortuna MD.
Licensure Intermediate care; Residential care.
Beds ICF 48; Residential care 57. *Private
Pay Patients* 15%. *Certified* Medicaid.

Owner Nonprofit organization/foundation
(Sisters of Saint Benedict Inc).
Staff RNs; LPNs; Nurses' aides; Physical
therapists; Activities coordinators; Dietitians.
Affiliation Roman Catholic.
Facilities Dining room; Physical therapy
room; Activities room; Chapel; Crafts room;
Laundry room; Barber/Beauty shop; Library.
Activities Arts & crafts; Cards; Games;
Reading groups; Prayer groups; Movies;
Shopping trips; Pet therapy.

Berne

Chalet Village
1065 Parkway St, Berne, IN 46711
(219) 589-2127
Admin Mike Evans. *Dir of Nursing* Shirley
Ellis RN. *Medical Dir* Dr Brendan Smith.
Licensure Intermediate care. *Beds* ICF 80.
Private Pay Patients 60%. *Certified*
Medicaid.
Owner Proprietary corp.
Staff Physicians 6 (ft); RNs 2 (ft), 1 (pt);
LPNs 5 (ft), 2 (pt); Nurses' aides 14 (ft), 7
(pt); Physical therapists 3 (pt); Reality
therapists 3 (pt); Recreational therapists 3
(pt); Occupational therapists 3 (pt); Speech
therapists 3 (pt); Activities coordinators 1
(ft); Dietitians 1 (ft); Ophthalmologists 1
(pt); Podiatrists 1 (pt); Audiologists 1 (pt).
Activities Arts & crafts; Cards; Games;
Reading groups; Prayer groups; Movies;
Shopping trips; Dances/Social/Cultural
gatherings; Intergenerational programs; Pet
therapy; Community events.

Swiss Village Inc
W Main St, Berne, IN 46711
(219) 589-3173
Admin Daryl L Martin. *Dir of Nursing*
LaDene Lehman. *Medical Dir* Dr Robert
Boze.
Licensure Intermediate care; Residential care;
Assisted residential care; Independent living
apartments. *Beds* ICF 108; Residential &
assisted residential care 135; Independent
living apts 84. *Private Pay Patients* 95%.
Certified Medicaid.
Owner Nonprofit organization/foundation.
Admissions Requirements Minimum age 62;
Medical examination.
Staff RNs 7 (ft), 3 (pt); LPNs 10 (ft), 1 (pt);
Nurses' aides 37 (ft), 39 (pt); Activities
coordinators 3 (ft), 3 (pt); Dietitians 1 (pt).
Affiliation Mennonite.
Facilities Dining room; Activities room;
Chapel; Crafts room; Laundry room; Barber/
Beauty shop; Library.
Activities Arts & crafts; Cards; Games;
Reading groups; Prayer groups; Movies;
Shopping trips; Dances/Social/Cultural
gatherings; Field trips; Exercise classes.

Bicknell

Bicknell Health Care
204 W 3rd St, Bicknell, IN 47512
(812) 735-3021
Admin Mary Alyce Cullop.
Medical Dir Dr B G O'Dell; Dr R W Rompf.
Licensure Intermediate care. *Beds* ICF 47.
Certified Medicaid.
Owner Proprietary corp.
Admissions Requirements Medical
examination.
Staff Physicians 2 (pt); RNs 1 (ft), 1 (pt);
LPNs 3 (ft), 3 (pt); Nurses' aides 13 (ft), 4
(pt); Physical therapists 1 (pt); Activities
coordinators 1 (ft); Dietitians 1 (ft);
Ophthalmologists 2 (pt); Podiatrists 1 (pt);
Dentists 2 (pt).
Facilities Dining room; Physical therapy
room; Activities room; Crafts room; Laundry
room; Barber/Beauty shop; Library;
Conference room; Supplementary nutrition
room.

Activities Arts & crafts; Cards; Games;
Reading groups; Prayer groups; Movies;
Shopping trips; Dances/Social/Cultural
gatherings; Birthday parties.

Bloomfield

Bloomfield Health Care Center
PO Box 111, 150 N Seminary, Bloomfield, IN
47424
(812) 384-4448
Admin Jan Ann Caudill. *Dir of Nursing*
Yvonne Deckard. *Medical Dir* Owen
Batterton.
Licensure Intermediate care; Alzheimer's care.
Beds ICF 60. *Private Pay Patients* 40%.
Certified Medicaid.
Owner Proprietary corp (Central Health Care
Management).
Admissions Requirements Minimum age 18;
Medical examination; Physician's request.
Staff Physicians 4 (pt); RNs 1 (ft); LPNs 3
(ft), 3 (pt); Nurses' aides 14 (ft), 6 (pt);
Physical therapists 1 (pt); Activities
coordinators 1 (ft); Dietitians 1 (ft), 1 (pt);
Ophthalmologists 1 (pt); Podiatrists 1 (pt).
Facilities Dining room; Physical therapy
room; Activities room; Laundry room;
Barber/Beauty shop.
Activities Arts & crafts; Cards; Games;
Reading groups; Movies; Shopping trips;
Dances/Social/Cultural gatherings;
Intergenerational programs; Pet therapy.

Bloomington

Bloomington Convalescent Center
PO Box 970, 714 S Rogers St, Bloomington,
IN 47401
(812) 336-6893
Admin Rodney L McBride. *Dir of Nursing*
Chris Johns RN. *Medical Dir* George Lewis
MD.
Licensure Skilled care; Intermediate care;
Retirement. *Beds* SNF 33; ICF 135.
Certified Medicaid; Medicare.
Owner Nonprofit corp.
Admissions Requirements Minimum age 18;
Medical examination; Physician's request.
Staff Physicians 1 (ft); RNs 5 (ft); LPNs 21
(ft), 7 (pt); Nurses' aides 43 (ft), 10 (pt);
Physical therapists 1 (ft); Recreational
therapists 2 (ft), 1 (pt); Occupational
therapists 1 (pt); Speech therapists 1 (pt);
Dietitians 1 (pt); Ophthalmologists 1 (pt);
Ophthalmologists 1 (pt); Podiatrists 1 (pt);
Dentists 1 (pt).
Facilities Dining room; Physical therapy
room; Activities room; Crafts room; Barber/
Beauty shop.
Activities Arts & crafts; Cards; Games;
Reading groups; Prayer groups; Movies;
Shopping trips; Dances/Social/Cultural
gatherings.

Fontanbleu Nursing Center
3305 S Hwy 37, Bloomington, IN 47401
(812) 332-4437
Admin Douglas V Lynch. *Dir of Nursing* Julia
Dutton RN. *Medical Dir* Steven Lewallen
MD.
Licensure Skilled care; Intermediate care;
Alzheimer's care. *Beds* SNF 101; ICF 100.
Certified Medicaid; Medicare.
Owner Proprietary corp (Beverly Enterprises).
Admissions Requirements Minimum age 18.

Hoosier Hills Health Care Center
120 E Miller Dr, Bloomington, IN 47401
(812) 336-1055
Admin Warren Hotte.
Licensure Intermediate care. *Beds* ICF 40.
Certified Medicaid.
Owner Proprietary corp (Waverly Group).
Admissions Requirements Minimum age 18;
Medical examination.

Staff RNs 1 (ft); LPNs 4 (pt); Nurses' aides 7 (ft), 6 (pt); Activities coordinators 1 (ft); Dietitians 1 (pt).
Facilities Dining room; Activities room; Crafts room.
Activities Arts & crafts; Games; Reading groups; Prayer groups; Movies; Shopping trips; Dances/Social/Cultural gatherings.

Hospitality House Inc
PO Box 427, 1100 S Curry Pike, Bloomington, IN 47402-0427
(812) 339-1657
Admin Caroline Lin. *Dir of Nursing* Jean Wagner RN. *Medical Dir* S LeWallen MD.
Licensure Skilled care; Intermediate care; Alzheimer's care. *Beds* SNF 52; ICF 140. *Certified* Medicaid; Medicare.
Owner Proprietary corp.
Admissions Requirements Minimum age 18; Medical examination; Physician's request.
Staff Physicians 4 (pt); RNs 3 (ft), 6 (pt); LPNs 12 (ft), 1 (pt); Nurses' aides 68 (ft), 7 (pt); Physical therapists 1 (pt); Recreational therapists 1 (pt); Occupational therapists 1 (pt); Speech therapists 1 (pt); Activities coordinators 1 (ft), 4 (pt); Dietitians 1 (pt); Ophthalmologists 3 (pt); Podiatrists 1 (pt); Dentists 1 (pt); Optometrists 1 (pt).
Languages Chinese.
Facilities Dining room; Physical therapy room; Activities room; Chapel; Crafts room; Laundry room; Barber/Beauty shop; Family room.
Activities Arts & crafts; Cards; Games; Reading groups; Prayer groups; Movies; Shopping trips; Dances/Social/Cultural gatherings; Parties; Spelling bees.

Meadowood
2455 Tamarack Trail, Bloomington, IN 47401
(812) 336-7060
Admin G Randy Hornstein.
Licensure Skilled care; Residential care. *Beds* SNF 25; Residential care 14.

Bluffton

Cooper Community Care Center
1509 Fort Wayne Rd, Bluffton, IN 46714
(219) 824-2434
Admin Gary L Maller.
Licensure Skilled care; Intermediate care. *Beds* SNF 33; ICF 71. *Certified* Medicaid; Medicare.
Owner Proprietary corp (Community Care Centers).

Meadowvale Care Center
1529 W Lancaster St, Bluffton, IN 46714
(219) 824-4320, 824-4689 FAX
Admin Rev Glenn V Propst. *Dir of Nursing* Maria Lund RN. *Medical Dir* Dr Gerald L Miller.
Licensure Intermediate care. *Beds* ICF 120. *Private Pay Patients* 40%. *Certified* Medicaid.
Owner Proprietary corp (Nationwide Management Inc).
Admissions Requirements Medical examination; Physician's request.
Staff Physicians 4 (pt); RNs 2 (ft); LPNs 9 (ft), 5 (pt); Nurses' aides 25 (ft), 12 (pt); Activities coordinators 1 (ft), 1 (pt); Dietitians 1 (pt).
Facilities Dining room; Activities room; Crafts room; Laundry room; Barber/Beauty shop; Library; TV lounge; Critical care wing.
Activities Arts & crafts; Cards; Games; Reading groups; Movies; Shopping trips; Dances/Social/Cultural gatherings; Intergenerational programs; Cooking; Baking; Sewing.

West Haven Health Care
1001 S Clark Ave, Bluffton, IN 46714
(219) 824-0326
Admin Lona S Maboy.

Medical Dir Dr George Merkle.
Licensure Intermediate care. *Beds* ICF 40. *Certified* Medicaid.
Owner Proprietary corp (Beverly Enterprises).
Admissions Requirements Minimum age 18; Medical examination.
Staff RNs 2 (pt); LPNs 3 (ft), 2 (pt); Nurses' aides 4 (ft), 4 (pt); Activities coordinators 1 (ft); Dietitians 1 (pt).
Facilities Dining room; Activities room; Laundry room; Barber/Beauty shop.
Activities Arts & crafts; Games; Reading groups; Prayer groups; Movies; Shopping trips; Dances/Social/Cultural gatherings; Weekly bus rides.

Boonville

Baker's Rest Haven
305 E North St, Boonville, IN 47601
(812) 897-2810
Admin David L Batts.
Medical Dir Ramona J Betz.
Licensure Intermediate care. *Beds* ICF 60. *Certified* Medicaid.
Owner Proprietary corp.
Admissions Requirements Minimum age 18; Medical examination; Physician's request.
Staff RNs 2 (ft), 3 (pt); LPNs 5 (ft), 1 (pt); Nurses' aides 15 (ft), 5 (pt); Activities coordinators 1 (ft); Dietitians 1 (pt).
Facilities Dining room; Activities room; Chapel; Crafts room; Laundry room; Barber/Beauty shop.
Activities Arts & crafts; Games; Reading groups; Prayer groups; Movies; Shopping trips; Dances/Social/Cultural gatherings; Field trips such as circus, plays, & concerts.

Boonville Convalescent Center Inc
725 S 2nd St, Boonville, IN 47601
(812) 897-1375
Admin Gloria Glore.
Licensure Intermediate care. *Beds* ICF 107. *Certified* Medicaid.
Owner Proprietary corp.

Brazil

Clay County Health Center Inc
1408 E Hendrix St, Brazil, IN 47834
(812) 433-4111
Admin Wilma I Ellison.
Medical Dir Rahim Farid.
Licensure Skilled care; Intermediate care. *Beds* SNF 39; ICF 60. *Certified* Medicaid; Medicare.
Owner Proprietary corp (Forum Group).
Facilities Dining room; Physical therapy room; Activities room; Crafts room; Laundry room; Barber/Beauty shop.
Activities Arts & crafts; Cards; Games; Reading groups; Prayer groups; Movies.

Holly Hill Health Care Facility
RR 17 Box 130, 110 S Murphy, Brazil, IN 47834
(812) 446-2636
Admin Bruce Gooding. *Dir of Nursing* Candy Clerk. *Medical Dir* Curt Oehler.
Licensure Intermediate care. *Beds* ICF 103. *Private Pay Patients* 60%. *Certified* Medicaid.
Owner Privately owned.
Admissions Requirements Medical examination.
Staff Physicians 6 (pt); RNs 1 (ft); LPNs 7 (ft); Nurses' aides 23 (ft), 5 (pt); Physical therapists 1 (pt); Reality therapists 1 (pt); Recreational therapists 1 (pt); Occupational therapists 1 (pt); Speech therapists 1 (pt); Activities coordinators 1 (ft), 1 (pt); Dietitians 1 (ft), 1 (pt); Ophthalmologists 1 (pt); Podiatrists 1 (pt); Audiologists 1 (pt).
Facilities Dining room; Physical therapy room; Activities room; Crafts room; Laundry room; Barber/Beauty shop.

Activities Arts & crafts; Cards; Games; Reading groups; Prayer groups; Movies; Shopping trips; Dances/Social/Cultural gatherings; Pet therapy.

Bremen

Bremen Health Care Center
316 Woodies Ln, Bremen, IN 46506
(219) 546-3494
Admin P William Triplett. *Dir of Nursing* Linda Rozwarski RN. *Medical Dir* Dr Robert Kolbe.
Licensure Intermediate care. *Beds* ICF 82. *Private Pay Patients* 40%. *Certified* Medicaid.
Owner Proprietary corp.
Admissions Requirements Medical examination.
Staff Physicians 7 (pt); RNs 2 (ft); LPNs 6 (ft), 2 (pt); Nurses' aides 27 (ft), 16 (pt); Physical therapists 1 (pt); Activities coordinators 1 (ft), 1 (pt); Dietitians 1 (pt); Podiatrists 1 (pt).
Facilities Dining room; Activities room; Crafts room; Laundry room; Barber/Beauty shop; Library.
Activities Arts & crafts; Cards; Games; Reading groups; Prayer groups; Movies; Shopping trips; Dances/Social/Cultural gatherings; Pet therapy.

Brookville

Elsie M Dreyer Nursing Home II
11049 S R 101, Brookville, IN 47012
(317) 647-2527
Admin Janet Stevens Hendricks.
Licensure Intermediate care. *Beds* ICF 75.

Elsie Dryer Nursing Home I
273 Main St, Brookville, IN 47012
(317) 647-6231
Admin E F Horton.
Medical Dir Dr William Stitt.
Licensure Intermediate care. *Beds* ICF 48. *Certified* Medicaid.
Admissions Requirements Medical examination; Physician's request.
Staff Physicians 4 (pt); RNs 1 (pt); LPNs 3 (ft), 1 (pt); Nurses' aides 7 (ft), 13 (pt); Activities coordinators 1 (ft).
Facilities Dining room.
Activities Arts & crafts; Cards; Reading groups; Prayer groups; Movies.

Brownsburg

Brownsburg Health Care Center
1010 Hornaday Rd, Brownsburg, IN 46112
(317) 852-3123, 852-2211 FAX
Admin Mike Cahill. *Dir of Nursing* Jennifer Gordon. *Medical Dir* Malcom Scamihorn.
Licensure Skilled care; Intermediate care; Alzheimer's care. *Beds* SNF 53; ICF 105; Alzheimer's care 20. *Private Pay Patients* 45%. *Certified* Medicaid; Medicare.
Owner Proprietary corp (Cardinal).

Brownstown

Hoosier Christian Village
621 S Sugar, Brownstown, IN 47220
(812) 358-2504
Admin Charles W McCormick.
Licensure Skilled care; Intermediate care; Comprehensive care. *Beds* SNF 36; ICF 49; Comprehensive care 12. *Certified* Medicaid; Medicare.
Owner Nonprofit corp (Christian Homes).

Butler

Hotel Butler Residential Center
117 S Broadway, Butler, IN 46721
(219) 868-2161

Admin Elvia Stickney.
Medical Dir Peggy Beyer MD.
Licensure Residential care. *Beds* Residential care 40. *Private Pay Patients* 10%.
Owner Proprietary corp (Central Health Care Management Co).
Admissions Requirements Minimum age 18; Medical examination.
Staff RNs 1 (pt); Activities coordinators 1 (pt); Dietitians 1 (pt).
Facilities Dining room; Activities room; Laundry room.
Activities Arts & crafts; Cards; Games; Reading groups; Prayer groups; Movies; Shopping trips; Dances/Social/Cultural gatherings; Intergenerational programs; Pet therapy.

Meadowhaven Health Care Center
PO Box 399, 520 W Liberty St, Butler, IN 46721
(219) 868-2164, 868-2166 FAX
Admin Raymond R Schlatter. *Dir of Nursing* Kay Meyer. *Medical Dir* Dr Laverne Miller.
Licensure Intermediate care. *Beds* ICF 101. *Private Pay Patients* 45%. *Certified* Medicaid.
Owner Proprietary corp (MDI Limited Partnership).
Admissions Requirements Minimum age 18; Medical examination; Physician's request.
Staff Physicians 6 (pt); RNs 1 (ft); LPNs 5 (ft); Nurses' aides 14 (ft), 11 (pt); Physical therapists 1 (pt); Activities coordinators 1 (ft); Dietitians 1 (pt); Podiatrists 1 (pt).
Facilities Dining room; Physical therapy room; Activities room; Laundry room; Barber/Beauty shop; Library.
Activities Arts & crafts; Cards; Games; Reading groups; Prayer groups; Movies; Shopping trips; Pet therapy.

Carmel

Carmel Care Center
118 Medical Dr, Carmel, IN 46032
(317) 844-4211, 846-5343 FAX
Admin Linda S Parkes. *Dir of Nursing* Susan Tillett. *Medical Dir* Norman Fogle MD.
Licensure Skilled care; Intermediate care; Alzheimer's care; Assisted living. *Beds* SNF 164; ICF 212. *Private Pay Patients* 37%. *Certified* Medicaid; Medicare.
Owner Proprietary corp.
Admissions Requirements Minimum age 18; Medical examination.
Staff Physicians 60 (pt); RNs 12 (ft), 3 (pt); LPNs 30 (ft), 3 (pt); Nurses' aides 90 (ft), 6 (pt); Physical therapists 2 (pt); Occupational therapists 1 (pt); Speech therapists 1 (pt); Activities coordinators 4 (ft), 1 (pt); Dietitians 1 (pt); Ophthalmologists 1 (pt); Podiatrists 1 (pt); Audiologists 1 (pt).
Facilities Dining room; Physical therapy room; Activities room; Chapel; Crafts room; Laundry room; Barber/Beauty shop; Library; Ventilator care; Respiratory care/Oximetry monitoring; IV therapy; Peritoneal dialysis.
Activities Arts & crafts; Cards; Games; Reading groups; Prayer groups; Movies; Dances/Social/Cultural gatherings; Intergenerational programs; Pet therapy; Special occasion outings; Cooking.

Lakeview Health Care Center
2907 E 136th St, Carmel, IN 46032
(317) 846-0265
Admin Steven L Dehne.
Medical Dir Dr Stephen Pennal; Dr Violet Woods White.
Licensure Intermediate care; Retirement; Alzheimer's care. *Beds* ICF 39. *Certified* Medicaid.
Owner Privately owned.
Admissions Requirements Minimum age 18; Medical examination; Physician's request.

Staff Physicians 1 (pt); RNs 1 (ft); LPNs 3 (ft), 3 (pt); Nurses' aides 12 (ft), 3 (pt); Recreational therapists 1 (pt); Activities coordinators 1 (ft); Dietitians 1 (pt).
Facilities Dining room; Activities room; Crafts room; Laundry room; Barber/Beauty shop.
Activities Arts & crafts; Cards; Games; Reading groups; Prayer groups; Movies; Shopping trips; Dances/Social/Cultural gatherings.

Manor House of Carmel
116 Medical Dr, Carmel, IN 46032
(317) 844-4211
Admin Greg Starnes. *Dir of Nursing* Linda Greene RN. *Medical Dir* Norman Fogle MD.
Licensure Skilled care; Intermediate care; Alzheimer's care. *Beds* SNF 99; ICF 163. *Certified* Medicare.
Owner Privately owned.
Admissions Requirements Minimum age 18; Medical examination.
Staff Physicians 30 (pt); RNs 3 (ft), 3 (pt); LPNs 4 (ft), 6 (pt); Nurses' aides 26 (ft), 14 (pt); Physical therapists 1 (pt); Occupational therapists 1 (pt); Speech therapists 1 (pt); Activities coordinators 1 (ft); Dietitians 1 (pt); Ophthalmologists 1 (pt); Podiatrists 1 (pt).
Facilities Dining room; Physical therapy room; Activities room; Chapel; Crafts room; Laundry room; Barber/Beauty shop; Library.
Activities Arts & crafts; Cards; Games; Reading groups; Movies; Shopping trips; Dances/Social/Cultural gatherings.

Summer Trace Retirement Communities
12999 N Pennsylvania, Carmel, IN 46032
(317) 848-2448
Admin Charles Lentz. *Dir of Nursing* Linda Hutslar RN. *Medical Dir* Dr Cliff Fedders.
Licensure Skilled care; Intermediate care; Assisted living. *Beds* Comprehensive care 60; Assisted living 30. *Private Pay Patients* 100%.
Owner Proprietary corp (Beverly Enterprises).
Admissions Requirements Minimum age 18; Medical examination; Physician's request.
Staff RNs 2 (ft), 1 (pt); LPNs 4 (ft), 3 (pt); Nurses' aides 7 (ft), 8 (pt); Physical therapists 1 (pt); Occupational therapists 1 (pt); Speech therapists 1 (pt); Activities coordinators 1 (ft); Dietitians 1 (pt); Podiatrists 1 (pt); Other staff 4 (ft), 3 (pt).
Facilities Dining room; Physical therapy room; Activities room; Chapel; Crafts room; Barber/Beauty shop; Library; Gazebo; Lake; Solarium; Exercise room; Bank.
Activities Arts & crafts; Cards; Games; Reading groups; Prayer groups; Movies; Shopping trips; Dances/Social/Cultural gatherings; Pet therapy; Lunch club; Gardening.

Center Point

Macanell Nursing Home Inc
Rte 2 Box 139, Center Point, IN 47840
(812) 835-3041
Admin Hugh W McCann.
Licensure Intermediate care. *Beds* ICF 67. *Certified* Medicaid.
Owner Proprietary corp.

Centerville

Pinehurst Nursing Home
Box 188, Centerville, IN 47330
(317) 855-3424
Admin Charlotte E LeGere.
Licensure Intermediate care; Comprehensive care. *Beds* ICF 79; Comprehensive care 2. *Certified* Medicaid.
Owner Privately owned.

Chandler

Medco Center of Chandler
RR 2 Box 39, Chandler, IN 47610
(812) 925-3381
Admin Barbara Cash.
Medical Dir Linda Roland.
Licensure Intermediate care. *Beds* ICF 74. *Certified* Medicaid.
Owner Proprietary corp (Unicare).
Admissions Requirements Medical examination; Physician's request.
Facilities Dining room; Physical therapy room; Activities room; Barber/Beauty shop.
Activities Arts & crafts; Cards; Games; Prayer groups; Movies; Shopping trips; Dances/Social/Cultural gatherings.

Charlestown

Longworth Villa
PO Box 9, Charlestown, IN 47111
(812) 256-3371
Admin William K Daugherty.
Licensure Intermediate care. *Beds* ICF 65. *Certified* Medicaid.
Owner Proprietary corp.
Admissions Requirements Minimum age 18; Medical examination.
Staff RNs 1 (pt); LPNs 2 (ft); Nurses' aides 20 (ft), 3 (pt); Activities coordinators 1 (ft); Dietitians 1 (ft); 1 (ft).
Facilities Dining room; Activities room; Chapel; Crafts room; Laundry room; Barber/Beauty shop.
Activities Arts & crafts; Cards; Games; Reading groups; Prayer groups; Movies; Shopping trips; Dances/Social/Cultural gatherings.

Chesterfield

Miller's Merry Manor Inc
524 Anderson Rd, Chesterfield, IN 46017
(317) 378-0213
Admin William C Carter.
Licensure Intermediate care. *Beds* ICF 60.

Chesterton

Chesterton Health Care Center
PO Box 598, 1620 S Old State Rd 49, Chesterton, IN 46304
(219) 926-8301
Admin C Jane Graves.
Licensure Skilled care; Intermediate care. *Beds* SNF 53; ICF 47.

Cicero

Cicero Children's Center Inc
69 N Harrison, PO Box 217, Cicero, IN 46034
(317) 934-4393
Admin Lane Guttman.
Licensure Developmentally disabled. *Beds* 28.
Admissions Requirements Minimum age 0-21; Medical examination.
Staff RNs 1 (pt); LPNs 1 (ft); Nurses' aides 18 (pt); Activities coordinators 1 (ft); Dietitians 1 (pt).
Facilities Dining room; Activities room; Laundry room.

Clarksville

Clarksville Healthcare Center
586 Eastern Blvd, Clarksville, IN 47130
(812) 282-6663
Admin Steve E Robison.
Medical Dir Dr Claude Meyer.
Licensure Skilled care; Intermediate care. *Beds* SNF 87; ICF 108. *Certified* Medicaid; Medicare.
Owner Proprietary corp (ARA).

Admissions Requirements Minimum age 18.
Staff Physicians 1 (pt); RNs 3 (ft); LPNs 12 (ft), 4 (pt); Nurses' aides 30 (ft), 15 (pt); Physical therapists 1 (ft); Recreational therapists 1 (ft), 1 (pt); Occupational therapists 1 (ft); Speech therapists 1 (ft); Activities coordinators 1 (ft); Dietitians 1 (ft); Audiologists 1 (ft); Dentists 1 (pt).
Facilities Dining room; Physical therapy room; Activities room; Crafts room; Laundry room; Barber/Beauty shop.
Activities Arts & crafts; Cards; Games; Reading groups; Shopping trips; Dances/ Social/Cultural gatherings.

Corydon Nursing Home
101 Potters Ln, Clarksville, IN 47130
(812) 738-2190
Admin Inez M LeSaux. *Dir of Nursing* Bob Fehrenbach. *Medical Dir* George Estill MD.
Licensure Intermediate care. *Beds* 40. *Certified* Medicaid.
Owner Proprietary corp (Beverly Enterprises).
Admissions Requirements Minimum age 18; Medical examination; Physician's request.
Staff LPNs; Nurses' aides; Activities coordinators.
Facilities Dining room; Activities room; Crafts room; Laundry room; Barber/Beauty shop.
Activities Arts & crafts; Cards; Games; Reading groups; Prayer groups; Movies; Shopping trips; Dances/Social/Cultural gatherings.

Medco Center of Clarksville
517 N Hallmark Dr, Clarksville, IN 47130
(812) 282-8406
Admin Sharon Schroder.
Medical Dir E'Austin B Johnson MD.
Licensure Skilled care; Intermediate care. *Beds* SNF 61; ICF 62. *Certified* Medicaid; Medicare.
Owner Proprietary corp (Unicare).
Admissions Requirements Medical examination.
Staff RNs 4 (ft), 1 (pt); LPNs 10 (ft), 2 (pt); Nurses' aides 31 (ft), 1 (pt); Physical therapists; Occupational therapists; Speech therapists; Activities coordinators 2 (ft); Dietitians; Social workers; Qualified medical assistants 4 (ft), 1 (pt).
Facilities Dining room; Physical therapy room; Laundry room; Barber/Beauty shop; Living room; 2 TV lounges.
Activities Arts & crafts; Cards; Games; Prayer groups; Movies; Shopping trips; Dances/ Social/Cultural gatherings.

Wedgewood Manor Healthcare Center
101 Potters Ln, Clarksville, IN 47130
(812) 948-0808
Admin Beatrice Siee.
Licensure Skilled care; Intermediate care. *Beds* SNF 25; ICF 75.

Westminster Healthcare Center
2200 Greentree N, Clarksville, IN 47130
(812) 282-5911
Admin Ronald C Hoffman.
Licensure Skilled care; Intermediate care. *Beds* SNF 47; ICF 47. *Certified* Medicare.
Owner Proprietary corp.

Clinton

Clinton Nursing Home
700 S Main, Clinton, IN 47842
(317) 832-8388
Admin Joyce D Burton. *Dir of Nursing* Donna Pinegar. *Medical Dir* Dr Joel Elias.
Licensure Intermediate care. *Beds* ICF 40. *Private Pay Patients* 2%. *Certified* Medicaid.
Owner Proprietary corp (Beverly Enterprises).
Admissions Requirements Minimum age 18; Medical examination; Physician's request.
Staff RNs 1 (ft); LPNs 6 (ft); Nurses' aides 10 (ft); Activities coordinators 1 (ft).

Facilities Dining room; Activities room; Laundry room; Library.
Activities Arts & crafts; Cards; Games; Reading groups; Prayer groups; Movies; Shopping trips; Dances/Social/Cultural gatherings; Intergenerational programs; Pet therapy; Parties; Holiday celebrations.

Vermillion Convalescent Center
1705 S Main St, Box 1A, Clinton, IN 47842
(317) 832-3573
Admin David J Olson.
Medical Dir S F Swaim MD.
Licensure Skilled care; Intermediate care. *Beds* SNF 22; ICF 99. *Certified* Medicaid; Medicare.
Owner Proprietary corp.
Staff Physicians 6 (pt); RNs 5 (ft), 3 (pt); LPNs 13 (ft), 6 (pt); Nurses' aides 35 (ft), 10 (pt); Physical therapists 1 (pt); Speech therapists 1 (pt); Activities coordinators 2 (ft); Dietitians 1 (pt); Podiatrists 1 (pt); Audiologists 1 (pt); Dentists 1 (pt).
Facilities Dining room; Physical therapy room; Activities room; Crafts room; Laundry room; Barber/Beauty shop; Library.
Activities Arts & crafts; Cards; Games; Reading groups; Prayer groups; Movies; Shopping trips; Dances/Social/Cultural gatherings.

Cloverdale

Houston Health Care Inc
PO Box 247, 34 S Main St, Cloverdale, IN 46120
(317) 795-4260
Admin Janice M Tribbett. *Dir of Nursing* Joan Tucker RN. *Medical Dir* Dr Keith Ernst.
Licensure Intermediate care. *Beds* ICF 40. *Certified* Medicaid.
Owner Proprietary corp.
Admissions Requirements Medical examination; Physician's request.
Staff Physicians 1 (pt); RNs 2 (ft), 1 (pt); LPNs 2 (ft); Nurses' aides 10 (ft), 4 (pt); Activities coordinators 1 (ft); Ophthalmologists 1 (pt).
Languages German.
Facilities Dining room; Activities room; Laundry room; Barber/Beauty shop.
Activities Arts & crafts; Cards; Games; Reading groups; Prayer groups; Movies; Shopping trips; Dances/Social/Cultural gatherings; Exercise class.

Columbia City

Columbia City Community Care Center
RR 9, Columbia City, IN 46725
(219) 248-8141
Admin Phillip E Couch. *Dir of Nursing* Linda Orcutt. *Medical Dir* David Hurley MD.
Licensure Skilled care; Intermediate care. *Beds* SNF 24; ICF 58. *Certified* Medicaid; Medicare; VA approved.
Owner Proprietary corp.
Admissions Requirements Medical examination; Physician's request.
Staff RNs 1 (ft), 2 (pt); LPNs 4 (ft), 5 (pt); Nurses' aides 15 (ft), 2 (pt); Physical therapists 1 (pt); Activities coordinators 1 (ft); Dietitians 1 (pt); Ophthalmologists 1 (pt); Social Services 1 (ft); Dentists 1 (pt).
Facilities Dining room; Physical therapy room; Activities room; Laundry room; Barber/Beauty shop.
Activities Arts & crafts; Cards; Games; Reading groups; Prayer groups; Movies; Shopping trips; Dances/Social/Cultural gatherings; Bowling; Church services.

Columbia City Nursing Home
522 N Line St, Columbia City, IN 46725
(219) 248-8216
Admin Michael H Heet.

Licensure Intermediate care. *Beds* ICF 40. *Certified* Medicaid.
Owner Proprietary corp (Beverly Enterprises).

Miller's Merry Manor Inc
710 W Ellsworth St, Columbia City, IN 46725
(219) 248-8101
Admin William E Voit.
Licensure Skilled care; Intermediate care. *Beds* SNF 37; ICF 77. *Certified* Medicaid; Medicare.
Owner Proprietary corp (Millers Merry Manor).

Columbus

Bartholomew County Home
2525 Illinois, Columbus, IN 47201
(812) 372-7370
Admin Diane Burford.
Licensure Residential care. *Beds* 31.

Columbus Convalescent Center
2100 Midway St, Columbus, IN 47201
(812) 372-8447
Admin Diane L Dodge.
Licensure Skilled care; Intermediate care. *Beds* SNF 77; ICF 158. *Certified* Medicaid; Medicare.
Owner Proprietary corp (Hillhaven Corp).

Cottonwood Manor
5480 E 25th St, Columbus, IN 47203
(812) 372-6136
Admin Kimberly L Page. *Dir of Nursing* Kim Freeman. *Medical Dir* Dr Charles M Hatcher.
Licensure Intermediate care; Alzheimer's care. *Beds* ICF 40. *Private Pay Patients* 20%. *Certified* Medicaid.
Owner Proprietary corp (Beverly Enterprises).
Admissions Requirements Minimum age 18.
Staff RNs 1 (pt); LPNs 6 (ft); Nurses' aides 13 (ft), 3 (pt); Physical therapists 2 (pt); Recreational therapists 1 (ft); Occupational therapists 2 (pt); Activities coordinators 1 (ft); Dietitians 1 (pt).
Facilities Dining room; Activities room; Crafts room; Laundry room.
Activities Arts & crafts; Cards; Games; Reading groups; Prayer groups; Movies; Shopping trips; Dances/Social/Cultural gatherings; Intergenerational programs; Pet therapy.

Four Seasons Retirement & Health Care Center
1901 Taylor Rd, Columbus, IN 47203
(812) 372-8481
Admin Marcia G Life. *Dir of Nursing* Paulette Wessel. *Medical Dir* Charles Hatcher MD.
Licensure Intermediate care; Residential care. *Beds* ICF 63; Residential 120. *Certified* Private pay.
Owner Nonprofit corp (Baptist Homes).
Admissions Requirements Minimum age 62; Medical examination.
Staff Physicians 1 (pt); RNs 1 (ft), 5 (pt); LPNs 8 (ft), 3 (pt); Nurses' aides 20 (ft), 1 (pt); Dietitians 1 (ft); Ophthalmologists 1 (pt); QMAs 4 (ft), 1 (pt).
Facilities Dining room; Activities room; Chapel; Crafts room; Laundry room; Barber/ Beauty shop; Library.
Activities Arts & crafts; Cards; Games; Reading groups; Prayer groups; Movies; Shopping trips; Dances/Social/Cultural gatherings; Bible study; Bridge; Euchre.

Connersville

Connersville Nursing Home
2600 N Grand Ave, Connersville, IN 47331
(317) 825-9771
Admin Vanessa R Wilson. *Dir of Nursing* Clara Monroe RN. *Medical Dir* George Ellis MD.

Licensure Intermediate care. *Beds* ICF 40.
Certified Medicaid.
Owner Proprietary corp (Beverly Enterprises).
Admissions Requirements Medical
examination.
Staff RNs 1 (ft), 1 (pt); LPNs 2 (ft), 5 (pt);
Nurses' aides 7 (ft), 4 (pt); Activities
coordinators 1 (ft); Dietitians 1 (pt).
Facilities Dining room; Activities room;
Crafts room; Laundry room.
Activities Arts & crafts; Cards; Games;
Reading groups; Prayer groups; Movies;
Shopping trips; Dances/Social/Cultural
gatherings; Outdoor activities.

Heartland of Connersville
2500 Iowa Ave, Connersville, IN 47331
(317) 825-7514
Admin Madge L Fosdick. *Dir of Nursing*
Joanna Dearth. *Medical Dir* Jag Patel MD.
Licensure Intermediate care. *Beds* ICF 50.
Certified Medicaid.
Owner Proprietary corp (National Heritage).
Admissions Requirements Minimum age 18;
Medical examination; Physician's request.
Staff RNs 1 (ft); LPNs 3 (ft), 4 (pt); Nurses'
aides 14 (ft), 9 (pt); Activities coordinators 1
(pt); Dietitians 1 (pt).
Facilities Dining room; Activities room;
Crafts room; Laundry room; Barber/Beauty
shop.
Activities Arts & crafts; Cards; Games;
Reading groups; Prayer groups; Movies;
Shopping trips; Dances/Social/Cultural
gatherings; Family/resident dinners; Exercise
groups.

Lincoln Lodge Nursing Center
1039 E 5th St, Connersville, IN 47331
(317) 825-2121
Admin Goldie O'Neal.
Licensure Skilled care; Intermediate care. *Beds*
SNF 51; ICF 50.

Lincoln Manor Nursing Center
1029 E 5th St, Connersville, IN 47331
(317) 825-0543
Admin Chester O'Neal Jr. *Dir of Nursing*
Carolyn Sears RN. *Medical Dir* Usha Patel
MD.
Licensure Intermediate care; Retirement. *Beds*
ICF 100. *Certified* Medicaid.
Owner Proprietary corp (Cardinal
Development).
Admissions Requirements Minimum age 18;
Medical examination; Physician's request.
Staff Physicians 1 (pt); RNs 2 (ft); LPNs 9
(ft); Nurses' aides 33 (ft); Activities
coordinators 1 (ft), 1 (pt); Dietitians 1 (pt).
Facilities Dining room; Activities room;
Crafts room; Laundry room; Barber/Beauty
shop.
Activities Arts & crafts; Cards; Games;
Reading groups; Prayer groups; Movies;
Shopping trips; Dances/Social/Cultural
gatherings.

Corydon

Indian Creek Convalescent Center
240 Beechmont Dr, Corydon, IN 47112
(812) 738-8127
Admin Donald Ingle.
Medical Dir Dr Bruce Burton.
Licensure Intermediate care. *Beds* ICF 140.
Certified Medicaid.
Owner Proprietary corp.
Admissions Requirements Physician's request.
Staff RNs 3 (ft); LPNs 12 (ft); Activities
coordinators 2 (ft).
Facilities Dining room; Physical therapy
room; Activities room; Crafts room; Laundry
room; Barber/Beauty shop.
Activities Arts & crafts; Cards; Games;
Reading groups; Prayer groups; Movies;
Shopping trips; Dances/Social/Cultural
gatherings.

Covington

Covington Manor Health Care Center
1600 E Liberty, Covington, IN 47932
(317) 793-4818
Admin Joseph D Henderson. *Dir of Nursing*
Vanda Phelps RN. *Medical Dir* Max
Huffman MD.
Licensure Skilled care; Intermediate care;
Comprehensive care. *Beds* SNF 42; ICF 62;
Comprehensive care 40. *Private Pay Patients*
40%. *Certified* Medicaid; Medicare.
Owner Proprietary corp (Healthcare
Associates).
Admissions Requirements Minimum age 18;
Medical examination; Physician's request.
Staff Physicians; RNs; LPNs; Nurses' aides;
Physical therapists; Activities coordinators;
Dietitians.
Facilities Dining room; Physical therapy
room; Activities room; Crafts room; Laundry
room; Barber/Beauty shop; Library.
Activities Arts & crafts; Cards; Games; Prayer
groups; Movies; Shopping trips; Dances/
Social/Cultural gatherings; Pet therapy;
Exercise.

Crawfordsville

Ben Hur Home
1375 S Grant Ave, Crawfordsville, IN 47933
(317) 362-0905
Admin Janice M Tribbett. *Dir of Nursing*
Debbie Shirar RN. *Medical Dir* Carl B
Howland MD.
Licensure Skilled care; Intermediate care. *Beds*
SNF 43; ICF 132. *Certified* Medicaid;
Medicare.
Owner Proprietary corp.
Staff Physicians; RNs; LPNs; Nurses' aides;
Activities coordinators; Dietitians;
Ophthalmologists.
Facilities Dining room; Activities room;
Crafts room; Laundry room; Barber/Beauty
shop; Ceramic room with kiln.
Activities Arts & crafts; Cards; Games;
Reading groups; Prayer groups; Movies;
Shopping trips; Dances/Social/Cultural
gatherings; Ceramics.

Carmen Nursing Home
817 N Whitlock Ave, Crawfordsville, IN
47933
(317) 362-8590
Admin Larry E Gray. *Dir of Nursing* Linda
Orsulak RN. *Medical Dir* S R Marri MD.
Licensure Intermediate care; Alzheimer's care.
Beds ICF 40. *Private Pay Patients* 35%.
Certified Medicaid.
Owner Proprietary corp (Beverly Enterprises).
Admissions Requirements Medical
examination.
Staff Physicians 1 (pt); RNs 1 (ft); LPNs 5
(ft); Nurses' aides 14 (ft); Physical therapists
1 (pt); Activities coordinators 1 (ft);
Dietitians 1 (pt).
Facilities Dining room; Activities room;
Laundry room.
Activities Arts & crafts; Cards; Games;
Reading groups; Prayer groups; Movies;
Dances/Social/Cultural gatherings;
Intergenerational programs; Pet therapy.

Houston Health Care Inc—Crawfordsville
1371 S Grant Ave, Crawfordsville, IN 47933
(317) 362-0965
Admin Mary Ruth Houston.
Licensure Intermediate care. *Beds* ICF 61.
Certified Medicaid.
Owner Proprietary corp.

Lane House
1000 Lane Ave, Crawfordsville, IN 47933
(317) 362-4815
Admin Mary Jane Surface.
Licensure Intermediate care. *Beds* ICF 60.
Certified Medicaid.

Owner Proprietary corp (National Heritage).
Admissions Requirements Medical
examination; Physician's request.
Staff RNs 2 (ft), 1 (pt); LPNs 2 (ft), 1 (pt);
Nurses' aides 18 (ft), 5 (pt); Activities
coordinators 1 (ft), 1 (pt); Dietitians 1 (pt).
Facilities Dining room; Chapel; Laundry
room; Barber/Beauty shop.
Activities Arts & crafts; Cards; Games; Prayer
groups; Movies; Shopping trips; Dances/
Social/Cultural gatherings.

Williamsburg Healthcare Inc
1609 Lafayette Rd, Crawfordsville, IN 47933
(317) 364-0363
Admin Kae Gallear. *Dir of Nursing* Rebecca
Pefley RN. *Medical Dir* Dr Carl B Howland;
Dr William H Leech.
Licensure Skilled care; Intermediate care. *Beds*
SNF 82; ICF 32. *Certified* Medicaid;
Medicare.
Owner Proprietary corp (Houston
Companies).
Admissions Requirements Medical
examination; Physician's request.
Facilities Dining room; Physical therapy
room; Activities room; Crafts room; Barber/
Beauty shop; Library; Ventilator unit.
Activities Arts & crafts; Cards; Games;
Reading groups; Prayer groups; Movies; Pet
therapy; Ceramics.

Crown Point

Colonial Nursing Home
119 N Indiana Ave, Crown Point, IN 46307
(219) 663-2532, 663-2533 FAX
Admin Jonathan L Doty MA. *Dir of Nursing*
Joyce Bales. *Medical Dir* Joseph Kacmar
MD.
Licensure Intermediate care. *Beds* ICF 40.
Certified Medicaid.
Owner Proprietary corp (J B Hook Inc).
Staff Physicians 1 (pt); RNs 1 (ft); LPNs 2
(ft), 1 (pt); Nurses' aides 11 (ft); Activities
coordinators 1 (pt); Dietitians 1 (pt);
Podiatrists 1 (pt).
Activities Cards; Games; Prayer groups;
Movies; Shopping trips; Exercise; Sing-
alongs.

Lake County Convalescent Home
2900 W 93rd Ave, Crown Point, IN 46307
(219) 769-3537, 769-1708 FAX
Admin Lawrence R Parducci HFA. *Dir of
Nursing* Pearl Novak RN. *Medical Dir* J C
Espino MD.
Licensure Skilled care; Intermediate care;
Residential care; Alzheimer's care. *Beds*
SNF 45; ICF 405; Residential care 34.
Private Pay Patients 40%. *Certified*
Medicaid; Medicare.
Owner Publicly owned.
Admissions Requirements Minimum age 18;
Medical examination.
Staff Physicians 1 (ft), 3 (pt); RNs 16 (ft), 7
(pt); LPNs 15 (ft), 1 (pt); Nurses' aides 161
(ft), 15 (pt); Recreational therapists 6 (ft), 1
(pt); Activities coordinators 1 (ft); Dietitians
1 (pt); Pharmacists 1 (ft), 1 (pt); Pharmacy
technicians 2 (ft); Lab technicians 1 (ft);
Central supply technicians 1 (ft), 1 (pt).
Languages Polish, German, Serbo-Croatian,
Lithuanian, Italian, Spanish.
Facilities Dining room; Physical therapy
room; Activities room; Chapel; Crafts room;
Barber/Beauty shop; Library.
Activities Arts & crafts; Cards; Games;
Reading groups; Prayer groups; Movies;
Shopping trips; Dances/Social/Cultural
gatherings; Intergenerational programs; Pet
therapy; Adult education; Bowling; Resident
council; Alzheimer activities.

Lutheran Home of Northwest Indiana Inc
1200 E Luther Dr, Crown Point, IN 46307
(219) 663-3860, 769-1145 Merrillville, (312)
895-8866 Chicago, (219) 662-3070 FAX

Admin Wayne A Hahn. *Dir of Nursing*
Mildred Lundstrom RN. *Medical Dir* Dr
Arthur Beckman, Crown Point Clinic.
Licensure Intermediate care; Retirement. *Beds*
ICF 191. *Private Pay Patients* 65%. *Certified*
Medicaid.
Owner Nonprofit corp.
Admissions Requirements Medical
examination.
Staff Physicians; RNs 4 (ft), 10 (pt); LPNs 2
(ft), 2 (pt); Nurses' aides 13 (ft), 50 (pt);
Physical therapists 1 (pt); Activities
coordinators 1 (ft); Dietitians 1 (pt);
Ophthalmologists 1 (pt); Podiatrists 1 (pt);
Dentists 1 (pt); Qualified medication aides
19 (ft), 7 (pt).
Affiliation Lutheran.
Facilities Dining room; Physical therapy
room; Activities room; Chapel; Crafts room;
Laundry room; Barber/Beauty shop; Library;
Enclosed courtyard.
Activities Arts & crafts; Cards; Games;
Reading groups; Prayer groups; Movies;
Shopping trips; Dances/Social/Cultural
gatherings; Pet therapy.

St Anthony Home
Main & Franciscan Rd, Crown Point, IN
46307
(219) 738-2100, 662-6161 FAX
Admin Steve Bardpczi. *Dir of Nursing* Patricia
Johnson. *Medical Dir* Mary D Carroll MD.
Licensure Skilled care; Intermediate care;
Residential care; Alzheimer's care. *Beds*
SNF 37; ICF 192. *Certified* Medicaid;
Medicare.
Owner Nonprofit organization/foundation.
Staff RNs 11 (ft), 5 (pt); LPNs 12 (ft), 6 (pt);
Nurses' aides 55 (ft), 18 (pt); Reality
therapists 1 (ft); Activities coordinators 2
(ft); Dietitians 1 (ft); QMAs 18 (ft), 5 (pt).
Affiliation Roman Catholic.
Facilities Dining room; Activities room;
Chapel; Crafts room; Barber/Beauty shop.
Activities Arts & crafts; Cards; Games;
Reading groups; Prayer groups; Movies;
Shopping trips; Dances/Social/Cultural
gatherings; Intergenerational programs; Pet
therapy.

Culver

Miller's Merry Manor Inc
730 School St, Culver, IN 46511
(219) 842-3337
Admin Lynn Reynolds.
Licensure Intermediate care. *Beds* ICF 66.
Certified Medicaid.
Owner Proprietary corp.

Cynthiana

Country Haven Healthcare
PO Box 367, 11121 North St, Cynthiana, IN
47612
(812) 845-2731
Admin Linda Crowe. *Dir of Nursing* Charlotte
Hall LPN. *Medical Dir* Randall Sholtz MD.
Licensure Intermediate care. *Beds* ICF 75.
Private Pay Patients 0%. *Certified* Medicaid.
Owner Privately owned.
Admissions Requirements Medical
examination; Physician's request.
Staff RNs; LPNs; Nurses' aides; Activities
coordinators; Dietitians; Podiatrists.
Facilities Dining room; Activities room;
Laundry room; Barber/Beauty shop.
Activities Arts & crafts; Cards; Games;
Reading groups; Prayer groups; Movies;
Shopping trips; Dances/Social/Cultural
gatherings; Intergenerational programs.

Dale

Community Care Center of Dale
PO Box 297, Hwy 68 W, Dale, IN 47523
(812) 937-4442
Admin Melvin D Hamrick.
Medical Dir Becky Price.
Licensure Intermediate care. *Beds* ICF 60.
Certified Medicaid.
Owner Proprietary corp (Community Care
Centers).
Staff RNs 2 (ft); LPNs 5 (ft), 1 (pt); Nurses'
aides 14 (ft), 6 (pt); Activities coordinators 1
(pt); Dietitians 1 (pt).
Languages German.
Facilities Dining room; Activities room;
Crafts room; Laundry room; Barber/Beauty
shop.
Activities Cards; Games; Reading groups;
Movies; Shopping trips; Dances/Social/
Cultural gatherings.

Professional Care Nursing Center
RR 2, Box 315, 2000 North Rd, Dale, IN
47523
(812) 937-4489
Admin Jo Junod.
Medical Dir Mario Leon MD.
Licensure Intermediate care. *Beds* ICF 60.
Certified Medicaid.
Owner Proprietary corp (Unicare).
Admissions Requirements Minimum age 18;
Medical examination.
Staff Physicians 4 (pt); RNs 1 (ft), 2 (pt);
Nurses' aides 15 (ft), 5 (pt); Physical
therapists 1 (pt); Activities coordinators 1
(ft); Dietitians 1 (pt); Ophthalmologists 1
(pt); Podiatrists 1 (pt); Dentists 1 (pt).
Facilities Dining room; Activities room;
Chapel; Crafts room; Laundry room; Barber/
Beauty shop.
Activities Cards; Games; Reading groups;
Prayer groups; Dances/Social/Cultural
gatherings.

Danville

Cardinal Healthcare of Danville
Rd 3 S, 400 E, Danville, IN 46122
(317) 745-5184
Admin Suzanne Mervis.
Licensure Skilled care; Intermediate care. *Beds*
SNF 29; ICF 70. *Certified* Medicaid.

Hendricks County Home
865 E Main, Danville, IN 46122
(317) 745-9317
Licensure Residential care. *Beds* 31.
Owner Publicly owned.
Admissions Requirements Minimum age 18;
Medical examination; Physician's request.
Staff Nurses' aides 3 (ft), 1 (pt).
Facilities Dining room; Laundry room;
Barber/Beauty shop.
Activities Arts & crafts; Cards; Games.

Medco Center of Danville
255 Meadow Dr, Danville, IN 46122
(317) 745-5451
Admin John Singleton.
Licensure Skilled care; Intermediate care. *Beds*
SNF 58; ICF 45. *Certified* Medicaid;
Medicare.
Owner Proprietary corp (Unicare).

Primrose Manor
337 W Lincoln St, Danville, IN 46122
(317) 745-5861
Admin Kevin Imlay. *Dir of Nursing* Donna
Boyer LPN. *Medical Dir* Larry Lovall MD.
Licensure Intermediate care. *Beds* ICF 40.
Certified Medicaid.
Owner Proprietary corp (Beverly Enterprises).
Admissions Requirements Medical
examination; Physician's request.

Staff Physicians 1 (pt); RNs 1 (ft); LPNs 3
(ft), 2 (pt); Nurses' aides 7 (ft), 1 (pt);
Occupational therapists 1 (pt); Activities
coordinators 1 (ft); Dietitians 1 (pt).
Facilities Dining room; Activities room;
Laundry room.
Activities Arts & crafts; Cards; Games;
Reading groups; Prayer groups; Movies;
Shopping trips; Dances/Social/Cultural
gatherings.

Decatur

Decatur Community Care Center
PO Box 421, Decatur, IN 46733
(219) 724-2191
Admin Ron Farmer.
Medical Dir Dr Zwick.
Licensure Skilled care; Intermediate care. *Beds*
SNF 34; ICF 94. *Certified* Medicaid.
Owner Proprietary corp (Community Care
Centers).
Admissions Requirements Medical
examination; Physician's request.
Staff RNs 1 (ft), 2 (pt); LPNs 5 (ft), 4 (pt);
Nurses' aides 13 (ft), 24 (pt); Activities
coordinators 1 (ft), 1 (pt).
Facilities Dining room; Physical therapy
room; Activities room; Laundry room;
Barber/Beauty shop.
Activities Arts & crafts; Cards; Games;
Reading groups; Movies.

Delphi

Delphi Nursing Home
RR 4 Box 143A, 1433 S Washington St,
Delphi, IN 46923
(317) 564-3123
Admin Linda Neskov.
Medical Dir Dr Seese.
Licensure Intermediate care. *Beds* ICF 40.
Certified Medicaid.
Owner Proprietary corp (Beverly Enterprises).
Admissions Requirements Medical
examination; Physician's request.
Staff RNs 2 (ft); LPNs 1 (ft), 1 (pt); Nurses'
aides 8 (ft), 8 (pt); Activities coordinators 1
(pt); Dietitians 1 (pt).

St Elizabeth Healthcare Center
701 Armory Rd, Delphi, IN 46923
(317) 564-6380
Admin Janet E LaPointe. *Dir of Nursing*
Peggy Bryant RN. *Medical Dir* T Neal Petry
MD; Eldon Baker MD; Brian Doggett MD.
Licensure Skilled care; Intermediate care;
Alzheimer's care. *Beds* SNF 20; ICF 40.
Certified Medicaid; Medicare.
Owner Nonprofit corp.
Admissions Requirements Minimum age 18;
Medical examination; Physician's request.
Staff RNs 3 (ft); LPNs 8 (ft); Nurses' aides 20
(ft); Physical therapists 3 (pt); Recreational
therapists 1 (pt); Occupational therapists 1
(pt); Activities coordinators 2 (ft).
Affiliation Roman Catholic.
Facilities Dining room; Physical therapy
room; Activities room; Chapel; Crafts room;
Laundry room; Barber/Beauty shop; Large
enclosed patio.
Activities Arts & crafts; Cards; Games;
Reading groups; Prayer groups; Movies;
Shopping trips; Dances/Social/Cultural
gatherings; Pet therapy; Plant therapy.

Dillsboro

Dillsboro Manor
Box 37 Lenover St, Dillsboro, IN 47018
(812) 432-5226
Admin John Race.
Medical Dir Ivan T Lindgren; Judy Gatzke.
Licensure Skilled care; Intermediate care. *Beds*
SNF 36; ICF 77. *Certified* Medicaid;
Medicare.

Owner Proprietary corp.
Admissions Requirements Minimum age 18;
Medical examination; Physician's request.
Staff Physicians 1 (pt); RNs 4 (ft); LPNs 4
(ft); Nurses' aides 60 (ft); Physical therapists
1 (pt); Activities coordinators 2 (ft);
Dietitians 1 (pt); Ophthalmologists 1 (pt).
Facilities Dining room; Physical therapy
room; Activities room; Chapel; Crafts room;
Laundry room; Barber/Beauty shop; Library.
Activities Arts & crafts; Cards; Games;
Reading groups; Prayer groups; Movies;
Shopping trips; Dances/Social/Cultural
gatherings.

Ross Manor
Lenover St, Dillsboro, IN 47018
(812) 432-3114
Admin Beth E Ingram.
Licensure Comprehensive care. *Beds*
Comprehensive care 49.

Dunkirk

Miller's Merry Manor Inc
PO Box 265, Dunkirk, IN 47336
(317) 768-7537
Admin Laura T Mihankhah. *Dir of Nursing*
Carol Suro RN. *Medical Dir* Dr Frank
Bonser; Dr James C Hutchinson.
Licensure Intermediate care. *Beds* ICF 62.
Certified Medicaid.
Owner Proprietary corp (Millers Merry
Manor).
Admissions Requirements Minimum age 21;
Medical examination; Physician's request.
Staff RNs 2 (ft), 1 (pt); LPNs 4 (ft), 3 (pt);
Nurses' aides 10 (ft), 9 (pt); Activities
coordinators 1 (ft).
Facilities Dining room; Activities room;
Crafts room; Laundry room; Barber/Beauty
shop.
Activities Arts & crafts; Cards; Games;
Reading groups; Prayer groups; Movies;
Shopping trips; Dances/Social/Cultural
gatherings.

Dyer

Meridian Nursing Center—Dyer
601 Sheffield Ave, Dyer, IN 46311
(219) 322-2273
Admin John W Stewart Jr.
Licensure Skilled care; Intermediate care;
Comprehensive care. *Beds* SNF 70; ICF 58;
Comprehensive care 12.
Owner Proprietary corp (Meridian
Healthcare).

Regency Place of Dyer
2300 Great Lakes Dr, Dyer, IN 46311
(219) 322-3555
Admin Jeffrey K Toutant. *Dir of Nursing*
Katheleen Garton RN. *Medical Dir* Dr
Melvin Hirsch.
Licensure Skilled care; Intermediate care. *Beds*
SNF 144; ICF 6.
Owner Proprietary corp (Lucas Corp).
Staff RNs; LPNs; Nurses' aides.

East Chicago

Lake County Rehabilitation Center Inc
5025 McCook Ave, East Chicago, IN 46312
(219) 397-0380
Admin Estella Watkins. *Dir of Nursing* Mary
Gilbert. *Medical Dir* Napoleon Santos MD.
Licensure Skilled care; Intermediate care. *Beds*
SNF 60; ICF 62. *Certified* Medicaid;
Medicare.
Owner Nonprofit organization/foundation.
Admissions Requirements Minimum age 18;
Medical examination; Physician's request.
Staff Physicians 3 (pt); RNs 2 (ft), 3 (pt);
LPNs 5 (ft), 6 (pt); Nurses' aides 29 (ft), 3
(pt); Activities coordinators 2 (ft); Dietitians
1 (pt).

Languages Spanish.
Facilities Dining room; Activities room;
Crafts room; Laundry room; Barber/Beauty
shop.
Activities Arts & crafts; Cards; Games;
Reading groups; Prayer groups; Movies;
Shopping trips; Dances/Social/Cultural
gatherings; Intergenerational programs; Pet
therapy.

Edinburg

Faith Nursing Home
30 N Eisenhower Dr, Edinburg, IN 46124
(812) 526-2626
Admin J D Carota. *Dir of Nursing* Crystal Y
DeVillez. *Medical Dir* Dr William Province.
Licensure Intermediate care; Alzheimer's care.
Beds ICF 34. *Certified* Medicaid.
Owner Proprietary corp (The Nepenthe
Group).
Admissions Requirements Medical
examination; Physician's request.
Staff LPNs; Nurses' aides; Activities
coordinators; Dietitians.
Facilities Dining room; Activities room;
Crafts room; Laundry room; Library.
Activities Arts & crafts; Cards; Games;
Reading groups; Prayer groups; Movies;
Shopping trips; Dances/Social/Cultural
gatherings; Intergenerational programs; Pet
therapy.

Elkhart

Americana Healthcare Center
343 S Nappanee St, Elkhart, IN 46514
(219) 295-0096
Admin Margot Parr.
Licensure Skilled care; Intermediate care. *Beds*
SNF 22; ICF 77. *Certified* Medicaid;
Medicare.
Owner Proprietary corp (Manor Care).
Facilities Dining room; Physical therapy
room; Activities room; Chapel; Crafts room;
Laundry room; Barber/Beauty shop; Library.
Activities Arts & crafts; Cards; Games;
Reading groups; Prayer groups; Movies;
Shopping trips; Dances/Social/Cultural
gatherings.

Elkhart Healthcare Center
PO Box 1107, 1400 W Franklin St, Elkhart,
IN 46516
(219) 293-0511
Admin Lawrence Raymond Chasson. *Dir of
Nursing* Gertrude Cutchin RN. *Medical Dir*
Verlin Houck MD.
Licensure Skilled care; Intermediate care. *Beds*
SNF 31; ICF 134. *Certified* Medicaid.
Owner Proprietary corp (ARA).
Admissions Requirements Minimum age 19;
Medical examination.
Staff RNs 2 (ft), 1 (pt); LPNs 5 (ft); Nurses'
aides 15 (ft), 10 (pt); Activities coordinators;
Dietitians; QMRPs 1 (ft).
Facilities Dining room; Physical therapy
room; Activities room; Crafts room; Barber/
Beauty shop; Library; Conference room.
Activities Arts & crafts; Cards; Games;
Reading groups; Prayer groups; Movies;
Shopping trips; Dances/Social/Cultural
gatherings; Bowling trips; Field trips.

Fountainview Place
1001 W Hively Ave, Elkhart, IN 46517
(219) 294-7641
Admin Barbara Rhodes.
Medical Dir R G Harswell.
Licensure Skilled care; Intermediate care;
Comprehensive care. *Beds* SNF 116; ICF
182; Comprehensive care 29. *Certified*
Medicaid; Medicare.
Owner Proprietary corp (Beverly Enterprises).
Admissions Requirements Medical
examination; Physician's request.

Staff RNs 17 (ft), 8 (pt); LPNs 16 (ft), 10 (pt);
Nurses' aides 72 (ft), 11 (pt); Physical
therapists 1 (ft), 1 (pt); Occupational
therapists 1 (ft), 1 (pt); Speech therapists 1
(pt); Activities coordinators 2 (ft), 2 (pt);
Dietitians 1 (pt); Dentists 1 (pt).
Facilities Dining room; Physical therapy
room; Activities room; Chapel; Crafts room;
Laundry room; Barber/Beauty shop; Library.
Activities Arts & crafts; Cards; Games;
Reading groups; Prayer groups; Movies;
Shopping trips; Dances/Social/Cultural
gatherings.

Hubbard Hill Estates Inc
28070 County Rd 24, Elkhart, IN 46517
(219) 295-6260
Admin Floran Mast. *Dir of Nursing* Charlene
Haines RN.
Licensure Residential care; Comprehensive
care. *Beds* Residential care 94;
Comprehensive care 22.
Admissions Requirements Minimum age 62;
Medical examination.
Staff RNs 1 (ft); LPNs 2 (ft), 1 (pt); Nurses'
aides 3 (ft), 6 (pt); Activities coordinators 1
(ft); Dietitians 1 (pt).
Affiliation Missionary Church.
Facilities Dining room; Activities room;
Chapel; Crafts room; Laundry room; Barber/
Beauty shop; Library.
Activities Arts & crafts; Cards; Games; Prayer
groups; Movies; Shopping trips; Dances/
Social/Cultural gatherings.

Medco Center of Elkhart
2600 Morehouse Ave, Elkhart, IN 46514
(219) 295-8800
Admin Judith A DeBartolo.
Medical Dir Dr R G Horswell.
Licensure Intermediate care; Comprehensive
care. *Beds* ICF 68; Comprehensive care 6.
Certified Medicaid.
Owner Proprietary corp (Unicare).

Meridian Nursing Center—East Lake
1900 Jeanwood Dr, Elkhart, IN 46514
(219) 264-1133
Admin Eunice Taylor. *Dir of Nursing* Susan
Callender. *Medical Dir* Dr T M Kolakovich.
Licensure Skilled care; Intermediate care. *Beds*
SNF 24; ICF 136. *Private Pay Patients* 40%.
Certified Medicaid; Medicare.
Owner Proprietary corp (Meridian
Healthcare).
Admissions Requirements Minimum age 18;
Medical examination; Physician's request.
Facilities Dining room; Physical therapy
room; Activities room; Laundry room;
Barber/Beauty shop.
Activities Arts & crafts; Cards; Games;
Reading groups; Prayer groups; Movies;
Shopping trips; Dances/Social/Cultural
gatherings; Intergenerational programs; Pet
therapy.

Oak Manor Nursing Home
3226 E Jackson Blvd, Elkhart, IN 46516
(901) 352-5317
Admin Larry Hardy.
Licensure Intermediate care. *Beds* ICF 50.
Certified Medicaid.

Valley View Health Care Center
333 W Mishawaka Rd, Elkhart, IN 46517
(219) 293-1550
Admin Eunice A Little. *Dir of Nursing* Betty
Howard RN. *Medical Dir* T Davis MD.
Licensure Intermediate care; Alzheimer's care.
Beds ICF 100. *Certified* Medicaid.
Owner Proprietary corp.
Admissions Requirements Minimum age 65;
Medical examination.
Staff RNs 3 (ft), 1 (pt); LPNs 7 (ft), 1 (pt);
Nurses' aides 30 (ft), 10 (pt); Activities
coordinators 1 (ft), 1 (pt); Dietitians 1 (pt).

Facilities Dining room; Physical therapy room; Activities room; Crafts room; Laundry room; Barber/Beauty shop; Resident lounge.
Activities Arts & crafts; Cards; Games; Reading groups; Prayer groups; Movies; Shopping trips; Dances/Social/Cultural gatherings.

Elwood

Dickey Nursing Home Inc
PO Box 28, 1007 N 9th St, Elwood, IN 46036
(317) 552-7308
Admin Terrill S Dickey. Dir of Nursing Brenda Willhoite RN. Medical Dir Thomas P Mengelt MD.
Licensure Skilled care; Intermediate care. Beds SNF 30; ICF 70. Certified Medicaid; Medicare.
Owner Proprietary corp.
Admissions Requirements Minimum age 18; Medical examination; Physician's request.
Staff Physicians 1 (pt); RNs 4 (ft), 1 (pt); LPNs 7 (ft), 1 (pt); Nurses' aides 33 (ft), 6 (pt); Physical therapists; Speech therapists 1 (pt); Activities coordinators 2 (ft); Dietitians 1 (pt); Podiatrists 1 (pt); Audiologists 1 (pt).
Facilities Dining room; Physical therapy room; Activities room; Crafts room; Laundry room; Barber/Beauty shop; Library.
Activities Arts & crafts; Cards; Games; Reading groups; Prayer groups; Movies; Dances/Social/Cultural gatherings; Intergenerational programs; Pet therapy; Resident council.

Parkview Convalescent Centre
N 19th St, Elwood, IN 46036
(317) 552-9884
Admin Bart Bingham.
Licensure Intermediate care. Beds ICF 92. Certified Medicaid.
Owner Privately owned.

Evansville

Arcadia Care Manor
1100 N Read St, Evansville, IN 47710
(812) 424-8295
Admin Judith Bates. Dir of Nursing Regina Boorman. Medical Dir Dr Rick Crawford.
Licensure Intermediate care. Beds ICF 36. Certified Medicaid.
Owner Proprietary corp.
Admissions Requirements Medical examination; Physician's request.
Staff RNs; LPNs; Nurses' aides; Activities coordinators; Dietitians.
Facilities Dining room.
Activities Arts & crafts; Cards; Games; Movies; Shopping trips; Pet therapy.

Bethel Manor
6015 Kratzville Rd, Evansville, IN 47710
(812) 425-8182
Admin David R Kast.
Licensure Intermediate care; Residential care. Beds ICF 66; Residential care 8. Certified Medicaid.
Owner Proprietary corp.
Admissions Requirements Medical examination.
Staff RNs 5 (ft); LPNs 4 (ft); Nurses' aides 21 (ft); Physical therapists 1 (pt); Reality therapists 1 (pt); Recreational therapists 1 (ft); Occupational therapists 1 (pt); Speech therapists 1 (pt); Activities coordinators 1 (ft); Dietitians 1 (ft), 1 (pt).
Affiliation Seventh-Day Adventist.
Facilities Dining room; Physical therapy room; Activities room; Chapel; Laundry room; Barber/Beauty shop.
Activities Arts & crafts; Games; Reading groups; Prayer groups; Movies; Shopping trips; Dances/Social/Cultural gatherings.

Braun's Nursing Home Inc
909 1st Ave, Evansville, IN 47710
(812) 423-6214
Admin Ruth H Braun LPN.
Licensure Intermediate care. Beds ICF 85. Certified Medicaid.
Owner Proprietary corp.

Brentwood Convalescent Center
30 E Chandler Ave, Evansville, IN 47713
(812) 423-6019
Admin Norman L Hunter.
Licensure Skilled care; Intermediate care. Beds SNF 62; ICF 60.

Christopher East Living Center
4301 Washington Ave, Evansville, IN 47715
(812) 477-8971
Admin Dorothy Wolf.
Licensure Skilled care; Intermediate care. Beds SNF 53; ICF 146. Certified Medicaid; Medicare.
Owner Proprietary corp (ARA).

Columbia Nursing Plaza Inc
621 W Columbia St, Evansville, IN 47710
(812) 428-5678, 428-5690 FAX
Admin Tom O'Niones, AIT; Tom Slaubaugh, District Dir. Dir of Nursing Barbara Tumey RN. Medical Dir Richard Wagner MD.
Licensure Skilled care; Intermediate care; Alzheimer's care. Beds SNF 37; ICF 127; Alzheimer's Unit 23. Private Pay Patients 30%. Certified Medicaid; Medicare.
Owner Proprietary corp (Hillhaven Corp).
Admissions Requirements Medical examination; Physician's request.
Staff RNs 3 (ft), 1 (pt); LPNs 15 (ft), 2 (pt); Physical therapists 2 (pt); Occupational therapists 1 (pt); Activities coordinators 1 (ft), 2 (pt); Dietitians 1 (pt); QMAs 43 (ft), 4 (pt).
Affiliation Civitan.
Facilities Dining room; Physical therapy room; Activities room; Chapel; Crafts room; Laundry room; Barber/Beauty shop.
Activities Arts & crafts; Cards; Games; Reading groups; Prayer groups; Movies; Shopping trips; Dances/Social/Cultural gatherings; Intergenerational programs; Pet therapy.

Evansville Protestant Home Inc
3701 Washington Ave, Evansville, IN 47715
(812) 476-3360
Admin Dorothy L Zehner. Dir of Nursing Donna Evans RN. Medical Dir Randall Stoltz MD.
Licensure Residential care; Comprehensive care. Beds Residential care 144; Comprehensive care 102. Private Pay Patients 100%.
Owner Nonprofit corp.
Admissions Requirements Minimum age 65; Medical examination.
Staff Physicians 1 (pt); RNs 10 (ft), 2 (pt); LPNs 8 (ft), 6 (pt); Nurses' aides 30 (ft), 8 (pt); Physical therapists 1 (pt); Activities coordinators 2 (ft), 1 (pt); Dietitians 1 (pt).
Affiliation Church of Christ.
Facilities Dining room; Physical therapy room; Activities room; Crafts room; Laundry room; Barber/Beauty shop; Library.
Activities Arts & crafts; Cards; Games; Reading groups; Prayer groups; Movies; Shopping trips; Intergenerational programs; Pet therapy.

Gertha's Nursing Center Inc
617 Oakley St, Evansville, IN 47710
(812) 423-4491
Admin Steve T Gossman. Dir of Nursing Julie Schrieber. Medical Dir Dr Richard Wagner.
Licensure Skilled care; Intermediate care. Beds SNF 45; ICF 110. Certified Medicaid; Medicare.
Owner Proprietary corp.

Admissions Requirements Minimum age 16; Medical examination; Physician's request.
Staff RNs 3 (ft), 1 (pt); LPNs 10 (ft), 4 (pt); Nurses' aides 54 (ft), 8 (pt); Recreational therapists 3 (ft); Activities coordinators 1 (ft); Dietitians 1 (ft).
Facilities Dining room; Physical therapy room; Activities room; Crafts room; Laundry room; Barber/Beauty shop; Library.
Activities Arts & crafts; Cards; Games; Reading groups; Prayer groups; Movies; Dances/Social/Cultural gatherings.

Good Samaritan Home Inc
PO Box 2788, 601 N Boeke, Evansville, IN 47728-0788
(812) 476-4912
Admin David H Roberts III. Dir of Nursing Charlotte Weigman.
Licensure Intermediate care; Residential care. Beds ICF 138; Residential care 28. Certified Medicaid.
Owner Nonprofit corp.
Admissions Requirements Medical examination.
Affiliation United Church of Christ.
Facilities Dining room; Physical therapy room; Activities room; Crafts room; Laundry room; Barber/Beauty shop.
Activities Arts & crafts; Cards; Games; Reading groups; Prayer groups; Movies; Shopping trips; Dances/Social/Cultural gatherings.

Holiday Home of Evansville
1201 W Buena Vista Rd, Evansville, IN 47710
(812) 429-0700
Admin Donnie L Hester.
Medical Dir Dr William Gentry.
Licensure Skilled care; Intermediate care; Residential care. Beds SNF 31; ICF 142; Residential 36. Certified Medicaid; Medicare.
Owner Proprietary corp.
Admissions Requirements Minimum age 65; Medical examination; Physician's request.
Staff RNs 10 (ft); LPNs 18 (ft); Nurses' aides 60 (ft); Physical therapists 4 (ft); Activities coordinators 1 (ft), 1 (pt); Dietitians 1 (ft); Audiologists 1 (pt); Speech pathologists 1 (ft).
Facilities Dining room; Physical therapy room; Activities room; Chapel; Crafts room; Laundry room; Barber/Beauty shop; Library.
Activities Arts & crafts; Cards; Games; Reading groups; Prayer groups; Movies; Shopping trips; Dances/Social/Cultural gatherings.

McCurdy Residential Center Inc
101 SE 1st St, Evansville, IN 47708
(812) 425-1041
Admin James Ward.
Medical Dir Lawrene Judy MD.
Licensure Intermediate care; Residential care. Beds ICF 213; Residential care 262. Certified Medicaid.
Owner Proprietary corp.
Admissions Requirements Minimum age 18; Medical examination.
Staff Physicians 1 (pt); RNs 6 (ft), 1 (pt); LPNs 26 (ft), 10 (pt); Nurses' aides 24 (ft), 12 (pt); Activities coordinators 1 (ft); Dietitians 1 (ft); Ophthalmologists 1 (pt); Podiatrists 1 (pt); Dentists 1 (pt).
Facilities Dining room; Activities room; Chapel; Crafts room; Laundry room; Barber/Beauty shop; Library; Men's lounge; Theatre.
Activities Arts & crafts; Cards; Games; Reading groups; Prayer groups; Movies; Shopping trips; Dances/Social/Cultural gatherings; Ceramics; Chapel services; Current events.

Medco Center of Evansville—North Inc
650 Fairway Dr, Evansville, IN 47710
(812) 425-5243
Admin James Allan Scheller.

Medical Dir Dr Robert Davidson.
Licensure Skilled care; Intermediate care. *Beds* SNF 35; ICF 116. *Certified* Medicaid; Medicare; VA.
Owner Proprietary corp (Unicare).
Admissions Requirements Medical examination.
Staff Physicians; RNs; LPNs; Nurses' aides; Physical therapists; Reality therapists; Recreational therapists; Occupational therapists; Speech therapists; Activities coordinators; Dietitians; Ophthalmologists; Podiatrists; Dentists.
Facilities Dining room; Physical therapy room; Activities room; Crafts room; Laundry room; Barber/Beauty shop; Library; Living room; Quiet rooms.
Activities Arts & crafts; Cards; Games; Reading groups; Prayer groups; Movies; Shopping trips; Dances/Social/Cultural gatherings; Baseball; Basketball; Philharmonic tickets.

Parkview Convalescent Center
2819 N Saint Joseph Ave, Evansville, IN 47712
(812) 424-2941, 428-3429 FAX
Admin Linda C Dickenson. *Dir of Nursing* Juanita J Kent. *Medical Dir* Dr Wallace Adye.
Licensure Skilled care; Intermediate care. *Beds* SNF 17; ICF 84. *Private Pay Patients* 22%. *Certified* Medicaid; Medicare.
Owner Proprietary corp (National Heritage).
Admissions Requirements Minimum age 17; Medical examination; Physician's request.
Staff RNs 4 (ft), 1 (pt) LPNs 8 (ft); Nurses' aides 20 (ft), 1 (pt); Physical therapists; Activities coordinators 1 (ft); Dietitians; QMAs 1 (ft), 1 (pt).
Facilities Dining room; Physical therapy room; Activities room; Barber/Beauty shop; Quiet room; Enclosed courtyard.
Activities Arts & crafts; Cards; Games; Reading groups; Prayer groups; Movies; Shopping trips; Dances/Social/Cultural gatherings; Intergenerational programs; Pet therapy; Gardening.

Pine Haven Nursing Home
3400 Stocker Dr, Evansville, IN 47712
(812) 424-8100
Admin Ruth C Smith RN. *Dir of Nursing* Judy Carr LPN. *Medical Dir* William Sutton MD.
Licensure Intermediate care. *Beds* ICF 96. *Certified* Medicaid.
Owner Proprietary corp.
Admissions Requirements Minimum age 50; Medical examination; Physician's request.
Staff RNs; LPNs; Nurses' aides; Activities coordinators; Dietitians; Ophthalmologists.
Facilities Dining room; Activities room; Chapel; Crafts room; Laundry room; Barber/Beauty shop.
Activities Arts & crafts; Cards; Games; Reading groups; Prayer groups; Movies; Shopping trips; Dances/Social/Cultural gatherings.

Regina Continuing Care Center
3900 Washington Ave, Evansville, IN 47715
(812) 479-4226
Admin Ann M Morrow.
Medical Dir Julian D Present MD.
Licensure Skilled care; Intermediate care. *Beds* SNF 100; ICF 54. *Certified* Medicaid; Medicare.
Admissions Requirements Minimum age 18; Medical examination.
Staff Physicians 1 (pt); RNs 4 (ft), 5 (pt); LPNs 8 (ft), 5 (pt); Nurses' aides 37 (ft), 13 (pt); Physical therapists 1 (pt); Occupational therapists 1 (pt); Speech therapists 1 (pt); Activities coordinators 1 (pt); Dietitians 1 (pt); Podiatrists 1 (pt); Dentists 1 (pt).
Affiliation Roman Catholic.

Facilities Dining room; Physical therapy room; Activities room; Chapel; Crafts room; Laundry room; Barber/Beauty shop; Library.
Activities Arts & crafts; Cards; Games; Reading groups; Prayer groups; Movies; Dances/Social/Cultural gatherings.

St John's Home for the Aged
1236 Lincoln Ave, Evansville, IN 47714
(812) 464-3607
Admin Sr Amedee Maxwell.
Medical Dir Sr Julie.
Licensure Intermediate care. *Beds* ICF 90. *Certified* Medicaid.
Owner Nonprofit corp.
Admissions Requirements Minimum age 60; Medical examination; Physician's request.
Staff RNs 2 (ft), 2 (pt); LPNs 6 (ft), 7 (pt); Nurses' aides 25 (ft), 17 (pt); Physical therapists 1 (pt); Occupational therapists 1 (pt); Speech therapists 1 (pt); Activities coordinators 1 (ft); Dietitians 1 (pt).
Languages Spanish, French.
Affiliation Roman Catholic.
Facilities Dining room; Physical therapy room; Activities room; Chapel; Crafts room; Laundry room; Barber/Beauty shop; Library.
Activities Arts & crafts; Cards; Games; Reading groups; Prayer groups; Movies; Shopping trips; Dances/Social/Cultural gatherings; Exercise; Music therapy.

Woodbridge Health Care Center
816 N 1st Ave, Evansville, IN 47710
(812) 426-2841, 422-8364 FAX
Admin David Chada. *Dir of Nursing* Suzanne Kiefer RN. *Medical Dir* Robert Barnes MD.
Licensure Intermediate care. *Beds* ICF 92. *Certified* Medicaid.
Owner Proprietary corp (Beverly Enterprises).
Admissions Requirements Minimum age 19; Medical examination; Physician's request.
Staff RNs 3 (ft); LPNs 5 (ft); Nurses' aides 20 (ft); Physical therapists 1 (pt); Occupational therapists 1 (pt); Speech therapists 1 (pt); Activities coordinators 1 (ft); Dietitians 1 (pt); Ophthalmologists 1 (pt); Podiatrists 1 (pt).
Facilities Dining room; Activities room; Laundry room; Barber/Beauty shop; Library.
Activities Arts & crafts; Cards; Games; Reading groups; Prayer groups; Movies; Shopping trips; Fall festival shrine temple; Field trip.

Ferdinand

Scenic Hills Care Center
311 E 1st St, Ferdinand, IN 47532
(812) 367-2299
Admin Patricia Standley.
Licensure Intermediate care; Comprehensive care. *Beds* ICF 32; Comprehensive care 26.

Flora

Brethren's Home of Indiana Inc
RR 2, Box 97, Flora, IN 46929
(219) 967-4571
Admin Gaye Davenport. *Dir of Nursing* Nancy Doud. *Medical Dir* Flora Family Physicians.
Licensure Intermediate care; Retirement. *Beds* ICF 86; Retirement apts 25. *Private Pay Patients* 67%. *Certified* Medicaid.
Owner Nonprofit organization/foundation.
Admissions Requirements Minimum age 60; Medical examination; Physician's request.
Staff Physicians 2 (pt); RNs 3 (ft), 1 (pt); LPNs 5 (ft), 3 (pt); Nurses' aides 20 (ft), 20 (pt); Activities coordinators 1 (ft), 1 (pt); Dietitians 1 (pt).
Affiliation Church of the Brethren.

Facilities Dining room; Activities room; Chapel; Laundry room; Barber/Beauty shop.
Activities Arts & crafts; Cards; Games; Reading groups; Prayer groups; Movies; Shopping trips; Dances/Social/Cultural gatherings; Intergenerational programs; Pet therapy.

Fort Wayne

Byron Health Center
RR 13, 12101 Lima Rd, Fort Wayne, IN 46818
(219) 637-3166
Admin Thomas Katsanis.
Licensure Intermediate care; Residential care. *Beds* ICF 467; Residential 55. *Certified* Medicaid.
Owner Publicly owned.
Admissions Requirements Minimum age 18; Medical examination; Physician's request.
Staff Physicians 1 (ft), 2 (pt); RNs 10 (ft), 1 (pt); LPNs 40 (ft); Nurses' aides 153 (ft), 12 (pt); Physical therapists 1 (ft); Recreational therapists 6 (ft); Occupational therapists 1 (ft); Speech therapists 1 (ft); Activities coordinators 1 (ft); Dietitians 1 (ft), 1 (pt); Ophthalmologists 1 (pt); Podiatrists 2 (pt); Optometrist 1 (pt).
Facilities Dining room; Physical therapy room; Activities room; Chapel; Crafts room; Laundry room; Barber/Beauty shop; Library.
Activities Arts & crafts; Cards; Games; Reading groups; Prayer groups; Movies; Shopping trips; Dances/Social/Cultural gatherings.

Covington Manor Nursing Center
5700 Wilkie Dr, Fort Wayne, IN 46804
(219) 432-7556, 436-0386 FAX
Admin Susan Junk. *Dir of Nursing* Susan Bosselman. *Medical Dir* Thomas Van Den Driessche MD.
Licensure Intermediate care. *Beds* ICF 121. *Private Pay Patients* 60%. *Certified* Medicaid.
Owner Proprietary corp (Shive Nursing Centers Inc).
Admissions Requirements Medical examination; Physician's request.
Staff Physicians 1 (pt); RNs 4 (ft), 7 (pt); LPNs 4 (ft), 5 (pt); Nurses' aides 35 (ft), 20 (pt); Physical therapists 1 (pt); Occupational therapists 1 (pt); Speech therapists 1 (pt); Activities coordinators 1 (pt); Dietitians 1 (pt); Ophthalmologists 1 (pt); Podiatrists 1 (pt); Audiologists 1 (pt).
Facilities Dining room; Physical therapy room; Activities room; Laundry room; Barber/Beauty shop; Library.
Activities Arts & crafts; Cards; Games; Reading groups; Prayer groups; Movies; Shopping trips; Dances/Social/Cultural gatherings; Intergenerational programs; Pet therapy.

Fort Wayne Nursing Home
2402 N Beacon, Fort Wayne, IN 46805
(219) 484-3415
Admin Patricia P Shea. *Dir of Nursing* Marvin Hormann. *Medical Dir* Robert Lohman MD.
Licensure Intermediate care. *Beds* ICF 40. *Certified* Medicaid.
Owner Proprietary corp.
Admissions Requirements Minimum age 19; Medical examination; Physician's request.
Staff Physicians; RNs; LPNs; Nurses' aides; Activities coordinators; Dietitians.
Facilities Dining room; Activities room; Laundry room; Living room; Therapy room; Fenced-in yard.
Activities Arts & crafts; Cards; Games; Reading groups; Prayer groups; Movies; Shopping trips; Dances/Social/Cultural gatherings; Luncheons; Special event programs; Bingo.

Golden Years Homestead Inc
8300 Maysville Rd, Fort Wayne, IN 46815
(219) 749-9655
Admin Thomas G Garman. *Dir of Nursing*
Rebecca Housman RN. *Medical Dir* Dr
Philip Schubert.
Licensure Intermediate care; Alzheimer's care;
Retirement. *Beds* ICF 85. *Private Pay
Patients* 60%. *Certified* Medicaid.
Owner Nonprofit corp.
Admissions Requirements Minimum age 62;
Medical examination.
Staff Physicians 1 (pt); RNs 4 (ft), 3 (pt);
LPNs 2 (ft), 4 (pt); Recreational therapists 1
(ft); Activities coordinators 1 (ft); Dietitians
1 (pt).
Affiliation Church of Christ.
Facilities Dining room; Physical therapy
room; Activities room; Chapel; Crafts room;
Laundry room; Barber/Beauty shop; Library;
Enclosed courtyard with gazebo and rabbits;
16-bed dementia unit.
Activities Arts & crafts; Cards; Games;
Reading groups; Prayer groups; Movies;
Shopping trips; Dances/Social/Cultural
gatherings; Intergenerational programs; Pet
therapy.

Heritage Manor Health Care Center
7519 Winchester Rd, Fort Wayne, IN 46819
(219) 747-7435
Admin Kim Hughes.
Medical Dir William Aeschlimen MD.
Licensure Intermediate care; Retirement. *Beds*
ICF 80. *Certified* Medicaid.
Owner Proprietary corp.
Admissions Requirements Minimum age 18;
Medical examination; Physician's request.
Staff Physicians 1 (pt); RNs 2 (ft), 1 (pt);
LPNs 3 (ft), 3 (pt); Nurses' aides 8 (ft), 14
(pt); Activities coordinators 1 (ft); Dietitians
1 (pt); Podiatrists 1 (pt); Dentists 1 (pt).
Facilities Dining room; Activities room;
Laundry room; Barber/Beauty shop.
Activities Arts & crafts; Cards; Games;
Reading groups; Movies; Shopping trips.

Heritage Manor—North
1010 W Washington Center Rd, Fort Wayne,
IN 46825
(219) 489-2552
Admin Michael Ianucilli. *Dir of Nursing*
Georgia Toedt RN.
Licensure Intermediate care; Retirement;
Alzheimer's care. *Beds* ICF 81. *Certified*
Medicaid.
Owner Proprietary corp.
Admissions Requirements Minimum age 18;
Medical examination.
Staff RNs 4 (ft), 4 (pt); LPNs 6 (ft), 6 (pt);
Nurses' aides 14 (ft), 16 (pt); Activities
coordinators 1 (ft); Dietitians 1 (pt).
Facilities Dining room; Physical therapy
room; Activities room; Crafts room; Laundry
room; Barber/Beauty shop; Private quiet
lounge.
Activities Arts & crafts; Cards; Games;
Reading groups; Prayer groups; Movies;
Dances/Social/Cultural gatherings.

Indian Village Health Center Inc
2237 Engle Rd, Fort Wayne, IN 46809
(219) 747-2353
Admin Ronda K Rennalls LPN. *Dir of
Nursing* Janice Ridings LPN. *Medical Dir*
Dr Robert Voorhees.
Licensure Intermediate care; Comprehensive
care. *Beds* ICF 36; Comprehensive care 1.
Certified Medicaid.
Owner Proprietary corp.
Admissions Requirements Medical
examination; Physician's request.
Staff Physicians 1 (ft); LPNs 4 (ft), 5 (pt);
Nurses' aides 12 (ft); Recreational therapists
1 (pt); Activities coordinators 1 (pt).

Facilities Dining room; Activities room;
Laundry room; Barber/Beauty shop.
Activities Games; Reading groups; Prayer
groups; Movies; Shopping trips; Bowling.

Lawton Nursing Home
1649 Spy Run Ave, Fort Wayne, IN 46805
(219) 422-8520
Admin Glen D Snorf.
Medical Dir L Bayazit MD.
Licensure Intermediate care; Comprehensive
care. *Beds* ICF 96; Comprehensive care 37.
Certified Medicaid.
Owner Proprietary corp (Life Care Center).
Admissions Requirements Medical
examination; Physician's request.
Staff RNs 5 (ft); LPNs 3 (ft), 3 (pt); Nurses'
aides 26 (ft), 3 (pt); Activities coordinators 1
(ft), 2 (pt); Dietitians 1 (pt); Podiatrists 1
(pt); Dentists 1 (pt).
Facilities Dining room; Activities room;
Laundry room; Barber/Beauty shop.
Activities Arts & crafts; Cards; Games;
Reading groups; Prayer groups; Movies;
Shopping trips; Dances/Social/Cultural
gatherings.

Lutheran Homes Inc
6701 S Anthony Blvd, Fort Wayne, IN 46816
(219) 447-1591
Admin Robert Scheimann.
Licensure Intermediate care; Residential care;
Comprehensive care. *Beds* ICF 275;
Residential 120; Comprehensive care 1.
Certified Medicaid.
Owner Proprietary corp.
Admissions Requirements Minimum age 62;
Medical examination.
Affiliation Lutheran.
Facilities Dining room; Physical therapy
room; Activities room; Chapel; Crafts room;
Laundry room; Barber/Beauty shop; Library.
Activities Arts & crafts; Cards; Games;
Reading groups; Prayer groups; Movies;
Shopping trips; Dances/Social/Cultural
gatherings.

Medco Center of Fort Wayne
3811 Parnell Ave, Fort Wayne, IN 46805
(219) 482-4651
Admin Steve Reed.
Licensure Skilled care; Intermediate care. *Beds*
SNF 41; ICF 53. *Certified* Medicaid;
Medicare.
Owner Proprietary corp (Unicare).

Medco Plaza of Fort Wayne
3636 Newport, Fort Wayne, IN 46805
(219) 483-8175
Admin Patty L Akins.
Licensure Intermediate care. *Beds* ICF 110.

Miller's Merry Manor Inc
5544 E State Blvd, Fort Wayne, IN 46815
(219) 749-9506
Admin Erin Acker. *Dir of Nursing* Liz
Furniss. *Medical Dir* Dr Richard Kelty.
Licensure Skilled care; Intermediate care. *Beds*
SNF 20; ICF 57. *Private Pay Patients* 40%.
Certified Medicaid; Medicare.
Owner Proprietary corp (Caremet Inc).
Admissions Requirements Medical
examination; Physician's request.
Staff RNs 5 (ft); LPNs 5 (ft), 1 (pt); Nurses'
aides 10 (ft), 4 (pt); Physical therapists 1
(pt); Occupational therapists 1 (pt); Speech
therapists 1 (pt); Activities coordinators 1
(ft); Dietitians.
Facilities Dining room; Physical therapy
room; Activities room; Crafts room; Laundry
room; Barber/Beauty shop.
Activities Arts & crafts; Cards; Games;
Reading groups; Prayer groups; Movies;
Shopping trips; Dances/Social/Cultural
gatherings; Intergenerational programs; Pet
therapy.

Regency Place of Fort Wayne
6006 Brandy Chase Cove, Fort Wayne, IN
46815
(219) 486-3001
Admin Patricia Augustine.
Licensure Skilled care; Intermediate care;
Residential care. *Beds* SNF 57; ICF 97;
Residential care 6.
Owner Proprietary corp (Lucas Corp).

Riverview Care Center
2827 Northgate Blvd, Fort Wayne, IN 46835
(219) 485-9691
Admin Joseph E Weingartner. *Dir of Nursing*
Sheila Benner. *Medical Dir* Kann Physicians
MD.
Licensure Skilled care; Intermediate care;
Residential; Comprehensive care. *Beds* SNF
30; ICF 30; ICF/MR 3; Comprehensive care
60; Residential 65. *Certified* Medicaid.
Owner Proprietary corp.
Admissions Requirements Minimum age 18;
Medical examination.
Staff Physicians 4 (pt); RNs 3 (ft), 2 (pt);
LPNs 12 (ft), 8 (pt); Nurses' aides 35 (ft), 15
(pt); Physical therapists 1 (pt); Recreational
therapists 1 (pt); Occupational therapists 1
(pt); Speech therapists 1 (pt); Activities
coordinators 1 (ft), 1 (pt); Dietitians 1 (ft);
Ophthalmologists 1 (pt); Podiatrists 1 (pt);
Dentists 1 (pt); QMRAs 1 (pt).
Facilities Dining room; Physical therapy
room; Activities room; Chapel; Crafts room;
Laundry room; Barber/Beauty shop;
Rathskeller.
Activities Arts & crafts; Cards; Games;
Reading groups; Prayer groups; Movies;
Shopping trips; Dances/Social/Cultural
gatherings; Outings to plays; Bus trips;
Happy hour.

St Anne Home
1900 Randallia Dr, Fort Wayne, IN 46805
(219) 484-5555
Admin Mary E Haverstick. *Dir of Nursing*
Dolores Helmsing RN. *Medical Dir* Gerald
R Nolan MD.
Licensure Skilled care; Intermediate care;
Retirement. *Beds* SNF 53; ICF 101.
Certified Medicaid.
Owner Nonprofit organization/foundation.
Admissions Requirements Medical
examination.
Staff RNs 6 (ft), 2 (pt); LPNs 11 (ft), 4 (pt);
Nurses' aides 52 (ft), 5 (pt); Physical
therapists 1 (pt); Activities coordinators 1
(ft); Dietitians 1 (pt); Ophthalmologists 1
(pt).
Affiliation Roman Catholic.
Facilities Dining room; Physical therapy
room; Activities room; Chapel; Crafts room;
Laundry room; Barber/Beauty shop; Library.
Activities Arts & crafts; Cards; Games;
Reading groups; Prayer groups; Movies;
Shopping trips; Dances/Social/Cultural
gatherings.

Summit House
2440 Bowser Ave, Fort Wayne, IN 46803
(219) 745-4508
Admin Fred Taylor. *Dir of Nursing* Beth
Kennedy. *Medical Dir* Dr Lohman.
Licensure Intermediate care; Residential. *Beds*
ICF 58; Residential 24. *Certified* Medicaid.
Owner Proprietary corp (US Care Corp).
Admissions Requirements Minimum age 18;
Medical examination.
Staff RNs 1 (ft); LPNs 3 (ft), 3 (pt); Nurses'
aides 10 (ft), 5 (pt); Activities coordinators 1
(ft).
Facilities Dining room; Physical therapy
room; Activities room; Chapel; Crafts room;
Barber/Beauty shop; Library.
Activities Arts & crafts; Cards; Games;
Reading groups; Prayer groups; Movies;
Shopping trips; Dances/Social/Cultural
gatherings.

Three Rivers Convalescent Center
2940 N Clinton St, Fort Wayne, IN 46805
(219) 484-0602
Admin Barbara G Armstrong.
Medical Dir Dr Robert Vorhees.
Licensure Skilled care; Intermediate care. *Beds*
SNF 50; ICF 94. *Certified* Medicaid;
Medicare.
Owner Proprietary corp (Beverly Enterprises).
Admissions Requirements Medical
examination; Physician's request.
Staff Physicians 1 (ft); Physical therapists 1
(ft); Reality therapists 1 (ft); Recreational
therapists 1 (ft); Occupational therapists 1
(ft); Speech therapists 1 (ft); Activities
coordinators 1 (ft); Dietitians 1 (ft);
Podiatrists 1 (ft); Dentists 1 (ft).
Facilities Dining room; Physical therapy
room; Activities room; Crafts room; Laundry
room; Barber/Beauty shop; Occupational
therapy room.
Activities Arts & crafts; Cards; Games;
Reading groups; Prayer groups; Movies;
Shopping trips; Dances/Social/Cultural
gatherings.

Towne House Retirement Community
2209 Saint Joe Center Rd, Fort Wayne, IN
46825
(219) 483-3116
Admin B Daniel Carr.
Licensure Intermediate care; Residential care.
Beds ICF 99; Residential 210.
Owner Nonprofit organization/foundation
(Baptist Homes).

University Park Nursing Center
1400 Medical Park Dr, Fort Wayne, IN 46825
(219) 484-1558, 484-9518 FAX
Admin Michael E Blake, Sr Admin. *Dir of
Nursing* C Suzie Wilhelm RN. *Medical Dir*
John Wallace MD, Geriatrics Inc.
Licensure Intermediate care; Alzheimer's care.
Beds ICF 98; Alzheimer's care secured unit
23. *Private Pay Patients* 45%. *Certified*
Medicaid.
Owner Proprietary corp (Shive Nursing
Centers).
Admissions Requirements Minimum age 21;
Medical examination.
Staff Physicians 5 (pt); RNs 3 (ft), 1 (pt);
LPNs 6 (ft), 3 (pt); Nurses' aides 30 (ft), 25
(pt); Physical therapists 1 (pt); Occupational
therapists 1 (pt); Speech therapists 1 (pt);
Activities coordinators 1 (ft), 2 (pt);
Dietitians 1 (pt); Podiatrists 1 (pt).
Facilities Dining room; Activities room;
Crafts room; Laundry room; Barber/Beauty
shop; Library.
Activities Arts & crafts; Cards; Games;
Reading groups; Prayer groups; Movies;
Shopping trips; Dances/Social/Cultural
gatherings; Intergenerational programs; Pet
therapy.

Anthony Wayne Living Center
2626 Fairfield Ave, Fort Wayne, IN 46807
(219) 744-4211
Admin Dee Anna Smallman. *Dir of Nursing*
Vary Fischer RN. *Medical Dir* John Nill.
Licensure Skilled care; Intermediate care. *Beds*
SNF 63; ICF 63. *Certified* Medicaid;
Medicare.
Owner Proprietary corp.
Admissions Requirements Minimum age 19;
Medical examination; Physician's request.
Staff RNs 4 (ft); LPNs 8 (ft), 2 (pt); Nurses'
aides 10 (ft), 3 (pt); Physical therapists 1 (ft);
Occupational therapists 1 (ft); Speech
therapists 1 (ft); Activities coordinators 1
(ft); Dietitians 1 (pt); Podiatrists 1 (pt);
Social service 1 (pt).
Facilities Dining room; Physical therapy
room; Activities room; Crafts room; Laundry
room; Barber/Beauty shop.
Activities Arts & crafts; Cards; Games;
Reading groups; Prayer groups; Movies;
Dances/Social/Cultural gatherings.

Willow Ridge Living Center
2001 Hobson Rd, Fort Wayne, IN 46805
(219) 484-9557
Admin Craig S Schuler.
Medical Dir Dr E Bolander.
Licensure Skilled care; Intermediate care;
Comprehensive care. *Beds* SNF 89; ICF 90;
Comprehensive care 1. *Certified* Medicaid;
Medicare.
Owner Proprietary corp (ARA).
Admissions Requirements Minimum age 18;
Medical examination.
Staff Physicians 4 (pt); RNs 8 (ft), 2 (pt);
LPNs 10 (ft), 3 (pt); Nurses' aides 34 (ft), 9
(pt); Physical therapists 1 (ft), 1 (pt);
Recreational therapists 1 (ft); Occupational
therapists 1 (pt); Speech therapists 1 (pt);
Activities coordinators 1 (ft); Dietitians 1
(ft); Ophthalmologists 1 (pt); Podiatrists 1
(pt); Audiologists 1 (pt); Dentists 1 (pt).
Facilities Dining room; Physical therapy
room; Activities room; Chapel; Crafts room;
Laundry room; Barber/Beauty shop; Library.
Activities Arts & crafts; Cards; Games;
Reading groups; Prayer groups; Movies;
Shopping trips; Dances/Social/Cultural
gatherings.

Woodview Healthcare Inc
3420 E State St, Fort Wayne, IN 46805
(219) 484-3120
Admin John August.
Licensure Skilled care; Intermediate care. *Beds*
SNF 33; ICF 71104. *Certified* Medicaid;
Medicare.
Owner Proprietary corp.
Facilities Dining room; Physical therapy
room; Activities room; Crafts room; Laundry
room; Barber/Beauty shop.
Activities Arts & crafts; Cards; Games;
Reading groups; Movies; Shopping trips;
Dances/Social/Cultural gatherings.

Fowler

Green-Hill Manor Inc
501 N Lincoln Ave, Fowler, IN 47944
(317) 884-1470
Admin Edith Dexter; Connie Brouillette.
Licensure Intermediate care. *Beds* ICF 42.
Certified Medicaid.
Owner Proprietary corp.

Francesville

Parkview Haven
PO Box 797, Ada at Brooks St, Francesville,
IN 47946
(219) 567-9149
Admin Benjamin L Metz. *Dir of Nursing*
Laurel Widmer. *Medical Dir* Charles
Heinsen.
Licensure Residential care; Comprehensive
care. *Beds* Residential care 8;
Comprehensive care 39. *Certified* Medicaid.
Owner Nonprofit organization/foundation.
Admissions Requirements Minimum age 65;
Medical examination.
Staff RNs 1 (ft), 3 (pt); LPNs 1 (ft), 2 (pt);
Nurses' aides 3 (ft), 14 (pt); Activities
coordinators 1 (pt); Dietitians 1 (pt); Social
service 1 (pt).
Affiliation Apostolic Christian.
Facilities Dining room; Physical therapy
room; Activities room; Chapel; Crafts room;
Laundry room; Barber/Beauty shop; Library.
Activities Arts & crafts; Games; Reading
groups; Prayer groups; Movies; Shopping
trips.

Frankfort

Clinton House Inc
809 W Freeman St, Frankfort, IN 46041
(317) 654-8783
Admin Laura L Peterson.

Licensure Skilled care; Intermediate care. *Beds*
SNF 21; ICF 100. *Certified* Medicaid.
Owner Proprietary corp.

Frankfort Nursing Home
1234 Rossville Ave, Frankfort, IN 46041
(317) 654-8118
Admin Evelyn Tidler. *Dir of Nursing* Cheryl
Moore RN. *Medical Dir* Dr Arthur Dannin.
Licensure Intermediate care. *Beds* ICF 40.
Certified Medicaid.
Owner Proprietary corp (Beverly Enterprises).
Admissions Requirements Minimum age 18;
Medical examination; Physician's request.
Staff Physicians 1 (pt); RNs 2 (ft), 1 (pt);
LPNs 3 (ft), 2 (pt); Nurses' aides 6 (ft), 8
(pt); Activities coordinators 1 (ft); Dietitians
1 (ft); Ophthalmologists 1 (pt); Dentists 1
(pt).
Facilities Dining room; Activities room;
Crafts room; Laundry room.
Activities Arts & crafts; Cards; Games;
Reading groups; Prayer groups; Movies;
Dances/Social/Cultural gatherings; Monthly
theme parties; Church services.

Parkview Home
RR 2 Box 26, Frankfort, IN 46041
(317) 659-3803
Admin Dorothy Schriefer, LPN.
Licensure Residential care. *Beds* 40.
Admissions Requirements Medical
examination; Physician's request.
Staff LPNs 1 (ft); Activities coordinators 1
(pt); Dietitians 1 (pt).
Facilities Dining room; Activities room;
Chapel; Laundry room; Barber/Beauty shop;
Library.
Activities Games; Reading groups; Prayer
groups; Movies; Shopping trips.

Wesley Manor
1555 N Main St, Frankfort, IN 46041
(317) 659-1811
Admin Kenneth D Adkins. *Dir of Nursing*
Debbie Lineback.
Licensure Residential care; Comprehensive
care. *Beds* Residential care 231;
Comprehensive care 128.
Owner Nonprofit corp.
Admissions Requirements Minimum age 60.
Staff Physicians 1 (pt); RNs 4 (ft), 1 (pt);
LPNs 9 (ft), 1 (pt); Nurses' aides 13 (ft), 23
(pt); Physical therapists 1 (pt); Activities
coordinators 4 (ft), 1 (pt); Dietitians 1 (pt);
Staff 120 (ft).
Affiliation Methodist.
Facilities Dining room; Physical therapy
room; Activities room; Chapel; Crafts room;
Laundry room; Barber/Beauty shop; Library;
Woodshop; Ceramics; Gift shop; Art studio;
Photo studio.
Activities Arts & crafts; Cards; Games;
Reading groups; Prayer groups; Movies;
Shopping trips; Dances/Social/Cultural
gatherings; Swimming pool; Bowling alley;
Free 18 hole golf.

Franklin

Franklin Healthcare Centre
1285 W Jefferson St, Franklin, IN 46131
(317) 736-9113
Admin Virginia Roberts. *Dir of Nursing* Vicki
Northcot. *Medical Dir* Dr Wm Province.
Licensure Skilled care; Intermediate care. *Beds*
SNF 63; ICF 60. *Certified* Medicaid;
Medicare.
Owner Proprietary corp (ARA).
Staff RNs 4 (ft), 1 (pt); LPNs 10 (ft), 2 (pt);
Nurses' aides 26 (ft), 12 (pt); Physical
therapists 1 (pt); Recreational therapists 1
(ft); Occupational therapists 1 (pt); Speech
therapists 1 (pt); Activities coordinators 1
(ft); Dietitians 1 (pt).

Franklin Nursing Home
1130 N Main St, Franklin, IN 46131
(317) 736-8214
Admin Rose Hepler. *Dir of Nursing* Linda
Fox LPN. *Medical Dir* William Province
MD.
Licensure Intermediate care; Alzheimer's care.
Beds ICF 40. *Private Pay Patients* 28%.
Certified Medicaid.
Owner Proprietary corp (Beverly Enterprises).
Admissions Requirements Medical
examination; Physician's request.
Staff RNs 1 (pt); LPNs 3 (ft); Nurses' aides 6
(ft), 2 (pt); Activities coordinators 1 (ft);
Dietitians.
Facilities Dining room; Activities room;
Crafts room; Laundry room.
Activities Arts & crafts; Cards; Games;
Reading groups; Prayer groups; Movies;
Shopping trips; Dances/Social/Cultural
gatherings; Intergenerational programs; Pet
therapy.

Franklin United Methodist Home
1070 W Jefferson St, Franklin, IN 46131
(317) 736-7185
Admin Rev Robert Allred. *Dir of Nursing* Pat
Deer. *Medical Dir* William Province II.
Licensure Skilled care; Intermediate care;
Residential retirement care; Alzheimer's
care. *Beds* Swing beds SNF/ICF 101;
Retirement units 459.
Owner Nonprofit corp.
Admissions Requirements Minimum age 62;
Medical examination.
Staff Physicians 1 (pt); RNs 4 (ft), 3 (pt);
LPNs 13 (ft), 2 (pt); Nurses' aides 41 (ft), 8
(pt); Physical therapists 1 (pt); Dietitians 1
(pt); Podiatrists 1 (pt).
Affiliation United Methodist.
Facilities Dining room; Physical therapy
room; Activities room; Chapel; Crafts room;
Laundry room; Barber/Beauty shop; Library;
Wood craft room; Greenhouse; Ping-Pong;
Pool; Shuffleboard; Post Office; Bank; Buses;
Wheelchair van; Art studio.
Activities Arts & crafts; Cards; Games;
Reading groups; Prayer groups; Movies;
Shopping trips; Dances/Social/Cultural
gatherings; Intergenerational programs; Pet
therapy; Music; Gardening; Swimming.

Homeview Center of Franklin
PO Box 464, 651 S State St, Franklin, IN
46131
(317) 736-6414
Admin Timothy H Nix. *Dir of Nursing*
Margaret Kelley RN. *Medical Dir* George
Small MD.
Licensure Intermediate care; Comprehensive
care. *Beds* ICF 60; Comprehensive care 10.
Certified Medicaid.
Owner Proprietary corp.
Admissions Requirements Minimum age 18;
Medical examination; Physician's request.
Staff Physicians; RNs; LPNs; Nurses' aides;
Activities coordinators; Dietitians;
Ophthalmologists.
Facilities Dining room; Activities room;
Laundry room; Barber/Beauty shop;
Lounges.
Activities Arts & crafts; Cards; Games;
Reading groups; Prayer groups; Movies;
Shopping trips; Dances/Social/Cultural
gatherings; Exercise.

Welcome Nursing Home
1109 N Main St, Franklin, IN 46131
(317) 736-7041
Admin Linda J Crowe. *Dir of Nursing* Katie
Lou Morris RN. *Medical Dir* William D
Province MD.
Licensure Intermediate care. *Beds* ICF 69.
Certified Medicaid.
Owner Privately owned.
Admissions Requirements Medical
examination.

Staff Physicians 1 (pt); RNs 1 (ft); LPNs 2
(ft), 1 (pt); Nurses' aides 18 (ft), 5 (pt);
Activities coordinators 1 (pt); Dietitians 1
(pt).
Facilities Dining room; Activities room;
Laundry room.
Activities Arts & crafts; Cards; Games;
Reading groups; Prayer groups; Movies;
Dances/Social/Cultural gatherings.

Freelandville

Freelandville Community Home
Box 288, Hwy 58, Freelandville, IN 47535
(812) 328-2134
Admin Roger M Stalker. *Dir of Nursing* Janet
Clinkenbeard RN. *Medical Dir* Dr B G
Odell.
Licensure Intermediate care. *Beds* ICF 50.
Private Pay Patients 80%. *Certified*
Medicaid.
Owner Nonprofit organization/foundation.
Admissions Requirements Medical
examination.
Staff RNs 2 (ft), 1 (pt); LPNs 2 (ft), 3 (pt);
Nurses' aides 20 (ft), 6 (pt); Activities
coordinators 1 (ft), 1 (pt); Dietitians.
Facilities Dining room; Activities room;
Crafts room; Laundry room; Barber/Beauty
shop.
Activities Arts & crafts; Cards; Games;
Reading groups; Prayer groups; Movies;
Shopping trips; Dances/Social/Cultural
gatherings; Pet therapy; Volunteer program;
Community support.

French Lick

Medco Center of French Lick
Hwy 145 & College Ave, French Lick, IN
47432
(812) 936-9991
Admin Connie S Kellams. *Dir of Nursing*
Mary Pankey RN. *Medical Dir* Terry
Nofziger MD.
Licensure Skilled care; Intermediate care. *Beds*
SNF 42; ICF 42. *Private Pay Patients* 10%.
Certified Medicaid; Medicare; VA.
Owner Proprietary corp (Unicare).
Admissions Requirements Medical
examination.
Facilities Dining room; Physical therapy
room; Barber/Beauty shop.
Activities Arts & crafts; Cards; Games;
Reading groups; Movies; Shopping trips;
Dances/Social/Cultural gatherings;
Intergenerational programs; Pet therapy;
Church services.

Medco Springs of French Lick
RR 2 Box 51, French Lick, IN 47432
(812) 936-9901
Admin Teresa Wininger.
Licensure Intermediate care. *Beds* ICF 58.
Certified Medicaid.
Owner Proprietary corp (Unicare).

Garrett

Miller's Merry Manor Inc
1367 S Randolph, Garrett, IN 46738
(219) 357-5174
Admin David Zehr RN.
Medical Dir Bryce Treadwall MD.
Licensure Intermediate care. *Beds* ICF 63.
Certified Medicaid.
Owner Proprietary corp (Millers Merry
Manor).
Admissions Requirements Minimum age 18;
Medical examination; Physician's request.
Staff Physicians 1 (pt); RNs 2 (ft); LPNs 2
(ft), 1 (pt); Nurses' aides 5 (ft), 15 (pt);
Physical therapists 1 (pt); Speech therapists
1 (pt); Activities coordinators 1 (ft);
Dietitians 1 (ft).

Facilities Dining room; Physical therapy
room; Crafts room; Laundry room; Barber/
Beauty shop.
Activities Arts & crafts; Cards; Games;
Reading groups; Prayer groups; Movies;
Shopping trips; Dances/Social/Cultural
gatherings.

Gary

Greens Geriatric Health Center Inc
2052 Delaware St, Gary, IN 46407
(219) 886-1513
Admin Horace Brown. *Dir of Nursing* Jimma
Graves. *Medical Dir* Dr Bayne Spotwood.
Licensure Intermediate care; Retirement. *Beds*
ICF 35. *Private Pay Patients* 1%. *Certified*
Medicaid.
Owner Proprietary corp.
Admissions Requirements Medical
examination; Physician's request.
Staff Physicians; RNs; LPNs 8 (ft); Nurses'
aides 12 (ft), 8 (pt); Activities coordinators 1
(ft); Dietitians 1 (pt); Podiatrists 1 (pt).
Facilities Dining room; Activities room;
Laundry room.
Activities Arts & crafts; Cards; Games;
Reading groups; Movies; Shopping trips;
Dances/Social/Cultural gatherings; Pet
therapy; Cosmetics classes; Square dancing.

Simmons Loving Care Health Facility
PO Box 1675, 700 E 21st Ave, Gary, IN
46407
(219) 882-2563
Admin Herberta B Miller; Anna L Simmons.
Licensure Intermediate care. *Beds* ICF 46.
Certified Medicaid.
Owner Privately owned.

West Side Health Care Center
353 Tyler St, Gary, IN 46402
(219) 886-7070
Admin Gerald Rothenberg.
Licensure Intermediate care. *Beds* ICF 214.
Certified Medicaid.
Owner Proprietary corp (Meridian
Healthcare).

Wildwood Manor Inc
1964 Clark Rd, Gary, IN 46404
(219) 949-9640
Admin A Joann Johnson. *Dir of Nursing*
Lydia M King. *Medical Dir* Dr Daniel T
Ramker.
Licensure Skilled care. *Beds* SNF 120.
Certified Medicaid; Medicare.
Owner Proprietary corp.
Admissions Requirements Minimum age 21;
Medical examination; Physician's request.
Staff Physicians 5 (pt); RNs 3 (ft), 1 (pt);
LPNs 12 (ft), 2 (pt); Nurses' aides 41 (ft), 10
(pt); Physical therapists 1 (pt); Occupational
therapists 2 (pt); Activities coordinators 2
(ft); Dietitians 1 (ft), 2 (pt);
Ophthalmologists 1 (pt).
Facilities Dining room; Physical therapy
room; Activities room; Chapel; Laundry
room; Barber/Beauty shop.
Activities Arts & crafts; Cards; Games;
Reading groups; Prayer groups; Movies;
Shopping trips; Dances/Social/Cultural
gatherings.

Wildwood Manor Mount Inc
386 Mount St, Gary, IN 46406
(219) 949-5600
Admin Paula T Flores. *Dir of Nursing* May O
Gonzalez RN. *Medical Dir* Daniel T
Ramker MD.
Licensure Intermediate care. *Beds* ICF 69.
Certified Medicaid.
Owner Proprietary corp.
Admissions Requirements Minimum age 18;
Medical examination; Physician's request.
Staff Physicians 2 (pt); RNs 1 (ft); LPNs 4
(ft), 3 (pt); Nurses' aides 18 (ft), 5 (pt);
Physical therapists 1 (pt); Occupational

therapists 1 (pt); Speech therapists 1 (pt); Activities coordinators 1 (ft); Dietitians 1 (pt); Ophthalmologists 1 (pt); Podiatrists 1 (pt); Dentists 1 (pt).
Languages Spanish.
Facilities Dining room; Activities room; Crafts room; Laundry room; Barber/Beauty shop.
Activities Arts & crafts; Cards; Games; Reading groups; Prayer groups; Movies; Shopping trips; Dances/Social/Cultural gatherings; Bingo; Shuffle board; Community outings.

Gas City

Twin City Nursing Home
627 East-North H St, Gas City, IN 46933
(317) 674-8516
Admin Donna Imlay.
Licensure Skilled care; Intermediate care; Comprehensive care. *Beds* SNF 23; ICF 68; Comprehensive care 7. *Certified* Medicaid.
Owner Proprietary corp.

Gaston

Procare Development Center
502 N Madison St, Gaston, IN 47342
(317) 358-3324
Admin Harold K Behm. *Dir of Nursing* JoAnne Johnstone. *Medical Dir* Dr Thaker.
Licensure Intermediate care for mentally retarded. *Beds* ICF/MR 75. *Certified* Medicaid.
Owner Proprietary corp.
Admissions Requirements Minimum age 18; Medical examination.
Staff RNs 1 (ft); LPNs 5 (ft); Nurses' aides 40 (ft); Recreational therapists 5 (ft); Speech therapists 1 (ft); Dietitians 1 (ft).
Facilities Dining room; Physical therapy room; Laundry room.

Goshen

Crystal Valley Care Center
1101 W Lincoln Ave, Goshen, IN 46526
(219) 533-8090
Admin Scott Piotrowicz. *Dir of Nursing* Joetta Pegues. *Medical Dir* Dr William Weybright.
Licensure Intermediate care. *Beds* ICF 40. *Private Pay Patients* 40%. *Certified* Medicaid.
Owner Proprietary corp (Waverly Group).
Admissions Requirements Physician's request.
Staff Physicians 1 (ft); LPNs 4 (ft), 2 (pt); Nurses' aides 10 (ft), 5 (pt); Activities coordinators 1 (pt); Dietitians 1 (pt); Podiatrists 1 (pt).
Facilities Dining room; Activities room; Laundry room.
Activities Arts & crafts; Cards; Games; Reading groups; Prayer groups; Movies; Shopping trips; Dances/Social/Cultural gatherings; Pet therapy.

Fountainview Place—Goshen
2400 College Ave, Goshen, IN 46526
(219) 533-0351
Admin James L Norton. *Dir of Nursing* Betty Brooks RN. *Medical Dir* Donald L Minter MD.
Licensure Skilled care; Intermediate care; Comprehensive. *Beds* SNF 49; ICF 78; Comprehensive 19. *Certified* Medicaid; Medicare.
Owner Proprietary corp (Beverly Enterprises).
Admissions Requirements Minimum age 18; Medical examination; Physician's request.
Staff Physicians 1 (pt); RNs 6 (ft), 1 (pt); LPNs 13 (ft), 2 (pt); Nurses' aides 27 (ft), 12 (pt); Physical therapists 1 (pt); Occupational therapists 1 (pt); Speech therapists 1 (pt); Activities coordinators 1 (ft), 1 (pt); Dietitians 1 (pt).

Languages Ukranian.
Facilities Dining room; Physical therapy room; Activities room; Chapel; Crafts room; Laundry room; Barber/Beauty shop; Library.
Activities Arts & crafts; Cards; Games; Reading groups; Prayer groups; Movies; Shopping trips; Dances/Social/Cultural gatherings.

Greencroft Nursing Center
PO Box 819, 1225 Greencroft Dr, Goshen, IN 46526
(219) 534-1546
Admin Wayne A Badskey. *Dir of Nursing* Dee Detweiler RN. *Medical Dir* Donald L Minter MD.
Licensure Skilled care; Intermediate care; Retirement. *Beds* SNF 50; ICF 130. *Certified* Medicaid; Medicare.
Owner Proprietary corp.
Admissions Requirements Minimum age 18; Medical examination.
Staff Physicians 1 (pt); RNs 7 (ft), 5 (pt); LPNs 13 (ft), 7 (pt); Nurses' aides 57 (ft), 33 (pt); Physical therapists 2 (pt); Speech therapists 1 (pt); Activities coordinators 3 (ft); Dietitians 1 (ft), 1 (pt).
Affiliation Mennonite.
Facilities Dining room; Physical therapy room; Activities room; Laundry room; Barber/Beauty shop; Library.
Activities Arts & crafts; Games; Reading groups; Prayer groups; Movies; Exercise; Bible study; Hymn singing; Current events.

Gosport

Gosport Nursing Home
27 S 7th St, Gosport, IN 47433
(812) 879-4242
Admin Fred J Ponton.
Licensure Intermediate care. *Beds* ICF 74. *Certified* Medicaid.
Owner Proprietary corp.

Greencastle

Asbury Towers
102 W Poplar St, Greencastle, IN 46135
(317) 653-5148
Admin James L Ray. *Dir of Nursing* June Conrad. *Medical Dir* Steve Kissel MD.
Licensure Intermediate care; Residential/ Assisted care; Independent living; Alzheimer's care. *Beds* ICF 39; Residential/ Assisted care 77; Independent living units 15. *Private Pay Patients* 100%.
Owner Nonprofit corp.
Admissions Requirements Minimum age 65; Medical examination.
Staff RNs 2 (ft); LPNs 2 (ft), 4 (pt); Nurses' aides 14 (ft), 3 (pt); Activities coordinators 1 (ft); Dietitians 1 (pt); Ophthalmologists 1 (pt); Podiatrists 1 (pt).
Affiliation Methodist.
Facilities Dining room; Activities room; Laundry room; Barber/Beauty shop; Library; 8 lounges; Game room.
Activities Arts & crafts; Cards; Games; Reading groups; Prayer groups; Movies; Shopping trips; Dances/Social/Cultural gatherings; Intergenerational programs.

Greencastle Nursing Home
815 E Tacoma Dr, Greencastle, IN 46135
(317) 653-8280
Admin Kathryn A Lemmon. *Dir of Nursing* Eva Keen RN. *Medical Dir* Warren Macy MD.
Licensure Intermediate care. *Beds* ICF 40. *Certified* Medicaid.
Owner Proprietary corp (Beverly Enterprises).
Staff RNs 1 (pt); LPNs 2 (ft), 1 (pt); Nurses' aides 8 (ft), 2 (pt); Activities coordinators 1 (ft); Dietitians 1 (pt).

Facilities Dining room; Activities room; Laundry room.
Activities Arts & crafts; Cards; Games; Reading groups; Prayer groups; Movies; Shopping trips; Dances/Social/Cultural gatherings.

Heritage House Convalescent Center of Putnam County Inc
PO Box 178, 1601 Hospital Dr, Greencastle, IN 46135-0178
(317) 653-2602
Admin Allen W Goodman. *Dir of Nursing* Laura Long RN. *Medical Dir* Dr Kissell; Dr Johnson.
Licensure Skilled care; Intermediate care; Alzheimer's care. *Beds* SNF 59; ICF 60. *Certified* Medicaid; Medicare.
Owner Proprietary corp.
Admissions Requirements Medical examination; Physician's request.
Facilities Dining room; Physical therapy room; Activities room; Chapel; Laundry room; Barber/Beauty shop.
Activities Arts & crafts; Cards; Games; Reading groups; Prayer groups; Movies; Shopping trips; Dances/Social/Cultural gatherings.

Shady Creek Health Care Facility
PO Box 524, 1306 S Bloomington St, Greencastle, IN 46135
(317) 653-2406
Admin Helen P Roe. *Dir of Nursing* Kathryn Lawson RN. *Medical Dir* Gregory Larken MD.
Licensure Intermediate care. *Beds* ICF 40. *Certified* Medicaid.
Owner Proprietary corp.
Admissions Requirements Minimum age 18; Physician's request.
Staff RNs 1 (ft); LPNs 4 (ft), 3 (pt); Nurses' aides 10 (ft), 2 (pt); Recreational therapists 1 (ft), 1 (pt); Activities coordinators 1 (ft), 2 (pt); Dietitians 1 (ft).
Facilities Dining room; Activities room; Crafts room; Active programing areas.
Activities Arts & crafts; Cards; Games; Reading groups; Prayer groups; Movies; Shopping trips; Dances/Social/Cultural gatherings; Active programing for MR/DD.

Sunset Manor Nursing Home
1109 S Indiana St, Greencastle, IN 46135
(317) 653-3143
Admin Brian L Cross.
Licensure Intermediate care. *Beds* ICF 79. *Certified* Medicaid.
Owner Proprietary corp.
Staff RNs 2 (ft).
Facilities Dining room; Activities room; Laundry room.
Activities Cards; Games; Reading groups.

Greenfield

Brandywine Manor
745 N Swope, Greenfield, IN 46140
(317) 462-9221, 462-3400 FAX
Admin Tim Tapp. *Dir of Nursing* Becky Stroud. *Medical Dir* Hal Rhynearson MD.
Licensure Skilled care; Intermediate care. *Beds* SNF 49; ICF 83. *Private Pay Patients* 22%. *Certified* Medicaid; Medicare.
Owner Proprietary corp (Beverly Enterprises).
Admissions Requirements Medical examination; Physician's request.
Staff Physicians 1 (pt); RNs 2 (ft), 2 (pt); LPNs 13 (ft); Nurses' aides 40 (ft); Physical therapists 1 (pt); Occupational therapists 1 (pt); Speech therapists 1 (pt); Activities coordinators 1 (ft), 1 (pt); Dietitians 1 (pt); Ophthalmologists 1 (pt); Podiatrists 1 (pt); Audiologists 1 (pt).
Facilities Dining room; Physical therapy room; Activities room; Chapel; Crafts room; Laundry room; Barber/Beauty shop; Lounge areas.

Activities Arts & crafts; Cards; Games;
Reading groups; Prayer groups; Movies;
Shopping trips; Dances/Social/Cultural
gatherings; Intergenerational programs; Pet
therapy.

Crescent Manor
1310 E Main, Greenfield, IN 46140
(317) 462-4344
Admin Linda Vest. *Dir of Nursing* Alice K
Wilson. *Medical Dir* Hal Rhynearson MD.
Licensure Intermediate care. *Beds* ICF 40.
Private Pay Patients 35%. *Certified*
Medicaid.
Owner Proprietary corp (Waverley Group).
Admissions Requirements Minimum age 18;
Medical examination; Physician's request.
Staff Physicians 1 (pt); RNs 1 (pt); LPNs 3
(ft), 4 (pt); Nurses' aides 5 (ft), 4 (pt);
Activities coordinators 1 (ft); Dietitians 1
(pt).
Facilities Dining room; Activities room;
Crafts room.
Activities Arts & crafts; Cards; Games;
Reading groups; Prayer groups; Movies;
Shopping trips; Dances/Social/Cultural
gatherings; Intergenerational programs; Pet
therapy.

Regency Place of Greenfield
200 Green Meadows Dr, Greenfield, IN 46140
(317) 462-3311
Admin Edward L Hastings. *Dir of Nursing*
Sue Folkenerg. *Medical Dir* Gary Sharp MD.
Licensure Skilled care; Intermediate care;
Residential care; Comprehensive care;
Alzheimer's care. *Beds* SNF 59; ICF 143;
Residential care 6; Comprehensive care 22.
Certified Medicaid; Medicare.
Owner Proprietary corp (Lucas Corp).
Admissions Requirements Minimum age 21;
Medical examination; Physician's request.
Staff Physicians 1 (pt); RNs 10 (ft), 1 (pt);
LPNs 15 (ft), 6 (pt); Nurses' aides 55 (ft), 45
(pt); Physical therapists 1 (ft); Occupational
therapists 1 (pt); Speech therapists 1 (pt);
Activities coordinators 1 (ft); Dietitians 1
(pt).
Facilities Dining room; Physical therapy
room; Activities room; Chapel; Crafts room;
Laundry room; Barber/Beauty shop; Library;
Courtyard.
Activities Arts & crafts; Cards; Games;
Reading groups; Prayer groups; Movies;
Shopping trips; Dances/Social/Cultural
gatherings.

Sugar Creek Convalescent Center
5430 W US 40, Greenfield, IN 46140
(317) 894-3301
Admin Lisa Slomovitz.
Medical Dir Monica Brunelle MD.
Licensure Skilled care; Intermediate care;
Retirement; Alzheimer's care. *Beds* SNF 40;
ICF 30; Retirement 16. *Private Pay Patients*
17%. *Certified* Medicaid; Medicare.
Owner Proprietary corp (Beverly Enterprises).
Staff Physicians 1 (ft); RNs 6 (ft), 1 (pt);
LPNs 6 (ft), 2 (pt); Nurses' aides 27 (ft), 3
(pt); Physical therapists 1 (ft); Occupational
therapists 1 (pt); Speech therapists 1 (pt);
Activities coordinators 1 (ft); Dietitians 1
(ft); Ophthalmologists 1 (pt); Podiatrists 1
(pt); Audiologists 1 (pt).
Facilities Dining room; Physical therapy
room; Activities room; Chapel; Crafts room;
Laundry room; Barber/Beauty shop; Library.
Activities Arts & crafts; Cards; Games;
Reading groups; Prayer groups; Movies;
Shopping trips; Dances/Social/Cultural
gatherings; Intergenerational programs; Pet
therapy.

Greensburg

Heritage House of Greensburg
410 Park Rd, Greensburg, IN 47240
(812) 663-7543

Admin Martha Waltz. *Dir of Nursing* Chrystal
Pershor.
Licensure Skilled care; Intermediate care;
Residential. *Beds* SNF 74; ICF 90;
Residential care 36. *Certified* Medicaid;
Medicare.
Owner Proprietary corp.
Admissions Requirements Medical
examination; Physician's request.
Staff RNs; LPNs; Nurses' aides; Dietitians.
Facilities Dining room; Physical therapy
room; Activities room; Crafts room; Laundry
room; Barber/Beauty shop; Library.
Activities Arts & crafts; Cards; Games;
Reading groups; Prayer groups; Movies;
Shopping trips.

North Lincoln Village
1420 N Lincoln St, Greensburg, IN 47240
(812) 663-7503
Admin Vanessa Wilson. *Dir of Nursing* Ed
Bryan. *Medical Dir* Greg Wiseman.
Licensure Skilled care; Intermediate care. *Beds*
SNF 11; ICF 29. *Private Pay Patients* 18%.
Certified Medicaid; Medicare.
Owner Proprietary corp (Beverly Enterprises).
Staff Physicians; RNs 2 (ft); LPNs 4 (ft), 1
(pt); Nurses' aides; Physical therapists;
Recreational therapists 1 (ft); Activities
coordinators 1 (ft); Dietitians 1 (pt);
Ophthalmologists; Podiatrists.
Facilities Dining room; Activities room;
Laundry room.
Activities Arts & crafts; Cards; Games;
Reading groups; Prayer groups; Movies;
Shopping trips; Dances/Social/Cultural
gatherings.

Odd Fellows Home
Rte 8, Greensburg, IN 47240
(812) 663-8553
Admin Jon W Kohlmeier. *Dir of Nursing*
Theresa Ripperger. *Medical Dir* Dr James
Miller.
Licensure Intermediate care; Residential. *Beds*
ICF 89; Residential care 22. *Certified*
Medicaid.
Owner Nonprofit corp.
Staff RNs 3 (ft), 1 (pt); LPNs 5 (ft), 3 (pt);
Nurses' aides 50 (ft), 15 (pt); Physical
therapists 1 (ft); Speech therapists 1 (pt);
Activities coordinators 1 (ft), 1 (pt);
Dietitians 1 (pt); Ophthalmologists 1 (pt);
Podiatrists 1 (pt).
Affiliation Independent Order of Odd Fellows
& Rebekahs.
Activities Arts & crafts; Cards; Games;
Reading groups; Prayer groups; Movies;
Shopping trips; Dances/Social/Cultural
gatherings.

Greentown

Century Villa Health Care
705 N Meridian, Greentown, IN 46936
(317) 628-3377
Admin Janet H Lemler. *Dir of Nursing*
Catherine Gale. *Medical Dir* Ken Ridgeway.
Licensure Intermediate care. *Beds* ICF 90.
Certified Medicaid.
Owner Privately owned.
Admissions Requirements Minimum age 18.
Facilities Dining room; Activities room;
Crafts room; Laundry room; Barber/Beauty
shop; Gift shop.
Activities Arts & crafts; Cards; Games;
Reading groups; Prayer groups; Movies;
Shopping trips; Dances/Social/Cultural
gatherings; Intergenerational programs.

Greenwood

Greenwood Convalescent Center
PO Box 1317, 937 Fry Rd, Greenwood, IN
46142
(317) 881-3535

Admin Patsy Van Sickel. *Dir of Nursing* Dee
Gee. *Medical Dir* Dr George Small.
Licensure Intermediate care. *Beds* ICF 137.
Private Pay Patients 50%. *Certified*
Medicaid.
Owner Privately owned.
Staff RNs 2 (ft), 1 (pt); LPNs 9 (ft), 1 (pt);
Nurses' aides 26 (ft), 4 (pt); Activities
coordinators 1 (ft), 1 (pt); Dietitians 1 (ft).
Facilities Dining room; Activities room;
Laundry room; Barber/Beauty shop; Library.
Activities Arts & crafts; Cards; Games;
Reading groups; Prayer groups; Movies;
Shopping trips; Dances/Social/Cultural
gatherings; Intergenerational programs; Pet
therapy.

Greenwood Village South
295 Village Ln, Greenwood, IN 46143
(317) 881-2591
Admin Michael F Mitchum. *Dir of Nursing*
Nancy Eckle. *Medical Dir* Dr Joseph Young.
Licensure Skilled care; Intermediate care;
Retirement. *Beds* SNF 43; ICF 48;
Retirement 380. *Private Pay Patients* 10%.
Certified Medicaid; Medicare.
Owner Nonprofit corp.
Admissions Requirements Medical
examination; Physician's request.
Staff Physicians 1 (pt); RNs 7 (ft), 5 (pt);
LPNs 5 (ft), 2 (pt); Nurses' aides 38 (ft), 9
(pt); Physical therapists (contracted); Speech
therapists 1 (pt); Activities coordinators 1
(ft), 1 (pt); Dietitians 1 (ft);
Ophthalmologists 2 (pt).
Facilities Dining room; Physical therapy
room; Activities room; Chapel; Crafts room;
Laundry room; Barber/Beauty shop; Library.
Activities Arts & crafts; Cards; Games;
Reading groups; Prayer groups; Movies;
Shopping trips; Dances/Social/Cultural
gatherings; Intergenerational programs; Pet
therapy.

Regency Place of Greenwood
1400 W Main St, Greenwood, IN 46143
(317) 888-4948
Admin Karen F Exline. *Dir of Nursing*
Charlotte Wilkens. *Medical Dir* Constance
VanValer MD.
Licensure Skilled care; Intermediate care;
Alzheimer's care. *Beds* SNF 128; ICF 77;
Alzheimer's care 26. *Private Pay Patients*
40%. *Certified* Medicaid; Medicare.
Owner Proprietary corp (Lucas Corp).
Facilities Dining room; Physical therapy
room; Activities room; Crafts room; Barber/
Beauty shop.
Activities Arts & crafts; Cards; Games;
Reading groups; Prayer groups; Movies;
Shopping trips; Dances/Social/Cultural
gatherings; Intergenerational programs; Pet
therapy.

Hammond

Hammond Nursing Home
1402 E 173rd St, Hammond, IN 46324
(219) 844-4534
Admin Thelma Zabinski.
Licensure Intermediate care. *Beds* ICF 40.
Certified Medicaid.
Owner Proprietary corp (Beverly Enterprises).

Hanover

Hanover Nursing Center
RR 2, Hanover, IN 47243
(812) 866-2625
Admin Bob Dunn.
Licensure Skilled care; Intermediate care. *Beds*
SNF 40; ICF 111. *Certified* Medicaid.
Owner Proprietary corp (Forum Group).

Hartford City

Hartford City Community Care Center
715 N Mill St, Hartford City, IN 47348
(317) 348-2273
Admin Kenneth W Seiffertt. *Dir of Nursing*
Roxie Bole RN. *Medical Dir* Dr Thomas
Lee.
Licensure Intermediate care. *Beds* ICF 80.
Private Pay Patients 22%. *Certified*
Medicaid.
Owner Proprietary corp (Community Care
Centers Inc).
Admissions Requirements Medical
examination.
Staff RNs; LPNs; Nurses' aides; Activities
coordinators.
Facilities Dining room; Activities room;
Chapel; Laundry room; Barber/Beauty shop.
Activities Arts & crafts; Cards; Games;
Reading groups; Prayer groups; Movies;
Shopping trips.

Miller's Merry Manor Inc
0548 S 100 W, Hartford City, IN 47348
(317) 348-1072
Admin Robert D Lau.
Medical Dir Roger Frazier DO.
Licensure Intermediate care. *Beds* ICF 86.
Certified Medicaid.
Owner Proprietary corp (Millers Merry
Manor).
Admissions Requirements Minimum age 18;
Medical examination; Physician's request.
Staff RNs 3 (ft); LPNs 2 (ft), 2 (pt); Nurses'
aides 13 (ft), 3 (pt); Activities coordinators 1
(ft); Dietitians 1 (pt).
Facilities Dining room; Activities room;
Chapel; Laundry room; Barber/Beauty shop.
Activities Arts & crafts; Games; Reading
groups; Prayer groups; Movies; Dances/
Social/Cultural gatherings.

Highland

Highland Nursing Home
9630 5th St, Highland, IN 46322
(219) 924-6953
Admin Richard E Meriwether MSNA. *Dir of
Nursing* Peggy Kresich. *Medical Dir* Mona
Stern MD.
Licensure Intermediate care. *Beds* ICF 40.
Private Pay Patients 33%. *Certified*
Medicaid.
Owner Proprietary corp (Beverly Enterprises).
Admissions Requirements Medical
examination; Physician's request.
Staff Physicians 1 (pt); RNs 1 (pt); LPNs 6
(ft); Nurses' aides 12 (ft), 6 (pt); Activities
coordinators 1 (pt); Dietitians 1 (pt).
Languages Spanish.
Facilities Dining room; Activities room;
Laundry room.
Activities Arts & crafts; Cards; Games;
Reading groups; Prayer groups; Movies;
Shopping trips; Dances/Social/Cultural
gatherings; Intergenerational programs.

Hobart

Miller's Merry Manor Inc
2901 W 37th Ave, Hobart, IN 46342
(219) 942-2170
Admin Gary A Brubaker. *Dir of Nursing*
Sandra Jones RN. *Medical Dir* R Billena
MD.
Licensure Skilled care; Intermediate care. *Beds*
SNF 129; ICF 31. *Certified* Medicaid;
Medicare.
Owner Proprietary corp (Millers Merry
Manor).
Admissions Requirements Minimum age 18;
Medical examination; Physician's request.
Staff Physicians 1 (pt); RNs 10 (ft), 2 (pt);
LPNs 3 (ft), 9 (pt); Nurses' aides 29 (ft), 29
(pt); Physical therapists 1 (pt); Occupational
therapists 1 (pt); Speech therapists 1 (pt);

Activities coordinators 2 (ft), 1 (pt);
Dietitians 1 (pt); Ophthalmologists 1 (pt);
Podiatrists 1 (pt); Dentists 1 (pt);
Medication aides 8 (ft), 3 (pt).
Languages Spanish.
Facilities Dining room; Physical therapy
room; Activities room; Crafts room; Laundry
room; Barber/Beauty shop; 2 Resident
lounges.
Activities Arts & crafts; Cards; Games;
Reading groups; Prayer groups; Movies;
Shopping trips; Dances/Social/Cultural
gatherings; Recreational outings; Holiday
celebrations.

Sebo Heritage Manor Nursing Home
4410 W 49th Ave, Hobart, IN 46342
(219) 942-1507
Admin Justine Truchan.
Licensure Intermediate care. *Beds* ICF 54.
Certified Medicaid.
Owner Proprietary corp.

Hope

Ken-Joy Convalescent Center
133 Maple St, Hope, IN 47246
(812) 546-4814
Admin Jan Barger. *Dir of Nursing* Shirley
Thayer. *Medical Dir* Dr William Ryan.
Licensure Intermediate care. *Beds* ICF 34.
Private Pay Patients 12%. *Certified*
Medicaid.
Owner Proprietary corp (First Nepenthe
Partners).
Admissions Requirements Physician's request.
Staff RNs 1 (ft); LPNs 4 (ft), 2 (pt); Nurses'
aides 15 (ft); Recreational therapists 1 (ft);
Activities coordinators 1 (ft); Dietitians 1
(ft); Podiatrists 1 (pt).
Facilities Dining room; Activities room;
Laundry room.
Activities Arts & crafts; Cards; Games;
Reading groups; Prayer groups; Movies;
Shopping trips; Dances/Social/Cultural
gatherings; Intergenerational programs; Pet
therapy.

Miller's Merry Manor
PO Box 8, 7440 N, 825 E, Hope, IN 47246
(812) 546-4416
Admin Martin D Allgin Jr. *Dir of Nursing*
Angie Stam BSN. *Medical Dir* Forest
Daugherty MD.
Licensure Intermediate care. *Beds* ICF 74.
Private Pay Patients 26%.
Owner Proprietary corp (Caremet Inc).
Admissions Requirements Medical
examination; Physician's request.
Staff Physicians 1 (pt); RNs 2 (ft), 1 (pt);
LPNs 5 (ft), 5 (pt); Nurses' aides 26 (ft), 2
(pt); Activities coordinators 1 (ft), 1 (pt);
Dietitians 1 (pt).
Facilities Dining room; Activities room;
Crafts room; Laundry room; Barber/Beauty
shop.
Activities Arts & crafts; Cards; Games;
Reading groups; Prayer groups; Movies;
Shopping trips; Dances/Social/Cultural
gatherings; Intergenerational programs; Pet
therapy.

Huntingburg

Huntingburg Convalescent Center Inc
1712 Leland Dr, Huntingburg, IN 47542
(812) 683-4090
Admin Carl Ahrens. *Dir of Nursing* Margie
Bell. *Medical Dir* J G Ellison MD.
Licensure Skilled care; Intermediate care. *Beds*
SNF 38; ICF 114. *Certified* Medicaid;
Medicare.
Owner Proprietary corp.
Admissions Requirements Minimum age 18.
Staff Physicians 1 (pt); RNs 4 (ft), 6 (pt);
LPNs 2 (ft), 6 (pt); Nurses' aides 32 (pt);
Physical therapists 2 (pt); Reality therapists

1 (pt); Recreational therapists 1 (ft);
Occupational therapists 1 (pt); Speech
therapists 1 (pt); Activities coordinators 2
(ft); Dietitians 1 (pt); Ophthalmologists 1
(pt).
Facilities Dining room; Physical therapy
room; Activities room; Chapel; Crafts room;
Laundry room; Barber/Beauty shop.
Activities Arts & crafts; Cards; Games;
Reading groups; Prayer groups; Movies;
Shopping trips; Dances/Social/Cultural
gatherings.

Unicare Health Facility of Huntingburg
530 4th St, Huntingburg, IN 47542
(812) 683-2535
Admin Joe Junod Jr.
Medical Dir Theodore A Waflart.
Licensure Skilled care; Intermediate care. *Beds*
SNF 27; ICF 55. *Certified* Medicaid.
Owner Proprietary corp (Unicare).
Admissions Requirements Minimum age 18;
Medical examination; Physician's request.
Staff Physicians 1 (ft), 5 (pt); RNs 3 (ft);
LPNs 5 (pt); Nurses' aides 9 (ft), 3 (pt);
Physical therapists 2 (pt); Occupational
therapists 2 (pt); Activities coordinators 1
(ft); Dietitians 1 (ft); Podiatrists 1 (ft);
Dentists 1 (ft).
Facilities Dining room; Physical therapy
room; Activities room; Chapel; Crafts room;
Laundry room; Barber/Beauty shop; Library;
Meeting rooms.
Activities Arts & crafts; Cards; Games;
Reading groups; Prayer groups; Movies;
Shopping trips; Dances/Social/Cultural
gatherings.

Huntington

Miller's Merry Manor Inc
1500 Grant St, Huntington, IN 46750
(219) 356-5713
Admin Greg Spaulding.
Medical Dir S E Cape MD.
Licensure Skilled care; Intermediate care. *Beds*
SNF 37; ICF 132. *Certified* Medicaid;
Medicare.
Owner Proprietary corp (Millers Merry
Manor).
Admissions Requirements Minimum age 18.
Staff Physicians 12 (pt); RNs 10 (ft), 4 (pt);
LPNs 5 (ft), 4 (pt); Nurses' aides 38 (ft), 16
(pt); Occupational therapists 1 (pt);
Activities coordinators 2 (ft); Dietitians 1
(ft).
Facilities Dining room; Physical therapy
room; Activities room; Crafts room; Laundry
room; Barber/Beauty shop.
Activities Arts & crafts; Cards; Games;
Reading groups; Prayer groups; Movies;
Shopping trips; Dances/Social/Cultural
gatherings.

Norwood Nursing Center
3720 N Norwood Rd, Huntington, IN 46750
(219) 356-1252
Admin Suzanne Whitted.
Medical Dir Dr Richard Blair.
Licensure Intermediate care; Comprehensive
care. *Beds* ICF 60; Comprehensive car 36.
Certified Medicaid.
Owner Proprietary corp (Shive Nursing
Centers).
Staff RNs 2 (ft), 2 (pt); LPNs 3 (ft), 3 (pt);
Nurses' aides 15 (ft), 23 (pt); Physical
therapists 1 (pt); Activities coordinators 1
(ft); Dietitians 1 (pt); Podiatrists 1 (pt);
Dentists 1 (pt).
Facilities Dining room; Physical therapy
room; Activities room; Laundry room;
Barber/Beauty shop.
Activities Arts & crafts; Cards; Games;
Reading groups; Prayer groups; Movies;
Shopping trips; Dances/Social/Cultural
gatherings.

Indianapolis

Alpha Home
1910 N Senate Ave, Indianapolis, IN 46202
(317) 923-1518
Admin Sherlee Butler.
Licensure Intermediate care. *Beds* ICF 86.
  Certified Medicaid.
Owner Proprietary corp.

Altenheim Community United Church Homes Inc
3525 E Hanna Ave, Indianapolis, IN 46227
(317) 788-4261
Admin William Boothe.
Licensure Skilled care; Intermediate care;
  Residential care. *Beds* SNF 25; ICF 47;
  Residential care 104.

American Village
2026 E 54th St, Indianapolis, IN 46220
(317) 253-6950
Admin Julianne Robinson. *Dir of Nursing*
  Jann Beery RN. *Medical Dir* Dr Robert
  Rudicell.
Licensure Skilled care; Intermediate care;
  Assisted living. *Beds* SNF 28; ICF 76;
  Assisted living 52. *Certified* Medicaid;
  Medicare.
Owner Proprietary corp (CommuniCare Inc).
Admissions Requirements Minimum age 18;
  Medical examination.
Staff Physicians (contracted); RNs 2 (ft), 1
  (pt); LPNs 6 (ft), 2 (pt); Nurses' aides 14
  (ft), 5 (pt); Physical therapists (contracted);
  Recreational therapists 1 (ft); Occupational
  therapists (contracted); Speech therapists
  (contracted); Dietitians 1 (ft);
  Ophthalmologists (contracted); Podiatrists
  (contracted); Audiologists (contracted).
Facilities Dining room; Physical therapy
  room; Activities room; Chapel; Crafts room;
  Laundry room; Barber/Beauty shop; Family
  rooms.
Activities Arts & crafts; Cards; Games;
  Reading groups; Prayer groups; Movies;
  Shopping trips; Dances/Social/Cultural
  gatherings; Intergenerational programs; Pet
  therapy; Cooking class.

Americana Healthcare Center—Indianapolis
5600 E 16th St, Indianapolis, IN 46218
(317) 356-0911
Admin Jeff A Cooper.
Licensure Skilled care; Intermediate care. *Beds*
  SNF 61; ICF 59. *Certified* Medicaid;
  Medicare.
Owner Proprietary corp (Manor Care).

Americana Healthcare Center—Indianapolis Midtown
2010 N Capitol Ave, Indianapolis, IN 46202
(317) 924-5821
Admin Christine Martin.
Licensure Skilled care; Intermediate care. *Beds*
  SNF 102; ICF 51. *Certified* Medicaid;
  Medicare.
Owner Proprietary corp (Manor Care).
Admissions Requirements Minimum age 18;
  Medical examination; Physician's request.
Facilities Dining room; Physical therapy
  room; Activities room; Barber/Beauty shop;
  Library.
Activities Arts & crafts; Cards; Games;
  Reading groups; Prayer groups; Movies;
  Shopping trips.

Americana Healthcare Center—Indianapolis North
8350 Naab Rd, Indianapolis, IN 46260
(317) 872-1110
Admin Gerrald McGowan.
Licensure Skilled care; Intermediate care;
  Comprehensive care. *Beds* SNF 94; ICF 79;
  Comprehensive care 54. *Certified* Medicaid;
  Medicare.
Owner Proprietary corp (Manor Care).

Americana Healthcare Center South
8549 S Madison Ave, Indianapolis, IN 46227-0779
(317) 881-9164
Admin Everett Rickert.
Licensure Skilled care; Intermediate care. *Beds*
  SNF 60; ICF 60.
Owner Proprietary corp (Manor Care).

Autumn Care of Castleton
7630 E 86th St, Indianapolis, IN 46256-9263
(317) 845-0032
Admin James C Ruthrauff.
Licensure Skilled care; Intermediate care. *Beds*
  SNF 60; ICF 60.

Barton House
505 N Delaware St, Indianapolis, IN 46204
(317) 634-9382
Admin Audrey Bonner.
Licensure Intermediate care. *Beds* ICF 120.
  Certified Medicaid.
Owner Proprietary corp.

Bethany Village Nursing Home
3518 Shelby St, Indianapolis, IN 46227
(317) 783-4042
Admin Stephen Harris.
Licensure Skilled care; Intermediate care. *Beds*
  SNF 50; ICF 50. *Certified* Medicaid.
Owner Proprietary corp.

Broad Ripple Nursing Home
6127 N College Ave, Indianapolis, IN 46220
(317) 257-8392
Admin John Niemeyer. *Dir of Nursing* Doris
  Koebbe. *Medical Dir* Robert Nation MD.
Licensure Intermediate care. *Beds* ICF 50.
  Private Pay Patients 56%. *Certified*
  Medicaid.
Owner Proprietary corp (Beverly Enterprises).
Admissions Requirements Minimum age 21;
  Medical examination.
Staff Physicians 1 (pt); RNs 1 (ft); LPNs 3
  (ft), 3 (pt); Nurses' aides 9 (ft), 6 (pt);
  Occupational therapists (consultant); Speech
  therapists (consultant); Activities
  coordinators (consultant); Dietitians
  (consultant); Ophthalmologists (consultant);
  Podiatrists (consultant); Audiologists
  (consultant).
Facilities Dining room; Activities room;
  Laundry room; Barber/Beauty shop.
Activities Arts & crafts; Cards; Games;
  Reading groups; Prayer groups; Movies;
  Shopping trips; Dances/Social/Cultural
  gatherings.

Brookview Manor
7145 E 21st St, Indianapolis, IN 46219
(317) 356-0977
Admin Carolyn Kindler.
Medical Dir Dr Fred Hendricks.
Licensure Skilled care; Intermediate care. *Beds*
  SNF 50; ICF 94. *Certified* Medicaid;
  Medicare.
Owner Proprietary corp (Beverly Enterprises).
Admissions Requirements Minimum age 18;
  Medical examination.
Staff Physicians 1 (ft); RNs 7 (ft); LPNs 30
  (ft); Nurses' aides 99 (ft); Physical therapists
  1 (ft), 3 (pt); Reality therapists 1 (ft);
  Recreational therapists 1 (ft); Occupational
  therapists 2 (ft); Speech therapists 1 (ft);
  Activities coordinators 2 (ft); Dietitians 1
  (ft), 1 (pt); Ophthalmologists 1 (pt);
  Podiatrists 1 (pt).
Facilities Dining room; Physical therapy
  room; Activities room; Chapel; Crafts room;
  Laundry room; Barber/Beauty shop; Library.
Activities Arts & crafts; Cards; Games;
  Reading groups; Prayer groups; Movies;
  Shopping trips; Dances/Social/Cultural
  gatherings.

Cambridge Health Care Center
8530 Township Line Rd, Indianapolis, IN
46260
(317) 876-9955

Admin Karen Talbot.
Licensure Comprehensive care. *Beds*
  Comprehensive care 143.

Capital Care Healthcare Center
2115 N Central Ave, Indianapolis, IN 46202
(317) 923-9844
Admin Donna J Byrd. *Dir of Nursing* Sue
  Ganguly. *Medical Dir* Melvin Baird MD.
Licensure Intermediate care. *Beds* ICF 60.
  Private Pay Patients 1%. *Certified* Medicaid.
Owner Proprietary corp (Cloverleaf Healthcare
  Services).
Admissions Requirements Minimum age 18;
  Medical examination; Physician's request.
Staff RNs 1 (ft); LPNs 5 (ft); Nurses' aides 13
  (ft), 2 (pt); Activities coordinators 1 (ft);
  Dietitians 1 (ft).
Facilities Dining room; Activities room;
  Laundry room; Barber/Beauty shop.
Activities Arts & crafts; Cards; Games;
  Reading groups; Prayer groups; Movies;
  Shopping trips; Dances/Social/Cultural
  gatherings; Intergenerational programs; Pet
  therapy; Church group activities.

Cedar Crest Health Center Inc
1924 Wellesley Blvd, Indianapolis, IN 46219
(317) 353-6270
Admin Diane Flack.
Medical Dir Roudolph Rouhana MD.
Licensure Skilled care; Intermediate care. *Beds*
  SNF 70; ICF 70. *Certified* Medicaid;
  Medicare.
Owner Proprietary corp.
Admissions Requirements Minimum age 18;
  Medical examination; Physician's request.
Staff RNs 5 (ft), 1 (pt); LPNs 15 (ft), 5 (pt);
  Nurses' aides 47 (ft), 4 (pt); Physical
  therapists 1 (ft); Recreational therapists 1
  (ft); Occupational therapists 1 (pt); Speech
  therapists 1 (pt); Activities coordinators 2
  (ft); Dietitians 1 (pt); Podiatrists 1 (pt);
  Audiologists 1 (pt); Dentists 1 (pt).
Facilities Dining room; Physical therapy
  room; Activities room; Chapel; Crafts room;
  Barber/Beauty shop; Library.
Activities Arts & crafts; Cards; Games;
  Reading groups; Prayer groups; Movies;
  Shopping trips; Dances/Social/Cultural
  gatherings.

Central Healthcare Center
55 W 33rd St, Indianapolis, IN 46208
(317) 927-2461
Admin Karyn Price.
Licensure Intermediate care. *Beds* ICF 88.
  Certified Medicaid; Medicare.
Owner Proprietary corp (ARA).
Admissions Requirements Minimum age 18;
  Medical examination.
Facilities Dining room; Physical therapy
  room; Activities room; Barber/Beauty shop.
Activities Arts & crafts; Cards; Games;
  Reading groups; Prayer groups; Movies;
  Shopping trips; Dances/Social/Cultural
  gatherings.

Churchman Manor
2860 Churchman Ave, Indianapolis, IN 46203
(317) 787-3451
Admin Thomas E Dobbins.
Licensure Skilled care; Intermediate care. *Beds*
  SNF 78; ICF 40. *Certified* Medicaid;
  Medicare.
Owner Proprietary corp (Beverly Enterprises).

Community Healthcare of Indianapolis
PO Box 88356, Indianapolis, IN 46203
(317) 926-0254
Admin Kathleen N Rynard.
Licensure Skilled care; Intermediate care. *Beds*
  SNF 35; ICF 35. *Certified* Medicaid.
Owner Proprietary corp.

Continental Convalescent Center
344 S Ritter Ave, Indianapolis, IN 46219
(317) 359-5515
Admin Jill S Johnston.

Licensure Skilled care. *Beds* SNF 54. *Certified* Medicaid.
Owner Proprietary corp (Beverly Enterprises).

Country Trace Healthcare Center
2140 W 86th St, Indianapolis, IN 46260
(317) 872-7211
Admin Karen E Spitznagel.
Licensure Skilled care; Intermediate care. *Beds* SNF 105; ICF 92. *Certified* Medicaid; Medicare.
Owner Proprietary corp (ARA).

Coventry Manor
8400 Clear Vista Dr, Indianapolis, IN 46256
(317) 845-0464
Admin Ruth E Hanlon. *Dir of Nursing* Marilyn Price RN. *Medical Dir* Dr David Pletzer.
Licensure Skilled care; Intermediate care; Retirement. *Beds* SNF 68; ICF 64. *Certified* Medicaid; Medicare.
Owner Proprietary corp (Millers Merry Manor).
Admissions Requirements Medical examination; Physician's request.
Facilities Dining room; Physical therapy room; Activities room; Chapel; Crafts room; Laundry room; Barber/Beauty shop; Library.
Activities Arts & crafts; Cards; Games; Reading groups; Prayer groups; Movies; Shopping trips; Dances/Social/Cultural gatherings; Monthly family nights.

Crestview Health Care Facility
1118 E 46th St, Indianapolis, IN 46205
(317) 257-1571
Admin Anne E Johnson.
Licensure Intermediate care. *Beds* ICF 50. *Certified* Medicaid.
Owner Proprietary corp.

Decatur Nursing & Rehabilitation Center
4851 Tincher Rd, Indianapolis, IN 46241
(317) 856-4851
Admin Debbie Williams, Senior Admin. *Dir of Nursing* Penny Dyer RN. *Medical Dir* Strobes MD.
Licensure Skilled care; Intermediate care. *Beds* SNF 19; ICF 67. *Private Pay Patients* 20%. *Certified* Medicaid; Medicare.
Owner Proprietary corp (Harborside Healthcare).
Admissions Requirements Medical examination.
Staff RNs 3 (ft), 1 (pt); LPNs 9 (ft), 1 (pt); Nurses' aides 30 (ft), 15 (pt); Physical therapists; Activities coordinators 1 (ft), 1 (pt); Dietitians.
Facilities Dining room; Physical therapy room; Activities room; Chapel; Laundry room; Barber/Beauty shop.
Activities Arts & crafts; Cards; Games; Reading groups; Prayer groups; Movies; Shopping trips; Dances/Social/Cultural gatherings; Intergenerational programs; Pet therapy.

Del Mar Nursing Home Inc
709 S Lynhurst Dr, Indianapolis, IN 46241
(317) 243-3109
Admin Margaret Ann Cronin.
Medical Dir Robert Dwyer.
Licensure Intermediate care. *Beds* ICF 40. *Certified* Medicaid.
Owner Proprietary corp (Beverly Enterprises).
Admissions Requirements Minimum age 18; Medical examination; Physician's request.
Staff Physicians; RNs; LPNs 5 (ft); Activities coordinators 1 (ft); Dietitians 1 (pt); Ophthalmologists 1 (pt); Podiatrists 1 (pt); Dentists 1 (pt).
Facilities Dining room; Activities room; Laundry room; Barber/Beauty shop.
Activities Arts & crafts; Cards; Games; Reading groups; Prayer groups; Movies; Shopping trips; Dances/Social/Cultural gatherings.

Delaware Health Care Facility
1910 N Delaware, Indianapolis, IN 46202
(317) 925-2393
Admin Gary A Loveless. *Dir of Nursing* Don Fugett. *Medical Dir* Dr Robert Lebow.
Licensure Intermediate care; Alzheimer's care. *Beds* ICF 42. *Private Pay Patients* 5%. *Certified* Medicaid.
Owner Proprietary corp (Sycamore Enterprises).
Admissions Requirements Minimum age 18; Medical examination; Physician's request.
Staff LPNs 4 (ft); Nurses' aides 10 (ft), 2 (pt); Activities coordinators 1 (pt).
Facilities Dining room; Laundry room; Large yard.
Activities Arts & crafts; Games; Reading groups; Movies; Shopping trips; Dances/Social/Cultural gatherings; Intergenerational programs.

Dove Tree Nursing Home
118 N Delaware, Indianapolis, IN 46204
(219) 485-8157
Admin Ron McSorley. *Dir of Nursing* Pauline Forte RN.
Licensure Intermediate care. *Beds* ICF 100. *Certified* Medicaid.
Owner Proprietary corp.
Admissions Requirements Medical examination; Physician's request.
Staff Physicians; RNs; LPNs; Nurses' aides; Activities coordinators; Dietitians; Ophthalmologists 1 (pt).
Facilities Dining room; Activities room; Chapel; Crafts room; Laundry room; Barber/Beauty shop; Privacy room for families.
Activities Arts & crafts; Cards; Games; Reading groups; Prayer groups; Movies; Shopping trips; Dances/Social/Cultural gatherings; Ceramic classes.

Eagle Valley Healthcare Center
3017 Valley Farms Rd, Indianapolis, IN 46224
(317) 293-2555
Admin Sherry Simons. *Dir of Nursing* Pat Cleavenger. *Medical Dir* Dr Carl Otten.
Licensure Intermediate care. *Beds* ICF 120. *Certified* Medicaid; Medicare.
Owner Proprietary corp (ARA Living Centers).
Admissions Requirements Minimum age 18; Medical examination; Physician's request.
Staff Physicians 1 (ft); RNs 5 (ft); LPNs 7 (ft); Nurses' aides 30 (ft); Physical therapists 1 (ft); Occupational therapists 1 (ft); Speech therapists 1 (ft); Activities coordinators 2 (ft); Dietitians 1 (ft); QMRPs 1 (ft), 10 (pt).
Facilities Dining room; Physical therapy room; Activities room; Crafts room; Laundry room; Barber/Beauty shop; Smoking lounge; Outside fenced patio; Gazebo.
Activities Arts & crafts; Cards; Games; Reading groups; Prayer groups; Movies; Shopping trips; Dances/Social/Cultural gatherings; Cooking.

Eastside Healthcare Center
1302 N Lesley Ave, Indianapolis, IN 46219
(317) 353-8061
Admin Kristina Simpson.
Medical Dir Linda Stropes MD.
Licensure Skilled care; Intermediate care. *Beds* SNF 89; ICF 90. *Certified* Medicaid; Medicare.
Owner Proprietary corp (ARA).
Admissions Requirements Minimum age 18.
Staff RNs 5 (ft); LPNs 10 (ft); Nurses' aides 48 (ft), 10 (pt); Physical therapists 1 (ft); Occupational therapists 1 (ft); Speech therapists 1 (ft); Activities coordinators 2 (ft); Dietitians 1 (ft); Podiatrists 1 (ft); Dentists 1 (ft).
Facilities Dining room; Physical therapy room; Activities room; Crafts room; Laundry room; Barber/Beauty shop; Library.

Activities Arts & crafts; Cards; Games; Reading groups; Prayer groups; Movies; Shopping trips; Dances/Social/Cultural gatherings; Reality orientation; Exercises.

Emerson Nursing Home
3420 N Emerson Ave, Indianapolis, IN 46218
(317) 546-9567
Admin Vincent B Farrell.
Medical Dir Dr Linda Stropes.
Licensure Intermediate care. *Beds* ICF 40. *Private Pay Patients* 1%. *Certified* Medicaid.
Owner Proprietary corp (Beverly Enterprises).
Staff RNs 1 (ft); LPNs 4 (ft), 2 (pt); Nurses' aides 10 (ft), 3 (pt); Physical therapists (contracted); Activities coordinators 1 (ft); Dietitians.
Facilities Dining room; Activities room; Laundry room; Barber/Beauty shop.
Activities Arts & crafts; Cards; Games; Reading groups; Prayer groups; Movies; Shopping trips; Dances/Social/Cultural gatherings; Intergenerational programs; Pet therapy.

Forum at the Crossing
8505 Woodfield Crossing Blvd, Indianapolis, IN 46240
(317) 257-7406
Admin James Thurston.
Licensure Skilled care; Intermediate care; Residential care. *Beds* SNF 30; ICF 30; Residential care 14.

Fountainview Place
5353 E Raymond, Indianapolis, IN 46203
(317) 353-8015
Admin David A Moberg. *Dir of Nursing* Patricia Sanders RN. *Medical Dir* John Karedes MD.
Licensure Skilled care; Intermediate care; Alzheimer's care. *Beds* SNF 95; ICF 128. *Private Pay Patients* 15%. *Certified* Medicaid; Medicare.
Owner Proprietary corp (Beverly Enterprises).
Admissions Requirements Minimum age 18; Medical examination; Physician's request.
Facilities Dining room; Physical therapy room; Activities room; Chapel; Crafts room; Laundry room; Barber/Beauty shop; Library.
Activities Arts & crafts; Cards; Games; Reading groups; Prayer groups; Movies; Shopping trips; Dances/Social/Cultural gatherings; Intergenerational programs; Pet therapy.

Frame House Manor
1316 N Tibbs, Indianapolis, IN 46222
(317) 634-8330
Admin David L McCarroll.
Licensure Intermediate care. *Beds* ICF 89. *Certified* Medicaid.
Owner Proprietary corp.

Frame Nursing Home Inc
373 N Holmes Ave, Indianapolis, IN 46222
(317) 634-7846
Admin Mark R McCarroll.
Licensure Intermediate care. *Beds* ICF 89. *Certified* Medicaid.
Owner Proprietary corp.
Admissions Requirements Medical examination; Physician's request.
Staff Physicians 1 (pt); RNs 1 (ft); LPNs 5 (ft); Nurses' aides 45 (ft); Physical therapists 1 (pt); Occupational therapists 1 (pt); Activities coordinators 2 (ft); Dietitians 1 (pt); Ophthalmologists 1 (pt); Podiatrists 1 (pt).
Facilities Dining room; Activities room; Crafts room; Laundry room; Barber/Beauty shop.
Activities Arts & crafts; Cards; Games; Reading groups; Prayer groups; Movies; Shopping trips; Dances/Social/Cultural gatherings; Camping trips; Courtesy van.

Garfield Park Health Facility
3895 S Keystone Ave, Indianapolis, IN 46227-3540
(317) 787-5364
Admin Diane M Gooden. *Dir of Nursing* Joan Bader. *Medical Dir* Thomas Spolyar MD.
Licensure Intermediate care. *Beds* ICF 81. *Private Pay Patients* 60%. *Certified* Medicaid.
Owner Proprietary corp (Oakwood Corp).
Admissions Requirements Medical examination; Physician's request.
Staff RNs 1 (ft); LPNs 6 (ft), 1 (pt); Nurses' aides 24 (ft); Recreational therapists (contracted); Activities coordinators 1 (ft), 1 (pt); Dietitians 1 (ft); Podiatrists.
Facilities Dining room; Physical therapy room; Activities room; Crafts room; Laundry room; Barber/Beauty shop; Library.
Activities Arts & crafts; Cards; Games; Reading groups; Prayer groups; Movies; Shopping trips; Dances/Social/Cultural gatherings; Intergenerational programs; Pet therapy.

Greenbriar Manor
8181 Harcourt Rd, Indianapolis, IN 46260
(317) 872-7261
Admin Douglas Singh.
Licensure Skilled care; Intermediate care. *Beds* SNF 74; ICF 76. *Certified* Medicaid; Medicare.
Owner Proprietary corp (Beverly Enterprises).

Anthony Hall Nursing Home
505 N Delaware St, Indianapolis, IN 46204-1503
(317) 925-7917
Admin Warren Hotte. *Dir of Nursing* Carolyn Scalf. *Medical Dir* Dan Hurley MD.
Licensure Intermediate care. *Beds* ICF 23. *Certified* Medicaid.
Owner Proprietary corp.
Staff RNs 1 (ft); LPNs 1 (ft), 2 (pt); Nurses' aides 10 (ft); Occupational therapists 1 (pt); Dietitians 1 (pt); Ophthalmologists 1 (pt); Dentists 1 (pt).
Facilities Dining room; Activities room.
Activities Arts & crafts; Cards; Games; Reading groups; Prayer groups; Movies; Shopping trips; Dances/Social/Cultural gatherings.

Hallmark Manor Nursing Home
6851 E 10th St, Indianapolis, IN 46219
(317) 357-5373
Admin Julia Nickels.
Licensure Intermediate care. *Beds* ICF 62.
Owner Proprietary corp (Beverly Enterprises).

Hoosier Village
5300 W 96th St, Indianapolis, IN 46268
(317) 873-3349
Admin Hilda Johnson.
Licensure Comprehensive care; Residential care. *Beds* Comprehensive care 70; Residential 112.
Owner Nonprofit organization/foundation (Baptist Home).
Admissions Requirements Medical examination.
Staff RNs 6 (ft), 1 (pt); LPNs 2 (ft), 1 (pt); Nurses' aides 30 (ft), 11 (pt); Physical therapists 1 (pt); Speech therapists 1 (pt); Podiatrists 1 (pt).
Facilities Dining room; Activities room; Chapel; Crafts room; Laundry room; Barber/Beauty shop; Library.
Activities Arts & crafts; Cards; Games; Reading groups; Prayer groups; Movies; Shopping trips; Dances/Social/Cultural gatherings.

Hooverwood
7001 Hoover Rd, Indianapolis, IN 46260
(317) 251-2261, 251-2266 FAX
Admin Jeffrey F Stern. *Dir of Nursing* Barbara Horner. *Medical Dir* Patrick Healey.
Licensure Skilled care; Intermediate care; Day care; Alzheimer's care. *Beds* SNF 93; ICF 70. *Private Pay Patients* 36%. *Certified* Medicaid; Medicare.
Owner Nonprofit organization/foundation.
Admissions Requirements Minimum age 65.
Staff Physicians 2 (pt); RNs 7 (ft), 10 (pt); LPNs 6 (ft), 2 (pt); Nurses' aides 30 (ft), 30 (pt); Physical therapists 1 (ft); Recreational therapists 2 (ft), 1 (pt); Occupational therapists 1 (pt); Speech therapists 1 (ft); Activities coordinators 2 (ft), 1 (pt); Dietitians 1 (ft).
Languages German.
Affiliation Jewish.
Facilities Dining room; Physical therapy room; Activities room; Chapel; Crafts room; Laundry room; Barber/Beauty shop; Library.
Activities Arts & crafts; Cards; Games; Reading groups; Prayer groups; Movies; Shopping trips; Dances/Social/Cultural gatherings; Intergenerational programs; Pet therapy; Recreational therapy; Sheltered workshop.

Houston Village Inc
PO Box 229043, 5055 W 52nd St, Indianapolis, IN 46222
(317) 293-8823
Admin Esther Houston. *Dir of Nursing* Sara Habegger. *Medical Dir* Dr Armstrong, Dr Karimi, Dr Bojrab.
Licensure Intermediate care. *Beds* ICF 39. *Certified* Medicaid.
Owner Proprietary corp.
Staff Physicians 3 (pt); LPNs 4 (ft), 2 (pt); Nurses' aides 4 (ft), 3 (pt).
Facilities Dining room; Activities room; Barber/Beauty shop.
Activities Arts & crafts; Cards; Games; Reading groups; Prayer groups; Movies; Shopping trips.

Indianapolis Retirement Home Inc
1731 N Capitol Ave, Indianapolis, IN 46202
(317) 924-5830
Admin Eileene Stevens HFA. *Dir of Nursing* Mary Ayers RN. *Medical Dir* Dr Steve Hartman.
Licensure Intermediate care; Independent retirement living. *Beds* ICF 22; Independent retirement living 33. *Certified* Medicaid.
Owner Nonprofit corp.
Admissions Requirements Minimum age 65; Females only or married couples; Medical examination.
Staff Physicians 1 (pt); RNs 1 (ft); LPNs 6 (ft), 2 (pt); Nurses' aides 6 (ft), 6 (pt); Activities coordinators 1 (ft); Dietitians 1 (pt).
Facilities Dining room; Activities room; Chapel; Crafts room; Laundry room; Barber/Beauty shop; Library; Solarium.
Activities Arts & crafts; Cards; Games; Reading groups; Prayer groups; Movies; Shopping trips; Dances/Social/Cultural gatherings; Intergenerational programs; Pet therapy.

Keystone Healthcare Center
2630 S Keystone Ave, Indianapolis, IN 46203
(317) 787-8951
Admin Jeanne List HFA. *Dir of Nursing* Jamie Ginder RN. *Medical Dir* Dr Thomas Spolyar.
Licensure Intermediate care. *Beds* ICF 55. *Private Pay Patients* 36%. *Certified* Medicaid.
Owner Privately owned (Central Healthcare Management).
Admissions Requirements Medical examination.
Staff Physicians 1 (pt); RNs 1 (ft); LPNs 2 (ft), 1 (pt); Nurses' aides 20 (ft), 3 (pt); Physical therapists; Activities coordinators 1 (ft); Dietitians 1 (pt); Podiatrists 1 (pt).

Facilities Dining room; Activities room; Laundry room; Barber/Beauty shop; Library.
Activities Arts & crafts; Cards; Games; Prayer groups; Movies; Dances/Social/Cultural gatherings; Intergenerational programs; Pet therapy.

Lakeview Manor Inc
45 Beachway Dr, Indianapolis, IN 46224
(317) 243-3721
Admin Thomas F Tyson Jr. *Dir of Nursing* Peggy Steinsberger RN. *Medical Dir* A Alan Fischer MD.
Licensure Skilled care; Intermediate care; Alzheimer's care. *Beds* SNF 43; ICF 144. *Certified* Medicaid; Medicare.
Owner Proprietary corp.
Admissions Requirements Minimum age 50; Medical examination.
Staff Physicians 13 (pt); RNs 7 (ft), 7 (pt); LPNs 11 (ft), 1 (pt); Nurses' aides 77 (ft), 7 (pt); Physical therapists 1 (ft), 1 (pt); Recreational therapists 1 (ft), 1 (pt); Occupational therapists 1 (pt); Speech therapists 1 (pt); Activities coordinators 1 (ft), 1 (pt); Dietitians 1 (pt); Ophthalmologists 1 (pt); Podiatrists 1 (pt); Dentists 1 (pt).
Facilities Dining room; Physical therapy room; Activities room; Chapel; Crafts room; Laundry room; Barber/Beauty shop; 5 Lounges; Outside courtyards.
Activities Arts & crafts; Cards; Games; Reading groups; Prayer groups; Movies; Shopping trips; Dances/Social/Cultural gatherings; Cooking; Ceramics; Exercise group; Wood working.

Lawrence Manor Nursing Home
8935 E 46th St, Indianapolis, IN 46226
(317) 898-1515
Admin Mark R Feeser.
Medical Dir Karen Dawes.
Licensure Intermediate care. *Beds* ICF 60. *Certified* Medicaid.
Owner Proprietary corp.
Staff RNs 1 (ft); LPNs 2 (ft); Nurses' aides 18 (ft), 7 (pt); Activities coordinators 1 (ft); Dietitians 1 (pt).
Facilities Dining room; Laundry room; Barber/Beauty shop.
Activities Arts & crafts; Games; Reading groups; Prayer groups; Shopping trips.

Lockerbie Healthcare Center
1629-33 N College Ave, Indianapolis, IN 46202
(317) 924-3239
Admin Roy L Anderson. *Dir of Nursing* Ellen Bidgood RN.
Licensure Intermediate care; Alzheimer's care. *Beds* ICF 79. *Certified* Medicaid.
Owner Proprietary corp.
Admissions Requirements Minimum age 21; Medical examination; Physician's request.
Staff Physicians 4 (pt); RNs 1 (ft); LPNs 8 (ft); Nurses' aides 30 (ft); Physical therapists 1 (pt); Recreational therapists 1 (pt); Occupational therapists 1 (pt); Speech therapists 1 (pt); Activities coordinators 1 (ft); Dietitians 1 (ft), 1 (pt); Ophthalmologists 1 (pt); Podiatrists 1 (pt); Dentists 1 (pt).
Facilities Dining room; Activities room; Crafts room; Laundry room; Barber/Beauty shop.
Activities Arts & crafts; Cards; Games; Reading groups; Prayer groups; Movies; Shopping trips; Dances/Social/Cultural gatherings; Outings.

Lynhurst Healthcare Center
5225 W Morris, Indianapolis, IN 46241
(317) 244-3251
Admin Linda Sisson. *Dir of Nursing* Shirley Arnold. *Medical Dir* Bryan Benedict.
Licensure Intermediate care. *Beds* ICF 41. *Private Pay Patients* 5%. *Certified* Medicaid.

Owner Proprietary corp.
Admissions Requirements Minimum age 18.
Staff RNs 1 (ft); LPNs 3 (ft); Nurses' aides 10 (ft); Activities coordinators 1 (ft); Dietitians 1 (pt).
Facilities Dining room; Activities room; Laundry room.
Activities Arts & crafts; Cards; Games; Prayer groups; Movies; Shopping trips; Dances/Social/Cultural gatherings; Intergenerational programs.

Mapleton Health Care Facility Inc
3650 Central Ave, Indianapolis, IN 46205
(317) 925-1453
Admin Tena Blakemora.
Medical Dir Dr Lord; Dr Lebow; Dr Strapts.
Licensure Intermediate care. *Beds* 52. *Certified* Medicaid.
Admissions Requirements Minimum age 18; Medical examination; Physician's request.
Staff Physicians 3 (ft); RNs 1 (ft); LPNs 3 (ft), 1 (pt); Nurses' aides 14 (ft); Activities coordinators 1 (ft); Dietitians 1 (pt); Ophthalmologists 1 (pt); Podiatrists 1 (pt); Dentists 1 (pt).
Facilities Dining room; Activities room; Laundry room; Barber/Beauty shop.
Activities Arts & crafts; Cards; Games; Reading groups; Prayer groups; Movies; Shopping trips; Dances/Social/Cultural gatherings.

Marion County Healthcare Center
11850 Brookville Rd, Indianapolis, IN 46239
(317) 862-6631
Admin Jack Musker. *Dir of Nursing* Char Price. *Medical Dir* Dan Hurley MD.
Licensure Skilled care; Intermediate care; Residential care; Alzheimer's care. *Beds* SNF 93; ICF 216; Residential 66. *Certified* Medicaid; Medicare.
Owner Publicly owned.
Admissions Requirements Minimum age 18; Medical examination; Physician's request.
Staff Physicians 3 (ft); RNs 5 (ft); LPNs 30 (ft); Nurses' aides 80 (ft); Physical therapists 1 (ft); Recreational therapists 1 (ft); Occupational therapists 1 (ft); Speech therapists 1 (pt); Activities coordinators 5 (ft); Dietitians 2 (ft); Ophthalmologists 1 (ft); Podiatrists 1 (ft).
Facilities Dining room; Physical therapy room; Activities room; Chapel; Crafts room; Laundry room; Barber/Beauty shop; Library.
Activities Arts & crafts; Cards; Games; Reading groups; Prayer groups; Movies; Shopping trips; Dances/Social/Cultural gatherings.

Marquette Manor
8140 Township Line Rd, Indianapolis, IN 46260
(317) 875-9700, 875-7504 FAX
Admin Carl L Wilkins. *Dir of Nursing* Ruth Leverett. *Medical Dir* Dr Thomas Lord.
Licensure Skilled care; Intermediate care; Retirement. *Beds* SNF 39; ICF 39. *Certified* Medicare.
Owner Nonprofit corp.
Admissions Requirements Minimum age 62 in residential; Medical examination; Physician's request.
Staff RNs; LPNs; Nurses' aides; Physical therapists; Recreational therapists; Occupational therapists; Speech therapists; Activities coordinators; Dietitians; Podiatrists; Audiologists.
Facilities Dining room; Physical therapy room; Activities room; Chapel; Crafts room; Laundry room; Barber/Beauty shop; Library; Wood shop.
Activities Arts & crafts; Cards; Games; Reading groups; Prayer groups; Movies; Shopping trips; Dances/Social/Cultural gatherings; Intergenerational programs; Pet therapy.

Maryfair Manor
3640 Central Ave, Indianapolis, IN 46205
(317) 925-2317
Admin Kathleen B Voll. *Dir of Nursing* Minnie Leath. *Medical Dir* Robert Lebow MD.
Licensure Skilled care; Intermediate care. *Beds* SNF 61; ICF 52. *Certified* Medicaid; Medicare.
Owner Proprietary corp.
Admissions Requirements Minimum age 18; Medical examination; Physician's request.
Staff Physicians 5 (ft); RNs 1 (ft); LPNs 5 (ft); Nurses' aides 12 (ft); Physical therapists 1 (ft); Recreational therapists 1 (ft), 1 (pt); Activities coordinators 1 (ft); Dietitians 1 (pt); Ophthalmologists 1 (pt); Podiatrists; Dentists 1 (pt).
Facilities Dining room; Physical therapy room; Activities room; Crafts room; Laundry room; Library.
Activities Arts & crafts; Cards; Games; Reading groups; Prayer groups; Movies; Shopping trips; Dances/Social/Cultural gatherings.

Meridian Nursing Home
2102 S Meridian St, Indianapolis, IN 46225
(317) 786-9426
Admin Cindy Neville.
Licensure Intermediate care. *Beds* ICF 44. *Certified* Medicaid.
Owner Proprietary corp (Beverly Enterprises).

Miller's Merry Manor Community
1651 N Campbell St, Indianapolis, IN 46218
(317) 357-8040
Admin Karen Warner.
Licensure Intermediate care. *Beds* ICF 114.
Owner Proprietary corp (Caremet Inc).

Miller's Merry Manor Inc
1700 N Illinois St, Indianapolis, IN 46202
(317) 924-1325
Admin Sandra K Ballenger. *Dir of Nursing* Betty Charpentier RN. *Medical Dir* Hugh Thatcher Jr MD.
Licensure Skilled care; Intermediate care. *Beds* SNF 102; ICF 51. *Certified* Medicaid; Medicare.
Owner Proprietary corp (Millers Merry Manor).
Admissions Requirements Minimum age 18; Medical examination; Physician's request.
Staff Physicians 15 (pt); RNs 5 (ft), 2 (pt); LPNs 14 (ft), 5 (pt); Nurses' aides 49 (ft), 12 (pt); Physical therapists 1 (pt); Occupational therapists 1 (pt); Speech therapists 1 (pt); Activities coordinators 3 (ft); Dietitians 1 (pt); Ophthalmologists 1 (pt); Podiatrists 1 (pt); Dentists 1 (pt).
Facilities Dining room; Physical therapy room; Activities room; Chapel; Crafts room; Laundry room; Barber/Beauty shop.
Activities Arts & crafts; Cards; Games; Reading groups; Prayer groups; Movies; Shopping trips; Dances/Social/Cultural gatherings.

Mt Zion Geriatric Center
3549 Boulevard Pl, Indianapolis, IN 46208
(317) 925-9681
Admin Lula Paige-Baxter RN.
Licensure Intermediate care. *Beds* ICF 104. *Certified* Medicaid.
Owner Proprietary corp.

North Willow Center
2002 W 86th St, Indianapolis, IN 46260
(317) 872-8811
Admin Patricia Krofft.
Licensure Intermediate care for mentally retarded. *Beds* ICF/MR 208. *Certified* Medicaid.
Owner Proprietary corp (Beverly Enterprises).

Admissions Requirements Minimum age 18.
Staff RNs; LPNs; Nurses' aides; Physical therapists; Recreational therapists; Occupational therapists; Speech therapists; Activities coordinators; Dietitians.

Northwest Manor Health Care Center
6640 W 34th St, Indianapolis, IN 46224
(317) 293-4930
Admin Jennifer A Knoll RN.
Licensure Skilled care; Intermediate care. *Beds* SNF 90; ICF 48. *Certified* Medicaid; Medicare.
Owner Proprietary corp.

Parkview Manor Nursing Home
PO Box 55046, Indianapolis, IN 46205-0046
(317) 253-3278
Admin Gregory A Holstein.
Licensure Intermediate care. *Beds* ICF 40. *Certified* Medicaid.
Owner Proprietary corp (Cloverleaf Enterprises).

Pleasant View Lodge
PO Box 36248, Indianapolis, IN 46236
(317) 335-2159
Admin Margaret McCreary. *Dir of Nursing* Eula Moore. *Medical Dir* Greg Bojrab MD.
Licensure Intermediate care. *Beds* ICF 48. *Certified* Medicaid.
Owner Privately owned.
Admissions Requirements Minimum age 18; Medical examination; Physician's request.
Staff Physicians; RNs; LPNs; Nurses' aides; Physical therapists (contracted); Reality therapists (contracted); Recreational therapists (contracted); Occupational therapists (contracted); Speech therapists (contracted); Activities coordinators; Dietitians; Ophthalmologists; Podiatrists.
Facilities Dining room; Physical therapy room; Activities room; Chapel; Laundry room; Barber/Beauty shop.
Activities Arts & crafts; Cards; Games; Reading groups; Prayer groups; Movies; Shopping trips.

Regency Place of Castleton
5226 E 82nd St, Indianapolis, IN 46250
(317) 842-6668
Admin Thomas M Mullins.
Medical Dir Erin Hattabaugh.
Licensure Skilled care; Intermediate care. *Beds* SNF 77; ICF 83.
Owner Proprietary corp (Lucas Corp).
Staff Physicians 1 (pt); RNs 6 (ft), 6 (pt); LPNs 12 (ft), 6 (pt); Nurses' aides 30 (ft); Physical therapists 1 (ft); Recreational therapists 1 (ft); Occupational therapists 1 (ft); Speech therapists 1 (pt); Activities coordinators 1 (ft); Dietitians 1 (pt).

Riley Health Care Facility
901 N East St, Indianapolis, IN 46202
(317) 635-2648
Admin Linda Wilkinson.
Licensure Intermediate care. *Beds* ICF 40.

Ritter Healthcare Center
1301 N Ritter, Indianapolis, IN 46219
(317) 353-9465
Admin Michael R Butler.
Licensure Skilled care; Intermediate care. *Beds* SNF 67; ICF 92. *Certified* Medicaid; Medicare.
Owner Proprietary corp (ARA).

Rural Health Care Facility
1747 N Rural St, Indianapolis, IN 46218
(317) 635-1355
Admin Claude A Shuee.
Licensure Intermediate care. *Beds* ICF 50. *Certified* Medicaid.
Owner Proprietary corp.
Admissions Requirements Medical examination.

Staff RNs 1 (ft); LPNs 4 (ft), 1 (pt); Activities coordinators 1 (ft); Dietitians 1 (ft); Ophthalmologists 1 (pt); Podiatrists 1 (pt); Audiologists 1 (pt); Dentists 1 (pt).
Facilities Dining room; Activities room; Crafts room; Laundry room; Barber/Beauty shop.
Activities Arts & crafts; Cards; Games; Prayer groups; Movies; Shopping trips; Dances/Social/Cultural gatherings.

St Augustine Home for the Aged
2345 W 86th St, Indianapolis, IN 46260
(317) 872-6420
Admin Sr Regina Loftus.
Medical Dir Sr Catherine.
Licensure Intermediate care; Residential care. *Beds* ICF 63; Residential care 32. *Certified* Medicaid.
Owner Nonprofit corp.
Admissions Requirements Minimum age 60; Medical examination.
Affiliation Roman Catholic.
Facilities Dining room; Physical therapy room; Activities room; Chapel; Crafts room; Laundry room; Barber/Beauty shop; Library.
Activities Arts & crafts; Cards; Games; Prayer groups; Movies; Shopping trips.

St Paul Baptist Church Home for the Aged
1141-45 N Sheffield Ave, Indianapolis, IN 46222
(317) 637-2429
Admin Anderson T Dailey.
Licensure Intermediate care. *Beds* ICF 48. *Certified* Medicaid.
Owner Nonprofit organization/foundation.
Admissions Requirements Minimum age 18; Medical examination; Physician's request.
Staff Physicians 2 (pt); RNs 1 (ft); LPNs 1 (ft), 2 (pt); Nurses' aides 7 (ft), 12 (pt); Activities coordinators 1 (ft); Dietitians 1 (pt); Ophthalmologists 1 (pt); Podiatrists 1 (pt); Dentists 1 (pt).
Affiliation Baptist.

St Vincent New Hope
8450 N Payne Rd, Indianapolis, IN 46268
(317) 872-4210, 872-4210, ext 246 FAX
Admin Robert Cannon. *Dir of Nursing* Marilynn Marshall RN. *Medical Dir* Daniel Shull MD.
Licensure Intermediate care for mentally retarded; Group homes. *Beds* ICF/MR 200. *Private Pay Patients* 2%. *Certified* Medicaid.
Owner Nonprofit corp (Daughters of Charity National Health System).
Admissions Requirements Minimum age 18-50; Medical examination.
Staff RNs 10 (ft), 2 (pt); LPNs 12 (ft), 7 (pt); Nurses' aides 56 (ft), 11 (pt); Physical therapists 3 (ft); Recreational therapists 5 (ft); Occupational therapists 4 (ft); Speech therapists 3 (ft); Activities coordinators 1 (ft); Dietitians 1 (ft).
Facilities Dining room; Physical therapy room; Activities room; Chapel; Crafts room; Laundry room; Barber/Beauty shop; Library; Bank; Pool; Outpatient neuro rehabilitative facility.
Activities Arts & crafts; Cards; Games; Reading groups; Prayer groups; Movies; Shopping trips; Dances/Social/Cultural gatherings; Intergenerational programs; Pet therapy; Volunteer program; Vocational therapy; Recreational therapy; Group, individual, and family counseling.

Scott Manor Nursing Home Inc
3402 N Schofield Ave, Indianapolis, IN 46218
(317) 925-6038, 925-1264
Admin Dr Leonard Scott, Donald L Golder. *Dir of Nursing* Rosella Majors. *Medical Dir* Dr Linda Stropes, Dr Robert Lebow.
Licensure Intermediate care. *Beds* ICF 41. *Certified* Medicaid.
Owner Proprietary corp.

Admissions Requirements Medical examination; Physician's request.
Staff RNs 1 (ft); LPNs 3 (ft), 2 (pt); Nurses' aides 10 (ft), 10 (pt); Activities coordinators 1 (ft); Dietitians 1 (pt).
Facilities Dining room; Activities room; Crafts room; Laundry room; Barber/Beauty shop.
Activities Arts & crafts; Cards; Games; Reading groups; Prayer groups; Movies; Shopping trips.

Sherwood Convalescent Home
3208 N Sherman Dr, Indianapolis, IN 46218
(317) 545-6017
Admin Sarah M Beasley.
Medical Dir Dr Debra Carter Bluitt.
Licensure Intermediate care. *Beds* ICF 51. *Certified* Medicaid.
Owner Proprietary corp.
Admissions Requirements Minimum age 19; Medical examination.
Staff RNs 2 (ft); LPNs 3 (ft), 2 (pt); Nurses' aides 10 (ft), 2 (pt); Activities coordinators 1 (ft); Dietitians 1 (pt).
Facilities Dining room; Activities room; Laundry room; Barber/Beauty shop.
Activities Arts & crafts; Cards; Games; Prayer groups; Movies; Shopping trips; Dances/Social/Cultural gatherings.

Southeastern Nursing Home
4743 Southeastern Ave, Indianapolis, IN 46203
(317) 356-0901
Admin Daniel J Pittman. *Dir of Nursing* Gloria Spiker. *Medical Dir* Dr Linda Stropes.
Licensure Intermediate care. *Beds* ICF 40. *Certified* Medicaid.
Owner Proprietary corp (Beverly Enterprises).
Admissions Requirements Medical examination.
Staff Physicians 3 (pt); LPNs 5 (ft); Nurses' aides 13 (ft), 3 (pt).
Languages Italian.
Facilities Dining room; Activities room; Crafts room; Laundry room; Barber/Beauty shop.
Activities Arts & crafts; Cards; Games; Reading groups; Movies; Shopping trips; Dances/Social/Cultural gatherings; Bingo.

Southside Healthcare Center
525 E Thompson Rd, Indianapolis, IN 46227
(317) 787-8253
Admin Janice A Reed. *Dir of Nursing* Anita James RN. *Medical Dir* Linda Stropes MD.
Licensure Skilled care; Intermediate care. *Beds* SNF 33; ICF 122. *Private Pay Patients* 7%. *Certified* Medicaid; Medicare.
Owner Privately owned (Evergreen HealthCare Ltd LP).
Admissions Requirements Medical examination; Physician's request.
Staff Physicians 1 (ft); RNs 4 (ft); LPNs 10 (ft); Nurses' aides 30 (ft); Physical therapists 1 (ft); Occupational therapists 1 (pt); Speech therapists 1 (pt); Activities coordinators 2 (ft); Dietitians 1 (pt); Podiatrists 1 (pt).
Facilities Dining room; Physical therapy room; Activities room; Crafts room; Laundry room; Barber/Beauty shop; Library.
Activities Arts & crafts; Games; Prayer groups; Movies; Shopping trips.

Stone Manor Convalescent Center
8201 W Washington St, Indianapolis, IN 46231
(317) 244-6848
Admin Deborah Sweet Williams.
Medical Dir Dr Reyes.
Licensure Intermediate care; Alzheimer's care. *Beds* ICF 103. *Certified* Medicaid.
Owner Proprietary corp.
Admissions Requirements Minimum age 18; Females only.

Staff Physicians; RNs; LPNs; Nurses' aides; Physical therapists; Recreational therapists; Occupational therapists; Speech therapists; Activities coordinators; Dietitians; Podiatrists.
Facilities Dining room; Physical therapy room; Activities room; Crafts room; Laundry room; Barber/Beauty shop.
Activities Arts & crafts; Cards; Games; Reading groups; Prayer groups; Movies; Shopping trips; Dances/Social/Cultural gatherings.

Three Sisters Healthcare Center
6130 N Michigan Rd, Indianapolis, IN 46208
(317) 253-3486
Admin Mamie Beamon. *Dir of Nursing* Irezean Thomas. *Medical Dir* Dr Robert LeBow.
Licensure Intermediate care; Respite care; Alzheimer's care. *Beds* ICF 100. *Private Pay Patients* 7%. *Certified* Medicaid.
Owner Proprietary corp.
Admissions Requirements Minimum age 18; Medical examination; Physician's request.
Staff RNs 1 (ft), 1 (pt); LPNs 4 (ft), 2 (pt); Nurses' aides 20 (ft), 4 (pt); Activities coordinators 1 (ft).
Facilities Dining room; Physical therapy room; Activities room; Chapel; Laundry room; Barber/Beauty shop; Courtyard.
Activities Arts & crafts; Cards; Games; Prayer groups; Movies; Dances/Social/Cultural gatherings; Intergenerational programs; Pet therapy; Bible study; Religious services.

Warren Park Nursing Home
6855 E 10th St, Indianapolis, IN 46219
(317) 353-9666
Admin Glenda Owens.
Medical Dir Dr Clarence Thomas.
Licensure Intermediate care. *Beds* ICF 40. *Certified* Medicaid.
Owner Proprietary corp (Beverly Enterprises).
Admissions Requirements Minimum age 18; Medical examination; Physician's request.
Staff RNs 1 (pt); LPNs 3 (ft), 2 (pt); Nurses' aides 4 (ft), 8 (pt); Recreational therapists 1 (ft); Activities coordinators 1 (ft); Dietitians 1 (pt).
Facilities Dining room; Activities room; Laundry room.
Activities Arts & crafts; Cards; Games; Reading groups; Prayer groups; Movies; Shopping trips; Dances/Social/Cultural gatherings.

Westminster Village North Inc
11050 Presbyterian Dr, Indianapolis, IN 46236
(317) 823-6841
Admin Karen Marie Bridges. *Dir of Nursing* Joan Gritter. *Medical Dir* Dr Robert Nation.
Licensure Skilled care; Intermediate care; Residential care; Alzheimer's care. *Beds* SNF 39; ICF 38; Residential care 35. *Certified* Medicaid; Medicare.
Owner Proprietary corp.
Admissions Requirements Minimum age 55; Medical examination.
Staff Physicians 1 (ft); RNs 3 (ft), 1 (pt); LPNs 9 (ft); Nurses' aides 28 (ft); Physical therapists 1 (ft); Activities coordinators 1 (ft); Dietitians 2 (ft), 1 (pt); Ophthalmologists 1 (pt).
Facilities Dining room; Physical therapy room; Activities room; Crafts room; Laundry room; Barber/Beauty shop.
Activities Arts & crafts; Cards; Games; Reading groups; Prayer groups; Movies; Shopping trips.

Westside Village Health Center
8616 W 10th St, Indianapolis, IN 46234
(317) 271-1020, 273-1444 FAX
Admin Ronald E Davis. *Dir of Nursing* Becky Nash RN BSN. *Medical Dir* Dr Joseph C Kirlin.

Licensure Intermediate care; Retirement. *Beds*
ICF 59; Retirement 200. *Private Pay
Patients* 65%. *Certified* Medicaid.
Owner Privately owned.
Admissions Requirements Minimum age 62;
Medical examination; Physician's request.
Staff RNs 1 (ft); LPNs 3 (ft), 1 (pt); Activities
coordinators 1 (ft); Dietitians 1 (pt); Nurses
aides & QMAs 18 (ft).
Facilities Dining room; Physical therapy
room; Activities room; Chapel; Crafts room;
Laundry room; Barber/Beauty shop; Library.
Activities Arts & crafts; Cards; Games;
Reading groups; Prayer groups; Movies;
Shopping trips; Dances/Social/Cultural
gatherings; Intergenerational programs; Pet
therapy.

Westview Nursing Home
5435 W 38th St, Indianapolis, IN 46254
(317) 293-2266
Admin Joseph Paul Castro. *Dir of Nursing*
Barb Weddle. *Medical Dir* Dr Fred Brooks.
Licensure Intermediate care. *Beds* ICF 44.
Certified Medicaid.
Owner Proprietary corp (Beverly Enterprises).
Admissions Requirements Minimum age 18;
Medical examination.
Staff RNs; LPNs; Nurses' aides; Recreational
therapists; Social services.
Facilities Dining room; Laundry room;
Barber/Beauty shop.
Activities Arts & crafts; Cards; Games; Prayer
groups; Movies; Shopping trips; Dances/
Social/Cultural gatherings.

Jasonville

Shakamak Good Samaritan Center
800 E Ohio St, Jasonville, IN 47438
(812) 666-2226
Admin Lois I Jensen. *Dir of Nursing* Ada P
Nuckolls. *Medical Dir* Dr Forrest Buell.
Licensure Skilled care; Intermediate care. *Beds*
SNF 32; ICF 63. *Private Pay Patients* 60%.
Certified Medicaid; Medicare.
Owner Nonprofit corp (Evangelical Lutheran/
Good Samaritan Society).
Admissions Requirements Minimum age 18;
Medical examination; Physician's request.
Staff Physicians 15 (pt); RNs 10 (pt); LPNs
30 (pt); Nurses' aides 60 (pt); Physical
therapists 1 (pt); Occupational therapists 1
(pt); Speech therapists 1 (pt); Activities
coordinators 1 (pt); Dietitians 1 (pt);
Podiatrists 2 (pt); Audiologists 1 (pt).
Affiliation Lutheran.
Facilities Dining room; Physical therapy
room; Activities room; Chapel; Crafts room;
Laundry room; Barber/Beauty shop; Library.
Activities Arts & crafts; Cards; Games;
Reading groups; Prayer groups; Movies;
Shopping trips; Dances/Social/Cultural
gatherings; Intergenerational programs; Pet
therapy.

Jasper

Jasper Nursing Center Inc
PO Box 1068, 2909 Howard Dr, Jasper, IN
47546
(812) 482-6161
Admin John L Wehrle. *Dir of Nursing* Loretta
Posey RN. *Medical Dir* Francis Gootee MD.
Licensure Intermediate care; Alzheimer's care.
Beds ICF 138; Alzheimer's care 28. *Certified*
Medicaid.
Owner Proprietary corp.
Admissions Requirements Minimum age 18.
Staff RNs 1 (ft); LPNs 5 (ft); Nurses' aides 30
(ft); Physical therapists 1 (pt); Activities
coordinators 2 (ft).
Facilities Dining room; Physical therapy
room; Activities room; Laundry room;
Barber/Beauty shop; Alzheimer's wing.

Activities Arts & crafts; Cards; Games;
Reading groups; Prayer groups; Movies;
Shopping trips; Dances/Social/Cultural
gatherings; Pet therapy.

North Wood Good Samaritan Center
2515 Newton St, Jasper, IN 47546
(812) 482-1722
Admin David McDaniel. *Dir of Nursing* Judy
Pund RN. *Medical Dir* Jeffry Rendel MD.
Licensure Skilled care; Intermediate care;
Supervised self-care; Alzheimer's care;
Retirement. *Beds* SNF 22; ICF 85;
Supervised self-care 28. *Private Pay Patients*
65%. *Certified* Medicaid; Medicare.
Owner Nonprofit corp (Evangelical Lutheran/
Good Samaritan Society).
Admissions Requirements Medical
examination; Physician's request.
Staff Physicians 1 (pt); RNs 2 (ft), 12 (pt);
LPNs 12 (pt); Nurses' aides 38 (pt); Physical
therapists 1 (pt); Recreational therapists 1
(pt); Occupational therapists 1 (pt); Speech
therapists 1 (pt); Activities coordinators 1
(pt); Dietitians 1 (pt).
Languages German.
Affiliation Lutheran.
Activities Arts & crafts; Cards; Games;
Reading groups; Prayer groups; Movies;
Shopping trips; Dances/Social/Cultural
gatherings; Intergenerational programs; Pet
therapy.

Providence Home
520 W 9th St, Jasper, IN 47546
(812) 482-6603
Admin Fr Thaddeus Sztuczko.
Medical Dir Julia Burress.
Licensure Intermediate care. *Beds* ICF 66.
Certified Medicaid.
Owner Nonprofit organization/foundation.
Admissions Requirements Minimum age 18;
Males only.
Staff Physicians 1 (pt); RNs 4 (pt); LPNs 3
(pt); Nurses' aides 6 (pt).
Facilities Dining room; Activities room;
Chapel; Crafts room; Laundry room; Barber/
Beauty shop; Library.
Activities Arts & crafts; Cards; Games; Prayer
groups; Movies; Shopping trips; Dances/Social/
Cultural gatherings; Bowling; Picnics;
Outings.

Jeffersonville

Hillcrest Healthcare Center
203 Sparks Ave, Jeffersonville, IN 47130
(812) 283-7918
Admin Stuart Reed.
Medical Dir Leonardo Ramus MD.
Licensure Skilled care; Intermediate care. *Beds*
SNF 51; ICF 170. *Certified* Medicaid;
Medicare.
Owner Proprietary corp (ARA).
Admissions Requirements Minimum age 18;
Medical examination; Physician's request.
Staff Physicians 3 (ft); RNs 6 (ft), 6 (pt);
LPNs 18 (ft), 10 (pt); Nurses' aides 31 (ft),
15 (pt); Physical therapists 2 (ft), 1 (pt);
Recreational therapists 1 (ft), 3 (pt);
Occupational therapists 1 (pt); Speech
therapists 1 (pt); Activities coordinators 1
(ft); Dietitians 1 (ft); Ophthalmologists 1
(pt); Podiatrists 1 (pt); Audiologists 1 (pt);
Dentists 1 (pt).
Facilities Dining room; Physical therapy
room; Activities room; Chapel; Crafts room;
Laundry room; Barber/Beauty shop; Library.
Activities Arts & crafts; Cards; Games;
Reading groups; Prayer groups; Movies;
Shopping trips; Dances/Social/Cultural
gatherings.

Jeffersonville Nursing Home
1720 E 8th St, Jeffersonville, IN 47130
(812) 282-5102

Admin Lynn Allyn Snow. *Dir of Nursing*
Gloria Montano RN. *Medical Dir* Dr Gene
Pierce.
Licensure Intermediate care. *Beds* ICF 40.
Certified Medicaid.
Owner Proprietary corp (Beverly Enterprises).
Admissions Requirements Minimum age 18;
Medical examination.
Staff RNs 1 (ft); LPNs 3 (ft), 3 (pt); Nurses'
aides 12 (ft), 4 (pt); Activities coordinators 1
(ft).
Facilities Dining room; Activities room;
Laundry room.
Activities Arts & crafts; Cards; Games; Prayer
groups; Movies; Dances/Social/Cultural
gatherings.

Twilight Nursing Home Inc
418 W Riverside Dr, Jeffersonville, IN 47130
(812) 283-6401
Admin Delilah J Swaney.
Licensure Intermediate care. *Beds* 11.

Kendallville

Kendallville Manor Healthcare Center
PO Box 488, 1802 Dowling St, Kendallville,
IN 46755
(219) 347-4374
Admin Nancy Daniel. *Dir of Nursing* Linda
Tilghman RN. *Medical Dir* Terry Gaff MD.
Licensure Intermediate care. *Beds* ICF 60.
Certified Medicaid.
Owner Proprietary corp (Cloverleaf Healthcare
Services Inc).
Admissions Requirements Medical
examination.
Staff RNs 2 (ft), 1 (pt); LPNs 3 (ft), 2 (pt);
Nurses' aides 14 (ft), 6 (pt); Activities
coordinators 1 (ft), 1 (pt); Dietitians 1 (pt).
Facilities Dining room; Physical therapy
room; Activities room; Laundry room;
Barber/Beauty shop.
Activities Arts & crafts; Cards; Games;
Reading groups; Prayer groups; Movies;
Shopping trips; Dances/Social/Cultural
gatherings; Intergenerational programs; Pet
therapy.

Kendallville Nursing Home
1433 S Main St, Kendallville, IN 46755
(219) 347-3612
Admin Sandra L Perry.
Medical Dir Dr C F Stallman.
Licensure Intermediate care. *Beds* ICF 40.
Certified Medicaid.
Owner Proprietary corp (Beverly Enterprises).
Admissions Requirements Medical
examination; Physician's request.
Staff RNs 1 (ft); LPNs 1 (ft), 1 (pt); Nurses'
aides 6 (ft), 10 (pt); Activities coordinators 1
(ft); Dietitians 1 (pt); Podiatrists 1 (pt).
Facilities Dining room; Activities room;
Laundry room.
Activities Arts & crafts; Cards; Games; Prayer
groups; Movies; Field trips; Special outings;
Picnics.

Shepherd of the Hill
US 6 & CR 1000 E, Kendallville, IN 46755
(219) 347-2256
Admin Judy Zirkelbach. *Dir of Nursing* Linda
Yoder. *Medical Dir* Dr Warrener.
Licensure Intermediate care; Residential care;
Retirement. *Beds* ICF 94; Residential care
32; Retirement 165. *Private Pay Patients*
50%. *Certified* Medicaid.
Owner Nonprofit corp (Lutheran Homes Inc).
Admissions Requirements Medical
examination.
Staff RNs 2 (ft), 1 (pt); LPNs 6 (ft), 4 (pt);
Nurses' aides 18 (ft), 10 (pt); Activities
coordinators 2 (ft); Dietitians 1 (ft), 1 (pt).
Languages German.
Affiliation Lutheran.
Facilities Dining room; Physical therapy
room; Activities room; Chapel; Crafts room;
Laundry room; Barber/Beauty shop; Library.

Activities Arts & crafts; Cards; Games; Prayer groups; Movies; Shopping trips; Intergenerational programs; Pet therapy.

Kentland

Kentland Nursing Home
620 E Washington St, Kentland, IN 47951
(219) 474-6741
Admin Christine Schrader. *Dir of Nursing* Lynette DeWitt LPN. *Medical Dir* Basil Datzman MD.
Licensure Intermediate care. *Beds* ICF 40. *Certified* Medicaid.
Owner Proprietary corp (Beverly Enterprises).
Admissions Requirements Minimum age 18; Medical examination; Physician's request.
Staff RNs 1 (pt); LPNs 3 (ft); Nurses' aides 12 (ft), 4 (pt); Recreational therapists 1 (pt); Activities coordinators 1 (pt); Dietitians 1 (pt).
Facilities Dining room; Activities room; Laundry room.
Activities Arts & crafts; Cards; Games; Reading groups; Prayer groups; Movies; Shopping trips; Dances/Social/Cultural gatherings.

Knightsville

Harty Nursing Home
PO Box D, Knightsville, IN 47857
(812) 446-2309
Admin Nita Mayle.
Licensure Intermediate care; Comprehensive care; Alzheimer's care; Retirement. *Beds* SNF 70; Comprehensive care 1. *Certified* Medicaid.
Staff RNs 1 (ft); LPNs 3 (ft); Nurses' aides 30 (ft); Activities coordinators 1 (ft); Dietitians 1 (pt).
Facilities Dining room; Activities room; Chapel; Crafts room; Laundry room; Barber/Beauty shop.
Activities Arts & crafts; Cards; Games; Reading groups; Prayer groups; Movies; Shopping trips.

Knox

Countryside Place
RR 3, Box 6, 300 E Culver Rd, Knox, IN 46534
(219) 772-6248
Admin Randy R Barghahn.
Medical Dir Walter Fritz.
Licensure Skilled care; Alzheimer's care; Retirement. *Beds* SNF 78. *Certified* Medicaid; Medicare.
Owner Proprietary corp (Beverly Enterprises).
Admissions Requirements Minimum age 18; Medical examination; Physician's request.
Staff RNs 4 (ft), 2 (pt); LPNs 3 (ft); Nurses' aides 19 (ft), 9 (pt); Physical therapists 1 (pt); Speech therapists 1 (pt); Activities coordinators 2 (pt); Dietitians 1 (ft); Podiatrists 1 (pt); Dentists 1 (pt).
Facilities Dining room; Physical therapy room; Activities room; Crafts room; Laundry room; Barber/Beauty shop.
Activities Arts & crafts; Cards; Games; Reading groups; Prayer groups; Movies; Shopping trips; Dances/Social/Cultural gatherings.

Wintersong Village of Knox
PO Box 337, Knox, IN 46534-0337
(219) 772-5826
Admin Patti Richardson.
Licensure Skilled care; Intermediate care; Comprehensive care. *Beds* SNF 18; ICF 27; Comprehensive care 5.

Kokomo

Americana Healthcare Center
3518 S LaFountain, Kokomo, IN 46901
(317) 453-4666
Admin Dorothy Fordyce.
Licensure Skilled care; Intermediate care; Comprehensive care; Alzheimer's care; Retirement. *Beds* SNF 35; ICF 69; Comprehensive care 1. *Certified* Medicaid; Medicare.
Owner Proprietary corp (Manor Care).

Forest Park Healthcare Center
2233 W Jefferson St, Kokomo, IN 46901
(317) 457-9175
Admin Susan S Cox. *Dir of Nursing* Diane Olmstead RN. *Medical Dir* Dr Artis.
Licensure Skilled care; Intermediate care; Medicare. *Beds* SNF 87; ICF 108; Medicare 36. *Certified* Medicaid; Medicare.
Owner Proprietary corp (Evergreen Health Care Ltd).
Staff RNs; LPNs; Nurses' aides; Physical therapists; Activities coordinators; Social service; Admissions directors; Maintenance directors; Housekeeping; Laundry supervisors.
Activities Arts & crafts; Cards; Games; Reading groups; Prayer groups; Movies; Shopping trips; Dances/Social/Cultural gatherings; Van trips; Pizza parties; Birthday parties.

Kokomo Nursing Home—Greentree Manor
1560 S Plate St, Kokomo, IN 46901
(317) 452-8934
Admin Linda Crowe. *Dir of Nursing* Julie Miller RN. *Medical Dir* Richard Bowling MD.
Licensure Intermediate care. *Beds* ICF 40. *Certified* Medicaid.
Owner Proprietary corp (Waverly Group).
Admissions Requirements Minimum age 18; Medical examination; Physician's request.
Staff RNs 1 (ft); LPNs 1 (ft), 4 (pt); Nurses' aides 9 (ft), 4 (pt); Activities coordinators 1 (ft); Dietitians 1 (pt).
Languages Spanish, Sign.
Facilities Dining room; Activities room; Laundry room; Barber/Beauty shop.
Activities Arts & crafts; Cards; Games; Reading groups; Prayer groups; Movies; Shopping trips; Dances/Social/Cultural gatherings; Birthday parties by McDonalds; Pizza parties by Pizza Hut.

Sycamore Village Health Center
2905 W Sycamore, Kokomo, IN 46901
(317) 452-5491
Admin Jean Wanders.
Licensure Intermediate care; Alzheimer's care. *Beds* ICF 201. *Certified* Medicaid.
Owner Proprietary corp (Beverly Enterprises).

Windsor Estates of Kokomo
429 W Lincoln Rd, Kokomo, IN 46902
(317) 453-5600, 455-0110 FAX
Admin Julie Guest. *Dir of Nursing* Norma Ault RN. *Medical Dir* James Whitfield MD.
Licensure Skilled care; Intermediate care. *Beds* SNF 58; ICF 57. *Private Pay Patients* 35%. *Certified* Medicaid; Medicare.
Owner Proprietary corp (Hillhaven Corp).
Admissions Requirements Medical examination.
Staff Physicians; RNs 4 (ft), 2 (pt); LPNs 16 (ft), 8 (pt); Nurses' aides 31 (ft), 23 (pt); Physical therapists (contracted); Occupational therapists (contracted); Speech therapists (contracted); Activities coordinators 1 (ft), 1 (pt); Dietitians 1 (pt); Ophthalmologists (contracted); Podiatrists (contracted).
Facilities Dining room; Physical therapy room; Activities room; Laundry room; Barber/Beauty shop.

Ladoga

Autumn Care of Ladoga
1001 E Main St, Ladoga, IN 47954
(317) 942-2223
Admin Steven M Still.
Licensure Skilled care; Intermediate care. *Beds* SNF 21; ICF 74. *Certified* Medicaid.
Owner Proprietary corp (Autumn Corp).

Lafayette

Comfort Retirement & Nursing Home Inc
312 N 8th St, Lafayette, IN 47901
(317) 742-8455
Admin Richard E Linson.
Licensure Intermediate care. *Beds* ICF 46. *Certified* Medicaid.

Indiana Pythian Home
1501 S 18th St, Lafayette, IN 47905
(317) 474-1405
Admin Richard W Bartnik. *Dir of Nursing* Lori Sickler RN. *Medical Dir* Eleanor Filmer MD.
Licensure Intermediate care; Residential care. *Beds* ICF 75; Residential care 43. *Certified* Medicaid.
Owner Nonprofit organization/foundation.
Admissions Requirements Minimum age 18; Medical examination; Physician's request.
Staff Physicians 1 (pt); RNs 1 (ft), 1 (pt); LPNs 5 (ft), 1 (pt); Nurses' aides 12 (ft), 6 (pt); Activities coordinators 1 (ft), 1 (pt); Dietitians 1 (pt).
Affiliation Knights of Pythias.
Facilities Dining room; Activities room; Chapel; Crafts room; Laundry room; Barber/Beauty shop; Library.
Activities Arts & crafts; Cards; Games; Reading groups; Prayer groups; Movies; Shopping trips; Dances/Social/Cultural gatherings; Intergenerational programs; Pet therapy.

Lafayette Healthcare Center
1903 Union St, Lafayette, IN 47901
(317) 447-9431
Admin Terry Johnson.
Medical Dir Dr Eleanor Filmer.
Licensure Skilled care; Intermediate care. *Beds* SNF 69; ICF 133. *Certified* Medicaid; Medicare.
Owner Proprietary corp (ARA Living Centers).
Admissions Requirements Medical examination.
Staff Physicians 1 (ft); RNs 2 (ft); LPNs 6 (ft), 3 (pt); Nurses' aides 58 (ft), 3 (pt); Physical therapists 1 (ft); Occupational therapists 1 (pt); Speech therapists 1 (pt); Activities coordinators 1 (ft), 1 (pt); Dietitians 1 (ft); Podiatrists 1 (pt); Audiologists 1 (pt); Dentists 1 (pt).
Facilities Dining room; Physical therapy room; Activities room; Chapel; Crafts room; Laundry room; Barber/Beauty shop; Library.
Activities Arts & crafts; Cards; Games; Reading groups; Prayer groups; Movies; Shopping trips; Dances/Social/Cultural gatherings.

Murdock Manor
2201 Cason St, Lafayette, IN 47901
(317) 447-4102
Admin Betty J Montgomery.
Licensure Skilled care; Intermediate care; Comprehensive care. *Beds* SNF 62; ICF 31; Comprehensive care 18. *Certified* Medicaid; Medicare.

Admissions Requirements Medical examination; Physician's request.
Staff Physicians 1 (pt); RNs 6 (ft), 4 (pt); LPNs 3 (ft), 4 (pt); Nurses' aides 25 (ft), 7 (pt); Physical therapists 1 (ft), 1 (pt); Occupational therapists 1 (ft), 1 (pt); Speech therapists 1 (pt); Activities coordinators 1 (ft); Dietitians 1 (ft).
Facilities Dining room; Physical therapy room; Activities room; Crafts room; Barber/Beauty shop.
Activities Arts & crafts; Cards; Games; Reading groups; Prayer groups; Movies; Dances/Social/Cultural gatherings.

Regency Place of Lafayette
300 Windy Hill Dr, Lafayette, IN 47905
(317) 477-7791
Admin David M Lennartz. *Dir of Nursing* Linda Marshall.
Licensure Skilled care; Intermediate care; Alzheimer's care. *Beds* SNF 52; ICF 102. *Certified* Medicaid; Medicare.
Owner Proprietary corp (Lucas Corp).
Admissions Requirements Minimum age 18; Medical examination.
Staff RNs 5 (ft), 3 (pt); LPNs 15 (ft), 7 (pt); Nurses' aides 38 (ft), 14 (pt); Physical therapists 1 (pt); Activities coordinators 2 (ft); Dietitians 1 (ft).
Facilities Dining room; Physical therapy room; Activities room; Crafts room; Laundry room; Barber/Beauty shop; Library; Resident/Family lounges.
Activities Arts & crafts; Cards; Games; Reading groups; Prayer groups; Movies; Shopping trips; Dances/Social/Cultural gatherings; Residents lunch club.

St Anthony Health Care
1205 N 14th St, Lafayette, IN 47904
(317) 423-4861
Admin Becky Thompson Weaver. *Dir of Nursing* Heidi Whitus RN. *Medical Dir* James Pickerill MD.
Licensure Intermediate care. *Beds* ICF 80. *Certified* Medicaid.
Owner Privately owned.
Admissions Requirements Medical examination; Physician's request.
Staff Physicians 1 (pt); RNs 5 (ft); LPNs 5 (ft), 3 (pt); Nurses' aides 20 (ft), 5 (pt); Physical therapists 1 (pt); Occupational therapists 1 (pt); Speech therapists 1 (pt); Activities coordinators 1 (ft); Dietitians 1 (pt); Ophthalmologists 1 (pt); Podiatrists 1 (pt).
Affiliation Roman Catholic.
Facilities Dining room; Physical therapy room; Activities room; Chapel; Crafts room; Laundry room; Barber/Beauty shop.
Activities Arts & crafts; Cards; Games; Reading groups; Prayer groups; Movies; Dances/Social/Cultural gatherings; Daily mass.

St Elizabeth Hospital Medical Center Skilled Nursing Unit
PO Box 7501, 1501 Hartford St, Lafayette, IN 47903
(317) 423-6260, 742-5764 FAX
Admin Mariellen M Neudeck. *Dir of Nursing* Virginia Klinker RN. *Medical Dir* Brice E Fitzgerald MD.
Licensure Skilled care. *Beds* SNF 27. *Private Pay Patients* 50%. *Certified* Medicaid; Medicare.
Owner Nonprofit corp (Sisters of Saint Francis Health Services Inc).
Admissions Requirements Minimum age 15; Medical examination; Physician's request.
Staff RNs 8 (ft), 1 (pt); LPNs 4 (ft), 1 (pt); Nurses' aides 14 (ft), 1 (pt); Activities coordinators 1 (pt).
Languages Interpreters available.
Affiliation Roman Catholic.

Facilities Dining room; Physical therapy room; Activities room; Chapel; Barber/Beauty shop; 3 Suites for families of cancer patients.
Activities Arts & crafts; Games; Reading groups; Movies; Pet therapy.

South Street Health Care Center
1123 E South St, Lafayette, IN 47901
(317) 742-6904
Admin Theresa A Dellwo.
Medical Dir Dr Mary Ade.
Licensure Intermediate care. *Beds* ICF 40. *Certified* Medicaid.
Owner Proprietary corp (Beverly Enterprises).
Admissions Requirements Medical examination; Physician's request.
Staff RNs 1 (pt); LPNs 3 (ft); Nurses' aides 5 (ft), 8 (pt); Activities coordinators 1 (pt); Dietitians 1 (pt).
Facilities Dining room; Activities room; Laundry room.
Activities Arts & crafts; Cards; Games; Reading groups; Prayer groups; Movies; Shopping trips; Dances/Social/Cultural gatherings.

LaFontaine

Shangri-La Health Care Center
604 Rennaker St, LaFontaine, IN 46940
(317) 981-2081, 662-9350, 981-4954 FAX
Admin Rita Holloway. *Dir of Nursing* Terry Dollar. *Medical Dir* Fred Poehler MD.
Licensure Intermediate care; Alzheimer's care. *Beds* ICF 90. *Certified* Medicaid.
Owner Proprietary corp.
Admissions Requirements Minimum age 18; Medical examination; Physician's request.
Staff Physicians 1 (pt); RNs 2 (ft); LPNs 4 (ft); Nurses' aides 30 (ft); Activities coordinators 1 (ft); Dietitians 1 (ft).
Facilities Dining room; Activities room; Crafts room; Laundry room; Barber/Beauty shop.
Activities Arts & crafts; Cards; Games; Reading groups; Prayer groups; Movies; Shopping trips; Dances/Social/Cultural gatherings; Intergenerational programs; Pet therapy.

Lagrange

LaGrange Nursing Home
Rte 5 Box 74, Lagrange, IN 46761
(219) 463-7455
Admin Donna L Kennedy, acting.
Medical Dir Debra Rose.
Licensure Intermediate care; Comprehensive care. *Beds* ICF 32; Comprehensive care 6. *Certified* Medicaid.
Owner Proprietary corp (Beverly Enterprises).
Admissions Requirements Medical examination; Physician's request.
Staff Physicians 1 (pt); RNs 1 (ft); LPNs 3 (pt); Nurses' aides 7 (ft), 2 (pt); Activities coordinators 1 (ft); Dietitians 1 (pt); Ophthalmologists 1 (pt); Podiatrists 1 (pt); Audiologists 1 (pt); Dentists 1 (pt).
Facilities Dining room; Activities room; Crafts room; Laundry room.
Activities Arts & crafts; Cards; Games; Reading groups; Prayer groups; Movies; Shopping trips; Dances/Social/Cultural gatherings.

Miller's Merry Manor Inc
State Rd 9 N, Lagrange, IN 46761
(219) 463-2172, (616) 651-4968
Admin Grace M Karst RN. *Dir of Nursing* Karen S Hyska RN. *Medical Dir* M Reed Taylor MD.
Licensure Skilled care; Intermediate care; Comprehensive. *Beds* SNF 54; ICF 113; Comprehensive 35. *Certified* Medicaid; Medicare.

Owner Proprietary corp (Millers Merry Manor).
Admissions Requirements Minimum age 18; Medical examination; Physician's request.
Staff RNs 6 (ft), 4 (pt); LPNs 16 (ft), 2 (pt); Nurses' aides 28 (ft), 20 (pt); Physical therapists 1 (pt); Activities coordinators 2 (ft); Dietitians 1 (ft); Ophthalmologists 1 (pt).
Facilities Dining room; Physical therapy room; Activities room; Chapel; Crafts room; Laundry room; Barber/Beauty shop.
Activities Arts & crafts; Cards; Games; Reading groups; Prayer groups; Movies; Shopping trips; Dances/Social/Cultural gatherings.

LaPorte

Countryside Place
1700 I St, LaPorte, IN 46350
(219) 362-6234
Admin Lawrence Beall. *Dir of Nursing* Joyce Nicholson.
Licensure Skilled care; Intermediate care. *Beds* SNF 39; ICF 60. *Certified* Medicaid; Medicare.
Owner Proprietary corp (Beverly Enterprises).

Fountainview Terrace
1900 Andrew Ave, LaPorte, IN 46350
(219) 362-7014
Admin Edward Y Given Jr. *Dir of Nursing* Pat Barnes. *Medical Dir* Dr Mark Ballard.
Licensure Skilled care; Intermediate care; Residential care. *Beds* SNF 64; ICF 114; Residential care 16. *Private Pay Patients* 20%. *Certified* Medicaid; Medicare.
Owner Proprietary corp (Beverly Enterprises).
Admissions Requirements Medical examination; Physician's request.
Staff RNs 6 (ft), 1 (pt); LPNs 5 (ft), 2 (pt); Nurses' aides 35 (ft), 25 (pt); Physical therapists 1 (pt); Speech therapists 1 (pt); Activities coordinators 1 (ft); Dietitians 1 (pt).
Languages Spanish, German, Polish.
Facilities Dining room; Physical therapy room; Activities room; Chapel; Crafts room; Laundry room; Barber/Beauty shop; Library.
Activities Arts & crafts; Cards; Games; Reading groups; Prayer groups; Movies; Shopping trips; Dances/Social/Cultural gatherings; Intergenerational programs.

Lawrenceburg

Shady Nook Care Center
36 Valley Dr, Lawrenceburg, IN 47025
(812) 537-0930
Admin Daniel McMullen.
Licensure Intermediate care; Comprehensive care. *Beds* ICF 100; Comprehensive care 1. *Certified* Medicaid.

Terrace View
403 Bielby Rd, Lawrenceburg, IN 47025
(812) 537-1132
Admin Howard Goodman.
Licensure Skilled care; Intermediate care. *Beds* SNF 41; ICF 82. *Certified* Medicaid; Medicare.

Leavenworth

Todd Dickey Medical Center
PO Box 134, A & 2nd Sts, Leavenworth, IN 47137
(812) 739-2292
Admin Floyd Shewmaker.
Licensure Intermediate care. *Beds* ICF 78. *Certified* Medicaid; Medicare.
Owner Proprietary corp (Unicare).

Lebanon

English Nursing Home
1015 N Lebanon St, Lebanon, IN 46052
(317) 482-5880
Admin Patty Akins.
Medical Dir Kimberly Byrd.
Licensure Intermediate care. *Beds* ICF 36.
   Certified Medicaid.
Owner Proprietary corp.
Admissions Requirements Minimum age 21.
Staff LPNs; Nurses' aides; Activities
   coordinators; Dietitians.
Facilities Dining room; Activities room;
   Crafts room; Laundry room; Barber/Beauty
   shop.
Activities Arts & crafts; Games; Movies;
   Dances/Social/Cultural gatherings.

Essex Manor
301 W Essex, Lebanon, IN 46052
(317) 482-1950
Admin Roxanne S Bagozzi. *Dir of Nursing*
   Cathy Ash RN. *Medical Dir* Dallas Coate
   MD.
Licensure Intermediate care; Day care;
   Respite care. *Beds* ICF 40. *Certified*
   Medicaid.
Owner Proprietary corp (Beverly Enterprises).
Admissions Requirements Medical
   examination; Physician's request.
Staff Physicians 1 (pt); RNs 1 (ft); LPNs 3
   (ft), 3 (pt); Nurses' aides 8 (ft), 6 (pt);
   Physical therapists; Occupational therapists 1
   (pt); Speech therapists 1 (pt); Activities
   coordinators 1 (ft); Dietitians;
   Ophthalmologists; Podiatrists; Audiologists.
Facilities Dining room; Activities room;
   Crafts room; Laundry room; Barber/Beauty
   shop; Library.
Activities Arts & crafts; Cards; Games;
   Reading groups; Prayer groups; Movies;
   Shopping trips; Dances/Social/Cultural
   gatherings; Intergenerational programs; Pet
   therapy; Pontoon boat rides; Picnics; Fishing
   trips.

Kingsbury Rehabilitation & Retirement Centre
1585 Perryworth Rd, Lebanon, IN 46052
(317) 482-6391, 873-5333
Admin Toni C James.
Medical Dir Dr Ben Park.
Licensure Skilled care; Intermediate care. *Beds*
   SNF 30; ICF 100. *Private Pay Patients* 50%.
   Certified Medicaid; Medicare.
Owner Proprietary corp.
Admissions Requirements Minimum age 21;
   Medical examination; Physician's request.
Staff Physicians 1 (pt); RNs 2 (ft); LPNs 6
   (ft), 3 (pt); Physical therapists 1 (pt);
   Recreational therapists 1 (pt); Occupational
   therapists 1 (ft); Speech therapists 1 (ft);
   Activities coordinators 1 (ft), 1 (pt);
   Dietitians 1 (ft); Podiatrists 1 (pt).
Facilities Dining room; Physical therapy
   room; Activities room; Laundry room;
   Barber/Beauty shop.
Activities Arts & crafts; Cards; Games;
   Reading groups; Prayer groups; Movies.

Parkwood Health Care Inc
1001 N Grant St, Lebanon, IN 46052
(317) 482-6400
Admin Arthur O Dickerson.
Licensure Intermediate care. *Beds* 133.
   Certified Medicaid.
Staff RNs 2 (ft), 3 (pt); LPNs 3 (ft), 2 (pt);
   Nurses' aides 29 (ft), 18 (pt); Physical
   therapists; Speech therapists; Activities
   coordinators; Dietitians; Podiatrists;
   Audiologists; Qualified medical assistants 11
   (ft), 6 (pt).
Facilities Dining room; Physical therapy
   room; Activities room; Laundry room;
   Barber/Beauty shop.
Activities Arts & crafts; Games; Reading
   groups; Prayer groups; Movies.

Lewisville

Lewisville Hotel for Senior Citizens
Box 98, US 40, Lewisville, IN 47352
(317) 987-7952
Admin Sarah Vollmer; Nancy Nicoletta.
Licensure Residential care. *Beds* 32.

Liberty

Hillcrest Estates
215 W High St, Liberty, IN 47353
(317) 458-5117
Admin Betty L Bussen. *Dir of Nursing* Fannye
   Embry. *Medical Dir* Dr John T Hinton.
Licensure Intermediate care. *Beds* ICF 60.
   Certified Medicaid.
Owner Proprietary corp (Sycamore
   Enterprises).
Admissions Requirements Minimum age 19;
   Medical examination; Physician's request.
Staff RNs 2 (ft); LPNs 4 (ft); Nurses' aides 9
   (ft), 4 (pt); Activities coordinators 1 (pt);
   Dietitians 1 (pt).
Facilities Dining room; Activities room;
   Laundry room; Barber/Beauty shop.
Activities Arts & crafts; Cards; Games;
   Reading groups; Prayer groups; Movies;
   Shopping trips; Dances/Social/Cultural
   gatherings.

Park Manor Nursing Home
409 E Union St, Liberty, IN 47353
(317) 458-6194
Admin Elaine Stubbs RN. *Dir of Nursing*
   Donna Marling LPN. *Medical Dir* Dr C G
   Clarkson.
Licensure Intermediate care. *Beds* ICF 22.
   Certified Medicaid.
Owner Privately owned.
Admissions Requirements Minimum age 18;
   Females only.
Staff RNs 1 (pt); LPNs 4 (ft); Nurses' aides 12
   (ft), 2 (pt); Activities coordinators 1 (ft), 1
   (pt); Dietitians 1 (pt).
Facilities Dining room; Activities room;
   Barber/Beauty shop.
Activities Arts & crafts; Cards; Games;
   Reading groups; Prayer groups; Movies;
   Shopping trips; Dances/Social/Cultural
   gatherings.

Ligonier

Heritage Manor Health Care Center of Ligonier
400 Pontiac St, Ligonier, IN 46767
(219) 894-7118
Admin Keith Ambrose.
Licensure Intermediate care. *Beds* ICF 61.

Kenney Health Care
200 Kenney Cir Dr, Ligonier, IN 46767
(219) 894-7131, 894-7133 FAX
Admin Maribelle S Dyer. *Dir of Nursing* June
   Styborski RN. *Medical Dir* Robert C Stone
   MD.
Licensure Skilled care; Intermediate care;
   Retirement. *Beds* SNF 27; ICF 40.
   Retirement apts 25. *Private Pay Patients*
   60%. *Certified* Medicaid; Medicare.
Owner Privately owned.
Admissions Requirements Minimum age 18;
   Physician's request.
Staff Physicians 1 (pt); RNs 1 (ft), 5 (pt);
   LPNs 2 (ft), 3 (pt); Nurses' aides 11 (ft), 3
   (pt); Physical therapists 2 (pt); Recreational
   therapists 1 (ft), 1 (pt); Occupational
   therapists 1 (pt); Speech therapists 1 (pt);
   Dietitians 1 (pt); Podiatrists 1 (pt).
Facilities Dining room; Physical therapy
   room; Activities room; Laundry room;
   Barber/Beauty shop.
Activities Arts & crafts; Cards; Games;
   Reading groups; Prayer groups; Movies; Pet
   therapy.

Linton

Glenburn Rest Haven Home Inc
RR 2, Glenburn Rd, Linton, IN 47441
(812) 847-2221
Admin William T Fisher.
Licensure Intermediate care. *Beds* ICF 154.
   Certified Medicaid.

Linton Nursing Home
1501 E 'A' St, Linton, IN 47441
(812) 847-4426
Admin Michael H Leistner.
Medical Dir William Powers; Peggy
   Southwood.
Licensure Intermediate care. *Beds* ICF 40.
   Certified Medicaid.
Owner Proprietary corp (Beverly Enterprises).
Admissions Requirements Minimum age 18;
   Medical examination.
Staff RNs 1 (pt); LPNs 6 (ft); Nurses' aides 6
   (ft), 4 (pt); Physical therapists 1 (pt); Speech
   therapists 1 (pt); Activities coordinators 1
   (ft); Dietitians 1 (pt); Ophthalmologists 1
   (pt).
Facilities Dining room; Activities room;
   Crafts room; Laundry room.
Activities Arts & crafts; Cards; Games;
   Reading groups; Prayer groups; Movies;
   Shopping trips; Dances/Social/Cultural
   gatherings.

Logansport

Camelot Care Centers
1555 Commerce St, Logansport, IN 46947
(219) 753-0404
Admin Rita Holloway. *Dir of Nursing* Rita
   Hollingsworth RN. *Medical Dir* E R
   Luxenberg MD.
Licensure Intermediate care. *Beds* ICF 75.
   Certified Medicaid.
Owner Proprietary corp.
Admissions Requirements Minimum age 0-2
   months (Health care facility for children).
Staff Physicians 1 (pt); RNs 2 (ft); LPNs 2
   (ft), 4 (pt); Physical therapists 1 (pt);
   Occupational therapists 1 (pt); Activities
   coordinators 1 (ft); Dietitians 1 (pt).
Facilities Dining room; Physical therapy
   room; Activities room; Crafts room; Laundry
   room.
Activities Arts & crafts; Games; Reading
   groups; Movies; Shopping trips; Dances/
   Social/Cultural gatherings; School programs;
   Sheltered workshop program.

Chase Centeer
2 Chase Park, Logansport, IN 46947
(219) 753-4137
Admin David J Krizmanich.
Licensure Skilled care; Intermediate care;
   Comprehensive care. *Beds* SNF 41; ICF 174;
   Comprehensive care 18. *Certified* Medicaid;
   Medicare.

Miller's Merry Manor
200 26th St, Logansport, IN 46947
(219) 722-4006
Admin Gregory L Fassett. *Dir of Nursing* Joan
   Baker RN. *Medical Dir* Dr Edward Wilson.
Licensure Skilled care; Intermediate care. *Beds*
   SNF 54; ICF 96. *Private Pay Patients* 40%.
   Certified Medicaid; Medicare.
Owner Proprietary corp (Caremet Inc).
Admissions Requirements Minimum age 18;
   Medical examination; Physician's request.
Staff RNs 9 (ft), 2 (pt); LPNs 9 (ft), 10 (pt);
   Nurses' aides 26 (ft), 16 (pt); Physical
   therapists 1 (ft); Activities coordinators 2
   (ft).
Facilities Dining room; Physical therapy
   room; Activities room; Laundry room;
   Barber/Beauty shop.

Activities Arts & crafts; Cards; Games; Prayer groups; Movies; Shopping trips; Dances/Social/Cultural gatherings; Intergenerational programs.

Neal Home
2518 George St, Logansport, IN 46947
(219) 753-3920
Admin Mary L Strahle.
Licensure Home for aged. *Beds* 20.
Admissions Requirements Females only.

Woodland Acres/Cass County Home
RR 4 Box 121, Logansport, IN 46947
(219) 753-2791
Admin Mary Jo Jacko. *Dir of Nursing* Dorothy Foust, County nurse.
Licensure Intermediate care. *Beds* ICF 23. *Private Pay Patients* 11%. *Certified* Medicaid; Medicare.
Owner Publicly owned.
Admissions Requirements Medical examination.
Staff Cooks 2 (ft); Housekeepers 1 (ft); Laundry attendants 1 (ft); Vocational attendants 1 (ft), 1 (pt); County nurses.
Facilities Dining room; Laundry room; Barber/Beauty shop; Garden.
Activities Cards; Games; Reading groups; Prayer groups; Movies; Shopping trips; Dances/Social/Cultural gatherings; Pet therapy.

Loogootee

Gentle Care of Loogootee
RR 4, Hwy 550, Loogootee, IN 47553
(812) 295-3624
Admin Lana Wells. *Dir of Nursing* Margaret Spaulding RN. *Medical Dir* Dr James Poirier.
Licensure Intermediate care; Alzheimer's care. *Beds* ICF 36. *Certified* Medicaid.
Owner Proprietary corp (Gentle Care Inc).
Admissions Requirements Medical examination; Physician's request.
Staff Physicians 5 (pt); RNs 2 (ft), 1 (pt); LPNs 3 (ft), 3 (pt); Nurses' aides 6 (ft), 6 (pt); Physical therapists 1 (pt); Speech therapists 1 (pt); Activities coordinators 1 (pt); Dietitians 1 (pt); Podiatrists 1 (pt).
Facilities Dining room; Activities room; Laundry room; Picnic area.
Activities Arts & crafts; Cards; Games; Reading groups; Prayer groups; Movies; Shopping trips; Dances/Social/Cultural gatherings; Pet therapy; Gardening; Outdoor walks and games; Alzheimer's support group.

Loogootee Nursing Center
PO Box 117, Loogootee, IN 47553
(812) 295-2101
Admin Barbara A Knepp. *Dir of Nursing* Shirley Yoder RN. *Medical Dir* J Poirier MD.
Licensure Skilled care; Intermediate care. *Beds* SNF 29; ICF 31. *Private Pay Patients* 70%. *Certified* Medicaid; Medicare.
Owner Privately owned.
Admissions Requirements Minimum age 18; Medical examination; Physician's request.
Facilities Dining room; Physical therapy room; Activities room; Laundry room; Barber/Beauty shop.
Activities Arts & crafts; Cards; Games; Reading groups; Prayer groups; Movies; Shopping trips; Dances/Social/Cultural gatherings; Intergenerational programs; Pet therapy.

Poplar Valley Living Center
313 Poplar St, Loogootee, IN 47553
(812) 295-4433
Admin Stan Bedker.
Licensure Skilled care; Intermediate care; Comprehensive care. *Beds* SNF 27; ICF 33; Comprehensive care 2.

Lowell

Lowell Healthcare Center
255 Burnham St, Lowell, IN 46356
(219) 696-7791
Admin Marcia J Quale. *Dir of Nursing* Beth Swank RN. *Medical Dir* Randall Hile MD.
Licensure Intermediate care. *Beds* ICF 100. *Private Pay Patients* 35%. *Certified* Medicaid.
Owner Proprietary corp.
Admissions Requirements Minimum age 18; Medical examination.
Staff Physicians 1 (ft), 2 (pt); RNs 3 (ft), 1 (pt); LPNs 6 (ft); Nurses' aides 20 (ft), 20 (pt); Activities coordinators 1 (ft), 1 (pt); Dietitians 1 (ft); Ophthalmologists 1 (pt); Podiatrists 1 (pt).
Facilities Dining room; Activities room; Crafts room; Laundry room; Barber/Beauty shop; Lounges.
Activities Arts & crafts; Cards; Games; Reading groups; Prayer groups; Movies; Shopping trips; Dances/Social/Cultural gatherings; Intergenerational programs; Pet therapy; Reality orientation program; Resident council; Family counseling; Volunteer program.

Lynn

Parrott's Home
304 W Sherman St, PO Box 347, Lynn, IN 47355
(317) 874-4281
Admin Maxine Parrott.
Licensure Residential care. *Beds* 5.

Lyons

Lyons Convalescent Center
PO Box 247, Lyons, IN 47443
(812) 659-1440
Admin Linda P Drew. *Dir of Nursing* Lynette Evans RN. *Medical Dir* Dr William Powers.
Licensure Skilled care; Intermediate care. *Beds* SNF 17; ICF 53. *Certified* Medicaid; Medicare.
Owner Proprietary corp.
Admissions Requirements Physician's request.
Facilities Dining room; Physical therapy room; Activities room; Laundry room; Barber/Beauty shop.
Activities Arts & crafts; Cards; Games; Reading groups; Prayer groups; Movies; Shopping trips; Dances/Social/Cultural gatherings; Pet therapy.

Madison

Clifty Falls Convalescent Center
950 Cross Ave, Madison, IN 47250
(812) 273-4640
Admin Aliene Breitenbach. *Dir of Nursing* Cathy Spry. *Medical Dir* Robert Ellis MD.
Licensure Skilled care; Intermediate care. *Beds* SNF 52; ICF 64.
Owner Proprietary corp.
Admissions Requirements Minimum age 18; Medical examination; Physician's request.
Staff RNs 3 (ft), 3 (pt); LPNs 4 (ft), 6 (pt); Nurses' aides 35 (ft), 30 (pt); Activities coordinators.
Facilities Dining room; Physical therapy room; Activities room; Laundry room; Barber/Beauty shop.
Activities Arts & crafts; Cards; Games; Reading groups; Prayer groups; Movies; Shopping trips; Dances/Social/Cultural gatherings.

Madison Nursing Home
1945 Cragmont St, Madison, IN 47250
(812) 273-4696
Admin W R Scott James.

Licensure Intermediate care. *Beds* ICF 40. *Certified* Medicaid.
Owner Proprietary corp (Beverly Enterprises).
Admissions Requirements Minimum age 18.
Staff RNs 1 (pt); LPNs 2 (ft), 1 (pt); Nurses' aides 5 (ft), 5 (pt); Activities coordinators 1 (pt); Dietitians 1 (pt).
Facilities Dining room; Activities room; Laundry room.
Activities Arts & crafts; Cards; Games; Movies.

River Valley Living Center
702-710 Elm St, Madison, IN 47250
(812) 265-2286
Admin Clara E McGinnis. *Dir of Nursing* Mary Ann Williams RN. *Medical Dir* Robert Johnson MD.
Licensure Intermediate care. *Beds* ICF 32. *Private Pay Patients* 12%. *Certified* Medicaid.
Owner Nonprofit corp (Adventist Living Centers).
Admissions Requirements Minimum age 18; Medical examination.
Staff RNs 1 (ft); LPNs 3 (ft), 1 (pt); Nurses' aides 7 (ft), 5 (pt); Activities coordinators 1 (ft).
Affiliation Seventh-Day Adventist.
Facilities Dining room; Activities room; Laundry room; Barber/Beauty shop.
Activities Arts & crafts; Cards; Games; Reading groups; Prayer groups; Movies; Shopping trips; Dances/Social/Cultural gatherings; Pet therapy; Picnics.

Marion

Bradner Village Health Care Center Inc
505 Bradner Ave, Marion, IN 46952
(317) 662-3981
Admin Jim J Walts.
Licensure Skilled care; Intermediate care; Comprehensive care. *Beds* SNF 48; ICF 153; Comprehensive care 99. *Certified* Medicaid.

Colonial Oaks Health Care Center
4725 S Colonial Oaks Dr, Marion, IN 46953
(317) 674-9791, 674-7117 FAX
Admin Penny J Keihn. *Dir of Nursing* Patricia Rigsbee RN. *Medical Dir* Miles Donaldson MD.
Licensure Skilled care; Intermediate care; Retirement. *Beds* SNF 32; ICF 88; Retirement 72. *Private Pay Patients* 48%. *Certified* Medicaid; Medicare.
Owner Proprietary corp (United Heritage Inc).
Admissions Requirements Minimum age 18; Medical examination; Physician's request.
Staff Physicians 1 (pt); RNs 5 (ft), 8 (pt); LPNs 8 (ft), 6 (pt); Nurses' aides 37 (ft), 14 (pt); Physical therapists 2 (pt); Speech therapists 1 (pt); Activities coordinators 1 (ft); Dietitians 1 (pt); Audiologists 1 (pt).
Languages Sign, German.
Facilities Dining room; Physical therapy room; Activities room; Crafts room; Laundry room; Barber/Beauty shop; Library.
Activities Arts & crafts; Cards; Games; Reading groups; Prayer groups; Movies; Shopping trips; Dances/Social/Cultural gatherings; Intergenerational programs; Pet therapy; Community projects; Educational programs; Recreational outings; Music; Exercise; Spiritual care.

Flinn Memorial Home
614 W 14th St, Marion, IN 46953-2199
(317) 664-0618
Admin David W Pennybacker. *Dir of Nursing* Jeri Curtis. *Medical Dir* Dr Ramesh Patel.
Licensure Intermediate care; Residential care; Comprehensive care. *Beds* ICF 78; Residential care 76; Comprehensive care 2. *Certified* Medicaid.
Owner Nonprofit corp (National Benevolent Association).

Admissions Requirements Minimum age 70; Medical examination.
Staff Physicians 1 (pt); RNs 1 (ft); LPNs 5 (ft), 3 (pt); Nurses' aides 20 (ft), 12 (pt); Physical therapists 1 (pt); Occupational therapists 1 (pt); Speech therapists 1 (pt); Activities coordinators 3 (ft); Dietitians 1 (pt); Podiatrists 1 (pt).
Affiliation Disciples of Christ.
Facilities Dining room; Physical therapy room; Activities room; Chapel; Crafts room; Laundry room; Barber/Beauty shop; Library.
Activities Arts & crafts; Games; Reading groups; Prayer groups; Movies; Shopping trips.

Golden Age Nursing Home
1800 Kem Rd, Marion, IN 46952
(317) 664-4573
Admin Amy Lambertson. *Dir of Nursing* Ruthann Richwine. *Medical Dir* Dr R Patel.
Licensure Intermediate care. *Beds* ICF 80. *Certified* Medicaid.
Owner Proprietary corp (Forum Grp).
Admissions Requirements Medical examination; Physician's request.
Staff RNs 2 (ft), 1 (pt); LPNs 2 (ft), 3 (pt); Nurses' aides 16 (ft), 9 (pt); Activities coordinators 1 (ft); Dietitians 1 (ft).
Facilities Dining room; Activities room; Crafts room; Laundry room; Barber/Beauty shop.
Activities Arts & crafts; Cards; Games; Reading groups; Prayer groups; Movies; Shopping trips; Dances/Social/Cultural gatherings.

Riverview Manor Nursing Home
221 N Washington St, Marion, IN 46952
(317) 664-0612
Admin Barbara Winters.
Licensure Intermediate care. *Beds* ICF 103. *Certified* Medicaid.
Owner Proprietary corp (Forum Grp).

Wesleyan Health Care Center
518 W 36th St, Marion, IN 46953
(317) 674-3371
Admin Gary L Ott. *Dir of Nursing* Theresa Lewis. *Medical Dir* Charles Yale MD.
Licensure Intermediate care. *Beds* ICF 154. *Private Pay Patients* 20%. *Certified* Medicaid.
Owner Privately owned.
Admissions Requirements Medical examination; Physician's request.
Staff Physicians 12 (ft), 5 (pt); RNs 4 (ft), 1 (pt); LPNs 6 (ft), 5 (pt); Nurses' aides 27 (ft), 13 (pt); Physical therapists 1 (pt); Speech therapists 1 (pt); Activities coordinators 1 (ft); Ophthalmologists 1 (pt); Podiatrists 1 (pt); Audiologists 1 (pt).
Facilities Dining room; Physical therapy room; Activities room; Chapel; Crafts room; Laundry room; Barber/Beauty shop; Library; Ceramic kiln; Progressive care unit; Special care unit.
Activities Arts & crafts; Cards; Games; Reading groups; Prayer groups; Movies; Shopping trips; Dances/Social/Cultural gatherings; Pet therapy; Ceramics.

Markle

Markle Health Care
5730 N 550 W, Markle, IN 46770
(219) 758-2131
Admin John R Siela.
Licensure Intermediate care. *Beds* ICF 66.

Martinsville

Dixon Home Care Center
60 E Harrison St, Martinsville, IN 46151
(317) 342-1744
Admin Ruth E Denny.
Licensure Intermediate care. *Beds* 17.

Grandview Convalescent Center
1959 E Columbus St, Martinsville, IN 46151
(317) 342-7114
Admin Patricia A Walker. *Dir of Nursing* Lynn Warner. *Medical Dir* Gary Midla DO.
Licensure Intermediate care. *Beds* ICF 100. *Private Pay Patients* 40%. *Certified* Medicaid.
Owner Privately owned.
Admissions Requirements Medical examination; Physician's request.
Staff RNs 2 (ft); LPNs 6 (ft), 2 (pt); Physical therapists 1 (pt); Reality therapists 1 (pt); Recreational therapists 1 (pt); Occupational therapists 1 (pt); Speech therapists 1 (pt); Activities coordinators 1 (ft), 1 (pt); Dietitians 1 (pt); Ophthalmologists 1 (pt); Podiatrists 1 (pt); Audiologists 1 (pt).
Facilities Dining room; Activities room; Crafts room; Laundry room; Barber/Beauty shop.
Activities Arts & crafts; Cards; Games; Reading groups; Prayer groups; Movies; Shopping trips; Dances/Social/Cultural gatherings; Intergenerational programs; Pet therapy.

Grandview Living Center
2009 E Columbus St, Martinsville, IN 46151
(317) 342-6101
Admin Shirleen Shockley.
Licensure Intermediate care. *Beds* ICF 34.

Heritage House Convalescent Center
2055 Heritage Dr, Martinsville, IN 46151
(317) 342-3305
Admin Margaret J Dillman. *Dir of Nursing* Kathy Fetherolf. *Medical Dir* Robert C Beesley MD.
Licensure Skilled care; Intermediate care. *Beds* SNF 59; ICF 60. *Certified* Medicaid; Medicare.
Owner Proprietary corp.
Admissions Requirements Minimum age 18; Medical examination.
Staff RNs 4 (ft), 1 (pt); LPNs 6 (ft), 1 (pt); Nurses' aides 41 (ft), 1 (pt); Physical therapists 1 (pt); Speech therapists 1 (pt); Activities coordinators 1 (ft), 1 (pt); Dietitians 1 (pt).
Facilities Dining room; Physical therapy room; Activities room; Crafts room; Laundry room; Barber/Beauty shop; Library.
Activities Arts & crafts; Cards; Games; Reading groups; Prayer groups; Movies; Shopping trips; Dances/Social/Cultural gatherings.

Kennedy Living Center
PO Box 1676, 301 W Harrison St, Martinsville, IN 46151
(317) 342-6636
Admin Michael W Terhorst. *Dir of Nursing* Sherry Easterday. *Medical Dir* George Ostheimer MD.
Licensure Intermediate care; Residential care. *Beds* ICF 78; Residential care 35. *Certified* Medicaid.
Owner Nonprofit organization/foundation (National Benevolent Association of Christian Homes).
Admissions Requirements Minimum age 62; Medical examination.
Staff Physicians 1 (pt); RNs 3 (ft); LPNs 8 (ft); Nurses' aides 21 (ft), 4 (pt); Activities coordinators 1 (ft); Dietitians 1 (pt); QMAs 9 (ft).
Affiliation Disciples of Christ.
Facilities Dining room; Activities room; Chapel; Crafts room; Laundry room; Barber/Beauty shop; Library.
Activities Arts & crafts; Cards; Games; Reading groups; Prayer groups; Movies; Shopping trips; Dances/Social/Cultural gatherings; Intergenerational programs.

Merrillville

Lincolnshire Health Care Center
8380 Virginia St, Merrillville, IN 46410
(219) 769-9009
Admin Lawrence A Beall.
Licensure Skilled care; Intermediate care. *Beds* SNF 50; ICF 50.

Merrillville Convalescent Center
601 W 61st Ave, Merrillville, IN 46410
(219) 980-5950
Admin Thomas Bell.
Licensure Skilled care. *Beds* SNF 180. *Certified* Medicaid; Medicare.

Southlake Care Center
8800 Virginia Pl, Merrillville, IN 46410
(219) 736-1310
Admin Alyce Jantz.
Licensure Skilled care; Intermediate care. *Beds* SNF 94; ICF 135.
Owner Proprietary corp (Beverly Enterprises).

Town Centre Health Care
7250 Arthur Blvd, Merrillville, IN 46410
(219) 736-2900
Admin Ruth Brockman.

Michigan City

Beach Cliff Lodge Nursing Home
1001 Lake Shore Dr, Michigan City, IN 46360
(219) 872-0120
Admin Janice Butcher RN.
Medical Dir Maurice Miller.
Licensure Intermediate care. *Beds* ICF 21. *Certified* Medicaid.
Admissions Requirements Minimum age 21; Medical examination; Physician's request.
Staff RNs 2 (ft), 1 (pt); Nurses' aides 4 (ft), 3 (pt); Activities coordinators 1 (pt).
Facilities Dining room; Activities room; Laundry room.
Activities Arts & crafts; Cards; Games; Reading groups; Prayer groups; Shopping trips.

Lakeside Health Center Inc
802 Hwy 20 E, Michigan City, IN 46360
(219) 872-7251
Admin Dorothy Snavley.
Licensure Intermediate care. *Beds* 64. *Certified* Medicaid.

Michigan City Health Care
1101 E Coolspring Ave, Michigan City, IN 46360
(219) 874-5211
Admin Debra Juarez. *Dir of Nursing* Lois J Kubica RN. *Medical Dir* Myron Berkston MD.
Licensure Skilled care; Intermediate care; Alzheimer's care. *Beds* SNF 66; ICF 198. *Private Pay Patients* 30%. *Certified* Medicaid; Medicare.
Owner Proprietary corp.
Admissions Requirements Medical examination.
Staff Physicians 1 (ft); RNs 7 (ft), 5 (pt); LPNs; Nurses' aides; Physical therapists 1 (ft); Reality therapists; Recreational therapists 1 (ft); Occupational therapists 1 (ft); Speech therapists 2 (ft); Activities coordinators 1 (ft); Dietitians 2 (ft); Ophthalmologists; Podiatrists 1 (ft).
Facilities Dining room; Physical therapy room; Activities room; Chapel; Crafts room; Laundry room; Barber/Beauty shop; Library; Guest rooms.
Activities Arts & crafts; Cards; Prayer groups; Shopping trips; Dances/Social/Cultural gatherings; Pet therapy.

Red Oaks Healthcare Center
910 S Carroll Ave, Michigan City, IN 46360
(219) 872-0696

Admin Terri Hastings. *Dir of Nursing* Claudia Christensen RN. *Medical Dir* Amos Arney MD.
Licensure Skilled care; Intermediate care. *Beds* SNF 58; ICF 58. *Private Pay Patients* 22%. *Certified* Medicaid; Medicare.
Owner Proprietary corp (ARA Living Centers).
Admissions Requirements Minimum age 18; Medical examination; Physician's request.
Staff RNs 6 (ft), 3 (pt); LPNs 5 (ft), 2 (pt); Nurses' aides 31 (ft), 6 (pt); Physical therapists (contracted); Occupational therapists (contracted); Speech therapists (contracted); Activities coordinators 1 (ft), 1 (pt); Dietitians (contracted); Ophthalmologists (contracted); Podiatrists (contracted).
Facilities Dining room; Physical therapy room; Activities room; Chapel; Laundry room; Barber/Beauty shop.
Activities Arts & crafts; Cards; Games; Reading groups; Prayer groups; Shopping trips; Dances/Social/Cultural gatherings; Intergenerational programs; Pet therapy.

Wedow Private Home Care
602 Spring St, Michigan City, IN 46360
(219) 879-0140
Admin Wilbur E Wedow. *Dir of Nursing* Louella Clark RN.
Licensure Residential care. *Beds* Residential 17.
Owner Privately owned.
Admissions Requirements Females only; Medical examination.
Staff Physicians; RNs; Nurses' aides; Activities coordinators; Dietitians.
Languages Polish.
Facilities Dining room; Activities room; Laundry room; Barber/Beauty shop.
Activities Arts & crafts; Cards; Games; Movies; Shopping trips.

Middletown

Miller's Merry Manor
Box 160, Middletown, IN 47356
(317) 354-2278
Admin John Winenger. *Dir of Nursing* Kathy Hagensieker RN. *Medical Dir* Dr Allen Neal.
Licensure Intermediate care; Adult day care; Respite care; Alzheimer's care. *Beds* ICF 64. *Private Pay Patients* 48%. *Certified* Medicaid.
Owner Proprietary corp (Caremet Inc).
Admissions Requirements Minimum age 21; Medical examination.
Staff RNs 2 (ft); LPNs 3 (ft), 1 (pt); Nurses' aides 10 (ft), 10 (pt); Activities coordinators 1 (ft); Dietitians 1 (pt).
Facilities Dining room; Activities room; Crafts room; Laundry room; Barber/Beauty shop; Patio.
Activities Arts & crafts; Cards; Games; Reading groups; Prayer groups; Movies; Shopping trips; Dances/Social/Cultural gatherings; Intergenerational programs; Pet therapy.

Milan

Milan Healthcare Center
Carr St, Milan, IN 47031
(812) 654-2231
Admin Ted Merrick.
Licensure Intermediate care. *Beds* ICF 65. *Certified* Medicaid.
Owner Proprietary corp (Forum Group).
Staff RNs; LPNs; Nurses' aides; Activities coordinators.
Facilities Dining room; Activities room; Laundry room; Barber/Beauty shop.
Activities Arts & crafts; Cards; Games; Prayer groups; Movies; Shopping trips; Dances/Social/Cultural gatherings.

Milford

Lakeland Loving Care Center Inc
PO Box 767, Milford, IN 46542
(219) 658-9455
Admin Diane K Shenefield. *Dir of Nursing* Sandra Twombly RN. *Medical Dir* S D Strycker MD.
Licensure Intermediate care. *Beds* ICF 60. *Private Pay Patients* 60%. *Certified* Medicaid.
Owner Proprietary corp.
Admissions Requirements Medical examination.
Staff RNs 2 (ft), 1 (pt); LPNs 2 (ft), 3 (pt); Nurses' aides 21 (ft), 9 (pt); Activities coordinators 1 (ft); Dietitians 1 (pt).
Facilities Dining room; Activities room; Crafts room; Laundry room; Barber/Beauty shop; Children's day care center.
Activities Arts & crafts; Cards; Games; Reading groups; Prayer groups; Movies; Shopping trips; Intergenerational programs.

Mishawaka

Countryside Place
811 E 12th St, Mishawaka, IN 46544
(219) 259-1917
Admin Christine Schrader. *Dir of Nursing* Jeanette Newton-McKnight. *Medical Dir* Dr James Serwatka.
Licensure Skilled care; Intermediate care. *Beds* SNF 56; ICF 46. *Certified* Medicaid; Medicare.
Owner Proprietary corp (Beverly Enterprises).
Admissions Requirements Medical examination; Physician's request.
Staff Physicians 3 (ft); RNs 4 (ft); LPNs 10 (ft); Nurses' aides 75 (ft); Physical therapists 1 (ft); Reality therapists 1 (ft); Recreational therapists 1 (ft); Occupational therapists 1 (ft); Speech therapists 1 (ft); Activities coordinators 1 (ft); Dietitians 1 (ft); Ophthalmologists 1 (ft); Podiatrists 1 (ft); Audiologists 1 (ft).
Facilities Dining room; Physical therapy room; Activities room; Crafts room; Laundry room; Barber/Beauty shop.
Activities Arts & crafts; Cards; Games; Reading groups; Prayer groups; Movies; Shopping trips; Dances/Social/Cultural gatherings; Intergenerational programs; Pet therapy.

Fountainview Place of Mishawaka
609 W Tanglewood Ln, Mishawaka, IN 46544
(219) 277-2500
Admin Randi Kiphen.
Medical Dir David Clayton MD.
Licensure Skilled care; Intermediate care; Residential care. *Beds* SNF 44; ICF 84; Residential care 19. *Certified* Medicaid; Medicare.
Owner Proprietary corp (Beverly Enterprises).
Staff RNs 1 (ft), 1 (pt); LPNs 10 (ft), 4 (pt); Nurses' aides 22 (ft), 19 (pt); Physical therapists 1 (pt); Occupational therapists 1 (ft); Speech therapists 1 (pt); Activities coordinators 1 (ft); Qualified medication aides 3 (ft), 8 (pt).
Facilities Dining room; Physical therapy room; Activities room; Chapel; Crafts room; Barber/Beauty shop.
Activities Arts & crafts; Cards; Games; Reading groups; Prayer groups; Movies; Shopping trips; Dances/Social/Cultural gatherings.

St Joseph's Care Center—Melrose
601 S Russell St, Mishawaka, IN 46544
(219) 259-5050
Admin Judith Jelinski RN.
Licensure Intermediate care. *Beds* ICF 38. *Certified* Medicaid.
Admissions Requirements Minimum age 18; Medical examination; Physician's request.

Staff RNs 2 (ft); LPNs 2 (ft); Nurses' aides 8 (ft), 23 (pt); Recreational therapists 1 (ft), 1 (pt); Activities coordinators 1 (ft).
Facilities Dining room; Activities room; Crafts room.
Activities Arts & crafts; Cards; Games; Reading groups; Prayer groups; Shopping trips.

Mitchell

Mitchell Manor
PO Box 277, RR 4, Box 383, Mitchell, IN 47446
(812) 849-2221
Admin Larry Carlson. *Dir of Nursing* Brenda Houchin RN.
Licensure Skilled care; Intermediate care. *Beds* SNF 33; ICF 162. *Certified* Medicaid.
Owner Proprietary corp (Life Care Centers of America).
Admissions Requirements Minimum age 21; Physician's request.
Facilities Dining room; Physical therapy room; Activities room; Crafts room; Barber/Beauty shop.
Activities Arts & crafts; Cards; Games; Reading groups; Prayer groups; Movies; Shopping trips; Dances/Social/Cultural gatherings.

Williams Health Facility
Hwy 37 S, Mitchell, IN 47446
(812) 849-2221
Admin Wayne Williams.
Beds 44.

Monticello

Lake View Home
800 W Norway Rd, Monticello, IN 47960
(219) 583-3242
Admin Ora Rumple.
Licensure Residential care. *Beds* 28.

Monticello Community Healthcare Center
RR 6, 1120 N Main St, Monticello, IN 47960
(219) 583-7073
Admin Greg Cochran.
Licensure Skilled care; Intermediate care; Residential care. *Beds* SNF 63; ICF 111; Residential care 32. *Certified* Medicaid; Medicare.
Owner Proprietary corp (ARA Living Centers).

Mooresville

Miller's Merry Manor Inc
259 W Harrison, Mooresville, IN 46158
(317) 831-6272
Admin Eric J Wiedeman.
Licensure Intermediate care. *Beds* ICF 99. *Certified* Medicaid.
Owner Proprietary corp (Millers Merry Manor).

Morgantown

Henderson Nursing Home Inc
140 W Washington St, Morgantown, IN 46160
(812) 597-4418
Admin Karen Henderson.
Licensure Intermediate care. *Beds* ICF 41.

Henderson Nursing Home Inc
140 W Washington St, Morgantown, IN 46160
(812) 597-4418
Admin Karen Henderson.
Medical Dir Gary Midla DO.
Licensure Intermediate care. *Beds* 41. *Certified* Medicaid.
Admissions Requirements Medical examination.

Staff Physicians 1 (ft); RNs 1 (pt); LPNs 3 (ft), 1 (pt); Nurses' aides 15 (ft), 5 (pt); Activities coordinators 1 (ft); Dietitians 1 (pt).
Facilities Dining room; Activities room; Crafts room; Laundry room; Library.
Activities Arts & crafts; Cards; Games; Reading groups; Prayer groups; Movies; Shopping trips; Dances/Social/Cultural gatherings.

Morristown

Morristown Healthcare
210 S Washington St, Morristown, IN 46161
(317) 763-6012
Admin Eileen Stevens.
Licensure Intermediate care. *Beds* ICF 63. *Certified* Medicaid.

Mount Vernon

Medco Center of Mt Vernon
1415 Country Club Rd, Mount Vernon, IN 47620
(812) 838-6554
Admin Lillie Branam.
Licensure Intermediate care. *Beds* ICF 123. *Certified* Medicaid.
Owner Proprietary corp (Unicare).
Admissions Requirements Minimum age 18; Medical examination.
Facilities Dining room; Physical therapy room; Activities room; Chapel; Crafts room; Laundry room; Barber/Beauty shop.
Activities Arts & crafts; Cards; Games; Reading groups; Prayer groups; Movies; Shopping trips; Dances/Social/Cultural gatherings.

Mulberry

Mulberry Lutheran Home
RR 1 Box 46, Mulberry, IN 46058
(317) 296-2911
Admin Mark Neubacher.
Medical Dir Grayson B Davis.
Licensure Intermediate care; Residential care/ Assisted living; Independent living; Comprehensive care. *Beds* ICF 6; Residential care/Assisted living 42; Independent living apts 12; Comprehensive care 81. *Certified* Medicaid.
Admissions Requirements Medical examination.
Staff Physicians 1 (pt); RNs 3 (ft), 2 (pt); LPNs 3 (ft), 1 (pt); Nurses' aides 26 (ft), 26 (pt); Physical therapists 1 (pt); Activities coordinators 2 (ft), 1 (pt); Dietitians 1 (ft); Dentists 1 (pt).
Affiliation Lutheran.
Facilities Dining room; Physical therapy room; Activities room; Chapel; Crafts room; Laundry room; Barber/Beauty shop; Library; Ceramics room.
Activities Arts & crafts; Cards; Games; Reading groups; Prayer groups; Movies; Shopping trips; Bingo.

Muncie

Chateau Convalescent Centre
2400 Chateau Dr, Muncie, IN 47303
(317) 747-9044
Admin Betty J Hickey.
Licensure Intermediate care. *Beds* ICF 102. *Certified* Medicaid.
Owner Proprietary corp.

Countryside Healthcare
PO Box 3070, 4400 Burlington Pike, Muncie, IN 47302
(317) 284-0502
Admin Mary Jo Crutcher.
Licensure Intermediate care. *Beds* ICF 40.

Delaware County Health Center
7524 E Jackson, Muncie, IN 47302
(317) 747-7820
Admin Michael Whitcomb. *Dir of Nursing* Barbara King RN. *Medical Dir* Dr Robert Suer.
Licensure Intermediate care; Residential. *Beds* ICF 48; Residential 24. *Certified* Medicaid; Medicare.
Owner Publicly owned.
Admissions Requirements Medical examination; Physician's request.
Staff Physicians 2 (ft); RNs 2 (ft), 1 (pt); LPNs 6 (ft), 4 (pt); Nurses' aides 18 (ft), 8 (pt); Activities coordinators 2 (ft); Dietitians 1 (pt); Ophthalmologists 1 (pt); Podiatrists 1 (pt); QMA 12 (ft), 3 (pt).
Facilities Dining room; Physical therapy room; Activities room; Crafts room; Laundry room; Barber/Beauty shop; Library.
Activities Arts & crafts; Cards; Games; Reading groups; Prayer groups; Movies; Shopping trips; Dances/Social/Cultural gatherings.

Fountainview Place
2701 Lyn-Mar Dr, Muncie, IN 47302
(317) 286-5979
Admin Shirley Lake.
Medical Dir Arnold Carter MD.
Licensure Skilled care; Intermediate care; Comprehensive care. *Beds* SNF 71; ICF 72; Comprehensive care 6. *Certified* Medicaid; Medicare.
Owner Proprietary corp (Beverly Enterprises).
Admissions Requirements Medical examination.
Staff Physical therapists 1 (ft); Occupational therapists 1 (ft); Speech therapists 1 (pt); Activities coordinators 1 (ft).
Facilities Dining room; Physical therapy room; Activities room; Chapel; Crafts room; Laundry room; Barber/Beauty shop.
Activities Arts & crafts; Cards; Games; Reading groups; Prayer groups; Movies; Shopping trips; Dances/Social/Cultural gatherings.

Muncie Health Care Center Inc
PO Box 112, 4301 N Walnut St, Muncie, IN 47305
(317) 282-0053
Admin David A Davis.
Licensure Skilled care; Intermediate care. *Beds* SNF 25; ICF 135. *Certified* Medicaid.

Northeast Healthcare Center of Muncie
505 N Gavin St, Muncie, IN 47304
(317) 289-1915
Admin Diana J Peckham. *Dir of Nursing* Karen Baty RN. *Medical Dir* Larry Cole MD.
Licensure Intermediate care. *Beds* ICF 42. *Certified* Medicaid.
Owner Privately owned.
Admissions Requirements Minimum age 18; Medical examination; Physician's request.
Staff Physicians; RNs; LPNs; Nurses' aides; Activities coordinators; Dietitians; Ophthalmologists.
Facilities Dining room; Activities room; Laundry room; Barber/Beauty shop.
Activities Arts & crafts; Cards; Games; Reading groups; Prayer groups; Movies; Shopping trips; Dances/Social/Cultural gatherings; Fishing trips; Concert trips.

Parkview Nursing Center
2200 White River Blvd, Muncie, IN 47303
(317) 289-3341
Admin Sandra Maikranz.
Medical Dir Dr Michael Seidle.
Licensure Skilled care; Intermediate care. *Beds* SNF 53; ICF 48. *Certified* Medicaid; Medicare.
Owner Proprietary corp (Unicare).
Admissions Requirements Minimum age 21; Medical examination; Physician's request.

Staff Physicians 1 (pt); RNs 5 (ft); LPNs 8 (ft); Nurses' aides 34 (ft), 8 (pt); Physical therapists; Speech therapists; Activities coordinators 1 (ft); Podiatrists.
Facilities Dining room; Physical therapy room; Activities room; Crafts room; Laundry room; Barber/Beauty shop; Lounge area.
Activities Arts & crafts; Cards; Reading groups; Prayer groups; Movies; Shopping trips; Bi-monthly newspaper; Exercise groups; Chapel twice weekly in lounge area.

Rosewood Manor
PO Box 3070, 5200 S Burlington Pike, Muncie, IN 47307
(317) 288-5082
Admin Sandy J Ford.
Licensure Intermediate care. *Beds* 50. *Certified* Medicaid.
Owner Proprietary corp.

Sylvester Nursing Home
RR 2, Box 79, Muncie, IN 47302
(317) 284-8283
Admin Kevin S Jeffers.
Medical Dir Larry G Cole MD.
Licensure Intermediate care. *Beds* 40. *Certified* Medicaid.
Admissions Requirements Medical examination.
Staff RNs 1 (pt); LPNs 2 (ft); Nurses' aides 17 (ft), 3 (pt); Activities coordinators 1 (ft); Dietitians 1 (pt).
Facilities Dining room; Activities room; Laundry room; Barber/Beauty shop.
Activities Arts & crafts; Games; Prayer groups; Movies; Shopping trips; Dances/Social/ Cultural gatherings.

Westminster Village Muncie Inc
5801 Bethel Ave, Muncie, IN 47304
(317) 288-2155
Admin Elizabeth DeVoe. *Dir of Nursing* Wanda Walters. *Medical Dir* Michael Seidle MD.
Licensure Skilled care; Residential care. *Beds* SNF 76; Residential care 227. *Private Pay Patients* 100%. *Certified* Medicare.
Owner Nonprofit organization/foundation.
Admissions Requirements Minimum age 62; Medical examination; Physician's request.
Staff Physicians; RNs; LPNs; Nurses' aides; Physical therapists; Speech therapists; Activities coordinators; Dietitians; Podiatrists; Audiologists.
Facilities Dining room; Physical therapy room; Activities room; Chapel; Crafts room; Laundry room; Barber/Beauty shop; Library; Pharmacy; Bank; Lounges.
Activities Arts & crafts; Cards; Games; Reading groups; Prayer groups; Movies; Shopping trips; Dances/Social/Cultural gatherings; Intergenerational programs; Pet therapy.

Woodland Nursing Home
3820 W Jackson St, Muncie, IN 47304
(317) 289-3451
Admin Anna J Powless.
Licensure Skilled care; Intermediate care. *Beds* SNF 31; ICF 90. *Certified* Medicaid; Medicare.
Owner Proprietary corp.

Munster

Munster Med-Inn
7935 Calumet Ave, Munster, IN 46321
(219) 836-8300
Admin Jean T Robinson Benavides. *Dir of Nursing* Diane Noe RN. *Medical Dir* William H Hehemann MD.
Licensure Skilled care; Intermediate care; Residential care; Comprehensive care. *Beds* SNF 208; ICF 48; Residential 30; Comprehensive care 2. *Private Pay Patients* 32%. *Certified* Medicaid; Medicare.
Owner Proprietary corp.

Admissions Requirements Minimum age 18; Medical examination; Physician's request.
Staff RNs 4 (ft), 7 (pt); LPNs 19 (ft), 2 (pt); Nurses' aides 106 (ft), 23 (pt); Physical therapists 1 (ft); Occupational therapists 1 (ft); Speech therapists 1 (ft); Activities coordinators 1 (ft); Dietitians 1 (ft), 1 (pt); COTAs 2 (ft); P T aides 5 (ft), 2 (pt); Activity aides 2 (ft), 2 (pt).
Languages Spanish, Polish.
Facilities Dining room; Physical therapy room; Activities room; Laundry room; Barber/Beauty shop; Library; Occupational therapy room; Speech therapy room; Lounges on all floors.
Activities Arts & crafts; Cards; Games; Prayer groups; Movies; Shopping trips; Dances/Social/Cultural gatherings; Intergenerational programs; Pet therapy; Reality orientation; Church services; Exercise groups; Glamour hour; Cooking club.

Nappanee

Lu Ann Nursing Home
952 W Walnut St, Nappanee, IN 46550
(219) 773-4119
Admin John L Mellinger. *Dir of Nursing* Dominica K Beath. *Medical Dir* V T Houck MD.
Licensure Intermediate care; Alzheimer's care. *Beds* ICF 50. *Certified* Medicaid.
Owner Privately owned.
Staff RNs 3 (ft), 2 (pt); LPNs 2 (ft), 1 (pt); Nurses' aides 10 (ft), 3 (pt); Dietitians 1 (ft); Ophthalmologists 1 (pt).
Facilities Dining room; Activities room; Chapel; Crafts room; Laundry room; Barber/Beauty shop; Library.
Activities Arts & crafts; Cards; Games; Reading groups; Prayer groups; Movies; Dances/Social/Cultural gatherings.

Nashville

Brown County Community Care Center Inc
Fred Henderson Dr, PO Box 667, Nashville, IN 47448
(812) 988-6666
Admin Virginia Burt.
Medical Dir Tim Alward.
Licensure Intermediate care. *Beds* ICF 70. *Certified* Medicaid.
Owner Proprietary corp (Community Care Centers).
Staff RNs 1 (ft), 1 (pt); LPNs 3 (ft), 1 (pt); Nurses' aides 10 (ft), 9 (pt); Activities coordinators 1 (ft); Dietitians 1 (pt).
Facilities Dining room; Activities room; Laundry room; Barber/Beauty shop.
Activities Arts & crafts; Cards; Games; Reading groups; Prayer groups; Shopping trips; Dances/Social/Cultural gatherings.

New Albany

Green Valley Convalescent Center
3118 Green Valley Rd, New Albany, IN 47150
(812) 945-2341, 945-0089 FAX
Admin Peter Graves. *Dir of Nursing* JoAnn Ehalt RN. *Medical Dir* Howard Pope MD.
Licensure Skilled care; Intermediate care; Comprehensive care; Retirement. *Beds* SNF 120; ICF 120; Comprehensive care 8; Retirement apts 12. *Private Pay Patients* 23%. *Certified* Medicaid; Medicare.
Owner Proprietary corp (Consolidated Resources Health Care Fund I).
Admissions Requirements Minimum age 18; Medical examination; Physician's request.
Staff Physicians 31 (pt); RNs 6 (ft), 1 (pt); LPNs 27 (ft), 5 (pt); Nurses' aides 75 (ft), 3 (pt); Physical therapists 1 (pt); Speech therapists 1 (pt); Activities coordinators 2 (ft); Dietitians 1 (pt); Audiologists 1 (pt);

Qualified medicine aides 4 (ft); Clinical psychologists 1 (pt); Dentists 1 (pt); Pharmacists 1 (pt); Medical records consultants 1 (pt).
Facilities Dining room; Physical therapy room; Activities room; Crafts room; Laundry room; Barber/Beauty shop; Patio; Sun room.
Activities Arts & crafts; Cards; Games; Reading groups; Prayer groups; Movies; Shopping trips; Dances/Social/Cultural gatherings; Intergenerational programs; Pet therapy.

Lincoln Hills of New Albany
PO Box 603, New Albany, IN 47150-0603
(812) 948-1311
Admin Roger Ambrose. *Dir of Nursing* Ila White RN. *Medical Dir* Dr Kenneth Brown; Dr John Paris.
Licensure Intermediate care; Alzheimer's care. *Beds* ICF 200. *Private Pay Patients* 30%. *Certified* Medicaid.
Owner Privately owned.
Admissions Requirements Minimum age 18; Medical examination; Physician's request.
Staff RNs 4 (ft); LPNs 8 (ft); Nurses' aides 50 (ft), 20 (pt); Physical therapists 1 (ft); Activities coordinators 3 (ft); Dietitians 1 (ft).
Facilities Dining room; Physical therapy room; Activities room; Chapel; Laundry room; Barber/Beauty shop.
Activities Arts & crafts; Cards; Games; Reading groups; Prayer groups; Movies; Shopping trips; Dances/Social/Cultural gatherings; Pet therapy.

New Albany Nursing Home
1919 Bono Rd, New Albany, IN 47150
(812) 944-4404
Admin Sandra Spencer.
Licensure Intermediate care. *Beds* ICF 40. *Certified* Medicaid.
Owner Proprietary corp (Beverly Enterprises).

Providence Retirement Home
703 E Spring St, New Albany, IN 47150
(812) 945-5221
Admin Sr Barbara Ann Zeller. *Dir of Nursing* David Conley RN. *Medical Dir* Eli Hallal MD.
Licensure Residential care; Comprehensive care; Alzheimer's care; Adult day care. *Beds* Residential 67; Comprehensive care 28.
Owner Nonprofit organization/foundation.
Admissions Requirements Minimum age 50; Medical examination.
Staff Physicians; RNs; LPNs; Nurses' aides; Activities coordinators; Dietitians.
Affiliation Roman Catholic.
Facilities Dining room; Activities room; Chapel; Crafts room; Laundry room; Barber/Beauty shop.
Activities Arts & crafts; Cards; Games; Reading groups; Prayer groups; Movies; Shopping trips; Dances/Social/Cultural gatherings.

Rolling Hills Health Care Center
3625 St Joseph Rd, New Albany, IN 47150
(812) 948-0670, 948-6222 FAX
Admin Judie C Scobee. *Dir of Nursing* C C Young. *Medical Dir* John Paris MD.
Licensure Intermediate care; Alzheimer's care. *Beds* ICF 100. *Private Pay Patients* 25%. *Certified* Medicaid.
Owner Proprietary corp (Nationwide Management).
Admissions Requirements Medical examination; Physician's request.
Staff RNs; LPNs; Nurses' aides; Activities coordinators.
Facilities Dining room; Physical therapy room; Activities room; Laundry room; Barber/Beauty shop.
Activities Arts & crafts; Cards; Games; Prayer groups; Movies; Shopping trips; Dances/Social/Cultural gatherings; Pet therapy.

New Carlisle

Hamilton Grove
31869 Chicago Trail, New Carlisle, IN 46552
(219) 654-3118
Admin Joseph S Dzwonar.
Medical Dir Robert Fenstermacher MD.
Licensure Intermediate care; Residential care; Comprehensive care. *Beds* ICF 9; Residential care 90; Comprehensive care 25. *Certified* Medicaid.
Owner Proprietary corp (Community Care Centers).
Admissions Requirements Minimum age 65.
Staff RNs 4 (ft); LPNs 12 (ft); Nurses' aides 30 (ft), 8 (pt); Recreational therapists 2 (ft), 2 (pt); Activities coordinators 1 (ft); Dietitians 1 (pt).
Affiliation Methodist.
Facilities Dining room; Physical therapy room; Activities room; Chapel; Crafts room; Laundry room; Barber/Beauty shop; Library; Commisary; Greenhouse.
Activities Arts & crafts; Cards; Games; Reading groups; Prayer groups; Movies; Shopping trips; Dances/Social/Cultural gatherings.

Miller's Merry Manor
PO Box 660, 220 E Dunn Rd, New Carlisle, IN 46552
(219) 654-7244
Admin Jerome H Ouding MSW.
Medical Dir Dr Ralph Inabnit. *Licensure* Intermediate care. *Beds* ICF 70.
Owner Proprietary corp (Caremet Inc).
Staff Physicians 1 (pt); RNs 2 (ft), 3 (pt); LPNs 5 (ft); Nurses' aides 12 (ft), 10 (pt); Physical therapists 1 (ft), 1 (pt); Reality therapists 1 (pt); Recreational therapists 1 (pt); Occupational therapists 1 (pt); Speech therapists 1 (pt); Activities coordinators 1 (ft), 1 (pt); Dietitians 1 (pt); Ophthalmologists 1 (pt); Dentists 1 (pt).

New Castle

Heritage House of New Castle
1023 N 20th St, New Castle, IN 47362
(317) 529-9694
Admin Sally A Schutte.
Licensure Skilled care; Intermediate care. *Beds* SNF 37; ICF 74. *Certified* Medicaid; Medicare.
Owner Proprietary corp.

Holly Hill Nursing Home
901 N 16th St, New Castle, IN 47362
(317) 529-4695
Admin Teresa Hosier. *Dir of Nursing* Donna Nelson. *Medical Dir* Bruce Ippel MD.
Licensure Intermediate care. *Beds* ICF 40. *Certified* Medicaid.
Owner Proprietary corp (Beverly Enterprises).
Admissions Requirements Minimum age 18; Physician's request.
Staff Physicians 1 (ft); RNs 1 (ft); LPNs 4 (ft), 2 (pt); Nurses' aides 10 (ft), 3 (pt); Activities coordinators 1 (ft); Dietitians 1 (pt); Ophthalmologists 1 (pt); Podiatrists 1 (pt).
Facilities Dining room; Laundry room.
Activities Arts & crafts; Cards; Games; Reading groups; Prayer groups; Movies; Shopping trips; Dances/Social/Cultural gatherings; Pet therapy.

New Castle Community Care Center
115 N 10th St, New Castle, IN 47362
(317) 529-2703
Admin Paul Rhodes.
Licensure Intermediate care. *Beds* ICF 60. *Certified* Medicaid.
Owner Proprietary corp (ARA Living Centers).

New Castle Healthcare Center
990 N 16th St, New Castle, IN 47362
(317) 521-0230

Admin Tim Herber.
Medical Dir Dr Rains.
Licensure Skilled care; Intermediate care. *Beds* SNF 51; ICF 144. *Private Pay Patients* 10%. *Certified* Medicaid; Medicare.
Owner Proprietary corp (PAFCO Enterprises).
Admissions Requirements Minimum age 21.
Staff Physicians 9 (pt); Dietitians.
Facilities Dining room; Physical therapy room; Activities room; Crafts room; Laundry room; Barber/Beauty shop.
Activities Arts & crafts; Cards; Games; Prayer groups; Movies; Shopping trips; Dances/Social/Cultural gatherings; Intergenerational programs; Pet therapy.

Oakwood Health Care Center
1000 N 16th St, New Castle, IN 47362
(317) 521-1420
Admin Christy Tompkins RN. *Dir of Nursing* Bonnie Culver RN. *Medical Dir* Cloyd Dye MD.
Licensure Skilled care. *Beds* SNF 36. *Certified* Medicaid; Medicare.
Owner Proprietary corp.
Admissions Requirements Medical examination; Physician's request.
Staff RNs 2 (ft), 4 (pt); LPNs 5 (ft), 2 (pt); Nurses' aides 15 (ft), 7 (pt); Activities coordinators 1 (pt); Dietitians 1 (pt).
Facilities Dining room; Physical therapy room; Activities room; Laundry room; Barber/Beauty shop.
Activities Arts & crafts; Cards; Games; Reading groups; Prayer groups; Movies; Dances/Social/Cultural gatherings; Intergenerational programs; Pet therapy.

New Haven

Brighton Hall Nursing Center
1201 Daly Dr, New Haven, IN 46774
(219) 749-0413
Admin Robert Shambaugh. *Dir of Nursing* Ruth Etzer. *Medical Dir* Geriatrics Inc.
Licensure Skilled care; Intermediate care. *Beds* SNF 42; ICF 78. *Certified* Medicaid; Medicare.
Owner Proprietary corp (Shive Nursing Centers Inc).
Admissions Requirements Minimum age 21.
Facilities Dining room; Physical therapy room; Activities room; Crafts room; Laundry room; Barber/Beauty shop; Library.
Activities Arts & crafts; Cards; Games; Reading groups; Prayer groups; Movies; Shopping trips; Dances/Social/Cultural gatherings; Intergenerational programs; Pet therapy.

Newburgh

Medco Center of Newburgh
4255 Medwel Dr, Newburgh, IN 47630
(812) 853-2993
Admin Susan Bookout.
Licensure Intermediate care; Residential care. *Beds* ICF 112; Residential care 8. *Certified* Medicaid.
Owner Proprietary corp (Unicare).

Newburgh Health Care & Residential Center
10466 Pollack Ave, Newburgh, IN 47630
(812) 853-2931
Admin Ron W O Wong.
Licensure Intermediate care. *Beds* 114. *Certified* Medicaid.
Owner Proprietary corp (Beverly Enterprises).

Woodlands Convalescent Center
PO Box 400, 4088 Frame Rd, Newburgh, IN 47630-0400
(812) 853-9567
Admin Janice Richey.
Licensure Skilled care; Intermediate care. *Beds* SNF 30; ICF 38.

Noblesville

Harbour Manor Care Center of St John's
1667 Sheridan Rd, Noblesville, IN 46060
(317) 773-9205
Admin Gerard Bodalski.
Licensure Intermediate care. *Beds* ICF 87.

Manor House at Riverview
395 Westfield Rd, 4th Fl, Noblesville, IN 46060
(317) 773-7699
Admin Joseph Trueblood. *Dir of Nursing* Debbie Baker RN. *Medical Dir* William Wander MD.
Licensure Skilled care; Intermediate care. *Beds* SNF 34; ICF 26.
Owner Proprietary corp.
Staff RNs; LPNs; Nurses' aides; Physical therapists; Reality therapists; Recreational therapists; Occupational therapists; Speech therapists; Activities coordinators; Dietitians.

Noblesville Healthcare Center
295 Westfield Rd, Noblesville, IN 46060
(317) 773-3760
Admin Gerard S Bodalski. *Dir of Nursing* Betty Hall. *Medical Dir* Walter Beaver MD.
Licensure Skilled care; Intermediate care; Alzheimer's care. *Beds* SNF 77; ICF 118. *Certified* Medicaid; Medicare.
Owner Proprietary corp (ARA Living Centers).
Admissions Requirements Medical examination; Physician's request.
Staff Physicians; RNs; LPNs; Nurses' aides; Physical therapists; Reality therapists; Recreational therapists; Occupational therapists; Speech therapists; Activities coordinators; Dietitians; Ophthalmologists; Podiatrists; Dentists.
Languages French.
Facilities Dining room; Physical therapy room; Activities room; Crafts room; Laundry room; Barber/Beauty shop; Living rooms; Private rooms for visits.
Activities Arts & crafts; Cards; Games; Reading groups; Prayer groups; Movies; Shopping trips; Dances/Social/Cultural gatherings; Sewing; Gardening.

Noblesville Nursing Home
1391 Greenfield Pike, Noblesville, IN 46060
(317) 773-1264
Admin Mary Jo Powers.
Licensure Intermediate care. *Beds* ICF 40. *Certified* Medicaid.
Owner Proprietary corp (Beverly Enterprises).
Staff RNs 1 (ft); LPNs 1 (ft), 1 (pt); Nurses' aides 10 (ft), 7 (pt); Activities coordinators 1 (ft); Dietitians 1 (pt); Podiatrists 1 (pt).

North Manchester

Peabody Retirement Community
400 W 7th St, North Manchester, IN 46962
(219) 982-8616
Admin Richard M Craig. *Dir of Nursing* Julie Snyder RN. *Medical Dir* Park Adams MD.
Licensure Intermediate care; Residential care. *Beds* ICF 150; Residential care 122. *Private Pay Patients* 80%. *Certified* Medicaid.
Owner Nonprofit corp.
Admissions Requirements Minimum age 65.
Affiliation Presbyterian.
Facilities Dining room; Physical therapy room; Activities room; Chapel; Crafts room; Laundry room; Barber/Beauty shop; Library.
Activities Arts & crafts; Cards; Games; Reading groups; Prayer groups; Movies; Shopping trips; Dances/Social/Cultural gatherings; Intergenerational programs.

Timbercrest—Church of the Brethren Home Inc
PO Box 501, East St, North Manchester, IN 46962
(219) 982-2118

Admin David Lawrenz. *Dir of Nursing* Laverne Mitmoen RN.
Licensure Intermediate care; Residential care. *Beds* ICF 46; Residential 144. *Certified* Medicaid.
Owner Nonprofit corp.
Admissions Requirements Minimum age 65; Medical examination.
Staff RNs 2 (ft); LPNs 4 (ft), 6 (pt); Nurses' aides 12 (ft), 20 (pt); Activities coordinators 1 (ft); Dietitians 1 (ft), 3 (pt).
Affiliation Church of the Brethren.
Facilities Dining room; Activities room; Chapel; Crafts room; Laundry room; Barber/Beauty shop; Library.
Activities Arts & crafts; Cards; Games; Reading groups; Prayer groups; Movies; Shopping trips; Dances/Social/Cultural gatherings.

North Vernon

Community Care Center of North Vernon
PO Box 640, 1200 W O & M Ave, North Vernon, IN 47265
(812) 346-7570
Admin Dawn L Black.
Licensure Skilled care; Intermediate care. *Beds* SNF 25; ICF 83. *Certified* Medicaid.
Owner Proprietary corp (Community Care Centers).

North Vernon Nursing Home
801 N Elm St, North Vernon, IN 47265
(812) 346-4942
Admin Frances J Cherry RN. *Dir of Nursing* V Gelene Lawdermilt. *Medical Dir* J B Schuck MD.
Licensure Intermediate care. *Beds* ICF 40. *Private Pay Patients* 1%. *Certified* Medicaid.
Owner Proprietary corp (Beverly Enterprises).
Admissions Requirements Minimum age 18.
Staff Physicians 6 (pt); RNs 1 (ft), 1 (pt); LPNs 2 (ft), 3 (pt); Nurses' aides 6 (ft), 4 (pt); Activities coordinators 1 (ft); Dietitians 1 (pt); Ophthalmologists 1 (pt); Podiatrists 1 (pt).
Facilities Dining room; Activities room; Laundry room; Barber/Beauty shop.
Activities Arts & crafts; Cards; Games; Reading groups; Prayer groups; Movies; Shopping trips; Dances/Social/Cultural gatherings; Intergenerational programs; Pet therapy.

Oakland City

Good Samaritan Home Inc
210 N Gibson St, Oakland City, IN 47560
(812) 749-4774
Admin Jeff Padgett. *Dir of Nursing* Jane Rusher. *Medical Dir* Dr Gehlhausen.
Licensure Intermediate care. *Beds* ICF 114. *Certified* Medicaid.
Owner Proprietary corp.
Admissions Requirements Minimum age 18; Medical examination.
Staff Physicians 5 (pt); RNs 3 (ft); LPNs 9 (ft) 48 (ft); Physical therapists 1 (pt); Activities coordinators 1 (ft); Dietitians 1 (pt); Ophthalmologists 1 (pt); Dentists 1 (pt); Social Services 1 (ft).
Facilities Dining room; Physical therapy room; Activities room; Chapel; Crafts room; Laundry room; Barber/Beauty shop; Library; TV room.
Activities Arts & crafts; Cards; Games; Reading groups; Prayer groups; Movies; Shopping trips; Dances/Social/Cultural gatherings.

Oaktown

Oak Village Inc
PO Box 270, 4th & School Sts, Oaktown, IN 47561
(812) 745-2360, 745-6302 FAX
Admin Kay Melvin. *Dir of Nursing* Lynda Parker. *Medical Dir* Dr Odell.
Licensure Intermediate care. *Beds* ICF 50. *Private Pay Patients* 50%. *Certified* Medicaid.
Owner Nonprofit corp.
Admissions Requirements Minimum age 18; Medical examination; Physician's request.
Staff Physicians 1 (pt); RNs 2 (ft), 2 (pt); LPNs 2 (ft), 2 (pt); Nurses' aides 15 (ft), 15 (pt); Activities coordinators 1 (ft); Dietitians 1 (ft).
Facilities Dining room; Activities room; Crafts room; Laundry room; Barber/Beauty shop; Library; Courtyard; Patio; Rose garden; Whirlpool tub.
Activities Arts & crafts; Cards; Games; Reading groups; Prayer groups; Movies; Shopping trips; Dances/Social/Cultural gatherings; Intergenerational programs; Pet therapy; Nature trips.

Odon

Bertha D Garten Ketcham Memorial Center Inc
601 E Race St, Odon, IN 47562
(812) 636-4920
Admin Terri L Shimer. *Dir of Nursing* Debra Ramsey RN.
Licensure Intermediate care. *Beds* ICF 62. *Certified* Medicaid.
Owner Nonprofit corp.
Admissions Requirements Minimum age 18; Medical examination.
Staff RNs 6 (ft); LPNs 5 (ft); Nurses' aides 20 (ft), 5 (pt); Activities coordinators 1 (ft); Dietitians 1 (pt).
Facilities Dining room; Activities room; Crafts room; Laundry room; Barber/Beauty shop.
Activities Arts & crafts; Cards; Games; Reading groups; Prayer groups; Movies; Shopping trips; Dances/Social/Cultural gatherings.

Osgood

Manderley Health Care Center
PO Box 135, US Hwy 421 S, Osgood, IN 47037
(812) 689-4143
Admin Charles F Negangard. *Dir of Nursing* Janet Burdsall. *Medical Dir* Dr Thomas Barley.
Licensure Intermediate care. *Beds* ICF 71. *Certified* Medicaid.
Owner Proprietary corp.
Admissions Requirements Minimum age 18; Medical examination.
Staff RNs 1 (ft), 1 (pt); LPNs 5 (ft); Nurses' aides 31 (ft), 3 (pt); Activities coordinators 1 (ft), 1 (pt); Dietitians 1 (pt).
Facilities Dining room; Activities room; Chapel; Crafts room; Barber/Beauty shop; Library; Living room.
Activities Arts & crafts; Cards; Games; Reading groups; Prayer groups; Movies; Shopping trips; Dances/Social/Cultural gatherings; Intergenerational programs; Pet therapy.

Ossian

Ossian Health Care
PO Box 589, 215 Davis Rd, Ossian, IN 46777
(219) 622-7821, 622-4370 FAX
Admin Gary S Cooke. *Dir of Nursing* Elaine Beck RN. *Medical Dir* J P Cripe MD.
Licensure Skilled care; Intermediate care. *Beds* SNF 34; ICF 66. *Private Pay Patients* 48%. *Certified* Medicaid; Medicare.
Owner Proprietary corp (Nationwide Management Inc).
Admissions Requirements Medical examination.
Staff RNs 3 (ft), 5 (pt); LPNs 6 (ft), 2 (pt); Nurses' aides 24 (ft), 5 (pt); Activities coordinators 1 (ft), 1 (pt).
Facilities Dining room; Physical therapy room; Activities room; Barber/Beauty shop; Library.
Activities Arts & crafts; Games; Reading groups; Prayer groups; Movies; Dances/Social/Cultural gatherings; Intergenerational programs.

Otterbein

Otterbein Care Center
PO Box 580, Otterbein, IN 47970
(317) 583-4468
Admin Elaine Brouillette.
Licensure Intermediate care. *Beds* ICF 60.

Owensville

Owensville Convalescent Center Inc
PO Box 368, Hwy 165 W, Owensville, IN 47665
(812) 729-7901
Admin Eugene Hall. *Dir of Nursing* Lisa A Hall RN.
Licensure Intermediate care. *Beds* ICF 68. *Certified* Medicaid.
Owner Proprietary corp (Cloverleaf Healthcare Services).
Admissions Requirements Medical examination.
Staff RNs 2 (ft); LPNs 3 (ft), 5 (pt); Nurses' aides 15 (ft), 11 (pt); Physical therapists 1 (pt); Activities coordinators 1 (pt); Dietitians 1 (pt); Ophthalmologists 1 (pt); Medical directors 1 (pt).
Facilities Dining room; Laundry room; Barber/Beauty shop; Lounge.
Activities Arts & crafts; Games; Reading groups; Prayer groups; Movies; Shopping trips; Dances/Social/Cultural gatherings.

Oxford

Edgewood Healthcare
State Rd 55, Oxford, IN 47971
(317) 385-2291
Admin Robert C Blackford. *Dir of Nursing* Dorsa Ann Sherman RN.
Licensure Intermediate care. *Beds* ICF 56. *Certified* Medicaid.
Owner Proprietary corp.
Admissions Requirements Medical examination.
Staff RNs 2 (ft); LPNs 3 (ft); Nurses' aides 15 (ft); Activities coordinators 1 (ft).
Facilities Dining room; Activities room; Crafts room; Laundry room; Barber/Beauty shop; Library.
Activities Arts & crafts; Cards; Games; Reading groups; Prayer groups; Movies; Shopping trips; Dances/Social/Cultural gatherings.

Paoli

Paoli Nursing Home
RR 4 Box 139, Paoli, IN 47454
(812) 723-3000
Admin Teresa Kellams.
Medical Dir Margaret McKnight.
Licensure Intermediate care. *Beds* ICF 40. *Certified* Medicaid.
Owner Proprietary corp (Beverly Enterprises).
Admissions Requirements Minimum age 19; Medical examination; Physician's request.

Staff Physicians 1 (pt); RNs 1 (ft); LPNs 2 (ft); Nurses' aides 10 (ft), 5 (pt); Activities coordinators 1 (ft); Dietitians 1 (pt).
Facilities Dining room; Activities room; Chapel; Crafts room; Laundry room.
Activities Arts & crafts; Cards; Games; Reading groups; Prayer groups; Movies; Shopping trips; Dances/Social/Cultural gatherings; Exercises; Art & travel clubs.

Parker City

Chrystal's Country Home Inc
Randolph St, Parker City, IN 47368
(317) 468-8280
Admin Robert E Steele.
Licensure Intermediate care. *Beds* ICF 99. *Certified* Medicaid.

Pendleton

Rawlins House Inc
PO Box 119, 300 J H Walker Dr, Pendleton, IN 46064
(317) 778-7501
Admin Steven D Costerison.
Medical Dir Robert C Beeson MD.
Licensure Intermediate care. *Beds* 134. *Certified* Medicaid.
Owner Proprietary corp.
Admissions Requirements Physician's request.
Staff Physicians 1 (pt); RNs 2 (ft); LPNs 6 (ft), 5 (pt); Nurses' aides 17 (ft), 22 (pt); Activities coordinators 1 (ft), 2 (pt); Dietitians 1 (ft), 1 (pt).
Facilities Dining room; Activities room; Laundry room; Barber/Beauty shop; Sun room.
Activities Arts & crafts; Cards; Games; Reading groups; Shopping trips; Dances/Social/Cultural gatherings.

Peru

Miller's Merry Manor Inc
317 Blair Pike, Peru, IN 46970
(317) 473-4426
Admin Roger Gunther.
Licensure Skilled care; Intermediate care. *Beds* SNF 43; ICF 155. *Certified* Medicaid; Medicare.
Owner Proprietary corp (Millers Merry Manor).

Peru Nursing Home
390 West Blvd, Peru, IN 46970
(317) 473-4900
Admin Dale G Parker.
Licensure Intermediate care. *Beds* ICF 40. *Certified* Medicaid.
Owner Proprietary corp (Beverly Enterprises).

Petersburg

Petersburg Healthcare Center
Box 100, Pike Ave, Petersburg, IN 47567
(812) 354-8833
Admin W R Scott James.
Licensure Skilled care; Intermediate care. *Beds* SNF 42; ICF 92. *Certified* Medicaid; Medicare.
Owner Proprietary corp (Beverly Enterprises).

Plainfield

Autumn Care of Clark's Creek
PO Box 7, 3700 Clark's Creek Rd, Plainfield, IN 46168
(317) 839-6577
Admin Dale N Maryfield. *Dir of Nursing* Frances Boone RN. *Medical Dir* David M Hadley MD.
Licensure Skilled care; Intermediate care. *Beds* SNF 59; ICF 140. *Certified* Medicaid; Medicare.
Owner Proprietary corp (Autumn Corp).

Admissions Requirements Minimum age 18; Medical examination; Physician's request.
Staff Physicians 1 (ft); RNs 4 (ft), 1 (pt); LPNs 11 (ft), 3 (pt); Nurses' aides 68 (ft), 8 (pt); Physical therapists 1 (ft); Occupational therapists 1 (pt); Speech therapists 1 (pt); Activities coordinators 5 (ft), 1 (pt); Dietitians 1 (pt); Ophthalmologists 1 (pt); Dentists 1 (pt).
Facilities Dining room; Physical therapy room; Activities room; Crafts room; Laundry room; Barber/Beauty shop; Lounges.
Activities Arts & crafts; Cards; Games; Reading groups; Prayer groups; Movies; Shopping trips; Dances/Social/Cultural gatherings.

Vinewood Nursing Home
404 N Vine St, Plainfield, IN 46168
(317) 839-0154
Admin Eileene C Stevens.
Licensure Intermediate care; Comprehensive care. *Beds* ICF 27; Comprehensive care 13. *Certified* Medicaid.

Plymouth

Mayflower Nursing Home
309 Kingston Dr, Plymouth, IN 46563
(219) 936-9025
Admin Paul F Duranczyk. *Dir of Nursing* Geraldine Kubaszyk. *Medical Dir* James Robertson MD.
Licensure Intermediate care. *Beds* ICF 40. *Certified* Medicaid.
Owner Proprietary corp (Beverly Enterprises).
Admissions Requirements Minimum age 18; Medical examination; Physician's request.
Staff RNs 1 (ft), 1 (pt); LPNs 4 (ft); Nurses' aides 7 (ft), 2 (pt); Activities coordinators 1 (ft).
Facilities Dining room; Activities room; Laundry room.
Activities Arts & crafts; Cards; Games; Reading groups; Prayer groups; Movies; Shopping trips; Dances/Social/Cultural gatherings.

Miller's Merry Manor Inc
PO Box 498, 600 W Oakhill Ave, Plymouth, IN 46563
(219) 936-9981
Admin Christy Clark.
Licensure Skilled care; Intermediate care; Comprehensive care. *Beds* SNF 33; ICF 106; Comprehensive care 27. *Certified* Medicaid; Medicare.
Owner Proprietary corp (Millers Merry Manor).

Pilgrim Manor Rehabilitation & Convalescent Center
222 Parkview St, Plymouth, IN 46563
(219) 936-9943
Admin G Dean Byers.
Licensure Skilled care; Intermediate care; Comprehensive care. *Beds* SNF 37; ICF 52; Comprehensive care 1. *Certified* Medicaid; Medicare.

Portage

Fountainview Place
3175 Lancer St, Portage, IN 46368
(219) 762-9571
Admin Glenn N Wagner.
Licensure Skilled care; Intermediate care; Residential care; Alzheimer's care. *Beds* SNF 71; ICF 127; Residential care 6; Alzheimer's care 22. *Private Pay Patients* 13%. *Certified* Medicaid; Medicare.
Owner Proprietary corp (Beverly Enterprises).
Admissions Requirements Minimum age 18.
Staff Physicians 1 (pt); RNs 8 (ft), 2 (pt); LPNs 16 (ft), 4 (pt); Nurses' aides 70 (ft), 10 (pt); Physical therapists 1 (ft), 1 (pt);

Occupational therapists 1 (pt); Speech therapists 1 (pt); Activities coordinators 2 (ft); Dietitians 1 (pt); Podiatrists 1 (pt).
Languages Spanish.
Facilities Dining room; Physical therapy room; Activities room; Chapel; Crafts room; Laundry room; Barber/Beauty shop; Library.
Activities Arts & crafts; Cards; Games; Reading groups; Prayer groups; Movies; Shopping trips; Dances/Social/Cultural gatherings; Intergenerational programs; Pet therapy.

Miller's Merry Manor Inc
5909 Lute Rd, Portage, IN 46368
(219) 763-2273, 763-7218 FAX
Admin Marsha Parry. *Dir of Nursing* Geri Kubaszyk. *Medical Dir* Dr John Crise.
Licensure Skilled care; Intermediate care. *Beds* SNF 22; ICF 44. *Private Pay Patients* 40%. *Certified* Medicaid; Medicare.
Owner Proprietary corp (Caremet Inc).
Admissions Requirements Minimum age 18; Medical examination; Physician's request.
Staff RNs 3 (ft), 3 (pt); LPNs 3 (ft), 3 (pt); Nurses' aides 20 (ft), 10 (pt); Physical therapists 2 (pt); Recreational therapists 1 (pt); Occupational therapists 1 (pt); Speech therapists 1 (pt); Activities coordinators 1 (ft); Dietitians 1 (pt).
Facilities Dining room; Physical therapy room; Activities room; Crafts room; Laundry room; Barber/Beauty shop; Separate resident lounges; Living rooms with skylights; Private and semi-private rooms.
Activities Arts & crafts; Cards; Games; Reading groups; Prayer groups; Movies; Shopping trips; Dances/Social/Cultural gatherings; Pet therapy.

Portland

Portland Community Care Center—East
PO Box 1012, 510 W High St, Portland, IN 47371
(219) 726-6591
Admin William DeRome. *Dir of Nursing* Betty Hisey RN.
Licensure Intermediate care. *Beds* ICF 60. *Certified* Medicaid.
Owner Proprietary corp (Community Care Centers).
Admissions Requirements Medical examination; Physician's request.
Staff RNs; LPNs; Nurses' aides; Activities coordinators.
Languages Spanish.
Facilities Dining room; Activities room; Crafts room; Laundry room; Barber/Beauty shop.
Activities Arts & crafts; Cards; Games; Prayer groups; Movies; Shopping trips; Dances/Social/Cultural gatherings.

Portland Community Care Center—West
PO Box 1012, 200 N Park St, Portland, IN 47371
(219) 726-9441
Admin Dixie B May.
Medical Dir Dr Eugene Gillum.
Licensure Skilled care; Intermediate care. *Beds* SNF 24; ICF 70. *Certified* Medicaid.
Owner Proprietary corp (Community Care Centers).
Admissions Requirements Minimum age 18; Medical examination.
Staff RNs; LPNs; Nurses' aides; Speech therapists; Activities coordinators; Dietitians.
Facilities Dining room; Activities room; Crafts room; Laundry room; Barber/Beauty shop.
Activities Arts & crafts; Cards; Games; Reading groups; Prayer groups; Movies.

Poseyville

Allison Healthcare Corp
PO Box 549, Corner of Locust & Pine Sts, Poseyville, IN 47633
(812) 874-2814
Admin Debra Johnson. *Dir of Nursing* Kathleen Johnson. *Medical Dir* Dr C Burkett.
Licensure Intermediate care. *Beds* ICF 39. *Certified* Medicaid.
Owner Proprietary corp.
Admissions Requirements Minimum age 18; Medical examination; Physician's request; Chest X-ray; Mantoux.
Facilities Dining room; Activities room; Laundry room; Barber/Beauty shop; Fenced yard.
Activities Arts & crafts; Cards; Games; Reading groups; Prayer groups; Movies; Shopping trips; Dances/Social/Cultural gatherings; Pet therapy.

Princeton

Forest Del Convalescent Center
1020 W Vine St, Princeton, IN 47670
(812) 385-5238
Admin Terry Miller.
Licensure Skilled care; Intermediate care. *Beds* SNF 28; ICF 88. *Certified* Medicaid.
Admissions Requirements Minimum age 18; Medical examination; Physician's request.
Staff Physicians 1 (pt); Reality therapists 1 (pt); Recreational therapists 1 (pt); Activities coordinators 1 (pt); Dietitians 1 (pt); Ophthalmologists 1 (pt); Podiatrists 1 (pt); Dentists 1 (pt).
Facilities Dining room; Activities room; Crafts room; Laundry room; Barber/Beauty shop; TV lounge & entertainment center.
Activities Arts & crafts; Cards; Games; Reading groups; Prayer groups; Movies; Shopping trips; Dances/Social/Cultural gatherings; Trips out of facility.

Holiday Manor
Rte 4, 6th Ave, Princeton, IN 47670
(812) 385-5288
Admin Robert Lovell.
Licensure Intermediate care. *Beds* ICF 91. *Certified* Medicaid.
Admissions Requirements Minimum age 18.
Staff RNs 3 (ft), 1 (pt); LPNs 4 (ft); Nurses' aides 20 (ft), 4 (pt); Activities coordinators 1 (ft); Dietitians 1 (pt); Ophthalmologists 1 (pt); Podiatrists 1 (pt); Dentists 1 (pt).
Facilities Dining room; Activities room; Laundry room; Barber/Beauty shop.
Activities Arts & crafts; Cards; Games; Reading groups; Prayer groups; Movies; Shopping trips; Dances/Social/Cultural gatherings.

Rensselear

Rensselaer Care Center
1109 E Grace, Rensselear, IN 47978
(219) 866-4181
Admin Eleanor White.
Licensure Skilled care; Intermediate care. *Beds* SNF 43; ICF 137. *Certified* Medicaid.

Richmond

Cherish Nursing Center
1811 S 9th St, Richmond, IN 47374
(317) 962-8175
Admin Bonnie R Newkirk. *Dir of Nursing* Patricia Sabados. *Medical Dir* Dr James R Daggy.
Licensure Intermediate care. *Beds* ICF 59. *Certified* Medicaid.
Owner Proprietary corp.
Admissions Requirements Minimum age 18; Medical examination; Physician's request.

Staff Physicians 1 (pt); RNs 1 (ft); LPNs 5 (ft), 4 (pt); Nurses' aides 10 (ft), 9 (pt); Activities coordinators 1 (ft); Dietitians 1 (pt).
Facilities Dining room; Activities room; Laundry room; Library service.
Activities Arts & crafts; Cards; Games; Reading groups; Prayer groups; Movies; Shopping trips; Dances/Social/Cultural gatherings.

Friends Fellowship Community Inc
2030 Chester Blvd, Richmond, IN 47374
(317) 962-6546
Admin Jeffrey L Baxter. *Dir of Nursing* Linda Mann RN. *Medical Dir* Dr Francis B Warrick.
Licensure Residential care; Comprehensive care. *Beds* Residential care 218; Comprehensive care 70. *Private Pay Patients* 100%.
Owner Nonprofit organization/foundation.
Admissions Requirements Medical examination.
Staff RNs 7 (ft), 3 (pt); LPNs 6 (ft), 2 (pt); Nurses' aides 24 (ft), 4 (pt); Physical therapists 1 (pt); Activities coordinators 1 (ft); Dietitians 1 (pt).
Affiliation Society of Friends.
Facilities Dining room; Physical therapy room; Activities room; Crafts room; Laundry room; Barber/Beauty shop; Library.
Activities Arts & crafts; Cards; Games; Reading groups; Prayer groups; Movies; Shopping trips; Dances/Social/Cultural gatherings; Intergenerational programs; Pet therapy.

Golden Rule Nursing Center
2001 US Hwy 27 S, Richmond, IN 47473
(317) 966-7681
Admin Brian Bailey. *Dir of Nursing* Joyce Kidd. *Medical Dir* C G Clarkson MD.
Licensure Skilled care; Intermediate care. *Beds* SNF 68; ICF 108. *Private Pay Patients* 20%. *Certified* Medicaid; Medicare.
Owner Proprietary corp (Beverly Enterprises).
Admissions Requirements Minimum age 18; Medical examination.
Staff RNs 5 (ft), 1 (pt); LPNs 14 (ft), 2 (pt); Nurses' aides 60 (ft), 10 (pt); Physical therapists 1 (ft); Recreational therapists 2 (pt); Occupational therapists 1 (pt); Speech therapists 1 (pt); Activities coordinators 1 (ft); Dietitians 1 (pt).
Languages German.
Facilities Dining room; Physical therapy room; Activities room; Chapel; Crafts room; Laundry room; Barber/Beauty shop; Library; Occupational and speech therapy room.
Activities Arts & crafts; Cards; Games; Reading groups; Prayer groups; Movies; Shopping trips; Dances/Social/Cultural gatherings; Intergenerational programs; Pet therapy.

Heritage House of Richmond
2070 Chester Blvd, Richmond, IN 47374
(317) 962-3543
Admin Linda Dotson.
Medical Dir Dr Glen Ramsdell.
Licensure Skilled care; Intermediate care. *Beds* SNF 37; ICF 82. *Certified* Medicaid; Medicare.
Admissions Requirements Minimum age 19; Medical examination; Physician's request.
Staff RNs 5 (ft), 1 (pt); LPNs 7 (ft), 3 (pt); Nurses' aides 49 (ft); Physical therapists 1 (ft); Activities coordinators 1 (ft), 1 (pt).
Facilities Dining room; Physical therapy room; Activities room; Crafts room; Laundry room; Barber/Beauty shop.
Activities Arts & crafts; Cards; Games; Reading groups; Prayer groups; Movies; Dances/Social/Cultural gatherings.

Heritage Regency Inc
2050 Chester Blvd, Richmond, IN 47374
(317) 935-4440
Admin Pamela Traumbauer.
Licensure Skilled care; Intermediate care. *Beds* SNF 47; ICF 84.

Jenkins Hall
1401 Chester Blvd, Richmond, IN 47374
(317) 983-3200
Admin Jo Ann Bechtel. *Dir of Nursing* Rose Mary Patterson. *Medical Dir* Dr Patrick Anderson.
Licensure Intermediate care. *Beds* ICF 58. *Private Pay Patients* 50%. *Certified* Medicaid.
Owner Nonprofit corp.
Admissions Requirements Minimum age 19.
Staff RNs 5 (ft); LPNs 6 (ft); Nurses' aides 16 (ft); Dietitians 1 (ft).
Facilities Dining room; Activities room; Chapel; Crafts room; Laundry room; Barber/Beauty shop; Library.
Activities Arts & crafts; Cards; Games; Reading groups; Prayer groups; Movies; Dances/Social/Cultural gatherings; Pet therapy.

Oak Ridge Convalescent Center
1042 Oak Dr, Richmond, IN 47374
(317) 966-7788
Admin Curtis Pittinger.
Medical Dir Francis B Warrick MD.
Licensure Skilled care; Intermediate care. *Beds* SNF 64; ICF 58. *Certified* Medicaid; Medicare.
Owner Proprietary corp (Beverly Enterprises).
Admissions Requirements Minimum age 18; Medical examination; Physician's request.
Staff RNs 5 (ft); LPNs 11 (ft), 2 (pt); Nurses' aides 37 (ft), 11 (pt); Physical therapists 2 (ft); Recreational therapists 1 (ft); Occupational therapists 2 (pt); Speech therapists 1 (pt); Activities coordinators 1 (ft); Dietitians 1 (pt); Podiatrists 1 (pt); Dentists 1 (pt).
Facilities Dining room; Physical therapy room; Activities room; Chapel; Crafts room; Laundry room; Barber/Beauty shop; Library; Occupational therapy room; Speech therapy room.
Activities Arts & crafts; Cards; Games; Reading groups; Prayer groups; Movies; Shopping trips; Dances/Social/Cultural gatherings.

Spring Grove Care Center
2302 Chester Blvd, Richmond, IN 47374
(317) 962-0043
Admin Gregory S Ehlers. *Dir of Nursing* Phyllis Quinn. *Medical Dir* Frances Warrick MD.
Licensure Intermediate care; Alzheimer's care. *Beds* ICF 40. *Private Pay Patients* 30%. *Certified* Medicaid.
Owner Proprietary corp (Waverly Group).
Admissions Requirements Minimum age 18; Medical examination; Physician's request.
Staff RNs 1 (ft); LPNs 4 (ft), 1 (pt); Nurses' aides 12 (ft), 2 (pt); Activities coordinators 1 (pt).
Facilities Dining room; Activities room; Crafts room; Laundry room; Barber/Beauty shop; Courtyard.
Activities Arts & crafts; Cards; Games; Reading groups; Prayer groups; Movies; Shopping trips; Dances/Social/Cultural gatherings; Intergenerational programs; Outdoor activities (fishing, ball games); Family counseling.

Rising Sun

Rising Sun Care Center
Rte 2 Box 171A, Rising Sun, IN 47040
(812) 438-2219
Admin Marian Spurlock. *Dir of Nursing* Mary Zeiser. *Medical Dir* Ivan Lindgren.

Licensure Intermediate care. *Beds* ICF 58. *Certified* Medicaid.
Owner Proprietary corp (Southeastern Health Care Inc).
Staff RNs; LPNs; Nurses' aides; Activities coordinators.
Facilities Dining room; Laundry room; Barber/Beauty shop.
Activities Arts & crafts; Cards; Games; Prayer groups; Movies; Dances/Social/Cultural gatherings.

Rochester

Canterbury Manor
RR 6, Court Rd 50 N, Rochester, IN 46975
(219) 223-4331
Admin Carl William Miller II.
Licensure Intermediate care. *Beds* ICF 157. *Certified* Medicaid.

Rochester Nursing Home
240 E 18th St, Rochester, IN 46975
(219) 223-5100
Admin Michael J Beach.
Licensure Intermediate care. *Beds* ICF 40. *Certified* Medicaid.
Owner Proprietary corp (Beverly Enterprises).

Rockport

Miller's Merry Manor Inc
PO Box 167, Rockport, IN 47635
(812) 649-2276
Admin Mary McDowell.
Licensure Skilled care; Intermediate care. *Beds* SNF 32; ICF 62. *Certified* Medicaid.
Owner Proprietary corp (Millers Merry Manor).

Rockville

Lee Alan Bryant Health Care Facilities Inc
Box 7, RR 1, Rockville, IN 47872
(317) 569-6654
Admin Bette A Hein. *Dir of Nursing* Carole Ladendorf. *Medical Dir* Dr Richard Bloomer.
Licensure Intermediate care; Residential care; Alzheimer's care. *Beds* ICF 80; Residential 156. *Certified* Medicaid.
Owner Proprietary corp.
Admissions Requirements Medical examination; Physician's request.
Staff Physicians 6 (pt); RNs 1 (ft); LPNs 8 (ft), 8 (pt); Nurses' aides 24 (ft), 14 (pt); Physical therapists 1 (pt); Speech therapists 1 (pt); Activities coordinators 2 (pt); Dietitians 1 (pt); Ophthalmologists 1 (pt); Podiatrists 1 (pt); Dentists 1 (pt).
Facilities Dining room; Physical therapy room; Activities room; Chapel; Crafts room; Laundry room; Barber/Beauty shop; Library; 186 acres of grounds; Fishing area.
Activities Arts & crafts; Cards; Games; Reading groups; Prayer groups; Movies; Shopping trips; Dances/Social/Cultural gatherings; Field trips; Outings; Bus.

Castle Shannon Nursing Home
Box 251, RR 3, Rockville, IN 47872
(317) 569-6526
Admin Mary Jane Kirkman. *Dir of Nursing* Nancy Newlin. *Medical Dir* Richard Bloomer MD.
Licensure Intermediate care. *Beds* ICF 40. *Certified* Medicaid.
Owner Proprietary corp (Beverly Enterprises).
Admissions Requirements Minimum age 18; Medical examination; Physician's request.
Staff LPNs 4 (ft), 2 (pt); Nurses' aides 6 (ft), 9 (pt); Activities coordinators 1 (ft).
Facilities Dining room; Activities room; Laundry room.
Activities Arts & crafts; Cards; Games; Reading groups; Prayer groups; Movies; Shopping trips.

Parke County Nursing Home Inc
RR 3, Box 260, Rockville, IN 47872
(317) 569-6700
Admin Gerald Ball.
Licensure Intermediate care. *Beds* ICF 58.
 Certified Medicaid.
Admissions Requirements Minimum age 18;
 Medical examination.
Staff RNs 2 (pt); LPNs 3 (ft), 3 (pt); Nurses'
 aides 30 (ft); Recreational therapists 1 (ft);
 Activities coordinators 1 (ft); Dietitians 1
 (pt).
Facilities Dining room; Activities room;
 Crafts room; Laundry room; Barber/Beauty
 shop.
Activities Arts & crafts; Cards; Games;
 Reading groups; Prayer groups; Movies;
 Shopping trips; Dances/Social/Cultural
 gatherings.

Roselawn

Lake Holiday Manor
PO Box 230, 10325 County Line Rd,
 Roselawn, IN 46310
(219) 345-5211, 345-2465 FAX
Admin Dorothy M Huston. *Dir of Nursing*
 Ruthann Richwine. *Medical Dir* Roy
 Kingma MD.
Licensure Intermediate care; Residential care;
 Alzheimer's care. *Beds* ICF 95; Residential
 care 20. *Private Pay Patients* 20%. *Certified*
 Medicaid.
Owner Proprietary corp (John K Freeman).
Admissions Requirements Minimum age 18;
 Medical examination; Physician's request.
Staff RNs 2 (ft); LPNs 1 (ft), 2 (pt); Nurses'
 aides 20 (ft), 20 (pt); Activities coordinators
 1 (ft), 1 (pt); Dietitians 1 (pt).
Facilities Dining room; Activities room;
 Chapel; Crafts room; Laundry room; Barber/
 Beauty shop.
Activities Arts & crafts; Cards; Games;
 Reading groups; Movies; Shopping trips;
 Dances/Social/Cultural gatherings; Pet
 therapy.

Rossville

Milner Community Health Care Inc
State Rd 26 E Box 15, Rossville, IN 46065
(317) 379-2112, 296-3099
Admin Karen L Barrick. *Dir of Nursing* Lucy
 Coghill. *Medical Dir* Dr Gordon D Welk.
Licensure Intermediate care. *Beds* ICF 96.
 Certified Medicaid.
Owner Nonprofit organization/foundation.
Admissions Requirements Minimum age 18;
 Medical examination; Physician's request.
Staff RNs 6 (ft); LPNs 3 (ft); Nurses' aides 30
 (ft), 5 (pt); Activities coordinators 1 (ft), 1
 (pt); Dietitians (consultant).
Facilities Dining room; Physical therapy
 room; Activities room; Chapel; Crafts room;
 Laundry room; Barber/Beauty shop; Library.
Activities Arts & crafts; Cards; Games;
 Reading groups; Prayer groups; Movies;
 Shopping trips; Dances/Social/Cultural
 gatherings; Pet therapy.

Rushville

Hillside Haven Nursing Home
424 N Perkins St, Rushville, IN 46173
(317) 932-3024
Admin Catherine Coffman. *Dir of Nursing*
 Jackie Foist. *Medical Dir* Dr Gilbert Ortiz.
Licensure Intermediate care. *Beds* ICF 28.
 Certified Medicaid.
Owner Proprietary corp.
Admissions Requirements Medical
 examination.
Staff Physicians 1 (pt); RNs 1 (pt); LPNs 2
 (ft), 2 (pt); Nurses' aides 7 (ft), 5 (pt);
 Activities coordinators 1 (ft); Dietitians 1

Facilities Dining room; Activities room;
 Laundry room; Porch.
Activities Arts & crafts; Cards; Games;
 Reading groups; Prayer groups; Movies;
 Shopping trips; Dances/Social/Cultural
 gatherings; Exercise class.

Rush Health Care Management Inc
1300 N Main St, Rushville, IN 46173
(317) 932-4111
Admin Jack Shaefer.
Licensure Skilled care. *Beds* SNF 22.

Rush Memorial Hospital—Swing Bed Unit
1300 N Main St, Rushville, IN 46173
(317) 932-4111, 932-3705 FAX
Admin Mr Hartley. *Dir of Nursing* Mary Jo
 Keith.
Licensure Skilled care. *Beds* SNF 22. *Certified*
 Medicare.
Owner Proprietary corp.
Admissions Requirements Physician's request.
Staff Physicians; RNs; LPNs; Nurses' aides;
 Physical therapists; Speech therapists;
 Activities coordinators; Dietitians.
Facilities Dining room; Physical therapy
 room; Activities room; Chapel.
Activities Arts & crafts; Cards; Games;
 Reading groups; Movies.

Rushville Millers Merry Manor
612 E 11th St, Rushville, IN 46173
(317) 932-4127
Admin Ronald A Green. *Dir of Nursing* Gwen
 Walters RNC. *Medical Dir* D W Ellis MD.
Licensure Skilled care; Intermediate care;
 Residential care. *Beds* SNF 33; ICF 137;
 Residential care 5. *Private Pay Patients* 29%.
 Certified Medicaid; Medicare.
Owner Proprietary corp (Caremet Inc).
Admissions Requirements Minimum age 18;
 Medical examination.
Staff RNs 6 (ft), 4 (pt); LPNs 6 (ft), 2 (pt);
 Nurses' aides; Activities coordinators 2 (ft),
 1 (pt).
Facilities Dining room; Physical therapy
 room; Activities room; Laundry room;
 Barber/Beauty shop; Library; Game room.
Activities Arts & crafts; Cards; Games;
 Reading groups; Prayer groups; Movies;
 Shopping trips; Dances/Social/Cultural
 gatherings.

Salem

Meadow View Health Care Center
Homer & Anson Sts, Salem, IN 47167
(812) 883-4681
Admin Connie S Kellams. *Dir of Nursing*
 Margaret Kerns. *Medical Dir* Donald Martin
 MD.
Licensure Skilled care; Intermediate care. *Beds*
 SNF 39; ICF 95. *Certified* Medicaid;
 Medicare.
Owner Proprietary corp (Unicare).
Admissions Requirements Minimum age 18.
Staff Physicians; RNs; LPNs; Nurses' aides;
 Physical therapists; Speech therapists;
 Activities coordinators; Dietitians;
 Ophthalmologists.
Facilities Dining room; Physical therapy
 room; Activities room; Laundry room;
 Barber/Beauty shop.
Activities Arts & crafts; Cards; Games; Prayer
 groups; Movies; Shopping trips; Dances/
 Social/Cultural gatherings.

San Pierre

Little Company of Mary Health Facility Inc
Rte 1 Box 22A, San Pierre, IN 46374
(219) 828-4111
Admin Thomas H Kramer. *Dir of Nursing*
 Doris Boisvert RN. *Medical Dir* A N
 Damodaran MD.
Licensure Intermediate care; Alzheimer's care.
 Beds ICF 200. *Certified* Medicaid.

Owner Nonprofit corp.
Admissions Requirements Minimum age 18;
 Medical examination.
Staff RNs 3 (ft), 3 (pt); LPNs 2 (ft), 1 (pt);
 Nurses' aides 60 (ft), 30 (pt); Activities
 coordinators 1 (ft).
Languages Polish, Czech.
Affiliation Roman Catholic.
Facilities Dining room; Activities room;
 Chapel; Crafts room; Laundry room; Barber/
 Beauty shop; Library; Ceramics room; Social
 room; Family dining room.
Activities Arts & crafts; Cards; Games;
 Movies; Shopping trips.

Scottsburg

Scott Villa Living Center
RR 1, Box 45, Scottsburg, IN 47170
(812) 752-3499
Admin Clara E McGinnis. *Dir of Nursing*
 Ruth A Young. *Medical Dir* Marvin L
 McClain MD.
Licensure Skilled care; Intermediate care. *Beds*
 SNF 20; ICF 50. *Certified* Medicaid;
 Medicare.
Owner Nonprofit corp (Adventist Living
 Centers).
Admissions Requirements Minimum age 18;
 Medical examination; Physician's request.
Staff RNs 3 (ft); LPNs 10 (ft), 3 (pt); Nurses'
 aides 20 (ft), 4 (pt); Physical therapists 1
 (pt); Ophthalmologists 1 (pt).
Affiliation Seventh-Day Adventist.
Facilities Dining room; Physical therapy
 room; Activities room; Crafts room; Laundry
 room; Barber/Beauty shop.
Activities Arts & crafts; Cards; Games;
 Reading groups; Prayer groups; Movies;
 Shopping trips; Dances/Social/Cultural
 gatherings.

Scottsburg Nursing Home
1100 N Gardner St, Scottsburg, IN 47170
(812) 752-5065
Admin JoAnne Kreis. *Dir of Nursing* Sondra
 Johnson RN. *Medical Dir* Dr M McClain.
Licensure Intermediate care. *Beds* ICF 40.
 Certified Medicaid.
Owner Proprietary corp (Beverly Enterprises).
Admissions Requirements Medical
 examination.
Staff Physicians; LPNs; Nurses' aides;
 Recreational therapists; Activities
 coordinators; Dietitians; Ophthalmologists;
 Podiatrists.
Facilities Dining room; Activities room;
 Barber/Beauty shop.
Activities Arts & crafts; Cards; Games;
 Reading groups; Prayer groups; Movies;
 Shopping trips; Dances/Social/Cultural
 gatherings.

Williams Manor
10 Todd Dr, Scottsburg, IN 47170
(812) 752-5663
Admin Barbara K Fleener.
Medical Dir Dr William Scott.
Licensure Intermediate care. *Beds* ICF 84.
 Certified Medicaid.
Admissions Requirements Minimum age 18;
 Medical examination; Physician's request.
Staff Physicians 7 (pt); RNs 1 (ft), 1 (pt);
 LPNs 4 (ft), 3 (pt); Recreational therapists 1
 (ft); Activities coordinators 1 (pt); Dietitians
 1 (pt).
Facilities Dining room; Physical therapy
 room; Activities room; Laundry room;
 Barber/Beauty shop; Conference room.
Activities Arts & crafts; Cards; Games;
 Reading groups; Prayer groups; Movies;
 Shopping trips; Dances/Social/Cultural
 gatherings; Picnics.

Sellersburg

Maple Manor Christian Home Inc—Adult Division
643 W Utica St, Sellersburg, IN 47172
(812) 246-4846
Admin A L Flohr. *Dir of Nursing* Linda Carroll LPN. *Medical Dir* R E Robertson MD.
Licensure Intermediate care; Retirement. *Beds* ICF 17. *Private Pay Patients* 58%. *Certified* Medicaid.
Owner Nonprofit corp.
Admissions Requirements Minimum age 18; Medical examination; Physician's request.
Staff Physicians 1 (pt); RNs 1 (pt); LPNs 3 (ft), 5 (pt); Nurses' aides 9 (ft), 3 (pt); Activities coordinators 1 (ft); Dietitians 1 (pt); Other staff 8 (ft), 3 (pt).
Affiliation Church of Christ.
Facilities Dining room; Activities room; Chapel; Crafts room; Laundry room; Barber/Beauty shop; Library.
Activities Arts & crafts; Cards; Games; Reading groups; Prayer groups; Shopping trips; Dances/Social/Cultural gatherings; Intergenerational programs; Pet therapy.

Seymour

Community Care Center of Seymour
PO Box 769, Rte 7, US 31, Seymour, IN 47274
(812) 523-3000
Admin Barbara J Tumey RN.
Licensure Intermediate care. *Beds* ICF 100.

Jackson Park Convalescent Center
PO Box 705, 707 Jackson Park Dr, Seymour, IN 47274
(812) 522-2416
Admin Mary C Driver RN. *Dir of Nursing* Vicki Myers RN. *Medical Dir* Paul E Page DO.
Licensure Skilled care; Intermediate care. *Beds* SNF 45; ICF 104. *Private Pay Patients* 30%. *Certified* Medicaid.
Owner Proprietary corp (Heritage House of Seymour).
Staff Physicians 1 (ft); RNs 5 (ft), 2 (pt); LPNs 14 (ft), 3 (pt); Nurses' aides 45 (ft), 10 (pt); Physical therapists 1 (ft); Activities coordinators 2 (ft); Dietitians 1 (ft).
Facilities Dining room; Physical therapy room; Activities room; Chapel; Laundry room; Barber/Beauty shop.
Activities Arts & crafts; Games; Reading groups; Prayer groups; Movies; Shopping trips; Intergenerational programs; Pet therapy.

Lutheran Community Home Inc
111 W Church Ave, Seymour, IN 47274
(812) 522-5927
Admin Donald Bruce. *Dir of Nursing* Jeanne Corcoran. *Medical Dir* Kenneth Bobb MD.
Licensure Intermediate care; Residential care. *Beds* ICF 82; Residential care 20. *Certified* Medicaid.
Owner Nonprofit corp.
Admissions Requirements Medical examination.
Affiliation Lutheran.
Facilities Dining room; Activities room; Chapel; Crafts room; Laundry room; Barber/Beauty shop; Library.
Activities Arts & crafts; Cards; Games; Reading groups; Prayer groups; Movies; Shopping trips; Dances/Social/Cultural gatherings; Intergenerational programs; Baking.

Shelbyville

Haven Heritage House Children's Center
2325 S Miller St, Shelbyville, IN 46176
(317) 392-3287
Admin Lou Ann Blake. *Dir of Nursing* Marie Strobel RN MSN. *Medical Dir* Craig Moorman MD, Pediatrician.
Licensure Skilled care for mentally retarded. *Beds* Skilled care for mentally retarded 135. *Certified* Medicaid.
Owner Proprietary corp.
Staff Physicians; RNs; LPNs; Nurses' aides; Physical therapists; Occupational therapists; Speech therapists; Activities coordinators; Dietitians.

Heritage House Convalescent Center
2309 S Miller St, Shelbyville, IN 46176
(317) 398-9781
Admin Linda C Kuhn.
Licensure Skilled care; Intermediate care. *Beds* SNF 55; ICF 98. *Certified* Medicaid; Medicare.

Heritage Manor Inc
2311 S Miller St, Shelbyville, IN 46176
(317) 398-9777
Admin Ellave Miles. *Dir of Nursing* Ruth Garner. *Medical Dir* Dr Douglas Carter.
Licensure Comprehensive care. *Beds* Comprehensive care 95.
Owner Privately owned.
Admissions Requirements Medical examination; Physician's request.
Staff RNs; LPNs; Nurses' aides; Dietitians.
Facilities Dining room; Physical therapy room; Activities room; Crafts room; Laundry room; Barber/Beauty shop.
Activities Arts & crafts; Cards; Games; Reading groups; Prayer groups; Movies; Shopping trips.

Sheridan

Sheridan Health Care Center Inc
PO Box 31, Sheridan, IN 46069
(317) 758-4426
Admin Jeanne Roeder.
Licensure Intermediate care. *Beds* ICF 80. *Certified* Medicaid.

Sheridan Special Care Center Inc
PO Box 9, 903 Sheridan Ave, Sheridan, IN 46069
(317) 758-5330
Admin Betty C Poshusta. *Dir of Nursing* Shirley Jeffers. *Medical Dir* Mark Ambre MD.
Licensure Intermediate care for mentally retarded. *Beds* ICF/MR 50. *Certified* Medicaid.
Owner Proprietary corp.
Admissions Requirements Medical examination.
Staff Physicians 1 (pt); RNs 1 (ft); LPNs 4 (ft); Nurses' aides 18 (ft); Physical therapists 1 (pt); Occupational therapists 1 (pt); Speech therapists 1 (pt); Activities coordinators 1 (ft); Dietitians 1 (pt).
Facilities Dining room; Physical therapy room; Activities room; Crafts room; Laundry room.
Activities Arts & crafts; Cards; Games; Reading groups; Prayer groups; Movies; Shopping trips; Dances/Social/Cultural gatherings.

South Bend

Carlyle Health Care Center
5024 Western Ave, South Bend, IN 46619
(219) 288-1464
Admin Sharon L Fiorella. *Dir of Nursing* Claudia Hays. *Medical Dir* Hancel Foley MD.
Licensure Skilled care; Intermediate care; Alzheimer's care. *Beds* SNF 52; ICF 191. *Certified* Medicaid; Medicare.
Owner Proprietary corp.
Admissions Requirements Minimum age 18; Medical examination; Physician's request.
Staff Physicians 1 (pt); RNs 7 (ft), 3 (pt); LPNs 15 (ft), 4 (pt); Nurses' aides 60 (ft), 5 (pt); Recreational therapists 4 (ft); Activities coordinators 2 (ft); Dietitians 1 (pt).
Facilities Dining room; Physical therapy room; Activities room; Chapel; Crafts room; Laundry room; Barber/Beauty shop; Respiratory services.
Activities Arts & crafts; Cards; Games; Reading groups; Prayer groups; Movies; Shopping trips; Dances/Social/Cultural gatherings.

Greensprings Manor Healthcare
1106 S 20th St, South Bend, IN 46615
(219) 288-6282, 234-2908 FAX
Admin Marlene C Newell RN. *Dir of Nursing* Cindy Owens RN BSN. *Medical Dir* Dr Armand Rigaux.
Licensure Skilled care; Intermediate care. *Beds* SNF 21; ICF 63. *Private Pay Patients* 38%. *Certified* Medicaid; Medicare.
Owner Proprietary corp (Health Concepts Corp).
Admissions Requirements Minimum age 18; Medical examination; Physician's request.
Staff RNs 4 (ft), 2 (pt); LPNs 4 (ft), 3 (pt); Nurses' aides 16 (ft), 8 (pt); Physical therapists 1 (pt); Occupational therapists 1 (pt); Speech therapists 1 (pt); Activities coordinators 1 (ft); Dietitians 1 (pt); Podiatrists (contracted).
Facilities Dining room; Physical therapy room; Activities room; Chapel; Laundry room; Barber/Beauty shop; Dining room for feeders and confused patients.
Activities Arts & crafts; Cards; Games; Reading groups; Prayer groups; Movies; Shopping trips; Dances/Social/Cultural gatherings; Intergenerational programs; Pet therapy.

Healthwin Hospital
20531 Darden Rd, South Bend, IN 46637
(219) 272-0100
Admin Michael J Roman.
Licensure Skilled care; Intermediate care. *Beds* SNF 33; ICF 110. *Certified* Medicaid; Medicare.
Owner Publicly owned.

Medco Center of South Bend
1950 E Ridgedale Rd, South Bend, IN 46614
(219) 291-6722
Admin Richard E Lewis.
Medical Dir Dr Zia Chowhan.
Licensure Skilled care; Intermediate care. *Beds* SNF 21; ICF 225. *Certified* Medicaid; Medicare.
Owner Proprietary corp (Unicare).
Admissions Requirements Medical examination; Physician's request.
Staff RNs 8 (ft), 15 (pt); LPNs 7 (ft), 5 (pt); Physical therapists 1 (pt); Activities coordinators 3 (ft), 1 (pt); Dietitians 1 (ft).
Facilities Dining room; Physical therapy room; Activities room; Laundry room; Barber/Beauty shop.
Activities Arts & crafts; Cards; Games; Reading groups; Prayer groups; Movies; Shopping trips; Dances/Social/Cultural gatherings.

Meridian Nursing Center—Cardinal
1121 E LaSalle, South Bend, IN 46601
(219) 287-6501
Admin Chris Mueller.
Licensure Skilled care; Intermediate care. *Beds* SNF 62; ICF 229. *Certified* Medicaid; Medicare.
Owner Proprietary corp (Meridian Healthcare).

Meridian Nursing Center—River Park
915 27th St, South Bend, IN 46615
(219) 287-1016

Admin William A Beghtel. *Dir of Nursing* Jo Ann Dake RN. *Medical Dir* Dr Debra McClain.
Licensure Intermediate care. *Beds* ICF 44. *Certified* Medicaid.
Owner Proprietary corp (Meridian Healthcare).
Facilities Dining room; Activities room; Barber/Beauty shop.

Milton Home
206 E Marion St, South Bend, IN 46601
(219) 233-0165
Admin Rosemary Ward.
Licensure Residential care; Comprehensive care. *Beds* Residential care 5; Comprehensive care 16.
Owner Proprietary corp (Meridan Healthcare).

Northwood Nursing Home
328 N Notre Dame Ave, South Bend, IN 46617
(219) 232-4486
Admin Nancy B Shugars. *Dir of Nursing* Susan Ingle. *Medical Dir* Armand J Rigaux MD.
Licensure Intermediate care. *Beds* ICF 40. *Private Pay Patients* 30%. *Certified* Medicaid.
Owner Proprietary corp (Beverly Enterprises).
Admissions Requirements Medical examination; Physician's request.
Staff RNs 1 (ft), 1 (pt); LPNs 3 (ft), 1 (pt); Nurses' aides 13 (ft), 1 (pt); Activities coordinators 1 (ft); Dietitians 1 (pt).
Facilities Dining room; Laundry room; Dayroom.
Activities Arts & crafts; Cards; Games; Reading groups; Prayer groups; Movies; Shopping trips; Pet therapy.

Regency Place of South Bend
52654 N Ironwood Rd, South Bend, IN 46635
(219) 277-8710
Admin Mark Willkom.
Licensure Skilled care; Intermediate care. *Beds* SNF 23; ICF 121.
Owner Proprietary corp (Lucas Corp).

St Joseph's Care Center—Morningside
18325 Bailey Ave, South Bend, IN 46637
(219) 272-6410
Admin Rose Ann Antkowiak. *Dir of Nursing* Karalee Eltzroth. *Medical Dir* Dr T Barbour.
Licensure Intermediate care. *Beds* ICF 40. *Private Pay Patients* 25%. *Certified* Medicaid.
Owner Nonprofit organization/foundation (Holy Cross Health Systems).
Admissions Requirements Minimum age 18; Medical examination; Physician's request.
Staff RNs 1 (ft); LPNs 3 (ft); Nurses' aides 12 (ft), 1 (pt); Activities coordinators 1 (ft); Dietitians 1 (ft).
Affiliation Roman Catholic.
Facilities Dining room; Activities room; Chapel; Laundry room; Barber/Beauty shop; Large yard.
Activities Arts & crafts; Cards; Games; Reading groups; Prayer groups; Movies; Shopping trips; Dances/Social/Cultural gatherings; Intergenerational programs; Pet therapy.

St Joseph's Care Center—Notre Dame
1024 N Notre Dame, South Bend, IN 46617
(219) 234-3179
Admin Judith Rice. *Dir of Nursing* Jeanette Pamachena. *Medical Dir* Dr Logan Dunlap.
Licensure Intermediate care. *Beds* ICF 24. *Certified* Medicaid.
Owner Nonprofit corp (Holy Cross Health Systems).
Admissions Requirements Minimum age 18; Medical examination.
Staff RNs 1 (ft); LPNs 3 (ft); Nurses' aides 8 (ft); Activities coordinators 1 (pt); Dietitians 1 (pt); Social workers 1 (pt).

Activities Arts & crafts; Cards; Games; Reading groups; Prayer groups; Shopping trips; Dances/Social/Cultural gatherings.

St Joseph's Care Center West
4600 W Washington Ave, South Bend, IN 46619
(219) 282-1294
Admin Dolores M Wisniewski. *Dir of Nursing* Evelyn Troub RN. *Medical Dir* Thomas Barbour MD.
Licensure Intermediate care. *Beds* ICF 180. *Certified* Medicaid.
Owner Nonprofit corp (Holy Cross Health Systems).
Admissions Requirements Minimum age 18; Medical examination; Physician's request.
Staff Physicians; RNs 4 (ft), 2 (pt); LPNs 4 (ft), 2 (pt); Nurses' aides 50 (ft); Occupational therapists 1 (ft); Activities coordinators 3 (ft); Dietitians 1 (ft).
Languages Polish.
Affiliation Roman Catholic.
Facilities Dining room; Activities room; Chapel; Crafts room; Laundry room; Barber/Beauty shop; Library.
Activities Arts & crafts; Cards; Games; Reading groups; Prayer groups; Movies; Shopping trips; Dances/Social/Cultural gatherings.

St Paul's Retirement Community
3602 S Ironwood Dr, South Bend, IN 46614
(219) 291-8205
Admin Joseph M Doran. *Dir of Nursing* Lena Weldon RN. *Medical Dir* Thomas Barbour MD.
Licensure Skilled care; Intermediate care; Residential care. *Beds* SNF 39; ICF 39; Residential care 103. *Certified* Medicaid; Medicare.
Owner Nonprofit corp.
Admissions Requirements Minimum age 55; Medical examination; Physician's request.
Staff Physicians 1 (pt); RNs 5 (ft); LPNs 9 (ft); Nurses' aides 24 (ft); Physical therapists 1 (pt); Recreational therapists 1 (ft); Occupational therapists 1 (pt); Speech therapists 1 (pt); Activities coordinators 1 (ft); Dietitians 1 (pt); Ophthalmologists 1 (pt); Podiatrists 1 (pt).
Facilities Dining room; Physical therapy room; Activities room; Chapel; Crafts room; Laundry room; Barber/Beauty shop; Library.
Activities Arts & crafts; Cards; Games; Reading groups; Prayer groups; Movies; Shopping trips; Dances/Social/Cultural gatherings.

Spencer

Owen County Home
RR 3, Box 124, Spencer, IN 47460
(812) 829-3492
Admin Ruthie Gray.
Beds 31.

Spencer Health Care Center
RR 2 Box 77, Spencer, IN 47460
(812) 879-4275
Admin Maida Pierson. *Dir of Nursing* Laura Lighter. *Medical Dir* Dr LeBow.
Licensure Intermediate care; Alzheimer's care. *Beds* ICF 46. *Certified* Medicaid.
Owner Privately owned.
Admissions Requirements Minimum age 2; Medical examination.
Staff Physicians 5 (pt); RNs 1 (pt); LPNs 2 (ft), 4 (pt); Nurses' aides 5 (ft), 1 (pt); Activities coordinators 1 (pt); Dietitians 1 (pt); Ophthalmologists 1 (pt); Dentists 1 (pt); DDS 1 (pt).
Facilities Dining room; Activities room; Chapel; Crafts room; Laundry room; Barber/Beauty shop; Library.

Activities Arts & crafts; Cards; Games; Reading groups; Prayer groups; Movies; Shopping trips; Dances/Social/Cultural gatherings.

Sullivan

Miller's Merry Manor
PO Box 525, W Wolfe St, Sullivan, IN 47882
(812) 268-6361
Admin Donald C Hunt.
Licensure Skilled care; Intermediate care. *Beds* SNF 49; ICF 126. *Certified* Medicaid.
Owner Proprietary corp (Millers Merry Manor).

Sullivan Convalescent Center
PO Box 447, Old US 41 N, Sullivan, IN 47882
(812) 268-3351
Admin Joyce A Tribby. *Dir of Nursing* Vanessa Thompson RN. *Medical Dir* Betty Dukes MD.
Licensure Intermediate care. *Beds* ICF 60. *Private Pay Patients* 35%. *Certified* Medicaid.
Owner Privately owned.
Admissions Requirements Medical examination; Physician's request.
Staff RNs 1 (ft); LPNs 6 (ft); Nurses' aides 20 (ft); Physical therapists 1 (ft); Activities coordinators 1 (ft).
Facilities Dining room; Activities room; Laundry room; Barber/Beauty shop; Library; Lounges.
Activities Arts & crafts; Cards; Games; Reading groups; Prayer groups; Movies; Dances/Social/Cultural gatherings; Pet therapy.

Village Nursing Home
975 N Section St, Sullivan, IN 47882
(812) 268-6810
Admin Richard W Bartnik.
Medical Dir Betty Dukes MD.
Licensure Intermediate care. *Beds* ICF 40. *Certified* Medicaid.
Owner Proprietary corp (Beverly Enterprises).
Admissions Requirements Minimum age 18; Medical examination; Physician's request.
Staff Physicians 1 (pt); LPNs 3 (ft), 2 (pt); Nurses' aides 6 (ft), 7 (pt); Physical therapists 1 (pt); Reality therapists 1 (pt); Recreational therapists 1 (pt); Speech therapists 1 (pt); Activities coordinators 1 (ft), 1 (pt); Dietitians 1 (pt); Ophthalmologists 1 (pt); Podiatrists 1 (pt); Dentists 1 (pt).
Facilities Dining room; Laundry room; Barber/Beauty shop.
Activities Arts & crafts; Cards; Games; Reading groups; Prayer groups; Movies; Shopping trips; Dances/Social/Cultural gatherings.

Summitville

Summit Convalescent Center
RR 1, Box 398, Summitville, IN 46070
(317) 536-2261, 536-2262 FAX
Admin Cindi Cooper. *Dir of Nursing* Joan Stone. *Medical Dir* Williams C Van Ness II MD.
Licensure Intermediate care. *Beds* ICF 34. *Certified* Medicaid.
Owner Privately owned.
Admissions Requirements Minimum age 18; Medical examination; Physician's request.
Staff Physicians 1 (pt); LPNs 3 (ft), 1 (pt); Nurses' aides 6 (ft), 2 (pt); Activities coordinators 1 (pt); Dietitians 1 (pt).
Facilities Dining room; Activities room; Crafts room; Laundry room; Barber/Beauty shop.

Activities Arts & crafts; Cards; Games; Reading groups; Prayer groups; Movies; Shopping trips; Dances/Social/Cultural gatherings; Intergenerational programs; Pet therapy.

Syracuse

Miller's Merry Manor Inc
PO Box 8, Pickwick Dr & Old St Rd 13, Syracuse, IN 46567
(219) 457-4401
Admin Judy A Warner.
Licensure Skilled care; Intermediate care. *Beds* SNF 22; ICF 44.

Tell City

Lincoln Hills Nursing Home
402 19th St, Tell City, IN 47586
(812) 547-3427
Admin William M Scheller.
Medical Dir Stephen Syler MD.
Licensure Intermediate care. *Beds* ICF 165. *Certified* Medicaid.
Owner Proprietary corp (Beverly Enterprises).
Admissions Requirements Minimum age 18; Medical examination; Physician's request.
Staff RNs 2 (ft), 1 (pt); LPNs 7 (ft); Nurses' aides 40 (ft), 27 (pt); Physical therapists 1 (ft); Activities coordinators 2 (ft); Dietitians 1 (pt).
Facilities Dining room; Physical therapy room; Activities room; Chapel; Crafts room; Laundry room; Barber/Beauty shop.
Activities Arts & crafts; Cards; Games; Reading groups; Prayer groups; Movies; Shopping trips; Dances/Social/Cultural gatherings.

Terre Haute

Countryside Nursing Center
1001 Springhill Rd, Terre Haute, IN 47802
(812) 238-2441
Admin Ivaetta McCammon.
Licensure Skilled care; Intermediate care. *Beds* SNF 34; ICF 86.

Davis Gardens Health Center
1120 Davis Ave, Terre Haute, IN 47802
(812) 232-7533
Admin Scott M McQuinn. *Dir of Nursing* Adah Y Roads RN. *Medical Dir* Dr John Freed.
Licensure Skilled care; Intermediate care; Assisted and independent living. *Beds* SNF 20; ICF 58; Assisted and independent living apartments 249. *Private Pay Patients* 63%. *Certified* Medicaid; Medicare.
Owner Nonprofit organization/foundation.
Admissions Requirements Medical examination; Physician's request.
Staff Physicians 1 (pt); RNs 4 (ft); LPNs 10 (ft); Nurses' aides 30 (ft); Physical therapists 1 (pt); Occupational therapists 1 (pt); Speech therapists 1 (pt); Activities coordinators 1 (ft); Dietitians 1 (pt); Podiatrists 1 (pt).
Facilities Dining room; Physical therapy room; Crafts room; Laundry room; Barber/Beauty shop; Library; Lounge.
Activities Arts & crafts; Cards; Games; Reading groups; Prayer groups; Movies; Shopping trips; Dances/Social/Cultural gatherings; Pet therapy.

Ewing Nursing Home
504 S 15th St, Terre Haute, IN 47807
(812) 232-3663
Admin Judith M Weathers. *Dir of Nursing* Karla M Clayton. *Medical Dir* James Walsh.
Licensure Intermediate care. *Beds* ICF 18. *Certified* Medicaid.
Owner Privately owned.
Admissions Requirements Medical examination; Physician's request.

Staff RNs 1 (pt); LPNs 5 (ft); Nurses' aides 4 (ft); Activities coordinators 1 (pt); Dietitians 1 (pt); Ophthalmologists 1 (pt) (consultant); Podiatrists 1 (pt) (consultant); Dentists 1 (pt) (consultant).
Facilities Dining room; Activities room; Laundry room; Barber/Beauty shop.
Activities Arts & crafts; Cards; Games; Reading groups; Prayer groups; Shopping trips; Dances/Social/Cultural gatherings; Pet therapy; Grand Sisters program.

Maplewood Manor
500 Maple Ave, Terre Haute, IN 47804
(812) 234-7702, 238-2413 FAX
Admin Don Cozort. *Dir of Nursing* Renay Harvey. *Medical Dir* Beth Kellum.
Licensure Skilled care; Intermediate care. *Beds* SNF 60; ICF 189. *Certified* Medicaid; Medicare.
Owner Proprietary corp (Beverly Enterprises).
Admissions Requirements Minimum age 18.
Staff Physicians; RNs; LPNs; Nurses' aides; Physical therapists; Recreational therapists; Speech therapists; Activities coordinators; Dietitians.
Facilities Dining room; Physical therapy room; Activities room; Laundry room; Barber/Beauty shop.
Activities Arts & crafts; Games; Reading groups; Movies; Shopping trips; Dances/Social/Cultural gatherings.

Meadows Manor Inc
3300 Poplar, Terre Haute, IN 47803
(812) 235-6281
Admin Sandy Francis. *Dir of Nursing* Anita Hightshoe. *Medical Dir* Dr James Walsh.
Licensure Intermediate care. *Beds* ICF 103.
Owner Privately owned (Sunset Harbor).
Admissions Requirements Physician's request.
Staff RNs; LPNs; Nurses' aides; Physical therapists; Recreational therapists; Activities coordinators; Dietitians.
Facilities Dining room; Physical therapy room; Activities room; Laundry room; Barber/Beauty shop; Library.
Activities Arts & crafts; Cards; Games; Reading groups; Prayer groups; Movies; Pet therapy.

Meadows Manor North Inc
3150 N 7th St, Terre Haute, IN 47804
(812) 466-5217
Admin Nancy F Applegate. *Dir of Nursing* Annette Jenkins RN. *Medical Dir* James Buechler MD.
Licensure Skilled care; Alzheimer's care; Retirement. *Beds* SNF 100. *Certified* Medicaid; Medicare.
Owner Proprietary corp.
Admissions Requirements Minimum age 17; Medical examination.
Staff Physicians 1 (ft), 38 (pt); RNs 6 (ft); LPNs 25 (ft); Nurses' aides 40 (ft); Physical therapists 1 (ft); Recreational therapists 1 (ft); Occupational therapists 1 (ft); Speech therapists 1 (ft); Activities coordinators 2 (ft); Dietitians 1 (ft); Ophthalmologists; Podiatrists; Dentists; Social Services 2 (ft); Beauticians 2 (ft); Medical Records 1 (ft).
Languages Italian, German, Sign.
Facilities Dining room; Physical therapy room; Activities room; Chapel; Crafts room; Laundry room; Barber/Beauty shop; Library; Lounges.
Activities Arts & crafts; Cards; Games; Reading groups; Prayer groups; Movies; Shopping trips; Dances/Social/Cultural gatherings; Pet related activities.

Terre Haute Nursing Home
830 S 6th St, Terre Haute, IN 47807
(812) 232-7102
Admin Patricia A Dunn. *Dir of Nursing* Amy Neff RN. *Medical Dir* Vasumati Patel MD.
Licensure Intermediate care. *Beds* ICF 40. *Private Pay Patients* 8%. *Certified* Medicaid.

Owner Proprietary corp (Waverly Group).
Admissions Requirements Medical examination; Physician's request.
Staff LPNs; Nurses' aides; Activities coordinators.
Facilities Dining room; Laundry room; Barber/Beauty shop.
Activities Arts & crafts; Cards; Games; Reading groups; Prayer groups; Movies; Shopping trips; Dances/Social/Cultural gatherings; Intergenerational programs; Pet therapy; Special holiday events.

Vigo County Home
3500 Maple Ave, Terre Haute, IN 47804
(812) 238-8375
Admin Robert D Wallace.
Medical Dir W L Loewenstein MD.
Licensure Intermediate care. *Beds* ICF 200. *Certified* Medicaid.
Owner Publicly owned.
Admissions Requirements Medical examination; Physician's request.
Staff Physicians 1 (pt); RNs 6 (ft); LPNs 28 (ft); Nurses' aides 66 (ft); Physical therapists 1 (pt); Reality therapists 1 (pt); Recreational therapists 3 (ft); Occupational therapists 1 (pt); Speech therapists 1 (pt); Activities coordinators 1 (ft); Dietitians 1 (ft); Ophthalmologists 1 (pt); Podiatrists 1 (pt); Dentists 1 (pt).
Facilities Dining room; Physical therapy room; Activities room; Chapel; Crafts room; Laundry room; Barber/Beauty shop.
Activities Arts & crafts; Cards; Games; Reading groups; Prayer groups; Movies; Shopping trips; Dances/Social/Cultural gatherings.

Webster's Rest Home
513-515 N 14th St, Terre Haute, IN 47807
(812) 232-4571
Admin Rachel Webster.
Licensure Intermediate care. *Beds* 10. *Certified* Medicaid.

Westridge Health Care
120 W Margaret Ave, Terre Haute, IN 47802
(812) 232-3311
Admin Lowell Gene Buck. *Dir of Nursing* Robina Darkis RN. *Medical Dir* W McIntosh MD.
Licensure Skilled care; Intermediate care; Alzheimer's care. *Beds* SNF 21; ICF 97. *Certified* Medicaid; Medicare.
Owner Nonprofit corp (First Humanics Inc).
Admissions Requirements Minimum age 18; Medical examination; Physician's request.
Staff Physicians 1 (pt); RNs 5 (ft), 1 (pt); LPNs 8 (ft), 6 (pt); Nurses' aides 26 (ft), 8 (pt); Physical therapists 1 (pt); Reality therapists 1 (pt); Recreational therapists 1 (pt); Occupational therapists 1 (pt); Speech therapists 1 (pt); Activities coordinators 1 (pt); Dietitians 1 (pt); Ophthalmologists 1 (pt); Podiatrists 1 (pt); Audiologists 1 (pt).
Facilities Dining room; Physical therapy room; Activities room; Laundry room; Barber/Beauty shop.
Activities Arts & crafts; Cards; Games; Prayer groups; Movies; Shopping trips; Dances/Social/Cultural gatherings; Pet therapy.

Tipton

Miller's Merry Manor
PO Box 265, 4-H Rd, Tipton, IN 46072
(317) 675-8791
Admin Rita Lynell Fox RN.
Licensure Intermediate care. *Beds* ICF 102. *Certified* Medicaid.
Owner Proprietary corp (Millers Merry Manor).
Admissions Requirements Minimum age 19; Medical examination; Physician's request.

Staff RNs 3 (ft); LPNs 3 (ft); Nurses' aides 20 (ft), 15 (pt); Physical therapists 1 (pt); Speech therapists 1 (pt); Activities coordinators 1 (ft), 1 (pt); Dietitians 1 (pt); Audiologists 1 (pt).
Facilities Dining room; Physical therapy room; Activities room; Crafts room; Laundry room; Barber/Beauty shop; Library.
Activities Arts & crafts; Cards; Games; Reading groups; Prayer groups; Movies; Dances/Social/Cultural gatherings.

Tipton Nursing Home
701 E Jefferson St, Tipton, IN 46072
(317) 675-4024
Admin Carolyn Sue Nevin MSW HFA. *Dir of Nursing* Martha Clouser. *Medical Dir* Jessie Cooperider.
Licensure Intermediate care. *Beds* ICF 40. *Private Pay Patients* 30%. *Certified* Medicaid.
Owner Proprietary corp (Beverly Enterprises).
Admissions Requirements Medical examination; Physician's request.
Staff Physicians 1 (pt); RNs 1 (ft); LPNs 4 (ft); Nurses' aides 7 (ft), 7 (pt); Physical therapists 1 (pt); Occupational therapists 1 (pt); Activities coordinators 1 (pt); Dietitians 1 (pt); Ophthalmologists 1 (pt); Podiatrists 1 (pt).
Facilities Dining room; Barber/Beauty shop; Backyard.
Activities Arts & crafts; Cards; Games; Reading groups; Prayer groups; Movies; Dances/Social/Cultural gatherings; Intergenerational programs; Services by local churches.

Upland

University Nursing Center
PO Box 3000, 1512 S University Blvd, Upland, IN 46989-3000
(317) 998-2761
Admin Emily Hayes Garvin. *Dir of Nursing* June K Lewis. *Medical Dir* Thomas Lee MD.
Licensure Skilled care; Intermediate care. *Beds* SNF 37; ICF 44. *Certified* Medicaid; Medicare.
Owner Proprietary corp (Hillhaven Corp).
Admissions Requirements Medical examination; Physician's request.
Staff RNs 2 (pt); LPNs 4 (ft), 4 (pt); Nurses' aides 15 (ft), 20 (pt); Physical therapists 1 (pt); Activities coordinators 1 (ft); Dietitians 1 (pt).
Facilities Dining room; Physical therapy room; Activities room; Laundry room; Barber/Beauty shop.
Activities Arts & crafts; Cards; Games; Prayer groups; Movies; Dances/Social/Cultural gatherings.

Valparaiso

Canterbury Place
251 East Dr, Valparaiso, IN 46383
(219) 462-6158
Admin Harlyne Hilliker Joy. *Dir of Nursing* Tammy Rowe. *Medical Dir* Robert Harvey MD.
Licensure Skilled care; Intermediate care. *Beds* SNF 51; ICF 51. *Certified* Medicaid; Medicare.
Owner Proprietary corp (Beverly Enterprises).
Admissions Requirements Minimum age 18.
Staff RNs 3 (ft), 2 (pt); LPNs 6 (ft), 4 (pt); Nurses' aides 20 (ft), 15 (pt); Recreational therapists 1 (ft); Activities coordinators 1 (ft).
Facilities Dining room; Physical therapy room; Activities room; Laundry room; Barber/Beauty shop.
Activities Arts & crafts; Cards; Games; Reading groups; Prayer groups; Movies; Dances/Social/Cultural gatherings.

Pavilion Healthcare Center of Valparaiso
606 Wall St, Valparaiso, IN 46383
(219) 464-4976, 464-3612 FAX
Admin Albert W Estes. *Dir of Nursing* Carolyn Siar RN. *Medical Dir* Joel L Hull MD; Owen H Lucas MD.
Licensure Skilled care; Intermediate care. *Beds* SNF 96; ICF 96. *Private Pay Patients* 27%. *Certified* Medicaid; Medicare.
Owner Proprietary corp.
Admissions Requirements Minimum age 18; Medical examination; Physician's request.
Staff RNs 9 (ft), 2 (pt); LPNs 11 (ft); Nurses' aides 48 (ft), 12 (pt); Physical therapists 1 (pt); Recreational therapists 1 (pt); Occupational therapists 1 (pt); Speech therapists 1 (pt); Activities coordinators 1 (ft); Dietitians 1 (pt); Ophthalmologists 1 (pt); Podiatrists 1 (pt); Audiologists 1 (pt); Respiratory therapists 8 (ft), 3 (pt).
Facilities Dining room; Physical therapy room; Activities room; Crafts room; Laundry room; Barber/Beauty shop; Ventilator unit.
Activities Arts & crafts; Cards; Games; Reading groups; Prayer groups; Movies; Shopping trips; Dances/Social/Cultural gatherings; Intergenerational programs; Pet therapy.

Whispering Pines
3301 N Calumet Ave, Valparaiso, IN 46383
(219) 462-0508
Admin James L Norton. *Dir of Nursing* Michele Kaplon-Perkins RN BSN. *Medical Dir* Michael Weiss MD.
Licensure Skilled care; Intermediate care. *Beds* SNF 39; ICF 152. *Private Pay Patients* 50%. *Certified* Medicaid; Medicare.
Owner Nonprofit organization/foundation.
Admissions Requirements Medical examination; Physician's request.
Staff Physicians 1 (ft); RNs 7 (ft), 5 (pt); LPNs 6 (ft), 5 (pt); Nurses' aides 60 (ft), 45 (pt); Physical therapists 1 (ft); Occupational therapists 1 (ft); Speech therapists 1 (pt); Activities coordinators 3 (ft), 1 (pt); Dietitians 1 (pt).
Facilities Dining room; Physical therapy room; Activities room; Chapel; Crafts room; Laundry room; Barber/Beauty shop; Library.
Activities Arts & crafts; Cards; Games; Reading groups; Prayer groups; Movies; Shopping trips; Dances/Social/Cultural gatherings; Intergenerational programs; Pet therapy.

Willows Rehabilitation Center
1000 Elizabeth, Valparaiso, IN 46383
(219) 464-4858, 477-4746 FAX
Admin LuAnn Nebelung. *Dir of Nursing* Marlene Versteeg. *Medical Dir* Dr James Chiu.
Licensure Skilled care; Intermediate care. *Beds* SNF 50; ICF 50. *Private Pay Patients* 38%. *Certified* Medicaid; Medicare.
Owner Proprietary corp (National Heritage).
Admissions Requirements Minimum age 18; Medical examination; Physician's request.
Staff RNs 4 (ft), 1 (pt); LPNs 3 (ft), 1 (pt); Nurses' aides 40 (ft), 20 (pt); Physical therapists 2 (pt); Recreational therapists 1 (ft), 1 (pt); Occupational therapists 1 (pt); Speech therapists 2 (pt); Activities coordinators 1 (ft); Dietitians 1 (pt).
Facilities Dining room; Physical therapy room; Laundry room; Barber/Beauty shop.
Activities Arts & crafts; Cards; Games; Reading groups; Prayer groups; Movies; Shopping trips; Dances/Social/Cultural gatherings; Intergenerational programs.

Versailles

Silver Bell Nursing Home
RR 2 Box 106, Versailles, IN 47402
(812) 689-6222

Admin Phyllis Fields; Linda McDole, Asst. *Dir of Nursing* Eula Busteed. *Medical Dir* Dr Alan P Culbreth.
Licensure Intermediate care. *Beds* ICF 23. *Private Pay Patients* 40%. *Certified* Medicaid.
Owner Privately owned.
Admissions Requirements Medical examination; Physician's request.
Staff Physicians; RNs 1 (pt); LPNs 3 (ft), 1 (pt); Nurses' aides 5 (ft), 1 (pt); Activities coordinators 1 (ft), 2 (pt); Dietitians (contracted).
Facilities Dining room; Activities room; Laundry room.
Activities Arts & crafts; Cards; Games; Prayer groups; Shopping trips; Dances/Social/Cultural gatherings; Pet therapy.

Vevay

Swiss Villa Living Center
RR 3, Box 169A, Vevay, IN 47043
(812) 427-2803
Admin Anita Sue Craig. *Dir of Nursing* Cathy Hart RN. *Medical Dir* Ivan Lindgren MD.
Licensure Intermediate care. *Beds* ICF 100. *Certified* Medicaid.
Owner Nonprofit corp (Adventist Living Centers).
Admissions Requirements Minimum age 18; Medical examination; Physician's request.
Staff RNs 3 (ft); LPNs 6 (ft); Nurses' aides; Activities coordinators 1 (ft).
Affiliation Seventh-Day Adventist.
Facilities Dining room; Laundry room; Barber/Beauty shop.
Activities Arts & crafts; Cards; Games; Reading groups; Prayer groups; Movies.

Vincennes

Crestview Convalescent Home
3801 Old Bruceville Rd, Vincennes, IN 47591
(812) 882-1783
Admin Douglas H Herrold. *Dir of Nursing* Debra Parish. *Medical Dir* Daniel J Combs MD.
Licensure Skilled care; Intermediate care. *Beds* SNF 82; ICF 134. *Certified* Medicaid; Medicare.
Owner Proprietary corp (Hillhaven Corp).
Admissions Requirements Medical examination; Physician's request.
Staff Physicians; RNs; LPNs; Nurses' aides; Physical therapists; Speech therapists; Activities coordinators; Dietitians; Ophthalmologists; Podiatrists.
Facilities Dining room; Physical therapy room; Activities room; Chapel.
Activities Arts & crafts; Cards; Games; Reading groups; Prayer groups; Movies; Shopping trips; Dances/Social/Cultural gatherings.

Vincennes Healthcare
PO Box 903, 1202 S 16th St, Vincennes, IN 47591
(812) 882-8292
Admin Frank Harrell.
Licensure Intermediate care. *Beds* ICF 66. *Certified* Medicaid.

Willow Manor Convalescent Center Inc
1321 Willow St, Vincennes, IN 47591
(812) 882-1136
Admin Judith Ann Drieman.
Licensure Skilled care; Intermediate care. *Beds* SNF 19; ICF 123. *Certified* Medicaid; Medicare.
Owner Proprietary corp (Cloverleaf Healthcare).

Wabash

Manor Care Division of Miller's Merry Manor
RR 2, Mill Creek Pike, Wabash, IN 46992
(219) 563-4121
Admin Lesley Garrison.
Medical Dir James Haughn MD.
Licensure Intermediate care. *Beds* ICF 39.
 Certified Medicaid.
Owner Proprietary corp (Millers Merry
 Manor).
Admissions Requirements Minimum age 18;
 Medical examination; Physician's request.
Staff RNs 1 (ft); LPNs 2 (ft), 2 (pt); Nurses'
 aides 5 (ft), 6 (pt); Activities coordinators 1
 (ft).
Facilities Dining room; Activities room;
 Laundry room; Barber/Beauty shop.
Activities Arts & crafts; Games; Movies;
 Shopping trips; Daily living classes.

Miller's Merry Manor Inc
1035 Manchester Ave, Wabash, IN 46992
(219) 563-7427
Admin Gerry Conway. *Dir of Nursing* Karen
 Middleton RN. *Medical Dir* Dr James
 Haughn.
Licensure Skilled care; Intermediate care. *Beds*
 SNF 27; ICF 75. *Certified* Medicaid;
 Medicare.
Owner Proprietary corp (Caremet Inc).
Admissions Requirements Medical
 examination; Physician's request.
Staff RNs 4 (ft), 8 (pt); LPNs 9 (ft), 3 (pt);
 Nurses' aides 24 (ft), 14 (pt); Activities
 coordinators 2 (pt).
Facilities Dining room; Physical therapy
 room; Activities room; Laundry room;
 Barber/Beauty shop.
Activities Arts & crafts; Cards; Games; Prayer
 groups; Movies; Shopping trips.

Vernon Manor Children's Home
1955 S Vernon St, Wabash, IN 46992
(219) 563-8438, 563-6747 FAX
Admin Jocelyn Ravenscroft. *Dir of Nursing*
 Mary Ann Hire. *Medical Dir* Dr P Shah.
Licensure Skilled care. *Beds* SNF 136.
 Certified Medicaid.
Owner Nonprofit organization/foundation.
Admissions Requirements Minimum age birth.
Staff Physicians 2 (pt); RNs 4 (ft), 3 (pt);
 LPNs 9 (ft), 3 (pt); Nurses' aides 30 (ft), 35
 (pt); Physical therapists 1 (pt); Activities
 coordinators 2 (pt); Dietitians 1 (pt);
 Ophthalmologists 1 (pt); Podiatrists 1 (pt);
 Audiologists 1 (pt).
Facilities Dining room; Physical therapy
 room; Activities room; Laundry room;
 Ventilator unit.
Activities Arts & crafts; Games; Reading
 groups; Movies; Dances/Social/Cultural
 gatherings; Pet therapy.

Wabash Healthcare Center
600 Washington St, Wabash, IN 46992
(219) 563-8402
Admin Carla Bowyer. *Dir of Nursing* Barbara
 Branson. *Medical Dir* Family Physicians
 Associated.
Licensure Skilled care; Intermediate care;
 Intermediate care for mentally retarded.
 Beds SNF 29; Swing beds ICF/ICF MR 79.
 Certified Medicaid; Medicare.
Owner Proprietary corp (Pafco Enterprises
 Inc).
Admissions Requirements Medical
 examination; Physician's request.
Staff Physicians 14 (pt); RNs 4 (ft), 4 (pt);
 LPNs 6 (ft), 2 (pt); Nurses' aides 24 (ft), 6
 (pt); Physical therapists 2 (pt); Occupational
 therapists 1 (pt); Speech therapists 1 (pt);
 Activities coordinators 1 (ft), 1 (pt);
 Dietitians 1 (pt); Ophthalmologists 1 (pt);
 Podiatrists 1 (pt); Audiologists 1 (pt).

Facilities Dining room; Physical therapy
 room; Activities room; Crafts room; Laundry
 room; Barber/Beauty shop; Library; Resident
 lounges.
Activities Arts & crafts; Cards; Games;
 Reading groups; Prayer groups; Movies;
 Shopping trips; Dances/Social/Cultural
 gatherings; Intergenerational programs; Pet
 therapy; Outings.

Wakarusa

Miller's Merry Manor Inc
PO Box 710, 300 N Washington, Wakarusa,
 IN 46573
(219) 862-4511
Admin Gerald R Hirschy.
Licensure Intermediate care. *Beds* ICF 66.

Waldron

Waldron Health Care Home Inc
PO Box 371, North Main St, Waldron, IN
 46182
(317) 525-4371
Admin Dwain R Kuhn. *Dir of Nursing* Carol
 Shurig. *Medical Dir* James Peters.
Licensure Intermediate care; Residential care.
 Beds ICF 20; Residential 63/20. *Certified*
 Medicaid.
Owner Proprietary corp.
Staff RNs 1 (ft); LPNs 3 (ft), 2 (pt); Nurses'
 aides 15 (ft), 20 (pt); Activities coordinators;
 Dietitians 1 (ft), 1 (pt).
Facilities Dining room; Activities room;
 Laundry room; Barber/Beauty shop.
Activities Arts & crafts; Cards; Games;
 Reading groups; Prayer groups; Movies;
 Shopping trips.

Walkerton

Miller's Merry Manor Inc
Walkerton Trail, Walkerton, IN 46574
(219) 586-3133
Admin Patrick Boyle.
Licensure Intermediate care. *Beds* ICF 124.
 Certified Medicaid.
Owner Proprietary corp (Millers Merry
 Manor).

Warren

United Methodist Memorial Home
PO Box 326, Warren, IN 46792
(219) 375-2201
Admin Philip E Souder. *Dir of Nursing* Lois
 Spahr RN. *Medical Dir* Gerald Miller MD.
Licensure Intermediate care; Residential care;
 Comprehensive nursing care. *Beds* ICF 185;
 Residential care 442; Comprehensive care
 28.
Admissions Requirements Minimum age 65;
 Medical examination; Physician's request.
Staff Physicians 7 (pt); RNs 14 (ft); LPNs 12
 (ft); Nurses' aides 112 (ft); Physical
 therapists 2 (ft), 1 (pt); Recreational
 therapists 2 (ft); Occupational therapists 5
 (ft); Activities coordinators 2 (ft), 1 (pt);
 Dietitians 1 (pt); Ophthalmologists 1 (pt);
 Podiatrists 1 (pt).
Affiliation Methodist.
Facilities Dining room; Physical therapy
 room; Activities room; Chapel; Crafts room;
 Laundry room; Barber/Beauty shop; Library;
 Dentist office; Eye clinic; Post office;
 Medical clinic on-site.
Activities Arts & crafts; Cards; Games;
 Reading groups; Prayer groups; Movies;
 Shopping trips; Dances/Social/Cultural
 gatherings.

Warsaw

Mason Health Care Facility Inc
900 Provident Dr, Warsaw, IN 46580
(219) 267-6309
Admin Carlyle L Mason. *Dir of Nursing*
 Gracie Freeman. *Medical Dir* Harold Mason
 MD.
Licensure Skilled care; Intermediate care. *Beds*
 SNF 25; ICF 64. *Certified* Medicaid;
 Medicare.
Owner Proprietary corp.
Admissions Requirements Minimum age 18;
 Medical examination; Physician's request.
Staff RNs 5 (ft), 3 (pt); LPNs 2 (ft), 3 (pt);
 Nurses' aides 24 (ft), 7 (pt); Physical
 therapists 1 (pt); Recreational therapists 1
 (pt); Activities coordinators 1 (ft), 2 (pt);
 Dietitians 1 (pt); Ophthalmologists 1 (pt);
 Dentists 1 (pt).
Facilities Dining room; Physical therapy
 room; Activities room; Crafts room; Laundry
 room; Barber/Beauty shop.
Activities Arts & crafts; Cards; Games;
 Reading groups; Shopping trips.

Miller's Merry Manor Inc
PO Box 377, Country Farm Rd, Warsaw, IN
 46580
(219) 267-8196
Admin Bruce Mehlhop.
Licensure Skilled care; Intermediate care. *Beds*
 SNF 33; ICF 121. *Certified* Medicaid;
 Medicare.
Owner Proprietary corp (Millers Merry
 Manor).
Admissions Requirements Minimum age 18;
 Medical examination; Physician's request.

Prairie View Rest Home Inc
300 E Prairie St, Warsaw, IN 46580
(219) 267-8922
Admin N Charlene Bradbury. *Dir of Nursing*
 Carol Brazo RN. *Medical Dir* YuDu Chen
 MD.
Licensure Intermediate care. *Beds* ICF 126.
 Certified Medicaid.
Owner Proprietary corp.
Admissions Requirements Minimum age 18;
 Medical examination; Physician's request.
Staff Physicians 1 (pt); RNs 4 (ft), 4 (pt);
 LPNs 6 (ft); Nurses' aides 25 (ft), 15 (pt);
 Physical therapists 1 (pt); Activities
 coordinators 2 (ft); Dietitians 1 (pt).
Facilities Dining room; Physical therapy
 room; Activities room; Barber/Beauty shop;
 2 Lounges; Enclosed courtyard; Quiet room;
 Wheelchair lift van & station wagon.
Activities Arts & crafts; Cards; Games; Prayer
 groups; Movies; Shopping trips; Dances/
 Social/Cultural gatherings; Trips to zoo;
 Botanical gardens; Travelogues.

Warsaw Nursing Home
2402 E Center St, Warsaw, IN 46580
(219) 269-1152
Admin Patricia Beam. *Dir of Nursing* Robert
 Nilsen RN. *Medical Dir* Yu du Chen MD.
Licensure Intermediate care. *Beds* ICF 40.
 Certified Medicaid.
Owner Proprietary corp (Beverly Enterprises).
Admissions Requirements Minimum age 18.
Staff RNs 1 (pt); LPNs 3 (ft); Nurses' aides 6
 (ft), 3 (pt); Activities coordinators 1 (pt).
Facilities Dining room; Activities room;
 Laundry room.
Activities Arts & crafts; Cards; Games;
 Dances/Social/Cultural gatherings.

Washington

**Eastgate Manor Nursing & Residential Center
Inc**
Hwy 50 E, PO Box 470, Washington, IN
 47501
(812) 254-3301
Admin Merle James Ward.

Licensure Intermediate care. *Beds* ICF 82. *Certified* Medicaid.
Owner Proprietary corp (Unicare).
Admissions Requirements Minimum age 18; Medical examination; Physician's request.
Staff RNs 3 (ft), 2 (pt); LPNs 3 (ft), 6 (pt); Nurses' aides 30 (ft), 10 (pt); Physical therapists 1 (pt); Activities coordinators 1 (ft); Dietitians 1 (pt); Ophthalmologists 1 (pt); Dentists 1 (pt).
Facilities Dining room; Physical therapy room; Activities room; Laundry room; Barber/Beauty shop.
Activities Arts & crafts; Cards; Games; Reading groups; Prayer groups; Movies; Shopping trips; Dances/Social/Cultural gatherings.

Hillside Manor
PO Box 654, Washington, IN 47501
(812) 254-7159
Admin John F Helm.
Medical Dir Dr T W Davis.
Licensure Intermediate care. *Beds* ICF 27. *Certified* Medicaid.
Admissions Requirements Medical examination; Physician's request.
Staff RNs 1 (ft), 1 (pt); LPNs 1 (ft), 1 (pt); Nurses' aides 7 (ft), 5 (pt); Physical therapists 1 (pt); Activities coordinators 1 (ft).
Facilities Dining room; Laundry room.
Activities Arts & crafts; Cards; Games; Reading groups; Shopping trips.

Prairie Village Living Center
1401 Hwy 57 S, Washington, IN 47501
(812) 254-4516
Admin Stephanie Atwood.
Medical Dir Donald Hall MD.
Licensure Intermediate care. *Beds* ICF 121. *Certified* Medicaid.
Owner Nonprofit corp (Adventist Living Centers).
Admissions Requirements Minimum age 18.
Staff Physicians 5 (pt); RNs 3 (ft); LPNs 6 (ft); Nurses' aides 40 (ft); Physical therapists 1 (pt); Activities coordinators 2 (ft); Dietitians 1 (pt); Ophthalmologists 1 (pt); Podiatrists 1 (pt); Dentists 1 (pt).
Affiliation Seventh-Day Adventist.
Facilities Dining room; Physical therapy room; Activities room; Laundry room; Barber/Beauty shop.
Activities Arts & crafts; Cards; Games; Reading groups; Prayer groups; Shopping trips.

West Lafayette

George Davis Manor
1051 Cumberland Ave, West Lafayette, IN 47906
(317) 463-2571
Admin Gail A Brown. *Dir of Nursing* Judy Cox RN. *Medical Dir* Dr Thomas J Stolz.
Licensure Intermediate care; Residential care. *Beds* ICF 59; Residential care 103. *Certified* Medicaid.
Owner Nonprofit corp (Service Frontiers Inc).
Admissions Requirements Minimum age 18; Medical examination.
Staff RNs 2 (ft), 1 (pt); LPNs 7 (ft); Nurses' aides 25 (ft), 3 (pt); Activities coordinators 1 (ft); Dietitians 1 (pt).
Facilities Dining room; Physical therapy room; Activities room; Crafts room; Laundry room; Barber/Beauty shop; Library; Lounge.
Activities Arts & crafts; Cards; Games; Reading groups; Prayer groups; Movies; Shopping trips; Dances/Social/Cultural gatherings.

Heritage Healthcare
3400 Soldiers Home Rd, West Lafayette, IN 47906
(317) 463-1541, 463-4592 FAX

Admin Judith K Rauch. *Dir of Nursing* Raelene Wing. *Medical Dir* Dr Thomas Stolz.
Licensure Skilled care; Intermediate care. *Beds* SNF 23; ICF 122. *Private Pay Patients* 45%. *Certified* Medicaid; Medicare.
Owner Proprietary corp (Life Care Centers of America).
Admissions Requirements Minimum age 18; Medical examination; Physician's request.
Staff Physicians 1 (pt); RNs 2 (ft), 4 (pt); LPNs 6 (ft), 2 (pt); Nurses' aides 65 (ft), 25 (pt); Physical therapists 2 (pt); Occupational therapists 1 (pt); Speech therapists 1 (pt); Activities coordinators 2 (ft), 2 (pt); Dietitians 1 (ft).
Facilities Dining room; Physical therapy room; Activities room; Crafts room; Laundry room; Barber/Beauty shop; Library.
Activities Arts & crafts; Cards; Games; Reading groups; Prayer groups; Movies; Shopping trips; Dances/Social/Cultural gatherings; Intergenerational programs; Pet therapy.

Indiana Veterans Home
3851 N River Rd, West Lafayette, IN 47906
(317) 463-1502
Admin Colonel Robert Hinds. *Dir of Nursing* Patricia L Query RN. *Medical Dir* Ben E Crouse MD.
Licensure Intermediate care; Retirement; Alzheimer's care. *Beds* ICF 800.
Owner Publicly owned.
Admissions Requirements Medical examination.
Staff Physicians 3 (ft), 2 (pt); RNs 42 (ft), 7 (pt); LPNs 28 (ft), 3 (pt); Nurses' aides 182 (ft), 10 (pt); Physical therapists 1 (ft); Reality therapists 8 (ft), 4 (pt); Occupational therapists 1 (ft); Speech therapists 1 (pt); Activities coordinators 1 (ft); Dietitians 4 (ft); Podiatrists 1 (pt); Audiologists 1 (ft); Other staff 269 (ft), 16 (pt).
Facilities Dining room; Physical therapy room; Activities room; Chapel; Crafts room; Laundry room; Barber/Beauty shop; Library.
Activities Arts & crafts; Cards; Games; Reading groups; Prayer groups; Movies; Shopping trips; Dances/Social/Cultural gatherings; Intergenerational programs.

Tippecanoe Villa
5308 N 50 W, West Lafayette, IN 47906
(317) 423-9240
Admin C Haan.
Licensure Residential care. *Beds* 121.

Westminster Village West Lafayette Inc
2741 N Salisbury St, West Lafayette, IN 47906
(317) 463-7546
Admin John J Morrison. *Dir of Nursing* Trudy Risemas RN. *Medical Dir* Eleanor H Filmer MD.
Licensure Skilled care; Retirement. *Beds* SNF 38. *Certified* Medicare.
Owner Nonprofit corp.
Admissions Requirements Minimum age 62; Medical examination.
Staff Physicians 1 (pt); RNs 4 (ft), 2 (pt); LPNs 1 (ft), 1 (pt); Nurses' aides 13 (ft), 8 (pt); Physical therapists 1 (pt); Occupational therapists 1 (pt); Speech therapists 1 (pt); Activities coordinators 1 (ft); Dietitians 1 (pt); Ophthalmologists 1 (pt); Podiatrists 1 (pt); Qualified medication aides 6 (pt); Dentists 1 (pt).
Facilities Dining room; Physical therapy room; Activities room; Chapel; Crafts room; Laundry room; Barber/Beauty shop; Library; Branch bank; General store; Exercise room; Club room.
Activities Arts & crafts; Cards; Games; Reading groups; Prayer groups; Movies; Shopping trips; Dances/Social/Cultural gatherings; Trips.

Westfield

Westfield Village
776 N Union, Westfield, IN 46074
(317) 896-2515
Admin Donna J Imlay. *Dir of Nursing* June Loor. *Medical Dir* Dr Robert Habig.
Licensure Skilled care; Intermediate care. *Beds* SNF 18; ICF 62. *Certified* Medicaid; Medicare.
Owner Proprietary corp (Hillhaven Corp).

Whiting

Hammond-Whiting Convalescent Center
1000 114th St, Whiting, IN 46394
(219) 659-2770
Admin Paul Asselin.
Medical Dir K Pahuja MD.
Licensure Intermediate care. *Beds* ICF 80. *Certified* Medicaid.
Owner Proprietary corp (National Heritage).
Admissions Requirements Minimum age 65; Medical examination; Physician's request.
Staff RNs 2 (ft), 6 (pt); LPNs 1 (ft); Nurses' aides 20 (ft), 12 (pt); Activities coordinators 1 (ft).
Facilities Dining room; Activities room; Laundry room; Barber/Beauty shop; TV lounge.
Activities Arts & crafts; Cards; Games; Prayer groups; Movies; Dances/Social/Cultural gatherings.

Williamsport

Country Care
200 Short St, Williamsport, IN 47993
(317) 762-6111
Admin Merridy J Dillman RN. *Dir of Nursing* M Jean Fields RN. *Medical Dir* Hugo A Brenner MD.
Licensure Intermediate care. *Beds* ICF 108. *Certified* Medicaid.
Owner Privately owned (First Nepenthe Partners).
Admissions Requirements Minimum age 16; Medical examination; Physician's request.
Staff Physicians 6 (ft); RNs 1 (ft); LPNs 4 (ft); Nurses' aides 49 (ft); Activities coordinators 1 (ft); Dietitians 1 (ft); Ophthalmologists 1 (ft); Podiatrists 1 (ft); Audiologists 1 (ft).
Facilities Dining room; Physical therapy room; Activities room; Crafts room; Laundry room; Barber/Beauty shop.
Activities Arts & crafts; Cards; Games; Reading groups; Prayer groups; Movies; Shopping trips; Dances/Social/Cultural gatherings.

Winamac

Pulaski Health Care Center
PO Box 347, 624 E 13th St, Winamac, IN 46996-1117
(219) 946-3394
Admin Daniel Dolezal.
Licensure Comprehensive care. *Beds* Comprehensive care 60.

Winamac Nursing Home
515 E 13th St, Winamac, IN 46996
(219) 946-6143
Admin Ray Welsh. *Dir of Nursing* Diana Vesh. *Medical Dir* Rex Allman MD.
Licensure Intermediate care. *Beds* ICF 40. *Private Pay Patients* 30%. *Certified* Medicaid.
Owner Proprietary corp (Beverly Enterprises).
Staff Physicians (consultant); RNs 1 (ft), 1 (pt); LPNs 2 (ft), 2 (pt); Nurses' aides 7 (ft), 3 (pt); Activities coordinators 1 (ft); Dietitians (consultant); Ophthalmologists (consultant); Podiatrists (consultant).

Facilities Dining room; Activities room; Laundry room; Barber/Beauty shop.
Activities Arts & crafts; Cards; Games; Reading groups; Prayer groups; Movies; Dances/Social/Cultural gatherings; Pet therapy.

Winchester

Community Care Center of Winchester
County Rd 100 E, Winchester, IN 47394
(317) 584-5084
Admin Stanley Wilkins.
Licensure Intermediate care; Comprehensive care. *Beds* ICF 50; Comprehensive care 16.

Randolph Nursing Home
701 S Oak St, Winchester, IN 47394
(317) 584-2201
Admin Patricia Sue Sneed.
Licensure Skilled care; Intermediate care. *Beds* SNF 29; ICF 65. *Certified* Medicaid.
Owner Proprietary corp (Forum Group).

Winona Lake

Grace Village Health Care Facility
PO Box 337, Winona Lake, IN 46590
(219) 372-6100

Admin Sherwood V Durkee. *Dir of Nursing* Nancy Derry RN.
Licensure Intermediate care; Residential care; Alzheimer's care. *Beds* ICF 33; Residential 17. *Certified* Medicaid.
Owner Nonprofit corp.
Admissions Requirements Minimum age 65; Medical examination; Physician's request.
Staff RNs; LPNs; Nurses' aides; Activities coordinators; Dietitians.
Affiliation Church of the Brethren.
Facilities Dining room; Physical therapy room; Activities room; Chapel; Crafts room; Laundry room; Barber/Beauty shop; Library.
Activities Arts & crafts; Games; Reading groups; Prayer groups; Movies; Shopping trips.

Yorktown

Yorktown Health Care Center Inc
PO Box 188, 500 Andrews Rd, Yorktown, IN 47396
(317) 759-7740
Admin Margaret J Hunley.
Licensure Skilled care; Intermediate care. *Beds* SNF 27; ICF 73.

Zionsville

Village Christian Parke
675 S Ford Rd, Zionsville, IN 46077
(317) 873-5205
Admin H Joseph Seidel. *Dir of Nursing* Evelyn Hudson. *Medical Dir* Ben Park.
Licensure Intermediate care; Residential care. *Beds* ICF 71; Residential care 261. *Private Pay Patients* 80%. *Certified* Medicaid.
Owner Nonprofit organization/foundation (Christian Homes).
Admissions Requirements Minimum age 60; Medical examination.
Staff RNs 5 (ft); LPNs 6 (ft); Nurses' aides 20 (ft); Activities coordinators 5 (ft).
Facilities Dining room; Activities room; Chapel; Crafts room; Laundry room; Barber/Beauty shop; Library.
Activities Arts & crafts; Cards; Games; Reading groups; Prayer groups; Movies; Shopping trips; Dances/Social/Cultural gatherings; Intergenerational programs; Pet therapy.

IOWA

Ackley

United Presbyterian Home
1020 2nd Ave, Ackley, IA 50601
(515) 847-3531
Admin Iva Griep.
Medical Dir Lisa Ubben.
Licensure Intermediate care; Residential care.
  Beds ICF 55; Residential care 40. *Certified*
  Medicaid.
Owner Nonprofit corp.
Admissions Requirements Medical
  examination.
Staff RNs 2 (ft); LPNs 5 (pt); Nurses' aides 20
  (ft), 26 (pt); Activities coordinators 1 (ft);
  Dietitians 1 (pt).
Languages German.
Affiliation Presbyterian.
Facilities Dining room; Activities room;
  Chapel; Crafts room; Barber/Beauty shop.
Activities Arts & crafts; Cards; Games;
  Reading groups; Prayer groups; Movies;
  Shopping trips; Dances/Social/Cultural
  gatherings; Church services; Bible study.

Adair

Adair Community Health Center
608 North St, Adair, IA 50002
(515) 742-3205
Admin Linda S Hemminger RN. *Dir of
  Nursing* Jolene Hinrichs LPN. *Medical Dir*
  Judy Schwenneker LPN.
Licensure Intermediate care. *Beds* ICF 48.
  Certified Medicaid.
Owner Nonprofit corp.
Admissions Requirements Medical
  examination; Physician's request.
Staff RNs 3 (pt); LPNs 5 (ft), 2 (pt); Nurses'
  aides 10 (ft), 13 (pt); Activities coordinators
  1 (pt).
Facilities Dining room; Activities room;
  Laundry room; Barber/Beauty shop.
Activities Arts & crafts; Cards; Games;
  Reading groups; Prayer groups; Movies;
  Shopping trips; Dances/Social/Cultural
  gatherings; Picnics; Plant flowers; Cooking.

Adel

Adel Acres Care Center
1919 Greene St, Adel, IA 50003
(515) 993-4511
Admin Pam Lancial. *Dir of Nursing* Karen
  Klisaris.
Licensure Intermediate care. *Beds* ICF 59.
  Certified Medicaid.
Owner Privately owned.
Admissions Requirements Medical
  examination.
Staff RNs 1 (ft), 1 (pt); LPNs 1 (ft), 3 (pt);
  Nurses' aides 10 (ft), 15 (pt); Activities
  coordinators; Dietitians.

Facilities Dining room; Laundry room;
  Barber/Beauty shop.
Activities Arts & crafts; Cards; Games;
  Reading groups; Prayer groups; Movies;
  Shopping trips; Dances/Social/Cultural
  gatherings.

Afton

Afton Care Center
805 W Pearl, Afton, IA 50830
(515) 347-8416
Admin Mary Cochran.
Licensure Intermediate care. *Beds* ICF 60.
  Certified Medicaid.

Akron

Akron City Convalescent Care Center
276 South St, Box 847, Akron, IA 51001
(712) 568-2422
Admin Jerold J Dykstra. *Dir of Nursing* Jan
  Pritchett RN. *Medical Dir* K Miller DO.
Licensure Skilled care; Intermediate care;
  Assisted living apartments. *Beds* SNF 26;
  ICF 34; Assisted living apts 6. *Private Pay
  Patients* 50%. *Certified* Medicaid; Medicare.
Owner Nonprofit organization/foundation.
Admissions Requirements Medical
  examination; Physician's request.
Staff Physicians 2 (pt); RNs 5 (ft), 4 (pt);
  LPNs 2 (ft), 1 (pt); Nurses' aides 12 (ft), 17
  (pt); Physical therapists 1 (pt); Speech
  therapists 1 (pt); Activities coordinators 1
  (ft), 1 (pt); Dietitians 1 (pt); Podiatrists 1
  (pt); Audiologists 1 (pt).
Languages Dutch, German.
Facilities Dining room; Physical therapy
  room; Activities room; Chapel; Crafts room;
  Laundry room; Barber/Beauty shop.
Activities Arts & crafts; Cards; Games;
  Reading groups; Movies; Shopping trips; Pet
  therapy; Music.

Albert City

Pleasant View Home
410 S 3rd St, Albert City, IA 50510
(712) 843-2238
Admin Dorothy Nordlund. *Dir of Nursing*
  Connie Hansen RN.
Licensure Intermediate care. *Beds* ICF 50.
  Private Pay Patients 73%. *Certified*
  Medicaid.
Owner Proprietary corp.
Admissions Requirements Minimum age 18;
  Medical examination; Physician's request.
Staff RNs 3 (ft), 1 (pt); LPNs 1 (ft), 2 (pt);
  Nurses' aides 12 (ft), 7 (pt); Physical
  therapists 1 (pt); Activities coordinators 1
  (ft); Dietitians 1 (pt); Podiatrists 1 (pt).
Facilities Dining room; Physical therapy
  room; Activities room; Crafts room; Laundry
  room; Barber/Beauty shop; Library.

Activities Arts & crafts; Cards; Games;
  Reading groups; Prayer groups; Movies;
  Shopping trips; Dances/Social/Cultural
  gatherings; Intergenerational programs; Pet
  therapy.

Albia

Albia Manor
Box 250, S Florence, Albia, IA 52531
(515) 932-2721
Admin Bernice E Butler. *Dir of Nursing*
  Brenda Ouyahia RN.
Licensure Intermediate care. *Beds* ICF 94.
  Private Pay Patients 20%. *Certified*
  Medicaid.
Owner Nonprofit corp (Mercy Health
  Initiatives).
Admissions Requirements Medical
  examination; Physician's request.
Staff RNs 2 (ft); LPNs 9 (ft); Nurses' aides 33
  (ft); Physical therapists (consultant); Reality
  therapists (consultant); Recreational
  therapists (consultant); Occupational
  therapists (consultant); Speech therapists
  (consultant); Activities coordinators 1 (ft), 1
  (pt); Dietitians (consultant).
Facilities Dining room; Physical therapy
  room; Barber/Beauty shop.
Activities Arts & crafts; Games; Reading
  groups; Prayer groups; Movies; Shopping
  trips; Dances/Social/Cultural gatherings;
  Intergenerational programs; Pet therapy.

Algona

Algona Manor Care Center
2221 E McGregor, Algona, IA 50511
(515) 295-3505
Admin George E Lewis.
Licensure Intermediate care. *Beds* ICF 46.

Good Samaritan Center
214 W Kennedy St, Algona, IA 50511
(515) 295-2414
Admin John E Kern. *Dir of Nursing* Marilyn
  Stevens.
Licensure Intermediate care; Alzheimer's care.
  Beds ICF 121. *Certified* Medicaid.
Owner Nonprofit corp (Evangelical Lutheran/
  Good Samaritan Society).
Languages German.
Affiliation Lutheran.
Facilities Dining room; Physical therapy
  room; Activities room; Crafts room; Laundry
  room; Barber/Beauty shop.
Activities Arts & crafts; Cards; Games;
  Reading groups; Prayer groups; Movies;
  Dances/Social/Cultural gatherings.

Allison

Allison Health Care Center
RR 1, PO Box 89A, 900 7th St W, Allison, IA
  50602
(319) 267-2791

Admin Steven P Wendler. *Dir of Nursing*
Victor Palmer RN.
Licensure Intermediate care. *Beds* ICF 80.
Private Pay Patients 40%. *Certified*
Medicaid; VA.
Owner Proprietary corp (ABCM Corp).
Admissions Requirements Minimum age 18;
Medical examination; Physician's request.
Staff RNs 1 (ft); LPNs 5 (ft), 4 (pt); Nurses'
aides 24 (ft), 14 (pt); Physical therapists
(consultant); Occupational therapists
(consultant); Speech therapists (consultant);
Activities coordinators 1 (ft); Dietitians
(consultant).
Languages German.
Facilities Dining room; Physical therapy
room; Activities room; Barber/Beauty shop;
Library.
Activities Arts & crafts; Cards; Games; Prayer
groups; Movies.

Altoona

Altoona Manor Care Center
200 7th Ave SW, Altoona, IA 50009
(515) 967-4267
Admin Rex V Logan.
Licensure Intermediate care. *Beds* ICF 114.
Certified Medicaid.
Owner Proprietary corp (National Heritage).

Amana

Colonial Manor
PO Box 160, Hwy 220 W, Amana, IA 52203
(319) 622-3131
Admin B H Otte. *Dir of Nursing* Marlys
Floyd. *Medical Dir* Dr C E Barryhill.
Licensure Intermediate care. *Beds* ICF 56.
Certified Medicaid.
Owner Proprietary corp.
Admissions Requirements Minimum age 16.
Staff Physicians 1 (pt); RNs 1 (ft); LPNs 5
(ft), 2 (pt); Nurses' aides 25 (ft), 4 (pt);
Physical therapists 1 (pt); Reality therapists
1 (pt); Recreational therapists 1 (pt);
Occupational therapists 1 (pt); Speech
therapists 1 (pt); Activities coordinators 1
(ft); Dietitians 1 (pt); Podiatrists 1 (pt);
Audiologists 1 (pt).
Languages German.
Facilities Dining room; Physical therapy
room; Activities room; Chapel; Crafts room;
Laundry room; Barber/Beauty shop.
Activities Arts & crafts; Cards; Games;
Reading groups; Prayer groups; Movies;
Dances/Social/Cultural gatherings;
Intergenerational programs; Pet therapy.

Ames

Mary Greeley Medical Center
117 11th St, Ames, IA 50010
(515) 239-2011
Admin Phyllis Crouse.
Licensure Skilled care. *Beds* SNF 20.

Green Hills Health Center
2210 Hamilton Dr, Ames, IA 50010
(515) 296-5100
Admin Joel D Nelson.
Licensure Intermediate care. *Beds* ICF 8.

North Grand Care Center
3440 Grand Ave, Ames, IA 50010
(515) 232-3426
Admin Joan Erickson.
Licensure Intermediate care. *Beds* ICF 100.
Certified Medicaid.
Admissions Requirements Medical
examination.
Staff RNs 5 (ft), 2 (pt); LPNs 3 (ft), 2 (pt);
Nurses' aides 25 (ft), 15 (pt); Physical
therapists 1 (ft), 1 (pt); Reality therapists 1
(pt); Recreational therapists 1 (ft), 1 (pt);
Occupational therapists 1 (pt); Speech

therapists 1 (pt); Activities coordinators 1
(ft); Dietitians 11 (ft); Podiatrists 1 (pt);
Audiologists 1 (pt).
Facilities Dining room; Physical therapy
room; Activities room; Chapel; Crafts room;
Laundry room; Barber/Beauty shop; Library;
TV lounges.
Activities Arts & crafts; Cards; Games;
Reading groups; Prayer groups; Movies;
Shopping trips; Dances/Social/Cultural
gatherings; Individualized activities.

Northcrest Retirement Community
1801 20th St, Ames, IA 50010
(515) 232-6760
Admin Larry L Allen. *Dir of Nursing* Marilyn
Hovick.
Licensure Intermediate care; Residential care;
Retirement. *Beds* ICF 18; Residential care
10; Retirement 125.
Owner Nonprofit organization/foundation.
Admissions Requirements Minimum age 62;
Medical examination.
Staff RNs; LPNs; Nurses' aides; Activities
coordinators; Dietitians.
Affiliation Baptist.
Facilities Dining room; Activities room;
Chapel; Crafts room; Laundry room; Barber/
Beauty shop; Library.
Activities Arts & crafts; Cards; Games;
Reading groups; Prayer groups; Movies;
Shopping trips; Dances/Social/Cultural
gatherings; Intergenerational programs; Pet
therapy.

Riverside Manor
1204 S 4th, Ames, IA 50010
(515) 233-2903
Admin Lee V Livingston.
Licensure Intermediate care. *Beds* ICF 59.
Certified Medicaid.

Anamosa

Anamosa Care Center
1209 E 3rd St, Anamosa, IA 52205
(319) 462-4356
Admin Darlene M Sissel.
Licensure Intermediate care. *Beds* ICF 76.
Certified Medicaid.

Anita

Colonial Manor
1000 Hillcrest Dr, Anita, IA 50020
(712) 762-3219
Admin Kent J Jorgensen.
Licensure Intermediate care. *Beds* ICF 65.
Certified Medicaid.
Owner Proprietary corp (Waverly Group).

Ankeny

Sunny View Care Center
410 NW Ash Dr, Ankeny, IA 50021
(515) 964-1101
Admin Bonnie Ballard. *Dir of Nursing* Cris
Mary RN. *Medical Dir* Dr Dennis Hopkins.
Licensure Intermediate care. *Beds* ICF 75.
Private Pay Patients 60%. *Certified*
Medicaid.
Owner Proprietary corp.
Admissions Requirements Minimum age 18;
Medical examination; Physician's request.
Staff RNs; LPNs; Nurses' aides; Activities
coordinators; Dietitians.
Facilities Dining room; Activities room;
Laundry room; Barber/Beauty shop;
Lounges; Offices.
Activities Arts & crafts; Cards; Games;
Reading groups; Prayer groups; Movies;
Shopping trips; Dances/Social/Cultural
gatherings; Intergenerational programs; Pet
therapy; Volunteer program.

Aplington

Maple Manor Nursing Home
345 Parrott, Aplington, IA 50604
(319) 347-2309
Admin Sally Aukes.
Licensure Intermediate care; Residential care.
Beds ICF 38; Residential care 20. *Certified*
Medicaid.
Admissions Requirements Medical
examination.
Staff RNs 1 (pt); LPNs 4 (pt); Nurses' aides
23 (pt); Physical therapists 1 (pt);
Occupational therapists 1 (pt); Activities
coordinators 2 (pt); Dietitians 1 (pt).
Facilities Dining room; Physical therapy
room; Activities room; Laundry room;
Barber/Beauty shop.
Activities Arts & crafts; Cards; Games;
Reading groups; Prayer groups; Movies;
Shopping trips.

Armstrong

Valley Vue Care Center
2nd Ave, Armstrong, IA 50514
(712) 864-3567
Admin Mary Tirevold.
Licensure Intermediate care. *Beds* ICF 50.
Certified Medicaid.
Owner Proprietary corp (ABCM Corp).

Atlantic

Atlantic Care Center
PO Box 270, Atlantic, IA 50022
(712) 243-3952
Admin Connie S Byrd.
Medical Dir Dr Keith Swanson.
Licensure Intermediate care. *Beds* ICF 123.
Certified Medicaid.
Owner Proprietary corp (Mercy Health
Initiatives).
Staff RNs 1 (ft); LPNs 8 (ft), 3 (pt); Nurses'
aides 18 (ft), 18 (pt); Physical therapists 1
(pt); Speech therapists 1 (pt); Activities
coordinators 1 (ft), 1 (pt); Dietitians 1 (pt);
Ophthalmologists 1 (pt); Podiatrists 1 (pt);
Audiologists 1 (pt); Dentists 1 (pt).

Cass County Memorial Hospital
1501 E 10th St, Atlantic, IA 50022
(712) 243-3250
Admin Patricia Markham.
Licensure Skilled care. *Beds* SNF 10.

Heritage House
1200 Brookridge Cir, Atlantic, IA 50022
(712) 243-1850
Admin Dennis Crouse. *Dir of Nursing* Barbara
Fischer RN. *Medical Dir* Mark Johnson
MD.
Licensure Intermediate care; Residential care;
Independent living; Apartments. *Beds* ICF
46; Residential care 15; Independent living
57; Apts 31. *Private Pay Patients* 80%.
Certified Medicaid.
Owner Nonprofit corp (Wesley Retirement
Services Inc).
Admissions Requirements Minimum age 55;
Medical examination.
Staff Physicians (contracted); RNs 1 (ft), 2
(pt); LPNs 4 (ft), 4 (pt); Nurses' aides 18
(ft), 11 (pt); Physical therapists (contracted);
Recreational therapists 1 (ft); Occupational
therapists (contracted); Speech therapists
(contracted); Activities coordinators 1 (ft);
Dietitians (contracted); Podiatrists
(contracted); Audiologists (contracted).
Affiliation Methodist.
Facilities Dining room; Physical therapy
room; Activities room; Chapel; Crafts room;
Laundry room; Barber/Beauty shop; Library;
Recreation room; Lounges; Leisure-walk
around grounds.

Activities Arts & crafts; Cards; Games; Reading groups; Prayer groups; Movies; Shopping trips; Dances/Social/Cultural gatherings; Intergenerational programs; Pet therapy.

Audubon

Friendship Home
714 N Division St, Audubon, IA 50025
(712) 563-2651
Admin Norman Hjelmeland. *Dir of Nursing* Judy Malmberg RN.
Licensure Intermediate care; Residential care. *Beds* ICF 69; Residential care 86. *Certified* Medicaid.
Owner Nonprofit organization/foundation.
Admissions Requirements Minimum age 60; Medical examination.
Staff Physicians; RNs; LPNs; Nurses' aides; Physical therapists; Activities coordinators; Dietitians.
Facilities Dining room; Physical therapy room; Activities room; Chapel; Crafts room; Laundry room; Barber/Beauty shop; Library.
Activities Arts & crafts; Cards; Games; Reading groups; Prayer groups; Movies; Shopping trips; Dances/Social/Cultural gatherings; Pet therapy.

Aurelia

Sunset Knoll Inc
5th & Spruce, Aurelia, IA 51005
(712) 434-2294
Admin Orin L Nelson. *Dir of Nursing* Joleen Goergen. *Medical Dir* Richard Berge MD.
Licensure Intermediate care; Residential care. *Beds* ICF 48; Residential care 20. *Private Pay Patients* 75%. *Certified* Medicaid.
Owner Proprietary corp.
Admissions Requirements Minimum age 50; Medical examination; Physician's request.
Staff Physicians 1 (pt); RNs 3 (ft); LPNs 3 (ft), 1 (pt); Nurses' aides 22 (ft), 4 (pt); Physical therapists 1 (pt); Activities coordinators 2 (pt); Dietitians 1 (pt).
Facilities Dining room; Physical therapy room; Activities room; Chapel; Barber/ Beauty shop.
Activities Arts & crafts; Cards; Games; Reading groups; Prayer groups; Movies; Shopping trips.

Avoca

Colonial Manor
1100 Chestnut St, Avoca, IA 51521
(712) 343-2665
Admin Suzie Nelson.
Medical Dir Lois Zobrist.
Licensure Intermediate care. *Beds* ICF 46. *Certified* Medicaid.
Owner Proprietary corp (Mercy Health Initiatives).
Staff RNs 2 (ft); LPNs 4 (ft); Nurses' aides 18 (ft); Activities coordinators 1 (ft).
Facilities Dining room; Laundry room; Barber/Beauty shop.
Activities Arts & crafts; Cards; Games; Reading groups; Prayer groups; Movies; Shopping trips; Dances/Social/Cultural gatherings.

Bancroft

Heritage Home of Bancroft
E Ramsey, Bancroft, IA 50517
(515) 885-2463
Admin Jeanne M Kinney.
Licensure Intermediate care. *Beds* ICF 39. *Certified* Medicaid.

Battle Creek

Willow Dale Care Center
Hwy 175, Battle Creek, IA 51006
(712) 365-4332
Admin Wilma McClellan. *Dir of Nursing* Anne Beery RN.
Licensure Intermediate care. *Beds* ICF 61. *Certified* Medicaid.
Owner Proprietary corp (ABCM Corp).
Admissions Requirements Medical examination; Physician's request.
Staff RNs 1 (ft), 2 (pt); LPNs 2 (ft), 2 (pt); Nurses' aides 12 (ft), 10 (pt); Activities coordinators 1 (ft); Dietitians 1 (pt).
Facilities Dining room; Physical therapy room; Activities room; Crafts room; Laundry room; Barber/Beauty shop.
Activities Arts & crafts; Cards; Games; Reading groups; Prayer groups; Movies; Shopping trips; Dances/Social/Cultural gatherings.

Baxter

Colonial Manor
407 East St, Baxter, IA 50028
(515) 227-3602
Admin Glenn Van Zante.
Medical Dir Beverley Van Zante.
Licensure Intermediate care. *Beds* ICF 65. *Certified* Medicaid.
Owner Privately owned.
Admissions Requirements Minimum age 20; Medical examination; Physician's request.
Staff Physicians; RNs 2 (ft), 2 (pt); LPNs 1 (ft); Nurses' aides 12 (ft), 13 (pt); Activities coordinators 1 (ft); Dietitians 1 (pt).
Languages German.
Facilities Dining room; Physical therapy room; Activities room; Chapel; Crafts room; Laundry room; Barber/Beauty shop.
Activities Arts & crafts; Cards; Games; Reading groups; Prayer groups; Movies; Shopping trips; Dances/Social/Cultural gatherings.

Bayard

Bayard Care Center
PO Box 310, Bayard, IA 50029
(712) 651-2085
Admin Dixie A Christensen.
Licensure Intermediate care. *Beds* ICF 50. *Certified* Medicaid.
Owner Proprietary corp (Mercy Health Initiatives).

Bedford

Bedford Manor
100 S W Pearl, Bedford, IA 50833
(712) 523-2161
Admin Dorothy McLeod.
Licensure Intermediate care. *Beds* ICF 64. *Certified* Medicaid.
Owner Proprietary corp (Mercy Health Initiatives).

Belle Plaine

Beverly Manor Convalescent Center
1505 Sunset Dr, Belle Plaine, IA 52208
(319) 444-2500
Admin Dorie Tammen.
Medical Dir Linda Meeks.
Licensure Intermediate care; Alzheimer's care. *Beds* ICF 70. *Certified* Medicaid.
Owner Proprietary corp (Mercy Health Initiatives).
Admissions Requirements Medical examination.
Staff RNs; LPNs; Nurses' aides; Activities coordinators.

Facilities Dining room; Laundry room; Barber/Beauty shop.
Activities Arts & crafts; Cards; Games; Reading groups; Prayer groups; Movies; Shopping trips; Dances/Social/Cultural gatherings.

Bellevue

Mill Valley Care Center
1201 Park St, Bellevue, IA 52031
(319) 872-5521
Admin Glinda Ernst. *Dir of Nursing* Auerle Bevan RN. *Medical Dir* Thomas F Garland MD.
Licensure Intermediate care. *Beds* ICF 68. *Certified* Medicaid.
Owner Proprietary corp.
Admissions Requirements Minimum age 18; Medical examination; Physician's request.
Staff RNs; LPNs; Nurses' aides; Activities coordinators.
Facilities Dining room; Physical therapy room; Activities room; Chapel; Laundry room; Barber/Beauty shop.
Activities Arts & crafts; Cards; Games; Reading groups; Prayer groups; Movies; Shopping trips; Dances/Social/Cultural gatherings.

Belmond

Belmond Health Care Center
1107 7th St NE, Belmond, IA 50421
(515) 444-3915
Admin Opal M Ellingston.
Licensure Intermediate care. *Beds* ICF 86. *Certified* Medicaid.
Owner Proprietary corp (ABCM Corp).

Bettendorf

Bettendorf Health Care Center
2730 Crow Creek Rd, Bettendorf, IA 52722
(319) 332-7463
Admin Steven Dowd.
Licensure Intermediate care. *Beds* ICF 101. *Certified* Medicaid.

Iowa Masonic Nursing Home
2500 Grant St, Bettendorf, IA 52722
(319) 359-9171, 359-9173 FAX
Admin James C Tourville, Exec Dir. *Dir of Nursing* Beverly Simkins RN. *Medical Dir* Dr Gerald Goettsch.
Licensure Intermediate care; Independent living; Alzheimer's care. *Beds* ICF 79; Independent living units 40. *Private Pay Patients* 44%. *Certified* Medicaid.
Owner Nonprofit organization/foundation.
Admissions Requirements Medical examination; Physician's request.
Staff Physicians 1 (pt); RNs 3 (ft); LPNs 2 (ft), 4 (pt); Nurses' aides 23 (ft), 7 (pt); Physical therapists (consultant); Reality therapists 1 (ft); Occupational therapists (consultant); Speech therapists (consultant); Activities coordinators 1 (ft); Dietitians (consultant); Ophthalmologists 1 (pt); Podiatrists 1 (pt).
Affiliation Masons.
Facilities Dining room; Physical therapy room; Activities room; Chapel; Crafts room; Laundry room; Barber/Beauty shop; Library; Game room.
Activities Arts & crafts; Cards; Games; Reading groups; Prayer groups; Movies; Shopping trips; Dances/Social/Cultural gatherings; Intergenerational programs; Pet therapy.

Bloomfield

Bloomfield Care Center
800 N Davis, Bloomfield, IA 52537
(515) 664-2699

Admin Janet Schwieger.
Licensure Intermediate care; Alzheimer's care.
Beds ICF 104. *Certified* Medicaid.
Owner Proprietary corp (ABCM Corp).
Staff RNs 1 (ft); LPNs 10 (ft), 1 (pt); Nurses'
aides 15 (ft), 19 (pt); Physical therapists 1
(pt); Occupational therapists 1 (pt);
Activities coordinators 1 (ft), 1 (pt);
Dietitians 1 (pt); Podiatrists.
Facilities Dining room; Physical therapy
room; Activities room; Chapel; Crafts room;
Barber/Beauty shop; Library; Picnic shelter;
TV area.
Activities Arts & crafts; Cards; Games;
Reading groups; Prayer groups; Movies;
Shopping trips; Dances/Social/Cultural
gatherings.

Davis County Hospital
507 N Madison, Bloomfield, IA 52537
(515) 664-2145
Admin William H Koellner.
Licensure Intermediate care. *Beds* ICF 32.

Boone

Eastern Star Masonic Home
715 Mamie Eisenhower Ave, Boone, IA 50036
(515) 432-5274
Admin Dennis Bock.
Licensure Intermediate care; Residential care.
Beds ICF 58; Residential care 118. *Certified*
Medicaid.
Affiliation Order of Eastern Star.

Evangelical Free Church Home
112 W 4th St, Boone, IA 50036
(515) 432-1393
Admin Rev Dwight M Schmidt.
Licensure Intermediate care. *Beds* ICF 120.
Certified Medicaid.
Affiliation Evangelical Free Church.

Ledges Manor
1400 22nd St, Boone, IA 50036
(515) 432-5580
Admin Lee V Livingston.
Licensure Intermediate care. *Beds* ICF 94.
Certified Medicaid.
Admissions Requirements Minimum age 18.
Staff RNs 2 (ft); LPNs 4 (ft), 3 (pt); Physical
therapists 20 (ft), 14 (pt); Activities
coordinators 1 (ft), 1 (pt).
Facilities Dining room; Activities room;
Crafts room; Laundry room; Barber/Beauty
shop.
Activities Arts & crafts; Cards; Games;
Reading groups; Prayer groups; Movies;
Shopping trips.

Britt

Westview Care Center
445 8th Ave SW, Britt, IA 50423
(515) 843-3835
Admin Becky L Smit. *Dir of Nursing* Dolores
Boehnke RN. *Medical Dir* Norman D Thede
MD.
Licensure Intermediate care. *Beds* ICF 59.
Private Pay Patients 45%. *Certified*
Medicaid.
Owner Proprietary corp (ABCM Corp).
Admissions Requirements Medical
examination; Physician's request.
Staff Physicians; RNs; LPNs; Nurses' aides;
Physical therapists; Occupational therapists;
Speech therapists; Activities coordinators;
Dietitians; Ophthalmologists; Podiatrists;
Audiologists.
Facilities Dining room; Activities room;
Laundry room; Barber/Beauty shop;
Lounges.
Activities Arts & crafts; Cards; Games;
Reading groups; Prayer groups; Movies;
Dances/Social/Cultural gatherings;
Intergenerational programs; Pet therapy;
Religious services.

Brooklyn

Brookhaven Nursing Home
406 North St, Brooklyn, IA 52211
(515) 522-9263
Admin Sandra Luft. *Dir of Nursing* Shirley
Mathes RN.
Licensure Intermediate care. *Beds* ICF 45.
Certified Medicaid.
Admissions Requirements Medical
examination.
Staff RNs 2 (ft), 1 (pt); LPNs 1 (ft), 1 (pt);
Nurses' aides 7 (ft), 10 (pt); Physical
therapists 1 (pt); Speech therapists 1 (pt);
Activities coordinators 1 (ft); Dietitians 1
(pt); Podiatrists 1 (pt).
Facilities Dining room; Laundry room;
Barber/Beauty shop.
Activities Arts & crafts; Cards; Games;
Reading groups; Prayer groups; Movies.

Buffalo Center

Timely Mission Nursing Home
109 Mission Dr, Buffalo Center, IA 50424
(515) 562-2494
Admin Murray D Berggren.
Licensure Intermediate care. *Beds* ICF 58.
Certified Medicaid.

Burlington

Burlington Care Center
2610 S 5th, Burlington, IA 52601
(319) 753-2841
Admin Robert Richard. *Dir of Nursing* Roxy
Richard.
Licensure Intermediate care. *Beds* ICF 103.
Certified Medicaid.
Owner Proprietary corp.
Admissions Requirements Minimum age 18.
Staff RNs 3 (ft), 1 (pt); LPNs 5 (ft), 5 (pt);
Nurses' aides 30 (ft), 18 (pt); Physical
therapists 1 (pt); Occupational therapists 1
(pt); Speech therapists 1 (pt); Activities
coordinators 1 (ft), 1 (pt); Dietitians 1 (pt);
Ophthalmologists 1 (pt); Dentists 1 (pt).
Facilities Dining room; Physical therapy
room; Activities room; Chapel; Crafts room;
Laundry room; Barber/Beauty shop.
Activities Arts & crafts; Cards; Games;
Reading groups; Prayer groups; Movies;
Shopping trips; Pet therapy.

Burlington Medical Center
602 N 3rd St, Burlington, IA 52601
(319) 753-3011
Admin Glen L Heagle.
Licensure Skilled care. *Beds* SNF 24.

Burlington Medical Center
602 N 3rd St, Burlington, IA 52601
(319) 753-3011
Admin Glen L Heagle.
Licensure Intermediate care. *Beds* ICF 96.
Owner Proprietary corp (Health One Health
Care).

Burlington Medical Center—Klein Unit
2910 Madison Ave, Burlington, IA 52601
(319) 752-5461
Admin Richard Miller. *Dir of Nursing* Carolyn
Mackey RN. *Medical Dir* Burton Stone MD.
Licensure Skilled care; Intermediate care. *Beds*
SNF 24; ICF 125. *Certified* Medicaid;
Medicare.
Owner Nonprofit corp.
Admissions Requirements Medical
examination; Physician's request.
Staff Physicians; RNs; LPNs; Nurses' aides;
Physical therapists; Reality therapists;
Recreational therapists; Occupational
therapists; Speech therapists; Activities
coordinators; Dietitians; Ophthalmologists;
Podiatrists; Dentists.

Facilities Dining room; Physical therapy
room; Activities room; Chapel; Crafts room;
Laundry room; Barber/Beauty shop; Library.
Activities Arts & crafts; Cards; Games;
Reading groups; Prayer groups; Movies;
Shopping trips; Dances/Social/Cultural
gatherings.

Elm View Care Center
715 Shoquoquon Dr, Burlington, IA 52601
(319) 752-4525
Admin James P Kelley. *Dir of Nursing* Linda
Gerdner RN.
Licensure Intermediate care; Alzheimer's care.
Beds ICF 146. *Certified* Medicaid.
Owner Proprietary corp (Hillhaven Corp).
Admissions Requirements Medical
examination; Physician's request.
Staff RNs; LPNs; Nurses' aides; Physical
therapists 1 (pt); Activities coordinators;
Dietitians 1 (pt).
Facilities Dining room; Physical therapy
room; Activities room; Chapel; Crafts room;
Laundry room; Barber/Beauty shop.
Activities Arts & crafts; Cards; Games;
Reading groups; Prayer groups; Movies;
Shopping trips; Dances/Social/Cultural
gatherings.

**St Francis Continuing Care & Nursing Home
Center**
210 S 5th St, Burlington, IA 52601
(319) 752-4564
Admin Wanda Hale. *Dir of Nursing* Janice
Smith RN.
Licensure Skilled care; Intermediate care;
Independent living units. *Beds* SNF 29; ICF
59; Independent living units 13. *Certified*
Medicaid; Medicare.
Owner Nonprofit corp.
Admissions Requirements Minimum age 18;
Medical examination; Physician's request.
Staff RNs 2 (ft), 7 (pt); LPNs 4 (ft), 2 (pt);
Nurses' aides 19 (ft), 20 (pt); Physical
therapists 1 (ft), 1 (pt); Occupational
therapists 1 (pt); Speech therapists 1 (pt);
Activities coordinators 1 (ft), 1 (pt);
Dietitians 1 (ft), 1 (pt).
Languages Spanish.
Affiliation Roman Catholic.
Facilities Dining room; Physical therapy
room; Activities room; Chapel; Crafts room;
Laundry room; Barber/Beauty shop; Library.
Activities Arts & crafts; Cards; Games;
Reading groups; Prayer groups; Movies;
Shopping trips; Dances/Social/Cultural
gatherings; Community programs; Festivals;
Picnics.

Wood Lake Group Home
1901 Racine, Burlington, IA 52601
(319) 752-9838
Admin Janelle Bangert.
Licensure Intermediate care for mentally
retarded. *Beds* ICF/MR 16.

Carlisle

Carlisle Care Center
680 Cole St, Carlisle, IA 50047
(515) 989-0871
Admin Kathy Holdsworth. *Dir of Nursing*
Roslie Hunt RN.
Licensure Intermediate care; Residential care.
Beds ICF 89; Residential care 12. *Certified*
Medicaid.
Owner Proprietary corp.
Admissions Requirements Medical
examination; Physician's request.
Staff RNs 2 (ft); LPNs 4 (ft), 1 (pt); Nurses'
aides 18 (ft), 17 (pt); Physical therapists 1
(pt); Speech therapists 1 (pt); Activities
coordinators 1 (ft), 1 (pt); Dietitians 1 (pt);
Ophthalmologists 1 (pt).
Facilities Dining room; Physical therapy
room; Activities room; Laundry room;
Barber/Beauty shop; Library.

Activities Arts & crafts; Games; Reading groups; Prayer groups; Movies.

Carroll

Carroll Health Center
2241 N West St, Carroll, IA 51401
(712) 792-9284
Admin Marty F Hoffman.
Licensure Intermediate care. *Beds* ICF 141.
Certified Medicaid.

Carroll Manor
500 Valley Dr, Carroll, IA 51401
(712) 792-9281
Admin Jim Feauto. *Dir of Nursing* Jayne Hanson. *Medical Dir* John Carroll.
Licensure Intermediate care. *Beds* ICF 51.
Private Pay Patients 50%. *Certified* Medicaid.
Owner Proprietary corp (National Heritage).
Staff Physicians; RNs 3 (ft), 4 (pt); LPNs 1 (ft), 1 (pt); Nurses' aides 16 (ft); Physical therapists 1 (pt); Reality therapists (consultant); Recreational therapists (consultant); Occupational therapists (consultant); Speech therapists (consultant); Activities coordinators 1 (ft); Dietitians 1 (pt); Ophthalmologists (consultant); Podiatrists (consultant); Audiologists (consultant).
Facilities Dining room; Activities room; Chapel; Crafts room; Laundry room; Barber/Beauty shop.
Activities Arts & crafts; Cards; Games; Reading groups; Prayer groups; Movies; Shopping trips; Dances/Social/Cultural gatherings; Intergenerational programs; Pet therapy; "Care-Ring" program.

St Anthony Nursing Home
S Clark St, Carroll, IA 51401
(712) 792-3581, 792-3581, ext 240 FAX
Admin Robert D Blincow. *Dir of Nursing* Wanda L Stephenson RN. *Medical Dir* J R Larkin MD.
Licensure Intermediate care; Retirement. *Beds* ICF 79; Retirement units 50. *Private Pay Patients* 50%. *Certified* Medicaid.
Owner Nonprofit corp (Health One Health Care).
Admissions Requirements Medical examination.
Staff Physicians (consultant); RNs 4 (ft), 1 (pt); LPNs 2 (ft), 2 (pt); Nurses' aides 18 (ft), 10 (pt); Physical therapists 3 (ft); Recreational therapists 1 (ft); Speech therapists 1 (pt); Dietitians 2 (ft).
Affiliation Roman Catholic.
Facilities Dining room; Activities room; Chapel; Crafts room; Laundry room; Barber/Beauty shop.
Activities Arts & crafts; Cards; Games; Reading groups; Prayer groups; Movies; Shopping trips; Dances/Social/Cultural gatherings; Intergenerational programs; Pet therapy.

Cascade

Shady Rest Care Center
700 N Johnson St, Cascade, IA 52033
(319) 852-3277
Admin Jean M Lynch.
Medical Dir William J Mehrl; Lorraine Takes.
Licensure Intermediate care. *Beds* ICF 70.
Certified Medicaid.
Owner Proprietary corp.
Admissions Requirements Medical examination; Physician's request.
Staff RNs 3 (ft), 2 (pt); LPNs 2 (ft), 2 (pt); Nurses' aides 13 (ft), 17 (pt); Physical therapists; Activities coordinators 1 (ft), 1 (pt); Dietitians 1 (pt).
Facilities Dining room; Physical therapy room; Activities room; Chapel; Crafts room; Laundry room; Barber/Beauty shop.

Activities Arts & crafts; Cards; Games; Prayer groups; Movies; Dances/Social/Cultural gatherings.

Cedar Falls

Cedar Falls Health Care Center
1728 W 8th, Cedar Falls, IA 50613
(319) 277-2437
Admin Gloria Heathman. *Dir of Nursing* Linda Ahlhelm.
Licensure Intermediate care. *Beds* ICF 100.
Private Pay Patients 35%. *Certified* Medicaid.
Owner Proprietary corp (Waverly Group).
Admissions Requirements Minimum age 18; Medical examination; Physician's request.
Staff RNs; LPNs; Nurses' aides; Physical therapists; Occupational therapists; Activities coordinators; Dietitians; Podiatrists.
Facilities Dining room; Physical therapy room; Activities room; Laundry room; Barber/Beauty shop.
Activities Arts & crafts; Cards; Games; Reading groups; Prayer groups; Movies; Dances/Social/Cultural gatherings; Intergenerational programs; Pet therapy.

Cedar Falls Lutheran Home
7511 University Ave, Cedar Falls, IA 50613
(319) 268-0401
Admin Patricia Welton.
Licensure Intermediate care; Residential care. *Beds* ICF 118; Residential care 66. *Certified* Medicaid.
Owner Nonprofit corp.
Affiliation Lutheran.

Sartori Memorial Hospital
6th & College, Cedar Falls, IA 50613
(319) 266-3584
Admin Verna Klinkenberg.
Licensure Skilled care. *Beds* SNF 18. *Certified* Medicaid; Medicare.
Owner Nonprofit organization/foundation.
Admissions Requirements Physician's request.
Staff Physicians; RNs; LPNs; Nurses' aides; Physical therapists; Recreational therapists; Occupational therapists; Speech therapists; Activities coordinators; Dietitians; Ophthalmologists; Podiatrists; Dentists.
Facilities Dining room; Physical therapy room; Activities room; Chapel; Crafts room; Library.
Activities Arts & crafts; Cards; Games; Reading groups; Movies.

Western Home
420 E 11th St, Cedar Falls, IA 50613
(319) 277-2141, 277-5158 FAX
Admin William K Appelgate. *Dir of Nursing* LaVonne Edwards RN. *Medical Dir* Dr Richard Frankhauser.
Licensure Intermediate care; Residential care; Independent living; Alzheimer's care. *Beds* ICF 68; Residential care 76; Independent living 106. *Private Pay Patients* 78%. *Certified* Medicaid; Medicare.
Owner Nonprofit organization/foundation.
Admissions Requirements Minimum age 60; Medical examination.
Staff RNs 5 (ft), 2 (pt); LPNs 12 (ft), 1 (pt); Nurses' aides 38 (ft), 29 (pt); Physical therapists 1 (pt); Activities coordinators 1 (ft); Dietitians 1 (pt); Podiatrists 1 (pt).
Affiliation Methodist.
Facilities Dining room; Physical therapy room; Activities room; Chapel; Crafts room; Laundry room; Barber/Beauty shop; Library; Large room with kitchen for family gatherings.
Activities Arts & crafts; Cards; Games; Reading groups; Prayer groups; Movies; Shopping trips; Dances/Social/Cultural gatherings; Intergenerational programs; Pet therapy.

Windsor Care Center
2305 Crescent Dr, Cedar Falls, IA 50613
(319) 268-0489
Admin H Jeanita Virchow.
Licensure Intermediate care. *Beds* ICF 100.
Certified Medicaid.
Owner Proprietary corp (Mercy Health Initiatives).
Admissions Requirements Medical examination.
Staff RNs 1 (ft), 3 (pt); LPNs 4 (ft), 6 (pt); Nurses' aides 20 (ft), 15 (pt); Activities coordinators 1 (ft), 1 (pt); Dietitians 1 (ft).
Facilities Dining room; Physical therapy room; Activities room; Laundry room; Barber/Beauty shop.
Activities Arts & crafts; Cards; Games; Reading groups; Prayer groups; Movies; Shopping trips; Dances/Social/Cultural gatherings.

Cedar Rapids

Americana Healthcare Center
1940 1st Ave NE, Cedar Rapids, IA 52402
(319) 364-5151
Admin Richard L Colby.
Licensure Skilled care; Intermediate care for mentally retarded; Residential care. *Beds* SNF 10; ICF/MR 12; Residential care 57. *Certified* Medicaid; Medicare.
Owner Proprietary corp (Manor Care Inc).

Hallmar, Mercy Medical Center
701 10th St SE, Cedar Rapids, IA 52403
(319) 398-6241, 398-6386
Admin A J Tinker.
Licensure Intermediate care; Respite care. *Beds* ICF 47; Respite care 15. *Private Pay Patients* 100%.
Owner Nonprofit organization/foundation.
Admissions Requirements Medical examination; Physician's request.
Staff RNs 2 (ft); LPNs 8 (ft); Nurses' aides 15 (ft); Recreational therapists 1 (ft); Activities coordinators 1 (pt); Secretaries 2 (ft).
Languages Czech, German.
Affiliation Roman Catholic.
Facilities Dining room; Physical therapy room; Activities room; Chapel; Crafts room; Laundry room; Barber/Beauty shop; Library.
Activities Arts & crafts; Cards; Games; Reading groups; Prayer groups; Movies; Shopping trips; Dances/Social/Cultural gatherings; Intergenerational programs; Pet therapy.

Heritage Acres
200 Clive Dr SW, Cedar Rapids, IA 52404
(319) 396-7171
Admin Cordell Poldberg. *Dir of Nursing* Connie Arens.
Licensure Intermediate care; Alzheimer's care. *Beds* ICF 201. *Certified* Medicaid.
Owner Nonprofit organization/foundation (Britwill Co).
Admissions Requirements Minimum age 16; Medical examination.
Staff RNs 6 (ft); LPNs 20 (ft), 2 (pt); Nurses' aides 58 (ft), 11 (pt); Physical therapists 2 (pt); Recreational therapists 1 (pt); Occupational therapists 1 (pt); Speech therapists 1 (pt); Activities coordinators 1 (ft); Dietitians 2 (ft); Ophthalmologists 1 (pt); Podiatrists 1 (pt); Audiologists 1 (pt).
Facilities Dining room; Physical therapy room; Activities room; Crafts room; Laundry room; Barber/Beauty shop.
Activities Arts & crafts; Cards; Games; Reading groups; Prayer groups; Movies; Shopping trips; Dances/Social/Cultural gatherings; Intergenerational programs; Pet therapy.

Living Center East
1220 5th Ave S, Cedar Rapids, IA 52403
(319) 366-8701

Licensure Intermediate care; Intermediate care for mentally retarded. *Beds* ICF 92; ICF/MR 26. *Certified* Medicaid.
Staff RNs 3 (ft); LPNs 3 (ft), 5 (pt); Nurses' aides 12 (ft), 30 (pt); Occupational therapists 1 (pt); Speech therapists 1 (pt); Activities coordinators 1 (ft); Dietitians 1 (pt).
Facilities Dining room; Physical therapy room; Activities room; Barber/Beauty shop.
Activities Arts & crafts; Cards; Games; Reading groups; Prayer groups; Movies; Shopping trips; Dances/Social/Cultural gatherings.

Living Center West
1040 4th Ave, Cedar Rapids, IA 52403
(319) 366-8714
Admin Jean Westerbeck.
Licensure Intermediate care. *Beds* ICF 120.

Meth-Wick Manor
1224 13th St NW, Cedar Rapids, IA 52405
(319) 365-9171
Medical Dir Jo A Gruenwald.
Licensure Intermediate care. *Beds* ICF 65. *Certified* Medicaid.
Admissions Requirements Minimum age 55; Medical examination.
Staff Physicians 1 (pt); RNs 1 (ft), 5 (pt); LPNs 6 (pt); Nurses' aides 16 (ft), 11 (pt); Physical therapists 1 (pt); Occupational therapists 1 (pt); Speech therapists 1 (pt); Activities coordinators 1 (ft); Dietitians 1 (ft); Podiatrists 1 (pt); Audiologists 1 (pt); Dentists 1 (pt).
Affiliation Methodist.
Facilities Dining room; Physical therapy room; Activities room; Chapel; Crafts room; Laundry room; Barber/Beauty shop; Library; Gift shop; Exercise room; Kitchen; Snack room; Patio; Garages; Numerous lounges.
Activities Arts & crafts; Games; Prayer groups; Movies; Shopping trips; Dances/Social/Cultural gatherings; Dining out; Exercise class; Weight control groups; Resident assemblies; Bake sales; Bazaars; Garage sales.

Northbrook Manor Care Center
6420 Council St NE, Cedar Rapids, IA 52402
(319) 393-1447
Admin Janice M Tague.
Licensure Intermediate care. *Beds* ICF 130. *Certified* Medicaid.

St Luke's Methodist Hospital
1026 A Ave NE, Cedar Rapids, IA 52402
(319) 369-7211
Admin Samuel T Wallace.
Licensure Skilled care. *Beds* SNF 28.
Affiliation Methodist.

Centerville

Centerville Care Center
1208 Cross St, Centerville, IA 52544
(515) 856-8651
Admin Mari R Wuekker.
Licensure Intermediate care. *Beds* ICF 69. *Certified* Medicaid.
Owner Proprietary corp (Mercy Health Initiatives).

Golden Age Care Center
1915 S 18th, Centerville, IA 52544
(515) 856-2757
Admin Todd B Hanson. *Dir of Nursing* Marilyn Vanderlinden RN.
Licensure Intermediate care. *Beds* ICF 128. *Private Pay Patients* 35%. *Certified* Medicaid.
Owner Proprietary corp (ABCM Corp).
Admissions Requirements Medical examination; Physician's request.
Staff RNs 2 (ft); LPNs 8 (ft), 2 (pt); Nurses' aides 45 (ft); Physical therapists 1 (pt); Activities coordinators 1 (ft), 1 (pt); Dietitians; Podiatrists 1 (pt); Audiologists 1 (pt).

Facilities Dining room; Activities room; Laundry room; Barber/Beauty shop.
Activities Arts & crafts; Cards; Games; Prayer groups; Movies; Dances/Social/Cultural gatherings; Events open to community.

St Joseph Mercy Hospital
RR 3, Centerville, IA 52544
(515) 437-4111
Admin William Assell.
Licensure Intermediate care. *Beds* ICF 6.

Chariton

Chariton Manor
N 7th St, Chariton, IA 50049
(515) 774-5921
Admin Stanley Vanderwoude.
Licensure Intermediate care. *Beds* ICF 130. *Certified* Medicaid.
Owner Proprietary corp (Mercy Health Initiatives).

Charles City

Burling House
910 1st Ave, Charles City, IA 50616
(515) 228-4182
Admin Barbara Roeder.
Licensure Intermediate care for mentally retarded. *Beds* ICF/MR 12.

Chautauqua Guest Home 1
120 Chautauqua Ave, Charles City, IA 50616
(515) 228-6512
Admin David F Ayers. *Dir of Nursing* Judy Kelly RN.
Licensure Intermediate care. *Beds* ICF 84. *Certified* Medicaid.
Owner Proprietary corp.
Admissions Requirements Minimum age 16; Medical examination; Physician's request.
Staff RNs 2 (ft); LPNs 2 (ft), 3 (pt); Nurses' aides 11 (ft), 20 (pt); Activities coordinators 1 (ft), 1 (pt).
Facilities Dining room; Activities room; Crafts room; Laundry room; Barber/Beauty shop; Library.
Activities Arts & crafts; Cards; Games; Reading groups; Prayer groups; Movies; Shopping trips; Dances/Social/Cultural gatherings.

Chautauqua Guest Home 2
602 11th St, Charles City, IA 50616
(515) 228-2353
Admin David F Ayers. *Dir of Nursing* Edward Kielsmeier RN. *Medical Dir* D L Trefz MD.
Licensure Skilled care. *Beds* SNF 75. *Certified* Medicaid; Medicare.
Owner Proprietary corp.
Admissions Requirements Minimum age 16; Medical examination.
Staff RNs 4 (ft), 1 (pt); LPNs 1 (ft), 1 (pt); Activities coordinators 1 (ft), 1 (pt).
Facilities Dining room; Physical therapy room; Activities room; Barber/Beauty shop.
Activities Arts & crafts; Cards; Games; Reading groups; Prayer groups; Movies; Shopping trips; Dances/Social/Cultural gatherings.

Chautauqua Guest Home 3
302 9th St, Charles City, IA 50616
(515) 228-5351
Admin Mary A Heeren.
Licensure Intermediate care. *Beds* ICF 74. *Certified* Medicaid.

Comprehensive Systems Inc
1700 Clark St, Charles City, IA 50616
(515) 228-6155
Admin Richard Turpin. *Dir of Nursing* Christine Gohr RN.
Licensure Intermediate care for mentally retarded; Foster care; RCF-MR. *Beds* ICF/MR 12; Foster care 86; RCF-MR 67. *Certified* Medicaid.

Owner Nonprofit organization/foundation.
Admissions Requirements Medical examination.
Staff RNs 2 (ft), 4 (pt); LPNs 4 (ft), 2 (pt); Recreational therapists 2 (ft); Dietitians 2 (ft); Direct care staff 100 (ft), 150 (pt).
Facilities Dining room; Physical therapy room; Activities room; Chapel; Crafts room; Laundry room.
Activities Arts & crafts; Cards; Games; Reading groups; Prayer groups; Movies; Shopping trips; Dances/Social/Cultural gatherings; Community activities; Special education in public school system; Vocational training; Sheltered workshop; Employment.

Salsbury Baptist Home
807 5th St, Charles City, IA 50616
(515) 228-1612
Admin Randall L Parks.
Licensure Intermediate care; Residential care; Alzheimer's care. *Beds* ICF 51; Residential care 39. *Certified* Medicaid.
Owner Nonprofit corp (American Baptist Homes).
Admissions Requirements Minimum age 55; Medical examination; Physician's request.
Staff RNs 2 (ft), 2 (pt); LPNs 2 (ft), 2 (pt); Nurses' aides 20 (ft), 15 (pt); Occupational therapists 1 (pt); Activities coordinators 1 (ft), 1 (pt); Dietitians 1 (pt); Podiatrists 1 (pt).
Affiliation Baptist.
Facilities Dining room; Physical therapy room; Activities room; Chapel; Crafts room; Laundry room; Barber/Beauty shop; Library.
Activities Arts & crafts; Cards; Games; Reading groups; Prayer groups; Movies; Shopping trips; Reading program for school children.

Cherokee

Cherokee Villa
1011 Roosevelt, Cherokee, IA 51012
(712) 225-5189
Admin Judith Streufert.
Licensure Intermediate care. *Beds* ICF 72. *Certified* Medicaid.
Owner Proprietary corp (Mercy Health Initiatives).
Admissions Requirements Medical examination; Physician's request.
Staff RNs 1 (ft); LPNs 1 (ft); Nurses' aides 1 (ft); Physical therapists 1 (pt); Occupational therapists 1 (pt); Speech therapists 1 (pt); Activities coordinators 1 (ft); Dietitians 1 (pt).
Facilities Dining room; Physical therapy room; Activities room; Chapel; Crafts room; Laundry room; Barber/Beauty shop.
Activities Arts & crafts; Cards; Games; Reading groups; Prayer groups; Movies; Shopping trips.

Countryside Estates
921 Riverview Dr, Cherokee, IA 51012
(712) 225-5724
Admin William R Livingston.
Medical Dir Karen Riedemann.
Licensure Intermediate care. *Beds* ICF 102. *Certified* Medicaid.
Owner Privately owned.
Admissions Requirements Minimum age 16; Medical examination.
Staff RNs 2 (ft), 1 (pt); LPNs 3 (ft), 2 (pt); Nurses' aides 25 (ft), 8 (pt); Physical therapists 1 (pt); Occupational therapists 1 (pt); Speech therapists 1 (pt); Activities coordinators 1 (ft); Dietitians 1 (pt); Ophthalmologists 1 (pt); Podiatrists 1 (pt).
Facilities Dining room; Physical therapy room; Activities room; Chapel; Crafts room; Laundry room; Barber/Beauty shop.

Activities Arts & crafts; Cards; Games;
Reading groups; Prayer groups; Movies;
Shopping trips; Dances/Social/Cultural
gatherings; Humanities class.

Hilltop Care Center
725 N 2nd, Cherokee, IA 51012
(712) 225-2561
Admin Marilyn M Peck. *Dir of Nursing*
Patricia Johansen RN BSN.
Licensure Intermediate care. *Beds* ICF 50.
Private Pay Patients 25%. *Certified*
Medicaid.
Owner Proprietary corp (ABCM Corp).
Admissions Requirements Minimum age 18;
Medical examination; Physician's request.
Staff RNs 2 (ft), 1 (pt); LPNs 2 (ft), 2 (pt);
Nurses' aides 14 (ft), 3 (pt); Physical
therapists; Activities coordinators; Dietitians.
Languages Sign.
Facilities Dining room; Activities room;
Laundry room.
Activities Arts & crafts; Cards; Games;
Reading groups; Prayer groups; Movies;
Shopping trips; Dances/Social/Cultural
gatherings; Intergenerational programs.

Clarence

Clarence Nursing Home
2nd & Smith, Clarence, IA 52216
(319) 452-3262
Admin Mavis Y Johnson. *Dir of Nursing*
Karla Ruther. *Medical Dir* George Utley
MD.
Licensure Intermediate care; Retirement. *Beds*
ICF 46. *Certified* Medicaid.
Owner Nonprofit corp.
Staff RNs 1 (ft), 1 (pt); LPNs 2 (pt); Nurses'
aides 12 (ft), 7 (pt); Physical therapists 1
(pt); Recreational therapists 1 (ft);
Occupational therapists 1 (pt); Activities
coordinators 1 (ft); Dietitians 1 (pt);
Podiatrists 1 (pt).
Facilities Dining room; Activities room;
Laundry room; Barber/Beauty shop; Library.
Activities Arts & crafts; Cards; Games;
Reading groups; Prayer groups; Movies;
Dances/Social/Cultural gatherings.

Clarinda

Bethesda Care Center
600 Manor Dr, Clarinda, IA 51632
(712) 542-5161
Admin Alan Cooper. *Dir of Nursing* Linda
Hutchinson RN. *Medical Dir* Dr James
Eaves.
Licensure Intermediate care. *Beds* ICF 117.
Private Pay Patients 40%. *Certified*
Medicaid.
Owner Proprietary corp (MTC West).
Staff Physicians; RNs; LPNs; Nurses' aides;
Physical therapists (consultant); Recreational
therapists; Occupational therapists; Speech
therapists; Activities coordinators; Dietitians
(consultant); Audiologists.

Goldenrod Manor Care Center
225 W La Perla, Clarinda, IA 51632
(712) 542-5621
Admin Marjorie Spry. *Dir of Nursing* Sharon
McCalla.
Licensure Intermediate care. *Beds* ICF 51.
Private Pay Patients 60%. *Certified*
Medicaid.
Owner Proprietary corp.
Admissions Requirements Medical
examination; Physician's request.
Facilities Dining room; Physical therapy
room; Activities room; Crafts room; Laundry
room; Barber/Beauty shop.
Activities Arts & crafts; Cards; Games;
Reading groups; Prayer groups; Movies;
Shopping trips; Dances/Social/Cultural
gatherings; Intergenerational programs; Pet
therapy.

Clarion

Clarion Care Center
110 13th Ave SW, Clarion, IA 50525
(515) 532-2893
Admin Cordell Poldberg.
Medical Dir Cindy Waage.
Licensure Intermediate care; Residential care;
Alzheimer's care. *Beds* ICF 89; Residential
care 3. *Certified* Medicaid.
Owner Proprietary corp (Quality Health Care
Specialists Inc).
Admissions Requirements Minimum age 16;
Physician's request.
Staff RNs 5 (ft); LPNs 4 (ft); Nurses' aides 25
(ft), 9 (pt); Physical therapists 1 (pt); Reality
therapists 1 (pt); Recreational therapists 1
(pt); Occupational therapists 1 (pt); Speech
therapists 1 (pt); Activities coordinators 1
(ft), 1 (pt); Dietitians 1 (pt);
Ophthalmologists 1 (pt); Podiatrists 1 (pt);
Dentists 1 (pt).
Facilities Dining room; Physical therapy
room; Activities room; Crafts room; Laundry
room; Barber/Beauty shop; Library.
Activities Arts & crafts; Cards; Games;
Reading groups; Prayer groups; Movies;
Shopping trips; Dances/Social/Cultural
gatherings.

Clarksville

Community Nursing Home
115 N Hilton, Clarksville, IA 50619
(319) 278-4900
Admin Janice I Cook. *Dir of Nursing* Diane
Gohr RN. *Medical Dir* Dr Michael Berstler.
Licensure Intermediate care; Retirement;
Residential care. *Beds* ICF 53; Retirement
apts 28; Residential care 13. *Private Pay
Patients* 53%. *Certified* Medicaid.
Owner Proprietary corp.
Admissions Requirements Minimum age 16;
Medical examination; Physician's request.
Staff Physicians 9 (pt); RNs 1 (ft); LPNs 2
(ft), 3 (pt); Nurses' aides 10 (ft), 15 (pt);
Physical therapists 1 (pt); Speech therapists
1 (pt); Activities coordinators 1 (ft), 1 (pt);
Dietitians 1 (pt); Podiatrists 1 (pt); Social
workers 1 (pt).
Facilities Dining room; Physical therapy
room; Activities room; Crafts room; Laundry
room; Barber/Beauty shop; Library cart.
Activities Arts & crafts; Cards; Games;
Reading groups; Prayer groups; Movies;
Shopping trips; Dances/Social/Cultural
gatherings; Intergenerational programs; Pet
therapy; Grief class.

Clear Lake

Oakwood Care Center
400 Hwy 18 W, Clear Lake, IA 50428
(515) 357-5244
Admin William C Platts.
Licensure Intermediate care. *Beds* ICF 90.
Certified Medicaid.
Owner Proprietary corp (ABCM Corp).

Clearfield

Clearview Home
Box 174, Clearfield, IA 50840
(515) 336-2333
Admin Gary J Routh.
Medical Dir Vicky Leonard.
Licensure Intermediate care; Alzheimer's care.
Beds ICF 36. *Certified* Medicaid.
Owner Privately owned.
Staff Physicians; RNs; LPNs; Nurses' aides;
Physical therapists; Occupational therapists;
Speech therapists; Activities coordinators;
Dietitians; Pharmacist.
Facilities Dining room; Physical therapy
room; Activities room; Chapel; Laundry
room; Barber/Beauty shop.

Activities Arts & crafts; Cards; Games;
Reading groups; Prayer groups; Movies;
Shopping trips; Dances/Social/Cultural
gatherings.

Clinton

Alverno Health Care Facility
849 13th Ave N, Clinton, IA 52732
(319) 242-1521
Admin Sr Ruth Cox. *Dir of Nursing* Pauline
Kaufman RN.
Licensure Intermediate care; Alzheimer's care.
Beds ICF 136. *Certified* Medicaid.
Owner Nonprofit corp.
Admissions Requirements Minimum age 60.
Staff RNs 7 (ft), 4 (pt); LPNs 6 (ft), 5 (pt);
Nurses' aides 45 (ft), 12 (pt); Activities
coordinators 1 (ft), 3 (pt); Dietitians 1 (pt).
Affiliation Roman Catholic.
Facilities Dining room; Physical therapy
room; Activities room; Chapel; Crafts room;
Laundry room; Barber/Beauty shop; Library;
Alzheimer's cafe.
Activities Arts & crafts; Cards; Games;
Reading groups; Prayer groups; Movies;
Shopping trips; Dances/Social/Cultural
gatherings; Intergenerational programs; Pet
therapy; SDAT support group.

Clinton Retirement Village
2604 N 4th St, Clinton, IA 52732
(319) 243-6600
Admin Diane Sarich.
Medical Dir Diana Van Wychen.
Licensure Intermediate care. *Beds* ICF 150.
Certified Medicaid.
Owner Proprietary corp (Hillhaven Corp).
Admissions Requirements Medical
examination; Physician's request.
Staff Physicians; RNs 1 (ft), 2 (pt); LPNs 5
(ft), 3 (pt); Nurses' aides 19 (ft), 16 (pt);
Activities coordinators 1 (ft).
Facilities Dining room; Physical therapy
room; Activities room; Chapel; Crafts room;
Laundry room; Barber/Beauty shop.
Activities Cards; Games; Reading groups;
Prayer groups; Movies; Dances/Social/
Cultural gatherings.

Jane Lamb Health Center
638 S Bluff Blvd, Clinton, IA 52732
Admin Mark D Richardson.
Licensure Skilled care; Intermediate care. *Beds*
SNF 18; ICF 64. *Certified* Medicaid.
Owner Nonprofit corp.
Admissions Requirements Medical
examination; Physician's request.
Staff RNs 3 (ft), 4 (pt); LPNs 1 (ft), 3 (pt);
Nurses' aides 9 (ft), 16 (pt); Physical
therapists 3 (pt); Occupational therapists 1
(pt); Speech therapists 1 (pt); Activities
coordinators 1 (ft); Dietitians 1 (ft);
Audiologists 1 (pt).
Facilities Dining room; Activities room;
Crafts room; Laundry room; Barber/Beauty
shop.
Activities Arts & crafts; Cards; Games;
Reading groups; Prayer groups; Movies;
Shopping trips; Dances/Social/Cultural
gatherings.

St Joseph Mercy Hospital
1410 N 4th St, Clinton, IA 52732
(319) 243-5900
Admin Ronald R Reed.
Licensure Skilled care. *Beds* SNF 15.

Wyndcrest Nursing Home
600 14th Ave N, Clinton, IA 52732
(319) 243-3200
Admin Thomas J Carpe.
Licensure Intermediate care. *Beds* ICF 95.
Certified Medicaid.

Columbus Junction

Colonial Manor—Columbus Junction
814 Springer, Columbus Junction, IA 52838
(319) 728-2276
Admin Karen Schroeder.
Medical Dir Betty Hamilton.
Licensure Intermediate care. *Beds* ICF 60.
Certified Medicaid.
Owner Proprietary corp (Mercy Health
Initiatives).
Admissions Requirements Medical
examination; Physician's request.
Staff Physicians 2 (pt); RNs 6 (ft); LPNs 3
(ft); Nurses' aides 10 (ft), 15 (pt); Physical
therapists 1 (pt); Speech therapists 1 (pt);
Activities coordinators 1 (ft); Dietitians 1
(ft).
Facilities Dining room; Physical therapy
room; Activities room; Chapel; Crafts room;
Laundry room; Barber/Beauty shop; Library.
Activities Arts & crafts; Cards; Games;
Reading groups; Prayer groups; Movies;
Shopping trips; Dances/Social/Cultural
gatherings.

Conrad

Oakview Home
RR 1 Box 66A, Conrad, IA 50621
(515) 366-2212
Admin Bonnie Switzer.
Licensure Intermediate care; Residential care.
Beds ICF 38; Residential care 8. *Certified*
Medicaid.

Coon Rapids

Thomas Rest Haven
217 Main St, Coon Rapids, IA 50058
(712) 684-2253
Admin George D Bentley.
Licensure Intermediate care. *Beds* ICF 62.

Coralville

Lantern Park Care Center
915 N 20th Ave, Coralville, IA 52241
(319) 351-8440
Admin Robert L Solinger.
Licensure Intermediate care. *Beds* ICF 100.
Certified Medicaid.
Owner Proprietary corp (Mercy Health
Initiatives).

Corning

Colonial Manor
Northgate Dr, Corning, IA 50841
(515) 322-4061
Admin Terry Cooper. *Dir of Nursing* Norma
Camden RN.
Licensure Intermediate care. *Beds* ICF 64.
Certified Medicaid.
Owner Proprietary corp (Mercy Health
Initiatives).
Admissions Requirements Medical
examination; Physician's request.
Staff RNs 1 (ft), 1 (pt); LPNs 4 (ft); Nurses'
aides 20 (ft), 2 (pt); Activities coordinators 1
(ft); Dietitians 1 (pt).
Facilities Dining room; Physical therapy
room; Activities room; Chapel; Barber/
Beauty shop; Family room.
Activities Arts & crafts; Cards; Games;
Reading groups; Prayer groups; Movies;
Dances/Social/Cultural gatherings.

Correctionville

Colonial Manor of Correctionville
1116 E Hwy 20, Correctionville, IA 51106
(712) 372-4466
Admin Marsha Sedlecek.
Medical Dir Nancy Jacobs.

Licensure Intermediate care. *Beds* ICF 65.
Certified Medicaid.
Owner Proprietary corp (Mercy Health
Initiatives).
Admissions Requirements Medical
examination; Physician's request.
Staff RNs; LPNs; Nurses' aides; Activities
coordinators; Dietitians; Social workers.
Facilities Dining room; Chapel; Laundry
room; Barber/Beauty shop.
Activities Arts & crafts; Cards; Games;
Reading groups; Prayer groups; Movies;
Shopping trips; Dances/Social/Cultural
gatherings; Individualized for each patient.

Corydon

Corydon Care Center
745 E South St, Corydon, IA 50060
(515) 872-1590
Admin Connie E Morris. *Dir of Nursing* Quita
Bethards. *Medical Dir* Dr Keith Garber.
Licensure Intermediate care. *Beds* ICF 79.
Private Pay Patients 40%. *Certified*
Medicaid.
Owner Nonprofit corp (Mercy Health
Initiatives).
Admissions Requirements Medical
examination.
Staff RNs 1 (ft), 2 (pt); LPNs 5 (ft), 2 (pt);
Nurses' aides 13 (ft), 12 (pt); Physical
therapists 1 (pt); Recreational therapists 1
(pt); Occupational therapists 1 (pt); Speech
therapists 1 (pt); Activities coordinators 1
(ft), 1 (pt); Dietitians 1 (pt); Podiatrists 1
(pt); Audiologists 1 (pt).
Facilities Dining room; Activities room;
Chapel; Crafts room; Laundry room; Barber/
Beauty shop; Library.
Activities Arts & crafts; Cards; Games;
Reading groups; Prayer groups; Movies;
Shopping trips; Dances/Social/Cultural
gatherings; Intergenerational programs; Pet
therapy.

Council Bluffs

Bethany Lutheran Home
7 Elliott St, Council Bluffs, IA 51503
(712) 328-9500
Admin M Sue Mortensen. *Dir of Nursing* Joan
Burten RN.
Licensure Intermediate care; Alzheimer's care.
Beds ICF 121. *Certified* Medicaid.
Owner Nonprofit corp.
Admissions Requirements Medical
examination.
Staff RNs 5 (ft), 5 (pt); LPNs 5 (ft), 4 (pt);
Nurses' aides 28 (ft), 22 (pt); Physical
therapists 1 (ft), 1 (pt); Recreational
therapists 1 (ft); Occupational therapists 1
(pt); Speech therapists 1 (pt); Activities
coordinators 1 (ft), 1 (pt); Dietitians 1 (pt);
Ophthalmologists 1 (pt); Podiatrists 1 (pt).
Affiliation Lutheran.
Facilities Dining room; Physical therapy
room; Activities room; Chapel; Laundry
room; Barber/Beauty shop.
Activities Arts & crafts; Cards; Games;
Reading groups; Prayer groups; Movies;
Shopping trips; Dances/Social/Cultural
gatherings.

Council Bluffs Care Center
2452 N Broadway, Council Bluffs, IA 51503
(712) 323-7135; 323-7161 FAX
Admin Diane M Sarich. *Dir of Nursing* Carol
Richards. *Medical Dir* Dr Marsh.
Licensure Intermediate care. *Beds* ICF 150.
Private Pay Patients 13%. *Certified*
Medicaid.
Owner Proprietary corp (Magellan
Investments).
Admissions Requirements Medical
examination; Physician's request.

Staff RNs 3 (ft), 2 (pt); LPNs 8 (ft), 2 (pt);
Nurses' aides 51 (ft), 3 (pt); Recreational
therapists 1 (ft); Activities coordinators 1
(ft); Dietitians 1 (ft).
Facilities Dining room; Physical therapy
room; Activities room; Barber/Beauty shop.
Activities Arts & crafts; Cards; Games;
Reading groups; Prayer groups; Movies;
Shopping trips; Dances/Social/Cultural
gatherings.

Jennie Edmundson Memorial Hospital
933 E Pierce, Council Bluffs, IA 51503
(712) 328-6000
Admin Edward R Lynn.
Licensure Skilled care. *Beds* SNF 25.

Indian Hills Nursing Center
1600 McPherson, Council Bluffs, IA 51501
(712) 322-9285
Admin Lawrence R Cotton.
Licensure Intermediate care. *Beds* ICF 166.
Certified Medicaid.

Mercy Hospital
800 Mercy Dr, Council Bluffs, IA 51502
(712) 328-5500
Admin Mervin M Riepe.
Licensure Skilled care. *Beds* SNF 18.

Cresco

Cresco Care Center
RR 2, Vernon Rd, Cresco, IA 52136
(319) 547-3580
Admin Dale Weaver.
Licensure Intermediate care. *Beds* ICF 73.
Certified Medicaid.

Evans Memorial Home
1010 N Elm, Cresco, IA 52136
(319) 547-2364
Admin Jerome Erdahl. *Dir of Nursing*
Marlene Ferrie.
Licensure Intermediate care; Retirement. *Beds*
ICF 65; Retirement 7. *Private Pay Patients*
60%. *Certified* Medicaid.
Owner Nonprofit corp.
Admissions Requirements Medical
examination; Physician's request.
Staff RNs 1 (ft), 4 (pt); LPNs 4 (pt); Nurses'
aides 5 (ft), 24 (pt); Physical therapists 1
(pt); Recreational therapists 1 (pt);
Occupational therapists 1 (pt); Speech
therapists 1 (pt); Activities coordinators 1
(ft), 1 (pt); Dietitians 1 (pt); Podiatrists 1
(pt).
Facilities Dining room; Physical therapy
room; Activities room; Chapel; Crafts room;
Laundry room; Barber/Beauty shop.
Activities Arts & crafts; Cards; Games;
Reading groups; Prayer groups; Movies;
Shopping trips; Dances/Social/Cultural
gatherings; Pet therapy.

Creston

Care Center of Iowa Inc
1000 E Howard, Creston, IA 50801
(515) 782-5012
Admin Stanley Boyle.
Licensure Intermediate care. *Beds* ICF 71.
Certified Medicaid.
Admissions Requirements Medical
examination; Physician's request.
Staff RNs 2 (ft); LPNs 4 (ft); Nurses' aides 24
(ft); Occupational therapists 1 (pt); Activities
coordinators 1 (ft); Dietitians 1 (pt);
Audiologists 1 (pt).
Facilities Dining room; Activities room;
Chapel; Crafts room; Laundry room.
Activities Arts & crafts; Cards; Games;
Reading groups; Prayer groups; Movies;
Shopping trips.

Creston Manor
1001 Cottonwood, Creston, IA 50801
(515) 782-8511

Admin William Robinson.
Licensure Intermediate care. *Beds* ICF 74.
  Certified Medicaid.
Owner Proprietary corp (Beverly Enterprises).

Dallas Center

Spurgeon Manor
PO Box 500, Dallas Center, IA 50063
(515) 992-3735
Admin Floyd J Haldeman.
Licensure Intermediate care; Residential care.
  Beds ICF 17; Residential care 30. *Certified*
  Medicaid.

Danville

Danville Care Center
Birch & Seymour, Danville, IA 52623
(319) 392-4259
Admin Michael W Hocking.
Licensure Intermediate care. *Beds* ICF 40.
  Certified Medicaid.

Davenport

Americana Healthcare Center
815 E Locust, Davenport, IA 52803
(319) 324-3276, 324-8844 FAX
Admin June L Price. *Dir of Nursing* Marion
  Tritz. *Medical Dir* Dr Dean Bunting.
Licensure Skilled care; Intermediate care. *Beds*
  Swing beds SNF/ICF 110. *Certified*
  Medicaid; Medicare.
Owner Proprietary corp (Manor Care Inc).
Admissions Requirements Medical
  examination; Physician's request.
Staff Physicians 1 (pt); RNs 5 (ft), 3 (pt);
  LPNs 6 (ft), 2 (pt); Nurses' aides 30 (ft), 7
  (pt); Physical therapists 3 (pt); Occupational
  therapists 1 (pt); Speech therapists 1 (pt);
  Activities coordinators 1 (ft), 2 (pt);
  Dietitians (contracted).
Facilities Dining room; Physical therapy
  room; Activities room; Crafts room; Laundry
  room; Barber/Beauty shop; Library.
Activities Arts & crafts; Cards; Games;
  Reading groups; Prayer groups; Movies;
  Shopping trips; Dances/Social/Cultural
  gatherings; Intergenerational programs; Pet
  therapy.

Davenport Good Samaritan Center
700 Waverly Rd, Davenport, IA 52804
(319) 324-1651, 324-7418 FAX
Admin Todd L Jacobsen. *Dir of Nursing*
  Paula Clarke RN. *Medical Dir* Monte L
  Skaufle MD.
Licensure Intermediate care; Alzheimer's care.
  Beds ICF 211. *Certified* Medicaid.
Owner Nonprofit corp (Evangelical Lutheran/
  Good Samaritan Society).
Admissions Requirements Minimum age 16;
  Medical examination.
Staff RNs; LPNs; Nurses' aides; Physical
  therapists; Activities coordinators; Dietitians.
Facilities Dining room; Physical therapy
  room; Activities room; Chapel; Laundry
  room; Barber/Beauty shop.
Activities Arts & crafts; Cards; Games; Prayer
  groups; Movies; Shopping trips; Dances/
  Social/Cultural gatherings; Intergenerational
  programs; Pet therapy.

Davenport Lutheran Home
1130 W 53rd St, Davenport, IA 52806
(319) 391-5342
Admin Fern Werning. *Dir of Nursing* Connie
  Noel.
Licensure Intermediate care; Alzheimer's care.
  Beds ICF 98; Alzheimer's unit 26. *Private
  Pay Patients* 15%. *Certified* Medicaid.
Owner Nonprofit organization/foundation
  (Lutheran Home for the Aged Association).
Admissions Requirements Minimum age 65.

Staff Physicians 1 (pt); RNs 3 (ft), 1 (pt);
  LPNs 10 (ft), 3 (pt); Nurses' aides 32 (ft), 6
  (pt); Physical therapists; Activities
  coordinators 2 (ft), 1 (pt); Dietitians 1 (pt).
Affiliation Lutheran.
Facilities Dining room; Physical therapy
  room; Activities room; Chapel; Crafts room;
  Laundry room; Barber/Beauty shop.
Activities Arts & crafts; Cards; Games;
  Reading groups; Prayer groups; Movies;
  Dances/Social/Cultural gatherings.

Fejervary Health Care Center
800 E Rusholme, Davenport, IA 52803
(319) 322-1668
Admin Lawrence Campana.
Licensure Intermediate care. *Beds* ICF 118.
  Certified Medicaid.

HDC Residential Center
6430 Linwood Ct, Davenport, IA 52806
Admin Karen Steen.
Licensure Intermediate care for mentally
  retarded. *Beds* ICF/MR 54.

Kahl Home for the Aged & Infirm
1101 W 9th St, Davenport, IA 52804
(319) 324-1621
Admin Sr M T Kathleen Dominick. *Dir of
  Nursing* Sr Michael Joseph RN. *Medical Dir*
  John Collins MD.
Licensure Skilled care; Intermediate care;
  Alzheimer's care. *Beds* SNF 40; ICF 101.
  Private Pay Patients 74%. *Certified*
  Medicaid; Medicare.
Owner Nonprofit corp (Carmelite Sisters).
Admissions Requirements Minimum age 64;
  Medical examination.
Staff RNs 4 (ft), 1 (pt); LPNs 13 (ft), 1 (pt);
  Nurses' aides 56 (ft), 3 (pt); Activities
  coordinators 2 (ft); Dietitians 1 (ft);
  Chaplains 1 (pt).
Affiliation Roman Catholic.
Facilities Dining room; Physical therapy
  room; Activities room; Chapel; Crafts room;
  Laundry room; Barber/Beauty shop; Library.
Activities Arts & crafts; Cards; Games; Prayer
  groups; Movies; Shopping trips; Dances/
  Social/Cultural gatherings; Pet therapy.

Meadow Lawn Nursing Center
4656 W Kimberly Rd, Davenport, IA 52806-
7111
(319) 391-5150, 391-5151
Admin Cathie Flanagan. *Dir of Nursing*
  Wanda Petersen.
Licensure Intermediate care. *Beds* ICF 65.
  Private Pay Patients 12%. *Certified*
  Medicaid.
Owner Proprietary corp.
Staff RNs 2 (ft); LPNs 3 (ft); Nurses' aides 18
  (ft), 4 (pt); Physical therapists (consultant);
  Activities coordinators 1 (ft); Dietitians
  (consultant).

Oak Terrace Care Center
PO Box 2309, Davenport, IA 52803-2309
(319) 323-8021
Admin Marcus L Jarrett.
Licensure Intermediate care. *Beds* ICF 49.
  Certified Medicaid.

Ridgecrest Retirement Village
4130 Northwest Blvd, Davenport, IA 52806
(319) 391-3430
Admin Dr Paul R Ausherman, Exec Dir; Sam
  E Johnson.
Medical Dir Beverly McLean.
Licensure Skilled care; Intermediate care;
  Residential care. *Beds* SNF 14; ICF 105;
  Residential care 18. *Certified* Medicaid;
  Medicare.
Owner Nonprofit corp.
Admissions Requirements Physician's request.
Staff RNs 6 (ft), 4 (pt); LPNs 11 (ft), 6 (pt);
  Nurses' aides 58 (ft), 16 (pt); Physical
  therapists 1 (pt); Occupational therapists 1

(pt); Speech therapists 1 (pt); Activities
  coordinators 2 (ft), 1 (pt); Dietitians 1 (pt);
  Ophthalmologists 1 (pt).
Facilities Dining room; Physical therapy
  room; Activities room; Chapel; Crafts room;
  Barber/Beauty shop.
Activities Arts & crafts; Cards; Games;
  Reading groups; Prayer groups; Movies;
  Shopping trips; Dances/Social/Cultural
  gatherings.

Royal Neighbor Home
4760 Rockingham Rd, Davenport, IA 52802
(319) 322-3591
Admin Evelyn Pealstrom.
Licensure Intermediate care; Residential care.
  Beds ICF 14; Residential care 54.

St Luke Hospital
1227 E Rusholme, Davenport, IA 52803
(319) 326-6512
Admin James R Stuhler.
Licensure Skilled care. *Beds* SNF 18.

Dayton

Grandview Care Center
508 2nd St NE, Dayton, IA 50530
(515) 547-2288
Admin Kristi Ott. *Dir of Nursing* Kristi Ott.
  Medical Dir Dr E DeHaan.
Licensure Intermediate care. *Beds* ICF 50.
  Certified Medicaid.
Owner Proprietary corp (Waverly Group).
Admissions Requirements Physician's request.
Staff RNs 2 (ft); LPNs 2 (ft); Nurses' aides 15
  (ft), 10 (pt); Physical therapists 1 (pt);
  Recreational therapists 1 (pt); Speech
  therapists 1 (pt); Activities coordinators 1
  (ft); Dietitians 1 (pt); Podiatrists 1 (pt);
  Dentists 1 (pt).
Facilities Dining room; Physical therapy
  room; Activities room; Crafts room; Laundry
  room; Barber/Beauty shop.
Activities Arts & crafts; Cards; Games;
  Reading groups; Prayer groups; Movies;
  Shopping trips; Dances/Social/Cultural
  gatherings.

Decorah

M A Barthell Order of Eastern Star Home
911 Ridgewood Dr, Decorah, IA 52101
(319) 382-8787
Admin Gary Gavle.
Medical Dir Sharon Kidd.
Licensure Intermediate care. *Beds* ICF 46.
Admissions Requirements Physician's request.
Staff RNs 2 (ft), 1 (pt); LPNs 5 (pt); Nurses'
  aides 6 (ft), 10 (pt); Activities coordinators 1
  (ft), 1 (pt); Dietitians 1 (pt).
Affiliation Order of Eastern Star.
Facilities Dining room; Physical therapy
  room; Activities room; Chapel; Crafts room;
  Laundry room; Barber/Beauty shop; Library.
Activities Arts & crafts; Cards; Games;
  Reading groups; Prayer groups; Movies;
  Shopping trips; Dances/Social/Cultural
  gatherings.

Aase Haugen Homes Inc
PO Box 510, 4 Ohio St, Decorah, IA 52101
(319) 382-3603
Admin Steve E Moss. *Dir of Nursing* Janeen
  Iverson.
Licensure Intermediate care; Residential care.
  Beds ICF 146; Residential care 13. *Private
  Pay Patients* 50%. *Certified* Medicaid.
Owner Nonprofit organization/foundation.
Admissions Requirements Medical
  examination; Physician's request.
Staff Physicians 9 (pt); RNs 6 (ft), 3 (pt);
  LPNs 4 (ft), 3 (pt); Nurses' aides 42 (ft), 28
  (pt); Physical therapists 1 (pt); Recreational
  therapists 3 (ft); Speech therapists 1 (pt);
  Activities coordinators 1 (ft); Dietitians 1
  (pt); Podiatrists 1 (pt).

Affiliation Lutheran.
Facilities Dining room; Physical therapy room; Activities room; Chapel; Crafts room; Barber/Beauty shop.
Activities Arts & crafts; Cards; Games; Reading groups; Prayer groups; Movies; Shopping trips; Dances/Social/Cultural gatherings; Intergenerational programs; Pet therapy.

Oneota Riverview Care Facility
Rte 6 Box 19, Decorah, IA 52101
(319) 382-9691
Admin Marlys E Cook. *Dir of Nursing* Shirley Szabo RN. *Medical Dir* Kevin Locke MD.
Licensure Intermediate care; Residential care; Community living. *Beds* ICF 36; Residential care 55; Community living 8. *Private Pay Patients* 5%. *Certified* Medicaid; Medicare.
Owner Nonprofit organization/foundation.
Admissions Requirements Minimum age 18; Medical examination; Physician's request.
Staff Physicians; RNs; LPNs; Nurses' aides; Physical therapists; Occupational therapists; Speech therapists; Activities coordinators; Dietitians; Ophthalmologists; Podiatrists; Audiologists; Educators.
Languages German, Norwegian.
Facilities Dining room; Activities room; Chapel; Crafts room; Laundry room; Barber/Beauty shop; Library; Rehabilitation room.
Activities Arts & crafts; Cards; Games; Reading groups; Prayer groups; Movies; Shopping trips; Dances/Social/Cultural gatherings; Intergenerational programs; Pet therapy.

Denison

Denison Care Center
RR 1, Box 188, Ridge Rd, Denison, IA 51442
(712) 263-5611
Admin Helen L Andersen. *Dir of Nursing* Pamela Walker RN.
Licensure Intermediate care; Alzheimer's care. *Beds* ICF 50. *Private Pay Patients* 50%. *Certified* Medicaid.
Owner Proprietary corp (Waverly Group).
Admissions Requirements Medical examination; Physician's request.
Staff RNs; LPNs; Nurses' aides; Physical therapists; Speech therapists (contracted); Activities coordinators; Dietitians (contracted); Ophthalmologists (contracted); Podiatrists (contracted); Audiologists (contracted).
Facilities Dining room; Physical therapy room; Activities room; Laundry room; Barber/Beauty shop.
Activities Arts & crafts; Cards; Games; Reading groups; Movies; Shopping trips; Intergenerational programs.

Eventide Lutheran Home
114 S 20th St, Denison, IA 51442
(712) 263-3114
Admin Arvin G Schmidt. *Dir of Nursing* Beth Neumann RN. *Medical Dir* Donald Soll MD.
Licensure Intermediate care; Residential care; Alzheimer's care. *Beds* ICF 71; Residential care 69. *Private Pay Patients* 60%. *Certified* Medicaid.
Owner Nonprofit organization/foundation.
Admissions Requirements Minimum age 62.
Staff RNs 6 (ft); LPNs 12 (ft); Nurses' aides 36 (ft), 10 (pt); Physical therapists 1 (pt); Recreational therapists 1 (ft); Occupational therapists 1 (pt); Speech therapists 1 (pt); Activities coordinators 2 (ft); Dietitians 1 (pt).
Languages German.
Affiliation Lutheran.
Facilities Dining room; Physical therapy room; Activities room; Chapel; Crafts room; Barber/Beauty shop.

Activities Arts & crafts; Cards; Games; Reading groups; Prayer groups; Movies; Shopping trips; Dances/Social/Cultural gatherings; Intergenerational programs; Pet therapy.

Denver

Denver Sunset Home
PO Box 383, 235 N Mill, Denver, IA 50622
(319) 984-5372
Admin Denise R Willig. *Dir of Nursing* Pat Bergeron. *Medical Dir* Dr K Megivern.
Licensure Intermediate care. *Beds* ICF 41. *Private Pay Patients* 66%. *Certified* Medicaid; Medicare.
Owner Nonprofit corp.
Admissions Requirements Medical examination; Physician's certification.
Staff RNs 1 (ft), 1 (pt); LPNs 3 (ft), 2 (pt); Nurses' aides 8 (ft), 8 (pt); Activities coordinators 1 (ft).
Facilities Dining room; Physical therapy room; Activities room; Laundry room; Barber/Beauty shop.
Activities Arts & crafts; Cards; Games; Reading groups; Prayer groups; Movies; Dances/Social/Cultural gatherings.

Des Moines

Bethphage No 1
4220 E Douglas, Des Moines, IA 50317
(515) 262-7799
Admin Ann Sexton.
Licensure Intermediate care for mentally retarded. *Beds* ICF/MR 8.

Bethphage No 2
4216 Easton Blvd, Des Moines, IA 50317
(515) 263-0453
Admin Ann Sexton.
Licensure Intermediate care for mentally retarded. *Beds* ICF/MR 8.

Bethphage No 3
3114 E 42nd St, Des Moines, IA 50317
(515) 263-8959
Admin Ann Sexton.
Licensure Intermediate care for mentally retarded. *Beds* ICF/MR 8.

Calvin Manor
4210 Hickman Rd, Des Moines, IA 50310
(515) 277-6141
Admin Richard J Shaffer.
Licensure Intermediate care. *Beds* ICF 59. *Certified* Medicaid.

Celebrity Care Center
721 16th St, Des Moines, IA 50314
(515) 244-8131
Admin Harold J Lynch.
Licensure Intermediate care; Residential care. *Beds* ICF 50; ICF Residential care 8. *Certified* Medicaid.
Owner Proprietary corp.
Facilities Dining room; Activities room; Crafts room; Laundry room; Barber/Beauty shop.
Activities Arts & crafts; Cards; Games; Reading groups; Prayer groups; Movies; Shopping trips; Dances/Social/Cultural gatherings.

Commonwealth Care Center
5608 SW 9th St, Des Moines, IA 50315
(515) 285-3070
Admin George Cristofis.
Licensure Intermediate care. *Beds* ICF 99. *Certified* Medicaid.

Community Living
1200 Williams St, Des Moines, IA 50317
(515) 265-5315
Admin Virginia Bradish.
Licensure Intermediate care for mentally retarded. *Beds* ICF/MR 8.

Community Living—Alpha
3333 E University, Des Moines, IA 50317
(515) 263-9109
Admin Virginia Bradish.
Licensure Intermediate care for mentally retarded. *Beds* ICF/MR 8.

Community Living—Beta
3337 E University, Des Moines, IA 50317
(515) 263-9109
Admin Virginia Bradish.
Licensure Intermediate care for mentally retarded. *Beds* ICF/MR 8.

Craigmont Care Center
2348 E 9th St, Des Moines, IA 50316
(515) 262-9303
Admin Kathy Holdsworth.
Licensure Intermediate care. *Beds* ICF 93. *Certified* Medicaid.

Crystal Manor Care Center
2501 24th St, Des Moines, IA 50310
(515) 279-1138
Admin Sandy Brand.
Licensure Intermediate care. *Beds* ICF 80. *Certified* Medicaid.

Des Moines General Hospital Skilled Nursing Facility
603 E 12th, Des Moines, IA 50307
(515) 263-4171
Admin Roy W Wright. *Dir of Nursing* Marilyn Rhodes. *Medical Dir* Michael Tobin DO.
Licensure Skilled care. *Beds* SNF 15. *Certified* Medicaid; Medicare.
Owner Nonprofit organization/foundation.
Admissions Requirements Medical examination; Physician's request.
Facilities Dining room; Physical therapy room; Activities room; Chapel.
Activities Arts & crafts; Games; Movies.

Heather Manor
600 E 5th St, Des Moines, IA 50316
(515) 243-6195
Admin Dean Schager. *Dir of Nursing* Lauretta Anderson.
Licensure Intermediate care. *Beds* ICF 44.
Owner Nonprofit corp (Life Care Services Corp).
Admissions Requirements Minimum age 62; Medical examination; Physician's request.
Staff Physicians 1 (pt); RNs 1 (ft), 3 (pt); LPNs 1 (ft), 4 (pt); Nurses' aides 6 (ft), 8 (pt); Physical therapists 1 (pt); Occupational therapists 1 (pt); Speech therapists 1 (pt); Activities coordinators 1 (pt); Dietitians 1 (pt); Podiatrists 1 (pt); Dentists 1 (pt).
Facilities Dining room; Activities room; Chapel; Crafts room; Laundry room; Barber/Beauty shop; Library.
Activities Arts & crafts; Cards; Games; Reading groups; Prayer groups; Movies; Shopping trips; Dances/Social/Cultural gatherings.

Hillside Convalescent Center
233 University Ave, Des Moines, IA 50314
(515) 284-1280
Admin Donna Lane. *Dir of Nursing* Cathy Thayer. *Medical Dir* Roy W Overton MD.
Licensure Skilled care; Intermediate care. *Beds* SNF 54; ICF 108. *Private Pay Patients* 30%. *Certified* Medicaid; Medicare.
Owner Privately owned (HEA of Iowa).
Admissions Requirements Medical examination; Physician's request.
Staff Physicians; RNs; LPNs; Nurses' aides; Physical therapists (contracted); Occupational therapists (contracted); Speech therapists (contracted); Activities coordinators; Dietitians (contracted); Ophthalmologists (contracted); Podiatrists (contracted); Audiologists (contracted).
Facilities Dining room; Physical therapy room; Activities room; Crafts room; Laundry room; Barber/Beauty shop.

Activities Arts & crafts; Cards; Games; Reading groups; Prayer groups; Movies; Shopping trips; Dances/Social/Cultural gatherings.

Iowa Jewish Senior Life Center
900 Polk Blvd, Des Moines, IA 50312
(515) 255-5433
Admin Michael D Kelner.
Medical Dir Stanton Danielson MD.
Licensure Skilled care; Intermediate care; Residential care. *Beds* SNF 15; ICF 35; Residential care 15. *Certified* Medicaid; Medicare.
Admissions Requirements Minimum age 18; Medical examination.
Staff Physicians 2 (pt); RNs 2 (ft), 8 (pt); LPNs 3 (ft), 1 (pt); Nurses' aides 12 (ft), 15 (pt); Physical therapists 1 (pt); Recreational therapists 1 (ft); Occupational therapists 1 (pt); Speech therapists 1 (pt); Activities coordinators 1 (ft); Dietitians 1 (ft), 1 (pt); Podiatrists 2 (pt).
Affiliation Jewish.
Facilities Dining room; Chapel; Crafts room; Laundry room; Barber/Beauty shop.
Activities Arts & crafts; Games; Reading groups; Prayer groups; Movies; Shopping trips; Dances/Social/Cultural gatherings; Theatre; Restaurants; Bus rides; Pet visitation; Resident council.

Iowa Lutheran Hospital
University at Penn, Des Moines, IA 50316
(515) 283-5305
Admin Eric C Bundgaard.
Licensure Skilled care. *Beds* SNF 16.

Karen Acres Nursing Home
3605 Elm Dr, Des Moines, IA 50322
(515) 276-4969
Admin Jo Anne Arndt. *Dir of Nursing* Cynthia Dabrico RN. *Medical Dir* Dr Lester Beachy.
Licensure Intermediate care. *Beds* ICF 38. *Private Pay Patients* 60%. *Certified* Medicaid.
Owner Proprietary corp (Celebrity Manor).
Admissions Requirements Medical examination; Physician's request.
Staff RNs 1 (ft), 2 (pt); LPNs 1 (ft), 1 (pt); Nurses' aides 8 (ft), 3 (pt); Activities coordinators 1 (pt).
Facilities Dining room; Activities room; Laundry room; Barber/Beauty shop; Library.
Activities Arts & crafts; Cards; Games; Reading groups; Prayer groups; Movies; Dances/Social/Cultural gatherings; Intergenerational programs; Pet therapy.

Luther Park Health Center
1555 Hull Ave, Des Moines, IA 50316
(515) 262-5639
Admin Dennis D Garland. *Dir of Nursing* Marcella Drannen Rn. *Medical Dir* Roy Overton MD.
Licensure Skilled care; Intermediate care; Retirement. *Beds* SNF 60; ICF 60. *Certified* Medicaid; Medicare.
Owner Nonprofit corp.
Admissions Requirements Minimum age 16; Medical examination; Physician's request.
Staff Physicians; RNs 10 (ft), 2 (pt); LPNs 10 (ft); Nurses' aides 40 (ft), 10 (pt); Physical therapists 1 (ft); Recreational therapists 2 (ft); Occupational therapists 1 (pt); Speech therapists 1 (pt); Dietitians 1 (pt); Ophthalmologists; Chaplains 2 (pt); Social workers 1 (ft), 1 (pt); Volunteer coordinators 1 (ft); Admissions coordinators 1 (ft).
Affiliation Lutheran.
Facilities Dining room; Physical therapy room; Activities room; Chapel; Crafts room; Laundry room; Barber/Beauty shop; Library.
Activities Arts & crafts; Cards; Games; Reading groups; Prayer groups; Movies; Shopping trips; Dances/Social/Cultural gatherings.

Mercy Hospital Medical Center
6th & University, Des Moines, IA 50314
(515) 247-3121
Admin Sr Patricia Sullivan.
Licensure Skilled care. *Beds* SNF 15.

New Oaks Care Center
3806 Easton Blvd, Des Moines, IA 50317
(515) 265-1474
Admin Larry R Rodgers.
Medical Dir Jan Summers.
Licensure Intermediate care. *Beds* ICF 51. *Certified* Medicaid.
Owner Privately owned.
Admissions Requirements Medical examination; Physician's request.
Staff RNs 1 (pt); LPNs 4 (ft), 3 (pt); Nurses' aides 12 (ft), 5 (pt); Activities coordinators 1 (ft); Dietitians 1 (ft), 1 (pt); Therapy aide 1 (ft).
Facilities Dining room; Laundry room; Barber/Beauty shop.
Activities Cards; Games; Reading groups; Prayer groups; Movies; Shopping trips; Ball games.

Parkridge Manor
2755 Parkridge Ave, Des Moines, IA 50317
(515) 265-5348
Admin Theodora Q Kracht.
Licensure Intermediate care. *Beds* ICF 74. *Certified* Medicaid.
Owner Proprietary corp (Mercy Health Initiatives).

Ramsey Home
1611 27th St, Des Moines, IA 50310
(515) 274-3612
Admin Ernest T DeHaven.
Medical Dir Robert Shires MD.
Licensure Skilled care; Intermediate care; Residential care. *Beds* SNF 12; ICF 66; Residential care 70. *Certified* Medicaid.
Owner Nonprofit corp (National Benevolent Association of Christian Homes).
Admissions Requirements Minimum age 65; Medical examination.
Staff RNs 2 (ft); LPNs 4 (ft), 5 (pt); Nurses' aides 19 (ft), 4 (pt); Physical therapists 1 (pt); Activities coordinators 2 (ft); Dietitians 1 (pt).
Affiliation Disciples of Christ.
Facilities Dining room; Activities room; Chapel; Crafts room; Laundry room; Barber/Beauty shop; Library.
Activities Arts & crafts; Cards; Games; Reading groups; Prayer groups; Movies; Shopping trips; Dances/Social/Cultural gatherings; Pet therapy program.

Riverview Care Center
701 Riverview, Des Moines, IA 50316
(515) 266-1106
Admin Ronald E Osby.
Licensure Intermediate care. *Beds* ICF 138. *Certified* Medicaid.
Owner Proprietary corp (ABCM Corp).

Scottish Rite Park
2909 Woodland Ave, Des Moines, IA 50312
(515) 274-4614
Admin Steve Lockwood. *Dir of Nursing* Carol Winchester.
Licensure Intermediate care; Residential care; Apartments. *Beds* ICF 41; Residential care 19; Apts 197. *Private Pay Patients* 100%.
Owner Nonprofit corp.
Admissions Requirements Minimum age 55; Medical examination; Financial statement.
Staff RNs; LPNs; Nurses' aides; Recreational therapists; Activities coordinators.
Affiliation Masons.
Facilities Dining room; Activities room; Crafts room; Laundry room; Barber/Beauty shop; Library.
Activities Arts & crafts; Cards; Games; Reading groups; Prayer groups; Movies; Intergenerational programs; Pet therapy.

Valley View Village
2571 Guthrie Ave, Des Moines, IA 50317
(515) 265-2571
Admin Dennis L Howe. *Dir of Nursing* Denice Shipley RN.
Licensure Intermediate care; Retirement. *Beds* ICF 79. *Certified* Medicaid.
Admissions Requirements Medical examination; Physician's request.
Staff RNs; LPNs; Nurses' aides; Activities coordinators.
Facilities Dining room; Activities room; Chapel; Crafts room; Barber/Beauty shop; Library.
Activities Arts & crafts; Cards; Games; Reading groups; Prayer groups; Movies; Shopping trips; Dances/Social/Cultural gatherings.

Wesley Acres
3520 Grand, Des Moines, IA 50312
(515) 271-6500
Admin Marie Mealiff.
Medical Dir Dr Robet Knox.
Licensure Intermediate care; Residential care. *Beds* ICF 59; Residential care 62. *Certified* Medicaid.
Admissions Requirements Minimum age 60; Medical examination.
Staff Physicians 1 (pt); RNs 2 (ft), 14 (pt); LPNs 3 (pt); Nurses' aides 22 (ft), 16 (pt); Activities coordinators 2 (ft); Dietitians 1 (ft).
Affiliation Methodist.
Facilities Dining room; Physical therapy room; Activities room; Chapel; Crafts room; Laundry room; Barber/Beauty shop; Library.
Activities Arts & crafts; Games; Reading groups; Movies; Shopping trips.

Dewitt

Dewitt Community Hospital
1118 11th St, Dewitt, IA 52742
(319) 659-3242
Admin Bruce Marlow.
Licensure Intermediate care. *Beds* ICF 50.

Donnellson

Donnellson Manor Care Center
901 State St, Donnellson, IA 52625
(319) 835-5621
Admin Michael S Dowell.
Medical Dir Nancy Bunnell.
Licensure Intermediate care. *Beds* ICF 73. *Certified* Medicaid.
Facilities Dining room; Activities room; Crafts room; Laundry room; Barber/Beauty shop.
Activities Arts & crafts; Cards; Games; Reading groups; Prayer groups; Movies; Dances/Social/Cultural gatherings.

Dows

Dows Care Center
909 Rowan Rd, Dows, IA 50071
(515) 852-4147
Admin Kathleen Remillard. *Dir of Nursing* Charlotte Brim RN.
Licensure Intermediate care. *Beds* ICF 50. *Private Pay Patients* 50%. *Certified* Medicaid.
Owner Proprietary corp (Five Star Care Corp).
Admissions Requirements Medical examination.
Staff RNs 3 (ft), 2 (pt); LPNs 2 (ft), 1 (pt); Nurses' aides 12 (ft), 10 (pt); Physical therapists (contracted); Recreational therapists (contracted); Occupational therapists (contracted); Speech therapists (contracted); Activities coordinators 1 (ft), 1 (pt); Dietitians 1 (pt); Ophthalmologists (contracted); Podiatrists (contracted); Audiologists (contracted).

Facilities Dining room; Activities room; Chapel; Laundry room; Barber/Beauty shop.
Activities Arts & crafts; Cards; Games; Reading groups; Prayer groups; Movies; Dances/Social/Cultural gatherings.

Dubuque

Bethany Home
1005 Lincoln Ave, Dubuque, IA 52001
(319) 556-5233
Admin Patricia L Gabrielson. *Dir of Nursing* Cris Kirsch. *Medical Dir* Dr Mark Liaboe.
Licensure Intermediate care; Residential care; Alzheimer's care. *Beds* ICF 55; Residential care 70. *Private Pay Patients* 75%. *Certified* Medicaid.
Owner Nonprofit corp.
Admissions Requirements Medical examination.
Staff RNs; LPNs; Nurses' aides; Activities coordinators; Dietitians.
Affiliation Presbyterian.
Facilities Dining room; Activities room; Chapel; Crafts room; Laundry room; Barber/Beauty shop.
Activities Arts & crafts; Cards; Games; Reading groups; Movies; Shopping trips; Dances/Social/Cultural gatherings; Intergenerational programs.

Dubuque Health Care Center
2935 Kaufman, Dubuque, IA 52001
(319) 556-0673
Admin Joyce L Post.
Licensure Intermediate care. *Beds* ICF 108. *Certified* Medicaid.
Owner Proprietary corp (Mercy Health Initiatives).
Admissions Requirements Minimum age 16; Physician's request.
Staff Recreational therapists 1 (ft); Activities coordinators 3 (pt).
Facilities Dining room; Physical therapy room; Activities room; Crafts room; Barber/Beauty shop.
Activities Arts & crafts; Cards; Games; Reading groups; Prayer groups; Movies; Shopping trips; Dances/Social/Cultural gatherings.

Ennoble Manor Care Center
2000 Pasadena Dr, Dubuque, IA 52001
(319) 557-1076
Admin Joan Sutherland.
Licensure Intermediate care. *Beds* ICF 102. *Certified* Medicaid.

Finley Hospital
350 N Grandview Ave, Dubuque, IA 52001
(319) 589-2413
Admin Stephen C Hanson.
Licensure Skilled care. *Beds* SNF 17.

Heritage Manor
4885 Asbury Rd, Dubuque, IA 52001
(319) 583-6447
Admin Mary J Bailey. *Dir of Nursing* Debra Hillard. *Medical Dir* John P Viner MD.
Licensure Intermediate care; Retirement. *Beds* ICF 75; Retirement apts 10. *Private Pay Patients* 45%. *Certified* Medicaid.
Owner Proprietary corp.
Admissions Requirements Minimum age 18; Medical examination; Physician's request.
Staff RNs 2 (ft), 2 (pt); LPNs 3 (ft), 1 (pt); Nurses' aides 24 (ft), 13 (pt); Dietitians 1 (pt); Recreational therapists; Activities coordinators 1 (ft), 1 (pt).
Facilities Dining room; Activities room; Chapel; Crafts room; Laundry room; Barber/Beauty shop; Library; Large deck.
Activities Arts & crafts; Cards; Games; Reading groups; Prayer groups; Movies; Shopping trips; Dances/Social/Cultural gatherings; Intergenerational programs; Pet therapy; Picnics; Sight-seeing trips; Teas.

Hills & Dales Child Development Center
1011 Davis, Dubuque, IA 52001
(319) 556-7878
Admin Janet Imhof. *Dir of Nursing* Kathy Derga RN.
Licensure Intermediate care for mentally retarded. *Beds* ICF/MR 42. *Private Pay Patients* 0%. *Certified* Medicaid.
Owner Proprietary corp.
Admissions Requirements Medical examination.
Staff RNs; LPNs; Physical therapists; Occupational therapists; Speech therapists; Activities coordinators; Dietitians.
Facilities Dining room; Activities room; Laundry room.
Activities Arts & crafts; Games; Prayer groups; Movies; Shopping trips; Bowling; Swimming; Camp.

Julien Care Facility
13066 Seippel Rd, Dubuque, IA 52001
(319) 583-1791
Admin Betty Kremer.
Licensure Intermediate care. *Beds* ICF 9.

Luther Manor
3131 Hillcrest Rd, Dubuque, IA 52001
(319) 588-1413
Admin Mark Noble.
Licensure Intermediate care. *Beds* ICF 86. *Certified* Medicaid.
Affiliation Lutheran.

Manor Care Nursing Center
901 W 3rd St, Dubuque, IA 52001
(319) 556-1163
Admin Cathleen Lehmann.
Licensure Skilled care. *Beds* SNF 92. *Certified* Medicaid; Medicare.
Owner Proprietary corp (Manor Care Inc).

Mercy Health Center Skilled Nursing Unit
Mercy Dr, Dubuque, IA 52001
(319) 589-8000, 589-8000 FAX
Admin Sr Helen Huewe OSF. *Dir of Nursing* Joan Hentges RN. *Medical Dir* Catherine Crall MD, contracted.
Licensure Skilled care. *Beds* SNF 20. *Private Pay Patients* 0%. *Certified* Medicaid; Medicare.
Owner Nonprofit corp (Mercy Health Services).
Admissions Requirements Medical examination; Physician's request.
Staff RNs 6 (ft), 7 (pt); LPNs 2 (ft), 1 (pt); Nurses' aides 6 (ft), 5 (pt); Physical therapists (hospital staff); Occupational therapists (hospital staff); Speech therapists (hospital staff); Activities coordinators (hospital staff); Dietitians (hospital staff).
Affiliation Roman Catholic.
Facilities Dining room; Physical therapy room; Activities room; Chapel; Crafts room.
Activities Arts & crafts; Cards; Games; Movies; Dances/Social/Cultural gatherings.

Stonehill Care Center
3485 Windsor Ave, Dubuque, IA 52001
(319) 557-7180
Admin Sr Delores Ullrich. *Dir of Nursing* Victoria Anderegg RN.
Licensure Intermediate care; Residential care; Alzheimer's care. *Beds* ICF 168; Residential care 82. *Certified* Medicaid.
Owner Nonprofit corp.
Admissions Requirements Minimum age 60; Medical examination.
Staff RNs 7 (ft), 13 (pt); LPNs 4 (ft), 14 (pt); Nurses' aides 35 (ft), 66 (pt); Activities coordinators 2 (ft); Dietitians 1 (pt).
Affiliation Roman Catholic.
Facilities Dining room; Physical therapy room; Activities room; Chapel; Crafts room; Laundry room; Barber/Beauty shop; Library; Greenhouse.

Activities Arts & crafts; Cards; Games; Reading groups; Prayer groups; Movies; Shopping trips; Dances/Social/Cultural gatherings; Exercise class; Bible class; Creative writing; Plant therapy.

Sunnycrest Manor
2375 Roosevelt St, Dubuque, IA 52001
(319) 583-1781
Admin Millard M Darlene.
Licensure Intermediate care; Intermediate care for mentally retarded. *Beds* ICF 104; ICF/MR 32.

Dumont

Dumont Nursing Home
921 3rd St, Dumont, IA 50625
(515) 857-3401
Admin Edna Reiners.
Licensure Intermediate care; Residential care. *Beds* ICF 44; Residential care 5. *Certified* Medicaid.
Owner Proprietary corp (ABCM Corp).

Dunlap

Dunlap Care Center
1403 Harrison Rd, Dunlap, IA 51529
(712) 643-2121
Admin Rodney A Hirchert.
Licensure Intermediate care. *Beds* ICF 73. *Certified* Medicaid.
Owner Proprietary corp (Mercy Health Initiatives).

Dyersville

Oakcrest Manor & Skilled Nursing Unit—St Mary's Unit
1111 3rd St SW, Mercy Health Center, Dyersville, IA 52001
(319) 875-7101, 543-2935 FAX
Admin Sr Helen Huewe OSF. *Dir of Nursing* Kathy Ripple RN. *Medical Dir* Robert Tomas MD, contracted.
Licensure Skilled care; Intermediate care. *Beds* SNF 3; ICF 40. *Private Pay Patients* 60%. *Certified* Medicaid; Medicare.
Owner Nonprofit organization/foundation (Mercy Health Services).
Admissions Requirements Medical examination.
Staff RNs 3 (ft), 5 (pt); LPNs 3 (pt); Nurses' aides 7 (ft), 16 (pt); Physical therapists 1 (pt); Occupational therapists (hospital staff); Speech therapists (hospital staff); Activities coordinators 3 (pt); Dietitians (hospital staff).
Affiliation Roman Catholic.
Facilities Dining room; Physical therapy room; Activities room; Chapel; Crafts room; Laundry room; Barber/Beauty shop; Library.
Activities Arts & crafts; Cards; Games; Reading groups; Prayer groups; Movies; Shopping trips; Dances/Social/Cultural gatherings; Intergenerational programs; Pet therapy; Visits to other nursing homes.

Dysart

Sunnycrest Nursing Center
401 Crisman, Dysart, IA 52224
(319) 476-2400
Admin Susan Loeb. *Dir of Nursing* Rebecca Ohrt RN. *Medical Dir* Dr Pathan.
Licensure Intermediate care. *Beds* ICF 67. *Private Pay Patients* 40%. *Certified* Medicaid.
Owner Privately owned (Quality Health Care Specialists).
Admissions Requirements Medical examination.

Staff Physicians; RNs; LPNs; Nurses' aides;
Physical therapists; Recreational therapists;
Occupational therapists; Activities
coordinators; Dietitians; Podiatrists;
Audiologists.
Facilities Dining room; Physical therapy
room; Activities room; Crafts room; Laundry
room; Barber/Beauty shop.
Activities Arts & crafts; Cards; Games;
Reading groups; Prayer groups; Movies;
Dances/Social/Cultural gatherings; Pet
therapy.

Eagle Grove

Rotary Ann Home
620 SE 5th St, Eagle Grove, IA 50533
(515) 448-5124
Admin Michael D Van Sickle. *Dir of Nursing*
Rodean Frakes.
Licensure Intermediate care; Residential care.
Beds ICF 51; Residential care 50. *Private
Pay Patients* 60%. *Certified* Medicaid.
Owner Nonprofit organization/foundation.
Admissions Requirements Minimum age 60;
Medical examination.
Staff RNs 5 (ft), 2 (pt); LPNs 4 (ft), 2 (pt);
Nurses' aides 20 (ft), 10 (pt); Recreational
therapists 2 (ft); Dietitians 1 (ft).
Facilities Dining room; Physical therapy
room; Activities room; Crafts room; Barber/
Beauty shop.
Activities Arts & crafts; Cards; Games;
Reading groups; Prayer groups; Movies;
Dances/Social/Cultural gatherings.

Earlham

Earlham Manor Care Center
201 Center St, Earlham, IA 50072
(515) 758-2244
Admin Karen G Reed.
Medical Dir Mary O Ralston.
Licensure Intermediate care. *Beds* ICF 29.
Certified Medicaid; Medicare.
Owner Proprietary corp (Quality Health Care
Specialists Inc).
Admissions Requirements Minimum age 16.
Staff RNs; Nurses' aides; Physical therapists;
Activities coordinators; Dietitians;
Ophthalmologists; Podiatrists.
Facilities Dining room; Laundry room;
Barber/Beauty shop.
Activities Arts & crafts; Cards; Games;
Reading groups; Prayer groups; Movies;
Shopping trips; Dances/Social/Cultural
gatherings.

Earling

Little Flower Haven
Hwy 37 W, Earling, IA 51530
(712) 747-3301
Admin David Hoffmann.
Licensure Intermediate care. *Beds* ICF 61.
Certified Medicaid.

Edgewood

Edgewood Convalescent Home
Bell St, Edgewood, IA 52042
(319) 928-6461
Admin Mildred Robinson.
Licensure Intermediate care. *Beds* ICF 59.
Certified Medicaid.
Admissions Requirements Medical
examination.
Staff RNs 1 (ft), 1 (pt); LPNs 4 (pt); Nurses'
aides 4 (ft), 12 (pt); Recreational therapists 1
(pt); Occupational therapists 1 (pt); Speech
therapists 1 (pt); Activities coordinators 1
(ft); Dietitians 1 (ft), 1 (pt);
Ophthalmologists 1 (pt); Podiatrists 1 (pt);
Audiologists 1 (pt); Dentists 1 (pt).

Facilities Dining room; Physical therapy
room; Activities room; Chapel; Crafts room;
Laundry room; Barber/Beauty shop.
Activities Arts & crafts; Cards; Games;
Reading groups; Prayer groups; Movies;
Dances/Social/Cultural gatherings.

Eldora

Eldora Manor
1510 22nd St, Eldora, IA 50627
(515) 858-3491
Admin Terry Cooper. *Dir of Nursing* Gladys
Peterson.
Licensure Intermediate care. *Beds* ICF 70.
Private Pay Patients 45%. *Certified*
Medicaid.
Owner Nonprofit corp (Mercy Health
Initiatives).
Admissions Requirements Minimum age 21;
Medical examination.
Staff RNs 3 (ft); LPNs 3 (ft), 1 (pt); Nurses'
aides 20 (ft), 6 (pt); Activities coordinators 1
(ft), 1 (pt); Social workers 1 (pt).
Facilities Dining room; Physical therapy
room; Activities room; Laundry room;
Barber/Beauty shop.
Activities Arts & crafts; Cards; Games;
Reading groups; Prayer groups; Movies;
Shopping trips; Dances/Social/Cultural
gatherings; Intergenerational programs;
Adopt-a-grandparent.

Valley View Nursing Center
2313 15th Ave, Eldora, IA 50627
(515) 858-5422
Admin Debra Hightshoe.
Licensure Intermediate care; Residential care.
Beds ICF 64; Residential care 16. *Certified*
Medicaid.
Owner Proprietary corp (Mercy Health
Initiatives).

Elk Horn

Salem Lutheran Home
2024 College St, Elk Horn, IA 51531
(712) 764-4201
Admin Mark Edward.
Medical Dir Beverly Kleen.
Licensure Intermediate care; Residential care.
Beds ICF 100; Residential care 62. *Certified*
Medicaid.
Owner Nonprofit corp.
Admissions Requirements Minimum age 16;
Medical examination; Physician's request.
Staff RNs; LPNs; Nurses' aides; Physical
therapists; Dietitians.
Affiliation Lutheran.
Facilities Dining room; Physical therapy
room; Activities room; Chapel; Crafts room;
Laundry room; Barber/Beauty shop.
Activities Arts & crafts; Cards; Games;
Reading groups; Prayer groups; Movies;
Shopping trips; Dances/Social/Cultural
gatherings.

Elkader

Elkader Care Center
116 Reimer St, Elkader, IA 52043
(319) 245-1620
Admin Glen J O'Loughlin.
Licensure Intermediate care. *Beds* ICF 51.
Certified Medicaid.
Admissions Requirements Minimum age 18;
Medical examination.
Staff RNs 1 (ft); LPNs 2 (ft), 3 (pt); Nurses'
aides 4 (ft), 11 (pt); Activities coordinators 1
(ft); Dietitians 1 (pt).
Facilities Dining room; Chapel; Laundry
room; Barber/Beauty shop.
Activities Arts & crafts; Cards; Games;
Reading groups; Prayer groups; Movies;
Shopping trips.

Elma

Colonial Manor 45
9th & Maple, Elma, IA 50628
(515) 393-2134
Admin Jerome Erdahl. *Dir of Nursing* Sheila
Kobliska RN. *Medical Dir* Dr Curtis Rainy.
Licensure Intermediate care. *Beds* ICF 62.
Certified Medicaid.
Owner Proprietary corp.
Admissions Requirements Minimum age 21;
Medical examination; Physician's request.
Staff Physicians 1 (pt); RNs 1 (ft), 1 (pt);
LPNs 1 (ft), 3 (pt); Nurses' aides 7 (ft), 21
(pt); Physical therapists 1 (pt); Recreational
therapists 1 (pt); Occupational therapists 1
(pt); Speech therapists 1 (pt); Activities
coordinators 2 (ft); Dietitians 1 (pt);
Ophthalmologists 1 (pt); Podiatrists 1 (pt);
Social worker 1 (pt); Dentists 1 (pt).
Facilities Dining room; Physical therapy
room; Activities room; Chapel; Crafts room;
Laundry room; Barber/Beauty shop; Library.
Activities Arts & crafts; Cards; Games;
Reading groups; Prayer groups; Movies;
Shopping trips; Dances/Social/Cultural
gatherings.

Emmetsburg

Emmetsburg Care Center
PO Box 490, Emmetsburg, IA 50536
(712) 852-4266
Admin Lyman D Bailey.
Medical Dir Nina J Jurries.
Licensure Intermediate care; Alzheimer's care.
Beds ICF 88. *Certified* Medicaid.
Owner Proprietary corp.
Admissions Requirements Minimum age 16;
Medical examination.
Staff RNs 2 (ft), 1 (pt); LPNs 5 (ft), 5 (pt);
Nurses' aides 30 (ft), 20 (pt); Physical
therapists 1 (pt); Reality therapists 2 (ft);
Recreational therapists 2 (ft); Occupational
therapists 1 (pt); Speech therapists 1 (pt);
Activities coordinators 2 (ft), 1 (pt);
Dietitians 1 (pt); Ophthalmologists 1 (pt);
Podiatrists 1 (pt).
Facilities Dining room; Physical therapy
room; Activities room; Chapel; Crafts room;
Laundry room; Barber/Beauty shop; Library.
Activities Arts & crafts; Cards; Games;
Reading groups; Prayer groups; Movies;
Shopping trips; Dances/Social/Cultural
gatherings.

Kathleen's Residential Care
1505 E 5th St, Emmetsburg, IA 50536
(712) 852-2267
Admin Marvin R Curry.
Licensure Intermediate care for mentally
retarded. *Beds* ICF/MR 14.

Lakeside Lutheran Home
N Lawler St, Emmetsburg, IA 50536
(712) 852-4060
Admin Robert Owen.
Licensure Intermediate care. *Beds* ICF 60.
Certified Medicaid.
Owner Nonprofit corp.
Affiliation Lutheran.

Estherville

Good Samaritan Center
1646 5th Ave N, Estherville, IA 51334
(712) 362-3522
Admin Bruce L Radtke.
Medical Dir Erla Scherschligt.
Licensure Intermediate care; Retirement;
Alzheimer's care. *Beds* ICF 141. *Certified*
Medicaid.
Owner Nonprofit corp (Evangelical Lutheran/
Good Samaritan Society).
Admissions Requirements Minimum age 16;
Medical examination; Physician's request.

Staff RNs 3 (ft), 3 (pt); LPNs 2 (ft), 6 (pt); Nurses' aides 30 (ft), 32 (pt); Physical therapists 1 (pt); Activities coordinators 1 (ft); Dietitians 1 (ft).
Facilities Dining room; Activities room; Chapel; Crafts room; Laundry room; Barber/Beauty shop.
Activities Arts & crafts; Games; Reading groups; Prayer groups; Movies; Dances/Social/Cultural gatherings.

Rosewood Manor
1720 1st Ave N, Estherville, IA 51334
(712) 362-3594
Admin Jeanne M Hofstader.
Medical Dir Dianne Howard.
Licensure Intermediate care. *Beds* ICF 55.
Owner Proprietary corp.
Admissions Requirements Medical examination.
Staff RNs 2 (ft); LPNs 4 (ft), 1 (pt); Nurses' aides 10 (ft), 5 (pt); Physical therapists 1 (pt); Recreational therapists 1 (pt); Activities coordinators 1 (ft); Dietitians 1 (pt); Podiatrists 1 (pt).
Facilities Dining room; Physical therapy room; Activities room; Chapel; Crafts room; Laundry room; Barber/Beauty shop.
Activities Arts & crafts; Cards; Games; Reading groups; Prayer groups; Movies.

Exira

Exira Care Center
409 S Carthage, Exira, IA 50076
(712) 268-5393
Admin Curt B Mardesen.
Licensure Intermediate care. *Beds* ICF 66.
Certified Medicaid.

Fairfield

Nelson Nursing Home
809 W Taylor, Fairfield, IA 52556
(515) 472-6126
Admin Sheri L Glassford.
Licensure Intermediate care. *Beds* ICF 63.
Certified Medicaid.

Parkview Care Center
RFD 1 Box 193, Fairfield, IA 52556
(515) 472-5022
Admin Christie L Six.
Medical Dir Connie Ferrell.
Licensure Intermediate care. *Beds* ICF 112.
Certified Medicaid.
Owner Proprietary corp.
Staff RNs; LPNs; Nurses' aides; Activities coordinators 2 (ft).

Fayette

Maple Crest Manor
RR 1 Box 132X, Fayette, IA 52142
(319) 425-3336
Admin Richard L Ford. *Dir of Nursing* Joyce Dahlquist.
Licensure Intermediate care. *Beds* ICF 60.
Certified Medicaid.
Owner Proprietary corp.
Admissions Requirements Minimum age 16; Medical examination; Physician's request.
Staff RNs; LPNs; Nurses' aides; Physical therapists; Occupational therapists; Speech therapists; Activities coordinators; Dietitians; Podiatrists.
Facilities Dining room; Physical therapy room; Activities room; Crafts room; Laundry room; Barber/Beauty shop.
Activities Arts & crafts; Cards; Games; Reading groups; Prayer groups; Movies; Dances/Social/Cultural gatherings.

Fonda

Fonda Care Center
6th & Queen Ave, Fonda, IA 50540
(712) 288-4441
Admin Betty J Cunningham. *Dir of Nursing* Jane Bierstedt RN.
Licensure Intermediate care. *Beds* ICF 49.
Certified Medicaid.
Admissions Requirements Minimum age 49; Medical examination; Physician's request.
Staff Physicians 1 (pt); RNs 2 (ft); LPNs 1 (ft), 1 (pt); Nurses' aides 10 (ft), 10 (pt); Physical therapists 1 (pt); Occupational therapists 1 (pt); Speech therapists 1 (pt); Activities coordinators 1 (ft); Dietitians 1 (pt); Podiatrists 1 (pt); Audiologists 1 (pt); Dentists 1 (pt).
Facilities Dining room; Physical therapy room; Activities room; Laundry room; Barber/Beauty shop.
Activities Arts & crafts; Cards; Games; Reading groups; Movies; Shopping trips.

Fontanelle

Fontanelle Good Samaritan Center
326 Summerset St, Fontanelle, IA 50846
(515) 745-4201
Admin Jane Mohror. *Dir of Nursing* Twilah Tipling RN.
Licensure Intermediate care; Retirement. *Beds* ICF 63. *Certified* Medicaid.
Owner Nonprofit corp (Evangelical Lutheran/ Good Samaritan Society).
Admissions Requirements Medical examination; Physician's request.
Staff RNs; LPNs; Nurses' aides; Activities coordinators.
Facilities Dining room; Physical therapy room; Activities room; Laundry room; Barber/Beauty shop.
Activities Cards; Games; Reading groups; Movies; Mental stimulation; Music; Demonstrations.

Forest City

Good Samaritan Center
606 S 7th, Forest City, IA 50436
(515) 582-2232
Admin Nancy Demmel. *Dir of Nursing* Dolores Nelson.
Licensure Intermediate care. *Beds* ICF 64. *Certified* Medicaid.
Owner Nonprofit corp (Evangelical Lutheran/ Good Samaritan Society).
Admissions Requirements Medical examination.
Staff RNs 3 (ft), 6 (pt); LPNs 4 (pt); Nurses' aides 12 (ft), 15 (pt); Activities coordinators 1 (pt).
Affiliation Lutheran.
Facilities Dining room; Activities room; Chapel; Laundry room; Barber/Beauty shop; Library.
Activities Games; Reading groups; Prayer groups; Movies; Dances/Social/Cultural gatherings.

North Central Human Services
101 Kelly's Ct, Forest City, IA 50436
(515) 582-3050
Licensure Intermediate care for mentally retarded. *Beds* ICF/MR 24.

Fort Dodge

Ellen's Convalescent Health Center
1305 N 22nd St, Fort Dodge, IA 50501
(515) 955-4145
Admin James Kratovil. *Dir of Nursing* Mrs Anderson.
Licensure Intermediate care; Residential care. *Beds* ICF 80; Residential care 18. *Certified* Medicaid.

Owner Proprietary corp.
Admissions Requirements Minimum age 13; Medical examination; Physician's request.
Staff RNs 3 (ft), 2 (pt); LPNs 4 (ft), 3 (pt); Nurses' aides 20 (ft), 8 (pt); Activities coordinators 2 (ft), 2 (pt); Dietitians 1 (pt).
Facilities Dining room; Physical therapy room; Activities room; Chapel; Crafts room; Laundry room; Barber/Beauty shop; Library.
Activities Arts & crafts; Cards; Games; Reading groups; Prayer groups; Movies; Shopping trips; Dances/Social/Cultural gatherings.

Fort Dodge Villa Care Center
2721 10th Ave N, Fort Dodge, IA 50501
(515) 576-7525
Admin Dori Smith. *Dir of Nursing* Sue Evers RN BSN. *Medical Dir* Dr John Sear.
Licensure Intermediate care; Residential care. *Beds* ICF 93; Residential care 14. *Private Pay Patients* 40%. *Certified* Medicaid.
Owner Proprietary corp (Quality Health Care Specialists Inc).
Admissions Requirements Medical examination; Physician's request.
Staff RNs 6 (ft), 7 (pt); LPNs 2 (ft); Nurses' aides 25 (ft), 15 (pt); Recreational therapists 1 (ft); Occupational therapists (contracted); Speech therapists (contracted); Activities coordinators 1 (ft); Dietitians 1 (pt); Podiatrists 1 (pt); Audiologists (contracted).
Facilities Dining room; Physical therapy room; Activities room; Crafts room; Laundry room; Barber/Beauty shop; Library.
Activities Arts & crafts; Cards; Games; Reading groups; Prayer groups; Movies; Shopping trips; Dances/Social/Cultural gatherings; Pet therapy.

Friendship Haven Inc
S Kenyon Rd, Fort Dodge, IA 50501
(515) 573-2121
Admin Rev Paul G Bousfield. *Dir of Nursing* Sally Young. *Medical Dir* James Metzger, Health Svcs Dir.
Licensure Intermediate care; Residential care; Alzheimer's care. *Beds* ICF 241; Residential care 352. *Certified* Medicaid.
Owner Nonprofit corp.
Admissions Requirements Minimum age 65; Medical examination.
Staff RNs 21 (ft); LPNs 9 (ft); Nurses' aides 130 (ft); Physical therapists 1 (ft); Activities coordinators 1 (ft); Dietitians 1 (ft); Ophthalmologists 1 (ft); Podiatrists 1 (ft); Audiologists 1 (ft).
Affiliation United Methodist.
Facilities Dining room; Physical therapy room; Activities room; Chapel; Crafts room; Laundry room; Barber/Beauty shop; Library; Kitchen; Coffee shop & small cafeteria; Gift shop & thrift shop; Swimming pool; Jacuzzi.
Activities Arts & crafts; Cards; Games; Reading groups; Prayer groups; Movies; Shopping trips; Dances/Social/Cultural gatherings; Intergenerational programs; Pet therapy; College classes; Exercise; Swimming.

Marian Home
2400 6th Ave N, Fort Dodge, IA 50501
(515) 576-1138
Admin Gerald J Bruening. *Dir of Nursing* Mary Bruening.
Licensure Intermediate care; Independent apartments. *Beds* ICF 97; Independent apts 29. *Private Pay Patients* 50%. *Certified* Medicaid.
Owner Nonprofit organization/foundation.
Staff RNs 5 (ft), 7 (pt); LPNs 5 (pt); Nurses' aides 15 (ft), 29 (pt); Physical therapists 2 (ft), 1 (pt); Occupational therapists 1 (pt); Speech therapists 1 (pt); Activities coordinators 2 (ft); Dietitians 1 (pt).
Affiliation Roman Catholic.

Facilities Dining room; Physical therapy room; Activities room; Chapel; Crafts room; Laundry room; Barber/Beauty shop.

Activities Arts & crafts; Cards; Games; Reading groups; Prayer groups; Movies; Shopping trips; Dances/Social/Cultural gatherings; Intergenerational programs; Pet therapy.

Park Manor Care Center
728 14th Ave N, Fort Dodge, IA 50501
(515) 576-7226
Admin Mary Lou Madsen. *Dir of Nursing* Doris Friesth.
Licensure Intermediate care. *Beds* ICF 100. *Private Pay Patients* 11%. *Certified* Medicaid.
Owner Proprietary corp (Five Star Care Corp).
Admissions Requirements Minimum age 21.
Staff RNs; LPNs; Nurses' aides; Physical therapists (contracted); Speech therapists (contracted); Activities coordinators; Dietitians (consultant); Ophthalmologists (contracted); Podiatrists (contracted); Audiologists (contracted).
Facilities Dining room; Physical therapy room; Activities room; Laundry room; Barber/Beauty shop; Family room.
Activities Arts & crafts; Cards; Games; Reading groups; Prayer groups; Movies; Shopping trips; Dances/Social/Cultural gatherings.

Fort Madison

Fort Madison Nursing Care Center
1702 41st St, Fort Madison, IA 52627
(319) 372-8021
Admin Sr Donna Venteicher.
Medical Dir Betty Lucas.
Licensure Intermediate care. *Beds* ICF 108. *Certified* Medicaid.
Owner Proprietary corp.
Admissions Requirements Minimum age 16; Medical examination.
Staff RNs 5 (ft), 2 (pt); LPNs 2 (ft), 1 (pt); Nurses' aides 18 (ft), 19 (pt); Physical therapists 1 (pt); Occupational therapists 1 (pt); Speech therapists 1 (pt); Activities coordinators; Dietitians 1 (pt); Ophthalmologists 1 (pt); Podiatrists 1 (pt).
Facilities Dining room; Physical therapy room; Activities room; Chapel; Crafts room; Laundry room; Barber/Beauty shop.
Activities Arts & crafts; Cards; Games; Reading groups; Prayer groups; Movies; Shopping trips; Dances/Social/Cultural gatherings.

Fredericksburg

Sunrise Guest Home
Lyons Rd, Fredericksburg, IA 50630
(319) 237-5323
Admin Sharon Jan Ploeger.
Licensure Intermediate care; Alzheimer's care. *Beds* ICF 37. *Certified* Medicaid.
Owner Proprietary corp.
Admissions Requirements Minimum age 16.
Staff RNs 1 (ft); LPNs 3 (ft); Nurses' aides 20 (ft); Speech therapists 1 (ft); Activities coordinators 1 (ft); Dietitians 1 (ft).
Facilities Dining room; Physical therapy room; Activities room; Crafts room; Laundry room; Barber/Beauty shop; Library.
Activities Arts & crafts; Cards; Games; Reading groups; Prayer groups; Movies; Dances/Social/Cultural gatherings.

Garner

Concord Care Center
1375 Division St, Garner, IA 50438
(515) 923-2677
Admin Debra Roberts. *Dir of Nursing* Mary Feuling RN. *Medical Dir* L R Fuller MD.

Licensure Intermediate care. *Beds* ICF 66. *Certified* Medicaid.
Owner Proprietary corp (ABCM Corp).
Admissions Requirements Medical examination.
Staff RNs 1 (ft), 1 (pt); LPNs 4 (ft); Nurses' aides 15 (ft), 10 (pt); Physical therapists 1 (pt); Activities coordinators 1 (ft); Dietitians 1 (pt).
Facilities Dining room; Activities room; Chapel; Barber/Beauty shop.
Activities Cards; Games; Reading groups; Prayer groups; Movies; Dances/Social/Cultural gatherings.

George

George Good Samaritan Center
Box 608, 324 1st Ave N, George, IA 51237
(712) 475-3391
Admin Nancy Demmel. *Dir of Nursing* Cathy Huff. *Medical Dir* Dr Hoffman.
Licensure Intermediate care; Retirement. *Beds* ICF 48; Retirement 6. *Private Pay Patients* 54%. *Certified* Medicaid.
Owner Nonprofit corp (Evangelical Lutheran/ Good Samaritan Society).
Admissions Requirements Minimum age 16; Medical examination; Physician's certification of need.
Staff RNs 1 (ft), 4 (pt); LPNs 4 (pt); Nurses' aides 24 (pt); Activities coordinators 1 (ft).
Affiliation Lutheran.
Facilities Dining room; Physical therapy room; Activities room; Chapel; Crafts room; Laundry room; Barber/Beauty shop.
Activities Arts & crafts; Games; Reading groups; Prayer groups; Movies.

Gladbrook

Westbrook Acres
RR 4 Box 35, Gladbrook, IA 50635
(515) 473-2016
Admin Loretta L Larson.
Licensure Intermediate care. *Beds* ICF 33. *Certified* Medicaid.

Glenwood

Glen Haven Home
302 6th St, Glenwood, IA 51534
(712) 527-3101
Admin Monte L McVey.
Licensure Intermediate care. *Beds* ICF 90. *Certified* Medicaid.

Glenwood State Hospital & School
711 S Vine St, Glenwood, IA 51534
(712) 527-4811
Admin William E Campbell. *Dir of Nursing* Barb Slama. *Medical Dir* John Thomas MD.
Licensure Intermediate care for mentally retarded. *Beds* ICF/MR 851. *Private Pay Patients* 0%. *Certified* Medicaid; Medicare.
Owner Publicly owned.
Staff Physicians 8 (ft); RNs 42 (ft); Nurses' aides 631 (ft); Physical therapists 2 (ft); Recreational therapists 12 (ft); Occupational therapists 2 (ft); Speech therapists 5 (ft); Activities coordinators 2 (ft); Dietitians 5 (ft); Ophthalmologists (contracted); Podiatrists (contracted); Audiologists 1 (ft).
Facilities Dining room; Physical therapy room; Activities room; Chapel; Crafts room; Laundry room; Barber/Beauty shop; Library.
Activities Arts & crafts; Cards; Games; Prayer groups; Movies; Shopping trips; Dances/ Social/Cultural gatherings.

Hillside Manor
114 E Green St, Glenwood, IA 51534
(712) 527-4841
Admin Jon Buchholz. *Dir of Nursing* Linda Heywood RN; Donna Mackey RN. *Medical Dir* Robet K Fryzek MD.

Licensure Intermediate care; Intermediate care for mentally retarded. *Beds* ICF 67; ICF/MR 112. *Certified* Medicaid.
Owner Privately owned.
Admissions Requirements Minimum age 19.
Staff Physicians 1 (pt); RNs 4 (ft), 1 (pt); LPNs 6 (ft); Nurses' aides 55 (ft); Physical therapists 1 (pt); Recreational therapists 10 (ft); Occupational therapists 1 (pt); Speech therapists 1 (pt); Activities coordinators 2 (ft); Dietitians 1 (pt).
Facilities Dining room; Physical therapy room; Activities room; Crafts room; Laundry room; Barber/Beauty shop.
Activities Arts & crafts; Cards; Games; Movies; Shopping trips; Dances/Social/ Cultural gatherings.

Gowrie

Gowrie Manor
1808 Main St, Gowrie, IA 50543
(515) 352-3912
Admin Christine Wolf.
Medical Dir Bev Swedlund.
Licensure Intermediate care; Retirement. *Beds* ICF 51. *Certified* Medicaid; Medicare.
Owner Proprietary corp (ABCM Corp).
Admissions Requirements Medical examination; Physician's request.
Staff RNs 2 (ft); LPNs 5 (ft), 1 (pt); Nurses' aides 14 (ft), 3 (pt); Activities coordinators 1 (ft), 1 (pt); Dietitians 1 (pt).
Facilities Dining room; Activities room; Laundry room; Barber/Beauty shop.
Activities Arts & crafts; Cards; Games; Reading groups; Prayer groups; Movies; Dances/Social/Cultural gatherings.

Granger

Granger Manor
2001 Kennedy St, Granger, IA 50109
(515) 999-2588
Admin Michael Feauto.
Medical Dir Josephine Kanniainen.
Licensure Intermediate care. *Beds* ICF 67. *Certified* Medicaid.
Owner Proprietary corp (National Heritage).
Staff RNs 2 (ft); LPNs 4 (ft); Nurses' aides 20 (ft); Physical therapists 4 (ft); Recreational therapists 1 (ft); Occupational therapists 1 (ft); Speech therapists 1 (ft); Activities coordinators 1 (ft); Dietitians 1 (ft); Ophthalmologists 1 (ft); Podiatrists 1 (ft).
Facilities Dining room; Physical therapy room; Activities room; Crafts room; Laundry room; Barber/Beauty shop.
Activities Arts & crafts; Cards; Games; Reading groups; Prayer groups; Shopping trips; Dances/Social/Cultural gatherings.

Greene

Mathers Nursing Home
108 S High St, Greene, IA 50636
(515) 823-4531
Admin Alberta Mathers. *Dir of Nursing* Linda Schroeder RN.
Licensure Intermediate care. *Beds* ICF 25. *Certified* Medicaid.
Owner Privately owned.
Admissions Requirements Minimum age 18; Medical examination; Physician's request.
Staff RNs 1 (ft); LPNs 2 (pt); Nurses' aides 2 (ft), 12 (pt); Activities coordinators 1 (pt); Dietary 1 (ft), 2 (pt); Housekeeping 2 (pt); Laundry 2 (pt).
Facilities Dining room; Physical therapy room; Activities room; Laundry room; Barber/Beauty shop.
Activities Arts & crafts; Cards; Games; Reading groups; Prayer groups; Movies; Dances/Social/Cultural gatherings.

Greenfield

Greenfield Manor
615 SE Kent, Greenfield, IA 50849
(515) 743-6131
Admin Helen L Martin. *Dir of Nursing* Esther Ramsey.
Licensure Intermediate care. *Beds* ICF 57. *Certified* Medicaid.
Owner Proprietary corp.
Admissions Requirements Medical examination; Physician's request.
Staff RNs 1 (ft), 2 (pt); LPNs 3 (ft), 1 (pt); Nurses' aides 16 (ft), 4 (pt); Activities coordinators 2 (pt); Dietitians 1 (pt).
Facilities Dining room; Physical therapy room; Activities room.
Activities Arts & crafts; Cards; Games; Reading groups; Prayer groups; Movies; Dances/Social/Cultural gatherings.

Grinnell

Friendship Manor Care Center
79 6th Ave, Grinnell, IA 50112
(515) 236-6511
Admin Patrick T Luft.
Licensure Intermediate care. *Beds* ICF 77. *Certified* Medicaid.

Mayflower Home
616 Broad St, Grinnell, IA 50112
(515) 236-6151
Admin Ted Mokricky. *Dir of Nursing* Karen Choate RN.
Licensure Intermediate care; Residential care; Retirement. *Beds* ICF 26; Residential care 34; Retirement 190. *Private Pay Patients* 85%. *Certified* Medicaid.
Owner Nonprofit corp.
Admissions Requirements Minimum age 55; Medical examination.
Staff RNs 3 (ft), 2 (pt); LPNs 1 (ft); Nurses' aides 9 (ft), 10 (pt); Activities coordinators 1 (ft), 1 (pt).
Affiliation United Church of Christ.
Facilities Dining room; Physical therapy room; Activities room; Chapel; Crafts room; Laundry room; Barber/Beauty shop; Library.
Activities Arts & crafts; Cards; Games; Reading groups; Prayer groups; Movies; Shopping trips; Dances/Social/Cultural gatherings; Intergenerational programs; Pet therapy.

St Francis Manor
2021 4th Ave, Grinnell, IA 50112
(515) 236-7592
Admin Dion Schrack. *Dir of Nursing* Connie Thomas.
Licensure Intermediate care; Retirement; Alzheimer's care. *Beds* ICF 74; Retirement apts 32. *Certified* Medicaid.
Owner Nonprofit corp.
Admissions Requirements Medical examination; Physician's request.
Staff RNs 3 (ft), 2 (pt); LPNs 5 (ft), 1 (pt); Nurses' aides 20 (ft), 6 (pt); Activities coordinators 2 (ft).
Facilities Dining room; Physical therapy room; Activities room; Chapel; Crafts room; Laundry room; Barber/Beauty shop.
Activities Arts & crafts; Cards; Games; Reading groups; Prayer groups; Movies; Shopping trips; Dances/Social/Cultural gatherings; Intergenerational programs; Pet therapy.

Griswold

Griswold Care Center Inc
106 Harrison St, Griswold, IA 51535
(712) 778-2534
Admin Lisa J Glasgo.
Licensure Intermediate care. *Beds* ICF 62. *Certified* Medicaid.

Grundy Center

Grundy Care Center
1st & "J" Ave, Grundy Center, IA 50638
(319) 824-5436
Admin LuAnn Modlin. *Dir of Nursing* Carol Bethke.
Licensure Intermediate care. *Beds* ICF 47. *Certified* Medicaid.
Owner Proprietary corp (Waverly Group).
Admissions Requirements Medical examination; Physician's request.
Staff LPNs 4 (ft); Activities coordinators 1 (ft).
Facilities Dining room; Physical therapy room; Activities room; Laundry room; Barber/Beauty shop.
Activities Arts & crafts; Cards; Games; Reading groups; Prayer groups; Movies; Shopping trips; Dances/Social/Cultural gatherings.

Grundy County Memorial Hospital
E "J" Ave, Grundy Center, IA 50638
Admin Loretta Jamerson.
Licensure Intermediate care. *Beds* ICF 55. *Certified* Medicaid; Medicare.
Owner Publicly owned.
Admissions Requirements Medical examination.
Staff Physicians 3 (ft); RNs 1 (ft), 1 (pt); LPNs 2 (ft), 1 (pt); Nurses' aides 12 (ft), 5 (pt); Physical therapists 1 (pt); Occupational therapists 1 (pt); Speech therapists 1 (pt); Activities coordinators 1 (ft); Dietitians 1 (pt); Podiatrists 1 (pt); Dentists 1 (pt); Urologists 1 (pt).
Facilities Dining room; Physical therapy room; Activities room; Laundry room.
Activities Arts & crafts; Games; Reading groups; Prayer groups; Movies; Dances/Social/Cultural gatherings.

Guthrie Center

New Homestead
RR 2 Box 13, Guthrie Center, IA 50115
(515) 747-2204
Admin Keith A Jennings. *Dir of Nursing* Gertrude Heise.
Licensure Intermediate care. *Beds* ICF 66. *Certified* Medicaid.
Owner Nonprofit corp.
Admissions Requirements Medical examination.
Staff RNs; LPNs; Nurses' aides; Physical therapists; Recreational therapists; Occupational therapists; Speech therapists; Activities coordinators; Dietitians.
Facilities Dining room; Physical therapy room; Activities room; Crafts room; Laundry room; Barber/Beauty shop.
Activities Arts & crafts; Cards; Games; Reading groups; Prayer groups; Movies; Dances/Social/Cultural gatherings.

Guttenberg

Guttenberg Care Center
400 Acre St, Guttenberg, IA 52052
(319) 252-2281
Admin Lou Ann Wikan.
Licensure Intermediate care. *Beds* ICF 93. *Certified* Medicaid.
Owner Proprietary corp (ABCM Corp).

Hampton

Franklin General Hospital
1720 Central Ave E, Hampton, IA 50441
(515) 456-4721, 456-2652 FAX
Admin Gary Busack. *Dir of Nursing* Joan Leiran RN. *Medical Dir* Surendra Seth MD.
Licensure Skilled care; Intermediate care; Acute care. *Beds* ICF 52; Swing beds Acute/SNF. *Private Pay Patients* 50%. *Certified* Medicaid; Medicare.
Owner Publicly owned.
Admissions Requirements Medical examination.
Staff Physicians 4 (pt); RNs 1 (ft), 3 (pt); LPNs 3 (pt); Nurses' aides 12 (ft), 11 (pt); Physical therapists 1 (pt); Occupational therapists (contracted); Speech therapists (contracted); Activities coordinators 1 (ft); Dietitians 1 (pt).
Facilities Dining room; Activities room; Chapel; Crafts room; Barber/Beauty shop; Park.
Activities Arts & crafts; Games; Reading groups; Prayer groups; Movies; Dances/Social/Cultural gatherings; Intergenerational programs; Dinner program for residents and guests; Auxiliary.

Franklin Nursing Home
105 1st Ave SW, Hampton, IA 50441
(515) 456-4724
Licensure Intermediate care. *Beds* 73. *Certified* Medicaid.

Hampton Care Center
700 2nd St SE, Hampton, IA 50441
(515) 456-4701
Admin Claudia Boeding.
Licensure Intermediate care. *Beds* ICF 97. *Certified* Medicaid.
Owner Proprietary corp (ABCM Corp).

Harlan

Baptist Memorial Home
2104 12th St, Harlan, IA 51537
(712) 755-5174
Admin John W Lusk. *Dir of Nursing* Arleatta Bartelsen RN.
Licensure Intermediate care; Residential care; Apartments. *Beds* ICF 71; Residential care 54; Apts 22. *Certified* Medicaid.
Owner Nonprofit corp (American Baptist Homes of the Midwest).
Admissions Requirements Minimum age 18; Medical examination; Physician's request.
Staff RNs 9 (ft); LPNs 8 (ft); Nurses' aides 39 (ft); Physical therapists 1 (pt); Speech therapists 1 (pt); Activities coordinators 2 (ft); Dietitians 1 (pt); Podiatrists 1 (pt); Audiologists 1 (pt).
Languages Danish.
Affiliation Baptist.
Facilities Dining room; Physical therapy room; Activities room; Chapel; Laundry room; Barber/Beauty shop; Library.
Activities Arts & crafts; Cards; Games; Reading groups; Movies; Shopping trips; Intergenerational programs; Pet therapy.

Hartley

Community Memorial Hospital
8th Ave W, Hartley, IA 51346
(712) 728-2428
Admin Thomas J Snyder.
Licensure Intermediate care. *Beds* ICF 43.

Hawarden

Hass Hillcrest Care Center
2121 Ave L, Hawarden, IA 51023
(712) 552-1074
Admin Dorinda Martin.
Medical Dir Marral Sheldon.
Licensure Intermediate care. *Beds* ICF 58. *Certified* Medicaid.
Owner Proprietary corp.
Admissions Requirements Medical examination; Physician's request.

Staff RNs 1 (ft); LPNs 2 (ft), 4 (pt); Nurses' aides 4 (ft), 30 (pt); Occupational therapists 1 (ft); Activities coordinators 1 (ft); Dietitians 1 (ft); Ophthalmologists 1 (pt).
Facilities Dining room; Physical therapy room; Activities room; Chapel; Laundry room; Barber/Beauty shop; Quiet room.
Activities Cards; Games; Reading groups; Prayer groups; Movies; Shopping trips; Dances/Social/Cultural gatherings.

Hills

Atrium Village
Brady & 3rd, Hills, IA 52235
(319) 679-2224
Admin Jessie Diers.
Licensure Intermediate care; Retirement. *Beds* ICF 20.
Owner Nonprofit corp.
Admissions Requirements Females only.
Staff RNs 2 (ft), 2 (pt); LPNs 2 (ft); Nurses' aides 4 (ft), 4 (pt); Activities coordinators 1 (pt).
Facilities Dining room; Physical therapy room; Activities room; Chapel; Laundry room; Barber/Beauty shop.
Activities Arts & crafts; Cards; Games; Reading groups; Prayer groups; Movies; Shopping trips.

Holstein

Holstein Good Samaritan Center
505 W 2nd, Holstein, IA 51025
(712) 368-4304
Admin John C Ashton. *Dir of Nursing* Genny Clark.
Licensure Intermediate care; ICF/Alzheimer's care. *Beds* ICF 46; Alzheimer's unit 14. *Certified* Medicaid.
Owner Nonprofit corp (Evangelical Lutheran/ Good Samaritan Society).
Staff Physicians; RNs; LPNs; Nurses' aides; Physical therapists; Occupational therapists; Speech therapists; Activities coordinators; Dietitians; Ophthalmologists; Podiatrists; Audiologists; Art therapists.
Languages German.
Affiliation Lutheran.
Facilities Dining room; Physical therapy room; Activities room; Chapel; Crafts room; Laundry room; Barber/Beauty shop; Library.
Activities Arts & crafts; Cards; Games; Reading groups; Prayer groups; Movies; Shopping trips; Dances/Social/Cultural gatherings; Intergenerational programs; Pet therapy.

Hull

Pleasant Acres
309 Railroad, Hull, IA 51239
(712) 439-2758
Admin Rebecca A Jones. *Dir of Nursing* Helen DeStigter RN.
Licensure Intermediate care. *Beds* ICF 50. *Certified* Medicaid.
Owner Proprietary corp (Waverly Group).
Admissions Requirements Medical examination; Physician's request.
Facilities Dining room; Physical therapy room; Laundry room; Barber/Beauty shop.
Activities Arts & crafts; Cards; Games; Reading groups; Prayer groups; Movies; Shopping trips; Dances/Social/Cultural gatherings; Bingo.

Humboldt

Humboldt Care Center—North
1111 11th Ave N, Humboldt, IA 50548
(515) 332-2623
Admin Deborah Johnson.
Licensure Intermediate care. *Beds* ICF 100. *Certified* Medicaid.
Admissions Requirements Medical examination; Physician's request.
Staff RNs 4 (ft), 4 (pt); Nurses' aides 30 (ft), 20 (pt); Activities coordinators 1 (ft), 1 (pt); Dietitians 1 (pt).
Facilities Dining room; Physical therapy room; Activities room; Crafts room; Laundry room; Barber/Beauty shop.
Activities Arts & crafts; Cards; Games; Reading groups; Prayer groups; Movies; Shopping trips; Dances/Social/Cultural gatherings.

Humboldt Care Center—South
Hwy 169 S, Humboldt, IA 50548
(515) 332-4104
Admin Deborah Johnson.
Licensure Intermediate care. *Beds* ICF 50. *Certified* Medicaid.
Admissions Requirements Physician's request.
Facilities Dining room; Physical therapy room; Activities room; Crafts room; Laundry room; Barber/Beauty shop.
Activities Arts & crafts; Cards; Games; Reading groups; Prayer groups; Movies; Shopping trips; Dances/Social/Cultural gatherings.

Ida Grove

Morningside Care Center
600 Morningside Ave, Ida Grove, IA 51445
(712) 364-3327
Admin Gary Harter.
Medical Dir Jagne Harter.
Licensure Intermediate care. *Beds* ICF 72. *Certified* Medicaid.
Staff RNs 1 (ft); LPNs 3 (ft), 3 (pt); Physical therapists 1 (pt); Activities coordinators 1 (ft); Dietitians 1 (pt); Audiologists 1 (pt); Dentists 1 (pt).
Facilities Dining room; Physical therapy room; Activities room; Laundry room; Barber/Beauty shop.
Activities Arts & crafts; Cards; Games; Reading groups; Prayer groups; Movies; Shopping trips; Dances/Social/Cultural gatherings.

Independence

East Towne Care Center
1700 3rd St N, Independence, IA 50644
(319) 334-7015
Admin Debra J Heldt.
Medical Dir Mrs Crawford.
Licensure Intermediate care. *Beds* ICF 55. *Certified* Medicaid.
Staff RNs 1 (pt); LPNs 4 (ft), 3 (pt); Nurses' aides 7 (ft), 20 (pt); Physical therapists 1 (pt); Recreational therapists 1 (pt); Occupational therapists 1 (pt); Speech therapists 1 (pt); Activities coordinators 1 (ft); Dietitians 1 (pt); Ophthalmologists 1 (pt); Podiatrists 1 (pt); Dentists 1 (pt).
Facilities Dining room; Physical therapy room; Barber/Beauty shop.
Activities Arts & crafts; Cards; Games; Reading groups; Prayer groups; Movies; Shopping trips; Dances/Social/Cultural gatherings.

Independence Care Center
1610 3rd St N, Independence, IA 50644
(319) 334-6039
Admin Debra J Heldt.
Licensure Intermediate care. *Beds* ICF 101. *Certified* Medicaid.

People's Nursing Care Center
803 E 1st St, Independence, IA 50644
(319) 334-6071
Admin Betty Meehan.
Licensure Intermediate care. *Beds* ICF 59. *Certified* Medicaid.

Indianola

Indianola Good Samaritan Center—East
708 S Jefferson, Indianola, IA 50125
(515) 961-2596
Admin Lanny Ward. *Dir of Nursing* Rosie Hunt.
Licensure Intermediate care. *Beds* ICF 101. *Private Pay Patients* 30%. *Certified* Medicaid.
Owner Nonprofit corp (Evangelical Lutheran/ Good Samaritan Society).
Admissions Requirements Medical examination.
Staff RNs 4 (ft), 2 (pt); LPNs 3 (ft), 3 (pt); Nurses' aides 23 (ft), 20 (pt); Physical therapists 1 (pt); Occupational therapists 1 (pt); Speech therapists 1 (pt); Activities coordinators 1 (ft); Dietitians 1 (ft).
Facilities Dining room; Physical therapy room; Activities room; Chapel; Crafts room; Laundry room; Barber/Beauty shop.
Activities Arts & crafts; Cards; Games; Reading groups; Prayer groups; Movies; Shopping trips; Dances/Social/Cultural gatherings.

Indianola Good Samaritan Center—West
709 S Jefferson, Indianola, IA 50125
(515) 961-2596
Admin Lanny Ward. *Dir of Nursing* Rosie Hunt.
Licensure Intermediate care. *Beds* ICF 41. *Private Pay Patients* 30%. *Certified* Medicaid.
Owner Nonprofit corp (Evangelical Lutheran/ Good Samaritan Society).
Admissions Requirements Medical examination.
Staff RNs 2 (ft); LPNs 3 (ft), 1 (pt); Nurses' aides 14 (ft), 12 (pt); Physical therapists 1 (pt); Recreational therapists 3 (ft); Occupational therapists 1 (pt); Speech therapists 1 (pt); Activities coordinators 1 (ft); Dietitians 1 (ft).
Facilities Dining room; Physical therapy room; Activities room; Chapel; Crafts room; Laundry room; Barber/Beauty shop.
Activities Arts & crafts; Cards; Games; Reading groups; Prayer groups; Movies; Shopping trips; Dances/Social/Cultural gatherings; Intergenerational programs.

Westview Care Center
1900 W 3rd Pl, Indianola, IA 50125
(515) 961-3189
Admin Deborah Swihart.
Licensure Intermediate care. *Beds* ICF 83. *Certified* Medicaid.
Owner Proprietary corp (ABCM Corp).

Iowa City

Beverly Manor Convalescent Center
605 Greenwood Dr, Iowa City, IA 52240
(319) 338-7912
Licensure Intermediate care. *Beds* ICF 87. *Certified* Medicaid.
Owner Proprietary corp (Magellan Investments).
Admissions Requirements Medical examination.
Staff RNs 5 (ft), 4 (pt); LPNs 2 (ft), 1 (pt); Nurses' aides 16 (ft), 16 (pt); Physical therapists 1 (pt); Activities coordinators 1 (ft), 1 (pt); Dietitians 1 (pt).
Facilities Dining room; Physical therapy room; Activities room; Crafts room; Laundry room; Barber/Beauty shop; Library; Outside patio.
Activities Arts & crafts; Cards; Games; Reading groups; Prayer groups; Movies; Shopping trips; Dances/Social/Cultural gatherings; Pet days; Visits by school children; Outings to restaurants.

Iowa City Care Center
3565 Rochester Ave, Iowa City, IA 52240
(319) 351-7460
Admin Vern Tott. *Dir of Nursing* Mary
Trentz. *Medical Dir* Glenys Williams MD.
Licensure Intermediate care; Alzheimer's care.
Beds ICF 89. *Private Pay Patients* 50%.
Certified Medicaid.
Owner Proprietary corp (Waverly Group).
Admissions Requirements Physician's request.
Staff Physicians 1 (pt); RNs 2 (ft), 2 (pt);
LPNs 5 (ft), 2 (pt); Nurses' aides 17 (ft), 8
(pt); Physical therapists 1 (pt); Occupational
therapists 1 (pt); Speech therapists 1 (pt);
Activities coordinators 1 (ft), 1 (pt);
Dietitians 1 (pt); Ophthalmologists 1 (pt);
Podiatrists 1 (pt); Audiologists 1 (pt).
Facilities Dining room; Physical therapy
room; Activities room; Chapel; Crafts room;
Laundry room; Barber/Beauty shop; Library.
Activities Arts & crafts; Cards; Games;
Reading groups; Prayer groups; Movies;
Shopping trips; Dances/Social/Cultural
gatherings; Intergenerational programs; Pet
therapy.

Oaknoll Retirement Residence
701 Oaknoll Dr, Iowa City, IA 52240
(319) 351-1720
Admin Felicia Hope.
Licensure Skilled care; Intermediate care. *Beds*
SNF 32; ICF 16. *Certified* Medicare.

Iowa Falls

Heritage Care Center
2320 Washington Ave, Iowa Falls, IA 50126
(515) 648-4250
Admin Marian L Long.
Licensure Intermediate care. *Beds* ICF 72.
Certified Medicaid.
Admissions Requirements Minimum age 18;
Medical examination; Physician's request.
Staff RNs 1 (ft); LPNs 3 (ft); Nurses' aides 11
(ft), 7 (pt); Physical therapists 1 (pt);
Recreational therapists 1 (ft); Occupational
therapists 1 (pt); Speech therapists 1 (pt);
Activities coordinators 1 (ft); Dietitians 1
(pt).
Facilities Dining room; Physical therapy
room; Activities room; Laundry room;
Barber/Beauty shop; Library.
Activities Arts & crafts; Cards; Games;
Reading groups; Prayer groups; Movies;
Shopping trips; Dances/Social/Cultural
gatherings.

Scenic City Manor
Manor Dr & Fremont, Iowa Falls, IA 50126
(515) 648-4671
Admin Glenn O Doupe.
Licensure Intermediate care. *Beds* ICF 61.
Certified Medicaid.

Jefferson

Greene County Medical Center
1000 W Lincolnway, Jefferson, IA 50129
(515) 386-2114, 386-3695 FAX
Admin Todd Linden; Karen Bossard, Asst/
Patient Svcs Dir.
Medical Dir Ken R Friday MD.
Licensure Intermediate care. *Beds* ICF 74.
Certified Medicaid; Medicare.
Owner Publicly owned.
Admissions Requirements Physician's request.
Staff RNs 3 (ft), 4 (pt); LPNs 3 (ft), 6 (pt);
Nurses' aides 13 (ft), 11 (pt); Physical
therapists 1 (ft); Occupational therapists 1
(pt); Speech therapists 1 (pt); Activities
coordinators 1 (ft); Dietitians 1 (ft);
Ophthalmologists 1 (pt); Podiatrists 1 (pt);
Audiologists 1 (pt).

Facilities Dining room; Physical therapy
room; Chapel; Barber/Beauty shop.
Activities Arts & crafts; Cards; Games;
Reading groups; Prayer groups; Movies;
Dances/Social/Cultural gatherings.

Jefferson Manor
100 E Sunset, Jefferson, IA 50129
(515) 386-4107
Admin Janet Proctor.
Licensure Intermediate care. *Beds* ICF 93.
Certified Medicaid.
Owner Proprietary corp (National Heritage).

Johnston

Children's Habilitation Center
5900 Pioneer Pkwy, Johnston, IA 50131
(515) 270-2205
Admin Clay Kennedy.
Medical Dir Sayeed Hussain MD.
Licensure Skilled care; Intermediate care for
mentally retarded. *Beds* SNF 19; ICF/MR
44. *Certified* Medicaid.
Admissions Requirements Minimum age Birth.
Staff RNs 9 (ft), 3 (pt); LPNs 8 (ft), 5 (pt);
Nurses' aides 15 (ft), 22 (pt); Physical
therapists 1 (ft); Recreational therapists 1
(ft); Occupational therapists 1 (ft); Speech
therapists 1 (pt); Activities coordinators 1
(ft); Dietitians 1 (pt); Dentists 2 (pt).
Facilities Dining room; Physical therapy
room; Activities room; Crafts room; Laundry
room; Barber/Beauty shop; Library; Game
room.
Activities Arts & crafts; Cards; Games;
Reading groups; Prayer groups; Movies;
Shopping trips; Dances/Social/Cultural
gatherings; Specific skill training in self-care,
prevocational, computers.

Bishop Drumm Care Center
5837 Winwood Dr, Johnston, IA 50131
(515) 270-1100
Admin Jospeh H Schulte.
Licensure Intermediate care. *Beds* ICF 120.
Certified Medicaid.
Affiliation Roman Catholic.

Kalona

Pleasantview Home
811 3rd St, Kalona, IA 52247
(319) 656-2421
Admin Francis B Harvey. *Dir of Nursing*
Phyllis Litwiller.
Licensure Intermediate care; Residential care;
Independent living; Low stimulus unit. *Beds*
ICF 60; Residential care 70; Low stimulus
unit 11; Independent living 30. *Certified*
Medicaid.
Owner Nonprofit corp.
Admissions Requirements Medical
examination.
Staff RNs; LPNs; Nurses' aides; Recreational
therapists; Activities coordinators; Dietitians.
Affiliation Mennonite.
Facilities Dining room; Physical therapy
room; Activities room; Barber/Beauty shop;
Spacious grounds; Van (wheelchair).
Activities Arts & crafts; Games; Prayer groups;
Shopping trips; Bible study; Quilting; Dinner
trips.

Kanawha

Kanawha Community Home
130 N 6th St, Kanawha, IA 50447
(515) 762-3302
Admin JoAnn Hunt RN. *Dir of Nursing*
Ethelene Jackson RN.
Licensure Intermediate care; Alzheimer's care.
Beds ICF 52. *Certified* Medicaid.
Owner Proprietary corp.
Admissions Requirements Medical
examination; Physician's request.

Staff RNs 2 (ft), 1 (pt); LPNs 1 (ft), 1 (pt);
Nurses' aides 5 (ft), 20 (pt); Physical
therapists (contracted); Occupational
therapists (consultant); Speech therapists
(consultant); Activities coordinators 1 (ft);
Dietitians (consultant); Audiologists
(contracted).
Facilities Dining room; Physical therapy
room; Activities room; Laundry room;
Barber/Beauty shop.
Activities Arts & crafts; Games; Prayer groups;
Movies; Intergenerational programs.

Keokuk

Keokuk Area Hospital
1600 Morgan St, Keokuk, IA 52632
(319) 524-7150
Admin Allan W Zastrow.
Licensure Skilled care. *Beds* SNF 12.

Keokuk Convalescent Center
500 Messenger Rd, Keokuk, IA 52632
(319) 524-5321
Admin Leona C Varner.
Licensure Skilled care; Intermediate care. *Beds*
SNF 21; ICF 105. *Certified* Medicaid;
Medicare.

River Hills in Keokuk
3140 Plank Rd, Keokuk, IA 52632
(319) 524-5772
Admin Lela June Barnes. *Dir of Nursing* Mary
Jo Woods RN.
Licensure Intermediate care. *Beds* ICF 63.
Private Pay Patients 50%. *Certified*
Medicaid.
Owner Proprietary corp.
Admissions Requirements Minimum age 18;
Medical examination; Physician's request.
Staff RNs 2 (ft), 1 (pt); LPNs 3 (ft), 1 (pt);
Nurses' aides 11 (ft), 16 (pt); Physical
therapists 1 (pt); Speech therapists 1 (pt);
Activities coordinators 1 (ft); Dietitians 1
(pt).
Facilities Dining room; Activities room;
Chapel; Laundry room; Barber/Beauty shop.
Activities Arts & crafts; Cards; Games;
Reading groups; Prayer groups; Dances/
Social/Cultural gatherings; Intergenerational
programs; Pet therapy.

Keosauqua

Van Buren Good Samaritan Center
Dodge & County Rd, Keosauqua, IA 52565
(319) 293-3761
Admin Tim Skardal. *Dir of Nursing* Linda
Corman.
Licensure Intermediate care. *Beds* ICF 75.
Private Pay Patients 33%. *Certified*
Medicaid.
Owner Nonprofit corp (Evangelical Lutheran/
Good Samaritan Society).
Admissions Requirements Minimum age 16;
Medical examination; Physician's request.
Staff RNs 3 (ft), 1 (pt); LPNs 3 (ft), 1 (pt);
Nurses' aides 10 (ft), 33 (pt); Activities
coordinators 1 (ft).
Affiliation Lutheran.
Facilities Dining room; Physical therapy
room; Activities room; Chapel; Crafts room;
Laundry room; Barber/Beauty shop.
Activities Arts & crafts; Cards; Games;
Reading groups; Prayer groups; Movies;
Shopping trips; Dances/Social/Cultural
gatherings; Pet therapy; Bible study.

Keota

Maplewood Manor Inc
County Line Rd, Keota, IA 52248
(515) 636-3400
Admin Constance C Ferrell. *Dir of Nursing*
Sheila Horras.

Licensure Intermediate care; Retirement. *Beds* ICF 54. *Private Pay Patients* 57%. *Certified* Medicaid; VA.
Owner Proprietary corp.
Admissions Requirements Medical examination; Physician's request.
Staff RNs 1 (ft), 7 (pt); Nurses' aides 10 (ft), 18 (pt); Physical therapists 1 (pt); Occupational therapists 1 (pt); Speech therapists 1 (pt); Activities coordinators 1 (ft); Dietitians 1 (pt); Podiatrists 1 (pt); Audiologists 1 (pt).
Facilities Dining room; Physical therapy room; Activities room; Crafts room; Laundry room; Barber/Beauty shop; Library.
Activities Arts & crafts; Cards; Games; Reading groups; Prayer groups; Movies; Shopping trips; Dances/Social/Cultural gatherings; Intergenerational programs; Pet therapy.

Keystone

Keystone Nursing Care Center
5th St E, Keystone, IA 52249
(319) 442-3234
Admin Susan Rieck.
Licensure Intermediate care. *Beds* ICF 45.

Kingsley

Colonial Manor
PO Box 407, 305 W 3rd, Kingsley, IA 51028
(712) 378-2400
Admin Donna L Enderlin.
Medical Dir Kate Henrich.
Licensure Intermediate care. *Beds* ICF 43. *Certified* Medicaid.
Owner Proprietary corp (Mercy Health Initiatives).
Admissions Requirements Minimum age 18; Medical examination; Physician's request.
Staff RNs; LPNs; Nurses' aides; Activities coordinators.
Facilities Dining room; Physical therapy room; Activities room; Chapel; Crafts room; Laundry room; Barber/Beauty shop; Library.
Activities Arts & crafts; Cards; Games; Reading groups; Prayer groups; Movies; Shopping trips; Dances/Social/Cultural gatherings; Adopt-a-grandparent.

Knoxville

Griffin Nursing Center
606 N 7th St, Knoxville, IA 50138
(515) 842-2187
Admin Hazel M Griffin.
Licensure Intermediate care. *Beds* ICF 65. *Certified* Medicaid.

West Ridge Manor
1201 W Jackson St, Knoxville, IA 50138
(515) 842-3153
Admin Denna M Ford.
Licensure Intermediate care. *Beds* ICF 78. *Certified* Medicaid.
Owner Proprietary corp (Mercy Health Initiatives).

Lake City

Shady Oaks
Hwy 175 W, Lake City, IA 51449
(712) 464-3106
Admin Lois Nadine Lindsay. *Dir of Nursing* Michelle Steinkamp RN. *Medical Dir* Paul Ferguson MD.
Licensure Skilled care; Intermediate care. *Beds* SNF 28; ICF 111. *Certified* Medicaid; Medicare.
Owner Privately owned.
Admissions Requirements Medical examination; Physician's request.

Staff Physicians 7 (pt); RNs 4 (ft), 13 (pt); LPNs 3 (ft), 5 (pt); Nurses' aides 14 (ft), 28 (pt); Physical therapists 1 (pt); Occupational therapists 1 (pt); Speech therapists 1 (pt); Activities coordinators 1 (ft), 1 (pt); Dietitians 1 (pt); Ophthalmologists 1 (pt); Pharmacists 1 (pt); Dentists 1 (pt); Social Services 1 (pt).
Facilities Dining room; Physical therapy room; Activities room; Crafts room; Laundry room; Barber/Beauty shop; Game room; Sun room; Conference room; Courtyard & gazebo; Fitness trail.
Activities Arts & crafts; Cards; Games; Reading groups; Prayer groups; Movies; Shopping trips; Exercise.

Lake Mills

Lake Mills Care Center
406 S 10th Ave E, Lake Mills, IA 50450
(515) 592-4900
Admin Naomi O Merryman.
Licensure Intermediate care. *Beds* ICF 101. *Certified* Medicaid.
Owner Proprietary corp (ABCM Corp).

Lake Park

Lake Park Care Center
1304 S Market, Lake Park, IA 51347
(712) 832-3691
Admin Robert J Hinz.
Licensure Intermediate care. *Beds* ICF 51. *Certified* Medicaid.

Lamoni

Lamoni Manor
215 S Oak St, Lamoni, IA 50140
(515) 784-3388
Admin Marlys Mathiesen. *Dir of Nursing* Velma Gleason RN.
Licensure Intermediate care. *Beds* ICF 51. *Certified* Medicaid.
Owner Proprietary corp (Mercy Health Initiatives).
Admissions Requirements Minimum age 16; Medical examination; Physician's request.
Staff RNs 2 (ft), 1 (pt); LPNs 2 (ft); Nurses' aides 13 (ft), 9 (pt); Physical therapists 1 (pt); Speech therapists 1 (pt); Activities coordinators 1 (ft); Dietitians 1 (pt); Audiologists 1 (pt); Dentists 1 (pt).
Facilities Dining room; Activities room; Laundry room; Barber/Beauty shop; Library.
Activities Arts & crafts; Cards; Games; Prayer groups; Movies; Shopping trips.

Lansing

Thornton Manor Nursing Home
1329 Main Ave, Lansing, IA 52151
(319) 538-4236
Admin Stephen H Haas. *Dir of Nursing* G Jane Hawes RN.
Licensure Intermediate care; Alzheimer's care. *Beds* ICF 60. *Certified* Medicaid.
Owner Nonprofit organization/foundation.
Admissions Requirements Medical examination.
Staff RNs 4 (ft); LPNs 4 (ft), 1 (pt); Nurses' aides 20 (ft), 7 (pt); Activities coordinators 1 (ft), 1 (pt); 10 (ft), 8 (pt) Social worker 1 (ft).
Facilities Dining room; Physical therapy room; Activities room; Chapel; Crafts room; Laundry room; Barber/Beauty shop.
Activities Arts & crafts; Cards; Games; Reading groups; Prayer groups; Movies; Shopping trips; Dances/Social/Cultural gatherings.

LaPorte City

Colonial Manor
Hwy 218 N, LaPorte City, IA 50651
(319) 342-2125
Licensure Intermediate care. *Beds* ICF 46. *Certified* Medicaid.
Owner Proprietary corp (Mercy Health Initiatives).
Admissions Requirements Minimum age 18; Medical examination; Physician's request.
Staff RNs 1 (ft); LPNs 3 (ft); Nurses' aides 5 (ft), 5 (pt); Physical therapists 1 (pt); Occupational therapists 1 (pt); Speech therapists 1 (pt); Activities coordinators 1 (ft); Dietitians 1 (pt); Podiatrists 1 (pt); Audiologists 1 (pt); Dentists 1 (pt).
Facilities Dining room; Laundry room; Barber/Beauty shop.
Activities Arts & crafts; Cards; Games; Reading groups; Prayer groups; Movies; Shopping trips; Dances/Social/Cultural gatherings; Weekly music therapy.

Laurens

Hovenden Memorial Good Samaritan Center
304 E Veterans Rd, Laurens, IA 50554
(712) 845-4915
Admin Cynthia L Fraser.
Licensure Intermediate care; Residential care. *Beds* ICF 42; Residential care 9. *Certified* Medicaid.
Owner Nonprofit corp (Evangelical Lutheran/Good Samaritan Society).

Le Mars

Abbey of LeMars
320 1st Ave SE, LeMars, IA 51031
(712) 546-7844
Admin Donald Butcher.
Licensure Intermediate care. *Beds* ICF 18.

Brentwood Good Samaritan Center
Hwy 3 E, Le Mars, IA 51031
(712) 546-4101
Admin Cameron L Liebenow.
Licensure Intermediate care. *Beds* ICF 65. *Certified* Medicaid.
Owner Nonprofit corp (Evangelical Lutheran/Good Samaritan Society).

Plymouth Manor Care Center
954 7th Ave SE, Le Mars, IA 51031
(712) 546-7831
Admin Marilyn K Kennedy.
Licensure Intermediate care. *Beds* ICF 83. *Certified* Medicaid.

Lenox

Lenox Care Center
111 E Van Buren, Lenox, IA 50851
(515) 333-2226
Admin Virginia Bennett. *Dir of Nursing* Mary Walter.
Licensure Intermediate care. *Beds* ICF 53. *Private Pay Patients* 35%. *Certified* Medicaid.
Owner Proprietary corp (Waverly Group).
Admissions Requirements Medical examination; Physician's request.
Staff RNs; LPNs; Nurses' aides; Physical therapists; Occupational therapists; Activities coordinators; Dietitians; Audiologists.
Facilities Dining room; Physical therapy room; Activities room; Laundry room; Barber/Beauty shop.
Activities Cards; Games; Reading groups; Prayer groups; Movies; Hay rides; Square dances; Car rides; Wheelchair walks.

Leon

Leon Care Center
200 Northern Ave, Leon, IA 50144
(515) 446-4833
Admin Gary D Martin. *Dir of Nursing*
Allyson Reynolds LPN.
Licensure Intermediate care. *Beds* ICF 61.
Certified Medicaid.
Owner Proprietary corp.
Admissions Requirements Medical
examination.
Staff RNs 1 (pt); LPNs 3 (ft), 2 (pt); Nurses'
aides 8 (ft), 11 (pt); Physical therapists 1
(pt); Activities coordinators 2 (pt); Dietitians
1 (pt).
Facilities Dining room; Activities room;
Crafts room; Laundry room; Barber/Beauty
shop.
Activities Arts & crafts; Cards; Games;
Reading groups; Prayer groups; Movies.

Westview Acres Care Center
PO Box 140, Leon, IA 50144
(515) 446-4165
Admin C Dean Dyke. *Dir of Nursing* Roberta
Brown.
Licensure Intermediate care. *Beds* ICF 91.
Private Pay Patients 43%. *Certified*
Medicaid.
Owner Proprietary corp (ABCM Corp).
Admissions Requirements Minimum age 16;
Medical examination; Physician's request.
Staff RNs 1 (ft); LPNs 8 (ft); Nurses' aides 23
(ft); Physical therapists 1 (pt); Speech
therapists 1 (pt); Activities coordinators 1
(ft), 1 (pt); Dietitians 1 (ft).
Facilities Dining room; Physical therapy
room; Laundry room; Barber/Beauty shop.
Activities Arts & crafts; Games; Reading
groups; Prayer groups; Movies; Dances/
Social/Cultural gatherings; Intergenerational
programs.

Logan

Westmont Care Center
314 S Elm, Logan, IA 51546
(712) 644-2922
Licensure Intermediate care; Residential care.
Beds ICF 73; Residential care 26. *Certified*
Medicaid.

Lone Tree

Lone Tree Health Care Center
Pioneer Rd, Lone Tree, IA 52755
(319) 629-4255
Admin Dale Van Dewater.
Licensure Intermediate care. *Beds* ICF 46.
Certified Medicaid.

Madrid

Madrid Home for the Aging
613 W North St, Madrid, IA 50156
(515) 795-3007
Admin William R Thayer; Betsy Warburton,
Asst. *Dir of Nursing* Carol Mallory RN.
Licensure Skilled care; Intermediate care;
Residential care; Alzheimer's care. *Beds*
SNF 40; ICF 99; Residential care 36.
Certified Medicaid; Medicare.
Owner Nonprofit corp.
Admissions Requirements Minimum age 16;
Medical examination.
Staff RNs; LPNs; Nurses' aides; Physical
therapists; Reality therapists; Recreational
therapists; Occupational therapists; Speech
therapists; Activities coordinators; Dietitians.
Facilities Dining room; Physical therapy
room; Activities room; Chapel; Crafts room;
Laundry room; Barber/Beauty shop; Library.

Activities Arts & crafts; Cards; Games;
Reading groups; Prayer groups; Movies;
Shopping trips; Dances/Social/Cultural
gatherings.

Malvern

Nishna Care Center
903 2nd Ave, Malvern, IA 51551
(712) 624-8300
Admin Geraldine A Reid. *Dir of Nursing* Rita
Maloney. *Medical Dir* Dr Fryek.
Licensure Intermediate care; Retirement;
Alzheimer's care. *Beds* ICF 51. *Certified*
Medicaid; Medicare.
Owner Privately owned.
Staff Physicians 5 (ft); RNs 1 (ft); LPNs 3 (ft);
Nurses' aides 12 (ft), 14 (pt); Physical
therapists 1 (ft); Reality therapists 1 (ft).
Facilities Dining room; Physical therapy
room; Activities room; Chapel; Crafts room;
Laundry room; Barber/Beauty shop; Library.
Activities Cards; Games; Reading groups;
Prayer groups; Movies; Shopping trips;
Dances/Social/Cultural gatherings.

Manchester

**Delaware County Memorial Hospital &
Memorial Care Center**
709 W Main, Manchester, IA 52057
(319) 927-7340
Admin Paul Albright; Lon Butikofer RN
PhDC, Asst. *Dir of Nursing* Jeanne Huber
RN. *Medical Dir* R R Boom MD.
Licensure Skilled care; Intermediate care. *Beds*
Swing beds SNF/ICF 37. *Private Pay
Patients* 50%. *Certified* Medicaid; Medicare.
Owner Publicly owned.
Admissions Requirements Minimum age 16;
Medical examination; Physician's request.
Staff RNs 4 (ft); LPNs 2 (ft), 1 (pt); Nurses'
aides 11 (ft), 6 (pt); Physical therapists 2 (ft);
Occupational therapists 1 (pt); Speech
therapists 1 (pt); Activities coordinators 1
(ft); Dietitians 1 (ft).
Facilities Dining room; Physical therapy
room; Activities room; Crafts room; Laundry
room; Barber/Beauty shop.
Activities Arts & crafts; Cards; Games;
Reading groups; Prayer groups; Movies;
Shopping trips; Dances/Social/Cultural
gatherings; Intergenerational programs; Pet
therapy.

Good Neighbor Home
105 McCarren Dr, Manchester, IA 52057
(319) 927-3907
Admin Stanley J Schryba. *Dir of Nursing*
Shirley Ross RN.
Licensure Intermediate care. *Beds* ICF 106.
Private Pay Patients 62%. *Certified*
Medicaid.
Owner Nonprofit corp.
Admissions Requirements Medical
examination; Physician's request.
Staff RNs 2 (ft), 3 (pt); LPNs 3 (ft), 5 (pt);
Nurses' aides 27 (ft), 18 (pt); Physical
therapists 2 (pt); Activities coordinators 2
(pt); Dietitians 1 (pt).
Affiliation Evangelical Lutheran.
Facilities Dining room; Physical therapy
room; Activities room; Chapel; Crafts room;
Barber/Beauty shop; Library.
Activities Arts & crafts; Cards; Games;
Reading groups; Prayer groups; Movies;
Shopping trips; Dances/Social/Cultural
gatherings; Intergenerational programs; Pet
therapy; Volunteer program.

Manilla

Manilla Manor
158 N 5th St, Manilla, IA 51454
(712) 654-6812
Admin Dana Jorgensen.

Licensure Intermediate care. *Beds* ICF 64.
Certified Medicaid.

Manly

Manly Care Center
Hwy 9 E, Manly, IA 50456
(515) 454-2223
Admin Claudia Abbott.
Medical Dir Dr Richard Munns.
Licensure Intermediate care. *Beds* ICF 69.
Certified Medicaid.
Owner Proprietary corp (Mercy Health
Initiatives).
Admissions Requirements Minimum age 21;
Medical examination; Physician's request.
Staff RNs 2 (ft), 3 (pt); LPNs 2 (ft), 2 (pt);
Nurses' aides 16 (ft), 10 (pt); Activities
coordinators 1 (ft); Dietitians 1 (pt).
Facilities Dining room; Physical therapy
room; Activities room; Crafts room; Laundry
room; Barber/Beauty shop; Library.
Activities Arts & crafts; Cards; Games;
Movies; Dances/Social/Cultural gatherings.

Manning

Manning Plaza
402 Main St, Manning, IA 51455
(712) 653-2422
Admin Ed Hackman. *Dir of Nursing* Aloha
Enenbach RN. *Medical Dir* Dr P L Myer.
Licensure Intermediate care. *Beds* ICF 58.
Private Pay Patients 50%. *Certified*
Medicaid.
Owner Nonprofit organization/foundation.
Admissions Requirements Minimum age 18;
Medical examination; Physician's request.
Staff Physicians 3 (pt); RNs 1 (ft), 2 (pt);
LPNs 4 (ft), 3 (pt); Physical therapists 1 (pt);
Recreational therapists 1 (ft), 1 (pt); Speech
therapists 1 (pt); Activities coordinators 1
(ft), 1 (pt); Dietitians 1 (pt); Podiatrists 1
(pt); Audiologists 1 (pt).
Facilities Dining room; Physical therapy
room; Activities room; Crafts room; Laundry
room.
Activities Arts & crafts; Cards; Games;
Reading groups; Prayer groups; Movies.

Manson

Manson Good Samaritan
1402 Main, Manson, IA 50563
(712) 469-3908
Admin Gail Blocker. *Dir of Nursing* Ella
Fistler. *Medical Dir* Dr Worthen.
Licensure Intermediate care; Adult day care.
Beds ICF 50. *Private Pay Patients* 50%.
Certified Medicaid.
Owner Nonprofit corp (Evangelical Lutheran/
Good Samaritan Society).
Admissions Requirements Medical
examination; Physician's request.
Staff RNs 2 (ft); LPNs 4 (ft); Nurses' aides 16
(ft); Physical therapists 1 (pt); Activities
coordinators 1 (ft); Dietitians 1 (pt);
Podiatrists 1 (pt).
Affiliation Lutheran.
Facilities Dining room; Physical therapy
room; Activities room; Chapel; Laundry
room; Barber/Beauty shop; Living area.
Activities Arts & crafts; Games; Reading
groups; Prayer groups; Movies; Dances/
Social/Cultural gatherings; Intergenerational
programs; Baking.

Mapleton

Maple Heights
Sunrise Ave, Mapleton, IA 51034
(712) 882-1680
Admin Eddie L Wright.
Licensure Intermediate care. *Beds* ICF 64.
Certified Medicaid.

Maquoketa

Crestridge
1015 Wesley Dr, Maquoketa, IA 52060
(319) 652-4968
Admin Holly Myatt.
Medical Dir Judy Herkleman.
Licensure Intermediate care. *Beds* ICF 101.
Certified Medicaid.
Owner Proprietary corp.
Admissions Requirements Medical
examination; Physician's request.
Staff RNs 3 (ft), 2 (pt); LPNs 6 (pt); Nurses'
aides 45 (pt); Activities coordinators 2 (ft).
Facilities Dining room; Physical therapy
room; Activities room; Chapel; Crafts room;
Laundry room; Barber/Beauty shop; Library;
Wheelchair height soda & liquor bar.
Activities Arts & crafts; Cards; Games;
Reading groups; Prayer groups; Movies;
Shopping trips; Dances/Social/Cultural
gatherings; Lots of entertainment type
groups.

Jackson County Public Hospital
700 W Grove St, Maquoketa, IA 52060
(319) 652-2474
Admin Karl C Schroeder. *Dir of Nursing*
Marcella Bormahl RN.
Licensure Skilled care. *Beds* SNF 18.
Owner Publicly owned.
Staff RNs 2 (ft), 1 (pt); LPNs 3 (ft), 1 (pt);
Nurses' aides 4 (ft), 7 (pt); Physical
therapists 1 (ft), 1 (pt); Recreational
therapists 1 (pt); Speech therapists 1 (pt);
Dietitians 1 (ft).

Maquoketa Care Center
McKinsey Rd, Maquoketa, IA 52060
(319) 652-5195
Admin Betty L Reed.
Medical Dir Edra Clasen.
Licensure Intermediate care. *Beds* ICF 66.
Certified Medicaid.
Owner Proprietary corp.
Admissions Requirements Minimum age 18;
Medical examination; Physician's request.
Staff RNs 1 (ft), 2 (pt); LPNs 2 (ft), 4 (pt);
Nurses' aides 10 (ft), 17 (pt); Activities
coordinators 2 (ft); Dietitians 1 (pt).
Facilities Dining room; Activities room;
Crafts room; Laundry room; Barber/Beauty
shop.
Activities Arts & crafts; Cards; Games;
Reading groups; Prayer groups; Movies;
Shopping trips; Dances/Social/Cultural
gatherings.

Marengo

Rose Haven Nursing Home
1500 Franklyn Ave, Marengo, IA 52301
(319) 642-5533
Admin David Yearian.
Medical Dir Alice Prince.
Licensure Intermediate care. *Beds* ICF 58.
Certified Medicaid.
Owner Privately owned.
Admissions Requirements Minimum age 16;
Medical examination.
Staff RNs 2 (ft), 2 (pt); LPNs 2 (ft); Nurses'
aides 17 (ft), 8 (pt); Physical therapists 1
(pt); Activities coordinators 1 (ft); Dietitians
1 (pt).
Facilities Dining room; Activities room;
Chapel; Crafts room; Laundry room; Barber/
Beauty shop.
Activities Arts & crafts; Cards; Games;
Reading groups; Prayer groups; Movies;
Shopping trips; Dances/Social/Cultural
gatherings.

Marion

Abbe Center for Community Care
1860 County Home Rd, Marion, IA 52302-
9753
(319) 398-3534
Admin Daniel E Strellner.
Medical Dir Richard Hodge, James Bell, Steve
Runde; Merry Elliott.
Licensure Intermediate care; Residential care.
Beds ICF 32; Residential care 327. *Certified*
Medicaid.
Owner Nonprofit corp.
Admissions Requirements Minimum age 16;
Medical examination; Physician's request.
Staff Physicians 3 (pt); RNs 6 (ft), 3 (pt);
LPNs 4 (ft), 4 (pt); Nurses' aides 30 (ft), 20
(pt); Recreational therapists 4 (ft); Activities
coordinators 3 (ft); Dietitians 1 (pt);
Ophthalmologists 1 (pt); Psychiatrist 1 (pt).
Facilities Dining room; Activities room;
Crafts room; Laundry room; Barber/Beauty
shop; Dayroom.
Activities Arts & crafts; Cards; Games;
Reading groups; Movies; Shopping trips;
Dances/Social/Cultural gatherings; Group
therapy.

Crestview Acres
1485 Grand Ave, Marion, IA 52302
(319) 377-4823
Admin Vivian M DeGreef. *Dir of Nursing*
Alice M Shea RN.
Licensure Intermediate care. *Beds* ICF 129.
Certified Medicaid.
Owner Proprietary corp (Quality Health Care
Specialists Inc).
Admissions Requirements Medical
examination.
Staff RNs 3 (ft); LPNs 8 (ft), 1 (pt); Nurses'
aides 41 (ft); Physical therapists 1 (pt);
Occupational therapists 1 (pt); Speech
therapists 1 (pt); Activities coordinators 2
(ft); Dietitians 1 (pt); Podiatrists 1 (pt).
Facilities Dining room; Physical therapy
room; Activities room; Chapel; Crafts room;
Laundry room; Barber/Beauty shop.
Activities Arts & crafts; Cards; Games;
Reading groups; Prayer groups; Movies;
Dances/Social/Cultural gatherings.

Linn Manor Care Center
1140 Elim Dr, Marion, IA 52302
(319) 377-4611
Admin Grant L Hagen.
Licensure Intermediate care. *Beds* ICF 44.
Certified Medicaid.

Willow Garden Care Center
455 31st St, Marion, IA 52302
(319) 377-7363, 377-6022 FAX
Admin Sharon Vogel. *Dir of Nursing* Marty
Scharff. *Medical Dir* Dr Louvar.
Licensure Intermediate care. *Beds* ICF 91.
Private Pay Patients 65%. *Certified*
Medicaid.
Owner Nonprofit corp (AHF-Iowa-Kentucky
Inc).
Admissions Requirements Medical
examination; Physician's request.
Staff RNs 7 (ft); LPNs 9 (ft), 1 (pt); Nurses'
aides 25 (ft), 7 (pt); Physical therapists 1
(pt); Occupational therapists 1 (pt); Speech
therapists 1 (pt); Activities coordinators 1
(ft), 1 (pt); Dietitians 1 (pt).
Facilities Dining room; Physical therapy
room; Activities room; Crafts room; Laundry
room; Barber/Beauty shop; Library; 3
Outdoor patios.
Activities Arts & crafts; Cards; Games;
Reading groups; Prayer groups; Movies;
Shopping trips; Dances/Social/Cultural
gatherings; Intergenerational programs; Pet
therapy.

Winslow House
3456 Indian Creek Rd, Marion, IA 52302
(319) 377-8296

Admin Barry Morrissey.
Licensure Intermediate care. *Beds* ICF 50.
Certified Medicaid.

Marshalltown

Grandview Heights
910 E Olive St, Marshalltown, IA 50158
(515) 752-4581
Admin Lila M Koonce.
Licensure Intermediate care. *Beds* ICF 129.
Certified Medicaid.

Marshall County Care Facility
2369 Jessup Ave, Marshalltown, IA 50158
(515) 752-3694
Admin Marian Malloy. *Dir of Nursing* Delaine
Aves RN.
Licensure Intermediate care; Residential care.
Beds ICF 80; Residential care 64. *Certified*
Medicaid.
Owner Nonprofit organization/foundation.
Admissions Requirements Minimum age 16;
Medical examination; Physician's request.
Staff RNs 4 (ft); LPNs 5 (ft), 3 (pt); Nurses'
aides 37 (ft), 12 (pt); Physical therapists 1
(pt); Recreational therapists 3 (pt); Activities
coordinators 1 (ft); Dietitians 1 (pt);
Pharmacists 1 (pt); Social workers 1 (pt).
Facilities Dining room; Physical therapy
room; Activities room; Chapel; Crafts room;
Laundry room; Barber/Beauty shop; Library.
Activities Arts & crafts; Cards; Games;
Reading groups; Prayer groups; Movies;
Shopping trips; Dances/Social/Cultural
gatherings; Bowling; Flea markets; Fishing;
Cooking; Kitchen band; School.

Marshalltown Manor Care Center
2206 S Center St, Marshalltown, IA 50158
(515) 752-4553
Admin Niel Froning.
Medical Dir Brenda Thompson.
Licensure Intermediate care. *Beds* ICF 82.
Certified Medicaid.
Owner Proprietary corp (Mercy Health
Initiatives).
Admissions Requirements Minimum age 18;
Medical examination.
Staff RNs 5 (ft), 2 (pt); LPNs 2 (ft), 1 (pt);
Nurses' aides 30 (ft), 5 (pt); Activities
coordinators 1 (ft), 1 (pt).
Facilities Dining room; Activities room;
Laundry room; Barber/Beauty shop.
Activities Arts & crafts; Cards; Games;
Reading groups; Prayer groups; Movies;
Shopping trips; Dances/Social/Cultural
gatherings; Bingo.

Marshalltown Medical Surgical Center Skilled Nursing Facility
3 S 4th Ave, Marshalltown, IA 50158
(515) 752-2738
Admin Omar Varan. *Dir of Nursing* Roberta
Brandenberg RN; Dorothy Stanley, Nurse
Mgr. *Medical Dir* Dr Michael Mirovsky.
Licensure Skilled care. *Beds* SNF 26. *Certified*
Medicaid; Medicare.
Owner Nonprofit corp.
Admissions Requirements Minimum age 16;
Medical examination; Physician's request.
Staff Physicians 40 (ft); RNs 4 (ft), 3 (pt);
LPNs 4 (ft), 7 (pt); Nurses' aides 7 (ft), 12
(pt); Physical therapists 3 (ft); Occupational
therapists 1 (ft); Speech therapists
(consultant); Activities coordinators 1 (pt);
Dietitians 3 (pt); Ophthalmologists 6 (ft);
Podiatrists 2 (ft); Audiologists (consultant);
Ward clerks 1 (ft), 4 (pt).
Facilities Dining room; Physical therapy
room; Activities room; Chapel; Crafts room;
Laundry room; Barber/Beauty shop; Library.
Activities Arts & crafts; Cards; Games; Prayer
groups; Movies; Pet therapy.

Villa del Sol
2401 S 2nd St, Marshalltown, IA 50158
(515) 752-1553

Admin Janice Plahn. *Dir of Nursing* LeeAnn Goecke RN. *Medical Dir* Cindy Geater.
Licensure Intermediate care; Residential care. *Beds* ICF 88; Residential care 29. *Certified* Medicaid.
Owner Privately owned.
Admissions Requirements Minimum age 16; Medical examination.
Staff RNs; LPNs; Nurses' aides; Activities coordinators.
Facilities Dining room; Activities room; Barber/Beauty shop.
Activities Arts & crafts; Games; Reading groups; Prayer groups; Movies; Intergenerational programs; Pet therapy.

Mason City

Americana Healthcare Center
222 S Pierce Ave, Mason City, IA 50401
(515) 423-3355
Admin Glen E Bandel. *Dir of Nursing* Mary Jane Birkholz. *Medical Dir* Bruce Harlan.
Licensure Skilled care. *Beds* SNF 77. *Private Pay Patients* 66%. *Certified* Medicaid; Medicare.
Owner Proprietary corp (Manor Health Care Corp).
Facilities Dining room; Physical therapy room; Activities room; Laundry room; Barber/Beauty shop.

Cerro Gordo County Care Facility
RR 1, Mason City, IA 50401
(515) 421-3128
Admin Monica M Murray.
Licensure Intermediate care. *Beds* ICF 15.

Good Shepherd Geriatric Center
302 2nd St NE, Mason City, IA 50401
(515) 424-1740
Admin Barry Miller.
Licensure Skilled care; Intermediate care; Residential care. *Beds* SNF 20; ICF 236; Residential care 10. *Certified* Medicaid; Medicare.

Heritage Care Center
501 S Kentucky, Mason City, IA 50401
(515) 423-2121
Admin Angela A Klus. *Dir of Nursing* Maggie Caldwell RN. *Medical Dir* A E McMahon MD.
Licensure Skilled care; Intermediate care. *Beds* Swing beds SNF/ICF 110. *Certified* Medicaid; Medicare; VA.
Owner Proprietary corp (ABCM Corp).
Admissions Requirements Minimum age 16; Medical examination; Physician's request.
Staff RNs 5 (ft); LPNs 10 (ft); Nurses' aides 52 (ft); Physical therapists (consultant); Occupational therapists (consultant); Speech therapists (consultant); Activities coordinators 2 (ft).
Facilities Dining room; Physical therapy room; Activities room; Laundry room; Barber/Beauty shop.
Activities Arts & crafts; Cards; Games; Reading groups; Prayer groups; Movies; Shopping trips; Dances/Social/Cultural gatherings.

I O O F Home
1037 19th St SW, Mason City, IA 50401
(515) 423-0428
Admin Helen Dumont. *Dir of Nursing* Sylvia Lloyd. *Medical Dir* Dr Harlan.
Licensure Intermediate care; Residential care. *Beds* ICF 64; Residential care 25. *Private Pay Patients* 60%. *Certified* Medicaid.
Owner Nonprofit corp.
Admissions Requirements Medical examination.
Staff Physicians 2 (pt); RNs 3 (ft), 1 (pt); LPNs 6 (ft), 1 (pt); Nurses' aides 25 (ft), 9 (pt); Physical therapists 1 (pt); Occupational

therapists 1 (pt); Speech therapists 1 (pt); Activities coordinators 2 (ft), 1 (pt); Dietitians 1 (pt).
Affiliation Independent Order of Odd Fellows & Rebekahs.
Facilities Dining room; Physical therapy room; Activities room; Chapel; Crafts room; Laundry room; Barber/Beauty shop.
Activities Arts & crafts; Cards; Games; Reading groups; Prayer groups; Movies; Shopping trips; Dances/Social/Cultural gatherings; Intergenerational programs; Pet therapy.

McGregor

Great River Care Center
Hwy 18 S, McGregor, IA 52044
(319) 873-3527
Admin Glen J O'Loughlin.
Licensure Intermediate care. *Beds* ICF 51. *Certified* Medicaid.
Admissions Requirements Minimum age 18; Medical examination.
Staff RNs 1 (ft), 2 (pt); LPNs 4 (pt); Nurses' aides 3 (ft), 20 (pt); Activities coordinators 1 (ft); Dietitians 1 (pt).
Facilities Dining room; Physical therapy room; Laundry room; Barber/Beauty shop.
Activities Arts & crafts; Cards; Games; Prayer groups; Shopping trips; Dances/Social/Cultural gatherings.

Mechanicsville

Mechanicsville Care Center
206 4th St, Mechanicsville, IA 52306
(319) 432-7235
Admin Helen B Shelden.
Licensure Intermediate care. *Beds* ICF 69. *Certified* Medicaid.
Owner Proprietary corp (Mercy Health Initiatives).

Mediapolis

Bethesda Care Center
608 Prairie St, Mediapolis, IA 52637
(319) 394-3991
Admin Joan A Egan. *Dir of Nursing* Norma Poland. *Medical Dir* Dr J F Roules.
Licensure Intermediate care; Retirement. *Beds* ICF 62; Retirement 4. *Private Pay Patients* 40%. *Certified* Medicaid.
Owner Proprietary corp (Meritcare Inc).
Admissions Requirements Medical examination; Physician's request.
Staff RNs 2 (ft), 4 (pt); LPNs 3 (ft), 3 (pt); Nurses' aides 15 (ft), 13 (pt); Activities coordinators 1 (ft), 1 (pt); Dietitians 1 (pt).
Facilities Dining room; Physical therapy room; Activities room; Crafts room; Laundry room; Barber/Beauty shop.
Activities Arts & crafts; Cards; Games; Reading groups; Prayer groups; Movies; Shopping trips; Dances/Social/Cultural gatherings; Intergenerational programs; Pet therapy.

Milford

Milford Nursing Center
1600 13th St, Milford, IA 51351
(712) 338-4742
Admin Sandra Bertelsen. *Dir of Nursing* Peg Reck.
Licensure Intermediate care. *Beds* ICF 50. *Private Pay Patients* 68%. *Certified* Medicaid.
Owner Privately owned.
Admissions Requirements Medical examination.
Staff RNs 2 (ft); LPNs 3 (ft); Nurses' aides 9 (ft), 8 (pt); Dietitians 1 (pt).

Facilities Dining room; Activities room; Chapel; Crafts room; Laundry room; Barber/Beauty shop.
Activities Arts & crafts; Cards; Games; Reading groups; Prayer groups; Movies; Shopping trips; Dances/Social/Cultural gatherings; Intergenerational programs; Pet therapy.

Missouri Valley

Longview Home
1010 Longview Rd, Missouri Valley, IA 51555
(712) 642-2264
Admin John Sherer. *Dir of Nursing* Diane Nuzum RN.
Licensure Intermediate care. *Beds* ICF 78. *Certified* Medicaid; VA.
Owner Privately owned.
Staff RNs 1 (ft), 1 (pt); LPNs 4 (ft), 2 (pt); Nurses' aides 20 (ft), 10 (pt); Activities coordinators 2 (ft).
Facilities Dining room; Physical therapy room; Activities room; Chapel; Crafts room; Laundry room; Barber/Beauty shop.
Activities Arts & crafts; Cards; Games; Reading groups; Prayer groups; Movies; Shopping trips; Dances/Social/Cultural gatherings.

Mitchellville

Mitchell Village Care Center
114 Carter St, Mitchellville, IA 50169
(515) 967-3726
Admin Roberta Nye. *Dir of Nursing* Linda Wunn RN. *Medical Dir* Stan Haag MD.
Licensure Intermediate care. *Beds* ICF 65. *Private Pay Patients* 30%. *Certified* Medicaid.
Owner Proprietary corp (Quality Health Care Specialists Inc).
Admissions Requirements Medical examination; Physician's request.
Staff Physicians 1 (pt); RNs 1 (ft); LPNs 5 (ft); Nurses' aides 18 (ft); Physical therapists 1 (pt); Reality therapists 1 (ft); Recreational therapists 1 (ft); Occupational therapists 1 (pt); Speech therapists 1 (pt); Activities coordinators 1 (ft); Dietitians 1 (pt); Ophthalmologists 1 (pt); Podiatrists 1 (pt); Audiologists 1 (pt).
Facilities Dining room; Physical therapy room; Activities room; Laundry room; Barber/Beauty shop.
Activities Arts & crafts; Cards; Games; Reading groups; Prayer groups; Movies; Shopping trips; Dances/Social/Cultural gatherings; Intergenerational programs; Pet therapy.

Montezuma

Senior Home
Meadow Lane Dr, Montezuma, IA 50171
(515) 623-5497
Admin Ted Powell. *Dir of Nursing* Jeri Creswell RN.
Licensure Intermediate care. *Beds* ICF 51. *Certified* Medicaid.
Owner Proprietary corp.
Admissions Requirements Medical examination.
Staff RNs 1 (ft), 3 (pt); LPNs 2 (ft), 3 (pt); Nurses' aides 8 (ft), 10 (pt); Activities coordinators 1 (ft).
Facilities Dining room; Laundry room; Barber/Beauty shop.
Activities Arts & crafts; Cards; Games; Reading groups; Prayer groups; Movies.

Monticello

Senior Home
500 Pine Haven Dr, Monticello, IA 52310
(319) 465-5415

Licensure Intermediate care. *Beds* ICF 133. *Certified* Medicaid.
Admissions Requirements Medical examination; Physician's request.
Staff RNs 2 (ft), 3 (pt); LPNs 2 (ft), 4 (pt); Nurses' aides 10 (ft), 24 (pt); Physical therapists; Occupational therapists; Speech therapists; Activities coordinators 1 (ft), 1 (pt); Dietitians; Audiologists; Dentists; Social workers.
Facilities Dining room; Physical therapy room; Activities room; Chapel; Laundry room; Barber/Beauty shop; Library.
Activities Arts & crafts; Cards; Games; Reading groups; Prayer groups; Movies; Shopping trips; Dances/Social/Cultural gatherings.

Montrose

Montrose Health Center
300 S 7th St, Montrose, IA 52639
(319) 463-5438
Admin Sr Donna Venteicher.
Licensure Intermediate care; Residential care. *Beds* ICF 60; Residential care 20. *Certified* Medicaid.
Admissions Requirements Minimum age 16; Medical examination.
Staff RNs 2 (ft), 3 (pt); LPNs 1 (ft), 2 (pt); Nurses' aides 16 (ft), 6 (pt); Activities coordinators 2 (ft).
Facilities Dining room; Activities room; Crafts room; Laundry room; Barber/Beauty shop; Examination room.
Activities Arts & crafts; Cards; Games; Reading groups; Prayer groups; Movies; Shopping trips; Dances/Social/Cultural gatherings.

Morning Sun

Morning Sun Care Center
Washington-Manor Rd, Morning Sun, IA 52640
(319) 868-7751
Admin Barbara Hirt. *Dir of Nursing* Nancy Wagner RN.
Licensure Intermediate care. *Beds* ICF 60. *Certified* Medicaid.
Owner Proprietary corp.
Staff RNs 2 (ft), 1 (pt); LPNs 2 (ft); Nurses' aides 10 (ft), 7 (pt); Physical therapists; Activities coordinators 1 (ft); Dietitians 1 (pt).
Facilities Dining room; Activities room; Laundry room; Barber/Beauty shop; Library.
Activities Arts & crafts; Games; Reading groups; Prayer groups; Movies; Dances/Social/Cultural gatherings.

Mount Ayr

Clearview Home
406 W Washington St, Mount Ayr, IA 50854
(515) 464-2240
Admin Richard C Routh.
Licensure Intermediate care. *Beds* ICF 97. *Certified* Medicaid.

Mt Ayr Health Care Center
Hwy 2 E, Mount Ayr, IA 50854
(515) 464-3204
Admin Lester W Gross.
Licensure Intermediate care. *Beds* ICF 53. *Certified* Medicaid.
Admissions Requirements Minimum age 18; Medical examination; Physician's request.
Staff Physicians; RNs; LPNs; Nurses' aides; Physical therapists; Activities coordinators; Dietitians; Ophthalmologists; Audiologists; Dentists.
Facilities Dining room; Physical therapy room; Activities room; Chapel; Crafts room; Laundry room; Barber/Beauty shop; Library; Woodworking shop.

Activities Arts & crafts; Cards; Games; Reading groups; Prayer groups; Movies; Shopping trips; Dances/Social/Cultural gatherings.

Mount Pleasant

Henry County Memorial Hospital Long-Term Care Unit
Saunders Pk, Mount Pleasant, IA 52641
(319) 385-3141
Admin Robert A Miller. *Dir of Nursing* Ava Seibert RN.
Licensure Skilled care; Intermediate care. *Beds* SNF 10; ICF 21. *Certified* Medicaid; Medicare.
Owner Publicly owned.
Admissions Requirements Medical examination; Physician's request.
Staff RNs 2 (ft); LPNs 4 (pt); Nurses' aides 12 (pt); Physical therapists 3 (ft); Occupational therapists 1 (pt); Speech therapists 1 (pt); Activities coordinators 1 (ft); Dietitians 1 (ft); Podiatrists 1 (pt).
Facilities Dining room; Physical therapy room; Activities room; Laundry room.
Activities Arts & crafts; Cards; Games; Reading groups; Prayer groups; Movies; Shopping trips; Dances/Social/Cultural gatherings; Pet therapy.

Mapleleaf Healthcare Center
701 Mapleleaf Dr, Mount Pleasant, IA 52641
(319) 385-2293
Admin Dale L Showalter. *Dir of Nursing* Dona Harloff.
Licensure Intermediate care; Retirement. *Beds* ICF 84. *Private Pay Patients* 50%. *Certified* Medicaid.
Owner Proprietary corp.
Admissions Requirements Minimum age 16; Medical examination; Physician's request.
Staff RNs 3 (ft), 2 (pt); LPNs 3 (ft), 2 (pt); Nurses' aides 22 (ft), 8 (pt); Activities coordinators 1 (ft), 1 (pt).
Facilities Dining room; Physical therapy room; Activities room; Chapel; Crafts room; Laundry room; Barber/Beauty shop; Child care center.
Activities Arts & crafts; Cards; Games; Reading groups; Prayer groups; Movies; Shopping trips; Dances/Social/Cultural gatherings; Intergenerational programs.

Pleasant Manor Care Center
413 Broadway, Mount Pleasant, IA 52641
(319) 385-8095
Admin Barry Miller.
Licensure Intermediate care; Alzheimer's care. *Beds* ICF 50. *Certified* Medicaid.
Owner Proprietary corp.
Admissions Requirements Minimum age 18; Medical examination; Physician's request.
Staff RNs 3 (ft); LPNs 1 (ft), 1 (pt); Nurses' aides 8 (ft), 8 (pt); Activities coordinators 1 (ft).
Facilities Dining room; Activities room; Laundry room; Barber/Beauty shop.
Activities Arts & crafts; Cards; Games; Reading groups; Prayer groups; Dances/Social/Cultural gatherings.

Mount Vernon

Hallmark Care Center
Hwy 30 & 1, Mount Vernon, IA 52314
(319) 895-8891
Admin Peggy Chensvold.
Licensure Intermediate care. *Beds* ICF 68. *Certified* Medicaid.
Owner Proprietary corp (ABCM Corp).
Admissions Requirements Minimum age 18; Medical examination; Physician's request.
Staff Physical therapists; Reality therapists; Recreational therapists; Occupational therapists; Speech therapists; Activities coordinators 1 (ft); Dietitians 1 (ft).

Facilities Dining room; Physical therapy room; Activities room; Crafts room; Laundry room; Barber/Beauty shop; Library.
Activities Arts & crafts; Cards; Games; Reading groups; Prayer groups; Movies; Dances/Social/Cultural gatherings.

Muscatine

Bethesda Care Center
3440 Mulberry Ave, Muscatine, IA 52761
(319) 263-2194
Admin Cheryl M Guild. *Dir of Nursing* Arlene Clark RN. *Medical Dir* Dr John Ellis.
Licensure Intermediate care; Retirement. *Beds* ICF 130; Retirement apts 18. *Private Pay Patients* 52%. *Certified* Medicaid.
Owner Proprietary corp (Meritcare/MTC West).
Admissions Requirements Medical examination; Physician's request.
Staff RNs 5 (ft), 4 (pt); LPNs 6 (ft); Nurses' aides 38 (ft), 17 (pt); Physical therapists (consultant); Activities coordinators 1 (ft), 3 (pt); Dietitians (consultant); Social workers 1 (ft).
Facilities Dining room; Physical therapy room; Activities room; Chapel; Laundry room; Barber/Beauty shop.
Activities Arts & crafts; Cards; Games; Prayer groups; Movies; Shopping trips; Dances/Social/Cultural gatherings; Intergenerational programs; Pet therapy.

Lutheran Home
Hershey Ave, Muscatine, IA 52761
(319) 263-1241
Admin Raymond F Poe.
Licensure Skilled care; Intermediate care. *Beds* SNF 25; ICF 121. *Certified* Medicaid.
Admissions Requirements Medical examination; Physician's request.
Staff RNs 4 (ft), 2 (pt); LPNs 7 (ft); Nurses' aides 70 (ft), 30 (pt); Occupational therapists 1 (ft); Activities coordinators 1 (ft).
Affiliation Lutheran.
Facilities Dining room; Physical therapy room; Activities room; Chapel; Crafts room; Laundry room; Barber/Beauty shop; Library.
Activities Arts & crafts; Cards; Games; Reading groups; Movies; Shopping trips; Dances/Social/Cultural gatherings; Bible study.

Muscatine Care Center
2002 Cedar St, Muscatine, IA 52761
(319) 264-2023
Admin Sharon Schumaker. *Dir of Nursing* Karen Schnell.
Licensure Intermediate care. *Beds* ICF 100. *Certified* Medicaid.
Owner Privately owned.
Admissions Requirements Medical examination; Physician's request.
Staff RNs; LPNs; Nurses' aides; Activities coordinators.
Facilities Dining room; Activities room; Crafts room; Laundry room; Barber/Beauty shop.
Activities Arts & crafts; Cards; Games; Reading groups; Prayer groups; Movies; Shopping trips; Intergenerational programs; Pet therapy.

Muscatine General Hospital
1501 Cedar St, Muscatine, IA 52761
(319) 264-9100
Admin Jonathan Goble.
Licensure Skilled care. *Beds* SNF 5.

Nevada

Rolling Green Village
100 6th St, Nevada, IA 50201
(515) 382-6556
Admin Karen J Harrison. *Dir of Nursing* Mary Wathen.

Licensure Intermediate care. *Beds* ICF 69. *Certified* Medicaid.
Owner Proprietary corp (ABCM Corp).
Admissions Requirements Medical examination; Physician's request.
Staff RNs 1 (ft); LPNs 4 (ft), 2 (pt); Nurses' aides 16 (ft), 4 (pt); Activities coordinators 1 (ft); Dietitians 1 (pt); Podiatrists 1 (pt).
Languages Spanish.
Facilities Dining room; Activities room; Crafts room; Laundry room; Barber/Beauty shop.
Activities Arts & crafts; Cards; Games; Reading groups; Prayer groups; Movies; Shopping trips; Dances/Social/Cultural gatherings; Wine & cheese parties; Senior citizens luncheon; Pet therapy.

Story County Hospital
630 6th St, Nevada, IA 50201
(515) 382-2111
Admin Phillip Cline. *Dir of Nursing* Nancy Haas RN. *Medical Dir* Dr Pandu Bonthala.
Licensure Intermediate care; Alzheimer's care. *Beds* ICF 80. *Certified* Medicaid; Medicare.
Owner Proprietary corp (Health One Health Care).
Admissions Requirements Medical examination; Physician's request.
Staff RNs 3 (ft); LPNs 8 (ft), 4 (pt); Physical therapists 1 (ft), 1 (pt); Recreational therapists 1 (ft); Occupational therapists 1 (pt); Speech therapists 1 (pt); Activities coordinators 2 (ft); Dietitians 1 (ft); Ophthalmologists 1 (pt); Podiatrists 1 (pt).
Facilities Dining room; Physical therapy room; Activities room; Chapel; Laundry room; Barber/Beauty shop.
Activities Arts & crafts; Cards; Games; Reading groups; Prayer groups; Movies; Shopping trips; Dances/Social/Cultural gatherings.

New Hampton

Health Care Manor
S 4th St, New Hampton, IA 50659
(515) 394-4154
Licensure Intermediate care; Residential care. *Beds* ICF 88; Residential care 15. *Certified* Medicaid.
Admissions Requirements Medical examination; Physician's request.
Staff RNs 1 (ft), 1 (pt); LPNs 1 (ft), 5 (pt); Nurses' aides 15 (ft), 10 (pt); Physical therapists 1 (pt); Occupational therapists 1 (pt); Speech therapists 1 (pt); Activities coordinators 1 (ft), 1 (pt); Dietitians 1 (ft).
Facilities Dining room; Physical therapy room; Activities room; Crafts room; Laundry room; Barber/Beauty shop; Separate lounge area.
Activities Arts & crafts; Cards; Games; Reading groups; Prayer groups; Shopping trips; Dances/Social/Cultural gatherings.

New Hampton Care Center
530 S Linn, New Hampton, IA 50659
(515) 394-3151
Admin Bonnie L Hubka.
Licensure Intermediate care. *Beds* ICF 50. *Certified* Medicaid.

New London

New London Care Center
Pine St, New London, IA 52645
(319) 367-5753
Admin Michael W Hocking.
Licensure Intermediate care. *Beds* ICF 51. *Certified* Medicaid.

New Sharon

New Sharon Care Center
Park at Cherry, New Sharon, IA 50207
(515) 637-4031

Admin Mardith Wood.
Medical Dir Linda Williams.
Licensure Intermediate care. *Beds* ICF 63. *Certified* Medicaid.
Owner Proprietary corp (Mercy Health Initiatives).
Admissions Requirements Minimum age 18; Medical examination; Physician's request.
Staff RNs 2 (ft); LPNs 2 (ft), 1 (pt); Nurses' aides 35 (ft), 15 (pt); Activities coordinators 1 (ft).
Facilities Dining room; Physical therapy room; Activities room; Crafts room; Laundry room; Barber/Beauty shop.
Activities Arts & crafts; Cards; Games; Reading groups; Prayer groups; Movies; Dances/Social/Cultural gatherings; Church services.

Newell

Newell Good Samaritan Center
415 W Hwy 7, Newell, IA 50568
(712) 272-3327
Admin Cynthia L Fraser.
Licensure Intermediate care. *Beds* ICF 50. *Certified* Medicaid.
Owner Nonprofit corp (Evangelical Lutheran/ Good Samaritan Society).

Newton

Embassy Manor Care Center
200 S 8th Ave E, Newton, IA 50208
(515) 792-7440
Admin Sandra L Dean.
Licensure Intermediate care. *Beds* ICF 101. *Certified* Medicaid.

Heritage Manor Care Center
1743 S 8th Ave E, Newton, IA 50208
(515) 792-5680
Admin Paul A Livingston. *Dir of Nursing* Sue Peterson.
Licensure Intermediate care. *Beds* ICF 62. *Private Pay Patients* 85%. *Certified* Medicaid.
Owner Proprietary corp.
Admissions Requirements Minimum age as required by law; Medical examination.
Staff RNs 2 (ft), 2 (pt); LPNs 1 (ft), 2 (pt); Nurses' aides 15 (ft), 6 (pt); Physical therapists 1 (pt); Recreational therapists 1 (pt); Occupational therapists 1 (pt); Speech therapists 1 (pt); Activities coordinators 1 (ft); Dietitians 1 (pt).
Facilities Dining room; Physical therapy room; Activities room; Crafts room; Laundry room; Barber/Beauty shop; Fireplace; Examination room.
Activities Arts & crafts; Cards; Games; Reading groups; Prayer groups; Movies; Shopping trips; Dances/Social/Cultural gatherings; Intergenerational programs; Pet therapy; Bowling.

Jasper County Care Facility
RR 4 Box 68, Newton, IA 50208
(515) 792-2000
Admin Elizabeth M Clayton. *Dir of Nursing* Janet Johnson RN. *Medical Dir* John Ferguson MD.
Licensure Intermediate care; Intermediate care for mentally retarded; Residential care. *Beds* ICF 45; ICF/MR 28; Residential care 43. *Private Pay Patients* 13%. *Certified* Medicaid.
Owner Publicly owned.
Admissions Requirements Minimum age 18; Medical examination; Physician's request.
Staff Physicians (consultant); RNs 4 (ft), 1 (pt); LPNs 4 (ft), 4 (pt); Nurses' aides 30 (ft), 33 (pt); Physical therapists (consultant); Recreational therapists 3 (ft); Occupational therapists (consultant); Speech therapists (consultant); Dietitians (consultant); Ophthalmologists (consultant); Podiatrists

(consultant); Audiologists (consultant); Psychiatrists (consultant); Psychologists (consultant).
Facilities Dining room; Physical therapy room; Activities room; Chapel; Crafts room; Laundry room; Barber/Beauty shop; Library; Occupational therapy room; Gym; Workshop; Living skills; Outdoor park; Wheelchair outdoor walk; Wheelchair swing.
Activities Arts & crafts; Cards; Games; Reading groups; Prayer groups; Movies; Shopping trips; Dances/Social/Cultural gatherings; Intergenerational programs; Pet therapy; Camping; Canoeing; Picnics.

Nelson Manor
1500 1st Ave E, Newton, IA 50208
(515) 792-1443
Admin Mary Ann Shaw. *Dir of Nursing* Ann Lutz.
Licensure Intermediate care. *Beds* ICF 36. *Certified* Medicaid.
Owner Privately owned.
Admissions Requirements Medical examination.
Staff RNs 2 (ft), 1 (pt); LPNs 1 (ft), 1 (pt); Nurses' aides 14 (ft); Physical therapists 1 (pt); Occupational therapists 1 (pt); Speech therapists 1 (pt); Activities coordinators 1 (pt); Dietitians 1 (pt); Ophthalmologists 1 (pt); Podiatrists 1 (pt).
Facilities Laundry room.
Activities Arts & crafts; Cards; Games; Reading groups; Prayer groups; Movies.

Nora Springs

Nora Springs Care Center
Hwy 18 W, Nora Springs, IA 50458
(515) 749-5331
Admin Michael J Fox. *Dir of Nursing* Rose Kuppinger.
Licensure Intermediate care. *Beds* ICF 60. *Private Pay Patients* 50%. *Certified* Medicaid.
Owner Proprietary corp (ABCM Corp).
Admissions Requirements Physician's request.
Staff RNs 1 (ft), 1 (pt); LPNs 4 (ft), 2 (pt); Nurses' aides 9 (ft), 7 (pt); Activities coordinators 1 (ft), 1 (pt); Dietitians 1 (pt).
Facilities Dining room; Physical therapy room; Activities room; Chapel; Crafts room; Laundry room; Barber/Beauty shop.
Activities Arts & crafts; Cards; Games; Reading groups; Prayer groups; Movies; Shopping trips; Dances/Social/Cultural gatherings.

North English

English Valley Nursing Care Center
PO Box 430, North English, IA 52316
(319) 664-3257
Admin Audrey Weldon.
Licensure Intermediate care. *Beds* ICF 67. *Certified* Medicaid.

Northwood

Lutheran Retirement Home Inc
700 10th St N, Northwood, IA 50459
(515) 324-1712
Admin James Tweeten. *Dir of Nursing* Dianne Zaiser RN.
Licensure Intermediate care. *Beds* ICF 81. *Certified* Medicaid.
Owner Nonprofit corp.
Admissions Requirements Minimum age 16; Medical examination.
Staff RNs 3 (ft), 4 (pt); LPNs 2 (ft), 5 (pt); Nurses' aides 10 (ft), 30 (pt); Activities coordinators 1 (ft), 2 (pt).
Affiliation Lutheran.
Facilities Dining room; Physical therapy room; Activities room; Chapel; Crafts room; Laundry room; Barber/Beauty shop.

Activities Arts & crafts; Cards; Games; Reading groups; Prayer groups; Movies; Chapel services; One-to-one visits; Reading & writing letters; Reality orientation group; Baking.

Norwalk

Norwalk Manor
921 Sunset Dr, Norwalk, IA 50211
(515) 981-0604
Admin Sharon K Dietz.
Medical Dir Edith Manley.
Licensure Intermediate care. *Beds* ICF 51. *Certified* Medicaid.
Owner Proprietary corp (National Heritage).
Admissions Requirements Medical examination; Physician's request.
Staff LPNs; Nurses' aides; Activities coordinators; Dietitians.
Facilities Dining room; Laundry room; Barber/Beauty shop.
Activities Arts & crafts; Cards; Games; Reading groups; Prayer groups; Movies; Shopping trips; Dances/Social/Cultural gatherings.

Regency Care Center
815 High Rd, Norwalk, IA 50211
(515) 981-4269
Admin Robert H Richardson.
Medical Dir Margaret Beener.
Licensure Intermediate care. *Beds* ICF 101. *Certified* Medicare.
Owner Proprietary corp.
Admissions Requirements Minimum age 65; Medical examination; Physician's request.
Staff RNs; LPNs; Nurses' aides; Physical therapists; Occupational therapists; Speech therapists; Activities coordinators; Dietitians; Ophthalmologists; Podiatrists; Dentists.
Facilities Dining room; Physical therapy room; Activities room; Crafts room; Laundry room; Barber/Beauty shop; Fireplace living room.
Activities Arts & crafts; Cards; Games; Reading groups; Prayer groups; Movies; Shopping trips; Dances/Social/Cultural gatherings.

Oakland

Oakland Manor Nursing Home
737 North Hwy, Oakland, IA 51560
(712) 482-6403
Admin Carolee Hamblin.
Medical Dir Gladys Pierce.
Licensure Intermediate care. *Beds* ICF 67. *Certified* Medicaid.
Owner Proprietary corp.
Admissions Requirements Medical examination.
Staff RNs; LPNs; Nurses' aides; Activities coordinators.
Facilities Dining room; Physical therapy room; Activities room; Chapel; Crafts room; Laundry room; Barber/Beauty shop.
Activities Arts & crafts; Cards; Games; Reading groups; Prayer groups; Movies; Shopping trips; Dances/Social/Cultural gatherings.

Odebolt

Colonial Manor of Odebolt
Hwy 39, Odebolt, IA 51458
(712) 668-4867
Admin Jack Lavelle.
Licensure Intermediate care. *Beds* ICF 64. *Certified* Medicaid.
Owner Proprietary corp (Mercy Health Initiatives).

Oelwein

Grandview HealthCare Center
800 5th St SE, Oelwein, IA 50662
(319) 283-1908
Admin Alexa Mayner. *Dir of Nursing* Jan Sringer RN. *Medical Dir* D B Jack MD.
Licensure Intermediate care; Adult day care; Respite care. *Beds* ICF 83. *Private Pay Patients* 45%. *Certified* Medicaid.
Owner Proprietary corp (ABCM Corp).
Admissions Requirements Minimum age 16; Medical examination; Physician's request.
Facilities Dining room; Physical therapy room; Activities room; Laundry room.
Activities Arts & crafts; Cards; Games; Reading groups; Prayer groups; Movies; Dances/Social/Cultural gatherings; Intergenerational programs; Pet therapy.

Oelwein Care Center
600 7th St SE, Oelwein, IA 50662
(319) 283-2794
Admin Betty J Baum. *Dir of Nursing* Sharon Reay RN. *Medical Dir* D B Jack MD.
Licensure Intermediate care; Adult Day Care; Alzheimer's care. *Beds* ICF 61. *Private Pay Patients* 48%. *Certified* Medicaid.
Owner Proprietary corp (Nursing Care Management).
Admissions Requirements Minimum age 18; Medical examination.
Staff Physicians 1 (pt); RNs 1 (ft), 1 (pt); LPNs 3 (ft), 3 (pt); Nurses' aides 11 (ft), 14 (pt); Physical therapists 2 (pt); Speech therapists 1 (pt); Activities coordinators 1 (ft); Dietitians 1 (pt); Podiatrists 1 (pt); Audiologists 1 (pt).
Facilities Dining room; Physical therapy room; Activities room; Chapel; Crafts room; Laundry room; Barber/Beauty shop.
Activities Arts & crafts; Cards; Games; Reading groups; Prayer groups; Movies; Shopping trips; Dances/Social/Cultural gatherings; Pet therapy.

Ogden

Ogden Manor
625 E Oak, Ogden, IA 50212
(515) 275-2481
Admin Charlene Cox. *Dir of Nursing* Ruth Bryant RN.
Licensure Intermediate care. *Beds* ICF 57. *Private Pay Patients* 50%. *Certified* Medicaid.
Owner Proprietary corp (Lee Livingston).
Admissions Requirements Medical examination.
Staff RNs 2 (ft); LPNs 2 (pt); Nurses' aides 10 (ft), 15 (pt); Activities coordinators 1 (ft); Dietitians 1 (pt).
Facilities Dining room; Physical therapy room; Activities room; Chapel; Crafts room; Laundry room; Barber/Beauty shop.
Activities Arts & crafts; Cards; Games; Reading groups; Prayer groups; Movies; Shopping trips; Dances/Social/Cultural gatherings; Intergenerational programs; Pet therapy; Bake & taste.

Onawa

Elmwood Care Center
222 N 15th St, Onawa, IA 51040
(712) 423-2510
Admin Kirk Snelson.
Licensure Intermediate care. *Beds* ICF 99. *Certified* Medicaid.

Orange City

Heritage House
519 Albany Ave SE, Orange City, IA 51041
(712) 737-4002

Admin Beth Haarsma. *Dir of Nursing* Muriel Ravestein.
Licensure Intermediate care. *Beds* ICF 50. *Certified* Medicaid.
Owner Proprietary corp.
Admissions Requirements Minimum age 16; Medical examination; Physician's request.
Staff RNs 1 (ft), 2 (pt); LPNs 3 (ft), 2 (pt); Nurses' aides 9 (ft), 14 (pt); Physical therapists 1 (pt); Recreational therapists 2 (pt); Activities coordinators 1 (ft); Dietitians 1 (pt).
Facilities Dining room; Physical therapy room; Activities room; Chapel; Crafts room; Laundry room; Barber/Beauty shop; Library.
Activities Arts & crafts; Cards; Games; Reading groups; Prayer groups; Movies; Intergenerational programs; Pet therapy.

Orange City Municipal Hospital
115 4th St NW, Orange City, IA 51041
(712) 737-4984
Admin Stephen Goeser.
Licensure Intermediate care. *Beds* ICF 13.

Osage

Faith Lutheran Home
914 Davidson Dr, Osage, IA 50461
(515) 732-5511
Admin John P Lienemann.
Licensure Intermediate care. *Beds* ICF 60.

Maple Manor
830 S 5th St, Osage, IA 50461
(515) 732-5520
Admin Gloria Heathman. *Dir of Nursing* Shirley Stille.
Licensure Intermediate care. *Beds* ICF 77. *Certified* Medicaid.
Owner Proprietary corp (Waverly Group).
Admissions Requirements Medical examination; Physician's request.
Staff RNs 2 (ft); LPNs 3 (ft), 1 (pt); Nurses' aides 12 (ft), 10 (pt); Activities coordinators 1 (ft), 1 (pt).
Facilities Dining room; Activities room; Barber/Beauty shop.
Activities Arts & crafts; Games; Prayer groups; Movies.

Osceola

Osceola Leisure Manor
Hwy 68 N, Osceola, IA 50213
(515) 342-6061
Admin Ruth Stephens.
Licensure Intermediate care. *Beds* ICF 101. *Certified* Medicaid.
Owner Proprietary corp (Mercy Health Initiatives).

Oskaloosa

Mahaska Manor
914 N 12th St, Oskaloosa, IA 52577
(515) 673-9408
Admin Linda K Arterburn.
Medical Dir Gretchen Updegraff.
Licensure Intermediate care. *Beds* ICF 103. *Certified* Medicaid.
Owner Proprietary corp.
Staff RNs; LPNs; Nurses' aides; Physical therapists; Recreational therapists; Occupational therapists; Speech therapists; Activities coordinators; Dietitians; Ophthalmologists; Podiatrists; Dentists; Social workers.
Facilities Dining room; Activities room; Laundry room; Barber/Beauty shop; TV lounge.
Activities Arts & crafts; Cards; Games; Reading groups; Prayer groups; Dances/Social/Cultural gatherings.

Pleasant Park Manor
1514 High Ave, Oskaloosa, IA 52577
(515) 673-7032
Admin Eugene Mott.
Licensure Intermediate care. *Beds* ICF 92.
  Certified Medicaid.

Siesta Park Retirement Home
1302 High Ave W, Oskaloosa, IA 52577
(515) 672-2474
Admin Jean Erickson.
Licensure Intermediate care. *Beds* ICF 37.

Ossian

Ossian Senior Hospice
PO Box 98, Ossian, IA 52161
(319) 532-9440
Admin Helen M Allen.
Licensure Intermediate care. *Beds* ICF 38.
  Certified Medicaid.
Admissions Requirements Minimum age 21;
  Medical examination; Physician's request.
Staff Physicians 2 (pt); RNs 2 (ft), 2 (pt);
  LPNs 3 (pt); Nurses' aides 5 (ft), 14 (pt);
  Physical therapists 1 (pt); Activities
  coordinators 1 (pt).
Facilities Dining room; Physical therapy
  room; Activities room; Chapel; Laundry
  room; Barber/Beauty shop.
Activities Arts & crafts; Cards; Games;
  Reading groups; Prayer groups; Movies;
  Dances/Social/Cultural gatherings.

Ottumwa

Crest Group Home
433 N Weller, Ottumwa, IA 52501
(515) 682-4624
Admin Judith A Madden.
Licensure Intermediate care for mentally
  retarded. *Beds* ICF/MR 15. *Private Pay
  Patients* 1%. *Certified* Medicaid; Medicare.
Owner Nonprofit corp (American Baptist
  Homes of the Midwest).
Admissions Requirements Minimum age 18;
  Medical examination; Physician's request.
Staff LPNs 1 (ft); Activities coordinators 1
  (ft); Dietitians 1 (ft).
Affiliation Baptist.
Facilities Dining room; Activities room;
  Laundry room; Living room.
Activities Arts & crafts; Cards; Games;
  Movies; Shopping trips.

Good Samaritan Center
2035 W Chester Ave, Ottumwa, IA 52501
(515) 682-8041
Admin Ronald K Moegenburg. *Dir of Nursing*
  Florence McCutchen.
Licensure Intermediate care. *Beds* ICF 126.
  Certified Medicaid.
Owner Nonprofit corp (Evangelical Lutheran/
  Good Samaritan Society).
Staff RNs 3 (ft), 4 (pt); LPNs 3 (ft), 3 (pt);
  Nurses' aides 16 (ft), 41 (pt); Activities
  coordinators 1 (ft).
Affiliation Lutheran.
Facilities Dining room; Physical therapy
  room; Activities room; Chapel; Crafts room;
  Laundry room; Barber/Beauty shop.
Activities Arts & crafts; Cards; Games;
  Reading groups; Movies; Dances/Social/
  Cultural gatherings.

Ottumwa Manor
927 E Pennsylvania, Ottumwa, IA 52501
(515) 684-4594
Admin Helen Jo Broerman.
Licensure Intermediate care. *Beds* ICF 101.
  Certified Medicaid.

Ottumwa Regional Health Center
1001 E Pennsylvania, Ottumwa, IA 52501
(515) 682-7511
Admin Clarence B Cory. *Dir of Nursing* Colee
  Hospers.

Licensure Skilled care. *Beds* SNF 14. *Certified*
  Medicaid; Medicare.
Owner Nonprofit organization/foundation.

Ridgewood Care Center Inc
1977 Albia Rd, Ottumwa, IA 52501
(515) 683-3111
Admin Kay Dudycha.
Licensure Intermediate care; Residential care.
  Beds ICF 54; Residential care 16. *Certified*
  Medicaid.
Owner Proprietary corp (Mercy Health
  Initiatives).

Sunnyslope Care Center
Rte 1, E Steller, Ottumwa, IA 52501
(515) 684-6524
Admin Ruth K Weaver. *Dir of Nursing* Judith
  A Lee.
Licensure Intermediate care. *Beds* ICF 61.
  Certified Medicaid.
Owner Publicly owned.

Panora

Craft Care Center
805 E Main, Panora, IA 50216
(515) 755-2700
Admin Donna Johnston.
Medical Dir JoAnn Ostby.
Licensure Intermediate care. *Beds* ICF 108.
  Certified Medicaid.
Owner Proprietary corp (Mercy Health
  Initiatives).
Admissions Requirements Medical
  examination.
Staff RNs 3 (ft), 2 (pt); LPNs 4 (ft), 3 (pt);
  Nurses' aides 30 (ft), 30 (pt); Physical
  therapists 1 (pt); Recreational therapists 2
  (ft); Occupational therapists 1 (pt); Speech
  therapists 1 (pt); Activities coordinators 1
  (ft); Dietitians 1 (pt); Ophthalmologists 1
  (pt); Podiatrists 1 (pt); Dentists 1 (pt).
Facilities Dining room; Activities room;
  Crafts room; Laundry room; Barber/Beauty
  shop; Library.
Activities Arts & crafts; Cards; Games;
  Reading groups; Prayer groups; Movies;
  Shopping trips; Dances/Social/Cultural
  gatherings.

Paullina

Wide View Rest Home
423 Willow St, Paullina, IA 51046
(712) 448-3455
Admin Tom V Nelson.
Licensure Intermediate care. *Beds* ICF 41.
  Certified Medicaid.

Pella

Pella Community Hospital
404 Jefferson St, Pella, IA 50219
(515) 628-3150
Admin John Harmeling.
Licensure Intermediate care. *Beds* ICF 61.

Perry

Memorial Masonic Home
3000 E Willis Ave, Perry, IA 50220
(515) 465-5316
Admin LuCinda L Friess. *Dir of Nursing* Deb
  Jamison RN. *Medical Dir* Dr Steven Sohn.
Licensure Skilled care; Intermediate care;
  Residential care; Independent living;
  Alzheimer's care. *Beds* Swing beds SNF/ICF
  48; Residential care 28; Independent living
  9. *Private Pay Patients* 80%. *Certified*
  Medicaid; Medicare.
Owner Nonprofit organization/foundation.
Admissions Requirements Medical
  examination; Must be an Iowa Mason or
  dependent.

Staff RNs 2 (ft); LPNs 6 (ft), 2 (pt); Nurses'
  aides 20 (ft), 5 (pt); Physical therapists
  (contracted); Reality therapists (contracted);
  Recreational therapists (contracted);
  Occupational therapists (contracted); Speech
  therapists (contracted); Activities
  coordinators 2 (ft), 1 (pt); Dietitians
  (contracted); Ophthalmologists (contracted);
  Podiatrists (contracted); Audiologists
  (contracted).
Affiliation Masons.
Facilities Dining room; Physical therapy
  room; Activities room; Chapel; Crafts room;
  Laundry room; Barber/Beauty shop; Library.
Activities Arts & crafts; Cards; Games;
  Reading groups; Prayer groups; Movies;
  Shopping trips; Dances/Social/Cultural
  gatherings; Intergenerational programs; Pet
  therapy.

Perry Lutheran Home
2323 E Willis Ave, Perry, IA 50220
(515) 465-5342
Admin Stephen F King. *Dir of Nursing* Robin
  McCauley RN.
Licensure Intermediate care; Residential care;
  Alzheimer's care. *Beds* ICF 108; Residential
  care 4. *Certified* Medicaid.
Owner Nonprofit organization/foundation.
Admissions Requirements Medical
  examination; Physician's request.
Affiliation Lutheran.
Facilities Dining room; Activities room;
  Chapel; Crafts room; Laundry room; Barber/
  Beauty shop.
Activities Arts & crafts; Cards; Games;
  Reading groups; Prayer groups; Movies;
  Shopping trips; Dances/Social/Cultural
  gatherings.

Perry Manor
2625 E Iowa St, Perry, IA 50220
(515) 465-5349
Admin Ruth Owen. *Dir of Nursing* Lila
  Rohde. *Medical Dir* Dr S Sohn.
Licensure Intermediate care. *Beds* ICF 54.
  Private Pay Patients 55%. *Certified*
  Medicaid.
Owner Proprietary corp (Drew Inc).
Admissions Requirements Minimum age 21;
  Medical examination; Physician's request.
Staff Physicians; RNs; LPNs; Nurses' aides;
  Physical therapists; Activities coordinators.
Facilities Dining room; Physical therapy
  room; Activities room; Laundry room;
  Barber/Beauty shop.
Activities Arts & crafts; Cards; Games;
  Reading groups; Prayer groups; Movies;
  Shopping trips; Dances/Social/Cultural
  gatherings; Intergenerational programs; Pet
  therapy.

Pleasant Valley

Riverview Manor Nursing Home
Spencer Rd, Pleasant Valley, IA 52767
(319) 332-4600
Admin Susan Morton RN. *Dir of Nursing*
  Kathleen Grimes LPN.
Licensure Intermediate care. *Beds* ICF 51.
  Certified Medicaid.
Owner Proprietary corp.
Admissions Requirements Minimum age 16;
  Medical examination; Physician's request.
Staff RNs 1 (ft); LPNs 3 (ft), 3 (pt); Nurses'
  aides 8 (ft), 7 (pt); Activities coordinators 1
  (ft).
Facilities Dining room; Physical therapy
  room; Activities room; Laundry room;
  Barber/Beauty shop.
Activities Arts & crafts; Cards; Games;
  Reading groups; Prayer groups; Movies;
  Shopping trips; Dances/Social/Cultural
  gatherings.

Pleasantville

Pleasant Care Living Center
PO Box 570, Pleasantville, IA 50225
(515) 848-5718
Admin Eric Gabrielson.
Medical Dir Judy Sparks.
Licensure Intermediate care. *Beds* ICF 57.
   Certified Medicaid.
Owner Proprietary corp.
Admissions Requirements Physician's request.
Staff RNs; LPNs; Nurses' aides; Activities
   coordinators; Dietitians.
Facilities Dining room; Activities room;
   Crafts room; Laundry room; Barber/Beauty
   shop.
Activities Arts & crafts; Games; Reading
   groups; Prayer groups; Movies.

Pocahontas

Pocahontas Manor
700 NW 7th, Pocahontas, IA 50574
(712) 335-3386
Admin Berniece E Milne.
Licensure Intermediate care. *Beds* ICF 92.
   Certified Medicaid.
Owner Proprietary corp (Diversicare Corp of
   America).

Polk City

Polk City Manor
Rte 2, 1002 NW 114th St, Polk City, IA
   50226
(515) 984-6201
Admin John Hougen. *Dir of Nursing* Christine
   Opfer RN.
Licensure Intermediate care. *Beds* ICF 68.
   Certified Medicaid.
Owner Proprietary corp (National Heritage).
Admissions Requirements Minimum age 18;
   Medical examination; Physician's request.
Staff RNs 1 (ft); LPNs 3 (ft), 1 (pt); Nurses'
   aides 16 (ft), 7 (pt); Activities coordinators 1
   (ft), 1 (pt).
Facilities Dining room; Activities room;
   Crafts room; Laundry room; Barber/Beauty
   shop; Library; Wine & cheese.
Activities Arts & crafts; Cards; Games;
   Reading groups; Prayer groups; Movies;
   Shopping trips; Dances/Social/Cultural
   gatherings; Van rides.

Pomeroy

Pomeroy Care Center
303 E 7th St, Pomeroy, IA 50575
(712) 468-2241
Admin Susan Juilfs. *Dir of Nursing* Judy
   Weller RN. *Medical Dir* John Rhodes MD.
Licensure Intermediate care. *Beds* ICF 48.
   Private Pay Patients 65%. *Certified*
   Medicaid.
Owner Proprietary corp.
Admissions Requirements Medical
   examination; Physician's request.
Staff Physicians 5 (pt); RNs 1 (ft), 2 (pt);
   LPNs 1 (ft), 3 (pt); Nurses' aides 6 (ft), 18
   (pt); Physical therapists (consultant); Speech
   therapists 1 (pt); Activities coordinators 2
   (pt); Dietitians (consultant);
   Ophthalmologists 1 (pt); Podiatrists 1 (pt);
   Audiologists 1 (pt); Dentists 1 (pt).
Facilities Dining room; Activities room;
   Crafts room; Laundry room; Barber/Beauty
   shop; Library.
Activities Arts & crafts; Cards; Games;
   Reading groups; Prayer groups; Movies;
   Shopping trips; Dances/Social/Cultural
   gatherings; Intergenerational programs.

Postville

Community Memorial Hospital
Oak Dr & Hospital Rd, Postville, IA 52162-
   0519
(319) 864-7431
Admin Linda Petersen. *Dir of Nursing* Debra
   Vondersitt RN. *Medical Dir* Milton F
   Kiesau MD.
Licensure Intermediate care; Acute care. *Beds*
   ICF 8; Acute care 34; Swing beds SNF/ICF
   26. *Certified* Medicaid; Medicare.
Owner Publicly owned.
Admissions Requirements Medical
   examination; Physician's request.
Staff RNs 4 (ft), 8 (pt); LPNs 2 (ft), 6 (pt);
   Nurses' aides 2 (ft), 3 (pt); Physical
   therapists 1 (pt); Occupational therapists 1
   (pt); Speech therapists 1 (pt); Activities
   coordinators 1 (ft); Dietitians 1 (ft).
Facilities Dining room; Activities room;
   Chapel.
Activities Arts & crafts; Cards; Games;
   Reading groups.

Good Samaritan Center
PO Box 716, 400 County Line Rd, Postville,
   IA 52162
(319) 864-7425
Admin Fran Gruenhaupt. *Dir of Nursing*
   Raletta Thomas RN.
Licensure Intermediate care. *Beds* ICF 60.
   Certified Medicaid.
Owner Nonprofit corp (Evangelical Lutheran/
   Good Samaritan Society).
Admissions Requirements Minimum age 18;
   Medical examination; Physician's request.
Staff RNs 1 (ft), 2 (pt); LPNs 3 (ft), 3 (pt);
   Nurses' aides 10 (ft), 17 (pt); Activities
   coordinators 1 (ft), 1 (pt).
Affiliation Lutheran.
Facilities Dining room; Activities room;
   Chapel; Crafts room; Laundry room; Barber/
   Beauty shop; Library; Lounges.
Activities Arts & crafts; Cards; Games; Prayer
   groups; Shopping trips; Dances/Social/
   Cultural gatherings; Conversation hour;
   Thursday night entertainment; Walking
   program.

Prairie City

Clearview Manor
501 N Sherman, Prairie City, IA 50228
(515) 994-2173
Admin Larry R Rodgers.
Licensure Intermediate care. *Beds* ICF 80.
   Certified Medicaid.

Primghar

Primghar Care Center
980 Cedar St, Primghar, IA 51245
(712) 757-3655
Admin James C Streufert.
Licensure Intermediate care. *Beds* ICF 40.
   Certified Medicaid.

Red Oak

Red Oak Good Samaritan Center
201 Alix Ave, Red Oak, IA 51566
(712) 623-3170
Admin Arthur H Hess.
Licensure Intermediate care. *Beds* ICF 76.
   Certified Medicaid.
Owner Nonprofit corp (Evangelical Lutheran/
   Good Samaritan Society).

Vista Gardens Nursing Home
1600 Summit, Red Oak, IA 51566
(712) 623-5156
Admin Mark A Anderson. *Dir of Nursing*
   Ruth Waldemer RN.
Licensure Intermediate care. *Beds* ICF 68.
   Certified Medicaid.

Staff RNs 3 (ft); LPNs 7 (ft), 1 (pt); Nurses'
   aides 14 (ft), 5 (pt); Physical therapists 1 (ft);
   Activities coordinators 1 (ft); Dietitians 1
   (pt).
Facilities Dining room; Physical therapy
   room; Activities room; Laundry room;
   Barber/Beauty shop; Sitting area/lounge.
Activities Arts & crafts; Cards; Games;
   Reading groups; Prayer groups; Movies;
   Music programs.

Reinbeck

Parkview Manor Inc
1009 3rd St, Reinbeck, IA 50669
(319) 345-2221
Admin Linda R Gould. *Dir of Nursing* Lois
   Stephan.
Licensure Intermediate care. *Beds* ICF 56.
   Private Pay Patients 66%. *Certified*
   Medicaid.
Owner Publicly owned.
Admissions Requirements Medical
   examination.
Facilities Dining room; Physical therapy
   room; Activities room; Crafts room; Laundry
   room; Barber/Beauty shop.
Activities Arts & crafts; Cards; Games;
   Reading groups; Prayer groups; Movies;
   Shopping trips; Dances/Social/Cultural
   gatherings; Intergenerational programs; Pet
   therapy.

Remsen

Happy Siesta Nursing Home
Lincoln at Kennedy, Remsen, IA 51050
(712) 786-1117
Admin Sandy Anderson.
Medical Dir Shirley Stowater.
Licensure Intermediate care. *Beds* ICF 61.
   Certified Medicaid.
Owner Proprietary corp.
Admissions Requirements Physician's request.
Staff RNs 2 (ft), 2 (pt); LPNs 1 (ft), 5 (pt);
   Nurses' aides 6 (ft), 14 (pt); Activities
   coordinators 3 (pt); Dietitians 1 (pt).
Affiliation Roman Catholic.
Facilities Dining room; Activities room;
   Chapel; Laundry room; Barber/Beauty shop.
Activities Arts & crafts; Cards; Games;
   Reading groups; Prayer groups; Movies;
   Shopping trips; Dances/Social/Cultural
   gatherings.

Riceville

Riceville Community Rest Home
Rte 1 Box 40, Riceville, IA 50466
(515) 985-2606
Admin Lavonne M Mayer.
Medical Dir Linda Weida.
Licensure Intermediate care. *Beds* ICF 49.
   Certified Medicaid.
Owner Nonprofit corp.
Admissions Requirements Minimum age 18;
   Medical examination; Physician's request.
Staff RNs 1 (ft), 2 (pt); LPNs 1 (ft), 2 (pt);
   Nurses' aides 3 (ft), 17 (pt); Activities
   coordinators 1 (ft), 1 (pt); Dietitians 1 (pt).
Activities Arts & crafts; Cards; Games;
   Reading groups; Prayer groups; Movies;
   Dances/Social/Cultural gatherings.

Rock Rapids

Lyon Manor
1010 S Union, Rock Rapids, IA 51246
(712) 472-3748
Admin Janet Hromalko. *Dir of Nursing* Linda
   Breuker.
Licensure Intermediate care. *Beds* ICF 51.
   Private Pay Patients 50%. *Certified*
   Medicaid.
Owner Nonprofit corp (Mercy Health
   Initiatives).

Admissions Requirements Minimum age 16.
Staff Physicians 3 (ft); RNs 2 (ft); LPNs 7 (pt); Nurses' aides 10 (ft), 15 (pt); Physical therapists 1 (pt); Activities coordinators 1 (ft); Dietitians 1 (ft); Ophthalmologists 1 (pt); Audiologists 1 (pt).
Facilities Dining room; Physical therapy room; Activities room; Chapel; Crafts room; Laundry room; Barber/Beauty shop.
Activities Arts & crafts; Cards; Games; Reading groups; Prayer groups; Movies; Shopping trips; Dances/Social/Cultural gatherings; Intergenerational programs; Pet therapy.

Rock Rapids Health Centre
703 S Union, Rock Rapids, IA 51246
(712) 472-2585
Admin Daniel Boyle.
Licensure Intermediate care; Residential care. *Beds* ICF 65; Residential care 12. *Certified* Medicaid.

Rock Valley

Hegg Memorial Health Center
1200 21st Ave, Rock Valley, IA 51247
(712) 476-5305
Admin Justin Cassel. *Dir of Nursing* Sandra Ver Steeg.
Licensure Intermediate care. *Beds* ICF 94. *Certified* Medicaid.
Owner Privately owned.
Admissions Requirements Medical examination; Physician's request.
Staff Physicians 3 (ft); RNs 1 (ft), 3 (pt); LPNs 5 (ft), 5 (pt); Nurses' aides 13 (ft), 31 (pt); Activities coordinators 3 (pt); Dietitians 1 (pt).
Facilities Dining room; Activities room; Chapel; Barber/Beauty shop.
Activities Arts & crafts; Cards; Games; Reading groups; Prayer groups; Movies; Dances/Social/Cultural gatherings.

Rockwell

Rockwell Community Nursing Home
707 E Elm, Rockwell, IA 50469
(515) 822-3203
Admin Richard Blake. *Dir of Nursing* James Hutzell. *Medical Dir* Suzan Adams.
Licensure Intermediate care. *Beds* ICF 52. *Private Pay Patients* 40-60%. *Certified* Medicaid.
Owner Proprietary corp.
Staff RNs; LPNs; Nurses' aides; Activities coordinators; Dietitians.
Facilities Dining room; Physical therapy room; Activities room; Crafts room; Barber/Beauty shop.
Activities Arts & crafts; Cards; Games; Reading groups; Prayer groups; Movies; Shopping trips.

Rockwell City

Sunny Knoll Care Centre
135 Warner, Rockwell City, IA 50579
(712) 297-8918
Licensure Intermediate care. *Beds* ICF 41. *Certified* Medicaid.
Admissions Requirements Minimum age 18; Medical examination; Physician's request.
Staff RNs 1 (ft), 1 (pt); LPNs 2 (pt); Nurses' aides 4 (ft), 10 (pt); Physical therapists 1 (pt); Activities coordinators 1 (pt).
Facilities Dining room; Physical therapy room; Activities room; Laundry room; Barber/Beauty shop.
Activities Arts & crafts; Games; Reading groups; Prayer groups; Movies; Shopping trips.

Rolfe

Rolfe Care Center
303 2nd St, Rolfe, IA 50581
(712) 848-3351
Admin A E Sluiter.
Licensure Intermediate care. *Beds* ICF 33. *Certified* Medicaid.
Owner Privately owned.
Admissions Requirements Medical examination; Physician's request.
Staff RNs 1 (ft); LPNs 1 (ft), 1 (pt); Nurses' aides 4 (ft), 12 (pt); Activities coordinators 1 (pt).
Facilities Dining room; Physical therapy room; Laundry room; Library.
Activities Arts & crafts; Cards; Games; Reading groups; Movies.

Ruthven

Ruthven Community Care Center
Mitchell St, Ruthven, IA 51358
(712) 837-5411
Admin Alice J Miller.
Licensure Intermediate care. *Beds* ICF 50.

Sac City

Loring Hospital
Highland Ave, Sac City, IA 50583
(712) 662-7105
Admin Terry J DeJong.
Licensure Intermediate care. *Beds* ICF 21.

Park View Care Center
601 Park Ave, Sac City, IA 50583
(712) 662-3818
Admin Kent Mertens.
Licensure Intermediate care. *Beds* ICF 77. *Certified* Medicaid.
Owner Proprietary corp (ABCM Corp).

Saint Ansgar

St Ansgar Good Samaritan Center
701 E 4th St, Saint Ansgar, IA 50472
(515) 736-4912
Admin Tim Moe. *Dir of Nursing* Roberta Howard. *Medical Dir* Mark Johnson MD.
Licensure Intermediate care. *Beds* ICF 76. *Certified* Medicaid.
Owner Nonprofit corp (Evangelical Lutheran/ Good Samaritan Society).
Admissions Requirements Minimum age 16.
Staff Physicians 1 (pt); RNs 2 (ft), 4 (pt); LPNs 1 (ft), 3 (pt); Nurses' aides 8 (ft), 33 (pt); Physical therapists 1 (pt); Occupational therapists 1 (pt); Activities coordinators 1 (ft); Dietitians 1 (pt); Ophthalmologists 1 (pt); Podiatrists 1 (pt).
Facilities Dining room; Physical therapy room; Activities room; Chapel; Crafts room; Laundry room; Barber/Beauty shop; Library.
Activities Arts & crafts; Cards; Games; Reading groups; Prayer groups; Movies; Shopping trips; Dances/Social/Cultural gatherings.

Sanborn

Prairie View Home
Hwy 18, Sanborn, IA 51248
(712) 729-3228
Admin John Mulder. *Dir of Nursing* Marcia Morgan.
Licensure Intermediate care. *Beds* ICF 73. *Private Pay Patients* 65%. *Certified* Medicaid.
Owner Proprietary corp.
Admissions Requirements Medical examination.
Staff RNs 1 (ft), 1 (pt); LPNs 5 (ft), 2 (pt); Nurses' aides 20 (ft), 16 (pt); Physical therapists 1 (pt); Activities coordinators 1 (ft), 1 (pt); Dietitians 1 (pt).

Facilities Dining room; Activities room; Chapel; Crafts room; Laundry room; Barber/Beauty shop; Library; Physician exam room.
Activities Arts & crafts; Cards; Games; Reading groups; Prayer groups; Movies.

Sergeant Bluff

Clock Tower Village
206 Port Neal Rd, Sergeant Bluff, IA 51054
(712) 943-3837, 943-9738 FAX
Admin Irene TerHaar. *Dir of Nursing* Sandra Van Fossen. *Medical Dir* Dr Katheryn Opheim.
Licensure Skilled care; Intermediate care. *Beds* SNF 31; ICF 29. *Private Pay Patients* 30%. *Certified* Medicaid; Medicare.
Owner Privately owned.
Facilities Dining room; Physical therapy room; Activities room; Crafts room; Laundry room; Barber/Beauty shop.

Seymour

Seymour Care Center
E 4th & Morgan, Seymour, IA 52590
(515) 898-2294
Admin R Alan Griffith.
Licensure Intermediate care. *Beds* ICF 51. *Certified* Medicaid.

Sheffield

Sheffield Care Center
PO Box 400, 100 Bennett Dr, Sheffield, IA 50475
(515) 892-4691
Admin Sandra L Lehr. *Dir of Nursing* Gwen Suntken.
Licensure Intermediate care; Residential care. *Beds* ICF 56; Residential care 4. *Private Pay Patients* 60%. *Certified* Medicaid.
Owner Nonprofit corp.
Staff RNs 1 (ft), 3 (pt); LPNs 3 (ft), 2 (pt); Nurses' aides 16 (ft), 10 (pt); Activities coordinators 1 (ft), 2 (pt); Dietitians 1 (pt).
Facilities Dining room; Physical therapy room; Activities room; Chapel; Crafts room; Laundry room; Barber/Beauty shop; Library.
Activities Arts & crafts; Cards; Games; Reading groups; Prayer groups; Movies; Shopping trips; Dances/Social/Cultural gatherings; Intergenerational programs; Pet therapy.

Sheldon

Northwest Iowa Health Center
118 N 7th, Sheldon, IA 51201
(712) 324-5041
Admin Mark V Dagoberg. *Dir of Nursing* Virginia Harson RN.
Licensure Intermediate care. *Beds* ICF 54. *Certified* Medicaid.
Owner Nonprofit corp.
Admissions Requirements Medical examination; Physician's request.
Staff Physicians 2 (ft); RNs 1 (ft), 2 (pt); LPNs 2 (ft), 10 (pt); Nurses' aides 5 (ft), 30 (pt); Physical therapists 1 (ft); Occupational therapists 1 (pt); Speech therapists 1 (pt); Activities coordinators 1 (ft), 1 (pt); Dietitians 1 (ft); Ophthalmologists 1 (pt); Podiatrists 1 (pt).
Languages Dutch.
Facilities Dining room; Physical therapy room; Activities room; Laundry room; Barber/Beauty shop; Library.
Activities Arts & crafts; Cards; Games; Prayer groups; Movies.

Shell Rock

Shell Rock Care Center
Kelly St & Waverly Rd, Shell Rock, IA 50670
(319) 885-4341
Admin Karen Habenight.
Medical Dir Marilyn K DeWitt.
Licensure Intermediate care; Alzheimer's care.
Beds ICF 56. *Certified* Medicaid.
Owner Proprietary corp.
Admissions Requirements Medical
examination; Physician's request.
Staff RNs 1 (pt); LPNs 4 (ft), 3 (pt); Nurses'
aides 10 (ft), 22 (pt); Physical therapists 1
(pt); Recreational therapists 1 (pt);
Occupational therapists 1 (pt); Speech
therapists 1 (pt); Activities coordinators 1
(ft); Dietitians 1 (pt); Ophthalmologists 1
(pt); Podiatrists 1 (pt).
Languages Spanish.
Facilities Dining room; Physical therapy
room; Activities room; Crafts room; Laundry
room; Barber/Beauty shop.
Activities Arts & crafts; Cards; Games;
Reading groups; Prayer groups; Movies;
Shopping trips; Dances/Social/Cultural
gatherings; Boat trips; Picnics; Barbeques.

Shenandoah

Elm Heights—Parkcrest
1203 S Elm, Shenandoah, IA 51601
(712) 246-4627
Admin Shirley M Teachout. *Dir of Nursing*
Alison Hutt RN.
Licensure Intermediate care; Residential care.
Beds ICF 48; Residential care 14. *Certified*
Medicaid.
Owner Nonprofit corp.
Admissions Requirements Medical
examination.
Staff Physicians; RNs; LPNs; Nurses' aides;
Physical therapists; Recreational therapists;
Occupational therapists; Speech therapists;
Activities coordinators; Dietitians;
Ophthalmologists.
Facilities Dining room; Activities room;
Barber/Beauty shop.
Activities Arts & crafts; Cards; Games;
Reading groups; Prayer groups; Movies;
Shopping trips; Dances/Social/Cultural
gatherings.

Garden View Care Center
1200 W Nishna Rd, Shenandoah, IA 51601
(712) 246-4515
Admin Dennis Dewild.
Licensure Intermediate care. Beds ICF 101.
Certified Medicaid.
Staff Physicians 8 (pt); RNs 1 (ft); LPNs 12
(ft); Nurses' aides 23 (ft), 11 (pt); Physical
therapists 4 (pt); Speech therapists 1 (pt);
Activities coordinators 1 (pt); Dietitians 1
(pt); Podiatrists 1 (pt); Dentists 2 (pt).
Facilities Dining room; Physical therapy
room; Activities room; Laundry room;
Barber/Beauty shop.
Activities Arts & crafts; Cards; Games;
Reading groups; Prayer groups; Movies;
Shopping trips; Dances/Social/Cultural
gatherings.

Sibley

Country View Manor Inc
100 Cedar Ln, Sibley, IA 51249
(712) 754-2568
Admin Lois J Werdal. *Dir of Nursing* Carol
Rice RN.
Licensure Intermediate care. Beds ICF 64.
Certified Medicaid.
Owner Proprietary corp.
Admissions Requirements Medical
examination; Physician's request.
Staff RNs 2 (ft), 3 (pt); LPNs 3 (pt); Nurses'
aides 9 (ft), 20 (pt); Activities coordinators 2
(pt).

Facilities Dining room; Activities room;
Chapel; Crafts room; Laundry room; Barber/
Beauty shop; Porch.
Activities Arts & crafts; Cards; Games;
Reading groups; Movies; Shopping trips;
Dances/Social/Cultural gatherings; Bingo;
Memorial services; Trips; Exercises; Reality
orientation.

Sibley Care Center
700 9th Ave N, Sibley, IA 51249
(712) 754-3629
Admin Leann Dohlman RN.
Licensure Intermediate care. Beds ICF 51.
Certified Medicaid.

Sidney

Sidney Health Center
Hwy 275 S, Sidney, IA 51652
(712) 374-2693
Admin Steve Fister.
Licensure Intermediate care. Beds ICF 100.
Certified Medicaid.

Sigourney

Manor House Care Center
1212 S Stuart, Sigourney, IA 52591
(515) 622-2142
Admin Chris Wolf. *Dir of Nursing* Susan
Mertz.
Licensure Intermediate care. Beds ICF 80.
Private Pay Patients 10%. *Certified*
Medicaid.
Owner Proprietary corp (ABCM Corp).
Admissions Requirements Medical
examination; Physician's request.
Staff RNs 2 (ft), 2 (pt); LPNs 4 (ft); Nurses'
aides 25 (ft), 5 (pt); Activities coordinators 1
(ft), 1 (pt); Dietary staff 5 (ft), 5 (pt).
Facilities Dining room; Physical therapy
room; Activities room; Crafts room; Laundry
room; Barber/Beauty shop.
Activities Arts & crafts; Cards; Games;
Reading groups; Prayer groups; Movies;
Shopping trips; Dances/Social/Cultural
gatherings.

Sigourney Care Center
900 S Stone, Sigourney, IA 52591
(515) 622-2971
Admin JoAnn J Schefers. *Dir of Nursing*
Marilyn Waechter.
Licensure Intermediate care; Residential care.
Beds ICF 55; Residential care 6. *Certified*
Medicaid.
Owner Proprietary corp.
Admissions Requirements Medical
examination.
Staff RNs 2 (ft), 1 (pt); LPNs 3 (ft), 3 (pt);
Nurses' aides 10 (ft), 10 (pt); Physical
therapists 1 (pt); Occupational therapists 1
(pt); Speech therapists 1 (pt); Activities
coordinators 1 (pt); Dietitians 1 (pt).
Languages German.
Facilities Dining room; Physical therapy
room; Activities room; Crafts room; Laundry
room; Barber/Beauty shop.
Activities Arts & crafts; Cards; Games;
Reading groups; Prayer groups; Movies;
Shopping trips; Dances/Social/Cultural
gatherings.

Sioux Center

Sioux Center Community Hospital
605 S Main Ave, Sioux Center, IA 51250
(712) 722-1271
Admin Kevin Schmidt.
Licensure Intermediate care. Beds ICF 69.

Sioux City

Casa De Paz
2121 W 19th St, Sioux City, IA 51103
(712) 233-3127
Admin Gregory A Andersen.
Licensure Intermediate care. Beds ICF 95.
Certified Medicaid.
Owner Proprietary corp (Waverly Group).

Countryside Retirement Home
6120 Morningside Ave, Sioux City, IA 51106
(712) 276-3000
Admin Karl Luther. *Dir of Nursing* Lorraine
Edmunds.
Licensure Intermediate care; Retirement. Beds
ICF 160; Retirement 28. *Certified* Medicaid.
Owner Nonprofit organization/foundation.
Admissions Requirements Minimum age 55;
Medical examination; Physician's request.
Staff RNs 10 (ft), 3 (pt); LPNs 8 (ft), 1 (pt);
Nurses' aides 55 (ft), 12 (pt); Activities
coordinators 1 (ft); Dietitians 1 (ft).
Facilities Dining room; Physical therapy
room; Activities room; Crafts room; Laundry
room; Barber/Beauty shop; Library.
Activities Arts & crafts; Cards; Games;
Reading groups; Prayer groups; Movies;
Shopping trips; Dances/Social/Cultural
gatherings; Intergenerational programs; Pet
therapy.

Courage Homes
5945 Morningside Ave, Sioux City, IA 51106
(712) 276-9113
Admin James Mascarello.
Licensure Intermediate care for mentally
retarded. Beds ICF/MR 45.

Hallmark Care Center
3800 Indian Hills Dr, Sioux City, IA 51104
(712) 239-5025
Admin Thomas J Swanson.
Licensure Intermediate care. Beds ICF 50.
Certified Medicaid.

Holy Spirit Retirement Home
1701 W 25th St, Sioux City, IA 51103
(712) 252-2726
Admin Phyllis J Peters.
Licensure Intermediate care. Beds ICF 94.
Certified Medicaid.

Indian Hills Care Center
1800 Indian Hills Dr, Sioux City, IA 51104
(712) 239-4582
Admin Cheryl Swanson.
Licensure Intermediate care. Beds ICF 196.
Certified Medicaid.
Owner Proprietary corp (Mercy Health
Initiatives).

Julia's Valley Manor
3901 Green Ave, Sioux City, IA 51106
(712) 252-0114
Admin Julia M Tott. *Dir of Nursing* Cynthia J
Christiansen BSN RN.
Licensure Intermediate care. Beds ICF 50.
Certified Medicaid.
Owner Privately owned.
Admissions Requirements Minimum age 18;
Medical examination; Physician's request.
Staff RNs 1 (ft), 1 (pt); LPNs 2 (ft), 2 (pt);
Nurses' aides 10 (ft), 5 (pt); Activities
coordinators 1 (ft); Dietitians 1 (pt).
Facilities Dining room; Physical therapy
room; Activities room; Chapel; Crafts room;
Laundry room; Barber/Beauty shop; Movie
lounge.
Activities Arts & crafts; Cards; Games; Prayer
groups; Movies; Shopping trips; Dances/
Social/Cultural gatherings; Bingo; Auctions;
Exercises; Music.

Matney's Morningside Manor
3420 S Lakeport Rd, Sioux City, IA 51106
(712) 276-4311
Admin Linda K Holben.

Licensure Intermediate care. *Beds* ICF 103.
  Certified Medicaid.
Admissions Requirements Medical
  examination.
Staff RNs 2 (ft), 3 (pt); LPNs 1 (ft), 9 (pt);
  Nurses' aides 16 (ft), 16 (pt); Activities
  coordinators 1 (ft), 1 (pt); Dietitians 1 (pt).
Facilities Dining room; Physical therapy
  room; Activities room; Crafts room; Laundry
  room; Barber/Beauty shop.
Activities Arts & crafts; Cards; Games;
  Reading groups; Prayer groups; Movies;
  Shopping trips; Dances/Social/Cultural
  gatherings.

Matney's Westside Manor
1414 Casselman, Sioux City, IA 51103
(712) 258-0896
Admin John Buck.
Medical Dir Paula Nelson.
Licensure Intermediate care. *Beds* ICF 104.
  Certified Medicaid.
Owner Proprietary corp.
Admissions Requirements Minimum age 21;
  Medical examination; Physician's request.
Staff RNs 6 (ft), 2 (pt); LPNs 1 (ft), 2 (pt);
  Nurses' aides 22 (ft), 6 (pt); Activities
  coordinators 2 (ft); Dietitians 1 (pt).
Facilities Dining room; Activities room;
  Crafts room; Laundry room; Barber/Beauty
  shop; Library.
Activities Arts & crafts; Cards; Games;
  Reading groups; Prayer groups; Movies;
  Shopping trips; Dances/Social/Cultural
  gatherings.

Park View Home No 1
2800 Lincoln Way, Sioux City, IA 51106
(712) 274-2252
Admin James Mascarello.
Licensure Intermediate care for mentally
  retarded. *Beds* ICF/MR 45.

Sunrise Manor
5501 Gordon Dr E, Sioux City, IA 51106
(712) 276-3821
Admin John Gerwulf.
Medical Dir Kathy Gothier.
Licensure Intermediate care; Residential care.
  Beds ICF 90; Residential care 130. *Certified*
  Medicaid.
Owner Nonprofit corp.
Admissions Requirements Minimum age 62.
Staff RNs 8 (ft); LPNs 1 (ft); Nurses' aides 38
  (ft); Recreational therapists 2 (ft).
Facilities Dining room; Physical therapy
  room; Activities room; Chapel; Crafts room;
  Laundry room; Barber/Beauty shop; Library.
Activities Arts & crafts; Cards; Games;
  Reading groups; Prayer groups; Movies;
  Shopping trips; Dances/Social/Cultural
  gatherings.

Westwood Convalescent & Rest Home
3201 Stone Park Blvd, Sioux City, IA 51104
(712) 258-0135
Admin Janine J Hatch.
Licensure Intermediate care. *Beds* ICF 85.
  Certified Medicaid.
Owner Proprietary corp (Mercy Health
  Initiatives).

Sioux Rapids

Sioux Care Center
702 Blake St, Sioux Rapids, IA 50585
(712) 283-2302
Admin Sandra Tielbur.
Medical Dir Jacki Bertness.
Licensure Intermediate care. *Beds* ICF 35.
  Certified Medicare.
Owner Proprietary corp.
Admissions Requirements Physician's request.
Staff RNs 1 (ft), 1 (pt); LPNs 6 (pt); Nurses'
  aides 13 (pt); Activities coordinators 1 (ft).
Facilities Dining room; Activities room;
  Crafts room; Laundry room; Barber/Beauty
  shop.

Activities Arts & crafts; Cards; Games;
  Reading groups; Prayer groups; Movies;
  Shopping trips; Dances/Social/Cultural
  gatherings.

Solon

Solon Nursing Care Center
523 E 5th St, Solon, IA 52333
(319) 644-3492
Admin Joy D Mote.
Licensure Intermediate care. *Beds* ICF 68.
  Certified Medicaid.

Spencer

Longhouse Residence
711 W 11th St, Spencer, IA 51301
(712) 262-2344
Admin Jim Manzer.
Medical Dir Kathy Pettitt.
Licensure Intermediate care; Residential care.
  Beds ICF 138; Residential care 60. *Certified*
  Medicaid.
Owner Privately owned.
Staff RNs 7 (ft), 2 (pt); LPNs 3 (ft), 3 (pt);
  Nurses' aides 30 (ft), 10 (pt); Physical
  therapists 1 (pt); Recreational therapists 4
  (pt); Activities coordinators 1 (ft).
Facilities Dining room; Activities room;
  Laundry room; Barber/Beauty shop.
Activities Arts & crafts; Cards; Games;
  Reading groups; Prayer groups; Movies;
  Shopping trips; Dances/Social/Cultural
  gatherings.

St Luke's Lutheran Home
Saint Luke Dr, Spencer, IA 51301
(712) 262-5931
Admin Lyle E Peters.
Medical Dir Dr Frink; Dr Fieselmann.
Licensure Intermediate care. *Beds* ICF 116.
  Certified Medicaid.
Staff Physicians 9 (ft); RNs 2 (ft), 7 (pt);
  LPNs 3 (ft), 5 (pt); Nurses' aides 30 (ft), 19
  (pt); Physical therapists 1 (pt); Recreational
  therapists 3 (pt); Speech therapists 1 (pt);
  Activities coordinators 1 (ft); Dietitians 1
  (pt); Audiologists 1 (pt); Dentists 1 (pt).
Affiliation Lutheran.
Facilities Dining room; Physical therapy
  room; Activities room; Chapel; Crafts room;
  Laundry room; Barber/Beauty shop; Library.
Activities Arts & crafts; Cards; Games;
  Reading groups; Prayer groups; Movies;
  Shopping trips; Dances/Social/Cultural
  gatherings.

Spencer Municipal Hospital
114 E 12th St, Spencer, IA 51301
(712) 264-6111
Admin James L Striepe.
Licensure Skilled care. *Beds* SNF 14.

Stacyville

Stacyville Community Nursing Home
RR 1 Box 4C, Stacyville, IA 50476
(515) 737-2215
Admin Anita Adams.
Licensure Intermediate care; Residential care.
  Beds ICF 47; Residential care 18. *Certified*
  Medicaid.
Owner Nonprofit corp.
Admissions Requirements Medical
  examination.
Staff RNs 1 (ft); LPNs 4 (pt); Nurses' aides 10
  (ft), 12 (pt); Activities coordinators 1 (ft), 1
  (pt).
Facilities Dining room; Physical therapy
  room; Activities room; Laundry room;
  Barber/Beauty shop.
Activities Arts & crafts; Cards; Games; Prayer
  groups; Movies; Dances/Social/Cultural
  gatherings; Flower gardens.

Stanton

Stanton Care Center
213 Halland Ave, Stanton, IA 51573
(712) 829-2727
Admin Louise Hart.
Medical Dir Allen Hart; Louise Hart.
Licensure Intermediate care; Residential care.
  Beds ICF 31; Residential care 30. *Certified*
  Medicaid.
Admissions Requirements Minimum age 18;
  Medical examination; Physician's request.
Staff Physicians; RNs; LPNs; Nurses' aides;
  Physical therapists; Recreational therapists;
  Speech therapists; Activities coordinators;
  Dietitians; Ophthalmologists; Podiatrists;
  Audiologists.
Facilities Dining room; Physical therapy
  room; Activities room; Chapel; Crafts room;
  Laundry room; Barber/Beauty shop; Library.
Activities Arts & crafts; Cards; Games; Prayer
  groups; Movies; Dances/Social/Cultural
  gatherings.

State Center

State Center Manor
703 NW 3rd St, State Center, IA 50247
(515) 483-2812
Admin Anne Fiscus.
Licensure Intermediate care. *Beds* ICF 51.
  Certified Medicaid.

Storm Lake

Buena Vista Manor
1325 N Lake, Storm Lake, IA 50588
(712) 732-3254
Admin Patricia J Richard. *Dir of Nursing*
  Barbara Smith; Marilyn Spooner.
Licensure Intermediate care. *Beds* ICF 100.
  Certified Medicaid.
Owner Proprietary corp.
Admissions Requirements Medical
  examination; Physician's request.
Staff RNs 5 (ft); LPNs 5 (ft), 4 (pt); Nurses'
  aides 28 (ft), 4 (pt); Physical therapists 1
  (pt); Activities coordinators 1 (ft), 1 (pt);
  Dietitians 1 (pt).
Facilities Dining room; Physical therapy
  room; Activities room; Chapel; Crafts room;
  Laundry room; Barber/Beauty shop.
Activities Arts & crafts; Cards; Games;
  Reading groups; Prayer groups; Movies;
  Shopping trips; Dances/Social/Cultural
  gatherings; Intergenerational programs; Pet
  therapy.

Methodist Manor
4th at Larchwood, Storm Lake, IA 50588
(712) 732-1120
Admin Blaine Donaldson.
Licensure Intermediate care; Residential care.
  Beds ICF 93; Residential care 88. *Certified*
  Medicaid.
Admissions Requirements Minimum age 55;
  Medical examination.
Staff Physicians 14 (pt); RNs 4 (ft), 3 (pt);
  LPNs 5 (ft), 4 (pt); Nurses' aides 19 (ft), 16
  (pt); Physical therapists 1 (ft), 1 (pt);
  Recreational therapists 1 (ft); Speech
  therapists 1 (pt); Activities coordinators 1
  (ft); Dietitians 1 (pt); Podiatrists 2 (pt);
  Audiologists 1 (pt); Dentists 2 (pt).
Affiliation Methodist.
Facilities Dining room; Physical therapy
  room; Activities room; Chapel; Crafts room;
  Laundry room; Barber/Beauty shop; Library.
Activities Arts & crafts; Cards; Games;
  Reading groups; Prayer groups; Movies;
  Shopping trips; Dances/Social/Cultural
  gatherings.

Story City

Bethany Manor
212 Lafayette St, Story City, IA 50248
(515) 733-4325
Admin Mark A Teigland.
Medical Dir Ruth Gabrielson.
Licensure Intermediate care; Alzheimer's care.
Beds ICF 167. *Certified* Medicaid.
Owner Nonprofit corp.
Staff RNs 12 (ft), 2 (pt); LPNs 5 (ft), 2 (pt);
Nurses' aides 40 (ft), 35 (pt); Physical
therapists 1 (ft); Activities coordinators 1
(ft); Dietitians 1 (pt); Activity aide 2 (ft);
Social worker 1 (ft); Volunteer coordinator 1
(ft); Dietary aides 18 (ft); Cooks 5 (ft).
Affiliation Lutheran.
Activities Arts & crafts; Games; Reading
groups; Prayer groups; Movies; Shopping
trips; Dances/Social/Cultural gatherings.

Stratford

Stratford Care Center
PO Box 370, 1200 Hwy 175 E, Stratford, IA
50249
(515) 838-2795
Admin Deb Hightshoe. *Dir of Nursing* Karla
Lyle BSN.
Licensure Intermediate care. Beds ICF 70.
Private Pay Patients 39%. *Certified*
Medicaid.
Owner Nonprofit corp (Mercy Health
Initiatives).
Admissions Requirements Minimum age 21;
Medical examination; Physician's request.
Staff RNs 2 (ft); LPNs 2 (ft), 1 (pt); Activities
coordinators 1 (ft).
Facilities Dining room; Physical therapy
room; Activities room; Laundry room;
Barber/Beauty shop.
Activities Arts & crafts; Cards; Games;
Movies; Dances/Social/Cultural gatherings;
Intergenerational programs.

Strawberry Point

Lutheran Home
313 Elkader St, Strawberry Point, IA 52076
(319) 933-6037
Admin Joan Kelley. *Dir of Nursing* Deb
Schloss RN. *Medical Dir* Craig Thompson
MD.
Licensure Skilled care; Intermediate care;
Independent living; Alzheimer's care. Beds
SNF 21; ICF 71; Independent living 40.
Certified Medicaid; Medicare.
Owner Nonprofit corp.
Admissions Requirements Medical
examination; Physician's request.
Staff RNs 10 (ft), 6 (pt); LPNs 3 (ft); Nurses'
aides 40 (ft), 23 (pt); Physical therapists 1
(pt); Occupational therapists 1 (pt); Speech
therapists 1 (pt); Activities coordinators 3
(ft); Dietitians 1 (pt); Ophthalmologists 1
(pt); Podiatrists 1 (pt).
Languages Sign.
Affiliation Lutheran.
Facilities Dining room; Physical therapy
room; Activities room; Chapel; Crafts room;
Laundry room; Barber/Beauty shop; Library.
Activities Arts & crafts; Cards; Games;
Reading groups; Prayer groups; Movies;
Shopping trips; Dances/Social/Cultural
gatherings.

Stuart

Community Care Center
1603 S 7th, Stuart, IA 50250
(515) 523-2815
Admin Mary Ellen Gilman. *Dir of Nursing*
Lori Poe RN. *Medical Dir* Dr D E Taylor.
Licensure Intermediate care; Retirement. Beds
ICF 60. *Private Pay Patients* 60%. *Certified*
Medicaid.

Owner Proprietary corp (Community Care
Centers).
Admissions Requirements Medical
examination.
Staff Physicians; RNs; LPNs; Nurses' aides;
Physical therapists; Recreational therapists;
Speech therapists; Activities coordinators;
Dietitians; Podiatrists; Audiologists.
Facilities Dining room; Physical therapy
room; Activities room; Chapel; Crafts room;
Laundry room; Barber/Beauty shop; Library;
Day care.
Activities Arts & crafts; Cards; Games;
Reading groups; Prayer groups; Movies;
Shopping trips; Dances/Social/Cultural
gatherings; Intergenerational programs; Pet
therapy; Spelling bee; Current events;
Residents' council; Field trips; Diner's club;
"Lunch Bunch"; Quilt shows.

Sumner

Hillcrest Home Inc
915 W 1st St, Sumner, IA 50674
(319) 578-8591
Admin Eunice A Neil RN. *Dir of Nursing*
Junever Heying RN.
Licensure Intermediate care; Independent
living apartments. Beds ICF 86; Independent
living apts 10. *Private Pay Patients* 60%.
Certified Medicaid.
Owner Nonprofit organization/foundation.
Admissions Requirements Medical
examination.
Staff RNs 4 (ft); LPNs 5 (ft); Nurses' aides 15
(ft), 23 (pt); Physical therapists (consultant);
Activities coordinators; Dietitians
(consultant).
Facilities Dining room; Physical therapy
room; Activities room; Chapel; Crafts room;
Laundry room; Barber/Beauty shop.
Activities Arts & crafts; Games; Reading
groups; Prayer groups; Movies; Shopping
trips; Dances/Social/Cultural gatherings.

Sutherland

Millie's Rest Home
506 4th St, Sutherland, IA 51058
(712) 446-3857
Admin Kent D Walton.
Licensure Intermediate care. Beds ICF 44.
Certified Medicaid.

Tabor

Tabor Manor Care Center
400 Main St, Tabor, IA 51653
(712) 629-2645
Admin Leonard B Worcester.
Medical Dir Shirley Maxwell.
Licensure Intermediate care. Beds ICF 63.
Certified Medicaid.
Owner Privately owned.
Admissions Requirements Medical
examination; Physician's request.
Staff RNs; LPNs; Nurses' aides; Physical
therapists; Reality therapists; Recreational
therapists; Occupational therapists; Activities
coordinators; Dietitians.
Facilities Dining room; Physical therapy
room; Laundry room; Barber/Beauty shop.
Activities Arts & crafts; Games; Reading
groups; Prayer groups; Movies; Dances/
Social/Cultural gatherings.

Tama

Sunny Hill Care Center
Hwy 63 N, Tama, IA 52339
(515) 484-4061
Admin Rosemary Schrack LPN. *Dir of
Nursing* Sandra Roeder LPN.
Licensure Intermediate care; Retirement. Beds
ICF 51. *Certified* Medicaid.
Owner Proprietary corp.

Admissions Requirements Medical
examination.
Staff RNs 1 (pt); LPNs 3 (ft), 1 (pt); Nurses'
aides; Physical therapists (consultant);
Occupational therapists (consultant); Speech
therapists (consultant); Activities
coordinators 1 (ft); Dietitians 1 (pt);
Podiatrists (consultant); Audiologists
(consultant); Pharmacist (consultant).
Languages German, Czech.
Facilities Dining room; Chapel; Crafts room;
Laundry room; Barber/Beauty shop;
Activities room with kitchen.
Activities Arts & crafts; Cards; Games;
Reading groups; Prayer groups; Movies;
Shopping trips; Dances/Social/Cultural
gatherings; Intergenerational programs; Pet
therapy; Baking.

Tipton

Cedar Manor
1200 Mulberry, Tipton, IA 52772
(319) 886-2133
Admin Nicki J Aikman.
Medical Dir Cathy Ford.
Licensure Intermediate care. Beds ICF 55.
Certified Medicaid.
Owner Nonprofit organization/foundation.
Staff RNs 3 (ft); LPNs 1 (ft), 2 (pt); Nurses'
aides 17 (ft), 10 (pt); Physical therapists 1
(pt); Activities coordinators 3 (pt); Dietitians
1 (pt); Ophthalmologists 1 (pt).
Facilities Dining room; Physical therapy
room; Activities room; Laundry room;
Barber/Beauty shop; Library.
Activities Arts & crafts; Cards; Games;
Reading groups; Prayer groups; Movies;
Dances/Social/Cultural gatherings; Bowling;
Volleyball; Shuffleboard.

Titonka

Titonka Care Center
Hwy P-64, Box 2, Titonka, IA 50480
(515) 928-2600
Admin Murray D Berggren.
Licensure Intermediate care. Beds ICF 51.
Certified Medicaid.

Toledo

Bethesda Care Center
Grandview Dr, Toledo, IA 52342
(515) 484-9922
Admin Paul M Whisler. *Dir of Nursing*
Marlene Kajer RN.
Licensure Intermediate care; Retirement. Beds
ICF 99. *Certified* Medicaid.
Owner Nonprofit corp (Bethesda Care
Centers).
Admissions Requirements Minimum age 16;
Medical examination.
Staff RNs 1 (ft), 1 (pt); LPNs 5 (ft); Nurses'
aides 25 (ft); Activities coordinators 1 (ft), 1
(pt).
Facilities Dining room; Physical therapy
room; Activities room; Chapel; Crafts room;
Laundry room; Barber/Beauty shop; Library;
Living room.
Activities Arts & crafts; Cards; Games;
Reading groups; Prayer groups; Movies;
Shopping trips; Dances/Social/Cultural
gatherings.

Traer

Sunrise Hill Care Center
909 6th St, Traer, IA 50675
(319) 478-2730
Admin Karen Brezina.
Medical Dir Kathy Hark.
Licensure Intermediate care. Beds ICF 64.
Certified Medicaid.
Owner Proprietary corp.

Staff RNs 2 (ft), 2 (pt); LPNs 2 (ft), 2 (pt);
Activities coordinators 1 (ft); Dietitians 1
(pt).
Facilities Dining room; Activities room;
Chapel; Crafts room; Laundry room; Barber/
Beauty shop.
Activities Arts & crafts; Cards; Games;
Reading groups; Movies; Baking.

Tripoli

Tripoli Nursing Home
604 3rd St SW, Tripoli, IA 50676
(319) 882-4269
Admin Ruby K Greenlees.
Licensure Intermediate care. *Beds* ICF 22.
Certified Medicaid.
Admissions Requirements Physician's request.
Staff Physicians 4 (pt); RNs 3 (pt); LPNs 2
(pt); Nurses' aides 4 (ft), 11 (pt); Activities
coordinators 1 (pt); Dietitians 1 (pt).
Facilities Dining room; Activities room;
Crafts room; Laundry room; Main lobby.
Activities Arts & crafts; Cards; Games;
Reading groups; Movies; Shopping trips;
Church groups.

Urbandale

Quality Health Care Center
4614 NW 84th St, Urbandale, IA 50322
(515) 270-6838
Admin JoAnn P Webb.
Medical Dir Dr Roy Overton.
Licensure Intermediate care. *Beds* ICF 120.
Certified Medicaid.
Admissions Requirements Medical
examination.
Staff RNs 3 (ft), 1 (pt); LPNs 5 (ft), 2 (pt);
Nurses' aides 25 (ft); Activities coordinators
2 (ft); Dietitians 1 (pt).
Facilities Dining room; Physical therapy
room; Activities room; Chapel; Laundry
room; Barber/Beauty shop.
Activities Arts & crafts; Cards; Games;
Reading groups; Movies.

Villisca

Villisca Good Samaritan Center
Central & Redmond, Villisca, IA 50864
(712) 826-9592
Admin Loren H Clayton.
Licensure Intermediate care. *Beds* ICF 65.
Certified Medicaid.

Vinton

Virginia Gay Hospital Inc
502 N 9th Ave, Vinton, IA 52349
(319) 472-2348, 472-2144 FAX
Admin Mark S Hearn. *Dir of Nursing* Sandra
Studebaker RN. *Medical Dir* S L Anthony
MD.
Licensure Intermediate care. *Beds* ICF 58.
Private Pay Patients 60%. *Certified*
Medicaid; Medicare.
Owner Nonprofit organization/foundation.
Staff RNs 1 (ft), 2 (pt); LPNs 1 (ft), 6 (pt);
Nurses' aides 47 (pt); Physical therapists;
Dietitians.
Facilities Dining room; Physical therapy
room; Activities room; Laundry room;
Barber/Beauty shop; Adjoined to an acute
care hospital & medical clinic.
Activities Arts & crafts; Cards; Games; Prayer
groups; Movies; Shopping trips; Dances/
Social/Cultural gatherings; Pet therapy.

Lutheran Home for the Aged
1301 2nd Ave, Vinton, IA 52349
(319) 472-4751
Admin Louis E Betts.
Medical Dir Linda Cole.
Licensure Intermediate care; Alzheimer's care.
Beds ICF 61. *Certified* Medicaid.

Owner Nonprofit corp.
Admissions Requirements Minimum age 65;
Medical examination.
Staff RNs 1 (ft), 2 (pt); LPNs 3 (ft), 5 (pt);
Nurses' aides 13 (ft), 13 (pt); Activities
coordinators 1 (ft); Dietitians 1 (pt).
Affiliation Lutheran.
Facilities Dining room; Physical therapy
room; Activities room; Chapel; Laundry
room; Barber/Beauty shop.
Activities Arts & crafts; Cards; Games;
Reading groups; Prayer groups; Movies;
Shopping trips; Dances/Social/Cultural
gatherings; Current events; Manicures.

Wall Lake

Twilight Acres Inc
6th & Melrose Ave, Wall Lake, IA 51466
(712) 664-2488
Admin Lauretta Skarin.
Medical Dir Nadine Peters.
Licensure Intermediate care; Residential care;
Alzheimer's care. *Beds* ICF 70; Residential
care 18. *Certified* Medicaid.
Owner Nonprofit corp.
Admissions Requirements Medical
examination.
Staff RNs 3 (ft), 3 (pt); LPNs 3 (ft), 2 (pt);
Nurses' aides 15 (ft), 13 (pt); Activities
coordinators 2 (ft).
Facilities Dining room; Physical therapy
room; Activities room; Chapel; Crafts room;
Laundry room; Barber/Beauty shop.
Activities Arts & crafts; Cards; Games;
Reading groups; Prayer groups; Movies;
Shopping trips; Dances/Social/Cultural
gatherings; Wine party; Dining out; Picnics;
Fishing trips.

Wapello

Wapello Nursing Home
Hwy 61 S, Wapello, IA 52653
(319) 523-2001
Admin James Keldgord.
Licensure Intermediate care. *Beds* ICF 54.
Certified Medicaid.

Washington

Halcyon House
1015 S Iowa Ave, Washington, IA 52353
(319) 653-3523
Admin Brian C Peterson.
Medical Dir Sue Knight.
Licensure Intermediate care; Residential care;
Alzheimer's care. *Beds* ICF 29; Residential
care 15. *Certified* Medicaid.
Owner Nonprofit corp.
Staff RNs; LPNs; Nurses' aides; Physical
therapists; Activities coordinators.
Affiliation Methodist.
Facilities Dining room; Physical therapy
room; Activities room; Chapel; Crafts room;
Laundry room; Barber/Beauty shop; Library;
Gardening; Potlucks; Programs.
Activities Arts & crafts; Cards; Games;
Reading groups; Movies; Shopping trips;
Dances/Social/Cultural gatherings.

United Presbyterian Home
1203 E Washington St, Washington, IA 52353
(319) 653-5473
Admin Richard R Colby. *Dir of Nursing*
Janice Yotty RN.
Licensure Intermediate care; Residential care.
Beds ICF 36; Residential care 16. *Certified*
Medicaid.
Owner Nonprofit organization/foundation.
Admissions Requirements Minimum age 62;
Medical examination.

Staff RNs 4 (ft), 1 (pt); LPNs 2 (pt); Nurses'
aides 16 (ft), 4 (pt); Physical therapists 1
(pt); Occupational therapists 1 (pt); Speech
therapists 1 (pt); Activities coordinators 1
(ft), 1 (pt); Dietitians 1 (pt).
Affiliation Presbyterian.
Facilities Dining room; Physical therapy
room; Activities room; Chapel; Crafts room;
Laundry room; Barber/Beauty shop; Library.
Activities Arts & crafts; Cards; Games;
Reading groups; Prayer groups; Movies;
Dances/Social/Cultural gatherings.

Washington Care Center
601 E Polk St, Washington, IA 52353
(319) 653-6526
Admin Jenny Kennedy. *Dir of Nursing* Greta
Wells.
Licensure Intermediate care. *Beds* ICF 125.
Certified Medicaid.
Owner Proprietary corp.
Admissions Requirements Medical
examination; Physician's request.
Staff RNs 6 (ft); LPNs 3 (ft), 3 (pt); Nurses'
aides 26 (ft), 18 (pt); Activities coordinators
2 (ft).
Facilities Dining room; Physical therapy
room; Activities room; Laundry room;
Barber/Beauty shop.
Activities Arts & crafts; Cards; Games;
Reading groups; Prayer groups; Movies;
Dances/Social/Cultural gatherings.

Waterloo

Allen Memorial Hospital
1825 Logan Ave, Waterloo, IA 50703
(319) 235-3941
Admin Larry W Pugh.
Licensure Skilled care. *Beds* SNF 20.

Americana Healthcare Center
201 W Ridgeway Ave, Waterloo, IA 50701
(319) 234-7777, 234-7779 FAX
Admin Vickie J Meester. *Dir of Nursing*
Cheryl Wilson. *Medical Dir* Ronald Roth
MD.
Licensure Skilled care. *Beds* SNF 67. *Certified*
Medicaid; Medicare.
Owner Proprietary corp (Manor Care Inc).
Admissions Requirements Physician's request.
Staff RNs 5 (ft), 1 (pt); LPNs 5 (ft), 4 (pt);
Nurses' aides 19 (ft), 7 (pt); Physical
therapists 2 (pt); Occupational therapists 1
(pt); Speech therapists 1 (pt); Activities
coordinators 1 (ft), 1 (pt); Dietitians 1 (ft).
Facilities Dining room; Physical therapy
room; Activities room; Crafts room; Laundry
room; Barber/Beauty shop; Library.
Activities Arts & crafts; Cards; Games;
Reading groups; Prayer groups; Movies;
Shopping trips; Dances/Social/Cultural
gatherings; Intergenerational programs; Pet
therapy.

Black Hawk County Health Care
1407 Independence Ave, Waterloo, IA 50703
(319) 291-2567
Licensure Intermediate care. *Beds* 120.
Certified Medicaid.
Admissions Requirements Medical
examination; Physician's request.
Staff RNs 2 (ft); LPNs 12 (ft), 2 (pt); Nurses'
aides 40 (ft); Physical therapists 1 (pt);
Reality therapists 1 (pt); Recreational
therapists 1 (ft); Occupational therapists 1
(pt); Speech therapists 1 (pt); Activities
coordinators 1 (ft); Dietitians 1 (ft);
Podiatrists 1 (pt); Dentists 2 (pt).
Facilities Dining room; Activities room;
Chapel; Crafts room; Laundry room; Barber/
Beauty shop.
Activities Arts & crafts; Cards; Games;
Reading groups; Prayer groups; Movies;
Shopping trips; Dances/Social/Cultural
gatherings.

Country View
1410 W Dunkerton Rd, Waterloo, IA 50701
(319) 291-2509
Admin Albert R Maricle.
Licensure Intermediate care; Intermediate care
for mentally retarded. *Beds* ICF 165; ICF/
MR 45.

Covenant Medical Center
2101 Kimball, Waterloo, IA 50702
(319) 291-3131
Admin Raymond Burfeind.
Licensure Skilled care. *Beds* SNF 18.

Covenant Medical Center
3421 W 9th St, Waterloo, IA 50702
(319) 236-4190
Admin Roger S Schuler. *Dir of Nursing* Ellen
Stapella RN. *Medical Dir* Richard Corton
MD.
Licensure Skilled care. *Beds* SNF 44. *Private
Pay Patients* 5%. *Certified* Medicaid;
Medicare.
Owner Nonprofit organization/foundation.
Admissions Requirements Minimum age 20;
Medical examination; Physician's request;
Mainly accomodates patients transferred
from facility's own units.
Staff Physicians 19 (pt); RNs 10 (ft), 6 (pt);
LPNs 15 (ft), 4 (pt); Nurses' aides 9 (ft), 7
(pt); Physical therapists 2 (ft); Recreational
therapists 1 (pt); Occupational therapists 1
(pt); Speech therapists 1 (pt); Activities
coordinators 1 (pt); Dietitians 2 (ft);
Ophthalmologists 1 (pt); Podiatrists 1 (pt).
Affiliation Roman Catholic.
Facilities Dining room; Physical therapy
room; Activities room; Chapel; Crafts room;
Ventilator dependent care; Coma
stimulation.
Activities Arts & crafts; Cards; Games;
Reading groups; Prayer groups; Pet therapy.

Friendship Village
600 Park Ln, Waterloo, IA 50702
(319) 291-8100
Admin Mary B O'Brien.
Licensure Skilled care; Intermediate care;
Residential care. *Beds* SNF 16; ICF 33;
Residential care 18. *Certified* Medicaid;
Medicare.

Harmony House Health Care Center
2950 W Shaulis Rd, Waterloo, IA 50701
(319) 234-4495
Admin Daniel M Larmore MS.
Medical Dir Ronald Roth MD; Walter
Verduyn MD.
Licensure Skilled care; Intermediate care;
Intermediate care for mentally retarded.
Beds ICF/MR 68; Swing beds SNF/ICF 46.
Private Pay Patients 70%. *Certified*
Medicaid; Medicare.
Owner Proprietary corp (ABCM Corp).
Admissions Requirements Minimum age 16;
Medical examination; Physician's request.
Staff Physicians 18 (pt); RNs 6 (ft), 2 (pt);
LPNs 10 (ft), 8 (pt); Nurses' aides 66 (ft), 20
(pt); Physical therapists 3 (ft), 2 (pt);
Recreational therapists 6 (ft); Occupational
therapists 2 (ft), 1 (pt); Speech therapists 2
(ft), 2 (pt); Activities coordinators 3 (ft);
Dietitians 1 (ft); Ophthalmologists 1 (pt);
Podiatrists 1 (pt); Audiologists 1 (pt).
Facilities Dining room; Physical therapy
room; Activities room; Crafts room; Laundry
room; Barber/Beauty shop; Library; Living
rooms; Brain-injury unit.
Activities Arts & crafts; Cards; Games;
Reading groups; Prayer groups; Movies;
Shopping trips; Dances/Social/Cultural
gatherings; Intergenerational programs; Pet
therapy; Exercise; Music therapy.

Parkview Gardens Care Center
310 Upland Dr, Waterloo, IA 50701
(319) 234-4423
Admin John A Jackson.

Licensure Intermediate care. *Beds* ICF 160.
Certified Medicaid.
Owner Proprietary corp (Mercy Health
Initiatives).

Ravenwood Health Care Center
2651 Saint Francis Dr, Waterloo, IA 50702
(319) 232-6808
Admin Gordon Kline.
Licensure Intermediate care. *Beds* ICF 196.
Certified Medicaid.
Owner Proprietary corp (Mercy Health
Initiatives).

Waukon

Northgate Care Center
10th Ave NW, Waukon, IA 52172
(319) 568-3493
Admin Lou Ann Wikan. *Dir of Nursing*
Maxine Connor RN. *Medical Dir* Dr B R
Withers.
Licensure Intermediate care; Retirement. *Beds*
ICF 51. *Private Pay Patients* 30%. *Certified*
Medicaid.
Owner Proprietary corp (ABCM Corp).
Admissions Requirements Minimum age 18;
Medical examination.
Staff RNs 2 (ft), 1 (pt); LPNs 4 (ft), 3 (pt);
Nurses' aides 11 (ft), 7 (pt); Activities
coordinators 1 (ft); Dietitians (consultant);
Social workers (consultant).
Facilities Dining room; Activities room;
Laundry room; Barber/Beauty shop.
Activities Arts & crafts; Cards; Games;
Reading groups; Prayer groups; Movies;
Dances/Social/Cultural gatherings.

Waukon Good Samaritan Center
21 E Main St, Waukon, IA 52172
(319) 568-3447
Admin Jay E Johnson.
Licensure Intermediate care; Residential care.
Beds ICF 100; Residential care 11. *Certified*
Medicaid.
Owner Nonprofit corp (Evangelical Lutheran/
Good Samaritan Society).

Waverly

Bartel's Lutheran Home
1922 5th Ave NW, Waverly, IA 50677
(319) 352-4540
Admin Terry D Dandy.
Licensure Intermediate care; Residential care.
Beds ICF 146; Residential care 96. *Certified*
Medicaid.
Staff RNs 5 (ft), 1 (pt); LPNs 9 (ft), 11 (pt);
Nurses' aides 29 (ft), 64 (pt); Activities
coordinators 1 (ft); Dietitians 1 (pt).
Affiliation Lutheran.
Facilities Dining room; Activities room;
Chapel; Crafts room; Laundry room; Barber/
Beauty shop; Library.
Activities Arts & crafts; Cards; Games;
Reading groups; Prayer groups; Movies;
Shopping trips; Dances/Social/Cultural
gatherings.

Wayland

Parkview Home
102 N Jackson, Wayland, IA 52654
(319) 256-3525
Admin Kelly R Overton.
Medical Dir Donna Heisner.
Licensure Intermediate care; Residential care.
Beds ICF 30; Residential care 19. *Certified*
Medicaid.
Owner Nonprofit organization/foundation.
Staff RNs 1 (ft); LPNs 3 (ft); Nurses' aides 11
(ft); Recreational therapists 1 (ft); Activities
coordinators 1 (ft); Dietitians 1 (pt).
Affiliation Mennonite.
Facilities Dining room; Physical therapy
room; Activities room; Chapel; Crafts room;
Laundry room; Barber/Beauty shop; Library.

Activities Arts & crafts; Cards; Games;
Reading groups; Prayer groups; Movies;
Shopping trips.

Webster City

Crestview Manor
2401 S Des Moines, Webster City, IA 50595
(515) 832-2727
Admin Joe H Sherman.
Medical Dir Lanette Patch.
Licensure Intermediate care; Senior citizen
apartments. *Beds* ICF 84; Senior citizen apts
22. *Certified* Medicaid.
Owner Privately owned.
Admissions Requirements Medical
examination.
Staff RNs; LPNs; Nurses' aides; Activities
coordinators.
Facilities Dining room; Laundry room;
Barber/Beauty shop.
Activities Arts & crafts; Games; Reading
groups; Prayer groups; Movies.

Southfield Care Center
2416 S Des Moines St, Webster City, IA
50595
(515) 832-3881
Admin Diana Shefveland.
Medical Dir Mary Halgrim.
Licensure Intermediate care. *Beds* ICF 88.
Certified Medicaid.
Owner Privately owned.
Admissions Requirements Minimum age 45;
Medical examination.
Staff RNs 1 (ft), 5 (pt); LPNs 1 (ft); Nurses'
aides 25 (ft), 6 (pt); Activities coordinators 1
(ft).
Facilities Dining room; Activities room;
Laundry room; Barber/Beauty shop.
Activities Arts & crafts; Cards; Games;
Reading groups; Prayer groups; Movies;
Shopping trips; Dances/Social/Cultural
gatherings.

Wellman

Parkview Manor
516 13th St, Wellman, IA 52356
(319) 646-2911
Admin Jerry Nicholls.
Medical Dir Dr Dwight Kauffman.
Licensure Intermediate care; Residential care.
Beds ICF 94; Residential care 23. *Certified*
Medicaid.
Admissions Requirements Medical
examination; Physician's request.
Staff RNs 4 (ft), 4 (pt); LPNs 1 (ft), 1 (pt);
Nurses' aides 21 (ft), 10 (pt); Physical
therapists 1 (pt); Activities coordinators 1
(ft), 2 (pt); Dietitians 1 (pt).
Facilities Dining room; Physical therapy
room; Activities room; Laundry room;
Barber/Beauty shop.
Activities Arts & crafts; Games; Reading
groups; Prayer groups; Movies; Shopping
trips; Dances/Social/Cultural gatherings.

West Bend

West Bend Care Center
203 4th St NW, West Bend, IA 50597
(515) 887-4071
Admin Phyllis Fandel.
Licensure Intermediate care. *Beds* ICF 56.
Certified Medicaid.

West Branch

Crestview Care Center
Oliphant & Northside Dr, West Branch, IA
52358
(319) 643-2551
Admin Cheryl J Mercer.

Licensure Intermediate care. *Beds* ICF 65.
Certified Medicaid.
Owner Proprietary corp (Mercy Health
Initiatives).

West Des Moines

Fountain West Health Center
1501 Office Park Rd, West Des Moines, IA
50265
(515) 223-1223
Admin Gary A Tiemeyer.
Licensure Intermediate care; Residential care.
Beds ICF 156; Residential care 38. *Certified*
Medicaid.

Woodbury West Care Center
1211 Vine St, West Des Moines, IA 50265
(515) 223-1251
Admin Jerry Bell.
Medical Dir Dr R Overton.
Licensure Intermediate care. *Beds* ICF 214.
Certified Medicaid.
Owner Proprietary corp.
Admissions Requirements Minimum age 18.
Staff RNs 15 (ft); LPNs 15 (ft); Nurses' aides
40 (ft); Activities coordinators 3 (ft);
Dietitians 1 (ft); Ophthalmologists 1 (ft);
Podiatrists 1 (ft).
Facilities Dining room; Physical therapy
room; Activities room; Chapel; Crafts room;
Laundry room; Barber/Beauty shop; Library.
Activities Arts & crafts; Cards; Games;
Reading groups; Prayer groups; Movies;
Shopping trips; Dances/Social/Cultural
gatherings; Intergenerational programs.

West Liberty

Simpson Memorial Home
1001 N Miller St, West Liberty, IA 52776
(319) 627-4775
Admin Jack L McIntosh.
Licensure Intermediate care. *Beds* ICF 63.
Certified Medicaid.

West Point

West Point Care Center
N 6th & Ave G, West Point, IA 52656
(319) 837-6117
Admin Patricia M Mumme. *Dir of Nursing*
Judith F Kirberg. *Medical Dir* David Hull
DO.
Licensure Intermediate care; Alzheimer's care.
Beds ICF; Alzheimer's care 51. *Certified*
Medicaid.
Owner Privately owned.
Admissions Requirements Minimum age 16;
Medical examination.
Staff RNs 2 (ft), 1 (pt); LPNs 3 (ft), 1 (pt);
Nurses' aides 10 (ft), 5 (pt); Physical
therapists; Activities coordinators 1 (ft);
Dietitians 1 (pt).
Facilities Dining room; Physical therapy
room; Activities room; Chapel; Crafts room;
Laundry room; Barber/Beauty shop.
Activities Arts & crafts; Cards; Games;
Reading groups; Prayer groups; Movies;
Shopping trips; Dances/Social/Cultural
gatherings; Pet therapy.

West Union

West Union Good Samaritan Center
300 Hall St, West Union, IA 52175
(319) 422-3814
Admin Terrance M McGinnity. *Dir of Nursing*
Kathleen Berns RN.
Licensure Intermediate care; Retirement. *Beds*
ICF 71. *Certified* Medicaid.
Owner Nonprofit corp (Evangelical Lutheran/
Good Samaritan Society).
Admissions Requirements Medical
examination; Physician's request.

Staff RNs 2 (ft), 4 (pt); LPNs 1 (ft), 5 (pt);
Nurses' aides 12 (ft), 18 (pt); Activities
coordinators 1 (ft).
Affiliation Lutheran.
Facilities Dining room; Activities room;
Chapel; Crafts room; Laundry room; Barber/
Beauty shop.
Activities Arts & crafts; Cards; Games;
Reading groups; Prayer groups; Movies;
Shopping trips; Dances/Social/Cultural
gatherings.

Wheatland

Wheatland Manor
515 E Lincolnway, Wheatland, IA 52777
(319) 374-1295
Admin Marilin Spangler. *Dir of Nursing* Sue
Klaas. *Medical Dir* Dr John Meyer.
Licensure Intermediate care. *Beds* ICF 51.
Certified Medicaid.
Owner Privately owned.
Admissions Requirements Medical
examination; Physician's request.
Facilities Dining room; Laundry room;
Barber/Beauty shop.
Activities Arts & crafts; Cards; Games;
Reading groups; Prayer groups; Movies.

Whiting

Pleasant View
200 Shannon Dr, Whiting, IA 51063
(712) 458-2417
Admin Ruth M Jordan.
Medical Dir Dr John L Garred.
Licensure Intermediate care. *Beds* ICF 106.
Certified Medicaid.
Admissions Requirements Minimum age 16;
Medical examination.
Staff Physicians 6 (pt); RNs 1 (ft), 7 (pt);
LPNs 1 (ft), 3 (pt); Nurses' aides 15 (ft), 20
(pt); Physical therapists 1 (pt); Activities
coordinators 1 (ft), 2 (pt); Dietitians 1 (pt).
Facilities Dining room; Physical therapy
room; Activities room; Chapel; Crafts room;
Laundry room; Barber/Beauty shop; Library.
Activities Arts & crafts; Cards; Games;
Reading groups; Prayer groups; Movies;
Shopping trips; Dances/Social/Cultural
gatherings.

Williamsburg

Williamsburg Care Center
104 Court St, Williamsburg, IA 52361
(319) 668-2311
Admin Kenneth H Gibson.
Licensure Intermediate care. *Beds* ICF 44.
Certified Medicaid.
Owner Proprietary corp (ABCM Corp).

Wilton

Wilton Nursing Home
415 E Prairie, Wilton, IA 52778
(319) 732-2086
Admin L R Buroker.
Licensure Intermediate care. *Beds* ICF 34.

Winfield

Sunrise Terrace
706 W Central Ave, Winfield, IA 52659
(319) 257-3303
Admin Stanley Schryba.
Licensure Intermediate care. *Beds* ICF 64.
Certified Medicaid.
Admissions Requirements Medical
examination.
Staff RNs 2 (ft), 5 (pt); LPNs 1 (ft), 1 (pt);
Nurses' aides 12 (ft), 7 (pt); Activities
coordinators 1 (ft).

Facilities Dining room; Physical therapy
room; Activities room; Chapel; Laundry
room; Barber/Beauty shop.
Activities Arts & crafts; Cards; Games;
Reading groups; Prayer groups; Movies;
Shopping trips; Dances/Social/Cultural
gatherings.

Winterset

Bethesda Care Center
1015 W Summitt, Winterset, IA 50273
(515) 462-1711
Admin Eva McDonald.
Licensure Intermediate care; Residential care.
Beds ICF 80; Residential care 19. *Certified*
Medicaid.
Owner Nonprofit corp (Bethesda Care
Centers).
Admissions Requirements Minimum age 16;
Medical examination; Physician's request.
Staff RNs 1 (ft), 2 (pt); LPNs 6 (ft), 3 (pt);
Nurses' aides 22 (ft), 12 (pt); Activities
coordinators 2 (ft).
Facilities Dining room; Physical therapy
room; Activities room; Chapel; Crafts room;
Laundry room; Barber/Beauty shop; Library.
Activities Arts & crafts; Cards; Games;
Reading groups; Prayer groups; Movies;
Shopping trips; Dances/Social/Cultural
gatherings; Baking & cooking classes.

Winterset Care Center—North
411 E Lane St, Winterset, IA 50273
(515) 462-1571
Admin Richard Meyer.
Licensure Intermediate care. *Beds* ICF 98.
Certified Medicaid.

Winterset Care Center South
715 S 2nd Ave, Winterset, IA 50273
(515) 462-4040
Admin Barbara A Woodworth. *Dir of Nursing*
Linda Wise RN.
Licensure Intermediate care. *Beds* ICF 49.
Private Pay Patients 25%. *Certified*
Medicaid.
Owner Proprietary corp (Quality Health Care
Specialists Corp).
Admissions Requirements Medical
examination; Physician's request.
Staff RNs 1 (ft); LPNs 2 (ft), 4 (pt); Nurses'
aides 7 (ft), 7 (pt); Physical therapists
(contracted); Occupational therapists
(contracted); Speech therapists (contracted);
Activities coordinators 1 (ft); Dietitians
(contracted); Podiatrists (contracted);
Recreational therapy aides 1 (ft), 1 (pt).
Facilities Dining room; Physical therapy
room; Activities room; Crafts room; Laundry
room; Barber/Beauty shop; Library; Chapel;
TV room.
Activities Arts & crafts; Cards; Games;
Reading groups; Prayer groups; Movies.

Woodbine

Rose Vista Home
1109 Normal St, Woodbine, IA 51579
(712) 647-2010
Admin Eugene Sherer.
Medical Dir Debbie Tiffey.
Licensure Intermediate care. *Beds* ICF 82.
Certified Medicaid.
Owner Proprietary corp.
Staff RNs 3 (ft); LPNs 3 (ft); Nurses' aides 22
(ft), 10 (pt); Activities coordinators 2 (ft);
Dietitians 1 (pt).
Facilities Dining room; Physical therapy
room; Activities room; Crafts room; Laundry
room; Barber/Beauty shop; Library.
Activities Arts & crafts; Cards; Games;
Reading groups; Prayer groups; Movies;
Shopping trips; Dances/Social/Cultural
gatherings.

Woodward

Parkview Manor Care Center
706 Cedar Ave, Woodward, IA 50276
(515) 438-2568
Admin Karen Reed. *Dir of Nursing* Edith
 Cerar LPN.
Licensure Intermediate care. *Beds* ICF 39.
 Certified Medicaid.
Owner Proprietary corp (Quality Health Care
 Specialists Inc).

Admissions Requirements Minimum age 16;
 Medical examination.
Staff LPNs 2 (ft), 1 (pt); Nurses' aides 7 (ft), 5
 (pt); Activities coordinators 1 (ft).
Facilities Dining room; Laundry room;
 Barber/Beauty shop.
Activities Arts & crafts; Cards; Games;
 Reading groups; Movies; Shopping trips;
 Dances/Social/Cultural gatherings.

Woodward State Hospital & School
Box 600, Woodward, IA 50276
(515) 438-2600

Admin Michael J Davis.
Licensure Intermediate care for mentally
 retarded. *Beds* ICF/MR 640.

Zearing

Colonial Manor
404 E Garfield, Zearing, IA 50278
(515) 487-7631
Admin John Walser.
Licensure Intermediate care. *Beds* ICF 56.
 Certified Medicaid.

KANSAS

Abilene

Abilene Nursing Center
705 N Brady, Abilene, KS 67410
(913) 263-1431
Admin Sandra Hoffman. *Dir of Nursing* Pam Jackson. *Medical Dir* J Dennis Biggs MD.
Licensure Intermediate care; Adult day care. *Beds* ICF 90. *Certified* Medicare.
Owner Proprietary corp (Beverly Enterprises).
Admissions Requirements Minimum age 16; Medical examination.
Staff Physicians; RNs 3 (ft), 1 (pt); LPNs 5 (ft); Nurses' aides 30 (ft), 5 (pt); Physical therapists 1 (pt); Reality therapists 1 (pt); Recreational therapists 1 (pt); Occupational therapists 1 (pt); Speech therapists 1 (pt); Activities coordinators 1 (ft); Dietitians 1 (pt).
Facilities Dining room; Physical therapy room; Activities room; Chapel; Crafts room; Laundry room; Barber/Beauty shop.
Activities Arts & crafts; Cards; Games; Reading groups; Prayer groups; Movies; Shopping trips; Dances/Social/Cultural gatherings; Intergenerational programs; Pet therapy.

Highland Care Home
1601 W 1st St, Abilene, KS 67410
(913) 263-2070
Admin Betty Ade.
Medical Dir Viola Aker.
Licensure Intermediate care. *Beds* ICF 42. *Certified* Medicaid.
Owner Proprietary corp.
Admissions Requirements Minimum age 18; Medical examination.
Staff RNs 1 (ft); LPNs 1 (ft), 1 (pt); Nurses' aides 8 (ft), 8 (pt); Physical therapists 1 (pt); Reality therapists 1 (pt); Recreational therapists 1 (pt); Occupational therapists 1 (pt); Speech therapists 1 (pt); Activities coordinators 1 (ft); Dietitians 1 (pt); Audiologists 1 (pt).
Facilities Dining room; Physical therapy room; Activities room; Chapel; Crafts room; Laundry room; Barber/Beauty shop.
Activities Arts & crafts; Cards; Games; Reading groups; Prayer groups; Movies; Shopping trips.

Alma

Alma Manor
234 Manor Cir, Alma, KS 66401
(913) 765-3318
Admin Linda Montgomery.
Licensure Intermediate care. *Beds* ICF 76. *Certified* Medicaid.
Owner Proprietary corp.
Admissions Requirements Medical examination; Physician's request.
Staff RNs; LPNs; Nurses' aides; Activities coordinators; Dietitians.
Facilities Dining room; Physical therapy room; Activities room; Chapel; Crafts room; Laundry room; Barber/Beauty shop; Library.

Activities Arts & crafts; Cards; Games; Reading groups; Prayer groups; Movies; Shopping trips; Dances/Social/Cultural gatherings.

Altamont

Arkhaven at Altamont
Box 770, Altamont, KS 67330-0770
(316) 784-5346
Admin Jacqueline Reimers.
Licensure Intermediate care. *Beds* ICF 46. *Certified* Medicaid.
Owner Proprietary corp.

Andover

Andover Health Care Center Inc
621 W 21, Andover, KS 67002
(316) 733-5376
Admin Brian S Warren.
Licensure Skilled care. *Beds* SNF 120. *Certified* Medicaid; Medicare.
Owner Proprietary corp.

Anthony

Life Care of Anthony
212 N 5th, Anthony, KS 67003
(316) 842-5103
Admin Nancy Rice.
Medical Dir Dr Jeff Bond.
Licensure Intermediate care. *Beds* ICF 60. *Certified* Medicaid.
Owner Proprietary corp (Lifecare Centers of Kansas Inc).
Admissions Requirements Minimum age 18; Physician's request.
Staff Physicians 1 (pt); RNs 1 (ft); LPNs 4 (ft); Nurses' aides 16 (ft); Physical therapists 1 (ft); Recreational therapists 1 (ft); Occupational therapists 1 (ft); Speech therapists 1 (ft); Dietitians 1 (ft); Ophthalmologists 1 (ft); Podiatrists 1 (ft).
Facilities Dining room; Physical therapy room; Activities room; Crafts room; Laundry room; Barber/Beauty shop.
Activities Arts & crafts; Cards; Games; Reading groups; Prayer groups; Movies; Dances/Social/Cultural gatherings; Sightseeing trips.

Arkansas City

Arkansas City Presbyterian Manor
1711 N 4th St, Arkansas City, KS 67005
(316) 442-8700
Admin Jacquita M Dodson. *Dir of Nursing* Wanda Howard.
Licensure Intermediate care; Retirement. *Beds* ICF 60. *Certified* Medicaid.
Owner Nonprofit corp (Presbyterian Manors of Mid-America).
Admissions Requirements Minimum age 65; Medical examination; Physician's request.

Staff Physicians 6 (pt); RNs 2 (ft), 1 (pt); LPNs 4 (ft), 2 (pt); Nurses' aides 20 (ft), 3 (pt); Physical therapists 1 (pt); Occupational therapists 1 (pt); Speech therapists 1 (pt); Activities coordinators 1 (ft); Dietitians 1 (ft); Ophthalmologists 1 (pt).
Affiliation Presbyterian.
Facilities Dining room; Physical therapy room; Activities room; Chapel; Laundry room; Barber/Beauty shop; Library.
Activities Arts & crafts; Cards; Games; Reading groups; Prayer groups; Shopping trips.

Medicalodge East of Arkansas City
203 E Osage, Arkansas City, KS 67005
(316) 442-9300
Admin Donna McGlasson. *Dir of Nursing* Paula Danes. *Medical Dir* Dr Jerry Old.
Licensure Intermediate care. *Beds* ICF 90. *Certified* Medicaid.
Owner Proprietary corp (Medicalodges Inc).
Admissions Requirements Medical examination; Physician's request.
Facilities Dining room; Physical therapy room; Activities room; Chapel; Crafts room; Laundry room; Barber/Beauty shop.
Activities Arts & crafts; Cards; Games; Reading groups; Prayer groups; Movies; Shopping trips; Dances/Social/Cultural gatherings; Intergenerational programs; Pet therapy.

Medicalodge North of Arkansas City
2575 Greenway, Arkansas City, KS 67005
(316) 442-1120
Admin Karen Richards.
Medical Dir Robert Yoachim MD.
Licensure Intermediate care; Alzheimer's care. *Beds* ICF 80. *Certified* Medicaid.
Owner Proprietary corp (Medicalodges Inc).
Admissions Requirements Minimum age 16; Medical examination.
Staff Physicians 1 (pt); RNs 1 (ft), 1 (pt); LPNs 2 (ft), 2 (pt); Nurses' aides 24 (ft), 2 (pt); Physical therapists 1 (pt); Occupational therapists 1 (pt); Speech therapists 1 (pt); Activities coordinators 1 (ft); Dietitians 1 (pt); Ophthalmologists 1 (pt); Podiatrists 1 (pt).
Facilities Dining room; Physical therapy room; Activities room; Chapel; Crafts room; Laundry room; Barber/Beauty shop; Library; Separate dining for alert residents.
Activities Arts & crafts; Cards; Games; Reading groups; Prayer groups; Movies; Dances/Social/Cultural gatherings; Bingo; Rides.

Arma

Gentry House
PO Box 789, 3rd & Melvin, Arma, KS 66712
(316) 347-4103
Admin Jay Brooks. *Dir of Nursing* Judith Marsh.
Licensure Intermediate care; Alzheimer's care. *Beds* ICF 95. *Certified* Medicaid.

Owner Proprietary corp (Quality Health Care Inc).
Admissions Requirements Medical examination; Physician's request.
Staff RNs; LPNs; Nurses' aides; Physical therapists; Activities coordinators; Dietitians; Chaplains (on call).
Facilities Dining room; Physical therapy room; Activities room; Crafts room; Laundry room; Barber/Beauty shop; Living room; Alzheimer's wing.
Activities Arts & crafts; Cards; Games; Prayer groups; Movies; Dances/Social/Cultural gatherings; Intergenerational programs; Pet therapy.

Ashland

Fountain View Villa
528 W 8th St, Ashland, KS 67831
(316) 635-2311
Admin Sandra Y Butler. *Dir of Nursing* Marla Williamson RN.
Licensure Intermediate care. *Beds* ICF 36. *Certified* Medicaid.
Owner Publicly owned.
Admissions Requirements Minimum age 16; Medical examination; Physician's request.
Staff RNs 2 (ft), 1 (pt); Nurses' aides 10 (ft), 3 (pt); Activities coordinators 1 (ft).
Facilities Dining room; Physical therapy room; Activities room; Chapel; Crafts room; Laundry room; Barber/Beauty shop; Living room.
Activities Arts & crafts; Cards; Games; Prayer groups; Movies; Coffee club; Bible study.

Atchison

Atchison Senior Village
1419 N 6th St, Atchison, KS 66002
(913) 367-1905
Admin Mary Mason Clay.
Medical Dir Janey Lykins.
Licensure Intermediate care. *Beds* ICF 50. *Certified* Medicaid.
Owner Publicly owned.
Admissions Requirements Minimum age 16; Medical examination; Physician's request.
Staff Physicians 1 (pt); RNs 1 (pt); LPNs 6 (ft), 3 (pt); Nurses' aides 21 (ft); Physical therapists 1 (pt); Activities coordinators 2 (ft); Dietitians 1 (pt); Pharmacist 1 (pt).
Facilities Dining room; Physical therapy room; Activities room; Chapel; Crafts room; Laundry room; Barber/Beauty shop.
Activities Arts & crafts; Cards; Games; Reading groups; Prayer groups; Movies; Shopping trips; Dances/Social/Cultural gatherings; Senior Olympics.

Medicalodge of Atchison
1637 Riley, Box A, Atchison, KS 66002
(913) 367-6066
Admin Janieve Rodriguez. *Dir of Nursing* Sue Butzin RN. *Medical Dir* John Eplee MD.
Licensure Skilled care; Intermediate care. *Beds* SNF 54; ICF 46. *Private Pay Patients* 40%. *Certified* Medicaid; Medicare.
Owner Proprietary corp (Medicalodges Inc).
Admissions Requirements Minimum age 65; Medical examination; Physician's request.
Staff Physicians 1 (ft); RNs 1 (ft), 1 (pt); LPNs 8 (ft); Nurses' aides 29 (ft), 2 (pt); Physical therapists 1 (ft); Occupational therapists 1 (pt); Speech therapists 1 (pt); Activities coordinators 1 (ft); Dietitians 1 (pt); Ophthalmologists 1 (pt); Podiatrists 1 (pt); Audiologists 1 (pt).
Facilities Dining room; Physical therapy room; Activities room; Chapel; Laundry room; Barber/Beauty shop.
Activities Arts & crafts; Cards; Games; Reading groups; Prayer groups; Movies; Shopping trips; Dances/Social/Cultural gatherings; Intergenerational programs; Pet therapy.

Atwood

Good Samaritan Center
650 Lake Rd, Box 216, Atwood, KS 67730
(913) 626-3253
Admin Henry Reith.
Licensure Intermediate care. *Beds* ICF 50. *Certified* Medicaid.
Owner Proprietary corp (Evangelical Lutheran/Good Samaritan Society).
Admissions Requirements Medical examination; Physician's request.
Staff RNs 1 (pt); LPNs 4 (ft); Nurses' aides 17 (ft); Occupational therapists 1 (pt); Activities coordinators 2 (ft).
Facilities Dining room; Physical therapy room; Activities room; Laundry room; Barber/Beauty shop.
Activities Arts & crafts; Cards; Games; Reading groups; Prayer groups; Movies; Shopping trips; Dances/Social/Cultural gatherings.

Augusta

Seal Residential Care Home
620 Osage St C-11, Augusta, KS 67010-1250
(303) 456-1181
Admin Margaret Seal.
Licensure Intermediate care. *Beds* 2.
Owner Proprietary corp.

Walnut Valley Manor
2100 N Ohio, Augusta, KS 67010
(316) 775-6333
Admin Harrison Warner.
Medical Dir Dorothy Leedom.
Licensure Intermediate care. *Beds* ICF 50. *Certified* Medicaid.
Owner Privately owned.
Admissions Requirements Minimum age 18; Medical examination; Physician's request.
Staff Physicians; LPNs; Nurses' aides; Activities coordinators; Ophthalmologists.
Facilities Dining room; Physical therapy room; Activities room; Crafts room; Laundry room; Barber/Beauty shop.
Activities Arts & crafts; Cards; Games; Reading groups; Prayer groups; Movies; Shopping trips; Dances/Social/Cultural gatherings.

Baldwin City

Orchard Lane Nursing Facility
1223 Orchard Ln, Baldwin City, KS 66006
(913) 594-6492
Admin Mary Ann Culley.
Licensure Intermediate care. *Beds* ICF 48. *Certified* Medicaid.
Owner Publicly owned.
Admissions Requirements Medical examination; Physician's request.
Staff RNs; LPNs; Nurses' aides; Activities coordinators; Dietitians.
Facilities Dining room; Physical therapy room; Activities room; Chapel; Crafts room; Laundry room; Barber/Beauty shop; Library.
Activities Arts & crafts; Cards; Games; Reading groups; Prayer groups; Movies; Shopping trips; Dances/Social/Cultural gatherings.

Baxter Springs

Midwest Nursing Center
217 E 14th St, Baxter Springs, KS 66713
(316) 856-2662
Admin Laurie Hamill. *Dir of Nursing* Linde Myer. *Medical Dir* C B Smith DO.
Licensure Intermediate care. *Beds* ICF 50. *Certified* Medicaid.
Owner Privately owned (Vetter Health Services Inc).
Admissions Requirements Medical examination; Physician's request.

Staff RNs; LPNs; Nurses' aides; Activities coordinators.
Facilities Dining room; Physical therapy room; Activities room; Chapel; Crafts room; Laundry room; Barber/Beauty shop.
Activities Arts & crafts; Cards; Games; Reading groups; Prayer groups; Movies; Shopping trips.

Quaker Hill Manor
RR 1, Baxter Springs, KS 66713
(316) 848-3797
Admin James E Galbraith.
Medical Dir Zina Hopkins.
Licensure Intermediate care. *Beds* ICF 36. *Certified* Medicaid.
Owner Privately owned.
Admissions Requirements Minimum age 16; Medical examination.
Staff LPNs 3 (ft); Nurses' aides 12 (ft), 1 (pt).
Facilities Dining room; Physical therapy room; Activities room; Laundry room.
Activities Arts & crafts; Reading groups; Prayer groups; Movies; Shopping trips.

Belle Plaine

Paradise Valley Living Center
801 N Logan, Belle Plaine, KS 67013
(316) 488-2228
Admin Martha M Speer. *Dir of Nursing* Karen Pracht LPN.
Licensure Intermediate care. *Beds* ICF 50. *Certified* Medicaid.
Owner Nonprofit corp (Adventist Living Centers Inc).
Admissions Requirements Medical examination; Physician's request.
Staff RNs 1 (pt); LPNs 1 (ft), 3 (pt); Nurses' aides 8 (ft), 10 (pt); Physical therapists 1 (pt); Recreational therapists 1 (pt); Occupational therapists 1 (pt); Speech therapists 1 (pt); Activities coordinators 1 (ft); Dietitians 1 (pt); Ophthalmologists 1 (pt); Podiatrists 1 (pt).
Affiliation Seventh-Day Adventist.
Facilities Dining room; Physical therapy room; Activities room; Chapel; Laundry room; Barber/Beauty shop; Library.
Activities Arts & crafts; Cards; Games; Reading groups; Prayer groups; Movies; Shopping trips; Dances/Social/Cultural gatherings.

Belleville

Belleville Health Care Center
2626 Wesleyan Dr, Belleville, KS 66935
(913) 527-5636, 527-5419 FAX
Admin Sandra Boyles. *Dir of Nursing* Shirley LeBlanc.
Licensure Intermediate care. *Beds* ICF 90. *Private Pay Patients* 57%. *Certified* Medicaid.
Owner Proprietary corp (Nationwide Management Inc).
Admissions Requirements Medical examination; Physician's request.
Staff RNs 5 (ft), 1 (pt); LPNs 5 (ft), 1 (pt); Nurses' aides 27 (ft), 10 (pt); Physical therapists; Occupational therapists 1 (pt); Speech therapists 1 (pt); Activities coordinators 2 (ft), 1 (pt); Dietitians 1 (pt).
Facilities Dining room; Physical therapy room; Activities room; Crafts room; Laundry room; Barber/Beauty shop; Private quiet room.
Activities Arts & crafts; Cards; Games; Reading groups; Prayer groups; Movies; Shopping trips; Dances/Social/Cultural gatherings; Pet therapy.

Heartland Care Center—Belleville
500 W 23rd St, Belleville, KS 66935
(913) 527-2242
Admin Karen Stierlan.

Licensure Intermediate care. *Beds* ICF 88.
  Certified Medicaid.
Owner Proprietary corp.

Beloit

Hilltop Lodge Inc Nursing Home
815 N Independence, Beloit, KS 67420
(913) 738-3516
Admin Harold E Heidrick.
Licensure Intermediate care. *Beds* ICF 131.
  Certified Medicaid.
Owner Proprietary corp.
Admissions Requirements Minimum age 18;
  Medical examination; Physician's request.
Staff Physicians 6 (pt); RNs 5 (pt); LPNs 5
  (pt); Nurses' aides 20 (ft), 15 (pt); Physical
  therapists 1 (pt); Recreational therapists 1
  (ft); Occupational therapists 1 (pt); Speech
  therapists 1 (pt); Activities coordinators 1
  (ft); Dietitians 1 (pt); Ophthalmologists 1
  (pt); Podiatrists 1 (pt); Audiologists 1 (pt);
  Dentists 1 (pt).
Facilities Dining room; Physical therapy
  room; Activities room; Chapel; Crafts room;
  Laundry room; Barber/Beauty shop; Library.
Activities Arts & crafts; Cards; Games;
  Reading groups; Prayer groups; Movies;
  Shopping trips; Dances/Social/Cultural
  gatherings.

Blue Rapids

Blue Valley Nursing Home Inc
710 Southwest Ave, Blue Rapids, KS 66411
(913) 226-7777
Admin Bertha Jane Harden. *Dir of Nursing*
  Jean Crane LPN.
Licensure Intermediate care. *Beds* ICF 60.
  Private Pay Patients 50%. *Certified*
  Medicaid.
Owner Nonprofit corp.
Admissions Requirements Medical
  examination; Physician's request.
Staff RNs 1 (pt); LPNs 6 (ft); Nurses' aides 16
  (ft), 3 (pt); Activities coordinators 1 (ft);
  Dietitians 4 (ft); Other staff 16 (ft).
Facilities Dining room; Physical therapy
  room; Activities room; Chapel; Crafts room;
  Laundry room; Barber/Beauty shop.
Activities Arts & crafts; Cards; Games; Prayer
  groups; Movies; Shopping trips; Pet therapy.

Bonner Springs

Bonner Health Center
520 E Morse, Bonner Springs, KS 66012
(913) 441-2515
Admin Donna B Foster. *Dir of Nursing*
  Juanita Flaggard LPN. *Medical Dir* Mark
  Peterson.
Licensure Intermediate care. *Beds* ICF 50.
  Private Pay Patients 12%. *Certified*
  Medicaid.
Owner Proprietary corp (Beverly Enterprises).
Admissions Requirements Minimum age 16;
  Medical examination; Physician's request.
Staff Physicians (consultant); LPNs 3 (ft), 2
  (pt); Nurses' aides 12 (ft), 2 (pt); Physical
  therapists (consultant); Occupational
  therapists (consultant); Speech therapists
  (consultant); Activities coordinators 1 (ft);
  Dietitians (consultant); Ophthalmologists
  (consultant); Podiatrists (consultant);
  Audiologists (consultant).
Facilities Dining room; Physical therapy
  room; Activities room; Laundry room;
  Barber/Beauty shop.
Activities Arts & crafts; Cards; Games;
  Reading groups; Prayer groups; Movies;
  Shopping trips; Dances/Social/Cultural
  gatherings; Intergenerational programs; Pet
  therapy.

Kaw Valley Manor
510 E Morse Ave, Bonner Springs, KS 66012
(913) 441-2444
Admin James Hetherington. *Dir of Nursing*
  Sandi Lebrecht.
Licensure Intermediate care. *Beds* ICF 108.
  Private Pay Patients 18%. *Certified*
  Medicaid.
Owner Proprietary corp (Beverly Enterprises).
Admissions Requirements Medical
  examination; Physician's request.
Staff RNs 1 (ft); LPNs 8 (ft); Nurses' aides 30
  (ft), 10 (pt); Activities coordinators.
Facilities Dining room; Physical therapy
  room; Activities room; Crafts room; Laundry
  room; Barber/Beauty shop; Library;
  Conference room.
Activities Arts & crafts; Cards; Games;
  Reading groups; Prayer groups; Movies;
  Dances/Social/Cultural gatherings.

Bucklin

Hill Top House
PO Box 248, 505 W Elm, Bucklin, KS 67834
(316) 826-3202
Admin Bert L Earls.
Licensure Intermediate care. *Beds* ICF 50.
  Certified Medicaid.
Owner Publicly owned.

Buhler

Buhler Sunshine Home Inc
412 W "C" Ave, Buhler, KS 67522
(316) 543-2251
Admin Luther H Dietz. *Dir of Nursing* Shirley
  Ediger.
Licensure Intermediate care; Retirement. *Beds*
  ICF 43; Retirement 25. *Certified* Medicaid.
Owner Nonprofit organization/foundation.
Admissions Requirements Minimum age 64.
Staff Physicians 1 (pt); RNs 1 (ft), 1 (pt);
  LPNs 2 (ft), 1 (pt); Nurses' aides 8 (ft), 11
  (pt); Physical therapists 1 (ft); Recreational
  therapists 1 (ft); Occupational therapists 1
  (pt); Speech therapists 1 (pt); Activities
  coordinators 1 (ft); Dietitians 1 (ft);
  Podiatrists 1 (pt); Audiologists 1 (pt).
Affiliation Mennonite.
Facilities Dining room; Physical therapy
  room; Activities room; Chapel; Crafts room;
  Laundry room; Barber/Beauty shop; Library.
Activities Arts & crafts; Cards; Games;
  Reading groups; Prayer groups; Movies;
  Shopping trips; Dances/Social/Cultural
  gatherings; Intergenerational programs; Pet
  therapy.

Burlingame

Santa Fe Trail Nursing Center
401 Prospect Pl, Box 6, Burlingame, KS
66413
(913) 654-3391
Admin Marion E Smith. *Dir of Nursing*
  Shirley D Bloomquist.
Licensure Intermediate care; Alzheimer's care.
  Beds ICF 50. *Private Pay Patients* 28%.
  Certified Medicaid.
Owner Proprietary corp.
Admissions Requirements Minimum age 17;
  Medical examination; Physician's request.
Staff RNs 1 (pt); LPNs 5 (ft); Nurses' aides 15
  (ft), 3 (pt); Activities coordinators 1 (ft);
  Dietitians.
Facilities Dining room; Physical therapy
  room; Activities room; Chapel; Crafts room;
  Laundry room; Barber/Beauty shop; Library.
Activities Arts & crafts; Cards; Games;
  Reading groups; Prayer groups; Movies;
  Shopping trips; Dances/Social/Cultural
  gatherings; Intergenerational programs; Pet
  therapy; Church services; Birthday
  celebrations; "Senior Prom".

Burlington

Golden Age Lodge of Burlington
Box 43, Cross & Jarboe, Burlington, KS 66839
(316) 364-2117
Admin Patti Young.
Licensure Intermediate care. *Beds* ICF 96.
  Certified Medicaid.
Owner Proprietary corp (Medicalodges Inc).

Caldwell

Leisure Center
415 S Osage, Caldwell, KS 67022
(316) 845-6495
Admin Dorothy Robertson RN. *Dir of Nursing*
  Sherry Stephens RN. *Medical Dir* Jim Blunk
  DO.
Licensure Intermediate care. *Beds* ICF 48.
  Private Pay Patients 67%. *Certified*
  Medicaid.
Owner Proprietary corp (Lifecare Centers of
  Kansas).
Admissions Requirements Medical
  examination; Physician's request.
Staff RNs 1 (ft), 1 (pt); LPNs 3 (ft); Nurses'
  aides 8 (ft), 3 (pt); Physical therapists;
  Activities coordinators 1 (ft), 1 (pt);
  Dietitians.
Languages Czech, Sign.
Facilities Dining room; Physical therapy
  room; Activities room; Chapel; Laundry
  room; Barber/Beauty shop.
Activities Arts & crafts; Games; Reading
  groups; Prayer groups; Movies; Shopping
  trips; Dances/Social/Cultural gatherings;
  Resident council; Monthly resident/employee
  meal; Monthly family night; Volunteer
  program.

Caney

Caney Nursing Center
615 S High, Caney, KS 67333
(316) 879-2929
Admin Rosemary Standiferd. *Dir of Nursing*
  Kay Foulk. *Medical Dir* Dr Mike Salrin.
Licensure Intermediate care. *Beds* ICF 40.
  Certified Medicaid.
Owner Privately owned (Lifecare Centers of
  Kansas Inc).
Admissions Requirements Minimum age 16;
  Medical examination; Physician's request.
Staff RNs; LPNs; Nurses' aides; Activities
  coordinators.
Facilities Dining room; Physical therapy
  room; Activities room; Crafts room; Laundry
  room; Barber/Beauty shop.
Activities Arts & crafts; Cards; Games;
  Reading groups; Prayer groups; Movies;
  Humanities program through Coffeyville
  Community College.

Canton

Shiloh Manor of Canton Inc
601 S Kansas, Box 67, Canton, KS 67428
(913) 628-4403
Admin Jeffrey J Birnbaum. *Dir of Nursing* Jo
  Colgin. *Medical Dir* Dr Claassen.
Licensure Intermediate care; Retirement. *Beds*
  ICF 60; Retirement duplexes. *Private Pay
  Patients* 55%. *Certified* Medicaid.
Owner Nonprofit organization/foundation.
Admissions Requirements Minimum age 16;
  Medical examination.
Staff RNs 1 (pt); LPNs 3 (ft); Nurses' aides 17
  (ft), 3 (pt); Physical therapists; Activities
  coordinators 1 (ft); Dietitians.
Languages German.
Affiliation Lutheran.
Facilities Dining room; Physical therapy
  room; Activities room; Chapel; Crafts room;
  Laundry room; Barber/Beauty shop; Library.

Activities Arts & crafts; Cards; Games;
Reading groups; Prayer groups; Movies;
Shopping trips; Dances/Social/Cultural
gatherings; Intergenerational programs; Pet
therapy.

Cedar Vale

Cedar Vale Nursing Center
100 River Rd, Cedar Vale, KS 67024
(316) 758-2248
Admin Marjorie R Lampson.
Licensure Intermediate care. *Beds* ICF 50.
Certified Medicaid.
Owner Proprietary corp (Beverly Enterprises).
Staff LPNs 2 (ft), 1 (pt); Nurses' aides 10 (ft),
2 (pt); Activities coordinators 1 (ft), 1 (pt).
Facilities Dining room; Physical therapy
room; Activities room; Chapel; Laundry
room; Barber/Beauty shop.
Activities Arts & crafts; Cards; Games;
Reading groups; Prayer groups; Movies;
Shopping trips; Dances/Social/Cultural
gatherings.

Chanute

Applewood Care Center Inc
302 S Denman, Chanute, KS 66720
(316) 431-7300
Admin Cheryl Borjas. *Dir of Nursing* Landa
Hughes.
Licensure Intermediate care. *Beds* ICF 50.
Certified Medicaid.
Owner Proprietary corp.
Admissions Requirements Minimum age 18;
Medical examination.
Staff RNs 1 (ft), 1 (pt); LPNs 3 (ft), 3 (pt);
Nurses' aides 6 (ft), 3 (pt); Activities
coordinators 2 (ft), 1 (pt).
Languages Spanish.
Facilities Dining room; Physical therapy
room; Activities room; Crafts room; Laundry
room; Barber/Beauty shop.
Activities Arts & crafts; Games; Reading
groups; Prayer groups; Movies; Shopping
trips; Dances/Social/Cultural gatherings.

Arolyn Heights Nursing Home
1709 W 7th, Chanute, KS 66720
(316) 431-9200
Admin Brenda Corbett. *Dir of Nursing* Julie
Dickens RN.
Licensure Intermediate care. *Beds* ICF 49.
Certified Medicaid.
Owner Privately owned.
Admissions Requirements Medical
examination.
Staff RNs 1 (ft), 3 (pt); LPNs 2 (ft), 1 (pt);
Nurses' aides 12 (ft), 3 (pt); Physical
therapists 1 (ft); Reality therapists 1 (pt);
Recreational therapists 1 (ft); Dietitians 1
(ft); Dentists 1 (pt).
Facilities Dining room; Physical therapy
room; Activities room; Chapel; Crafts room;
Laundry room; Barber/Beauty shop.
Activities Arts & crafts; Cards; Games;
Reading groups; Prayer groups; Movies;
Shopping trips; Dances/Social/Cultural
gatherings.

Bethesda Nursing Center
530 W 14th, Chanute, KS 66720
(316) 431-4940
Admin David Cantril. *Dir of Nursing* Joan K
Augustine. *Medical Dir* Albert A Kihm MD.
Licensure Intermediate care. *Beds* ICF 90.
Certified Medicaid.
Owner Proprietary corp (Hillhaven Corp).
Admissions Requirements Medical
examination; Physician's request.
Staff RNs 2 (ft); LPNs 5 (ft), 2 (pt); Nurses'
aides 20 (ft), 5 (pt); Activities coordinators 1
(ft).
Languages Spanish.

Facilities Dining room; Physical therapy
room; Activities room; Chapel; Laundry
room; Barber/Beauty shop.
Activities Arts & crafts; Cards; Games; Prayer
groups; Movies; Dances/Social/Cultural
gatherings.

Heritage Health Care Center
1630 W 2nd, Chanute, KS 66720
(316) 431-4151
Admin Sonja Ann Emerson. *Dir of Nursing*
Judy Hallbauer.
Licensure Intermediate care; Alzheimer's care.
Beds ICF 105. *Private Pay Patients* 35%.
Certified Medicaid.
Owner Privately owned.
Admissions Requirements Minimum age 16;
Medical examination; Physician's request.
Staff RNs 1 (ft); LPNs 4 (ft), 1 (pt); Nurses'
aides 20 (ft), 10 (pt); Activities coordinators
2 (ft).
Facilities Dining room; Physical therapy
room; Activities room; Chapel; Laundry
room; Barber/Beauty shop; Alzheimer's unit.
Activities Arts & crafts; Cards; Games;
Reading groups; Prayer groups; Movies;
Shopping trips; Dances/Social/Cultural
gatherings; Pet therapy.

Chapman

Chapman Valley Manor
1009 N Marshall, Chapman, KS 67431
(913) 922-6594
Admin Thomas L Canfield.
Licensure Intermediate care. *Beds* ICF 60.
Certified Medicaid.
Owner Proprietary corp.

Cheney

Cheney Golden Age Home Inc
724 N Jefferson, Cheney, KS 67025
(316) 542-3691
Admin Teresa Bogner. *Dir of Nursing*
Kathleen May RN. *Medical Dir* Randall
Fahrenholtz MD.
Licensure Intermediate care. *Beds* ICF 60.
Certified Medicaid.
Owner Proprietary corp.
Admissions Requirements Minimum age 18;
Medical examination.
Staff Physicians 6 (pt); RNs 2 (ft), 1 (pt);
LPNs 2 (ft), 1 (pt); Nurses' aides 14 (ft), 6
(pt); Physical therapists 1 (ft); Occupational
therapists 1 (pt); Speech therapists 1 (pt);
Activities coordinators 1 (ft); Dietitians 1
(ft).
Languages German.
Facilities Dining room; Physical therapy
room; Activities room; Laundry room;
Barber/Beauty shop.
Activities Arts & crafts; Cards; Games;
Reading groups; Prayer groups; Movies;
Shopping trips; Dances/Social/Cultural
gatherings.

Cherryvale

Cherryvale Medi-Lodge
PO Box 188, Cherryvale, KS 67335
(316) 336-2102
Admin Sandra Sue Hale.
Licensure Intermediate care. *Beds* ICF 51.
Certified Medicaid.
Owner Proprietary corp.
Admissions Requirements Medical
examination; Physician's request.
Staff Physicians 1 (pt); RNs 1 (pt); LPNs 2
(ft); Nurses' aides 19 (ft), 1 (pt); Activities
coordinators 1 (ft).
Facilities Dining room; Physical therapy
room; Activities room; Chapel; Crafts room;
Laundry room; Barber/Beauty shop; Library.

Activities Arts & crafts; Cards; Games;
Reading groups; Prayer groups; Movies;
Shopping trips; Dances/Social/Cultural
gatherings.

Cimarron

Heritage of Cimarron
PO Box 249, Cimarron, KS 67835-0249
(316) 855-3498
Admin Shellee Kay Nordhus.
Licensure Intermediate care. *Beds* ICF 44.
Certified Medicaid.
Owner Proprietary corp (Vetter Health
Services Inc).

Clay Center

Clay Center Presbyterian Manor
924 8th St, Clay Center, KS 67432
(913) 632-5646
Admin Mariel Kolle.
Licensure Intermediate care. *Beds* ICF 25.
Certified Medicaid.
Owner Nonprofit corp.
Affiliation Presbyterian.

Medicalodge of Clay Center
PO Box 517, 715 Liberty, Clay Center, KS
67432
(913) 632-5696
Admin Rosemary Gonser.
Medical Dir Eltanis Volen.
Licensure Skilled care; Intermediate care. *Beds*
SNF 40; ICF 56. *Certified* Medicaid.
Owner Proprietary corp (Medicalodges Inc).
Admissions Requirements Minimum age 16;
Medical examination; Physician's request.
Staff RNs 1 (ft), 2 (pt); LPNs 4 (ft); Nurses'
aides 25 (ft), 5 (pt); Physical therapists 2 (ft);
Occupational therapists 1 (pt); Activities
coordinators 1 (ft); Dietitians 1 (pt).
Facilities Dining room; Physical therapy
room; Activities room; Crafts room; Laundry
room; Barber/Beauty shop; 2 Quiet rooms
which serve many purposes including chapel.
Activities Arts & crafts; Cards; Games;
Reading groups; Prayer groups; Movies;
Shopping trips; Dances/Social/Cultural
gatherings; Van trips.

Clearwater

Ninnescah Manor Inc
620 Wood St, Clearwater, KS 67026
(316) 584-2271, 584-2277 FAX
Admin Marlis J Felber. *Dir of Nursing* L
Tjaden. *Medical Dir* A J Wray MD.
Licensure Intermediate care. *Beds* ICF 60.
Private Pay Patients 60%. *Certified*
Medicaid.
Owner Proprietary corp.
Admissions Requirements Medical
examination; Physician's request.
Staff RNs 2 (ft); LPNs 3 (pt); Nurses' aides 12
(ft), 2 (pt); Physical therapists (consultant);
Occupational therapists (consultant); Speech
therapists (consultant); Activities
coordinators 1 (ft); Dietitians (consultant);
Ophthalmologists (consultant); Podiatrists
(consultant); Audiologists (consultant).
Facilities Dining room; Physical therapy
room; Activities room; Crafts room; Laundry
room; Barber/Beauty shop; TV room for
smokers; Solarium; Sun room.
Activities Arts & crafts; Cards; Games; Prayer
groups; Movies; Shopping trips; Dances/
Social/Cultural gatherings; Volunteer group;
Community involvement.

Clifton

Estelle's Nursing Home
RR 1 Box 219, Strand St, Clifton, KS 66937
(913) 455-3522

Admin Kenneth DeLude. *Dir of Nursing* Judy Chaput LPN.
Licensure Intermediate care. *Beds* ICF 32. *Private Pay Patients* 40%. *Certified* Medicaid.
Owner Privately owned.
Admissions Requirements Minimum age 16; Medical examination; Physician's request.
Staff LPNs 1 (ft); Nurses' aides 9 (ft), 2 (pt); Activities coordinators 1 (pt).
Facilities Dining room; Physical therapy room; Activities room; Laundry room; Barber/Beauty shop.
Activities Arts & crafts; Games; Prayer groups; Movies; Shopping trips.

Clyde

Park Villa
114 S High, Clyde, KS 66938
(913) 446-2818
Admin Jane A Magaw. *Dir of Nursing* Jacque Smith.
Licensure Intermediate care. *Beds* ICF 50. *Private Pay Patients* 75%. *Certified* Medicaid.
Owner Nonprofit corp.
Admissions Requirements Minimum age 17; Medical examination; Physician's request.
Staff RNs 2 (ft); LPNs 3 (ft); Nurses' aides 10 (ft), 8 (pt); Physical therapists 1 (ft); Occupational therapists 1 (pt); Speech therapists 1 (pt); Activities coordinators 1 (ft); Dietitians 1 (pt); Podiatrists 1 (pt); Audiologists 1 (pt).
Facilities Dining room; Physical therapy room; Activities room; Chapel; Crafts room; Laundry room; Barber/Beauty shop.
Activities Arts & crafts; Cards; Games; Reading groups; Prayer groups; Movies; Shopping trips; Dances/Social/Cultural gatherings; Intergenerational programs; Pet therapy.

Coffeyville

Medicalodge East of Coffeyville
720 W 1st, Coffeyville, KS 67337
(316) 251-3705
Admin Diane Close. *Dir of Nursing* Lynn Hatton RN. *Medical Dir* Kenneth Parker.
Licensure Intermediate care; Alzheimer's care. *Beds* ICF 44. *Certified* Medicaid.
Owner Proprietary corp (Medicalodges Inc).
Staff RNs; LPNs; Nurses' aides; Activities coordinators.
Facilities Dining room; Physical therapy room; Laundry room; Barber/Beauty shop.
Activities Arts & crafts; Games; Reading groups; Prayer groups; Movies; Shopping trips; Dances/Social/Cultural gatherings.

Medicalodge West of Coffeyville
2910 Midland Ave, Coffeyville, KS 67337
(316) 251-2420
Admin James E Pede. *Dir of Nursing* Rhonda Craven. *Medical Dir* Dr Gibbs.
Licensure Skilled care; Intermediate care; Retirement. *Beds* SNF 44; ICF 136. *Certified* Medicaid.
Owner Proprietary corp (Medicalodges Inc).
Admissions Requirements Minimum age 16; Medical examination; Physician's request.
Facilities Dining room; Physical therapy room; Activities room; Chapel; Laundry room; Barber/Beauty shop.
Activities Arts & crafts; Cards; Games; Reading groups; Prayer groups; Movies; Shopping trips; Dances/Social/Cultural gatherings.

Sunny View Adult Care Home
14th & Roosevelt, Coffeyville, KS 67337
(316) 251-4032
Admin Jane Guy RN. *Dir of Nursing* Mykka Mangan. *Medical Dir* James Wilson MD.

Licensure Intermediate care. *Beds* ICF 49. *Private Pay Patients* 20%. *Certified* Medicaid.
Owner Proprietary corp (Gary Marvine).
Admissions Requirements Minimum age 18; Medical examination; Physician's request.
Staff RNs 2 (ft); LPNs 1 (ft); Nurses' aides 18 (ft), 2 (pt); Physical therapists (consultant); Activities coordinators 1 (ft); Dietitians (consultant).
Languages Spanish.
Facilities Dining room; Physical therapy room; Activities room; Laundry room; Barber/Beauty shop.
Activities Arts & crafts; Games; Reading groups; Prayer groups; Movies; Shopping trips; Dances/Social/Cultural gatherings; Garden club.

Colby

Good Samaritan Home
Rte 1 Box 1, Colby, KS 67701
(913) 462-7564
Admin Kenneth H Wagner.
Licensure Intermediate care. *Beds* 46. *Certified* Medicaid.

Lantern Park Manor
105 E College Dr, Colby, KS 67701
(913) 462-6721
Admin Larry L Booth. *Dir of Nursing* Carol Steward RN. *Medical Dir* Asher Dahl MD.
Licensure Intermediate care. *Beds* ICF 70. *Certified* Medicaid.
Owner Proprietary corp (Beverly Enterprises).
Admissions Requirements Minimum age 18.
Staff RNs 5 (ft), 1 (pt); LPNs 3 (ft); Nurses' aides 25 (ft); Activities coordinators 1 (ft).
Facilities Dining room; Physical therapy room; Activities room; Laundry room; Barber/Beauty shop.
Activities Arts & crafts; Cards; Games; Reading groups; Prayer groups; Movies; Shopping trips; Dances/Social/Cultural gatherings; Rhythm band; Gardening.

Thomas County Care Center
350 S Range, Colby, KS 67701
(913) 462-8295
Admin Sonny Ellis-Sprick. *Dir of Nursing* Joan Jamison. *Medical Dir* Dr Rex Kolste.
Licensure Intermediate care; Adult day care. *Beds* ICF 42. *Certified* Medicaid.
Owner Publicly owned.
Admissions Requirements Medical examination; Physician's request.
Staff Physicians 4 (pt); RNs 1 (ft), 2 (pt); LPNs 3 (ft), 2 (pt); Nurses' aides 11 (ft), 11 (pt); Physical therapists 1 (pt); Occupational therapists; Speech therapists; Activities coordinators 1 (ft), 1 (pt); Dietitians 1 (pt); Ophthalmologists 1 (pt); Podiatrists 1 (pt); Audiologists 1 (pt); Social workers 1 (pt); Rehabilitation aides.
Facilities Dining room; Physical therapy room; Activities room; Laundry room; Barber/Beauty shop; Quiet lounge; Van.
Activities Arts & crafts; Cards; Games; Reading groups; Prayer groups; Movies; Shopping trips; Dances/Social/Cultural gatherings; Pet therapy; Rhythm band; Picnics in park; Volunteer program; Religious activities.

Coldwater

Pioneer Lodge
3rd & Frisco, Coldwater, KS 67029
(316) 582-2123
Admin Ernest K Parker.
Medical Dir Lorena Friend.
Licensure Intermediate care. *Beds* ICF 52. *Certified* Medicaid.
Owner Proprietary corp.

Staff RNs 2 (pt); LPNs 1 (ft); Nurses' aides 15 (ft), 5 (pt); Physical therapists 1 (pt); Occupational therapists 1 (pt); Speech therapists 1 (pt); Activities coordinators 1 (ft); Dietitians 1 (pt); Podiatrists 1 (pt).
Facilities Dining room; Physical therapy room; Activities room; Chapel; Crafts room; Laundry room; Barber/Beauty shop.
Activities Arts & crafts; Cards; Games; Reading groups; Prayer groups; Movies; Shopping trips.

Columbus

Medicalodge of Columbus
101 N Lee, Columbus, KS 66725
(316) 429-2134
Admin Cathy J Bowman.
Licensure Intermediate care. *Beds* ICF 100. *Certified* Medicaid.
Owner Proprietary corp (Medicalodges Inc).

Colwich

Colwich Health Center
5th & Colwich, Colwich, KS 67030
(316) 796-0919
Admin Sharon Kuepker. *Dir of Nursing* Sharry Turner. *Medical Dir* Dr David Hufford.
Licensure Intermediate care; Retirement. *Beds* ICF 60. *Certified* Medicaid.
Owner Proprietary corp.
Admissions Requirements Medical examination.
Staff RNs 1 (ft), 3 (pt); LPNs 2 (ft), 1 (pt); Nurses' aides 12 (ft), 8 (pt); Recreational therapists 1 (ft), 1 (pt); Activities coordinators 1 (ft), 1 (pt).
Facilities Dining room; Physical therapy room; Activities room; Crafts room; Laundry room; Barber/Beauty shop.
Activities Arts & crafts; Cards; Games; Movies; Shopping trips; Dances/Social/Cultural gatherings.

Concordia

Concordia Nursing Center
825 E 7th, Concordia, KS 66901
(913) 243-3497
Admin Eva L Schwab.
Licensure Intermediate care. *Beds* ICF 48. *Certified* Medicaid.
Owner Privately owned (Lifecare Centers of Kansas Inc).
Admissions Requirements Medical examination; Physician's request.
Staff RNs 1 (pt); LPNs 1 (ft); Nurses' aides 20 (ft), 2 (pt); Activities coordinators 1 (pt).
Facilities Dining room; Physical therapy room; Activities room; Chapel; Laundry room; Barber/Beauty shop; Library.
Activities Arts & crafts; Cards; Games; Reading groups; Prayer groups; Movies; Shopping trips.

Mt Joseph Inc
Rte 1, 1110 W 11th, Concordia, KS 66901
(913) 243-1347
Admin Gretchen Storey Barclay.
Medical Dir Charlotte Wineinger.
Licensure Intermediate care. *Beds* ICF 125. *Certified* Medicaid.
Owner Nonprofit corp.
Admissions Requirements Physician's request.
Staff RNs 4 (ft), 3 (pt); LPNs 3 (ft), 2 (pt); Nurses' aides 40 (ft), 15 (pt); Physical therapists 1 (pt); Recreational therapists 1 (pt); Activities coordinators 2 (ft).
Affiliation Roman Catholic.
Facilities Dining room; Physical therapy room; Activities room; Chapel; Crafts room; Barber/Beauty shop; Library.
Activities Arts & crafts; Cards; Games; Prayer groups; Movies.

Sunset Nursing Center
620 Second Ave, Concordia, KS 66901
(913) 243-2720
Admin Dennis W Knapp.
Licensure Intermediate care; Retirement. *Beds*
ICF 58.
Owner Nonprofit corp.
Admissions Requirements Minimum age 65;
Medical examination.
Staff RNs 3 (ft), 1 (pt); LPNs 2 (pt); Nurses'
aides 15 (ft), 11 (pt).
Affiliation Baptist.
Facilities Dining room; Physical therapy
room; Activities room; Chapel; Crafts room;
Laundry room; Barber/Beauty shop; Library.
Activities Arts & crafts; Cards; Games;
Reading groups; Prayer groups; Movies;
Shopping trips; Dances/Social/Cultural
gatherings.

Conway Springs

Spring View Manor Inc
500 S 8th, Conway Springs, KS 67031
(316) 456-2285
Admin Virginia C Winter. *Dir of Nursing*
Jennella Stitt, HSS. *Medical Dir* Dr L Will.
Licensure Intermediate care. *Beds* ICF 60.
Certified Medicaid.
Owner Proprietary corp.
Admissions Requirements Minimum age 18;
Medical examination.
Staff Physicians 1 (pt); RNs 1 (pt); LPNs 2
(ft); Nurses' aides 14 (ft); Physical therapists
1 (pt); Reality therapists 1 (pt); Recreational
therapists 1 (ft); Occupational therapists 1
(ft), 1 (pt); Activities coordinators 1 (ft);
Dietitians 1 (ft).
Facilities Dining room; Physical therapy
room; Activities room; Chapel; Crafts room;
Laundry room; Barber/Beauty shop.
Activities Arts & crafts; Cards; Games;
Reading groups; Prayer groups; Movies;
Shopping trips; Dances/Social/Cultural
gatherings; Intergenerational programs; Pet
therapy.

Cottonwood Falls

Chase County Nursing Center
612 Walnut, Cottonwood Falls, KS 66845
(316) 273-6360
Admin Earlene Lind. *Dir of Nursing* Barbara
Wente. *Medical Dir* Dr Bobby Ellis.
Licensure Intermediate care. *Beds* ICF 69.
Certified Medicaid.
Owner Proprietary corp (Beverly Enterprises).
Admissions Requirements Medical
examination; Physician's request.
Staff RNs 1 (pt); LPNs 5 (ft); Nurses' aides 18
(ft), 3 (pt); Physical therapists 1 (pt);
Occupational therapists 1 (pt); Speech
therapists 1 (pt); Activities coordinators 1
(ft); Dietitians 1 (pt); Social Services 1 (ft).
Languages Spanish.
Facilities Dining room; Physical therapy
room; Activities room; Chapel; Crafts room;
Laundry room; Barber/Beauty shop; Library.
Activities Arts & crafts; Cards; Games;
Reading groups; Prayer groups; Movies;
Shopping trips; Dances/Social/Cultural
gatherings.

Council Grove

Country Club Home
PO Box 319, 400 Sunset Dr, Council Grove,
KS 66846
(316) 767-5172
Admin Carole Downes. *Dir of Nursing* Bonnie
Thomas RN.
Licensure Intermediate care. *Beds* ICF 100.
Private Pay Patients 50%. *Certified*
Medicaid.
Owner Proprietary corp (Hillhaven Corp).

Admissions Requirements Medical
examination.
Staff RNs 4 (ft); LPNs 4 (ft); Nurses' aides 23
(ft), 13 (pt); Physical therapists (consultant);
Activities coordinators 1 (ft); Dietitians.
Facilities Dining room; Physical therapy
room; Activities room; Laundry room;
Barber/Beauty shop; Patio.
Activities Arts & crafts; Cards; Games; Prayer
groups; Movies; Intergenerational programs.

Cunningham

Hilltop Manor Inc
PO Box 8, Saint Leo Rd, Cunningham, KS
67035
(316) 298-2781
Admin Izena Monk. *Dir of Nursing* Sonja
McGregor.
Licensure Intermediate care. *Beds* ICF 76.
Certified Medicaid.
Owner Proprietary corp.
Admissions Requirements Medical
examination; Physician's request.
Staff RNs 2 (ft), 2 (pt); LPNs 1 (ft); Nurses'
aides 32 (ft); Physical therapists 1 (pt);
Recreational therapists; Occupational
therapists 1 (pt); Speech therapists 1 (pt);
Activities coordinators; Dietitians 1 (pt);
Podiatrists 1 (pt).
Facilities Dining room; Physical therapy
room; Activities room; Crafts room; Laundry
room; Barber/Beauty shop.
Activities Arts & crafts; Cards; Games;
Reading groups; Prayer groups; Movies;
Shopping trips; Dances/Social/Cultural
gatherings.

Delphos

Delphos Rest Home Inc
405 N Custer, Delphos, KS 67436
(913) 523-4234
Admin Carmelita J Berndt. *Dir of Nursing*
Eileen Boatwright RN.
Licensure Intermediate care. *Beds* ICF 34.
Private Pay Patients 80%. *Certified*
Medicaid.
Owner Proprietary corp.
Admissions Requirements Medical
examination.
Staff RNs 1 (ft); LPNs 1 (ft); Nurses' aides 11
(ft), 9 (pt); Physical therapists 1 (pt);
Occupational therapists 1 (pt); Activities
coordinators 1 (ft); Dietitians 1 (pt).
Facilities Dining room; Physical therapy
room; Activities room; Laundry room;
Barber/Beauty shop.
Activities Arts & crafts; Games; Reading
groups; Prayer groups; Movies; Pet therapy.

Derby

Westview Manor
445 N Westview, Derby, KS 67037
(316) 788-3739
Admin John A Nicholas. *Dir of Nursing* Pat
Mills RN. *Medical Dir* Roger L Thomas
DO.
Licensure Skilled care; Intermediate care;
Retirement; Alzheimer's care. *Beds* SNF 60;
ICF 60. *Certified* Medicaid.
Owner Proprietary corp.
Admissions Requirements Minimum age 21;
Medical examination; Physician's request.
Staff Physicians 35 (pt); RNs 4 (ft), 4 (pt);
LPNs 4 (ft), 6 (pt); Nurses' aides 35 (ft), 25
(pt); Physical therapists 2 (pt); Reality
therapists 1 (pt); Recreational therapists 1
(ft), 1 (pt); Occupational therapists 1 (pt);
Speech therapists 1 (pt); Activities
coordinators 1 (ft); Dietitians 1 (pt);
Ophthalmologists 1 (pt); Podiatrists 1 (pt);
Dentists 1 (pt).

Facilities Dining room; Physical therapy
room; Activities room; Crafts room; Laundry
room; Barber/Beauty shop; Library.
Activities Arts & crafts; Cards; Games;
Reading groups; Prayer groups; Movies;
Shopping trips; Dances/Social/Cultural
gatherings; Other outings with N/C transport
provided.

DeSoto

Regency Health Care Center
33600 W 85th St, DeSoto, KS 66018
(913) 585-1845
Admin Wylene Nibarger.
Medical Dir Christopher Murray DO.
Licensure Intermediate care. *Beds* ICF 50.
Certified Medicaid.
Owner Proprietary corp (Regency Health Care
Centers Inc).
Admissions Requirements Minimum age 21;
Medical examination; Physician's request.
Staff RNs 1 (pt); LPNs 8 (ft); Nurses' aides 7
(ft), 2 (pt); Recreational therapists 1 (ft);
Activities coordinators 1 (ft); Art therapist 1
(pt).
Facilities Dining room; Physical therapy
room; Activities room; Crafts room; Laundry
room; Barber/Beauty shop.
Activities Arts & crafts; Cards; Games;
Reading groups; Prayer groups; Movies;
Shopping trips; Dances/Social/Cultural
gatherings; Bingo; Church; Senior citizens;
Pets (dog, cats, rabbit); Garden.

Dexter

Grouse Valley Manor
S Main & Grouse Box 98, Dexter, KS 67038
(316) 876-5421
Admin Hazel P Young.
Licensure Intermediate care. *Beds* ICF 48.
Certified Medicaid.
Owner Proprietary corp.

Dodge City

Good Samaritan Center
501 W Beeson, Dodge City, KS 67801
(316) 227-7512
Admin William B Bender. *Dir of Nursing*
Moya Peterson.
Licensure Intermediate care; Retirement. *Beds*
ICF 85; Retirement apts 6. *Private Pay
Patients* 30%. *Certified* Medicaid.
Owner Nonprofit corp (Evangelical Lutheran/
Good Samaritan Society).
Admissions Requirements Medical
examination; Physician's request.
Staff RNs 1 (ft); LPNs 4 (ft), 2 (pt); Nurses'
aides 26 (ft), 11 (pt); Activities coordinators
1 (ft); Dietitians 1 (ft).
Facilities Dining room; Physical therapy
room; Activities room; Chapel; Crafts room;
Laundry room; Barber/Beauty shop;
Solarium; Living room.
Activities Arts & crafts; Games; Prayer groups;
Movies; Shopping trips; Pet therapy.

Trinity Manor Adult Care Home
510 Frontview, Dodge City, KS 67801
(316) 227-8551
Admin Barbara R Schroeder. *Dir of Nursing*
Maida Waldman RN. *Medical Dir* R C
Trotter MD.
Licensure Skilled care; Intermediate care;
Retirement. *Beds* SNF 30; ICF 53;
Retirement apts 46. *Private Pay Patients*
75%. *Certified* Medicaid.
Owner Nonprofit corp.
Admissions Requirements Medical
examination.
Staff RNs 7 (ft), 5 (pt); LPNs 2 (ft), 2 (pt);
Nurses' aides 26 (ft), 5 (pt); Physical
therapists; Dietitians.
Languages Spanish.

Affiliation Methodist.
Facilities Dining room; Physical therapy room; Activities room; Chapel; Crafts room; Laundry room; Barber/Beauty shop.
Activities Arts & crafts; Cards; Games; Reading groups; Prayer groups; Movies; Dances/Social/Cultural gatherings.

Douglass

Medicalodge of Douglass
9541 S Hwy 77, Douglass, KS 67039
(316) 746-2157
Admin Sandy Nesler. *Dir of Nursing* Kelly Winter. *Medical Dir* Dr Dale Anderson.
Licensure Intermediate care. *Beds* ICF 60. *Private Pay Patients* 50%. *Certified* Medicaid.
Owner Proprietary corp (Medicalodges Inc).
Admissions Requirements Minimum age 18; Medical examination; Physician's request.
Staff RNs; LPNs; Nurses' aides; Physical therapists; Activities coordinators; Dietitians.
Facilities Dining room; Physical therapy room; Activities room; Laundry room; Barber/Beauty shop.
Activities Arts & crafts; Cards; Games; Reading groups; Prayer groups; Movies; Shopping trips; Dances/Social/Cultural gatherings; Intergenerational programs; Pet therapy.

Downs

Downs Nursing Center
Rte 2, 1218 Kansas Ave, Downs, KS 67437
(913) 454-3321
Admin Jacqueline A Williams. *Dir of Nursing* Mary Moreland RN. *Medical Dir* Burton Cox DO.
Licensure Skilled care. *Beds* SNF 6. *Certified* Medicaid.
Owner Proprietary corp (Beverly Enterprises).
Staff RNs 3 (ft); LPNs 3 (ft), 3 (pt); Nurses' aides 16 (ft); Activities coordinators 1 (ft).
Facilities Dining room; Physical therapy room; Activities room; Crafts room; Laundry room; Barber/Beauty shop.
Activities Arts & crafts; Cards; Games; Reading groups; Prayer groups; Movies; Shopping trips; Dances/Social/Cultural gatherings.

Easton

Easton Manor
Hwy 192, Box 279, Easton, KS 66020
(913) 773-8254
Admin Martha Hegarty.
Medical Dir Penny L Wilson.
Licensure Intermediate care. *Beds* ICF 60. *Certified* Medicaid.
Owner Proprietary corp.
Staff Physicians 4 (pt); RNs 2 (ft), 1 (pt); LPNs 3 (ft); Nurses' aides 13 (ft), 1 (pt); Physical therapists 1 (pt); Occupational therapists 1 (pt); Speech therapists 1 (pt); Activities coordinators 1 (ft); Ophthalmologists 1 (pt); Podiatrists 1 (pt); Dentists 1 (pt).
Facilities Dining room; Physical therapy room; Activities room; Crafts room; Laundry room; Barber/Beauty shop.
Activities Arts & crafts; Cards; Games; Reading groups; Dances/Social/Cultural gatherings.

Edwardsville

Edwardsville Convalescent Center
750 Blake, Edwardsville, KS 66111
(913) 422-5832
Admin Barbara B Taff.
Licensure Intermediate care. *Beds* ICF 50. *Certified* Medicaid.
Owner Proprietary corp (Beverly Enterprises).

Edwardsville Manor
751 Blake, Edwardsville, KS 66111
(913) 441-1900
Admin Pat Keller.
Licensure Intermediate care. *Beds* ICF 100. *Certified* Medicaid.
Owner Proprietary corp (Beverly Enterprises).

Parkway Care Home
749 Blake, Edwardsville, KS 66111
(913) 422-5952
Admin Lois Ann Gulick.
Licensure Intermediate care. *Beds* ICF 50. *Certified* Medicaid.
Owner Proprietary corp (Beverly Enterprises).

El Dorado

El Dorado Nursing Center
900 Country Club Ln, El Dorado, KS 67042
(316) 321-4444
Admin James Knight.
Licensure Intermediate care. *Beds* ICF 85. *Certified* Medicaid.
Owner Proprietary corp (Life Care Centers of Kansas Inc).
Admissions Requirements Medical examination; Physician's request.
Staff RNs 2 (ft), 1 (pt); LPNs 3 (ft); Nurses' aides 16 (ft), 4 (pt); Activities coordinators 1 (ft).
Facilities Dining room; Physical therapy room; Activities room; Laundry room; Barber/Beauty shop.
Activities Arts & crafts; Cards; Games; Movies; Shopping trips; Dances/Social/ Cultural gatherings; Adopt-a-grandparent; Resident council; Family council.

Knutson Manor Nursing Center
1313 S High, El Dorado, KS 67042
(316) 321-4140
Admin Elizabeth L Heinrich. *Dir of Nursing* Brenda Poe RN.
Licensure Skilled care; Intermediate care; Alzheimer's care. *Beds* SNF 60; ICF 57. *Certified* Medicaid; Medicare.
Owner Nonprofit corp.
Admissions Requirements Medical examination; Physician's request.
Staff RNs 4 (ft); LPNs 4 (ft); Nurses' aides 43 (ft); Physical therapists 1 (pt); Occupational therapists 1 (pt); Speech therapists 1 (pt); Activities coordinators; Dietitians 1 (pt); Podiatrists 1 (pt).
Facilities Dining room; Physical therapy room; Activities room; Chapel; Laundry room; Barber/Beauty shop; Library.
Activities Arts & crafts; Cards; Games; Reading groups; Prayer groups; Movies; Shopping trips; Dances/Social/Cultural gatherings.

Ellinwood

Woodhaven Care Center
510 W 7th St, Ellinwood, KS 67526
(316) 564-2337
Admin John E Tanner.
Licensure Intermediate care. *Beds* ICF 59. *Certified* Medicaid.
Staff RNs 1 (ft); LPNs 1 (ft); Nurses' aides 15 (ft), 5 (pt); Physical therapists 1 (pt); Occupational therapists 1 (pt); Speech therapists 1 (pt); Activities coordinators 1 (ft); Dietitians 1 (pt); Audiologists 1 (pt).
Facilities Dining room; Physical therapy room; Activities room; Crafts room; Laundry room; Barber/Beauty shop; Quiet room.
Activities Arts & crafts; Cards; Games; Reading groups; Prayer groups; Movies; Shopping trips; Dances/Social/Cultural gatherings.

Ellis

Ellis Good Samaritan Center
1100 Spruce, Ellis, KS 67637
(913) 726-3101
Admin John R Binder Jr.
Licensure Intermediate care. *Beds* ICF 59. *Certified* Medicaid.
Owner Nonprofit corp (Evangelical Lutheran/ Good Samaritan Society).
Affiliation Lutheran.

Ellsworth

Ellsworth Good Samaritan Center—Villa Hope
870 S Hwy 14 Box 47, Ellsworth, KS 67439
(913) 472-3146
Admin Juliene Saxon. *Dir of Nursing* Mary Lou Pflughoeft RN.
Licensure Intermediate care; Retirement. *Beds* ICF 48. *Certified* Medicaid.
Owner Proprietary corp (Evangelical Lutheran/Good Samaritan Society).
Admissions Requirements Minimum age 20; Medical examination.
Staff RNs 2 (ft); LPNs 2 (pt); Nurses' aides 10 (ft), 4 (pt); Physical therapists 1 (pt); Reality therapists 1 (pt); Occupational therapists 1 (pt); Speech therapists 1 (pt); Activities coordinators 1 (ft); Dietitians 1 (pt); Podiatrists 1 (pt); Dentists 1 (pt).
Affiliation Lutheran.
Facilities Dining room; Physical therapy room; Activities room; Chapel; Crafts room; Laundry room; Barber/Beauty shop; Library.
Activities Arts & crafts; Cards; Games; Reading groups; Prayer groups; Movies; Shopping trips; Dances/Social/Cultural gatherings.

Ellsworth Good Samaritan Village—Villa Grace
870 S Hwy 14, Ellsworth, KS 67439
(913) 472-3167
Admin Roger R Thompson. *Dir of Nursing* Mary Lou Pflughoeft.
Licensure Intermediate care; Retirement. *Beds* ICF 116; Retirement 17. *Private Pay Patients* 52%. *Certified* Medicaid.
Owner Nonprofit corp (Evangelical Lutheran/ Good Samaritan Society).
Admissions Requirements Medical examination; Physician's request.
Staff RNs 7 (ft); LPNs 4 (ft), 1 (pt); Nurses' aides 32 (ft), 8 (pt); Physical therapists 1 (pt); Occupational therapists 1 (pt); Speech therapists 1 (pt); Activities coordinators 2 (ft); Dietitians 1 (ft); Podiatrists 1 (pt); Audiologists 1 (pt).
Languages Spanish.
Affiliation Lutheran.
Facilities Dining room; Physical therapy room; Activities room; Chapel; Crafts room; Laundry room; Barber/Beauty shop; Library.
Activities Cards; Games; Reading groups; Prayer groups; Movies; Dances/Social/ Cultural gatherings.

Emporia

Emporia Presbyterian Manor Inc
2300 Industrial Rd, Emporia, KS 66801
(316) 343-2613
Admin Floyd Born. *Dir of Nursing* Beverly Sparks.
Licensure Skilled care; Retirement. *Beds* SNF 60. *Certified* Medicaid.
Owner Proprietary corp (Presbyterian Manors of Mid America Inc).
Admissions Requirements Physician's request.
Staff RNs; LPNs; Nurses' aides; Activities coordinators; Dietitians.
Affiliation Presbyterian.
Facilities Dining room; Physical therapy room; Activities room; Chapel; Crafts room; Laundry room; Barber/Beauty shop; Library.

Activities Arts & crafts; Cards; Games; Reading groups; Prayer groups; Movies; Shopping trips; Dances/Social/Cultural gatherings.

Flint Hills Manor
1620 Wheeler, Emporia, KS 66801
(316) 342-3280
Admin William "Buck" Fischer. *Dir of Nursing* Paula Zook LPN. *Medical Dir* John P Brookhouse, MD.
Licensure Intermediate care. *Beds* ICF 81. *Private Pay Patients* 40%. *Certified* Medicaid.
Owner Proprietary corp (Beverly Enterprises).
Admissions Requirements Physician's request.
Staff RNs 1 (pt); LPNs 6 (ft); Nurses' aides 30 (ft); Recreational therapists 1 (ft); Occupational therapists 1 (pt); Speech therapists 1 (pt); Activities coordinators 1 (ft); Dietitians 1 (pt).
Languages Sign.
Facilities Dining room; Physical therapy room; Activities room; Chapel; Crafts room; Laundry room; Barber/Beauty shop.
Activities Arts & crafts; Games; Reading groups; Prayer groups; Movies; Shopping trips; Dances/Social/Cultural gatherings; Intergenerational programs; Pet therapy.

Heritage Manor of Emporia
221 W Logan, Emporia, KS 66801
(316) 342-4212
Admin Linda Jackson. *Dir of Nursing* Janet Maltby LPN.
Licensure Intermediate care. *Beds* ICF 105. *Certified* Medicaid.
Owner Proprietary corp (National Heritage).
Admissions Requirements Minimum age 18.
Facilities Dining room; Physical therapy room; Activities room; Chapel; Crafts room; Barber/Beauty shop.
Activities Arts & crafts; Cards; Games; Reading groups; Prayer groups; Movies; Dances/Social/Cultural gatherings.

Holiday Resort Inc
2700 W 30th, Emporia, KS 66801
(316) 343-9285
Admin Gregory C Stuart.
Licensure Skilled care. *Beds* SNF 60. *Certified* Medicaid; Medicare.
Owner Proprietary corp.

Meadowview Care Center
315 S Commercial, Emporia, KS 66801
(316) 342-3656
Admin Linda Slead. *Dir of Nursing* Elizabeth Stafford. *Medical Dir* Kendall Wright.
Licensure Intermediate care. *Beds* ICF 55. *Private Pay Patients* 50%. *Certified* Medicaid.
Owner Proprietary corp.
Admissions Requirements Minimum age 18; Medical examination; Physician's request.
Staff RNs 1 (ft); LPNs 4 (ft); Nurses' aides 20 (ft); Physical therapists (contracted); Activities coordinators 1 (ft); Dietitians.
Facilities Dining room; Physical therapy room; Activities room; Crafts room; Laundry room; Barber/Beauty shop.
Activities Arts & crafts; Cards; Games; Reading groups; Prayer groups; Movies; Shopping trips; Dances/Social/Cultural gatherings; Intergenerational programs; Pet therapy.

Enterprise

Enterprise Estates Nursing Center
Crestview Dr, Enterprise, KS 67441
(913) 934-2278
Admin Lester E Young. *Dir of Nursing* Dorothy Wilson RN. *Medical Dir* J Steven Schwarting MD; Donald C Rorabaugh MD.
Licensure Intermediate care. *Beds* ICF 52. *Private Pay Patients* 60%. *Certified* Medicaid.

Owner Nonprofit corp.
Admissions Requirements Minimum age 18; Medical examination; Physician's request.
Staff RNs 2 (ft); LPNs 4 (ft); Nurses' aides 20 (ft), 5 (pt); Physical therapists; Dietitians.
Facilities Dining room; Physical therapy room; Activities room; Laundry room; Barber/Beauty shop.
Activities Cards; Games; Reading groups; Prayer groups; Movies; Pet therapy.

Erie

Arkhaven at Erie
330 N Main, Erie, KS 66733
(316) 224-5301
Admin Ernestine C Anselmi. *Dir of Nursing* Carole A Hastong RN.
Licensure Intermediate care; Alzheimer's care. *Beds* ICF 43. *Certified* Medicaid.
Owner Privately owned (Health Care Systems Inc).
Staff RNs 2 (ft); LPNs 1 (ft), 1 (pt); Nurses' aides 10 (ft), 6 (pt); Activities coordinators 1 (ft).
Facilities Dining room; Physical therapy room; Activities room; Chapel; Laundry room; Barber/Beauty shop; Library.
Activities Arts & crafts; Cards; Games; Reading groups; Prayer groups; Movies; Shopping trips.

Eskridge

Heritage Village of Eskridge
505 N Main, Eskridge, KS 66423
(913) 449-2294
Admin Nancy Fischer.
Medical Dir Dr William Wade.
Licensure Intermediate care. *Beds* ICF 60. *Certified* Medicaid.
Owner Proprietary corp (Beverly Enterprises).
Admissions Requirements Minimum age 18; Medical examination; Physician's request.
Staff Physicians 1 (pt); RNs 1 (ft); LPNs 4 (ft); Nurses' aides 15 (ft), 4 (pt); Physical therapists 1 (pt); Recreational therapists 1 (pt); Speech therapists 1 (pt); Activities coordinators 1 (ft); Dietitians 1 (pt); Ophthalmologists 1 (pt); Podiatrists 1 (pt); Dentists 1 (pt); Psychiatrist 1 (pt).
Facilities Dining room; Physical therapy room; Activities room; Chapel; Crafts room; Laundry room; Barber/Beauty shop; Library.
Activities Arts & crafts; Cards; Games; Reading groups; Prayer groups; Movies; Shopping trips; Dances/Social/Cultural gatherings.

Eudora

Eudora Nursing Center
PO Box 400, 1415 Maple, Eudora, KS 66025
(913) 542-2176
Admin Civil Gray. *Dir of Nursing* Sylvia Neis RN.
Licensure Intermediate care; Retirement. *Beds* ICF 100; Retirement duplex 1. *Certified* Medicaid.
Owner Proprietary corp.
Admissions Requirements Medical examination; Physician's request; Geriatric or disabled.
Staff RNs 3 (ft), 1 (pt); LPNs 3 (ft); Nurses' aides; Activities coordinators 1 (ft); Social workers 1 (ft); Physical therapy aides 4 (ft).
Languages French.
Facilities Dining room; Physical therapy room; Activities room; Chapel; Crafts room; Laundry room; Barber/Beauty shop; Library; Outside fenced area; Outside walkways.
Activities Arts & crafts; Cards; Games; Reading groups; Prayer groups; Movies; Pet therapy.

Eureka

Medicalodge of Eureka
1020 N School, Eureka, KS 67045
(316) 583-7418
Admin Jeanne Mertens.
Medical Dir Vivian Mitchell.
Licensure Intermediate care. *Beds* ICF 92. *Certified* Medicaid.
Owner Proprietary corp (Medicalodges Inc).
Admissions Requirements Minimum age 16; Medical examination; Physician's request.
Staff RNs 1 (ft); LPNs 5 (ft); Activities coordinators 1 (ft), 1 (pt).
Facilities Dining room; Physical therapy room; Activities room; Crafts room; Laundry room; Barber/Beauty shop; Library.
Activities Arts & crafts; Cards; Games; Reading groups; Prayer groups; Movies; Shopping trips; Dances/Social/Cultural gatherings.

Regency Health Care Center
1406 N Elm, Eureka, KS 67045
(316) 583-5630
Admin Rosalie L Garrison. *Dir of Nursing* Karen Stilwell LPN. *Medical Dir* Terry Morris DO.
Licensure Intermediate care. *Beds* ICF 48. *Private Pay Patients* 44%. *Certified* Medicaid.
Owner Proprietary corp (Regency Health Care Centers Inc).
Admissions Requirements Minimum age 16; Medical examination; Physician's request.
Staff LPNs 1 (ft), 4 (pt); Nurses' aides 15 (ft), 5 (pt); Physical therapists (consultant); Occupational therapists (consultant); Speech therapists (consultant); Activities coordinators 1 (ft); Dietitians (consultant); Audiologists (consultant).
Facilities Dining room; Physical therapy room; Activities room; Crafts room; Laundry room; Barber/Beauty shop; Library; Family room.
Activities Arts & crafts; Cards; Games; Reading groups; Prayer groups; Movies; Shopping trips; Dances/Social/Cultural gatherings; Intergenerational programs; Pet therapy; Church services.

Florence

Regency Health Care Center
9th & Marion, Florence, KS 66851
(316) 878-4440
Admin Madeline Teufel.
Medical Dir Larona Loveless.
Licensure Intermediate care. *Beds* ICF 60. *Certified* Medicaid.
Owner Proprietary corp (Regency Health Care Centers Inc).
Admissions Requirements Minimum age 21.
Staff Physicians 1 (pt); RNs 1 (ft); LPNs 3 (ft); Nurses' aides 18 (ft); Physical therapists 1 (pt); Recreational therapists 1 (pt); Occupational therapists 2 (ft); Activities coordinators 1 (ft); Dietitians 1 (ft); Ophthalmologists 1 (pt); Podiatrists 1 (pt).
Facilities Dining room; Physical therapy room; Activities room; Chapel; Crafts room; Laundry room; Barber/Beauty shop; Library.
Activities Arts & crafts; Cards; Games; Prayer groups; Movies; Shopping trips; ADL skills training; Living skills training; Fishing outings; Swimming; Playing pool; Bowling.

Fort Scott

Arkhaven at Fort Scott
737 Heylman, Fort Scott, KS 66701
(316) 223-1620
Admin Cynthia Lipe.
Medical Dir Jacqueline Vann.
Licensure Intermediate care. *Beds* ICF 60. *Certified* Medicaid.

Owner Proprietary corp (Health Care
Systems).
Admissions Requirements Minimum age 19;
Medical examination; Physician's request.
Staff RNs; LPNs; Nurses' aides; Physical
therapists; Reality therapists; Recreational
therapists; Occupational therapists; Speech
therapists; Activities coordinators; Dietitians;
Ophthalmologists; Podiatrists.
Facilities Dining room; Physical therapy
room; Activities room; Crafts room; Laundry
room; Barber/Beauty shop.
Activities Arts & crafts; Cards; Games; Prayer
groups; Movies; Dances/Social/Cultural
gatherings; Cooking; Gardening; Self
improvement.

Fort Scott Manor
736 Heylman, Fort Scott, KS 66701
(316) 223-3120
Admin Vicky L Killinger.
Medical Dir Amy Wiggans.
Licensure Intermediate care. *Beds* ICF 53.
Certified Medicaid.
Owner Proprietary corp.
Staff RNs 3 (ft); LPNs 2 (ft), 2 (pt); Physical
therapists 1 (pt); Occupational therapists 1
(pt); Speech therapists 1 (pt); Activities
coordinators 1 (ft); Dietitians 1 (pt);
Podiatrists 1 (pt); Dentists 1 (pt).
Facilities Dining room; Physical therapy
room; Activities room; Crafts room; Laundry
room; Barber/Beauty shop.
Activities Arts & crafts; Cards; Games;
Reading groups; Prayer groups; Shopping
trips; Dances/Social/Cultural gatherings.

Medicalodge of Fort Scott
PO Box 1135, 915 S Horton, Fort Scott, KS
66701
(316) 223-0210
Admin Leona Miller.
Licensure Intermediate care. *Beds* ICF 107.
Certified Medicaid.
Owner Proprietary corp (Medicalodges Inc).

Fowler

Fowler Nursing Home
512 E 5th, Fowler, KS 67844
(316) 646-5215
Admin Penny Turner.
Medical Dir Barbara Whitney.
Licensure Intermediate care. *Beds* 38.
Certified Medicaid.
Owner Publicly owned.
Admissions Requirements Minimum age 16;
Physician's request.
Staff RNs 3 (ft); LPNs 2 (ft); Nurses' aides 20
(ft), 15 (pt); Physical therapists 1 (pt);
Occupational therapists 1 (pt); Speech
therapists 1 (pt); Activities coordinators 1
(ft), 1 (pt); Podiatrists 1 (pt).
Languages Spanish.
Facilities Dining room; Physical therapy
room; Activities room; Chapel; Laundry
room; Barber/Beauty shop.
Activities Cards; Games; Prayer groups;
Movies; Shopping trips; Dances/Social/
Cultural gatherings.

Frankfort

Frankfort Community Care Home Inc
510 Walnut, Frankfort, KS 66427
(913) 292-4442
Admin Linnea Brandt.
Medical Dir Shirley Anderson.
Licensure Intermediate care. *Beds* ICF 60.
Certified Medicaid.
Owner Nonprofit corp.
Admissions Requirements Physician's request.
Staff RNs; LPNs; Nurses' aides; Physical
therapists; Recreational therapists;
Occupational therapists; Speech therapists;
Activities coordinators; Dietitians.

Facilities Dining room; Physical therapy
room; Activities room; Chapel; Laundry
room; Barber/Beauty shop; Storm shelter.
Activities Arts & crafts; Cards; Games;
Reading groups; Prayer groups; Movies;
Shopping trips; Dances/Social/Cultural
gatherings; Music; Church services; Picnics;
Fishing.

Fredonia

Hillcrest Manor
PO Box 306, Fredonia, KS 66736
(316) 378-4163
Admin Lillian L Ghramm.
Medical Dir Mary E Walker.
Licensure Intermediate care. *Beds* ICF 50.
Certified Medicaid.
Owner Proprietary corp (Beverly Enterprises).
Admissions Requirements Minimum age 16;
Medical examination.
Staff RNs; LPNs; Nurses' aides; Activities
coordinators; Medication aide.
Facilities Dining room; Physical therapy
room; Activities room; Chapel; Crafts room;
Laundry room; Barber/Beauty shop.
Activities Arts & crafts; Cards; Games;
Movies.

Frontenac

Sunset Manor Inc
206 S Dittmann, Frontenac, KS 66762
(316) 231-7340
Admin Raymond R Knaup.
Licensure Intermediate care. *Beds* ICF 150.
Certified Medicaid.
Owner Proprietary corp.

Galena

Barker Rest Home
109 W Empire, Galena, KS 66739
(316) 783-5048
Admin Barbara Link.
Licensure Intermediate care. *Beds* ICF 50.
Certified Medicaid.
Owner Proprietary corp.

Galena Manor
8th & Keller, Galena, KS 66739
(316) 783-1383
Admin Marjorie A Abraham. *Dir of Nursing*
Pat Kinder. *Medical Dir* Stephen J Bazzano
DO.
Licensure Intermediate care; Adult day care;
Alzheimer's care. *Beds* ICF 60; Adult day
care 5. *Private Pay Patients* 20%. *Certified*
Medicaid.
Owner Proprietary corp (Americare Systems
Inc).
Admissions Requirements Minimum age 18;
Medical examination; Physician's request.
Staff LPNs 4 (ft), 2 (pt); Nurses' aides 14 (ft),
4 (pt); Recreational therapists 1 (ft);
Occupational therapists 1 (ft); Activities
coordinators 1 (ft); Dietitians 1 (ft);
Podiatrists 1 (pt).
Languages Sign.
Facilities Dining room; Physical therapy
room; Activities room; Crafts room; Laundry
room; Barber/Beauty shop; Quiet room;
Fenced patio.
Activities Arts & crafts; Cards; Games;
Reading groups; Prayer groups; Movies;
Dances/Social/Cultural gatherings; Pet
therapy; Coffee klatch; Popcorn party.

Garden City

Garden Valley Retirement Village
1505 E Spruce, Garden City, KS 67846
(316) 275-9651
Admin Alfred C Hill. *Dir of Nursing* Norma
Caldwell. *Medical Dir* James Greenwood
MD.

Licensure Skilled care; Intermediate care;
Retirement. *Beds* SNF 45; ICF 87;
Retirement 90. *Private Pay Patients* 66%.
Certified Medicaid; Medicare.
Owner Nonprofit corp.
Admissions Requirements Medical
examination; Physician's request.
Staff Physicians 3 (pt); RNs 4 (ft), 3 (pt);
LPNs 4 (ft), 2 (pt); Nurses' aides 24 (ft), 6
(pt); Physical therapists 3 (ft), 1 (pt);
Occupational therapists 1 (pt); Speech
therapists 1 (pt); Activities coordinators 2
(ft); Dietitians 1 (pt); Podiatrists 1 (pt);
Audiologists 1 (pt).
Languages Spanish.
Affiliation Mennonite.
Facilities Dining room; Physical therapy
room; Activities room; Chapel; Crafts room;
Laundry room; Barber/Beauty shop; Library;
Enclosed privacy patio.
Activities Arts & crafts; Cards; Games;
Reading groups; Prayer groups; Movies;
Dances/Social/Cultural gatherings;
Intergenerational programs.

Terrace Garden Care Center
Box 955, Garden City, KS 67846
(316) 276-7643
Admin David J Cerveny.
Licensure Intermediate care. *Beds* ICF 98.
Certified Medicaid.
Owner Proprietary corp (Vetter Health
Services Inc).
Admissions Requirements Minimum age 18;
Medical examination; Physician's request.
Facilities Dining room; Physical therapy
room; Activities room; Laundry room;
Barber/Beauty shop.
Activities Arts & crafts; Cards; Games;
Reading groups; Prayer groups; Movies;
Shopping trips; Dances/Social/Cultural
gatherings.

Gardner

Bedford Nursing Center
223 Bedford, Gardner, KS 66030
(913) 884-6520
Admin Bonita Schockey. *Dir of Nursing*
Patricia Marstall LPN, HSS. *Medical Dir*
Thomen Reece MD.
Licensure Intermediate care; Retirement
cottages. *Beds* ICF 82; Retirement cottages
10. *Private Pay Patients* 20%. *Certified*
Medicaid.
Owner Proprietary corp (Beverly Enterprises).
Admissions Requirements Minimum age 16;
Medical examination; Physician's request.
Staff LPNs; Nurses' aides; Psychiatrists.
Facilities Dining room; Physical therapy
room; Activities room; Chapel; Laundry
room; Barber/Beauty shop; Library; Mental
health unit.
Activities Arts & crafts; Cards; Games;
Reading groups; Prayer groups; Movies;
Dances/Social/Cultural gatherings; Pet
therapy.

Garnett

Arkhaven at Garnett
RR 2, Box 306, W 7th St, Garnett, KS 66032
(913) 448-6884
Admin Barbara Watkins. *Dir of Nursing*
Kathleen McNutt.
Licensure Intermediate care. *Beds* ICF 49.
Private Pay Patients 20%. *Certified*
Medicaid.
Owner Proprietary corp (Health Care Systems
Inc).
Admissions Requirements Minimum age 55.
Staff RNs 1 (ft); LPNs 2 (ft); Nurses' aides 7
(ft), 6 (pt); Physical therapists 1 (pt); Reality
therapists 1 (pt); Occupational therapists 1
(pt); Speech therapists 1 (pt); Activities
coordinators 1 (ft); Dietitians 1 (ft).

Facilities Dining room; Physical therapy room; Activities room; Chapel; Crafts room; Laundry room; Barber/Beauty shop.
Activities Arts & crafts; Cards; Games; Reading groups; Prayer groups; Shopping trips; Dances/Social/Cultural gatherings; Pet therapy.

Golden Heights Living Center
101 N Pine, Garnett, KS 66032
(913) 448-2434
Admin Jon M Covault.
Medical Dir Debbie Bangs.
Licensure Intermediate care. *Beds* ICF 55. *Certified* Medicaid.
Owner Proprietary corp (Vetter Health Services Inc).
Admissions Requirements Minimum age 16; Medical examination.
Staff RNs 1 (ft), 1 (pt); LPNs 3 (ft); Nurses' aides 15 (ft); Activities coordinators 1 (ft).
Facilities Dining room; Physical therapy room; Activities room; Crafts room; Laundry room; Barber/Beauty shop.
Activities Arts & crafts; Cards; Games; Reading groups; Prayer groups; Movies; Shopping trips; Dances/Social/Cultural gatherings.

Girard

Heritage
PO Box 66, 511 N Western, Girard, KS 66743
(316) 724-8288
Admin John Twarog.
Licensure Intermediate care. *Beds* ICF 106. *Certified* Medicaid.
Owner Proprietary corp.

Glasco

Nicol Home Inc
PO Box 68, Spears & Buffalo Sts, Glasco, KS 67445
(913) 568-2251
Admin Janette Nonamaker. *Dir of Nursing* Janice Fief RN.
Licensure Intermediate care. *Beds* ICF 32. *Certified* Medicaid.
Owner Nonprofit corp.
Staff RNs 1 (ft); LPNs 3 (ft); Nurses' aides 15 (ft); Occupational therapists 1 (pt); Activities coordinators 1 (ft).
Facilities Dining room; Physical therapy room; Activities room; Laundry room; Barber/Beauty shop; Library.
Activities Arts & crafts; Cards; Games; Reading groups; Movies; Dances/Social/Cultural gatherings.

Goddard

Medicalodge of Goddard
501 Easy, Goddard, KS 67052
(316) 794-8635
Admin James E Dyck.
Licensure Intermediate care. *Beds* ICF 80. *Certified* Medicaid.
Owner Proprietary corp (Medicalodges Inc).

Goessel

Bethesda Home
408-412 E Main, Goessel, KS 67053
(316) 367-2291
Admin Ralph L Garrison.
Licensure Intermediate care. *Beds* ICF 83. *Certified* Medicaid.
Owner Nonprofit corp.

Goodland

Golden West Skills Center
108 Aspen Rd, Goodland, KS 67735
(913) 899-2322
Admin Vicki Baker.

Licensure Intermediate care for mentally retarded. *Beds* ICF/MR 53. *Certified* Medicaid.
Owner Proprietary corp (Beverly Enterprises).

Sherman County Good Samaritan Center
208 W 2nd, Goodland, KS 67735
(913) 899-7517
Admin David Cecil. *Dir of Nursing* Pat Graves.
Licensure Intermediate care. *Beds* ICF 60. *Private Pay Patients* 53%. *Certified* Medicaid.
Owner Nonprofit corp (Evangelical Lutheran/Good Samaritan Society).
Admissions Requirements Medical examination.
Staff RNs 3 (pt); LPNs 5 (ft), 2 (pt); Nurses' aides 17 (ft), 5 (pt); Physical therapists 1 (pt); Activities coordinators 1 (ft); Dietitians 1 (ft).
Facilities Dining room; Physical therapy room; Activities room; Chapel; Crafts room; Laundry room; Barber/Beauty shop.
Activities Arts & crafts; Cards; Games; Reading groups; Prayer groups; Movies; Shopping trips; Pet therapy.

Great Bend

Cherry Village
1401 Cherry Ln, Great Bend, KS 67530
(316) 792-2165
Admin Clarence M Johansen.
Medical Dir Pamla S Lewis.
Licensure Skilled care; Alzheimer's care; Retirement. *Beds* ICF 95. *Certified* Medicaid.
Owner Proprietary corp.
Admissions Requirements Minimum age 18; Medical examination; Physician's request.
Staff RNs 6 (ft), 2 (pt); LPNs 5 (ft); Nurses' aides 24 (ft), 6 (pt); Physical therapists 1 (ft); Recreational therapists 1 (pt).
Facilities Dining room; Physical therapy room; Activities room; Barber/Beauty shop; Crafts room; Laundry room; Barber/Beauty shop.
Activities Arts & crafts; Cards; Games; Prayer groups; Movies.

Great Bend Manor
1560 K-96 Hwy, Great Bend, KS 67530
(316) 792-2448
Admin Tom A Hermansen.
Licensure Intermediate care; Personal care. *Beds* ICF 110; Personal care 50. *Certified* Medicaid.
Owner Proprietary corp (National Heritage).

Greensburg

Lifecare of Greensburg
723 S Elm, Greensburg, KS 67054
(316) 723-3328
Admin Peggy J Adee. *Dir of Nursing* Irene Monroe LPN.
Licensure Intermediate care; Retirement; Alzheimer's care. *Beds* ICF 50. *Certified* Medicaid.
Owner Proprietary corp (Life Care Centers of Kansas Inc).
Admissions Requirements Minimum age 16.
Staff Physicians 2 (ft); RNs 3 (ft); LPNs 3 (ft); Physical therapists 2 (ft); Activities coordinators 1 (ft).
Facilities Dining room; Physical therapy room; Activities room; Chapel; Crafts room; Laundry room; Barber/Beauty shop.
Activities Arts & crafts; Games; Reading groups; Prayer groups; Movies; Shopping trips; Dances/Social/Cultural gatherings.

Halstead

Regency Health Care Center
915 McNair St, Halstead, KS 67056
(316) 835-2276
Admin Frank Taylor. *Dir of Nursing* Andrea Hall RN.
Licensure Intermediate care. *Beds* ICF 90. *Certified* Medicaid.
Owner Proprietary corp (Regency Health Care Centers Inc).
Admissions Requirements Minimum age 18; Medical examination; Physician's request.
Staff Physicians 25 (pt); RNs 3 (ft), 2 (pt); LPNs 5 (ft), 3 (pt); Nurses' aides 40 (ft); Physical therapists 1 (pt); Recreational therapists 1 (pt); Occupational therapists 1 (pt); Speech therapists 1 (pt); Activities coordinators 1 (ft); Dietitians 1 (pt); Ophthalmologists 1 (pt).
Facilities Dining room; Physical therapy room; Activities room; Crafts room; Laundry room; Barber/Beauty shop; Library.
Activities Arts & crafts; Cards; Games; Reading groups; Prayer groups; Movies; Shopping trips.

Harper

Lifecare of Harper
615 W 12th, Harper, KS 67058
(316) 896-2914
Admin Judy Curry. *Dir of Nursing* Carla Pence HHS. *Medical Dir* Dr Ralph Bellar.
Licensure Intermediate care. *Beds* ICF 52. *Certified* Medicaid; Medicare.
Owner Proprietary corp (Lifecare Centers of Kansas Inc).
Admissions Requirements Medical examination.
Facilities Dining room; Physical therapy room; Activities room; Crafts room; Laundry room; Barber/Beauty shop.
Activities Arts & crafts; Cards; Games; Reading groups; Prayer groups; Movies; Shopping trips; Dances/Social/Cultural gatherings; Intergenerational programs.

Hartford

Hartford Manor
413 E Exchange, Hartford, KS 66854
(316) 392-5523
Admin Brenda Sherwood. *Dir of Nursing* Virginia Sorenson. *Medical Dir* K R Hunter MD.
Licensure Intermediate care for mentally retarded. *Beds* ICF/MR 50. *Certified* Medicaid.
Owner Proprietary corp.
Admissions Requirements Minimum age 18; Medical examination.
Staff Physicians 1 (pt); RNs 1 (ft); LPNs 2 (ft); Nurses' aides 65 (ft), 7 (pt); Physical therapists 1 (pt); Occupational therapists 1 (pt); Speech therapists 1 (pt); Activities coordinators 1 (ft); Dietitians 1 (pt); Podiatrists 1 (pt); Social worker 1 (ft).
Facilities Dining room; Physical therapy room; Activities room; Crafts room; Laundry room; Barber/Beauty shop; Training facilities.
Activities Arts & crafts; Cards; Games; Reading groups; Movies; Shopping trips; Dances/Social/Cultural gatherings; Training in all areas of personal care & independent living.

Haven

Lifecare Training Center at Haven
216 N Topeka, Haven, KS 67543
(316) 465-2249
Admin Roman K Freundorfer.
Medical Dir Virginia Brawner.

Licensure Intermediate care for mentally retarded. *Beds* ICF/MR 76. *Certified* Medicaid.
Owner Proprietary corp (Life Care Centers of Kansas).
Admissions Requirements Minimum age 18.
Staff Physicians; RNs; LPNs; Nurses' aides; Physical therapists; Recreational therapists; Occupational therapists; Speech therapists; Activities coordinators; Dietitians; Ophthalmologists; Dentists.
Facilities Dining room; Physical therapy room; Activities room; Laundry room; Barber/Beauty shop.
Activities Arts & crafts; Cards; Games; Reading groups; Prayer groups; Movies; Shopping trips; Dances/Social/Cultural gatherings.

Haviland

Lifecare Rehabilitation Center
200 Main St, Haviland, KS 67059
(316) 862-5291
Admin Bertha Tuttle. *Dir of Nursing* Bertha M Tuttle RN.
Licensure Intermediate care. *Beds* ICF 50. *Certified* Medicaid.
Owner Proprietary corp (Life Care Centers of Kansas Inc).
Admissions Requirements Minimum age 18; Medical examination.
Staff Physicians; RNs; LPNs; Nurses' aides; Physical therapists; Occupational therapists; Speech therapists; Activities coordinators; Dietitians; Ophthalmologists; Podiatrists; Dentists.
Facilities Dining room; Physical therapy room; Activities room; Crafts room; Laundry room; Barber/Beauty shop; Quiet room.
Activities Arts & crafts; Cards; Games; Prayer groups; Movies; Shopping trips; Dances/ Social/Cultural gatherings.

Hays

Hays Good Samaritan Center
27th & Canal, Hays, KS 67601
(913) 625-7331
Admin Elaine Metzger. *Dir of Nursing* Sheila Rupp, RN.
Licensure Intermediate care. *Beds* ICF 88. *Private Pay Patients* 33%. *Certified* Medicaid.
Owner Nonprofit corp (Evangelical Lutheran/ Good Samaritan Society).
Admissions Requirements Medical examination; Physician's request.
Staff RNs 3 (ft), 1 (pt); LPNs 6 (ft), 3 (pt); Nurses' aides 15 (ft), 11 (pt); Activities coordinators 1 (ft); Social services 1 (ft); Food services supervisor 1 (ft); Restorative aides 2 (ft).
Languages German.
Affiliation Lutheran.
Facilities Dining room; Physical therapy room; Activities room; Chapel; Laundry room; Barber/Beauty shop; In-service.
Activities Arts & crafts; Cards; Games; Reading groups; Prayer groups; Movies; Shopping trips; Dances/Social/Cultural gatherings; Intergenerational programs; Pet therapy; Restorative therapy; Pastoral counseling.

St John's of Hays
2403 Canterbury, Hays, KS 67601
(913) 628-3241
Admin Carl L Noyes. *Dir of Nursing* Joyce Jacobs. *Medical Dir* Joe Ramsey.
Licensure Skilled care. *Beds* SNF 60. *Private Pay Patients* 42%. *Certified* Medicaid.
Owner Nonprofit corp (Saint John's Rest Home Corp).
Staff Physicians 1 (pt); RNs 2 (ft), 2 (pt); LPNs 3 (ft), 3 (pt); Nurses' aides; Physical therapists 1 (ft); Occupational therapists 1

(pt); Speech therapists 1 (pt); Activities coordinators 1 (ft); Dietitians 1 (ft); Audiologists 1 (pt).
Languages German.
Affiliation Roman Catholic.
Facilities Dining room; Physical therapy room; Activities room; Chapel; Laundry room; Barber/Beauty shop.
Activities Arts & crafts; Cards; Games; Reading groups; Prayer groups; Movies; Shopping trips; Dances/Social/Cultural gatherings; Intergenerational programs; Pet therapy.

Haysville

Green Meadows Nursing Center
215 N Lamar St, Haysville, KS 67060
(316) 524-3211
Admin Ed Brass. *Dir of Nursing* Donna Malia RN. *Medical Dir* R D Magsalin MD.
Licensure Skilled care; Intermediate care. *Beds* SNF 50; ICF 100. *Certified* Medicaid; Medicare.
Owner Proprietary corp (Hillhaven Corp).
Admissions Requirements Minimum age; Medical examination; Physician's request.
Staff RNs 4 (ft), 2 (pt); LPNs 12 (ft), 3 (pt); Nurses' aides 36 (ft), 10 (pt); Physical therapists 1 (pt); Recreational therapists 1 (ft); Occupational therapists 1 (pt); Speech therapists 1 (pt); Activities coordinators 1 (ft); Dietitians 1 (pt); Podiatrists 1 (pt).
Facilities Dining room; Physical therapy room; Activities room; Laundry room; Barber/Beauty shop.
Activities Arts & crafts; Cards; Games; Reading groups; Prayer groups; Movies; Shopping trips; Dances/Social/Cultural gatherings; Reality orientation; Remotivation groups; Music therapy.

Herington

Lutheran Home Inc
2 E Ash St, Herington, KS 67449
(913) 258-2283
Admin William D Peterson.
Licensure Intermediate care. *Beds* ICF 100. *Certified* Medicaid.
Owner Nonprofit corp.
Affiliation Lutheran.

Hesston

Schowalter Villa
Box 5000, 200 W Cedar, Hesston, KS 67062
(316) 327-4261
Admin Leo G Schmidt. *Dir of Nursing* Joyce Bedsworth RN. *Medical Dir* Paul Fransen MD.
Licensure Intermediate care; Retirement community. *Beds* ICF 67; Retirement community 175-180. *Private Pay Patients* 70%. *Certified* Medicaid.
Owner Nonprofit corp (Mennonite Board of Missions and Charities Inc).
Admissions Requirements Medical examination; Physician's request.
Staff RNs 3 (ft), 5 (pt); LPNs 2 (pt); Physical therapists (consultant); Occupational therapists (consultant); Speech therapists (consultant); Activities coordinators 1 (ft); Dietitians (consultant); Podiatrists (consultant); Audiologists (consultant).
Affiliation Mennonite.
Facilities Dining room; Physical therapy room; Activities room; Chapel; Crafts room; Laundry room; Barber/Beauty shop; Library.
Activities Cards; Games; Reading groups; Prayer groups; Movies; Shopping trips; Dances/Social/Cultural gatherings.

Hiawatha

Heritage Manor of Hiawatha
RR 2, Iowa St, Hiawatha, KS 66434
(913) 742-7465
Admin Judith Floyd.
Medical Dir Dr Larson.
Licensure Intermediate care. *Beds* ICF 100. *Certified* Medicaid.
Owner Proprietary corp (National Heritage).
Admissions Requirements Minimum age 16; Physician's request.
Staff RNs 1 (ft), 1 (pt); LPNs 5 (ft); Physical therapists 2 (ft); Activities coordinators 1 (ft).
Facilities Dining room; Physical therapy room; Activities room; Chapel; Crafts room; Laundry room; Barber/Beauty shop; Library.
Activities Arts & crafts; Games; Prayer groups; Movies.

Oak Ridge Acres
201 Sioux, Hiawatha, KS 66434
(913) 742-2149
Admin Georgia A Loyd. *Dir of Nursing* Tracy Britt HSS. *Medical Dir* Delbert Larson MD.
Licensure Intermediate care; Adult day care. *Beds* ICF 49. *Private Pay Patients* 55%. *Certified* Medicaid.
Owner Proprietary corp (Adult Care Management Corp).
Admissions Requirements Minimum age 16; Medical examination; Physician's request.
Staff RNs 1 (ft), 1 (pt); LPNs 4 (ft), 1 (pt); Nurses' aides 10 (ft), 5 (pt); Activities coordinators 1 (ft); Dietitians 1 (ft).
Facilities Dining room; Physical therapy room; Activities room; Crafts room; Laundry room; Barber/Beauty shop; Adult day care program.
Activities Arts & crafts; Cards; Games; Reading groups; Prayer groups; Movies; Shopping trips; Dances/Social/Cultural gatherings; Intergenerational programs; Pet therapy.

Highland

Collier Manor
PO Box 117, South Ave, Highland, KS 66035
(913) 442-3217
Admin Bette J Fritch.
Licensure Intermediate care. *Beds* ICF 50. *Certified* Medicaid.
Owner Proprietary corp (Adult Care Management Corp).

Hill City

Dawson Place Inc
208 W Prout, Hill City, KS 67642
(913) 674-3414
Admin Ladonna Hensley.
Licensure Intermediate care. *Beds* ICF 55. *Certified* Medicaid.
Owner Proprietary corp.

Hillsboro

Parkside Homes Inc
200 Willow Rd, Hillsboro, KS 67063
(316) 947-2301
Admin Luella Janzen. *Dir of Nursing* Elva Penner.
Licensure Intermediate care; Retirement; Alzheimer's care. *Beds* ICF 60; Retirement apts 19. *Private Pay Patients* 45%. *Certified* Medicaid.
Owner Nonprofit organization/foundation.
Admissions Requirements Minimum age 62 (exceptions may be board approved); Medical examination; Physician's request.
Staff RNs 2 (ft), 7 (pt); LPNs 1 (ft), 2 (pt); Nurses' aides 8 (ft), 27 (pt); Physical therapists (consultant); Activities coordinators 1 (pt); Dietitians (consultant).

Languages German.
Affiliation Mennonite.
Facilities Dining room; Physical therapy room; Activities room; Crafts room; Laundry room; Barber/Beauty shop; Family dining room; Quiet room; Counseling room; Mini store; Wander guard.
Activities Arts & crafts; Games; Reading groups; Prayer groups; Movies; Shopping trips; Intergenerational programs; Outings to restaurants; Picnics; Bible studies; Musical programs; Coffee breaks; Psychosocial programs.

Hoisington

Regency Health Care Center
272 W Cheyenne, Hoisington, KS 67544
(316) 653-4141
Admin Thomas L Hoban.
Licensure Intermediate care. *Beds* ICF 70. *Certified* Medicaid.
Owner Proprietary corp (Regency Health Care Center Inc).

Holton

Jackson County Nursing Home Inc
1121 W 7th, Holton, KS 66436
(913) 364-3164
Admin Suzanne Misenhelter. *Dir of Nursing* Karen McCrory. *Medical Dir* Carlos Chavez MD.
Licensure Intermediate care. *Beds* ICF 80. *Certified* Medicaid.
Owner Nonprofit corp.
Activities Arts & crafts; Cards; Games; Reading groups; Prayer groups; Movies; Shopping trips; Dances/Social/Cultural gatherings; Intergenerational programs; Pet therapy.

Merry Manor Corp
100 Topeka, Holton, KS 66436
(913) 364-3840
Admin Mary Ann Kirk. *Dir of Nursing* Theresa Kirk.
Licensure Intermediate care; Retirement. *Beds* ICF 60; Retirement 3. *Private Pay Patients* 75%. *Certified* Medicaid.
Owner Proprietary corp.
Admissions Requirements Medical examination; Physician's request.
Staff RNs 1 (pt); LPNs 5 (ft), 1 (pt); Nurses' aides 16 (ft); Activities coordinators 1 (ft); Dietitians 1 (pt).
Facilities Dining room; Physical therapy room; Activities room; Laundry room; Barber/Beauty shop.
Activities Arts & crafts; Games; Reading groups; Prayer groups; Movies; Shopping trips; Dances/Social/Cultural gatherings; Pet therapy.

Horton

Tri-County Manor Nursing Center
1890 Euclid, Horton, KS 66439
(913) 486-2697
Admin Rhonda Parks.
Medical Dir Dr Edgardo Francisco.
Licensure Intermediate care. *Beds* ICF 110. *Certified* Medicaid.
Admissions Requirements Minimum age 16; Medical examination; Physician's request.
Staff Physicians 5 (pt); RNs 2 (pt); LPNs 6 (ft), 2 (pt); Nurses' aides 34 (ft), 6 (pt); Physical therapists 1 (pt); Occupational therapists 1 (pt); Speech therapists 1 (pt); Activities coordinators 1 (ft); Dietitians 1 (pt); Ophthalmologists 1 (pt); Podiatrists 1 (pt); Audiologists 1 (pt); Dentists 1 (pt).
Facilities Dining room; Physical therapy room; Activities room; Crafts room; Laundry room; Barber/Beauty shop; Library.

Activities Arts & crafts; Cards; Games; Reading groups; Prayer groups; Shopping trips; Dances/Social/Cultural gatherings; Musical programs; Scenic bus rides.

Howard

Howard Twilight Manor
PO Box 237, Hwy 99, Howard, KS 67349
(316) 374-2495
Admin Mary J Smith.
Licensure Intermediate care. *Beds* ICF 50. *Certified* Medicaid.
Owner Publicly owned.
Admissions Requirements Minimum age 16; Medical examination; Physician's request.
Staff RNs 1 (pt); LPNs 3 (ft); Nurses' aides 20 (ft); Activities coordinators 1 (ft).
Facilities Dining room; Physical therapy room; Activities room; Chapel; Laundry room; Barber/Beauty shop.
Activities Arts & crafts; Cards; Games; Reading groups; Prayer groups; Movies; Shopping trips; Dances/Social/Cultural gatherings.

Hugoton

Pioneer Manor
PO Box 758, Hugoton, KS 67951
(316) 544-2023
Admin Leo L Buss. *Dir of Nursing* Cindy Kuder RN. *Medical Dir* Dr Larry Balzer.
Licensure Intermediate care. *Beds* ICF 56. *Certified* Medicaid.
Owner Publicly owned.
Admissions Requirements Minimum age 45; Medical examination; Physician's request.
Staff Physicians 1 (pt); RNs 3 (ft); LPNs 2 (ft); Nurses' aides 12 (ft), 6 (pt); Speech therapists 1 (pt); Activities coordinators 1 (ft), 1 (pt); Dietitians 7 (ft), 2 (pt); Podiatrists 1 (pt).
Facilities Dining room; Physical therapy room; Activities room; Chapel; Crafts room; Laundry room; Barber/Beauty shop.
Activities Arts & crafts; Games; Reading groups; Prayer groups; Movies; Shopping trips; Dances/Social/Cultural gatherings; Make floats for county fair; Make Chamber of Commerce annual banquet decorations.

Humboldt

Pinecrest Nursing Home
1020 Pine, Humboldt, KS 66748
(316) 473-2393
Admin Carolyn J Moore. *Dir of Nursing* Barbara Heady RN.
Licensure Intermediate care. *Beds* ICF 52. *Private Pay Patients* 35%. *Certified* Medicaid.
Owner Privately owned.
Admissions Requirements Minimum age 16; Medical examination; Physician's request.
Staff RNs; LPNs; Nurses' aides; Physical therapists; Occupational therapists; Activities coordinators; Dietitians; Podiatrists.
Languages Spanish.
Facilities Dining room; Physical therapy room; Activities room; Chapel; Crafts room; Laundry room; Barber/Beauty shop; Library.
Activities Arts & crafts; Cards; Games; Reading groups; Movies; Shopping trips; Dances/Social/Cultural gatherings; Intergenerational programs; Pet therapy.

Hutchinson

Golden Plains Health Care Center
1202 E 23rd, Hutchinson, KS 67502
(316) 669-9393
Admin Mary E Stuart.
Medical Dir W C Goodpasture MD.

Licensure Skilled care; Intermediate care. *Beds* SNF 60; ICF 56. *Certified* Medicaid; Medicare.
Owner Privately owned.
Admissions Requirements Minimum age 16; Medical examination; Physician's request.
Staff Physicians 1 (ft); RNs 8 (ft), 4 (pt); LPNs 4 (ft), 2 (pt); Nurses' aides 45 (ft), 10 (pt); Physical therapists 1 (ft); Speech therapists 1 (ft); Activities coordinators 1 (ft); Dietitians 1 (pt); Ophthalmologists 1 (pt); Podiatrists 1 (pt); Audiologists 1 (pt); Dentists 1 (pt).
Facilities Dining room; Physical therapy room; Activities room; Laundry room; Barber/Beauty shop; Library.
Activities Arts & crafts; Cards; Games; Reading groups; Prayer groups; Movies; Dances/Social/Cultural gatherings.

Hutchinson Good Samaritan Center
810 E 30th, Hutchinson, KS 67501
(316) 663-1189
Admin Shelly Henderson.
Licensure Intermediate care. *Beds* ICF 90. *Certified* Medicaid.
Owner Nonprofit corp (Evangelical Lutheran/ Good Samaritan Society).
Admissions Requirements Minimum age 21.
Staff RNs 3 (ft); LPNs 3 (ft); Nurses' aides 30 (ft); Activities coordinators 1 (ft), 1 (pt).
Affiliation Lutheran.
Facilities Dining room; Physical therapy room; Activities room; Chapel; Crafts room; Laundry room; Barber/Beauty shop; Library.
Activities Arts & crafts; Cards; Games; Reading groups; Prayer groups; Movies; Shopping trips; Bell choir; Adopt-a-grandparent program.

Hutchinson Heights
4000 N Monroe, Hutchinson, KS 67502
(316) 669-8522
Admin Mary Oberle.
Medical Dir Doris Coats Gray.
Licensure Intermediate care for mentally retarded. *Beds* ICF/MR 15. *Certified* Medicaid.
Owner Nonprofit organization/foundation.
Admissions Requirements Minimum age 18; Medical examination; Physician's request.
Staff Physicians 1 (pt); RNs 3 (ft), 2 (pt); LPNs 1 (pt); Nurses' aides 20 (ft), 3 (pt); Occupational therapists 1 (pt); Speech therapists 1 (pt); Activities coordinators 2 (pt); Dietitians 1 (pt); Podiatrists 1 (pt).
Affiliation Presbyterian.
Facilities Dining room; Physical therapy room; Activities room; Laundry room.
Activities Arts & crafts; Cards; Games; Reading groups; Prayer groups; Movies; Shopping trips; Dances/Social/Cultural gatherings.

Oakwood Villa Care Center
2301 N Severance, Hutchinson, KS 67502
(316) 662-0597
Admin Sunny Z Brooks.
Medical Dir Dr Savage.
Licensure Intermediate care. *Beds* ICF 100. *Certified* Medicaid.
Owner Proprietary corp (Pinnacle Care Corp).
Admissions Requirements Minimum age 18; Medical examination.
Staff RNs 4 (ft); LPNs 8 (ft); Nurses' aides 30 (ft); Reality therapists 1 (ft); Recreational therapists 1 (ft); Activities coordinators 1 (ft); Dietitians 1 (ft).
Facilities Dining room; Physical therapy room; Activities room; Chapel; Crafts room; Laundry room; Barber/Beauty shop.
Activities Arts & crafts; Cards; Games; Reading groups; Prayer groups; Movies; Shopping trips; Dances/Social/Cultural gatherings; Fishing; Barbeques; Shuffleboard; Horseshoes.

Rebekah—Odd Fellow Care Home
PO Box 175, Rte 1, Hutchinson, KS 67501
(316) 663-3839
Admin Wanda I Carter. *Dir of Nursing*
Regena McFarland. *Medical Dir* David
Hanson MD.
Licensure Intermediate care; Retirement. *Beds*
59. *Certified* Medicaid.
Owner Nonprofit organization/foundation.
Admissions Requirements Minimum age 18.
Staff RNs 3 (ft); LPNs 2 (ft), 1 (pt); Physical
therapists 1 (ft); Reality therapists 1 (ft);
Occupational therapists 1 (ft); Speech
therapists 1 (ft); Activities coordinators 1
(ft); Dietitians 1 (ft); Dentists 1 (ft).
Affiliation Independent Order of Odd Fellows
& Rebekahs.
Facilities Dining room; Physical therapy
room; Activities room; Laundry room;
Barber/Beauty shop.
Activities Arts & crafts; Cards; Games;
Reading groups; Prayer groups; Movies;
Shopping trips; Dances/Social/Cultural
gatherings; Field trips; Dining out.

Silver Oak Health Center
2813 S Broadacres Rd, Hutchinson, KS 67501
(316) 663-2829
Admin Wanda Carter.
Licensure Intermediate care. *Beds* ICF 59.
Certified Medicaid.
Owner Proprietary corp.

Wesley Towers Inc
700 Monterey Pl, Hutchinson, KS 67502
(316) 663-9175
Admin Louise Edge. *Dir of Nursing* Lorraine
Lanzrath RN.
Licensure Intermediate care; Retirement. *Beds*
ICF 130.
Owner Nonprofit corp.
Admissions Requirements Medical
examination.
Staff RNs 6 (ft), 5 (pt); Nurses' aides 22 (ft), 3
(pt); Activities coordinators 1 (ft); Dietitians
1 (ft).
Affiliation Methodist.
Facilities Dining room; Physical therapy
room; Activities room; Chapel; Crafts room;
Laundry room; Barber/Beauty shop; Library;
Mens woodwork shop; Weaving room;
Therapy/exercise pool; Home health services;
Dental office; Gardening; Meals on wheels.
Activities Arts & crafts; Cards; Games;
Reading groups; Prayer groups; Movies;
Shopping trips; Dances/Social/Cultural
gatherings; Swimming & fishing outings;
Golf; Exercise classes; Weaving; Quilting.

Independence

Colonial Lodge Nursing Home
1000 W Mulberry, Independence, KS 67301
(316) 331-8420, 331-0223 FAX
Admin Cynthia Neises. *Dir of Nursing* Jodi
Foster RN. *Medical Dir* Charles Empson
MD.
Licensure Skilled care. *Beds* SNF 6; ICF 49.
Private Pay Patients 4%. *Certified* Medicaid;
Medicare.
Owner Proprietary corp (Hillhaven Corp).
Admissions Requirements Physician's request.
Staff RNs 4 (ft); LPNs 2 (ft), 4 (pt); Nurses'
aides 17 (ft), 4 (pt); Activities coordinators 1
(ft); Dietitians 1 (ft).
Facilities Dining room; Physical therapy
room; Activities room; Chapel; Crafts room;
Laundry room; Barber/Beauty shop.
Activities Arts & crafts; Cards; Games;
Reading groups; Prayer groups; Movies;
Dances/Social/Cultural gatherings;
Intergenerational programs; Pet therapy.

Colonial Terrace
PO Box 467, Independence, KS 67301
(316) 331-8432
Admin Kelli Hagan.

Licensure Intermediate care. *Beds* ICF 50.
Certified Medicaid.
Owner Proprietary corp (Hillhaven Corp).

Glenwood Estate
621 S 2nd, Independence, KS 67301
(316) 331-2260
Admin Marilyn D Botts.
Licensure Intermediate care. *Beds* ICF 43.
Certified Medicaid.
Owner Privately owned.
Admissions Requirements Minimum age 16;
Medical examination; Physician's request.
Staff RNs; LPNs; Nurses' aides; Physical
therapists; Recreational therapists;
Occupational therapists; Speech therapists;
Activities coordinators; Dietitians;
Ophthalmologists; Podiatrists; Audiologists;
Dentists.
Facilities Dining room; Physical therapy
room; Crafts room; Laundry room; Barber/
Beauty shop.
Activities Arts & crafts; Cards; Games;
Reading groups; Prayer groups; Movies;
Dances/Social/Cultural gatherings.

Manor Nursing Home
614 S 8th, Independence, KS 67301
(316) 331-0511
Admin James N Riddles.
Licensure Intermediate care. *Beds* ICF 60.
Certified Medicaid.
Owner Privately owned.
Affiliation Lutheran.

Inman

Pleasant View Home
108 N Walnut, Inman, KS 67546
(316) 585-6411
Admin Donald G Ratzloff. *Dir of Nursing*
Dolores Hedrich.
Licensure Intermediate care; Personal care.
Beds ICF 67; Personal care 20. *Certified*
Medicaid.
Owner Nonprofit corp.
Admissions Requirements Medical
examination.
Languages German.
Facilities Dining room; Physical therapy
room; Activities room; Chapel; Crafts room;
Laundry room; Barber/Beauty shop; Library.
Activities Arts & crafts; Cards; Games;
Reading groups; Prayer groups; Movies;
Dances/Social/Cultural gatherings.

Iola

Arkhaven at Iola
1336 N Walnut, Iola, KS 66749
(316) 365-6989
Admin Luella Weems.
Licensure Intermediate care. *Beds* ICF 106.
Certified Medicaid.
Owner Proprietary corp.

Countryside Estates
600 E Garfield, Iola, KS 66749
(316) 365-3183
Admin Roberta Childers.
Licensure Intermediate care. *Beds* ICF 90.
Certified Medicaid.
Owner Proprietary corp (Beverly Enterprises).

Tara Gardens Personal Care Home
1110 E Carpenter, Iola, KS 66749
(319) 365-3107
Admin Steart Lallman. *Dir of Nursing*
Rosemary Davis LPN.
Licensure Intermediate care. *Beds* 45.
Certified Medicaid.
Admissions Requirements Minimum age 16.
Staff RNs 1 (pt); LPNs 2 (ft); Nurses' aides 10
(ft); Physical therapists 1 (pt); Reality
therapists 1 (pt); Recreational therapists 1
(pt); Occupational therapists 1 (pt); Speech

therapists 1 (pt); Activities coordinators 1
(pt); Dietitians 1 (pt); Podiatrists 1 (pt);
Audiologists 1 (pt).
Facilities Dining room; Physical therapy
room; Activities room; Chapel; Crafts room;
Laundry room; Barber/Beauty shop.
Activities Arts & crafts; Cards; Games;
Reading groups; Prayer groups; Movies;
Shopping trips.

Jamestown

Cheyenne Lodge Nursing Home
716 Cedar, Jamestown, KS 66948
(913) 439-6211
Admin Ella Thurston RN. *Dir of Nursing*
Evelyn Gray RN. *Medical Dir* C J Harwood
MD.
Licensure Intermediate care. *Beds* ICF 54.
Private Pay Patients 50%. *Certified*
Medicaid.
Owner Proprietary corp.
Admissions Requirements Minimum age 16;
Medical examination.
Staff RNs 1 (ft); LPNs 2 (ft), 1 (pt); Nurses'
aides 11 (ft), 2 (pt); Activities coordinators 1
(ft).
Facilities Dining room; Physical therapy
room; Activities room; Chapel; Crafts room;
Laundry room; Barber/Beauty shop.
Activities Arts & crafts; Cards; Games;
Reading groups; Prayer groups; Movies;
Shopping trips; Dances/Social/Cultural
gatherings; Intergenerational programs; Pet
therapy; Bingo.

Junction City

Good Samaritan Center
416 W Spruce, Junction City, KS 66441
(913) 238-1187
Admin Joyce Ploussard. *Dir of Nursing*
Deanna Byers RN.
Licensure Intermediate care; Alzheimer's care.
Beds ICF 60. *Certified* Medicaid.
Owner Nonprofit corp (Evangelical Lutheran/
Good Samaritan Society).
Admissions Requirements Medical
examination; Physician's request.
Staff RNs 1 (ft); LPNs 2 (ft), 4 (pt); Nurses'
aides 9 (ft), 9 (pt); Horticulture therapists 1
(ft), 1 (pt); Social worker 1 (ft).
Affiliation Lutheran.
Facilities Dining room; Physical therapy
room; Activities room; Chapel; Laundry
room; Barber/Beauty shop; Library.
Activities Arts & crafts; Cards; Games;
Reading groups; Prayer groups; Movies;
Shopping trips; Dances/Social/Cultural
gatherings; Pet therapy.

Valley View Professional Care Center
1417 W Ash, Junction City, KS 66441
(913) 762-2162
Admin Richard S Jung. *Dir of Nursing* Norma
J Bush RN.
Licensure Skilled care; Retirement. *Beds* SNF
129. *Certified* Medicaid; Medicare.
Owner Proprietary corp.
Admissions Requirements Minimum age 18;
Medical examination; Physician's request.
Staff Physicians 1 (pt); RNs 6 (ft); LPNs 11
(ft); Nurses' aides 46 (ft), 1 (pt); Physical
therapists 1 (ft), 1 (pt); Speech therapists 1
(pt); Activities coordinators 1 (ft); Dietitians
1 (pt).
Languages Spanish, German, Korean.
Facilities Dining room; Physical therapy
room; Activities room; Chapel; Crafts room;
Laundry room; Barber/Beauty shop; Library.
Activities Arts & crafts; Cards; Games;
Reading groups; Prayer groups; Movies;
Shopping trips; Dances/Social/Cultural
gatherings.

Valley Vista Care Center
1115 W 14th St, Junction City, KS 66441
(913) 238-2128
Admin Charles V Cobb. *Dir of Nursing* Joleen
  Curran RN. *Medical Dir* Alex Scott MD.
Licensure Intermediate care. *Beds* ICF 52.
  Certified Medicaid.
Owner Proprietary corp.
Admissions Requirements Minimum age 18;
  Medical examination; Physician's request.
Staff RNs 1 (ft); LPNs 6 (ft); Nurses' aides 11
  (ft), 3 (pt); Activities coordinators 3 (ft).
Facilities Dining room; Physical therapy
  room; Activities room; Chapel; Crafts room;
  Laundry room; Barber/Beauty shop.
Activities Arts & crafts; Cards; Games;
  Reading groups; Prayer groups; Movies;
  Shopping trips; Dances/Social/Cultural
  gatherings.

Kansas City

Bryant-Butler-Kitchen Nursing Home
PO Box 171828, Kansas City, KS 66117
(913) 321-7725
Admin John Oliva.
Licensure Intermediate care. *Beds* 100.
  Certified Medicaid.
Owner Nonprofit corp.

Kansas City Presbyterian Manor
7850 Freeman, Kansas City, KS 66112
(913) 334-3666
Admin Marcia L Schuler. *Dir of Nursing*
  Vinetta S Belden. *Medical Dir* John A
  Mallory MD.
Licensure Skilled care; Intermediate care;
  Personal care; Alzheimer's care. *Beds* SNF
  21; ICF 123; Personal care 36. *Private Pay
  Patients* 85%. *Certified* Medicaid.
Owner Nonprofit corp (Presbyterian Manors
  of Mid-America Inc).
Admissions Requirements Minimum age 65;
  Medical examination.
Staff RNs 8 (ft), 2 (pt); LPNs 8 (ft); Nurses'
  aides 36 (ft), 3 (pt); Physical therapists 1
  (pt); Occupational therapists 1 (pt); Speech
  therapists 1 (pt); Activities coordinators 1
  (ft), 1 (pt).
Affiliation Presbyterian.
Facilities Dining room; Physical therapy
  room; Activities room; Chapel; Crafts room;
  Laundry room; Barber/Beauty shop; Library;
  8 Lounges; Alzheimer's unit with courtyard.
Activities Arts & crafts; Cards; Games;
  Reading groups; Prayer groups; Movies;
  Shopping trips; Pet therapy.

Manor of Kansas City
3231 N 61st, Kansas City, KS 66104
(913) 299-1770
Admin Debra Biehl. *Dir of Nursing* Jeannette
  McClean RN. *Medical Dir* Robert Potter
  MD.
Licensure Intermediate care; Alzheimer's care.
  Beds ICF 80. *Private Pay Patients* 65%.
  Certified Medicaid.
Owner Proprietary corp (National Heritage).
Staff LPNs 5 (ft), 2 (pt); Nurses' aides 14 (ft),
  3 (pt); Activities coordinators 1 (ft).
Facilities Dining room; Physical therapy
  room; Activities room; Crafts room; Laundry
  room; Barber/Beauty shop; Whirlpool;
  Wanderguard system.
Activities Arts & crafts; Cards; Games;
  Reading groups; Prayer groups; Movies;
  Shopping trips; Dances/Social/Cultural
  gatherings; Pet therapy.

Medicalodge East of Kansas City
6261 Leavenworth Rd, Kansas City, KS 66104
(913) 299-9722
Admin Richard A Shillcutt.
Licensure Intermediate care. *Beds* ICF 75.
  Certified Medicaid.
Owner Proprietary corp (Medicalodges Inc).

Medicalodge North of Kansas City
6500 Greeley, Kansas City, KS 66104
(913) 334-0200
Admin Cindy Frakes. *Dir of Nursing* Inez
  Woods RN. *Medical Dir* Robert Potter MD.
Licensure Skilled care; Intermediate care;
  Adult day care. *Beds* SNF 50; ICF 50.
  Private Pay Patients 15%. *Certified*
  Medicaid; Medicare.
Owner Proprietary corp (Medicalodges Inc).
Admissions Requirements Minimum age 18;
  Medical examination; Physician's request.
Staff Physicians 2 (pt); RNs 2 (ft), 2 (pt);
  LPNs 8 (ft), 2 (pt); Nurses' aides 40 (ft), 15
  (pt); Activities coordinators 2 (ft).
Languages German, Spanish.
Facilities Dining room; Physical therapy
  room; Activities room; Crafts room; Laundry
  room; Barber/Beauty shop.
Activities Arts & crafts; Cards; Games;
  Reading groups; Prayer groups; Movies;
  Shopping trips; Dances/Social/Cultural
  gatherings; Intergenerational programs; Pet
  therapy.

Medicalodge South of Kansas City
6501 Greeley, Kansas City, KS 66104
(913) 334-5252
Admin Lloyd Grimmett.
Licensure Intermediate care. *Beds* ICF 106.
  Certified Medicaid.
Owner Proprietary corp (Medicalodges Inc).
Admissions Requirements Medical
  examination; Physician's request.
Staff Physicians 2 (pt); RNs 1 (ft), 1 (pt);
  LPNs 5 (ft); Nurses' aides 22 (ft), 1 (pt);
  Physical therapists 1 (pt); Reality therapists
  1 (pt); Recreational therapists 1 (pt);
  Occupational therapists 1 (pt); Speech
  therapists 1 (pt); Activities coordinators 1
  (ft), 1 (pt); Dietitians 1 (pt); Podiatrists 1
  (pt); Audiologists 1 (pt); Dentists 1 (pt).
Facilities Dining room; Physical therapy
  room; Activities room; Chapel; Crafts room;
  Laundry room; Barber/Beauty shop; Library.
Activities Arts & crafts; Cards; Games;
  Reading groups; Prayer groups; Movies;
  Shopping trips.

Providence Place Inc
8909 Parallel Pkwy, Kansas City, KS 66112
(913) 299-3030
Admin J Tim Allin. *Dir of Nursing* Diana
  Johnson RN BSN. *Medical Dir* Miguel Parra
  MD.
Licensure Skilled care; Intermediate care;
  Alzheimer's care. *Beds* SNF 30; ICF 60.
  Private Pay Patients 85%. *Certified*
  Medicare.
Owner Proprietary corp (Health Care
  Facilities Inc).
Admissions Requirements Minimum age 16;
  Medical examination; Physician's request.
Staff Physicians; RNs 4 (ft), 1 (pt); LPNs 6
  (ft), 1 (pt); Nurses' aides 25 (ft), 9 (pt);
  Physical therapists 1 (pt); Recreational
  therapists 1 (pt); Occupational therapists 1
  (pt); Speech therapists 1 (pt); Activities
  coordinators 1 (ft); Dietitians 1 (pt);
  Podiatrists 1 (pt); Audiologists 1 (pt).
Languages Spanish, Polish, Croatian.
Affiliation Roman Catholic.
Facilities Dining room; Physical therapy
  room; Activities room; Chapel; Crafts room;
  Laundry room; Barber/Beauty shop.
Activities Arts & crafts; Cards; Games;
  Reading groups; Prayer groups; Movies;
  Shopping trips; Dances/Social/Cultural
  gatherings; Intergenerational programs; Pet
  therapy; Music therapy.

St Joseph Care Center
759 Vermont Ave, Kansas City, KS 66101
(913) 621-6800, 621-4803 FAX
Admin Jerry Ney. *Dir of Nursing* Mary P
  Harris. *Medical Dir* William Taylor MD.

Licensure Skilled care; Intermediate care;
  Independent living; Alzheimer's care. *Beds*
  SNF 65; ICF 136; Independent living 31.
  Private Pay Patients 17%. *Certified*
  Medicaid; Medicare.
Owner Nonprofit corp (Catholic Housing
  Services Inc).
Admissions Requirements Minimum age 16;
  Medical examination; Physician's request.
Staff Physicians 8 (pt); RNs 3 (ft), 3 (pt);
  LPNs 23 (ft), 5 (pt); Nurses' aides 81 (ft), 3
  (pt); Physical therapists 2 (pt); Occupational
  therapists 2 (pt); Speech therapists 2 (pt);
  Activities coordinators 1 (ft); Dietitians 1
  (ft); Podiatrists 1 (pt); Recreational aids 2
  (ft), 1 (pt); Rehabilitation Assistants.
Languages Croatian, Spanish, Polish.
Affiliation Roman Catholic.
Facilities Dining room; Physical therapy
  room; Activities room; Chapel; Crafts room;
  Laundry room; Barber/Beauty shop; Library;
  Gift shop; Thrift shop.
Activities Arts & crafts; Cards; Games;
  Reading groups; Movies; Shopping trips;
  Dances/Social/Cultural gatherings;
  Intergenerational programs; Pet therapy;
  Ceramics; Exercise; Pastoral services;
  Rehabilitation program.

Kensington

Prairie Haven Nursing Home
PO Box 248, N Hwy 36, Kensington, KS
  66951
(913) 476-2623
Admin Merlyn L Watts.
Licensure Intermediate care. *Beds* ICF 58.
  Certified Medicaid.
Owner Proprietary corp (Beverly Enterprises).
Admissions Requirements Medical
  examination; Physician's request.
Staff RNs 2 (ft), 1 (pt); Nurses' aides 15 (ft), 1
  (pt); Activities coordinators 1 (ft).
Facilities Dining room; Physical therapy
  room; Activities room; Laundry room;
  Barber/Beauty shop.
Activities Arts & crafts; Cards; Games;
  Reading groups; Prayer groups; Shopping
  trips; Dances/Social/Cultural gatherings.

Kingman

Lifecare of Kingman
310 W Copeland, Kingman, KS 67068
(316) 532-2223
Admin Judith M Williams. *Dir of Nursing*
  Doris Simons.
Licensure Intermediate care. *Beds* ICF 87.
  Certified Medicaid.
Owner Proprietary corp (Lifecare Centers of
  Kansas Inc).
Admissions Requirements Medical
  examination.
Facilities Dining room; Physical therapy
  room; Activities room; Laundry room;
  Barber/Beauty shop.
Activities Arts & crafts; Cards; Games;
  Reading groups; Prayer groups; Movies;
  Shopping trips; Dances/Social/Cultural
  gatherings.

Wheatlands Health Care Center
750 W Washington, Kingman, KS 67068
(316) 532-5801
Admin Jerry L Korbe.
Licensure Skilled care. *Beds* SNF 60.
Owner Nonprofit corp.

Kinsley

Medicalodge of Kinsley
Box 65-A, W 6th & Winchester, Kinsley, KS
  67547
(316) 659-2156
Admin Carolyn Walker. *Dir of Nursing* Beth
  Blackwell.

Licensure Intermediate care. *Beds* ICF 94. *Certified* Medicaid.
Owner Proprietary corp (Medicalodges Inc).
Admissions Requirements Minimum age 45; Medical examination; Physician's request.
Staff RNs 3 (ft); LPNs 4 (ft); Nurses' aides 22 (ft), 1 (pt); Activities coordinators 2 (ft).
Facilities Dining room; Physical therapy room; Activities room; Chapel; Laundry room; Barber/Beauty shop; Kitchen.
Activities Arts & crafts; Games; Prayer groups; Shopping trips; Dances/Social/Cultural gatherings; Discussion groups; Hygiene groups.

Kiowa

Lifecare of Kiowa
1020 Main, Kiowa, KS 67070
(316) 825-4732
Admin Vivian Diel. *Dir of Nursing* Pat Hockett.
Licensure Intermediate care. *Beds* ICF 45. *Certified* Medicaid.
Owner Proprietary corp (Lifecare Centers of Kansas Inc).
Admissions Requirements Medical examination; Physician's request.
Staff RNs 1 (pt); LPNs 2 (ft), 1 (pt); Nurses' aides 12 (ft), 2 (pt); Activities coordinators 1 (ft).
Facilities Dining room; Physical therapy room; Activities room; Chapel; Laundry room; Barber/Beauty shop; Exam room.
Activities Arts & crafts; Cards; Games; Reading groups; Prayer groups; Movies; Shopping trips; Dances/Social/Cultural gatherings; School & community activities.

LaCrosse

Rush County Nursing Home
701 W 6th St, LaCrosse, KS 67548
(913) 222-2574
Admin Joanna Wilson RN BSN. *Dir of Nursing* Diana Torres LPN, HSS.
Licensure Intermediate care. *Beds* ICF 60. *Private Pay Patients* 70%. *Certified* Medicaid.
Owner Nonprofit organization/foundation.
Admissions Requirements Medical examination.
Staff RNs 1 (ft), 1 (pt); Nurses' aides 13 (ft), 5 (pt); Activities coordinators 1 (ft).
Affiliation Lutheran.
Facilities Dining room; Physical therapy room; Activities room; Chapel; Crafts room; Laundry room; Barber/Beauty shop; Library; Quiet room.
Activities Arts & crafts; Cards; Games; Reading groups; Prayer groups; Movies; Shopping trips; Dances/Social/Cultural gatherings; Intergenerational programs; Pet therapy; Reality orientation.

LaCygne

Swan Manor Inc
215 N Broadway, LaCygne, KS 66040
(913) 757-4414
Admin Daniel F Widner.
Medical Dir Robert Banks MD.
Licensure Intermediate care. *Beds* ICF 36. *Certified* Medicaid.
Owner Nonprofit corp.
Staff Physicians 1 (pt); RNs 1 (pt); LPNs 1 (ft), 1 (pt); Physical therapists 1 (pt); Reality therapists 1 (pt); Recreational therapists 1 (pt); Occupational therapists 1 (pt); Speech therapists 1 (pt); Activities coordinators 1 (pt); Dietitians 1 (pt); Podiatrists 1 (pt); Audiologists 1 (pt); Dentists 1 (pt).
Facilities Dining room; Physical therapy room; Activities room; Crafts room; Laundry room; Barber/Beauty shop.

Activities Arts & crafts; Cards; Games; Reading groups; Prayer groups; Movies.

Lakin

High Plains Retirement Village
607 Court Pl, Lakin, KS 67860
(316) 355-7836
Admin Steven S Reimer.
Licensure Intermediate care. *Beds* ICF 40. *Certified* Medicaid.
Owner Publicly owned.

Lansing

Colonial Manor Nursing & Care Center
PO Box 250, Holiday Plaza, Lansing, KS 66043
(913) 727-1284
Admin Diana Corpstein. *Dir of Nursing* LaRinda McConnaughey LPN.
Licensure Intermediate care. *Beds* ICF 60. *Certified* Medicaid.
Owner Proprietary corp (Beverly Enterprises).
Admissions Requirements Minimum age 16; Medical examination; Physician's request.
Staff LPNs 5 (ft); Nurses' aides 20 (ft), 5 (pt); Physical therapists; Activities coordinators 1 (ft).
Facilities Dining room; Physical therapy room; Activities room; Chapel; Crafts room; Laundry room; Barber/Beauty shop; Library; Private conference room.
Activities Cards; Games; Reading groups; Prayer groups; Movies; Shopping trips; Dances/Social/Cultural gatherings; Bingo.

Larned

Hammond Holiday Home
1114 W 11th St, Larned, KS 67550
(316) 285-6914
Admin Charles E Hatfield. *Dir of Nursing* Sherri Burger. *Medical Dir* Dr V R Cade.
Licensure Intermediate care; Retirement; Alzheimer's care. *Beds* ICF 100. *Certified* Medicaid.
Owner Proprietary corp (Hillhaven Corp).
Admissions Requirements Minimum age 16; Medical examination; Physician's request.
Staff Physicians 1 (ft); RNs 8 (ft); LPNs 1 (ft); Nurses' aides 40 (ft); Physical therapists 1 (pt); Occupational therapists 1 (pt); Speech therapists 1 (pt); Activities coordinators 1 (ft); Dietitians 1 (ft); Podiatrists 1 (pt).
Facilities Dining room; Physical therapy room; Activities room; Chapel; Crafts room; Laundry room; Barber/Beauty shop.
Activities Arts & crafts; Cards; Games; Reading groups; Prayer groups; Movies; Dances/Social/Cultural gatherings.

Lawrence

Brandon Woods
1501 Inverness Dr, Lawrence, KS 66046
(913) 843-4571
Admin Jim Maddox.
Medical Dir Joan Brunfield.
Licensure Skilled care; Assisted living; Retirement. *Beds* SNF 60; Assisted living 20; Retirement apartments 100. *Private Pay Patients* 80%. *Certified* Medicaid.
Owner Proprietary corp (Retirement Management Company Inc).
Staff RNs 5 (ft); LPNs 15 (ft); Nurses' aides 20 (ft); Physical therapists (consultant); Occupational therapists 1 (pt); Speech therapists 1 (pt); Activities coordinators 2 (ft), 1 (pt); Dietitians (consultant); Ophthalmologists 1 (pt); Podiatrists 1 (pt); Audiologists 1 (pt).
Facilities Dining room; Physical therapy room; Activities room; Chapel; Crafts room; Laundry room; Barber/Beauty shop.

Activities Arts & crafts; Cards; Games; Reading groups; Prayer groups; Movies; Shopping trips; Dances/Social/Cultural gatherings; Intergenerational programs; Pet therapy.

Cedar Wood Living Center
205 N Michigan, Lawrence, KS 66044
(913) 843-8934
Admin Sharon O'Banion. *Dir of Nursing* Kathy King HSS. *Medical Dir* Carl Inzerillo MD.
Licensure Intermediate care. *Beds* ICF 50. *Certified* Medicaid.
Owner Nonprofit corp (Adventist Living Centers Inc).
Admissions Requirements Minimum age 14; Medical examination.
Staff RNs; LPNs; Nurses' aides; Physical therapists; Activities coordinators; Dietitians; Podiatrists.
Facilities Dining room; Physical therapy room; Laundry room; Barber/Beauty shop.
Activities Arts & crafts; Cards; Games; Reading groups; Prayer groups; Movies; Dances/Social/Cultural gatherings; Intergenerational programs; Pet therapy.

Colonial Manor
3015 W 31st, Lawrence, KS 66044
(913) 842-7282
Admin K J Langlais. *Dir of Nursing* Louise Yarbro RN. *Medical Dir* Dr John Gravino.
Licensure Skilled care. *Beds* SNF 96. *Private Pay Patients* 20%. *Certified* Medicaid; Medicare.
Owner Proprietary corp (Beverly Enterprises).
Admissions Requirements Medical examination; Physician's request.
Staff RNs 5 (ft), 1 (pt); LPNs 9 (ft), 1 (pt); Nurses' aides 40 (ft); Physical therapists 1 (ft); Recreational therapists 1 (ft); Occupational therapists 1 (ft); Speech therapists 1 (ft); Activities coordinators 1 (ft); Dietitians 1 (ft); Podiatrists (contracted); Audiologists (contracted).
Facilities Dining room; Physical therapy room; Activities room; Crafts room; Laundry room; Barber/Beauty shop; Library.
Activities Arts & crafts; Cards; Games; Reading groups; Prayer groups; Movies; Shopping trips; Dances/Social/Cultural gatherings; Intergenerational programs; Pet therapy.

Heritage Manor of Lawrence
1800 W 27th St, Lawrence, KS 66044
(913) 842-3162
Admin Ruth Faulk.
Licensure Intermediate care. *Beds* ICF 99. *Certified* Medicaid.
Owner Proprietary corp (National Heritage).

Lawrence Presbyterian Manor
1429 Kasold, Lawrence, KS 66044
(913) 841-4262
Admin Phillip M Levi Jr.
Licensure Skilled care. *Beds* SNF 60. *Certified* Medicaid.
Owner Privately owned.
Admissions Requirements Minimum age 65; Medical examination.
Staff RNs 2 (ft), 1 (pt); Nurses' aides 24 (pt); Physical therapists 2 (pt); Occupational therapists 2 (pt); Speech therapists 2 (pt); Activities coordinators 1 (ft); Dietitians 1 (ft); Ophthalmologists 1 (pt); Dentists 1 (pt).
Affiliation Presbyterian.
Facilities Dining room; Physical therapy room; Activities room; Chapel; Crafts room; Laundry room; Barber/Beauty shop; Library; Covered parking.

Valley View Care Home
2518 Ridge Ct, Lawrence, KS 66044
(913) 842-2610
Admin Doris Faye McAfee. *Dir of Nursing* Judity Harkins RN.

Licensure Intermediate care. *Beds* ICF 61.
Certified Medicaid.
Owner Publicly owned.
Staff RNs 1 (ft); LPNs 8 (ft); Nurses' aides 24 (ft); Activities coordinators 1 (ft).
Facilities Dining room; Physical therapy room; Activities room; Crafts room; Laundry room; Barber/Beauty shop.
Activities Arts & crafts; Cards; Games; Reading groups.

Leavenworth

Leavenworth County Convalescent Infirmary
Broadway & Rees, Leavenworth, KS 66048
(913) 682-4501
Admin Thomas V McEvoy. *Dir of Nursing* Elizabeth J Brown RN.
Licensure Skilled care; Intermediate care. *Beds* SNF 47; ICF 34. *Certified* Medicaid.
Owner Publicly owned.
Admissions Requirements Minimum age 18; Medical examination; Physician's request.
Staff Physicians 1 (pt); RNs 4 (ft), 1 (pt); LPNs 4 (ft), 2 (pt); Nurses' aides 26 (ft), 4 (pt); Physical therapists 1 (pt); Recreational therapists 1 (ft); Occupational therapists 1 (pt); Speech therapists 1 (pt); Dietitians 1 (pt).
Facilities Dining room; Physical therapy room; Activities room; Laundry room; Barber/Beauty shop.
Activities Arts & crafts; Cards; Games; Reading groups; Prayer groups; Shopping trips; Dances/Social/Cultural gatherings.

Medicalodge of Leavenworth
1503 Ohio, Leavenworth, KS 66048
(913) 682-1844
Admin Kathleen Lantz. *Dir of Nursing* Nancy Watkins RN.
Licensure Skilled care; Intermediate care. *Beds* SNF 36; ICF 84. *Certified* Medicaid; Medicare.
Owner Proprietary corp (Medicalodges Inc).
Admissions Requirements Medical examination; Physician's request.
Staff Physicians 1 (ft); RNs 4 (ft), 2 (pt); LPNs 4 (ft), 5 (pt); Nurses' aides 43 (ft), 2 (pt); Physical therapists; Reality therapists; Recreational therapists; Occupational therapists; Speech therapists; Activities coordinators 1 (ft); Dietitians; Ophthalmologists 1 (pt).
Facilities Dining room; Physical therapy room; Activities room; Chapel; Crafts room; Laundry room; Barber/Beauty shop; Library.
Activities Arts & crafts; Cards; Games; Prayer groups; Movies; Shopping trips; Dances/Social/Cultural gatherings; Baseball games; Picnics.

Lenexa

Delmar Gardens of Lenexa
9701 Monrovia, Lenexa, KS 66215
(913) 492-1130
Admin Sandra McGinnis. *Dir of Nursing* Kathleen Stone RN. *Medical Dir* Thomas Williams MD.
Licensure Skilled care; Intermediate care; Alzheimer's care; Retirement. *Beds* SNF 190; ICF 60. *Certified* Medicaid; Medicare.
Owner Proprietary corp (Delmar Gardens Enterprises).
Admissions Requirements Medical examination; Physician's request.
Staff Physicians 4 (ft); RNs 10 (ft), 7 (pt); LPNs 8 (ft), 1 (pt); Nurses' aides 64 (ft), 11 (pt); Physical therapists 1 (ft); Recreational therapists 2 (ft), 1 (pt); Occupational therapists 1 (pt); Speech therapists 1 (pt); Dietitians 1 (ft); Podiatrists 1 (pt); Audiologists 1 (pt).
Facilities Dining room; Physical therapy room; Activities room; Chapel; Crafts room; Laundry room; Barber/Beauty shop; Library.

Activities Arts & crafts; Cards; Games; Reading groups; Games; Movies; Shopping trips; Dances/Social/Cultural gatherings; Intergenerational programs; Pet therapy.

Lakeview Village Inc
9100 Park, Lenexa, KS 66215
(913) 888-1900
Admin Lowell E Strahan.
Licensure Intermediate care. *Beds* ICF 21.
Owner Nonprofit corp.
Admissions Requirements Minimum age 62; Medical examination.
Staff RNs 2 (ft), 1 (pt); LPNs 1 (ft), 3 (pt); Nurses' aides 12 (ft); Recreational therapists 1 (ft); Activities coordinators 1 (ft); Dietitians 1 (pt); Podiatrists 1 (pt); Dentists 1 (pt).
Facilities Dining room; Physical therapy room; Activities room; Chapel; Crafts room; Laundry room; Barber/Beauty shop; Library.
Activities Arts & crafts; Cards; Games; Reading groups; Prayer groups; Movies; Shopping trips; Dances/Social/Cultural gatherings.

Leonardville

Leonardville Nursing Home
PO Box 148, Hwy 24, Leonardville, KS 66449
(913) 293-5246
Admin Sandra S Hageman.
Licensure Intermediate care. *Beds* ICF 60.
Certified Medicaid.
Owner Nonprofit corp.

Leoti

Golden Acres Nursing Home
Earl & 7th, Leoti, KS 67861
(316) 375-4600
Admin Jerry Korbe.
Licensure Intermediate care. *Beds* 30.
Certified Medicaid.
Owner Publicly owned.
Admissions Requirements Minimum age 65.
Staff RNs 1 (pt); LPNs 1 (ft), 1 (pt); Nurses' aides 13 (ft), 2 (pt); Physical therapists 1 (pt); Activities coordinators 1 (ft).
Facilities Dining room; Physical therapy room; Activities room; Chapel; Barber/Beauty shop.
Activities Arts & crafts; Games; Reading groups; Prayer groups; Movies.

Liberal

Liberal Good Samaritan Center
2160 Zinnia Ln, Liberal, KS 67901
(316) 624-3831
Admin Bonnie L Monnier. *Dir of Nursing* Diane Balzer. *Medical Dir* Dr Norvan Harris.
Licensure Intermediate care; Independent living apartments. *Beds* ICF 98; Independent living apts 2. *Private Pay Patients* 96%. *Certified* Medicaid.
Owner Nonprofit corp (Evangelical Lutheran/Good Samaritan Society).
Admissions Requirements Medical examination; Physician's request.
Languages Spanish.
Affiliation Lutheran.
Facilities Dining room; Physical therapy room; Activities room; Chapel; Crafts room; Laundry room; Barber/Beauty shop; Library.
Activities Arts & crafts; Cards; Games; Reading groups; Prayer groups; Movies; Shopping trips; Dances/Social/Cultural gatherings; Intergenerational programs.

Victorian Manor
Box 1006, 1501 S Holly, Liberal, KS 67901
(316) 624-0130
Admin Kevin Reimer.

Licensure Intermediate care. *Beds* ICF 44.
Owner Proprietary corp.

Lincoln

Mid-America Nursing Center of Lincoln
922 N 5th St, Lincoln, KS 67455
(913) 524-4428
Admin Joyce Watts.
Medical Dir Colleen Vance.
Licensure Intermediate care. *Beds* ICF 60.
Certified Medicaid.
Owner Proprietary corp.
Staff RNs 1 (ft), 1 (pt); LPNs 2 (ft), 1 (pt); Nurses' aides 10 (ft), 4 (pt); Activities coordinators 1 (ft), 3 (pt).
Facilities Dining room; Physical therapy room; Activities room; Chapel; Crafts room; Laundry room; Barber/Beauty shop; Library.
Activities Arts & crafts; Cards; Games; Reading groups; Prayer groups; Movies; Dances/Social/Cultural gatherings.

Lindsborg

Bethany Home Association
321 N Chestnut, Lindsborg, KS 67456
(913) 227-2721
Admin William P Carlson. *Dir of Nursing* Jane Nelson.
Licensure Intermediate care; Self care; Retirement. *Beds* ICF 130; Self care cottages 38. *Private Pay Patients* 78%. *Certified* Medicaid.
Owner Nonprofit organization/foundation.
Admissions Requirements Minimum age 65; Medical examination; Physician's request.
Staff RNs 6 (ft), 1 (pt); LPNs 4 (ft), 2 (pt); Nurses' aides 60 (ft), 20 (pt); Physical therapists 1 (pt); Activities coordinators 2 (ft); Dietitians 1 (pt).
Languages Swedish.
Affiliation Lutheran.
Facilities Dining room; Physical therapy room; Activities room; Chapel; Crafts room; Laundry room; Barber/Beauty shop; Library.
Activities Arts & crafts; Cards; Games; Reading groups; Prayer groups; Movies; Shopping trips; Intergenerational programs; Pet therapy.

White Cross Health Center
PO Box 389, Lindsborg, KS 67456
(913) 668-2251
Admin William Taylor.
Medical Dir Tammy Wiegert.
Licensure Intermediate care. *Beds* ICF 53.
Certified Medicaid.
Owner Proprietary corp.
Staff RNs; LPNs; Nurses' aides; Activities coordinators.
Facilities Dining room; Physical therapy room; Laundry room; Barber/Beauty shop.
Activities Arts & crafts; Cards; Reading groups; Movies; Shopping trips; Dances/Social/Cultural gatherings.

Linn

Linn Community Nursing Home Inc
314 W 3rd St, Linn, KS 66953
(913) 348-5551
Admin Sonia S DeRusseau.
Medical Dir Carol Rahe.
Licensure Intermediate care; Retirement. *Beds* ICF 77. *Certified* Medicaid.
Owner Nonprofit corp.
Admissions Requirements Minimum age 55.
Staff RNs 1 (pt); LPNs 4 (ft); Nurses' aides 37 (pt); Activities coordinators 2 (pt); Social service coordinator 2 (pt).
Languages German.
Affiliation Lutheran.
Facilities Dining room; Physical therapy room; Activities room; Crafts room; Laundry room; Barber/Beauty shop; Quiet room.

Activities Arts & crafts; Cards; Games; Prayer groups; Movies; Shopping trips; Dances/ Social/Cultural gatherings; Birthday parties; Bingo.

Little River

Sandstone Heights
Box 50A, 440 State St, Little River, KS 67457
(316) 897-6266
Admin Michael Rajewski.
Licensure Intermediate care. *Beds* ICF 55. *Certified* Medicaid.
Owner Publicly owned.
Admissions Requirements Medical examination.
Staff RNs 1 (pt); LPNs 5 (ft); Nurses' aides 15 (ft), 5 (pt); Activities coordinators 1 (ft).
Facilities Dining room; Physical therapy room; Activities room; Laundry room; Barber/Beauty shop.
Activities Arts & crafts; Cards; Games; Prayer groups; Movies; Shopping trips; Dances/ Social/Cultural gatherings.

Logan

Logan Manor Nursing Home
108 S Adams, Logan, KS 67646
(913) 689-4201
Admin Elizabeth Charlton.
Licensure Intermediate care. *Beds* ICF 50. *Certified* Medicaid.
Owner Publicly owned.

Louisburg

Southridge Manor Care Home
PO Box 339, 12th & Broadway, Louisburg, KS 66053
(913) 837-2916
Admin Richard G Summers.
Medical Dir Barborah Spies MD.
Licensure Intermediate care. *Beds* ICF 42. *Certified* Medicaid.
Owner Proprietary corp (Americare Systems Inc).
Admissions Requirements Physician's request.
Staff RNs 1 (ft); LPNs 2 (ft), 1 (pt); Nurses' aides 8 (ft), 5 (pt); Physical therapists 1 (pt); Occupational therapists 1 (pt); Speech therapists 1 (pt); Activities coordinators 1 (ft); Dietitians 1 (pt); Dentists 1 (pt).
Facilities Dining room; Physical therapy room; Activities room; Chapel; Laundry room; Barber/Beauty shop.
Activities Arts & crafts; Cards; Games; Reading groups; Prayer groups; Shopping trips; Dances/Social/Cultural gatherings.

Lucas

Lucas Nursing Center
PO Box 68, 414 N Main, Lucas, KS 67648
(913) 525-6215
Admin Celia Anschutz. *Dir of Nursing* Cynthia Bricker.
Licensure Intermediate care. *Beds* ICF 50. *Private Pay Patients* 40%. *Certified* Medicaid.
Owner Proprietary corp (Life Care Centers of Kansas).
Admissions Requirements Medical examination; Physician's request.
Staff RNs 2 (pt); LPNs 1 (ft); Nurses' aides 16 (ft), 4 (pt); Activities coordinators 1 (ft).
Facilities Dining room; Physical therapy room; Activities room; Laundry room; Barber/Beauty shop.
Activities Arts & crafts; Cards; Games; Prayer groups; Movies; Shopping trips; Dances/ Social/Cultural gatherings.

Lyndon

Hilltop Home
PO Box W, 131 W 14th St, Lyndon, KS 66451
(913) 828-3111
Admin Brad Fischer.
Licensure Intermediate care. *Beds* ICF 54. *Certified* Medicaid.
Owner Proprietary corp.

Lyons

Lyons Good Samaritan Center
1311 S Douglas, Lyons, KS 67554
(316) 257-5163
Admin Leora Carl Phillips.
Licensure Intermediate care. *Beds* ICF 85. *Certified* Medicaid.
Owner Proprietary corp (Evangelical Lutheran/Good Samaritan Society).
Admissions Requirements Medical examination; Physician's request.
Staff RNs 4 (ft), 1 (pt); LPNs 3 (ft), 4 (pt); Nurses' aides 23 (ft), 10 (pt); Activities coordinators 1 (ft), 1 (pt).
Languages Spanish.
Affiliation Lutheran.
Facilities Dining room; Physical therapy room; Activities room; Chapel; Crafts room; Laundry room; Barber/Beauty shop; Library; Dayrooms.
Activities Arts & crafts; Games; Reading groups; Prayer groups; Movies; Shopping trips; Dances/Social/Cultural gatherings; Outings; Picnics; Church services; Music therapy.

Macksville

Achenbach Learning Center
PO Box 128, Macksville, KS 67557
(316) 296-4421
Admin Bernard Turnbaugh.
Licensure Intermediate care for mentally retarded. *Beds* 51. *Certified* Medicaid.
Owner Proprietary corp (Beverly Enterprises).

Parkview Learning Center
117 N Spickard, Macksville, KS 67557
(316) 348-3665
Admin Anne Robinson.
Licensure Intermediate care for mentally retarded. *Beds* ICF/MR 54. *Certified* Medicaid.
Owner Proprietary corp (Beverly Enterprises).

Madison

Madison Manor
PO Box 277, Bluestem Dr, Madison, KS 66860
(316) 437-2470
Admin Mary L Cookson. *Dir of Nursing* Patti Young LPN.
Licensure Intermediate care. *Beds* ICF 55. *Certified* Medicaid.
Owner Nonprofit corp.
Admissions Requirements Physician's request.
Staff LPNs 6 (ft); Nurses' aides 11 (ft), 5 (pt); Activities coordinators 1 (ft); Certified rest aides 3 (ft); Medical records 1 (ft); Medication aides 3 (pt).
Facilities Dining room; Physical therapy room; Activities room; Chapel; Laundry room; Barber/Beauty shop.
Activities Arts & crafts; Cards; Games; Reading groups; Prayer groups; Movies; Shopping trips.

Manhattan

College Hill Skilled Nursing Center
2423 Kimball, Manhattan, KS 66502
(913) 539-7671

Admin Douglas W Frihart. *Dir of Nursing* Jan Bennett RN. *Medical Dir* Phil Hostetter MD & Palmer Meed MD.
Licensure Skilled care; Intermediate care. *Beds* SNF 56; ICF 50. *Certified* Medicaid; Medicare.
Owner Privately owned.
Admissions Requirements Medical examination; Physician's request.
Staff Physicians 2 (pt); RNs 3 (ft), 1 (pt); LPNs 8 (ft), 6 (pt); Nurses' aides 23 (ft), 5 (pt); Physical therapists 1 (pt); Occupational therapists 1 (pt); Speech therapists 1 (pt); Activities coordinators 1 (ft); Dietitians 1 (pt); CPTAs 1 (ft).
Facilities Dining room; Physical therapy room; Activities room; Crafts room; Laundry room; Barber/Beauty shop; Library; Quiet room; Piano; Flower garden; Courtyard.
Activities Arts & crafts; Cards; Games; Reading groups; Prayer groups; Movies; Dances/Social/Cultural gatherings; Bus rides; Cooking class; Field trips; Humane society visits; Happy hour.

Meadowlark Hills
2121 Meadowlark Rd, Manhattan, KS 66502
(913) 537-4610
Admin Roger Closson.
Medical Dir Dr P Meek & Dr W Durkee.
Licensure Skilled care. *Beds* SNF 60. *Certified* Medicaid; Medicare.
Owner Nonprofit corp.
Admissions Requirements Minimum age 65; Medical examination; Physician's request.
Staff RNs 1 (ft), 5 (pt); LPNs 2 (ft), 1 (pt); Nurses' aides 13 (ft), 6 (pt); Activities coordinators 2 (ft), 1 (pt).
Facilities Dining room; Physical therapy room; Activities room; Crafts room; Laundry room; Barber/Beauty shop; Library.
Activities Arts & crafts; Cards; Games; Reading groups; Prayer groups; Movies; Dances/Social/Cultural gatherings.

Wharton Manor
2101 Claflin Rd, Manhattan, KS 66502
(913) 776-0636
Admin Norman G Wallace. *Dir of Nursing* Betty Coles RN. *Medical Dir* Drs Mosiers.
Licensure Intermediate care; Alzheimer's care. *Beds* ICF 60. *Private Pay Patients* 48%. *Certified* Medicaid.
Owner Nonprofit organization/foundation.
Admissions Requirements Medical examination.
Staff RNs 1 (ft); LPNs 7 (ft); Nurses' aides 23 (ft); Physical therapists (consultant); Recreational therapists 1 (ft); Occupational therapists (consultant); Speech therapists (consultant); Activities coordinators 1 (ft); Dietitians (consultant); Audiologists (consultant).
Facilities Dining room; Physical therapy room; Activities room; Chapel; Crafts room; Laundry room; Barber/Beauty shop; Library; Large multi-purpose room with stage, lights, PA system; Alzheimer's patients walk areas; Arts and crafts room.
Activities Arts & crafts; Cards; Games; Reading groups; Prayer groups; Movies; Shopping trips; Dances/Social/Cultural gatherings; Intergenerational programs; Pet therapy; Field trips in Care-A-Van bus.

Marion

Marion Manor
1500 E Lawrence St, Marion, KS 66861
(316) 382-2191
Admin Kenneth Vinduska.
Licensure Intermediate care. *Beds* ICF 80. *Certified* Medicaid.
Owner Proprietary corp (Beverly Enterprises).
Staff RNs 1 (ft), 3 (pt); LPNs 1 (ft), 1 (pt); Nurses' aides 10 (ft), 10 (pt); Physical therapists 1 (pt); Reality therapists 1 (pt);

Recreational therapists 1 (pt); Occupational therapists 1 (pt); Speech therapists 1 (pt); Activities coordinators 1 (ft), 1 (pt); Dietitians 1 (pt).
Facilities Dining room; Physical therapy room; Activities room; Crafts room; Laundry room; Barber/Beauty shop.
Activities Arts & crafts; Cards; Games; Reading groups; Prayer groups; Movies; Shopping trips; Dances/Social/Cultural gatherings.

Marquette

Riverview Estates Inc
202 S Washington St, Marquette, KS 67464
(316) 546-2211
Admin Nancy Riggs.
Licensure Intermediate care. *Beds* ICF 52. *Certified* Medicaid.
Staff RNs 3 (pt); LPNs 1 (pt); Nurses' aides 10 (ft), 9 (pt); Physical therapists 1 (pt); Occupational therapists 1 (pt); Speech therapists 1 (pt); Activities coordinators 1 (ft); Dietitians 1 (pt); Ophthalmologists 1 (pt); Dentists 1 (pt).
Facilities Dining room; Physical therapy room; Activities room; Chapel; Crafts room; Laundry room; Barber/Beauty shop.
Activities Arts & crafts; Cards; Games; Reading groups; Prayer groups; Movies; Shopping trips; Dances/Social/Cultural gatherings; Van for handicapped.

Marysville

Marshall County Nursing Center
1906 North St, Marysville, KS 66508
(913) 562-5321
Admin Anne Bradford.
Medical Dir Carolyn Whitlinger.
Licensure Intermediate care. *Beds* ICF 49. *Certified* Medicaid.
Owner Proprietary corp.
Facilities Dining room; Physical therapy room; Activities room; Laundry room.
Activities Arts & crafts; Cards; Games; Reading groups; Prayer groups; Movies; Shopping trips; Dances/Social/Cultural gatherings.

Mary Marshall Manor Inc
810 N 18th St, Marysville, KS 66508
(913) 562-5325
Admin Dorothy L Welch. *Dir of Nursing* Janell Johnson. *Medical Dir* Dr Donald Argo.
Licensure Intermediate care; Alzheimer's care. *Beds* ICF 93. *Private Pay Patients* 67%. *Certified* Medicaid.
Owner Proprietary corp.
Admissions Requirements Medical examination; Physician's request.
Staff RNs; LPNs; Nurses' aides; Physical therapists (consultant); Recreational therapists; Dietitians (consultant).
Facilities Dining room; Physical therapy room; Activities room; Chapel; Crafts room; Laundry room; Barber/Beauty shop; TV room.
Activities Arts & crafts; Cards; Games; Reading groups; Prayer groups; Movies; Shopping trips; Dances/Social/Cultural gatherings; Intergenerational programs; Pet therapy.

McPherson

Autumnwood Villa
PO Box 1314, McPherson, KS 67460
(316) 241-5360
Admin Linda B Tolley. *Dir of Nursing* Mysel Shoemaker. *Medical Dir* Dr Thomas Billings.
Licensure Intermediate care; Alzheimer's care. *Beds* ICF 94. *Certified* Medicaid.

Owner Proprietary corp (Eagle Health Care Corp).
Admissions Requirements Minimum age 18; Medical examination; Physician's request.
Staff LPNs; Nurses' aides; Physical therapists; Activities coordinators 1 (ft); Dietitians 1 (ft).
Facilities Dining room; Physical therapy room; Activities room; Chapel; Crafts room; Laundry room; Barber/Beauty shop; Quiet room.
Activities Arts & crafts; Cards; Games; Reading groups; Prayer groups; Movies; Shopping trips; Dances/Social/Cultural gatherings; Intergenerational programs; Pet therapy; Outings to eat; Volunteer programs.

Cedars Inc
1021 Cedars Dr, McPherson, KS 67460
(316) 241-0919
Admin Madonna Reynolds; LeRoy C Weddle CEO. *Dir of Nursing* Kathy Duerkson RN.
Licensure Intermediate care; Apartment living. *Beds* ICF 120; Apartment living 133. *Private Pay Patients* 73%. *Certified* Medicaid.
Owner Nonprofit corp.
Admissions Requirements Minimum age 60; Medical examination; Physician's request.
Staff RNs 3 (ft), 1 (pt); LPNs 7 (ft), 5 (pt); Nurses' aides 32 (ft), 9 (pt); Physical therapists 1 (pt); Activities coordinators 2 (ft); Dietitians 1 (ft).
Languages Spanish.
Affiliation Church of the Brethren.
Facilities Dining room; Physical therapy room; Activities room; Chapel; Laundry room; Barber/Beauty shop; Library; Living room.
Activities Arts & crafts; Cards; Games; Reading groups; Prayer groups; Movies; Shopping trips; Dances/Social/Cultural gatherings; Bible study.

Mac House
225 S Hickory, McPherson, KS 67460
(316) 241-6780
Admin Larry Elmquist.
Licensure Intermediate care for mentally retarded. *Beds* ICF/MR 6. *Certified* Medicaid.
Owner Nonprofit corp.
Admissions Requirements Minimum age 18.
Staff RNs 1 (pt); Nurses' aides 2 (ft), 2 (pt); Activities coordinators 1 (ft); Medical aides 5 (ft).
Facilities Dining room; Activities room; Laundry room.
Activities Arts & crafts; Cards; Games; Movies; Shopping trips; Dances/Social/Cultural gatherings; Work activity; Day program.

Meade

Lone Tree Lodge
PO Box 340, 407 E Rainbelt, Meade, KS 67864
(316) 873-2146
Admin Darrell K Webb. *Dir of Nursing* Agnes Wiens RN.
Licensure Intermediate care. *Beds* ICF 56. *Private Pay Patients* 55%. *Certified* Medicaid.
Owner Nonprofit corp.
Admissions Requirements Minimum age 17; Medical examination; Physician's request.
Staff RNs 2 (ft), 3 (pt); LPNs 2 (ft), 2 (pt); Nurses' aides; Physical therapists 1 (pt); Occupational therapists 1 (pt); Speech therapists 1 (pt); Activities coordinators 1 (ft); Dietitians 1 (pt); Ophthalmologists 1 (pt); Audiologists 1 (pt).
Affiliation Mennonite.

Facilities Dining room; Physical therapy room; Activities room; Barber/Beauty shop.
Activities Arts & crafts; Cards; Games; Reading groups; Prayer groups; Movies; Shopping trips.

Medicine Lodge

Lifecare Manor
601 N Cedar, Medicine Lodge, KS 67104
(316) 886-3886
Admin William D Parker. *Dir of Nursing* Vicki Honas. *Medical Dir* Dr Stucky.
Licensure Intermediate care; Alzheimer's care. *Beds* ICF 60. *Private Pay Patients* 60%. *Certified* Medicaid.
Owner Proprietary corp (Lifecare of Kansas).
Admissions Requirements Minimum age 50; Medical examination; Physician's request.
Staff RNs 1 (ft), 2 (pt); LPNs 1 (ft); Nurses' aides 11 (ft), 2 (pt); Physical therapists 1 (ft); Recreational therapists 1 (ft); Occupational therapists 1 (pt); Activities coordinators 1 (ft); Dietitians 1 (ft); Podiatrists 1 (pt); Audiologists 1 (pt).
Languages Spanish.
Facilities Dining room; Physical therapy room; Activities room; Chapel; Crafts room; Laundry room; Barber/Beauty shop; Library.
Activities Arts & crafts; Cards; Games; Reading groups; Prayer groups; Movies; Shopping trips; Dances/Social/Cultural gatherings; Intergenerational programs; Pet therapy.

Lifecare Training Center of Medicine Lodge
106 W Stolp, Medicine Lodge, KS 67104
(316) 886-3425
Admin John M Vanhook.
Medical Dir Joyce Range.
Licensure Intermediate care for mentally retarded. *Beds* ICF/MR 49. *Certified* Medicaid.
Owner Proprietary corp (Life Care Centers of Kansas Inc).
Admissions Requirements Minimum age 21.
Staff RNs 1 (ft), 1 (pt); LPNs 1 (ft); Nurses' aides 10 (ft); Dietitians 1 (pt).
Facilities Dining room; Physical therapy room; Activities room; Chapel; Crafts room; Laundry room; Barber/Beauty shop.
Activities Arts & crafts; Cards; Games; Reading groups; Prayer groups; Movies; Shopping trips; Dances/Social/Cultural gatherings.

Merriam

Trinity Lutheran Manor
9700 W 62nd St, Merriam, KS 66203
(913) 384-0800
Admin Willa J Hughes. *Dir of Nursing* Deronda Davis RN. *Medical Dir* Mohan Gollerkeri MD.
Licensure Skilled care. *Beds* SNF 120. *Private Pay Patients* 70%. *Certified* Medicaid; Medicare.
Owner Nonprofit corp.
Admissions Requirements Minimum age 18.
Staff Physicians 1 (ft); RNs 5 (ft), 4 (pt); LPNs 2 (ft), 3 (pt); Nurses' aides 36 (ft), 2 (pt); Physical therapists 1 (ft), 1 (pt); Recreational therapists 2 (ft); Occupational therapists 1 (pt); Speech therapists 1 (pt); Activities coordinators 2 (ft); Dietitians 1 (pt); Ophthalmologists 1 (pt); Podiatrists 1 (pt); Audiologists 1 (pt).
Languages French, Spanish, Latin.
Affiliation Lutheran.
Facilities Dining room; Physical therapy room; Activities room; Chapel; Crafts room; Laundry room; Barber/Beauty shop; Living rooms; Quiet room; Exercise room.
Activities Arts & crafts; Cards; Games; Reading groups; Prayer groups; Movies; Shopping trips; Intergenerational programs; Pet therapy.

Minneapolis

Minneapolis Good Samaritan Center
816 Argyle, Minneapolis, KS 67467
(913) 392-2162
Admin Richard Elliott. *Dir of Nursing* Shelly
Doris.
Licensure Intermediate care; Retirement. *Beds*
ICF 93; Retirement 6. *Private Pay Patients*
45%. *Certified* Medicaid.
Owner Nonprofit corp (Evangelical Lutheran/
Good Samaritan Society).
Admissions Requirements Medical
examination; Physician's request.
Staff RNs 3 (ft), 2 (pt); LPNs 3 (ft), 5 (pt);
Nurses' aides 22 (ft), 16 (pt); Physical
therapists 1 (ft), 1 (pt); Activities
coordinators 1 (ft), 1 (pt).
Affiliation Lutheran.
Facilities Dining room; Physical therapy
room; Activities room; Chapel; Crafts room;
Laundry room; Barber/Beauty shop.
Activities Arts & crafts; Cards; Games;
Reading groups; Prayer groups; Movies;
Shopping trips; Dances/Social/Cultural
gatherings; Intergenerational programs; Pet
therapy.

Minneola

Minneola Nursing Home
PO Box 10, 207 Chestnut, Minneola, KS
67865
(316) 885-4238
Admin Lou A Esplund.
Medical Dir Lori Skeen.
Licensure Intermediate care. *Beds* ICF 50.
Certified Medicaid.
Owner Publicly owned.
Admissions Requirements Minimum age 16;
Physician's request.
Staff Physicians 1 (pt); RNs 1 (pt); LPNs 6
(ft); Nurses' aides 12 (ft), 4 (pt); Physical
therapists 1 (pt); Recreational therapists 1
(pt); Occupational therapists 1 (pt);
Activities coordinators 1 (pt); Dietitians 1
(pt).
Facilities Dining room; Physical therapy
room; Activities room; Chapel; Crafts room;
Laundry room; Barber/Beauty shop; Kitchen.
Activities Arts & crafts; Cards; Prayer groups;
Movies; Shopping trips; Dances/Social/
Cultural gatherings.

Moline

Elk Manor Home
Rte 1 Box 7, Walnut St, Moline, KS 67353
(316) 647-3235
Admin Bruce R Smith. *Dir of Nursing* Frances
Roper.
Licensure Intermediate care. *Beds* ICF 41.
Certified Medicaid.
Owner Publicly owned.
Admissions Requirements Medical
examination; Physician's request.
Staff RNs 1 (pt); LPNs 3 (ft), 1 (pt); Nurses'
aides 9 (ft), 5 (pt); Physical therapists 1 (ft);
Occupational therapists 1 (pt); Activities
coordinators 1 (ft); Dietitians 1 (ft).
Facilities Dining room; Physical therapy
room; Laundry room; Barber/Beauty shop;
Sun room.
Activities Arts & crafts; Cards; Games;
Reading groups; Prayer groups; Movies;
Shopping trips; Dances/Social/Cultural
gatherings; Visiting musical groups.

Montezuma

Bethel Home Inc
Rte 1, Aztec St, Montezuma, KS 67867
(316) 846-2241
Admin Marion D Becker.
Medical Dir Alma Wiens.

Licensure Intermediate care. *Beds* ICF 48.
Certified Medicaid.
Owner Nonprofit corp.
Admissions Requirements Physician's request.
Staff RNs 1 (ft); LPNs 1 (ft), 5 (pt); Nurses'
aides 10 (ft), 11 (pt); Physical therapists 2
(pt); Recreational therapists 1 (pt); Activities
coordinators 1 (ft), 1 (pt); Dietitians 3 (ft), 4
(pt).
Affiliation Mennonite.
Facilities Dining room; Physical therapy
room; Activities room; Chapel; Crafts room;
Laundry room; Barber/Beauty shop; Library.
Activities Arts & crafts; Games; Reading
groups; Prayer groups; Shopping trips;
Dances/Social/Cultural gatherings.

Moran

Moran Manor
RR 1 Box 53, Moran, KS 66755
(316) 237-4309
Admin Sandra S Northcutt.
Licensure Intermediate care. *Beds* ICF 42.
Certified Medicaid.
Owner Proprietary corp (Americare Systems
Inc).
Admissions Requirements Minimum age 16;
Medical examination.
Staff RNs 1 (ft); LPNs 1 (ft), 2 (pt); Nurses'
aides 11 (ft), 6 (pt); Physical therapists 1 (ft),
1 (pt); Occupational therapists 1 (pt); Speech
therapists 1 (pt); Activities coordinators 1
(ft), 1 (pt); Dietitians 1 (pt); Podiatrists 1
(pt); Dentists 1 (pt).
Facilities Dining room; Physical therapy
room; Activities room; Laundry room;
Barber/Beauty shop.
Activities Arts & crafts; Cards; Games;
Reading groups; Prayer groups; Movies;
Shopping trips; Dances/Social/Cultural
gatherings.

Mound City

Sugar Valley Home Inc
W Main, Mound City, KS 66056
(913) 795-2231
Admin Wes W Worthington. *Dir of Nursing*
Sharon Willard RN.
Licensure Intermediate care; Alzheimer's care.
Beds ICF 60. *Certified* Medicaid.
Owner Proprietary corp.
Admissions Requirements Minimum age 18;
Medical examination.
Staff RNs 2 (ft); LPNs 3 (ft); Nurses' aides 19
(ft); Activities coordinators 1 (ft).
Facilities Dining room; Physical therapy
room; Activities room; Laundry room;
Barber/Beauty shop; Library.
Activities Arts & crafts; Cards; Games;
Reading groups; Prayer groups; Movies;
Shopping trips; Dances/Social/Cultural
gatherings.

Moundridge

Memorial Home for the Aged
PO Box 29, Moundridge, KS 67107
(316) 345-2901
Admin Jerry Unruh. *Dir of Nursing* Pat Rupp
RN. *Medical Dir* Dr W E Kaufman.
Licensure Intermediate care; Assisted self-care;
Retirement. *Beds* ICF 50; assisted self-care
36. *Certified* Medicaid.
Owner Nonprofit corp.
Admissions Requirements Minimum age 60.
Staff RNs 2 (ft), 2 (pt); LPNs 1 (ft), 3 (pt);
Nurses' aides 3 (ft), 22 (pt); Activities
coordinators 1 (ft).
Affiliation Mennonite.
Facilities Dining room; Physical therapy
room; Activities room; Chapel; Crafts room;
Laundry room; Barber/Beauty shop; Library.

Activities Arts & crafts; Games; Reading
groups; Movies; Dances/Social/Cultural
gatherings.

Moundridge Manor
PO Box 800, Moundridge, KS 67107
(316) 345-6364
Admin Bernard Regehr.
Medical Dir Dr W Kauffman.
Licensure Intermediate care. *Beds* ICF 67.
Certified Medicaid.
Owner Nonprofit corp.
Admissions Requirements Minimum age 16;
Medical examination; Physician's request.
Staff RNs 1 (ft), 1 (pt); LPNs 4 (ft), 3 (pt);
Nurses' aides 23 (ft); Speech therapists 1
(pt); Activities coordinators 1 (ft).
Affiliation Mennonite.
Facilities Dining room; Physical therapy
room; Activities room; Crafts room; Laundry
room; Barber/Beauty shop.
Activities Arts & crafts; Games; Reading
groups; Prayer groups.

Mount Hope

Mt Hope Nursing Center
704 E Main, Mount Hope, KS 67108
(316) 667-2431
Admin Patricia J Elliott RN.
Medical Dir J M Steck MD.
Licensure Intermediate care; Retirement. *Beds*
ICF 62. *Certified* Medicaid.
Owner Nonprofit corp.
Admissions Requirements Minimum age 16;
Medical examination; Physician's request.
Staff RNs 1 (ft), 1 (pt); LPNs 1 (ft), 1 (pt);
Activities coordinators 1 (ft).
Facilities Dining room; Physical therapy
room; Activities room; Chapel; Crafts room;
Laundry room; Barber/Beauty shop.
Activities Arts & crafts; Cards; Games;
Reading groups; Prayer groups; Movies;
Shopping trips; Dances/Social/Cultural
gatherings.

Mulvane

Villa Maria Inc
116 S Central, Mulvane, KS 67110
(316) 777-1129
Admin Sr M M Wappelharst. *Dir of Nursing*
Sr Justine Busch RN. *Medical Dir* Leslie H
Cobb MD.
Licensure Intermediate care. *Beds* ICF 66.
Certified Medicaid.
Owner Nonprofit corp.
Admissions Requirements Minimum age 65;
Medical examination; Physician's request.
Staff RNs 2 (ft); LPNs 4 (ft), 2 (pt); Nurses'
aides 18 (ft), 2 (pt); Physical therapists 1 (ft),
1 (pt); Recreational therapists 1 (pt);
Occupational therapists 1 (pt); Speech
therapists 1 (pt); Activities coordinators 1
(ft); Dietitians 1 (ft); Dietitians 1 (pt);
Podiatrists 1 (pt).
Affiliation Roman Catholic.
Facilities Dining room; Physical therapy
room; Activities room; Chapel; Laundry
room; Barber/Beauty shop; Library.
Activities Arts & crafts; Cards; Games;
Reading groups; Prayer groups; Movies;
Dances/Social/Cultural gatherings.

Neodesha

Golden Keys Nursing Home
Box 350, 221 Mill, Neodesha, KS 66757
(316) 325-2639
Admin Phyllis C Cunningham. *Dir of Nursing*
Toni Barnhart RN. *Medical Dir* Bert
Chronister MD.
Licensure Intermediate care. *Beds* ICF 64.
Private Pay Patients 75%. *Certified*
Medicaid.
Owner Publicly owned.

Admissions Requirements Minimum age 18;
Medical examination; Physician's request.
Staff RNs 1 (ft); LPNs 3 (ft); Nurses' aides 20
(ft), 5 (pt); Physical therapists (consultant);
Recreational therapists 1 (ft); Activities
coordinators 1 (ft); Dietitians (consultant);
CFMs 1 (ft).
Facilities Dining room; Physical therapy
room; Activities room; Crafts room; Laundry
room; Barber/Beauty shop; Library.
Activities Arts & crafts; Cards; Games;
Reading groups; Prayer groups; Movies;
Dances/Social/Cultural gatherings.

Neodesha Nursing Home
1626 N 8th, Neodesha, KS 66757
(316) 325-3088
Admin Sherri R Brown. *Dir of Nursing* Jolene
Ramey.
Licensure Intermediate care. *Beds* ICF 50.
Certified Medicaid.
Owner Proprietary corp (Life Care Centers of
Kansas Inc).
Staff RNs 2 (ft); LPNs 2 (ft); Nurses' aides 19
(ft); Activities coordinators 1 (ft).
Facilities Dining room; Physical therapy
room; Activities room; Chapel; Crafts room;
Laundry room; Barber/Beauty shop.
Activities Arts & crafts; Cards; Games;
Reading groups; Prayer groups; Movies;
Shopping trips; Bingo.

Newton

Bethel Home for Aged
222 S Pine, Newton, KS 67114
(316) 283-4014
Admin Thomas C Wentz. *Dir of Nursing*
Esther M McDonald RN.
Licensure Intermediate care; Retirement. *Beds*
ICF 67. *Certified* Medicaid.
Owner Nonprofit corp.
Admissions Requirements Minimum age 62 or
w/special permission; Medical examination.
Staff RNs 3 (ft), 2 (pt); LPNs 2 (ft), 1 (pt);
Nurses' aides 10 (ft), 8 (pt); Physical
therapists 2 (pt); Occupational therapists 1
(pt); Speech therapists 1 (pt); Activities
coordinators 1 (ft); Dietitians 1 (pt);
Medication aides 8 (ft), 3 (pt); Social
services 1 (ft).
Languages German.
Affiliation Mennonite.
Facilities Dining room; Activities room;
Chapel; Crafts room; Laundry room; Barber/
Beauty shop; Library.
Activities Arts & crafts; Cards; Games;
Reading groups; Prayer groups; Movies;
Shopping trips; Dances/Social/Cultural
gatherings; Sing-along; Worship hour; Bible
class; Birthday parties.

Friendly Acres Inc
PO Box 648, 200 SW 14th St, Newton, KS
67114
(316) 283-4770
Admin Mina M Coulter; Mike Kaufmann,
Exec Dir. *Dir of Nursing* Bonnie Krenning.
Medical Dir Dr Paul Fransen.
Licensure Intermediate care; Personal care;
Retirement; Assisted living. *Beds* ICF 144;
Personal care 44; Retirement cottages 71.
Private Pay Patients 56%. *Certified*
Medicaid.
Owner Nonprofit corp.
Admissions Requirements Minimum age 62;
Medical examination.
Staff Physicians 2 (pt); RNs 7 (ft); LPNs 9
(ft), 2 (pt); Nurses' aides 50 (ft), 18 (pt);
Physical therapists 3 (ft); Recreational
therapists 1 (ft); Occupational therapists 1
(pt); Speech therapists 1 (pt); Dietitians 1
(pt); Podiatrists 1 (pt); Audiologists 1 (pt).
Affiliation United Methodist.
Facilities Dining room; Physical therapy
room; Activities room; Chapel; Crafts room;
Laundry room; Barber/Beauty shop; Library.

Activities Arts & crafts; Cards; Games;
Reading groups; Prayer groups; Movies;
Dances/Social/Cultural gatherings;
Intergenerational programs.

Kansas Christian Home Inc
1035 SE 3rd St, Newton, KS 67114
(316) 283-6600
Admin Dana A Froelich.
Licensure Intermediate care. *Beds* ICF 107.
Certified Medicaid.
Owner Nonprofit corp.

Newton Presbyterian Manor
1200 E 7th, Newton, KS 67114
(316) 283-5400
Admin William P Palmer. *Dir of Nursing*
Marion Schroeder.
Licensure Intermediate care; Retirement;
Alzheimer's care. *Beds* ICF 60. *Certified*
Medicaid.
Owner Nonprofit corp.
Admissions Requirements Minimum age 65;
Medical examination.
Staff RNs 2 (ft); LPNs 4 (ft); Nurses' aides;
Occupational therapists; Activities
coordinators; Dietitians.
Affiliation Presbyterian.
Facilities Dining room; Physical therapy
room; Activities room; Chapel; Crafts room;
Laundry room; Barber/Beauty shop; Library.
Activities Arts & crafts; Shopping trips;
Dances/Social/Cultural gatherings; Music
therapy; Horticultural therapy; Chapel
services.

Norton

Andbe Home Inc
201 W Crane, Norton, KS 67654
(913) 877-2601
Admin Wilma Winder RN. *Dir of Nursing*
Jackie Rutherford RN.
Licensure Intermediate care. *Beds* ICF 100.
Certified Medicaid.
Owner Nonprofit corp.
Admissions Requirements Minimum age 16;
Medical examination.
Staff RNs 2 (ft); LPNs 7 (ft), 3 (pt); Nurses'
aides 40 (ft); Physical therapists 1 (pt);
Activities coordinators 1 (ft); Dietitians 1
(pt); CPTAs 2 (pt).
Facilities Dining room; Physical therapy
room; Activities room; Chapel; Crafts room;
Laundry room; Barber/Beauty shop.
Activities Arts & crafts; Cards; Games;
Reading groups; Prayer groups; Movies;
Shopping trips; Dances/Social/Cultural
gatherings.

Nortonville

Village Villa Nursing Home
Walnut & Taggart, Box 346, Nortonville, KS
66060
(913) 886-6400
Admin Linda Ronnebaum. *Dir of Nursing*
Diane Babcock RN. *Medical Dir* James V
Rider DO.
Licensure Intermediate care. *Beds* ICF 50.
Certified Medicaid.
Owner Proprietary corp.
Admissions Requirements Minimum age 18;
Medical examination; Physician's request.
Staff Physicians 6 (pt); RNs 2 (ft), 1 (pt);
LPNs 1 (ft), 3 (pt); Nurses' aides 5 (ft), 3
(pt); Activities coordinators 1 (pt); Podiatrists
1 (pt); Medication aides 8 (pt); Social worker
1 (pt); Social service 1 (pt).
Facilities Dining room; Physical therapy
room; Activities room; Crafts room; Laundry
room; Barber/Beauty shop; Sun room with
TV; Quiet room.

Activities Arts & crafts; Cards; Games;
Reading groups; Prayer groups; Movies;
Bible study by volunteers; Womens support
groups; News time & visiting; Music time &
singing.

Oakley

Oakley Manor
615 Price, Oakley, KS 67748
(913) 672-3115
Admin Joan Wesswl. *Dir of Nursing*
Rosemary Davis LPN.
Licensure Intermediate care. *Beds* ICF 42.
Certified Medicaid.
Owner Proprietary corp (Beverly Enterprises).
Admissions Requirements Minimum age 16.
Staff RNs 1 (pt); LPNs 2 (ft), 1 (pt); Nurses'
aides 16 (ft), 4 (pt); Physical therapists 1 (ft);
Activities coordinators 1 (ft).
Facilities Dining room; Physical therapy
room; Laundry room; Barber/Beauty shop.
Activities Arts & crafts; Games; Prayer groups;
Movies; Shopping trips; Dances/Social/
Cultural gatherings.

Oberlin

Decatur County Good Samaritan Center
108 E Ash, Oberlin, KS 67749
(913) 475-2245
Admin Troy Lerseth.
Medical Dir Dr Ren Whitacker.
Licensure Intermediate care; Personal care.
Beds ICF 71; Personal care 8. *Certified*
Medicaid.
Owner Nonprofit corp (Evangelical Lutheran/
Good Samaritan Society).
Admissions Requirements Minimum age 35;
Medical examination; Physician's request.
Staff Physicians 4 (pt); RNs 3 (pt); LPNs 4
(pt); Nurses' aides 35 (pt); Physical
therapists 1 (pt); Activities coordinators 1
(ft), 2 (pt).
Affiliation Lutheran.
Facilities Dining room; Physical therapy
room; Activities room; Chapel; Laundry
room; Barber/Beauty shop.
Activities Arts & crafts; Cards; Games;
Reading groups; Prayer groups; Movies;
Shopping trips; Dances/Social/Cultural
gatherings.

Olathe

Delmar Gardens of Olathe Inc
2150 Delmar Gardens Plaza, Olathe, KS
66062
(913) 764-0331
Admin Katharyn Link.
Licensure Skilled care. *Beds* SNF 235.
Certified Medicaid; Medicare.
Owner Proprietary corp.

Johnson County Nursing Center
301-C S Clairborne St, Olathe, KS 66062
(913) 782-0272
Admin Kenneth Betterton.
Licensure Intermediate care. *Beds* ICF 104.
Certified Medicaid.
Owner Publicly owned.

Johnson County Residential Care Facility
1125 W Spruce, Olathe, KS 66061
(913) 780-1306
Admin Karen Croman.
Licensure Intermediate care. *Beds* ICF 39.
Certified Medicaid.
Owner Publicly owned.

Olathe Good Samaritan Center
572 E Park, Olathe, KS 66061
(913) 782-1372
Admin Michael Adkins.
Licensure Intermediate care. *Beds* ICF 161.
Certified Medicaid.

Owner Nonprofit corp (Evangelical Lutheran/ Good Samaritan Society).
Admissions Requirements Minimum age 18; Medical examination; Physician's request.
Staff RNs 4 (ft); LPNs 10 (ft); Nurses' aides 50 (ft), 20 (pt); Activities coordinators 1 (ft).
Affiliation Lutheran.
Facilities Dining room; Physical therapy room; Activities room; Chapel; Crafts room; Laundry room; Barber/Beauty shop; Library; Plant room.
Activities Arts & crafts; Cards; Games; Reading groups; Prayer groups; Movies; Shopping trips; Dances/Social/Cultural gatherings.

Olathe Nursing Home
625 N Lincoln, Olathe, KS 66061
(913) 782-1311
Admin Kathy Wilcox.
Medical Dir Ronald LaHue DO.
Licensure Intermediate care. *Beds* ICF 54. *Certified* Medicaid.
Owner Proprietary corp.
Admissions Requirements Minimum age 60; Medical examination.
Staff LPNs 2 (ft), 1 (pt); Nurses' aides 13 (ft); Physical therapists 1 (ft); Activities coordinators 1 (ft).
Facilities Dining room; Physical therapy room; Activities room; Chapel; Laundry room; Barber/Beauty shop.
Activities Arts & crafts; Cards; Prayer groups; Movies; Shopping trips.

Regency Health Care Center
400 S Rogers Rd, Olathe, KS 66062
(913) 782-3350
Admin Sally A Gates. *Dir of Nursing* Carol Browning. *Medical Dir* Robert Nottingham.
Licensure Skilled care; Intermediate care. *Beds* SNF 55; ICF 54. *Certified* Medicaid; Medicare.
Owner Proprietary corp (Regency Health Care Centers Inc).
Admissions Requirements Minimum age 16; Medical examination.
Staff RNs 5 (ft); LPNs 8 (ft), 6 (pt); Nurses' aides 19 (ft), 4 (pt); Physical therapists 1 (pt); Recreational therapists 1 (ft); Occupational therapists 1 (pt); Speech therapists 1 (pt); Activities coordinators 1 (ft); Dietitians 1 (pt); Ophthalmologists 1 (pt); Podiatrists 1 (pt); Dentists 1 (pt).
Facilities Dining room; Physical therapy room; Activities room; Crafts room; Laundry room; Barber/Beauty shop.
Activities Arts & crafts; Cards; Games; Reading groups; Prayer groups; Movies; Shopping trips; Dances/Social/Cultural gatherings.

Royal Terrace Care Center Inc
201 E Flaming Dr, Olathe, KS 66061
(913) 829-2273
Admin John S May.
Licensure Skilled care; Personal care. *Beds* SNF 118; Personal care 30. *Certified* Medicaid; Medicare.
Owner Proprietary corp.

Onaga

Golden Acres
500 Western St, Onaga, KS 66521
(913) 889-4227
Admin Connie Ellis.
Licensure Intermediate care. *Beds* ICF 55. *Certified* Medicaid.
Owner Proprietary corp (Beverly Enterprises).

Osage City

Osage Manor Inc
10th & Main St, Osage City, KS 66523
(913) 528-4262

Admin Bruce Struble. *Dir of Nursing* Irene Hasenbank RN.
Licensure Intermediate care. *Beds* ICF 67. *Certified* Medicaid.
Owner Proprietary corp.
Staff RNs 1 (ft); LPNs 3 (ft); Nurses' aides 20 (ft), 4 (pt); Recreational therapists 1 (ft); Occupational therapists 1 (ft); Activities coordinators 1 (ft).
Facilities Dining room; Physical therapy room; Chapel; Crafts room; Laundry room; Barber/Beauty shop.
Activities Arts & crafts; Cards; Games; Reading groups; Prayer groups; Movies; Dances/Social/Cultural gatherings; Fishing trips with picnic; Watermelon feeds; Ice cream social; Pot luck suppers; Country/ western bands; Balloon lift offs; Movies.

Peterson Nursing Home
630 Holliday, Osage City, KS 66523
(913) 528-4420
Admin Crystal M Peterson.
Medical Dir Peggy L Lira.
Licensure Intermediate care. *Beds* ICF 60. *Certified* Medicaid.
Owner Proprietary corp.
Admissions Requirements Medical examination; Physician's request.
Staff RNs; LPNs; Nurses' aides; Activities coordinators; Dietitians.
Facilities Dining room; Physical therapy room; Activities room; Chapel; Crafts room; Laundry room; Barber/Beauty shop.
Activities Arts & crafts; Cards; Games; Reading groups; Prayer groups; Movies; Shopping trips; Dances/Social/Cultural gatherings; Resident council.

Osawatomie

Heritage Manor of Osawatomie
1615 Parker Ave, Osawatomie, KS 66064
(913) 755-4165
Admin Patricia Cranston. *Dir of Nursing* Catherine McRoberts RN. *Medical Dir* Robert E Banks MD.
Licensure Skilled care; Intermediate care; Alzheimer's care. *Beds* SNF 48; ICF 98. *Certified* Medicaid; Medicare.
Owner Proprietary corp (National Heritage).
Admissions Requirements Minimum age 16; Medical examination; Physician's request.
Staff Physicians 5 (pt); RNs 4 (ft), 1 (pt); LPNs 8 (ft), 2 (pt); Nurses' aides 27 (ft), 8 (pt); Physical therapists 2 (pt); Recreational therapists 2 (ft); Occupational therapists 1 (pt); Speech therapists 1 (pt); Activities coordinators 1 (ft); Dietitians 1 (pt); Ophthalmologists 1 (pt); Dentists 1 (pt).
Facilities Dining room; Physical therapy room; Activities room; Chapel; Crafts room; Laundry room; Barber/Beauty shop; Library.
Activities Arts & crafts; Cards; Games; Reading groups; Prayer groups; Movies; Shopping trips; Dances/Social/Cultural gatherings.

Osawatomie Rest Home
1615 Parker, Osawatomie, KS 66064
(913) 755-4165
Licensure Intermediate care. *Beds* 24. *Certified* Medicaid.
Owner Proprietary corp.

Osborne

Parkview Care Center
811 N 1st St, Osborne, KS 67473
(913) 346-2114
Admin Betty Jo Banks.
Medical Dir Cindy Hyde.
Licensure Intermediate care; Alzheimer's care. *Beds* ICF 104. *Certified* Medicaid.
Owner Proprietary corp.
Admissions Requirements Physician's request.

Staff RNs 1 (ft), 3 (pt); LPNs 4 (ft); Nurses' aides 1 (ft); Activities coordinators 2 (ft), 2 (pt); Dietitians 1 (ft).
Facilities Dining room; Physical therapy room; Activities room; Chapel; Crafts room; Laundry room; Barber/Beauty shop; Library.
Activities Arts & crafts; Cards; Games; Reading groups; Prayer groups; Movies; Shopping trips; Dances/Social/Cultural gatherings.

Oskaloosa

Cherokee Lodge Adult Care Home
700 Cherokee, Box 307, Oskaloosa, KS 66066
(913) 863-2108
Admin Garry Swords.
Licensure Intermediate care. *Beds* ICF 100. *Certified* Medicaid.
Owner Proprietary corp.

Oswego

Villa of Oswego
Rte 2 Box 26, Ohio St, Oswego, KS 67356
(316) 795-4429
Admin Sherrie Addis.
Medical Dir Judith Marsh.
Licensure Intermediate care; Alzheimer's care. *Beds* ICF 60. *Certified* Medicaid.
Owner Proprietary corp (Health Haven Company).
Admissions Requirements Minimum age 18; Medical examination; Physician's request.
Staff RNs 2 (ft), 1 (pt); LPNs 3 (ft); Nurses' aides 20 (ft), 5 (pt); Physical therapists 1 (pt); Occupational therapists 1 (pt); Speech therapists 1 (pt); Activities coordinators 1 (ft); Dietitians 1 (pt); Ophthalmologists 1 (pt); Podiatrists 1 (pt).
Facilities Dining room; Physical therapy room; Activities room; Crafts room; Laundry room; Barber/Beauty shop; Library.
Activities Arts & crafts; Cards; Games; Reading groups; Prayer groups; Movies; Shopping trips; Dances/Social/Cultural gatherings.

Ottawa

Crestview Nursing Home
1002 W 7th St Terr, Ottawa, KS 66067
(913) 242-3454
Admin Cathy Wallace.
Licensure Intermediate care. *Beds* ICF 51. *Certified* Medicaid.
Owner Proprietary corp (Health Care Systems Inc).

Ottawa Retirement Village
1100 W 15th, Ottawa, KS 66067
(913) 242-5399
Admin John Howe. *Dir of Nursing* Daniel Everly.
Licensure Intermediate care; Retirement. *Beds* ICF 120; Retirement 50. *Private Pay Patients* 60%. *Certified* Medicaid; Medicare.
Owner Privately owned.
Admissions Requirements Medical examination.
Staff RNs 5 (ft); LPNs 2 (ft), 2 (pt); Nurses' aides 40 (ft); Activities coordinators 1 (ft).
Facilities Dining room; Physical therapy room; Activities room; Crafts room; Laundry room; Barber/Beauty shop; Quiet room; Courtyard.
Activities Arts & crafts; Cards; Games; Reading groups; Prayer groups; Movies; Shopping trips; Dances/Social/Cultural gatherings; Intergenerational programs; Pet therapy; Van rides; Picnics.

Overbrook

Brookside Manor
Hwy 56 & Wester Heights, Overbrook, KS 66524
(913) 665-7124
Admin Clifford E Fischer.
Medical Dir Judy Bagby.
Licensure Skilled care; Intermediate care; Retirement. *Beds* SNF 50; ICF 50. *Certified* Medicaid; Medicare.
Owner Proprietary corp.
Admissions Requirements Medical examination.
Staff Physicians 1 (pt); RNs 4 (ft); LPNs 4 (ft), 2 (pt); Nurses' aides 35 (ft), 10 (pt); Physical therapists 1 (pt); Occupational therapists 1 (pt); Speech therapists 1 (pt); Activities coordinators 1 (ft), 1 (pt); Dietitians 1 (pt); Dentists 1 (pt).
Facilities Dining room; Physical therapy room; Activities room; Chapel; Crafts room; Laundry room; Barber/Beauty shop; Visitors lounge.
Activities Arts & crafts; Cards; Games; Reading groups; Prayer groups; Movies; Shopping trips; Dances/Social/Cultural gatherings.

Overland Park

Conser House
7829 Conser, Overland Park, KS 66204
(913) 381-6623
Admin Yolanda Hargett.
Licensure Intermediate care for mentally retarded. *Beds* ICF/MR 10. *Certified* Medicaid.
Owner Nonprofit corp.
Admissions Requirements Minimum age 18; Medical examination; Physician's request.
Staff Physicians 4 (pt); RNs 1 (ft); Nurses' aides 25 (ft); Physical therapists 1 (pt); Occupational therapists 1 (pt); Speech therapists 1 (pt); Dietitians 1 (pt).
Facilities Dining room; Activities room; Laundry room.
Activities Arts & crafts; Cards; Games; Prayer groups; Movies; Shopping trips; Dances/ Social/Cultural gatherings.

Delmar Gardens of Overland Park
12100 W 109th St, Overland Park, KS 66210
(913) 469-4210, 469-4279 FAX
Admin Richard Carlson. *Dir of Nursing* Cheryl Hoerl RN. *Medical Dir* Dr Fred Farris.
Licensure Skilled care; Respite care; Hospice care. *Beds* SNF 120. *Private Pay Patients* 65%. *Certified* Medicaid; Medicare.
Owner Proprietary corp (Delmar Gardens Enterprises).
Admissions Requirements Minimum age 18; Medical examination; Physician's request.
Staff RNs 1 (ft), 3 (pt); LPNs 2 (ft), 3 (pt); Nurses' aides 10 (ft), 7 (pt); Physical therapists; Activities coordinators 1 (ft); Dietitians 1 (ft); Certified medication aides 2 (ft).
Facilities Dining room; Physical therapy room; Activities room; Chapel; Crafts room; Laundry room; Barber/Beauty shop; Library.
Activities Arts & crafts; Cards; Games; Reading groups; Prayer groups; Movies; Shopping trips; Dances/Social/Cultural gatherings; Intergenerational programs; Pet therapy.

Healthcare Center at the Forum
3501 W 95th St, Overland Park, KS 66206
(913) 648-4500
Admin Ronald G Barrett.
Licensure Skilled care. *Beds* SNF 90.
Owner Proprietary corp (Forum Group Inc).

Indian Creek Nursing Center
6515 W 103rd, Overland Park, KS 66212
(913) 642-5545
Admin Philip Thompson. *Dir of Nursing* Dixie Byrnes.
Licensure Skilled care; Alzheimer's care. *Beds* SNF 120. *Certified* Medicare.
Owner Proprietary corp (Hillhaven Corp).
Admissions Requirements Minimum age 16; Medical examination; Physician's request.
Staff Physicians; RNs; LPNs; Nurses' aides; Physical therapists; Reality therapists; Recreational therapists; Occupational therapists; Speech therapists; Activities coordinators; Dietitians; Ophthalmologists; Podiatrists; Dentists.
Facilities Dining room; Physical therapy room; Activities room; Crafts room; Laundry room; Barber/Beauty shop.
Activities Arts & crafts; Cards; Games; Reading groups; Prayer groups; Movies.

Indian Meadows Nursing Center
6505 W 103rd, Overland Park, KS 66212
(913) 649-5110
Admin Linda Nelson. *Dir of Nursing* Michelle Boudreaux RN. *Medical Dir* Dr Norman Marvin.
Licensure Skilled care. *Beds* SNF 120. *Certified* Medicaid.
Owner Proprietary corp (Hillhaven Corp).
Admissions Requirements Minimum age 16; Medical examination; Physician's request.
Staff Physicians; RNs; LPNs; Nurses' aides; Physical therapists; Recreational therapists; Occupational therapists; Speech therapists; Dietitians; Ophthalmologists.
Facilities Dining room; Physical therapy room; Activities room; Crafts room; Laundry room; Barber/Beauty shop.
Activities Arts & crafts; Cards; Games; Reading groups; Prayer groups; Movies; Shopping trips.

Life Care Center of Overland Park
7541 NE Switzer Rd, Overland Park, KS 66214
(913) 631-2273
Admin Darlene Zuber.
Medical Dir Dr Philip Boyer.
Licensure Skilled care; Intermediate care. *Beds* SNF 93; ICF 80. *Certified* Medicare.
Owner Proprietary corp (Life Care Center of America Inc).
Admissions Requirements Medical examination.
Staff RNs 4 (ft), 1 (pt); LPNs 8 (ft), 3 (pt); Nurses' aides 52 (ft), 3 (pt); Physical therapists 1 (pt); Occupational therapists 1 (pt); Speech therapists 1 (pt); Activities coordinators 1 (ft); Dietitians 1 (ft); Podiatrists 1 (pt); Audiologists 1 (pt); Dentists 1 (pt).
Facilities Dining room; Physical therapy room; Activities room; Crafts room; Laundry room; Barber/Beauty shop; Library.
Activities Arts & crafts; Cards; Games; Reading groups; Movies; Dances/Social/ Cultural gatherings; Zoo.

Manor Care Nursing Center
5211 W 103rd St, Overland Park, KS 66207
(913) 383-2569
Admin Johnson.
Licensure Skilled care; Personal care. *Beds* SNF 120; Personal care 60. *Certified* Medicaid; Medicare.
Owner Proprietary corp (Manor Care).

Overland Park Manor
6501 W 75th St, Overland Park, KS 66204
(913) 383-9866
Admin Jackie Tuohig. *Dir of Nursing* Debbie Greenlee. *Medical Dir* Arthur Snow MD.
Licensure Skilled care; Intermediate care; Personal care. *Beds* SNF 58; ICF 42. *Certified* Medicare.
Owner Nonprofit organization/foundation.

Admissions Requirements Minimum age 20; Medical examination.
Staff Physicians 1 (ft); RNs 5 (ft); LPNs 8 (ft), 3 (pt); Nurses' aides 20 (ft), 4 (pt); Physical therapists (contracted); Occupational therapists (contracted); Speech therapists (contracted); Activities coordinators 1 (ft), 1 (pt); Dietitians (contracted); Ophthalmologists (contracted); Podiatrists (contracted); Audiologists (contracted); LaundryHousekeeping; Dietary.
Languages Spanish.
Affiliation Seventh-Day Adventist.
Facilities Dining room; Physical therapy room; Activities room; Chapel; Crafts room; Laundry room; Barber/Beauty shop; Library.
Activities Arts & crafts; Cards; Games; Reading groups; Prayer groups; Movies; Dances/Social/Cultural gatherings; Intergenerational programs; Pet therapy; Bookmobile.

Villa St Joseph
11901 Rosewood, Overland Park, KS 66209
(913) 345-1745
Admin Dianne Doctor.
Licensure Skilled care. *Beds* SNF 90. *Certified* Medicaid; Medicare.
Owner Nonprofit corp.

Oxford

Riverview Manor Inc
200 S Ohio, Oxford, KS 67119
(316) 455-2214
Admin Carol Sue Wilkerson.
Licensure Intermediate care; Retirement. *Beds* ICF 50. *Certified* Medicaid.
Owner Nonprofit corp.
Admissions Requirements Medical examination; Physician's request.
Staff RNs; LPNs; Nurses' aides.
Facilities Dining room; Physical therapy room; Activities room; Chapel; Laundry room; Barber/Beauty shop.
Activities Arts & crafts; Games; Prayer groups; Movies; Shopping trips.

Paola

Country Haven Adult Care Center
908 N Pearl, Paola, KS 66071
(913) 294-4308
Admin Joseph A Hornick. *Dir of Nursing* Patricia Dunlap.
Licensure Intermediate care; Adult day care. *Beds* ICF 80. *Certified* Medicaid.
Owner Proprietary corp (Americare Systems Inc).
Admissions Requirements Medical examination.
Staff LPNs 6 (ft); Nurses' aides 16 (ft); Activities coordinators 1 (ft).
Facilities Dining room; Physical therapy room; Activities room; Chapel; Crafts room; Laundry room; Barber/Beauty shop; Library; Humor room.
Activities Arts & crafts; Cards; Games; Reading groups; Prayer groups; Movies; Shopping trips; Pet therapy; Intergenerational programs.

Medicalodge of Paola
501 Assembly Ln, Box C, Paola, KS 66071
(913) 294-3345
Admin Allen Floyd.
Licensure Intermediate care. *Beds* ICF 96. *Certified* Medicaid.
Owner Proprietary corp (Medicalodges Inc).

Pine Crest Haven
1004 N Pearl, Paola, KS 66071
(913) 294-2404
Admin Beverly Hinchcliff.
Licensure Intermediate care. *Beds* ICF 50. *Certified* Medicaid.
Owner Proprietary corp.

Parsons

Elmhaven
1315 S 15th, Parsons, KS 67357
(316) 421-1320
Admin Patricia L Woodworth. *Dir of Nursing*
Kim McMunn RN.
Licensure Intermediate care; Licensed day
care; Retirement. *Beds* ICF 60. *Certified*
Medicaid.
Owner Privately owned.
Admissions Requirements Minimum age 16;
Medical examination.
Staff RNs 4 (ft), 4 (pt); Nurses' aides 10 (ft), 1
(pt); Activities coordinators 3 (ft).
Facilities Dining room; Physical therapy
room; Activities room; Laundry room;
Barber/Beauty shop.
Activities Arts & crafts; Cards; Games;
Reading groups; Prayer groups; Movies;
Shopping trips; Dances/Social/Cultural
gatherings; Cooking classes.

Heritage Home
1400 S 15th, Parsons, KS 67357
(316) 421-1430
Admin Jeannie Nichols.
Medical Dir F N Stephens DO.
Licensure Intermediate care. *Beds* ICF 60.
Certified Medicaid.
Owner Privately owned.
Admissions Requirements Minimum age 18;
Medical examination; Physician's request.
Staff RNs 1 (ft), 1 (pt); LPNs 1 (pt); Nurses'
aides 11 (ft), 2 (pt); Activities coordinators 2
(ft).
Facilities Dining room; Physical therapy
room; Activities room; Chapel; Crafts room;
Laundry room; Barber/Beauty shop.
Activities Arts & crafts; Cards; Games;
Reading groups; Prayer groups; Movies;
Shopping trips; Dances/Social/Cultural
gatherings.

Miner Nursing Home
814 Walnut, Parsons, KS 67357
(316) 236-7248
Admin Donna J McGlasson. *Dir of Nursing*
Judy Fromm RN.
Licensure Intermediate care. *Beds* ICF 41.
Certified Medicaid.
Owner Proprietary corp.
Admissions Requirements Minimum age 18;
Medical examination; Physician's request.
Staff RNs 1 (ft); LPNs 1 (pt); Nurses' aides 12
(ft), 2 (pt); Physical therapists 1 (pt); Reality
therapists 1 (pt); Recreational therapists 1
(pt); Occupational therapists 1 (pt); Speech
therapists 1 (pt); Activities coordinators 1
(ft); Dietitians 1 (pt); Podiatrists 1 (pt).
Facilities Dining room; Physical therapy
room; Activities room; Chapel; Crafts room;
Laundry room; Barber/Beauty shop; Library.
Activities Arts & crafts; Cards; Games;
Reading groups; Prayer groups; Movies;
Shopping trips; Dances/Social/Cultural
gatherings.

Parsons Good Samaritan Center
709 Leawood Dr, Parsons, KS 67357
(316) 421-1110
Admin Julie Marko. *Dir of Nursing* Joy
Wolgamott.
Licensure Intermediate care; Alzheimer's care.
Beds ICF 66. *Private Pay Patients* 50%.
Certified Medicaid.
Owner Nonprofit corp (Evangelical Lutheran/
Good Samaritan Society).
Admissions Requirements Minimum age 21;
Medical examination; Physician's request.
Staff RNs 3 (ft); LPNs 4 (ft); Nurses' aides 17
(ft), 3 (pt); Activities coordinators 1 (ft).
Affiliation Lutheran.
Facilities Dining room; Physical therapy
room; Activities room; Chapel; Crafts room;
Laundry room; Barber/Beauty shop.
Activities Arts & crafts; Cards; Games;
Reading groups; Movies; Shopping trips.

Parsons Presbyterian Manor
3501 Dirr, Parsons, KS 67357
(316) 421-1450
Admin Thomas L Gengler. *Dir of Nursing*
Dennis Riggs. *Medical Dir* Dr Dan Pauls.
Licensure Intermediate care; Home health-self
care; Retirement. *Beds* ICF 41; Home
health-self care 22. *Certified* Medicaid.
Owner Nonprofit corp.
Admissions Requirements Minimum age 65;
Medical examination; Physician's request.
Staff RNs 2 (ft); LPNs 2 (ft), 2 (pt); Nurses'
aides 18 (ft), 6 (pt); Physical therapists 1 (ft);
Recreational therapists 1 (ft), 1 (pt);
Activities coordinators 1 (ft), 1 (pt);
Dietitians 1 (ft).
Affiliation Presbyterian.
Facilities Dining room; Physical therapy
room; Activities room; Chapel; Crafts room;
Laundry room; Barber/Beauty shop; Library.
Activities Arts & crafts; Games; Prayer groups;
Movies; Shopping trips; Dances/Social/
Cultural gatherings.

Westbrook Manor Nursing Center
3500 W Broadway, Parsons, KS 67357
(316) 421-4180
Admin Wade Patton.
Licensure Intermediate care. *Beds* ICF 96.
Certified Medicaid.
Owner Privately owned.

Peabody

Peabody Memorial Nursing Home Inc
407 N Locust, Peabody, KS 66866
(316) 983-2152
Admin Shirley E Smith. *Dir of Nursing* Jane
Voth RN. *Medical Dir* Dr Ruth Sherman.
Licensure Intermediate care; Retirement. *Beds*
ICF 76. *Certified* Medicaid.
Owner Nonprofit corp.
Admissions Requirements Medical
examination.
Staff RNs 3 (ft), 2 (pt); LPNs 3 (ft), 1 (pt);
Activities coordinators 1 (ft), 1 (pt).
Facilities Dining room; Physical therapy
room; Chapel; Laundry room; Barber/Beauty
shop.
Activities Arts & crafts; Games; Reading
groups; Prayer groups; Movies; Shopping
trips.

Westview Nursing Center
4th & Peabody, Peabody, KS 66866
(316) 983-2165
Admin Teresa Sharp.
Medical Dir Dorothy Rhodes.
Licensure Intermediate care. *Beds* ICF 52.
Certified Medicaid.
Owner Proprietary corp (Beverly Enterprises).
Staff RNs 3 (ft); Nurses' aides 10 (ft), 3 (pt).
Facilities Dining room; Physical therapy
room; Activities room; Laundry room;
Barber/Beauty shop.
Activities Arts & crafts; Cards; Games;
Reading groups; Prayer groups; Movies;
Shopping trips; Dances/Social/Cultural
gatherings.

Phillipsburg

Evergreen Health Center
E Hwy 36, Box 628, Phillipsburg, KS 67661
(913) 543-5209
Admin Leonard Morfitt. *Dir of Nursing* Anne
Gower.
Licensure Intermediate care. *Beds* ICF 67.
Certified Medicaid.
Owner Proprietary corp.
Admissions Requirements Minimum age 18;
Medical examination; Physician's request.
Staff RNs 2 (ft); LPNs 3 (ft), 2 (pt); Nurses'
aides 3 (pt); Activities coordinators.
Facilities Dining room; Physical therapy
room; Activities room; Crafts room; Laundry
room; Barber/Beauty shop; Quiet room.

Activities Arts & crafts; Cards; Games;
Reading groups; Prayer groups; Movies;
Shopping trips; Dances/Social/Cultural
gatherings.

Phillips County Home
784 6th St, Phillipsburg, KS 67661
(913) 543-2131
Admin Sondra K Kester.
Licensure Intermediate care. *Beds* ICF 30.
Certified Medicaid.
Owner Publicly owned.
Staff LPNs 1 (ft), 2 (pt); Recreational
therapists 1 (pt); Activities coordinators 1
(ft).
Facilities Dining room; Laundry room;
Barber/Beauty shop.

Pittsburg

Beverly Nursing Center
1005 Centennial, Pittsburg, KS 66762
(316) 231-1120
Admin Wilma Van Houten.
Medical Dir Robin Nelson.
Licensure Intermediate care. *Beds* ICF 100.
Certified Medicaid.
Owner Proprietary corp (Beverly Enterprises).
Admissions Requirements Minimum age 18;
Medical examination; Physician's request.
Staff Physicians 1 (ft); RNs 3 (ft); LPNs 3 (ft);
Physical therapists 1 (ft); Reality therapists 1
(ft); Recreational therapists 1 (ft);
Occupational therapists 1 (ft); Speech
therapists 1 (ft); Activities coordinators 1
(ft); Dietitians 1 (ft); Podiatrists 1 (ft).
Facilities Dining room; Physical therapy
room; Activities room; Crafts room; Laundry
room; Barber/Beauty shop.
Activities Arts & crafts; Cards; Games;
Reading groups; Prayer groups; Movies;
Shopping trips; Dances/Social/Cultural
gatherings; Outings; Shopping; Fishing trips;
Picnics.

Medicalodge North of Pittsburg
2614 N Joplin, Pittsburg, KS 66762
(316) 231-3670
Admin Pamela Gould.
Licensure Skilled care; Intermediate care. *Beds*
SNF 32; ICF 48. *Certified* Medicaid;
Medicare.
Owner Proprietary corp (Medicalodges Inc).
Admissions Requirements Medical
examination.
Staff RNs 2 (ft); LPNs 5 (ft); Nurses' aides 25
(ft); Activities coordinators 1 (ft).
Facilities Dining room; Physical therapy
room; Activities room; Chapel; Crafts room;
Laundry room; Barber/Beauty shop.
Activities Arts & crafts; Cards; Games;
Reading groups; Prayer groups; Movies;
Shopping trips; Dances/Social/Cultural
gatherings.

Medicalodge South of Pittsburg
2520 S Rouse, Pittsburg, KS 66762
(316) 231-0300
Admin Karen Briggs. *Dir of Nursing* Jeanette
Redick. *Medical Dir* Dr G W Pogson.
Licensure Skilled care; Intermediate care. *Beds*
SNF 49; ICF 51. *Private Pay Patients* 40%.
Certified Medicaid; Medicare.
Owner Proprietary corp (Medicalodges Inc).
Admissions Requirements Medical
examination; Physician's request.
Staff Physicians 1 (ft); RNs 10 (ft); LPNs 8
(ft); Nurses' aides 40 (ft); Physical therapists
1 (ft); Occupational therapists 1 (ft); Speech
therapists 1 (ft); Activities coordinators 1
(ft); Dietitians 1 (ft).
Facilities Dining room; Physical therapy
room; Activities room; Chapel; Crafts room;
Laundry room; Barber/Beauty shop;
Hospitality room.

Activities Arts & crafts; Cards; Games;
Reading groups; Prayer groups; Movies;
Shopping trips; Dances/Social/Cultural
gatherings; Intergenerational programs; Pet
therapy.

New Horizons of Pittsburg
2702 N Joplin, Pittsburg, KS 66762
(316) 231-3910
Admin Jan Blevins.
Licensure Intermediate care for mentally
retarded. *Beds* ICF/MR 88. *Certified*
Medicaid.
Owner Proprietary corp (Medicalodges Inc).

Shields Adult Care Home Inc
2420 S Rouse, Pittsburg, KS 66762
(316) 231-5590
Admin Wilfred C Shields. *Dir of Nursing*
Gretchen Belfield RN. *Medical Dir* D M
Halsinger MD.
Licensure Intermediate care for mentally
retarded. *Beds* ICF/MR 50. *Certified*
Medicaid.
Owner Proprietary corp.
Admissions Requirements Minimum age 18;
Ambulatory only.
Staff Physicians 1 (pt); RNs 1 (ft); LPNs 2
(ft); Nurses' aides 30 (ft); Physical therapists
1 (pt); Occupational therapists 1 (pt); Speech
therapists 1 (pt); Activities coordinators 1
(ft); Dietitians 1 (pt); Ophthalmologists 1
(pt); Podiatrists 1 (pt); Dentists 1 (pt);
Psychologists 1 (ft); Social workers 1 (ft).
Facilities Dining room; Physical therapy
room; Activities room; Chapel; Crafts room;
Laundry room; Barber/Beauty shop; Library.
Activities Arts & crafts; Cards; Games;
Reading groups; Prayer groups; Movies;
Shopping trips; Dances/Social/Cultural
gatherings.

Plainville

Rooks County Home
1000 S Washington, Plainville, KS 67663
(913) 434-2846
Admin Forrest Burkholder.
Licensure Intermediate care. *Beds* ICF 52.
Certified Medicaid.
Owner Publicly owned.

Pleasanton

Pleasant View Manor Inc
1005 W 15th, Box 169, Pleasanton, KS 66075
(913) 352-8455
Admin Pamela K Sheets.
Medical Dir Dr Fred Dunlap.
Licensure Intermediate care. *Beds* ICF 50.
Certified Medicaid.
Owner Proprietary corp.
Admissions Requirements Minimum age 16;
Medical examination.
Staff Physicians 1 (pt); RNs 1 (pt); LPNs 2
(ft); Nurses' aides 20 (ft); Physical therapists
1 (pt); Occupational therapists 1 (pt); Speech
therapists 1 (pt); Activities coordinators 1
(pt); Dietitians 1 (pt); Ophthalmologists 1
(pt); Podiatrists 1 (pt); Audiologists 1 (pt);
Dentists 1 (pt).
Facilities Dining room; Physical therapy
room; Activities room; Chapel; Crafts room;
Laundry room; Barber/Beauty shop; Library.
Activities Arts & crafts; Cards; Games;
Reading groups; Prayer groups; Movies;
Shopping trips; Dances/Social/Cultural
gatherings.

Pratt

Lifecare of Pratt
1221 Larimer, Pratt, KS 67124
(316) 672-6541
Admin Barbara L Frazier. *Dir of Nursing*
Tracy Cavanaugh RN.

Licensure Intermediate care. *Beds* ICF 87.
Certified Medicaid.
Owner Proprietary corp (Life Care Centers of
Kansas).
Admissions Requirements Medical
examination.

Siesta Home of Pratt Inc
227 S Howard, Pratt, KS 67124
(316) 672-5971
Admin Linda M Young. *Dir of Nursing* Deb
Toombs RN.
Licensure Intermediate care. *Beds* ICF 55.
Certified Medicaid.
Owner Proprietary corp.
Admissions Requirements Medical
examination; Physician's request.
Staff RNs 2 (ft); LPNs 1 (ft); Nurses' aides 15
(ft); Physical therapists 1 (pt); Occupational
therapists 1 (pt); Speech therapists 1 (pt);
Activities coordinators 1 (ft); Dietitians 1
(pt); Podiatrists.
Facilities Dining room; Physical therapy
room; Activities room; Chapel; Crafts room;
Laundry room; Barber/Beauty shop.
Activities Arts & crafts; Cards; Games;
Reading groups; Prayer groups; Movies;
Shopping trips; Dances/Social/Cultural
gatherings; Joy rides.

Prescott

Prescott Country View Nursing Home
PO Box 37, Hwy 239, Prescott, KS 66767
(913) 471-4315
Admin Betty S Keiser. *Dir of Nursing* Mary
Smith; Debbie Diehl. *Medical Dir* Dr R R
Nichols.
Licensure Intermediate care. *Beds* ICF 50.
Private Pay Patients 70%. *Certified*
Medicaid.
Owner Publicly owned.
Admissions Requirements Minimum age 20;
Medical examination.
Staff Physicians 3 (pt); RNs 1 (pt); LPNs 3
(ft), 2 (pt); Nurses' aides 17 (ft), 8 (pt);
Physical therapists 1 (pt); Occupational
therapists 1 (pt); Speech therapists 1 (pt);
Activities coordinators 1 (pt); Dietitians 1
(pt); Ophthalmologists 1 (pt); Podiatrists 1
(pt); Audiologists 1 (pt).
Facilities Dining room; Physical therapy
room; Activities room; Chapel; Crafts room;
Laundry room; Barber/Beauty shop.
Activities Arts & crafts; Cards; Games; Prayer
groups; Movies; Dances/Social/Cultural
gatherings; Pet therapy; Volunteer program.

Pretty Prairie

Prairie Sunset Home
601 E Main, Pretty Prairie, KS 67570
(316) 459-6822
Admin Janice Krehbiel.
Licensure Intermediate care. *Beds* ICF 45.
Certified Medicaid.
Owner Nonprofit corp.

Protection

Protection Valley Manor
600 S Broadway, Protection, KS 67127
(316) 622-4261
Admin Rex Maris. *Dir of Nursing* Frances
Edmonston.
Licensure Intermediate care; Alzheimer's care.
Beds ICF 50. *Private Pay Patients* 26%.
Certified Medicaid.
Owner Publicly owned.
Admissions Requirements Medical
examination; Physician's request.
Staff RNs 1 (pt); LPNs 1 (ft), 1 (pt); Nurses'
aides 12 (ft), 6 (pt); Physical therapists 1 (ft);
Activities coordinators 1 (ft); Dietitians 1
(ft).

Facilities Dining room; Physical therapy
room; Activities room; Chapel; Crafts room;
Laundry room; Barber/Beauty shop;
Alzheimer's; Van.
Activities Arts & crafts; Cards; Games;
Reading groups; Prayer groups; Movies;
Shopping trips; Dances/Social/Cultural
gatherings.

Richmond

Oakhaven Nursing Center
340 South St, Richmond, KS 66080
(913) 835-6135
Admin Mary Sue Cox. *Dir of Nursing* Barbara
Neal RN.
Licensure Intermediate care; Alzheimer's care.
Beds ICF 53. *Certified* Medicaid.
Owner Publicly owned.
Admissions Requirements Minimum age 16;
Medical examination; Physician's request.
Staff RNs 2 (ft), 1 (pt); LPNs 2 (ft); Nurses'
aides 20 (ft), 10 (pt); Activities coordinators
1 (ft); Dietitians 1 (pt).
Facilities Dining room; Physical therapy
room; Activities room; Chapel; Crafts room;
Laundry room; Barber/Beauty shop; Library;
Greenhouse.
Activities Arts & crafts; Cards; Games;
Reading groups; Prayer groups; Movies;
Shopping trips; Dances/Social/Cultural
gatherings.

Rose Hill

Heritage Village of Rose Hill
601 N Rose Hill Rd, Rose Hill, KS 67133
(316) 776-2194
Admin Debra A Houk.
Licensure Intermediate care. *Beds* ICF 60.
Certified Medicaid.
Owner Proprietary corp (Beverly Enterprises).

Rossville

Rossville Valley Manor
600 Perry, Rossville, KS 66533-0787
(913) 584-6104
Admin Aaron D Kelley Jr. *Dir of Nursing* Lisa
S Landis RN. *Medical Dir* Myron
Leinwetter DO.
Licensure Intermediate care; Alzheimer's care.
Beds ICF 91. *Private Pay Patients* 55%.
Certified Medicaid.
Owner Proprietary corp.
Staff Physicians 1 (pt); RNs 2 (ft); LPNs 8
(ft); Nurses' aides 25 (ft); Physical therapists
1 (pt); Speech therapists 1 (pt); Activities
coordinators 2 (ft); Dietitians 1 (pt).
Facilities Dining room; Physical therapy
room; Activities room; Crafts room; Laundry
room; Barber/Beauty shop.
Activities Arts & crafts; Cards; Games;
Reading groups; Prayer groups; Movies;
Shopping trips; Dances/Social/Cultural
gatherings; Intergenerational programs; Pet
therapy.

Russell

Ala Fern Nursing Home
225 E Jewell, Russell, KS 67665
(913) 483-6555
Admin Helen E Janes.
Medical Dir Karleen Wolf.
Licensure Intermediate care. *Beds* ICF 46.
Certified Medicaid.
Owner Proprietary corp (Americare Systems
Inc).
Admissions Requirements Minimum age 18;
Medical examination; Physician's request.
Staff Physicians 4 (pt); RNs 2 (ft); LPNs 2
(ft); Nurses' aides 10 (ft), 2 (pt); Physical
therapists 1 (pt); Recreational therapists 1
(ft); Occupational therapists 1 (pt); Speech
therapists 1 (pt); Activities coordinators 2

(ft); Dietitians 1 (pt); Ophthalmologists 1 (pt); Audiologists 1 (pt); Psychologist 1 (pt); Social worker 1 (pt).
Facilities Dining room; Physical therapy room; Activities room; Chapel; Laundry room; Barber/Beauty shop; Library; TV lounge; Quiet room.
Activities Arts & crafts; Cards; Games; Reading groups; Prayer groups; Movies; Shopping trips; Dances/Social/Cultural gatherings; Sunday school; Church services; Individual & group therapy.

Wheatland Nursing
320 S Lincoln, Russell, KS 67665
(913) 483-5364
Admin Janice Kay Schertz. *Dir of Nursing* Brenda Marcus.
Licensure Intermediate care. *Beds* ICF 70. *Private Pay Patients* 33%. *Certified* Medicaid.
Owner Proprietary corp (Americare Systems Inc).
Admissions Requirements Medical examination.
Staff RNs 1 (ft); LPNs 4 (ft); Nurses' aides 20 (ft), 10 (pt); Physical therapists 1 (pt); Reality therapists 1 (pt); Recreational therapists 1 (pt); Occupational therapists 1 (pt); Speech therapists 1 (pt); Activities coordinators 1 (ft); Dietitians (consultant); Ophthalmologists (consultant); Podiatrists (consultant); Audiologists (consultant).
Languages German.
Facilities Dining room; Physical therapy room; Activities room; Crafts room; Laundry room; Barber/Beauty shop.
Activities Arts & crafts; Cards; Games; Reading groups; Prayer groups; Movies; Shopping trips; Dances/Social/Cultural gatherings; Intergenerational programs; Pet therapy.

Sabetha

Apostolic Christian Home
511 Paramount, Sabetha, KS 66534
(913) 284-3471
Admin John E Lehman. *Dir of Nursing* Ann Kent RN. *Medical Dir* Kevin P Kennally.
Licensure Intermediate care; Adult day care; Retirement. *Beds* ICF 91; Retirement 87. *Private Pay Patients* 78%. *Certified* Medicaid.
Owner Nonprofit corp.
Staff RNs 3 (ft), 8 (pt); LPNs 1 (ft), 5 (pt); Nurses' aides 10 (ft), 24 (pt); Physical therapists (consultant); Reality therapists (consultant); Recreational therapists 1 (ft); Occupational therapists (consultant); Speech therapists (consultant); Activities coordinators (consultant); Dietitians (consultant); Ophthalmologists (consultant); Podiatrists (consultant); Audiologists (consultant).
Affiliation Apostolic Christian.
Facilities Dining room; Physical therapy room; Activities room; Chapel; Crafts room; Laundry room; Barber/Beauty shop; Library; Branch bank.
Activities Arts & crafts; Cards; Games; Reading groups; Prayer groups; Movies; Shopping trips; Dances/Social/Cultural gatherings; Pet therapy.

Fountain Villa Care Center
913 Dakota, Sabetha, KS 66534
(913) 284-3418
Admin Marlin M Johnson.
Licensure Intermediate care. *Beds* ICF 60. *Certified* Medicaid.
Owner Proprietary corp.
Admissions Requirements Medical examination.
Staff RNs 1 (ft); LPNs 1 (ft); Nurses' aides 19 (ft), 9 (pt); Physical therapists 2 (pt); Reality therapists 1 (ft); Occupational therapists 1

(pt); Speech therapists 1 (pt); Activities coordinators 1 (pt); Dietitians 1 (ft), 1 (pt); Dentists 1 (pt).
Facilities Dining room; Physical therapy room; Activities room; Crafts room; Laundry room; Barber/Beauty shop; Library.
Activities Arts & crafts; Cards; Games; Reading groups; Prayer groups; Movies; Shopping trips; Dances/Social/Cultural gatherings.

Sabetha Manor
1441 Oregon St, Sabetha, KS 66534
(913) 284-3411
Admin Homer R Branham. *Dir of Nursing* Roma Hervey RN. *Medical Dir* Gregg Wenger MD.
Licensure Intermediate care; Alzheimer's care. *Beds* ICF 60. *Private Pay Patients* 25%. *Certified* Medicaid.
Owner Proprietary corp (Americare Systems Inc).
Admissions Requirements Minimum age 17; Medical examination.
Staff Physicians 3 (pt); RNs 2 (ft); LPNs 2 (ft), 2 (pt); Nurses' aides 10 (ft), 7 (pt); Physical therapists 3 (pt); Recreational therapists 1 (ft); Occupational therapists 1 (pt); Speech therapists 1 (pt); Activities coordinators 1 (ft); Dietitians 1 (pt); Ophthalmologists 1 (pt); Podiatrists 1 (pt); Audiologists 1 (pt).
Facilities Dining room; Physical therapy room; Activities room; Crafts room; Laundry room; Barber/Beauty shop.
Activities Arts & crafts; Cards; Games; Reading groups; Prayer groups; Movies; Shopping trips; Dances/Social/Cultural gatherings; Intergenerational programs; Pet therapy.

Saint Francis

Good Samaritan Village
S Side Hwy 36, Box 747, Saint Francis, KS 67756
(913) 332-2531
Admin Michael H Fleming.
Licensure Intermediate care. *Beds* ICF 57. *Certified* Medicaid.
Owner Nonprofit corp (Evangelical Lutheran/ Good Samaritan Society).
Affiliation Lutheran.

Saint John

Hearthstone Nursing Center
4th & Sante Fe, Saint John, KS 67576
(316) 549-3541
Admin Susan Kersenbrock. *Dir of Nursing* Michelle Hatfield LPN HSS. *Medical Dir* F J Farmer III.
Licensure Intermediate care. *Beds* ICF 68. *Certified* Medicaid.
Owner Proprietary corp (Beverly Enterprises).
Admissions Requirements Medical examination.
Staff LPNs 3 (ft); Nurses' aides 23 (ft); Activities coordinators 1 (ft).
Facilities Dining room; Physical therapy room; Activities room; Laundry room; Barber/Beauty shop; 2 Living rooms; Feeder room.
Activities Arts & crafts; Cards; Games; Reading groups; Prayer groups; Movies; Shopping trips; Dances/Social/Cultural gatherings; Intergenerational programs; Pet therapy.

Saint Marys

St Marys Manor
206 Grand Ave, Saint Marys, KS 66536
(913) 437-2286
Admin Michael E McCrite.

Licensure Intermediate care. *Beds* ICF 50. *Certified* Medicaid.
Owner Proprietary corp.

Saint Paul

Living Skills Center
5th & Lafayette Box 27, Saint Paul, KS 66771
(316) 449-2277
Admin Judity Foebe.
Medical Dir Asha Verma MD.
Licensure Intermediate care for mentally retarded. *Beds* ICF/MR 60. *Certified* Medicaid.
Owner Proprietary corp (Beverly Enterprises).
Admissions Requirements Minimum age 18; Medical examination; Physician's request.
Staff Physicians 1 (pt); RNs 1 (ft); LPNs 1 (ft); Nurses' aides 25 (ft), 15 (pt); Physical therapists 1 (pt); Recreational therapists 1 (ft); Occupational therapists 1 (pt); Speech therapists 1 (pt); Activities coordinators 1 (ft); Dietitians 1 (pt); Ophthalmologists 1 (pt); Podiatrists 1 (pt); Audiologists 1 (pt); Dentists 1 (pt).
Facilities Dining room; Physical therapy room; Activities room; Crafts room; Laundry room; Barber/Beauty shop.
Activities Arts & crafts; Cards; Games; Reading groups; Prayer groups; Movies; Shopping trips; Dances/Social/Cultural gatherings; Special Olympics.

Salina

College Park Village
Box 217, 2925 Florida Ave, Salina, KS 67401
(913) 8256954
Admin Alice Canfield.
Licensure Intermediate care. *Beds* ICF 60.
Owner Proprietary corp.

Kenwood View Nursing Home
900 Elmhurst Blvd, Salina, KS 67401
(913) 825-5471
Admin Bob Hodge.
Licensure Skilled care. *Beds* SNF 94. *Certified* Medicaid.
Owner Proprietary corp.

Salina Nursing Center
1007 Johnstown, Salina, KS 67401
(913) 823-7107
Admin Joleen Hasker. *Dir of Nursing* Dorienne Sleek. *Medical Dir* Dr Shafer.
Licensure Skilled care; Intermediate care. *Beds* SNF 28; ICF 78. *Private Pay Patients* 35%. *Certified* Medicaid; Medicare.
Owner Proprietary corp (Pinnacle Care Corp).
Admissions Requirements Medical examination.
Facilities Dining room; Physical therapy room; Activities room; Chapel; Crafts room; Laundry room; Barber/Beauty shop; Gazebo; Garden area; Courtyard.
Activities Arts & crafts; Cards; Games; Reading groups; Prayer groups; Movies; Shopping trips; Dances/Social/Cultural gatherings; Intergenerational programs; Pet therapy; Gardening.

Salina Presbyterian Manor
2601 E Crawford, Salina, KS 67401
(913) 825-1366
Admin James C Moore. *Dir of Nursing* Betty L Roberts RN.
Licensure Skilled care; Retirement. *Beds* SNF 60; Retirement 95. *Private Pay Patients* 93%. *Certified* Medicaid.
Owner Nonprofit organization/foundation (Presbyterian Manors Inc).
Admissions Requirements Minimum age 65; Medical examination; Physician's request.

Staff RNs 4 (ft), 1 (pt); LPNs 1 (ft), 1 (pt);
Nurses' aides 16 (ft), 7 (pt); Physical
therapists (consultant); Activities
coordinators 1 (ft); CMAs 4 (ft), 2 (pt);
Physical therapy aides 1 (ft).
Affiliation Presbyterian.
Facilities Dining room; Physical therapy
room; Activities room; Chapel; Crafts room;
Laundry room; Barber/Beauty shop; Library.
Activities Arts & crafts; Cards; Games;
Reading groups; Prayer groups; Movies;
Shopping trips; Dances/Social/Cultural
gatherings; Pet therapy.

Shalimar Plaza Nursing Home
2054 Lambertson Ln, Salina, KS 67401
(913) 827-5589
Admin Alice M Canfield.
Medical Dir Brenda Ward.
Licensure Intermediate care. *Beds* ICF 46.
Certified Medicaid.
Owner Proprietary corp.
Admissions Requirements Minimum age 21;
Medical examination; Physician's request.
Staff RNs 1 (pt); LPNs 3 (ft), 3 (pt); Nurses'
aides 12 (ft), 2 (pt); Physical therapists 1
(pt); Recreational therapists 1 (ft);
Occupational therapists 1 (pt); Activities
coordinators 1 (ft); Dietitians 1 (pt).
Facilities Dining room; Physical therapy
room; Activities room; Crafts room; Laundry
room; Barber/Beauty shop.
Activities Arts & crafts; Games; Reading
groups; Prayer groups; Movies; Dances/
Social/Cultural gatherings.

Windsor Estates Nursing Home
623 S 3rd, Salina, KS 67401
(913) 825-6757
Admin Fae Mann.
Medical Dir Dr Lou Forster.
Licensure Skilled care. *Beds* SNF 60. *Certified*
Medicaid; Medicare.
Owner Proprietary corp.
Facilities Dining room; Physical therapy
room; Activities room; Crafts room; Laundry
room; Barber/Beauty shop.
Activities Arts & crafts; Cards; Games;
Reading groups; Prayer groups; Movies;
Shopping trips; Dances/Social/Cultural
gatherings.

Scott City

Park Lane Nursing Home
13th & College, Scott City, KS 67871
(316) 872-2148
Admin Gregory W Uhruh.
Licensure Intermediate care. *Beds* ICF 84.
Certified Medicaid.
Admissions Requirements Medical
examination; Physician's request.
Staff RNs 2 (ft), 1 (pt); LPNs 2 (ft), 1 (pt);
Nurses' aides 21 (ft), 9 (pt); Physical
therapists 1 (pt); Activities coordinators 1
(ft); Dietitians 1 (pt).
Facilities Dining room; Physical therapy
room; Activities room; Chapel; Crafts room;
Laundry room; Barber/Beauty shop.
Activities Arts & crafts; Cards; Games;
Reading groups; Prayer groups; Movies;
Shopping trips; Dances/Social/Cultural
gatherings.

Sedan

Pleasant Valley Manor
PO Box 40, 623 E Elm St, Sedan, KS 67361
(316) 725-3154
Admin Carmaleta J Lorenz.
Medical Dir Nancy Turner.
Licensure Intermediate care. *Beds* ICF 67.
Certified Medicaid.
Owner Proprietary corp (Americare Systems
Inc).
Admissions Requirements Medical
examination; Physician's request.

Staff RNs 1 (pt); LPNs 4 (ft), 2 (pt); Nurses'
aides 21 (ft); Physical therapists 1 (pt);
Reality therapists 1 (pt); Recreational
therapists 1 (pt); Speech therapists 1 (pt);
Activities coordinators 1 (ft); Podiatrists 1
(pt); Dentists 1 (pt).
Facilities Dining room; Physical therapy
room; Activities room; Chapel; Crafts room;
Laundry room; Barber/Beauty shop.
Activities Arts & crafts; Games; Prayer groups;
Movies; Bowling; Bus trips.

Sedgwick

Sedgwick Convalescent Center
712 Monroe Box 49, Sedgwick, KS 67135
(316) 772-5185
Admin Jan K Collins. *Dir of Nursing* Nita
King RN.
Licensure Intermediate care. *Beds* ICF 95.
Certified Medicaid.
Owner Proprietary corp (Hillhaven Corp).
Admissions Requirements Medical
examination; Physician's request.
Staff RNs 2 (ft), 1 (pt); LPNs 4 (ft); Nurses'
aides 23 (ft); Physical therapists 1 (pt);
Occupational therapists 1 (pt); Speech
therapists 1 (pt); Activities coordinators 1
(ft).
Facilities Dining room; Physical therapy
room; Activities room; Crafts room; Barber/
Beauty shop.
Activities Arts & crafts; Cards; Games;
Reading groups; Prayer groups; Movies;
Dances/Social/Cultural gatherings.

Seneca

Country View Estates
512 Community Dr, Seneca, KS 66538
(913) 336-3528
Admin Edna Jane Werner. *Dir of Nursing*
Janet Hermesch RN.
Licensure Intermediate care. *Beds* ICF 75.
Private Pay Patients 68%. *Certified*
Medicaid.
Owner Proprietary corp (Life Care Centers of
America).
Admissions Requirements Minimum age 16;
Medical examination.
Staff RNs 2 (ft); LPNs 4 (ft), 1 (pt); Nurses'
aides 12 (ft), 17 (pt); Activities coordinators
1 (ft), 1 (pt); Dietitians 1 (pt).
Facilities Dining room; Physical therapy
room; Activities room; Laundry room;
Barber/Beauty shop.
Activities Arts & crafts; Cards; Games;
Reading groups; Prayer groups; Movies;
Dances/Social/Cultural gatherings;
Intergenerational programs; Pet therapy.

Crestview Manor
808 N 8th, Seneca, KS 66538
(913) 336-2156
Admin Arlene Wessel.
Licensure Intermediate care. *Beds* ICF 50.
Certified Medicaid.
Owner Proprietary corp.

Sharon Springs

Prairie Manor Rest Home
HCL Box 20, 408 E 6th, Sharon Springs, KS
67758
(913) 852-4244
Admin Roberta O'Leary. *Dir of Nursing* Ruby
Voth RN.
Licensure Intermediate care. *Beds* ICF 28.
Private Pay Patients 39%. *Certified*
Medicaid.
Owner Publicly owned.
Admissions Requirements Medical
examination.
Staff Physicians; RNs 1 (ft), 1 (pt); LPNs 2
(ft); Nurses' aides 9 (ft), 6 (pt); Physical
therapists; Reality therapists; Recreational

therapists 1 (ft), 1 (pt); Occupational
therapists; Speech therapists; Activities
coordinators 1 (ft), 1 (pt); Dietitians 2 (ft), 2
(pt); Ophthalmologists; Podiatrists;
Audiologists.
Facilities Dining room; Physical therapy
room; Activities room; Laundry room;
Barber/Beauty shop.
Activities Arts & crafts; Cards; Games;
Reading groups; Prayer groups; Movies;
Shopping trips; Dances/Social/Cultural
gatherings; Intergenerational programs; Pet
therapy; Special holiday events.

Shawnee

Sharonlane Inc
10315 Johnson Dr, Shawnee, KS 66203
(913) 631-8200
Admin Katharine Ensign. *Dir of Nursing* Betty
C Price RN.
Licensure Intermediate care. *Beds* ICF 66.
Owner Nonprofit corp (Adventist Health
Systems).
Staff RNs 3 (ft), 1 (pt); LPNs 2 (ft); Nurses'
aides 20 (ft), 2 (pt); Activities coordinators 1
(ft).
Facilities Dining room; Physical therapy
room; Activities room; Laundry room;
Barber/Beauty shop; Library.
Activities Arts & crafts; Cards; Games;
Reading groups; Prayer groups; Movies.

Shawnee Mission

Faith Handicap Village 1, 2, 3
14155 W 113th St, Shawnee Mission, KS
66215
(913) 469-5566
Admin Richard L Schmitz. *Dir of Nursing*
Judie Gornetzki RN.
Licensure Intermediate care for mentally
retarded. *Beds* ICF/MR 45. *Certified*
Medicaid.
Owner Nonprofit corp.
Admissions Requirements Minimum age 18.
Staff RNs 1 (pt); LPNs 2 (pt); Nurses' aides
25 (ft), 4 (pt); Physical therapists 1 (pt);
Speech therapists 1 (pt); Activities
coordinators 1 (ft); Dietitians 1 (pt);
Recreation aides 6 (pt); Dietary aides 3 (pt);
House managers 3 (pt); Social worker 1 (pt).
Facilities Dining room; Activities room;
Laundry room.
Activities Arts & crafts; Games; Shopping
trips; Special Olympics.

Smith Center

Bethesda Care Center
117 W 1st St Box 369, Smith Center, KS
66967
(913) 282-6696
Admin Shirley Steen. *Dir of Nursing* Leigh
Berthol. *Medical Dir* Dr V W Steinkruger.
Licensure Intermediate care. *Beds* ICF 83.
Certified Medicaid.
Owner Proprietary corp.
Admissions Requirements Medical
examination.
Staff RNs 1 (ft); LPNs 2 (ft); Nurses' aides 40
(ft).
Facilities Dining room; Physical therapy
room; Activities room; Chapel; Crafts room;
Laundry room; Barber/Beauty shop; Library.
Activities Arts & crafts; Cards; Games;
Reading groups; Prayer groups; Movies;
Shopping trips.

South Haven

Wheatland Lodge
PO Box 198, South Haven, KS 67140
(316) 892-5513
Admin Arif Haider.
Medical Dir Denise Showman.

Licensure Intermediate care. *Beds* ICF 50.
Certified Medicaid.
Owner Publicly owned.
Admissions Requirements Physician's request.
Staff RNs 1 (ft), 2 (pt); LPNs 2 (ft), 1 (pt);
Nurses' aides 19 (ft), 7 (pt); Physical
therapists 1 (ft); Reality therapists 1 (ft);
Recreational therapists 1 (ft); Occupational
therapists 1 (ft); Activities coordinators 1
(ft).
Facilities Dining room; Physical therapy
room; Activities room; Chapel; Crafts room;
Laundry room; Barber/Beauty shop;
Smoking lounge.
Activities Arts & crafts; Cards; Games;
Reading groups; Prayer groups; Movies;
Shopping trips; Dances/Social/Cultural
gatherings; Exercise; Picnic trips.

South Hutchinson

Mennonite Friendship Manor Inc
600 W Blanchard, South Hutchinson, KS
67505
(316) 663-7175
Admin Allen L Holsopple. *Dir of Nursing*
Bette Hirst RN.
Licensure Intermediate care; Retirement. *Beds*
ICF 120; Retirement apts 64. *Private Pay
Patients* 60%. *Certified* Medicaid.
Owner Nonprofit organization/foundation.
Admissions Requirements Medical
examination; Physician's request.
Staff RNs 10 (ft), 4 (pt); LPNs 8 (ft), 4 (pt);
Nurses' aides 45 (ft), 10 (pt); Physical
therapists 1 (pt); Occupational therapists 1
(pt); Speech therapists 1 (pt); Activities
coordinators 2 (ft), 2 (pt); Dietitians 1 (ft), 1
(pt); Audiologists 1 (pt); Music therapists.
Languages Spanish, German.
Affiliation Mennonite.
Facilities Dining room; Physical therapy
room; Activities room; Chapel; Crafts room;
Laundry room; Barber/Beauty shop; Library.
Activities Arts & crafts; Cards; Games;
Reading groups; Prayer groups; Movies;
Shopping trips; Dances/Social/Cultural
gatherings; Intergenerational programs; Pet
therapy; Chime choir & rhythm band.

Spring Hill

Spring Hill Nursing Center
251 Wilson Ave, Spring Hill, KS 66083
(913) 686-3100
Admin Frances Ann Keearns.
Medical Dir Golda Colles.
Licensure Intermediate care. *Beds* ICF 50.
Certified Medicaid.
Owner Privately owned (Life Care Centers of
Kansas Inc).
Admissions Requirements Medical
examination; Physician's request.
Staff LPNs 3 (ft), 1 (pt); Nurses' aides 12 (ft),
5 (pt); Physical therapists 1 (pt);
Recreational therapists 1 (pt); Occupational
therapists 1 (pt); Speech therapists 1 (pt);
Activities coordinators 1 (ft); Dietitians 1
(pt).
Facilities Dining room; Physical therapy
room; Activities room; Crafts room; Laundry
room; Barber/Beauty shop; Library.
Activities Arts & crafts; Cards; Games;
Reading groups; Prayer groups; Movies;
Shopping trips; Dances/Social/Cultural
gatherings.

Stafford

Leisure Homestead Association
405 E Grand, Stafford, KS 67578
(316) 234-5208
Admin Jennifer Younie. *Dir of Nursing*
Maradean Cox.

Licensure Intermediate care; Retirement. *Beds*
ICF 60; Retirement apts 12. *Private Pay
Patients* 70%. *Certified* Medicaid.
Owner Nonprofit organization/foundation.
Admissions Requirements Minimum age 16;
Medical examination; Physician's request.
Staff RNs 1 (ft); LPNs 3 (ft), 1 (pt); Nurses'
aides 18 (ft), 2 (pt); Physical therapists
(consultant); Occupational therapists 1 (pt);
Speech therapists 1 (pt); Activities
coordinators 1 (ft), 1 (pt); Dietitians 1 (pt);
Audiologists 1 (pt).
Facilities Dining room; Physical therapy
room; Activities room; Laundry room;
Barber/Beauty shop.
Activities Arts & crafts; Cards; Games;
Reading groups; Prayer groups; Movies;
Shopping trips; Dances/Social/Cultural
gatherings; Intergenerational programs; Pet
therapy.

Sterling

Sterling Presbyterian Manor
204 W Washington, Sterling, KS 67579
(319) 278-3651
Admin Sadie P Goodwin. *Dir of Nursing* Dee
Fabin RN.
Licensure Intermediate care; Retirement. *Beds*
ICF 60. *Certified* Medicaid.
Owner Nonprofit corp.
Admissions Requirements Minimum age 65;
Females only.
Staff RNs 4 (ft); LPNs 3 (ft); Nurses' aides 25
(ft), 3 (pt); Activities coordinators 1 (ft).
Affiliation Presbyterian.
Facilities Dining room; Physical therapy
room; Activities room; Chapel; Crafts room;
Laundry room; Barber/Beauty shop; Library.
Activities Arts & crafts; Cards; Games;
Reading groups; Prayer groups; Movies;
Shopping trips; Dances/Social/Cultural
gatherings.

Stockton

Solomon Valley Manor
315 S Ash, Stockton, KS 67669
(913) 425-6109
Admin Betty Locke.
Medical Dir Kris Glendening.
Licensure Intermediate care. *Beds* ICF 50.
Certified Medicaid.
Owner Proprietary corp.
Staff RNs; LPNs; Nurses' aides; Physical
therapists; Activities coordinators; Dietitians.
Facilities Dining room; Laundry room;
Barber/Beauty shop.
Activities Games; Prayer groups; Movies.

Syracuse

Hamilton County Rest Home
E "G" St, Syracuse, KS 67878
(316) 384-7780
Admin Kathryn D Zimmett.
Medical Dir Dr C E Petterson.
Licensure Intermediate care. *Beds* ICF 21.
Certified Medicaid.
Owner Publicly owned.
Admissions Requirements Minimum age 21;
Medical examination; Physician's request.
Staff Physicians 2 (pt); RNs 2 (pt); LPNs 2
(ft); Nurses' aides 7 (ft), 8 (pt); Physical
therapists 1 (pt); Activities coordinators 1
(ft), 1 (pt); Dietitians 1 (pt);
Ophthalmologists 1 (pt); Podiatrists 1 (pt);
Dentists 1 (pt).
Facilities Dining room; Physical therapy
room; Activities room; Chapel; Crafts room;
Laundry room; Barber/Beauty shop.
Activities Arts & crafts; Cards; Games;
Reading groups; Prayer groups; Movies;
Shopping trips; Dances/Social/Cultural
gatherings.

Tonganoxie

Tonganoxie Nursing Center
Box 940, 1010 E St, Tonganoxie, KS 66086
(913) 845-2777
Admin Lois Gulick. *Dir of Nursing* Fran
Marquardt.
Licensure Intermediate care. *Beds* ICF 50.
Private Pay Patients 28%. *Certified*
Medicaid.
Owner Proprietary corp (Beverly Enterprises).
Staff LPNs 7 (ft); Nurses' aides 45 (ft);
Recreational therapists 1 (ft); Occupational
therapists 1 (ft); Activities coordinators 1
(ft); Dietitians.

Topeka

Aldersgate Village Health Unit
3220 Albright Dr, Topeka, KS 66614
(913) 478-9440
Admin Janice M Jenkins. *Dir of Nursing* Pam
Lynch. *Medical Dir* Larry Rumans MD.
Licensure Skilled care; Personal care;
Alzheimer's care. *Beds* SNF 60; Personal
care 55. *Certified* Medicaid.
Owner Nonprofit corp.
Admissions Requirements Minimum age 16;
Medical examination; Physician's request.
Staff Physicians 2 (pt); RNs 4 (ft), 4 (pt);
LPNs 7 (ft); Nurses' aides 18 (ft), 8 (pt);
Physical therapists 1 (pt); Occupational
therapists 1 (pt); Speech therapists 1 (pt);
Activities coordinators 3 (ft), 2 (pt);
Dietitians 1 (ft), 1 (pt); Ophthalmologists 1
(pt); Podiatrists 1 (pt); Dentists 1 (pt);
Massage Therapists 1 (pt).
Affiliation Methodist.
Facilities Dining room; Physical therapy
room; Activities room; Chapel; Crafts room;
Laundry room; Barber/Beauty shop; Library;
Outpatient clinic rooms; Dental office;
Sundries shop; Wood shop; Spa; Handicap
kitchen; Enclosed outdoor patios.
Activities Arts & crafts; Cards; Games;
Reading groups; Prayer groups; Movies;
Shopping trips; Dances/Social/Cultural
gatherings; Pet therapy; Music therapy;
Men's breakfast; Ladies' tea; Creative
cooking; Exercise classes; Spelling bee;
Quizical quizzes; Play reading; Gardening;
Resident council; Van rides.

Brewster Place
1205 W 29th St, Topeka, KS 66611
(913) 267-1667
Admin Ronald A Schmoller. *Dir of Nursing*
Virginia Tevis. *Medical Dir* Dr Michael
Atwood.
Licensure Skilled care; Alzheimer's care;
Retirement. *Beds* SNF 77; Retirement apts
265. *Private Pay Patients* 90%. *Certified*
Medicaid; Medicare.
Owner Nonprofit organization/foundation.
Admissions Requirements Minimum age 62.
Staff Physicians 1 (pt); RNs 5 (ft), 10 (pt);
LPNs 2 (ft), 1 (pt); Nurses' aides 24 (ft), 15
(pt); Physical therapists 1 (pt); Reality
therapists 1 (ft); Recreational therapists 1
(ft); Occupational therapists 1 (pt); Speech
therapists 1 (pt); Activities coordinators 1
(ft); Dietitians 1 (pt); Podiatrists 1 (pt);
Audiologists 1 (pt).
Affiliation Congregational.
Facilities Dining room; Physical therapy
room; Activities room; Chapel; Crafts room;
Laundry room; Barber/Beauty shop; Library.
Activities Arts & crafts; Cards; Games;
Reading groups; Prayer groups; Movies;
Shopping trips; Dances/Social/Cultural
gatherings; Intergenerational programs; Pet
therapy.

Briarcliff Manor Inc
3224 W 29th St, Topeka, KS 66614
(913) 272-2601
Admin Mary Ann Warren.

Topeka / KANSAS / 445

Medical Dir Dr William Wade.
Licensure Intermediate care. *Beds* ICF 60.
  Certified Medicaid.
Owner Proprietary corp.
Admissions Requirements Medical
  examination; Physician's request.
Staff RNs 1 (pt); LPNs 4 (ft), 2 (pt); Nurses'
  aides 15 (ft), 4 (pt); Physical therapists 1
  (pt); Activities coordinators 1 (ft); Dietitians
  1 (pt).
Facilities Dining room; Physical therapy
  room; Activities room; Crafts room; Laundry
  room; Barber/Beauty shop; TV room; Quiet
  room; Sitting room.
Activities Arts & crafts; Cards; Games;
  Reading groups; Prayer groups; Movies;
  Shopping trips; Dances/Social/Cultural
  gatherings; Community speakers.

Brighton Place North
1301 N Jefferson, Topeka, KS 66608
(913) 233-5127
Admin David S Tuttle. *Dir of Nursing* Patricia
  Hinton. *Medical Dir* Glenn O Bair MD.
Licensure Intermediate care. *Beds* ICF 34.
  Certified Medicaid.
Owner Proprietary corp.
Admissions Requirements Minimum age 18;
  Medical examination; Physician's request.
Staff Physicians 2 (pt); RNs 1 (pt); LPNs 5
  (ft), 1 (pt); Nurses' aides 7 (ft), 1 (pt);
  Activities coordinators 1 (ft); Dietitians 3
  (ft), 1 (pt).
Facilities Dining room; Physical therapy
  room; Activities room; Laundry room;
  Barber/Beauty shop.
Activities Arts & crafts; Cards; Games;
  Shopping trips; Dances/Social/Cultural
  gatherings; Church visits; Bingo.

Brighton Place West Inc
331 Oakley, Topeka, KS 66606
(913) 232-1212
Admin Mary Ann Perry. *Dir of Nursing* Betty
  Bryan LPN. *Medical Dir* Joan Sehdev MD.
Licensure Intermediate care; Alzheimer's care.
  Beds ICF 50. *Certified* Medicaid.
Owner Privately owned.
Admissions Requirements Minimum age 50;
  Medical examination; Physician's request.
Staff RNs 1 (pt); LPNs 4 (ft); Nurses' aides 11
  (ft); Physical therapists 1 (pt); Recreational
  therapists 1 (ft); Activities coordinators 1
  (pt); Social workers 1 (ft).
Facilities Dining room; Physical therapy
  room; Activities room; Crafts room; Laundry
  room; Barber/Beauty shop; Library.
Activities Arts & crafts; Cards; Games;
  Reading groups; Prayer groups; Movies;
  Shopping trips; Dances/Social/Cultural
  gatherings.

Countryside Health Center
3401 Seward, Topeka, KS 66616
(913) 234-6147
Admin Nancy A Kirk.
Licensure Intermediate care. *Beds* ICF 60.
  Certified Medicaid.
Owner Proprietary corp.

Eventide Convalescent Center Inc
2015 E 10th, Topeka, KS 66607
(913) 233-8918
Admin M Mac Austin.
Medical Dir Dr Robert Jacoby.
Licensure Skilled care; Intermediate care. *Beds*
  SNF 50; ICF 50. *Certified* Medicaid;
  Medicare.
Owner Proprietary corp.
Admissions Requirements Medical
  examination; Physician's request.
Staff Physicians 1 (pt); RNs 2 (ft); LPNs 7
  (ft), 1 (pt); Nurses' aides 25 (ft); Physical
  therapists 1 (pt); Occupational therapists 1
  (pt); Speech therapists 1 (pt); Activities
  coordinators 2 (ft); Dietitians 1 (ft), 1 (pt);
  Ophthalmologists 1 (pt); Podiatrists 1 (pt);
  Audiologists 1 (pt); Dentists 1 (pt).

Facilities Dining room; Physical therapy
  room; Activities room; Chapel; Crafts room;
  Laundry room; Barber/Beauty shop; Library.
Activities Arts & crafts; Cards; Games;
  Reading groups; Prayer groups; Shopping
  trips; Dances/Social/Cultural gatherings.

Fairlawn Heights Nursing Center
5400 W 7th, Topeka, KS 66606
(913) 272-6880
Admin Virginia Eaton. *Dir of Nursing* Elaine
  L Luce RN. *Medical Dir* Dr Doug Gardner.
Licensure Intermediate care. *Beds* ICF 70.
  Certified Medicaid.
Owner Proprietary corp.
Admissions Requirements Minimum age 18;
  Medical examination; Physician's request.
Staff RNs 1 (ft); LPNs 3 (ft), 6 (pt); Nurses'
  aides 15 (ft), 10 (pt); Physical therapists 1
  (pt); Occupational therapists; Activities
  coordinators 1 (ft), 1 (pt); Dietitians 1 (pt).
Facilities Dining room; Physical therapy
  room; Activities room; Crafts room; Laundry
  room; Barber/Beauty shop.
Activities Arts & crafts; Cards; Games;
  Reading groups; Prayer groups; Movies;
  Shopping trips; Dances/Social/Cultural
  gatherings; Reminiscence therapy.

Glendale Manor
1334 Buchanan, Topeka, KS 66604
(913) 235-6258
Admin L Sue Starkebaum. *Dir of Nursing*
  John Gregory Dempewolf LPN/HSS.
  Medical Dir Dr Q Sufi.
Licensure Intermediate care. *Beds* ICF 53.
  Private Pay Patients 40%. *Certified*
  Medicaid.
Owner Proprietary corp (Care Centers Inc).
Admissions Requirements Medical
  examination.
Staff RNs 1 (pt); LPNs 6 (ft); Nurses' aides 11
  (ft), 1 (pt); Physical therapists 1 (ft);
  Activities coordinators 1 (pt); CMAs 6 (ft), 1
  (pt); Social services coordinator 1 (pt).
Facilities Dining room; Physical therapy
  room; Activities room; Crafts room; Laundry
  room; Barber/Beauty shop; Library.
Activities Arts & crafts; Cards; Games;
  Reading groups; Prayer groups; Movies;
  Shopping trips; Dances/Social/Cultural
  gatherings; Intergenerational programs; Pet
  therapy.

Hillhaven of Topeka
711 Garfield, Topeka, KS 66606
(913) 357-6121, 357-1143 FAX
Admin Doug Frihart. *Dir of Nursing* Ruth
  Johnson RN. *Medical Dir* Jorge Herrera
  MD.
Licensure Skilled care; Intermediate care. *Beds*
  SNF 58; ICF 116. *Private Pay Patients* 17%.
  Certified Medicaid; Medicare.
Owner Proprietary corp (Hillhaven Corp).
Admissions Requirements Minimum age 16;
  Medical examination; Physician's request.
Staff RNs 6 (ft); LPNs 13 (ft), 3 (pt); Nurses'
  aides 52 (ft), 12 (pt); Physical therapists 1
  (ft); Occupational therapists 1 (ft); Activities
  coordinators 2 (ft); Dietitians; CPTAs 1 (ft),
  1 (pt).
Facilities Dining room; Physical therapy
  room; Activities room; Crafts room; Barber/
  Beauty shop.
Activities Arts & crafts; Cards; Games; Prayer
  groups; Movies; Shopping trips; Dances/
  Social/Cultural gatherings.

Indian Trails Mental Health Living Center
1112 SE Republican Ave, Topeka, KS 66607
(913) 233-0588
Admin Tanya Williamson. *Dir of Nursing*
  Robbie Davies BSN RN. *Medical Dir* Dr
  Glenn O Bair.
Licensure Intermediate care; Crisis
  stabilization. *Beds* ICF 82; Crisis
  stabilization 6. *Certified* Medicaid.

Owner Proprietary corp (Golden Years Health
  Care Services Inc).
Admissions Requirements Minimum age 16;
  Medical examination; Physician's request.
Staff Physicians 3 (pt); RNs 1 (ft), 1 (pt);
  LPNs 15 (ft), 1 (pt); Nurses' aides 18 (ft);
  Physical therapists 1 (pt); Occupational
  therapists 1 (pt); Speech therapists 1 (pt);
  Activities coordinators 3 (ft); Dietitians 1
  (pt); Podiatrists 1 (pt); Audiologists 1 (pt).
Facilities Dining room; Physical therapy
  room; Activities room; Crafts room; Laundry
  room; Barber/Beauty shop; Library.
Activities Arts & crafts; Cards; Games;
  Reading groups; Prayer groups; Movies;
  Shopping trips; Dances/Social/Cultural
  gatherings; Intergenerational programs; Pet
  therapy; Self-improvement program.

Manor Care Topeka
2515 SW Wanamaker, Topeka, KS 66614
(913) 271-6808
Admin Laurie McMillan. *Dir of Nursing* Joyce
  Conner. *Medical Dir* Jeff Rhodes.
Licensure Skilled care; Intermediate care;
  Alzheimer's care. *Beds* Swing beds SNF/ICF
  114; Alzheimer's unit 30. *Private Pay
  Patients* 60%. *Certified* Medicaid; Medicare.
Owner Proprietary corp (Manor Health Care
  Corp).
Admissions Requirements Medical
  examination; Physician's request.
Staff RNs 8 (ft), 1 (pt); LPNs 15 (ft), 3 (pt);
  Nurses' aides 32 (ft), 12 (pt); Physical
  therapists 1 (ft); Recreational therapists 1
  (ft); Activities coordinators 1 (ft).
Facilities Dining room; Physical therapy
  room; Activities room; Crafts room; Barber/
  Beauty shop.
Activities Arts & crafts; Cards; Games;
  Reading groups; Prayer groups; Movies;
  Shopping trips; Dances/Social/Cultural
  gatherings; Intergenerational programs; Pet
  therapy.

Manor of Topeka Inc
4101 Martin Dr, Topeka, KS 66609
(913) 267-3100
Admin Sharon L Durrell.
Licensure Intermediate care; Retirement;
  Alzheimer's care. *Beds* ICF 120. *Certified*
  Medicaid.
Owner Proprietary corp.
Admissions Requirements Minimum age 55;
  Medical examination; Physician's request.
Staff RNs 2 (ft); LPNs 9 (ft); Nurses' aides 30
  (ft); Physical therapists 2 (ft); Reality
  therapists 1 (ft); Recreational therapists 1
  (ft); Occupational therapists 1 (ft); Speech
  therapists 1 (ft); Activities coordinators 2
  (ft); Dietitians 1 (ft); Ophthalmologists 1 (ft).
Facilities Dining room; Physical therapy
  room; Activities room; Chapel; Crafts room;
  Laundry room; Barber/Beauty shop;
  Whirlpool.
Activities Arts & crafts; Cards; Games;
  Reading groups; Prayer groups; Movies;
  Shopping trips; Dances/Social/Cultural
  gatherings; Supper clubs.

McCrite Plaza Health Center
1610 W 37th St, Topeka, KS 66611
(913) 267-2960
Admin Joan Russell.
Licensure Skilled care; Intermediate care. *Beds*
  SNF 46; ICF 74. *Certified* Medicaid;
  Medicare.
Owner Proprietary corp.

North Towne Manor
1035 SW Wanamaker, Topeka, KS 66615
(316) 682-1612
Admin Bonita Williams.
Medical Dir Jacquelyn Maloney.
Licensure Intermediate care. *Beds* ICF 100.
  Certified Medicaid.
Owner Privately owned.

Admissions Requirements Medical
examination; Physician's request.
Staff RNs 1 (ft); LPNs 5 (ft); Nurses' aides 25
(ft).
Facilities Dining room; Physical therapy
room; Activities room; Chapel; Crafts room;
Laundry room; Barber/Beauty shop.
Activities Arts & crafts; Games; Prayer groups;
Movies; Shopping trips; Dances/Social/
Cultural gatherings.

Pioneer Village I
2201 SE 25th, Topeka, KS 66605
(913) 267-2927
Admin Kari Ebeling. *Dir of Nursing* Linda
McWilliams RN. *Medical Dir* William Wade
DO.
Licensure Intermediate care for mentally
retarded. *Beds* ICF/MR 15. *Certified*
Medicaid.
Owner Nonprofit corp.
Admissions Requirements Minimum age 18;
Medical examination.
Staff Physicians 1 (ft); RNs 1 (ft); LPNs 2 (ft);
Nurses' aides 12 (ft), 3 (pt); Physical
therapists 1 (pt); Occupational therapists 1
(pt); Speech therapists 1 (pt); Activities
coordinators 1 (ft); Dietitians 1 (pt);
Podiatrists 1 (pt).
Languages Sign.
Facilities Dining room; Laundry room.
Activities Arts & crafts; Cards; Games;
Movies; Shopping trips; Dances/Social/
Cultural gatherings; Special Olympics.

Pioneer Village II
2125 SE 25th, Topeka, KS 66605
(913) 267-2927
Admin Kari Ebeling. *Dir of Nursing* Linda
McWilliams RN. *Medical Dir* William Wade
DO.
Licensure Intermediate care for mentally
retarded. *Beds* ICF/MR 15. *Certified*
Medicaid.
Owner Nonprofit corp.
Admissions Requirements Minimum age 18;
Medical examination.
Staff Physicians 1 (ft); RNs 1 (ft); LPNs 2 (ft);
Nurses' aides 11 (ft), 2 (pt); Physical
therapists 1 (pt); Occupational therapists 1
(pt); Speech therapists 1 (pt); Activities
coordinators 1 (ft); Dietitians 1 (pt);
Podiatrists 1 (pt).
Languages Sign.
Facilities Dining room; Laundry room.
Activities Arts & crafts; Cards; Games;
Movies; Shopping trips; Dances/Social/
Cultural gatherings; Special Olympics.

Pioneer Village III
2201 SE 25th, Topeka, KS 66605
(913) 267-2927
Admin Steve Garrett. *Dir of Nursing* Linda
McWilliams RN.
Licensure Intermediate care for mentally
retarded. *Beds* ICF/MR 15. *Certified*
Medicaid.
Owner Nonprofit corp.
Staff RNs 1 (ft); LPNs 2 (pt); Nurses' aides 58
(ft); Recreational therapists 1 (ft).

Pioneer Village IV
2117 SE 25th, Topeka, KS 66605
(913) 267-2927
Admin Kari Ebeling. *Dir of Nursing* Linda
McWilliams RN. *Medical Dir* William Wade
DO.
Licensure Intermediate care for mentally
retarded. *Beds* ICF/MR 15. *Certified*
Medicaid.
Owner Nonprofit corp.
Admissions Requirements Minimum age 16;
Medical examination.
Staff Physicians 1 (ft); RNs 1 (ft); LPNs 2 (ft);
Nurses' aides 11 (ft), 2 (pt); Physical
therapists 1 (pt); Occupational therapists 1

(pt); Speech therapists 1 (pt); Activities
coordinators 1 (ft); Dietitians 1 (pt);
Podiatrists 1 (pt).
Languages Sign.
Facilities Dining room; Laundry room.
Activities Arts & crafts; Cards; Games;
Movies; Shopping trips; Dances/Social/
Cultural gatherings; Special Olympics.

Rolling Hills Health Center
2400 Urish Rd, Topeka, KS 66614
(913) 273-5001
Admin Jim Klausman.
Licensure Skilled care; Intermediate care. *Beds*
SNF 60; ICF 60. *Certified* Medicaid;
Medicare.
Owner Proprietary corp.

Samaritan Home
2075 Fillmore, Topeka, KS 66604
(913) 234-0548
Admin Linda Sue Starkebaum.
Medical Dir Joan Sehdeu MD.
Licensure Intermediate care. *Beds* ICF 77.
Certified Medicaid.
Owner Proprietary corp.
Admissions Requirements Minimum age 22;
Medical examination; Physician's request.
Staff RNs 1 (pt); LPNs 4 (ft); Nurses' aides 23
(ft); Physical therapists 1 (pt); Occupational
therapists 1 (pt); Activities coordinators 1
(ft); Dietitians 1 (pt).
Facilities Dining room; Physical therapy
room; Activities room; Chapel; Crafts room;
Laundry room; Library.
Activities Arts & crafts; Cards; Games;
Reading groups; Prayer groups; Movies;
Shopping trips; Dances/Social/Cultural
gatherings.

Topeka Convalescent Center
515 Horne St, Topeka, KS 66606
(913) 233-2321
Admin Nancy A Kirk. *Dir of Nursing* Julie
Weber. *Medical Dir* Eric Voth MD.
Licensure Skilled care; Intermediate care. *Beds*
SNF 58; ICF 42. *Certified* Medicaid;
Medicare.
Owner Proprietary corp.
Admissions Requirements Physician's request.
Staff Physicians 2 (pt); RNs 3 (ft), 1 (pt);
LPNs 6 (ft); Nurses' aides 25 (ft), 5 (pt);
Physical therapists 1 (ft); Recreational
therapists 1 (ft); Occupational therapists 1
(pt); Speech therapists 1 (pt); Activities
coordinators 1 (ft), 1 (pt); Dietitians 1 (pt);
Ophthalmologists 1 (pt); Podiatrists 1 (pt);
Dentists 1 (pt).
Facilities Dining room; Physical therapy
room; Activities room; Crafts room; Laundry
room; Barber/Beauty shop; Library.
Activities Arts & crafts; Cards; Games;
Reading groups; Prayer groups; Movies;
Shopping trips; Dances/Social/Cultural
gatherings.

Topeka Presbyterian Manor Inc
4712 W 6th St, Topeka, KS 66606
(913) 272-6510
Admin Thomas Gengler.
Medical Dir Jo Neill.
Licensure Skilled care; Intermediate care;
Alzheimer's care; Retirement. *Beds* SNF 62;
ICF 65. *Certified* Medicaid.
Owner Nonprofit corp.
Admissions Requirements Minimum age 65;
Medical examination.
Staff RNs 8 (ft), 8 (pt); LPNs 12 (ft), 4 (pt);
Nurses' aides 35 (ft), 15 (pt); Physical
therapists 2 (ft), 2 (pt); Reality therapists 1
(pt); Recreational therapists 1 (pt);
Occupational therapists 1 (ft); Speech
therapists 1 (pt); Activities coordinators 3
(ft); Dietitians 1 (ft); Ophthalmologists 1
(pt); Podiatrists 1 (pt); Dentists 1 (pt); Social
workers 2 (ft); Chaplains 1 (ft).
Affiliation Presbyterian.

Facilities Dining room; Physical therapy
room; Activities room; Chapel; Crafts room;
Laundry room; Barber/Beauty shop; Library.
Activities Arts & crafts; Cards; Games;
Reading groups; Prayer groups; Movies;
Shopping trips; Dances/Social/Cultural
gatherings.

United Methodist Home
1135 College Ave, Topeka, KS 66604
(913) 234-0421
Admin A Lowell Geelan. *Dir of Nursing*
Gergory Duncan RNC.
Licensure Intermediate care; Retirement;
Alzheimer's care. *Beds* ICF 110. *Certified*
Medicaid.
Owner Nonprofit corp.
Admissions Requirements Minimum age 65;
Medical examination; Physician's request.
Staff Physicians 2 (pt); RNs 7 (ft), 4 (pt);
LPNs 8 (ft), 4 (pt); Nurses' aides 34 (ft), 9
(pt); Physical therapists 1 (pt); Reality
therapists 1 (pt); Recreational therapists 1
(ft); Occupational therapists 1 (pt); Speech
therapists 1 (pt); Activities coordinators 1
(ft); Dietitians 1 (ft); Ophthalmologists 1
(pt); Podiatrists 1 (pt); Dentists 1 (pt).
Affiliation Methodist.
Facilities Dining room; Physical therapy
room; Activities room; Chapel; Crafts room;
Laundry room; Barber/Beauty shop; Library.
Activities Arts & crafts; Cards; Games;
Reading groups; Prayer groups; Movies;
Shopping trips; Dances/Social/Cultural
gatherings.

Westwood Manor
5015 W 28th St, Topeka, KS 66614
(913) 273-0886
Admin Andrea Graham.
Licensure Intermediate care. *Beds* ICF 54.
Certified Medicaid.
Owner Proprietary corp.

Woodland Health Center
440 Woodland, Topeka, KS 66607
(913) 233-0544
Admin Dee Klausman. *Dir of Nursing* Peggy
Lemon RN. *Medical Dir* Jeffrey Rhoads
MD; Scott Teeter MD.
Licensure Skilled care; Intermediate care. *Beds*
SNF 57; ICF 50. *Certified* Medicaid.
Owner Proprietary corp.
Admissions Requirements Minimum age 16;
Medical examination; Physician's request.
Staff RNs 3 (ft), 2 (pt); LPNs 5 (ft), 4 (pt);
Nurses' aides 30 (ft), 2 (pt); Physical
therapists 1 (pt); Occupational therapists 1
(pt); Activities coordinators 1 (ft); Dietitians
1 (ft); Social worker 1 (ft).
Facilities Dining room; Physical therapy
room; Activities room; Crafts room; Laundry
room; Barber/Beauty shop; Living room.
Activities Arts & crafts; Cards; Games;
Reading groups; Prayer groups; Movies;
Shopping trips; Dances/Social/Cultural
gatherings.

Tribune

Helmwood Care Home
311 E Harper, Box 190, Tribune, KS 67879
(316) 376-4225
Admin Margaret McAllister.
Medical Dir W F Werner MD.
Licensure Intermediate care. *Beds* ICF 32.
Certified Medicaid.
Owner Privately owned.
Admissions Requirements Minimum age 18.
Staff RNs 2 (ft); LPNs 1 (ft); Nurses' aides 10
(ft), 3 (pt); Physical therapists; Recreational
therapists; Activities coordinators 1 (ft);
Dentists 1 (pt).
Facilities Dining room; Physical therapy
room; Activities room; Chapel; Crafts room;
Barber/Beauty shop.

Activities Arts & crafts; Cards; Games; Reading groups; Prayer groups; Movies; Shopping trips; Dances/Social/Cultural gatherings.

Ulysses

Western Prairie Care Home
300 E Maize, Ulysses, KS 67880
(316) 356-3331, 356-1982 RAX
Admin Paul A Florquist. *Dir of Nursing* Becky Cameron.
Licensure Intermediate care; Alzheimer's care. *Beds* ICF 69. *Private Pay Patients* 35%. *Certified* Medicaid.
Owner Publicly owned.
Admissions Requirements Minimum age 16; Physician's request.
Staff RNs 6 (ft), 4 (pt); LPNs 3 (ft), 1 (pt); Nurses' aides 30 (ft), 10 (pt); Physical therapists 1 (ft), 1 (pt); Recreational therapists 1 (ft), 1 (pt); Activities coordinators 1 (ft); Dietitians 1 (ft).
Facilities Dining room; Physical therapy room; Activities room; Chapel; Crafts room; Laundry room; Barber/Beauty shop; Library.
Activities Arts & crafts; Games; Reading groups; Prayer groups; Movies; Shopping trips; Intergenerational programs; Bingo; Variety of church activities.

Uniontown

Marmaton Valley Home
Box 22, Hwy K-3 & 54, Uniontown, KS 66779
(316) 756-4629
Admin Debra Jackson.
Medical Dir Marsha Kumalae.
Licensure Intermediate care. *Beds* ICF 40. *Certified* Medicaid.
Owner Proprietary corp.
Admissions Requirements Minimum age 18.
Staff RNs 2 (pt); LPNs 1 (ft), 2 (pt); Nurses' aides 12 (ft), 7 (pt); Physical therapists 1 (ft); Activities coordinators 1 (ft); Dietitians 6 (ft).
Facilities Dining room; Physical therapy room; Activities room; Laundry room; Barber/Beauty shop.
Activities Arts & crafts; Games; Prayer groups; Movies; Shopping trips.

Valley Center

New Horizons of Valley Center
821 3rd St Terr, Valley Center, KS 67147
(316) 755-1288
Admin Paula Calabrese.
Medical Dir Helen Chamberlain.
Licensure Intermediate care for mentally retarded. *Beds* ICF/MR 100. *Certified* Medicaid.
Owner Proprietary corp (Medicalodges Inc).
Admissions Requirements Minimum age 17; Medical examination.
Staff Physicians 1 (pt); RNs 2 (ft), 2 (pt); LPNs 7 (ft); Nurses' aides 50 (ft); Physical therapists 1 (pt); Recreational therapists 1 (ft); Occupational therapists 1 (pt); Speech therapists 1 (pt); Activities coordinators 1 (ft); Dietitians 1 (ft); Ophthalmologists 1 (pt); Podiatrists 1 (pt); Resident care 7 (ft).
Facilities Dining room; Physical therapy room; Activities room; Crafts room; Laundry room; Barber/Beauty shop.
Activities Arts & crafts; Cards; Games; Reading groups; Movies; Shopping trips; Dances/Social/Cultural gatherings; Special Olympics.

Valley Falls

Valley Health Care Center Inc
12th & Sycamore, Valley Falls, KS 66088
(913) 945-3832

Admin Scott Klausman.
Licensure Intermediate care. *Beds* ICF 80. *Certified* Medicaid.
Owner Proprietary corp.

Victoria

St Johns Rest Home
701 7th St, Victoria, KS 67671
(913) 735-2208
Admin Donald D Curl. *Dir of Nursing* Artis Perret RN. *Medical Dir* Dr Pira Rochanayon.
Licensure Intermediate care; Retirement; Alzheimer's care. *Beds* ICF 90. *Certified* Medicaid.
Owner Nonprofit organization/foundation.
Admissions Requirements Medical examination; Physician's request.
Staff RNs; LPNs; Nurses' aides; Physical therapists; Reality therapists; Recreational therapists; Occupational therapists; Speech therapists; Activities coordinators; Dietitians.
Languages German.
Affiliation Roman Catholic.
Facilities Dining room; Physical therapy room; Activities room; Chapel; Crafts room; Laundry room; Barber/Beauty shop.
Activities Arts & crafts; Cards; Games; Reading groups; Prayer groups; Movies; Shopping trips; Dances/Social/Cultural gatherings.

Wakeeney

Heartland Manor—Wakeeney
320 South Ave, Wakeeney, KS 67672
(913) 743-2913
Admin Irma G Ell.
Licensure Intermediate care. *Beds* ICF 50. *Certified* Medicaid.
Owner Privately owned.

Wakefield

Heritage Village of Wakefield
6th & Grove, Wakefield, KS 67487
(913) 461-5417
Admin Cheryl Blanken.
Medical Dir Gloria Hohman.
Licensure Intermediate care; Retirement. *Beds* ICF 50. *Certified* Medicaid.
Owner Proprietary corp (Beverly Enterprises).
Admissions Requirements Medical examination; Physician's request.
Staff Physicians; LPNs; Nurses' aides; Physical therapists; Occupational therapists; Speech therapists; Activities coordinators; Dietitians; Ophthalmologists; Podiatrists.
Facilities Dining room; Physical therapy room; Activities room; Chapel; Crafts room; Laundry room; Barber/Beauty shop; Library.
Activities Arts & crafts; Cards; Games; Reading groups; Prayer groups; Movies; Shopping trips.

Wamego

Valley Vista Good Samaritan Center
2011 Grandview Dr, Wamego, KS 66547
(913) 456-9482
Admin Robin Lowery.
Licensure Intermediate care. *Beds* ICF 50. *Certified* Medicaid.
Owner Nonprofit corp (Evangelical Lutheran/ Good Samaritan Society).
Affiliation Lutheran.

Washington

Centennial Homestead Inc
311 E 2nd, Washington, KS 66968
(913) 325-2361
Admin Deloris Syring. *Dir of Nursing* Terry A Severin RN.

Licensure Intermediate care. *Beds* ICF 50. *Certified* Medicaid.
Owner Proprietary corp.
Admissions Requirements Minimum age 16; Physician's request.
Staff Physicians 1 (pt); RNs 1 (ft); LPNs 4 (ft), 1 (pt); Nurses' aides 17 (ft), 5 (pt); Physical therapists 1 (pt); Speech therapists 1 (pt); Activities coordinators 1 (ft); Dietitians 4 (ft), 6 (pt); Ophthalmologists 1 (pt); Podiatrists 1 (pt).
Facilities Dining room; Physical therapy room; Activities room; Crafts room; Laundry room; Barber/Beauty shop; Library.
Activities Arts & crafts; Cards; Games; Reading groups; Prayer groups; Movies; Shopping trips.

Wathena

Colonial Manor Nursing & Care Center
RR 1 Hwy 36, Wathena, KS 66090
(913) 989-3141
Admin Candace Browne. *Dir of Nursing* Cynthia Claywell RN.
Licensure Intermediate care. *Beds* ICF 60. *Certified* Medicaid.
Owner Proprietary corp (Beverly Enterprises).
Staff RNs; LPNs; Nurses' aides; Physical therapists; Occupational therapists; Speech therapists; Activities coordinators.
Facilities Dining room; Physical therapy room; Activities room; Laundry room; Barber/Beauty shop.
Activities Cards; Games; Movies; Dances/ Social/Cultural gatherings.

Waverly

Sunset Manor
128 S Pearson Ave, Box 246, Waverly, KS 66871
(913) 733-2744
Admin Melinda J Arb. *Dir of Nursing* Eunice Bowersox.
Licensure Intermediate care. *Beds* ICF 50. *Certified* Medicaid.
Owner Proprietary corp.
Admissions Requirements Medical examination.
Staff RNs 2 (ft); LPNs 1 (pt); Nurses' aides 9 (ft), 8 (pt); Activities coordinators 1 (ft); Social service designees 1 (pt); Restorative aides; CMAs 4 (ft), 1 (pt).
Facilities Dining room; Physical therapy room; Activities room; Laundry room; Barber/Beauty shop.
Activities Arts & crafts; Cards; Games; Reading groups; Prayer groups; Movies; Shopping trips; Dances/Social/Cultural gatherings.

Wellington

Cedar View Good Samaritan Center
1600 W 8th, Wellington, KS 67152
(316) 326-2232
Admin Jim Cowan.
Licensure Intermediate care. *Beds* ICF 97. *Certified* Medicaid.
Owner Nonprofit corp (Evangelical Lutheran/ Good Samaritan Society).
Admissions Requirements Medical examination; Physician's request.
Affiliation Lutheran.
Facilities Dining room; Physical therapy room; Activities room; Chapel; Crafts room; Laundry room; Barber/Beauty shop.
Activities Arts & crafts; Cards; Games; Reading groups; Prayer groups; Movies; Shopping trips.

Lifecare of Wellington
102 W Botkin, Wellington, KS 67152
(316) 326-7437
Admin Jere Schwerdfieger.

Licensure Intermediate care. *Beds* ICF 60.
Certified Medicaid.
Owner Proprietary corp (Life Care Centers of
Kansas Inc).

Wellsville

Wellsville Manor Care Center
304 W 7th, Wellsville, KS 66092
(913) 883-4101
Admin Louis A Huff.
Licensure Intermediate care. *Beds* ICF 60.
Certified Medicaid.
Owner Proprietary corp.

Westmoreland

Westy Community Care Home Inc
RR 1 Box 9, Westmoreland, KS 66549
(913) 457-2130
Admin Virginia Roggenkamp.
Medical Dir Dr Thomas Dechairo.
Licensure Intermediate care. *Beds* ICF 60.
Certified Medicaid.
Owner Nonprofit corp.
Admissions Requirements Medical
examination; Physician's request.
Staff RNs 1 (ft); LPNs 1 (ft), 3 (pt); Nurses'
aides 14 (ft), 8 (pt); Physical therapists 1
(pt); Occupational therapists 1 (pt); Speech
therapists 1 (pt); Activities coordinators 1
(ft); Dietitians 1 (pt); Ophthalmologists 1
(pt); Audiologists 1 (pt); Dentists 1 (pt).
Facilities Dining room; Physical therapy
room; Activities room; Crafts room; Laundry
room; Barber/Beauty shop.
Activities Arts & crafts; Cards; Games;
Reading groups; Prayer groups; Movies;
Shopping trips; Dances/Social/Cultural
gatherings.

Whitewater

Wheat State Manor Inc
601 S Main, Whitewater, KS 67154
(316) 799-2181
Admin Janet Chapman. *Dir of Nursing*
Dorothy Pratt RN. *Medical Dir* Paul
Fransen MD.
Licensure Intermediate care. *Beds* ICF 66.
Private Pay Patients 54%. *Certified*
Medicaid.
Owner Nonprofit organization/foundation.
Admissions Requirements Minimum age 16;
Medical examination; Physician's request.
Staff RNs 1 (ft), 6 (pt); LPNs 2 (ft), 3 (pt);
Nurses' aides 7 (ft), 22 (pt); Physical
therapists 1 (pt); Reality therapists 1 (pt);
Recreational therapists 1 (pt); Occupational
therapists 1 (pt); Speech therapists 1 (pt);
Activities coordinators 1 (ft), 1 (pt);
Dietitians 1 (ft); Podiatrists 1 (pt);
Audiologists 1 (pt).
Facilities Dining room; Physical therapy
room; Activities room; Crafts room; Laundry
room; Barber/Beauty shop; Library.
Activities Arts & crafts; Cards; Games;
Reading groups; Prayer groups; Movies;
Shopping trips; Dances/Social/Cultural
gatherings; Intergenerational programs; Pet
therapy.

Wichita

Catholic Care Center
45th & Woodlawn, Wichita, KS 67220
(316) 681-2118, 681-0398 FAX
Admin Michael E Smith. *Dir of Nursing*
Patricia Ryan RN. *Medical Dir* Ernie
Chaney MD.
Licensure Skilled care; Intermediate care;
Alzheimer's care; AIDS care. *Beds* SNF 60;
ICF 120. *Certified* Medicaid; Medicare.
Owner Nonprofit corp (Catholic Charities).
Admissions Requirements Minimum age 18;
Medical examination; Physician's request.

Staff Physicians 1 (pt); RNs 12 (ft); LPNs 9
(ft); Nurses' aides 58 (ft), 10 (pt); Physical
therapists (contracted); Reality therapists 1
(pt); Recreational therapists 2 (pt);
Occupational therapists 1 (pt); Speech
therapists 1 (pt); Activities coordinators 2
(ft); Dietitians 1 (ft); Ophthalmologists 1
(pt); Podiatrists 1 (pt); Audiologists 1 (pt).
Languages Spanish, Hindi, Vietnamese.
Affiliation Roman Catholic.
Facilities Dining room; Physical therapy
room; Activities room; Chapel; Crafts room;
Laundry room; Barber/Beauty shop; Library.
Activities Arts & crafts; Cards; Games;
Reading groups; Prayer groups; Movies;
Shopping trips; Dances/Social/Cultural
gatherings; Intergenerational programs; Pet
therapy; Validation therapy; Reminiscence
therapy.

Cherry Creek Village Nursing Center
8100 E Pawnee, Wichita, KS 67207
(316) 684-1313
Admin Linda J Reash. *Dir of Nursing* Mary
Jane Schneider. *Medical Dir* Dr Robert
Fowler.
Licensure Skilled care; Intermediate care;
Retirement. *Beds* SNF 46; ICF 96. *Certified*
Medicaid.
Owner Privately owned.
Admissions Requirements Minimum age 16;
Medical examination; Physician's request.
Staff RNs 3 (ft); LPNs 3 (ft); Activities
coordinators 2 (ft).
Facilities Dining room; Physical therapy
room; Activities room; Chapel; Crafts room;
Laundry room; Barber/Beauty shop;
Ceramics area.
Activities Arts & crafts; Cards; Games;
Reading groups; Prayer groups; Movies;
Shopping trips; Dances/Social/Cultural
gatherings.

Christ Villa Nursing Center
1555 N Meridian, Wichita, KS 67203
(316) 942-8471
Admin Tom Nevills. *Dir of Nursing* Faye
Clements. *Medical Dir* Ed Hett MD.
Licensure Skilled care; Intermediate care;
Retirement. *Beds* SNF 60; ICF 58. *Certified*
Medicaid; Medicare.
Owner Publicly owned.
Admissions Requirements Medical
examination; Physician's request.
Staff Physicians 2 (ft); RNs 6 (ft); LPNs 8 (ft);
Nurses' aides 40 (ft); Physical therapists 1
(pt); Recreational therapists 1 (pt);
Occupational therapists 1 (pt); Speech
therapists 1 (pt); Activities coordinators 1
(ft); Ophthalmologists 1 (pt); Podiatrists 1
(pt).
Affiliation Church of Christ.
Facilities Dining room; Physical therapy
room; Activities room; Chapel; Crafts room;
Laundry room; Barber/Beauty shop; Library.
Activities Arts & crafts; Cards; Games;
Reading groups; Prayer groups; Movies;
Shopping trips; Dances/Social/Cultural
gatherings.

Heartland Rehabilitation Center
3410 E Funston St, Wichita, KS 67218
(316) 685-1341
Admin Carol O'Tool.
Medical Dir Ann Hatfield.
Licensure Intermediate care. *Beds* ICF 81.
Certified Medicaid.
Owner Privately owned.
Admissions Requirements Minimum age 18;
Medical examination.
Staff RNs 1 (ft), 3 (pt); LPNs 5 (ft), 3 (pt);
Nurses' aides 12 (ft), 4 (pt); Activities
coordinators 1 (ft); Social workers 1 (ft).
Facilities Dining room; Physical therapy
room; Activities room; Laundry room;
Barber/Beauty shop; Game room; Smoking
room; Quiet room.

Activities Arts & crafts; Cards; Games;
Reading groups; Movies; Shopping trips;
Dances/Social/Cultural gatherings; Psyche
therapy groups; Role play groups; Exercise
groups; Social interaction groups.

Heritage Lakewood Health Care Center
1319 Seville, Wichita, KS 67209
(316) 722-6916
Admin Maria Gillespie.
Licensure Intermediate care; Retirement. *Beds*
ICF 100. *Certified* Medicaid.
Owner Proprietary corp (National Heritage).
Admissions Requirements Medical
examination.
Staff LPNs 9 (ft); Nurses' aides 25 (ft);
Activities coordinators 1 (ft).
Facilities Dining room; Physical therapy
room; Activities room; Crafts room; Laundry
room; Barber/Beauty shop.
Activities Arts & crafts; Cards; Games;
Reading groups; Prayer groups; Movies;
Dances/Social/Cultural gatherings.

Hillhaven Wichita
932 N Topeka St, Wichita, KS 67214
(316) 262-4261
Admin Keith M Hart. *Dir of Nursing* JoEva
Blair MN. *Medical Dir* Robert Fowler MD.
Licensure Skilled care; Intermediate care. *Beds*
SNF 58; ICF 116. *Certified* Medicaid;
Medicare.
Owner Proprietary corp (Hillhaven Corp).
Admissions Requirements Physician's request.
Staff RNs 7 (ft), 2 (pt); LPNs 18 (ft), 6 (pt);
Nurses' aides 58 (ft), 13 (pt); Physical
therapists 1 (ft); Occupational therapists 1
(ft); Speech therapists 1 (ft); Activities
coordinators 2 (ft); Dietitians 1 (ft).
Facilities Dining room; Physical therapy
room; Activities room; Crafts room; Barber/
Beauty shop.
Activities Arts & crafts; Cards; Games;
Reading groups; Prayer groups; Movies;
Shopping trips; Dances/Social/Cultural
gatherings.

Homestead Health Center Inc
2133 S Elizabeth, Wichita, KS 67213
(316) 262-4473
Admin Bill Lee Shook. *Dir of Nursing* Kathi S
Beeton RN.
Licensure Intermediate care; Retirement. *Beds*
ICF 80. *Certified* Medicaid.
Owner Nonprofit corp.
Admissions Requirements Medical
examination; Physician's request.
Staff RNs; LPNs; Nurses' aides; Activities
coordinators.
Affiliation Baptist.
Facilities Dining room; Physical therapy
room; Activities room; Crafts room; Laundry
room; Barber/Beauty shop.
Activities Arts & crafts; Cards; Games;
Reading groups; Prayer groups; Movies;
Shopping trips; Dances/Social/Cultural
gatherings; Family parties.

Kansas Masonic Home
401 S Seneca, Wichita, KS 67213
(316) 267-0271
Admin Jerry B Lindenbaum. *Dir of Nursing*
Betty Fry RN. *Medical Dir* Dr John Kleady.
Licensure Skilled care; Retirement. *Beds* SNF
120. *Certified* Medicaid; Medicare.
Owner Nonprofit corp.
Admissions Requirements Minimum age 65;
Medical examination.
Staff Physicians 1 (pt); RNs 6 (ft); LPNs 14
(ft); Nurses' aides 50 (ft); Physical therapists
1 (pt); Recreational therapists 1 (pt);
Occupational therapists 1 (ft); Activities
coordinators 4 (ft), 1 (pt); Dietitians 1 (ft).
Affiliation Masons.
Facilities Dining room; Physical therapy
room; Activities room; Chapel; Crafts room;
Laundry room; Barber/Beauty shop; Library.

Activities Arts & crafts; Cards; Games; Reading groups; Prayer groups; Movies; Shopping trips; Dances/Social/Cultural gatherings; Current events; Religious events; Fraternal events; Masonic Lodge on premises.

Larksfield Place
2828 N Governeour, Wichita, KS 67226
(316) 682-7920
Admin Bob Bethell.
Licensure Skilled care; Intermediate care. *Beds* SNF 56; ICF 18. *Certified* Medicare.
Owner Nonprofit corp.

Lincoln East Nursing Home
4007 E Lincoln, Wichita, KS 67218
(316) 683-7588
Admin Mary Lou Shaft. *Dir of Nursing* Angelia Polk LPN.
Licensure Intermediate care; Alzheimer's care; Retirement. *Beds* ICF 60. *Certified* Medicaid.
Owner Proprietary corp (Beverly Enterprises).
Admissions Requirements Medical examination.
Staff RNs; LPNs; Nurses' aides; Recreational therapists; Activities coordinators; Dietitians.
Facilities Dining room; Physical therapy room; Activities room; Chapel; Crafts room; Laundry room; Barber/Beauty shop; Library.
Activities Arts & crafts; Cards; Games; Reading groups; Prayer groups; Movies; Shopping trips; Dances/Social/Cultural gatherings; Quilting; Ceramics.

Manor Care Nursing Center of Wichita
7101 E 21 N, Wichita, KS 67206
(316) 684-8018
Admin Tony Stork.
Licensure Skilled care. *Beds* SNF 116. *Certified* Medicaid; Medicare.
Owner Proprietary corp (Manor Care).

Medicalodge of Wichita
2280 S Minneapolis, Wichita, KS 67211
(316) 265-5693
Admin Nadene Oller. *Dir of Nursing* Patricia Swartz RN. *Medical Dir* R D Magsalin MD.
Licensure Skilled care. *Beds* SNF 100. *Certified* Medicaid; Medicare.
Owner Proprietary corp (Medicalodges Inc).
Admissions Requirements Minimum age 18; Medical examination.
Staff Physicians 1 (pt); RNs 4 (ft), 1 (pt); LPNs 8 (ft), 4 (pt); Nurses' aides 32 (ft), 4 (pt); Physical therapists 1 (ft), 1 (pt); Reality therapists 1 (pt); Recreational therapists 2 (ft); Occupational therapists 1 (pt); Speech therapists 1 (pt); Activities coordinators 1 (ft); Dietitians 8 (ft), 2 (pt); Ophthalmologists 1 (pt); Podiatrists 1 (pt); Dentists 1 (pt).
Languages Spanish.
Facilities Dining room; Physical therapy room; Activities room; Chapel; Crafts room; Laundry room; Barber/Beauty shop; Library.
Activities Arts & crafts; Cards; Games; Reading groups; Prayer groups; Movies; Shopping trips; Dances/Social/Cultural gatherings.

Northeast Health Care Center
5005 E 21st St N, Wichita, KS 67208
(316) 685-9291
Admin Kathy A Crosswhite.
Medical Dir Dr Robert Fowler.
Licensure Skilled care. *Beds* SNF 116. *Certified* Medicare.
Owner Proprietary corp (National Heritage).
Admissions Requirements Medical examination; Physician's request.
Staff RNs 6 (ft); LPNs 8 (ft); Nurses' aides 30 (ft); Physical therapists 1 (pt); Occupational therapists 1 (pt); Speech therapists 1 (pt); Activities coordinators 1 (pt); Dietitians 1 (ft), 1 (pt); Ophthalmologists 1 (pt); Podiatrists 1 (pt).

Parkway Health Care Center
2840 S Hillside, Wichita, KS 67216
(316) 684-7777
Admin Rose A Hand.
Licensure Intermediate care. *Beds* ICF 57. *Certified* Medicaid.
Owner Proprietary corp (Beverly Enterprises).
Admissions Requirements Minimum age 18.
Staff Physicians 3 (pt); RNs 1 (ft); LPNs 2 (ft); Nurses' aides 14 (ft), 2 (pt); Physical therapists 1 (pt); Reality therapists 1 (pt); Occupational therapists 1 (pt); Activities coordinators 1 (ft); Dietitians 1 (pt).
Facilities Dining room; Physical therapy room; Activities room; Chapel; Laundry room; Barber/Beauty shop.
Activities Arts & crafts; Cards; Games; Reading groups; Prayer groups; Movies; Shopping trips; Dances/Social/Cultural gatherings.

Regency Health Care Center
1432 N Waco, Wichita, KS 67203
(316) 262-8481
Admin Linda Karling.
Medical Dir Dr A J Wray.
Licensure Skilled care; Intermediate care. *Beds* SNF 35; ICF 92. *Certified* Medicaid.
Owner Proprietary corp (Regency Health Care Centers Inc).
Admissions Requirements Medical examination; Physician's request.
Facilities Dining room; Physical therapy room; Activities room; Chapel; Crafts room; Laundry room; Barber/Beauty shop; Library.
Activities Arts & crafts; Games; Reading groups; Prayer groups; Movies; Dances/Social/Cultural gatherings.

Sandpiper Bay Healthcare Center
5808 W 8th, Wichita, KS 67212
(316) 945-3606
Admin Jane E Smith.
Licensure Skilled care; Intermediate care. *Beds* SNF 55; ICF 55. *Certified* Medicaid.
Owner Proprietary corp.

Terrace Gardens Nursing Center
1315 N West St, Wichita, KS 67203
(316) 943-2132
Admin Chester R West. *Dir of Nursing* Carol Trow; Linda Farrar. *Medical Dir* Dr Jon Kardatzke.
Licensure Skilled care; Intermediate care; Personal care; Retirement. *Beds* SNF 39; ICF 106; Personal care 104; Retirement apts 120. *Private Pay Patients* 95%. *Certified* Medicaid; Medicare.
Owner Proprietary corp.
Admissions Requirements Medical examination; Physician's request.
Staff Physicians 1 (pt); RNs 2 (ft); LPNs 9 (ft), 1 (pt); Nurses' aides 48 (ft), 12 (pt); Physical therapists 1 (pt); Occupational therapists 1 (pt); Speech therapists 1 (pt); Activities coordinators 4 (ft); Dietitians 1 (pt); Podiatrists 1 (pt); Audiologists 1 (pt); Security 1 (ft), 1 (pt).
Languages Spanish.
Facilities Dining room; Physical therapy room; Activities room; Chapel; Crafts room; Laundry room; Barber/Beauty shop; Library.
Activities Arts & crafts; Cards; Games; Reading groups; Prayer groups; Movies; Shopping trips; Dances/Social/Cultural gatherings; Intergenerational programs; Pet therapy.

Wichita Presbyterian Manor
4700 W 13th, Wichita, KS 67212
(316) 942-7456
Admin David M Beck. *Dir of Nursing* Dorene Ruth. *Medical Dir* Richard Egelhof MD.
Licensure Skilled care; Independent living & assisted living with home health care; Alzheimer's care. *Beds* SNF 60; Independent living & assisted living 128. *Private Pay Patients* 80%. *Certified* Medicaid.

Owner Nonprofit corp.
Admissions Requirements Minimum age 65; Medical examination; Physician's request.
Staff Physicians 1 (pt); RNs 5 (ft), 2 (pt); LPNs 3 (ft); Nurses' aides 30 (ft); Physical therapists 1 (pt); Occupational therapists 1 (pt); Speech therapists 1 (pt); Activities coordinators 2 (ft); Dietitians 1 (ft); Ophthalmologists 1 (pt); Podiatrists 1 (pt); Dentists 1 (pt).
Languages Spanish.
Affiliation Presbyterian.
Facilities Dining room; Physical therapy room; Activities room; Chapel; Crafts room; Laundry room; Barber/Beauty shop; Library; Enclosed courtyards; Private patios.
Activities Arts & crafts; Cards; Games; Reading groups; Prayer groups; Movies; Shopping trips; Dances/Social/Cultural gatherings; Religious/Spiritual; Support groups.

Woodlawn Nursing Home
1600 S Woodlawn, Wichita, KS 67218
(316) 683-4628
Admin John T Wills.
Licensure Skilled care; Intermediate care. *Beds* SNF 56; ICF 67. *Certified* Medicaid; Medicare.
Owner Proprietary corp.

Wilson

Wilson Nursing Home
PO Box 160, 611 31st St, Wilson, KS 67490
(913) 658-2505
Admin Barbara J Hladek.
Licensure Intermediate care. *Beds* ICF 50. *Certified* Medicaid.
Owner Proprietary corp (Beverly Enterprises).

Winfield

Cumbernauld Village
716 Tweed, Winfield, KS 67156
(316) 221-4141
Admin Thomas Bechtel.
Licensure Intermediate care. *Beds* ICF 38.
Owner Proprietary corp.

Good Samaritan Village
1320 Wheat Rd, Winfield, KS 67156
(316) 221-4660
Admin Richard L Osborne.
Licensure Intermediate care; Retirement. *Beds* ICF 98. *Certified* Medicaid.
Owner Nonprofit corp (Evangelical Lutheran/ Good Samaritan Society).
Admissions Requirements Minimum age 16; Medical examination; Physician's request.
Staff RNs 1 (ft); LPNs 2 (ft), 6 (pt); Nurses' aides 25 (ft), 20 (pt); Recreational therapists 3 (ft); Activities coordinators 1 (ft).
Affiliation Lutheran.
Facilities Dining room; Physical therapy room; Activities room; Chapel; Crafts room; Laundry room; Barber/Beauty shop; Library.
Activities Arts & crafts; Cards; Games; Reading groups; Prayer groups; Movies; Shopping trips; Dances/Social/Cultural gatherings.

Heritage House Nursing Home
2720 E 12th St, Winfield, KS 67156
(316) 221-9120
Admin James J O'Leary. *Dir of Nursing* Lore Vickens LPN HSS. *Medical Dir* Seavard Denkke MD.
Licensure Intermediate care. *Beds* ICF 59. *Certified* Medicaid.
Owner Privately owned.
Admissions Requirements Medical examination; Physician's request.
Staff RNs 1 (ft); LPNs 3 (ft); Nurses' aides; Physical therapists 1 (ft); Speech therapists 1 (ft); Activities coordinators 2 (ft); Dietitians 1 (ft).

Facilities Dining room; Physical therapy room; Activities room; Chapel; Laundry room; Barber/Beauty shop.
Activities Arts & crafts; Cards; Games; Reading groups; Prayer groups; Movies.

New Horizons of Winfield
2802 E Hwy 160, Winfield, KS 67156
(316) 221-1747
Admin Mary Kent.
Medical Dir Gloria Anderson Health Service Supv.
Licensure Intermediate care for mentally retarded. *Beds* ICF/MR 81. *Certified* Medicaid.
Owner Proprietary corp (Medicalodges Inc).

Winfield Rest Haven Inc
1611 Ritchie, Winfield, KS 67156
(316) 221-9290
Admin Linda Voth.
Medical Dir Dr S S Daehnke.

Licensure Intermediate care. *Beds* ICF 52.
Owner Nonprofit corp.
Admissions Requirements Medical examination; Physician's request.
Staff RNs 1 (ft), 1 (pt); LPNs 1 (ft), 1 (pt); Physical therapists 1 (pt); Occupational therapists 1 (pt); Speech therapists 1 (pt); Dietitians 1 (pt).
Affiliation Church of Christ.
Facilities Dining room; Physical therapy room; Activities room; Crafts room; Laundry room; Barber/Beauty shop.
Activities Arts & crafts; Cards; Games; Reading groups; Prayer groups; Movies; Shopping trips.

Yates Center

Regency Health Care Center
801 S Fry St, Yates Center, KS 66783
(316) 625-2111

Admin Dorothy V Kester.
Medical Dir Beverly Saubers.
Licensure Intermediate care. *Beds* ICF 104. *Certified* Medicaid.
Owner Proprietary corp (Regency Health Care Centers Inc).
Admissions Requirements Medical examination; Physician's request.
Staff RNs 3 (ft); LPNs 3 (ft), 2 (pt); Nurses' aides 24 (ft), 4 (pt); Activities coordinators 2 (ft), 1 (pt).
Facilities Dining room; Physical therapy room; Activities room; Laundry room; Barber/Beauty shop.
Activities Arts & crafts; Cards; Games; Reading groups; Prayer groups; Movies; Shopping trips.

KENTUCKY

Albany

Twin Lakes Nursing Home
404 Washington St, Albany, KY 42602
(606) 387-6623
Admin Deanna D Loy.
Licensure Intermediate care. *Beds* ICF 52.
 Certified Medicaid.
Owner Proprietary corp.
Admissions Requirements Medical
 examination; Physician's request.
Staff Physicians 5 (ft); RNs 1 (ft); LPNs 8 (ft);
 Nurses' aides 21 (ft); Physical therapists;
 Speech therapists; Activities coordinators 1
 (ft); Dietitians.
Facilities Dining room; Activities room;
 Crafts room; Laundry room.
Activities Arts & crafts; Cards; Games;
 Reading groups; Prayer groups; Movies;
 Shopping trips; Dances/Social/Cultural
 gatherings.

Ashland

Artrips Personal Care Home
3000 Central Ave, Ashland, KY 41101
(606) 325-3244
Admin Maggie Artrip.
Licensure Personal care. *Beds* Personal care
 16.
Owner Privately owned.
Admissions Requirements Minimum age 21;
 Medical examination; Physician's request.
Staff Nurses' aides 6 (pt); Activities
 coordinators 2 (pt); Dietitians 1 (pt).
Facilities Dining room; Activities room;
 Laundry room; Quiet/Reading area; TV
 room.
Activities Cards; Games; Reading groups;
 Prayer groups; Dances/Social/Cultural
 gatherings.

Elmwood Village of Ashland
PO Box 1291, 5400 Apple Blossom Ln,
 Ashland, KY 41105-1291
(606) 324-2161
Admin R Morris Stafford.
Medical Dir W Rex Duff MD.
Licensure Skilled care; Intermediate care;
 Personal care; Adult day care. *Beds* SNF 48;
 ICF 99; Personal 14. *Certified* Medicaid;
 Medicare.
Owner Nonprofit corp.
Admissions Requirements Medical
 examination; Physician's request.
Staff Physicians 5 (pt); RNs 2 (ft), 5 (pt);
 LPNs 20 (ft), 4 (pt); Nurses' aides 70 (ft), 10
 (pt); Physical therapists 1 (pt); Recreational
 therapists 2 (ft), 1 (pt); Speech therapists 1
 (pt); Activities coordinators 1 (ft); Dietitians
 1 (pt); Ophthalmologists 1 (pt); Dentists 1
 (pt).
Facilities Dining room; Physical therapy
 room; Activities room; Chapel; Crafts room;
 Laundry room; Barber/Beauty shop; Library;
 Covered patio.

Activities Arts & crafts; Cards; Games;
 Reading groups; Prayer groups; Movies;
 Dances/Social/Cultural gatherings.

**King's Daughters & Sons Home for Aged Men
& Women**
1100 Bath Ave, Ashland, KY 41101
(606) 324-0343
Admin Frances Lyons.
Licensure Personal care. *Beds* Personal care
 36.
Owner Proprietary corp.
Staff Nurses' aides 3 (ft); Activities
 coordinators 1 (pt); Dietitians 1 (pt).
Affiliation King's Daughters & Sons.
Facilities Dining room; Activities room;
 Chapel; Laundry room; Barber/Beauty shop;
 Library.
Activities Cards; Games; Prayer groups.

Riverview Homes
38 Russell Rd, Ashland, KY 41101
(606) 836-3551
Admin Sheila Lemaster.
Licensure Personal care. *Beds* Personal care
 78.
Owner Proprietary corp.
Staff Physicians 2 (ft); Nurses' aides 18 (ft);
 Speech therapists 1 (pt); Activities
 coordinators 1 (ft); Dietitians 1 (pt);
 Podiatrists 1 (pt).
Facilities Dining room; Activities room;
 Crafts room; Laundry room.
Activities Arts & crafts; Games; Prayer groups;
 Shopping trips; Dances/Social/Cultural
 gatherings.

Auburn

Auburn Nursing Center Inc
PO Box 128, 139 Pearl St, Auburn, KY 42206
(502) 542-4111
Admin Grover A Corum. *Dir of Nursing*
 Barbara Ramsey. *Medical Dir* Dr Dewey
 Wood.
Licensure Skilled care; Intermediate care;
 Retirement. *Beds* SNF 30; ICF 36;
 Retirement 7. *Private Pay Patients* 60%.
 Certified Medicaid; Medicare.
Owner Proprietary corp.
Admissions Requirements Medical
 examination.
Staff Physicians (consultant); RNs; LPNs;
 Nurses' aides; Physical therapists
 (consultant); Reality therapists (consultant);
 Recreational therapists (consultant);
 Occupational therapists (consultant); Speech
 therapists (consultant); Activities
 coordinators; Dietitians; Ophthalmologists
 (consultant); Podiatrists (consultant);
 Audiologists (consultant).
Facilities Dining room; Activities room;
 Laundry room; Barber/Beauty shop; Library.
Activities Arts & crafts; Cards; Games;
 Reading groups; Prayer groups; Movies;
 Shopping trips; Dances/Social/Cultural
 gatherings; Intergenerational programs; Pet
 therapy.

Augusta

Bracken Center Inc
Rte 1 Box 418, Augusta, KY 41002
(606) 256-2156
Admin Philip A Gilkison. *Dir of Nursing*
 Janet Bradford. *Medical Dir* Milton Brindley
 MD.
Licensure Intermediate care; Personal care.
 Beds ICF 32; Personal care 50. *Certified*
 Medicaid.
Owner Proprietary corp.
Admissions Requirements Physician's request.
Staff RNs 1 (pt); LPNs 3 (ft); Nurses' aides 20
 (ft), 5 (pt); Activities coordinators 1 (ft).
Facilities Dining room; Activities room;
 Crafts room; Laundry room; Barber/Beauty
 shop.
Activities Arts & crafts; Cards; Games; Prayer
 groups; Movies; Shopping trips.

Barbourville

Valley Park Convalescent Center
117 Shelby St, Barbourville, KY 40906
(606) 546-5136
Admin Judy Scott.
Medical Dir Dr Harold Bushey.
Licensure Skilled care; Intermediate care. *Beds*
 SNF 15; ICF 104. *Certified* Medicaid.
Owner Proprietary corp (Health Systems).
Admissions Requirements Medical
 examination; Physician's request.
Staff Physicians 7 (ft); RNs 5 (ft); LPNs 11
 (ft); Nurses' aides 45 (ft); Physical therapists
 1 (pt); Speech therapists 1 (pt); Activities
 coordinators 2 (ft); Dietitians 12 (ft);
 Dentists 1 (ft).
Facilities Dining room; Physical therapy
 room; Activities room; Laundry room;
 Barber/Beauty shop.
Activities Arts & crafts; Games; Reading
 groups; Prayer groups; Shopping trips.

Bardstown

Colonial House
708 Bartley Ave, Bardstown, KY 40004
(502) 348-9260
Admin Heather Halfacre. *Dir of Nursing* D
 Sue Smith.
Licensure Intermediate care; Personal care.
 Beds ICF 60; Personal care 36. *Certified*
 Medicaid.
Owner Proprietary corp (EPI Corp).
Staff RNs; LPNs; Nurses' aides; Activities
 coordinators; Dietitians.
Facilities Dining room; Activities room;
 Crafts room; Laundry room; Barber/Beauty
 shop; Library.
Activities Arts & crafts; Cards; Games;
 Reading groups; Prayer groups; Movies;
 Shopping trips; Dances/Social/Cultural
 gatherings; Intergenerational programs; Pet
 therapy.

Federal Hill Manor Nursing/Convalescent Center
PO Box 349, Old Bloomfield Rd, Bardstown, KY 40004
(502) 348-4220
Admin Cliff Lake.
Licensure Skilled care; Intermediate care; Personal care. *Beds* SNF 15; ICF 79; Personal care 6. *Certified* Medicaid; Medicare.
Owner Proprietary corp.

Beattyville

Lee County Constant Care Inc
245 Lumber St, Beattyville, KY 41311
(606) 464-3611
Admin Joanne Benton.
Medical Dir Dr J M Smith & Dr A L Taulbee.
Licensure Intermediate care; Personal care. *Beds* ICF 93; Personal care 12. *Certified* Medicaid.
Owner Publicly owned.
Staff RNs 2 (ft), 1 (pt); LPNs 2 (ft); Nurses' aides 25 (ft), 2 (pt); Activities coordinators 2 (ft); Dietitians 1 (pt).
Facilities Dining room; Activities room; Crafts room; Laundry room; Barber/Beauty shop.
Activities Arts & crafts; Games; Reading groups; Movies; Shopping trips; Dances/ Social/Cultural gatherings.

Beaver Dam

Beaver Dam Health Care Manor
Rte 4, Hwy 231, Beaver Dam, KY 42320
(502) 274-9646
Admin Donna Bratcher NHA.
Medical Dir Kathy Drone.
Licensure Intermediate care; Personal care. *Beds* ICF 58; ICF/MR Personal 50. *Certified* Medicaid.
Owner Proprietary corp (Adventist Living Centers).
Admissions Requirements Minimum age 18; Medical examination; Physician's request.
Staff Physicians 6 (ft); LPNs 6 (ft); Nurses' aides 65 (ft), 3 (pt); Activities coordinators 1 (ft).
Facilities Dining room; Activities room; Chapel; Crafts room; Laundry room; Barber/ Beauty shop.
Activities Arts & crafts; Games; Reading groups; Prayer groups; Movies; Shopping trips; Dances/Social/Cultural gatherings; Homemaker club; Supper club; Cooking class; Storytelling.

Bedford

Trimble Nursing Center
Hwy 42, Box 24, Bedford, KY 40006
(502) 255-3244, 255-3245 FAX
Admin Terrie Hill MA. *Dir of Nursing* Rosemary Crittendon. *Medical Dir* Dr Ben Kutnicki.
Licensure Intermediate care. *Beds* ICF 60. *Private Pay Patients* 4%. *Certified* Medicaid.
Owner Proprietary corp (Louden & Co).
Admissions Requirements Physician's request.
Staff Physicians (available); RNs 1 (ft); LPNs 2 (ft); Nurses' aides 15 (ft); Physical therapists (contracted); Activities coordinators 1 (ft); Dietitians 1 (ft); Ophthalmologists (contracted); Podiatrists (contracted).
Facilities Dining room; Activities room; Barber/Beauty shop; Library; Garden.
Activities Games; Reading groups; Prayer groups; Movies; Pet therapy.

Benton

Britthaven of Benton
PO Box 385, US Hwy 641 S, Benton, KY 42025
(502) 527-3296
Admin Donald R Jury.
Medical Dir C R Freeman MD.
Licensure Intermediate care; Personal care. *Beds* ICF 76; Personal 24. *Certified* Medicaid.
Owner Proprietary corp (Hillhaven Corp).
Admissions Requirements Medical examination; Physician's request.
Staff LPNs 2 (ft); Physical therapists 1 (pt); Reality therapists 1 (pt); Speech therapists 1 (pt); Activities coordinators 1 (pt); Dietitians 1 (pt); Podiatrists 1 (pt); Audiologists 1 (pt); Dentists 1 (pt).
Facilities Dining room; Activities room; Laundry room; Barber/Beauty shop.
Activities Arts & crafts; Cards; Games; Reading groups; Shopping trips.

Lake Haven Health Care Center Inc
PO Box 385, US 641 S, Benton, KY 42025
(502) 527-3296
Admin Donald R Jury. *Dir of Nursing* M S Newton RN. *Medical Dir* C R Freeman.
Licensure Intermediate care; Personal care. *Beds* ICF 76; Personal 24. *Certified* Medicaid.
Owner Proprietary corp (Britthaven Inc).
Admissions Requirements Minimum age 18; Physician's request.
Staff RNs 1 (ft); LPNs 4 (ft), 2 (pt); Nurses' aides 27 (ft), 12 (pt); Physical therapists 1 (pt); Activities coordinators 1 (ft); Dietitians 1 (pt); Ophthalmologists 1 (pt); Dentists 1 (pt).
Facilities Dining room; Activities room; Laundry room; Barber/Beauty shop.
Activities Arts & crafts; Cards; Games; Reading groups; Prayer groups; Shopping trips; Dances/Social/Cultural gatherings.

Marshall County Hospital & LTC
502 George McClain Dr, Benton, KY 42025
(502) 527-1336
Admin Marjorie Newton RN. *Dir of Nursing* Patricia H Myers RN. *Medical Dir* Clark Harris MD.
Licensure Intermediate care. *Beds* ICF 34. *Private Pay Patients* 29%. *Certified* Medicaid; Medicare.
Owner Publicly owned.
Admissions Requirements Physician's request.
Staff Physicians 1 (pt); RNs 3 (pt); LPNs 1 (ft), 3 (pt); Nurses' aides 9 (ft), 3 (pt); Physical therapists 1 (ft); Speech therapists 1 (pt); Activities coordinators 1 (ft); Dietitians 1 (ft); Ophthalmologists 1 (pt); Podiatrists 1 (pt); Dentists 1 (pt).
Facilities Dining room; Physical therapy room; Activities room; Chapel; Crafts room; Barber/Beauty shop.
Activities Arts & crafts; Games; Reading groups; Prayer groups; Shopping trips; Dances/Social/Cultural gatherings; Intergenerational programs; Pet therapy.

Berea

Berea Health Care Center
Rte 1, Berea, KY 40403
(606) 986-4710
Admin Audrey Runda.
Medical Dir Clifford Kerby MD.
Licensure Intermediate care; Alzheimer's care. *Beds* ICF 40. *Certified* Medicaid.
Owner Proprietary corp.
Admissions Requirements Medical examination.
Staff RNs 1 (ft); LPNs 2 (ft); Nurses' aides 20 (ft), 4 (pt); Occupational therapists 1 (pt); Activities coordinators 1 (ft); Dietitians 1 (pt).
Facilities Dining room; Activities room.
Activities Arts & crafts; Cards; Games; Reading groups; Prayer groups; Movies.

Berea Hospital—Skilled Nursing Facility
PO Box 128, Estill St, Berea, KY 40403
(606) 986-3151
Admin David E Burgio.
Licensure Skilled care. *Beds* SNF 37. *Certified* Medicaid; Medicare.
Owner Nonprofit corp.

Booneville

Owsley County Health Care Center
PO Box 539, Hwy 11, Booneville, KY 41314
(606) 593-6302
Admin Judy Terry. *Dir of Nursing* Connie Alexander. *Medical Dir* W E Becknell MD.
Licensure Intermediate care; Personal care. *Beds* ICF 91; Personal care 10. *Private Pay Patients* 5%. *Certified* Medicaid.
Owner Nonprofit organization/foundation.
Admissions Requirements Medical examination.
Staff Physicians 2 (ft); RNs 2 (ft); LPNs 6 (ft); Nurses' aides 50 (ft); Activities coordinators 1 (ft); Dietitians 1 (ft).
Facilities Dining room; Activities room; Crafts room; Laundry room; Barber/Beauty shop.
Activities Arts & crafts; Games; Reading groups; Prayer groups; Movies; Shopping trips; Dances/Social/Cultural gatherings; Intergenerational programs.

Bowling Green

Britthaven of Bowling Green
PO Box 1719, 5079 Scottsville Rd, Bowling Green, KY 42102-1719
(502) 782-1125
Admin James Craig White.
Licensure Skilled care; Intermediate care; Personal care. *Beds* SNF 30; ICF 88; Personal 58. *Certified* Medicaid.
Owner Proprietary corp (Hillhaven Corp).
Facilities Dining room; Physical therapy room; Activities room; Chapel; Crafts room; Laundry room; Barber/Beauty shop.
Activities Arts & crafts; Cards; Games; Prayer groups; Movies; Shopping trips; Dances/ Social/Cultural gatherings.

Colonial Manor Nursing Home
2365 Nashville Rd, Bowling Green, KY 42101
(502) 842-1641
Admin Scarlotte Freeman.
Medical Dir Harold West MD.
Licensure Skilled care; Intermediate care. *Beds* SNF 38; ICF 10. *Certified* Medicaid; Medicare.
Owner Proprietary corp (Tullock Management).
Staff RNs 3 (ft), 3 (pt); LPNs 2 (ft), 3 (pt); Nurses' aides 21 (ft), 3 (pt); Physical therapists 1 (pt); Speech therapists 1 (pt); Activities coordinators 1 (pt); Dietitians 1 (pt).
Facilities Dining room; Activities room.
Activities Arts & crafts; Cards; Games; Movies.

Fern Terrace Lodge of Bowling Green
1030 Shive Ln, Bowling Green, KY 42101
(502) 781-6784
Admin Marcia McEwen.
Medical Dir Monica Blair.
Licensure Personal care; Day care. *Beds* Personal care 114.
Owner Proprietary corp.
Admissions Requirements Minimum age 47; Medical examination.
Staff Nurses' aides 18 (ft), 2 (pt).

Facilities Dining room; Laundry room;
Barber/Beauty shop.
Activities Arts & crafts; Cards; Games;
Reading groups; Prayer groups; Movies;
Shopping trips; Dances/Social/Cultural
gatherings.

Medco Center of Bowling Green
1561 Newton Ave, Bowling Green, KY 42101
(502) 842-1611
Admin Cathy Abell.
Licensure Intermediate care. Beds ICF 66.
Certified Medicaid.
Owner Proprietary corp (Unicare).
Admissions Requirements Medical
examination.
Staff Physicians 23 (ft); RNs 1 (ft), 1 (pt);
LPNs 5 (ft), 3 (pt); Nurses' aides 26 (ft);
Speech therapists 1 (ft); Activities
coordinators 1 (ft); Dietitians 1 (ft);
Podiatrists 1 (ft); Audiologists 1 (ft); Dentists
1 (ft).
Facilities Dining room; Laundry room;
Barber/Beauty shop.
Activities Arts & crafts; Cards; Games;
Reading groups; Movies; Shopping trips;
Dances/Social/Cultural gatherings.

Panorama
PO Box 1113, US 231 W, Morgantown Rd,
Bowling Green, KY 42101
(502) 782-7770
Admin Tony Staynings. Dir of Nursing
Elizabeth Wansack. Medical Dir Dr Larry
Green.
Licensure Intermediate care for mentally
retarded. Beds ICF/MR 58. Certified
Medicaid.
Owner Privately owned.
Staff Physicians 1 (pt); RNs 2 (ft); LPNs 3
(ft), 2 (pt); Nurses' aides 1 (ft); Physical
therapists 1 (ft); Recreational therapists 2
(ft); Occupational therapists 2 (ft); Speech
therapists 2 (ft); Dietitians 1 (pt).
Facilities Dining room; Physical therapy
room; Activities room; Crafts room; Laundry
room; Library; Occupational therapy room;
Speech therapy rooms.
Activities Arts & crafts; Cards; Games;
Reading groups; Prayer groups; Movies;
Shopping trips; Dances/Social/Cultural
gatherings; Community activities; Visits to
other communities.

Rosewood Manor Health Care Center
550 High St, Bowling Green, KY 42101
(502) 843-3296
Admin Carmen Downing.
Licensure Skilled care; Intermediate care. Beds
SNF 29; ICF 157. Certified Medicaid;
Medicare.
Owner Proprietary corp (Hillhaven Corp).

Brandenburg

Medco Center of Brandenburg
814 Old Ekron Rd, Brandenburg, KY 40108
(502) 422-2148
Admin Greg L Lowhorn. Dir of Nursing
Karen Bonn RN. Medical Dir Charles
Conley DO.
Licensure Intermediate care; Personal care.
Beds ICF 51; Personal care 13. Certified
Medicaid.
Owner Proprietary corp (Unicare).
Facilities Dining room; Laundry room;
Barber/Beauty shop.

Brodhead

Sowder Nursing Home Inc
7190 W Main St, Brodhead, KY 40409
(606) 758-8711
Admin Linda L Whitt. Dir of Nursing Ann
Taylor RN.

Licensure Intermediate care; Personal care.
Beds ICF 82; Personal 10. Private Pay
Patients 22%. Certified Medicaid.
Owner Proprietary corp.
Admissions Requirements Minimum age 16;
Medical examination; Physician's request.
Staff RNs 1 (ft); LPNs 5 (ft), 1 (pt); Nurses'
aides 38 (ft), 2 (pt); Physical therapists 1
(pt); Activities coordinators 1 (ft); Dietitians
1 (pt).
Facilities Dining room; Activities room;
Barber/Beauty shop; Library; Outdoor
garden; Picnic area.
Activities Arts & crafts; Games; Reading
groups; Prayer groups; Movies; Dances/
Social/Cultural gatherings; Homemaker's
club; Exercise group.

Brownsville

Joywells
PO Box 510, 234 E Main Cross St,
Brownsville, KY 42210
(502) 597-2159
Admin Marie Parsley.
Licensure Personal care. Beds Personal care
37.
Owner Nonprofit corp.

Burkesville

Cumberland Valley Manor
PO Box 433, S Main St, Burkesville, KY
42717
(502) 864-4315
Admin Tim Hicks.
Medical Dir Dr Robert Flowers.
Licensure Intermediate care; Personal care.
Beds ICF 64; Personal 16. Certified
Medicaid.
Owner Nonprofit corp.
Admissions Requirements Physician's request.
Staff Physicians 5 (ft); RNs 1 (ft); LPNs 6 (ft),
4 (pt); Nurses' aides 11 (ft), 9 (pt); Activities
coordinators 1 (ft), 1 (pt); Dietitians 1 (pt).
Facilities Dining room; Activities room;
Chapel; Crafts room; Laundry room; Barber/
Beauty shop; Country store.
Activities Arts & crafts; Cards; Games; Prayer
groups; Movies; Shopping trips; Dances/
Social/Cultural gatherings.

Butler

Grants Lake IC Home
305 Taylor St, Butler, KY 41006
(606) 472-2217
Admin Kathleen Mueller. Dir of Nursing
Kathleen Mueller. Medical Dir Dr Stephen
Scott.
Licensure Intermediate care. Beds ICF 32.
Private Pay Patients 33%. Certified
Medicaid.
Owner Proprietary corp.
Admissions Requirements Medical
examination; Physician's request.
Staff Physicians 1 (ft); RNs 1 (ft); LPNs 3 (ft);
Nurses' aides 20 (ft); Physical therapists 1
(ft); Recreational therapists 1 (ft); Speech
therapists 1 (ft); Activities coordinators 1
(ft); Dietitians 1 (ft); Podiatrists 1 (ft);
Dentists; Eye care.
Facilities Dining room; Activities room;
Crafts room; Laundry room; Barber/Beauty
shop.
Activities Arts & crafts; Games; Reading
groups; Prayer groups; Movies; Dances/
Social/Cultural gatherings; Pet therapy;
Religious activities.

Grants Lake Rest Home
PO Box 231, 305 Taylor St, Butler, KY 41006
(606) 472-2217
Admin Julia A Poe. Dir of Nursing Betty
Hornbeck LPN.

Licensure Intermediate care. Beds ICF 32.
Certified Medicaid.
Owner Proprietary corp.
Admissions Requirements Medical
examination; Physician's request.
Staff RNs 1 (ft); LPNs 2 (ft), 1 (pt); Nurses'
aides 11 (ft), 6 (pt); Activities coordinators 1
(ft).
Facilities Dining room; Activities room.
Activities Arts & crafts; Cards; Games;
Reading groups; Prayer groups; Dances/
Social/Cultural gatherings; Story hour with
local children.

Cadiz

Shady Lawn Nursing Home
Rte 1 Box 22, Cerulean Rd, Cadiz, KY 42211
(502) 522-3236
Admin Raymond C Lafser.
Medical Dir Dr William Anderson.
Licensure Intermediate care. Beds ICF 50.
Certified Medicaid; Medicare.
Owner Proprietary corp (Unicare).
Admissions Requirements Medical
examination; Physician's request.
Staff RNs 2 (ft), 2 (pt); LPNs 4 (ft), 2 (pt);
Nurses' aides 12 (ft), 9 (pt); Activities
coordinators 1 (pt); Dietitians 1 (ft).
Facilities Dining room; Activities room;
Chapel; Crafts room; Laundry room; Barber/
Beauty shop; Lobby; Movie room; TV room.
Activities Arts & crafts; Games; Prayer groups;
Movies; Dances/Social/Cultural gatherings;
Social get-togethers; Birthday parties;
Holiday parties.

Trigg County Manor Personal Care Home
Shelby St, Cadiz, KY 42211
(502) 522-3711
Admin Dorothy Tooke.
Licensure Personal care. Beds Personal care
68.
Owner Proprietary corp.
Admissions Requirements Minimum age 15;
Medical examination; Physician's request.
Staff LPNs 1 (ft); Nurses' aides 23 (ft);
Activities coordinators 1 (ft).
Facilities Dining room; Activities room;
Laundry room; Barber/Beauty shop; Library.
Activities Arts & crafts; Cards; Games;
Reading groups; Prayer groups; Movies;
Shopping trips; Dances/Social/Cultural
gatherings.

Calhoun

McLean County General Hospital Inc
200 Hwy 81 N, Calhoun, KY 42327
(502) 273-5252
Admin Mynette Dennis RN. Dir of Nursing
Mynette Dennis RN. Medical Dir Leighton
Larsson MD.
Licensure Skilled care; Intermediate care;
Dual care/Acute care. Beds SNF 8; ICF 9;
Dual care/Acute care 9. Certified Medicaid;
Medicare.
Owner Proprietary corp.
Admissions Requirements Medical
examination; Physician's request.
Staff Physicians 2 (ft); RNs 5 (ft); LPNs 7 (ft);
Nurses' aides 8 (ft); Physical therapists
(consultant); Occupational therapists 1 (ft);
Speech therapists 1 (ft); Dietitians 1 (ft).
Facilities Dining room; Physical therapy
room; Activities room; Chapel; Crafts room;
Laundry room; Barber/Beauty shop; Library;
Home health program; 24-hour ambulance
service.
Activities Arts & crafts; Cards; Games;
Reading groups; Prayer groups; Movies;
Shopping trips; Dances/Social/Cultural
gatherings; Intergenerational programs; Pet
therapy.

Riverside Healthcare
PO Box 438, Calhoun, KY 42327
(502) 273-5289, 273-3794 FAX
Admin Terry Tackett. *Dir of Nursing* Trudy
Bell RN. *Medical Dir* W Edward
Shuttleworth MD.
Licensure Intermediate care; Personal care.
Beds ICF 51; Personal care 33. *Private Pay
Patients* 15%. *Certified* Medicaid.
Owner Proprietary corp (Hillhaven Corp).
Staff Physicians; RNs; LPNs; Nurses' aides;
Physical therapists; Speech therapists;
Activities coordinators; Dietitians.
Facilities Dining room; Physical therapy
room; Activities room; Crafts room; Laundry
room; Barber/Beauty shop.
Activities Arts & crafts; Cards; Games;
Reading groups; Movies; Dances/Social/
Cultural gatherings; Pet therapy.

Sunny Acres
PO Box 7, Hwy 81 N, Calhoun, KY 42327
(502) 273-3113
Admin Jan Ferguson.
Licensure Personal care. *Beds* Personal care
32. *Private Pay Patients* 0%.
Owner Proprietary corp.

Calvert City

Calvert City Convalescent Center
PO Box 7, 5th Ave, Calvert City, KY 42029
(502) 395-4124
Admin Omer Hille.
Licensure Intermediate care; Personal care.
Beds ICF 95; Personal 5. *Certified*
Medicaid.
Owner Nonprofit corp.

Oakview Manor Health Care Center
Rte 1 Box 125, Calvert City, KY 42029
(502) 898-6288
Admin Terry Skaggs.
Licensure Skilled care; Intermediate care;
Personal care. *Beds* SNF 13; ICF 83;
Personal care 22. *Certified* Medicaid.
Owner Proprietary corp (Hillhaven Corp).

Campbellsville

Medco Center of Campbellsville
1980 Old Greensburg Rd, Campbellsville, KY
42718
(502) 465-3506, 465-3507 FAX
Admin Amaryllis B Lobb. *Dir of Nursing*
Mary Jane Karns RN. *Medical Dir* Forest F
Shiely.
Licensure Intermediate care. *Beds* ICF 67.
Private Pay Patients 6%. *Certified* Medicaid.
Owner Proprietary corp (Unicare).
Admissions Requirements Medical
examination.
Staff Physicians 8 (ft); RNs 1 (ft); LPNs 5 (ft);
Nurses' aides 25 (ft); Physical therapists 1
(ft); Speech therapists 1 (ft); Activities
coordinators 1 (ft), 1 (pt); Dietitians 1 (ft);
Ophthalmologists 3 (pt); Podiatrists 1 (pt).
Facilities Dining room; Physical therapy
room; Activities room; Crafts room; Laundry
room; Barber/Beauty shop; Library; Front
porch; Yard; Outside activity areas.
Activities Arts & crafts; Cards; Games;
Reading groups; Prayer groups; Movies;
Shopping trips; Dances/Social/Cultural
gatherings; Intergenerational programs; Pet
therapy.

Metzmeier Nursing Home
700 N Central Ave, Campbellsville, KY 42718
(502) 465-4321
Admin Don Metzmeier.
Medical Dir Roy E Wilson MD.
Licensure Skilled care; Intermediate care. *Beds*
SNF 48; ICF 23. *Certified* Medicaid;
Medicare.
Owner Proprietary corp.

Staff Physicians 14 (pt); RNs 2 (ft), 1 (pt);
LPNs 7 (ft), 1 (pt); Nurses' aides 24 (ft), 12
(pt); Speech therapists 1 (pt); Activities
coordinators 1 (ft); Dietitians;
Ophthalmologists; Dentists 5 (pt).
Facilities Dining room; Physical therapy
room; Activities room; Laundry room;
Barber/Beauty shop.
Activities Arts & crafts; Cards; Games;
Reading groups; Prayer groups; Movies;
Shopping trips; Dances/Social/Cultural
gatherings.

Carlisle

Johnson-Mathers Nursing Home
2323 Concrete Rd, Box 232, Carlisle, KY
40311
(606) 289-7181
Admin Robert W Hester Jr. *Dir of Nursing*
Pam Garrison RN. *Medical Dir* Jack T
Morford MD.
Licensure Skilled care; Intermediate care;
Personal care. *Beds* SNF 13; ICF 26;
Personal 4; Swing beds SNF/ICF 12.
Certified Medicaid; Medicare.
Owner Nonprofit corp.
Admissions Requirements Medical
examination; Physician's request.
Staff RNs 2 (ft), 4 (pt); LPNs 5 (ft); Nurses'
aides 24 (ft), 26 (pt); Physical therapists 1
(pt); Activities coordinators 1 (ft); Dietitians
1 (pt).
Facilities Dining room; Physical therapy
room; Activities room; Chapel; Laundry
room; Barber/Beauty shop.
Activities Arts & crafts; Cards; Games;
Reading groups; Prayer groups; Movies;
Dances/Social/Cultural gatherings; Residents
council.

Carrollton

Carrollton Manor
205 5th St, Carrollton, KY 41008
(502) 732-5528
Admin Cathy C Vinson.
Licensure Personal care. *Beds* Personal care
32.
Owner Proprietary corp.

Green Valley Health Care Center
1206 11th St, Carrollton, KY 41008
(502) 732-6683
Admin Susan Carlisle. *Dir of Nursing* Valecia
Penick RN.
Licensure Intermediate care; Personal care.
Beds ICF 55; Personal 8.
Owner Proprietary corp.
Staff RNs 1 (ft); LPNs 1 (ft); Physical
therapists 1 (ft); Speech therapists 1 (ft);
Activities coordinators 1 (ft); Dietitians 1
(pt); Ophthalmologists 1 (pt); Audiologists 1
(pt); Dentists 1 (pt).
Facilities Dining room; Activities room;
Laundry room; Library.
Activities Arts & crafts; Cards; Games;
Reading groups; Prayer groups; Dances/
Social/Cultural gatherings.

Central City

Sparks Nursing Center
PO Box 387, Central City, KY 42345
(502) 754-4838
Admin Lula Wade.
Licensure Personal care. *Beds* Personal care
88.
Owner Privately owned.
Admissions Requirements Physician's request.
Staff LPNs; Activities coordinators; Dietitians.
Facilities Dining room; Activities room;
Crafts room; Laundry room; Barber/Beauty
shop.

Activities Arts & crafts; Cards; Games;
Reading groups; Prayer groups; Movies; Pet
therapy.

Clinton

Clinton-Hickman County Hospital—IC/PC Facility
359 Washington St, Clinton, KY 42031
(502) 653-2461
Admin William B Little.
Licensure Intermediate care; Personal care.
Beds ICF 46; Personal care 10. *Certified*
Medicaid.
Owner Nonprofit corp.

West Kentucky Manor
106 Padgett Dr, Clinton, KY 42031
(502) 653-2011
Admin Sharon Boaz.
Medical Dir Hazel Litesy.
Licensure Intermediate care; Personal care.
Beds ICF 86; Personal care 10. *Certified*
Medicaid.
Owner Proprietary corp.
Staff Physicians 3 (pt); RNs 1 (pt); LPNs 2
(ft), 1 (pt); Nurses' aides 40 (ft), 3 (pt);
Physical therapists 1 (pt); Activities
coordinators 1 (ft); Dietitians 1 (ft).
Facilities Dining room; Physical therapy
room; Activities room; Crafts room.
Activities Arts & crafts; Cards; Games;
Reading groups; Prayer groups; Movies;
Shopping trips; Dances/Social/Cultural
gatherings.

Cloverport

Tindles Personal Care Home
PO Box 108, Hwy 105, Cloverport, KY 40111
(502) 788-3723
Admin Sue Tindle; Ray Tindle.
Medical Dir Sue Tindle.
Licensure Personal care. *Beds* Personal care
40.
Owner Privately owned.
Admissions Requirements Minimum age 16;
Medical examination; Physician's request.
Staff Nurses' aides.
Facilities Dining room; Activities room;
Laundry room.
Activities Arts & crafts; Cards; Games;
Reading groups; Prayer groups; Shopping
trips; Picnics; Dinners; Bible study.

Columbia

Goodin's Rest Home
Rte 3, Columbia, KY 42728
(502) 384-2630
Admin Bertha Goodin.
Licensure Personal care. *Beds* 5.

Summit Manor
400 Bomar Heights, Columbia, KY 42728
(502) 384-2153
Admin Brenda C Williams. *Dir of Nursing*
Carol Edwards. *Medical Dir* Dr James
Salato.
Licensure Skilled care; Intermediate care. *Beds*
SNF 38; ICF 66. *Certified* Medicaid;
Medicare.
Owner Proprietary corp.
Facilities Dining room; Physical therapy
room; Activities room; Laundry room;
Barber/Beauty shop; 2 Lounges.
Activities Arts & crafts; Games; Reading
groups; Prayer groups; Movies; Shopping
trips.

Corbin

Christian Health Center
PO Box 1304, Master St & Commonwealth
Ave, Corbin, KY 40701
(606) 528-2886

Admin William Collins.
Licensure Intermediate care; Personal care. *Beds* ICF 98; Personal care 17.
Owner Nonprofit corp (Christian Church Campuses).

Hillcrest Nursing Home
PO Box 556, Rte 7, Corbin, KY 40701
(606) 528-8917
Admin Carolyn Smith.
Medical Dir Elmer G Prewitt MD.
Licensure Skilled care; Intermediate care. *Beds* SNF 41; ICF 79. *Certified* Medicaid; Medicare.
Owner Proprietary corp (Health Systems).
Admissions Requirements Medical examination.
Staff Physicians 8 (ft); RNs 5 (ft); LPNs 9 (ft); Nurses' aides 44 (ft); Physical therapists 1 (ft); Speech therapists 1 (pt); Activities coordinators 1 (ft); Dietitians 1 (pt); Dentists 3 (pt).
Facilities Dining room; Physical therapy room; Activities room; Crafts room; Barber/Beauty shop.
Activities Arts & crafts; Cards; Games; Reading groups; Prayer groups; Movies; Dances/Social/Cultural gatherings.

Mountain Laurel Manor
PO Box 1190, Rte 7 Box 349, Corbin, KY 40701
(606) 528-8822
Admin Cathy J Willis. *Dir of Nursing* Betty Carter LPN. *Medical Dir* Dr Elmer G Prewitt.
Licensure Intermediate care. *Beds* ICF 50. *Certified* Medicaid.
Owner Proprietary corp (Health Systems).
Admissions Requirements Medical examination.
Staff Physicians 8 (ft); RNs 1 (pt); LPNs 3 (ft); Nurses' aides 10 (ft), 11 (pt); Activities coordinators 1 (ft); Dietitians 3 (ft), 2 (pt); Supervisors 1 (ft).
Facilities Dining room; Laundry room.
Activities Arts & crafts; Cards; Games; Reading groups; Movies; Shopping trips.

Covington

Covington Ladies Home
702 Garrard St, Covington, KY 41011
(606) 431-6913
Admin Judy Gilbert.
Licensure Personal care. *Beds* Personal care 36.
Owner Proprietary corp.
Admissions Requirements Minimum age 65; Females only; Medical examination.
Staff LPNs 3 (ft); Nurses' aides 6 (ft), 3 (pt); Activities coordinators 1 (ft).
Facilities Dining room; Activities room; Chapel; Laundry room.
Activities Arts & crafts; Cards; Games; Prayer groups; Movies; Shopping trips.

Garrard Convalescent Home
425 Garrard St, Covington, KY 41011
(606) 581-9393
Admin Ralph Stacy.
Medical Dir Dr F B Rodriquez.
Licensure Skilled care; Intermediate care. *Beds* SNF 41; ICF 22. *Certified* Medicaid; Medicare.
Owner Proprietary corp.
Staff Physicians 1 (pt); RNs 2 (ft), 1 (pt); LPNs 5 (ft); Nurses' aides 28 (ft), 2 (pt); Physical therapists 1 (pt); Speech therapists 1 (pt); Activities coordinators 1 (ft); Dietitians 1 (pt); Ophthalmologists 1 (pt); Podiatrists 1 (pt); Dentists 1 (pt).
Facilities Dining room; Activities room; Laundry room.
Activities Arts & crafts; Cards; Reading groups; Prayer groups; Dances/Social/Cultural gatherings; Trips to zoo.

Rosedale Manor
4250 Glenn Ave, Covington, KY 41015-1699
(606) 431-2244
Admin Arthur W Urlage. *Dir of Nursing* Kathy Knight RN.
Licensure Intermediate care; Personal care. *Beds* ICF 142; Personal 66. *Certified* Medicaid.
Owner Nonprofit corp.
Admissions Requirements Medical examination; Physician's request.
Staff RNs 1 (ft); LPNs 10 (ft); Activities coordinators 1 (ft); Dietitians 1 (ft).
Facilities Dining room; Activities room; Chapel; Crafts room; Laundry room; Barber/Beauty shop; Library; Outdoor grounds.
Activities Arts & crafts; Cards; Games; Reading groups; Prayer groups; Movies; Shopping trips; Dances/Social/Cultural gatherings; Field trips; Shuffleboard; Picnics; Fishing; Ball games; Bingo; Birthday parties.

St Charles Care Center
500 Farrell Dr, Covington, KY 41011
(606) 331-3224
Admin Sr Mary Luann Bender. *Dir of Nursing* Sr Mary Delrita Glaser. *Medical Dir* Dr Ralph Huller.
Licensure Skilled care; Intermediate care; Retirement; Alzheimer's care. *Beds* SNF 54; ICF 93. *Certified* Medicaid; Medicare.
Owner Nonprofit corp.
Staff RNs; LPNs; Nurses' aides; Physical therapists; Recreational therapists; Activities coordinators; Dietitians.
Facilities Dining room; Physical therapy room; Activities room; Chapel; Crafts room; Laundry room; Barber/Beauty shop; Library.
Activities Arts & crafts; Cards; Games; Reading groups; Prayer groups; Movies; Shopping trips; Dances/Social/Cultural gatherings.

St John's Nursing Home
800 Highland Ave, Covington, KY 41011
(606) 491-3800
Admin Alfred Mollozzi. *Dir of Nursing* Cheryl Menninger RN. *Medical Dir* Dr David Suetholtz.
Licensure Skilled care; Intermediate care; Personal care. *Beds* SNF 58; ICF 269; Personal care 63. *Certified* Medicaid; Medicare.
Owner Nonprofit corp (Pavillion Care Centers).
Admissions Requirements Minimum age 18.
Staff RNs 2 (ft); LPNs 29 (ft); Nurses' aides 169 (ft); Physical therapists 1 (ft); Speech therapists 1 (ft); Activities coordinators 1 (ft); Dietitians 2 (ft).
Facilities Dining room; Physical therapy room; Activities room; Chapel; Crafts room; Barber/Beauty shop; Respiratory therapy; Speech therapy.
Activities Arts & crafts; Cards; Games; Reading groups; Prayer groups; Movies; Shopping trips; Dances/Social/Cultural gatherings; Traveling wheelchair volleyball team.

Cynthiana

Edgemont Manor Nursing Home
Monticello Heights, Cynthiana, KY 41031
(606) 234-4595
Admin Rita Glascock.
Licensure Personal care; Nursing home. *Beds* Personal care 2; Nursing home 68.
Owner Proprietary corp.

Grand Haven Nursing Home
RR 3, Rodgers Park, Cynthiana, KY 41031
(606) 234-2050
Admin Martha Brown.
Medical Dir Anna Ruth McLoney.
Licensure Intermediate care. *Beds* ICF 54. *Certified* Medicaid.
Owner Proprietary corp.

Admissions Requirements Medical examination.
Staff RNs 1 (ft), 1 (pt); LPNs 1 (ft), 3 (pt); Nurses' aides 8 (ft), 13 (pt); Activities coordinators 1 (ft); Dietitians 1 (ft).
Facilities Dining room; Physical therapy room; Activities room; Laundry room; Barber/Beauty shop.
Activities Games; Prayer groups; Movies; Shopping trips; Dances/Social/Cultural gatherings.

Harrison Memorial Hospital
PO Box 250, Millersburg Pike, Cynthiana, KY 41031
(606) 234-2300
Admin James R Farris. *Dir of Nursing* Bettye Marshall RN. *Medical Dir* Richard Allen MD.
Licensure Skilled care; Intermediate care. *Beds* SNF 16; ICF 8. *Certified* Medicaid; Medicare.
Owner Nonprofit corp.
Admissions Requirements Medical examination; Physician's request.
Staff RNs 27 (ft), 7 (pt); LPNs 21 (ft), 2 (pt); Nurses' aides 32 (ft), 3 (pt); Physical therapists 1 (ft); Activities coordinators 1 (ft); Dietitians 1 (ft).
Facilities Dining room; Activities room; Outdoor patio.
Activities Cards; Games; Reading groups; Prayer groups; Movies; Dances/Social/Cultural gatherings.

Martin's Rest Home
321 Oddville Ave, Cynthiana, KY 41031
(606) 234-1683
Admin Martha R Brown.
Licensure Personal care. *Beds* Personal care 51.
Owner Proprietary corp.
Staff Nurses' aides 11 (ft), 4 (pt); Dietitians 1 (pt).
Facilities Dining room; Activities room; Laundry room.
Activities Games; Shopping trips; Dances/Social/Cultural gatherings.

Shady Lawn Home
108 Miller St, Cynthiana, KY 41031
(606) 234-2606
Admin Martha Brown.
Licensure Personal care. *Beds* Personal care 75.
Owner Proprietary corp.

Danville

Autumnfield of Danville
203 Bruce Ct, Danville, KY 40422
(606) 236-9292
Admin Shirley Quisenberry.
Licensure Intermediate care; Personal care. *Beds* ICF 74; Personal 16.
Owner Proprietary corp (OMG Corp).

Friendship House Fellowship Home
642 N 3rd St, Danville, KY 40422
(606) 236-3972
Admin Timothy W Struttmann. *Dir of Nursing* Martha Gray. *Medical Dir* R Quinn Bailey MD.
Licensure Skilled care; Intermediate care; Personal care. *Beds* SNF; ICF 54; Personal care 6. *Certified* Medicaid; Medicare.
Owner Proprietary corp (Hillhaven Corp).
Admissions Requirements Minimum age 18.
Staff Physicians 12 (pt); RNs 5 (ft), 2 (pt); LPNs 15 (ft), 1 (pt); Nurses' aides 36 (ft), 10 (pt); Physical therapists 1 (pt); Recreational therapists 1 (pt); Occupational therapists 1 (pt); Speech therapists 1 (pt); Activities coordinators 1 (ft); Dietitians 1 (pt); Ophthalmologists 1 (pt); Podiatrists 1 (pt); Audiologists 1 (pt).

Facilities Dining room; Activities room; Laundry room; Barber/Beauty shop.
Activities Arts & crafts; Cards; Reading groups; Prayer groups; Movies; Shopping trips; Pet therapy.

Dawson Springs

Dawson Springs Health Care Center
PO Box 338, 100 Ramsey St, Dawson Springs, KY 42408
(502) 797-8131
Admin Deborah Johnson. *Dir of Nursing* Ruth Barnett RN. *Medical Dir* Dr Herbert Chaney.
Licensure Skilled care; Intermediate care. *Beds* SNF 20; ICF 60. *Certified* Medicaid; Medicare; JCAH; VA.
Owner Proprietary corp (National Health Corp).
Staff Physicians 2 (pt); RNs 4 (ft); LPNs 7 (ft); Nurses' aides 22 (ft), 7 (pt); Physical therapists 1 (pt); Speech therapists 1 (pt); Activities coordinators 1 (ft); Dietitians 1 (pt).
Facilities Dining room; Physical therapy room; Activities room; Laundry room; Barber/Beauty shop.
Activities Arts & crafts; Games; Movies.

New Dawson Springs Nursing Home
PO Box 580, 213 Water St, Dawson Springs, KY 42408
(502) 797-2025, 797-5682
Admin Linda S Thomas.
Licensure Intermediate care; Personal care. *Beds* ICF 69; Personal care 35. *Certified* Medicaid.
Owner Proprietary corp.
Admissions Requirements Medical examination.
Staff RNs 2 (ft), 1 (pt); LPNs 5 (ft); Nurses' aides 50 (ft); Activities coordinators 1 (ft); Resident services directors 1 (ft); Dietary managers 1 (ft), 1 (pt).
Facilities Dining room; Laundry room.
Activities Arts & crafts; Cards; Games; Reading groups; Prayer groups; Movies; Shopping trips; Dances/Social/Cultural gatherings; Pet therapy; Church services.

Dry Ridge

Dry Ridge Personal Care Home
Taft Hwy, Dry Ridge, KY 41035
(606) 824-6164
Admin Ronald B Bennett.
Licensure Personal care. *Beds* Personal care 64.
Owner Proprietary corp.

Edmonton

Harper's Home for the Aged
CASS 905, 7410 Greensburg Rd, Edmonton, KY 42129
(502) 432-5202
Admin Dinah Cassady.
Licensure Personal care. *Beds* Personal care 29.
Owner Proprietary corp.
Admissions Requirements Minimum age 16; Medical examination.
Staff Nurses' aides 5 (ft); Activities coordinators 1 (ft).
Facilities Dining room; Laundry room.
Activities Arts & crafts; Cards; Games; Movies; Shopping trips; Dances/Social/Cultural gatherings; Church services; Activities for visually & hearing impaired.

Metcalfe County Nursing Home
PO Box 115, Skyline Dr, Edmonton, KY 42129
(502) 432-2921
Admin Lee G Bidwell. *Dir of Nursing* Debbie Acree.

Licensure Intermediate care; Personal care; Alzheimer's care. *Beds* ICF 71; Personal care 30. *Private Pay Patients* 3%. *Certified* Medicaid.
Owner Publicly owned.
Staff RNs 1 (ft); LPNs 5 (ft); Nurses' aides 30 (ft); Speech therapists 1 (ft); Dietitians 1 (ft).
Facilities Dining room; Activities room; Crafts room; Laundry room; Barber/Beauty shop.
Activities Arts & crafts; Cards; Games; Reading groups; Prayer groups; Movies; Shopping trips; Dances/Social/Cultural gatherings.

Elizabethtown

The Healthcare Center
106 Diecks Dr, Elizabethtown, KY 42701
(502) 737-2738
Admin Mary Lou Dearner. *Dir of Nursing* Rosie Hildesheim. *Medical Dir* Dr P Gerrard.
Licensure Skilled care; Independent and assisted living. *Beds* SNF 60; Independent and assisted living apartments 67. *Certified* Medicaid; Medicare.
Owner Nonprofit corp (Presbyterian Homes & Services of Kentucky Inc).
Staff RNs 4 (ft); LPNs 12 (ft); Nurses' aides 20 (ft); Activities coordinators 1 (ft).
Facilities Dining room; Physical therapy room; Activities room; Barber/Beauty shop; Lounges.
Activities Arts & crafts; Cards; Games; Reading groups; Prayer groups; Movies; Shopping trips; Dances/Social/Cultural gatherings; Intergenerational programs; Pet therapy; Exercise classes; Religious services.

Heartland Healthcare Center
510 Pennsylvania Ave, Elizabethtown, KY 42701
(502) 769-3314
Admin Sarah Lovell. *Dir of Nursing* Jerilyn Oakes. *Medical Dir* William Godfrey.
Licensure Intermediate care. *Beds* ICF 67. *Private Pay Patients* 6%. *Certified* Medicaid.
Owner Proprietary corp (Complete Care Inc).
Admissions Requirements Minimum age 18; Medical examination; Physician's request.
Facilities Dining room; Activities room.
Activities Arts & crafts; Games; Prayer groups; Movies; Dances/Social/Cultural gatherings; Intergenerational programs; Pet therapy.

Medco Center of Elizabethtown
1101 Woodland Dr, Elizabethtown, KY 42701
(502) 765-6106
Admin Rebecca S Weaver. *Dir of Nursing* Ida Watts. *Medical Dir* Dr Godfrey.
Licensure Intermediate care; Personal care. *Beds* ICF 50; Personal 16. *Certified* Medicaid.
Owner Proprietary corp (Unicare).
Admissions Requirements Medical examination.
Staff RNs 1 (ft); LPNs 4 (ft); Nurses' aides 10 (ft), 10 (pt); Activities coordinators 1 (ft).
Facilities Dining room; Physical therapy room; Activities room; Barber/Beauty shop.
Activities Arts & crafts; Cards; Games; Reading groups; Prayer groups; Movies; Shopping trips; Dances/Social/Cultural gatherings; Outings.

Woodland Terrace Health Care Facility
PO Box 1, 1117 Woodland Dr, Elizabethtown, KY 42701
(502) 769-2363
Admin Ellen S Stafford. *Dir of Nursing* Trina Ready. *Medical Dir* David T Lewis.
Licensure Skilled care; Intermediate care; Personal care. *Beds* SNF 50; ICF 62; Personal care 6. *Private Pay Patients* 8%. *Certified* Medicaid; Medicare.
Owner Proprietary corp (First Healthcare Corp).

Admissions Requirements Medical examination.
Staff Physicians 1 (pt); RNs 4 (ft), 2 (pt); LPNs 9 (ft), 4 (pt); Nurses' aides 35 (ft), 7 (pt); Physical therapists; Speech therapists 1 (pt); Activities coordinators 1 (ft); Dietitians 1 (pt); Podiatrists 1 (pt).
Facilities Dining room; Physical therapy room; Activities room; Laundry room; Barber/Beauty shop.
Activities Arts & crafts; Cards; Games; Reading groups; Prayer groups; Movies; Shopping trips; Dances/Social/Cultural gatherings; Pet therapy; Exercise.

Elkhorn City

Mountain View Health Care Center
PO Box 650, US Hwy 197, Elkhorn City, KY 41522
(606) 754-4134
Admin Sharon K Hall.
Licensure Intermediate care; Personal care. *Beds* ICF 106; Personal 20. *Certified* Medicaid.
Owner Proprietary corp (Angell Group).

Elkton

Country Manor of Todd County
PO Box 427, Allensville Rd, Elkton, KY 42220
(502) 265-5321
Admin Nancy K Bolster.
Licensure Personal care. *Beds* Personal care 94.
Owner Proprietary corp.

Falmouth

Falmouth Rest Home
406 Barkley St, Falmouth, KY 41040
(606) 654-4341
Admin Ruth Sharp. *Dir of Nursing* Stella Richardson, Supv.
Licensure Personal care. *Beds* Personal care 28. *Certified* Medicaid; Medicare.
Owner Privately owned (Jowin Inc).
Staff Physicians; LPNs; Nurses' aides; Dietitians.
Facilities Dining room; Activities room; Laundry room; Private and semi-private rooms available.
Activities Arts & crafts; Cards; Games; Prayer groups; Movies.

Sharp's Personal Care Home
307 Maple Ave, Falmouth, KY 41040
(606) 654-8294
Admin Donna R West. *Dir of Nursing* Ruth Sharp. *Medical Dir* Ruth Sharp.
Licensure Personal care. *Beds* Personal care 22. *Private Pay Patients* 20%. *Certified* Medicaid.
Owner Privately owned.
Admissions Requirements Medical examination.
Staff LPNs; Nurses' aides; Activities coordinators; Dietitians.
Facilities Dining room; Activities room; Laundry room.
Activities Arts & crafts; Cards; Games; Reading groups; Prayer groups; Movies; Shopping trips; Pet therapy.

Flatwoods

Oakmont Manor
1100 Grandview Dr, Flatwoods, KY 41139
(606) 836-3187
Admin June Setser. *Dir of Nursing* Barbara McKinney RN. *Medical Dir* Oren Justice MD.
Licensure Intermediate care. *Beds* ICF 85. *Certified* Medicaid.
Owner Proprietary corp.

Admissions Requirements Medical examination; Physician's request.
Staff Physicians 5 (pt); RNs 1 (ft); LPNs 5 (ft), 2 (pt); Nurses' aides 20 (ft), 10 (pt); Recreational therapists 1 (ft); Dietitians 1 (pt); Podiatrists 1 (pt).
Facilities Dining room; Activities room; Crafts room; Laundry room; Barber/Beauty shop.
Activities Arts & crafts; Games; Reading groups; Prayer groups; Movies; Shopping trips; Dances/Social/Cultural gatherings.

Flemingsburg

Pioneer Trace Nursing Home
115 Pioneer Trace, Flemingsburg, KY 41041
(606) 845-2131
Admin Mary Ann Campbell. *Dir of Nursing* Kathy Catron.
Licensure Intermediate care; Personal care. *Beds* ICF 89; Personal care 6. *Private Pay Patients* 20%. *Certified* Medicaid.
Owner Proprietary corp.
Admissions Requirements Physician's request.
Staff Physicians 4 (ft); RNs 3 (ft); LPNs 4 (ft), 1 (pt); Nurses' aides 25 (ft), 10 (pt); Activities coordinators 1 (ft); Dietitians 1 (pt).
Facilities Dining room; Activities room; Chapel; Crafts room; Barber/Beauty shop.
Activities Arts & crafts; Reading groups; Prayer groups; Movies; Intergenerational programs.

Florence

Florence Park Care Center
6975 Burlington Pike, Florence, KY 41042
(606) 525-0007, 525-8995 FAX
Admin William J Krech II. *Dir of Nursing* Donna Geromes RNC. *Medical Dir* William Reutman MD.
Licensure Skilled care; Intermediate care; Alzheimer's care. *Beds* SNF 30; ICF 120. *Certified* Medicare.
Owner Proprietary corp.
Admissions Requirements Physician's request.
Staff Physicians 1 (pt); RNs 6 (ft), 1 (pt); LPNs 17 (ft), 4 (pt); Nurses' aides 74 (ft), 18 (pt); Physical therapists 1 (pt); Recreational therapists 2 (ft), 3 (pt); Occupational therapists 1 (pt); Speech therapists 1 (pt); Activities coordinators 1 (ft); Dietitians 1 (pt); Ophthalmologists 1 (pt); Podiatrists 1 (pt); Audiologists 1 (pt); Music therapists 1 (pt).
Facilities Dining room; Physical therapy room; Activities room; Crafts room; Laundry room; Barber/Beauty shop; Library; Outdoor garden walkway with video camera surveillance for Alzheimer's patients; Nurse assistant training center; Clinical site for university programs.
Activities Arts & crafts; Cards; Games; Reading groups; Prayer groups; Movies; Shopping trips; Dances/Social/Cultural gatherings; Intergenerational programs; Pet therapy.

Woodspoint Nursing Home
7300 Woodspoint Dr, Florence, KY 41042
(606) 371-5731
Admin Ken Urlage.
Licensure Skilled care; Intermediate care. *Beds* SNF 50; ICF 101. *Certified* Medicaid; Medicare.
Owner Nonprofit corp.
Facilities Dining room; Physical therapy room; Activities room; Chapel; Laundry room; Barber/Beauty shop.
Activities Arts & crafts; Cards; Games; Reading groups; Prayer groups; Movies; Shopping trips; Dances/Social/Cultural gatherings.

Fordsville

Medco Center of Fordsville
PO Box 205, Fordsville, KY 42343
(502) 276-3603
Admin Kara Meredith. *Dir of Nursing* Hettie Johnson.
Licensure Intermediate care. *Beds* ICF 67. *Certified* Medicaid.
Owner Proprietary corp (Unicare).
Admissions Requirements Physician's request.
Staff RNs 1 (ft); LPNs 4 (ft).
Facilities Dining room; Laundry room.
Activities Arts & crafts; Cards; Games; Reading groups; Prayer groups; Movies; Shopping trips; Dances/Social/Cultural gatherings.

Fort Thomas

Carmel Manor
Carmel Manor Rd, Fort Thomas, KY 41075
(606) 781-5111
Admin Sr Ann Kruskamp.
Medical Dir Dr Edward Stratman.
Licensure Personal care. *Beds* Personal care 99.
Owner Proprietary corp.
Admissions Requirements Minimum age 65; Medical examination.
Staff Physicians 2 (pt); RNs 2 (ft); LPNs 6 (pt); Nurses' aides 55 (ft), 7 (pt); Activities coordinators 1 (ft); Dietitians 1 (pt).
Affiliation Roman Catholic.
Facilities Dining room; Physical therapy room; Activities room; Chapel; Crafts room; Laundry room; Barber/Beauty shop; Library; Coffee shop.
Activities Arts & crafts; Cards; Games; Prayer groups; Movies; Shopping trips; Dances/Social/Cultural gatherings.

Horizon House II
435 River Rd, Fort Thomas, KY 41075
(606) 781-5662
Admin Vickie Anderson.
Licensure Intermediate care for mentally retarded.
Owner Nonprofit corp.

Frankfort

Bradford Square
1040 US 127 S, Frankfort, KY 40601
(502) 875-5600
Admin Deborah Ison. *Dir of Nursing* Virgie Babalmuradi. *Medical Dir* Jerald Dudney MD.
Licensure Skilled care; Intermediate care; Personal care. *Beds* SNF 25; ICF 50; Personal care 25. *Certified* Medicaid; Medicare.
Owner Proprietary corp (Senior Care Inc).
Admissions Requirements Medical examination; Physician's request.
Staff Physicians 10 (pt); RNs 3 (ft), 1 (pt); LPNs 4 (ft), 2 (pt); Nurses' aides 25 (ft), 10 (pt); Physical therapists 1 (ft); Speech therapists 1 (pt); Activities coordinators 1 (ft); Dietitians 1 (ft); Podiatrists 1 (pt).
Facilities Dining room; Physical therapy room; Activities room; Crafts room; Laundry room; Barber/Beauty shop.
Activities Arts & crafts; Cards; Games; Reading groups; Prayer groups; Movies; Shopping trips; Dances/Social/Cultural gatherings; Pet therapy.

Franklin Manor
Old Soldiers Ln, Frankfort, KY 40601
(502) 875-7272
Admin Steve Ramsey.
Medical Dir Dr William McElwain.
Licensure Skilled care; Intermediate care. *Beds* SNF 50; ICF 50. *Certified* Medicaid; Medicare.
Owner Proprietary corp (Beverly Enterprises).

Admissions Requirements Medical examination.
Staff RNs 2 (ft), 3 (pt); LPNs 7 (ft), 1 (pt); Nurses' aides 30 (ft), 1 (pt); Physical therapists 1 (ft), 1 (pt); Speech therapists 1 (pt); Activities coordinators 1 (ft); Dietitians 1 (ft).
Facilities Dining room; Physical therapy room; Activities room; Crafts room; Laundry room; Barber/Beauty shop; Lobby/Lounge.
Activities Arts & crafts; Games; Reading groups; Prayer groups; Dances/Social/Cultural gatherings.

Franklin

Franklin Personal Care
214 S College St, Franklin, KY 42134
(502) 586-5995
Admin Hector Rivas.
Licensure Personal care. *Beds* Personal care 28.
Owner Proprietary corp.

Lewis Memorial Methodist Home
2905 Bowling Green Rd, Franklin, KY 42134
(502) 586-3461
Admin Dorothy C Clark.
Licensure Personal care. *Beds* Personal care 23.
Owner Nonprofit corp.
Affiliation Methodist.

Medco Center of Franklin
PO Box 367, 414 Robey St, Franklin, KY 42134
(502) 586-7141
Admin Clifton Lake. *Dir of Nursing* Carol Frye RN. *Medical Dir* J M Pulliam MD.
Licensure Intermediate care; Alzheimer's care. *Beds* ICF 98. *Certified* Medicaid.
Owner Proprietary corp (Unicare).
Admissions Requirements Medical examination; Physician's request.
Staff RNs 1 (ft); LPNs 10 (ft); Nurses' aides 30 (ft); Physical therapists 1 (pt), 2 (pt); Recreational therapists 1 (ft), 1 (pt); Speech therapists 1 (ft), 1 (pt); Dietitians 1 (ft).
Facilities Dining room; Physical therapy room; Activities room; Crafts room; Laundry room; Barber/Beauty shop.
Activities Arts & crafts; Cards; Games; Reading groups; Prayer groups; Movies; Dances/Social/Cultural gatherings.

Fulton

Haws Memorial Nursing Home
Holiday Ln, Fulton, KY 42041
(502) 472-1971
Admin Marvin Hayes.
Licensure Skilled care. *Beds* SNF 60. *Certified* Medicaid; Medicare.
Owner Proprietary corp.
Facilities Dining room; Physical therapy room; Activities room; Crafts room; Barber/Beauty shop; Library.
Activities Arts & crafts; Games; Reading groups; Movies; Dances/Social/Cultural gatherings.

Parkway Manor
309 N Highland Dr, Fulton, KY 42041
(502) 472-3386
Admin Joanne Harper.
Licensure Intermediate care. *Beds* ICF 20. *Certified* Medicaid.
Owner Proprietary corp.
Staff Physicians 4 (ft); RNs 2 (pt); LPNs 1 (ft), 1 (pt); Nurses' aides 8 (ft), 2 (pt); Activities coordinators 1 (ft); Dietitians 1 (pt).
Facilities Dining room; Laundry room; Barber/Beauty shop.
Activities Arts & crafts; Cards; Games; Dances/Social/Cultural gatherings.

Georgetown

Dover Manor Nursing Home
112 Dover Dr, Georgetown, KY 40324
(502) 863-9529
Admin Tracey L Martin.
Medical Dir Laura Shields.
Licensure Intermediate care; Personal care.
  Beds ICF 85; Personal care 10. *Certified*
  Medicaid.
Owner Privately owned.
Admissions Requirements Medical
  examination.
Staff RNs 1 (ft); LPNs 7 (ft); Nurses' aides 50
  (ft); Activities coordinators 1 (pt); Dietitians
  1 (pt).
Facilities Dining room; Activities room;
  Chapel; Crafts room; Laundry room; Barber/
  Beauty shop.
Activities Arts & crafts; Cards; Games;
  Reading groups; Prayer groups; Movies;
  Dances/Social/Cultural gatherings.

Springhaven Nursing Care
102 Pocahantas Trail, Georgetown, KY
  40324-1196
(502) 863-3696, 863-3983
Admin Gordon Poppell.
Licensure Skilled care; Intermediate care. *Beds*
  SNF 15; ICF 35. *Certified* Medicaid;
  Medicare.
Owner Proprietary corp.

Glasgow

Barren County Health Care Center
300 Westwood, Glasgow, KY 42141
(502) 651-9131
Admin Steve Brown.
Licensure Intermediate care. *Beds* ICF 94.
  Certified Medicaid.
Owner Proprietary corp.

Glasgow Health Care Facility
220 Westwood St, Glasgow, KY 42141
(502) 651-6661
Admin Georgene H Fraley. *Dir of Nursing*
  Marcella Fox RN.
Licensure Intermediate care; Personal care.
  Beds ICF 60; Personal care 40. *Certified*
  Medicaid.
Owner Proprietary corp (EPI Corp).
Facilities Dining room.
Activities Arts & crafts; Cards; Games;
  Reading groups; Prayer groups; Movies;
  Shopping trips.

Glasgow State—ICF
State Ave, Glasgow, KY 42141
(502) 651-2151
Admin John E Broadbent. *Dir of Nursing*
  Doris Oliver RN. *Medical Dir* Phillip Bale
  MD.
Licensure Intermediate care. *Beds* ICF 100.
  Certified Medicaid.
Owner Publicly owned.
Admissions Requirements Medical
  examination.
Staff Physicians 3 (pt); RNs 2 (ft); LPNs 16
  (ft); Nurses' aides 30 (ft), 1 (pt); Physical
  therapists 1 (pt); Recreational therapists 3
  (ft); Activities coordinators 1 (ft); Dietitians
  1 (ft), 1 (pt).
Facilities Dining room; Activities room;
  Crafts room; Laundry room; Barber/Beauty
  shop; Library.
Activities Arts & crafts; Cards; Games;
  Reading groups; Movies; Shopping trips.

Glenview Manor
1002 Glenview Dr, Glasgow, KY 42141
(502) 651-8332
Admin Kay Bush. *Dir of Nursing* Jessica Shaw
  RN. *Medical Dir* Dr John Asriel.
Licensure Intermediate care. *Beds* ICF 60.
  Certified Medicaid.
Owner Privately owned.

Admissions Requirements Minimum age 30;
  Medical examination; Physician's request.
Staff RNs 1 (ft); LPNs 3 (ft), 2 (pt); Nurses'
  aides 18 (ft), 10 (pt); Activities coordinators
  1 (ft), 1 (pt); Dietitians 1 (ft).
Facilities Dining room; Activities room;
  Crafts room; Laundry room; Barber/Beauty
  shop.
Activities Arts & crafts; Cards; Games;
  Reading groups; Prayer groups; Movies;
  Shopping trips; Dances/Social/Cultural
  gatherings.

Homewood Health Care Center
PO Box 297, Homewood Blvd, Glasgow, KY
  42141
(502) 651-6126
Admin Emogene C Stephens. *Dir of Nursing*
  Janie Tharp RN. *Medical Dir* Dr William
  Marrs.
Licensure Skilled care; Intermediate care;
  Personal care. *Beds* SNF 80; ICF 114;
  Personal care 12. *Certified* Medicaid;
  Medicare.
Owner Proprietary corp (National Health
  Corp).
Admissions Requirements Medical
  examination; Physician's request.
Staff RNs 3 (ft), 8 (pt); LPNs 10 (ft), 16 (pt);
  Nurses' aides 70 (ft), 30 (pt); Physical
  therapists 1 (ft); Speech therapists 1 (ft);
  Activities coordinators 1 (ft), 4 (pt);
  Dietitians 1 (ft).
Facilities Dining room; Physical therapy
  room; Activities room; Chapel; Crafts room;
  Laundry room; Barber/Beauty shop.
Activities Arts & crafts; Cards; Games;
  Reading groups; Prayer groups; Movies;
  Shopping trips; Dances/Social/Cultural
  gatherings.

Grayson

Carter Health Care Center
PO Box 904, Old US 60 E, Grayson, KY
  41143
(606) 474-7835
Admin Van Baldwin.
Licensure Intermediate care. *Beds* ICF 120.
Owner Proprietary corp.

Greensburg

Green Hill Manor
213 Industrial Rd, Greensburg, KY 42743
(502) 932-4241
Admin Geneva Marcum.
Medical Dir Patricia Sutton.
Licensure Intermediate care; Personal care.
  Beds ICF 118; Personal care 8. *Certified*
  Medicaid.
Owner Proprietary corp (Beverly Enterprises).
Admissions Requirements Medical
  examination.
Staff RNs 3 (ft); LPNs 8 (ft); Nurses' aides 40
  (ft), 6 (pt); Occupational therapists 1 (ft);
  Activities coordinators 1 (ft).
Facilities Dining room; Activities room;
  Laundry room; Barber/Beauty shop.
Activities Arts & crafts; Cards; Games;
  Reading groups; Prayer groups; Movies;
  Shopping trips; Dances/Social/Cultural
  gatherings; Fishing trips; Picnics at parks;
  Outings to amusement parks.

McDowell Skilled Nursing Facility
PO Box 202, 202-206 Milby St, Greensburg,
  KY 42743
(502) 932-4211, 932-4211 FAX
Admin William Dowe. *Dir of Nursing* Pam
  Bills RN. *Medical Dir* Robert Shuffett MD.
Licensure Skilled care; Intermediate care. *Beds*
  SNF 12; Swing beds SNF/ICF 10. *Private
  Pay Patients* 1%. *Certified* Medicaid;
  Medicare.
Owner Publicly owned.

Admissions Requirements Medical
  examination; Physician's request.
Staff Physicians 1 (pt); RNs 3 (ft); LPNs 4
  (ft); Nurses' aides 3 (ft); Physical therapists
  (contracted); Speech therapists 1 (pt);
  Activities coordinators 1 (ft); Dietitians 1
  (pt).
Facilities Dining room; Physical therapy
  room; Activities room; Laundry room;
  Barber/Beauty shop; Patio.
Activities Arts & crafts; Cards; Games;
  Reading groups; Movies; Intergenerational
  programs; Church services; Resident council.

Greenville

Maple Manor Health Care Center
515 Greene Dr, Greenville, KY 42345
(502) 338-5400
Admin Martha S Rhoads.
Medical Dir C J Shipp MD.
Licensure Intermediate care; Personal care.
  Beds ICF 88; Personal 18. *Certified*
  Medicaid.
Owner Proprietary corp (Hillhaven Corp).
Staff RNs 2 (ft); LPNs 5 (ft), 4 (pt); Nurses'
  aides 33 (ft), 5 (pt); Physical therapists 1
  (pt); Speech therapists 1 (pt); Activities
  coordinators 1 (ft); Dietitians 1 (pt).
Facilities Dining room; Activities room;
  Chapel; Crafts room; Laundry room; Barber/
  Beauty shop.
Activities Arts & crafts; Cards; Games;
  Reading groups; Prayer groups; Movies;
  Shopping trips; Dances/Social/Cultural
  gatherings.

Belle Meade Home
PO Box 565, 521 Greene Dr, Greenville, KY
  42345
(502) 338-1523
Admin Emily Neff. *Dir of Nursing* Rebecca
  Hammonds. *Medical Dir* Dr Gary Givens.
Licensure Intermediate care; Personal care.
  Beds ICF 62; Personal care 30. *Private Pay
  Patients* 48%. *Certified* Medicaid.
Owner Privately owned.
Staff Physicians 1 (ft); RNs 1 (ft); LPNs 7 (ft);
  Nurses' aides 28 (ft); Activities coordinators
  1 (ft); Dietitians 1 (ft).
Facilities Dining room; Activities room;
  Laundry room; Barber/Beauty shop.
Activities Arts & crafts; Cards; Games; Prayer
  groups; Movies; Shopping trips; Dances/
  Social/Cultural gatherings; Pet therapy.

Muhlenberg Community Hospital
PO Box 387, 440 Hopkinsville St, Greenville,
  KY 42345
(502) 338-4211
Admin C J Perry.
Medical Dir Andre J Wininger.
Licensure Skilled care; Acute care; Alzheimer's
  care. *Beds* SNF 30; Acute care 100. *Certified*
  Medicaid; Medicare.
Owner Nonprofit organization/foundation.
Admissions Requirements Medical
  examination; Physician's request.
Staff Physicians 30 (ft), 4 (pt); RNs 3 (ft), 3
  (pt); LPNs 16 (ft); Nurses' aides 6 (ft);
  Physical therapists 2 (ft); Recreational
  therapists 1 (ft); Speech therapists 1 (pt);
  Activities coordinators 1 (ft); Dietitians 1
  (ft).
Languages Spanish, German.
Facilities Dining room; Physical therapy
  room; Activities room; Chapel; Barber/
  Beauty shop; Library; Courtyards.
Activities Arts & crafts; Cards.

Poplar Grove Rest Home
512 W Campbell St, Greenville, KY 42345
(502) 338-4592
Admin Onedia Owens.
Medical Dir Dr King.
Licensure Personal care. *Beds* Personal care
  42.
Owner Proprietary corp.

Admissions Requirements Minimum age 18; Medical examination.
Staff LPNs 1 (ft); Nurses' aides 9 (ft); Activities coordinators 1 (pt); Dietitians 1 (pt).
Facilities Dining room; Laundry room.
Activities Arts & crafts; Cards; Games; Reading groups; Prayer groups; Movies; Shopping trips; Dances/Social/Cultural gatherings.

Hardinsburg

Medco Center of Hardinsburg
Rte 1 Box 134, Hardinsburg, KY 40143
(502) 756-2159
Admin Ann Snyder. *Dir of Nursing* Norma Combs.
Licensure Intermediate care. *Beds* ICF 63. *Certified* Medicaid.
Owner Proprietary corp (Unicare).
Admissions Requirements Minimum age 18.
Facilities Dining room; Laundry room; Barber/Beauty shop.
Activities Arts & crafts; Cards; Games; Prayer groups; Movies; Dances/Social/Cultural gatherings.

Harlan

Harlan Appalachian Regional Hospital—ECF
Martin Fork Rd, Harlan, KY 40831
(606) 573-1400
Admin Vernon Rucke.
Licensure Acure care; Psychiatric care. *Beds* Acute care 159; Psychiatric care 20. *Certified* Medicaid; Medicare.
Owner Proprietary corp.

Harlan Nursing Home
Mounted Rte 1, Hwy 421, Harlan, KY 40831
(606) 573-7250
Admin Connie Moren. *Dir of Nursing* Leta Holden RN. *Medical Dir* Elmer Prewitt MD.
Licensure Skilled care; Intermediate care. *Beds* SNF 24; ICF 119. *Certified* Medicaid; Medicare; VA.
Owner Proprietary corp (Health Systems).
Admissions Requirements Physician's request.
Staff Physicians 5 (pt); RNs 5 (ft), 1 (pt); LPNs 9 (ft), 5 (pt); Nurses' aides 36 (ft), 14 (pt); Activities coordinators 1 (ft); Dietary manager 1 (ft); Dietary (consultant); Social services (consultant).
Facilities Dining room; Activities room; Crafts room; Laundry room; Barber/Beauty shop; Resident lounge; Outdoor patio/garden.
Activities Arts & crafts; Games; Reading groups; Prayer groups; Movies; Shopping trips; Dances/Social/Cultural gatherings; Music; Pet therapy; Special events; Television.

Harrodsburg

Harrodsburg Health Care Manor
PO Box 39, 853 Lexington Rd, Harrodsburg, KY 40330
(606) 734-7791
Admin Elizabeth Logue.
Licensure Intermediate care; Personal care. *Beds* ICF 106; Personal care 6. *Certified* Medicaid.
Owner Proprietary corp (Hillhaven Corp).
Staff RNs; LPNs; Nurses' aides; Physical therapists; Occupational therapists; Speech therapists; Activities coordinators; Dietitians.
Facilities Dining room; Activities room; Crafts room; Laundry room; Barber/Beauty shop; Outside gazebo.
Activities Arts & crafts; Cards; Games; Prayer groups; Movies.

Hartford

Professional Care Home
114 McMurry Ave, Hartford, KY 42347
(502) 298-7437
Admin Patricia Donald. *Dir of Nursing* Frances Coble RN.
Licensure Intermediate care. *Beds* ICF 129. *Certified* Medicaid.
Owner Proprietary corp.
Staff Physicians 5 (ft); RNs 1 (ft); LPNs 7 (ft), 2 (pt); Nurses' aides 24 (ft), 14 (pt); Physical therapists 2 (pt); Speech therapists 1 (pt); Activities coordinators 1 (ft), 1 (pt); Dietitians 1 (ft); Audiologists 1 (pt); Dietary 11 (ft); Housekeeping & laundry 11 (ft); Maintenance 1 (ft); Certified medication aides 6 (ft); Administration 2 (ft).
Facilities Dining room; Activities room; Chapel; Crafts room; Laundry room; Barber/Beauty shop.
Activities Arts & crafts; Cards; Games; Reading groups; Prayer groups; Movies; Shopping trips; Dances/Social/Cultural gatherings; Hawaiian Luau; Family picnics; Fall festival.

Hazard

Hazard Nursing Home
PO Box 1329, Airport Industrial Site, Hazard, KY 41701
(606) 439-2306
Admin Debra K Reynolds.
Medical Dir Cordell Williams MD.
Licensure Skilled care; Intermediate care. *Beds* SNF 36; ICF 114. *Certified* Medicaid; Medicare.
Owner Proprietary corp (Health Systems).
Facilities Dining room; Physical therapy room; Activities room; Crafts room; Laundry room; Barber/Beauty shop.
Activities Arts & crafts; Games; Reading groups; Prayer groups.

Henderson

Henderson Rest Home
864 Watson Ln, Henderson, KY 42420
(502) 826-2394
Admin Gail Willingham RN.
Medical Dir Dr Jack Bland.
Licensure Personal care. *Beds* Personal care 64.
Owner Proprietary corp.
Admissions Requirements Medical examination.
Staff RNs 1 (ft); Nurses' aides 1 (ft); Recreational therapists 1 (ft).
Facilities Dining room; Laundry room.
Activities Arts & crafts; Cards; Games; Reading groups; Prayer groups; Movies; Shopping trips; Dances/Social/Cultural gatherings.

Medco Center of Henderson
2500 N Elm St, Henderson, KY 42420
(502) 826-9794
Admin Lavine Terry. *Dir of Nursing* Joyce Klutey RN.
Licensure Intermediate care. *Beds* ICF 100. *Certified* Medicaid; Medicare.
Owner Proprietary corp (Unicare).

Redbanks
851 Kimsey Ln, Henderson, KY 42420
(502) 826-6436
Admin Marilyn Manon Byrd. *Dir of Nursing* Angela Stewart; Joyce Williams. *Medical Dir* Dr Kenneth Eblen.
Licensure Skilled care; Intermediate care; Personal care; Adult day care. *Beds* SNF 76; ICF 146; Personal care 49; Adult day care 11. *Private Pay Patients* 10%. *Certified* Medicaid; Medicare.
Owner Nonprofit organization/foundation.

Admissions Requirements Minimum age 16; Medical examination; Physician's request.
Staff Physicians 23 (pt); RNs 5 (ft), 3 (pt); LPNs 10 (ft); Nurses' aides 85 (ft), 30 (pt); Physical therapists 1 (ft), 1 (pt); Speech therapists 2 (pt); Activities coordinators 1 (ft); Dietitians 1 (pt); Podiatrists 2 (pt); Audiologists 1 (pt).
Facilities Dining room; Physical therapy room; Activities room; Chapel; Laundry room; Barber/Beauty shop; Library.
Activities Arts & crafts; Cards; Games; Reading groups; Prayer groups; Movies; Shopping trips; Dances/Social/Cultural gatherings.

Highland Heights

Lakeside Place
3510 Alexandria Pike, Highland Heights, KY 41076
(606) 441-1100
Admin Richard S Kidd. *Dir of Nursing* Betty Ward RN. *Medical Dir* Stephen Scott MD.
Licensure Skilled care; Intermediate care; Personal care. *Beds* SNF 40; ICF 236; Personal care 38. *Private Pay Patients* 18%. *Certified* Medicaid; Medicare.
Owner Nonprofit corp.
Admissions Requirements Medical examination; Physician's request.
Staff RNs 3 (ft), 3 (pt); LPNs 30 (ft), 3 (pt); Nurses' aides 120 (ft); Activities coordinators 2 (ft), 2 (pt); Dietitians 1 (ft).
Facilities Dining room; Physical therapy room; Activities room; Chapel; Crafts room; Laundry room; Barber/Beauty shop; Library.
Activities Arts & crafts; Cards; Games; Reading groups; Prayer groups; Movies; Dances/Social/Cultural gatherings; Pet therapy.

Hindman

June Buchanan Primary Care Center
PO Box 471, Hindman, KY 41822
(606) 785-3175
Admin Don Dunn.
Medical Dir Dr Denzil G Barker.
Licensure Primary care. *Certified* Medicaid; Medicare.
Owner Nonprofit corp (Appalachian Regional Health Care).
Staff Physicians 3 (ft); RNs 1 (ft); LPNs 2 (ft); Speech therapists 1 (pt); Dietitians 1 (pt).
Languages Spanish, Sign.
Facilities Dining room; Lab; ER; Pharmacy; Radiology.

Knott County Nursing Home
HCR 60, Box 985, Hindman, KY 41822
(606) 785-5011
Admin Margaret Noble.
Medical Dir George A Sullivan MD.
Licensure Skilled care; Intermediate care. *Beds* SNF 29; ICF 53. *Certified* Medicaid; Medicare.
Owner Proprietary corp (Health Systems).
Staff Physicians 5 (ft); RNs 3 (ft); LPNs 12 (ft); Nurses' aides 28 (ft); Activities coordinators 1 (ft); Dietitians 1 (ft); Dentists 1 (ft).
Facilities Dining room; Physical therapy room; Activities room; Crafts room; Laundry room; Barber/Beauty shop; Library.
Activities Arts & crafts; Cards; Games; Reading groups; Prayer groups; Movies; Shopping trips.

Hodgenville

Sunrise Manor Nursing Home
Phillips Ln, Rte 3, Hodgenville, KY 42748
(502) 358-3103
Admin Hilda Harned.
Medical Dir Glenn Catlett MD.

Licensure Skilled care; Intermediate care. *Beds*
SNF 43; ICF 79. *Certified* Medicaid;
Medicare.
Owner Proprietary corp.
Admissions Requirements Medical
examination.
Staff Physicians 1 (pt); RNs 5 (ft); LPNs 5
(ft), 3 (pt); Nurses' aides 40 (ft), 8 (pt);
Physical therapists 1 (ft); Occupational
therapists; Speech therapists; Activities
coordinators 1 (ft); Dietitians.
Facilities Dining room; Physical therapy
room; Activities room; Chapel; Laundry
room; Barber/Beauty shop; TV room.
Activities Arts & crafts; Cards; Games;
Reading groups; Prayer groups; Dances/
Social/Cultural gatherings.

Hopkinsville

Brookfield Manor
Richard St/Henderson, Box 711, Hopkinsville,
KY 42240
(502) 886-8185
Admin Sue Winders.
Licensure Personal care. *Beds* Personal care
78.
Owner Proprietary corp.
Staff LPNs 1 (ft); Nurses' aides 14 (ft);
Activities coordinators 1 (ft); Dietitians 1
(pt).
Facilities Dining room; Activities room;
Laundry room; Barber/Beauty shop.
Activities Arts & crafts; Cards; Games;
Reading groups; Prayer groups.

Christian Health Center
200 Sterling Dr, Hopkinsville, KY 42240
(502) 885-1166
Admin Nancy H Steele.
Medical Dir Guinn Cost MD.
Licensure Skilled care; Intermediate care;
Personal care. *Beds* SNF 30; ICF 82;
Personal care 4. *Certified* Medicaid;
Medicare.
Owner Nonprofit corp (Christian Church
Campuses).
Staff RNs 3 (ft), 3 (pt); LPNs 11 (ft), 5 (pt);
Nurses' aides 24 (ft), 19 (pt); Physical
therapists 1 (pt); Recreational therapists 1
(ft); Speech therapists 1 (pt); Activities
coordinators 1 (ft); Dietitians 1 (pt);
Podiatrists 1 (pt); Dentists 1 (pt).
Facilities Dining room; Physical therapy
room; Activities room; Chapel; Crafts room;
Laundry room; Barber/Beauty shop.
Activities Arts & crafts; Cards; Games;
Reading groups; Prayer groups; Movies;
Shopping trips; Dances/Social/Cultural
gatherings.

Covingtons Convalescent Center
115 Cayce St, Hopkinsville, KY 42240
(502) 886-4403, 886-6773
Admin William Earl Covington.
Medical Dir Palmer Covington.
Licensure Intermediate care; Personal care.
Beds ICF 72; Personal 25. *Certified*
Medicaid.
Owner Privately owned.
Activities Arts & crafts; Cards; Games;
Reading groups; Prayer groups; Movies;
Shopping trips; Dances/Social/Cultural
gatherings.

Gainesville Manor
PO Box 4004, Rte 9, Hopkinsville, KY 42240
(502) 886-0258
Admin Ida Woodard.
Medical Dir Dr J W Frazier.
Licensure Personal care. *Beds* Personal care
102.
Owner Proprietary corp.
Admissions Requirements Minimum age 18;
Medical examination; Physician's request.

Staff Physicians; LPNs 1 (ft), 1 (pt); Nurses'
aides 20 (ft), 2 (pt); Activities coordinators 1
(ft); Dietitians 1 (pt); Ophthalmologists 2
(pt); Audiologists 1 (pt); Dentists 1 (pt).
Facilities Dining room; Activities room;
Crafts room; Laundry room; Library.
Activities Arts & crafts; Cards; Games;
Reading groups; Prayer groups; Shopping
trips; Dances/Social/Cultural gatherings.

Pennyrile Home
502 Noel Ave, Hopkinsville, KY 42240
(502) 885-9100
Admin Phyllis Burke.
Licensure Personal care. *Beds* Personal care
94.
Owner Proprietary corp.

Pinecrest Manor
950 Highpoint Dr, Hopkinsville, KY 42240
(502) 885-1151
Admin Resanda S Austin.
Medical Dir Dr Robert Rose.
Licensure Skilled care; Intermediate care. *Beds*
SNF 10; ICF 105. *Certified* Medicaid;
Medicare.
Owner Proprietary corp (Sunbelt Healthcare
Centers Inc).
Admissions Requirements Minimum age 21;
Physician's request.
Staff Physicians 19 (pt); RNs 3 (ft), 2 (pt);
LPNs 7 (ft), 12 (pt); Nurses' aides 26 (ft), 14
(pt); Physical therapists 1 (ft); Speech
therapists 1 (pt); Activities coordinators 1
(ft); Dietitians 1 (ft).
Affiliation Seventh-Day Adventist.
Facilities Dining room; Physical therapy
room; Activities room; Crafts room; Laundry
room; Barber/Beauty shop.
Activities Arts & crafts; Games; Reading
groups; Prayer groups; Movies; Dances/
Social/Cultural gatherings.

**Western State Hospital Intermediate Care
Facility**
621 Las Vegas Dr, Hopkinsville, KY 42240
(502) 886-4431
Admin Gloria Tyson. *Dir of Nursing* Debbie
Johannes. *Medical Dir* Dr Randol Fielder.
Licensure Intermediate care. *Beds* ICF 144.
Private Pay Patients 1%. *Certified* Medicaid;
Medicare.
Owner Nonprofit corp.
Staff Physicians 3 (pt); RNs 4 (ft); LPNs 13
(ft); Nurses' aides 76 (ft); Physical therapists
1 (ft); Activities coordinators 1 (ft); Social
workers 2 (ft).
Facilities Dining room; Physical therapy
room; Activities room; Barber/Beauty shop.
Activities Arts & crafts; Cards; Games;
Shopping trips; Dances/Social/Cultural
gatherings; Exercise; Music; Reminiscing;
Occupational therapy program.

Hyden

**Lewis Health Care Facilities Inc—Hyden
Manor**
PO Box 618, Hyden, KY 41749
(606) 672-2940
Admin Melissa Lewis Sparks. *Dir of Nursing*
Kathy Mills. *Medical Dir* Dr Steven Spadey.
Licensure Skilled care; Intermediate care;
Personal care; Adult day care; Alzheimer's
care. *Beds* SNF 32; ICF 31; Personal care
20. *Private Pay Patients* 10%. *Certified*
Medicaid; Medicare.
Owner Proprietary corp.
Staff Physicians 1 (ft); RNs 2 (ft), 1 (pt);
LPNs; Nurses' aides 25 (ft), 3 (pt); Physical
therapists 1 (ft); Activities coordinators 1
(ft); Dietitians 1 (pt); Respiratory therapists.
Facilities Dining room; Physical therapy
room; Laundry room; Barber/Beauty shop;
Adult day care.
Activities Arts & crafts; Games; Prayer groups;
Movies; Shopping trips; Pet therapy.

Independence

Regency Manor
5716 Madison Pike, Independence, KY 41051
(606) 356-9294
Admin Patricia C Schroer.
Medical Dir Melva Jean Elbert.
Licensure Personal care. *Beds* Personal care
50.
Owner Proprietary corp.
Admissions Requirements Minimum age 18;
Medical examination.
Staff Nurses' aides 9 (ft); Activities
coordinators 1 (ft).
Facilities Dining room; Activities room;
Crafts room; Barber/Beauty shop.
Activities Arts & crafts; Cards; Games; Prayer
groups; Movies; Dances/Social/Cultural
gatherings.

Irvine

Irvine Health Care Center
411 Wallace Dr, Irvine, KY 40336
(606) 723-5153
Admin Nona L Bush. *Dir of Nursing* Faye
Mullins LPN. *Medical Dir* Jerry Brackett
MD.
Licensure Intermediate care; Personal care.
Beds ICF 78; Personal care 18. *Certified*
Medicaid.
Owner Proprietary corp (Unicare).
Admissions Requirements Medical
examination; Physician's request.
Staff Physicians; RNs; LPNs; Nurses' aides;
Physical therapists; Speech therapists.
Facilities Dining room; Activities room;
Crafts room; Laundry room; Barber/Beauty
shop.
Activities Arts & crafts; Games; Prayer groups;
Movies; Pet therapy.

Jackson

Nim Henson Geriatric Center
PO Box 636, Jetts Subdivision, Jackson, KY
41339
(606) 666-2456
Admin Kenny Noble. *Dir of Nursing* Betsy
Henson RN. *Medical Dir* Dr Emanuel C
Turner.
Licensure Skilled care; Intermediate care. *Beds*
SNF 30; ICF 92. *Certified* Medicaid;
Medicare.
Owner Publicly owned.
Staff Physicians; RNs; LPNs; Nurses' aides;
Physical therapists; Activities coordinators;
Dietitians.
Facilities Dining room; Laundry room;
Barber/Beauty shop.
Activities Arts & crafts; Cards; Games;
Reading groups; Prayer groups; Movies;
Shopping trips; Pet therapy.

Jamestown

Fair Oaks Nursing Home
PO Box 140, Hwy 127, Jamestown, KY 42629
(502) 343-2101
Admin Don Hamlin.
Licensure Intermediate care. *Beds* ICF 94.
Certified Medicaid.
Owner Proprietary corp.

Jeffersontown

Louisville Lutheran Home
10617 E Watterson Trail, Jeffersontown, KY
40299
(502) 267-7403
Admin James Thomason. *Dir of Nursing*
Shirley Andrew.
Licensure Intermediate care; Personal care.
Beds ICF 70; Personal care 28. *Certified*
Medicaid.
Owner Nonprofit corp.

Admissions Requirements Medical examination; Physician's request.
Staff RNs 1 (pt); LPNs 4 (ft); Nurses' aides 18 (ft); Recreational therapists 1 (ft); Dietitians 1 (pt).
Affiliation Lutheran.
Facilities Dining room; Physical therapy room; Activities room; Chapel; Laundry room; Barber/Beauty shop; Library.
Activities Arts & crafts; Cards; Games; Reading groups; Prayer groups; Movies; Shopping trips; Dances/Social/Cultural gatherings.

Jenkins

Letcher County Golden Years Rest Home
PO Box 867, Lakeside Dr, Jenkins, KY 41537
(606) 832-2123
Admin James F Tackett.
Medical Dir Anita Taylor.
Licensure Personal care. Beds Personal care 44.
Owner Nonprofit corp.
Admissions Requirements Medical examination.
Staff LPNs 1 (ft); Nurses' aides 11 (ft).
Facilities Dining room; Activities room; Chapel; Laundry room; Barber/Beauty shop.
Activities Arts & crafts; Cards; Games; Prayer groups; Shopping trips; Dances/Social/Cultural gatherings.

Jonesville

Jonesville Rest Home
Rte 36, Jonesville, KY 41052
(606) 824-4610
Admin Leon Tuttle; Wanda Sue Tuttle.
Licensure Personal care. Beds Personal care 26.
Owner Proprietary corp.

Kuttawa

Hilltop Nursing Home
Lake Barkley Dr, Kuttawa, KY 42055
(502) 388-7611
Admin Nancy J Adams.
Licensure Intermediate care; Personal care. Beds ICF 96; Personal 32. Certified Medicaid.
Owner Proprietary corp.
Admissions Requirements Medical examination.
Staff RNs 2 (ft); LPNs 6 (ft); Nurses' aides 54 (ft), 2 (pt); Speech therapists 1 (ft); Activities coordinators 1 (ft); Dietitians 1 (ft).
Facilities Dining room; Activities room; Crafts room; Laundry room; Barber/Beauty shop.
Activities Arts & crafts; Cards; Games; Reading groups; Prayer groups; Movies; Shopping trips; Dances/Social/Cultural gatherings.

LaCenter

Life Care Center of LaCenter
PO Bwx 269, 5th & Pine Sts, LaCenter, KY 42056
(502) 665-5681
Admin Marilyn D Ingram.
Licensure Intermediate care; Personal care. Beds ICF 70; Personal care 21. Certified Medicaid.
Owner Proprietary corp (Life Care Centers of America).
Staff Physicians 3 (pt); RNs 1 (ft); LPNs 4 (ft); Nurses' aides 33 (ft); Recreational therapists 1 (pt); Speech therapists 1 (pt); Activities coordinators 1 (ft); Dietitians 1 (pt).

Facilities Dining room; Laundry room; Barber/Beauty shop.
Activities Arts & crafts; Games; Movies; Shopping trips; Dances/Social/Cultural gatherings.

Lackey

Golden Years Rest Home
HC 80, Box 25, Lackey, KY 41643
(606) 946-2220
Admin Hugh Henegar Jr.
Medical Dir Alberta G Deaton.
Licensure Personal care. Beds Personal care 84.
Owner Proprietary corp.
Admissions Requirements Minimum age 18; Medical examination; Physician's request.
Staff Physicians 3 (ft), 1 (pt); LPNs 1 (ft); Nurses' aides 16 (ft), 4 (pt); Activities coordinators 1 (ft), 1 (pt); Dietitians 1 (ft), 1 (pt); Ophthalmologists 1 (pt); Audiologists 1 (pt); Dentists 1 (pt).
Facilities Dining room; Activities room; Laundry room; Barber/Beauty shop.
Activities Arts & crafts; Cards; Games; Reading groups; Prayer groups; Movies; Shopping trips; Dances/Social/Cultural gatherings.

LaGrange

Cedar Lake Lodge
PO Box 289, 3301 Jericho Rd, LaGrange, KY 40031
(502) 222-7157
Admin Clyde D Lang.
Medical Dir Rose Marie Miller.
Licensure Intermediate care for mentally retarded. Beds ICF/MR 76. Certified Medicaid.
Owner Nonprofit corp.
Affiliation Lutheran.
Facilities Dining room; Physical therapy room; Activities room; Chapel; Crafts room.
Activities Arts & crafts; Games; Prayer groups; Movies; Shopping trips; Dances/Social/Cultural gatherings.

Lancaster

Garrard County Home for Senior Citizens
308 W Maple St, Lancaster, KY 40444
(606) 792-2112
Admin W David MacCool.
Medical Dir Paul J Sides MD.
Licensure Intermediate care; Personal care. Beds ICF 16; Personal care 32.
Owner Proprietary corp.
Admissions Requirements Minimum age 21; Medical examination.
Staff RNs 1 (pt); LPNs 2 (ft), 2 (pt); Nurses' aides 6 (ft); Activities coordinators 1 (ft); Dietitians 1 (pt); Social worker 1 (pt).
Facilities Dining room; Activities room; Laundry room; Barber/Beauty shop.
Activities Arts & crafts; Games; Reading groups; Prayer groups; Movies; Shopping trips.

Garrard County Memorial Hospital—SNF
308 W Maple St, Lancaster, KY 40444
(606) 792-2112
Admin W David MacCool.
Licensure Skilled care; Intermediate care. Beds SNF 34; ICF 18. Certified Medicaid; Medicare.
Owner Nonprofit corp.

Lawrenceburg

Heritage Hall
Box 349, 331 S Main, Lawrenceburg, KY 40342
(502) 839-7246

Admin Fran Cole. Dir of Nursing Fran Cole RN. Medical Dir William P McElwain.
Licensure Intermediate care; Personal care. Beds ICF 80; Personal care 32. Certified Medicaid.
Owner Proprietary corp.
Admissions Requirements Minimum age 16; Medical examination.
Staff RNs 4 (ft), 1 (pt); LPNs 2 (ft); Nurses' aides 40 (ft); Physical therapists 1 (pt); Speech therapists 1 (pt); Activities coordinators 1 (ft); Dietitians 1 (pt).
Facilities Dining room; Physical therapy room; Activities room; Chapel; Crafts room; Laundry room; Barber/Beauty shop; Library; 5 Patient lounge areas; Park; Courtyard; 2 outdoor patio areas.
Activities Arts & crafts; Cards; Games; Reading groups; Prayer groups; Movies; Shopping trips; Dances/Social/Cultural gatherings.

Sunset Hill Home for Aged & Infirm
1428 Tyrone Rd, Lawrenceburg, KY 40342
(502) 839-4835
Admin William Crabb.
Licensure Personal care. Beds Personal care 16.
Owner Nonprofit corp.

Lebanon

Cedars of Lebanon Rest Home
S Harrison, Lebanon, KY 40033
(502) 692-3121
Admin Sandra Creech.
Licensure Intermediate care; Personal care. Beds ICF 81; Personal 13. Certified Medicaid.
Owner Proprietary corp (Hillhaven Corp).

Spring View Nursing Home
353 W Walnut St, Lebanon, KY 40033
(502) 692-3161
Admin Gary Foster.
Medical Dir Tina Fenwick.
Licensure Nursing home; Alzheimer's care. Beds Nursing home 38.
Owner Proprietary corp.
Admissions Requirements Minimum age 60; Medical examination; Physician's request.
Staff RNs 1 (ft); LPNs 5 (ft); Nurses' aides 9 (ft), 3 (pt); Activities coordinators 1 (ft); Dietitians 1 (pt).
Facilities Dining room; Physical therapy room; Activities room; Chapel; Crafts room; Laundry room; Barber/Beauty shop.
Activities Arts & crafts; Cards; Games; Reading groups; Prayer groups; Movies; Shopping trips; Dances/Social/Cultural gatherings; Music therapy; Gardening.

Leitchfield

Grayson Manor Nursing Home
349 E Lake Dr, Leitchfield, KY 42754
(502) 259-4028
Admin Suzanne E Givan. Dir of Nursing Linda Duke RN.
Licensure Skilled care; Intermediate care; Personal care. Beds SNF 6; ICF 76; Personal care 30. Certified Medicaid; Medicare.
Owner Nonprofit corp.
Admissions Requirements Medical examination; Physician's request.
Staff RNs 2 (ft), 1 (pt); LPNs 4 (ft), 2 (pt); Nurses' aides 14 (ft); Speech therapists 1 (pt); Activities coordinators 1 (ft); Dietitians 1 (pt).
Facilities Dining room; Activities room; Chapel; Crafts room; Laundry room; Barber/Beauty shop.
Activities Arts & crafts; Cards; Games; Reading groups; Prayer groups; Movies; Shopping trips; Dances/Social/Cultural gatherings.

Leitchfield Health Care Manor
PO Box 466, 186 Wallace Ave, Leitchfield,
KY 42754
(502) 259-4036
Admin Margaret Ann Embry.
Medical Dir Margaret Ann Embry.
Licensure Intermediate care; Personal care.
Beds ICF 56; Personal care 12. *Certified*
Medicaid.
Owner Nonprofit corp (Adventist Living
Centers).
Admissions Requirements Medical
examination; Physician's request.
Staff RNs 1 (pt); LPNs 2 (ft), 1 (pt); Activities
coordinators 1 (ft); Dietitians 1 (ft).
Facilities Dining room; Laundry room;
Barber/Beauty shop.
Activities Arts & crafts; Cards; Games;
Reading groups; Prayer groups; Movies;
Shopping trips; Dances/Social/Cultural
gatherings.

Lewisport

Hancock County Rest Haven
Drawer G, Lewisport, KY 42351
(502) 295-6825
Admin Carla K Jones.
Licensure Personal care. *Beds* Personal care
78. *Certified* Medicaid.
Owner Proprietary corp.
Admissions Requirements Minimum age 18;
Medical examination; TB test.
Staff Nurses' aides 10 (ft), 11 (pt); Activities
coordinators 1 (ft).
Facilities Dining room; Activities room;
Laundry room.
Activities Arts & crafts; Cards; Games;
Reading groups; Prayer groups; Movies;
Shopping trips; Dances/Social/Cultural
gatherings; Reality & Socialization Groups;
Church services provided by 3 different
denominations.

Lexington

Arnett Pritchett Foundation Home
319 Duke Rd, Lexington, KY 40502
(606) 266-6031
Admin Carolyn Danks.
Licensure Personal care. *Beds* Personal care
16.
Owner Proprietary corp.

Ashland Terrace
475 S Ashland Ave, Lexington, KY 40502
(606) 266-2581
Admin Leona Coleman.
Licensure Personal care. *Beds* Personal care
22.
Owner Nonprofit corp.

Bluegrass Personal Care Home
627 W 4th St, Lexington, KY 40508
(606) 252-5031
Admin Inge Petit.
Licensure Personal care. *Beds* Personal care
40.
Owner Proprietary corp.

Breckinridge Health Care Inc
1500 Trent Blvd, Lexington, KY 40515
(606) 272-2273
Admin Patricia A Taylor. *Dir of Nursing*
Claire Schuster RN. *Medical Dir* Samuel
Scott MD.
Licensure Skilled care; Intermediate care;
Alzheimer's care. *Beds* SNF 50; ICF 100.
Private Pay Patients 35-40%. *Certified*
Medicaid; Medicare.
Owner Nonprofit organization/foundation.
Admissions Requirements Physician's request.
Staff RNs 4 (ft), 3 (pt); LPNs 10 (ft), 5 (pt);
Nurses' aides 43 (ft), 20 (pt); Physical
therapists 1 (pt); Recreational therapists 1

(ft); Occupational therapists 1 (pt); Speech
therapists 1 (pt); Activities coordinators 1
(ft); Dietitians 1 (pt).
Facilities Dining room; Physical therapy
room; Activities room; Crafts room; Laundry
room; Barber/Beauty shop; Library.
Activities Arts & crafts; Cards; Games;
Reading groups; Prayer groups; Movies;
Shopping trips; Dances/Social/Cultural
gatherings; Intergenerational programs; Pet
therapy.

Breckinridge Health Care Inc
1500 Trent Blvd, Lexington, KY 40515
(606) 253-2558
Admin Patricia A Taylor.
Licensure Skilled care; Intermediate care. *Beds*
SNF 50; ICF 100.
Owner Proprietary corp.

Darby Square
2770 Palumbo Dr, Lexington, KY 40509
(606) 263-2410
Admin Margarette Scanlon. *Dir of Nursing*
Sharon McCart.
Licensure Skilled care; Intermediate care. *Beds*
SNF 10; ICF 110. *Certified* Medicaid;
Medicare.
Owner Nonprofit corp (Pinnacle Care Corp).
Admissions Requirements Medical
examination; Physician's request.
Staff Physicians; RNs; LPNs; Nurses' aides;
Physical therapists; Occupational therapists;
Speech therapists; Activities coordinators;
Dietitians; Ophthalmologists; Podiatrists.
Languages Spanish.
Facilities Dining room; Physical therapy
room; Activities room; Crafts room; Laundry
room; Barber/Beauty shop.
Activities Arts & crafts; Cards; Games;
Reading groups; Prayer groups; Movies;
Shopping trips; Dances/Social/Cultural
gatherings; Intergenerational programs; Pet
therapy; Open house; Town meetings.

Excepticon—Lexington Campus
1321 Trent Blvd, Lexington, KY 40502
(606) 272-3496
Admin Jeffrey M Cross.
Licensure Intermediate care for mentally
retarded. *Beds* 180. *Certified* Medicaid.
Owner Proprietary corp.
Admissions Requirements Minimum age 18;
Medical examination.
Staff Physicians 2 (pt); RNs 2 (pt); LPNs 7
(pt); Nurses' aides 45 (ft), 9 (pt); Physical
therapists 1 (pt); Recreational therapists 3
(ft); Occupational therapists 2 (ft); Speech
therapists 1 (ft); Dietitians 1 (ft); Dentists 1
(pt).
Facilities Dining room; Activities room;
Crafts room; Laundry room.
Activities Arts & crafts; Games; Movies;
Shopping trips; Dances/Social/Cultural
gatherings.

Glen Arvin Personal Care Home
444 Glen Arvin Ave, Lexington, KY 40508
(606) 255-4606
Admin Edna E Calloway.
Licensure Personal care. *Beds* Personal care
23. *Private Pay Patients* 5%. *Certified*
Medicaid; Medicare.
Owner Privately owned.
Admissions Requirements Minimum age 16;
Medical examination; Physician's request.
Staff Physicians; Nurses' aides; Physical
therapists; Dietitians.
Facilities Dining room; Activities room;
Crafts room; Laundry room.
Activities Arts & crafts; Cards; Games; Prayer
groups; Movies; Shopping trips; Dances/
Social/Cultural gatherings; Pet therapy.

Harrison's Sanitorium
1537 N Limestone, Lexington, KY 40505
(606) 252-6673

Admin Beverly Turner. *Dir of Nursing*
Margaret L Harrison RN. *Medical Dir*
James W Mathews MD.
Licensure Skilled care; Alzheimer's care. *Beds*
SNF 77. *Certified* Medicaid; Medicare.
Owner Proprietary corp.
Admissions Requirements Physician's request.
Staff RNs 5 (ft); LPNs 7 (ft); Nurses' aides 30
(ft); Physical therapists 1 (ft); Reality
therapists 1 (ft); Occupational therapists 1
(pt); Speech therapists 1 (ft), 1 (pt); Activities
coordinators 1 (ft), 1 (pt); Dietitians 1 (pt);
Ophthalmologists 1 (pt); Dentists 1 (pt).
Facilities Dining room; Physical therapy
room; Activities room; Chapel; Crafts room;
Laundry room; Barber/Beauty shop.
Activities Arts & crafts; Cards; Games;
Movies; Shopping trips; Dances/Social/
Cultural gatherings.

Hayden's Personal Care Home
553 E 3rd St, Lexington, KY 40508
(606) 233-1944
Admin Lula Hayden.
Licensure Personal care. *Beds* Personal care
36.
Owner Proprietary corp.

Homestead Nursing Center
1608 Versailles Rd, Lexington, KY 40504
(606) 252-0871
Admin Joni Tyrer.
Licensure Skilled care; Intermediate care. *Beds*
SNF 111; ICF 25. *Certified* Medicaid;
Medicare.
Owner Proprietary corp.

Kiva House
201 Mechanic, Lexington, KY 40507-1096
(606) 252-3676
Admin Nancy Washbaugh.
Licensure Personal care. *Beds* 28.

Lexington Country Place
700 Mason Headley Rd, Lexington, KY 40504
(606) 259-3486
Admin David K Rice.
Medical Dir Kenneth C Tufts MD.
Licensure Skilled care; Intermediate care. *Beds*
SNF 107; ICF 4. *Certified* Medicaid;
Medicare.
Owner Proprietary corp.
Admissions Requirements Minimum age 16;
Medical examination; Physician's request.
Staff RNs 6 (ft), 1 (pt); Nurses' aides 42 (ft);
Physical therapists 1 (ft); Recreational
therapists 1 (ft); Speech therapists 1 (pt);
Dietitians 1 (ft); Podiatrists 1 (pt).
Facilities Dining room; Physical therapy
room; Activities room; Crafts room; Laundry
room; Barber/Beauty shop; Library.
Activities Arts & crafts; Cards; Games;
Reading groups; Prayer groups; Movies;
Shopping trips; Dances/Social/Cultural
gatherings.

Lexington Manor Health Care
353 Waller Ave, Lexington, KY 40504
(606) 252-3558, 233-0192 FAX
Admin Olive M Allen.
Medical Dir Max Crocker MD.
Licensure Skilled care; Intermediate care;
Alzheimer's unit. *Beds* SNF 52; ICF 108;
Alzheimer unit 20. *Private Pay Patients* 54%.
Certified Medicaid; Medicare.
Owner Proprietary corp (Hillhaven Corp).
Admissions Requirements Minimum age 18;
Medical examination; Physician's request.
Staff Physicians 24 (pt); RNs 3 (ft); LPNs 16
(ft), 5 (pt); Nurses' aides 48 (ft), 7 (pt);
Physical therapists 2 (ft); Recreational
therapists 1 (pt); Occupational therapists 1
(pt); Speech therapists 1 (pt); Activities
coordinators 1 (ft), 2 (pt); Dietitians 1 (ft);
Ophthalmologists 1 (pt); Podiatrists 1 (pt);
Dentists 1 (pt); Opticians 1 (pt);
Psychiatrists 1 (pt); Beauticians 1 (pt);
Barbers 1 (pt); Social workers 1 (ft).

Facilities Dining room; Physical therapy room; Activities room; Crafts room; Laundry room; Barber/Beauty shop; Enclosed courtyard.
Activities Arts & crafts; Cards; Games; Reading groups; Prayer groups; Movies; Shopping trips; Dances/Social/Cultural gatherings; Intergenerational programs; Pet therapy; Family support groups.

Mayfair Manor Convalescent Center
3300 Tates Creek Rd, Lexington, KY 40502
(606) 266-2126
Admin Renee H Martin. *Dir of Nursing* Marge Peter. *Medical Dir* Kenneth Tufts MD.
Licensure Skilled care; Nursing home. *Beds* SNF 50; Nursing home 50. *Certified* Medicaid; Medicare.
Owner Proprietary corp (National Heritage).
Admissions Requirements Physician's request.
Staff RNs 4 (ft), 2 (pt); LPNs 10 (ft), 4 (pt); Nurses' aides 25 (ft), 20 (pt); Physical therapists 1 (ft), 1 (pt); Activities coordinators 1 (ft), 2 (pt); Dietitians 1 (ft).
Facilities Dining room; Physical therapy room; Activities room; Crafts room; Laundry room; Barber/Beauty shop; Library.
Activities Arts & crafts; Cards; Games; Reading groups; Prayer groups; Movies; Shopping trips; Dances/Social/Cultural gatherings.

Meadowbrook Health Care Center
2020 Cambridge Dr, Lexington, KY 40504
(606) 252-6747
Admin Jerry Rogers.
Licensure Intermediate care; Personal care. *Beds* ICF 106; Personal 34. *Certified* Medicaid.
Owner Proprietary corp.
Admissions Requirements Medical examination.
Staff Physicians 10 (pt); RNs 1 (ft), 1 (pt); LPNs 5 (ft), 2 (pt); Nurses' aides 40 (ft), 9 (pt); Physical therapists 2 (pt); Speech therapists 1 (pt); Activities coordinators 1 (ft); Dietitians 1 (ft); Podiatrists 1 (pt); Dentists 1 (pt).
Facilities Dining room; Activities room; Crafts room; Laundry room; Barber/Beauty shop; Library; Sun rooms.
Activities Arts & crafts; Cards; Games; Reading groups; Prayer groups; Movies; Shopping trips; Dances/Social/Cultural gatherings.

Rose Manor Intermediate Care Facility
3057 Cleveland Rd, Lexington, KY 40505
(606) 299-4117
Admin Alfred E McGregor. *Dir of Nursing* Anne Cropper. *Medical Dir* Ellis Taylor MD; Dr Halburt.
Licensure Intermediate care. *Beds* ICF 34. *Private Pay Patients* 15%. *Certified* Medicaid; Medicare.
Owner Privately owned.
Admissions Requirements Minimum age 18.
Staff Physicians 1 (ft); RNs 1 (ft); LPNs 1 (ft); Nurses' aides 21 (ft); Activities coordinators 1 (ft); Dietitians 1 (ft).
Languages Sign.
Facilities Dining room; Activities room; Laundry room; Barber/Beauty shop.
Activities Arts & crafts; Cards; Games; Prayer groups; Movies; Shopping trips; Dances/Social/Cultural gatherings; Pet therapy.

Sayre Christian Village Nursing Home
3840 Camelot Dr, Lexington, KY 40503
(606) 273-7575
Admin M Eileen Burberry. *Dir of Nursing* Linda Cummins RN. *Medical Dir* Dr Jeff Foxx.
Licensure Intermediate care; Personal care; Alzheimer's care. *Beds* ICF 105; Personal care 4. *Private Pay Patients* 30%. *Certified* Medicaid.

Owner Nonprofit corp (Christian Benevolent Outreach Inc).
Admissions Requirements Physician's request.
Staff RNs 3 (ft), 1 (pt); LPNs 8 (ft), 3 (pt); Nurses' aides 38 (ft), 7 (pt); Activities coordinators 1 (ft), 2 (pt); Dietitians 1 (pt).
Affiliation Church of Christ.
Facilities Dining room; Activities room; Chapel; Crafts room; Laundry room; Barber/Beauty shop; Library; Wander-guard system.
Activities Arts & crafts; Cards; Games; Reading groups; Prayer groups; Movies; Shopping trips; Intergenerational programs; Pet therapy.

Tates Creek Health Care Center
3576 Pimlico Pkwy, Lexington, KY 40502
(606) 272-0608
Admin Donna Goodman. *Dir of Nursing* Tonia Harris RN. *Medical Dir* Dr Richard French.
Licensure Intermediate care; Personal care. *Beds* ICF 100; Personal care 36. *Certified* Medicaid.
Owner Proprietary corp.
Admissions Requirements Females only; Physician's request.
Staff Physicians 20 (pt); RNs 1 (ft), 1 (pt); LPNs 5 (ft), 4 (pt); Nurses' aides 37 (ft), 8 (pt); Physical therapists 2 (pt); Speech therapists 1 (pt); Activities coordinators 1 (ft), 1 (pt); Dietitians 1 (ft); Ophthalmologists 1 (pt); Podiatrists 1 (pt); Dentists 2 (pt).
Facilities Dining room; Activities room; Crafts room; Laundry room; Barber/Beauty shop; Library; Florida room; Van.
Activities Arts & crafts; Cards; Games; Reading groups; Prayer groups; Movies; Shopping trips; Dances/Social/Cultural gatherings.

YWCA Arnett Pritchett Foundation Home
319 Duke Rd, Lexington, KY 40502
(606) 266-6031
Admin Carolyn Danks.
Licensure Personal care. *Beds* 14.
Owner Nonprofit organization/foundation.
Admissions Requirements Minimum age 65; Females only.
Staff Nurses' aides 8 (ft); Recreational therapists 1 (ft); Activities coordinators 1 (ft); Dietitians 1 (ft).
Facilities Dining room; Activities room; Laundry room; Library; Home type atmosphere; Private rooms.
Activities Arts & crafts; Cards; Games; Reading groups; Prayer groups; Movies; Shopping trips; Dances/Social/Cultural gatherings; Exercise groups; Pet therapy.

Liberty

Green River Rest Home
PO Box G, Liberty, KY 42539
(606) 787-9256
Admin Wendell Ann Burris.
Licensure Personal care. *Beds* Personal care 24.
Owner Nonprofit corp.

London

Laurel Heights Home for the Elderly
208 W 12th St, London, KY 40741
(606) 684-4155
Admin Melinda Helton. *Dir of Nursing* Martha Burns RN.
Licensure Skilled care; Intermediate care; Personal care. *Beds* SNF 42; ICF 101; Personal care 54. *Certified* Medicaid; Medicare.
Owner Nonprofit corp.
Admissions Requirements Medical examination.

Staff Physicians 1 (pt); RNs 3 (ft), 1 (pt); LPNs; Nurses' aides; Physical therapists 1 (pt); Speech therapists 1 (pt); Activities coordinators 1 (ft); Dietitians 1 (pt).
Facilities Dining room; Physical therapy room; Activities room; Chapel; Crafts room; Laundry room; Barber/Beauty shop; Library.
Activities Arts & crafts; Cards; Games; Reading groups; Prayer groups; Movies; Shopping trips; Dances/Social/Cultural gatherings.

Louisa

J J Jordan Geriatric Center
PO Box 726, E Clayton Ln, Louisa, KY 41230
(606) 638-4586, 638-9881
Admin David McKenzie.
Medical Dir Lloyd Browning MD & Norman Edwards MD.
Licensure Skilled care; Intermediate care; Personal care. *Beds* SNF 22; ICF 82; Personal care 16. *Certified* Medicaid; Medicare.
Owner Proprietary corp.
Admissions Requirements Physician's request.
Staff Physicians 2 (pt); RNs 3 (ft); LPNs 5 (ft); Nurses' aides 40 (ft); Physical therapists 1 (ft); Speech therapists 1 (pt); Activities coordinators 1 (ft); Dietitians 1 (pt); Dentists 1 (pt).
Facilities Dining room; Physical therapy room; Activities room; Laundry room; Barber/Beauty shop.
Activities Arts & crafts; Cards; Games; Movies; Shopping trips.

Louisville

Baptist Home East
3001 Hounz Ln, Louisville, KY 40222
(502) 426-5531
Admin Larry Jack Butler. *Dir of Nursing* Virginia Hancock.
Licensure Intermediate care; Personal care. *Beds* ICF 90; Personal 20. *Certified* Medicaid.
Owner Nonprofit corp.
Admissions Requirements Medical examination; Physician's request.
Staff RNs 1 (ft); LPNs 4 (ft); Nurses' aides 25 (ft), 15 (pt); Activities coordinators 2 (ft), 1 (pt); Dietitians 1 (ft).
Affiliation Baptist.
Facilities Dining room; Activities room; Chapel; Crafts room; Laundry room; Barber/Beauty shop; Library.
Activities Arts & crafts; Cards; Games; Reading groups; Prayer groups; Movies; Shopping trips; Dances/Social/Cultural gatherings.

Bashford East Health Care Facility
3535 Bardstown Rd, Louisville, KY 40218
(502) 459-1400
Admin Patricia Holland.
Medical Dir Dr Charles Severs.
Licensure Skilled care; Intermediate care. *Beds* SNF 35; ICF 97. *Certified* Medicaid; Medicare.
Owner Proprietary corp (Hillhaven Corp).
Staff RNs; LPNs; Nurses' aides; Physical therapists; Occupational therapists; Speech therapists; Activities coordinators; Dietitians.
Facilities Dining room; Physical therapy room; Laundry room; Barber/Beauty shop.
Activities Arts & crafts; Cards; Games; Prayer groups; Shopping trips; Dances/Social/Cultural gatherings.

Briarwood Nursing & Convalescent Center
4300 Hazelwood Ave, Louisville, KY 40215
(502) 367-6139
Admin Mary B Campbell.
Licensure Skilled care; Intermediate care. *Beds* SNF 37; ICF 39. *Certified* Medicaid; Medicare.

Owner Proprietary corp.

Britthaven of South Louisville
9600 Lamborne Blvd, Louisville, KY 40272
(502) 935-7284
Admin Joanna Palmer. *Dir of Nursing* Nancy
  Gooch. *Medical Dir* Barry Schlossberg MD.
Licensure Intermediate care. *Beds* ICF 128.
  Certified Medicaid.
Owner Proprietary corp (Britthaven Inc).
Staff Physicians 1 (pt); RNs 1 (ft); LPNs 1
  (ft); Nurses' aides 1 (ft); Physical therapists 1
  (pt); Occupational therapists 1 (pt); Speech
  therapists 1 (pt); Activities coordinators 1
  (ft); Dietitians 1 (ft); Ophthalmologists 1
  (pt).

Brownsboro Hills Nursing Home
2141 Sycamore Ave, Louisville, KY 40206
(502) 895-5417
Admin Harold V Bomar Jr.
Licensure Nursing home. *Beds* Nursing home
  96.
Owner Proprietary corp.

Christian Health Center
920 S 4th St, Louisville, KY 40203
(502) 583-6533
Admin Keith R Knapp. *Dir of Nursing* Linda
  Kempf RN. *Medical Dir* Dr Kenneth
  Holtzappl; Dr John C Wright.
Licensure Skilled care; Intermediate care;
  Personal care; Retirement. *Beds* SNF 14;
  ICF 106; Personal care 6; Retirement 440.
  Private Pay Patients 30%. *Certified*
  Medicaid; Medicare.
Owner Nonprofit corp (Christian Church
  Homes of Kentucky Inc).
Admissions Requirements Medical
  examination.
Staff Physicians 12 (pt); RNs 5 (ft), 4 (pt);
  LPNs 8 (ft), 6 (pt); Nurses' aides 45 (ft), 15
  (pt); Physical therapists 1 (ft); Occupational
  therapists 1 (ft); Speech therapists 1 (ft);
  Activities coordinators 1 (ft); Dietitians 1
  (ft); Podiatrists 1 (pt).
Affiliation Disciples of Christ.
Facilities Dining room; Physical therapy
  room; Activities room; Chapel; Crafts room;
  Laundry room; Barber/Beauty shop; Library.
Activities Arts & crafts; Cards; Games;
  Reading groups; Prayer groups; Movies;
  Shopping trips; Dances/Social/Cultural
  gatherings; Intergenerational programs; Pet
  therapy.

Christopher—East Health Care Facility
4200 Browns Ln, Louisville, KY 40220
(502) 459-8900
Admin Margaret Wulf Brown.
Licensure Skilled care; Intermediate care;
  Personal care. *Beds* SNF 100; ICF 50;
  Personal 50.
Owner Proprietary corp (Health Care and
  Retirement Corp).

Eastern Star Home in Kentucky
923 Cherokee Rd, Louisville, KY 40204
(502) 451-3535
Admin Martha R Durbin. *Dir of Nursing*
  Connie Fitzer LPN. *Medical Dir* J Michael
  Ray.
Licensure Intermediate care; Personal care.
  Beds ICF 18; Personal care 24. *Private Pay
  Patients* 100%.
Owner Nonprofit organization/foundation.
Admissions Requirements Minimum age 65;
  Medical examination.
Staff RNs 2 (pt); LPNs 1 (ft); Nurses' aides 9
  (ft), 9 (pt); Activities coordinators 1 (ft).
Affiliation Order of Eastern Star.
Facilities Dining room; Activities room;
  Chapel; Laundry room; Barber/Beauty shop.
Activities Arts & crafts; Cards; Games;
  Reading groups; Prayer groups; Movies;
  Shopping trips; Dances/Social/Cultural
  gatherings; Pet therapy.

Episcopal Church Home
1201 Lyndon Ln, Louisville, KY 40222
(502) 425-8840
Admin J T Horton.
Licensure Intermediate care; Personal care.
  Beds ICF 93; Personal 127. *Certified*
  Medicaid.
Owner Proprietary corp.
Affiliation Episcopal.

Fair Lodge Health Care Center
4522 Winnrose Way, Louisville, KY 40211
(502) 778-5063
Admin O Howard Silvers.
Medical Dir James E Redmon MD.
Licensure Personal care. *Beds* Personal care
  141.
Owner Proprietary corp.
Admissions Requirements Minimum age 21;
  Medical examination; Physician's request.
Staff Physicians 1 (ft); LPNs 1 (ft); Nurses'
  aides 15 (ft); Activities coordinators 1 (ft);
  Dietitians 1 (ft); Ophthalmologists 1 (ft).
Facilities Dining room; Activities room;
  Laundry room.
Activities Arts & crafts; Cards; Games; Prayer
  groups.

Filson Care Home
1550 Raydale Dr, Louisville, KY 40219
(502) 968-6600, 966-9218 FAX
Admin Deanna Reid. *Dir of Nursing*
  Bernadette Stewart. *Medical Dir* Dr John
  Lach.
Licensure Intermediate care. *Beds* ICF 110.
  Private Pay Patients 25%. *Certified*
  Medicaid.
Owner Proprietary corp.
Admissions Requirements Medical
  examination; Physician's request.
Staff RNs 1 (ft); LPNs 4 (ft); Nurses' aides 38
  (ft); Physical therapists 1 (pt); Activities
  coordinators 1 (ft); Dietitians 1 (ft), 1 (pt);
  Podiatrists 1 (pt).
Facilities Dining room; Physical therapy
  room; Activities room; Crafts room; Laundry
  room; Barber/Beauty shop; Library.
Activities Arts & crafts; Cards; Games;
  Reading groups; Prayer groups; Movies;
  Shopping trips; Dances/Social/Cultural
  gatherings; Pet therapy.

Four Courts
2100 Millvale Rd, Louisville, KY 40205
(502) 451-0990
Admin Sharon H Sizemore. *Dir of Nursing*
  Freda G Manion RN. *Medical Dir* Harold
  Kramer MD.
Licensure Intermediate care; Personal care.
  Beds ICF 59; Personal care 16. *Certified*
  Medicaid; Medicare.
Owner Nonprofit corp.
Admissions Requirements Medical
  examination.
Facilities Dining room; Physical therapy
  room; Activities room; Chapel; Crafts room;
  Laundry room; Barber/Beauty shop; Library.
Activities Arts & crafts; Cards; Games;
  Reading groups; Movies; Shopping trips;
  Dances/Social/Cultural gatherings.

Franciscan Health Care Center
3625 Fern Valley Rd, Louisville, KY 40219
(502) 964-3381
Admin Suzanne Mervis.
Licensure Skilled care; Intermediate care. *Beds*
  SNF 19; ICF 131.
Owner Proprietary corp.

Georgetown Manor
900 Gagel Ave, Louisville, KY 40216
(502) 368-5827
Admin Tim Herber. *Dir of Nursing* Debbie
  Bonner. *Medical Dir* John Lach MD.
Licensure Skilled care; Intermediate care. *Beds*
  SNF 96; ICF 24. *Private Pay Patients* 50%.
  Certified Medicaid; Medicare.
Owner Nonprofit corp (Pinnacle Care Corp).

Admissions Requirements Minimum age 16;
  Medical examination; Physician's request.
Staff RNs 6 (ft), 9 (pt); LPNs 14 (ft), 7 (pt);
  Nurses' aides 37 (ft), 49 (pt); Physical
  therapists 3 (ft); Occupational therapists 2
  (ft); Speech therapists 1 (ft), 1 (pt); Activities
  coordinators 2 (ft); Dietitians 1 (pt).
Facilities Dining room; Physical therapy
  room; Activities room; Barber/Beauty shop;
  Rehabilitation department; Head trauma
  unit.
Activities Arts & crafts; Games; Prayer groups;
  Movies; Shopping trips; Dances/Social/
  Cultural gatherings; Pet therapy; Swimming;
  Dining out.

**Hazelwood Intermediate Care Facility/Mental
Retardation**
1800 Bluegrass Ave, Louisville, KY 40214
(502) 361-2301
Admin Fred Sapp, Dir. *Dir of Nursing* Carol
  Wyckoff MSN. *Medical Dir* Teresita Layug
  MD.
Licensure Intermediate care for mentally
  retarded. *Beds* ICF/MR 220. *Private Pay
  Patients* 1%.
Owner Publicly owned.
Admissions Requirements Minimum age 6;
  Physically and mentally handicapped.
Staff Physicians 3 (ft); RNs 23 (ft), 1 (pt);
  LPNs 28 (ft), 7 (pt); Nurses' aides 202 (ft),
  17 (pt); Physical therapists 4 (pt);
  Recreational therapists 3 (ft); Occupational
  therapists 2 (ft), 1 (pt); Speech therapists 3
  (ft); Activities coordinators 3 (ft); Dietitians
  3 (ft).
Languages Sign.
Facilities Dining room; Physical therapy
  room; Activities room; Chapel; Crafts room;
  Laundry room; Barber/Beauty shop; Library.
Activities Arts & crafts; Cards; Games;
  Movies; Shopping trips; Dances/Social/
  Cultural gatherings; Intergenerational
  programs.

Health Center of the Forum at Brookside
200 Brookside Dr, Louisville, KY 40243
(502) 245-3048
Admin William Hulsey. *Dir of Nursing* Shirley
  Bealmear RN. *Medical Dir* Stephen
  Applegate MD.
Licensure Skilled care; Personal care. *Beds*
  SNF 40; Personal care 20. *Private Pay
  Patients* 90%. *Certified* Medicare.
Owner Proprietary corp (Forum Group).
Admissions Requirements Medical
  examination; Physician's request.
Staff Physicians 1 (ft); RNs 8 (ft); LPNs 10
  (ft); Nurses' aides 30 (ft); Physical therapists
  1 (ft); Reality therapists 1 (ft); Recreational
  therapists 1 (ft); Speech therapists 1 (ft);
  Activities coordinators 1 (ft); Dietitians 2
  (ft); Podiatrists 1 (ft).
Facilities Dining room; Activities room;
  Crafts room; Laundry room; Barber/Beauty
  shop; Nature trail.
Activities Arts & crafts; Cards; Games;
  Reading groups; Prayer groups; Movies;
  Shopping trips; Dances/Social/Cultural
  gatherings; Intergenerational programs; Pet
  therapy.

Hillcreek Manor
3116 Breckenridge Ln, Louisville, KY 40220
(502) 459-9120, 454-3666 FAX
Admin William Scheller. *Dir of Nursing* Patsy
  Martin RN. *Medical Dir* Dr Kenneth Hodge.
Licensure Skilled care; Intermediate care;
  Intermediate care for mentally retarded;
  Personal care. *Beds* SNF 28; ICF 62; ICF/
  MR 60; Personal care 55. *Certified*
  Medicaid; Medicare.
Owner Proprietary corp (Beverly Enterprises).
Admissions Requirements Minimum age 16;
  Medical examination; Physician's request.
Staff Physicians 2 (pt); RNs 7 (ft), 2 (pt);
  LPNs 19 (ft), 2 (pt); Nurses' aides 66 (ft), 13
  (pt); Physical therapists 1 (ft); Occupational

therapists 1 (pt); Speech therapists 1 (pt); Activities coordinators 2 (ft); Dietitians 1 (ft); Ophthalmologists 1 (pt); Podiatrists 1 (pt); Audiologists 1 (pt).

Facilities Dining room; Physical therapy room; Activities room; Chapel; Crafts room; Laundry room; Barber/Beauty shop; Library.

Activities Arts & crafts; Cards; Games; Reading groups; Prayer groups; Movies; Shopping trips; Dances/Social/Cultural gatherings; Intergenerational programs; Pet therapy; Weekly religious services; Resident volunteer program.

Home of the Innocents
485 E Gray St, Louisville, KY 40202
(502) 239-6368
Admin David A Graves.
Medical Dir Suzanne Hite.
Licensure Skilled care; Intermediate care. *Beds* Swing beds SNF/ICF 40. *Certified* Medicaid; Medicare.
Owner Proprietary corp.
Admissions Requirements Must be between ages birth-17.
Staff RNs 5 (ft), 1 (pt); LPNs 12 (ft), 1 (pt); Nurses' aides 24 (ft), 14 (pt); Physical therapists (consultant); Occupational therapists 1 (ft); Speech therapists (consultant); Activities coordinators 1 (ft); Dietitians (consultant); CPTAs 2 (ft).
Facilities Dining room; Physical therapy room; Activities room; Family visitation room.
Activities Arts & crafts; Cards; Games; Movies; Shopping trips; Dances/Social/Cultural gatherings; Intergenerational programs; Pet therapy.

Rose Anna Hughes Presbyterian Home
2120 Buechel Bank Rd, Louisville, KY 40218
(502) 491-3695, 499-3592 FAX
Admin Lisa Herzberg. *Dir of Nursing* Zana Thomas LPN. *Medical Dir* Harold Haller.
Licensure Personal care; Assisted living. *Beds* Personal care 32; Assisted living 30. *Private Pay Patients* 85%.
Owner Nonprofit organization/foundation (Presbyterian Homes & Services of Kentucky).
Admissions Requirements Minimum age 62; Medical examination; Physician's request.
Staff LPNs 1 (ft); Nurses' aides 4 (ft), 3 (pt); Activities coordinators 1 (ft); CMTs 3 (ft), 2 (pt).
Affiliation Presbyterian.
Facilities Dining room; Activities room; Chapel; Crafts room; Laundry room; Barber/Beauty shop; Library.
Activities Arts & crafts; Cards; Games; Reading groups; Prayer groups; Movies; Shopping trips; Dances/Social/Cultural gatherings; Pet therapy.

Jefferson Manor
1801 Lynn Way, Louisville, KY 40222
(502) 426-4513
Admin Deborah Bell.
Medical Dir Robert L Nold Sr MD.
Licensure Skilled care; Intermediate care. *Beds* SNF 30; ICF 70.
Owner Proprietary corp.
Admissions Requirements Medical examination; Physician's request.
Staff RNs 5 (ft), 3 (pt); LPNs 7 (ft), 7 (pt); Nurses' aides 25 (ft), 25 (pt); Physical therapists 2 (pt); Speech therapists 1 (pt); Activities coordinators 2 (ft); Dietitians 1 (pt); Podiatrists 1 (pt); Dentists 1 (pt); Respiratory therapists 4 (ft), 2 (pt).
Facilities Dining room; Physical therapy room; Activities room; Crafts room; Laundry room; Barber/Beauty shop; Library.
Activities Arts & crafts; Cards; Games; Reading groups; Prayer groups; Movies; Shopping trips; Dances/Social/Cultural gatherings; Wine & cheese parties; Family dinners; Guest luncheons.

Jewish Hospital Skilled Nursing Facility
217 E Chestnut St, Louisville, KY 40202
(502) 587-4412
Admin Patricia Bryan Burge.
Licensure Skilled care. *Beds* SNF 12.
Owner Proprietary corp.

Kings Daughters & Sons Home
1705 Stevens Ave, Louisville, KY 40205
(502) 451-7330
Admin Edward L Holley.
Medical Dir Shelby J Simpson.
Licensure Skilled care; Intermediate care; Personal care. *Beds* SNF 66; ICF 88; Personal care 15. *Certified* Medicaid; Medicare.
Owner Proprietary corp.
Admissions Requirements Medical examination; Physician's request.
Staff Physicians 2 (pt); RNs 4 (ft); LPNs 12 (ft); Nurses' aides 65 (ft); Physical therapists 1 (ft); Speech therapists 1 (pt); Activities coordinators 1 (ft); Dietitians 1 (ft); Ophthalmologists 1 (pt); Podiatrists 1 (pt); Dentists 1 (pt).
Affiliation King's Daughters & Sons.
Facilities Dining room; Physical therapy room; Activities room; Chapel; Crafts room; Laundry room; Barber/Beauty shop; Library.
Activities Arts & crafts; Cards; Games; Reading groups; Prayer groups; Movies; Dances/Social/Cultural gatherings.

Klondike Manor
3802 Klondike Ln, Louisville, KY 40218
(502) 452-1579, 452-2111 FAX
Admin Mary Jo Slahta. *Dir of Nursing* Pam Skrine. *Medical Dir* Dr John Lach Jr.
Licensure Intermediate care. *Beds* ICF 62. *Private Pay Patients* 70%. *Certified* Medicaid.
Owner Proprietary corp (Senior Care Inc).
Admissions Requirements Medical examination; Physician's request.
Staff RNs 1 (ft), 1 (pt); LPNs 3 (ft), 3 (pt); Nurses' aides 14 (ft), 10 (pt); Physical therapists contracted; Activities coordinators 1 (ft), 1 (pt); Dietitians contracted; Podiatrists contracted; Optometrists contracted; Dentists contracted.
Facilities Dining room; Laundry room; Barber/Beauty shop; Lounge; Private areas; Courtyard.
Activities Arts & crafts; Cards; Games; Reading groups; Prayer groups; Movies; Shopping trips; Dances/Social/Cultural gatherings; Intergenerational programs; Pet therapy.

Louisville Protestant Althenheim
936 Barrett Ave, Louisville, KY 40204
(502) 584-7417
Admin Joan E Walcutt NHA. *Dir of Nursing* Doris McGraw.
Licensure Intermediate care; Personal care. *Beds* ICF 12; Personal 46.
Owner Nonprofit corp.
Admissions Requirements Minimum age 65; Medical examination; Physician's request.
Staff RNs 1 (ft); LPNs 2 (ft); Nurses' aides 9 (ft), 3 (pt); Activities coordinators 1 (ft); Dietitians 1 (ft); CMT 5 (ft), 1 (pt); CPM 1 (ft).
Facilities Dining room; Activities room; Chapel; Crafts room; Laundry room; Barber/Beauty shop; Library.
Activities Arts & crafts; Cards; Games; Reading groups; Prayer groups; Movies; Shopping trips; Dances/Social/Cultural gatherings.

Lyndon Lane Nursing Center
1101 Lyndon Ln, Louisville, KY 40222
(502) 425-0331
Admin Joseph R Hagan. *Dir of Nursing* Mary A Reardon. *Medical Dir* Eric Hilgeford.

Licensure Skilled care; Intermediate care. *Beds* SNF 29; ICF 136. *Private Pay Patients* 5%. *Certified* Medicaid; Medicare.
Owner Proprietary corp (Beverly Enterprises).
Admissions Requirements Medical examination; Physician's request.
Staff Physicians 1 (pt); RNs 4 (ft); LPNs 15 (ft), 1 (pt); Nurses' aides 44 (ft); Physical therapists 3 (pt); Occupational therapists 1 (ft); Speech therapists 2 (pt); Activities coordinators 1 (ft), 1 (pt); Dietitians 1 (ft); Podiatrists 1 (pt).
Facilities Dining room; Physical therapy room; Activities room; Laundry room; Barber/Beauty shop.
Activities Arts & crafts; Cards; Games; Reading groups; Prayer groups; Movies; Shopping trips; Dances/Social/Cultural gatherings; Pet therapy.

Marian Home—Ursuline Sisters
3105 Lexington Rd, Louisville, KY 40206
(502) 893-0121
Admin Sr Assumpta Devine OSU. *Dir of Nursing* Sr Patricia Ann Thompson OSU. *Medical Dir* Walter L Thompson MD.
Licensure Intermediate care; Personal care. *Beds* ICF 55; Personal care 15. *Certified* Medicaid.
Owner Nonprofit organization/foundation.
Admissions Requirements Females only; Medical examination; Physician's request.
Staff RNs 2 (pt); LPNs 5 (ft); Nurses' aides 24 (ft), 4 (pt); Activities coordinators 1 (pt).
Affiliation Roman Catholic.
Facilities Dining room; Chapel; Crafts room; Laundry room; Barber/Beauty shop; Library.
Activities Arts & crafts; Cards; Games; Reading groups; Prayer groups; Movies; Shopping trips; Dances/Social/Cultural gatherings; Intergenerational programs.

Masonic Widows & Orphans Home
3701 Frankfort Ave, Louisville, KY 40207
(502) 897-4907
Admin Sally A Bowers. *Dir of Nursing* Sue Rouse RN. *Medical Dir* Steven Shelton MD.
Licensure Skilled care; Intermediate care; Personal care. *Beds* SNF 38; ICF 130; Personal care 129. *Private Pay Patients* 0%.
Owner Nonprofit organization/foundation.
Admissions Requirements Minimum age 60.
Staff Physicians 4 (pt); RNs 8 (ft), 1 (pt); LPNs 13 (ft), 2 (pt); Nurses' aides 48 (ft), 26 (pt); Activities coordinators 3 (ft); Dietitians 1 (ft).
Affiliation Masons.
Facilities Dining room; Activities room; Chapel; Crafts room; Laundry room; Barber/Beauty shop.
Activities Arts & crafts; Games; Prayer groups; Movies; Shopping trips; Dances/Social/Cultural gatherings; Intergenerational programs; Pet therapy.

Meadows—East
2529 Six Mile Ln, Louisville, KY 40220
(502) 491-5560
Admin Debra Finneran.
Licensure Intermediate care; Personal care. *Beds* ICF 128; Personal 70. *Certified* Medicaid.
Owner Proprietary corp.

Meadows—South
1120 Cristland Rd, Louisville, KY 40214
(502) 367-0104
Admin Kathy Fellonneau. *Dir of Nursing* Betty Seaton. *Medical Dir* Dr Charles Severs; Dr Manuel Brown.
Licensure Intermediate care; Personal care. *Beds* ICF 100; Personal care 32. *Private Pay Patients* 44%. *Certified* Medicaid.
Owner Proprietary corp.
Admissions Requirements Medical examination.
Staff RNs 2 (pt); LPNs 7 (ft), 2 (pt); Activities coordinators 2 (ft).

Facilities Dining room; Activities room; Laundry room; Barber/Beauty shop.
Activities Arts & crafts; Cards; Games; Reading groups; Movies; Dances/Social/Cultural gatherings; Pet therapy; Church groups.

Meadowview Nursing & Convalescent Center
9701 Whipps Mill Rd, Louisville, KY 40223
(502) 426-2778
Admin Todd Taylor.
Medical Dir A J Perez MD.
Licensure Intermediate care. *Beds* ICF 132.
Certified Medicaid.
Owner Proprietary corp.
Admissions Requirements Minimum age 21; Medical examination; Physician's request.

Melrose Manor Health Care Center
4331 Churchman Ave, Louisville, KY 40215
(502) 367-6489
Admin Jack Czerkiewicz. *Dir of Nursing* Doris Allison RN. *Medical Dir* Dr Antolin Perez.
Licensure Skilled care; Intermediate care; Nursing home; Alzheimer's care. *Beds* SNF 6; ICF 24; Nursing home 15. *Private Pay Patients* 80%. *Certified* Medicaid; Medicare.
Owner Privately owned.
Admissions Requirements Minimum age 18.
Staff Physicians 1 (pt); RNs 2 (ft); LPNs 3 (ft), 2 (pt); Nurses' aides 12 (ft), 8 (pt); Activities coordinators 1 (ft).
Facilities Dining room; Laundry room; Barber/Beauty shop; Wheelchair accessible floor plan.
Activities Arts & crafts; Games; Reading groups; Prayer groups; Movies; Shopping trips; Dances/Social/Cultural gatherings; Pet therapy.

Charles P Moorman Home for Women
966 Cherokee Rd, Louisville, KY 40204
(502) 451-4424
Admin Lois Irwin RN. *Dir of Nursing* M R Rand RN.
Licensure Personal care. *Beds* Personal care 81.
Owner Nonprofit corp.
Admissions Requirements Females only.
Staff Physicians 1 (ft); RNs 2 (ft); Nurses' aides 10 (ft); Activities coordinators 1 (ft); Dietitians 1 (ft).
Facilities Dining room.
Activities Arts & crafts; Cards; Games; Reading groups; Prayer groups; Movies; Shopping trips.

Mt Holly Nursing Home
446 Mount Holly Ave, Louisville, KY 40206
(502) 897-1646
Admin William M Scheller. *Dir of Nursing* Myra Fuller RN. *Medical Dir* Dr Eric Hilgeford.
Licensure Skilled care; Nursing home; Alzheimer's care. *Beds* SNF 20; Nursing home 92. *Certified* Medicaid; Medicare.
Owner Proprietary corp (Beverly Enterprises).
Admissions Requirements Physician's request.
Staff Physicians; RNs; LPNs; Nurses' aides; Physical therapists; Recreational therapists; Occupational therapists; Speech therapists; Activities coordinators; Dietitians; Ophthalmologists; Podiatrists; Dentists.
Facilities Dining room; Physical therapy room; Activities room; Crafts room; Laundry room; Barber/Beauty shop; Library.
Activities Arts & crafts; Cards; Games; Prayer groups; Movies; Shopping trips; Dances/Social/Cultural gatherings.

Nazareth Home
2000 Newburg Rd, Louisville, KY 40205
(502) 459-9681
Admin Sr Gwen McMahon. *Dir of Nursing* Rebecca Wilson. *Medical Dir* Russell May MD.

Licensure Skilled care; Intermediate care; Personal care. *Beds* SNF 14; ICF 104; Personal care 50. *Certified* Medicaid; Medicare.
Owner Nonprofit corp.
Staff Physicians 2 (pt); RNs 7 (ft); LPNs 9 (ft), 7 (pt); Nurses' aides 41 (ft), 15 (pt); Physical therapists 1 (pt); Speech therapists 1 (pt); Activities coordinators 3 (ft); Dietitians 1 (pt); Ophthalmologists 1 (pt); Dentists 2 (pt).
Affiliation Roman Catholic.
Facilities Dining room; Physical therapy room; Activities room; Chapel; Crafts room; Laundry room; Barber/Beauty shop; Library.
Activities Arts & crafts; Cards; Games; Reading groups; Prayer groups; Movies; Shopping trips; Dances/Social/Cultural gatherings.

Northfield Manor Health Care Facility
6000 Hunting Rd, Louisville, KY 40222
(502) 426-1425
Admin Nedra J Devine.
Medical Dir Terry Hagan MD.
Licensure Skilled care; Intermediate care. *Beds* SNF 49; ICF 71. *Certified* Medicaid.
Owner Proprietary corp (Hillhaven Corp).
Staff Physicians 20 (pt); RNs 4 (ft), 2 (pt); LPNs 4 (ft), 6 (pt); Nurses' aides 32 (ft), 8 (pt); Activities coordinators 1 (ft); Dietitians 1 (ft); Podiatrists 1 (pt); Dentists 1 (pt).
Facilities Dining room; Physical therapy room; Activities room; Laundry room; Barber/Beauty shop.
Activities Arts & crafts; Cards; Games; Prayer groups; Movies; Dances/Social/Cultural gatherings.

Parkway Medical Center
1155 Eastern Pkwy, Louisville, KY 40217
(502) 636-5241
Admin Joseph E Okruhlica. *Dir of Nursing* Barbara Kremer-Schmitt RN. *Medical Dir* Truman DeMunbrun MD.
Licensure Skilled care; Intermediate care. *Beds* SNF 168; ICF 84. *Certified* Medicaid; Medicare.
Owner Privately owned.
Admissions Requirements Physician's request.
Staff Physicians 2 (pt); Physical therapists 1 (ft); Occupational therapists 1 (pt); Speech therapists 1 (ft); Activities coordinators 1 (ft); Dietitians 1 (pt); Podiatrists 1 (pt).
Facilities Dining room; Physical therapy room; Activities room; Chapel; Crafts room; Barber/Beauty shop; Dental unit; X-ray department; Coffee shop; Pharmacy with gift shop.
Activities Arts & crafts; Cards; Games; Reading groups; Prayer groups; Movies; Shopping trips; Dances/Social/Cultural gatherings; Intergenerational programs; Pet therapy.

Parr's Rest Home
969 Cherokee Rd, Louisville, KY 40204
(502) 451-5440
Admin Ruth Cushenberry.
Medical Dir Doris Pipkin MD.
Licensure Personal care. *Beds* Personal care 80.
Owner Proprietary corp.
Admissions Requirements Minimum age 65; Medical examination.
Staff Physicians; RNs; Nurses' aides 8 (ft), 1 (pt); Activities coordinators 1 (pt); Podiatrists 1 (pt).
Facilities Dining room; Activities room; Chapel; Crafts room; Laundry room; Barber/Beauty shop.
Activities Arts & crafts; Cards; Games; Reading groups; Prayer groups; Movies; Shopping trips; Dances/Social/Cultural gatherings.

Pavilion Health Care Center
432 E Jefferson St, Louisville, KY 40202
(502) 583-2851
Admin William H Wallen. *Dir of Nursing* Carol Canary RN. *Medical Dir* James Redmon MD.
Licensure Skilled care; Intermediate care. *Beds* SNF 62; ICF/MR 124. *Certified* Medicaid; Medicare.
Owner Proprietary corp (Pavilion Health Care Centers).
Admissions Requirements Medical examination.
Staff RNs 10 (ft), 4 (pt); LPNs 16 (ft), 6 (pt); Nurses' aides 60 (ft), 20 (pt); Physical therapists 1 (ft); Occupational therapists 2 (ft); Speech therapists 1 (pt); Activities coordinators 11 (ft); Dietitians 1 (ft).
Facilities Dining room; Physical therapy room; Activities room; Laundry room; Barber/Beauty shop.
Activities Arts & crafts; Cards; Games; Reading groups; Prayer groups; Movies; Shopping trips; Dances/Social/Cultural gatherings.

Pine Tree Villa
4604 Lowe Rd, Louisville, KY 40220
(502) 451-1401, 451-1381 FAX
Admin Betty A Hoehn. *Dir of Nursing* Marge Eskridge. *Medical Dir* Drs Peters; Stober; Copley; Dunaway.
Licensure Intermediate care; Personal care. *Beds* ICF 70; Personal care 133. *Private Pay Patients* 90%. *Certified* Medicaid.
Owner Proprietary corp (Meadows Group).
Admissions Requirements Medical examination.
Staff RNs 4 (ft); LPNs 8 (ft); Nurses' aides 46 (ft), 5 (pt); Activities coordinators 2 (ft); Dietitians 3 (ft).
Facilities Dining room; Activities room; Chapel; Crafts room; Laundry room; Barber/Beauty shop.
Activities Arts & crafts; Cards; Games; Reading groups; Prayer groups; Movies; Shopping trips; Dances/Social/Cultural gatherings.

Pleasant Place Home for Care
12800 Dixie Hwy, Louisville, KY 40272
(502) 937-4965
Admin B J Miles.
Licensure Personal care. *Beds* Personal care 58.
Owner Proprietary corp.

Sacred Heart Home
2120 Payne St, Louisville, KY 40206
(502) 895-9425
Admin Mark Pastura.
Medical Dir Betty Gallahue LPN.
Licensure Personal care. *Beds* Personal care 64.
Owner Nonprofit corp.
Admissions Requirements Minimum age 65; Medical examination.
Staff LPNs 2 (ft); Nurses' aides 4 (ft), 8 (pt); Activities coordinators 1 (ft); Dietitians 1 (ft); Ophthalmologists 1 (ft); Pastoral Care Director 1 (ft); Chaplain 1 (ft).
Affiliation Roman Catholic.
Facilities Dining room; Activities room; Chapel; Laundry room; Barber/Beauty shop; Library.
Activities Arts & crafts; Cards; Games; Reading groups; Prayer groups; Movies; Shopping trips; Dances/Social/Cultural gatherings; Pet therapy; Resident council.

St Matthews Manor
227 Browns Ln, Louisville, KY 40207
(502) 893-2595
Admin Herschel B Sedoris. *Dir of Nursing* Barbara Hiland RN. *Medical Dir* Eric Hilgeford MD.
Licensure Skilled care; Nursing home. *Beds* SNF 20; Nursing home 105.

Owner Proprietary corp (Beverly Enterprises).
Admissions Requirements Medical examination.
Staff RNs 12 (ft), 12 (pt); LPNs 1 (ft); Nurses' aides 45 (ft), 6 (pt); Physical therapists 1 (pt); Activities coordinators 1 (ft); Dietitians 1 (ft); Podiatrists 1 (pt).
Facilities Dining room; Physical therapy room; Activities room; Crafts room; Laundry room; Barber/Beauty shop; Library.
Activities Arts & crafts; Cards; Games; Prayer groups; Movies; Shopping trips; Dances/Social/Cultural gatherings.

W W Spradling Rest Home
726 S Preston, Louisville, KY 40203
(502) 585-2426
Admin William H Brown Jr.
Licensure Personal care. *Beds* Personal care 24.
Owner Nonprofit corp.

Summerfield Manor Nursing Home
1877 Farnsley Rd, Louisville, KY 40216
(502) 448-8622
Admin James Morris.
Licensure Intermediate care. *Beds* ICF 179. *Certified* Medicaid.
Owner Proprietary corp.

James S Taylor Memorial Home
1015 Magazine St, Louisville, KY 40203
(502) 589-2827
Admin Paul A Ferry Jr. *Dir of Nursing* Brenda Gilmet.
Licensure Intermediate care. *Beds* ICF 122. *Private Pay Patients* 10%.
Owner Nonprofit organization/foundation.
Staff RNs 2 (ft); LPNs 5 (ft); Nurses' aides 40 (ft); Activities coordinators 2 (ft); Dietitians 1 (ft).

Treyton Oak Towers
211 W Oak St, Louisville, KY 40203
(502) 589-3211
Admin Stewart A Ingram.
Licensure Skilled care. *Beds* SNF 60.
Owner Proprietary corp.

Twinbrook Nursing Home
3526 Dutchmans Ln, Louisville, KY 40205
(502) 452-6331
Admin Brad McCoy.
Licensure Skilled care; Nursing home. *Beds* SNF 25; Nursing home 62. *Certified* Medicaid; Medicare.
Owner Proprietary corp.

Wesley Manor Nursing Center & Retirement Community
PO Box 19258, 5012 E Manslick Rd, Louisville, KY 40219
(502) 969-3277
Admin Edward D Brandeberry. *Dir of Nursing* Joyce Wells. *Medical Dir* John Stober MD.
Licensure Skilled care; Intermediate care; Personal care. *Beds* SNF 10; ICF 58; Personal 39. *Certified* Medicaid; Medicare.
Owner Nonprofit corp.
Admissions Requirements Minimum age 65; Medical examination; Physician's request.
Staff RNs; LPNs; Nurses' aides; Activities coordinators; Dietitians.
Affiliation Methodist.
Facilities Dining room; Physical therapy room; Activities room; Chapel; Crafts room; Laundry room; Barber/Beauty shop; Library.
Activities Arts & crafts; Cards; Games; Reading groups; Prayer groups; Movies; Shopping trips; Dances/Social/Cultural gatherings.

Westminster Terrace—Rose Anna Hughes Campus
2116-2120 Buechel Bank Rd, Louisville, KY 40218
(502) 499-9383
Admin James Walsh. *Dir of Nursing* Joyce Wells. *Medical Dir* Harold Haller MD.

Licensure Skilled care; Intermediate care; Personal care; Retirement. *Beds* SNF 31; ICF 81; Personal care 32; Retirement apts 84. *Certified* Medicaid; Medicare.
Owner Nonprofit organization/foundation.
Admissions Requirements Minimum age 62.
Staff Physicians 1 (ft); RNs 6 (ft), 2 (pt); LPNs 11 (ft), 4 (pt); Nurses' aides 41 (ft), 17 (pt); Physical therapists 1 (pt); Activities coordinators 3 (ft); Ophthalmologists 1 (pt).
Affiliation Presbyterian.
Facilities Dining room; Physical therapy room; Activities room; Chapel; Crafts room; Laundry room; Barber/Beauty shop; Library.
Activities Arts & crafts; Cards; Games; Reading groups; Prayer groups; Movies; Shopping trips; Dances/Social/Cultural gatherings; Intergenerational programs; Pet therapy.

Ludlow

Madonna Manor
2344 Amsterdam Rd, Ludlow, KY 41016
(606) 341-3981
Admin Sr M Charles Wolking.
Licensure Intermediate care. *Beds* 38. *Certified* Medicaid.
Owner Nonprofit corp.

Madisonville

Brown Rest Home
384 Thompson Ave, Madisonville, KY 42431
(502) 821-5294
Admin Larry Brown.
Licensure Intermediate care; Personal care. *Beds* ICF 100; Personal 48. *Certified* Medicaid.
Owner Proprietary corp.
Admissions Requirements Medical examination.
Staff RNs 1 (pt); LPNs 6 (ft); Nurses' aides 50 (ft), 20 (pt); Speech therapists 1 (pt); Dietitians 1 (pt).
Facilities Dining room; Activities room; Crafts room; Laundry room.
Activities Arts & crafts; Cards; Games; Prayer groups; Movies; Shopping trips; Dances/Social/Cultural gatherings.

Clinic Convalescent Center
55 E North St, Madisonville, KY 42431
(502) 821-1492
Admin Coleen Lovell. *Dir of Nursing* Jo Ann Ashby RN. *Medical Dir* Dan Martin MD.
Licensure Skilled care. *Beds* SNF 66. *Certified* Medicaid; Medicare.
Owner Proprietary corp.
Admissions Requirements Physician's request.
Staff Physicians 20 (pt); RNs 3 (ft); LPNs 7 (ft), 4 (pt); Nurses' aides 24 (ft), 4 (pt); Recreational therapists 1 (pt); Activities coordinators 1 (ft); Dietitians 1 (ft), 1 (pt); Dentists 3 (pt).
Facilities Dining room; Physical therapy room; Activities room; Crafts room; Barber/Beauty shop.
Activities Arts & crafts; Cards; Games; Prayer groups; Dances/Social/Cultural gatherings.

Kentucky Rest Haven
419 N Seminary St, Madisonville, KY 42431
(502) 821-5564
Admin Danny Belcher.
Licensure Skilled care; Intermediate care. *Beds* SNF 54; ICF 40. *Certified* Medicaid; Medicare.
Owner Proprietary corp (National Health Corp).

Madisonville Manor
Franklin & Givens Sts, Madisonville, KY 42431
(502) 821-2155
Admin John Bard.

Licensure Personal care. *Beds* Personal care 86.
Owner Proprietary corp.

Senior Citizens Nursing Home
PO Box 743, US Rte 41A & Pride Ave, Madisonville, KY 42431
(502) 821-1813
Admin Sandra Higgins.
Medical Dir Dr Richard Dodds.
Licensure Skilled care; Intermediate care. *Beds* SNF 32; ICF 54. *Certified* Medicaid; Medicare.
Owner Proprietary corp.
Admissions Requirements Medical examination; Physician's request.
Facilities Dining room; Physical therapy room; Laundry room; Barber/Beauty shop; Library.
Activities Cards; Games; Movies; Shopping trips; Dances/Social/Cultural gatherings.

Manchester

Laurel Creek Health Care Center
Rte 2 Box 254, Manchester, KY 40962
(606) 598-6163
Admin Everett Ben Bays.
Licensure Intermediate care; Personal care. *Beds* ICF 106; Personal care 12. *Certified* Medicaid.
Owner Proprietary corp (Angell Group).

Memorial Hospital Inc—SNF
401 Memorial Dr, Manchester, KY 40962
(606) 598-5104, 598-7008 FAX
Admin Bruce Wickwire. *Dir of Nursing* Jeff Joiner RN. *Medical Dir* Lee Meadows MD.
Licensure Skilled care. *Beds* SNF 11. *Private Pay Patients* 0%. *Certified* Medicaid; Medicare.
Owner Nonprofit corp.
Admissions Requirements Physician's request.
Staff Physicians 12 (ft); RNs 2 (ft); LPNs 3 (ft); Nurses' aides 6 (ft); Physical therapists (contracted); Activities coordinators 1 (pt); Dietitians (contracted).
Affiliation Seventh-Day Adventist.
Facilities Physical therapy room; Activities room; Chapel; Laundry room.
Activities Movies; Pet therapy; Music.

Marion

Crittenden County Convalescence Center
Rte 2, Moore & Watson Sts, Marion, KY 42064
(502) 965-2218
Admin Marie Yates. *Dir of Nursing* Gail Fowler RN. *Medical Dir* Dr Greg Maddux.
Licensure Intermediate care; Personal care. *Beds* ICF 101; Personal care 6. *Private Pay Patients* 10%. *Certified* Medicaid.
Owner Privately owned.
Admissions Requirements Medical examination; Physician's request.
Staff Physicians 4 (pt); RNs 2 (ft); LPNs 4 (ft); Nurses' aides 60 (ft); Physical therapists 1 (pt); Recreational therapists 1 (ft); Speech therapists 1 (pt); Activities coordinators 1 (ft); Dietitians 1 (ft).
Facilities Dining room; Activities room; Laundry room; Barber/Beauty shop; Courtyard.
Activities Arts & crafts; Games; Prayer groups; Movies; Shopping trips; Dances/Social/Cultural gatherings; Pet therapy.

Mayfield

Fern Terrace Lodge of Mayfield
PO Box 325, Hwy 45 N, Mayfield, KY 42066
(502) 247-3259
Admin Kathryn P Baer; A Loudean Austin Asst.
Medical Dir A Loudean Austin.

Licensure Personal care. *Beds* Personal care 140. *Certified* Medicaid.
Owner Proprietary corp.
Admissions Requirements Minimum age 42; Medical examination.
Staff Nurses' aides; Recreational therapists; Activities coordinators; Dietitians.
Facilities Dining room; Activities room; Laundry room; Barber/Beauty shop; Library.
Activities Arts & crafts; Cards; Games; Reading groups; Prayer groups; Dances/Social/Cultural gatherings; Pet therapy.

Green Acres Healthcare
402 W Farthing St, Mayfield, KY 42066
(502) 247-6477
Admin Samuel Gray. *Dir of Nursing* Sharon Jameson RN. *Medical Dir* Dr Wayne Williams.
Licensure Intermediate care; Personal care. *Beds* ICF 24; Personal care 49. *Private Pay Patients* 40%. *Certified* Medicaid.
Owner Proprietary corp.
Admissions Requirements Minimum age 50; Medical examination; Physician's request.
Staff RNs 1 (ft); LPNs 1 (ft); Nurses' aides 15 (ft); Physical therapists 1 (pt); Activities coordinators 1 (ft); Dietitians 1 (ft); Other staff.
Facilities Dining room; Activities room; Crafts room; Laundry room; Barber/Beauty shop; Library.
Activities Arts & crafts; Cards; Games; Reading groups; Prayer groups; Movies; Shopping trips; Dances/Social/Cultural gatherings; Intergenerational programs; Pet therapy.

Heritage Manor Healthcare Center
4th & Indiana Ave, Mayfield, KY 42066
(502) 247-0200
Admin Lanny Harvey.
Licensure Skilled care; Intermediate care. *Beds* SNF 42; ICF 58. *Certified* Medicaid; Medicare.
Owner Proprietary corp.

Meadowview Retirement Home
Rte 7 Box 64, Mayfield, KY 42066
(502) 345-2116
Admin Barbara Lamb.
Licensure Personal care. *Beds* Personal care 24.
Owner Proprietary corp.

Mills Manor
500 Beck Ln, Mayfield, KY 42066
(502) 247-7890, 247-8653 FAX
Admin Jerry F Medanich. *Dir of Nursing* Teresa Chambers RN. *Medical Dir* Charles Howard MD.
Licensure Intermediate care. *Beds* ICF 98. *Certified* Medicaid.
Owner Nonprofit corp (Sunbelt Healthcare Centers Inc).
Admissions Requirements Minimum age 21.
Staff RNs 3 (ft); LPNs 9 (ft), 2 (pt); Nurses' aides 35 (ft), 10 (pt); Physical therapists 1 (pt); Speech therapists 1 (pt); Activities coordinators 1 (ft); Dietitians 1 (pt); Other staff 12 (ft), 4 (pt).
Affiliation Seventh-Day Adventist.
Facilities Dining room; Physical therapy room; Activities room; Crafts room; Laundry room; Barber/Beauty shop.
Activities Arts & crafts; Cards; Games; Reading groups; Prayer groups; Movies; Pet therapy.

Skyview Personal Care Home
Rte 4, Mayfield, KY 42066
(502) 623-6696
Admin Nancy Riley.
Licensure Personal care. *Beds* 40.
Owner Proprietary corp.

Maysville

Maysville Extended Care Facility
Rte 2, Maysville, KY 41056
(606) 564-4085
Admin Teresa G Lewis. *Dir of Nursing* Susan Price RN.
Licensure Skilled care; Intermediate care. *Beds* SNF 18; ICF 82. *Certified* Medicaid.
Owner Proprietary corp.
Staff Physicians 10 (pt); RNs 2 (ft), 1 (pt); LPNs 8 (ft), 2 (pt); Nurses' aides 30 (ft), 10 (pt); Physical therapists 1 (pt); Speech therapists 1 (pt); Activities coordinators 1 (ft), 1 (pt); Dietitians 1 (pt).
Facilities Dining room; Activities room; Laundry room; Barber/Beauty shop.
Activities Arts & crafts; Cards; Games; Reading groups; Prayer groups; Movies; Shopping trips; Dances/Social/Cultural gatherings.

Melber

Melber Rest Home
Rte 1, General Delivery, Melber, KY 42069
(502) 856-3210
Admin Bonnie Milgate.
Licensure Personal care. *Beds* Personal care 10.
Owner Proprietary corp.
Admissions Requirements Minimum age 16; Medical examination.
Staff Nurses' aides 2 (ft); Dietitians 1 (ft).
Facilities Dining room; Activities room; Laundry room.
Activities Arts & crafts; Cards; Games; Prayer groups; Shopping trips; Dances/Social/Cultural gatherings.

Middlesboro

Ruby's Rest Home
504 S 24th St, Middlesboro, KY 40965
(606) 248-1540
Admin Ruby J Lake. *Dir of Nursing* Mary Frances Smith. *Medical Dir* Dr Maria Hortillosa.
Licensure Personal care; Alzheimer's care. *Beds* Personal care 64. *Private Pay Patients* 5%. *Certified* Medicaid.
Owner Privately owned.
Admissions Requirements Minimum age 30; Medical examination; Physician's request.
Staff Physicians 1 (pt); LPNs 2 (pt); Nurses' aides 14 (pt); Activities coordinators 1 (pt); Dietitians 1 (pt).
Affiliation Baptist.
Facilities Dining room; Activities room; Chapel; Crafts room; Laundry room; Library.
Activities Arts & crafts; Cards; Games; Reading groups; Prayer groups; Movies; Shopping trips; Dances/Social/Cultural gatherings; Pet therapy.

Monticello

Dishman Personal Care Home
Warsham Ln, Monticello, KY 42633
(606) 348-6201
Admin Christine Bybee Goff.
Licensure Personal care. *Beds* Personal care 49.
Owner Proprietary corp.

Hicks Golden Years Nursing Home
Rte 4 Box 121, Monticello, KY 42633
(606) 348-6034
Admin Darrell Hicks.
Medical Dir Glenda Turner.
Licensure Intermediate care; Personal care. *Beds* ICF 55; Personal care 5. *Certified* Medicaid.
Owner Privately owned.

Staff RNs 2 (ft); LPNs 1 (ft); Nurses' aides 20 (ft), 4 (pt); Activities coordinators 2 (ft); Dietitians 1 (ft), 1 (pt).
Facilities Dining room; Activities room; Chapel; Laundry room; Barber/Beauty shop.
Activities Arts & crafts; Cards; Games; Reading groups; Prayer groups; Movies; Shopping trips; Dances/Social/Cultural gatherings.

Morehead

Life Care Center of Morehead
PO Box 654, 933 N Tolliver Rd, Morehead, KY 40351
(606) 784-7518
Admin Virginia H Saunders. *Dir of Nursing* Danica Ellington RN. *Medical Dir* J Hunter Black MD.
Licensure Skilled care; Intermediate care; Personal care; Nursing home. *Beds* SNF 21; ICF 67; Personal care 14; Nursing home 9. *Certified* Medicaid; Medicare.
Owner Proprietary corp (Life Care Centers of America).
Admissions Requirements Minimum age 16; Medical examination; Physician's request.
Staff RNs 2 (ft), 1 (pt); Nurses' aides 39 (ft), 8 (pt); Activities coordinators 1 (ft); Social services director 1 (ft).
Facilities Dining room; Activities room; Chapel; Crafts room; Laundry room; Barber/Beauty shop.
Activities Arts & crafts; Games; Prayer groups; Dances/Social/Cultural gatherings; Residents council; Gourmet club.

Morganfield

Higgins Learning Center
PO Box 374, Hwy 141 N, Morganfield, KY 42437
(502) 389-0822
Admin Robert R Rupsch. *Dir of Nursing* Reva S Brown. *Medical Dir* Joel Haffner MD.
Licensure Intermediate care for mentally retarded. *Beds* ICF/MR 56. *Private Pay Patients* 0%. *Certified* Medicaid; Medicare.
Owner Proprietary corp (Res-Care Health Services).
Admissions Requirements Minimum age 7.
Staff Physicians 1 (ft); RNs 1 (ft), 1 (pt); LPNs 5 (ft); Nurses' aides 40 (ft); Physical therapists 1 (ft), 1 (pt); Recreational therapists 2 (ft); Occupational therapists 1 (ft), 2 (pt); Speech therapists 2 (ft); Dietitians 1 (pt).
Facilities Dining room; Physical therapy room; Activities room; Crafts room; Laundry room; Library.
Activities Arts & crafts; Cards; Games; Prayer groups; Movies; Shopping trips; Dances/Social/Cultural gatherings.

Medco Center of Morganfield
Rte 5 Box 24A, Morganfield, KY 42437
(502) 389-3513
Admin Wanda J Jones.
Licensure Intermediate care. *Beds* ICF 60. *Certified* Medicaid.
Owner Proprietary corp (Unicare).

Morgantown

Lakeview Nursing Home
Warren St, Box 159, Morgantown, KY 42261
(502) 526-3368
Admin Ralph Eaton. *Dir of Nursing* Alice Forgy RN. *Medical Dir* Dr Richard T C Wan.
Licensure Skilled care; Intermediate care; Personal care. *Beds* SNF 38; ICF 96; Personal care 35. *Certified* Medicaid; Medicare.
Owner Proprietary corp (National Heritage).

Admissions Requirements Medical examination; Physician's request.
Staff Physicians 3 (ft); RNs 7 (ft); LPNs 5 (ft); Nurses' aides 6 (ft), 8 (pt); Physical therapists 2 (ft); Recreational therapists 2 (ft); Speech therapists 1 (ft); Activities coordinators 1 (ft); Dietitians 1 (ft).
Facilities Dining room; Physical therapy room; Activities room; Crafts room; Laundry room; Barber/Beauty shop.
Activities Arts & crafts; Cards; Games; Reading groups; Prayer groups; Movies; Shopping trips; Dances/Social/Cultural gatherings.

Mount Sterling

Mary Chiles Hospital
PO Box 7, 50 Sterling Ave, Mount Sterling, KY 40353
(606) 498-1220
Admin Alan Newberry.
Licensure Skilled care; Intermediate care for mentally retarded. *Beds* SNF 40; ICF/MR 7. *Certified* Medicaid; Medicare.
Owner Nonprofit corp.

Annie Walker Nursing Home
PO Box 639, Bridgett Dr, Mount Sterling, KY 40353
(606) 498-6397
Admin Marcella Knowles. *Dir of Nursing* Maxine O Huddleston. *Medical Dir* Dr Robert J Salisbury.
Licensure Intermediate care; Personal care. *Beds* ICF 42; Personal care 8. *Private Pay Patients* 3%. *Certified* Medicaid.
Owner Privately owned.
Admissions Requirements Medical examination.
Staff LPNs 2 (ft), 2 (pt); Nurses' aides 15 (ft), 2 (pt); Physical therapists 1 (pt); Activities coordinators 1 (ft); Dietitians (consultant); Podiatrists 1 (pt).
Facilities Dining room; Activities room; Laundry room; Semi-private rooms.
Activities Arts & crafts; Games; Reading groups; Shopping trips; Dances/Social/Cultural gatherings; Weekly church services.

Windsor Care Center
PO Box 346, Rte 460, Windsor Square, Mount Sterling, KY 40353
(606) 498-3343
Admin James Stephens.
Licensure Intermediate care; Personal care. *Beds* ICF 58; Personal care 2. *Certified* Medicaid.
Owner Proprietary corp (Hillhaven Corp).

Mount Vernon

Rockcastle County Hospital
Rte 4 Box 28, Mount Vernon, KY 40456
(606) 256-2195
Admin Wayne Stewart.
Medical Dir Cindy Burton.
Licensure Skilled care. *Beds* SNF 32. *Certified* Medicaid; Medicare.
Owner Nonprofit corp.
Admissions Requirements Medical examination.
Staff Physicians 5 (ft); RNs 8 (ft); LPNs 12 (ft); Nurses' aides 16 (ft); Physical therapists 2 (ft); Recreational therapists 2 (ft); Speech therapists 1 (ft); Activities coordinators 1 (ft); Dietitians 2 (ft); Audiologists 1 (pt); Respiratory therapists 25 (ft).
Facilities Dining room; Physical therapy room; Activities room; Chapel; Crafts room; Barber/Beauty shop; Library.
Activities Arts & crafts; Cards; Games; Reading groups; Prayer groups; Movies; Shopping trips; Dances/Social/Cultural gatherings; Home trips.

Munfordville

Hart County Personal Care Home
Riverview Ct, Munfordville, KY 42765
(502) 524-4194
Admin Donna Cruse.
Licensure Personal care. *Beds* Personal care 54.
Owner Proprietary corp (Angell Group).
Admissions Requirements Minimum age 16; Medical examination.
Staff Nurses' aides 11 (ft); Activities coordinators; Dietitians.
Facilities Dining room; Laundry room; Barber/Beauty shop.
Activities Recreation in afternoon.

Murray

Fern Terrace Lodge of Murray
1505 Stadium View Dr, Murray, KY 42071
(502) 753-7109
Admin Glada Dodd RN.
Licensure Personal care; Day care. *Beds* Personal care 103. *Certified* Medicaid.
Owner Privately owned.
Admissions Requirements Minimum age 50; Medical examination; Physician's request.
Staff LPNs 1 (ft); Nurses' aides 10 (ft), 4 (pt); Activities coordinators 1 (pt).
Facilities Dining room; Activities room; Laundry room; Barber/Beauty shop.
Activities Arts & crafts; Cards; Games; Prayer groups; Shopping trips; Dances/Social/Cultural gatherings; Bingo.

Murray-Calloway County Hospital Convalescent Division
803 Poplar St, Murray, KY 42071
(502) 753-5131
Admin James Stuart Poston. *Dir of Nursing* Bonna Yates RN.
Licensure Skilled care; Intermediate care. *Beds* SNF 20; ICF 20. *Certified* Medicaid; Medicare.
Owner Nonprofit corp.
Staff Physicians 35 (ft); RNs 2 (ft), 1 (pt); LPNs 8 (ft), 1 (pt); Nurses' aides 12 (ft); Physical therapists 3 (ft); Speech therapists 1 (pt); Activities coordinators 1 (ft); Dietitians 2 (ft); Ophthalmologists 1 (ft); Podiatrists 1 (pt); Dentists 2 (ft).
Facilities Dining room; Physical therapy room; Activities room; Chapel; Laundry room; Barber/Beauty shop; Library.
Activities Arts & crafts; Cards; Games; Reading groups; Prayer groups; Movies; Shopping trips; Dances/Social/Cultural gatherings; Pet therapy; Cooking club.

West View Nursing Home
PO Box 165, 1401 S 16th St, Murray, KY 42071
(502) 753-1304
Admin Lowell K Beck.
Licensure Skilled care; Intermediate care. *Beds* SNF 56; ICF 118. *Certified* Medicaid; Medicare.
Owner Proprietary corp.

Nerinx

Loretto Motherhouse Infirmary
Hwy 152, Nerinx, KY 40049
(502) 865-5811
Admin Sr Kay Carlew. *Dir of Nursing* Sr Marie Lourde Steckler RN.
Licensure Intermediate care. *Beds* ICF 63. *Certified* Medicaid.
Owner Nonprofit corp.
Admissions Requirements Females only; Medical examination; Physician's request.
Staff Physicians 2 (ft); RNs 2 (ft); LPNs 4 (ft); Nurses' aides 30 (ft); Activities coordinators 1 (ft); Dietitians 1 (ft).
Affiliation Roman Catholic.

Facilities Dining room; Physical therapy room; Activities room; Chapel; Laundry room; Barber/Beauty shop.
Activities Arts & crafts; Games; Prayer groups; Movies; Shopping trips; Pet therapy; Coffee & conversation.

New Castle

Homestead Nursing Center of New Castle Inc
Box 329, New Castle, KY 40050
(502) 845-2861
Admin Gregory John Patterson.
Medical Dir Dr R Houston.
Licensure Intermediate care. *Beds* ICF 60. *Certified* Medicaid.
Owner Proprietary corp.
Admissions Requirements Minimum age 16.
Staff Physicians 4 (ft); RNs 2 (ft); LPNs 2 (ft); Nurses' aides 22 (ft); Physical therapists 1 (ft); Recreational therapists 1 (ft); Activities coordinators 1 (ft); Dietitians 1 (ft); Dentists 1 (ft).
Facilities Dining room; Activities room; Crafts room; Laundry room; Barber/Beauty shop; Library.
Activities Arts & crafts; Cards; Games; Reading groups; Prayer groups; Movies; Dances/Social/Cultural gatherings.

Newport

Baptist Convalescent Center
120 Main St, Newport, KY 41071
(606) 581-1938
Admin Rev Lee Hopkins. *Dir of Nursing* Lawanna Jones RN. *Medical Dir* Dr Doris Spegal.
Licensure Skilled care; Intermediate care. *Beds* SNF 59; ICF 108. *Private Pay Patients* 53%. *Certified* Medicaid; Medicare.
Owner Nonprofit corp.
Admissions Requirements Medical examination.
Staff Physicians 1 (pt); RNs 4 (ft), 2 (pt); LPNs 10 (ft), 5 (pt); Nurses' aides 47 (ft), 19 (pt); Physical therapists 3 (pt); Activities coordinators 1 (ft); Dietitians 1 (ft).
Affiliation Baptist.
Facilities Dining room; Physical therapy room; Activities room; Chapel; Crafts room; Laundry room; Barber/Beauty shop.
Activities Arts & crafts; Cards; Games; Shopping trips; Dances/Social/Cultural gatherings; Exercise class; Birthday parties; Sing-alongs; Discussion group; Religious activities; Media presentations; Holiday events; Resident council.

Nicholasville

Rose Terrace Lodge
401 N 2nd St, Nicholasville, KY 40356
(606) 885-3821
Admin Sharon Reynolds.
Licensure Personal care. *Beds* Personal care 36.
Owner Privately owned.

Royal Manor
100 Sparks Ave, Nicholasville, KY 40356
(606) 885-4171
Admin Marlin K Sparks. *Dir of Nursing* Shannon Allen. *Medical Dir* Wayne Marlowe.
Licensure Intermediate care; Personal care. *Beds* ICF 73; Personal care 10. *Private Pay Patients* 25%. *Certified* Medicaid.
Owner Proprietary corp.
Admissions Requirements Physician's request.
Staff RNs 1 (ft); LPNs 7 (ft); Nurses' aides 26 (ft), 5 (pt); Physical therapists 1 (pt); Occupational therapists 1 (pt); Speech therapists 1 (pt); Activities coordinators 1 (ft); Dietitians 1 (pt).

Facilities Dining room; Laundry room.
Activities Arts & crafts; Games; Reading
groups; Movies.

North Middletown

Lovely's Rest Home
PO Box 114, North Middletown, KY 40357
(606) 362-4560
Admin Allean Platt.
Licensure Personal care. *Beds* 11.
Owner Proprietary corp.

Owensboro

Carmel Home
2501 Old Hartford Rd, Owensboro, KY 42303
(502) 683-0227
Admin Sr Mary Catherine DCJ. *Dir of
Nursing* Sarah Kamuf RN.
Licensure Intermediate care; Personal care.
Beds ICF 36; Personal care 79. *Certified*
Medicaid.
Owner Nonprofit corp (Carmelite Sisters).
Admissions Requirements Minimum age over
60 preferred; Medical examination.
Staff RNs 3 (ft); LPNs 7 (ft), 1 (pt); Nurses'
aides 30 (ft), 2 (pt); Activities coordinators 1
(ft); Dietitians (consultant).
Affiliation Roman Catholic.
Facilities Dining room; Activities room;
Chapel; Crafts room; Laundry room; Barber/
Beauty shop; Library; Guest rooms; Sitting
rooms.
Activities Arts & crafts; Cards; Games;
Reading groups; Prayer groups; Movies;
Shopping trips; Dances/Social/Cultural
gatherings; Pet therapy; Happy hour; Bible
study; Lunch out; Exercise;
Interdenominational services.

Fern Terrace Lodge of Owensboro
45 Woodford Ave, Owensboro, KY 42301
(502) 684-7171
Admin Gertrude P Cagle.
Medical Dir Gertrude P Cagle.
Licensure Personal care; Day care. *Beds*
Personal care 68. *Certified* Medicaid.
Owner Privately owned.
Admissions Requirements Minimum age 40;
Medical examination.
Staff Nurses' aides 6 (ft), 3 (pt).
Facilities Dining room; Activities room;
Chapel; Crafts room; Laundry room; Barber/
Beauty shop; Outside patio; Enclosed gazebo
& porch.
Activities Arts & crafts; Cards; Games;
Reading groups; Prayer groups; Movies;
Shopping trips; Dances/Social/Cultural
gatherings.

Wendell Foster Center
PO Box 1668, 815 Triplett St, Owensboro,
KY 42302-1668
(502) 683-4517
Admin Robert G Mobley.
Medical Dir Anne H Hopwood MD.
Licensure Intermediate care for mentally
retarded. *Beds* ICF/MR 63. *Certified*
Medicaid.
Owner Nonprofit corp.
Admissions Requirements Minimum age 16;
Medical examination; Physician's request.
Staff Physicians 1 (ft); RNs 2 (ft); LPNs 7 (ft),
1 (pt); Nurses' aides 2 (ft); Physical
therapists 1 (ft); Recreational therapists 1
(ft); Occupational therapists 1 (ft); Speech
therapists 1 (ft); Dietitians 1 (ft).
Facilities Dining room; Physical therapy
room; Activities room; Chapel; Crafts room;
Laundry room; Barber/Beauty shop; Library.
Activities Arts & crafts; Cards; Games;
Reading groups; Prayer groups; Movies;
Shopping trips; Dances/Social/Cultural
gatherings.

Mary Harding Home
2410 W 7th St, Owensboro, KY 42301-1814
(502) 684-5459
Admin Cynthia Murray.
Medical Dir Janet Martin LPN Nurses
Consultant.
Licensure Personal care; Alzheimer's care.
Beds Personal care 12. *Certified* Medicaid;
Medicare.
Owner Nonprofit corp.
Admissions Requirements Medical
examination; Physician's request.
Staff Physicians 6; Nurses' aides 3; Activities
coordinators 1; Dietitians 3.
Affiliation Baptist.
Facilities Dining room; Activities room;
Laundry room.
Activities Arts & crafts; Cards; Games;
Reading groups; Prayer groups; Dances/
Social/Cultural gatherings.

Hermitage Manor Nursing Home
1614 Parrish Ave, Owensboro, KY 42301
(502) 684-4559
Admin Jack T Wells.
Medical Dir Sarah Kamuf.
Licensure Skilled care; Intermediate care;
Nursing home. *Beds* SNF 20; ICF 38;
Nursing home 22.
Owner Proprietary corp.
Staff RNs 1 (ft), 1 (pt); LPNs 3 (ft), 3 (pt);
Nurses' aides 13 (ft), 12 (pt); Activities
coordinators 1 (ft); Dietitians 1 (ft).
Facilities Dining room; Activities room;
Crafts room; Laundry room; Barber/Beauty
shop.
Activities Arts & crafts; Cards; Games;
Reading groups; Prayer groups; Movies;
Shopping trips; Dances/Social/Cultural
gatherings.

Hillcrest Health Care Center
3740 Old Hartford Rd, Owensboro, KY 42301
(502) 684-7259
Admin Shelia Stallings.
Licensure Skilled care; Intermediate care. *Beds*
SNF 32; ICF 124. *Certified* Medicaid;
Medicare.
Owner Proprietary corp (Hillhaven Corp).

Mary Kendall Ladies Home
199 Phillips Ct, Owensboro, KY 42301
(502) 683-5044
Admin Donna Anderson.
Licensure Personal care. *Beds* 22.
Admissions Requirements Females only;
Medical examination.
Staff Nurses' aides 4 (ft), 4 (pt); Activities
coordinators 1 (pt); Dietitians 1 (pt).
Facilities Dining room; Laundry room.
Activities Arts & crafts; Cards; Games;
Reading groups; Prayer groups; Shopping
trips; Weekly church service; Sunday school.

Leisure Years Nursing Home
1205 Leitchfield Rd, Owensboro, KY 42303
(502) 684-0464, 684-5575 FAX
Admin Flora J Norsworthy. *Dir of Nursing*
Theresa Hagan. *Medical Dir* Dr James
Litsey.
Licensure Intermediate care; Personal care.
Beds ICF 125; Personal care 59. *Certified*
Medicaid.
Owner Proprietary corp.
Staff Physicians 45 (pt); RNs 2 (ft), 1 (pt);
LPNs 8 (ft); Nurses' aides 47 (ft), 18 (pt);
Physical therapists 1 (pt); Speech therapists
1 (pt); Activities coordinators 1 (ft);
Dietitians 1 (pt); Podiatrists 1 (pt).
Facilities Dining room; Physical therapy
room; Activities room; Laundry room;
Barber/Beauty shop.
Activities Arts & crafts; Cards; Games;
Reading groups; Prayer groups; Movies;
Shopping trips; Dances/Social/Cultural
gatherings; Intergenerational programs; Pet
therapy.

Medco Center of Owensboro
2420 W 3rd St, Owensboro, KY 42301
(502) 685-3141, 684-3126 FAX
Admin Gregory E Wells. *Dir of Nursing*
Dolores Huff RN. *Medical Dir* Dr Gary
Wahl.
Licensure Skilled care; Intermediate care. *Beds*
SNF 43; ICF 89. *Private Pay Patients* 25%.
Certified Medicaid; Medicare; VA.
Owner Proprietary corp (Unicare).
Admissions Requirements Medical
examination; Physician's request.
Staff Physicians 1 (pt); RNs 4 (ft), 4 (pt);
LPNs 12 (ft), 8 (pt); Nurses' aides 30 (ft), 20
(pt); Physical therapists 1 (ft); Speech
therapists 1 (pt); Activities coordinators 1
(ft), 1 (pt); Dietitians 1 (ft); Podiatrists 1
(pt); Respiratory therapists 1 (pt).
Facilities Dining room; Physical therapy
room; Activities room; Laundry room;
Barber/Beauty shop.
Activities Arts & crafts; Cards; Games;
Reading groups; Prayer groups; Movies;
Shopping trips; Dances/Social/Cultural
gatherings; Intergenerational programs; Pet
therapy.

Rosedale Rest Home
415 Sutton Ln, Owensboro, KY 42301
(502) 684-6753
Admin April Ziemer. *Dir of Nursing* Teresa
Snyder.
Licensure Personal care; Alzheimer's care.
Beds Personal care 50.
Owner Privately owned.
Admissions Requirements Minimum age 21;
Medical examination; Physician's request.
Staff LPNs; Nurses' aides; Activities
coordinators; Dietitians.
Facilities Dining room; Activities room;
Chapel; Crafts room; Laundry room; Barber/
Beauty shop; Lawn swings.
Activities Arts & crafts; Cards; Games; Prayer
groups; Movies; Shopping trips; Dances/
Social/Cultural gatherings; Intergenerational
programs; Pet therapy; Field trips; Outside
games.

Owenton

Owenton Manor Inc
PO Box 492, Owenton, KY 40359
(502) 484-5721
Admin Bernard T Poe.
Licensure Intermediate care. *Beds* 100.
Certified Medicaid.
Owner Proprietary corp.
Admissions Requirements Minimum age 18;
Medical examination; Physician's request.
Staff RNs 3 (ft); LPNs 4 (ft); Nurses' aides 45
(ft); Physical therapists 1 (pt); Speech
therapists 1 (pt); Activities coordinators 1
(ft); Dietitians 1 (pt); Ophthalmologists 1
(pt); Podiatrists 1 (pt).
Facilities Dining room; Activities room;
Crafts room; Laundry room; Barber/Beauty
shop.
Activities Arts & crafts; Cards; Games; Prayer
groups; Movies; Dances/Social/Cultural
gatherings.

Owingsville

Colonial Rest Home
E Main St, Owingsville, KY 40360
(606) 674-2222
Admin Emery V Goodpaster & Joetta Y
Goodpaster.
Licensure Personal care. *Beds* 26.
Owner Proprietary corp.

Hilltop Lodge
E High St, Box 448, Owingsville, KY 40360
(606) 674-6062
Admin Jerry Maze.

Licensure Intermediate care. *Beds* 39.
   Certified Medicaid.
Owner Proprietary corp.

Ridgeway Manor
PO Box 38, Owingsville, KY 40360
(606) 674-6613
Admin Thomas Maze.
Licensure Intermediate care. *Beds* ICF 60.
   Certified Medicaid.
Owner Proprietary corp.

Paducah

Life Care Center of Paducah
600 N 4th St, Paducah, KY 42001
(502) 442-3568
Admin Marilyn Ingram. *Dir of Nursing*
   Loudel Paul RN.
Licensure Intermediate care; Personal care.
   Beds ICF 102; Personal care 40. *Certified*
   Medicaid.
Owner Proprietary corp (Life Care Centers of
   America).
Staff RNs 3 (ft); LPNs 13 (ft); Nurses' aides
   37 (ft), 15 (pt); Physical therapists 2 (ft);
   Speech therapists 1 (ft); Activities
   coordinators 1 (ft); Dietitians 1 (ft);
   Ophthalmologists 1 (ft); Podiatrists 1 (ft).
Facilities Dining room; Activities room;
   Chapel; Crafts room; Barber/Beauty shop;
   Library.
Activities Arts & crafts; Cards; Games; Prayer
   groups; Movies; Shopping trips; Dances/
   Social/Cultural gatherings.

McElrath Rest Home
517 S 5th St, Paducah, KY 42001
(502) 442-2600
Admin Anna Mae McElrath.
Licensure Personal care. *Beds* 11.
Owner Proprietary corp.

Medco Center of Paducah
867 McGuire Ave, Paducah, KY 42001
(502) 442-6168
Admin Rose Moss.
Licensure Intermediate care. *Beds* ICF 108.
   Certified Medicaid.
Owner Proprietary corp (Unicare).

Parkview Convalescent Center
544 Lone Oak Rd, Paducah, KY 42001
(502) 443-6543
Admin Sandra J Dick.
Licensure Skilled care; Intermediate care. *Beds*
   SNF 78; ICF 48. *Certified* Medicaid;
   Medicare.
Owner Proprietary corp (National Heritage).

Riverfront Terrace
PO Box 1137, 501 N 3rd St, Paducah, KY
   42002-1137
(502) 444-9661, 444-3916 FAX
Admin Jim Grady. *Dir of Nursing* Cindy
   Garrett RN. *Medical Dir* Frank Allen
   Shemwell MD.
Licensure Intermediate care. *Beds* ICF 100.
   Certified Medicaid; Medicare.
Owner Proprietary corp (Hillhaven Corp).
Admissions Requirements Medical
   examination; Physician's request.
Staff Physicians 5 (ft); RNs 2 (ft); LPNs 6 (ft),
   1 (pt); Nurses' aides 38 (ft); Physical
   therapists 1 (ft); Reality therapists 1 (ft);
   Occupational therapists 1 (ft); Speech
   therapists 1 (ft); Activities coordinators 1
   (ft); Dietitians 1 (ft); Ophthalmologists 1 (ft);
   Podiatrists 1 (ft); Audiologists 1 (ft).
Facilities Dining room; Activities room;
   Crafts room; Laundry room; Barber/Beauty
   shop; Library.
Activities Arts & crafts; Cards; Games;
   Reading groups; Prayer groups; Movies;
   Shopping trips; Dances/Social/Cultural
   gatherings; Intergenerational programs; Pet
   therapy.

Superior Care Home
3100 Clay St, Paducah, KY 42001
(502) 442-6884
Admin Barbara Davis.
Licensure Intermediate care. *Beds* ICF 85.
   Certified Medicaid.
Owner Proprietary corp.

Paintsville

Paintsville Health Care Center
610 F M Stafford Ave, Paintsville, KY 41240
(606) 789-5576
Admin Franklin Davidson. *Dir of Nursing*
   Charlotte Porter.
Licensure Personal care. *Beds* Personal care
   56.
Owner Proprietary corp.
Staff Nurses' aides 8 (ft), 1 (pt); Activities
   coordinators 1 (ft); Dietitians 1 (ft).
Facilities Dining room; Activities room;
   Chapel; Laundry room.
Activities Arts & crafts; Cards; Games;
   Movies; Shopping trips; Dances/Social/
   Cultural gatherings.

Paris

Bourbon Heights Nursing Home
2000 S Main St, Paris, KY 40361
(606) 987-5750
Admin Emmett R Davis Jr.
Licensure Skilled care; Intermediate care;
   Personal care; Nursing home. *Beds* SNF 10;
   ICF 30; Personal care 17; Nursing home 32.
   Certified Medicaid.
Owner Nonprofit corp.

Parker's Lake

Cumberland Manor Rest Home
HC 84, Box 200, Parker's Lake, KY 42634
(606) 376-5951
Admin Mary A Gordon.
Licensure Personal care. *Beds* Personal care
   49.
Owner Proprietary corp.
Admissions Requirements Minimum age 16;
   Medical examination.
Staff LPNs 1 (ft); Nurses' aides 8 (ft).
Facilities Dining room; Laundry room.
Activities Games; Prayer groups; Dances/
   Social/Cultural gatherings.

Pembroke

Medco Center of Pembroke
Hwy 41, Pembroke, KY 42266
(502) 475-4227
Admin Brenda Dye.
Medical Dir J C Woodall.
Licensure Intermediate care. *Beds* ICF 64.
   Certified Medicaid.
Owner Proprietary corp (Unicare).
Staff LPNs 7 (ft); Nurses' aides 20 (ft); Speech
   therapists 1 (pt); Activities coordinators 1
   (ft); Dietitians 1 (pt); Dentists 1 (pt).
Facilities Dining room; Activities room;
   Laundry room.
Activities Arts & crafts; Cards; Games;
   Reading groups; Prayer groups; Movies;
   Shopping trips; Dances/Social/Cultural
   gatherings.

Pewee Valley

Friendship Manor Nursing Home
7400 LaGrange Rd, Pewee Valley, KY 40056
(502) 241-8821
Admin Beth Pearman. *Dir of Nursing* Irene
   Walper.
Licensure Intermediate care; Nursing home.
   Beds ICF 40; Nursing home 54. *Certified*
   Medicaid.
Owner Nonprofit corp.

Admissions Requirements Medical
   examination; Physician's request.
Staff Physicians 5 (ft); RNs 4 (ft); LPNs 6 (ft);
   Nurses' aides 27 (ft); Activities coordinators
   1 (ft).
Affiliation Seventh-Day Adventist.
Facilities Dining room; Physical therapy
   room; Activities room; Chapel; Crafts room;
   Laundry room; Barber/Beauty shop.
Activities Arts & crafts; Games; Reading
   groups; Prayer groups; Movies; Shopping
   trips.

Phelps

Phelps Community Medical Center
PO Box 424, Hwy 194, Phelps, KY 41553
(606) 456-8725
Admin Jesse L Frye. *Dir of Nursing* Patricia
   Elaine Hatfield. *Medical Dir* Ronald Mann.
Licensure Intermediate care; Personal care.
   Beds ICF 118; Personal care 6. *Private Pay
   Patients* 3%. *Certified* Medicaid.
Owner Proprietary corp.
Admissions Requirements Medical
   examination.
Staff Physicians; RNs (consultant); LPNs;
   Nurses' aides; Activities coordinators;
   Dietitians; Podiatrists.
Facilities Dining room; Activities room;
   Chapel; Crafts room; Laundry room; Barber/
   Beauty shop.
Activities Arts & crafts; Cards; Games; Prayer
   groups; Movies; Shopping trips; Dances/
   Social/Cultural gatherings; Intergenerational
   programs.

Philpot

Bishop Soenneker Home
9545 Ky 144, Philpot, KY 42366
(502) 281-4881
Admin Sr Raymonde Carrat.
Licensure Personal care. *Beds* Personal care
   68.
Owner Proprietary corp.

Knottsville Home
Rte 1, Philpot, KY 42366
(502) 281-4881
Admin Sr Raymonde Carrot.
Licensure Personal care. *Beds* 68.
Owner Nonprofit corp.

Pikeville

Mountain Manor Nursing Home
182 S Mayo Trail, Pikeville, KY 41501
(606) 437-7327, 437-7396 FAX
Admin Susan R Arnold. *Dir of Nursing* Faye
   Morris. *Medical Dir* James D Adams MD.
Licensure Skilled care; Intermediate care. *Beds*
   SNF 43; ICF 63. *Certified* Medicaid;
   Medicare.
Owner Proprietary corp.
Facilities Dining room; Laundry room;
   Barber/Beauty shop.
Activities Arts & crafts; Prayer groups;
   Shopping trips.

Parkview Manor
360 Douglas Pkwy, Pikeville, KY 41501
(606) 639-4840
Admin Tim Daugherty.
Licensure Intermediate care. *Beds* ICF 120.
Owner Proprietary corp.

Pineville

Britthaven of Pineville
Rte 1 Box 102, Pineville, KY 40977
(606) 337-7071, 337-6862 FAX
Admin Damont Drake. *Dir of Nursing* Cheryl
   Barnard. *Medical Dir* C C Moore MD.

Licensure Intermediate care; Personal care.
Beds ICF 114; Personal care 8. *Private Pay
Patients* 4%. *Certified* Medicaid.
Owner Proprietary corp (Britthaven Inc).
Admissions Requirements Minimum age 18;
Medical examination; Physician's request.
Staff Physicians 8 (ft); RNs 2 (ft); LPNs 9 (ft),
2 (pt); Nurses' aides 30 (ft), 15 (pt);
Activities coordinators 1 (ft); Dietitians 1
(pt); Ophthalmologists 1 (pt).
Facilities Dining room; Activities room;
Laundry room; Barber/Beauty shop; 2 TV
lounges.
Activities Arts & crafts; Cards; Games;
Reading groups; Prayer groups; Movies;
Sing-alongs; Picnics.

Prestonsburg

Mountain Manor of Prestonburg
17 College Ln, Prestonsburg, KY 41653
(606) 886-2378
Admin Goldie Rorrer.
Licensure Intermediate care. Beds ICF 56.
Certified Medicaid.
Owner Proprietary corp.
Admissions Requirements Medical
examination; Physician's request.
Staff Physicians 5 (ft); RNs 1 (ft); LPNs 2 (ft),
1 (pt); Nurses' aides 16 (ft); Activities
coordinators 1 (ft); Dietitians 1 (pt); Dentists
5 (pt).
Facilities Dining room; Physical therapy
room; Activities room; Crafts room; Laundry
room; Barber/Beauty shop.
Activities Arts & crafts; Cards; Games;
Reading groups; Prayer groups; Movies;
Shopping trips; Dances/Social/Cultural
gatherings.

Riverview Manor Nursing Home
1020 Circle Dr, Prestonsburg, KY 41653
(606) 886-9178
Admin Charlotte Slone.
Licensure Skilled care; Intermediate care. Beds
SNF 56; ICF 60. *Certified* Medicaid;
Medicare.
Owner Proprietary corp.

Princeton

Highlands Homes
PO Box 590, Stevens Ave, Princeton, KY
42445
(502) 365-3254
Admin Jo Ann Capps.
Licensure Personal care. Beds Personal care
88.
Owner Proprietary corp.
Staff LPNs 2 (ft); Nurses' aides 22 (ft), 4 (pt);
Recreational therapists 1 (ft).
Facilities Dining room; Activities room;
Laundry room.
Activities Arts & crafts; Games; Prayer groups.

Princeton Health Care Manor
1333 W Main, Princeton, KY 42445
(502) 365-3541
Admin Mary Jewel Alexander. *Dir of Nursing*
Wanda Babb LPN.
Licensure Intermediate care; Personal care.
Beds ICF 104; Personal care 8. *Private Pay
Patients* 20%. *Certified* Medicaid.
Owner Proprietary corp (Sunbelt Health Care
Centers).
Admissions Requirements Minimum age 16.
Staff RNs 2 (pt); LPNs 3 (ft), 1 (pt); Nurses'
aides 40 (ft), 4 (pt); Physical therapists 1 (ft);
Speech therapists 1 (ft); Activities
coordinators 1 (ft); Dietitians 1 (pt).
Facilities Dining room; Physical therapy
room; Activities room; Crafts room; Laundry
room; Barber/Beauty shop.
Activities Arts & crafts; Games; Shopping
trips.

Prospect

Britthaven of Prospect
PO Box 147, 6301 Bass Rd, Prospect, KY
40059
(502) 228-8359
Admin Linda L Riffe. *Dir of Nursing*
Ernestine Williams. *Medical Dir* Dr A J
Perez.
Licensure Intermediate care. Beds ICF 100.
Certified Medicaid.
Owner Proprietary corp (Britthaven Inc).
Admissions Requirements Medical
examination.
Staff RNs 1 (ft), 1 (pt); LPNs 5 (ft); Nurses'
aides 30 (ft), 10 (pt); Activities coordinators
1 (ft), 1 (pt); Dietitians 1 (ft).
Facilities Dining room; Activities room;
Chapel; Crafts room; Laundry room; Barber/
Beauty shop; Library.
Activities Arts & crafts; Games; Reading
groups; Prayer groups; Movies; Shopping
trips; Dances/Social/Cultural gatherings.

Providence

Country Meadows Rest Haven
Rte 1 Box 98, Providence, KY 42450
(502) 667-2682
Admin Loeta Tow.
Licensure Personal care. Beds Personal care
50.
Owner Proprietary corp.

Shemwell Nursing Home
805 Princeton St, Providence, KY 42450
(502) 667-2023
Admin Billie C Cole.
Licensure Nursing home. Beds Nursing home
22.
Owner Proprietary corp.

Radcliff

North Hardin Nursing & Convalescent Center
599 Rogersville Rd, Radcliff, KY 40160
(502) 351-2999
Admin Donald D Irwin.
Licensure Skilled care; Intermediate care. Beds
SNF 30; ICF 90.
Owner Proprietary corp.

Richmond

Crestview Personal Care Home
131 S Meadowlark Dr, Richmond, KY 40475
(606) 623-5031
Admin Mary K Ousley. *Dir of Nursing* Donna
J Jessie LPN. *Medical Dir* Dr John
Gillespie.
Licensure Personal care. Beds Personal care
50. *Private Pay Patients* 6%. *Certified*
Medicaid; Medicare.
Owner Proprietary corp (EPI).
Staff Physicians 25 (ft); LPNs 1 (ft); Nurses'
aides 1 (ft), 1 (pt); Physical therapists 1 (pt);
Recreational therapists 1 (pt); Occupational
therapists 1 (pt); Speech therapists 1 (pt);
Activities coordinators 1 (ft), 1 (pt);
Dietitians 1 (ft); Podiatrists 1 (pt).
Facilities Dining room; Laundry room.
Activities Arts & crafts; Cards; Games;
Reading groups; Prayer groups; Movies;
Shopping trips; Dances/Social/Cultural
gatherings; Intergenerational programs; Pet
therapy.

Kenwood House
130 S Meadowlark Dr, Richmond, KY 40475
(606) 623-9472
Admin Mary K Ousley.
Licensure Skilled care; Intermediate care;
Personal care. Beds SNF 23; ICF 70;
Personal care 15. *Certified* Medicaid;
Medicare.
Owner Proprietary corp.

Madison Manor
Meadowlark Dr, Richmond, KY 40475
(606) 623-3564
Admin Karen Kelley.
Licensure Intermediate care; Personal care.
Beds ICF 96; Personal care 5. *Certified*
Medicaid.
Owner Proprietary corp.

Russell

Russell Convalescent Home
PO Box 457, Russell, KY 41169
(606) 836-5616
Admin Carolyn Baumgarden; Oscar
Baumgarden.
Licensure Personal care. Beds Personal care
28. *Certified* Medicaid.
Owner Proprietary corp.

Russellville

Russellville Health Care Manor
683 E 3rd St, Russellville, KY 42276
(502) 726-9049
Admin Alyce C Robinson. *Dir of Nursing*
Vera Hadden.
Licensure Intermediate care; Personal care.
Beds ICF 104; Personal care 8. *Private Pay
Patients* 14%. *Certified* Medicaid.
Owner Proprietary corp (Sunbelt Healthcare
Centers Inc).
Staff LPNs 4 (ft), 1 (pt); Nurses' aides 46 (ft),
2 (pt); Activities coordinators 1 (ft);
Dietitians 1 (ft).
Facilities Dining room; Activities room;
Crafts room; Laundry room; Barber/Beauty
shop; Library.

Saint Catherine

Sansbury Memorial Infirmary
Hwy 150, Bardstown Rd, Saint Catherine, KY
40061
(606) 336-3974
Admin Sr Ann Robert Gray.
Licensure Intermediate care; Personal care.
Beds ICF 36; Personal 28. *Certified*
Medicare.
Admissions Requirements Females only.
Staff Physicians 2 (pt); RNs 1 (ft); LPNs 5
(ft); Nurses' aides 18 (ft); Dietitians 1 (ft).
Affiliation Roman Catholic.

Salem

Salem Nursing Home
PO Box 216, Hayden Ave, Hwy 723, Salem,
KY 42078
(502) 988-2388
Admin Carol Roberts. *Dir of Nursing* Janet
Kemper RN. *Medical Dir* Stephen Burkhart
MD.
Licensure Skilled care. Beds SNF 50. *Certified*
Medicaid; Medicare.
Owner Privately owned.
Staff Physicians 2 (pt); RNs 4 (ft), 1 (pt);
LPNs 7 (ft), 1 (pt); Physical therapists 1 (pt);
Speech therapists 1 (pt); Activities
coordinators 1 (ft); Dietitians 1 (pt).
Facilities Dining room; Activities room.
Activities Arts & crafts; Cards; Games;
Reading groups; Prayer groups.

Salyersville

Mountain Valley Rest Home
Box 445, Salyersville, KY 41465
(606) 349-2014
Admin Bethel Stephens.
Licensure Personal care. Beds Personal care
32.
Owner Privately owned.

Salyersville Health Care Center
PO Box 819, Hwy 114, Salyersville, KY 41465
(606) 349-6181
Admin Thomas E Hummer.
Licensure Intermediate care; Personal care;
Day care. *Beds* ICF 147; Personal care 21.
Certified Medicaid.
Owner Proprietary corp (Unicare).

Sanders

Valley Haven Nursing Home
McDaniel St, Sanders, KY 41083
(502) 347-9355
Admin Patricia Boots.
Licensure Personal care. *Beds* Personal care
45.
Owner Proprietary corp.
Admissions Requirements Minimum age 16;
Males only; Medical examination;
Physician's request.
Staff Physicians 1 (pt); Nurses' aides 4 (ft);
Activities coordinators 2 (ft); Dietitians 1
(ft).
Facilities Dining room; Activities room;
Laundry room.
Activities Cards; Games; Movies; Shopping
trips.

Science Hill

Hilltop Rest Home
2391 W Hwy 635, Science Hill, KY 42553
(606) 423-2555
Admin Ida M Dick.
Licensure Personal care. *Beds* Personal care
40.
Owner Proprietary corp.

Scottsville

Friendship Manor
824 N 4th St, Scottsville, KY 42164
(502) 237-5182
Admin Stephen Foster.
Licensure Personal care. *Beds* Personal care
40.
Owner Proprietary corp.

Hillcrest Nursing Home
515 Water St, Scottsville, KY 42164
(502) 237-3485
Admin Helois West.
Licensure Personal care. *Beds* Personal care
36.
Owner Privately owned (Edmond Braham &
Thomas McKinney).
Admissions Requirements Minimum age 18;
Medical examination.
Staff LPNs 1 (ft); Nurses' aides 10 (ft);
Activities coordinators 1 (ft).
Facilities Dining room; Activities room;
Laundry room.
Activities Arts & crafts; Cards; Games; Prayer
groups; Movies; Dances/Social/Cultural
gatherings; Pet therapy.

Hillview Manor
Hillview Dr, Scottsville, KY 42164
(502) 237-4164
Admin Gary Rose.
Licensure Intermediate care; Personal care.
Beds ICF 50; Personal care 34. *Private Pay
Patients* 10%.
Owner Nonprofit organization/foundation.
Admissions Requirements Minimum age 16;
Medical examination; Physician's request.
Staff RNs 1 (pt); Nurses' aides 35 (ft);
Activities coordinators 1 (ft), 2 (pt).
Facilities Dining room; Laundry room.
Activities Arts & crafts; Cards; Games;
Reading groups; Prayer groups; Movies;
Shopping trips; Dances/Social/Cultural
gatherings.

Sebree

Colonial Terrace Intermediate Care
S Church St, Sebree, KY 42455
(502) 835-2533
Admin Kathy Crowley. *Dir of Nursing* Connie
Cobb LPN. *Medical Dir* Jason Samuel MD.
Licensure Intermediate care; Personal care.
Beds ICF 80; Personal care 23. *Certified*
Medicaid.
Owner Proprietary corp.
Admissions Requirements Minimum age 20;
Medical examination; Physician's request.
Staff Physicians 7 (pt); RNs 1 (pt); LPNs 3
(ft); Nurses' aides 30 (ft), 10 (pt); Speech
therapists 1 (pt); Activities coordinators 2
(ft), 1 (pt); Dietitians 1 (pt);
Ophthalmologists 1 (pt); Dentists 1 (pt).
Facilities Dining room; Activities room;
Chapel; Crafts room; Laundry room; Barber/
Beauty shop.
Activities Arts & crafts; Cards; Games; Prayer
groups; Movies; Shopping trips; Dances/
Social/Cultural gatherings; Bingo; Barbeques;
Fish fries; Paper money auction.

Shelbyville

Colonial Hall Manor
PO Box 219, 920 Henry Clay St (40065),
Shelbyville, KY 40066-0219
(502) 633-4762
Admin Francis Clark.
Licensure Personal care. *Beds* Personal care
57.
Owner Proprietary corp.
Staff RNs 1 (ft); LPNs 1 (pt); Nurses' aides 18
(ft); Activities coordinators 1 (ft); Dietitians
1 (pt).
Facilities Dining room; Activities room;
Chapel; Crafts room; Laundry room;
Library.
Activities Arts & crafts; Cards; Games;
Reading groups; Prayer groups; Movies;
Shopping trips.

Crestview Healthcare Center
Rte 6 Box 382, Shelbyville, KY 40065
(502) 633-2454
Admin Jeanette Pope. *Dir of Nursing* Shelby
Simpson RN. *Medical Dir* Donald Chatham
MD.
Licensure Nursing home. *Beds* Nursing home
58. *Private Pay Patients* 100%.
Owner Proprietary corp (Senior Care Inc).
Admissions Requirements Medical
examination; Physician's request.
Staff Physicians 12 (pt); RNs 1 (ft); LPNs 2
(ft), 2 (pt); Nurses' aides 16 (ft), 12 (pt);
Physical therapists 1 (pt); Speech therapists
1 (pt); Activities coordinators 1 (ft);
Dietitians 1 (pt); Podiatrists 1 (pt).
Facilities Dining room; Physical therapy
room; Activities room; Chapel; Laundry
room; Barber/Beauty shop.
Activities Arts & crafts; Games; Reading
groups; Prayer groups; Movies; Shopping
trips; Dances/Social/Cultural gatherings; Pet
therapy.

Old Masons' Home of Kentucky
PO Box 909, US Hwy 60 E, Shelbyville, KY
40065
(502) 633-3486
Admin O J Simpson.
Licensure Intermediate care; Personal care.
Beds ICF 20; Personal care 130. *Certified*
Medicaid.
Owner Nonprofit corp.
Affiliation Masons.

Shelby Manor Health Center
US 60 W, 9 Village Plaza, Shelbyville, KY
40065
(502) 633-2691
Admin Carolyn Fegenbush.

Licensure Intermediate care; Personal care.
Beds ICF 63; Personal care 68. *Certified*
Medicaid.
Owner Proprietary corp.

Shepherdsville

Colonial House of Shepherdsville
Star Rte Box 64, Shepherdsville, KY 40165
(502) 543-7042
Admin Sarah M Simpson RN.
Licensure Personal care. *Beds* Personal care
62.
Owner Proprietary corp.

Patterson's Pleasant View Personal Care Home
Hwy 44 E & Loyd's Ln, Shepherdsville, KY
40165
(502) 543-7995
Admin Pamela Hawkins.
Licensure Personal care. *Beds* Personal care
13.
Owner Proprietary corp.

Shively

Rockford Manor
4700 Quinn Dr, Shively, KY 40216
(502) 448-5850
Admin Carol Ann Bottoms.
Licensure Intermediate care. *Beds* ICF 120.
Certified Medicaid.
Owner Proprietary corp.

Smithland

Livingston County Rest Home
Rudd & Walnut St, Smithland, KY 42081
(502) 928-2137
Admin Dathel Ramage; Nora E Ramage. *Dir
of Nursing* Reba Matthews. *Medical Dir*
Reba Matthews.
Licensure Personal care. *Beds* Personal care
38. *Private Pay Patients* 2%. *Certified*
Medicare.
Owner Publicly owned.
Admissions Requirements Minimum age 16;
Medical examination.
Staff Nurses' aides 15 (ft), 2 (pt); Activities
coordinators 1 (ft); Dietitians 1 (pt).
Facilities Dining room; Activities room;
Chapel; Laundry room; Barber/Beauty shop.
Activities Arts & crafts; Games; Reading
groups; Prayer groups; Movies.

Somerset

Britthaven of Somerset
Bourne Ave & Central Ave, Somerset, KY
42501
(606) 679-7421
Admin Laura T Mihankhah.
Licensure Skilled care; Intermediate care;
Personal care. *Beds* SNF 23; ICF 129;
Personal care 12. *Certified* Medicaid;
Medicare.
Owner Proprietary corp (Britthaven Inc).

Colonial Care Home
202 N Main St, Somerset, KY 42501
(606) 679-1504
Admin Joan O Johnson.
Licensure Personal care. *Beds* Personal care
50.
Owner Proprietary corp.
Admissions Requirements Minimum age 45;
Medical examination; Physician's request.
Staff Nurses' aides 7 (ft), 4 (pt); Dietitians 2
(ft), 2 (pt).
Facilities Dining room; Activities room;
Laundry room.
Activities Arts & crafts; Games; Reading
groups; Prayer groups; Shopping trips.

Crestview Personal Care Home
235 S Richardson, Somerset, KY 42501
(606) 678-8927
Admin Patricia Tarter RN. *Dir of Nursing*
Venus B Tanamachi RN.
Licensure Personal care. *Beds* Personal care
30.
Owner Proprietary corp.
Admissions Requirements Minimum age 16;
Females only; Medical examination.
Staff RNs; Nurses' aides; Activities
coordinators; Dietitians.
Facilities Dining room; Activities room;
Chapel; Crafts room; Laundry room;
Library.
Activities Arts & crafts; Cards; Games;
Reading groups; Prayer groups; Movies.

Midtown Care Home
106 Gover St, Somerset, KY 42501
(606) 679-8331
Admin Brenda Abbott. *Dir of Nursing* Eileen
Brown RN. *Medical Dir* Dr Stephen Kiteck.
Licensure Intermediate care. *Beds* ICF 123.
Private Pay Patients 17%. *Certified*
Medicaid.
Owner Proprietary corp.
Admissions Requirements Medical
examination; Physician's request.
Staff Physicians 19 (pt); RNs 2 (ft); LPNs 8
(ft), 2 (pt); Nurses' aides 38 (ft), 4 (pt);
Physical therapists (contracted); Reality
therapists (contracted); Recreational
therapists (contracted); Occupational
therapists (contracted); Speech therapists
(contracted); Activities coordinators 1 (ft);
Dietitians 1 (pt).
Facilities Dining room; Activities room;
Laundry room; Barber/Beauty shop.
Activities Arts & crafts; Games; Prayer groups;
Movies; Shopping trips.

Oakwood Intermediate Care Facility
US 27 S, Somerset, KY 42501
(606) 679-4361
Admin Mary Warman. *Dir of Nursing* Cindy
Marcum. *Medical Dir* Alberto Jayme MD.
Licensure Intermediate care for mentally
retarded. *Beds* ICF/MR 420. *Certified*
Medicaid; Medicare.
Owner Publicly owned.
Admissions Requirements Minimum age 6;
Primary diagnosis must be mental
retardation.
Staff Physicians 1 (ft), 1 (pt); RNs 17 (ft);
LPNs 15 (ft); Physical therapists 1 (ft);
Recreational therapists 1 (ft); Occupational
therapists 2 (ft); Speech therapists 2 (pt);
Activities coordinators 1 (ft); Dietitians 2
(ft), 1 (pt); Audiologists 1 (pt); Aides 457
(ft), 77 (pt); Dentists 1 (pt).
Facilities Dining room; Physical therapy
room; Activities room; Laundry room;
Barber/Beauty shop; Library.
Activities Arts & crafts; Cards; Games;
Movies; Shopping trips; Dances/Social/
Cultural gatherings; Intergenerational
programs.

Sunrise Manor Nursing Home
200 Norfleet Dr, Somerset, KY 42501
(606) 678-5104
Admin David Pendley.
Licensure Skilled care; Intermediate care. *Beds*
SNF 58; ICF 35. *Certified* Medicaid;
Medicare.
Owner Proprietary corp (Unicare).

South Shore

South Shore Health Care Center
PO Box 489, James E Hannah Dr, South
Shore, KY 41175
(606) 932-6266
Admin Theresa S Bauer.
Medical Dir Dr Grant Stevenson.
Licensure Intermediate care. *Beds* ICF 60.
Certified Medicaid; Medicare.

Owner Privately owned (Sterling Health Care).
Staff Physicians 2 (ft); RNs 2 (ft); LPNs 5 (ft);
Nurses' aides; Physical therapists 1 (ft);
Recreational therapists 1 (ft); Speech
therapists 1 (ft); Activities coordinators 1
(ft); Dietitians 1 (ft); Podiatrists (contracted);
Audiologists (contracted).
Facilities Dining room; Activities room;
Crafts room; Laundry room; Barber/Beauty
shop; Library.
Activities Arts & crafts; Cards; Games;
Reading groups; Prayer groups; Movies;
Shopping trips; Dances/Social/Cultural
gatherings; Intergenerational programs; Pet
therapy.

South Williamson

**Appalachian Regional Hospital Skilled Nursing
Facility**
2000 Central Ave, South Williamson, KY
41503
(606) 237-1725
Admin Karen Reed NHA. *Dir of Nursing*
Josie Stone RN. *Medical Dir* Charles Smith
DO.
Licensure Skilled care. *Beds* SNF 40. *Private
Pay Patients* 0%. *Certified* Medicaid;
Medicare.
Owner Nonprofit corp.
Admissions Requirements Physician's request.
Facilities Dining room; Physical therapy
room; Activities room; Chapel; Barber/
Beauty shop; Ventilators; Trachs; IV
therapy.

Springfield

Medco Center of Springfield
120 E Grundy Ave, Springfield, KY 40069
(606) 336-7771, 336-7800 FAX
Admin Violet Elliott. *Dir of Nursing* Donnie L
Cocanovgher. *Medical Dir* Brian Wells MD.
Licensure Intermediate care. *Beds* ICF 70.
Private Pay Patients 21%. *Certified*
Medicaid.
Owner Proprietary corp (Unicare).
Admissions Requirements Minimum age 21.
Staff LPNs 3 (ft), 1 (pt); Nurses' aides 24 (ft);
Physical therapists; Activities coordinators 1
(ft); Dietitians.
Facilities Dining room; Activities room;
Laundry room; Barber/Beauty shop; Living
room.
Activities Arts & crafts; Cards; Games;
Reading groups; Prayer groups; Movies;
Shopping trips; Dances/Social/Cultural
gatherings.

Stanford

Fort Logan Hospital
124 Portman Ave, Stanford, KY 40484
(606) 365-2187
Admin Terry C Powers.
Licensure Skilled care. *Beds* SNF 30. *Certified*
Medicaid; Medicare.
Owner Nonprofit corp.

Stanford House
Harmon Heights, Stanford, KY 40484
(606) 365-2141
Admin Lisa Mullen.
Medical Dir Dr Joseph Middleton.
Licensure Intermediate care. *Beds* ICF 98.
Certified Medicaid.
Owner Proprietary corp (Beverly Enterprises).
Staff Physicians 5 (pt); RNs 1 (pt); LPNs 6
(ft), 1 (pt); Nurses' aides 23 (ft); Activities
coordinators 1 (ft); Dietitians 1 (pt); Dentists
1 (pt).
Facilities Dining room; Physical therapy
room; Activities room; Laundry room;
Barber/Beauty shop.

Activities Arts & crafts; Cards; Games;
Reading groups; Movies; Shopping trips;
Dances/Social/Cultural gatherings.

Stanton

Stanton Nursing Center
Rte 2 Box 620, Derickson Rd, Stanton, KY
40380
(606) 663-2846
Admin Janice Jones. *Dir of Nursing* Imogene
Lane.
Licensure Intermediate care; Personal care.
Beds ICF 81; Personal care 9. *Private Pay
Patients* 2%.
Owner Proprietary corp (Unicare).
Admissions Requirements Medical
examination; Physician's request.
Staff Physicians 3 (pt); RNs 1 (ft); LPNs 2
(ft), 3 (pt); Nurses' aides 31 (ft), 10 (pt);
Physical therapists 2 (pt); Activities
coordinators 1 (ft); Dietitians 1 (pt);
Podiatrists 1 (pt); Other staff 15 (ft), 3 (pt).
Facilities Dining room; Activities room;
Laundry room; Barber/Beauty shop; Lounge.
Activities Arts & crafts; Cards; Games;
Reading groups; Prayer groups; Movies;
Shopping trips; Dances/Social/Cultural
gatherings; Intergenerational programs.

Sturgis

Sturgis Community Rest Home
7th & Main St, Sturgis, KY 42459-0304
(502) 333-5508
Admin Minnie Sue Thompson.
Licensure Personal care. *Beds* Personal care
27.
Owner Proprietary corp.
Admissions Requirements Medical
examination.
Staff Physicians 1 (pt); Nurses' aides 3 (ft), 3
(pt); Activities coordinators 1 (ft); Dietitians
1 (pt).
Facilities Dining room; Activities room;
Chapel; Crafts room; Laundry room; Barber/
Beauty shop.
Activities Arts & crafts; Games; Prayer groups;
Movies; Shopping trips; Dances/Social/
Cultural gatherings.

Tompkinsville

Monroe Health Care Facility
706 N Magnolia, Tompkinsville, KY 42167
(502) 487-6135
Admin Nikki Wright.
Licensure Skilled care; Intermediate care;
Personal care. *Beds* SNF 23; ICF 79;
Personal care 18. *Certified* Medicaid;
Medicare.
Owner Proprietary corp.

Vanceburg

Vanceburg Health Care
PO Box 297, Vanceburg, KY 41179
(606) 796-3046
Admin Eugena Forman.
Medical Dir Greg Dick; Joan Pollitt.
Licensure Intermediate care; Personal care.
Beds ICF 94; Personal 16. *Certified*
Medicaid.
Owner Proprietary corp (Beverly Enterprises).
Admissions Requirements Medical
examination.
Staff Physicians 1 (pt); RNs 1 (ft); LPNs 7
(ft); Nurses' aides 32 (ft); Activities
coordinators 1 (ft); Dietitians 1 (pt).
Facilities Dining room; Activities room;
Laundry room; Barber/Beauty shop; Patient
lounge.
Activities Arts & crafts; Cards; Games;
Reading groups; Prayer groups; Movies;
Shopping trips; Dances/Social/Cultural
gatherings.

Versailles

Taylor Manor Nursing Home
PO Drawer D, Berry Ave, Versailles, KY 40383
(606) 873-4201
Admin Sr Mary Virginia Sayers SJW. *Dir of Nursing* Sr Ann Curran RN.
Licensure Intermediate care; Personal care; Nursing home. *Beds* ICF 18; Personal care 24; Nursing home 40.
Owner Nonprofit corp.
Admissions Requirements Minimum age 50; Medical examination.
Staff Physicians 6 (pt); RNs 1 (ft), 2 (pt); LPNs 4 (ft), 3 (pt); Nurses' aides 21 (ft), 3 (pt); Activities coordinators 1 (ft), 1 (pt); Dietitians 1 (pt); CMA; Nurse aides 5 (ft).
Affiliation Roman Catholic.
Facilities Dining room; Activities room; Chapel; Crafts room; Barber/Beauty shop.
Activities Arts & crafts; Cards; Games; Prayer groups; Shopping trips; Dances/Social/Cultural gatherings.

Woodford Memorial Hospital Intermediate Care Facility
360 Amsden Ave, Versailles, KY 40383
(606) 873-3111
Admin Mark L Reynolds.
Licensure Intermediate care. *Beds* ICF 23.
Owner Proprietary corp.

Villa Hills

Madonna Manor
2344 Amsterdam Rd, Villa Hills, KY 41017
(606) 341-3981
Admin Sr M Charles Wolking.
Licensure Intermediate care; Personal care. *Beds* ICF 35; Personal care 25.
Owner Proprietary corp.

Waynesburg

Waynesburg Rest Home
PO Box 68, Waynesburg, KY 40489
(606) 379-2614
Admin Reva Reynolds.
Licensure Personal care. *Beds* Personal care 28.
Owner Proprietary corp.
Admissions Requirements Minimum age 30; Physician's request.
Staff Nurses' aides 10 (ft); Recreational therapists 3 (pt); Activities coordinators 2 (pt); Dietitians 1 (pt).
Facilities Dining room; Activities room; Laundry room; Barber/Beauty shop.

West Liberty

Morgan County Appalachian Regional Hospital
PO Box 579, West Liberty, KY 41472-0579
(606) 743-3186
Admin Raymond Rowlett. *Dir of Nursing* E Pearl Blackburn RN. *Medical Dir* James D Frederick MD.
Licensure Skilled care. *Beds* SNF 15; Swing beds SNF/ICF 4. *Private Pay Patients* 0%. *Certified* Medicaid; Medicare.

Owner Nonprofit corp.
Admissions Requirements Medical examination; Physician's request.
Staff Physicians 7 (ft); RNs 5 (ft); LPNs 3 (ft); Nurses' aides 4 (ft); Physical therapists 1 (ft); Activities coordinators 1 (ft); Dietitians 1 (ft).
Facilities Dining room; Physical therapy room.
Activities Arts & crafts; Prayer groups.

West Liberty Health Care Center Inc
PO Box 219, Rte 5 Wells Hill, West Liberty, KY 41472
(606) 743-3846
Admin Pam Burton. *Dir of Nursing* Sue Vancleave.
Licensure Intermediate care. *Beds* ICF 29. *Private Pay Patients* 20%. *Certified* Medicaid.
Owner Proprietary corp.
Staff Physicians 1 (pt); RNs 1 (pt); LPNs 2 (ft); Nurses' aides 10 (ft), 1 (pt); Activities coordinators 1 (ft); Dietitians 1 (pt); Ophthalmologists 1 (pt); Podiatrists 1 (pt); Audiologists 1 (pt).
Facilities Dining room; Activities room; Laundry room.
Activities Arts & crafts; Cards; Games; Reading groups; Movies.

Williamsburg

Williamsburg Nursing Home
PO Box 719, Rte 4, Williamsburg, KY 40769
(606) 549-4321
Admin Bryan Barton.
Licensure Skilled care; Intermediate care. *Beds* SNF 30; ICF 70. *Certified* Medicaid; Medicare.
Owner Proprietary corp (Health Systems).

Williamstown

Grant Manor Inc
201 Kimberly Ln, Williamstown, KY 41097
(606) 824-7803
Admin Julia Poe.
Licensure Intermediate care. *Beds* ICF 60.
Owner Proprietary corp.

Winchester

Winchester Manor Health Care Center
200 White Dr, Winchester, KY 40391
(606) 744-1800, 744-0285 FAX
Admin Damie U Castle. *Dir of Nursing* Kathy Florence. *Medical Dir* Dr Harold Moberly.
Licensure Skilled care; Intermediate care; Personal care. *Beds* SNF 50; ICF 137; Personal care 9. *Private Pay Patients* 30%. *Certified* Medicaid; Medicare.
Owner Proprietary corp (Hillhaven Corp).
Admissions Requirements Minimum age 18; Medical examination; Physician's request.
Staff Physicians (contracted); RNs 3 (ft), 1 (pt); LPNs 16 (ft), 2 (pt); Nurses' aides; Physical therapists 2 (ft); Occupational therapists 1 (pt); Speech therapists 1 (pt); Activities coordinators 2 (ft); Dietitians 1 (ft); Ophthalmologists (contracted);

Podiatrists (contracted); Audiologists (contracted); Developmental coordinators 1 (ft); BSWs 1 (ft).
Facilities Dining room; Physical therapy room; Activities room; Crafts room; Laundry room; Barber/Beauty shop.
Activities Arts & crafts; Cards; Games; Reading groups; Prayer groups; Movies; Shopping trips; Dances/Social/Cultural gatherings; Pet therapy.

Woodburn

Hopkins Nursing Facility
College St, Woodburn, KY 42170
(502) 529-2853
Admin Scarlotte Freeman. *Dir of Nursing* Lynnda McPeak. *Medical Dir* J M Pulliam MD.
Licensure Skilled care; Intermediate care. *Beds* SNF 21; ICF 29. *Private Pay Patients* 5%. *Certified* Medicaid; Medicare.
Owner Proprietary corp.
Admissions Requirements Physician's request.
Staff RNs 3 (ft), 1 (pt); LPNs 4 (ft), 1 (pt); Recreational therapists 1 (ft); Activities coordinators 1 (ft); Dietitians 1 (ft).
Facilities Dining room; Activities room; Crafts room; Laundry room.
Activities Arts & crafts; Cards; Games; Reading groups; Prayer groups; Movies.

Twilight Personal Care Home
Clark St, Woodburn, KY 42170
(502) 529-2962
Admin Jack Wofford.
Licensure Personal care. *Beds* 25.

Woodburn Personal Care Home
PO Box 118, 311 Clark St, Woodburn, KY 42170-0118
(502) 529-2962
Admin Mildred Gergory.
Licensure Personal care. *Beds* Personal care 25.
Owner Proprietary corp.

Wurtland

Wurtland Health Care Center
100 Wurtland Ave, Wurtland, KY 41144
(606) 836-1956
Admin Carl W Cotton. *Dir of Nursing* Clara Parker. *Medical Dir* Dr Oren Justice.
Licensure Intermediate care. *Beds* ICF 126. *Certified* Medicaid.
Owner Proprietary corp.
Staff Physicians 4 (pt); RNs 1 (pt); LPNs 10 (ft); Nurses' aides 25 (ft); Physical therapists 1 (pt); Recreational therapists 2 (ft); Speech therapists 1 (pt); Activities coordinators 1 (ft); Dietitians 1 (pt); Ophthalmologists 1 (pt); Podiatrists 1 (pt); Dentists 1 (pt).
Facilities Dining room; Physical therapy room; Activities room; Crafts room; Laundry room; Barber/Beauty shop; Library.
Activities Arts & crafts; Cards; Games; Reading groups; Prayer groups; Movies; Shopping trips; Dances/Social/Cultural gatherings; Rock-n-roll jamboree; 2 Festivals.

LOUISIANA

Abbeville

Abbeville Heritage Manor
2403 Alonzo St, Abbeville, LA 70510
(318) 893-6140
Admin Freddie J Arceneaux. *Dir of Nursing*
Evelyn Hollier. *Medical Dir* Donna
Augustus.
Licensure Skilled care; Intermediate care. *Beds*
Swing beds SNF/ICF 60. *Private Pay*
Patients 20%. *Certified* Medicaid; Medicare.
Owner Proprietary corp (Health Care Capital
Inc).
Admissions Requirements Medical
examination.
Staff RNs 1 (ft); LPNs 6 (ft); Nurses' aides 35
(ft), 3 (pt); Activities coordinators 1 (ft);
Dietitians 1 (ft).
Languages French.
Facilities Dining room; Laundry room;
Barber/Beauty shop.
Activities Arts & crafts; Cards; Games;
Reading groups; Prayer groups; Movies;
Shopping trips; Dances/Social/Cultural
gatherings; Intergenerational programs; Pet
therapy.

Acadia

Acadia Manor Nursing Home
PO Box 726, 1200 Daniel St, Acadia, LA
71001
(318) 263-2025
Admin E E Letlow Jr.
Licensure Skilled care. *Beds* SNF 125.

Alexandria

**Annie Mae Matthews Memorial Nursing
Home**
PO Box 12910, 5100 Jackson St, Alexandria,
LA 71315-2910
(318) 445-5215, 448-9414
Admin Lynda C Lambdin.
Licensure Intermediate care. *Beds* ICF 159.
Certified Medicaid.

Heritage Manor No 2
3343 Masonic Dr, Alexandria, LA 71301
(318) 445-5058
Admin Wayne L Morris. *Dir of Nursing* Betty
Setliff. *Medical Dir* William M Brown.
Licensure Skilled care; Intermediate care. *Beds*
SNF 60; ICF 64. *Private Pay Patients* 20%.
Certified Medicaid; Medicare.
Owner Proprietary corp.
Admissions Requirements Medical
examination; Physician's request.
Staff RNs 2 (ft), 2 (pt); LPNs 14 (ft), 4 (pt);
Nurses' aides 38 (ft), 4 (pt); Physical
therapists; Activities coordinators 1 (ft);
Dietitians.
Languages French.
Facilities Dining room; Physical therapy
room; Activities room; Chapel; Crafts room;
Laundry room; Barber/Beauty shop; Library;
Whirlpool baths.

Activities Arts & crafts; Cards; Games;
Reading groups; Prayer groups; Movies;
Shopping trips; Dances/Social/Cultural
gatherings; Intergenerational programs; Pet
therapy.

Heritage Manor of Alexandria No 1
5115 McArthur Dr, Alexandria, LA 71301
(318) 442-2340
Admin Katherine R Simpson.
Licensure Intermediate care. *Beds* ICF 56.
Certified Medicaid.
Owner Proprietary corp (National Heritage).

Heritage Manor of Alexandria North
1709 Odom St, Alexandria, LA 71301
(318) 445-6355
Admin Otey M Dear. *Dir of Nursing* Peggy
Bihm RN. *Medical Dir* Dr M R Khokhar.
Licensure Intermediate care. *Beds* ICF 75.
Certified Medicaid.
Owner Proprietary corp (National Heritage).
Admissions Requirements Medical
examination.
Staff RNs 1 (ft); LPNs 5 (ft), 4 (pt); Nurses'
aides 21 (ft), 6 (pt); Activities coordinators 1
(ft); Dietitians.
Languages French.
Facilities Dining room; Laundry room;
Barber/Beauty shop.
Activities Arts & crafts; Cards; Games; Prayer
groups; Movies; Shopping trips; Dances/
Social/Cultural gatherings.

Louisiana Special Education Center
PO Drawer 7797, Alexandria, LA 71306
(318) 487-5484
Admin Dr Aline R Cicardo. *Dir of Nursing*
Mona Yarno RN. *Medical Dir* Dr L J
Credeur.
Licensure Intermediate care for
orthopaedically handicapped. *Beds* ICFH 75.
Private Pay Patients 0%. *Certified* Medicaid.
Owner Publicly owned.
Admissions Requirements Minimum age 3;
Medical examination.
Staff Physicians 6 (pt); RNs 3 (ft), 2 (pt);
LPNs 4 (ft), 3 (pt); Physical therapists
(consultants); Occupational therapists 1 (pt);
Speech therapists 2 (ft); Activities
coordinators 1 (pt); Dietitians (consultant);
Audiologists 1 (pt).
Facilities Dining room; Physical therapy
room; Activities room; Crafts room; Laundry
room; Barber/Beauty shop; Library.
Activities Arts & crafts; Cards; Games;
Reading groups; Movies; Shopping trips;
Individualized education; Family
involvement.

Naomi Heights Nursing Home
2421 E Texas Ave, Alexandria, LA 71301
(318) 443-5638
Admin Finley C Matthews Jr.
Licensure Intermediate care. *Beds* ICF 143.
Certified Medicaid.
Staff RNs 3 (ft); LPNs 7 (ft), 1 (pt); Nurses'
aides 26 (ft); Dietitians 1 (pt).

Facilities Dining room; Activities room;
Laundry room; Barber/Beauty shop.
Activities Arts & crafts; Prayer groups;
Movies; Shopping trips; Dances/Social/
Cultural gatherings.

Pecan Grove Training Center
PO Box 1827, 5000 Lower 3rd St, Alexandria,
LA 71309
(318) 448-0291
Admin C L Miller. *Dir of Nursing* Diane Sant
RN. *Medical Dir* L J Credeur.
Licensure Intermediate care for mentally
retarded. *Beds* ICF/MR 120. *Private Pay*
Patients 0%. *Certified* Medicaid.
Owner Privately owned.
Admissions Requirements Minimum age 5-40;
Medical examination; Physician's request;
IQ below 70.
Staff Physicians; RNs; LPNs; Recreational
therapists; Occupational therapists; Speech
therapists; Activities coordinators; Dietitians.
Facilities Dining room; Physical therapy
room; Activities room; Crafts room; Laundry
room; Barber/Beauty shop; Playground;
Swimming pool; Semi-private rooms;
Medical services.
Activities Arts & crafts; Games; Movies;
Shopping trips; Dances/Social/Cultural
gatherings; Individualized training programs.

Pleasant Manor Nursing Home
5908 Skye St, Alexandria, LA 71303
(318) 445-5984
Admin Mark Thompson.
Licensure Intermediate care. *Beds* ICF 120.
Certified Medicaid.

Regency House
5131 Masonic Dr, Alexandria, LA 71301
(318) 473-9057
Admin Mary McCampbell.
Beds 72.

St Mary's Residential Training School
PO Box 7768, Alexandria, LA 71306
(318) 445-6443
Admin Sr M Antoinette Baroncini. *Dir of*
Nursing Charlotte Cull RN. *Medical Dir* L J
Credeur MD.
Licensure Intermediate care for mentally
retarded. *Beds* ICF/MR 152. *Certified*
Medicaid.
Owner Nonprofit corp.
Admissions Requirements Minimum age 3-21;
Medical examination; Must be ambulatory.
Staff Physicians 4 (pt); RNs 2 (ft); LPNs 4
(ft), 1 (pt); Nurses' aides 5 (ft); Physical
therapists 1 (pt); Recreational therapists 2
(ft); Occupational therapists 1 (pt); Speech
therapists 2 (ft), 1 (pt); Activities
coordinators 1 (ft); Dietitians 1 (ft);
Ophthalmologists 1 (pt); Audiologists 1 (pt);
Social workers 3 (ft); Dentists 1 (pt);
Psychologists 2 (ft), 1 (pt).
Languages Italian.
Affiliation Roman Catholic.

Facilities Dining room; Physical therapy room; Activities room; Chapel; Crafts room; Laundry room; Barber/Beauty shop; Library; Health care clinic; Psychology department; Gymnasium; School; Occupational therapy clinic; Speech therapy clinic; Prevocational building; Covered walkways; Concrete sidewalks; Recreation pavilion; Greenhouse; Softball stadium; Basketball court; Tennis court; Playgrounds; 2 swimming pools; Picnic area with picnic tables; Media center.
Activities Arts & crafts; Cards; Games; Movies; Shopping trips; Dances/Social/ Cultural gatherings; Active treatment; Prevocational skills; Life skills; Volunteer program; Educational program; Recreational programs; Entertainment programs; Outings; Special Olympics; Boy & Girl Scout troops.

Wilshire Manor Nursing Home
1225 Windsor Pl, Alexandria, LA 71303
(318) 445-9356
Admin Bob Marshall.
Licensure Intermediate care. *Beds* ICF 110.
Certified Medicaid.

Amite

Amite Nursing Home Inc
PO Box 219, 709 E North Pl, Amite, LA 70422
(504) 748-9464
Admin Patricia Fruge.
Licensure Intermediate care. *Beds* ICF 100.
Certified Medicaid.

Hood Memorial Hospital—Skilled Nursing Facility
301 W Walnut St, Amite, LA 70422
(504) 748-9485
Admin A D Richardson.
Licensure Skilled care.

Arabi

Maison Orleans Nursing Home
2310 Mehle Ave, Arabi, LA 70032
(504) 279-0401
Admin Frank T Stewart Jr.
Licensure Intermediate care. *Beds* ICF 154.
Certified Medicaid.

St Ann's Convalescent Home
633 Mehle St, Arabi, LA 70032
(504) 279-4461
Admin James R Wingate.
Licensure Intermediate care. *Beds* ICF 76.
Certified Medicaid.

Arcadia

Arcadia Baptist Home
PO Box 599, 1109 6th St, Arcadia, LA 71001
(318) 263-9581
Admin Leamon Best.
Licensure Intermediate care. *Beds* ICF 120.
Certified Medicaid.
Affiliation Baptist.

Arnaudville

J Michael Morrow Memorial Nursing Home
PO Box 670, Hwy 740, Arnaudville, LA 70512
(318) 754-7703
Admin Wanda Hebert.
Beds 124.

St Luke General Hospital
PO Box 110, Arnaudville, LA 70512
(318) 754-5112
Admin Thomas J McElree.
Licensure Skilled care; Intermediate care. *Beds* Swing beds SNF/ICF 33.

Baker

Baker Manor Nursing Home
PO Box 419, 3612 Baker Blvd, Baker, LA 70714
(504) 778-0573
Admin Randye Watson.
Licensure Intermediate care. *Beds* ICF 136.
Certified Medicaid.
Owner Proprietary corp.
Staff LPNs 10 (ft), 2 (pt); Nurses' aides 47 (ft), 2 (pt); Activities coordinators 1 (ft); Dietitians 1 (ft).
Facilities Dining room; Activities room; Crafts room; Laundry room; Barber/Beauty shop.
Activities Arts & crafts; Cards; Games; Reading groups; Prayer groups; Movies; Shopping trips; Dances/Social/Cultural gatherings.

Basile

Basile Care Center Inc
PO Drawer 38, Basile, LA 70515
(318) 432-6663
Admin Joseph P Young NHA. *Dir of Nursing* Bernice G Young RN. *Medical Dir* Dr Bobby Deshotel.
Licensure Intermediate care. *Beds* ICF 78.
Private Pay Patients 10%. *Certified* Medicaid.
Owner Privately owned.
Admissions Requirements Medical examination.
Staff Physicians 3 (ft); RNs 2 (ft); LPNs 8 (ft); Nurses' aides 25 (ft); Physical therapists 1 (ft); Activities coordinators; Dietitians.
Languages French.
Facilities Dining room; Activities room; Crafts room; Laundry room; Barber/Beauty shop; Large front porch; Shady area with benches; Large fenced-in backyard.
Activities Arts & crafts; Cards; Games; Reading groups; Prayer groups; Movies; Dances/Social/Cultural gatherings.

Bastrop

Cherry Ridge Guest Care Center
PO Box 941, 1800 Cherry Ridge Rd, Bastrop, LA 71220
(318) 281-6933
Admin Richard E Boyter. *Dir of Nursing* Patsy Bing. *Medical Dir* Jack Noble MD.
Licensure Intermediate care; Alzheimer's care. *Beds* ICF 110. *Certified* Medicaid.
Owner Proprietary corp.
Admissions Requirements Medical examination; Physician's request.
Staff Physicians 1 (pt); RNs 2 (ft); LPNs 10 (ft); Nurses' aides 34 (ft); Physical therapists 1 (pt); Speech therapists 1 (pt); Activities coordinators 1 (ft); Dietitians 1 (pt).
Facilities Dining room; Activities room; Chapel; Crafts room; Laundry room; Barber/ Beauty shop.
Activities Arts & crafts; Cards; Games; Reading groups; Prayer groups; Movies; Shopping trips; Dances/Social/Cultural gatherings.

Hickory Manor Nursing Home Inc
PO Box 69, 360 W Hickory Ave, Bastrop, LA 71221
(318) 281-6523
Admin Betty Sisson.
Medical Dir Dr Bruce Wheeler.
Licensure Intermediate care. *Beds* ICF 104.
Certified Medicaid.
Admissions Requirements Minimum age 21.
Staff Physicians 10 (pt); RNs 1 (ft); LPNs 9 (ft), 3 (pt); Nurses' aides 20 (ft); Physical therapists 1 (pt); Activities coordinators 1 (ft); Dietitians 1 (ft); Ophthalmologists 2 (pt); Dentists 2 (pt).

Facilities Dining room; Physical therapy room; Activities room; Chapel; Crafts room; Laundry room; Barber/Beauty shop.
Activities Arts & crafts; Cards; Games; Prayer groups; Movies; Shopping trips; Dances/ Social/Cultural gatherings.

Hillview Nursing Home Inc
PO Box 667, 105 Alvin St, Bastrop, LA 71220
(318) 281-0322
Admin Doris V Johnston.
Medical Dir Patrica Watson.
Licensure Intermediate care. *Beds* ICF 120.
Certified Medicaid.
Staff RNs 1 (ft); LPNs 10 (ft); Nurses' aides 40 (ft); Physical therapists 1 (pt); Dietitians 1 (ft).
Facilities Dining room; Physical therapy room; Activities room; Crafts room; Laundry room.
Activities Arts & crafts; Cards; Games; Reading groups; Prayer groups; Movies; Shopping trips; Dances/Social/Cultural gatherings.

Summerlin Lane Nursing Home
1408 Summerlin Ln, Bastrop, LA 71220
(318) 281-5188
Admin David Holland.
Medical Dir Dianne Anders.
Licensure Intermediate care. *Beds* ICF 100.
Certified Medicaid.
Owner Privately owned.
Admissions Requirements Medical examination.
Staff RNs; LPNs; Nurses' aides; Recreational therapists; Activities coordinators; Dietitians.
Facilities Dining room; Physical therapy room; Activities room; Crafts room; Laundry room; Barber/Beauty shop.
Activities Arts & crafts; Games; Reading groups; Movies; Shopping trips; Dances/ Social/Cultural gatherings.

Baton Rouge

Acadian House Care Center
4005 North Blvd, Baton Rouge, LA 70806
(504) 387-5934
Admin James E Morris.
Licensure Intermediate care. *Beds* ICF 184.
Certified Medicaid.

Baton Rouge Extensive Care
4914 McClelland Dr, Baton Rouge, LA 70806
(504) 356-3551
Admin Ed Hannie.
Licensure Intermediate care. *Beds* ICF 123.
Certified Medicaid.

Baton Rouge General Medical Center Skilled Nursing Facility
3600 Florida Blvd, Baton Rouge, LA 70806
(504) 387-7295
Admin George Munn Jr.
Licensure Skilled care. *Beds* SNF 46.

Baton Rouge Health Care Center
5550 Thomas Rd, Baton Rouge, LA 70807
(504) 774-2141
Admin Lena Johnson.
Beds 172.

Baton Rouge Heritage House Nursing Home II
1335 Wooddale Blvd, Baton Rouge, LA 70806
(504) 924-2851
Admin Tom R Reeses.
Medical Dir Virginia Philmon.
Licensure Intermediate care. *Beds* ICF 160.
Certified Medicaid.
Owner Proprietary corp.
Admissions Requirements Medical examination.
Staff RNs; LPNs; Nurses' aides; Physical therapists; Speech therapists; Activities coordinators; Dietitians.

Facilities Dining room; Activities room;
Chapel; Crafts room; Laundry room; Barber/
Beauty shop.
Activities Arts & crafts; Cards; Games;
Reading groups; Prayer groups; Movies;
Shopping trips; Dances/Social/Cultural
gatherings.

Ollie Steele Burden Manor
4200 Essen Ln, Baton Rouge, LA 70809
(504) 926-0091
Admin Ken Cormier. *Dir of Nursing* Marie
Thibodeaux RN.
Licensure Intermediate care. *Beds* ICF 72.
Private Pay Patients 100%.
Owner Nonprofit organization/foundation
(Franciscan Missionaries of Our Lady).
Admissions Requirements Medical
examination.
Staff RNs 2 (ft); LPNs 6 (ft), 2 (pt); Nurses'
aides 15 (ft), 13 (pt); Activities coordinators
1 (ft); Dietitians 1 (pt).
Languages French.
Facilities Dining room; Physical therapy
room; Activities room; Chapel; Crafts room;
Laundry room; Barber/Beauty shop; Sun
room; Courtyard; Parlors.
Activities Arts & crafts; Cards; Games; Prayer
groups; Movies; Shopping trips; Dances/
Social/Cultural gatherings; Intergenerational
programs; Pet therapy.

Capitol Nursing Home
11546 Florida Blvd, Baton Rouge, LA 70815
(504) 275-0474
Admin Elaine Daniel.
Medical Dir Kathy Hagan.
Licensure Intermediate care. *Beds* ICF 85.
Certified Medicaid.
Admissions Requirements Physician's request.
Staff RNs 1 (ft), 1 (pt); LPNs 7 (ft); Nurses'
aides 25 (ft); Activities coordinators 1 (ft);
Dietitians 1 (ft), 1 (pt).
Facilities Dining room; Activities room;
Chapel; Crafts room; Laundry room; Barber/
Beauty shop; Library.
Activities Arts & crafts; Cards; Games;
Reading groups; Prayer groups; Movies;
Shopping trips; Dances/Social/Cultural
gatherings.

Care Center
11188 Florida Blvd, Baton Rouge, LA 70815
(504) 275-7570
Admin Lorie Greenwald.
Medical Dir Dannette Craft.
Licensure Intermediate care. *Beds* ICF 106.
Certified Medicaid.
Owner Proprietary corp.
Admissions Requirements Medical
examination.
Staff RNs 1 (ft); LPNs 5 (ft), 3 (pt); Nurses'
aides 64 (ft), 6 (pt); Activities coordinators 1
(ft); Dietitians 1 (pt).
Facilities Dining room; Activities room;
Crafts room; Laundry room; Barber/Beauty
shop.
Activities Arts & crafts; Cards; Games;
Reading groups; Prayer groups; Movies;
Shopping trips; Dances/Social/Cultural
gatherings.

Convention Street Nursing Center
4660 Convention St, Box 65274, Baton
Rouge, LA 70896
(504) 926-5884
Admin Rebecca Barnett.
Licensure Intermediate care. *Beds* ICF 54.
Certified Medicaid.

Flannery Oaks Guest House
1642 N Flannery Rd, Baton Rouge, LA 70815
(504) 275-6393
Admin Dun Stockwell.
Beds 164.

Heritage Manor of Baton Rouge
9301 Oxford Place Dr, Baton Rouge, LA
70809
(504) 291-8474
Admin Raymond Cook.
Beds 176.
Owner Proprietary corp (National Heritage).

Hillhaven Nursing Center—East
4100 North Blvd, Baton Rouge, LA 70806
(504) 387-6704
Admin William Kimbro.
Medical Dir M Landry.
Licensure Intermediate care. *Beds* ICF 123.
Certified Medicaid.
Owner Proprietary corp (Hillhaven Corp).
Admissions Requirements Minimum age 25;
Medical examination; Physician's request.
Staff RNs 2 (ft); LPNs 10 (ft), 3 (pt); Nurses'
aides 32 (ft); Activities coordinators 1 (ft);
Dietitians 1 (ft).
Languages French.
Facilities Dining room; Activities room;
Laundry room; Barber/Beauty shop.
Activities Arts & crafts; Cards; Games;
Reading groups; Prayer groups; Movies;
Shopping trips; Dances/Social/Cultural
gatherings.

Hillhaven Nursing Center—West
170 W Washington St, Baton Rouge, LA
70802
(504) 343-8770
Admin Gerald Colston.
Licensure Intermediate care. *Beds* ICF 85.
Certified Medicaid.
Owner Proprietary corp (Hillhaven Corp).

Jefferson Manor Nursing Home
9919 Jefferson Hwy, Baton Rouge, LA 70809
(504) 293-1434
Admin Stan Passman.
Licensure Intermediate care. *Beds* ICF 122.
Certified Medicaid.
Staff RNs 1 (ft); LPNs 6 (ft); Nurses' aides 26
(ft); Physical therapists 1 (pt); Reality
therapists 1 (pt); Recreational therapists 1
(pt); Occupational therapists 1 (pt); Speech
therapists 1 (pt); Activities coordinators 1
(ft), 1 (pt); Dietitians 1 (pt);
Ophthalmologists 1 (pt); Podiatrists 1 (pt);
Dentists 1 (pt).
Facilities Dining room; Physical therapy
room; Activities room; Chapel; Crafts room;
Laundry room; Barber/Beauty shop; Library.
Activities Arts & crafts; Cards; Games; Prayer
groups; Movies; Shopping trips; Dances/
Social/Cultural gatherings.

Louisiana Guest House of Baton Rouge
7414 Sumrall Dr, Baton Rouge, LA 70812
(504) 356-0644
Admin Robert Nance. *Dir of Nursing* Teresa
Harris RN.
Licensure Intermediate care. *Beds* ICF 144.
Certified Medicaid.
Owner Proprietary corp.
Admissions Requirements Medical
examination.
Staff Physicians 1 (ft); RNs 1 (ft); LPNs 9 (ft),
32 (pt); Nurses' aides 22 (ft), 11 (pt);
Activities coordinators 1 (ft), 1 (pt);
Dietitians 1 (pt).
Facilities Dining room; Activities room;
Crafts room; Laundry room; Barber/Beauty
shop; Doctor's office.
Activities Arts & crafts; Cards; Games;
Reading groups; Prayer groups; Movies;
Shopping trips; Dances/Social/Cultural
gatherings.

**Medical Center of Baton Rouge Skilled
Nursing Facility**
17000 Medical Center Blvd, Baton Rouge, LA
70816
(504) 292-2470
Admin William Anderson.
Licensure Skilled care. *Beds* SNF 6.

Oakley House Care Center
4363 Convention St, Baton Rouge, LA 70806
(504) 383-6134
Admin Cindy Quirk.
Licensure Intermediate care. *Beds* ICF 141.
Certified Medicaid.

**Our Lady of the Lake Regional Medical Center
Skilled Nursing**
5000 Hennessy Blvd, Baton Rouge, LA 70809
(504) 765-6565
Admin Robert C Davidge.
Licensure Skilled care.

Retirement Center
14686 Old Hammond Hwy, Baton Rouge, LA
70816
(504) 272-9339
Admin Sheila Kimbro. *Dir of Nursing* Pat
Chance. *Medical Dir* Pat Chance.
Licensure Skilled care; Intermediate care;
Apartments. *Beds* Swing beds SNF/ICF 80;
Apts 38. *Private Pay Patients* 100%.
Owner Privately owned.
Admissions Requirements Medical
examination.
Staff RNs 1 (ft); LPNs 7 (ft); Nurses' aides 28
(ft); Activities coordinators 1 (ft).
Languages French.
Facilities Dining room; Activities room;
Chapel; Crafts room; Laundry room; Barber/
Beauty shop; Library; Individually heated &
air-conditioned rooms; Whirlpool baths.
Activities Arts & crafts; Cards; Games;
Reading groups; Prayer groups; Movies;
Shopping trips; Dances/Social/Cultural
gatherings; Intergenerational programs;
Monthly family support group.

St James Place Nursing Care Center
333 Lee Dr, Baton Rouge, LA 70808
(504) 769-1407, 769-9641 FAX
Admin Bill Bivens. *Dir of Nursing* Fay Ashley
RN. *Medical Dir* Maurice Nassar MD.
Licensure Skilled care; Alzheimer's care;
Retirement. *Beds* SNF 60; Retirement apts
190. *Private Pay Patients* 100%.
Owner Nonprofit organization/foundation.
Admissions Requirements Minimum age 18;
Medical examination.
Staff Physicians; RNs 4 (ft); LPNs 11 (ft);
Nurses' aides 20 (ft); Physical therapists
(contracted); Occupational therapists
(contracted); Speech therapists (contracted);
Activities coordinators 1 (ft); Dietitians 1
(ft); Ophthalmologists (consultant);
Podiatrists (consultant); Audiologists
(consultant).
Affiliation Episcopal.
Facilities Dining room; Physical therapy
room; Activities room; Crafts room; Laundry
room; Barber/Beauty shop; Library.
Activities Arts & crafts; Cards; Games;
Reading groups; Prayer groups; Movies;
Shopping trips; Dances/Social/Cultural
gatherings; Intergenerational programs; Pet
therapy.

Sterling Place
3888 North Blvd, Baton Rouge, LA 70806
(504) 344-3551
Admin Natalie McCauley.
Medical Dir Connie Harig.
Licensure Intermediate care; Alzheimer's care;
Retirement. *Beds* ICF 114. Certified
Medicaid.
Owner Nonprofit corp.
Admissions Requirements Medical
examination.
Staff Physicians 1 (ft); RNs 1 (ft); LPNs;
Nurses' aides 16 (ft), 3 (pt); Physical
therapists 1 (pt); Speech therapists 1 (pt);
Activities coordinators 1 (ft); Dietitians 1
(ft).
Facilities Dining room; Activities room;
Crafts room; Laundry room; Barber/Beauty
shop.

Activities Arts & crafts; Cards; Games; Reading groups; Prayer groups; Movies; Shopping trips; Dances/Social/Cultural gatherings.

Bernice

Pinecrest Manor Nursing Home
101 Reeves St, Bernice, LA 71222
(318) 285-7600
Admin Denise C Festervan. *Dir of Nursing* Linda Tucker RN. *Medical Dir* W C Reeves MD.
Licensure Intermediate care. *Beds* ICF 126. *Private Pay Patients* 20%. *Certified* Medicaid.
Owner Privately owned (Tommy Bankston, Helen Campbell, Charles Bice, Harvey Marcus, T R Price).
Staff RNs 1 (ft), 1 (pt); LPNs 9 (ft), 2 (pt); Nurses' aides 32 (ft), 6 (pt); Activities coordinators 1 (ft).
Languages German.
Facilities Dining room; Activities room; Chapel; Laundry room; Barber/Beauty shop; Flower garden.
Activities Arts & crafts; Cards; Games; Reading groups; Prayer groups; Movies; Shopping trips; Dances/Social/Cultural gatherings; Intergenerational programs; Pet therapy.

Bienville

Bienville General Hospital
PO Drawer 599, 810 Pine St, Bienville, LA 71001
(318) 263-2044
Admin Hoye A Bowman.
Licensure Skilled care; Intermediate care. *Beds* Swing beds SNF/ICF 30.

Bogalusa

Rest Haven Nursing Home
1301 Harrison St, Bogalusa, LA 70427
(504) 732-3909
Admin Gary Stafford. *Dir of Nursing* Ivy N Hill RN. *Medical Dir* Dr R A Casama.
Licensure Intermediate care. *Beds* ICF 205. *Private Pay Patients* 15%. *Certified* Medicaid.
Owner Privately owned (Alan V Barnett & John Gum).
Staff RNs 2 (ft); LPNs 16 (ft), 2 (pt); Nurses' aides 40 (ft), 20 (pt); Activities coordinators 1 (ft); Dietitians (consultant); SSDs 1 (ft).

Bossier City

Bossier Health Care Center
2901 Douglas St, Bossier City, LA 71111
(318) 747-2700
Admin Melvin Stallcup. *Dir of Nursing* Connie Kurz RN. *Medical Dir* T A Riley MD.
Licensure Intermediate care. *Beds* ICF 142. *Certified* Medicaid; Medicare.
Owner Proprietary corp.
Admissions Requirements Minimum age 18.
Staff Physicians; RNs; LPNs; Nurses' aides; Physical therapists; Recreational therapists; Speech therapists; Activities coordinators; Dietitians; Ophthalmologists; Podiatrists; Dentists.
Facilities Dining room; Activities room; Chapel; Crafts room; Laundry room; Barber/Beauty shop.
Activities Arts & crafts; Cards; Games; Reading groups; Prayer groups; Movies; Shopping trips; Dances/Social/Cultural gatherings.

Bossier Medical Center Skilled Nursing Facility
2105 Airline Dr, Bossier City, LA 71111
(318) 741-6139
Admin Ellen T Kyle NHA. *Dir of Nursing* Beth Montano RN. *Medical Dir* Charles Powers MD.
Licensure Skilled care. *Beds* SNF 10. *Private Pay Patients* 10%. *Certified* Medicare.
Owner Publicly owned.
Admissions Requirements Medical examination.
Staff RNs 1 (ft), 2 (pt); LPNs 3 (ft), 3 (pt); Nurses' aides 1 (ft), 3 (pt); Physical therapists 2 (ft); Occupational therapists 1 (pt); Speech therapists 1 (pt); Activities coordinators 1 (pt); Dietitians 1 (ft).
Facilities Dining room; Distinct part of hospital Orthopaedic/Neurology unit.

Garden Court Nursing Center Inc
4405 Airline Dr, Bossier City, LA 71111
(318) 747-5440
Admin Sam Teague.
Beds 64.

Heritage Manor of Bossier City
2575 N Airline Dr, Bossier City, LA 71111
(318) 746-7542
Admin Brian Martin.
Licensure Intermediate care. *Beds* ICF 64. *Certified* Medicaid.
Owner Proprietary corp (National Heritage).

Pilgrim Manor of Bossier City—North
1524 Doctors Dr, Bossier City, LA 71111
(318) 742-1623
Admin Ronald Hines.
Licensure Intermediate care. *Beds* ICF 179. *Certified* Medicare.
Owner Proprietary corp.
Admissions Requirements Medical examination; Physician's request.
Staff RNs 3 (ft); LPNs 21 (ft), 2 (pt); Nurses' aides 60 (ft); Activities coordinators 1 (ft).
Languages Spanish.
Facilities Dining room; Activities room; Chapel; Laundry room; Barber/Beauty shop; Library.
Activities Cards; Games; Reading groups; Movies; Shopping trips; Dances/Social/Cultural gatherings.

Pilgrim Manor of Bossier City—South
1525 Fullilove Dr, Bossier City, LA 71112
(318) 742-5420
Admin Byron Neal Hines.
Licensure Intermediate care. *Beds* ICF 96. *Certified* Medicaid.

Riverview Care Center
4820 Medical Dr, Bossier City, LA 71112
(318) 747-1857
Admin N June Owens. *Dir of Nursing* Marie Mayo. *Medical Dir* David Henry.
Licensure Intermediate care. *Beds* ICF 151. *Private Pay Patients* 40%. *Certified* Medicaid.
Owner Proprietary corp.
Admissions Requirements Medical examination; Physician's request.
Staff RNs 2 (ft), 1 (pt); LPNs 11 (ft); Nurses' aides 40 (ft); Physical therapists; Activities coordinators 1 (ft); Dietitians.
Facilities Dining room; Activities room; Crafts room; Barber/Beauty shop; Library.
Activities Arts & crafts; Cards; Games; Reading groups; Prayer groups; Movies; Shopping trips; Dances/Social/Cultural gatherings; Pet therapy.

Breaux Bridge

Gary Memorial Hospital
210 Champagne St, Breaux Bridge, LA 70517-0357
(318) 332-2178

Admin James C Morrogh.
Licensure Skilled care; Intermediate care.

St Agnes Nursing Home
PO Box 10, Latiolais Rd, Breaux Bridge, LA 70517
Admin Kenneth Landry.
Beds 120.

Bunkie

Bayou Vista Manor
PO Box 270, 323 Evergreen Rd, Bunkie, LA 71322
(318) 346-2080
Admin Jodie Russo.
Licensure Intermediate care. *Beds* ICF 174. *Certified* Medicaid.

Bunkie General Hospital
PO Box 380, Evergreen Hwy, Bunkie, LA 71322
(318) 346-6681
Admin Ray A Lemoine.
Licensure Skilled care; Intermediate care.

Calhoun

Marion Nursing Home
452 Pine Hills Dr, Calhoun, LA 71225
(318) 292-4514
Admin Stan Beeson.
Medical Dir Susan Hiser.
Licensure Intermediate care. *Beds* ICF 77. *Certified* Medicaid.
Owner Privately owned.
Admissions Requirements Minimum age 17; Medical examination.
Staff Physicians 1 (pt); RNs 1 (ft), 1 (pt); LPNs 9 (ft); Nurses' aides; Activities coordinators 2 (ft), 1 (pt); Dietitians 1 (ft), 1 (pt).
Facilities Dining room; Activities room; Laundry room; Barber/Beauty shop.
Activities Arts & crafts; Cards; Games; Reading groups; Prayer groups; Movies; Shopping trips; Dances/Social/Cultural gatherings.

Cameron

South Cameron Hospital
Rte 1 Box 277, Cameron, LA 70631
(318) 775-5786
Admin H K Hopper.
Licensure Skilled care; Intermediate care.

Carencro

Evangeline Oaks Guest House
PO Box 548, 240 Arceneaux Rd, Carencro, LA 70520
(318) 896-9227
Admin Frankie LaFleur.
Beds 152.

Center Point

Oak Haven Nursing Home Inc
PO Box 198, Hwy 107, Center Point, LA 71323
(318) 253-4601
Admin Linda Brittain.
Licensure Intermediate care. *Beds* ICF 104. *Certified* Medicaid.
Staff Physicians 1 (pt); RNs 1 (ft), 1 (pt); LPNs 5 (ft), 3 (pt); Nurses' aides 25 (ft), 11 (pt); Activities coordinators 1 (ft); Dietitians 1 (pt); Dentists 1 (pt).
Facilities Dining room; Crafts room; Laundry room; Barber/Beauty shop.
Activities Arts & crafts; Cards; Games; Prayer groups; Shopping trips; Dances/Social/Cultural gatherings.

Church Point

Acadia—St Landry Guest Home Inc
830 S Broadway St, Church Point, LA 70525
(318) 684-6316
Admin Milton Seilhan. *Dir of Nursing* Angela
Fusilier RN.
Licensure Intermediate care. *Beds* ICF 126.
Private Pay Patients 9%. *Certified* Medicaid.
Owner Proprietary corp.
Admissions Requirements Medical
examination; Physician's request.
Staff RNs 2 (ft); LPNs 10 (ft); Nurses' aides
39 (ft), 10 (pt); Activities coordinators 1 (ft);
Dietitians 1 (pt).
Languages French.
Facilities Dining room; Chapel; Laundry
room; Barber/Beauty shop.
Activities Arts & crafts; Cards; Games; Prayer
groups; Movies; Dances/Social/Cultural
gatherings; Religious services & activities.

Acadia—St Landry Hospital
810 S Broadway, Church Point, LA 70525
(318) 684-5435
Admin Alcus Trahan.
Licensure Skilled care; Intermediate care. *Beds*
Swing beds SNF/ICF 30.

Clinton

Grace Nursing Home
PO Box 945, Hwy 67 S, Clinton, LA 70722
(504) 683-8533
Admin Martin M Stott.
Medical Dir Maydee Rushing.
Licensure Intermediate care. *Beds* ICF 128.
Owner Proprietary corp.
Admissions Requirements Medical
examination.
Staff Physicians 1 (pt); RNs 1 (ft), 1 (pt);
LPNs 6 (ft), 3 (pt); Nurses' aides 37 (ft), 8
(pt); Physical therapists 1 (pt); Reality
therapists 1 (pt); Recreational therapists 1
(pt); Occupational therapists 1 (pt); Speech
therapists 1 (pt); Activities coordinators 1
(ft); Dietitians 1 (pt).
Facilities Dining room; Activities room;
Crafts room; Laundry room; Barber/Beauty
shop.
Activities Arts & crafts; Games; Reading
groups; Prayer groups; Movies; Shopping
trips; Dances/Social/Cultural gatherings.

Colfax

Grant Manor Nursing Center
366 Webb Smith Dr, Colfax, LA 71417
(318) 627-3207, 448-0604 FAX
Admin Betty Thibodaux. *Dir of Nursing*
Virginia Wallace. *Medical Dir* Alfred Krake.
Licensure Intermediate care. *Beds* ICF 140.
Private Pay Patients 10%. *Certified*
Medicaid.
Owner Proprietary corp.
Admissions Requirements Minimum age 18;
Medical examination.
Staff RNs 1 (ft), 1 (pt); LPNs 12 (ft); Nurses'
aides 50 (ft); Physical therapists; Activities
coordinators 1 (ft); Dietitians.
Facilities Dining room; Activities room;
Crafts room; Laundry room; Barber/Beauty
shop; Library.
Activities Arts & crafts; Games; Reading
groups; Prayer groups; Shopping trips;
Dances/Social/Cultural gatherings; Pet
therapy.

Columbia

Caldwell Memorial Hospital
410 Main St, Columbia, LA 71418
(318) 649-7261
Admin Georgia Martin.
Licensure Skilled care; Intermediate care.

Citizens Medical Center
PO Box 1079, 165 S, Columbia, LA 71418
(318) 649-6106
Admin Ewell D Singleton.
Licensure Skilled care; Intermediate care.

Columbia Heights Nursing Home Inc
1612 Hwy 165 S, Columbia, LA 71418
(318) 649-2702
Admin Robert H Causey. *Dir of Nursing*
Mona L Dostch RN. *Medical Dir* Dr P S
Shroff.
Licensure Intermediate care; Retirement. *Beds*
ICF 169; Retirement apts 4. *Certified*
Medicaid.
Owner Proprietary corp.
Admissions Requirements Medical
examination.
Staff Physicians 6 (ft); RNs 2 (ft); LPNs 13
(ft); Nurses' aides 55 (ft); Physical therapists
1 (ft); Occupational therapists 1 (ft); Speech
therapists 1 (ft); Activities coordinators 3
(ft); Dietitians 1 (ft); Ophthalmologists 1 (ft).
Facilities Dining room; Physical therapy
room; Activities room; Chapel; Crafts room;
Laundry room; Barber/Beauty shop; Library.
Activities Arts & crafts; Cards; Games;
Reading groups; Prayer groups; Movies;
Shopping trips.

Columbia State School
PO Box 1559, Louisiana Hwy 850, Columbia,
LA 71435
(318) 649-2385
Admin Gene I Barrow.
Medical Dir Sylvia Malcomb.
Licensure Intermediate care for mentally
retarded. *Beds* ICF/MR 32. *Certified*
Medicaid.
Owner Publicly owned.
Admissions Requirements Minimum age 3;
Medical examination.
Staff Physicians 3 (pt); RNs 1 (ft); LPNs 1
(ft); Physical therapists 1 (pt); Occupational
therapists 1 (pt); Speech therapists 1 (ft);
Dietitians 1 (ft); Dentists 1 (pt).
Facilities Dining room; Physical therapy
room; Activities room; Laundry room;
Library; Adaptive physical education &
diagnostic areas.
Activities Cards; Games; Reading groups;
Movies; Shopping trips; Dances/Social/
Cultural gatherings.

Coushatta

L S Huckabay Memorial Hospital
PO Box 369, 309 Marvelle, Coushatta, LA
71019
(318) 932-5786
Admin Ronnie Cox.
Licensure Skilled care; Intermediate care. *Beds*
Swing beds SNF/ICF 102.

Senior Citizens Center
1110 Ringgold Ave, Coushatta, LA 71019
(318) 932-5202
Admin Len Stephens. *Dir of Nursing* Frances
Hutson.
Licensure Intermediate care. *Beds* ICF 83.
Certified Medicaid.
Admissions Requirements Medical
examination.
Staff RNs 1 (ft); LPNs 4 (ft), 1 (pt); Nurses'
aides 18 (ft), 5 (pt); Physical therapists 1
(pt); Activities coordinators 1 (ft); Dietitians
1 (pt).
Facilities Dining room; Activities room;
Laundry room; Barber/Beauty shop.
Activities Cards; Games; Prayer groups;
Movies; Shopping trips; Dances/Social/
Cultural gatherings.

Springville Nursing Center
PO Box 469, 2423 Springville Rd, Coushatta,
LA 71019
(318) 932-5066

Admin Len W Stephens. *Dir of Nursing* Loyce
V Plunkett RN.
Licensure Intermediate care. *Beds* ICF 74.
Certified Medicaid.
Admissions Requirements Medical
examination.
Staff RNs 1 (ft); LPNs 4 (ft), 1 (pt); Nurses'
aides 18 (ft), 3 (pt); Physical therapists 1
(pt); Activities coordinators 1 (ft); Dietitians
1 (pt).
Facilities Dining room; Activities room;
Laundry room; Barber/Beauty shop.
Activities Arts & crafts; Games; Prayer groups;
Movies; Shopping trips; Dances/Social/
Cultural gatherings; Field trips.

Covington

Forest Manor Nursing Home
PO Box 779, Madisonville Hwy, Covington,
LA 70434
(504) 892-6900
Admin John Franzke.
Medical Dir Brook McDonald.
Licensure Intermediate care. *Beds* ICF 192.
Certified Medicaid.
Owner Proprietary corp.
Staff RNs; LPNs; Nurses' aides; Activities
coordinators; Dietitians.
Activities Arts & crafts; Cards; Games;
Reading groups; Prayer groups; Movies;
Shopping trips.

**Skilled Nursing Facility of St Tammany Parish
Hospital**
1202 S Tyler St, Covington, LA 70433
(504) 898-4414
Admin James Bingham. *Dir of Nursing* Phyllis
W Pond RN BSN, Extended Care Dir.
Medical Dir P Craig Parker MD.
Licensure Skilled care. *Beds* SNF 12. *Certified*
Medicaid; Medicare.
Owner Nonprofit corp.
Admissions Requirements Medical
examination; Physician's request.
Staff Physicians (contracted); RNs 1 (ft), 2
(pt); LPNs 6 (ft); Nurses' aides 5 (ft);
Physical therapists (contracted); Speech
therapists (contracted); Activities
coordinators 1 (pt); Dietitians 1 (ft); Speech
pathologists (contracted).
Facilities Dining room; Physical therapy
room; Activities room; Crafts room.
Activities Arts & crafts; Cards; Games;
Dances/Social/Cultural gatherings.

Crowley

Bayou Village Nursing Center
1101 Southeastern Ave, Crowley, LA 70526
(318) 783-2740
Admin DAvid Grotefend.
Licensure Intermediate care. *Beds* ICF 102.
Certified Medicaid.

Christian Villa Nursing Home
PO Drawer 540, 1120 W Hutchinson Ave,
Crowley, LA 70527-0540
(318) 783-5533
Admin Willie Maynard Jr. *Dir of Nursing*
Carolyn Toussaint. *Medical Dir* J C
Dauphin MD.
Licensure Intermediate care. *Beds* ICF 73.
Private Pay Patients 2%. *Certified* Medicaid.
Owner Nonprofit organization/foundation.
Admissions Requirements Medical
examination; Physician's request.
Staff Physicians 1 (ft); RNs 1 (ft); LPNs 8 (ft);
Nurses' aides 32 (ft); Activities coordinators
1 (ft); Dietitians 1 (ft).
Languages French.
Facilities Dining room; Laundry room.
Activities Arts & crafts; Cards; Games; Prayer
groups; Movies; Shopping trips.

Crowley Guest House
PO Box 1274, 1400 E Elm St, Crowley, LA
  70526
(318) 783-8101
Admin Brenda Holden.
Medical Dir H Lawrence Gardiner MD.
Licensure Intermediate care. *Beds* ICF 124.
  Certified Medicaid.
Owner Proprietary corp (US Care Corp).
Admissions Requirements Medical
  examination; Physician's request.
Staff Physicians 1 (ft); RNs 1 (ft); LPNs 9 (ft),
  1 (pt); Nurses' aides 20 (ft), 5 (pt); Physical
  therapists 1 (pt); Activities coordinators 1
  (ft).
Facilities Dining room; Activities room;
  Chapel; Crafts room; Laundry room;
  Library.
Activities Arts & crafts; Cards; Games; Prayer
  groups; Movies; Dances/Social/Cultural
  gatherings.

Heritage Manor of Crowley
PO Drawer 1547, 1526 N Ave I, Crowley, LA
  70526
(318) 783-2363
Admin Marian A Trahan.
Licensure Intermediate care. *Beds* ICF 57.
  Certified Medicaid.
Owner Proprietary corp (National Heritage).
Admissions Requirements Medical
  examination.
Staff RNs 1 (ft); LPNs 3 (ft), 4 (pt); Nurses'
  aides 40 (ft), 3 (pt); Activities coordinators 1
  (ft); Dietitians 1 (pt).
Facilities Dining room; Laundry room;
  Barber/Beauty shop.
Activities Arts & crafts; Cards; Games;
  Reading groups; Prayer groups; Movies;
  Shopping trips; Dances/Social/Cultural
  gatherings.

Cut Off

South Lafourche Nursing Center
202 E 28th St, Cut Off, LA 70345
(504) 693-8677
Admin Cletus M Solar.
Medical Dir Dr Seludd.
Licensure Intermediate care. *Beds* ICF 126.
  Certified Medicaid.
Admissions Requirements Medical
  examination.
Staff Physicians 1 (ft); RNs 1 (ft); LPNs 6 (ft);
  Nurses' aides 26 (ft); Physical therapists 1
  (ft); Occupational therapists 1 (pt); Speech
  therapists 1 (pt); Activities coordinators 1
  (ft); Dietitians 1 (pt); Ophthalmologists 1
  (pt); Podiatrists 1 (pt); Audiologists 1 (pt);
  Dentists 1 (pt).
Facilities Dining room; Physical therapy
  room; Activities room; Chapel; Crafts room;
  Laundry room; Barber/Beauty shop; Library.
Activities Arts & crafts; Games; Prayer groups;
  Movies; Shopping trips; Dances/Social/
  Cultural gatherings.

Delhi

Delhi Guest Home
203 Rancher St, Delhi, LA 71232
(318) 878-5106
Admin Archie B Clayton Jr.
Medical Dir Lessie Boyett.
Licensure Intermediate care for mentally
  retarded. *Beds* ICF/MR 145. *Certified*
  Medicaid; Medicare.
Owner Proprietary corp.
Admissions Requirements Minimum age 14.
Staff RNs 1 (ft); LPNs 7 (ft); Nurses' aides 2
  (pt); Recreational therapists 3 (ft);
  Occupational therapists 1 (pt); Speech
  therapists 1 (pt); Activities coordinators 7
  (ft); Dietitians 1 (ft).

Facilities Dining room; Activities room;
  Laundry room; Barber/Beauty shop.
Activities Arts & crafts; Games; Reading
  groups; Movies; Shopping trips; Dances/
  Social/Cultural gatherings.

Richland Nursing Home
504 N Charter St, Delhi, LA 71232
(318) 878-2417
Admin Allen S Brown.
Licensure Intermediate care. *Beds* ICF 87.
  Certified Medicaid.
Staff RNs 1 (ft); LPNs 6 (ft); Nurses' aides 18
  (ft); Physical therapists; Activities
  coordinators; Ophthalmologists; Dentists.
Facilities Dining room; Barber/Beauty shop.
Activities Arts & crafts; Cards; Games;
  Reading groups; Prayer groups; Movies.

Richland Parish Hospital
507 Cincinnati St, Delhi, LA 71232
(318) 878-5171
Admin Michael E Cooper.
Licensure Skilled care; Intermediate care. *Beds*
  Swing beds SNF/ICF 75.

Denham Springs

Golden Age Nursing Home
Rte 5 Box 574, 4-H Club Rd, Denham
  Springs, LA 70726
(504) 665-5544
Admin Bobby Messina.
Medical Dir Louise Corkern.
Licensure Intermediate care. *Beds* ICF 175.
  Certified Medicaid.
Staff Physicians 9 (pt); RNs 1 (ft), 1 (pt);
  LPNs 10 (ft), 3 (pt); Nurses' aides 27 (ft), 23
  (pt); Physical therapists 1 (pt); Occupational
  therapists 1 (pt); Speech therapists 1 (pt);
  Activities coordinators 1 (ft), 1 (pt);
  Dietitians 1 (pt); Ophthalmologists 1 (pt);
  Podiatrists 1 (pt); Dentists 1 (pt).
Facilities Dining room; Physical therapy
  room; Activities room; Crafts room; Laundry
  room; Barber/Beauty shop; Sun room.
Activities Arts & crafts; Cards; Games;
  Reading groups; Prayer groups; Movies;
  Shopping trips; Dances/Social/Cultural
  gatherings; Field trips.

Harvest Manor Nursing Home
9171 Cockerham Rd, Denham Springs, LA
  70726
(504) 665-8946
Admin Bobby L Beebe.
Medical Dir Bebe Sylar.
Licensure Intermediate care. *Beds* ICF 178.
  Certified Medicaid.
Owner Proprietary corp.
Admissions Requirements Medical
  examination.
Staff RNs 2 (ft), 2 (pt); LPNs 8 (ft), 2 (pt);
  Nurses' aides 19 (ft); Activities coordinators
  1 (ft); Dietitians 1 (ft).
Facilities Dining room; Activities room;
  Laundry room; Barber/Beauty shop.
Activities Prayer groups; Movies; Dances/
  Social/Cultural gatherings.

DeQuincy

DeQuincy Memorial Hospital
110 W 4th St, DeQuincy, LA 70633
(318) 768-1200
Admin Luther J Lewis.
Licensure Skilled care; Intermediate care. *Beds*
  Swing beds SNF/ICF 50.

Greenhill Nursing Home
PO Box 1219, 602 N Division, DeQuincy, LA
  70633
(318) 786-2466
Admin Gale Lewis.
Licensure Intermediate care. *Beds* ICF 80.
  Certified Medicaid.

DeRidder

Beauregard Nursing Home Inc
PO Box 250, 1420 Blankenship Dr, DeRidder,
  LA 70630
(318) 463-9022
Admin Richard Newell.
Licensure Intermediate care. *Beds* ICF 142.
  Certified Medicaid.

Westwood Manor Nursing Home Inc
714 High School Dr, DeRidder, LA 70634
(318) 463-6293
Admin Benson W Sylvest.
Licensure Intermediate care. *Beds* ICF 100.
  Certified Medicaid.

Destrehan

Evangeline of Ormond
PO Box 1057, 1940 Ormond Blvd, Destrehan,
  LA 70047
(504) 764-1793, 764-1374 FAX
Admin Nannette Alba. *Dir of Nursing* Theresa
  Meyer RN. *Medical Dir* Dr James Roger.
Licensure Skilled care; Intermediate care. *Beds*
  Swing beds SNF/ICF 148. *Private Pay
  Patients* 35%. *Certified* Medicaid; Medicare.
Owner Proprietary corp (Evangeline Health
  Care).
Admissions Requirements Physician's request.
Staff RNs; LPNs; Nurses' aides; Physical
  therapists; Activities coordinators; Dietitians.
Facilities Dining room; Activities room;
  Barber/Beauty shop.
Activities Arts & crafts; Cards; Games;
  Reading groups; Prayer groups; Movies;
  Dances/Social/Cultural gatherings.

Donaldsonville

D'Ville House Inc
PO Box 688, Vatican Dr, Donaldsonville, LA
  70346
(504) 473-8614
Admin John Gum Jr.
Licensure Intermediate care. *Beds* ICF 142.
  Certified Medicaid.

Prevost Memorial Hospital
301 Memorial Dr, Donaldsonville, LA 70346
(504) 473-7931
Admin Harold J Ramirez.
Beds 35.

Erath

Morris Lahasky Nursing Home
PO Box 323, 501 E Conrad, Erath, LA 70533
(318) 937-6752
Admin Hazel Hebert.
Medical Dir Dr Bernard Lahasky.
Licensure Intermediate care. *Beds* ICF 129.
  Certified Medicaid.
Staff Physicians 6 (ft); RNs 1 (ft), 1 (pt);
  Nurses' aides 32 (ft), 5 (pt); Physical
  therapists 1 (pt); Activities coordinators 1
  (ft); Dietitians 1 (pt).
Languages French.
Facilities Dining room; Physical therapy
  room; Activities room; Chapel; Crafts room;
  Laundry room; Barber/Beauty shop.
Activities Arts & crafts; Cards; Games;
  Reading groups; Prayer groups; Movies;
  Shopping trips; Dances/Social/Cultural
  gatherings.

Eunice

Eunice Care Center Inc
1100 Nile St, Eunice, LA 70535
(318) 457-2681
Admin Gwen A Hebert. *Dir of Nursing* Jane
  Vidmire RN. *Medical Dir* Dr Brian Heinen.

Licensure Intermediate care. *Beds* ICF 200. *Private Pay Patients* 12%. *Certified* Medicaid.
Owner Nonprofit organization/foundation.
Admissions Requirements Medical examination; Physician's request.
Staff Physicians 1 (pt); RNs 1 (ft), 2 (pt); LPNs; Nurses' aides; Activities coordinators 2 (ft); Dietitians 1 (pt).
Languages French (Creole).
Facilities Dining room; Activities room; Laundry room; Barber/Beauty shop; Smoking lobby.
Activities Arts & crafts; Cards; Games; Prayer groups; Movies; Shopping trips; Dances/Social/Cultural gatherings; Intergenerational programs.

Moosa Memorial Hospital
PO Box 1026, Eunice, LA 70535
(318) 457-5244
Admin Douglas C Longman.
Licensure Skilled care; Intermediate care.

Farmerville

Chateau D'Arbonne Nursing Care Center
PO Box 733, 813 N Main St, Farmerville, LA 71241
(318) 368-2256
Admin Bruce Hall.
Beds 138.

Lakeview Nursing Home Inc
PO Box 206, 110 W Hill St, Farmerville, LA 71241
(318) 368-3103
Admin Ed Boudreaux. *Dir of Nursing* Carol Kennedy RN.
Licensure Intermediate care. *Beds* ICF 114. *Certified* Medicaid.
Admissions Requirements Medical examination.
Staff RNs 2 (ft); LPNs 10 (ft); Nurses' aides 35 (ft); Physical therapists 1 (pt); Recreational therapists 1 (ft); Activities coordinators 1 (ft); Dietitians 1 (ft).
Facilities Dining room; Physical therapy room; Activities room; Crafts room; Laundry room; Barber/Beauty shop.
Activities Arts & crafts; Cards; Games; Reading groups; Prayer groups; Movies; Shopping trips; Dances/Social/Cultural gatherings.

Ferriday

Concordia Parish Rest Home
411 N EE Wallace Blvd, Ferriday, LA 71334
(318) 757-2181
Admin Floyd Thornhill.
Licensure Intermediate care. *Beds* ICF 60. *Certified* Medicaid.

Heritage Manor of Ferriday
PO Box 392, Hwy 65 N, Ferriday, LA 71334
(318) 757-8671
Admin Tommy L Massey.
Licensure Intermediate care. *Beds* ICF 120. *Certified* Medicaid.
Owner Proprietary corp (National Heritage).

Franklin

Franklin Nursing Home
1907 Chinaberry St, Franklin, LA 70538
(318) 828-1918
Admin Ben Rawls.
Licensure Intermediate care. *Beds* ICF 120. *Certified* Medicaid.

Franklinton

Good Samaritans Nursing Home Inc
605 Hilltop Ave, Franklinton, LA 70438
(504) 839-6706

Admin Reuben Cornist.
Beds 78.

Heritage Manor of Franklinton
PO Box 568, Hwy 16, Franklinton, LA 70438
(504) 839-4491
Admin Harold Smith. *Dir of Nursing* Charlotte Sheridan RN. *Medical Dir* Dr Gerald Foret.
Licensure Intermediate care; Alzheimer's care. *Beds* ICF 121. *Private Pay Patients* 20%. *Certified* Medicaid; Medicare.
Owner Proprietary corp (National Heritage).
Admissions Requirements Medical examination.
Staff Physicians 6 (ft); RNs 1 (ft); LPNs 14 (ft); Nurses' aides 60 (ft); Physical therapists 2 (ft); Recreational therapists 1 (ft); Occupational therapists 1 (ft); Speech therapists 1 (ft); Activities coordinators 1 (ft); Dietitians 1 (ft); Ophthalmologists 3 (ft); Podiatrists 1 (ft); Audiologists 1 (ft).
Facilities Dining room; Activities room; Crafts room; Laundry room; Barber/Beauty shop; Library.
Activities Arts & crafts; Cards; Games; Reading groups; Prayer groups; Movies; Shopping trips; Dances/Social/Cultural gatherings; Intergenerational programs; Pet therapy; Art classes.

Riverside Medical Center
PO Box 528, Franklinton, LA 70438
(504) 839-4431
Admin James E Cathey Jr.
Licensure Skilled care; Intermediate care.

Galliano

Lady of the Sea General Hospital
PO Box 68, Galliano, LA 70354
(504) 632-6401
Admin Barney Falgout.
Licensure Skilled care; Intermediate care. *Beds* Swing beds SNF/ICF 78.

Gonzales

Acadian Nursing Home
711 W Cornerview Rd, Gonzales, LA 70737
(504) 644-6581
Admin Robert Rotolo.
Licensure Intermediate care. *Beds* ICF 102. *Certified* Medicaid.

Heritage Manor of Gonzales
905 W Cornerview Rd, Gonzales, LA 70737
(504) 644-5358
Admin Ollie Hymel.
Licensure Intermediate care. *Beds* ICF 124. *Certified* Medicaid.
Owner Proprietary corp (National Heritage).

Riverview Skilled Nursing Facility
1125 Hwy 30 W, Gonzales, LA 70737
(504) 647-5000
Admin N Phillip Bennett.
Licensure Skilled care. *Beds* SNF 8.

Greensburg

St Helena Parish Hospital
PO Box 337, 100 Kendrick St, Greensburg, LA 70441

St Helena Parish Nursing Home
PO Box 700, Hwy 43, Greensburg, LA 70441
(504) 222-4102
Admin Jean-Paul LeJeune.
Beds 72.

Gretna

Meadowcrest Living Center
535 Commerce St, Gretna, LA 70053
(504) 393-9595
Admin Schober Roberts.

Beds 167.
Owner Proprietary corp (ARA Living Centers).

Hammond

Audubon Living Center
1300 Derek Dr, Hammond, LA 70401
(504) 542-8570
Admin Ann Dittlinger.
Beds 120.

Belle Maison Nursing Home
301 7th Ward Medical Plaza, Hammond, LA 70401
(504) 542-0110
Admin E P Guitreau Jr.
Medical Dir Collins P Lipcomb MD.
Licensure Intermediate care. *Beds* ICF 181. *Certified* Medicaid.
Admissions Requirements Medical examination.
Staff Physicians; RNs 3 (ft); LPNs 10 (ft); Nurses' aides 65 (ft); Physical therapists; Reality therapists; Recreational therapists 1 (ft); Speech therapists; Activities coordinators 1 (ft); Dietitians; Podiatrists.
Facilities Dining room; Physical therapy room; Activities room; Chapel; Crafts room; Laundry room; Barber/Beauty shop; Library.
Activities Arts & crafts; Cards; Games; Reading groups; Prayer groups; Movies; Dances/Social/Cultural gatherings.

Hammond Nursing Home
501 Old Covington Hwy, Hammond, LA 70403
(504) 542-1200
Admin Ray A Naquin. *Dir of Nursing* Fay White. *Medical Dir* Merlin Allen.
Licensure Intermediate care. *Beds* ICF 120. *Private Pay Patients* 30%. *Certified* Medicaid.
Owner Proprietary corp.
Admissions Requirements Medical examination; Physician's request.
Staff RNs 1 (ft); LPNs 9 (ft), 1 (pt); Nurses' aides 41 (ft), 6 (pt); Activities coordinators 1 (ft).
Facilities Dining room; Activities room; Crafts room; Laundry room; Barber/Beauty shop.
Activities Arts & crafts; Cards; Games; Reading groups; Prayer groups; Movies; Shopping trips; Dances/Social/Cultural gatherings; Intergenerational programs; Pet therapy.

Hammond State School
Rte 3 Box 165-P, Hammond, LA 70401
(504) 567-3111
Admin Austin H Glass.
Licensure Intermediate care for mentally retarded. *Beds* 750. *Certified* Medicaid.

Heritage Manor of Hammond
800 S Oak St, Hammond, LA 70401
(504) 345-2226
Admin Mike Wunnenberg.
Licensure Intermediate care. *Beds* ICF 108. *Certified* Medicaid.
Owner Proprietary corp (National Heritage).

Seventh Ward General Hospital—Skilled Nursing Facility
PO Box 2668, Hammond, LA 70443
(504) 345-2700, 549-4171 FAX
Admin James Cathey. *Dir of Nursing* Paula Hymel. *Medical Dir* Merlin Allen.
Licensure Skilled care. *Beds* SNF 26. *Private Pay Patients* 0%. *Certified* Medicare.
Owner Nonprofit corp.
Admissions Requirements Physician's request.
Staff Physicians 70 (ft), 37 (pt); RNs 3 (ft), 2 (pt); LPNs 7 (ft), 6 (pt); Nurses' aides 5 (ft), 4 (pt); Physical therapists 4 (ft);

Occupational therapists 1 (ft); Speech therapists 1 (pt); Activities coordinators 1 (ft); Dietitians 3 (ft), 1 (pt).
Facilities Activities room.

Westpark Community Hospital—Skilled Nursing Facility
1900 S Morrison Blvd, Hammond, LA 70403
(504) 542-7777
Admin Roy E Nichols.
Licensure Skilled care.

Harahan

Healthsouth Rehabilitation Center of New Orleans
405 Folse St, Harahan, LA 70123
(504) 737-8982
Admin Anthony Tanner.
Beds 80.

Harrisonburg

Harrisonburg Nursing Center
PO Box 307, Sicily St, Harrisonburg, LA 71340
(318) 744-5954
Admin Beth Willis.
Licensure Intermediate care. *Beds* ICF 104.
Certified Medicaid.

Harvey

Acadian Oaks Living Center
1020 Manhattan Blvd, Harvey, LA 70058
(504) 362-2020
Admin Ken Pitts.
Medical Dir David Euans.
Licensure Skilled care; Intermediate care. *Beds* 104. *Certified* Medicaid; Medicare.
Owner Proprietary corp (ARA Living Centers).
Admissions Requirements Medical examination; Physician's request.
Staff RNs 2 (ft); LPNs 12 (ft), 4 (pt); Nurses' aides 35 (ft); Physical therapists 1 (pt); Speech therapists 1 (pt); Activities coordinators 1 (pt); Dietitians 1 (pt); Podiatrists 1 (pt); Dentists 1 (pt).
Facilities Dining room; Activities room; Barber/Beauty shop.
Activities Arts & crafts; Cards; Games; Reading groups; Prayer groups.

Manhattan Manor Guest House
2233 8th St, Harvey, LA 70058
(504) 362-9522
Admin Ken Pitts.
Medical Dir Nancy Hembree.
Licensure Intermediate care; Alzheimer's care. *Beds* ICF 100. *Certified* Medicaid.
Owner Proprietary corp (ARA Living Centers).
Staff Physicians 1 (pt); RNs 1 (ft); LPNs 10 (ft); Nurses' aides 50 (ft); Physical therapists 1 (pt); Speech therapists 1 (pt); Activities coordinators 1 (ft); Dietitians 1 (pt); Ophthalmologists 1 (pt); Dentists 1 (pt).
Languages French, German.
Facilities Dining room; Activities room; Crafts room; Laundry room; Barber/Beauty shop.
Activities Arts & crafts; Cards; Games; Reading groups; Prayer groups; Movies; Shopping trips; Dances/Social/Cultural gatherings.

Haynesville

Heritage Nursing Center
112-114 Bailey St, Haynesville, LA 71038
(318) 624-1166
Admin John L Savagge Jr. *Dir of Nursing* Rhonda Ward. *Medical Dir* Dr E Butler.
Licensure Intermediate care. *Beds* ICF 38.
Certified Medicaid.

Owner Proprietary corp.
Staff RNs 1 (ft); LPNs 5 (ft); Nurses' aides 13 (ft); Activities coordinators 1 (ft); Dietitians 1 (ft).
Facilities Dining room; Activities room; Crafts room; Laundry room; Barber/Beauty shop.
Activities Arts & crafts; Cards; Games; Reading groups; Prayer groups.

North Claiborne Hospital
Hwy 79 S, Haynesville, LA 71038
(318) 624-0441
Admin Helen M Sharp.
Licensure Skilled care; Intermediate care. *Beds* Swing beds SNF/ICF 32.

Hessmer

Hessmer Nursing Home Inc
Rte 1 Box 61, Hessmer, LA 71341
(318) 563-4246
Admin Nell Oliver. *Dir of Nursing* Nathlie Lemoine. *Medical Dir* F P Bordelon Jr MD.
Licensure Intermediate care. *Beds* ICF 92.
Certified Medicaid.
Owner Proprietary corp.
Admissions Requirements Minimum age 18.
Staff RNs 1 (ft); LPNs 7 (ft); Nurses' aides 6 (ft); Activities coordinators; Dietitians.
Languages French.
Facilities Dining room; Activities room; Chapel; Crafts room; Laundry room; Barber/Beauty shop.
Activities Arts & crafts; Cards; Games; Reading groups; Prayer groups; Movies; Shopping trips.

Hineston

Fair Oaks Nursing Home
PO Box 32, Hwy 121, Hineston, LA 71438
(318) 793-2368
Admin Connie Swayze. *Dir of Nursing* Kay Gaskins. *Medical Dir* Dr Roy Harding.
Licensure Intermediate care. *Beds* ICF 66.
Certified Medicaid; Medicare.
Owner Privately owned.
Admissions Requirements Medical examination; Physician's request.
Staff Physicians 1 (pt); RNs 1 (ft); LPNs 4 (ft), 3 (pt); Nurses' aides 19 (ft), 9 (pt); Physical therapists 1 (pt); Dietitians (consultant).
Facilities Dining room; Activities room; Crafts room; Laundry room; Library.
Activities Arts & crafts; Cards; Games; Prayer groups; Movies; Shopping trips.

Homer

Claiborne Manor Nursing Home Inc
PO Box 307, Hwy 79 N, Homer, LA 71040
(318) 927-3586
Admin Bill Copeland.
Beds 138.

Presbyterian Village of Homer Inc
PO Box 149, Minden Hwy, Homer, LA 71040
(318) 927-3352
Admin Robert L McGaha.
Medical Dir Betty Smith.
Licensure Intermediate care. *Beds* ICF 79.
Certified Medicaid.
Admissions Requirements Physician's request.
Staff Physicians 3 (pt); RNs 2 (ft); LPNs 7 (ft); Nurses' aides 20 (ft); Recreational therapists 1 (ft), 1 (pt); Activities coordinators 1 (pt); Dietitians 1 (pt); Dentists 1 (pt).
Affiliation Presbyterian.

Houma

Evangeline Village Nursing Home
400 Monarch Dr, Houma, LA 70360
(504) 876-5692
Admin Reginald Harvey.
Beds 120.

Heritage Manor of Houma
1701 Polk St, Houma, LA 70360
(504) 851-2307
Admin Homer Rodgers.
Beds 120.
Owner Proprietary corp (National Heritage).

Houma Health Care
107 S Hollywood Rd, Houma, LA 70360
(504) 876-3250
Admin Diwana Sanders. *Dir of Nursing* Norma Macks. *Medical Dir* Saul Landry.
Licensure Intermediate care; Alzheimer's care. *Beds* ICF 105. *Private Pay Patients* 15%. *Certified* Medicaid.
Owner Privately owned.
Admissions Requirements Medical examination.
Staff Physicians; RNs 3 (ft); LPNs 6 (pt); Nurses' aides 10 (ft), 20 (pt); Activities coordinators 1 (ft); Dietitians 1 (ft).
Languages French.
Facilities Dining room; Activities room; Chapel; Crafts room; Laundry room; Barber/Beauty shop.
Activities Cards; Games; Prayer groups; Movies; Dances/Social/Cultural gatherings; Intergenerational programs.

Southdown Care Center
1395 W Tunnel Blvd, Houma, LA 70360
(504) 872-4553
Admin Madeline Giroir.
Licensure Intermediate care. *Beds* ICF 198.
Certified Medicaid.

Terrebonne General Medical Center
936 E Main St, Houma, LA 70360
(504) 873-4141
Admin Alex B Smith.

Iota

Southwest Louisiana State School
PO Box 218, Iota, LA 70543
(318) 779-3305, 824-6250
Admin Samuel K McDaniel. *Dir of Nursing* Gale Morgan RN.
Licensure Intermediate care for mentally retarded. *Beds* ICF/MR. *Certified* Medicaid; Medicare.
Owner Publicly owned.
Admissions Requirements Minimum age 5; Medical examination.
Staff Physicians 2 (pt); RNs 3 (ft); LPNs 3 (pt); Physical therapists 2 (pt); Recreational therapists 1 (ft); Occupational therapists 1 (pt); Speech therapists 3 (ft); Activities coordinators 1 (ft); Dietitians 1 (ft); Podiatrists 1 (pt).
Languages French.
Facilities Dining room; Physical therapy room; Activities room; Crafts room; Laundry room; Barber/Beauty shop; Library; Training/therapy room.
Activities Arts & crafts; Cards; Games; Prayer groups; Movies; Shopping trips; Dances/Social/Cultural gatherings; Habilitation training.

Jackson

Louisiana War Veterans Home
PO Box 748, Jackson, LA 70748
(504) 634-5265
Admin J E Donovan. *Dir of Nursing* Barbara Anthony. *Medical Dir* Tomas Alvera.

Licensure Intermediate care; Domiciliary care; Alzheimer's care. *Beds* ICF 187; Domiciliary 50. *Private Pay Patients* 8%. *Certified* VA.
Owner Publicly owned.
Admissions Requirements Medical examination.
Staff Physicians 2 (ft); RNs 9 (ft); LPNs 17 (ft); Nurses' aides; Physical therapists 1 (ft); Recreational therapists 2 (ft); Occupational therapists 1 (ft); Activities coordinators 1 (ft); Dietitians 1 (ft).
Facilities Dining room; Physical therapy room; Activities room; Chapel; Crafts room; Laundry room; Barber/Beauty shop; Library.
Activities Arts & crafts; Cards; Games; Reading groups; Prayer groups; Movies; Shopping trips; Dances/Social/Cultural gatherings; Behavior modification program.

Villa Feliciana Chronic Disease Hospital & Rehabilitation Center
PO Box 438, Jackson, LA 70748
(504) 634-7793
Admin John A London.
Licensure Skilled care; Intermediate care. *Beds* 610. *Certified* Medicaid; Medicare.

Jeanerette

Maison Teche Nursing Center
PO Box 960, Hwy 182 W, Jeanerette, LA 70544
(318) 276-4514
Admin John Winnfield Murphy.
Beds 121.

Jefferson

Jefferson Healthcare Center
2200 Jefferson Hwy, Jefferson, LA 70121
(504) 837-3144
Admin Patrick Foret.
Licensure Intermediate care. *Beds* ICF 288. *Certified* Medicaid.
Owner Proprietary corp (ARA Living Centers).

Ochsner Foundation Hospital—Skilled Nursing Facility
1516 Jefferson Hwy, Jefferson, LA 70121
(504) 838-3555, 837-0977 FAX
Admin Kathleen B Carter RN MSN. *Dir of Nursing* Corliss Dixon RN HN; Linda S Matessino. *Medical Dir* Susan Vogel MD.
Licensure Skilled care. *Beds* SNF 31. *Private Pay Patients* 1%. *Certified* Medicare.
Owner Nonprofit organization/foundation.
Admissions Requirements Minimum age 18; Medical examination; Physician's request.
Staff Physicians 1 (pt); RNs 3 (ft); LPNs 9 (ft), 1 (pt); Nurses' aides 11 (ft); Physical therapists 1 (ft); Recreational therapists; Occupational therapists 1 (ft); Speech therapists 1 (pt); Activities coordinators 1 (ft); Dietitians 1 (pt).
Languages Spanish.
Facilities Dining room; Physical therapy room; Activities room; Laundry room; Barber/Beauty shop; Library.
Activities Arts & crafts; Cards; Games; Prayer groups; Movies.

Jena

Golden Age Nursing Center
PO Drawer 1366, Aimwell Rd, Jena, LA 71342-1366
(318) 992-4175
Admin V Lynn Conn.
Medical Dir Betty Guynes.
Licensure Intermediate care. *Beds* ICF 88. *Certified* Medicaid.
Owner Proprietary corp.
Admissions Requirements Medical examination.
Staff RNs 1 (ft); LPNs; Nurses' aides 22 (ft).

Facilities Dining room; Laundry room; Barber/Beauty shop.
Activities Arts & crafts; Cards; Games; Reading groups; Prayer groups; Movies; Shopping trips; Dances/Social/Cultural gatherings.

La Salle Nursing Home Inc
PO Drawer 1510, Hwy 84 W, Jena, LA 71342
(318) 992-6627
Admin W J Nunnally.
Medical Dir Suzanne Harris.
Licensure Intermediate care. *Beds* ICF 133. *Certified* Medicaid.
Owner Nonprofit corp.
Admissions Requirements Minimum age 18; Medical examination.
Staff Physicians 4 (pt); RNs 3 (ft); LPNs 13 (ft); Nurses' aides 56 (ft), 5 (pt); Activities coordinators 1 (ft); Dietitians 1 (ft).
Facilities Dining room; Activities room; Crafts room; Barber/Beauty shop; Library.
Activities Arts & crafts; Cards; Games; Reading groups; Prayer groups; Movies; Shopping trips; Dances/Social/Cultural gatherings.

LaSalle General Hospital
PO Box 1388, Hwy 84 W, Jena, LA 71342-1388
(318) 992-8231
Admin Mary M Denton.
Licensure Skilled care; Intermediate care. *Beds* SNF 10.

Jennings

Jefferson Davis Nursing Home
PO Box 757, 1338 N Cutting Ave, Jennings, LA 70546
(318) 824-3165
Admin Jeanne P Qualey. *Dir of Nursing* Tamea Robert RN. *Medical Dir* Louis Shirley MD.
Licensure Intermediate care. *Beds* ICF 135. *Certified* Medicaid.
Owner Proprietary corp.
Admissions Requirements Medical examination; Physician's request.
Staff RNs 2 (ft), 1 (pt); LPNs 12 (ft), 2 (pt); Nurses' aides 35 (ft), 18 (pt); Physical therapists 1 (pt); Activities coordinators 1 (ft); Dietitians 1 (pt); Podiatrists 1 (pt).
Languages French.
Facilities Dining room; Physical therapy room; Activities room; Crafts room; Laundry room; Barber/Beauty shop; Library.
Activities Arts & crafts; Cards; Games; Reading groups; Prayer groups; Movies; Shopping trips; Dances/Social/Cultural gatherings; GED classes.

Jennings American Legion Hospital Skilled Nursing Facility
PO Box 1027, 1634 Elton Rd, Jennings, LA 70546
(318) 824-2490
Admin Terry J Terrebonne.
Licensure Skilled care. *Beds* SNF 4.

Jennings Guest House
203 S Louise, Jennings, LA 70546
(318) 824-2466
Admin Jennifer Meyer. *Dir of Nursing* Margaret Duhon.
Licensure Intermediate care. *Beds* ICF 152. *Private Pay Patients* 15%. *Certified* Medicaid.
Owner Proprietary corp (Louisiana Guest House).
Admissions Requirements Medical examination.
Staff RNs; LPNs; Nurses' aides; Activities coordinators.
Languages Cajun, French.

Facilities Dining room; Laundry room; Barber/Beauty shop.
Activities Arts & crafts; Games; Prayer groups; Movies; Dances/Social/Cultural gatherings.

Jonesboro

Carter Nursing Home Inc
503 W Main, Jonesboro, LA 71251
(318) 259-2729
Admin Catherine Walsworth.
Licensure Intermediate care. *Beds* ICF 51. *Certified* Medicaid.

Jackson Manor Nursing Home
PO Box 669, Hwy 167 S, Jonesboro, LA 71251
(318) 259-7386
Admin Charles E Pogue.
Licensure Intermediate care. *Beds* ICF 84. *Certified* Medicaid.

Jackson Parish Hospital
PO Box 685, 600 Beech Springs Rd, Jonesboro, LA 71251
(318) 259-4435
Admin Larry J Ayres.
Licensure Skilled care; Intermediate care.

Wyatt Manor Nursing Home
PO Drawer L, Hwy 505, Jonesboro, LA 71251
(318) 259-2590
Admin Harold L Hickey. *Dir of Nursing* Lyn Branch.
Licensure Intermediate care. *Beds* ICF 62. *Private Pay Patients* 5%. *Certified* Medicaid; Medicare.
Owner Proprietary corp.
Admissions Requirements Minimum age 25; Medical examination.
Staff Physicians 2 (ft), 62 (pt); RNs 1 (ft), 62 (pt); LPNs 6 (ft); Nurses' aides 19 (ft); Activities coordinators 1 (ft); Dietitians 1 (ft).
Facilities Dining room; Activities room; Crafts room; Laundry room.
Activities Arts & crafts; Cards; Games; Reading groups; Prayer groups; Movies; Shopping trips; Dances/Social/Cultural gatherings.

Kaplan

Heritage Manor of Kaplan
1300 W 8th St, Kaplan, LA 70548
(318) 643-7302
Admin Barbara B Hair. *Dir of Nursing* Cheryl Gaspard. *Medical Dir* George P Des Ormeaux.
Licensure Intermediate care. *Beds* ICF 120. *Private Pay Patients* 14%. *Certified* Medicaid.
Owner Proprietary corp (National Heritage).
Admissions Requirements Medical examination.
Staff RNs 1 (ft); LPNs 13 (ft), 2 (pt); Nurses' aides 40 (ft); Activities coordinators 1 (ft); Dietitians 1 (pt).
Languages French.
Facilities Dining room; Chapel; Laundry room; Barber/Beauty shop.
Activities Arts & crafts; Cards; Games; Prayer groups; Movies; Shopping trips; Dances/Social/Cultural gatherings; Intergenerational programs; Care ring program.

Abrom Kaplan Memorial Hospital
1310 W 7th St, Kaplan, LA 70548
(318) 643-8300
Admin Maxie Borne.
Licensure Skilled care; Intermediate care.

Vermilion Health Care Center
Rte 2 Box 100, Kaplan, LA 70548
(318) 643-1949
Admin Al Breaux Jr. *Dir of Nursing* Darlene Deshotels sRN. *Medical Dir* Dr George Desormeaux.

Licensure Intermediate care. *Beds* ICF 120.
Certified Medicaid.
Owner Privately owned.
Admissions Requirements Physician's request.
Staff RNs 1 (ft); LPNs 10 (pt); Nurses' aides
35 (ft), 4 (pt); Activities coordinators 1 (ft).
Languages French.
Facilities Dining room; Activities room;
Chapel; Crafts room; Barber/Beauty shop.
Activities Arts & crafts; Cards; Games;
Reading groups; Prayer groups; Movies;
Shopping trips; Dances/Social/Cultural
gatherings.

Kenner

Chateau Living Center
716 Village Rd, Kenner, LA 70065
(504) 464-0604
Admin John Silliter.
Beds 300.
Owner Proprietary corp (ARA Living
Centers).

St Jude Skilled Nursing Facility
180 W Esplanade Ave, Kenner, LA 70065
(504) 464-8085
Admin John W McDaniel.
Licensure Skilled care. *Beds* SNF 12.

Waldon Health Care Center
2401 Idaho St, Kenner, LA 70062
(504) 466-0222
Admin Greg Tortorich. *Dir of Nursing* JoAnn
Trader. *Medical Dir* Dr Deabate.
Licensure Skilled care; Intermediate care. *Beds*
SNF 40; Swing beds SNF/ICF 165. *Private
Pay Patients* 10%. *Certified* Medicaid;
Medicare.
Owner Proprietary corp (ARA Living
Centers).
Admissions Requirements Medical
examination; Physician's request.
Staff RNs 5 (ft), 5 (pt); LPNs 15 (ft), 7 (pt);
Nurses' aides 60 (ft); Activities coordinators
1 (ft); Dietitians.
Facilities Dining room; Activities room;
Crafts room; Laundry room; Barber/Beauty
shop; Arthritis care; Wanderer security
system; Courtyard; 2 TV rooms.
Activities Arts & crafts; Cards; Games;
Reading groups; Prayer groups; Movies;
Shopping trips; Dances/Social/Cultural
gatherings; Intergenerational programs; Pet
therapy.

Kentwood

Kentwood Manor Nursing Home Inc
PO Box 67, Hwy 38 W, Kentwood, LA 70444
(504) 229-2112
Admin Willie Murl Rogers.
Licensure Intermediate care; Alzheimer's care.
Beds ICF 134. *Certified* Medicaid;
Medicare.
Owner Proprietary corp.
Admissions Requirements Medical
examination.
Staff Physicians; RNs; LPNs; Nurses' aides;
Physical therapists; Reality therapists;
Recreational therapists; Speech therapists;
Activities coordinators; Dietitians;
Ophthalmologists; Podiatrists; Dentists.
Facilities Dining room; Physical therapy
room; Activities room; Laundry room;
Barber/Beauty shop.
Activities Arts & crafts; Games; Prayer groups;
Movies; Shopping trips; Dances/Social/
Cultural gatherings.

Kinder

Allen Parish Hospital
Hwy 190 W, Kinder, LA 70648
(318) 738-2527
Admin Joseph Darbonne Jr.

Licensure Skilled care; Intermediate care. *Beds*
Swing beds SNF/ICF 39.

Kinder Nursing Home
PO Box 1270, Hwy 165 N, Kinder, LA 70698
(318) 738-5671
Admin Ronald Smith.
Licensure Intermediate care. *Beds* ICF 100.
Certified Medicaid.
Admissions Requirements Minimum age 30;
Medical examination; Physician's request.
Staff RNs 1 (ft), 1 (pt); LPNs 8 (ft), 2 (pt);
Nurses' aides 25 (ft), 8 (pt); Activities
coordinators 1 (ft); Dietitians 1 (pt).
Facilities Dining room; Activities room;
Laundry room; Barber/Beauty shop.
Activities Arts & crafts; Games; Prayer groups;
Movies.

Lafayette

Acadiana Nursing Home
408 SE Evangeline Thruway, Lafayette, LA
70501
(318) 235-9976
Admin Guy Sarver. *Dir of Nursing* Irene
Tilbury.
Licensure Intermediate care. *Beds* ICF 92.
Certified Medicaid.
Owner Privately owned.
Staff Physicians 1 (ft); RNs 1 (ft); LPNs 6 (ft);
Nurses' aides 35 (ft); Physical therapists 2
(ft); Speech therapists 1 (ft); Activities
coordinators 1 (ft); Dietitians 1 (ft).
Languages French.
Facilities Dining room; Activities room;
Chapel; Laundry room; Barber/Beauty shop;
Library.
Activities Arts & crafts; Cards; Games;
Reading groups; Prayer groups; Movies;
Shopping trips; Dances/Social/Cultural
gatherings.

Amelia Manor Nursing Home Inc
903 Center St, Lafayette, LA 70501
(318) 234-7331
Admin J B Sarver. *Dir of Nursing* Debra
Goodly RN. *Medical Dir* Lonn Guidry MD.
Licensure Intermediate care; Alzheimer's care.
Beds ICF 150. *Private Pay Patients* 10%.
Certified Medicaid.
Owner Proprietary corp.
Admissions Requirements Minimum age 40;
Medical examination.
Staff Physicians 6 (pt); RNs 1 (ft); LPNs 10
(ft), 3 (pt); Nurses' aides 50 (ft), 8 (pt);
Physical therapists 1 (pt); Recreational
therapists 1 (ft); Occupational therapists 1
(pt); Speech therapists 1 (pt); Activities
coordinators 1 (ft); Dietitians 1 (pt).
Languages French.
Facilities Dining room; Laundry room;
Barber/Beauty shop.
Activities Arts & crafts; Games; Movies;
Intergenerational programs.

Bethany MHS Health Care Center
PO Box 2308, 406 Saint Julien St, Lafayette,
LA 70502
(318) 234-2459
Admin Ken Cormier. *Dir of Nursing* Donna B
Gardiner LPN. *Medical Dir* Dr Zerben
Bienvenu.
Licensure Intermediate care; Retirement;
Alzheimer's care. *Beds* ICF 42; Retirement
5. *Certified* Medicaid.
Owner Nonprofit organization/foundation.
Admissions Requirements Females only;
Medical examination; Physician's request.
Staff Physicians 7 (pt); LPNs 4 (ft), 3 (pt);
Nurses' aides 8 (ft), 9 (pt); Activities
coordinators 1 (pt); Dietitians 1 (ft), 1 (pt);
Chaplains.
Languages French.
Affiliation Roman Catholic.

Facilities Dining room; Activities room;
Chapel; Crafts room; Laundry room; Barber/
Beauty shop; Grounds with benches and
swings.
Activities Arts & crafts; Cards; Games;
Reading groups; Prayer groups; Movies;
Shopping trips; Dances/Social/Cultural
gatherings; Intergenerational programs;
Religious services.

Cornerstone Village Infirmary
308 Sideny Martin Rd, Lafayette, LA 70507
(318) 237-3040
Beds 73.

Hamilton Medical Center Hospital—Skilled Nursing Facility
2810 Ambassador Caffery Pkwy, Lafayette, LA
70506
(318) 981-2949
Admin John E Smithhisler.
Licensure Skilled care. *Beds* SNF 13.

Heritage Manor Lafayette
325 Bacque Crescent Dr, Lafayette, LA 70501
(318) 232-0299
Admin Hollie K Owens.
Licensure Intermediate care. *Beds* ICF 60.
Certified Medicaid.
Owner Proprietary corp (National Heritage).
Admissions Requirements Medical
examination.
Staff Physicians 1 (pt); RNs 1 (ft); LPNs 7
(ft), 2 (pt); Nurses' aides 20 (ft), 3 (pt);
Physical therapists 1 (pt); Reality therapists
1 (pt); Recreational therapists 1 (pt);
Occupational therapists 1 (pt); Speech
therapists 1 (pt); Activities coordinators 1
(ft); Dietitians 1 (pt); Podiatrists 1 (pt);
Audiologists 1 (pt); Dentists 1 (pt).
Facilities Dining room; Activities room;
Laundry room; Barber/Beauty shop.
Activities Arts & crafts; Cards; Games;
Reading groups; Prayer groups; Movies;
Shopping trips; Dances/Social/Cultural
gatherings.

Lady of the Oaks Nursing Home
1005 Landry Rd, Lafayette, LA 70503
(318) 232-6370
Admin William Friedman. *Dir of Nursing*
Anita Conner RN.
Licensure Intermediate care. *Beds* ICF 101.
Certified Medicaid.
Admissions Requirements Medical
examination; Physician's request.
Staff RNs 1 (ft); LPNs 4 (ft), 5 (pt); Nurses'
aides 18 (ft), 10 (pt); Physical therapists 1
(pt); Speech therapists 1 (pt); Activities
coordinators 1 (ft); Dietitians 1 (pt).
Facilities Dining room; Activities room;
Crafts room; Laundry room; Barber/Beauty
shop; Solarium.
Activities Arts & crafts; Cards; Games;
Reading groups; Prayer groups; Movies;
Dances/Social/Cultural gatherings.

Lafayette General Medical Center Skilled Nursing Facility
1214 Coolidge Ave, Lafayette, LA 70505
(318) 261-7381
Admin James Michael Ramsay.
Licensure Skilled care.

Lafayette Guest House—East
811 Martin Luther King Jr Dr, Lafayette, LA
70501
(318) 233-2375
Admin Bill Copeland. *Dir of Nursing* Debra
Goodly. *Medical Dir* Dr Donald Reed.
Licensure Intermediate care. *Beds* ICF 130.
Certified Medicaid.
Owner Proprietary corp (US Care Corp).
Admissions Requirements Minimum age 18.
Staff RNs; LPNs; Nurses' aides; Physical
therapists; Reality therapists; Recreational
therapists; Occupational therapists; Speech
therapists; Activities coordinators; Dietitians;
Dentists.

Languages Creole, French.
Facilities Dining room; Activities room; Chapel; Laundry room; Barber/Beauty shop.
Activities Arts & crafts; Cards; Games; Movies; Shopping trips; Dances/Social/ Cultural gatherings.

Lafayette Guest House—West
809 Martin Luther King Jr Dr, Lafayette, LA 70501
(318) 233-6855
Admin Mark Stutes.
Medical Dir Dr Charles Dugal.
Licensure Intermediate care. *Beds* ICF 206. *Certified* Medicaid.
Owner Proprietary corp (US Care Corp).
Admissions Requirements Physician's request.
Staff Physicians 1 (ft); RNs 1 (ft), 1 (pt); LPNs 16 (ft); Nurses' aides 21 (ft); Physical therapists; Reality therapists; Dietitians 1 (pt); Ophthalmologists 1 (pt); Podiatrists 1 (pt); Audiologists 1 (pt); Dentists 1 (pt).

Oakwood Village Nurse Care Center
2500 E Simcoe St, Lafayette, LA 70501
(318) 233-7115
Admin Gordon Doine.
Medical Dir Kearney Veazey.
Licensure Intermediate care. *Beds* ICF 160. *Certified* Medicaid.
Owner Proprietary corp.
Admissions Requirements Minimum age 18; Medical examination; Physician's request.
Staff RNs 1 (ft); LPNs 10 (ft), 9 (pt); Nurses' aides 42 (ft), 11 (pt); Recreational therapists 1 (ft); Activities coordinators 1 (ft), 1 (pt); Dietitians 1 (pt); Social service director 1 (ft).
Languages French, Arabic.
Facilities Dining room; Laundry room; Barber/Beauty shop; Library; Living room-Activities room-Chapel; Movie theater.
Activities Arts & crafts; Cards; Games; Reading groups; Prayer groups; Movies; Dances/Social/Cultural gatherings; Monthly birthday parties.

Our Lady of Lourdes Regional Medical Center—Skilled Nursing Facility
611 Saint Landry St, Lafayette, LA 70506
(318) 231-2100
Admin Dudley Romero.
Licensure Skilled care. *Beds* SNF 25.

Lake Charles

Lake Charles Care Center
2701 Ernest St, Lake Charles, LA 70601
(318) 439-0336
Admin Jane Grimes.
Beds 136.
Owner Proprietary corp (Hillhaven Corp).

Martin dePorres Nursing Home Inc
200 Teal St, Lake Charles, LA 70602
(318) 439-5761
Admin Robert Leonards.
Licensure Intermediate care. *Beds* ICF 249. *Certified* Medicaid.
Affiliation Roman Catholic.

Moss Bluff Manor
Rte 1 Box 1310, Lake Charles, LA 70601
(318) 436-9527
Admin Frederick Doine. *Dir of Nursing* Mary Guillory. *Medical Dir* Dr Charles Fellows.
Licensure Intermediate care. *Beds* ICF 92. *Private Pay Patients* 10%. *Certified* Medicaid.
Owner Proprietary corp (Geriatrics Inc).
Admissions Requirements Physician's request.
Staff RNs; LPNs; Nurses' aides; Physical therapists; Reality therapists; Recreational therapists; Occupational therapists; Speech therapists; Activities coordinators; Dietitians; Ophthalmologists; Podiatrists; Audiologists.

Facilities Dining room; Activities room; Crafts room; Laundry room; Barber/Beauty shop.
Activities Arts & crafts; Cards; Games; Prayer groups; Movies; Dances/Social/Cultural gatherings; Intergenerational programs.

Oak Park Care Center
2717 1st Ave, Lake Charles, LA 70601
(318) 478-2920
Admin Muriel L Bates. *Dir of Nursing* Rosemary Stambaugh. *Medical Dir* Gerald Mouton; John Digelia.
Licensure Intermediate care; Alzheimer's care. *Beds* ICF 177. *Private Pay Patients* 35%. *Certified* Medicaid.
Owner Nonprofit organization/foundation.
Staff RNs 2 (ft); LPNs 15 (ft), 2 (pt); Nurses' aides 75 (ft), 10 (pt); Physical therapists 1 (pt); Activities coordinators 2 (ft); Dietitians 1 (pt).
Languages French.
Affiliation Assembly of God.
Activities Arts & crafts; Cards; Games; Reading groups; Prayer groups; Movies; Shopping trips; Dances/Social/Cultural gatherings; Intergenerational programs; Pet therapy.

Resthaven Nursing Center
4532 Sale Ln, Lake Charles, LA 70605
(318) 477-6371
Admin Sereitha M McGee.
Medical Dir Alecia Shatluck.
Licensure Intermediate care. *Beds* ICF 160. *Certified* Medicaid.
Owner Proprietary corp.
Admissions Requirements Medical examination; Physician's request.
Staff Physicians 1 (pt); RNs 1 (ft); LPNs 8 (ft); Nurses' aides 45 (ft); Physical therapists 1 (pt); Occupational therapists 1 (pt); Speech therapists 1 (pt); Activities coordinators 1 (ft); Dietitians 1 (pt).
Languages French.
Facilities Dining room; Activities room; Laundry room; Barber/Beauty shop.
Activities Games; Prayer groups; Movies; Shopping trips; Dances/Social/Cultural gatherings.

Robinswood School
200 Ave C, Lake Charles, LA 70601
(318) 436-6664
Admin Gordon Propst. *Dir of Nursing* Toni Schell RN. *Medical Dir* Melvin Morris MD.
Licensure Intermediate care for mentally retarded. *Beds* ICF/MR 120. *Certified* Medicaid.
Owner Proprietary corp (Multicare Management).
Admissions Requirements Minimum age 18; Medical examination.
Languages Creole.
Facilities Dining room; Physical therapy room; Activities room; Crafts room; Laundry room; Barber/Beauty shop; Library; Gym; Classrooms; OT.
Activities Arts & crafts; Cards; Games; Reading groups; Prayer groups; Movies; Shopping trips; Dances/Social/Cultural gatherings; Community activities.

Rosewood Nursing Center Inc
543 15th St, Lake Charles, LA 70601
(318) 439-8338
Admin Louis Charles.
Licensure Intermediate care. *Beds* ICF 129. *Certified* Medicaid.

Lake Providence

East Carroll Care Center Inc
Rte 2 Box 73, Lake Providence, LA 71254
(318) 559-4050
Admin Glenn Tanner.
Beds 122.

Shady Lake Nursing Home
Box 426, Mill St, Lake Providence, LA 71254
(318) 559-2248
Admin Don Temple.
Medical Dir Virginia Ratcliff.
Licensure Intermediate care. *Beds* ICF 100. *Certified* Medicaid.
Staff RNs 1 (ft); LPNs 8 (ft); Nurses' aides 22 (ft); Activities coordinators 1 (ft); Dietitians 1 (ft).
Facilities Dining room; Physical therapy room; Activities room; Laundry room; Barber/Beauty shop.
Activities Arts & crafts; Cards; Games; Prayer groups; Movies; Shopping trips; Dances/ Social/Cultural gatherings.

LaPlace

Twin Oaks Nursing & Convalescent Home
1881 W 5th St, LaPlace, LA 70068
(504) 652-9538
Admin Janet Beaman.
Medical Dir S J St Martin MD.
Licensure Intermediate care. *Beds* 152. *Certified* Medicaid.
Admissions Requirements Medical examination; Physician's request.
Staff Physicians 1 (pt); RNs 1 (ft); LPNs 15 (ft); Nurses' aides 45 (ft); Physical therapists 1 (pt); Activities coordinators 1 (ft); Dietitians 1 (pt); Podiatrists 1 (pt); Dentists 1 (pt).
Facilities Dining room; Activities room; Barber/Beauty shop.
Activities Arts & crafts; Games; Dances/Social/Cultural gatherings.

Leesville

Byrd Memorial Hospital
1020 Feritta Blvd, Leesville, LA 71446
(318) 239-9041
Admin Greg Griffith.
Licensure Skilled care; Intermediate care. *Beds* Swing beds SNF/ICF 70.

Kurthwood Manor Nursing Home
PO Box 270, Kurthwood Rd, Leesville, LA 71446
(318) 239-6578
Admin Geneva Laughlin.
Licensure Intermediate care. *Beds* ICF 142. *Certified* Medicaid.

Leesville State School
401 W Texas St, Leesville, LA 71446
(318) 239-2687
Admin Joseph Martinez.
Licensure Intermediate care for mentally retarded. *Beds* 96. *Certified* Medicaid.

Pine Haven Nursing Home Inc
Rte 2 Box 145, Hawks Rd, Leesville, LA 71446
(318) 463-8778
Admin Charles Allen.
Licensure Intermediate care. *Beds* ICF 52. *Certified* Medicaid.

Luling

St Charles Hospital
PO Box 87, Paul Mallard Rd, Luling, LA 70070
(504) 785-6242
Admin Fred Martinez.
Licensure Skilled care; Intermediate care. *Beds* Swing beds SNF/ICF 50.

St Charles Manor Nursing Center Inc
PO Box 1098, 1108 Paul Maillard Rd, Luling, LA 70070
(504) 785-8271
Admin Diane Gaston.
Medical Dir Irene Ham.

Licensure Intermediate care. *Beds* ICF 189.
Certified Medicaid.
Admissions Requirements Medical
examination; Physician's request.
Staff Physicians 1 (pt); RNs 2 (ft), 3 (pt);
LPNs 10 (ft); Nurses' aides 37 (ft), 13 (pt);
Activities coordinators 1 (ft).
Facilities Dining room; Laundry room;
Barber/Beauty shop.
Activities Arts & crafts; Cards; Games; Prayer
groups; Movies; Dances/Social/Cultural
gatherings.

Lutcher

Riverlands Health Care Center
PO Drawer CC, 720 River Rd, Lutcher, LA
70071
(504) 869-5725
Admin Sam E Narrow Jr.
Licensure Intermediate care. *Beds* ICF 128.
Certified Medicaid.

St James Parish Hospital
PO Box 430, 2471 Louisiana Ave, Lutcher,
70071
(504) 869-5512, 869-4956 FAX
Admin Harry St Pierre Jr. *Dir of Nursing*
Joan Murray RN.
Licensure Skilled care. *Beds* SNF 10.
Owner Publicly owned.
Staff RNs; LPNs; Nurses' aides; Physical
therapists; Dietitians.

Mamou

Savoy Care Center Inc
801 Poinciana Ave, Mamou, LA 70554
(318) 468-0348
Admin Frank P Savoy III. *Dir of Nursing*
Laurelle Fuselier RN.
Licensure Intermediate care. *Beds* ICF 98.
Certified Medicaid.
Owner Nonprofit organization/foundation.
Admissions Requirements Medical
examination.
Staff Physicians; RNs; LPNs; Nurses' aides;
Physical therapists; Occupational therapists;
Speech therapists; Activities coordinators;
Dietitians.
Languages French.
Facilities Dining room; Activities room;
Chapel; Crafts room; Laundry room; Barber/
Beauty shop.
Activities Arts & crafts; Cards; Games; Prayer
groups; Movies; Shopping trips; Dances/
Social/Cultural gatherings.

Savoy Medical Center Skilled Nursing Unit
801 Poinciana Ave, Mamou, LA 70554
(318) 468-5261
Admin J E Richardson.
Licensure Skilled care. *Beds* SNF 32.

Mandeville

Pontchartrain Guest House
PO Box 338, Hwy 190 & Atlin, Mandeville,
LA 70448
(504) 626-8581
Admin Ronald A Goux.
Medical Dir Karen Jones.
Licensure Intermediate care; Alzheimer's care.
Beds ICF 182. *Certified* Medicaid;
Medicare.
Owner Privately owned.
Admissions Requirements Medical
examination.
Staff RNs 1 (ft); LPNs 8 (ft), 2 (pt); Nurses'
aides 35 (ft); Activities coordinators 2 (ft);
Dietitians 1 (ft).
Facilities Dining room; Activities room;
Chapel; Crafts room; Laundry room; Barber/
Beauty shop.

Activities Arts & crafts; Cards; Games;
Reading groups; Prayer groups; Movies;
Shopping trips; Dances/Social/Cultural
gatherings.

Mansfield

DeSoto General Hospital
PO Box 672, 207 Jefferson St, Mansfield, LA
71052
(318) 872-4610
Admin Robert Taylor.
Licensure Skilled care; Intermediate care. *Beds*
Swing beds SNF/ICF 60.

Heritage Manor of Mansfield
102 E Schley St, Mansfield, LA 71052
(318) 872-3733
Admin Richard Valentine.
Licensure Intermediate care. *Beds* ICF 135.
Certified Medicaid.
Owner Proprietary corp (National Heritage).

Mansura

Rio Sol Nursing Home Inc
PO Box 85, Prevot & Zylenne Sts, Mansura,
LA 71350
(318) 964-2198
Admin Dorothy S Roy.
Licensure Intermediate care. *Beds* ICF 92.
Certified Medicaid.

Many

Heritage Manor of Many No 1
PO Box 360, Natchitoches Hwy, Many, LA
71449
(318) 256-9233
Admin Edwin E Teal. *Dir of Nursing* Doris
Everett. *Medical Dir* Dr Gregory P Founds.
Licensure Intermediate care. *Beds* ICF 128.
Private Pay Patients 18%. *Certified*
Medicaid.
Owner Proprietary corp (National Heritage).
Admissions Requirements Medical
examination; Physician's request.
Staff Physicians; RNs 2 (ft); LPNs 10 (ft);
Nurses' aides 45 (ft); Physical therapists
(contracted); Activities coordinators 1 (ft);
Dietitians.
Facilities Dining room; Activities room;
Chapel; Crafts room; Laundry room; Barber/
Beauty shop.
Activities Arts & crafts; Cards; Games;
Reading groups; Prayer groups; Movies.

Heritage Manor of Many No 2
PO Box 360, Middle Creek Rd, Many, LA
71449
(318) 256-6281
Admin Judy Procell. *Dir of Nursing* Renee
Blake. *Medical Dir* Greg Founds MD.
Licensure Intermediate care. *Beds* ICF 60.
Certified Medicaid.
Owner Proprietary corp (National Heritage).
Admissions Requirements Medical
examination; Physician's request.
Staff RNs 1 (ft); LPNs 5 (ft), 3 (pt); Nurses'
aides 18 (ft), 3 (pt); Activities coordinators 1
(ft).
Facilities Dining room; Activities room;
Laundry room; Barber/Beauty shop.
Activities Arts & crafts; Games; Prayer groups;
Movies; Shopping trips; Dances/Social/
Cultural gatherings; Religious services;
Resident council; Sunshine club; Care ring.

Marksville

Colonial Nursing Home Inc
413 N Washington St, Marksville, LA 71351
(318) 253-4556
Admin Nell Oliver. *Dir of Nursing* Karen
Barbin RN.

Licensure Intermediate care. *Beds* ICF 104.
Certified Medicaid.
Owner Privately owned.
Admissions Requirements Minimum age 18.
Staff RNs 1 (ft); LPNs 7 (ft); Nurses' aides 25
(ft); Activities coordinators 1 (ft); Dietitians
1 (pt).
Languages French.
Facilities Dining room; Activities room;
Chapel; Crafts room; Laundry room; Barber/
Beauty shop.
Activities Arts & crafts; Cards; Games;
Reading groups; Prayer groups; Movies;
Shopping trips; Dances/Social/Cultural
gatherings.

Humana Hospital Marksville
PO Box 255, Hwy 107, Marksville, LA 71351
(318) 253-8611
Admin Lloyd Dupuy.
Licensure Skilled care; Intermediate care.

Valley View Health Care Facility
PO Box 535, Mansur Hwy, Marksville, LA
71351
(318) 253-6553
Admin Donna Caubarreaux. *Dir of Nursing*
Rosanne Brochard.
Licensure Intermediate care. *Beds* ICF 100.
Private Pay Patients 8%. *Certified* Medicaid.
Owner Proprietary corp.
Admissions Requirements Medical
examination.
Staff Physicians; RNs; LPNs; Nurses' aides;
Physical therapists; Activities coordinators;
Dietitians.
Facilities Dining room; Activities room;
Laundry room; Barber/Beauty shop.
Activities Arts & crafts; Cards; Games;
Reading groups; Prayer groups; Movies;
Shopping trips; Dances/Social/Cultural
gatherings; Pet therapy.

Marrero

Heritage Manor Marrero
5301 August Ln, Marrero, LA 70072
(504) 341-3658
Admin Vickie Hughes.
Licensure Intermediate care. *Beds* ICF 134.
Certified Medicaid.
Owner Proprietary corp (National Heritage).

Wynhoven Health Care Center
1050 Ave D, Marrero, LA 70072
(504) 347-0777
Admin Sr Joanne Upjohn CSC. *Dir of Nursing*
Audrey Johosky RN. *Medical Dir* Farrell
Nicholson MD.
Licensure Skilled care; Intermediate care. *Beds*
Swing beds SNF/ICF 178. *Private Pay
Patients* 30%. *Certified* Medicaid; Medicare.
Owner Nonprofit corp (Archdiocese of New
Orleans).
Admissions Requirements Medical
examination; Physician's request.
Staff Physicians (visiting); RNs 3 (ft); LPNs
24 (ft); Nurses' aides 51 (ft), 10 (pt);
Physical therapists (contracted);
Occupational therapists (contracted); Speech
therapists (contracted); Activities
coordinators; Dietitians (contracted);
Ophthalmologists (contracted); Podiatrists
(contracted).
Languages French, Spanish.
Facilities Dining room; Physical therapy
room; Activities room; Chapel; Crafts room;
Laundry room; Barber/Beauty shop; Library;
TV room; Patios.
Activities Arts & crafts; Cards; Games;
Reading groups; Prayer groups; Movies;
Dances/Social/Cultural gatherings; Pet
therapy; Children's groups.

Mer Rouge

Oak Woods
PO Box 263, 3802 Davenport Ave, Mer
  Rouge, LA 71261
(318) 647-3691
Admin Ted Parker. *Dir of Nursing* Carolyn
  Costello. *Medical Dir* Dr Joe Williams.
Licensure Skilled care; Intermediate care. *Beds*
  SNF 80; ICF 86. *Certified* Medicaid;
  Medicare.
Owner Nonprofit organization/foundation.
Admissions Requirements Medical
  examination; Physician's request.
Staff Physicians 1 (pt); RNs 1 (ft), 2 (pt);
  LPNs 22 (ft); Nurses' aides 44 (ft); Physical
  therapists 1 (pt); Activities coordinators 1
  (ft); Dietitians 1 (ft).
Facilities Dining room; Physical therapy
  room; Activities room; Chapel; Crafts room;
  Laundry room; Barber/Beauty shop; Library.
Activities Arts & crafts; Cards; Games;
  Reading groups; Prayer groups; Movies;
  Shopping trips; Dances/Social/Cultural
  gatherings.

Merryville

Merryville Nursing Center
PO Drawer C, Bryan St, Merryville, LA 70653
(318) 825-6181
Admin James O Graham.
Licensure Intermediate care. *Beds* ICF 70.
  Certified Medicaid.

Metairie

Austin's Rest Haven Nursing Home
3601 Houma Blvd No 810, Metairie, LA
  70006-4301
(512) 453-6658
Licensure Nursing. *Beds* Nursing 80.

Colonial Oaks Living Center
4312 Ithaca St, Metairie, LA 70006
(504) 887-6414
Admin George Fischer. *Dir of Nursing* Mary
  Garcia. *Medical Dir* Dr Samuel Greenberg.
Licensure Intermediate care; Respite care;
  Alzheimer's care. *Beds* ICF 110. *Private Pay
  Patients* 70%. *Certified* Medicaid.
Owner Proprietary corp (ARA Living
  Centers).
Admissions Requirements Medical
  examination; Physician's request.
Staff Physicians 1 (pt); RNs 3 (ft), 1 (pt);
  LPNs 5 (ft), 5 (pt); Nurses' aides 40 (ft);
  Physical therapists (contracted);
  Occupational therapists 1 (pt); Speech
  therapists 1 (pt); Activities coordinators 1
  (ft); Dietitians 1 (ft); Ophthalmologists 1
  (pt); Podiatrists 1 (pt).
Languages Spanish.
Facilities Dining room; Activities room;
  Crafts room; Laundry room; Barber/Beauty
  shop; Whirlpool; Lounges; Patio; Wanderer
  security system.
Activities Arts & crafts; Cards; Games; Prayer
  groups; Movies; Shopping trips; Dances/
  Social/Cultural gatherings; Intergenerational
  programs; Pet therapy.

**East Jefferson Hospital Skilled Nursing
Facility**
4200 Houma Blvd, Metairie, LA 70011
(504) 456-5000
Admin Peter J Betts.
Licensure Skilled care.

Metairie Health Care Center
6401 Riverside St, Metairie, LA 70003
(504) 885-8611
Admin David Hargrave.
Licensure Intermediate care. *Beds* ICF 202.
  Certified Medicaid.
Owner Proprietary corp (ARA Living
  Centers).

St Anthony's Nursing Home Inc
6001 Airline Hwy, Metairie, LA 70003
(504) 733-8448
Admin John S Morvant Jr.
Medical Dir Joyce Ferrier.
Licensure Intermediate care; Alzheimer's care.
  Beds ICF 124. *Certified* Medicaid.
Owner Proprietary corp.
Admissions Requirements Medical
  examination; Physician's request.
Staff Physicians 4 (ft); RNs 1 (ft); LPNs 10
  (ft), 3 (pt); Nurses' aides 65 (ft), 22 (pt);
  Physical therapists 1 (pt); Activities
  coordinators 1 (ft); Dietitians 1 (ft), 1 (pt);
  Podiatrists 1 (pt).
Languages French, Spanish, Italian.
Facilities Dining room; Activities room;
  Laundry room; Barber/Beauty shop.
Activities Arts & crafts; Cards; Games; Prayer
  groups; Movies; Dances/Social/Cultural
  gatherings.

Minden

Evergreen Manor
PO Drawer 1177, Rte 3, Minden, LA 71055-
  1177
(318) 377-5405
Admin Harold D Knowles. *Dir of Nursing*
  Penny Thomas RN; Laulie Hobbs RN.
Licensure Intermediate care for mentally
  retarded. *Beds* ICF/MR 96. *Certified*
  Medicaid.
Owner Nonprofit corp.
Admissions Requirements Minimum age 15;
  Medical examination.
Staff Physicians 1 (pt); RNs 2 (ft); LPNs 9
  (ft), 2 (pt); Nurses' aides; Physical therapists
  1 (pt); Recreational therapists 1 (ft);
  Occupational therapists 1 (pt); Speech
  therapists 1 (pt); Activities coordinators 1
  (ft); Dietitians 1 (ft); Ophthalmologists 1
  (pt); Podiatrists 1 (pt); Dentists 1 (pt).
Affiliation Presbyterian.
Facilities Dining room; Physical therapy
  room; Activities room; Chapel; Crafts room;
  Laundry room; Barber/Beauty shop; Dental
  clinic.
Activities Arts & crafts; Games; Prayer groups;
  Movies; Shopping trips; Dances/Social/
  Cultural gatherings.

Meadowview Nursing Home
400 Meadowview Rd, Minden, LA 71055
(318) 377-1011
Admin Ruby Edmonds.
Medical Dir Karen Carter.
Licensure Intermediate care. *Beds* ICF 230.
  Certified Medicaid.
Owner Proprietary corp (National Heritage).
Admissions Requirements Minimum age 60;
  Medical examination.
Staff Physicians 1 (pt); RNs 3 (ft); LPNs 17
  (ft), 5 (pt); Nurses' aides 74 (ft), 9 (pt);
  Physical therapists 1 (pt); Occupational
  therapists 1 (pt); Speech therapists 1 (pt);
  Activities coordinators 2 (ft); Dietitians 1
  (ft).
Facilities Dining room; Activities room;
  Chapel; Crafts room; Laundry room; Barber/
  Beauty shop; Atrium.
Activities Arts & crafts; Cards; Games;
  Reading groups; Prayer groups; Movies;
  Shopping trips; Dances/Social/Cultural
  gatherings.

**Minden Medical Center Skilled Nursing
Facility**
1 Medical Plaza, Minden, LA 71055
(318) 377-2321
Admin George E French III.
Licensure Skilled care. *Beds* SNF 16.

Town & Country Nursing Center
PO Box 892, 614 Weston St, Minden, LA
  71058-0892
(318) 377-5145
Admin Walter Ledig.

Licensure Intermediate care. *Beds* 128.
  Certified Medicaid.

Town & Country Nursing Center Inc
PO Box 892, 614 Weston St, Minden, LA
  71058-0892
(318) 377-5145

Monroe

Cottage Healthcare Inc
2700 Georgia St, Monroe, LA 71202
(318) 387-2700
Admin Claudia Winkler. *Dir of Nursing* Betty
  Bishop RN. *Medical Dir* Bruce Wheeler
  MD.
Licensure Intermediate care. *Beds* ICF 94.
  Certified Medicaid.
Admissions Requirements Medical
  examination.
Staff Physicians 1 (ft), 4 (pt); RNs 1 (ft), 2
  (pt); LPNs 10 (ft), 3 (pt); Nurses' aides 20
  (ft), 4 (pt); Physical therapists 1 (ft), 1 (pt);
  Reality therapists 1 (ft); Recreational
  therapists 1 (ft); Occupational therapists 1
  (pt); Speech therapists 1 (pt); Activities
  coordinators 1 (ft), 1 (pt); Dietitians 1 (ft), 1
  (pt); Ophthalmologists 1 (pt); Podiatrists 1
  (pt); Dentists 1 (pt).
Facilities Dining room; Physical therapy
  room; Activities room; Chapel; Crafts room;
  Laundry room.
Activities Arts & crafts; Cards; Games;
  Reading groups; Prayer groups; Movies;
  Shopping trips; Dances/Social/Cultural
  gatherings.

Mary Goss Nursing Home Inc
3300 White St, Monroe, LA 71203
(318) 323-9013
Admin Louise G Tucker.
Licensure Intermediate care. *Beds* ICF 92.
  Certified Medicaid.

Lincoln Park Healthcare Inc
4600 Burg Jones Ln, Monroe, LA 71202
(318) 322-3100
Admin Lisa Dixon.
Licensure Intermediate care. *Beds* ICF 96.
  Certified Medicaid.

Monroe Manor Nursing Center
4201 S Grand, Monroe, LA 71202
(318) 325-8244
Admin Robert M Many.
Licensure Intermediate care. *Beds* ICF 108.
  Certified Medicaid.
Owner Proprietary corp (National Heritage).

North Monroe Healthcare
PO Box 8490, 4385 Old Sterlington Rd,
  Monroe, LA 71211
(318) 322-2000
Admin James C Houston.
Beds 80.

Oaks
1000 McKeen Dr, Monroe, LA 71201
(318) 387-5300
Admin Sherry K Mullin.
Licensure Skilled care. *Beds* SNF 180.
Owner Proprietary corp (Woodlawn Manor
  Inc).

Riverside Nursing Home Inc
PO Bwx 1841, 3001 S Grand, Monroe, LA
  71202-4199
(318) 388-3200
Admin Donnice Reynolds.
Licensure Intermediate care. *Beds* ICF 166.
  Certified Medicaid.
Owner Proprietary corp; Privately owned.
Admissions Requirements Medical
  examination; Physician's request.
Staff Physicians 1 (pt); RNs 1 (ft), 1 (pt);
  LPNs 12 (ft), 3 (pt); Nurses' aides 30 (ft), 12
  (pt); Activities coordinators 2 (ft); Dietitians
  1 (ft).

Facilities Dining room; Physical therapy room; Activities room; Chapel; Crafts room; Laundry room; Barber/Beauty shop.
Activities Arts & crafts; Cards; Games; Reading groups; Prayer groups; Movies; Shopping trips; Dances/Social/Cultural gatherings.

St Francis Medical Center Skilled Nursing Care Unit
PO Box 1901, 309 Jackson St, Monroe, LA 71210-1901
(318) 362-4158
Admin Sr Anne Marie Twohig. *Dir of Nursing* Janice Finley RN. *Medical Dir* Dr Doyle Hamilton.
Licensure Skilled care. *Beds* SNF 27. *Private Pay Patients* 1%. *Certified* Medicare.
Owner Nonprofit organization/foundation (Franciscan Missionaries of Our Lady).
Admissions Requirements Minimum age 18; Medical examination; Physician's request.
Staff RNs 5 (ft), 1 (pt); LPNs 9 (ft); Nurses' aides 10 (ft); Physical therapists 1 (pt); Occupational therapists 1 (pt); Speech therapists 1 (pt); Activities coordinators 1 (pt); Dietitians 1 (pt).
Facilities Dining room; Activities room; Crafts room; Library; Whirlpool room; Private rooms.
Activities Arts & crafts; Cards; Games; Reading groups; Prayer groups; Pet therapy; Music therapy.

St Joseph's Home for Infirm & Aged
2301 Sterlington Rd, Monroe, LA 71211-6057
(318) 323-3426
Admin Joy Anderson.
Medical Dir Symira Cupit.
Licensure Intermediate care. *Beds* ICF 132. *Certified* Medicaid.
Owner Nonprofit corp (Sisters of Charity of the Incarnate Word).
Admissions Requirements Medical examination; Physician's request.
Staff RNs 3 (ft); LPNs 16 (ft), 3 (pt); Nurses' aides 36 (ft), 3 (pt); Activities coordinators 1 (ft).
Affiliation Roman Catholic.
Facilities Dining room; Activities room; Chapel; Crafts room; Laundry room; Barber/Beauty shop.
Activities Arts & crafts; Cards; Games; Reading groups; Prayer groups; Movies; Shopping trips.

Shady Oaks
4310 S Grand St, Monroe, LA 71201
(318) 322-2616
Admin Daniel Mathis. *Dir of Nursing* Caroline Bennett. *Medical Dir* Dr Doyle Hamilton.
Licensure Intermediate care; Alzheimer's care. *Beds* ICF 104. *Private Pay Patients* 5%. *Certified* Medicaid.
Owner Proprietary corp (Affiliated Nursing Homes).
Admissions Requirements Medical examination; Physician's request.
Staff Physicians 10 (pt); RNs 1 (ft); LPNs 7 (ft), 2 (pt); Nurses' aides 19 (ft), 10 (pt); Physical therapists 1 (pt); Reality therapists 1 (pt); Recreational therapists 1 (pt); Occupational therapists 1 (pt); Speech therapists 1 (pt); Activities coordinators 1 (ft); Dietitians 1 (pt); Ophthalmologists 1 (pt); Podiatrists 1 (pt); Audiologists 1 (pt); Dentists 1 (pt).
Facilities Dining room; Activities room; Chapel; Crafts room; Laundry room; Barber/Beauty shop.
Activities Arts & crafts; Cards; Games; Reading groups; Prayer groups; Movies; Shopping trips; Dances/Social/Cultural gatherings; Pet therapy; Alzheimer's family support group.

Morgan City

St Mary Guest Home
PO Box 2563, 740 Justa St, Morgan City, LA 70381
(504) 384-1726
Admin Randall Wilson.
Licensure Intermediate care. *Beds* ICF 87. *Certified* Medicaid.
Owner Proprietary corp (Beverly Enterprises).

Napoleonville

Assumption General Hospital
PO Drawer 546, Whittaker Ln, Napoleonville, LA 70390
(504) 369-7241
Admin Jean Paul LeJeune.
Licensure Skilled care; Intermediate care. *Beds* Swing beds SNF/ICF 34.

Assumption Health Care Center
PO Box 669, Hwy 402, Napoleonville, LA 70390
(504) 369-6011
Admin Barbara A Solar. *Dir of Nursing* Doris Arboneaux. *Medical Dir* Dr Charles Bolotte.
Licensure Skilled care; Intermediate care. *Beds* Swing beds SNF/ICF 186. *Private Pay Patients* 6%. *Certified* Medicaid; Medicare.
Owner Privately owned.
Admissions Requirements Medical examination.
Staff RNs; LPNs; Nurses' aides; Activities coordinators.
Facilities Dining room; Activities room; Chapel; Crafts room; Laundry room; Barber/Beauty shop; Library.
Activities Arts & crafts; Cards; Games; Reading groups; Prayer groups; Movies; Shopping trips; Dances/Social/Cultural gatherings.

Natchitoches

Evangeline of Natchitoches
PO Box 2299, 750 Keyser Ave, Natchitoches, LA 71457
(318) 352-8779
Admin Joseph Kitchens.
Licensure Intermediate care. *Beds* ICF 102. *Certified* Medicaid.

Natchitoches Manor
720 Keyser Ave, Natchitoches, LA 71457
(318) 352-8296
Admin Tom Matherne.
Medical Dir Dr I L Campbell.
Licensure Intermediate care. *Beds* ICF 160. *Certified* Medicaid.
Owner Proprietary corp (National Heritage).
Staff RNs 2 (ft), 1 (pt); LPNs 6 (ft); Nurses' aides 25 (ft); Activities coordinators 1 (ft); Dietitians 1 (pt).
Facilities Dining room; Physical therapy room; Activities room; Crafts room; Laundry room; Barber/Beauty shop.
Activities Arts & crafts; Cards; Games; Reading groups; Prayer groups; Movies; Shopping trips; Dances/Social/Cultural gatherings.

Natchitoches Parish Hospital—Long-Term Care Unit
PO Box 2009, 501 Keyser Dr, Natchitoches, LA 71457
(318) 352-1250
Admin Eugene Spillman.
Licensure Intermediate care. *Beds* ICF 110. *Certified* Medicaid.
Owner Publicly owned.
Staff Physicians 5 (ft); RNs 9 (ft); LPNs 9 (ft); Nurses' aides 10 (ft); Speech therapists 1 (ft); Activities coordinators 2 (ft); Dietitians 1 (ft).

Facilities Dining room; Physical therapy room; Activities room; Chapel; Barber/Beauty shop.
Activities Arts & crafts; Games; Reading groups.

New Iberia

Azalea Villa Nursing Home
PO Box 9766, 1002 Admiral Doyle, New Iberia, LA 70562-9766
(318) 364-5472
Admin Norma D Dupre.
Medical Dir Dr J C Musso.
Licensure Intermediate care. *Beds* ICF 150. *Certified* Medicaid.
Admissions Requirements Medical examination; Physician's request.
Facilities Dining room; Activities room; Laundry room; Barber/Beauty shop.
Activities Arts & crafts; Cards; Games; Reading groups; Prayer groups; Movies; Shopping trips; Dances/Social/Cultural gatherings.

Consolata Home
2319 E Main St, New Iberia, LA 70560
(318) 365-8226
Admin David Landry. *Dir of Nursing* Madonna Thibodeaux. *Medical Dir* Dr Oscar Alvarez.
Licensure Intermediate care. *Beds* ICF 114. *Private Pay Patients* 30%. *Certified* Medicaid.
Owner Nonprofit organization/foundation (Diocese of Lafayette).
Admissions Requirements Medical examination; Physician's request.
Staff RNs 1 (ft), 2 (pt); LPNs 7 (ft), 7 (pt); Nurses' aides 36 (ft), 9 (pt); Activities coordinators 1 (ft); Dietitians 1 (pt).
Languages French.
Affiliation Roman Catholic.
Facilities Dining room; Activities room; Chapel; Laundry room; Barber/Beauty shop.
Activities Arts & crafts; Cards; Games; Prayer groups; Movies; Dances/Social/Cultural gatherings; Intergenerational programs; Pet therapy.

Dautrive Hospital Skilled Nursing Facility
PO Box 11210, 600 N Lewis St, New Iberia, LA 70562-1210
(318) 365-7311
Admin Clay B Hurley.
Licensure Skilled care. *Beds* SNF 10.

Heritage Manor New Iberia North
PO Box 9459, New Iberia, LA 70562-9459
(318) 365-2466
Admin Larry Viator.
Licensure Intermediate care. *Beds* ICF 121. *Certified* Medicaid.
Owner Proprietary corp (National Heritage).

Heritage Manor New Iberia South
PO Box 984, 600 Bayard St, New Iberia, LA 70560
(318) 365-3441
Admin Harvey W Koenig II.
Licensure Intermediate care. *Beds* ICF 80. *Certified* Medicaid.
Owner Proprietary corp (National Heritage).

New Orleans

Bethany Home
2535 Esplanade Ave, New Orleans, LA 70119
(504) 949-1738
Admin Joan Coates. *Dir of Nursing* Elizabeth Sturdevant. *Medical Dir* William LaCorte MD.
Licensure Skilled care; Intermediate care. *Beds* 117. *Certified* Medicaid.
Owner Nonprofit corp.
Admissions Requirements Minimum age 65; Medical examination.

Staff RNs 2 (ft); LPNs 11 (ft), 6 (pt); Nurses' aides 35 (ft), 13 (pt); Activities coordinators 1 (ft).
Facilities Dining room; Physical therapy room; Activities room; Library.
Activities Arts & crafts; Cards; Games; Prayer groups; Movies.

Chateau de Notre Dame
2832 Burdette St, New Orleans, LA 70125
(504) 866-2741
Admin Kathleen E Dollymore. *Dir of Nursing* Carol Hirsch RN. *Medical Dir* Dr Fred Hunter.
Licensure Skilled care; Retirement; Group home. *Beds* SNF 180; Retirement apts 115; Group home 6 units. *Certified* Medicare.
Owner Nonprofit organization/foundation.
Staff Physicians; RNs 4 (ft), 1 (pt); LPNs 16 (ft), 5 (pt); Nurses' aides 48 (ft), 22 (pt); Physical therapists 2 (ft); Activities coordinators 4 (ft); Dietitians 1 (ft); Podiatrists 1 (pt).
Facilities Dining room; Physical therapy room; Activities room; Chapel; Laundry room; Barber/Beauty shop; Library; Dayrooms.
Activities Arts & crafts; Cards; Games; Reading groups; Prayer groups; Movies; Shopping trips; Dances/Social/Cultural gatherings; Religious services.

Covenant Home
5919 Magazine St, New Orleans, LA 70115
(504) 897-6216
Admin J Erik Engberg.
Medical Dir Howard Russell MD.
Licensure Intermediate care. *Beds* ICF 84. *Certified* Medicaid.
Admissions Requirements Medical examination; Physician's request.
Staff RNs 1 (ft); LPNs 7 (ft), 3 (pt); Nurses' aides 25 (ft), 3 (pt); Activities coordinators 1 (ft).
Facilities Dining room; Physical therapy room; Activities room; Chapel; Crafts room; Laundry room; Barber/Beauty shop; Library.
Activities Arts & crafts; Cards; Games; Prayer groups; Movies.

CPC Coliseum Medical Center Skilled Nursing Facility
3601 Coliseum St, New Orleans, LA 70115
(504) 897-9700
Admin Jane Blake.
Licensure Skilled care. *Beds* SNF 42. *Certified* Medicare.

Crescent City Health Care Center
1420 General Taylor, New Orleans, LA 70115
(504) 895-7755
Admin Jacqueline Fulda.
Beds 216.
Owner Proprietary corp (Beverly Enterprises).

Easthaven Care Center
9660 Lake Forest Blvd, New Orleans, LA 70127
(504) 244-9013
Admin Arthur Arnold. *Dir of Nursing* Barbara Deris. *Medical Dir* Dr Tamar Acikalin.
Licensure Skilled care; Intermediate care; Alzheimer's care. *Beds* SNF 35; ICF 250. *Private Pay Patients* 12%. *Certified* Medicaid; Medicare.
Owner Proprietary corp (Health Care Capital).
Admissions Requirements Minimum age 18.
Staff Physicians 10 (pt); RNs 2 (ft), 4 (pt); LPNs 20 (ft), 10 (pt); Nurses' aides 80 (ft), 20 (pt); Physical therapists 1 (pt); Speech therapists 1 (pt); Activities coordinators 3 (ft); Dietitians 1 (pt); Podiatrists 1 (pt).
Facilities Dining room; Activities room; Crafts room; Laundry room; Barber/Beauty shop; Library.

Activities Arts & crafts; Cards; Games; Reading groups; Prayer groups; Movies; Shopping trips; Dances/Social/Cultural gatherings.

Ferncrest Manor Nursing Home
14500 Hayne Blvd, New Orleans, LA 70128
(504) 246-1426
Admin Kathy McEnaney.
Beds 194.

F Edward Hebert Hospital—SNF
1 Sanctuary Dr, New Orleans, LA 70114
(504) 363-2664
Admin Patricia Miller. *Dir of Nursing* Barbara Riley RN. *Medical Dir* Frank Wagner MD.
Licensure Skilled care. *Beds* SNF 44. *Certified* Medicare.
Owner Proprietary corp.
Admissions Requirements Medical examination; Physician's request.
Staff RNs 4 (ft), 20 (pt); LPNs 8 (ft), 20 (pt); Nurses' aides 3 (ft), 20 (pt); Physical therapists 2 (ft), 20 (pt); Recreational therapists 1 (ft), 20 (pt); Occupational therapists 2 (ft), 20 (pt); Speech therapists 5 (ft), 4 (pt); Dietitians 1 (ft), 20 (pt).
Facilities Dining room; Physical therapy room; Activities room; Chapel; Laundry room; Barber/Beauty shop.
Activities Arts & crafts; Cards; Games; Reading groups; Prayer groups; Movies.

Hotel Dieu Hospital Skilled Nursing Facility
2021 Perdido St, New Orleans, LA 70112
(504) 588-3000
Admin Christopher D Sammons.
Licensure Skilled care. *Beds* SNF 31.

Lafon Nursing Home of the Holy Family
6900 Chef Menteur Hwy, New Orleans, LA 70126
(504) 246-1100
Admin Sr Ann Elise Sonnier. *Dir of Nursing* Christell Morrison RN. *Medical Dir* Dr William Stallworth.
Licensure Intermediate care. *Beds* ICF 171. *Private Pay Patients* 33%. *Certified* Medicaid; Medicare.
Owner Nonprofit corp.
Admissions Requirements Medical examination; Physician's request.
Staff Physicians 2 (pt); RNs 2 (ft), 7 (pt); LPNs 17 (ft), 4 (pt); Nurses' aides 56 (ft), 6 (pt); Physical therapists (consultant); Dietitians 1 (ft); Ophthalmologists 1 (pt); Podiatrists 1 (pt).
Affiliation Roman Catholic.
Facilities Dining room; Physical therapy room; Activities room; Chapel; Crafts room; Laundry room; Barber/Beauty shop; Library.
Activities Arts & crafts; Cards; Games; Reading groups; Prayer groups; Movies; Shopping trips.

Lafon United Methodist Nursing Home
4021 Cadillac St, New Orleans, LA 70122
(504) 288-2314
Admin Edward J Lang. *Dir of Nursing* Winniefred A Jones RN.
Licensure Intermediate care. *Beds* ICF 104. *Certified* Medicaid; Medicare.
Owner Nonprofit organization/foundation (United Methodist Church Louisiana Conference).
Admissions Requirements Medical examination; Physician's request.
Staff Physicians; RNs; LPNs; Nurses' aides; Activities coordinators; Dietitians.
Affiliation Methodist.
Facilities Dining room; Activities room; Chapel; Crafts room; Laundry room; Barber/Beauty shop.
Activities Arts & crafts; Cards; Games; Reading groups; Dances/Social/Cultural gatherings.

Les Fontaines Retirement Community
13001 Chef Menteur Hwy, New Orleans, LA 70129
(504) 254-5700, 254-7120 FAX
Admin Janett T Loeb. *Dir of Nursing* Angela Lowe.
Licensure Intermediate care. *Beds* ICF 217. *Private Pay Patients* 35%. *Certified* Medicaid.
Owner Privately owned.
Staff Physicians 20 (pt); RNs 1 (ft); LPNs 10 (ft); Activities coordinators 1 (ft), 1 (pt); Podiatrists 2 (pt); Audiologists 1 (pt).
Languages Spanish, French.
Facilities Dining room; Crafts room; Laundry room; Barber/Beauty shop.
Activities Arts & crafts; Cards; Games; Reading groups; Prayer groups; Movies; Shopping trips; Dances/Social/Cultural gatherings; Intergenerational programs.

Lutheran Home of New Orleans
6400 Hayne Blvd, New Orleans, LA 70126
(504) 246-7900
Admin Thomas E Schuetz.
Licensure Intermediate care. *Beds* ICF 208. *Certified* Medicaid.
Affiliation Lutheran.

Maison Hospitaliere
1220 Dauphine St, New Orleans, LA 70116
(504) 524-4309
Admin Joyce Flynn.
Licensure Intermediate care. *Beds* ICF 91. *Certified* Medicaid.

Maison Orleans II
13500 Chef Menteur Hwy, New Orleans, LA 70129
(504) 254-9431
Admin Wayne Landry. *Dir of Nursing* Ronny Monterio RN. *Medical Dir* Gordon McHardy MD.
Licensure Intermediate care; Alzheimer's unit. *Beds* ICF 207. *Certified* Medicaid.
Owner Proprietary corp.
Admissions Requirements Medical examination.
Staff Physicians 2 (pt); RNs 1 (ft); LPNs; Nurses' aides; Physical therapists 1 (pt); Recreational therapists 3 (ft); Speech therapists 1 (pt); Activities coordinators 1 (ft); Dietitians 1 (ft); Ophthalmologists 1 (pt); Dentists 1 (pt).
Languages Vietnamese, Spanish.
Facilities Dining room; Physical therapy room; Activities room; Crafts room; Laundry room; Barber/Beauty shop; Greenhouse.
Activities Arts & crafts; Cards; Games; Reading groups; Prayer groups; Movies; Shopping trips; Dances/Social/Cultural gatherings.

Mary Joseph Residence—Little Sisters of the Poor
4201 Woodland Dr, New Orleans, LA 70114
(504) 394-2200
Admin Sr Mary Vincent Mannion. *Dir of Nursing* Sr Clare. *Medical Dir* Henry White MD.
Licensure Intermediate care; Retirement. *Beds* ICF 122. *Certified* Medicaid.
Owner Nonprofit corp.
Admissions Requirements Minimum age 62.
Staff Physicians 5 (pt); RNs 4 (ft); LPNs 8 (ft), 6 (pt); Nurses' aides 30 (ft), 8 (pt); Physical therapists 1 (pt); Recreational therapists 1 (ft), 1 (pt); Speech therapists 1 (pt); Activities coordinators 1 (ft); Dietitians 1 (pt); Ophthalmologists 1 (pt); Podiatrists 1 (pt); Dentists 1 (pt).
Affiliation Roman Catholic.
Facilities Dining room; Physical therapy room; Activities room; Chapel; Crafts room; Laundry room; Barber/Beauty shop; Library.

Activities Arts & crafts; Cards; Games; Reading groups; Prayer groups; Movies; Shopping trips; Dances/Social/Cultural gatherings.

Mercy Hospital Skilled Nursing Facility
301 N Jefferson Davis Pkwy, New Orleans, LA 70119
(504) 486-7361
Admin Gary J Blan.
Licensure Skilled care. *Beds* SNF 275.

New Orleans Home & Rehabilitation Center
612 Henry Clay Ave, New Orleans, LA 70118
(504) 896-1315
Admin Harry A Cicero Sr NHA. *Dir of Nursing* Jackie Beary. *Medical Dir* Henry Rothschild MD.
Licensure Skilled care; Intermediate care; Alzheimer's care. *Beds* SNF 101; ICF 101. *Certified* Medicaid; Medicare.
Owner Publicly owned.
Admissions Requirements Minimum age 18; Medical examination; Physician's request.
Staff RNs 8 (ft); LPNs 22 (ft); Nurses' aides 59 (ft); Recreational therapists 1 (ft); Speech therapists 1 (ft).
Facilities Dining room; Physical therapy room; Activities room; Chapel; Crafts room; Laundry room; Barber/Beauty shop; Library.
Activities Arts & crafts; Cards; Games; Reading groups; Prayer groups; Movies; Shopping trips; Dances/Social/Cultural gatherings.

Pendleton Memorial Methodist Hospital—Skilled Nursing Facility
5620 Read Blvd, New Orleans, LA 70127
(504) 244-5100
Admin Carol Beck.
Licensure Skilled care. *Beds* SNF 18.

Poydras Home
5354 Magazine St, New Orleans, LA 70115
(504) 897-0535
Admin Georgia P Horne. *Dir of Nursing* Maureen Cutillo. *Medical Dir* Dr John Phillips.
Licensure Intermediate care. *Beds* ICF 44.
Owner Nonprofit organization/foundation.
Admissions Requirements Females only; Medical examination.
Staff Physicians 1 (pt); RNs 1 (ft), 2 (pt); LPNs 2 (ft), 5 (pt); Nurses' aides 8 (ft), 4 (pt); Activities coordinators 1 (pt); Dietitians 1 (pt); Social worker 1 (pt); Food Service Supervisor 1 (ft); Kitchen 3 (ft), 4 (pt); Housekeeper 2 (ft); Secretary 1 (ft); Maintenance 1 (ft).
Facilities Dining room; Activities room; Chapel; Crafts room; Laundry room; Barber/Beauty shop; Library.
Activities Arts & crafts; Cards; Games; Prayer groups; Movies; Shopping trips; Social activities.

Prayer Tower Rest Home
3316 Pine St, New Orleans, LA 70125
(504) 486-1235
Admin Thelma D Harper. *Dir of Nursing* Lucille Cavitt. *Medical Dir* Dr Shelton Barnes.
Licensure Intermediate care. *Beds* ICF 104. *Certified* Medicaid; Medicare.
Owner Proprietary corp.
Admissions Requirements Medical examination; Physician's request.
Staff Physicians 2 (ft); RNs 2 (ft); LPNs 10 (ft); Nurses' aides 30 (ft); Physical therapists 1 (ft); Activities coordinators 3 (ft); Dietitians 1 (ft); Podiatrists 1 (ft).
Facilities Dining room; Physical therapy room; Activities room; Chapel; Crafts room; Laundry room; Barber/Beauty shop.

Activities Arts & crafts; Cards; Games; Reading groups; Prayer groups; Movies; Shopping trips; Dances/Social/Cultural gatherings; Intergenerational programs; Pet therapy.

St Anna's Asylum
1823 Prytania St, New Orleans, LA 70130
(504) 523-3466
Admin Barbara S Nicolas.
Beds 88.
Owner Nonprofit corp.

St Charles Health Care Center
1539 Delachaise St, New Orleans, LA 70115
(504) 895-3953
Admin Ben J Wimberly.
Licensure Skilled care; Intermediate care. *Beds* 99. *Certified* Medicaid; Medicare.

St Margaret's Daughters Nursing Home
6220 Chartres St, New Orleans, LA 70117
(504) 279-6414
Admin Patricia Heintz. *Dir of Nursing* Diane Candebat RN. *Medical Dir* Henry Rothschild MD.
Licensure Intermediate care. *Beds* ICF 111. *Private Pay Patients* 30%. *Certified* Medicaid.
Owner Nonprofit organization/foundation.
Admissions Requirements Females only; Medical examination; Physician's request.
Staff Physicians; RNs; LPNs; Nurses' aides; Activities coordinators; Dietitians (consultant).
Affiliation Roman Catholic.
Facilities Dining room; Physical therapy room; Activities room; Chapel; Crafts room; Laundry room; Barber/Beauty shop.
Activities Arts & crafts; Cards; Games; Reading groups; Prayer groups; Movies; Shopping trips; Dances/Social/Cultural gatherings.

Southern Baptist Hospital—Skilled Nursing Facility
2700 Napoleon Ave, New Orleans, LA 70115
(504) 899-9311, 897-4593 FAX
Admin Byron Harrell CEO. *Dir of Nursing* Tara Foto.
Licensure Skilled care; Respite care. *Beds* SNF 37. *Private Pay Patients* 1%. *Certified* Medicare.
Owner Nonprofit organization/foundation.
Admissions Requirements Medical examination; Physician's request.
Staff Physicians; RNs 7 (ft); LPNs 12 (ft); Nurses' aides 10 (ft); Physical therapists 10 (ft); Recreational therapists 1 (ft); Occupational therapists 1 (ft); Speech therapists 1 (ft); Activities coordinators 1 (ft), 1 (pt); Dietitians 1 (ft), 1 (pt); Ophthalmologists 6 (ft); Podiatrists 3 (ft); Audiologists 1 (ft).
Languages Spanish, French.
Facilities Dining room; Physical therapy room; Activities room; Chapel; Crafts room; Laundry room; Barber/Beauty shop; Library.
Activities Arts & crafts; Cards; Games; Prayer groups; Dances/Social/Cultural gatherings; Intergenerational programs; Pet therapy.

Touro Infirmary
1401 Foucher St, New Orleans, LA 70115
(504) 897-7011
Admin Barth A Weinberg.
Beds 33.

Touro Shakespeare Home
2621 General Meyer Ave, New Orleans, LA 70114
(504) 366-9881
Admin Paul Lumbi. *Dir of Nursing* Mary Preen. *Medical Dir* Dr Michael Lavigne.
Licensure Intermediate care; Adult day care; Alzheimer's care. *Beds* ICF 119; Adult day care 26. *Private Pay Patients* 10%. *Certified* Medicaid.
Owner Publicly owned.

Admissions Requirements Medical examination; Physician's request.
Staff Physicians 1 (ft); RNs 2 (ft); LPNs 14 (ft); Nurses' aides 38 (ft); Recreational therapists 1 (ft); Activities coordinators 1 (ft); Dietitians 1 (pt); Ophthalmologists 1 (pt); Podiatrists 1 (pt).
Facilities Dining room; Physical therapy room; Activities room; Chapel; Crafts room; Laundry room; Barber/Beauty shop; Library; Waiting room; Lawn with benches.
Activities Arts & crafts; Cards; Games; Reading groups; Prayer groups; Movies; Shopping trips; Dances/Social/Cultural gatherings; Intergenerational programs; Pet therapy; Bingo.

Willow Wood New Orleans Home for Jewish Aged
3701 Behrman Pl, New Orleans, LA 70114
(504) 367-5640
Admin Byron S Arbeit.
Licensure Skilled care; Intermediate care. *Beds* 101. *Certified* Medicaid; Medicare.
Affiliation Jewish.

Woodland Village Health Care Center
5301 Tullis Dr, New Orleans, LA 70131
(504) 394-5807
Admin Jeff Dungan.
Beds 186.

New Roads

Lakeview Manor Nursing Home
PO Box 320, 400 Hospital Rd, New Roads, LA 70760
(504) 638-4404
Admin Myron Chatelain. *Dir of Nursing* Phyllis Chatelain.
Licensure Intermediate care. *Beds* ICF 120. *Certified* Medicaid.
Owner Proprietary corp.
Staff RNs 1 (ft); LPNs 7 (ft), 2 (pt); Nurses' aides 27 (ft), 5 (pt); Activities coordinators 1 (ft); Dietitians 1 (pt).
Facilities Dining room; Activities room; Laundry room; Barber/Beauty shop; 2 TV lobbies; 2 Patios.
Activities Arts & crafts; Cards; Games; Prayer groups; Movies; Shopping trips.

Pointe Coupee General Hospital
PO Box 578, 2202 False River Dr, New Roads, LA 70760
(504) 638-6331
Admin Joseph Gallo.
Licensure Skilled care; Intermediate care.

Pointe Coupee Parish Nursing Home
2202-A Hospital Rd, New Roads, LA 70760
(504) 638-4431
Admin Betty L Vosburg. *Dir of Nursing* Pamela M Firmin RN.
Licensure Intermediate care. *Beds* ICF 120. *Certified* Medicaid.
Owner Publicly owned.
Admissions Requirements Medical examination.
Staff RNs 2 (ft); LPNs 10 (ft), 7 (pt); Nurses' aides 39 (ft), 5 (pt); Physical therapists 1 (pt); Speech therapists 1 (pt); Activities coordinators 1 (ft); Dietitians 1 (ft); Dentists 1 (pt).
Languages French.
Facilities Dining room; Physical therapy room; Activities room; Crafts room; Laundry room; Barber/Beauty shop; Library.
Activities Arts & crafts; Cards; Games; Reading groups; Prayer groups; Movies; Shopping trips; Dances/Social/Cultural gatherings.

Newellton

St Charles Nursing Home
PO Box 508, Newellton, LA 71357
(318) 467-9442
Admin Louise Crane.
Licensure Intermediate care. *Beds* 56.
Certified Medicaid.

Tensas Care Center
PO Box 508, 903 Verona St, Newellton, LA
71357
(318) 467-5919
Admin Joe R Kitchens. *Dir of Nursing*
Christine A Hulett RN.
Licensure Intermediate care. *Beds* ICF 61.
Certified Medicaid.
Owner Nonprofit corp (Newellton
Development Corp).
Admissions Requirements Medical
examination; Physician's request.
Staff Physicians 3 (pt); RNs 1 (ft); LPNs 4
(ft), 2 (pt); Nurses' aides 13 (ft), 5 (pt);
Activities coordinators 1 (ft); Dietitians 1
(pt); Clerical 1 (ft).
Facilities Dining room; Crafts room; Barber/
Beauty shop; TV Room.
Activities Arts & crafts; Games; Prayer groups;
Movies.

Oak Grove

Carroll Nursing Home Inc
PO Box 788, N Castleman St, Oak Grove, LA
71263
(318) 428-3249
Admin Lisa Cox.
Licensure Intermediate care. *Beds* ICF 106.
Certified Medicaid.
Admissions Requirements Medical
examination; Physician's request.
Staff Physicians 1 (pt); RNs 1 (ft); LPNs 7
(ft), 1 (pt); Nurses' aides 40 (ft), 3 (pt);
Recreational therapists 1 (ft); Activities
coordinators 1 (ft); Dietitians 1 (pt); Dentists
1 (pt).
Facilities Dining room; Activities room;
Crafts room; Laundry room; Barber/Beauty
shop; Library.
Activities Arts & crafts; Cards; Games;
Reading groups; Prayer groups; Movies;
Shopping trips; Dances/Social/Cultural
gatherings.

West Carroll Memorial Care Center
PO Box 748, 522 Ross, Oak Grove, LA 71263
(318) 428-3237
Admin Raymond Morris.
Beds 29.

West Carroll Memorial Hospital
522 Ross St, Oak Grove, LA 71263
(318) 428-3237
Admin Raymond R Morris.
Licensure Skilled care; Intermediate care. *Beds*
Swing beds SNF/ICF 21.

Oakdale

Allen Oaks
PO Box 683, 6 East Ave, Oakdale, LA 71463
(318) 335-1469
Admin Michael R Hathorn. *Dir of Nursing*
Tammy Moore. *Medical Dir* George B
Mowad MD.
Licensure Intermediate care. *Beds* ICF 91.
Owner Privately owned.
Admissions Requirements Medical
examination.
Staff Physicians 1 (ft), 3 (pt); RNs 1 (ft);
LPNs 4 (ft); Nurses' aides 11 (ft); Physical
therapists 1 (ft); Recreational therapists 1
(pt); Activities coordinators 1 (ft); Dietitians
1 (ft).

Facilities Dining room; Activities room;
Laundry room; Barber/Beauty shop.
Activities Arts & crafts; Games; Movies;
Dances/Social/Cultural gatherings.

Humana Hospital Oakdale
130 N Hospital Dr, Oakdale, LA 71463
(318) 335-3700
Admin Louis J Deumite.
Licensure Skilled care; Intermediate care. *Beds*
Swing beds SNF/ICF 12.

Oberlin

St Francis Nursing Home of Oberlin Inc
1001 Industrial Park Dr, Oberlin, LA 70655
(318) 639-2934
Admin Nealan J Rider.
Beds 100.

Olla

Hardtner Medical Center
Hwy 165 S, Olla, LA 71465
Admin M L Barksdale.
Licensure Skilled care; Intermediate care. *Beds*
Swing beds SNF/ICF 47.

Opelousas

**Doctors Hospital of Opelousas—Skilled
Nursing Facility**
5101 Hwy 167 S, Opelousas, LA 70570
(318) 948-2102
Admin Nancy Lee Scrugham.
Licensure Skilled care. *Beds* SNF 8.

**Opelousas General Hospital—Skilled Nursing
Facility**
520 Prudhomme Ln, Opelousas, LA 70570
(318) 948-5113
Admin Gary I Keller.
Licensure Skilled care. *Beds* SNF 14.

Opelousas Health Care
328 W Grolee St, Opelousas, LA 70570
(318) 942-7588
Admin Mary E Thurmond.
Medical Dir James McCarthy; Rosemary Roy.
Licensure Intermediate care. *Beds* ICF 71.
Certified Medicaid.
Owner Proprietary corp (Southeastern Health
Care Inc).
Admissions Requirements Medical
examination.
Staff Physicians 1 (pt); RNs 1 (ft); LPNs 6
(ft), 3 (pt); Activities coordinators 1 (ft);
Dietitians 1 (pt).
Languages French.
Facilities Dining room; Laundry room;
Barber/Beauty shop.
Activities Arts & crafts; Cards; Games; Prayer
groups; Movies; Dances/Social/Cultural
gatherings.

Our Lady of Prompt Succor Nursing Home
751 Prudhomme Ln, Opelousas, LA 70570
(318) 948-3634
Admin Sr Margaret M Lafleur.
Medical Dir Dr Donald Gremillion.
Licensure Intermediate care. *Beds* ICF 80.
Certified Medicaid.
Staff RNs 4 (ft); LPNs 6 (ft), 2 (pt); Nurses'
aides 30 (ft), 4 (pt); Physical therapists 1
(pt); Speech therapists 1 (pt); Activities
coordinators 1 (pt); Dietitians 1 (pt);
Audiologists 1 (pt); Dentists 1 (pt).
Affiliation Roman Catholic.
Facilities Dining room; Activities room;
Chapel; Laundry room; Barber/Beauty shop.
Activities Arts & crafts; Cards; Games;
Reading groups; Prayer groups; Shopping
trips; Dances/Social/Cultural gatherings.

Senior Village Nursing Home
160 Durcharme Rd, Opelousas, LA 70570
(318) 948-4486

Admin Susan Bourgogne.
Licensure Intermediate care. *Beds* ICF 240.
Certified Medicaid.
Owner Proprietary corp (National Heritage).

Patterson

QC II Nursing Care Center of Patterson
PO Box 2099, 910 Lisa St, Patterson, LA
70392
(504) 395-4563
Admin Amanda Landry.
Beds 131.

Pine Prairie

Prairie Manor Nursing Home
PO Box 500, Edwin Elliott Dr, Pine Prairie,
LA 70576
(318) 599-2031
Admin Martha Miller.
Beds 80.

Pineville

Camellia Garden Nursing Home
701 Bayou Marie Rd, Pineville, LA 71360
(318) 445-4251
Admin Ralph Hargrove. *Dir of Nursing* Kathy
Baker RN.
Licensure Intermediate care. *Beds* ICF 93.
Certified Medicaid.
Owner Proprietary corp.
Admissions Requirements Minimum age 16;
Medical examination; Physician's request.
Staff Physicians 1 (ft), 8 (pt); RNs 1 (ft);
LPNs 6 (ft), 3 (pt); Nurses' aides 20 (ft), 10
(pt); Physical therapists 1 (pt); Speech
therapists 1 (pt); Activities coordinators 1
(ft); Dietitians 1 (pt).
Languages French.
Facilities Dining room; Activities room;
Laundry room; Barber/Beauty shop.
Activities Arts & crafts; Cards; Games;
Reading groups; Prayer groups; Movies;
Shopping trips; Dances/Social/Cultural
gatherings.

Hilltop Nursing Center No 1
PO Box 3067, PO Box 3067, Pineville, LA
71361
(318) 442-9552
Admin Juanita B Kelley.
Medical Dir Dr Grover Bahm.
Licensure Intermediate care. *Beds* ICF 98.
Certified Medicaid.
Admissions Requirements Medical
examination; Physician's request.
Staff Physicians 1 (ft), 6 (pt); RNs 2 (ft);
LPNs 10 (ft); Nurses' aides 25 (ft), 4 (pt);
Physical therapists 1 (pt); Activities
coordinators 1 (ft); Dietitians 1 (pt).
Facilities Dining room; Activities room;
Laundry room; Barber/Beauty shop.
Activities Arts & crafts; Cards; Games; Prayer
groups; Movies; Shopping trips; Dances/
Social/Cultural gatherings.

Hilltop Nursing Center No 2
PO Box 4177, 1100 Bayou Marie Rd,
Pineville, LA 71360
(318) 487-9400
Admin Carole Swain.
Medical Dir Carrie Graves.
Licensure Intermediate care. *Beds* ICF 102.
Certified Medicaid.
Owner Proprietary corp.
Admissions Requirements Minimum age 21;
Medical examination; Physician's request.
Staff RNs 1 (ft), 2 (pt); LPNs 6 (ft), 4 (pt);
Nurses' aides 28 (ft); Activities coordinators
1 (ft); Dietitians 1 (pt).
Facilities Dining room; Activities room;
Laundry room; Barber/Beauty shop.
Activities Arts & crafts; Cards; Games; Prayer
groups; Movies; Shopping trips; Dances/
Social/Cultural gatherings.

Homage Manor Nursing Home
708 Mercer Dr, Pineville, LA 71360-3671
(318) 339-7374
Admin Floyd Thornhill.
Licensure Intermediate care. *Beds* ICF 54.
   Certified Medicaid.

Lakeland Nursing Home
PO Box 4300, Hillsdale Dr, Pineville, LA
   71361
(318) 448-0141
Admin Herman P Marshall.
Licensure Intermediate care. *Beds* ICF 140.
   Certified Medicaid.

Pilgrim Manor of Pineville
PO Box 4208, 200 Gordon St, Pineville, LA
   71360
(318) 442-8343
Admin Sharon Burns.
Medical Dir Ken Rose.
Licensure Intermediate care; Alzheimer's care.
   Beds ICF 152. *Certified* Medicaid.
Owner Privately owned.
Staff RNs 1 (ft), 1 (pt); LPNs 14 (ft), 1 (pt);
   Nurses' aides 56 (ft), 3 (pt); Physical
   therapists 1 (pt); Activities coordinators 1
   (ft).
Languages French.
Facilities Dining room; Activities room;
   Chapel; Crafts room; Laundry room; Barber/
   Beauty shop.
Activities Arts & crafts; Cards; Games;
   Reading groups; Prayer groups; Movies;
   Shopping trips; Dances/Social/Cultural
   gatherings.

Pinecrest State School
PO Drawer 191, Pineville, LA 71360
(318) 640-0754
Admin Coates Stuckey.
Licensure Intermediate care for mentally
   retarded. *Beds* 1688. *Certified* Medicaid.

Plain Dealing

Whispering Pines Nursing Home
PO Box 147, Plain Dealing, LA 71064
(318) 326-4259
Admin Louis A Dye Sr.
Licensure Intermediate care. *Beds* ICF 89.
   Certified Medicaid.

Plaquemine

Iberville Living Center
1601 River West Dr, Plaquemine, LA 70764
(504) 687-0240
Admin John Denis Badeaux. *Dir of Nursing*
   Yvonne Hasten RN. *Medical Dir* Dr B F
   Trosclair.
Licensure Intermediate care; Alzheimer's care.
   Beds ICF 180. *Certified* Medicaid;
   Medicare; VA.
Owner Proprietary corp (ARA Living
   Centers).
Admissions Requirements Minimum age 16.
Staff RNs 2 (ft); LPNs 8 (ft), 1 (pt); Nurses'
   aides 18 (ft), 1 (pt); Activities coordinators 1
   (ft); Dietitians 1 (ft).
Languages French.
Facilities Dining room; Physical therapy
   room; Activities room; Chapel; Crafts room;
   Laundry room; Barber/Beauty shop; Library;
   Van with wheelchair lift.
Activities Arts & crafts; Cards; Games; Prayer
   groups; Movies; Shopping trips; Dances/
   Social/Cultural gatherings; Outings to
   participate in local activities.

Plaquemine Manor Nursing Home Inc
PO Box 487, 1202 Ferdinand St, Plaquemine,
   LA 70764
(504) 387-1345
Admin David Cook.
Licensure Intermediate care. *Beds* ICF 106.
   Certified Medicaid.

**River West Medical Center—Skilled Nursing
Facility**
1725 River W Dr, Plaquemine, LA 70764
(504) 687-9222
Admin Ricky Blunschi.
Licensure Skilled care.

Plaucheville

Avoyelles Manor Inc
Rte 1 Box 215, Hwy 107—Dupont,
   Plaucheville, LA 71362
(318) 922-3404
Admin CArolos Martinez.
Licensure Intermediate care. *Beds* ICF 104.
   Certified Medicaid.

Pleasant Hill

North Sabine Nursing Home Inc
Rte 1 Box 168, Pleasant Hill, LA 71065
(318) 796-3316
Admin Elizabeth Durr.
Licensure Intermediate care. *Beds* ICF 92.
   Certified Medicaid.

Pollock

Woods Haven Senior Citizens Home
PO Box 469, Pollock, LA 71467
(318) 765-3557
Admin Rev H P Tarpley.
Licensure Intermediate care. *Beds* ICF 103.
   Certified Medicaid.
Owner Proprietary corp.
Admissions Requirements Medical
   examination.
Staff RNs; LPNs; Nurses' aides; Activities
   coordinators; Dietitians.
Facilities Dining room; Activities room;
   Laundry room; Barber/Beauty shop.
Activities Arts & crafts; Cards; Games;
   Reading groups; Prayer groups; Movies;
   Shopping trips; Dances/Social/Cultural
   gatherings.

Port Allen

Port Allen Care Center Inc
403 15th St, Port Allen, LA 70767
(504) 346-8815
Admin Ed Hannie.
Licensure Intermediate care. *Beds* ICF 125.
   Certified Medicaid.

Quitman

Pine Hill Senior Citizens Home Inc
Rte 2 Box 75, Pinehill Dr, Quitman, LA
   71268
(318) 259-4829
Admin Maxine Roberson.
Licensure Intermediate care. *Beds* ICF 80.
   Certified Medicaid.

Raceland

Raceland Health Care
PO Box 430, 4302 Hwy 1, Raceland, LA
   70394
(504) 537-3569
Admin Diwana Sanders NHA. *Dir of Nursing*
   Marcie Guidry RN. *Medical Dir* Michael
   Marcello MD.
Licensure Intermediate care. *Beds* ICF 82.
   Certified Medicaid.
Owner Privately owned (Solo Nursing Home
   Partnership).
Admissions Requirements Medical
   examination.
Staff RNs 1 (ft); LPNs 9 (ft); Nurses' aides 36
   (ft); Physical therapists 2 (ft); Speech
   therapists 1 (ft); Activities coordinators 1
   (ft); Dietitians 1 (ft); Ophthalmologists 1 (ft);
   Podiatrists 1 (ft).

Languages Cajun French, Spanish.
Facilities Dining room; Chapel; Laundry
   room; Barber/Beauty shop.
Activities Arts & crafts; Cards; Games;
   Reading groups; Prayer groups; Movies;
   Shopping trips; Dances/Social/Cultural
   gatherings; Intergenerational programs.

**St Anne General Hospital—Skilled Nursing
Facility**
PO Box 440, Twin Oaks Dr, Raceland, LA
   70394
(504) 537-6841
Admin Milton D Bourgeois Jr.
Licensure Skilled care. *Beds* SNF 20.

Rayne

Rayne-Branch Hospital
301 S Chevis, Rayne, LA 70578
(318) 334-2665
Admin Dale Moore.
Beds 63.

Rayne Guest Home Inc
308 Amelia St, Rayne, LA 70578
(318) 334-5111
Admin LeRoy Richard.
Licensure Intermediate care. *Beds* ICF 120.
   Certified Medicaid.

Rayville

Colonial Manor Guest House
PO Box 874, 505 E 4th St, Rayville, LA
   71269
(318) 728-3251
Admin David E Barr.
Licensure Intermediate care. *Beds* ICF 134.
   Certified Medicaid.

Community Comfort Cottage Nursing Home
PO Box 60, 717 Madeline, Rayville, LA 71269
(318) 728-5373
Admin Claude H Minor Sr. *Dir of Nursing*
   Fransic Slack RN. *Medical Dir* Nettie Lee
   LPN.
Licensure Skilled care; Intermediate care. *Beds*
   SNF 5; ICF 80. *Certified* Medicaid;
   Medicare.
Owner Nonprofit organization/foundation.
Admissions Requirements Medical
   examination.
Staff RNs; LPNs; Nurses' aides; Activities
   coordinators; Dietitians.
Facilities Dining room; Activities room;
   Chapel; Laundry room; Barber/Beauty shop.
Activities Arts & crafts; Games; Reading
   groups; Prayer groups; Movies; Shopping
   trips; Dances/Social/Cultural gatherings; Pet
   therapy.

Rayville Guest House
PO Box 875, Rayville, LA 71269
(318) 728-2089
Admin Gary E Bickham. *Dir of Nursing*
   Wanda Sharbono RN.
Licensure Intermediate care. *Beds* ICF 125.
   Certified Medicaid.
Owner Privately owned.
Admissions Requirements Medical
   examination.
Staff RNs 1 (ft), 1 (pt); LPNs 8 (ft), 2 (pt);
   Nurses' aides 15 (ft), 29 (pt); Activities
   coordinators 1 (ft); Dietitians 1 (pt); Social
   services 1 (ft); Ward clerks 2 (ft), 1 (pt);
   Maintenance 1 (ft); Housekeeping & laundry
   7 (ft), 2 (pt); Dietary department 5 (ft), 5
   (pt).
Facilities Dining room; Chapel; Laundry
   room; Barber/Beauty shop.
Activities Arts & crafts; Games; Prayer groups;
   Movies; Shopping trips; Dances/Social/
   Cultural gatherings.

Richland Parish Hospital
Greer Rd, Rayville, LA 71269

Admin Michael E Cooper.
Licensure Skilled care; Intermediate care.

Ringgold

Ringgold Nursing Care Center Inc
PO Box 828, Kenneth St, Ringgold, LA 71068
(318) 894-9181
Admin James L Collins.
Beds 125.

Ruston

Alpine Guest Care Center
PO Box 1385, Hwy 80 E, Ruston, LA 71273
(318) 255-6492
Admin Elton E Dugan.
Licensure Intermediate care. *Beds* ICF 137.
  Certified Medicaid.

Longleaf Nurse Care Center Inc
PO Box 849, Hwy 80 E, Ruston, LA 71270
(318) 255-5001
Admin Buddy White.
Licensure Intermediate care. *Beds* ICF 92.
  Certified Medicaid.

Towne Oaks Nursing Center
1405 White St, Ruston, LA 71270
(318) 255-4400
Admin Bill Copeland.
Licensure Intermediate care. *Beds* 119.
  Certified Medicaid.

Saint Bernard

Fernandez Nursing Home Inc
Hwy 46, 2725 Bayou Rd, Saint Bernard, LA
  70085
(504) 682-0131
Admin M R Fernandez.
Beds 80.

Poydras Manor Nursing Home
Rte 3 Box 132, Massicott St, Saint Bernard,
  LA 70085
(504) 682-0012
Admin Gary Allen.
Licensure Intermediate care. *Beds* ICF 36.
  Certified Medicaid.

St Rita's Nursing Home
Rte 2 Box 1050 Hwy 46, Saint Bernard, LA
  70085
(504) 682-2650
Admin James R Wingate.
Beds 80.

Saint Francisville

Idlewood Nursing Home
PO Box 490, Saint Francisville, LA 70775
(504) 635-3346
Admin Mary Ann Gustin.
Licensure Intermediate care. *Beds* ICF 128.
  Certified Medicaid.

Saint Martinville

St Martinville Nursing Home
PO Box 787, 200 Claire Dr, Saint Martinville,
  LA 70582
(318) 394-6044
Admin Eula Dutton.
Licensure Intermediate care. *Beds* ICF 146.
  Certified Medicaid.

Shreveport

Autumn Leaves Care Center of Shreveport
PO Box 18294, 205 Idema St, Shreveport, LA
  71138
(318) 688-0961
Admin Judith Glover.
Beds 140.

Centenary Heritage Manor
225 Wyandotte St, Shreveport, LA 71101
(318) 221-3591
Admin Debbie Mayo.
Medical Dir Mary Johnson.
Licensure Intermediate care. *Beds* ICF 101.
  Certified Medicaid.
Owner Proprietary corp (National Heritage).
Admissions Requirements Medical
  examination; Physician's request.
Staff Physicians; RNs; LPNs; Nurses' aides;
  Physical therapists; Speech therapists;
  Activities coordinators; Dietitians;
  Ophthalmologists.
Facilities Dining room; Laundry room;
  Barber/Beauty shop.
Activities Arts & crafts; Cards; Games;
  Reading groups; Prayer groups; Movies;
  Shopping trips; Dances/Social/Cultural
  gatherings.

Eden Gardens Nursing Center
7923 Line Ave, Shreveport, LA 71106
(318) 865-0261
Admin Richard E Anderson. *Dir of Nursing*
  Donna Areaux RN. *Medical Dir* C R Teagle
  MD.
Licensure Intermediate care. *Beds* ICF 74.
  Certified Medicaid.
Owner Proprietary corp.
Admissions Requirements Medical
  examination.
Staff RNs 2 (ft); LPNs 11 (ft); Nurses' aides
  45 (ft); Activities coordinators 1 (ft);
  Dietitians 1 (pt).
Facilities Dining room; Activities room;
  Laundry room.
Activities Arts & crafts; Cards; Games;
  Reading groups; Prayer groups; Movies;
  Shopping trips; Dances/Social/Cultural
  gatherings.

Glen Oaks Home
1524 Glen Oak Pl, Shreveport, LA 71103
(318) 222-6333
Admin Emma Jean McCarty.
Medical Dir Nora McCoy.
Licensure Intermediate care. *Beds* ICF 61.
  Certified Medicaid.
Owner Nonprofit corp.
Admissions Requirements Minimum age 65;
  Medical examination.
Staff Physicians 1 (pt); RNs 1 (ft); LPNs 3
  (ft), 3 (pt); Nurses' aides 18 (ft), 1 (pt);
  Physical therapists 1 (pt); Activities
  coordinators 2 (ft); Dietitians 1 (pt);
  Ophthalmologists 1 (pt); Dentists 1 (pt).
Facilities Dining room; Activities room;
  Laundry room; Barber/Beauty shop.
Activities Arts & crafts; Cards; Games; Prayer
  groups; Movies; Shopping trips; Dances/
  Social/Cultural gatherings; Field trips.

Glen Retirement Village
403 E Flournoy Lucas Rd, Shreveport, LA
  71115
(318) 798-3500, 798-7730 FAX
Admin Peggy Newell. *Dir of Nursing* Linda
  McWaters. *Medical Dir* Dr Robert Henry.
Licensure Intermediate care; Retirement. *Beds*
  ICF 120; Retirement 25. *Private Pay
  Patients* 72%. *Certified* Medicaid.
Owner Nonprofit corp (Glen Retirement
  System).
Admissions Requirements Minimum age 62;
  Medical examination; Physician's request.
Staff Physicians 1 (pt); RNs 1 (ft), 1 (pt);
  LPNs 10 (ft), 8 (pt); Nurses' aides 39 (ft), 18
  (pt); Physical therapists 1 (pt); Activities
  coordinators 1 (ft); Dietitians 1 (pt);
  Ophthalmologists 1 (pt); Podiatrists 1 (pt);
  Dentists 1 (pt).
Languages Greek, Yiddish, Italian, Spanish,
  French.
Facilities Dining room; Physical therapy
  room; Activities room; Crafts room; Laundry
  room; Barber/Beauty shop; Library; Gift
  shop.

Activities Arts & crafts; Cards; Games;
  Reading groups; Movies; Shopping trips;
  Intergenerational programs; Pet therapy;
  Fishing tournament.

Guest Care Center at Spring Lake
8622 Line Ave, Shreveport, LA 71106
(318) 868-4126
Admin Daryl Edwards.
Beds 105.

Guest House
9225 Normandie Dr, Shreveport, LA 71118
(318) 686-0515, 687-0311 FAX
Admin Edward Forrest. *Dir of Nursing* Wanda
  Smith RN. *Medical Dir* Dr Robert Braswell.
Licensure Intermediate care. *Beds* ICF 117.
  Certified Medicaid.
Owner Proprietary corp (Convalescent
  Services).
Admissions Requirements Medical
  examination; Physician's request.
Staff RNs 1 (ft), 1 (pt); LPNs 8 (ft); Nurses'
  aides 36 (ft), 6 (pt); Activities coordinators 1
  (ft).
Facilities Dining room; Laundry room;
  Barber/Beauty shop.
Activities Arts & crafts; Games; Reading
  groups; Prayer groups; Movies; Shopping
  trips; Dances/Social/Cultural gatherings.

Harmony House Nursing Home Inc
PO Box 37573, 1825 Laurel St, Shreveport,
  LA 71103
(318) 424-5251
Admin Darrell Price.
Licensure Intermediate care. *Beds* ICF 115.
  Certified Medicaid.
Staff Physicians 2 (pt); RNs 1 (ft); LPNs 6
  (ft), 2 (pt); Nurses' aides 30 (ft); Physical
  therapists 1 (pt); Speech therapists 1 (ft), 1
  (pt); Activities coordinators 1 (ft); Dietitians
  1 (ft); Ophthalmologists 1 (pt); Audiologists
  1 (pt); Dentists 1 (ft).

Heritage Manor of Westwood
PO Box 9289, 1 Westwood Cir, Shreveport,
  LA 71109
(318) 631-1846
Admin David Gaither.
Licensure Intermediate care. *Beds* ICF 142.
  Certified Medicaid.
Owner Proprietary corp (National Heritage).

Heritage Manor Shreveport
1536 Claiborne St, Shreveport, LA 71103
(318) 631-3426
Admin Sandra Elliott.
Licensure Intermediate care. *Beds* ICF 86.
  Certified Medicaid.
Owner Proprietary corp (National Heritage).

Heritage Manor South
PO Box 9984, 9712 Mansfield Rd, Shreveport,
  LA 71118
(318) 687-2080
Admin Harold J Gamburg.
Beds 145.
Owner Proprietary corp (National Heritage).

Live Oak
600 E Flournoy Lucas Rd, Shreveport, LA
  71115
(318) 797-1900
Admin Jay P Irby.
Medical Dir Dr Fred Robberson.
Licensure Intermediate care; Alzheimer's care;
  Retirement. *Beds* ICF 130. *Certified*
  Medicaid.
Owner Nonprofit corp.
Admissions Requirements Minimum age 62;
  Medical examination; Physician's request.
Staff Physicians 1 (pt); RNs 2 (ft), 1 (pt);
  LPNs 14 (ft), 5 (pt); Nurses' aides 26 (ft), 12
  (pt); Physical therapists 1 (pt); Reality
  therapists 1 (ft); Recreational therapists 1
  (pt); Occupational therapists 1 (ft); Activities
  coordinators 2 (ft); Dietitians 1 (pt);
  Ophthalmologists 1 (pt).

Facilities Dining room; Physical therapy room; Activities room; Chapel; Crafts room; Laundry room; Barber/Beauty shop; Library; Convenience store; Gift shop.
Activities Arts & crafts; Cards; Games; Reading groups; Prayer groups; Movies; Shopping trips; Dances/Social/Cultural gatherings.

Magnolia Manor Nursing Home Inc
1411 Claiborne Ave, Shreveport, LA 71103
(318) 868-4421
Admin Melvin Stallcup.
Licensure Intermediate care. *Beds* ICF 98. *Certified* Medicaid.

Midway Manor Nursing Home Inc
2150 Midway St, Shreveport, LA 71108
(318) 635-9720
Admin Ken Calhoun.
Medical Dir Dr J F Hawkins.
Licensure Intermediate care. *Beds* ICF 212. *Certified* Medicaid.
Admissions Requirements Medical examination.
Staff RNs 4 (ft); LPNs 16 (ft), 2 (pt); Nurses' aides 58 (ft), 12 (pt); Activities coordinators 2 (ft); Dietitians 2 (ft).
Facilities Dining room; Activities room; Crafts room; Laundry room; Barber/Beauty shop.
Activities Arts & crafts; Cards; Games; Prayer groups; Movies; Shopping trips; Dances/ Social/Cultural gatherings.

Nursecare of Shreveport
1736 Irving Pl, Shreveport, LA 71101
(318) 221-1983
Admin Patricia T Daron. *Dir of Nursing* Ann Shideler. *Medical Dir* Robert Braswell MD.
Licensure Intermediate care; Independent living. *Beds* ICF 228; Independent living apts 8. *Private Pay Patients* 45%. *Certified* Medicaid.
Owner Proprietary corp.
Admissions Requirements Minimum age Adult; Medical examination; Physician's request.
Staff Physicians; RNs; LPNs; Nurses' aides; Physical therapists (available); Occupational therapists (available); Speech therapists (available); Activities coordinators; Dietitians; Ophthalmologists (available); Podiatrists (available); Audiologists (available); Chaplains; Physical therapy aides.
Facilities Dining room; Activities room; Chapel; Barber/Beauty shop.
Activities Arts & crafts; Cards; Games; Prayer groups; Movies; Dances/Social/Cultural gatherings; Intergenerational programs; Pet therapy; Spiritual program.

Pierremont Heritage Manor
725 Mitchell Ln, Shreveport, LA 71106
(318) 868-2789
Admin Carolyn Fultz. *Dir of Nursing* Betty Youngblood. *Medical Dir* Dr David Henry.
Licensure Intermediate care. *Beds* ICF 196. *Certified* Medicaid.
Owner Proprietary corp (National Heritage).
Admissions Requirements Minimum age 53; Medical examination.
Staff RNs 3 (ft); LPNs 16 (ft), 2 (pt); Nurses' aides 54 (ft), 4 (pt); Activities coordinators 2 (ft); Dietitians 1 (ft).
Facilities Dining room; Activities room; Crafts room; Laundry room; Barber/Beauty shop; Library.
Activities Arts & crafts; Cards; Games; Reading groups; Prayer groups; Movies; Shopping trips; Dances/Social/Cultural gatherings; Picnics; Fishing trips; Baseball games.

Roseview Nursing Center Inc
3405 Mansfield Rd, Shreveport, LA 71103
(318) 222-3100

Admin Mary Ann Wade.
Licensure Intermediate care. *Beds* ICF 124. *Certified* Medicaid.

Shreveport Manor Guest Care
3302 Mansfield Rd, Shreveport, LA 71103
(318) 222-9482
Admin Michael Mathis.
Licensure Intermediate care. *Beds* ICF 124. *Certified* Medicaid.

South Park Guest Care Center
3050 Baird Rd, Shreveport, LA 71138-0739
(318) 688-1010
Admin Claude Pasquier.
Licensure Intermediate care. *Beds* ICF 128. *Certified* Medicaid.

Virginia Hall Nursing Home
2715 Virginia Ave, Shreveport, LA 71103
(318) 425-3247
Admin Rosalind B Foster.
Licensure Skilled care; Intermediate care. *Beds* 155. *Certified* Medicaid; Medicare.

Booker T Washington Nursing Home
PO Box 6021, 610 Turner Ln, Shreveport, LA 71106
(318) 869-2524
Admin Hattie Mae Scott Blunt.
Licensure Intermediate care. *Beds* ICF 54. *Certified* Medicaid.

Simmesport

Bayou Chateau Nursing Center
Rte 1 Box 390, Hwy 1 S, Simmesport, LA 71369
(318) 941-2294
Admin Dorothy Anne Lacour. *Dir of Nursing* Lela Normand. *Medical Dir* Leon F Beridon MD.
Licensure Intermediate care; Alzheimer's care. *Beds* ICF 104. *Certified* Medicaid.
Owner Proprietary corp.
Admissions Requirements Medical examination; Physician's request.
Staff Physicians 1 (pt); RNs 1 (ft); LPNs 8 (ft), 4 (pt); Nurses' aides; Activities coordinators 1 (ft); Dietitians 1 (ft).
Languages French.
Facilities Dining room; Activities room; Crafts room; Laundry room; Barber/Beauty shop; Library; Sun & recreation rooms; Lounges.
Activities Arts & crafts; Cards; Games; Reading groups; Prayer groups; Movies; Shopping trips; Dances/Social/Cultural gatherings.

Slidell

Greenbriar Nursing & Convalescent Home
505 Roberts Rd, Slidell, LA 70458
(504) 643-6900
Admin Ron Floyd.
Licensure Intermediate care. *Beds* ICF 174. *Certified* Medicaid.

Guest House of Slidell
1051 Robert Rd, Slidell, LA 70458
(504) 643-5630
Admin Ron Floyd.
Licensure Intermediate care. *Beds* ICF 116. *Certified* Medicaid.

New Medico Neurologic Rehabilitation Center of the Gulf Coast
1400 Lindberg Dr, Slidell, LA 70458
(504) 641-4985
Admin James A Hunter Sr.
Beds 118.

Northshore Living Center
106 Medical Center Dr, Slidell, LA 70461
(504) 643-0307
Admin John D Ferguson.
Beds 120.

Springhill

Fountain View Nursing Home
PO Box 813, 215 1st St NE, Springhill, LA 71075
(318) 539-3527
Admin L M Cadenhead Jr.
Licensure Intermediate care. *Beds* ICF 133. *Certified* Medicaid.

Humana Hospital Springhill
PO Box 917, 2001 Humana Dr, Springhill, LA 71075
(318) 539-9161
Admin Ronald P O'Neal.
Licensure Skilled care; Intermediate care. *Beds* Swing beds SNF/ICF 86.

Sterlington

Sterlington Hospital
PO box 567, Hwy 2, Sterlington, LA 71280
(318) 665-2526
Admin Larry A Jones.
Licensure Skilled care; Intermediate care.

Sulphur

High Hope Care Center
PO Box 1460, High Hope Rd, Sulphur, LA 70664-1460
(318) 527-8140
Admin Paul C Reed. *Dir of Nursing* Denise Ardon RN. *Medical Dir* Dr H B Lovejoy.
Licensure Intermediate care. *Beds* ICF 101. *Certified* Medicaid.
Owner Proprietary corp.
Admissions Requirements Minimum age 18; Medical examination.
Staff Physicians; RNs; LPNs; Nurses' aides; Physical therapists; Reality therapists; Speech therapists; Activities coordinators; Dietitians.
Languages French.
Facilities Dining room; Activities room; Crafts room; Laundry room; Barber/Beauty shop.
Activities Arts & crafts; Cards; Games; Prayer groups; Movies; Shopping trips; Dances/ Social/Cultural gatherings.

Holly Hill House Nursing Home
100 Kingston Rd, Sulphur, LA 70663
(318) 625-5843
Admin Raymond Green.
Medical Dir C L Fellows MD.
Licensure Skilled care. *Beds* SNF 235. *Certified* Medicaid; Medicare.
Admissions Requirements Medical examination; Physician's request.
Staff Physicians 1 (ft), 1 (pt); LPNs 18 (ft), 5 (pt); Nurses' aides 40 (ft), 10 (pt); Physical therapists 1 (pt); Occupational therapists 1 (pt); Speech therapists 1 (pt); Activities coordinators 2 (ft); Dietitians 1 (ft); Podiatrists 1 (pt); Audiologists 1 (pt); Dentists 1 (pt).
Facilities Dining room; Activities room; Chapel; Crafts room; Laundry room; Barber/ Beauty shop; Library.
Activities Arts & crafts; Cards; Games; Reading groups; Prayer groups; Movies; Shopping trips; Dances/Social/Cultural gatherings; Pet therapy.

Tallulah

Delta Haven Nursing Home
201 Lee St, Tallulah, LA 71282
(318) 574-4621
Admin Richard Snow NHA MA. *Dir of Nursing* Marla Cummins RN.
Licensure Intermediate care for mentally retarded. *Beds* ICF 146. *Certified* Medicaid.
Owner Proprietary corp.

Admissions Requirements Medical examination.
Staff RNs; LPNs; Nurses' aides; Activities coordinators.
Facilities Dining room; Activities room; Chapel; Crafts room; Laundry room; Barber/Beauty shop.
Activities Arts & crafts; Cards; Games; Reading groups; Movies; Exercise; Music; Church.

Madison Parish Home for the Aged
PO Box 1739, Tallulah, LA 71282
(318) 574-1541
Admin Georgia Mae C Johnson.
Medical Dir Reba Rinicker.
Licensure Intermediate care. *Beds* ICF 43. *Certified* Medicaid; Medicare.
Owner Nonprofit corp.
Admissions Requirements Medical examination; Physician's request.
Staff Physicians 4 (pt); RNs 1 (ft); LPNs 3 (ft), 3 (pt); Nurses' aides 8 (ft), 4 (pt); Activities coordinators 1 (ft); Dietitians 1 (pt).
Affiliation Baptist.
Facilities Dining room; Activities room; Laundry room.
Activities Arts & crafts; Cards; Games; Prayer groups; Shopping trips.

Thibodaux

Audubon Guest House
2110 Audubon Ave, Thibodaux, LA 70301
(504) 446-3109
Admin Earl Thibodaux.
Beds 180.
Owner Proprietary corp (National Heritage).

Heritage Manor Thibodaux
1300 Lafourche Dr, Thibodaux, LA 70301
(504) 446-1332
Admin Ann Thibodaux.
Licensure Intermediate care. *Beds* ICF 58. *Certified* Medicaid.
Owner Proprietary corp (National Heritage).

Lafourche Home for the Aged & Infirm Inc
1002 Tiger Dr, Thibodaux, LA 70301
(504) 447-2205
Admin Ann Howell.
Medical Dir Richard A Morvant MD.
Licensure Intermediate care. *Beds* ICF 64. *Certified* Medicaid.
Owner Nonprofit corp.
Admissions Requirements Medical examination.
Staff RNs 1 (ft), 1 (pt); LPNs 4 (ft), 3 (pt); Nurses' aides 35 (ft), 15 (pt); Activities coordinators 1 (ft); Dietitians 1 (ft).
Facilities Dining room; Activities room; Crafts room; Laundry room; Barber/Beauty shop.
Activities Arts & crafts; Cards; Games; Prayer groups; Movies; Shopping trips; Dances/Social/Cultural gatherings.

Thibodaux Hospital & Health Centers
PO Box 1118, 602 N Acadia Rd, Thibodaux, LA 70302
(504) 447-5500, 447-0794 FAX
Admin Joel J Champagne. *Dir of Nursing* Roberta Crochet RN. *Medical Dir* Dr Billy W Hillman; Dr Michael Cooper, Chief of SNF.
Licensure Skilled care. *Beds* SNF 6. *Certified* Medicare.
Owner Publicly owned.
Admissions Requirements Physician's request.
Staff RNs; LPNs; Nurses' aides; Physical therapists; Speech therapists; Activities coordinators; Dietitians.
Languages French.
Facilities Dining room; Physical therapy room; Chapel.
Activities Arts & crafts; Cards; Games; Movies.

Tioga

Tioga Manor Nursing Center
PO Box 1097, 5201 Shreveport Hwy, Tioga, LA 71477
(318) 640-3014
Admin Iris Winegeart. *Dir of Nursing* Karen Z Williams RN BS. *Medical Dir* Jajinda Verma MD.
Licensure Intermediate care. *Beds* ICF 62. *Certified* Medicaid.
Owner Privately owned.
Admissions Requirements Medical examination; Physician's request.
Staff Physicians 6 (pt); RNs 1 (ft), 1 (pt); LPNs 8 (ft), 3 (pt); Nurses' aides 40 (ft), 7 (pt); Physical therapists 1 (pt); Speech therapists 1 (pt); Dietitians 1 (pt).
Facilities Dining room; Activities room; Barber/Beauty shop; Library.
Activities Arts & crafts; Cards; Games; Reading groups; Prayer groups; Movies; Shopping trips; Dances/Social/Cultural gatherings; Pet shows; Exercise classes.

Ville Platte

Humana Hospital Ville Platte
800 E Main St, Ville Platte, LA 70586
(318) 363-5684
Admin James C Colligan.
Licensure Skilled care; Intermediate care. *Beds* Swing beds SNF/ICF 49.

Maison de Sante Inc
220 S Thompson St, Ville Platte, LA 70586
(318) 363-5532
Admin Cecil Reed.
Licensure Intermediate care. *Beds* ICF 217. *Certified* Medicaid.

Violet

Simmon's Nursing Home Inc
2309 A St, Violet, LA 70092
(504) 682-2505, 682-2506
Admin Jeannie J Simmons. *Dir of Nursing* Rosemary James RN. *Medical Dir* Dr Rodney Huddleston.
Licensure Skilled care; Intermediate care. *Beds* Swing beds SNF/ICF 48. *Private Pay Patients* 10%. *Certified* Medicaid; Medicare.
Owner Proprietary corp.
Admissions Requirements Medical examination.
Staff Physicians 2 (pt); RNs 1 (ft), 1 (pt); LPNs 6 (ft), 2 (pt); Nurses' aides 10 (ft); Physical therapists 1 (pt); Recreational therapists 1 (pt); Activities coordinators 1 (ft).
Facilities Dining room; Activities room; Laundry room.
Activities Arts & crafts; Games; Reading groups; Prayer groups; Movies.

Vivian

Heritage Manor of Vivian
Rte 1 Box 111, Camp Rd, Vivian, LA 71082
(318) 375-2203
Admin Michella Bricker. *Dir of Nursing* Melinda Baker RN. *Medical Dir* John Haymes MD.
Licensure Intermediate care. *Beds* ICF 80. *Certified* Medicaid.
Owner Proprietary corp (National Heritage).
Admissions Requirements Medical examination; Physician's request.
Staff Physicians 3 (pt); RNs 1 (ft); LPNs 4 (ft), 1 (pt); Nurses' aides 16 (ft), 4 (pt); Physical therapists 1 (pt); Occupational therapists 1 (pt); Activities coordinators 1 (ft); Dietitians 1 (pt).
Facilities Dining room; Activities room; Chapel; Crafts room; Laundry room; Barber/Beauty shop; Library.

Activities Arts & crafts; Cards; Games; Movies; Shopping trips; Dances/Social/Cultural gatherings.

Welsh

Welsh General Hospital
PO Box 918, 410 Simmons St, Welsh, LA 70591
(318) 734-2555
Admin Ron Piccone.
Licensure Skilled care; Intermediate care.

Welsh Nursing Facility
PO Box 918, 410 S Simmons St, Welsh, LA 70591-0918
(318) 734-2555
Admin Robert Watkins.
Licensure Intermediate care. *Beds* ICF 60. *Certified* Medicaid.

West Monroe

G B Cooley Services
PO Box 93, Rte 8, 364 Cooley Rd, West Monroe, LA 71291
(318) 396-6300, 396-6300, ext 179 FAX
Admin H Larry Parks. *Dir of Nursing* Jeanette Gibson. *Medical Dir* Warren Daniel MD.
Licensure Intermediate care for mentally retarded; Community homes. *Beds* ICF/MR 85; Community homes 10. *Private Pay Patients* 0%. *Certified* Medicaid.
Owner Publicly owned.
Admissions Requirements Minimum age 6; Medical examination.
Staff Physicians 1 (pt); RNs 1 (pt); LPNs 5 (ft); Physical therapists 1 (pt); Recreational therapists 1 (ft); Occupational therapists 1 (ft); Speech therapists 2 (ft); Activities coordinators 1 (ft); Dietitians 1 (ft).
Facilities Dining room; Physical therapy room; Activities room; Crafts room; Laundry room; Library.
Activities Arts & crafts; Games; Movies; Shopping trips; Dances/Social/Cultural gatherings; Special Olympics; Active treatment.

Glenwood Regional Medical Center Skilled Nursing Facility
McMillan & Thomas Rd, West Monroe, LA 71291
(318) 329-4200
Admin Joe Maggio.
Licensure Skilled care. *Beds* SNF 13.

Ridgecrest Nursing Home
100 Landrum Dr, West Monroe, LA 71291
(318) 387-2577
Admin Barbara A Jones. *Dir of Nursing* Carolyn Walters. *Medical Dir* Dr Bruce Wheeler, consultant.
Licensure Intermediate care. *Beds* ICF 114. *Private Pay Patients* 8%. *Certified* Medicaid; Medicare.
Owner Privately owned (Affiliated Nursing Homes).
Admissions Requirements Medical examination; Physician's request.
Staff RNs 1 (ft); LPNs 8 (ft); Nurses' aides 34 (ft); Activities coordinators 1 (ft); Dietitians 1 (pt); Food service supervisors.
Facilities Dining room; Activities room; Crafts room; Laundry room; Barber/Beauty shop; Whirlpool.
Activities Arts & crafts; Cards; Games; Reading groups; Prayer groups; Movies; Shopping trips; Dances/Social/Cultural gatherings; Pet therapy; Fishing; Talent shows; Religious activities.

West Monroe Guest House Inc
PO Box 465, 1007 Glenwood Dr, West Monroe, LA 71291
(318) 387-3900
Admin Beth Coplin.

Licensure Intermediate care. *Beds* ICF 182.
  Certified Medicaid.

Winnfield

Autumn Leaves Nursing Home
PO Box 591, 1400 W Court St, Winnfield, LA
  71483
(318) 628-4152
Admin Jimmy Dale Zimmerman.
Licensure Intermediate care. *Beds* ICF 114.
  Certified Medicaid.

Humana Hospital Winn Parish
301 W Boundary St, Winnfield, LA 71483
(318) 628-2721
Admin Lloyd C Dupuy.
Licensure Skilled care; Intermediate care. *Beds*
  Swing beds SNF/ICF 22.

Parkview Guest Care Center
PO Box 1353, 915 1st St, Winnfield, LA
  71483
(318) 628-3533
Admin Ron Frazier.
Licensure Intermediate care. *Beds* ICF 110.
  Certified Medicaid.

Winnsboro

Franklin Guest Home Inc
2400 Ellis St, Winnsboro, LA 71295
(318) 435-5026
Admin Lois J Evans.
Licensure Intermediate care. *Beds* ICF 108.
  Certified Medicaid.

Golden Doors of Franklin Parish Inc
804 Polk St, Winnsboro, LA 71295
(318) 435-5118
Admin Henry C Bullock. *Dir of Nursing* Alice
  F Roberts.
Licensure Intermediate care; Alzheimer's care.
  Beds ICF 110. *Private Pay Patients* 15%.
  Certified Medicaid.

Owner Proprietary corp.
Admissions Requirements Medical
  examination 90 L E PSCR.
Staff RNs 1 (ft); LPNs 7 (ft), 1 (pt); Nurses'
  aides 50 (ft), 6 (pt); Speech therapists 1 (pt);
  Activities coordinators 1 (ft); Dietitians 1
  (ft).
Facilities Dining room; Activities room;
  Laundry room; Barber/Beauty shop;
  Conversation areas; Courtyards with gazebos
  and walking paths.
Activities Arts & crafts; Cards; Games; Prayer
  groups; Movies; Shopping trips; Dances/
  Social/Cultural gatherings; Pet therapy.

King's Guest Home Inc
PO Box 878, 1216 Prairie St, Winnsboro, LA
  71295
(318) 435-5194
Admin Lloyd Posey.
Licensure Intermediate care. *Beds* ICF 99.
  Certified Medicaid.

Winnsboro Manor Nursing Center
PO Box 879, Lone Cedar Rd, Winnsboro, LA
  71295
(318) 435-4536
Admin James D Sikes.
Licensure Intermediate care. *Beds* ICF 113.
  Certified Medicaid.

Wisner

Mary Anna Nursing Home Inc
PO Box 776, Hwy 15 S, Wisner, LA 71378
(318) 724-7244
Admin Candace Sanders.
Licensure Intermediate care. *Beds* ICF 81.
  Certified Medicaid.

Rosalie Nursing Home Inc
PO Box 190, Natchez St, Wisner, LA 71378
(318) 724-7493
Admin Peggy Juneau. *Dir of Nursing* Barbara
  Harris RN.

Licensure Intermediate care. *Beds* ICF 75.
  Certified Medicaid; Medicare.
Owner Proprietary corp.
Admissions Requirements Medical
  examination.
Staff RNs 1 (ft); LPNs 4 (ft), 1 (pt); Nurses'
  aides 22 (ft), 3 (pt); Activities coordinators 1
  (pt); Dietitians 1 (pt).
Facilities Dining room; Activities room;
  Crafts room; Laundry room.
Activities Arts & crafts; Cards; Games;
  Reading groups; Prayer groups; Movies;
  Shopping trips; Dances/Social/Cultural
  gatherings; Bingo; Fishing trips/fries; Car
  excursions.

Zachary

Lane Memorial Hospital Geriatric Unit
6300 Main St, Zachary, LA 70791
(504) 658-4000
Admin Charlie L Massey. *Dir of Nursing*
  Linda Long RN. *Medical Dir* Wayne
  Gravois MD.
Licensure Intermediate care. *Beds* ICF 39.
  Certified Medicaid.
Owner Publicly owned.
Staff Physicians 30 (ft), 50 (pt); RNs 1 (ft);
  LPNs 3 (ft), 2 (pt); Nurses' aides 4 (pt);
  Physical therapists 1 (ft); Activities
  coordinators 1 (pt); Dietitians 1 (ft);
  Ophthalmologists 1 (pt).
Facilities Dining room; Physical therapy
  room; Activities room; Barber/Beauty shop.
Activities Arts & crafts; Games; Prayer groups;
  Shopping trips; Dances/Social/Cultural
  gatherings; Intergenerational programs.

Zachary Manor Nursing Home
6161 Main St, Zachary, LA 70791
(504) 654-6893
Admin George Gordon.
Licensure Intermediate care. *Beds* ICF 110.
  Certified Medicaid.

MAINE

Abbot

Abbot Group Home
PO Box 141, West Rd, Abbot, ME 04406
(207) 876-3703
Admin Leigh Wiley.
Licensure Intermediate care for mentally
  retarded. *Beds* ICF/MR 6. *Certified*
  Medicaid.
Owner Nonprofit corp.
Admissions Requirements Minimum age 18.
Staff Activities coordinators 2 (pt); Dietitians
  1 (ft); QMPP 1 (pt); Administration 3 (pt).
Facilities Dining room; Activities room;
  Laundry room; Library; Living room; TV
  room; Kitchen; Large yard.
Activities Arts & crafts; Games; Reading
  groups; Movies; Shopping trips; Dances/
  Social/Cultural gatherings; Bowling;
  Camping; Picnics; Museums; Community
  activities.

Albion

Bethany Inc
PO Box 198, Hussey Rd, Albion, ME 04910
(207) 437-4294
Admin Kathryn Sawtelle.
Licensure Intermediate care. *Beds* ICF 25.
  Certified Medicaid.

Athens

Athens Group Home
PO Box 142, Brighton Rd, Athens, ME 04912
(207) 654-2629
Admin Christy Provost.
Licensure Intermediate care for mentally
  retarded. *Beds* ICF/MR 6.
Owner Nonprofit organization/foundation.
Staff ADL Counselors 7 (ft), 1 (pt).

Auburn

Auburn Nursing Home
185 Summer St, Auburn, ME 04240
(207) 786-0676
Admin Donald Powers. *Dir of Nursing* Karen
  Fortin. *Medical Dir* Dr Wolf.
Licensure Intermediate care. *Beds* ICF 46.
  Private Pay Patients 20%. *Certified*
  Medicaid.
Owner Privately owned.
Staff RNs 4 (ft); LPNs 3 (ft), 1 (pt); Nurses'
  aides 15 (ft), 6 (pt); Activities coordinators 1
  (ft).
Languages French.
Facilities Dining room; Physical therapy
  room; Activities room; Laundry room;
  Barber/Beauty shop.
Activities Arts & crafts; Cards; Games;
  Reading groups; Prayer groups; Movies;
  Shopping trips; Dances/Social/Cultural
  gatherings; Pet therapy; Weekly visits with
  school children.

Bolster Heights Health Care Facility
26 Bolster St, Auburn, ME 04210
(207) 784-1364
Admin Gerrald Frenette.
Licensure Intermediate care. *Beds* ICF 94.
  Certified Medicaid.

Clover Manor Inc
440 Minot Ave, Auburn, ME 04210
(207) 784-3573
Admin Cynthia Quinlan. *Dir of Nursing*
  Deanne Doherty. *Medical Dir* Dr Ned
  Claxton.
Licensure Skilled care; Intermediate care;
  Alzheimer's units; Child day care; Personal
  adult day care; Congregate housing. *Beds*
  SNF 5; ICF 120; Hospice beds 5; Child day
  care 20; Personal adult day care 20;
  Congregate housing 91. *Certified* Medicaid.
Owner Proprietary corp.
Staff Physicians 2 (pt); RNs 7 (ft), 5 (pt);
  LPNs 6 (ft), 3 (pt); Nurses' aides 52 (ft), 33
  (pt); Physical therapists 1 (ft); Occupational
  therapists 1 (pt); Speech therapists 1 (pt);
  Activities coordinators 1 (ft); Dietitians 1
  (ft), 1 (pt).
Facilities Dining room; Physical therapy
  room; Activities room; Crafts room; Laundry
  room; Barber/Beauty shop; Greenhouse.
Activities Arts & crafts; Cards; Games;
  Reading groups; Prayer groups; Movies;
  Shopping trips; Dances/Social/Cultural
  gatherings; Cocktail parties.

Good Shepherd Health Care Facility
200 Stetson Rd, Seville Park Plaza, Auburn,
ME 04210
(207) 782-3922
Admin Steven F Sasseville.
Medical Dir Anne Lacourse.
Licensure Intermediate care. *Beds* ICF 20.
  Certified Medicaid.
Owner Proprietary corp.
Admissions Requirements Medical
  examination; Physician's request.
Staff RNs 1 (ft); LPNs 3 (ft), 1 (pt); Nurses'
  aides 9 (ft); Recreational therapists 1 (pt).
Languages French.
Facilities Dining room; Activities room;
  Laundry room; Barber/Beauty shop.
Activities Arts & crafts; Cards; Games; Prayer
  groups; Movies; Shopping trips; Dances/
  Social/Cultural gatherings.

Lovelett Health Care Center
392 Turner St, Auburn, ME 04210
(207) 784-4773
Admin Ann Lally.
Licensure Intermediate care. *Beds* ICF 22.
  Certified Medicaid.

Promenade Health Care Facility
27 Charles St, Auburn, ME 04210
(207) 782-1621
Admin Donald C Johnson, acting.
Medical Dir Rita Wilson.
Licensure Intermediate care. *Beds* ICF 29.
  Certified Medicaid.

Staff RNs; LPNs; Nurses' aides; Activities
  coordinators; Podiatrists.
Facilities Dining room; Laundry room.
Activities Arts & crafts; Cards; Games; Prayer
  groups; Movies; Shopping trips.

Schooner Estates—Seville Park Plaza
200 Stetson Rd, Auburn, ME 04210
(207) 784-2900, ext 136
Admin Gail L Sasseville. *Dir of Nursing*
  Sandra James. *Medical Dir* Dr Albert
  Shems.
Licensure Intermediate care; Assisted living.
  Beds ICF 37; Assisted living units 73.
  Private Pay Patients 75%. *Certified*
  Medicaid.
Owner Proprietary corp.
Admissions Requirements Minimum age 55.
Staff RNs; LPNs; Nurses' aides; Physical
  therapists (contracted); Activities
  coordinators; Dietitians.
Languages French.
Facilities Dining room; Physical therapy
  room; Activities room; Chapel; Crafts room;
  Laundry room; Barber/Beauty shop; Library;
  Pub.
Activities Arts & crafts; Cards; Games;
  Reading groups; Prayer groups; Movies;
  Shopping trips; Dances/Social/Cultural
  gatherings; Pet therapy.

Augusta

Augusta Convalescent Center
187 Eastern Ave, Augusta, ME 04330
(207) 622-3121
Admin Rosemary Rowe.
Licensure Intermediate care. *Beds* ICF 78.
  Certified Medicaid.
Owner Proprietary corp (Hillhaven Corp).

Augusta Mental Health Institute
PO Box 724, Arsenal St, Augusta, ME 04330
(207) 289-7200
Admin William C Daumueller.
Medical Dir Jose Castellanos MD.
Licensure Intermediate care; Acute care. *Beds*
  ICF 70; Acute care 16. *Certified* Medicaid.
Staff Physicians 1 (ft); RNs 3 (ft), 1 (pt);
  LPNs 6 (ft); Nurses' aides 39 (ft); Physical
  therapists 1 (pt); Recreational therapists 1
  (ft); Dietitians 1 (pt).
Facilities Dining room; Physical therapy
  room; Chapel; Crafts room; Laundry room;
  Barber/Beauty shop; Library; Gift shop;
  Canteen.
Activities Arts & crafts; Cards; Games;
  Reading groups; Movies; Shopping trips;
  Dances/Social/Cultural gatherings.

Maine Veterans Home
Cony Rd, Box 901, Augusta, ME 04330
(207) 622-2454
Admin William Carney.
Licensure Intermediate care. *Beds* ICF 120.

Williams Health Care—Glenridge
Glenridge Dr, Augusta, ME 04330
(207) 623-2593
Admin Nola B Ribe. *Dir of Nursing* Judy
McGrail RN. *Medical Dir* Roy Miller MD.
Licensure Intermediate care. *Beds* ICF 120.
Certified Medicaid; Medicare.
Owner Nonprofit corp.
Admissions Requirements Medical
examination; Physician's request.
Staff RNs 6 (ft), 7 (pt); LPNs 2 (ft), 1 (pt);
Nurses' aides 39 (ft), 9 (pt); Physical
therapists 1 (ft); Activities coordinators 1
(ft); Dietitians 1 (ft).
Languages French.
Facilities Dining room; Physical therapy
room; Activities room; Chapel; Crafts room;
Laundry room; Barber/Beauty shop.
Activities Arts & crafts; Cards; Games;
Reading groups; Prayer groups; Movies;
Dances/Social/Cultural gatherings.

Williams Health Care—Gray Birch
Gray Birch Dr, Augusta, ME 04330
(207) 622-6228
Admin Gregory B Gravel. *Dir of Nursing*
Charlene Dorsky RN. *Medical Dir* Roy
Miller MD.
Licensure Skilled care; Intermediate care. *Beds*
SNF 20; ICF 100. *Certified* Medicaid;
Medicare.
Owner Nonprofit corp.
Admissions Requirements Medical
examination; Physician's request.
Staff RNs 6 (ft), 3 (pt); LPNs 2 (ft), 1 (pt);
Nurses' aides 39 (ft), 7 (pt); Physical
therapists 1 (ft); Reality therapists 1 (pt);
Recreational therapists 1 (ft), 4 (pt);
Activities coordinators 1 (ft); Dietitians 1
(pt).
Languages French.
Facilities Dining room; Physical therapy
room; Activities room; Crafts room; Laundry
room; Barber/Beauty shop.
Activities Arts & crafts; Cards; Games;
Reading groups; Prayer groups; Movies;
Dances/Social/Cultural gatherings.

Bangor

Bangor City Nursing Facility
103 Texas Ave, Bangor, ME 04401
(207) 947-4557
Admin Judith B Roscetti. *Dir of Nursing*
Sharon Miner RN. *Medical Dir* Edward
Babcock MD.
Licensure Skilled care; Intermediate care. *Beds*
Swing beds SNF/ICF 56. *Certified* Medicaid;
Medicare.
Owner Publicly owned.
Admissions Requirements Medical
examination.
Staff Physicians 1 (pt); RNs 3 (ft), 6 (pt);
LPNs 4 (ft), 6 (pt); Nurses' aides 19 (ft), 20
(pt); Physical therapists 1 (ft); Activities
coordinators 1 (ft); Dietitians 1 (pt).
Facilities Dining room; Physical therapy
room; Activities room; Crafts room; Laundry
room; Barber/Beauty shop.
Activities Arts & crafts; Cards; Games;
Reading groups; Prayer groups; Movies;
Shopping trips; Dances/Social/Cultural
gatherings; Intergenerational programs; Pet
therapy.

Bangor Convalescent Center
516 Mount Hope Ave, Bangor, ME 04401
(207) 947-6131
Admin Gloria Rice.
Medical Dir Michael Bruhel MD.
Licensure Intermediate care. *Beds* ICF 78.
Certified Medicaid.
Owner Proprietary corp (Hillhaven Corp).
Admissions Requirements Medical
examination.

Staff Physicians 12 (pt); RNs 2 (ft), 1 (pt);
LPNs 8 (ft), 2 (pt); Nurses' aides 25 (ft), 10
(pt); Physical therapists 1 (pt); Occupational
therapists 1 (pt); Speech therapists 1 (pt);
Activities coordinators 1 (ft), 1 (pt);
Dietitians 1 (ft), 1 (pt).
Facilities Dining room; Physical therapy
room; Activities room; Crafts room; Laundry
room; Barber/Beauty shop; Library; Living
rooms.
Activities Arts & crafts; Cards; Games;
Reading groups; Prayer groups; Movies;
Shopping trips; Dances/Social/Cultural
gatherings; Field trips; Family dinners.

Bangor Mental Health Institute
PO Box 926, 656 State St, Bangor, ME 04401
(207) 941-4289
Admin N Lawrence Ventura. *Dir of Nursing*
Franes Vanecek, Asst. *Medical Dir* Roger M
Wilson MD.
Licensure Intermediate care; Acute care;
Psychiatric care; Alzheimer's care. *Beds* ICF
130; Acute care 17; Psychiatric care 135.
Certified Medicaid.
Owner Publicly owned.
Staff Physicians 5 (ft), 5 (pt); RNs 46 (ft);
LPNs 27 (ft); Nurses' aides 226 (ft); Physical
therapists 1 (ft); Reality therapists 1 (ft);
Recreational therapists 2 (ft); Occupational
therapists 1 (ft).
Facilities Dining room; Physical therapy
room; Activities room; Chapel; Crafts room;
Laundry room; Barber/Beauty shop; Library;
Occupational therapy; Home living skills
area.
Activities Arts & crafts; Cards; Games;
Reading groups; Prayer groups; Movies;
Shopping trips; Dances/Social/Cultural
gatherings.

Eastern Maine Medical Center (Ross Division)
489 State St, Bangor, ME 04401
(207) 945-8570
Admin Ruth Tozier RN. *Dir of Nursing*
Florence Fenton RN. *Medical Dir* Phillip
Mossman MD.
Licensure Skilled care; Retirement. *Beds* SNF
15; Retirement 14. *Certified* Medicaid;
Medicare.
Owner Nonprofit organization/foundation.
Admissions Requirements Medical
examination; Physician's request.
Staff Physicians 1 (pt); RNs 5 (ft), 4 (pt);
Nurses' aides 7 (ft), 8 (pt); Physical
therapists 1 (ft); Recreational therapists 1
(ft); Occupational therapists 1 (ft); Speech
therapists 1 (ft); Activities coordinators 1
(ft); Dietitians 1 (ft); Ophthalmologists 1
(pt); Podiatrists 1 (pt); Audiologists 1 (pt).
Languages French.
Facilities Dining room; Physical therapy
room; Activities room; Chapel; Crafts room;
Laundry room; Barber/Beauty shop.
Activities Arts & crafts; Cards; Games;
Movies; Dances/Social/Cultural gatherings;
Pet therapy.

Pine Street Group Home
188 Pine St, Bangor, ME 04401
(207) 947-6634
Admin Ellen Hoyt.
Licensure Intermediate care for mentally
retarded. *Beds* ICF/MR 6. *Certified*
Medicaid.
Owner Privately owned.
Admissions Requirements Minimum age 21;
Medical examination; Physician's request.
Staff Recreational therapists 1 (ft).
Facilities Dining room; Activities room;
Laundry room.
Activities Arts & crafts; Cards; Games;
Movies; Shopping trips; Dances/Social/
Cultural gatherings.

Stillwater Health Care
335 Stillwater Ave, Bangor, ME 04401
(207) 947-1111

Admin Gerard H Cyr.
Medical Dir Dr Henry Atkins.
Licensure Intermediate care. *Beds* ICF 67.
Certified Medicaid.
Owner Proprietary corp.
Facilities Dining room; Physical therapy
room; Activities room; Chapel; Laundry
room; Barber/Beauty shop.
Activities Arts & crafts; Cards; Games;
Reading groups; Prayer groups; Movies;
Shopping trips; Picnics.

Taylor Hospital
268 Stillwater Ave, Bangor, ME 04401
(207) 942-5286
Admin Donald A Mayer.
Medical Dir Koster K Peter DO.
Licensure Intermediate care; Acute care. *Beds*
ICF 38; Acute care 55. *Certified* Medicaid.
Admissions Requirements Physician's request.
Staff RNs 2 (ft); LPNs 5 (ft); Nurses' aides 14
(ft); Physical therapists 1 (pt); Activities
coordinators 1 (pt); Dietitians 1 (ft).
Facilities Dining room; Activities room;
Chapel; Laundry room.
Activities Arts & crafts; Cards; Games;
Movies; Shopping trips.

Westgate Manor
750 Union St, Bangor, ME 04401
(207) 942-7336
Admin Susan C Cirone. *Dir of Nursing* Elaine
Brown RN. *Medical Dir* Henry Atkins MD.
Licensure Intermediate care; Alzheimer's care.
Beds ICF 113. *Private Pay Patients* 30%.
Certified Medicaid.
Owner Proprietary corp (Hillhaven Corp).
Admissions Requirements Medical
examination; Physician's request.
Staff RNs 5 (ft); LPNs 5 (ft); Nurses' aides 35
(ft); Activities coordinators 2 (ft); Dietitians
1 (pt).
Facilities Dining room; Barber/Beauty shop.
Activities Arts & crafts; Cards; Games; Prayer
groups; Movies; Shopping trips; Dances/
Social/Cultural gatherings; Intergenerational
programs; Pet therapy.

Bar Harbor

Sonogee Estates
Eden St, Box 156, Bar Harbor, ME 04609
(207) 288-5800
Admin Donna Cameron RN.
Licensure Intermediate care. *Beds* ICF 83.
Certified Medicaid.
Owner Proprietary corp.
Admissions Requirements Minimum age 60;
Physician's request.
Staff RNs 5 (ft); LPNs 9 (ft); Nurses' aides 35
(ft), 8 (pt); Activities coordinators 2 (ft);
Dietitians 1 (ft).
Facilities Dining room; Physical therapy
room; Activities room; Chapel; Crafts room;
Laundry room; Barber/Beauty shop.
Activities Arts & crafts; Cards; Games;
Reading groups; Prayer groups; Movies;
Shopping trips; Dances/Social/Cultural
gatherings.

Summit House Health Center
Norman Rd, Bar Harbor, ME 04609
(207) 288-5856
Admin David Waldron.
Licensure Intermediate care. *Beds* ICF 80.
Certified Medicaid.

Bath

Bath Nursing Home
PO Box 138, Winship St, Bath, ME 04530
(207) 443-9772
Admin Mark A Lowell.
Medical Dir Anthony Keating MD.
Licensure Intermediate care. *Beds* ICF 72.
Certified Medicaid.
Owner Proprietary corp (Hillhaven Corp).

Admissions Requirements Medical
examination; Physician's request.
Staff Physicians 16 (pt); RNs 3 (ft), 4 (pt);
LPNs 3 (ft), 2 (pt); Nurses' aides 22 (ft), 12
(pt); Physical therapists; Occupational
therapists; Speech therapists; Activities
coordinators 1 (ft), 1 (pt); Dietitians 1 (pt);
Ophthalmologists 3 (pt); Podiatrists 1 (pt);
Dentists 3 (pt).
Facilities Dining room; Physical therapy
room; Activities room; Chapel; Crafts room;
Laundry room; Barber/Beauty shop.
Activities Arts & crafts; Cards; Games;
Reading groups; Prayer groups; Movies;
Shopping trips; Dances/Social/Cultural
gatherings.

Hillhouse Convalescent Home
Box 98, Whiskeag Rd, Bath, ME 04530
(207) 443-6301
Admin Marjorie Voorhees.
Licensure Intermediate care. *Beds* 37.
Certified Medicaid.

Belfast

Bradbury Manor
32 High St, Belfast, ME 04915
(207) 338-3666
Admin Edward A Bonenfant.
Licensure Intermediate care. *Beds* ICF 56.
Certified Medicaid.

Tallpines Health Care Facility
20 Wight St, Belfast, ME 04915
(207) 338-4117, 338-4118 FAX
Admin Elizabeth B Barnaby RN. *Dir of
Nursing* Kathie Ball RN. *Medical Dir* David
Loxterkamp MD.
Licensure Intermediate care. *Beds* ICF 70.
Private Pay Patients 30-32%. *Certified*
Medicaid.
Owner Nonprofit corp (Max-Parry Associates).
Admissions Requirements Minimum age 21;
Medical examination; Physician's request.
Staff Physicians 10 (ft); RNs 6 (ft), 5 (pt);
LPNs 5 (ft), 2 (pt); Nurses' aides 30 (ft), 17
(pt); Physical therapists (consultant);
Occupational therapists (consultant); Speech
therapists (consultant); Dietitians
(consultant); Ophthalmologists (consultant);
Podiatrists 1 (pt); Reality therapistsActivities
coordinators 1 (ft), 1 (pt).
Languages Swedish, French, German.
Facilities Dining room; Physical therapy
room; Activities room; Chapel; Crafts room;
Laundry room; Barber/Beauty shop; Library;
2 solariums; Nature trail; Raised bed
gardens; Patio; Family room.
Activities Arts & crafts; Cards; Games;
Reading groups; Prayer groups; Movies;
Shopping trips; Dances/Social/Cultural
gatherings; Intergenerational programs; Pet
therapy; Rhythm band; Community
activities.

Biddeford

Greenhill Residence
1 Green St, Biddeford, ME 04005
(207) 282-3741
Admin Donna Whitten.
Licensure Intermediate care for mentally
retarded. *Beds* ICF/MR 6.
Admissions Requirements Minimum age 16;
Medical examination; Physician's request.
Staff RNs 1 (pt); Activities coordinators 1 (ft).
Facilities Dining room; Activities room;
Laundry room.
Activities Arts & crafts; Cards; Games;
Movies; Shopping trips; Dances/Social/
Cultural gatherings.

Riverwood Health Care Center
PO Box 364, 355 Pool St, Biddeford, ME
04005
(207) 283-3646

Admin Daniel Sowerby. *Dir of Nursing* Linda
Owen RN.
Licensure Intermediate care; Alzheimer's care.
Beds ICF 61. *Certified* Medicaid.
Owner Proprietary corp.
Admissions Requirements Medical
examination.
Staff RNs 5 (ft), 2 (pt); LPNs 4 (ft), 3 (pt);
Nurses' aides 14 (ft), 8 (pt); Activities
coordinators 1 (ft), 1 (pt); Medical
technicians 2 (ft).
Languages French, Greek.
Facilities Dining room; Physical therapy
room; Activities room; Chapel; Crafts room;
Laundry room; Barber/Beauty shop; Library.
Activities Arts & crafts; Cards; Games;
Reading groups; Prayer groups; Movies;
Shopping trips; Dances/Social/Cultural
gatherings.

St Andre Health Care Facility
407 Pool St, Biddeford, ME 04005
(207) 282-5171
Admin Sr Madeleine D'Anjou. *Dir of Nursing*
Cecile Rossignol RN. *Medical Dir* Leslie
Tripp MD.
Licensure Intermediate care. *Beds* ICF 96.
Private Pay Patients 30%. *Certified*
Medicaid.
Owner Nonprofit corp.
Admissions Requirements Medical
examination.
Staff Physicians 1 (pt); RNs 6 (ft), 9 (pt);
LPNs 4 (ft), 7 (pt); Nurses' aides 34 (ft), 25
(pt); Physical therapists 2 (pt); Activities
coordinators 2 (ft); Dietitians 1 (pt);
Ophthalmologists 1 (pt); Podiatrists 1 (pt).
Languages French.
Affiliation Roman Catholic.
Facilities Dining room; Physical therapy
room; Activities room; Chapel; Crafts room;
Laundry room; Barber/Beauty shop; Library.
Activities Arts & crafts; Cards; Games;
Reading groups; Prayer groups; Movies;
Shopping trips; Dances/Social/Cultural
gatherings; Intergenerational programs; Pet
therapy; Books on tape.

Southridge Living Center
PO Box 388, Biddeford, ME 04005-0388
(207) 282-4138
Admin Beth Beaudin Ham.
Medical Dir M P Houle MD.
Licensure Intermediate care. *Beds* ICF 125.
Certified Medicaid.
Owner Proprietary corp (Continental Health
Service Management).
Staff RNs 5 (ft); LPNs 11 (ft); Nurses' aides
36 (ft); Activities coordinators 2 (ft);
Dietitians 2 (ft).
Facilities Dining room; Physical therapy
room; Activities room; Chapel; Crafts room;
Laundry room; Barber/Beauty shop.
Activities Arts & crafts; Cards; Games;
Reading groups; Prayer groups; Movies;
Shopping trips; Dances/Social/Cultural
gatherings.

Trull Nursing Home
PO Box 1245, 15 May St, Biddeford, ME
04005
(207) 284-4507
Admin Marion Stickney.
Licensure Intermediate care. *Beds* ICF 49.
Certified Medicaid.

Bingham

Somerset Manor Inc
PO Box 449, Owen St, Bingham, ME 04920
(207) 672-4041
Admin Karen Lynne Leupold. *Dir of Nursing*
Molly Williams.
Licensure Intermediate care. *Beds* ICF 34.
Certified Medicaid.
Owner Proprietary corp (Continental Health
Service Management).

Staff RNs 2 (ft); LPNs 2 (ft), 1 (pt); Nurses'
aides 10 (ft), 14 (pt).
Facilities Dining room; Activities room;
Laundry room; Barber/Beauty shop.
Activities Arts & crafts; Cards; Games;
Reading groups; Prayer groups; Movies;
Shopping trips; Dances/Social/Cultural
gatherings; Van rides.

Boothbay Harbor

St Andrews Hospital Gregory Wing
3rd St Andrews Ln, Boothbay Harbor, ME
04538
(207) 633-2121
Admin Karen Fiducia.
Licensure Skilled care; Intermediate care;
Acute care. *Beds* ICF 30; Acute care 16;
Swing beds SNF/ICF 6.

Brewer

**Brewer Convalescent Center—Head Injury
Treatment Program**
74 Parkway S, Brewer, ME 04412
(207) 989-7300, 989-7199, (800) 445-2141,
(207) 989-4240 FAX
Admin Penelope H Sargent. *Dir of Nursing*
David Hamlin RN. *Medical Dir* Richard
Sagall MD.
Licensure Skilled care; Intermediate care. *Beds*
SNF 12; ICF 100. *Certified* Medicaid;
Medicare.
Owner Proprietary corp (Hillhaven Corp).
Staff Physicians 1 (ft), 4 (pt); RNs 10 (ft);
LPNs 12 (ft), 3 (pt); Nurses' aides 40 (ft), 20
(pt); Physical therapists 1 (ft); Recreational
therapists 1 (ft); Occupational therapists 1
(ft); Speech therapists 1 (ft); Activities
coordinators 2 (ft), 1 (pt); Dietitians 1 (ft);
Ophthalmologists 1 (pt); Podiatrists 1 (pt);
Audiologists 1 (pt).
Languages French.
Facilities Dining room; Physical therapy
room; Activities room; Chapel; Crafts room;
Laundry room; Barber/Beauty shop; Library.
Activities Arts & crafts; Cards; Games;
Reading groups; Prayer groups; Movies;
Shopping trips; Dances/Social/Cultural
gatherings; Intergenerational programs; Pet
therapy.

Eddington Group Home
RFD 2 Box 82, Brewer, ME 04412
(207) 989-1303
Admin Jacqueline Allen. *Dir of Nursing* Gail
Sinclair RN.
Licensure Intermediate care for mentally
retarded. *Beds* ICF/MR 6. *Certified*
Medicaid.
Owner Nonprofit corp.
Admissions Requirements Minimum age 18;
Medical examination.
Staff RNs 1 (pt); Nurses' aides 12 (ft); Speech
therapists 1 (pt); Activities coordinators 1
(ft); Dietitians 1 (pt).
Activities Arts & crafts; Cards; Games;
Reading groups; Prayer groups; Movies;
Shopping trips; Dances/Social/Cultural
gatherings.

Bridgton

Bridgton Health Care Center
PO Box 330, Portland St, Bridgton, ME 04009
(207) 647-8821
Admin Elaine Hicks.
Licensure Intermediate care. *Beds* ICF 70.

Good Neighbors Inc
PO Box 119, S High St, Bridgton, ME 04009
(207) 647-8244
Admin Dale Zebulske.
Licensure Intermediate care for mentally
retarded. *Beds* ICF/MR 12. *Certified*
Medicaid.

Brunswick

Brunswick Convalescent Center
70 Baribeau Dr, Brunswick, ME 04011
(207) 725-4379
Admin Vicki N White.
Medical Dir E Schmidt MD.
Licensure Intermediate care. *Beds* ICF 82.
  Certified Medicaid.
Admissions Requirements Medical
  examination.
Staff RNs 3 (ft), 4 (pt); LPNs 1 (ft), 7 (pt);
  Nurses' aides 21 (ft), 28 (pt); Activities
  coordinators 1 (ft); Dietitians 1 (ft).
Facilities Dining room; Activities room;
  Crafts room; Laundry room; Barber/Beauty
  shop; Library.
Activities Arts & crafts; Reading groups;
  Prayer groups; Movies; Shopping trips;
  Dances/Social/Cultural gatherings.

Brunswick Manor
26-28 Cumberland St, Brunswick, ME 04011
(207) 725-5801
Admin Kathleen A McGhee. *Dir of Nursing*
  Marion A Roy RN.
Licensure Intermediate care. *Beds* ICF 51.
  Certified Medicaid.
Owner Privately owned.
Admissions Requirements Physician's request.
Staff RNs; LPNs; Nurses' aides; Activities
  coordinators; Dietitians.
Facilities Activities room; Laundry room;
  Barber/Beauty shop; Library.
Activities Arts & crafts; Cards; Games;
  Reading groups; Prayer groups; Movies;
  Shopping trips; Dances/Social/Cultural
  gatherings; Resident council.

Mere Point Nursing Home
Mere Point Rd, Brunswick, ME 04011
(207) 725-2870
Admin Theodore A Hussey.
Licensure Intermediate care. *Beds* ICF 26.
  Certified Medicaid.

Regional Memorial Hospital
58 Baribeau Dr, Brunswick, ME 04011
(207) 729-0181
Admin Herbert Paris.
Medical Dir Dr Montegut.
Licensure Skilled care; Acute care. *Beds* SNF
  8; Acute care 90. *Certified* Medicaid;
  Medicare.
Owner Nonprofit corp.
Admissions Requirements Medical
  examination.
Staff RNs 2 (ft), 2 (pt); LPNs 1 (ft), 2 (pt);
  Nurses' aides 4 (ft), 2 (pt); Activities
  coordinators 1 (pt).
Languages French.
Facilities Dining room; Physical therapy
  room; Activities room.
Activities Arts & crafts; Cards; Games;
  Movies; Shopping trips; Home cooked
  meals.

Calais

Barnard Nursing Home
Palmer St Ext, Calais, ME 04619
(207) 454-2366
Admin Edward Fournier.
Medical Dir Ann Lyons.
Licensure Intermediate care. *Beds* ICF 100.
  Certified Medicaid.
Owner Privately owned.
Staff RNs; LPNs; Nurses' aides; Activities
  coordinators; Dietitians.
Facilities Dining room; Activities room;
  Crafts room; Laundry room; Barber/Beauty
  shop.
Activities Arts & crafts; Cards; Games;
  Reading groups; Prayer groups; Movies;
  Shopping trips; Dances/Social/Cultural
  gatherings; Student reading; Volunteer
  programs; Cooking.

Camden

Camden Community Health Care Center
108 Elm St, Camden, ME 04843
(207) 236-8381
Admin Jefferson Ackor. *Dir of Nursing*
  Marjorie Smith RN.
Licensure Skilled care; Intermediate care;
  Alzheimer's care. *Beds* SNF 20; ICF 178.
  Certified Medicaid; Medicare; VA.
Owner Nonprofit corp.
Admissions Requirements Medical
  examination; Physician's request.
Staff Physicians 2 (pt); RNs 3 (ft), 10 (pt);
  LPNs 2 (ft), 10 (pt); Nurses' aides 80 (ft), 40
  (pt); Physical therapists 3 (ft), 2 (pt);
  Occupational therapists 2 (ft), 2 (pt); Speech
  therapists 2 (ft), 1 (pt); Activities
  coordinators 1 (ft), 3 (pt); Dietitians 1 (pt);
  Ophthalmologists 2 (pt); Podiatrists 1 (ft);
  Dentists 3 (pt).
Facilities Dining room; Physical therapy
  room; Activities room; Chapel; Crafts room;
  Laundry room; Barber/Beauty shop; Library;
  Outdoor patio; Park & BBQ area.
Activities Arts & crafts; Cards; Games;
  Reading groups; Prayer groups; Movies;
  Shopping trips; Dances/Social/Cultural
  gatherings.

Camden Nursing Home
19 Mountain St, Camden, ME 04843
(207) 236-2900
Admin Krista S Weber. *Dir of Nursing*
  Thelma Dean RN. *Medical Dir* Dr Paul
  Cox.
Licensure Intermediate care. *Beds* ICF 29.
  Certified Medicaid.
Owner Proprietary corp (Kenneth J Weber).
Admissions Requirements Minimum age 65.
Staff RNs 1 (ft), 1 (pt); LPNs 2 (ft), 2 (pt);
  Nurses' aides 13 (ft), 3 (pt); Physical
  therapists 1 (pt); Activities coordinators 1
  (ft); Dietitians 1 (pt); Podiatrists 1 (pt).
Facilities Dining room; Activities room;
  Laundry room.
Activities Arts & crafts; Cards; Games;
  Reading groups; Prayer groups; Movies;
  Shopping trips; Dances/Social/Cultural
  gatherings; Intergenerational programs; Pet
  therapy.

Canton

Victorian Villa Nursing Home
PO Box 636, Canton, ME 04221
(207) 597-2115
Admin Aiden E Redding. *Dir of Nursing*
  Barbara Williamson RN. *Medical Dir* Leslie
  Harding MD.
Licensure Intermediate care. *Beds* ICF 56.
  Private Pay Patients 10%. *Certified*
  Medicaid.
Owner Proprietary corp (Redding Homes Inc).
Staff RNs 3 (ft), 1 (pt); LPNs 5 (ft), 1 (pt);
  Nurses' aides 28 (ft), 1 (pt); Activities
  coordinators 1 (ft); Dietitians 1 (ft).
Facilities Dining room; Laundry room;
  Barber/Beauty shop.
Activities Arts & crafts; Cards; Games;
  Reading groups; Prayer groups; Movies;
  Dances/Social/Cultural gatherings.

Cape Elizabeth

Viking Nursing Facility Inc
126 Scott Dyer Rd, Cape Elizabeth, ME
04107
(207) 767-3373
Admin Duane Rancourt. *Dir of Nursing* Susan
  Ryder.
Licensure Intermediate care. *Beds* ICF 60.
  Certified Medicaid.
Owner Proprietary corp.
Staff RNs 4 (ft), 5 (pt); LPNs 2 (ft), 4 (pt);
  Nurses' aides 14 (ft), 19 (pt).

Facilities Dining room; Activities room;
  Laundry room; Barber/Beauty shop.
Activities Arts & crafts; Cards; Games;
  Reading groups; Prayer groups; Movies;
  Shopping trips.

Caribou

Caribou Nursing Home
10 Bernadette St, Caribou, ME 04736
(207) 498-3102
Admin Michael Cyr.
Licensure Intermediate care. *Beds* ICF 110.
  Certified Medicaid.
Admissions Requirements Medical
  examination.
Staff RNs 1 (ft), 7 (pt); LPNs 1 (ft), 10 (pt);
  Nurses' aides 16 (ft), 67 (pt); Physical
  therapists 1 (ft); Activities coordinators 2
  (ft); Dietitians 6 (ft), 9 (pt).
Facilities Dining room; Physical therapy
  room; Activities room; Crafts room; Laundry
  room; Barber/Beauty shop.
Activities Arts & crafts; Cards; Games; Prayer
  groups; Movies; Dances/Social/Cultural
  gatherings.

Coopers Mills

Country Manor Nursing Home
PO Box 76, Coopers Mills, ME 04341
(204) 549-7471
Admin Barbara Baranello. *Dir of Nursing*
  Linda Bradford RN.
Licensure Intermediate care. *Beds* ICF 54.
  Certified Medicaid.
Owner Proprietary corp.
Admissions Requirements Minimum age 65;
  Medical examination; Physician's request.
Staff RNs 2 (ft), 1 (pt); LPNs 1 (ft), 2 (pt);
  Nurses' aides 12 (ft), 9 (pt); Activities
  coordinators 1 (pt).
Facilities Dining room; Activities room;
  Laundry room.
Activities Arts & crafts; Cards; Games;
  Reading groups; Prayer groups; Movies;
  Shopping trips.

Sheepscot Valley Health Center
Main St, Coopers Mills, ME 04341
(207) 549-7581
Admin David N Fenton.

Danforth

Danforth Habilitation Residential Center
Maple St, Danforth, ME 04424
(207) 448-2327
Admin Cecil Williams.
Licensure Intermediate care for mentally
  retarded. *Beds* ICF/MR 13. *Certified*
  Medicaid.

Danforth Nursing Home Inc
PO Box 145, Depot St, Danforth, ME 04424
(207) 448-2383
Admin Pamela DeWitt. *Dir of Nursing* Vicki
  Little. *Medical Dir* Dr Ted Sussman.
Licensure Intermediate care. *Beds* ICF 17.
  Certified Medicaid.
Owner Proprietary corp.
Staff Physicians; RNs; LPNs; Nurses' aides;
  Physical therapists; Reality therapists;
  Recreational therapists; Occupational
  therapists; Speech therapists; Activities
  coordinators; Dietitians; Podiatrists.
Facilities Dining room; Activities room;
  Crafts room; Laundry room.
Activities Arts & crafts; Cards; Games;
  Reading groups.

Deer Isle

Island Nursing Home
Rte 15 Box 124, Deer Isle, ME 04627
(207) 348-2351

Admin Laura Griffin. *Dir of Nursing* Arlene Hasbell. *Medical Dir* Dr Daniel.
Licensure Intermediate care. *Beds* ICF 50. *Certified* Medicaid.
Owner Nonprofit corp.
Admissions Requirements Minimum age 16; Physician's request.
Staff RNs 2 (ft), 1 (pt); LPNs 3 (ft), 2 (pt); Nurses' aides 23 (ft), 15 (pt); Speech therapists 1 (pt); Activities coordinators 1 (ft), 1 (pt); Dietitians 1 (pt).
Facilities Dining room; Activities room; Crafts room; Laundry room; Barber/Beauty shop; Library.
Activities Arts & crafts; Cards; Games; Reading groups; Prayer groups; Movies; Shopping trips; Dine out trips.

Island Nursing Home Inc
PO Box 124, Rte 15, Deer Isle, ME 04627
(207) 348-2351
Admin Laura C Griffin. *Dir of Nursing* Rhonda Carlin RN. *Medical Dir* Daniel Rissi MD.
Licensure Intermediate care. *Beds* ICF 50. *Private Pay Patients* 35%. *Certified* Medicaid.
Owner Nonprofit corp.
Admissions Requirements Minimum age 18; Medical examination; Physician's request.
Staff RNs 3 (ft); LPNs 3 (ft); Physical therapists; Speech therapists; Activities coordinators 1 (ft), 1 (pt); Dietitians; Podiatrists.
Facilities Dining room; Activities room; Crafts room; Laundry room; Barber/Beauty shop; Library.
Activities Arts & crafts; Cards; Games; Reading groups; Prayer groups; Movies; Shopping trips; Intergenerational programs; Pet therapy.

Dexter

Dexter Nursing Home
PO Box 347, 64 Park St, Dexter, ME 04930
(207) 924-5516
Admin Donald J Palleschi. *Dir of Nursing* Marcia Young.
Licensure Intermediate care. *Beds* ICF 66. *Private Pay Patients* 14%. *Certified* Medicaid.
Owner Proprietary corp (First Atlantic Corp).
Admissions Requirements Medical examination; Physician's request.
Staff Physicians; RNs; LPNs; Nurses' aides; Physical therapists; Recreational therapists; Activities coordinators; Dietitians; Podiatrists.
Facilities Dining room; Physical therapy room; Activities room; Laundry room; Barber/Beauty shop.
Activities Arts & crafts; Cards; Games; Reading groups; Prayer groups; Movies; Shopping trips; Dances/Social/Cultural gatherings; Intergenerational programs; Pet therapy; Adopt-a-grandparent.

Dixfield

Dixfield Health Care Center
100 Weld St, Dixfield, ME 04224
(207) 562-4922
Admin Carolyn Farley.
Licensure Intermediate care. *Beds* ICF 55. *Certified* Medicaid.
Owner Proprietary corp (Hillhaven Corp).

Dover-Foxcroft

Hibbard Nursing Home
Guilford Rd, Dover-Foxcroft, ME 04426
(207) 564-8129
Admin Jane M Hibbard.
Medical Dir L J Stitham MD.

Licensure Skilled care; Intermediate care. *Beds* SNF 12; ICF 90. *Certified* Medicaid; Medicare.
Staff Physicians 10 (ft), 3 (pt); RNs 3 (ft), 3 (pt); LPNs 4 (ft), 2 (pt); Nurses' aides 31 (ft), 13 (pt); Physical therapists 1 (ft); Speech therapists 1 (pt); Activities coordinators 2 (ft); Dietitians 1 (pt); Ophthalmologists 1 (pt); Podiatrists 1 (pt); Dentists 1 (pt).
Facilities Dining room; Physical therapy room; Activities room; Crafts room; Laundry room; Barber/Beauty shop; Library.
Activities Arts & crafts; Cards; Games; Reading groups; Prayer groups; Movies; Shopping trips; Dances/Social/Cultural gatherings.

Eagle Lake

Eagle Lake Home
Church St, Eagle Lake, ME 04739
(207) 444-5152
Admin Mark S Plourde. *Dir of Nursing* Jeanne Charette RN.
Licensure Intermediate care. *Beds* ICF 60. *Certified* Medicaid.
Owner Nonprofit corp.
Admissions Requirements Minimum age 16; Medical examination; Physician's request.
Staff RNs 7 (ft), 1 (pt); LPNs 1 (ft), 1 (pt); Nurses' aides 12 (ft), 30 (pt); Recreational therapists 1 (ft); Speech therapists 1 (pt); Activities coordinators 1 (ft); Dietitians 1 (ft); Ophthalmologists 1 (pt); Podiatrists 1 (pt).
Languages French.
Facilities Dining room; Physical therapy room; Activities room; Chapel; Crafts room; Laundry room; Barber/Beauty shop; Library.
Activities Arts & crafts; Cards; Games; Reading groups; Movies; Shopping trips; Dances/Social/Cultural gatherings.

Eastport

Eastport Memorial Nursing Home
23 Boynton St, Eastport, ME 04631
(207) 853-2531
Admin John Wood. *Dir of Nursing* Dolly Newcomb. *Medical Dir* Stephen Austin.
Licensure Intermediate care. *Beds* ICF 26. *Certified* Medicaid.
Owner Nonprofit organization/foundation.
Admissions Requirements Physician's request.
Staff RNs 3 (ft); LPNs 1 (ft), 2 (pt); Nurses' aides 6 (ft), 15 (pt); Dietitians.
Facilities Dining room; Activities room; Crafts room; Laundry room; Barber/Beauty shop.
Activities Games; Reading groups; Movies; Dances/Social/Cultural gatherings.

Ellsworth

Collier's Health Care Center
PO Box 544, Ellsworth, ME 04605
(207) 667-9336
Admin William L Collier. *Dir of Nursing* Sigrid Stevens. *Medical Dir* Dr Joseph LaCasce.
Licensure Intermediate care. *Beds* ICF 44. *Certified* Medicaid.
Owner Proprietary corp.
Admissions Requirements Medical examination.
Staff RNs 2 (ft); LPNs 4 (ft), 5 (pt); Nurses' aides 21 (ft), 5 (pt); Activities coordinators 1 (pt).
Languages French.
Facilities Activities room; Laundry room.
Activities Arts & crafts; Cards; Games; Prayer groups; Movies; Special meals.

Ellsworth Convalescent Center
38 Court St, Ellsworth, ME 04605
(207) 667-9036

Admin Mitchell Rousseau.
Medical Dir Charles Alexander MD.
Licensure Intermediate care. *Beds* ICF 94. *Certified* Medicaid.
Admissions Requirements Medical examination; Physician's request.
Staff RNs 4 (ft), 1 (pt); LPNs 5 (ft), 2 (pt); Nurses' aides 39 (ft); Physical therapists 1 (pt); Speech therapists 1 (pt); Activities coordinators 1 (ft); Dietitians 1 (ft).
Facilities Dining room; Physical therapy room; Activities room; Laundry room; Barber/Beauty shop; Library.
Activities Arts & crafts; Cards; Games; Reading groups; Prayer groups; Movies; Shopping trips; Dances/Social/Cultural gatherings.

Fairfield

Klearview Manor
RR 1 Box 640, Fairfield, ME 04937
(207) 453-2112
Admin Daniel Nimon.
Licensure Intermediate care for mentally retarded. *Beds* ICF/MR 29.
Owner Proprietary corp (Continental Health Service Management).

Pleasant Hill Health Facility
Mountain Ave, Box 318, Fairfield, ME 04937
(207) 453-2511
Admin Carey Davis.
Medical Dir Marion Strickland MD.
Licensure Intermediate care; Retirement. *Beds* ICF 95. *Certified* Medicaid.
Staff RNs 4 (ft); LPNs 6 (ft), 3 (pt); Nurses' aides 32 (ft), 10 (pt); Activities coordinators 1 (ft), 1 (pt); Dietitians 1 (pt).
Facilities Dining room; Activities room; Crafts room; Barber/Beauty shop.
Activities Arts & crafts; Cards; Games; Reading groups; Prayer groups; Movies; Shopping trips; Dances/Social/Cultural gatherings; Cooking; Gardening.

Falmouth

Falmouth by the Sea
191 Foreside Rd, Falmouth, ME 04105
(207) 781-4714
Admin Craig G Coffin. *Dir of Nursing* Susan Bernier. *Medical Dir* Dr Hardy.
Licensure Intermediate care. *Beds* ICF 70. *Certified* Medicaid.
Owner Proprietary corp (First Atlantic Corp).

Farmington

Edgewood Manor
70 N Main St, Farmington, ME 04938
(207) 778-3386
Admin Paula Varney.
Medical Dir K Gooch MD.
Licensure Intermediate care. *Beds* ICF 58. *Certified* Medicaid.
Owner Proprietary corp (Continental Health Service Management).
Admissions Requirements Medical examination; Physician's request.
Staff RNs 4 (ft), 2 (pt); LPNs 6 (ft), 2 (pt); Nurses' aides 23 (ft), 16 (pt); Physical therapists 1 (pt); Recreational therapists 1 (ft); Activities coordinators 1 (ft); Dietitians 1 (pt).
Facilities Dining room; Activities room; Chapel; Crafts room; Laundry room; Barber/Beauty shop; Library.
Activities Arts & crafts; Cards; Games; Reading groups; Prayer groups; Movies; Shopping trips; Dances/Social/Cultural gatherings.

Orchard Park Living Center
18 Orchard St, Farmington, ME 04938
(207) 778-4416
Admin Jill M Berry.

Medical Dir Paul Taylor MD.
Licensure Intermediate care. *Beds* ICF 35. *Certified* Medicaid.
Owner Proprietary corp (Continental Health Service Management).
Admissions Requirements Medical examination.
Staff RNs 1 (ft), 1 (pt); LPNs 3 (ft), 3 (pt); Nurses' aides 10 (ft), 8 (pt); Activities coordinators 1 (pt).
Facilities Dining room; Laundry room.
Activities Arts & crafts; Cards; Games; Reading groups; Prayer groups; Movies; Shopping trips; Dances/Social/Cultural gatherings.

Our House
8 Anson St, Farmington, ME 04938
(207) 778-2602
Admin Kathleen Cordes.
Licensure Intermediate care for mentally retarded. *Beds* ICF/MR 6. *Certified* Medicaid.
Owner Nonprofit corp.
Admissions Requirements Minimum age 18; Medical examination; Physician's request.
Staff Activities coordinators 1 (pt); Residential counselors 5 (ft), 3 (pt); QMRP 1 (ft).
Facilities Dining room; Laundry room; Normal household setting; In-town location; Pool.
Activities Arts & crafts; Games; Movies; Shopping trips; Dances/Social/Cultural gatherings; Instruction & supervision in activities of daily living.

Sandy River Nursing Care Center
RFD 4 Box 5121, Farmington, ME 04938
(207) 778-6591, 778-4542 FAX
Admin Phyllis Hager. *Dir of Nursing* Clara Labbe; Gloria Dean. *Medical Dir* Anne Hunter MD.
Licensure Intermediate care. *Beds* ICF 95. *Certified* Medicaid.
Owner Proprietary corp.
Admissions Requirements Minimum age 16; Medical examination; Physician's request.
Staff RNs; LPNs; Nurses' aides; Activities coordinators.
Facilities Dining room; Physical therapy room; Activities room; Barber/Beauty shop.
Activities Arts & crafts; Cards; Games; Reading groups; Prayer groups; Dances/ Social/Cultural gatherings; Intergenerational programs; Pet therapy.

Fort Fairfield

Aroostook Medical Center—Community General Hospital Division
3 Green St, Fort Fairfield, ME 04742
(207) 472-3811
Admin William E Nettles. *Dir of Nursing* Brenda Roope RN. *Medical Dir* Arthur Pendleton MD.
Licensure Skilled care; Intermediate care; Acute care. *Beds* SNF 10; ICF 16; Acute care 33. *Certified* Medicaid; Medicare.
Owner Nonprofit organization/foundation.
Admissions Requirements Medical examination; Physician's request.
Staff RNs 2 (ft), 1 (pt); LPNs 2 (ft), 5 (pt); Nurses' aides 11 (ft), 12 (pt); Activities coordinators 1 (pt); Dietitians 1 (pt).
Languages French, Spanish.
Facilities Dining room; Activities room; Barber/Beauty shop.
Activities Arts & crafts; Cards; Games; Movies; Shopping trips; Dances/Social/ Cultural gatherings; Dining out.

Fort Kent

Forest Hill Manor Inc
20 Bolduc Ave, Fort Kent, ME 04743
(207) 834-3915

Admin James Levasseur. *Dir of Nursing* Rosanne Paradis RN.
Licensure Intermediate care. *Beds* ICF 45. *Certified* Medicaid.
Owner Proprietary corp.
Admissions Requirements Medical examination; Physician's request.
Staff RNs 4 (ft), 1 (pt); LPNs 2 (ft), 1 (pt); Nurses' aides 26 (ft); Activities coordinators 1 (ft).
Languages French.
Facilities Dining room; Activities room; Chapel; Crafts room; Laundry room; Barber/ Beauty shop.
Activities Arts & crafts; Cards; Prayer groups; Movies.

Freeport

Freeport Nursing Home
PO Box K, 3 East St, Freeport, ME 04032
(207) 865-4713, 865-9075 FAX
Admin Douglas Neal Powers. *Dir of Nursing* Shelly M Lezer. *Medical Dir* Michael Bither.
Licensure Intermediate care. *Beds* ICF 60. *Private Pay Patients* 30%. *Certified* Medicaid.
Owner Privately owned (Elaine & David Hicks).
Admissions Requirements Medical examination.
Staff RNs 6 (ft); LPNs 5 (ft); Nurses' aides 21 (ft); Activities coordinators 1 (ft), 1 (pt); Dietitians.
Languages French, German.
Facilities Dining room; Activities room; Crafts room; Laundry room; Barber/Beauty shop; Swimming pool.
Activities Arts & crafts; Cards; Games; Reading groups; Prayer groups; Movies; Shopping trips; Dances/Social/Cultural gatherings; Intergenerational programs; Pet therapy.

Freeport Towne Square I
Lower Main St, Freeport, ME 04032
(207) 865-4876
Admin William Hughes.
Licensure Intermediate care for mentally retarded. *Beds* ICF/MR 6.

Freeport Towne Square II
Lower Main St, Freeport, ME 04032
(207) 865-6060
Admin William Hughes.
Licensure Intermediate care for mentally retarded. *Beds* ICF/MR 8.

Hawthorne House
Old County Rd, Freeport, ME 04032
(207) 865-4782
Admin Sandra Tate. *Dir of Nursing* Sandra Keith RN.
Licensure Intermediate care. *Beds* ICF 82. *Certified* Medicaid.
Owner Proprietary corp (Rousseau Enterprises).
Admissions Requirements Medical examination.
Staff RNs 4 (ft); LPNs 4 (ft); Nurses' aides 14 (ft); Activities coordinators 1 (ft).
Languages French.
Facilities Dining room; Activities room; Crafts room; Laundry room; Barber/Beauty shop.
Activities Arts & crafts; Games; Reading groups; Prayer groups; Movies; Shopping trips; Dances/Social/Cultural gatherings.

Fryeburg

Fryeburg Health Care Center
77 Fairview Dr, Fryeburg, ME 04037
(207) 935-3351
Admin James H Dutton.
Licensure Intermediate care. *Beds* ICF 82. *Certified* Medicaid.

Hicks Nursing Home
PO Box 170, 27 Oxford St, Fryeburg, ME 04037
(207) 935-2985
Admin Erna Hicks.
Licensure Intermediate care. *Beds* ICF 27. *Certified* Medicaid.

Gardiner

Gardiner Group Home
23 River Rd, Gardiner, ME 04345
(207) 582-7355
Admin Peter Miller.
Licensure Intermediate care for mentally retarded. *Beds* ICF/MR 6.

Kennebec Valley Medical Center Gardiner Division
150 Dresden Ave, Gardiner, ME 04345
(207) 582-1700
Admin Warren C Kessler.
Licensure Skilled care; Acute care. *Beds* SNF 19; Acute care 10.

Merrill Memorial Manor
146 Dresden Ave, Gardiner, ME 04345
(207) 582-2114
Admin William P Cullen. *Dir of Nursing* Barbara Seaman. *Medical Dir* Dr Stanley Painter.
Licensure Intermediate care; Alzheimer's care. *Beds* ICF 64. *Certified* Medicaid.
Owner Proprietary corp.
Admissions Requirements Minimum age 60.
Staff RNs 2 (ft); LPNs 3 (ft), 2 (pt); Nurses' aides 13 (ft), 15 (pt); Activities coordinators 1 (ft); Dietitians 1 (pt).
Languages French.
Facilities Dining room; Activities room; Chapel; Crafts room; Laundry room; Barber/ Beauty shop; Library.
Activities Arts & crafts; Cards; Games; Reading groups; Prayer groups; Movies; Shopping trips; Dances/Social/Cultural gatherings.

Robinson's Health Care Facility
PO Box 478, 284 Brunswick Ave, Gardiner, ME 04345
(207) 582-6250
Admin Carol Sharp. *Dir of Nursing* Barbara Gray RN.
Licensure Intermediate care. *Beds* ICF 50. *Certified* Medicare.
Owner Privately owned.
Staff RNs 2 (ft), 3 (pt); LPNs 2 (pt); Nurses' aides 12 (ft), 17 (pt); Activities coordinators 1 (pt); Dietitians 1 (pt); Social service 1 (pt).
Languages Russian, French.
Facilities Dining room; Physical therapy room; Activities room; Laundry room.
Activities Arts & crafts; Games; Reading groups; Prayer groups; Movies.

Gorham

Gorham House
50 New Portland Rd, Gorham, ME 04038
(207) 839-5757, 839-6203 FAX
Admin Joseph Hogan. *Dir of Nursing* Judy King. *Medical Dir* Dr Delaney.
Licensure Intermediate care; Assisted living; Independent living; Alzheimer's care; Adult day care. *Beds* ICF 46; Assisted living 72; Independent living apts 24. *Private Pay Patients* 88%. *Certified* Medicaid.
Owner Proprietary corp (Gillis, Hand, Hogan).
Staff Physicians 2 (pt); RNs 5 (ft); LPNs 8 (ft); Nurses' aides 32 (ft); Physical therapists 2 (pt); Recreational therapists 2 (ft); Occupational therapists 1 (pt); Speech therapists 1 (pt); Activities coordinators 1 (ft); Dietitians 1 (pt); Podiatrists 1 (pt).

Facilities Dining room; Physical therapy room; Activities room; Chapel; Crafts room; Laundry room; Barber/Beauty shop; Library; Patios; Porches; Guest room; Child day care.
Activities Arts & crafts; Cards; Games; Reading groups; Prayer groups; Movies; Shopping trips; Dances/Social/Cultural gatherings; Intergenerational programs; Pet therapy.

Greene

Greene Acres Manor
PO Box 180, Rte 202, Greene, ME 04236
(207) 946-5225
Admin Paul T Andrews. *Dir of Nursing* Pauline Bockus.
Licensure Intermediate care; Geriatric-psychiatric care. *Beds* ICF 59. *Certified* Medicaid.
Owner Proprietary corp.
Admissions Requirements Physician's request.
Staff Physicians; RNs; LPNs; Nurses' aides; Physical therapists; Recreational therapists; Speech therapists; Activities coordinators; Dietitians; Podiatrists; Audiologists; Behavior modification therapist.
Languages French.
Facilities Dining room; Activities room; Crafts room; Laundry room.
Activities Arts & crafts; Cards; Games; Reading groups; Prayer groups; Movies; Shopping trips; Dances/Social/Cultural gatherings; Intergenerational programs; Pet therapy; Behavior modification.

Greenville

Mid-Maine Medical Center—Charles A Dean Memorial Hospital
Pritham Ave, Greenville, ME 04441
(207) 695-2223
Admin David B Manahan.
Licensure Intermediate care; Acute care. *Beds* ICF 36; Acute care 14. *Certified* Medicaid.

Hartland

Sanfield Manor
PO Box 234, Main St, Hartland, ME 04943
(207) 938-2616
Admin Carroll P Marston.
Medical Dir Marion Strickland MD.
Licensure Intermediate care. *Beds* ICF 47. *Certified* Medicaid.
Owner Proprietary corp (Continental Heatlh Service Management).
Staff RNs 1 (ft), 1 (pt); LPNs 3 (ft); Nurses' aides 26 (ft); Activities coordinators 1 (ft); Social workers 1 (ft).
Facilities Dining room; Physical therapy room; Laundry room.
Activities Arts & crafts; Cards; Games; Prayer groups.

Houlton

Crest View Manor Inc
RFD 2 Box 26, Calais Rd, Houlton, ME 04730
(207) 532-3498
Admin Phyllis S Hersey RN. *Dir of Nursing* Darlene McLaughlin RN.
Licensure Intermediate care; Boarding care. *Beds* ICF 22; Boarding care 17. *Private Pay Patients* 0%. *Certified* Medicaid; Medicare.
Owner Proprietary corp (George Dugal).
Admissions Requirements Medical examination; Physician's request.
Staff Physicians (consultant); RNs 1 (ft); LPNs 3 (ft); Nurses' aides 9 (ft); Physical therapists (consultant); Activities coordinators 1 (ft); Dietitians (consultant); Podiatrists (consultant); Social services 1 (ft).
Languages French.

Facilities Dining room; Physical therapy room; Activities room; Laundry room.
Activities Arts & crafts; Cards; Games; Reading groups; Prayer groups; Movies; Shopping trips; Dances/Social/Cultural gatherings; Intergenerational programs; Pet therapy; Barbecues; Rides.

Gardiner Nursing Home
PO Box 520, 8 Holland St, Houlton, ME 04730
(702) 532-3323
Admin Mark Anderson.
Licensure Intermediate care. *Beds* ICF 60. *Certified* Medicaid.
Staff RNs 1 (ft); LPNs 4 (ft), 3 (pt); Nurses' aides 30 (ft), 4 (pt); Activities coordinators 1 (ft); Dietitians 1 (pt).
Facilities Dining room; Activities room; Laundry room; Barber/Beauty shop; Library.
Activities Arts & crafts; Cards; Games; Reading groups; Prayer groups; Movies; Dances/Social/Cultural gatherings.

Houlton Regional Hospital
20 Hartford St, Houlton, ME 04730
(207) 532-9471
Admin Bradley C Bean.
Medical Dir Donald Brushett MD.
Licensure Skilled care; Acute care. *Beds* SNF 24; Acute care 65. *Certified* Medicaid; Medicare.
Owner Nonprofit corp.
Admissions Requirements Medical examination; Physician's request.
Staff Physicians 1 (pt); RNs 1 (ft), 1 (pt); LPNs 5 (ft), 5 (pt); Nurses' aides 5 (ft), 9 (pt); Physical therapists 3 (pt); Occupational therapists 1 (pt); Activities coordinators 1 (ft); Dietitians 1 (pt).
Facilities Dining room; Activities room; Crafts room; Laundry room.
Activities Arts & crafts; Cards; Games; Reading groups; Prayer groups; Movies.

Houlton Residential Center
45 School St, Houlton, ME 04730
(207) 532-9446
Admin Ron Langworthy.
Licensure Intermediate care for mentally retarded. *Beds* ICF/MR 28. *Certified* Medicaid.
Owner Nonprofit corp.
Admissions Requirements Minimum age 18.
Staff RNs 1 (ft); LPNs 1 (ft), 6 (pt); Nurses' aides 20 (ft), 20 (pt); Activities coordinators 1 (ft).
Facilities Dining room; Physical therapy room; Activities room; Crafts room; Laundry room.
Activities Arts & crafts; Cards; Games; Movies; Shopping trips; Dances/Social/Cultural gatherings.

Madigan Estates
93 Military St, Houlton, ME 04730
(207) 532-6593
Admin Brenda L Brown. *Dir of Nursing* Carol Swallow RN.
Licensure Intermediate care. *Beds* ICF 55. *Certified* Medicaid.
Owner Privately owned.
Admissions Requirements Medical examination.
Staff Physicians 8 (pt); RNs 3 (ft); LPNs 6 (ft); Nurses' aides 25 (ft); Recreational therapists 1 (ft); Activities coordinators 1 (ft); Dietitians 1 (ft); Dentists 1 (pt).
Facilities Dining room; Activities room; Laundry room; Barber/Beauty shop.
Activities Arts & crafts; Cards; Games; Reading groups; Prayer groups; Movies; Shopping trips; Dances/Social/Cultural gatherings.

Park Street Group Home
7 Park St, Houlton, ME 04730
(207) 532-7150

Admin Terry Hutchinson.
Licensure Intermediate care for mentally retarded. *Beds* ICF/MR 6. *Certified* Medicaid.
Owner Nonprofit corp.
Admissions Requirements Minimum age 18.
Staff RNs; Activities coordinators; Dietitians.
Facilities Dining room; Activities room; Laundry room.
Activities Arts & crafts; Cards; Games; Reading groups; Movies; Shopping trips; Dances/Social/Cultural gatherings.

Howland

Cummings Health Care Facility Inc
Crocker St Ext, Box 307, Howland, ME 04448
(207) 732-4121
Admin Fern P Cummings. *Dir of Nursing* Susan Bailey RN.
Licensure Intermediate care. *Beds* ICF 43. *Certified* Medicaid.
Owner Privately owned.
Admissions Requirements Physician's request.
Staff RNs 6 (ft); LPNs 3 (ft); Nurses' aides 25 (ft); Activities coordinators 1 (ft); Dietitians 1 (ft).
Facilities Dining room; Physical therapy room; Activities room; Chapel; Crafts room; Laundry room; Barber/Beauty shop.
Activities Arts & crafts; Cards; Games; Reading groups; Prayer groups; Movies; Shopping trips.

Island Falls

One Sewall Street
Sewall St, Box 127, Island Falls, ME 04747
(207) 463-2156
Admin Sonja Burleigh.
Licensure Intermediate care for mentally retarded. *Beds* ICF/MR 6. *Certified* Medicaid.
Owner Nonprofit corp.
Admissions Requirements Minimum age 20; Medical examination; Physician's request.
Staff Speech therapists; Activities coordinators 1 (pt); Direct care staff 6 (ft), 7 (pt).
Facilities Dining room; Activities room; Laundry room.
Activities Arts & crafts; Cards; Games; Movies; Shopping trips; Dances/Social/Cultural gatherings; Hiking club; Outing club; Cross country ski team; Running races.

Jackman

Jackman Region Health Center
Rte 201, Main St, Jackman, ME 04945
(207) 668-2691
Admin Marcia Seavey. *Dir of Nursing* Marcia Seavey. *Medical Dir* Patricia Doyle MD.
Licensure Intermediate care. *Beds* ICF 18. *Certified* Medicaid; Medicare.
Owner Nonprofit corp.
Admissions Requirements Medical examination.
Staff Physicians 1 (ft); RNs 3 (pt); LPNs 1 (pt); Nurses' aides 8 (ft), 11 (pt); Activities coordinators; Dietitians; Ophthalmologists.
Languages French.
Facilities Dining room; Activities room; Laundry room; Library; Sitting room.
Activities Cards; Games; Prayer groups; Movies; Dances/Social/Cultural gatherings; Maple sugar parties; Pets.

Northland Manor
Main St, Jackman, ME 04945
(207) 668-3221
Admin Bertha Norris.
Licensure Intermediate care for mentally retarded. *Beds* ICF/MR 20.
Owner Proprietary corp (Continental Health Service Management).

Admissions Requirements Minimum age 18; Medical examination.
Staff RNs 1 (ft); LPNs 3 (ft); Nurses' aides 10 (ft), 3 (pt); Activities coordinators 1 (ft); Dietitians 1 (pt).
Facilities Dining room; Activities room; Laundry room.
Activities Arts & crafts; Cards; Games; Reading groups; Prayer groups; Movies; Shopping trips.

Jonesport

Resthaven Nursing Home
Ocean St, Jonesport, ME 04649
(207) 497-5948, 497-5608 FAX
Admin LaVonne M Lamson. Dir of Nursing Carol Umphenour RN. Medical Dir Dr Don Caruso.
Licensure Intermediate care. Beds ICF 22. Private Pay Patients 1%. Certified Medicaid.
Owner Nonprofit organization/foundation.
Admissions Requirements Medical examination; Physician's request.
Staff RNs 1 (ft); LPNs 3 (ft); Nurses' aides 13 (ft), 6 (pt); Activities coordinators 1 (pt); Dietitians 1 (pt).
Affiliation Latter Day Saints.
Facilities Dining room; Activities room; Laundry room; Barber/Beauty shop.
Activities Arts & crafts; Games; Reading groups; Prayer groups; Movies.

Kennebunk

Beachwood
77 Brown St, Kennebunk, ME 04043
(207) 985-7959
Admin Karen Miller.
Licensure Intermediate care for mentally retarded. Beds ICF/MR 6.
Admissions Requirements Medical examination.
Staff RNs 1 (pt); Physical therapists 1 (pt); Occupational therapists 1 (pt); Speech therapists 1 (pt); Activities coordinators 1 (ft); Dietitians 1 (pt).
Facilities Dining room; Laundry room.
Activities Arts & crafts; Games; Movies; Shopping trips; Dances/Social/Cultural gatherings.

Kennebunk Nursing Home
158 Ross Rd, Kennebunk, ME 04043
(207) 985-7141
Admin Patricia Small.
Licensure Intermediate care. Beds ICF 65. Certified Medicaid.
Owner Proprietary corp (Hillhaven Corp).
Admissions Requirements Medical examination; Physician's request.
Staff RNs 3 (ft), 4 (pt); LPNs 2 (ft), 3 (pt); Nurses' aides 17 (ft), 16 (pt); Physical therapists 1 (pt); Recreational therapists 1 (ft); Speech therapists 1 (pt); Activities coordinators 1 (ft); Dietitians 1 (pt); Podiatrists 1 (pt).
Facilities Dining room; Physical therapy room; Activities room; Crafts room; Laundry room; Barber/Beauty shop; Library.
Activities Arts & crafts; Cards; Games; Reading groups; Prayer groups; Movies; Shopping trips.

Kezar Falls

Greenhill Farm
Rte 2 Box 421, Kezar Falls, ME 04047
(207) 625-8644
Admin Brenda Mitchell.
Licensure Intermediate care for mentally retarded. Beds ICF/MR 6.
Admissions Requirements Minimum age 18; Medical examination; Physician's request.
Staff RNs; Activities coordinators 1 (ft).

Facilities Dining room; Activities room; Crafts room; Laundry room.
Activities Arts & crafts; Cards; Games; Reading groups; Shopping trips; Dances/Social/Cultural gatherings.

Kittery

Homestead Inc
RFD 1, Box 735, Kittery, ME 03904
(207) 439-2100
Admin David Sowerby.
Medical Dir Dr William Gilbert.
Licensure Intermediate care. Beds ICF 61. Certified Medicaid.
Admissions Requirements Minimum age 55; Medical examination.
Staff RNs 2 (ft), 2 (pt); LPNs 2 (ft), 3 (pt); Nurses' aides 13 (ft), 17 (pt); Physical therapists; Reality therapists 1 (ft); Occupational therapists; Speech therapists; Activities coordinators 1 (ft); Social workers 1 (ft).
Facilities Dining room; Activities room; Barber/Beauty shop.
Activities Arts & crafts; Prayer groups; Movies; Shopping trips; Dances/Social/Cultural gatherings; Happy hour; Church service; Bingo; Cooking club; Exercise.

Lewiston

D'Youville Pavilion
102 Campus Ave, Lewiston, ME 04240
(207) 783-1471
Admin Roger Dumont. Dir of Nursing Kathy Murphy. Medical Dir Dr Betty Kennedy.
Licensure Skilled care; Intermediate care; Retirement. Beds SNF 30; ICF 250. Private Pay Patients 10%. Certified Medicaid; Medicare.
Owner Nonprofit corp.
Admissions Requirements Minimum age 18; Medical examination; Physician's request.
Staff RNs 12 (ft), 5 (pt); LPNs 18 (ft), 10 (pt); Nurses' aides 100 (ft), 80 (pt); Physical therapists 1 (pt); Occupational therapists 1 (pt); Speech therapists 1 (pt); Activities coordinators 5 (ft), 1 (pt); Dietitians 1 (pt); Podiatrists 1 (pt).
Languages French.
Affiliation Roman Catholic.
Facilities Dining room; Physical therapy room; Activities room; Chapel; Crafts room; Laundry room; Barber/Beauty shop.
Activities Arts & crafts; Cards; Games; Reading groups; Prayer groups; Movies; Shopping trips; Dances/Social/Cultural gatherings; Intergenerational programs.

Marshwood Nursing Care Center
Roger Ave, Lewiston, ME 04240
(207) 784-0108
Admin Joseph N Sirdis. Dir of Nursing H Noel. Medical Dir Dr S Rosenblatt.
Licensure Intermediate care. Beds ICF 120. Certified Medicaid.
Owner Proprietary corp.
Admissions Requirements Minimum age 18.
Staff RNs 7 (ft), 6 (pt); LPNs 1 (ft), 3 (pt); Recreational therapists 7 (pt); Activities coordinators 1 (ft); Dietitians 1 (pt).
Languages French.
Facilities Dining room; Physical therapy room; Activities room; Crafts room; Laundry room; Barber/Beauty shop.
Activities Arts & crafts; Cards; Games; Reading groups; Prayer groups; Movies; Shopping trips; Dances/Social/Cultural gatherings.

Montello Manor
540 College St, Lewiston, ME 04240
(207) 783-2039
Admin Stephen Marsden.
Medical Dir John Mendros.

Licensure Skilled care; Intermediate care. Beds SNF 69; ICF 72. Certified Medicaid; Medicare.
Staff Physicians 1 (pt); RNs 15 (ft), 5 (pt); LPNs 9 (ft), 2 (pt); Nurses' aides 30 (ft), 20 (pt); Physical therapists 2 (pt); Occupational therapists 1 (pt); Speech therapists 1 (pt); Activities coordinators 2 (pt); Dietitians 1 (pt); Ophthalmologists 1 (pt); Podiatrists 1 (pt); Dentists 1 (pt).
Facilities Dining room; Physical therapy room; Activities room; Crafts room; Laundry room; Barber/Beauty shop.
Activities Arts & crafts; Cards; Games; Reading groups; Prayer groups; Movies; Shopping trips; Dances/Social/Cultural gatherings; Newsletter.

Russell Park Manor
158-178 Russell St, Lewiston, ME 04240
(207) 786-0691
Admin Maurice Labbe.
Licensure Skilled care; Intermediate care. Beds SNF 30; ICF 90.

St Casimir Health Care Facility
69 Horton St, Lewiston, ME 04240
(207) 784-5273
Admin Charles Cook.
Licensure Intermediate care. Beds ICF 23. Certified Medicaid.
Staff LPNs 3 (ft), 2 (pt); Nurses' aides 7 (ft), 5 (pt); Activities coordinators 1 (ft).
Affiliation Roman Catholic.
Facilities Dining room; Activities room; Crafts room; Laundry room.
Activities Arts & crafts; Cards; Games; Prayer groups; Movies; Shopping trips; Dances/Social/Cultural gatherings; Various outings.

Lincoln

Colonial Acres Nursing Home
Workman Terrace, Lincoln, ME 04457
(207) 794-6534
Admin R Eugene Libby.
Medical Dir Bourcard Nesin MD.
Licensure Skilled care; Intermediate care. Beds Swing beds SNF/ICF 78. Certified Medicaid.
Admissions Requirements Medical examination; Physician's request.
Staff RNs 3 (ft), 3 (pt); LPNs 4 (ft), 2 (pt); Nurses' aides 23 (ft), 25 (pt); Activities coordinators 1 (ft).
Facilities Dining room; Physical therapy room; Activities room; Chapel; Crafts room; Laundry room; Barber/Beauty shop.
Activities Arts & crafts; Cards; Games; Reading groups; Prayer groups; Movies; Shopping trips; Dances/Social/Cultural gatherings.

Penobscot Valley Hospital
Box 368, Transalpine Rd, Lincoln, ME 04457
(207) 794-3321
Admin Ronald Victory.
Licensure Skilled care; Acute care. Beds SNF 9; Acute care.

Lisbon

Lamp Nursing Home
RFD 2, Box 133, Lisbon Rd, Lisbon, ME 04250
(207) 353-4318
Admin Irene LaMarche.
Medical Dir Joseph M Mendes MD.
Licensure Intermediate care. Beds ICF 36. Certified Medicaid.
Admissions Requirements Medical examination.
Staff RNs 3 (ft); LPNs 1 (pt); Nurses' aides 13 (ft), 6 (pt); Physical therapists; Speech therapists; Activities coordinators 1 (ft); Dietitians 1 (pt); Podiatrists; Dentists.

Facilities Dining room; Activities room;
Crafts room; Barber/Beauty shop; Library.
Activities Arts & crafts; Cards; Games;
Reading groups; Prayer groups; Movies;
Shopping trips; Dances/Social/Cultural
gatherings.

Livermore Falls

Pomeroy Hill Nursing Home
RFD 1, Fiorica Rd, Livermore Falls, ME
04254
(207) 897-6748
Admin Arthur Upton.
Medical Dir Dr Joseph DeGrinney.
Licensure Intermediate care. *Beds* ICF 60.
Certified Medicaid.
Staff RNs 5 (ft), 2 (pt); LPNs 3 (ft), 4 (pt);
Nurses' aides 17 (ft), 17 (pt); Physical
therapists 1 (pt); Reality therapists 1 (ft);
Recreational therapists 1 (ft); Occupational
therapists 1 (pt); Activities coordinators 1
(ft); Dietitians 1 (pt); Podiatrists 1 (pt).
Facilities Dining room; Physical therapy
room; Activities room; Crafts room; Laundry
room; Barber/Beauty shop.
Activities Arts & crafts; Cards; Games;
Reading groups; Prayer groups; Movies;
Shopping trips; Dances/Social/Cultural
gatherings; Outside trips.

Lubec

Oceanview Nursing Home
48 Washington St, Lubec, ME 04652
(207) 733-4900
Admin Margaret Brown. *Dir of Nursing*
Marilyn Bullock RN. *Medical Dir* Dr Robert
G MacBride.
Licensure Intermediate care. *Beds* ICF 50.
Private Pay Patients 10%. *Certified*
Medicaid.
Owner Proprietary corp (Max-Parry
Associates).
Admissions Requirements Physician's request.
Staff Physicians 3 (ft); RNs 2 (ft); LPNs 5 (ft);
Nurses' aides 19 (ft); Physical therapists;
Activities coordinators 1 (ft); Dietitians;
Podiatrists 1 (ft).
Facilities Dining room; Activities room;
Barber/Beauty shop.
Activities Arts & crafts; Cards; Games;
Reading groups; Prayer groups; Movies;
Shopping trips; Dances/Social/Cultural
gatherings; Volunteer program.

Machias

Marshall Health Care Facility
High St Ext, Machias, ME 04654
(207) 255-3387
Admin Vaughn Marshall.
Medical Dir Karl V Larson MD.
Licensure Intermediate care. *Beds* ICF 66.
Certified Medicaid.
Admissions Requirements Medical
examination.
Staff Physicians 4 (pt); RNs 4 (ft), 3 (pt);
LPNs 2 (ft), 1 (pt); Nurses' aides 42 (ft).
Facilities Dining room; Activities room;
Chapel; Crafts room; Laundry room; Barber/
Beauty shop; Library.
Activities Arts & crafts; Cards; Games;
Reading groups; Prayer groups; Movies.

Madawaska

Highview Manor
40 Riverview St, Madawaska, ME 04756
(207) 728-3338
Admin George Dugal.
Licensure Intermediate care. *Beds* ICF 78.
Certified Medicaid.

Madison

Maplecrest Living Center
174 Main St, Madison, ME 04950
(207) 696-8225
Admin Lynn Jordan.
Licensure Intermediate care. *Beds* ICF 58.
Certified Medicaid.
Owner Proprietary corp (Continental Health
Service Management).
Staff RNs 2 (ft), 1 (pt); LPNs 3 (ft), 1 (pt);
Nurses' aides 20 (ft), 10 (pt); Recreational
therapists 1 (ft).

Mars Hill

TAMC—Aroostook Health Center Division
Highland Ave, Mars Hill, ME 04758
(207) 768-4915
Admin Gerald Pope. *Dir of Nursing* Lucy
Folts RN. *Medical Dir* Eric Nicholas MD.
Licensure Skilled care; Intermediate care. *Beds*
SNF 15; ICF 55. *Private Pay Patients* 7%.
Certified Medicaid; Medicare.
Owner Publicly owned.
Staff Physicians 2 (ft); RNs 3 (ft), 2 (pt);
LPNs 11 (ft), 3 (pt); Nurses' aides 25 (ft), 27
(pt); Physical therapists 1 (pt); Speech
therapists 1 (pt); Activities coordinators 2
(ft); Dietitians 1 (ft), 1 (pt); Podiatrists 1
(pt).
Facilities Dining room; Physical therapy
room; Activities room; Laundry room;
Barber/Beauty shop.
Activities Arts & crafts; Cards; Games;
Reading groups; Prayer groups; Movies;
Shopping trips; Dances/Social/Cultural
gatherings; Intergenerational programs.

Milbridge

Narraguagus Bay Health Care Facility
Main St, Milbridge, ME 04658
(207) 546-2371
Admin Larry M Brown.
Medical Dir Carl Aselton MD.
Licensure Intermediate care. *Beds* ICF 65.
Certified Medicaid.
Owner Proprietary corp (Beverly Enterprises).
Admissions Requirements Medical
examination.
Staff RNs 1 (ft); LPNs 2 (ft), 6 (pt); Nurses'
aides 12 (ft), 20 (pt); Physical therapists;
Speech therapists; Activities coordinators 1
(ft); Dietitians.
Facilities Dining room; Physical therapy
room; Activities room; Crafts room; Laundry
room; Barber/Beauty shop.
Activities Arts & crafts; Cards; Games;
Reading groups; Prayer groups; Movies;
Shopping trips; Dances/Social/Cultural
gatherings.

Millinocket

Katahdin Nursing Home
22 Walnut St, Millinocket, ME 04462
(207) 723-4711
Admin Donald J Palleschi. *Dir of Nursing*
Elaine Niles.
Licensure Intermediate care. *Beds* ICF 50.
Certified Medicaid.
Owner Proprietary corp.
Staff RNs 3 (ft); LPNs 2 (ft); Nurses' aides 23
(ft); Activities coordinators 1 (ft); Social
service 1 (ft).
Languages French.
Facilities Dining room; Physical therapy
room; Activities room; Laundry room.
Activities Arts & crafts; Cards; Games;
Reading groups; Prayer groups; Movies;
Shopping trips; Dances/Social/Cultural
gatherings; Outings.

North Berwick

North Berwick Nursing Home
PO Box 730, 45 Elm St, North Berwick, ME
03906
(207) 676-2242
Admin Jean Gardner RN.
Licensure Intermediate care. *Beds* ICF 48.
Certified Medicaid.

North Vassalboro

Volmer Nursing Home
RFD 1, Box 1190, North Vassalboro, ME
04962
(207) 873-2040
Admin Roland E Drouin.
Licensure Intermediate care. *Beds* ICF 30.
Certified Medicaid.
Staff RNs 1 (ft); LPNs 2 (ft); Nurses' aides 9
(ft), 6 (pt); Activities coordinators 1 (ft);
Dietitians 1 (ft), 1 (pt).
Facilities Dining room; Activities room;
Crafts room; Laundry room; Barber/Beauty
shop; Library.
Activities Arts & crafts; Cards; Games; Prayer
groups; Shopping trips.

North Windham

Ledgewood Manor Inc
PO Box 760, 200 Rte 115, North Windham,
ME 04062
(207) 892-2261
Admin Edison H Bennett. *Dir of Nursing*
Rachael Coleman.
Licensure Intermediate care. *Beds* ICF 60.
Private Pay Patients 12%. *Certified*
Medicaid.
Owner Proprietary corp.
Staff Physicians; RNs; LPNs; Nurses' aides;
Activities coordinators.
Facilities Dining room; Physical therapy
room; Activities room; Crafts room; Laundry
room; Barber/Beauty shop.
Activities Arts & crafts; Games; Reading
groups; Movies; Pet therapy.

Norway

Norway Convalescent Center
Marion Ave, Norway, ME 04268
(207) 743-7075
Admin Robert Armstrong.
Licensure Intermediate care. *Beds* ICF 72.
Certified Medicaid.
Owner Proprietary corp (Hillhaven Corp).
Admissions Requirements Minimum age 16;
Medical examination.
Staff RNs 4 (ft), 2 (pt); LPNs 3 (ft), 3 (pt);
Nurses' aides 15 (ft), 23 (pt); Physical
therapists 1 (pt); Activities coordinators 1
(ft), 1 (pt); Dietitians 1 (pt).
Facilities Dining room; Physical therapy
room; Activities room; Laundry room;
Barber/Beauty shop.
Activities Arts & crafts; Cards; Games;
Reading groups; Prayer groups; Movies;
Shopping trips; Dances/Social/Cultural
gatherings.

Old Orchard Beach

Elms Residence Nursing Home
28 Portland Ave, Old Orchard Beach, ME
04064
(207) 934-2174
Admin Roger Painchaud.
Licensure Intermediate care. *Beds* ICF 26.
Certified Medicaid.
Staff RNs 3 (ft); LPNs 2 (ft); Nurses' aides 6
(ft), 10 (pt); Activities coordinators 1 (ft).

Facilities Dining room; Activities room; Crafts room; Laundry room.
Activities Arts & crafts; Cards; Games; Reading groups; Movies; Dances/Social/ Cultural gatherings.

Orono

Orono Nursing Home Inc
PO Box 430, 117 Bennoch Rd, Orono, ME 04473
(207) 866-4914
Admin William C Shirley. *Dir of Nursing* Carleen Caswell RN. *Medical Dir* Michael Bruehl MD.
Licensure Skilled care; Intermediate care. *Beds* SNF 12; ICF 100. *Private Pay Patients* 40%. *Certified* Medicaid; Medicare.
Owner Proprietary corp.
Staff Physicians 6 (pt); RNs 8 (ft), 3 (pt); LPNs 8 (ft), 4 (pt); Nurses' aides 60 (ft), 15 (pt); Physical therapists 1 (pt); Recreational therapists 2 (pt); Occupational therapists 1 (pt); Speech therapists 1 (pt); Activities coordinators 1 (ft); Dietitians 1 (pt); Podiatrists 1 (pt).
Facilities Dining room; Physical therapy room; Activities room; Laundry room; Barber/Beauty shop.
Activities Arts & crafts; Cards; Games; Reading groups; Prayer groups; Movies; Shopping trips; Dances/Social/Cultural gatherings.

Treats Falls House
2 Hill St, Orono, ME 04473
(207) 866-3769
Admin Dick Valentine.
Licensure Intermediate care for mentally retarded. *Beds* ICF/MR 20. *Certified* Medicaid.
Admissions Requirements Minimum age 18; Medical examination.
Staff Physicians 1 (pt); RNs 1 (pt); LPNs 1 (pt); Nurses' aides 23 (ft); Physical therapists 1 (pt); Occupational therapists 1 (pt); Activities coordinators 1 (pt); Dietitians 1 (pt).
Facilities Dining room; Activities room; Crafts room; Laundry room.
Activities Arts & crafts; Cards; Games; Movies; Shopping trips; Dances/Social/ Cultural gatherings.

Orrington

Orrington Group Home
RFD 2, Box 125, Orrington, ME 04474
(207) 825-3557
Admin Patrick Rager.
Licensure Intermediate care for mentally retarded. *Beds* ICF/MR 6. *Certified* Medicaid.

Patten

Resthaven Health Care Facility
PO Box 240, Patten, ME 04765
(207) 528-2200
Admin Justine Michaud. *Dir of Nursing* Dianne Lane. *Medical Dir* Ronald Blum.
Licensure Intermediate care. *Beds* ICF 25. *Private Pay Patients* 2%. *Certified* Medicaid.
Owner Proprietary corp (Central Maine Health Ventures).
Admissions Requirements Medical examination.
Staff Physicians 2 (pt); RNs 2 (pt); LPNs 1 (ft), 1 (pt); Nurses' aides 8 (ft), 6 (pt); Activities coordinators 1 (pt); Dietitians 1 (pt).
Facilities Dining room; Activities room; Laundry room.
Activities Arts & crafts; Cards; Games; Reading groups; Prayer groups; Intergenerational programs; Pet therapy.

Penobscot

Penobscot Nursing Home
Main St, Penobscot, ME 04476
(207) 326-4344
Admin Wendell Dennison. *Dir of Nursing* Elizabeth Sawyer RN. *Medical Dir* Dr Dale Walter.
Licensure Intermediate care. *Beds* ICF 98. *Certified* Medicaid.
Owner Proprietary corp.
Staff RNs 3 (ft); LPNs 13 (ft); Nurses' aides 27 (ft); Physical therapists 1 (ft); Occupational therapists 1 (ft); Activities coordinators 1 (ft); Dietitians 1 (ft).
Facilities Dining room; Physical therapy room; Activities room; Crafts room; Laundry room; Barber/Beauty shop.
Activities Arts & crafts; Cards; Games; Reading groups; Prayer groups; Movies; Foliage tours; Outings.

24 Katahdin Street
Katahdin St, Penobscot, ME 04765
(207) 528-2929
Admin Rebecca Baltzer.
Licensure Intermediate care for mentally retarded. *Beds* ICF/MR 6. *Certified* Medicaid; Medicare.
Owner Nonprofit organization/foundation.
Admissions Requirements Minimum age 18; Medical examination; Physician's request.
Facilities Dining room; Activities room; Crafts room; Laundry room.
Activities Arts & crafts; Cards; Games; Reading groups; Movies; Shopping trips; Dances/Social/Cultural gatherings; Hikes; Trips; Swimming; Walk/jog races; Nature groups; Hobby clubs; Social/sexuality club.

Pittsfield

Pittsfield Convalescent Center
Leighton St, Pittsfield, ME 04967
(207) 487-3182
Admin Kathy Crawford.
Licensure Intermediate care. *Beds* ICF 28. *Certified* Medicaid.
Owner Proprietary corp (Hillhaven Corp).

Sebasticook Valley Health Care Facility
PO Box 339, Leighton St, Pittsfield, ME 04967
(207) 487-3131
Admin Barbara Steller. *Dir of Nursing* Cheryl West RN.
Licensure Intermediate care. *Beds* ICF 64. *Certified* Medicaid.
Owner Privately owned.
Admissions Requirements Physician's request.
Staff RNs 2 (ft), 1 (pt); LPNs 5 (ft), 1 (pt); Nurses' aides 25 (ft), 13 (pt); Activities coordinators 1 (ft).
Facilities Dining room; Physical therapy room; Activities room; Laundry room; Barber/Beauty shop; Library.
Activities Arts & crafts; Cards; Games; Reading groups; Prayer groups; Movies; Shopping trips; Dances/Social/Cultural gatherings; Remotivation groups.

Portland

Barron Center
1145 Brighton Ave, Portland, ME 04102
(207) 774-2623
Admin Anthony Forgione. *Dir of Nursing* Jeanne Delicata RN. *Medical Dir* Benjamin Zolou MD.
Licensure Skilled care; Intermediate care; Retirement; Alzheimer's care. *Beds* SNF 20; ICF 165. *Certified* Medicaid; Medicare.
Owner Publicly owned.
Admissions Requirements Minimum age 18; Medical examination; Physician's request.

Staff Physicians 4 (ft); RNs 18 (ft); LPNs 16 (ft); Nurses' aides 92 (ft); Physical therapists 3 (ft); Recreational therapists 6 (ft); Occupational therapists 1 (pt); Speech therapists 1 (pt); Dietitians 1 (pt); Ophthalmologists 1 (pt); Dentists 1 (pt).
Facilities Dining room; Physical therapy room; Activities room; Chapel; Crafts room; Laundry room; Barber/Beauty shop.
Activities Arts & crafts; Cards; Games; Reading groups; Prayer groups; Movies; Shopping trips; Dances/Social/Cultural gatherings.

Devonshire Nursing Care Center
68 Devonshire St, Portland, ME 04103
(207) 772-2893
Admin Paula Curtis Everett.
Licensure Intermediate care. *Beds* ICF 149. *Certified* Medicaid.

Emery Street Community Residence
72 Emery St, Portland, ME 04102
(207) 772-6332
Admin Lisa J MacDonald.
Licensure Intermediate care for mentally retarded. *Beds* ICF/MR 6. *Certified* Medicaid.

Jewish Home for the Aged
158 North St, Portland, ME 04101
(207) 772-5456
Admin C Gail MacLean.
Licensure Skilled care; Intermediate care. *Beds* SNF 18; ICF 70. *Certified* Medicaid; Medicare.
Affiliation Jewish.

New England Rehabilitation Hospital of Portland
13 Charles St, Portland, ME 04102
(207) 775-4000
Admin Gregg Stanley.
Licensure Skilled care; Acute care. *Beds* SNF 55; Acute care 25.

St Joseph's Manor
1133 Washington Ave, Portland, ME 04103
(207) 797-0600
Admin Ronald Tardif. *Dir of Nursing* Maureen Brennan RN.
Licensure Intermediate care; Adult day care. *Beds* ICF 200; Adult day care 20-30. *Private Pay Patients* 20%. *Certified* Medicaid.
Owner Nonprofit corp.
Admissions Requirements Medical examination; Physician's request.
Staff RNs; LPNs; Nurses' aides; Activities coordinators; Dietitians.
Languages French.
Affiliation Roman Catholic.
Facilities Dining room; Physical therapy room; Activities room; Chapel; Crafts room; Laundry room; Barber/Beauty shop.
Activities Arts & crafts; Cards; Games; Reading groups; Movies; Shopping trips; Intergenerational programs.

Seaside Nursing & Retirement Home
850 Baxter Blvd, Portland, ME 04103
(207) 774-7878
Admin Cynthia Farley.
Licensure Skilled care; Intermediate care; Boarding care. *Beds* SNF 38; ICF 76; Boarding care 38. *Certified* Medicaid.

Woodfords Group Home I
342 Woodfords St, Portland, ME 04103
(207) 871-1209
Admin Daniel Bonner.
Licensure Intermediate care for mentally retarded. *Beds* ICF/MR 6. *Certified* Medicaid.

Woodfords Group Home II
388 Woodfords St, Portland, ME 04103
(207) 774-3331
Admin Melvin Richards.

Licensure Intermediate care for mentally retarded. *Beds* 4. *Certified* Medicaid.

Pownal

Pineland Center
PO Box C, Pownal, ME 04069
(207) 688-4811
Admin Spencer A Moore PhD. *Dir of Nursing* Julie L Biggs RN. *Medical Dir* Hecter A Arrache MD.
Licensure Intermediate care for mentally retarded. *Beds* ICF/MR 295. *Certified* Medicaid.
Owner Publicly owned.
Admissions Requirements Minimum age 5; Physician's request; Court commitment.
Staff Physicians 3 (ft), 1 (pt); RNs 19 (ft), 1 (pt); LPNs 14 (ft), 1 (pt); Nurses' aides 300 (ft), 2 (pt); Physical therapists 3 (ft); Recreational therapists 4 (ft); Occupational therapists 6 (ft); Speech therapists 3 (ft); Dietitians 1 (ft).
Facilities Dining room; Physical therapy room; Activities room; Chapel; Crafts room; Laundry room; Barber/Beauty shop; Library.
Activities Arts & crafts; Games; Prayer groups; Movies; Shopping trips; Dances/Social/ Cultural gatherings; Developmental training centers.

Presque Isle

Aroostook Residential Center
PO Box 1285, Presque Isle, ME 04769
(207) 764-2010
Admin Terry L Sandusky.
Licensure Intermediate care for mentally retarded. *Beds* ICF/MR 13. *Certified* Medicaid.
Owner Publicly owned.
Admissions Requirements Minimum age 16.
Staff Physicians 1 (pt); RNs 1 (pt); Occupational therapists 1 (pt); Speech therapists 1 (pt); Activities coordinators 1 (pt); Dietitians 1 (pt).
Facilities Dining room; Activities room; Laundry room; Library.
Activities Arts & crafts; Games; Movies; Shopping trips; Dances/Social/Cultural gatherings; Swimming.

Presque Isle Nursing Home Inc
162 Academy St, Presque Isle, ME 04769
(207) 764-0145
Admin Paul Cyr.
Licensure Intermediate care. *Beds* ICF 82. *Certified* Medicaid.

Rockland

Rockland Convalescent Center
201 Camden St, Rockland, ME 04841
(207) 596-6423
Admin Rosanne Tousignant.
Licensure Intermediate care. *Beds* ICF 61. *Certified* Medicaid.
Owner Proprietary corp (Hillhaven Corp).

Rumford

Cozy Inn Nursing Home
Eaton Hill Rd, Box 430, Rumford, ME 04276
(207) 364-7863
Admin John Ford.
Medical Dir David Phillips MD.
Licensure Intermediate care. *Beds* ICF 57. *Certified* Medicaid.
Staff RNs 6 (ft); LPNs 3 (ft); Nurses' aides 27 (ft); Activities coordinators 1 (ft); Dietitians 1 (pt).
Facilities Dining room; Activities room; Chapel; Crafts room; Laundry room; Barber/ Beauty shop.
Activities Arts & crafts; Cards; Games; Prayer groups; Movies.

Saco

Evergreen Manor
328 North St, Saco, ME 04072
(207) 282-5161
Medical Dir Andre Fortier MD.
Licensure Intermediate care. *Beds* ICF 42. *Private Pay Patients* 29%. *Certified* Medicaid.
Owner Proprietary corp.
Staff RNs 2 (ft), 3 (pt); LPNs 3 (ft), 5 (pt); Nurses' aides 15 (ft), 11 (pt); Recreational therapists 1 (ft); Activities coordinators 1 (ft).
Languages French.
Facilities Dining room; Activities room; Chapel; Crafts room; Laundry room; Barber/ Beauty shop; Library.
Activities Arts & crafts; Cards; Games; Reading groups; Prayer groups; Movies; Shopping trips; Dances/Social/Cultural gatherings.

Saint Albans

Square Road Group Home
Rte 1 Box 2265, Square Rd, Saint Albans, ME 04971
(207) 938-2046
Admin Christy Provost.
Licensure Intermediate care for mentally retarded. *Beds* ICF/MR 6.
Owner Nonprofit organization/foundation.
Admissions Requirements Minimum age 18; Medical examination.
Staff ADL staff 7 (ft), 2 (pt).
Facilities Dining room; Activities room; Laundry room; Home setting.
Activities Arts & crafts; Cards; Games; Reading groups; Movies; Shopping trips; Dances/Social/Cultural gatherings.

Sanford

Greenwood Center
384 Main St, Sanford, ME 04073
(207) 324-2273
Admin Christine Boisvert.
Licensure Intermediate care. *Beds* ICF 96. *Certified* Medicaid.

Hillcrest Manor Skilled Care Div
Hillcrest Dr, Sanford, ME 04073
(207) 324-4310
Admin Peter Booth.
Medical Dir Carl E Richards MD.
Licensure Skilled care; Intermediate care. *Beds* SNF 25; ICF 77. *Certified* Medicaid; Medicare.
Admissions Requirements Medical examination; Physician's request.
Staff RNs 3 (ft), 6 (pt); LPNs 9 (ft), 8 (pt); Nurses' aides 27 (ft), 12 (pt); Physical therapists 3 (pt); Recreational therapists 1 (ft); Occupational therapists 1 (pt); Speech therapists 1 (pt); Activities coordinators 1 (ft); Dietitians 1 (pt); Audiologists 1 (pt).
Facilities Dining room; Physical therapy room; Activities room; Laundry room; Barber/Beauty shop.
Activities Arts & crafts; Cards; Games; Reading groups; Movies; Shopping trips; Dances/Social/Cultural gatherings.

Maine Stay Nursing Home
291 Main St, Sanford, ME 04073
(207) 324-7999
Admin Doyle T Sowerby.
Licensure Intermediate care; Lodging care. *Beds* ICF 42; Lodging care 11. *Certified* Medicaid.
Staff RNs 3 (ft); LPNs 2 (ft), 2 (pt); Nurses' aides 17 (ft); Activities coordinators 1 (ft), 1 (pt); Dietitians 1 (pt); Podiatrists 1 (pt).
Facilities Dining room; Activities room; Chapel; Crafts room; Laundry room; Barber/ Beauty shop.

Activities Arts & crafts; Cards; Games; Reading groups; Prayer groups; Movies; Shopping trips; Dances/Social/Cultural gatherings.

Sanford Health Care Facility
179 Main St, Sanford, ME 04073
(207) 324-6818
Admin Doyle Sowerby.
Licensure Intermediate care. *Beds* ICF 31. *Certified* Medicaid.

Scarborough

Casa Inc
PO Box 58, 148 Gorham Rd, Scarborough, ME 04074
(207) 883-6333
Admin Anne D Walsh Walp. *Dir of Nursing* Dorothy Bender RN.
Licensure Intermediate care for mentally retarded. *Beds* ICF/MR 8. *Certified* Medicaid.
Owner Nonprofit corp.
Admissions Requirements Minimum age 8-15; Medical examination; Physician's request.
Staff RNs 1 (ft); LPNs 3 (ft), 2 (pt); Nurses' aides 6 (ft), 6 (pt); Recreational therapists 1 (pt).
Facilities Dining room; Activities room; Laundry room.
Activities Arts & crafts; Games; Reading groups; Movies; Shopping trips; Dances/ Social/Cultural gatherings.

Skowhegan

Cedar Ridge Inc
RR 1 Box 1283, Skowhegan, ME 04976
(207) 474-9686
Admin David Sylvester.
Medical Dir Robert Kaschub MD.
Licensure Intermediate care. *Beds* ICF 50. *Certified* Medicaid.
Admissions Requirements Medical examination.
Staff RNs 3 (ft), 1 (pt); LPNs 3 (ft); Nurses' aides 35 (ft); Physical therapists 1 (pt); Recreational therapists 1 (ft); Activities coordinators 1 (ft); Dietitians 1 (ft).
Facilities Dining room; Physical therapy room; Activities room; Crafts room; Laundry room; Barber/Beauty shop.
Activities Arts & crafts; Cards; Games; Reading groups; Prayer groups; Movies; Shopping trips; Dances/Social/Cultural gatherings.

Woodlawn (First Allied)
PO Box 600, Skowhegan, ME 04976
(207) 474-9300
Admin Anthony Belliveau Jr.
Licensure Intermediate care. *Beds* ICF 50. *Certified* Medicaid.

South Paris

Market Square Health Care Center
12 Market Square, South Paris, ME 04281
(207) 743-7086
Admin Richard H Hooper.
Licensure Intermediate care. *Beds* ICF 109. *Certified* Medicaid.
Staff Physicians 6 (pt); RNs 6 (ft); LPNs 12 (ft); Occupational therapists 1 (pt); Speech therapists 1 (pt); Activities coordinators 1 (ft); Dietitians 1 (ft); Ophthalmologists 1 (pt); Podiatrists 1 (pt); Audiologists 1 (pt); Dentists 1 (pt).
Facilities Dining room; Physical therapy room; Activities room; Crafts room; Laundry room; Library.
Activities Arts & crafts; Cards; Games; Reading groups; Prayer groups; Movies; Shopping trips; Dances/Social/Cultural gatherings.

South Portland

Hillside Nursing Home
25 Smith St, South Portland, ME 04106-2237
(207) 799-2245
Dir of Nursing Rita Adams RN. *Medical Dir*
Douglas Hill MD.
Licensure Intermediate care. *Beds* ICF 18.
Certified Medicaid.
Owner Proprietary corp.
Admissions Requirements Medical
examination; Physician's request.
Staff Physicians 1 (pt); RNs 1 (ft); LPNs 5
(pt); Nurses' aides 4 (ft), 6 (pt); Activities
coordinators 1 (pt); Dietitians 1 (pt);
Podiatrists 1 (pt).
Facilities Dining room; Activities room;
Crafts room; Laundry room.
Activities Arts & crafts; Cards; Games;
Reading groups; Prayer groups; Shopping
trips; Dances/Social/Cultural gatherings.

Manden Nursing Home
1060 Broadway, South Portland, ME 04106
(207) 799-1945
Admin Dawn Wursthorne.
Licensure Intermediate care. *Beds* 10.
Certified Medicaid.

South Portland Nursing Home Inc
42 Anthoine St, Box 2413, South Portland,
ME 04106
(207) 799-8561
Admin Donald Johnson.
Licensure Intermediate care. *Beds* ICF 73.
Certified Medicaid.

South Windham

Swampscotta Nursing Home
Rte 302, 233 Roosevelt Trail, South
Windham, ME 04082
(207) 892-6922
Admin Florence Mayberry.
Medical Dir Walter Penta MD.
Licensure Intermediate care. *Beds* ICF 36.
Certified Medicaid.

Strong

Strong Nursing Home
PO Box 249, Main St, Strong, ME 04983
(207) 684-3341
Admin Glenna Barden. *Dir of Nursing* Mary
Evelyn Gregor RN.
Licensure Intermediate care for mentally
retarded. *Beds* ICF/MR 20. *Private Pay
Patients* 0%. *Certified* Medicaid; Medicare.
Owner Proprietary corp.
Admissions Requirements Psychological
evaluation.
Staff RNs; LPNs; Nurses' aides; Physical
therapists; Occupational therapists; Speech
therapists; Activities coordinators; Dietitians.
Facilities Dining room; Physical therapy
room; Activities room; Crafts room; Laundry
room.
Activities Arts & crafts; Cards; Games;
Reading groups; Movies; Shopping trips;
Intergenerational programs; Pet therapy.

Sullivan

Maplecrest Nursing Home
Rte 1 Box 50, Sullivan, ME 04689
(207) 422-3345
Admin Martha Scott. *Dir of Nursing* Joyce D
Jamison RN. *Medical Dir* Dr Richard
LaRocco; Dr Kerri Crowley.
Licensure Intermediate care; Alzheimer's care.
Beds ICF 34. *Certified* Medicaid.
Owner Proprietary corp.
Admissions Requirements Medical
examination; Physician's request.

Staff Physicians 2 (pt); RNs 1 (ft); LPNs 1
(ft), 1 (pt); Nurses' aides 12 (ft), 2 (pt);
Physical therapists 1 (pt); Activities
coordinators 1 (ft), 1 (pt); Dietitians 1 (pt);
Dentists 1 (pt); MSWs 1 (ft).
Facilities Dining room; Activities room;
Crafts room; Laundry room.
Activities Arts & crafts; Cards; Games;
Reading groups; Movies.

Topsham

Amenity Manor
29 Elm St, Topsham, ME 04086
(207) 725-7495
Admin Susan J Gajewski.
Licensure Intermediate care. *Beds* ICF 69.
Certified Medicaid.

Gregory House
1 Middlesex Rd, Topsham, ME 04086
(207) 729-8251
Admin Linda Grondin.
Licensure Intermediate care for mentally
retarded. *Beds* ICF/MR 8. *Certified*
Medicaid.
Admissions Requirements Minimum age 18.
Activities Arts & crafts; Cards; Games;
Reading groups; Prayer groups; Movies;
Shopping trips; Dances/Social/Cultural
gatherings.

Upper Frenchville

St Joseph Nursing Home
PO Box K, Main St, Upper Frenchville, ME
04784
(207) 543-6252
Admin Clovis Daigle. *Dir of Nursing* Roberta
Guerrette. *Medical Dir* Dr Zui Sun Tao.
Licensure Intermediate care; Alzheimer's care.
Beds ICF 40. *Certified* Medicaid.
Owner Proprietary corp.
Admissions Requirements Females only;
Medical examination; Physician's request.
Staff Physicians 1 (pt); RNs 1 (ft), 2 (pt);
LPNs 3 (ft); Nurses' aides 21 (ft); Activities
coordinators 1 (pt); Dietitians 1 (pt);
Ophthalmologists 1 (pt); Podiatrists 1 (pt);
Audiologists 1 (pt).
Affiliation Roman Catholic.
Facilities Dining room; Physical therapy
room; Activities room; Chapel; Crafts room;
Laundry room; Barber/Beauty shop; Library.
Activities Games; Movies; Dances/Social/
Cultural gatherings.

Van Buren

Borderview Manor Inc
90 State St, Van Buren, ME 04785
(207) 868-5211
Admin John B Pelletier. *Dir of Nursing*
Maxima A Corriveau RN.
Licensure Intermediate care; Boarding care;
Alzheimer's care. *Beds* ICF 82; Boarding
care 36. *Certified* Medicaid.
Owner Proprietary corp.
Staff RNs; LPNs; Nurses' aides; Activities
coordinators; Dietitians.
Languages French.
Facilities Dining room; Physical therapy
room; Activities room; Chapel; Crafts room;
Laundry room; Barber/Beauty shop.
Activities Arts & crafts; Cards; Games; Prayer
groups; Movies; Shopping trips; Dances/
Social/Cultural gatherings.

Waldoboro

Fieldcrest Manor Nursing Home
Depot St, Box 34, Waldoboro, ME 04572
(207) 832-5343
Admin Barry Spellman. *Dir of Nursing* Phyllis
Tonry. *Medical Dir* Jack Waterman MD.

Licensure Intermediate care. *Beds* ICF 70.
Certified Medicaid.
Owner Proprietary corp (Hillhaven Corp).
Staff Physicians 9 (pt); RNs 2 (ft), 4 (pt);
LPNs 3 (ft), 4 (pt); Nurses' aides 20 (ft), 23
(pt); Activities coordinators 1 (ft); Dietitians
1 (pt); Podiatrists 1 (pt).
Facilities Dining room; Physical therapy
room; Activities room; Laundry room;
Barber/Beauty shop.
Activities Arts & crafts; Games; Reading
groups; Prayer groups; Movies; Shopping
trips; Dances/Social/Cultural gatherings.

Waterville

Colonial House Manor
110 College Ave, Waterville, ME 04901
(207) 873-0641
Admin Rev Bruce Alexander. *Dir of Nursing*
Lillian Phillips RN. *Medical Dir* John M
Szala DO.
Licensure Intermediate care. *Beds* ICF 74.
Certified Medicaid.
Owner Proprietary corp (Hillhaven Corp).
Admissions Requirements Medical
examination; Physician's request.
Staff Physicians 19 (pt); RNs 3 (ft), 2 (pt);
LPNs 2 (ft), 4 (pt); Nurses' aides; Activities
coordinators 1 (ft); Dietitians 1 (pt); Social
workers 1 (ft).
Languages French.
Facilities Dining room; Activities room;
Chapel; Crafts room; Laundry room; Barber/
Beauty shop; Library.
Activities Arts & crafts; Cards; Games;
Reading groups; Prayer groups; Movies;
Shopping trips; Dances/Social/Cultural
gatherings.

Lakewood Manor
220 Kennedy Memorial Dr, Waterville, ME
04901
(207) 873-5125
Admin Norma Pearl.
Medical Dir Dr Stanley Beckerman.
Licensure Intermediate care. *Beds* ICF 75.
Certified Medicaid.
Staff Physicians 14 (pt); RNs 5 (ft), 1 (pt);
LPNs 4 (ft), 4 (pt); Nurses' aides 26 (ft), 5
(pt); Physical therapists 1 (pt); Reality
therapists 1 (pt); Recreational therapists 1
(pt); Occupational therapists 1 (pt); Speech
therapists 1 (pt); Activities coordinators 1
(ft); Dietitians 1 (pt); Ophthalmologists 1
(pt); Podiatrists 1 (pt); Audiologists 1 (pt);
Dentists 1 (pt).
Facilities Dining room; Physical therapy
room; Activities room; Chapel; Crafts room;
Laundry room; Barber/Beauty shop; Library;
Living rooms.
Activities Arts & crafts; Cards; Games;
Reading groups; Prayer groups; Movies;
Shopping trips; Dances/Social/Cultural
gatherings; Bean & cheese parties.

Mt St Joseph Nursing Home
Highwood St, Waterville, ME 04901
(207) 873-0705
Admin Patricia Berger. *Dir of Nursing*
Jeannette Leighton RN.
Licensure Intermediate care; Alzheimer's care.
Beds ICF 78. *Private Pay Patients* 22%.
Certified Medicaid.
Owner Nonprofit corp.
Admissions Requirements Physician's request.
Staff RNs 4 (ft), 2 (pt); LPNs 7 (ft), 2 (pt);
Nurses' aides 45 (ft), 4 (pt); Physical
therapists 1 (pt); Activities coordinators 1
(ft), 1 (pt); Dietitians 1 (ft).
Languages French.
Affiliation Roman Catholic.
Facilities Dining room; Physical therapy
room; Activities room; Chapel; Crafts room;
Laundry room; Barber/Beauty shop.

Activities Arts & crafts; Cards; Games;
Reading groups; Prayer groups; Movies;
Shopping trips; Dances/Social/Cultural
gatherings; Pet therapy.

Waterville Convalescent Center
Cool St, Waterville, ME 04901
(207) 873-0721
Admin Rita R Low.
Licensure Intermediate care. *Beds* ICF 77.
Certified Medicaid.
Owner Proprietary corp (Hillhaven Corp).

Western Avenue Residence
101 Western Ave, Waterville, ME 04901
(207) 872-8195
Admin Patricia Geary.
Licensure Intermediate care for mentally
retarded. *Beds* ICF/MR 6.

West Paris

Ledgeview Nursing Home
Rte 26 Box 3420, West Paris, ME 04289
(207) 674-2250
Admin Lawrence Wilday.
Medical Dir Thomas Nangle MD.
Licensure Intermediate care. *Beds* ICF 125.
Certified Medicaid.
Admissions Requirements Medical
examination; Physician's request.
Staff RNs 2 (ft), 5 (pt); LPNs 8 (ft), 4 (pt);
Nurses' aides 34 (ft), 27 (pt); Physical
therapists 1 (pt); Speech therapists 1 (pt);
Activities coordinators 2 (ft); Dietitians 1
(pt); Podiatrists 1 (pt); Audiologists 1 (pt);
Dentists 1 (pt).
Affiliation Seventh-Day Adventist.
Facilities Dining room; Physical therapy
room; Activities room; Chapel; Crafts room;
Laundry room; Barber/Beauty shop; Library;
Dental.
Activities Arts & crafts; Cards; Games;
Reading groups; Prayer groups; Movies;
Shopping trips; Dances/Social/Cultural
gatherings; Day trips; Cookouts.

West Scarborough

Pine Point Nursing Care Center
Pine Point Rd, Box 127, West Scarborough,
ME 04074
(207) 883-2468
Admin Pierre Morneault.
Licensure Intermediate care. *Beds* ICF 62.
Certified Medicaid.

Winthrop

Heritage Manor Inc
RFD 3 Box 1220, Old Lewiston Rd,
Winthrop, ME 04364
(207) 377-8453
Admin Jessie E Jacques. *Dir of Nursing*
Alberta Chick RN. *Medical Dir* Dr R E
Barron.
Licensure Intermediate care; Alzheimer's care.
Beds ICF 61. *Certified* Medicaid.
Owner Proprietary corp (Continental Health
Service Management).
Staff RNs 2 (ft), 1 (pt); LPNs 2 (ft), 6 (pt);
Nurses' aides 15 (ft), 10 (pt); Recreational
therapists 1 (ft); Activities coordinators 1
(ft); Dietitians 1 (pt); Social worker 1 (ft).
Facilities Dining room; Activities room;
Crafts room; Laundry room; Barber/Beauty
shop.
Activities Arts & crafts; Cards; Games;
Reading groups; Prayer groups; Movies;
Shopping trips; Dances/Social/Cultural
gatherings.

Nicholson's Nursing Home
11 Western Ave, Winthrop, ME 04364
(207) 377-8184
Admin Constance Burnham.
Licensure Intermediate care. *Beds* ICF 46.
Certified Medicaid.

Yarmouth

Brentwood Manor
122 Portland St, Yarmouth, ME 04096
(207) 846-9021
Admin Robert Lezer.
Licensure Intermediate care. *Beds* ICF 78.
Certified Medicaid.
Owner Proprietary corp (Hillhaven Corp).

Coastal Manor
10 W Main St, Yarmouth, ME 04096
(207) 846-5013
Admin Cindy N Scott. *Dir of Nursing*
Dorothy Smith RN.
Licensure Intermediate care; Retirement;
Alzheimer's care. *Beds* ICF 46; Retirement
6. *Certified* Medicaid.
Owner Privately owned.
Staff Physicians 6 (pt); RNs 2 (ft), 5 (pt);
LPNs 1 (ft); Nurses' aides 15 (ft), 15 (pt);
Activities coordinators 1 (ft); Dietitians 1
(pt); Podiatrists 1 (pt); Audiologists 1 (pt).
Facilities Dining room; Laundry room.
Activities Arts & crafts; Cards; Games;
Reading groups; Prayer groups; Movies;
Shopping trips; Dances/Social/Cultural
gatherings; Intergenerational programs; Pet
therapy.

York

York Hospital
15 Hospital Dr, York, ME 03909
(207) 363-4321
Admin Jud Knox. *Dir of Nursing* Jill Fargo
RN.
Licensure Skilled care; Acute care. *Beds* SNF
18; Acute care 61. *Certified* Medicare.
Owner Nonprofit corp.
Facilities Dining room; Physical therapy
room; Activities room; Barber/Beauty shop.
Activities Arts & crafts; Cards; Games;
Movies; Shopping trips.

York Harbor

Harbor Home
PO Box 96, Norwood Farms Rd, York
Harbor, ME 03911
(207) 363-2422
Admin Marcella Sowerby.
Licensure Intermediate care. *Beds* ICF 79.
Certified Medicaid.
Facilities Dining room; Laundry room;
Barber/Beauty shop.
Activities Arts & crafts; Cards; Games;
Reading groups; Prayer groups; Movies;
Shopping trips; Dances/Social/Cultural
gatherings.

MARYLAND

Adelphi

Hillhaven Nursing Center Inc
3210 Powder Mill Rd, Adelphi, MD 20783
(301) 937-3939
Admin Joyce A Malin NHA. *Dir of Nursing*
Judy Dolecek RN. *Medical Dir* Charles
Benner MD.
Licensure Skilled care; Intermediate care. *Beds*
Swing beds SNF/ICF 60. *Certified* Medicaid;
Medicare.
Owner Proprietary corp.
Staff RNs 5 (ft), 2 (pt); LPNs 2 (ft), 2 (pt);
Nurses' aides 17 (ft), 10 (pt); Physical
therapists 1 (pt); Recreational therapists 1
(pt); Occupational therapists 1 (ft); Speech
therapists 1 (pt); Activities coordinators 2
(ft); Dietitians 1 (pt); Ophthalmologists 1
(pt); Podiatrists 1 (pt).
Facilities Dining room; Physical therapy
room; Activities room; Crafts room; Laundry
room; Barber/Beauty shop; Library;
Nourishment room.
Activities Arts & crafts; Cards; Games;
Reading groups; Prayer groups; Movies;
Shopping trips; Dances/Social/Cultural
gatherings; Intergenerational programs; Pet
therapy; Dining out club; Resident council.

Presidential Woods Health Care Center
1801 Metzerott Rd, Adelphi, MD 20783
(301) 434-0500
Admin Ray Hepner. *Dir of Nursing* Nancy L
Petersen RN. *Medical Dir* Paul DeVore
MD.
Licensure Skilled care; Intermediate care;
Alzheimer's care. *Beds* Comprehensive care
218. *Certified* Medicaid; Medicare.
Owner Proprietary corp (Health Care &
Retirement Corp).
Admissions Requirements Minimum age 18.
Staff RNs 4 (ft), 2 (pt); LPNs 10 (ft); Nurses'
aides 90 (ft); Physical therapists 1 (ft);
Recreational therapists 2 (ft); Occupational
therapists 1 (ft); Speech therapists 1 (ft);
Dietitians 2 (ft).
Languages Spanish.
Facilities Dining room; Physical therapy
room; Activities room; Crafts room; Laundry
room; Barber/Beauty shop.
Activities Arts & crafts; Cards; Games;
Reading groups; Prayer groups; Movies;
Shopping trips; Dances/Social/Cultural
gatherings.

Annapolis

Annapolis Convalescent Center
900 Van Buren St, Annapolis, MD 21403
(301) 267-8653
Admin Helen Ray. *Dir of Nursing* Charlotte
Stouder. *Medical Dir* Richard Hochman
MD.
Licensure Skilled care. *Beds* SNF 91. *Certified*
Medicaid; Medicare.
Owner Proprietary corp.
Admissions Requirements Minimum age 14.

Staff RNs 4 (ft), 1 (pt); LPNs 5 (ft), 5 (pt);
Nurses' aides 26 (ft), 16 (pt); Physical
therapists 2 (pt); Recreational therapists 1
(ft), 1 (pt); Dietitians 1 (pt).
Facilities Dining room; Physical therapy
room; Laundry room; Barber/Beauty shop;
Living room.
Activities Arts & crafts; Games; Reading
groups; Prayer groups; Movies; Pet therapy.

Ginger Cove
4000 River Crescent Dr, Annapolis, MD
21401
(301) 266-7300
Admin David M Zwald. *Dir of Nursing*
Barbara O Smith RN. *Medical Dir* John
Jackson MD.
Licensure Skilled care; Intermediate care;
Retirement. *Beds* SNF 29; ICF 14;
Retirement 325. *Certified* Medicare.
Owner Nonprofit corp.
Admissions Requirements Minimum age 62;
Medical examination.
Staff RNs; LPNs; Nurses' aides; Physical
therapists 1 (pt); Recreational therapists 1
(ft); Activities coordinators 1 (ft); Dietitians
1 (pt).
Languages Spanish, French.
Facilities Dining room; Physical therapy
room; Activities room; Chapel; Crafts room;
Laundry room; Barber/Beauty shop; Library;
Auditorium; Indoor pool; Fitness center;
Cocktail lounge; Bank; Convenience store;
Arts & crafts studio; Card & game room.
Activities Arts & crafts; Cards; Games;
Reading groups; Prayer groups; Movies;
Shopping trips; Dances/Social/Cultural
gatherings; Intergenerational programs; Pet
therapy.

Arnold

Bay Manor Nursing Home Inc
305 College Pkwy, Arnold, MD 21012
(301) 757-2069
Admin Vickie Fila. *Dir of Nursing* Chris
Ellzey RN. *Medical Dir* Dr C V Cyriac.
Licensure Intermediate care. *Beds* ICF 74.
Certified Medicaid.
Owner Proprietary corp.
Admissions Requirements Medical
examination; Physician's request.
Staff Physicians 1 (ft); RNs 2 (ft), 4 (pt);
LPNs 5 (pt); Nurses' aides 28 (ft); Physical
therapists; Occupational therapists; Speech
therapists; Activities coordinators 2 (pt);
Dietitians.
Facilities Dining room; Laundry room; TV
room.
Activities Arts & crafts; Cards; Games;
Reading groups; Prayer groups; Movies;
Shopping trips; Dances/Social/Cultural
gatherings; Music; Resident council;
Cooking; Exercise.

Chesapeake Manor Extended Care
305 College Parkway, Arnold, MD 21012
(301) 974-1761

Admin Vicki Lee Fila.
Medical Dir C V Cyriac MD.
Licensure Comprehensive care. *Beds*
Comprehensive care 100.
Owner Proprietary corp.

Baltimore

Alice Manor
2095 Rockrose Ave, Baltimore, MD 21211
(301) 243-7458
Admin Joseph Devadoss.
Medical Dir L Kemper Owens MD.
Licensure Intermediate care; Adult day care.
Beds ICF 36; Adult day care 7. *Certified*
Medicaid.
Owner Proprietary corp.
Admissions Requirements Minimum age 14;
Medical examination.
Staff Physicians; RNs; LPNs; Nurses' aides;
Activities coordinators; Dietitians.
Activities Arts & crafts; Cards; Games;
Reading groups; Prayer groups; Movies;
Shopping trips; Dances/Social/Cultural
gatherings.

Armacost Nursing Home Inc
812 Regester Ave, Baltimore, MD 21239
(301) 377-5225
Admin Ira D Greene. *Dir of Nursing* Barbara
Harris RN. *Medical Dir* Mark Davis MD.
Licensure Intermediate care; Alzheimer's care.
Beds ICF 45. *Private Pay Patients* 15%.
Certified Medicaid.
Owner Proprietary corp.
Admissions Requirements Minimum age 21;
Medical examination.
Staff RNs 2 (ft), 2 (pt); LPNs 3 (ft), 1 (pt);
Nurses' aides 11 (ft), 11 (pt); Physical
therapists (consultant); Activities
coordinators 1 (ft); Dietitians (consultant).
Facilities Dining room; Activities room.
Activities Arts & crafts; Cards; Games; Prayer
groups; Movies; Shopping trips; Dances/
Social/Cultural gatherings; Intergenerational
programs; Pet therapy; Theater and museum
trips.

Ashburton Nursing Home
3520 N Hilton Rd, Baltimore, MD 21215
(301) 466-2400
Admin Teresa M Kelly.
Medical Dir Allan H Macht MD.
Licensure Comprehensive care. *Beds*
Comprehensive care 41. *Certified* Medicaid.
Owner Proprietary corp.
Admissions Requirements Minimum age 21;
Medical examination; Physician's request.
Staff Physicians 1 (ft); RNs 2 (ft); LPNs 1 (ft),
3 (pt); Nurses' aides 7 (ft), 4 (pt); Physical
therapists 1 (ft); Reality therapists 1 (ft);
Recreational therapists 1 (ft); Speech
therapists 1 (pt); Activities coordinators 1
(ft); Dietitians 1 (pt); Ophthalmologists 1
(pt); Podiatrists 1 (pt); Dentists 1 (pt).

Facilities Dining room; Physical therapy
room; Activities room; Laundry room.
Activities Arts & crafts; Cards; Games;
Reading groups; Prayer groups; Shopping
trips; Dances/Social/Cultural gatherings;
Outdoor picnics; Various trips.

Belair Convalesarium
6116 Belair Rd, Baltimore, MD 21206
(301) 426-1424
Admin Robert R Ross.
Medical Dir Luis E Rivera MD.
Licensure Skilled care; Intermediate care. *Beds*
Comprehensive care 200. *Certified*
Medicaid; Medicare.
Owner Proprietary corp.

Brighton Manor Nursing & Geriatric Center
1501 N Dukeland St, Baltimore, MD 21216
(301) 945-7433, 945-7461 FAX
Admin Darrell H Reich Jr NHA. *Dir of
Nursing* Fannie Lewis RN. *Medical Dir*
Warren Smith MD.
Licensure Intermediate care. *Beds* ICF 104.
Certified Medicaid.
Owner Nonprofit corp (Lutheran Healthcare
Corp).
Admissions Requirements Medical
examination.
Staff Physicians 5 (pt); RNs 4 (ft), 2 (pt);
LPNs 4 (ft), 2 (pt); Nurses' aides 30 (ft), 2
(pt); Physical therapists (contracted); Reality
therapists 1 (pt); Recreational therapists 1
(pt); Occupational therapists 1 (pt); Speech
therapists 1 (pt); Activities coordinators 1
(ft); Dietitians 1 (pt); Ophthalmologists 1
(pt); Podiatrists 1 (pt); Audiologists 1 (pt).
Affiliation Lutheran.
Activities Arts & crafts; Cards; Games; Prayer
groups; Movies; Shopping trips; Dances/
Social/Cultural gatherings; Intergenerational
programs; Pet therapy; Exercise program.

Canton Harbor Nursing Centre
1300 S Ellwood Ave, Baltimore, MD 21224
(301) 342-6644
Admin Stanley Savitz.
Medical Dir Michael Plott MD.
Licensure Comprehensive care; Domiciliary
care. *Beds* Comprehensive care 120;
Domiciliary care 30.
Owner Proprietary corp.

**Walter P Carter Center—Mental Retardation
Unit**
630 W Fayette St, Baltimore, MD 21201
(301) 528-2139
Admin Dr Patricia Whitmore.
Medical Dir George Lentz MD.
Licensure Intermediate care for mentally
retarded. *Beds* ICF/MR 12. *Certified*
Medicaid.
Owner Publicly owned.
Admissions Requirements Minimum age 18.
Staff Physicians; RNs; LPNs; Recreational
therapists; Occupational therapists; Speech
therapists; Activities coordinators; Dietitians.
Languages Spanish.
Facilities Dining room; Activities room;
Crafts room; Laundry room.
Activities Arts & crafts; Cards; Games;
Reading groups; Prayer groups; Movies;
Shopping trips; Dances/Social/Cultural
gatherings.

Century Home Inc
102 N Paca St, Baltimore, MD 21201
(301) 727-2050
Admin Oscar Newman.
Medical Dir Hollis Seunarine MD.
Licensure Intermediate care. *Beds* ICF 82.
Certified Medicaid.
Owner Proprietary corp.
Admissions Requirements Minimum age 17.
Staff Physicians; RNs; LPNs; Nurses' aides;
Physical therapists; Speech therapists;
Activities coordinators; Dietitians;
Ophthalmologists; Podiatrists; Dentists.

Facilities Dining room; Activities room.
Activities Arts & crafts; Cards; Games;
Reading groups; Prayer groups; Movies;
Shopping trips.

Community Care Nursing & Geriatric Center
730 Ashburton St, Baltimore, MD 21216
(301) 945-1601, 362-7915 FAX
Admin Marie Okronley LNHA. *Dir of Nursing*
Bonnie Williams RN. *Medical Dir* Dr Abdul
Qureshi.
Licensure Skilled care; Intermediate care. *Beds*
SNF 70; ICF 59. *Private Pay Patients* 12%.
Certified Medicaid; Medicare.
Owner Nonprofit corp (Lutheran Healthcare
Corp).
Admissions Requirements Medical
examination.
Staff Physicians 5 (pt); RNs 4 (ft); LPNs;
Nurses' aides 42 (ft), 10 (pt); Physical
therapists 2 (pt); Recreational therapists 2
(ft); Occupational therapists 2 (pt); Speech
therapists 2 (pt); Activities coordinators 1
(ft); Dietitians 2 (pt); Ophthalmologists;
Podiatrists 1 (ft); Audiologists 1 (ft).
Facilities Physical therapy room; Chapel;
Crafts room; Barber/Beauty shop.
Activities Arts & crafts; Cards; Games;
Reading groups; Prayer groups; Movies;
Intergenerational programs; Pet therapy.

Crawford Retreat Inc
2117 Denison St, Baltimore, MD 21216
(301) 566-0160
Admin Marie A Fox.
Medical Dir Edward Hunt Jr MD.
Licensure Intermediate care. *Beds*
Comprehensive care 22. *Certified* Medicaid.
Owner Proprietary corp.

Deaton Hospital & Medical Center
611 S Charles St, Baltimore, MD 21230
(301) 547-8500, 752-2920 FAX
Admin Errol G Newport. *Dir of Nursing*
Donna L Leister. *Medical Dir* Herbert L
Muncie Jr MD.
Licensure Skilled care; Intermediate care;
Chronic care. *Beds* Swing beds SNF/ICF
180; Chronic care 180. *Private Pay Patients*
1%. *Certified* Medicaid; Medicare.
Owner Nonprofit corp.
Admissions Requirements Minimum age 14;
Medical examination; Physician's request.
Staff Physicians 2 (pt); RNs 34 (ft); LPNs 31
(ft); Nurses' aides 169 (ft); Physical
therapists 2 (ft); Recreational therapists 4
(ft); Occupational therapists 2 (ft); Speech
therapists 1 (pt); Activities coordinators 1
(ft); Dietitians 3 (ft); Podiatrists 2 (pt).
Affiliation Lutheran.
Facilities Dining room; Physical therapy
room; Activities room; Chapel; Crafts room;
Laundry room; Barber/Beauty shop;
Ventilator unit.
Activities Arts & crafts; Games; Reading
groups; Prayer groups; Movies; Shopping
trips; Pet therapy.

**Deaton Hospital & Medical Center of Christ
Lutheran Church—South**
3001 S Hanover St, Baltimore, MD 21230
(301) 347-3547
Admin Noel Kroncke.
Medical Dir Julian Reed MD.
Licensure Chronic care; Comprehensive care.
Beds Chronic care 59; Comprehensive care
20.
Owner Nonprofit corp.

Eastpoint Nursing Home
1046 Old N Point Rd, Baltimore, MD 21224
(301) 282-0100
Admin Cesare Tapino.
Medical Dir Joseph Cameron MD.
Licensure Comprehensive care. *Beds*
Comprehensive care 150.
Owner Proprietary corp.

Fairmount Nursing Center
100 N Broadway, Baltimore, MD 21231
(301) 732-0456
Admin Carolynne Adams.
Medical Dir Corazon Vergara-Soares MD.
Licensure Comprehensive care. *Beds*
Comprehensive care 50.
Owner Proprietary corp.

**Francis Scott Key Hospital Center/Mason F
Lord Nursing Facility**
5200 Eastern Ave, Baltimore, MD 21224
(301) 550-0756
Admin Cleve Laub Jr. *Dir of Nursing* Anita
Langford RN. *Medical Dir* Edmund
Beachum MD.
Licensure Chronic care; Comprehensive care;
Adult day care. *Beds* Chronic care 45;
Comprehensive care 171; Adult day care 36.
Certified Medicaid; Medicare.
Owner Publicly owned.
Admissions Requirements Minimum age 14;
Females only; Medical examination;
Physician's request.
Staff Physicians 1 (ft), 5 (pt); RNs 15 (ft), 1
(pt); LPNs 6 (ft); Nurses' aides 96 (ft);
Physical therapists 3 (ft); Recreational
therapists 4 (ft); Occupational therapists 3
(ft); Speech therapists 1 (pt); Dietitians 1
(ft); Podiatrists 1 (pt).
Languages Greek.
Facilities Dining room; Physical therapy
room; Activities room; Chapel; Crafts room;
Laundry room; Library Occupational therapy
room; Clinics; Adult day care.
Activities Arts & crafts; Cards; Games;
Reading groups; Prayer groups; Movies;
Shopping trips; Dances/Social/Cultural
gatherings.

Franklin Court Nursing Center
607 Pennsylvania Ave, Baltimore, MD 21201
(301) 728-3344
Admin Grace Lewis.
Medical Dir Richard Tyson.
Licensure Intermediate care. *Beds* ICF 122.
Certified Medicaid.
Owner Proprietary corp (ARA Living
Centers).
Admissions Requirements Minimum age 21;
Medical examination; Physician's request.
Staff Physicians 5 (pt); RNs 4 (ft), 1 (pt);
LPNs 10 (ft), 3 (pt); Nurses' aides 43 (ft);
Physical therapists 2 (pt); Speech therapists
1 (pt); Activities coordinators 1 (pt);
Dietitians 1 (pt); Ophthalmologists 1 (pt);
Podiatrists 1 (pt); Dentists 1 (pt).
Facilities Dining room; Physical therapy
room; Activities room; Barber/Beauty shop.
Activities Arts & crafts; Cards; Games;
Reading groups; Prayer groups; Movies;
Shopping trips; Dances/Social/Cultural
gatherings.

Frederick Villa Nursing Center
711 Academy Rd, Baltimore, MD 21228
(301) 788-3300, 788-6453 FAX
Admin Lois A McGovern. *Dir of Nursing*
Robyn Baginski RN DN. *Medical Dir* Julian
W Reed MD.
Licensure Skilled care; Intermediate care. *Beds*
Swing beds SNF/ICF 125. *Certified*
Medicaid; Medicare.
Owner Privately owned (Henry Reitberger).
Staff RNs 1 (ft), 6 (pt); LPNs 9 (ft); Nurses'
aides 2 (ft), 22 (pt); Physical therapists 1
(pt); Occupational therapists 1 (pt); Speech
therapists 1 (pt); Dietitians; Podiatrists 1
(pt).
Facilities Dining room; Physical therapy
room; Activities room; Laundry room;
Barber/Beauty shop.
Activities Arts & crafts; Cards; Games;
Reading groups; Prayer groups; Movies;
Shopping trips; Dances/Social/Cultural
gatherings; Intergenerational programs; Pet
therapy.

Friedler's Nursing Home
2449 Shirley Ave, Baltimore, MD 21215
(301) 466-0061
Admin Ellis Friedler. *Dir of Nursing* Josephine Mungin. *Medical Dir* Manuel Levin MD.
Licensure Intermediate care. *Beds* ICF 31. *Certified* Medicaid.
Owner Privately owned.
Staff Physicians 2 (pt); RNs 1 (ft); LPNs 2 (ft), 1 (pt); Nurses' aides 11 (ft); Activities coordinators 1 (ft); Dietitians 1 (pt); Ophthalmologists 1 (pt); Podiatrists 1 (pt).
Facilities Dining room; Activities room; Chapel; Laundry room.
Activities Arts & crafts; Cards; Games; Prayer groups; Movies; Shopping trips; Dances/Social/Cultural gatherings; Pet therapy.

Garrison Nursing Home Inc
2803 Garrison Blvd, Baltimore, MD 21216
(301) 367-6726
Admin Teresa M Friend. *Dir of Nursing* Gwendolyn Lopez-Rodriquez. *Medical Dir* Edward Hunt Jr MD.
Licensure Intermediate care. *Beds* ICF 22. *Certified* Medicaid.
Owner Proprietary corp.
Admissions Requirements Minimum age 45; Medical examination; Physician's request.
Staff Physicians 1 (ft); RNs 1 (ft); LPNs 4 (ft); Nurses' aides 6 (ft); Activities coordinators 1 (pt); Dietitians 1 (pt).
Facilities Dining room; Activities room; Laundry room.
Activities Arts & crafts; Cards; Games; Reading groups; Prayer groups; Trips to senior center weekly.

Granada Nursing Center
4017 Liberty Heights Ave, Baltimore, MD 21207
(301) 542-5306
Admin Robert T DeFontes.
Medical Dir Hollis Seunarine MD.
Licensure Intermediate care. *Beds* ICF 112. *Certified* Medicaid.
Owner Proprietary corp (Health Care & Retirement Corp).

Greenwood Acres Nursing Home
3706 Nortonia Rd, Baltimore, MD 21216
(301) 947-1444
Admin Delzora S Johnson.
Medical Dir Shaukat Y Kahn MD.
Licensure Intermediate care. *Beds* ICF 23. *Certified* Medicaid.
Owner Proprietary corp.

Harford Gardens Convalescent Center Inc
4700 Harford Rd, Baltimore, MD 21214
(301) 254-3012
Admin Janice Mattare.
Medical Dir E Ellsworth Cook MD.
Licensure Intermediate care. *Beds* ICF 58. *Certified* Medicaid.
Owner Proprietary corp.
Staff Physicians 1 (ft); RNs; LPNs; Nurses' aides; Physical therapists; Recreational therapists; Speech therapists; Activities coordinators; Dietitians; Ophthalmologists; Dentists.
Facilities Dining room; Laundry room.
Activities Arts & crafts; Cards; Games; Reading groups; Prayer groups; Movies; Shopping trips; Dances/Social/Cultural gatherings.

Haven Nursing Home
3939 Penhurst Ave, Baltimore, MD 21215
(301) 664-9535
Admin Evelyn Bennett.
Medical Dir Swadesh Bmatiani MD.
Licensure Intermediate care. *Beds* 22. *Certified* Medicaid.
Owner Proprietary corp.
Admissions Requirements Minimum age 45; Medical examination; Physician's request.

Staff Physicians 1 (pt); RNs 1 (ft), 1 (pt); LPNs 3 (ft), 2 (pt); Nurses' aides 6 (ft); Recreational therapists 1 (ft); Activities coordinators 1 (ft); Dietitians 1 (pt); Podiatrists 1 (pt).
Facilities Dining room; Activities room; Crafts room; Laundry room.
Activities Arts & crafts; Cards; Games; Reading groups; Prayer groups; Movies; Shopping trips; Dances/Social/Cultural gatherings.

Hayes Care Home
3001 Garrison Blvd, Baltimore, MD 21216
(301) 542-9694
Admin Queen E Hayes. *Dir of Nursing* Carolyn Ennis. *Medical Dir* Dr Fabio Banegura.
Licensure Intermediate care; Domiciliary care. *Beds* ICF 15; Domicilliary care 4. *Private Pay Patients* 0%. *Certified* Medicaid; Medicare.
Owner Privately owned.
Admissions Requirements Medical examination; Physician's request.
Staff Physicians 2 (pt); RNs 2 (ft); LPNs 3 (ft), 2 (pt); Nurses' aides 4 (ft), 1 (pt); Physical therapists 1 (pt); Recreational therapists 1 (pt); Activities coordinators 1 (ft); Dietitians 1 (pt).
Facilities Dining room; Activities room; Crafts room; Laundry room; Library.
Activities Arts & crafts; Cards; Games; Reading groups; Prayer groups; Movies; Shopping trips; Dances/Social/Cultural gatherings.

Highland Health Facility—Mental Retardation Unit
5200 Eastern Ave, Bldg D, Baltimore, MD 21224
(301) 276-7000
Admin Delores M Miller.
Medical Dir Patricia Mildvan MD.
Licensure Intermediate care for mentally retarded. *Beds* ICF/MR 99. *Certified* Medicaid.
Owner Publicly owned.
Admissions Requirements Closed admissions at this time.
Staff Physicians 1 (ft); RNs 3 (ft); LPNs 14 (ft); Nurses' aides 59 (ft); Physical therapists 1 (pt); Recreational therapists 1 (ft); Occupational therapists 1 (pt); Speech therapists 1 (pt); Activities coordinators 1 (ft); Dietitians 1 (ft).
Facilities Dining room; Physical therapy room; Activities room; Crafts room; Laundry room.
Activities Arts & crafts; Games; Movies; Shopping trips; Dances/Social/Cultural gatherings.

Hurwitz House
133 Slade Ave, Baltimore, MD 21208
(301) 466-8700
Admin Peggy L Warner.
Medical Dir Noel List MD.
Licensure Intermediate care. *Beds* ICF 23. *Certified* Medicaid.
Owner Nonprofit corp.
Admissions Requirements Minimum age 60; Medical examination.
Staff LPNs 3 (ft), 3 (pt); Nurses' aides 3 (ft), 3 (pt).
Affiliation Jewish.
Facilities Dining room; Activities room; Laundry room.
Activities Arts & crafts; Cards; Games; Reading groups; Movies; Shopping trips.

Inns of Evergreen—Central
140 W Lafayette Ave, Baltimore, MD 21217
(301) 523-3400
Admin Roslyn Scott. *Dir of Nursing* Patricia Woolson RN. *Medical Dir* Richard F Tyson MD.

Licensure Intermediate care. *Beds* ICF 264. *Certified* Medicaid.
Owner Proprietary corp (Evergreen Health Group).
Staff Physicians 9 (pt); RNs 5 (ft), 1 (pt); LPNs 20 (ft), 3 (pt); Nurses' aides 140 (ft), 20 (pt); Physical therapists 4 (pt); Recreational therapists 5 (pt); Speech therapists 1 (pt); Dietitians 1 (ft); Ophthalmologists 1 (pt); Podiatrists 1 (pt); Dentists 1 (pt).
Facilities Dining room; Physical therapy room; Activities room; Chapel; Crafts room; Laundry room; Barber/Beauty shop; Library; Art gallery.
Activities Arts & crafts; Cards; Games; Reading groups; Prayer groups; Movies; Dances/Social/Cultural gatherings; Outside activities; Trips.

Inns of Evergreen—Northeast
5837 Belair Rd, Baltimore, MD 21206
(301) 483-5800
Admin Susan Mooneyham. *Dir of Nursing* Peggy Nearhoof RN. *Medical Dir* Albert Bradley MD.
Licensure Skilled care; Intermediate care. *Beds* Comprehensive care 100. *Certified* Medicaid; Medicare.
Owner Proprietary corp (Evergreen Health Group Inc).
Facilities Dining room; Activities room; Laundry room.
Activities Arts & crafts; Games; Prayer groups; Movies.

Inns of Evergreen—Northwest
2525 W Belvedere Ave, Baltimore, MD 21215
(301) 367-9100
Admin Thomas Keiser.
Medical Dir Leon Kochman MD.
Licensure Skilled care; Intermediate care. *Beds* Comprehensive care 170. *Certified* Medicaid; Medicare.
Owner Proprietary corp (Evergreen Health Group).

Inns of Evergreen—South
1213 Light St, Baltimore, MD 21230
(301) 727-1600
Admin Sandra Minnerick. *Dir of Nursing* Sandra Williams RN. *Medical Dir* C Thomas Folkemer MD.
Licensure Intermediate care. *Beds* ICF 314. *Certified* Medicaid.
Owner Proprietary corp (Evergreen Health Group).
Admissions Requirements Minimum age 21; Medical examination; Physician's request.
Staff Physicians 12 (pt); RNs 9 (ft), 2 (pt); LPNs 15 (ft), 5 (pt); Nurses' aides 90 (ft), 20 (pt); Physical therapists 3 (pt); Recreational therapists 1 (ft); Speech therapists 1 (pt); Activities coordinators 6 (ft); Dietitians 1 (pt); Ophthalmologists 1 (pt); Podiatrists 1 (pt); Dentists 1 (pt).
Facilities Dining room; Physical therapy room; Activities room; Chapel; Crafts room; Laundry room; Barber/Beauty shop; Library.
Activities Arts & crafts; Cards; Games; Reading groups; Prayer groups; Movies; Shopping trips; Dances/Social/Cultural gatherings.

Inns of Evergreen—West
333 Harlem Ln, Baltimore, MD 21228
(301) 744-1020
Admin Lisa Stone. *Dir of Nursing* Alice Lepson. *Medical Dir* James McPhillips.
Licensure Skilled care; Intermediate care. *Beds* 96. *Certified* Medicaid; Medicare.
Owner Proprietary corp (Evergreen Health Group).

Ivy Hall Geriatric Center
1300 Windlass Dr, Baltimore, MD 21220
(301) 687-1383, 687-1693 FAX

Admin Darell R Cammack Jr. *Dir of Nursing* Barbara Anderson. *Medical Dir* Tarique Firozi MD.
Licensure Skilled care; Intermediate care; Adult day care; Alzheimer's care. *Beds* SNF 30; ICF 90; Adult day care 30. *Private Pay Patients* 25%. *Certified* Medicaid; Medicare.
Owner Privately owned.
Admissions Requirements Minimum age 18; Medical examination; Physician's request.
Staff Physicians 6 (pt); RNs 5 (ft), 2 (pt); LPNs 10 (ft), 2 (pt); Nurses' aides 35 (ft), 15 (pt); Physical therapists 1 (pt); Reality therapists 1 (pt); Recreational therapists 1 (pt); Occupational therapists 1 (pt); Speech therapists 1 (pt); Activities coordinators 2 (ft), 1 (pt); Dietitians 1 (pt); Ophthalmologists 1 (pt); Podiatrists 2 (pt); Audiologists 1 (pt).
Facilities Dining room; Physical therapy room; Activities room; Crafts room; Laundry room; Barber/Beauty shop; Library; Quiet room; Sprinkler system; Smoke detectors; Automatic alarm to fire department.
Activities Arts & crafts; Cards; Games; Reading groups; Prayer groups; Movies; Shopping trips; Dances/Social/Cultural gatherings; Intergenerational programs; Pet therapy; Picnics; Current events; Family dinners.

Jenkins Memorial Inc
1000 S Caton Ave, Baltimore, MD 21229
(301) 644-7100
Admin Sr Veronica Tinseth. *Dir of Nursing* Nina Cheuvront RN. *Medical Dir* John F Hartman MD.
Licensure Skilled care; Comprehensive care. *Beds* SNF 83; Comprehensive care 43. *Certified* Medicaid; Medicare.
Owner Nonprofit corp.
Admissions Requirements Medical examination.
Staff RNs 1 (ft), 2 (pt); RNs 3 (ft), 3 (pt); LPNs 8 (ft), 2 (pt); Nurses' aides 40 (ft), 19 (pt); Physical therapists 2 (pt); Activities coordinators 2 (ft), 1 (pt); Dietitians 1 (pt); Ophthalmologists 1 (pt); Podiatrists 1 (pt).
Affiliation Roman Catholic.
Facilities Dining room; Physical therapy room; Activities room; Chapel; Crafts room; Laundry room; Barber/Beauty shop; Library.
Activities Arts & crafts; Cards; Games; Reading groups; Prayer groups; Movies; Shopping trips; Dances/Social/Cultural gatherings.

Jewish Convalescent Center—Scotts Level
7920 Scotts Level Rd, Baltimore, MD 21208
(301) 521-3600
Admin Margaret Sybert.
Medical Dir A A Silver MD.
Licensure Skilled care; Intermediate care. *Beds* 151. *Certified* Medicaid; Medicare.
Owner Nonprofit corp.
Affiliation Jewish.

Kenesaw Nursing Home Inc
2601 Roslyn Ave, Baltimore, MD 21216
(301) 466-3900
Admin Doris P Gordon.
Medical Dir Edward Hunt Jr MD.
Licensure Intermediate care. *Beds* ICF 27. *Certified* Medicaid.
Owner Proprietary corp.

Kenson Nursing Home
2914-2922 Arunah Ave, Baltimore, MD 21216
(301) 947-3566
Admin Benjamin Roffman.
Medical Dir S Liau MD.
Licensure Intermediate care. *Beds* 38. *Certified* Medicaid.
Owner Proprietary corp.
Admissions Requirements Minimum age 12.
Staff Physicians 2 (ft); RNs 2 (ft); LPNs 11 (ft); Nurses' aides 10 (ft); Physical therapists 1 (ft); Reality therapists 1 (ft); Recreational

therapists 1 (ft); Occupational therapists 1 (ft); Speech therapists 1 (ft); Activities coordinators 2 (ft); Dietitians 1 (ft); Ophthalmologists 1 (ft); Podiatrists 1 (ft); Audiologists 1 (ft); Dentists 1 (ft).
Facilities Dining room; Activities room; Chapel; Crafts room; Laundry room.
Activities Arts & crafts; Cards; Games; Reading groups; Prayer groups; Movies; Shopping trips; Dances/Social/Cultural gatherings.

Keswick Home for Incurables of Baltimore City
700 W 40th St, Baltimore, MD 21211-2199
(301) 235-8860, 235-7425 FAX
Admin Brooks R Major. *Dir of Nursing* Hilary Klein. *Medical Dir* Isabelle MacGregor MD.
Licensure Skilled care; Domiciliary care; Adult day care; Alzheimer's care. *Beds* SNF 221; Domiciliary care 46; Adult day care 50. *Certified* Medicaid; Medicare.
Owner Nonprofit organization/foundation.
Admissions Requirements Minimum age 18; Medical examination.
Staff Physicians 1 (ft), 19 (pt); RNs 24 (ft); LPNs 22 (ft); Nurses' aides 127 (ft); Physical therapists 1 (ft); Recreational therapists 3 (ft); Occupational therapists 3 (ft), 1 (pt); Speech therapists 2 (pt); Dietitians 1 (ft), 1 (pt); Ophthalmologists 1 (pt); Podiatrists 1 (pt); Audiologists 1 (pt); Dentists 1 (pt).
Facilities Dining room; Physical therapy room; Activities room; Chapel; Crafts room; Laundry room; Barber/Beauty shop; Library.
Activities Arts & crafts; Cards; Games; Reading groups; Prayer groups; Movies; Shopping trips; Dances/Social/Cultural gatherings; Intergenerational programs; Pet therapy; Children's hour.

Key Circle Hospice Inc
1214 Eutaw Pl, Baltimore, MD 21217
(301) 523-7800
Admin Bertram Zimmerman. *Dir of Nursing* Howard G Chaney RNs. *Medical Dir* E Ellsworth Cook MD.
Licensure Intermediate care. *Beds* ICF 121. *Certified* Medicaid.
Owner Proprietary corp.
Admissions Requirements Minimum age 18; Medical examination; Physician's request.
Staff Physicians 1 (pt); RNs 1 (ft), 1 (pt); LPNs 6 (ft), 2 (pt); Nurses' aides 40 (ft), 42 (pt); Activities coordinators 1 (ft), 1 (pt); Dietitians 1 (pt); Social worker 1 (ft).
Languages Russian, Hungarian.
Facilities Dining room; Physical therapy room; Activities room; Laundry room; Barber/Beauty shop.
Activities Arts & crafts; Cards; Games; Prayer groups; Movies; Shopping trips; Dances/Social/Cultural gatherings; Exercise group.

Lake Drive Nursing Home Inc
200 E Lexington St, Baltimore, MD 21202-3522
(301) 669-4444
Admin Wallace Dow.
Medical Dir Arthur Lebson MD.
Licensure Intermediate care. *Beds* 50. *Certified* Medicaid.
Owner Proprietary corp.

Levindale Hebrew Geriatric Center & Hospital Inc
2434 W Belvedere Ave, Baltimore, MD 21215
(301) 466-8700
Admin Stanford A Alliker. *Dir of Nursing* Barbara Keiser RN, Nursing Svcs V Pres. *Medical Dir* Steven A Levenson MD.
Licensure Skilled care; Intermediate care; Chronic hospital; Alzheimer's care. *Beds* SNF 155; ICF 65; Chronic hospital 63. *Certified* Medicaid; Medicare.
Owner Nonprofit organization/foundation.
Admissions Requirements Medical examination.

Staff Physicians 5 (ft); RNs 20 (ft); LPNs 46 (ft); Nurses' aides 101 (ft); Physical therapists 3 (ft); Reality therapists 1 (pt); Occupational therapists 2 (ft), 1 (pt); Dietitians 2 (ft), 1 (pt); Creative arts therapists 3 (ft); Physical therapy aides 1 (ft); Psychologists 1 (pt).
Languages Yiddish, Hebrew.
Affiliation Jewish.
Facilities Dining room; Physical therapy room; Activities room; Chapel; Crafts room; Laundry room; Barber/Beauty shop.
Activities Arts & crafts; Cards; Games; Reading groups; Prayer groups; Movies; Shopping trips; Dances/Social/Cultural gatherings.

Lincoln Convalescent Center Inc
1217 W Fayette St, Baltimore, MD 21223
(301) 727-3947
Admin Mildred L Pipkin.
Medical Dir Ali Baykalar MD.
Licensure Skilled care; Intermediate care. *Beds* 224. *Certified* Medicaid.
Owner Proprietary corp.

Manor Care Rossville
6600 Ridge Rd, Baltimore, MD 21237
(301) 574-4950, 574-0895 FAX
Admin Patricia Megary. *Dir of Nursing* Marley Nicolas. *Medical Dir* Samuel J Westrick MD.
Licensure Skilled care; Intermediate care. *Beds* SNF 41; ICF 163. *Certified* Medicaid; Medicare.
Owner Proprietary corp (Manor Care Inc).
Admissions Requirements Must be younger than 16.
Staff RNs 7 (ft), 4 (pt); LPNs 16 (ft), 18 (pt); Nurses' aides 73 (ft), 13 (pt); Activities coordinators 1 (ft); Physical therapy assistants 1 (ft); Food service managers 1 (ft).
Facilities Dining room; Physical therapy room; Activities room; Laundry room; Barber/Beauty shop.
Activities Arts & crafts; Games; Reading groups; Prayer groups; Movies; Dances/Social/Cultural gatherings; Pet therapy.

Stella Maris
2300 Dulaney Valley Rd, Baltimore, MD 21092
(301) 252-4500
Admin Sr Louis Mary Battle RSM. *Dir of Nursing* Joan Conroy RN. *Medical Dir* Eddie Nakhuda MD.
Licensure Skilled care; Retirement; Alzheimer's care. *Beds* SNF 438; Retirement 200. *Private Pay Patients* 50%. *Certified* Medicaid; Medicare.
Owner Nonprofit organization/foundation.
Admissions Requirements Minimum age 65; Medical examination; Physician's request.
Staff Physicians 2 (pt); RNs 25 (ft), 60 (pt); LPNs 6 (ft), 7 (pt); Nurses' aides 181 (ft), 30 (pt); Physical therapists 1 (ft); Occupational therapists 2 (pt); Speech therapists 1 (pt); Activities coordinators 10 (ft), 6 (pt); Dietitians 4 (ft).
Affiliation Roman Catholic.
Facilities Dining room; Physical therapy room; Activities room; Chapel; Crafts room; Laundry room; Barber/Beauty shop; Library; Auditorium; Happy Hollow room.
Activities Arts & crafts; Cards; Games; Reading groups; Prayer groups; Movies; Shopping trips; Dances/Social/Cultural gatherings; Intergenerational programs; Pet therapy.

Maryland Baptist Aged Home
2801 Rayner Ave, Baltimore, MD 21216
(301) 624-3694
Admin Angeline Byrd; Lillian Moore, Asst. *Dir of Nursing* Christine Stanley. *Medical Dir* Hollis Seunarine MD.

Licensure Intermediate care. *Beds* ICF 33.
Private Pay Patients 1%. *Certified* Medicaid.
Owner Nonprofit organization/foundation.
Admissions Requirements Medical
examination; Physician's request.
Staff Physicians; RNs 1 (ft); LPNs 2 (ft), 2
(pt); Nurses' aides 9 (ft), 3 (pt); Recreational
therapists 1 (pt); Activities coordinators 1
(ft); Dietitians 1 (ft); Ophthalmologists 1
(pt); Podiatrists 1 (pt); Dentists 1 (pt).
Affiliation Baptist.
Facilities Dining room; Activities room;
Laundry room.
Activities Arts & crafts; Cards; Games;
Reading groups; Prayer groups; Movies;
Shopping trips; Pet therapy; Community
trips.

**Maryland Intensive Behavior Management
Program**
630 W Fayette St, Baltimore, MD 21228
(301) 328-2358
Admin Mark Quinn.
Medical Dir Dr Olmpia Aybar.
Licensure Intermediate care for mentally
retarded. *Beds* 12. *Certified* Medicaid.
Owner Publicly owned.
Admissions Requirements Minimum age 18.
Staff Physicians 1 (ft); RNs 3 (ft); LPNs 1 (ft);
Nurses' aides 1 (ft); Reality therapists 1 (pt);
Recreational therapists 1 (ft); Occupational
therapists 1 (ft); Speech therapists 1 (pt);
Activities coordinators 1 (ft); Dietitians 1
(pt); Podiatrists 1 (pt).
Facilities Dining room; Activities room;
Crafts room; Laundry room; Barber/Beauty
shop.
Activities Arts & crafts; Games; Movies;
Shopping trips; Dances/Social/Cultural
gatherings.

Melchor Nursing Home
2327 N Charles St, Baltimore, MD 21218
(301) 235-8997
Admin P Ramona Fearins.
Medical Dir Lawrence Blob MD.
Licensure Intermediate care. *Beds* ICF 50.
Certified Medicaid.
Owner Proprietary corp.
Admissions Requirements Minimum age 18;
Medical examination; Physician's request.
Facilities Dining room; Activities room;
Laundry room.
Activities Arts & crafts; Cards; Games;
Reading groups; Prayer groups; Movies;
Shopping trips; Dances/Social/Cultural
gatherings.

Meridian Long Green
115 E Melrose Ave, Baltimore, MD 21212
(301) 435-9073, 435-6842 FAX
Admin Deborah Skwiercz. *Dir of Nursing*
Elaine Hale-Barlow. *Medical Dir* Norma R
Freeman.
Licensure Skilled care; Intermediate care;
Domiciliary care. *Beds* Swing beds SNF/ICF
146; Domiciliary care 10. *Certified*
Medicaid; Medicare.
Owner Proprietary corp (Meridian
Healthcare).
Staff Physicians; RNs; LPNs; Nurses' aides;
Physical therapists; Reality therapists;
Recreational therapists; Occupational
therapists; Speech therapists; Activities
coordinators; Dietitians; Ophthalmologists;
Podiatrists; Audiologists.
Facilities Dining room; Physical therapy
room; Activities room; Crafts room; Laundry
room; Barber/Beauty shop; Library; Lounge
areas; Large screen TVs.
Activities Arts & crafts; Cards; Games; Prayer
groups; Movies; Shopping trips; Dances/
Social/Cultural gatherings; Pet therapy;
Religious services.

Meridian Nursing Center—Caton Manor
3330 Wilkens Ave, Baltimore, MD 21229
(301) 525-1544

Admin Michael Marin.
Medical Dir Herbert Levickas MD.
Licensure Skilled care; Intermediate care. *Beds*
Comprehensive care 184. *Certified*
Medicaid; Medicare.
Owner Proprietary corp (Meridian
Healthcare).
Admissions Requirements Minimum age 14;
Medical examination.
Facilities Dining room; Activities room;
Laundry room; Barber/Beauty shop.
Activities Arts & crafts; Cards; Games;
Reading groups; Prayer groups; Movies;
Shopping trips; Dances/Social/Cultural
gatherings.

Meridian Nursing Center—Cromwell
8710 Emge Rd, Baltimore, MD 21234
(301) 661-5955
Admin Jeffrey Berenbach.
Medical Dir Marion Kowaleski MD.
Licensure Skilled care; Intermediate care. *Beds*
173. *Certified* Medicaid; Medicare.
Owner Proprietary corp (Meridian
Healthcare).

Meridian Nursing Center—Hamilton
6040 Harford Rd, Baltimore, MD 21214
(301) 426-8855
Admin Karen Pressman.
Medical Dir Ingeborg Fromm MD.
Licensure Skilled care; Intermediate care. *Beds*
104. *Certified* Medicaid; Medicare.
Owner Proprietary corp (Meridian
Healthcare).

Meridian Nursing Center—Heritage
7232 German Hill Rd, Baltimore, MD 21222
(301) 282-6310
Admin Pamela E Fisher. *Dir of Nursing* Rita
Stewart. *Medical Dir* Theodore C Patterson
MD.
Licensure Skilled care; Intermediate care;
Domiciliary care; Alzheimer's care. *Beds*
Comprehensive care 177; Domiciliary care
4. *Certified* Medicaid; Medicare.
Owner Proprietary corp (Meridian
Healthcare).
Admissions Requirements Medical
examination.
Staff Physicians 1 (pt); RNs 8 (ft), 4 (pt) 13C
8 (ft), 13 (pt); Nurses' aides 45 (ft), 40 (pt);
Activities coordinators 4 (ft).
Facilities Dining room; Physical therapy
room; Activities room; Crafts room; Laundry
room; Barber/Beauty shop; TV Lounges.
Activities Arts & crafts; Cards; Games; Prayer
groups; Movies; Shopping trips; Dances/
Social/Cultural gatherings; College courses;
Intergenerational programs.

Meridian Nursing Center—Homewood
6000 Bellona Ave, Baltimore, MD 21212
(301) 323-4223
Admin Joseph R Fuchs. *Dir of Nursing* Mary
Ann Rodavitch RN. *Medical Dir* Anthony
Carozza MD.
Licensure Skilled care. *Beds* SNF 127.
Certified Medicaid; Medicare.
Owner Proprietary corp (Meridian
Healthcare).
Admissions Requirements Medical
examination.
Staff Physicians 1 (pt); RNs 6 (ft), 9 (pt);
LPNs 8 (ft), 4 (pt); Nurses' aides 35 (ft), 23
(pt); Physical therapists 2 (pt); Occupational
therapists 1 (pt); Speech therapists 1 (pt);
Activities coordinators 2 (ft); Dietitians 1
(pt).
Facilities Dining room; Physical therapy
room; Activities room; Crafts room; Laundry
room; Barber/Beauty shop.
Activities Arts & crafts; Cards; Games;
Reading groups; Prayer groups; Movies;
Shopping trips; Dances/Social/Cultural
gatherings.

Meridian Nursing Center—Loch Raven
8720 Emge Rd, Baltimore, MD 21234
(301) 668-1961, 882-5082 FAX
Admin Brian H Klausmeyer. *Dir of Nursing*
Doris J Hokemeyer. *Medical Dir* Dr Voung
Vu Nguyen.
Licensure Skilled care; Intermediate care. *Beds*
Swing beds SNF/ICF 130. *Private Pay
Patients* 27%. *Certified* Medicaid; Medicare;
VA.
Owner Proprietary corp (Meridian
Healthcare).
Admissions Requirements Medical
examination.
Staff Physicians 1 (pt); RNs 3 (ft), 6 (pt);
LPNs 10 (ft), 6 (pt); Nurses' aides 30 (ft), 22
(pt); Physical therapists (consultant);
Occupational therapists (consultant); Speech
therapists (consultant); Activities
coordinators 2 (ft); Dietitians 1 (pt);
Ophthalmologists (consultant); Podiatrists
(consultant).
Facilities Dining room; Physical therapy
room; Activities room; Crafts room; Laundry
room; Barber/Beauty shop; Dining lounge;
Courtyard; Two visitor's lounges.
Activities Arts & crafts; Cards; Games;
Reading groups; Prayer groups; Movies;
Shopping trips; Dances/Social/Cultural
gatherings; Intergenerational programs; Pet
therapy; Adopt-a-grandparent program.

Meridian Nursing Center—Perring Parkway
1801 Wentworth Rd, Baltimore, MD 21234
(301) 661-5717
Admin Lucy Monninger.
Medical Dir Anthony Carozza MD.
Licensure Skilled care; Intermediate care. *Beds*
130. *Certified* Medicaid; Medicare.
Owner Proprietary corp (Meridian
Healthcare).

Milford Manor Nursing Home
4204 Old Milford Mill Rd, Baltimore, MD
21208
(301) 486-1500
Admin Earl Raffel. *Dir of Nursing* Beth
Yarnold RN. *Medical Dir* Barry Gold MD.
Licensure Skilled care. *Beds* SNF 99. *Certified*
Medicaid; Medicare.
Owner Proprietary corp.
Admissions Requirements Medical
examination.
Staff RNs 3 (ft), 1 (pt); LPNs 7 (ft), 1 (pt);
Nurses' aides 42 (ft); Physical therapists;
Recreational therapists; Speech therapists;
Activities coordinators; Dietitians;
Podiatrists; Dentists.
Languages Yiddish, Hebrew, Russian,
German.
Affiliation Jewish.
Facilities Dining room; Physical therapy
room; Activities room; Chapel; Crafts room;
Laundry room; Barber/Beauty shop; TV
lounges.
Activities Arts & crafts; Cards; Games;
Reading groups; Prayer groups; Movies;
Shopping trips; Dances/Social/Cultural
gatherings.

Mt Vernon Care Center
808 Saint Paul St, Baltimore, MD 21202
(301) 685-6766
Admin Harvey S Perle. *Dir of Nursing*
Theresa Peet. *Medical Dir* Alex Enrique
MD.
Licensure Intermediate care. *Beds* ICF 137.
Certified Medicaid; VA.
Owner Proprietary corp.
Admissions Requirements Minimum age 21;
Medical examination.
Staff Physicians 5 (pt); RNs 4 (ft); LPNs 11
(ft); Nurses' aides 64 (ft); Physical therapists
1 (pt); Reality therapists 1 (pt); Speech
therapists 1 (pt); Activities coordinators 1
(ft), 2 (pt); Dietitians 1 (ft);
Ophthalmologists 1 (pt); Podiatrists 1 (pt);
Dentists 1 (pt).

Facilities Dining room; Physical therapy room; Activities room; Library.
Activities Arts & crafts; Cards; Games; Reading groups; Prayer groups; Movies; Dances/Social/Cultural gatherings.

Northwest Nursing & Convalescent Center
4601 Pall Mall Rd, Baltimore, MD 21215
(301) 664-5551
Admin Z W Hunter. *Dir of Nursing* June Heseldach RN. *Medical Dir* Arthur Lebson MD.
Licensure Intermediate care. *Beds* ICF 91. *Certified* Medicaid.
Owner Proprietary corp.
Admissions Requirements Minimum age 21; Medical examination.
Staff RNs 6 (ft); LPNs 10 (ft), 4 (pt); Nurses' aides 60 (ft), 15 (pt); Activities coordinators 1 (ft).
Facilities Dining room; Physical therapy room; Activities room; Crafts room.
Activities Arts & crafts; Cards; Games; Reading groups; Prayer groups; Movies; Shopping trips; Dances/Social/Cultural gatherings.

Park Manor Nursing Home
1802 Eutaw Pl, Baltimore, MD 21217
(301) 523-4370
Admin Henry Goldbaum.
Medical Dir Richard Tyson MD.
Licensure Intermediate care. *Beds* ICF 50. *Certified* Medicaid.
Owner Proprietary corp.

Pleasant Manor Nursing & Convalescent Center
4615 Park Heights Ave, Baltimore, MD 21215
(301) 542-4800
Admin Henry Reitberger acting.
Medical Dir Jamie Punzalan MD.
Licensure Skilled care; Intermediate care. *Beds* 137. *Certified* Medicaid; Medicare.
Owner Proprietary corp.

Poplar Manor Nursing Home
3313 Poplar St, Baltimore, MD 21216
(301) 566-1300
Admin Sheila Jones. *Dir of Nursing* Shirly Wright. *Medical Dir* Hollis Seunarine MD.
Licensure Skilled care; Intermediate care. *Beds* Comprehensive care 157. *Certified* Medicaid; Medicare.
Owner Proprietary corp.
Admissions Requirements Physician's request.
Staff Physicians 1 (ft), 1 (pt); RNs 6 (ft), 1 (pt); LPNs 8 (ft), 3 (pt); Nurses' aides 36 (ft), 6 (pt); Physical therapists; Speech therapists 1 (pt); Activities coordinators 1 (ft); Dietitians 1 (pt); Ophthalmologists 1 (pt).
Facilities Dining room; Physical therapy room; Activities room; Laundry room; Barber/Beauty shop; Outside community activities; Wheelchair van; Physical therapy room.
Activities Arts & crafts; Cards; Games; Reading groups; Prayer groups; Movies; Shopping trips; Dances/Social/Cultural gatherings.

Riverview Nursing Centre
1 Eastern Ave, Baltimore, MD 21221
(301) 574-1400
Admin Wayne K DeFontes.
Medical Dir B W Sollod MD.
Licensure Intermediate care. *Beds* ICF 308. *Certified* Medicaid.
Owner Proprietary corp.
Admissions Requirements Minimum age 14; Medical examination.
Staff Physicians 2 (pt); RNs 8 (ft), 2 (pt); LPNs 20 (ft), 10 (pt); Nurses' aides 150 (ft), 30 (pt); Physical therapists 2 (ft); Recreational therapists 3 (ft), 2 (pt); Speech therapists 1 (pt); Activities coordinators 1

(ft), 2 (pt); Dietitians 1 (pt); Ophthalmologists 1 (pt); Podiatrists 1 (pt); Audiologists 1 (pt); Dentists 1 (pt).
Facilities Dining room; Physical therapy room; Activities room; Chapel; Crafts room; Laundry room; Barber/Beauty shop; Library.
Activities Arts & crafts; Cards; Games; Reading groups; Prayer groups; Movies; Shopping trips; Dances/Social/Cultural gatherings.

Roland Park Place Inc
830 W 40th St, Baltimore, MD 21211
(301) 243-5800
Admin Frank Bailey. *Dir of Nursing* Donna Srichley RN. *Medical Dir* K A Peter Van Berkum MD.
Licensure Intermediate care; Domiciliary care. *Beds* ICF 48; Domiciliary care 10. *Certified* Medicare.
Owner Nonprofit corp.
Admissions Requirements Medical examination.
Staff Physicians 2 (pt); RNs 6 (ft); Physical therapists 1 (ft); Recreational therapists 1 (ft); Activities coordinators 1 (ft); Dietitians 1 (pt); Podiatrists 1 (pt); Audiologists 1 (pt).
Affiliation Lutheran.
Facilities Dining room; Physical therapy room; Activities room; Crafts room; Laundry room; Barber/Beauty shop; Library; Den; Board room.
Activities Arts & crafts; Cards; Games; Reading groups; Prayer groups; Movies; Dances/Social/Cultural gatherings.

St Luke Lutheran Home
7600 Clays Ln, Baltimore, MD 21207
(301) 298-1400
Admin Stanley D Selenski.
Medical Dir Darold Beard MD.
Licensure Domiciliary care; Comprehensive care. *Beds* Domiciliary care 54; Comprehensive care 67. *Certified* Medicaid.
Owner Nonprofit corp.
Admissions Requirements Medical examination.
Staff Physicians 1 (ft), 5 (pt); RNs 2 (ft), 3 (pt); LPNs 4 (ft), 2 (pt); Nurses' aides 17 (ft), 17 (pt); Physical therapists 2 (pt); Activities coordinators 1 (ft), 1 (pt); Dietitians 1 (ft); Ophthalmologists 1 (pt).
Affiliation Lutheran.
Facilities Dining room; Physical therapy room; Activities room; Chapel; Crafts room; Laundry room; Barber/Beauty shop; Library.
Activities Arts & crafts; Cards; Games; Reading groups; Prayer groups; Movies; Shopping trips; Dances/Social/Cultural gatherings; Bible study.

Seton Hill Manor
501 W Franklin St, Baltimore, MD 21201
(301) 837-4990, 783-0149 FAX
Admin Barbara P Potts MSW. *Dir of Nursing* Jessie Rodgers. *Medical Dir* Philip Konits MD.
Licensure Skilled care; Intermediate care; AIDS unit. *Beds* SNF 142; ICF 218; AIDS unit 26. *Private Pay Patients* 3%. *Certified* Medicaid; Medicare.
Owner Proprietary corp.
Admissions Requirements Medical examination; Physician's request.
Staff Physicians 15 (pt); RNs 12 (ft); LPNs 17 (ft); Nurses' aides 129 (ft); Physical therapists 1 (ft); Recreational therapists 7 (ft); Speech therapists 1 (pt); Activities coordinators 1 (ft); Dietitians 1 (ft), 2 (pt); Ophthalmologists 1 (ft); Podiatrists 2 (ft); Audiologists 1 (ft).
Facilities Dining room; Physical therapy room; Activities room; Chapel; Crafts room; Laundry room; Barber/Beauty shop; Library.
Activities Arts & crafts; Cards; Games; Reading groups; Prayer groups; Movies; Shopping trips; Dances/Social/Cultural gatherings; Bus trips; Sporting events.

Union Memorial Extended Care
201 E University Parkway, Baltimore, MD 21218
Admin Barbara Gustke.
Licensure Extended care. *Beds* Extended care 31.

Uplands Home for Church Women
4501 Old Frederick Rd, Baltimore, MD 21229
(301) 945-1900
Admin Richard Buck.
Medical Dir Dr Alva Baker.
Licensure Domiciliary care. *Beds* 48.
Owner Nonprofit corp.
Admissions Requirements Minimum age 65; Females only; Medical examination; Physician's request.
Staff Physicians 1 (pt); RNs 1 (ft); LPNs 2 (ft), 2 (pt); Nurses' aides 6 (ft), 5 (pt); Activities coordinators 1 (pt); Dietitians 1 (pt).
Affiliation Episcopal.
Facilities Dining room; Activities room; Chapel; Crafts room; Laundry room; Barber/Beauty shop; Library.
Activities Arts & crafts; Cards; Games; Movies; Shopping trips; Dances/Social/Cultural gatherings.

Villa St Michael Nursing & Retirement Center
4800 Seton Dr, Baltimore, MD 21215
(301) 358-3903, 358-0432 FAX
Admin Basil F (Bud) Boyce FACHCA. *Dir of Nursing* Helen R Nelson RNC. *Medical Dir* Harold Bob MD.
Licensure Skilled care; Intermediate care. *Beds* SNF 14; ICF 165. *Certified* Medicaid; Medicare.
Owner Proprietary corp.
Admissions Requirements Minimum age 18; Medical examination; Physician's request.
Staff Physicians 12 (pt); RNs 9 (pt); LPNs 15 (pt); Nurses' aides 65 (pt); Physical therapists 1 (ft); Recreational therapists 1 (ft); Occupational therapists 1 (pt); Speech therapists 1 (pt); Activities coordinators 1 (ft); Dietitians 1 (ft), 1 (pt); Ophthalmologists 1 (pt); Podiatrists 1 (pt); Audiologists 1 (pt).
Facilities Dining room; Physical therapy room; Activities room; Chapel; Crafts room; Laundry room; Barber/Beauty shop; Library.
Activities Arts & crafts; Cards; Games; Reading groups; Prayer groups; Movies; Shopping trips; Dances/Social/Cultural gatherings; Intergenerational programs; Pet therapy.

Bel Air

Bel Air Convalescent Center Inc
410 MacPhail Rd, Bel Air, MD 21014
(301) 879-1120
Admin Phyllis M Kelley.
Medical Dir Andrew Nowakowski MD.
Licensure Skilled care; Intermediate care. *Beds* Comprehensive care 155. *Certified* Medicaid; Medicare.
Owner Proprietary corp.
Staff Physicians 14 (pt); RNs 11 (pt); Nurses' aides 80 (ft); Physical therapists 3 (pt); Recreational therapists 2 (pt); Speech therapists 1 (pt); Activities coordinators 1 (pt); Dietitians 1 (pt); Podiatrists 1 (pt); Dentists 1 (pt).
Facilities Dining room; Physical therapy room; Laundry room; Barber/Beauty shop; Lounges.
Activities Arts & crafts; Cards; Games; Reading groups; Prayer groups; Movies; Shopping trips; Dances/Social/Cultural gatherings.

Berlin

Berlin Nursing Home
PO Box 799, US 50 at Rte 113, Berlin, MD 21811
(301) 641-4400, 641-0011 FAX
Admin Gary N Crowley. *Dir of Nursing* Jeannine Hooper RN. *Medical Dir* Federico G Arthes MD.
Licensure Skilled care; Intermediate care; Intermediate care for mentally retarded; Domiciliary care. *Beds* Comprehensive care 184; Domiciliary care 18. *Private Pay Patients* 33%. *Certified* Medicaid; Medicare.
Owner Privately owned.
Admissions Requirements Medical examination; Physician's request.
Staff Physicians 1 (pt); RNs 8 (ft), 2 (pt); LPNs 6 (ft), 2 (pt); Nurses' aides 80 (ft), 20 (pt); Physical therapists; Activities coordinators 1 (ft); Dietitians 1 (pt).
Facilities Dining room; Physical therapy room; Activities room; Laundry room; Barber/Beauty shop; Library.
Activities Arts & crafts; Cards; Games; Reading groups; Prayer groups; Movies; Dances/Social/Cultural gatherings; Intergenerational programs; Pet therapy.

Bethesda

Carriage Hill—Bethesda Inc
5215 Cedar Lane Ave, Bethesda, MD 20814
(301) 897-5500
Admin Ruth Reynolds. *Dir of Nursing* Claire Malden RN. *Medical Dir* John Umhau MD.
Licensure Skilled care. *Beds* SNF 81.
Owner Proprietary corp.
Admissions Requirements Minimum age 18; Medical examination.
Staff Physicians 35 (pt); RNs 14 (pt); LPNs 3 (pt); Nurses' aides 36 (pt); Physical therapists 3 (pt); Speech therapists 1 (pt); Activities coordinators 3 (pt); Dietitians 1 (pt); Ophthalmologists 6 (pt); Podiatrists 1 (pt); Dentists 4 (pt).
Languages Spanish, French, German.
Facilities Dining room; Physical therapy room; Activities room; Chapel; Crafts room; Laundry room; Barber/Beauty shop; Library.
Activities Arts & crafts; Cards; Games; Reading groups; Prayer groups; Movies; Dances/Social/Cultural gatherings.

Fernwood House Retirement & Nursing Center
6530 Democracy Blvd, Bethesda, MD 20817
(301) 530-9000
Admin Sandra L Wood.
Medical Dir J Blaine Fitzgerald MD.
Licensure Skilled care; Intermediate care. *Beds* 100. *Certified* Medicaid; Medicare.
Owner Proprietary corp.

Grosvenor Health Care Center
5721 Grosvenor Ln, Bethesda, MD 20814
(301) 530-1600, 493-5329 FAX
Admin Donna R Rinehart. *Dir of Nursing* Marilyn Kohler. *Medical Dir* Dr John Tauber.
Licensure Skilled care; Intermediate care. *Beds* SNF 72; ICF 108. *Certified* Medicaid; Medicare.
Owner Proprietary corp.
Staff Physicians 1 (pt); RNs 8 (ft); LPNs 8 (ft), 4 (pt); Nurses' aides 46 (ft); Physical therapists 1 (pt); Activities coordinators 2 (ft), 1 (pt); Dietitians 1 (pt).
Facilities Dining room; Physical therapy room; Activities room; Crafts room; Laundry room; Barber/Beauty shop.
Activities Arts & crafts; Cards; Games; Movies; Shopping trips.

Boonsboro

Reeders Memorial Home
141 S Main St, Boonsboro, MD 21713
(301) 432-5457
Admin Marilyn Young.
Medical Dir R Lawrence Kugler MD.
Licensure Skilled care; Intermediate care. *Beds* Comprehensive care 200. *Certified* Medicaid.
Owner Nonprofit corp.

Braddock Heights

Vindobona Nursing Home Inc
6012 Jefferson Blvd, Braddock Heights, MD 21714
(301) 371-7160
Admin Nayoda E Kefauver. *Dir of Nursing* Brenda Esterly. *Medical Dir* Dr Wayne Allgaier.
Licensure Skilled care. *Beds* SNF 64. *Certified* Medicaid; Medicare.
Owner Proprietary corp.
Admissions Requirements Minimum age 18; Medical examination.
Staff Physicians; RNs 5 (ft), 2 (pt); LPNs 7 (ft), 3 (pt); Nurses' aides 20 (ft), 21 (pt); Physical therapists (consultant); Recreational therapists 1 (ft); Occupational therapists (consultant); Speech therapists (consultant); Activities coordinators 1 (ft); Dietitians 1 (pt); Ophthalmologists (consultant); Podiatrists (monthly).
Facilities Dining room; Physical therapy room; Activities room; Crafts room; Laundry room; Barber/Beauty shop.
Activities Arts & crafts; Cards; Games; Reading groups; Prayer groups; Movies; Shopping trips; Pet therapy; Volunteer groups; Group band; Lunch outings; Bingo.

Brooklyn Park

Meridian Nursing Center—Hammonds
Hammonds Ln & Robinswood Rd, Brooklyn Park, MD 21225
(301) 636-3400
Admin Deborah Skwiercz. *Dir of Nursing* Margaret Schmitt RN. *Medical Dir* E H Weiss MD.
Licensure Skilled care; Intermediate care. *Beds* SNF 50; ICF 79. *Certified* Medicaid; Medicare.
Owner Proprietary corp (Meridian Healthcare).
Admissions Requirements Medical examination.
Staff Physicians 1 (pt); RNs 6 (ft), 4 (pt); LPNs 5 (ft), 5 (pt); Nurses' aides 45 (ft), 20 (pt); Physical therapists 1 (ft); Occupational therapists 1 (pt); Speech therapists 1 (pt); Activities coordinators 1 (ft), 1 (pt); Dietitians 1 (ft); Ophthalmologists 1 (ft); Podiatrists 1 (ft); Dentists 1 (ft).
Facilities Dining room; Physical therapy room; Activities room; Barber/Beauty shop.
Activities Arts & crafts; Cards; Games; Reading groups; Prayer groups; Movies; Shopping trips; Dances/Social/Cultural gatherings; Bingo.

Cambridge

Glasgow Nursing Home
311 Glenburn Ave, Cambridge, MD 21613
(301) 228-3780
Admin Esther Russell. *Dir of Nursing* Barbara Rolf RN. *Medical Dir* Michael Moskewicz MD.
Licensure Intermediate care. *Beds* ICF 35. *Certified* Medicaid.
Owner Proprietary corp.
Admissions Requirements Physician's request.

Staff Physicians 2 (pt); RNs 1 (ft), 2 (pt); LPNs 3 (ft), 3 (pt); Nurses' aides 9 (ft), 5 (pt); Dietitians 1 (pt).
Facilities Dining room; Laundry room; Barber/Beauty shop.
Activities Arts & crafts; Games; Reading groups; Prayer groups; Movies.

Mallard Bay
PO Box 919, Cambridge, MD 21613
(301) 228-9191
Admin Faye Lucas. *Dir of Nursing* Vickie Cox. *Medical Dir* E Ayliffe.
Licensure Skilled care; Intermediate care. *Beds* SNF 60; ICF 120. *Certified* Medicaid; Medicare.
Owner Proprietary corp (Genesis Health Ventures).
Admissions Requirements Minimum age 18; Medical examination.
Staff RNs 18 (ft), 4 (pt); Nurses' aides 50 (ft), 35 (pt); Physical therapists (consultant); Activities coordinators 2 (ft); Dietitians (consultant).
Facilities Dining room; Physical therapy room; Activities room; Crafts room; Laundry room; Barber/Beauty shop.
Activities Arts & crafts; Cards; Games; Reading groups; Prayer groups; Movies; Shopping trips; Dances/Social/Cultural gatherings; Intergenerational programs; Pet therapy.

Catonsville

Charlestown Retirement Community
711 Maiden Choice Ln, Catonsville, MD 21228
(301) 247-3400, 247-7881 FAX
Admin Robert R Rigel. *Dir of Nursing* Joyce Carberry RN. *Medical Dir* Dr Gary Applebaum.
Licensure Skilled care; Intermediate care; Retirement. *Beds* Swing beds SNF/ICF 61; Retirement 1000. *Private Pay Patients* 98%. *Certified* Medicaid.
Owner Nonprofit corp.
Admissions Requirements Minimum age 62; Physician's request.
Staff Physicians 1 (ft), 1 (pt); Physical therapists; Dietitians.
Facilities Dining room; Physical therapy room; Activities room; Crafts room; Laundry room; Barber/Beauty shop.
Activities Arts & crafts; Cards; Games; Reading groups; Prayer groups; Movies; Shopping trips; Pet therapy.

Forest Haven Nursing Home
315 Ingleside Ave, Catonsville, MD 21228
(301) 747-7425
Admin Faye L Maguire. *Dir of Nursing* Mary Schell RN. *Medical Dir* Harold Bob MD.
Licensure Skilled care. *Beds* SNF 172. *Certified* Medicaid; Medicare.
Owner Proprietary corp.
Admissions Requirements Medical examination.
Staff RNs 5 (ft), 1 (pt); LPNs 16 (ft), 2 (pt); Nurses' aides 66 (ft); Physical therapists 1 (pt); Speech therapists; Activities coordinators 3 (ft); Dietitians 1 (pt); Ophthalmologists 1 (pt); Podiatrists 1 (pt); Dentists 1 (pt).
Facilities Dining room; Physical therapy room; Activities room; Chapel; Crafts room; Barber/Beauty shop.
Activities Arts & crafts; Cards; Games; Reading groups; Prayer groups; Movies; Shopping trips; Dances/Social/Cultural gatherings.

Meridian Nursing Center—Catonsville
16 Fusting Ave, Catonsville, MD 21228
(301) 747-1800
Admin Irv Winebrenner.
Medical Dir Herbert J Levickas.

Licensure Skilled care; Intermediate care. *Beds* Comprehensive care 160. *Certified* Medicaid; Medicare.
Owner Proprietary corp (Meridian Healthcare).
Staff Physicians 1 (pt); RNs 5 (ft), 5 (pt); LPNs 8 (ft), 4 (pt); Nurses' aides 58 (ft), 20 (pt); Speech therapists; Activities coordinators 2 (ft); Dietitians 1 (pt); Ophthalmologists; Podiatrists; Dentists.
Facilities Dining room; Physical therapy room; Activities room; Crafts room; Laundry room; Barber/Beauty shop.
Activities Arts & crafts; Cards; Games; Prayer groups; Movies; Shopping trips; Dances/ Social/Cultural gatherings.

Ridgeway Manor Inc
5734 Edmondson Ave, Catonsville, MD 21228
(301) 747-5250
Admin John E Burleigh Jr.
Medical Dir William Goodman MD.
Licensure Intermediate care. *Beds* ICF 45. *Certified* Medicaid.
Owner Proprietary corp.
Staff Physicians 2 (pt); RNs 1 (ft), 3 (pt); LPNs 1 (ft), 8 (pt); Nurses' aides 7 (ft), 15 (pt); Physical therapists 1 (pt); Reality therapists 1 (pt); Recreational therapists 3 (pt); Occupational therapists 1 (pt); Speech therapists 1 (pt); Activities coordinators 1 (pt); Dietitians 1 (pt); Ophthalmologists 1 (pt); Podiatrists 1 (pt); Audiologists 1 (pt); Dentists 1 (pt).
Facilities Dining room; Physical therapy room; Activities room; Crafts room; Laundry room; Barber/Beauty shop; Library.
Activities Arts & crafts; Cards; Games; Reading groups; Prayer groups; Movies; Shopping trips.

St Joseph's Nursing Home
1222 Tugwell Dr, Catonsville, MD 21228
(301) 747-0026
Admin Sr Carolyn Carne. *Dir of Nursing* Sr Krystyna Mroczek RN. *Medical Dir* J Nelson McKay MD.
Licensure Intermediate care. *Beds* ICF 40. *Certified* Medicaid.
Owner Nonprofit corp.
Admissions Requirements Medical examination.
Staff Physicians 1 (ft), 3 (pt); RNs 3 (ft), 2 (pt); LPNs 1 (ft), 2 (pt); Nurses' aides 10 (ft), 25 (pt); Physical therapists 1 (pt); Recreational therapists 1 (ft); Activities coordinators 1 (ft); Dietitians 1 (ft); Dentists 1 (pt); Psychologist 1 (pt).
Languages Polish.
Affiliation Roman Catholic.
Facilities Dining room; Activities room; Chapel; Crafts room; Laundry room; Barber/ Beauty shop; Library; Enclosed outdoor porch; 3 Acre grounds.
Activities Arts & crafts; Cards; Games; Reading groups; Prayer groups; Movies; Dances/Social/Cultural gatherings; Picnics; Musical events; Daily mass & rosary.

Summit Nursing Home Inc
98 Smithwood Ave, Catonsville, MD 21228
(301) 747-3287
Admin Lawrence J Repetti.
Medical Dir James E Rowe MD.
Licensure Skilled care. *Beds* SNF 141. *Certified* Medicare.
Owner Proprietary corp.
Staff RNs 7 (ft), 20 (pt); LPNs 2 (ft), 9 (pt); Nurses' aides 103 (ft), 24 (pt); Physical therapists 1 (pt); Recreational therapists 1 (ft); Speech therapists 1 (pt); Activities coordinators 1 (ft); Dietitians 1 (pt); Podiatrists 1 (pt); Dentists 1 (pt).
Facilities Dining room; Physical therapy room; Activities room; Chapel; Crafts room; Laundry room; Barber/Beauty shop.

Activities Arts & crafts; Games; Reading groups; Prayer groups; Movies; Dances/ Social/Cultural gatherings.

Tawes/Bland Bryant Nursing Center
Wade Ave, Spring Grove Hospital, Catonsville, MD 21228
(301) 455-7603
Admin Haywood R Ammons.
Medical Dir Carl Fischer MD.
Licensure Comprehensive care. *Beds* Comprehensive care 240. *Certified* Medicaid; Medicare.
Owner Publicly owned.

Centreville

Meridian Nursing Center—Corsica Hills
PO Box 50, Rte 213 Box 50, Centreville, MD 21617
(301) 758-2323
Admin Margaret Miller.
Medical Dir John Smith Jr MD.
Licensure Skilled care; Intermediate care. *Beds* Comprehensive care 180. *Certified* Medicaid; Medicare.
Owner Proprietary corp (Meridian Healthcare).

Charlotte Hall

Charlotte Hall Veterans Home
Rte 2 Box 5, Charlotte Hall, MD 20622
(301) 884-8171, 884-8036 FAX
Admin Stewart R Seitz. *Dir of Nursing* Sharry Busser. *Medical Dir* John Weigel MD.
Licensure Skilled care; Intermediate care; Domiciliary care. *Beds* Swing beds SNF/ICF 140; Domiciliary care 112. *Private Pay Patients* 35%. *Certified* Medicaid; Medicare.
Owner Publicly owned.
Admissions Requirements Minimum age 18; Medical examination; Physician's request; Must be Maryland resident and an honorably discharged veteran.
Staff Physicians 4 (pt); RNs 13 (ft); LPNs 15 (ft); Nurses' aides 53 (ft); Physical therapists 3 (pt); Reality therapists 1 (ft); Recreational therapists 1 (ft); Occupational therapists 1 (pt); Speech therapists 1 (pt); Activities coordinators 1 (ft); Dietitians 1 (ft); Ophthalmologists 1 (pt); Podiatrists 1 (pt); Audiologists 1 (pt).
Facilities Dining room; Physical therapy room; Activities room; Chapel; Laundry room; Barber/Beauty shop; Library; Ping Pong tables, pool table, large screen TV & card tables in recreation room; Dental care suite.
Activities Arts & crafts; Cards; Games; Reading groups; Prayer groups; Movies; Shopping trips; Dances/Social/Cultural gatherings; Intergenerational programs; Pet therapy; Outings; Baseball games; Community events.

Chestertown

Magnolia Hall Inc
Morgnec Rd, Chestertown, MD 21620
(301) 778-4550
Admin Pauline E Lindauer RN. *Dir of Nursing* Carol A Miller RN. *Medical Dir* Harry P Ross MD.
Licensure Intermediate care. *Beds* ICF 74. *Private Pay Patients* 65%. *Certified* Medicaid.
Owner Publicly owned.
Admissions Requirements Minimum age 16; Medical examination; Physician's request.
Staff RNs 3 (ft), 2 (pt); LPNs 6 (ft); Nurses' aides 40 (ft), 20 (pt); Recreational therapists 1 (ft); Activities coordinators 1 (ft).
Facilities Dining room; Physical therapy room; Activities room; Chapel; Crafts room; Laundry room; Barber/Beauty shop.

Activities Arts & crafts; Cards; Games; Reading groups; Prayer groups; Movies; Shopping trips; Dances/Social/Cultural gatherings; Intergenerational programs; Pet therapy.

Cheverly

Gladys Spellman Nursing Center
2900 Mercy Ln, Cheverly, MD 20785
(301) 341-3350
Admin Roger D Larson.
Medical Dir Don Yablondwitz MD.
Licensure Skilled care; Intermediate care. *Beds* SNF 20; ICF 80. *Certified* Medicaid; Medicare.
Owner Proprietary corp.
Admissions Requirements Minimum age 16.
Staff RNs 14 (ft); LPNs 11 (ft); Nurses' aides 24 (ft); Reality therapists 1 (ft); Recreational therapists 2 (ft); Dietitians 5 (pt).
Facilities Dining room; Physical therapy room; Activities room; Crafts room; Barber/ Beauty shop.
Activities Arts & crafts; Games; Reading groups; Prayer groups; Movies; Dances/ Social/Cultural gatherings.

Chevy Chase

Bethesda Retirement Nursing Center
8700 Jones Mill Rd, Chevy Chase, MD 20815
(301) 657-8686
Admin Jeanetta M Manuel.
Medical Dir J Blaine Fitzgerald MD.
Licensure Comprehensive care. *Beds* Comprehensive care 166. *Certified* Medicare.
Owner Proprietary corp.
Admissions Requirements Minimum age 16; Medical examination.
Staff RNs 19 (ft); LPNs 3 (ft); Nurses' aides 55 (ft); Physical therapists 1 (pt); Recreational therapists 3 (ft); Occupational therapists 1 (pt); Speech therapists 1 (pt); Activities coordinators 1 (ft); Dietitians 1 (pt); Podiatrists 1 (pt); Audiologists 1 (pt); Dentists 1 (pt).
Facilities Dining room; Physical therapy room; Activities room; Chapel; Crafts room; Barber/Beauty shop; Library; Lounges; Lobbies; Patios.
Activities Arts & crafts; Cards; Games; Reading groups; Prayer groups; Movies; Shopping trips; Dances/Social/Cultural gatherings.

Clinton

Bradford Oaks Nursing & Retirement Centre
7520 Surratts Rd, Clinton, MD 20735
(301) 856-1660
Admin Roger J Tartaglia Sr. *Dir of Nursing* Pat Semple. *Medical Dir* Frank Ryan.
Licensure Skilled care. *Beds* SNF 120. *Certified* Medicaid; Medicare.
Owner Proprietary corp (Savoy Health Care Corp).
Staff RNs 5 (ft); LPNs 13 (ft); Nurses' aides 28 (ft); Physical therapists 1 (ft); Recreational therapists 2 (ft); Occupational therapists 1 (ft); Speech therapists 1 (ft); Activities coordinators 1 (ft); Dietitians 1 (ft); Ophthalmologists 1 (ft); Podiatrists 1 (ft); Audiologists 1 (ft).
Facilities Dining room; Physical therapy room; Activities room; Laundry room; Barber/Beauty shop; Library.
Activities Arts & crafts; Cards; Reading groups; Movies; Pet therapy.

Clinton Convalescent Center
9211 Stuart Ln, Clinton, MD 20735
(301) 868-3600
Admin Roger Tartaglia.
Medical Dir Frank Ryan MD.

Licensure Skilled care; Intermediate care. *Beds* 275. *Certified* Medicaid; Medicare.
Owner Proprietary corp (Beverly Enterprises).
Staff RNs 15 (pt); LPNs 24 (pt); Nurses' aides 150 (pt); Physical therapists 2 (pt); Speech therapists 1 (ft); Activities coordinators 4 (ft), 1 (pt); Dietitians 1 (ft).
Facilities Dining room; Physical therapy room; Activities room; Chapel; Crafts room; Laundry room; Barber/Beauty shop.
Activities Arts & crafts; Cards; Games; Reading groups; Prayer groups; Movies; Dances/Social/Cultural gatherings.

Pineview Manor Extended Care Centre
9106 Pineview Ln, Clinton, MD 20735
(301) 856-2930, 856-0577 FAX
Admin Owen M Schwartz. *Dir of Nursing* Edna L Douglas. *Medical Dir* Elie A Sayan MD.
Licensure Skilled care; Intermediate care; Alzheimer's care. *Beds* SNF 128; ICF 62. *Private Pay Patients* 20%. *Certified* Medicaid; Medicare.
Owner Proprietary corp.
Facilities Dining room; Physical therapy room; Activities room; Chapel; Crafts room; Laundry room; Barber/Beauty shop.
Activities Arts & crafts; Cards; Games; Reading groups; Prayer groups; Movies; Shopping trips; Dances/Social/Cultural gatherings; Intergenerational programs; Pet therapy.

Cockeysville

Broadmead
13801 York Rd, Cockeysville, MD 21030
(301) 527-1900
Admin Thomas Mondloch. *Dir of Nursing* Debra Titus. *Medical Dir* Charles Ellicott MD.
Licensure Comprehensive care; Domiciliary care. *Beds* Comprehensive care 72; Domiciliary care 35. *Certified* Medicare.
Owner Nonprofit corp.
Admissions Requirements Minimum age 65; Medical examination.
Staff Physicians 3 (pt); RNs 8 (ft), 11 (pt); LPNs 5 (ft), 1 (pt); Nurses' aides 20 (ft), 15 (pt); Physical therapists 1 (pt); Recreational therapists 1 (pt); Occupational therapists 1 (pt); Speech therapists 1 (pt); Activities coordinators 1 (pt); Dietitians 1 (pt); Ophthalmologists 1 (pt); Dentists 1 (pt).
Affiliation Society of Friends.
Facilities Dining room; Physical therapy room; Activities room; Crafts room; Laundry room; Barber/Beauty shop; Library.
Activities Arts & crafts; Cards; Games; Reading groups; Prayer groups; Movies; Shopping trips; Dances/Social/Cultural gatherings.

Maryland Masonic Homes
300 International Cir, Cockeysville, MD 21030
(301) 527-1111
Admin George A Dailey NHA. *Dir of Nursing* Marie Slaysman RN. *Medical Dir* Paul Rivas MD.
Licensure Domiciliary care; Comprehensive care. *Beds* Domiciliary care 100; Comprehensive care 120.
Owner Nonprofit organization/foundation.
Admissions Requirements Minimum age 60; Medical examination.
Staff Physicians 1 (pt); RNs 1 (ft), 2 (pt); LPNs 5 (ft), 3 (pt); Nurses' aides 30 (ft), 2 (pt); Physical therapists 1 (pt); Recreational therapists 1 (pt); Speech therapists 1 (pt); Activities coordinators 2 (ft); Podiatrists 1 (pt); Dentists 1 (pt); Social workers 1 (ft).
Affiliation Masons.
Facilities Dining room; Physical therapy room; Activities room; Chapel; Crafts room; Laundry room; Barber/Beauty shop; Library.

Activities Arts & crafts; Cards; Games; Reading groups; Prayer groups; Movies; Shopping trips; Dances/Social/Cultural gatherings; Fraternal oriented activities; Picnics; Watermelon parties.

Columbia

Lorien Nursing & Rehabilitation Center
6334 Cedar Ln, Columbia, MD 21044
(301) 531-5300, 531-5608 FAX
Admin Louis G Grimmel. *Dir of Nursing* Carol Gibbons RN BSN. *Medical Dir* Jerome Hantman MD.
Licensure Skilled care; Intermediate care. *Beds* Swing beds SNF/ICF 247. *Private Pay Patients* 35%. *Certified* Medicaid; Medicare.
Owner Proprietary corp.
Staff Physicians 40 (pt); RNs 9 (ft), 15 (pt); LPNs 12 (ft), 14 (pt); Nurses' aides 60 (ft), 45 (pt); Physical therapists 1 (ft); Occupational therapists 1 (ft); Speech therapists 1 (ft); Activities coordinators 3 (ft); Dietitians 1 (ft); Podiatrists 1 (ft); Audiologists 1 (pt).
Facilities Dining room; Physical therapy room; Activities room; Chapel; Laundry room; Barber/Beauty shop.
Activities Arts & crafts; Games; Reading groups; Prayer groups; Movies.

Crisfield

McCready Comprehensive Care Unit
Hall Hwy, Crisfield, MD 21817
(301) 968-1200, ext 225
Admin Geraldine Schmidlin. *Dir of Nursing* Deb Pope RN. *Medical Dir* Dr Sterling.
Licensure Skilled care; Intermediate care. *Beds* Swing beds SNF/ICF 6. *Private Pay Patients* 1%. *Certified* Medicaid; Medicare.
Owner Nonprofit organization/foundation.
Admissions Requirements Physician's request; Must have 3 days acute hospital care prior to admission.
Staff Physicians 2 (ft), 1 (pt); RNs 2 (ft); LPNs 4 (ft), 1 (pt); Nurses' aides 6 (ft); Physical therapists 2 (ft); Speech therapists 1 (ft); Activities coordinators 1 (ft); Dietitians 1 (ft); Ophthalmologists (consultant); Podiatrists (consultant); Audiologists (consultant); RealityRecreationOccupational therapists 1 (ft).
Facilities Physical therapy room; Activities room; Chapel; Barber/Beauty shop.
Activities Arts & crafts; Cards; Games; Reading groups; Movies; Dances/Social/Cultural gatherings.

Alice Byrd Tawes Nursing Home
201 Hall Hwy, Crisfield, MD 21817
(301) 968-1200
Admin Novella Bozman. *Dir of Nursing* Dottie Edwards. *Medical Dir* James Sterling MD.
Licensure Skilled care; Intermediate care. *Beds* Swing beds SNF/ICF 64. *Private Pay Patients* 1%. *Certified* Medicaid; Medicare.
Owner Nonprofit organization/foundation.
Admissions Requirements Medical examination.
Staff Physicians 2 (pt); RNs 4 (ft), 4 (pt); LPNs 5 (ft), 3 (pt); Nurses' aides 17 (ft), 13 (pt); Activities coordinators 2 (ft); Dietitians 1 (pt).
Facilities Dining room; Activities room; Crafts room; Laundry room; Barber/Beauty shop.
Activities Arts & crafts; Games; Reading groups; Prayer groups; Movies; Shopping trips; Dances/Social/Cultural gatherings.

Crofton

Crofton Convalescent Center
2131 Davidsonville Rd, Crofton, MD 21114
(301) 721-1000
Admin Philip Gordon. *Dir of Nursing* Dorothy L Cox RN. *Medical Dir* Max C Frank MD.
Licensure Skilled care. *Beds* SNF 144. *Private Pay Patients* 40%. *Certified* Medicaid; Medicare.
Owner Privately owned.
Admissions Requirements Medical examination; Physician's request.
Staff RNs 7 (ft), 10 (pt); LPNs 14 (ft), 4 (pt); Nurses' aides 51 (ft), 15 (pt); Physical therapists 3 (pt); Occupational therapists 1 (pt); Speech therapists 1 (pt); Activities coordinators 3 (pt); Dietitians 1 (pt); Podiatrists 5 (pt).
Languages French, Sign.
Facilities Dining room; Physical therapy room; Activities room; Chapel; Laundry room; Barber/Beauty shop; Library.
Activities Arts & crafts; Cards; Games; Reading groups; Prayer groups; Movies; Shopping trips; Dances/Social/Cultural gatherings; Pet therapy; Non-credit community college courses.

Crownsville

Fairfield Nursing Center Inc
1454 Fairfield Loop Rd, Crownsville, MD 21032
(301) 923-6820, 987-5818 FAX
Admin Kathy Gilzherzer. *Dir of Nursing* Rosemary Mewhorr. *Medical Dir* Dr Scott Rifkin.
Licensure Skilled care; Intermediate care. *Beds* Swing beds SNF/ICF 142. *Private Pay Patients* 36%. *Certified* Medicaid; Medicare.
Owner Nonprofit corp (National Care Facilities).
Admissions Requirements Minimum age 18; Medical examination.
Staff Physicians 6 (ft); RNs 12 (ft); LPNs 20 (ft); Nurses' aides 62 (ft); Physical therapists 1 (pt); Recreational therapists 1 (pt); Occupational therapists 1 (pt); Speech therapists 1 (pt); Activities coordinators 1 (ft); Dietitians 1 (pt); Podiatrists 1 (pt); Audiologists 1 (pt).
Facilities Dining room; Physical therapy room; Activities room; Crafts room; Laundry room; Barber/Beauty shop; Library.
Activities Arts & crafts; Cards; Games; Reading groups; Movies; Shopping trips; Dances/Social/Cultural gatherings; Intergenerational programs; Pet therapy.

Cumberland

Allegany County Nursing Home
PO Box 599, Furnace Rd, Cumberland, MD 21502
(301) 777-5941, 777-2300 FAX
Admin Bertie M Stotler.
Medical Dir Dr Robustiano J Barrera.
Licensure Intermediate care. *Beds* ICF 153. *Certified* Medicaid.
Owner Publicly owned.
Staff Physicians 1 (ft), 1 (pt); RNs 4 (ft), 2 (pt); LPNs 10 (ft), 9 (pt); Nurses' aides 29 (ft), 27 (pt); Physical therapists 1 (ft); Activities coordinators 1 (ft), 1 (pt); Dietitians 1 (ft); Podiatrists 1 (ft); Dentists 1 (ft).
Facilities Dining room; Physical therapy room; Activities room; Crafts room; Laundry room; Barber/Beauty shop.
Activities Arts & crafts; Cards; Games; Prayer groups; Movies; Dances/Social/Cultural gatherings; Birthday parties.

Joseph D Brandenburg Center
PO Box 1722, Country Club Rd, Cumberland,
MD 21502
(301) 777-2256
Admin Dennis George acting.
Medical Dir Gary Wagoner MD.
Licensure Intermediate care for mentally
retarded. *Beds* ICF/MR 50. *Certified*
Medicaid.
Owner Publicly owned.
Admissions Requirements Minimum age 18.
Staff Physicians 1 (pt); RNs 6 (ft); LPNs 3
(ft); Physical therapists 1 (pt); Recreational
therapists 2 (ft); Occupational therapists 1
(ft); Speech therapists 1 (ft), 1 (pt);
Audiologists 2 (pt).
Facilities Dining room; Physical therapy
room; Activities room; Crafts room; Laundry
room; Barber/Beauty shop; Library.
Activities Arts & crafts; Games; Movies;
Shopping trips; Dances/Social/Cultural
gatherings.

Cumberland Nursing Center
510 Winifred Rd, Cumberland, MD 21502
(301) 724-6066
Admin Shirley E Paulus.
Medical Dir Peter B Halmos.
Licensure Skilled care; Intermediate care. *Beds*
135. *Certified* Medicaid.
Owner Proprietary corp (Beverly Enterprises).

Lions Manor Nursing Home
Seton Dr Ext, Cumberland, MD 21502
(301) 722-6272
Admin Leo J Bechtold. *Dir of Nursing* Nancy
J Miller RN. *Medical Dir* Vimala A
Ranjithan MD.
Licensure Skilled care; Intermediate care. *Beds*
Swing beds SNF/ICF 101. *Private Pay
Patients* 25%. *Certified* Medicaid; Medicare.
Owner Nonprofit organization/foundation.
Admissions Requirements Minimum age 14;
Medical examination; Physician's request.
Staff Physicians 1 (pt); RNs 5 (ft), 3 (pt);
LPNs 4 (ft), 5 (pt); Nurses' aides 34 (ft), 7
(pt); Physical therapists 1 (pt); Recreational
therapists 1 (pt); Occupational therapists
(consultant); Speech therapists (consultant);
Activities coordinators 2 (ft); Dietitians 1
(pt); Ophthalmologists (consultant);
Podiatrists (consultant); Audiologists
(consultant); Social service directors 1 (ft).
Languages Spanish.
Facilities Dining room; Physical therapy
room; Activities room; Crafts room; Laundry
room; Barber/Beauty shop; Library;
Wheelchair van.
Activities Arts & crafts; Cards; Games;
Reading groups; Prayer groups; Movies;
Shopping trips; Dances/Social/Cultural
gatherings; Resident council.

Denton

Caroline Nursing Home Inc
520 Kerr Ave, Denton, MD 21629
(301) 479-2130
Admin Karen L Potter.
Medical Dir David Smith MD.
Licensure Skilled care; Intermediate care. *Beds*
76. *Certified* Medicaid; Medicare.
Owner Nonprofit corp.
Admissions Requirements Minimum age 18.
Staff Physicians 6 (pt); RNs 4 (ft), 4 (pt);
LPNs 4 (ft), 5 (pt); Nurses' aides 24 (ft), 26
(pt); Physical therapists 1 (pt); Occupational
therapists 1 (pt); Speech therapists 1 (pt);
Activities coordinators 1 (ft); Dietitians 1
(pt); Ophthalmologists 1 (pt); Podiatrists 1
(pt); Dentists 1 (pt).
Facilities Dining room; Physical therapy
room; Activities room; Chapel; Crafts room;
Laundry room; Barber/Beauty shop.
Activities Arts & crafts; Cards; Games;
Reading groups; Prayer groups; Movies;
Shopping trips.

Wesleyan Health Care Center Inc
PO Box 400, 280 Camp Rd, Denton, MD
21629
(301) 479-4400
Admin Shirley Smith.
Medical Dir Philip Felipe MD.
Licensure Comprehensive care. *Beds*
Comprehensive care 120.
Owner Proprietary corp (US Care Corp).

Easton

William Hill Manor Health Care Center
501 Dutchman's Ln, Easton, MD 21601
(301) 822-8888, 820-9438 FAX
Admin Donna S Taylor. *Dir of Nursing*
Donna D Ignatavicius MS RN. *Medical Dir*
Albert T Dawkins MD.
Licensure Skilled care; Intermediate care;
Continuing care retirement. *Beds* Swing beds
SNF/ICF 95; Continuing care retirement
200. *Private Pay Patients* 88%. *Certified*
Medicaid; Medicare.
Owner Proprietary corp.
Admissions Requirements Minimum age 55;
Medical examination; Physician's request.
Staff Physicians 1 (pt); RNs 6 (ft), 7 (pt);
LPNs 6 (ft), 7 (pt); Nurses' aides 25 (ft), 10
(pt); Physical therapists 1 (pt); Occupational
therapists 1 (pt); Speech therapists 1 (pt);
Activities coordinators 3 (ft); Dietitians 1
(pt); Podiatrists 1 (pt).
Facilities Dining room; Physical therapy
room; Activities room; Laundry room;
Barber/Beauty shop.
Activities Arts & crafts; Cards; Games;
Reading groups; Prayer groups; Movies;
Dances/Social/Cultural gatherings;
Intergenerational programs; Pet therapy;
Guest speakers; Special dinners; Parties;
Exercise classes.

Memorial Hospital at Easton
219 S Washington St, Easton, MD 21601
(301) 822-1000, 822-7369 FAX
Admin Charles H Gersdorf. *Dir of Nursing*
Patricia Noble RN MS. *Medical Dir* Albert
T Dawkins MD.
Licensure Skilled care; Intermediate care. *Beds*
Swing beds SNF/ICF 33. *Private Pay
Patients* 39%. *Certified* Medicaid; Medicare.
Owner Nonprofit corp.
Admissions Requirements Minimum age 14;
Medical examination; Physician's request.
Staff Physicians 1 (pt); RNs 3 (ft); LPNs 2
(ft), 1 (pt); Nurses' aides 14 (ft); Physical
therapists 3 (ft); Occupational therapists 2
(ft); Speech therapists 1 (ft); Activities
coordinators 1 (ft), 1 (pt); Dietitians 3 (ft);
Podiatrists 1 (pt).
Facilities Dining room; Physical therapy
room; Activities room.
Activities Arts & crafts; Cards; Games;
Reading groups; Prayer groups; Movies.

Meridian Nursing Center—The Pines
Rte 50 & Dutchman's Ln, Easton, MD 21601
(301) 822-4000
Admin Bruce Levin.
Medical Dir Stephen P Carney MD.
Licensure Skilled care; Intermediate care;
Domiciliary care. *Beds* Comprehensive care
205; Domiciliary care 8. *Certified* Medicaid;
Medicare.
Owner Proprietary corp (Meridian
Healthcare).

Edgewater

Pleasant Living Convalescent Center
144 Washington Rd, Edgewater, MD 21037
(301) 956-5000
Admin Howard Waltz Jr. *Dir of Nursing*
Nancy Youngblood RN. *Medical Dir* Jon B
Lowe MD.
Licensure Skilled care; Intermediate care. *Beds*
120. *Certified* Medicaid; Medicare.

Owner Proprietary corp.
Admissions Requirements Minimum age 14;
Medical examination; Physician's request.
Staff Physicians 17 (pt); RNs 6 (ft), 4 (pt);
LPNs 5 (ft), 7 (pt); Nurses' aides 37 (ft), 28
(pt); Physical therapists 1 (pt); Recreational
therapists 1 (ft); Speech therapists 1 (pt);
Activities coordinators 2 (ft); Dietitians 1
(pt); Ophthalmologists 1 (pt); Podiatrists 1
(pt); Dentists 1 (pt).
Facilities Dining room; Physical therapy
room; Activities room; Chapel; Crafts room;
Laundry room; Barber/Beauty shop; Library.
Activities Arts & crafts; Cards; Games;
Reading groups; Prayer groups; Movies;
Shopping trips; Dances/Social/Cultural
gatherings; Picnic outings; Dining affair
twice monthly, local restaurants provide
their specialty & wine w/their chef &
assistants.

Elkton

Devine Haven Convalescent Center
224 E Main St, Elkton, MD 21921
(301) 398-4550
Admin Sharon Fox.
Medical Dir S Ralph Andrews Jr MD.
Licensure Intermediate care. *Beds* ICF 43.
Certified Medicaid.
Owner Proprietary corp.

Laurelwood Nursing Center
100 Laurel Dr, Elkton, MD 21921
(301) 398-8800
Admin Kimberly M Carr.
Medical Dir Joseph Lanzi MD.
Licensure Comprehensive care. *Beds*
Comprehensive care 133.
Owner Proprietary corp (Genesis Health
Ventures).

Ellicott City

Bon Secours Extended Care
3000 N Ridge Rd, Ellicott City, MD 21043
(301) 461-6660
Admin Leslie D Goldschmidt. *Dir of Nursing*
Wanda Murray RN. *Medical Dir* William
Flowers.
Licensure Skilled care; Intermediate care. *Beds*
Swing beds SNF/ICF 99. *Private Pay
Patients* 60%. *Certified* Medicaid; Medicare.
Owner Nonprofit corp (Bon Secours Health
Systems).
Admissions Requirements Minimum age 14;
Physician's request.
Staff Physicians 1 (pt); RNs 7 (ft), 7 (pt);
LPNs 6 (ft), 4 (pt); Physical therapists 1 (pt);
Recreational therapists 1 (ft), 2 (pt);
Occupational therapists 1 (pt); Speech
therapists 1 (pt); Dietitians 1 (pt);
Ophthalmologists 1 (pt); Podiatrists 1 (pt);
Audiologists 1 (pt).
Affiliation Roman Catholic.
Facilities Dining room; Physical therapy
room; Activities room; Chapel; Crafts room;
Laundry room; Barber/Beauty shop; Library.
Activities Arts & crafts; Cards; Games;
Reading groups; Prayer groups; Movies;
Shopping trips; Dances/Social/Cultural
gatherings; Intergenerational programs; Pet
therapy.

Forest Hill

Bel Forest Nursing & Rehabilitation Center
109 Forest Valley Dr, Forest Hill, MD 21050
(301) 838-0101
Admin Amy Rothert. *Dir of Nursing* Margaret
Nickles RN. *Medical Dir* David Dunn MD.
Licensure Skilled care. *Beds* SNF 148.
Certified Medicaid; Medicare.
Owner Privately owned.

Staff RNs; LPNs; Nurses' aides; Physical
therapists; Recreational therapists;
Occupational therapists; Speech therapists;
Activities coordinators; Dietitians;
Ophthalmologists; Podiatrists.
Facilities Dining room; Physical therapy
room; Activities room; Crafts room; Laundry
room; Barber/Beauty shop; Lawns; Gardens;
Patios.
Activities Arts & crafts; Cards; Games;
Reading groups; Prayer groups; Movies;
Dances/Social/Cultural gatherings;
Intergenerational programs; Pet therapy.

Forestville

**Regency Nursing & Rehabilitation Treatment
Center**
7420 Marlboro Pike, Forestville, MD 20747
(301) 736-0240
Admin Robert C Bristol. *Dir of Nursing* Vera
Thorn. *Medical Dir* Glen Edgecomb MD.
Licensure Comprehensive care; Alzheimer's
care. *Beds* Comprehensive care 160. *Private
Pay Patients* 50%. *Certified* Medicaid;
Medicare.
Owner Proprietary corp (Regency Health
Service Inc).
Admissions Requirements Minimum age 14;
Medical examination.
Staff RNs 5 (ft), 6 (pt); LPNs 7 (ft), 4 (pt);
Nurses' aides 50 (ft), 25 (pt); Physical
therapists 1 (pt); Recreational therapists 1
(pt); Occupational therapists 1 (pt); Speech
therapists 1 (pt); Activities coordinators 1
(ft), 1 (pt); Dietitians 1 (ft).
Facilities Dining room; Physical therapy
room; Activities room; Crafts room; Laundry
room; Barber/Beauty shop; Library.
Activities Arts & crafts; Cards; Games;
Reading groups; Prayer groups; Movies;
Shopping trips; Dances/Social/Cultural
gatherings; Intergenerational programs; Pet
therapy.

Fort Washington

Fort Washington Rehabilitation Center
12021 Livingston Rd, Fort Washington, MD
20744
(301) 292-0300
Admin Randall Hixson. *Dir of Nursing* Diana
Adinig RN. *Medical Dir* William Furst MD.
Licensure Skilled care; Intermediate care. *Beds*
150. *Certified* Medicaid; Medicare.
Owner Proprietary corp.
Admissions Requirements Minimum age 14;
Medical examination.
Staff Physicians 7 (pt); RNs 8 (ft), 3 (pt);
LPNs 9 (ft), 3 (pt); Nurses' aides 30 (ft), 7
(pt); Physical therapists 1 (ft); Reality
therapists 1 (ft); Recreational therapists 2
(ft); Occupational therapists 1 (ft); Speech
therapists 1 (pt); Activities coordinators 1
(ft); Dietitians 1 (ft); Ophthalmologists 1
(pt); Podiatrists 1 (pt); Dentists 1 (pt).
Facilities Dining room; Physical therapy
room; Activities room; Crafts room; Laundry
room; Barber/Beauty shop.
Activities Arts & crafts; Cards; Games;
Reading groups; Prayer groups; Movies;
Shopping trips; Dances/Social/Cultural
gatherings.

Frederick

Citizens Nursing Home of Frederick County
2200 Rosemont Ave, Frederick, MD 21701
(301) 694-1550
Admin William P Hill Jr.
Medical Dir B O Thomas Jr MD.
Licensure Skilled care; Intermediate care. *Beds*
170. *Certified* Medicaid; Medicare.
Owner Publicly owned.

Staff Physicians 1 (pt); RNs 12 (ft), 8 (pt);
LPNs 7 (ft), 10 (pt); Nurses' aides 50 (ft), 35
(pt); Physical therapists 2 (pt); Speech
therapists 1 (pt); Activities coordinators 1
(ft); Dietitians 1 (ft), 1 (pt).
Facilities Dining room; Physical therapy
room; Activities room; Chapel; Crafts room;
Laundry room; Barber/Beauty shop; Library.
Activities Arts & crafts; Cards; Games;
Reading groups; Prayer groups; Movies;
Shopping trips.

Frederick Health Care Center
30 N Place, Frederick, MD 21701-6200
(301) 695-6618, 695-7329 FAX
Admin Robert D Sands. *Dir of Nursing*
Margaret Derr RN. *Medical Dir* Leroy T
Davis MD.
Licensure Skilled care; Intermediate care;
Domiciliary care; Alzheimer's care. *Beds*
SNF 22; ICF 76; Domiciliary care 22.
Certified Medicaid; Medicare.
Owner Proprietary corp (Beverly Enterprises).
Admissions Requirements Medical
examination; Physician's request.
Staff RNs 6 (ft), 1 (pt); LPNs 7 (ft), 1 (pt);
Nurses' aides 32 (ft), 16 (pt); Physical
therapists 1 (pt); Recreational therapists 1
(pt); Occupational therapists 1 (pt); Speech
therapists 1 (pt); Activities coordinators 1
(ft); Dietitians 1 (ft); Ophthalmologists 1
(pt); Podiatrists 1 (pt); Audiologists 1 (pt).
Languages Korean, Hebrew, German.
Facilities Dining room; Physical therapy
room; Activities room; Crafts room; Laundry
room; Barber/Beauty shop; Private dining
room for all domiciliary residents; Patio;
Lobby; Security system on doors.
Activities Arts & crafts; Cards; Games; Prayer
groups; Movies; Dances/Social/Cultural
gatherings; Intergenerational programs; Pet
therapy.

Northampton Manor Inc
200 E 16th St, Frederick, MD 21701
(301) 662-8700
Admin Louis Vogel.
Medical Dir George Smith Jr MD.
Licensure Comprehensive care. *Beds*
Comprehensive care 106.
Owner Proprietary corp.

Frostburg

**Frostburg Community Hospital Extended Care
Facility**
48 Tarn Terr, Frostburg, MD 21502
Admin William Udovich.
Licensure Extended care. *Beds* Extended care
10.

Frostburg Village of Allegany County
1 Kaylor Cir, Corner of Rte 36 & Rte 40,
Frostburg, MD 21532
(301) 689-2425
Admin Leo J Cyr. *Dir of Nursing* Phyllis
Roque RN. *Medical Dir* S L Sandhir MD.
Licensure Skilled care; Adult day care;
Retirement; Alzheimer's care. *Beds* SNF
170; Adult day care 24. *Certified* Medicaid;
Medicare.
Owner Nonprofit corp (Tressler-Lutheran
Services Association).
Admissions Requirements Minimum age 65.
Staff RNs; LPNs; Nurses' aides; Recreational
therapists; Activities coordinators; Dietitians.
Affiliation Lutheran.
Facilities Dining room; Physical therapy
room; Activities room; Chapel; Crafts room;
Laundry room; Barber/Beauty shop; Library.
Activities Arts & crafts; Cards; Games;
Reading groups; Prayer groups; Movies;
Shopping trips; Dances/Social/Cultural
gatherings.

Gaithersburg

Herman M Wilson Health Care Center
201-301 Russell Ave, Gaithersburg, MD
20760
(301) 330-3000
Admin Alan W Porterfield.
Medical Dir Henry Scruggs MD.
Licensure Skilled care; Intermediate care. *Beds*
Comprehensive care 285. *Certified*
Medicaid; Medicare.
Owner Nonprofit corp.

Garrison

Garrison Valley Center Inc
9600 Reisterstown Rd, Garrison, MD 21055
(301) 363-3337
Admin Ida M Campanella. *Dir of Nursing*
Josephine Mungin RN. *Medical Dir* Allan H
Macht MD.
Licensure Intermediate care. *Beds* ICF 76.
Certified Medicaid.
Owner Proprietary corp.
Admissions Requirements Minimum age 16;
Medical examination; Physician's request.
Staff Physicians 2 (ft); RNs 3 (ft); LPNs 4 (ft),
4 (pt); Physical therapists 1 (pt); Activities
coordinators 1 (ft); Dietitians 1 (pt).
Facilities Dining room; Physical therapy
room; Activities room; Chapel; Crafts room;
Laundry room; Library.
Activities Arts & crafts; Cards; Games; Prayer
groups; Movies; Shopping trips.

Glen Arm

Notchcliff
11630 Glen Arm Rd, Glen Arm, MD 21057
(301) 592-5310
Admin Carol A Baker. *Dir of Nursing* Dot
Schwemmer. *Medical Dir* Dr David
McClure.
Licensure Intermediate care; Retirement. *Beds*
ICF 16; Retirement apts and cottages 215.
Owner Privately owned.
Staff Physicians (consultant); RNs 3 (ft), 6
(pt); LPNs 1 (ft), 2 (pt); Nurses' aides 5 (ft),
6 (pt); Physical therapists (consultant);
Recreational therapists (consultant);
Occupational therapists (consultant); Speech
therapists (consultant); Activities
coordinators 1 (ft); Dietitians (consultant);
Ophthalmologists (consultant); Podiatrists
(consultant).
Facilities Dining room; Physical therapy
room; Activities room; Chapel; Crafts room;
Laundry room; Barber/Beauty shop; Library;
Country store; Hobby room; Exercise room;
Cafe; Transportation; Private gardening
areas; Full-service bank; Pub room.
Activities Arts & crafts; Cards; Games;
Reading groups; Prayer groups; Movies;
Shopping trips; Dances/Social/Cultural
gatherings; Intergenerational programs; Pet
therapy.

Glen Burnie

Arundel Geriatric & Nursing Center
7355 Furnace Branch Rd E, Glen Burnie, MD
21061
(301) 766-3460
Admin Vida Sullivan. *Dir of Nursing* Mary Jo
Neal. *Medical Dir* Edward Hunt Jr.
Licensure Intermediate care. *Beds* ICF 115.
Certified Medicaid.
Owner Proprietary corp.
Admissions Requirements Minimum age 14.
Staff RNs; LPNs; Nurses' aides; Recreational
therapists; Activities coordinators.

Facilities Dining room; Activities room; Laundry room.
Activities Arts & crafts; Cards; Games; Reading groups; Prayer groups; Movies; Shopping trips; Dances/Social/Cultural gatherings.

Maryland Manor of Glen Burnie
7575 E Howard St, Glen Burnie, MD 21061
(301) 768-8200
Admin Paul J Robertson.
Medical Dir Peter Rheinstein MD.
Licensure Skilled care. *Beds* SNF 99. *Certified* Medicaid; Medicare.
Owner Proprietary corp.
Admissions Requirements Minimum age 18; Medical examination.
Staff Physicians; RNs; LPNs; Nurses' aides; Physical therapists; Speech therapists; Activities coordinators; Dietitians; Ophthalmologists; Podiatrists; Dentists.
Facilities Dining room; Physical therapy room; Activities room; Chapel; Crafts room; Laundry room; Barber/Beauty shop; Library.
Activities Arts & crafts; Cards; Games; Reading groups; Prayer groups; Movies; Shopping trips; Dances/Social/Cultural gatherings.

North Arundel Nursing & Convalescent Center
313 Hospital Dr, Glenburnie, MD 21061
(301) 761-1222
Admin Shirley McKnight. *Dir of Nursing* Barbara N Terry RN. *Medical Dir* Mustafa C Oz MD.
Licensure Skilled care; Intermediate care; Domiciliary care; Alzheimer's care. *Beds* Swing beds SNF/ICF 121; Domiciliary care 10; Alzheimer's care. *Private Pay Patients* 40%. *Certified* Medicaid; Medicare.
Owner Proprietary corp (Health Care Management Corp).
Admissions Requirements Medical examination; Physician's request.
Staff Physicians (consultant); RNs 9 (ft); LPNs 8 (ft); Nurses' aides 6 (ft); Physical therapists (consultant); Speech therapists (consultant); Activities coordinators; Dietitians; Podiatrists (monthly visit).
Facilities Dining room; Physical therapy room; Activities room; Crafts room; Laundry room; Barber/Beauty shop; Library.
Activities Arts & crafts; Cards; Games; Reading groups; Prayer groups; Movies; Shopping trips; Dances/Social/Cultural gatherings; Pet therapy.

Grantsville

Goodwill Mennonite Home Inc
Dorsey Hotel Rd, Grantsville, MD 21536
(301) 895-5194
Admin R Henry Diller.
Medical Dir George Stoltzfus MD.
Licensure Intermediate care. *Beds* ICF 81. *Certified* Medicaid.
Owner Nonprofit corp.
Admissions Requirements Medical examination.
Staff RNs 1 (ft); LPNs 5 (ft); Nurses' aides 20 (ft); Activities coordinators 1 (ft).
Affiliation Mennonite.
Facilities Dining room; Physical therapy room; Activities room; Chapel; Crafts room; Laundry room; Barber/Beauty shop.
Activities Arts & crafts; Games; Movies.

Greenbelt

Greenbelt Nursing Center
7010 Greenbelt Rd, Greenbelt, MD 20770
(301) 345-9595
Admin Bret Stine. *Dir of Nursing* Bonnie Baker RN. *Medical Dir* David Granite.

Licensure Skilled care; Intermediate care. *Beds* Comprehensive care 132. *Certified* Medicaid; Medicare.
Owner Proprietary corp (Unicare).
Admissions Requirements Minimum age 18.
Staff RNs 5 (ft), 5 (pt); LPNs 9 (ft), 9 (pt); Nurses' aides 50 (ft), 25 (pt); Physical therapists 1 (ft); Recreational therapists 1 (ft); Occupational therapists 1 (ft); Speech therapists 1 (ft); Activities coordinators 1 (ft); Dietitians 1 (ft); Podiatrists 1 (pt).
Facilities Dining room; Physical therapy room; Barber/Beauty shop.
Activities Arts & crafts; Cards; Games; Reading groups; Prayer groups; Movies; Shopping trips; Dances/Social/Cultural gatherings.

Hagerstown

Avalon Manor Inc
Rte 8 Box 35, Marsh Pike & Eden Rd, Hagerstown, MD 21740
(301) 739-9360
Admin Stuart Reiker.
Medical Dir William Lesh MD.
Licensure Intermediate care. *Beds* ICF 221. *Certified* Medicaid.
Owner Proprietary corp.
Admissions Requirements Minimum age 14; Medical examination; Physician's request.
Staff Physicians 4 (pt); RNs 7 (ft); LPNs 19 (ft); Nurses' aides 94 (ft), 3 (pt); Recreational therapists 1 (ft), 2 (pt); Activities coordinators 1 (ft); Dietitians 1 (ft).
Facilities Dining room; Activities room; Crafts room; Laundry room; Barber/Beauty shop; Library.
Activities Arts & crafts; Cards; Games; Prayer groups; Movies; Shopping trips; Dances/Social/Cultural gatherings; Ceramics.

Clearview Nursing Home Inc
Rte 3 Box 144, Hagerstown, MD 21740
(301) 582-1654
Admin Ronald Sohl.
Medical Dir John D Wilson MD.
Licensure Intermediate care. *Beds* ICF 49. *Certified* Medicaid.
Owner Proprietary corp.

Coffman Home for the Aging Inc
1304 Pennsylvania Ave, Hagerstown, MD 21740
(301) 733-2914
Admin Ruth Yvonne Eyler.
Medical Dir J D Wilson MD.
Licensure Intermediate care. *Beds* ICF 51. *Certified* Medicaid.
Owner Publicly owned.

Colton Villa Nursing Center
750 Dual Hwy, Hagerstown, MD 21740
(301) 797-4020
Admin Christopher Johns.
Medical Dir Vasant Datta.
Licensure Skilled care; Intermediate care. *Beds* 160. *Certified* Medicaid; Medicare.
Owner Proprietary corp (Beverly Enterprises).
Admissions Requirements Minimum age 18; Medical examination; Physician's request.
Staff Physicians 1 (pt); RNs 8 (ft), 3 (pt); LPNs 9 (ft), 3 (pt); Nurses' aides 60 (ft), 4 (pt); Physical therapists 1 (pt); Speech therapists 2 (pt); Activities coordinators 2 (ft); Dietitians 1 (pt); Podiatrists 1 (pt).
Facilities Dining room; Activities room; Laundry room; Barber/Beauty shop.
Activities Arts & crafts; Cards; Games; Reading groups; Prayer groups; Movies; Shopping trips; Dances/Social/Cultural gatherings.

Garlock Memorial Convalescent Home Inc
241 S Prospect St, Hagerstown, MD 21740
(301) 733-3310
Admin Stuart Ricker.

Medical Dir Sidney Novenstein MD.
Licensure Intermediate care. *Beds* ICF 37. *Certified* Medicaid.
Owner Proprietary corp.

Potomac Center
1380 Marshall St, Hagerstown, MD 21740
(301) 791-4650
Admin Steven J Smith.
Medical Dir J Ramsey Farah MD.
Licensure Intermediate care for mentally retarded. *Beds* ICF/MR 150. *Certified* Medicaid.
Owner Publicly owned.

Ravenwood Lutheran Village
1183 Luther Dr, Hagerstown, MD 21740
(301) 790-1000
Admin Annie P Dunbar.
Medical Dir Sidney Novenstein MD.
Licensure Skilled care; Intermediate care. *Beds* 86. *Certified* Medicaid; Medicare.
Owner Nonprofit corp (Tressler-Lutheran Services Association).
Affiliation Lutheran.

Washington County Hospital Extended Care Facility
251 E Antietam St, Hagerstown, MD 21740
(301) 790-8000
Admin Linda Kaufman.
Licensure Extended care. *Beds* Extended care 23.

Western Maryland Center
1500 Pennsylvania Ave, Hagerstown, MD 21740
(301) 791-4400
Admin Carl A Fischer MD. *Dir of Nursing* Natalie Rook RN MS. *Medical Dir* Fatima Mohiuddin MD.
Licensure Skilled care; Intermediate care. *Beds* Swing beds SNF/ICF 52. *Private Pay Patients* 0%. *Certified* Medicaid; Medicare.
Owner Nonprofit organization/foundation.
Staff Physicians 4 (ft); RNs; LPNs; Activities coordinators 1 (ft); Dietitians 1 (ft).

Havre de Grace

Brevin Nursing Home Inc
421 S Union Ave, Havre de Grace, MD 21078
(301) 939-1740
Admin Jerrold F Bress.
Medical Dir Gunther Hirsch MD.
Licensure Intermediate care. *Beds* ICF 40. *Certified* Medicaid.
Owner Proprietary corp.

Citizens Nursing Home of Harford County
415 S Market St, Havre de Grace, MD 21078
(301) 939-5500
Admin John C Fisher.
Medical Dir John D Yun MD.
Licensure Skilled care; Intermediate care. *Beds* 200. *Certified* Medicaid; Medicare.
Owner Publicly owned.
Admissions Requirements Minimum age 14; Medical examination; Physician's request.
Staff RNs 4 (ft), 6 (pt); LPNs 14 (ft), 11 (pt); Nurses' aides 48 (ft), 42 (pt); Activities coordinators 1 (ft); Dietitians 1 (ft).
Facilities Dining room; Physical therapy room; Activities room; Chapel; Crafts room; Laundry room; Barber/Beauty shop; Enclosed courtyard.
Activities Arts & crafts; Cards; Games; Prayer groups; Movies; Shopping trips; Dances/Social/Cultural gatherings; Outside entertainment; College programs.

Hyattsville

Carroll Manor Inc
4922 LaSalle Rd, Hyattsville, MD 20782
(301) 864-2333

Admin Sr Jeanette Lindsay. *Dir of Nursing* Eileen Blaustein RN. *Medical Dir* Thomas Curtin MD.
Licensure Skilled care; Intermediate care; Domiciliary care. *Beds* ICF 215; Swing beds SNF/ICF 20; Domiciliary care 17. *Private Pay Patients* 37%. *Certified* Medicaid; Medicare.
Owner Nonprofit corp.
Admissions Requirements Medical examination.
Staff Physicians 1 (pt); RNs 7 (ft), 10 (pt); LPNs 10 (ft), 3 (pt); Physical therapists (contracted); Recreational therapists 1 (ft); Occupational therapists 1 (ft); Speech therapists (contracted); Activities coordinators 1 (ft); Dietitians 1 (ft); Podiatrists (contracted); GAs and CMAs 67 (ft), 29 (pt).
Affiliation Roman Catholic.
Facilities Dining room; Physical therapy room; Activities room; Chapel; Crafts room; Laundry room; Barber/Beauty shop; Library.
Activities Arts & crafts; Cards; Games; Reading groups; Prayer groups; Movies; Shopping trips; Dances/Social/Cultural gatherings; Intergenerational programs; Pet therapy.

Hyattsville Manor
6500 Riggs Ave, Hyattsville, MD 20783
(301) 559-0300
Admin Elliot M Roth. *Dir of Nursing* Ronald Bowlyou. *Medical Dir* Myron Lenkin MD.
Licensure Skilled care; Intermediate care; Alzheimer's care. *Beds* SNF 10; ICF 140. *Certified* Medicaid; Medicare.
Owner Proprietary corp (Health Care & Retirement Corp).
Admissions Requirements Minimum age 16.
Staff Physicians 1 (pt); RNs 8 (ft); LPNs 12 (ft), 4 (pt); Nurses' aides 25 (ft), 10 (pt); Physical therapists 1 (pt); Recreational therapists 1 (ft); Occupational therapists 1 (pt); Speech therapists 1 (pt); Activities coordinators 1 (ft); Dietitians 1 (ft); Ophthalmologists 1 (pt).
Facilities Dining room; Physical therapy room; Activities room; Crafts room; Laundry room; Barber/Beauty shop.
Activities Arts & crafts; Cards; Games; Reading groups; Prayer groups; Movies; Shopping trips; Dances/Social/Cultural gatherings.

Madison Manor Nursing Home
5801 42nd Ave, Hyattsville, MD 20781
(301) 864-8800
Admin Mayther Brackins. *Dir of Nursing* Brenda Mauney Rian. *Medical Dir* B Arora MD.
Licensure Intermediate care. *Beds* ICF 27. *Certified* Medicaid.
Owner Proprietary corp.
Admissions Requirements Medical examination.
Staff Physicians 3 (ft), 1 (pt); RNs 1 (ft); LPNs 3 (ft), 3 (pt); Nurses' aides 5 (ft), 5 (pt); Activities coordinators 1 (ft); Dietitians 1 (ft); Ophthalmologists 1 (pt).
Facilities Dining room; Activities room; Laundry room.
Activities Arts & crafts; Games; Reading groups; Shopping trips.

Sacred Heart Home
5805 Queens Chapel Rd, Hyattsville, MD 20782
(301) 277-6500
Admin Sr Mary Agnes Fahrland.
Medical Dir Ibrahim Khatri MD.
Licensure Intermediate care. *Beds* ICF 102. *Certified* Medicaid.
Owner Nonprofit corp.

Kensington

Circle Manor Nursing Home
10231 Carroll Pl, Kensington, MD 20895
(301) 949-0230
Admin Gary Sudhalter. *Dir of Nursing* Judy Pelton RN. *Medical Dir* Barry Rosenbaum MD; Dr Shargel.
Licensure Intermediate care; Alzheimer's care. *Beds* ICF 86. *Certified* Medicaid.
Owner Proprietary corp.
Admissions Requirements Medical examination.
Staff RNs 3 (ft), 1 (pt); LPNs 4 (ft), 4 (pt); Nurses' aides 30 (ft), 5 (pt); Physical therapists 1 (pt); Recreational therapists 1 (ft); Occupational therapists 1 (pt); Speech therapists 1 (pt); Activities coordinators 1 (ft); Dietitians 1 (pt).
Facilities Dining room; Activities room; Laundry room; Barber/Beauty shop.
Activities Arts & crafts; Games; Reading groups; Prayer groups; Movies; Dances/Social/Cultural gatherings; Summerfest picnic; Holiday parties.

Kensington Gardens Nursing Center
3000 McComas Ave, Kensington, MD 20895
(301) 933-0060, 942-3008 FAX
Admin Vincent P McCubbin. *Dir of Nursing* Joseph P Freeman Jr. *Medical Dir* John Merindino; David Kessler.
Licensure Skilled care. *Beds* SNF 170. *Private Pay Patients* 50%. *Certified* Medicaid; Medicare.
Owner Privately owned.
Staff Physicians 3 (ft); RNs 19 (ft), 4 (pt); LPNs 12 (ft), 4 (pt); Nurses' aides 20 (ft); Physical therapists 1 (ft), 2 (pt); Occupational therapists 1 (ft); Speech therapists 1 (ft); Activities coordinators 1 (ft), 2 (pt); Dietitians 1 (ft); Podiatrists 1 (ft); Dentists 1 (ft).
Facilities Dining room; Physical therapy room; Activities room; Crafts room; Laundry room; Barber/Beauty shop; Library.
Activities Arts & crafts; Cards; Games; Reading groups; Prayer groups; Movies; Shopping trips; Dances/Social/Cultural gatherings; Intergenerational programs; Pet therapy.

La Plata

Charles County Nursing Home
Rte 488 Box 1320, La Plata, MD 20646
(301) 934-1900
Admin Lester Clough. *Dir of Nursing* Barbara Howard RN. *Medical Dir* Paul Prichett MD.
Licensure Skilled care; Intermediate care; Adult day care; Retirement. *Beds* Comprehensive care 105; Adult day care 24. *Certified* Medicaid; Medicare.
Owner Publicly owned.
Facilities Dining room; Physical therapy room; Activities room; Chapel; Crafts room; Laundry room; Barber/Beauty shop.
Activities Arts & crafts; Cards; Games; Reading groups; Prayer groups; Movies; Dances/Social/Cultural gatherings.

Meridian Nursing Center—LaPlata
1 Magnolia Dr, LaPlata, MD 20646
(301) 934-4001
Admin Bruce Goodpaster.
Medical Dir Daniel Howell MD.
Licensure Comprehensive care. *Beds* Comprehensive care 149.
Owner Proprietary corp (Meridian Healthcare).

Lanham

Magnolia Gardens Nursing Home
8200 Good Luck Rd, Lanham, MD 20801
(301) 552-2000
Admin Margaret O'Hara.
Medical Dir Leon Levitsky MD.
Licensure Skilled care; Intermediate care. *Beds* 104. *Certified* Medicaid; Medicare.
Owner Proprietary corp.

Largo

Largo Manor Care
Rte 2, 600 Largo Rd, Largo, MD 20772
(301) 350-5555
Admin Barry Grofic. *Dir of Nursing* Ruth O'Neill. *Medical Dir* Norton Elson MD.
Licensure Skilled care; Intermediate care. *Beds* Swing beds SNF/ICF 120. *Certified* Medicaid; Medicare.
Owner Proprietary corp (Manor Care Inc).
Admissions Requirements Minimum age 16.
Staff Physicians; RNs; LPNs; Nurses' aides; Physical therapists; Reality therapists; Recreational therapists; Occupational therapists; Speech therapists; Activities coordinators; Dietitians; Ophthalmologists; Podiatrists; Dentists.
Facilities Dining room; Physical therapy room; Activities room; Barber/Beauty shop; Library.
Activities Arts & crafts; Cards; Games; Reading groups; Prayer groups; Movies; Shopping trips; Dances/Social/Cultural gatherings.

Laurel

Bureau of Habilitation Services—Forest Haven
3360 Center Ave, Laurel, MD 20707
(301) 725-3600
Admin Clifford Hubbard.
Medical Dir Robert L Baird MD.
Licensure Intermediate care for mentally retarded. *Beds* (day treatment center). *Certified* Medicaid.
Owner Publicly owned.
Admissions Requirements Admission closed.
Staff Physicians 7 (ft); RNs 28 (ft); LPNs 18 (ft); Physical therapists 8 (ft); Recreational therapists 10 (ft); Occupational therapists 5 (ft); Speech therapists 3 (ft); Dietitians 3 (ft); Ophthalmologists 1 (ft); Podiatrists 1 (ft); Dentists 1 (ft).
Facilities Dining room; Physical therapy room; Activities room; Chapel; Crafts room; Laundry room; Barber/Beauty shop; Comprehensive complex.
Activities Arts & crafts; Cards; Games; Reading groups; Prayer groups; Movies; Shopping trips; Dances/Social/Cultural gatherings.

Golden Oaks Nursing Home Inc
9001 Cherry Ln, Laurel, MD 20708
(301) 498-8558, 792-2462 FAX
Admin Shirley Blumenfeld. *Dir of Nursing* Kathy Whitson. *Medical Dir* Dr Margolis.
Licensure Skilled care; Alzheimer's care. *Beds* SNF 130. *Certified* Medicaid; Medicare.
Owner Proprietary corp.
Staff Physicians; RNs; LPNs; Nurses' aides; Physical therapists; Reality therapists; Recreational therapists; Occupational therapists; Speech therapists; Activities coordinators; Dietitians; Podiatrists.
Facilities Dining room; Activities room; Crafts room; Laundry room; Barber/Beauty shop.
Activities Arts & crafts; Cards; Games; Reading groups; Prayer groups; Movies; Shopping trips; Dances/Social/Cultural gatherings; Intergenerational programs; Pet therapy.

Greater Laurel Nursing Home
14200 Laurel Park Dr, Laurel, MD 20707
(301) 792-4717 Baltimore, (202) 953-7980
Washington
Admin Stanley Savitz. *Dir of Nursing* Elaine
Lesher RN. *Medical Dir* Gregory Compton
MD.
Licensure Skilled care; Intermediate care;
Alzheimer's care. *Beds* SNF 47; ICF 130.
Certified Medicaid; Medicare.
Owner Privately owned.
Admissions Requirements Medical
examination.
Staff Physicians 7 (ft); RNs 3 (ft), 9 (pt);
LPNs 14 (ft), 7 (pt); Nurses' aides 51 (ft), 33
(pt); Physical therapists 1 (ft); Reality
therapists 1 (pt); Recreational therapists 3
(ft); Occupational therapists 1 (pt); Speech
therapists 1 (pt); Activities coordinators 3
(ft); Dietitians 1 (pt); Podiatrists
(consultant); Certified medicine aides 10 (ft),
5 (pt).
Facilities Dining room; Physical therapy
room; Activities room; Crafts room; Laundry
room; Barber/Beauty shop.
Activities Arts & crafts; Cards; Games;
Reading groups; Prayer groups; Movies;
Shopping trips; Dances/Social/Cultural
gatherings; Intergenerational programs; Pet
therapy.

Leonardtown

St Mary's Nursing Center
PO Box 518, Peabody St, Leonardtown, MD
20650
(301) 475-5681
Admin George E Smith NHA. *Dir of Nursing*
Monalea C Potter RN. *Medical Dir* David
Fedderly MD.
Licensure Skilled care; Intermediate care;
Alzheimer's care. *Beds* Swing beds SNF/ICF
148. *Private Pay Patients* 38%. *Certified*
Medicaid; Medicare.
Owner Nonprofit organization/foundation.
Admissions Requirements Minimum age 14;
Physician's request.
Staff Physicians 1 (pt); RNs 3 (ft), 8 (pt);
LPNs 11 (ft), 8 (pt); Nurses' aides 40 (ft), 18
(pt); Physical therapists (contracted); Reality
therapists (contracted); Recreational
therapists (contracted); Occupational
therapists (contracted); Speech therapists
(contracted); Activities coordinators 1 (ft);
Dietitians 1 (pt).
Facilities Dining room; Activities room;
Chapel; Crafts room; Laundry room; Barber/
Beauty shop; Library; Resident gift shop;
Volunteer program.
Activities Arts & crafts; Cards; Games;
Reading groups; Prayer groups; Movies;
Dances/Social/Cultural gatherings;
Intergenerational programs; Pet therapy;
Gran-pals program; Volunteer program.

Lexington Park

Bayside Nursing Center
1500 Great Mills Rd, Lexington Park, MD
20653
(301) 863-7244
Admin Jean Moulds. *Dir of Nursing* Gerri
Metcalf. *Medical Dir* James Boyd.
Licensure Skilled care; Intermediate care. *Beds*
SNF 65; ICF 60. *Private Pay Patients* 20%.
Certified Medicaid; Medicare.
Owner Proprietary corp (Genesis Health
Ventures).
Admissions Requirements Physician's request.
Staff RNs 4 (ft), 1 (pt); LPNs 10 (ft), 5 (pt);
Nurses' aides 29 (ft), 19 (pt); Physical
therapists (contracted); Occupational
therapists (contracted); Speech therapists
(contracted); Activities coordinators 1 (ft);
Dietitians (contracted).

Facilities Dining room; Physical therapy
room; Activities room; Barber/Beauty shop;
2 Outdoor courtyards.
Activities Arts & crafts; Cards; Games;
Reading groups; Prayer groups; Movies;
Shopping trips; Dances/Social/Cultural
gatherings; Intergenerational programs.

Lonaconing

Egle Nursing Home
57 Jackson St, Lonaconing, MD 21539
(301) 463-5451
Admin Vera Clark Egle.
Medical Dir Donald Manger MD.
Licensure Intermediate care. *Beds* ICF 24.
Certified Medicaid.
Owner Proprietary corp.
Admissions Requirements Minimum age 16;
Medical examination; MIMR screening.
Staff Physicians; RNs; LPNs; Nurses' aides;
Physical therapists; Reality therapists;
Recreational therapists; Occupational
therapists; Speech therapists; Activities
coordinators; Dietitians; Ophthalmologists;
Podiatrists; Audiologists; Dentists; Social
workers.
Facilities Dining room; Physical therapy
room; Activities room; Crafts room; Laundry
room; Living room.
Activities Arts & crafts; Cards; Games;
Reading groups; Prayer groups; Movies;
Shopping trips; Dances/Social/Cultural
gatherings; Pet therapy; Ombudsman
program.

Manchester

Longview Nursing Home Inc
3332 Main St, Box 390, Manchester, MD
21102-0390
(301) 239-7139
Admin Martha J Tarutis. *Dir of Nursing* Gay
I Rohr RN. *Medical Dir* Wilbur H Foard
MD.
Licensure Skilled care. *Beds* SNF 57. *Private
Pay Patients* 36%. *Certified* Medicaid;
Medicare.
Owner Privately owned.
Staff RNs 4 (ft), 3 (pt); LPNs 3 (ft), 3 (pt);
Nurses' aides 18 (ft), 4 (pt); Activities
coordinators 1 (ft), 2 (pt).
Facilities Dining room; Physical therapy
room; Activities room; Crafts room; Laundry
room; Barber/Beauty shop.
Activities Arts & crafts; Cards; Games;
Reading groups; Prayer groups; Movies;
Shopping trips; Dances/Social/Cultural
gatherings; Intergenerational programs; Pet
therapy.

Millersville

Knollwood Manor Inc
PO Box 408, 899 Cecil Ave, Millersville, MD
21108
(301) 987-1644
Admin James Hayden.
Medical Dir Paul S Rhodes MD.
Licensure Skilled care; Intermediate care. *Beds*
97. *Certified* Medicaid; Medicare.
Owner Proprietary corp (Concord Healthcare
Corp).
Admissions Requirements Minimum age 14;
Medical examination; Physician's request.
Staff Physicians 1 (ft); RNs 4 (ft); LPNs 6 (ft);
CNA 32 (ft); CMA 3 (ft).
Facilities Dining room; Activities room;
Barber/Beauty shop.
Activities Arts & crafts; Cards; Games;
Reading groups; Prayer groups; Movies;
Shopping trips; Dances/Social/Cultural
gatherings; Activities Program.

Mitchellville

Collington Episcopal Life Care Center
10450 Lottsford Rd, Mitchellville, MD 20716
(301) 925-9601
Admin Gail Cohn.
Licensure Comprehensive care. *Beds*
Comprehensive care 38.

Villa Rosa Nursing Home
3800 Lottsford Vista Rd, Mitchellville, MD
20716
(301) 459-4700
Admin Rev Anthony Dal Balcon. *Dir of
Nursing* Marion Bendt RN. *Medical Dir*
Ciro Montanez MD.
Licensure Skilled care; Intermediate care. *Beds*
101.
Owner Nonprofit organization/foundation.
Admissions Requirements Minimum age 14;
Medical examination; Physician's request.
Staff RNs 3 (ft), 1 (pt); LPNs 6 (ft), 1 (pt);
Nurses' aides 39 (ft), 3 (pt); Occupational
therapists 1 (ft), 3 (pt); Dietitians 1 (pt).
Languages Italian, Portuguese, Spanish,
German, French.
Affiliation Roman Catholic.
Activities Arts & crafts; Cards; Games;
Reading groups; Prayer groups; Movies;
Shopping trips; Dances/Social/Cultural
gatherings.

Mount Airy

Pleasant View Nursing Home of Mt Airy Inc
4101 Baltimore National Pike, Mount Airy,
MD 21771
(301) 829-0800
Admin Karen A Nichols. *Dir of Nursing*
Patricia Keaton. *Medical Dir* Melvin
Kordon MD.
Licensure Intermediate care. *Beds* ICF 104.
Certified Medicaid.
Admissions Requirements Physician's request.
Staff Physicians; RNs 3 (ft), 1 (pt); LPNs 7
(ft), 7 (pt); Nurses' aides 24 (ft), 24 (pt);
Recreational therapists; Occupational
therapists; Activities coordinators 1 (ft);
Dietitians 1 (ft); Ophthalmologists 1 (pt);
Dentists.
Facilities Dining room; Activities room;
Crafts room; Laundry room; Barber/Beauty
shop Hair care room; Library Mobile.
Activities Arts & crafts; Cards; Games;
Reading groups; Prayer groups; Movies;
Dances/Social/Cultural gatherings.

Oakland

Cuppett & Weeks Nursing Home
706 E Alder St, Oakland, MD 21550
(301) 334-2319
Admin James E Cuppett. *Dir of Nursing*
Charee Reckner. *Medical Dir* Walter
Naumann MD.
Licensure Intermediate care. *Beds* ICF 155.
Private Pay Patients 2%. *Certified* Medicaid;
Medicare.
Owner Privately owned.
Admissions Requirements Minimum age 14;
Medical examination.
Staff Physicians (consultant); RNs 3 (ft), 1
(pt); LPNs 9 (ft), 1 (pt); Nurses' aides;
Physical therapists 2 (ft), 1 (pt); Activities
coordinators 1 (ft); Dietitians 1 (ft);
Ophthalmologists (consultant); Podiatrists
(consultant); Audiologists (consultant).
Facilities Dining room; Physical therapy
room; Activities room; Crafts room; Laundry
room; Barber/Beauty shop.
Activities Arts & crafts; Cards; Games;
Reading groups; Prayer groups; Movies;
Dances/Social/Cultural gatherings.

Dennett Road Manor Inc
1113 Mary Dr, Mountain Lake Park, Oakland, MD 21550
(301) 334-8346
Admin Thomas U Cuppett.
Medical Dir James H Feaster Jr MD.
Licensure Intermediate care. *Beds* ICF 107. *Certified* Medicaid.
Owner Proprietary corp.
Admissions Requirements Minimum age 60; Medical examination; Physician's request.
Staff Physicians 10 (pt); RNs 5 (ft), 1 (pt); LPNs 5 (ft), 2 (pt); Nurses' aides 23 (ft), 27 (pt); Activities coordinators 2 (ft); Dietitians 1 (ft), 1 (pt); Podiatrists 1 (pt); Dentists 1 (pt).
Facilities Dining room; Activities room; Crafts room; Laundry room; Barber/Beauty shop; Library.
Activities Arts & crafts; Games; Reading groups; Prayer groups; Movies.

Olney

Brooke Grove Nursing Home
18430 Brooke Grove Rd, Olney, MD 20832
(301) 924-4475
Admin Florence Hallman. *Dir of Nursing* Marge Jennings RN. *Medical Dir* Charles Ligon MD.
Licensure Intermediate care; Retirement. *Beds* ICF 99. *Certified* Medicaid.
Owner Nonprofit corp.
Staff Physicians 1 (ft), 1 (pt); RNs 6 (ft), 3 (pt); LPNs 2 (ft), 1 (pt); Nurses' aides 27 (ft), 16 (pt); Recreational therapists 2 (ft); Activities coordinators 1 (ft); Dietitians 1 (pt).
Facilities Dining room; Physical therapy room; Activities room; Laundry room; Barber/Beauty shop.
Activities Games; Prayer groups; Shopping trips; Restaurants.

Sharon Nursing Home
18201 Marden Ln, Olney, MD 20832
(301) 924-4475
Admin Gloria Folkenberg.
Medical Dir Charles Ligon MD.
Licensure Intermediate care. *Beds* ICF 48. *Certified* Medicaid.
Owner Nonprofit corp.

Owings Mills

Baptist Home of Maryland Del Inc
10729 Park Heights Ave, Owings Mills, MD 21117-3098
(301) 484-3324
Admin Randal N Fowler.
Medical Dir Dr John G Lavin.
Licensure Intermediate care; Domiciliary care. *Beds* ICF 17; Domiciliary care 47. *Private Pay Patients* 100%.
Owner Nonprofit corp.
Admissions Requirements Minimum age 65; Medical examination.
Staff Physicians; RNs; LPNs; Nurses' aides; Physical therapists; Recreational therapists; Occupational therapists; Activities coordinators; Dietitians; Ophthalmologists.
Facilities Dining room; Activities room; Chapel; Crafts room; Laundry room; Barber/Beauty shop; Gift shop.
Activities Arts & crafts; Prayer groups; Movies; Shopping trips; Music; Physical education.

Rosewood Center
Rosewood Ln, Owings Mills, MD 21117-2999
(301) 363-0300, 356-5783 FAX
Admin Allan M Radinsky PhD. *Dir of Nursing* Mary Jane Peitersen MS CNA. *Medical Dir* Allan Wolins MD.
Licensure Intermediate care for mentally retarded. *Beds* ICF/MR 626. *Private Pay Patients* 0%. *Certified* Medicaid.

Owner Publicly owned.
Admissions Requirements Minimum age 16.
Staff Physicians 9 (ft), 4 (pt); RNs 33 (ft); LPNs 58 (ft); Physical therapists 4 (ft), 2 (pt); Recreational therapists 7 (ft); Occupational therapists 9 (ft), 4 (pt); Speech therapists; Activities coordinators 2 (ft); Dietitians 7 (ft), 2 (pt); Direct care workers 610 (ft), 56 (pt); Psychologists 15 (ft), 1 (pt).
Facilities Dining room; Physical therapy room; Laundry room; Library; Active treatment; Day programs.
Activities Movies; Shopping trips; Dances/Social/Cultural gatherings; Intergenerational programs.

Pikesville

Augsburg Lutheran Home of Maryland
6811 Campfield Rd, Pikesville, MD 21207
(301) 486-4573
Admin Norman O Payne.
Medical Dir Abdul Quereshi MD.
Licensure Comprehensive care; Domiciliary care. *Beds* Comprehensive care 136; Domiciliary care 5. *Certified* Medicaid.
Owner Nonprofit corp.
Admissions Requirements Minimum age 65; Medical examination.
Staff Physicians 1 (ft); RNs 2 (ft), 5 (pt); LPNs 6 (ft), 5 (pt); Nurses' aides 22 (ft), 15 (pt); Physical therapists 1 (ft); Reality therapists 1 (ft); Recreational therapists 1 (ft); Speech therapists 1 (ft); Activities coordinators 1 (ft); Dietitians 1 (ft); Ophthalmologists 1 (ft); Podiatrists 1 (ft); Dentists 2 (ft).
Affiliation Lutheran.
Facilities Dining room; Activities room; Chapel; Crafts room; Laundry room; Barber/Beauty shop; Library.
Activities Arts & crafts; Cards; Games; Reading groups; Prayer groups; Movies; Shopping trips; Dances/Social/Cultural gatherings.

Pikesville Nursing & Convalescent Center
7 Sudbrook Ln, Pikesville, MD 21208
(301) 486-8771
Admin Fred DiBartolo.
Medical Dir Dr Harold Bob.
Licensure Skilled care; Intermediate care. *Beds* 174. *Certified* Medicaid; Medicare.
Owner Proprietary corp.
Admissions Requirements Minimum age 14; Medical examination.
Staff RNs 6 (ft); LPNs 12 (ft), 5 (pt); Nurses' aides 60 (ft), 23 (pt); Physical therapists 1 (pt); Recreational therapists 1 (ft); Activities coordinators 1 (ft).
Affiliation Jewish.
Facilities Dining room; Physical therapy room; Activities room; Chapel; Barber/Beauty shop; Library; Four separate TV lounges (one on each unit).
Activities Arts & crafts; Prayer groups; Movies; Numerous volunteer groups provide entertainment.

Pocomoke City

Hartley Hall Inc
1006 Market St, Pocomoke City, MD 21851
(301) 957-2266
Admin Rebecca Sutton.
Medical Dir Paul Fleury MD.
Licensure Comprehensive care. *Beds* Comprehensive care 70. *Certified* Medicaid; Medicare.
Owner Nonprofit corp.
Admissions Requirements Minimum age 16.
Staff Physicians 3 (pt); RNs 1 (ft), 3 (pt); LPNs 2 (ft), 6 (pt); Nurses' aides 20 (ft), 7 (pt); Physical therapists 1 (pt); Speech therapists 1 (pt); Activities coordinators 1 (ft); Dietitians 1 (pt); Ophthalmologists 1 (pt); Dentists 1 (pt).

Facilities Dining room; Physical therapy room; Activities room; Chapel; Laundry room; Barber/Beauty shop.
Activities Arts & crafts; Cards; Games; Reading groups; Prayer groups; Movies; Shopping trips; Dances/Social/Cultural gatherings.

Potomac

Manor Care Potomac
10714 Potomac Tennis Ln, Potomac, MD 20854
(301) 299-2273
Admin Cherilyn Poulsen.
Medical Dir James Brodsky MD.
Licensure Comprehensive care. *Beds* Comprehensive care 106.
Owner Nonprofit corp.

Prince Frederick

Calvert County Nursing Center
85 Hospital Rd, Prince Frederick, MD 20678
(301) 535-2300
Admin Scotty Ann Lawyer. *Dir of Nursing* Priscilla Baker RN. *Medical Dir* Thomas Lusby MD.
Licensure Skilled care; Intermediate care. *Beds* Swing beds SNF/ICF 100. *Private Pay Patients* 30%. *Certified* Medicaid.
Owner Nonprofit corp.
Admissions Requirements Medical examination; Physician's request.
Staff RNs 5 (ft), 5 (pt); LPNs 6 (ft), 5 (pt); Nurses' aides 26 (ft), 31 (pt); Dietitians 1 (pt).
Facilities Dining room; Activities room; Chapel; Barber/Beauty shop.
Activities Arts & crafts; Cards; Games; Reading groups; Prayer groups; Movies; Dances/Social/Cultural gatherings.

Calvert House Corp
Rte 1 Box 1, Prince Frederick, MD 20678
(301) 535-0984
Admin Helen P Marsellas.
Medical Dir George J Weems MD.
Licensure Intermediate care. *Beds* ICF 50. *Certified* Medicaid.
Owner Proprietary corp.
Admissions Requirements Minimum age 14; Medical examination; Physician's request.
Staff Physicians 3 (pt); RNs 3 (ft); LPNs 2 (ft); Nurses' aides 22 (ft), 2 (pt); Physical therapists 1 (pt); Activities coordinators 1 (ft); Dietitians 1 (pt); Podiatrists 1 (pt); Dentists 1 (pt).
Facilities Dining room; Physical therapy room; Laundry room.
Activities Arts & crafts; Cards; Games; Prayer groups; Movies.

Princess Anne

Manokin Manor
Rte 3 Box 10C, Princess Anne, MD 21853
(301) 651-0011
Admin Edward Winship.
Medical Dir Charles Stegman MD.
Licensure Comprehensive care. *Beds* Comprehensive care 81.
Owner Proprietary corp.

Randallstown

Chapel Hill Convalescent Home
4511 Roboson Rd, Randallstown, MD 21133
(301) 922-2443, 655-9491 FAX
Admin Frances Gosnay. *Dir of Nursing* Jackie Hann. *Medical Dir* Dr Renzo Ricci.
Licensure Intermediate care; Alzheimer's care. *Beds* ICF 71. *Private Pay Patients* 28%. *Certified* Medicaid.
Owner Proprietary corp.

Admissions Requirements Medical
examination; Physician's request.
Staff Physicians 9 (pt); RNs 1 (ft), 3 (pt);
LPNs 4 (ft), 1 (pt); Nurses' aides 29 (ft), 5
(pt); Physical therapists 1 (pt); Occupational
therapists 1 (pt); Speech therapists 1 (pt);
Activities coordinators 1 (ft); Dietitians 1
(pt); Ophthalmologists 2 (pt); Podiatrists 2
(pt).
Facilities Dining room; Physical therapy
room; Activities room; Crafts room; Laundry
room; Barber/Beauty shop; Library.
Activities Arts & crafts; Cards; Games;
Reading groups; Prayer groups; Movies;
Dances/Social/Cultural gatherings; Bus trips;
Special luncheons; Pool parties.

Meridian Nursing Center—Randallstown
9109 Liberty Rd, Randallstown, MD 21133
(301) 655-7373, 655-0579 FAX
Admin Richard D Hanauer. *Dir of Nursing*
Carol C Whilden RN. *Medical Dir* H Gerald
Oster MD.
Licensure Skilled care; Intermediate care;
Alzheimer's care. *Beds* SNF 70; ICF 250.
Certified Medicaid; Medicare; VA.
Owner Proprietary corp (Meridian
Healthcare).
Admissions Requirements Medical
examination.
Staff Physicians 40 (pt); RNs 8 (ft), 4 (pt);
LPNs 14 (ft), 13 (pt); Nurses' aides 90 (ft),
10 (pt); Physical therapists 1 (pt);
Occupational therapists 1 (pt); Speech
therapists 1 (pt); Activities coordinators 1
(ft); Dietitians 1 (ft), 1 (pt);
Ophthalmologists 1 (pt); Podiatrists 1 (pt);
Audiologists 1 (pt).
Facilities Dining room; Physical therapy
room; Activities room; Crafts room; Barber/
Beauty shop; Library.
Activities Arts & crafts; Cards; Games;
Reading groups; Prayer groups; Movies;
Shopping trips; Dances/Social/Cultural
gatherings; Intergenerational programs; Pet
therapy.

Old Court Nursing Center
5412 Old Court Rd, Randallstown, MD 21133
(301) 922-3200
Admin Albert H Radtke.
Medical Dir Michael Perlman MD.
Licensure Skilled care; Intermediate care. *Beds*
144. *Certified* Medicaid; Medicare.
Owner Proprietary corp.

Reisterstown

Cherrywood Extended Care Centre
12020 Reisterstown Rd, Reisterstown, MD
21136
(301) 833-3974, 833-3976
Admin Patricia Rodenhauser.
Medical Dir Dr C E McWilliams.
Licensure Comprehensive care. *Beds*
Comprehensive care 125. *Certified*
Medicaid.
Owner Proprietary corp.
Admissions Requirements Minimum age 21;
Medical examination; Physician's request.
Staff Physicians 1 (ft), 1 (pt); RNs 4 (ft), 2
(pt); LPNs 6 (ft), 3 (pt); Nurses' aides 21
(ft), 8 (pt); Physical therapists 1 (pt);
Recreational therapists 1 (ft); Occupational
therapists 1 (pt); Speech therapists 1 (pt);
Dietitians 1 (pt); Ophthalmologists 1 (pt);
Podiatrists 1 (pt); Audiologists 1 (pt);
Dentists 1 (pt).

Ommret
314 Cherry Chapel Rd, Reisterstown, MD
21136
(301) 747-0689
Admin Kathy Gelzhiser.
Medical Dir David Moseman.
Licensure Intermediate care. *Beds* 34.
Certified Medicaid.
Owner Proprietary corp.

Admissions Requirements Minimum age 14;
Medical examination; Physician's request.
Staff Physicians 1 (pt); RNs 1 (ft), 1 (pt);
LPNs 3 (ft), 3 (pt); Nurses' aides 8 (ft);
Activities coordinators 1 (ft); Dietitians 1
(pt).
Facilities Dining room; Activities room.
Activities Arts & crafts; Games; Reading
groups; Prayer groups.

Towson Convalescent Home Inc
12020 Reisterstown Rd, Reisterstown, MD
21136
(301) 296-3191
Admin Lee S Rose.
Licensure Intermediate care. *Beds* 34.
Owner Proprietary corp.
Staff RNs 2 (ft), 1 (pt); LPNs 4 (pt); Nurses'
aides 24 (ft), 3 (pt); Activities coordinators 1
(pt); Dietitians 1 (pt).
Facilities Dining room; Activities room.
Activities Arts & crafts; Games; Prayer groups;
Movies.

Rockville

Collingswood Nursing Center
299 Hurley Ave, Rockville, MD 20850
(301) 762-8900
Admin Sarah Chamberlain.
Medical Dir Walter Goozh MD.
Licensure Skilled care; Intermediate care;
Alzheimer's care. *Beds* Comprehensive care
159. *Certified* Medicaid; Medicare.
Owner Proprietary corp (T J Rock).
Staff RNs 8 (ft), 6 (pt); LPNs 4 (ft), 2 (pt);
Nurses' aides 38 (ft), 11 (pt); Physical
therapists 1 (pt); Activities coordinators 1
(ft); Dietitians 1 (pt).
Facilities Dining room; Physical therapy
room; Activities room; Laundry room;
Barber/Beauty shop.
Activities Arts & crafts; Cards; Games;
Reading groups; Prayer groups; Movies;
Dances/Social/Cultural gatherings.

Hebrew Home of Greater Washington
6121 Montrose Rd, Rockville, MD 20852
(301) 881-0300
Admin Frank Balistrieri. *Dir of Nursing*
Judith Braun RN. *Medical Dir* Dinishbkai
Patel MD.
Licensure Skilled care; Intermediate care;
Adult day care; Alzheimer's care. *Beds*
Comprehensive care 550; Adult day care 30.
Certified Medicaid; Medicare.
Owner Nonprofit organization/foundation.
Admissions Requirements Minimum age 65
(long term); 40 (short stay); Medical
examination.
Staff Physicians 5 (ft); RNs 11 (ft), 9 (pt);
LPNs 21 (ft), 5 (pt); Nurses' aides 160 (ft),
30 (pt); Physical therapists 3 (ft), 1 (pt);
Recreational therapists 4 (ft), 6 (pt);
Occupational therapists 2 (ft); Speech
therapists 1 (ft); Activities coordinators 1
(ft), 1 (pt); Dietitians 2 (ft);
Ophthalmologists 10 (pt); Podiatrists 1 (pt);
Dentists 1 (pt); Physiatrists 1 (pt).
Languages Yiddish, Hebrew, Russian,
German, Hungarian, Polish.
Affiliation Jewish.
Facilities Dining room; Physical therapy
room; Activities room; Chapel; Crafts room;
Laundry room; Barber/Beauty shop; Library;
Soda shop; Occupatinal therapy room; Social
hall.
Activities Arts & crafts; Cards; Games;
Reading groups; Prayer groups; Movies;
Shopping trips; Dances/Social/Cultural
gatherings; Outside lunches; Day camp.

National Lutheran Home for the Aged
9701 Viers Dr, Rockville, MD 20850
(301) 424-9560
Admin Richard Reichard.
Medical Dir Thomas Dooley MD.

Licensure Skilled care; Intermediate care;
Independent living. *Beds* Swing beds SNF/
ICF 300; Independent living 75. *Certified*
Medicaid; Medicare.
Owner Nonprofit corp.
Affiliation Lutheran.

Potomac Valley Nursing Center
1235 Potomac Valley Rd, Rockville, MD
20850
(301) 762-0700
Admin Roxanne L Stigers RN LNHA. *Dir of
Nursing* Penny Brasher RN. *Medical Dir*
Henry Scruggs D.
Licensure Skilled care; Intermediate care;
Alzheimer's care. *Beds* 171. *Certified*
Medicaid; Medicare.
Owner Proprietary corp (T J Rock).
Admissions Requirements Minimum age 18.
Staff RNs 8 (ft), 20 (pt); LPNs 2 (ft), 4 (pt);
Nurses' aides 56 (ft), 18 (pt); Physical
therapists 2 (pt); Occupational therapists;
Speech therapists; Activities coordinators 2
(ft), 2 (pt); Dietitians; Ophthalmologists;
Podiatrists; 1 (pt) Chaplains; Supportive
staff; Laundry; Dietary.
Facilities Physical therapy room; Activities
room; Chapel; Crafts room; Laundry room;
Barber/Beauty shop; Library.
Activities Arts & crafts; Cards; Games;
Reading groups; Prayer groups; Movies;
Shopping trips; Dances/Social/Cultural
gatherings.

Rockville Nursing Home Inc
303 Adclare Rd, Rockville, MD 20850
(301) 279-9000
Admin Ray Cromwell.
Medical Dir Frauke Westphal MD.
Licensure Skilled care; Intermediate care. *Beds*
100. *Certified* Medicaid; Medicare.
Owner Nonprofit corp.

Shady Grove Adventist Nursing Center
9701 Medical Center Dr, Rockville, MD
20850
(301) 424-6400
Admin Richard Balogh. *Dir of Nursing* Ron
Bowlyow RN. *Medical Dir* Gary Langston
MD.
Licensure Skilled care; Domiciliary care. *Beds*
SNF 120; Domiciliary care 30. *Certified*
Medicaid; Medicare.
Owner Nonprofit corp.
Admissions Requirements Minimum age 18;
Physician's request.
Staff RNs; LPNs; Nurses' aides; Physical
therapists; Recreational therapists;
Occupational therapists; Speech therapists;
Activities coordinators; Dietitians;
Ophthalmologists; Podiatrists; Audiologists.
Affiliation Seventh-Day Adventist.
Facilities Dining room; Physical therapy
room; Activities room; Crafts room; Laundry
room; Barber/Beauty shop; Library.
Activities Arts & crafts; Cards; Games;
Reading groups; Prayer groups; Movies;
Shopping trips; Intergenerational programs;
Pet therapy.

Sabillasville

Victor Cullen Center
6000 Cullen Dr, Sabillasville, MD 21780
(301) 241-3131
Admin Steven M Haigh.
Medical Dir Robert Brull MD.
Licensure Intermediate care for mentally
retarded. *Beds* ICF/MR 97. *Certified*
Medicaid; Medicare.
Owner Publicly owned.
Admissions Requirements Minimum age 18.
Staff RNs; LPNs; Recreational therapists;
Occupational therapists; Speech therapists;
Dietitians.

Facilities Dining room; Activities room;
Chapel; Crafts room; Library.
Activities Arts & crafts; Movies; Shopping
trips; Dances/Social/Cultural gatherings.

Salisbury

Deer's Head Center
PO Box 2018, Emerson Ave, Salisbury, MD
21801
(301) 543-4000
Admin N David Outten. *Dir of Nursing*
Theresa Myer RN. *Medical Dir* Loenard
Maldve MD.
Licensure Comprehensive care; Chronic care.
Beds Comprehensive care 12; Chronic care
188. *Certified* Medicaid; Medicare.
Owner Publicly owned.
Admissions Requirements Physician's request.
Staff Physicians 1 (ft); RNs 3 (ft); LPNs 3 (ft);
Nurses' aides 2 (ft); Physical therapists 1 (ft);
Recreational therapists 1 (ft); Occupational
therapists 1 (ft); Speech therapists 1 (ft);
Activities coordinators 1 (ft); Dietitians 1
(ft); Ophthalmologists 1 (pt); Dentists 1 (pt).
Facilities Dining room; Physical therapy
room; Activities room; Chapel; Crafts room;
Laundry room; Barber/Beauty shop; Library.
Activities Arts & crafts; Cards; Games;
Reading groups; Prayer groups; Movies;
Shopping trips; Dances/Social/Cultural
gatherings.

Holly Center
PO Box 2358, Snow Hill Rd, Salisbury, MD
21801
(301) 546-2181
Admin Dr Frank Gibson.
Medical Dir Hilda Houlihan MD.
Licensure Intermediate care for mentally
retarded. *Beds* ICF/MR 250. *Certified*
Medicaid.
Owner Publicly owned.

River Walk Manor
105 Times Square, Salisbury, MD 21801
(301) 749-2474
Admin Robyn Drechsler.
Medical Dir Thomas C Hill Jr MD.
Licensure Intermediate care. *Beds* ICF 150.
Certified Medicaid.
Owner Proprietary corp.
Admissions Requirements Physician's request.
Staff RNs 4 (ft), 2 (pt); LPNs 13 (ft), 6 (pt);
Nurses' aides 47 (ft), 5 (pt).
Facilities Dining room; Physical therapy
room; Activities room; Crafts room; Laundry
room; Barber/Beauty shop; Dayroom on
each floor.
Activities Arts & crafts; Cards; Games;
Reading groups; Prayer groups; Movies;
Shopping trips; Dances/Social/Cultural
gatherings.

Salisbury Nursing Home
US 50 at Civic Ave, Salisbury, MD 21801
(301) 749-1466
Admin Janet Giordano.
Medical Dir Earl Beardsley MD.
Licensure Comprehensive care; Domiciliary
care. *Beds* Comprehensive care 350;
Domiciliary care 9. *Certified* Medicaid;
Medicare.
Owner Proprietary corp.
Admissions Requirements Minimum age 14;
Physician's request.
Staff Physicians 2 (pt); RNs 23 (pt); LPNs 12
(pt); Nurses' aides 80 (pt); Physical
therapists 1 (pt); Activities coordinators 1
(pt); Dietitians 1 (pt).
Facilities Dining room; Physical therapy
room; Activities room; Crafts room; Laundry
room; Barber/Beauty shop; Library.
Activities Arts & crafts; Cards; Games;
Reading groups; Prayer groups; Movies;
Shopping trips.

Wicomico Nursing Home
PO Box 2378, Booth St, Salisbury, MD 21801
(301) 742-8896
Admin Mary E Schwartz. *Dir of Nursing* Jane
Insley. *Medical Dir* Andrew Mithcell MD.
Licensure Skilled care. *Beds* SNF 82. *Certified*
Medicaid; Medicare.
Owner Nonprofit organization/foundation.
Admissions Requirements Minimum age 14;
Medical examination; Physician's request.
Staff RNs 4 (ft), 3 (pt); LPNs 5 (ft), 3 (pt);
Nurses' aides 22 (ft), 17 (pt); Physical
therapists 1 (pt); Activities coordinators 1
(ft), 1 (pt); Dietitians 1 (pt).
Facilities Dining room; Physical therapy
room; Activities room; Laundry room;
Barber/Beauty shop.
Activities Arts & crafts; Cards; Games;
Reading groups; Prayer groups; Movies;
Shopping trips; Dances/Social/Cultural
gatherings.

Sandy Spring

Friends Nursing Home Inc
17340 Quaker Ln, Sandy Spring, MD 20860
(301) 924-4900
Admin Nicholas Mason, Asst.
Medical Dir Donald Lewis MD.
Licensure Skilled care. *Beds* SNF 80. *Certified*
Medicaid; Medicare.
Owner Nonprofit corp.
Staff Physicians 1 (pt); RNs 2 (ft), 12 (pt);
LPNs 2 (ft); Nurses' aides 35 (ft), 10 (pt);
Physical therapists 1 (ft); Recreational
therapists 1 (ft), 2 (pt); Speech therapists 1
(pt); Dietitians 1 (pt); Podiatrists 1 (pt).
Affiliation Society of Friends.
Facilities Dining room; Physical therapy
room; Activities room; Crafts room; Laundry
room; Barber/Beauty shop; Library.
Activities Arts & crafts; Cards; Games;
Reading groups; Prayer groups; Movies;
Shopping trips.

Severna Park

Meridian Nursing Center—Severna Park
24 Truck House Rd, Severna Park, MD 21146
(301) 544-4220
Admin Richard Kincaid.
Medical Dir Thomas Walsh MD.
Licensure Comprehensive care. *Beds*
Comprehensive care 141.
Owner Proprietary corp (Meridian
Healthcare).

Silver Spring

Carriage Hill—Silver Spring
9101 2nd Ave, Silver Spring, MD 20910
(301) 588-5544
Admin Flora Luckett.
Medical Dir John Umhau MD.
Licensure Comprehensive care. *Beds*
Comprehensive care 107. *Certified*
Medicare.
Owner Proprietary corp.

Colonial Villa Nursing Home
12325 New Hampshire Ave, Silver Spring,
MD 20904
(301) 622-4600
Admin Steven H Haynal. *Dir of Nursing*
Marjorie Beheydt RN. *Medical Dir* Marian
Chung.
Licensure Skilled care; Intermediate care;
Retirement; Alzheimer's care. *Beds* 92.
Certified Medicaid; Medicare.
Owner Proprietary corp (Beverly Enterprises).
Admissions Requirements Minimum age 14;
Medical examination.

Staff RNs 15 (ft); LPNs 4 (ft); Nurses' aides
25 (ft); Recreational therapists 1 (ft);
Activities coordinators 1 (ft); Dietitians 1
(ft); Housekeeping; Dietary; Laundry;
General office.
Facilities Dining room; Physical therapy
room; Activities room; Crafts room; Laundry
room; Barber/Beauty shop; Living room;
Independent living area (12 beds).
Activities Arts & crafts; Cards; Games;
Reading groups; Prayer groups; Movies;
Shopping trips; Dances/Social/Cultural
gatherings.

Fairland Nursing & Rehabilitation Center
2101 Fairland Rd, Silver Spring, MD 20904
(301) 384-6161
Admin Carol Baker.
Medical Dir Thomas Ward MD.
Licensure Skilled care; Intermediate care. *Beds*
83. *Certified* Medicaid; Medicare.
Owner Proprietary corp.

Fox Chase Rehabilitation & Nursing Center
2015 East-West Hwy, Silver Spring, MD
20910
(301) 587-2400
Admin Barbara W Siegfried. *Dir of Nursing*
Patricia Stanley. *Medical Dir* Dr Goozh.
Licensure Skilled care. *Beds* SNF 75. *Private
Pay Patients* 55%. *Certified* Medicaid;
Medicare.
Owner Proprietary corp (Renaissance
Healthcare Corp).
Admissions Requirements Minimum age 14;
Medical examination; Physician's request.
Staff Physicians 1 (pt); RNs 2 (ft), 1 (pt);
LPNs 8 (ft), 1 (pt); Nurses' aides 25 (ft);
Physical therapists 1 (ft); Reality therapists 1
(pt); Recreational therapists 1 (ft);
Occupational therapists 1 (pt); Speech
therapists 1 (pt); Activities coordinators 1
(ft); Dietitians 1 (pt); Ophthalmologists 1
(pt); Podiatrists 1 (pt); Audiologists 1 (pt).
Facilities Dining room; Physical therapy
room; Activities room; Laundry room;
Barber/Beauty shop.
Activities Arts & crafts; Cards; Games;
Reading groups; Prayer groups; Movies;
Dances/Social/Cultural gatherings;
Intergenerational programs; Pet therapy.

Great Oaks Center
3100 Gracefield Rd, Silver Spring, MD 20904-
1899
(301) 595-5000
Admin Marvin Malcotti PhD.
Medical Dir Stefanio Kenessey MD.
Licensure Intermediate care for mentally
retarded. *Beds* ICF/MR 500. *Certified*
Medicaid.
Owner Publicly owned.
Staff Physicians 2 (ft), 1 (pt); RNs 33 (ft), 4
(pt); LPNs 8 (ft); Nurses' aides 297 (ft);
Physical therapists 5 (ft); Recreational
therapists 26 (ft); Occupational therapists 5
(ft); Speech therapists 6 (ft); Activities
coordinators 2 (ft); Dietitians 4 (ft);
Podiatrists 1 (ft).
Facilities Dining room; Activities room;
Laundry room.
Activities Arts & crafts; Cards; Games;
Movies; Shopping trips; Dances/Social/
Cultural gatherings.

Medlantic Manor at Layhill
2601 Bel Pre Rd, Silver Spring, MD 20906
(301) 598-6000
Admin Irvin Gershowitz.
Medical Dir Raymond Benack MD.
Licensure Skilled care; Intermediate care. *Beds*
100. *Certified* Medicaid.
Owner Proprietary corp.
Admissions Requirements Minimum age 18;
Medical examination.

Staff RNs 7 (ft), 6 (pt); LPNs 1 (ft), 2 (pt); Nurses' aides 43 (ft); Physical therapists 2 (pt); Recreational therapists 1 (pt); Speech therapists 1 (pt); Activities coordinators 1 (ft); Dietitians 1 (pt); Podiatrists 1 (pt).
Facilities Dining room; Activities room; Crafts room; Laundry room; Barber/Beauty shop.
Activities Arts & crafts; Cards; Games; Reading groups; Prayer groups; Movies; Shopping trips; Dances/Social/Cultural gatherings.

Meridian Nursing & Rehabilitation Center
3227 Bel Pre Rd, Silver Spring, MD 20906
(301) 871-2000, 871-2031 FAX
Admin Roger Larson. *Dir of Nursing* Sarahjean Thompson. *Medical Dir* Robert Fields.
Licensure Skilled care; Intermediate care. *Beds* SNF 34; ICF 106. *Private Pay Patients* 50%.
Owner Proprietary corp (Meridian Healthcare).
Staff RNs 8 (ft), 10 (pt); LPNs; Nurses' aides 20 (ft), 24 (pt); Activities coordinators 3 (ft); Dietitians 1 (ft).

Sylvan Manor Health Care Center
2700 Barker St, Silver Spring, MD 20910
(301) 565-0300
Admin Patricia K Queen.
Medical Dir Martin Shargel MD.
Licensure Comprehensive care. *Beds* Comprehensive care 138. *Certified* Medicaid.
Owner Proprietary corp.

Althea Woodland Nursing Home
1000 Daleview Dr, Silver Spring, MD 20901
(301) 434-2646
Admin Ron Carsell. *Dir of Nursing* R Robertson RN. *Medical Dir* B Fitzgerald MD.
Licensure Comprehensive care. *Beds* Comprehensive care 52.
Owner Proprietary corp.
Admissions Requirements Minimum age 18; Medical examination.
Staff Physicians 8 (pt); RNs 4 (ft), 2 (pt); LPNs 1 (ft); Nurses' aides 25 (ft), 1 (pt); Physical therapists 2 (pt); Recreational therapists 1 (ft); Occupational therapists 1 (pt); Speech therapists 1 (pt); Activities coordinators 1 (ft); Dietitians 1 (ft); Ophthalmologists 1 (pt); Podiatrists 1 (pt); Dentists 1 (pt).
Facilities Dining room; Activities room; Crafts room; Laundry room; Barber/Beauty shop.
Activities Arts & crafts; Cards; Games; Reading groups; Prayer groups; Movies; Shopping trips; Dances/Social/Cultural gatherings.

Snow Hill

Harrison House
430 W Market St, Snow Hill, MD 21863
(301) 632-3755
Admin E Thomas Sterling. *Dir of Nursing* Rebecca Wheaton. *Medical Dir* Dorothy C Holzworth RN.
Licensure Comprehensive care. *Beds* Comprehensive care 62. *Certified* Medicaid; Medicare.
Owner Proprietary corp.
Admissions Requirements Minimum age 14; Medical examination; Physician's request.
Staff Physicians 3 (pt); RNs 3 (pt); LPNs 5 (ft), 4 (pt); Nurses' aides 24 (ft), 11 (pt); Physical therapists 1 (pt); Speech therapists 1 (pt); Activities coordinators 1 (ft); Dietitians 1 (pt); Ophthalmologists 1 (pt).
Facilities Dining room; Physical therapy room; Activities room; Laundry room; Barber/Beauty shop.

Activities Arts & crafts; Cards; Games; Reading groups; Prayer groups; Movies; Shopping trips.

Sykesville

Fairhaven Nursing Home
7200 3rd Ave, Sykesville, MD 21784
(301) 795-8800
Admin James Melhorn.
Medical Dir Alva Baker MD.
Licensure Comprehensive care. *Beds* Comprehensive care 104.
Owner Nonprofit corp.

Sykesville Eldercare Center
7309 2nd Ave, Sykesville, MD 21784
(301) 795-1100, 795-0029 FAX
Admin Robert L Killett NHA. *Dir of Nursing* Mary E Killett RNC DN. *Medical Dir* Jose' Chapulle MD.
Licensure Skilled care; Intermediate care. *Beds* SNF 52; ICF 87. *Private Pay Patients* 30%. *Certified* Medicaid; Medicare.
Owner Proprietary corp.
Admissions Requirements Minimum age 21; Medical examination.
Staff RNs 6 (ft), 5 (pt); LPNs 10 (ft), 5 (pt); Nurses' aides 41 (ft), 5 (pt); Activities coordinators 2 (ft), 1 (pt).
Facilities Dining room; Physical therapy room; Activities room; Crafts room; Laundry room; Barber/Beauty shop; Private and semi-private rooms and mini-suites.
Activities Arts & crafts; Cards; Games; Reading groups; Prayer groups; Movies; Shopping trips; Pet therapy.

Takoma Park

Heritage Healthcare Center
7525 Carroll Ave, Takoma Park, MD 20012
(301) 270-4200
Admin Patricia Doherty. *Dir of Nursing* Kitty Brown RN. *Medical Dir* Myron Lenkin MD.
Licensure Comprehensive care. *Beds* Comprehensive care 102. *Certified* Medicaid; Medicare.
Owner Proprietary corp (Beverly Enterprises).
Admissions Requirements Medical examination; Physician's request.
Staff RNs 6 (ft), 9 (pt); LPNs 1 (ft), 6 (pt); Nurses' aides 29 (ft), 24 (pt); Physical therapists 1 (ft), 1 (pt); Recreational therapists 1 (ft), 1 (pt); Occupational therapists 1 (pt); Speech therapists 1 (pt); Activities coordinators 1 (ft); Dietitians 1 (pt).
Facilities Dining room; Physical therapy room; Activities room; Crafts room; Laundry room; Barber/Beauty shop; Library.
Activities Arts & crafts; Cards; Games; Reading groups; Prayer groups; Movies; Shopping trips; Dances/Social/Cultural gatherings; Intergenerational activities; Pets on wheels.

Towson

Cardinal Shehan Center
Dulaney Valley Rd, Towson, MD 21204
(301) 252-4500
Admin Sr Louis Mary Battle RSM. *Dir of Nursing* Joan Conroy RN. *Medical Dir* Eddie Nakhuda MD.
Licensure Skilled care; Retirement; Alzheimer's care. *Beds* SNF 438; Retirement 200. *Private Pay Patients* 50%. *Certified* Medicaid; Medicare.
Owner Nonprofit organization/foundation.
Admissions Requirements Minimum age 65; Medical examination; Physician's request.
Staff Physicians 2 (pt); RNs 25 (ft), 60 (pt); LPNs 6 (ft), 7 (pt); Nurses' aides 181 (ft), 30 (pt); Physical therapists 1 (ft); Occupational

therapists 2 (pt); Speech therapists 1 (pt); Activities coordinators 10 (ft), 6 (pt); Dietitians 4 (ft).
Affiliation Roman Catholic.
Facilities Dining room; Physical therapy room; Activities room; Chapel; Crafts room; Laundry room; Barber/Beauty shop; Library; Auditorium; Happy Hollow room.
Activities Arts & crafts; Cards; Games; Reading groups; Prayer groups; Movies; Shopping trips; Dances/Social/Cultural gatherings; Intergenerational programs; Pet therapy.

Edenwald
800 Southerly Rd, Towson, MD 21204
(301) 339-6000, 583-8786 FAX
Admin Vlasta Stadler LNHA; Jeanne Miecznikoski, Assoc Dir. *Dir of Nursing* Cecilia Frank RN. *Medical Dir* Marcellino Albuerne MD, Principal Physician.
Licensure Intermediate care; Domiciliary care; Retirement. *Beds* ICF 67; Domiciliary care 48; Retirement 300. *Private Pay Patients* 100%.
Owner Nonprofit corp.
Admissions Requirements Minimum age 62; Medical examination.
Staff RNs 3 (ft), 2 (pt); LPNs 4 (ft), 3 (pt); Nurses' aides 25 (ft), 5 (pt); Physical therapists 2 (pt); Occupational therapists 1 (pt); Speech therapists 1 (pt); Activities coordinators 1 (ft), 2 (pt); Dietitians; Podiatrists 1 (pt); Audiologists 1 (pt).
Languages German.
Facilities Dining room; Physical therapy room; Activities room; Crafts room; Laundry room; Barber/Beauty shop; Library; Bank; Store; Bus; Van; Cafeteria.
Activities Arts & crafts; Cards; Games; Reading groups; Prayer groups; Movies; Shopping trips; Dances/Social/Cultural gatherings; Intergenerational programs; Pet therapy.

Holly Hill Manor Inc
531 Stevenson Ln, Towson, MD 21204
(301) 823-5310
Admin M L Cursey Jr. *Dir of Nursing* Theresa Walter RN.
Licensure Intermediate care. *Beds* ICF 55. *Certified* Medicaid.
Owner Proprietary corp.
Admissions Requirements Medical examination.
Staff RNs 4 (ft), 2 (pt); LPNs 2 (ft), 2 (pt); Nurses' aides 17 (ft), 10 (pt); Activities coordinators 1 (ft).
Facilities Dining room; Activities room; Barber/Beauty shop.
Activities Arts & crafts; Games; Reading groups; Prayer groups; Movies; Dances/Social/Cultural gatherings; Intergenerational programs; Pet therapy.

Manor Care of Ruxton
7001 Charles St, Towson, MD 21204
(301) 821-9600
Admin Robert Harris.
Medical Dir Walter T Kees MD.
Licensure Comprehensive care. *Beds* Comprehensive care 212. *Certified* Medicaid; Medicare.
Owner Proprietary corp (Manor Care Inc).
Staff Physicians; RNs; LPNs; Nurses' aides; Physical therapists 1 (ft); Reality therapists 3 (ft); Recreational therapists 3 (ft); Occupational therapists 2 (pt); Speech therapists 1 (ft); Activities coordinators 3 (ft); Dietitians 2 (ft); Podiatrists 1 (ft); Audiologists 1 (ft); Dentists 1 (ft).
Facilities Dining room; Physical therapy room; Activities room; Crafts room; Laundry room; Barber/Beauty shop; Library.
Activities Arts & crafts; Cards; Games; Reading groups; Prayer groups; Movies; Shopping trips; Dances/Social/Cultural gatherings.

Manor Care of Towson
509 E Joppa Rd, Towson, MD 21204
(301) 828-9494
Admin Norma Walters.
Medical Dir Walter T Kees MD.
Licensure Comprehensive care. *Beds*
Comprehensive care 127. *Certified*
Medicaid; Medicare.
Owner Proprietary corp (Manor Care Inc).
Admissions Requirements Medical
examination.
Staff Physicians 1 (pt); RNs 7 (ft), 10 (pt);
LPNs 3 (ft), 2 (pt); Nurses' aides 28 (ft), 23
(pt); Recreational therapists 1 (ft), 1 (pt);
Audiologists 8 (ft), 8 (pt).
Facilities Dining room; Physical therapy
room; Activities room; Crafts room; Laundry
room; Barber/Beauty shop.
Activities Arts & crafts; Cards; Games;
Reading groups; Prayer groups; Movies;
Shopping trips; Dances/Social/Cultural
gatherings.

Meridian Nursing Center—Multi-Medical
7700 York Rd, Towson, MD 21204
(301) 821-5500
Admin Ron Rothstein. *Dir of Nursing* Bonnie
Brill. *Medical Dir* Henry Babbitt MD.
Licensure Comprehensive care; Domiciliary
care. *Beds* Comprehensive care 113;
Domiciliary care 7. *Certified* Medicare.
Owner Proprietary corp (Meridian
Healthcare).
Admissions Requirements Minimum age 15.
Staff RNs 7 (ft), 2 (pt); LPNs 9 (ft), 4 (pt);
Nurses' aides 75 (ft), 20 (pt); Physical
therapists 2 (ft); Recreational therapists 3
(ft); Occupational therapists 1 (ft); Speech
therapists 1 (pt); Dietitians 1 (ft).
Facilities Dining room; Physical therapy
room; Activities room; Laundry room;
Barber/Beauty shop.
Activities Arts & crafts; Cards; Games;
Movies; Shopping trips; Dances/Social/
Cultural gatherings.

**Dulaney Towson Nursing & Convalescent
Center**
111 West Rd, Towson, MD 21204
(301) 828-6500
Admin William Boyer Jr.
Medical Dir Charles O'Donnell MD.
Licensure Skilled care; Intermediate care. *Beds*
151. *Certified* Medicaid; Medicare.
Owner Proprietary corp (Health Care &
Retirement Corp).

Westernport

Moran Manor
200 Clayton Ave, Westernport, MD 21562
(301) 359-3006, 359-9388 FAX
Admin Monica L Mason LNHA; Dona
Cantafio, Asst. *Dir of Nursing* Harriet
Moore. *Medical Dir* Jesus H Tan MD.

Licensure Intermediate care; Adult medical
day care. *Beds* ICF 130; Adult medical day
care 30. *Certified* Medicaid.
Owner Proprietary corp (Magnolia
Management Inc).
Admissions Requirements Medical
examination.
Staff Physicians 2 (pt); RNs 5 (ft), 3 (pt);
LPNs 8 (ft), 1 (pt); Nurses' aides 29 (ft), 34
(pt); Physical therapists 2 (pt); Occupational
therapists 1 (pt); Speech therapists 1 (pt);
Activities coordinators 2 (pt); Dietitians 2
(pt); Podiatrists 1 (pt); Audiologists 1 (pt).
Facilities Dining room; Physical therapy
room; Activities room; Crafts room; Laundry
room; Barber/Beauty shop; TV rooms;
Lounges; Dayrooms.
Activities Arts & crafts; Cards; Games;
Reading groups; Prayer groups; Movies;
Shopping trips; Dances/Social/Cultural
gatherings; Intergenerational programs; Pet
therapy.

Westminster

Carroll Lutheran Nursing Home
200 St Luke's Cir, Westminster, MD 21157
(301) 876-7925
Admin Martha Coleman.
Medical Dir John Lehigh MD.
Licensure Comprehensive care. *Beds*
Comprehensive care 99.
Owner Nonprofit corp.

**Westminster Villa Nursing & Convalescent
Center**
1234 Washington Rd, Westminster, MD
21157
(301) 848-0700
Admin Lorrie Custodio.
Medical Dir Daniel Welliver MD.
Licensure Skilled care; Intermediate care. *Beds*
170. *Certified* Medicaid; Medicare.
Owner Proprietary corp (Beverly Enterprises).

Wheaton

Manor Care of Wheaton
11901 Georgia Ave, Wheaton, MD 20902
(301) 942-2500
Admin Bonny Young. *Dir of Nursing* Elaine
Fairweather RN. *Medical Dir* Walter Goozh
MD.
Licensure Skilled care. *Beds* SNF 102.
Certified Medicare.
Owner Proprietary corp (Manor Care Inc).
Admissions Requirements Minimum age 16;
Medical examination.
Facilities Dining room; Physical therapy
room; Activities room; Laundry room;
Barber/Beauty shop; Library; Living room;
Lobby.
Activities Arts & crafts; Cards; Games;
Reading groups; Prayer groups; Movies;
Shopping trips; Dances/Social/Cultural
gatherings; Resident council; Monthly
newsletter.

Randolph Hills Nursing Home
4011 Randolph Rd, Wheaton, MD 20902
(301) 933-2500
Admin Harvey R Wertlieb.
Medical Dir Dr Ayrumin; Dr Shargel.
Licensure Skilled care; Intermediate care. *Beds*
95. *Certified* Medicaid; Medicare.
Owner Proprietary corp.
Admissions Requirements Minimum age 14;
Medical examination; Physician's request.
Staff RNs 13 (ft); LPNs 2 (ft); Nurses' aides
33 (ft); Physical therapists 1 (ft);
Recreational therapists 1 (ft); Occupational
therapists 1 (pt); Speech therapists 1 (pt);
Activities coordinators 2 (ft); Dietitians 1
(pt); Ophthalmologists 1 (pt); Podiatrists 1
(pt); Dentists 1 (pt).
Facilities Dining room; Physical therapy
room; Activities room; Crafts room; Laundry
room; Barber/Beauty shop; Library.
Activities Arts & crafts; Cards; Games;
Reading groups; Prayer groups; Movies;
Shopping trips; Dances/Social/Cultural
gatherings.

University Convalescent & Nursing Home Inc
901 Arcola Ave, Wheaton, MD 20902
(301) 649-2400
Admin Marvin Rabovsky.
Medical Dir Myron L Lenkin MD.
Licensure Comprehensive care. *Beds*
Comprehensive care 159. *Certified*
Medicaid; Medicare.
Owner Proprietary corp.
Admissions Requirements Minimum age 16;
Medical examination.
Staff RNs 25 (ft), 8 (pt); LPNs 10 (ft), 2 (pt);
Nurses' aides 65 (ft), 5 (pt); Physical
therapists 1 (ft).
Facilities Dining room; Physical therapy
room; Activities room; Crafts room; Barber/
Beauty shop.
Activities Arts & crafts; Cards; Games;
Reading groups; Prayer groups; Movies;
Dances/Social/Cultural gatherings; Resident
council.

Williamsport

Williamsport Nursing Home
154 N Artizan St, Williamsport, MD 21795
(301) 223-7971
Admin Patricia Kirstein.
Medical Dir John Melnick.
Licensure Intermediate care. *Beds* ICF 97.
Certified Medicaid.
Owner Nonprofit corp.
Staff Physicians 2 (pt); RNs 6 (ft), 3 (pt);
LPNs 6 (ft), 3 (pt); Nurses' aides 60 (ft), 8
(pt); Physical therapists 1 (pt); Speech
therapists 1 (pt); Activities coordinators 2
(ft); Dietitians 1 (pt); Podiatrists 1 (pt).
Facilities Dining room; Activities room;
Crafts room; Laundry room; Barber/Beauty
shop.
Activities Arts & crafts; Cards; Games;
Movies; Wheelchair accessible van.

MASSACHUSETTS

Abington

Mildred Alford Nursing Home
81 Birch St, Abington, MA 02351
(617) 878-4660
Admin Norman Messier.
Licensure Skilled care; Intermediate care. *Beds*
SNF 47; ICF 52. *Certified* Medicaid.

Colony House Healthcare Nursing Home
277 Washington St, Abington, MA 02351
(617) 871-0200
Admin Michael T Barry. *Dir of Nursing* Claire
Kelly RN. *Medical Dir* Edward Welch MD.
Licensure Skilled care; Intermediate care. *Beds*
SNF 36; ICF 66. *Certified* Medicaid.
Owner Proprietary corp (First Healthcare
Corp).
Admissions Requirements Medical
examination.
Staff RNs 2 (ft), 15 (pt); LPNs 1 (ft), 8 (pt);
Nurses' aides 7 (ft), 40 (pt); Physical
therapists 1 (pt); Occupational therapists 1
(pt); Speech therapists 1 (pt); Activities
coordinators 1 (ft); Dietitians 1 (pt);
Ophthalmologists 1 (pt).
Facilities Dining room; Activities room;
Crafts room; Laundry room; Barber/Beauty
shop.
Activities Arts & crafts; Cards; Games;
Reading groups; Prayer groups; Movies;
Shopping trips; Dances/Social/Cultural
gatherings; Reality orientation program;
Creative reflections grooming groups;
Restorative feeding program.

Acton

**Suburban Manor Convalescent & Nursing
Home**
1 Great Rd, Acton, MA 01720
(617) 263-9101
Admin Vincent M Polo.
Licensure Skilled care; Intermediate care. *Beds*
SNF 81; ICF 41. *Certified* Medicaid;
Medicare.

Acushnet

Acushnet Nursing Home
127 S Main St, Acushnet, MA 02740
(617) 995-1857
Admin Mary G Loughlin.
Medical Dir Lorraine Travers LPN.
Licensure Intermediate care. *Beds* ICF 28.
Certified Medicaid.
Owner Proprietary corp.
Admissions Requirements Minimum age 30;
Physician's request.
Staff RNs 1 (pt); LPNs 6 (pt); Nurses' aides;
Physical therapists 1 (pt); Speech therapists
1 (pt); Activities coordinators 1 (pt);
Dietitians 1 (pt); Ophthalmologists 1 (pt);
Dentists 1 (pt).
Languages Portuguese.

Facilities Dining room; Activities room;
Crafts room; Laundry room.
Activities Arts & crafts; Games; Reading
groups; Prayer groups; Movies; Dances/
Social/Cultural gatherings.

Adams

Adams Rest Home Inc
17 Commercial St, Adams, MA 01220
(413) 743-1132
Admin Lucy C Bassi.
Licensure Rest home. *Beds* Rest home 45.

Agawam

Heritage Hall East
464 Main St, Agawam, MA 01001
(413) 786-8000
Admin Earl Woomer Jr.
Licensure Skilled care; Functional
rehabilitative and treatment unit; Sub-acute
unit. *Beds* SNF 123; 43. *Private Pay Patients*
20%. *Certified* Medicaid; Medicare.
Owner Proprietary corp (Genesis Health
Ventures).
Staff Physicians; RNs; LPNs; Nurses' aides;
Physical therapists; Recreational therapists;
Occupational therapists; Speech therapists;
Activities coordinators; Dietitians;
Ophthalmologists; Podiatrists; Audiologists;
Social workers.
Facilities Dining room; Physical therapy
room; Activities room; Chapel; Crafts room;
Laundry room; Barber/Beauty shop;
Daycare; Occupational therapy room; Speech
therapy room.
Activities Arts & crafts; Cards; Games;
Reading groups; Prayer groups; Movies;
Shopping trips; Dances/Social/Cultural
gatherings; Intergenerational programs; Pet
therapy.

Heritage Hall North Nursing Home
55 Cooper St, Agawam, MA 01001
(413) 786-8000
Admin Regina T Bossig RN. *Dir of Nursing*
Linda Wells RN. *Medical Dir* Vincent
Barnaba MD.
Licensure Intermediate care; Rest home. *Beds*
ICF 62; Rest home 62. *Certified* Medicaid.
Owner Proprietary corp (Genesis Health
Ventures).
Admissions Requirements Minimum age 21;
Medical examination.
Staff Physicians; RNs; LPNs; Nurses' aides;
Physical therapists; Recreational therapists;
Occupational therapists; Speech therapists;
Activities coordinators; Dietitians;
Ophthalmologists; Podiatrists; Audiologists.
Languages Italian, Polish, French.
Facilities Dining room; Activities room;
Crafts room; Laundry room; Barber/Beauty
shop; Library.

Activities Arts & crafts; Cards; Games;
Reading groups; Prayer groups; Movies;
Shopping trips; Dances/Social/Cultural
gatherings; Intergenerational programs; Pet
therapy.

Heritage Hall South Nursing Home
PO Box 347, 100 Harvey Johnson Dr,
Agawam, MA 01001
(413) 786-8000
Admin Darrell A Carlson. *Dir of Nursing*
Linda Alston. *Medical Dir* Vincent Barnaba.
Licensure Skilled care; Intermediate care;
Retirement. *Beds* SNF 82; ICF 40;
Retirement 60. *Private Pay Patients* 30%.
Certified Medicaid; Medicare.
Owner Proprietary corp (Genesis Health
Ventures).
Admissions Requirements Minimum age 18.
Staff RNs; LPNs; Nurses' aides; Physical
therapists; Reality therapists; Recreational
therapists; Occupational therapists; Speech
therapists; Activities coordinators; Dietitians;
Podiatrists.
Facilities Dining room; Physical therapy
room; Activities room; Chapel; Crafts room;
Laundry room; Barber/Beauty shop; Library.
Activities Arts & crafts; Cards; Games;
Reading groups; Movies; Shopping trips;
Dances/Social/Cultural gatherings;
Intergenerational programs; Pet therapy;
Latch key intergenerational program.

Heritage Hall West
61 Cooper St, Agawam, MA 01001
(413) 786-8000
Admin Kathleen Roop. *Dir of Nursing* Kareen
Delskey. *Medical Dir* Vincent Barnaba.
Licensure Skilled care. *Beds* SNF 164. *Private
Pay Patients* 20%. *Certified* Medicaid;
Medicare.
Owner Proprietary corp (Genesis Health
Ventures).
Admissions Requirements Minimum age 21.
Staff Physicians 1 (pt); RNs 9 (ft), 10 (pt);
LPNs 6 (ft), 6 (pt); Nurses' aides 57 (ft), 21
(pt); Physical therapists 1 (pt); Occupational
therapists 1 (pt); Speech therapists 1 (pt);
Activities coordinators 2 (ft); Dietitians 1
(pt); Podiatrists 1 (pt); Audiologists 1 (pt);
Staff development RNs 1 (pt);
Administrative RNs 3 (ft).
Languages French, Polish, Russian, Spanish.
Facilities Dining room; Physical therapy
room; Activities room; Chapel; Barber/
Beauty shop; Solariums; IV unit.
Activities Arts & crafts; Games; Reading
groups; Prayer groups; Movies;
Intergenerational programs; Pet therapy.

Amesbury

Hillside Rest Home
29 Hillside Ave, Amesbury, MA 01913
(617) 388-1010
Admin William E Ring.
Licensure Rest home. *Beds* Rest home 28.
Owner Privately owned.

Maplewood Manor Nursing Home
6 Morrill Pl, Amesbury, MA 01913
(617) 388-3500
Admin Robert M Shaughnessy. *Dir of Nursing*
Nancy Piecewicz RN. *Medical Dir* Barrie
Paster MD.
Licensure Skilled care; Intermediate care;
Alzheimer's care. *Beds* SNF 60; ICF 60.
Certified Medicaid; Medicare.
Owner Proprietary corp.
Admissions Requirements Minimum age 21.
Staff Physicians 2 (pt); RNs 6 (ft), 14 (pt);
LPNs 8 (ft), 7 (pt); Nurses' aides 34 (ft), 27
(pt); Physical therapists 1 (pt); Recreational
therapists 1 (ft), 5 (pt); Occupational
therapists 1 (pt); Speech therapists 1 (pt);
Activities coordinators 1 (ft); Dietitians 1
(pt).
Facilities Dining room; Physical therapy
room; Activities room; Chapel; Crafts room;
Laundry room; Barber/Beauty shop; TV
rooms.
Activities Arts & crafts; Cards; Games;
Reading groups; Prayer groups; Movies;
Shopping trips; Dances/Social/Cultural
gatherings; Exercise; Restaurant outings;
Sight-seeing; Musical entertainment.

**Merrimack Valley Nursing & Rehabilitation
Center**
22 Maple St, Amesbury, MA 01913
(508) 388-4682, 388-6979 FAX
Admin Monique M Dosogne. *Dir of Nursing*
Sandra Axelrod. *Medical Dir* Dr Mark Bean.
Licensure Skilled care; Intermediate care. *Beds*
SNF 30; ICF 94. *Private Pay Patients* 17%.
Certified Medicaid; Medicare.
Owner Proprietary corp (Mariner Health Care
Inc).
Staff RNs; LPNs; Nurses' aides; Physical
therapists 1 (pt); Speech therapists 1 (pt);
Activities coordinators 1 (ft); Dietitians 1
(pt); Podiatrists 1 (pt).
Facilities Dining room; Physical therapy
room; Laundry room; Barber/Beauty shop;
Resident lounges; Activity areas.
Activities Arts & crafts; Cards; Games;
Reading groups; Prayer groups; Movies;
Shopping trips; Dances/Social/Cultural
gatherings; Intergenerational programs; Pet
therapy.

Amherst

Amherst Nursing Home Inc
150 University Dr, Amherst, MA 01002
(413) 256-8185
Admin Sharon E Meyers RN. *Dir of Nursing*
Bettie S Kravetz. *Medical Dir* Dr Daniel
Clapp.
Licensure Skilled care; Intermediate care. *Beds*
SNF 41; ICF 40. *Private Pay Patients* 30%.
Certified Medicaid.
Owner Proprietary corp.
Admissions Requirements Minimum age 21.
Staff RNs; LPNs; Nurses' aides; Recreational
therapists; Activities coordinators.
Languages Spanish, French, Chinese, German.
Facilities Dining room; Physical therapy
room; Activities room; Laundry room;
Barber/Beauty shop.
Activities Arts & crafts; Cards; Games;
Reading groups; Prayer groups; Movies;
Shopping trips; Dances/Social/Cultural
gatherings; Intergenerational programs; Pet
therapy.

Andover

Academy Manor of Andover
89 Morton St, Andover, MA 01810
(508) 475-0944
Admin David Solomont. *Dir of Nursing*
Edwina Arsenault RN. *Medical Dir* Edward
Braddus MD.

Licensure Skilled care; Intermediate care. *Beds*
SNF; ICF 85. *Certified* Medicaid;
Medicare.
Owner Proprietary corp.
Admissions Requirements Medical
examination; Physician's request.
Staff RNs 11 (ft); LPNs 12 (ft), 8 (pt); Nurses'
aides 55 (ft), 3 (pt); Physical therapists
(consultants); Recreational therapists 1 (ft), 2
(pt); Occupational therapists 2 (ft); Speech
therapists 1 (pt); Activities coordinators 1
(ft); Dietitians 1 (pt); Podiatrists 1 (pt);
Music therapists 1 (ft).
Languages Spanish; Hebrew.
Facilities Dining room; Physical therapy
room; Laundry room; Barber/Beauty shop;
Library; Activities/crafts room.
Activities Arts & crafts; Cards; Games;
Reading groups; Prayer groups; Movies;
Shopping trips; Dances/Social/Cultural
gatherings; Intergenerational programs.

Randolph House Nursing Home
102 Burnham Rd, Andover, MA 01810
(617) 475-2092
Admin Frank Andreoli.
Licensure Intermediate care. *Beds* ICF 16.
Certified Medicaid.
Owner Proprietary corp.

Arlington

**Park Avenue Nursing, Convalescent &
Retirement Home**
146 Park Ave, Arlington, MA 02174
(617) 648-9530
Admin Joseph J Alessandroni.
Licensure Skilled care; Intermediate care. *Beds*
SNF 40; ICF 40. *Certified* Medicaid.
Owner Proprietary corp.

Wellington Manor Nursing Home
8 Wellington St, Arlington, MA 02174
(617) 648-7300
Admin Mary A Carroll.
Licensure Intermediate care. *Beds* ICF 42.
Certified Medicaid.
Owner Proprietary corp.

Ashburnham

Ashburnham Rest Home Inc
97 Platts Rd, Ashburnham, MA 01466
(617) 827-6851
Admin Geraldine McQuoid.
Licensure Rest home. *Beds* Rest home 17.

Collins Rest Home Inc
10 Lawrence St, Ashburnham, MA 01430
(508) 827-4351
Admin Louise A Gilligan.
Licensure Level II CSF. *Beds* Level II CSF
20. *Certified* Medicaid.
Owner Proprietary corp.
Admissions Requirements Minimum age 50;
Medical examination; Physician's request.
Staff RNs; LPNs; Nurses' aides; Activities
coordinators; Dietitians (consultant); Social
workers.
Facilities Dining room; Activities room;
Laundry room.
Activities Arts & crafts; Games; Prayer groups;
Shopping trips; Pet therapy.

Ashland

Ashland Manor Nursing Home
25 Central St, Ashland, MA 01721
(617) 881-1044
Admin Sabina Milman.
Licensure Intermediate care. *Beds* ICF 29.
Certified Medicaid.
Owner Privately owned.

Mill Pond Rest Home
84 Myrtle St, Ashland, MA 01721
(617) 881-1360

Admin Thomas E Woods.
Licensure Rest home. *Beds* Rest home 27.
Owner Proprietary corp.
Admissions Requirements Minimum age 50;
Medical examination.
Staff LPNs 1 (ft); Nurses' aides 1 (ft);
Activities coordinators 1 (pt); Dietitians 1
(pt).
Facilities Dining room; Activities room;
Laundry room; Barber/Beauty shop.
Activities Arts & crafts; Cards; Games; Prayer
groups; Movies; Shopping trips; Dances/
Social/Cultural gatherings.

Athol

Quabbin Valley Convalescent Center Inc
821 Daniel Shays Hwy, Athol, MA 01331
(617) 249-3717
Admin Eleanor M Giaquinto.
Licensure Skilled care; Intermediate care. *Beds*
SNF 41; ICF 89. *Certified* Medicaid.
Owner Proprietary corp.

Tully Brook Rest Home
232 N Orange Rd, Athol, MA 01331
(617) 249-4482
Admin Helen M Bisbee.
Licensure Rest home. *Beds* Rest home 9.
Owner Privately owned.

Attleboro

Bristol Nursing Home
1000 Oak Hill Ave, Attleboro, MA 02703
(617) 222-6410
Admin Darrold Endres. *Dir of Nursing* Denise
Laboissonniere RN. *Medical Dir* Harry
Mayer MD.
Licensure Intermediate care. *Beds* ICF 68.
Private Pay Patients 12%. *Certified*
Medicaid.
Owner Privately owned.
Admissions Requirements Medical
examination.
Staff Physicians; RNs; LPNs; Nurses' aides;
Physical therapists; Recreational therapists;
Occupational therapists; Speech therapists;
Activities coordinators; Dietitians;
Ophthalmologists.
Facilities Dining room; Activities room;
Chapel; Crafts room; Laundry room; Barber/
Beauty shop; Library.
Activities Arts & crafts; Cards; Games;
Reading groups; Prayer groups; Movies;
Shopping trips; Dances/Social/Cultural
gatherings.

Pleasant Manor Nursing Home
193-195 Pleasant St, Attleboro, MA 02703
(617) 222-4950
Admin Joyce Pinto.
Medical Dir J Allen Bryer MD.
Licensure Skilled care; Intermediate care. *Beds*
SNF 82; ICF 51. *Certified* Medicaid;
Medicare.
Owner Proprietary corp (Beverly Enterprises).
Admissions Requirements Minimum age 21;
Medical examination; Physician's request.
Staff Physicians 1 (pt); RNs 8 (ft), 4 (pt);
LPNs 4 (ft), 9 (pt); Nurses' aides 25 (ft), 20
(pt); Physical therapists 2 (pt); Reality
therapists 1 (ft); Occupational therapists 1
(pt); Speech therapists 1 (pt); Activities
coordinators 2 (ft); Dietitians 1 (pt);
Ophthalmologists 1 (pt); Podiatrists 1 (pt).
Facilities Dining room; Physical therapy
room; Activities room; Chapel; Crafts room;
Laundry room; Barber/Beauty shop.
Activities Arts & crafts; Cards; Games;
Reading groups; Prayer groups; Movies;
Shopping trips; Dances/Social/Cultural
gatherings.

Pleasant Street Rest Home Inc
144 Pleasant St, Attleboro, MA 02703
(617) 222-1532

Admin Juliana M Morin.
Medical Dir Jane Chadwick.
Licensure Rest home. *Beds* Rest home 60.
Certified Medicaid.
Owner Proprietary corp.
Admissions Requirements Medical
examination; Physician's request.
Staff Physicians 1 (pt); RNs 1 (pt); LPNs 1
(ft); Nurses' aides 6 (ft); Recreational
therapists 1 (ft); Activities coordinators 1
(ft); Dietitians 1 (pt); Ophthalmologists 1
(pt).
Languages French, Portuguese.
Facilities Dining room; Activities room;
Crafts room; Laundry room; Barber/Beauty
shop.
Activities Arts & crafts; Cards; Games; Prayer
groups; Shopping trips; Music entertainment.

Ridgewood Court Nursing Home
27 George St, Attleboro, MA 02703
(508) 226-1650
Admin Thomas F Meade III. *Dir of Nursing*
Rosemary Dolan RN. *Medical Dir* Craig
Hobsen MD.
Licensure Skilled care; Intermediate care. *Beds*
SNF 80; ICF 40. *Private Pay Patients* 13%.
Certified Medicaid; Medicare.
Owner Proprietary corp (Beverly Enterprises).
Admissions Requirements Medical
examination; Physician's request.
Staff RNs 10 (ft); LPNs 10 (ft); Nurses' aides
45 (ft); Physical therapists; Occupational
therapists; Speech therapists; Activities
coordinators 2 (ft); Dietitians;
Ophthalmologists; Podiatrists; Audiologists.
Facilities Dining room; Physical therapy
room; Activities room; Chapel; Crafts room;
Laundry room; Barber/Beauty shop.
Activities Arts & crafts; Cards; Games;
Reading groups; Prayer groups; Movies;
Shopping trips; Dances/Social/Cultural
gatherings; Pet therapy.

Victorian Mansion Retirement Home
574 Newport Ave, Attleboro, MA 02703
(617) 761-5115
Admin Jodie Seidl.
Licensure Rest home. *Beds* 18.

Ayer

Woodford of Ayer Nursing Home
PO Box 220, 15 Winthrop Ave, Ayer, MA
01432
(508) 772-0409
Dir of Nursing Linda Colleton. *Medical Dir*
Dr George Geibel.
Licensure Intermediate care. *Beds* ICF 71.
Private Pay Patients 12%. *Certified*
Medicaid.
Owner Privately owned.
Admissions Requirements Minimum age 21;
Medical examination; Physician's request.
Staff Physicians 5 (pt); RNs 3 (ft); LPNs 6
(ft); Nurses' aides 21 (ft), 14 (pt); Activities
coordinators 1 (ft); Dietitians 1 (pt);
Podiatrists 1 (pt).
Languages Spanish.
Facilities Dining room; Activities room;
Crafts room; Laundry room; Barber/Beauty
shop.
Activities Arts & crafts; Cards; Games;
Reading groups; Prayer groups; Movies;
Shopping trips; Dances/Social/Cultural
gatherings; Intergenerational programs; Pet
therapy.

Barnstable

Cape Regency Nursing Home
120 S Main St, Barnstable, MA 02632
(508) 778-1835
Admin Charles Peterman.
Licensure Skilled care; Intermediate care. *Beds*
SNF 80; ICF 40.
Owner Proprietary corp.

**New Medico Rest & Skilled Nursing Center at
Lewis Bay**
89 Lewis Bay Rd, Barnstable, MA 02601
(508) 775-7601
Admin Darlene R Meetze.
Medical Dir Arthur Bickford MD.
Licensure Skilled care; Intermediate care. *Beds*
SNF 82; ICF 60. Certified Medicaid;
Medicare.
Owner Privately owned.
Admissions Requirements Minimum age 21;
Medical examination; Physician's request.
Facilities Dining room; Physical therapy
room; Activities room; Laundry room;
Barber/Beauty shop; Library.
Activities Arts & crafts; Cards; Games;
Reading groups; Prayer groups; Movies;
Shopping trips; Dances/Social/Cultural
gatherings; Remotivation; Sensitivity
stimulation; Exercise to music; Radio
interviews; Annual fair.

Resthaven Nursing Home
82 School St, Barnstable, MA 02601
(617) 775-3616
Admin Nicholas H Thisse. *Dir of Nursing*
Barbara V Massoni RN. *Medical Dir* Arthur
F Bickford MD.
Licensure Intermediate care. *Beds* ICF 44.
Owner Proprietary corp.
Admissions Requirements Minimum age 21;
Medical examination.
Staff Physicians 1 (pt); RNs 2 (ft), 2 (pt);
LPNs 2 (ft); Nurses' aides 7 (ft), 6 (pt);
Physical therapists 1 (pt); Activities
coordinators 1 (ft); Dietitians 1 (pt);
Ophthalmologists 1 (pt).
Facilities Dining room; Physical therapy
room; Activities room; Crafts room; Laundry
room.
Activities Arts & crafts; Cards; Games;
Reading groups; Prayer groups; Movies;
Shopping trips; Shopping trips; Dining out.

Whitehall Manor Nursing Home
Rte 28 Box 979, 850 Falmouth Rd,
Barnstable, MA 02601
(617) 775-6662
Admin Edward J Clark.
Medical Dir Dr Forrest Beame.
Licensure Skilled care; Intermediate care. *Beds*
SNF 36; ICF 69. Certified Medicaid;
Medicare.
Owner Proprietary corp.
Staff Physicians; RNs 25 (ft); LPNs 6 (ft);
Nurses' aides 60 (ft); Physical therapists;
Reality therapists 1 (ft); Recreational
therapists 4 (ft); Occupational therapists 2
(pt); Speech therapists 1 (pt); Activities
coordinators 2 (pt); Dietitians 1 (ft);
Ophthalmologists 1 (pt); Podiatrists 1 (pt);
Dentists 1 (ft).
Facilities Dining room; Physical therapy
room; Activities room; Chapel; Crafts room;
Laundry room; Barber/Beauty shop; Library.
Activities Arts & crafts; Cards; Games;
Reading groups; Prayer groups; Movies;
Shopping trips; Dances/Social/Cultural
gatherings.

Whitehall Pavilion Nursing Home
Box 979, Barnstable, MA 02601
(617) 775-6663
Licensure Skilled care. *Beds* SNF 82.

Barre

Christian Hill Rest Home
Christian Hill Dr, Barre, MA 01005
(617) 355-4491
Admin May E Danahy.
Licensure Rest home. *Beds* 18.

Bedford

Carleton-Willard Village Nursing Center
100 Old Billerica Rd, Bedford, MA 01730
(617) 275-8700
Admin Michon M Kelliher.
Medical Dir John W Bergin MD.
Licensure Skilled care; Intermediate care; Rest
home. *Beds* SNF 80; ICF 40; Rest home 80.
Owner Nonprofit corp.
Admissions Requirements Minimum age 65;
Medical examination; Physician's request.
Staff Physicians 1 (ft); RNs 6 (ft), 16 (pt);
LPNs 10 (ft), 15 (pt); Nurses' aides 46 (ft),
23 (pt); Physical therapists 2 (ft);
Recreational therapists 1 (ft); Occupational
therapists; Activities coordinators 2 (ft);
Dietitians 1 (ft).
Facilities Dining room; Physical therapy
room; Activities room; Crafts room; Laundry
room; Barber/Beauty shop; Library.
Activities Arts & crafts; Cards; Games;
Reading groups; Prayer groups; Movies;
Shopping trips; Dances/Social/Cultural
gatherings; Day trips; Workshop; Ceramics.

Belchertown

Belchertown State School
Box 446, Belchertown, MA 01007
(413) 326-3111
Admin William Jones.
Medical Dir Aran Kasparyan MD.
Licensure Intermediate care for mentally
retarded. *Beds* 415. Certified Medicaid.
Owner Publicly owned.
Admissions Requirements Minimum age 6.
Staff Physicians 3 (ft); RNs 50 (ft), 2 (pt);
LPNs 52 (ft), 10 (pt); Nurses' aides 243 (ft),
9 (pt); Physical therapists 4 (ft); Recreational
therapists 27 (ft), 15 (pt); Occupational
therapists 6 (ft), 1 (pt); Speech therapists 14
(ft); Dietitians 4 (ft); Dentists 1 (ft).
Facilities Dining room; Physical therapy
room; Activities room; Chapel; Crafts room;
Laundry room; Barber/Beauty shop; Library.
Activities Arts & crafts; Cards; Games;
Reading groups; Prayer groups; Movies;
Shopping trips; Dances/Social/Cultural
gatherings.

Belmont

Belmont Manor Nursing Home Inc
34 Agassiz Ave, Belmont, MA 02178
(617) 489-1200
Admin Stewart A Karger. *Dir of Nursing* Zofia
Mierzua-Nycz. *Medical Dir* David Barrasso
MD.
Licensure Skilled care; Intermediate care;
Alzheimer's care. *Beds* SNF 57; ICF 62.
Private Pay Patients 70%. *Certified*
Medicaid.
Owner Proprietary corp.
Staff RNs; LPNs; Nurses' aides; Recreational
therapists.
Languages French, Spanish, Italian,
Portuguese.
Facilities Dining room; Physical therapy
room; Activities room; Chapel; Laundry
room; Barber/Beauty shop.
Activities Arts & crafts; Cards; Games;
Reading groups; Prayer groups; Movies;
Shopping trips; Dances/Social/Cultural
gatherings; Intergenerational programs; Pet
therapy.

Beverly

Beverly Nursing Home
40 Heather St, Beverly, MA 01915
(617) 927-6220
Admin James F Smith.
Licensure Skilled care; Intermediate care. *Beds*
SNF 84; ICF 80. Certified Medicaid;
Medicare.

Owner Proprietary corp (Greenery Rehabilitation Group Inc).

Blueberry Hill Healthcare Nursing Home
75 Brimbal Ave, Beverly, MA 01915
(617) 927-2020
Admin Arthur O'Leary.
Medical Dir F Carbone MD.
Licensure Skilled care; Intermediate care. *Beds* SNF 80; ICF 54. *Certified* Medicaid; Medicare.
Owner Proprietary corp.
Staff Physicians 19 (pt); RNs 6 (ft), 10 (pt); LPNs 2 (ft), 8 (pt); Nurses' aides 16 (ft), 28 (pt); Physical therapists 1 (pt); Occupational therapists 1 (pt); Speech therapists 1 (pt); Activities coordinators 2 (ft); Dietitians 1 (pt); Ophthalmologists 1 (pt); Podiatrists 2 (pt); Audiologists 1 (pt); Dentists 1 (pt).
Facilities Dining room; Physical therapy room; Activities room; Chapel; Crafts room; Laundry room; Barber/Beauty shop; Library.
Activities Arts & crafts; Cards; Games; Reading groups; Prayer groups; Movies; Shopping trips; Dances/Social/Cultural gatherings.

Girdler House
78 Lothrop St, Beverly, MA 01915
(617) 922-0346
Admin Margaret Shea.
Medical Dir M Sadie Reid.
Licensure Self care. *Beds* 11.
Owner Nonprofit organization/foundation.
Admissions Requirements Minimum age 65; Females only; Medical examination; Physician's request.
Staff RNs 3 (pt); LPNs 1 (pt); Nurses' aides 1 (pt).
Facilities Dining room; Activities room; Laundry room; Barber/Beauty shop; Library.
Activities Cards; Games; Movies; Shopping trips; Dances/Social/Cultural gatherings.

Ledgewood Nursing Care Center
87 Herrick St, Beverly, MA 01915
(617) 921-1392
Admin Laurie Roberto.
Licensure Skilled care; Intermediate care. *Beds* SNF 82; ICF 40.

Mediplex of Beverly: A Long-Term Care Facility
265 Essex St, Beverly, MA 01915
(617) 927-3260
Admin Scott Dickinson. *Dir of Nursing* Mrs Myers RN. *Medical Dir* Dr Taylor.
Licensure Skilled care; Intermediate care. *Beds* SNF 80; ICF 110. *Certified* Medicaid; Medicare.
Owner Proprietary corp (Mediplex Inc).
Admissions Requirements Minimum age 16; Medical examination.
Staff RNs 10 (ft), 6 (pt); LPNs 8 (ft), 18 (pt); Nurses' aides 38 (ft), 46 (pt); Physical therapists 1 (pt); Reality therapists 1 (pt); Recreational therapists 3 (ft); Occupational therapists 1 (pt); Speech therapists 1 (pt); Activities coordinators 1 (ft); Dietitians 1 (pt); Ophthalmologists 1 (pt); Podiatrists 1 (pt); Dentists 1 (pt); Social workers 2 (ft).
Facilities Dining room; Physical therapy room; Activities room; Chapel; Crafts room; Barber/Beauty shop; Library.
Activities Arts & crafts; Cards; Games; Reading groups; Prayer groups; Movies; Shopping trips; Dances/Social/Cultural gatherings.

Billerica

Country View Nursing Home
80 Boston Rd, Billerica, MA 01862
(508) 667-2166
Admin Marjorie A Cohenno. *Dir of Nursing* Betsey Griffin.

Licensure Skilled care; Intermediate care. *Beds* SNF 41; ICF 80. *Private Pay Patients* 25%. *Certified* Medicaid.
Owner Proprietary corp (Life Care Centers of America).
Staff RNs; LPNs; Nurses' aides; Physical therapists; Recreational therapists; Occupational therapists; Activities coordinators; Dietitians; Podiatrists.
Facilities Dining room; Activities room; Chapel; Crafts room; Laundry room; Barber/ Beauty shop.
Activities Arts & crafts; Cards; Games; Reading groups; Prayer groups; Movies; Shopping trips; Dances/Social/Cultural gatherings; Intergenerational programs; Pet therapy.

Northeast Pediatric Care
PO Box E, 78 Boston Rd, Billerica, MA 01862
(617) 667-5123
Admin Charles W Merriam Jr.
Licensure Skilled care. *Beds* SNF 80. *Certified* Medicaid.
Owner Proprietary corp.

Simmons Nursing Home Inc
317 Boston Rd, Billerica, MA 01862
(617) 663-3538
Admin Christine C Silva.
Medical Dir Dr John Q Marshall.
Licensure Intermediate care; Alzheimer's care. *Beds* ICF 44. *Certified* Medicare.
Owner Proprietary corp.
Admissions Requirements Females only; Medical examination.
Staff Physicians 6 (ft); RNs 2 (ft); LPNs 7 (ft); Nurses' aides 20 (ft); Recreational therapists 2 (ft); Activities coordinators 1 (ft); Dietitians 2 (ft).
Facilities Dining room; Activities room; Crafts room; Laundry room.
Activities Arts & crafts; Cards; Games; Reading groups; Prayer groups; Movies; Shopping trips; Dances/Social/Cultural gatherings; Cookouts; Dances.

Blackstone

Blackstone Nursing Home
8 Butler St, Blackstone, MA 01504
(617) 883-5818
Admin Beverly J McIntyre RN. *Dir of Nursing* Janice Flinton RN.
Licensure Intermediate care; Alzheimer's care. *Beds* ICF 33. *Certified* Medicaid.
Owner Proprietary corp.
Admissions Requirements Minimum age 25.
Staff Physicians 1 (pt); RNs 2 (ft), 2 (pt); LPNs 4 (ft), 4 (pt); Nurses' aides 12 (ft), 5 (pt); Physical therapists 1 (pt); Recreational therapists 1 (ft); Occupational therapists 1 (pt); Speech therapists 1 (pt); Activities coordinators 1 (pt); Dietitians 1 (pt); Ophthalmologists 1 (pt); Podiatrists 1 (pt); Dentists 1 (pt).
Languages French.
Facilities Dining room; Activities room; Barber/Beauty shop.
Activities Arts & crafts; Cards; Games; Reading groups; Prayer groups; Movies; Shopping trips; Dances/Social/Cultural gatherings; Exercise groups.

Boston

Almeida Rest Home
69 Robeson St, Jamaica Plain, Boston, MA 02130
(617) 522-1904
Admin Vernard N Granderson.
Licensure Rest home. *Beds* Rest home 30.
Owner Privately owned.

Arborway Manor Inc
55 Burroughs St, Boston, MA 02130
(617) 524-2155

Admin Marilyn M Martin. *Dir of Nursing* Donna Cassio.
Licensure Intermediate care. *Beds* ICF 32. *Private Pay Patients* 15%.
Owner Proprietary corp.
Admissions Requirements Medical examination; Physician's request.
Facilities Dining room; Activities room; Crafts room; Laundry room; Barber/Beauty shop.
Activities Arts & crafts; Cards; Games; Reading groups; Prayer groups; Movies; Shopping trips; Dances/Social/Cultural gatherings.

Auburn House Nursing Home
9 Revere St, Boston, MA 02130
(617) 524-2822
Admin Jane G Spear.
Licensure Intermediate care. *Beds* 71. *Certified* Medicaid.
Admissions Requirements Minimum age 21; Medical examination; Physician's request.
Staff Physicians 2 (pt); RNs 1 (ft), 3 (pt); LPNs 2 (ft), 4 (pt); Nurses' aides 14 (ft), 4 (pt); Physical therapists 1 (pt); Recreational therapists 1 (ft), 1 (pt); Occupational therapists 1 (pt); Speech therapists 1 (pt); Dietitians 1 (pt); Podiatrists 1 (pt); Dentists 1 (pt).
Facilities Dining room; Activities room; Crafts room; Laundry room; Library.
Activities Arts & crafts; Cards; Games; Reading groups; Prayer groups; Movies; Shopping trips; Dances/Social/Cultural gatherings.

Bayside Nursing Home
804 E 7th St, Boston, MA 02127
(617) 268-1833
Admin Joseph Vilimas Jr.
Licensure Skilled care; Intermediate care. *Beds* SNF 51; ICF 52. *Certified* Medicaid.
Owner Proprietary corp.

Beatrice Catherine Rest Home
47 Ocean St, Boston, MA 02124
(617) 825-4862
Admin Marguerite I Munster.
Licensure Rest home. *Beds* 18.
Admissions Requirements Minimum age 75; Females only.
Staff RNs 2 (ft); Nurses' aides 4 (ft), 1 (pt); Activities coordinators 1 (pt).
Facilities Activities room; Laundry room.
Activities Arts & crafts; Cards; Games; Movies; Exercises.

Boston Home Inc
2049-2061 Dorchester Ave, Boston, MA 02124
(617) 825-3905
Admin Cletus A Carr. *Dir of Nursing* Irene Reynolds RN. *Medical Dir* Eugene F McAuliffe MD.
Licensure Skilled care. *Beds* SNF 42. *Certified* Medicaid.
Owner Nonprofit corp.
Admissions Requirements Minimum age 21; Females only; Medical examination; Physician's request.
Staff Physicians 4 (pt); RNs 1 (ft), 7 (pt); LPNs 4 (ft), 2 (pt); Nurses' aides 17 (ft), 15 (pt); Physical therapists 1 (pt); Occupational therapists 1 (pt); Activities coordinators 1 (ft); Dietitians 1 (pt); Ophthalmologists 1 (pt); Podiatrists 1 (pt); Dentists 1 (pt); Rehabilitation aides 1 (ft); Social workers 1 (ft).
Facilities Physical therapy room; Activities room; Chapel; Barber/Beauty shop; Library.
Activities Arts & crafts; Cards; Games; Reading groups; Prayer groups; Movies; Shopping trips; Dances/Social/Cultural gatherings; Resident run store.

Bradlee Rest Home
33 Bradlee St, Boston, MA 02124
(617) 436-3560
Admin Toni L Bullock.
Licensure Rest home. *Beds* 17.

Burgoyne Rest Home
53 Hartford St, Dorchester, Boston, MA 02125
(617) 445-1868
Admin Willard L Basler.
Licensure Rest home. *Beds* Rest home 11.
Owner Privately owned.
Admissions Requirements Minimum age 21.
Facilities Activities room.
Activities Movies.

Circle Manor Nursing Home
29 Chestnut Hill Ave, Boston, MA 02135
(617) 254-7655
Admin Clifford F Blake. *Dir of Nursing* Margaret Brennan RN.
Licensure Intermediate care. *Beds* ICF 64. *Certified* Medicaid.
Owner Proprietary corp.
Admissions Requirements Medical examination.
Staff Physicians; RNs 1 (ft), 3 (pt); LPNs 6 (pt); Nurses' aides 11 (ft), 9 (pt); Physical therapists; Recreational therapists 1 (ft); Dietitians.
Facilities Dining room; Activities room; Chapel; Crafts room; Laundry room; Barber/Beauty shop.
Activities Arts & crafts; Cards; Games; Reading groups; Prayer groups; Movies; Shopping trips; Dances/Social/Cultural gatherings.

Corey Hill Nursing Home
249 Corey Rd, Boston, MA 02135
(617) 734-7138
Admin Louis Dronge.
Medical Dir Dr Herbert Leventhal.
Licensure Intermediate care. *Beds* ICF 43. *Certified* Medicaid.
Owner Proprietary corp.
Admissions Requirements Minimum age 60; Medical examination; Physician's request.
Staff RNs 2 (ft), 1 (pt); LPNs 2 (ft), 1 (pt); Nurses' aides 14 (ft), 6 (pt); Activities coordinators 1 (ft); Dietitians 1 (pt).

Cushing Retirement Home
20 Cushing Ave, Dorchester, Boston, MA 02125
(617) 436-9608
Admin Natalie I Batchelder.
Licensure Rest home. *Beds* Rest home 36. *Certified* Medicaid.
Owner Proprietary corp.

Deutsches Altenheim Inc
2222 Centre St, West Roxbury, Boston, MA 02132
(617) 325-1230
Admin Donna Lee McLean. *Dir of Nursing* Carolyn Anderson RN. *Medical Dir* Dr Robert Mullins.
Licensure Intermediate care. *Beds* ICF 40. *Certified* Medicaid.
Owner Nonprofit corp.
Admissions Requirements Minimum age 65; Medical examination; Physician's request.
Staff RNs 3 (ft), 1 (pt); LPNs 3 (ft), 1 (pt); Nurses' aides 10 (ft), 9 (pt); Activities coordinators 1 (ft); Dietitians 1 (pt).
Languages German.
Affiliation German Ladies Aid Society.
Facilities Dining room; Activities room; Chapel; Crafts room; Laundry room; Barber/Beauty shop; Library; 12 Acres.
Activities Arts & crafts; Cards; Games; Reading groups; Prayer groups; Movies; Shopping trips; Dances/Social/Cultural gatherings; Reality orientation; Choir; German cultural activities.

Don Orione Nursing Home
111 Orient Ave, Boston, MA 02128
(617) 569-2100
Admin Rev Rocco Crescenzi.
Licensure Skilled care; Intermediate care. *Beds* SNF 107; ICF 83. *Certified* Medicaid.
Owner Proprietary corp.

Edgewood Convalescent Home
637 Washington St, Boston, MA 02124
(617) 436-6210
Admin Lawrence M Osterweil.
Medical Dir Mark Ostrem MD.
Licensure Skilled care; Intermediate care. *Beds* SNF 48; ICF 50. *Certified* Medicaid.
Owner Proprietary corp (First Healthcare Corp).
Admissions Requirements Physician's request.
Staff RNs 5 (ft); LPNs 5 (ft); Nurses' aides 30 (ft), 15 (pt); Physical therapists 1 (pt); Recreational therapists 1 (ft), 1 (pt); Occupational therapists 1 (pt); Speech therapists 1 (pt); Dietitians 1 (pt); Ophthalmologists 1 (pt); Podiatrists 1 (pt); Dentists 1 (pt).
Facilities Dining room; Physical therapy room; Activities room; Crafts room; Laundry room; Barber/Beauty shop.
Activities Arts & crafts; Cards; Games; Reading groups; Prayer groups; Movies; Shopping trips.

Elizabeth Carelton House
2055 Columbus Ave, Boston, MA 02119
(617) 522-2100
Admin Hilda Jane Miller.
Licensure Intermediate care. *Beds* 110. *Certified* Medicaid.

Elm Hill Nursing Home
237-241 Walnut Ave, Boston, MA 02119
(617) 427-4798
Admin Francis V Dargon.
Licensure Intermediate care. *Beds* ICF 53. *Certified* Medicaid.
Owner Proprietary corp.

Englewood Nursing Home
27 Howland St, Boston, MA 02121
(617) 442-6735
Admin Lillian B Granderson.
Licensure Intermediate care. *Beds* ICF 35. *Certified* Medicaid.
Owner Privately owned.

Fairfax Rest Home
15 Fairfax St, Boston, MA 02124
(617) 265-8431
Admin Andrew Basler.
Licensure Rest home. *Beds* 17.

Fairmount Rest Home Inc
172 Fairmount Ave, Hyde Park, Boston, MA 02136
(617) 361-5150
Admin Mildred Marden.
Licensure Rest home. *Beds* 32.
Owner Proprietary corp.

Forestdale Nursing Home
240 Savin Hill Ave, Boston, MA 02125-04
(617) 322-1716
Admin Clyde L Tyler Jr.
Licensure Intermediate care. *Beds* 69. *Certified* Medicaid.

Goddard House, A Retirement & Nursing Home
201 S Huntington Ave, Boston, MA 02130
(617) 522-3080, 522-1035 FAX
Admin Elizabeth Wood. *Dir of Nursing* Janet Fuller RN. *Medical Dir* John Jainchill MD.
Licensure Skilled care; Intermediate care; Rest home. *Beds* SNF 41; ICF 40; Rest home 63. *Certified* Medicaid.
Owner Nonprofit organization/foundation.
Admissions Requirements Minimum age 60; Medical examination.

Staff Physicians (attending); RNs 6 (ft), 7 (pt); LPNs 6 (ft), 7 (pt); Nurses' aides 33 (ft), 14 (pt); Physical therapists (consultant); Occupational therapists (consultant); Speech therapists (consultant); Activities coordinators 1 (ft); Dietitians (consultant); Ophthalmologists (available); Podiatrists (available); Audiologists (available).
Facilities Dining room; Physical therapy room; Activities room; Crafts room; Laundry room; Barber/Beauty shop; Library.
Activities Arts & crafts; Cards; Games; Reading groups; Prayer groups; Movies; Shopping trips; Dances/Social/Cultural gatherings; Intergenerational programs; Pet therapy.

Grampian Nursing Home
33 Grampian Way, Dorchester, Boston, MA 02125
(617) 436-3331
Admin Louis Furash.
Medical Dir Kathleen A Maffie.
Licensure Intermediate care. *Beds* ICF 26. *Certified* Medicaid; Medicare.
Owner Proprietary corp.
Admissions Requirements Minimum age 18; Females only; Medical examination; Physician's request.
Staff Physicians 4 (pt); RNs 2 (pt); LPNs 3 (ft), 3 (pt); Nurses' aides 8 (ft), 5 (pt); Physical therapists 1 (pt); Reality therapists 1 (pt); Recreational therapists 1 (pt); Occupational therapists 1 (pt); Speech therapists 1 (pt); Activities coordinators 1 (pt); Dietitians 1 (pt); Ophthalmologists 1 (pt); Podiatrists 1 (pt); Dentists 1 (pt).
Languages French.
Facilities Laundry room; Barber/Beauty shop.
Activities Arts & crafts; Cards; Games; Reading groups; Movies; Shopping trips; Dances/Social/Cultural gatherings.

Greenery Rehabilitation & Skilled Nursing Center
99-111 Chestnut Hill Ave, Boston, MA 02135
(617) 787-3390
Admin Jeannine Carroll. *Dir of Nursing* Elizabeth Berry. *Medical Dir* William Garvin MD.
Licensure Skilled care. *Beds* SNF 201. *Certified* Medicaid; Medicare.
Owner Proprietary corp.
Admissions Requirements Minimum age 15; Medical examination.
Staff Physicians 2 (ft), 2 (pt); RNs 26 (ft); LPNs 26 (ft); Nurses' aides 88 (ft); Physical therapists 17 (ft); Recreational therapists 10 (ft); Occupational therapists 12 (ft); Speech therapists 15 (ft); Dietitians 1 (ft); Ophthalmologists 1 (pt); Podiatrists 1 (pt); Dentists 1 (pt); Special education 6 (ft); Neuropsychologists 6 (ft); Behavioral therapists 3 (ft); Vocational rehabilitation therapists 6 (ft).
Languages French, Spanish.
Facilities Dining room; Physical therapy room; Activities room; Crafts room; Laundry room; Barber/Beauty shop; Library; Vocational rehabilitation; Special education classrooms.
Activities Arts & crafts; Cards; Games; Reading groups; Prayer groups; Movies; Shopping trips; Dances/Social/Cultural gatherings.

Hale House
273 Clarendon St, Boston, MA 02116
(617) 536-3726
Admin Carolyn Widen.
Medical Dir Christine Wolford.
Licensure Rest home. *Beds* Rest home 60.
Owner Proprietary corp.
Admissions Requirements Minimum age 65; Medical examination.
Staff RNs 2 (ft); LPNs 6 (pt); Nurses' aides 1 (ft), 1 (pt); Activities coordinators 1 (pt).

Facilities Dining room; Activities room; Laundry room; Barber/Beauty shop; Library.
Activities Cards; Games; Reading groups; Movies; Shopping trips; Dances/Social/Cultural gatherings.

Haven Nursing Home
1780 Columbia Rd, Boston, MA 02127-3414
(617) 524-3150
Admin Elizabeth J Argus.
Licensure Intermediate care. *Beds* ICF 20. *Certified* Medicaid.
Owner Privately owned.

Hyde Park Convalescent Home
113 Central Ave, Boston, MA 02136
(617) 361-2388
Admin Arthur D Kruskall.
Licensure Skilled care; Intermediate care. *Beds* SNF 25; ICF 28. *Certified* Medicaid.
Owner Proprietary corp.
Staff RNs 6 (ft), 2 (pt); LPNs 4 (ft), 3 (pt); Nurses' aides 23 (ft), 8 (pt).
Facilities Dining room; Activities room; Crafts room; Laundry room; Barber/Beauty shop.
Activities Arts & crafts; Cards; Games; Reading groups; Prayer groups; Movies; Shopping trips; Dances/Social/Cultural gatherings; Mens club; Cooking club; Garden club; Exercise bike club.

Jamaica Towers Nursing Home
174 Forest Hills St, Boston, MA 02130
(617) 522-1550
Admin Donna Andrews-Alley.
Medical Dir Saripalli V Subbaraju MD.
Licensure Skilled care; Intermediate care. *Beds* SNF 80; ICF 40. *Certified* Medicaid; Medicare.
Owner Proprietary corp.
Admissions Requirements Minimum age 21; Physician's request.
Staff Physicians 18 (pt); RNs 5 (ft), 2 (pt); LPNs 7 (ft), 9 (pt); Nurses' aides 60 (ft), 1 (pt); Physical therapists 1 (pt); Occupational therapists 1 (pt); Speech therapists 1 (pt); Activities coordinators 2 (ft); Dietitians 1 (pt); Ophthalmologists 1 (pt); Podiatrists 1 (pt); Audiologists 1 (pt); Dentists 1 (pt).
Facilities Dining room; Physical therapy room; Activities room; Crafts room; Laundry room; Barber/Beauty shop.
Activities Arts & crafts; Cards; Games; Reading groups; Prayer groups; Movies; Shopping trips; Dances/Social/Cultural gatherings.

Ellen James Rest Home
42 Elm Hill Ave, Roxbury, Boston, MA 02121
(617) 427-7464
Admin Jeanette Savoie.
Licensure Rest home. *Beds* Rest home 40.
Owner Proprietary corp.

Long-Term Care at Neponset—Ashmont Manor
45 Coffey St, Boston, MA 02122
(617) 282-9700
Admin Peter S Gordon.
Medical Dir Sharon Acker.
Licensure Intermediate care. *Beds* ICF 77.
Owner Proprietary corp.
Staff RNs 2 (ft), 1 (pt); LPNs 5 (ft), 6 (pt); Nurses' aides 20 (ft), 20 (pt); Physical therapists 1 (pt); Reality therapists 2 (ft); Recreational therapists 2 (ft), 2 (pt); Occupational therapists 1 (pt); Activities coordinators 1 (ft); Dietitians 1 (pt).
Facilities Dining room; Activities room; Crafts room; Laundry room; Barber/Beauty shop.
Activities Arts & crafts; Cards; Games; Reading groups; Prayer groups; Movies; Shopping trips; Dances/Social/Cultural gatherings.

Long-Term Care at Neponset—Bostonian Nursing Care Center
337 Neponset Ave, Dorchester, Boston, MA 02122
(617) 265-2350
Admin Thomas F Healy.
Medical Dir John Jainchill MD.
Licensure Skilled care; Intermediate care. *Beds* SNF 80; ICF 29. *Certified* Medicaid.
Owner Proprietary corp.
Admissions Requirements Minimum age 21; Medical examination; Physician's request.
Staff RNs 4 (ft), 2 (pt); LPNs 10 (ft), 7 (pt); Nurses' aides 24 (ft), 26 (pt); Activities coordinators 2 (ft), 2 (pt).
Facilities Dining room; Activities room; Crafts room; Barber/Beauty shop; Gift shop; Cafe.
Activities Arts & crafts; Cards; Games; Reading groups; Prayer groups; Movies; Shopping trips; Dances/Social/Cultural gatherings; Ceramics; Cooking; Field trips; Barbeques.

Long-Term Care at Neponset—Neponset Hall
35 Coffey St, Dorchester, Boston, MA 02122
(617) 282-3600
Admin Peter S Gordon.
Medical Dir Sharon Acker.
Licensure Intermediate care. *Beds* ICF 98.
Owner Proprietary corp.
Staff RNs 2 (ft), 2 (pt); LPNs 5 (ft), 6 (pt); Nurses' aides 20 (ft), 25 (pt); Physical therapists 1 (pt); Reality therapists 1 (ft), 1 (pt); Recreational therapists 1 (ft), 1 (pt); Occupational therapists 1 (pt); Activities coordinators 1 (ft); Dietitians 1 (pt).
Facilities Dining room; Activities room; Laundry room; Barber/Beauty shop.
Activities Arts & crafts; Cards; Games; Reading groups; Prayer groups; Movies; Shopping trips; Dances/Social/Cultural gatherings.

Malden Nursing Home
240 Savin Hill Ave, Boston, MA 02125-1012
(617) 324-2620
Admin Clyde L Tyler Jr.
Licensure Intermediate care. *Beds* 52.
Certified Medicaid.

Marco Polo Rest Home Inc
Box 501, Boston, MA 02128
(617) 567-7500
Admin Richard J Diamond.
Medical Dir Glenn Rothfeld MD.
Licensure Rest home. *Beds* Rest home 62.
Owner Proprietary corp.
Admissions Requirements Minimum age 45; Medical examination.
Staff Nurses' aides 4 (ft), 6 (pt); Activities coordinators 1 (pt).
Facilities Dining room; Activities room; Laundry room.
Activities Arts & crafts; Cards; Games; Dances/Social/Cultural gatherings.

Marian Manor
130 Dorchester St, South Boston, Boston, MA 02127
(617) 268-3333
Admin Sr Andre Marie. *Dir of Nursing* Anne Marie Perry RN. *Medical Dir* Ernesto Waingortin MD.
Licensure Skilled care; Intermediate care; Rest home. *Beds* SNF 171; ICF 187; Rest home 18. *Certified* Medicaid.
Owner Nonprofit organization/foundation.
Admissions Requirements Minimum age 65; Physician's request.
Staff Physicians; RNs; LPNs; Nurses' aides; Physical therapists; Reality therapists; Recreational therapists; Occupational therapists; Speech therapists; Activities coordinators; Dietitians; Ophthalmologists; Podiatrists; Dentists.
Languages Spanish, Lithuanian, Polish.
Affiliation Roman Catholic.

Facilities Dining room; Physical therapy room; Activities room; Chapel; Crafts room; Laundry room; Barber/Beauty shop; Library.
Activities Arts & crafts; Cards; Games; Reading groups; Prayer groups; Movies; Shopping trips; Dances/Social/Cultural gatherings.

Martin Nursing Home
415 Columbia Rd, Boston, MA 02125
(617) 436-4170
Admin Susanna Sheppard.
Licensure Intermediate care. *Beds* 150.
Certified Medicaid.

Med Inn & Parker Hill—SNF
53 Parker Hill Ave, Boston, MA 02120
(617) 232-9370
Admin Thomas Sheridan.
Licensure Skilled care. *Beds* SNF 41.

Melville Rest Home
3 Melville Ave, Dorchester, Boston, MA 02124
(617) 288-5816
Admin Margaret T Murray.
Medical Dir Dr Boderick.
Licensure Rest home. *Beds* Rest home 23.
Owner Privately owned.
Admissions Requirements Minimum age 18; Medical examination.
Staff LPNs 1 (pt); Activities coordinators 1 (pt).
Facilities Dining room; Activities room; Laundry room; Kitchen.
Activities Arts & crafts; Cards; Games; Reading groups; Prayer groups; Movies; Shopping trips; Dances/Social/Cultural gatherings.

Miltonview Nursing Home
150 River St, Mattapan, Boston, MA 02126
(617) 296-0140
Admin Roger Dillingham.
Licensure Intermediate care. *Beds* ICF 64.
Certified Medicaid.
Owner Proprietary corp.

Mary Murphy Nursing Home
70 Rockview St, Boston, MA 02130
(617) 524-6200
Admin Louis J Furash.
Medical Dir Dr Louis Kassler.
Licensure Intermediate care. *Beds* ICF 91.
Certified Medicaid.
Owner Proprietary corp.
Admissions Requirements Minimum age 21; Medical examination; Physician's request.
Staff Physicians 4 (pt); RNs 2 (ft), 2 (pt); LPNs 4 (ft), 2 (pt); Nurses' aides 18 (ft), 8 (pt); Physical therapists 1 (pt); Recreational therapists 1 (pt); Speech therapists 1 (pt); Activities coordinators 1 (ft), 1 (pt); Dietitians 1 (pt); Ophthalmologists 1 (pt); Podiatrists 1 (pt); Dentists 1 (pt).
Activities Arts & crafts; Cards; Games; Reading groups; Prayer groups; Movies; Shopping trips.

Nelson Manor Nursing Home
3 Aspinwall Rd, Dorchester, Boston, MA 02124
(617) 288-4100
Admin Barbara Cohen.
Licensure Intermediate care. *Beds* ICF 47.
Certified Medicaid.
Owner Proprietary corp.

North End Community Nursing Home
70 Fulton St, Boston, MA 02109
(617) 367-3750
Admin Audrey F Aschiero.
Licensure Skilled care; Intermediate care. *Beds* SNF 80; ICF 60.

Norwegian Old Peoples Home
1205 Centre St, Boston, MA 02131
(617) 325-9439
Admin Arnold N Harklow.

Licensure Rest home. *Beds* Rest home 18.
Owner Proprietary corp.

Oak Haven Nursing Home
74 Howland St, Boston, MA 02121
(617) 427-8080
Admin Loretta Murphy.
Licensure Intermediate care. *Beds* ICF 38.
Certified Medicaid.
Owner Proprietary corp.

Oakwood Long Term Care Center
142 Bigelow St, Boston, MA 02135
(617) 782-3424
Admin Norman P Michaud Jr.
Licensure Intermediate care. *Beds* ICF 143.
Certified Medicaid.
Owner Proprietary corp.

Park Dale Rest Home
36 Elm Hill Ave, Boston, MA 02121
(617) 427-9649
Admin L B Granderson.
Licensure Rest home. *Beds* Rest home 27.
Owner Privately owned.

Parkwell Health Care Center: A Skilled Nursing Facility
745 Truman Hwy, Boston, MA 02136
(617) 361-8300
Admin Patrick O'Connor.
Licensure Skilled care; Intermediate care. *Beds* SNF 82; ICF 42. *Certified* Medicaid; Medicare.
Owner Privately owned.

Presentation Manor Nursing Home
10 Bellamy St, Boston, MA 02135
(617) 782-8113
Admin Robert D Whitkin. *Dir of Nursing* Nancy Laffey RN. *Medical Dir* Ralph Porter MD.
Licensure Skilled care; Intermediate care. *Beds* SNF 61; ICF 61. *Certified* Medicaid.
Owner Proprietary corp (Hillhaven Corp).
Admissions Requirements Medical examination; Physician's request.
Staff Physicians 16 (pt); Physical therapists 1 (pt); Speech therapists 1 (pt); Activities coordinators 1 (ft); Dietitians 1 (pt); Ophthalmologists 1 (pt); Podiatrists 1 (pt).
Languages Spanish, Creole.
Facilities Dining room; Activities room; Chapel; Crafts room; Laundry room; Barber/ Beauty shop.
Activities Arts & crafts; Cards; Games; Reading groups; Prayer groups; Movies; Shopping trips; Dances/Social/Cultural gatherings; Intergenerational programs; Pet therapy.

Provident Nursing Home
1501 Commonwealth Ave, Boston, MA 02135
(617) 782-1320
Admin Mary A Carroll. *Dir of Nursing* Charlene Ayers. *Medical Dir* Jeffrey Kang MD.
Licensure Intermediate care for mentally retarded. *Beds* ICF/MR 100. *Certified* Medicaid.
Owner Proprietary corp.
Admissions Requirements Minimum age 65 or Waiver; Medical examination.
Staff Physicians 5 (pt); RNs 15 (ft); Nurses' aides 73 (ft); Recreational therapists 2 (ft); Occupational therapists 1 (ft); Activities coordinators 1 (ft); Dietitians 1 (pt); Podiatrists 1 (pt).
Facilities Dining room; Activities room; Crafts room; Laundry room; Barber/Beauty shop.
Activities Arts & crafts; Cards; Games; Reading groups; Movies; Shopping trips; Dances/Social/Cultural gatherings.

Resthaven Corporation
120 Fisher Ave, Boston, MA 02120
(617) 738-1500
Admin Roy Fitzsimmons.

Licensure Skilled care; Intermediate care. *Beds* SNF 160; ICF 80. *Certified* Medicaid.
Owner Proprietary corp.

Riverside Nursing Home
405 River St, Boston, MA 02126
(617) 296-5585
Admin Stephen J Kelly.
Medical Dir Barbra Collins.
Licensure Skilled care; Alzheimer's care. *Beds* SNF 85. *Certified* Medicaid.
Owner Proprietary corp.
Admissions Requirements Minimum age 65.
Staff RNs 8 (ft); LPNs 10 (pt); Nurses' aides 20 (ft), 10 (pt); Physical therapists 1 (pt); Recreational therapists 3 (ft); Occupational therapists 1 (pt); Activities coordinators 1 (ft); Dietitians 1 (pt); Ophthalmologists 1 (pt); Podiatrists 1 (pt); Dentists 1 (pt).
Languages French.
Facilities Dining room; Activities room; Chapel; Crafts room; Laundry room; Barber/ Beauty shop.
Activities Arts & crafts; Cards; Games; Reading groups; Prayer groups; Movies; Shopping trips; Dances/Social/Cultural gatherings.

Rodger Rest Home
54 Bowdoin St, Dorchester, Boston, MA 02124
(617) 825-1771
Admin Lillian B Granderson.
Licensure Rest home. *Beds* Rest home 20.
Owner Privately owned.

Roxbury Home for Aged Women
1215 Centre St, Roslindale, Boston, MA 02131
(617) 323-0373
Admin Alice Runci.
Medical Dir Dr Alice Rogado.
Licensure Rest home. *Beds* Rest home 24.
Owner Proprietary corp.
Admissions Requirements Minimum age 65; Females only; Medical examination.
Staff Physicians 1 (pt); RNs 1 (pt); LPNs 1 (ft), 1 (pt); Nurses' aides 7 (pt); Activities coordinators 1 (pt); Dietitians 1 (pt); Ophthalmologists 1 (pt); Podiatrists 1 (pt); Audiologists 1 (pt); Dentists 1 (pt).

St Joseph's Manor
321 Centre St, Boston, MA 02122
(617) 825-6320
Admin Sr James Frances Powers.
Licensure Rest home. *Beds* Rest home 77.
Owner Proprietary corp.
Admissions Requirements Minimum age 70; Females only; Medical examination; Physician's request.
Staff RNs 1 (pt); LPNs 1 (ft); Activities coordinators 1 (ft); Dietitians 1 (pt); Podiatrists 1 (pt).
Affiliation Roman Catholic.
Facilities Dining room; Activities room; Chapel; Laundry room; Barber/Beauty shop.
Activities Arts & crafts; Cards; Games; Reading groups; Prayer groups; Movies; Shopping trips; Dances/Social/Cultural gatherings.

Sheriff Manor Nursing Home
176 Humboldt Ave, Boston, MA 02121
(617) 445-5224
Admin Roger T Dillingham.
Licensure Intermediate care. *Beds* ICF 60. *Certified* Medicaid.
Owner Proprietary corp.

Sherrill House Inc
135 S Huntington Ave, Boston, MA 02130
(617) 731-2400
Admin Donald M Powell. *Dir of Nursing* Betty Mollica. *Medical Dir* Dr Jens Tougorg.
Licensure Skilled care; Intermediate care. *Beds* SNF 123; ICF 41. *Certified* Medicaid; Medicare.
Owner Proprietary corp.

Staff RNs 15 (ft), 10 (pt); LPNs 10 (ft), 10 (pt); Nurses' aides 60 (ft), 30 (pt).
Facilities Dining room; Physical therapy room; Activities room; Chapel; Crafts room; Laundry room; Barber/Beauty shop; Library.
Activities Arts & crafts; Cards; Games; Reading groups; Prayer groups; Movies; Shopping trips.

South Cove Manor
120 Shawmut Ave, Boston, MA 02118
(617) 423-0590
Admin Nancy Hsu. *Dir of Nursing* Katherine (Kay) Walsh. *Medical Dir* Dr Albert Yee.
Licensure Skilled care; Intermediate care. *Beds* SNF 40; ICF 60. *Private Pay Patients* 4%. *Certified* Medicaid.
Owner Nonprofit corp.
Admissions Requirements Physician's request.
Staff Physicians; RNs; LPNs; Nurses' aides; Physical therapists; Occupational therapists; Activities coordinators; Dietitians; Podiatrists; Dentists.
Languages Chinese, Spanish.
Facilities Dining room; Physical therapy room; Activities room; Laundry room; Barber/Beauty shop; Chinese or American kitchen.
Activities Arts & crafts; Cards; Games; Reading groups; Prayer groups; Movies; Shopping trips; Dances/Social/Cultural gatherings; Intergenerational programs.

Stadium Manor Nursing Home
461 Walnut Ave, Boston, MA 02130
(617) 522-1170
Admin Ann McDonnell.
Licensure Intermediate care. *Beds* ICF 120. *Certified* Medicaid.
Owner Proprietary corp.

Star of David Convalescent Home
1100 VFW Pkwy, Boston, MA 02132
(617) 325-8100
Admin Richard Sabounjiam.
Medical Dir Dr Joseph Pines.
Licensure Skilled care; Intermediate care. *Beds* SNF 77; ICF 69. *Certified* Medicaid.
Owner Proprietary corp (First Healthcare Corp).
Admissions Requirements Medical examination.
Staff RNs 18 (ft); LPNs 6 (ft); Nurses' aides 38 (ft); Physical therapists 2 (ft), 1 (pt); Reality therapists 2 (ft); Occupational therapists 1 (pt); Speech therapists 1 (pt); Activities coordinators 1 (ft), 2 (pt); Dietitians 1 (pt).
Facilities Dining room; Physical therapy room; Activities room; Chapel; Crafts room; Laundry room; Barber/Beauty shop; Library; Lounges; Auditorium.
Activities Arts & crafts; Cards; Reading groups; Prayer groups; Movies; Shopping trips; Dances/Social/Cultural gatherings.

Union Square Nursing Center
533 Cambridge St, Boston, MA 02134
(617) 782-2053
Admin John J O'Meara. *Dir of Nursing* Richard Levesque RN CNAA. *Medical Dir* Walter Lee MD.
Licensure Intermediate care. *Beds* ICF 150. *Certified* Medicaid.
Owner Proprietary corp.
Admissions Requirements Minimum age 21; Medical examination.
Staff Physicians 12 (pt); RNs 5 (ft), 3 (pt); LPNs 3 (ft), 8 (pt); Nurses' aides 24 (ft), 1 (pt); Physical therapists 1 (pt); Recreational therapists 2 (pt); Occupational therapists 1 (pt); Speech therapists 1 (pt); Activities coordinators 1 (ft); Dietitians 1 (pt); Ophthalmologists 1 (pt); Podiatrists 1 (pt); Audiologists 1 (pt); Rehabilitation assistants 1 (ft).

Facilities Dining room; Activities room; Laundry room; Barber/Beauty shop.
Activities Arts & crafts; Cards; Games; Reading groups; Movies; Shopping trips.

VFW Parkway Nursing Home
1190 VFW Pkwy, Boston, MA 02132
(617) 325-1688
Admin Thomas E Martin.
Licensure Skilled care; Intermediate care. *Beds* SNF 91; ICF 49. *Certified* Medicaid.
Owner Proprietary corp (First Healthcare Corp).

Wayne Manor Nursing Home
133 Hancock St, Boston, MA 02125
(617) 265-5220
Admin Barbara Cohen.
Licensure Intermediate care. *Beds* ICF 78. *Certified* Medicaid.
Owner Proprietary corp.

West Roxbury Manor Nursing Home
5060 Washington St, Boston, MA 02132
(617) 323-5440
Admin John Spears.
Medical Dir James Harrison MD.
Licensure Skilled care; Intermediate care. *Beds* SNF 37; ICF 39. *Certified* Medicaid.
Owner Proprietary corp (First Healthcare Corp).
Admissions Requirements Minimum age 50; Medical examination; Physician's request.
Staff Physicians 12 (pt); RNs 5 (ft); LPNs 8 (ft); Nurses' aides 25 (ft); Physical therapists 1 (pt); Reality therapists 1 (pt); Recreational therapists 1 (ft), 1 (pt); Occupational therapists 1 (pt); Speech therapists 1 (pt); Activities coordinators 1 (ft); Dietitians 1 (pt); Ophthalmologists 1 (pt); Podiatrists 1 (pt); Audiologists 1 (pt); Dentists 1 (pt).
Facilities Dining room; Laundry room; Library.
Activities Arts & crafts; Cards; Games; Reading groups; Movies; Shopping trips; Dances/Social/Cultural gatherings.

Frank Wood Convalescent Home
1135 Morton St, Boston, MA 02126
(617) 298-8003
Admin Dennis F Sullivan.
Licensure Skilled care. *Beds* SNF 62. *Certified* Medicaid; Medicare.
Owner Proprietary corp.

Bradford

Lenox Nursing Home Inc
378 S Main St, Bradford, MA 01830
(508) 374-7953
Admin Denise T Allen. *Dir of Nursing* Tina M O'Sullivan LPN. *Medical Dir* Dr Forrest Milden.
Licensure Intermediate care. *Beds* ICF 27. *Certified* Medicaid.
Owner Proprietary corp.
Activities Arts & crafts; Cards; Games; Reading groups; Prayer groups; Movies; Shopping trips; Dances/Social/Cultural gatherings; Intergenerational programs; Pet therapy.

Braintree

Braintree Manor
1102 Washington St, Braintree, MA 02184
(617) 848-3100
Admin Elizabeth A Pattavina. *Dir of Nursing* Judith Arredondo. *Medical Dir* Mark S Ostrem.
Licensure Skilled care. *Beds* SNF 192. *Private Pay Patients* 18%. *Certified* Medicaid.
Owner Proprietary corp.
Admissions Requirements Minimum age 20; Medical examination; Physician's request.
Languages Polish.

Facilities Dining room; Physical therapy room; Activities room; Crafts room; Barber/ Beauty shop; Library; Child care.
Activities Arts & crafts; Cards; Games; Reading groups; Prayer groups; Movies; Shopping trips; Dances/Social/Cultural gatherings; Intergenerational programs; Pet therapy; Adopt-a-grandparent.

Franklin Nursing Home
149 Franklin St, Braintree, MA 02184
(617) 843-3136
Admin Andrew J Comeau. *Dir of Nursing* Gloria Del Pico LPN. *Medical Dir* Floyd Wolff MD.
Licensure Intermediate care. *Beds* ICF 27. *Private Pay Patients* 0%. *Certified* Medicaid.
Owner Proprietary corp.
Admissions Requirements Females only; Medical examination.
Staff RNs 5 (pt); LPNs 2 (ft), 3 (pt); Nurses' aides 7 (ft), 4 (pt); Physical therapists 1 (pt); Activities coordinators 1 (pt); Dietitians 1 (pt).
Facilities Dining room; Activities room; Laundry room.
Activities Arts & crafts; Cards; Games; Reading groups; Prayer groups; Movies; Dances/Social/Cultural gatherings; Pet therapy.

Franvale Nursing Home
20 Pond St, Braintree, MA 02184
(617) 848-1616, 848-8813 FAX
Admin David Bond. *Dir of Nursing* Joan Chamberlain. *Medical Dir* Dr Iraj Aghdasi.
Licensure Skilled care; Intermediate care. *Beds* SNF 51; ICF 40. *Private Pay Patients* 7%. *Certified* Medicaid; Medicare.
Owner Proprietary corp.
Admissions Requirements Medical examination; Physician's request.
Staff Physicians 14 (pt); RNs 5 (ft), 18 (pt); LPNs 17 (pt); Nurses' aides 21 (ft), 36 (pt); Physical therapists 1 (ft), 1 (pt); Reality therapists 1 (pt); Recreational therapists 1 (ft), 1 (pt); Occupational therapists 1 (pt); Activities coordinators 1 (ft), 1 (pt); Dietitians 1 (pt); Podiatrists 1 (pt).
Languages Spanish, French, Creole, Polish.
Facilities Dining room; Physical therapy room; Activities room; Crafts room; Laundry room; Barber/Beauty shop.
Activities Arts & crafts; Cards; Games; Reading groups; Prayer groups; Movies; Shopping trips; Dances/Social/Cultural gatherings; Intergenerational programs; Pet therapy; Theater.

Hollingsworth House Nursing & Retirement
1120 Washington St, Braintree, MA 02185
(617) 848-3100
Admin Elizabeth A Pattavina. *Dir of Nursing* Margaret Nelson RN. *Medical Dir* Mark Ostrem MD.
Licensure Intermediate care. *Beds* ICF 120. *Certified* Medicaid.
Owner Proprietary corp.
Admissions Requirements Minimum age 60.
Staff RNs 16 (ft), 4 (pt); LPNs 12 (ft), 6 (pt); Nurses' aides 15 (ft), 20 (pt); Physical therapists 1 (pt); Recreational therapists 4 (ft), 2 (pt); Activities coordinators 1 (ft); Dietitians 1 (pt); Hairdresser 1 (pt); Barber 1 (pt).
Facilities Dining room; Activities room; Crafts room; Barber/Beauty shop; Library.
Activities Arts & crafts; Cards; Games; Reading groups; Prayer groups; Movies; Shopping trips; Dances/Social/Cultural gatherings; Slide shows; Happy hour.

Resthaven Nursing Home
155 Quincy Ave, Braintree, MA 02184
(617) 843-2155
Admin Ruth E Houde.

Licensure Skilled care; Intermediate care. *Beds* SNF 49; ICF 24. *Certified* Medicaid.
Activities Arts & crafts; Games; Reading groups; Prayer groups; Movies.

John Scott House Nursing & Rehabilitation Center
233 Middle St, Braintree, MA 02184
(617) 843-1860
Admin Michael Welch.
Licensure Skilled care; Intermediate care. *Beds* SNF 107; ICF 93. *Certified* Medicaid; Medicare.
Owner Proprietary corp.

Elihu White Nursing & Rehabilitation Center
95 Commercial St, Braintree, MA 02184
(617) 848-3678, 848-0933 FAX
Admin Florence E Logan. *Dir of Nursing* Diane Hoffman RN. *Medical Dir* Peter Barrett MD.
Licensure Skilled care; Intermediate care. *Beds* SNF 80; ICF 112. *Certified* Medicaid; Medicare.
Owner Proprietary corp (Samuel & Florence E Logan).
Staff Physical therapists; Occupational therapists; Speech therapists; Activities coordinators; Dietitians; Podiatrists.
Facilities Dining room; Physical therapy room; Activities room; Barber/Beauty shop; Courtyard.
Activities Arts & crafts; Cards; Games; Reading groups; Prayer groups; Movies; Dances/Social/Cultural gatherings.

Brewster

Brewster Manor Nursing & Retirement Home
873 Harwich Rd, Brewster, MA 02631
(617) 896-7046
Admin David Maloney. *Dir of Nursing* Elinore Swansen RN. *Medical Dir* Carol Topolewski MD.
Licensure Skilled care; Intermediate care. *Beds* SNF 121; ICF 82. *Certified* Medicaid.
Owner Proprietary corp.
Staff Physicians 1 (pt); RNs 21 (ft), 8 (pt); LPNs 6 (ft), 1 (pt); Nurses' aides 47 (ft), 25 (pt); Physical therapists 1 (pt); Reality therapists 2 (pt); Recreational therapists 1 (ft), 2 (pt); Occupational therapists 1 (pt); Speech therapists 1 (pt); Activities coordinators 1 (ft), 1 (pt); Dietitians 1 (pt); Ophthalmologists 1 (pt); Podiatrists 1 (pt).
Facilities Dining room; Physical therapy room; Activities room; Chapel; Crafts room; Laundry room; Barber/Beauty shop; Library.
Activities Arts & crafts; Cards; Games; Reading groups; Prayer groups; Movies; Shopping trips; Dances/Social/Cultural gatherings.

Bridgewater

Bridgewater Nursing Home
16 Pleasant St, Bridgewater, MA 02324
(617) 697-4616
Admin Margaret Pomeroy.
Licensure Intermediate care. *Beds* ICF 43. *Certified* Medicaid.
Owner Proprietary corp.

Brockton

Braemoor Nursing Home Inc
34 N Pearl St, Brockton, MA 02401
(508) 586-3696
Admin Michael J Roland. *Dir of Nursing* Mary Brooks RN. *Medical Dir* Dr Craig Warnick.
Licensure Skilled care; Intermediate care. *Beds* SNF 80; ICF 40. *Certified* Medicaid; Medicare.
Owner Proprietary corp.

Staff Physicians 3 (pt); RNs 4 (ft), 4 (pt); LPNs 10 (ft), 8 (pt); Nurses' aides 40 (ft), 20 (pt); Physical therapists 1 (ft); Occupational therapists (consultant); Speech therapists (consultant); Activities coordinators 1 (ft); Dietitians (consultant); Ophthalmologists (consultant); Podiatrists (consultant); Audiologists (consultant).
Facilities Dining room; Physical therapy room; Activities room; Chapel; Crafts room; Laundry room; Barber/Beauty shop; Library.
Activities Arts & crafts; Cards; Games; Reading groups; Prayer groups; Movies; Shopping trips; Dances/Social/Cultural gatherings; Intergenerational programs; Pet therapy.

Brockwood Health Care Nursing Home
PO Box 4156, 227 W Elm St, Brockton, MA 02401
(617) 583-2203
Admin Mary J Tomlinson.
Licensure Intermediate care. *Beds* ICF 50. *Certified* Medicaid.
Owner Proprietary corp.
Admissions Requirements Minimum age 21; Medical examination; Physician's request.
Staff RNs 2 (ft), 1 (pt); LPNs 1 (ft), 2 (pt); Nurses' aides 10 (ft), 4 (pt); Recreational therapists 1 (pt); Dietitians 1 (pt).
Facilities Dining room; Activities room; Laundry room.
Activities Arts & crafts; Cards; Games; Reading groups; Prayer groups; Movies; Shopping trips; Dances/Social/Cultural gatherings; Outside dinners.

Brockton Ridge Long-Term Care Center
130 Quincy Ave, Brockton, MA 02402
(617) 588-4700
Admin Martha A Munies.
Licensure Skilled care; Intermediate care. *Beds* SNF 84; ICF 41. *Certified* Medicaid.
Owner Proprietary corp.

Embassy House Health Care Nursing Home
2 Beaumont Ave, Brockton, MA 02402
(617) 588-8550
Admin James Morris.
Medical Dir Dr Elliot Korim.
Licensure Skilled care; Intermediate care. *Beds* SNF 82; ICF 41. *Certified* Medicaid; Medicare.
Owner Proprietary corp (First Healthcare Corp).
Admissions Requirements Minimum age 21; Medical examination; Physician's request.
Staff Physicians 15 (pt); RNs 14 (ft), 18 (pt); LPNs 5 (ft), 8 (pt); Nurses' aides 14 (ft), 38 (pt); Physical therapists 1 (pt); Recreational therapists 1 (pt); Occupational therapists 1 (pt); Speech therapists 1 (pt); Activities coordinators 1 (ft), 1 (pt); Dietitians 1 (pt); Podiatrists 1 (pt); Dentists 1 (pt).
Facilities Dining room; Physical therapy room; Activities room; Crafts room; Laundry room; Barber/Beauty shop; Library; TV rooms; Solariums.
Activities Arts & crafts; Cards; Games; Reading groups; Prayer groups; Movies; Shopping trips; Dances/Social/Cultural gatherings; Fishing for men; Bus tours.

Green Oak Nursing Home
947 N Main St, Brockton, MA 02401
(617) 587-9367
Admin Shirley Lajoie. *Dir of Nursing* Virginia Foster.
Licensure Intermediate care. *Beds* ICF 83. *Certified* Medicaid.
Owner Nonprofit organization/foundation.
Admissions Requirements Minimum age 40; Females only.
Staff RNs 2 (ft); LPNs 4 (ft), 6 (pt); Nurses' aides 17 (ft), 8 (pt); Recreational therapists 1 (ft), 1 (pt); Dietitians 1 (pt); Social worker 1 (ft).
Languages French.

Facilities Dining room; Activities room; Crafts room; Laundry room; Barber/Beauty shop.
Activities Arts & crafts; Cards; Games; Reading groups; Prayer groups; Movies; Shopping trips; Dances/Social/Cultural gatherings.

Lutheran Home of Brockton Inc
888 N Main St, Brockton, MA 02401
(617) 587-6556
Admin Rev William S Eaton. *Dir of Nursing* Carol Glazier RN. *Medical Dir* Mayer Rubenstein MD.
Licensure Skilled care; Intermediate care; Outpatient Geriatric Center. *Beds* SNF 82; ICF 41. *Certified* Medicaid.
Owner Proprietary corp.
Admissions Requirements Minimum age 65; Medical examination.
Staff Physicians 1 (pt); RNs 3 (ft), 14 (pt); LPNs 12 (ft), 4 (pt); Nurses' aides 36 (ft), 23 (pt); Physical therapists 3 (ft); Reality therapists 1 (ft), 1 (pt); Activities coordinators 1 (ft); Social workers 1 (ft).
Affiliation Lutheran.
Facilities Dining room; Physical therapy room; Activities room; Chapel; Crafts room; Laundry room; Barber/Beauty shop; Library.
Activities Arts & crafts; Games; Reading groups; Prayer groups; Movies; Shopping trips; Dances/Social/Cultural gatherings; Music; Short plays; Dancing shows; In-house shopping.

Madalawn Nursing Home
1330 Main St, Brockton, MA 02401
(617) 583-1070
Admin Thomas F Shields.
Licensure Intermediate care. *Beds* ICF 50. *Certified* Medicaid.
Owner Proprietary corp.

Regent Park Long-Term Care Center
41 Libbey St, Brockton, MA 02402
(617) 588-1450
Admin Ross H Galasso. *Dir of Nursing* Nancy McComas RN. *Medical Dir* Peter C Roos MD.
Licensure Skilled care; Intermediate care. *Beds* SNF 60; ICF 60. *Certified* Medicaid.
Owner Proprietary corp.
Admissions Requirements Medical examination; Physician's request.
Staff RNs 4 (ft), 5 (pt); LPNs 7 (ft), 5 (pt); Nurses' aides 29 (ft); Physical therapists 1 (pt); Occupational therapists 1 (pt); Activities coordinators 2 (ft); Dietitians 1 (ft).
Facilities Dining room; Activities room; Laundry room; Barber/Beauty shop; Dayrooms.
Activities Arts & crafts; Cards; Games; Reading groups; Prayer groups; Movies; Shopping trips; Dances/Social/Cultural gatherings.

St Joseph Manor
215 Thatcher St, Brockton, MA 02402
(617) 583-5834
Admin Sr Geraldine Nevaras.
Licensure Skilled care; Intermediate care. *Beds* SNF 40; ICF 80. *Certified* Medicaid.
Owner Proprietary corp.

Village Rest Home of Brockton
197 W Chestnut St, Brockton, MA 02401
(508) 583-0040
Admin Nenita T Elevado.
Medical Dir Karl Stammen.
Licensure Community support. *Beds* Community support 14.
Owner Privately owned.
Admissions Requirements Minimum age 40; Females only; Medical examination; Physician's request.

Staff Physicians; RNs; Nurses' aides; Recreational therapists; Activities coordinators; Dietitians; Podiatrists (consultant).
Facilities Dining room; Laundry room.
Activities Cards; Games; Prayer groups; Church groups.

West Acres Nursing Home
804 Pleasant St, Brockton, MA 02401
(617) 583-6000
Admin John Soule.
Licensure Skilled care; Intermediate care. *Beds* SNF 82; ICF 44. *Certified* Medicaid; Medicare.
Owner Proprietary corp.

Woodridge House
596 Summer St, Brockton, MA 02402
(508) 586-1467
Admin Vincent Bettes. *Dir of Nursing* Sandra Bell. *Medical Dir* Dr Poor.
Licensure Skilled care; Intermediate care. *Beds* SNF 83; ICF 42. *Private Pay Patients* 10%. *Certified* Medicaid; Medicare.
Owner Proprietary corp (First Healthcare Corp).
Activities Arts & crafts; Cards; Games; Reading groups; Prayer groups; Movies; Shopping trips; Dances/Social/Cultural gatherings; Pet therapy.

Brookline

Brentwood Nursing Home Inc
34-36 Francis St, Brookline, MA 02146
(617) 277-0722
Admin Mary Kathryn Bittner. *Dir of Nursing* Vivian Evers RN.
Licensure Intermediate care. *Beds* ICF 23.
Owner Proprietary corp.
Staff Physicians 1 (pt); RNs 2 (ft), 3 (pt); LPNs 2 (ft); Nurses' aides 8 (ft), 6 (pt); Activities coordinators 1 (pt); Dietitians 1 (pt).
Languages French.
Activities Cards; Games; Reading groups; Prayer groups; Movies.

Chamberlain Nursing Home
123 Gardner Rd, Brookline, MA 02146
(617) 277-0225
Admin Barbara A Smith.
Licensure Intermediate care. *Beds* ICF 27. *Certified* Medicaid.
Owner Proprietary corp.
Staff RNs 2 (ft), 1 (pt); LPNs 1 (ft); Nurses' aides 4 (ft), 2 (pt); Activities coordinators 1 (ft); Dietitians 1 (pt).
Facilities Dining room; Activities room; Laundry room.
Activities Arts & crafts; Games; Movies; Shopping trips; Dances/Social/Cultural gatherings; Overnight trips.

City View Nursing Home Inc
PO Box 446, 232 Summit Ave, Brookline, MA 02146-0004
(617) 232-8266
Admin Leon Backenroth.
Licensure Intermediate care. *Beds* 80. *Certified* Medicaid.

Coolidge Corner Convalescent Center
30 Webster St, Brookline, MA 02146
(617) 734-2300
Admin Martha B Armstrong.
Licensure Skilled care; Intermediate care. *Beds* SNF 105; ICF 105.

Franida House Nursing Home
123 Gardner Rd, Brookline, MA 02146-4570
(617) 522-8714
Admin Barbara A Smith.
Licensure Intermediate care. *Beds* ICF 22. *Certified* Medicaid.
Owner Proprietary corp.

Mason Terrace Rest Home
12 Mason Terrace, Brookline, MA 02146
(617) 277-0655
Admin Elaine K Porter.
Licensure Rest home. *Beds* Rest home 26.
 Certified Medicaid.
Owner Proprietary corp.
Admissions Requirements Minimum age 30;
 Medical examination; Physician's request.
Staff Nurses' aides 4 (ft), 2 (pt); Activities
 coordinators 1 (pt).
Facilities Dining room; Activities room.
Activities Arts & crafts; Cards; Games;
 Reading groups.

Park Marion Nursing Center
99 Park St, Brookline, MA 02146
(617) 731-1050
Admin James S Mamary.
Licensure Skilled care; Alzheimer's care. *Beds*
 SNF 120. *Certified* Medicaid.
Owner Proprietary corp.
Admissions Requirements Medical
 examination; Physician's request.
Staff RNs 18 (ft); Nurses' aides 54 (ft);
 Physical therapists 1 (ft); Recreational
 therapists 1 (ft); Occupational therapists 1
 (ft); Speech therapists 1 (ft); Activities
 coordinators 1 (ft); Dietitians 1 (ft);
 Ophthalmologists 1 (ft).
Languages French, Spanish.
Facilities Dining room; Physical therapy
 room; Activities room; Crafts room; Laundry
 room; Barber/Beauty shop.
Activities Arts & crafts; Cards; Games;
 Reading groups; Prayer groups; Movies;
 Shopping trips; Dances/Social/Cultural
 gatherings.

Wellman House Rest Home
35-37 Winchester St, Brookline, MA 02146
(617) 277-4081
Admin Albert V Reynolds.
Licensure Rest home. *Beds* Rest home 20.
Owner Privately owned.

Winthrop Road Rest Home
24 Winthrop Rd, Brookline, MA 02146
(617) 277-5504
Admin Arthur V Reynolds.
Licensure Rest home. *Beds* Rest home 31.
Owner Proprietary corp.

Cambridge

Cambridge Homes
360 Mount Auburn St, Cambridge, MA 02138
(617) 876-0369
Admin Miriam S Klapper. *Dir of Nursing*
 Lorraine Nicholls. *Medical Dir* Dr Aram
 Tomasian.
Licensure Intermediate care; Retirement
 home. *Beds* ICF 12; Retirement home 38.
Owner Nonprofit organization/foundation.
Admissions Requirements Minimum age 65;
 Medical examination.
Staff RNs 1 (ft), 1 (pt); LPNs 2 (ft), 2 (pt);
 Nurses' aides; Activities coordinators 1 (ft);
 Dietitians 1 (pt).
Facilities Dining room; Activities room;
 Crafts room; Laundry room; Barber/Beauty
 shop; Library; Guest bedroom.
Activities Arts & crafts; Cards; Games;
 Reading groups; Prayer groups; Movies;
 Shopping trips; Dances/Social/Cultural
 gatherings; Intergenerational programs; Pet
 therapy; Lectures.

Cambridge Nursing Home
1 Russell St, Cambridge, MA 02140
(617) 491-6110
Admin Joseph Deveau.
Licensure Skilled care; Intermediate care. *Beds*
 SNF 39; ICF 80. *Certified* Medicaid.
Owner Proprietary corp.

Cantabridgia Health Care Nursing Facility
195 Prospect St, Cambridge, MA 02139
(617) 491-6363
Admin Barry Chiler. *Dir of Nursing* Eileen
 Ireton.
Licensure Skilled care; Intermediate care. *Beds*
 SNF 49; ICF 50. *Certified* Medicaid.
Owner Proprietary corp.
Admissions Requirements Minimum age 21.
Staff RNs; LPNs; Nurses' aides; Physical
 therapists; Reality therapists; Recreational
 therapists; Occupational therapists; Activities
 coordinators; Dietitians; Ophthalmologists.
Languages Portuguese.
Facilities Dining room; Activities room;
 Crafts room; Laundry room; Barber/Beauty
 shop.
Activities Arts & crafts; Cards; Games;
 Reading groups; Prayer groups; Movies;
 Shopping trips; Dances/Social/Cultural
 gatherings.

Jane Elizabeth House Nursing Home
6 Prentiss St, Cambridge, MA 02140
(617) 491-7086
Admin Bradley McDermott.
Licensure Intermediate care. *Beds* ICF 53.
 Certified Medicaid.
Owner Proprietary corp.

Harvard Manor Nursing Home
273 Harvard St, Cambridge, MA 02139
(617) 547-4291
Admin Saul Tobias.
Medical Dir M Norah Murray.
Licensure Intermediate care. *Beds* ICF 95.
 Certified Medicaid.
Owner Proprietary corp.
Admissions Requirements Minimum age 45;
 Medical examination.
Staff RNs 3 (ft); LPNs 7 (ft); Nurses' aides 25
 (ft); Recreational therapists 1 (ft); Dietitians
 1 (ft).
Facilities Activities room; Laundry room.
Activities Arts & crafts; Cards; Games; Prayer
 groups; Movies; Shopping trips; Dances/
 Social/Cultural gatherings.

Mayor Michael J Neville Manor
650 Concord Ave, Cambridge, MA 02138
(617) 492-6310
Admin James G Mulcahy. *Dir of Nursing*
 Teresa Clunan RN. *Medical Dir* Ilan P
 Abrams MD.
Licensure Skilled care; Intermediate care. *Beds*
 SNF 96; ICF 83. *Certified* Medicaid.
Owner Publicly owned.
Admissions Requirements Minimum age 21;
 Medical examination.
Staff Physicians 1 (pt); RNs 7 (ft), 5 (pt);
 LPNs 10 (ft), 6 (pt); Nurses' aides 41 (ft), 16
 (pt); Physical therapists 1 (ft); Recreational
 therapists 3 (ft); Occupational therapists 1
 (pt); Speech therapists 1 (pt); Dietitians 1
 (pt); Ophthalmologists 1 (pt); Podiatrists 1
 (pt); Dentists 1 (pt).
Facilities Dining room; Physical therapy
 room; Activities room; Laundry room;
 Barber/Beauty shop; Library; Gift shop.
Activities Arts & crafts; Cards; Games;
 Reading groups; Prayer groups; Movies;
 Shopping trips; Dances/Social/Cultural
 gatherings; Bus trips.

Vernon Hall Inc
8 Dana St, Cambridge, MA 02138
(617) 864-4267
Admin Patricia G O'Callagher.
Licensure Skilled care; Intermediate care. *Beds*
 SNF 41; ICF 42. *Certified* Medicaid.
Owner Proprietary corp.

Canton

Hellenic Nursing Home for the Aged
601 Sherman St, Canton, MA 02021-2098
(617) 828-7450

Admin Mary Jarvis. *Dir of Nursing* Denise
 Murray. *Medical Dir* Dr George A Hasiotis.
Licensure Skilled care; Intermediate care. *Beds*
 SNF 80; ICF 80. *Certified* Medicaid.
Owner Nonprofit corp.
Admissions Requirements Minimum age 60;
 Physician's request.
Staff RNs; LPNs; Nurses' aides; Physical
 therapists 1 (pt); Recreational therapists 3
 (ft), 1 (pt); Occupational therapists 1 (pt);
 Speech therapists 1 (pt); Activities
 coordinators 1 (ft); Dietitians 1 (pt);
 Ophthalmologists 1 (pt); Podiatrists 1 (pt);
 Audiologists 1 (pt).
Languages Greek.
Affiliation Hellenic Women's Benevolent
 Society.
Facilities Dining room; Physical therapy
 room; Activities room; Chapel; Crafts room;
 Laundry room; Barber/Beauty shop; Library.
Activities Arts & crafts; Cards; Games;
 Reading groups; Prayer groups; Movies;
 Shopping trips; Dances/Social/Cultural
 gatherings; Intergenerational programs; Pet
 therapy.

**Massachusetts Hospital School Skilled Nursing
Facility**
3 Randolph St, Canton, MA 02021
(617) 828-2440
Admin John Britt.
Licensure Skilled care. *Beds* SNF 78.
Owner Publicly owned.

Centerville

Centerville Nursing Home
22 Richardson Rd, Centerville, MA 02632
(508) 775-5050
Admin Ronald W Morris. *Dir of Nursing*
 Wilhelmina Cuff RN.
Licensure Skilled care. *Beds* SNF 110.
 Certified Medicaid.
Owner Proprietary corp.
Staff Physicians 1 (ft), 4 (pt); RNs 34 (ft), 14
 (pt); LPNs 3 (ft), 4 (pt); Nurses' aides 43
 (ft), 15 (pt); Occupational therapists 1 (ft), 1
 (pt); Speech therapists 1 (pt); Activities
 coordinators 1 (ft); Dietitians 1 (ft);
 Podiatrists 1 (pt).
Facilities Dining room; Physical therapy
 room; Activities room; Crafts room; Laundry
 room; Barber/Beauty shop.
Activities Arts & crafts; Cards; Games;
 Reading groups; Prayer groups; Movies;
 Dances/Social/Cultural gatherings; Pet
 therapy.

Charlton

Charlton Manor Rest Home Inc
RR 1 Box 131, Town Farm Rd, Charlton, MA
 01507
(617) 248-5136
Admin Caroline G Iandoli.
Licensure Rest home. *Beds* Rest home 35.
Owner Proprietary corp.

Masonic Home
PO Box 1000, Masonic Hill Rd, Charlton, MA
 01507
(508) 248-7344
Admin James L Parker. *Dir of Nursing* Carol
 J Mason RN. *Medical Dir* Edmond Koury
 MD.
Licensure Intermediate care; Rest home. *Beds*
 ICF 100; Rest home 69. *Private Pay Patients*
 50%. *Certified* Medicaid.
Owner Nonprofit organization/foundation.
Admissions Requirements Minimum age 65;
 Medical examination.
Staff Physicians 2 (pt); RNs 6 (ft), 6 (pt);
 LPNs 6 (ft), 6 (pt); Nurses' aides 40 (ft), 20
 (pt); Physical therapists 1 (pt); Reality
 therapists 1 (pt); Recreational therapists 2

(pt); Occupational therapists 1 (pt);
Activities coordinators 1 (ft); Dietitians 1
(ft); Podiatrists 1 (pt); Audiologists 1 (pt).
Affiliation Masons.
Facilities Dining room; Physical therapy
room; Activities room; Chapel; Crafts room;
Laundry room; Barber/Beauty shop; Library.
Activities Arts & crafts; Cards; Games;
Reading groups; Prayer groups; Movies;
Shopping trips; Dances/Social/Cultural
gatherings; Intergenerational programs; Pet
therapy.

Chatham

Liberty Commons
390 Orleans Rd, Chatham, MA 02650
(508) 945-4611, 945-2245 FAX
Admin Michele O'Brien. *Dir of Nursing* Ann
Lavallee. *Medical Dir* Jean-Paul Aucoin.
Licensure Skilled care; Intermediate care;
Alzheimer's care. *Beds* SNF 80; ICF 40.
Private Pay Patients 45%. *Certified*
Medicaid; Medicare.
Owner Proprietary corp.
Staff RNs; LPNs; Nurses' aides; Physical
therapists 2 (pt); Recreational therapists 1
(ft); Occupational therapists 1 (pt); Speech
therapists 1 (pt); Activities coordinators 1
(ft); Dietitians 1 (pt); Ophthalmologists 1
(pt); Podiatrists 1 (pt).
Facilities Dining room; Physical therapy
room; Activities room; Chapel; Crafts room;
Laundry room; Barber/Beauty shop; Library.
Activities Arts & crafts; Cards; Games;
Reading groups; Prayer groups; Movies;
Shopping trips; Dances/Social/Cultural
gatherings; Intergenerational programs; Pet
therapy; Alzheimer's program.

Chelmsford

Palm Manor Nursing Home
40 Parkhurst Rd, Chelmsford, MA 01824
(617) 256-3151
Admin Robert Noonan.
Medical Dir Dr Thomas Fitzpatrick.
Licensure Skilled care; Intermediate care. *Beds*
SNF 38; ICF 82. *Certified* Medicaid.
Owner Proprietary corp.
Facilities Dining room; Physical therapy
room; Activities room; Chapel; Laundry
room; Barber/Beauty shop; Library.
Activities Arts & crafts; Cards; Games;
Reading groups; Prayer groups; Movies;
Shopping trips; Dances/Social/Cultural
gatherings.

Sunny Acres Nursing Home
254 Billerica Rd, Chelmsford, MA 01824
(617) 256-0231
Admin Shirley Schwartz.
Licensure Skilled care; Intermediate care. *Beds*
SNF 48; ICF 33. *Certified* Medicaid.
Owner Proprietary corp.

Chelsea

Chelsea Jewish Nursing Home
17 Lafayette Ave, Chelsea, MA 02150
(617) 884-6766
Admin Barry Berman.
Licensure Skilled care; Intermediate care. *Beds*
SNF 82; ICF 41. *Certified* Medicaid.
Owner Proprietary corp.
Affiliation Jewish.

Cottage Manor Nursing Home
148 Shawmut St, Chelsea, MA 02150
(617) 889-2250
Admin Marjorie A Manichello.
Licensure Intermediate care. *Beds* ICF 34.
Certified Medicaid.
Owner Proprietary corp.
Admissions Requirements Minimum age 21;
Medical examination.

Staff RNs 2 (ft); LPNs 4 (pt); Nurses' aides 9
(ft), 4 (pt); Recreational therapists 1 (ft);
Activities coordinators 1 (ft); Dietitians 1
(pt).
Facilities Dining room; Activities room;
Crafts room; Laundry room; Barber/Beauty
shop.
Activities Arts & crafts; Cards; Games;
Reading groups; Prayer groups; Movies;
Shopping trips; Dances/Social/Cultural
gatherings.

Soldiers' Home in Massachusetts
91 Crest Ave, Chelsea, MA 02150
(617) 884-5660, 884-1162 FAX
Admin William D Thompson. *Dir of Nursing*
Silva Gerety RN. *Medical Dir* George
Smithy MD.
Licensure Skilled care; Rehabilitation;
Alzheimer's care; Acute care; OPO dorm.
Beds SNF 88; Rehabilitation 10; Alzheimer's
care 12; Acute care 34; OPO dorm 360.
Private Pay Patients 0%. *Certified* Medicare;
VA.
Owner Publicly owned.
Admissions Requirements Medical
examination; Must be an Armed Forces
veteran and a Massachusetts citizen.
Staff Physicians 7 (ft), 15 (pt); RNs 50 (ft), 10
(pt); LPNs 25 (ft), 5 (pt); Nurses' aides 32
(ft), 8 (pt); Physical therapists 2 (ft);
Recreational therapists 3 (ft); Activities
coordinators 1 (ft); Dietitians 2 (ft);
Ophthalmologists 2 (pt); Podiatrists 2 (pt);
Chaplain 2 (ft), 1 (pt).
Languages Spanish.
Facilities Dining room; Physical therapy
room; Activities room; Chapel; Barber/
Beauty shop; Library.
Activities Arts & crafts; Cards; Games; Prayer
groups; Movies; Shopping trips; Dances/
Social/Cultural gatherings; Pet therapy.

Chicopee

Birch Manor Nursing Home
44 New Lombard Rd, Chicopee, MA 01020
(413) 592-7738
Admin Mary L Harris (Shea).
Medical Dir Trudy Atteridge.
Licensure Intermediate care. *Beds* ICF 56.
Certified Medicaid.
Owner Proprietary corp.
Staff RNs; LPNs; Nurses' aides; Activities
coordinators.
Activities Arts & crafts; Cards; Games;
Reading groups; Prayer groups; Movies;
Shopping trips; Dances/Social/Cultural
gatherings.

Chicopee Municipal Home
820 Front St, Chicopee, MA 01020
(413) 598-8455
Admin David F Leitl. *Dir of Nursing*
Margaret Yopak RN. *Medical Dir* Raymond
Gagnon MD.
Licensure Intermediate care. *Beds* ICF 74.
Private Pay Patients .01%. *Certified*
Medicaid.
Owner Publicly owned.
Admissions Requirements Minimum age 60;
Medical examination.
Staff RNs 4 (ft), 2 (pt); LPNs 5 (ft), 1 (pt);
Nurses' aides 22 (ft), 10 (pt); Recreational
therapists 1 (ft); Dietitians 1 (pt).
Languages French, Polish, Spanish.
Facilities Dining room; Activities room;
Chapel; Crafts room; Laundry room; Barber/
Beauty shop; Library.
Activities Arts & crafts; Cards; Games;
Reading groups; Prayer groups; Movies;
Dances/Social/Cultural gatherings; Pet
therapy.

Elms Manor Nursing Home
269 Moore St, Chicopee, MA 01013
(413) 592-7736
Admin Jospeh P Kennedy.

Licensure Intermediate care; Rest home. *Beds*
ICF 53; Rest home 32. *Certified* Medicaid.
Owner Proprietary corp.
Admissions Requirements Minimum age 21.
Staff RNs 2 (ft); LPNs 2 (ft), 5 (pt); Nurses'
aides 10 (ft), 8 (pt); Physical therapists 1
(pt); Reality therapists 1 (pt); Recreational
therapists 1 (ft); Occupational therapists 1
(pt); Speech therapists 1 (pt); Activities
coordinators 1 (ft); Dietitians 1 (pt);
Podiatrists 1 (pt).
Facilities Dining room; Activities room;
Laundry room; Barber/Beauty shop.
Activities Arts & crafts; Cards; Games;
Reading groups; Prayer groups; Movies;
Shopping trips; Dances/Social/Cultural
gatherings.

Willimansett East Nursing Home
11 Saint Anthony St, Chicopee, MA 01013
(413) 536-2540
Admin Virginia F Matosky RN NHA. *Dir of
Nursing* Eileen C Plante RN. *Medical Dir*
William J Dean Jr MD.
Licensure Skilled care; Intermediate care;
Alzheimer's care. *Beds* SNF 128; ICF 60.
Certified Medicaid; Medicare.
Owner Proprietary corp (Genesis Health
Ventures).
Staff RNs; LPNs; Nurses' aides; Physical
therapists; Recreational therapists;
Occupational therapists; Speech therapists;
Activities coordinators; Dietitians;
Ophthalmologists; Podiatrists; Audiologists.
Languages Polish, French, Spanish,
Portuguese.
Facilities Dining room; Physical therapy
room; Activities room; Chapel; Crafts room;
Laundry room; Barber/Beauty shop; Library.
Activities Arts & crafts; Cards; Games;
Reading groups; Prayer groups; Movies;
Dances/Social/Cultural gatherings;
Intergenerational programs; Pet therapy;
Painting classes.

Willimansett West Nursing Home
546 Chicopee St, Chicopee, MA 01013
(413) 536-2540
Admin Rosemary J Dubuc RN. *Dir of Nursing*
Mona Simard RN. *Medical Dir* William
Dean.
Licensure Skilled care; Intermediate care. *Beds*
SNF 43; ICF 60. *Certified* Medicaid;
Medicare.
Owner Proprietary corp (Genesis Health
Ventures).
Admissions Requirements Medical
examination; Physician's request.
Staff RNs; LPNs; Nurses' aides; Physical
therapists; Recreational therapists;
Occupational therapists; Speech therapists;
Activities coordinators; Dietitians;
Ophthalmologists; Podiatrists.
Languages Polish, French, Spanish,
Portuguese.
Facilities Dining room; Physical therapy
room; Activities room; Crafts room; Laundry
room; Barber/Beauty shop.
Activities Arts & crafts; Cards; Games;
Reading groups; Prayer groups; Movies;
Shopping trips; Dances/Social/Cultural
gatherings; Intergenerational programs; Pet
therapy.

Clinton

Clinton Home for Aged People
271 Church St, Clinton, MA 01510
(617) 365-4872
Admin Marjorie C Stake.
Licensure Rest home. *Beds* Rest home 12.
Owner Proprietary corp.
Admissions Requirements Minimum age 65;
Medical examination.
Staff RNs 1 (pt).
Facilities Dining room; Living room.

Clinton Manor Nursing Home
250 Main St, Clinton, MA 01510
(617) 368-0171
Admin Anne B Roy. *Dir of Nursing* Patricia P
Dwyer. *Medical Dir* Dr Allan Ramey.
Licensure Skilled care; Intermediate care;
Alzheimer's care. *Beds* SNF 49; ICF 30.
Certified Medicaid.
Owner Proprietary corp.
Admissions Requirements Medical
examination; Physician's request.
Staff RNs; LPNs; Nurses' aides; Activities
coordinators; Dietitians.
Languages Italian.
Facilities Dining room; Physical therapy
room; Laundry room; Barber/Beauty shop.
Activities Arts & crafts; Cards; Games;
Reading groups; Prayer groups; Movies;
Dances/Social/Cultural gatherings; Garden;
Cooking; Trivia; One on one visits; Slides;
Pet therapy; Adopt-a-grandparent program;
Pen & palette sittercise & more.

Ferguson Rest Home
88 Walnut St, Clinton, MA 01510
(617) 365-3552
Admin Duncan Ferguson.
Medical Dir Dr William Jacobson.
Licensure Rest home. *Beds* Rest home 17.
Certified Medicaid.
Owner Privately owned.
Admissions Requirements Minimum age 60;
Females only; Medical examination;
Physician's request.
Staff Physicians 1 (ft); RNs 1 (ft); Nurses'
aides 6 (pt); Recreational therapists 1 (ft);
Activities coordinators 1 (ft); Dietitians 1
(ft); Ophthalmologists 1 (ft).
Facilities Dining room; Activities room;
Crafts room; Barber/Beauty shop; Library.
Activities Arts & crafts; Cards; Games;
Movies; Shopping trips.

Cohasset

**Cohasset Knoll Skilled Nursing &
Rehabilitation**
Rte 3A, Chief Justice Hwy, Cohasset, MA
02025
(617) 383-9060
Admin Robert M Dufresne.
Medical Dir Albert Cline.
Licensure Skilled care. *Beds* SNF 80. *Certified*
Medicare.
Owner Proprietary corp (Beverly Enterprises).
Admissions Requirements Minimum age 21;
Medical examination; Physician's request.
Staff Physicians 16 (pt); RNs 5 (ft), 4 (pt);
LPNs 2 (ft), 3 (pt); Nurses' aides 21 (ft), 20
(pt); Physical therapists 1 (pt); Occupational
therapists 1 (pt); Speech therapists 1 (pt);
Activities coordinators 1 (ft), 1 (pt);
Dietitians 1 (pt); Podiatrists 2 (pt); Dentists
1 (pt).
Facilities Dining room; Physical therapy
room; Activities room; Crafts room; Laundry
room; Barber/Beauty shop; Library; Sitting
rooms.
Activities Arts & crafts; Cards; Games;
Reading groups; Prayer groups; Movies;
Shopping trips; Dances/Social/Cultural
gatherings.

Ripley Road Nursing Home Inc
25 Ripley Rd, Cohasset, MA 02025
(617) 383-0419
Admin Kathleen R Logan.
Licensure Intermediate care. *Beds* ICF 22.
Certified Medicaid.
Owner Proprietary corp.

Concord

Rivercrest Long-Term Care Facility
80 Deaconess Rd, Concord, MA 01742
(617) 369-5151
Admin Cathy B Smith.

Medical Dir Dr Henry Vaillant.
Licensure Skilled care; Intermediate care;
Retirement. *Beds* SNF 41; ICF 39. *Certified*
Medicaid; Medicare.
Owner Nonprofit corp.
Admissions Requirements Minimum age 65.
Staff Physicians 3 (pt); RNs 8 (ft), 21 (pt);
LPNs 9 (ft), 2 (pt); Nurses' aides 20 (ft), 19
(pt); Physical therapists 1 (pt); Reality
therapists 1 (ft); Occupational therapists 1
(pt); Speech therapists 1 (pt); Activities
coordinators 1 (ft); Dietitians 1 (ft);
Ophthalmologists 1 (pt).
Affiliation Methodist.
Facilities Dining room; Physical therapy
room; Activities room; Chapel; Crafts room;
Barber/Beauty shop; Library.
Activities Arts & crafts; Cards; Games;
Reading groups; Prayer groups; Movies;
Shopping trips; Dances/Social/Cultural
gatherings.

Walden House Healthcare Nursing Home
785 Main St, Concord, MA 01742
(617) 369-6889
Admin Ira R Lipshutz. *Dir of Nursing* Helen
McNabola RN. *Medical Dir* Mary Donald
MD.
Licensure Skilled care; Intermediate care. *Beds*
SNF 82; ICF 41. *Certified* Medicaid;
Medicare.
Owner Proprietary corp (First Healthcare
Corp).
Admissions Requirements Medical
examination; Physician's request.
Staff RNs 6 (ft), 12 (pt); LPNs 4 (ft), 5 (pt);
Nurses' aides 30 (ft), 10 (pt); Physical
therapists 1 (pt); Recreational therapists 2
(ft); Occupational therapists 1 (pt); Speech
therapists 1 (pt); Activities coordinators 1
(ft); Dietitians 1 (pt); Ophthalmologists 1
(pt).
Languages Spanish, Portuguese.
Facilities Dining room; Physical therapy
room; Activities room; Chapel; Crafts room;
Laundry room; Barber/Beauty shop; Library.
Activities Arts & crafts; Cards; Games; Prayer
groups; Movies; Shopping trips; Dances/
Social/Cultural gatherings.

Dalton

Curtis Manor Retirement Home
83 Curtis Ave, Dalton, MA 01226
(413) 684-0218
Admin Fred D Daniel.
Licensure Rest home. *Beds* Rest home 23.
Owner Privately owned.

Dalton Nursing Home Inc
265 Main St, Dalton, MA 01226
(413) 684-3212
Admin Susan Bonak.
Medical Dir Wilfren A Blais MD.
Licensure Skilled care. *Beds* SNF 77. *Certified*
Medicaid.
Owner Proprietary corp.
Staff RNs 3 (ft), 4 (pt); LPNs 5 (ft), 5 (pt);
Nurses' aides 14 (ft), 19 (pt); Physical
therapists 2 (ft); Activities coordinators 1
(ft); Dietitians 1 (pt); Podiatrists 1 (pt).
Facilities Dining room; Physical therapy
room; Activities room; Crafts room; Laundry
room; Barber/Beauty shop.
Activities Arts & crafts; Games; Reading
groups; Prayer groups; Movies; Shopping
trips; Dances/Social/Cultural gatherings.

Danvers

Cedar Glen Nursing Home
44 Summer St, Danvers, MA 01923
(617) 774-6955
Admin Lindael A Barrington.
Licensure Skilled care; Intermediate care; Rest
home. *Beds* SNF 40; ICF 36; Rest home 24.
Certified Medicaid.

Owner Privately owned.

Danvers Twin Oaks Nursing Home
63 Locust St, Danvers, MA 01923
(508) 777-0011
Admin Maureen E Buckley. *Dir of Nursing*
Gail Harrington RN. *Medical Dir* John
Hazelton MD.
Licensure Skilled care; Intermediate care. *Beds*
SNF 65; ICF 36. *Certified* Medicaid;
Medicare.
Owner Proprietary corp.
Staff RNs; LPNs; Nurses' aides; Physical
therapists; Recreational therapists;
Occupational therapists; Speech therapists;
Activities coordinators; Dietitians.
Facilities Dining room; Physical therapy
room; Activities room; Crafts room; Laundry
room; Barber/Beauty shop; Dayrooms.
Activities Arts & crafts; Cards; Games;
Reading groups; Prayer groups; Movies;
Shopping trips; Dances/Social/Cultural
gatherings; Intergenerational programs;
Hospitality program.

Heritage House Nursing Home
11 Sylvan St, Danvers, MA 01923
(617) 774-1763
Admin David W Bittner.
Licensure Intermediate care. *Beds* ICF 46.
Certified Medicaid.
Owner Proprietary corp.
Admissions Requirements Minimum age 21.
Staff RNs 2 (ft), 4 (pt); LPNs 2 (ft), 6 (pt);
Nurses' aides 6 (ft), 12 (pt); Recreational
therapists 1 (pt); Activities coordinators 1
(ft), 1 (pt); Dietitians 1 (pt);
Ophthalmologists 1 (pt).
Facilities Dining room; Activities room;
Laundry room.
Activities Arts & crafts; Cards; Games;
Reading groups; Prayer groups; Movies;
Shopping trips; Dances/Social/Cultural
gatherings.

**Charles V Hogan Regional Center & John T
Berry Rehabilitation Center**
PO Box A, Danvers, MA 01937
(617) 774-5000
Admin Edward W Budelmann. *Dir of Nursing*
Dorothy Mullen. *Medical Dir* Zsuzanna
Dallos MD.
Licensure Intermediate care for mentally
retarded. *Beds* 325. *Certified* Medicaid.
Owner Publicly owned.
Staff Physicians; RNs; LPNs; Physical
therapists; Recreational therapists;
Occupational therapists; Speech therapists;
Activities coordinators; Dietitians;
Ophthalmologists; Podiatrists.
Facilities Dining room; Physical therapy
room; Activities room; Chapel; Crafts room;
Laundry room; Barber/Beauty shop; Library.
Activities Arts & crafts; Cards; Games;
Reading groups; Prayer groups; Movies;
Shopping trips; Dances/Social/Cultural
gatherings.

Hunt Nursing & Retirement Home Inc
90 Lindall St, Danvers, MA 01923
(617) 777-3740
Admin Barbara Whalen.
Medical Dir B Geoffrey Piken MD.
Licensure Skilled care; Intermediate care. *Beds*
SNF 80; ICF 40. *Certified* Medicaid.
Owner Proprietary corp (Hannover
Healthcare).
Admissions Requirements Minimum age 60.
Staff Physicians 3 (pt); RNs 18 (pt); LPNs 6
(pt); Nurses' aides 65 (pt); Physical
therapists 1 (pt); Recreational therapists 1
(pt); Occupational therapists 1 (pt); Speech
therapists 1 (pt); Activities coordinators 2
(pt); Dietitians 1 (pt); Ophthalmologists 1
(pt); Podiatrists 1 (pt); Audiologists 1 (pt);
Dentists 1 (pt).

Facilities Dining room; Physical therapy room; Activities room; Crafts room; Laundry room; Barber/Beauty shop; Library; Patios.
Activities Arts & crafts; Cards; Games; Reading groups; Prayer groups; Movies; Shopping trips; Dances/Social/Cultural gatherings; Community program.

Liberty Pavilion Nursing Home
56 Liberty St, Danvers, MA 01923
(617) 777-2700
Admin M Jean Heffernan. *Dir of Nursing* Melba Wharton. *Medical Dir* John Hazelton MD.
Licensure Skilled care; Intermediate care. *Beds* SNF 80; ICF 80. *Certified* Medicaid; Medicare.
Owner Proprietary corp (Greenery Rehabilitation Group Inc).
Admissions Requirements Minimum age 18; Medical examination; Physician's request.
Staff Physicians 25 (pt); RNs 6 (ft), 5 (pt); LPNs 7 (ft), 4 (pt); Nurses' aides 31 (ft), 70 (pt); Physical therapists 1 (pt); Occupational therapists 1 (pt); Speech therapists 1 (pt); Activities coordinators 1 (ft); Dietitians 1 (pt); Ophthalmologists 1 (pt); Podiatrists 1 (pt); Dentists 1 (pt); Psychiatrists 1 (pt).
Facilities Dining room; Physical therapy room; Activities room; Crafts room; Laundry room; Barber/Beauty shop.
Activities Arts & crafts; Cards; Games; Reading groups; Prayer groups; Movies; Dances/Social/Cultural gatherings.

New England Home for the Deaf
154 Water St, Danvers, MA 01923
(508) 774-0445 Voice/TTY
Admin Eddy F Laird. *Dir of Nursing* Linda Minsky.
Licensure Rest home. *Beds* Rest home 30. *Private Pay Patients* 5%. *Certified* Medicaid.
Owner Nonprofit corp.
Admissions Requirements Minimum age 50; Medical examination; Physician's request.
Staff RNs 1 (ft); LPNs 1 (ft); Nurses' aides 6 (ft); Activities coordinators 4 (ft).
Languages Sign.
Facilities Dining room; Activities room; Crafts room; Laundry room; Barber/Beauty shop; Library; Foyer; parlor; Multi-purpose room.
Activities Arts & crafts; Cards; Games; Reading groups; Prayer groups; Movies; Shopping trips; Dances/Social/Cultural gatherings; Intergenerational programs; Pet therapy.

Dartmouth

Brandon Woods Long-Term Care Facility
567 Dartmouth St, Dartmouth, MA 02748
(617) 997-7787
Admin Robert E Arsenault. *Dir of Nursing* Elaine Tetreault RN. *Medical Dir* James W Ross MD.
Licensure Skilled care; Intermediate care; Retirement; Alzheimer's care. *Beds* SNF 71; ICF 37. *Certified* Medicaid.
Owner Proprietary corp.
Admissions Requirements Minimum age 65; Medical examination.
Staff RNs; LPNs; Nurses' aides; Physical therapists; Recreational therapists; Occupational therapists; Speech therapists; Activities coordinators; Dietitians.
Facilities Dining room; Physical therapy room; Activities room; Chapel; Crafts room; Laundry room; Barber/Beauty shop.
Activities Arts & crafts; Cards; Games; Prayer groups; Movies; Shopping trips; Dances/Social/Cultural gatherings.

Country Rest Home
PO Box P85, 263 Bakerville Rd, Dartmouth, MA 02748
(617) 992-9280
Admin Elsie M Niemac.

Licensure Rest home. *Beds* Rest home 25.
Owner Privately owned.

Dartmouth Manor Rest Home
70 State Rd, North Dartmouth, Dartmouth, MA 02747
(617) 993-9255
Admin James Casey.
Licensure Rest home. *Beds* Rest home 25.
Owner Proprietary corp.

Harborview Manor—A Long-Term Care Facility
173 Smith Neck Rd, Dartmouth, MA 02748
(617) 992-8901
Admin Robert Sugar. *Dir of Nursing* Sandra Wrench. *Medical Dir* Dr Stewart Kirknedy.
Licensure Intermediate care. *Beds* ICF 29. *Certified* Medicaid.
Owner Proprietary corp (Meritcare).
Admissions Requirements Medical examination.
Staff Physicians 1 (ft); RNs 2 (ft), 2 (pt); LPNs 2 (ft); Nurses' aides 7 (ft), 7 (pt); Activities coordinators 1 (ft); Dietitians 1 (ft); Ophthalmologists 1 (pt).
Languages French, Spanish, Portuguese.
Affiliation Roman Catholic.
Facilities Dining room; Crafts room; Laundry room; Barber/Beauty shop; Library.
Activities Arts & crafts; Cards; Games; Reading groups; Prayer groups; Movies; Shopping trips; Dances/Social/Cultural gatherings.

Dedham

Eastwood Care Center A Long-Term Care Facility
1007 East St, Dedham, MA 02026
(617) 329-1520
Admin Wayne Pultman.
Licensure Skilled care; Intermediate care. *Beds* SNF 42; ICF 103. *Certified* Medicaid.
Owner Proprietary corp (Meritcare).

Deerfield

Hillside Nursing Home
N Hillside Rd, Deerfield, MA 01373
(413) 665-2200
Admin Robert S Page Jr.
Licensure Intermediate care. *Beds* ICF 54. *Certified* Medicaid.
Owner Proprietary corp.

Dighton

Dighton Nursing Center
907 Centre St, Dighton, MA 02764
(617) 669-6741
Admin Michael F Cummings.
Licensure Intermediate care. *Beds* ICF 30. *Certified* Medicaid.
Owner Proprietary corp.

Dorchester

Ann's Rest Home
66 Bowdoin Ave, Dorchester, MA 02121
(617) 825-1793
Admin Willard L Basler. *Dir of Nursing* Joan Taglieri.
Licensure Intermediate care; Intermediate care for mentally retarded. *Beds* ICF 13. *Private Pay Patients* 10%. *Certified* Medicaid.
Owner Privately owned (Willard L Basler).
Admissions Requirements Minimum age 21.
Staff RNs 1 (pt); Recreational therapists 1 (pt); Activities coordinators 1 (pt); Dietitians 1 (pt).
Facilities Dining room; Activities room.
Activities Arts & crafts; Cards; Games; Movies; Shopping trips; Dances/Social/Cultural gatherings.

Highland Rest Home
516 Warren St, Dorchester, MA 02121
(617) 427-6640
Admin Barbara Wade. *Dir of Nursing* Frances Valentine.
Licensure Intermediate care. *Beds* ICF 41. *Certified* Medicaid.
Owner Privately owned.
Admissions Requirements Medical examination.
Staff RNs 1 (pt); LPNs 1 (ft); Nurses' aides 5 (ft), 4 (pt); Activities coordinators 1 (pt); Dietitians 1 (pt).
Facilities Dining room; Activities room; Laundry room.
Activities Arts & crafts; Cards; Games; Movies; Shopping trips; Dances/Social/Cultural gatherings.

Duxbury

Bay Path at Duxbury Nursing Rehabilitation
308 Kings Town Way, Duxbury, MA 02332
(617) 585-5561
Admin George D Spagholia.
Licensure Skilled care; Intermediate care. *Beds* SNF 80; ICF 40.
Owner Privately owned.

Duxbury House Nursing Home
298 Kings Town Way, Duxbury, MA 02332
(617) 585-2397
Admin Ruth St John.
Licensure Intermediate care. *Beds* ICF 23. *Certified* Medicaid.
Owner Privately owned.
Admissions Requirements Minimum age 21; Medical examination; Physician's request.
Staff RNs 1 (ft); LPNs 4 (ft); Activities coordinators 1 (ft).
Facilities Dining room; Activities room; Laundry room.
Activities Arts & crafts; Cards; Games; Prayer groups; Movies; Shopping trips; Dances/Social/Cultural gatherings.

East Boston

New Medico Rest & Skilled Nursing Center at Columbus
910 Saratoga St, East Boston, MA 02128
(617) 569-1157
Admin Valerie Williamson Gingras. *Dir of Nursing* Denise Kress. *Medical Dir* Carl Sterpi.
Licensure Skilled care; Intermediate care. *Beds* SNF 54; ICF 56. *Private Pay Patients* 0%. *Certified* Medicaid; Medicare.
Owner Proprietary corp (New Medico Associates).
Admissions Requirements Minimum age 21.
Staff Physicians; RNs; LPNs; Nurses' aides; Physical therapists; Recreational therapists; Occupational therapists; Speech therapists; Activities coordinators; Dietitians.
Facilities Dining room; Physical therapy room; Activities room; Chapel; Crafts room; Laundry room; Barber/Beauty shop.
Activities Arts & crafts; Cards; Games; Reading groups; Prayer groups; Movies; Shopping trips; Dances/Social/Cultural gatherings.

East Bridgewater

Forge Pond Nursing Home
66 Central St, East Bridgewater, MA 02333
(617) 378-7227
Admin James J Morris. *Dir of Nursing* Claire Wheeer RN. *Medical Dir* George Gagne MD.
Licensure Skilled care; Intermediate care. *Beds* SNF 82; ICF 41. *Certified* Medicaid.
Owner Proprietary corp (First Healthcare Corp).

Admissions Requirements Minimum age 21; Medical examination; Physician's request.
Staff Physicians 2 (pt); RNs 3 (ft), 5 (pt); LPNs 3 (ft), 10 (pt); Nurses' aides 29 (ft), 31 (pt); Physical therapists 1 (pt); Occupational therapists 1 (pt); Speech therapists 1 (pt); Activities coordinators 2 (ft); Dietitians 1 (pt); Ophthalmologists 1 (pt); Podiatrists 1 (pt); Dentists 1 (pt).
Facilities Dining room; Activities room; Crafts room; Laundry room; Barber/Beauty shop; Screened porch; Outside patio; Gardens.
Activities Arts & crafts; Cards; Games; Reading groups; Prayer groups; Movies; Shopping trips; Dances/Social/Cultural gatherings.

Westview Rest Home
446 West St, East Bridgewater, MA 02333
(617) 378-2451
Admin Robert W Carey Jr.
Licensure Rest home. *Beds* Rest home 18.
Owner Privately owned.

East Longmeadow

Chestnut Hill Nursing Home
32 Chestnut St, East Longmeadow, MA 01028
(413) 525-1893
Admin Bonnie Davis.
Licensure Skilled care; Intermediate care. *Beds* SNF 82; ICF 41.
Owner Proprietary corp.

East Longmeadow Nursing Home
305 Maple St, East Longmeadow, MA 01028
(413) 525-6361
Admin Russell J Firewicz. *Dir of Nursing* Barbara Owczarski RN. *Medical Dir* John Quinn MD.
Licensure Skilled care; Intermediate care. *Beds* SNF 78; ICF 41. *Private Pay Patients* 57%. *Certified* Medicaid; Medicare.
Owner Proprietary corp (Hannover Healthcare).
Admissions Requirements Minimum age 21; Medical examination; Physician's request.
Staff Physicians 1 (pt); RNs 5 (ft), 13 (pt); LPNs 2 (ft), 3 (pt); Nurses' aides 24 (ft), 44 (pt); Physical therapists 1 (pt); Occupational therapists 1 (pt); Speech therapists 1 (pt); Activities coordinators 2 (ft); Dietitians 1 (pt); Ophthalmologists 1 (pt); Podiatrists 1 (pt); Audiologists 1 (pt).
Languages Spanish, Polish.
Facilities Dining room; Physical therapy room; Activities room; Crafts room; Laundry room; Barber/Beauty shop.
Activities Arts & crafts; Cards; Games; Reading groups; Prayer groups; Movies; Shopping trips; Dances/Social/Cultural gatherings; Intergenerational programs; Pet therapy.

Mediplex of East Longmeadow
135 Benton Dr, East Longmeadow, MA 01028
(413) 525-3336
Admin Earle Lerner.
Licensure Skilled care; Intermediate care. *Beds* SNF 127; ICF 45.
Owner Proprietary corp.

Easthampton

Hampshire Manor Nursing Home
Rte 10, Easthampton, MA 01027
(413) 584-2213
Admin David LaBroad.
Licensure Intermediate care. *Beds* ICF 42. *Certified* Medicaid.
Owner Proprietary corp.

Easton

Stonehill Manor Nursing Home
231 Main St, Easton, MA 02356
(617) 238-6511
Admin Arthur S Logan. *Dir of Nursing* Elaine Rogers LPN.
Licensure Intermediate care. *Beds* ICF 26. *Certified* Medicaid.
Owner Privately owned.
Admissions Requirements Minimum age 21; Females only; Medical examination.
Staff Physicians 5 (pt); RNs 2 (pt); LPNs 5 (pt); Nurses' aides 12 (pt); Physical therapists 1 (pt); Activities coordinators 1 (pt); Dietitians 1 (pt); Ophthalmologists 1 (pt); Podiatrists 1 (pt); Dentists 1 (pt).
Facilities Dining room; Activities room; Laundry room.
Activities Arts & crafts; Cards; Games; Reading groups; Prayer groups; Movies; Shopping trips; Dances/Social/Cultural gatherings.

Village Rest Home
22 Main St, Easton, MA 02356
(617) 238-7262
Admin Carol L Audette.
Licensure Rest home. *Beds* Rest home 14.
Owner Privately owned.
Admissions Requirements Females only; Medical examination; Physician's request.
Staff LPNs 1 (pt); Nurses' aides 5 (pt); Dietitians 1 (pt).
Facilities Dining room; Activities room; Laundry room.
Activities Arts & crafts; Cards; Games; Movies; Shopping trips; Dances/Social/Cultural gatherings.

Everett

Parkway Manor Nursing Home
13 School St, Everett, MA 02149
(617) 387-1200
Admin Lillian M Murray. *Dir of Nursing* Carol Dondero. *Medical Dir* Dr Willard Nalchajian.
Licensure Intermediate care. *Beds* ICF 57. *Certified* Medicaid.
Owner Privately owned.
Admissions Requirements Minimum age 21; Physician's request.
Staff Physicians 1 (pt); RNs 2 (ft), 2 (pt); LPNs 6 (ft), 2 (pt); Nurses' aides 15 (ft), 10 (pt); Activities coordinators 1 (ft); Dietitians 1 (pt).
Facilities Dining room; Activities room.
Activities Arts & crafts; Cards; Games; Reading groups; Prayer groups; Movies; Dances/Social/Cultural gatherings.

Woodlawn Manor Nursing Home
289 Elm St, Everett, MA 02149
(617) 387-6557
Admin Patrick O'Connor.
Licensure Skilled care; Intermediate care. *Beds* SNF 83; ICF 61. *Certified* Medicaid.
Owner Proprietary corp (Oakwood Living Center).

Fairhaven

Bailie's Rest Home
125 New Boston Rd, Fairhaven, MA 02719
(617) 993-4106
Admin Eleanor M Charpentier.
Licensure Rest home. *Beds* 12.

Center Green Rest Home
109 Green St, Fairhaven, MA 02719
(617) 994-7653
Licensure Rest home. *Beds* Rest home 27.
Owner Proprietary corp.
Admissions Requirements Minimum age 18; Medical examination.

Staff LPNs 1 (pt); Nurses' aides 3 (ft), 3 (pt); Activities coordinators 1 (pt); Dietitians 1 (pt); Podiatrists 1 (pt).
Facilities Dining room; Activities room; Laundry room.
Activities Arts & crafts; Cards; Games; Movies; Shopping trips; Dances/Social/Cultural gatherings.

McCormack Rest Home
88 Fort St, Fairhaven, MA 02719
(617) 993-3277
Admin Teresa Ann Vieira.
Licensure Rest home. *Beds* Rest home 13.
Owner Proprietary corp.

Nichols House Nursing Home
184 Main St, Fairhaven, MA 02719
(617) 997-3193
Admin William C Moloney Jr.
Medical Dir Edward D Mackler MD.
Licensure Skilled care; Intermediate care. *Beds* SNF 48; ICF 52. *Certified* Medicaid; Medicare.
Owner Proprietary corp (First Healthcare Corp).
Staff RNs 8 (ft), 5 (pt); LPNs 6 (ft), 3 (pt); Nurses' aides 31 (ft), 17 (pt); Reality therapists 1 (ft); Occupational therapists 1 (pt); Speech therapists 1 (pt); Activities coordinators 2 (ft), 1 (pt); Dietitians 1 (pt); Ophthalmologists 1 (pt); Podiatrists 1 (pt); Audiologists 1 (pt); Dentists 1 (pt).
Facilities Dining room; Physical therapy room; Activities room; Laundry room; Barber/Beauty shop; Library.
Activities Arts & crafts; Cards; Games; Reading groups; Prayer groups; Movies; Shopping trips; Dances/Social/Cultural gatherings.

Our Lady's Haven
71 Center St, Fairhaven, MA 02719
(617) 999-4561
Admin Sandra Sylvia.
Licensure Skilled care; Intermediate care. *Beds* SNF 38; ICF 72. *Certified* Medicaid.
Owner Nonprofit corp.
Admissions Requirements Minimum age 65; Medical examination.
Staff Physicians; RNs 3 (ft), 8 (pt); LPNs 6 (ft), 12 (pt); Nurses' aides 35 (ft), 13 (pt); Physical therapists; Reality therapists; Recreational therapists; Occupational therapists; Speech therapists; Activities coordinators 1 (pt); Dietitians; Ophthalmologists; Podiatrists; Dentists.
Affiliation Roman Catholic.
Facilities Dining room; Physical therapy room; Activities room; Chapel; Crafts room; Laundry room; Barber/Beauty shop; Library.
Activities Arts & crafts; Cards; Games; Reading groups; Prayer groups; Movies; Shopping trips; Dances/Social/Cultural gatherings.

Fall River

Catholic Memorial Home
2446 Highland Ave, Fall River, MA 02720
(617) 679-0011
Admin Sr Shawn Flynn. *Dir of Nursing* Jean M Quigley RNBSN. *Medical Dir* Robert J Rubano MD.
Licensure Skilled care; Intermediate care. *Beds* SNF 116; ICF 172. *Certified* Medicaid; Medicare.
Owner Nonprofit corp.
Admissions Requirements Minimum age 65; Medical examination; Physician's request.
Staff RNs 5 (ft), 15 (pt); LPNs 14 (ft), 19 (pt); Nurses' aides 100 (ft), 73 (pt); Reality therapists 1 (ft); Activities coordinators 6 (ft), 1 (pt).
Languages Portuguese, French, Spanish.
Affiliation Roman Catholic.

Facilities Dining room; Physical therapy room; Activities room; Chapel; Crafts room; Laundry room; Barber/Beauty shop; Library; Wood shop; Dentist office.
Activities Arts & crafts; Cards; Games; Reading groups; Prayer groups; Movies; Shopping trips; Dances/Social/Cultural gatherings; Gourmet cooking class.

Cliff Gables Nursing Home
423 Middle St, Fall River, MA 02724
(617) 678-4855
Admin Mary M Schroeder.
Licensure Intermediate care. *Beds* ICF 36. *Certified* Medicaid.
Owner Proprietary corp.

Cliff Haven Nursing Home
745 Highland Ave, Fall River, MA 02720
(617) 674-3354
Admin Mary M Schroeder.
Licensure Intermediate care. *Beds* ICF 31. *Certified* Medicaid.
Owner Proprietary corp.

Cliff Heights Nursing Home
635 Rock St, Fall River, MA 02720
(617) 674-7509
Admin Mary M Schroeder.
Licensure Intermediate care. *Beds* ICF 33. *Certified* Medicaid.
Owner Proprietary corp.

Cliff Lawn Nursing Home
851 Highland Ave, Fall River, MA 02720
(617) 678-6100
Admin Mary M Schroeder.
Licensure Intermediate care. *Beds* ICF 26. *Certified* Medicaid.
Owner Proprietary corp.

Cliff Manor Nursing Home
431 Rock St, Fall River, MA 02720
(617) 678-8011
Admin Mary M Schroeder.
Licensure Intermediate care. *Beds* ICF 37. *Certified* Medicaid.
Owner Proprietary corp.

Crawford House Convalescent Home
273 Oak Grove Ave, Fall River, MA 02723
(617) 679-4866
Admin Susan A Cohen.
Licensure Skilled care; Intermediate care. *Beds* SNF 42; ICF 82. *Certified* Medicaid.
Owner Proprietary corp (First Healthcare Corp).

Crestwood Convalescent Home
170 Oak Grove Ave, Fall River, MA 02723
(617) 678-5234
Admin Joyce Pinto.
Licensure Skilled care; Intermediate care. *Beds* SNF 53; ICF 49. *Certified* Medicaid.
Owner Proprietary corp (First Healthcare Corp).

Fall River Jewish Home
538 Robeson St, Fall River, MA 02720
(508) 679-6172
Admin Janet B Smith. *Dir of Nursing* Anne Zygiel RN. *Medical Dir* Harvey Reback MD.
Licensure Skilled care; Intermediate care. *Beds* SNF 32; ICF 28. *Certified* Medicaid; Medicare.
Owner Nonprofit corp.
Admissions Requirements Medical examination; Physician's request.
Languages Portuguese.
Affiliation Jewish.
Facilities Dining room; Physical therapy room; Activities room; Chapel; Laundry room; Barber/Beauty shop.
Activities Arts & crafts; Cards; Games; Reading groups; Prayer groups; Movies; Shopping trips; Dances/Social/Cultural gatherings; Intergenerational programs; Pet therapy.

Fall River Nursing Home Inc
1748 Highland Ave, Fall River, MA 02720
(617) 675-1131
Admin James A Jackson.
Medical Dir N Kenneth Shand MD.
Licensure Skilled care; Intermediate care. *Beds* SNF 123; ICF 41. *Certified* Medicaid.
Owner Proprietary corp.
Admissions Requirements Minimum age 16.
Staff Physicians 1 (pt); RNs 14 (ft), 5 (pt); LPNs 11 (ft), 5 (pt); Nurses' aides 48 (ft), 31 (pt); Physical therapists 1 (ft), 1 (pt); Recreational therapists 1 (ft), 2 (pt); Occupational therapists 1 (pt); Dietitians 1 (pt); Podiatrists 2 (pt); Dentists 1 (pt).
Facilities Dining room; Physical therapy room; Activities room; Chapel; Crafts room; Laundry room; Barber/Beauty shop; Library.
Activities Arts & crafts; Cards; Games; Reading groups; Prayer groups; Movies; Shopping trips; Dances/Social/Cultural gatherings.

Hanover House Retirement Facility
391 Hanover St, Fall River, MA 02720
(617) 675-7583
Admin Elizabeth C Shay.
Licensure Rest home. *Beds* Rest home 35.
Owner Privately owned.

Highland Manor Nursing Home Inc
761 Highland Ave, Fall River, MA 02720
(617) 679-1411
Admin Michael F Cummings.
Licensure Intermediate care. *Beds* ICF 26. *Certified* Medicaid.
Owner Proprietary corp.

Home for Aged People
1168 Highland Ave, Fall River, MA 02720
(617) 679-0144
Admin Joanne E O'Day.
Licensure Intermediate care; Rest home. *Beds* ICF 24; Rest home 35.
Owner Proprietary corp.
Admissions Requirements Minimum age 68; Medical examination; Physician's request.

Kimwell Health Care Center A Skilled Nursing Facility
495 New Boston Rd, Fall River, MA 02720
(617) 679-0106
Admin Arthur Taylor. *Dir of Nursing* Sharon Lounsbury. *Medical Dir* N Kenneth Shand MD.
Licensure Skilled care; Intermediate care. *Beds* SNF 82; ICF 42. *Certified* Medicaid; Medicare.
Owner Privately owned.
Admissions Requirements Medical examination.
Staff Physicians 3 (pt); RNs 8 (ft), 2 (pt); LPNs 7 (ft), 8 (pt); Nurses' aides 20 (ft), 27 (pt); Physical therapists 1 (pt); Reality therapists 1 (pt); Recreational therapists 2 (ft), 2 (pt); Occupational therapists 1 (pt); Speech therapists 1 (pt); Dietitians 1 (pt); Ophthalmologists 1 (pt); Podiatrists 1 (pt); Dentists 1 (pt).
Facilities Dining room; Physical therapy room; Activities room; Chapel; Crafts room; Laundry room; Barber/Beauty shop; Library.
Activities Arts & crafts; Cards; Games; Reading groups; Prayer groups; Movies; Shopping trips; Dances/Social/Cultural gatherings.

Rose Hawthorne Lathrop Home
1600 Bay St, Fall River, MA 02724
(508) 673-2322
Admin Sr M Joseph OP. *Dir of Nursing* Sr M Christopher OP. *Medical Dir* Robert J Rubano MD.
Licensure Intermediate care. *Beds* ICF 35. *Certified* Medicaid.
Owner Nonprofit organization/foundation (Servants of Relief for Incurable Cancer).

Admissions Requirements Terminal cancer patients only.
Staff Physicians 1 (pt); RNs 3 (ft), 1 (pt); LPNs 1 (ft); Nurses' aides 7 (ft), 1 (pt); Dietitians 1 (pt).
Languages French, Portuguese.
Affiliation Roman Catholic.
Facilities Dining room; Chapel; Laundry room; Barber/Beauty shop.
Activities Arts & crafts; Cards; Games; Movies; Pet therapy; Picnics.

Rosewood Rest Home
547 Highland Ave, Fall River, MA 02720
(617) 678-6075
Admin Joanne Enos.
Licensure Rest home. *Beds* Rest home 57.
Owner Proprietary corp (First Healthcare Corp).
Admissions Requirements Minimum age 21; Medical examination.
Staff Nurses' aides 6 (ft), 6 (pt); Activities coordinators 1 (ft); Dietitians 1 (pt); Ophthalmologists 1 (pt); Podiatrists 1 (pt); Dentists 1 (pt).
Facilities Dining room; Activities room; Laundry room; Barber/Beauty shop.
Activities Arts & crafts; Cards; Games; Reading groups; Prayer groups; Movies; Shopping trips; Dances/Social/Cultural gatherings.

Falmouth

Falmouth Nursing Home
545 Main St, Falmouth, MA 02540
(508) 548-3800, 548-2712 FAX
Admin John J Hedderson. *Dir of Nursing* Jean E Throckmorton RN. *Medical Dir* Virginia Biddle MD.
Licensure Skilled care; Intermediate care; Alzlheimer's care; Alzheimer's care. *Beds* SNF 81; ICF 40. *Certified* Medicaid.
Owner Proprietary corp.
Admissions Requirements Minimum age 21; Medical examination.
Staff Physicians 1 (pt); RNs 5 (ft), 8 (pt); LPNs 11 (ft), 4 (pt); Nurses' aides 63 (ft), 16 (pt); Physical therapists 1 (pt); Recreational therapists 3 (ft); Occupational therapists 1 (pt); Speech therapists 1 (pt); Activities coordinators 1 (ft); Dietitians 1 (pt); Ophthalmologists 1 (pt); Podiatrists 1 (pt); Dentists 1 (pt).
Facilities Dining room; Physical therapy room; Activities room; Chapel; Crafts room; Laundry room; Barber/Beauty shop; Preschool for employees; Dental services; Alzheimer's unit; Bus with handicap ramp.
Activities Arts & crafts; Cards; Games; Reading groups; Prayer groups; Movies; Shopping trips; Dances/Social/Cultural gatherings; Intergenerational programs; Pet therapy.

Freedom Crest Nursing Home
359 Jones Rd, Falmouth, MA 02540
(508) 457-9000, 457-9002 FAX
Admin Darlene Meetze. *Dir of Nursing* Robert McMahon. *Medical Dir* John Howard.
Licensure Skilled care; Intermediate care. *Beds* SNF 80; ICF 40. *Certified* Medicaid; Medicare.
Owner Privately owned.
Staff RNs; LPNs; Nurses' aides; Physical therapists; Occupational therapists; Speech therapists; Activities coordinators; Dietitians.
Facilities Dining room; Physical therapy room; Activities room; Chapel; Crafts room; Laundry room; Barber/Beauty shop.
Activities Arts & crafts; Cards; Games; Reading groups; Prayer groups; Movies; Shopping trips; Dances/Social/Cultural gatherings; Intergenerational programs; Pet therapy.

Royal Megansett Nursing Home
209 County Rd, Falmouth, MA 02556
(508) 563-5913
Admin David J Carboneau. *Dir of Nursing*
Ann Bailey. *Medical Dir* Dr Virginia Biddle.
Licensure Intermediate care; Retirement. *Beds*
ICF 74; Retirement 10. *Certified* Medicaid.
Owner Proprietary corp.
Facilities Dining room; Physical therapy
room; Activities room; Crafts room; Laundry
room; Barber/Beauty shop.
Activities Arts & crafts; Cards; Games;
Reading groups; Prayer groups; Movies;
Shopping trips; Dances/Social/Cultural
gatherings; Intergenerational programs; Pet
therapy.

Fitchburg

**Birchwood Care Center A Long-Term Care
Facility**
1199 John Fitch Hwy, Fitchburg, MA 01420
(617) 345-0146
Admin Lawrence Solomini.
Licensure Skilled care; Intermediate care. *Beds*
SNF 40; ICF 120. *Certified* Medicaid;
Medicare.
Owner Proprietary corp (Meritcare).

Grand View Rest Home
55 Garnet St, Fitchburg, MA 01420
(617) 342-3030
Admin Donald F Richards.
Medical Dir Dr Parnes.
Licensure Rest home. *Beds* Rest home 21.
Owner Privately owned.
Admissions Requirements Minimum age 30;
Medical examination.
Staff RNs 1 (pt); Nurses' aides 4 (ft), 3 (pt);
Activities coordinators 1 (pt); Dietitians 1
(pt).
Facilities Dining room; Activities room;
Laundry room.
Activities Arts & crafts; Cards; Games;
Reading groups; Prayer groups; Movies;
Shopping trips; Dances/Social/Cultural
gatherings.

High Street Rest Home
69 High St, Fitchburg, MA 01420
(617) 342-7962
Admin Kathryn E Salafia.
Licensure Rest home. *Beds* Rest home 16.
Owner Privately owned.

Highlands, L T C Center
50 Nichols Rd, Fitchburg, MA 01420
(508) 343-4411
Admin Robin Churray-Rousseau.
Licensure Skilled care; Intermediate care. *Beds*
SNF 76; ICF 92.
Owner Proprietary corp.

Hillcrest Nursing Home
94 Summer St, Fitchburg, MA 01420
(617) 343-3530
Admin Lisa V Allen. *Dir of Nursing* Elizabeth
Sigmon. *Medical Dir* Raymond Wolejko.
Licensure Skilled care; Intermediate care. *Beds*
SNF 69; ICF 27. *Certified* Medicaid.
Owner Proprietary corp (First Healthcare
Corp).
Admissions Requirements Minimum age 21;
Medical examination; Physician's request.
Staff RNs 6 (ft), 4 (pt); LPNs 5 (ft), 5 (pt);
Nurses' aides 20 (ft), 25 (pt); Physical
therapists 1 (pt); Occupational therapists 1
(pt); Speech therapists 1 (pt); Activities
coordinators 1 (ft), 1 (pt); Dietitians 1 (pt);
Ophthalmologists 4 (pt); Podiatrists 1 (pt);
Dentists 1 (pt).
Facilities Dining room; Physical therapy
room; Activities room; Chapel; Crafts room;
Laundry room; Barber/Beauty shop; Library.
Activities Arts & crafts; Cards; Games;
Reading groups; Prayer groups; Movies;
Shopping trips; Dances/Social/Cultural
gatherings.

James Manor Rest Home
222 South St, Fitchburg, MA 01420
(617) 342-5041
Admin Rosalyn J Piro.
Licensure Rest home. *Beds* Rest home 28.
Owner Privately owned.

Magnolia Rest Home Inc
159 Summer St, Fitchburg, MA 01420
(617) 342-5372
Admin Paul Gully Jr.
Medical Dir Eric L Knutson.
Licensure Rest home. *Beds* Rest home 16.
Owner Proprietary corp.
Admissions Requirements Minimum age 50.
Staff Physicians 1 (ft); LPNs 1 (pt); Nurses'
aides 6 (pt); Dietitians 2 (pt); Podiatrists 1
(ft); Dentists 1 (ft).
Facilities Dining room; Activities room;
Crafts room; Laundry room.
Activities Arts & crafts; Cards; Games;
Reading groups.

Mystic Nursing & Rehabilitation Center
360 Electric Ave, Fitchburg, MA 01420
(617) 342-3242
Admin Catherine F Rowlands. *Dir of Nursing*
Jacqueline Woicieschowski. *Medical Dir* Eric
Knutson MD.
Licensure Skilled care. *Beds* SNF 99. *Certified*
Medicaid; Medicare.
Owner Proprietary corp.
Admissions Requirements Medical
examination; Physician's request.
Staff Physicians 1 (pt); RNs 4 (ft), 9 (pt);
LPNs 5 (ft), 2 (pt); Nurses' aides 17 (ft), 22
(pt); Physical therapists 1 (pt); Occupational
therapists 1 (pt); Speech therapists 1 (pt);
Activities coordinators 1 (ft); Dietitians 1
(pt); Ophthalmologists 1 (pt); Podiatrists 1
(pt); Recreational assistants 1 (ft), 2 (pt);
Rehabilitation assistants 1 (pt).
Facilities Dining room; Physical therapy
room; Activities room; Laundry room;
Barber/Beauty shop.
Activities Arts & crafts; Cards; Games;
Reading groups; Prayer groups; Movies;
Shopping trips; Dances/Social/Cultural
gatherings.

Tower Hill Rest Home
PO Box 943, 20 Myrtle Ave, Fitchburg, MA
01420
(508) 342-4242
Admin Pauline J Stockwell.
Medical Dir Dr Babineau.
Licensure Intermediate care. *Beds* ICF 21.
Private Pay Patients 1%. *Certified* Medicaid;
Medicare.
Owner Privately owned.
Admissions Requirements Minimum age 55;
Medical examination; Physician's request.
Staff LPNs 1 (pt); Nurses' aides 1 (ft), 4 (pt);
Activities coordinators 1 (ft); Dietitians 1
(pt); Cooks, housekeepers 1 (ft), 1 (pt).
Languages French, Spanish, Finnish.
Affiliation Roman Catholic.
Facilities Dining room; Activities room;
Crafts room; Laundry room; Barber/Beauty
shop; Smoking room.
Activities Arts & crafts; Cards; Games;
Reading groups; Prayer groups; Movies;
Shopping trips; Dances/Social/Cultural
gatherings; Pet therapy; Exercise groups.

Foxborough

Doolittle Home Inc
16 Bird St, Foxborough, MA 02035
(617) 543-2131
Admin Deanna J Willis. *Dir of Nursing* Sheila
Miller RN. *Medical Dir* Dr John
MacDonald.
Licensure Intermediate care; Rest home. *Beds*
ICF 9; Rest home 24. *Certified* Medicare.
Owner Nonprofit corp.
Admissions Requirements Minimum age 65.

Staff Physicians 1 (pt); RNs 2 (ft), 3 (pt);
LPNs 1 (ft), 8 (pt); Nurses' aides 3 (ft), 5
(pt); Physical therapists 1 (pt); Recreational
therapists 1 (pt); Activities coordinators 1
(pt); Dietitians 1 (pt); Ophthalmologists 1
(pt); Podiatrists 1 (pt); Dentists 1 (pt).
Affiliation Unitarian Universalist.
Facilities Dining room; Crafts room; Laundry
room; Barber/Beauty shop.
Activities Arts & crafts; Games; Prayer groups;
Shopping trips.

Van Dora Nursing Home
67 Central St, Foxborough, MA 02035
(617) 543-8000
Admin Joseph G Ranieri.
Licensure Intermediate care. *Beds* ICF 67.
Certified Medicaid.
Owner Proprietary corp.

Framingham

Carlyle Nursing Home Inc
342 Winter St, Framingham, MA 01701
(617) 879-6100
Admin Caroline M Kreshpane.
Licensure Intermediate care. *Beds* ICF 43.
Certified Medicaid.
Owner Proprietary corp.

Colonial House Nursing Home
11 Arbetter Dr, Framingham, MA 01701
(617) 877-3300
Admin Rita Frankel.
Licensure Intermediate care. *Beds* ICF 33.

Countryside Nursing Home Inc
153 Winter St, Framingham, MA 01701
(617) 872-5250
Admin John L Steacie.
Licensure Intermediate care. *Beds* ICF 30.
Certified Medicaid.
Owner Proprietary corp.
Admissions Requirements Females only.
Staff RNs 1 (ft); LPNs 4 (pt); Nurses' aides 30
(pt); Physical therapists 1 (pt); Occupational
therapists 1 (pt); Speech therapists 1 (pt);
Activities coordinators 1 (ft); Dietitians 1
(pt).
Facilities Dining room; Activities room;
Laundry room.
Activities Arts & crafts; Cards; Games; Prayer
groups; Shopping trips.

Kathleen Daniel Health Care SNF
485 Franklin St, Framingham, MA 01701
(617) 872-8801
Admin Barbara Iarrobino. *Dir of Nursing* Joan
Parent. *Medical Dir* Arthur Freedman MD.
Licensure Skilled care; Intermediate care. *Beds*
SNF 82; ICF 42. *Certified* Medicaid;
Medicare.
Owner Privately owned.
Staff Physicians 20 (pt); RNs 10 (ft), 4 (pt);
LPNs 6 (ft), 6 (pt); Nurses' aides 35 (ft), 17
(pt); Physical therapists 1 (pt); Reality
therapists 2 (ft); Recreational therapists 2
(ft), 2 (pt); Occupational therapists 1 (pt);
Speech therapists 1 (pt); Activities
coordinators 1 (ft); Dietitians 1 (pt);
Ophthalmologists 1 (pt); Podiatrists 1 (pt);
Audiologists 1 (pt); Dentists 1 (pt);
Psychologists 1 (pt).
Facilities Dining room; Physical therapy
room; Activities room; Chapel; Crafts room;
Laundry room; Barber/Beauty shop.
Activities Arts & crafts; Cards; Games;
Reading groups; Prayer groups; Movies;
Shopping trips; Dances/Social/Cultural
gatherings.

Edgell Rest Home
248 Edgell Rd, Framingham, MA 01701
(617) 875-5454
Admin James J Battles.
Licensure Rest home. *Beds* Rest home 18.
Owner Proprietary corp.

Framingham Nursing Home
517 Winter St, Framingham, MA 01701
(617) 875-0607
Admin Beverly McIntyre.
Medical Dir Pramod Chira MD.
Licensure Skilled care. *Beds* SNF 43. *Certified* Medicaid.
Owner Proprietary corp.
Admissions Requirements Minimum age 21; Medical examination.
Staff Physicians 1 (pt); RNs 4 (ft); LPNs 4 (ft); Nurses' aides 20 (ft); Physical therapists 1 (pt); Reality therapists 1 (pt); Recreational therapists 1 (pt), 1 (pt); Occupational therapists 1 (pt); Speech therapists 1 (pt); Activities coordinators 1 (pt); Dietitians 1 (pt); Ophthalmologists 1 (pt); Podiatrists 1 (pt); Dentists 1 (pt).
Facilities Dining room; Activities room; Crafts room; Laundry room.
Activities Arts & crafts; Cards; Games; Reading groups; Prayer groups; Movies; Shopping trips; Dances/Social/Cultural gatherings.

Heritage L T Health Care Center
9 Arbetter Dr, Framingham, MA 01701
(617) 877-3300
Admin Rita Frankel.
Licensure Skilled care. *Beds* SNF 40.

Resident Care Nursing Home
PO Box 887, 228 Concord St, Framingham, MA 01701
(617) 237-2799
Admin Ethel Peters.
Licensure Intermediate care. *Beds* ICF 91. *Certified* Medicaid.
Owner Proprietary corp.
Staff RNs 4 (ft), 2 (pt); LPNs 4 (ft), 4 (pt); Nurses' aides 15 (ft), 10 (pt); Physical therapists 1 (pt); Recreational therapists 1 (pt); Activities coordinators 1 (ft), 1 (pt); Dietitians 1 (pt); Ophthalmologists 1 (pt); Podiatrists 1 (pt); Audiologists 1 (pt); Dentists 1 (pt).

St Patricks Manor Inc
863 Central St, Framingham, MA 01701
(508) 879-8000, 626-1604 FAX
Admin Sr M Joseph Augustine. *Dir of Nursing* Carol M Regan RN. *Medical Dir* Dr Donald E Love.
Licensure Skilled care; Intermediate care; Alzheimer's care. *Beds* SNF 249; ICF 83. *Private Pay Patients* 59%. *Certified* Medicaid.
Owner Nonprofit corp.
Admissions Requirements Medical examination.
Staff Physicians 11 (pt); RNs 32 (ft); LPNs 22 (ft); Nurses' aides 154 (ft); Physical therapists 1 (ft); Recreational therapists 1 (pt); Occupational therapists 2 (pt); Speech therapists 1 (pt); Activities coordinators 7 (ft); Dietitians 1 (ft), 1 (pt); Ophthalmologists 1 (pt); Podiatrists 2 (pt); Psychologists 2 (pt); Neurologists 1 (pt).
Affiliation Roman Catholic.
Facilities Dining room; Physical therapy room; Activities room; Chapel; Crafts room; Laundry room; Barber/Beauty shop; Library; Coffee shop/Pub.
Activities Arts & crafts; Cards; Games; Reading groups; Prayer groups; Movies; Shopping trips; Dances/Social/Cultural gatherings; Intergenerational programs; Pet therapy; Religious services.

Winter Gables Rest Home
68 Griffin, Framingham, MA 01701
(617) 879-6100
Admin Caroline M Kreshpane.
Licensure Rest home. *Beds* 30.

Franklin

Franklin House Healthcare
130 Chestnut St, Franklin, MA 02035
(508) 528-4600
Admin Michael B Lincoln. *Dir of Nursing* Diane Paster.
Licensure Skilled care; Intermediate care. *Beds* SNF 41; ICF 41. *Private Pay Patients* 15%. *Certified* Medicaid.
Owner Proprietary corp (Hillhaven Corp).
Admissions Requirements Minimum age 21; Medical examination; Physician's request.
Staff RNs 12 (ft), 5 (pt); LPNs 7 (pt); Nurses' aides 4 (ft), 30 (pt); Physical therapists 1 (pt); Occupational therapists 1 (pt); Activities coordinators 1 (ft), 1 (pt); Dietitians 1 (ft); Ophthalmologists 1 (pt); Podiatrists 1 (pt); Audiologists 1 (pt).
Facilities Dining room; Activities room; Crafts room; Laundry room; Barber/Beauty shop.
Activities Arts & crafts; Cards; Games; Prayer groups; Movies; Shopping trips; Dances/Social/Cultural gatherings; Pet therapy.

Gardner

Eastwood Pines Nursing Home
Eastwood Cir, Gardner, MA 01440
(617) 632-8776
Admin Abe Treshinsky.
Licensure Skilled care; Intermediate care. *Beds* SNF 78; ICF 50. *Certified* Medicaid; Medicare.
Owner Proprietary corp.

Forest Manor Rest Home
381 E Broadway, Gardner, MA 01440
(617) 632-6175
Admin Pauline LeBlanc.
Medical Dir Dr John Denman.
Licensure Rest home. *Beds* Rest home 13.
Owner Proprietary corp.
Admissions Requirements Minimum age 18.
Staff Physicians 1 (ft); LPNs 1 (ft); Podiatrists 1 (pt); Dentists 1 (pt).
Facilities Dining room; Activities room; Laundry room.
Activities Arts & crafts; Cards; Games; Prayer groups; Movies; Shopping trips.

Gardner Manor Nursing Home
155 Green St, Gardner, MA 01440
(508) 632-2900
Admin Linda A Brooke. *Dir of Nursing* Kathleen Cormier. *Medical Dir* William Damon.
Licensure Skilled care; Intermediate care. *Beds* SNF 38; ICF 36. *Certified* Medicare.
Owner Proprietary corp.
Admissions Requirements Minimum age 18; Physician's request.
Staff Physicians; RNs; LPNs; Nurses' aides; Activities coordinators.
Languages Polish, French, Spanish.
Facilities Dining room; Physical therapy room; Activities room; Laundry room; Barber/Beauty shop.
Activities Arts & crafts; Cards; Games; Prayer groups; Movies; Intergenerational programs.

Wachusett Manor Nursing Home
32 Hospital Hill Rd, Gardner, MA 01440
(508) 632-5477
Admin John P Zoltowski. *Dir of Nursing* Judith Rose RN. *Medical Dir* Diane Rahman MD.
Licensure Intermediate care. *Beds* ICF 89. *Private Pay Patients* 8%. *Certified* Medicaid.
Owner Privately owned.
Admissions Requirements Minimum age 60; Medical examination; Physician's request.
Staff RNs; LPNs; Nurses' aides; Activities coordinators; Dietitians.
Languages French.

Facilities Dining room; Activities room; Crafts room; Laundry room; Barber/Beauty shop.
Activities Arts & crafts; Cards; Games; Reading groups; Prayer groups; Movies; Shopping trips; Dances/Social/Cultural gatherings; Intergenerational programs; Pet therapy.

Gloucester

Greycliff at Cape Ann Convalescent Center
272 Washington St, Gloucester, MA 01930
(617) 281-0333
Admin John A Holt.
Medical Dir Dr Douglas Fiero.
Licensure Skilled care; Intermediate care. *Beds* SNF 52; ICF 49. *Certified* Medicaid.
Owner Proprietary corp (Beverly Enterprises).
Admissions Requirements Medical examination.
Staff RNs 5 (ft), 2 (pt); LPNs 3 (ft), 3 (pt); Nurses' aides 20 (ft), 25 (pt); Physical therapists 1 (pt); Occupational therapists 1 (pt); Activities coordinators 2 (ft); Dietitians 1 (pt); Podiatrists 1 (pt).
Facilities Dining room; Activities room; Crafts room; Laundry room; Barber/Beauty shop; Library.
Activities Arts & crafts; Cards; Games; Reading groups; Prayer groups; Movies; Shopping trips; Dances/Social/Cultural gatherings.

Shore Cliff Retirement Home
PO Box 5390, Shore & Cliff Rds, Gloucester, MA 01930
(617) 525-3456
Admin Mary L Barnett.
Licensure Rest home. *Beds* Rest home 28.
Owner Proprietary corp.
Admissions Requirements Minimum age 65; Medical examination.
Staff RNs 2 (ft); LPNs 5 (pt); Nurses' aides 1 (ft), 3 (pt); Activities coordinators 1 (pt).
Facilities Dining room; Activities room; Laundry room; Barber/Beauty shop; Library.
Activities Arts & crafts; Cards; Games; Reading groups; Prayer groups; Movies; Shopping trips; Dances/Social/Cultural gatherings; Field trips; Exercise program.

Grafton

Crescent Manor Rest Home
5 Crescent St, Grafton, MA 01519
(508) 839-2124
Admin Mary C Brewer. *Dir of Nursing* Lisa C Coates.
Licensure Rest home. *Beds* Rest home 58. *Certified* Medicaid; Medicare.
Owner Privately owned.
Admissions Requirements Medical examination.
Staff Physicians; RNs; LPNs; Nurses' aides; Activities coordinators; Dietitians; Podiatrists.
Facilities Dining room; Activities room; Crafts room; Laundry room; Barber/Beauty shop.
Activities Arts & crafts; Cards; Games; Reading groups; Prayer groups; Movies; Shopping trips; Dances/Social/Cultural gatherings; Intergenerational programs; Pet therapy.

Edgewood Nursing Home Inc
23 N Brigham Hill Rd, Grafton, MA 01519
(617) 839-4980
Admin Burton K Lipsky.
Licensure Intermediate care. *Beds* ICF 36. *Certified* Medicaid.
Owner Proprietary corp.
Admissions Requirements Minimum age 16.
Staff RNs 1 (pt); LPNs 2 (ft), 4 (pt); Nurses' aides 4 (ft), 4 (pt); Activities coordinators 1 (pt); Dietitians 1 (pt).

Facilities Dining room; Activities room; Laundry room; Barber/Beauty shop.
Activities Arts & crafts; Cards; Games; Reading groups; Prayer groups; Movies; Dances/Social/Cultural gatherings.

Keith Hill Nursing Home Inc
44 Old Upton Rd, Grafton, MA 01519
(617) 839-2195
Admin Richard J Carlson.
Licensure Skilled care; Intermediate care. *Beds* SNF 22; ICF 21. *Certified* Medicaid.
Owner Proprietary corp.

Great Barrington

Great Barrington Healthcare Nursing Home
148 Maple Ave, Great Barrington, MA 01230
(413) 528-3320
Admin Melvin J Hitt.
Licensure Skilled care; Intermediate care. *Beds* SNF 39; ICF 67. *Certified* Medicaid; Medicare.
Owner Proprietary corp (First Healthcare Corp).

Timberlyn Heights Nursing Home
320 Maple Ave, Great Barrington, MA 01230
(413) 528-2650
Admin Edward M Lenz.
Medical Dir Joanne Marshall.
Licensure Skilled care; Intermediate care. *Beds* SNF 39; ICF 39. *Certified* Medicaid.
Owner Proprietary corp (First Healthcare Corp).
Facilities Dining room; Physical therapy room; Activities room; Chapel; Laundry room; Barber/Beauty shop.
Activities Arts & crafts; Cards; Games; Reading groups; Prayer groups; Movies; Shopping trips; Dances/Social/Cultural gatherings.

Willowood Nursing & Retirement Facility
Christian Hill Rd, Great Barrington, MA 01230
(413) 528-4560, 528-5691 FAX
Admin Melvin J Hitt. *Dir of Nursing* Mary Anne Jones RN MEd. *Medical Dir* Dr Richard Clarke.
Licensure Skilled care; Intermediate care. *Beds* SNF 120; ICF 60. *Private Pay Patients* 17%. *Certified* Medicaid; Medicare.
Owner Proprietary corp.
Admissions Requirements Minimum age 21; Medical examination.
Staff Physicians 9 (pt); RNs 11 (ft), 4 (pt); LPNs 13 (ft), 7 (pt); Nurses' aides 49 (ft), 23 (pt); Physical therapists 1 (pt); Occupational therapists 1 (pt); Speech therapists 1 (pt); Activities coordinators 1 (ft); Dietitians 1 (pt); Podiatrists 1 (pt).
Facilities Dining room; Physical therapy room; Activities room; Crafts room; Laundry room; Barber/Beauty shop; Ventilator care unit.
Activities Arts & crafts; Cards; Games; Reading groups; Prayer groups; Movies; Shopping trips; Dances/Social/Cultural gatherings; Intergenerational programs; Pet therapy; Religious services.

Greenfield

Buckley Nursing Home
PO Box 1436, Greenfield, MA 01302
(413) 774-3143
Admin Myron W Sibley Jr.
Licensure Skilled care; Intermediate care. *Beds* SNF 80; ICF 40.

Charlene Manor Extended Care Facility
130 Colrain Rd, Greenfield, MA 01301
(413) 774-3724
Admin Timothy V Cotz.

Licensure Skilled care; Intermediate care. *Beds* SNF 82; ICF 41.
Owner Privately owned.

Franklin Nursing Home
329 Conway St, Greenfield, MA 01301
(413) 772-0811
Admin Doris Garbose.
Licensure Skilled care; Intermediate care. *Beds* SNF 129; ICF 121. *Certified* Medicaid; Medicare.
Owner Proprietary corp.
Admissions Requirements Physician's request.
Staff RNs; LPNs; Nurses' aides; Recreational therapists; Occupational therapists; Activities coordinators; Dietitians.
Facilities Dining room; Physical therapy room; Activities room; Barber/Beauty shop.
Activities Arts & crafts; Cards; Games; Reading groups; Prayer groups; Movies; Shopping trips; Dances/Social/Cultural gatherings; Intergenerational programs.

Pioneer Valley Manor Rest Home
148 Montague City Rd, Greenfield, MA 01301
(413) 773-8589
Admin Roberta C Bryant.
Licensure Rest home. *Beds* Rest home 37.
Owner Privately owned.

Poet's Seat Nursing Home
359 High St, Greenfield, MA 01301
(413) 774-6318
Admin Robert H Claflin. *Dir of Nursing* Kathleen Murphy. *Medical Dir* Spencer Flo.
Licensure Skilled care. *Beds* SNF 63. *Private Pay Patients* 29%. *Certified* Medicaid; Medicare.
Owner Proprietary corp.
Staff RNs 4 (ft), 4 (pt); LPNs 1 (ft), 2 (pt); Nurses' aides 20 (ft), 3 (pt); Activities coordinators 2 (ft); Dietitians 1 (pt); Podiatrists 1 (pt).
Languages French, Polish, Sign.
Facilities Dining room; Physical therapy room; Activities room; Laundry room; Barber/Beauty shop; Library; Whirlpool bath.
Activities Arts & crafts; Cards; Games; Reading groups; Prayer groups; Movies; Shopping trips; Dances/Social/Cultural gatherings; Pet therapy.

Groton

Children's Extended Care Center
22 Hillside Ave, Groton, MA 01450
(617) 448-3388
Admin Carol S Lobron MS. *Dir of Nursing* Debra Willard RN. *Medical Dir* I Leslie Rubin MD.
Licensure Skilled care. *Beds* SNF 71. *Certified* Medicaid.
Owner Nonprofit corp.
Admissions Requirements Through Massachusetts Department of Public Health.
Staff Physicians 3 (pt); RNs 11 (ft), 11 (pt); LPNs 7 (ft), 11 (pt); Nurses' aides 31 (ft), 43 (pt); Physical therapists 3 (ft); Occupational therapists 1 (ft); Speech therapists 1 (pt); Dietitians 1 (pt); Podiatrists 1 (pt).

Hale Convalescent & Nursing Home Inc
58 Main St, Groton, MA 01472
(617) 448-6802
Admin Francis M Andreoli.
Licensure Intermediate care. *Beds* ICF 36. *Certified* Medicaid.
Owner Proprietary corp.

Hadley

Shady Lawn Rest Home Inc
90 Middle St, Hadley, MA 01035
(413) 584-4018
Admin Anna W Thompson.

Medical Dir David Artzerounian; Peter Betjemann.
Licensure Rest home; Alzheimer's care. *Beds* Rest home 23. *Certified* Medicaid.
Owner Proprietary corp.
Admissions Requirements Minimum age 36; Medical examination.
Staff Physicians 1 (pt); LPNs 1 (ft), 1 (pt); Nurses' aides 7 (ft), 2 (pt); Physical therapists 1 (pt); Activities coordinators 1 (pt); Dietitians 1 (pt); Ophthalmologists 1 (pt).
Languages Polish, Spanish.
Facilities Dining room; Activities room; Chapel; Laundry room; Barber/Beauty shop; Library.
Activities Arts & crafts; Cards; Games; Prayer groups; Shopping trips; Lunch trips; Trips to flower shows; Parks; Picnics; Dinner trips.

Hampden

Mary Lyon Nursing Home
34 Main St, Hampden, MA 01036
(413) 566-5511
Admin Nancy Varinoski.
Medical Dir Dr Fred Schwendenmann.
Licensure Skilled care; Intermediate care. *Beds* SNF 40; ICF 60. *Certified* Medicaid; Medicare.
Owner Proprietary corp.
Admissions Requirements Minimum age 16; Medical examination; Physician's request.
Staff Physicians 12 (ft); RNs 6 (ft), 10 (pt); LPNs 5 (ft), 6 (pt); Nurses' aides 24 (ft), 11 (pt); Physical therapists 1 (ft), 1 (pt); Occupational therapists 1 (pt); Speech therapists 1 (pt); Activities coordinators 1 (ft); Dietitians 1 (pt).
Languages French, Spanish, Italian.
Facilities Dining room; Physical therapy room; Activities room; Laundry room; Barber/Beauty shop.
Activities Arts & crafts; Cards; Games; Prayer groups; Movies; Shopping trips; Dances/Social/Cultural gatherings.

Hanover

Mill Pond Rest Home
974 Main St, Hanover, MA 02339
(617) 871-0171
Admin Edward R Hammond Jr. *Dir of Nursing* Donna Buckley RN.
Licensure Rest home. *Beds* Rest home 38.
Owner Proprietary corp.
Admissions Requirements Minimum age 55; Medical examination; Physician's request.
Staff Nurses' aides 10 (ft), 4 (pt); Recreational therapists 1 (pt); Activities coordinators 1 (pt); Dietitians 1 (pt).
Facilities Dining room; Activities room; Chapel; Barber/Beauty shop.
Activities Cards; Games; Movies; Shopping trips; Dances/Social/Cultural gatherings.

North River Nursing Home
Box 11, Washington St, Pembroke, Hanover, MA 02339
(617) 826-4521
Admin Maryanne Sullivan.
Licensure Intermediate care. *Beds* ICF 41. *Certified* Medicaid.
Owner Proprietary corp.

Hardwick

Hilltop Rest Home
31 Prospect St, Gilbertville, Hardwick, MA 01031
(413) 477-6601
Admin Richard J Muise.
Licensure Rest home. *Beds* Rest home 22.
Owner Proprietary corp.

Haverhill

Baker Katz Nursing Home
194 Boardman St, Haverhill, MA 01830
(617) 373-5697
Admin David M Baker.
Licensure Intermediate care. *Beds* ICF 77.
Certified Medicaid.
Owner Proprietary corp.

Churchview Health Center Retirement Home
35-37 Arlington St, Box 150, Haverhill, MA
01830
(617) 372-3675
Admin Ann Azzarito.
Medical Dir Arnold George MD.
Licensure Rest home. *Beds* 22.
Admissions Requirements Minimum age 21;
Medical examination; Physician's request.
Facilities Dining room; Activities room;
Laundry room.
Activities Arts & crafts; Prayer groups.

Hannah Duston Long-Term Health Care Center
126 Monument St, Haverhill, MA 01832
(617) 373-1747
Admin David Lewis. *Dir of Nursing* Arline
Martin RN. *Medical Dir* Thomas Hayes
MD.
Licensure Skilled care; Intermediate care. *Beds*
SNF 40; ICF 40. *Certified* Medicaid;
Medicare.
Owner Privately owned.
Admissions Requirements Medical
examination.
Facilities Dining room; Physical therapy
room; Activities room; Laundry room;
Barber/Beauty shop.
Activities Arts & crafts; Cards; Games;
Reading groups; Prayer groups; Movies;
Shopping trips; Dances/Social/Cultural
gatherings; Intergenerational programs; Pet
therapy.

Glynn Memorial Home
61 Brown St, Haverhill, MA 01830
(617) 374-2378
Admin Stanley T Trocki Jr. *Dir of Nursing*
Janine Bloomfield RN. *Medical Dir* Dr
Charles Chaput.
Licensure Intermediate care. *Beds* ICF 48.
Certified Medicaid.
Owner Publicly owned.
Admissions Requirements Minimum age 21.
Staff RNs 4 (ft), 2 (pt); LPNs 4 (ft), 1 (pt);
Nurses' aides 18 (ft), 4 (pt); Activities
coordinators 1 (ft); Dietitians 1 (pt).
Languages Polish, French.
Facilities Dining room; Activities room;
Chapel; Crafts room; Laundry room; Barber/
Beauty shop; Library.
Activities Arts & crafts; Cards; Games;
Reading groups; Prayer groups; Movies;
Shopping trips; Dances/Social/Cultural
gatherings.

Haverhill Manor Nursing Home
100 Lawrence St, Haverhill, MA 01830
(617) 374-0356
Admin Laura M Roy. *Dir of Nursing* Jane
Merrow. *Medical Dir* Charles Chaput.
Licensure Skilled care; Intermediate care. *Beds*
SNF 47; ICF 53. *Certified* Medicaid.
Owner Proprietary corp (American Health
Center Inc).
Admissions Requirements Minimum age 21;
Physician's request.
Staff Physicians 1 (pt); RNs 8 (ft), 2 (pt);
LPNs 12 (ft), 4 (pt); Nurses' aides 22 (ft), 5
(pt); Physical therapists 1 (pt); Occupational
therapists 1 (pt); Speech therapists 1 (pt);
Activities coordinators 1 (ft); Dietitians 1
(pt); Ophthalmologists 1 (pt); Podiatrists 1
(pt).
Facilities Dining room; Physical therapy
room; Activities room; Laundry room;
Barber/Beauty shop; TV room.

Activities Arts & crafts; Cards; Games;
Reading groups; Prayer groups; Movies;
Shopping trips; Dances/Social/Cultural
gatherings; Community events; Outings;
Lunch groups; Fairs; Sports; Pets;
Gardening.

Kenoza Hillcrest Nursing Home
Box 6306, Haverhill, MA 01831-6306
(617) 373-5121
Admin Charles H Rinne.
Licensure Intermediate care. *Beds* ICF 22.
Certified Medicaid.
Owner Proprietary corp (American Health
Center Inc).

Kenoza Manor Convalescent Center
190 North Ave, Haverhill, MA 01830
(617) 372-7700
Admin Timothy G Barry. *Dir of Nursing*
Darlene Ryan. *Medical Dir* Dr David Byrne.
Licensure Skilled care; Intermediate care. *Beds*
SNF 40; ICF 60. *Certified* Medicare.
Owner Proprietary corp (American Health
Center Inc).
Admissions Requirements Minimum age 18;
Physician's request.
Staff Physicians 12 (pt); RNs 6 (ft), 3 (pt);
LPNs 7 (ft), 2 (pt); Nurses' aides 29 (ft), 13
(pt); Physical therapists 1 (pt); Recreational
therapists 1 (pt); Occupational therapists 1
(pt).
Facilities Dining room; Activities room;
Crafts room; Laundry room; Barber/Beauty
shop.
Activities Arts & crafts; Cards; Games;
Reading groups; Prayer groups; Movies;
Shopping trips; Dances/Social/Cultural
gatherings; Continental breakfast; Dance
exercise class; Mens group; Sensory
stimulation; Bowling; Basketball; Painting;
Baking.

Lakeview House Nursing Home
PO Box 1598, Haverhill, MA 01831-2298
(617) 372-1081
Admin Jon D Guarino.
Licensure Skilled care; Rest home. *Beds* SNF
22; Rest home 65. *Certified* Medicaid.
Owner Proprietary corp.

Oxford Manor Nursing Home
689 Main St, Haverhill, MA 01830
(508) 373-1131
Admin Beth Casso. *Dir of Nursing* Kathleen
Silva RN. *Medical Dir* David Byrne MD.
Licensure Skilled care; Intermediate care. *Beds*
SNF 60; ICF 60. *Certified* Medicaid;
Medicare.
Owner Proprietary corp (Cushman
Management Associates Inc).
Admissions Requirements Minimum age 21.
Staff RNs; LPNs; Nurses' aides; Physical
therapists; Recreational therapists;
Occupational therapists; Speech therapists;
Dietitians.
Facilities Dining room; Physical therapy
room; Activities room; Laundry room;
Barber/Beauty shop.
Activities Arts & crafts; Cards; Games;
Reading groups; Prayer groups; Movies;
Shopping trips; Dances/Social/Cultural
gatherings; Intergenerational programs; Pet
therapy.

Scott's Rest Home
69 Keeley St, Haverhill, MA 01830-6694
(617) 374-4535
Admin Eva M Scott.
Licensure Retirement home. *Beds* Retirement
home 10.
Owner Privately owned.
Admissions Requirements Minimum age 60;
Medical examination; Physician's request.
Staff Physicians; LPNs; Nurses' aides.
Facilities Dining room; Laundry room;
Barber/Beauty shop.
Activities Arts & crafts; Cards; Games.

Stevens Bennett
337 Main St, Haverhill, MA 01830
(508) 374-8861
Admin Sandra A Favor. *Dir of Nursing* Diane
McNally RN. *Medical Dir* Dr David Byrne.
Licensure Skilled care. *Beds* SNF 30. *Certified*
Medicaid; Medicare.
Owner Nonprofit organization/foundation.
Admissions Requirements Minimum age 65;
Females only; Medical examination;
Physician's request.
Staff Physicians 1 (ft); RNs 1 (pt); Nurses'
aides 2 (ft), 6 (pt); Activities coordinators 1
(ft); Dietitians 1 (pt).
Facilities Dining room; Activities room;
Crafts room; Laundry room; Barber/Beauty
shop; Library.
Activities Arts & crafts; Games; Movies.

Union Mission Nursing Home Inc
150 Water St, Haverhill, MA 01830
(617) 374-0707
Admin Dr Eugene Tillock. *Dir of Nursing*
Marcia Kent RN. *Medical Dir* Ulrich Ehrig
MD.
Licensure Skilled care; Intermediate care. *Beds*
SNF 121; ICF 39; Social day care program
M-F; Respite care for short-term admissions.
Certified Medicaid.
Owner Nonprofit corp.
Admissions Requirements Medical
examination; Physician's request.
Staff Physicians 15 (pt); RNs 8 (ft); LPNs 6
(ft); Nurses' aides 48 (ft); Physical therapists
1 (pt); Recreational therapists 1 (ft);
Occupational therapists 1 (pt); Speech
therapists 1 (pt); Activities coordinators 1
(ft); Dietitians 1 (pt); Ophthalmologists 1
(pt); Podiatrists 3 (pt); Dentists 2 (pt).
Facilities Dining room; Physical therapy
room; Activities room; Crafts room; Barber/
Beauty shop; Library; Lounges.
Activities Arts & crafts; Cards; Games;
Reading groups; Prayer groups; Movies;
Shopping trips; Dances/Social/Cultural
gatherings; Continuing education.

Griffin White Home
170 Main St, Haverhill, MA 01830
(617) 372-1501
Admin Harold MacFarlane.
Licensure Rest home. *Beds* Rest home 16.
Owner Nonprofit corp.
Admissions Requirements Minimum age 60;
Males only & married couples.

Hingham

Deering Nursing Home Inc
1192 Main St, Hingham, MA 02043
(617) 749-2285
Admin Lorraine A Starr.
Licensure Intermediate care. *Beds* ICF 54.
Certified Medicaid.
Owner Proprietary corp.

New England Friends Home
Turkey Hill Ln, Hingham, MA 02043
(617) 749-3556
Admin David H Lowa.
Licensure Rest home. *Beds* Rest home 15.
Owner Proprietary corp.
Affiliation Society of Friends.
Facilities Dining room; Activities room;
Library.
Activities Cards; Games; Prayer groups;
Movies; Dances/Social/Cultural gatherings.

Queen Anne Nursing Home Inc
50 Recreation Park Dr, Hingham, MA 02043
(617) 749-4983
Admin Peter H Starr.
Licensure Skilled care; Intermediate care. *Beds*
SNF 41; ICF 53. *Certified* Medicaid;
Medicare.
Owner Proprietary corp.

Hinsdale

Ashmere Manor Nursing Home
George Schnopp Rd, Hinsdale, MA 01235
(413) 655-2929, 655-2092 FAX
Admin J Michael Rivers. *Dir of Nursing* Jo
Ann Danforth. *Medical Dir* Michael J
Murray MD.
Licensure Skilled care; Intermediate care;
Alzheimer's care. *Beds* SNF 22; ICF 60.
Private Pay Patients 18%. *Certified*
Medicaid.
Owner Privately owned.
Admissions Requirements Medical
examination; Physician's request.
Staff Physicians (consultants); RNs 4 (ft), 2
(pt); LPNs 9 (ft), 2 (pt); Nurses' aides 25
(ft), 4 (pt); Physical therapists (consultant);
Occupational therapists (consultant); Speech
therapists (consultant); Activities
coordinators 1 (ft), 1 (pt); Dietitians
(consultant); Podiatrists (consultant).
Languages Polish, Italian.
Facilities Dining room; Physical therapy
room; Activities room; Crafts room; Laundry
room; Barber/Beauty shop; Outside visiting
areas.
Activities Arts & crafts; Cards; Games;
Reading groups; Prayer groups; Movies;
Shopping trips; Dances/Social/Cultural
gatherings; Intergenerational programs; Pet
therapy; Picnics; Fishing.

Holbrook

Holbrook Nursing Home
45 S Franklin St, Holbrook, MA 02343
(617) 767-1915
Admin Margaret Pomeroy.
Licensure Intermediate care. *Beds* ICF 41.
Certified Medicaid.
Owner Proprietary corp.

Holden

Holden Nursing Home Inc
32 Mayo Rd, Holden, MA 01520
(617) 829-4327
Admin Robert G Oriol.
Medical Dir Henry Kramer.
Licensure Skilled care; Intermediate care. *Beds*
SNF 40; ICF 48. *Certified* Medicaid.
Owner Proprietary corp.
Admissions Requirements Minimum age 21;
Medical examination; Physician's request.
Staff Physicians 1 (pt); RNs 6 (ft), 6 (pt);
LPNs 4 (ft), 5 (pt); Nurses' aides 23 (ft), 18
(pt); Physical therapists 1 (ft); Recreational
therapists 1 (ft); Occupational therapists 1
(pt); Dietitians 2 (ft), 1 (pt).
Facilities Dining room; Physical therapy
room; Activities room; Chapel; Laundry
room; Barber/Beauty shop; Library.
Activities Arts & crafts; Cards; Games;
Reading groups; Prayer groups; Movies;
Shopping trips; Dances/Social/Cultural
gatherings; Church services.

Holliston

Holliston Manor Nursing Home
84 Elm St, Holliston, MA 01746
(617) 429-4566
Admin V Jean Cohen.
Medical Dir John LaRossa MD.
Licensure Intermediate care. *Beds* ICF 40.
Certified Medicaid.
Owner Proprietary corp.
Admissions Requirements Minimum age 21.
Staff Physicians 3 (pt); RNs 1 (ft), 4 (pt);
LPNs 1 (ft), 3 (pt); Nurses' aides 7 (ft), 6
(pt); Physical therapists 1 (pt); Activities
coordinators 1 (ft); Dietitians 1 (pt);
Podiatrists 1 (pt).

Facilities Dining room; Activities room.
Activities Arts & crafts; Games; Prayer groups;
Movies; Shopping trips; Dances/Social/
Cultural gatherings.

Holyoke

Buckley Nursing & Retirement Home
282 Cabot St, Holyoke, MA 01040
(413) 538-7470
Admin William M Hartt. *Dir of Nursing*
Margaret Thieme RN. *Medical Dir* Philip
Dean MD.
Licensure Skilled care; Intermediate care. *Beds*
SNF 68; ICF 34. *Certified* Medicaid;
Medicare.
Owner Proprietary corp (Buckley Nursing
Home Inc).
Admissions Requirements Minimum age 18;
Medical examination; Physician's request.
Staff Physicians; RNs; LPNs; Nurses' aides;
Physical therapists; Reality therapists;
Recreational therapists; Occupational
therapists; Speech therapists; Activities
coordinators; Dietitians; Ophthalmologists;
Podiatrists.
Facilities Dining room; Physical therapy
room; Activities room; Crafts room; Laundry
room; Barber/Beauty shop; Library.
Activities Arts & crafts; Cards; Games;
Reading groups; Movies; Shopping trips;
Dances/Social/Cultural gatherings;
Intergenerational programs.

Chapel Hill Nursing Home
100 Locust St, Holyoke, MA 01040
(413) 536-3435
Admin Mary F Uschmann.
Licensure Skilled care. *Beds* SNF 61. *Certified*
Medicaid.
Owner Proprietary corp.

Holyoke Geriatric & Convalescent Center
45 Lower Westfield Rd, Holyoke, MA 01040
(413) 536-8110
Admin Edward C Brunelle. *Dir of Nursing*
Patricia Silver. *Medical Dir* Robert Mausel
MD.
Licensure Skilled care; Intermediate care. *Beds*
SNF 120; ICF 120. *Private Pay Patients* 9%.
Certified Medicaid; Medicare.
Owner Publicly owned.
Admissions Requirements Minimum age 21;
Physician's request.
Staff Physicians 14 (pt); RNs 20 (ft); LPNs 24
(ft); Nurses' aides 125 (ft); Physical
therapists 2 (ft); Recreational therapists 7
(ft); Occupational therapists 2 (ft); Speech
therapists 1 (pt); Activities coordinators 1
(ft); Dietitians 1 (ft); Ophthalmologists 1
(pt); Podiatrists 3 (pt).
Languages French, Polish, Spanish.
Facilities Dining room; Physical therapy
room; Activities room; Chapel; Crafts room;
Barber/Beauty shop; Library.
Activities Arts & crafts; Cards; Games;
Reading groups; Prayer groups; Movies;
Shopping trips; Intergenerational programs;
Pet therapy.

Holyoke Nursing Home
1913 Northampton St, Holyoke, MA 01040
(413) 536-7110
Admin Theodore P Baldwin. *Dir of Nursing*
Susan Brooks RN. *Medical Dir* Norman
Halpern MD.
Licensure Skilled care; Intermediate care. *Beds*
SNF 50; ICF 50. *Certified* Medicaid.
Owner Proprietary corp.
Staff RNs 3 (ft), 3 (pt); LPNs 6 (ft), 2 (pt);
Nurses' aides 28 (ft), 9 (pt); Activities
coordinators 1 (ft); Dietitians 1 (pt).
Facilities Dining room; Physical therapy
room; Activities room; Chapel; Crafts room;
Laundry room; Barber/Beauty shop.

Activities Arts & crafts; Cards; Games;
Reading groups; Prayer groups; Movies;
Shopping trips; Dances/Social/Cultural
gatherings.

Loomis House Inc
298 Jarvis Ave, Holyoke, MA 01040
(413) 538-7551, 536-2024 FAX
Admin Carol C Katz. *Dir of Nursing* Terry
Peltier RN. *Medical Dir* David Clinton MD.
Licensure Skilled care; Intermediate care;
Independent & assisted living. *Beds* SNF 41;
ICF 39; Independent & assisted living 74.
Private Pay Patients 50%. *Certified*
Medicaid; Medicare.
Owner Nonprofit organization/foundation.
Admissions Requirements Minimum age 18;
Medical examination; Physician's request.
Staff RNs; LPNs; Nurses' aides; Physical
therapists; Recreational therapists; Activities
coordinators; Dietitians.
Languages Polish, French, Spanish, Greek,
Sign.
Facilities Dining room; Physical therapy
room; Activities room; Laundry room;
Barber/Beauty shop.
Activities Arts & crafts; Cards; Games;
Reading groups; Prayer groups; Movies;
Shopping trips; Dances/Social/Cultural
gatherings; Intergenerational programs; Pet
therapy.

Mt St Vincent Home
Holy Family Rd, Holyoke, MA 01040
(413) 532-3246, 532-0309 FAX
Admin Patricia A Tiernan. *Dir of Nursing*
Ana Nunez RN BSN. *Medical Dir* Michael
A Rosner MD.
Licensure Skilled care; Intermediate care. *Beds*
SNF 43; ICF 82. *Certified* Medicaid.
Owner Nonprofit corp.
Admissions Requirements Medical
examination.
Staff Physicians 1 (pt); RNs 5 (ft), 8 (pt);
LPNs 3 (ft), 4 (pt); Nurses' aides 36 (ft), 14
(pt); Physical therapists 1 (pt); Recreational
therapists 1 (ft); Occupational therapists 1
(pt); Activities coordinators 1 (ft); Dietitians
1 (pt).
Languages Polish, French, Spanish.
Affiliation Roman Catholic.
Facilities Dining room; Physical therapy
room; Activities room; Chapel; Crafts room;
Laundry room; Barber/Beauty shop; Library;
Auditorium; Sundeck.
Activities Arts & crafts; Cards; Games;
Reading groups; Prayer groups; Movies;
Shopping trips; Dances/Social/Cultural
gatherings.

New Medico RSNC at Brook Wood
260 Easthampton Rd, Holyoke, MA 01040
(413) 538-7941
Admin Wayne D Brown. *Dir of Nursing*
Kathryn Hervieux. *Medical Dir* Dr Shawki
Konazi.
Licensure Skilled care; Intermediate care. *Beds*
SNF 82; ICF 82. *Certified* Medicaid;
Medicare.
Owner Proprietary corp.
Admissions Requirements Physician's request.
Staff Physicians 1 (pt); RNs 8 (ft), 8 (pt);
LPNs 9 (ft), 5 (pt); Nurses' aides 48 (ft), 27
(pt); Physical therapists 1 (pt); Occupational
therapists 1 (pt); Speech therapists 1 (pt);
Activities coordinators 1 (ft), 2 (pt);
Dietitians 1 (pt); Podiatrists 1 (pt); Dentists
1 (pt).
Facilities Dining room; Physical therapy
room; Activities room; Chapel; Crafts room;
Laundry room; Barber/Beauty shop.
Activities Arts & crafts; Cards; Games;
Reading groups; Prayer groups; Movies;
Shopping trips; Dances/Social/Cultural
gatherings.

Oak Manor Nursing Home
19 Quirk Ave, Holyoke, MA 01040
(413) 532-1415
Admin Eleanor L David.
Licensure Intermediate care. *Beds* ICF 60.
 Certified Medicaid.
Owner Proprietary corp.

Hopedale

Adin Manor Convalescent Home
34 Adin St, Hopedale, MA 01747
(617) 473-0171
Admin James M Tracy.
Medical Dir Faheem Farooq MD.
Licensure Intermediate care; Alzheimer's care.
 Beds ICF 56. *Certified* Medicaid.
Owner Proprietary corp.
Admissions Requirements Minimum age 21;
 Medical examination.
Staff Physicians 4 (pt); RNs 2 (ft); LPNs 8
 (ft), 2 (pt); Nurses' aides 20 (ft); Physical
 therapists 1 (pt); Recreational therapists 1
 (pt); Occupational therapists 1 (pt); Speech
 therapists 1 (pt); Activities coordinators 1
 (ft); Dietitians 1 (pt); Ophthalmologists 1
 (pt); Podiatrists 1 (pt); Dentists.
Facilities Dining room; Activities room;
 Laundry room; Barber/Beauty shop; Library.
Activities Arts & crafts; Cards; Games;
 Reading groups; Prayer groups; Movies;
 Shopping trips; Dances/Social/Cultural
 gatherings.

Hopedale Garden Nursing Home
325 S Main St, Hopedale, MA 01747
(617) 473-9600
Admin Sidney Croll.
Licensure Skilled care; Intermediate care. *Beds*
 SNF 37; ICF 33. *Certified* Medicaid.
Owner Proprietary corp.

Hudson

Hudson Health Care
53 Church St, Hudson, MA 01749
(508) 562-6906
Admin Beverly Singer. *Dir of Nursing* Cynthia
 J Brown. *Medical Dir* Michele Ricard MD.
Licensure Intermediate care. *Beds* ICF 43.
 Certified Medicaid.
Owner Proprietary corp.
Admissions Requirements Minimum age 55;
 Medical examination.
Staff RNs 3 (ft), 3 (pt); LPNs 2 (ft), 4 (pt);
 Nurses' aides 9 (ft), 6 (pt); Activities
 coordinators 1 (pt); Dietitians 1 (pt).
Languages Portuguese.
Facilities Activities room; Laundry room;
 Barber/Beauty shop.
Activities Arts & crafts; Cards; Games;
 Reading groups; Prayer groups;
 Intergenerational programs; Pet therapy.

Huntington

Governor's House Nursing Home
66 Broad St, Huntington, MA 01085
(413) 562-5464
Admin Charlene Whitaker. *Dir of Nursing*
 Cynthia Puza. *Medical Dir* Paul Bothner
 MD.
Licensure Skilled care; Intermediate care. *Beds*
 SNF 40; ICF 60. *Private Pay Patients* 30%.
 Certified Medicaid; Medicare.
Owner Proprietary corp (Concord Health Care
 Corp).
Admissions Requirements Minimum age 21;
 Medical examination; Physician's request.
Staff RNs 3 (ft), 2 (pt); LPNs 7 (ft), 2 (pt);
 Physical therapists 1 (pt); Occupational
 therapists 1 (pt); Speech therapists
 (consultant); Activities coordinators 1 (ft), 1
 (pt); Dietitians 1 (pt); Ophthalmologists
 (consultant); Podiatrists (consultant);
 Audiologists (consultant).

Languages Spanish.
Facilities Dining room; Physical therapy
 room; Activities room; Crafts room; Laundry
 room; Barber/Beauty shop; Classroom;
 Conference room.
Activities Arts & crafts; Cards; Games;
 Reading groups; Prayer groups; Movies;
 Shopping trips; Dances/Social/Cultural
 gatherings; Intergenerational programs; Pet
 therapy; Outings with staff; Family support
 group.

Hyannis

Fraser Rest Home of Hyannis
349 Sea St, Hyannis, MA 02601
(617) 775-4881
Admin Audrey Cornell.
Licensure Intermediate care. *Beds* ICF 37.
 Certified Medicaid.
Owner Proprietary corp.
Admissions Requirements Minimum age 21.
Staff RNs 1 (pt); LPNs 1 (ft); Nurses' aides 10
 (ft); Activities coordinators 1 (ft); Dietitians
 1 (pt).
Facilities Dining room; Activities room;
 Crafts room.
Activities Arts & crafts; Cards; Games;
 Reading groups; Prayer groups; Movies;
 Shopping trips; Dances/Social/Cultural
 gatherings.

Hyde Park

Village Manor
25 Alpine St, Hyde Park, MA 02126
(617) 361-5400, 364-1124 FAX
Admin Scott Elsass. *Dir of Nursing* Steve
 Kolodziej RN. *Medical Dir* Dr David Chen.
Licensure Skilled care; Intermediate care. *Beds*
 SNF 82; ICF 41. *Private Pay Patients* 20%.
 Certified Medicaid; Medicare.
Owner Nonprofit corp.
Admissions Requirements Minimum age 45;
 Medical examination; Physician's request.
Staff Physicians 1 (pt); RNs 7 (ft), 3 (pt);
 LPNs 11 (ft), 5 (pt); Nurses' aides 35 (ft), 25
 (pt); Physical therapists 1 (pt); Reality
 therapists 1 (pt); Recreational therapists 1
 (pt); Occupational therapists 1 (pt); Speech
 therapists 1 (pt); Activities coordinators 3
 (ft); Dietitians 1 (ft); Ophthalmologists 1
 (pt); Podiatrists 1 (pt); Audiologists 1 (pt).
Languages French, Italian, Greek.
Facilities Dining room; Physical therapy
 room; Activities room; Chapel; Crafts room;
 Laundry room; Barber/Beauty shop; Library.
Activities Arts & crafts; Cards; Games;
 Reading groups; Prayer groups; Movies;
 Shopping trips; Dances/Social/Cultural
 gatherings; Intergenerational programs; Pet
 therapy.

Ipswich

**Stephen Caldwell Memorial Convalescent
Home Inc**
15 Green St, Ipswich, MA 01938
(617) 356-5460
Admin Jeannette D Connor. *Dir of Nursing*
 Donald Frances RN. *Medical Dir* Thomas
 Sullivan MD.
Licensure Skilled care. *Beds* SNF 60. *Certified*
 Medicaid; Medicare.
Owner Nonprofit corp.
Admissions Requirements Minimum age 21;
 Medical examination; Physician's request.
Staff Physicians 10 (pt); RNs 5 (ft), 3 (pt);
 LPNs 6 (pt); Nurses' aides 15 (ft), 7 (pt);
 Physical therapists 1 (pt); Occupational
 therapists 1 (pt); Speech therapists 1 (pt);
 Activities coordinators 2 (ft); Dietitians 1
 (pt); Ophthalmologists 1 (pt); Podiatrists 1
 (pt); Dentists 2 (pt).

Facilities Dining room; Physical therapy
 room; Activities room; Barber/Beauty shop;
 Library.
Activities Arts & crafts; Cards; Games;
 Reading groups; Prayer groups; Movies;
 Shopping trips; Dances/Social/Cultural
 gatherings.

Coburn Charitable Society
20 N Main St, Ipswich, MA 01938
(617) 356-3571
Admin Helen Fraga.
Licensure Rest home. *Beds* Rest home 9.
Owner Nonprofit corp.
Admissions Requirements Minimum age 60;
 Medical examination.
Staff LPNs 1 (pt); Nurses' aides 1 (ft), 1 (pt);
 Ophthalmologists 1 (pt).
Facilities Dining room; Activities room;
 Laundry room.
Activities Shopping trips.

Jamaica Plain

Armenian Nursing Home
431 Pond St, Jamaica Plain, MA 02130
(617) 522-2600
Admin Ira R Lipshute MPA. *Dir of Nursing*
 Suzanne O'Brien. *Medical Dir* Terrance
 Murphy MD.
Licensure Skilled care; Intermediate care. *Beds*
 SNF 41; ICF 42. *Private Pay Patients* 10%.
 Certified Medicaid.
Owner Nonprofit corp.
Admissions Requirements Minimum age 65;
 Medical examination.
Staff Physicians 1 (pt); RNs 4 (ft); LPNs 6
 (ft); Nurses' aides 25 (ft); Physical therapists
 1 (pt); Recreational therapists 2 (ft);
 Occupational therapists 1 (pt); Speech
 therapists 1 (pt); Activities coordinators 1
 (ft); Dietitians 1 (pt); Podiatrists 1 (pt).
Languages Armenian, Russian, Spanish,
 French, Arabic, Turkish.
Facilities Dining room; Activities room;
 Crafts room; Laundry room; Barber/Beauty
 shop.
Activities Arts & crafts; Cards; Games;
 Reading groups; Prayer groups; Movies;
 Shopping trips; Dances/Social/Cultural
 gatherings; Intergenerational programs; Van
 outings.

Bradley Nursing Home
495 Walnut Ave, Jamaica Plain, MA 02130
(617) 522-0660
Admin Joseph C Novak. *Dir of Nursing* Hazel
 Butler RN. *Medical Dir* Solomon Freedman.
Licensure Intermediate care. *Beds* ICF 26.
 Private Pay Patients 2%. *Certified* Medicaid;
 Medicare.
Owner Proprietary corp.
Admissions Requirements Females only;
 Medical examination.
Staff Physicians 4 (pt); RNs 1 (ft), 1 (pt);
 LPNs 2 (ft), 4 (pt); Nurses' aides 11 (ft), 2
 (pt); Physical therapists 1 (pt); Reality
 therapists 1 (pt); Recreational therapists 1
 (pt); Activities coordinators 1 (pt); Dietitians
 1 (pt); Ophthalmologists 1 (pt); Podiatrists 1
 (pt).
Facilities Activities room; Laundry room.
Activities Games; Prayer groups; Movies;
 Dances/Social/Cultural gatherings.

Mt Pleasant Home
301 S Huntington Ave, Jamaica Plain, MA
 02130
(617) 522-7600
Admin Harriet H Caton. *Dir of Nursing*
 Karen Noonan. *Medical Dir* Dr John
 Jainehill.
Licensure Intermediate care. *Beds* ICF 44.
 Certified Medicaid; Medicare.
Owner Nonprofit organization/foundation.
Admissions Requirements Medical
 examination.

Staff LPNs 2 (ft); Nurses' aides 4 (ft); Recreational therapists 1 (ft); Dietitians 1 (pt); Podiatrists 1 (pt).
Activities Games; Reading groups; Prayer groups; Movies; Shopping trips; Dances/ Social/Cultural gatherings.

Tudor House Nursing Home Corp
81 S Huntington Ave, Jamaica Plain, MA 02130
(617) 277-2633
Admin Dr Herbert D Fisher.
Licensure Intermediate care. *Beds* ICF 43. *Certified* Medicaid.
Owner Proprietary corp.

Kingston

Blueberry Hill Rest Home
15 Foster Ln, Kingston, MA 02364
(617) 585-3657
Admin Bonnie Robinson.
Medical Dir Bonnie Robinson.
Licensure Rest home; Alzheimer's care. *Beds* Rest home 15. *Certified* Medicaid.
Owner Proprietary corp.
Admissions Requirements Minimum age 50; Males only; Medical examination.
Staff Physicians 2 (ft); LPNs 1 (ft); Nurses' aides 10 (ft); Recreational therapists 1 (ft); Activities coordinators 1 (ft); Dietitians 1 (ft); Ophthalmologists 2 (ft); Podiatrists 1 (ft); Dentists 2 (ft).
Facilities Dining room; Activities room; Laundry room.
Activities Arts & crafts; Cards; Games; Reading groups; Prayer groups; Movies; Shopping trips; Dances/Social/Cultural gatherings.

Lakeville

Island Terrace Nursing Home
PO Box 1237, Lakeville, MA 02347
(508) 947-0151
Admin Brenton L Tolles. *Dir of Nursing* Lucille Tolles. *Medical Dir* Stuart Silliker.
Licensure Skilled care; Intermediate care. *Beds* SNF 44; ICF 33. *Private Pay Patients* 40%. *Certified* Medicaid.
Owner Proprietary corp.
Staff RNs; LPNs; Nurses' aides; Physical therapists; Occupational therapists; Activities coordinators; Dietitians; Podiatrists.
Activities Arts & crafts; Games; Reading groups; Prayer groups; Pet therapy.

Meadowview Nursing Home
18 Crooked Ln, Lakeville, MA 02347
(508) 947-2793
Admin Ora Mae Torres.
Licensure Intermediate care. *Beds* ICF 29. *Certified* Medicaid.
Owner Proprietary corp.
Staff RNs; LPNs; Nurses' aides; Physical therapists; Recreational therapists; Activities coordinators; Dietitians; Podiatrists.
Facilities Dining room; Activities room.
Activities Arts & crafts; Cards; Games; Prayer groups; Movies; Shopping trips; Pet therapy.

Lancaster

River Terrace Healthcare Nursing Home
Rte 117, Ballard Hill Rd, Lancaster, MA 01523
(617) 365-4538
Admin Linda E Weldon. *Dir of Nursing* Phyllis Mortimer RN. *Medical Dir* Dr Robert Fraser.
Licensure Skilled care; Intermediate care. *Beds* SNF 41; ICF 41. *Certified* Medicaid.
Owner Proprietary corp (First Healthcare Corp).

Lawrence

Anlaw Nursing Home
555 S Union St, Lawrence, MA 01843
(508) 682-5281
Admin John Spears. *Dir of Nursing* Eileen Conley RN. *Medical Dir* Roger LeTourneau MD.
Licensure Skilled care; Intermediate care. *Beds* SNF 44; ICF 46. *Private Pay Patients* 10%. *Certified* Medicaid.
Owner Proprietary corp (First Healthcare Corp).
Admissions Requirements Medical examination.
Staff RNs 5 (ft); LPNs 10 (ft); Nurses' aides 35 (ft); Physical therapists 1 (pt); Reality therapists 1 (pt); Recreational therapists 1 (pt); Occupational therapists 1 (pt); Speech therapists 1 (pt); Activities coordinators 1 (ft); Dietitians 1 (pt); Podiatrists 1 (pt).
Facilities Dining room; Activities room; Crafts room; Laundry room; Barber/Beauty shop.
Activities Arts & crafts; Cards; Games; Reading groups; Prayer groups; Movies; Shopping trips; Dances/Social/Cultural gatherings; Intergenerational programs; Pet therapy.

Berkeley Retirement Home
150 Berkeley St, Lawrence, MA 01841
(617) 682-1614
Admin Nancy J Herrmann.
Medical Dir Edward Broaddus MD.
Licensure Intermediate care; Rest home. *Beds* ICF 5; Rest home 27.
Owner Proprietary corp.
Admissions Requirements Minimum age 70; Medical examination.
Staff Physicians 1 (pt); RNs 1 (ft); LPNs 5 (pt); Nurses' aides 5 (pt); Recreational therapists 1 (pt); Activities coordinators 1 (pt); Dietitians 1 (pt); Podiatrists 1 (pt).
Facilities Dining room; Activities room; Chapel; Crafts room; Laundry room; Barber/ Beauty shop; Library.
Activities Arts & crafts; Cards; Games; Reading groups; Prayer groups; Movies; Shopping trips; Dances/Social/Cultural gatherings.

German Old Folks Home Inc
374 Howard St, Lawrence, MA 01841
(617) 682-5593
Admin Estelle Champagne.
Licensure Rest home. *Beds* Rest home 31. *Certified* Medicaid.
Owner Nonprofit corp.
Admissions Requirements Minimum age 50; Medical examination; Physician's request.
Staff RNs 1 (pt); Nurses' aides 7 (pt); Reality therapists 1 (pt); Recreational therapists 1 (pt); Dietitians 1 (pt).
Facilities Dining room; Activities room; Crafts room; Laundry room.
Activities Arts & crafts; Cards; Games; Prayer groups; Movies; Shopping trips; Dances/ Social/Cultural gatherings.

MI Nursing & Restorative Center
0 Bennington St, Lawrence, MA 01841
(508) 685-6321
Admin Bruce Freeman. *Dir of Nursing* Ernest Griffiths. *Medical Dir* Alan Miller MD.
Licensure Skilled care; Intermediate care; Alzheimer's skilled nursing facility; Congregate housing; Adult day care. *Beds* SNF 167; ICF 42; Alzheimer's SNF 41; Congregate housing 305. *Certified* Medicaid; Medicare.
Owner Nonprofit organization/foundation.
Admissions Requirements Medical examination; Physician's request.
Staff Physicians 18 (pt); RNs 20 (ft), 10 (pt); LPNs 40 (ft), 30 (pt); Nurses' aides 80 (ft), 50 (pt); Physical therapists 6 (ft), 1 (pt); Recreational therapists 4 (ft); Occupational

therapists 1 (ft), 1 (pt); Speech therapists 1 (pt); Activities coordinators 1 (ft); Dietitians 2 (ft).
Languages Spanish, French, Lebanese, Italian.
Affiliation Roman Catholic.
Facilities Dining room; Physical therapy room; Activities room; Chapel; Crafts room; Barber/Beauty shop.
Activities Arts & crafts; Cards; Games; Prayer groups; Movies; Dances/Social/Cultural gatherings; Intergenerational programs; Pet therapy.

Town Manor Nursing Home
55 Lowell St, Lawrence, MA 01840
(617) 688-6056
Admin Thomas Dresser.
Licensure Skilled care; Intermediate care. *Beds* SNF 45; ICF 60. *Certified* Medicaid.
Owner Proprietary corp (First Healthcare Corp).

Wood Mill Convalescent Home
800 Essex St, Lawrence, MA 01841
(617) 686-2994
Admin Ray D'Aiuto. *Dir of Nursing* Joanne Ferguson. *Medical Dir* Dr Walter Jacobs.
Licensure Skilled care; Intermediate care. *Beds* SNF 48; ICF 46. *Certified* Medicaid.
Owner Proprietary corp (First Healthcare Corp).
Admissions Requirements Minimum age 21; Medical examination; Physician's request.
Staff Physicians; RNs 5 (ft); LPNs 6 (pt); Nurses' aides 31 (ft), 5 (pt); Physical therapists; Occupational therapists; Activities coordinators; Dietitians.
Languages Spanish.
Facilities Dining room; Physical therapy room; Activities room; Crafts room; Laundry room; Barber/Beauty shop.
Activities Arts & crafts; Cards; Games; Reading groups; Prayer groups; Movies; Shopping trips; Dances/Social/Cultural gatherings.

Lee

Berkshire Hills North
190 Prospect St, Lee, MA 01238
(413) 243-2010, 243-4462 FAX
Admin Paul R Chernov. *Dir of Nursing* Marcia Bush. *Medical Dir* Eugene Heyman.
Licensure Skilled care; Intermediate care. *Beds* SNF 46; ICF 30. *Private Pay Patients* 29%. *Certified* Medicaid.
Owner Privately owned.
Admissions Requirements Medical examination; Physician's request.
Staff Physicians 1 (ft), 4 (pt); RNs 3 (ft), 3 (pt); LPNs 11 (ft), 2 (pt); Nurses' aides 25 (ft), 1 (pt); Physical therapists 1 (ft); Recreational therapists 1 (ft), 1 (pt); Occupational therapists 1 (pt); Speech therapists 1 (pt); Dietitians 1 (pt); Podiatrists 1 (pt).
Languages Spanish.
Facilities Dining room; Physical therapy room; Activities room; Laundry room; Barber/Beauty shop.
Activities Arts & crafts; Games; Reading groups; Prayer groups; Movies; Shopping trips; Dances/Social/Cultural gatherings; Intergenerational programs; Pet therapy.

Lenox

Edgecombe Nursing Home
40 Sunset Ave, Lenox, MA 02140
(413) 637-0622, 637-4030 FAX
Admin Thomas J Romeo. *Dir of Nursing* Cheryl Leeman Saunders BSN. *Medical Dir* Dr Asta Potter.
Licensure Skilled care; Intermediate care. *Beds* SNF 28; ICF 95. *Certified* Medicaid.
Owner Proprietary corp.

Admissions Requirements Minimum age 18; Medical examination; Physician's request.
Staff RNs 3 (ft), 6 (pt); LPNs 5 (ft), 10 (pt); Nurses' aides 28 (ft), 25 (pt); Physical therapists 2 (pt); Occupational therapists 1 (pt); Activities coordinators 1 (ft), 1 (pt); Dietitians 1 (ft); Podiatrists 1 (pt).
Facilities Dining room; Physical therapy room; Barber/Beauty shop.
Activities Arts & crafts; Cards; Games; Reading groups; Prayer groups; Movies; Shopping trips; Dances/Social/Cultural gatherings; Intergenerational programs.

Valley View Nursing Home
PO Box 963, 540 Pittsfield Rd, Lenox, MA 01240
(413) 637-1221
Admin Kathy M Fuller.
Licensure Intermediate care. *Beds* ICF 140. *Certified* Medicaid.
Owner Proprietary corp.
Staff Physicians 2 (pt); RNs 3 (ft), 2 (pt); LPNs 6 (ft), 4 (pt); Nurses' aides 25 (ft), 17 (pt); Occupational therapists 1 (pt); Activities coordinators 1 (ft); Dietitians 1 (pt); Ophthalmologists 1 (pt); Podiatrists 1 (pt); Dentists 1 (pt).
Facilities Dining room; Physical therapy room; Activities room; Chapel; Crafts room; Laundry room; Barber/Beauty shop; Library.
Activities Arts & crafts; Cards; Games; Reading groups; Prayer groups; Movies; Shopping trips; Dances/Social/Cultural gatherings; Exercise program.

Leominster

Fairlawn Nursing Home
370 West St, Leominster, MA 01453
(508) 537-0771
Admin James M Oliver. *Dir of Nursing* Judith Raichle RN. *Medical Dir* Edward Kamens MD.
Licensure Skilled care; Intermediate care. *Beds* SNF 81; ICF 40. *Private Pay Patients* 40%. *Certified* Medicaid; Medicare.
Owner Proprietary corp.
Admissions Requirements Minimum age 21.
Staff Physicians 15 (pt); RNs 6 (ft); LPNs 70 (ft); Physical therapists 2 (ft); Reality therapists 1 (pt); Recreational therapists 1 (pt); Occupational therapists 1 (pt); Speech therapists 1 (pt); Activities coordinators 2 (ft); Dietitians 1 (pt); Ophthalmologists 1 (pt); Podiatrists 1 (pt); Audiologists 1 (pt).
Facilities Dining room; Physical therapy room; Activities room; Crafts room; Laundry room; Barber/Beauty shop; Library.
Activities Arts & crafts; Cards; Games; Reading groups; Prayer groups; Movies; Shopping trips; Dances/Social/Cultural gatherings; Pet therapy.

Fairmount Rest Home
34 Fairmount St, Leominster, MA 01453
(617) 537-5472
Admin Mary A Gagne.
Licensure Rest home. *Beds* Rest home 20.
Owner Proprietary corp.

Homestead Rest Home
226 Main St, Leominster, MA 01453
(617) 537-7202
Admin Richard J Ryan.
Licensure Rest home. *Beds* Rest home 21.
Owner Privately owned.
Admissions Requirements Medical examination; Physician's request.
Facilities Dining room; Laundry room; Barber/Beauty shop.
Activities Arts & crafts; Cards; Games; Movies; Shopping trips.

Keystone Nursing Home
44 Keystone Dr, Leominster, MA 01453
(508) 537-9327

Admin Joseph Rizzo. *Dir of Nursing* Marie Lanzillotti. *Medical Dir* John J Murphy MD.
Licensure Skilled care; Intermediate care. *Beds* SNF 42; ICF 64. *Certified* Medicaid; Medicare.
Owner Proprietary corp.
Admissions Requirements Physician's request.
Staff RNs; LPNs; Nurses' aides; Physical therapists; Reality therapists; Recreational therapists; Occupational therapists; Speech therapists; Activities coordinators; Dietitians; Ophthalmologists; Podiatrists; Dentists.
Languages French, Italian, Finnish, Spanish.
Facilities Dining room; Physical therapy room; Activities room; Chapel; Crafts room; Laundry room; Barber/Beauty shop; Library; Solarium.
Activities Arts & crafts; Cards; Games; Reading groups; Prayer groups; Movies; Shopping trips; Dances/Social/Cultural gatherings; Intergenerational programs; Pet therapy.

Nancy Patch Retirement Home
16 Pearl St, Leominster, MA 01453
(617) 537-3022
Admin Kathleen Flanagan Bergeron. *Dir of Nursing* Helen Kline RN.
Licensure Rest home. *Beds* Rest home 12.
Owner Nonprofit corp.
Admissions Requirements Minimum age 65; Medical examination.
Staff Physicians; RNs; Nurses' aides; Activities coordinators; Dietitians; Ophthalmologists.
Facilities Dining room; Activities room; Laundry room; Barber/Beauty shop.
Activities Arts & crafts; Cards; Games; Reading groups; Prayer groups; Movies; Shopping trips; Dances/Social/Cultural gatherings.

Village Rest Home
446 Main St, Leominster, MA 01453
(617) 534-6270
Admin Matilda Iandoli.
Licensure Rest home. *Beds* Rest home 25.
Owner Proprietary corp.
Admissions Requirements Minimum age 32.
Staff LPNs 1 (ft); Nurses' aides 5 (ft); Recreational therapists 1 (ft); Activities coordinators 1 (ft); Ophthalmologists 1 (ft).
Facilities Dining room; Activities room; Crafts room; Laundry room; Barber/Beauty shop; Library.
Activities Arts & crafts; Cards; Games; Reading groups; Prayer groups; Movies; Shopping trips; Dances/Social/Cultural gatherings.

Lexington

Dana Home of Lexington
2027 Massachusetts Ave, Lexington, MA 02173
(617) 861-0131
Admin Showkat Rafi.
Licensure Rest home. *Beds* Rest home 15.
Owner Nonprofit organization/foundation.
Staff Activities coordinators; Dietitians.
Activities Arts & crafts; Cards; Games; Movies.

East Village Nursing Home
140 Emerson Gardens Rd, Lexington, MA 02173
(617) 861-8630
Admin Donna M Hayes.
Licensure Skilled care; Intermediate care. *Beds* SNF 82; ICF 76. *Certified* Medicaid.
Owner Proprietary corp (Beverly Enterprises).

Fairlawn Nursing Home Inc
265 Lowell St, Lexington, MA 02173
(617) 862-7640

Admin Loretta A Moresco. *Dir of Nursing* Janet Shannon RN, Supv. *Medical Dir* Robert Stewart MD.
Licensure Intermediate care. *Beds* ICF 104. *Private Pay Patients* 100%.
Owner Proprietary corp.
Admissions Requirements Minimum age 21; Medical examination; Physician's request.
Staff RNs 8 (ft), 1 (pt); LPNs 2 (ft), 1 (pt); Nurses' aides; Physical therapists (consultant); Recreational therapists 1 (pt); Activities coordinators 1 (ft); Dietitians (consultant).
Facilities Dining room; Physical therapy room; Activities room; Laundry room; Barber/Beauty shop; Library.
Activities Arts & crafts; Cards; Games; Reading groups; Prayer groups; Movies; Shopping trips; Dances/Social/Cultural gatherings; Intergenerational programs; Pet therapy; Recreation therapy; Support services.

Mediplex of Lexington—Long-Term Care Facility
178 Lowell St, Lexington, MA 02173
(617) 862-7400
Admin Robert F Belluche.
Licensure Skilled care; Intermediate care. *Beds* SNF 142; ICF 60. *Certified* Medicaid.
Owner Proprietary corp.

Pine Knoll Nursing Home
30 Watertown St, Lexington, MA 02173
(617) 862-8151
Admin Edward F Cataldo.
Licensure Skilled care. *Beds* SNF 81. *Certified* Medicaid; Medicare.
Owner Proprietary corp.
Admissions Requirements Physician's request.
Staff RNs; LPNs; Nurses' aides; Physical therapists; Occupational therapists; Speech therapists; Activities coordinators; Dietitians; Ophthalmologists; Dentists.
Languages Greek, French.
Facilities Dining room; Physical therapy room; Activities room; Chapel; Crafts room; Laundry room; Barber/Beauty shop.
Activities Arts & crafts; Cards; Games; Reading groups; Prayer groups; Movies; Shopping trips.

Lincoln

Lincoln Rest Home
Farrar Rd, Lincoln, MA 01773
(617) 259-8128
Admin Joseph S Sulomont.
Licensure Rest home. *Beds* 12.

Littleton

Littleton House
191 Foster St, Littleton, MA 01460
(508) 486-3512
Admin Leonard Small. *Dir of Nursing* Sheila Walsh. *Medical Dir* Dr Thomas Fitzpatrick.
Licensure Intermediate care. *Beds* ICF 120. *Certified* Medicaid.
Owner Proprietary corp (Lifecare Centers of America).
Admissions Requirements Medical examination; Physician's request.
Staff Physicians 6 (pt); RNs 2 (pt); LPNs 8 (pt); Nurses' aides 15 (ft), 18 (pt); Physical therapists 1 (pt); Recreational therapists 1 (ft), 1 (pt); Occupational therapists 1 (pt); Speech therapists 1 (pt); Activities coordinators 1 (ft); Dietitians 1 (pt); Ophthalmologists 1 (pt); Podiatrists 2 (pt); Audiologists 1 (pt).
Facilities Dining room; Activities room; Chapel; Crafts room; Laundry room; Barber/Beauty shop; Library.

Activities Arts & crafts; Cards; Games; Reading groups; Prayer groups; Movies; Shopping trips; Dances/Social/Cultural gatherings; Intergenerational programs.

Longmeadow

Jewish Nursing Home of Western Massachusetts
770 Converse St, Longmeadow, MA 01106
(413) 567-6211, 567-0175 FAX
Admin Howard L Braverman. *Dir of Nursing* Teresa Sherman RN. *Medical Dir* Irving Hoff MD.
Licensure Skilled care; Intermediate care; Retirement; Alzheimer's care. *Beds* SNF 160; ICF 40; Retirement units 48. *Private Pay Patients* 17%. *Certified* Medicaid; Medicare.
Owner Nonprofit organization/foundation.
Admissions Requirements Minimum age 21; Medical examination.
Staff Physicians 1 (ft); RNs 15 (ft), 8 (pt); LPNs 12 (ft), 6 (pt); Nurses' aides 70 (ft), 15 (pt); Physical therapists 1 (pt); Occupational therapists 1 (pt); Speech therapists 1 (pt); Activities coordinators 2 (ft), 2 (pt); Dietitians 1 (pt); Podiatrists 2 (pt).
Languages Hebrew, Yiddish.
Affiliation Jewish.
Facilities Dining room; Physical therapy room; Activities room; Chapel; Barber/Beauty shop; Library.
Activities Arts & crafts; Cards; Games; Reading groups; Prayer groups; Movies; Shopping trips; Dances/Social/Cultural gatherings; Intergenerational programs; Pet therapy.

Lowell

Arcadia Nursing Home
841 Merrimack St, Lowell, MA 01854
(617) 459-0546
Admin Isabel R Donovan.
Licensure Skilled care; Intermediate care. *Beds* SNF 82; ICF 60. *Certified* Medicaid.
Owner Proprietary corp (Ads Management Inc).

Battles Home
236 Fairmount St, Lowell, MA 01852
(617) 453-2531
Admin Clifford R Jennings; Catherine F Bastien. *Dir of Nursing* Kathy Lemay, consultant.
Licensure Rest home. *Beds* Rest home 12. *Private Pay Patients* 100%.
Owner Nonprofit corp.
Admissions Requirements Males only; Medical examination.
Staff RNs; Nurses' aides; Recreational therapists; Occupational therapists; Activities coordinators; Dietitians; Ophthalmologists; Podiatrists.
Languages French, Sign.
Facilities Dining room; Activities room; Laundry room; Barber/Beauty shop; Library.
Activities Cards; Movies; Dances/Social/Cultural gatherings; Intergenerational programs.

Colonial Rest Home
945 Middlesex St, Lowell, MA 01851
(617) 454-5644
Admin Elliott C Williams.
Licensure Rest home. *Beds* 22.

D'Youville Manor Nursing Home
981 Varnum Ave, Lowell, MA 01854
(508) 455-5681
Admin Sr Pauline Beauchesne. *Dir of Nursing* Ruth MacKinnon RN. *Medical Dir* Stephen R Brovender MD.
Licensure Skilled care; Intermediate care; Adult day care. *Beds* SNF 84; ICF 112; Adult day care 20. *Certified* Medicaid.

Owner Nonprofit corp.
Admissions Requirements Medical examination; Physician's request.
Staff RNs 3 (ft), 6 (pt); LPNs 12 (ft), 22 (pt); Nurses' aides 43 (ft), 37 (pt); Physical therapists 1 (pt); Recreational therapists 1 (ft); Occupational therapists 1 (ft); Activities coordinators 1 (ft); Dietitians 1 (ft); Ophthalmologists 6 (pt); Social workers 1 (ft), 1 (pt).
Affiliation Roman Catholic.
Facilities Dining room; Physical therapy room; Activities room; Chapel; Crafts room; Laundry room; Barber/Beauty shop; Library; Podiatrist's room; Pastoral room.
Activities Arts & crafts; Cards; Games; Reading groups; Prayer groups; Movies; Shopping trips; Dances/Social/Cultural gatherings; Music movement; Daily Mass.

Fairhaven Nursing Home
476 Varnum Ave, Lowell, MA 01854
(508) 458-3388
Admin Lita I Noel. *Dir of Nursing* Rita Levesque RN. *Medical Dir* William Mast MD.
Licensure Skilled care; Intermediate care. *Beds* SNF 70; ICF 96. *Private Pay Patients* 17%. *Certified* Medicaid.
Owner Nonprofit organization/foundation.
Admissions Requirements Minimum age 21.
Staff RNs 7 (ft), 7 (pt); LPNs 12 (ft), 5 (pt); Nurses' aides 35 (ft), 27 (pt); Physical therapists 1 (pt); Occupational therapists 1 (pt); Speech therapists 1 (pt); Activities coordinators 1 (ft); Dietitians 1 (pt); Podiatrists 1 (pt).
Languages French.
Facilities Dining room; Physical therapy room; Activities room; Crafts room; Laundry room; Barber/Beauty shop; Library.
Activities Arts & crafts; Cards; Games; Reading groups; Prayer groups; Movies; Shopping trips; Dances/Social/Cultural gatherings; Pet therapy.

Glenwood Convalescent Home
577 Varnum Ave, Lowell, MA 01854
(617) 454-5444
Admin Marie A Wells.
Medical Dir Dr Susan Black.
Licensure Intermediate care. *Beds* ICF 101. *Certified* Medicaid.
Owner Proprietary corp (First Healthcare Corp).
Admissions Requirements Minimum age 21; Medical examination; Physician's request.
Staff RNs; LPNs; Nurses' aides; Physical therapists; Reality therapists; Recreational therapists; Occupational therapists; Speech therapists; Activities coordinators; Dietitians; Ophthalmologists; Podiatrists; Dentists.
Facilities Dining room; Activities room; Crafts room; Barber/Beauty shop.
Activities Arts & crafts; Cards; Games; Reading groups; Prayer groups; Movies; Shopping trips; Dances/Social/Cultural gatherings.

Merrimack River Valley House
520 Fletcher St, Lowell, MA 01854
(508) 452-6071
Admin Jane I Bellegarde.
Licensure Residential care; Respite care. *Beds* Residential care 24; Respite care 1. *Private Pay Patients* 100%.
Owner Nonprofit corp.
Admissions Requirements Minimum age 62; Females only; Medical examination; Must be a Greater Lowell resident.
Staff Physicians (consultant); LPNs 1 (ft); Dietitians (consultant); Podiatrists (consultant); Recreational therapists Activities coordinators 1 (pt); Resident assistants 6 (ft), 3 (pt).

Facilities Dining room; Activities room; Crafts room; Laundry room; Barber/Beauty shop; Library; Private rooms; Common areas.
Activities Arts & crafts; Cards; Games; Reading groups; Prayer groups; Movies; Shopping trips; Dances/Social/Cultural gatherings; Intergenerational programs; Pet therapy; Cooking; Entertainment; Current events; Resident council; Religious services.

New Medico Skilled Nursing Center—Christian Hill
19 Varnum St, Lowell, MA 01850
(617) 454-5644
Admin Frank P Miller. *Dir of Nursing* Rachel Eiserman. *Medical Dir* Lawrence Newman MD.
Licensure Skilled care; Intermediate care. *Beds* SNF 120; ICF 40. *Certified* Medicaid; Medicare.
Owner Privately owned.
Staff RNs 9 (ft), 12 (pt); LPNs 17 (ft), 11 (pt); Nurses' aides 46 (ft), 37 (pt); Physical therapists 1 (pt); Activities coordinators 1 (ft); Dietitians 2 (ft).
Facilities Dining room; Physical therapy room; Activities room; Chapel; Crafts room; Laundry room; Barber/Beauty shop.
Activities Arts & crafts; Cards; Games; Reading groups; Prayer groups; Movies; Shopping trips; Dances/Social/Cultural gatherings.

Northwood Convalescent Center
1010 Varnum Ave, Lowell, MA 01854
(508) 458-8773
Admin Wendy LaBate. *Dir of Nursing* Lillian Dozois RN. *Medical Dir* Dr John Janas.
Licensure Skilled care; Intermediate care. *Beds* SNF 82; ICF 41. *Certified* Medicaid; Medicare.
Owner Proprietary corp (Oakwood Living Center).
Admissions Requirements Medical examination.
Staff Physicians 5 (pt); RNs; LPNs; Physical therapists 1 (pt); Recreational therapists 2 (ft), 1 (pt); Occupational therapists 1 (pt); Speech therapists 1 (pt); Activities coordinators 1 (ft); Dietitians 1 (pt); Podiatrists 1 (pt); Dentists 1 (pt).
Facilities Dining room; Physical therapy room; Activities room; Crafts room; Laundry room; Barber/Beauty shop.
Activities Arts & crafts; Cards; Games; Reading groups; Prayer groups; Movies; Shopping trips; Dances/Social/Cultural gatherings; Intergenerational programs; Pet therapy.

Princeton House Rest Home
94-100 Priceton Blvd, Lowell, MA 01853
(617) 458-4056
Admin Jeanette F Savoie.
Licensure Rest home. *Beds* Rest home 53.
Owner Proprietary corp.

St Johns Nursing Home of Lowell
500 Wentworth Ave, Lowell, MA 01850
(617) 458-1271
Admin Raymond V Mailloux. *Dir of Nursing* Janet Sweeney. *Medical Dir* Edward Saba MD.
Licensure Skilled care; Intermediate care; Alzheimer's care. *Beds* SNF 69; ICF 34. *Certified* Medicaid; Medicare.
Owner Nonprofit corp.
Staff Physicians; RNs; LPNs; Nurses' aides; Physical therapists; Occupational therapists; Speech therapists; Activities coordinators; Dietitians; Ophthalmologists; Podiatrists; Dentists.
Languages Spanish, Portuguese.
Facilities Dining room; Activities room; Chapel; Crafts room; Laundry room; Barber/Beauty shop.

Activities Arts & crafts; Cards; Games; Reading groups; Prayer groups; Movies; Shopping trips; Dances/Social/Cultural gatherings.

Town & Country Nursing Home
915 Westford St, Lowell, MA 01851
(508) 459-7262, 970-3692 FAX
Admin Alex E Struzziero. *Dir of Nursing* Joan Soulard RN. *Medical Dir* Lawrence Newman MD.
Licensure Intermediate care; Alzheimer's care. *Beds* ICF 50. *Private Pay Patients* 32%. *Certified* Medicaid.
Owner Proprietary corp.
Admissions Requirements Minimum age 16; Medical examination; Physician's request.
Staff RNs; LPNs; Nurses' aides; Physical therapists; Activities coordinators; Dietitians.
Facilities Dining room; Activities room; Laundry room; Barber/Beauty shop.
Activities Arts & crafts; Cards; Games; Reading groups; Prayer groups; Movies; Shopping trips; Dances/Social/Cultural gatherings; Pet therapy.

Willow Manor Nursing Home
30 Princeton Blvd, Lowell, MA 01851
(617) 454-8086
Admin S Joseph S Solomont.
Licensure Skilled care; Intermediate care. *Beds* SNF 42; ICF 47. *Certified* Medicaid.
Owner Proprietary corp.

Lynn

Abbott House Nursing Home
28 Essex St, Lynn, MA 01902
(617) 595-5500
Admin Kenneth D Bane.
Licensure Skilled care. *Beds* SNF 47. *Certified* Medicaid; Medicare.
Owner Proprietary corp.

Alba Nursing Home
12 Park St, Lynn, MA 01905
(617) 599-3993
Admin William A Sherman, Jr.
Licensure Intermediate care. *Beds* ICF 34. *Certified* Medicaid.
Owner Proprietary corp.

Atlantic Rest Home
60 Atlantic St, Lynn, MA 01902
(617) 598-0609
Admin Dolores J Cummings.
Licensure Rest home. *Beds* Rest home 21.
Owner Proprietary corp.
Admissions Requirements Minimum age 60; Females only; Medical examination; Physician's request.
Staff Nurses' aides 3 (ft), 5 (pt); Podiatrists.
Facilities Dining room.
Activities Cards; Games.

Ann Carroll Nursing Home
66 Johnson St, Lynn, MA 01902
(617) 592-5849
Admin Robert Douglas. *Dir of Nursing* Marilyn Arsenault LPN.
Licensure Intermediate care. *Beds* ICF 28. *Certified* Medicaid.
Owner Proprietary corp.
Admissions Requirements Medical examination; Physician's request.
Staff Physicians 3 (pt); LPNs 3 (pt); Nurses' aides 5 (pt); Physical therapists 1 (pt); Recreational therapists 1 (pt); Activities coordinators 1 (pt); Dietitians 1 (pt); Podiatrists 1 (pt); Audiologists 1 (pt).
Facilities Dining room; Activities room; Laundry room; Dining rooms double as activity rooms for services & crafts.
Activities Arts & crafts; Cards; Games; Reading groups; Prayer groups; Shopping trips; Dances/Social/Cultural gatherings.

Crestview Manor Nursing Home
72 Nahant St, Lynn, MA 01902
(617) 598-6363
Admin William A Sherman Jr.
Licensure Intermediate care. *Beds* ICF 29. *Certified* Medicaid.
Owner Proprietary corp.

Joseph B Devlin Public Medical Institute
179 Holyoke St, Lynn, MA 01905
(617) 595-3743
Admin Garry Mayo. *Dir of Nursing* Barbara Spencer RN. *Medical Dir* Stephen P Weglarz MD.
Licensure Skilled care; Alzheimer's care. *Beds* SNF 54. *Certified* Medicaid.
Owner Publicly owned.
Admissions Requirements Physician's request.
Staff Physicians 1 (pt); RNs 4 (ft), 3 (pt); LPNs 2 (ft), 3 (pt); Nurses' aides 26 (ft); Physical therapists 1 (pt); Occupational therapists 1 (pt); Activities coordinators 1 (ft); Dietitians 1 (pt).
Facilities Dining room; Activities room; Laundry room; Barber/Beauty shop.
Activities Arts & crafts; Games; Reading groups; Prayer groups; Movies; Dances/Social/Cultural gatherings.

Essex Convalescent Home
94 Franklin St, Lynn, MA 01902
(617) 592-7758
Admin William Mantzoukas. *Dir of Nursing* Clestorine Madden RN. *Medical Dir* James Gottschall MD.
Licensure Intermediate care; Alzheimer's care. *Beds* ICF 62. *Certified* Medicaid.
Owner Proprietary corp.
Admissions Requirements Minimum age 40; Medical examination.
Staff RNs 3 (ft), 3 (pt); LPNs 1 (pt); Nurses' aides 14 (ft), 8 (pt); Physical therapists 1 (pt); Recreational therapists 1 (pt); Activities coordinators 1 (pt); Dietitians 1 (pt).
Languages Greek, Spanish, French.
Facilities Dining room; Activities room; Laundry room.
Activities Arts & crafts; Cards; Games; Reading groups; Prayer groups; Movies; Shopping trips.

Harbor Hill Manor Rest Home
13 Essex St, Lynn, MA 01902
(617) 595-7644
Admin Gretchen A Potter.
Licensure Rest home. *Beds* Rest home 22. *Certified* Medicaid.
Owner Proprietary corp.
Admissions Requirements Medical examination.
Facilities Dining room; Activities room; Laundry room.
Activities Arts & crafts; Cards; Games; Shopping trips.

Lawrence Manor Nursing Home
26 Henry Ave, Lynn, MA 01902
(617) 595-2941
Admin Albert Dukatz.
Licensure Intermediate care. *Beds* ICF 39. *Certified* Medicaid.
Owner Privately owned.

Lynn Convalescent Home & Infirmary
655 Boston St, Lynn, MA 01905
(617) 593-4347
Admin Donald P Dixon.
Medical Dir Dr Milton Helsel.
Licensure Intermediate care; Rest home. *Beds* ICF 75; Rest home 30. *Certified* Medicaid.
Owner Publicly owned.
Admissions Requirements Medical examination; Physician's request.
Staff Physicians 1 (pt); RNs 9 (ft); LPNs 4 (ft); Nurses' aides 30 (ft); Physical therapists 1 (pt); Occupational therapists 1 (pt); Activities coordinators 1 (ft), 1 (pt); Dietitians 1 (pt).

Facilities Activities room; Laundry room.
Activities Arts & crafts; Games; Prayer groups; Movies.

Lynn Home for Elderly Persons
Atlantic Terrace, Lynn, MA 01902
(617) 593-8099
Admin Lawrence D Carlson.
Medical Dir G Fred Jackson MD.
Licensure Rest home. *Beds* Rest home 39.
Owner Proprietary corp.
Admissions Requirements Minimum age 65; Medical examination.
Staff RNs 1 (pt); LPNs 1 (ft), 4 (pt); Nurses' aides 3 (ft), 5 (pt); Activities coordinators 1 (ft).
Facilities Dining room; Activities room; Crafts room; Laundry room; Barber/Beauty shop; Library; Sewing room; Card room; Ceramic shop.
Activities Arts & crafts; Cards; Games; Reading groups; Prayer groups; Movies; Shopping trips; Dances/Social/Cultural gatherings; Ceramics; Cooking.

Lynn Shore Rest Home
37 Breed St, Lynn, MA 01902
(617) 595-7110
Admin Dolores J Cummings.
Licensure Rest home. *Beds* Rest home 34.
Owner Privately owned.
Admissions Requirements Minimum age 60; Medical examination; Physician's request.
Staff Nurses' aides 3 (ft), 3 (pt); Podiatrists.
Facilities Dining room; Activities room.
Activities Cards; Games.

New Medico Rehabilitation & Skilled Nursing Center Lenox Hill
70 Granite St, Lynn, MA 01904
(617) 581-2400
Admin Brian K Sullivan.
Licensure Skilled care; Intermediate care. *Beds* SNF 123; ICF 95. *Certified* Medicaid; Medicare.
Owner Proprietary corp.

Phillips Manor Nursing Home
28 Linwood Rd, Lynn, MA 01905
(617) 592-8000
Admin Anna Freehling.
Licensure Intermediate care. *Beds* ICF 20. *Certified* Medicaid.
Owner Proprietary corp.

Pine Hill Rest Home
341 Linwood St, Lynn, MA 01905
(617) 598-6256
Admin Charles Dandaneau.
Licensure Rest home. *Beds* 12.

Malden

Bartlett Manor Nursing Home
180 Summer St, Malden, MA 02148
(617) 321-4157
Admin Ann Azzarrito. *Dir of Nursing* Donna Hurd RN.
Licensure Intermediate care. *Beds* ICF 40. *Certified* Medicaid.
Owner Proprietary corp.
Admissions Requirements Medical examination; Physician's request.
Staff RNs 2 (ft), 3 (pt); LPNs 2 (pt); Nurses' aides 8 (ft), 6 (pt); Activities coordinators 1 (pt).
Languages French.
Facilities Dining room; Activities room.
Activities Arts & crafts; Cards; Games; Prayer groups; Shopping trips; Dances/Social/Cultural gatherings.

Buchanon Nursing Home Inc
190 Summer St, Malden, MA 02148
(617) 321-4157
Admin Ann Azzarito.
Medical Dir Lillian McCarthy.

Licensure Intermediate care. *Beds* ICF 35.
 Certified Medicaid; Medicare.
Owner Proprietary corp.
Admissions Requirements Females only.
Staff RNs 2 (ft); LPNs 3 (ft); Nurses' aides 12
 (ft); Activities coordinators.
Facilities Dining room; Activities room;
 Crafts room; Laundry room.
Activities Arts & crafts; Cards; Games;
 Dances/Social/Cultural gatherings; Van rides.

Care Well Manor Nursing Home
203 Summer St, Malden, MA 02148
(617) 324-3663
Admin Neil B McCole.
Licensure Intermediate care. *Beds* ICF 23.
 Certified Medicaid.
Owner Proprietary corp.
Admissions Requirements Minimum age 21;
 Females only; Medical examination.
Staff RNs 1 (ft); LPNs 1 (ft), 2 (pt); Nurses'
 aides 3 (ft), 4 (pt); Activities coordinators;
 Dietitians.
Facilities Dining room; Activities room;
 Crafts room; Laundry room.
Activities Arts & crafts; Cards; Games;
 Reading groups; Prayer groups; Movies;
 Shopping trips; Dances/Social/Cultural
 gatherings; Outings for lunches & dinners.

Davenport Memorial Home
70 Salem St, Malden, MA 02148
(617) 324-0150
Admin Beth E Walsh.
Licensure Rest home. *Beds* Rest home 21.
Owner Nonprofit organization/foundation.
Admissions Requirements Minimum age 65;
 Medical examination.
Staff RNs 1 (pt); LPNs 1 (pt); Nurses' aides 6
 (pt).
Facilities Dining room; Laundry room;
 Barber/Beauty shop; Library; Social rooms.
Activities Games; Movies; Shopping trips;
 Dances/Social/Cultural gatherings.

Dexter House Nursing Facility
120 Main St, Malden, MA 02148
(617) 324-5600
Admin Corolyn E Lassiter.
Licensure Skilled care; Intermediate care. *Beds*
 SNF 100; ICF 30. *Certified* Medicaid.
Owner Proprietary corp (Beverly Enterprises).
Admissions Requirements Minimum age 21;
 Medical examination; Physician's request.
Staff Physicians 1 (pt); RNs 13 (ft); LPNs 9
 (ft); Nurses' aides 55 (ft); Physical therapists
 1 (ft); Reality therapists 1 (ft); Recreational
 therapists 1 (ft); Occupational therapists 1
 (pt); Speech therapists 1 (pt); Dietitians 1
 (ft); Ophthalmologists 1 (pt); Podiatrists 1
 (pt); Audiologists 1 (pt); Dentists 1 (pt);
 Social workers 1 (ft).
Facilities Dining room; Physical therapy
 room; Activities room; Crafts room; Barber/
 Beauty shop; Library.
Activities Arts & crafts; Cards; Games;
 Reading groups; Prayer groups; Movies;
 Shopping trips; Dances/Social/Cultural
 gatherings.

Malden Home for Aged Persons
578 Main St, Malden, MA 02148
(617) 321-3740
Admin Bridget Burke.
Medical Dir H Portman MD.
Licensure Intermediate care; Rest home. *Beds*
 ICF 6; Rest home 19.
Owner Nonprofit corp.
Admissions Requirements Minimum age 65;
 Females only; Medical examination.
Staff RNs 2 (ft), 1 (pt); LPNs 4 (pt); Nurses'
 aides 2 (ft), 4 (pt); Activities coordinators 1
 (pt); Dietitians 1 (pt).
Facilities Dining room; Activities room;
 Crafts room; Laundry room; Barber/Beauty
 shop; Store.
Activities Arts & crafts; Cards; Games;
 Shopping trips; Annual fair.

Mansion Rest Home
14 Rockland Ave, Malden, MA 02148
(617) 322-4634
Admin Reta C MacKinnon.
Licensure Rest home. *Beds* Rest home 27.
 Certified Medicaid.
Owner Privately owned.

McFadden Memorial Manor
341 Forest St, Malden, MA 02148
(617) 322-1700
Admin Garry E Dixon.
Licensure Intermediate care. *Beds* ICF 61.
 Certified Medicaid.
Owner Publicly owned.

San Filippo Rest Home Inc
53 James St, Malden, MA 02148
(617) 324-7233
Admin Carol Wallace. *Dir of Nursing*
 Elizabeth Banks.
Licensure Rest home. *Beds* Rest home 17.
 Certified Medicaid; Medicare.
Owner Proprietary corp.
Admissions Requirements Medical
 examination.
Staff Physicians 3 (pt); LPNs 1 (pt); Nurses'
 aides 3 (ft), 3 (pt); Activities coordinators 1
 (pt); Dietitians 1 (pt); Ophthalmologists 1
 (pt).
Languages Italian.
Facilities Dining room; Activities room;
 Laundry room.
Activities Arts & crafts; Cards; Games;
 Dances/Social/Cultural gatherings.

Manchester

Oakwood Nursing Home
601 Summer St, Manchester, MA 01944
(508) 526-4653
Admin Donna M Crabtree. *Dir of Nursing*
 Marie Toye RN. *Medical Dir* Gregory
 Bazylewicz MD.
Licensure Intermediate care. *Beds* ICF 20.
 Private Pay Patients 100%.
Owner Proprietary corp (Beverly Enterprises).
Admissions Requirements Medical
 examination.
Staff RNs 3 (ft), 2 (pt); LPNs 5 (ft), 2 (pt);
 Nurses' aides 7 (ft), 2 (pt); Physical
 therapists; Activities coordinators 1 (ft);
 Dietitians 1 (ft); Private duty nurses.
Facilities Dining room; Laundry room; Living
 room; Solarium.
Activities Arts & crafts; Cards; Games;
 Reading groups; Prayer groups; Movies;
 Dances/Social/Cultural gatherings;
 Intergenerational programs; Pet therapy;
 Current events; Group cooking; Varied
 entertainment.

Marblehead

Devereux House Nursing Home
39 Lafayette St, Marblehead, MA 01945
(617) 631-6120
Admin Kenneth D Bane. *Dir of Nursing* Clara
 M Donahue RN. *Medical Dir* Dr Elliot
 Strauss.
Licensure Skilled care. *Beds* SNF 64. *Certified*
 Medicaid.
Owner Proprietary corp.
Admissions Requirements Minimum age 18.
Staff Physicians 13 (pt); RNs 9 (ft); LPNs 7
 (ft); Nurses' aides 19 (ft), 18 (pt); Physical
 therapists 1 (pt); Reality therapists 1 (ft), 2
 (pt); Recreational therapists 1 (ft), 2 (pt);
 Occupational therapists 1 (pt); Speech
 therapists 1 (pt); Activities coordinators;
 Dietitians 1 (pt); Ophthalmologists 2 (pt);
 Podiatrists 3 (pt); Dentists 4 (pt).
Facilities Dining room; Physical therapy
 room; Activities room; Chapel; Crafts room;
 Laundry room; Barber/Beauty shop; Library;
 Patio.

Activities Arts & crafts; Cards; Games;
 Reading groups; Prayer groups; Movies;
 Shopping trips; Dances/Social/Cultural
 gatherings.

Lafayette Convalescent Home
25 Lafayette St, Marblehead, MA 01945
(617) 631-4535
Admin William E Mantzoukas.
Licensure Skilled care; Intermediate care. *Beds*
 SNF 32; ICF 33. *Certified* Medicaid.
Owner Proprietary corp.

Marlborough

Bolton Manor Nursing Home
400 Bolton Rd, Marlborough, MA 01752
(617) 481-6123
Admin Laurie L Finnegan. *Dir of Nursing*
 Elizabeth Mocklow RN.
Licensure Skilled care; Intermediate care. *Beds*
 SNF 80; ICF 80. *Certified* Medicaid.
Owner Proprietary corp (First Healthcare
 Corp).
Admissions Requirements Minimum age 50.
Staff RNs; LPNs; Nurses' aides; Activities
 coordinators; Dietitians.
Languages French, Portuguese, Spanish.
Facilities Dining room; Physical therapy
 room; Activities room; Chapel; Crafts room;
 Laundry room; Barber/Beauty shop.
Activities Arts & crafts; Cards; Games;
 Reading groups; Prayer groups; Movies;
 Shopping trips; Dances/Social/Cultural
 gatherings.

Pine Grove Rest Home
455 Northboro Rd, Marlborough, MA 01752
(617) 481-6562
Admin Alice M McGee.
Medical Dir Dr C Levin.
Licensure Rest home. *Beds* Rest home 28.
Owner Privately owned.
Admissions Requirements Minimum age 25;
 Males only; Medical examination;
 Physician's request.
Staff RNs 1 (ft); Nurses' aides 4 (ft);
 Recreational therapists 1 (pt).
Languages French, Spanish.
Facilities Dining room; Activities room;
 Crafts room; Laundry room; Library.
Activities Arts & crafts; Cards; Games;
 Movies; Shopping trips; Dances/Social/
 Cultural gatherings; Holiday parties; Bingo.

Westridge Health Care Center Nursing Home
121 Northboro Rd, Marlborough, MA 01752
(617) 485-4040
Admin Philip Quillard.
Medical Dir Dr Richard McMahon.
Licensure Skilled care; Intermediate care;
 Alzheimer's care. *Beds* SNF 139; ICF 57.
 Certified Medicaid; Medicare.
Owner Proprietary corp (First Healthcare
 Corp).
Admissions Requirements Medical
 examination.
Staff RNs 8 (ft), 6 (pt); LPNs 15 (ft), 5 (pt);
 Nurses' aides 41 (ft), 30 (pt); Physical
 therapists 1 (ft); Recreational therapists 3
 (pt); Occupational therapists 1 (pt); Speech
 therapists 1 (pt); Activities coordinators 1
 (ft); Dietitians 1 (pt); Ophthalmologists 1
 (pt); Podiatrists 1 (pt); Dentists 1 (pt).
Facilities Dining room; Physical therapy
 room; Activities room; Chapel; Crafts room;
 Laundry room; Barber/Beauty shop; Library.
Activities Arts & crafts; Cards; Games;
 Reading groups; Prayer groups; Movies;
 Shopping trips; Dances/Social/Cultural
 gatherings.

Mashpee

Pilgrim's Pride Nursing Home
Rte 28, 161 Falmouth Rd, Mashpee, MA
02649
(508) 477-1310
Admin Bruce Kaiser. *Dir of Nursing* Norene
Pucci RN. *Medical Dir* Abraham Dietz MD.
Licensure Skilled care; Intermediate care. *Beds*
SNF 60; ICF 60. *Private Pay Patients* 20%.
Certified Medicaid.
Owner Privately owned.
Admissions Requirements Minimum age 21;
Medical examination; Physician's request.
Staff Physicians 1 (pt); RNs 5 (ft), 1 (pt);
LPNs 6 (ft), 5 (pt); Nurses' aides 30 (ft), 15
(pt); Activities coordinators 2 (ft); Dietitians
1 (pt).
Facilities Dining room; Physical therapy
room; Activities room; Chapel; Crafts room;
Laundry room; Barber/Beauty shop; Library.
Activities Arts & crafts; Cards; Games;
Reading groups; Prayer groups; Movies;
Shopping trips; Dances/Social/Cultural
gatherings; Intergenerational programs; Pet
therapy.

Mattapoisett

Mattapoisett Nursing Home
79 North St, Mattapoisett, MA 02739
(508) 758-2512
Admin Edward J Turcotte-Shamski. *Dir of
Nursing* Linda J Turcotte-Shamski RN.
Medical Dir Dr John Howard.
Licensure Intermediate care. *Beds* ICF 42.
Private Pay Patients 15%. *Certified*
Medicaid.
Owner Proprietary corp.
Admissions Requirements Minimum age 22.
Staff RNs 2 (ft), 5 (pt); LPNs 1 (ft), 1 (pt);
Nurses' aides 9 (ft), 18 (pt); Activities
coordinators 1 (pt); Dietitians 1 (pt); Social
workers 1 (pt).
Languages Portuguese, Cape Verdian.
Facilities Dining room; TV room.
Activities Arts & crafts; Cards; Games; Prayer
groups; Movies; Shopping trips; Dances/
Social/Cultural gatherings; Pet therapy.

Medfield

Med-Vale Nursing Home
519 Main St, Medfield, MA 02052
(508) 359-6050
Admin Maureen T Murran NHA. *Dir of
Nursing* Darlene Saffran RN, Health Svc
Supv. *Medical Dir* A Stagg MD.
Licensure Intermediate care; Respite care.
Beds ICF 49. *Private Pay Patients* 7%.
Certified Medicaid.
Owner Proprietary corp (Five-Nineteen Main
Street Inc).
Admissions Requirements Minimum age 21.
Staff Physicians (consultant); RNs 1 (ft); LPNs
4 (ft), 3 (pt); Nurses' aides 17 (ft), 10 (pt);
Physical therapists (consultant); Reality
therapists (consultant); Recreational
therapists (consultant); Occupational
therapists (consultant); Speech therapists
(consultant); Activities coordinators 1 (ft);
Dietitians (consultant); Ophthalmologists
(consultant); Podiatrists (consultant);
Audiologists (consultant).
Facilities Laundry room.
Activities Arts & crafts; Cards; Games;
Reading groups; Prayer groups; Movies;
Shopping trips; Dances/Social/Cultural
gatherings.

Medford

Emery Retirement & Convalescent Home
34 Grove St, Medford, MA 02155
(617) 488-7117
Admin Thomas J McNulty Jr.
Licensure Intermediate care. *Beds* ICF 31.
Certified Medicaid.
Owner Nonprofit organization/foundation.

Magoun Manor Nursing Home
68 Magoun Ave, Medford, MA 02155
(617) 395-007
Admin Richard Kaffenberger.
Licensure Intermediate care. *Beds* ICF 29.
Certified Medicaid.
Owner Proprietary corp.
Admissions Requirements Medical
examination; Physician's request.
Staff RNs; LPNs; Nurses' aides; Recreational
therapists; Activities coordinators; Dietitians
1 (pt); Podiatrists 1 (pt).
Facilities Dining room; Activities room;
Crafts room; Laundry room.
Activities Arts & crafts; Cards; Games;
Reading groups; Prayer groups; Movies;
Shopping trips; Dances/Social/Cultural
gatherings; Bowling; Life program.

Rest Haven Nursing Home
96 Mystic St, Medford, MA 02155
(617) 396-3632
Admin Eleanor Larkin.
Licensure Intermediate care. *Beds* ICF 33.
Certified Medicaid; Medicare.
Owner Proprietary corp.

Winthrop House Nursing Home
300 Winthrop St, Medford, MA 02155
(617) 396-4400
Admin John H Rossetti. *Dir of Nursing*
Angela Derrivan RN. *Medical Dir* Ralph
Goldstein MD.
Licensure Skilled care; Intermediate care. *Beds*
SNF 82; ICF 60. *Certified* Medicaid.
Owner Privately owned.
Admissions Requirements Physician's request.
Staff RNs 9 (ft), 5 (pt); LPNs 3 (ft), 5 (pt);
Nurses' aides 39 (ft), 12 (pt).
Facilities Dining room; Physical therapy
room; Activities room; Chapel; Barber/
Beauty shop.
Activities Arts & crafts; Games; Prayer groups;
Movies; Dances/Social/Cultural gatherings.

Medway

Mary-Land Rest Home
17 Holliston St, Medway, MA 02053
(617) 533-2900
Admin Gertrude A O'Connor.
Licensure Rest home. *Beds* Rest home 32.
Certified Medicaid.
Owner Proprietary corp.
Admissions Requirements Minimum age 50;
Medical examination.
Staff RNs 1 (pt); Nurses' aides 5 (ft), 2 (pt);
Activities coordinators 1 (ft).
Languages French.
Facilities Dining room; Laundry room.
Activities Arts & crafts; Cards; Games;
Reading groups; Prayer groups; Movies;
Shopping trips; Dances/Social/Cultural
gatherings; Parties; Cookouts; Trips.

Medway Country Manor Nursing Home
Holliston St, Medway, MA 02053
(617) 533-6634
Admin John Peters.
Licensure Skilled care; Intermediate care. *Beds*
SNF 40; ICF 42. *Certified* Medicaid.
Owner Proprietary corp.

Melrose

Elmhurst Nursing Home
743 Main St, Melrose, MA 02176
(617) 662-7500
Admin Grace C Young.
Licensure Intermediate care. *Beds* ICF 43.
Certified Medicaid.
Owner Proprietary corp (Beverly Enterprises).

Fitch Rest Home
75 Lake Ave, Melrose, MA 02176
(617) 665-0521
Admin Joyce M Lamb. *Dir of Nursing* Rose
Pica RN.
Licensure Rest home. *Beds* Rest home 28.
Owner Nonprofit corp.
Admissions Requirements Minimum age 65;
Medical examination.
Staff Physicians 1 (pt); RNs 1 (ft); LPNs 4
(pt); Nurses' aides 7 (pt); Activities
coordinators 1 (pt); Dietitians 1 (pt).
Facilities Dining room; Activities room;
Crafts room; Barber/Beauty shop.
Activities Cards; Games; Movies; Shopping
trips.

MacKenzie Nursing Home Inc
24 Vine St, Melrose, MA 02176
(617) 665-4419
Admin Harry G Meline. *Dir of Nursing* Jean
Wentworth, Health Svcs Supv. *Medical Dir*
Dr S Chawla, consultant.
Licensure Intermediate care. *Beds* ICF 29.
Private Pay Patients 0%. *Certified* Medicaid.
Owner Proprietary corp.
Admissions Requirements Minimum age 55;
Females only; Medical examination;
Physician's request.
Staff RNs 1 (ft), 2 (pt); LPNs 2 (pt); Nurses'
aides; Activities coordinators 1 (ft);
Dietitians 1 (pt).
Facilities Dining room; Activities room;
Laundry room; Library; Visiting beautician.
Activities Arts & crafts; Cards; Games;
Reading groups; Prayer groups; Movies;
Shopping trips; Dances/Social/Cultural
gatherings.

**Melrose Care Center A Long-Term Care
Facility**
40 Martin St, Melrose, MA 02176
(617) 665-7050
Admin Elizabeth O'Brien.
Medical Dir Dr M Akbarian.
Licensure Skilled care; Intermediate care. *Beds*
Swing beds SNF/ICF 106. *Certified*
Medicaid; Medicare.
Owner Proprietary corp (Meritcare).
Admissions Requirements Medical
examination.
Staff Physicians 3 (pt); RNs 13 (ft), 10 (pt);
LPNs 4 (ft), 2 (pt); Nurses' aides 20 (ft), 26
(pt); Physical therapists 2 (pt); Occupational
therapists 1 (pt); Speech therapists 1 (pt);
Activities coordinators 1 (ft), 1 (pt);
Dietitians 1 (pt); Podiatrists 1 (pt);
Audiologists 1 (pt); Dentists 1 (pt).
Facilities Dining room; Physical therapy
room; Activities room; Crafts room; Laundry
room; Barber/Beauty shop.
Activities Arts & crafts; Cards; Games;
Reading groups; Prayer groups; Movies;
Shopping trips.

Normandy House Nursing Home
15 Green St, Melrose, MA 02176
(617) 665-3950
Admin Bonnie-Jean McLean.
Licensure Skilled care; Intermediate care. *Beds*
SNF 41; ICF 41. *Certified* Medicaid.
Owner Proprietary corp.

Oosterman Melrose Rest Home
93 Laurel St, Melrose, MA 02176
(617) 665-3188
Admin Troy Oosterman. *Dir of Nursing*
Gladys Foster RN.
Licensure Rest home. *Beds* Rest home 20.
Owner Privately owned.
Admissions Requirements Females only;
Medical examination; Physician's request.
Staff RNs 1 (pt); Nurses' aides 4 (ft), 6 (pt);
Dietitians 2 (ft).
Facilities Dining room; Activities room;
Crafts room; Laundry room; Library.
Activities Arts & crafts; Cards; Games;
Movies; Shopping trips.

Tuell Nursing Home Inc
92 Franklin St, Melrose, MA 02176
(617) 665-0764
Admin Francis J Cummings. *Dir of Nursing*
Ruth Bougas RN.
Licensure Intermediate care. *Beds* 28.
Certified Medicaid.
Owner Proprietary corp.
Admissions Requirements Females only.
Staff RNs 1 (ft), 4 (pt); LPNs 4 (pt); Nurses'
aides 6 (ft), 8 (pt); Physical therapists 1 (pt);
Activities coordinators 1 (pt); Dietitians 1
(pt); Ophthalmologists 1 (pt).
Facilities Dining room; Activities room.
Activities Arts & crafts; Cards; Games;
Reading groups; Prayer groups; Movies.

Merrimac

Serenity Rest Home
7 Wendy Way, Merrimac, MA 01860-2115
(617) 251-4420
Admin Henry H Martell.
Licensure Rest home. *Beds* 21.

Methuen

Blenwood Nursing Home
302 Broadway, Methuen, MA 01844
(617) 682-8113
Admin Denise A Thisse.
Licensure Intermediate care. *Beds* ICF 41.
Certified Medicaid.
Owner Proprietary corp.

Broadway Convalescent Home
281 Broadway, Methuen, MA 01844
(617) 682-5373
Admin Linda E Weldon.
Licensure Skilled care; Intermediate care. *Beds*
SNF 23; ICF 29. *Certified* Medicaid.
Owner Proprietary corp (First Healthcare
Corp).
Admissions Requirements Minimum age 21.
Staff RNs; LPNs; Nurses' aides; Activities
coordinators.
Facilities Dining room; Activities room;
Laundry room; Barber/Beauty shop.
Activities Arts & crafts; Cards; Games;
Reading groups; Prayer groups; Movies;
Shopping trips; Dances/Social/Cultural
gatherings; Intergenerational programs; Pet
therapy.

McGowan Nursing Home
489 Prospect St, Methuen, MA 01844
(617) 682-4342
Admin Mary R Kim.
Licensure Intermediate care. *Beds* ICF 41.
Certified Medicaid.
Owner Proprietary corp.

Methuen Nursing & Rehabilitation Center
480 Jackson St, Methuen, MA 01844
(508) 686-3906, 687-6007 FAX
Admin Diane Tessier-Efstathiou. *Dir of*
Nursing Adrien Ginchereau RN. *Medical*
Dir Stephen Chastain.
Licensure Skilled care; Intermediate care. *Beds*
SNF 43; ICF 62. *Private Pay Patients* 18%.
Certified Medicaid; Medicare.
Owner Proprietary corp (Mariner Health
Care).
Admissions Requirements Minimum age 21;
Medical examination; Physician's request.
Staff Physicians (contracted); RNs 5 (ft), 7
(pt); LPNs 6 (ft), 7 (pt); Nurses' aides 35
(ft), 10 (pt); Physical therapists 1 (ft);
Recreational therapists (contracted);
Occupational therapists (contracted); Speech
therapists (contracted); Activities
coordinators 2 (ft); Dietitians (contracted);
Ophthalmologists (contracted); Podiatrists
(contracted); Audiologists (contracted).
Languages Italian.

Facilities Dining room; Physical therapy
room; Activities room; Crafts room; Laundry
room; Barber/Beauty shop; Library; Fenced-
in yard.
Activities Arts & crafts; Cards; Games;
Reading groups; Prayer groups; Movies;
Shopping trips; Dances/Social/Cultural
gatherings; Intergenerational programs; Pet
therapy.

Henry C Nevins Home Inc
10 Ingalls Ct, Methuen, MA 01844
(617) 682-7611
Admin Kenneth C Mermer.
Licensure Skilled care; Intermediate care. *Beds*
SNF 82; ICF 60. *Certified* Medicaid.
Owner Proprietary corp.

Middleborough

Alpha Village Long-Term Care Facility
PO Box 798, Middleborough, MA 02346
(617) 947-8632
Admin Ora Mae Torres.
Licensure Intermediate care. *Beds* ICF 50.
Certified Medicaid.
Owner Proprietary corp.
Admissions Requirements Elderly people
requiring Level III care.
Staff RNs; LPNs; Nurses' aides; Recreational
therapists; Activities coordinators; Dietitians;
Social workers.
Languages Portuguese.
Facilities Dining room; Activities room.
Activities Arts & crafts; Cards; Games;
Movies; Shopping trips; Dances/Social/
Cultural gatherings.

Fair Havens Rest Home Inc
334 Marion Rd, Middleborough, MA 02346
(617) 947-1660
Admin Sharon Copeland.
Medical Dir Carol Sologaistoa.
Licensure Rest home. *Beds* Rest home 28.
Certified Medicaid; Medicare.
Owner Nonprofit corp.
Admissions Requirements Minimum age 45;
Medical examination.
Staff LPNs 2 (ft); Nurses' aides 10 (ft), 10
(pt); Reality therapists 1 (ft); Recreational
therapists 1 (ft); Activities coordinators 1
(ft).
Affiliation Lutheran.
Facilities Dining room; Activities room;
Chapel; Crafts room; Laundry room; Barber/
Beauty shop; Library.
Activities Arts & crafts; Cards; Games; Prayer
groups; Movies; Shopping trips; Dances/
Social/Cultural gatherings.

Greenlawn Nursing Home
14 E Grove St, Middleborough, MA 02346
(617) 947-1172
Admin Andrew Comeau.
Medical Dir Shirley Dionne.
Licensure Intermediate care. *Beds* ICF 47.
Certified Medicaid.
Owner Privately owned.
Admissions Requirements Minimum age 18;
Medical examination.
Staff LPNs; Nurses' aides; Physical therapists;
Recreational therapists; Occupational
therapists; Speech therapists; Dietitians.
Facilities Dining room; Activities room;
Laundry room.
Activities Arts & crafts; Cards; Games;
Reading groups; Prayer groups; Movies;
Shopping trips; Dances/Social/Cultural
gatherings; School sessions.

Ann Lewis Rest Home Inc
98 S Main St, Middleborough, MA 02346
(508) 947-2155
Admin Carol A Cheli. *Dir of Nursing* Sheila
Moquin LPN. *Medical Dir* Dr Silliker.
Licensure Rest home. *Beds* Rest home 24.
Certified Medicaid.
Owner Proprietary corp.

Admissions Requirements Females only;
Medical examination; Physician's request.
Staff Physicians 1 (ft); LPNs 1 (ft); Nurses'
aides 5 (ft); Recreational therapists 1 (ft);
Activities coordinators 1 (ft); Dietitians;
Podiatrists 1 (ft).
Facilities Dining room; Activities room;
Laundry room; Barber/Beauty shop.
Activities Arts & crafts; Cards; Games; Prayer
groups; Movies; Shopping trips.

Middleboro Rest Home
5 Barrows St, Middleborough, MA 02346
(617) 947-4120
Admin Robert A Jackson.
Licensure Rest home. *Beds* Rest home 17.
Owner Proprietary corp.
Staff Physicians 1 (pt); RNs 6 (pt); Nurses'
aides 2 (ft), 2 (pt); Recreational therapists 1
(pt); Dietitians 1 (pt); Podiatrists 1 (pt);
Dentists 1 (pt).
Facilities Dining room; Activities room;
Laundry room.
Activities Arts & crafts; Cards; Games;
Reading groups; Prayer groups; Shopping
trips; Dances/Social/Cultural gatherings.

**New Medico Rehabilitation & Skilled Nursing
Center Forest Manor**
Isaac St, Middleborough, MA 02346
(508) 947-9295
Admin William Capser.
Medical Dir Sylvio Landry MD.
Licensure Skilled care; Intermediate care. *Beds*
SNF 83; ICF 41. *Certified* Medicaid;
Medicare.
Owner Privately owned.
Languages Sign.
Facilities Dining room; Physical therapy
room; Activities room; Crafts room; Laundry
room; Barber/Beauty shop.
Activities Arts & crafts; Cards; Games;
Reading groups; Prayer groups; Movies;
Shopping trips; Dances/Social/Cultural
gatherings.

Oak Hill Nursing Home
76 North St, Middleborough, MA 02346
(617) 947-4775
Admin Brian D Brown.
Medical Dir Bernard Beuthner.
Licensure Skilled care; Intermediate care. *Beds*
SNF 81; ICF 45. *Certified* Medicaid;
Medicare.
Owner Proprietary corp (Beverly Enterprises).
Facilities Dining room; Physical therapy
room; Activities room; Crafts room; Laundry
room; Barber/Beauty shop; Library.
Activities Arts & crafts; Cards; Games;
Reading groups; Prayer groups; Movies;
Dances/Social/Cultural gatherings.

Hannah B G Shaw Home for the Aged Inc
PO Box 390, 299 Wareham St,
Middleborough, MA 02346
(617) 947-1184
Admin Lenore Baldwin. *Dir of Nursing*
Thelma Hayden RN.
Licensure Intermediate care; Rest home. *Beds*
ICF 8; Rest home 42.
Owner Nonprofit corp.
Admissions Requirements Minimum age 65;
Medical examination.
Staff RNs 1 (ft), 5 (pt); LPNs 2 (ft), 3 (pt);
Nurses' aides 2 (ft), 2 (pt); Activities
coordinators 1 (ft), 1 (pt); Dietitians 1 (pt).
Facilities Dining room; Activities room;
Chapel; Crafts room; Laundry room; Barber/
Beauty shop; Library.
Activities Arts & crafts; Cards; Games;
Reading groups; Prayer groups; Movies;
Shopping trips; Dances/Social/Cultural
gatherings.

Milford

Blaire House Long-Term Care Facility
20 Claflin St, Milford, MA 01757
(508) 473-1272, 634-3943 FAX
Admin Martha A Forsher MS BSN RN. *Dir of Nursing* Josephine Rogers RN. *Medical Dir* Faheem Faroog MD.
Licensure Skilled care; Respite care. *Beds* SNF 61. *Private Pay Patients* 15%. *Certified* Medicaid; Medicare.
Owner Proprietary corp (Elder Care Services).
Admissions Requirements Minimum age 40; Medical examination; Physician's request.
Staff RNs 1 (ft), 4 (pt); LPNs 6 (ft), 4 (pt); Nurses' aides 22 (ft), 17 (pt); Physical therapists 1 (pt); Occupational therapists 1 (ft), 1 (pt); Speech therapists 1 (pt); Activities coordinators 1 (ft); Ophthalmologists 1 (pt); Podiatrists 1 (pt).
Facilities Dining room; Physical therapy room; Activities room; Crafts room; Laundry room; Barber/Beauty shop.
Activities Arts & crafts; Cards; Games; Prayer groups; Movies; Shopping trips; Dances/Social/Cultural gatherings; Intergenerational programs; Pet therapy.

Geriatric Authority of Milford Nursing Home
Countryside Dr, Milford, MA 01757
(617) 473-0435
Admin Michael R Smith.
Licensure Skilled care; Intermediate care. *Beds* SNF 39; ICF 34. *Certified* Medicaid.
Owner Publicly owned.

Milford Manor Rest Home Inc
16 Claflin St, Milford, MA 01757
(617) 473-2896
Admin Kalida R Patel.
Licensure Rest home. *Beds* Rest home 27.
Owner Proprietary corp.
Admissions Requirements Minimum age 30; Medical examination; Physician's request.
Staff Physicians 2 (pt); LPNs 1 (pt); Nurses' aides 4 (ft), 4 (pt); Activities coordinators 1 (ft); Dietitians 1 (pt); Podiatrists 1 (pt).
Facilities Dining room; Activities room; Crafts room; Laundry room.
Activities Arts & crafts; Cards; Games; Reading groups; Prayer groups; Shopping trips; Dances/Social/Cultural gatherings.

Millbury

New Pine Grove Villa Nursing Home
5 Rhodes St, Millbury, MA 01527
(617) 865-9490
Admin Steven L Hochhauser. *Dir of Nursing* Terry Kitteredge. *Medical Dir* Dr Susan Moran.
Licensure Intermediate care. *Beds* ICF 41. *Certified* Medicaid.
Owner Proprietary corp.
Admissions Requirements Minimum age 18; Physician's request.
Staff Physicians; RNs; LPNs; Nurses' aides; Activities coordinators; Dietitians.
Facilities Dining room; Activities room; Laundry room.
Activities Arts & crafts; Cards; Games; Reading groups; Prayer groups; Movies; Shopping trips; Dances/Social/Cultural gatherings.

Providence House Nursing Home of Milbury
29 Main St, Millbury, MA 01527
(617) 865-6106
Admin Karen A Koprowski.
Licensure Skilled care; Intermediate care; Rest home. *Beds* SNF 40; ICF 60; Rest home 42. *Certified* Medicaid.
Owner Proprietary corp.

Millis

Willowbrook Manor Rest Home
71 Union St, Millis, MA 02054
(617) 376-5083
Admin Gabriel Gabrielli.
Licensure Rest home. *Beds* Rest home 36.
Owner Proprietary corp.

Milton

Milton Health Care Facility A Skilled Nursing Facility
1200 Brush Hill Rd, Milton, MA 02186
(617) 333-0600
Admin Donald Gresh.
Licensure Skilled care; Intermediate care. *Beds* SNF 80; ICF 60; Rest home 20.
Owner Privately owned.

Montgomery

Mountain View Nursing Home
RFD 1, Montgomery, MA 01085
(413) 562-0097
Admin Mary F Uschmann.
Licensure Intermediate care. *Beds* ICF 27. *Certified* Medicaid.
Owner Proprietary corp.

Nahant

Jesmond Nursing Home
271 Nahant Rd, Nahant, MA 01908
(617) 581-0420
Admin Rosemary C Costin. *Dir of Nursing* Elizabeth Dubin. *Medical Dir* Elliot Strauss.
Licensure Skilled care; Intermediate care. *Beds* SNF 29; ICF 28. *Private Pay Patients* 75%. *Certified* Medicaid.
Owner Proprietary corp.
Admissions Requirements Medical examination; Physician's request.
Staff Physicians 1 (ft); RNs 4 (ft), 1 (pt); LPNs 5 (ft), 1 (pt); Nurses' aides 13 (ft), 8 (pt); Physical therapists 1 (pt); Reality therapists 1 (pt); Recreational therapists 1 (ft); Occupational therapists 1 (pt); Speech therapists 1 (pt); Activities coordinators 1 (ft); Dietitians 1 (pt); Ophthalmologists (contracted); Podiatrists (contracted); Audiologists (contracted).
Facilities Dining room; Physical therapy room; Activities room; Crafts room; Laundry room; Barber/Beauty shop; Library.
Activities Arts & crafts; Cards; Games; Reading groups; Prayer groups; Movies; Dances/Social/Cultural gatherings; Intergenerational programs; Pet therapy; Restaurant trips.

Nantucket

Our Island Home
East Creek Rd, Nantucket, MA 02554
(508) 228-0462
Admin John Marshall. *Dir of Nursing* Eleanor E MacVicar RN. *Medical Dir* Christian Briggs.
Licensure Skilled care; Intermediate care. *Beds* SNF 22; ICF 23. *Private Pay Patients* 40%. *Certified* Medicaid.
Owner Publicly owned.
Admissions Requirements Medical examination; Physician's request.
Staff Physicians 5 (pt); RNs 3 (ft), 3 (pt); LPNs 2 (pt); Nurses' aides 14 (ft), 8 (pt); Physical therapists (consultant); Recreational therapists 1 (ft); Occupational therapists 1 (pt); Dietitians (consultant); Ophthalmologists 1 (pt); Podiatrists 1 (pt); Audiologists 1 (pt).
Languages Portuguese.
Facilities Dining room; Physical therapy room; Activities room; Chapel; Crafts room; Laundry room; Barber/Beauty shop.
Activities Arts & crafts; Cards; Games; Reading groups; Prayer groups; Movies; Shopping trips; Dances/Social/Cultural gatherings; Intergenerational programs; Pet therapy.

Natick

Brittany Convalescent Home
168 W Central St, Natick, MA 01760
(617) 327-1262, (508) 655-1000
Admin Angela Matzilevich. *Dir of Nursing* Barbara Kane RN. *Medical Dir* Dr Alan Engel.
Licensure Skilled care; Intermediate care; Retirement. *Beds* SNF 40; ICF 40; Retirement 36. *Private Pay Patients* 25%. *Certified* Medicaid.
Owner Proprietary corp (Hillhaven Corp).
Admissions Requirements Minimum age 20.
Staff Physicians; RNs 3 (ft), 5 (pt); LPNs 3 (ft), 1 (pt); Nurses' aides 24 (ft), 10 (pt); Physical therapists 1 (pt); Reality therapists 1 (pt); Recreational therapists 1 (ft); Occupational therapists 1 (pt); Speech therapists 1 (pt); Activities coordinators 1 (ft); Dietitians 1 (pt); Dentists 1 (pt).
Facilities Dining room; Physical therapy room; Activities room; Crafts room; Laundry room; Barber/Beauty shop.
Activities Arts & crafts; Cards; Games; Reading groups; Prayer groups; Movies; Shopping trips; Dances/Social/Cultural gatherings; Intergenerational programs; Pet therapy.

Nims Rest Home
38 Fiske St, Natick, MA 01760
(617) 653-0382
Admin Helen Nims.
Medical Dir Muriel Baim.
Licensure Rest home. *Beds* Rest home 21.
Owner Privately owned.
Admissions Requirements Minimum age 35; Medical examination; Physician's request.
Staff RNs 1 (pt); Nurses' aides 4 (ft); Dietitians 1 (ft); Podiatrists 1 (pt).
Facilities Dining room; Activities room; Laundry room.
Activities Arts & crafts; Cards; Games; Prayer groups; Shopping trips; Dances/Social/Cultural gatherings; A group comes the first of every month for singing & prayers.

Phillips House Nursing Home
10 Phillips St, Natick, MA 01760
(617) 653-1543
Admin Robert L Douglas.
Licensure Intermediate care. *Beds* 9.

Riverbend Convalescent Center
34 Lincoln St, South Natick, Natick, MA 01760
(617) 653-8330
Admin Beverly McIntyre RN. *Dir of Nursing* Cynthia Wade RN.
Licensure Intermediate care; Alzheimer's care. *Beds* ICF 55. *Certified* Medicaid.
Owner Proprietary corp.
Staff Physicians 1 (pt); RNs 4 (ft); LPNs 3 (ft), 1 (pt); Nurses' aides 20 (ft), 6 (pt); Physical therapists 1 (pt); Recreational therapists 2 (ft); Occupational therapists 1 (pt); Speech therapists 1 (pt); Dietitians 1 (pt); Ophthalmologists 1 (pt); Podiatrists 1 (pt); Dentists 1 (pt); Social services 1 (pt).
Facilities Dining room; Activities room; Crafts room; Laundry room; Barber/Beauty shop; Library.
Activities Arts & crafts; Cards; Games; Reading groups; Movies; Shopping trips; Dances/Social/Cultural gatherings; Drama club takes musicals to other homes & hospitals.

Needham

Briarwood Convalescent Center
26 Garfield St, Needham, MA 02192
(617) 449-4040
Admin Dan Micherone. *Dir of Nursing* Mary
M Morrissey RN. *Medical Dir* Simon
Weitzman MD.
Licensure Skilled care; Intermediate care. *Beds*
SNF 80; ICF 40. *Certified* Medicaid.
Owner Proprietary corp (First Healthcare
Corp).
Admissions Requirements Minimum age 65;
Medical examination.
Facilities Dining room; Physical therapy
room; Activities room; Chapel; Crafts room;
Barber/Beauty shop.
Activities Arts & crafts; Cards; Games;
Reading groups; Prayer groups; Movies;
Shopping trips; Dances/Social/Cultural
gatherings; Luncheons; Residents council;
Music therapy.

Daystar Home
1180 Great Plain Ave, Needham, MA 02192
(617) 449-1149
Admin Ethel F Blettner.
Licensure Rest home. *Beds* 20.

Needham/Hamilton House Convalescent Center
141 Chestnut St, Needham, MA 02192
(617) 444-9114
Admin Larry Osterweil.
Medical Dir John Fernald MD & Asha
Wallace MD.
Licensure Skilled care; Intermediate care. *Beds*
SNF 41; ICF 39. *Certified* Medicaid;
Medicare.
Owner Proprietary corp.
Admissions Requirements Minimum age 21.
Staff RNs 6 (ft), 9 (pt); LPNs 2 (ft), 2 (pt);
Nurses' aides 18 (ft), 34 (pt).
Facilities Dining room; Physical therapy
room; Activities room; Chapel; Crafts room;
Laundry room; Barber/Beauty shop.
Activities Arts & crafts; Cards; Games;
Reading groups; Prayer groups; Movies;
Shopping trips; Dances/Social/Cultural
gatherings.

Skilled Nursing Facility at North Hill
865 Central Ave, Needham, MA 02192
(617) 444-9910
Admin Patrick T Zoerner. *Dir of Nursing*
Barbara Gerstein RN. *Medical Dir* Simon
Weitzman MD.
Licensure Skilled care; Intermediate care;
Retirement. *Beds* SNF 40; ICF 20. *Certified*
Medicaid; Medicare.
Owner Proprietary corp.
Admissions Requirements Medical
examination; Physician's request.
Staff Physicians 1 (pt); RNs 6 (ft), 7 (pt);
LPNs 2 (ft), 3 (pt); Nurses' aides 20 (ft), 8
(pt); Physical therapists 1 (ft), 1 (pt);
Recreational therapists 1 (ft); Activities
coordinators 1 (pt); Dietitians 1 (pt); Social
workers 1 (pt).
Facilities Dining room; Physical therapy
room; Activities room; Crafts room; Barber/
Beauty shop; Library; Pool; Extensive
walkways.
Activities Arts & crafts; Cards; Games;
Reading groups; Prayer groups; Movies;
Shopping trips; Dances/Social/Cultural
gatherings; Restaurant trips.

New Bedford

Bedford Village Nursing Home Inc
9 Pope St, New Bedford, MA 02740
(617) 997-3358
Admin Michael Cummings.
Licensure Intermediate care. *Beds* ICF 73.
Certified Medicaid.
Owner Proprietary corp.

Blaire House of New Bedford
397 County St, New Bedford, MA 02740
(508) 997-9396, 990-3336 FAX
Admin Linda R Valenzano. *Dir of Nursing*
Ruth Mendonca RN. *Medical Dir* Sheldon
Davis MD.
Licensure Skilled care; Intermediate care. *Beds*
SNF 82; ICF 41. *Certified* Medicaid;
Medicare.
Owner Proprietary corp (Elder Care Services
Inc).
Admissions Requirements Minimum age 65;
Medical examination.
Staff RNs; LPNs; Nurses' aides; Physical
therapists; Recreational therapists;
Occupational therapists; Speech therapists;
Activities coordinators; Dietitians;
Ophthalmologists.
Facilities Dining room; Physical therapy
room; Activities room; Crafts room; Laundry
room; Barber/Beauty shop.
Activities Arts & crafts; Cards; Games;
Reading groups; Prayer groups; Movies;
Shopping trips; Dances/Social/Cultural
gatherings; Intergenerational programs; Pet
therapy.

Hallmark Nursing Home of New Bedford
1123 Rockdale Ave, New Bedford, MA 02740
(617) 997-7448
Admin Mark S Nussman. *Dir of Nursing*
Nancy S Clark RN.
Licensure Skilled care; Intermediate care. *Beds*
SNF 41; ICF 83. *Certified* Medicaid.
Owner Proprietary corp (First Healthcare
Corp).
Admissions Requirements Minimum age 16;
Medical examination; Physician's request.
Staff Physicians 5 (pt); Physical therapists 1
(pt); Reality therapists 1 (ft); Recreational
therapists 1 (pt); Occupational therapists 1
(pt); Speech therapists 1 (pt); Activities
coordinators 1 (ft), 1 (pt); Dietitians 1 (pt);
Ophthalmologists 1 (pt); Podiatrists 1 (pt);
Dentists 1 (pt).
Languages Portuguese, German.
Facilities Dining room; Activities room;
Crafts room; Laundry room; Barber/Beauty
shop.
Activities Arts & crafts; Cards; Games;
Reading groups; Prayer groups; Movies;
Shopping trips; Dances/Social/Cultural
gatherings.

Havenwood Rest Home
251 Walnut St, New Bedford, MA 02740
(617) 994-3120
Admin Donald L Di Santi.
Licensure Rest home. *Beds* Rest home 41.
Certified Medicaid; Medicare.
Owner Proprietary corp.
Admissions Requirements Minimum age 21.
Staff Physicians 1 (pt); LPNs 1 (pt); Nurses'
aides 4 (ft), 2 (pt); Activities coordinators 1
(pt); Dietitians 1 (pt); Ophthalmologists 1
(pt).
Languages Spanish, Portuguese.
Facilities Dining room; Activities room;
Laundry room; Barber/Beauty shop; TV
room.
Activities Arts & crafts; Cards; Games;
Shopping trips; Dances/Social/Cultural
gatherings.

Kristen Beth Nursing Home Inc
713 Shawmut Ave, New Bedford, MA 02746
(617) 999-6456
Admin Antonio T Moniz.
Medical Dir Dr John Barnes.
Licensure Skilled care; Intermediate care. *Beds*
SNF 36; ICF 57. *Certified* Medicaid.
Owner Proprietary corp.
Admissions Requirements Minimum age 21.
Staff RNs 6 (ft); LPNs 5 (ft), 2 (pt); Nurses'
aides 37 (ft); Physical therapists 1 (pt);
Occupational therapists 1 (pt); Speech

therapists 1 (pt); Dietitians 1 (pt);
Ophthalmologists 1 (pt); Podiatrists 1 (pt);
Dentists 1 (pt).
Facilities Dining room; Physical therapy
room; Activities room; Crafts room; Laundry
room; Barber/Beauty shop.
Activities Arts & crafts; Cards; Games;
Reading groups; Prayer groups; Movies;
Shopping trips; Dances/Social/Cultural
gatherings.

New Bedford Jewish Convalescent Home
200 Hawthorn St, New Bedford, MA 02740
(617) 997-9314
Admin Estelle R Shanbrun.
Licensure Skilled care; Intermediate care. *Beds*
SNF 40; ICF 40. *Certified* Medicaid;
Medicare.
Owner Nonprofit corp.
Admissions Requirements Minimum age 22.
Languages Portuguese, Polish, Yiddish,
Hebrew.
Affiliation Jewish.
Facilities Dining room; Physical therapy
room; Activities room; Chapel; Crafts room;
Barber/Beauty shop; Library; Patio.
Activities Arts & crafts; Cards; Games;
Reading groups; Prayer groups; Movies;
Shopping trips; Dances/Social/Cultural
gatherings; Birthday parties; Music; Lunch
outings; Pet therapy; Cooking; Baking.

Plainview Long-Term Care Facility
875 Plainville Rd, New Bedford, MA 02745
(617) 995-8229
Admin Almerinda Jorge.
Licensure Rest home. *Beds* Rest home 26.
Owner Proprietary corp.

Rita's Rest Home
49 Desautels St, New Bedford, MA 02745
(617) 992-6074
Admin Rita Rouke.
Licensure Rest home. *Beds* Rest home 10.
Owner Proprietary corp.

Sacred Heart Nursing Home
359 Summer St, New Bedford, MA 02740
(508) 996-6751
Admin Sr Blandine d'Amours. *Dir of Nursing*
Sr Theresa Bergeron. *Medical Dir* Dr
William A Jeffrey.
Licensure Skilled care; Intermediate care. *Beds*
SNF 147; ICF 70. *Private Pay Patients* 10%.
Certified Medicaid.
Owner Nonprofit corp.
Admissions Requirements Minimum age 65;
Medical examination; Physician's request.
Staff Physicians 1 (pt); RNs 11 (ft), 9 (pt);
LPNs 23 (ft), 11 (pt); Nurses' aides 83 (ft),
12 (pt); Physical therapists 5 (ft), 1 (pt);
Reality therapists 1 (ft); Recreational
therapists 4 (ft); Occupational therapists 1
(pt); Speech therapists 1 (pt); Activities
coordinators 1 (ft); Dietitians 1 (pt);
Podiatrists 2 (pt); Dentists 1 (pt).
Languages French, Portuguese, Polish.
Affiliation Roman Catholic.
Facilities Dining room; Physical therapy
room; Activities room; Chapel; Crafts room;
Laundry room; Barber/Beauty shop; Library;
Remotivation room.
Activities Arts & crafts; Cards; Games;
Reading groups; Prayer groups; Movies;
Shopping trips; Dances/Social/Cultural
gatherings.

Savoy Convalescent Home
670 County St, New Bedford, MA 02740
(508) 994-2400
Admin Nancy A Winer. *Dir of Nursing*
Hannah Ameral RN. *Medical Dir* Dr
William Jeffrey.
Licensure Skilled care. *Beds* SNF 39. *Certified*
Medicaid; Medicare.
Owner Proprietary corp.

Admissions Requirements Minimum age 21;
Females only; Medical examination;
Physician's request.
Facilities Dining room; Laundry room.
Activities Arts & crafts; Cards; Games;
Reading groups; Prayer groups; Movies;
Dances/Social/Cultural gatherings;
Intergenerational programs; Pet therapy.

Taber Street Nursing Home
19 Taber St, New Bedford, MA 02740
(617) 997-0791
Admin Laurence Reed. *Dir of Nursing*
Kathleen M Douris RN.
Licensure Intermediate care; Alzheimer's care.
Beds ICF 56. *Certified* Medicaid.
Owner Proprietary corp (Beverly Enterprises).
Admissions Requirements Minimum age 65;
Medical examination.
Staff Physicians 1 (pt); RNs 3 (ft), 2 (pt);
LPNs 2 (ft), 2 (pt); Nurses' aides 15 (ft), 10
(pt); Activities coordinators 1 (ft); Dietitians
1 (pt); Podiatrists 1 (pt).
Languages Portuguese, French.
Affiliation Episcopal.
Facilities Dining room; Activities room;
Chapel; Crafts room; Laundry room; Barber/
Beauty shop; Library.
Activities Arts & crafts; Cards; Games;
Reading groups; Prayer groups; Movies;
Shopping trips; Dances/Social/Cultural
gatherings.

Newburyport

Brigham Manor Convalescent Home
77 High St, Newburyport, MA 01950
(617) 462-4221
Admin Scott Ullrich. *Dir of Nursing* Claire
Lawrence.
Licensure Intermediate care. *Beds* ICF 64.
Certified Medicaid.
Owner Proprietary corp (First Healthcare
Corp).
Admissions Requirements Medical
examination.
Staff RNs; LPNs; Nurses' aides; Activities
coordinators; Dietitians.
Facilities Dining room; Barber/Beauty shop;
Porch.
Activities Arts & crafts; Cards; Games;
Reading groups; Prayer groups; Movies;
Shopping trips; Dances/Social/Cultural
gatherings.

Country Manor Convalescent Home
180 Low St, Newburyport, MA 01950
(617) 465-5361
Admin Clyde Tyler. *Dir of Nursing* Marion
Chabot RN. *Medical Dir* Dr Christopher
Harris.
Licensure Skilled care; Intermediate care. *Beds*
SNF 82; ICF 41. *Certified* Medicaid.
Owner Proprietary corp (First Healthcare
Corp).
Admissions Requirements Minimum age 21;
Medical examination; Physician's request.
Staff Physicians 1 (pt); RNs 4 (ft), 4 (pt);
LPNs 4 (ft), 2 (pt); Nurses' aides 23 (ft), 11
(pt); Physical therapists 1 (pt); Occupational
therapists 1 (pt); Activities coordinators 1
(ft), 1 (pt); Dietitians 1 (pt).
Facilities Dining room; Activities room;
Chapel; Laundry room; Barber/Beauty shop.
Activities Arts & crafts; Games; Reading
groups; Prayer groups; Movies; Shopping
trips.

Newbury Port Society Home for Aged Women
75 High St, Newburyport, MA 01950
(617) 465-7102
Admin Susanne Roaf Flaherty.
Licensure Rest home. *Beds* Rest home 10.
Owner Nonprofit organization/foundation.
Admissions Requirements Minimum age 65;
Females only; Medical examination.
Staff RNs; Nurses' aides; Podiatrists.

Facilities Dining room; Laundry room;
Barber/Beauty shop.
Activities Arts & crafts; Cards; Games;
Movies; Shopping trips; Dances/Social/
Cultural gatherings.

Newburyport Society Home for Aged Men
361 High St, Newburyport, MA 01950
(617) 465-7091
Admin Patricia C Messinger.
Licensure Rest home. *Beds* Rest home 9.
Owner Nonprofit organization/foundation.
Admissions Requirements Minimum age 65;
Males only; Medical examination.
Staff RNs; Nurses' aides; Dietitians.
Facilities Dining room; Activities room;
Laundry room.

Port Rehabilitation & Skilled Nursing Center
Hale & Low Sts, Newburyport, MA 01950
(617) 462-7373
Admin Robert J Basek.
Licensure Skilled care. *Beds* SNF 102.

Newton

Baptist Home of Massachusetts
66 Commonwealth Ave, Newton, MA 02167
(617) 969-9380
Admin Cathy B Smith.
Medical Dir Allen Ergel MD.
Licensure Intermediate care. *Beds* 131.
Certified Medicaid.
Admissions Requirements Minimum age 65;
Medical examination.
Staff Physicians 1 (pt); RNs 7 (ft), 1 (pt);
LPNs 3 (ft), 4 (pt); Nurses' aides 21 (ft), 4
(pt); Physical therapists 1 (pt); Recreational
therapists 1 (ft); Occupational therapists 1
(pt); Activities coordinators 1 (ft), 1 (pt);
Dietitians 1 (pt); Ophthalmologists 1 (pt);
Podiatrists 1 (pt); Audiologists 1 (pt);
Dentists 1 (pt).
Affiliation Baptist.
Facilities Dining room; Activities room;
Chapel; Crafts room; Laundry room; Barber/
Beauty shop; Library.
Activities Arts & crafts; Games; Reading
groups; Prayer groups; Movies; Shopping
trips; Dances/Social/Cultural gatherings;
Field trips.

Braeburn Nursing Home
20 Kinmonth Rd, Newton, MA 02168
(617) 332-8481
Admin Salvatore Freddura.
Licensure Intermediate care. *Beds* ICF 84.

Chetwynde Convalescent Home
1660 Washington St, Newton, MA 02165
(617) 244-1137
Admin Kathleen McKenna.
Licensure Intermediate care. *Beds* ICF 32.
Certified Medicaid.
Owner Proprietary corp (Beverly Enterprises).

Chetwynde Nursing Home
1650 Washington St, Newton, MA 02165
(617) 244-5407
Admin Stephen E Maxam.
Licensure Skilled care; Intermediate care. *Beds*
SNF 38; ICF 37. *Certified* Medicaid.
Owner Proprietary corp (Beverly Enterprises).

Elliot Manor Nursing Home
25 Mechanic St, Newton, MA 02164
(617) 527-1750
Admin Andrew Comeau. *Dir of Nursing* Ann
Keon RN. *Medical Dir* Dr Carl Levison.
Licensure Intermediate care. *Beds* ICF 53.
Certified Medicaid.
Owner Proprietary corp.
Admissions Requirements Minimum age 21;
Medical examination; Physician's request.
Staff RNs 3 (ft), 3 (pt); LPNs 2 (ft), 1 (pt);
Nurses' aides 18 (ft), 6 (pt); Recreational
therapists 1 (ft), 1 (pt); Dietitians 1 (pt).

Activities Arts & crafts; Games; Reading
groups; Prayer groups; Movies; Shopping
trips.

Garland Rest Home
217 Bellevue St, Newton, MA 02158
(617) 527-0381
Admin Rosemary Omelite.
Licensure Rest home. *Beds* Rest home 9.
Owner Privately owned.

Heathwood Nursing & Retirement Home
188 Florence St, Chestnut Hill, Newton, MA
02167
(617) 332-4730
Admin Joanne Cooper. *Dir of Nursing*
Marjorie O'Neill. *Medical Dir* Dr Bana.
Licensure Intermediate care; Residential care;
Alzheimer's care. *Beds* ICF 34; Residential
care 40. *Private Pay Patients* 100%.
Owner Proprietary corp (Beverly Enterprises).
Admissions Requirements Minimum age 65.
Staff RNs; LPNs; Nurses' aides; Recreational
therapists; Activities coordinators; Dietitians.
Facilities Dining room; Activities room;
Laundry room; Barber/Beauty shop; Library.
Activities Arts & crafts; Cards; Games;
Reading groups; Prayer groups; Movies;
Shopping trips; Dances/Social/Cultural
gatherings; Intergenerational programs; Pet
therapy.

Lakeview Rest Home
38 Lake Ave, Newton, MA 02159
(617) 244-9179
Admin N Joan Sterndale.
Licensure Rest home. *Beds* Rest home 12.
Owner Proprietary corp.
Admissions Requirements Medical
examination; Physician's request.
Staff RNs 1 (pt); Nurses' aides 2 (pt);
Activities coordinators 1 (pt); Dietitians 1
(pt).
Facilities Activities room; Library; Solarium;
Gazebo.
Activities Cards; Games; Movies; Dances/
Social/Cultural gatherings; Music.

Mediplex of Newton—Long-Term Care Facility
2101 Washington St, Newton, MA 02162
(617) 969-4660
Admin Joanne Mukerjee.
Licensure Skilled care; Intermediate care. *Beds*
SNF 135; ICF 55. *Certified* Medicaid.
Owner Proprietary corp (Mediplex Inc).

Mt Ida Rest Home
32 Newtonville Ave, Newton, MA 02158
(617) 527-5657
Admin John Keeney. *Dir of Nursing* Ann
Lennihan RN.
Licensure Rest home. *Beds* Rest home 18.
Certified Medicaid; Medicare.
Owner Privately owned.
Admissions Requirements Minimum age 21;
Males only.
Staff Physicians; RNs; LPNs; Nurses' aides;
Recreational therapists; Activities
coordinators; Dietitians; Ophthalmologists;
Podiatrists; Dentists; Social workers.
Facilities Dining room; Physical therapy
room; Activities room; Laundry room;
Barber/Beauty shop.
Activities Arts & crafts; Cards; Games;
Reading groups; Prayer groups; Movies;
Shopping trips; Dances/Social/Cultural
gatherings; Cooking classes.

Pelham House Nursing Home
45 Pelham St, Newton, MA 02159
(617) 527-5833
Admin Barry Chiler. *Dir of Nursing* Gail
Bekebrede. *Medical Dir* Dr Mark Rohrer.
Licensure Intermediate care; Retirement;
Alzheimer's care. *Beds* ICF 19; Retirement
6. *Certified* Medicaid.
Owner Proprietary corp.
Admissions Requirements Minimum age 21.

Staff Physicians 1 (pt); RNs 3 (ft); LPNs 2 (ft), 2 (pt); Nurses' aides 1 (ft), 2 (pt); Physical therapists 1 (pt); Reality therapists 1 (pt); Recreational therapists 1 (ft); Occupational therapists 1 (pt); Speech therapists 1 (pt); Activities coordinators 1 (ft); Dietitians 1 (pt); Ophthalmologists 1 (pt); Podiatrists 1 (pt); Dentists 1 (pt).
Facilities Dining room; Activities room; Crafts room; Laundry room; Barber/Beauty shop; Library.
Activities Arts & crafts; Cards; Games; Reading groups; Prayer groups; Movies; Shopping trips; Dances/Social/Cultural gatherings; Entertainment.

Vanderklish Hall Nursing Home
929 Beacon St, Newton, MA 02159
(617) 244-5063
Admin Duncan Vanderklish. *Dir of Nursing* Nancy Kirrane RN.
Licensure Intermediate care. *Beds* ICF 22.
Owner Proprietary corp.
Admissions Requirements Medical examination; Physician's request.
Staff RNs 3 (ft), 2 (pt); LPNs 1 (ft), 1 (pt); Nurses' aides 1 (ft), 6 (pt); Recreational therapists 1 (pt); Dietitians 1 (pt).
Activities Arts & crafts; Cards; Games; Reading groups; Prayer groups; Movies.

Newton Centre

Eliot Falls Nursing Home
PO Box 431, Newton Centre, MA 02153
(617) 653-1543
Admin Robert L Douglas.
Licensure Intermediate care. *Beds* ICF 13. *Certified* Medicaid.
Owner Proprietary corp.

North Adams

Homestead Rest Home
215 E Main St, North Adams, MA 01247
(413) 663-6885
Admin Henry Dargie.
Licensure Rest home. *Beds* Rest home 36.
Owner Proprietary corp.

Willowood Nursing Home of North Adams
175 Franklin St, North Adams, MA 01247
(413) 664-4041
Admin Christopher S Duncan. *Dir of Nursing* Susan Chalifoux RN. *Medical Dir* Douglas Herr MD.
Licensure Skilled care; Intermediate care. *Beds* SNF 41; ICF 42. *Certified* Medicaid.
Owner Proprietary corp.
Staff RNs; LPNs; Nurses' aides; Physical therapists; Occupational therapists; Activities coordinators; Dietitians.
Facilities Dining room; Physical therapy room; Activities room; Laundry room; Barber/Beauty shop.
Activities Arts & crafts; Cards; Games; Prayer groups; Movies.

North Andover

New Medico Rehabilitation & Skilled Nursing Center—Stevens Hall
75 Park St, North Andover, MA 01845
(617) 685-3372
Admin John H Keeney.
Medical Dir Matthew Cushing MD.
Licensure Skilled care; Intermediate care. *Beds* SNF 82; ICF 40. *Certified* Medicaid; Medicare.
Owner Proprietary corp.
Admissions Requirements Minimum age 21.
Staff Physicians 1 (ft), 4 (pt); RNs 7 (ft), 12 (pt); LPNs 5 (ft), 4 (pt); Nurses' aides 27 (ft), 13 (pt); Physical therapists 1 (ft); Recreational therapists 1 (ft); Occupational therapists 1 (pt); Speech therapists 1 (pt);

Activities coordinators 1 (ft); Dietitians 1 (pt); Ophthalmologists 2 (pt); Podiatrists 2 (pt); Audiologists 1 (pt); Dentists 1 (pt).
Facilities Dining room; Physical therapy room; Activities room; Crafts room; Laundry room; Barber/Beauty shop; Library; TV rooms; Sitting rooms.
Activities Arts & crafts; Cards; Games; Reading groups; Prayer groups; Movies; Shopping trips; Dances/Social/Cultural gatherings; Bowling; Happy hour; Traveling store; Various bus trips; Sunday ice cream; Parties; Morning coffee, tea, hot chocolate, donuts, English muffins.

Prescott House Nursing Home
140 Prescott St, North Andover, MA 01845
(617) 685-8086
Admin John M Harris. *Dir of Nursing* Kathleen Melia RN. *Medical Dir* Edward Broaddus MD.
Licensure Skilled care; Intermediate care. *Beds* SNF 70; ICF 56. *Certified* Medicaid.
Owner Proprietary corp.
Admissions Requirements Minimum age 21.
Staff Physicians 1 (pt); RNs 15 (ft); LPNs 9 (ft); Nurses' aides 37 (ft); Physical therapists 1 (pt); Recreational therapists 1 (ft), 1 (pt); Occupational therapists 1 (pt); Speech therapists 1 (pt); Activities coordinators 1 (ft); Dietitians 1 (pt).
Facilities Dining room; Physical therapy room; Activities room; Crafts room; Laundry room; Barber/Beauty shop; Library.
Activities Arts & crafts; Cards; Games; Reading groups; Prayer groups; Movies; Shopping trips; Dances/Social/Cultural gatherings.

North Attleboro

Madonna Manor Nursing Home
85 N Washington St, North Attleboro, MA 02760
(508) 699-2740
Admin Martha J Daneault.
Medical Dir Joshua Gutman MD.
Licensure Skilled care; Intermediate care. *Beds* SNF 39; ICF 82. *Certified* Medicaid.
Owner Nonprofit corp.
Admissions Requirements Must require Level II or Level III Care.
Staff RNs 6 (ft), 9 (pt); LPNs 4 (ft), 10 (pt); Nurses' aides 10 (ft), 30 (pt); Physical therapists 1 (ft); Recreational therapists 1 (ft), 3 (pt); Activities coordinators 1 (ft), 3 (pt); Dietitians 4 (ft), 12 (pt).
Affiliation Roman Catholic.
Facilities Dining room; Physical therapy room; Activities room; Chapel; Laundry room; Barber/Beauty shop; Library.
Activities Arts & crafts; Cards; Games; Reading groups; Prayer groups; Movies; Shopping trips; Dances/Social/Cultural gatherings.

North Easton

Easton—Lincoln Nursing Home
184 Lincoln St, North Easton, MA 02356
(508) 238-7053
Admin Colleen Lovering. *Dir of Nursing* Jane Redmond. *Medical Dir* Lawrence Hotes MD.
Licensure Skilled care; Intermediate care. *Beds* SNF 41; ICF 47. *Certified* Medicaid; Medicare.
Owner Proprietary corp (Oakwood Living Center).
Admissions Requirements Minimum age 21; Medical examination.
Staff RNs; LPNs; Nurses' aides; Physical therapists; Occupational therapists; Speech therapists; Activities coordinators; Dietitians; Ophthalmologists; Podiatrists.
Languages French.

Facilities Dining room; Physical therapy room; Activities room; Laundry room; Barber/Beauty shop; Library.
Activities Arts & crafts; Cards; Games; Reading groups; Prayer groups; Movies; Dances/Social/Cultural gatherings; Pet therapy.

Happiness House Rest Home
5 Gaslight Ln, North Easton, MA 02356
(617) 746-2982
Admin Harry McCabe.
Licensure Rest home. *Beds* 36.
Admissions Requirements Medical examination; Physician's request.
Staff LPNs 2 (pt); Recreational therapists 1 (pt); Activities coordinators 1 (pt).
Facilities Dining room; Activities room; Crafts room.
Activities Arts & crafts; Cards; Games; Prayer groups; Movies; Shopping trips.

North Falmouth

Fraser Rest Home of Falmouth
PO Box 347, North Falmouth, MA 02550
(617) 563-3522
Admin Caleb Fraser.
Licensure Rest home. *Beds* Rest home 23.
Owner Proprietary corp.

North Quincy

Oceanside Nursing Home
445 Quincy Shore Dr, North Quincy, MA 02171
(617) 328-4618
Admin Harry J Minassian. *Dir of Nursing* Kathleen Lally. *Medical Dir* Floyd Wolff MD.
Licensure Intermediate care; Alzheimer's care. *Beds* ICF 23. *Private Pay Patients* 20%. *Certified* Medicaid.
Owner Proprietary corp.
Admissions Requirements Minimum age 21.
Staff Physicians; RNs; LPNs; Nurses' aides; Physical therapists; Recreational therapists; Speech therapists; Activities coordinators; Dietitians; Podiatrists.
Languages Armenian, Turkish.
Facilities Dining room; Activities room; Barber/Beauty shop.
Activities Arts & crafts; Cards; Games; Reading groups; Prayer groups; Movies; Shopping trips; Dances/Social/Cultural gatherings; Pet therapy.

North Reading

Meadow View Convalescent Home
134 North St, North Reading, MA 01864
(617) 944-1107
Admin Scott E Stone. *Dir of Nursing* Dianna Veno. *Medical Dir* Dr John Kidd.
Licensure Skilled care; Intermediate care. *Beds* SNF 52; ICF 49. *Certified* Medicaid.
Owner Proprietary corp (First Healthcare Corp).
Admissions Requirements Minimum age 21.
Staff Physicians; RNs; LPNs; Nurses' aides; Physical therapists; Recreational therapists; Occupational therapists; Speech therapists; Activities coordinators; Dietitians; Ophthalmologists; Dentists.
Facilities Dining room; Activities room; Crafts room; Laundry room; Barber/Beauty shop.
Activities Arts & crafts; Cards; Games; Reading groups; Prayer groups; Movies; Shopping trips; Dances/Social/Cultural gatherings.

Northampton

Hampshire County Long-Term Care Facility
River Rd, Northampton, MA 01053
(413) 584-8457
Admin Edwin Warner.
Licensure Skilled care. *Beds* SNF 120.
Owner Publicly owned.

New Medico Rehabilitation & Skilled Nursing Center at Pioneer Valley
548 Elm St, Northampton, MA 01060
(413) 586-3150, 584-7720
Admin Douglas Motter. *Dir of Nursing* Betty Podolak. *Medical Dir* Dr Mitchell Tenerowicz.
Licensure Skilled care; Intermediate care. *Beds* SNF 43; ICF 82. *Certified* Medicaid; Medicare.
Owner Proprietary corp (New Medico Associates).
Staff Physicians 2 (pt); RNs 14 (ft), 14 (pt); LPNs 11 (ft), 8 (pt); Nurses' aides 36 (ft), 17 (pt); Physical therapists 3 (ft); Recreational therapists 2 (ft); Occupational therapists 3 (ft); Speech therapists 3 (ft); Activities coordinators 2 (ft); Dietitians 1 (pt).
Languages Sign.
Facilities Dining room; Physical therapy room; Activities room; Laundry room; Barber/Beauty shop; Family visiting room; ADL kitchen; Adult head injury rehabilitation unit.
Activities Arts & crafts; Cards; Games; Reading groups; Prayer groups; Movies; Shopping trips; Dances/Social/Cultural gatherings; Intergenerational programs; Pet therapy; Exercise programs.

Northampton Nursing Home Inc
737 Bridge Rd, Northampton, MA 01060
(413) 586-3300
Admin John Mahoney.
Medical Dir Bernard St John DO.
Licensure Skilled care; Intermediate care. *Beds* SNF 41; ICF 82. *Certified* Medicaid.
Owner Proprietary corp.
Admissions Requirements Minimum age 6 months; Medical examination; Physician's request.
Staff Physicians 1 (pt); RNs 16 (ft), 15 (pt); LPNs 12 (ft), 17 (pt); Nurses' aides 20 (ft), 23 (pt); Physical therapists 3 (ft); Occupational therapists 2 (pt); Speech therapists 1 (pt); Activities coordinators 1 (ft), 1 (pt); Dietitians 1 (pt); Podiatrists 3 (pt); Dentists 1 (pt).
Facilities Dining room; Physical therapy room; Activities room; Chapel; Crafts room; Laundry room; Barber/Beauty shop; Library.
Activities Arts & crafts; Cards; Games; Reading groups; Prayer groups; Movies; Shopping trips; Dances/Social/Cultural gatherings.

Pine Rest Nursing Home
5 Franklin St, Northampton, MA 01060
(413) 584-2369
Admin Leon L Dickinson.
Medical Dir Donald B Rogers MD.
Licensure Intermediate care. *Beds* 47. *Certified* Medicaid.
Staff RNs 1 (ft); LPNs 3 (ft), 2 (pt); Nurses' aides 12 (ft), 6 (pt); Activities coordinators 1 (ft); Dietitians 1 (pt).
Facilities Dining room; Activities room; Library.
Activities Arts & crafts; Cards; Games; Reading groups; Movies; Shopping trips; Dances/Social/Cultural gatherings.

Rockridge at Laurel Park
25 Coles Meadow Rd, Northampton, MA 01060
(413) 586-2902
Admin Dorothea V Munro. *Dir of Nursing* Patricia Sokop. *Medical Dir* Dr Richard Berkman.
Licensure Rest home. *Beds* Rest home 61. *Private Pay Patients* 92%. *Certified* Medicaid.
Owner Nonprofit organization/foundation (New England Deaconess Association).
Admissions Requirements Minimum age 65; Medical examination.
Staff RNs 1 (ft), 5 (pt); LPNs 5 (pt); Nurses' aides 2 (ft), 4 (pt); Activities coordinators 1 (ft); Dietitians 1 (pt); Podiatrists 1 (pt).
Facilities Dining room; Activities room; Chapel; Crafts room; Laundry room; Barber/Beauty shop; Library; Private rooms; Nature trail.
Activities Arts & crafts; Cards; Games; Prayer groups; Movies; Shopping trips; Dances/Social/Cultural gatherings; Pet therapy.

Northborough

Grangers Nursing Home
112 W Main St, Northborough, MA 01532
(508) 393-2382
Admin Matthew Serafin RN MA LNHA. *Dir of Nursing* Pearl Gibbs RN. *Medical Dir* Christian W Aussenheimer MD.
Licensure Skilled care; Intermediate care. *Beds* SNF 14; ICF 19. *Private Pay Patients* 1%. *Certified* Medicaid.
Owner Proprietary corp.
Admissions Requirements Minimum age 16.
Staff Physicians 5 (pt); RNs 2 (ft), 4 (pt); LPNs 1 (ft), 2 (pt); Nurses' aides; Physical therapists 1 (pt); Occupational therapists 1 (pt); Speech therapists 1 (pt); Activities coordinators 1 (pt); Dietitians 1 (pt); Ophthalmologists 1 (pt); Podiatrists 1 (pt); Audiologists 1 (pt).
Languages Portuguese.
Facilities Dining room; Activities room; Laundry room; Barber/Beauty shop; Library.
Activities Arts & crafts; Cards; Games; Reading groups; Prayer groups; Movies; Shopping trips; Dances/Social/Cultural gatherings; Intergenerational programs.

Northboro Rest Home
238 W Main St, Northborough, MA 01532
(617) 393-2368
Admin Timothy J Coburn.
Licensure Rest home. *Beds* Rest home 20.
Owner Proprietary corp.

Thornton Nursing Home
238 1/2 W Main St, Northborough, MA 01532
(617) 393-2368
Admin Sylvia Riccardi.
Licensure Skilled care; Intermediate care. *Beds* SNF 42; ICF 42. *Certified* Medicaid.
Owner Proprietary corp.

Northbridge

Beaumont Nursing Home
85 Beaumont Dr, Northbridge, MA 01534
(617) 234-9771
Admin Daniel J Salmon.
Medical Dir James Kuehan MD.
Licensure Skilled care; Intermediate care. *Beds* SNF 82; ICF 60. *Certified* Medicaid; Medicare.
Owner Proprietary corp.
Staff Physicians; RNs; LPNs; Nurses' aides; Physical therapists; Recreational therapists; Occupational therapists; Speech therapists; Activities coordinators; Dietitians; Ophthalmologists; Podiatrists; Audiologists; Dentists.
Facilities Dining room; Physical therapy room; Activities room; Crafts room; Laundry room; Barber/Beauty shop; Library.

Northbridge Nursing Home
2356 Providence Rd, Northbridge, MA 01534
(508) 234-4641

Admin James M Tracy. *Dir of Nursing* Barbara C Stone. *Medical Dir* Dr Lester Mietkiewicz.
Licensure Skilled care; Intermediate care; Retirement. *Beds* SNF 58; ICF 60. *Private Pay Patients* 20%. *Certified* Medicaid; Medicare.
Owner Proprietary corp (Oakwood Living Centers).
Staff Physicians 10 (pt); RNs 5 (ft), 2 (pt); LPNs 10 (ft), 10 (pt); Nurses' aides 40 (ft), 30 (pt); Physical therapists 1 (ft), 1 (pt); Occupational therapists 1 (ft), 1 (pt); Speech therapists 1 (pt); Activities coordinators 1 (ft), 1 (pt); Dietitians 1 (pt); Ophthalmologists 1 (pt); Podiatrists 1 (pt).
Facilities Dining room; Physical therapy room; Laundry room; Barber/Beauty shop; Library; Private & semi-private rooms.
Activities Arts & crafts; Games; Reading groups; Prayer groups; Movies; Shopping trips; Dances/Social/Cultural gatherings; Intergenerational programs.

Norton

Country Haven Nursing Home
184 Mansfield Ave, Norton, MA 02766
(617) 285-7745
Admin John J Ribiero.
Licensure Skilled care; Intermediate care. *Beds* SNF 40; ICF 54. *Certified* Medicaid.
Owner Proprietary corp.

Daggett-Crandall-Newcomb Home
55 Newland St, Norton, MA 02766
(508) 285-3264, 285-7944
Admin Cheryl J Larson. *Dir of Nursing* Pauline Christie. *Medical Dir* Dr Timothy Whiting.
Licensure Retirement home. *Beds* Retirement home 30. *Private Pay Patients* 100%. *Certified* Medicare.
Owner Nonprofit organization/foundation.
Admissions Requirements Minimum age 65; Medical examination; Physician's request.
Staff Physicians 1 (ft); RNs 1 (ft), 4 (pt); LPNs 3 (pt); Nurses' aides 1 (ft), 11 (pt); Physical therapists 1 (pt); Activities coordinators 1 (ft); Dietitians 1 (pt).
Facilities Dining room; Activities room; Barber/Beauty shop.
Activities Arts & crafts; Cards; Games; Movies; Shopping trips; Pet therapy; Church service.

Old Colony Road Rest Home Inc
377 Old Colony Rd, Norton, MA 02766-2099
(508) 222-1074
Admin Robert J Devlin.
Licensure Rest home. *Beds* Rest home 50. *Private Pay Patients* 20%. *Certified* Medicaid.
Owner Proprietary corp.
Admissions Requirements Minimum age 40.
Facilities Dining room; Activities room; Crafts room; Laundry room; Barber/Beauty shop.
Activities Arts & crafts; Cards; Games; Reading groups; Prayer groups; Movies; Shopping trips; Dances/Social/Cultural gatherings; Intergenerational programs; Pet therapy.

Norwell

Norwell Knoll Nursing Home
329 Washington St, Norwell, MA 02061
(617) 659-4901
Admin Brian G Geany.
Medical Dir Dr Clifford Ward.
Licensure Skilled care; Intermediate care. *Beds* SNF 40; ICF 40. *Certified* Medicaid.
Owner Proprietary corp.
Admissions Requirements Medical examination; Physician's request.

Staff Physicians 22 (pt); RNs 7 (ft); LPNs 2 (ft); Nurses' aides 32 (ft), 6 (pt); Physical therapists 1 (pt); Recreational therapists 1 (ft); Occupational therapists 1 (pt); Speech therapists 1 (pt); Activities coordinators 1 (ft); Dietitians 1 (pt); Ophthalmologists 1 (pt); Podiatrists 1 (pt); Audiologists 1 (pt); Dentists 1 (pt).
Facilities Dining room; Physical therapy room; Activities room; Chapel; Crafts room; Laundry room; Barber/Beauty shop.
Activities Arts & crafts; Cards; Games; Reading groups; Prayer groups; Movies; Shopping trips; Dances/Social/Cultural gatherings; Fashion shows.

Stetson Manor Nursing Home
12 Barstow Ave, Norwell, MA 02061
(617) 826-2311
Admin Rena Driscoll.
Licensure Intermediate care. *Beds* ICF 20. *Certified* Medicaid.
Owner Proprietary corp.

Norwood

Charlwell House
305 Walpole St, Norwood, MA 02062
(617) 762-7700
Admin Stephen L Esdale. *Dir of Nursing* Susan Chace RN. *Medical Dir* Prya Nandi MD.
Licensure Skilled care; Intermediate care; Alzheimer's care. *Beds* SNF 41; ICF 83. *Certified* Medicaid; Medicare.
Owner Proprietary corp (Cavan Health Centers).
Staff Physicians 1 (pt); RNs 10 (ft), 15 (pt); LPNs 15 (ft), 10 (pt); Nurses' aides 60 (ft), 25 (pt); Physical therapists 1 (pt); Reality therapists 1 (pt); Recreational therapists 1 (pt); Occupational therapists 1 (pt); Speech therapists 1 (pt); Activities coordinators 3 (ft); Dietitians 1 (pt); Ophthalmologists 1 (pt); Podiatrists 1 (pt); Audiologists 1 (pt); Dentists 1 (pt).
Facilities Dining room; Physical therapy room; Activities room; Crafts room; Laundry room; Barber/Beauty shop; Library; Meeting room.
Activities Arts & crafts; Cards; Games; Reading groups; Prayer groups; Movies; Shopping trips; Dances/Social/Cultural gatherings; Intergenerational programs; Pet therapy.

Colonial Care Center A Long-Term Care Facility
460 Washington St, Norwood, MA 02062
(617) 769-2200
Admin Thomas Daley. *Dir of Nursing* F Palmieri RN. *Medical Dir* Dr P Nandi.
Licensure Skilled care; Intermediate care. *Beds* SNF 139; ICF 46. *Certified* Medicaid.
Owner Proprietary corp (Meritcare).
Staff RNs; LPNs; Nurses' aides; Physical therapists; Recreational therapists; Occupational therapists; Speech therapists; Activities coordinators; Dietitians.

Denny House Nursing Home Inc
86 Saunders Rd, Norwood, MA 02062
(617) 762-4426
Admin Maurice M Denny. *Dir of Nursing* Maureen Miller LPN.
Licensure Intermediate care. *Beds* ICF 38. *Certified* Medicaid.
Owner Proprietary corp.
Admissions Requirements Minimum age 35; Medical examination; Physician's request.
Staff LPNs 3 (ft), 3 (pt); Nurses' aides 6 (ft), 2 (pt); Activities coordinators 1 (ft); Dietitians 1 (pt); LSW 1 (pt).

Facilities Dining room; Activities room; Laundry room.
Activities Arts & crafts; Cards; Games; Reading groups; Prayer groups; Movies; Shopping trips; Dances/Social/Cultural gatherings; Shows; Singing & dancing; Guitar & accordion players.

Ellis Nursing Center
135 Ellis Ave, Norwood, MA 02062
(617) 762-6880
Admin Mark W Tobin. *Dir of Nursing* Elizabeth Goughan RN.
Licensure Skilled care; Intermediate care; Alzheimer's care. *Beds* SNF 113; ICF 78. *Certified* Medicaid; Medicare.
Owner Proprietary corp.
Admissions Requirements Minimum age 21; Physician's request.
Staff Physicians; RNs 14 (ft); LPNs 12 (ft); Nurses' aides 75 (ft); Physical therapists; Occupational therapists 1 (pt); Speech therapists; Activities coordinators 4 (ft); Dietitians.
Languages Italian, Yiddish, French, Spanish.
Facilities Dining room; Physical therapy room; Activities room; Chapel; Crafts room; Laundry room; Barber/Beauty shop; Library.
Activities Arts & crafts; Cards; Games; Reading groups; Prayer groups; Movies; Shopping trips; Dances/Social/Cultural gatherings.

Norwood Nursing Home
767 Washington St, Norwood, MA 02062
(617) 769-3704
Admin Kathleen F McKenna. *Dir of Nursing* Carol B Quinn RN. *Medical Dir* John O'Day MD; Melvin Schwartz MD.
Licensure Intermediate care. *Beds* ICF 48. *Private Pay Patients* 100%.
Owner Proprietary corp (Beverly Enterprises).
Staff RNs 4 (ft), 3 (pt); LPNs 5 (ft), 3 (pt); Nurses' aides; Activities coordinators 1 (ft); Dietitians 1 (pt).
Facilities Dining room; Activities room; Barber/Beauty shop; Library.
Activities Arts & crafts; Cards; Games; Reading groups; Movies; Shopping trips; Entertainment; Dinner parties.

Victoria Haven Nursing Facility
137 Nichols St, Norwood, MA 02062
(617) 762-0858
Admin Larry J LeBlanc.
Licensure Intermediate care. *Beds* ICF 31. *Certified* Medicaid.
Owner Proprietary corp.

Oak Bluffs

Marthas Vineyard Hospital—Skilled & Intermediate Care Facility
Linton Ln, Oak Bluffs, MA 02557
(617) 693-0410
Admin Robert L Langlois.
Licensure Skilled care; Intermediate care. *Beds* SNF 20; ICF 20. *Certified* Medicaid.
Owner Privately owned.

Orleans

Orleans Convalescent & Retirement Home
Daley Terr, Orleans, MA 02563
(617) 255-2328
Admin Peter J Meade.
Licensure Intermediate care. *Beds* ICF 50. *Certified* Medicaid.
Owner Proprietary corp.

Oxbridge

Sunnyside Rest Home
Old Millville Rd, Oxbridge, MA 01569
(617) 278-3357
Admin Dorothy F Moore.

Licensure Intermediate care for mentally retarded. *Beds* 37.

Oxford

Sandalwood Convalescent Home
3 Pine St, Oxford, MA 01540
(617) 987-8417
Admin Jill R Andring.
Licensure Skilled care; Intermediate care. *Beds* SNF 25; ICF 52. *Certified* Medicaid.
Owner Proprietary corp (First Healthcare Corp).

Palmer

Monson State Hospital
Box F, Palmer, MA 01069
(413) 283-3411
Admin Ron Rosen.
Licensure Intermediate care for mentally retarded. *Beds* 851. *Certified* Medicaid.
Owner Publicly owned.

Palmer House Healthcare Nursing Home
Shearer St, Palmer, MA 01069
(413) 283-8361
Admin Ted J Purdy.
Licensure Intermediate care. *Beds* ICF 61. *Certified* Medicaid.
Owner Proprietary corp (First Healthcare Corp).

Peabody

Farnsworth Nursing Home
28 Bowditch St, Peabody, MA 01960
(617) 532-0768
Admin Gerald Swartz.
Licensure Intermediate care. *Beds* ICF 74. *Certified* Medicaid.
Owner Proprietary corp.

Parkside Rest Home
210 Lowell St, Peabody, MA 01960-4201
(617) 388-2446
Admin William L Twomey.
Licensure Rest home. *Beds* 30.

Peabody Glen Nursing Care Center
199 Andover St, Peabody, MA 01960
(508) 531-0772
Admin Scott W Kardenetz.
Licensure Skilled care. *Beds* SNF 20.

Pilgrim Rehabilitation & Skilled Nursing Center
96 Forest St, Peabody, MA 01960-3999
(617) 884-8383, (508) 532-0303, (508) 531-6112 FAX
Admin W Bruce Glass. *Dir of Nursing* Dianne Crone. *Medical Dir* Stephen Price MD.
Licensure Skilled care. *Beds* SNF 144. *Certified* Medicaid; Medicare.
Owner Proprietary corp (Hanover Healthcare).
Staff RNs 11 (ft), 8 (pt); LPNs 15 (ft), 8 (pt); Physical therapists 2 (ft), 2 (pt); Recreational therapists 48 (ft), 46 (pt); Occupational therapists 2 (ft), 2 (pt); Speech therapists 1 (ft), 1 (pt); Activities coordinators 2 (ft), 1 (pt); Dietitians 1 (pt); Audiologists 1 (pt).
Languages Spanish, Portuguese.
Facilities Dining room; Physical therapy room; Activities room; Chapel; Crafts room; Barber/Beauty shop; Library; Enclosed courtyard.
Activities Arts & crafts; Cards; Games; Reading groups; Prayer groups; Movies; Shopping trips; Dances/Social/Cultural gatherings; Intergenerational programs; Pet therapy.

Rainbow Nursing Home
210 Lowell St, Peabody, MA 01960
(617) 531-2499
Admin Ann Azzarito. *Dir of Nursing* Gail Cochran RN.

Licensure Intermediate care. *Beds* ICF 35.
Certified Medicaid.
Owner Proprietary corp.
Admissions Requirements Minimum age 18;
Medical examination.
Staff RNs 1 (ft), 1 (pt); LPNs 3 (ft); Nurses'
aides 5 (ft); Activities coordinators 1 (pt);
Dietitians 1 (pt).
Facilities Dining room; Activities room;
Chapel; Crafts room; Laundry room.
Activities Arts & crafts; Cards; Games;
Reading groups; Prayer groups; Movies;
Shopping trips; Dances/Social/Cultural
gatherings.

Pepperell

Freeman Nursing Home
17 Main St, Pepperell, MA 01463
(508) 433-2461
Admin Esther P Elliott. *Dir of Nursing* Linda
Sheehan LPN. *Medical Dir* Wayne J Byrnes
MD.
Licensure Intermediate care. *Beds* ICF 17.
Certified Medicaid.
Owner Privately owned.
Staff RNs 2 (pt); LPNs 1 (ft), 3 (pt); Nurses'
aides 5 (ft), 6 (pt); Recreational therapists 1
(pt); Activities coordinators 1 (pt); Dietitians
1 (pt).
Activities Arts & crafts; Cards; Games;
Reading groups; Prayer groups; Movies;
Shopping trips; Dances/Social/Cultural
gatherings; Pet therapy.

Park Manor Nursing Home
13 Park St, Pepperell, MA 01463
(617) 433-2490
Admin Esther P Elliott. *Dir of Nursing* Debra
P Walsh RN.
Licensure Intermediate care. *Beds* ICF 32.
Certified Medicaid.
Owner Privately owned.
Admissions Requirements Minimum age 40;
Medical examination.
Staff RNs 1 (ft), 1 (pt); LPNs 1 (ft), 2 (pt);
Nurses' aides 8 (ft), 5 (pt); Recreational
therapists 1 (pt); Activities coordinators 1
(pt); Dietitians 1 (pt).
Facilities Dining room; Activities room;
Laundry room.
Activities Arts & crafts; Cards; Games;
Reading groups; Prayer groups; Movies;
Shopping trips; Dances/Social/Cultural
gatherings; Cookouts; Picnics; Swimming;
Hay rides; Sleigh rides.

Pittsfield

Berkshire Nursing Home Inc
360 W Housatonic St, Pittsfield, MA 01201
(413) 442-4841
Admin Michael Stroetzel.
Licensure Skilled care; Intermediate care. *Beds*
SNF 51; ICF 33. Certified Medicaid.
Owner Proprietary corp.

Berkshire Place
89 South St, Pittsfield, MA 01201
(413) 445-4056
Admin Robrt L Betit.
Licensure Intermediate care; Rest home. *Beds*
ICF 9; Rest home 29. Certified Medicaid.
Owner Nonprofit organization/foundation.
Admissions Requirements Minimum age 65;
Females only; Medical examination.
Staff RNs 8 (pt); LPNs 4 (ft); Nurses' aides 1
(ft), 4 (pt); Physical therapists 1 (pt);
Recreational therapists 1 (pt); Activities
coordinators 1 (pt); Dietitians 1 (pt);
Podiatrists 1 (pt).
Facilities Dining room; Laundry room;
Barber/Beauty shop.
Activities Arts & crafts; Cards; Games;
Shopping trips; Dances/Social/Cultural
gatherings.

Edgewood Rest Home
50 Edgewood Rd, Pittsfield, MA 01201
(413) 442-1004
Admin Dorothy E Studley.
Licensure Rest home. *Beds* 13.

Mt Greylock Extended Care Facility
North St, Pittsfield, MA 01201
(413) 499-7186
Admin Bruce Gendron.
Licensure Skilled care; Intermediate care. *Beds*
SNF 60; ICF 40.

**Springside of Pittsfield Long-Term Care
Facility**
255 Lebanon Ave, Pittsfield, MA 01201
(413) 499-2334
Admin Kathleen Nichols.
Licensure Skilled care; Intermediate care. *Beds*
SNF 40; ICF 60. Certified Medicaid.
Owner Proprietary corp.

Bertha M Young Rest Home
261 South St, Pittsfield, MA 01201
(413) 448-8801
Admin Doris T Hogan.
Licensure Rest home. *Beds* Rest home 18.
Owner Privately owned.

Plainville

Plainville Nursing Home
PO Box 1807, Plainville, MA 02762
(617) 695-1434
Admin Louis Furash. *Dir of Nursing* Jane
Sellmayer.
Licensure Intermediate care. *Beds* ICF 60.
Certified Medicaid.
Owner Proprietary corp.
Admissions Requirements Physician's request.
Staff RNs; LPNs; Nurses' aides; Activities
coordinators 1 (ft); Dietitians 1 (pt).
Facilities Dining room; Activities room;
Chapel; Crafts room; Laundry room; Barber/
Beauty shop; Library.
Activities Arts & crafts; Cards; Games;
Reading groups; Prayer groups; Movies;
Shopping trips; Dances/Social/Cultural
gatherings.

Plymouth

Beverly Manor of Plymouth Nursing Home
19 Obery St, Plymouth, MA 02360
(508) 747-4790
Admin Ira R Lipshutz.
Licensure Skilled care; Intermediate care. *Beds*
SNF 60; ICF 41.
Owner Proprietary corp (Beverly Enterprises).

**Mayflower House Nursing Home & Child Care
Center**
123 South St, Plymouth, MA 02360
(617) 746-4343
Admin Gerald Labourne. *Dir of Nursing*
Marie McDonald.
Licensure Skilled care; Intermediate care;
Child care unit. *Beds* SNF 62; ICF 62.
Certified Medicaid; Medicare.
Owner Proprietary corp (Oakwood Living
Center).
Admissions Requirements Minimum age 21;
Medical examination; Physician's request.
Staff Physicians 1 (pt); RNs 23 (ft), 5 (pt);
LPNs 10 (ft); Nurses' aides 60 (ft), 20 (pt);
Physical therapists 1 (ft), 1 (pt); Recreational
therapists 1 (ft); Occupational therapists 1
(ft), 1 (pt); Speech therapists 2 (pt);
Activities coordinators 1 (ft); Dietitians 1
(pt).
Facilities Dining room; Physical therapy
room; Activities room; Laundry room;
Barber/Beauty shop; Library.
Activities Arts & crafts; Cards; Games;
Reading groups; Prayer groups; Movies;
Shopping trips; Dances/Social/Cultural
gatherings.

Newfield House Convalescent Home
19 Newfield St, Plymouth, MA 02360
(617) 746-2912
Admin Geoffrey T Stewart. *Dir of Nursing*
Catherine D Maher RN.
Licensure Intermediate care. *Beds* ICF 100.
Owner Proprietary corp.
Facilities Dining room; Physical therapy
room; Activities room; Laundry room;
Barber/Beauty shop.
Activities Arts & crafts; Cards; Games;
Reading groups; Prayer groups; Movies;
Dances/Social/Cultural gatherings.

Pilgrim Manor
60 Stafford St, Plymouth, MA 02360
(617) 746-7016
Admin Bonnie A Burke. *Dir of Nursing*
Kalina Vendetti. *Medical Dir* John T O'Neil
MD.
Licensure Skilled care; Intermediate care. *Beds*
SNF 120; ICF 56. Certified Medicaid;
Medicare.
Owner Proprietary corp.
Staff Physicians 1 (pt); RNs 8 (ft), 9 (pt);
LPNs 5 (ft), 11 (pt); Nurses' aides 40 (ft), 49
(pt); Physical therapists 2 (pt); Recreational
therapists 2 (ft), 1 (pt); Occupational
therapists 1 (pt); Speech therapists 1 (pt);
Activities coordinators 1 (pt); Dietitians 1
(pt); Ophthalmologists 2 (pt); Dentists 1 (pt).
Facilities Dining room; Physical therapy
room; Activities room; Chapel; Crafts room;
Barber/Beauty shop; Library.
Activities Arts & crafts; Cards; Games;
Reading groups; Prayer groups; Movies;
Shopping trips; Dances/Social/Cultural
gatherings; Intergenerational programs; Pet
therapy.

Plymouth Nursing Home
35 Warren Ave, Plymouth, MA 02360
(617) 746-2085
Admin Salvatore Freddura.
Licensure Intermediate care. *Beds* ICF 37.
Certified Medicaid.
Owner Privately owned.
Admissions Requirements Minimum age 21;
Physician's request.
Staff LPNs 1 (ft), 2 (pt); Nurses' aides 6 (ft), 3
(pt); Activities coordinators 1 (ft).
Facilities Dining room; Activities room;
Laundry room.
Activities Arts & crafts; Cards; Games; Prayer
groups; Movies; Dances/Social/Cultural
gatherings; Special Olympics.

Provincetown

Cape End Manor
100 Alden St, Provincetown, MA 02657
(508) 487-0235
Admin George Spagnolia. *Dir of Nursing* Ruth
Dutra RN. *Medical Dir* Brian O'Malley MD.
Licensure Intermediate care; Alzheimer's care.
Beds ICF 57. *Private Pay Patients* 18%.
Certified Medicaid.
Owner Publicly owned.
Admissions Requirements Minimum age 21.
Staff Physicians 1 (pt); RNs 2 (ft), 3 (pt);
LPNs 3 (ft), 1 (pt); Nurses' aides 17 (ft), 10
(pt); Physical therapists 1 (pt); Recreational
therapists 1 (ft); Activities coordinators 1
(ft); Dietitians 1 (pt); Podiatrists 1 (pt).
Languages Portuguese, Spanish, French,
Italian.
Facilities Dining room; Activities room;
Crafts room; Laundry room.
Activities Arts & crafts; Cards; Games;
Reading groups; Prayer groups; Movies;
Shopping trips; Dances/Social/Cultural
gatherings; Intergenerational programs; Pet
therapy.

Quincy

John Adams Nursing Home
211 Franklin St, Quincy, MA 02169
(617) 479-0837
Admin Muriel F Finn.
Licensure Skilled care. *Beds* SNF 65. *Certified*
Medicaid.
Owner Privately owned.

Arlington Green Eldercare
210 Arlington St, Quincy, MA 02170
(617) 773-6362
Admin Vincent J Pattavina.
Licensure Intermediate care. *Beds* ICF 21.
Certified Medicaid.
Owner Proprietary corp.

Crestview Healthcare Facility
86 Greenleaf St, Quincy, MA 02169
(617) 479-2978
Admin Mark S Logan. *Dir of Nursing* Paula
DaForno. *Medical Dir* Floyd Wolff MD.
Licensure Intermediate care; Alzheimer's care.
Beds ICF 49. *Private Pay Patients* 30%.
Certified Medicaid.
Owner Proprietary corp.
Admissions Requirements Minimum age 50;
Medical examination; Physician's request.
Staff Physicians 1 (pt); RNs 2 (ft), 1 (pt);
LPNs 4 (ft), 4 (pt); Nurses' aides 10 (ft), 20
(pt); Physical therapists 1 (pt); Reality
therapists 1 (pt); Recreational therapists 1
(pt); Occupational therapists 1 (pt); Speech
therapists 1 (pt); Activities coordinators 2
(ft); Dietitians 1 (pt); Podiatrists 1 (pt).
Facilities Dining room; Activities room;
Chapel; Crafts room; Laundry room; Barber/
Beauty shop; Library.
Activities Arts & crafts; Cards; Games;
Reading groups; Prayer groups; Movies;
Shopping trips; Dances/Social/Cultural
gatherings; Intergenerational programs; Pet
therapy; Van tours.

Friel Nursing Home Inc
58 Beach St, Quincy, MA 02170
(617) 479-7722
Admin Isabel Friel.
Licensure Intermediate care. *Beds* ICF 29.

Merrymount Manor Nursing Home
38 Edgemere Rd, Quincy, MA 02169
(617) 472-1704
Admin F Roy Fitzsimmons.
Licensure Intermediate care. *Beds* ICF 23.
Certified Medicaid.
Owner Proprietary corp.
Staff RNs 1 (ft), 1 (pt); LPNs 2 (ft), 2 (pt);
Nurses' aides 4 (ft), 8 (pt); Dietitians 1 (pt).
Facilities Dining room; Laundry room;
Library.
Activities Arts & crafts; Cards; Games;
Reading groups; Movies; Shopping trips;
Dances/Social/Cultural gatherings.

Presidential Convalescent Home Inc
43 Old Colony Ave, Quincy, MA 02170
(617) 471-0155
Admin Carl A Awed.
Medical Dir Dr Joseph Carella.
Licensure Skilled care; Intermediate care. *Beds*
SNF 43; ICF 46. *Certified* Medicaid.
Owner Proprietary corp.
Staff RNs 8 (ft), 3 (pt); LPNs 3 (ft), 4 (pt);
Nurses' aides 27 (ft); Physical therapists 1
(pt); Occupational therapists 1 (pt); Speech
therapists 1 (pt); Activities coordinators 1
(ft), 1 (pt); Dietitians 1 (pt);
Ophthalmologists 1 (pt); Podiatrists 1 (pt);
Dentists 1 (pt).
Facilities Dining room; Activities room;
Crafts room; Laundry room; Barber/Beauty
shop.
Activities Arts & crafts; Cards; Games;
Reading groups; Prayer groups; Movies;
Shopping trips; Dances/Social/Cultural
gatherings.

Quincy Nursing Home
11 Thomas J McGrath Hwy, Quincy, MA
02169
(617) 479-2820
Admin Ruth A Harris.
Licensure Skilled care; Intermediate care. *Beds*
SNF 69; ICF 70. *Certified* Medicaid;
Medicare.
Owner Proprietary corp (First Healthcare
Corp).

William B Rice Eventide Home
215 Adams St, Quincy, MA 02169
(617) 472-8300
Admin Priscilla Urann.
Licensure Intermediate care. *Beds* ICF 53.
Certified Medicaid.
Owner Nonprofit corp.

Robbin House Convalescent Home
205 Elm St, Quincy, MA 02169
(617) 471-1750
Admin Timothy D Brainerd. *Dir of Nursing*
Jane Kimball.
Licensure Skilled care; Intermediate care. *Beds*
SNF 49; ICF 65. *Certified* Medicaid.
Owner Proprietary corp (First Healthcare
Corp).
Admissions Requirements Medical
examination.
Facilities Dining room; Laundry room; Patio.
Activities Arts & crafts; Cards; Games;
Reading groups; Prayer groups; Movies;
Shopping trips; Dances/Social/Cultural
gatherings; Therapeutic groups.

Randolph

Hollywell Health Care Center
975 N Main St, Randolph, MA 02368
(617) 963-8800
Admin Donald Gresh.
Licensure Skilled care; Intermediate care. *Beds*
SNF 106; ICF 33. *Certified* Medicaid;
Medicare.
Owner Privately owned.

Seth Mann Home for the Aged II
349 N Main St, Randolph, MA 02368
(617) 963-9116
Admin Evelyn McLeer.
Licensure Rest home. *Beds* Rest home 5.
Owner Proprietary corp.

Raynham Center

Taunton Female Charity Association Inc
PO Box 704, Raynham Center, MA 02768
(617) 824-7747
Admin Mary A Contreras.
Licensure Rest home. *Beds* Rest home 12.
Owner Proprietary corp.
Admissions Requirements Females only.

Reading

Daniel's House Nursing Home
59 Middlesex Ave, Reading, MA 01867
(617) 944-4410
Admin Leo R Curtin.
Licensure Intermediate care. *Beds* ICF 30.
Certified Medicaid.
Owner Proprietary corp.

Somerset Nursing Home
1364 Main St, Reading, MA 01867
(617) 942-1210
Admin Melanie Kosich.
Licensure Skilled care; Intermediate care. *Beds*
SNF 82; ICF 41.

Revere

Annmark Nursing Home
133 Salem St, Revere, MA 02151
(617) 322-4861

Admin Elena A Bean. *Dir of Nursing* Donna
M Brown RN. *Medical Dir* Haren Desai
MD.
Licensure Skilled care; Intermediate care. *Beds*
SNF 80; ICF 60. *Certified* Medicaid.
Owner Proprietary corp.
Admissions Requirements Medical
examination; Physician's request.
Staff RNs 8 (ft), 3 (pt); LPNs 11 (ft), 6 (pt);
Nurses' aides 58 (ft), 8 (pt); Physical
therapists 1 (pt); Recreational therapists 2
(ft); Occupational therapists 1 (pt); Speech
therapists 1 (pt); Activities coordinators 1
(ft); Dietitians 1 (pt); Ophthalmologists 1
(pt); Podiatrists 1 (pt); Audiologists 1 (pt);
Dentists 1 (pt).
Languages Spanish, Italian, Polish.
Facilities Dining room; Physical therapy
room; Activities room; Crafts room; Laundry
room; Barber/Beauty shop; Library;
Dayrooms; TV rooms; Conference room.
Activities Arts & crafts; Cards; Games;
Reading groups; Prayer groups; Movies;
Shopping trips; Dances/Social/Cultural
gatherings; Intergenerational programs; Pet
therapy; Monthly buffet luncheons; Birthday
parties.

AtlantiCare Nursing Home
204 Proctor Ave, Revere, MA 02151
(617) 286-3100, 286-4109 FAX
Admin Alvin Haase. *Dir of Nursing* Ken King
RN. *Medical Dir* Richard Zizza MD.
Licensure Skilled care; Intermediate care. *Beds*
SNF 82; ICF 41. *Private Pay Patients* 20%.
Certified Medicaid; Medicare.
Owner Proprietary corp.
Admissions Requirements Minimum age 40;
Medical examination; Physician's request;
Hospital referred.
Staff Physicians 7 (pt); RNs 6 (ft), 7 (pt);
LPNs 8 (ft), 7 (pt); Nurses' aides 24 (ft), 19
(pt); Physical therapists 1 (pt); Occupational
therapists 1 (pt); Activities coordinators 1
(ft); Dietitians 1 (ft); Ophthalmologists 1
(pt); Podiatrists 1 (pt); Audiologists 1 (pt).
Languages Italian.
Facilities Dining room; Physical therapy
room; Activities room; Crafts room; Laundry
room; Barber/Beauty shop; Handicapped
garden area; Private and semi-private rooms.
Activities Arts & crafts; Cards; Games;
Reading groups; Prayer groups; Movies;
Shopping trips; Dances/Social/Cultural
gatherings; Intergenerational programs; Pet
therapy.

Oak Island Skilled Nursing Center
400 Revere Beach Blvd, Revere, MA 02151
(617) 284-1958
Admin Dorothy King. *Dir of Nursing* Carol
Smith. *Medical Dir* Carl Sterpi.
Licensure Skilled care; Intermediate care. *Beds*
SNF 66; ICF 70. *Private Pay Patients* 1%.
Certified Medicaid.
Owner Proprietary corp.
Admissions Requirements Medical
examination; Physician's request.
Staff Physicians; RNs; LPNs; Nurses' aides;
Physical therapists; Reality therapists;
Recreational therapists; Occupational
therapists; Speech therapists; Activities
coordinators; Dietitians; Ophthalmologists;
Podiatrists; Audiologists.
Languages Italian, Spanish, Creole.
Facilities Dining room; Physical therapy
room; Activities room; Crafts room; Laundry
room; Barber/Beauty shop.
Activities Arts & crafts; Cards; Games;
Reading groups; Prayer groups; Movies;
Shopping trips; Dances/Social/Cultural
gatherings; Intergenerational programs; Pet
therapy.

Rockland

Del Manor Nursing Home Inc
54 Webster St, Rockland, MA 02370
(617) 871-0555
Admin Kimberly A Edmands. *Dir of Nursing*
Ann Hession RN. *Medical Dir* Brian Battista
MD.
Licensure Skilled care. *Beds* SNF 110.
Certified Medicaid.
Owner Proprietary corp.

Linden Nursing & Retirement Home
167 W Water St, Rockland, MA 02370
(617) 878-3728
Admin Arthur S Logan.
Licensure Intermediate care. *Beds* ICF 19.
Certified Medicaid.
Owner Privately owned.

South Shore Nursing Facility
115 North Ave, Rockland, MA 02370
(617) 878-3308
Admin Charles O Williams Jr. *Dir of Nursing*
Susan Keaney RN. *Medical Dir* John
Carpenter MD.
Licensure Skilled care; Intermediate care. *Beds*
SNF 40; ICF 44. *Private Pay Patients* 18%.
Certified Medicaid; Medicare.
Owner Proprietary corp.
Admissions Requirements Minimum age 55.
Staff RNs 5 (ft), 13 (pt); LPNs 2 (ft), 2 (pt);
Nurses' aides 24 (ft), 14 (pt); Physical
therapists 1 (pt); Recreational therapists 1
(ft); Occupational therapists 1 (pt); Speech
therapists 1 (pt); Activities coordinators 1
(ft); Dietitians 1 (pt); Ophthalmologists 1
(pt); Podiatrists 1 (pt); Audiologists 1 (pt).
Facilities Dining room; Physical therapy
room; Activities room; Crafts room; Laundry
room; Barber/Beauty shop; Library; Living
room with TV.
Activities Arts & crafts; Cards; Games;
Reading groups; Prayer groups; Movies;
Shopping trips; Dances/Social/Cultural
gatherings; Intergenerational programs; Pet
therapy.

Tiffany Rest & Retirement Home
5 Union St, Rockland, MA 02370
(617) 878-3757
Admin Diane B Gillis.
Licensure Rest home. *Beds* Rest home 43.
Certified Medicaid.
Owner Privately owned.
Admissions Requirements Minimum age 50.
Staff LPNs 1 (ft), 1 (pt); Nurses' aides 3 (ft), 3
(pt).
Facilities Dining room; Laundry room;
Library.
Activities Arts & crafts; Cards; Games; Prayer
groups; Movies; Shopping trips.

Tiffany II Rest Home
56 W Water St, Rockland, MA 02370
(617) 878-0676
Admin Donna M Zaccardi.
Licensure Rest home. *Beds* Rest home 16.
Owner Privately owned.

Rockport

Den-Mar Nursing Home
44 South St, Rockport, MA 01966
(508) 546-6311
Admin Michael P Takesian. *Dir of Nursing*
Dorothy Harnish. *Medical Dir* Dr John
Gale.
Licensure Skilled care; Intermediate care;
Alzheimer's care. *Beds* SNF 38; ICF 42.
Private Pay Patients 28%. Certified
Medicaid.
Owner Proprietary corp (Hillhaven Corp).
Admissions Requirements Medical
examination.

Staff RNs 4 (ft), 2 (pt); LPNs 6 (ft), 2 (pt);
Nurses' aides 12 (ft), 19 (pt); Physical
therapists 1 (pt); Occupational therapists 1
(pt); Activities coordinators 1 (ft), 1 (pt);
Dietitians 1 (ft); Podiatrists 1 (pt).
Facilities Dining room; Activities room;
Laundry room; Barber/Beauty shop.
Activities Arts & crafts; Games; Reading
groups; Prayer groups; Movies; Shopping
trips; Dances/Social/Cultural gatherings;
Cooking; Awareness & exercise group;
Manicures; Residents council; For Men Only
group.

Roslindale

Recuperative Center
1245 Centre St, Roslindale, MA 02131
(617) 325-5400
Admin Kenneth Mermer. *Dir of Nursing* M
Elizabeth Hern. *Medical Dir* Lester
Steinberg MD.
Licensure Skilled care. *Beds* SNF 81. *Private
Pay Patients* 25%. Certified Medicaid;
Medicare.
Owner Nonprofit corp.
Admissions Requirements Minimum age 21.
Staff Physicians 1 (pt); RNs 15 (ft), 10 (pt);
LPNs 2 (ft), 2 (pt); Nurses' aides 20 (ft), 20
(pt); Physical therapists 3 (ft); Recreational
therapists 1 (ft); Occupational therapists 1
(ft), 1 (pt); Speech therapists (consultant);
Activities coordinators 1 (pt); Dietitians 1
(pt); Podiatrists (consultant).
Languages Yiddish, Hebrew, Russian, Polish,
Creole.
Facilities Dining room; Physical therapy
room; Activities room; Chapel; Crafts room;
Laundry room; Barber/Beauty shop; Library.
Activities Arts & crafts; Cards; Games;
Reading groups; Prayer groups; Movies;
Intergenerational programs; Pet therapy.

Rowley

Sea View Nursing Home
76 Central St, Rowley, MA 01969
(508) 948-2552
Admin Mrs Comley. *Dir of Nursing* Mary E
Mighill RNC. *Medical Dir* Dr Sideris Baer.
Licensure Intermediate care. *Beds* ICF 61.
Private Pay Patients 50-60%. Certified
Medicaid.
Owner Proprietary corp.
Staff Physicians (consultants); RNs 3 (ft), 8
(pt); LPNs 1 (ft), 7 (pt); Nurses' aides 16
(ft), 20 (pt); Physical therapists 1 (pt);
Reality therapists 1 (pt); Recreational
therapists (consultant); Occupational
therapists (consultant); Speech therapists
(consultant); Activities coordinators 1 (ft), 1
(pt); Dietitians 1 (pt); Podiatrists 1 (pt).
Languages German, French.
Facilities Greenhouse.
Activities Arts & crafts; Cards; Games;
Reading groups; Prayer groups; Movies;
Shopping trips; Dances/Social/Cultural
gatherings; Intergenerational programs; Pet
therapy; Gardening & plant care.

Roxbury

Gardner House Rest Home
47 Centre St, Roxbury, MA 02119
(617) 445-1727
Admin Phillip P Cohen. *Dir of Nursing* Annie
Johnson. *Medical Dir* Annie Johnson.
Licensure Rest home. *Beds* Rest home 24.
Private Pay Patients 1%. Certified Medicaid;
Medicare.
Owner Nonprofit corp.
Admissions Requirements Medical
examination Geriatric.

Staff Physicians; RNs; Nurses' aides;
Occupational therapists; Activities
coordinators; Dietitians; Ophthalmologists;
Podiatrists.
Languages Greek, Spanish.
Facilities Dining room; Activities room;
Crafts room; Laundry room.
Activities Arts & crafts; Cards; Games;
Reading groups; Prayer groups; Movies;
Shopping trips; Dances/Social/Cultural
gatherings; Intergenerational programs.

Rutland

**Rutland Heights Hospital—Skilled Nursing
Facility**
86 Maple St, Rutland, MA 01543
(413) 886-4711
Admin William R Goyelte. *Dir of Nursing*
Bonnie Fauteux. *Medical Dir* Priscilla Hele
MD.
Licensure Skilled care. *Beds* SNF 36; Respite
4. Certified Medicaid; Medicare.
Owner Publicly owned.
Admissions Requirements Minimum age 16;
Physician's request.
Staff Physicians 4 (ft); RNs; Physical
therapists 1 (ft); Recreational therapists 2
(ft); Occupational therapists 1 (ft); Speech
therapists 1 (ft); Dietitians 2 (ft);
Ophthalmologists 1 (pt).
Facilities Dining room; Physical therapy
room; Activities room; Crafts room; Barber/
Beauty shop; Library.
Activities Arts & crafts; Cards; Games; Prayer
groups; Movies; Shopping trips; Dances/
Social/Cultural gatherings.

Salem

Bertran Home for Aged Men
29 Washington Sq, Salem, MA 01970
(617) 744-1002
Admin Marion T Mayer.
Licensure Rest home. *Beds* Rest home 16.
Owner Privately owned.
Admissions Requirements Males only.

Brookhouse Home for Aged Women
180 Derby St, Salem, MA 01970
(617) 744-0219
Admin William L Ives.
Licensure Rest home. *Beds* Rest home 36.
Owner Proprietary corp.

Newhall Nursing Home
7 Carpenter St, Salem, MA 01970
(617) 744-3844
Admin Gertrude Labrecque.
Licensure Intermediate care. *Beds* ICF 47.
Certified Medicaid.
Owner Proprietary corp.
Admissions Requirements Minimum age 21;
Medical examination; Physician's request.
Staff RNs 3 (pt); LPNs 4 (ft), 2 (pt); Nurses'
aides 13 (ft), 6 (pt); Activities coordinators;
Dietitians.
Facilities Dining room; Activities room.
Activities Arts & crafts; Cards; Games;
Reading groups; Prayer groups; Movies;
Shopping trips.

**Shaughnessy-Kaplan Rehabilitation Skilled
Nursing Facility**
Dove Ave, Salem, MA 01970
(617) 745-9000
Admin Frederick R Boss. *Dir of Nursing*
Linda Henlotter RN. *Medical Dir* Frederic
O Buckley Jr MD.
Licensure Skilled care. *Beds* SNF 40;
Rehabilitation 120. Certified Medicaid;
Medicare.
Owner Publicly owned.
Admissions Requirements Physician's request.

Staff Physicians; RNs; LPNs; Nurses' aides;
Physical therapists; Reality therapists;
Recreational therapists; Occupational
therapists; Speech therapists; Activities
coordinators; Dietitians.
Facilities Dining room; Physical therapy
room; Activities room; Chapel; Crafts room;
Barber/Beauty shop.
Activities Arts & crafts; Cards; Games;
Reading groups; Prayer groups; Movies;
Shopping trips; Dances/Social/Cultural
gatherings.

Salisbury

Greenleaf House Nursing Home
335 Elm St, Salisbury, MA 01952
(508) 462-3111
Admin Marcella A Costin. *Dir of Nursing*
Darlene Ryan RN. *Medical Dir* Dr Charles
Schissel.
Licensure Intermediate care. *Beds* ICF 60.
Private Pay Patients 33%. *Certified*
Medicaid.
Owner Proprietary corp.
Admissions Requirements Minimum age 21;
Medical examination; Physician's request.
Staff Physicians (consultant); RNs 3 (ft), 3
(pt); LPNs 3 (ft), 4 (pt); Nurses' aides 14
(ft), 6 (pt); Physical therapists 1 (pt);
Recreational therapists 1 (pt); Occupational
therapists (consultant); Dietitians 1 (pt);
Ophthalmologists (consultant); Podiatrists
(consultant).
Facilities Dining room; Activities room;
Crafts room; Laundry room; Barber/Beauty
shop; Library; Summer porch; Semi-private
rooms with baths.
Activities Arts & crafts; Cards; Games;
Reading groups; Prayer groups; Movies;
Shopping trips; Dances/Social/Cultural
gatherings; Pet therapy; Beauty magic;
Religious services; Van rides.

Sandisfield

New Boston Nursing Home Inc
Rte 57, Sandisfield, MA 01255
(413) 258-4731
Admin Kenneth P Lewis.
Licensure Intermediate care. *Beds* ICF 51.
Certified Medicaid.
Owner Proprietary corp.

Sandwich

Cape Heritage Nursing Home
37 Rte 6A, Sandwich, MA 02563
(508) 888-8222
Admin Keith Lombardi. *Dir of Nursing*
Virginia Robinson. *Medical Dir* Dr William
Bowers.
Licensure Skilled care; Intermediate care. *Beds*
SNF 82; ICF 41. *Private Pay Patients* 15-
20%. *Certified* Medicaid; Medicare.
Owner Proprietary corp (Oakwood Living
Centers).
Admissions Requirements Minimum age 21;
Physician's request.
Staff Physicians; RNs; LPNs; Nurses' aides;
Physical therapists; Recreational therapists;
Occupational therapists; Speech therapists;
Activities coordinators; Dietitians
(consultant); Ophthalmologists (consultant);
Podiatrists (consultant); Audiologists
(consultant).
Languages Italian, Polish, Portuguese.
Facilities Dining room; Physical therapy
room; Activities room; Chapel; Crafts room;
Laundry room; Barber/Beauty shop; Library;
Open courtyard.
Activities Arts & crafts; Cards; Games;
Reading groups; Prayer groups; Movies;
Shopping trips; Dances/Social/Cultural
gatherings; Pet therapy.

Fraser Rest Home of Sandwich
125 Old Main Rd, Sandwich, MA 02563
(617) 888-0880
Admin Charles R Fraser.
Licensure Rest home. *Beds* Rest home 20.
Owner Proprietary corp.

Saugus

Abbey Hill Nursing Home
163 Hamilton St, Saugus, MA 01906
(617) 233-2522
Admin Patrick J Fahy. *Dir of Nursing* Agnes
Wilson. *Medical Dir* Dr Margaret Simon.
Licensure Intermediate care. *Beds* ICF 30.
Private Pay Patients 25%. *Certified*
Medicaid.
Owner Proprietary corp.
Admissions Requirements Minimum age 55.
Staff RNs 3 (pt); LPNs 1 (ft), 3 (pt); Nurses'
aides 8 (ft), 10 (pt); Physical therapists 1
(pt); Activities coordinators 1 (ft); Dietitians
1 (pt); Podiatrists 1 (pt).
Facilities Dining room; Activities room;
Laundry room.
Activities Arts & crafts; Cards; Games;
Reading groups; Prayer groups; Movies;
Shopping trips; Dances/Social/Cultural
gatherings.

**Louise Caroline Rehabilitation & Nursing
Center**
266 Lincoln Ave, Saugus, MA 01906
(617) 233-6830
Admin Thomas Schroot.
Medical Dir Terrance O'Malley MD.
Licensure Skilled care; Intermediate care. *Beds*
SNF 42; ICF 38. *Certified* Medicaid;
Medicare.
Owner Proprietary corp.
Admissions Requirements Minimum age 65.
Staff Physicians 6 (pt); RNs 5 (ft), 9 (pt);
LPNs 4 (ft), 2 (pt); Nurses' aides 22 (ft), 19
(pt); Physical therapists 1 (pt); Recreational
therapists 1 (pt); Occupational therapists 1
(pt); Speech therapists 1 (pt); Activities
coordinators 1 (ft); Dietitians 2 (pt).
Facilities Dining room; Physical therapy
room; Activities room; Crafts room; Laundry
room; Barber/Beauty shop.
Activities Arts & crafts; Cards; Games;
Reading groups; Prayer groups; Movies;
Shopping trips; Restaurant outings.

North Shore Convalescent Home
73 Chestnut St, Saugus, MA 01906
(617) 233-8123
Admin Carolyn E Lassiter.
Medical Dir J Stanley Carp MD.
Licensure Skilled care; Intermediate care. *Beds*
SNF 52; ICF 52. *Certified* Medicaid.
Owner Proprietary corp (First Healthcare
Corp).
Admissions Requirements Minimum age 21.
Staff Nurses' aides 60 (ft); Physical therapists
1 (pt); Reality therapists 1 (pt); Recreational
therapists 2 (ft), 1 (pt); Occupational
therapists 1 (pt); Speech therapists 1 (pt);
Activities coordinators 1 (ft); Dietitians 1
(ft); Ophthalmologists 1 (pt); Podiatrists 1
(pt); Audiologists 1 (pt); Dentists 1 (pt).
Facilities Dining room; Physical therapy
room; Activities room; Chapel; Crafts room;
Laundry room; Barber/Beauty shop.
Activities Arts & crafts; Cards; Games;
Reading groups; Prayer groups; Movies;
Shopping trips; Dances/Social/Cultural
gatherings.

Scituate

Cardigan Nursing Home
59 Country Way, Scituate, MA 02040
(617) 545-9477
Admin John H Hilton Jr.

Licensure Intermediate care. *Beds* ICF 65.
Certified Medicaid.
Owner Proprietary corp.

Scituate Ocean Manor Nursing Home
309 Driftway, Scituate, MA 02066
(617) 545-1370
Admin Patricia M Allard.
Medical Dir Tod Forman MD.
Licensure Skilled care; Intermediate care. *Beds*
SNF 29; ICF 88. *Certified* Medicaid.
Owner Privately owned.
Staff Physicians 2 (pt); RNs 5 (ft), 12 (pt);
LPNs 6 (ft), 9 (pt); Nurses' aides 22 (ft), 53
(pt); Physical therapists 2 (ft), 1 (pt);
Recreational therapists 2 (ft); Occupational
therapists 1 (pt); Speech therapists 1 (pt);
Activities coordinators 1 (ft), 1 (pt);
Dietitians 1 (pt); Ophthalmologists 1 (pt);
Podiatrists 1 (pt); Audiologists 1 (pt);
Dentists 1 (pt).
Facilities Dining room; Physical therapy
room; Activities room; Chapel; Crafts room;
Laundry room; Barber/Beauty shop; Library.
Activities Arts & crafts; Cards; Games;
Reading groups; Prayer groups; Movies;
Shopping trips; Dances/Social/Cultural
gatherings.

Sharon

Sharon Manor Nursing Home
259 Norwood St, Sharon, MA 02067
(617) 784-6781
Admin Thomas D Ward.
Licensure Skilled care. *Beds* SNF 58. *Certified*
Medicaid; Medicare.
Owner Proprietary corp.

Shelburne Falls

Anchorage Nursing Home
Mohawk Trail, Shelburne Falls, MA 01370
(413) 625-2305
Admin Francis B Caldwell. *Dir of Nursing*
Marion Stafford.
Licensure Intermediate care. *Beds* ICF 35.
Private Pay Patients 50%.
Owner Proprietary corp.
Staff RNs 2 (ft); LPNs 5 (ft); Nurses' aides 20
(ft), 5 (pt); Activities coordinators 1 (ft);
Dietitians 1 (pt); Podiatrists 1 (pt).

La Belle's Rest Home
3 High St, Shelburne Falls, MA 01370
(413) 625-6560
Admin Patricia D Driscoll.
Licensure Rest home. *Beds* Rest home 32.
Certified Medicaid; Medicare.
Owner Privately owned.
Admissions Requirements Minimum age 18.
Staff RNs; LPNs; Nurses' aides; Activities
coordinators; Dietitians; Ophthalmologists.
Facilities Dining room; Activities room;
Laundry room.
Activities Arts & crafts; Cards; Games;
Reading groups; Prayer groups; Movies;
Shopping trips; Dances/Social/Cultural
gatherings.

Shrewsbury

Shrewsbury Nursing Home Inc
66 South St, Shrewsbury, MA 01545
(617) 845-6786
Admin Betty L Stratford.
Licensure Skilled care; Intermediate care. *Beds*
SNF 82; ICF 41. *Certified* Medicaid.
Owner Proprietary corp.

Somerset

**Clifton Geriatric Center Long-Term Care
Facility**
500 Wilbur Ave, Somerset, MA 02725
(617) 675-7589

Admin Clifton O Greenwood.
Licensure Skilled care; Intermediate care. *Beds* SNF 80; ICF 50. *Certified* Medicaid.
Owner Proprietary corp.

Somerville

Chandler Manor Rest Home
38 Chandler St, Somerville, MA 02144
(617) 666-1519
Admin Janina Elmaleh.
Licensure Rest home. *Beds* Rest home 21.
Owner Privately owned.

Clarendon Hill Nursing Home
1323 Broadway, Somerville, MA 02144
(617) 623-6700
Admin Burton F Faulkner Jr.
Licensure Intermediate care. *Beds* ICF 58.
Certified Medicaid.
Owner Proprietary corp.

Jeanne Jugan Residence
186 Highland Ave, Somerville, MA 02143
(617) 776-4420
Admin Sr Gertrude Mary Maiorino. *Dir of Nursing* Sr Claire Lynch. *Medical Dir* Dr Schaffer.
Licensure Skilled care; Intermediate care; Residential care; Retirement. *Beds* SNF 25; ICF 31; Residential care 39; Retirement 27.
Private Pay Patients 5%. *Certified* Medicaid.
Owner Nonprofit corp.
Admissions Requirements Minimum age 65.
Staff Physicians 5 (pt); RNs 5 (ft); LPNs 2 (ft); Nurses' aides 15 (ft); Physical therapists 2 (pt); Recreational therapists 2 (ft), 1 (pt); Occupational therapists 2 (pt); Dietitians 1 (pt); Ophthalmologists 1 (pt); Podiatrists 1 (pt).
Facilities Dining room; Physical therapy room; Activities room; Chapel; Crafts room; Laundry room; Barber/Beauty shop; Library.
Activities Arts & crafts; Cards; Games; Reading groups; Prayer groups; Movies; Shopping trips; Dances/Social/Cultural gatherings; Intergenerational programs; Pet therapy.

Mary Ellen Nursing Home
170 Highland Ave, Somerville, MA 02143
(617) 625-7764
Admin Martha L Ditucci.
Licensure Intermediate care. *Beds* 23.
Certified Medicaid.

Prospect Hill Manor Nursing Home
37 Munroe St, Somerville, MA 02143
(617) 666-9891
Admin Richard S Percoco. *Dir of Nursing* June Baker.
Licensure Intermediate care. *Beds* ICF 40.
Certified Medicaid.
Owner Proprietary corp.
Staff RNs; LPNs; Nurses' aides; Speech therapists; Activities coordinators; Dietitians; Ophthalmologists; Dentists.
Activities Arts & crafts; Cards; Games; Picnics.

Reagan's Resident Care Facility
174 Morrison Ave, Somerville, MA 02144
(617) 666-0380
Admin Victoria Stone. *Dir of Nursing* Dorothy Bradley.
Licensure Rest home. *Beds* Rest home 38.
Certified Medicaid; SSI.
Owner Proprietary corp.
Admissions Requirements Medical examination; Physician's request.
Staff Physicians (consultants); LPNs; Nurses' aides; Activities coordinators; Dietitians; Social workers.
Facilities Dining room; Activities room; TV rooms; Porch; Yard.
Activities Arts & crafts; Cards; Games; Prayer groups; Shopping trips.

Somerville Home for the Aged
117 Summer St, Somerville, MA 02143
(617) 776-0664
Admin Elsa E Lewis RN, Exec Dir.
Licensure Retirement home. *Beds* Retirement home 59. *Private Pay Patients* 50%. *Certified* Medicaid.
Owner Nonprofit corp.
Admissions Requirements Minimum age 65; Medical examination; Physician's request.
Staff Nurses' aides 4 (ft), 2 (pt); Dietitians 1 (pt); Podiatrists 1 (pt); Audiologists 1 (pt).
Facilities Dining room; Activities room; Chapel; Laundry room; Barber/Beauty shop; Library.
Activities Arts & crafts; Games; Reading groups; Prayer groups; Movies; Shopping trips; Dances/Social/Cultural gatherings.

Sunrise Nursing Home Inc
26 Adams St, Somerville, MA 02145
(617) 625-2233
Admin Jacob M Volensky.
Licensure Intermediate care. *Beds* ICF 40.
Certified Medicaid.
Owner Proprietary corp.

South Boston

Harbor Inn Nursing Home Inc
1380 Columbia Rd, South Boston, MA 02127
(617) 268-5450, 268-3463 FAX
Admin Lillian Ruth Talcof. *Dir of Nursing* Hinda Abrams RN. *Medical Dir* Veronica Boderick MD.
Licensure Intermediate care. *Beds* ICF 111.
Private Pay Patients 12%. *Certified* Medicaid.
Owner Proprietary corp.
Admissions Requirements Minimum age 30.
Staff RNs 3 (ft); LPNs 4 (ft), 2 (pt); Nurses' aides 23 (ft), 6 (pt); Physical therapists (contracted); Recreational therapists 1 (ft); Dietitians 1 (pt); Podiatrists 1 (pt).
Languages Polish, Italian, Yiddish, French, Lithuanian.
Facilities Dining room; Activities room; Chapel; Crafts room; Laundry room; Barber/Beauty shop; Public library distributes books & magazines.
Activities Arts & crafts; Cards; Games; Reading groups; Prayer groups; Movies; Shopping trips; Dances/Social/Cultural gatherings; Intergenerational programs; Pet therapy; Dining out.

South Dennis

Eagle Pond Nursing Home
PO Box 208, 1 Love Ln, South Dennis, MA 02660
(508) 385-6034
Admin David P Jasinski. *Dir of Nursing* Priscilla M Cabral RN. *Medical Dir* Dr Arthur F Bickford.
Licensure Skilled care; Intermediate care. *Beds* SNF 41; ICF 60. *Certified* Medicare.
Owner Proprietary corp (First Healthcare Corp).
Admissions Requirements Minimum age 18; Medical examination.
Facilities Dining room; Physical therapy room; Activities room; Laundry room; Barber/Beauty shop; Library; Ice cream parlor/Pub; Child day care; Security devices.
Activities Arts & crafts; Cards; Games; Prayer groups; Movies; Shopping trips; Dances/Social/Cultural gatherings; Intergenerational programs; Pet therapy; Current events club; Van outings.

South Hadley

Falls Nursing Home
18 Hartford St, South Hadley, MA 01075
(413) 538-8403

Admin Ann F Maher.
Licensure Intermediate care. *Beds* ICF 44.
Certified Medicaid.

Meadowood Skilled Nursing Facility & Intermediate Care Facility
573 Granby Rd, South Hadley, MA 01075
(413) 532-2200
Licensure Skilled care; Intermediate care. *Beds* SNF 40; ICF 40.

South Yarmouth

Windsor Nursing Home
265 N Main St, South Yarmouth, MA 02664
(508) 394-3514
Admin Judith A Welling. *Dir of Nursing* Diane Daley. *Medical Dir* Robert Snell MD.
Licensure Skilled care. *Beds* SNF 120.
Certified Medicaid; Medicare.
Owner Proprietary corp (Hannover Healthcare).
Admissions Requirements Minimum age 21; Physician's request.
Staff Physicians 1 (pt); RNs 3 (ft), 12 (pt); LPNs 4 (pt); Nurses' aides 16 (ft), 25 (pt); Physical therapists 1 (pt); Occupational therapists 1 (pt); Speech therapists 1 (pt); Activities coordinators 2 (ft); Dietitians 1 (pt); Podiatrists 1 (pt).
Facilities Dining room; Physical therapy room; Activities room; Chapel; Crafts room; Laundry room; Barber/Beauty shop; Adult day health.
Activities Arts & crafts; Games; Movies; Dances/Social/Cultural gatherings; Intergenerational programs; Pet therapy; Current events; Sensory.

Southbridge

Providence House Nursing Home of South Bridge
84 Chapin St, Southbridge, MA 01550
(617) 765-9133
Admin Barbara Kowalski.
Licensure Skilled care; Intermediate care. *Beds* SNF 125; ICF 101. *Certified* Medicaid.
Owner Proprietary corp.

Spencer

Lincoln Hill Manor Rest Home
53 Lincoln St, Spencer, MA 01562
(617) 885-3338
Admin Joan M Lynds.
Medical Dir Dr Richard Fowler.
Licensure Rest home. *Beds* Rest home 30.
Owner Privately owned.
Admissions Requirements Minimum age 30; Medical examination; Physician's request.
Staff Physicians 5 (ft); RNs 1 (pt); Recreational therapists 1 (ft); Dietitians 1 (pt); Podiatrists 1 (pt).
Facilities Dining room; Laundry room.
Activities Cards; Games; Reading groups; Prayer groups.

Springfield

Beech Manor Rest Home
38 Warner St, Springfield, MA 01118
(413) 733-7162
Admin Ellen N Rice. *Dir of Nursing* Nathan Rice. *Medical Dir* Nathan Rice.
Licensure Intermediate care; Intermediate care for mentally retarded. *Beds* ICF 9; ICF/MR 3. *Private Pay Patients* 30%. *Certified* Medicaid; Medicare.
Owner Privately owned (Nathan Rice).
Admissions Requirements Minimum age 45; Females only.
Staff RNs 1 (ft); Activities coordinators 1 (pt).
Languages Swedish.

Facilities Dining room; Sitting room.
Activities Arts & crafts; Cards; Games;
Reading groups; Prayer groups; Movies;
Shopping trips.

Blue Spruce Rest Home
175 Bowdoin St, Springfield, MA 01109
(413) 739-2373
Admin Nathan H Rice RN BS; Ellen N Rice
LPN. *Dir of Nursing* Nathan H Rice RN BS.
Licensure Rest home. *Beds* Rest home 19.
Private Pay Patients 0%.
Owner Proprietary corp.
Admissions Requirements Medical
examination; Physician's request.
Staff Physicians (contracted); RNs; LPNs;
Nurses' aides; Activities coordinators;
Dietitians (consultant); Podiatrists
(contracted).
Facilities Dining room; Activities room;
Laundry room; Barber/Beauty shop; Library.
Activities Arts & crafts; Games; Prayer groups;
Shopping trips; Pet therapy; Bingo.

Campbell's Ingersoll Rest Home
29 Ingersoll Grove St, Springfield, MA 01109
(413) 732-1068
Admin Collin A Campbell. *Dir of Nursing*
Marilyn Campbell.
Licensure Rest home. *Beds* Rest home 36.
Certified Medicaid.
Owner Proprietary corp.
Admissions Requirements Minimum age 50;
Medical examination.
Staff RNs; Nurses' aides; Activities
coordinators; Dietitians; Social services.
Facilities Dining room; Activities room;
Crafts room; Laundry room.
Activities Arts & crafts; Cards; Games;
Reading groups; Prayer groups; Movies.

Chapin Center Skilled Nursing Facility
200 Kendall St, Springfield, MA 01104
(413) 737-4756
Admin David E Carlson.
Medical Dir Alphonse Calvanese MD.
Licensure Skilled care; Intermediate care. *Beds*
SNF 80; ICF 80. *Certified* Medicaid.
Owner Proprietary corp (Genesis Health
Ventures).
Admissions Requirements Minimum age 55;
Medical examination; Physician's request.
Staff Physicians 13 (pt); RNs 5 (ft), 10 (pt);
LPNs 7 (ft), 8 (pt); Nurses' aides 31 (ft), 22
(pt); Physical therapists 1 (pt) Occupational
therapists 1 (pt); Speech therapists 1 (pt);
Activities coordinators 1 (ft); Dietitians 1
(pt); Ophthalmologists 1 (pt); Podiatrists 1
(pt); Dentists 1 (pt).
Facilities Dining room; Physical therapy
room; Activities room; Crafts room; Barber/
Beauty shop.
Activities Arts & crafts; Cards; Games;
Reading groups; Prayer groups; Movies;
Dances/Social/Cultural gatherings; Reality
orientation.

Chestnut Knoll Inc
471 Chestnut St, Springfield, MA 01107
(413) 732-7817
Admin Sandra Golec.
Licensure Intermediate care; Rest home. *Beds*
ICF 13; Rest home 35.
Owner Nonprofit corp.
Admissions Requirements Minimum age 65;
Medical examination.
Staff Physicians 1 (pt); RNs 1 (ft); LPNs 4
(ft); Nurses' aides 6 (ft); Activities
coordinators; Dietitians 1 (pt);
Ophthalmologists; Podiatrists.
Facilities Dining room; Activities room;
Chapel; Laundry room; Barber/Beauty shop;
Library; Private rooms.
Activities Cards; Games; Reading groups;
Movies; Shopping trips; Dances/Social/
Cultural gatherings; Gardening.

Crescent Hill Nursing Home
370 Pine St, Springfield, MA 01105
(413) 781-5290
Admin Dennis K McKenna.
Medical Dir Jack Skelskie MD.
Licensure Skilled care; Intermediate care. *Beds*
SNF 41; ICF 129. *Certified* Medicaid.
Owner Proprietary corp.
Admissions Requirements Minimum age 16.
Staff Physicians 21 (pt); RNs 6 (ft), 2 (pt);
LPNs 8 (ft), 8 (pt); Nurses' aides 24 (ft), 27
(pt); Physical therapists 2 (ft), 1 (pt); Reality
therapists 1 (ft), 1 (pt); Occupational
therapists 1 (pt); Speech therapists 1 (pt);
Activities coordinators 2 (ft); Dietitians 1
(pt); Ophthalmologists 1 (pt); Podiatrists 1
(pt); Audiologists 1 (pt); Dentists 1 (pt).
Facilities Dining room; Physical therapy
room; Activities room; Crafts room; Laundry
room; Barber/Beauty shop.
Activities Arts & crafts; Cards; Games;
Reading groups; Prayer groups; Movies;
Shopping trips; Dances/Social/Cultural
gatherings.

Evergreen Place A Rest Home
PO Box 80871, Springfield, MA 01138-0971
(413) 737-5964
Admin Warren C Laborde. *Dir of Nursing*
Shirley J Laborde.
Licensure Rest home. *Beds* Rest home 18.
Certified Medicaid.
Owner Privately owned.
Admissions Requirements Minimum age 21;
Medical examination; Physician's request.
Staff RNs.
Facilities Dining room; Activities room;
Crafts room; Laundry room; Barber/Beauty
shop.
Activities Arts & crafts; Cards; Games; Prayer
groups; Shopping trips.

Hahn Rest Home
178 Thompson St, Springfield, MA 01109
(413) 737-5124
Admin Kathleen M Hahn.
Licensure Rest home. *Beds* 13.

Hampden House Retirement Home
190 Kendall St, Springfield, MA 01104
(413) 733-6617
Admin Bestey Brooks. *Dir of Nursing*
Alphonse Calvanese.
Licensure Rest home. *Beds* Rest home 160.
Owner Proprietary corp (Genesis Health
Ventures).
Admissions Requirements Minimum age 50;
Medical examination.
Staff LPNs 3 (ft), 2 (pt); Nurses' aides 9 (ft), 1
(pt); Activities coordinators 1 (ft); Dietitians
1 (ft).
Facilities Dining room; Activities room;
Laundry room; Barber/Beauty shop.
Activities Arts & crafts; Games; Reading
groups; Prayer groups; Movies; Shopping
trips; Dances/Social/Cultural gatherings.

Hilltop Rest Home
103 Bowdoin St, Springfield, MA 01109
(413) 739-6377
Admin Edith Gibby.
Licensure Rest home. *Beds* Rest home 19.
Owner Proprietary corp.

Hurstdale Rest Home
181 Acorn St, Springfield, MA 01109
(413) 734-0177
Admin M Z Barksdale.
Medical Dir Dr Jack Skelskie.
Licensure Rest home. *Beds* Rest home 15.
Owner Privately owned.
Admissions Requirements Minimum age 21;
Medical examination; Physician's request.
Staff Physicians 1 (pt); RNs 1 (pt); LPNs 2
(pt); Nurses' aides 2 (pt); Recreational
therapists 1 (pt); Occupational therapists 1
(pt); Activities coordinators 1 (pt); Dietitians
1 (pt); Podiatrists 1 (pt).

Affiliation Afro-American.
Facilities Dining room; Activities room;
Crafts room; Laundry room; Library.
Activities Arts & crafts; Cards; Games;
Reading groups; Prayer groups; Shopping
trips; Dances/Social/Cultural gatherings.

Maple Hill Rest Home
156 Mill St, Springfield, MA 01108
(413) 737-2148
Admin Michael H Joseph.
Licensure Rest home. *Beds* Rest home 32.
Owner Proprietary corp.

Pine Manor Nursing Home
1190 Liberty St, Springfield, MA 01104
(413) 781-0831
Admin Joseph P Kennedy Jr.
Licensure Intermediate care. *Beds* ICF 101.
Certified Medicaid.
Owner Proprietary corp.
Admissions Requirements Minimum age 21;
Medical examination.
Facilities Dining room; Activities room;
Laundry room; Barber/Beauty shop.
Activities Arts & crafts; Cards; Games;
Movies; Shopping trips; Dances/Social/
Cultural gatherings.

Primus Mason Manor Rest Home
74 Walnut St, Springfield, MA 01105
(413) 733-1571
Admin Elizabeth L Hogan.
Licensure Rest home. *Beds* Rest home 20.
Owner Proprietary corp.
Admissions Requirements Minimum age 60;
Medical examination; Physician's request.
Staff Physicians 1 (pt); LPNs 1 (pt); Nurses'
aides 2 (pt); Activities coordinators 1 (pt);
Dietitians 1 (pt); Ophthalmologists 1 (pt);
Podiatrists 1 (pt); Dentists.
Facilities Dining room; Activities room;
Laundry room; Barber/Beauty shop; Library.
Activities Arts & crafts; Cards; Games;
Movies; Shopping trips; Dances/Social/
Cultural gatherings.

Ring Nursing Home East
215 Bicentennial Hwy, Springfield, MA 01118
(413) 734-1133
Admin James T Clifford.
Licensure Skilled care. *Beds* SNF 20.

Ring Nursing Home—Ridgewood
22 Ridgewood Pl, Springfield, MA 01105
(413) 734-1111
Admin Matthew J Leahey.
Licensure Intermediate care. *Beds* ICF 126.
Certified Medicaid.
Owner Proprietary corp.
Staff RNs 1 (ft), 1 (pt); LPNs 7 (ft), 7 (pt);
Nurses' aides 25 (ft), 18 (pt); Activities
coordinators 1 (ft), 1 (pt); Dietitians 1 (pt).
Facilities Dining room; Physical therapy
room; Activities room; Chapel; Laundry
room; Barber/Beauty shop.
Activities Arts & crafts; Cards; Games;
Reading groups; Prayer groups; Movies;
Dances/Social/Cultural gatherings.

Ring Nursing Home—South
155 Mill St, Springfield, MA 01105
(413) 734-1122, 731-7642 FAX
Admin Jean Clifford RN NHA. *Dir of Nursing*
Lois A Madden RN NP. *Medical Dir* Jay
Ungar MD.
Licensure Skilled care; Intermediate care. *Beds*
SNF 38; ICF 72. *Private Pay Patients* 30%.
Certified Medicaid.
Owner Proprietary corp (Morril Stone Ring).
Admissions Requirements Medical
examination; Physician's request.
Staff Physicians 1 (pt); RNs 6 (ft), 2 (pt);
LPNs 5 (ft), 2 (pt); Nurses' aides 28 (ft), 30
(pt); Physical therapists 1 (pt); Reality
therapists 1 (ft); Recreational therapists 1
(ft); Occupational therapists 1 (pt); Activities
coordinators 1 (ft); Dietitians 1 (pt).
Languages French, Italian, Spanish, Chinese.

Facilities Dining room; Physical therapy room; Activities room; Crafts room; Laundry room; Barber/Beauty shop; Library; Child day care.
Activities Arts & crafts; Cards; Games; Reading groups; Prayer groups; Movies; Shopping trips; Dances/Social/Cultural gatherings; Intergenerational programs; Art/ Ceramics classes.

Springfield Municipal Hospital
1400 State St, Springfield, MA 01109
(413) 787-6700
Admin George H Lane.
Licensure Skilled care; Intermediate care. *Beds* 438. *Certified* Medicaid.
Admissions Requirements Medical examination; Physician's request.
Facilities Dining room; Physical therapy room; Activities room; Chapel; Crafts room; Laundry room; Barber/Beauty shop; Library.
Activities Arts & crafts; Cards; Games; Prayer groups; Movies; Shopping trips; Dances/ Social/Cultural gatherings.

Spruce Manor Nursing Home
388 Central St, Springfield, MA 01105
(413) 734-4986
Admin Myrna E Wynn.
Licensure Intermediate care. *Beds* ICF 150. *Certified* Medicaid.
Owner Proprietary corp.

Stone Acre Rest Home Inc
120 Mill St, Springfield, MA 01108
(413) 734-3054
Admin Conrad E Wertheim.
Licensure Rest home. *Beds* 26.
Admissions Requirements Minimum age 21; Medical examination.
Staff Physicians 1 (pt); LPNs 1 (ft); Nurses' aides 3 (ft), 1 (pt); Activities coordinators 1 (pt); Dietitians 1 (pt).
Facilities Dining room; Activities room; Crafts room; Laundry room; Barber/Beauty shop.
Activities Cards; Games; Movies; Shopping trips.

Stoneham

Arnold House Incorporated
490 William St, Stoneham, MA 02180
(617) 438-1116
Admin Loretta Marino.
Licensure Intermediate care. *Beds* ICF 22. *Private Pay Patients* 100%.
Owner Proprietary corp.
Staff RNs 1 (ft), 6 (pt); LPNs 2 (ft), 3 (pt); Nurses' aides 3 (ft), 8 (pt); Activities coordinators 2 (pt); Dietitians 1 (pt).
Facilities Dining room; Activities room; Crafts room; Laundry room; Barber/Beauty shop; Library.
Activities Arts & crafts; Cards; Games; Reading groups; Prayer groups; Movies; Shopping trips; Dances/Social/Cultural gatherings; Intergenerational programs; Pet therapy.

Bear Hill Nursing Center at Wakefield
Enter 11 North St, Stoneham, MA 02180
(617) 438-8515
Admin George W Seabrook.
Medical Dir John Danis MD.
Licensure Skilled care; Intermediate care. *Beds* SNF 84; ICF 41.
Owner Proprietary corp.
Admissions Requirements Minimum age 21; Physician's request.
Staff Physicians; RNs 10 (ft); LPNs 10 (ft); Nurses' aides 30 (ft); Physical therapists 1 (pt); Reality therapists 1 (pt); Recreational therapists 2 (ft); Occupational therapists 1 (pt); Speech therapists 1 (pt); Activities coordinators 1 (ft); Dietitians 1 (pt); Ophthalmologists 1 (pt); Podiatrists 1 (pt); Audiologists 1 (pt); Dentists 1 (pt).

Facilities Dining room; Physical therapy room; Activities room; Chapel; Crafts room; Laundry room; Barber/Beauty shop; Library; Pub; Greenhouse; Cinema.
Activities Arts & crafts; Cards; Games; Reading groups; Prayer groups; Movies; Shopping trips; Dances/Social/Cultural gatherings.

Fuller House
32 Franklin St, Stoneham, MA 02180
(617) 438-0580
Admin Janet Theriault. *Dir of Nursing* Karen Sherry RN. *Medical Dir* Dr Clara Lennox.
Licensure Rest home. *Beds* Rest home 12. *Certified* Medicare.
Owner Proprietary corp.
Admissions Requirements Minimum age 65; Females only; Medical examination; Physician's request.
Staff Physicians 1 (pt); RNs 1 (pt); Dietitians 1 (pt); Podiatrists 1 (pt).
Facilities Dining room; Activities room; Laundry room; Library.
Activities Reading groups; Shopping trips; Intergenerational programs.

Sunshine Nursing Home
12 Benton St, Stoneham, MA 02180
(617) 438-9305
Admin Lillian I Price. *Dir of Nursing* Ellen Lomastro. *Medical Dir* Dr Francis Hinnendoel.
Licensure Intermediate care. *Beds* ICF 36. *Private Pay Patients* 33%. *Certified* Medicaid.
Owner Proprietary corp.
Admissions Requirements Minimum age 18; Medical examination; Physician's request.
Staff RNs 3 (ft), 1 (pt); LPNs 2 (ft), 3 (pt); Nurses' aides 6 (ft), 12 (pt); Physical therapists (consultant); Occupational therapists (consultant); Speech therapists (consultant); Activities coordinators 1 (ft); Dietitians; Podiatrists (consultant); Audiologists (consultant).
Facilities Dining room; Activities room; Crafts room; Laundry room; Barber/Beauty shop.
Activities Arts & crafts; Cards; Games; Reading groups; Prayer groups; Movies; Shopping trips; Intergenerational programs.

Stoughton

Blue Hills Convalescent Home
1044 Park St, Stoughton, MA 02072
(617) 344-7300
Admin Judith D Cunningham. *Dir of Nursing* Barbara Despres RN. *Medical Dir* Dr Peter Roos.
Licensure Skilled care; Intermediate care. *Beds* SNF 41; ICF 60. *Certified* Medicaid.
Owner Proprietary corp (Hillhaven Corp).
Admissions Requirements Minimum age 21.
Staff RNs; LPNs; Nurses' aides; Physical therapists; Recreational therapists; Occupational therapists; Speech therapists; Activities coordinators; Dietitians; Ophthalmologists; Podiatrists; Audiologists.
Facilities Dining room; Activities room; Laundry room; Barber/Beauty shop.
Activities Arts & crafts; Cards; Games; Reading groups; Prayer groups; Movies; Shopping trips; Dances/Social/Cultural gatherings; Intergenerational programs; Pet therapy.

Norfolk Nursing Home
94 Prospect St, Stoughton, MA 02072
(617) 344-3645
Admin Catherine Warner.
Licensure Intermediate care. *Beds* ICF 59. *Certified* Medicaid.
Owner Proprietary corp.

Weekes Rest Home Inc
239 Pleasant St, Stoughton, MA 02072
(617) 344-2451
Admin Bernice Weekes. *Dir of Nursing* Ellie Berkowitz. *Medical Dir* Dr Vina Joshi.
Licensure Rest home. *Beds* Rest home 20. *Certified* Medicaid; Medicare.
Owner Proprietary corp.
Admissions Requirements Medical examination.
Staff Physicians; RNs; LPNs; Nurses' aides; Activities coordinators; Dietitians; Ophthalmologists; Podiatrists; Audiologists.
Facilities Dining room; Activities room; Laundry room.
Activities Arts & crafts; Cards; Games; Reading groups; Prayer groups; Movies; Shopping trips; Dances/Social/Cultural gatherings; Intergenerational programs; Pet therapy.

Stow

Stow Rest Home
Wheeler Rd, Stow, MA 01775
(617) 897-7923
Admin Charles L Alves.
Licensure Rest home. *Beds* Rest home 18.
Owner Privately owned.

Whitney Homestead Rest Home
Great Rd, Stow, MA 01775
(617) 756-1515
Admin Bonnie Fredette.
Licensure Rest home. *Beds* Rest home 25.
Owner Proprietary corp.

Sudbury

Sudbury Pines Nursing Home
642 Boston Post Rd, Sudbury, MA 01776
(508) 443-9000
Admin Roberta C Henderson. *Dir of Nursing* Ellen Pennington RN. *Medical Dir* Dr Melvyn Kramer.
Licensure Skilled care; Intermediate care; Respite care; Alzheimer's care. *Beds* SNF 39; ICF 43. *Private Pay Patients* 100%.
Owner Proprietary corp.
Admissions Requirements Minimum age 21.
Staff Physicians 1 (pt); RNs 7 (ft), 3 (pt); LPNs 5 (ft), 3 (pt); Nurses' aides 31 (ft), 20 (pt); Physical therapists 1 (pt); Reality therapists 1 (pt); Recreational therapists 1 (pt); Occupational therapists 1 (pt); Activities coordinators 1 (ft), 2 (pt); Dietitians 1 (pt); Podiatrists 1 (pt).
Languages French, Italian, Spanish, Portuguese, Hebrew, Sign.
Facilities Dining room; Activities room; Crafts room; Laundry room; Barber/Beauty shop; Wanderer security system; IV therapy; Respite care; Child day care.
Activities Arts & crafts; Cards; Games; Reading groups; Prayer groups; Movies; Shopping trips; Dances/Social/Cultural gatherings; Intergenerational programs; Pet therapy; Resident council; Monthly newspaper; Current events; Baking; Reality orientation; 24-hr family visitation; Feeding improvement program.

Sunderland

Cozy Corner Nursing Home Inc
PO Box 405, Old Amherst Rd, Sunderland, MA 01375
(413) 665-2740
Admin I James Bednarski III.
Medical Dir Samuel Hunter MD.
Licensure Intermediate care. *Beds* ICF 57. *Certified* Medicaid.
Owner Proprietary corp.
Admissions Requirements Minimum age 21; Medical examination.

Staff Physicians 14 (pt); RNs 4 (ft), 3 (pt); LPNs 1 (ft), 1 (pt); Nurses' aides 12 (ft), 8 (pt); Physical therapists 1 (pt); Recreational therapists 1 (pt); Occupational therapists 1 (pt); Speech therapists 1 (pt); Activities coordinators 1 (ft); Dietitians 1 (pt); Podiatrists 1 (pt); Dentists 1 (pt).
Facilities Dining room; Activities room; Chapel; Crafts room; Laundry room; Barber/Beauty shop.
Activities Arts & crafts; Cards; Games; Reading groups; Prayer groups; Movies; Shopping trips.

Swampscott

Jewish Rehabilitation Center for Aged of the North Shore Inc
330 Paradise Rd, Swampscott, MA 01907
(617) 598-5310
Admin Greg Acqua. Dir of Nursing Carolann Crowe. Medical Dir David Levy MD.
Licensure Skilled care; Intermediate care; Alzheimer's care. Beds SNF 84; ICF 87. Certified Medicaid.
Owner Nonprofit organization/foundation.
Admissions Requirements Minimum age 65; Medical examination; Physician's request.
Staff Physicians 1 (pt); RNs 12 (ft), 6 (pt); LPNs 7 (ft), 9 (pt); Nurses' aides 58 (ft), 15 (pt); Physical therapists 1 (pt); Recreational therapists 3 (ft), 2 (pt); Occupational therapists 1 (pt); Speech therapists 1 (pt); Activities coordinators 1 (ft); Dietitians 1 (ft); Ophthalmologists 1 (pt); Podiatrists 1 (pt); Dentists 1 (pt).
Affiliation Jewish.
Facilities Dining room; Physical therapy room; Activities room; Chapel; Crafts room; Laundry room; Barber/Beauty shop; Library.
Activities Arts & crafts; Cards; Games; Reading groups; Prayer groups; Movies.

Swansea

Country Gardens Nursing Home
2045 Grand Army Hwy, Swansea, MA 02777
(617) 379-9700
Admin Elizabeth Wood. Dir of Nursing Elaine A Downs RN. Medical Dir Dr Daniel Sullivan.
Licensure Skilled care. Beds SNF 86. Certified Medicaid; Medicare.
Owner Proprietary corp (First Healthcare Corp).
Languages Portuguese.
Facilities Dining room; Physical therapy room; Activities room; Chapel; Laundry room; Barber/Beauty shop.
Activities Arts & crafts; Cards; Games; Reading groups; Prayer groups; Movies; Dances/Social/Cultural gatherings; Outings.

Gardner's Grove Nursing Home
924 Gardner's Neck Rd, Swansea, MA 02777
(508) 674-1717
Admin Burton K Lipsky.
Licensure Intermediate care. Beds ICF 27. Certified Medicaid.
Owner Proprietary corp.

Taunton

Paul A Dever State School
PO Box 4003, 1380 Bay St, Taunton, MA 02780
(508) 824-5881
Licensure Skilled care. Beds 20.
Owner Publicly owned.

Hartshorn House Retirement Home
68 Dean St, Taunton, MA 02780
(617) 822-0070
Admin Susan C Burnett.
Licensure Rest home. Beds Rest home 51.

Longmeadow of Taunton A Skilled Nursing Facility
68 Dean St, Rear, Taunton, MA 02780
(508) 824-1467
Admin Susan M Corman.
Licensure Skilled care; Intermediate care. Beds SNF 40; ICF 60. Certified Medicaid.
Owner Privately owned.

Marian Manor of Taunton
33 Summer St, Taunton, MA 02780
(617) 822-4885
Admin Thomas F Healy.
Licensure Skilled care; Intermediate care. Beds SNF 75; ICF 41. Certified Medicaid.
Owner Proprietary corp.

Taunton Nursing Home
350 Norton Ave, Taunton, MA 02780
(617) 822-6404
Admin Peter F Tardo.
Licensure Intermediate care; Rest home. Beds ICF 20; 19. Certified Medicaid.
Owner Publicly owned.

Wedgemere Convalescent Home
146 Dean St, Taunton, MA 02780
(617) 823-0767
Admin Ruth A Vital. Dir of Nursing Mary Hennique RN. Medical Dir David Pottier MD.
Licensure Skilled care. Beds SNF 82. Certified Medicaid; Medicare.
Owner Proprietary corp (Beverly Enterprises).
Admissions Requirements Minimum age 21.
Staff RNs 5 (ft); LPNs 8 (ft), 4 (pt); Nurses' aides 20 (ft), 16 (pt); Recreational therapists 1 (ft); Dietitians 2 (pt).
Facilities Dining room; Physical therapy room; Activities room; Crafts room; Laundry room; Barber/Beauty shop; Library.
Activities Arts & crafts; Cards; Games; Reading groups; Prayer groups; Movies; Shopping trips; Dances/Social/Cultural gatherings; Pet visits.

Templeton

Baldwinville Nursing Home
Hospital Rd, Baldwinville, Templeton, MA 01436
(617) 939-2196
Admin Leighton S Cheney.
Licensure Skilled care; Intermediate care. Beds SNF 41; ICF 41. Certified Medicaid.
Owner Proprietary corp.

Tewksbury

Blaire House Long-Term Care Facility Tewksbury
10 Erlin Terr, Tewksbury, MA 01876
(617) 851-3121
Admin Karol A Vitale.
Licensure Skilled care; Intermediate care. Beds SNF 81; ICF 43. Certified Medicaid; Medicare.
Owner Proprietary corp.

Upton

Knowlton Manor Nursing Home
145 Main St, Box 453, Upton, MA 01587
(508) 529-6983
Admin Anthony D'Amore. Dir of Nursing Francis O'Bara RN. Medical Dir Dr Aussenheimer.
Licensure Intermediate care. Beds ICF 37. Private Pay Patients 16%. Certified Medicaid.
Owner Privately owned.
Admissions Requirements Minimum age 50; Females only; Medical examination; Physician's request.

Staff RNs 2 (ft), 2 (pt); LPNs 1 (ft), 3 (pt); Nurses' aides 7 (ft), 10 (pt); Recreational therapists 1 (pt); Activities coordinators 1 (pt); Dietitians 1 (pt).
Facilities Dining room; Activities room; Laundry room; Barber/Beauty shop.
Activities Arts & crafts; Cards; Games; Reading groups; Prayer groups; Movies; Shopping trips; Pet therapy.

Waban

Braeburn Nursing Home
20 Kinmonth Rd, Waban, MA 02168
(617) 332-8481
Admin Peter H DiFoggio. Dir of Nursing Roberta S Golledge.
Licensure Intermediate care. Beds ICF 84. Certified Medicaid.
Owner Proprietary corp.
Admissions Requirements Minimum age 40; Medical examination.
Staff RNs 7 (ft), 3 (pt); LPNs 1 (pt); Nurses' aides 27 (ft), 4 (pt); Activities coordinators 1 (ft); Dentists 1 (pt).
Languages Italian, Spanish, French.
Facilities Dining room; Physical therapy room; Activities room; Chapel; Crafts room; Laundry room; Barber/Beauty shop; Library.
Activities Arts & crafts; Cards; Games; Reading groups; Prayer groups; Movies; Shopping trips; Dances/Social/Cultural gatherings.

Wakefield

Greenview Manor Nursing Home
Bathol St, Wakefield, MA 01880
(617) 245-7600, 245-2238 FAX
Admin Judith J Gordon. Dir of Nursing Norene Gachignard RN. Medical Dir Alexander Latty MD.
Licensure Skilled care; Intermediate care. Beds SNF 48; ICF 60. Private Pay Patients 25%. Certified Medicaid.
Owner Proprietary corp (Winthrop Realty Trust).
Admissions Requirements Minimum age 60; Medical examination; Physician's request.
Staff Physicians 22 (pt); RNs 7 (ft), 3 (pt); LPNs 5 (ft), 8 (pt); Nurses' aides 28 (ft), 22 (pt); Physical therapists 1 (pt); Recreational therapists 2 (pt); Occupational therapists 1 (pt); Speech therapists; Activities coordinators 1 (ft); Dietitians 1 (pt); Ophthalmologists 4 (pt); Podiatrists 5 (pt).
Facilities Dining room; Physical therapy room; Activities room; Laundry room; Barber/Beauty shop; Wander security system.
Activities Arts & crafts; Games; Reading groups; Prayer groups; Movies; Shopping trips; Dances/Social/Cultural gatherings; Intergenerational programs; Pet therapy.

Greenwood Nursing Home
90 Greenwood St, Wakefield, MA 01880
(617) 246-0211
Admin Merna E Morse. Dir of Nursing Claire Carter. Medical Dir Dr John Kidd.
Licensure Intermediate care. Beds ICF 36. Certified Medicaid.
Owner Proprietary corp.
Admissions Requirements Medical examination.
Staff RNs; LPNs; Nurses' aides; Recreational therapists; Dietitians.
Facilities Dining room; Activities room.
Activities Arts & crafts; Cards; Games; Reading groups; Movies; Dances/Social/Cultural gatherings; Pet therapy.

Kirkwood Nursing Home
202 Main St, Wakefield, MA 01880
(617) 245-4129
Admin Bettiann Wells.

Licensure Intermediate care. *Beds* ICF 32.
Certified Medicaid.
Owner Proprietary corp.

Oosterman's Rest Home
706 Main St, Wakefield, MA 01880
(617) 245-4778
Admin Troy P Oosterman. *Dir of Nursing*
Gladys Foster RN.
Licensure Rest home. *Beds* Rest home 19.
Owner Proprietary corp.
Admissions Requirements Females only;
Physician's request.
Staff RNs 1 (ft); LPNs 2 (ft); Nurses' aides 6
(ft); Activities coordinators 1 (ft); Dietitians
1 (ft); Ophthalmologists 1 (ft).
Facilities Dining room; Activities room;
Laundry room.
Activities Cards; Prayer groups; Movies;
Exercise.

Wallaston

Friel Nursing Home Inc
58 Beach St, Wallaston, MA 02170
(617) 479-7722
Admin Isabel Friel RN. *Dir of Nursing* Isabel
Friel RN.
Licensure Intermediate care. *Beds* ICF 29.
Certified Medicaid.
Owner Proprietary corp.
Admissions Requirements Females only;
Medical examination.
Staff Physicians 1 (pt); RNs 1 (ft), 3 (pt);
LPNs 1 (ft), 2 (pt); Nurses' aides 5 (ft), 10
(pt); Physical therapists 1 (pt); Reality
therapists 1 (pt); Recreational therapists 1
(ft); Activities coordinators 1 (ft); Dietitians
1 (pt).
Facilities Dining room; Laundry room.
Activities Arts & crafts; Cards; Games;
Reading groups; Prayer groups; Movies;
Shopping trips; Dances/Social/Cultural
gatherings; Entertainment; Parties.

Waltham

Abbey Forest Nursing Home
50 Forest St, Waltham, MA 02154
(617) 893-3453
Admin Patrick J Fahy.
Licensure Intermediate care. *Beds* ICF 37.
Certified Medicaid.
Owner Privately owned.

Hopkins Nursing Home Inc
508 Lexington St, Waltham, MA 02154
(617) 893-7841
Admin Paul G Hopkins.
Licensure Intermediate care. *Beds* ICF 19.
Certified Medicaid.
Owner Proprietary corp.

Larchwood Lodge Nursing Home Inc
221 Worcester Ln, Waltham, MA 02154
(617) 894-4720
Admin G Paul Hopkins.
Licensure Intermediate care. *Beds* ICF 32.
Certified Medicaid.
Owner Proprietary corp.

Lee Rest Home
222 Bacon St, Waltham, MA 02154
(617) 894-0645
Admin William F Lee.
Licensure Rest home. *Beds* Rest home 27.
Owner Proprietary corp.

Leland Home
21 Newton St, Waltham, MA 02154
(617) 893-2557
Admin Joan Turner.
Medical Dir David Duhme MD.
Licensure Intermediate care; Rest home. *Beds*
ICF 8; Rest home 33. *Certified* Medicare.
Owner Nonprofit corp.
Admissions Requirements Minimum age 65;
Medical examination; Physician's request.

Staff Physicians 32 (pt); RNs 1 (ft), 32 (pt);
LPNs 1 (ft), 32 (pt); Nurses' aides 1 (ft), 32
(pt); Physical therapists 32 (pt); Reality
therapists 32 (pt); Dentists 1 (pt).
Facilities Dining room; Laundry room;
Barber/Beauty shop; Library; Library
services.
Activities Cards; Games; Dances/Social/
Cultural gatherings.

Maristhill Nursing Home
66 Newton St, Waltham, MA 02154
(617) 893-0240
Admin Janet C Murphy. *Dir of Nursing* Jackie
Wojciechowski. *Medical Dir* Dr Joseph
Riley.
Licensure Skilled care; Intermediate care;
Alzheimer's care. *Beds* SNF 82; ICF 41.
Certified Medicaid.
Owner Nonprofit corp.
Admissions Requirements Minimum age 60;
Medical examination.
Staff Physicians; RNs; LPNs; Nurses' aides;
Physical therapists; Occupational therapists;
Speech therapists; Activities coordinators;
Dietitians; Ophthalmologists; Podiatrists;
Audiologists; COTAs.
Affiliation Roman Catholic.
Facilities Dining room; Physical therapy
room; Activities room; Chapel; Crafts room;
Laundry room; Barber/Beauty shop; Library;
Visiting rooms.
Activities Arts & crafts; Cards; Games;
Reading groups; Prayer groups; Movies;
Shopping trips; Dances/Social/Cultural
gatherings; Intergenerational programs; Pet
therapy; Theatre; Happy hour.

Meadow Green Nursing Center
45 Woburn St, Waltham, MA 02154
(617) 899-8600, 899-3124 FAX
Admin David L Bell. *Dir of Nursing* Ellen
Batting RN. *Medical Dir* Gerald Harris MD.
Licensure Skilled care; Intermediate care. *Beds*
SNF 82; ICF 41. *Private Pay Patients* 55%.
Certified Medicaid.
Owner Privately owned.
Staff RNs 10 (ft), 4 (pt); LPNs 15 (ft), 5 (pt);
Nurses' aides 40 (ft), 20 (pt); Physical
therapists 2 (ft); Recreational therapists 2
(ft); Occupational therapists 1 (pt); Speech
therapists 1 (pt); Activities coordinators 1
(ft); Dietitians 1 (pt); Podiatrists 1 (pt);
Audiologists 1 (pt).
Facilities Dining room; Physical therapy
room; Activities room; Chapel; Barber/
Beauty shop; Library; Gift shop.
Activities Arts & crafts; Cards; Games;
Reading groups; Prayer groups; Movies;
Shopping trips; Pet therapy.

Piety Corner Nursing Home
325 Bacon St, Waltham, MA 02154
(617) 894-5264
Admin Guy D'Amore.
Licensure Intermediate care. *Beds* ICF 34.
Certified Medicaid.
Owner Privately owned.

Prospect Hill Nursing Home
31 Woodland Rd, Waltham, MA 02154
(617) 893-6916
Admin Vasco A Lima Jr.
Medical Dir Albert Levinson.
Licensure Intermediate care. *Beds* ICF 28.
Certified Medicaid; Medicare.
Owner Privately owned.
Admissions Requirements Females only;
Medical examination; Physician's request.
Staff RNs 1 (ft); LPNs 4 (ft); Nurses' aides 6
(ft); Physical therapists 1 (pt); Reality
therapists 1 (pt); Recreational therapists 1
(pt); Occupational therapists 1 (pt); Speech
therapists 1 (pt); Activities coordinators 1
(ft); Dietitians 1 (pt); Ophthalmologists 1
(pt); Dentists 1 (pt).
Languages French, Spanish.

Facilities Dining room; Activities room;
Laundry room.
Activities Arts & crafts; Cards; Games;
Reading groups; Prayer groups; Movies;
Shopping trips; Dances/Social/Cultural
gatherings.

Reservoir Nursing Home Inc
1841 Trapelo Rd, Waltham, MA 02154
(617) 890-5000
Admin Theodore W Vathally.
Licensure Skilled care; Intermediate care. *Beds*
SNF 80; ICF 40. *Certified* Medicaid;
Medicare.
Owner Proprietary corp.

Varnum Park Rest Home
249 Bacon St, Waltham, MA 02154
(617) 894-3320
Admin William F Lee.
Licensure Rest home. *Beds* Rest home 32.
Owner Proprietary corp.

Wareham

Cape Cod Nursing & Retirement Home
Lewis Point Rd, Wareham, MA 02532
(617) 759-5752
Admin Lori N Charles. *Dir of Nursing* Mary
Rainville RN. *Medical Dir* Dr W Bowers.
Licensure Intermediate care; Alzheimer's care.
Beds ICF 97. *Certified* Medicaid.
Owner Proprietary corp (Beverly Enterprises
Inc).
Admissions Requirements Minimum age 21;
Medical examination.
Staff RNs 4 (ft), 2 (pt); LPNs 8 (ft), 4 (pt);
Nurses' aides 10 (ft), 10 (pt); Recreational
therapists 1 (ft); Activities coordinators 1
(pt); Dietitians 1 (pt).
Languages Chinese.
Facilities Dining room; Activities room;
Laundry room; Barber/Beauty shop; Outdoor
walks; Putting green.
Activities Arts & crafts; Cards; Games;
Reading groups; Prayer groups; Dances/
Social/Cultural gatherings; Exercise groups.

Roland Thatcher Nursing Home
Main St, Wareham, MA 02571
(617) 295-1040
Admin Margaret T Murray.
Licensure Skilled care; Intermediate care. *Beds*
SNF 43; ICF 65. *Certified* Medicaid.
Owner Proprietary corp.

Waterford Manor Rest Home
2 Depot St, Wareham, MA 02538
(617) 295-1440
Admin James A Hughes.
Licensure Rest home. *Beds* Rest home 16.
Owner Privately owned.

Warren

Buckwell Rest Home
PO Box 413, Warren, MA 01083-0413
(413) 267-9285
Admin Jane Delaney.
Licensure Rest home. *Beds* Rest home 17.
Owner Proprietary corp.

Washington

Maple View Nursing Home
Lover's Lane Rd, Washington, MA 01223
(413) 623-8936
Admin Toni Meddaugh.
Licensure Intermediate care. *Beds* ICF 57.
Certified Medicaid.
Owner Proprietary corp.

Watertown

Charlesgate Manor Convalescent Home Inc
590 Main St, Watertown, MA 02172
(617) 924-1966

Admin Frances E Olson. *Dir of Nursing*
Marcia Resnik RN. *Medical Dir* Mark B
Rohrer MD.
Licensure Skilled care; Intermediate care. *Beds*
SNF 50; ICF 52. *Private Pay Patients* 29%.
Certified Medicaid.
Owner Proprietary corp.
Admissions Requirements Medical
examination; Physician's request.
Staff Physicians 3 (pt); RNs 5 (ft), 6 (pt);
LPNs 7 (ft); Nurses' aides 30 (ft), 12 (pt);
Physical therapists 1 (pt); Occupational
therapists 1 (pt); Speech therapists 1 (pt);
Activities coordinators 1 (ft), 1 (pt);
Dietitians 1 (pt); Ophthalmologists 1 (pt);
Podiatrists 1 (pt).
Facilities Dining room; Physical therapy
room; Activities room; Chapel; Laundry
room; Barber/Beauty shop.
Activities Arts & crafts; Cards; Games;
Reading groups; Prayer groups; Movies.

Emerson Convalescent Home
59 Coolidge Hill Rd, Watertown, MA 02172
(617) 924-1130
Admin Norman J Duffy. *Dir of Nursing* Clare
McNally RN. *Medical Dir* Alan M Barron
MD.
Licensure Skilled care; Intermediate care. *Beds*
SNF 81; ICF 82. *Certified* Medicaid.
Owner Proprietary corp.
Admissions Requirements Minimum age 60;
Medical examination.
Staff RNs 8 (ft), 6 (pt); LPNs 11 (ft), 10 (pt);
Physical therapists 2 (ft); Reality therapists 1
(ft); Recreational therapists 2 (ft), 2 (pt);
Occupational therapists 1 (ft); Activities
coordinators 1 (ft); Dietitians 1 (pt).
Facilities Dining room; Physical therapy
room; Activities room; Chapel; Crafts room;
Laundry room; Barber/Beauty shop.
Activities Arts & crafts; Cards; Games;
Reading groups; Prayer groups; Movies;
Shopping trips; Dances/Social/Cultural
gatherings.

Marshall Home
120 Mount Auburn St, Watertown, MA 02172
(617) 924-4510
Admin Ann M Leffert.
Licensure Rest home. *Beds* Rest home 19.
Private Pay Patients 98%. *Certified*
Medicaid.
Owner Nonprofit corp.
Staff RNs 1 (pt); Activities coordinators 1
(pt).
Facilities Dining room; Activities room;
Laundry room; Barber/Beauty shop; Living
rooms; Patio; Sitting room.
Activities Arts & crafts; Cards; Games;
Movies; Shopping trips; Dances/Social/
Cultural gatherings; Intergenerational
programs; Exercise class.

Wayland

Kathryn Barton Nursing Home
373 Commonwealth Rd, Wayland, MA 01778
(617) 653-5401
Admin Barry E Conway.
Medical Dir Joyce Vettraino MD.
Licensure Skilled care. *Beds* SNF 55. *Certified*
Medicaid; Medicare.
Owner Proprietary corp.
Staff Physicians 1 (pt); RNs 4 (ft), 3 (pt);
LPNs 2 (ft), 6 (pt); Nurses' aides 24 (ft), 12
(pt); Physical therapists 1 (pt); Speech
therapists 1 (pt); Activities coordinators 1
(ft); Dietitians 1 (pt); Podiatrists 1 (pt);
Dentists 1 (pt).
Facilities Dining room; Physical therapy
room; Crafts room; Laundry room; Barber/
Beauty shop.

Activities Arts & crafts; Games; Prayer groups;
Movies; Shopping trips; Dances/Social/
Cultural gatherings; Sculpture group;
Painting class; Weekly cookout in summer;
Musical group; Exercise aerobics.

Cochituate Nursing Home Inc
188 Commonwealth Rd, Wayland, MA 01778
(617) 653-8500
Admin Alan A Guidrey. *Dir of Nursing*
Sandra O'Leary RN.
Licensure Intermediate care. *Beds* ICF 40.
Certified Medicaid.
Owner Proprietary corp.
Admissions Requirements Minimum age 65.
Staff RNs 3 (ft), 2 (pt); LPNs 4 (ft), 1 (pt);
Nurses' aides 8 (ft), 8 (pt); Activities
coordinators 1 (ft); Dietitians 1 (pt).
Facilities Dining room; Physical therapy
room; Activities room; Laundry room;
Barber/Beauty shop.
Activities Arts & crafts; Cards; Games;
Reading groups; Shopping trips; Dances/
Social/Cultural gatherings.

Webster

Lanessa Extended Care Facility
751 School St, Webster, MA 01570
(508) 949-1334, 949-0647 FAX
Admin Mark Berman.
Licensure Skilled care; Intermediate care. *Beds*
SNF 41; ICF 41. *Certified* Medicaid.
Facilities Dining room; Physical therapy
room; Activities room; Crafts room; Laundry
room; Barber/Beauty shop.
Activities Arts & crafts; Cards; Games;
Reading groups; Prayer groups; Movies;
Shopping trips; Dances/Social/Cultural
gatherings; Intergenerational programs; Pet
therapy.

Oakwood Convalescent Home
86 Hartley St, Webster, MA 01570
(617) 943-3889
Admin Daniel A O'Neil.
Licensure Skilled care; Intermediate care. *Beds*
SNF 41; ICF 40. *Certified* Medicaid.
Owner Proprietary corp (First Healthcare
Corp).
Admissions Requirements Minimum age 21.
Staff Physicians; RNs 4 (ft), 2 (pt); LPNs 3
(ft), 4 (pt); Nurses' aides; Physical therapists;
Occupational therapists; Speech therapists;
Activities coordinators; Dietitians;
Ophthalmologists; Podiatrists; Audiologists;
Dentists.
Facilities Dining room; Activities room;
Chapel; Laundry room; Barber/Beauty shop.
Activities Arts & crafts; Cards; Games;
Reading groups; Movies; Shopping trips;
Dances/Social/Cultural gatherings.

Webster House Long Term Care Facility
749 School St, Webster, MA 01570
(617) 949-0644
Admin Jeanne M Care.
Licensure Intermediate care. *Beds* ICF 43.

Webster Manor Long-Term Care Facility
745 School St, Webster, MA 01570
(508) 949-0644, 949-0647 FAX
Admin Carol Singh. *Dir of Nursing* Catherine
Boyer. *Medical Dir* Dr George Nasinnyk.
Licensure Skilled care; Intermediate care. *Beds*
SNF 82; ICF 41. *Private Pay Patients* 12%.
Certified Medicaid; Medicare.
Owner Proprietary corp.
Admissions Requirements Minimum age 21;
Medical examination.
Staff Physicians; RNs; LPNs; Nurses' aides;
Physical therapists; Recreational therapists;
Occupational therapists; Activities
coordinators; Dietitians; Ophthalmologists;
Podiatrists.

Facilities Dining room; Physical therapy
room; Activities room; Crafts room; Laundry
room; Barber/Beauty shop; Private and semi-
private rooms with balconies.
Activities Arts & crafts; Cards; Games;
Reading groups; Prayer groups; Movies;
Dances/Social/Cultural gatherings;
Intergenerational programs; Pet therapy.

Wellesley

Newton & Wellesley Nursing Home
694 Worcester Rd, Wellesley, MA 02181
(617) 237-6400
Admin Edmond A Perregaux III. *Dir of
Nursing* Mary Gallo RN. *Medical Dir* David
Kaufman MD.
Licensure Skilled care; Intermediate care;
Alzheimer's care. *Beds* SNF 60; ICF 60.
Certified Medicaid; Medicare.
Owner Proprietary corp (First Healthcare
Corp).
Admissions Requirements Medical
examination.
Staff RNs 8 (ft), 10 (pt); LPNs 6 (ft), 4 (pt);
Nurses' aides 20 (ft), 30 (pt); Recreational
therapists 3 (ft); Dietitians 1 (pt).
Languages French, Italian, Yiddish, Spanish.
Facilities Dining room; Activities room;
Crafts room; Laundry room; Barber/Beauty
shop.
Activities Arts & crafts; Cards; Games;
Reading groups; Prayer groups; Movies;
Shopping trips; Dances/Social/Cultural
gatherings; Music therapy.

Elizabeth Seton Residence
125 Oakland St, Wellesley, MA 02181
(617) 237-2161
Admin Sr Catherine Hanlon.
Licensure Skilled care; Intermediate care. *Beds*
SNF 41; ICF 24. *Certified* Medicaid.
Owner Proprietary corp.

Wellesley Manor Nursing Home
878 Worcester St, Wellesley, MA 02181
(617) 235-6699
Admin Marilyn Morgan. *Dir of Nursing* Eileen
Tucker RN. *Medical Dir* Stephen Peabody
MD.
Licensure Skilled care. *Beds* SNF 97. *Certified*
Medicaid; Medicare.
Owner Proprietary corp (Beverly Enterprises).
Staff RNs; LPNs; Nurses' aides; Physical
therapists (consultant); Recreational
therapists (consultant); Occupational
therapists (consultant); Speech therapists
(consultant); Activities coordinators;
Dietitians (consultant).
Facilities Dining room; Physical therapy
room; Activities room; Crafts room; Laundry
room; Barber/Beauty shop.
Activities Arts & crafts; Cards; Games;
Reading groups; Prayer groups; Movies;
Shopping trips; Dances/Social/Cultural
gatherings; Intergenerational programs; Pet
therapy; Elder arts network.

West Boylston

Oakdale Nursing Home
76 N Main St, West Boylston, MA 01539
(617) 835-6076
Admin David H Oriol.
Licensure Skilled care; Intermediate care. *Beds*
SNF 40; ICF 40. *Certified* Medicaid.
Owner Proprietary corp.

West Brookfield

Brook Haven Rest Home
Main St, West Brookfield, MA 01585
(617) 867-3325
Admin Madaline D Smith-Papison.
Licensure Rest home. *Beds* Rest home 22.
Owner Privately owned.

Quaboag Nursing Home
30 Main St, West Brookfield, MA 01585
(508) 867-7716, 867-2074 FAX
Admin Frederick White. *Dir of Nursing*
Barbara Potter RN. *Medical Dir* Orhan
Under MD.
Licensure Skilled care; Intermediate care;
Alzheimer's care. *Beds* SNF 83; ICF 46.
Certified Medicaid; Medicare.
Owner Proprietary corp (GHM Inc).
Admissions Requirements Minimum age 30.
Staff RNs 5 (ft), 14 (pt); LPNs 5 (ft), 9 (pt);
Nurses' aides 32 (ft), 31 (pt); Physical
therapists 1 (pt); Occupational therapists 1
(pt); Activities coordinators 1 (ft), 2 (pt);
Dietitians 1 (pt).
Languages French, Polish.
Facilities Dining room; Physical therapy
room; Activities room; Chapel; Crafts room;
Laundry room; Barber/Beauty shop; Books
from local library.
Activities Arts & crafts; Cards; Games;
Reading groups; Prayer groups; Movies;
Shopping trips; Dances/Social/Cultural
gatherings; Intergenerational programs; Pet
therapy; Happy hour; Reality orientation
group.

Westbrook Heights Rest Home
Rte 9 Box 581, Brookfield Rd, West
Brookfield, MA 01585
(413) 867-2062
Admin Annette M Dorman. *Dir of Nursing*
Sue Farrelly RN. *Medical Dir* Richard
Fowler MD.
Licensure Skilled care. *Beds* SNF 26. *Private
Pay Patients* 0%. *Certified* Medicaid;
Medicare.
Owner Privately owned.
Admissions Requirements Minimum age 35;
Medical examination; Physician's request.
Staff Physicians; RNs; Nurses' aides;
Activities coordinators; Dietitians;
Ophthalmologists; Podiatrists.
Facilities Dining room; Activities room;
Crafts room; Laundry room; Barber/Beauty
shop; Picnic area.
Activities Arts & crafts; Cards; Games;
Reading groups; Prayer groups; Movies;
Shopping trips; Dances/Social/Cultural
gatherings; Pet therapy; Outdoor activities.

West Newton

Newton Convalescent Home
25 Armory St, West Newton, MA 02368
(617) 969-2300
Admin George Elkins. *Dir of Nursing* Debbie
Johnson RN. *Medical Dir* David Kaufman
MD.
Licensure Skilled care; Intermediate care. *Beds*
SNF 82; ICF 41. *Private Pay Patients* 18%.
Certified Medicare.
Owner Proprietary corp (Beverly Enterprises).
Staff RNs 8 (ft), 2 (pt); LPNs 6 (ft); Nurses'
aides 36 (ft); Physical therapists 1 (pt);
Recreational therapists 2 (ft); Occupational
therapists 1 (pt); Speech therapists 1 (pt);
Activities coordinators 1 (ft); Dietitians 1
(pt); Podiatrists 1 (pt); Audiologists 1 (pt).
Activities Arts & crafts; Cards; Games;
Reading groups; Prayer groups; Movies;
Shopping trips; Dances/Social/Cultural
gatherings; Intergenerational programs; Pet
therapy.

West Roxbury

Stonehedge Convalescent Center Inc
5 Redlands Rd, West Roxbury, MA 02132
(617) 327-6325, 327-8204 FAX
Admin John J O'Meara. *Dir of Nursing*
Kathleen Prindeville. *Medical Dir* Dr
Thomas Monahan.
Licensure Skilled care; Intermediate care. *Beds*
SNF 39; ICF 40. *Private Pay Patients* 25%.
Certified Medicaid.

Owner Proprietary corp (CAPS).
Admissions Requirements Minimum age 21;
Medical examination; Physician's request.
Staff Physicians 3 (pt); RNs 12 (pt); LPNs 7
(pt); Nurses' aides 28 (pt); Physical
therapists 1 (pt); Occupational therapists 1
(pt); Speech therapists 1 (pt); Activities
coordinators 2 (pt); Dietitians 1 (pt);
Podiatrists 1 (pt).
Facilities Dining room; Activities room;
Chapel; Crafts room; Laundry room; Barber/
Beauty shop.
Activities Arts & crafts; Cards; Games;
Reading groups; Prayer groups; Movies;
Shopping trips; Dances/Social/Cultural
gatherings; Intergenerational programs; Pet
therapy.

West Springfield

Riverdale Gardens Nursing Home
42 Prospect Ave, West Springfield, MA 01089
(413) 733-3151
Admin James Cameron McNeill. *Dir of
Nursing* Laurie A McNeill.
Licensure Skilled care; Intermediate care;
Alzheimer's care. *Beds* SNF 84; ICF 84.
Private Pay Patients 50%. *Certified*
Medicaid; Medicare.
Owner Nonprofit organization/foundation.
Facilities Dining room; Physical therapy
room; Activities room; Crafts room; Laundry
room; Barber/Beauty shop; Library.
Activities Arts & crafts; Cards; Games;
Reading groups; Prayer groups; Movies;
Shopping trips; Dances/Social/Cultural
gatherings; Intergenerational programs; Pet
therapy.

West Springfield Nursing Home
PO Box 1017, 217 Westfield St, West
Springfield, MA 01090
(413) 788-6126
Admin Thomas R Bertrand. *Dir of Nursing*
Martha McNamara RN. *Medical Dir* Dr
George Reynolds.
Licensure Skilled care; Intermediate care. *Beds*
SNF 80; ICF 40. *Private Pay Patients* 25%.
Certified Medicaid.
Owner Proprietary corp (M Cerveny Corp).
Admissions Requirements Minimum age 22.
Staff Physicians 1 (ft); RNs 10 (ft), 6 (pt);
LPNs 2 (ft), 7 (pt); Nurses' aides 30 (ft), 30
(pt); Physical therapists 1 (pt); Recreational
therapists 1 (ft); Occupational therapists 1
(pt); Speech therapists 1 (pt); Activities
coordinators 1 (pt); Dietitians 1 (pt);
Ophthalmologists 1 (pt); Podiatrists 1 (pt).
Facilities Dining room; Activities room;
Crafts room; Laundry room; Barber/Beauty
shop.
Activities Arts & crafts; Cards; Games;
Reading groups; Prayer groups; Movies;
Shopping trips; Pet therapy.

Westborough

**Beaumont at the Willows A Skilled Nursing
Facility**
1 Lyman St, Westborough, MA 01581
(617) 366-9933
Admin Ivan S Yamamoto. *Dir of Nursing*
Karen Brennan RN.
Licensure Skilled care; Intermediate care;
Retirement. *Beds* SNF 80; ICF 60. *Certified*
Medicaid; Medicare.
Owner Proprietary corp.
Staff RNs 11 (ft), 1 (pt); LPNs 10 (ft), 6 (pt);
Nurses' aides 32 (ft), 25 (pt); Recreational
therapists 3 (ft); Activities coordinators 3
(ft).
Facilities Dining room; Physical therapy
room; Activities room; Laundry room;
Barber/Beauty shop.
Activities Arts & crafts; Games; Reading
groups; Prayer groups; Movies; Shopping
trips; Dances/Social/Cultural gatherings.

Westborough Nursing Home
Colonial Dr, Westborough, MA 01581
(617) 366-9131
Admin Eugene Belle.
Medical Dir Robert Klugman MD.
Licensure Skilled care; Intermediate care. *Beds*
SNF 82; ICF 41. *Certified* Medicaid;
Medicare.
Owner Proprietary corp (First Healthcare
Corp).
Staff RNs 6 (ft), 14 (pt); LPNs 4 (ft), 5 (pt);
Nurses' aides 28 (ft), 28 (pt); Activities
coordinators 2 (ft), 1 (pt).
Facilities Dining room; Physical therapy
room; Activities room; Crafts room; Laundry
room; Barber/Beauty shop.
Activities Arts & crafts; Cards; Games;
Reading groups; Prayer groups; Movies;
Shopping trips; Dances/Social/Cultural
gatherings.

Westfield

Barnard Rest Home
160 Franklin St, Westfield, MA 01085
(413) 562-2931
Admin Ivan K Barnard.
Licensure Rest home. *Beds* Rest home 84.
Owner Proprietary corp.

Valley View Nursing Home Inc
PO Box 578, 37 Feedings Hills Rd, Westfield,
MA 01085
(413) 568-2341
Admin C Lee Verrill. *Dir of Nursing* Lucille
Harding RN. *Medical Dir* George Reynolds
MD.
Licensure Skilled care. *Beds* SNF 80. *Certified*
Medicaid.
Owner Proprietary corp (Cerveny).
Admissions Requirements Minimum age 21.
Staff Physicians; RNs; LPNs; Nurses' aides;
Physical therapists; Reality therapists;
Recreational therapists; Occupational
therapists; Speech therapists; Activities
coordinators; Dietitians; Ophthalmologists;
Podiatrists; Audiologists.
Facilities Dining room; Activities room;
Crafts room; Laundry room; Barber/Beauty
shop.
Activities Arts & crafts; Cards; Games;
Reading groups; Prayer groups; Movies;
Shopping trips; Dances/Social/Cultural
gatherings; Intergenerational programs.

Westfield Manor Nursing Home
60 E Silver St, Westfield, MA 01085
(413) 562-5122
Admin Mark R Ellsworth.
Medical Dir Ms Simmons.
Licensure Skilled care; Intermediate care. *Beds*
SNF 42; ICF 62. *Certified* Medicaid.
Owner Privately owned.
Admissions Requirements Minimum age 16;
Medical examination.
Staff RNs; LPNs; Nurses' aides; Physical
therapists; Occupational therapists; Activities
coordinators; Dietitians; Ophthalmologists.
Languages Spanish, Polish.
Facilities Dining room; Activities room;
Chapel; Laundry room; Barber/Beauty shop.
Activities Arts & crafts; Cards; Games;
Reading groups; Prayer groups; Movies;
Shopping trips; Dances/Social/Cultural
gatherings.

Westford

Westford Nursing Home
39 Main St, Westford, MA 01824
(617) 692-4787
Admin Katherine Lemay. *Dir of Nursing*
Kathleen Chambers. *Medical Dir* Thomas
Fitzpatrick MD.
Licensure Intermediate care. *Beds* ICF 58.
Private Pay Patients 10%. *Certified*
Medicaid.

Owner Proprietary corp (Solomont Family).
Admissions Requirements Medical examination; Physician's request.
Staff Physicians 1 (pt); RNs 1 (ft), 3 (pt); LPNs 3 (ft), 5 (pt); Nurses' aides 10 (ft), 16 (pt); Physical therapists 1 (pt); Occupational therapists 1 (pt); Speech therapists 1 (pt); Activities coordinators 1 (ft); Dietitians 1 (pt).
Facilities Dining room; Activities room; Barber/Beauty shop.
Activities Arts & crafts; Cards; Games; Reading groups; Prayer groups; Movies; Shopping trips; Dances/Social/Cultural gatherings; Intergenerational programs; Pet therapy.

Westminster

Maranatha Rest Home
99 State Rd W, Westminster, MA 01473
(508) 632-0985
Admin Jean Plummer.
Licensure Intermediate care. *Beds* ICF 12. *Certified* Medicaid; Medicare.
Owner Privately owned.
Admissions Requirements Minimum age 50; Medical examination.
Staff Nurses' aides 3 (ft), 1 (pt).
Facilities Dining room; Activities room; Laundry room; Library.
Activities Arts & crafts; Cards; Games; Prayer groups; Shopping trips; Dances/Social/Cultural gatherings.

Weston

Campion Residence & Renewal Center
319 Concord Rd, Weston, MA 02193
(617) 894-0751
Admin Rev Richard T Cleary. *Dir of Nursing* Jayne Strunk RN. *Medical Dir* Dr John E Doherty.
Licensure Skilled care; Retirement. *Beds* SNF 15.
Owner Nonprofit corp.
Admissions Requirements Males only.
Staff Physicians 1 (pt); RNs 4 (ft), 3 (pt); LPNs 1 (ft); Nurses' aides 2 (ft), 3 (pt); Physical therapists 1 (pt); Activities coordinators 1 (ft); Dietitians 1 (ft).
Languages Spanish.
Affiliation Roman Catholic.
Facilities Dining room; Physical therapy room; Activities room; Chapel; Crafts room; Laundry room; Barber/Beauty shop; Library.
Activities Arts & crafts; Cards; Games; Prayer groups; Movies; Special trips & outings.

Weston Manor Nursing & Retirement
75 Norumbega Rd, Weston, MA 02193
(617) 891-6100
Admin Walter F Connor.
Medical Dir Jerome Tanzer MD.
Licensure Skilled care; Intermediate care. *Beds* SNF 120; ICF 40. *Certified* Medicaid.
Owner Proprietary corp.
Staff Physicians 1 (pt); RNs 8 (ft), 9 (pt); LPNs 4 (ft), 3 (pt); Nurses' aides 25 (ft), 35 (pt); Physical therapists 2 (pt); Recreational therapists 2 (ft); Occupational therapists 1 (pt); Speech therapists 1 (pt); Activities coordinators 1 (ft); Dietitians 1 (pt); Ophthalmologists 1 (pt); Podiatrists 1 (pt); Audiologists 1 (pt); Dentists 1 (pt).
Facilities Dining room; Physical therapy room; Activities room; Chapel; Crafts room; Laundry room; Barber/Beauty shop.
Activities Arts & crafts; Cards; Games; Reading groups; Movies; Shopping trips; Dances/Social/Cultural gatherings.

Weymouth

Colonial Nursing & Rehabilitation Center
125 Broad St, Weymouth, MA 02188
(617) 337-3121
Admin Brian J McKenna.
Licensure Skilled care; Intermediate care. *Beds* SNF 122; ICF 89. *Certified* Medicaid; Medicare.
Owner Proprietary corp.

Elizabeth Catherine Retirement Facility
27 Front St, Weymouth, MA 02188
(617) 335-2596
Admin Paul D Grady.
Licensure Rest home. *Beds* SNF Rest home 34.
Owner Privately owned.

Logan Healthcare Facility—Skilled Nursing Facility
861 Main St, Weymouth, MA 02190
(617) 337-0678
Admin Jori K Logan.
Licensure Skilled care; Intermediate care. *Beds* SNF 34; ICF 36. *Certified* Medicaid.
Owner Privately owned.

Samuel Marcus Nursing & Retirement Home
28 Front St, Weymouth, MA 02188
(617) 337-9074
Admin Arthur S Logan.
Licensure Intermediate care. *Beds* ICF 22. *Certified* Medicaid.
Owner Privately owned.

Pond Meadow Healthcare Facility Nursing Home
188 Summer St, Weymouth, MA 02188
(617) 337-6900
Admin Robert C Nolan.
Licensure Skilled care; Intermediate care. *Beds* SNF 44; ICF 44. *Certified* Medicaid.
Owner Proprietary corp.

Pope Nursing Home
140 Webb St, Weymouth, MA 02188
(617) 335-4352
Admin Larry J LeBlanc.
Licensure Intermediate care. *Beds* ICF 37. *Certified* Medicaid.
Owner Proprietary corp.

Whittaker Rest Home
46 Union St, Weymouth, MA 02190
(617) 335-5885
Admin Robert S Whittaker.
Licensure Rest home. *Beds* Rest home 34.
Owner Privately owned.

Whitman

Brae Burn Nursing Home
146 South Ave, Whitman, MA 02382
(617) 447-5541
Admin Peter J O'Reilly. *Dir of Nursing* Elaine Hawley RN.
Licensure Intermediate care. *Beds* ICF 60. *Certified* Medicaid.
Owner Proprietary corp.
Admissions Requirements Minimum age.
Staff RNs; LPNs; Nurses' aides; Physical therapists; Recreational therapists; Speech therapists; Activities coordinators; Dietitians; Podiatrists.
Facilities Dining room; Activities room; Laundry room.
Activities Arts & crafts; Cards; Games; Reading groups; Prayer groups; Movies; Shopping trips; Dances/Social/Cultural gatherings.

Wilbraham

Hampton Hills Nursing Home
PO Box 657, 9 Maple St, Wilbraham, MA 01095
(413) 596-2411

Admin Amelia Fournier.
Licensure Skilled care; Intermediate care. *Beds* SNF 82; ICF 41.

Williamsburg

Sunny Acres Nursing Home
Rte 9, Haydenville, Williamsburg, MA 01039
(413) 268-3612
Admin James R Wade.
Licensure Intermediate care. *Beds* ICF 30. *Certified* Medicaid.
Owner Proprietary corp.

Williamstown

Rest Haven Rest Home Inc
PO Box 286, 84 Spring St, Williamstown, MA 01267
(413) 743-2115
Admin Sandra L Bisson.
Medical Dir Dr Ronald Durning.
Licensure Rest home. *Beds* 29. *Certified* Medicaid; Medicare.
Owner Proprietary corp.
Admissions Requirements Minimum age 40; Medical examination.
Staff Physicians; RNs; Nurses' aides; Physical therapists; Activities coordinators; Dietitians; Ophthalmologists; Podiatrists; Dentists.
Languages Polish.
Facilities Dining room; Activities room; Laundry room.
Activities Arts & crafts; Cards; Games; Reading groups; Prayer groups; Shopping trips.

Sweet Brook Nursing Home Inc
Cold Spring Rd, Williamstown, MA 01267
(413) 458-8127
Admin Elaine K Neely. *Dir of Nursing* Connie Hvizda RN. *Medical Dir* Dr Robert Wicksman.
Licensure Skilled care; Retirement. *Beds* SNF 123. *Certified* Medicaid; Medicare.
Owner Proprietary corp.
Admissions Requirements Minimum age 18.

Willowood Nursing Home of Williamstown
Adams Rd, Williamstown, MA 01267
(413) 458-2111
Admin David L Johnson. *Dir of Nursing* Rhonda Hartlage. *Medical Dir* Dr Ronald Durning.
Licensure Skilled care. *Beds* SNF 72. *Certified* Medicaid.
Owner Proprietary corp.
Admissions Requirements Minimum age 18; Medical examination.
Staff Physicians 3 (pt); RNs 2 (ft), 2 (pt); LPNs 7 (ft), 1 (pt); Nurses' aides 213 (ft), 4 (pt); Physical therapists 1 (pt); Recreational therapists 1 (pt); Occupational therapists 1 (pt); Speech therapists 1 (pt); Activities coordinators 2 (ft); Dietitians 1 (ft), 1 (pt); Ophthalmologists 1 (pt); Podiatrists 1 (pt); Social workers 1 (pt).
Facilities Dining room; Physical therapy room; Activities room; Crafts room; Laundry room; Barber/Beauty shop.
Activities Arts & crafts; Cards; Games; Reading groups; Prayer groups; Movies; Shopping trips; Dances/Social/Cultural gatherings.

Winchendon

Hillside Rest Home
547 Central St, Winchendon, MA 01475
(617) 297-2333
Admin Stanley S Smith.
Licensure Intermediate care. *Beds* ICF 18. *Certified* Medicaid; Medicare.
Owner Proprietary corp.
Admissions Requirements Minimum age Elderly; Medical examination.

Staff Physicians; RNs; Activities coordinators; Dietitians; Ophthalmologists.
Facilities Dining room; Activities room; Crafts room; Laundry room.
Activities Arts & crafts; Cards; Games; Reading groups; Prayer groups; Movies; Shopping trips; Dances/Social/Cultural gatherings.

Open Arms Nursing Home
163 Brown St, Winchendon, MA 01475
(508) 297-2458
Admin Edith A Hallet. *Dir of Nursing* Barbara Sibley.
Licensure Intermediate care. *Beds* ICF 43. *Private Pay Patients* 15%. *Certified* Medicaid.
Owner Proprietary corp.
Admissions Requirements Minimum age 55; Medical examination.
Staff RNs 3 (ft), 2 (pt); LPNs 2 (pt); Nurses' aides 6 (ft), 10 (pt); Activities coordinators 1 (ft); Dietitians.
Facilities Dining room; Activities room; Crafts room; Laundry room; Barber/Beauty shop.
Activities Arts & crafts; Cards; Games; Reading groups; Prayer groups; Movies; Shopping trips; Dances/Social/Cultural gatherings; Intergenerational programs.

Winchester

Aberjona Nursing Center Inc
184 Swanton St, Box 490, Winchester, MA 01890
(617) 729-9370
Admin Robert Salter.
Licensure Skilled care; Intermediate care. *Beds* SNF 82; ICF 41. *Certified* Medicaid.

Winchester Mt Vernon House IV
110 Mount Vernon St, Winchester, MA 01890
(617) 729-0497
Admin Grace P Phillips.
Licensure Rest home. *Beds* Rest home 17.
Owner Proprietary corp.
Admissions Requirements Minimum age 65; Medical examination.
Staff RNs 1 (ft).
Facilities Dining room; Activities room; Crafts room; Laundry room; Barber/Beauty shop; Library.
Activities Games; Movies.

Winchester Nursing Center Inc
223 Swanton St, Box 490, Winchester, MA 01890
(617) 729-9595
Admin Richard Salter.
Licensure Skilled care; Intermediate care. *Beds* SNF 92; ICF 29. *Certified* Medicaid; Medicare.
Owner Proprietary corp.
Admissions Requirements Minimum age 25; Physician's request.
Staff Physicians; RNs; LPNs; Nurses' aides; Physical therapists; Recreational therapists; Occupational therapists; Speech therapists; Activities coordinators; Dietitians.
Languages French.
Facilities Dining room; Physical therapy room; Activities room; Crafts room; Laundry room; Barber/Beauty shop; Library.
Activities Arts & crafts; Cards; Games; Reading groups; Prayer groups; Movies; Shopping trips; Dances/Social/Cultural gatherings; Van trips.

Winthrop

Bay View Nursing Home
26 Sturgis St, Winthrop, MA 02152
(617) 846-2060, 846-3283 FAX
Admin Louise Boucher RN. *Dir of Nursing* Dorothy Copoulos RN.

Licensure Intermediate care. *Beds* ICF 78. *Private Pay Patients* 20%. *Certified* Medicaid.
Owner Proprietary corp (Bane Family Nursing Centers).
Admissions Requirements Minimum age 65.
Staff RNs 5 (ft), 2 (pt); LPNs 1 (ft), 4 (pt); Nurses' aides 14 (ft), 6 (pt); Physical therapists 1 (pt); Occupational therapists 1 (pt); Speech therapists 1 (pt); Activities coordinators 1 (ft); Dietitians 1 (pt); Ophthalmologists 1 (pt); Podiatrists 1 (pt).
Facilities Dining room; Activities room; Laundry room; Barber/Beauty shop; Front porch; Fenced backyard; Community center.
Activities Arts & crafts; Cards; Games; Prayer groups; Movies; Shopping trips; Intergenerational programs; Pet therapy; Barbecues; Breakfast club; Family dinners.

Cliff House Nursing Home Inc
PO Box 39, 170 Cliff Ave, Winthrop, MA 02152
(617) 846-0500
Admin Paul J LeMay. *Dir of Nursing* Jane Page RN. *Medical Dir* John Coyle MD.
Licensure Skilled care; Intermediate care. *Beds* SNF 31; ICF 57. *Certified* Medicaid.
Owner Proprietary corp.
Admissions Requirements Minimum age 21.
Staff Physicians 1 (pt); RNs 2 (ft); LPNs 12 (ft); Nurses' aides 48 (ft), 12 (pt); Physical therapists 1 (ft); Recreational therapists 1 (ft), 2 (pt); Occupational therapists 1 (pt); Speech therapists 1 (pt); Activities coordinators 1 (pt); Dietitians 1 (pt); Ophthalmologists 1 (pt); Podiatrists 1 (pt).
Languages Italian, Spanish, French.
Activities Arts & crafts; Cards; Games; Reading groups; Shopping trips; Pet therapy.

Governor Winthrop Nursing Home
142 Pleasant St, Winthrop, MA 02152
(617) 846-7750
Admin Robert D Wilkins. *Dir of Nursing* William Moore RN. *Medical Dir* Dr Coyle.
Licensure Skilled care; Intermediate care. *Beds* SNF 34; ICF 51. *Private Pay Patients* 2%. *Certified* Medicaid; Medicare.
Owner Proprietary corp.
Admissions Requirements Minimum age 35.
Staff Physicians 1 (pt); RNs 8 (ft), 2 (pt); LPNs 10 (ft), 2 (pt); Nurses' aides 40 (ft); Physical therapists 1 (pt); Occupational therapists 1 (pt); Speech therapists 1 (pt); Activities coordinators 1 (ft); Dietitians 1 (pt).
Facilities Dining room; Activities room; Laundry room; Barber/Beauty shop; Lounge; TV/Movie room.
Activities Arts & crafts; Games; Prayer groups; Movies; Dances/Social/Cultural gatherings; Intergenerational programs.

Woburn

Glendale Nursing Home
171 Cambridge Rd, Woburn, MA 01801
(617) 933-7080
Admin William E Lynskey.
Licensure Intermediate care. *Beds* ICF 49. *Certified* Medicaid.
Owner Proprietary corp.

New England Rehabilitation Hospital
Rehabilitation Way, Woburn, MA 01801
(617) 935-5050
Admin Sr Joan Cassidy.
Licensure Skilled care. *Beds* 120. *Certified* Medicaid; Medicare.

Tidd Home
74 Elm St, Woburn, MA 01801
(617) 933-0248
Admin Theresa N O'Connor MSM RD.
Licensure Retirement care. *Beds* Retirement care 14. *Private Pay Patients* 100%.
Owner Nonprofit corp.

Admissions Requirements Minimum age 65; Females only; Medical examination.
Staff Physicians; RNs; LPNs; Nurses' aides; Physical therapists; Reality therapists; Recreational therapists; Occupational therapists; Speech therapists; Activities coordinators; Dietitians; Ophthalmologists; Podiatrists; Audiologists.
Facilities Dining room; Laundry room; Library.
Activities Cards; Games; Prayer groups; Movies; Shopping trips; Dances/Social/Cultural gatherings; Intergenerational programs.

Woburn Nursing Center Inc
18 Frances St, Woburn, MA 01801
(617) 933-8175
Admin Edythe Salter. *Dir of Nursing* Patricia Devercaux RN. *Medical Dir* Thomas Hirschfeld MD.
Licensure Skilled care; Intermediate care. *Beds* SNF 71; ICF 39. *Certified* Medicaid.
Owner Proprietary corp.
Admissions Requirements Minimum age 21; Males only; Females only; Medical examination; Physician's request.
Staff Physicians 2 (pt); RNs 8 (ft); LPNs 8 (ft); Physical therapists 1 (pt); Recreational therapists 1 (pt); Occupational therapists 1 (pt); Activities coordinators 1 (ft); Dietitians 1 (ft); Ophthalmologists 1 (pt).
Facilities Dining room; Physical therapy room; Activities room; Crafts room; Barber/Beauty shop.
Activities Arts & crafts; Cards; Games; Reading groups; Prayer groups; Movies; Shopping trips; Dances/Social/Cultural gatherings.

Worcester

Armstrong Nursing Home
119 Forest St, Worcester, MA 01609
(617) 754-6190
Admin Robert D Brennan.
Medical Dir Dr Arthur Ward.
Licensure Intermediate care. *Beds* ICF 17. *Certified* Medicaid.
Owner Proprietary corp.
Admissions Requirements Minimum age 50; Males only; Medical examination; Physician's request.
Staff Physicians 1 (pt); RNs 1 (ft), 2 (pt); LPNs 1 (ft), 5 (pt); Nurses' aides 1 (ft), 2 (pt); Activities coordinators 1 (pt); Dietitians 1 (pt).
Facilities Dining room; Laundry room.
Activities Arts & crafts; Cards; Games; Movies; Shopping trips.

Bancroft House Healthcare Nursing Home
835 Main St, Worcester, MA 01610
(617) 757-6311
Admin Paul C Skarmos.
Medical Dir Carl Marsh MD.
Licensure Skilled care; Intermediate care. *Beds* SNF 29; ICF 91. *Certified* Medicaid; Medicare.
Owner Proprietary corp (First Healthcare Corp).
Admissions Requirements Minimum age 18.
Staff RNs 4 (ft), 13 (pt); LPNs 3 (ft), 6 (pt); Nurses' aides 19 (ft), 26 (pt); Activities coordinators 1 (ft), 1 (pt); 14 (ft), 16 (pt).
Facilities Dining room; Physical therapy room; Activities room; Crafts room; Laundry room; Barber/Beauty shop.
Activities Arts & crafts; Cards; Games; Reading groups; Prayer groups; Movies; Shopping trips; Dances/Social/Cultural gatherings.

Belmont Home
255 Belmont St, Worcester, MA 01605
(508) 799-1554, 799-1547 FAX
Admin Arthur Tirella. *Dir of Nursing* Carol Ford. *Medical Dir* Dr Horatio Turner.

Licensure Skilled care; Intermediate care; Rest home. *Beds* SNF 40; ICF 104; Rest home 40. *Private Pay Patients* 5%. *Certified* Medicaid.
Owner Publicly owned.
Admissions Requirements Minimum age 21; Medical examination.
Staff Physicians 4 (pt); RNs 6 (ft); LPNs 20 (ft), 1 (pt); Nurses' aides 55 (ft), 3 (pt); Physical therapists 1 (pt); Recreational therapists 1 (pt); Activities coordinators 1 (ft); Dietitians 1 (pt).
Facilities Dining room; Activities room; Chapel; Crafts room; Laundry room; Barber/Beauty shop; Library.
Activities Arts & crafts; Cards; Games; Reading groups; Prayer groups; Movies; Shopping trips; Dances/Social/Cultural gatherings; Intergenerational programs; Pet therapy.

Blaire House of Worcester
116 Houghton St, Worcester, MA 01604
(508) 791-5543, 755-2505 FAX
Admin John P Richwagen. *Dir of Nursing* Charlene Magliocca. *Medical Dir* Hooshang Poor.
Licensure Skilled care; Intermediate care; Alzheimer's unit. *Beds* SNF 37; ICF 38; Alzheimer's unit 12. *Private Pay Patients* 25%. *Certified* Medicaid.
Owner Proprietary corp (Elder Care Services).
Staff Physicians 12 (pt); RNs 3 (pt); LPNs 4 (pt); Nurses' aides 10 (ft), 13 (pt); Physical therapists 1 (pt); Occupational therapists 1 (pt); Activities coordinators 1 (ft), 2 (pt); Dietitians 1 (pt); Ophthalmologists 1 (pt); Podiatrists 1 (pt).
Facilities Dining room; Activities room; Crafts room; Barber/Beauty shop; Library; Security systems for Alzheimer's.
Activities Arts & crafts; Cards; Games; Reading groups; Prayer groups; Movies; Shopping trips; Dances/Social/Cultural gatherings; Intergenerational programs; Pet therapy.

Burncoat Plains Rest Home
572 Burncoat St, Worcester, MA 01606
(617) 755-6404
Admin William J Lange.
Licensure Rest home. *Beds* Rest home 35.
Owner Proprietary corp.

Castle Park Nursing Home
22-24 King St, Worcester, MA 01610
(617) 752-8910
Admin Janet P Waller RN LNHA. *Dir of Nursing* Rita Reilly RN.
Licensure Intermediate care. *Beds* ICF 30. *Certified* Medicaid.
Owner Privately owned.
Admissions Requirements Minimum age 60.
Staff RNs; LPNs; Nurses' aides; Activities coordinators; Dietitians.
Languages Greek, French.
Facilities Activities room; Laundry room; Barber/Beauty shop.
Activities Arts & crafts; Cards; Games; Prayer groups; Movies; Shopping trips.

Clark Manor Nursing Home Inc
1350 Main St, Worcester, MA 01603
(617) 791-4200
Admin Robert N Sibulkin.
Licensure Skilled care; Intermediate care. *Beds* SNF 96; ICF 66. *Certified* Medicaid.
Owner Proprietary corp.

Dalton Rest Home
453 Cambridge St, Worcester, MA 01610
(508) 756-7310
Admin William J Lange. *Dir of Nursing* Cynthia Carlo; Mary Grenier.
Licensure Intermediate care. *Beds* ICF 34. *Private Pay Patients* 2%. *Certified* Medicaid; Medicare.

Owner Nonprofit corp (Lange Rest Homes Inc).
Admissions Requirements Minimum age 50; Medical examination; Physician's request.
Staff Physicians (consultant); RNs 1 (pt); LPNs 1 (pt); Nurses' aides 6 (pt); Reality therapists 3 (pt); Recreational therapists 1 (pt); Activities coordinators 1 (pt); Dietitians 1 (pt); Ophthalmologists (consultant); Podiatrists (consultant).
Facilities Dining room; Activities room; Crafts room; Laundry room.
Activities Arts & crafts; Reading groups; Prayer groups; Shopping trips; Dances/Social/Cultural gatherings; Pet therapy.

Dodge Park Rest Home
101 Randolph Rd, Worcester, MA 01606
(617) 853-8180
Admin Anthony E Penny.
Licensure Rest home. *Beds* Rest home 60.
Owner Proprietary corp.

Donna Kay Rest Home
16 Marble St, Worcester, MA 01603
(617) 755-6667
Admin Barbara J Duffy.
Licensure Rest home. *Beds* Rest home 60. *Certified* Medicaid.
Owner Proprietary corp.
Admissions Requirements Minimum age 50; Physician's request.
Staff LPNs 1 (pt); Nurses' aides 10 (ft); Activities coordinators 1 (ft); Dietitians 1 (pt).
Facilities Dining room; Activities room; Laundry room; Barber/Beauty shop; Library.
Activities Arts & crafts; Cards; Games; Reading groups; Prayer groups; Movies; Shopping trips; Dances/Social/Cultural gatherings.

Elmwood Manor Nursing Home
21 Catherine St, Worcester, MA 01610
(617) 756-4875
Admin John G Bastille.
Licensure Intermediate care. *Beds* ICF 31. *Certified* Medicaid.
Owner Privately owned.
Admissions Requirements Physician's request.
Staff RNs 1 (pt); LPNs 3 (ft); Physical therapists 1 (pt); Recreational therapists 1 (pt); Occupational therapists 1 (pt); Speech therapists 1 (pt); Activities coordinators 1 (pt); Dietitians 1 (pt); Ophthalmologists 1 (pt); Podiatrists 1 (pt).
Languages Polish, French.
Facilities Dining room; Activities room; Crafts room; Barber/Beauty shop.
Activities Arts & crafts; Cards; Games; Movies; Shopping trips; Dances/Social/Cultural gatherings.

Evamor Manor
23 May St, Worcester, MA 01610
(617) 799-4043
Admin Josephine M Morrow.
Licensure Intermediate care. *Beds* 28. *Certified* Medicaid.
Admissions Requirements Minimum age 21; Medical examination; Physician's request.
Staff RNs 1 (pt); LPNs 1 (pt); Nurses' aides 3 (ft), 3 (pt); Activities coordinators 1 (pt); Dietitians 1 (pt).
Facilities Dining room; Activities room; Crafts room; Laundry room; Barber/Beauty shop; Library.
Activities Arts & crafts; Cards; Games; Reading groups; Prayer groups; Movies; Shopping trips; Dances/Social/Cultural gatherings.

Evans Manor Nursing Home
27 Tirrell St, Worcester, MA 01603
(617) 755-4255
Admin Clifton N LaFrenier.

Licensure Intermediate care. *Beds* ICF 18. *Certified* Medicaid.
Owner Privately owned.

Goddard House Home for Aged Men
1199 Main St, Worcester, MA 01602
(617) 753-4890
Admin Margaret P Naylor.
Licensure Rest home. *Beds* Rest home 32.
Owner Privately owned.
Admissions Requirements Minimum age 65; Medical examination.
Staff RNs; Activities coordinators; Dietitians.
Facilities Dining room; Activities room; Chapel; Crafts room; Laundry room; Barber/Beauty shop; Library; Living room.
Activities Arts & crafts; Cards; Games; Reading groups; Prayer groups; Movies; Shopping trips; Dances/Social/Cultural gatherings.

Greenery Extended Care Center
59 Acton St, Worcester, MA 01604
(617) 791-3147
Admin Steven Haase. *Dir of Nursing* Elizabeth Howard RN. *Medical Dir* Dr Robert McGan.
Licensure Skilled care; Intermediate care. *Beds* SNF 82; ICF 79. *Certified* Medicaid; Medicare.
Owner Proprietary corp (Greenery Rehab Grp).
Admissions Requirements Medical examination.
Staff Physicians 2 (pt); RNs 7 (ft), 3 (pt); LPNs 12 (ft), 5 (pt); Nurses' aides 60 (ft), 12 (pt); Physical therapists 8 (ft); Recreational therapists 5 (ft); Occupational therapists 9 (ft); Speech therapists 4 (ft); Activities coordinators 1 (ft).
Facilities Dining room; Physical therapy room; Activities room; Barber/Beauty shop; Library.
Activities Arts & crafts; Cards; Games; Reading groups; Prayer groups; Movies; Shopping trips; Dances/Social/Cultural gatherings.

Gronna Good Samaritan Center
The Lutheran Home of Worcester Inc, 26 Harvard St, Worcester, MA 01609
(701) 247-2902
Admin David Holmberg. *Dir of Nursing* Joyce Crowe. *Medical Dir* Debby Anderson.
Licensure Intermediate care. *Beds* ICF 58. *Certified* Medicaid.
Owner Nonprofit corp (Evangelical Lutheran/ Good Samaritan Society).
Admissions Requirements Medical examination.
Staff Physicians 1 (pt); RNs 1 (ft), 1 (pt); LPNs 3 (ft), 3 (pt); Nurses' aides 6 (ft), 16 (pt); Physical therapists 1 (pt); Activities coordinators 1 (ft); Dietitians 1 (pt).
Affiliation Lutheran.
Facilities Dining room; Activities room; Crafts room; Laundry room; Barber/Beauty shop.
Activities Arts & crafts; Cards; Games; Reading groups; Prayer groups; Movies; Shopping trips; Dances/Social/Cultural gatherings.

Hammond House Convalescent Home
18 Hammond St, Worcester, MA 01610
(508) 799-7991
Admin Linda M Murphy. *Dir of Nursing* Patricia J Scanlon. *Medical Dir* E Russell Yang.
Licensure Intermediate care. *Beds* ICF 70. *Private Pay Patients* 2%. *Certified* Medicaid.
Owner Proprietary corp (Hillhaven Corp).
Admissions Requirements Minimum age 65.
Staff Physicians 1 (pt); RNs 1 (ft); LPNs 3 (ft), 4 (pt); Nurses' aides 13 (ft), 13 (pt); Activities coordinators 1 (ft); Dietitians 1 (pt).
Languages Spanish.

Facilities Dining room; Activities room;
Chapel; Crafts room; Laundry room; Barber/
Beauty shop; Library.
Activities Arts & crafts; Cards; Games;
Reading groups; Prayer groups; Movies;
Shopping trips; Dances/Social/Cultural
gatherings; Intergenerational programs; Pet
therapy; Outside trips.

Harvard Nursing Home Inc
14 John St, Worcester, MA 01609
(617) 755-7268
Admin Richard J Carlson.
Licensure Intermediate care. *Beds* ICF 41.
Certified Medicaid.
Owner Privately owned.

Hermitage Nursing Home
383 Mill St, Worcester, MA 01602
(617) 791-8131
Admin David D Morrall.
Licensure Skilled care; Intermediate care. *Beds*
SNF 73; ICF 28. *Certified* Medicaid;
Medicare.
Owner Proprietary corp (Beverly Enterprises).

Highland Manor Rest Home
41 Lancaster St, Worcester, MA 01609
(617) 753-0184
Admin Richard B Bastille.
Licensure Rest home. *Beds* Rest home 30.
Owner Privately owned.
Admissions Requirements Minimum age 50;
Medical examination.
Staff LPNs 1 (pt); Nurses' aides 4 (ft), 4 (pt);
Activities coordinators 1 (pt); Dietitians 1
(pt).
Facilities Dining room; Activities room;
Laundry room.
Activities Arts & crafts; Cards; Games;
Movies; Shopping trips; Dances/Social/
Cultural gatherings.

Home for Aged Women
1183 Main St, Worcester, MA 01603
(617) 752-4628
Admin Hilda-Jane Miller.
Medical Dir Dr Horatio Turner.
Licensure Intermediate care; Rest home. *Beds*
ICF 12; Rest home 36. *Certified* Medicaid.
Owner Nonprofit organization/foundation.
Admissions Requirements Females only.
Staff Physicians; RNs; LPNs; Nurses' aides;
Recreational therapists; Activities
coordinators; Dietitians.
Facilities Dining room; Activities room;
Chapel; Crafts room; Laundry room; Barber/
Beauty shop; Library.
Activities Arts & crafts; Games; Prayer groups;
Movies; Shopping trips.

Homestead Hall
10 Homestead Ave, Worcester, MA 01610
(617) 755-7915
Admin Margaret P Naylor.
Licensure Rest home. *Beds* Rest home 30.
Owner Proprietary corp.

Jewish Home for the Aged
629 Salisbury St, Worcester, MA 01609
(617) 798-8653
Admin Marvin A Goldberg.
Licensure Skilled care; Intermediate care. *Beds*
SNF 81; ICF 60. *Certified* Medicaid;
Medicare.
Owner Proprietary corp.
Affiliation Jewish.

Knollwood Nursing Home
271 E Mountain St, Worcester, MA 01606
(508) 853-6910
Admin Paula Ann Kuzdzal. *Dir of Nursing*
Diane Inzerillo RN. *Medical Dir* Betsy
Moody MD.
Licensure Skilled care. *Beds* SNF 70. *Private
Pay Patients* 45%. *Certified* Medicaid;
Medicare.
Owner Proprietary corp (Concord Healthcare
Corp).

Admissions Requirements Physician's request.
Staff RNs 11 (ft), 2 (pt); LPNs 2 (ft), 2 (pt);
Nurses' aides 18 (ft), 2 (pt); Physical
therapists; Recreational therapists 2 (ft), 1
(pt); Activities coordinators 1 (ft); Dietitians.
Facilities Dining room; Physical therapy
room; Activities room; Laundry room;
Barber/Beauty shop.
Activities Arts & crafts; Cards; Games;
Reading groups; Prayer groups; Movies;
Shopping trips; Dances/Social/Cultural
gatherings; Intergenerational programs; Pet
therapy; Exercise class; Music therapy.

Linda Lee Rest Home
30 Institute Rd, Worcester, MA 01609
(617) 753-3718
Admin Olga C Burdett. *Dir of Nursing* Olga C
Burdett LPN. *Medical Dir* Dr Ageonavritis
Demosthenes.
Licensure Rest home. *Beds* Rest home 11.
Certified Medicaid.
Owner Privately owned.
Admissions Requirements Minimum age 21;
Females only; Medical examination;
Physician's request.
Staff Physicians 1 (ft); LPNs 2 (ft); Nurses'
aides 4 (ft); Activities coordinators 1 (ft);
Dietitians 1 (ft); Ophthalmologists 1 (ft).
Facilities Dining room; Activities room;
Laundry room.
Activities Arts & crafts; Cards; Games;
Reading groups; Movies; Shopping trips.

Lincoln Nursing Home
299 Lincoln St, Worcester, MA 01605
(617) 852-2000
Admin Maria J Troisi.
Licensure Skilled care; Intermediate care. *Beds*
SNF 82; ICF 48. *Certified* Medicaid;
Medicare.
Owner Proprietary corp.

Lutheran Home of Worcester Inc
26 Harvard St, Worcester, MA 01609
(508) 754-8877
Admin Rev David Holmberg. *Dir of Nursing*
Donna Cummings RN. *Medical Dir* Lorenzo
Campos MD.
Licensure Skilled care; Intermediate care; Rest
home. *Beds* SNF 69; ICF 60; Rest home 12.
Private Pay Patients 23%. *Certified*
Medicaid.
Owner Nonprofit organization/foundation.
Admissions Requirements Minimum age 65;
Medical examination.
Staff Physicians 1 (pt); RNs 5 (ft), 20 (pt);
LPNs 2 (ft), 9 (pt); Nurses' aides 24 (ft), 37
(pt); Physical therapists 1 (pt); Occupational
therapists 1 (pt); Activities coordinators 1
(ft); Dietitians 1 (pt).
Affiliation Lutheran.
Facilities Dining room; Physical therapy
room; Activities room; Chapel; Laundry
room; Barber/Beauty shop.
Activities Arts & crafts; Cards; Games;
Reading groups; Prayer groups; Movies;
Shopping trips; Dances/Social/Cultural
gatherings; Intergenerational programs.

Maple Hall Nursing Home
19 King St, Worcester, MA 01610
(617) 753-4380
Licensure Intermediate care. *Beds* 56.
Certified Medicaid.

Meadowbrook Manor Rest Home
PO Box 227, Greendale Station, 856 Main St,
Worcester, MA 01606-0227
(508) 756-7822
Admin Richard F Alarie. *Dir of Nursing* Joan
F Jewell. *Medical Dir* Dr Herbert S Jordan.
Licensure Community support facility. *Beds*
Community support 25. *Private Pay Patients*
1%. *Certified* Medicaid.
Owner Privately owned (Alarie-Ramsdell Rest
Home's).

Admissions Requirements Medical
examination.
Staff Physicians 1 (pt); RNs 1 (pt); Nurses'
aides 6 (pt); Recreational therapists 1 (pt);
Dietitians 1 (pt); Podiatrists 1 (pt).
Facilities Dining room; Activities room;
Laundry room.
Activities Arts & crafts; Cards; Games;
Reading groups; Prayer groups; Movies.

Mill Hill Nursing Home
215 Mill St, Worcester, MA 01602
(617) 791-3168
Admin Richard Johnson.
Licensure Skilled care; Intermediate care. *Beds*
SNF 39; ICF 62. *Certified* Medicaid.
Owner Privately owned.

Newton Manor Rest Home
710 Pleasant St, Worcester, MA 01602
(617) 753-4024
Admin Marie Callahan.
Licensure Rest home. *Beds* Rest home 25.
Certified Medicaid; Medicare.
Owner Privately owned.
Staff Physicians 1 (ft); RNs 1 (ft); Nurses'
aides 6 (ft); Activities coordinators 1 (ft).
Facilities Dining room; Laundry room;
Barber/Beauty shop; Library.
Activities Arts & crafts; Games; Reading
groups.

Notre Dame Long-Term Care Center
555 Plantation St, Worcester, MA 01605
(617) 852-1486
Admin Sr Margaret F Middleton. *Dir of
Nursing* Sr Barbara A Gubski RN. *Medical
Dir* James Morrison MD.
Licensure Skilled care; Intermediate care. *Beds*
SNF 18; ICF 33. *Private Pay Patients* 4%.
Certified Medicaid.
Owner Nonprofit corp.
Admissions Requirements Females only.
Staff RNs 2 (ft), 6 (pt); LPNs 3 (pt); Nurses'
aides 3 (ft), 15 (pt); Physical therapists 1
(pt); Recreational therapists 1 (ft), 2 (pt);
Occupational therapists 1 (pt); Dietitians 1
(ft); Podiatrists 1 (pt).
Affiliation Roman Catholic.
Activities Arts & crafts; Cards; Games;
Reading groups; Prayer groups; Movies;
Shopping trips; Dances/Social/Cultural
gatherings.

Odd Fellows Home of Massachusetts
104 Randolph Rd, Worcester, MA 01606
(617) 853-6687
Admin Deanne Willis. *Dir of Nursing* Shirley
Platts. *Medical Dir* Dr Steven R Rozak.
Licensure Intermediate care; Rest home. *Beds*
SNF 37; 38. *Certified* Medicaid.
Owner Nonprofit corp.
Admissions Requirements Medical
examination.
Staff Physicians 1 (pt); RNs 2 (ft); LPNs 3
(ft), 2 (pt); Nurses' aides 12 (ft), 6 (pt);
Physical therapists 1 (pt); Activities
coordinators 1 (ft); Dietitians 1 (pt).
Affiliation Independent Order of Odd Fellows
& Rebekahs.
Facilities Dining room; Activities room;
Chapel; Crafts room; Laundry room; Barber/
Beauty shop; Library.
Activities Arts & crafts; Cards; Games;
Reading groups; Prayer groups; Movies;
Shopping trips; Dances/Social/Cultural
gatherings; Trips.

Park Terrace Nursing & Rehabilitation Center
39 Queen St, Worcester, MA 01610
(617) 753-4791
Admin Linda K Benson. *Dir of Nursing* Marie
Lanzillotti RN. *Medical Dir* Dr Jeffrey Burl.
Licensure Skilled care; Intermediate care;
Alzheimer's care. *Beds* SNF 80; ICF 80.
Certified Medicaid; Medicare.
Owner Proprietary corp.

Admissions Requirements Minimum age 21;
Medical examination; Physician's request.
Staff Physicians 1 (pt); RNs 10 (ft); LPNs 10
(ft); Nurses' aides 50 (ft), 20 (pt); Physical
therapists 1 (ft), 1 (pt); Reality therapists 1
(ft); Recreational therapists 3 (ft);
Occupational therapists 1 (pt); Speech
therapists 1 (pt); Activities coordinators 1
(ft); Dietitians 1 (pt); Ophthalmologists 1
(pt); Podiatrists 1 (pt); Dentists 1 (pt);
Medical Records.
Facilities Dining room; Physical therapy
room; Activities room; Chapel; Crafts room;
Laundry room; Barber/Beauty shop; Patio w/
furniture.
Activities Arts & crafts; Cards; Games;
Reading groups; Prayer groups; Movies;
Shopping trips; Dances/Social/Cultural
gatherings; Birds & fish.

Providence House Nursing Home
119 Providence St, Worcester, MA 01604
(617) 791-7881
Admin Ann M Nadreau.
Licensure Skilled care; Intermediate care. *Beds*
SNF 40; ICF 120. *Certified* Medicaid;
Medicare.
Owner Proprietary corp.

Roselawn Manor Rest Home
60 Randolph Rd, Worcester, MA 01606
(617) 853-5140
Admin Ruth G Bopp.
Licensure Rest home. *Beds* Rest home 12.
Owner Privately owned.

St Francis Home
101 Plantation St, Worcester, MA 01604
(508) 755-8605
Admin Sr Jacquelyn Alix PFM. *Dir of Nursing*
Sr Frances Emond PFM. *Medical Dir*
Stanley L Kocot MD.
Licensure Skilled care; Intermediate care. *Beds*
SNF 100; ICF 37. *Private Pay Patients* 23%.
Certified Medicaid.
Owner Nonprofit organization/foundation.
Admissions Requirements Medical
examination.
Staff RNs 6 (ft), 5 (pt); LPNs 10 (ft), 8 (pt);
Nurses' aides 30 (ft), 20 (pt); Physical
therapists 2 (pt); Reality therapists 1 (ft), 2
(pt); Recreational therapists 1 (ft), 2 (pt);
Occupational therapists 1 (ft); Activities
coordinators 1 (ft); Dietitians 1 (ft).
Languages French.
Affiliation Roman Catholic.
Facilities Dining room; Physical therapy
room; Activities room; Chapel; Crafts room;
Laundry room; Barber/Beauty shop; Library.
Activities Arts & crafts; Cards; Games;
Reading groups; Prayer groups; Movies;
Shopping trips; Dances/Social/Cultural
gatherings; Intergenerational programs; Pet
therapy; Adopt-a-grandparent program.

Salisbury Nursing Home
25 Oriol Dr, Worcester, MA 01605
(617) 852-3330
Admin Stephen F Flanagan.
Licensure Skilled care; Intermediate care. *Beds*
SNF 80; ICF 80. *Certified* Medicaid.
Owner Proprietary corp.

Schussler Rest Home
PO Box 227, Greendale Station, 1 Schussler
Rd, Worcester, MA 01606-0227
(508) 757-6759
Admin Richard F Alarie. *Dir of Nursing* Eric
Dunphy RN. *Medical Dir* Dr Kenneth
Farbman.
Licensure Community support facility. *Beds*
Community support facility 25. *Private Pay
Patients* 2%. *Certified* Medicaid.
Owner Privately owned (Alarie-Ramsdell Rest
Homes).
Admissions Requirements Medical
examination.

Staff Physicians 1 (pt); RNs 1 (pt); Nurses'
aides 3 (pt), 3 (pt); Recreational therapists 1
(pt); Dietitians 1 (pt); Podiatrists 1 (pt).
Facilities Dining room; Activities room;
Laundry room.
Activities Arts & crafts; Cards; Games;
Reading groups; Prayer groups; Movies.

Smith Rest Home
25 Sturgis St, Worcester, MA 01605
(617) 755-8711
Admin Richard F Alarie.
Licensure Rest home. *Beds* Rest home 27.
Owner Privately owned.

Spring Valley Convalescent Home
81 Chatham St, Worcester, MA 01609
(617) 754-3276
Admin James M Meola.
Licensure Skilled care; Intermediate care. *Beds*
SNF 41; ICF 41. *Certified* Medicaid.
Owner Proprietary corp (First Healthcare
Corp).

Stonehouse Hill Nursing Home
PO Box 38, Worcester, MA 01602
(508) 755-5345
Admin Karen Wilkinson. *Dir of Nursing*
Linda Anderson. *Medical Dir* Dmetre
Tsagronis MD.
Licensure Intermediate care. *Beds* ICF 48.
Certified Medicaid.
Owner Proprietary corp (Hillhaven Corp).
Facilities Dining room; Activities room;
Laundry room.
Activities Arts & crafts; Cards; Games;
Reading groups; Prayer groups; Movies;
Shopping trips; Dances/Social/Cultural
gatherings; Pet therapy.

Wayside Nursing Home Inc
751 Grove St, Worcester, MA 01605
(617) 852-4365
Admin Barbara H Leasure.
Licensure Skilled care. *Beds* SNF 73. *Certified*
Medicaid; Medicare.
Owner Proprietary corp.

West Side House
35 Fruit St, Worcester, MA 01609
(508) 752-6763, 831-9920 FAX
Admin Kenneth L Sleeper. *Dir of Nursing*
Patricia Conefrey. *Medical Dir* Dr C B S
Patel.
Licensure Skilled care. *Beds* SNF 91. *Private
Pay Patients* 8%. *Certified* Medicaid.
Owner Proprietary corp (Elder Care Services).
Admissions Requirements Minimum age 65;
Primary diagnosis must be psychiatric.
Staff Physicians 6 (pt); RNs 24 (ft); LPNs 18
(ft); Nurses' aides 50 (ft); Physical therapists
1 (ft); Reality therapists 2 (pt); Recreational
therapists 4 (pt); Occupational therapists 1
(pt); Speech therapists 1 (pt); Activities
coordinators 1 (ft); Dietitians 1 (ft);
Ophthalmologists 1 (pt); Audiologists 1 (pt);
Dentists 1 (pt); Psychologists.
Facilities Dining room; Activities room;
Laundry room.
Activities Arts & crafts; Cards; Games;
Reading groups; Movies; Shopping trips;
Dances/Social/Cultural gatherings; Therapy
groups.

Winter Hill Rest Home
24 Chester St, Worcester, MA 01605
(617) 852-2438
Admin William J Lange.
Medical Dir Dr Carl Marsh.
Licensure Rest home. *Beds* Rest home 15.
Owner Proprietary corp.
Admissions Requirements Females only;
Medical examination; Physician's request.
Facilities Dining room; Activities room.
Activities Arts & crafts; Cards; Games;
Reading groups; Movies; Shopping trips;
Dances/Social/Cultural gatherings.

Wrentham

King's Daughters & Sons Home
PO Box 419, "Pond Home" 289 East St,
Wrentham, MA 02093
(508) 384-3531
Admin DeAnna E Willis. *Dir of Nursing*
Dorothy B Adams, Mgr. *Medical Dir* Robert
Kelliher.
Licensure Intermediate care; Retirement. *Beds*
ICF 6; Retirement 25. *Private Pay Patients*
100%.
Owner Nonprofit organization/foundation.
Admissions Requirements Minimum age 65;
Medical examination.
Staff Physicians 2 (pt); LPNs 6 (pt); Nurses'
aides 12 (pt); Physical therapists 1 (pt);
Activities coordinators 1 (pt); Dietitians 1
(pt); Ophthalmologists 1 (pt); Podiatrists 1
(pt); Hairdresser.
Facilities Dining room; Activities room;
Laundry room; Barber/Beauty shop; Library.
Activities Arts & crafts; Cards; Games;
Movies; Shopping trips; Dances/Social/
Cultural gatherings; Pet therapy.

Maples Convalescent Home
24 Common St, Wrentham, MA 02093
(617) 384-3481
Admin Caroline F Capachin.
Licensure Intermediate care. *Beds* ICF 50.
Certified Medicaid.
Owner Proprietary corp.
Admissions Requirements Minimum age 60;
Medical examination; Physician's request.
Staff RNs 1 (ft), 1 (pt); LPNs 3 (ft), 3 (pt);
Nurses' aides 9 (ft), 9 (pt); Activities
coordinators 1 (ft); Dietitians 1 (pt).
Facilities Dining room; Activities room;
Laundry room; Barber/Beauty shop.
Activities Arts & crafts; Cards; Games;
Reading groups; Prayer groups; Movies;
Shopping trips; Dances/Social/Cultural
gatherings.

Maples Nursing & Retirement Center
20 Common St, Wrentham, MA 02093
(617) 384-3481
Admin Caroline F Capachin.
Licensure Skilled care. *Beds* SNF 82.
Owner Privately owned.

Serenity Hill Nursing Home
655 Dedham St, Wrentham, MA 02093
(508) 384-3400
Admin DeAnna Willis. *Dir of Nursing* Anne
Marie Reilly. *Medical Dir* Hooshang Poor
MD.
Licensure Intermediate care. *Beds* ICF 44.
Private Pay Patients 30%. *Certified*
Medicaid.
Owner Proprietary corp.
Admissions Requirements Minimum age 60;
Medical examination; Physician's request.
Staff RNs 2 (ft), 1 (pt); LPNs 4 (ft), 1 (pt);
Nurses' aides 11 (ft), 4 (pt); Recreational
therapists 1 (ft); Dietitians 1 (pt).
Facilities Dining room; Laundry room.
Activities Arts & crafts; Cards; Games;
Reading groups; Prayer groups; Movies;
Shopping trips; Dances/Social/Cultural
gatherings; Intergenerational programs.

Sheldonville Nursing Home
PO Box 1050, 1022 West St, Wrentham, MA
02093
(617) 384-2421
Admin Joseph G Ranieri.
Licensure Intermediate care. *Beds* ICF 50.
Certified Medicaid.
Owner Privately owned.
Staff Physicians; RNs; LPNs; Nurses' aides;
Physical therapists; Reality therapists;
Recreational therapists; Occupational
therapists; Speech therapists; Activities
coordinators; Dietitians; Ophthalmologists;
Podiatrists; Audiologists; Dentists.

Facilities Dining room; Activities room; Chapel; Crafts room; Barber/Beauty shop; TV sitting room.

Activities Arts & crafts; Cards; Games; Reading groups; Prayer groups; Movies; Shopping trips; Dances/Social/Cultural gatherings.

MICHIGAN

Adrian

Adrian Health Care Center
130 Sand Creek Hwy, Adrian, MI 49221
Licensure Intermediate care. *Beds* ICF 120.
  Certified Medicaid.
Owner Proprietary corp (Beverly Enterprises).

Charlotte Stephenson Home
120 N Locust St, Adrian, MI 49221
Licensure Home for aged. *Beds* Home for
  aged 58.

Lenawee County Medical Care Facility
200 Sand Creek Hwy, Adrian, MI 49221
(517) 263-6794
Admin Mark C Wendt. *Dir of Nursing* Alice
  Schultz RN. *Medical Dir* Randall De
  Arment DO.
Licensure Skilled care; Alzheimer's care. *Beds*
  SNF 136. *Certified* Medicaid; Medicare.
Owner Publicly owned.
Admissions Requirements Medical
  examination; Physician's request.
Staff Physicians 1 (pt); RNs 6 (ft), 6 (pt);
  LPNs 6 (ft), 6 (pt); Nurses' aides 15 (ft), 58
  (pt); Physical therapists 1 (pt); Activities
  coordinators 1 (ft), 1 (pt); Dietitians 1 (pt);
  Ophthalmologists 1 (pt).
Languages Spanish, Polish, German.
Facilities Dining room; Physical therapy
  room; Activities room; Laundry room;
  Barber/Beauty shop.
Activities Arts & crafts; Cards; Games;
  Reading groups; Prayer groups; Movies;
  Shopping trips; Dances/Social/Cultural
  gatherings.

Lynwood Manor
730 Kimole Ln, Adrian, MI 49221
(517) 263-6771, 265-8599 FAX
Admin Katherine R Smith, acting. *Dir of
  Nursing* Sybil A Gamble RN. *Medical Dir*
  Michael McAuliffe MD.
Licensure Skilled care; Intermediate care. *Beds*
  Swing beds SNF/ICF 98. *Private Pay
  Patients* 25%. *Certified* Medicaid; Medicare.
Owner Proprietary corp (Health Enterprises
  Inc).
Admissions Requirements Minimum age 13;
  Medical examination; Physician's request.
Staff RNs 2 (ft), 3 (pt); LPNs 4 (ft), 5 (pt);
  Nurses' aides 10 (ft), 35 (pt); Recreational
  therapists 1 (ft); Activities coordinators 1
  (ft); Dietitians 1 (ft).
Languages Spanish.
Facilities Dining room; Physical therapy
  room; Activities room; Chapel; Crafts room;
  Barber/Beauty shop.
Activities Arts & crafts; Cards; Games; Prayer
  groups; Movies; Shopping trips; Pet therapy.

Provincial House—Adrian
700 Lakeshire Trail, Adrian, MI 49221
(517) 263-0781
Medical Dir Dr Michael Worzniak.
Licensure Skilled care. *Beds* SNF 117.
  Certified Medicaid; Medicare.
Owner Proprietary corp (Beverly Enterprises).

Admissions Requirements Medical
  examination; Physician's request.
Staff RNs 5 (ft), 1 (pt); LPNs 8 (ft); Physical
  therapists 1 (pt); Occupational therapists 1
  (pt); Speech therapists 1 (pt); Activities
  coordinators 1 (ft); Dietitians 1 (pt);
  Audiologists 1 (pt).
Facilities Dining room; Physical therapy
  room; Activities room; Barber/Beauty shop.
Activities Arts & crafts; Cards; Games;
  Reading groups; Prayer groups; Movies;
  Shopping trips; Dances/Social/Cultural
  gatherings.

Albion

Albion Manor Care Center
1000 W Erie St, Albion, MI 49224
(517) 629-5501
Medical Dir Dr Horace Davis.
Licensure Skilled care. *Beds* SNF 80. *Certified*
  Medicaid; Medicare.
Owner Proprietary corp (Vantage Healthcare).
Admissions Requirements Minimum age 15;
  Medical examination; Physician's request.
Staff Physicians 8 (pt); RNs 1 (ft), 2 (pt);
  LPNs 4 (ft), 5 (pt); Nurses' aides 26 (ft), 11
  (pt); Physical therapists 1 (pt); Occupational
  therapists 1 (pt); Speech therapists 1 (pt);
  Activities coordinators 1 (ft); Dietitians 1
  (pt); Dentists 1 (pt).
Facilities Dining room; Physical therapy
  room; Activities room; Crafts room; Laundry
  room; Barber/Beauty shop.
Activities Arts & crafts; Cards; Games;
  Reading groups; Prayer groups; Movies;
  Shopping trips; Dances/Social/Cultural
  gatherings.

Allegan

Allegan County Medical Care Facility
Rte 2, 3265 122nd Ave, Allegan, MI 49010
(616) 673-2102
Admin Keith M Miller.
Licensure Skilled care. *Beds* SNF 60. *Certified*
  Medicaid; Medicare.
Owner Publicly owned.

Pine Oaks Nursing Center
1200 Ely St, Allegan, MI 49010
Licensure Skilled care. *Beds* SNF 123.
  Certified Medicaid; Medicare.

Allen Park

Allen Park Convalescent Home
9150 Allen Rd, Allen Park, MI 48101
(313) 386-2150
Licensure Skilled care. *Beds* SNF 180.
  Certified Medicare.
Owner Proprietary corp (Health Care and
  Retirement Corp).

Inter-City Christian Manor
4600 Allen Rd, Allen Park, MI 48101
(313) 383-6226

Admin Robert G Hopper. *Dir of Nursing*
  Debbie Kuzma.
Licensure Intermediate care; Retirement. *Beds*
  ICF 17. *Private Pay Patients* 100%.
Owner Nonprofit corp.
Admissions Requirements Minimum age 62;
  Medical examination.
Staff RNs 5 (ft), 5 (pt); LPNs 2 (ft), 3 (pt);
  Nurses' aides 10 (ft), 10 (pt); Activities
  coordinators 1 (pt).
Affiliation Baptist.
Facilities Dining room; Activities room;
  Laundry room; Barber/Beauty shop; Library.
Activities Arts & crafts; Games; Prayer groups;
  Shopping trips.

Allendale

West Michigan Care Center
11007 Radcliff Dr, Allendale, MI 49401
(616) 895-6688
Admin Philip B Turlington. *Dir of Nursing*
  Lucille Omiljan. *Medical Dir* Roger Holman
  DO.
Licensure Skilled care. *Beds* SNF 60. *Private
  Pay Patients* 25%. *Certified* Medicaid;
  Medicare.
Owner Proprietary corp.
Admissions Requirements Minimum age 17.
Staff RNs 2 (ft), 3 (pt); LPNs 2 (ft), 5 (pt);
  Nurses' aides 10 (ft), 26 (pt); Activities
  coordinators.
Facilities Dining room; Physical therapy
  room; Activities room; Laundry room;
  Barber/Beauty shop.
Activities Arts & crafts; Cards; Games;
  Reading groups; Prayer groups; Movies;
  Dances/Social/Cultural gatherings; Pet
  therapy.

Alma

Michigan Masonic Home
1200 Wright Ave, Alma, MI 48801
(517) 463-3141
Admin Roger L Myers.
Medical Dir Dr Richard Remsberg.
Licensure Skilled care; Intermediate care;
  Home for aged; Independent living. *Beds*
  Swing beds SNF/ICF 204; Home for aged
  205; Independent living 16. *Certified*
  Medicaid; Medicare.
Owner Nonprofit corp.
Admissions Requirements Medical
  examination.
Staff Physicians 3 (ft); RNs 8 (ft); LPNs 55
  (ft); Nurses' aides 70 (ft); Physical therapists
  1 (ft); Recreational therapists 1 (ft);
  Occupational therapists 6 (ft); Dietitians 1
  (ft); Ophthalmologists 1 (ft); Podiatrists 1
  (ft); Dentists 1 (ft).
Affiliation Masons.
Facilities Dining room; Physical therapy
  room; Activities room; Chapel; Crafts room;
  Laundry room; Barber/Beauty shop; Library.
Activities Arts & crafts; Cards; Games;
  Reading groups; Prayer groups; Movies.

Wilcox Health Care Center
525 N State St, Alma, MI 48801
(517) 463-4000
Licensure Intermediate care. *Beds* ICF 45.
  Certified Medicaid.

Alpena

Peirce Nursing Home
1234 Golf Course Rd, Alpena, MI 49707
(517) 356-1030
Admin Donald J Wisniewski. *Dir of Nursing*
  Mary K Wisniewski. *Medical Dir* Dr Don
  Miller.
Licensure Intermediate care. *Beds* ICF 36.
  Private Pay Patients 25%. *Certified*
  Medicaid.
Owner Proprietary corp.
Admissions Requirements Physician's request.
Staff Physicians 1 (pt); RNs 1 (ft); LPNs 3
  (ft), 4 (pt); Nurses' aides 9 (ft), 5 (pt);
  Activities coordinators 1 (ft).
Facilities Dining room; Activities room;
  Crafts room; Laundry room.
Activities Arts & crafts; Cards; Games;
  Reading groups; Prayer groups; Movies; Pet
  therapy.

Provincial House—Alpena
301 Long Rapids Rd, Alpena, MI 49707
(517) 356-2194
Admin Sylvia Owens. *Dir of Nursing* Roma
  Dean RN.
Licensure Skilled care. *Beds* SNF 117.
  Certified Medicaid; Medicare.
Owner Proprietary corp (Beverly Enterprises).
Admissions Requirements Minimum age 18;
  Medical examination.
Staff RNs 6 (ft); LPNs 15 (ft); Nurses' aides
  100 (ft); Physical therapists 1 (ft); Speech
  therapists 1 (ft); Activities coordinators 1
  (ft); Dietitians 1 (ft); Ophthalmologists 1 (ft);
  Social workers 1 (ft).
Facilities Dining room; Physical therapy
  room; Activities room; Laundry room;
  Barber/Beauty shop; TV room.
Activities Arts & crafts; Cards; Games;
  Reading groups; Prayer groups; Movies;
  Shopping trips; Dances/Social/Cultural
  gatherings.

Ann Arbor

Glacier Hills
1200 Earhart Rd, Ann Arbor, MI 48105
(313) 769-6410, 769-3613 FAX
Admin Terri Durkin Williams RN NHA. *Dir
  of Nursing* Nancy Stickradt RN.
Licensure Skilled care; Home for aged;
  Alzheimer's care. *Beds* SNF 89; Home for
  aged 302. *Private Pay Patients* 80%. *Certified*
  Medicaid; Medicare.
Owner Nonprofit corp.
Admissions Requirements Minimum age 15.
Staff RNs 10 (ft), 8 (pt); LPNs 5 (ft), 2 (pt);
  Nurses' aides 40 (ft), 10 (pt); Physical
  therapists 1 (ft), 1 (pt); Occupational
  therapists 1 (ft), 1 (pt); Speech therapists 1
  (pt); Activities coordinators 1 (ft), 3 (pt);
  Dietitians 1 (ft); Podiatrists 1 (pt).
Facilities Dining room; Physical therapy
  room; Activities room; Laundry room;
  Barber/Beauty shop; Library; Bank; Gift
  shop.
Activities Arts & crafts; Games; Reading
  groups; Prayer groups; Movies; Shopping
  trips; Dances/Social/Cultural gatherings;
  Intergenerational programs; Pet therapy.

Hillside Terrace
1939 Jackson Ave, Ann Arbor, MI 48103
(313) 761-4451
Licensure Intermediate care; Home for aged.
  Beds ICF 23; Home for aged 88. *Certified*
  Medicaid.

Whitehall Convalescent Home
3370 Morgan Rd, Ann Arbor, MI 48108
(313) 971-3230
Dir of Nursing Mabel K Johnson RN. *Medical
  Dir* Russell Achison MD.
Licensure Intermediate care. *Beds* ICF 102.
  Certified Medicaid.
Admissions Requirements Minimum age 18;
  Medical examination; Physician's request.
Staff RNs 6 (ft), 2 (pt); LPNs 8 (ft), 2 (pt);
  Nurses' aides 60 (ft), 14 (pt); Physical
  therapists 1 (pt); Recreational therapists 1
  (ft); Activities coordinators 1 (ft); Dietitians
  1 (pt).
Facilities Dining room; Physical therapy
  room; Activities room; Crafts room; Laundry
  room; Barber/Beauty shop.
Activities Arts & crafts; Cards; Games;
  Reading groups; Prayer groups; Movies.

Woodmont of Ann Arbor
355 Huron View Blvd, Ann Arbor, MI 48103
(313) 761-3800
Admin Brenda L Smith. *Dir of Nursing*
  Lynnda Fleischman RN. *Medical Dir*
  William Silverstone DO.
Licensure Skilled care; Intermediate care. *Beds*
  SNF 36; ICF 35. *Private Pay Patients* 46%.
  Certified Medicaid; Medicare.
Owner Proprietary corp (Woodmont
  Healthcare Services Inc).
Admissions Requirements Minimum age 16;
  Medical examination; Physician's request.
Staff RNs 1 (ft), 4 (pt); LPNs 6 (ft), 4 (pt);
  Nurses' aides; Physical therapists 1 (pt);
  Reality therapists 1 (ft); Recreational
  therapists 1 (ft); Occupational therapists 1
  (pt); Speech therapists 1 (pt); Activities
  coordinators 1 (ft); Dietitians 1 (pt);
  Podiatrists 1 (pt).
Facilities Dining room; Physical therapy
  room; Activities room; Crafts room; Laundry
  room; Barber/Beauty shop.
Activities Arts & crafts; Cards; Games;
  Reading groups; Prayer groups; Movies;
  Dances/Social/Cultural gatherings;
  Intergenerational programs; Pet therapy.

Armada

Fair Acres Nursing Home
22600 Armada Ridge Rd, Armada, MI 48005
(313) 784-5322
Admin Diane M Ewald. *Dir of Nursing*
  Patricia Falk RN.
Licensure Intermediate care. *Beds* ICF 49.
  Certified Medicaid.
Owner Privately owned.
Admissions Requirements Minimum age 18;
  Medical examination; Physician's request.
Staff RNs 1 (ft), 3 (pt); LPNs 2 (ft), 3 (pt);
  Nurses' aides 10 (ft), 20 (pt); Activities
  coordinators 1 (ft); Dietitians 1 (pt).
Facilities Dining room; Activities room;
  Barber/Beauty shop; Beautiful grounds.
Activities Arts & crafts; Cards; Games;
  Reading groups; Prayer groups; Movies;
  Shopping trips; Dances/Social/Cultural
  gatherings.

Ashley

Maple Valley
211 W Wallace, Ashley, MI 48806
(517) 847-2011
Admin Sherry R Beck. *Dir of Nursing* Minnie
  Freed RN.
Licensure Intermediate care. *Beds* ICF 49.
  Private Pay Patients 38%. *Certified*
  Medicaid.
Owner Proprietary corp.
Admissions Requirements Medical
  examination; Physician's request.
Staff RNs 1 (ft); LPNs 3 (ft), 2 (pt); Nurses'
  aides 10 (ft), 13 (pt); Physical therapists
  (contracted); Dietitians.
Languages Slovak.

Facilities Dining room; Physical therapy
  room; Activities room; Crafts room; Laundry
  room; Barber/Beauty shop.
Activities Arts & crafts; Cards; Games;
  Reading groups; Prayer groups; Movies;
  Dances/Social/Cultural gatherings;
  Intergenerational programs; Pet therapy.

Bad Axe

Four Seasons Health Care
1167 E Hopson St, Bad Axe, MI 48413
Licensure Skilled care. *Beds* SNF 112.
  Certified Medicaid; Medicare.

Huron County Medical Care Facility
1116 S Van Dyke Rd, Bad Axe, MI 48413
(517) 269-6425
Admin Arthur J Woelke. *Dir of Nursing* Gwen
  McLachlan RN. *Medical Dir* R A Lockard
  MD.
Licensure Skilled care. *Beds* SNF 112.
  Certified Medicaid; Medicare.
Owner Publicly owned.
Admissions Requirements Medical
  examination; Physician's request.
Staff Physicians 2 (pt); RNs 6 (ft), 8 (pt);
  LPNs 6 (ft), 4 (pt); Nurses' aides 44 (ft), 20
  (pt); Physical therapists 1 (pt); Recreational
  therapists 1 (ft); Occupational therapists 1
  (pt); Speech therapists 1 (pt); Dietitians 1
  (ft).
Facilities Dining room; Physical therapy
  room; Activities room; Crafts room; Laundry
  room; Barber/Beauty shop.
Activities Arts & crafts; Cards; Games;
  Reading groups; Prayer groups; Movies;
  Dances/Social/Cultural gatherings; Bus tours;
  County fair; Gardening.

Sunny Acres Nursing Center Inc
2762 Pigeon Rd, Bad Axe, MI 48413
(517) 269-9138
Admin Patricia Patterson.
Medical Dir O Kay Seiting.
Licensure Intermediate care. *Beds* ICF 30.
  Certified Medicaid.
Owner Proprietary corp.
Admissions Requirements Medical
  examination.
Staff RNs 2 (ft), 2 (pt); LPNs 3 (ft), 5 (pt);
  Nurses' aides 2 (ft), 8 (pt); Activities
  coordinators 1 (pt); Dietitians 1 (ft).
Languages German, Polish.
Facilities Dining room; Activities room;
  Laundry room.
Activities Arts & crafts; Cards; Games;
  Reading groups; Prayer groups; Movies;
  Shopping trips; Dances/Social/Cultural
  gatherings.

Baldwin

Oak Village Care Center
Rte 2 Box 2258, 4153 S M-37, Baldwin, MI
  49304
(616) 745-4648d
Licensure Skilled care; Intermediate care. *Beds*
  Swing beds SNF/ICF 135. *Certified*
  Medicaid; Medicare.

Battle Creek

Arrowood Nursing Center
270 N Bedford Rd, Battle Creek, MI 49017
(616) 968-2296
Licensure Skilled care. *Beds* SNF 123.
  Certified Medicaid; Medicare.

Calhoun County Medical Care Facility
1150 E Michigan Ave, Battle Creek, MI 49017
(616) 962-5458
Admin Joanne J Konkle MSW CG. *Dir of
  Nursing* Kayla Vandegriff. *Medical Dir*
  Robert Oakes MD.

Licensure Skilled care; Alzheimer's care; Adult day care. *Beds* SNF 120. *Private Pay Patients* 5%. *Certified* Medicaid; Medicare. *Owner* Publicly owned.
Admissions Requirements Minimum age 18; Medical examination; Physician's request.
Staff Physicians 8 (pt); RNs 9 (ft), 4 (pt); LPNs 10 (ft), 7 (pt); Nurses' aides 42 (ft), 6 (pt); Physical therapists 1 (pt); Occupational therapists 1 (pt); Speech therapists 1 (pt); Activities coordinators 1 (pt); Dietitians 1 (pt); Ophthalmologists 1 (pt); Podiatrists 1 (pt); Audiologists 1 (pt).
Facilities Dining room; Physical therapy room; Activities room; Chapel; Crafts room; Laundry room; Barber/Beauty shop; Outdoor fenced courtyard.
Activities Arts & crafts; Cards; Games; Reading groups; Prayer groups; Movies; Shopping trips; Dances/Social/Cultural gatherings; Intergenerational programs; Pet therapy.

Mercy Pavilion of Battle Creek
80 N 20th St, Battle Creek, MI 49015
Licensure Skilled care; Home for aged. *Beds* SNF 77; Home for aged 64. *Certified* Medicaid; Medicare.

Provincial House—Battle Creek
111 Evergreen Rd, Battle Creek, MI 49017
Admin Helen Gastian.
Medical Dir Gerald Rutledge DO.
Licensure Skilled care. *Beds* SNF 117. *Certified* Medicaid; Medicare.
Owner Proprietary corp (Beverly Enterprises).
Admissions Requirements Medical examination; Physician's request.
Staff RNs 5 (ft), 1 (pt); LPNs 6 (ft), 4 (pt); Nurses' aides 32 (ft), 15 (pt); Activities coordinators 1 (ft); Dietitians 1 (ft).
Facilities Dining room; Physical therapy room; Activities room; Chapel; Crafts room; Laundry room; Barber/Beauty shop; Library.
Activities Arts & crafts; Cards; Games; Reading groups; Prayer groups; Movies; Shopping trips; Dances/Social/Cultural gatherings.

Riverside Manor
675 Wagner Dr, Battle Creek, MI 49017
(616) 962-6244
Admin Douglas Allen Hart. *Dir of Nursing* Carolyn Hess RN.
Licensure Intermediate care; Home for aged; Alzheimer's care. *Beds* ICF 99; Home for aged 8. *Private Pay Patients* 20-25%. *Certified* Medicaid.
Owner Proprietary corp.
Admissions Requirements Minimum age 15; Physician's request.
Staff RNs 2 (ft); LPNs 4 (ft), 5 (pt); Nurses' aides 30 (ft), 8 (pt); Activities coordinators 1 (ft), 1 (pt).
Facilities Dining room; Activities room; Chapel; Barber/Beauty shop; Library; 11-Bed Alzheimer's unit; Fenced-in outdoor area.
Activities Arts & crafts; Cards; Games; Prayer groups; Movies; Shopping trips; Dances/Social/Cultural gatherings; Intergenerational programs; Pet therapy; Religious services.

Springhill Manor
200 E Roosevelt Ave, Battle Creek, MI 49017
(616) 965-3327
Admin Betty J Martin. *Dir of Nursing* Donna D Bunce RN. *Medical Dir* Paul Diamante MD.
Licensure Skilled care. *Beds* SNF 65. *Certified* Medicaid; Medicare.
Owner Proprietary corp (Health Care and Retirement Corp).
Admissions Requirements Medical examination; Physician's request.
Staff RNs 4 (ft), 4 (pt); LPNs 2 (ft), 6 (pt); Nurses' aides 17 (ft), 20 (pt); Physical therapists 1 (pt); Speech therapists 1 (pt);

Activities coordinators 1 (ft); Dietitians 1 (ft); Ophthalmologists 1 (pt); Podiatrists 1 (pt).
Facilities Dining room; Laundry room; Barber/Beauty shop.
Activities Arts & crafts; Cards; Games; Reading groups; Prayer groups; Movies; Shopping trips; Dances/Social/Cultural gatherings; Bus tours twice per year.

Bay City

Bay Shores Nursing Care Center
3254 E Midland Rd, Bay City, MI 48706
(517) 686-3770, 686-9601 FAX
Admin Glenn J Porterfield. *Dir of Nursing* Carole Thomas RN. *Medical Dir* Dr Daniel T Webb.
Licensure Skilled care; Intermediate care. *Beds* SNF 46; ICF 80. *Private Pay Patients* 18%. *Certified* Medicaid; Medicare.
Owner Proprietary corp (International Healthcare Management).
Staff Physicians 1 (ft), 4 (pt); RNs 2 (ft), 3 (pt); LPNs 11 (ft), 4 (pt); Nurses' aides 34 (ft), 23 (pt); Physical therapists 1 (ft); Occupational therapists 1 (pt); Speech therapists 1 (pt); Activities coordinators 1 (ft), 1 (pt); Dietitians 1 (ft); Podiatrists 1 (pt).
Languages Polish.
Facilities Dining room; Physical therapy room; Activities room; Crafts room; Laundry room; Barber/Beauty shop.
Activities Arts & crafts; Games; Reading groups; Prayer groups; Movies; Shopping trips; Dances/Social/Cultural gatherings; Pet therapy.

Carriage House of Bay City
2394 Midland Rd, Bay City, MI 48706
(517) 684-2303
Admin Raphael J Dubay. *Dir of Nursing* Corinne Douglas RN.
Licensure Intermediate care. *Beds* ICF 127. *Private Pay Patients* 30%. *Certified* Medicaid.
Owner Proprietary corp.
Admissions Requirements Medical examination.
Staff RNs; LPNs; Nurses' aides; Recreational therapists; Activities coordinators; Dietitians.
Languages Spanish.
Facilities Dining room; Activities room; Crafts room; Barber/Beauty shop; Library.
Activities Arts & crafts; Cards; Games; Reading groups; Prayer groups; Movies; Shopping trips; Dances/Social/Cultural gatherings; Intergenerational programs; Pet therapy.

Hampton Manor
800 Mulholland Rd, Bay City, MI 48706
(517) 895-8539
Admin Nancy J Walker. *Dir of Nursing* Julie Osling RN. *Medical Dir* L Berta DO.
Licensure Skilled care. *Beds* SNF 51. *Certified* Medicaid; Medicare.
Owner Proprietary corp (Health Care and Retirement Corp).
Admissions Requirements Minimum age 18; Physician's request.
Staff RNs 1 (ft), 2 (pt); LPNs 3 (ft), 2 (pt); Nurses' aides 15 (ft), 11 (pt); Activities coordinators 1 (ft).
Facilities Dining room; Physical therapy room; Laundry room; Barber/Beauty shop.
Activities Arts & crafts; Cards; Games; Reading groups; Prayer groups; Movies; Shopping trips; Dances/Social/Cultural gatherings.

Rachel Sovereign Memorial Home
1014 Center Ave, Bay City, MI 48706
(517) 892-8493
Licensure Home for aged. *Beds* Home for aged 24.

Belding

Belding Christian Nursing Home
414 E State St, Belding, MI 48809
(616) 794-0406
Licensure Skilled care. *Beds* SNF 123. *Certified* Medicaid; Medicare.
Owner Proprietary corp (Miko Enterprises Inc).

Bellaire

Meadow Brook Medical Care Facility
Box 357, 4543 Scenic Hwy, Bellaire, MI 49615
(616) 533-8661
Admin Mrs LaVerne Sheneman RN. *Dir of Nursing* Patsy Marshall RN. *Medical Dir* Donald Bills DO.
Licensure Skilled care; Retirement. *Beds* SNF 113. *Certified* Medicaid; Medicare.
Owner Publicly owned.
Admissions Requirements Minimum age 15; Physician's request.
Staff Physicians 4 (pt); RNs 4 (ft), 5 (pt); LPNs 6 (ft), 5 (pt); Nurses' aides 52 (ft), 6 (pt); Physical therapists 1 (pt); Recreational therapists 1 (ft); Activities coordinators 1 (ft); Dietitians 1 (ft); Ophthalmologists 1 (pt); Podiatrists 1 (pt); Physical therapy aides 1 (pt) Recreational therapy aides 1 (pt).
Facilities Dining room; Physical therapy room; Activities room; Chapel; Crafts room; Laundry room; Barber/Beauty shop; Library; Bingo; Picnics; Fishing; Catholic mass; Theme dinners.
Activities Arts & crafts; Cards; Games; Movies; Dances/Social/Cultural gatherings.

Belleville

Van Buren Convalescent Center
44401 I-94 Service Dr, Belleville, MI 48111
(313) 697-8051
Licensure Skilled care. *Beds* SNF 222. *Certified* Medicaid; Medicare.
Owner Proprietary corp (International Healthcare Management).

Benton Harbor

Carson Retirement Home
1564 M63 N, Benton Harbor, MI 49022
Licensure Home for aged. *Beds* Home for aged 34.

Orchard Grove Extended Care Centre
1385 E Empire, Benton Harbor, MI 49022
(616) 925-0033, 925-2019 FAX
Admin Edward K Moghtader. *Dir of Nursing* Sally Gale Thorndike RN. *Medical Dir* Lynn Gray MD.
Licensure Intermediate care. *Beds* ICF 123. *Private Pay Patients* 10%. *Certified* Medicaid.
Owner Proprietary corp (Community Centre Group).
Admissions Requirements Minimum age 15; Medical examination.
Staff Physicians; RNs 4 (ft); LPNs 6 (ft); Nurses' aides 25 (ft); Physical therapists 1 (pt); Recreational therapists 1 (ft); Occupational therapists 1 (pt); Speech therapists 1 (pt); Activities coordinators 1 (ft); Dietitians 1 (ft); Ophthalmologists; Podiatrists; Audiologists.
Facilities Dining room; Physical therapy room; Activities room; Laundry room; Barber/Beauty shop.
Activities Arts & crafts; Cards; Games; Reading groups; Prayer groups; Movies; Shopping trips; Intergenerational programs; Pet therapy.

Berrien Center

Berrien General Hospital
6418 Deans Hill Rd, Berrien Center, MI 49102
(616) 471-7761
Medical Dir Dwain Silvernale MD.
Licensure Skilled care. *Beds* SNF 248.
  Certified Medicaid; Medicare.
Admissions Requirements Minimum age 18;
  Physician's request.
Staff Physicians 14 (ft), 1 (pt); RNs 7 (ft), 3
  (pt); LPNs 13 (ft), 7 (pt); Physical therapists
  2 (ft); Recreational therapists 1 (ft); Speech
  therapists 1 (pt); Activities coordinators 1
  (ft); Dietitians 1 (ft); Ophthalmologists 1
  (pt); Dentists 1 (pt).
Facilities Dining room; Physical therapy
  room; Activities room; Chapel; Crafts room;
  Laundry room; Barber/Beauty shop; Living
  center.
Activities Arts & crafts; Cards; Games;
  Reading groups; Prayer groups; Movies;
  Shopping trips; Dances/Social/Cultural
  gatherings.

Bry-Fern Care Center
Deans Hill, Berrien Center, MI 49102
(616) 473-4911
Medical Dir Dr Richard Roach.
Licensure Intermediate care. *Beds* ICF 62.
  Certified Medicaid.
Admissions Requirements Minimum age 15;
  Medical examination.
Staff RNs 3 (ft); LPNs 5 (ft); Nurses' aides 12
  (ft), 18 (pt); Physical therapists;
  Occupational therapists; Speech therapists;
  Activities coordinators 1 (ft); Dietitians 1
  (ft); Ophthalmologists.
Facilities Dining room; Activities room;
  Crafts room; Laundry room; Barber/Beauty
  shop; Library.
Activities Arts & crafts; Cards; Games;
  Reading groups; Prayer groups; Movies;
  Shopping trips; Dances/Social/Cultural
  gatherings.

Big Rapids

Altercare of Big Rapids
805 West Ave, Big Rapids, MI 49307
Licensure Skilled care; Home for aged. *Beds*
  SNF 50; Home for aged 58. *Certified*
  Medicaid; Medicare.

Greenridge Nursing Care
725 Fuller, Big Rapids, MI 49307
(616) 796-2631
Admin Janet L Worthington. *Dir of Nursing*
  Leona Spedoski RN.
Licensure Skilled care; Alzheimer's care. *Beds*
  SNF 126. *Certified* Medicaid; Medicare.
Owner Proprietary corp (Miko Enterprises
  Inc).
Admissions Requirements Minimum age 15;
  Medical examination; Physician's request.
Staff RNs 2 (ft), 3 (pt); LPNs 9 (ft); Nurses'
  aides 50 (ft), 20 (pt); Physical therapists 1
  (ft), 1 (pt); Occupational therapists 1 (pt);
  Speech therapists 1 (pt); Activities
  coordinators 1 (ft); Dietitians 1 (ft).
Facilities Dining room; Physical therapy
  room; Activities room; Crafts room; Laundry
  room; Barber/Beauty shop.
Activities Arts & crafts; Cards; Games;
  Reading groups; Prayer groups; Movies;
  Shopping trips; Dances/Social/Cultural
  gatherings.

Birmingham

Cambridge South
18200 W Thirteen Mile Rd, Birmingham, MI 48009
(313) 647-6500
Licensure Skilled care. *Beds* SNF 102.
  Certified Medicaid; Medicare.
Owner Proprietary corp (International
  Healthcare Management).

Georgian Bloomfield
2975 N Adams Rd, Birmingham, MI 48009-5546
(313) 645-2900
Medical Dir Dr John Dzuiba.
Licensure Skilled care. *Beds* SNF 274.
  Certified Medicare.
Owner Proprietary corp (Health Care and
  Retirement Corp).
Staff Physicians 7 (pt); RNs 16 (ft), 9 (pt);
  LPNs 8 (ft), 5 (pt); Nurses' aides 60 (ft), 18
  (pt); Recreational therapists 1 (ft), 1 (pt);
  Activities coordinators 1 (ft); Dietitians 1
  (ft), 1 (pt).
Facilities Dining room; Physical therapy
  room; Activities room; Chapel; Laundry
  room; Barber/Beauty shop.
Activities Arts & crafts; Cards; Games;
  Reading groups; Prayer groups; Movies;
  Dances/Social/Cultural gatherings.

Bloomfield Hills

Bloomfield Hills Care Center
PO Box 7008, Bloomfield Hills, MI 48302-7008
(313) 338-0345
Licensure Skilled care. *Beds* SNF 366.
  Certified Medicaid; Medicare.

Brae Burn Inc
1312 N Woodward Ave, Bloomfield Hills, MI 48013
(313) 644-8015
Admin Linda Kopietz. *Dir of Nursing* Judy
  Mills. *Medical Dir* Dr Harley J Robinson.
Licensure Intermediate care. *Beds* ICF 115.
  Private Pay Patients 100%. *Certified*
  Medicaid.
Owner Privately owned.
Admissions Requirements Physician's request.
Staff Physicians (private); RNs; LPNs; Nurses'
  aides; Physical therapists (independent);
  Recreational therapists; Dietitians;
  Ophthalmologists; Podiatrists; Audiologists.
Facilities Dining room on each floor; Barber/
  Beauty shop; Sun room.
Activities Arts & crafts; Cards; Games;
  Reading groups; Prayer groups; Movies;
  Shopping trips; Dances/Social/Cultural
  gatherings; Intergenerational programs; Pet
  therapy.

St Elizabeth Briarbank Home for the Aging
1315 N Woodward Ave, Box O, Bloomfield
Hills, MI 48013
Licensure Home for aged. *Beds* Home for
  aged 55.

Bloomingdale

Bethany Nursing Home
42235 County Rd 390, Bloomingdale, MI 49026
(616) 521-3383
Admin Delmon M Esh Jr. *Dir of Nursing*
  Imelda Fuster RN. *Medical Dir* Daniel
  Ekkens MD.
Licensure Skilled care. *Beds* SNF 78. *Certified*
  Medicaid; Medicare.
Owner Proprietary corp.
Admissions Requirements Minimum age 15;
  Medical examination; Physician's request.
Staff Physicians 1 (pt); RNs 3 (ft), 6 (pt);
  LPNs 3 (ft), 1 (pt); Nurses' aides 28 (ft), 12
  (pt); Physical therapists 1 (pt); Occupational
  therapists 1 (pt); Speech therapists 1 (pt);
  Activities coordinators 1 (ft), 1 (pt);
  Dietitians 1 (pt).
Languages Tagalog, Spanish.

Facilities Dining room; Physical therapy
  room; Activities room; Crafts room; Laundry
  room; Barber/Beauty shop; Library.
Activities Arts & crafts; Cards; Games;
  Reading groups; Prayer groups; Movies;
  Dances/Social/Cultural gatherings.

Bridgman

Jordan's Nursing Home
PO Box 607, 9935 Red Arrow Hwy,
Bridgman, MI 49106
(616) 465-3017
Admin Larry Olson.
Licensure Intermediate care. *Beds* ICF 105.
  Certified Medicaid.
Admissions Requirements Minimum age 15;
  Medical examination; Physician's request.
Staff Physicians 4 (pt); RNs 1 (ft), 4 (pt);
  LPNs 2 (ft), 4 (pt); Nurses' aides 31 (ft), 28
  (pt); Reality therapists 1 (ft); Recreational
  therapists 1 (ft); Activities coordinators 1
  (ft), 1 (pt); Dietitians 1 (ft); Dentists 1 (pt).
Facilities Dining room; Activities room;
  Chapel; Crafts room; Laundry room; Barber/
  Beauty shop.
Activities Arts & crafts; Games; Prayer groups;
  Movies.

Cadillac

Lakeview Lutheran Manor Nursing Home
460 Pearl St, Cadillac, MI 49601
(313) 775-0101
Medical Dir Wendell Hyink MD.
Licensure Skilled care. *Beds* SNF 218.
  Certified Medicaid; Medicare.
Admissions Requirements Minimum age 16;
  Medical examination; Physician's request.
Staff Physicians 1 (pt); RNs 7 (ft), 4 (pt);
  LPNs 16 (ft), 13 (pt); Nurses' aides 66 (ft),
  24 (pt); Physical therapists 1 (ft); Activities
  coordinators 1 (ft); Dietitians 1 (ft).
Facilities Dining room; Physical therapy
  room; Activities room; Crafts room; Barber/
  Beauty shop; 5 Lounges.
Activities Arts & crafts; Cards; Games;
  Reading groups; Prayer groups; Movies;
  Shopping trips; Dances/Social/Cultural
  gatherings.

Calumet

Apostolic Lutheran Home
637 Pine St, Calumet, MI 49913
Licensure Home for aged. *Beds* Home for
  aged 39.

Still Waters Community Elders Home
600 E Elm St, Calumet, MI 49913
Licensure Home for aged. *Beds* Home for
  aged 70.

Caro

Tuscola County Medical Care Facility
1285 Cleaver Rd, Caro, MI 48723
(517) 673-4117
Admin Darlene N Davidson. *Dir of Nursing*
  Nancy Hack RN BSN. *Medical Dir* Edward
  N Elmendorf MD.
Licensure Skilled care. *Beds* SNF 123.
  Certified Medicaid; Medicare.
Owner Publicly owned.
Admissions Requirements Minimum age 15;
  Medical examination; Physician's request.
Staff Physicians 1 (ft); RNs 5 (ft), 1 (pt);
  LPNs 4 (ft), 4 (pt); Nurses' aides 60 (ft), 25
  (pt); Physical therapists 1 (pt); Occupational
  therapists 1 (pt); Speech therapists 1 (pt);
  Activities coordinators 1 (pt); Dietitians 1
  (pt); Ophthalmologists 1 (pt); Podiatrists 1
  (pt); Dentists 1 (pt).
Facilities Dining room; Physical therapy
  room; Activities room; Chapel; Crafts room;
  Laundry room; Barber/Beauty shop.

Activities Arts & crafts; Cards; Games; Reading groups; Prayer groups; Movies; Shopping trips; Dances/Social/Cultural gatherings.

Cass City

Provincial House—Cass City
4782 Hospital Dr, Cass City, MI 48726
(517) 872-2174
Admin Alan J Sward.
Medical Dir Dr Zuzga.
Licensure Skilled care. *Beds* SNF 117.
Certified Medicaid; Medicare.
Owner Proprietary corp (Beverly Enterprises).
Staff Physicians 5 (pt); RNs 4 (ft), 2 (pt); LPNs 7 (ft), 2 (pt); Nurses' aides 57 (ft), 18 (pt); Physical therapists 1 (pt); Occupational therapists 1 (pt); Speech therapists 1 (pt); Activities coordinators 1 (ft); Dietitians 1 (pt); Ophthalmologists 1 (pt); Podiatrists 1 (pt); Dentists 1 (pt).
Facilities Dining room; Physical therapy room; Activities room; Crafts room; Laundry room; Barber/Beauty shop.
Activities Arts & crafts; Cards; Games; Reading groups; Movies; Shopping trips; Dances/Social/Cultural gatherings.

Cassopolis

Cass County Medical Care Facility
23770 Hospital St, Cassopolis, MI 49031
(616) 445-3801
Admin Norma J Weaver. *Dir of Nursing* Janet L Huffman RN. *Medical Dir* Aaron K Warren MD.
Licensure Skilled care. *Beds* SNF 80. *Certified* Medicaid; Medicare.
Owner Publicly owned.
Admissions Requirements Minimum age 16; Medical examination; Physician's request.
Staff Physicians 2 (pt); RNs 4 (ft), 1 (pt); LPNs 7 (ft), 2 (pt); Nurses' aides 39 (ft), 6 (pt); Physical therapists 1 (pt); Activities coordinators 1 (ft).
Languages German, Hungarian.
Facilities Dining room; Physical therapy room; Activities room; Chapel; Crafts room; Laundry room; Barber/Beauty shop.
Activities Arts & crafts; Cards; Games; Reading groups; Prayer groups; Movies; Dances/Social/Cultural gatherings.

Cedar Springs

Cedar Care Center Inc
400 Jeffery, Cedar Springs, MI 49319
Licensure Skilled care. *Beds* SNF 77. *Certified* Medicaid; Medicare.

Cedar Springs Nursing Center
RR 3, 280 Marie, Cedar Springs, MI 49319-9509
(616) 696-0170
Licensure Skilled care; Intermediate care. *Beds* 77. *Certified* Medicaid; Medicare.
Owner Proprietary corp (Miko Enterprises Inc).

Centerline

Father Murray Nursing Center
8444 Engleman, Centerline, MI 48015
(313) 755-2400
Admin Catherine T Bertolini. *Dir of Nursing* Nettie Rickerman RN. *Medical Dir* Barry Szczesny DO.
Licensure Skilled care. *Beds* SNF 234. *Certified* Medicaid; Medicare.
Owner Nonprofit corp.
Admissions Requirements Minimum age 16; Medical examination; Physician's request.
Languages Polish, Italian, German.

Facilities Dining room; Physical therapy room; Activities room; Laundry room; Barber/Beauty shop; Dentist office.
Activities Arts & crafts; Cards; Games; Reading groups; Prayer groups; Movies; Dances/Social/Cultural gatherings; Holiday parties including residents families.

Centreville

Fairview Medical Care Facility
PO Box 97, 441 E Main St, Centreville, MI 49032
(616) 467-9575
Admin Jeanette M Schirs. *Dir of Nursing* Hazel Hoffine RN. *Medical Dir* Dr Robert Smith.
Licensure Skilled care. *Beds* SNF 64. *Certified* Medicaid; Medicare.
Owner Publicly owned.
Admissions Requirements Medical examination; Physician's request.
Staff RNs 4 (ft); LPNs 8 (ft), 8 (pt); Nurses' aides 18 (ft), 8 (pt).
Facilities Dining room; Physical therapy room; Activities room; Chapel; Crafts room; Barber/Beauty shop; Occupational therapy room.
Activities Arts & crafts; Cards; Games; Reading groups; Prayer groups; Movies; Dances/Social/Cultural gatherings; Pet therapy.

Charlotte

Eaton County Medical Care Facility
530 W Beech St, Charlotte, MI 48813
(517) 543-2940
Licensure Skilled care. *Beds* SNF 100. *Certified* Medicaid; Medicare.
Owner Publicly owned.

Eaton Manor Inc
511 E Shepherd, Charlotte, MI 48813
(517) 543-4750
Admin Ray C Howard. *Dir of Nursing* Ray C Howard. *Medical Dir* Dr Vanator.
Licensure Intermediate care. *Beds* ICF 49. *Private Pay Patients* 36%. *Certified* Medicaid.
Owner Proprietary corp (Frank Wromski).
Admissions Requirements Minimum age 18; Medical examination; Physician's request.
Staff RNs 1 (ft); LPNs 2 (ft); Nurses' aides 6 (ft), 12 (pt); Activities coordinators 1 (ft); Dietitians.
Facilities Dining room; Activities room; Crafts room; Barber/Beauty shop.
Activities Arts & crafts; Cards; Games; Reading groups; Prayer groups; Movies; Dances/Social/Cultural gatherings; Intergenerational programs.

Cheboygan

Cheboygan Health Care Center
824 S Huron St, Cheboygan, MI 49721
(616) 627-4347
Admin Julie Jewell-Cole RN. *Dir of Nursing* Carole Goodwin RN. *Medical Dir* Richard Knecht MD.
Licensure Intermediate care; Home for aged. *Beds* ICF 112; Home for aged 8. *Private Pay Patients* 27%. *Certified* Medicaid.
Owner Nonprofit corp (International Elderly Care Inc).
Admissions Requirements Medical examination.
Staff RNs 3 (ft); LPNs 5 (ft), 7 (pt); Nurses' aides 34 (ft), 6 (pt); Activities coordinators 2 (ft); Dietitians 1 (ft).
Facilities Dining room; Laundry room; Barber/Beauty shop; Dayroom/Visiting lounge.

Activities Arts & crafts; Cards; Games; Reading groups; Prayer groups; Movies; Pet therapy.

Community Memorial Hospital—Extended Care Facility
748 S Main St, Cheboygan, MI 49721
(616) 627-5601
Admin Howard Purcell Jr. *Dir of Nursing* Sandra Dunlap RN. *Medical Dir* Michael Bacon DO.
Licensure Skilled care. *Beds* SNF 129. *Certified* Medicaid; Medicare.
Owner Nonprofit corp.
Admissions Requirements Medical examination; Physician's request.
Staff RNs 1 (ft), 4 (pt); LPNs 3 (ft), 5 (pt); Nurses' aides 12 (ft), 16 (pt); Physical therapists 1 (ft); Activities coordinators 1 (pt); Dietitians 1 (ft).
Facilities Dining room; Physical therapy room; Activities room; Crafts room; Barber/Beauty shop; Recreation room; 2 Outdoor patios; Fenced outdoor area.
Activities Arts & crafts; Cards; Games; Reading groups; Prayer groups; Movies; Shopping trips; Dances/Social/Cultural gatherings; Exercise class; Life review group; Annual picnic; Open house.

Chelsea

Chelsea United Methodist Retirement Home
805 W Middle St, Chelsea, MI 48118
(313) 475-8633, 475-5820 FAX
Admin James C Batten. *Dir of Nursing* Colleen Glynn RN. *Medical Dir* James Peggs MD.
Licensure Skilled care; Intermediate care; Retirement; Alzheimer's care. *Beds* SNF 110; ICF 173; Retirement apartments 26. *Private Pay Patients* 76%. *Certified* Medicaid; Medicare.
Owner Nonprofit corp.
Admissions Requirements Minimum age 62; Medical examination.
Staff RNs 4 (ft); LPNs 7 (ft); Nurses' aides 45 (ft); Physical therapists 1 (ft); Reality therapists 1 (ft); Recreational therapists 1 (ft); Occupational therapists 1 (ft); Speech therapists 1 (ft); Activities coordinators 5 (ft); Dietitians 1 (ft).
Affiliation United Methodist.
Facilities Dining room; Physical therapy room; Activities room; Chapel; Crafts room; Laundry room; Barber/Beauty shop; Library; Ice cream parlor; Ceramics shop; Woodworking shop.
Activities Arts & crafts; Cards; Games; Reading groups; Prayer groups; Movies; Shopping trips; Dances/Social/Cultural gatherings; Intergenerational programs; Pet therapy.

Chesaning

Chesaning Nursing Care Center
201 S Front St, Chesaning, MI 48616
(517) 845-6602
Admin Maria A Janveja. *Dir of Nursing* Jo Anne Nixon RN.
Licensure Intermediate care; Home for aged; Alzheimer's care. *Beds* ICF 39; Home for aged 12. *Private Pay Patients* 25%. *Certified* Medicaid.
Owner Proprietary corp.
Admissions Requirements Minimum age 18; Medical examination; Physician's request.
Staff Physicians 4 (pt); RNs 1 (ft), 2 (pt); LPNs 4 (ft), 3 (pt); Nurses' aides 12 (ft), 12 (pt); Physical therapists; Reality therapists; Activities coordinators 1 (ft), 1 (pt); Dietitians 1 (pt); Podiatrists.
Facilities Dining room; Physical therapy room; Laundry room; Barber/Beauty shop; Activities/Crafts room; Lounges.

Activities Arts & crafts; Cards; Games; Reading groups; Prayer groups; Movies; Shopping trips; Dances/Social/Cultural gatherings; Intergenerational programs; Exercise.

Clare

Clare Nursing Home
600 SE 4th St, Clare, MI 48617
(517) 386-7723
Admin Wilma Shurlow.
Medical Dir Dr E C Shurlow.
Licensure Skilled care. *Beds* SNF 129. *Certified* Medicaid; Medicare.
Staff RNs 2 (ft), 4 (pt); LPNs 12 (ft), 4 (pt); Nurses' aides 41 (ft), 36 (pt); Physical therapists 1 (pt); Speech therapists; Activities coordinators 1 (ft); Dietitians 1 (pt); Dentists.
Facilities Dining room; Physical therapy room; Activities room; Chapel; Crafts room; Laundry room; Barber/Beauty shop; 3 Dayrooms.
Activities Arts & crafts; Cards; Games; Reading groups; Prayer groups; Movies; Shopping trips; Dances/Social/Cultural gatherings.

Clarkston

Grovecrest Care Center of Clarkston
PO Box 9, Clarkston, MI 48016
(313) 674-0903
Admin Paul Ver Lee. *Dir of Nursing* Elaine Hines RN. *Medical Dir* Dr James Ver Lee.
Licensure Skilled care; Alzheimer's care. *Beds* SNF 120. *Certified* Medicaid; Medicare.
Owner Proprietary corp.
Admissions Requirements Minimum age 18.
Staff RNs 4 (ft), 6 (pt); LPNs 4 (ft), 11 (pt); Nurses' aides 42 (ft), 12 (pt); Physical therapists (contracted); Occupational therapists (contracted); Speech therapists (contracted); Activities coordinators 1 (ft); Dietitians (contracted); Dietary staff 7 (ft), 9 (pt); Housekeeping 11 (ft), 3 (pt).
Facilities Dining room; Physical therapy room; Activities room; Crafts room; Barber/Beauty shop; Library; Alzheimer's.
Activities Arts & crafts; Cards; Games; Reading groups; Prayer groups; Movies; Dances/Social/Cultural gatherings; Intergenerational programs; Pet therapy; Bedside activities.

Clawson

Cambridge North
535 N Main, Clawson, MI 48017
(313) 435-5200
Admin Barbara L Iseppi. *Dir of Nursing* Jane Brunt RN. *Medical Dir* Ronald Knauff DO.
Licensure Skilled care. *Beds* SNF 120. *Certified* Medicaid; Medicare.
Owner Proprietary corp (International Healthcare Management).
Staff Physicians; RNs; LPNs; Nurses' aides; Physical therapists; Recreational therapists; Speech therapists; Activities coordinators; Dietitians; Ophthalmologists; Dentists.
Facilities Dining room; Physical therapy room; Activities room; Crafts room; Barber/Beauty shop.
Activities Arts & crafts; Cards; Games; Prayer groups; Movies; Parties.

Clio

Clio Convalescent Center
13137 N Clio Rd, Clio, MI 48420
(313) 686-2600
Admin John Koncz; Pearl Fredell. *Dir of Nursing* Roberta Kennedy RN. *Medical Dir* Charles Claffey DO.

Licensure Intermediate care; Home for aged; Alzheimer's care. *Beds* ICF 133; Home for aged 4. *Private Pay Patients* 25%. *Certified* Medicaid.
Owner Privately owned.
Staff RNs; LPNs; Nurses' aides; Physical therapists; Speech therapists; Activities coordinators; Dietitians; Ophthalmologists; Podiatrists; Audiologists.
Facilities Dining room; Activities room; Laundry room; Barber/Beauty shop.
Activities Arts & crafts; Cards; Games; Reading groups; Prayer groups; Movies; Dances/Social/Cultural gatherings; Intergenerational programs; Pet therapy; Church programs.

Coldwater

Carriage Inn Convalescent Center
90 N Michigan Ave, Coldwater, MI 49036
(517) 278-4819
Admin F Harold Creal.
Medical Dir L J Creal.
Licensure Skilled care; Retirement; Alzheimer's care. *Beds* SNF 169; Retirement 60-80. *Certified* Medicaid; Medicare.
Owner Proprietary corp.
Admissions Requirements Medical examination.
Staff RNs; LPNs; Nurses' aides; Physical therapists; Occupational therapists; Speech therapists; Activities coordinators.
Facilities Dining room; Physical therapy room; Activities room; Crafts room; Laundry room; Barber/Beauty shop.
Activities Arts & crafts; Cards; Games; Reading groups; Prayer groups; Movies; Shopping trips; Dances/Social/Cultural gatherings; High school courses.

Maple Lawn Medical Care Facility
50 Sanderson Ln, Coldwater, MI 49036
(517) 279-9587
Admin C Eldon Loney. *Dir of Nursing* Darlene Starr. *Medical Dir* L F Chapman MD.
Licensure Skilled care. *Beds* SNF 114. *Certified* Medicaid; Medicare; VA.
Owner Publicly owned.
Admissions Requirements Physician's request.
Staff RNs 4 (ft), 2 (pt); LPNs 8 (ft), 10 (pt); Nurses' aides 31 (ft), 34 (pt); Activities coordinators 1 (pt).
Facilities Dining room; Physical therapy room; Activities room; Chapel; Crafts room; Laundry room; Barber/Beauty shop.
Activities Arts & crafts; Cards; Games; Reading groups; Prayer groups; Movies; Dances/Social/Cultural gatherings; Intergenerational programs.

Corunna

Griffin Home for the Aged
1042 N Shiawassee St, Corunna, MI 48817
Licensure Home for aged. *Beds* Home for aged 56.

Shiawassee County Medical Care Facility
729 S Norton St, Corunna, MI 48817
(517) 743-3491
Admin Anne Hark RN BA MS. *Dir of Nursing* Linda Gall RN BS MA. *Medical Dir* P J Moore MD.
Licensure Skilled care. *Beds* SNF 152. *Certified* Medicaid; Medicare.
Owner Publicly owned.
Admissions Requirements Minimum age 16; Medical examination; Physician's request.
Staff Physicians 2 (pt); RNs; LPNs 40 (ft); Nurses' aides 80 (ft); Physical therapists 1 (pt); Activities coordinators 1 (ft); Dietitians 1 (pt).
Facilities Dining room; Physical therapy room; Activities room; Chapel; Crafts room; Barber/Beauty shop.

Activities Arts & crafts; Cards; Games; Reading groups; Prayer groups; Movies.

Covington

Covington Rest Home
Box 167, Covington, MI 49919
Licensure Home for aged. *Beds* Home for aged 45.

Crystal Falls

Crystal Manor
400 Superior Ave, Crystal Falls, MI 49920
(906) 875-6663
Licensure Intermediate care. *Beds* ICF 71. *Certified* Medicaid.
Owner Nonprofit corp (Lutheran Health Systems).

Iron County Medical Care Facility
1523 W US 2, Crystal Falls, MI 49920
(906) 875-6671
Admin Chester E Pintarelli. *Dir of Nursing* Maxine M Tokoly RN. *Medical Dir* Robert F Han MD.
Licensure Skilled care. *Beds* SNF 109. *Certified* Medicaid; Medicare.
Owner Publicly owned.
Admissions Requirements Physician's request.
Staff Physicians 1 (pt); RNs 2 (ft), 5 (pt); LPNs 9 (ft), 3 (pt); Nurses' aides 38 (ft), 22 (pt); Physical therapists 2 (pt); Occupational therapists 2 (ft); Activities coordinators 1 (pt).
Facilities Dining room; Physical therapy room; Activities room; Chapel; Crafts room; Laundry room; Barber/Beauty shop; Library; Smoking & TV areas.
Activities Arts & crafts; Cards; Games; Reading groups; Prayer groups; Movies; Dances/Social/Cultural gatherings; Woodworking; Ceramics; Parties; Picnics; Fair outings.

Dearborn Heights

Dearborn Heights Health Care Center
26001 Ford Rd, Dearborn Heights, MI 48127
Licensure Skilled care. *Beds* SNF 151. *Certified* Medicare.
Owner Proprietary corp (Health Care and Retirement Corp).

Kenneth J Roney Convalescent Home
26505 Powers Ave, Dearborn Heights, MI 48125
Licensure Skilled care. *Beds* SNF 265. *Certified* Medicaid; Medicare.

Deckerville

Autumnwood of Deckerville
PO Box 1000, Deckerville, MI 48427
Licensure Skilled care. *Beds* SNF 120. *Certified* Medicaid; Medicare.

Detroit

Alpha Annex Nursing Center
609 E Grand Blvd, Detroit, MI 48207
(313) 923-0300
Licensure Skilled care; Intermediate care. *Beds* Swing beds SNF/ICF 103. *Certified* Medicaid; Medicare.

Alpha Manor Nursing Home
440 E Grand Blvd, Detroit, MI 48207
(313) 579-2900
Licensure Skilled care. *Beds* SNF 100. *Certified* Medicaid; Medicare.

Americare Convalescent Center
19211 Anglin, Detroit, MI 48234
(313) 893-9745

Admin Aysel Saglik RN, Adm/Owner. *Dir of Nursing* Barbara Fick RN. *Medical Dir* Hilda Jerius MD.
Licensure Skilled care; Intermediate care. *Beds* SNF 73; ICF 66. *Certified* Medicaid; Medicare.
Owner Privately owned.
Admissions Requirements Minimum age 40; Medical examination; Physician's request; Transfer papers; Chest X-ray.
Staff Physicians 1 (ft), 1 (pt); RNs 4 (ft), 3 (pt); LPNs 9 (ft), 5 (pt); Nurses' aides 60 (ft), 20 (pt); Physical therapists 1 (pt); Reality therapists 1 (ft); Recreational therapists 1 (ft), 3 (pt); Occupational therapists 1 (pt); Speech therapists 1 (pt); Activities coordinators 1 (ft); Dietitians 2 (ft), 1 (pt); Ophthalmologists 1 (pt); Podiatrists 2 (pt).
Facilities Dining room; Physical therapy room; Activities room; Crafts room; Laundry room; Barber/Beauty shop; Library.
Activities Arts & crafts; Cards; Games; Reading groups; Prayer groups; Movies; Shopping trips; Dances/Social/Cultural gatherings; Intergenerational programs; Pet therapy; Picnics; Walkathons; Family night; Restaurant visits.

Anchorage Convalescent Home Inc
13850 Grand River, Detroit, MI 48227
(313) 273-2470
Admin Virginia Sampson. *Dir of Nursing* Clabon Densley RN. *Medical Dir* Lawrence Usher DO.
Licensure Intermediate care. *Beds* ICF 53. *Certified* Medicaid.
Owner Proprietary corp.
Admissions Requirements Minimum age 18; Medical examination; Physician's request.
Staff RNs 1 (ft); LPNs 3 (ft), 2 (pt); Nurses' aides 20 (ft), 4 (pt); Physical therapists (contracted); Recreational therapists 1 (ft); Occupational therapists (contracted); Activities coordinators 1 (ft); Dietitians (consultant); Ophthalmologists (contracted); Podiatrists (contracted).
Facilities Dining room; Activities room; Laundry room; Barber/Beauty shop.
Activities Arts & crafts; Cards; Games; Reading groups; Prayer groups; Movies; Shopping trips; Dances/Social/Cultural gatherings.

Arbor Home
2501 W Grand Blvd, Detroit, MI 48208
Licensure Home for aged. *Beds* Home for aged 55.

Arnold Home Inc
18530 W Seven Mile Rd, Detroit, MI 48239
(313) 531-4001
Admin Chester E Pearson. *Dir of Nursing* Mildred Angelillo RN. *Medical Dir* Douglas J Wood MD.
Licensure Skilled care; Intermediate care; Home for aged; Alzheimer's care. *Beds* Swing beds SNF/ICF 224; Home for aged 165. *Certified* Medicaid; Medicare.
Owner Nonprofit corp.
Admissions Requirements Minimum age 15; Medical examination; Physician's request.
Staff Physicians 1 (ft), 2 (pt); RNs 3 (ft), 4 (pt); LPNs 20 (ft), 6 (pt); Nurses' aides 88 (ft); Physical therapists 1 (pt); Reality therapists 1 (pt); Recreational therapists 1 (ft), 1 (pt); Occupational therapists 1 (ft); Speech therapists 1 (pt); Activities coordinators 1 (ft); Dietitians 1 (ft); Podiatrists 1 (pt); Dentists 1 (pt).
Facilities Dining room; Physical therapy room; Activities room; Chapel; Crafts room; Laundry room; Barber/Beauty shop; Library; Pharmacy; Gift shop; Courtyard; Outdoor seating and walkways.

Activities Arts & crafts; Cards; Games; Reading groups; Prayer groups; Movies; Shopping trips; Dances/Social/Cultural gatherings; Pet therapy.

Avonside Nursing Home
791 E Grand Blvd, Detroit, MI 48207
(313) 9211-1332
Licensure Intermediate care. *Beds* 42. *Certified* Medicaid.

Barton Nursing Home
722 E Grand Blvd, Detroit, MI 48207
(313) 923-8080
Admin Daniel W James.
Medical Dir Eleanor James.
Licensure Intermediate care; Alzheimer's care. *Beds* ICF 50. *Certified* Medicaid.
Owner Proprietary corp.
Admissions Requirements Physician's request.
Staff RNs 1 (ft), 1 (pt); LPNs 2 (ft), 14 (pt); Nurses' aides 16 (ft), 8 (pt); Dietitians 1 (pt).
Languages Polish, Tagalog.
Facilities Dining room; Activities room; Crafts room; Barber/Beauty shop; Library.
Activities Arts & crafts; Cards; Games; Reading groups; Prayer groups; Movies; Shopping trips; Dances/Social/Cultural gatherings.

Boulevard Home for the Aged
570 E Grand Blvd, Detroit, MI 48207
Licensure Home for aged. *Beds* Home for aged 47.

Boulevard Temple United Methodist Retirement Home
2567 W Grand Blvd, Detroit, MI 48208
(313) 895-5340, 895-5970 FAX
Admin James R Weidman. *Dir of Nursing* Elisabeth Tullis RN. *Medical Dir* Caroline Blaum MD.
Licensure Intermediate care; Home for aged; Alzheimer's care. *Beds* ICF 124; Home for aged 45; Alzheimers care 11; Apts 33. *Private Pay Patients* 58%. *Certified* Medicaid.
Owner Nonprofit corp.
Admissions Requirements Minimum age 62; Medical examination; Physician's request X-ray report.
Staff Physicians 3 (pt); RNs 4 (ft); LPNs 3 (ft), 12 (pt); Nurses' aides 50 (ft), 60 (pt); Physical therapists 1 (pt); Occupational therapists 1 (pt); Speech therapists 1 (pt); Activities coordinators 2 (ft); Dietitians 1 (pt); Podiatrists 1 (pt).
Affiliation United Methodist.
Facilities Dining room; Physical therapy room; Activities room; Chapel; Crafts room; Laundry room; Barber/Beauty shop; Library; Roof-top garden; Medical clinic; Dental clinic.
Activities Arts & crafts; Cards; Games; Reading groups; Prayer groups; Movies; Shopping trips; Dances/Social/Cultural gatherings; Intergenerational programs; Pet therapy; Exercise program.

Broadstreet Nursing Center
12040 Broad St, Detroit, MI 48204
(313) 931-2800
Admin Diane M Haugh. *Dir of Nursing* Rita Jarrett RN. *Medical Dir* Fred Gold DO.
Licensure Skilled care; Intermediate care. *Beds* Swing beds SNF/ICF 97. *Certified* Medicaid; Medicare.
Owner Proprietary corp.
Admissions Requirements Minimum age 21; Physician's request.
Staff Physicians 1 (pt); RNs 1 (ft), 1 (pt); LPNs 7 (ft), 4 (pt); Nurses' aides 27 (ft), 11 (pt); Physical therapists 1 (pt); Occupational therapists 1 (pt); Speech therapists 1 (pt); Activities coordinators 1 (ft), 1 (pt); Dietitians 1 (pt); Ophthalmologists 1 (pt); Podiatrists 1 (pt); Dentists 1 (pt).

Facilities Dining room; Physical therapy room; Activities room; Laundry room; Barber/Beauty shop; Library.
Activities Arts & crafts; Cards; Games; Reading groups; Prayer groups; Movies; Shopping trips; Dances/Social/Cultural gatherings; Music therapy.

Cadillac Nursing Home
1533 Cadillac Blvd, Detroit, MI 48214
(313) 823-0435
Admin Hari Mali. *Dir of Nursing* Helen T Carroll RN. *Medical Dir* Donald Dreyfuss DO.
Licensure Skilled care. *Beds* SNF 97. *Private Pay Patients* 22%. *Certified* Medicaid; Medicare.
Owner Proprietary corp (Hari Mali).
Admissions Requirements Medical examination.
Staff Physicians 1 (pt); RNs 2 (ft), 2 (pt); LPNs 4 (ft), 3 (pt); Nurses' aides 38 (ft); Physical therapists 1 (pt); Activities coordinators 1 (ft); Dietitians 1 (pt); Ophthalmologists 1 (pt); Podiatrists 1 (pt).
Languages German, Italian, Spanish, Tagalog, French, Indian.
Facilities Dining room; Physical therapy room; Laundry room; Barber/Beauty shop.
Activities Arts & crafts; Cards; Games; Reading groups; Prayer groups; Movies; Shopping trips; Dances/Social/Cultural gatherings; Pet therapy; YMCA swim program; Sight-seeing; Ballgames; Religious services.

Chandler Haven
511 E Grand Blvd, Detroit, MI 48207
Licensure Home for aged. *Beds* Home for aged 108.

Cranbrook Geriatric Village
5000 E Seven Mile Rd, Detroit, MI 48234
(313) 366-8500
Licensure Skilled care. *Beds* SNF 91. *Certified* Medicaid; Medicare.
Admissions Requirements Minimum age 15; Medical examination; Physician's request.
Staff RNs; LPNs; Nurses' aides; Physical therapists 1 (pt); Occupational therapists 1 (pt); Activities coordinators 1 (ft); Dietitians 1 (pt).
Facilities Dining room; Physical therapy room; Activities room; Crafts room; Barber/Beauty shop.
Activities Arts & crafts; Cards; Games; Reading groups; Prayer groups; Movies; Shopping trips; Dances/Social/Cultural gatherings.

David Nursing Home
13241 W Chicago, Detroit, MI 48228
(313) 834-6670 & 834-1192
Licensure Skilled care. *Beds* SNF 57. *Certified* Medicaid; Medicare.

Detroiter Residence
2560 Woodward, Detroit, MI 48201
(313) 963-3545
Licensure Intermediate care. *Beds* 300. *Certified* Medicaid.
Staff Physicians 5 (pt); RNs 3 (ft); LPNs 18 (ft); Nurses' aides 150 (ft); Physical therapists 4 (ft); Reality therapists 2 (ft); Recreational therapists 4 (ft); Occupational therapists 1 (pt); Speech therapists 1 (pt); Activities coordinators 1 (ft); Dietitians 3 (ft), 1 (pt); Ophthalmologists 1 (pt); Podiatrists 1 (pt); Dentists 1 (pt).
Facilities Dining room; Physical therapy room; Activities room; Chapel; Crafts room; Laundry room; Barber/Beauty shop; Library.
Activities Arts & crafts; Games; Reading groups; Prayer groups; Shopping trips; Dances/Social/Cultural gatherings.

East Grand Nursing Home
130 E Grand Blvd, Detroit, MI 48207
(313) 824-8224

Licensure Intermediate care. *Beds* ICF 94.
Certified Medicaid.

Eastwood Nursing Center
626 E Grand Blvd, Detroit, MI 48207
(313) 923-5816
Admin Earl F Furbish. *Dir of Nursing* Lorene
Cook. *Medical Dir* Dr William Silverstone.
Licensure Skilled care; Intermediate care. *Beds*
SNF 47; ICF 39. *Private Pay Patients* 1%.
Certified Medicaid; Medicare.
Owner Privately owned (Camelot Enterprises).
Admissions Requirements Medical
examination; Physician's request.
Staff RNs 2 (ft), 1 (pt); LPNs 5 (ft), 3 (pt);
Nurses' aides 26 (ft), 15 (pt); Physical
therapists; Dietitians.
Facilities Dining room; Activities room;
Laundry room.
Activities Cards; Games; Reading groups;
Movies; Shopping trips.

Elmwood Geriatric Village
1881 E Grand Blvd, Detroit, MI 48211
(313) 922-1600
Admin Jacqueline E Nave. *Dir of Nursing*
Dorothy Cheit RN. *Medical Dir* Lawrence
Usher DO.
Licensure Skilled care. *Beds* SNF 120.
Certified Medicaid; Medicare.
Owner Privately owned.
Admissions Requirements Minimum age 18;
Medical examination; Physician's request.
Staff Physicians 2 (pt); RNs 2 (ft), 4 (pt);
LPNs 10 (ft), 10 (pt); Nurses' aides 30 (ft),
15 (pt); Activities coordinators 1 (ft).
Facilities Dining room; Physical therapy
room; Activities room; Chapel; Crafts room;
Laundry room; Barber/Beauty shop.
Activities Arts & crafts; Cards; Games;
Reading groups; Prayer groups; Movies;
Shopping trips; Dances/Social/Cultural
gatherings.

Evangelical Home—Detroit
6700 W Outer Dr, Detroit, MI 48235
(313) 836-1700
Admin Vito A Bommarito. *Dir of Nursing*
Jeanne Legge-Taylor RN. *Medical Dir*
Donald Visscher MD.
Licensure Skilled care; Home for aged. *Beds*
SNF 121; Home for aged 115. *Certified*
Medicaid; Medicare.
Owner Nonprofit corp.
Admissions Requirements Minimum age 60;
Medical examination.
Staff Physicians; RNs; LPNs; Nurses' aides;
Physical therapists; Occupational therapists;
Speech therapists; Activities coordinators;
Dietitians; Ophthalmologists; Dentists.
Affiliation Church of Christ.
Facilities Dining room; Physical therapy
room; Activities room; Chapel; Crafts room;
Laundry room; Barber/Beauty shop; Library.
Activities Arts & crafts; Games; Prayer groups;
Movies; Shopping trips; Dances/Social/
Cultural gatherings.

Fairlane Memorial Convalescent Home
15750 Joy Rd, Detroit, MI 48228
(313) 273-6850
Admin James R Branscum. *Dir of Nursing*
Ronda Kuzmanovich RN. *Medical Dir* Jack
Mayer DO.
Licensure Skilled care; Intermediate care;
Alzheimer's care. *Beds* Swing beds SNF/ICF
325. *Certified* Medicaid; Medicare.
Owner Proprietary corp.
Admissions Requirements Minimum age 18;
Physician's request.
Staff Physicians 4 (pt); RNs 4 (ft); LPNs 20
(ft); Nurses' aides 100 (ft); Physical
therapists 2 (ft); Reality therapists 3 (ft);
Recreational therapists 2 (ft); Occupational
therapists 1 (ft); Speech therapists 1 (ft);
Activities coordinators 1 (ft); Dietitians 1
(ft); Ophthalmologists 1 (ft); Podiatrists 1
(ft); Dentists 1 (ft).

Languages Polish.
Facilities Dining room; Physical therapy
room; Activities room; Chapel; Crafts room;
Laundry room; Barber/Beauty shop; Library.
Activities Arts & crafts; Cards; Games;
Reading groups; Prayer groups; Movies;
Shopping trips; Dances/Social/Cultural
gatherings.

Friendship Manor Nursing Home
3950 Beaubien Ave, Detroit, MI 48201
(313) 833-7600
Licensure Intermediate care. *Beds* ICF 170.
Certified Medicaid.

Grace Convalescent Center
18901 Meyers Rd, Detroit, MI 48235
(313) 864-8481
Licensure Skilled care; Intermediate care. *Beds*
Swing beds SNF/ICF 226. *Certified*
Medicaid; Medicare.

Great Lakes Care Center
12900 W Chicago, Detroit, MI 48228
(313) 491-6400
Licensure Intermediate care. *Beds* ICF 164.
Certified Medicaid.
Owner Proprietary corp (Beverly Enterprises).

Hadley Manor
535 E Grand Blvd, Detroit, MI 48207
(313) 923-2020
Admin Timothy Korlson. *Dir of Nursing*
Georgia Gray RN. *Medical Dir* William
Silverstone MD.
Licensure Intermediate care. *Beds* ICF 38.
Certified Medicaid.
Staff Physicians 1 (pt); RNs 1 (ft); LPNs 3
(ft), 4 (pt); Nurses' aides 20 (ft); Activities
coordinators 1 (ft); Dietitians 1 (pt);
Ophthalmologists 1 (pt); Dentists 1 (pt).
Facilities Dining room; Activities room;
Crafts room; Laundry room.
Activities Arts & crafts; Cards; Games; Prayer
groups; Movies; Shopping trips; Dances/
Social/Cultural gatherings; Outings.

Hamilton Nursing Home
590 E Grand Blvd, Detroit, MI 48207
(313) 921-1580
Licensure Skilled care. *Beds* SNF 64. *Certified*
Medicaid; Medicare.

Hannan House
4750 Woodward Ave, Detroit, MI 48201
Licensure Home for aged. *Beds* Home for
aged 49.

Hillcrest Convalescent Center
12535 Harper Ave, Detroit, MI 48213
(313) 371-5520
Licensure Skilled care; Intermediate care. *Beds*
Swing beds SNF/ICF 79. *Certified* Medicaid;
Medicare.
Owner Proprietary corp (Beverly Enterprises).

Ingleside Convalescent Center
9155 Woodward Ave, Detroit, MI 48202
(313) 872-1420
Licensure Intermediate care. *Beds* ICF 141.
Certified Medicaid.

Jewish Home for the Aged 2
19100 W Seven Mile Rd, Detroit, MI 48219
(313) 532-7112
Medical Dir William Solomon MD.
Licensure Skilled care. *Beds* SNF 212.
Certified Medicaid; Medicare.
Owner Nonprofit corp (Jewish Home for the
Aged).
Staff Physicians 1 (ft), 3 (pt); RNs 5 (ft), 4
(pt); LPNs 10 (ft), 3 (pt); Nurses' aides 77
(ft), 24 (pt); Physical therapists 1 (pt);
Occupational therapists 4 (ft); Speech
therapists 1 (pt); Activities coordinators 1
(ft); Dietitians 1 (pt); Ophthalmologists 1
(pt); Podiatrists 1 (pt); Dentists 1 (pt).
Affiliation Jewish.

Facilities Dining room; Physical therapy
room; Activities room; Chapel; Crafts room;
Laundry room; Barber/Beauty shop; Library.
Activities Arts & crafts; Cards; Games;
Reading groups; Prayer groups; Movies;
Shopping trips; Dances/Social/Cultural
gatherings.

Lakeland Convalescent Center
745-751 E Grand Blvd, Detroit, MI 48207
(313) 921-0998
Licensure Intermediate care. *Beds* ICF 92.
Certified Medicaid.

LaSalle Nursing Home
2411 W Grand Blvd, Detroit, MI 48208
(313) 897-5144
Admin Clair K Lewis. *Dir of Nursing* Pamela
McCants RN. *Medical Dir* Dr Auther
Cooper.
Licensure Intermediate care; Alzheimer's care.
Beds ICF 100. *Certified* Medicaid.
Owner Privately owned.
Admissions Requirements Minimum age 18;
Medical examination; Physician's request.
Staff Physicians 1 (ft), 2 (pt); RNs 5 (ft);
LPNs 10 (ft), 10 (pt); Nurses' aides 70 (ft), 5
(pt); Physical therapists 1 (ft); Recreational
therapists 1 (ft); Occupational therapists 1
(ft); Speech therapists 1 (ft); Activities
coordinators 1 (ft); Dietitians 1 (ft), 1 (pt);
Ophthalmologists 1 (ft); Podiatrists 1 (ft);
Dentists 1 (ft).
Languages Polish, Spanish, Tagalog.
Facilities Dining room; Physical therapy
room; Activities room; Crafts room; Laundry
room; Barber/Beauty shop; Library.
Activities Arts & crafts; Cards; Games;
Reading groups; Prayer groups; Movies;
Shopping trips.

Ozie LaTrece Home for the Aged
9298 Wyoming Ave, Detroit, MI 48204
Licensure Home for aged. *Beds* Home for
aged 40.

LaVilla Nursing Center
660 E Grand Blvd, Detroit, MI 48207
(313) 923-5800
Admin Pierce S Morton Jr.
Medical Dir Dr W Silverstone.
Licensure Skilled care; Intermediate care. *Beds*
Swing beds SNF/ICF 95. *Certified* Medicaid;
Medicare.
Owner Proprietary corp.
Admissions Requirements Minimum age 30;
Staff RNs; LPNs; Nurses' aides; Activities
coordinators.
Facilities Dining room; Activities room;
Barber/Beauty shop.
Activities Arts & crafts; Cards; Games;
Reading groups; Prayer groups; Movies;
Shopping trips; Dances/Social/Cultural
gatherings.

Law-Den Nursing Home
1640 Webb Ave, Detroit, MI 48206
(313) 867-1719
Admin Lawrence D Johnson.
Licensure Intermediate care. *Beds* ICF 100.
Certified Medicaid.
Owner Proprietary corp.
Admissions Requirements Minimum age 18;
Staff RNs 2 (ft); LPNs 8 (ft), 2 (pt); Nurses'
aides 42 (ft); Recreational therapists 1 (ft);
Activities coordinators 1 (ft); Dietitians 1
(pt).
Languages Spanish.
Facilities Dining room; Activities room;
Chapel; Crafts room; Laundry room.
Activities Arts & crafts; Cards; Games;
Reading groups; Prayer groups; Movies;
Dances/Social/Cultural gatherings; Baseball
games.

Lincoln Care Center
13001 W Chicago, Detroit, MI 48228
(313) 834-1204

Admin Genevieve Stratton. *Dir of Nursing*
Barbara Osborne RN. *Medical Dir* Raymond
Weitzman MD.
Licensure Skilled care. *Beds* SNF 118.
Certified Medicaid; Medicare.
Owner Proprietary corp.
Admissions Requirements Minimum age 18;
Medical examination; Physician's request.
Staff Physicians; RNs; LPNs; Nurses' aides;
Physical therapists; Reality therapists;
Recreational therapists; Occupational
therapists; Speech therapists; Activities
coordinators; Dietitians; Ophthalmologists;
Podiatrists; Audiologists.
Languages Zimbabwe, Spanish, Arabic.
Facilities Dining room; Physical therapy
room; Activities room; Crafts room; Laundry
room; Barber/Beauty shop.
Activities Arts & crafts; Cards; Games;
Reading groups; Prayer groups; Movies;
Shopping trips; Dances/Social/Cultural
gatherings; Intergenerational programs; Pet
therapy.

Luther Haven
464 E Grand Blvd, Detroit, MI 48207
(313) 579-2255
Admin Shela R Taylor. *Dir of Nursing* Jewel
D Vinson RN. *Medical Dir* A Bedell MD &
Associates.
Licensure Skilled care; Intermediate care;
Home for aged. *Beds* Swing beds SNF/ICF
89; Home for aged 52. *Private Pay Patients*
15%. *Certified* Medicaid; Medicare.
Owner Nonprofit corp (Lutheran Social
Services of Michigan).
Admissions Requirements Minimum age 65;
Medical examination.
Staff Physicians 1 (pt); RNs 2 (ft), 2 (pt);
LPNs 5 (ft), 5 (pt); Nurses' aides 27 (ft), 10
(pt); Physical therapists 1 (pt); Recreational
therapists 1 (pt); Occupational therapists 1
(pt); Speech therapists 1 (pt); Activities
coordinators 1 (ft); Dietitians 1 (pt);
Ophthalmologists 1 (pt); Podiatrists 1 (pt);
Dentists 1 (pt).
Affiliation Evangelical Lutheran.
Facilities Dining room; Physical therapy
room; Activities room; Chapel; Crafts room;
Laundry room; Barber/Beauty shop;
Lounges.
Activities Arts & crafts; Cards; Games;
Reading groups; Prayer groups; Movies;
Shopping trips; Dances/Social/Cultural
gatherings.

Madonna Nursing Center
15311 Schaefer St, Detroit, MI 48227
(313) 835-4775
Licensure Intermediate care. *Beds* ICF 138.
Certified Medicaid.
Owner Proprietary corp (International
Healthcare Management).

Medicos Health Care Center
22355 W Eight Mile Rd, Detroit, MI 48219
(313) 255-6450
Admin Shirley A St Souver. *Dir of Nursing* C
Littleton RN. *Medical Dir* Marvin Klein
MD.
Licensure Skilled care. *Beds* SNF 180.
Certified Medicaid; Medicare.
Owner Proprietary corp.
Admissions Requirements Minimum age 18.
Staff RNs 4 (ft), 4 (pt); LPNs 12 (ft), 10 (pt);
Nurses' aides 90 (ft), 10 (pt); Physical
therapists 1 (ft); Activities coordinators 1
(ft), 1 (pt); Dietitians 1 (pt); Podiatrists 1
(pt).
Facilities Dining room; Physical therapy
room; Activities room; Crafts room; Laundry
room; Barber/Beauty shop.
Activities Arts & crafts; Cards; Games; Prayer
groups; Movies; Shopping trips; Dances/
Social/Cultural gatherings.

Moroun Nursing Home
8045 E Jefferson Ave, Detroit, MI 48214
(313) 821-3525
Dir of Nursing Remedios Doctor RN.
Licensure Skilled care; Intermediate care. *Beds*
Swing beds SNF/ICF 189. *Certified*
Medicaid; Medicare.

New Detroit Nursing Center
716 E Grand Blvd, Detroit, MI 48207
(313) 923-0300
Admin Thelma J Scott. *Dir of Nursing* M
Miller RN. *Medical Dir* Dr M Williams.
Licensure Intermediate care. *Beds* ICF 50.
Certified Medicaid.
Owner Proprietary corp.
Admissions Requirements Minimum age 18;
Physician's request.
Staff Physicians 1 (pt); RNs 1 (ft), 1 (pt);
LPNs 3 (ft), 3 (pt); Nurses' aides 20 (ft), 20
(pt); Reality therapists 1 (pt); Recreational
therapists 1 (ft); Activities coordinators 1
(ft); Dietitians 1 (pt); Ophthalmologists 1
(pt); Dentists 1 (pt).
Facilities Dining room; Activities room;
Laundry room; Barber/Beauty shop.
Activities Arts & crafts; Cards; Games;
Reading groups; Prayer groups; Movies;
Shopping trips; Dances/Social/Cultural
gatherings.

Newlight Baptist Nursing Home
9500 Grand River Ave, Detroit, MI 48204
(313) 491-7920
Admin George B Talley. *Dir of Nursing* N
Blair RN. *Medical Dir* I Jan MD.
Licensure Skilled care; Intermediate care. *Beds*
Swing beds SNF/ICF 189. *Certified*
Medicaid; Medicare.
Owner Nonprofit corp.
Admissions Requirements Minimum age 18;
Medical examination; Physician's request.
Staff Physicians; RNs; LPNs; Nurses' aides;
Physical therapists; Reality therapists;
Recreational therapists; Activities
coordinators; Dietitians; Ophthalmologists;
Dentists.
Facilities Dining room; Physical therapy
room; Activities room; Chapel; Crafts room;
Laundry room; Barber/Beauty shop.
Activities Arts & crafts; Cards; Games;
Reading groups; Prayer groups; Movies;
Shopping trips; Dances/Social/Cultural
gatherings.

Northland Nursing Center
21630 Hessel, Detroit, MI 48219
(313) 534-8400
Licensure Skilled care. *Beds* SNF 110.
Certified Medicaid; Medicare.

Northwest Care Continuing Center
16181 Hubbell, Detroit, MI 48235
(313) 273-8764
Admin Martha N Little. *Dir of Nursing* W
Boone.
Licensure Skilled care; Intermediate care. *Beds*
SNF 104; ICF 50. *Private Pay Patients* 2%.
Certified Medicaid; Medicare.
Owner Proprietary corp (Tendercare Nursing
Home).
Admissions Requirements Minimum age 16;
Medical examination; Physician's request.
Staff RNs; LPNs; Nurses' aides; Activities
coordinators; Dietitians.
Facilities Dining room; Physical therapy
room; Activities room; Chapel; Crafts room;
Laundry room; Barber/Beauty shop; Library;
Portable service.
Activities Arts & crafts; Cards; Games;
Reading groups; Prayer groups; Movies;
Shopping trips; Dances/Social/Cultural
gatherings; Intergenerational programs.

Park Plaza Inc
2560 2nd Ave, Detroit, MI 48201
Licensure Home for aged. *Beds* Home for
aged 116.

Pembrook Nursing Center
9146 Woodward, Detroit, MI 48202
(313) 875-1263
Licensure Skilled care; Intermediate care. *Beds*
Swing beds SNF/ICF 195. *Certified*
Medicaid; Medicare.

Presbyterian Village of Detroit
17383 Garfield, Detroit, MI 48240
Licensure Skilled care; Home for aged. *Beds*
SNF 88; Home for aged 211. *Certified*
Medicaid; Medicare.

Qualicare Nursing Home
695 E Grand Blvd, Detroit, MI 48207
(313) 925-6655
Admin Jeri Ribant.
Medical Dir Jean Sherman.
Licensure Skilled care; Alzheimer's care. *Beds*
SNF 115. *Certified* Medicaid; Medicare.
Owner Proprietary corp.
Admissions Requirements Minimum age 21;
Medical examination; Physician's request.
Staff RNs; LPNs; Nurses' aides; Activities
coordinators; Dietitians.
Facilities Dining room; Physical therapy
room; Activities room; Crafts room; Barber/
Beauty shop.
Activities Arts & crafts; Cards; Games;
Reading groups; Prayer groups; Movies;
Shopping trips; Dances/Social/Cultural
gatherings.

Redford Geriatric Village
22811 W Seven Mile Rd, Detroit, MI 48219
(313) 534-1440
Admin W T Beardsley.
Medical Dir Lawrence Usher; V Farris.
Licensure Skilled care. *Beds* SNF 106.
Certified Medicaid; Medicare.
Owner Privately owned.
Admissions Requirements Minimum age 18;
Medical examination; Physician's request.
Staff Physicians; RNs; LPNs; Nurses' aides;
Physical therapists; Occupational therapists;
Speech therapists; Activities coordinators;
Dietitians; Ophthalmologists; Podiatrists;
Dentists.
Facilities Dining room; Physical therapy
room; Activities room; Crafts room; Laundry
room; Barber/Beauty shop.
Activities Arts & crafts; Cards; Games;
Reading groups; Prayer groups; Movies;
Shopping trips; Dances/Social/Cultural
gatherings; Lunch outings.

Regency Park Convalescent Center
5201 Conner Ave, Detroit, MI 48213
(313) 571-5555
Admin Beverly Court.
Medical Dir Pearlie Mae Brown.
Licensure Intermediate care; Alzheimer's care.
Beds ICF 234. *Certified* Medicaid.
Owner Proprietary corp.
Admissions Requirements Medical
examination; Physician's request.
Staff Physicians 1 (ft); RNs 1 (ft); LPNs 8 (ft),
2 (pt); Nurses' aides 50 (ft), 25 (pt); Physical
therapists 2 (ft); Activities coordinators 1
(ft); Dietitians 1 (ft); Ophthalmologists 1 (ft).
Facilities Dining room; Physical therapy
room; Activities room; Crafts room; Laundry
room; Barber/Beauty shop.
Activities Arts & crafts; Cards; Games;
Reading groups; Prayer groups; Movies;
Shopping trips; Dances/Social/Cultural
gatherings.

St Anne Convalescent Center
6232 Cadieux Rd, Detroit, MI 48224
(313) 886-2500
Admin Mary E Gallagher. *Dir of Nursing*
Catherine McEntee. *Medical Dir* Vishwanath
B Mali MD.
Licensure Skilled care; Intermediate care. *Beds*
Swing beds SNF/ICF 105. *Private Pay
Patients* 20%. *Certified* Medicaid; Medicare.
Owner Proprietary corp.

Admissions Requirements Medical
examination; Physician's request.
Staff RNs 5 (ft), 1 (pt); LPNs 5 (ft), 1 (pt);
Nurses' aides 31 (ft), 6 (pt); Activities
coordinators 1 (ft); Dietitians 1 (pt).
Languages Italian, Polish, Spanish.
Facilities Dining room; Physical therapy
room; Activities room; Chapel; Laundry
room.
Activities Arts & crafts; Cards; Games;
Reading groups; Prayer groups; Movies;
Shopping trips; Dances/Social/Cultural
gatherings; Pet therapy.

St Clare Convalescent Center
15063 Gratiot, Detroit, MI 48205
(313) 372-4065
Licensure Skilled care. *Beds* SNF 150.
Certified Medicaid; Medicare.

St John-Bon Secours Senior Community
18300 E Warren Ave, Detroit, MI 48224
Licensure Skilled care. *Beds* SNF 150.

St Josephs Home for the Aged
4800 Cadieux Rd, Detroit, MI 48224
(313) 882-3800
Licensure Home for aged. *Beds* Home for
aged 104.

St Martin Deporres Nursing Home
1880 E Grand Blvd, Detroit, MI 48211
(313) 925-6868
Licensure Skilled care; Intermediate care. *Beds*
Swing beds SNF/ICF 81. *Certified* Medicaid;
Medicare.
Affiliation Roman Catholic.

Torry Pines Home for the Aged
491 E Grand Blvd, Detroit, MI 48207
Licensure Home for aged. *Beds* Home for
aged 22.

Westwood Nursing Center
16588 Schaefer, Detroit, MI 48235
(313) 345-5000, 345-4036 FAX
Admin Robert A Malott. *Dir of Nursing* Jill A
Rogers. *Medical Dir* Robert Silverstone DO.
Licensure Skilled care; Intermediate care. *Beds*
SNF 69; ICF 70. *Certified* Medicaid;
Medicare.
Owner Proprietary corp.
Admissions Requirements Minimum age 21;
Medical examination; Physician's request.
Staff Physicians; RNs; LPNs; Nurses' aides;
Physical therapists; Recreational therapists;
Occupational therapists; Speech therapists;
Activities coordinators; Dietitians.
Facilities Dining room; Physical therapy
room; Activities room; Crafts room; Laundry
room; Barber/Beauty shop.
Activities Arts & crafts; Cards; Games;
Reading groups; Prayer groups; Movies;
Shopping trips; Dances/Social/Cultural
gatherings; Intergenerational programs.

Dimondale

St Lawrence Dimondale Center
4000 N Michigan Rd, Dimondale, MI 48821
(517) 646-6258
Admin Sr Mary Ricardo Gentle RSM. *Dir of
Nursing* Janet L Graham RN. *Medical Dir*
Rodman Jacobi MD.
Licensure Skilled care; Home for aged. *Beds*
SNF 177; Home for aged 1. *Certified*
Medicaid; Medicare.
Owner Nonprofit corp.
Admissions Requirements Medical
examination; Physician's request.
Staff Physicians; RNs 2 (ft), 3 (pt); LPNs 14
(ft), 2 (pt); Nurses' aides 35 (ft), 25 (pt);
Recreational therapists 1 (ft); Activities
coordinators 2 (ft); Dietitians 11 (ft);
Podiatrists; Dentists; Dermatologists.
Affiliation Roman Catholic.

Facilities Dining room; Physical therapy
room; Activities room; Chapel; Crafts room;
Laundry room; Barber/Beauty shop; Lobby;
Large garden area.
Activities Arts & crafts; Cards; Games;
Reading groups; Prayer groups; Movies;
Shopping trips; Dances/Social/Cultural
gatherings.

Douglas

Harbors Health Facility
130th Ave, Box 2, Douglas, MI 49406
Licensure Skilled care; Home for aged. *Beds*
SNF 35; Home for aged 63. *Certified*
Medicaid; Medicare.

Dowagiac

Dowagiac Nursing Home
610 Uneta St, Dowagiac, MI 49047
(616) 782-3471
Admin Alex Miskiewicz. *Dir of Nursing* Pat
Parker.
Licensure Skilled care. *Beds* SNF 150.
Certified Medicaid; Medicare.
Owner Nonprofit organization/foundation.
Admissions Requirements Minimum age 18;
Medical examination; Physician's request.
Staff RNs 7 (ft); LPNs 7 (ft), 8 (pt); Nurses'
aides 60 (ft), 25 (pt); Physical therapists 1
(pt); Recreational therapists 2 (ft); Speech
therapists 1 (pt); Activities coordinators 2
(ft); Dietitians 1 (pt); Ophthalmologists 1
(pt); Podiatrists 1 (pt).
Affiliation Roman Catholic.
Facilities Dining room; Physical therapy
room; Activities room; Chapel; Laundry
room; Barber/Beauty shop.
Activities Arts & crafts; Cards; Games;
Reading groups; Prayer groups; Movies;
Dances/Social/Cultural gatherings.

Durand

Durand Convalescent Center
8750 E Monroe Rd, Durand, MI 48429
(517) 288-3166
Licensure Skilled care. *Beds* SNF 159.
Certified Medicaid; Medicare.

East Jordan

Grandvue Medical Care Facility
1728 S Peninsula Rd, East Jordan, MI 49727
(616) 536-2286, 536-2476 FAX
Admin Regina Shaffer. *Dir of Nursing* Nancy
Carey RN. *Medical Dir* Robert Martin MD.
Licensure Skilled care; Intermediate care;
Supervised residential care. *Beds* Swing beds
SNF/ICF 73; Supervised residential care
beds 27. *Private Pay Patients* 20%. *Certified*
Medicaid; Medicare.
Owner Publicly owned.
Admissions Requirements Minimum age 15;
Medical examination; Physician's request.
Staff Physicians (contracted); RNs 5 (ft), 1
(pt); LPNs 5 (ft), 3 (pt); Nurses' aides 32
(ft), 8 (pt); Physical therapists 1 (pt);
Occupational therapists 1 (pt); Activities
coordinators 2 (ft), 1 (pt); Dietitians 1 (pt);
Podiatrists 1 (pt).
Facilities Dining room; Physical therapy
room; Activities room; Chapel; Laundry
room; Barber/Beauty shop; Fenced courtyard
with gazebo.
Activities Arts & crafts; Cards; Games;
Reading groups; Prayer groups; Movies;
Shopping trips; Dances/Social/Cultural
gatherings; Pet therapy.

East Lansing

Burcham Hills Retirement Center II
2700 Burcham Dr, East Lansing, MI 48823
(517) 351-8377, 351-1738 FAX
Admin Frank G Salimbene. *Dir of Nursing*
Janice Doxtader. *Medical Dir* Gordon
Baustian MD.
Licensure Skilled care; Intermediate care;
Home for aged; Alzheimer's care. *Beds*
Swing beds SNF/ICF 133; Home for aged
293. *Certified* Medicaid; Medicare.
Owner Nonprofit corp.
Staff RNs; LPNs; Nurses' aides; Physical
therapists; Recreational therapists;
Occupational therapists; Activities
coordinators; Dietitians; Ophthalmologists;
Podiatrists.
Facilities Dining room; Physical therapy
room; Activities room; Crafts room; Barber/
Beauty shop; Gift shop.
Activities Arts & crafts; Cards; Games;
Reading groups; Prayer groups; Movies;
Shopping trips; Dances/Social/Cultural
gatherings.

East Lansing Health Care Center
2815 Northwind Dr, East Lansing, MI 48823
(517) 332-0817
Medical Dir E Rittenhouse DO.
Licensure Intermediate care. *Beds* ICF 113.
Certified Medicaid.
Owner Proprietary corp (Waverly Group).
Admissions Requirements Minimum age 21;
Medical examination; Physician's request.
Staff RNs 3 (ft), 2 (pt); LPNs 4 (ft), 6 (pt);
Nurses' aides 38 (ft), 10 (pt); Activities
coordinators 1 (ft).
Facilities Dining room; Activities room;
Laundry room; Barber/Beauty shop.
Activities Arts & crafts; Cards; Games;
Reading groups; Prayer groups; Movies;
Shopping trips; Dances/Social/Cultural
gatherings.

Whitehills Health Care Center
1843 N Hagadorn Rd, East Lansing, MI
48823
(517) 332-5061
Licensure Skilled care. *Beds* SNF 115.
Certified Medicaid; Medicare.
Owner Proprietary corp (Waverly Group).

Escanaba

Christian Park Health Care Center
2415 5th Ave S, Escanaba, MI 49829
(906) 786-6907
Admin Daniel H Ross. *Dir of Nursing* Mary
Lou Lancour RN. *Medical Dir* John LeMire
MD.
Licensure Skilled care; Alzheimer's care. *Beds*
SNF 99. *Certified* Medicaid; Medicare.
Owner Proprietary corp.
Admissions Requirements Minimum age 15;
Medical examination.
Staff Physicians 17 (pt); RNs 3 (ft), 2 (pt);
LPNs 5 (ft), 11 (pt); Nurses' aides 20 (ft), 21
(pt); Physical therapists 1 (pt); Occupational
therapists 1 (pt); Speech therapists 1 (pt);
Activities coordinators 1 (ft), 1 (pt);
Dietitians 1 (pt); Ophthalmologists 1 (pt);
Podiatrists 1 (pt); Audiologists 1 (pt).
Activities Arts & crafts; Cards; Games;
Reading groups; Prayer groups; Movies;
Shopping trips; Dances/Social/Cultural
gatherings; Intergenerational programs; Pet
therapy.

Christian Park Village
2525 7th Ave S, Escanaba, MI 49829
(906) 786-0408
Admin Brian R Baum. *Dir of Nursing* Amy
Wilson RN. *Medical Dir* John LeMire MD.
Licensure Skilled care; Alzheimer's care. *Beds*
SNF 59. *Certified* Medicaid; Medicare.
Owner Proprietary corp.

Admissions Requirements Minimum age 15;
Medical examination.
Staff Physicians 17 (pt); RNs 2 (ft), 3 (pt);
LPNs 2 (ft), 5 (pt); Nurses' aides 9 (ft), 15
(pt); Physical therapists 1 (pt); Occupational
therapists 1 (pt); Speech therapists 1 (pt);
Activities coordinators 1 (ft), 1 (pt);
Dietitians 1 (pt); Ophthalmologists 1 (pt);
Podiatrists 1 (pt); Audiologists 1 (pt).
Facilities Dining room; Physical therapy
room; Activities room; Laundry room;
Barber/Beauty shop.
Activities Arts & crafts; Cards; Games;
Reading groups; Prayer groups; Movies;
Shopping trips; Dances/Social/Cultural
gatherings; Intergenerational programs; Pet
therapy.

Bishop Noa Home
624 Ludington St, Escanaba, MI 49829
(906) 786-5810
Admin Douglas G Heath. *Dir of Nursing* Sr
Laura Perry. *Medical Dir* Dr John LaMire.
Licensure Intermediate care; Home for aged.
Beds ICF 81; Home for aged 28. *Private Pay
Patients* 30%. *Certified* Medicaid.
Owner Nonprofit corp.
Admissions Requirements Minimum age 15;
Medical examination; Physician's request.
Staff RNs 2 (ft); LPNs 5 (ft), 5 (pt); Nurses'
aides 35 (ft), 17 (pt); Activities coordinators
1 (ft), 1 (pt).
Affiliation Roman Catholic.
Facilities Dining room; Activities room;
Chapel; Crafts room; Laundry room;
Library.
Activities Arts & crafts; Cards; Games;
Reading groups; Prayer groups; Movies;
Shopping trips; Dances/Social/Cultural
gatherings; Intergenerational programs; Pet
therapy; Bingo.

Essexville

Bay County Medical Care Facility
564 W Hampton Rd, Essexville, MI 48732
(517) 892-3591
Admin W R Mahoney. *Dir of Nursing* G
VanTol RN. *Medical Dir* B W Webb DO.
Licensure Skilled care. *Beds* SNF 206.
Certified Medicaid; Medicare.
Owner Publicly owned.
Admissions Requirements Medical
examination; Physician's request.
Staff Physicians; RNs; LPNs; Nurses' aides;
Physical therapists; Occupational therapists;
Speech therapists; Activities coordinators;
Dietitians; Ophthalmologists; Dentists.
Facilities Dining room; Physical therapy
room; Activities room; Chapel; Crafts room;
Barber/Beauty shop; Library.
Activities Arts & crafts; Cards; Games; Prayer
groups; Movies; Dances/Social/Cultural
gatherings.

Evart

Brown Nursing Home
PO Box 591, Evart, MI 49631-0591
(517) 236-7348
Licensure Intermediate care. *Beds* 50.
Certified Medicaid.

Fairview

Ausable Valley Home
Box 8, Maple Dr, Fairview, MI 48621
(517) 848-2241
Admin Wayne M Miller. *Dir of Nursing* Leta
Gerber RN. *Medical Dir* G Frailey MD.
Licensure Skilled care; Intermediate care;
Retirement. *Beds* Swing beds SNF/ICF 62.
Private Pay Patients 38%. *Certified*
Medicaid; Medicare.
Owner Nonprofit corp (Mennonite Board of
Missions).

Admissions Requirements Medical
examination; Physician's request.
Staff RNs 3 (ft), 3 (pt); LPNs 1 (ft), 5 (pt);
Nurses' aides 20 (ft), 10 (pt); Physical
therapists 1 (pt); Speech therapists 1 (pt);
Activities coordinators 1 (ft), 2 (pt);
Dietitians 1 (pt).
Languages German.
Affiliation Mennonite.
Facilities Dining room; Activities room;
Laundry room; Barber/Beauty shop.
Activities Arts & crafts; Games; Reading
groups; Prayer groups; Movies.

Farmington

Oak Hill Care Center
34225 Grand River, Farmington, MI 48024
(313) 477-7373
Licensure Skilled care. *Beds* SNF 137.
Certified Medicaid; Medicare.

Oak Hill Nursing Home Annex
34225 Grand River, Farmington, MI 48024
(313) 474-6750
Licensure Intermediate care. *Beds* 16.
Certified Medicaid.

St Benedict Nursing Home
23900 Orchard Lake Rd, Farmington, MI
48024-3450
(313) 554-2700
Licensure Intermediate care. *Beds* ICF 258.
Certified Medicaid.
Owner Proprietary corp (Beverly Enterprises).

Farmington Hills

Farmington Hills Inn
30350 W Twelve Mile Rd, Farmington Hills,
MI 48018
Licensure Home for aged. *Beds* Home for
aged 146.

Farmington Nursing Home
30405 Folsom Rd, Farmington Hills, MI
48024
(313) 477-7400
Admin Ruth Farrell. *Dir of Nursing* Barbara
Blair RN. *Medical Dir* Harold Wasserman
MD.
Licensure Skilled care; Alzheimer's care. *Beds*
SNF 179. *Certified* Medicaid; Medicare.
Owner Nonprofit corp.
Admissions Requirements Minimum age 18.
Facilities Dining room; Physical therapy
room; Activities room; Crafts room; Laundry
room; Barber/Beauty shop.
Activities Arts & crafts; Cards; Games; Prayer
groups; Movies; Dances/Social/Cultural
gatherings; Alzheimer's support group.

Williamsburg Care Center
21017 Middlebelt Rd, Farmington Hills, MI
48027
(313) 476-8300
Admin Marsha E Tomas. *Dir of Nursing*
Olivia Brenner. *Medical Dir* A Slaim.
Licensure Intermediate care; Alzheimer's care.
Beds ICF 112. *Private Pay Patients* 30%.
Certified Medicaid.
Owner Proprietary corp (Care Centers of
Michigan).
Admissions Requirements Minimum age 18;
Medical examination; Physician's request.
Staff Physicians 4 (ft); RNs 2 (ft); LPNs 15
(ft); Nurses' aides 54 (ft); Physical therapists
1 (ft); Occupational therapists 1 (pt);
Activities coordinators 1 (ft); Dietitians 1
(ft); Podiatrists 1 (pt).
Facilities Dining room; Physical therapy
room; Activities room; Laundry room;
Barber/Beauty shop; Library.
Activities Arts & crafts; Cards; Games;
Reading groups; Prayer groups; Movies;
Shopping trips; Dances/Social/Cultural
gatherings; Intergenerational programs; Pet

therapy; Resident council; Family council;
Music therapy; Art therapy; "Senior
Connection".

Farwell

Ardis Nursing Home
2532 Cadillac Dr, Farwell, MI 48622
(517) 588-9928
Admin Grant Walter.
Medical Dir C McGowen.
Licensure Skilled care; Intermediate care;
Alzheimer's care. *Beds* Swing beds SNF/ICF
71. *Certified* Medicaid; Medicare.
Owner Proprietary corp.
Admissions Requirements Minimum age 18;
Medical examination.
Staff RNs; LPNs; Nurses' aides; Physical
therapists; Recreational therapists;
Occupational therapists; Speech therapists;
Activities coordinators.
Languages Sign, Spanish.
Facilities Dining room; Physical therapy
room; Activities room; Crafts room; Laundry
room; Barber/Beauty shop.
Activities Arts & crafts; Cards; Games;
Reading groups; Prayer groups; Movies;
Dances/Social/Cultural gatherings.

Fenton

Crestmont Medical Care Facility
111 Trealout Dr, Fenton, MI 48430
(313) 629-4105
Medical Dir W Buchanan MD.
Licensure Skilled care. *Beds* SNF 132.
Certified Medicaid; Medicare.
Owner Proprietary corp (International
Healthcare Management).
Staff Physicians 6 (pt); RNs 8 (ft), 5 (pt);
LPNs 5 (ft); Nurses' aides 51 (ft), 14 (pt);
Physical therapists 1 (pt); Occupational
therapists 1 (pt); Speech therapists 1 (pt);
Activities coordinators 2 (ft); Dietitians 1
(pt); Podiatrists 1 (pt); Dentists 1 (pt);
Physical therapy assistants 1 (ft).
Facilities Dining room; Physical therapy
room; Activities room; Chapel; Crafts room;
Laundry room; Barber/Beauty shop; Family
room; Dayroom; Classroom.
Activities Arts & crafts; Cards; Games; Prayer
groups; Movies; Shopping trips; Dances/
Social/Cultural gatherings; Picnics; Happy
hour.

Elder House
202 W Shiawassee Ave, Fenton, MI 48430
(313) 629-6391
Licensure Home for aged. *Beds* Home for
aged 36.
Admissions Requirements Minimum age 60;
Medical examination; Physician's request.
Staff RNs 1 (pt); Nurses' aides 6 (ft);
Activities coordinators 1 (ft); Dietitians 1
(pt).
Facilities Dining room; Activities room;
Crafts room; Barber/Beauty shop; Library;
Outdoor activity area.
Activities Arts & crafts; Cards; Games;
Reading groups; Prayer groups; Movies;
Shopping trips; Dances/Social/Cultural
gatherings; Cookouts; Bowling.

Fenton Extended Care Center
512 Beach St, Fenton, MI 48430
(313) 629-4117
Licensure Intermediate care. *Beds* ICF 121.
Certified Medicaid.

Hammond Rest Home
700 S Adelaide St, Fenton, MI 48430
(313) 629-9641
Admin Anna M Charles. *Dir of Nursing* Anna
M Charles.
Licensure Intermediate care. *Beds* ICF 25.
Certified Medicaid.
Owner Proprietary corp.

Admissions Requirements Minimum age 15;
Females only; Medical examination.
Staff RNs 1 (ft), 1 (pt); LPNs 3 (ft), 4 (pt);
Nurses' aides 7 (ft), 4 (pt); Activities
coordinators 1 (ft); Dietitians 1 (pt).
Facilities Dining room; Activities room;
Laundry room.
Activities Arts & crafts; Cards; Games; Prayer
groups; Movies.

Ferndale

Coplin Manor Convalescent Home
PO Box 20097, Ferndale, MI 48220-0097
(313) 823-0330
Medical Dir Arthur Cooper DO.
Licensure Intermediate care. *Beds* ICF 38.
Certified Medicaid.
Admissions Requirements Minimum age 18;
Females only; Medical examination;
Physician's request.
Staff RNs; LPNs; Nurses' aides; Physical
therapists; Reality therapists; Recreational
therapists; Occupational therapists; Speech
therapists; Activities coordinators; Dietitians;
Ophthalmologists; Podiatrists; Audiologists;
Dentists.
Facilities Dining room; Physical therapy
room; Activities room; Crafts room; Laundry
room; Barber/Beauty shop.
Activities Arts & crafts; Cards; Games;
Reading groups; Prayer groups; Movies;
Shopping trips; Dances/Social/Cultural
gatherings.

Hilton Convalescent Home
3161 Hilton Rd, Ferndale, MI 48220
(313) 547-6227
Licensure Skilled care; Intermediate care. *Beds*
Swing beds SNF/ICF 78. *Certified* Medicaid;
Medicare.

Flint

Clara Barton Terrace
1801 E Atherton Rd, Flint, MI 48439
(313) 742-5850, 742-5853 FAX
Admin Diane Blick RN. *Dir of Nursing* Mary
Winch RN. *Medical Dir* Maurice Chapin
MD.
Licensure Intermediate care. *Beds* ICF 149.
Private Pay Patients 12%. *Certified*
Medicaid.
Owner Proprietary corp.
Admissions Requirements Minimum age 15;
Medical examination; Physician's request.
Staff RNs 4 (ft), 3 (pt); LPNs 9 (ft), 10 (pt);
Nurses' aides 50 (ft), 40 (pt); Activities
coordinators 1 (ft).
Facilities Dining room; Activities room;
Chapel; Crafts room; Laundry room; Barber/
Beauty shop; Library; Enclosed patio.
Activities Arts & crafts; Cards; Games;
Reading groups; Prayer groups; Movies;
Shopping trips; Dances/Social/Cultural
gatherings; Intergenerational programs; Pet
therapy.

Beecher Manor
702 S Ballenger Hwy, Flint, MI 48502
Licensure Intermediate care. *Beds* ICF 60.
Certified Medicaid.

Briarwood Manor Nursing Home
3011 N Center Rd, Flint, MI 48506
(313) 736-0600
Admin Glenn J Porterfield. *Dir of Nursing*
Leslie Goodell RN. *Medical Dir* Thomas E
Lewis MD.
Licensure Skilled care. *Beds* SNF 97. *Certified*
Medicaid; Medicare.
Owner Proprietary corp (Health Care and
Retirement Corp).
Admissions Requirements Minimum age 21;
Medical examination; Physician's request.

Staff RNs 2 (ft); LPNs 3 (ft), 10 (pt); Nurses'
aides 15 (ft), 25 (pt); Recreational therapists
1 (ft), 1 (pt); Activities coordinators.
Facilities Dining room; Physical therapy
room; Activities room; Laundry room;
Barber/Beauty shop.
Activities Cards; Games; Reading groups;
Prayer groups; Movies; Dances/Social/
Cultural gatherings.

Chateau Gardens
627 Begole St, Flint, MI 48503
(313) 234-1667
Medical Dir Richard Dykewicz MD.
Licensure Skilled care. *Beds* SNF 222.
Certified Medicaid; Medicare.
Admissions Requirements Physician's request.
Staff RNs 6 (ft), 8 (pt); LPNs 13 (ft), 2 (pt);
Nurses' aides 60 (ft), 33 (pt); Physical
therapists 1 (pt); Occupational therapists 1
(pt); Speech therapists 1 (pt); Activities
coordinators 1 (ft), 2 (pt); Dietitians 1 (pt).
Facilities Dining room; Physical therapy
room; Activities room; Chapel; Crafts room;
Laundry room; Barber/Beauty shop; Library.
Activities Arts & crafts; Cards; Games;
Reading groups; Prayer groups; Movies;
Shopping trips; Dances/Social/Cultural
gatherings.

Heritage Manor Nursing Center
G-3201 Beecher Rd, Flint, MI 48504
(313) 732-9200
Medical Dir Kenneth Jordan MD.
Licensure Skilled care. *Beds* SNF 180.
Certified Medicaid; Medicare.
Owner Proprietary corp (International
Healthcare Management).
Admissions Requirements Minimum age 17;
Medical examination; Physician's request.
Facilities Dining room; Physical therapy
room; Activities room; Library.
Activities Arts & crafts; Cards; Games;
Reading groups; Prayer groups; Movies;
Shopping trips; Dances/Social/Cultural
gatherings.

Kith Haven
G-1069 Ballenger Hwy, Flint, MI 48504
(313) 235-6676
Licensure Skilled care. *Beds* SNF 167.
Certified Medicaid; Medicare.

Marian Hall
529 Detroit St, Flint, MI 48502
Licensure Home for aged. *Beds* Home for
aged 116.

McFarlan Home
700 E Kearsley St, Flint, MI 48503
Licensure Home for aged. *Beds* Home for
aged 22.

Stockton House
720 Ann Arbor St, Flint, MI 48503
Licensure Home for aged. *Beds* Home for
aged 49.

Williams Home for the Aged
G-6384 N Dort Hwy, Flint, MI 48458
Licensure Home for aged. *Beds* Home for
aged 28.

Willowbrook Manor
G-4436 Beecher Rd, Flint, MI 48532
(313) 733-0290
Licensure Swing beds SNF/ICF 101. *Beds*
101. *Certified* Medicaid.

Flushing

Fostrian Manor
540 Sunnyside Dr, Flushing, MI 48433
(313) 659-5695
Licensure Skilled care. *Beds* SNF 101.
Certified Medicaid; Medicare.
Owner Proprietary corp (Health Care and
Retirement Corp).

Frankenmuth

Frankenmuth Convalescent Center
500 W Genesee, Frankenmuth, MI 48734
(517) 652-6101
Licensure Skilled care. *Beds* SNF 126.
Certified Medicaid; Medicare.

Lutheran Home
725 W Genesee, Frankenmuth, MI 48734
(517) 652-9951
Admin C Douglas Anderson.
Medical Dir J F Shetlar MD.
Licensure Skilled care; Home for aged;
Alzheimer's care. *Beds* SNF 112; Home for
aged 26. *Certified* Medicaid; Medicare.
Owner Proprietary corp (Vantage Healthcare).
Admissions Requirements Minimum age 65;
Medical examination.
Staff RNs 7 (ft), 14 (pt); LPNs 4 (pt); Nurses'
aides 24 (ft), 30 (pt); Physical therapists 1
(pt); Activities coordinators 1 (ft), 2 (pt);
Dietitians 1 (ft).
Languages German.
Affiliation Lutheran.
Facilities Dining room; Physical therapy
room; Activities room; Chapel; Crafts room;
Laundry room; Barber/Beauty shop; Library.
Activities Arts & crafts; Cards; Games;
Reading groups; Prayer groups; Movies;
Shopping trips; Dances/Social/Cultural
gatherings.

Frankfort

Benzie County Medical Care Facility
210 Maple St, Frankfort, MI 49635
(616) 352-9674
Admin Vickie Burlew RN. *Dir of Nursing*
Theresa Schmeichel RN. *Medical Dir* James
N Kaufman MD.
Licensure Skilled care. *Beds* SNF 62. *Certified*
Medicaid; Medicare.
Owner Publicly owned.
Admissions Requirements Minimum age 16;
Physician's request.
Staff Physicians 1 (ft); RNs 2 (ft), 3 (pt);
LPNs 4 (ft), 2 (pt); Nurses' aides 23 (ft), 6
(pt); Physical therapists 1 (pt); Activities
coordinators 1 (ft); Dietitians 1 (pt).
Facilities Dining room; Physical therapy
room; Activities room; Crafts room; Laundry
room; Barber/Beauty shop.
Activities Arts & crafts; Games; Reading
groups; Prayer groups; Movies; Shopping
trips; Dances/Social/Cultural gatherings.

Paul Oliver Memorial Hospital
224 Park Ave, Frankfort, MI 49635
Licensure Skilled care. *Beds* SNF 48. *Certified*
Medicaid; Medicare.

Fraser

Fraser Villa
33300 Utica Rd, Fraser, MI 48026
Licensure Skilled care; Home for aged. *Beds*
SNF 141; Home for aged 138. *Certified*
Medicaid; Medicare.

Fremont

Meadows Nursing Home
4554 W 48th St, Fremont, MI 49412
(616) 924-3990
Licensure Skilled care. *Beds* SNF 129.
Certified Medicaid; Medicare.

Newaygo Medical Care Facility
4465 W 48th St, Fremont, MI 49412
(616) 924-2020
Admin Michael B Shira. *Dir of Nursing*
Lorraine DeKan RN.
Licensure Skilled care; Alzheimer's care. *Beds*
SNF 116. *Certified* Medicaid; Medicare.
Owner Publicly owned.
Admissions Requirements Physician's request.

Staff Physicians 1 (pt); RNs 4 (ft), 6 (pt); LPNs 6 (ft), 5 (pt); Nurses' aides 35 (ft), 23 (pt); Physical therapists 1 (pt); Recreational therapists 1 (ft); Occupational therapists 1 (pt); Speech therapists 1 (pt); Activities coordinators 1 (ft); Dietitians 1 (pt); Ophthalmologists 1 (pt); Podiatrists 1 (pt); Dentists 1 (pt).
Facilities Dining room; Physical therapy room; Activities room; Crafts room; Laundry room; Barber/Beauty shop.
Activities Arts & crafts; Cards; Games; Reading groups; Prayer groups; Movies; Dances/Social/Cultural gatherings; Music therapy; Exercise classes.

Galesburg

Arboridge Care Center
1080 N 35th St, Galesburg, MI 49503
(616) 665-7043
Licensure Intermediate care. *Beds* ICF 93. *Certified* Medicaid.

Gaylord

Otsego County Memorial Hospital
825 N Center St, Gaylord, MI 49735
(517) 732-1731
Licensure Skilled care. *Beds* SNF 87. *Certified* Medicaid; Medicare.

Tender Care Gaylord
508 Random Ln, Gaylord, MI 49735
(517) 732-3508
Admin Frances Kuntz. *Dir of Nursing* Eleanor Leinonen RN. *Medical Dir* Irineo Matias MD.
Licensure Skilled care; Intermediate care. *Beds* SNF 50; ICF 70. *Certified* Medicaid; Medicare.
Owner Proprietary corp (Tendercare Nursing Home).
Admissions Requirements Minimum age 18; Medical examination.
Staff Physicians; RNs 4 (ft); LPNs 15 (ft); Nurses' aides 50 (ft); Physical therapists 1 (ft); Recreational therapists 1 (ft); Occupational therapists 1 (ft); Speech therapists 1 (ft); Activities coordinators 1 (ft); Dietitians 1 (ft); Ophthalmologists 1 (ft); Podiatrists 1 (ft).
Facilities Dining room; Physical therapy room; Activities room; Crafts room; Laundry room; Barber/Beauty shop; Patio; Ventilator care.
Activities Arts & crafts; Games; Reading groups; Prayer groups; Movies; Shopping trips; Family nights; Adopt-a-grandparent.

Gladwin

Gladwin Nursing Home
3270 Pratt Lake Rd, Gladwin, MI 48624
(517) 426-7275
Medical Dir H A Timreck MD.
Licensure Skilled care. *Beds* SNF 60. *Certified* Medicaid; Medicare.
Admissions Requirements Minimum age 15; Medical examination; Physician's request.
Staff RNs 4 (ft), 3 (pt); LPNs 2 (ft), 4 (pt); Nurses' aides 15 (ft), 7 (pt).
Facilities Dining room; Physical therapy room; Activities room.
Activities Arts & crafts; Cards; Games; Reading groups; Dances/Social/Cultural gatherings.

Gladwin Pines Nursing Home
1 River Ct, Gladwin, MI 48624
Licensure Skilled care; Home for aged. *Beds* SNF 43; Home for aged 21.

Goodells

St Clair County Medical Centre
8332 County Park Dr, Goodells, MI 48027
(313) 325-1291
Admin Cora M Urquhart. *Dir of Nursing* Cornelia Smith. *Medical Dir* Fredrick E Ludwig MD.
Licensure Skilled care. *Beds* SNF 75. *Private Pay Patients* 5%. *Certified* Medicaid; Medicare.
Owner Publicly owned.
Admissions Requirements Minimum age 15; Medical examination; Physician's request.
Staff Physicians 1 (pt); RNs 4 (ft), 2 (pt); LPNs 5 (ft), 2 (pt); Nurses' aides 20 (ft), 19 (pt); Physical therapists 1 (pt); Occupational therapists 1 (pt); Speech therapists 1 (pt); Activities coordinators 1 (ft); Dietitians 1 (pt); Ophthalmologists 1 (pt); Podiatrists 1 (pt); Audiologists 1 (pt).
Facilities Dining room; Physical therapy room; Activities room; Laundry room; Barber/Beauty shop; Library.
Activities Arts & crafts; Cards; Games; Reading groups; Prayer groups; Movies; Dances/Social/Cultural gatherings; Intergenerational programs; Pet therapy.

Grand Blanc

Grand Blanc Convalescent Center
8481 Holly Rd, Grand Blanc, MI 48439
(313) 694-1711, 694-9717 FAX
Admin Paul N Wright. *Dir of Nursing* Jeanette Goldstein RN. *Medical Dir* Dr Joseph T Batdorf.
Licensure Skilled care; Alzheimer's care. *Beds* SNF 140. *Private Pay Patients* 52%. *Certified* Medicaid; Medicare.
Owner Nonprofit corp.
Admissions Requirements Minimum age 25; Medical examination; Physician's request.
Staff RNs 10 (ft), 8 (pt); LPNs 5 (ft), 5 (pt); Nurses' aides 56 (ft), 48 (pt); Physical therapists 1 (pt); Recreational therapists 2 (ft); Occupational therapists 1 (pt); Activities coordinators 1 (ft), 1 (pt); Podiatrists 1 (pt).
Affiliation Roman Catholic.
Facilities Dining room; Physical therapy room; Activities room; Chapel; Crafts room; Barber/Beauty shop; Library; Lounges.
Activities Arts & crafts; Cards; Games; Reading groups; Prayer groups; Movies; Intergenerational programs; Pet therapy.

Riverbend Nursing Home
11941 Belsay Rd, Grand Blanc, MI 48439
(313) 694-1970
Admin M Ellen Knickerbocker. *Dir of Nursing* Rosemary E Sedgewick RN BSN. *Medical Dir* Thomas B Marwil MD.
Licensure Skilled care; Home for aged. *Beds* SNF 157; Home for aged 20. *Certified* Medicaid; Medicare.
Owner Proprietary corp.
Admissions Requirements Minimum age 16; Medical examination; Physician's request.
Staff Physicians 3 (pt); RNs 7 (ft), 4 (pt); LPNs 12 (ft), 8 (pt); Nurses' aides 55 (ft), 24 (pt); Physical therapists 1 (pt); Occupational therapists 1 (pt); Speech therapists 2 (pt); Activities coordinators 1 (ft); Dietitians 1 (ft), 1 (pt); Ophthalmologists 1 (pt); Dentists 1 (pt); Social workers 1 (ft).
Facilities Dining room; Physical therapy room; Activities room; Crafts room; Laundry room; Barber/Beauty shop; Library; Lounges.
Activities Arts & crafts; Cards; Games; Reading groups; Prayer groups; Movies; Shopping trips; Dances/Social/Cultural gatherings.

Grand Haven

Christian Haven
704 Pennoyer Ave, Grand Haven, MI 49417
Licensure Home for aged. *Beds* Home for aged 57.

North Ottawa Care Center
1615 S Despelder St, Grand Haven, MI 49417
(616) 842-0770
Licensure Skilled care. *Beds* SNF 64. *Certified* Medicaid; Medicare.

Riverside Nursing Centre
415 Friant, Grand Haven, MI 49417
(616) 842-4120
Admin Jeff Bandstra. *Dir of Nursing* Vicki Towne RN.
Licensure Intermediate care. *Beds* ICF 34. *Certified* Medicaid.
Owner Privately owned.
Admissions Requirements Minimum age 15; Medical examination; Physician's request.
Staff RNs 1 (ft), 1 (pt); LPNs 2 (ft), 3 (pt); Nurses' aides 8 (ft), 8 (pt); Activities coordinators 1 (ft).
Facilities Dining room; Activities room; Laundry room; Barber/Beauty shop.
Activities Arts & crafts; Cards; Games; Reading groups; Prayer groups; Movies; Shopping trips; Dances/Social/Cultural gatherings; Intergenerational programs; Pet therapy; Bingo.

Robbinswood—An Assisted Living Centre
1125 Robbins Rd, Grand Haven, MI 49417
(616) 842-1900
Admin Karen S Walsh. *Dir of Nursing* Cindy Wisman. *Medical Dir* Cindy Wisman.
Licensure Home for aged. *Beds* Home for aged 120. *Private Pay Patients* 77%. *Certified* Medicaid.
Owner Privately owned (CCG-Partner).
Admissions Requirements Minimum age 60; Medical examination.
Staff LPNs 1 (ft); Nurses' aides 5 (ft), 6 (pt); Activities coordinators 1 (ft); Dietitians 1 (ft).
Facilities Dining room; Activities room; Crafts room; Laundry room; Barber/Beauty shop; Library; Non-smoking & smoking lounges.
Activities Arts & crafts; Cards; Games; Prayer groups; Movies; Shopping trips; Dances/Social/Cultural gatherings; Intergenerational programs; Community education.

Shore Haven Nursing Home
900 S Beacon Blvd, Grand Haven, MI 49417
(616) 846-1850
Licensure Skilled care. *Beds* SNF 126. *Certified* Medicaid; Medicare.
Owner Proprietary corp (Beverly Enterprises).

Grand Rapids

Alpine Manor
1050 Four Mile Rd NW, Grand Rapids, MI 49504
(616) 784-0646
Medical Dir Dr James O'Brien.
Licensure Skilled care. *Beds* SNF 207. *Certified* Medicaid; Medicare.
Admissions Requirements Minimum age 17; Medical examination; Physician's request.
Staff Physicians 3 (pt); RNs 8 (ft), 4 (pt); LPNs 4 (ft), 11 (pt); Nurses' aides 52 (ft), 30 (pt); Physical therapists 1 (ft); Reality therapists 1 (ft); Recreational therapists 1 (ft).
Facilities Dining room; Physical therapy room; Activities room; Chapel; Crafts room; Laundry room; Barber/Beauty shop; Library; Cooking kitchen; Men's workshop.
Activities Arts & crafts; Cards; Games; Reading groups; Prayer groups; Movies; Shopping trips; Dances/Social/Cultural

gatherings; Outside visits to community functions; Bowling; Pet shows; Educational opportunities.

Cascade Care Center
1095 Medical Park Dr SE, Grand Rapids, MI 49506
(616) 949-7220
Admin Sylvia Jean Mosher. *Dir of Nursing* Edith Miller.
Licensure Skilled care. *Beds* SNF 123. *Certified* Medicare; Medicare.
Owner Proprietary corp (Miko Enterprises Inc).
Admissions Requirements Minimum age 18.
Staff RNs; LPNs; Nurses' aides; Physical therapists; Recreational therapists; Occupational therapists; Speech therapists; Activities coordinators.
Facilities Dining room; Physical therapy room; Activities room; Crafts room; Laundry room; Barber/Beauty shop.
Activities Arts & crafts; Cards; Games; Prayer groups; Movies; Shopping trips; Dances/ Social/Cultural gatherings.

Christian Nursing Center
2589 44th St SE, Grand Rapids, MI 49508-3877
(616) 452-8992 & 452-7206
Licensure Intermediate care. *Beds* 42. *Certified* Medicaid.

Christian Rest Home Association
1000 Edison Ave NW, Grand Rapids, MI 49504
(616) 453-2475
Admin John Rurter.
Medical Dir John Vander Molen MD.
Licensure Skilled care. *Beds* SNF 153. *Certified* Medicaid; Medicare.
Admissions Requirements Minimum age 15; Medical examination; Physician's request.
Staff RNs 1 (ft), 12 (pt); LPNs 1 (ft), 10 (pt); Nurses' aides 45 (ft), 45 (pt); Physical therapists 1 (ft); Recreational therapists 2 (ft), 1 (pt); Occupational therapists 1 (pt).
Facilities Dining room; Physical therapy room; Activities room; Chapel; Crafts room; Laundry room; Barber/Beauty shop; Library.
Activities Arts & crafts; Cards; Games; Reading groups; Prayer groups; Movies; Shopping trips; Dances/Social/Cultural gatherings.

M J Clark Memorial Home
1546 Sherman SE, Grand Rapids, MI 49506
(616) 452-7206
Licensure Skilled care; Home for aged. *Beds* SNF 111; Home for aged 237. *Certified* Medicaid; Medicare.

Grand Valley Nursing Center
4118 Kalamazoo Ave SE, Grand Rapids, MI 49508
(616) 455-7300
Medical Dir Dr Dirk Mouw.
Licensure Skilled care. *Beds* SNF 165. *Certified* Medicaid; Medicare.
Admissions Requirements Minimum age 3; Medical examination; Physician's request.
Staff RNs 9 (ft), 15 (pt); LPNs 10 (ft), 10 (pt); Nurses' aides 46 (ft), 38 (pt); Physical therapists 1 (ft); Recreational therapists 1 (ft); Occupational therapists 1 (ft); Speech therapists 1 (ft); Activities coordinators 1 (ft); Dietitians 1 (ft); Ophthalmologists 1 (pt); Podiatrists 1 (pt); Dentists 1 (pt); Social workers 2 (ft), 1 (pt); Psychologists 1 (ft).
Facilities Dining room; Physical therapy room; Activities room; Chapel; Crafts room; Barber/Beauty shop; Library.
Activities Arts & crafts; Cards; Games; Reading groups; Prayer groups; Movies; Shopping trips; Dances/Social/Cultural gatherings; Luncheon trips.

Grandview Resident Home for Senior Citizens
3460 Alpine Ave NW, Grand Rapids, MI 49504
Licensure Home for aged. *Beds* Home for aged 94.

Greenview Manor
1708 Leonard NE, Grand Rapids, MI 49505
(616) 456-7243
Admin Bill Hekker. *Dir of Nursing* Shirley Carter RN.
Licensure Skilled care. *Beds* SNF 69. *Certified* Medicaid; Medicare.
Owner Proprietary corp (Health Care and Retirement Corp).
Admissions Requirements Medical examination; Physician's request.
Facilities Dining room; Activities room; Crafts room; Laundry room; Barber/Beauty shop.
Activities Arts & crafts; Cards; Games; Reading groups; Prayer groups; Movies; Shopping trips; Dances/Social/Cultural gatherings.

Holland Home—Brown Home
1435 Fulton E, Grand Rapids, MI 49503
(616) 459-2717
Licensure Home for aged. *Beds* Home for aged 34.

Holland Home—Fulton Manor
1450 E Fulton Ave, Grand Rapids, MI 49503
(616) 459-3495
Admin Irvin G Van Dyke.
Medical Dir Joyce A Rottman.
Licensure Skilled care; Home for aged. *Beds* SNF 79; Home for aged 290. *Certified* Medicaid; Medicare.
Owner Nonprofit corp.
Admissions Requirements Minimum age 60; Medical examination.
Staff RNs; LPNs; Nurses' aides; Recreational therapists; Activities coordinators.
Languages Dutch.
Facilities Dining room; Physical therapy room; Activities room; Chapel; Crafts room; Laundry room; Barber/Beauty shop; Library.
Activities Arts & crafts; Cards; Games; Reading groups; Prayer groups; Movies; Shopping trips; Dances/Social/Cultural gatherings.

Holland Home—Raybrook Manor
2121 Raybrook Ave SE, Grand Rapids, MI 49506
(616) 949-6656
Admin Gary G Ellens. *Dir of Nursing* Margaret Dekker RN. *Medical Dir* Dr Keith Crane.
Licensure Skilled care; Home for aged. *Beds* SNF 101; Home for aged 179. *Certified* Medicaid; Medicare.
Owner Nonprofit corp.
Admissions Requirements Minimum age 16; Medical examination; Physician's request.
Staff RNs 7 (ft), 7 (pt); LPNs 11 (ft), 10 (pt); Nurses' aides 46 (ft), 31 (pt); Activities coordinators 2 (ft).
Languages Dutch.
Affiliation Christian Reformed.
Facilities Dining room; Physical therapy room; Activities room; Chapel; Crafts room; Laundry room; Barber/Beauty shop; Library.
Activities Arts & crafts; Cards; Games; Reading groups; Prayer groups; Movies; Shopping trips; Dances/Social/Cultural gatherings.

Jefferson Christian Nursing Home
2589 44th St SE, Grand Rapids, MI 49508-3877
(616) 452-9198
Licensure Intermediate care. *Beds* 30. *Certified* Medicaid.

Kent Community Hospital Long-Term Care Unit
750 Fuller Ave NE, Grand Rapids, MI 49503
(616) 774-3300
Licensure Skilled care; Intermediate care. *Beds* Swing beds SNF/ICF 484. *Certified* Medicaid; Medicare.

Lafayette Christian Nursing Center
1001 Lafayette SE, Grand Rapids, MI 49507
(616) 452-9673
Admin Doyle R Melton.
Medical Dir Maxine Rogers.
Licensure Intermediate care. *Beds* ICF 59. *Certified* Medicaid.
Owner Proprietary corp.
Staff Physicians 1 (pt); RNs 1 (ft); LPNs 3 (ft); Nurses' aides 8 (ft); Physical therapists 1 (pt); Recreational therapists 1 (ft); Activities coordinators 1 (ft); Dietitians 1 (pt); Ophthalmologists 1 (pt); Podiatrists 1 (pt); Dentists 1 (pt).
Facilities Dining room; Activities room; Laundry room; Barber/Beauty shop.
Activities Arts & crafts; Cards; Games; Dances/Social/Cultural gatherings.

Luther Home
1950 32nd St SE, Grand Rapids, MI 49508
(616) 243-0252
Licensure Skilled care. *Beds* SNF 125. *Certified* Medicaid; Medicare.
Owner Nonprofit corp (Lutheran Social Services of Michigan).
Affiliation Lutheran.

Michigan Christian Home
1845 Boston SE, Grand Rapids, MI 49506
(616) 245-9179
Admin Byron G Wild. *Dir of Nursing* Sue Vanderberg.
Licensure Skilled care; Home for aged; Retirement. *Beds* SNF 29; Home for aged 72; Retirement apartments 20. *Certified* Medicaid; Medicare.
Owner Nonprofit corp.
Admissions Requirements Minimum age 62; Medical examination.
Staff RNs; LPNs; Nurses' aides; Recreational therapists; Activities coordinators; Dietitians.
Affiliation Baptist.
Facilities Dining room; Activities room; Chapel; Crafts room; Laundry room; Barber/Beauty shop; Library.
Activities Arts & crafts; Cards; Games; Reading groups; Prayer groups; Movies; Shopping trips.

Olds Manor
201 Michigan NW, Grand Rapids, MI 49503
(616) 459-0101, 459-1055 FAX
Admin Dan Daniel. *Dir of Nursing* Jacki Collier. *Medical Dir* John N Campbell MD.
Licensure Intermediate care; Home for aged; Alzheimer's care. *Beds* ICF 44; Home for aged 150. *Certified* Medicaid.
Owner Proprietary corp.
Admissions Requirements Minimum age 60; Medical examination.
Staff Physicians 2 (pt); RNs 3 (ft), 1 (pt); LPNs 7 (ft), 4 (pt); Nurses' aides 12 (ft), 5 (pt); Activities coordinators 1 (ft), 1 (pt); Dietitians 1 (pt); Podiatrists 1 (pt).
Facilities Dining room; Activities room; Chapel; Crafts room; Laundry room; Barber/ Beauty shop; Library.
Activities Arts & crafts; Cards; Games; Reading groups; Prayer groups; Movies; Shopping trips; Dances/Social/Cultural gatherings; Intergenerational programs; Pet therapy.

Pilgrim Manor
2000 Leonard NE, Grand Rapids, MI 49505
(616) 458-1133
Admin Robert PM Johns. *Dir of Nursing* Sandra DeHaan. *Medical Dir* Dr Crane.

Licensure Skilled care; Home for aged. *Beds*
SNF 55; Home for aged 117. *Private Pay
Patients* 30%. *Certified* Medicaid; Medicare.
Owner Nonprofit organization/foundation.
Admissions Requirements Minimum age 62;
Medical examination.
Staff Physicians 1 (pt); RNs 2 (ft), 4 (pt);
LPNs 4 (ft), 5 (pt); Nurses' aides 21 (ft), 10
(pt); Activities coordinators 1 (ft); Dietitians
1 (pt); Podiatrists 1 (pt).
Affiliation United Church of Christ.
Facilities Dining room; Activities room;
Chapel; Crafts room; Laundry room; Barber/
Beauty shop; Library.
Activities Arts & crafts; Cards; Games;
Reading groups; Prayer groups; Movies;
Shopping trips; Dances/Social/Cultural
gatherings.

Porter Hills Presbyterian Village
3600 Fulton St E, Grand Rapids, MI 49506
(616) 949-4971
Admin David B Douma. *Dir of Nursing* Kay
Downs. *Medical Dir* Dr Grace.
Licensure Skilled care; Intermediate care;
Home for aged; Alzheimer's care. *Beds* SNF
81; Home for aged 210. *Certified* Medicaid;
Medicare.
Owner Nonprofit corp.
Admissions Requirements Minimum age 62;
Medical examination; Physician's request.
Staff RNs 3 (ft), 8 (pt); LPNs 4 (ft), 15 (pt);
Nurses' aides 8 (ft), 33 (pt); Activities
coordinators 3 (pt); Dietitians 1 (pt).
Affiliation Presbyterian.
Facilities Dining room; Physical therapy
room; Activities room; Chapel; Crafts room;
Laundry room; Barber/Beauty shop; Library.
Activities Arts & crafts; Cards; Games;
Reading groups; Prayer groups; Movies;
Shopping trips; Dances/Social/Cultural
gatherings.

Rest Haven Homes Inc
1424 Union NE, Grand Rapids, MI 49505
(616) 363-6819
Licensure Nursing home; Home for aged. *Beds*
Nursing home & home for aged 48. *Private
Pay Patients* 100%.

Sherbrooke Nursing Center
1157 Medical Park Dr SE, Grand Rapids, MI
49506
(616) 949-7310
Licensure Intermediate care. *Beds* ICF 71.
Owner Proprietary corp (Health Care and
Retirement Corp).

Springbrook Manor
2320 E Beltline SE, Grand Rapids, MI 49506
(616) 949-3000
Licensure Skilled care. *Beds* SNF 205.
Certified Medicaid; Medicare.
Owner Proprietary corp (Health Care and
Retirement Corp).

Villa Elizabeth
2100 Leonard NE, Grand Rapids, MI 49505
(616) 454-8273
Admin Sr Mary Norbertine Zacharias. *Dir of
Nursing* Mary Ann Greenhoe RN. *Medical
Dir* J D Maskill MD.
Licensure Skilled care; Retirement;
Alzheimer's care. *Beds* SNF 136. *Certified*
Medicaid; Medicare.
Owner Nonprofit corp.
Admissions Requirements Minimum age 65
Villa Elizabeth, 60 Country Villa; Medical
examination; Physician's request for Villa
Elizabeth.
Staff RNs 4 (ft), 8 (pt); LPNs 2 (ft), 6 (pt);
Nurses' aides 36 (ft), 38 (pt); Physical
therapists 1 (ft); Activities coordinators 2
(ft); Dietitians 1 (pt); Social worker 1 (ft);
Pastoral care 1 (ft).
Affiliation Roman Catholic.

Facilities Dining room; Physical therapy
room; Activities room; Chapel; Laundry
room; Barber/Beauty shop.
Activities Arts & crafts; Cards; Games;
Reading groups; Prayer groups; Movies;
Shopping trips; Parties.

Welcome Home for the Blind
1953 Monroe Ave NW, Grand Rapids, MI
49505
Licensure Home for aged. *Beds* Home for
aged 40.

Grandville

Brookcrest Nursing Home
3400 Wilson Ave SW, Grandville, MI 49418
(616) 534-5487
Licensure Skilled care. *Beds* SNF 153.
Certified Medicaid; Medicare.

Grass Lake

Cedar Knoll Rest Home
9230 Cedar Knoll Dr, Grass Lake, MI 49240
(517) 522-8471
Admin Janet M Smith. *Dir of Nursing* Donna
Myers. *Medical Dir* E E Vivirski MD.
Licensure Skilled care; Intermediate care. *Beds*
Swing beds SNF/ICF 169. *Certified*
Medicaid; Medicare.
Owner Proprietary corp.
Admissions Requirements Minimum age 16;
Medical examination; Physician's request.
Staff RNs 5 (ft), 1 (pt); LPNs 15 (ft), 3 (pt);
Nurses' aides 62 (ft), 3 (pt); Activities
coordinators 3 (ft).
Facilities Dining room; Physical therapy
room; Activities room; Crafts room; Laundry
room; Barber/Beauty shop.
Activities Arts & crafts; Cards; Games;
Reading groups; Prayer groups; Movies;
Shopping trips.

Grayling

Meadows of Grayling
2301 S Grayling Ave, Grayling, MI 49738
Licensure Skilled care. *Beds* SNF 120.
Certified Medicaid; Medicare.

Mercy Hospital—Grayling
1100 Michigan Ave, Grayling, MI 49738
(517) 348-5461
Licensure Skilled care. *Beds* SNF 130.
Certified Medicaid; Medicare.

Greenville

Greenville Care Center Inc
828 E Washington Ave, Greenville, MI 48838
(616) 754-7186
Admin Teresa L Lindsey. *Dir of Nursing*
Suzanne Thorlund RN. *Medical Dir* R B
Hammond DO.
Licensure Skilled care. *Beds* SNF 106.
Certified Medicaid; Medicare.
Owner Proprietary corp (Miko Enterprises
Inc).
Admissions Requirements Minimum age 16;
Medical examination; Physician's request.
Staff RNs 3 (ft), 2 (pt); LPNs 6 (ft), 4 (pt);
Nurses' aides 50 (ft), 20 (pt); Physical
therapists 1 (pt); Occupational therapists 1
(pt); Speech therapists 1 (pt); Activities
coordinators 1 (ft); Dietitians 1 (pt);
Podiatrists 1 (pt); Audiologists 1 (pt).
Facilities Dining room; Physical therapy
room; Activities room; Crafts room; Laundry
room; Barber/Beauty shop.
Activities Arts & crafts; Cards; Games;
Reading groups; Prayer groups; Movies;
Shopping trips; Dances/Social/Cultural
gatherings; Pet therapy.

United Memorial
615 S Bower St, Greenville, MI 48838
(616) 754-4691, 754-5054 FAX
Admin Mary L Boyd COO. *Dir of Nursing*
Helen E Harms RN.
Licensure Skilled care. *Beds* SNF 40. *Certified*
Medicaid; Medicare.
Owner Nonprofit corp.
Admissions Requirements Physician's request.
Staff RNs 4 (ft), 1 (pt); LPNs 6 (ft), 6 (pt);
Nurses' aides 16 (ft), 10 (pt); Physical
therapists; Activities coordinators 1 (ft);
Dietitians.
Facilities Dining room; Physical therapy
room; Activities room; Barber/Beauty shop.
Activities Arts & crafts; Cards; Games;
Reading groups; Prayer groups; Movies;
Shopping trips; Church service.

Grosse Pointe Woods

Grosse Pointe
21401 Mack Ave, Grosse Pointe Woods, MI
48236
(313) 778-0800
Licensure Skilled care. *Beds* SNF 80. *Certified*
Medicare.
Owner Proprietary corp (Health Care and
Retirement Corp).

Hamtramck

St Joseph Nursing Home
9400 Conant, Hamtramck, MI 48212
(313) 874-4500
Admin Rosanne Ruehlen. *Dir of Nursing*
Diane Cottle RN.
Licensure Skilled care; Alzheimer's care. *Beds*
SNF 170. *Certified* Medicaid; Medicare.
Owner Proprietary corp (Beverly Enterprises).
Admissions Requirements Medical
examination; Physician's request.
Staff RNs 7 (ft), 2 (pt); LPNs 18 (ft), 3 (pt);
Nurses' aides 48 (ft), 25 (pt); Physical
therapists 2 (pt); Speech therapists 1 (pt);
Activities coordinators 2 (ft); Dietitians 1
(ft), 2 (pt); Ophthalmologists 2 (pt).
Languages Polish, Arabic.
Facilities Dining room; Physical therapy
room; Activities room; Chapel; Crafts room;
Laundry room; Barber/Beauty shop.
Activities Arts & crafts; Cards; Games;
Reading groups; Prayer groups; Movies.

Hancock

Cypress Manor Nursing Home
1400 Poplar St, Hancock, MI 49930
(906) 482-6644
Admin Kathleen L Dube. *Dir of Nursing*
Miriam Kipina RN. *Medical Dir* Terry
Kinzel MD.
Licensure Intermediate care. *Beds* ICF 63.
Certified Medicaid.
Owner Proprietary corp (Health Concepts
Corp).
Admissions Requirements Minimum age 18;
Medical examination; Physician's request.
Staff Physicians 4 (ft); RNs 2 (ft); LPNs 4 (ft);
Nurses' aides 25 (ft); Physical therapists 1
(pt); Reality therapists 1 (pt); Recreational
therapists 1 (pt); Occupational therapists 1
(pt); Speech therapists 1 (pt); Activities
coordinators 1 (ft); Dietitians 1 (pt);
Ophthalmologists 1 (pt); Podiatrists 1 (pt);
Dentists 1 (pt).
Facilities Dining room; Physical therapy
room; Activities room; Laundry room;
Barber/Beauty shop.
Activities Arts & crafts; Cards; Games;
Reading groups; Prayer groups; Movies;
Shopping trips; Dances/Social/Cultural
gatherings.

596 / MICHIGAN / Hancock

Houghton County Medical Care Facility
1100 Quincy St, Hancock, MI 49930
(906) 482-5050
Medical Dir Hororatio Barrios MD.
Licensure Skilled care. *Beds* SNF 197.
 Certified Medicaid; Medicare.
Owner Publicly owned.
Admissions Requirements Minimum age 18;
 Medical examination; Physician's request.
Staff Physicians 9 (pt); RNs 8 (ft), 6 (pt);
 LPNs 7 (ft), 4 (pt); Nurses' aides 66 (ft), 14
 (pt); Physical therapists 1 (pt); Speech
 therapists 1 (pt); Activities coordinators 2
 (ft); Dietitians 1 (pt); Ophthalmologists 1
 (pt); Dentists 1 (pt).
Facilities Dining room; Physical therapy
 room; Activities room; Chapel; Crafts room;
 Barber/Beauty shop; Library.
Activities Arts & crafts; Cards; Games;
 Reading groups; Movies; Shopping trips;
 Dances/Social/Cultural gatherings.

Portage View Hospital
200 Michigan St, Hancock, MI 49930
(906) 482-1122
Admin James Bogan. *Dir of Nursing* Deb
 Young RN BSN. *Medical Dir* Marko V Belei
 MD.
Licensure Intermediate care. *Beds* ICF 30.
 Private Pay Patients 10%. *Certified*
 Medicaid; Medicare.
Owner Nonprofit organization/foundation.
Staff Physicians 1 (ft); RNs 1 (ft); LPNs 3 (ft),
 6 (pt); Nurses' aides 8 (ft), 6 (pt); Physical
 therapists 1 (ft); Speech therapists 1 (pt);
 Activities coordinators 1 (pt); Dietitians 1
 (pt); Audiologists 1 (pt).
Languages Finnish.
Facilities Dining room; Physical therapy
 room; Activities room; Chapel; Crafts room;
 Laundry room; Barber/Beauty shop; Library;
 Shaded grounds with barbecues.
Activities Arts & crafts; Cards; Games;
 Reading groups; Prayer groups; Movies;
 Shopping trips; Dances/Social/Cultural
 gatherings; Intergenerational programs; Pet
 therapy; Birthday parties; Sing alongs; Bingo;
 Religious services; Bus trips.

Harbor Beach

Harbor Beach Community Hospital
201 S 1st St, Harbor Beach, MI 48441
(517) 479-3201
Admin Pauline Siemen. *Dir of Nursing* Linda
 C Roggenbuck. *Medical Dir* William Benish
 MD.
Licensure Skilled care; Intermediate care. *Beds*
 Swing beds SNF/ICF 40. *Certified* Medicaid;
 Medicare.
Owner Nonprofit organization/foundation.
Admissions Requirements Minimum age 15.
Staff Physicians 5 (ft); RNs 1 (ft), 2 (pt);
 LPNs 3 (ft), 3 (pt); Nurses' aides 6 (ft), 14
 (pt); Physical therapists 1 (pt); Occupational
 therapists 1 (pt); Activities coordinators 1
 (ft); Dietitians 1 (ft).
Facilities Dining room; Barber/Beauty shop.
Activities Arts & crafts; Cards; Games;
 Reading groups; Prayer groups; Movies;
 Dances/Social/Cultural gatherings; Pet
 therapy.

Harbor Springs

Emmet County Medical Care Facility
750 E Main St, Harbor Springs, MI 49740
(616) 526-2161
Admin Paula Kobrzycki. *Dir of Nursing* Ann
 Bodzick. *Medical Dir* Richard A Knecht
 MD.
Licensure Skilled care. *Beds* SNF 110.
 Certified Medicaid; Medicare.
Owner Publicly owned.
Admissions Requirements Minimum age 16;
 Medical examination; Physician's request.

Staff Physicians 4 (pt); RNs 10 (ft), 4 (pt);
 LPNs 2 (ft); Nurses' aides 45 (ft), 12 (pt);
 Physical therapists 1 (pt); Occupational
 therapists 1 (pt); Speech therapists 1 (pt);
 Activities coordinators 2 (ft), 2 (pt);
 Dietitians 1 (ft); Ophthalmologists 1 (pt).
Facilities Dining room; Physical therapy
 room; Activities room; Chapel; Crafts room;
 Laundry room; Barber/Beauty shop.
Activities Arts & crafts; Cards; Games;
 Reading groups; Prayer groups; Movies;
 Dances/Social/Cultural gatherings.

Harper Woods

Cottage-Belmont Nursing Center
19840 Harper Ave, Harper Woods, MI 48225
(313) 881-9556
Admin William T Barr. *Dir of Nursing*
 Dorothy Pankowski RN.
Licensure Intermediate care; Alzheimer's care.
 Beds ICF 153.
Owner Nonprofit corp.
Admissions Requirements Minimum age 50;
 Medical examination; Physician's request.
Staff Physicians 5 (pt); RNs 5 (ft), 5 (pt);
 LPNs 5 (ft), 5 (pt); Nurses' aides 50 (ft), 25
 (pt); Physical therapists 2 (pt); Reality
 therapists 1 (pt); Recreational therapists 1
 (ft); Occupational therapists 1 (pt); Speech
 therapists 1 (pt); Activities coordinators 2
 (ft), 2 (pt); Dietitians 1 (pt);
 Ophthalmologists 1 (pt).
Languages Polish.
Activities Arts & crafts; Cards; Games;
 Reading groups; Prayer groups; Movies;
 Shopping trips; Dances/Social/Cultural
 gatherings.

Harrisville

Jamieson Nursing Home
790 S US 23, Box 369, Harrisville, MI 48740
(517) 724-6889
Admin Sally J Smith LPN. *Dir of Nursing*
 Jamie Lynn Smith RN.
Licensure Intermediate care. *Beds* ICF 51.
 Private Pay Patients 10%. *Certified*
 Medicaid.
Owner Proprietary corp.
Admissions Requirements Minimum age 15;
 Physician's request.
Staff Physicians 7 (ft); RNs 4 (ft); LPNs 6 (ft);
 Nurses' aides 30 (ft); Physical therapists
 (consultant); Reality therapists 1 (ft);
 Recreational therapists 1 (ft); Speech
 therapists (consultant); Activities
 coordinators 1 (ft); Dietitians 2 (ft);
 Ophthalmologists 1 (ft); Podiatrists 2 (ft).
Facilities Dining room; Physical therapy
 room; Activities room; Chapel; Crafts room;
 Laundry room; Barber/Beauty shop; Library.
Activities Arts & crafts; Cards; Games;
 Reading groups; Prayer groups; Movies;
 Shopping trips; Dances/Social/Cultural
 gatherings; Pet therapy.

Hart

Oceana County Medical Care Facility
701 E Main St, Hart, MI 49420
(616) 873-2148
Admin Bill Hekker. *Dir of Nursing* Donna
 Mikkelson RN. *Medical Dir* V Dale Barker
 MD.
Licensure Skilled care; Alzheimer's care. *Beds*
 SNF 113. *Private Pay Patients* 10%. *Certified*
 Medicaid; Medicare.
Owner Publicly owned.
Admissions Requirements Medical
 examination; Physician's request.
Facilities Dining room; Physical therapy
 room; Activities room; Crafts room; Laundry
 room; Barber/Beauty shop.

Activities Arts & crafts; Cards; Games;
 Reading groups; Prayer groups; Movies;
 Shopping trips; Dances/Social/Cultural
 gatherings; Intergenerational programs; Pet
 therapy.

Hastings

Provincial House—Hastings
240 E North St, Hastings, MI 49058
(616) 945-9564
Admin Joyce F Weinbrecht. *Dir of Nursing*
 Kay Rowley RN. *Medical Dir* Joseph C
 Roth DO.
Licensure Skilled care. *Beds* SNF 114.
 Certified Medicaid; Medicare.
Owner Proprietary corp (Beverly Enterprises).
Admissions Requirements Minimum age 16;
 Medical examination; Physician's request.
Staff Physicians 17 (pt); RNs 4 (ft), 5 (pt);
 LPNs 5 (ft), 3 (pt); Nurses' aides 35 (ft), 31
 (pt); Physical therapists 1 (pt); Occupational
 therapists 1 (ft); Speech therapists 1 (pt);
 Activities coordinators 1 (ft), 1 (pt);
 Dietitians 1 (ft); Ophthalmologists 1 (pt);
 Dentists 1 (pt).
Facilities Dining room; Physical therapy
 room; Activities room; Crafts room; Laundry
 room; Barber/Beauty shop.
Activities Arts & crafts; Cards; Games;
 Reading groups; Prayer groups; Movies;
 Shopping trips; Dances/Social/Cultural
 gatherings.

Thornapple Manor
2700 Nashville Rd, Hastings, MI 49058
(616) 945-2407
Admin Lynn Sommerfeld. *Dir of Nursing*
 Bonita Laverty RN. *Medical Dir* Lawrence
 Hawkings MD.
Licensure Skilled care. *Beds* SNF 138.
 Certified Medicaid; Medicare.
Owner Publicly owned.
Admissions Requirements Physician's request.
Staff RNs; LPNs; Nurses' aides; Physical
 therapists; Occupational therapists; Speech
 therapists; Activities coordinators; Dietitians;
 Ophthalmologists.
Facilities Dining room; Physical therapy
 room; Activities room; Crafts room; Laundry
 room; Barber/Beauty shop.

Highland Park

Park Geriatric Village
111 Ford Ave, Highland Park, MI 48203
(313) 883-3585
Admin Paul C Holliday. *Dir of Nursing* B
 Cash RN. *Medical Dir* E Pistain MD.
Licensure Skilled care. *Beds* SNF 134.
 Certified Medicaid; Medicare.
Owner Privately owned.
Admissions Requirements Minimum age 18;
 Medical examination; Physician's request.
Staff Physicians 2 (ft); RNs 3 (ft), 3 (pt);
 LPNs 7 (ft), 10 (pt); Nurses' aides 36 (ft), 25
 (pt); Activities coordinators 1 (ft).
Facilities Dining room; Physical therapy
 room; Activities room; Laundry room;
 Barber/Beauty shop; Library.
Activities Arts & crafts; Cards; Games;
 Reading groups; Prayer groups; Movies.

Royal Nursing Center
91 Glendale Ave, Highland Park, MI 48203
(313) 869-7711
Licensure Skilled care. *Beds* SNF 183.
 Certified Medicaid; Medicare.

St Luke's Episcopal Church Home
224 Highland Ave, Highland Park, MI 48203
(313) 868-1445
Admin David D Dieter, Exec Dir. *Dir of
 Nursing* Mary Caragay. *Medical Dir* Dr
 John Costea.

Licensure Intermediate care; Home for aged. *Beds* ICF 22; Home for aged 58. *Private Pay Patients* 55%. *Certified* Medicaid.
Owner Nonprofit corp.
Admissions Requirements Minimum age 65; Medical examination.
Staff Physicians 4 (pt); RNs 1 (ft), 3 (pt); LPNs 3 (ft), 4 (pt); Nurses' aides 15 (ft), 15 (pt); Activities coordinators 1 (ft), 1 (pt); Dietitians 1 (ft); Social workers 1 (ft).
Languages French, German, Polish.
Affiliation Episcopal.
Facilities Dining room; Activities room; Chapel; Crafts room; Barber/Beauty shop; Library.
Activities Arts & crafts; Cards; Games; Reading groups; Prayer groups; Movies; Shopping trips; Dances/Social/Cultural gatherings; Intergenerational programs; Pet therapy.

Hillman

Pineview of Hillman
631 Caring St, Hillman, MI 49746
Licensure Skilled care; Home for aged. *Beds* SNF 75; Home for aged 29. *Certified* Medicaid; Medicare.
Owner Proprietary corp (Hillhaven Corp).

Hillsdale

Hillsdale County Medical Care Facility
140 W Mechanic St, Hillsdale, MI 49242
(517) 439-9341
Admin Keith Van Oosterhout MD.
Medical Dir Dr Frank Monti.
Licensure Skilled care. *Beds* SNF 160. *Certified* Medicaid; Medicare.
Owner Publicly owned.
Admissions Requirements Minimum age 15; Medical examination; Physician's request.
Staff Physicians 1 (ft), 1 (pt); RNs 6 (ft), 2 (pt); LPNs 20 (ft), 10 (pt); Nurses' aides 50 (ft), 50 (pt); Physical therapists 1 (pt); Recreational therapists 3 (ft); Occupational therapists 1 (pt); Speech therapists 1 (pt); Activities coordinators 1 (ft); Dietitians 1 (ft); Ophthalmologists 1 (pt); Podiatrists 1 (pt); Dentists 1 (pt).
Facilities Dining room; Physical therapy room; Activities room; Chapel; Crafts room; Laundry room; Barber/Beauty shop.
Activities Arts & crafts; Cards; Games; Reading groups; Prayer groups; Movies; Dances/Social/Cultural gatherings.

Holland

Birchwood Manor—Holland
493 W 32nd St, Holland, MI 49423
(616) 396-1438
Licensure Skilled care. *Beds* SNF 111. *Certified* Medicaid; Medicare.
Owner Proprietary corp (Health Care and Retirement Corp).

Meadowbrook Care Center
280 W 40th, Holland, MI 49423
(616) 392-7161
Admin Richard A Myers. *Dir of Nursing* Bernice Catson. *Medical Dir* Dr Leppink.
Licensure Skilled care. *Beds* SNF 125. *Certified* Medicaid; Medicare.
Owner Proprietary corp (Beverly Enterprises).
Admissions Requirements Medical examination; Physician's request.
Staff Physicians 5 (pt); RNs 4 (ft), 4 (pt); LPNs 9 (ft), 6 (pt); Nurses' aides 75 (ft), 50 (pt); Physical therapists 1 (ft); Occupational therapists 1 (pt); Speech therapists 1 (pt); Activities coordinators 1 (ft), 1 (pt); Dietitians 1 (ft); Ophthalmologists 1 (pt); Podiatrists 1 (pt); Dentists 1 (pt).
Languages Dutch.

Facilities Dining room; Physical therapy room; Activities room; Laundry room; Barber/Beauty shop.
Activities Arts & crafts; Cards; Games; Reading groups; Prayer groups; Movies.

Resthaven Patrons
49 E 32nd St, Holland, MI 49423
Licensure Home for aged. *Beds* Home for aged 103.

Holly

Holly Convalescent Center
313 Sherwood St, Holly, MI 48442
(313) 634-9281
Admin Donald D Haney Jr. *Dir of Nursing* Alma Bylsma RN. *Medical Dir* Richard Cronk DO.
Licensure Intermediate care. *Beds* ICF 66. *Private Pay Patients* 20%. *Certified* Medicaid.
Owner Privately owned.
Admissions Requirements Medical examination; Physician's request.
Staff Physicians; RNs 2 (ft), 5 (pt); LPNs 2 (ft), 1 (pt); Nurses' aides 20 (ft), 12 (pt); Activities coordinators 1 (ft); Dietitians 1 (ft); Ophthalmologists (contracted); Podiatrists (contracted).
Facilities Dining room; Activities room; Crafts room; Laundry room; Barber/Beauty shop.
Activities Arts & crafts; Cards; Games; Prayer groups; Movies; Pet therapy.

Holt

Martin Luther—Holt Home
5091 Willoughby Rd, Holt, MI 48842
(517) 694-2144
Admin Ben Larsen. *Dir of Nursing* Marcelene Morris RN. *Medical Dir* Dr Elizabeth Imeson.
Licensure Skilled care. *Beds* SNF 84. *Certified* Medicaid; Medicare.
Owner Nonprofit organization/foundation.
Admissions Requirements Medical examination.
Staff RNs 3 (ft), 6 (pt); LPNs 2 (ft), 5 (pt); Nurses' aides 16 (ft), 45 (pt); Activities coordinators 1 (ft); Dietitians 1 (ft).
Affiliation Lutheran.
Facilities Dining room; Activities room; Crafts room; Barber/Beauty shop.
Activities Arts & crafts; Games; Reading groups; Prayer groups; Movies; Shopping trips.

Houghton Lake

King Nursing Home
PO Box 397, Houghton Lake, MI 48629
(517) 422-5153
Licensure Intermediate care. *Beds* ICF 49. *Certified* Medicaid.

Howell

Greenbriar Care Center
3003 W Grand River Ave, Howell, MI 48843
(517) 546-4210
Admin Sheryl Purcell. *Dir of Nursing* Kathy Bonfiglio RN. *Medical Dir* Edwin C Blumberg MD.
Licensure Skilled care. *Beds* SNF 189. *Certified* Medicaid; Medicare; VA.
Owner Proprietary corp.
Admissions Requirements Medical examination; Physician's request.
Facilities Dining room; Physical therapy room; Activities room; Crafts room; Laundry room; Barber/Beauty shop.

Activities Arts & crafts; Cards; Games; Reading groups; Prayer groups; Movies; Shopping trips; Dances/Social/Cultural gatherings.

Livingston Care Center
1333 W Grand River, Howell, MI 48843
(517) 548-1900
Admin Julie C Kaslly. *Dir of Nursing* Marlene Smith RN. *Medical Dir* Edwin C Blumberg DO.
Licensure Intermediate care; Home for aged; Apartments. *Beds* ICF 210; Home for aged 29; Apts 43. *Private Pay Patients* 23%. *Certified* Medicaid.
Owner Proprietary corp (Care Centers of Michigan).
Admissions Requirements Minimum age 16.
Staff Physicians 1 (ft); Physical therapists (contracted); Reality therapists (contracted); Recreational therapists (contracted); Occupational therapists (contracted); Speech therapists (contracted); Activities coordinators 2 (ft); Dietitians 1 (ft); Ophthalmologists (contracted); Podiatrists (contracted); Audiologists (contracted).
Facilities Dining room; Physical therapy room; Activities room; Crafts room; Laundry room; Barber/Beauty shop; Library; Fenced patios; Semi-private rooms.
Activities Arts & crafts; Cards; Games; Reading groups; Prayer groups; Movies; Intergenerational programs; Pet therapy.

Hubbell

Our Lady of Mercy Convalescent Home
1201 Grant St, Hubbell, MI 49934
(906) 296-3301 & 296-9601
Admin Raymond E Dube. *Dir of Nursing* Deborah Little RN. *Medical Dir* Dr Jerry Luoma; Dr Gary Mikel.
Licensure Intermediate care. *Beds* ICF 45. *Certified* Medicaid.
Owner Proprietary corp.
Admissions Requirements Minimum age 18; Medical examination.
Staff Physicians 2 (ft); RNs 2 (ft), 2 (pt); LPNs 1 (ft), 3 (pt); Nurses' aides 12 (ft), 7 (pt); Activities coordinators 1 (ft), 1 (pt); Dietitians 1 (pt).
Languages French, Croatian, Finnish.
Affiliation Roman Catholic.
Facilities Dining room; Activities room; Laundry room; Barber/Beauty shop; Library.
Activities Arts & crafts; Cards; Games; Reading groups; Prayer groups; Movies; Dances/Social/Cultural gatherings; Library services.

Hudsonville

Hudsonville Christian Nursing Home
3650 Van Buren St, Hudsonville, MI 49426
(616) 669-1520
Licensure Skilled care. *Beds* SNF 113. *Certified* Medicaid; Medicare.

Inkster

Advance Nursing Center Inc
2936 S John Daly Rd, Inkster, MI 48141
(313) 278-7272
Admin Roberta Caurdy. *Dir of Nursing* Minnie White. *Medical Dir* Donald Dreyfuss DO.
Licensure Skilled care; Intermediate care. *Beds* SNF 92. *Private Pay Patients* 10%. *Certified* Medicaid; Medicare; Blue Cross.
Owner Nonprofit corp.
Admissions Requirements Physician's request.
Staff Physicians 1 (pt); RNs 1 (ft), 4 (pt); LPNs 4 (ft), 4 (pt); Nurses' aides 34 (ft), 5 (pt); Activities coordinators 1 (ft), 2 (pt); Dietitians 1 (pt); Ophthalmologists 1 (pt); Podiatrists 1 (pt).

Facilities Dining room; Activities room; Chapel; Crafts room; Laundry room; Barber/Beauty shop.
Activities Arts & crafts; Cards; Games; Reading groups; Prayer groups; Movies; Shopping trips; Dances/Social/Cultural gatherings; Intergenerational programs.

Ionia

Ionia Manor
PO Box 509, Ionia, MI 48846
(616) 527-0080
Licensure Skilled care. *Beds* SNF 120. *Certified* Medicaid; Medicare.
Owner Proprietary corp (Health Care and Retirement Corp).

Riverside Correctional Facility—Comprehensive Care Unit
777 W Riverside Dr, Ionia, MI 48875
Licensure Skilled care. *Beds* SNF 150.

Iron Mountain

Freeman Convalescent Home Inc
PO Box 130, S US 2, Iron Mountain, MI 49801
(906) 774-1530
Admin Lois A Podgornik. *Dir of Nursing* Mary K Cahill. *Medical Dir* Paul Hayes MD.
Licensure Intermediate care; Alzheimer's care. *Beds* ICF 45. *Certified* Medicaid.
Owner Proprietary corp.
Admissions Requirements Medical examination; Physician's request.
Staff Physicians 1 (pt); RNs 1 (ft); LPNs; Nurses' aides 17 (ft), 4 (pt); Physical therapists (contracted); Recreational therapists (contracted); Occupational therapists (contracted); Speech therapists (contracted); Activities coordinators (contracted); Dietitians (contracted); Ophthalmologists (contracted); Podiatrists (contracted); Audiologists (contracted).
Languages Lebanese, Italian.
Facilities Dining room; Activities room; Chapel; Crafts room; Laundry room; Barber/Beauty shop; Library.
Activities Arts & crafts; Cards; Games; Reading groups; Prayer groups; Movies; Shopping trips; Dances/Social/Cultural gatherings; Intergenerational programs; Pet therapy.

Hyland Convalescent Home
601 E "G" St, Iron Mountain, MI 49801
(906) 774-9333
Licensure Intermediate care. *Beds* ICF 51. *Certified* Medicaid.

Iron River

Iron River Nursing Home
330 Lincoln Ave, Iron River, MI 49935
(906) 265-5168
Admin Philip Laturi. *Dir of Nursing* Karen Patton. *Medical Dir* Robert Han MD.
Licensure Intermediate care. *Beds* ICF 69. *Certified* Medicaid.
Owner Proprietary corp.
Staff LPNs 3 (ft), 3 (pt); Nurses' aides 18 (ft), 15 (pt); Activities coordinators 1 (ft), 1 (pt); Dietitians 1 (pt).

Ironwood

Hautamaki Westgate Rest Haven
1500 N Lowell St, Ironwood, MI 49938
(906) 932-3867
Licensure Intermediate care; Home for aged. *Beds* ICF 65; Home for aged 48. *Certified* Medicaid.

Josephson Nursing Home
634 E Ayer St, Ironwood, MI 49938
(906) 932-2006
Medical Dir Allen C Gorrilca MD.
Licensure Intermediate care. *Beds* ICF 47. *Certified* Medicaid.
Staff Physicians 9 (pt); RNs 1 (ft); LPNs 8 (pt); Nurses' aides 20 (ft), 30 (pt); Physical therapists 1 (pt); Reality therapists 1 (pt); Recreational therapists 1 (pt); Activities coordinators 1 (ft); Dietitians 1 (pt); Ophthalmologists 1 (pt); Podiatrists 1 (pt); Audiologists 1 (pt); Dentists 1 (pt).
Facilities Dining room; Activities room; Laundry room.
Activities Arts & crafts; Cards; Games; Reading groups; Prayer groups; Movies; Shopping trips; Dances/Social/Cultural gatherings; Fishing trips; Picnics; Swimming.

Ishpeming

Marquette County Medical Care Facility
PO Box 309, 200 W Saginaw St, Ishpeming, MI 49849
(906) 485-1061
Admin Bradley N Cory. *Dir of Nursing* Patricia Cornish RN. *Medical Dir* Dr Barbara Lyons.
Licensure Skilled care; Intermediate care. *Beds* Swing beds SNF/ICF 120. *Certified* Medicaid; Medicare.
Owner Publicly owned.
Admissions Requirements Minimum age 18; Males only; Females only; Medical examination.
Staff Physicians; RNs; LPNs; Nurses' aides; Physical therapists 1 (pt); Speech therapists 1 (pt); Activities coordinators 1 (ft); Dietitians 1 (ft); Podiatrists 1 (pt).
Facilities Dining room; Physical therapy room; Activities room; Chapel; Crafts room; Laundry room; Barber/Beauty shop.
Activities Arts & crafts; Cards; Games; Reading groups; Prayer groups; Movies; Dances/Social/Cultural gatherings; Pet therapy.

Mather Nursing Center
435 Stoneville Rd, Ishpeming, MI 49849
(906) 485-1073
Admin Sue Cieslinski. *Dir of Nursing* Judith Nagel. *Medical Dir* Barbara Lyons MD.
Licensure Skilled care. *Beds* SNF 122. *Certified* Medicaid; Medicare.
Owner Proprietary corp (Health Concepts Corp).
Staff Physicians; RNs; LPNs; Nurses' aides; Physical therapists; Reality therapists; Recreational therapists; Occupational therapists; Speech therapists; Activities coordinators; Dietitians; Podiatrists.
Facilities Dining room; Physical therapy room; Activities room; Crafts room; Laundry room; Barber/Beauty shop.
Activities Arts & crafts; Cards; Games; Reading groups; Prayer groups; Movies; Shopping trips; Dances/Social/Cultural gatherings.

Jackson

Countryside Care Center
2121 Robinson Rd, Jackson, MI 49203
Licensure Intermediate care; Home for aged. *Beds* ICF 59; Home for aged 56. *Certified* Medicaid.

Faith Haven Care Center
6531 W Michigan Ave, Jackson, MI 49201
(517) 750-3822
Licensure Skilled care; Intermediate care; Home for aged. *Beds* Swing beds SNF/ICF 88; Home for aged 20. *Certified* Medicaid; Medicare.
Owner Proprietary corp (Beverly Enterprises).

John George Home
1501 E Ganson, Jackson, MI 49202
(517) 783-4134
Admin Billie Ann Veit.
Licensure Home for aged. *Beds* Home for aged 27. *Certified* Medicaid.
Owner Nonprofit organization/foundation.
Admissions Requirements Minimum age 60; Males only; Medical examination.
Facilities Dining room; Laundry room; Library.

Highland Home
1948 Cooper St, Jackson, MI 49202
Licensure Home for aged. *Beds* Home for aged 23.

Jackson County Medical Care Facility
1715 Lansing Ave, Jackson, MI 49202
(517) 783-2726
Licensure Skilled care. *Beds* SNF 194. *Certified* Medicaid; Medicare.
Owner Publicly owned.

Jackson Friendly Home
435 W North St, Jackson, MI 49202
(517) 784-1377
Admin Sherry A Rainey.
Licensure Home for aged. *Beds* Home for aged 45. *Private Pay Patients* 100%.
Owner Nonprofit organization/foundation.
Admissions Requirements Minimum age 60; Females only; Medical examination.
Staff Nurses' aides; Activities coordinators; Podiatrists.
Facilities Dining room; Activities room; Crafts room; Laundry room; Barber/Beauty shop; Library; Private rooms.
Activities Arts & crafts; Games; Reading groups; Prayer groups; Movies; Dances/Social/Cultural gatherings.

Marlin Manor
434 W North St, Jackson, MI 49202
(517) 787-3250
Admin Herbert E Harrington. *Dir of Nursing* Kathleen Riske RN. *Medical Dir* Dale Schaeffer MD.
Licensure Skilled care. *Beds* SNF 100. *Certified* Medicaid; Medicare.
Owner Proprietary corp (Health Care and Retirement Corp).
Admissions Requirements Minimum age 18; Medical examination; Physician's request.
Staff RNs; LPNs; Nurses' aides; Physical therapists 1 (pt); Recreational therapists 1 (ft), 1 (pt); Occupational therapists 1 (pt); Speech therapists 1 (pt); Podiatrists.
Facilities Dining room; Physical therapy room; Activities room; Crafts room; Laundry room; Barber/Beauty shop.
Activities Arts & crafts; Cards; Games; Reading groups; Prayer groups; Movies; Shopping trips; Dances/Social/Cultural gatherings; Intergenerational programs.

Odd Fellow & Rebekah Home
2388 W Michigan Ave, Jackson, MI 49202
(517) 787-5140
Admin Ann E O'Dell. *Dir of Nursing* Pat Balaze RN.
Licensure Intermediate care; Home for aged. *Beds* ICF 50; Home for aged 20. *Certified* Medicaid.
Owner Nonprofit corp.
Admissions Requirements Minimum age 16; Medical examination.
Staff Physicians; RNs; LPNs; Nurses' aides; Recreational therapists; Activities coordinators; Dietitians; Ophthalmologists.
Affiliation Independent Order of Odd Fellows & Rebekahs.
Facilities Dining room; Physical therapy room; Activities room; Chapel; Crafts room; Laundry room; Barber/Beauty shop; Library.

Activities Arts & crafts; Cards; Games; Reading groups; Prayer groups; Movies; Shopping trips; Dances/Social/Cultural gatherings.

Vista Grande Villa
2251 Springport Rd, Jackson, MI 49202-1496
(517) 787-0222
Admin Donald Johansen. *Dir of Nursing* Blanche Knight RN. *Medical Dir* I H Butt MD.
Licensure Skilled care; Intermediate care; Life care retirement. *Beds* Swing beds SNF/ICF 60; Life care retirement 250. *Private Pay Patients* 0%. *Certified* Medicaid; Medicare.
Owner Nonprofit corp (Life Care Services Corp).
Admissions Requirements Minimum age 62; Medical examination.
Staff Physicians 1 (ft), 2 (pt); RNs 2 (ft), 5 (pt); LPNs 3 (ft), 8 (pt); Nurses' aides 18 (ft), 16 (pt); Physical therapists 1 (pt); Speech therapists 1 (pt); Activities coordinators 1 (ft), 2 (pt); Dietitians 1 (ft), 1 (pt); Ophthalmologists 1 (pt); Podiatrists 1 (pt).
Facilities Dining room; Physical therapy room; Activities room; Chapel; Crafts room; Laundry room; Barber/Beauty shop; Library; Pharmacy.
Activities Arts & crafts; Cards; Games; Reading groups; Prayer groups; Movies; Shopping trips; Dances/Social/Cultural gatherings; Scheduled transportation.

Jenison

Sunset Manor
725 Baldwin St, Jenison, MI 49428
Licensure Home for aged. *Beds* Home for aged 202.

Kalamazoo

Alamo Nursing Home Inc
8290 W "C" Ave, Kalamazoo, MI 49009
(616) 343-2587
Admin Catherine Preston. *Dir of Nursing* Carol Allor. *Medical Dir* E Robert Topp MD.
Licensure Skilled care; Intermediate care. *Beds* SNF 63; ICF 37. *Private Pay Patients* 10%. *Certified* Medicaid; Medicare.
Owner Proprietary corp.
Admissions Requirements Minimum age 15; Medical examination.
Staff Physicians; RNs; LPNs; Nurses' aides; Physical therapists; Activities coordinators; Dietitians.
Facilities Dining room; Physical therapy room; Activities room; Crafts room; Laundry room; Barber/Beauty shop; Library; TV rooms.
Activities Arts & crafts; Cards; Games; Reading groups; Prayer groups; Movies; Shopping trips; Dances/Social/Cultural gatherings; Intergenerational programs; Pet therapy; Reminiscing groups; Sensory groups.

Arboridge Care Center
1 Healthcare Plz, Kalamazoo, MI 49007
(616) 665-7043

Borgess Nursing Home
537 Chicago Ave, Kalamazoo, MI 49001
(616) 382-2392
Medical Dir Frank Harrell MD.
Licensure Skilled care. *Beds* SNF 121. *Certified* Medicaid; Medicare.
Admissions Requirements Minimum age 15; Medical examination; Physician's request.
Staff RNs 14 (ft); LPNs 8 (ft); Nurses' aides 100 (ft); Reality therapists 1 (pt); Recreational therapists 4 (ft); Occupational therapists 1 (pt); Activities coordinators 1 (ft); Dietitians 1 (ft).

Facilities Dining room; Physical therapy room; Activities room; Chapel; Crafts room; Laundry room; Barber/Beauty shop; Library.
Activities Arts & crafts; Cards; Games; Reading groups; Prayer groups; Movies; Dances/Social/Cultural gatherings; Outdoor picnics; Tours by bus.

Brookhaven Care Center
1701 Olmstead Rd, Kalamazoo, MI 49001
(616) 349-9694
Licensure Intermediate care. *Beds* ICF 50. *Certified* Medicaid.

Directors Hall
600 Golden Dr, Kalamazoo, MI 49001
Licensure Home for aged. *Beds* Home for aged 101.

Friendship Village
1400 N Drake Rd, Kalamazoo, MI 49007
(616) 381-0560
Medical Dir Dr Bennard Dowd.
Licensure Skilled care. *Beds* SNF 57. *Certified* Medicaid; Medicare.
Owner Nonprofit corp (Life Care Services Corp).
Admissions Requirements Minimum age 62; Medical examination; Physician's request.
Staff Physicians 3 (pt); RNs 1 (ft), 6 (pt); LPNs 4 (ft), 3 (pt); Nurses' aides 22 (ft), 8 (pt); Physical therapists 1 (pt); Speech therapists 1 (pt); Activities coordinators 1 (ft); Dietitians 1 (pt); Ophthalmologists 1 (pt); Podiatrists 1 (pt); Audiologists 1 (pt); Dentists 1 (pt).
Facilities Dining room; Physical therapy room; Activities room; Chapel; Crafts room; Laundry room; Barber/Beauty shop; Library.
Activities Arts & crafts; Cards; Games; Reading groups; Prayer groups; Movies; Shopping trips; Dances/Social/Cultural gatherings.

Park Village Pines
2920 Crystal Ln, Kalamazoo, MI 49009
Licensure Home for aged. *Beds* Home for aged 140.

Provincial House Kalamazoo
1701 S 11th St, Kalamazoo, MI 49009
(616) 375-2020
Admin Thomas M Bourisseau. *Dir of Nursing* Pat Bushouse. *Medical Dir* Simon Hoogendyk.
Licensure Skilled care. *Beds* SNF 117. *Certified* Medicaid; Medicare.
Owner Proprietary corp (Beverly Enterprises).
Admissions Requirements Medical examination; Physician's request.
Staff Physicians 23 (pt); RNs 4 (ft), 2 (pt); LPNs 8 (ft), 1 (pt); Nurses' aides 50 (ft), 5 (pt); Physical therapists 1 (pt); Recreational therapists 1 (pt); Occupational therapists 1 (pt); Speech therapists 1 (pt); Activities coordinators 1 (ft), 1 (pt); Dietitians 1 (ft); Ophthalmologists 1 (pt); Podiatrists 1 (pt).
Facilities Dining room; Physical therapy room; Activities room; Crafts room; Laundry room; Barber/Beauty shop; Library.
Activities Arts & crafts; Cards; Games; Reading groups; Prayer groups; Movies; Dances/Social/Cultural gatherings.

Provincial House of Portage
7855 Currier Dr, Kalamazoo, MI 49002
(616) 323-7748
Admin Terri Fowler. *Dir of Nursing* Judy Rome. *Medical Dir* Dr Dennis Konzen.
Licensure Skilled care. *Beds* SNF 120. *Certified* Medicaid; Medicare.
Owner Proprietary corp (Beverly Enterprises).
Admissions Requirements Medical examination; Physician's request.
Staff RNs 4 (ft), 6 (pt); LPNs 12 (ft), 4 (pt); Nurses' aides 40 (ft), 30 (pt); Physical therapists 1 (pt); Recreational therapists 1 (ft); Occupational therapists 1 (pt); Speech

therapists 1 (pt); Activities coordinators 1 (ft); Dietitians 1 (ft); Podiatrists 1 (pt); Audiologists 1 (pt).
Facilities Dining room; Physical therapy room; Activities room; Crafts room; Laundry room; Barber/Beauty shop.
Activities Arts & crafts; Cards; Games; Reading groups; Prayer groups; Movies; Shopping trips; Dances/Social/Cultural gatherings; Intergenerational programs; Pet therapy.

Ridgeview Manor
3625 W Michigan Ave, Kalamazoo, MI 49007
(616) 375-4550
Admin Donald J Kitchin. *Dir of Nursing* Mar Driskill. *Medical Dir* Dr J T Cerovski.
Licensure Skilled care; Intermediate care. *Beds* Swing beds SNF/ICF 180. *Certified* Medicaid; Medicare.
Owner Proprietary corp (Health Care and Retirement Corp).
Admissions Requirements Medical examination; Physician's request.
Staff RNs; LPNs; Nurses' aides; Activities coordinators; Dietitians.
Facilities Dining room; Physical therapy room; Activities room; Crafts room; Laundry room; Barber/Beauty shop.
Activities Arts & crafts; Cards; Games; Reading groups; Prayer groups; Movies; Shopping trips; Dances/Social/Cultural gatherings; Youth activities; College courses.

Senior Citizens—Merrill Residence
475 W Lovell St, Kalamazoo, MI 49007
Licensure Home for aged. *Beds* Home for aged 87.

Upjohn Community Nursing Home
2400 Portage St, Kalamazoo, MI 49001
(616) 381-4290
Admin Donna Menchinger. *Dir of Nursing* Donna Menchinger RN.
Licensure Skilled care; Retirement. *Beds* SNF 130. *Certified* Medicaid; Medicare.
Owner Nonprofit corp.
Admissions Requirements Medical examination; Physician's request.
Staff Physicians 1 (pt); RNs 6 (ft), 10 (pt); LPNs 5 (ft), 6 (pt); Nurses' aides 38 (ft), 61 (pt); Physical therapists 1 (pt); Occupational therapists 1 (ft); Activities coordinators 1 (ft); Dietitians 1 (ft); Volunteer coordinators 1 (pt).
Facilities Dining room; Physical therapy room; Activities room; Chapel; Crafts room; Laundry room; Barber/Beauty shop; Library.
Activities Arts & crafts; Cards; Games; Reading groups; Prayer groups; Movies; Shopping trips; Dances/Social/Cultural gatherings; Gardening; Baking.

Verdries Nursing Center
1430 Alamo Ave, Kalamazoo, MI 49007
(616) 349-2661
Licensure Intermediate care. *Beds* ICF 140. *Certified* Medicaid.
Owner Proprietary corp (Comprehensive Health Care Assn).

Westbrook Manor
6203 W Michigan Ave, Kalamazoo, MI 49009
(616) 375-1204
Admin William R Becker.
Medical Dir Helen Kroemlien.
Licensure Skilled care; Alzheimer's care. *Beds* SNF 101. *Certified* Medicaid; Medicare.
Owner Privately owned.
Admissions Requirements Medical examination.
Staff Physicians 2 (ft); RNs 2 (ft); LPNs 8 (ft); Nurses' aides 20 (ft); Occupational therapists 1 (ft); Activities coordinators 1 (ft); Dietitians 1 (ft); Ophthalmologists 1 (ft).
Facilities Dining room; Physical therapy room; Activities room; Crafts room; Laundry room; Barber/Beauty shop.

Activities Arts & crafts; Cards; Games; Reading groups; Prayer groups; Movies; Shopping trips; Dances/Social/Cultural gatherings.

Kalkaska

Kalkaska Memorial Health Center
PO Box 249, 419 S Coral, Kalkaska, MI 49646
(616) 258-9142
Admin Harvey Norris. *Dir of Nursing* Lynn Quail RN. *Medical Dir* Dr Richard E Hodgman.
Licensure Skilled care. *Beds* SNF 21. *Certified* Medicaid; Medicare.
Admissions Requirements Minimum age 15; Medical examination; Physician's request.
Staff Physicians 4 (pt); RNs 8 (pt); LPNs 10 (pt); Nurses' aides 6 (pt); Physical therapists 1 (ft); Activities coordinators 1 (pt); Dietitians 1 (pt); Podiatrists 1 (pt).
Facilities Physical therapy room; Activities room.
Activities Arts & crafts; Games; Reading groups; Prayer groups; Movies; Shopping trips; Dances/Social/Cultural gatherings.

Kawkawlin

Huron Woods Nursing Home
1395 S Huron Rd, Kawkawlin, MI 48631
(517) 684-3213
Licensure Intermediate care. *Beds* ICF 51. *Certified* Medicaid.

Kentwood

Christian Nursing Center Inc
2589 44th St SE, Kentwood, MI 49507
Licensure Intermediate care. *Beds* ICF 73. *Certified* Medicaid.

Kingsford

Americana Healthcare Center
1225 Woodward Ave, Kingsford, MI 49801
(906) 774-4805
Admin Helen R Roach. *Dir of Nursing* Dorothy Saler RN. *Medical Dir* Dr Donald J Jacobs.
Licensure Skilled care. *Beds* SNF 107. *Certified* Medicaid; Medicare.
Owner Proprietary corp (Manor Care).
Admissions Requirements Minimum age 17.
Staff RNs 1 (ft), 4 (pt); LPNs 1 (ft), 5 (pt); Nurses' aides 25 (ft), 30 (pt); Physical therapists 1 (pt); Activities coordinators; Dietitians 1 (pt).
Facilities Dining room; Physical therapy room; Activities room; Crafts room; Laundry room; Barber/Beauty shop.
Activities Arts & crafts; Cards; Games; Reading groups; Prayer groups; Movies; Shopping trips.

Lake Orion

Ortonville Nursing Home
PO Box 129, Lake Orion, MI 48035-0129
(313) 627-2420
Licensure Intermediate care. *Beds* ICF 51. *Certified* Medicaid.

Lakeview

Kelsey Memorial Hospital Inc
418 Washington Ave, Lakeview, MI 48850
(517) 352-7211, 352-6435 FAX
Admin Joseph M Smith. *Dir of Nursing* Nancy L Miner. *Medical Dir* John L London MD.
Licensure Skilled care; Acute care. *Beds* SNF 42; Acute care 52. *Private Pay Patients* 3%. *Certified* Medicaid; Medicare.

Owner Nonprofit organization/foundation.
Admissions Requirements Medical examination; Physician's request.
Staff Physicians 8 (ft); RNs 2 (ft), 1 (pt); LPNs 8 (ft), 7 (pt); Nurses' aides 7 (ft), 22 (pt); Physical therapists 1 (pt); Occupational therapists 1 (pt); Speech therapists 1 (pt); Activities coordinators 1 (ft); Dietitians 1 (pt); Podiatrists 1 (pt).
Facilities Dining room; Physical therapy room; Activities room; Barber/Beauty shop.
Activities Arts & crafts; Cards; Games; Reading groups; Prayer groups; Movies; Shopping trips; Dances/Social/Cultural gatherings; Intergenerational programs; Pet therapy; Picnics; Museum trips.

Lamont

Glenwood Christian Nursing Home
13030 44th Ave, Lamont, MI 49430
(616) 677-1243
Medical Dir Mary S Kitchel MD.
Licensure Skilled care. *Beds* SNF 66. *Certified* Medicaid; Medicare.
Owner Proprietary corp (Miko Enterprises Inc).
Admissions Requirements Minimum age 17; Medical examination; Physician's request.
Staff Physicians 7 (ft); RNs 11 (ft); LPNs 5 (ft); Nurses' aides 50 (ft); Physical therapists 1 (ft); Recreational therapists 1 (ft); Occupational therapists 1 (pt); Speech therapists 1 (pt); Activities coordinators 1 (ft); Dietitians 1 (ft); Ophthalmologists 1 (pt); Podiatrists 1 (pt); Dentists 1 (pt).
Facilities Dining room; Physical therapy room; Activities room; Crafts room; Laundry room; Barber/Beauty shop.
Activities Arts & crafts; Cards; Games; Reading groups; Prayer groups; Movies; Shopping trips.

L'Anse

Baraga County Memorial Hospital
770 N Main St, L'Anse, MI 49946
(906) 524-6166, 524-7147 FAX
Admin John P Tembreull. *Dir of Nursing* Mary E Hulkonen RN. *Medical Dir* Tamas A Lanczy MD.
Licensure Skilled care; Intermediate care. *Beds* Swing beds SNF/ICF 28. *Private Pay Patients* 5%. *Certified* Medicaid; Medicare.
Owner Publicly owned.
Admissions Requirements Minimum age 14; Medical examination; Physician's request.
Staff Physicians; RNs; LPNs; Nurses' aides; Physical therapists; Speech therapists; Activities coordinators; Dietitians.
Languages Finnish.
Facilities Dining room; Physical therapy room; Activities room; Crafts room; Barber/Beauty shop.
Activities Arts & crafts; Cards; Games; Prayer groups; Movies; Shopping trips; Dances/Social/Cultural gatherings; Intergenerational programs.

Winkler Nursing Home
833 Sicotte St, L'Anse, MI 49946
(906) 524-6531
Admin Catherine Kinsey. *Dir of Nursing* Jennie Jukkala RN. *Medical Dir* P E Carmody MD.
Licensure Skilled care. *Beds* SNF 59. *Certified* Medicaid; Medicare.
Owner Proprietary corp.
Admissions Requirements Medical examination; Only admitted by order of a physician.
Staff RNs 1 (ft), 3 (pt); LPNs 2 (ft), 5 (pt); Nurses' aides 18 (ft), 11 (pt); Activities coordinators 1 (ft), 1 (pt); Dietitians 1 (pt).

Facilities Dining room; Activities room; Crafts room; Laundry room.
Activities Arts & crafts; Cards; Games; Reading groups; Prayer groups; Movies; Shopping trips; Dances/Social/Cultural gatherings; Rides; Visit other facilities; Outings to lunch & dinner.

Lansing

Mary Avenue Care Center
1313 Mary Ave, Lansing, MI 48910
(517) 393-6130
Medical Dir Willard J Miller MD.
Licensure Skilled care. *Beds* SNF 134. *Certified* Medicaid; Medicare.
Owner Proprietary corp (Hillhaven Corp).
Admissions Requirements Minimum age 17; Medical examination; Physician's request.
Staff Physicians 2 (ft), 4 (pt); LPNs 6 (ft), 6 (pt); Nurses' aides 42 (ft), 16 (pt); Activities coordinators 1 (ft); Dietitians 1 (ft).
Facilities Dining room; Physical therapy room; Activities room; Laundry room.
Activities Arts & crafts; Reading groups; Movies; Dances/Social/Cultural gatherings.

Provincial House South
2100 Provincial Dr, Lansing, MI 48910
(517) 882-2458
Admin Markham T Farrell. *Dir of Nursing* Linda Wagner RN. *Medical Dir* Stephen Tepastee MD.
Licensure Skilled care. *Beds* SNF 120. *Certified* Medicaid; Medicare.
Owner Proprietary corp (Beverly Enterprises).
Staff Physicians 1 (pt); RNs 8 (ft), 2 (pt); LPNs 7 (ft), 5 (pt); Nurses' aides 45 (ft), 11 (pt); Physical therapists 1 (pt); Occupational therapists 1 (pt); Speech therapists 1 (pt); Activities coordinators 1 (ft); Dietitians 1 (pt); Ophthalmologists 1 (pt); Podiatrists 1 (pt); Dentists 1 (pt).
Facilities Dining room; Physical therapy room; Activities room; Crafts room; Laundry room; Barber/Beauty shop.
Activities Arts & crafts; Cards; Games; Reading groups; Prayer groups; Movies; Shopping trips; Dances/Social/Cultural gatherings.

Provincial House West
731 Starkweather Dr, Lansing, MI 48917
(517) 323-9133
Medical Dir Dr John Neuman.
Licensure Skilled care. *Beds* SNF 117. *Certified* Medicaid; Medicare.
Owner Proprietary corp (Beverly Enterprises).
Admissions Requirements Medical examination.
Staff Physicians 1 (ft), 14 (pt); RNs 4 (ft), 4 (pt); LPNs 4 (ft), 4 (pt); Nurses' aides 30 (ft), 35 (pt); Physical therapists 1 (pt); Occupational therapists 1 (pt); Speech therapists 1 (pt); Activities coordinators 1 (ft); Dietitians 1 (ft); Podiatrists 1 (pt); Dentists 1 (pt).
Facilities Dining room; Physical therapy room; Activities room; Laundry room; Barber/Beauty shop; TV lounge.
Activities Arts & crafts; Cards; Games; Reading groups; Prayer groups; Movies; Shopping trips; Dances/Social/Cultural gatherings; Musical programs.

Roselawn Manor
707 Armstrong Rd, Lansing, MI 48910
(517) 393-5680
Licensure Skilled care. *Beds* SNF 234. *Certified* Medicaid; Medicare.
Staff Physicians 4 (pt); RNs 8 (pt); LPNs 14 (pt); Physical therapists 1 (pt); Recreational therapists 3 (ft), 3 (pt); Occupational therapists 1 (pt); Speech therapists 1 (pt); Activities coordinators 1 (pt); Dietitians 2 (ft); Ophthalmologists 1 (pt); Podiatrists 1 (pt); Audiologists 1 (pt); Dentists 1 (pt).

Facilities Dining room; Physical therapy room; Activities room; Crafts room; Laundry room; Barber/Beauty shop.
Activities Arts & crafts; Cards; Games; Reading groups; Prayer groups; Movies; Shopping trips; Dances/Social/Cultural gatherings.

Willow Manor
510 W Willow St, Lansing, MI 48906
Licensure Home for aged. Beds Home for aged 40.

Lapeer

Ferguson Convalescent Home
239 S Main St, Lapeer, MI 48446
(313) 664-6611
Licensure Intermediate care; Home for aged. Beds ICF 91; Home for aged 20. Certified Medicaid.

Lapeer County Medical Care Facility
1455 Suncrest Dr, Lapeer, MI 48446
(313) 664-8571
Medical Dir Jules Reinhardt DO.
Licensure Skilled care. Beds SNF 162. Certified Medicaid; Medicare.
Owner Publicly owned.
Admissions Requirements Minimum age 16; Physician's request.
Staff Physicians 2 (pt); RNs 10 (ft), 1 (pt); LPNs 17 (ft), 12 (pt); Physical therapists 1 (pt); Recreational therapists 1 (ft); Occupational therapists 1 (pt); Speech therapists 1 (pt); Activities coordinators 1 (ft); Dietitians 1 (pt); Ophthalmologists 1 (pt); Podiatrists 1 (pt); Dentists 1 (pt).
Facilities Dining room; Physical therapy room; Activities room; Chapel; Laundry room; Barber/Beauty shop.
Activities Arts & crafts; Cards; Games; Reading groups; Prayer groups; Movies; Shopping trips; Dances/Social/Cultural gatherings.

Lawton

Lake View Community Nursing Home
99 Walker St, Lawton, MI 49065
(616) 624-4311
Admin Edward Alderman. Dir of Nursing Ms E Lanphear RN. Medical Dir E Lean MD.
Licensure Skilled care. Beds SNF 120. Certified Medicaid; Medicare.
Owner Nonprofit organization/foundation.
Admissions Requirements Minimum age 16; Medical examination; Physician's request.
Staff Physicians 3 (pt); RNs 3 (ft), 3 (pt); LPNs 6 (ft), 8 (pt); Nurses' aides 15 (ft), 35 (pt); Physical therapists 1 (pt); Speech therapists 1 (pt); Activities coordinators 1 (ft); Dietitians 1 (pt); Ophthalmologists 1 (pt).
Facilities Dining room; Physical therapy room; Activities room; Crafts room; Laundry room; Barber/Beauty shop.
Activities Arts & crafts; Cards; Games; Reading groups; Prayer groups; Movies; Dances/Social/Cultural gatherings.

Lincoln

Lincoln Haven Rest Home
950 Barlow Rd, Lincoln, MI 48742
(517) 736-8481
Licensure Intermediate care. Beds ICF 36. Certified Medicaid.

Linden

Stanmarie
9051 Silver Lake Rd, Linden, MI 48451
(313) 735-7413

Licensure Intermediate care; Home for aged. Beds ICF 60; Home for aged 2. Certified Medicaid.

Litchfield

Litchfield Nursing Centre Inc
527 Marshall Rd, Litchfield, MI 49252
(517) 542-2323
Admin Martha Brownlee. Dir of Nursing Billie Bushre.
Licensure Intermediate care; Alzheimer's care. Beds ICF 81. Certified Medicaid.
Owner Proprietary corp.
Admissions Requirements Minimum age 18; Medical examination.
Staff RNs 1 (ft), 1 (pt); LPNs 6 (ft), 4 (pt); Nurses' aides 18 (ft), 15 (pt); Recreational therapists 1 (ft).
Facilities Dining room; Activities room; Laundry room; Barber/Beauty shop.
Activities Arts & crafts; Cards; Games; Reading groups; Prayer groups.

Livonia

Camelot Hall Convalescent Center
35100 Ann Arbor Trail, Livonia, MI 48150
(313) 522-1444
Admin Nancy J Mix. Dir of Nursing Martha Felosak RN. Medical Dir David Miller MD.
Licensure Skilled care. Beds SNF 166. Certified Medicaid; Medicare; VA.
Owner Proprietary corp.
Admissions Requirements Minimum age 55; Medical examination; Physician's request.
Staff Physicians 3 (pt); RNs 10 (ft), 4 (pt); LPNs 12 (ft), 5 (pt); Nurses' aides 60 (ft), 10 (pt); Physical therapists 1 (ft); Recreational therapists 3 (ft); Occupational therapists 1 (pt); Speech therapists 1 (pt); Activities coordinators 1 (ft); Dietitians 1 (pt); Ophthalmologists 1 (pt); Restorative nursing 4 (ft).
Facilities Dining room; Physical therapy room; Activities room; Laundry room; Barber/Beauty shop; Library; Patio.
Activities Arts & crafts; Cards; Games; Reading groups; Prayer groups; Movies; Shopping trips; Dances/Social/Cultural gatherings; Field trips.

Dorvin Convalescent & Nursing Center
29270 Morlock Ave, Livonia, MI 48152
(313) 476-0550
Admin Julie Cameron Kaslly. Dir of Nursing Ellen Basmaji RN. Medical Dir Leslie Mandel MD.
Licensure Skilled care. Beds SNF 132. Certified Medicaid; Medicare.
Owner Proprietary corp (Health Care and Retirement Corp).
Admissions Requirements Medical examination.
Staff Physicians 2 (ft), 3 (pt); RNs 8 (ft), 5 (pt); LPNs 7 (ft), 3 (pt); Nurses' aides 80 (ft), 20 (pt); Physical therapists 2 (ft), 2 (pt); Reality therapists 1 (ft), 2 (pt); Recreational therapists 1 (ft), 2 (pt); Occupational therapists 2 (pt); Speech therapists 1 (pt); Activities coordinators 1 (ft), 2 (pt); Dietitians 1 (ft); Ophthalmologists 1 (pt); Podiatrists 1 (pt); Dentists 1 (pt).
Facilities Dining room; Physical therapy room; Activities room; Crafts room; Laundry room; Barber/Beauty shop; Library; 2 Lounges; Patio areas.
Activities Arts & crafts; Cards; Games; Reading groups; Prayer groups; Movies; Shopping trips; Dances/Social/Cultural gatherings; Religious services; Sensory stimulation; Current events; Pet therapy; Resident council; Volunteer program.

Livonia Nursing Center
28910 Plymouth Rd, Livonia, MI 48150
(313) 522-8970

Licensure Intermediate care. Beds ICF 88. Certified Medicaid.

Manoogian Manor
15775 Middlebelt Rd, Livonia, MI 48154
(313) 522-5780
Admin Harry Zartarian.
Licensure Home for aged. Beds Home for aged 60. Private Pay Patients 67%. Certified Medicaid.
Owner Nonprofit organization/foundation.
Admissions Requirements Minimum age 60; Medical examination.
Staff Nurses' aides 3 (ft); Activities coordinators 1 (ft); Dietitians 1 (ft).
Languages Armenian, French, Arabic, Turkish, and others.
Facilities Dining room; Activities room; Chapel; Crafts room; Laundry room; Barber/ Beauty shop; Library.
Activities Arts & crafts; Games; Movies; Shopping trips; Dances/Social/Cultural gatherings; Classes.

Marycrest Manor
15475 Middlebelt, Livonia, MI 48154
(313) 427-9175
Admin Sr Mary Innocent. Dir of Nursing Sr Mary Emily RN. Medical Dir John M Shuey MD.
Licensure Skilled care; Intermediate care. Beds Swing beds SNF/ICF 55. Certified Medicaid; Medicare.
Owner Nonprofit organization/foundation.
Staff Physicians 1 (ft); RNs 2 (ft); LPNs 3 (ft), 2 (ft); Nurses' aides 25 (ft), 4 (pt); Physical therapists 1 (pt); Recreational therapists 2 (ft); Speech therapists 1 (pt); Activities coordinators 1 (ft); Dietitians 1 (ft); Podiatrists 2 (pt).
Affiliation Roman Catholic.
Facilities Dining room; Physical therapy room; Activities room; Chapel; Crafts room; Laundry room; Barber/Beauty shop; Library.
Activities Arts & crafts; Cards; Games; Reading groups; Prayer groups; Movies; Pet therapy.

Middlebelt Nursing Centre
14900 Middlebelt Rd, Livonia, MI 48154
(313) 425-4200
Admin Charles A Gutkowski.
Medical Dir Donald Albert MD.
Licensure Intermediate care. Beds ICF 162. Certified Medicaid.
Owner Proprietary corp (International Healthcare Management).
Admissions Requirements Minimum age 16; Medical examination; Physician's request.
Staff Physicians 4 (pt); RNs 4 (ft), 6 (pt); LPNs 6 (ft), 4 (pt); Nurses' aides 70 (ft), 20 (pt); Reality therapists 2 (ft); Recreational therapists 2 (ft); Occupational therapists 1 (pt); Speech therapists 1 (pt); Activities coordinators 1 (ft); Dietitians 1 (ft), 1 (pt); Ophthalmologists 1 (pt); Podiatrists 1 (pt); Dentists 1 (pt).
Facilities Dining room; Physical therapy room; Activities room; Chapel; Crafts room; Laundry room; Barber/Beauty shop; Library.
Activities Arts & crafts; Cards; Games; Reading groups; Prayer groups; Movies; Shopping trips; Dances/Social/Cultural gatherings; Sports; Entertainment events; Fishing - outside facility; Marching in parades.

St Jude Convalescent Center
34350 Ann Arbor Trail, Livonia, MI 48150
(313) 261-4800
Licensure Skilled care. Beds SNF 64. Certified Medicaid; Medicare.
Affiliation Roman Catholic.

Trinity Park West
38910 Six Mile Rd, Livonia, MI 48152
Licensure Home for aged. Beds Home for aged 99.

University Convalescent & Nursing Home
28550 Five Mile Rd, Livonia, MI 48154
(313) 427-8270
Admin Kay Kermode. *Dir of Nursing* Linda
Hirschfield RN. *Medical Dir* George Pappas
DO.
Licensure Skilled care. *Beds* SNF 184.
Certified Medicaid; Medicare.
Owner Proprietary corp (Health Care and
Retirement Corp).
Admissions Requirements Medical
examination; Physician's request.
Staff RNs 12 (ft); LPNs 18 (ft); Nurses' aides
70 (ft); Physical therapists 1 (ft); Activities
coordinators 2 (ft), 1 (pt); Dietitians 1 (ft).
Languages French.
Facilities Dining room; Physical therapy
room; Activities room; Chapel; Crafts room;
Laundry room; Barber/Beauty shop.
Activities Arts & crafts; Cards; Games;
Reading groups; Prayer groups; Movies;
Shopping trips; Dances/Social/Cultural
gatherings.

Woodhaven of Livonia
29667 Wentworth Ave, Livonia, MI 48154
(313) 261-9000
Admin Randall W Gasser. *Dir of Nursing*
Anna Baraboll. *Medical Dir* Dr Mario Cote.
Licensure Assisted living. *Beds* Assisted living
66.
Owner Nonprofit corp.
Admissions Requirements Minimum age 60;
Medical examination.
Staff LPNs 1 (ft); Nurses' aides 10 (ft), 5 (pt);
Activities coordinators 2 (pt); Dietitians 1
(ft).
Affiliation Apostolic Christian Church.
Facilities Dining room; Activities room;
Crafts room; Laundry room; Barber/Beauty
shop; Library; Lounges.
Activities Arts & crafts; Cards; Games;
Reading groups; Movies; Shopping trips;
Dances/Social/Cultural gatherings; Pet
therapy.

Lowell

Cumberland Manor
PO Box 210, Lowell, MI 49331
Licensure Home for aged. *Beds* Home for
aged 148.

Lowell Medical Care Center
350 N Center St, Lowell, MI 49331
(616) 897-8473
Licensure Skilled care. *Beds* SNF 153.
Certified Medicaid; Medicare.

Ludington

Baywood Nursing Home
1000 E Tinkham Ave, Ludington, MI 49431
(616) 845-6291
Licensure Skilled care. *Beds* SNF 126.
Certified Medicaid; Medicare.
Owner Proprietary corp (Beverly Enterprises).

Oakview Medical Care Facility
1000 Diana, Ludington, MI 49431
(616) 845-5185
Admin Frederick A Hough. *Dir of Nursing* D
Dianne Eisenlohr. *Medical Dir* William F
Sutter MD.
Licensure Skilled care; Intermediate care. *Beds*
Swing beds SNF/ICF 76. *Private Pay
Patients* 15%. *Certified* Medicaid; Medicare.
Owner Publicly owned.
Admissions Requirements Physician's request.
Staff Physicians 2 (pt); RNs 5 (ft), 5 (pt);
LPNs 5 (ft), 4 (pt); Nurses' aides 24 (ft), 20
(pt); Physical therapists 1 (ft); Occupational
therapists 1 (pt); Dietitians 1 (ft).
Facilities Dining room; Physical therapy
room; Activities room; Crafts room; Barber/
Beauty shop; Library; Multi-purpose rooms.

Activities Arts & crafts; Cards; Games; Prayer
groups; Movies; Dances/Social/Cultural
gatherings; Tours.

Madison Heights

Cambridge East
31155 DeQuindre, Madison Heights, MI
48071
(313) 585-7010
Admin H L Ostrow. *Dir of Nursing* J Kowal
RN. *Medical Dir* Dr S Wollock.
Licensure Skilled care. *Beds* SNF 160.
Certified Medicaid; Medicare.
Owner Proprietary corp (International
Healthcare Management).
Staff RNs 10 (ft), 5 (pt); LPNs 10 (ft), 5 (pt);
Nurses' aides 125 (ft), 25 (pt); Activities
coordinators 1 (ft), 1 (pt).

Manistee

Manistee County Medical Care Facility
1505 E Parkdale Ave, Manistee, MI 49660
(616) 723-2543
Admin Mary D Hansen. *Dir of Nursing*
Barbara J Hansen RN. *Medical Dir* Dr
Raymond Schmoke.
Licensure Skilled care. *Beds* SNF 102.
Certified Medicaid; Medicare.
Owner Publicly owned.
Admissions Requirements Minimum age 15;
Medical examination; Physician's request.
Staff RNs 6 (ft), 6 (pt); LPNs 1 (ft), 7 (pt);
Nurses' aides 26 (ft), 34 (pt); Physical
therapists 1 (ft); Activities coordinators 1
(ft); Dietitians 1 (pt); Physical therapy aides
1 (pt).
Facilities Dining room; Physical therapy
room; Activities room; Chapel; Crafts room;
Laundry room; Barber/Beauty shop; Patio.
Activities Arts & crafts; Cards; Games;
Reading groups; Prayer groups; Movies;
Intergenerational programs; Pet therapy.

Manistee Heights Care Center
300 Care Center Dr, Manistee, MI 49660
(313) 723-6262
Admin Shirley Abfalter. *Dir of Nursing* Anne
Reed RN. *Medical Dir* Dr John Long DO.
Licensure Skilled care. *Beds* SNF 119.
Certified Medicaid; Medicare.
Owner Proprietary corp (Beverly Enterprises).
Admissions Requirements Minimum age 16;
Medical examination.
Staff RNs 6 (ft), 2 (pt); LPNs 3 (ft), 1 (pt);
Nurses' aides 40 (ft), 20 (pt); Recreational
therapists 1 (ft); Activities coordinators 1
(ft).
Facilities Dining room; Physical therapy
room; Activities room; Chapel; Crafts room;
Laundry room; Barber/Beauty shop; Patio.
Activities Arts & crafts; Cards; Games;
Reading groups; Prayer groups; Movies;
Shopping trips; Dances/Social/Cultural
gatherings.

Manistique

Schoolcraft Medical Care Facility
520 Main St, Manistique, MI 49854
(906) 341-6921, 341-6922
Admin Dennis K Boyd. *Dir of Nursing*
Charlottle Schwartz RN. *Medical Dir* Neil
Grossmikle MD.
Licensure Skilled care. *Beds* SNF 75. *Certified*
Medicaid; Medicare.
Owner Publicly owned.
Admissions Requirements Medical
examination; Physician's request.
Staff RNs 3 (ft); LPNs 8 (ft) 13E 41 (ft);
Recreational therapists 1 (ft).
Facilities Dining room; Physical therapy
room; Activities room; Chapel; Laundry
room; Barber/Beauty shop; TV areas;
Smoking areas.

Activities Arts & crafts; Cards; Games;
Reading groups; Prayer groups; Movies;
Shopping trips; Dances/Social/Cultural
gatherings; Exercise classes.

Maple City

Maple Valley Nursing Home
Rte 2 Box 7, Maple City, MI 49664
(616) 228-5895
Admin Daniel J Weber. *Dir of Nursing* Donna
Kasben RN. *Medical Dir* Dr William
Thomas.
Licensure Intermediate care. *Beds* ICF 25.
Private Pay Patients 15%. *Certified*
Medicaid.
Owner Proprietary corp.
Admissions Requirements Minimum age 15;
Medical examination; Physician's request.
Staff RNs 1 (ft), 1 (pt); LPNs 3 (ft), 1 (pt);
Nurses' aides 3 (ft), 3 (pt); Activities
coordinators 1 (ft); Dietitians 1 (ft).
Languages Polish, German, French.
Facilities Dining room; Activities room;
Chapel; Crafts room; Laundry room;
Garden.
Activities Arts & crafts; Cards; Games;
Reading groups; Prayer groups; Movies;
Dances/Social/Cultural gatherings;
Intergenerational programs.

Marlette

**Marlette Community Hospital Long-Term Care
Unit**
2770 Main St, Marlette, MI 48453
(517) 635-7491, 635-3181 FAX
Admin Darwin Root. *Dir of Nursing* Roberta
Schultze. *Medical Dir* Duane Smith MD.
Licensure Skilled care; Retirement. *Beds* SNF
43; Retirement 23. *Private Pay Patients* 5%.
Certified Medicaid; Medicare.
Owner Nonprofit organization/foundation.
Admissions Requirements Physician's request.
Staff Physicians 7 (ft), 4 (pt); RNs 1 (ft), 5
(pt); LPNs 3 (ft), 7 (pt); Nurses' aides 10
(ft), 16 (pt); Physical therapists 2 (pt);
Reality therapists 1 (pt); Recreational
therapists 1 (pt); Occupational therapists 1
(pt); Speech therapists 1 (pt); Activities
coordinators 1 (ft); Dietitians 2 (ft), 1 (pt);
Podiatrists 1 (pt).
Facilities Dining room; Physical therapy
room; Activities room; Chapel; Laundry
room; Barber/Beauty shop.
Activities Arts & crafts; Cards; Games;
Reading groups; Prayer groups; Movies;
Shopping trips; Pet therapy; Religous
services.

Marne

Birchwood Care Center
15140 16th Ave, Marne, MI 49435
(616) 667-1215
Admin Lawana S Parks. *Dir of Nursing*
Carolyn VanBoven RN. *Medical Dir* Earl
Reynolds DO.
Licensure Skilled care; Intermediate care;
Home for aged. *Beds* Swing beds SNF/ICF
198; Home for aged 41. *Certified* Medicaid;
Medicare.
Owner Proprietary corp (Hillhaven Corp).
Admissions Requirements Minimum age 16;
Medical examination; Physician's request.
Staff RNs 5 (ft), 2 (pt); LPNs 11 (ft), 8 (pt);
Nurses' aides 46 (ft), 22 (pt); Activities
coordinators 1 (ft), 3 (pt); Dietitians 1 (ft).
Facilities Dining room; Physical therapy
room; Activities room; Chapel; Crafts room;
Laundry room; Barber/Beauty shop; Library.
Activities Arts & crafts; Games; Reading
groups; Prayer groups; Movies; Dances/
Social/Cultural gatherings.

Marquette

Brooks Center Health Care Facility
PO Box 779, S Rte 41, Marquette, MI 49855
Admin Grace E McCarthy.
Medical Dir Benjamin T Ulep.
Licensure Intermediate care. *Beds* ICF 11.
Admissions Requirements Males only; Medical examination; Physician's request.
Staff Physicians 1 (ft); RNs 10 (ft); LPNs 4 (ft); Physical therapists; Reality therapists; Recreational therapists; Occupational therapists; Speech therapists; Activities coordinators; Dietitians 1 (pt); Ophthalmologists; Podiatrists; Audiologists; Dentists 1 (pt); Laboratory workers 1 (ft); Physical aides 1 (ft).

Norlite Nursing Centers of Marquette
701 Homestead St, Marquette, MI 49855
(906) 228-9252
Admin Maila Tiffany. *Dir of Nursing* Karen Maskus. *Medical Dir* William C Humphry.
Licensure Skilled care. *Beds* SNF 99. *Private Pay Patients* 30%. *Certified* Medicaid; Medicare.
Owner Proprietary corp.
Admissions Requirements Minimum age 18.
Staff Physicians 15 (pt); RNs 5 (ft); LPNs 11 (ft), 1 (pt); Nurses' aides 48 (ft), 1 (pt); Physical therapists 1 (ft); Reality therapists 1 (ft); Recreational therapists 1 (ft); Occupational therapists 1 (ft); Speech therapists 1 (ft); Activities coordinators 1 (ft); Ophthalmologists 1 (pt); Podiatrists 1 (pt); Audiologists 1 (pt).
Languages Finnish.
Facilities Dining room; Physical therapy room; Activities room; Crafts room; Barber/ Beauty shop.
Activities Arts & crafts; Cards; Games; Reading groups; Prayer groups; Movies; Shopping trips; Dances/Social/Cultural gatherings; Pet therapy.

Marshall

Marshall Manor
575 N Madison, Marshall, MI 49068
(616) 781-4281, 781-9290 FAX
Admin Deborah Culp. *Dir of Nursing* Bette Wozniak RN. *Medical Dir* Thomas Neidlinger MD.
Licensure Skilled care; Intermediate care. *Beds* SNF 71; ICF 71. *Private Pay Patients* 23%. *Certified* Medicaid; Medicare.
Owner Proprietary corp (Medilodge Corp).
Admissions Requirements Minimum age 15; Medical examination; Physician's request.
Staff RNs 3 (ft), 1 (pt); LPNs 5 (ft), 6 (pt); Nurses' aides 17 (ft), 16 (pt); Physical therapists 1 (pt); Recreational therapists 1 (ft); Occupational therapists 1 (pt); Speech therapists 1 (pt); Activities coordinators 1 (ft); Dietitians 1 (pt); Ophthalmologists 1 (pt); Podiatrists 1 (pt).
Facilities Dining room; Physical therapy room; Activities room; Chapel; Crafts room; Laundry room; Barber/Beauty shop.
Activities Arts & crafts; Cards; Games; Reading groups; Prayer groups; Movies; Shopping trips; Dances/Social/Cultural gatherings; Intergenerational programs; Pet therapy; Annual trip to county fair.

Provincial House Marshall
879 E Michigan Ave, Marshall, MI 49068
(616) 781-4251
Licensure Intermediate care. *Beds* ICF 114. *Certified* Medicaid.
Owner Proprietary corp (Beverly Enterprises).
Admissions Requirements Minimum age 15; Medical examination; Physician's request.
Staff Physicians 16 (pt); RNs 3 (ft), 3 (pt); LPNs 1 (ft), 9 (pt); Nurses' aides 24 (ft), 42 (pt); Physical therapists 1 (pt); Reality therapists 1 (pt); Recreational therapists 1

(ft); Occupational therapists 1 (pt); Speech therapists 1 (pt); Activities coordinators 1 (ft); Dietitians 1 (ft); Ophthalmologists 1 (pt); Podiatrists 1 (pt); Audiologists 1 (pt); Dentists 1 (pt).
Facilities Dining room; Physical therapy room; Activities room; Crafts room; Laundry room; Barber/Beauty shop.
Activities Arts & crafts; Cards; Games; Reading groups; Prayer groups; Movies; Dances/Social/Cultural gatherings.

Mayville

Fisher Convalescent Home
521 Ohmer Rd, M-24, Mayville, MI 48744
(517) 843-6185
Licensure Intermediate care. *Beds* ICF 38. *Certified* Medicaid.

McBain

Autumnwood of McBain
220 Hughston St, McBain, MI 49657
Licensure Skilled care; Home for aged. *Beds* SNF 75; Home for aged 10. *Certified* Medicaid; Medicare.

McMillan

Applewood Manor
Rte 3 Box 2347, McMillan, MI 49853
(906) 586-9641
Admin Peter D Costa. *Dir of Nursing* Grace Shepperd. *Medical Dir* Dr Neil Grossnickle.
Licensure Intermediate care. *Beds* ICF 30. *Private Pay Patients* 5%. *Certified* Medicaid.
Owner Proprietary corp.
Staff Physicians 1 (pt); RNs 1 (ft); LPNs 3 (ft), 3 (pt); Nurses' aides 8 (ft), 7 (pt); Activities coordinators 1 (ft); Dietitians 1 (pt); Podiatrists 1 (pt).

Menominee

Good Samaritan Home
501 2nd St, Menominee, MI 49858
(906) 863-9941
Admin Kathleen R Wall RN. *Dir of Nursing* Kathleen R Wall RN. *Medical Dir* Dr David Darcy.
Licensure Intermediate care; Home for aged; Alzheimer's care. *Beds* ICF 39; Home for aged 18. *Private Pay Patients* 12%. *Certified* Medicaid.
Owner Nonprofit corp.
Admissions Requirements Minimum age 16; Medical examination; Physician's request.
Staff RNs 2 (ft); Nurses' aides 18 (ft); Activities coordinators 1 (ft); Dietitians 1 (ft).
Facilities Dining room; Activities room; Crafts room; Barber/Beauty shop.
Activities Arts & crafts; Cards; Games; Reading groups; Prayer groups; Movies; Shopping trips; Dances/Social/Cultural gatherings; Intergenerational programs; Pet therapy; Reality orientation groups.

Midland

Midland Hospital Center
4005 Orchard Dr, Midland, MI 48670
(517) 839-3000
Admin C Fraser. *Dir of Nursing* J Wenglikowski RN. *Medical Dir* J Christopher Hough MD.
Licensure Skilled care. *Beds* SNF 287. *Certified* Medicaid; Medicare.
Owner Nonprofit corp.
Admissions Requirements Medical examination; Physician's request.
Staff Physicians 1 (pt); RNs 5 (ft), 6 (pt); LPNs 8 (ft), 9 (pt); Nurses' aides 7 (ft), 5 (pt); Physical therapists 3 (ft), 2 (pt);

Recreational therapists 1 (pt); Occupational therapists 6 (ft), 2 (pt); Speech therapists 3 (ft), 1 (pt); Dietitians 8 (pt); Podiatrists 1 (pt).
Facilities Dining room; Physical therapy room; Activities room; Chapel; Laundry room; Barber/Beauty shop.
Activities Arts & crafts; Cards; Games; Reading groups; Prayer groups; Movies; Dances/Social/Cultural gatherings; Cooking classes; Bowling; Fun & fitness classes.

Midland King's Daughter's Home
2410 Rodd St, Midland, MI 48640
Licensure Intermediate care; Home for aged. *Beds* ICF 31; Home for aged 30.

Provincial House—Midland
4900 Hedgewood, Midland, MI 48640
(517) 631-9670
Licensure Skilled care. *Beds* SNF 120. *Certified* Medicaid; Medicare.
Owner Proprietary corp (Beverly Enterprises).

Stratford Pines Nursing Home
2121 Rockwell Dr, Midland, MI 48640
Licensure Intermediate care; Home for aged. *Beds* ICF 64; Home for aged 40. *Certified* Medicaid.

Town & Country Nursing Home
3615 E Ashman St, Midland, MI 48640
(517) 631-0460
Medical Dir John E Vargas DO.
Licensure Skilled care. *Beds* SNF 153. *Certified* Medicaid; Medicare.
Admissions Requirements Medical examination; Physician's request.
Staff RNs 6 (ft), 1 (pt); LPNs 5 (ft), 8 (pt); Nurses' aides 17 (ft), 64 (pt); Activities coordinators 1 (ft); Dietitians 1 (pt).
Facilities Dining room; Activities room; Crafts room; Laundry room; Barber/Beauty shop.
Activities Arts & crafts; Cards; Games; Reading groups; Prayer groups; Shopping trips; Dances/Social/Cultural gatherings.

Milford

West Hickory Haven
3310 W Commerce Rd, Milford, MI 48042
(313) 685-1400
Admin Wanda Baad RN. *Dir of Nursing* Donna Beebe RN. *Medical Dir* William Kolbe DO.
Licensure Skilled care. *Beds* SNF 101. *Certified* Medicaid; Medicare.
Owner Proprietary corp.
Admissions Requirements Minimum age Geriatric; Medical examination.
Staff RNs 4 (ft), 4 (pt); LPNs 3 (ft), 14 (pt); Nurses' aides 10 (ft), 35 (pt); Physical therapists 1 (pt); Recreational therapists 1 (ft); Speech therapists 1 (pt); Activities coordinators 1 (ft), 1 (pt); Dietitians 1 (pt).
Facilities Dining room; Physical therapy room; Activities room; Barber/Beauty shop; Library.

Mio

White Oak Manor
PO Box 466, Mio, MI 48647
(517) 826-3983
Admin Peter Costa.
Medical Dir E Kauffman.
Licensure Intermediate care; Alzheimer's care. *Beds* ICF 28. *Certified* Medicaid.
Owner Privately owned.
Admissions Requirements Medical examination; Physician's request.
Staff Physicians 8 (pt); RNs 1 (ft); LPNs 5 (ft); Nurses' aides 12 (ft); Physical therapists 1 (pt); Speech therapists 1 (pt); Activities coordinators 1 (ft); Dietitians 4 (ft), 1 (pt); Ophthalmologists 1 (pt); Podiatrists 1 (pt).

Facilities Dining room; Activities room; Crafts room; Laundry room.
Activities Arts & crafts; Cards; Games; Reading groups; Prayer groups; Movies; Shopping trips; Dances/Social/Cultural gatherings.

Monroe

Beach Nursing Home
1215 N Telegraph Rd, Monroe, MI 48161
(313) 242-4848
Admin Joan Rasegan. *Dir of Nursing* Elaine Evans RN.
Licensure Skilled care; Alzheimer's care. *Beds* SNF 192. *Certified* Medicaid; Medicare.
Owner Proprietary corp (Beverly Enterprises).
Admissions Requirements Minimum age 18.
Staff RNs; LPNs; Nurses' aides; Activities coordinators 1 (ft), 2 (pt).
Facilities Dining room; Physical therapy room; Activities room; Barber/Beauty shop.
Activities Arts & crafts; Cards; Games; Reading groups; Prayer groups; Movies; Dances/Social/Cultural gatherings; Intergenerational groups; Adult education.

Frenchtown Convalescent Center
3250 N Monroe St, Monroe, MI 48161
(313) 243-5100, 243-5427 FAX
Admin Karen Palazzolo. *Dir of Nursing* Sandra Spangler. *Medical Dir* John Pasko MD.
Licensure Skilled care. *Beds* SNF 72; Swing beds SNF/basic/skilled swing beds 157. *Private Pay Patients* 17%. *Certified* Medicaid; Medicare.
Owner Proprietary corp (International Health Care Management).
Admissions Requirements Minimum age 16; Medical examination; Physician's request.
Staff Physicians 2 (pt); RNs 5 (ft), 2 (pt); LPNs 18 (ft), 6 (pt); Nurses' aides 60 (ft), 20 (pt); Physical therapists 3 (pt); Occupational therapists 1 (pt); Speech therapists 1 (pt); Activities coordinators 1 (ft); Dietitians 1 (pt); Ophthalmologists 1 (pt); Podiatrists 1 (pt).
Facilities Dining room; Physical therapy room; Activities room; Crafts room; Laundry room; Barber/Beauty shop.
Activities Arts & crafts; Cards; Games; Reading groups; Prayer groups; Movies; Shopping trips; Dances/Social/Cultural gatherings; Intergenerational programs; Pet therapy; Religious services.

Greenbrook Manor
481 Village Green Ln, Monroe, MI 48161
(517) 242-6282
Licensure Skilled care. *Beds* SNF 103. *Certified* Medicaid.

Lutheran Home
1236 S Monroe St, Monroe, MI 48161
(313) 241-9533
Admin Edward G Kurtz. *Dir of Nursing* Marie Schlump RN. *Medical Dir* John J Burroughs MD.
Licensure Skilled care; Intermediate care. *Beds* Swing beds SNF/ICF 102. *Certified* Medicaid; Medicare.
Owner Nonprofit corp.
Admissions Requirements Minimum age 62; Medical examination.
Affiliation Lutheran.
Facilities Dining room; Activities room; Chapel; Crafts room; Laundry room; Barber/Beauty shop.
Activities Arts & crafts; Cards; Games; Reading groups; Prayer groups; Movies; Shopping trips; Dances/Social/Cultural gatherings.

Monroe Convalescent Center
120 Maple Blvd, Monroe, MI 48161
(313) 242-5656

Admin Mary Jo Szandrowsky. *Dir of Nursing* Cathy Ledford RN. *Medical Dir* Dr Hyun Steward.
Licensure Intermediate care; Alzheimer's care. *Beds* ICF 70. *Certified* Medicaid.
Owner Proprietary corp.
Admissions Requirements Minimum age 16; Medical examination; Physician's request.
Staff Physicians 1 (pt); RNs 1 (ft), 2 (pt); LPNs 3 (ft), 6 (pt); Nurses' aides 13 (ft), 12 (pt); Physical therapists 1 (pt); Occupational therapists 1 (pt); Speech therapists 1 (pt); Activities coordinators 1 (ft); Dietitians 1 (pt); Ophthalmologists 1 (pt); Podiatrists 1 (pt); Dentists 1 (pt).
Facilities Dining room; Activities room; Crafts room; Laundry room; Barber/Beauty shop.
Activities Arts & crafts; Cards; Games; Reading groups; Prayer groups; Movies; Shopping trips.

Montrose

Mary James Nursing Home
13476 Duffield Rd, Montrose, MI 48457
(313) 639-6113
Medical Dir John T Block DO.
Licensure Skilled care. *Beds* SNF 63. *Certified* Medicaid; Medicare.
Admissions Requirements Minimum age 18; Medical examination; Physician's request.
Staff Physicians 2 (pt); RNs 3 (ft), 1 (pt); LPNs 1 (ft), 3 (pt); Nurses' aides 19 (ft), 17 (pt); Recreational therapists 1 (ft); Activities coordinators 1 (ft); Dietitians 1 (ft); Podiatrists 1 (pt).
Facilities Dining room.
Activities Arts & crafts; Cards; Games; Reading groups; Prayer groups; Movies; Shopping trips; Dances/Social/Cultural gatherings.

Montrose Nursing Home
9317 W Vienna Rd, Montrose, MI 48457
Admin Gale E Neff.
Licensure Intermediate care. *Beds* ICF 71. *Certified* Medicaid.
Owner Proprietary corp.
Admissions Requirements Minimum age 15; Medical examination.
Staff RNs 1 (ft), 1 (pt); LPNs 3 (ft), 5 (pt); Nurses' aides 20 (ft), 12 (pt); Activities coordinators 1 (ft); Dietitians 1 (pt).
Facilities Dining room; Activities room; Laundry room; Barber/Beauty shop.
Activities Arts & crafts; Cards; Games; Reading groups; Prayer groups; Movies; Shopping trips; Dances/Social/Cultural gatherings.

Mount Clemens

Martha T Berry Memorial Medical Care Facility
43533 Elizabeth Rd, Mount Clemens, MI 48043
(313) 469-5265
Admin Raymond D Pietrzak. *Dir of Nursing* Marjorie Kelley RN. *Medical Dir* Donald Dreyfuss DO.
Licensure Skilled care. *Beds* SNF 218. *Certified* Medicaid; Medicare.
Owner Publicly owned.
Admissions Requirements Medical examination; Physician's request.
Staff Physicians 2 (pt); RNs 17 (ft), 2 (pt); LPNs 14 (ft), 4 (pt); Nurses' aides 81 (ft), 13 (pt); Physical therapists 1 (ft); Recreational therapists 1 (ft); Occupational therapists 1 (pt); Speech therapists 1 (pt); Activities coordinators 1 (pt); Dietitians 1 (pt); Podiatrists 1 (pt).
Facilities Dining room; Physical therapy room; Activities room; Crafts room; Laundry room; Library.

Activities Arts & crafts; Cards; Games; Reading groups; Prayer groups; Movies; Shopping trips; Dances/Social/Cultural gatherings; Community parties; Musical groups; Basic adult education; Horticultural therapy; Exercise program; One-to-one contacts; Patient council; Picnics; Barbeques; Monthly newspaper & calendar.

Church of Christ Care Center
23575 Fifteen Mile Rd, Mount Clemens, MI 48043
(313) 791-2470
Admin Louis D Elliott.
Medical Dir Dr Stanley Pesta DO.
Licensure Intermediate care; Retirement. *Beds* ICF 130. *Certified* Medicaid.
Owner Nonprofit corp.
Admissions Requirements Physician's request.
Staff Physicians 1 (pt); RNs 6 (ft), 4 (pt); LPNs 7 (ft), 5 (pt); Nurses' aides 40 (ft), 30 (pt); Activities coordinators 1 (ft); Dietitians 1 (pt).
Affiliation Church of Christ.
Facilities Dining room; Activities room; Laundry room; Barber/Beauty shop.
Activities Arts & crafts; Cards; Games; Reading groups; Prayer groups; Movies.

Clinton-Aire Nursing Center
17001 Seventeen Mile Rd, Mount Clemens, MI 48044
(313) 286-7100
Medical Dir Sonjai Poonpanij MD.
Licensure Skilled care. *Beds* SNF 150. *Certified* Medicaid; Medicare.
Owner Proprietary corp (International Healthcare Management).
Admissions Requirements Minimum age 15.
Staff RNs 3 (ft), 6 (pt); LPNs 3 (ft), 11 (pt); Nurses' aides 37 (ft), 19 (pt); Physical therapists 1 (pt); Recreational therapists 1 (ft); Occupational therapists 1 (pt); Speech therapists 1 (pt); Activities coordinators 1 (ft); Dietitians 1 (ft); Ophthalmologists 1 (pt); Podiatrists 1 (pt); Dentists 1 (pt).
Facilities Dining room; Physical therapy room; Activities room; Chapel; Laundry room; Barber/Beauty shop.
Activities Arts & crafts; Cards; Games; Reading groups; Prayer groups; Movies; Shopping trips.

St Joseph Living Care Center
37700 Harper, Mount Clemens, MI 48043
(313) 468-0827
Medical Dir M Shiffman MD.
Licensure Intermediate care. *Beds* ICF 264. *Certified* Medicaid.
Owner Proprietary corp (International Healthcare Management).
Admissions Requirements Minimum age 17; Medical examination; Physician's request.
Staff Physicians 4 (pt); RNs 16 (ft), 4 (pt); LPNs 10 (ft), 3 (pt); Nurses' aides 120 (ft), 5 (pt); Physical therapists 1 (ft); Recreational therapists 1 (ft); Occupational therapists 1 (ft); Speech therapists 1 (pt); Activities coordinators 1 (ft); Dietitians 1 (pt); Ophthalmologists 2 (pt); Podiatrists 1 (pt); Dentists 3 (pt).
Facilities Dining room; Physical therapy room; Activities room; Chapel; Crafts room; Laundry room; Barber/Beauty shop; Library.
Activities Arts & crafts; Cards; Games; Reading groups; Prayer groups; Movies; Shopping trips; Dances/Social/Cultural gatherings.

Mount Pleasant

Isabella County Medical Care Facility
1222 North Dr, Mount Pleasant, MI 48858
(517) 772-1957, 773-4319 FAX
Admin John P Verwey. *Dir of Nursing* Lois S Rank RN. *Medical Dir* Dan C Dean DO.

Licensure Skilled care. *Beds* SNF 80. *Private Pay Patients* 10%. *Certified* Medicaid; Medicare.
Owner Publicly owned.
Admissions Requirements Minimum age 14; Physician's request.
Staff Physicians 30 (pt); RNs 8 (ft), 6 (pt); LPNs 6 (ft), 5 (pt); Nurses' aides 30 (ft), 14 (pt); Physical therapists 4 (ft); Occupational therapists 1 (ft); Speech therapists 1 (pt); Activities coordinators 1 (ft); Dietitians 1 (pt).
Facilities Dining room; Physical therapy room; Activities room; Chapel; Crafts room; Laundry room; Barber/Beauty shop.
Activities Arts & crafts; Cards; Games; Reading groups; Prayer groups; Movies; Shopping trips; Dances/Social/Cultural gatherings; Pet therapy.

Mt Pleasant Total Living Center
1524 Portabella Rd, Mount Pleasant, MI 48858
(517) 772-2967
Admin Rosemary Shuette. *Dir of Nursing* Beverly Curtiss RN. *Medical Dir* Dan Radawski MD.
Licensure Skilled care. *Beds* SNF 117. *Certified* Medicaid; Medicare.
Owner Proprietary corp (Beverly Enterprises).
Staff Physicians 5 (ft); RNs 3 (ft), 1 (pt); Nurses' aides 50 (ft), 10 (pt); Physical therapists 1 (ft); Occupational therapists 1 (pt); Speech therapists 1 (pt); Activities coordinators 1 (ft), 1 (pt); Dietitians 1 (ft); Ophthalmologists 1 (pt); Podiatrists 1 (pt); Dentists 1 (pt).
Facilities Dining room; Physical therapy room; Activities room; Laundry room; Barber/Beauty shop.
Activities Arts & crafts; Cards; Games; Reading groups; Prayer groups; Movies; Shopping trips; Dances/Social/Cultural gatherings.

Pleasant Manor
400 S Crapo St, Mount Pleasant, MI 48858
(517) 773-5918
Admin Sandra Caul. *Dir of Nursing* Shirley Schafer RN. *Medical Dir* Leo Wickert MD.
Licensure Skilled care; Alzheimer's care. *Beds* SNF 112. *Certified* Medicaid; Medicare.
Owner Proprietary corp.
Admissions Requirements Minimum age 15; Medical examination; Physician's request.
Staff RNs 4 (ft), 5 (pt); LPNs 6 (ft), 1 (pt); Physical therapists 1 (pt); Recreational therapists 1 (pt); Occupational therapists 1 (pt); Speech therapists 1 (pt); Activities coordinators 1 (ft); Dietitians 1 (ft), 1 (pt); Ophthalmologists 1 (pt); Podiatrists 1 (pt); Dentists 1 (pt).
Facilities Dining room; Physical therapy room; Activities room; Barber/Beauty shop; Library.
Activities Arts & crafts; Cards; Games; Reading groups; Prayer groups; Movies; Shopping trips; Dances/Social/Cultural gatherings; Exercise class; Stroke club; Monthly special event; Outings each week; Art study classes; Lunch outings.

Munising

Superior Health Haven
815 W Munising Ave, Munising, MI 49862
(906) 387-2096
Admin Barbara Moore.
Licensure Home for aged. *Beds* Home for aged 22. *Private Pay Patients* 21%. *Certified* Medicaid.
Owner Proprietary corp.
Admissions Requirements Medical examination.
Staff Nurses' aides 7 (ft), 4 (pt); Occupational therapists 1 (pt).
Languages Finnish.

Facilities Dining room; Activities room; Laundry room; Barber/Beauty shop.
Activities Cards; Games; Prayer groups; Shopping trips; Dances/Social/Cultural gatherings; Pet therapy.

Superior Shores Nursing Center
300 W City Park Dr, Munising, MI 49862
(906) 387-2273
Admin Denis C Harbath. *Dir of Nursing* LaVonne "Bonnie" Dietsche. *Medical Dir* Barbara E Lyons MD PC.
Licensure Skilled care; Intermediate care. *Beds* Swing beds SNF/ICF 106. *Private Pay Patients* 8%. *Certified* Medicaid; Medicare.
Owner Proprietary corp (Health Concepts Corp).
Admissions Requirements Minimum age 18; Physician's request.
Staff RNs 2 (ft), 3 (pt); LPNs 1 (ft), 12 (pt); Nurses' aides 23 (ft), 18 (pt); Physical therapists 1 (pt); Reality therapists 1 (ft); Speech therapists 1 (ft); Activities coordinators 1 (ft); Dietitians 1 (pt).
Facilities Dining room; Physical therapy room; Activities room; Laundry room; Barber/Beauty shop; Lounge.
Activities Arts & crafts; Cards; Games; Reading groups; Prayer groups; Movies; Shopping trips; Dances/Social/Cultural gatherings; Pet therapy.

Muskegon

Brookhaven Medical Care Facility
1890 Apple Ave, Muskegon, MI 49442
(616) 773-9146
Admin Bertram G Hanson. *Dir of Nursing* Wilma Overweg RN. *Medical Dir* Erwin Grasman MD.
Licensure Skilled care. *Beds* SNF 218. *Certified* Medicaid; Medicare.
Owner Publicly owned.
Admissions Requirements Minimum age 18; Physician's request.
Staff Physicians 2 (pt); RNs 9 (ft); LPNs 20 (ft), 16 (pt); Nurses' aides 48 (ft), 68 (pt); Physical therapists 1 (pt); Occupational therapists 1 (ft); Speech therapists 1 (pt); Activities coordinators 1 (ft); Dietitians 1 (ft); Podiatrists 1 (pt).
Facilities Dining room; Physical therapy room; Activities room; Chapel; Crafts room; Laundry room; Barber/Beauty shop; Large enclosed courtyard.
Activities Arts & crafts; Cards; Games; Reading groups; Prayer groups; Movies; Shopping trips; Dances/Social/Cultural gatherings.

Christian Convalescent Home
1275 Kenneth Ave, Muskegon, MI 49442
(616) 722-7165
Licensure Intermediate care. *Beds* ICF 49. *Certified* Medicaid.

Christian Home for the Aged
1691 Peck St, Muskegon, MI 49441
Licensure Home for aged. *Beds* Home for aged 50.

DeBoer Nursing Home
1684 Vulcan St, Muskegon, MI 49442
(616) 777-2511
Admin Samuel T DeBoer. *Dir of Nursing* Robert G Willis RN. *Medical Dir* Dale W Heeres MD.
Licensure Skilled care; Retirement. *Beds* SNF 90. *Certified* Medicaid; Medicare.
Owner Proprietary corp.
Admissions Requirements Medical examination; Physician's request.
Staff Physicians; RNs; LPNs; Nurses' aides; Physical therapists; Recreational therapists; Occupational therapists; Speech therapists; Activities coordinators; Dietitians; Ophthalmologists.

Facilities Dining room; Physical therapy room; Activities room; Chapel; Crafts room; Laundry room; Barber/Beauty shop; Library.
Activities Arts & crafts; Cards; Games; Reading groups; Prayer groups; Movies; Shopping trips.

Hermitage
1776 Vulcan St, Muskegon, MI 49442
Licensure Home for aged. *Beds* Home for aged 80.

Knollview Manor
1061 W Hackley Ave, Muskegon, MI 49441
(616) 755-2255
Licensure Skilled care. *Beds* SNF 107. *Certified* Medicaid; Medicare.
Owner Proprietary corp (Health Care and Retirement Corp).

Mercy Services for Aging—University Park
570 S Harvey St, Muskegon, MI 49442
(616) 773-9121
Licensure Skilled care. *Beds* SNF 99. *Private Pay Patients* 10%. *Certified* Medicaid; Medicare.
Owner Nonprofit organization/foundation (Mercy Services for Aging).
Admissions Requirements Minimum age 15; Medical examination; Physician's request.
Facilities Dining room; Physical therapy room; Activities room; Laundry room; Barber/Beauty shop; Ventilator unit.
Activities Arts & crafts; Cards; Games; Reading groups; Prayer groups; Movies; Intergenerational programs.

Muskegon Correctional Facility
2400 S Sheridan, Muskegon, MI 49442
Admin Diane Haynor.
Medical Dir Richard G Huff DO.
Licensure Skilled care. *Beds* 7.
Owner Publicly owned.
Admissions Requirements Minimum age 18; Males only; Medical examination; Physician's request.
Staff Physicians 1 (pt); RNs 8 (ft); Dietitians 1 (ft); Dentists 1 (ft); Physician's aides 1 (ft).
Facilities Physical therapy room; Activities room; Crafts room; Laundry room; Barber/Beauty shop; Library.
Activities Games; Movies.

Roosevelt Park Nursing Centre Inc
1300 Broadway, Muskegon, MI 49441
(616) 755-2221
Licensure Intermediate care. *Beds* ICF 69. *Certified* Medicaid.

Sherman Oaks Care Center
1380 E Sherman Blvd, Muskegon, MI 49444
(616) 733-2578
Admin Elsie Plank. *Dir of Nursing* Kay Houston. *Medical Dir* Gregory Sobczak MD.
Licensure Skilled care. *Beds* SNF 98. *Private Pay Patients* 5%. *Certified* Medicaid; Medicare.
Owner Proprietary corp (Beverly Enterprises).
Admissions Requirements Minimum age 18.
Staff RNs 2 (ft), 2 (pt); LPNs 5 (ft), 6 (pt); Nurses' aides 24 (ft), 24 (pt); Recreational therapists 1 (ft); Dietitians 1 (ft).
Facilities Dining room; Physical therapy room; Activities room; Barber/Beauty shop.
Activities Arts & crafts; Cards; Games; Reading groups; Prayer groups; Movies; Pet therapy.

Muskegon Heights

Park Manor Care Center
2333 Jarman St, Muskegon Heights, MI 49444
(616) 733-9423
Admin Robert A Van Rhee. *Dir of Nursing* Benjamin Bailey RN. *Medical Dir* Dr Craig Weiss.

Licensure Intermediate care. *Beds* ICF 27.
Private Pay Patients 10%. *Certified*
Medicaid.
Owner Proprietary corp (Manor Care).
Admissions Requirements Medical
examination; Physician's request.
Staff RNs 1 (ft); LPNs 3 (ft), 2 (pt); Nurses'
aides 5 (ft), 7 (pt); Activities coordinators 1
(ft); Dietitians 1 (ft).
Facilities Dining room; Activities room;
Crafts room; Laundry room.
Activities Arts & crafts; Games; Reading
groups; Prayer groups; Movies; Dances/
Social/Cultural gatherings; Intergenerational
programs.

New Baltimore

Presbyterian Village East
33875 Kiely Dr, New Baltimore, MI 48047
(313) 725-6030
Admin David M Miller.
Licensure Home for aged; Independent living.
Beds Home for aged 77; Independent living
apartments 52. *Private Pay Patients* 98%.
Owner Nonprofit corp (Presbyterian Village of
Detroit Inc).
Admissions Requirements Minimum age 65;
Medical examination.
Staff RNs 1 (pt); LPNs 1 (pt); Activities
coordinators 1 (ft); Dietitians 1 (pt).
Languages Polish, German.
Affiliation Presbyterian.
Facilities Dining room; Activities room;
Crafts room; Laundry room; Barber/Beauty
shop; Library; Private rooms and bath.
Activities Arts & crafts; Cards; Games;
Reading groups; Prayer groups; Movies;
Shopping trips; Dances/Social/Cultural
gatherings; Intergenerational programs;
Transportation, Parties.

Newberry

Helen Newberry Joy Hospital Annex
502 W Harrie St, Newberry, MI 49868
(906) 293-5181
Admin Tom Hicks.
Medical Dir Theresa Shiffutt.
Licensure Skilled care; Intermediate care. *Beds*
Swing beds SNF/ICF 69. *Certified* Medicaid;
Medicare.
Owner Publicly owned.
Staff RNs 1 (ft); LPNs 6 (ft), 4 (pt); Nurses'
aides 20 (ft), 10 (pt); Physical therapists 1
(ft); Recreational therapists 1 (ft);
Occupational therapists 1 (pt); Speech
therapists 1 (pt); Dietitians 1 (pt);
Ophthalmologists 1 (pt); Podiatrists 1 (pt);
Dentists 1 (pt).
Activities Arts & crafts; Cards; Games;
Reading groups; Prayer groups; Movies;
Shopping trips; Dances/Social/Cultural
gatherings.

Niles

Riveridge Manor Inc
1333 Wells St, Niles, MI 49120
(616) 684-1111
Admin Pauline M Westman, RN. *Dir of
Nursing* Helen Rhodes, RN.
Licensure Intermediate care; Home for aged.
Beds ICF 84; Home for aged 10. *Certified*
Medicaid.
Owner Proprietary corp.
Admissions Requirements Medical
examination; Physician's request.
Staff RNs 1 (ft); LPNs 5 (ft), 2 (pt); Nurses'
aides 46 (ft), 3 (pt); Activities coordinators 1
(ft).
Affiliation Seventh-Day Adventist.
Facilities Dining room; Activities room;
Laundry room; Barber/Beauty shop.
Activities Arts & crafts; Games; Reading
groups; Prayer groups; Movies.

Silverbrook Manor
911 S 3rd St, Niles, MI 49120
(616) 684-4320
Licensure Skilled care. *Beds* SNF 100.
Certified Medicaid; Medicare.

Woodfield Manor Inc
1211 State Line Rd, Niles, MI 49120
(616) 684-2810
Admin Phillip Stephan. *Dir of Nursing* Curt
Kause. *Medical Dir* James Speers.
Licensure Skilled care. *Beds* SNF 89. *Private
Pay Patients* 20%. *Certified* Medicaid;
Medicare.
Owner Proprietary corp.
Admissions Requirements Minimum age 15;
Medical examination; Physician's request.
Staff Physicians (consultant); RNs 4 (ft), 3
(pt); LPNs 2 (ft), 2 (pt); Nurses' aides 27
(ft); Physical therapists 1 (pt); Activities
coordinators 1 (ft); Dietitians 1 (ft);
Podiatrists 1 (pt).
Facilities Dining room; Activities room;
Crafts room; Laundry room; Barber/Beauty
shop.
Activities Arts & crafts; Cards; Games; Prayer
groups; Movies; Shopping trips; Dances/
Social/Cultural gatherings.

North Muskegon

Hillcrest Nursing Centre
695 Mitzi Dr, North Muskegon, MI 49445
(616) 744-1641
Licensure Intermediate care. *Beds* ICF 63.
Certified Medicaid.

Northcrest Living Centre
2650 Ruddiman St, North Muskegon, MI
49445
Licensure Home for aged. *Beds* Home for
aged 86.

Northport

Leelanau Memorial Hospital
S High St, Northport, MI 49670
(616) 386-5101
Admin Kathleen Putnam. *Dir of Nursing*
Kathy Garthern MSN. *Medical Dir* J M
Wood MD.
Licensure Skilled care. *Beds* SNF 94. *Certified*
Medicaid; Medicare.
Owner Nonprofit organization/foundation.
Staff Physicians 1 (pt); RNs 2 (ft), 2 (pt);
LPNs 7 (ft), 3 (pt); Nurses' aides 18 (ft), 6
(pt); Physical therapists 1 (pt); Activities
coordinators 1 (ft), 1 (pt); Dietitians 1 (pt).

Northville

Star Manor of Northville
520 W Main St, Northville, MI 48167
(313) 349-4290
Admin Donald J Nowka. *Dir of Nursing*
Constance J Nowka RN.
Licensure Intermediate care; Alzheimer's care.
Beds ICF 37. *Certified* Medicaid.
Owner Proprietary corp.
Admissions Requirements Minimum age 60;
Medical examination; Physician's request.
Staff Physicians 1 (pt); RNs 1 (ft); LPNs 3
(ft), 3 (pt); Nurses' aides 12 (ft); Activities
coordinators 1 (ft); Dietitians 1 (pt); Social
worker 1 (pt).
Facilities Dining room; Activities room;
Crafts room; Laundry room; Barber/Beauty
shop.
Activities Arts & crafts; Cards; Games;
Reading groups; Prayer groups; Movies;
Dances/Social/Cultural gatherings.

Novi

Novi Care Center
24500 Meadowbrook Rd, Novi, MI 48050
(313) 447-2000
Admin James L Tiffin. *Dir of Nursing* Kathy
Bonfiglio.
Licensure Intermediate care. *Beds* ICF 144.
Certified Medicaid.
Owner Proprietary corp (Beverly Enterprises).
Admissions Requirements Minimum age 15;
Medical examination.
Staff Physicians; RNs; LPNs; Nurses' aides;
Physical therapists; Recreational therapists;
Speech therapists; Dietitians;
Ophthalmologists; Podiatrists.
Facilities Dining room; Physical therapy
room; Activities room; Crafts room; Laundry
room; Barber/Beauty shop.
Activities Arts & crafts; Cards; Prayer groups;
Movies; Shopping trips.

Whitehall Convalescent Home
43455 W Ten Mile Rd, Novi, MI 48050
(313) 349-2200
Medical Dir R M Atchison MD.
Licensure Intermediate care. *Beds* ICF 82.
Certified Medicaid.
Admissions Requirements Minimum age 18;
Medical examination; Physician's request.
Staff RNs 4 (ft), 2 (pt); LPNs 2 (ft), 4 (pt);
Nurses' aides 50 (ft), 6 (pt); Recreational
therapists 1 (ft); Activities coordinators 1
(ft); Dietitians 1 (pt).
Affiliation Royal Order of Moose.
Facilities Dining room; Activities room;
Crafts room; Laundry room; Barber/Beauty
shop; Library.
Activities Arts & crafts; Cards; Games;
Reading groups; Prayer groups; Movies.

Whitehall Home
40875 Grand River, Novi, MI 48050
Licensure Home for aged. *Beds* Home for
aged 31.

Okemos

Ingham County Medical Care Facility
3860 Dobie Rd, Okemos, MI 48864
(517) 349-1050
Admin D Vande Vusse.
Medical Dir John Strandmark MD.
Licensure Skilled care. *Beds* SNF 204.
Certified Medicaid; Medicare.
Admissions Requirements Minimum age 12;
Medical examination; Physician's request.
Staff Physicians 3 (pt); RNs 15 (ft); LPNs 20
(ft); Nurses' aides 145 (ft); Physical
therapists 1 (pt); Recreational therapists 2
(ft), 1 (pt); Occupational therapists 1 (pt);
Speech therapists 3 (pt); Activities
coordinators 1 (ft); Dietitians 1 (ft);
Ophthalmologists 1 (pt); Podiatrists 1 (pt);
Dentists 1 (pt).
Facilities Dining room; Physical therapy
room; Activities room; Crafts room; Laundry
room; Barber/Beauty shop; Library.
Activities Arts & crafts; Cards; Games;
Reading groups; Prayer groups; Movies;
Shopping trips; Dances/Social/Cultural
gatherings.

Ontonagon

Maple Manor Nursing Center
102 2nd St, Ontonagon, MI 49953
Licensure Intermediate care. *Beds* ICF 64.
Certified Medicaid.

Ontonagon Memorial
601 S 7th St, Ontonagon, MI 49953
(906) 884-4134
Admin Jamos Richards. *Dir of Nursing*
Patricia A Webber. *Medical Dir* J P Strong
MD.

Licensure Skilled care; Acute care. *Beds* SNF
46; Acute care. *Private Pay Patients* 10%.
Certified Medicaid; Medicare.
Owner Publicly owned.
Admissions Requirements Minimum age
Adults; Medical examination; Physician's
request.
Staff Physicians 3 (pt); RNs 2 (ft), 4 (pt);
LPNs 1 (ft), 3 (pt); Nurses' aides 7 (ft), 18
(pt); Physical therapists 1 (pt); Activities
coordinators 1 (pt); Dietitians 1 (pt).
Languages Finnish.
Facilities Dining room; Physical therapy
room; Activities room; Crafts room; Laundry
room; Barber/Beauty shop.
Activities Arts & crafts; Games; Reading
groups; Prayer groups.

Ovid

Ovid Convalescent Manor
9480 M 21 W, Ovid, MI 48866
(517) 834-2228
Licensure Intermediate care. *Beds* ICF 63.
Certified Medicaid.

Owosso

Memorial Hospital Long-Term Care Unit
826 W King St, Owosso, MI 48867
Licensure Skilled care. *Beds* SNF 194.
Certified Medicaid; Medicare.

Palmer

Palmer Home for the Aged
PO Box 67, Isabella & M35, Palmer, MI
49871
Licensure Home for aged. *Beds* Home for
aged 65.

Perrinton

Fulton Medical Care Center
4735 Ranger Rd, Perrinton, MI 48871
Licensure Skilled care. *Beds* SNF 50. *Certified*
Medicaid; Medicare.

Petoskey

Bortz Health Care of Petoskey
1500 Spring St, Petoskey, MI 49770
(616) 347-5500
Admin Ray W Persall. *Dir of Nursing* Regina
Shafer RN. *Medical Dir* Bradley Haas MD.
Licensure Skilled care. *Beds* SNF 120.
Certified Medicaid; Medicare.
Owner Proprietary corp.
Admissions Requirements Minimum age 15;
Medical examination; Physician's request.
Staff RNs 6 (ft), 2 (pt); LPNs 7 (ft), 4 (pt);
Nurses' aides 28 (ft), 11 (pt); Activities
coordinators 1 (ft), 1 (pt).
Languages Tagalog.
Facilities Dining room; Physical therapy
room; Activities room; Laundry room;
Barber/Beauty shop.
Activities Games; Reading groups; Prayer
groups; Movies; Shopping trips; Dances/
Social/Cultural gatherings.

Pigeon

Scheurer Hospital—Long-Term Care Unit
170 N Caseville Rd, Pigeon, MI 48755
(517) 453-3223
Licensure Skilled care; Intermediate care. *Beds*
Swing beds SNF/ICF 19. *Certified* Medicaid;
Medicare.

Plainwell

Bridgewood Manor
PO Box 385, 320 Brigham St, Plainwell, MI
49080
(616) 685-5390
Licensure Skilled care. *Beds* SNF 124.
Certified Medicaid; Medicare.

Plainwell Pines Nursing Centre
3260 E "B" Ave, Plainwell, MI 49080
(616) 349-6649, 349-2520 FAX
Admin Gwendolyn E Parker. *Dir of Nursing*
Arlene A Dickenson RN. *Medical Dir*
Richard Kik DO.
Licensure Intermediate care. *Beds* ICF 58.
Private Pay Patients 10%. *Certified*
Medicaid.
Owner Privately owned.
Admissions Requirements Minimum age 21;
Medical examination; Physician's request.
Staff RNs 2 (ft), 2 (pt); LPNs 4 (ft), 2 (pt);
Nurses' aides 26 (pt); Activities coordinators
1 (pt); Dietitians 1 (ft).
Facilities Dining room; Activities room;
Laundry room.
Activities Arts & crafts; Cards; Games;
Reading groups; Prayer groups; Movies;
Shopping trips; Dances/Social/Cultural
gatherings; Intergenerational programs; Pet
therapy.

Plymouth

Plymouth Court
105 Haggerty Rd, Plymouth, MI 48170
(313) 455-0510
Admin Ralph Corvino. *Dir of Nursing*
Kathleen Hervian. *Medical Dir* Louis
Schwartz MD.
Licensure Skilled care; Alzheimer's care. *Beds*
SNF 129. *Certified* Medicare.
Owner Proprietary corp (Health Care and
Retirement Corp).
Admissions Requirements Minimum age 18;
Physician's request.

Plymouth Inn
205 Haggerty Rd, Plymouth, MI 48170
Licensure Home for aged. *Beds* Home for
aged 100.

West Trail Nursing Home
395 W Ann Arbor Trail, Plymouth, MI 48170
(313) 453-3983
Medical Dir Joseph Gadbaw MD.
Licensure Intermediate care. *Beds* ICF 46.
Certified Medicaid.
Admissions Requirements Medical
examination; Physician's request.
Staff Physicians 1 (pt); RNs 2 (ft); LPNs 3
(ft); Nurses' aides 14 (ft); Recreational
therapists 1 (ft); Activities coordinators 1
(ft); Dietitians 1 (ft); Podiatrists 1 (pt);
Dentists 1 (pt).
Facilities Dining room; Activities room;
Laundry room; Barber/Beauty shop; Library.
Activities Arts & crafts; Cards; Games;
Reading groups; Prayer groups; Movies;
Shopping trips; Dances/Social/Cultural
gatherings.

Pontiac

Bortz Health Care of Oakland
1255 W Silverbell, Pontiac, MI 48057
(313) 391-0900, 391-4019 FAX
Admin William T Beardsley. *Dir of Nursing*
Teri Sage RN. *Medical Dir* Timothy
Hramits MD.
Licensure Skilled care; Intermediate care;
Retirement. *Beds* SNF 49; ICF 57;
Retirement 12. *Private Pay Patients* 25%.
Certified Medicaid; Medicare.
Owner Privately owned (D J Bortz Jr).
Admissions Requirements Medical
examination; Physician's request.

Staff Physicians 2 (pt); RNs 3 (ft); LPNs 8
(ft), 3 (pt); Nurses' aides 22 (ft), 11 (pt);
Physical therapists; Activities coordinators 1
(ft), 1 (pt); Dietitians 1 (pt).
Facilities Dining room; Physical therapy
room; Activities room; Laundry room;
Barber/Beauty shop.
Activities Arts & crafts; Cards; Games;
Reading groups; Prayer groups; Movies;
Shopping trips; Dances/Social/Cultural
gatherings; Intergenerational programs; Pet
therapy; Cooking class; Exercise.

Evergreen Residential Care Home
54 Seneca, Pontiac, MI 48015
Licensure Home for aged. *Beds* Home for
aged 33.

Grovecrest Home for the Aged
121 Prall St, Pontiac, MI 48053
(313) 334-4732
Licensure Home for aged. *Beds* Home for
aged 57.

Lourdes Inc
2300 Watkins Lake Rd, Pontiac, MI 48054
(313) 674-2241
Admin Sr Frances Mary Kernasovich OP. *Dir
of Nursing* Elaine L Sawchuk RN BSN.
Medical Dir W P Richards MD.
Licensure Skilled care; Intermediate care. *Beds*
Swing beds SNF/ICF 108. *Private Pay
Patients* 75%. *Certified* Medicaid; Medicare.
Owner Nonprofit organization/foundation.
Admissions Requirements Minimum age 65;
Medical examination; Physician's request.
Staff Physicians 4 (pt); RNs 4 (ft), 8 (pt);
LPNs 6 (ft), 6 (pt); Nurses' aides 31 (ft), 15
(pt); Physical therapists 1 (pt); Activities
coordinators 1 (ft), 2 (pt); Dietitians 1 (ft);
Podiatrists 1 (pt); Dentists 1 (pt).
Affiliation Roman Catholic.
Facilities Dining room; Physical therapy
room; Activities room; Chapel; Crafts room;
Laundry room; Barber/Beauty shop; Library.
Activities Arts & crafts; Cards; Games;
Reading groups; Prayer groups; Movies;
Intergenerational programs; Pet therapy.

Oakland County Medical Care Facility
2200 N Telegraph Rd, Pontiac, MI 48053
(313) 858-1415
Admin James A Eddy.
Medical Dir Antonio Nucum MD.
Licensure Skilled care. *Beds* SNF 120.
Certified Medicaid; Medicare.
Owner Publicly owned.
Admissions Requirements Physician's request.
Staff Physicians 1 (ft), 1 (pt); RNs 9 (ft), 4
(pt); LPNs 6 (ft), 8 (pt); Nurses' aides 25
(ft), 40 (pt); Physical therapists 2 (pt);
Occupational therapists 1 (pt); Speech
therapists 1 (pt); Activities coordinators 1
(ft); Dietitians 2 (pt); Ophthalmologists 1
(pt); Podiatrists 1 (pt).
Facilities Dining room; Physical therapy
room; Activities room; Chapel; Crafts room;
Laundry room; Barber/Beauty shop; Library.
Activities Arts & crafts; Cards; Games;
Reading groups; Prayer groups; Movies;
Shopping trips; Dances/Social/Cultural
gatherings.

Pontiac Nursing Center
532 Orchard Lake Ave, Pontiac, MI 48053
(313) 338-7151
Admin Morsy F Morsy Sr Adm; Marianne
Mikkelsen, Barbara Lawson Asst Adm. *Dir
of Nursing* Marie Bell RN.
Licensure Skilled care. *Beds* SNF 360.
Certified Medicaid; Medicare.
Owner Proprietary corp (Beverly Enterprises).
Admissions Requirements Minimum age 15.
Staff Physicians 10 (pt); RNs 5 (ft); LPNs 22
(ft), 11 (pt); Nurses' aides 78 (ft), 5 (pt);
Physical therapists 1 (ft); Activities
coordinators 1 (ft); Dietitians 1 (ft).
Languages Arabic, Spanish, Tagalog.

Port Huron

Evangelical Home—Port Huron
5635 Lakeshore Rd, Port Huron, MI 48060
(313) 385-7447
Admin Katherine Schlichting RNC. *Dir of Nursing* Cathy Kuberski RNC. *Medical Dir* Douglas A Krause MD.
Licensure Skilled care; Alzheimer's care. *Beds* SNF 182; Alzheimer's care unit 12. *Certified* Medicaid; Medicare.
Owner Nonprofit organization/foundation (Evangelical Homes of Michigan).
Admissions Requirements Minimum age 18; Medical examination; Physician's request.
Staff RNs 10 (ft); LPNs 22 (ft); Nurses' aides 78 (ft); Physical therapists (consultant); Occupational therapists (consultant); Speech therapists (consultant); Activities coordinators 1 (ft), 1 (pt); Dietitians 2 (ft); Ophthalmologists (consultant); Podiatrists (consultant); Audiologists (consultant).
Affiliation United Church of Christ.
Facilities Dining room; Physical therapy room; Activities room; Crafts room; Laundry room; Barber/Beauty shop.
Activities Arts & crafts; Cards; Games; Reading groups; Prayer groups; Movies; Shopping trips; Dances/Social/Cultural gatherings; Pet therapy; Baking; Cooking.

Marwood Manor Nursing Home
1300 Beard, Port Huron, MI 48060
(313) 385-4594, 982-5369 FAX
Admin Peter Cangemi. *Dir of Nursing* Sherry Seeley RNC. *Medical Dir* Frederick E Ludwig MD.
Licensure Skilled care; Intermediate care; Alzheimer's care. *Beds* Swing beds SNF/ICF 252. *Private Pay Patients* 20%. *Certified* Medicaid; Medicare.
Owner Nonprofit organization/foundation.
Admissions Requirements Minimum age 17; Medical examination; Physician's request.
Staff RNs 5 (ft), 8 (pt); LPNs 17 (ft), 12 (pt); Nurses' aides 72 (ft), 30 (pt); Physical therapists (consultant); Occupational therapists 1 (pt); Speech therapists 1 (pt); Activities coordinators 2 (ft), 1 (pt); Dietitians 1 (pt).
Facilities Dining room; Physical therapy room; Activities room; Crafts room; Laundry room; Barber/Beauty shop; Library; Gift shop.
Activities Arts & crafts; Cards; Games; Prayer groups; Movies; Live bands; Cookouts; Christmas teas; Popcorn parties; Ice cream socials; Bingo; Wheelchair gardening; Resident council; Family council; Volunteer auxiliary.

Sanborn Gratiot Memorial Home
2732 Cherry St, Port Huron, MI 48060
Licensure Home for aged. *Beds* Home for aged 40.

Powers

Pinecrest Medical Care Facility
Box 603, Powers, MI 49874-0603
(906) 497-5244, 497-5005 FAX
Admin Gerald A Betters. *Dir of Nursing* Darlene Smith RN. *Medical Dir* Catherine Williams MD.
Licensure Skilled care. *Beds* SNF 160. *Certified* Medicaid; Medicare.
Owner Publicly owned.

Admissions Requirements Minimum age 14.
Staff Physicians 1 (ft); RNs 3 (ft), 3 (pt); LPNs 14 (ft), 12 (pt); Nurses' aides 42 (ft), 32 (pt); Physical therapists 1 (ft); Recreational therapists 1 (ft); Speech therapists 1 (ft); Dietitians 1 (ft); Podiatrists (contracted); Audiologists (contracted).
Facilities Dining room; Physical therapy room; Activities room; Chapel; Crafts room; Laundry room; Barber/Beauty shop.
Activities Arts & crafts; Cards; Games; Reading groups; Prayer groups; Movies; Shopping trips; Dances/Social/Cultural gatherings; Intergenerational programs; Pet therapy.

Redford

Cambridge West
18633 Beech Daly, Redford, MI 48240
(313) 255-1010, 255-5792 FAX
Admin Betty Foster-Powell. *Dir of Nursing* Christine Considine RN. *Medical Dir* David Rosenberg DO.
Licensure Skilled care. *Beds* SNF 121. *Private Pay Patients* 25%. *Certified* Medicaid; Medicare.
Owner Proprietary corp (International Healthcare Management).
Admissions Requirements Minimum age 15; Medical examination; Physician's request.
Staff Physicians (contracted); RNs 4 (ft), 1 (pt); LPNs 13 (ft), 4 (pt); Nurses' aides 31 (ft), 10 (pt); Physical therapists (contracted); Occupational therapists (contracted); Speech therapists (contracted); Activities coordinators 1 (ft); Dietitians 1 (pt); Ophthalmologists (contracted); Podiatrists (contracted); Audiologists (contracted).
Facilities Dining room; Physical therapy room; Activities room; Crafts room; Laundry room; Barber/Beauty shop; Library.
Activities Arts & crafts; Cards; Games; Reading groups; Prayer groups; Movies; Shopping trips; Dances/Social/Cultural gatherings; Intergenerational programs; Pet therapy.

Reed City

Reed City Hospital
7665 Patterson Rd, Reed City, MI 49677
(616) 832-3271
Admin Jack L Haybarker RPH. *Dir of Nursing* Richard Karns RN.
Licensure Skilled care. *Beds* SNF 110. *Certified* Medicaid; Medicare.
Owner Publicly owned.
Admissions Requirements Physician's request.
Staff Physicians; RNs; LPNs; Nurses' aides; Physical therapists; Occupational therapists; Speech therapists; Activities coordinators; Dietitians; Ophthalmologists; Dentists.
Facilities Dining room; Activities room.
Activities Arts & crafts; Cards; Games; Reading groups; Prayer groups.

Richmond

Medilodge of Richmond
34901 Division Rd, Richmond, MI 48062
(313) 727-7562
Licensure Intermediate care. *Beds* ICF 126. *Certified* Medicaid.

Riverview

Marian Manor Nursing Care Center
18591 Quarry Rd, Riverview, MI 48192
(313) 282-2100
Admin Alexander D Duonch. *Dir of Nursing* Virginia LePla RN. *Medical Dir* Gerald Lammers MD.
Licensure Skilled care. *Beds* SNF 140. *Certified* Medicaid; Medicare.

Owner Proprietary corp (International Healthcare Management).
Admissions Requirements Minimum age 18; Medical examination; Physician's request.
Staff Physicians 2 (ft), 1 (pt); RNs 4 (ft); LPNs 7 (ft), 3 (pt); Nurses' aides 23 (ft), 10 (pt); Physical therapists 1 (ft), 1 (pt); Reality therapists 1 (ft); Recreational therapists 1 (ft), 1 (pt); Occupational therapists 1 (ft); Speech therapists 1 (ft); Activities coordinators 1 (ft), 1 (pt); Dietitians 1 (ft), 1 (pt); Ophthalmologists 1 (pt); Podiatrists 1 (pt); Dentists 1 (pt).
Facilities Dining room; Physical therapy room; Activities room; Laundry room; Barber/Beauty shop; Library.
Activities Arts & crafts; Cards; Games; Reading groups; Prayer groups; Movies; Shopping trips; Dances/Social/Cultural gatherings; Off site trips; Zoo.

Rivergate Convalescent Center
14041 Pennsylvania, Riverview, MI 48192
(313) 284-7200
Licensure Skilled care. *Beds* SNF 223. *Certified* Medicaid; Medicare.

Rivergate Terrace
14141 Pennsylvania Rd, Riverview, MI 48192
(313) 284-8000, 283-6244
Licensure Intermediate care; Home for aged. *Beds* ICF 292; Home for aged 3. *Certified* Medicaid.

Rochester

Avondale Convalescent Home
1480 Walton Blvd, Rochester, MI 48063
(313) 651-4422
Admin Michael G Ardelean. *Dir of Nursing* Marsha Ackerman RN. *Medical Dir* C E Hendershott DO.
Licensure Skilled care; Alzheimer's care. *Beds* SNF 166. *Certified* Medicaid; Medicare.
Owner Privately owned.
Admissions Requirements Minimum age 16; Medical examination; Physician's request.
Staff RNs 4 (ft), 21 (pt); LPNs 2 (ft), 5 (pt); Nurses' aides 80 (ft); Physical therapists 1 (ft); Activities coordinators 1 (ft); Dietitians 1 (ft).
Facilities Dining room; Physical therapy room; Activities room; Chapel; Crafts room; Laundry room; Barber/Beauty shop; Library.
Activities Arts & crafts; Cards; Games; Reading groups; Prayer groups; Movies; Dances/Social/Cultural gatherings.

Rochester Hills

Mercy Bellbrook
873 W Avon Rd, Rochester Hills, MI 48063
Licensure Skilled care; Home for aged. *Beds* SNF 66; Home for aged 54. *Certified* Medicaid; Medicare.

Peachwood Inn
3500 W South Blvd, Rochester Hills, MI 48309
(313) 852-7800
Admin Victoria Cicone. *Dir of Nursing* Diane Howell. *Medical Dir* Dr Hollett.
Licensure Skilled care; Alzheimer's care. *Beds* SNF 186. *Certified* Medicare.
Owner Privately owned.
Admissions Requirements Minimum age 15; Physician's request.
Staff RNs; LPNs; Nurses' aides; Recreational therapists; Occupational therapists; Activities coordinators.
Facilities Dining room; Physical therapy room; Activities room; Chapel; Crafts room; Laundry room; Barber/Beauty shop; Library.

Activities Arts & crafts; Cards; Games; Reading groups; Prayer groups; Movies; Shopping trips; Dances/Social/Cultural gatherings; Intergenerational programs; Pet therapy.

Rogers City

Rogers City Hospital Long-Term Care Unit
555 N Bradley Hwy, Rogers City, MI 49779
(517) 734-2151, 734-4311 FAX
Admin Pamela MacFalda RN. *Dir of Nursing* Karen Meyers RN. *Medical Dir* Jesus Neri MD.
Licensure Skilled care. *Beds* SNF 49. *Private Pay Patients* 5%. *Certified* Medicaid; Medicare.
Owner Nonprofit organization/foundation.
Admissions Requirements Medical examination.
Staff Physicians 4 (ft); RNs 2 (ft), 2 (pt); LPNs 3 (ft), 3 (pt); Nurses' aides 6 (ft), 20 (pt); Activities coordinators 1 (ft); Ophthalmologists 1 (pt); Podiatrists 1 (pt).
Languages Polish.
Facilities Dining room; Physical therapy room; Activities room; Chapel; Crafts room; Barber/Beauty shop.
Activities Arts & crafts; Cards; Games; Reading groups; Prayer groups; Shopping trips; Dances/Social/Cultural gatherings; Intergenerational programs; Pet therapy.

Romeo

Medilodge of Romeo
309 S Bailey, Romeo, MI 48065
(313) 752-2581
Admin Sharon Lorey, Fac Mgr. *Dir of Nursing* Mary Marvin RN. *Medical Dir* A R Satyanathan MD.
Licensure Intermediate care. *Beds* ICF 33. *Private Pay Patients* 30%. *Certified* Medicaid.
Owner Proprietary corp.
Admissions Requirements Minimum age 17; Medical examination.
Staff Physicians 2 (ft); RNs 1 (ft); LPNs 3 (ft), 4 (pt); Nurses' aides 6 (ft), 7 (pt); Activities coordinators 1 (pt).
Languages Polish, German.
Facilities Dining room; Activities room; Crafts room; Laundry room; Barber/Beauty shop.
Activities Arts & crafts; Cards; Games; Reading groups; Prayer groups; Movies; Pet therapy.

Romeo Nursing Center
PO Box 306, 250 Denby St, Romeo, MI 48065
(313) 752-3571
Licensure Intermediate care. *Beds* ICF 35. *Certified* Medicaid.
Admissions Requirements Minimum age 18; Medical examination.
Staff Physicians 1 (ft); RNs 1 (ft), 2 (pt); LPNs 4 (pt); Nurses' aides 8 (ft), 6 (pt); Activities coordinators 1 (ft); Dietitians 1 (pt); Ophthalmologists 1 (pt); Podiatrists 1 (pt); Dentists 1 (pt).
Facilities Dining room; Activities room.
Activities Arts & crafts; Cards; Games; Dances/Social/Cultural gatherings.

Romulus

Apple Tree Lane Ltd
39000 Chase Rd, Romulus, MI 48174
(313) 941-1142
Licensure Intermediate care. *Beds* ICF 43. *Certified* Medicaid.

Rose City

Bortz Health Care of Rose City
517 W Page St, Rose City, MI 48654
(313) 685-25656
Licensure Skilled care. *Beds* SNF 140. *Certified* Medicaid; Medicare.

Roseville

Henry Ford Continuing Care—Roseville
25375 Kelly Rd, Roseville, MI 48066
(313) 773-6022, 771-2424 FAX
Admin Elizabeth Hynous RN BS. *Dir of Nursing* Mary Slago RN AD. *Medical Dir* R Danforth MD.
Licensure Skilled care; Intermediate care; Alzheimer's care. *Beds* SNF 25; Swing beds SNF/ICF 147; Alzheimer's care 15. *Private Pay Patients* 80%. *Certified* Medicare.
Owner Nonprofit corp.
Admissions Requirements Minimum age 18.
Languages Polish, Spanish, German.
Facilities Dining room; Physical therapy room; Activities room; Crafts room; Laundry room; Barber/Beauty shop; Small visitor's dining room; Closed head injury unit.
Activities Arts & crafts; Cards; Games; Reading groups; Prayer groups; Movies; Dances/Social/Cultural gatherings; Intergenerational programs; Pet therapy; Special outings.

Royal Oak

Alexander Continuing Care Center
718 W 4th St, Royal Oak, MI 48067
(313) 545-0571
Admin Helen Harmon. *Dir of Nursing* Beverly Bilge RN. *Medical Dir* Harold Wasserman MD.
Licensure Skilled care; Alzheimer's care. *Beds* SNF 96. *Certified* Medicaid; Medicare.
Owner Proprietary corp (Beverly Enterprises).
Admissions Requirements Minimum age 18; Medical examination; Physician's request.
Staff Physicians 1 (ft), 3 (pt); RNs 2 (ft), 2 (pt); LPNs 6 (pt); Nurses' aides 28 (ft), 4 (pt); Physical therapists 1 (ft), 1 (pt); Speech therapists 1 (pt); Activities coordinators 1 (ft), 1 (pt); Dietitians 1 (ft); Ophthalmologists 1 (pt); Podiatrists 1 (pt); Dentists 1 (pt).
Facilities Dining room; Physical therapy room; Laundry room.
Activities Arts & crafts; Cards; Games; Reading groups; Prayer groups; Movies; Shopping trips; Dances/Social/Cultural gatherings.

Oakland Care Center
3030 Greenfield Rd, Royal Oak, MI 48072
(313) 288-6610
Medical Dir Edwin Blumberg DO.
Licensure Skilled care. *Beds* SNF 151. *Certified* Medicaid; Medicare.
Admissions Requirements Minimum age 15.
Staff Physicians 1 (ft), 8 (pt); RNs 1 (ft), 6 (pt); LPNs 10 (ft), 6 (pt); Nurses' aides 36 (ft), 27 (pt); Physical therapists 1 (ft); Reality therapists 1 (pt); Recreational therapists 1 (pt); Occupational therapists 1 (pt); Speech therapists 1 (pt); Activities coordinators 1 (ft), 1 (pt); Dietitians 1 (ft); Ophthalmologists 2 (pt); Podiatrists 1 (pt); Audiologists 1 (pt); Dentists 2 (pt).
Facilities Dining room; Physical therapy room; Activities room; Crafts room; Laundry room; Barber/Beauty shop; Library.
Activities Arts & crafts; Cards; Games; Reading groups; Prayer groups; Movies; Shopping trips; Dances/Social/Cultural gatherings; Sight-seeing.

Saginaw

Home for the Aged
1446 S Washington, Saginaw, MI 48601
Licensure Home for aged. *Beds* Home for aged 25.

Hoyt Nursing Home
1202 Weiss St, Saginaw, MI 48602
Licensure Skilled care. *Beds* SNF 69. *Certified* Medicaid; Medicare.

Luther Manor Nursing Home
3161 Davenport St, Saginaw, MI 48602
(517) 799-1902
Admin Mr Gere L Ablett. *Dir of Nursing* Jean Roe. *Medical Dir* Dr Frederick Rosin.
Licensure Skilled care; Alzheimer's care. *Beds* SNF 98. *Certified* Medicaid; Medicare.
Owner Nonprofit corp (Lutheran Social Services of Michigan).
Admissions Requirements Medical examination; Physician's request.
Staff RNs 1 (ft), 6 (pt); LPNs 3 (ft), 6 (pt); Nurses' aides 28 (ft), 26 (pt); Chaplains 1 (ft).
Affiliation Lutheran.
Facilities Dining room; Activities room; Chapel; Crafts room; Barber/Beauty shop; In-house TV live broadcast M-F; Courtyards; Living room; 79 Private rooms.
Activities Arts & crafts; Cards; Games; Prayer groups; Movies; Shopping trips; Dances/ Social/Cultural gatherings.

Martin Luther—Saginaw Home
4322 Mackinaw Rd, Saginaw, MI 48603
(517) 792-8729
Admin Werner H Rosenbaum. *Dir of Nursing* Darlene Geiger RN. *Medical Dir* Dr James K Brasseur.
Licensure Skilled care; Intermediate care. *Beds* Swing beds SNF/ICF 71. *Certified* Medicaid; Medicare.
Owner Nonprofit corp (Martin Luther Memorial Home Inc).
Admissions Requirements Medical examination.
Staff RNs 2 (ft), 3 (pt); LPNs 3 (ft), 5 (pt); Nurses' aides 20 (ft), 20 (pt); Activities coordinators 2 (ft); Dietitians.
Languages German, Spanish.
Affiliation Lutheran.
Facilities Dining room; Physical therapy room; Activities room; Chapel; Crafts room; Laundry room; Barber/Beauty shop.
Activities Arts & crafts; Cards; Games; Prayer groups; Movies; Shopping trips; Dances/ Social/Cultural gatherings.

Maccabee Gardens Extended Care
2160 N Center Rd, Saginaw, MI 48603
(517) 799-2996
Admin Daniel Echler. *Dir of Nursing* Ann Phillips. *Medical Dir* Dr Ellis.
Licensure Skilled care. *Beds* SNF 98. *Certified* Medicaid; Medicare.
Owner Proprietary corp (Beverly Enterprises).
Admissions Requirements Minimum age 15.
Staff Physicians; RNs; LPNs; Nurses' aides; Physical therapists; Occupational therapists; Speech therapists; Activities coordinators; Dietitians.
Facilities Dining room; Physical therapy room; Activities room; Chapel; Crafts room; Barber/Beauty shop.
Activities Arts & crafts; Cards; Games; Reading groups; Prayer groups; Movies.

Saginaw Community Hospital
PO Box 6280, 3340 Hospital Rd, Saginaw, MI 48608-6280
(517) 790-1234
Licensure Skilled care; Intermediate care. *Beds* Swing beds SNF/ICF 297. *Certified* Medicaid; Medicare.

Saginaw Geriatric Home
1413 Gratiot, Saginaw, MI 48602
(517) 793-3471
Licensure Skilled care; Home for aged. *Beds*
SNF 55; Home for aged 58. *Certified*
Medicaid; Medicare.

St Francis Home
915 N River Rd, Saginaw, MI 48603
(517) 781-3150
Admin Sr Jane Marie. *Dir of Nursing* Ann
Suhr. *Medical Dir* Dr Ronald Jensen.
Licensure Skilled care. *Beds* SNF 100.
Certified Medicaid; Medicare.
Owner Nonprofit corp.
Admissions Requirements Medical
examination.
Staff RNs 13 (ft); LPNs 7 (ft); Nurses' aides
45 (pt); Physical therapists 1 (ft); Activities
coordinators 1 (ft); Dietitians 1 (ft);
Ophthalmologists 1 (ft).
Affiliation Roman Catholic.
Facilities Dining room; Physical therapy
room; Activities room; Chapel; Crafts room;
Laundry room; Barber/Beauty shop.
Activities Arts & crafts; Cards; Games;
Reading groups; Prayer groups; Movies.

Sun Valley Manor
2901 Galaxy Dr, Saginaw, MI 48601
(517) 777-5110
Admin Corinne Douglas RN. *Dir of Nursing*
Sally Carigan RN. *Medical Dir* James
Brasseur DO.
Licensure Skilled care; Home for aged. *Beds*
SNF 103; Home for aged 26. *Certified*
Medicaid; Medicare.
Owner Proprietary corp (Health Care and
Retirement Corp).
Admissions Requirements Medical
examination.
Staff RNs 4 (ft), 2 (pt); LPNs 10 (ft); Nurses'
aides 27 (ft), 29 (pt); Activities coordinators
1 (ft).
Facilities Dining room; Physical therapy
room; Activities room; Laundry room;
Barber/Beauty shop.
Activities Arts & crafts; Cards; Games;
Reading groups; Prayer groups; Movies;
Shopping trips; Dances/Social/Cultural
gatherings.

Saint Clair

Faith Medical Care Center
4220 S Hospital Dr, Saint Clair, MI 48079
(313) 329-4736
Medical Dir Gordon H Webb MD.
Licensure Skilled care. *Beds* SNF 125.
Certified Medicaid; Medicare.
Admissions Requirements Minimum age 16;
Medical examination.
Staff Physicians 14 (pt); RNs 4 (ft), 2 (pt);
LPNs 6 (ft), 4 (pt); Nurses' aides 39 (ft), 10
(pt); Recreational therapists 2 (ft); Activities
coordinators 1 (ft); Dietitians 2 (ft);
Podiatrists 1 (pt); Dentists 1 (pt).
Facilities Dining room; Activities room;
Crafts room; Laundry room; Barber/Beauty
shop.
Activities Arts & crafts; Cards; Games;
Reading groups; Prayer groups; Movies;
Dances/Social/Cultural gatherings.

Saint Clair Shores

St Mary's Nursing Home
22601 E Nine Mile Rd, Saint Clair Shores, MI
48080
(313) 772-4300
Admin C T Bertolini.
Medical Dir Harry Latos DO.
Licensure Skilled care; Intermediate care. *Beds*
Swing beds SNF/ICF 107. *Certified*
Medicaid; Medicare.
Owner Proprietary corp (Bon Secours Health
Systems).

Admissions Requirements Minimum age 15;
Medical examination; Physician's request.
Staff Physicians 2 (pt); RNs 5 (ft), 1 (pt);
LPNs 1 (ft), 6 (pt); Nurses' aides 30 (ft), 10
(pt); Physical therapists; Recreational
therapists; Occupational therapists; Speech
therapists; Dietitians; Ophthalmologists;
Podiatrists; Dentists.
Facilities Dining room; Physical therapy
room; Activities room; Laundry room;
Barber/Beauty shop.
Activities Arts & crafts; Cards; Games;
Reading groups; Prayer groups; Movies;
Shopping trips; Dances/Social/Cultural
gatherings.

Sisters of Bon Secours Nursing Care Center
26001 Jefferson Ave, Saint Clair Shores, MI
48081
Licensure Skilled care. *Beds* SNF 200.
Certified Medicaid; Medicare.

Saint Ignace

**Mackinac Straits Hospital Long-Term Care
Unit**
220 Burdette St, Saint Ignace, MI 49781
(906) 643-8585
Admin Frank Burgess. *Dir of Nursing* Thora A
Foster RN. *Medical Dir* Carl Hawkins MD.
Licensure Skilled care. *Beds* SNF 60. *Private
Pay Patients* 4%. *Certified* Medicaid;
Medicare.
Owner Nonprofit corp.
Admissions Requirements Medical
examination.
Staff Physicians 2 (ft); RNs 2 (ft), 2 (pt);
LPNs 4 (ft), 6 (pt); Nurses' aides 30 (ft), 6
(pt); Physical therapists (contracted); Speech
therapists (contracted); Activities
coordinators 1 (ft); Dietitians (contracted);
Audiologists 1 (pt).
Facilities Dining room; Physical therapy
room; Activities room; Chapel; Crafts room;
Barber/Beauty shop.
Activities Arts & crafts; Cards; Games; Prayer
groups; Movies; Dances/Social/Cultural
gatherings.

Saint Johns

Hazel I Findlay Country Manor
1101 S Scott Rd, Saint Johns, MI 48879
(517) 224-8936
Admin Mark Stapelman MBA NHA. *Dir of
Nursing* Mary Ann Bond RN.
Licensure Intermediate care. *Beds* ICF 108.
Certified Medicaid.
Owner Nonprofit corp.
Admissions Requirements Minimum age 15;
Medical examination; Physician's request.
Staff RNs 4 (ft), 1 (pt); LPNs 3 (ft), 8 (pt);
Nurses' aides 39 (ft), 24 (pt); Physical
therapists 1 (ft), 1 (pt); Recreational
therapists 2 (ft); Occupational therapists 1
(pt); Speech therapists 1 (pt); Dietitians 1
(pt); Ophthalmologists 1 (pt); Podiatrists 1
(pt); Social workers 1 (ft).
Languages Spanish.
Facilities Dining room; Physical therapy
room; Activities room; Crafts room; Barber/
Beauty shop; Library; Courtyards; Resident
gardens.
Activities Arts & crafts; Cards; Games;
Reading groups; Prayer groups; Movies;
Shopping trips; Dances/Social/Cultural
gatherings; King & Queen annually; Adult
education; Garden grant winner.

Saint Joseph

Shoreham Terrace
3425 Lakeshore Dr, Saint Joseph, MI 49085
(616) 983-6501
Admin Judith E Hoese. *Dir of Nursing* Mary
Bauer RN.

Licensure Skilled care. *Beds* SNF 112.
Certified Medicaid; Medicare.
Owner Proprietary corp (Beverly Enterprises).
Staff RNs; LPNs; Nurses' aides; Activities
coordinators.

Saint Louis

Schnepp Health Care Center
427 E Washington Ave, Saint Louis, MI
48880
(517) 681-5721
Admin Richard S Prestage. *Dir of Nursing*
Jeanne Wernette. *Medical Dir* Dr William
Thiemkey.
Licensure Skilled care; Intermediate care. *Beds*
Swing beds SNF/ICF 127. *Certified*
Medicaid; Medicare.
Owner Privately owned.
Admissions Requirements Physician's request.
Staff RNs 5 (ft), 2 (pt); LPNs 11 (ft), 4 (pt);
Nurses' aides 40 (ft), 29 (pt); Activities
coordinators 2 (ft), 2 (pt).
Facilities Dining room; Physical therapy
room; Activities room; Crafts room; Barber/
Beauty shop.
Activities Arts & crafts; Cards; Games;
Reading groups; Prayer groups; Movies;
Shopping trips; Pet therapy.

Westgate Manor Nursing Home
1149 W Monroe Rd, Saint Louis, MI 48880
(517) 681-3852
Admin Joyce Feldkamp. *Dir of Nursing*
Jeanne Wernette RN.
Licensure Skilled care. *Beds* SNF 81. *Certified*
Medicaid; Medicare.
Owner Proprietary corp.
Admissions Requirements Minimum age 15;
Medical examination; Physician's request.
Staff RNs; LPNs; Nurses' aides; Physical
therapists; Recreational therapists;
Occupational therapists; Speech therapists;
Activities coordinators; Dietitians;
Ophthalmologists.
Facilities Dining room; Activities room;
Barber/Beauty shop.
Activities Arts & crafts; Cards; Games;
Reading groups; Prayer groups; Movies;
Shopping trips; Dances/Social/Cultural
gatherings.

Saline

Evangelical Home—Saline
440 W Russell St, Saline, MI 48176
(313) 429-9401
Licensure Skilled care; Home for aged. *Beds*
SNF 215; Home for aged 56. *Certified*
Medicaid; Medicare.

Sandusky

Sanilac Medical Care Facility
137 N Elk, Sandusky, MI 48471
(313) 648-3017
Admin Kenneth L Fisher. *Dir of Nursing*
Judith Lakatos RN. *Medical Dir* L G Ellis
MD.
Licensure Skilled care. *Beds* SNF 84. *Private
Pay Patients* 10%. *Certified* Medicaid;
Medicare.
Owner Publicly owned.
Staff Physicians 8 (ft); RNs 5 (ft); LPNs 12
(ft), 2 (pt); Nurses' aides 42 (ft), 5 (pt);
Physical therapists 1 (pt); Occupational
therapists 1 (pt); Speech therapists 1 (pt);
Activities coordinators 2 (ft); Dietitians 1
(pt); Podiatrists 1 (pt); Audiologists 1 (pt).
Facilities Dining room; Physical therapy
room; Activities room; Chapel; Laundry
room; Barber/Beauty shop; Library.
Activities Arts & crafts; Cards; Games;
Reading groups; Movies; Dances/Social/
Cultural gatherings; Pet therapy.

Sault Sainte Marie

Chippewa County War Memorial Hospital Inc
500 Osborn Blvd, Sault Sainte Marie, MI
49783
(906) 635-4410
Admin Brian R Mitteer. *Dir of Nursing* Elaine
Woodward. *Medical Dir* E J Ranta MD.
Licensure Skilled care; Intermediate care. *Beds*
Swing beds SNF/ICF 138. *Certified*
Medicaid; Medicare.
Owner Publicly owned.
Admissions Requirements Medical
examination; Physician's request.
Staff Physicians 12 (pt); RNs 3 (ft); LPNs 3
(ft); Nurses' aides 15 (ft), 1 (pt); Physical
therapists 2 (pt); Occupational therapists 1
(ft); Activities coordinators 1 (ft); Dietitians
1 (ft); Dentists 1 (pt); Clerks 1 (ft).
Facilities Dining room; Physical therapy
room; Activities room; Chapel; Crafts room;
Barber/Beauty shop; Library.
Activities Arts & crafts; Cards; Games;
Reading groups; Prayer groups; Movies;
Shopping trips; Dances/Social/Cultural
gatherings; Senior living classes through the
community schools; Exercise class; Special
parties.

Provincial House Sault Sainte Marie
1011 Meridian, Sault Sainte Marie, MI 49783
(906) 635-1518
Admin Floyd Johnson. *Dir of Nursing* Cynthia
Jenkins. *Medical Dir* Phillip Niemi DO.
Licensure Skilled care; Intermediate care. *Beds*
Swing beds SNF/ICF 117. *Private Pay
Patients* 7%. *Certified* Medicaid; Medicare.
Owner Proprietary corp (Beverly Enterprises).
Admissions Requirements Minimum age 16.
Staff RNs 5 (ft), 2 (pt); LPNs 10 (ft), 3 (pt);
Nurses' aides 42 (ft), 14 (pt); Activities
coordinators 1 (ft); Dietitians 1 (pt);
Podiatrists 1 (pt).
Facilities Dining room; Physical therapy
room; Activities room; Crafts room; Laundry
room; Barber/Beauty shop.
Activities Arts & crafts; Cards; Games;
Reading groups; Prayer groups; Movies;
Dances/Social/Cultural gatherings;
Intergenerational programs; Pet therapy.

Sunset Manor
1501 W 6th Ave, Sault Sainte Marie, MI
49783
Licensure Home for aged. *Beds* Home for
aged 64.

South Haven

Countryside Nursing Home
120 Baseline Rd, South Haven, MI 49090
(616) 637-8411
Medical Dir Thomas Burns MD.
Licensure Intermediate care; Home for aged.
Beds ICF 81; Home for aged 28. *Certified*
Medicaid.
Admissions Requirements Medical
examination.
Staff RNs 3 (pt); LPNs 6 (ft), 2 (pt); Nurses'
aides 25 (ft), 20 (pt); Recreational therapists
1 (ft), 2 (pt); Activities coordinators 1 (ft);
Dietitians 1 (pt).
Facilities Dining room; Activities room;
Laundry room; Barber/Beauty shop.
Activities Arts & crafts; Cards; Games;
Reading groups; Prayer groups; Movies;
Shopping trips; Dances/Social/Cultural
gatherings.

Martin Luther Memorial Home—South Haven
PO box 690, 850 Phillips St, South Haven, MI
49090
(616) 637-5147
Admin Richard F Hennig. *Dir of Nursing*
Bunny Porter RN. *Medical Dir* Dale Morgan
MD.

Licensure Skilled care. *Beds* ICF 125
concurrent. *Private Pay Patients* 22%.
Certified Medicaid; Medicare.
Owner Nonprofit organization/foundation
(Martin Luther Memorial Home Inc).
Admissions Requirements Medical
examination; Physician's request.
Staff Physicians 8 (pt); RNs 4 (ft); LPNs 7
(ft), 2 (pt); Nurses' aides 50 (ft), 5 (pt);
Physical therapists 1 (pt); Occupational
therapists 1 (pt); Speech therapists 1 (pt);
Activities coordinators 1 (ft); Dietitians 1
(ft); Ophthalmologists 1 (pt); Podiatrists 1
(pt); Audiologists 1 (pt); Beautician 1 (pt).
Languages German.
Affiliation Lutheran.
Facilities Dining room; Physical therapy
room; Activities room; Chapel; Crafts room;
Laundry room; Barber/Beauty shop; Library.
Activities Arts & crafts; Cards; Games;
Reading groups; Prayer groups; Movies;
Intergenerational programs.

South Lyon

Martin Luther Memorial Home
305 Elm Pl, South Lyon, MI 48178
(313) 437-2048
Admin C Douglas Anderson. *Dir of Nursing*
Sally J Beckstein RN. *Medical Dir* Allan
Schwartz DO.
Licensure Skilled care; Intermediate care. *Beds*
SNF 44; ICF 36. *Certified* Medicaid;
Medicare.
Owner Nonprofit organization/foundation.
Admissions Requirements Minimum age HFA
65, ECF 0; Medical examination; Physician's
request ECF.
Staff Physicians 4 (pt); RNs 2 (ft), 6 (pt);
LPNs 3 (ft), 4 (pt); Nurses' aides 16 (ft), 7
(pt); Physical therapists; Activities
coordinators 1 (ft); Dietitians 1 (ft).
Languages German.
Affiliation Lutheran.
Facilities Dining room; Physical therapy
room; Activities room; Crafts room; Laundry
room; Barber/Beauty shop.
Activities Arts & crafts; Cards; Games;
Reading groups; Prayer groups; Movies; Pet
therapy; Ladies auxiliary.

Southfield

Cambridge Bedford
16240 W Twelve Mile Rd, Southfield, MI
48076
(313) 557-3333, 569-4834 FAX
Admin Karl Bartscht NAA. *Dir of Nursing*
Mary Richards RN BSN. *Medical Dir* R
Knauff DO.
Licensure Skilled care; Alzheimer's care. *Beds*
SNF 61. *Private Pay Patients* 100%.
Owner Proprietary corp (International
Healthcare Management Inc).
Admissions Requirements Physician's request.
Staff Physicians; RNs; LPNs; Nurses' aides;
Physical therapists; Occupational therapists;
Speech therapists; Activities coordinators;
Dietitians; Ophthalmologists; Podiatrists.
Facilities Dining room; Physical therapy
room; Activities room; Crafts room; Laundry
room; Barber/Beauty shop; Day/TV room.
Activities Arts & crafts; Cards; Games;
Reading groups; Prayer groups; Movies;
Shopping trips; Dances/Social/Cultural
gatherings; Intergenerational programs; Pet
therapy; Senior Olympics.

Franklin Manor Convalescent Center
26900 Franklin Rd, Southfield, MI 48034
(313) 352-7390
Licensure Intermediate care. *Beds* ICF 107.

Jewish Home for Aged—Prentis Manor
26051 Lahser, Southfield, MI 48034
(313) 352-2336

Admin Marcia Mittelman. *Dir of Nursing*
Sharon Furtaw. *Medical Dir* Marc Feldman.
Licensure Skilled care. *Beds* SNF 100. *Private
Pay Patients* 24%. *Certified* Medicaid;
Medicare.
Owner Nonprofit corp (Jewish Home for the
Aged).
Admissions Requirements Minimum age 65;
Physician's request.
Staff Physicians (contracted); RNs 9 (ft);
LPNs 9 (ft); Nurses' aides 38 (ft); Physical
therapists 1 (pt); Recreational therapists 1
(ft); Occupational therapists 1 (pt); Speech
therapists (contracted); Dietitians 1 (ft);
Ophthalmologists (contracted); Podiatrists
(contracted).
Affiliation Jewish.
Activities Arts & crafts; Cards; Games;
Reading groups; Prayer groups; Movies;
Dances/Social/Cultural gatherings;
Intergenerational programs; Pet therapy.

Lahser Hills Nursing Center
25300 Lahser Rd, Southfield, MI 48075
(313) 354-3222
Admin Belle Eisenberg. *Dir of Nursing* Dianne
Casagrande RN.
Licensure Skilled care. *Beds* SNF 161.
Certified Medicaid; Medicare.
Admissions Requirements Minimum age 60;
Medical examination; Physician's request.
Staff Physicians; RNs; LPNs; Nurses' aides;
Physical therapists; Occupational therapists;
Speech therapists; Activities coordinators;
Dietitians; Ophthalmologists; Podiatrists;
Dentists.
Facilities Dining room; Physical therapy
room; Activities room; Barber/Beauty shop.
Activities Arts & crafts; Cards; Games;
Reading groups; Prayer groups; Movies;
Shopping trips; Dances/Social/Cultural
gatherings.

Mt Vernon Nursing Center
26715 Greenfield Rd, Southfield, MI 48076
(313) 557-0050
Licensure Skilled care. *Beds* SNF 228.
Certified Medicaid; Medicare.

St Anne's Mead Nursing Facility
16106 W Twelve Mile Rd, Southfield, MI
48076
Licensure Skilled care; Home for aged. *Beds*
SNF 20; Home for aged 87.

Southfield Rehabilitation Hospital
22401 Foster Winter Dr, Southfield, MI
48075
(313) 569-1500
Admin Marcia Thomas-Brown. *Dir of Nursing*
Janet Rippy RN. *Medical Dir* J Chatfield
MD.
Licensure Skilled care; Rehabilitation hospital.
Beds SNF 75; Rehabilitation hospital 75.
Certified Medicaid; Medicare.
Owner Proprietary corp.
Admissions Requirements Minimum age 16;
Medical examination; Physician's request.
Staff Physicians 10 (ft); RNs 9 (ft), 13 (pt);
LPNs 15 (ft), 3 (pt); Nurses' aides 16 (ft), 8
(pt); Physical therapists 6 (ft), 2 (pt);
Occupational therapists 4 (ft), 1 (pt); Speech
therapists 3 (ft), 4 (pt).
Facilities Dining room; Physical therapy
room; Activities room; Crafts room; Laundry
room; Barber/Beauty shop.
Activities Arts & crafts; Cards; Games;
Reading groups; Prayer groups.

Southgate

Beverly Manor Convalescent Center
15400 Trenton Rd, Southgate, MI 48195
(313) 284-4620
Licensure Skilled care. *Beds* SNF 100.
Certified Medicaid; Medicare.
Owner Proprietary corp (Beverly Enterprises).

Spring Arbor

Arbor Manor Care Center
151 2nd St, Spring Arbor, MI 49283
(517) 750-1900
Admin Kevin J Ganton. *Dir of Nursing*
Barbara A. Buikema RN.
Licensure Skilled care; Home for aged. *Beds*
SNF 107; Home for aged 16. *Certified*
Medicaid; Medicare.
Owner Privately owned.
Admissions Requirements Minimum age 15;
Medical examination; Physician's request.
Staff Physicians 6 (pt); RNs 4 (ft), 4 (pt);
LPNs 7 (ft), 9 (pt); Nurses' aides 33 (ft), 25
(pt); Physical therapists 1 (pt); Recreational
therapists 1 (ft); Occupational therapists 1
(pt); Speech therapists 1 (pt); Activities
coordinators 1 (ft), 1 (pt); Dietitians 1 (ft), 1
(pt); Ophthalmologists 1 (pt); Social workers
1 (ft).
Languages Polish, Yiddish.
Facilities Dining room; Physical therapy
room; Activities room; Crafts room; Laundry
room; Barber/Beauty shop; Library;
Occupational Therapy.
Activities Arts & crafts; Cards; Games;
Reading groups; Prayer groups; Movies;
Shopping trips; Dances/Social/Cultural
gatherings; Bingo; Bible study; Music; Stroke
club; Mens club; Pet day; Church.

Springfield

Docsa Home for the Aged
565 General Ave, Springfield, MI 49015
Licensure Home for aged. *Beds* Home for
aged 147.

Standish

Standish Community Hospital
Box 579, 805 W Cedar, Standish, MI 48658
(517) 846-4521
Admin James J Polonis. *Dir of Nursing* Laurel
P Borylo RN. *Medical Dir* Antonio F
Mendiola Jr MD.
Licensure Skilled care; Alzheimer's care. *Beds*
SNF 77. *Certified* Medicaid; Medicare.
Owner Nonprofit corp.
Admissions Requirements Physician's request.
Staff Physicians 1 (ft); RNs 1 (ft); LPNs 8 (ft),
4 (pt); Nurses' aides 18 (ft), 9 (pt); Physical
therapists 1 (pt); Recreational therapists 1
(pt); Speech therapists 1 (pt); Dietitians 1
(pt).
Facilities Dining room; Physical therapy
room; Activities room; Crafts room; Barber/
Beauty shop.
Activities Arts & crafts; Cards; Games;
Reading groups; Prayer groups; Movies;
Shopping trips; Dances/Social/Cultural
gatherings.

Stephenson

Roubal Nursing Home
Rte 1 Box 32, Stephenson, MI 49887
(906) 753-2231
Admin William Rosner.
Medical Dir Karen Raether.
Licensure Intermediate care. *Beds* ICF 88.
Certified Medicaid.
Owner Proprietary corp.
Admissions Requirements Minimum age 18;
Medical examination; Physician's request.
Staff RNs 1 (ft), 1 (pt); LPNs 6 (ft), 6 (pt);
Nurses' aides 46 (ft), 15 (pt); Activities
coordinators 1 (ft), 2 (pt); Dietitians 1 (ft).
Facilities Dining room; Activities room;
Crafts room; Laundry room; Barber/Beauty
shop.
Activities Arts & crafts; Cards; Games;
Reading groups; Prayer groups; Movies;
Shopping trips; Dances/Social/Cultural
gatherings.

Sterling

Greenbriar Nursing Home
500 School Rd, Sterling, MI 48659
Admin John H Swaffield.
Medical Dir Gordon A Page Jr MD.
Licensure Skilled care. *Beds* SNF 104.
Certified Medicaid; Medicare.
Owner Proprietary corp.
Admissions Requirements Minimum age 15.
Staff Physical therapists 1 (pt); Occupational
therapists 1 (pt); Speech therapists 1 (pt);
Activities coordinators 1 (ft); Dietitians 1
(ft).
Facilities Dining room; Physical therapy
room; Activities room; Chapel; Crafts room;
Laundry room; Barber/Beauty shop.
Activities Arts & crafts; Cards; Games;
Reading groups; Prayer groups; Movies;
Shopping trips.

Sterling Heights

Evangelical Home—Sterling Heights
14900 Shore Line Dr, Sterling Heights, MI
48078
Licensure Skilled care; Home for aged. *Beds*
SNF 120; Home for aged 24. *Certified*
Medicaid; Medicare.

Nightingale North Nursing Home
14151 E Fifteen Mile Rd, Sterling Heights, MI
48077
(313) 939-0200
Licensure Skilled care; Home for aged. *Beds*
SNF 307; Home for aged 30. *Certified*
Medicaid; Medicare.

Polish Army Veterans Home
13707 Clinton River, Sterling Heights, MI
48078
Licensure Home for aged. *Beds* Home for
aged 30.

Stockbridge

Pleasantview Manor
406 W Main St, Stockbridge, MI 49285
(517) 851-7700
Admin Joyce A Novak. *Dir of Nursing*
Jennifer Rooney RN. *Medical Dir* Michael
Smith MD.
Licensure Intermediate care. *Beds* ICF 53.
Certified Medicaid.
Owner Proprietary corp.
Staff RNs 2 (ft); LPNs 2 (ft), 3 (pt); Nurses'
aides 13 (ft), 9 (pt); Activities coordinators 1
(ft).
Facilities Dining room; Activities room;
Crafts room; Barber/Beauty shop.
Activities Arts & crafts; Cards; Games;
Reading groups; Prayer groups; Movies;
Shopping trips; Dances/Social/Cultural
gatherings.

Sturgis

Thurston Woods Village
307 Spruce St, Sturgis, MI 49091
(616) 651-7841, 651-2050 FAX
Admin Marilyn Archer; J D Yoder, Exec Dir.
Dir of Nursing Violet Lahr. *Medical Dir* Dr
Olin Lepard; Dr Robert Smith.
Licensure Skilled care; Home for aged. *Beds*
SNF 118; Home for aged 90. *Private Pay
Patients* 20%. *Certified* Medicaid; Medicare.
Owner Nonprofit corp.
Admissions Requirements Minimum age 16;
Medical examination; Physician's request.
Staff Physicians 2 (pt); RNs 4 (ft), 3 (pt);
LPNs 9 (ft), 5 (pt); Nurses' aides 37 (ft), 16
(pt); Physical therapists 1 (pt); Reality
therapists 1 (pt); Recreational therapists 1
(pt); Occupational therapists 1 (pt); Speech
therapists 1 (pt); Activities coordinators 1

(ft); Dietitians 1 (pt); Ophthalmologists 1
(pt); Podiatrists 1 (pt); Audiologists 1 (pt);
Dentists 1 (pt).
Languages German, Spanish.
Affiliation Mennonite.
Facilities Dining room; Physical therapy
room; Activities room; Chapel; Crafts room;
Laundry room; Barber/Beauty shop.
Activities Arts & crafts; Cards; Games;
Reading groups; Prayer groups; Movies;
Shopping trips; Dances/Social/Cultural
gatherings; Intergenerational programs; Pet
therapy; Pontoon boat rides; Outdoor
recreation.

Tawas City

Iosco County Medical Care Facility
1201 Harris Ave, Tawas City, MI 48763
(517) 362-4424
Licensure Skilled care. *Beds* SNF 64. *Certified*
Medicaid; Medicare.
Owner Publicly owned.

Provinical House—Tawas City
400 W North St, Tawas City, MI 48763
(517) 362-8645
Licensure Skilled care. *Beds* SNF 120.
Certified Medicaid; Medicare.
Owner Proprietary corp (Beverly Enterprises).

Taylor

Park Nursing Center Inc
12575 Telegraph Rd, Taylor, MI 48180
(313) 287-4710
Admin Juanita W Brannock. *Dir of Nursing*
Carol O'Brien.
Licensure Skilled care. *Beds* SNF 265.
Certified Medicaid; Medicare.
Owner Proprietary corp.
Admissions Requirements Minimum age 15;
Medical examination; Physician's request.
Staff Physicians; RNs; LPNs; Nurses' aides;
Physical therapists; Recreational therapists;
Speech therapists; Activities coordinators;
Dietitians; Ophthalmologists; Podiatrists;
Dentists.
Languages French, Spanish, Polish.
Facilities Dining room; Physical therapy
room; Activities room; Crafts room; Laundry
room; Barber/Beauty shop.
Activities Arts & crafts; Cards; Games;
Reading groups; Movies; Shopping trips.

Pine Knoll Convalescent Center
23600 Northline Rd, Taylor, MI 48180
(313) 287-8580
Admin Diane Tackett. *Dir of Nursing* B
Shellhammer RN. *Medical Dir* M Elanjian
DO.
Licensure Skilled care; Alzheimer's care. *Beds*
SNF 142. *Certified* Medicaid; Medicare.
Owner Privately owned.
Admissions Requirements Minimum age 15;
Medical examination; Physician's request.
Staff RNs; LPNs; Nurses' aides; Physical
therapists; Reality therapists; Occupational
therapists; Speech therapists; Activities
coordinators; Dietitians; Ophthalmologists;
Dentists.
Facilities Dining room; Physical therapy
room; Activities room; Chapel; Crafts room;
Laundry room; Barber/Beauty shop;
Dayrooms.
Activities Arts & crafts; Cards; Games; Prayer
groups; Movies.

Taylor Living Center for Seniors
22970 Northline Rd, Taylor, MI 48180
Licensure Home for aged. *Beds* Home for
aged 120.

**Taylor Total Living Center For the
Developmentally Disabled**
22950 Northline Rd, Taylor, MI 48180

Licensure Skilled care. *Beds* SNF 150.
Certified Medicaid.
Owner Proprietary corp (Beverly Enterprises).

Tecumseh

Herrick Manor
500 E Pottawatamie St, Tecumseh, MI 49286
(517) 423-2141, ext 3260
Admin Philip M Sullivan, Pres CEO. *Dir of Nursing* Janet E Plambech RN BSN.
Medical Dir Daniel Doman DO.
Licensure Intermediate care. *Beds* ICF 25.
Private Pay Patients 25%. *Certified* Medicaid.
Owner Publicly owned.
Admissions Requirements Medical examination; Physician's request.
Staff Physicians; RNs 1 (ft); LPNs 2 (ft), 3 (pt); Nurses' aides 10 (ft), 7 (pt); Physical therapists; Occupational therapists; Speech therapists; Activities coordinators 1 (pt); Dietitians; Ophthalmologists; Podiatrists; Audiologists; Dentists.
Languages Spanish.
Facilities Dining room; Physical therapy room; Activities room; Chapel; Crafts room; Laundry room; Barber/Beauty shop; Hospital attached.
Activities Arts & crafts; Cards; Games; Reading groups; Prayer groups; Movies; Shopping trips; Dances/Social/Cultural gatherings; Intergenerational programs; Pet therapy; Tecumseh Civic Theatre programs; Volunteer program; Community participation; Vocational tech program.

Three Rivers

River Forest Nursing Care Center
55378 Wilbur Rd, Three Rivers, MI 49093
(616) 279-7441
Admin Ron Boothby. *Dir of Nursing* Don Makela. *Medical Dir* Dr Bas Mutnal.
Licensure Skilled care; Home for aged. *Beds* SNF 87; Home for aged 30. *Certified* Medicaid; Medicare.
Owner Nonprofit organization/foundation.
Admissions Requirements Minimum age 16; Medical examination; Physician's request.
Staff Physicians 6 (pt); RNs 2 (ft), 3 (pt); LPNs 5 (ft), 3 (pt); Nurses' aides 30 (ft), 20 (pt); Physical therapists 1 (pt); Recreational therapists 1 (pt); Occupational therapists 11 (pt); Speech therapists 1 (pt); Activities coordinators 1 (ft); Dietitians 1 (pt); Ophthalmologists 1 (pt); Podiatrists 1 (pt); Dentists 1 (pt).
Affiliation Roman Catholic.
Facilities Dining room; Physical therapy room; Activities room; Chapel; Crafts room; Laundry room; Barber/Beauty shop; Library.
Activities Arts & crafts; Cards; Games; Reading groups; Prayer groups; Movies; Shopping trips; Dances/Social/Cultural gatherings.

Three Rivers Manor
517 Erie St, Three Rivers, MI 49093
(616) 273-8661, 279-6173 FAX
Admin Char Baum. *Dir of Nursing* Bart Carrel. *Medical Dir* Shoon Lee MD.
Licensure Skilled care. *Beds* SNF 100. *Private Pay Patients* 13%. *Certified* Medicaid; Medicare.
Owner Proprietary corp (Health Care and Retirement Corp).
Admissions Requirements Minimum age 17.
Staff Physicians 6 (pt); RNs 3 (ft); LPNs 5 (ft), 3 (pt); Nurses' aides 24 (ft), 6 (pt); Physical therapists 1 (ft); Activities coordinators 1 (ft); Dietitians 1 (pt); Podiatrists 1 (pt).
Facilities Dining room; Physical therapy room; Activities room; Chapel; Crafts room; Laundry room; Barber/Beauty shop; Library.

Activities Arts & crafts; Cards; Games; Reading groups; Prayer groups; Movies; Shopping trips; Dances/Social/Cultural gatherings; Intergenerational programs; Pet therapy; Sensory stimulation; Continuing education (GED).

Traverse City

Birchwood Nursing Center
2950 Lafranier Rd, Traverse City, MI 49684
(616) 947-0506
Licensure Skilled care. *Beds* SNF 155.
Certified Medicaid; Medicare.
Owner Proprietary corp (Beverly Enterprises).

Bortz Health Care of Traverse City
2828 Concord, Traverse City, MI 49684
(616) 941-1200
Admin Lori Wells. *Dir of Nursing* Gertrude Timm RN. *Medical Dir* Mark Jackson MD.
Licensure Skilled care; Intermediate care. *Beds* SNF 39; ICF 57. *Private Pay Patients* 40%. *Certified* Medicaid; Medicare.
Owner Privately owned (D J Bortz).
Admissions Requirements Minimum age 15; Medical examination; Physician's request.
Staff Physicians 1 (ft); RNs 6 (ft), 1 (pt); LPNs 6 (ft), 4 (pt); Nurses' aides 35 (ft), 10 (pt); Physical therapists 1 (ft); Occupational therapists 1 (ft); Speech therapists 1 (ft); Activities coordinators 1 (ft), 2 (pt); Dietitians 1 (ft); Ophthalmologists 1 (ft); Podiatrists 1 (ft); Audiologists 1 (ft).
Facilities Dining room; Physical therapy room; Activities room; Crafts room; Laundry room; Barber/Beauty shop; Library; Enclosed courtyard; Dayrooms.
Activities Arts & crafts; Cards; Games; Reading groups; Prayer groups; Movies; Shopping trips; Dances/Social/Cultural gatherings; Intergenerational programs; Pet therapy.

Grand Traverse Medical Care Facility
410 S Elmwood, Traverse City, MI 49684
(616) 947-4750
Admin Leta R Amon, acting. *Dir of Nursing* Marilynn Bailey RN. *Medical Dir* Robert Johnson MD.
Licensure Skilled care; Alzheimer's care. *Beds* SNF 181. *Certified* Medicaid; Medicare.
Owner Publicly owned.
Admissions Requirements Minimum age 18; Medical examination; Physician's request.
Staff Physicians 1 (pt); RNs 8 (ft), 8 (pt); LPNs 9 (ft), 11 (pt); Nurses' aides 61 (ft), 43 (pt).
Facilities Dining room; Physical therapy room; Activities room; Chapel; Crafts room; Laundry room; Barber/Beauty shop.
Activities Arts & crafts; Cards; Games; Reading groups; Prayer groups; Movies; Shopping trips; Dances/Social/Cultural gatherings; Intergenerational programs; Pet therapy.

Provincial House—Traverse City
2585 S Lafranier Rd, Traverse City, MI 49684
(616) 947-9511
Admin Judy Petieff. *Dir of Nursing* Katie Thomos RN. *Medical Dir* Wm Thomos MD.
Licensure Skilled care. *Beds* SNF 120.
Certified Medicaid; Medicare.
Owner Proprietary corp (Beverly Enterprises).
Admissions Requirements Minimum age 15; Physician's request.
Staff Physicians 41 (pt); RNs 3 (ft), 1 (pt); LPNs 9 (ft), 4 (pt); Nurses' aides 108 (ft), 10 (pt); Physical therapists 1 (pt); Recreational therapists 1 (pt); Occupational therapists 2 (pt); Speech therapists 1 (pt); Activities coordinators 1 (pt); Dietitians 1 (pt); Ophthalmologists 1 (pt); Podiatrists 1 (pt).
Facilities Dining room; Physical therapy room; Activities room; Chapel; Crafts room; Laundry room; Barber/Beauty shop; Library.

Activities Arts & crafts; Games; Reading groups; Prayer groups; Movies.

Trenton

Balmoral Skilled Nursing Home
5500 Fort St, Trenton, MI 48183
(313) 675-1600
Medical Dir Dr S Kwasiborski.
Licensure Skilled care. *Beds* SNF 209.
Certified Medicaid; Medicare.
Owner Proprietary corp (Comprehensive Health Care Assn).
Admissions Requirements Minimum age 16.
Staff Physicians 50 (pt); RNs 5 (ft), 6 (pt); LPNs 7 (ft), 7 (pt); Nurses' aides 51 (ft), 14 (pt); Physical therapists 1 (pt); Occupational therapists 1 (pt); Speech therapists 1 (pt); Activities coordinators 1 (ft); Dietitians 1 (ft); Ophthalmologists 1 (pt); Podiatrists 1 (pt); Dentists 1 (pt).
Facilities Dining room; Physical therapy room; Activities room; Laundry room; Barber/Beauty shop; Library.
Activities Arts & crafts; Cards; Games; Prayer groups; Movies; Dances/Social/Cultural gatherings; Classes; Cooking.

Troy

Canton Care Center
803 W Big Beaver Rd, 353, Troy, MI 48084-4734
Licensure Intermediate care. *Beds* ICF 91.
Certified Medicaid.

Union Lake

West Winds Nursing Home
10765 Bogie Lake Rd, Union Lake, MI 48085
(313) 363-9400
Admin Daniel C Page.
Medical Dir J J Johnstone DO.
Licensure Intermediate care. *Beds* ICF 50.
Certified Medicaid.
Admissions Requirements Minimum age 60.
Staff Physicians 2 (pt); RNs 7 (ft); LPNs 3 (ft); Nurses' aides 13 (ft), 24 (pt); Physical therapists; Reality therapists; Recreational therapists; Occupational therapists; Speech therapists; Activities coordinators 1 (ft); Dietitians 1 (pt); Ophthalmologists; Podiatrists; Audiologists; Dentists.
Facilities Dining room; Activities room; Crafts room; Laundry room; Barber/Beauty shop.
Activities Arts & crafts; Cards; Games; Reading groups; Prayer groups; Movies; Dances/Social/Cultural gatherings.

Utica

Wil Mar Nursing Home
7700 McClellan, Utica, MI 48087
Licensure Intermediate care. *Beds* ICF 52.
Certified Medicaid.

Vassar

Vassar Rest Home
999 E Huron Ave, Vassar, MI 48768
Licensure Home for aged. *Beds* Home for aged 22.

Wakefield

Gogebic Medical Care Facility
Rte 1 Box 31, Wakefield, MI 49968
(906) 224-9811, 224-9841 FAX
Admin Donald G Hall. *Dir of Nursing* Gail Hellerstedt RN. *Medical Dir* Bruce D Gordon MD.
Licensure Skilled care; Intermediate care. *Beds* Swing beds SNF/ICF 109. *Private Pay Patients* 9%. *Certified* Medicaid; Medicare.

Owner Publicly owned.
Admissions Requirements Minimum age 15; Medical examination; Physician's request.
Staff Physicians 5 (pt); RNs 6 (ft), 5 (pt); LPNs 5 (ft), 8 (pt); Nurses' aides 39 (ft), 20 (pt); Physical therapists 1 (ft), 1 (pt); Reality therapists 2 (ft); Recreational therapists 1 (ft), 2 (pt); Activities coordinators 1 (ft); Dietitians 1 (ft); Ophthalmologists 1 (pt); Podiatrists 1 (pt); Audiologists 1 (pt); Dentists 1 (ft), 1 (pt).
Facilities Dining room; Physical therapy room; Activities room; Chapel; Crafts room; Laundry room; Barber/Beauty shop; Library.
Activities Arts & crafts; Games; Reading groups; Prayer groups; Movies; Shopping trips; Dances/Social/Cultural gatherings; Intergenerational programs; Pet therapy.

Warren

Abbey Convalescent Center
12250 E Twelve Mile Rd, Warren, MI 48093
(313) 751-6200
Admin Juanita A Majishe.
Medical Dir Barry Szczesny DO.
Licensure Intermediate care. *Beds* ICF 201.
Certified Medicaid.
Owner Proprietary corp (Beverly Enterprises).
Admissions Requirements Minimum age 21; Medical examination; Physician's request.
Staff Physicians; RNs 12 (ft); LPNs 14 (ft); Nurses' aides 40 (ft), 25 (pt); Physical therapists 1 (pt); Recreational therapists 2 (ft); Speech therapists 1 (pt); Activities coordinators 1 (ft); Dietitians 1 (pt); Ophthalmologists 1 (pt); Podiatrists 1 (pt); Audiologists 1 (pt); Dentists 1 (pt).
Facilities Dining room; Physical therapy room; Activities room; Laundry room; Barber/Beauty shop.
Activities Arts & crafts; Cards; Games; Reading groups; Prayer groups; Movies; Shopping trips; Dances/Social/Cultural gatherings.

Arbor Inn
14030 Fourteen Mile Rd, Warren, MI 48093
Licensure Home for aged. *Beds* Home for aged 146.

Autumn Woods Residential Health Care Facility
29800 Hoover Rd, Warren, MI 48093
Licensure Skilled care. *Beds* SNF 330.
Certified Medicaid; Medicare.

Bortz Health Care of Warren
11700 E Ten Mile Rd, Warren, MI 48089
(313) 759-5960
Licensure Skilled care. *Beds* SNF 304.
Certified Medicaid; Medicare.

Nightingale Nursing Home
11525 E Ten Mile Rd, Warren, MI 48078
(313) 739-5523
Admin Lois J Klaus. *Dir of Nursing* Martha Dettloff. *Medical Dir* Laurence O Ribiat DO.
Licensure Skilled care. *Beds* SNF 185. *Private Pay Patients* 10%. *Certified* Medicaid; Medicare.
Owner Proprietary corp (International Healthcare Management).
Admissions Requirements Minimum age 18.
Staff Physicians 1 (pt); RNs 2 (ft), 1 (pt); LPNs 14 (ft), 2 (pt); Nurses' aides 60 (ft), 20 (pt); Speech therapists 1 (pt); Activities coordinators 3 (ft); Dietitians 1 (pt); Podiatrists 1 (pt); Audiologists 1 (pt).
Languages Polish, Czech.
Facilities Dining room; Physical therapy room; Activities room; Barber/Beauty shop.
Activities Arts & crafts; Cards; Games; Reading groups; Prayer groups; Movies; Shopping trips; Dances/Social/Cultural gatherings.

St Anthony Nursing Center
31830 Ryan Rd, Warren, MI 48092
(313) 977-6700
Licensure Skilled care. *Beds* SNF 102.
Certified Medicaid; Medicare.
Owner Proprietary corp (International Healthcare Management).
Affiliation Roman Catholic.

Wayland

Sandy Creek Nursing Home
425 E Elm St, Wayland, MI 49348
(616) 792-2249
Admin Evelyn L Hampel. *Dir of Nursing* Bertha Tew RN. *Medical Dir* Steven Bergman DO.
Licensure Skilled care; Intermediate care; Foster care; Supportive care; Retirement. *Beds* Swing beds SNF/ICF 99; Supportive care 20. *Private Pay Patients* 33%. *Certified* Medicaid; Medicare.
Owner Proprietary corp.
Admissions Requirements Minimum age 16; Medical examination; Physician's request.
Staff RNs 4 (ft), 3 (pt); LPNs 8 (ft), 2 (pt); Nurses' aides 47 (ft), 40 (pt); Physical therapists (consultants); Activities coordinators 3 (ft); Dietitians (consultants); Social services (consultants).
Facilities Dining room; Physical therapy room; Activities room; Laundry room; Barber/Beauty shop.
Activities Arts & crafts; Games; Reading groups; Prayer groups; Movies; Outside musical groups; Sing-alongs.

Wayne

Leisure Village
31720 Van Born Rd, Wayne, MI 48184
Licensure Home for aged. *Beds* Home for aged 312.

Venoy Continued Care Center
3999 Venoy, Wayne, MI 48184
(313) 326-6600
Admin Walter P Grabda. *Dir of Nursing* Rosa Redmond. *Medical Dir* L Usher DO.
Licensure Skilled care; Intermediate care; Alzheimer's care. *Beds* SNF 105; ICF 105. *Private Pay Patients* 9%. *Certified* Medicaid; Medicare.
Owner Nonprofit corp (Amerigard).
Admissions Requirements Minimum age 18; Physician's request.
Staff Physicians 1 (pt); RNs 4 (ft), 2 (pt); LPNs 11 (ft), 12 (pt); Nurses' aides 107 (ft), 8 (pt); Physical therapists 2 (pt); Recreational therapists 1 (pt); Occupational therapists 1 (pt); Speech therapists 1 (pt); Activities coordinators 1 (ft); Dietitians 1 (ft); Ophthalmologists; Podiatrists; Audiologists.
Languages Spanish, Polish.
Facilities Dining room; Physical therapy room; Activities room; Laundry room; Barber/Beauty shop; Obs unit; Dementia unit.
Activities Arts & crafts; Cards; Games; Reading groups; Prayer groups; Movies; Shopping trips; Dances/Social/Cultural gatherings; Pet therapy.

Wayne Convalescent Center
34330 Van Born Rd, Wayne, MI 48184
(313) 721-0740
Admin Rozella Hardin NHA. *Dir of Nursing* Linda Bagozzi RN. *Medical Dir* Marvin Trimas DO.
Licensure Intermediate care. *Beds* ICF 53. *Private Pay Patients* 11%. *Certified* Medicaid.
Owner Proprietary corp (Cardinal Medical).
Admissions Requirements Minimum age 15; Medical examination; Physician's request.

Staff Physicians 3 (pt); RNs 3 (ft); LPNs 4 (ft); Nurses' aides 30 (ft); Physical therapists (consultant); Reality therapists (consultant); Recreational therapists (consultant); Occupational therapists (consultant); Speech therapists (consultant); Activities coordinators (consultant); Dietitians (consultant); Ophthalmologists (consultant); Podiatrists (consultant); Audiologists (consultant).
Languages Spanish.
Facilities Dining room; Activities room; Laundry room; Large yard.
Activities Arts & crafts; Cards; Games; Reading groups; Prayer groups; Movies; Shopping trips; Dances/Social/Cultural gatherings; Intergenerational programs; Pet therapy; Various other activities.

Wayne Living Center for Seniors
4425 Venoy Rd, Wayne, MI 48184
Licensure Home for aged. *Beds* Home for aged 120.

Wayne Living Center Nursing Care
4429 Venoy Rd, Wayne, MI 48184
Licensure Intermediate care. *Beds* ICF 99.
Owner Proprietary corp (Beverly Enterprises).

Wayne Total Living Center For the Developmentally Disabled
4427 Venoy Rd, Wayne, MI 48184
Licensure Skilled care. *Beds* SNF 150.
Certified Medicaid.
Owner Proprietary corp (Beverly Enterprises).

West Bloomfield

Bortz Health Care of West Bloomfield
6470 Alden Dr, West Bloomfield, MI 48033
(313) 363-4121
Admin F Taker.
Medical Dir Dr J Janicke.
Licensure Intermediate care. *Beds* ICF 85.
Certified Medicaid.
Admissions Requirements Minimum age 21.
Staff Physicians 1 (ft); RNs 1 (ft), 3 (pt); LPNs 2 (ft), 4 (pt); Nurses' aides 35 (ft); Activities coordinators 1 (ft); Dietitians 1 (pt); Ophthalmologists 1 (pt); Podiatrists 1 (pt); Dentists 1 (pt).
Facilities Dining room; Barber/Beauty shop.
Activities Arts & crafts; Games; Reading groups; Prayer groups; Movies.

Orchard Lake Resthaven
7277 Richardson Rd, West Bloomfield, MI 48033
(313) 363-7161
Admin Jo Ann Williams. *Dir of Nursing* Patricia Miller RN. *Medical Dir* Dr Andrew Berry.
Licensure Intermediate care. *Beds* ICF 50. *Private Pay Patients* 50%. *Certified* Medicaid.
Owner Proprietary corp.
Admissions Requirements Medical examination; Physician's request.
Staff Physicians 3 (pt); RNs 1 (ft); LPNs 2 (ft), 6 (pt); Nurses' aides 10 (ft), 10 (pt); Physical therapists 1 (pt); Recreational therapists 1 (pt); Activities coordinators 1 (ft); Dietitians 1 (pt); Ophthalmologists 1 (pt); Podiatrists 1 (pt).
Facilities Dining room; Activities room; Laundry room; Barber/Beauty shop.
Activities Arts & crafts; Cards; Games; Reading groups; Prayer groups; Movies; Dances/Social/Cultural gatherings; Pet therapy.

West Bloomfield Nursing & Convalescent Center
6445 W Maple Rd, West Bloomfield, MI 48033
Licensure Skilled care; Home for aged. *Beds* SNF 120; Home for aged 86.

Windemere
6950 Farmington Rd, West Bloomfield, MI 48322
Licensure Skilled care; Home for aged. *Beds* SNF 120; Home for aged 105.

West Branch

Bortz Health Care of West Branch
445 S Valley Rd, West Branch, MI 48661
(313) 345-3600
Admin Pats;y Hardaway NHA. *Dir of Nursing* Patricia Yost.
Licensure Skilled care; Intermediate care. *Beds* Swing beds SNF/ICF 93. *Certified* Medicaid; Medicare.
Owner Proprietary corp.
Admissions Requirements Medical examination; Physician's request.
Staff RNs 3 (ft), 1 (pt); LPNs 6 (ft), 1 (pt); Nurses' aides 25 (ft), 10 (pt); Activities coordinators 1 (ft), 1 (pt); Dietitians 1 (ft).
Facilities Dining room; Physical therapy room; Activities room; Chapel; Crafts room; Barber/Beauty shop; Library.
Activities Arts & crafts; Cards; Games; Reading groups; Prayer groups; Movies; Shopping trips; Dances/Social/Cultural gatherings; Garden clubs; Resident of the month; Annual king & queen.

Westland

Four Chaplains Convalescent Center
28349 Joy Rd, Westland, MI 48185
(313) 261-9500
Admin Dr Larry L Ruehlen. *Dir of Nursing* Diane Pryslak RN. *Medical Dir* Michael Gambel MD.
Licensure Skilled care; Intermediate care; Home for aged. *Beds* Swing beds SNF/ICF 111; Home for aged 50. *Certified* Medicaid; Medicare.
Owner Proprietary corp (Beverly Enterprises).
Admissions Requirements Minimum age 21; Medical examination; Physician's request.
Staff Physicians; RNs; LPNs; Nurses' aides; Physical therapists; Activities coordinators; Dietitians.
Facilities Dining room; Physical therapy room; Activities room; Chapel; Crafts room; Laundry room; Barber/Beauty shop; Library.
Activities Arts & crafts; Cards; Games; Reading groups; Prayer groups; Movies; Shopping trips; Dances/Social/Cultural gatherings; Exercises; Current events; Cooking classes.

Middlebelt-Hope Nursing Center
38410 Cherry Hill Rd, Westland, MI 48185
(313) 326-1200
Admin P Ostlund RN. *Dir of Nursing* S McCormack RN. *Medical Dir* J Mohtadi MD.
Licensure Skilled care. *Beds* SNF 142. *Private Pay Patients* 35%. *Certified* Medicaid; Medicare.
Owner Proprietary corp (International Healthcare Management).
Admissions Requirements Minimum age 15; Physician's request.
Staff Physicians 2 (pt); RNs 4 (ft), 1 (pt); LPNs 7 (ft), 5 (pt); Nurses' aides 54 (ft), 27 (pt); Physical therapists 1 (ft), 2 (pt); Recreational therapists 1 (ft), 2 (pt); Speech therapists 1 (pt); Activities coordinators 1 (ft); Dietitians 1 (pt); Podiatrists 1 (pt).
Facilities Dining room; Physical therapy room; Activities room; Crafts room; Laundry room; Barber/Beauty shop.
Activities Arts & crafts; Cards; Games; Reading groups; Prayer groups; Movies; Dances/Social/Cultural gatherings; Intergenerational programs; Pet therapy.

Nightingale West Nursing Home
8365 Newburgh Rd, Westland, MI 48185
(313) 261-5300
Licensure Intermediate care. *Beds* ICF 236. *Certified* Medicaid.

Westland Convalescent Center
36137 W Warren, Westland, MI 48185
(313) 728-6100
Admin Judith G Caroselli. *Dir of Nursing* Judith Smith RN BSN. *Medical Dir* Leonard Rosenberg DO.
Licensure Skilled care; Intermediate care; Alzheimer's care. *Beds* Swing beds SNF/ICF 230. *Certified* Medicaid; Medicare.
Owner Proprietary corp.
Admissions Requirements Minimum age 15; Medical examination; Physician's request.
Staff Physicians; RNs 20 (ft), 6 (pt); LPNs 16 (ft), 4 (pt); Nurses' aides 150 (ft); Physical therapists 1 (ft); Reality therapists 4 (ft); Recreational therapists; Occupational therapists 1 (ft); Speech therapists 1 (ft); Activities coordinators 3 (ft); Dietitians 2 (ft); Ophthalmologists 1 (pt); Podiatrists 2 (pt); Dentists 1 (pt).
Facilities Dining room; Physical therapy room; Activities room; Chapel; Crafts room; Laundry room; Barber/Beauty shop; Library; Private dining room.
Activities Arts & crafts; Cards; Games; Reading groups; Prayer groups; Movies; Shopping trips; Dances/Social/Cultural gatherings; Intergenerational programs; Pet therapy; M.S. club; Men's night.

Whitehall

Whitehall Manor
916 E Lewis, Whitehall, MI 49461
(616) 894-4056, 894-8579 FAX
Admin Paula R Herraiz. *Dir of Nursing* Marlene Easley. *Medical Dir* Albert D Engstrom MD.
Licensure Skilled care; Intermediate care. *Beds* SNF 61; ICF 64. *Private Pay Patients* 20%. *Certified* Medicaid; Medicare.
Owner Proprietary corp (Health Care and Retirement Corp).
Admissions Requirements Minimum age 15; Medical examination; Physician's request.
Staff Physicians 1 (ft), 4 (pt); RNs 4 (ft), 2 (pt); LPNs 6 (ft), 7 (pt); Nurses' aides 35 (ft), 15 (pt); Physical therapists 1 (pt); Occupational therapists 1 (pt); Speech therapists 1 (pt); Activities coordinators 1 (ft), 1 (pt); Dietitians 1 (ft), 1 (pt); Ophthalmologists 1 (pt); Podiatrists 1 (pt); Audiologists 1 (pt).
Facilities Dining room; Physical therapy room; Activities room; Crafts room; Laundry room; Barber/Beauty shop; Private and semi-private rooms.
Activities Arts & crafts; Cards; Games; Reading groups; Prayer groups; Movies; Shopping trips; Dances/Social/Cultural gatherings; Intergenerational programs; Pet therapy.

Whitmore Lake

Whitmore Lake Convalescent Center
8633 N Main St, Whitmore Lake, MI 48189
(313) 449-4431
Admin Sara J Schaden. *Dir of Nursing* Pamela J Thorp RN. *Medical Dir* George Fischmann MD.
Licensure Intermediate care. *Beds* ICF 212. *Certified* Medicaid.
Owner Proprietary corp.
Admissions Requirements Minimum age 15; Medical examination; Physician's request.
Staff Physicians 2 (pt); RNs 3 (ft), 7 (pt); LPNs 11 (ft), 3 (pt); Nurses' aides 35 (ft), 8 (pt); Activities coordinators 2 (pt); Dietitians 12 (ft), 5 (pt).

Facilities Dining room; Physical therapy room; Activities room; Laundry room; Barber/Beauty shop; Library; Privacy room; Gift shop.
Activities Arts & crafts; Cards; Games; Reading groups; Prayer groups; Movies; Dances/Social/Cultural gatherings; GED program; Outings; Pets in-house; Wood shop.

Woodhaven

Applewood Nursing Center
18500 Van Horn Rd, Woodhaven, MI 48183
(313) 676-7575
Medical Dir Craig Kwalton DO.
Licensure Skilled care. *Beds* SNF 150. *Certified* Medicaid; Medicare.
Admissions Requirements Medical examination; Physician's request.
Facilities Dining room; Physical therapy room; Activities room; Crafts room; Laundry room; Barber/Beauty shop.
Activities Arts & crafts; Cards; Games; Reading groups; Prayer groups; Movies; Dances/Social/Cultural gatherings.

Wyoming

Crestview Manor
625 36th St SW, Wyoming, MI 49509
(616) 531-0200
Licensure Skilled care; Home for aged. *Beds* SNF 80; Home for aged 13. *Certified* Medicaid; Medicare.
Owner Proprietary corp (Health Care and Retirement Corp).

Yale

Medilodge of Yale
90 Jean St, Yale, MI 48097
(313) 387-3226
Licensure Skilled care. *Beds* SNF 88. *Certified* Medicaid; Medicare.

Ypsilanti

Bortz Health Care of Ypsilanti
28 S Prospect St, Ypsilanti, MI 48198
(313) 483-6125
Admin Herbert E Harrington.
Medical Dir Athar Siddiqui MD.
Licensure Skilled care. *Beds* SNF 180. *Certified* Medicaid; Medicare.
Owner Proprietary corp.
Admissions Requirements Minimum age 18; Physician's request.
Staff Physicians 1 (pt); RNs 4 (ft); LPNs 15 (ft), 3 (pt); Physical therapists 1 (pt); Occupational therapists 1 (pt); Speech therapists 1 (pt); Activities coordinators 1 (ft); Dietitians 1 (pt); Ophthalmologists 1 (pt).
Facilities Dining room; Physical therapy room; Activities room; Crafts room; Barber/Beauty shop.
Activities Arts & crafts; Cards; Games; Reading groups; Prayer groups; Movies; Shopping trips; Dances/Social/Cultural gatherings.

Evergreen Hills Nursing Center
1045 Ware Ct, Ypsilanti, MI 48198
(313) 483-5421
Admin Patricia A Seeley. *Dir of Nursing* Patricia Yost RN. *Medical Dir* Charles Lyon DO.
Licensure Intermediate care. *Beds* ICF 108. *Private Pay Patients* 7%. *Certified* Medicaid.
Owner Proprietary corp.
Admissions Requirements Minimum age 21.
Staff Physicians 3 (pt); RNs 2 (ft); LPNs 7 (ft), 3 (pt); Nurses' aides 26 (ft), 2 (pt); Physical therapists 1 (pt); Occupational

therapists 1 (pt); Activities coordinators 1 (ft); Dietitians 1 (ft); Ophthalmologists 1 (pt); Podiatrists 1 (pt); Audiologists 1 (pt).
Languages Spanish.
Facilities Dining room; Physical therapy room; Activities room; Chapel; Crafts room; Laundry room; Barber/Beauty shop; Library.
Activities Arts & crafts; Cards; Games; Reading groups; Prayer groups; Movies; Shopping trips; Dances/Social/Cultural gatherings.

Gilbert Old Peoples Home of Ypsilanti
203 S Huron St, Ypsilanti, MI 48197
(313) 482-9498
Medical Dir William Edmunds MD.
Licensure Intermediate care; Home for aged. *Beds* ICF 32; Home for aged 40. *Certified* Medicaid.
Admissions Requirements Minimum age 65; Medical examination.
Facilities Dining room; Activities room; Laundry room; Barber/Beauty shop; Library.
Activities Arts & crafts; Games; Prayer groups; Movies; Shopping trips.

Huron Valley Nursing Care Facility
3201 Bemis Rd, Ypsilanti, MI 48197
(313) 434-7775
Licensure Intermediate care. *Beds* ICF 36. *Certified* Medicaid.

Zeeland

Haven Park Nursing Center
285 N State, Zeeland, MI 49464
(616) 772-4641
Admin Valerie Powell RN. *Dir of Nursing* Hazel Fik RN. *Medical Dir* Dr Nasim Yacob.
Licensure Skilled care. *Beds* SNF 153. *Certified* Medicaid; Medicare.
Owner Proprietary corp (Comprehensive Health Care Assn).
Admissions Requirements Medical examination; Physician's request.
Staff RNs; LPNs; Nurses' aides; Activities coordinators.
Languages Dutch.

Facilities Dining room; Physical therapy room; Activities room; Laundry room; Barber/Beauty shop.
Activities Arts & crafts; Cards; Games; Reading groups; Prayer groups; Movies.

Heritage Healthcare Centre
320 E Central Ave, Zeeland, MI 49464
(616) 772-9191
Admin Marsha Van Norman.
Medical Dir Marge Bergsma.
Licensure Intermediate care. *Beds* ICF 45. *Certified* Medicaid.
Owner Proprietary corp.
Admissions Requirements Medical examination; Physician's request.
Staff Physicians 1 (pt); RNs 1 (ft); LPNs 1 (ft), 6 (pt); Nurses' aides; Activities coordinators 2 (pt); Dietitians 1 (pt).
Facilities Dining room; Activities room; Chapel; Crafts room; Laundry room; Barber/Beauty shop; Library.
Activities Arts & crafts; Cards; Games; Prayer groups; Movies.

MINNESOTA

Ada

Ada Municipal Hospital
405 E 2nd Ave, Ada, MN 56510
(218) 784-2561
Admin Robert Cameron.
Licensure Skilled care. *Beds* SNF 53. *Certified*
Medicaid; Medicare.
Owner Publicly owned.

Ada 1
207 Jamison Dr, Ada, MN 56510
(218) 784-2219
Admin Dr Vernon C Nordmark.
Medical Dir Josette C Nordmark MD.
Licensure Intermediate care for mentally
retarded. *Beds* ICF/MR 6. *Certified*
Medicaid.
Owner Proprietary corp.
Admissions Requirements Minimum age 18;
Medical examination.
Staff RNs 1 (pt); Activities coordinators 1 (ft);
Direct care 3 (ft), 6 (pt).
Facilities Dining room; Laundry room.
Activities Arts & crafts; Cards; Games;
Movies; Shopping trips; Dances/Social/
Cultural gatherings; Community recreation.

Ada 2
21 E 4th Ave, Ada, MN 56510
(218) 784-2217
Admin Dr Vernon Nordmark.
Licensure Intermediate care for mentally
retarded. *Beds* ICF/MR 6. *Certified*
Medicaid.
Owner Proprietary corp.

Adams

Adams Group Home
407 6th St NW, Adams, MN 55909
(507) 582-3482
Admin Vicki Evenson.
Licensure Intermediate care for mentally
retarded. *Beds* ICF/MR 16. *Certified*
Medicaid.
Owner Proprietary corp.
Admissions Requirements Minimum age 16;
Medical examination.
Staff LPNs 3 (pt); Nurses' aides 8 (ft), 12 (pt).
Affiliation Lutheran.
Facilities Dining room; Laundry room.
Activities Arts & crafts; Cards; Games; Prayer
groups; Movies; Shopping trips; Dances/
Social/Cultural gatherings; Dinner out;
Concerts.

Adams Health Care Center
RR 2, Box 300, Adams, MN 55909
(507) 582-3263
Admin James Thalberg.
Licensure Skilled care. *Beds* SNF 66. *Certified*
Medicaid; Medicare.
Owner Publicly owned.

Adrian

Arnold Memorial Nursing Home
601 Louisiana Ave, Adrian, MN 56110-0279
(507) 483-2668
Admin Charlotte D Heitkamp. *Dir of Nursing*
Virginia B Simonich RN. *Medical Dir*
Timothy E Nealy MD.
Licensure Intermediate care. *Beds* ICF 41.
Private Pay Patients 40%. *Certified*
Medicaid.
Owner Publicly owned.
Admissions Requirements Physician's request.
Staff RNs 1 (ft), 1 (pt); LPNs 1 (ft), 3 (pt);
Nurses' aides 3 (ft), 15 (pt); Activities
coordinators 1 (ft), 1 (pt); Dietitians.
Facilities Dining room; Activities room;
Chapel; Crafts room; Laundry room; Barber/
Beauty shop; Wheelchair accessible garden.
Activities Arts & crafts; Cards; Games;
Reading groups; Prayer groups; Movies;
Shopping trips; Dances/Social/Cultural
gatherings; Pet therapy.

Ah Gwah Ching

Ah-Gwah-Ching Nursing Home
Ah Gwah Ching, MN 56430
(218) 547-1250
Admin John Grimley. *Dir of Nursing* Nancy
Dahl. *Medical Dir* Dr Burton Haugen.
Licensure Skilled care; Intermediate care. *Beds*
SNF 179; ICF 164. *Certified* Medicaid;
Medicare.
Owner Publicly owned.
Admissions Requirements Minimum age 65;
Medical examination.
Staff RNs 19 (ft), 2 (pt); LPNs 42 (ft); Nurses'
aides 88 (ft), 26 (pt); Physical therapists 2
(ft); Recreational therapists 13 (ft); Activities
coordinators 1 (ft); Dietitians 1 (ft);
Psychologists 2 (ft); Social workers 5 (ft);
RNPs (Geriatric Specialty) 1 (ft).
Facilities Dining room; Physical therapy
room; Activities room; Chapel; Crafts room;
Barber/Beauty shop.
Activities Arts & crafts; Cards; Games;
Reading groups; Prayer groups; Movies;
Shopping trips; Dances/Social/Cultural
gatherings; Pontoon rides; Fishing.

Lakeside Center
Ah Gwah Ching, MN 56430
(218) 547-1250
Admin John Grimley.
Licensure Supervised living. *Beds* Supervised
living 40.
Owner Nonprofit corp.

Aitkin

Aicota Nursing Home
850 2nd St NW, Aitkin, MN 56431
(218) 927-2164
Admin Barry Foss.

Licensure Skilled care; Intermediate care;
Medicare and Medicaid beds. *Beds* SNF 29;
ICF 51; Medicare & Medicaid beds 26.
Certified Medicaid; Medicare.
Owner Proprietary corp.

Aitkin Community Hospital
301 Minnesota Ave S, Aitkin, MN 56431
(218) 927-2121
Admin Patrick B Renner.
Licensure Skilled care; Boarding care. *Beds*
SNF 48; Boarding care 6. *Certified*
Medicaid; Medicare.
Owner Proprietary corp (Health One).

Oak Ridge Homes
316 2nd Ave SE, Aitkin, MN 56431
(218) 927-3946
Admin David Felske.
Licensure Intermediate care for mentally
retarded. *Beds* ICF/MR 12.
Owner Proprietary corp.

Albany

Mother of Mercy Nursing Home
Box 676, 320 Church Ave, Albany, MN 56307
(612) 845-2195
Admin Patrick F Mitchell. *Dir of Nursing*
Bertha Schiller.
Licensure Skilled care; Intermediate care;
Retirement. *Beds* SNF 72; ICF 12. *Certified*
Medicaid; Medicare.
Owner Proprietary corp.
Staff Physicians 1 (ft); RNs 3 (ft), 4 (pt);
LPNs 4 (ft), 3 (pt); Nurses' aides 33 (ft), 17
(pt); Physical therapists 1 (ft); Reality
therapists 4 (ft); Recreational therapists 4
(ft); Recreational therapists 4 (ft);
Occupational therapists 1 (pt); Speech
therapists 1 (pt); Activities coordinators 1
(ft); Dietitians 1 (ft).
Languages German.
Affiliation Roman Catholic.
Facilities Dining room; Physical therapy
room; Activities room; Chapel; Crafts room;
Laundry room; Barber/Beauty shop; Library.
Activities Arts & crafts; Cards; Games;
Reading groups; Prayer groups; Movies;
Shopping trips; Dances/Social/Cultural
gatherings; Fishing; Golf.

Albert Lea

Albert Lea Good Samaritan Center
Rte 2 Box 217, Albert Lea, MN 56007
(507) 373-0683
Admin Craig Johnsen.
Medical Dir Dr Thoburn Thompson.
Licensure Skilled care. *Beds* SNF 182.
Certified Medicaid; Medicare.
Owner Nonprofit corp (Evangelical Lutheran/
Good Samaritan Society).
Admissions Requirements Minimum age 16;
Medical examination; Physician's request.

Staff RNs 2 (ft), 9 (pt); LPNs 4 (ft), 7 (pt);
Nurses' aides 21 (ft), 83 (pt); Physical
therapists 1 (pt); Recreational therapists 4
(ft); Activities coordinators 1 (ft); Dietitians
1 (ft).
Affiliation Lutheran.
Facilities Dining room; Physical therapy
room; Activities room; Chapel; Crafts room;
Laundry room; Barber/Beauty shop; Library.
Activities Arts & crafts; Cards; Games;
Reading groups; Prayer groups; Movies;
Shopping trips; Dances/Social/Cultural
gatherings.

Crest Home of Albert Lea
1205 Garfield Ave, Albert Lea, MN 56007
(507) 373-0188
Admin Virginia Larson.
Licensure Intermediate care for mentally
retarded. *Beds* ICF/MR 15. *Certified*
Medicaid.
Owner Proprietary corp.
Staff RNs (consultant); Recreational therapists
(consultant); Speech therapists (consultant);
Dietitians (consultant).

Fountain Lake Treatment Center
408 Fountain St, Albert Lea, MN 56007
(507) 373-2384
Admin Neil Carolan.
Licensure Supervised living. *Beds* Supervised
living 93.
Owner Proprietary corp.

Golden Age Guest Home
601 E 5th St, Albert Lea, MN 56007
(507) 373-0949
Admin Laverne Marie Peters. *Dir of Nursing*
Viola Rynerson. *Medical Dir* Vicky
Thompson.
Licensure Board and care. *Beds* Board and
care 9. *Private Pay Patients* 2-4%. *Certified*
Medicare.
Owner Privately owned.
Admissions Requirements Minimum age 30.
Staff LPNs; Nurses' aides; Activities
coordinators.
Facilities Dining room; Activities room;
Laundry room.
Activities Arts & crafts; Cards; Games;
Movies; Shopping trips; Pet therapy;
Outings; Picnics; Transportation to church
by church bus; Bingo; Birthday parties;
Family gatherings.

Albert Lea Boarding Care Center
315 Park Ave, Albert Lea, MN 56007
(507) 373-9616
Admin Myrtle Dahl RN. *Dir of Nursing* Gail
Harty LPN; Myrtle Dahl RN.
Licensure Boarding care. *Beds* Boarding care
21.
Owner Privately owned.
Admissions Requirements Medical
examination; Physician's request.
Staff RNs 1 (ft); LPNs 1 (ft); Nurses' aides 13
(ft); Physical therapists; Activities
coordinators 1 (pt); Dietitians 1 (pt).
Facilities Dining room; Activities room;
Laundry room; Library.
Activities Arts & crafts; Cards; Games;
Reading groups; Prayer groups; Movies;
Shopping trips.

Rathjen House
RR 3 Box 45A, Albert Lea, MN 56007
(507) 373-6730
Admin Del Sand.
Licensure Supervised living. *Beds* Supervised
living 15.
Owner Proprietary corp.

St Johns Lutheran Home
901 Luther Pl, Albert Lea, MN 56007
(507) 373-8226
Admin Timothy J Samuelson.
Medical Dir L E Shelhamer MD.
Licensure Skilled care. *Beds* SNF 206.
Certified Medicaid; Medicare.

Owner Nonprofit corp.
Admissions Requirements Minimum age 21;
Medical examination; Physician's request.
Staff RNs 7 (ft), 9 (pt); LPNs 4 (ft), 13 (pt);
Nurses' aides 45 (ft), 60 (pt); Physical
therapists 3 (ft); Occupational therapists 2
(ft), 2 (pt); Speech therapists 1 (pt);
Activities coordinators 1 (pt); Dietitians 1
(ft).
Affiliation Lutheran.
Facilities Dining room; Physical therapy
room; Activities room; Chapel; Crafts room;
Laundry room; Barber/Beauty shop; Library.
Activities Arts & crafts; Cards; Games;
Reading groups; Prayer groups; Movies;
Shopping trips; Dances/Social/Cultural
gatherings.

Thorne Crest Retirement Center
1201 Garfield Ave, Albert Lea, MN 56007
(507) 373-2311
Admin Dale L Rippey.
Licensure Skilled care. *Beds* SNF 52. *Certified*
Medicaid; Medicare.
Owner Nonprofit corp (American Baptist
Homes).
Admissions Requirements Medical
examination.
Staff RNs 3 (ft), 5 (pt); LPNs 2 (ft), 4 (pt);
Nurses' aides 10 (ft), 20 (pt); Activities
coordinators 1 (ft), 2 (pt).
Affiliation Baptist.
Facilities Dining room; Physical therapy
room; Activities room; Chapel; Crafts room;
Laundry room; Barber/Beauty shop; Library.
Activities Arts & crafts; Cards; Games;
Reading groups; Prayer groups; Movies;
Shopping trips; Dances/Social/Cultural
gatherings.

Thorne-Crest South
617 10th St, Albert Lea, MN 56007
(507) 373-7600
Admin Dale Rippey. *Dir of Nursing* Judy
Eidness. *Medical Dir* Dr D Birkhofer.
Licensure Skilled care. *Beds* SNF 28. *Certified*
Medicaid; Medicare.
Owner Nonprofit corp (American Baptist
Homes).
Admissions Requirements Medical
examination.
Staff RNs 1 (ft), 1 (pt); LPNs 6 (pt); Activities
coordinators 1 (ft).
Activities Arts & crafts; Reading groups;
Prayer groups; Movies; Shopping trips;
Dances/Social/Cultural gatherings.

Woodvale V
1204 Plainview Ln, Albert Lea, MN 56007
(507) 373-7629
Admin Richard Turcotte.
Licensure Intermediate care for mentally
retarded. *Beds* ICF/MR 32. *Certified*
Medicaid.
Owner Proprietary corp.

Woodvale VII
PO Box 650, 1432 Spartan Ave, Albert Lea,
MN 56007
(507) 373-7629
Admin Richard Turcotte.
Licensure Intermediate care for mentally
retarded. *Beds* ICF/MR 10. *Certified*
Medicaid.
Owner Proprietary corp.

Alexandria

Bethany Home
1020 Lark St, Alexandria, MN 56308
(612) 762-1567
Admin Paul Collins. *Dir of Nursing* Virginia
Long. *Medical Dir* Dr Mark Odland.
Licensure Skilled care; Retirement;
Alzheimer's care. *Beds* SNF 181. *Certified*
Medicaid; Medicare.
Owner Nonprofit corp.

Admissions Requirements Medical
examination; Physician's request.
Staff RNs; LPNs; Nurses' aides; Physical
therapists 1 (ft); Activities coordinators 1
(ft); Dietitians 1 (ft); Chaplains 1 (ft).
Affiliation Lutheran.
Facilities Dining room; Physical therapy
room; Activities room; Chapel; Crafts room;
Laundry room; Barber/Beauty shop; Library;
Coffee shop.
Activities Arts & crafts; Cards; Games;
Reading groups; Prayer groups; Movies;
Shopping trips; Dances/Social/Cultural
gatherings.

Knute Nelson Memorial Home
420 12th Ave E, Alexandria, MN 56308
(612) 763-6653
Admin David L Sorbel.
Licensure Skilled care; Intermediate care. *Beds*
SNF 97; ICF 70. *Certified* Medicaid;
Medicare.
Owner Proprietary corp.

Project New Hope 1-5
PO Box 368, Quincy & Glendale, Alexandria,
MN 56308
(612) 763-6528
Admin Betty Schmitt. *Dir of Nursing* Laurie
Holm RN.
Licensure Intermediate care for mentally
retarded. *Beds* ICF/MR 30 (5 facilities of 6
residents each). *Private Pay Patients* 0%.
Certified Medicaid.
Owner Nonprofit corp.
Admissions Requirements Minimum age 15;
Medical examination.
Staff RNs 1 (ft); LPNs 1 (ft).
Facilities Dining room.
Activities Arts & crafts; Cards; Games;
Movies; Shopping trips; Dances/Social/
Cultural gatherings; Day programs in
community.

Project New Hope 6
1007 High St, Alexandria, MN 56308
(612) 763-6528
Admin Gerry Cascioli. *Dir of Nursing* Nancy
Scholl RN.
Licensure Intermediate care for mentally
retarded. *Beds* ICF/MR 6. *Certified*
Medicaid.
Owner Proprietary corp.
Admissions Requirements Minimum age 18;
Medical examination.
Staff RNs 1 (pt); LPNs 1 (pt).
Activities Arts & crafts; Cards; Games;
Reading groups; Movies; Shopping trips;
Dances/Social/Cultural gatherings.

Project New Hope 7
1108 W Meadow Ln, Alexandria, MN 56308
(612) 763-6528
Admin Gerry Cascioli. *Dir of Nursing* Nancy
Scholl RN.
Licensure Intermediate care for mentally
retarded. *Beds* ICF/MR 6. *Certified*
Medicaid.
Owner Proprietary corp.
Admissions Requirements Minimum age 18;
Medical examination.
Staff RNs 1 (pt); LPNs 1 (pt).
Activities Arts & crafts; Cards; Games;
Reading groups; Movies; Shopping trips;
Dances/Social/Cultural gatherings.

Annandale

Annandale Care Center
RR 4, Box 57, Hwy 24 E, Annandale, MN
55302
(612) 274-3737
Admin John Nelson.
Licensure Skilled care. *Beds* SNF 60. *Certified*
Medicaid; Medicare.
Owner Nonprofit corp.

Anoka

Anoka Maple Manor Care Center
1040 Madison St, Anoka, MN 55303
(612) 421-2311
Admin Steve Forster.
Licensure Skilled care. *Beds* SNF 127.
  Certified Medicaid; Medicare.
Owner Proprietary corp (Good Neighbor
  Services).

Twin Rivers Care Center
305 Fremont, Anoka, MN 55303
(612) 421-5660
Admin M Claire Melstrom. *Dir of Nursing*
  Laure Olson. *Medical Dir* Robert Sonntag
  MD.
Licensure Skilled care. *Beds* SNF 62. *Certified*
  Medicaid; Medicare.
Owner Proprietary corp (Beverly Enterprises).
Admissions Requirements Minimum age 18;
  Medical examination; Physician's request.
Staff RNs 6 (ft), 4 (pt); LPNs 8 (ft), 4 (pt);
  Nurses' aides 13 (ft), 14 (pt); Physical
  therapists 1 (ft); Recreational therapists 1
  (ft); Occupational therapists 1 (ft); Speech
  therapists 1 (pt); Activities coordinators 1
  (ft); Dietitians 1 (ft); Ophthalmologists
  (contracted); Podiatrists (contracted);
  Audiologists (contracted).
Facilities Dining room; Physical therapy
  room; Activities room; Barber/Beauty shop.
Activities Arts & crafts; Cards; Games;
  Reading groups; Prayer groups; Movies;
  Shopping trips; Dances/Social/Cultural
  gatherings; Intergenerational programs; Pet
  therapy.

Apple Valley

Apple Valley Health Center
14650 Garrett Ave, Apple Valley, MN 55124
(612) 431-7700
Admin Pearl A Lemieux. *Dir of Nursing* Lois
  A Duffy RN. *Medical Dir* E J English MD.
Licensure Skilled care; Retirement;
  Alzheimer's care. *Beds* SNF 200. *Certified*
  Medicaid; Medicare.
Owner Proprietary corp.
Admissions Requirements Minimum age 16;
  Medical examination.
Staff Physicians; RNs; LPNs; Nurses' aides;
  Physical therapists; Recreational therapists;
  Occupational therapists; Speech therapists;
  Activities coordinators; Dietitians.
Facilities Dining room; Physical therapy
  room; Activities room; Crafts room; Laundry
  room; Barber/Beauty shop; Therapeutic pool.
Activities Arts & crafts; Cards; Games;
  Reading groups; Prayer groups; Movies;
  Shopping trips; Dances/Social/Cultural
  gatherings.

Appleton

Appleton Municipal Hospital
30 S Behl St, Appleton, MN 56208
(612) 289-2400
Admin Mark Paulson. *Dir of Nursing* Marti
  Croatt. *Medical Dir* R V Kabatay MD.
Licensure Skilled care. *Beds* SNF 84. *Certified*
  Medicaid; Medicare.
Owner Publicly owned.
Admissions Requirements Females only;
  Medical examination.
Staff RNs 6 (ft); LPNs 10 (ft); Nurses' aides
  25 (ft); Activities coordinators 1 (ft).
Languages Norwegian.
Facilities Dining room; Physical therapy
  room; Activities room; Chapel; Crafts room;
  Laundry room; Barber/Beauty shop.
Activities Arts & crafts; Cards; Games;
  Reading groups; Prayer groups; Movies;
  Shopping trips; Dances/Social/Cultural
  gatherings.

Arden Hills

CR Homes on Cummings
1385 Cummings Ln, Arden Hills, MN 55112
(612) 636-7537
Admin James Nelson.
Licensure Intermediate care for mentally
  retarded. *Beds* ICF/MR 6. *Certified*
  Medicaid.
Owner Proprietary corp.

Johanna Shores
3220 Lake Johanna Blvd, Arden Hills, MN
  55112
(612) 631-6000
Admin Fred Strandberg.
Medical Dir Robert Blomberg MD.
Licensure Skilled care; Retirement. *Beds* SNF
  208; Retirement 178. *Certified* Medicaid;
  Medicare.
Owner Nonprofit organization/foundation.
Admissions Requirements Medical
  examination.
Staff Physicians; RNs; LPNs; Nurses' aides;
  Physical therapists; Recreational therapists;
  Occupational therapists; Speech therapists;
  Activities coordinators; Dietitians;
  Podiatrists; Dentists; X-ray technicians;
  Aquatics instructors.
Affiliation Presbyterian.
Facilities Dining room; Physical therapy
  room; Activities room; Chapel; Crafts room;
  Laundry room; Barber/Beauty shop; Library;
  Medical clinic (Ophthalmology, X-ray,
  Dental, Podiatry, Audiology, Speech);
  Swimming pool; Whirlpool.
Activities Arts & crafts; Cards; Games;
  Reading groups; Prayer groups; Movies;
  Shopping trips; Dances/Social/Cultural
  gatherings.

Argyle

Marshall County Group Homes Inc
PO Box D, Argyle, MN 56713
(218) 437-6695
Admin Sue C Holter. *Dir of Nursing* JoAnn
  Saunders. *Medical Dir* Mary Safranski.
Licensure Intermediate care for mentally
  retarded; Supportive living. *Beds* ICF/MR
  10; Supportive living 8. *Private Pay Patients*
  0%. *Certified* Medicaid.
Owner Nonprofit corp.
Admissions Requirements Medical
  examination.
Staff RNs 1 (pt); LPNs 1 (pt); Physical
  therapists (contracted); Occupational
  therapists (contracted); Dietitians
  (contracted); Audiologists (contracted);
  Resident programmers 11 (ft), 26 (pt).
Facilities Dining room; Activities room;
  Crafts room; Laundry room.
Activities Arts & crafts; Cards; Games; Prayer
  groups; Movies; Shopping trips; Dances/
  Social/Cultural gatherings; Pet therapy.

Arlington

Arlington Good Samaritan Center
411 7th Ave NW, Box 645, Arlington, MN
  55307
(612) 964-2251
Admin Dale Miller.
Licensure Intermediate care. *Beds* ICF 63.
  Certified Medicaid.
Owner Nonprofit corp (Evangelical Lutheran/
  Good Samaritan Society).
Affiliation Lutheran.

High Island Creek Residence
Box 334, Chestnut Dr, Arlington, MN 55307
(612) 964-5984
Admin Dennis Spurling.
Licensure Intermediate care for mentally
  retarded. *Beds* ICF/MR 15.
Owner Proprietary corp.

Ashby

Pelican Lake Health Care Center
305 Melba, Box 227, Ashby, MN 56309
(218) 747-2224
Admin Jon Ellefson.
Medical Dir Paul Jacobson MD.
Licensure Skilled care; Intermediate care;
  Alzheimer's care. *Beds* SNF 72; ICF 6.
  Certified Medicaid; Medicare.
Owner Proprietary corp.
Admissions Requirements Medical
  examination.
Staff Physicians 2 (ft); RNs 3 (ft); LPNs 2 (ft),
  5 (pt); Nurses' aides 4 (ft), 30 (pt); Activities
  coordinators 1 (ft), 1 (pt).
Facilities Dining room; Activities room;
  Crafts room; Laundry room; Barber/Beauty
  shop.
Activities Arts & crafts; Cards; Games;
  Reading groups; Prayer groups; Movies;
  Dances/Social/Cultural gatherings.

Atwater

Atwater House
5th & Minnesota Ave, Atwater, MN 56209
(612) 974-8070
Admin Kathryn Selseth-Kill. *Dir of Nursing*
  Linda Nelson RN. *Medical Dir* Ronald
  Holmgien MD.
Licensure Intermediate care for mentally
  retarded. *Beds* ICF/MR 15. *Certified*
  Medicaid.
Owner Proprietary corp.
Admissions Requirements Minimum age 18;
  Females only; Medical examination.
Staff Physicians 1 (pt); RNs 1 (pt); Activities
  coordinators 1 (ft).
Languages Spanish.
Facilities Dining room; Activities room;
  Laundry room.
Activities Arts & crafts; Cards; Games;
  Reading groups; Movies; Shopping trips;
  Dances/Social/Cultural gatherings; Travel.

Aurora

Salmi Boarding Home
Rte 1 Box 237-B, Aurora, MN 55705
(218) 638-2990
Admin Clyde E Salmi.
Licensure Intermediate care for mentally
  retarded. *Beds* ICF/MR 15. *Certified*
  Medicaid.
Owner Proprietary corp.

White Community Hospital
320 Hwy 110 E, Aurora, MN 55705
(218) 229-2211
Admin Albert Briggs.
Licensure Skilled care; Boarding care. *Beds*
  SNF 43; Boarding care 26. *Certified*
  Medicaid; Medicare.
Owner Proprietary corp.

Austin

Burr Oak Manor
400 10th Ave NW, Austin, MN 55912
(507) 433-7391
Admin Eugene Gustason. *Dir of Nursing*
  Jolene Alexander. *Medical Dir* Dr C Jones.
Licensure Skilled care; Intermediate care. *Beds*
  SNF 106; ICF 31. *Certified* Medicaid;
  Medicare.
Owner Proprietary corp (Hillhaven Corp).
Admissions Requirements Minimum age 18.
Staff RNs 3 (ft), 9 (pt); LPNs 2 (ft), 8 (pt);
  Nurses' aides 6 (ft), 9 (pt).
Facilities Dining room; Physical therapy
  room; Activities room; Crafts room; Barber/
  Beauty shop.
Activities Arts & crafts; Cards; Games; Prayer
  groups; Movies; Shopping trips; Dances/
  Social/Cultural gatherings.

Cedar I
PO Box 1047, 207 SW 1st Ave, Austin, MN 55912
(507) 433-7301
Admin Walter A Baldus.
Medical Dir Pam Ollman.
Licensure Intermediate care for mentally retarded. *Beds* ICF/MR 10. *Certified* Medicaid.
Owner Proprietary corp.
Admissions Requirements Minimum age 5.
Staff LPNs 2 (pt).
Activities Arts & crafts; Cards; Games; Movies; Shopping trips; Dances/Social/Cultural gatherings.

Cedar II
PO Box 1047, 601 13th Ave SE, Austin, MN 55912
(507) 433-7301
Admin Walter A Baldus.
Licensure Intermediate care for mentally retarded; Alzheimer's care. *Beds* ICF/MR 9. *Certified* Medicaid; Medicare.
Owner Proprietary corp.
Admissions Requirements Medical examination; Physician's request; Maximum age 25.
Staff RNs; LPNs; Nurses' aides; Physical therapists; Recreational therapists; Occupational therapists; Speech therapists; Activities coordinators; Dietitians.
Facilities Dining room; Activities room; Crafts room; Laundry room.
Activities Arts & crafts; Cards; Games; Reading groups; Movies; Shopping trips; Dances/Social/Cultural gatherings.

Cedar III
PO Box 1047, 1921 6th Ave NW, Austin, MN 55912
(507) 433-7301
Admin Walter A Baldus.
Medical Dir Pam Ollman.
Licensure Intermediate care for mentally retarded. *Beds* ICF/MR 6. *Certified* Medicaid.
Owner Proprietary corp.
Admissions Requirements Minimum age 5.
Staff LPNs 2 (pt).
Facilities Regular homes.
Activities Arts & crafts; Cards; Games; Movies; Shopping trips; Dances/Social/Cultural gatherings.

Cedar IV
PO Box 1047, 108 16th St SE, Austin, MN 55912
(507) 433-7301
Admin Walter A Baldus.
Medical Dir Pam Ollman.
Licensure Intermediate care for mentally retarded. *Beds* ICF/MR 6. *Certified* Medicaid.
Owner Proprietary corp.
Admissions Requirements Minimum age 5.
Staff LPNs 2 (pt).
Facilities Regular homes.

Comforcare Care Center
205 14th St NW, Austin, MN 55912
(507) 437-4526
Admin Dan Colgan. *Dir of Nursing* Michele Gemmel.
Licensure Skilled care. *Beds* SNF 45. *Certified* Medicaid; Medicare.
Owner Proprietary corp (Good Neighbor Services).
Admissions Requirements Medical examination; Physician's request.
Staff RNs 3 (ft); LPNs 1 (ft), 8 (pt); Nurses' aides 3 (ft), 20 (pt); Physical therapists 1 (pt); Recreational therapists 1 (ft), 1 (pt); Occupational therapists 1 (pt); Dietitians 1 (ft).
Facilities Dining room; Physical therapy room; Activities room; Crafts room; Barber/Beauty shop.

Activities Arts & crafts; Cards; Games; Reading groups; Prayer groups; Movies; Shopping trips; Dances/Social/Cultural gatherings; Resident council; Family council; Recreation program through community organizations & auxiliary.

Sacred Heart Hospice
1200 12th St SW, Austin, MN 55912
(507) 433-1808
Admin Nadine Pogons.
Medical Dir Dr Thomas Seery.
Licensure Skilled care. *Beds* SNF 59. *Certified* Medicaid; Medicare.
Owner Nonprofit organization/foundation.
Admissions Requirements Physician's request.
Staff RNs 1 (ft), 6 (pt); LPNs 13 (pt); Nurses' aides 34 (pt); Recreational therapists 2 (ft); Occupational therapists 1 (ft).
Affiliation Roman Catholic.

St Marks Lutheran Home
400 15th Ave SW, Austin, MN 55912
(507) 437-4594
Admin Glenn E Mair. *Dir of Nursing* Connie Priebe. *Medical Dir* Dr Reginald Isele.
Licensure Skilled care; Retirement; Alzheimer's care. *Beds* SNF 169; Retirement 75. *Certified* Medicaid; Medicare.
Owner Nonprofit organization/foundation.
Admissions Requirements Minimum age 18; Medical examination; Physician's request.
Staff Physicians 1 (pt); RNs 1 (ft), 14 (pt); LPNs 2 (ft), 13 (pt); Nurses' aides 125 (pt); Physical therapists 1 (pt); Recreational therapists 1 (pt); Activities coordinators 1 (pt); Dietitians 1 (pt).
Affiliation Lutheran.
Facilities Dining room; Physical therapy room; Activities room; Chapel; Crafts room; Laundry room; Barber/Beauty shop; Library; Child day care.
Activities Arts & crafts; Cards; Games; Reading groups; Prayer groups; Movies; Shopping trips; Dances/Social/Cultural gatherings.

Woodvale III
1209 1st St NE, Austin, MN 55912
(507) 437-7621
Admin Robert R Clark.
Licensure Intermediate care for mentally retarded. *Beds* ICF/MR 41. *Certified* Medicaid.
Owner Proprietary corp.
Admissions Requirements Minimum age 18; Medical examination.
Staff RNs 1 (pt); LPNs 1 (ft), 1 (pt); Recreational therapists 1 (ft).
Facilities Dining room; Laundry room.
Activities Arts & crafts; Cards; Games; Reading groups; Movies; Shopping trips; Dances/Social/Cultural gatherings.

Bagley

Greensview Health Care Center
Rte 1, Bagley, MN 56621
(218) 694-6552
Admin Jan Otness. *Dir of Nursing* Carmen Stinson RN. *Medical Dir* Rudd Thabes DO.
Licensure Skilled care; Retirement; Alzheimer's care. *Beds* SNF 70; Retirement apts 20. *Certified* Medicaid; Medicare.
Owner Proprietary corp (Health Dimensions Inc).
Admissions Requirements Medical examination; Physician's request.
Staff RNs; LPNs; Nurses' aides; Physical therapists; Reality therapists; Recreational therapists; Occupational therapists; Speech therapists; Activities coordinators; Dietitians.
Languages Norwegian.
Facilities Dining room; Physical therapy room; Activities room; Chapel; Crafts room; Laundry room; Barber/Beauty shop.

Activities Arts & crafts; Cards; Games; Reading groups; Prayer groups; Movies; Shopping trips; Dances/Social/Cultural gatherings; Intergenerational programs; Pet therapy.

Pine Ridge Residence
Box 29, 8th St & Hallan Ave, Bagley, MN 56621
(218) 694-6716
Admin Donald L Blooflat.
Licensure Intermediate care for mentally retarded. *Beds* ICF/MR 15. *Certified* Medicaid.
Owner Proprietary corp.
Admissions Requirements Minimum age 18; Medical examination.
Staff RNs 1 (pt); Physical therapists 1 (pt); Occupational therapists 1 (pt); Speech therapists 1 (pt); Dietitians 1 (pt); Podiatrists 1 (pt); 8 (ft), 4 (pt).
Facilities Dining room; Activities room; Crafts room; Laundry room.
Activities Arts & crafts; Cards; Games; Reading groups; Prayer groups; Movies; Shopping trips; Dances/Social/Cultural gatherings.

Balaton

Colonial Manor of Balaton
Hwy 14 E, Balaton, MN 56115
(507) 734-3511
Admin Paul E Bachschneider. *Dir of Nursing* Mary Lebert RN. *Medical Dir* Dr Steven Mulder.
Licensure Intermediate care. *Beds* ICF 78. *Private Pay Patients* 45%. *Certified* Medicaid.
Owner Proprietary corp (Beverly Enterprises).
Admissions Requirements Medical examination.
Staff Physicians 1 (pt); RNs 4 (ft); LPNs 4 (ft); Nurses' aides 20 (ft); Activities coordinators 1 (ft), 2 (pt); Dietitians 1 (pt); Podiatrists 1 (pt).
Facilities Dining room; Physical therapy room; Activities room; Chapel; Crafts room; Laundry room; Barber/Beauty shop; Library.
Activities Arts & crafts; Cards; Games; Reading groups; Prayer groups; Movies; Shopping trips; Dances/Social/Cultural gatherings; Intergenerational programs.

Barnesville

Barnesville Care Center
PO Box 129, 600 5th St SE, Barnesville, MN 56514
(218) 354-2254
Admin Michael D Pattee. *Dir of Nursing* Beth Desing RN.
Licensure Skilled care. *Beds* SNF 76. *Certified* Medicaid; Medicare.
Owner Proprietary corp (Good Neighbor Services).
Staff RNs 2 (ft), 3 (pt); LPNs 2 (ft), 7 (pt); Nurses' aides 12 (ft), 26 (pt); Recreational therapists 1 (ft), 1 (pt); Rehab nurses 4 (pt).
Facilities Dining room; Activities room; Crafts room; Laundry room; Barber/Beauty shop.
Activities Arts & crafts; Cards; Games; Reading groups; Prayer groups; Movies; Shopping trips; Dances/Social/Cultural gatherings.

Barrett

Barrett Care Center Inc
Hwy 55 & 59 S, Barrett, MN 56311
(612) 528-2527
Admin Betty DeClercq. *Dir of Nursing* Vi Melin RN. *Medical Dir* Dr Larry Rapp.

Licensure Intermediate care. *Beds* ICF 60.
Private Pay Patients 62%. *Certified*
Medicaid.
Owner Proprietary corp.
Admissions Requirements Medical
examination; Physician's request.
Staff RNs 3 (ft), 2 (pt); LPNs 2 (ft), 5 (pt);
Nurses' aides 12 (ft), 22 (pt); Physical
therapists 1 (pt); Recreational therapists 1
(pt); Activities coordinators 1 (ft); Dietitians
1 (pt).
Facilities Dining room; Activities room;
Crafts room; Laundry room; Barber/Beauty
shop.
Activities Arts & crafts; Cards; Games;
Reading groups; Prayer groups; Movies;
Dances/Social/Cultural gatherings;
Intergenerational programs.

Steffen Group Home
PO Box 63, Barrett, MN 56311
(612) 528-2533
Admin Julia Solein Mortenson.
Medical Dir Ronna Steffen.
Licensure Intermediate care for mentally
retarded. *Beds* ICF/MR 6. *Certified*
Medicaid.
Owner Privately owned.
Admissions Requirements Minimum age 18;
Medical examination.
Staff LPNs 1 (ft); Recreational therapists 1
(pt); Speech therapists 1 (pt); Activities
coordinators 1 (ft).
Facilities Dining room; Activities room;
Crafts room; Laundry room.
Activities Arts & crafts; Cards; Games;
Reading groups; Movies; Shopping trips;
Dances/Social/Cultural gatherings.

Battle Lake

Battle Lake Care Center
PO Box 68, Glenhaven Dr, Battle Lake, MN
56515
(218) 864-5231
Admin John Rieke. *Dir of Nursing* Mildred
Mitzel RN. *Medical Dir* Charles McGraw
MD.
Licensure Skilled care; Alzheimer's care. *Beds*
SNF 65. *Certified* Medicaid; Medicare.
Owner Proprietary corp (Good Neighbor
Services).
Admissions Requirements Medical
examination.
Staff RNs 2 (ft), 2 (pt); LPNs 5 (ft), 4 (pt);
Nurses' aides 18 (ft), 14 (pt); Physical
therapists 1 (pt); Recreational therapists 1
(ft); Speech therapists 1 (pt); Dietitians 1
(pt).
Facilities Dining room; Physical therapy
room; Activities room; Chapel; Crafts room;
Laundry room; Barber/Beauty shop.
Activities Arts & crafts; Cards; Games;
Reading groups; Prayer groups; Movies;
Shopping trips; Dances/Social/Cultural
gatherings.

Otter Tail Lake Residence
Rte 2 Box 258, Battle Lake, MN 56515
(218) 495-3292
Admin Mark E Tysver.
Licensure Intermediate care for mentally
retarded. *Beds* ICF/MR 12.
Owner Proprietary corp.

Otter Tail Nursing Home
Rte 2 Box 257, Battle Lake, MN 56515
(218) 495-2992
Admin Mark E Tysver. *Dir of Nursing* June
Shearer RN.
Licensure Intermediate care. *Beds* ICF 62.
Certified Medicaid.
Owner Proprietary corp (Beverly Enterprises).
Admissions Requirements Medical
examination; Physician's request.
Staff RNs 2 (ft), 2 (pt); LPNs 2 (ft), 4 (pt);
Nurses' aides 10 (ft), 18 (pt).

Facilities Dining room; Activities room;
Crafts room; Laundry room; Barber/Beauty
shop; Library.
Activities Arts & crafts; Cards; Games;
Reading groups; Prayer groups; Movies;
Shopping trips.

Baudette

Pioneer Nursing Home
Rte 1 Box 1180, Baudette, MN 56623
(218) 634-1588, 634-1307 FAX
Admin David A Nelson. *Dir of Nursing* Kay
M Schell. *Medical Dir* James Sutherland
MD.
Licensure Intermediate care. *Beds* ICF 52.
Private Pay Patients 28%. *Certified*
Medicaid.
Owner Publicly owned.
Admissions Requirements Physician's request.
Staff RNs 2 (ft), 2 (pt); LPNs 2 (ft), 4 (pt);
Nurses' aides 5 (ft), 18 (pt); Physical
therapists (consultant); Activities
coordinators 1 (ft), 2 (pt); Dietitians
(consultant); Physical therapy supervisors &
aides 1 (ft), 1 (pt); Dietary supervisors &
aides 2 (ft), 7 (pt).
Facilities Dining room; Physical therapy
room; Activities room; Chapel; Crafts room;
Dayroom; Sun porch; Yard with gazebo and
garden.
Activities Arts & crafts; Cards; Games;
Reading groups; Prayer groups; Movies;
Shopping trips; Dances/Social/Cultural
gatherings; Pet therapy.

Bayport

Croixdale Residence
334 N 7th Ave, Bayport, MN 55003
(612) 439-4946
Admin Margaret Day Juhl.
Licensure Boarding care. *Beds* Boarding care
50.
Owner Proprietary corp.

Belgrade

Belgrade Nursing Home
Box 340, Belgrade, MN 56312
(612) 254-8215
Admin Philip Lord.
Medical Dir G R Savelkoul MD.
Licensure Skilled care. *Beds* SNF 64. *Certified*
Medicaid; Medicare.
Owner Proprietary corp.
Admissions Requirements Minimum age 16;
Medical examination; Physician's request.
Staff Physicians 1 (pt); RNs 1 (ft), 3 (pt);
LPNs 1 (ft), 7 (pt); Physical therapists 1 (pt);
Speech therapists 1 (pt); Activities
coordinators 1 (ft), 2 (pt); Dietitians 1 (pt);
Dentists 1 (pt).
Facilities Dining room; Physical therapy
room; Activities room; Chapel; Crafts room;
Laundry room; Barber/Beauty shop; TV/
Dayroom.
Activities Arts & crafts; Cards; Games;
Reading groups; Prayer groups; Movies;
Shopping trips; Dances/Social/Cultural
gatherings; Outside entertainment groups.

Belle Plaine

Lutheran Home
611 W Main St, Belle Plaine, MN 56011
(612) 873-2215
Admin Lois M Dahlke. *Dir of Nursing* Rick
Krant. *Medical Dir* Dr Roger Hallgren.
Licensure Intermediate care; Intermediate care
for mentally retarded; Retirement. *Beds* ICF
128; ICF/MR 52; Retirement 27. *Certified*
Medicaid.
Owner Nonprofit organization/foundation.
Admissions Requirements Physician's request.

Affiliation Lutheran.
Activities Arts & crafts; Cards; Games;
Reading groups; Prayer groups; Movies;
Shopping trips; Dances/Social/Cultural
gatherings; Intergenerational programs.

Belview

Parkview Home
RR 1 Box 103AA, 401 County State Aid Hwy
9, Belview, MN 56214
(507) 938-4151
Admin Madonna C Keaveny. *Dir of Nursing*
Ruth Gjermundson RN. *Medical Dir* Steve
Medrud MD.
Licensure Skilled care. *Beds* SNF 62. *Private
Pay Patients* 48%. *Certified* Medicaid;
Medicare.
Owner Publicly owned.
Admissions Requirements Medical
examination.
Staff Physicians 1 (pt); RNs 3 (ft); LPNs 3
(ft), 3 (pt); Nurses' aides 13 (ft), 40 (pt);
Physical therapists 1 (pt); Speech therapists
1 (pt); Activities coordinators 3 (ft);
Dietitians 1 (pt).
Languages Swedish, Norwegian, German.
Facilities Dining room; Physical therapy
room; Activities room; Chapel; Crafts room;
Laundry room; Barber/Beauty shop; Library.
Activities Arts & crafts; Cards; Games;
Reading groups; Prayer groups; Movies;
Dances/Social/Cultural gatherings;
Intergenerational programs; Pet therapy.

Bemidji

Beltrami Nursing Home
1633 Delton Ave, Bemidji, MN 56601
(218) 751-1024
Admin Larry Schuette. *Dir of Nursing* Steve
Liebhard. *Medical Dir* Dr Gary Winkler.
Licensure Skilled care; Alzheimer's care. *Beds*
SNF 133. *Private Pay Patients* 20%. *Certified*
Medicaid; Medicare.
Owner Publicly owned.
Admissions Requirements Medical
examination; Physician's request.
Staff RNs 6 (ft), 3 (pt); LPNs 5 (ft), 13 (pt);
Nurses' aides 15 (ft), 56 (pt); Physical
therapists 1 (pt); Recreational therapists 1
(ft), 3 (pt); Occupational therapists 1 (pt);
Speech therapists 1 (pt); Activities
coordinators 1 (ft); Dietitians 1 (ft).
Languages Hawaiian, Chippewa, Norwegian.
Facilities Dining room; Physical therapy
room; Activities room; Crafts room; Laundry
room; Barber/Beauty shop; Library.
Activities Arts & crafts; Cards; Games;
Reading groups; Prayer groups; Movies;
Shopping trips; Dances/Social/Cultural
gatherings; Intergenerational programs; Pet
therapy.

**North Country Nursing & Rehabilitation
Center**
109 E 8th St, Bemidji, MN 56601
(218) 751-0220
Admin Eunice Ulshafer. *Dir of Nursing*
Colleen Lubken. *Medical Dir* James F Hatch
MD.
Licensure Skilled care. *Beds* SNF 78. *Private
Pay Patients* 15%. *Certified* Medicaid;
Medicare.
Owner Nonprofit corp.
Admissions Requirements Minimum age 18;
Physician's request.
Staff RNs 6 (ft), 4 (pt); LPNs 4 (ft), 11 (pt);
Nurses' aides 10 (ft), 30 (pt); Physical
therapists 3 (ft); Activities coordinators 1
(ft).
Facilities Dining room; Physical therapy
room; Activities room; Chapel; Barber/
Beauty shop.
Activities Arts & crafts; Cards; Games; Prayer
groups; Movies; Shopping trips; Pet therapy.

North Star Homes
2528 Park Ave, Bemidji, MN 56601
(218) 751-5876
Admin Judith M Thorson. *Dir of Nursing*
Jane Nelson PHN. *Medical Dir* Brian P
Livermore.
Licensure Intermediate care for mentally
retarded. *Beds* ICF/MR 14. *Private Pay
Patients* 0%. *Certified* Medicaid; Medicare.
Owner Nonprofit corp.
Admissions Requirements Minimum age 18;
Medical examination; Prefer physically
disabled clients over those with behavior
problems.
Languages Sign.
Activities Cards; Games; Movies; Shopping
trips; Dances/Social/Cultural gatherings;
Active treatment.

REM Beltrami
916 S 1st St, Bemidji, MN 56601
(218) 751-5830
Admin David Peterson.
Licensure Intermediate care for mentally
retarded. *Beds* ICF/MR 15.
Owner Proprietary corp.

REM Bemidji
Rte 5 Box 197E, Bemidji, MN 56601
(218) 586-2573
Admin David Petersen.
Licensure Intermediate care for mentally
retarded. *Beds* ICF/MR 10. *Certified*
Medicaid.
Owner Proprietary corp.
Admissions Requirements Minimum age 16;
Medical examination.
Facilities Dining room; Activities room;
Laundry room.
Activities Arts & crafts; Cards; Games;
Reading groups; Movies; Shopping trips;
Dances/Social/Cultural gatherings.

Spruce Woods Apartments
718 15th St NW, Bemidji, MN 55601
(218) 759-1223
Admin Del Sand.
Licensure Supervised living. *Beds* Supervised
living 14.
Owner Proprietary corp.

Benson

Meadowlane Healthcare Center
W Hwy 9, Benson, MN 56215
(612) 843-2225
Admin Dale Nibbe. *Dir of Nursing* Beverly
Ehret. *Medical Dir* Richard Horeka.
Licensure Skilled care; Intermediate care;
Board & care. *Beds* SNF 63; Board & care
31. *Private Pay Patients* 28%. *Certified*
Medicaid; Medicare.
Owner Proprietary corp (Beverly Enterprises).
Admissions Requirements Medical
examination; Physician's request.
Staff Physicians 3 (ft); RNs 2 (ft), 2 (pt);
LPNs 12 (ft); Nurses' aides 36 (ft), 6 (pt);
Physical therapists 1 (ft); Recreational
therapists 1 (ft); Occupational therapists 1
(ft); Speech therapists 1 (pt); Activities
coordinators 1 (ft); Dietitians 1 (ft), 1 (pt);
Audiologists 1 (pt).
Facilities Dining room; Physical therapy
room; Activities room; Crafts room; Laundry
room; Barber/Beauty shop.
Activities Arts & crafts; Cards; Games;
Reading groups; Prayer groups; Movies;
Dances/Social/Cultural gatherings;
Intergenerational programs.

Swift County Home
1650 Stone Ave, Benson, MN 56215
(612) 843-3509
Admin Margaret Demarce.
Licensure Intermediate care for mentally
retarded. *Beds* ICF/MR 10. *Certified*
Medicaid.
Owner Proprietary corp.

Big Lake

Residential Alternatives VII
150 Powell Cir W, Big Lake, MN 55309
(612) 263-6503
Admin Peter Jacobsen. *Dir of Nursing* Sharon
Robideau RN, consultant.
Licensure Intermediate care for mentally
retarded. *Certified* Medicare.
Owner Privately owned.
Admissions Requirements Minimum age 18.
Staff RNs.
Facilities Dining room; Activities room;
Laundry room.
Activities Arts & crafts; Games; Movies;
Shopping trips; Dances/Social/Cultural
gatherings.

Bigfork

Northern Itasca Health Care Center
258 Pine Tree Dr, Bigfork, MN 56628
(218) 743-3177
Admin Lillian M Krueger. *Dir of Nursing*
Pearl Aakhus. *Medical Dir* J Scrivner MD.
Licensure Skilled care. *Beds* SNF 40. *Certified*
Medicaid.
Owner Publicly owned.
Staff Physicians; RNs; LPNs; Nurses' aides;
Physical therapists; Activities coordinators;
Dietitians.
Facilities Dining room; Physical therapy
room; Activities room; Barber/Beauty shop.
Activities Arts & crafts; Cards; Games;
Reading groups; Prayer groups; Movies;
Shopping trips; Dances/Social/Cultural
gatherings.

Bird Island

Bird Island Manor Healthcare Center
421 S 11th St, Bird Island, MN 55310
(612) 365-4141
Admin Mark Rust.
Licensure Boarding care. *Beds* Boarding care
24. *Certified* Medicaid.
Owner Proprietary corp (Beverly Enterprises).

Biwabik

Merritt House
120 N 3rd Ave, Biwabik, MN 55708
(218) 865-6381
Admin David Salsman.
Licensure Supervised living. *Beds* Supervised
living 22.
Owner Proprietary corp.

Blackduck

Northern Pines Good Samaritan Center
Rte 1, Blackduck, MN 56630
(218) 835-4218
Admin Lane Anderson. *Dir of Nursing* Kalynn
Mayers.
Licensure Intermediate care. *Beds* ICF 70.
Private Pay Patients 25%. *Certified*
Medicare.
Owner Nonprofit corp (Evangelical Lutheran/
Good Samaritan Society).
Admissions Requirements Minimum age 18;
Medical examination; Physician's request.
Staff RNs 2 (ft), 2 (pt); LPNs 1 (ft), 6 (pt);
Nurses' aides 17 (ft), 20 (pt); Activities
coordinators 1 (ft).
Affiliation Lutheran.
Facilities Dining room; Physical therapy
room; Activities room; Chapel; Crafts room;
Laundry room; Barber/Beauty shop; Library.
Activities Arts & crafts; Cards; Games;
Reading groups; Prayer groups; Movies;
Shopping trips; Dances/Social/Cultural
gatherings; Intergenerational programs; Pet
therapy.

Blooming Prairie

Prairie Manor
220 3rd St NW, Blooming Prairie, MN 55917
(507) 583-4434
Admin Michelle Gemmel.
Medical Dir Mary Jane Simonson.
Licensure Skilled care. *Beds* SNF 82. *Certified*
Medicaid; Medicare.
Owner Proprietary corp.
Admissions Requirements Medical
examination; Physician's request.
Staff Physicians; RNs; LPNs; Nurses' aides;
Physical therapists; Reality therapists;
Recreational therapists; Activities
coordinators; Dietitians.
Facilities Dining room; Physical therapy
room; Activities room; Chapel; Crafts room;
Laundry room; Barber/Beauty shop; Family
visiting room; Resident's kitchen.
Activities Arts & crafts; Cards; Games;
Reading groups; Prayer groups; Movies;
Shopping trips; Dances/Social/Cultural
gatherings; Sing-alongs; Cooking; Church
services; Family nights; Picnics.

Bloomington

Bloomington Maple Manor
8916 Lyndale Ave S, Bloomington, MN 55420
(612) 881-5803
Admin James A Jasper. *Dir of Nursing* Mary
Mellenbruch RN. *Medical Dir* J P Carlson
MD.
Licensure Skilled care; Retirement. *Beds* SNF
63. *Certified* Medicaid; Medicare.
Owner Proprietary corp (Good Neighbor
Services).
Admissions Requirements Minimum age 16;
Medical examination; Physician's request.
Staff RNs 6 (ft), 5 (pt); LPNs 1 (ft), 3 (pt);
Nurses' aides 16 (ft), 21 (pt); Physical
therapists 1 (pt); Reality therapists 1 (ft);
Recreational therapists 1 (ft), 1 (pt);
Occupational therapists 1 (pt); Speech
therapists 1 (pt); Activities coordinators 1
(ft); Dietitians 1 (pt); Ophthalmologists 1
(pt); Podiatrists 1 (pt); Dentists 1 (pt).
Facilities Dining room; Physical therapy
room; Activities room; Laundry room;
Barber/Beauty shop.
Activities Arts & crafts; Cards; Games;
Reading groups; Prayer groups; Movies;
Shopping trips; Dances/Social/Cultural
gatherings; Music therapy.

Bloomington Nursing Home
9200 Nicollet Ave S, Bloomington, MN 55420
(612) 881-8676
Admin Jane Wright.
Medical Dir Dr Lorraine Kretchman.
Licensure Skilled care. *Beds* SNF 80. *Certified*
Medicaid; Medicare.
Owner Proprietary corp (Beverly Enterprises).
Admissions Requirements Minimum age 18;
Medical examination.
Staff Physicians 2 (pt); RNs 2 (ft), 8 (pt);
LPNs 6 (pt); Nurses' aides 9 (ft), 26 (pt);
Physical therapists 1 (pt); Recreational
therapists 1 (ft); Occupational therapists 1
(pt); Speech therapists 1 (pt); Dietitians 1
(ft); Podiatrists 1 (pt); Audiologists 1 (pt);
Dentists 1 (pt); Respiratory aides 2 (pt);
Social workers 1 (ft).
Facilities Dining room; Physical therapy
room; Activities room; Laundry room.
Activities Arts & crafts; Cards; Games;
Reading groups; Prayer groups; Movies;
Shopping trips; Dances/Social/Cultural
gatherings.

Bloomington Outreach Home
10633 Kell Ave S, Bloomington, MN 55437
(612) 881-2848
Admin Eileen L Harris.

Licensure Intermediate care for mentally retarded. *Beds* ICF/MR 6. *Certified* Medicare.
Owner Proprietary corp.
Admissions Requirements Minimum age 19; Medical examination.
Facilities Dining room; Activities room; Crafts room; Laundry room; Kitchen; 4 Bedrooms; 2 Baths.
Activities Arts & crafts; Cards; Games; Reading groups; Prayer groups; Movies; Shopping trips; Dances/Social/Cultural gatherings; Vacations.

Carlson Drake House
5414 W Old Shakopee Cir, Bloomington, MN 55437
(612) 888-5611
Admin Terry Schneider.
Licensure Supervised living. *Beds* Supervised living 12.
Owner Proprietary corp.

Eagle Nursing Home
401 W 95th St, Bloomington, MN 55420
(612) 888-9461
Admin William J Eagle.
Licensure Intermediate care for mentally retarded. *Beds* ICF/MR 80. *Certified* Medicaid.
Owner Proprietary corp.

Forestview Sunlen
400 E 99th St, Bloomington, MN 55420
(612) 888-0897
Admin Mary M Hill.
Licensure Intermediate care for mentally retarded. *Beds* ICF/MR 6. *Certified* Medicaid.
Owner Proprietary corp.

Friendship Village
8100 Highwood Dr, Bloomington, MN 55438
(612) 831-7500
Admin Shirley Barnes.
Medical Dir Paul Kaldor MD.
Licensure Skilled care. *Beds* SNF 66. *Certified* Medicare.
Owner Nonprofit corp (Life Care Services Corp).
Admissions Requirements Minimum age 62; Medical examination; Physician's request.
Staff Physicians 1 (ft); RNs 3 (ft), 4 (pt); LPNs 6 (ft), 4 (pt); Nurses' aides 21 (ft), 8 (pt); Physical therapists 1 (pt); Activities coordinators 1 (ft), 2 (pt); Dietitians 1 (ft); Podiatrists 1 (pt).
Facilities Dining room; Physical therapy room; Activities room; Chapel; Crafts room; Laundry room; Barber/Beauty shop; Library.
Activities Arts & crafts; Cards; Games; Reading groups; Prayer groups; Movies; Shopping trips; Dances/Social/Cultural gatherings.

Gerarda House
8706 Penn Ave S, Bloomington, MN 55431
(612) 888-9741
Admin Roberta Miller Rosenow.
Licensure Supervised living. *Beds* Supervised living 6.
Owner Proprietary corp.

Janus
8041 12th Ave S, Bloomington, MN 55420
(612) 854-8060
Admin Mary Jo Gaskins.
Licensure Supervised living. *Beds* Supervised living 24.
Owner Proprietary corp.

Martin Luther Manor
1401 E 100th St, Bloomington, MN 55420
(612) 888-7751
Admin Thomas Goeritz. *Dir of Nursing* Doris Larkin.

Licensure Skilled care; Intermediate care; Boarding care; Alzheimer's care. *Beds* SNF 120; ICF 38; Boarding care 60. *Certified* Medicaid; Medicare.
Owner Nonprofit corp (Minnesota Synod/ Lutheran Church Board).
Admissions Requirements Minimum age 18; Medical examination; Physician's request.
Staff Physical therapists 1 (ft); Recreational therapists 2 (ft); Occupational therapists 1 (ft); Speech therapists 1 (pt); Activities coordinators 1 (ft); Dietitians 1 (ft); Ophthalmologists 1 (pt); Podiatrists 1 (pt); Dentists 1 (pt).
Affiliation Lutheran.
Facilities Dining room; Physical therapy room; Activities room; Chapel; Crafts room; Laundry room; Barber/Beauty shop; Library; Adult Day Care.
Activities Arts & crafts; Cards; Games; Reading groups; Prayer groups; Movies; Shopping trips; Dances/Social/Cultural gatherings.

Penn Lake House
8743 Penn Ave S, Bloomington, MN 55431
(612) 881-9584
Admin Roberta Miller Rosenow.
Licensure Supervised living. *Beds* Supervised living 7.
Owner Proprietary corp.

REM Bloomington Inc
9201 Cedar Ave S, Bloomington, MN 55420
(612) 854-1800
Admin David Peterson.
Licensure Intermediate care for mentally retarded. *Beds* ICF/MR 15. *Certified* Medicaid.
Owner Proprietary corp.

St Luke's Group Home
1601 W Old Shakopee Rd, Bloomington, MN 55431
(612) 884-0768
Admin Norman Doeden.
Licensure Intermediate care for mentally retarded. *Beds* ICF/MR 12.
Owner Proprietary corp.

St Stephen Group Homes A & B
8450 France Ave S, Bloomington, MN 55431
(612) 831-0321, 831-7456
Admin Norman Doeden.
Medical Dir Jane Knudsen.
Licensure Intermediate care for mentally retarded. *Beds* ICF/MR 24. *Certified* Medicaid; Medicare.
Owner Proprietary corp.
Admissions Requirements Minimum age 18; Medical examination; Primary disability of MR.
Staff RNs 1 (pt); Residential counselors 10 (ft), 15 (pt).
Affiliation Lutheran.
Facilities Dining room; Activities room; Laundry room.
Activities Arts & crafts; Cards; Games; Movies; Shopping trips; Dances/Social/ Cultural gatherings; Community related for daily living skills.

Blue Earth

St Lukes Lutheran Home
1217 S Ramsey, Blue Earth, MN 56013
(507) 526-2184
Admin Mark G Robinson. *Dir of Nursing* Mary Jo Hill. *Medical Dir* Dr George Drexler.
Licensure Skilled care; Retirement; Alzheimer's care. *Beds* SNF 180. *Certified* Medicaid; Medicare.
Owner Proprietary corp.
Admissions Requirements Medical examination; Physician's request.

Staff Physicians; RNs; LPNs; Nurses' aides; Physical therapists; Recreational therapists; Occupational therapists; Speech therapists; Activities coordinators; Dietitians; Ophthalmologists; Podiatrists; Dentists.
Languages Norwegian, Danish.
Facilities Dining room; Physical therapy room; Activities room; Chapel; Crafts room; Laundry room; Barber/Beauty shop; Library.
Activities Arts & crafts; Cards; Games; Reading groups; Prayer groups; Movies; Shopping trips; Dances/Social/Cultural gatherings.

Brainerd

Bethany Good Samaritan Village
804 Wright St, Brainerd, MN 56401
(218) 829-1407
Admin Michael T Cranny.
Licensure Skilled care; Retirement. *Beds* SNF 160; Retirement apts 39. *Private Pay Patients* 55%. *Certified* Medicaid; Medicare.
Owner Nonprofit organization/foundation.
Admissions Requirements Medical examination; Physician's request.
Affiliation Evangelical Lutheran.
Facilities Dining room; Physical therapy room; Activities room; Crafts room; Laundry room; Barber/Beauty shop.
Activities Arts & crafts; Cards; Games; Reading groups; Movies; Shopping trips; Dances/Social/Cultural gatherings; Intergenerational programs; Pet therapy.

Brainerd Good Samaritan Center
803 Kingwood St, Brainerd, MN 56401
(218) 829-8711
Admin Mary Feig.
Medical Dir Dr Peter Dunphy.
Licensure Skilled care; Intermediate care; Boarding care. *Beds* SNF 24; ICF 12; Boarding care 32. *Certified* Medicaid.
Owner Proprietary corp (Evangelical Lutheran/Good Samaritan Society).
Admissions Requirements Medical examination; Physician's request.
Staff RNs 1 (ft), 4 (pt); LPNs 2 (ft), 7 (pt); Nurses' aides 6 (ft), 14 (pt); Activities coordinators 1 (ft), 2 (pt); Dietitians 1 (ft), 1 (pt).
Affiliation Lutheran.
Facilities Dining room; Activities room; Chapel; Crafts room; Laundry room; Barber/ Beauty shop; Library.
Activities Arts & crafts; Cards; Games; Reading groups; Prayer groups; Movies; Shopping trips; Dances/Social/Cultural gatherings.

Brainerd Regional Human Services Center
1777 Hwy 18 E, Brainerd, MN 56401
(218) 828-2201
Admin Harvey G Caldwell. *Dir of Nursing* Cheryl Bolles RN; Donna Peppel RN. *Medical Dir* Frederick Ferron MD.
Licensure Skilled care; Intermediate care; Intermediate care for mentally retarded; Psychiatric hospital. *Beds* SNF 28; ICF 33; ICF/MR 192; Psychiatric hospital 151. *Private Pay Patients* 10%. *Certified* Medicaid; Medicare.
Owner Publicly owned.
Staff Physicians 2 (ft), 13 (pt); RNs 44 (ft), 8 (pt); LPNs 40 (ft), 8 (pt); Nurses' aides 110 (ft), 24 (pt); Physical therapists 1 (pt); Recreational therapists 11 (ft), 1 (pt); Occupational therapists 1 (ft); Speech therapists 1 (pt); Activities coordinators 1 (ft); Dietitians 1 (ft); Ophthalmologists 1 (pt); Podiatrists 1 (pt); Audiologists 1 (pt).
Facilities Dining room; Physical therapy room; Activities room; Chapel; Crafts room; Laundry room; Barber/Beauty shop; Library; Chemical dependency program.

Activities Arts & crafts; Cards; Games; Movies; Shopping trips; Dances/Social/Cultural gatherings; Pet therapy.

Charis House
1008 S 10th St, Brainerd, MN 56401
(218) 828-4823
Admin John D Peterson.
Licensure Intermediate care for mentally retarded. *Beds* ICF/MR 12.
Owner Proprietary corp.

Charis House
1008 S 10th St, Brainerd, MN 58401
(218) 828-4823
Admin John D Peterson.
Licensure Skilled care. *Beds* SNF 12; ICF/MR 12. *Certified* Medicaid.
Owner Nonprofit corp.

Woodland Acres Health Care Center
100 Buffalo Hills Ln, Brainerd, MN 56401
(218) 829-1429, 829-6547 FAX
Admin Scot Allen. *Dir of Nursing* Carole Erickson RN. *Medical Dir* Dr Stephen Hanske.
Licensure Skilled care; Intermediate care; Retirement. *Beds* Swing beds SNF/ICF 80; Retirement apartments 117. *Private Pay Patients* 30%. *Certified* Medicaid; Medicare.
Owner Proprietary corp.
Admissions Requirements Medical examination; Physician's request.
Staff RNs 4 (ft), 2 (pt); LPNs 6 (ft), 5 (pt); Nurses' aides 20 (ft), 20 (pt); Physical therapists 1 (pt); Reality therapists (consultant); Recreational therapists (consultant); Occupational therapists (consultant); Speech therapists (consultant); Activities coordinators 1 (ft); Dietitians (consultant); Ophthalmologists (consultant); Podiatrists (consultant); Audiologists (consultant).
Facilities Dining room; Physical therapy room; Activities room; Chapel; Crafts room; Laundry room; Barber/Beauty shop.
Activities Arts & crafts; Cards; Games; Reading groups; Prayer groups; Movies; Shopping trips; Dances/Social/Cultural gatherings; Intergenerational programs; Pet therapy; One-to-one visitations.

Breckenridge

St Francis Home
501 Oak St, Breckenridge, MN 56520
(218) 643-7661
Admin Kalvin G Michels. *Dir of Nursing* Lori Nelson. *Medical Dir* Dr Dan Aguila.
Licensure Skilled care; Intermediate care; Adult day care. *Beds* SNF 86; ICF 38. *Private Pay Patients* 40%. *Certified* Medicaid; Medicare.
Owner Nonprofit corp (Franciscan Sisters Health Care Inc).
Admissions Requirements Medical examination; Physician's request.
Staff RNs 5 (ft); LPNs 5 (ft), 11 (pt); Nurses' aides 30 (ft), 27 (pt); Physical therapists (consultant); Occupational therapists 1 (ft); Dietitians 1 (ft).
Affiliation Roman Catholic.
Facilities Dining room; Physical therapy room; Activities room; Chapel; Crafts room; Laundry room; Barber/Beauty shop; Library.
Activities Arts & crafts; Cards; Games; Reading groups; Prayer groups; Movies; Shopping trips; Dances/Social/Cultural gatherings.

Wilkin County Group Home
732 5th St S, Breckenridge, MN 56520
(218) 643-5952
Admin Addie Kuznia-Kroshus, acting. *Dir of Nursing* Floss Kempfer RN.
Licensure Intermediate care for mentally retarded. *Beds* ICF/MR 6. *Certified* Medicaid.

Owner Proprietary corp.
Admissions Requirements Minimum age 18.
Facilities Dining room; Activities room; Laundry room.
Activities Arts & crafts; Cards; Games; Movies; Shopping trips; Dances/Social/Cultural gatherings.

Brooklyn Center

Brooklyn Center Outreach Home
507 69th Ave N, Brooklyn Center, MN 55430
(612) 561-9030
Admin Mary M Tjosvold.
Licensure Intermediate care for mentally retarded. *Beds* ICF/MR 6. *Certified* Medicaid.
Owner Proprietary corp.

Maranatha Baptist Care Center
5401 69th Ave N, Brooklyn Center, MN 55429
(612) 561-0477
Admin Joan Dikkers, acting. *Dir of Nursing* Nancy Brady. *Medical Dir* Bradley Johnson MD.
Licensure Skilled care; Retirement. *Beds* SNF 106; Retirement units 65. *Private Pay Patients* 35%. *Certified* Medicaid; Medicare.
Owner Nonprofit corp.
Admissions Requirements Minimum age 18.
Staff RNs; LPNs; Nurses' aides; Recreational therapists 3 (ft); Dietitians 1 (ft).
Affiliation Baptist.
Facilities Dining room; Physical therapy room; Activities room; Chapel; Barber/Beauty shop; Sun room.
Activities Arts & crafts; Games; Reading groups; Prayer groups; Movies; Shopping trips.

Residential Alternatives II
5449 Lyndale Ave N, Brooklyn Center, MN 55430
(612) 560-2220
Admin Peter Jacobson.
Licensure Intermediate care for mentally retarded. *Beds* ICF/MR 8. *Certified* Medicaid.
Owner Proprietary corp.

Brooklyn Park

Homeward Bound Brooklyn Park
7839 Brooklyn Blvd, Brooklyn Park, MN 55430
(612) 566-7860
Admin James Glasoe.
Licensure Intermediate care for mentally retarded. *Beds* ICF/MR 32. *Certified* Medicaid.
Owner Proprietary corp.

Residential Alternatives III
6525 Edgewood Ave N, Brooklyn Park, MN 55428
(612) 533-5104
Admin Peter Jacobson.
Licensure Intermediate care for mentally retarded. *Beds* ICF/MR 8. *Certified* Medicaid.
Owner Proprietary corp.

Shingle Creek Option
5624 73rd Ave N, Brooklyn Park, MN 55429
(612) 560-5330
Admin Betty Rosse.
Licensure Intermediate care for mentally retarded. *Beds* ICF/MR 15.
Owner Proprietary corp.

Brookston

Aneskarn IV
Star Rte Box 630, Brookston, MN 55711
(218) 879-3296
Admin Lawrence Tunell.

Licensure Intermediate care for mentally retarded; Supervised living. *Beds* ICF/MR 28; Supervised living 28. *Certified* Medicaid.
Owner Proprietary corp.

Hilltop Manor
Box 338, Brookston, MN 55711
(218) 453-5622
Admin Elizabeth Demenge.
Licensure Supervised living. *Beds* Supervised living 6. *Certified* Medicaid.
Owner Proprietary corp.
Admissions Requirements Minimum age 18; Medical examination.
Staff RNs 1 (pt); Activities coordinators 1 (pt).
Facilities Dining room; Activities room; Crafts room; Laundry room.
Activities Arts & crafts; Cards; Games; Reading groups; Prayer groups; Movies; Shopping trips; Dances/Social/Cultural gatherings.

Riverview Home I
PO Box 349, Brookston, MN 55711
(218) 453-5522
Admin John Anderson.
Licensure Supervised living. *Beds* Supervised living 30.
Owner Proprietary corp.

Browns Valley

Browns Valley Community Nursing Home
340 S Jefferson, Browns Valley, MN 56219
(612) 695-2166
Admin Mary Nell Zellner-Smith. *Dir of Nursing* Bunny Hoyt.
Licensure Intermediate care; Alzheimer's care. *Beds* ICF 63. *Private Pay Patients* 68%. *Certified* Medicaid.
Owner Proprietary corp.
Admissions Requirements Minimum age 18; Medical examination; Physician's request.
Staff Physicians 12 (pt); RNs 2 (ft), 1 (pt); LPNs 3 (ft), 2 (pt); Nurses' aides 17 (ft), 15 (pt); Physical therapists 1 (pt); Reality therapists 1 (pt); Recreational therapists 1 (ft), 3 (pt); Occupational therapists 1 (pt); Activities coordinators 1 (ft); Dietitians 1 (pt).
Facilities Dining room; Physical therapy room; Activities room; Crafts room; Laundry room; Barber/Beauty shop; Library.
Activities Arts & crafts; Cards; Games; Reading groups; Prayer groups; Movies; Shopping trips; Dances/Social/Cultural gatherings; Intergenerational programs.

Buffalo

Ebenezer Covenant Home
310 Lake Blvd, Buffalo, MN 55313
(612) 682-1434
Admin John Daniel Engels. *Dir of Nursing* Darlene A Nyquist RN. *Medical Dir* Dr Robert Sandeen.
Licensure Skilled care; Retirement. *Beds* SNF 65. *Certified* Medicaid; Medicare.
Owner Nonprofit corp (Covenant Benevolent Institute).
Admissions Requirements Medical examination.
Staff RNs 3 (ft), 3 (pt); LPNs 1 (ft), 4 (pt); Nurses' aides 12 (ft), 30 (pt); Activities coordinators 1 (ft), 2 (pt).
Affiliation Evangelical Covenant Church.
Facilities Dining room; Physical therapy room; Activities room; Chapel; Crafts room; Laundry room; Barber/Beauty shop; Library.
Activities Arts & crafts; Cards; Games; Reading groups; Prayer groups; Movies; Shopping trips; Dances/Social/Cultural gatherings.

REM—Buffalo Inc
914 3rd Ave NE, Buffalo, MN 55313
(612) 682-3960
Admin Deanna Benson.
Licensure Intermediate care for mentally retarded. *Beds* ICF/MR 15. *Certified* Medicaid.
Owner Proprietary corp.

Residential Alternatives I
303 Douglas Dr, Buffalo, MN 55313
(612) 682-4588
Admin Peter Jacobson.
Licensure Intermediate care for mentally retarded. *Beds* ICF/MR 6.
Owner Proprietary corp.

Residential Alternatives V
303 Douglas Dr, Buffalo, MN 55313
(612) 682-5868
Admin Peter Jacobson.
Licensure Intermediate care for mentally retarded. *Beds* ICF/MR 8. *Certified* Medicaid.
Owner Proprietary corp.

Retirement Center of Wright County
200 Park Ln, Buffalo, MN 55313
(612) 682-1131
Admin Ann R Dirks. *Dir of Nursing* Joyce Smith. *Medical Dir* Dr Robert Milligan.
Licensure Skilled care. *Beds* SNF 154. *Private Pay Patients* 50%. *Certified* Medicaid; Medicare.
Owner Nonprofit organization/foundation.
Admissions Requirements Medical examination; Physician's request.
Staff RNs 7 (ft), 1 (pt); LPNs 18 (ft), 6 (pt); Nurses' aides 36 (ft), 43 (pt); Activities coordinators 1 (ft).
Facilities Dining room; Physical therapy room; Activities room; Crafts room; Laundry room; Barber/Beauty shop; Enclosed courtyard.
Activities Arts & crafts; Cards; Games; Reading groups; Prayer groups; Movies; Shopping trips; Dances/Social/Cultural gatherings; Intergenerational programs; Pet therapy; Child day care; Adult day care.

Buffalo Lake

Buffalo Lake Nursing Home
PO Box 368, 703 W Yellowstone Trail, Buffalo Lake, MN 55314
(612) 833-5364
Admin Stanley Gallup. *Dir of Nursing* Janet Scharmer RN. *Medical Dir* Dan Huebert MD.
Licensure Intermediate care; Retirement. *Beds* ICF 66. *Certified* Medicaid.
Owner Proprietary corp.
Staff RNs 1 (ft), 2 (pt); LPNs 6 (ft); Nurses' aides 8 (ft), 24 (pt); Physical therapists 1 (pt); Activities coordinators 1 (ft); Dietitians 1 (ft).
Languages Swedish, Norwegian, German.
Facilities Dining room; Activities room; Laundry room; Barber/Beauty shop.
Activities Arts & crafts; Cards; Games; Reading groups; Prayer groups; Movies; Shopping trips; Dances/Social/Cultural gatherings.

Buhl

Mesabi Home
PO Box 703, 501 Jones Ave, Buhl, MN 55713
(218) 258-3253
Admin Betty Holmes.
Medical Dir Esther Lakso.
Licensure Intermediate care. *Beds* ICF 31. *Certified* Medicaid.
Owner Proprietary corp.
Admissions Requirements Medical examination; Physician's request.

Staff RNs 1 (ft), 2 (pt); LPNs 2 (pt); Nurses' aides 5 (ft), 6 (pt); Activities coordinators 1 (pt); Dietitians 1 (pt).
Facilities Dining room; Activities room; Laundry room; TV room.
Activities Arts & crafts; Cards; Games; Reading groups; Prayer groups; Movies; Shopping trips; Dances/Social/Cultural gatherings.

Burnsville

Ebenezer Ridges
13820 Community Dr, Burnsville, MN 55337
(612) 435-8116
Admin Mark Broman.
Licensure Skilled care. *Beds* SNF 104. *Certified* Medicaid; Medicare.
Owner Proprietary corp.

Kennelly House
12000 Kennelly Rd, Burnsville, MN 55337
(612) 894-3044
Admin Kathleen Pine.
Licensure Intermediate care for mentally retarded. *Beds* ICF/MR 8.
Owner Proprietary corp.

Caledonia

Caledonia Health Care Center
425 N Badger, Caledonia, MN 55921
(507) 724-3351
Admin Sr Elizabeth Amman.
Licensure Skilled care. *Beds* SNF 74. *Certified* Medicaid; Medicare.
Owner Nonprofit corp.

Houston County Group Home
109 S Winnebago St, Caledonia, MN 55921
(507) 724-5259
Admin Dennis Theede.
Medical Dir Janice Storlie.
Licensure Intermediate care for mentally retarded. *Beds* ICF/MR 13. *Certified* Medicaid.
Owner Proprietary corp.
Admissions Requirements Minimum age 18; Medical examination.
Staff RNs 1 (pt); LPNs 1 (pt); Activities coordinators 1 (ft), 2 (pt).
Facilities Dining room; Activities room; Laundry room.
Activities Arts & crafts; Cards; Games; Prayer groups; Movies; Shopping trips; Dances/ Social/Cultural gatherings.

Cambridge

Cambridge Health Care Center
548 1st Ave, Cambridge, MN 55008
(612) 689-2323
Admin Dale Thompson.
Medical Dir P S Sanders MD.
Licensure Skilled care. *Beds* SNF 157. *Certified* Medicaid; Medicare.
Owner Proprietary corp.
Admissions Requirements Medical examination; Physician's request.
Staff RNs 8 (ft); LPNs 5 (ft); Nurses' aides 40 (ft); Physical therapists 1 (ft); Occupational therapists 1 (ft); Speech therapists 1 (pt); Activities coordinators 1 (ft); Dietitians 1 (pt); Podiatrists 1 (pt); Audiologists 1 (pt); Dentists 1 (pt).
Facilities Dining room; Physical therapy room; Activities room; Chapel; Crafts room; Laundry room; Barber/Beauty shop; Library.
Activities Arts & crafts; Cards; Games; Reading groups; Prayer groups; Movies; Shopping trips; Dances/Social/Cultural gatherings; Resident council; Family council.

Grandview Christian Home
800 NW 2nd Ave, Cambridge, MN 55008
(612) 689-1474
Admin Greg Carlson.

Licensure Skilled care; Intermediate care; Boarding care. *Beds* SNF 90; ICF 45; Boarding care 63. *Certified* Medicaid; Medicare.
Owner Proprietary corp.

Residential Alternatives VI
RR 3 Box 268, Cambridge, MN 55008
(612) 689-3794
Admin Peter Jacobson.
Licensure Intermediate care for mentally retarded. *Beds* ICF/MR 6. *Certified* Medicaid.
Owner Proprietary corp.
Admissions Requirements Minimum age 18; Medical examination.
Staff RNs 1 (pt); Dietitians 1 (pt).

Canby

Canby Community Health Services
112 Saint Olaf Ave S, Canby, MN 56220
(507) 223-7277
Admin Robert J Salmon.
Medical Dir Robert T Olson MD.
Licensure Skilled care. *Beds* SNF 75. *Certified* Medicaid; Medicare.
Owner Proprietary corp.
Admissions Requirements Minimum age 16; Medical examination.
Staff Physicians 3 (ft); RNs 1 (ft), 3 (pt); LPNs 3 (ft), 10 (pt); Nurses' aides 9 (ft), 32 (pt); Physical therapists 1 (pt); Occupational therapists; Speech therapists 1 (pt); Activities coordinators 1 (ft), 2 (pt); Dietitians 1 (ft); Podiatrists 1 (pt); Dentists 1 (pt).
Facilities Dining room; Physical therapy room; Activities room; Chapel; Crafts room; Laundry room; Barber/Beauty shop; Library.
Activities Arts & crafts; Cards; Games; Reading groups; Prayer groups; Movies; Dances/Social/Cultural gatherings; Entertainment groups; Picnics.

REM Canby A & B
1201 Haarfagar Ave N, Canby, MN 56220
(507) 223-7271
Admin Craig Miller.
Licensure Intermediate care for mentally retarded. *Beds* ICF/MR 30. *Certified* Medicaid.
Owner Proprietary corp.

Cannon Falls

Cannon Falls Manor Nursing Home
300 N Dow St, Cannon Falls, MN 55009
(507) 263-4658
Admin Jeff Johnson. *Dir of Nursing* Roberta Fure. *Medical Dir* Lloyd Klefstad.
Licensure Skilled care; Intermediate care; Boarding care. *Beds* SNF 86; ICF 31; Boarding care 2. *Private Pay Patients* 40%. *Certified* Medicaid; Medicare.
Owner Proprietary corp.
Admissions Requirements Minimum age 16.
Staff Physicians 2 (ft); RNs 1 (ft), 6 (pt); LPNs 3 (ft), 6 (pt); Nurses' aides 7 (ft), 45 (pt); Physical therapists 1 (pt); Activities coordinators 1 (ft); Dietitians 1 (ft).
Facilities Dining room; Physical therapy room; Activities room; Laundry room; Barber/Beauty shop.
Activities Arts & crafts; Cards; Games; Reading groups; Prayer groups; Movies; Shopping trips; Dances/Social/Cultural gatherings.

Carlton

Carlton Nursing Home
810 3rd St, Carlton, MN 55718
(218) 384-4258
Admin Larry C Penk.
Medical Dir Dr Vickie Anderson.
Licensure Skilled care. *Beds* SNF 96. *Certified* Medicaid; Medicare.

Owner Proprietary corp.
Admissions Requirements Minimum age 16; Medical examination.
Staff Physicians 2 (pt); RNs 1 (ft), 3 (pt); LPNs 10 (pt); Nurses' aides 42 (pt); Physical therapists 1 (ft); Speech therapists 1 (pt); Activities coordinators 1 (pt); Dietitians 1 (pt); Ophthalmologists 1 (pt); Podiatrists 1 (pt); Dentists 1 (pt).
Facilities Dining room; Physical therapy room; Activities room; Crafts room; Laundry room; Barber/Beauty shop.
Activities Arts & crafts; Cards; Games; Reading groups; Prayer groups; Movies; Shopping trips; Dances/Social/Cultural gatherings.

Center City

Hazelden Foundation
Box 11, Pleasant Valley Rd, Center City, MN 55012
(612) 257-4010
Admin Harold A Swift.
Licensure Skilled care; Supervised living. *Beds* SNF 19; Supervised living 184. *Certified* Medicaid.
Owner Nonprofit organization/foundation.
Admissions Requirements Medical examination.
Staff Physicians 3 (ft); RNs 34 (ft); Recreational therapists 7 (ft); Occupational therapists 3 (ft); Dietitians 1 (ft).
Facilities Dining room; Crafts room; Laundry room; Barber/Beauty shop; Library; Recreational facility including swimming pool.
Activities Arts & crafts; Movies.

South Center Manor
508 Park Island, Center City, MN 55012
(612) 257-1686
Admin Lowell J Petersen. *Dir of Nursing* Caroline M Petersen.
Licensure Intermediate care for mentally retarded. *Beds* ICF/MR 15. *Private Pay Patients* 0%. *Certified* Medicaid; Medicare.
Owner Proprietary corp.
Admissions Requirements Minimum age 18.
Staff RNs 1 (pt); LPNs 1 (ft); Dietitians 1 (pt).
Facilities Dining room; Activities room; Crafts room; Laundry room.
Activities Arts & crafts; Cards; Games; Movies; Shopping trips.

Chaska

Auburn Manor
500 Walnut St N, Chaska, MN 55318
(612) 448-9303
Admin Marvel Heath. *Dir of Nursing* Eileen Veum. *Medical Dir* Dr David Willey.
Licensure Boarding care. *Beds* Boarding care 61. *Private Pay Patients* 50%.
Owner Nonprofit corp.
Admissions Requirements Medical examination.
Staff RNs 2 (ft), 3 (pt); LPNs 2 (ft), 9 (pt); Nurses' aides 12 (ft), 22 (pt); Activities coordinators 2 (ft), 1 (pt); Dietitians (consultant).
Languages German.
Affiliation Moravian.
Facilities Dining room; Activities room; Laundry room; Corridor living rooms; 74% of rooms are private.
Activities Arts & crafts; Cards; Games; Reading groups; Movies; Shopping trips; Dances/Social/Cultural gatherings; Study & discussion groups.

Chatfield

Chosen Valley Care Center
1102 Liberty St SE, Chatfield, MN 55923
(507) 867-4220
Admin Ruth Jensen.
Licensure Skilled care. *Beds* SNF 86. *Certified* Medicaid; Medicare.
Owner Publicly owned.

Chisago City

Chisago Lakes Hospital
11685 Lake Blvd N, Chisago City, MN 55013
(612) 257-2500
Admin Scott Wordelman.
Licensure Skilled care. *Beds* SNF 40. *Certified* Medicaid; Medicare.
Owner Publicly owned.

Linnea Residential Home
28770 Old Town Rd, Chisago City, MN 55013
(612) 257-2211
Admin Donna Hoverman.
Licensure Intermediate care for mentally retarded. *Beds* ICF/MR 12. *Certified* Medicaid.
Owner Proprietary corp.

Margaret S Parmly Residence
28210 Old Town Rd, Chisago City, MN 55013
(612) 257-5620
Admin Charles Zimmerman. *Dir of Nursing* Shari Larson.
Licensure Skilled care; Boarding care. *Beds* SNF 77; Boarding care 24. *Certified* Medicaid; Medicare.
Owner Nonprofit corp (MN Synod/Lutheran Church Board).
Admissions Requirements Minimum age 18; Medical examination; Physician's request.
Staff RNs 2 (ft), 6 (pt); LPNs 2 (ft), 12 (pt); Nurses' aides 10 (ft), 15 (pt); Recreational therapists 1 (ft), 2 (pt).
Facilities Dining room; Activities room; Chapel; Crafts room; Laundry room; Barber/ Beauty shop.
Activities Arts & crafts; Cards; Games; Reading groups; Prayer groups; Movies; Shopping trips; Dances/Social/Cultural gatherings.

Chisholm

Buchanan Nursing Home
PO Box 549, 30 1st St NW, Chisholm, MN 55719
(218) 254-3614
Admin John Buchanan.
Licensure Intermediate care. *Beds* ICF 39. *Certified* Medicaid.
Owner Proprietary corp.

Heritage Manor Health Care Center
321 NE 6th St, Chisholm, MN 55719
(218) 254-5765
Admin Robert Koepcke. *Dir of Nursing* Carol McVicars RN. *Medical Dir* Jack Greene MD.
Licensure Skilled care; Retirement. *Beds* SNF 76. *Certified* Medicaid; Medicare.
Owner Proprietary corp.
Admissions Requirements Medical examination; Physician's request.
Staff Physicians 9 (pt); RNs 3 (ft), 5 (pt); LPNs 2 (ft), 5 (pt); Nurses' aides 11 (ft), 22 (pt); Physical therapists 1 (pt); Occupational therapists 1 (pt); Speech therapists 1 (pt); Activities coordinators 1 (ft); Dietitians 1 (pt); Ophthalmologists 1 (pt).

Facilities Dining room; Physical therapy room; Activities room; Children's center.
Activities Arts & crafts; Games; Prayer groups; Movies; Shopping trips; Dances/Social/ Cultural gatherings; Field trips; Outings to restaurants; Cooking.

Range Center
PO Box 629, 1001 8th Ave NW, Chisholm, MN 55719
(218) 254-3347
Admin Neil Boyum.
Licensure Intermediate care for mentally retarded; Retirement. *Beds* ICF/MR 21. *Certified* Medicaid.
Owner Proprietary corp.
Admissions Requirements Physician's request; Social worker referral.
Staff RNs 1 (ft); LPNs 3 (pt); Physical therapists 1 (pt); Occupational therapists 1 (pt); Speech therapists 1 (ft).
Languages Sign.
Facilities Dining room; Physical therapy room; Crafts room; Laundry room; Library; Candle factory (DAC portion).
Activities Work activity; Habilitation services.

Range Center—Oakwood Home
28 NE 11th St, Chisholm, MN 55719
(218) 254-3347
Admin Neil Boyum.
Licensure Intermediate care for mentally retarded. *Beds* ICF/MR 6. *Certified* Medicaid.
Owner Proprietary corp.
Admissions Requirements Minimum age 3.
Staff RNs 1 (pt).
Facilities Dining room; Activities room; Laundry room.
Activities Arts & crafts; Cards; Games; Reading groups; Movies; Shopping trips; Dances/Social/Cultural gatherings.

Range Center Westwind
901 Center Dr, Chisholm, MN 55719
(218) 254-3347
Admin Timothy Larson.
Licensure Intermediate care for mentally retarded. *Beds* ICF/MR 8.
Owner Proprietary corp.

Circle Pines

Valor Lexington
9329 Dunlap Ave N, Circle Pines, MN 55014
(612) 786-8470
Admin Eileen Harris.
Licensure Intermediate care for mentally retarded. *Beds* ICF/MR 6.
Owner Proprietary corp.

Clara City

Clara City Community Nursing Home
1012 Division St N, Clara City, MN 56222
(612) 847-2221
Admin Mark Rossi.
Licensure Intermediate care. *Beds* ICF 95. *Certified* Medicaid.
Owner Publicly owned.
Admissions Requirements Medical examination; Physician's request.
Staff Physicians 3 (pt); RNs 2 (ft); LPNs 3 (ft), 6 (pt); Physical therapists 1 (pt); Activities coordinators 1 (ft); Dietitians 1 (pt).
Facilities Dining room; Physical therapy room; Activities room; Chapel; Crafts room; Laundry room; Barber/Beauty shop.
Activities Arts & crafts; Cards; Games; Reading groups; Movies; Shopping trips; Dances/Social/Cultural gatherings.

Clarissa

Central Todd County Care Center
Hwy 71, Near Oak St, Clarissa, MN 56440
(218) 756-3636
Admin Margaret Taggart. *Dir of Nursing* Judy
Ladwig RN.
Licensure Skilled care; Retirement. *Beds* SNF
78. *Certified* Medicaid; Medicare.
Owner Proprietary corp.
Admissions Requirements Minimum age 16;
Medical examination.
Staff RNs; LPNs; Nurses' aides; Activities
coordinators; Dietitians.
Facilities Dining room; Physical therapy
room; Activities room; Chapel; Crafts room;
Laundry room; Barber/Beauty shop; Library.
Activities Arts & crafts; Cards; Games;
Reading groups; Prayer groups; Movies;
Shopping trips; Dances/Social/Cultural
gatherings.

Clarkfield

Clarkfield Care Center
805 5th St, Clarkfield, MN 56223
(612) 669-7561
Admin Mark Rossi. *Dir of Nursing* Yvonne
Severson. *Medical Dir* Dr Charles
Pogemiller.
Licensure Intermediate care. *Beds* ICF 86.
Private Pay Patients 40%. *Certified*
Medicaid.
Owner Publicly owned.
Staff RNs 3 (pt); LPNs 2 (ft), 4 (pt); Nurses'
aides 5 (ft), 55 (pt); Physical therapists;
Activities coordinators 1 (ft); Dietitians.
Facilities Dining room; Activities room;
Barber/Beauty shop.
Activities Arts & crafts; Cards; Games;
Reading groups; Prayer groups; Movies;
Shopping trips; Intergenerational programs;
Pet therapy.

Clear Lake

High Point Lodge Care Center
Rte 1 Box 346, Clear Lake, MN 55319
(612) 743-2695
Admin Hazel L Bollinger. *Dir of Nursing*
Bernie Bieledeldt RN.
Licensure Intermediate care. *Beds* ICF 26.
Certified Medicaid.
Owner Proprietary corp.
Admissions Requirements Minimum age 18;
Medical examination; Physician's request.
Staff RNs 1 (pt); LPNs 3 (pt); Nurses' aides 9
(pt).
Facilities Dining room; Activities room;
Laundry room.
Activities Arts & crafts; Cards; Games;
Movies; Shopping trips; Dances/Social/
Cultural gatherings; Bowling; Boating;
Fishing.

Clearbrook

Good Samaritan Center
PO Box 47, Clearbrook, MN 56634
(218) 776-3157
Admin Craig Boeddeker. *Dir of Nursing*
Sherry Torgerson. *Medical Dir* Dr Frank
Drucker.
Licensure Skilled care. *Beds* SNF 93. *Private
Pay Patients* 21%. *Certified* Medicaid;
Medicare.
Owner Nonprofit corp (Evangelical Lutheran/
Good Samaritan Society).
Staff RNs 3 (ft), 4 (pt); LPNs 4 (ft), 9 (pt);
Nurses' aides 10 (ft), 42 (pt); Physical
therapists; Recreational therapists; Activities
coordinators 1 (ft); Dietitians.
Languages Norwegian.

Affiliation Evangelical Lutheran.
Activities Arts & crafts; Games; Reading
groups; Prayer groups; Movies; Shopping
trips; Dances/Social/Cultural gatherings;
Intergenerational programs; Pet therapy;
Chapel services; Reality orientation;
Remotivation.

Clinton

Clinton Good Samaritan Center
PO Box 379, Hwy 75, Cty Rd 6, Clinton, MN
56225
(612) 325-5414
Admin Patrick Kelly.
Licensure Intermediate care. *Beds* ICF 54.
Certified Medicaid.
Owner Nonprofit corp (Evangelical Lutheran/
Good Samaritan Society).
Staff RNs 1 (ft); LPNs 2 (ft), 1 (pt); Nurses'
aides 9 (ft), 11 (pt); Activities coordinators 1
(ft), 1 (pt).
Affiliation Lutheran.
Facilities Dining room; Activities room;
Laundry room.
Activities Arts & crafts; Cards; Games;
Reading groups.

Cloquet

Community Memorial Hospital
Skyline Blvd, Cloquet, MN 55720
(218) 879-4641
Admin James J Carroll.
Licensure Skilled care. *Beds* SNF 88. *Certified*
Medicaid; Medicare.
Owner Proprietary corp.

Pine Ridge Home 1
413 Broadway, Cloquet, MN 55720
(218) 879-3910
Admin David Felske.
Licensure Intermediate care for mentally
retarded. *Beds* ICF/MR 6. *Certified*
Medicaid.
Owner Proprietary corp.

Pine Ridge Home 2
16 11th St, Cloquet, MN 55720
(218) 879-8395
Admin David Felske.
Licensure Intermediate care for mentally
retarded. *Beds* ICF/MR 6. *Certified*
Medicaid.
Owner Proprietary corp.

Pine Ridge Home 3
1509 14th St, Cloquet, MN 55720
(218) 879-1281
Admin David Felske.
Licensure Intermediate care for mentally
retarded. *Beds* ICF/MR 13. *Certified*
Medicaid.
Owner Proprietary corp.

Cokato

Cokato Manor Inc
W Hwy 12, Cokato, MN 55321
(612) 286-2158
Admin Larry S Petersen. *Dir of Nursing* Jan
Gunnerson. *Medical Dir* Tracy Wolf MD.
Licensure Skilled care. *Beds* SNF 66. *Private
Pay Patients* 40%. *Certified* Medicaid;
Medicare.
Owner Proprietary corp.
Admissions Requirements Minimum age 16;
Medical examination; Physician's request.
Staff RNs 1 (ft), 4 (pt); LPNs 6 (pt); Nurses'
aides 8 (ft), 30 (pt); Physical therapists
(contracted); Occupational therapists
(contracted); Speech therapists (contracted);
Activities coordinators 3 (pt); Dietitians
(contracted).
Facilities Dining room; Physical therapy
room; Activities room; Laundry room;
Barber/Beauty shop.

Activities Arts & crafts; Cards; Games;
Reading groups; Prayer groups; Movies;
Shopping trips; Dances/Social/Cultural
gatherings; Intergenerational programs; Pet
therapy.

Warner Care Home 1
325 Swanson Ave, Cokato, MN 55321
(612) 286-2843
Admin Martin McGraw.
Licensure Intermediate care for mentally
retarded. *Beds* ICF/MR 15. *Certified*
Medicaid.
Owner Proprietary corp.

Warner Care Home 2
180 6th St W, Cokato, MN 55321
(612) 286-2955
Admin Martin McGraw.
Licensure Intermediate care for mentally
retarded. *Beds* ICF/MR 7. *Certified*
Medicaid.
Owner Proprietary corp.

Warner Care Home 3
370 W 3rd St, Cokato, MN 55321
(612) 286-5248
Admin Martin McGraw.
Licensure Intermediate care for mentally
retarded. *Beds* ICF/MR 7. *Certified*
Medicaid.
Owner Proprietary corp.

Cold Spring

Assumption Home
715 N 1st St, Cold Spring, MN 56320
(612) 685-3693
Admin Sr Mary Roger Andert OSB. *Dir of
Nursing* Jean Lamond. *Medical Dir* Dr
George Schoephoerster.
Licensure Skilled care. *Beds* SNF 95. *Private
Pay Patients* 40%. *Certified* Medicaid;
Medicare.
Owner Nonprofit corp.
Admissions Requirements Medical
examination; Physician's request.
Staff Physicians 1 (pt); RNs 5 (ft), 3 (pt);
LPNs 3 (ft), 10 (pt); Nurses' aides 17 (ft), 22
(pt); Physical therapists 1 (pt); Reality
therapists 1 (pt); Recreational therapists 1
(ft); Occupational therapists 1 (pt); Activities
coordinators 1 (ft); Dietitians 1 (pt).
Affiliation Roman Catholic.
Facilities Dining room; Physical therapy
room; Activities room; Chapel; Crafts room;
Barber/Beauty shop; Library.
Activities Arts & crafts; Cards; Games;
Reading groups; Prayer groups; Movies;
Shopping trips; Dances/Social/Cultural
gatherings.

Mother Teresa Home
101 10th Ave N, Cold Spring, MN 56320
(612) 685-8626
Admin George Boswell.
Licensure Intermediate care for mentally
retarded. *Beds* ICF/MR 14. *Certified*
Medicare.
Owner Nonprofit organization/foundation.
Admissions Requirements Minimum age 18.
Staff RNs 1 (pt); LPNs 1 (pt).
Affiliation Roman Catholic.
Facilities Dining room; Laundry room.
Activities Arts & crafts; Cards; Games;
Movies; Shopping trips; Dances/Social/
Cultural gatherings.

Columbia Heights

Crest View Lutheran Home
4444 Reservoir Blvd, Columbia Heights, MN
55421
(612) 782-1611
Admin Thomas W Paul. *Dir of Nursing* Pam
Klosner. *Medical Dir* Spencer Johnson.

Licensure Skilled care; Retirement. *Beds* SNF
122; Retirement 77-90. *Private Pay Patients*
43%. *Certified* Medicaid; Medicare.
Owner Nonprofit organization/foundation.
Admissions Requirements Minimum age 55 or
younger with board approval; Medical
examination.
Staff RNs 3 (ft), 8 (pt); LPNs 3 (ft), 8 (pt);
Nurses' aides 30 (ft), 50 (pt); Physical
therapists 1 (ft), 1 (pt); Recreational
therapists 3 (ft); Occupational therapists 1
(ft); Activities coordinators 1 (ft).
Affiliation Lutheran.
Facilities Dining room; Physical therapy
room; Activities room; Chapel; Crafts room;
Laundry room; Barber/Beauty shop; Library.
Activities Arts & crafts; Cards; Games;
Reading groups; Prayer groups; Movies;
Shopping trips; Intergenerational programs.

Cook

Cook Community Hospital
3rd St & Cedar Ave, Cook, MN 55723
(218) 666-5945
Admin Lineta Scott.
Medical Dir Margie Hyppa.
Licensure Skilled care. *Beds* SNF 41. *Certified*
Medicaid; Medicare.
Owner Publicly owned.
Admissions Requirements Physician's request.
Staff RNs 10 (ft), 7 (pt); LPNs 3 (ft), 7 (pt);
Nurses' aides 10 (ft), 14 (pt); Physical
therapists 1 (ft), 1 (pt); Occupational
therapists 1 (pt); Speech therapists 1 (pt);
Activities coordinators 1 (ft); Dietitians 2
(pt).
Languages Swedish, Finnish, German.
Facilities Dining room; Physical therapy
room; Activities room; Crafts room; Laundry
room; Barber/Beauty shop; Library.
Activities Arts & crafts; Cards; Games;
Reading groups; Prayer groups; Movies;
Shopping trips; Dances/Social/Cultural
gatherings.

Coon Rapids

Camilia Rose Convalescent Center
11800 Xeon Blvd NW, Coon Rapids, MN
55433
(612) 755-8400
Admin Norma Brendle. *Dir of Nursing* Janice
Villella RN. *Medical Dir* William Rodman
MD.
Licensure Skilled care; Retirement. *Beds* SNF
94; Retirement apts 72. *Certified* Medicaid;
Medicare.
Owner Proprietary corp.
Admissions Requirements Minimum age 16;
Medical examination; Physician's request.
Staff RNs 3 (ft), 10 (pt); LPNs 15 (pt);
Nurses' aides 10 (ft), 32 (pt); Physical
therapists 1 (ft); Recreational therapists 3
(ft); Occupational therapists 1 (ft); Speech
therapists 1 (pt); Dietitians 1 (ft).
Facilities Dining room; Chapel; Laundry
room; Barber/Beauty shop; Physical therapy
clinic; Occupational therapy clinic; Family
lounges.
Activities Arts & crafts; Cards; Games;
Reading groups; Prayer groups; Movies;
Shopping trips; Dances/Social/Cultural
gatherings; Music therapy; Lunch outings;
Picnics; Sensory stimulation groups.

Camilia Rose Group Home
11820 Xeon Blvd NW, Coon Rapids, MN
55433
(612) 755-8489, 754-0332 FAX
Admin Dr Mary M Tjosvold. *Dir of Nursing*
Virginia Naros.
Licensure Intermediate care for mentally
retarded. *Beds* ICF/MR 35. *Private Pay
Patients* 0%. *Certified* Medicaid.
Owner Proprietary corp.

Staff RNs 1 (pt); LPNs 3 (ft); Physical
therapists (consulted); Dietitians
(consultant); Direct care 69.
Activities Arts & crafts; Cards; Games;
Reading groups; Movies; Shopping trips;
Dances/Social/Cultural gatherings;
Independence training; Community
integration.

Community Living Inc—Cottage 6
2493 109th Ave NW, Coon Rapids, MN
55433
(612) 757-6248
Admin Jerry Gross.
Licensure Intermediate care for mentally
retarded. *Beds* ICF/MR 12.
Owner Proprietary corp.

Community Living Inc—Cottage 5
2483 109th Ave NW, Coon Rapids, MN
55433
(612) 757-4079
Admin Jerry Gross.
Licensure Intermediate care for mentally
retarded. *Beds* ICF/MR 12. *Certified*
Medicaid.
Owner Proprietary corp.

Demars Childrens Home
11777 Xeon Blvd, Coon Rapids, MN 55433
(612) 755-8174
Admin Dr Mary Tjosvold.
Licensure Intermediate care for mentally
retarded. *Beds* ICF/MR 20.
Owner Privately owned.
Admissions Requirements Minimum age 0-21;
Medical examination; Physician's request.
Staff RNs 1 (ft); LPNs 1 (ft); Nurses' aides 25
(ft); Physical therapists; Recreational
therapists 1 (ft); Occupational therapists 1
(ft); Dietitians.
Facilities Dining room; Physical therapy
room; Activities room; Crafts room; Laundry
room; Living room.
Activities Arts & crafts; Cards; Games;
Reading groups; Movies; Shopping trips;
Dances/Social/Cultural gatherings; Dance
therapy; Music therapy; Camp;
Communication groups; Learning groups;
Sports.

Park River Estates Care Center
9899 Avocet St NW, Coon Rapids, MN 55433
(612) 757-2320
Admin Steven Chies. *Dir of Nursing* Cindy
McClintock RN. *Medical Dir* Dr Mark
Brakke.
Licensure Skilled care; Intermediate care. *Beds*
SNF 91; ICF 13. *Certified* Medicaid;
Medicare.
Owner Proprietary corp.
Admissions Requirements Medical
examination; Physician's request.
Staff Physicians 2 (pt); RNs 1 (ft), 8 (pt);
LPNs 1 (ft), 12 (pt); Nurses' aides 34 (ft), 18
(pt); Physical therapists 1 (ft); Occupational
therapists 1 (pt); Activities coordinators 1
(ft); Dietitians 1 (pt).
Facilities Dining room; Physical therapy
room; Activities room; Chapel; Crafts room;
Laundry room; Barber/Beauty shop; Library.
Activities Arts & crafts; Cards; Games;
Reading groups; Prayer groups; Movies;
Shopping trips; Dances/Social/Cultural
gatherings.

Cosmos

Cosmos Healthcare Center
Neptune & Pegasus, Cosmos, MN 56228
(612) 877-7227
Admin Mark Rust.
Licensure Skilled care; Intermediate care. *Beds*
SNF 29; ICF 29. *Certified* Medicaid;
Medicare.
Owner Proprietary corp (Beverly Enterprises).

Cromwell

Villa Vista Inc
PO Box 98, N Hwy 73, Cromwell, MN 55726
(218) 644-3331
Admin Raymond M Lally. *Dir of Nursing* Gail
Dahl. *Medical Dir* Ricard Puumala.
Licensure Intermediate care; Alzheimer's care.
Beds ICF 51. *Private Pay Patients* 15%.
Certified Medicaid.
Owner Proprietary corp.
Admissions Requirements Medical
examination; Pre-admission screening.
Staff RNs 2 (ft); LPNs 4 (ft); Nurses' aides 25
(ft); Activities coordinators 2 (ft), 1 (pt);
Dietitians 1 (ft).
Languages Finnish.
Facilities Dining room; Activities room;
Crafts room; Laundry room; Barber/Beauty
shop; Wander-guard door alarm.
Activities Arts & crafts; Cards; Games;
Reading groups; Prayer groups; Movies;
Shopping trips; Dances/Social/Cultural
gatherings; Intergenerational programs.

Crookston

Crookston Group Home 1
315 Summit Ave, Crookston, MN 56716
(218) 281-7245
Admin Vernon C Nordmark PhD.
Medical Dir Josette C Nordmark MD.
Licensure Intermediate care for mentally
retarded. *Beds* ICF/MR 10. *Certified*
Medicaid.
Owner Proprietary corp.
Admissions Requirements Minimum age 18;
Medical examination.
Staff RNs 1 (pt); Activities coordinators 1 (ft).
Facilities Dining room; Activities room;
Laundry room.
Activities Arts & crafts; Cards; Games;
Movies; Shopping trips; Dances/Social/
Cultural gatherings.

Crookston Group Home 2
1423 Foskett, Crookston, MN 56716
(218) 281-1904
Admin Vernon C Nordmark PhD.
Medical Dir Josette C Nordmark MD.
Licensure Intermediate care for mentally
retarded. *Beds* ICF/MR 10. *Certified*
Medicaid.
Owner Proprietary corp.
Admissions Requirements Minimum age 18;
Females only.
Facilities Dining room; Activities room;
Laundry room.
Activities Arts & crafts; Cards; Games;
Movies; Shopping trips; Dances/Social/
Cultural gatherings.

Crookston Group Home 3
220 Johnson Pl, Crookston, MN 56716
(218) 281-5642
Admin Vernon C Nordmark PhD.
Medical Dir Josette C Nordmark MD.
Licensure Intermediate care for mentally
retarded. *Beds* ICF/MR 8. *Certified*
Medicaid.
Owner Proprietary corp.
Admissions Requirements Minimum age 18;
Medical examination.
Staff RNs 1 (pt); Activities coordinators 1 (ft);
Direct care.
Facilities Dining room; Activities room;
Laundry room.
Activities Arts & crafts; Cards; Games;
Movies; Shopping trips; Dances/Social/
Cultural gatherings; Community recreation.

Glenmore Recovery Center
PO Box 497, Crookston, MN 56716
(218) 281-3123
Admin Thomas C Lenertz.

Licensure Supervised living. *Beds* Supervised living 27.
Owner Proprietary corp.

Riverview Nursing Home
323 S Minnesota, Crookston, MN 56716
(218) 281-4682
Admin Thomas C Lenertz. *Dir of Nursing* Gloria Kaste. *Medical Dir* B Ring MD.
Licensure Skilled care; Intermediate care. *Beds* Swing beds SNF/ICF 100. *Certified* Medicaid; Medicare.
Owner Nonprofit organization/foundation.
Admissions Requirements Minimum age 16; Medical examination; Physician's request.
Staff Physicians; RNs; LPNs; Nurses' aides; Physical therapists; Occupational therapists; Speech therapists; Activities coordinators; Dietitians; Ophthalmologists (consultant); Podiatrists (consultant); Audiologists (consultant).
Languages Norwegian, French, German.
Facilities Dining room; Physical therapy room; Activities room; Chapel; Crafts room; Laundry room; Barber/Beauty shop.
Activities Arts & crafts; Cards; Games; Reading groups; Prayer groups; Movies; Shopping trips; Dances/Social/Cultural gatherings; Intergenerational programs; Pet therapy; One-on-one; Cooking.

Villa St Vincent
516 Walsh St, Crookston, MN 56716
(218) 281-3424
Admin Michael D Siekas. *Dir of Nursing* Judy Hulst RN. *Medical Dir* Charles Winjum MD.
Licensure Skilled care; Intermediate care. *Beds* SNF 80; ICF 95. *Private Pay Patients* 40%.
Owner Nonprofit organization/foundation.
Admissions Requirements Medical examination; Physician's request.
Staff Physicians 1 (pt); RNs 3 (ft), 3 (pt); LPNs 7 (ft), 5 (pt); Nurses' aides 30 (ft), 45 (pt); Recreational therapists 5 (ft); Occupational therapists 1 (ft); Dietitians 1 (pt).
Affiliation Roman Catholic.
Facilities Dining room; Physical therapy room; Activities room; Chapel; Crafts room; Laundry room; Barber/Beauty shop; Library; Darkroom; Kiln room.
Activities Arts & crafts; Cards; Games; Reading groups; Prayer groups; Movies; Shopping trips; Dances/Social/Cultural gatherings; Ceramics.

Crosby

Cuyuna Range District Nursing Home
320 E Main St, Crosby, MN 56441
(218) 546-5147, 546-6091 FAX
Admin Thomas F Reek. *Dir of Nursing* Kevin Olander. *Medical Dir* Dr Edward Rosenbaum.
Licensure Skilled care; Intermediate care. *Beds* Swing beds SNF/ICF 130. *Private Pay Patients* 24%. *Certified* Medicaid; Medicare.
Owner Publicly owned.
Admissions Requirements Medical examination.
Staff Physicians 1 (pt); RNs 5 (ft), 4 (pt); LPNs 6 (ft), 9 (pt); Nurses' aides 12 (ft), 43 (pt); Physical therapists 2 (ft); Activities coordinators 1 (ft); Dietitians 1 (ft); Social workers 1 (ft).
Facilities Dining room; Physical therapy room; Activities room; Chapel; Crafts room; Laundry room; Barber/Beauty shop; Wood shop; Wanderguard system.
Activities Arts & crafts; Cards; Games; Reading groups; Prayer groups; Movies; Shopping trips; Dances/Social/Cultural gatherings; Intergenerational programs; Pet therapy; Reality therapy; Sensory stimulation.

Crystal

Crystal Care Center
3245 Vera Cruz Ave N, Crystal, MN 55422
(612) 535-6260
Admin Patricia J Reller. *Dir of Nursing* Terri Ritten. *Medical Dir* Dr Keith Kubasch.
Licensure Skilled care; Alzheimer's care. *Beds* SNF 192. *Certified* Medicaid; Medicare.
Owner Nonprofit corp (Volunteers of America).
Admissions Requirements Minimum age 21; Medical examination; Physician's request.
Staff Physicians 1 (pt); RNs 12 (ft), 3 (pt); LPNs 13 (ft), 15 (pt); Nurses' aides 45 (ft), 25 (pt); Physical therapists 1 (ft), 2 (pt); Recreational therapists 4 (ft); Occupational therapists 2 (ft), 1 (pt); Activities coordinators 1 (ft); Dietitians 1 (pt).
Affiliation Volunteers of America.
Facilities Dining room; Physical therapy room; Activities room; Chapel; Crafts room; Laundry room; Barber/Beauty shop; Library.
Activities Arts & crafts; Cards; Games; Reading groups; Prayer groups; Movies; Shopping trips; Dances/Social/Cultural gatherings.

Dungarvin V Tyrothy
3157 Douglas Dr, Crystal, MN 55422
(612) 545-8757
Admin Diane Madden.
Licensure Intermediate care for mentally retarded. *Beds* ICF/MR 12. *Certified* Medicaid.
Owner Proprietary corp.
Staff RNs 1 (pt); Activities coordinators 1 (ft).
Facilities Laundry room.
Activities Games; Movies; Shopping trips; Dances/Social/Cultural gatherings.

Dassel

Dassel Lakeside Community Home
441 William Ave, Dassel, MN 55325
(612) 275-3433
Admin William D Ward.
Medical Dir Marilyn Nelson.
Licensure Intermediate care; Retirement; Alzheimer's care. *Beds* ICF 63. *Certified* Medicaid.
Owner Publicly owned.
Admissions Requirements Minimum age 16; Medical examination; Physician's request.
Staff RNs 2 (ft), 3 (pt); LPNs 5 (ft), 3 (pt); Nurses' aides 18 (ft), 20 (pt); Recreational therapists 1 (ft), 1 (pt); Activities coordinators 1 (ft); Dietitians 1 (pt).
Facilities Dining room; Activities room; Chapel; Crafts room; Laundry room; Barber/Beauty shop.
Activities Arts & crafts; Games; Reading groups; Prayer groups; Movies; Dances/Social/Cultural gatherings.

Dawson

Johnson Memorial Hospital & Home
Walnut St & Memorial Pl, Dawson, MN 56232
(612) 769-4323
Admin Mark Rinehardt.
Medical Dir Dr P W Maus.
Licensure Skilled care. *Beds* SNF 70. *Certified* Medicaid; Medicare.
Owner Publicly owned.
Admissions Requirements Medical examination.
Staff Physicians 2 (ft); RNs 1 (ft), 3 (pt); LPNs 4 (ft), 5 (pt); Nurses' aides 17 (ft), 22 (pt); Physical therapists 1 (pt); Occupational therapists 1 (ft); Activities coordinators 1 (ft); Dietitians 1 (pt); Dentists 2 (pt); Activity assistants 5 (ft).
Facilities Dining room; Physical therapy room; Activities room; Chapel; Barber/Beauty shop; Dayroom.

Activities Arts & crafts; Cards; Games; Reading groups; Prayer groups; Dances/ Social/Cultural gatherings; Weekly bingo.

Deer River

Homestead Nursing Home
1002 Comstock Dr, Deer River, MN 56636
(218) 246-2900
Admin William Eckblad. *Dir of Nursing* Sharyn Rohder. *Medical Dir* Dr L Karges.
Licensure Skilled care; Retirement. *Beds* SNF 50. *Private Pay Patients* 15%. *Certified* Medicaid; Medicare.
Owner Nonprofit organization/foundation.
Admissions Requirements Medical examination; Physician's request.
Staff Physicians 3 (ft), 3 (pt); RNs 2 (ft), 2 (pt); LPNs 5 (ft), 15 (pt); Nurses' aides 6 (ft), 25 (pt); Physical therapists 1 (ft); Occupational therapists 1 (pt); Speech therapists 1 (pt); Activities coordinators 1 (ft); Dietitians 1 (ft).
Languages Chippewa, Ojibway, Finnish.
Facilities Dining room; Physical therapy room; Activities room; Chapel; Crafts room; Barber/Beauty shop.
Activities Arts & crafts; Cards; Games; Reading groups; Prayer groups; Movies; Shopping trips; Dances/Social/Cultural gatherings; Intergenerational programs; Pet therapy; Outings.

Delano

Delano Healthcare Center
433 County Rd 30, Delano, MN 55328
(612) 479-2987
Admin Kristi Olmanson. *Dir of Nursing* Joann Hubbard.
Licensure Skilled care. *Beds* SNF 64. *Certified* Medicaid; Medicare.
Owner Proprietary corp (Beverly Enterprises).
Admissions Requirements Physician's request.
Staff RNs 3 (ft), 1 (pt); LPNs 2 (ft), 3 (pt); Nurses' aides 9 (ft), 31 (pt); Physical therapists 1 (ft); Recreational therapists 2 (ft); Occupational therapists 1 (ft); Speech therapists 1 (pt).
Facilities Dining room; Physical therapy room; Activities room; Barber/Beauty shop; Library; Patio.
Activities Arts & crafts; Cards; Games; Reading groups; Prayer groups; Movies; Shopping trips; Dances/Social/Cultural gatherings.

Dells Place Inc
235 S 2nd St, Delano, MN 55328
(612) 972-3664
Admin Vernon Wahlstrom.
Licensure Intermediate care for mentally retarded. *Beds* ICF/MR 9. *Certified* Medicaid.
Owner Proprietary corp.
Admissions Requirements Minimum age 18; Medical examination.
Staff RNs 1 (pt); Activities coordinators 1 (ft).
Facilities Dining room; Activities room; Laundry room; Kitchen; Living room; Dayroom.
Activities Arts & crafts; Cards; Games; Movies; Shopping trips; Dances/Social/ Cultural gatherings.

Detroit Lakes

Emmanuel Nursing Home
1415 Madison Ave, Detroit Lakes, MN 56501
(218) 847-4486
Admin Mark Hoplin.
Medical Dir Dr Bill Henke.
Licensure Skilled care; Retirement; Alzheimer's care. *Beds* SNF 144. *Certified* Medicaid; Medicare.
Owner Proprietary corp.

Staff RNs 6 (ft); LPNs 22 (ft); Nurses' aides 50 (ft), 40 (pt); Physical therapists 1 (ft), 1 (pt); Speech therapists 1 (pt); Activities coordinators 1 (ft); Dietitians 1 (ft).
Affiliation Lutheran.
Facilities Dining room; Physical therapy room; Activities room; Chapel; Crafts room; Laundry room; Barber/Beauty shop; Library.
Activities Arts & crafts; Cards; Games; Reading groups; Prayer groups; Movies; Shopping trips; Dances/Social/Cultural gatherings.

St Marys Nursing Center
1014 Lincoln Ave, Detroit Lakes, MN 56501
(218) 847-5611
Admin John Korzendorfer. *Dir of Nursing* Janet Green. *Medical Dir* Dr Robert Koschnik.
Licensure Skilled care; Alzheimer's care. *Beds* SNF 100. *Certified* Medicaid; Medicare.
Owner Nonprofit organization/foundation.
Admissions Requirements Minimum age 16; Medical examination; Physician's request.
Affiliation Roman Catholic.
Facilities Dining room; Physical therapy room; Activities room; Chapel; Crafts room; Barber/Beauty shop.
Activities Arts & crafts; Cards; Games; Prayer groups; Movies; Shopping trips; Dances/Social/Cultural gatherings; Intergenerational programs; Pet therapy.

Summit Home
920 Summit Ave, Box 169, Detroit Lakes, MN 56501
(218) 847-5642
Admin Thomas Reiffenberger.
Licensure Intermediate care for mentally retarded. *Beds* ICF/MR 9. *Certified* Medicaid.
Owner Proprietary corp.

West Home
PO Box 1355, 1118 West Ave, Detroit Lakes, MN 56502
(218) 847-5642, 847-7176 FAX
Admin Thomas Reiffenberger.
Licensure Intermediate care for mentally retarded; Retirement. *Beds* ICF/MR 9. *Certified* Medicaid.
Owner Nonprofit corp.
Admissions Requirements Minimum age 18; Medical examination.
Staff RNs; Human service technicians 7 (ft), 4 (pt).
Facilities Dining room; Activities room; Laundry room.
Activities Arts & crafts; Cards; Games; Reading groups; Prayer groups; Movies; Shopping trips; Dances/Social/Cultural gatherings; Intergenerational programs; Pet therapy.

Dodge Center

Fairview Nursing Home
Rte 1 Box 334, Dodge Center, MN 55927
(507) 374-2578
Admin Donald W Bakke.
Medical Dir O S Kulstad.
Licensure Skilled care. *Beds* SNF 72. *Certified* Medicaid; Medicare.
Owner Publicly owned.
Admissions Requirements Minimum age 16; Medical examination.
Staff RNs 3 (ft), 4 (pt); LPNs 3 (ft), 4 (pt); Nurses' aides 15 (ft), 23 (pt); Physical therapists 1 (pt); Occupational therapists 1 (pt); Activities coordinators 1 (ft); Dietitians 1 (ft).
Facilities Dining room; Physical therapy room; Activities room; Chapel; Laundry room; Barber/Beauty shop.
Activities Arts & crafts; Cards; Games; Prayer groups; Movies.

Woodvale Dodge Center
503 5th Ave NW, Dodge Center, MN 55927
(507) 374-2836
Admin Walter Baldus.
Licensure Intermediate care for mentally retarded. *Beds* ICF/MR 8. *Certified* Medicaid.
Owner Proprietary corp.

Duluth

ABC Community Services Inc
1707 Cliff Ave, Duluth, MN 55811
(218) 525-3075
Admin Mary Manion-Bick.
Licensure Intermediate care for mentally retarded. *Beds* ICF/MR 6. *Certified* Medicaid.
Owner Proprietary corp.

Aftenro Home
510 W College St, Duluth, MN 55811
(218) 728-6864
Admin Jerold Nugent. *Dir of Nursing* Cherlyn Morrison. *Medical Dir* Catherine Watt.
Licensure Intermediate care. *Beds* ICF 65. *Private Pay Patients* 45%. *Certified* Medicaid.
Owner Nonprofit organization/foundation.
Admissions Requirements Medical examination.
Staff RNs 1 (ft); LPNs 7 (ft); Nurses' aides 7 (ft); Dietitians 1 (ft).
Facilities Dining room; Activities room; Chapel; Crafts room; Laundry room; Barber/Beauty shop; Library.
Activities Arts & crafts; Cards; Games; Reading groups; Prayer groups; Movies; Shopping trips; Dances/Social/Cultural gatherings; Intergenerational programs.

Benedictine Health Center
935 Kenwood Ave, Duluth, MN 55811
(218) 723-6408
Admin Sr Armella Oblak.
Licensure Skilled care. *Beds* SNF 120.
Owner Proprietary corp.

Caromin House—Dodge
4620 Dodge St, Duluth, MN 55804
(218) 525-6995
Admin Trudy Carlson.
Licensure Intermediate care for mentally retarded. *Beds* ICF/MR 6. *Certified* Medicaid.
Owner Proprietary corp.
Admissions Requirements Minimum age 18.

Caromin House—Tioga
6009 Tioga St, Duluth, MN 55804
(218) 525-5650
Admin Trudy Carlson.
Licensure Intermediate care for mentally retarded. *Beds* ICF/MR 15. *Certified* Medicaid.
Owner Proprietary corp.
Admissions Requirements Minimum age 18; Females only.

Champion Childrens Home
1889 Lester River Rd, Duluth, MN 55804
(218) 525-1165
Admin Gordon Atol.
Licensure Supervised living. *Beds* Supervised living 16. *Certified* Medicaid.
Owner Proprietary corp.
Admissions Requirements Medical examination.
Staff RNs 1 (pt); LPNs 1 (ft), 1 (pt); Nurses' aides 2 (ft), 15 (pt); Dietitians 1 (pt).
Facilities Dining room; Activities room; Laundry room; Music room; Living room.
Activities Arts & crafts; Games; Reading groups; Movies; Shopping trips; Dances/Social/Cultural gatherings.

Duluth Regional Care Center 1
2232 E 1st St, Duluth, MN 55812
(218) 728-4347
Admin Clyde Johnson.
Licensure Intermediate care for mentally retarded. *Beds* ICF/MR 10. *Certified* Medicaid.
Owner Nonprofit corp.
Admissions Requirements Minimum age 17.
Facilities Dining room; Activities room; Laundry room.
Activities Cards; Games; Movies; Shopping trips; Dances/Social/Cultural gatherings.

Duluth Regional Care Center II
323 90th Ave W, Duluth, MN 55808
(218) 626-1784
Admin Clyde Johnson.
Licensure Intermediate care for mentally retarded. *Beds* ICF/MR 6. *Certified* Medicaid.
Owner Proprietary corp.
Admissions Requirements Minimum age 17; Medical examination.
Facilities Dining room; Activities room; Laundry room.
Activities Arts & crafts; Cards; Games; Movies; Shopping trips; Dances/Social/Cultural gatherings.

Duluth Regional Care Center III
631 W Skyline Blvd, Duluth, MN 55805
(218) 727-5984
Admin Clyde Johnson.
Licensure Intermediate care for mentally retarded; Retirement. *Beds* ICF/MR 10. *Certified* Medicaid.
Owner Nonprofit corp.
Admissions Requirements Minimum age 18.
Staff Program directors 1 (ft); Program coordinators 2 (ft); Program implementers 4 (ft).
Facilities 3 complete apartments.
Activities Cards; Games; Movies; Shopping trips; Dances/Social/Cultural gatherings; Daily living skills.

Duluth Regional Care Center IV
2502 W 2nd St, Duluth, MN 55806
(218) 727-4423
Admin Clyde Johnson.
Licensure Intermediate care for mentally retarded. *Beds* ICF/MR 6. *Certified* Medicaid.
Owner Proprietary corp.

EBI Inc
625 N 56th Ave W, Duluth, MN 55807
(218) 624-3122
Admin James Evans.
Licensure Supervised living. *Beds* Supervised living 6.
Owner Proprietary corp.

Chris Jensen Nursing Home
2501 Rice Lake Rd, Duluth, MN 55811
(218) 720-1500
Admin Ronald J Johnson. *Dir of Nursing* Beverly Nordwall. *Medical Dir* William A Stein MD.
Licensure Skilled care. *Beds* SNF 247. *Certified* Medicaid; Medicare.
Owner Publicly owned.
Admissions Requirements Minimum age 16.
Staff Physicians 3 (ft); RNs 10 (ft), 12 (pt); LPNs 17 (ft), 14 (pt); Nurses' aides 59 (ft), 71 (pt); Physical therapists 1 (ft); Activities coordinators 1 (ft); Dietitians 2 (ft).
Languages Finnish, Swedish.
Facilities Dining room; Physical therapy room; Activities room; Chapel; Crafts room; Barber/Beauty shop.
Activities Arts & crafts; Cards; Games; Reading groups; Prayer groups; Movies; Shopping trips; Dances/Social/Cultural gatherings.

Lake Haven Manor
7700 Grand Ave, Duluth, MN 55807
(218) 628-2341
Admin Robert D Sundberg. *Dir of Nursing*
Virginia McDonnell. *Medical Dir* Dr
Douglas J Hiza.
Licensure Skilled care. *Beds* SNF 132. *Private
Pay Patients* 30%. *Certified* Medicaid;
Medicare.
Owner Proprietary corp.
Admissions Requirements Minimum age 18;
Medical examination.
Staff RNs 1 (ft), 14 (pt); LPNs 1 (ft), 7 (pt);
Nurses' aides 5 (ft), 60 (pt); Physical
therapists 1 (ft), 2 (pt); Occupational
therapists 1 (ft), 2 (pt); Activities
coordinators 1 (ft); Dietitians 1 (pt).
Facilities Dining room; Physical therapy
room; Activities room; Chapel; Crafts room;
Laundry room; Barber/Beauty shop.
Activities Arts & crafts; Cards; Games;
Reading groups; Prayer groups; Movies;
Shopping trips; Intergenerational programs;
Pet therapy.

Lakeshore Lutheran Home
4002 London Rd, Duluth, MN 55804
(218) 525-1951
Admin Joyce M Underkofler. *Dir of Nursing*
Marilyn Moore. *Medical Dir* Dr Matthew
Eckman.
Licensure Skilled care; Intermediate care. *Beds*
SNF 177; ICF 53. *Certified* Medicaid;
Medicare.
Owner Nonprofit organization/foundation.
Admissions Requirements Medical
examination; Physician's request.
Staff RNs 9 (ft), 12 (pt); LPNs 13 (ft), 23 (pt);
Nurses' aides 77 (ft), 26 (pt); Physical
therapists 1 (ft), 3 (pt); Recreational
therapists 3 (ft); Occupational therapists 1
(pt); Activities coordinators 1 (ft); Dietitians
1 (pt).
Affiliation Lutheran.
Facilities Dining room; Physical therapy
room; Activities room; Chapel; Crafts room;
Laundry room; Barber/Beauty shop.
Activities Arts & crafts; Cards; Games;
Reading groups; Prayer groups; Movies;
Shopping trips; Dances/Social/Cultural
gatherings; Intergenerational programs; Sing-
alongs; Other musical activities; Theme
parties.

Nekton on Greysolon
3518 Greysolon Rd, Duluth, MN 55804
(218) 724-9373
Admin Joe Modec.
Licensure Intermediate care for mentally
retarded. *Beds* ICF/MR 6. *Certified*
Medicaid.
Owner Proprietary corp.
Admissions Requirements Minimum age 4;
Medical examination; Physician's request.
Staff Physicians 4 (pt); RNs 1 (pt); Physical
therapists 1 (pt); Recreational therapists 2
(pt); Occupational therapists 1 (pt); Speech
therapists 1 (pt); Activities coordinators 1
(pt); Dietitians 1 (pt); Ophthalmologists 1
(pt); Podiatrists 1 (pt); Audiologists 1 (pt);
Dentists 1 (pt).
Facilities Dining room; Activities room;
Laundry room; Library.
Activities Arts & crafts; Cards; Games;
Reading groups; Movies; Shopping trips;
Dances/Social/Cultural gatherings.

Nekton on London Road
4515 London Rd, Duluth, MN 55804
(218) 525-3632
Admin Joe Modec.
Licensure Intermediate care for mentally
retarded. *Beds* ICF/MR 6. *Certified*
Medicaid.
Owner Proprietary corp.

Nekton on Springvale
2214 Springvale Rd, Duluth, MN 55811
(218) 722-7280
Admin Joe Modec.
Licensure Intermediate care for mentally
retarded. *Beds* ICF/MR 6. *Certified*
Medicaid.
Owner Proprietary corp.

Nekton on Wallace
1702 Wallace Ave, Duluth, MN 55803
(218) 726-6224
Admin Joe Modec.
Licensure Intermediate care for mentally
retarded. *Beds* ICF/MR 6. *Certified*
Medicaid.
Owner Proprietary corp.

Park Point Manor
1601 St Louis Ave, Duluth, MN 55802
(218) 727-8651
Admin Mark Norgard. *Dir of Nursing* Shelly
Hanson. *Medical Dir* Dr Hiza.
Licensure Skilled care; Intermediate care;
Alzheimer's care. *Beds* SNF 216; ICF 24.
Certified Medicaid; Medicare.
Owner Proprietary corp.
Admissions Requirements Minimum age 16;
Medical examination; Physician's request.
Staff Physicians 1 (pt); RNs 8 (ft), 10 (pt);
LPNs 10 (ft), 20 (pt); Nurses' aides 70 (ft),
90 (pt); Physical therapists 3 (ft);
Recreational therapists 5 (ft); Occupational
therapists 1 (ft); Speech therapists 1 (pt);
Activities coordinators 1 (ft); Dietitians 1
(pt); Ophthalmologists 1 (pt).
Facilities Dining room; Physical therapy
room; Activities room; Chapel; Crafts room;
Laundry room; Barber/Beauty shop; Library;
Courtyard.
Activities Arts & crafts; Cards; Games;
Reading groups; Prayer groups; Movies;
Shopping trips; Dances/Social/Cultural
gatherings; Concerts; Horseback riding;
Swimming.

Residential Services of Northeast Minnesota I
PO Box 3008, Duluth, MN 55803-3008
(218) 728-6819
Admin Jon Nelson, acting.
Licensure Intermediate care for mentally
retarded. *Beds* ICF/MR 13. *Certified*
Medicaid.
Owner Proprietary corp.

Residential Services of Northeast Minnesota II
707 Arrowhead Rd, Duluth, MN 55811
(218) 728-6823
Admin Tim Mowbray.
Licensure Intermediate care for mentally
retarded. *Beds* ICF/MR 16. *Certified*
Medicaid.
Owner Proprietary corp.
Admissions Requirements Medical
examination.
Staff RNs 1 (pt); LPNs 1 (ft); Activities
coordinators 1 (ft).

**Residential Services of Northeast Minnesota
Inc III**
2320 Arrowhead Rd, Duluth, MN 55811
(218) 728-6823
Admin Timothy Mowbray.
Licensure Supervised living. *Beds* Supervised
living 6.
Owner Proprietary corp.

Surf & Sand Health Center
3910 Minnesota Ave, Duluth, MN 55802
(218) 727-8933
Admin William J Buchanan. *Dir of Nursing*
Lori Randa. *Medical Dir* Hadley Young.
Licensure Skilled care; Intermediate care. *Beds*
Swing beds SNF/ICF 56. *Private Pay
Patients* 37%. *Certified* Medicaid; Medicare.

Owner Proprietary corp.
Staff RNs 5 (ft), 3 (pt); LPNs 6 (ft); Nurses'
aides 20 (ft), 10 (pt); Physical therapists 1
(ft); Occupational therapists 1 (ft); Activities
coordinators 1 (ft).

Thunderbird House
229 N 4th Ave W, Duluth, MN 55806
(218) 727-1476
Admin Edwin J Benton.
Licensure Supervised living. *Beds* Supervised
living 10.
Owner Nonprofit corp.

Viewcrest Nursing Center
3111 Church St, Duluth, MN 55811
(218) 727-8801
Admin Thomas Buchanan. *Dir of Nursing*
Rose Jenny.
Licensure Skilled care. *Beds* SNF 139. *Private
Pay Patients* 25%. *Certified* Medicare.
Owner Proprietary corp.
Staff RNs 7 (ft); LPNs 17 (ft); Nurses' aides
66 (ft); Physical therapists 1 (ft);
Occupational therapists 1 (ft); Speech
therapists 1 (pt); Activities coordinators 2
(ft); Dietitians 1 (pt); Podiatrists 1 (pt).
Facilities Dining room; Physical therapy
room; Activities room; Crafts room; Laundry
room; Barber/Beauty shop.
Activities Arts & crafts; Cards; Games;
Reading groups; Prayer groups; Movies;
Shopping trips; Dances/Social/Cultural
gatherings; Intergenerational programs; Pet
therapy.

Wren House
1731 W 1st St, Duluth, MN 55806
(218) 722-2703
Admin Elwin J Benton.
Licensure Supervised living. *Beds* Supervised
living 10. *Certified* Medicaid; Medicare.
Owner Proprietary corp.

Eagan

Orvilla Inc
3430 Westcott Hills Dr, Eagan, MN 55123
(612) 454-8501
Admin James Driscoll.
Licensure Intermediate care for mentally
retarded. *Beds* ICF/MR 54. *Certified*
Medicaid.
Owner Proprietary corp.

East Grand Forks

East Grand Forks Group Home I
1924 5th Ave NW, East Grand Forks, MN
56721
(218) 773-7439
Admin Vernon C Nordmark PhD.
Medical Dir Josette C Nordmark.
Licensure Intermediate care for mentally
retarded. *Beds* ICF/MR 10. *Certified*
Medicaid.
Owner Proprietary corp.
Admissions Requirements Minimum age 15;
Medical examination.
Staff RNs 1 (pt); Activities coordinators 1
(pt).
Facilities Dining room; Laundry room; Living
area.
Activities Arts & crafts; Cards; Games;
Reading groups; Movies; Shopping trips;
Dances/Social/Cultural gatherings.

East Grand Forks Group Home II
2138 9th Ave NW, East Grand Forks, MN
56721
(218) 773-8338
Admin Vernon C Nordmark PhD.
Medical Dir Josette C Nordmark MD.
Licensure Intermediate care for mentally
retarded. *Beds* ICF/MR 8. *Certified*
Medicaid.
Owner Proprietary corp.

Admissions Requirements Minimum age 18;
Medical examination.
Staff RNs 1 (pt); Activities coordinators 1 (ft);
Direct care 6 (ft), 3 (pt).
Facilities Dining room; Activities room;
Laundry room.
Activities Arts & crafts; Cards; Games;
Movies; Shopping trips; Dances/Social/
Cultural gatherings; Community recreation.

Good Samaritan Center
1414 20th St NW, East Grand Forks, MN
56721
(218) 773-7484
Admin Sandra Bentley. *Dir of Nursing* Mary
Johnson RN. *Medical Dir* Dr Dale Moquist.
Licensure Skilled care; Retirement. *Beds* SNF
129. *Certified* Medicaid; Medicare.
Owner Nonprofit corp (Evangelical Lutheran/
Good Samaritan Society).
Admissions Requirements Minimum age 16;
Medical examination; Physician's request.
Staff RNs 4 (ft), 4 (pt); LPNs 6 (ft), 10 (pt);
Nurses' aides 34 (ft), 33 (pt); Activities
coordinators.
Affiliation Lutheran.
Facilities Dining room; Physical therapy
room; Activities room; Chapel; Laundry
room; Barber/Beauty shop.
Activities Arts & crafts; Cards; Games;
Reading groups; Prayer groups; Shopping
trips; Dances/Social/Cultural gatherings.

Eden Prairie

Castle Ridge Care Center
625 Prairie Center Dr, Eden Prairie, MN
55344
(612) 944-8982
Admin Jean Mulder. *Dir of Nursing* Lavonne
Seemann. *Medical Dir* David Olson MD.
Licensure Skilled care; Assisted living. *Beds*
SNF 60; Assisted living 21. *Private Pay
Patients* 49%. *Certified* Medicaid; Medicare.
Owner Nonprofit organization/foundation.
Admissions Requirements Minimum age 16;
Medical examination; Physician's request.
Staff RNs 5 (ft), 5 (pt); LPNs 3 (ft), 3 (pt);
Nurses' aides 19 (ft), 19 (pt); Physical
therapists 1 (ft); Recreational therapists 1
(ft), 1 (pt); Occupational therapists 1 (ft);
Speech therapists 1 (ft).
Facilities Dining room; Physical therapy
room; Activities room; Chapel; Crafts room;
Laundry room; Barber/Beauty shop.
Activities Arts & crafts; Cards; Games;
Reading groups; Prayer groups; Movies;
Shopping trips; Dances/Social/Cultural
gatherings; Pet therapy.

Fairview Receiving Center
9927 Valley View Dr, Eden Prairie, MN
55344
(612) 941-0200
Admin Sharon Lee-Foster.
Licensure Supervised living. *Beds* Supervised
living 19.
Owner Proprietary corp.

Muriel Humphrey Residence Charlson
8751 Preserve Blvd, Eden Prairie, MN 55344
(612) 941-5339
Admin Paul Jaeger.
Licensure Intermediate care for mentally
retarded. *Beds* ICF/MR 12.
Owner Proprietary corp.

Muriel Humphrey Residence Fraser
8761 Preserve Blvd, Eden Prairie, MN 55344
(612) 941-5376
Admin Paul Jaeger.
Licensure Intermediate care for mentally
retarded. *Beds* ICF/MR 12.
Owner Proprietary corp.

Muriel Humphrey Residence Westby
8771 Preserve Blvd, Eden Prairie, MN 55344
(612) 941-5361

Admin Paul Jaeger.
Licensure Intermediate care for mentally
retarded. *Beds* ICF/MR 12.
Owner Proprietary corp.

Pride Institute
14400 Martin Dr, Eden Prairie, MN 55344
(612) 934-7555
Admin Christopher Eskeli.
Licensure Supervised living. *Beds* Supervised
living 36.
Owner Proprietary corp.

Eden Valley

Valley Rest Home
PO Box 575, Eden Valley, MN 55329
(612) 453-6747
Admin Maryann Ruhland.
Licensure Boarding care. *Beds* Boarding care
21.
Owner Proprietary corp.

Edgerton

Edgebrook Rest Center Inc
505 Trosky Rd W, Edgerton, MN 56128
(507) 442-7121
Admin Larry Oberloh. *Dir of Nursing* Audrey
Vander Maten. *Medical Dir* Roland
Beckering MD.
Licensure Intermediate care; Retirement. *Beds*
ICF 61. *Certified* Medicaid.
Owner Proprietary corp.
Admissions Requirements Medical
examination; Physician's request.
Staff RNs 2 (ft), 3 (pt); LPNs 2 (ft), 3 (pt);
Nurses' aides 10 (ft), 20 (pt); Physical
therapists 1 (pt); Activities coordinators 1
(ft); Dietitians 1 (pt).
Languages Dutch.
Facilities Dining room; Activities room;
Chapel; Crafts room; Laundry room; Barber/
Beauty shop.
Activities Arts & crafts; Cards; Games;
Reading groups; Prayer groups; Movies;
Shopping trips; Dances/Social/Cultural
gatherings; Group trips; Zoo outings.

Edina

Edina Care Center
6200 Xerxes Ave S, Edina, MN 55423
(612) 925-4810
Admin Marie Nelson. *Dir of Nursing* Chris
Gorder. *Medical Dir* Dr William Meiches.
Licensure Skilled care; Intermediate care;
Alzheimer's care. *Beds* Swing beds SNF/ICF
161. *Private Pay Patients* 60%. *Certified*
Medicaid; Medicare.
Owner Nonprofit organization/foundation.
Admissions Requirements Physician's request.
Staff RNs 15 (ft); LPNs 20 (ft); Nurses' aides
110 (ft); Physical therapists 1 (ft);
Recreational therapists 3 (ft); Occupational
therapists 1 (ft).
Facilities Dining room; Physical therapy
room; Activities room; Chapel; Crafts room;
Laundry room; Barber/Beauty shop; Library;
Dental office.
Activities Arts & crafts; Cards; Games;
Reading groups; Prayer groups; Movies;
Shopping trips; Dances/Social/Cultural
gatherings.

Heritage of Edina
3456 Heritage Dr, Edina, MN 55435
(612) 927-5656
Admin Sylvia Triden.
Medical Dir Dr Albert Fetzek.
Licensure Nursing home. *Beds* Nursing home
121.
Owner Proprietary corp.

Staff RNs 3 (ft), 12 (pt); LPNs 2 (ft), 8 (pt);
Nurses' aides 17 (ft), 32 (pt); Physical
therapists 2 (ft); Speech therapists 1 (pt);
Activities coordinators 1 (ft); Dietitians 1
(ft); Podiatrists 1 (pt); Dentists 1 (pt).
Facilities Dining room; Physical therapy
room; Activities room; Chapel; Crafts room;
Laundry room; Barber/Beauty shop.
Activities Arts & crafts; Cards; Games;
Reading groups; Prayer groups; Movies;
Shopping trips; Dances/Social/Cultural
gatherings.

Nekton on William
5100 William Ave, Edina, MN 55436
(612) 925-3292
Admin Peter Sajevic.
Licensure Intermediate care for mentally
retarded. *Beds* ICF/MR 6. *Certified*
Medicaid.
Owner Proprietary corp.

Elk River

Elk River Nursing Home
400 Evans Ave, Elk River, MN 55330
(612) 441-1213
Admin Timothy J O'Brien.
Licensure Skilled care; Intermediate care;
Boarding care. *Beds* SNF 60; ICF 40;
Boarding care 20. *Certified* Medicaid;
Medicare.
Owner Nonprofit corp (Health One).

Shire—Dungarvin IV
9607 201st Ave NE, Elk River, MN 55330
(612) 441-6043
Admin Diane Madden.
Licensure Intermediate care for mentally
retarded. *Beds* ICF/MR 12. *Certified*
Medicaid.
Owner Proprietary corp.

Ellsworth

Parkview Manor Nursing Home
RR1, Box 152, Ellsworth, MN 56129
(507) 967-2482
Admin Michael Werner.
Licensure Intermediate care. *Beds* ICF 60.
Certified Medicaid.
Owner Publicly owned.
Admissions Requirements Medical
examination.
Staff RNs 1 (ft), 3 (pt); LPNs 1 (ft), 3 (pt);
Nurses' aides 8 (ft), 23 (pt); Physical
therapists 1 (pt); Activities coordinators 1
(ft), 1 (pt); Dietitians 1 (pt).
Languages German, Dutch.
Facilities Dining room; Physical therapy
room; Activities room; Crafts room; Laundry
room; Barber/Beauty shop.
Activities Arts & crafts; Cards; Games;
Reading groups; Prayer groups; Movies.

Ely

**Ely Bloomenson Community Hospital &
Nursing Home**
328 W Conan St, Ely, MN 55731
(218) 365-3271, 365-3064 FAX
Admin Larry Ravenberg. *Dir of Nursing* Mary
Reichensperger RN. *Medical Dir* Dr Walter
B Leino.
Licensure Skilled care. *Beds* SNF 99. *Certified*
Medicaid; Medicare.
Owner Nonprofit corp.
Admissions Requirements Minimum age 16;
Physician's request.
Staff Physicians 5 (pt); RNs 1 (ft), 1 (pt);
LPNs 7 (ft), 5 (pt); Nurses' aides 22 (ft), 16
(pt); Physical therapists 1 (ft); Speech
therapists 1 (pt); Activities coordinators 2
(ft), 3 (pt); Dietitians 1 (ft), 2 (pt);
Ophthalmologists 1 (pt).
Languages Finnish, Slavic, Swedish,
Norwegian, German, Italian.

Facilities Dining room; Physical therapy room; Activities room; Chapel; Crafts room; Laundry room; Barber/Beauty shop.
Activities Arts & crafts; Cards; Games; Reading groups; Prayer groups; Movies; Shopping trips; Dances/Social/Cultural gatherings; Pet therapy; Bingo; Outings.

Erhard

Peleske Group Home
RR 1 Box 197B, Erhard, MN 56534
(218) 758-2570
Admin Mike Lathrop.
Licensure Intermediate care for mentally retarded. *Beds* ICF/MR 8.
Owner Proprietary corp.

Erskine

Johnson Rest Home
Vance Ave N, Erskine, MN 56535
(218) 687-3955
Admin Palma C Johnson.
Licensure Boarding care. *Beds* Boarding care 8.
Owner Privately owned.

Pioneer Memorial Care Center
Hwy 59 & 2, Erskine, MN 56535
(218) 687-2365
Admin Dorothy Sandahl.
Licensure Skilled care; Intermediate care. *Beds* SNF 60; ICF 15. *Certified* Medicaid; Medicare.
Owner Proprietary corp.

Evansville

Crestview Manor Inc
RR1 Box 51, Evansville, MN 56326
(218) 948-2219
Admin Susan Loechler. *Dir of Nursing* Jackie Wenstrum. *Medical Dir* Dr James Lueders.
Licensure Skilled care; Retirement. *Beds* SNF 70; Retirement 30. *Certified* Medicaid; Medicare.
Owner Proprietary corp (Odell Nursing Management).
Admissions Requirements Medical examination; Physician's request.
Staff RNs 3 (ft), 2 (pt); LPNs 5 (ft); Nurses' aides 16 (ft), 16 (pt); Occupational therapists 2 (pt); Activities coordinators 1 (ft), 3 (pt); Dietitians 6 (ft), 6 (pt).
Facilities Dining room; Physical therapy room; Activities room; Crafts room; Laundry room; Barber/Beauty shop; Library.
Activities Arts & crafts; Cards; Games; Reading groups; Prayer groups; Movies; Shopping trips; Dances/Social/Cultural gatherings; Intergenerational programs.

Eveleth

Arrowhead Health Care Center
601 Grant Ave, Eveleth, MN 55734
(218) 744-2550
Admin Phyllis J King.
Licensure Skilled care. *Beds* SNF 122. *Certified* Medicaid; Medicare.
Owner Proprietary corp (Beverly Enterprises).

Eveleth Hospital Community & Nursing Care Unit
227 McKinley Ave, Eveleth, MN 55734
(218) 744-1950, 744-3868 FAX
Admin Dan Milbridge. *Dir of Nursing* Linda Kolocek. *Medical Dir* Dr D Werner.
Licensure Skilled care; Hospital. *Beds* SNF 24; Hospital 26. *Private Pay Patients* 20%. *Certified* Medicaid; Medicare.
Owner Nonprofit corp.
Admissions Requirements Medical examination; Physician's request.

Staff RNs 3 (ft), 5 (pt); LPNs 4 (ft), 1 (pt); Nurses' aides 10 (ft), 2 (pt); Activities coordinators 1 (ft); Dietitians 1 (ft).
Facilities Dining room; Activities room; Laundry room; Barber/Beauty shop.
Activities Cards; Games; Reading groups; Prayer groups; Movies.

Range Center—Birchwood Home
1016 W 1st St, Eveleth, MN 55734
(218) 254-3347
Admin Neil Boyum.
Licensure Intermediate care for mentally retarded. *Beds* ICF/MR 6. *Certified* Medicaid.
Owner Proprietary corp.

Excelsior

Excelsior Nursing Home
515 Division St, Excelsior, MN 55331
(612) 474-5488
Admin Joel Kelsh. *Dir of Nursing* Gwen Ladner. *Medical Dir* William Jefferies MD.
Licensure Skilled care; Intermediate care; Alzheimer's care. *Beds* Swing beds SNF/ICF 58. *Certified* Medicaid; Medicare.
Owner Proprietary corp (Beverly Enterprises).
Admissions Requirements Minimum age 18.
Staff Physicians; RNs; LPNs; Nurses' aides; Physical therapists; Occupational therapists; Speech therapists; Activities coordinators; Dietitians; Ophthalmologists; Podiatrists; Audiologists.
Facilities Dining room; Physical therapy room; Activities room; Laundry room; Barber/Beauty shop; Audible door alarms.
Activities Arts & crafts; Cards; Games; Reading groups; Prayer groups; Shopping trips; Intergenerational programs; Pet therapy.

Minnetonka Health Care Center Inc
20395 Summerville Rd, Excelsior, MN 55331
(612) 474-4474
Admin Kathleen Melin. *Dir of Nursing* Karen Sprinkel RN. *Medical Dir* Milton H Seifert MD.
Licensure Intermediate care. *Beds* ICF 21. *Certified* Medicaid; Medicare.
Owner Proprietary corp.
Admissions Requirements Minimum age 18; Medical examination; Physician's request.
Staff RNs 1 (ft), 1 (pt); LPNs 2 (ft), 1 (pt); Nurses' aides 2 (ft), 2 (pt); Activities coordinators 1 (pt); Dietitians 1 (pt).
Facilities Dining room; Activities room; Laundry room.
Activities Arts & crafts; Cards; Games; Reading groups; Prayer groups; Movies; Shopping trips; Dances/Social/Cultural gatherings; Bowling trips; Library trips.

Mt Olivet Rolling Acres
7200 Rolling Acres Rd, Excelsior, MN 55331
(612) 474-5974
Admin Gerald F Walsh.
Licensure Intermediate care for mentally retarded. *Beds* ICF/MR 70. *Certified* Medicaid.
Owner Nonprofit corp.

Fairfax

Fairfax Community Home
10th Ave SE, Fairfax, MN 55332
(507) 426-8241
Admin Judy Sandmann. *Dir of Nursing* Nancy Niebuhr. *Medical Dir* Dr Thomas Gilles.
Licensure Skilled care; Alzheimer's care. *Beds* SNF 65. *Certified* Medicaid; Medicare.
Owner Proprietary corp (Dennis Dirlam).
Admissions Requirements Minimum age 16; Physician's request.

Staff RNs 2 (ft), 3 (pt); LPNs 4 (ft), 6 (pt); Nurses' aides 15 (ft), 15 (pt); Physical therapists 1 (pt); Activities coordinators 1 (ft); Dietitians.
Facilities Dining room; Physical therapy room; Activities room; Chapel; Crafts room; Laundry room; Barber/Beauty shop.
Activities Arts & crafts; Cards; Games; Reading groups; Prayer groups; Movies; Dances/Social/Cultural gatherings; Intergenerational programs; Pet therapy; Therapeutic activities.

Fairmont

Fairmont Community Hospital
835 Johnson St, Fairmont, MN 56031
(507) 238-4254
Admin Gerry Gilbertson.
Medical Dir Gayle Hansen.
Licensure Skilled care; Alzheimer's care. *Beds* SNF 40. *Certified* Medicaid; Medicare.
Owner Proprietary corp.
Staff Physicians 16 (ft); RNs 19 (ft), 33 (pt); LPNs 8 (ft), 11 (pt); Nurses' aides 17 (ft), 28 (pt); Physical therapists 1 (ft), 1 (pt); Activities coordinators 1 (ft); Dietitians 1 (ft); Dentists 1 (ft).
Activities Arts & crafts; Cards; Games; Reading groups; Prayer groups; Movies; Shopping trips; Dances/Social/Cultural gatherings.

Lakeview Methodist Health Care Center
610 Summit Dr, Fairmont, MN 56031
(507) 238-6606
Admin Lloyd Swalve.
Medical Dir Dr H A Williamson.
Licensure Skilled care; Boarding care. *Beds* SNF 140; Boarding care 18. *Certified* Medicaid; Medicare.
Owner Proprietary corp.
Admissions Requirements Medical examination; Physician's request.
Staff RNs 5 (ft), 7 (pt); LPNs 8 (ft), 6 (pt); Nurses' aides 17 (ft), 36 (pt); Physical therapists 2 (ft); Reality therapists 1 (ft); Recreational therapists 2 (ft); Activities coordinators 1 (ft); Dietitians 1 (ft).
Affiliation Methodist.
Facilities Dining room; Physical therapy room; Activities room; Chapel; Laundry room; Barber/Beauty shop; Library.
Activities Arts & crafts; Cards; Games; Reading groups; Prayer groups; Movies; Shopping trips; Dances/Social/Cultural gatherings.

REM Fairmont A
107 Dorothy St, Fairmont, MN 56031
(507) 238-4751
Admin Douglas Miller.
Licensure Intermediate care for mentally retarded. *Beds* ICF/MR 15. *Certified* Medicaid.
Owner Proprietary corp.
Admissions Requirements Minimum age 16; Medical examination.
Staff Direct care 10 (ft), 14 (pt).
Facilities Dining room; Activities room; Crafts room; Laundry room.
Activities Arts & crafts; Cards; Games; Reading groups; Movies; Shopping trips; Dances/Social/Cultural gatherings.

REM Fairmont B
111 Dorothy St, Fairmont, MN 56031
(507) 238-4751
Admin Douglas Miller.
Medical Dir Gayle Zoch.
Licensure Intermediate care for mentally retarded. *Beds* ICF/MR 15. *Certified* Medicaid; Medicare.
Owner Nonprofit corp.
Admissions Requirements Minimum age 16; Medical examination.
Staff RNs 1 (pt); Activities coordinators 1 (pt).

Facilities Dining room; Activities room; Crafts room; Laundry room.
Activities Arts & crafts; Cards; Games; Movies; Shopping trips; Dances/Social/Cultural gatherings.

Faribault

Faribault Manor
1738 Hulett Ave, Faribault, MN 55021
(507) 334-3910
Admin Gordon Brueuer.
Medical Dir Dr Goode.
Licensure Skilled care. *Beds* SNF 94. *Certified* Medicaid; Medicare.
Owner Proprietary corp (Beverly Enterprises).
Admissions Requirements Minimum age 18.
Staff Physicians 1 (pt); RNs 3 (ft), 4 (pt); LPNs 6 (ft), 3 (pt); Nurses' aides 23 (ft), 19 (pt); Physical therapists 1 (pt); Reality therapists 1 (pt); Occupational therapists 1 (pt); Speech therapists 1 (pt); Activities coordinators 2 (ft), 1 (pt); Dietitians 1 (pt); Ophthalmologists 1 (pt); Podiatrists 1 (pt); Audiologists 1 (pt); Dentists 1 (pt).
Facilities Dining room; Physical therapy room; Activities room; Laundry room; Barber/Beauty shop.
Activities Arts & crafts; Cards; Games; Reading groups; Prayer groups; Movies; Shopping trips; Dances/Social/Cultural gatherings.

Faribault Regional Center
802 Circle Dr, Faribault, MN 55021
(507) 332-3000
Admin Rhonda Mulder NHA; William C Saufferer CEO. *Dir of Nursing* Mary Zabel. *Medical Dir* Iancu Foni MD.
Licensure Skilled care; Intermediate care for mentally retarded. *Beds* SNF 35; ICF/MR 500. *Certified* Medicaid; Medicare.
Owner Publicly owned.
Admissions Requirements Minimum age 18; Medical examination; Physician's request.
Staff Physicians 3 (ft), 3 (pt); RNs 31 (ft); LPNs 85 (ft); Nurses' aides 4 (ft); Recreational therapists 10 (ft); Occupational therapists 5 (ft); Speech therapists 6 (ft); Activities coordinators 8 (ft); Dietitians 3 (ft); Chaplains.
Facilities Dining room; Physical therapy room; Activities room; Chapel; Crafts room; Laundry room; Barber/Beauty shop; Library; Gymnasium.
Activities Arts & crafts; Games; Prayer groups; Movies; Shopping trips; Dances/Social/Cultural gatherings; Day program services; Active treatment.

Inisfail Childrens Home
921 SW 1st St, Faribault, MN 55021
(507) 334-1803
Admin Russell Kennedy.
Licensure Intermediate care for mentally retarded. *Beds* ICF/MR 16.
Owner Proprietary corp.

Kroegers House
122 NW 7th St, Faribault, MN 55021
(507) 332-7676
Admin Charles A Kroeger.
Licensure Intermediate care for mentally retarded. *Beds* ICF/MR 6.
Owner Proprietary corp.

Park Avenue Home
214 Park Ave, Faribault, MN 55021
(507) 334-7808
Admin Russell D Kennedy.
Licensure Intermediate care for mentally retarded. *Beds* ICF/MR 15.
Owner Privately owned.

Pleasant Manor Inc
PO Box 446, 27 Brand Ave, Faribault, MN 55021
(507) 334-2036

Admin David E Meillier. *Dir of Nursing* Pamela Kreager RN. *Medical Dir* Dr Robert C Speckhals.
Licensure Skilled care. *Beds* SNF 103. *Certified* Medicaid; Medicare.
Owner Proprietary corp.
Admissions Requirements Minimum age 18; Medical examination; Physician's request.
Staff RNs 3 (ft), 6 (pt); LPNs 9 (ft), 6 (pt); Nurses' aides 26 (ft), 28 (pt); Recreational therapists 3 (ft), 1 (pt).
Languages Bohemian, Norwegian.
Facilities Dining room; Physical therapy room; Activities room; Crafts room; Laundry room; Barber/Beauty shop.
Activities Arts & crafts; Cards; Games; Reading groups; Prayer groups; Movies; Shopping trips; Dances/Social/Cultural gatherings; Pet therapy.

Region Park Hall
1150 SW 3rd St, Faribault, MN 55021
(507) 334-2751
Admin Charles A Kroeger.
Licensure Intermediate care for mentally retarded. *Beds* ICF/MR 12. *Certified* Medicaid.
Owner Proprietary corp.

St Lucas Convalescent & Geriatric Center
503 E Division St, Faribault, MN 55021
(507) 334-4314
Admin Joseph Stanislav. *Dir of Nursing* Betty Judd RN. *Medical Dir* R P Meyer MD.
Licensure Skilled care; Retirement. *Beds* SNF 148. *Certified* Medicaid; Medicare.
Owner Proprietary corp.
Admissions Requirements Medical examination.
Staff RNs 7 (ft); LPNs 12 (ft); Nurses' aides 40 (ft); Physical therapists 1 (ft); Occupational therapists 1 (ft); Activities coordinators 3 (ft); Dietitians 1 (pt).
Affiliation Church of Christ.
Facilities Dining room; Physical therapy room; Activities room; Chapel; Crafts room; Laundry room; Barber/Beauty shop; Occupational therapy room.
Activities Arts & crafts; Cards; Games; Reading groups; Prayer groups; Movies; Shopping trips; Dances/Social/Cultural gatherings.

Seventh Street Home
216 7th St NW, Faribault, MN 55021
(507) 334-8985
Admin Russell Kennedy.
Licensure Intermediate care for mentally retarded. *Beds* ICF/MR 15. *Certified* Medicaid.
Owner Proprietary corp.

Farmington

Sanford Memorial Hospital
913 Main St, Farmington, MN 55024
(612) 463-7825
Admin Robert D Johnson. *Dir of Nursing* C Robin Schmitz RN. *Medical Dir* Dr Joseph Emond.
Licensure Skilled care; Intermediate care; General hospital. *Beds* SNF 60; ICF 5; General hospital 47. *Certified* Medicaid; Medicare.
Owner Proprietary corp.
Admissions Requirements Minimum age 50; Medical examination; Physician's request.
Staff RNs 1 (ft), 8 (pt); LPNs 2 (ft), 8 (pt); Nurses' aides 19 (ft), 22 (pt); Physical therapists 1 (ft); Activities coordinators 1 (ft), 1 (pt); Dietitians 1 (ft); Social worker 1 (ft).
Facilities Dining room; Physical therapy room; Activities room; Chapel; Crafts room; Laundry room; Barber/Beauty shop; Library.

Activities Arts & crafts; Cards; Games; Reading groups; Prayer groups; Movies; Shopping trips; Dances/Social/Cultural gatherings; Luncheon trips; Outings; Daytime trips (other than shopping).

Fergus Falls

Arlington Home
1505 S Arlington, Fergus Falls, MN 56537
(218) 736-7254
Admin Sr Latona Kalis.
Licensure Intermediate care for mentally retarded. *Beds* ICF/MR 6.
Owner Proprietary corp.

Broen Memorial Home
824 S Sheridan, Box 123, Fergus Falls, MN 56537
(218) 736-5441
Admin Ina M Larson. *Dir of Nursing* Becky Odden RN. *Medical Dir* Dr R Beck.
Licensure Skilled care; Boarding care. *Beds* SNF 149; Boarding care 58. *Certified* Medicaid; Medicare.
Owner Nonprofit corp.
Admissions Requirements Medical examination; Physician's request.
Staff RNs; LPNs; Nurses' aides.
Affiliation Lutheran.
Facilities Dining room; Physical therapy room; Activities room; Chapel; Crafts room; Laundry room; Barber/Beauty shop; Library.
Activities Arts & crafts; Games; Reading groups; Prayer groups; Movies; Shopping trips.

Cedar Home
527 W Cedar, Fergus Falls, MN 56537
(218) 736-7254
Admin Sr Latona Kalis.
Licensure Intermediate care for mentally retarded. *Beds* ICF/MR 6. *Certified* Medicaid; Medicare.
Owner Proprietary corp.

Douglas Home
720 W Douglas, Fergus Falls, MN 56537
(218) 736-2153
Admin Sr Latona Kalis.
Licensure Intermediate care for mentally retarded. *Beds* ICF/MR 6.
Owner Proprietary corp.

Fergus Falls Regional Treatment Center
Fir & Union Ave S, Fergus Falls, MN 56537
(218) 739-7200
Admin Elaine Timmer.
Licensure Intermediate care for mentally retarded. *Beds* ICF/MR 270. *Certified* Medicaid.
Owner Publicly owned.

Koep Group Home
PO Box 764, Fergus Falls, MN 56537
(218) 736-6312
Admin Ione Koep.
Medical Dir LaRie Hull.
Licensure Intermediate care for mentally retarded. *Beds* ICF/MR 8.
Owner Proprietary corp.
Admissions Requirements Minimum age 14; Medical examination; Physician's request.
Staff RNs 1 (pt); LPNs 1 (ft).
Facilities Dining room; Activities room; Crafts room; Laundry room.
Activities Cards; Games; Movies; Shopping trips; Dances/Social/Cultural gatherings; Developmental training.

Lake Region Nursing Home
PO Box 728, 712 S Cascade, Fergus Falls, MN 56538-0728
(218) 736-5475, 736-7283 FAX
Admin Edward J Mehl. *Dir of Nursing* Kay Kratochwill. *Medical Dir* Dr B E Money.

Licensure Skilled care; Intermediate care. *Beds* Swing beds SNF/ICF 44. *Certified* Medicaid; Medicare.
Owner Nonprofit corp.
Admissions Requirements Physician's request.
Staff RNs 5 (ft), 4 (pt); LPNs 6 (ft), 11 (pt); Nurses' aides 10 (ft), 15 (pt); Physical therapists 4 (ft); Occupational therapists 1 (ft), 1 (pt); Activities coordinators 1 (ft); Dietitians 1 (ft), 2 (pt).
Facilities Dining room; Physical therapy room; Activities room; Chapel; Crafts room; Laundry room; Barber/Beauty shop.
Activities Arts & crafts; Cards; Games; Reading groups; Prayer groups; Movies; Shopping trips; Pet therapy.

Pioneer Home Inc
1006 S Sheridan, Fergus Falls, MN 56537
(218) 739-3361
Admin Carmon D Jackson. *Dir of Nursing* Linda Bergerud BSN. *Medical Dir* David Bjork MD.
Licensure Skilled care; Retirement; Alzheimer's care; Adult day care. *Beds* SNF 110; Retirement 16. *Private Pay Patients* 50%. *Certified* Medicaid; Medicare.
Owner Nonprofit corp.
Admissions Requirements Minimum age 16.
Staff RNs 4 (ft), 3 (pt); LPNs 11 (ft), 1 (pt); Nurses' aides 38 (ft), 20 (pt); Physical therapists (contracted); Recreational therapists 2 (ft), 1 (pt); Occupational therapists 1 (pt); Speech therapists 1 (pt); Activities coordinators 1 (ft); Dietitians 1 (pt).
Affiliation Evangelical Lutheran.
Facilities Dining room; Physical therapy room; Activities room; Chapel; Crafts room; Laundry room; Barber/Beauty shop; Garden court; Craft kitchen.
Activities Arts & crafts; Cards; Games; Reading groups; Prayer groups; Movies; Shopping trips; Intergenerational programs; Pet therapy; Art class.

Piper Group Home
Rte 6 Box 167, Fergus Falls, MN 56537
(218) 736-6612
Admin Catherine Piper. *Dir of Nursing* JoAnn Ehlert.
Licensure Intermediate care for mentally retarded. *Beds* ICF/MR 6. *Private Pay Patients* 0%. *Certified* Medicaid.
Owner Privately owned.
Admissions Requirements Minimum age 18; Medical examination; Physician's request.
Staff Physicians (consultant); RNs; Physical therapists (consultant); Speech therapists (consultant); Dietitians (consultant); HSTs 2 (ft), 2 (pt).
Facilities Dining room; Activities room; Crafts room; Laundry room.
Activities Arts & crafts; Cards; Games; Movies; Shopping trips; Dances/Social/ Cultural gatherings.

Fertile

Fair Meadow Nursing Home
PO Box 8, Fertile, MN 56540
(218) 945-6194
Admin Barry J Robertson. *Dir of Nursing* Marian Cerkowniak. *Medical Dir* Bruce Ring MD.
Licensure Intermediate care. *Beds* ICF 83. *Certified* Medicaid.
Owner Publicly owned.
Staff RNs; LPNs; Nurses' aides; Activities coordinators.
Facilities Dining room; Physical therapy room; Activities room; Chapel; Crafts room; Laundry room; Barber/Beauty shop.
Activities Arts & crafts; Cards; Games; Reading groups; Movies; Shopping trips; Dances/Social/Cultural gatherings.

Foley

Foley Nursing Center
253 Pine St, Foley, MN 56329
(612) 968-6201
Admin Steve Oelrich. *Dir of Nursing* Dean Weber RN.
Licensure Skilled care. *Beds* SNF 117. *Private Pay Patients* 25%. *Certified* Medicaid; Medicare.
Owner Proprietary corp.
Admissions Requirements Minimum age 16; Medical examination; Physician's request.
Staff RNs 2 (ft), 7 (pt); LPNs 8 (ft), 6 (pt); Nurses' aides 15 (ft), 50 (pt); Physical therapists 1 (ft); Occupational therapists 1 (ft); Activities coordinators 1 (ft); Dietitians 1 (ft); Registered nurse practitioners 1 (pt).
Facilities Dining room; Physical therapy room; Activities room; Chapel; Crafts room; Laundry room; Barber/Beauty shop; Library; Country store; Day care.
Activities Arts & crafts; Cards; Games; Reading groups; Prayer groups; Movies; Shopping trips; Dances/Social/Cultural gatherings; Intergenerational programs; Pet therapy; Special birthday recognition; Volunteer program.

Forest Lake

Birchwood Health Care Center
604 NE 1st St, Forest Lake, MN 55025
(612) 464-5600
Admin Warren Ortenblad, acting. *Dir of Nursing* Voni Gervais. *Medical Dir* Carl Peikert.
Licensure Skilled care. *Beds* SNF 161. *Certified* Medicaid; Medicare.
Owner Proprietary corp.
Admissions Requirements Minimum age 16; Medical examination; Physician's request.
Staff Physicians 4 (pt); RNs 7 (ft), 10 (pt); LPNs 2 (ft), 15 (pt); Nurses' aides 22 (ft), 55 (pt); Physical therapists 2 (ft); Recreational therapists 1 (ft), 3 (pt); Occupational therapists 2 (ft); Speech therapists 1 (pt); Dietitians 1 (pt); Ophthalmologists 1 (pt); Podiatrists 1 (pt); Dentists 1 (pt).
Facilities Dining room; Physical therapy room; Activities room; Chapel; Crafts room; Laundry room; Barber/Beauty shop; Library.
Activities Arts & crafts; Cards; Games; Reading groups; Prayer groups; Movies; Shopping trips; Dances/Social/Cultural gatherings.

Fosston

Fosston Group Home
N Mark Ave, Fosston, MN 56542
(218) 435-6088
Admin Vernon C Nordmark PhD.
Medical Dir Josette C Nordmark MD.
Licensure Intermediate care for mentally retarded. *Beds* ICF/MR 10. *Certified* Medicaid.
Owner Proprietary corp.
Admissions Requirements Minimum age 18; Medical examination.
Staff RNs 1 (pt); Activities coordinators 1 (ft).
Facilities Dining room; Activities room; Laundry room.
Activities Arts & crafts; Cards; Games; Movies; Shopping trips; Dances/Social/ Cultural gatherings.

Fosston Municipal Hospital & Home
900 S Hilligoss Blvd E, Fosston, MN 56542
(218) 435-1133
Admin David Hubbard. *Dir of Nursing* Stefanie Reed RN. *Medical Dir* Wes Ofstedal MD.
Licensure Skilled care. *Beds* SNF 50. *Certified* Medicaid; Medicare.
Owner Proprietary corp.
Admissions Requirements Physician's request.

Staff Physicians; RNs; LPNs; Nurses' aides; Physical therapists; Recreational therapists; Occupational therapists; Speech therapists; Activities coordinators; Dietitians.
Facilities Dining room; Physical therapy room; Activities room; Chapel; Laundry room; Barber/Beauty shop; Library.
Activities Arts & crafts; Cards; Games; Reading groups; Prayer groups; Movies; Shopping trips; Dances/Social/Cultural gatherings.

Johnson Rest Home
516 2nd St NE, Fosston, MN 56542
(218) 435-1494
Admin Palma C Johnson.
Medical Dir Dr Haven.
Licensure Boarding care. *Beds* Boarding care 20. *Certified* Medicaid.
Owner Privately owned.
Admissions Requirements Medical examination; Physician's request.
Staff RNs 1 (ft), 1 (pt); LPNs 1 (pt); Nurses' aides 10 (pt); Recreational therapists 1 (ft); Dietitians 1 (pt).
Facilities Dining room; Activities room; Crafts room.
Activities Arts & crafts; Cards; Games; Reading groups; Prayer groups; Movies; Shopping trips; Dances/Social/Cultural gatherings.

Midway Care Center Inc
114 2nd St NE, Fosston, MN 56542
(218) 435-1272
Admin Allen G Potvin. *Dir of Nursing* Rosella Cormican RN. *Medical Dir* Paul Havens MD.
Licensure Intermediate care. *Beds* ICF 32. *Private Pay Patients* 15%. *Certified* Medicaid.
Owner Proprietary corp.
Admissions Requirements Minimum age 16; Medical examination; Physician's request.
Staff RNs 1 (ft); LPNs 3 (ft), 1 (pt); Nurses' aides 4 (ft), 4 (pt); Activities coordinators 1 (ft).
Facilities Dining room; Activities room; Laundry room; Barber/Beauty shop.
Activities Arts & crafts; Cards; Games; Reading groups; Prayer groups; Movies; Shopping trips; Dances/Social/Cultural gatherings; Intergenerational programs; Car outings.

Franklin

Franklin Healthcare Center
900 E 3rd St, Franklin, MN 55333
(507) 557-2211
Admin Scot D Spates. *Dir of Nursing* Alene Poss. *Medical Dir* Dr Kurt Angstman.
Licensure Skilled care. *Beds* SNF 58. *Private Pay Patients* 25%. *Certified* Medicaid; Medicare.
Owner Proprietary corp (Beverly Enterprises).
Admissions Requirements Minimum age 16; Medical examination; Physician's request.
Staff Physicians 5 (pt); RNs 2 (ft), 2 (pt); LPNs 5 (ft), 1 (pt); Nurses' aides 20 (ft), 15 (pt); Physical therapists 1 (pt); Speech therapists 1 (pt); Activities coordinators 1 (ft); Dietitians 1 (ft); Ophthalmologists 1 (pt); Podiatrists 1 (pt); Audiologists 1 (pt).
Facilities Dining room; Physical therapy room; Activities room; Chapel; Laundry room; Barber/Beauty shop; Fireside room.
Activities Cards; Games; Reading groups; Prayer groups; Movies; Dances/Social/ Cultural gatherings; Intergenerational programs; Pet therapy.

Frazee

Frazee Retirement Center
Box 96, 2nd St SW, Frazee, MN 56544
(218) 334-4501

Admin Robert B McTaggert. *Dir of Nursing* Jan Riewer. *Medical Dir* Dr J Emery.
Licensure Skilled care. *Beds* SNF 102. *Certified* Medicaid; Medicare.
Owner Proprietary corp.
Admissions Requirements Minimum age 18; Medical examination; Physician's request.
Staff RNs 3 (ft), 2 (pt); LPNs 6 (ft), 4 (pt); Nurses' aides 31 (ft), 26 (pt); Physical therapists 1 (pt); Speech therapists 1 (pt); Activities coordinators 1 (ft).
Facilities Dining room; Physical therapy room; Activities room; Chapel; Crafts room; Laundry room; Barber/Beauty shop.
Activities Arts & crafts; Cards; Games; Reading groups; Prayer groups; Movies; Shopping trips; Dances/Social/Cultural gatherings; Dinner outings.

Smith Group Home
Rte 1 Box 36, Frazee, MN 56544
(218) 334-5651
Admin Leona Smith.
Licensure Intermediate care for mentally retarded. *Beds* ICF/MR 7.
Owner Privately owned.
Admissions Requirements Minimum age 21; Females only.
Facilities Dining room; Laundry room.
Activities Arts & crafts; Cards; Games; Reading groups; Movies; Shopping trips; Dances/Social/Cultural gatherings; Vacations.

Fridley

Community Options
5384 NE 5th St, Fridley, MN 55421
(612) 572-2437
Admin Ranae Hanson.
Licensure Supervised living. *Beds* Supervised living 14.
Owner Proprietary corp.

Fridley Convalescent Home
7590 Lyric Ln, Fridley, MN 55432
(612) 786-7700
Admin Jackie Jedlicki.
Licensure Skilled care. *Beds* SNF 129. *Certified* Medicaid; Medicare.
Owner Nonprofit corp (Health One).

Lynwood Healthcare Center
5700 E River Rd, Fridley, MN 55432
(612) 571-3150
Admin Judy A Cline. *Dir of Nursing* Lacy Grivette. *Medical Dir* Michael E Clifford MD.
Licensure Skilled care; Intermediate care; Alzheimer's care. *Beds* Swing beds SNF/ICF 55. *Private Pay Patients* 28%. *Certified* Medicaid; Medicare.
Owner Proprietary corp (Beverly Enterprises).
Admissions Requirements Minimum age 18; Medical examination; Physician's request.
Staff RNs 5 (ft); LPNs 3 (ft), 2 (pt); Physical therapists 1 (pt); Recreational therapists 1 (ft); Occupational therapists 1 (pt); Speech therapists 1 (pt); Activities coordinators 1 (ft); Dietitians (consultant); Food service supervisors 1 (ft); Social workers 1 (ft); Environmental services 4 (ft).
Facilities Dining room; Physical therapy room; Activities room; Laundry room; Barber/Beauty shop; Occupational therapy room; Wanderguard system.
Activities Arts & crafts; Cards; Games; Prayer groups; Movies; Dances/Social/Cultural gatherings; Intergenerational programs; Pet therapy.

Fulda

Maple Lawn Nursing Home
400 7th St, Fulda, MN 56131
(507) 425-2571
Admin Lisa M Abicht.

Licensure Intermediate care. *Beds* ICF 62. *Certified* Medicaid.
Owner Proprietary corp.
Admissions Requirements Medical examination; Physician's request.
Staff RNs 1 (ft), 2 (pt); LPNs 8 (pt); Nurses' aides 6 (ft), 29 (pt); Reality therapists 3 (pt); Speech therapists 1 (pt); Activities coordinators 1 (ft); Dietitians 1 (pt).
Languages Sign.
Facilities Dining room; Activities room; Chapel; Crafts room; Laundry room.
Activities Arts & crafts; Cards; Games; Reading groups; Prayer groups; Movies; Shopping trips; Dances/Social/Cultural gatherings; Dining out; Football outings; County Fair exhibitors.

New Dawn Inc
307 S Lafayette Ave, Fulda, MN 56131
(507) 425-3278
Admin Stephen D Lee.
Medical Dir Kathy Thurston.
Licensure Intermediate care for mentally retarded; Retirement. *Beds* ICF/MR 15. *Certified* Medicaid.
Owner Proprietary corp.
Admissions Requirements Minimum age 18; Medical examination; Physician's request.
Staff RNs 1 (ft); LPNs 1 (ft); Nurses' aides 8 (ft); Physical therapists 1 (ft); Recreational therapists 1 (ft); Occupational therapists 1 (ft); Speech therapists 1 (ft); Dietitians 1 (ft).
Facilities Dining room; Activities room; Crafts room; Laundry room.
Activities Arts & crafts; Cards; Games; Movies; Shopping trips; Dances/Social/Cultural gatherings.

Gaylord

Gaylord Community Hospital & Nursing Home
640 3rd St, Gaylord, MN 55334
(612) 237-2905
Admin Glen Horejsi. *Dir of Nursing* Betty Henke RN. *Medical Dir* Dr H A Knoche.
Licensure Skilled care; Intermediate care; Retirement. *Beds* SNF 52; ICF 6. *Certified* Medicaid; Medicare.
Owner Publicly owned.
Admissions Requirements Minimum age 16; Medical examination; Physician's request.
Staff Physicians 5 (ft); RNs 2 (ft); LPNs 10 (ft); Nurses' aides 26 (ft); Physical therapists 1 (ft); Recreational therapists 1 (ft); Occupational therapists 1 (ft); Speech therapists 1 (ft); Activities coordinators 1 (ft); Dietitians 1 (ft).
Facilities Dining room; Physical therapy room; Activities room; Crafts room; Laundry room; Barber/Beauty shop; Library.
Activities Arts & crafts; Cards; Games; Prayer groups; Movies; Shopping trips; Dances/Social/Cultural gatherings.

Glencoe

Glencoe Area Health Center
705 E 18th St, Glencoe, MN 55336
(612) 864-3121, 864-4876 FAX
Admin John C Doidge; John E Robson, Exec Dir. *Dir of Nursing* Clenora Hoversten. *Medical Dir* Donald Rudy MD.
Licensure Skilled care. *Beds* SNF 110. *Private Pay Patients* 27%. *Certified* Medicaid; Medicare.
Owner Publicly owned.
Admissions Requirements Minimum age 16.
Staff RNs 9 (ft), 3 (pt); LPNs 8 (ft), 3 (pt); Nurses' aides 29 (ft), 26 (pt); Physical therapists 1 (ft); Occupational therapists 1 (pt); Speech therapists 1 (pt); Activities coordinators 1 (ft); Dietitians 1 (ft).
Facilities Dining room; Physical therapy room; Activities room; Chapel; Crafts room; Laundry room; Barber/Beauty shop; Library.

Activities Arts & crafts; Cards; Games; Reading groups; Prayer groups; Movies; Shopping trips; Dances/Social/Cultural gatherings; Intergenerational programs.

Glenwood

Glenwood Retirement Home Inc
719 SE 2nd St, Glenwood, MN 56334
(612) 634-5131
Admin Gordon H Amble. *Dir of Nursing* Mrs Bymere. *Medical Dir* Dr Schuster.
Licensure Skilled care; Intermediate care; Boarding care; Alzheimer's care. *Beds* SNF 53; ICF 12; Boarding care 35. *Certified* Medicaid; Medicare.
Owner Nonprofit organization/foundation.
Admissions Requirements Medical examination.
Affiliation Lutheran.
Facilities Dining room; Physical therapy room; Activities room; Chapel; Crafts room; Barber/Beauty shop; Library.
Activities Arts & crafts; Cards; Reading groups; Prayer groups; Movies; Dances/Social/Cultural gatherings.

Lakeview Care Center
Franklin at Lakeshore Dr, Glenwood, MN 56334
(612) 634-4553
Admin Ruth Gunderson. *Dir of Nursing* Jean Cosgriff RN. *Medical Dir* Dr Jeffrey Schlueter.
Licensure Skilled care. *Beds* SNF 69. *Certified* Medicaid; Medicare.
Owner Proprietary corp (Good Neighbor Services).
Admissions Requirements Minimum age 18; Medical examination; Physician's request.
Staff RNs 2 (ft), 2 (pt); LPNs 2 (ft), 3 (pt); Nurses' aides 11 (ft), 18 (pt); Physical therapists 1 (ft); Occupational therapists 1 (pt); Activities coordinators 1 (ft).
Facilities Dining room; Physical therapy room; Activities room; Chapel; Crafts room; Laundry room; Barber/Beauty shop.
Activities Arts & crafts; Cards; Games; Reading groups; Prayer groups; Movies; Shopping trips; Dances/Social/Cultural gatherings.

Golden Valley

Colonial Acres Health Care Center
5825 Saint Croix Ave, Golden Valley, MN 55422
(612) 544-1555
Admin Kathryn Witta.
Medical Dir Dr Roger Grimm.
Licensure Skilled care; Intermediate care. *Beds* 151. *Certified* Medicare.
Owner Nonprofit corp (Covenant Benevolent Institute).
Admissions Requirements Medical examination; Physician's request.
Staff Physicians 1 (pt); RNs 7 (ft), 13 (pt); LPNs 8 (ft), 8 (pt); Nurses' aides 21 (ft), 42 (pt); Physical therapists 1 (ft); Occupational therapists 1 (ft); Speech therapists 1 (pt); Activities coordinators 1 (ft); Dietitians 1 (pt).
Affiliation Evangelical Covenant Church.
Facilities Dining room; Physical therapy room; Activities room; Chapel; Crafts room; Laundry room; Barber/Beauty shop; Library.
Activities Arts & crafts; Games; Reading groups; Prayer groups; Movies; Shopping trips; Dances/Social/Cultural gatherings.

Courage Residence
3915 Golden Valley Rd, Golden Valley, MN 55422
(612) 588-0811, ext 300
Admin Kathy Bakkenist. *Dir of Nursing* Kathy Lytle. *Medical Dir* Dr Mark Moret.

Licensure Skilled care. *Beds* SNF 64. *Certified* Medicaid; Medicare.
Owner Nonprofit organization/foundation.
Admissions Requirements Minimum age 18.
Staff Physicians 5 (pt); RNs 3 (ft), 8 (pt); LPNs 2 (ft), 4 (pt); Nurses' aides 11 (ft), 20 (pt); Physical therapists 2 (ft), 1 (pt); Recreational therapists 2 (ft); Occupational therapists 3 (ft), 1 (pt); Speech therapists 1 (ft), 1 (pt); Dietitians 1 (ft); Podiatrists 1 (pt).
Facilities Dining room; Physical therapy room; Activities room; Chapel; Laundry room; Barber/Beauty shop.
Activities Arts & crafts; Cards; Games; Reading groups; Movies; Shopping trips; Dances/Social/Cultural gatherings.

Oasis
6739 Golden Valley Rd, Golden Valley, MN 55427
(612) 544-1447
Admin Henry Norton.
Licensure Supervised living. *Beds* Supervised living 18.
Owner Proprietary corp.

Trevilla of Golden Valley
7505 Country Club Rd, Golden Valley, MN 55427
(612) 545-0416
Admin Dorothy Sandahl. *Dir of Nursing* Corrine Pieper. *Medical Dir* Dr Towne.
Licensure Skilled care; Intermediate care; Alzheimer's care. *Beds* SNF 233; ICF 26. *Private Pay Patients* 23%. *Certified* Medicaid; Medicare.
Owner Proprietary corp (Unicare).
Admissions Requirements Minimum age 16.
Staff RNs; LPNs; Nurses' aides; Physical therapists (contracted); Recreational therapists; Occupational therapists; Speech therapists; Activities coordinators; Dietitians.
Facilities Dining room; Physical therapy room; Activities room; Chapel; Crafts room; Laundry room; Barber/Beauty shop; Library.
Activities Arts & crafts; Cards; Games; Reading groups; Prayer groups; Movies; Shopping trips; Dances/Social/Cultural gatherings; Intergenerational programs; Pet therapy.

Weldwood Health Care Center
5411 Circle Downs, Golden Valley, MN 55416
(612) 545-5633
Admin Janice L Palmer. *Dir of Nursing* Diane Sjogren. *Medical Dir* William Shimp MD.
Licensure Skilled care. *Beds* SNF 88. *Certified* Medicaid; Medicare.
Owner Proprietary corp (Good Neighbor Services).
Admissions Requirements Minimum age 18.
Staff Physicians; RNs 5 (ft), 3 (pt); LPNs 3 (ft), 4 (pt); Nurses' aides 11 (ft), 15 (pt); Physical therapists 2 (pt); Recreational therapists 2 (ft); Occupational therapists 2 (pt).
Facilities Dining room; Activities room; Crafts room; Laundry room; Barber/Beauty shop.
Activities Arts & crafts; Cards; Games; Reading groups; Prayer groups; Movies; Shopping trips; Dances/Social/Cultural gatherings; Camping trips.

Graceville

Grace Home
116 W 2nd St, Graceville, MN 56240
(612) 748-7261
Dir of Nursing Esperanza Viacrucis RN, temp. *Medical Dir* Dr Stanley Gallagher.
Licensure Intermediate care. *Beds* ICF 60. *Private Pay Patients* 60%. *Certified* Medicaid.
Owner Nonprofit organization/foundation.

Staff RNs 1 (ft), 1 (pt); LPNs 3 (ft), 4 (pt); Nurses' aides 13 (ft), 16 (pt); Activities coordinators 1 (ft).
Facilities Dining room; Physical therapy room; Activities room; Chapel; Crafts room; Laundry room; Barber/Beauty shop.
Activities Arts & crafts; Cards; Games; Reading groups; Movies; Dances/Social/Cultural gatherings.

Grand Marais

Cook County Northshore Hospital
Gunflint Trail, Grand Marais, MN 55604
(218) 387-1500
Admin Craig Kantos. *Dir of Nursing* Donna Clothier. *Medical Dir* Dr Bill Gallea.
Licensure Skilled care; Hospital. *Beds* SNF 47; Hospital 16. *Certified* Medicaid; Medicare.
Owner Publicly owned.
Staff RNs 1 (ft), 4 (pt); LPNs 1 (ft), 3 (pt); Nurses' aides 11 (ft), 12 (pt); Physical therapists 1 (ft); Activities coordinators 1 (ft); Dietitians 1 (pt).
Facilities Dining room; Physical therapy room; Activities room; Laundry room; Barber/Beauty shop.
Activities Arts & crafts; Cards; Games; Reading groups; Prayer groups; Movies; Shopping trips; Dances/Social/Cultural gatherings.

Grand Meadow

Meadow Manor Nursing Home
PO Box 365, 210 E Grand Ave, Grand Meadow, MN 55936
(507) 754-5212
Admin Robert A Lamp.
Medical Dir B D Westra MD.
Licensure Skilled care. *Beds* SNF 50. *Certified* Medicaid; Medicare.
Owner Publicly owned.
Admissions Requirements Minimum age 18; Medical examination; Physician's request.
Facilities Dining room; Physical therapy room; Activities room; Chapel; Crafts room; Laundry room; Barber/Beauty shop; Library.
Activities Arts & crafts; Cards; Games; Reading groups; Prayer groups; Movies; Shopping trips; Dances/Social/Cultural gatherings.

Grand Rapids

Esther House
213 11th St SE, Grand Rapids, MN 55744
(507) 931-1117
Admin Del Sand.
Licensure Supervised living. *Beds* Supervised living 15.
Owner Proprietary corp.

Itasca Medical Center C&NC Unit
126 1st Ave SE, Grand Rapids, MN 55744
(218) 326-3401, 326-3401, ext 333 FAX
Admin David G Triebes.
Medical Dir Vernon D Erickson MD.
Licensure Skilled care. *Beds* SNF 35. *Private Pay Patients* 20%. *Certified* Medicaid; Medicare.
Owner Publicly owned.
Admissions Requirements Physician's request.
Staff RNs 2 (ft), 1 (pt); LPNs 5 (ft), 14 (pt); Nurses' aides 8 (ft), 14 (pt); Physical therapists; Occupational therapists 1 (pt); Activities coordinators 1 (ft); Dietitians.
Facilities Dining room; Physical therapy room; Activities room; Chapel; Barber/Beauty shop.
Activities Arts & crafts; Cards; Games; Reading groups; Prayer groups; Movies; Dances/Social/Cultural gatherings;

Intergenerational programs; Pet therapy; Sensory integration; Cooking; Memory lane groups; Reminiscence.

Itasca Nursing Home
923 County Home Rd, Grand Rapids, MN 55744
(218) 326-0543
Admin Patrick McNeil. *Dir of Nursing* Don Gaalaas RN. *Medical Dir* Dr L E Karges.
Licensure Skilled care; Boarding care. *Beds* SNF 60; Boarding care 58. *Certified* Medicaid; Medicare.
Owner Publicly owned.
Admissions Requirements Minimum age 12; Medical examination.
Staff RNs 4 (ft), 2 (pt); LPNs 7 (ft), 8 (pt); Nurses' aides 22 (ft), 10 (pt); Physical therapists 1 (pt); Activities coordinators 1 (ft); Dietitians 1 (ft).
Facilities Dining room; Physical therapy room; Activities room; Chapel; Crafts room; Laundry room; Barber/Beauty shop.
Activities Arts & crafts; Cards; Games; Reading groups; Movies; Shopping trips; Dances/Social/Cultural gatherings.

Leisure Hills Inc
2801 S Pokegama, Grand Rapids, MN 55744
(218) 326-3431
Admin Ronald Evensen.
Licensure Skilled care. *Beds* SNF 124. *Certified* Medicaid; Medicare.
Owner Proprietary corp (Good Neighbor Services).

Granite Falls

Municipal Hospital & Granite Manor
345 10th Ave, Granite Falls, MN 56241
(612) 564-3111
Admin George Gerlach. *Dir of Nursing* Nancy St Sauver RN. *Medical Dir* Patti Kile MD.
Licensure Skilled care; Intermediate care. *Beds* SNF 48; ICF 16. *Certified* Medicaid; Medicare.
Owner Publicly owned.
Admissions Requirements Medical examination; Physician's request.
Facilities Dining room; Physical therapy room; Activities room; Laundry room; Barber/Beauty shop; Library.
Activities Arts & crafts; Cards; Games; Reading groups; Prayer groups; Movies; Shopping trips; Dances/Social/Cultural gatherings.

Project Turnabout
660 18th St, Granite Falls, MN 56241
(612) 564-4911
Admin William C Anderson.
Medical Dir Peggy Gatz.
Licensure Supervised living. *Beds* Supervised living 52.
Owner Proprietary corp.
Staff RNs 1 (ft); LPNs 3 (ft); Nurses' aides 4 (ft); Counselors 8 (ft).
Facilities Dining room; Activities room; Laundry room; Group therapy rooms; Lecture hall; Chemical dependency treatment.
Activities Arts & crafts; Movies.

Greenbush

Greenbush Community Hospital
152 5th St S, Greenbush, MN 56726
(218) 782-2131
Admin Maurice A Bertilrud.
Licensure Skilled care; Boarding care. *Beds* SNF 40; Boarding care 20.
Owner Proprietary corp.

Hallock

Kittson County Nursing Home
PO Box 700, 1010 S Birch, Hallock, MN
56728
(218) 843-2633
Admin John A Nelson.
Licensure Intermediate care. *Beds* ICF 36.
Certified Medicaid.
Owner Publicly owned.

Kittson Memorial Hospital
PO Box 700, 1010 S Birch, Hallock, MN
56728
(218) 843-3612
Admin Bruce Berg.
Licensure Skilled care; Intermediate care. *Beds*
SNF 40; ICF 55. *Certified* Medicaid;
Medicare.
Owner Proprietary corp.

Halstad

Halstad Lutheran Memorial Home
133 4th Ave E, Halstad, MN 56548
(218) 456-2105
Admin Kurt S Hansen.
Medical Dir Dr G Brown.
Licensure Intermediate care; Retirement. *Beds*
ICF 68.
Owner Proprietary corp.
Admissions Requirements Medical
examination; Physician's request.
Staff RNs 1 (pt); LPNs 7 (ft).
Affiliation Lutheran.
Facilities Dining room; Physical therapy
room; Activities room; Chapel; Crafts room;
Laundry room; Barber/Beauty shop; Library;
Garden & gazebo area.
Activities Arts & crafts; Cards; Games;
Reading groups; Prayer groups; Movies;
Shopping trips; Dances/Social/Cultural
gatherings.

Hancock

Parkview Home
762 Union Ave, Hancock, MN 56244
(612) 392-5212
Admin Sandra Lenertz.
Licensure Supervised living. *Beds* Supervised
living 15.
Owner Nonprofit corp.

Williams Home
539 Pacific Ave, Hancock, MN 56244
(612) 392-5803
Admin Sandra Lenertz.
Licensure Supervised living. *Beds* Supervised
living 16.
Owner Proprietary corp.

Harmony

Harmony Community Hospital
RR 1 Box 173, 815 Main Ave, Harmony, MN
55939
(507) 886-6566
Admin Greg Braun. *Dir of Nursing* Shirley
Browning RN. *Medical Dir* John D Nehring
MD.
Licensure Skilled care; General hospital;
Alzheimer's care. *Beds* SNF 45; General
hospital 14. *Certified* Medicaid; Medicare.
Owner Proprietary corp.
Admissions Requirements Medical
examination.
Staff Physicians 1 (ft); RNs 1 (ft), 1 (pt);
LPNs 2 (ft), 9 (pt); Nurses' aides 9 (ft), 18
(pt); Physical therapists 1 (pt); Activities
coordinators 1 (ft), 1 (pt); Dietitians 1 (pt);
Ophthalmologists 1 (pt); Podiatrists 1 (pt).
Facilities Dining room; Physical therapy
room; Activities room; Chapel; Crafts room;
Laundry room; Barber/Beauty shop.

Activities Arts & crafts; Cards; Games;
Reading groups; Prayer groups; Movies;
Dances/Social/Cultural gatherings.

Sunshine Place
135 Center St E, Harmony, MN 55939
(507) 886-2220
Admin Luwayne Ommen.
Licensure Intermediate care for mentally
retarded. *Beds* ICF/MR 10.
Owner Proprietary corp.
Activities Arts & crafts; Cards; Games;
Reading groups; Prayer groups; Movies;
Shopping trips; Dances/Social/Cultural
gatherings.

Hastings

Dakota County Receiving Center
1200 E 18th St, Bldg 1, Hastings, MN 55033
(612) 437-4209
Admin Joseph Swanson.
Licensure Supervised living. *Beds* Supervised
living 32.
Owner Proprietary corp.

Henry Hagen Residence
19845 Lillehei Ave, Hastings, MN 55033
(612) 437-9363
Admin Laura L Reynolds.
Licensure Intermediate care for mentally
retarded. *Beds* ICF/MR 6.
Owner Privately owned.
Admissions Requirements Minimum age 18;
Medical examination; Physician's request.
Staff RNs 1 (pt); Activities coordinators 1
(pt).
Facilities Dining room; Activities room;
Crafts room; Laundry room.
Activities Arts & crafts; Cards; Games;
Movies; Shopping trips; Dances/Social/
Cultural gatherings.

Haven Homes Health Center
930 W 16th St, Hastings, MN 55033
(612) 437-6176
Admin Rev Lester Fair. *Dir of Nursing*
Jeannie Menard. *Medical Dir* David Ecker
MD.
Licensure Skilled care. *Beds* SNF 107. *Private
Pay Patients* 35%. *Certified* Medicaid;
Medicare.
Owner Privately owned.
Admissions Requirements Minimum age 55;
Medical examination; Physician's request.
Staff RNs 5 (ft); LPNs 7 (ft); Nurses' aides 36
(ft); Physical therapists 1 (pt); Recreational
therapists 1 (ft); Occupational therapists 1
(pt); Dietitians 1 (ft).
Facilities Dining room; Physical therapy
room; Activities room; Chapel; Crafts room;
Barber/Beauty shop.
Activities Arts & crafts; Cards; Games;
Reading groups; Prayer groups; Movies;
Shopping trips; Dances/Social/Cultural
gatherings; Pet therapy.

Micoll Residence
926 W 2nd St, Hastings, MN 55033
(612) 437-1967
Admin James Driscoll.
Licensure Intermediate care for mentally
retarded. *Beds* ICF/MR 6.
Owner Proprietary corp.

Minnesota Veterans Home
1200 E 18th St, Hastings, MN 55033
(612) 437-3111
Admin Dennis Forsberg.
Medical Dir Ralph D Rayner MD.
Licensure Boarding care. *Beds* Boarding care
200.
Owner Publicly owned.
Admissions Requirements Medical
examination.
Staff Physicians 1 (pt); RNs 3 (ft); LPNs 5
(ft); Recreational therapists 1 (ft); Activities
coordinators 1 (ft); Dietitians 1 (pt);

Ophthalmologists 1 (pt); Podiatrists 1 (pt);
Dentists 1 (pt); Chiropractors 1 (pt); Social
workers 2 (ft); Counselors 2 (ft).
Facilities Dining room; Physical therapy
room; Activities room; Chapel; Crafts room;
Laundry room; Barber/Beauty shop; Library.
Activities Arts & crafts; Cards; Games;
Reading groups; Prayer groups; Movies;
Shopping trips; Dances/Social/Cultural
gatherings; Sports activities; Fishing trips;
Golf.

Regina Memorial Complex
1175 Nininger Rd, Hastings, MN 55033
(612) 437-3121
Admin John W Junkman. *Dir of Nursing*
Susan Simon RN. *Medical Dir* Dr James
Noreen.
Licensure Skilled care; Retirement;
Alzheimer's care. *Beds* SNF 61; Retirement
41. *Private Pay Patients* 50%. *Certified*
Medicaid; Medicare.
Owner Nonprofit corp.
Admissions Requirements Minimum age 55;
Medical examination; Physician's request.
Staff Physicians; RNs; LPNs; Nurses' aides;
Physical therapists; Activities coordinators;
Dietitians; Ophthalmologists; Podiatrists.
Facilities Dining room; Physical therapy
room; Activities room; Chapel; Crafts room;
Laundry room; Barber/Beauty shop; Library;
Woodshop; Pharmacy; Gift shop; Enclosed
patio; Game room with large screen TV;
Private courtyard.
Activities Arts & crafts; Cards; Games;
Reading groups; Prayer groups; Movies;
Shopping trips; Dances/Social/Cultural
gatherings; Intergenerational programs; Pet
therapy; Woodworking; Weaving; Discussion
groups; Religious services; Happy hour.

Hawley

Clay County Residence
1358 Main St, Hawley, MN 56549
(218) 483-4472
Admin Douglas E Johnson.
Licensure Intermediate care for mentally
retarded. *Beds* ICF/MR 8.
Owner Proprietary corp.
Admissions Requirements Minimum age 18;
Medical examination.
Staff RNs 1 (pt).
Facilities Dining room; Activities room;
Crafts room; Laundry room.
Activities Arts & crafts; Cards; Games;
Movies; Shopping trips.

Hayfield

Field Crest Nursing Home
Rte 2 Box 6A, Hayfield, MN 55940
(507) 477-3266
Admin Steven E Moss. *Dir of Nursing*
Dorothy Gesme RN. *Medical Dir* Dr Joan
Knight.
Licensure Skilled care. *Beds* SNF 84. *Certified*
Medicaid; Medicare.
Owner Publicly owned.
Admissions Requirements Medical
examination; Physician's request.
Staff Physicians 1 (pt); RNs 4 (ft), 5 (pt);
LPNs 4 (ft), 6 (pt); Nurses' aides 27 (ft), 16
(pt); Physical therapists 1 (pt); Activities
coordinators 1 (ft).
Facilities Dining room; Physical therapy
room; Activities room; Crafts room; Laundry
room; Barber/Beauty shop.
Activities Arts & crafts; Cards; Games;
Reading groups; Prayer groups; Movies;
Shopping trips; Dances/Social/Cultural
gatherings.

Hendricks

Hendricks Community Hospital
503 E Lincoln St, Hendricks, MN 56136
(507) 275-3134, 275-3135
Admin Betty Buseth. *Dir of Nursing* Barbara
Oerter. *Medical Dir* Dr LeRoy Mueller.
Licensure Skilled care; Intermediate care;
Boarding care. *Beds* SNF 40; ICF 16;
Boarding care 14. *Certified* Medicaid;
Medicare.
Owner Proprietary corp.
Admissions Requirements Medical
examination; Physician's request.
Staff Physicians 2 (ft); RNs 3 (ft), 5 (pt);
LPNs 1 (ft), 8 (pt); Nurses' aides 4 (ft), 40
(pt); Physical therapists 2 (pt); Activities
coordinators 1 (ft); Dietitians 1 (pt); Aides 1
(ft), 1 (pt).
Languages Norwegian, Danish, German.
Facilities Dining room; Physical therapy
room; Activities room; Chapel; Crafts room;
Laundry room.
Activities Arts & crafts; Cards; Games;
Reading groups; Prayer groups; Movies;
Shopping trips; Dances/Social/Cultural
gatherings; Bingo; Horseshoes; Bowling;
Sensory stimulation.

Henning

Henning Nursing Home
907 Marshall Ave, Henning, MN 56551
(218) 583-2965
Admin Richard A Cloeter. *Dir of Nursing*
Joan M Johnson. *Medical Dir* Jon Wigert
MD.
Licensure Skilled care. *Beds* SNF 64. *Private
Pay Patients* 29%. *Certified* Medicaid.
Owner Proprietary corp (Beverly Enterprises).
Admissions Requirements Minimum age 16;
Medical examination.
Staff RNs 2 (ft), 1 (pt); LPNs 5 (ft), 3 (pt);
Nurses' aides 14 (ft), 24 (pt); Activities
coordinators 1 (ft), 2 (pt).
Languages German, Norwegian.
Facilities Dining room; Activities room;
Crafts room; Laundry room.
Activities Arts & crafts; Cards; Games;
Reading groups; Prayer groups; Movies;
Shopping trips; Intergenerational programs.

Heron Lake

**Heron Lake Municipal Hospital & Community
Nursing Care**
9410 County Rd 9, Heron Lake, MN 56137
(507) 793-2346
Admin Michael Dulaney.
Licensure Intermediate care. *Beds* ICF 47.
Owner Nonprofit corp.

Hibbing

Golden Crest Nursing Home
2413 1st Ave, Hibbing, MN 55746
(218) 262-1081
Admin Terry J Rupar. *Dir of Nursing* Barbara
Quitberg. *Medical Dir* Bayard French MD.
Licensure Skilled care. *Beds* SNF 84. *Private
Pay Patients* 25%. *Certified* Medicaid;
Medicare.
Owner Proprietary corp (Beverly Enterprises).
Admissions Requirements Minimum age 16;
Medical examination; Physician's request.
Staff RNs 15 (ft); LPNs 7 (ft); Nurses' aides
75 (ft); Physical therapists; Activities
coordinators 1 (ft).
Facilities Dining room; Physical therapy
room; Activities room; Laundry room;
Barber/Beauty shop; Library.
Activities Arts & crafts; Cards; Games;
Movies; Shopping trips; Dances/Social/
Cultural gatherings; Evening activities;
Adopt-a-grandparent program.

Leisure Hills Healthcare Center
1500 3rd Ave E, Hibbing, MN 55746
(218) 263-7583
Admin Dolores M Paull.
Licensure Skilled care. *Beds* SNF 192.
Certified Medicaid; Medicare.
Owner Proprietary corp.

Range Center—Mapleview
506 W 47th St, Hibbing, MN 55746
(218) 254-8347
Admin Neil Boyum.
Licensure Intermediate care for mentally
retarded. *Beds* ICF/MR 6.
Owner Proprietary corp.

Hills

Tuff Memorial Home
RR 1, Box 10, Hills, MN 56138
(507) 962-3276
Admin Dana Dahlquist. *Dir of Nursing* Karen
Sandager RN. *Medical Dir* Dr L E Lyon.
Licensure Intermediate care; Retirement. *Beds*
ICF 52.
Owner Proprietary corp.
Admissions Requirements Minimum age 19;
Medical examination; Physician's request.
Staff RNs 2 (ft), 2 (pt); LPNs 1 (ft), 3 (pt);
Nurses' aides 4 (ft), 25 (pt); Activities
coordinators 1 (ft), 1 (pt); Dietitians 1 (pt).
Affiliation Lutheran.
Facilities Dining room; Chapel; Crafts room;
Laundry room; Barber/Beauty shop.
Activities Arts & crafts; Games; Reading
groups; Movies; Shopping trips; Dances/
Social/Cultural gatherings.

Hoffman

Hoffman Health Care Center
104 6th St, Box 337, Hoffman, MN 56339
(612) 986-2048
Admin Tim Swoboda. *Dir of Nursing* Debra
Nelson RN. *Medical Dir* Douglass Perkins
MD.
Licensure Skilled care. *Beds* SNF 54. *Certified*
Medicaid; Medicare.
Owner Proprietary corp (Good Neighbor
Services).
Admissions Requirements Medical
examination; Physician's request.
Staff RNs 1 (ft), 1 (pt); LPNs 2 (ft), 7 (pt);
Nurses' aides 7 (ft), 21 (pt); Physical
therapists (consultant); Occupational
therapists (consultant); Speech therapists
(consultant); Activities coordinators 1 (ft);
Dietitians (consultant).
Facilities Dining room; Physical therapy
room; Laundry room; Barber/Beauty shop;
Dayroom/Chapel; Activities/Crafts room.
Activities Arts & crafts; Cards; Games;
Reading groups; Prayer groups; Movies;
Shopping trips; Dances/Social/Cultural
gatherings; Intergenerational programs; Pet
therapy; Sensory stimulation; Exercises.

REM—Grant Inc
104 Kentucky Ave, Hoffman, MN 56339
(612) 925-5067
Admin Juanita Turner.
Licensure Supervised living. *Beds* Supervised
living 6.
Owner Proprietary corp.

REM—Hoffman Inc
117 S 6th St, Hoffman, MN 56339
(612) 986-2091
Admin Juanita Turner.
Licensure Intermediate care for mentally
retarded. *Beds* ICF/MR 8.
Owner Proprietary corp.

Hopkins

Chapel View Inc
615 Minnetonka Mills Rd, Hopkins, MN
55343
(612) 938-2761
Admin Steven J Fritzke. *Dir of Nursing*
Margaret Schroeder.
Licensure Skilled care; Retirement. *Beds* SNF
128. *Certified* Medicaid; Medicare.
Owner Nonprofit organization/foundation.
Admissions Requirements Minimum age 65.
Affiliation Methodist.
Facilities Dining room; Physical therapy
room; Activities room; Chapel; Crafts room;
Laundry room; Barber/Beauty shop; Library.
Activities Arts & crafts; Cards; Games;
Reading groups; Prayer groups; Movies;
Shopping trips; Dances/Social/Cultural
gatherings.

Edgewood Nursing Center
725 Second Ave S, Hopkins, MN 55343
(612) 935-3338
Admin Mark A Wiener.
Medical Dir April Anderson.
Licensure Skilled care; Alzheimer's care. *Beds*
SNF 183. *Certified* Medicaid; Medicare.
Owner Proprietary corp (Beverly Enterprises).
Admissions Requirements Medical
examination.
Staff Physicians; RNs; LPNs; Nurses' aides;
Physical therapists; Occupational therapists;
Speech therapists; Activities coordinators;
Dietitians; Ophthalmologists; Podiatrists;
Dentists.
Facilities Dining room; Physical therapy
room; Activities room; Crafts room; Laundry
room; Barber/Beauty shop; Library.
Activities Arts & crafts; Cards; Games;
Reading groups; Prayer groups; Movies;
Shopping trips; Dances/Social/Cultural
gatherings; Diners club.

Houston

Valley View Nursing Home
510 E Cedar St, Houston, MN 55943
(507) 895-3125
Admin Rick Buechner.
Licensure Intermediate care for mentally
retarded. *Beds* ICF/MR 68.
Owner Proprietary corp.

Howard Lake

Howard Lake Care Center
Box CC, Howard Lake, MN 55349
(612) 543-3800
Admin Timothy Ryden. *Dir of Nursing*
Marilyn Augle RN. *Medical Dir* Dr Mary
Stiles.
Licensure Skilled care. *Beds* SNF 73. *Certified*
Medicaid; Medicare.
Owner Proprietary corp (Good Neighbor
Services).
Admissions Requirements Minimum age 18;
Medical examination; Physician's request.
Staff RNs 2 (ft), 4 (pt); LPNs 3 (ft), 4 (pt);
Nurses' aides 8 (ft), 39 (pt); Physical
therapists 1 (pt); Occupational therapists 1
(pt); Speech therapists 1 (pt); Activities
coordinators 1 (ft); Dietitians 1 (pt).
Facilities Dining room; Physical therapy
room; Activities room; Laundry room;
Barber/Beauty shop; Dayroom; Courtyard.
Activities Arts & crafts; Cards; Games;
Reading groups; Movies; Shopping trips;
Dances/Social/Cultural gatherings;
Intergenerational programs; Bible studies.

Hugo

Dungarvin VIII
1443 Ash St, Hugo, MN 55428
(612) 429-8074

Admin Janice Carver.
Licensure Supervised living. *Beds* Supervised living 6.
Owner Proprietary corp.

Hutchinson

Aveyron Homes Inc
851 Dale St, Hutchinson, MN 55350
(612) 587-6277
Admin Rose Siegler.
Medical Dir Jane Larter.
Licensure Intermediate care for mentally retarded. *Beds* ICF/MR 14.
Owner Proprietary corp.
Admissions Requirements Minimum age; Medical examination.
Staff RNs 1 (pt).
Facilities Dining room; Activities room; Laundry room.
Activities Arts & crafts; Cards; Games; Movies; Shopping trips; Dances/Social/ Cultural gatherings.

Burns Manor Nursing Home
Rte 1 Box 205B, Hutchinson, MN 55350
(612) 587-4919
Admin Mavis J Geier.
Licensure Skilled care; Intermediate care. *Beds* SNF 115; ICF 14. *Certified* Medicaid; Medicare.
Owner Publicly owned.

International Falls

Falls Care Center
Hwy 11-71, International Falls, MN 56649
(218) 283-8313
Admin Rose M Matthews.
Medical Dir Charles Helleloid MD.
Licensure Skilled care. *Beds* SNF 100. *Certified* Medicaid; Medicare; VA.
Owner Proprietary corp (Good Neighbor Services).
Admissions Requirements Minimum age 18; Medical examination; Physician's request.
Staff RNs 4 (ft); LPNs 16 (ft); Nurses' aides 48 (ft); Activities coordinators 3 (ft); Social services 1 (ft).
Facilities Dining room; Activities room; Chapel; Crafts room; Laundry room; Barber/ Beauty shop.
Activities Arts & crafts; Cards; Games; Reading groups; Prayer groups; Movies; Shopping trips; Dances/Social/Cultural gatherings.

International Falls Group Home
2000 Spruce St, International Falls, MN 56649
(218) 285-7264
Admin Sandra Johnson.
Licensure Intermediate care for mentally retarded. *Beds* ICF/MR 12.
Owner Proprietary corp.

Inver Grove Heights

Careco Apartments
6115 Carmen Ave, Inver Grove Heights, MN 55075
(612) 451-1756
Admin Wendy S Johnson.
Licensure Intermediate care for mentally retarded. *Beds* ICF/MR 15.
Owner Proprietary corp.

Inver Grove Care Center
1301 50th St E, Inver Grove Heights, MN 55077
(612) 451-1853
Admin Caryl Crozier. *Dir of Nursing* Mary Petrie RN. *Medical Dir* Dr Anthony Ferrara.
Licensure Skilled care. *Beds* SNF 76. *Certified* Medicaid; Medicare.
Owner Proprietary corp (Good Neighbor Services).

Staff Physical therapists 2 (pt); Recreational therapists 2 (ft); Occupational therapists 1 (pt); Speech therapists 1 (pt); Dietitians.
Languages Spanish.
Facilities Dining room; Physical therapy room; Activities room; Chapel; Crafts room; Laundry room; Barber/Beauty shop; Patios; Dayroom; Semi-private rooms; Garden; Sidewalks.
Activities Arts & crafts; Cards; Games; Reading groups; Prayer groups; Movies; Shopping trips; Dances/Social/Cultural gatherings; Intergenerational programs; Pet therapy; Volunteer program.

Wedgewood Health Care
2060 Upper 55th St E, Inver Grove Heights, MN 55077
(612) 451-1881
Admin Edward W Lehmann Sr. *Dir of Nursing* Sandra VanBeck RN. *Medical Dir* Mary Wangness MD.
Licensure Skilled care; Intermediate care. *Beds* SNF 120; ICF 50. *Private Pay Patients* 40%. *Certified* Medicaid; Medicare.
Owner Proprietary corp.
Admissions Requirements Minimum age 16; Medical examination; Physician's request.
Staff RNs 7 (ft), 6 (pt); LPNs 6 (ft), 4 (pt); Nurses' aides 36 (ft), 48 (pt); Physical therapists 1 (ft); Occupational therapists 1 (pt); Speech therapists 1 (pt); Activities coordinators 3 (ft); Dietitians 1 (ft); Ophthalmologists 1 (pt); Podiatrists 1 (pt); Audiologists 1 (pt).
Facilities Dining room; Physical therapy room; Activities room; Chapel; Laundry room; Barber/Beauty shop.
Activities Arts & crafts; Cards; Games; Prayer groups; Movies; Shopping trips; Dances/ Social/Cultural gatherings; Intergenerational programs; Pet therapy.

Ivanhoe

Divine Providence Hospital & Home
PO Box G, Ivanhoe, MN 56142
(507) 694-1414
Admin Sr Mariette Ketterer. *Dir of Nursing* Jacquelyn Atkins. *Medical Dir* Dr M Bird.
Licensure Skilled care; Retirement. *Beds* SNF 51; Retirement 7. *Certified* Medicaid; Medicare.
Owner Nonprofit organization/foundation.
Admissions Requirements Minimum age 18; Medical examination; Physician's request.
Staff RNs 2 (ft), 2 (pt); LPNs 3 (ft), 5 (pt); Nurses' aides 12 (ft), 24 (pt); Physical therapists 1 (pt); Speech therapists 1 (pt); Activities coordinators 1 (ft), 2 (pt); Dietitians 1 (ft).
Languages Polish, German.
Affiliation Roman Catholic.
Facilities Dining room; Physical therapy room; Activities room; Chapel; Crafts room; Laundry room; Barber/Beauty shop; Library.
Activities Arts & crafts; Games; Reading groups; Prayer groups; Movies; Shopping trips; Dances/Social/Cultural gatherings; Intergenerational programs; Pet therapy.

Jackson

Good Samaritan Center
600 W Jackson, Jackson, MN 56143
(507) 847-3100
Admin Michael T Cranny. *Dir of Nursing* Lois Stensland. *Medical Dir* Dr Marianne Clinton.
Licensure Skilled care. *Beds* SNF 89. *Certified* Medicaid; Medicare.
Owner Nonprofit corp (Evangelical Lutheran/ Good Samaritan Society).
Staff Physicians 1 (pt); RNs 7 (ft), 4 (pt); LPNs 5 (ft), 2 (pt).
Affiliation Lutheran.

Facilities Dining room; Physical therapy room; Activities room; Chapel; Crafts room; Laundry room; Barber/Beauty shop; Library.
Activities Arts & crafts; Cards; Games; Reading groups; Prayer groups; Movies; Shopping trips; Dances/Social/Cultural gatherings.

Jackson Municipal Nursing Home
N Hwy, Jackson, MN 56143
(507) 847-2420
Admin Jeff Johnson, Asst. *Dir of Nursing* William Petersen RN. *Medical Dir* Dr G Alvero.
Licensure Intermediate care. *Beds* ICF 21. *Private Pay Patients* 60%. *Certified* Medicaid.
Owner Publicly owned.
Admissions Requirements Medical examination; Physician's request.
Staff Physicians 1 (pt); RNs 2 (pt); LPNs 3 (ft), 4 (pt); Nurses' aides 3 (ft), 8 (pt); Physical therapists 1 (pt); Activities coordinators 1 (ft); Dietitians 1 (pt).
Facilities Dining room; Physical therapy room; Activities room; Crafts room; Laundry room; Barber/Beauty shop.
Activities Arts & crafts; Cards; Games; Reading groups; Prayer groups; Movies; Dances/Social/Cultural gatherings; Pet therapy.

Janesville

Janesville Nursing Home
102 E North St, Janesville, MN 56048
(507) 234-5113
Admin Thomas C Lindh. *Dir of Nursing* Cynthia Cahill. *Medical Dir* David Pope MD.
Licensure Skilled care. *Beds* SNF 45. *Private Pay Patients* 35-40%. *Certified* Medicaid; Medicare.
Owner Publicly owned.
Admissions Requirements Physician's request.
Staff RNs 2 (ft), 1 (pt); LPNs 3 (ft), 3 (pt); Nurses' aides 10 (ft), 22 (pt); Physical therapists (consultant); Occupational therapists (consultant); Activities coordinators 1 (ft), 1 (pt); Dietitians (consultants); Audiologists (consultant).
Facilities Dining room; Activities room; Chapel; Crafts room; Laundry room; Barber/ Beauty shop.
Activities Arts & crafts; Cards; Games; Reading groups; Prayer groups; Movies; Shopping trips; Dances/Social/Cultural gatherings; Pet therapy; Religious services.

Jordan

Valleyview Health Care Center
4061 W 173rd St, Jordan, MN 55352
(612) 492-6160
Admin Ralph A Olinger. *Dir of Nursing* LaDonna Battcher RN. *Medical Dir* Theodore Groskreutz MD.
Licensure Skilled care; Intermediate care; Retirement. *Beds* SNF 75; ICF 27; Retirement 3. *Private Pay Patients* 23%. *Certified* Medicaid; Medicare.
Owner Proprietary corp.
Admissions Requirements Minimum age 21; Medical examination; Physician's request.
Staff Physicians 19 (pt); RNs 4 (ft), 3 (pt); LPNs 4 (ft), 11 (pt); Nurses' aides 24 (ft), 37 (pt); Physical therapists 1 (pt); Occupational therapists 1 (pt); Speech therapists 1 (pt); Activities coordinators 1 (ft); Dietitians 1 (pt); Ophthalmologists 1 (pt); Podiatrists 1 (pt).
Facilities Dining room; Physical therapy room; Activities room; Laundry room; Barber/Beauty shop.
Activities Arts & crafts; Cards; Games; Reading groups; Movies; Shopping trips.

Karlstad

Karlstad Memorial Nursing Center
3rd & Washington, Karlstad, MN 56732
(218) 436-2161
Admin Stanley Beaker. *Dir of Nursing* Donna Craigmile. *Medical Dir* Ruben Thorbus MD.
Licensure Skilled care; Intermediate care. *Beds* Swing beds SNF/ICF 71. *Private Pay Patients* 25%. *Certified* Medicaid; Medicare.
Owner Publicly owned.
Admissions Requirements Medical examination; Physician's request.
Staff Physicians 2 (ft), 2 (pt); RNs 1 (ft), 3 (pt); LPNs 5 (ft), 1 (pt); Nurses' aides 16 (ft), 31 (pt); Occupational therapists 1 (pt); Activities coordinators 1 (ft).
Affiliation Seventh-Day Adventist.
Facilities Dining room; Physical therapy room; Activities room; Chapel; Crafts room; Laundry room; Barber/Beauty shop.
Activities Arts & crafts; Cards; Games; Reading groups; Prayer groups; Movies; Shopping trips; Dances/Social/Cultural gatherings; Intergenerational programs; Pet therapy; One-on-one; Small groups.

Valley Group Home 2
Box 240, Main St S, Karlstad, MN 56732
(218) 436-2518
Admin Vernon C Nordmark PhD.
Medical Dir Josette C Nordmark MD.
Licensure Intermediate care for mentally retarded. *Beds* ICF/MR 10.
Owner Proprietary corp.
Admissions Requirements Minimum age 18; Medical examination.
Staff RNs 1 (pt); Activities coordinators 1 (ft).
Facilities Dining room; Activities room; Laundry room.
Activities Arts & crafts; Cards; Games; Movies; Shopping trips; Dances/Social/Cultural gatherings.

Kelliher

Kelliher Good Samaritan
PO Box 189, Kelliher, MN 56650
(218) 647-8258
Admin Raletta Thomas.
Licensure Intermediate care. *Beds* ICF 36. *Private Pay Patients* 32%. *Certified* Medicaid.
Owner Nonprofit corp (Evangelical Lutheran/Good Samaritan Society).
Admissions Requirements Medical examination.
Staff RNs 1 (ft); LPNs 3 (ft), 4 (pt); Nurses' aides 3 (ft), 9 (pt); Occupational therapists 1 (ft); Activities coordinators 1 (ft), 1 (pt); Dietitians 1 (ft), 8 (pt).
Affiliation Evangelical Lutheran.
Facilities Dining room; Activities room; Crafts room; Laundry room; Barber/Beauty shop; Rehabilitation; Social services.
Activities Arts & crafts; Cards; Games; Reading groups; Prayer groups; Movies; Shopping trips; Dances/Social/Cultural gatherings.

Kenyon

Kenyon Sunset Home
127 Gunderson Blvd, Kenyon, MN 55946
(507) 789-6134
Admin Gary E Flatgard. *Dir of Nursing* Beverly Olson RN. *Medical Dir* Dr William Walter.
Licensure Skilled care; Boarding care. *Beds* SNF 62; Boarding care 17. *Certified* Medicaid; Medicare.
Owner Proprietary corp.
Staff RNs; LPNs; Nurses' aides; Activities coordinators.
Affiliation Lutheran.

Facilities Dining room; Activities room; Chapel; Crafts room; Laundry room; Barber/Beauty shop.
Activities Arts & crafts; Cards; Games; Reading groups; Prayer groups; Movies; Dances/Social/Cultural gatherings.

Kerkhoven

Lindberg Rest Home
Kerkhoven, MN 56252
(612) 264-2601
Admin Florence E Lindberg.
Licensure Boarding care. *Beds* Boarding care 26.
Owner Privately owned.

Kimball

Madden Kimball Home
PO Box 129, Kimball, MN 55353
(612) 398-5678
Admin Dolores Madden. *Dir of Nursing* D Krengel RN.
Licensure Intermediate care for mentally retarded. *Beds* ICF/MR 32.
Owner Proprietary corp.
Admissions Requirements Minimum age 18; Medical examination.
Staff RNs; LPNs; Speech therapists; Dietitians.
Facilities Dining room; Activities room; Independent kitchens.
Activities Arts & crafts; Cards; Games; Shopping trips; Dances/Social/Cultural gatherings.

LaCrescent

Houston County—LaCrescent Home
1700 Lancer Blvd, LaCrescent, MN 55947
(507) 895-8111
Admin Dennis Theede.
Medical Dir Janice Larsen.
Licensure Intermediate care for mentally retarded. *Beds* ICF/MR 15.
Owner Proprietary corp.
Admissions Requirements Minimum age 3.
Staff RNs 1 (ft), 2 (pt); LPNs 1 (ft); Activities coordinators 3 (ft).
Facilities Dining room; Activities room; Laundry room.
Activities Arts & crafts; Cards; Games; Reading groups; Prayer groups; Movies; Shopping trips.

LaCrescent Healthcare Center
701 Main St, LaCrescent, MN 55947
(507) 895-4445
Admin Gale A Bruessel. *Dir of Nursing* Dixie Johnson RN. *Medical Dir* Dr Bruce Carlson.
Licensure Skilled care. *Beds* SNF 77. *Certified* Medicaid; Medicare.
Owner Proprietary corp (Beverly Enterprises).
Admissions Requirements Medical examination; Physician's request.
Staff RNs 4 (ft); LPNs 2 (ft), 8 (pt); Nurses' aides 6 (ft), 34 (pt); Physical therapists 1 (pt); Recreational therapists 1 (ft); Occupational therapists 1 (pt); Speech therapists 1 (pt).
Facilities Dining room; Physical therapy room; Activities room; Chapel; Crafts room; Laundry room; Barber/Beauty shop.
Activities Arts & crafts; Cards; Games; Prayer groups; Movies; Shopping trips; Dances/Social/Cultural gatherings; Birthday parties; Bingo; Happy hours; Memorial services.

Lafayette

Lafayette Good Samaritan Center
Box 19, Esther Ave, Lafayette, MN 56054
(507) 228-8238
Admin Lane Anderson. *Dir of Nursing* Julie Pace RN.

Licensure Intermediate care. *Beds* ICF 40.
Owner Nonprofit corp (Evangelical Lutheran/Good Samaritan Society).
Staff RNs 3 (ft); LPNs 4 (ft); Nurses' aides 18 (ft); Physical therapists 1 (ft); Activities coordinators 2 (ft); Dietitians 1 (ft).
Affiliation Lutheran.
Facilities Dining room; Activities room; Chapel; Crafts room; Laundry room; Barber/Beauty shop; Library.
Activities Arts & crafts; Cards; Games; Reading groups; Prayer groups; Movies; Shopping trips; Dances/Social/Cultural gatherings.

Lake City

Lake City Nursing Home
405 W Grant, Lake City, MN 55041
(612) 345-5366
Admin Donna Van Loon, Interim. *Dir of Nursing* Jeanette Hoops. *Medical Dir* Frank Thorngren MD.
Licensure Skilled care. *Beds* SNF 115. *Private Pay Patients* 36%. *Certified* Medicaid; Medicare.
Owner Publicly owned.
Admissions Requirements Medical examination.
Staff RNs 4 (ft), 6 (pt); LPNs 4 (ft), 17 (pt); Nurses' aides 15 (ft), 54 (pt); Activities coordinators 1 (ft); Dietitians 1 (ft).
Languages German, Norwegian.
Facilities Dining room; Physical therapy room; Activities room; Crafts room; Laundry room; Barber/Beauty shop.
Activities Arts & crafts; Cards; Games; Reading groups; Prayer groups; Movies; Shopping trips; Dances/Social/Cultural gatherings; Pet therapy.

River Oaks Health Care Center
815 N High St, Lake City, MN 55041
(612) 345-5336
Admin James E Range.
Licensure Nursing home; Boarding care. *Beds* Nursing home 19; Boarding care 19.
Owner Proprietary corp.
Admissions Requirements Minimum age 21; Medical examination.
Staff RNs 1 (ft), 1 (pt); LPNs 3 (ft), 3 (pt); Nurses' aides 10 (ft), 12 (pt); Recreational therapists 1 (pt); Activities coordinators 1 (pt); Dietitians 1 (pt).
Facilities Dining room; Activities room; Chapel; Crafts room; Family room.
Activities Arts & crafts; Cards; Games; Prayer groups; Movies; Shopping trips.

Seven Eleven North High
711 N High St, Lake City, MN 55041
(612) 345-2625
Admin Michael Weinandt.
Licensure Intermediate care for mentally retarded. *Beds* ICF/MR 8.
Owner Proprietary corp.
Admissions Requirements Minimum age 18.
Staff RNs 1 (pt); LPNs 1 (pt).
Facilities Dining room; Laundry room.

Lake Crystal

Lake Crystal Healthcare Center
202 Laclaire, Lake Crystal, MN 56055
(507) 726-2669
Admin Mark Jefferis.
Licensure Skilled care; Boarding care. *Beds* SNF 60; Boarding care 4. *Certified* Medicaid; Medicare.
Owner Proprietary corp (Thro Co).

Lake Elmo

Beeman Place
3819 Laverne Ave N, Lake Elmo, MN 55042
(612) 770-2224
Admin Jeffrey T Boston.

Licensure Supervised living. *Beds* Supervised living 15.
Owner Proprietary corp.

Nekton on Stillwater Lane
10092 Stillwater Ln, Lake Elmo, MN 55042
(612) 777-1907
Admin Steve Kodluboy. *Dir of Nursing* Jeanne Kube RN.
Licensure Intermediate care for mentally retarded. *Beds* ICF/MR 6.
Owner Proprietary corp.
Admissions Requirements Medical examination; Physician's request.
Staff RNs 1 (ft).
Languages Sign.
Facilities Dining room; Activities room; Laundry room.
Activities Arts & crafts; Cards; Games; Movies; Shopping trips; Dances/Social/ Cultural gatherings.

Lake Park

Sunnyside Nursing Home
Rte 2, Lake Park, MN 56554
(218) 238-5944
Admin Gary Ask.
Licensure Intermediate care. *Beds* ICF 63.
Owner Publicly owned.

Lakefield

Colonial Manor Nursing Home
RR 1 Box 370, Manor Dr, Lakefield, MN 56150
(507) 662-6646
Admin Geraldine Burmeister, acting. *Dir of Nursing* Lee Ann Bauer. *Medical Dir* B Carleton MD.
Licensure Intermediate care. *Beds* ICF 54.
Owner Publicly owned.
Admissions Requirements Medical examination; Physician's request.
Staff Physicians 2 (pt); RNs 1 (ft), 2 (pt); LPNs 3 (ft), 6 (pt); Nurses' aides 3 (ft), 20 (pt); Recreational therapists 1 (ft); Activities coordinators 1 (ft); Dietitians 1 (pt).
Facilities Dining room; Activities room; Chapel; Crafts room; Laundry room; Barber/ Beauty shop.
Activities Arts & crafts; Cards; Games; Reading groups; Prayer groups; Movies; Shopping trips; Dances/Social/Cultural gatherings.

Lakeville

Ebenezer Ridges Geriatric Care Center
13820 Community Dr, Lakeville, MN 55337
(612) 435-8116
Admin Mark Broman. *Dir of Nursing* Mary Hoeppner. *Medical Dir* Dr Brian Ebeling.
Licensure Skilled care. *Beds* SNF 104.
Certified Medicaid; Medicare.
Owner Nonprofit corp.
Admissions Requirements Minimum age 62; Medical examination.
Staff RNs 4 (ft), 14 (pt); LPNs 2 (ft), 10 (pt); Nurses' aides 15 (ft), 50 (pt); Physical therapists 1 (ft); Occupational therapists 1 (ft); Speech therapists 1 (pt); Activities coordinators 1 (pt); Dietitians 1 (ft).
Affiliation Lutheran.
Facilities Dining room; Physical therapy room; Crafts room; Laundry room; Barber/ Beauty room; Occupational therapy room; Multi-purpose room; Patio & garden area.
Activities Arts & crafts; Cards; Games; Prayer groups; Movies; Shopping trips; Dances/ Social/Cultural gatherings.

Zenith Apartments
20345 Iberia Ave W, Lakeville, MN 55044
(612) 469-4000
Admin James Driscoll.

Licensure Intermediate care for mentally retarded. *Beds* ICF/MR 15.
Owner Proprietary corp.

Lamberton

Valley View Manor
Rte 2 Box 86, Lamberton, MN 56152
(507) 752-7346
Admin James Broich. *Dir of Nursing* Arlene Nordby. *Medical Dir* Dr M L Schmitz.
Licensure Skilled care; Intermediate care. *Beds* SNF 65; ICF 15. *Private Pay Patients* 50%.
Certified Medicaid; Medicare.
Owner Publicly owned.
Admissions Requirements Minimum age 18; Medical examination; Physician's request.
Staff Physicians 4 (pt); RNs 1 (ft), 4 (pt); LPNs 3 (ft), 6 (pt); Nurses' aides 11 (ft), 39 (pt); Physical therapists 1 (pt); Recreational therapists 1 (ft), 2 (pt); Activities coordinators 1 (ft); Dietitians 1 (ft).
Languages German, Norwegian.
Facilities Dining room; Physical therapy room; Activities room; Chapel; Crafts room; Laundry room; Barber/Beauty shop.
Activities Arts & crafts; Cards; Games; Reading groups; Prayer groups; Movies; Shopping trips; Dances/Social/Cultural gatherings; Intergenerational programs; Pet therapy.

Le Center

Central Health Care Inc
444 N Cordova St, Le Center, MN 56057
(612) 357-2275
Admin Scott P Jackson. *Dir of Nursing* Roxie Dillon RN. *Medical Dir* Dr Michael Wilcox.
Licensure Skilled care; Intermediate care. *Beds* Swing beds SNF/ICF 110. *Private Pay Patients* 40%. *Certified* Medicaid; Medicare; VA.
Owner Privately owned.
Admissions Requirements Medical examination; Physician's request.
Staff RNs 3 (ft), 5 (pt); LPNs 4 (ft), 11 (pt); Nurses' aides 16 (ft), 48 (pt); Physical therapists 4 (pt); Recreational therapists; Speech therapists 1 (pt); Activities coordinators 1 (ft); Dietitians 1 (pt).
Facilities Dining room; Physical therapy room; Activities room; Chapel; Crafts room; Laundry room; Barber/Beauty shop; Library; Fenced picnic area; Medical clinic.
Activities Arts & crafts; Cards; Games; Reading groups; Prayer groups; Movies; Shopping trips; Dances/Social/Cultural gatherings; Pet therapy.

Le Sueur

Minnesota Valley Memorial Hospital
621 S 4th St, Le Sueur, MN 56058
(612) 665-3375
Admin John McClain.
Licensure Skilled care. *Beds* SNF 85. *Certified* Medicaid; Medicare.
Owner Proprietary corp.

Lester Prairie

Dungarvin XI Urlingford
512 1st Ave N, Lester Prairie, MN 55354
(612) 395-2518
Admin Larry Tunnell.
Licensure Intermediate care for mentally retarded. *Beds* ICF/MR 12.
Owner Proprietary corp.

Lewiston

Lewiston Villa
505 E Main St, Lewiston, MN 55952
(507) 523-2123

Admin Patrick Ogden. *Dir of Nursing* Debbie Black. *Medical Dir* Dr Donald Morris.
Licensure Skilled care. *Beds* SNF 50. *Private Pay Patients* 30%. *Certified* Medicaid; Medicare.
Owner Proprietary corp (Beverly Enterprises).
Admissions Requirements Minimum age 16; Medical examination; Physician's request.
Staff Physicians (contracted); RNs 1 (ft), 2 (pt); LPNs 5 (ft), 4 (pt); Nurses' aides 8 (ft), 20 (pt); Physical therapists (contracted); Occupational therapists (contracted); Speech therapists (contracted); Activities coordinators 1 (ft); Dietitians (contracted); Ophthalmologists (contracted); Podiatrists (contracted).
Facilities Dining room; Physical therapy room; Activities room; Chapel; Crafts room; Laundry room; Barber/Beauty shop; Library.
Activities Arts & crafts; Cards; Games; Reading groups; Prayer groups; Movies; Shopping trips; Dances/Social/Cultural gatherings; Outings.

Lindstrom

Therapeutic Community Residence
28150 Newberry Trail, Lindstrom, MN 55045
(612) 257-1507
Admin Daniel J McNally.
Licensure Intermediate care for mentally retarded. *Beds* ICF/MR 8.
Owner Proprietary corp.

Litchfield

Bethany Home
203 N Armstrong, Litchfield, MN 55355
(612) 693-2423
Admin Brandon Pietsch. *Dir of Nursing* Joan Kuechle RN. *Medical Dir* Dr Ted Loftness.
Licensure Boarding care. *Beds* Boarding care 52.
Owner Proprietary corp.
Admissions Requirements Medical examination; Physician's request.
Staff RNs; LPNs; Nurses' aides; Activities coordinators; Dietitians.
Affiliation Lutheran.
Facilities Dining room; Activities room; Chapel; Crafts room; Laundry room; Barber/ Beauty shop.
Activities Arts & crafts; Cards; Games; Reading groups; Prayer groups; Movies; Shopping trips; Dances/Social/Cultural gatherings.

Emmanuel Home
600 S Davis, Litchfield, MN 55355
(612) 693-2472
Admin Michael Boyle.
Medical Dir Cecil Leitch MD.
Licensure Skilled care. *Beds* SNF 120. *Certified* Medicaid; Medicare.
Owner Proprietary corp.
Staff RNs 10 (ft); LPNs 18 (ft); Nurses' aides 90 (ft); Physical therapists 1 (ft); Activities coordinators 1 (ft).
Affiliation Lutheran.
Facilities Dining room; Physical therapy room; Activities room; Chapel; Crafts room; Laundry room; Barber/Beauty shop.
Activities Arts & crafts; Cards; Games; Reading groups; Prayer groups; Movies; Shopping trips; Dances/Social/Cultural gatherings.

Meeker County Community Home
504 S Marshall, Litchfield, MN 55355
(612) 693-8836
Admin Bruce Thomes.
Licensure Intermediate care for mentally retarded. *Beds* ICF/MR 15.
Owner Proprietary corp.
Admissions Requirements Minimum age 18.
Staff RNs 1 (pt).

Facilities Dining room; Activities room; Laundry room; Living room; Kitchen.
Activities Arts & crafts; Cards; Games; Reading groups; Movies; Shopping trips; Dances/Social/Cultural gatherings.

Red Castle Home
405 N Armstrong, Litchfield, MN 55355
(612) 693-6381
Admin Del Sand.
Licensure Supervised living. *Beds* Supervised living 15.
Owner Privately owned.

Little Canada

Nekton on Sextant
332 Sextant, Little Canada, MN 55117
(612) 483-3093
Admin Steve Kodluboy.
Licensure Intermediate care for mentally retarded. *Beds* ICF/MR 6.
Owner Proprietary corp.

Little Falls

Christus Group Home
315 SW 6th St, Little Falls, MN 56345
(612) 632-2240
Admin Stephen Reger.
Licensure Intermediate care for mentally retarded. *Beds* ICF/MR 13.
Owner Proprietary corp.

Lutheran Senior Citizens Home Inc
1200 1st Ave NE, Little Falls, MN 56345
(612) 632-9211
Admin Hubert T Zyvoloski. *Dir of Nursing* Albina Perowitz. *Medical Dir* Dr Royden Belcher.
Licensure Skilled care; Alzheimer's care. *Beds* SNF 118. *Private Pay Patients* 33%.
Owner Nonprofit organization/foundation.
Admissions Requirements Physician's request.
Staff Physicians 1 (pt); RNs 3 (ft), 5 (pt); LPNs 8 (ft), 10 (pt); Nurses' aides 24 (ft), 32 (pt); Physical therapists 1 (ft), 1 (pt); Reality therapists; Recreational therapists; Activities coordinators 3 (ft), 2 (pt); Dietitians 1 (pt); Podiatrists 1 (pt); Audiologists 1 (pt).
Facilities Dining room; Physical therapy room; Activities room; Chapel; Crafts room; Laundry room; Barber/Beauty shop; Library; 5 Acre walking park.
Activities Arts & crafts; Cards; Games; Reading groups; Prayer groups; Movies; Shopping trips; Dances/Social/Cultural gatherings; Pet therapy; Annual ice cream social with 4 hours of continuous entertainment.

St Camillus Place
1100 SE 4th St, Little Falls, MN 56345
(612) 632-6894
Admin Sr Susan Knutson OSF.
Licensure Intermediate care for mentally retarded. *Beds* ICF/MR 14.
Owner Proprietary corp.

St Ottos Care Center
920 SE 4th St, Little Falls, MN 56345
(612) 632-9281
Admin Sr Susan Knutson OSF. *Dir of Nursing* Mary Cordts. *Medical Dir* James Gehant.
Licensure Skilled care; Adult day care. *Beds* SNF 150. *Private Pay Patients* 1%. *Certified* Medicaid; Medicare.
Owner Nonprofit corp (Franciscan Sisters Health Care).
Admissions Requirements Physician's request.
Staff RNs 2 (ft), 5 (pt); LPNs 8 (ft), 18 (pt); Nurses' aides 18 (ft), 55 (pt); Physical therapists 1 (ft); Occupational therapists 1 (ft); Activities coordinators 1 (ft); Dietitians 1 (ft).
Languages Polish, German.

Affiliation Roman Catholic.
Facilities Dining room; Physical therapy room; Activities room; Chapel; Crafts room; Laundry room; Barber/Beauty shop; Library.
Activities Arts & crafts; Cards; Games; Reading groups; Prayer groups; Movies; Shopping trips; Dances/Social/Cultural gatherings; Intergenerational programs; Pet therapy; Pastoral care.

White Shell
PO Box 101, Little Falls, MN 56345
(612) 632-4242
Admin Del Sand.
Licensure Supervised living. *Beds* Supervised living 15.
Owner Proprietary corp.

Littlefork

Littlefork Municipal Hospital
Box N, Littlefork, MN 56653
(218) 278-6634
Admin Calvin Olson.
Licensure Intermediate care. *Beds* ICF 40.
Owner Publicly owned.

Long Lake

Long Lake Nursing Home
345 S Brown Rd, Long Lake, MN 55356
(612) 473-2527
Admin Maryann P Mickelson. *Dir of Nursing* Beverly Wimmer. *Medical Dir* Dr Rolland Olson.
Licensure Skilled care; Intermediate care; Alzheimer's care. *Beds* Swing beds SNF/ICF 52. *Private Pay Patients* 10%. *Certified* Medicaid; Medicare.
Owner Proprietary corp (Beverly Enterprises).
Admissions Requirements Minimum age 60; Medical examination; Physician's request.
Staff RNs 5 (ft), 2 (pt); LPNs 3 (ft); Nurses' aides 15 (ft), 5 (pt); Activities coordinators 1 (ft); Dietitians (contracted); Ophthalmologists (contracted); Podiatrists (contracted); Audiologists (contracted).
Facilities Dining room; Physical therapy room; Activities room; Laundry room; Barber/Beauty shop; Wanderguard system.
Activities Arts & crafts; Cards; Games; Reading groups; Prayer groups; Movies; Shopping trips; Dances/Social/Cultural gatherings; Intergenerational programs; Pet therapy.

Orono Woodlands
Box 507, 2100 6th Ave N, Long Lake, MN 55356
(612) 473-0852
Admin Delores Wirak.
Licensure Intermediate care for mentally retarded. *Beds* ICF/MR 6.
Owner Proprietary corp.

Long Prairie

Long Prairie Memorial Hospital & Home
20 9th St SE, Long Prairie, MN 56347
(612) 732-2141, 732-3802 FAX
Admin Kathleen Konetzko. *Dir of Nursing* Roxanne Ostendorf. *Medical Dir* Dr James Burke.
Licensure Skilled care; Special care unit; Alzheimer's care. *Beds* SNF 123. *Private Pay Patients* 23%. *Certified* Medicaid; Medicare.
Owner Nonprofit organization/foundation.
Admissions Requirements Minimum age 18.
Staff RNs 4 (ft), 1 (pt); LPNs 7 (ft), 6 (pt); Nurses' aides 31 (ft), 35 (pt); Physical therapists 1 (ft); Speech therapists 1 (pt); Activities coordinators 1 (ft); Dietitians 1 (ft); Music therapists 1 (pt).
Facilities Dining room; Physical therapy room; Activities room; Chapel; Crafts room; Barber/Beauty shop.

Activities Arts & crafts; Cards; Games; Reading groups; Prayer groups; Movies; Dances/Social/Cultural gatherings; Intergenerational programs; Pet therapy.

Luverne

Mary J Brown Good Samaritan Center
110 S Walnut Ave, Luverne, MN 56156
(507) 283-2375
Admin Rev Daniel Fuelling.
Medical Dir Dr Larry Lyon.
Licensure Intermediate care; Boarding care. *Beds* ICF 66; Boarding care 4. *Certified* Medicaid.
Owner Nonprofit corp (Evangelical Lutheran/ Good Samaritan Society).
Admissions Requirements Medical examination.
Staff RNs 1 (ft), 2 (pt); LPNs 3 (ft), 2 (pt); Nurses' aides 10 (ft), 15 (pt); Physical therapists 2 (ft), 1 (pt); Activities coordinators 1 (ft), 1 (pt); Dietitians 1 (pt).
Affiliation Lutheran.
Facilities Dining room; Physical therapy room; Activities room; Chapel; Crafts room; Laundry room; Barber/Beauty shop.
Activities Arts & crafts; Cards; Games; Reading groups; Prayer groups; Movies; Shopping trips; Dances/Social/Cultural gatherings.

Luverne Residential Facility
107 S Blue Mound Ave, Luverne, MN 56156
(507) 283-4088
Admin Bill D Olson.
Licensure Intermediate care for mentally retarded. *Beds* ICF/MR 10.
Owner Proprietary corp.

Mabel

Green Lea Manor
PO Box 306, Mabel, MN 55954
(507) 493-5436
Admin Jon P Tagatz.
Licensure Intermediate care. *Beds* ICF 79.
Owner Publicly owned.
Staff RNs 2 (ft); LPNs 7 (ft); Nurses' aides 30 (ft), 15 (pt); Activities coordinators 1 (ft); Dietitians 1 (pt).

Madelia

Luther Memorial Home
221 6th St SW, Madelia, MN 56062
(507) 642-3271
Admin Timothy J Samuelson. *Dir of Nursing* Elizabeth Sondt. *Medical Dir* William Halverson MD.
Licensure Skilled care. *Beds* SNF 89. *Certified* Medicaid; Medicare.
Owner Nonprofit organization/foundation.
Admissions Requirements Medical examination.
Staff RNs 1 (ft), 3 (pt); LPNs 6 (ft); Activities coordinators 1 (ft), 1 (pt).
Affiliation Lutheran.
Facilities Dining room; Activities room; Chapel; Crafts room; Laundry room; Barber/Beauty shop; Library.
Activities Arts & crafts; Cards; Games; Reading groups; Prayer groups; Movies; Shopping trips; Dances/Social/Cultural gatherings.

REM Madelia
125 Drew Ave SE, Madelia, MN 56062
(507) 642-3153
Admin Douglas Miller.
Licensure Intermediate care for mentally retarded. *Beds* ICF/MR 15.
Owner Proprietary corp.

Madison

Madison Lutheran Home
900 2nd Ave, Madison, MN 56256
(612) 598-7536, 598-7559 FAX
Admin Joseph C Brown. *Dir of Nursing* Liz
Sether. *Medical Dir* Dr Frank Lasala.
Licensure Skilled care; Board and care;
Retirement. *Beds* SNF 140; Board and care
37; Retirement apts 35. *Private Pay Patients*
55%. *Certified* Medicaid; Medicare.
Owner Nonprofit organization/foundation.
Admissions Requirements Minimum age 16;
Medical examination; Physician's request.
Staff Physicians 1 (ft); RNs 1 (ft), 5 (pt);
LPNs 5 (ft), 5 (pt); Nurses' aides 35 (ft), 51
(pt); Occupational therapists 1 (pt);
Activities coordinators 1 (ft); Dietitians 1
(pt); DONs 1 (ft).
Affiliation Lutheran.
Facilities Dining room; Physical therapy
room; Activities room; Chapel; Crafts room;
Laundry room; Barber/Beauty shop; Library.
Activities Arts & crafts; Cards; Games;
Reading groups; Prayer groups; Movies;
Shopping trips; Dances/Social/Cultural
gatherings; Intergenerational programs; Pet
therapy; Community support; Volunteer
program.

Mahnomen

Mahnomen County & Village Hospital
414 W Jefferson, Mahnomen, MN 56557
(218) 935-2511
Admin Wallace Meid.
Licensure Skilled care. *Beds* SNF 48. *Certified*
Medicaid; Medicare.
Owner Publicly owned.

Mankato

Hillcrest Health Care Center
Rte 9 Box 3, Mankato, MN 56001
(507) 387-3491
Admin Dorothy Leduc.
Licensure Skilled care. *Beds* SNF 158.
Certified Medicaid; Medicare.
Owner Proprietary corp (Thro Co).

Horizon Home II
317-319 Hickory, Mankato, MN 56001
(507) 625-7879
Admin Mary Ann Watts.
Licensure Supervised living. *Beds* Supervised
living 14.
Owner Proprietary corp.

Mankato House Health Care Center
700 James Ave, Mankato, MN 56001
(507) 387-3491
Admin David Gislason.
Medical Dir Dr Harry Brauer.
Licensure Skilled care. *Beds* SNF 97. *Certified*
Medicaid; Medicare.
Owner Proprietary corp (Thro Co).
Admissions Requirements Minimum age 18;
Medical examination; Physician's request.
Staff Physicians 1 (pt); RNs 4 (ft), 11 (pt);
LPNs 6 (ft), 14 (pt); Nurses' aides 23 (ft), 26
(pt); Physical therapists 1 (pt); Recreational
therapists 2 (ft); Occupational therapists 1
(pt); Activities coordinators 1 (ft); Dietitians
1 (pt).

Mankato Lutheran Home
718 Mound Ave, Mankato, MN 56001
(507) 345-4576
Admin Kevin A Anderson. *Dir of Nursing*
Bonnie Betts. *Medical Dir* John J Heimark
MD.
Licensure Skilled care; Boarding care. *Beds*
SNF 45; Boarding care 24. *Certified*
Medicaid; Medicare.
Owner Nonprofit corp (MN Synod/Lutheran
Church Board).

Admissions Requirements Medical
examination; Physician's request.
Staff RNs 1 (ft), 4 (pt); LPNs 4 (ft), 6 (pt);
Nurses' aides 9 (ft), 10 (pt); Physical
therapists 1 (pt); Recreational therapists 3
(pt); Occupational therapists 1 (pt);
Activities coordinators 1 (ft); Dietitians 1
(ft).
Affiliation Lutheran.
Facilities Dining room; Physical therapy
room; Activities room; Crafts room; Laundry
room; Barber/Beauty shop.
Activities Arts & crafts; Cards; Games;
Reading groups; Prayer groups; Movies;
Dances/Social/Cultural gatherings.

Harry Meyering Center Inc
109 Homestead Dr, Mankato, MN 56001
(507) 387-8281
Admin Carol Lee.
Licensure Intermediate care for mentally
retarded. *Beds* ICF/MR 44.
Owner Nonprofit organization/foundation.
Admissions Requirements Minimum age 18;
Medical examination; Screening.
Staff LPNs 1 (ft), 1 (pt); Activities
coordinators 1 (ft).
Languages Sign.
Facilities Laundry room.
Activities Arts & crafts; Cards; Games;
Reading groups; Movies; Shopping trips;
Dances/Social/Cultural gatherings;
Community focused recreation.

Oaklawn Health Care Center
1112 Mulberry, Mankato, MN 56001
(507) 388-2913
Admin Chris Thro.
Licensure Skilled care. *Beds* SNF 63. *Certified*
Medicaid; Medicare.
Owner Proprietary corp (Thro Co)
Staff RNs; LPNs; Nurses' aides; Recreational
therapists; Activities coordinators; Dietitians.
Facilities Dining room.
Activities Arts & crafts; Cards; Games;
Reading groups; Prayer groups; Movies;
Shopping trips; Dances/Social/Cultural
gatherings.

REM Mankato—A
210 Thomas Dr, Mankato, MN 56001
(612) 387-3181
Admin Thomas Miller.
Licensure Intermediate care for mentally
retarded. *Beds* ICF/MR 15.
Owner Proprietary corp.
Admissions Requirements Minimum age 18;
Medical examination.
Staff RNs 1 (ft); LPNs 1 (pt).
Facilities Dining room; Activities room;
Laundry room.
Activities Arts & crafts; Cards; Games;
Movies; Shopping trips; Dances/Social/
Cultural gatherings; Sporting & other
community events.

REM Mankato B
206 Thomas Dr, Mankato, MN 56001
(507) 387-1635
Admin Thomas Miller.
Licensure Intermediate care for mentally
retarded. *Beds* ICF/MR 15.
Owner Proprietary corp.

REM Mankato C
204 Thomas Dr, Mankato, MN 56001
(507) 387-1638
Admin Thomas Miller.
Licensure Intermediate care for mentally
retarded. *Beds* ICF/MR 15.
Owner Proprietary corp.

Maple Grove

Dungarvin IX
10203 94th Ave, Maple Grove, MN 55369
(612) 425-2649
Admin Diane Madden.

Licensure Supervised living. *Beds* Supervised
living 6.
Owner Proprietary corp.

Residential Alternatives X
14850 75th Ave N, Maple Grove, MN 55369
(612) 420-5848
Admin Peter Jacobson.
Licensure Intermediate care for mentally
retarded. *Beds* ICF/MR 6.
Owner Proprietary corp.

Maple Plain

Haven Homes of Maple Plain
1520 Wyman Avenue, Maple Plain, MN
55359
(612) 479-1993
Admin Daniel Fair.
Medical Dir Jo Berger MD.
Licensure Skilled care; Retirement. *Beds* SNF
67. *Certified* Medicaid; Medicare.
Owner Proprietary corp.
Admissions Requirements Medical
examination; Physician's request.
Staff Physicians 8 (pt); RNs 2 (ft), 7 (pt);
LPNs 2 (ft), 3 (pt); Nurses' aides 4 (ft), 28
(pt); Physical therapists 1 (ft), 2 (pt);
Recreational therapists 1 (ft); Occupational
therapists 1 (pt); Speech therapists 1 (pt);
Dietitians 1 (pt); Ophthalmologists 1 (pt);
Podiatrists 1 (pt); Dentists 1 (pt).
Facilities Dining room; Physical therapy
room; Barber/Beauty shop.
Activities Arts & crafts; Cards; Games;
Reading groups; Movies.

Mapleton

Mapleton Community Home
301 Troendel St, Mapleton, MN 56065
(507) 524-3315
Admin Kevin King.
Medical Dir Dr John Lester.
Licensure Skilled care. *Beds* SNF 80. *Certified*
Medicaid; Medicare.
Owner Proprietary corp.
Admissions Requirements Medical
examination; Physician's request.
Staff RNs 2 (ft), 5 (pt); LPNs 10 (pt); Nurses'
aides 14 (ft), 38 (pt); Activities coordinators
1 (ft), 2 (pt); Dietitians 1 (pt).
Facilities Dining room; Activities room;
Chapel; Crafts room; Laundry room; Barber/
Beauty shop; Library.
Activities Arts & crafts; Cards; Games;
Reading groups; Prayer groups; Movies;
Shopping trips.

Maplewood

Maplewood Maple Manor Care Center
550 E Roselawn Ave, Maplewood, MN 55117
(612) 774-9765
Admin Claudia Sajevic. *Dir of Nursing* Mary
Flaherty. *Medical Dir* Leon Nesvacil MD.
Licensure Skilled care. *Beds* SNF 162.
Certified Medicaid; Medicare.
Owner Proprietary corp (Good Neighbor
Services).
Admissions Requirements Medical
examination; Physician's request.
Staff RNs 7 (ft), 15 (pt); LPNs 3 (ft), 10 (pt);
Nurses' aides 31 (ft), 49 (pt); Physical
therapists 1 (ft); Recreational therapists 3
(ft), 2 (pt); Occupational therapists 1 (ft);
Speech therapists 1 (ft); Dietitians 2 (pt);
Volunteer coordinators 1 (ft).
Facilities Dining room; Physical therapy
room; Activities room; Crafts room; Laundry
room; Barber/Beauty shop; Library; Meeting
rooms.
Activities Arts & crafts; Cards; Games;
Reading groups; Prayer groups; Movies;
Shopping trips; Dances/Social/Cultural
gatherings; Poetry; Art; Camping; Exercise.

Nekton on Frost
1695 Frost Ave, Maplewood, MN 55109
(612) 770-5370
Admin Peter Sajevic.
Licensure Intermediate care for mentally
retarded. *Beds* ICF/MR 6. *Certified*
Medicaid.
Owner Proprietary corp.

1778 Prosperity Inc
1778 Prosperity, Maplewood, MN 55109
(612) 777-8148
Admin Dennis Kastama.
Licensure Supervised living. *Beds* Supervised
living 6.
Owner Proprietary corp.

Sur La Rue de Skillman
373 Skillman Ave, Maplewood, MN 55117
(612) 488-6956
Admin Peter Sajevic.
Licensure Intermediate care for mentally
retarded. *Beds* ICF/MR 6. *Certified*
Medicaid.
Owner Proprietary corp.

Marshall

REM Marshall Inc A B C
1005 N 4th St, Marshall, MN 56258
(507) 537-1458
Admin Craig Miller.
Licensure Intermediate care for mentally
retarded. *Beds* ICF/MR 45.
Owner Proprietary corp.

Wiener Memorial Medical Center
300 S Bruce St, Marshall, MN 56258
(507) 532-9661
Admin Ronald L Jensen.
Licensure Skilled care. *Beds* SNF 76. *Certified*
Medicaid; Medicare.
Owner Publicly owned.

McIntosh

McIntosh Nursing Home Inc
700 NE Riverside, McIntosh, MN 56556
(218) 563-2715
Admin Curtis Jenson. *Dir of Nursing* Pam
Kerssen.
Licensure Skilled care; Alzheimer's care. *Beds*
SNF 89. *Private Pay Patients* 15%. *Certified*
Medicaid; Medicare.
Owner Proprietary corp.
Facilities Dining room; Physical therapy
room; Activities room; Chapel; Crafts room;
Laundry room; Barber/Beauty shop.
Activities Arts & crafts; Cards; Games;
Reading groups; Prayer groups; Movies;
Dances/Social/Cultural gatherings;
Intergenerational programs.

Riverside Board & Care
240 1st St NE, McIntosh, MN 56556
(218) 563-4451
Admin Dennis Ekeberg.
Licensure Boarding care. *Beds* Boarding care
11.
Owner Privately owned.

Melrose

Melrose Hospital & Pine Villa
11 N 5th Ave W, Melrose, MN 56352
(612) 256-4231
Admin Julia M Westendorf.
Licensure Skilled care. *Beds* SNF 75. *Certified*
Medicaid; Medicare.
Owner Publicly owned.

Menahga

Green Pine Acres Nursing Home
PO Box 130, Menahga, MN 56464
(218) 564-4101
Admin Clair Erickson.

Licensure Intermediate care. *Beds* ICF 91.
Owner Publicly owned.

Mendota Heights

DCI Dakota Adults
2031 S Victoria Rd, Mendota Heights, MN
55118
(612) 452-4295
Admin Kathleen Pine.
Licensure Intermediate care for mentally
retarded. *Beds* ICF/MR 12.
Owner Proprietary corp.

Milaca

Elim Home
730 2nd St SE, Milaca, MN 56353
(612) 983-2185
Admin Gary Weygant.
Medical Dir Dr Bruce Gersterkorn.
Licensure Skilled care. *Beds* SNF 119.
Certified Medicaid; Medicare.
Owner Proprietary corp.
Admissions Requirements Medical
examination; Physician's request.
Staff RNs 2 (ft), 8 (pt); LPNs 1 (ft), 5 (pt);
Nurses' aides 8 (ft), 57 (pt); Physical
therapists 1 (ft); Reality therapists 1 (ft);
Activities coordinators 1 (ft), 2 (pt);
Dietitians 1 (ft).
Affiliation Evangelical Free Church.
Facilities Dining room; Physical therapy
room; Activities room; Chapel; Crafts room;
Laundry room; Barber/Beauty shop; Library.
Activities Arts & crafts; Cards; Games;
Reading groups; Prayer groups; Movies;
Shopping trips; Dances/Social/Cultural
gatherings.

Stepping Stones Group Home
560 3rd Ave SE, Milaca, MN 56353
(612) 983-2550
Admin Glenn Anderson.
Licensure Intermediate care for mentally
retarded. *Beds* ICF/MR 8.
Owner Proprietary corp.

Minneapolis

Abbott Northwestern Hospital
800 E 28th St at Chicago Ave, Minneapolis,
MN 55422
(612) 874-4000
Admin Robert Spinner.
Licensure Nursing care. *Beds* Nursing care 18.
Owner Proprietary corp.

Aldrich Board & Care
3101 Aldrich Ave S, Minneapolis, MN 55408
(612) 825-4488
Admin D W Thistlewood. *Dir of Nursing* Pam
Hughs. *Medical Dir* Pam Hughs.
Licensure Intermediate care. *Beds* ICF 25.
Private Pay Patients 0%.
Owner Privately owned.
Admissions Requirements Females only.
Staff LPNs 1 (ft); Recreational therapists 1
(pt); Dietitians 1 (ft).
Facilities Dining room; Activities room;
Crafts room; Laundry room.
Activities Arts & crafts; Cards; Games;
Reading groups; Movies; Shopping trips;
Dances/Social/Cultural gatherings; Ball
games; Picnics.

Andrew Residence
1215 S 9th St, Minneapolis, MN 55404
(612) 333-0111
Admin Karen M Foy. *Dir of Nursing* Phyllis
Goranson.
Licensure Intermediate care. *Beds* ICF 212.
Private Pay Patients 1%. *Certified* Medicaid;
Medicare.
Owner Proprietary corp (Beverly Enterprises).

Admissions Requirements Minimum age 18;
Medical examination; Primary diagnosis of
mental illness.
Staff Physicians (contracted); RNs 6 (ft), 2
(pt); LPNs 1 (ft), 2 (pt); Dietitians; Leisure
services 6 (ft); Mental health staff 60 (ft), 20
(pt).
Facilities Dining room; Activities room;
Crafts room; Laundry room; Music room;
Instructional center; Kitchen for resident
cooking groups; Small house for groups and
practice of basic living skills.
Activities Arts & crafts; Cards; Games;
Reading groups; Movies; Shopping trips;
Basic living skills.

Angelus Convalescent Home
4544 4th Ave S, Minneapolis, MN 55409
(612) 827-3526
Admin Annette Thorson. *Dir of Nursing*
Theresa Thornton RN. *Medical Dir* John
Bjorklund MD.
Licensure Skilled care. *Beds* SNF 79. *Private
Pay Patients* 6%. *Certified* Medicaid;
Medicare.
Owner Proprietary corp (Beverly Enterprises).
Staff Physicians; RNs; LPNs; Nurses' aides;
Physical therapists 1 (pt); Recreational
therapists 1 (ft); Occupational therapists 1
(pt); Speech therapists 1 (pt); Dietitians 1
(pt); Podiatrists; Audiologists.

Augustana Home of Minneapolis
1007 E 14th St, Minneapolis, MN 55404
(612) 333-1551
Admin Robert Letich. *Dir of Nursing*
Margaret Sorenson. *Medical Dir* Henry
Quist MD.
Licensure Skilled care; Boarding care;
Alzheimer's care. *Beds* SNF 290; Boarding
care 92. *Certified* Medicaid; Medicare.
Owner Nonprofit organization/foundation.
Admissions Requirements Medical
examination; Physician's request.
Staff Physicians 1 (pt); RNs 17 (ft), 18 (pt);
LPNs 12 (ft), 8 (pt); Nurses' aides 58 (ft),
125 (pt); Physical therapists 3 (ft); Reality
therapists 2 (ft); Recreational therapists 8
(ft); Activities coordinators 1 (ft).
Affiliation Lutheran.
Facilities Dining room; Physical therapy
room; Activities room; Chapel; Crafts room;
Laundry room; Barber/Beauty shop.
Activities Arts & crafts; Cards; Games;
Reading groups; Prayer groups; Movies;
Shopping trips; Dances/Social/Cultural
gatherings.

Bannochie Nursing Home
3515 2nd Ave S, Minneapolis, MN 55408
(612) 822-3600
Admin Douglas W Bannochie.
Licensure Intermediate care. *Beds* ICF 43.
Owner Proprietary corp.

Baptist Residence
512 49th Ave N, Minneapolis, MN 55430
(612) 529-7747
Admin David Nelson, acting.
Licensure Intermediate care; Boarding care.
Beds ICF 34; Boarding care 53. *Certified*
Medicaid.
Owner Nonprofit corp (American Baptist
Homes).

Bethany Covenant Home
2309 Hayes St NE, Minneapolis, MN 55418
(612) 781-2691
Admin Neil Warnygora.
Medical Dir Darlene Vandermyde.
Licensure Intermediate care; Boarding care;
Retirement. *Beds* ICF 56; Boarding care 10;
Retireement 40.
Owner Nonprofit corp (Covenant Benevolent
Institute).
Admissions Requirements Minimum age 62;
Medical examination; Physician's request.

Staff RNs 3 (ft), 6 (pt); LPNs 1 (ft), 8 (pt);
Nurses' aides 7 (ft), 20 (pt); Physical
therapists 1 (pt); Activities coordinators 1
(ft), 2 (pt); Dietitians 1 (ft).
Languages Swedish, German.
Facilities Dining room; Activities room;
Chapel; Crafts room; Laundry room; Barber/
Beauty shop; Library; Parlor; Park.
Activities Arts & crafts; Games; Reading
groups; Prayer groups; Movies; Shopping
trips; Dances/Social/Cultural gatherings;
Sunday chapel services.

Birchwood Care Home
715 W 31st St, Minneapolis, MN 55408
(612) 823-7286
Admin Randal L Halemeyer.
Licensure Boarding care. *Beds* Boarding care
60.
Owner Proprietary corp.
Admissions Requirements Minimum age 21;
Medical examination; Physician's request.
Staff LPNs 3 (ft); Nurses' aides 2 (ft);
Activities coordinators 1 (ft), 1 (pt).
Facilities Dining room; Activities room;
Laundry room; Barber/Beauty shop.
Activities Arts & crafts; Cards; Games;
Reading groups; Prayer groups; Movies;
Shopping trips; Dances/Social/Cultural
gatherings; Community outings.

Charles Bronstien Home
2644 Fremont Ave S, Minneapolis, MN 55408
(612) 377-3710
Admin Norman Doeden.
Licensure Supervised living. *Beds* Supervised
living 6.
Owner Proprietary corp.

Bryn Mawr Health Care Center
275 Penn Ave N, Minneapolis, MN 55405
(612) 377-4723, 377-0294 FAX
Admin Mary C Rosch. *Dir of Nursing* Patricia
Braun RN. *Medical Dir* Susan Banick-
Moreland MD.
Licensure Skilled care; Intermediate care;
Hospice & extended care for AIDS patients;
Alzheimer's care. *Beds* Swing beds SNF/ICF
175. *Certified* Medicaid; Medicare.
Owner Privately owned.
Admissions Requirements Minimum age 16;
Medical examination; Physician's request.
Staff Physical therapists 3 (ft); Recreational
therapists 3 (ft); Occupational therapists 2
(ft); Speech therapists 1 (ft); Activities
coordinators 1 (ft); Dietitians 1 (ft).
Facilities Dining room; Physical therapy
room; Activities room; Laundry room;
Barber/Beauty shop.
Activities Arts & crafts; Cards; Games;
Reading groups; Prayer groups; Movies;
Shopping trips; Intergenerational programs;
Pet therapy; Psychosocial support for AIDS
patients.

Bywood East Health Care
3427 Central Ave NE, Minneapolis, MN
55418
(612) 788-9757
Admin Richard C Werner. *Dir of Nursing*
Mary Lundquist.
Licensure Boarding care. *Beds* Boarding care
105.
Owner Proprietary corp.
Admissions Requirements Minimum age 17.
Staff RNs 2 (ft), 3 (pt); LPNs 9 (ft), 10 (pt);
Nurses' aides 3 (ft); Activities coordinators 1
(ft); Dietitians 1 (pt).
Facilities Dining room; Activities room;
Crafts room; Barber/Beauty shop; Library;
Patio in yard.
Activities Arts & crafts; Cards; Games;
Reading groups; Prayer groups; Movies;
Shopping trips; Dances/Social/Cultural
gatherings; Breakfast club; Fishing trips;
Camping trips; Bus tours; Bowling team.

Camden Care Center
4659 Lyndale Ave N, Minneapolis, MN 55412
(612) 529-9152
Admin Richard Johnson.
Medical Dir Susan Thistlewood.
Licensure Intermediate care. *Beds* ICF 44.
Owner Proprietary corp.
Admissions Requirements Medical
examination.
Staff Physicians 1 (pt); RNs 2 (pt); LPNs 4
(pt); Nurses' aides 16 (pt); Physical
therapists 2 (pt); Occupational therapists 3
(pt); Activities coordinators 1 (pt); Dietitians
1 (pt); Ophthalmologists 1 (pt).
Facilities Dining room; Physical therapy
room; Laundry room; Barber/Beauty shop.
Activities Arts & crafts; Cards; Games;
Movies; Shopping trips.

Careview Home Inc
5517 Lyndale Ave S, Minneapolis, MN 55419
(612) 827-5677
Admin Tim Hokanson, acting.
Licensure Skilled care. *Beds* SNF 150.
Certified Medicaid; Medicare.
Owner Nonprofit corp.

Cedar Pines Nursing Home
2739 Cedar Ave, Minneapolis, MN 55407
(612) 724-5491
Admin Deborah L Rose, acting. *Dir of
Nursing* Adelle Winkels. *Medical Dir* Dr
Robert Breitenbucher.
Licensure Skilled care. *Beds* SNF 131.
Certified Medicaid; Medicare.
Owner Proprietary corp.
Admissions Requirements Medical
examination; Physician's request.
Facilities Dining room; Physical therapy
room; Activities room; Laundry room;
Barber/Beauty shop.
Activities Arts & crafts; Cards; Games;
Reading groups; Prayer groups; Movies;
Shopping trips; Dances/Social/Cultural
gatherings.

Central Care Center
1828 Central Ave NE, Minneapolis, MN
55418
(612) 781-3118
Admin Christie Hutchens. *Dir of Nursing* Ron
Kaylor. *Medical Dir* Dr John Doyle.
Licensure Skilled care. *Beds* SNF 149.
Certified Medicaid; Medicare.
Owner Proprietary corp (Beverly Enterprises).
Admissions Requirements Medical
examination.
Staff RNs; LPNs; Nurses' aides; Physical
therapists; Recreational therapists;
Occupational therapists; Speech therapists;
Activities coordinators; Dietitians.
Facilities Dining room; Physical therapy
room; Activities room; Crafts room; Laundry
room; Barber/Beauty shop.
Activities Arts & crafts; Cards; Games;
Reading groups; Prayer groups; Movies;
Shopping trips; Dances/Social/Cultural
gatherings.

Chateau Healthcare Center
2106 2nd Ave S, Minneapolis, MN 55404
(612) 874-1603
Admin Kara M Johnson.
Licensure Skilled care. *Beds* SNF 93. *Certified*
Medicaid; Medicare.
Owner Proprietary corp (Beverly Enterprises).
Staff Physicians 2 (pt); RNs 2 (ft); LPNs 3
(ft), 3 (pt); Nurses' aides; Physical therapists
1 (ft); Occupational therapists 1 (ft); Speech
therapists 1 (ft); Activities coordinators 1
(ft); Dietitians 1 (ft); Ophthalmologists;
Dentists.
Facilities Dining room; Physical therapy
room; Activities room; Laundry room;
Barber/Beauty shop.

Activities Arts & crafts; Cards; Games;
Reading groups; Prayer groups; Movies;
Shopping trips; Dances/Social/Cultural
gatherings.

Clara Doerr-Lindley Hall
1717 2nd Ave S, Minneapolis, MN 55403
(612) 870-4440
Admin David Wiencke.
Licensure Intermediate care for mentally
retarded. *Beds* ICF/MR 103.
Owner Proprietary corp.

Clifton House
301 Clifton Ave, Minneapolis, MN 55403
(612) 870-8111
Admin Neal H Frank Jr.
Licensure Intermediate care. *Beds* ICF 13.
Owner Proprietary corp.
Affiliation Christian Science.
Facilities Dining room; Laundry room;
Barber/Beauty shop; Library.
Activities Arts & crafts; Reading groups.

Ebenezer Caroline
110 E 18th St, Minneapolis, MN 55403
(612) 879-2800
Admin Wayne Ward.
Licensure Skilled care; Intermediate care. *Beds*
SNF 213; ICF 14. *Certified* Medicaid;
Medicare.
Owner Nonprofit corp (Ebenezer Society).

Ebenezer Hall
2545 Portland Ave S, Minneapolis, MN 55404
(612) 879-2200
Admin Paula Sparling.
Medical Dir Robert Tierney MD.
Licensure Intermediate care; Boarding care.
Beds ICF 33; Boarding care 139.
Owner Nonprofit corp (Ebenezer Society).
Admissions Requirements Minimum age 65.
Affiliation Lutheran.
Facilities Dining room; Physical therapy
room; Activities room; Chapel; Crafts room;
Laundry room; Barber/Beauty shop; Library.
Activities Arts & crafts; Cards; Games;
Reading groups; Prayer groups; Movies;
Shopping trips; Dances/Social/Cultural
gatherings.

Ebenezer Society Luther & Field
2636 Park Ave, Minneapolis, MN 55407
(612) 879-2200
Admin Barbara DeLa Hunt.
Medical Dir Robert Tierney MD.
Licensure Skilled care; Intermediate care. *Beds*
SNF 179; ICF 131. *Certified* Medicaid;
Medicare.
Owner Nonprofit corp (Ebenezer Society).
Admissions Requirements Minimum age 62.
Affiliation Lutheran.
Facilities Dining room; Physical therapy
room; Activities room; Chapel; Crafts room;
Laundry room; Barber/Beauty shop.
Activities Arts & crafts; Cards; Games;
Reading groups; Prayer groups; Movies;
Shopping trips; Dances/Social/Cultural
gatherings; Music therapy.

Elliot Avenue Boarding Care Home
1500 Elliot Ave S, Minneapolis, MN 55404
(612) 339-2291
Admin Barbara Bester.
Medical Dir Kimberly Louricas.
Licensure Boarding care. *Beds* Boarding care
15.
Owner Privately owned.
Admissions Requirements Minimum age 21;
Medical examination.
Staff RNs 1 (pt); LPNs 1 (ft), 1 (pt); Nurses'
aides 1 (ft), 1 (pt); Activities coordinators 1
(ft).
Facilities Dining room; Activities room.
Activities Arts & crafts; Cards; Games;
Reading groups; Movies; Shopping trips;
Dances/Social/Cultural gatherings; Exercise
group.

Emerson Boarding Care Home
2708 Emerson Ave S, Minneapolis, MN 55408
(612) 872-7100
Admin Barbara Bester.
Licensure Boarding care. *Beds* Boarding care 10.
Owner Proprietary corp.

Emerson Place North
2304 Emerson Ave N, Minneapolis, MN 55411
(612) 521-3679
Admin Mona Meinke.
Licensure Intermediate care. *Beds* ICF 65.
Owner Proprietary corp.
Admissions Requirements Physician's request.
Staff Physicians 2 (pt); RNs 3 (ft); LPNs 3 (ft); Nurses' aides 16 (ft), 16 (pt); Physical therapists 1 (pt); Recreational therapists 4 (ft); Occupational therapists 1 (ft), 2 (pt); Speech therapists 1 (pt); Dietitians 1 (pt); Ophthalmologists 1 (pt); Podiatrists 1 (pt); Dentists 1 (pt).
Facilities Dining room; Activities room; Crafts room; Laundry room; Occupational therapy room.
Activities Arts & crafts; Cards; Games; Reading groups; Prayer groups; Movies; Shopping trips; Dances/Social/Cultural gatherings.

First Christian Church Residence
2300 Stevens Ave S, Minneapolis, MN 55404
(612) 870-1811
Admin JoAnne Angier.
Medical Dir Janet Gulsuig.
Licensure Intermediate care; Boarding care. *Beds* ICF 65; Boarding care 4.
Owner Proprietary corp.
Staff RNs 6 (ft); LPNs 3 (ft); Nurses' aides 15 (ft); Activities coordinators 1 (ft).

Flambeau—Dungarvin XII
1446 W 34th St, Minneapolis, MN 55408
(612) 823-3927
Admin Diane Madden.
Licensure Intermediate care for mentally retarded. *Beds* ICF/MR 7.
Owner Proprietary corp.

Four Seasons Care Center—Metro
321 E 25th St, Minneapolis, MN 55404
(612) 874-1701
Admin William D McEachern. *Dir of Nursing* Jacqueline Oziuk. *Medical Dir* Dr Richard Pfohl.
Licensure Skilled care; Alzheimer's care. *Beds* SNF 114. *Certified* Medicaid; Medicare.
Owner Proprietary corp.
Admissions Requirements Minimum age 16; Medical examination.
Staff RNs 4 (ft), 1 (pt); LPNs 2 (ft), 1 (pt); Nurses' aides 26 (ft), 1 (pt); Occupational therapists 2 (pt); Speech therapists 1 (pt); Activities coordinators 1 (ft); Dietitians 1 (pt).
Facilities Dining room; Physical therapy room; Laundry room; Barber/Beauty shop; Library.
Activities Cards; Games; Reading groups; Prayer groups; Movies; Dances/Social/ Cultural gatherings; Pet therapy.

Franklin Place East
2100 1st Ave S, Minneapolis, MN 55404
(612) 874-1101
Admin Debra Campbell. *Dir of Nursing* Mary Kellett. *Medical Dir* Keith Kubasch.
Licensure Intermediate care. *Beds* ICF 35.
Owner Proprietary corp.
Admissions Requirements Minimum age 16; Medical examination.
Staff RNs 1 (ft), 2 (pt); LPNs 1 (ft), 2 (pt); Nurses' aides 10 (ft), 5 (pt); Recreational therapists 1 (ft); Occupational therapists 1 (ft); Dietitians 1 (ft).

Facilities Dining room; Activities room; Crafts room.
Activities Arts & crafts; Cards; Games; Reading groups; Movies; Shopping trips; Dances/Social/Cultural gatherings.

Grand Avenue Rest Home
3956 Grand Ave S, Minneapolis, MN 55409
(612) 824-1434
Admin Richard Johnson.
Medical Dir Nancy Winslow.
Licensure Boarding care. *Beds* Boarding care 21.
Owner Proprietary corp.

Hennepin County Detox Center
1800 Chicago Ave S, Minneapolis, MN 55404
(612) 347-6111
Admin Robert Olander.
Licensure Supervised living. *Beds* Supervised living 88.
Owner Publicly owned.

David Herman Health Care Center
2401 Chicago Ave S, Minneapolis, MN 55404
(612) 871-3661
Admin Sharon Gislason.
Medical Dir Thomas J Bloss MD.
Licensure Skilled care. *Beds* SNF 147. *Certified* Medicaid.
Owner Proprietary corp.
Admissions Requirements Minimum age 18; Medical examination; Physician's request.
Staff Physicians 3 (pt); RNs 9 (ft); LPNs 12 (ft), 2 (pt); Nurses' aides 51 (ft), 6 (pt); Physical therapists 3 (ft); Recreational therapists 3 (ft), 1 (pt); Occupational therapists 1 (ft), 1 (pt); Speech therapists 1 (pt); Activities coordinators 4 (ft); Dietitians 1 (pt); Ophthalmologists 1 (pt); Podiatrists 1 (pt); Audiologists 1 (pt); Directors 1 (pt); Clinical psychologists 1 (pt).
Facilities Dining room; Physical therapy room; Activities room; Chapel; Crafts room; Barber/Beauty shop; Library.
Activities Arts & crafts; Cards; Games; Movies; Dances/Social/Cultural gatherings; Birthday parties.

Horizon West Health Care
1620 Oak Park Ave N, Minneapolis, MN 55411
(612) 588-0804
Admin Margaret Stewart. *Dir of Nursing* Cindy Yaklich. *Medical Dir* Keith Kubasch.
Licensure Skilled care. *Beds* SNF 96. *Certified* Medicaid; Medicare.
Owner Proprietary corp.
Admissions Requirements Minimum age 18; Medical examination.
Staff RNs; LPNs; Nurses' aides; Physical therapists; Recreational therapists; Occupational therapists; Speech therapists; Dietitians; Ophthalmologists; Podiatrists; Dentists; Psychologists.
Facilities Dining room; Physical therapy room; Activities room; Crafts room; Laundry room; Barber/Beauty shop.
Activities Arts & crafts; Cards; Games; Reading groups; Prayer groups; Movies; Shopping trips; Dances/Social/Cultural gatherings.

Jones-Harrison Residence
3700 Cedar Lake Ave, Minneapolis, MN 55416
(612) 920-2030
Admin Gloria C Fiebiger. *Dir of Nursing* Leslie Martens. *Medical Dir* Dr John Cardle.
Licensure Skilled care; Boarding care. *Beds* SNF 66; Boarding care 97. *Certified* Medicaid; Medicare.
Owner Proprietary corp.
Admissions Requirements Medical examination; Physician's request.
Staff Physicians 2 (pt); RNs 6 (ft), 9 (pt); LPNs 5 (ft), 7 (pt); Nurses' aides 11 (ft), 17 (pt); Physical therapists 1 (pt); Recreational

therapists 2 (ft); Occupational therapists 1 (pt); Speech therapists 1 (pt); Dietitians 1 (pt); Ophthalmologists 1 (pt); Podiatrists 1 (pt); Dentists 1 (pt).
Facilities Dining room; Physical therapy room; Activities room; Chapel; Crafts room; Laundry room; Barber/Beauty shop; Library; Lounges; Living room.
Activities Arts & crafts; Cards; Games; Reading groups; Prayer groups; Movies; Shopping trips; Dances/Social/Cultural gatherings; Educational opportunities; Ceramics; Gardening.

Jorgensen House
3444 Girard Ave S, Minneapolis, MN 55408
(612) 825-8681
Admin Gerald Biese.
Licensure Intermediate care for mentally retarded; Supervised living. *Beds* ICF/MR 41; Supervised living 6.
Owner Nonprofit corp (Opportunity Workshop Inc).
Admissions Requirements Minimum age 18.
Staff RNs 1 (pt).
Facilities Dining room; Home setting.
Activities Arts & crafts; Cards; Games; Movies; Shopping trips; Pet therapy.

Bill Kelly House
3104 58th St E, Minneapolis, MN 55417
(612) 871-4131
Admin Henry W Norton Jr.
Licensure Supervised living. *Beds* Supervised living 23.
Owner Proprietary corp.

LaSalle Convalescent Home
1920 LaSalle Ave, Minneapolis, MN 55403
(612) 870-8611
Admin Paul Jenson. *Dir of Nursing* Bette Martinson RN. *Medical Dir* Dr John Dunn.
Licensure Skilled care; Intermediate care; Alzheimer's care. *Beds* SNF 106; ICF 33. *Certified* Medicaid; Medicare.
Owner Proprietary corp (Beverly Enterprises).
Admissions Requirements Medical examination; Physician's request.
Staff RNs 6 (ft), 3 (pt); LPNs 11 (ft), 7 (pt); Nurses' aides 28 (ft), 14 (pt); Physical therapists 2 (ft), 1 (pt); Reality therapists 1 (pt); Recreational therapists 1 (ft), 1 (pt); Occupational therapists 3 (ft), 2 (pt); Activities coordinators 1 (ft); Social workers 1 (ft), 1 (pt).
Languages Spanish, German, Polish.
Facilities Dining room; Physical therapy room; Activities room; Laundry room; Barber/Beauty shop; Library; Occupational therapy room.
Activities Arts & crafts; Cards; Games; Reading groups; Prayer groups; Movies; Shopping trips; Dances/Social/Cultural gatherings; Resident council; Therapeutic work programs.

Living Challenge
701 E 57th St, Minneapolis, MN 55417
(612) 827-2444
Admin Ade O Demehin.
Licensure Supervised living. *Beds* Supervised living 6.
Owner Proprietary corp.

Maria Home
420 Ridgewood Ave, Minneapolis, MN 55403
(612) 871-0805
Admin Sheldon Schneider.
Licensure Intermediate care for mentally retarded. *Beds* ICF/MR 9.
Owner Proprietary corp.
Admissions Requirements Minimum age 18; Medical examination.
Staff RNs 1 (pt); Activities coordinators 1 (pt); Counselors 2 (ft), 1 (pt).

Facilities Dining room; Activities room; Laundry room.
Activities Arts & crafts; Cards; Games; Movies; Shopping trips; Dances/Social/Cultural gatherings.

Medallion II Board & Lodge Home
2430 Pillsbury Ave S, Minneapolis, MN 55404
(612) 871-8306
Admin Robert Servold.
Licensure Intermediate care. *Beds* ICF 25. *Certified* Medicaid.
Owner Proprietary corp.
Admissions Requirements Minimum age 18.
Staff Cooks, Managers 1 (ft), 1 (pt); Housekeepers 2 (pt).
Facilities Dining room; Laundry room.

Metro Care Center
1300 Olson Memorial Hwy, Minneapolis, MN 55411
(612) 374-5660
Admin Gayle Sanders; Jeff Bomberger, Asst. *Dir of Nursing* Donna Barr. *Medical Dir* Dr Keith Kubasch.
Licensure Skilled care; Intermediate care; Alzheimer's care. *Beds* SNF 101; ICF 5. *Private Pay Patients* 3%. *Certified* Medicaid; Medicare.
Owner Proprietary corp (Beverly Enterprises).
Admissions Requirements Minimum age 16; Medical examination; Physician's request.
Staff RNs 8 (ft); LPNs 8 (ft); Nurses' aides 44 (ft); Physical therapists 2 (ft), 1 (pt); Recreational therapists 2 (ft), 2 (pt); Occupational therapists 2 (ft); Speech therapists 1 (ft); Activities coordinators 1 (ft); Dietitians 1 (ft); Ophthalmologists 1 (pt); Podiatrists 1 (pt); Audiologists 1 (pt); Psychologists 1 (pt).
Facilities Dining room; Physical therapy room; Activities room; Chapel; Crafts room; Laundry room; Barber/Beauty shop; Alzheimer's care; Huntington disease program; Closed head injury care; Young disabled adult care.
Activities Arts & crafts; Cards; Games; Reading groups; Prayer groups; Movies; Shopping trips; Dances/Social/Cultural gatherings; Intergenerational programs; Pet therapy; Huntington disease support groups.

Minnesota Masonic Home Care Center
11400 Normandale Blvd, Minneapolis, MN 55437
(612) 881-8665, 885-2419 FAX
Admin Amaryllys Thompson. *Dir of Nursing* Bert Gagnon. *Medical Dir* Dr Jan Tunghe.
Licensure Skilled care; Board and care. *Beds* SNF 157; Board and care 249. *Certified* Medicaid; Medicare.
Owner Proprietary corp.
Admissions Requirements Medical examination; Waiting list gives priority to Masons and Eastern Star members.
Staff Physicians; RNs; LPNs; Nurses' aides; Physical therapists; Recreational therapists; Occupational therapists; Activities coordinators; Dietitians; Ophthalmologists; Podiatrists; Audiologists.
Affiliation Masonic, Eastern Star.
Facilities Dining room; Physical therapy room; Activities room; Chapel; Crafts room; Laundry room; Barber/Beauty shop; Library.
Activities Arts & crafts; Cards; Games; Reading groups; Movies; Shopping trips; Dances/Social/Cultural gatherings.

Minnesota Veterans Home
5101 Minnehaha Ave S, Minneapolis, MN 55417
(612) 721-0600
Admin Jeff Smith. *Dir of Nursing* Jean Timmermann.
Licensure Nursing care; Boarding care; Alzheimer's care. *Beds* Nursing care 346; Boarding care 194.

Owner Publicly owned.
Admissions Requirements Medical examination; Physician's request.
Staff Physicians; RNs; LPNs; Nurses' aides; Physical therapists; Recreational therapists; Activities coordinators; Dietitians.
Facilities Dining room; Physical therapy room; Activities room; Chapel; Crafts room; Laundry room; Barber/Beauty shop; Library.
Activities Arts & crafts; Cards; Games; Reading groups; Movies; Shopping trips; Dances/Social/Cultural gatherings.

Mt Olivet Homes Inc
5517 Lyndale Ave S, Minneapolis, MN 55419
(612) 827-5677
Admin Tim Hokanson.
Licensure Intermediate care. *Beds* ICF 97.
Owner Proprietary corp.

Nekton on Minnehaha Park
3822 E 49th St, Minneapolis, MN 55417
(612) 729-5526
Admin Peter Sajevic.
Licensure Intermediate care for mentally retarded. *Beds* ICF/MR 6.
Owner Proprietary corp.

Nekton on Queen
614 Queen Ave S, Minneapolis, MN 55404
(612) 377-5587
Admin Peter J Sajevic Jr.
Licensure Intermediate care for mentally retarded. *Beds* ICF/MR 6.
Owner Proprietary corp.

New Visions Treatment Center
2605 2nd Ave S, Minneapolis, MN 55408
(612) 870-0441
Licensure Supervised living. *Beds* Supervised living 21.
Owner Proprietary corp.

Nicollet Health Care Center
4429 Nicollet Ave S, Minneapolis, MN 55409
(612) 827-5667
Admin Leon Rotering.
Medical Dir Stuart Lancer MD.
Licensure Skilled care; Intermediate care. *Beds* SNF 88; ICF 59. *Certified* Medicaid; Medicare.
Owner Proprietary corp (Good Neighbor Services).
Admissions Requirements Minimum age 16; Medical examination; Physician's request.
Facilities Dining room; Physical therapy room; Activities room; Crafts room; Laundry room; Barber/Beauty shop; Library.
Activities Arts & crafts; Cards; Games; Reading groups; Prayer groups; Movies; Shopping trips; Dances/Social/Cultural gatherings.

Nile Health Care Center
3720 23rd Ave S, Minneapolis, MN 55407
(612) 724-5495
Admin Deborah Rose. *Dir of Nursing* Adele Winkels. *Medical Dir* Dr Robert Breitenbucher.
Licensure Skilled care; Alzheimer's care. *Beds* SNF 125. *Certified* Medicaid; Medicare.
Owner Proprietary corp (Merle Nugent).
Admissions Requirements Medical examination; Physician's request.
Staff RNs 9 (ft); LPNs 11 (ft); Nurses' aides 44 (ft); Physical therapists 1 (ft); Occupational therapists 1 (ft); Speech therapists 1 (ft); Activities coordinators 1 (ft).
Facilities Dining room; Physical therapy room; Activities room; Crafts room; Laundry room; Barber/Beauty shop.
Activities Arts & crafts; Cards; Games; Reading groups; Prayer groups; Movies; Shopping trips; Dances/Social/Cultural gatherings; Pet therapy.

Northeast House Inc
1918 19th Ave, Minneapolis, MN 55418
(612) 789-8841
Admin Donald G Levin. *Dir of Nursing* Jeanette Oleary RN. *Medical Dir* Dr V K Arora.
Licensure Intermediate care for mentally retarded; Retirement. *Beds* ICF/MR 24.
Owner Proprietary corp.
Admissions Requirements Minimum age 30; Medical examination; Physician's request.
Staff Physicians 2 (pt); RNs 1 (ft), 1 (pt); LPNs 1 (pt); Physical therapists 2 (pt); Reality therapists 2 (pt); Recreational therapists 1 (ft); Occupational therapists 1 (pt); Speech therapists 1 (pt); Activities coordinators 2 (ft), 1 (pt); Dietitians 1 (pt); Ophthalmologists 1 (pt); Podiatrists 1 (pt); Dentists 2 (pt); Psychiatrists 2 (pt); Psychologists 2 (pt); Program directors 1 (ft).
Facilities Dining room; Activities room; Crafts room; Laundry room; 2-season screened porch; Nature trails.
Activities Arts & crafts; Cards; Games; Reading groups; Movies; Shopping trips; Dances/Social/Cultural gatherings.

Oak Grove Resident Treatment Center
131 Oak Grove, Minneapolis, MN 55403
(612) 871-5800
Admin Tom Paul.
Licensure Boarding care. *Beds* Boarding care 21.
Owner Proprietary corp.
Admissions Requirements Minimum age 30; Medical examination.
Staff LPNs 1 (ft), 2 (pt); Nurses' aides 1 (ft), 2 (pt); Reality therapists 2 (ft); Recreational therapists 1 (ft); Dietitians 1 (pt).
Facilities Dining room; Activities room; Crafts room; Laundry room.
Activities Arts & crafts; Cards; Games; Movies; Shopping trips; Dances/Social/Cultural gatherings.

Oakwood Residence Inc
3012 W 44th St, Minneapolis, MN 55410
(612) 924-0438
Admin Sandra L Singer.
Medical Dir Irene Moore.
Licensure Intermediate care for mentally retarded. *Beds* ICF/MR 15.
Owner Proprietary corp.
Admissions Requirements Minimum age 15.
Staff RNs 1 (pt); Activities coordinators 1 (ft).
Facilities Dining room; Laundry room.
Activities Arts & crafts; Cards; Games; Movies; Shopping trips; Programs for independent leisure skills in community.

Outreach Minneapolis—Stevens Group Home
5304 Stevens Ave S, Minneapolis, MN 55419
(612) 823-9241
Admin Eileen Harris.
Licensure Intermediate care for mentally retarded. *Beds* ICF/MR 6.
Owner Proprietary corp.
Admissions Requirements Minimum age 18; Medical examination.
Staff Physicians 1 (pt); RNs 1 (pt).
Affiliation Presbyterian.
Facilities Dining room; Activities room; Laundry room.
Activities Arts & crafts; Cards; Games; Prayer groups; Movies; Shopping trips; Dances/Social/Cultural gatherings.

Outreach Northeast Group Home
729 Adams St NE, Minneapolis, MN 55413
(612) 379-8897
Admin Eileen Harris. *Dir of Nursing* Carole Pitrowski RN.
Licensure Intermediate care for mentally retarded. *Beds* ICF/MR 7.
Owner Nonprofit corp.
Admissions Requirements Minimum age 18; Medical examination.
Staff RNs 1 (pt).

Facilities Dining room; Activities room;
Laundry room.
Activities Arts & crafts; Cards; Games;
Movies; Shopping trips; Dances/Social/
Cultural gatherings.

Pillsbury Board & Care Home
2500 Pillsbury Ave S, Minneapolis, MN
55404
(612) 872-8363
Admin Marilyn J Egge. *Dir of Nursing* Juanita
Campbell. *Medical Dir* Richard Pfohl MD.
Licensure Boarding care. *Beds* Boarding care
22. *Private Pay Patients* 0%. *Certified*
Medicaid.
Owner Proprietary corp.
Admissions Requirements Minimum age 21;
Medical examination; Physician's request.
Staff Physicians (consultant); RNs
(consultant); LPNs 2 (ft), 4 (pt); Nurses'
aides 1 (ft), 1 (pt); Activities coordinators 1
(ft); Dietitians (consultant); Podiatrists
(consultant).
Facilities Dining room; Laundry room.
Activities Arts & crafts; Cards; Games;
Reading groups; Prayer groups; Movies;
Shopping trips; Dances/Social/Cultural
gatherings; Pet therapy.

Queen Care Center
300 Queen Ave N, Minneapolis, MN 55405
(612) 374-3380, 374-2202 FAX
Admin David R Juhl. *Dir of Nursing* Barbara
Corsbie. *Medical Dir* Dr Susan Bannick
Mohrland.
Licensure Skilled care; Board and care. *Beds*
SNF 63; Board and care 12. *Certified*
Medicaid; Medicare.
Owner Proprietary corp (Med Care
Associates).
Admissions Requirements Minimum age 21.
Staff Physicians 1 (pt); RNs 3 (ft); LPNs 6
(ft); Nurses' aides 9 (ft), 9 (pt); Physical
therapists 1 (ft), 1 (pt); Recreational therapists 1
(ft), 1 (pt); Occupational therapists 1 (ft), 1
(pt); Speech therapists 1 (ft); Activities
coordinators 1 (ft); Dietitians 1 (ft);
Ophthalmologists 1 (pt); Podiatrists 1 (pt);
Audiologists 1 (pt).
Facilities Dining room; Physical therapy
room; Activities room; Laundry room;
Barber/Beauty shop.
Activities Arts & crafts; Cards; Games;
Reading groups; Movies; Shopping trips; Pet
therapy; AA meetings.

Redeemer Residence Inc
3111 Lyndale Ave S, Minneapolis, MN 55408
(612) 827-2555
Admin William E Brown. *Dir of Nursing*
Mary I Adams. *Medical Dir* Dr James
Struve.
Licensure Skilled care; Board and care. *Beds*
SNF 142; Board and care 17. *Certified*
Medicaid; Medicare.
Owner Nonprofit corp.
Admissions Requirements Minimum age 65;
Medical examination.
Staff RNs 8 (ft), 8 (pt); LPNs 5 (ft), 7 (pt);
Nurses' aides 44 (ft), 17 (pt); Physical
therapists 1 (ft), 1 (pt); Reality therapists 1
(ft); Recreational therapists 1 (ft);
Occupational therapists 1 (ft); Speech
therapists; Activities coordinators 1 (ft);
Dietitians (consultant); Ophthalmologists;
Podiatrists (monthly); Audiologists.
Languages Swedish, Norwegian, Filipino,
Spanish, Vietnamese.
Facilities Dining room; Physical therapy
room; Activities room; Chapel; Crafts room;
Laundry room; Barber/Beauty shop;
Whirlpool bath.
Activities Arts & crafts; Cards; Games;
Reading groups; Prayer groups; Movies;
Shopping trips; Dances/Social/Cultural
gatherings; Pet therapy; Financial counseling.

Reentry House
5812 Lyndale Ave S, Minneapolis, MN 55419
(612) 869-2411
Admin Terry Schneider.
Licensure Supervised living. *Beds* Supervised
living 28.
Owner Proprietary corp.

REM Lyndale Inc
2210 Lyndale Ave N, Minneapolis, MN 55411
(612) 522-6689
Admin David Petersen.
Medical Dir Laura Sissala.
Licensure Intermediate care for mentally
retarded. *Beds* ICF/MR 10.
Owner Proprietary corp.
Admissions Requirements Minimum age 18;
Males only.
Staff RNs 1 (pt).
Facilities Dining room; Laundry room.
Activities Arts & crafts; Cards; Games;
Reading groups; Prayer groups; Movies;
Shopping trips; Dances/Social/Cultural
gatherings; Sports.

REM Nicollet
5816-5818 Nicollet Ave S, Minneapolis, MN
55435
(612) 869-5538
Admin David Petersen.
Licensure Supervised living. *Beds* Supervised
living 6.
Owner Proprietary corp.

REM Pillsbury Inc
2311 Pillsbury Ave S, Minneapolis, MN
55404
(612) 871-1954
Admin Craig Miller.
Licensure Intermediate care for mentally
retarded. *Beds* ICF/MR 34.
Owner Proprietary corp.

REM Pleasant
2548 Pleasant Ave S, Minneapolis, MN 55404
(612) 872-7800
Admin Douglas Miller.
Licensure Intermediate care for mentally
retarded. *Beds* ICF/MR 15. *Certified*
Medicaid.
Owner Proprietary corp.

REM Southeast
1307 6th St SE, Minneapolis, MN 55414
(612) 378-1556
Admin Lynne Megan. *Dir of Nursing* Diane
Greig.
Licensure Intermediate care for mentally
retarded. *Beds* ICF/MR 10. *Certified*
Medicaid.
Owner Proprietary corp (REM Southeast).
Admissions Requirements Minimum age 50;
Medical examination; Physician's request.
Staff RNs; Dietitians.
Facilities Dining room; Laundry room; Living
room.
Activities Cards; Games; Movies; Shopping
trips; Dances/Social/Cultural gatherings;
Daily living skills training.

St Anns Residence
2120 Clinton Ave S, Minneapolis, MN 55404
(612) 871-0666
Admin Annette Rowland.
Licensure Intermediate care for mentally
retarded. *Beds* ICF/MR 30.
Owner Nonprofit organization/foundation.
Staff RNs 1 (ft); LPNs 1 (pt); Dietitians 1
(pt).
Facilities Dining room; Activities room;
Crafts room; Laundry room; Barber/Beauty
shop.
Activities Arts & crafts; Cards; Games;
Reading groups; Prayer groups; Movies;
Shopping trips; Dances/Social/Cultural
gatherings.

St Anthony Elder Center on Main
817 Main St NE, Minneapolis, MN 55413
(612) 379-1370
Admin David Westbrook. *Dir of Nursing*
Florence Zamor RN. *Medical Dir* Gene Ott
MD.
Licensure Skilled care. *Beds* SNF 150.
Certified Medicaid; Medicare.
Owner Nonprofit corp (Catholic Eldercare).
Admissions Requirements Medical
examination; Physician's request.
Staff RNs; LPNs; Nurses' aides; Physical
therapists; Recreational therapists;
Occupational therapists; Speech therapists;
Activities coordinators; Dietitians.
Languages Polish, German, Slavic, Russian,
French.
Affiliation Roman Catholic.
Facilities Dining room; Physical therapy
room; Activities room; Chapel; Crafts room;
Laundry room; Barber/Beauty shop; Library.
Activities Arts & crafts; Cards; Games;
Reading groups; Prayer groups; Movies;
Shopping trips; Dances/Social/Cultural
gatherings.

St Anthony Health Center
3700 Foss Rd NE, Minneapolis, MN 55421
(612) 788-9673
Admin Marian Post.
Licensure Skilled care. *Beds* SNF 154.
Certified Medicaid.
Owner Privately owned.

St Mary's Rehabilitation Center
2512 S 7th St, Minneapolis, MN 55454
(612) 337-4197
Admin Phyllis C Winters.
Licensure Skilled care; Intermediate care. *Beds*
SNF 98; ICF 51.
Owner Proprietary corp.

St Olaf Residence
2912 Fremont Ave N, Minneapolis, MN
55411
(612) 522-6561
Admin Richard F Holy. *Dir of Nursing* Mary
Lou Tkalcich. *Medical Dir* Dr LeRoy Geis.
Licensure Skilled care; Intermediate care;
Retirement. *Beds* SNF 92; ICF 93;
Retirement 62. *Private Pay Patients* 60%.
Certified Medicaid; Medicare.
Owner Nonprofit organization/foundation.
Admissions Requirements Medical
examination.
Staff Physicians 1 (ft); RNs 7 (ft), 4 (pt);
LPNs 7 (ft), 4 (pt); Nurses' aides 24 (ft), 10
(pt); Physical therapists 1 (pt); Reality
therapists 1 (ft); Recreational therapists 2
(ft); Occupational therapists 2 (pt); Speech
therapists 1 (pt); Activities coordinators 1
(ft); Dietitians 1 (pt).
Affiliation Lutheran.
Facilities Dining room; Physical therapy
room; Activities room; Chapel; Crafts room;
Laundry room; Barber/Beauty shop; Library.
Activities Arts & crafts; Cards; Games;
Reading groups; Prayer groups; Movies;
Shopping trips; Dances/Social/Cultural
gatherings; Intergenerational programs; Pet
therapy.

Salvation Army Harbor Light
706 1st Ave N, Minneapolis, MN 55403
(612) 338-0113
Admin Cpt Richard Rubottom.
Licensure Supervised living. *Beds* Supervised
living 60.
Owner Proprietary corp.

Southside Care Center
2644 Aldrich Ave S, Minneapolis, MN 55408
(612) 872-4233
Admin Marcy Kronfeld, acting.
Licensure Boarding care. *Beds* Boarding care
20.
Owner Proprietary corp.

Admissions Requirements Medical
examination.
Staff RNs 1 (pt); LPNs 2 (ft), 1 (pt); Nurses'
aides 2 (ft), 2 (pt); Recreational therapists 1
(ft); Activities coordinators 1 (pt); Dietitians
1 (pt).
Facilities Dining room; Activities room;
Laundry room; Barber/Beauty shop.
Activities Arts & crafts; Cards; Games; Prayer
groups.

Stevens Square
101 E 32nd St, Minneapolis, MN 55408
(612) 823-5201
Admin Rachel Rustad.
Licensure Intermediate care; Boarding care.
Beds ICF 38; Boarding care 28.
Owner Proprietary corp.

Tasks Unlimited Training Center
3020 Clinton Ave S, Minneapolis, MN 55408
(612) 823-0156
Admin Karl Hallsten.
Licensure Supervised living. Beds Supervised
living 12.
Owner Proprietary corp.

Teachers Homes Healthcare Center
2625 Park Ave, Minneapolis, MN 55407-1097
(612) 871-4594
Admin David Hjortland. Dir of Nursing
Marilyn Westlin.
Licensure Intermediate care; Retirement. Beds
ICF 13; Retirement Apts 90. Private Pay
Patients 100%.
Owner Nonprofit corp.
Admissions Requirements Minimum age 55;
Medical examination; Physician's request.
Staff RNs 2 (ft), 4 (pt); LPNs 2 (pt); Nurses'
aides 4 (pt); Activities coordinators 1 (pt);
Dietitians 1 (pt).
Facilities Dining room; Activities room;
Laundry room; Barber/Beauty shop; Library.
Activities Arts & crafts; Cards; Games;
Intergenerational programs.

Three Thirty Five Ridgewood
335 Ridgewood Ave S, Minneapolis, MN
55403
(612) 871-0805
Admin Sheldon Schneider.
Licensure Intermediate care for mentally
retarded. Beds ICF/MR 9.
Owner Proprietary corp.
Admissions Requirements Minimum age 18;
Medical examination.
Staff RNs 1 (pt); Activities coordinators 1
(pt); Counselors 1 (ft), 2 (pt).
Facilities Dining room; Activities room;
Laundry room.
Activities Arts & crafts; Cards; Games;
Movies; Shopping trips; Dances/Social/
Cultural gatherings.

2020 Adolescent Receiving Center
2414 7th St S, Minneapolis, MN 55454
(612) 371-6953
Admin Tom Collins.
Licensure Supervised living. Beds Supervised
living 14.
Owner Proprietary corp.

University Health Care Center
22 27th Ave SE, Minneapolis, MN 55414
(612) 332-4262
Admin Paula Kneisl. Dir of Nursing Joanna
Nordseth RN. Medical Dir John Mielke
MD.
Licensure Skilled care; Alzheimer's care. Beds
SNF 368. Certified Medicaid; Medicare.
Owner Proprietary corp (Good Neighbor
Services).
Admissions Requirements Minimum age 16;
Physician's request.
Staff Recreational therapists 2 (pt);
Occupational therapists 3 (ft); Speech
therapists 1 (ft); Activities coordinators 1
(ft); Dietitians 3 (ft); Counselors 4 (ft); Social
workers 10 (ft).

Facilities Dining room; Physical therapy
room; Activities room; Crafts room; Laundry
room; Barber/Beauty shop; Library.
Activities Arts & crafts; Cards; Games;
Reading groups; Prayer groups; Movies;
Shopping trips; Dances/Social/Cultural
gatherings; Community events.

Valor Kentucky
18115 30th Ave N, Minneapolis, MN 55447
(612) 535-3116
Admin Eileen Harris.
Licensure Intermediate care for mentally
retarded. Beds ICF/MR 6. Certified
Medicaid.
Owner Proprietary corp.

Valor Sunlen
6444 13th Ave S, Minneapolis, MN 55423
(612) 888-0897
Admin Eileen Harris.
Licensure Intermediate care for mentally
retarded. Beds ICF/MR 6.
Owner Proprietary corp.

Valor Vincent
9101 Erickson Ct, Minneapolis, MN 55428
(612) 861-4373
Admin Eileen Harris.
Licensure Intermediate care for mentally
retarded. Beds ICF/MR 6.
Owner Proprietary corp.

Venture Group Home
414 W Diamond Lake Rd, Minneapolis, MN
55419
(612) 824-8664
Admin Nancy Prindle-Stratton.
Licensure Intermediate care for mentally
retarded. Beds ICF/MR 6.
Owner Proprietary corp.

Walker Methodist Health Center
3737 Bryant Ave S, Minneapolis, MN 55409
(612) 827-5931
Admin Paul Mikelson. Dir of Nursing
Elizabeth Colloton. Medical Dir Dr Thomas
M Recht.
Licensure Skilled care; Retirement;
Alzheimer's care. Beds SNF 490. Certified
Medicaid; Medicare.
Owner Nonprofit corp.
Admissions Requirements Minimum age 65;
Medical examination; Physician's request.
Staff Physicians 1 (pt); RNs 29 (ft), 14 (pt);
LPNs 23 (ft), 14 (pt); Nurses' aides 115 (ft),
95 (pt); Recreational therapists 6 (ft), 1 (pt);
Occupational therapists; Speech therapists;
Activities coordinators 1 (ft); Dietitians 1
(ft); Ophthalmologists; Dentists.
Affiliation Methodist.
Facilities Dining room; Physical therapy
room; Activities room; Chapel; Crafts room;
Laundry room; Barber/Beauty shop; Library;
Terrace/Greenhouse.
Activities Arts & crafts; Cards; Games;
Reading groups; Prayer groups; Movies;
Shopping trips; Dances/Social/Cultural
gatherings; Support groups.

Wellspring Therapeutic Community
245 Clifton Ave, Minneapolis, MN 55403
(612) 870-3787
Admin Richard Duffin.
Licensure Supervised living. Beds Supervised
living 24.
Owner Proprietary corp.

Irene Whitney Center for Recovery
4954 Upton Ave S, Minneapolis, MN 55410
(612) 922-3825
Admin Betty Triliegi.
Licensure Supervised living. Beds Supervised
living 41.
Owner Proprietary corp.

Willows Convalescent Center Central
625 E 16th St, Minneapolis, MN 55404
(612) 332-3541

Admin Dorothy Ragland.
Medical Dir Henry Smith MD.
Licensure Skilled care; Boarding care. Beds
SNF 150; Boarding care 22. Certified
Medicaid; Medicare.
Owner Proprietary corp.
Admissions Requirements Minimum age 16;
Medical examination.
Staff RNs 10 (ft), 1 (pt); LPNs 6 (ft), 8 (pt);
Nurses' aides 22 (ft), 14 (pt); Physical
therapists 1 (ft); Recreational therapists 1
(ft); Occupational therapists 2 (ft); Speech
therapists 1 (pt); Activities coordinators 2
(ft); Dietitians 1 (pt); Podiatrists 1 (pt);
Social workers 3 (ft).
Facilities Dining room; Physical therapy
room; Activities room; Chapel; Crafts room;
Laundry room; Barber/Beauty shop; Library.
Activities Arts & crafts; Cards; Games;
Reading groups; Prayer groups; Movies;
Shopping trips; Dances/Social/Cultural
gatherings.

Willows Convalescent Center South
6130 Lyndale Ave S, Minneapolis, MN 55419
(612) 866-3095
Admin Sharon Klefsaas.
Medical Dir Diane Klefsaas.
Licensure Skilled care. Beds SNF 144.
Certified Medicaid; Medicare.
Owner Proprietary corp.
Admissions Requirements Minimum age 16;
Medical examination; Physician's request.
Staff RNs; LPNs; Nurses' aides; Physical
therapists; Reality therapists; Recreational
therapists; Occupational therapists; Speech
therapists; Activities coordinators; Dietitians;
Ophthalmologists; Podiatrists; Dentists.
Facilities Dining room; Physical therapy
room; Activities room; Laundry room;
Barber/Beauty shop.
Activities Arts & crafts; Cards; Games;
Reading groups; Prayer groups; Movies;
Shopping trips; Dances/Social/Cultural
gatherings.

Willows East Health Care Center
719 E 16th St, Minneapolis, MN 55404
(612) 339-7281
Admin Patrick J Rafferty.
Licensure Skilled care; Alzheimer's care. Beds
SNF 170. Certified Medicaid; Medicare.
Owner Proprietary corp.
Admissions Requirements Minimum age 18.
Staff RNs 12 (ft); LPNs 7 (ft); Nurses' aides
36 (ft); Physical therapists 1 (ft);
Recreational therapists 4 (ft); Occupational
therapists 1 (ft); Speech therapists 1 (pt).
Facilities Dining room; Physical therapy
room; Activities room; Chapel; Crafts room;
Laundry room; Barber/Beauty shop.
Activities Arts & crafts; Cards; Games;
Reading groups; Prayer groups; Movies;
Shopping trips; Dances/Social/Cultural
gatherings.

Yorkshire Manor
2200 Park Ave S, Minneapolis, MN 55404
(612) 871-2200, 871-2260 FAX
Admin Jenean Erickson. Dir of Nursing Pat
Hollenhorst RN. Medical Dir C Dwight
Townes MD.
Licensure Skilled care. Beds SNF 84. Certified
Medicaid; Medicare.
Owner Proprietary corp.
Admissions Requirements Medical
examination; Physician's request.
Staff RNs 3 (ft), 1 (pt); LPNs 3 (ft), 1 (pt);
Nurses' aides 12 (ft), 24 (pt); Physical
therapists 1 (pt); Recreational therapists 1
(ft); Occupational therapists 1 (pt); Activities
coordinators 1 (ft); Dietitians 1 (pt).
Facilities Dining room; Physical therapy
room; Activities room; Crafts room; Laundry
room.

Activities Arts & crafts; Cards; Games; Reading groups; Prayer groups; Movies; Shopping trips; Dances/Social/Cultural gatherings; Intergenerational programs; Pet therapy.

Minneota

Minneota Manor
700 N Monroe, Minneota, MN 56264
(507) 872-6166
Admin Rev Richard Erickson. *Dir of Nursing* Mary Ann Full. *Medical Dir* Dr Mary Bird.
Licensure Skilled care; Retirement. *Beds* SNF 87; Retirement 30. *Certified* Medicaid; Medicare.
Owner Proprietary corp.
Admissions Requirements Minimum age 16; Medical examination; Physician's request.
Staff RNs 2 (ft), 4 (pt); LPNs 3 (ft), 4 (pt); Nurses' aides 12 (ft), 49 (pt); Reality therapists 1 (pt); Activities coordinators 2 (ft), 1 (pt); Dietitians 1 (pt); Horticulture therapists 1 (pt).
Facilities Dining room; Activities room; Crafts room; Laundry room; Barber/Beauty shop.
Activities Arts & crafts; Cards; Games; Reading groups; Prayer groups; Movies; Shopping trips; Dances/Social/Cultural gatherings; Intergenerational programs; Pet therapy; Horticulture.

Minnetonka

Oak Terrace Nursing Home
14500 County Rd 62, Minnetonka, MN 55345
(612) 934-4100
Admin Rosemary H Wilder. *Dir of Nursing* Lynn Wiegand. *Medical Dir* Robert Breitenbucher MD.
Licensure Skilled care; Alzheimer's care. *Beds* SNF 322. *Private Pay Patients* 5%. *Certified* Medicaid; Medicare.
Owner Publicly owned.
Admissions Requirements Medical examination; Physician's request.
Staff Physicians 3 (pt); RNs 17 (ft), 6 (pt); LPNs 19 (ft), 4 (pt); Nurses' aides 76 (ft), 26 (pt); Physical therapists 1 (pt); Recreational therapists 5 (ft), 1 (pt); Occupational therapists 1 (ft); Speech therapists 1 (pt); Dietitians 2 (ft); Ophthalmologists 1 (pt); Podiatrists 1 (pt).
Facilities Dining room; Physical therapy room; Activities room; Chapel; Crafts room; Laundry room; Barber/Beauty shop; Library; Auditorium.
Activities Arts & crafts; Cards; Games; Reading groups; Prayer groups; Movies; Shopping trips; Dances/Social/Cultural gatherings; Intergenerational programs; Pet therapy; Swimming; Twins ballgames; Picnics; Behavior management.

Omegon Residential
2000 Hopkins Crossroads, Minnetonka, MN 55343
(612) 541-4738
Admin Barbara J Danielsen.
Licensure Supervised living. *Beds* Supervised living 26.
Owner Proprietary corp.

REM Minnetonka
21 Westwood Rd, Minnetonka, MN 55443
(612) 541-9421
Admin Douglas Miller.
Licensure Intermediate care for mentally retarded; Retirement. *Beds* ICF/MR 15.
Owner Proprietary corp.
Admissions Requirements Minimum age 16.
Staff RNs 1 (ft); Activities coordinators 1 (pt); Coordinators 8 (ft).

Facilities Dining room; Activities room; Laundry room.
Activities Arts & crafts; Cards; Games; Movies; Shopping trips.

Resa On Eden Prairie Rd
5601 County Rd 4, Minnetonka, MN 55343
(612) 933-3348
Admin Jean Searles.
Medical Dir Health Counseling, consultant.
Licensure Intermediate care for mentally retarded. *Beds* ICF/MR 6.
Owner Proprietary corp.
Admissions Requirements Minimum age 40.
Staff RNs 1 (pt).
Facilities Dining room; Laundry room; Library; Living room; Recreation room; Kitchen.
Activities Arts & crafts; Cards; Games; Reading groups; Movies; Shopping trips; Dances/Social/Cultural gatherings; Vacations; Church; Visitation; Walks; Fishing.

Valor Minnetonka
14212 Excelsior Blvd, Minnetonka, MN 55343
(612) 938-7203
Admin Eileen Harris.
Licensure Intermediate care for mentally retarded. *Beds* ICF/MR 6.
Owner Proprietary corp.

Montevideo

Clare Home
101 S 5th St, Montevideo, MN 56265
(612) 589-3077
Admin Sr Latona Kalis.
Licensure Supervised living. *Beds* Supervised living 6.
Owner Proprietary corp.

Luther Haven Nursing Home
1109 E Hwy 7, Montevideo, MN 56265
(612) 269-6517
Admin James Flaherty.
Licensure Skilled care; Intermediate care. *Beds* SNF 65; ICF 55. *Certified* Medicare; Medicaid.
Owner Proprietary corp (Health One).
Affiliation Lutheran.

REM Montevideo Inc
585 Gravel Rd, Montevideo, MN 56265
(612) 269-6479
Admin Craig R Miller.
Licensure Intermediate care for mentally retarded. *Beds* ICF/MR 15.
Owner Proprietary corp.
Admissions Requirements Minimum age 16; Medical examination; Physician's request.
Staff RNs 1 (pt); Nurses' aides 3 (ft), 8 (pt); Recreational therapists 1 (pt); Activities coordinators 1 (pt).
Facilities Dining room; Activities room; Laundry room.
Activities Arts & crafts; Cards; Games; Reading groups; Movies; Shopping trips; Dances/Social/Cultural gatherings; Camping; Bowling; Swimming; Fishing.

Montgomery

Siemers Board & Care
211 Spruce Ave, Montgomery, MN 56069
(612) 364-8831
Admin David Mann. *Dir of Nursing* Diane Dokken.
Licensure Boarding care. *Beds* Boarding care 12.
Owner Privately owned.
Admissions Requirements Medical examination.
Staff RNs 1 (pt); LPNs 1 (ft), 1 (pt); Nurses' aides 5 (pt); Dietitians 1 (pt).
Languages German, Czech.

Facilities Dining room; Activities room; Chapel; Laundry room.
Activities Arts & crafts; Cards; Games; Shopping trips; Dances/Social/Cultural gatherings.

Monticello

Monticello Big Lake
1104 E River St, Monticello, MN 55362
(612) 295-5116
Admin Barbara Schwintek. *Dir of Nursing* Olive Krahl. *Medical Dir* Dr Mathew Smorstok.
Licensure Skilled care; Alzheimer's care. *Beds* SNF 91. *Certified* Medicaid; Medicare.
Owner Publicly owned.
Admissions Requirements Minimum age 18; Medical examination; Physician's request.
Staff Physicians 1 (pt); RNs 2 (ft), 4 (pt); LPNs 11 (pt); Nurses' aides 5 (ft), 65 (pt); Physical therapists 1 (pt); Recreational therapists 1 (ft); Occupational therapists 1 (pt); Speech therapists 1 (pt); Dietitians 1 (ft); Ophthalmologists 1 (pt); Podiatrists 1 (pt); Audiologists 1 (pt).
Facilities Dining room; Activities room; Crafts room; Laundry room; Barber/Beauty shop.
Activities Arts & crafts; Cards; Games; Reading groups; Prayer groups; Movies; Shopping trips; Dances/Social/Cultural gatherings; Intergenerational programs; Pet therapy.

Moorhead

Alpha Home
PO Box 698, Moorhead, MN 56560-0698
(612) 796-5792
Admin Barbara Ulman.
Licensure Supervised living. *Beds* Supervised living 15. *Certified* Medicaid.
Owner Proprietary corp.
Admissions Requirements Minimum age 18.
Staff RNs 1 (pt); LPNs 1 (ft).
Facilities Dining room; Activities room; Crafts room; Laundry room.
Activities Arts & crafts; Cards; Games; Shopping trips; Dances/Social/Cultural gatherings.

Clay County Residence II
2842 Village Green Dr, Moorhead, MN 56560
(218) 233-5949
Admin Douglas Johnson.
Licensure Intermediate care for mentally retarded. *Beds* ICF/MR 6.
Owner Proprietary corp.
Admissions Requirements Minimum age 16; Medical examination.
Staff RNs 1 (ft).
Facilities Dining room; Activities room; Crafts room; Laundry room.
Activities Arts & crafts; Cards; Games; Movies; Shopping trips.

Eventide Lutheran Home
1405 7th St S, Moorhead, MN 56560
(218) 233-7508
Admin Helen Frampton. *Dir of Nursing* Sandi Pettersen. *Medical Dir* Dr John R Holten.
Licensure Skilled care; Intermediate care; Retirement; Alzheimer's care; Adult day care. *Beds* Swing beds SNF/ICF 195; Retirement apartments 46. *Private Pay Patients* 30%. *Certified* Medicaid; Medicare.
Owner Nonprofit organization/foundation.
Admissions Requirements Medical examination.
Staff RNs; LPNs; Nurses' aides; Physical therapists; Occupational therapists; Speech therapists; Activities coordinators; Dietitians.
Affiliation Lutheran.

Facilities Dining room; Physical therapy room; Activities room; Chapel; Crafts room; Laundry room; Barber/Beauty shop; Library; Formal dining room; Gift shop; Kaffe Hus.
Activities Arts & crafts; Cards; Games; Reading groups; Prayer groups; Movies; Shopping trips; Dances/Social/Cultural gatherings; Intergenerational programs; Pet therapy.

Gull Harbour Apartments
1702 Bel Sly Blvd, Moorhead, MN 56560
(218) 233-9436
Admin Del Sand.
Licensure Supervised living. *Beds* Supervised living 16.
Owner Proprietary corp.

Moorhead Healthcare Center
2810 N 2nd Ave, Moorhead, MN 56560
(218) 233-7578
Admin Joanne Hubbard, acting.
Medical Dir Dr Craychee.
Licensure Skilled care. *Beds* SNF 89. *Certified* Medicaid; Medicare.
Owner Proprietary corp (Beverly Enterprises).
Admissions Requirements Medical examination; Physician's request.
Facilities Dining room; Physical therapy room; Activities room; Chapel; Crafts room; Laundry room; Barber/Beauty shop.
Activities Arts & crafts; Cards; Games; Reading groups; Prayer groups; Movies; Shopping trips; Dances/Social/Cultural gatherings.

Valley Group Home 1
1330 2nd Ave N, Moorhead, MN 56560
(218) 236-9805
Admin Vernon C Nordmark Phd.
Medical Dir Josette Nordmark MD.
Licensure Intermediate care for mentally retarded. *Beds* ICF/MR 10.
Owner Proprietary corp.
Admissions Requirements Minimum age 18; Medical examination.
Staff RNs 1 (pt); Activities coordinators 1 (ft); Direct care 3 (ft), 8 (pt).
Facilities Dining room; Activities room; Laundry room.
Activities Arts & crafts; Cards; Games; Movies; Shopping trips; Dances/Social/Cultural gatherings.

Moose Lake

Mercy Hospital & Health Care Center
Box 469, Moose Lake, MN 55767
(218) 485-4481, 485-8800 FAX
Admin Leone J Riley. *Dir of Nursing* Joyce Bogenholm. *Medical Dir* Dr Ray Christensen.
Licensure Skilled care. *Beds* SNF 94. *Private Pay Patients* 17%. *Certified* Medicaid; Medicare.
Owner Publicly owned.
Admissions Requirements Minimum age 16; Physician's request.
Staff RNs 4 (ft), 10 (pt); LPNs 6 (ft), 7 (pt); Nurses' aides 10 (ft), 41 (pt); Physical therapists 3 (ft); Activities coordinators 1 (ft); Activity assistants 1 (pt), 2 (pt); Social workers 1 (ft); M-O secretaries 1 (ft), 3 (pt).
Languages Finnish, Polish.
Facilities Dining room; Physical therapy room; Activities room; Crafts room; Laundry room; Barber/Beauty shop.
Activities Arts & crafts; Cards; Games; Reading groups; Prayer groups; Movies; Shopping trips; Dances/Social/Cultural gatherings; Intergenerational programs; Pet therapy; Bible study.

Moose Lake Regional Treatment Center
1000 Lakeshore Dr, Moose Lake, MN 55767
(218) 485-4411
Admin Frank R Milczark.

Licensure Intermediate care for mentally retarded; Psychiatric hospital. *Beds* ICF/MR 101; Psychiatric hospital 460.
Owner Publicly owned.

Mora

Brighter Day Residence
620 N Wood St, Mora, MN 55051
(612) 679-3840
Admin Louis Nelson.
Licensure Intermediate care for mentally retarded. *Beds* ICF/MR 10.
Owner Proprietary corp.

Fireside Foster Inn
110 N 7th St, Mora, MN 55051
(612) 679-2822
Admin Robert Sandberg.
Licensure Board care & board lodging. *Beds* Board care & board lodging 29. *Certified* Medicaid.
Owner Proprietary corp.
Staff LPNs 1 (ft), 2 (pt); Nurses' aides 9 (pt); Activities coordinators 1 (pt); Dietitians 1 (pt).

Villa Health Care Center
Birch-Mor Medical Park, Mora, MN 55051
(612) 679-3016
Admin Jack L'Heureux. *Dir of Nursing* Marna Palmen. *Medical Dir* Larry Brettingen.
Licensure Skilled care; Retirement. *Beds* SNF 80; Retirement 45. *Private Pay Patients* 25%. *Certified* Medicaid; Medicare.
Owner Proprietary corp (Health Dimensions Inc).
Admissions Requirements Medical examination; Physician's request.
Staff RNs 2 (ft), 3 (pt); LPNs 3 (ft), 6 (pt); Nurses' aides 6 (ft), 47 (pt); Physical therapists 1 (pt); Occupational therapists 1 (pt); Activities coordinators 2 (ft), 1 (pt); Dietitians 1 (pt).
Facilities Dining room; Physical therapy room; Activities room; Crafts room; Laundry room; Barber/Beauty shop.
Activities Arts & crafts; Cards; Games; Reading groups; Prayer groups; Movies; Shopping trips; Dances/Social/Cultural gatherings; Reality orientation.

Morgan

Gil Mor Manor
RR 1, Morgan, MN 56266
(507) 249-3143
Admin Rita Sabatino.
Medical Dir C M Galvin.
Licensure Intermediate care. *Beds* ICF 49.
Owner Proprietary corp.
Admissions Requirements Physician's request.
Staff RNs 1 (ft); LPNs 4 (ft), 1 (pt); Nurses' aides 10 (ft), 10 (pt); Activities coordinators 1 (ft); Dietitians 1 (pt).
Facilities Dining room; Activities room; Chapel; Crafts room; Laundry room; Barber/Beauty shop; Library.
Activities Arts & crafts; Cards; Games; Reading groups; Prayer groups; Movies; Shopping trips.

Morris

Hoffman Home
210 W 7th, Morris, MN 56267
(612) 589-2057
Admin Sr Latona Kalis.
Licensure Intermediate care for mentally retarded. *Beds* ICF/MR 10. *Certified* Medicaid.
Owner Proprietary corp.

Kooda Home
1001 Scott Ave, Morris, MN 56267
(612) 589-1556
Admin Sr Latona Kalis.

Licensure Supervised living. *Beds* Supervised living 6.
Owner Proprietary corp.

Villa of St Francis Nursing Home
1001 Scott Ave, Morris, MN 56267
(612) 589-1133
Admin Luverne Hoffman. *Dir of Nursing* Mary Garmer. *Medical Dir* Dr Raymond Rossberg.
Licensure Skilled care; Intermediate care; Retirement; Alzheimer's care. *Beds* SNF 98; ICF 42. *Certified* Medicaid; Medicare.
Owner Proprietary corp.
Admissions Requirements Minimum age 16; Medical examination; Physician's request.
Staff Physicians 8 (pt); RNs 7 (pt); LPNs 8 (ft), 13 (pt); Nurses' aides 22 (ft), 44 (pt); Recreational therapists 1 (ft); Activities coordinators 1 (ft); Dietitians 1 (pt).
Affiliation Roman Catholic.
Facilities Dining room; Physical therapy room; Activities room; Chapel; Barber/Beauty shop.
Activities Arts & crafts; Cards; Games; Movies; Shopping trips; Discussion club; Bible discussion.

Mountain Lake

Eventide Home
810 3rd Ave, Mountain Lake, MN 56159
(507) 427-3221
Admin Jane Ramiller.
Licensure Intermediate care. *Beds* ICF 50. *Certified* Medicaid.
Owner Proprietary corp.

Mountain Lake Good Samaritan Village
745 Basinger Memorial Dr, Mountain Lake, MN 56159
(507) 427-2464
Admin Greg C Staudenmaier. *Dir of Nursing* Doris Oakland.
Licensure Intermediate care. *Beds* ICF 80. *Private Pay Patients* 60%. *Certified* Medicaid.
Owner Nonprofit corp (Evangelical Lutheran/ Good Samaritan Society).
Staff RNs 3 (ft); LPNs 8 (ft); Nurses' aides 20 (ft), 20 (pt); Physical therapists 1 (pt); Activities coordinators 1 (ft); Dietitians 1 (pt).
Affiliation Lutheran.
Facilities Dining room; Physical therapy room; Activities room; Chapel; Laundry room; Barber/Beauty shop.
Activities Arts & crafts; Cards; Games; Movies; Shopping trips; Intergenerational programs; Pet therapy; Adopt-a-grandparent.

New Brighton

Innsbruck Healthcare Center
2800 Hwy 694, New Brighton, MN 55112
(612) 633-1686
Admin Thomas Chamberlain.
Licensure Skilled care. *Beds* SNF 130. *Certified* Medicaid; Medicare.
Owner Proprietary corp (Beverly Enterprises).

New Brighton Care Center
550 8th St NW, New Brighton, MN 55112
(612) 633-7200
Admin Michael Chies. *Dir of Nursing* Arella Saretle.
Licensure Skilled care; Alzheimer's care. *Beds* SNF 64. *Certified* Medicaid; Medicare.
Owner Proprietary corp.
Admissions Requirements Physician's request.
Staff Physicians 3 (pt); RNs 5 (ft); LPNs 6 (ft); Nurses' aides 15 (ft); Physical therapists 1 (pt); Reality therapists 1 (pt); Recreational therapists 1 (pt); Occupational therapists 1 (pt); Speech therapists 1 (pt); Activities

coordinators 1 (ft); Dietitians 1 (ft), 1 (pt); Ophthalmologists 1 (pt); Podiatrists 1 (pt); Dentists 1 (pt).
Facilities Dining room; Activities room; Chapel; Crafts room; Barber/Beauty shop.
Activities Arts & crafts; Cards; Games; Reading groups; Prayer groups; Movies; Shopping trips.

Trevilla of New Brighton
825 1st Ave NW, New Brighton, MN 55112
(612) 633-7875
Admin Obie L Reese. *Dir of Nursing* Marcia Sager. *Medical Dir* Dr Mary Wangsness.
Licensure Skilled care. *Beds* SNF 189. *Private Pay Patients* 20%. *Certified* Medicaid; Medicare.
Owner Proprietary corp (Unicare).
Admissions Requirements Minimum age 16; Medical examination; Physician's request.
Staff Physicians 1 (pt); RNs; LPNs; Nurses' aides; Physical therapists; Reality therapists; Recreational therapists; Occupational therapists; Speech therapists; Activities coordinators.
Facilities Dining room; Physical therapy room; Activities room; Chapel; Crafts room; Laundry room; Barber/Beauty shop.
Activities Arts & crafts; Cards; Games; Reading groups; Prayer groups; Movies; Shopping trips; Dances/Social/Cultural gatherings; Intergenerational programs; Pet therapy.

New Hope

Ambassador Health Care Center
8100 Medicine Lake Rd, New Hope, MN 55427
(612) 544-4171
Admin Jonathon Lundberg. *Dir of Nursing* Shirley Stiener. *Medical Dir* Diane Dahl MD.
Licensure Skilled care. *Beds* SNF 114. *Certified* Medicaid; Medicare.
Owner Proprietary corp (Good Neighbor Services).
Admissions Requirements Minimum age 18; Medical examination.
Staff RNs 5 (ft), 7 (pt); LPNs 3 (ft), 12 (pt); Nurses' aides 21 (ft), 20 (pt); Physical therapists 1 (ft); Activities coordinators 1 (ft), 1 (pt); Social workers 1 (ft), 1 (pt).
Facilities Dining room; Physical therapy room; Activities room; Crafts room; Laundry room; Barber/Beauty shop; Occupational therapy room; Gazebo; Patio.
Activities Arts & crafts; Games; Reading groups; Prayer groups; Movies; Shopping trips; Dances/Social/Cultural gatherings.

Dungarvin VII
5820 Gettysburg Cir, New Hope, MN 55428
(612) 533-0563
Admin Julie Hanson.
Licensure Supervised living. *Beds* Supervised living 6.
Owner Proprietary corp.

Homeward Bound
4741 Zealand Ave N, New Hope, MN 55428
(612) 535-6171
Admin James L Glasoe.
Medical Dir Arnold Anderson MD.
Licensure Intermediate care for mentally retarded. *Beds* ICF/MR 64.
Owner Proprietary corp.
Staff RNs 3 (ft); LPNs 6 (ft), 12 (pt); Nurses' aides 14 (ft), 30 (pt); Physical therapists 1 (ft); Recreational therapists 1 (ft); Occupational therapists 2 (ft); Speech therapists 1 (ft); Activities coordinators 1 (ft).

North Ridge Care Center
5430 Boone Ave N, New Hope, MN 55428
(612) 536-7000

Admin Charles P Thompson. *Dir of Nursing* Catherine A Lloyd RN. *Medical Dir* Dr James J Pattee.
Licensure Skilled care; Retirement; Alzheimer's care. *Beds* SNF 559. *Certified* Medicaid; Medicare.
Owner Proprietary corp.
Admissions Requirements Medical examination; Physician's request.
Staff Physicians 1 (pt); RNs 38 (ft); LPNs 37 (ft), 40 (pt); Nurses' aides 85 (ft), 175 (pt); Physical therapists 1 (ft); Occupational therapists 1 (ft); Activities coordinators 1 (ft); Recreational aides 7 (ft), 15 (pt).
Facilities Dining room; Physical therapy room; Activities room; Chapel; Crafts room; Laundry room; Barber/Beauty shop; Dental office; Occupational therapy room.
Activities Arts & crafts; Cards; Games; Reading groups; Prayer groups; Movies; Shopping trips; Dances/Social/Cultural gatherings; Bazaars; Mini-golf course; Bell ringer band; Theatre group.

St Therese Home
8000 Bass Lake Rd, New Hope, MN 55428
(612) 537-4503
Admin Kenneth J Gallus.
Medical Dir C Dwight Townes; Dianne Crawford.
Licensure Skilled care; Intermediate care; Boarding care. *Beds* SNF 202; ICF 50; Boarding care 50. *Certified* Medicaid; Medicare.
Owner Proprietary corp.
Admissions Requirements Minimum age 65; Medical examination.
Staff RNs 4 (ft), 23 (pt); LPNs 2 (ft), 19 (pt); Nurses' aides 19 (ft), 131 (pt); Physical therapists 2 (ft), 2 (pt); Reality therapists 1 (ft); Recreational therapists 5 (ft), 3 (pt); Occupational therapists 1 (ft), 1 (pt); Speech therapists 1 (pt); Activities coordinators 1 (ft); Dietitians 1 (ft); Ophthalmologists 1 (pt); Podiatrists 1 (pt); Dentists 1 (pt); Pharmacists 1 (ft); Psychologists 11 (pt).
Affiliation Roman Catholic.
Facilities Dining room; Physical therapy room; Activities room; Chapel; Crafts room; Laundry room; Barber/Beauty shop; Library; Gift shop; Coffee shop.
Activities Arts & crafts; Cards; Games; Prayer groups; Movies; Dances/Social/Cultural gatherings; Rosary; Parties; Gardening.

New London

Glen Oaks Nursing Home
207 N Main St, New London, MN 56273
(612) 354-2231
Admin Larry E Juhl. *Dir of Nursing* Louise Ziemer RN. *Medical Dir* Jock A Guy MD.
Licensure Skilled care; Retirement. *Beds* SNF 62. *Certified* Medicaid; Medicare.
Owner Proprietary corp.
Admissions Requirements Minimum age 16; Medical examination.
Staff Physicians 1 (pt); RNs 4 (ft), 4 (pt); Nurses' aides 5 (ft), 31 (pt); Physical therapists 1 (pt); Occupational therapists 1 (pt); Activities coordinators 1 (ft); Dietitians 1 (pt).
Facilities Dining room; Physical therapy room; Activities room; Chapel; Crafts room; Laundry room; Barber/Beauty shop; Library.
Activities Arts & crafts; Cards; Games; Reading groups; Prayer groups; Movies; Shopping trips; Dances/Social/Cultural gatherings.

New Prague

Mala Strana Health Care Center
1001 Columbus Ave N, New Prague, MN 56071
(612) 758-2511

Admin Jacqueline J Henle. *Dir of Nursing* Fay Kohnert. *Medical Dir* Michael Wilcox MD.
Licensure Skilled care. *Beds* SNF 120. *Certified* Medicaid; Medicare.
Owner Proprietary corp (Thro Co).
Admissions Requirements Medical examination; Physician's request.
Languages Czech.
Facilities Dining room; Physical therapy room; Activities room; Chapel; Crafts room; Laundry room; Barber/Beauty shop; Library.
Activities Arts & crafts; Cards; Games; Reading groups; Prayer groups; Movies; Shopping trips; Dances/Social/Cultural gatherings.

New Richland

New Richland Care Center
312 NE 1st St, Box 477, New Richland, MN 56072
(507) 465-3292
Admin Jeffrey A Thorne. *Dir of Nursing* Barb Garrison. *Medical Dir* Dr John Tveite.
Licensure Skilled care. *Beds* SNF 60. *Private Pay Patients* 45%. *Certified* Medicaid; Medicare.
Owner Publicly owned.
Admissions Requirements Medical examination.
Staff RNs 2 (ft), 4 (pt); LPNs 8 (pt); Nurses' aides 3 (ft), 27 (pt); Activities coordinators 1 (ft).
Facilities Dining room; Physical therapy room; Activities room; Chapel; Crafts room; Laundry room; Barber/Beauty shop; Sun porch.
Activities Arts & crafts; Cards; Games; Reading groups; Prayer groups; Movies; Dances/Social/Cultural gatherings.

New Ulm

Brown County Detox & Evaluation Center
1417 S State St, New Ulm, MN 56073
(507) 359-9111
Admin Allen Alvig.
Licensure Supervised living. *Beds* Supervised living 6.
Owner Proprietary corp.

Eleven Seven
117 S Minnesota, New Ulm, MN 56073
(507) 359-7812
Admin Mark S Wiger.
Licensure Intermediate care for mentally retarded. *Beds* ICF/MR 8. *Private Pay Patients* 0%.
Owner Proprietary corp.
Staff RNs; Recreational therapists.

Highland Manor
405 N Highland Ave, New Ulm, MN 56073
(507) 359-2026
Admin Elroy E Ubl. *Dir of Nursing* Karen Stoite.
Licensure Skilled care. *Beds* SNF 98. *Certified* Medicaid; Medicare.
Owner Nonprofit organization/foundation.
Admissions Requirements Medical examination; Physician's request.
Languages German.
Facilities Dining room; Activities room; Crafts room; Laundry room; Barber/Beauty shop.
Activities Arts & crafts; Cards; Games; Reading groups; Prayer groups; Movies; Shopping trips; Dances/Social/Cultural gatherings.

MBW on Center
801 Center St, New Ulm, MN 56073
(507) 354-3808
Admin Mark Wiger.
Medical Dir Brenda Wiger.
Licensure Intermediate care for mentally retarded. *Beds* ICF/MR 8.

Owner Proprietary corp.
Staff RNs 1 (pt); Nurses' aides; Recreational therapists 4 (ft); Activities coordinators 1 (ft).

New Ulm CRF I
327 N German, New Ulm, MN 56073
(507) 359-2892
Admin D Bill Olson.
Medical Dir Devin Nelson.
Licensure Intermediate care for mentally retarded. *Beds* ICF/MR 6.
Owner Proprietary corp.
Admissions Requirements Minimum age 18; State screening.
Facilities Laundry room.

New Ulm CRF II
1708 N Garden, New Ulm, MN 56073
(507) 359-2892
Admin D Bill Olson.
Medical Dir Devin Nelson.
Licensure Intermediate care for mentally retarded. *Beds* ICF/MR 6.
Owner Proprietary corp.
Admissions Requirements Minimum age 18; State screening.
Facilities Laundry room.

New York Mills

Elders' Home Inc
Box 188, S Tousley Ave, New York Mills, MN 56567
(218) 385-2005
Admin Andrew Tumberg. *Dir of Nursing* Marion Hansen RN. *Medical Dir* Duane Ness MD.
Licensure Intermediate care. *Beds* ICF 70. *Private Pay Patients* 15%. *Certified* Medicaid.
Owner Nonprofit organization/foundation.
Staff RNs 2 (ft), 1 (pt); LPNs 6 (ft), 4 (pt); Nurses' aides 20 (ft), 10 (pt); Physical therapists.
Languages Finnish, Norwegian, Swedish, German.
Affiliation Lutheran.
Facilities Dining room; Physical therapy room; Activities room; Chapel; Crafts room; Laundry room; Barber/Beauty shop.
Activities Arts & crafts; Cards; Games; Reading groups; Prayer groups; Shopping trips.

Mills Community Home
S Tousley Ave, New York Mills, MN 56567
(218) 385-2000
Admin Andrew Tumberg. *Dir of Nursing* Esther Underdahl RN. *Medical Dir* Gary Robinson MD.
Licensure Intermediate care. *Beds* ICF 30. *Private Pay Patients* 100%.
Owner Publicly owned.
Admissions Requirements Medical examination; Physician's request.
Staff RNs 1 (ft), 1 (pt); LPNs 4 (ft), 2 (pt); Nurses' aides 3 (ft), 10 (pt); Occupational therapists 1 (ft).
Languages Finnish, German, Norwegian.
Facilities Dining room; Physical therapy room; Activities room; Crafts room.
Activities Arts & crafts; Cards; Games; Reading groups; Movies; Shopping trips.

Nopeming

Nopeming Nursing Home
Nopeming, MN 55810
(218) 628-2381
Admin Richard Jokinen. *Dir of Nursing* Mrs Nancy Parkko RN. *Medical Dir* Dr William Stein.
Licensure Skilled care; Alzheimer's care. *Beds* SNF 212. *Certified* Medicaid; Medicare.
Owner Publicly owned.

Admissions Requirements Medical examination; Physician's request.
Staff RNs 9 (ft), 8 (pt); LPNs 11 (ft), 30 (pt); Nurses' aides 44 (ft), 66 (pt); Physical therapists 1 (ft), 1 (pt); Activities coordinators 1 (ft); Dietitians 1 (ft), 1 (pt).
Languages Finnish, Polish, Swedish, Serbian, Slavic, Norwegian.
Facilities Dining room; Physical therapy room; Activities room; Chapel; Crafts room; Laundry room; Barber/Beauty shop; Library; Cafeteria.
Activities Arts & crafts; Cards; Games; Reading groups; Prayer groups; Movies; Shopping trips; Dances/Social/Cultural gatherings; Church; Band; Dining club.

North Branch

Green Acres Nursing Home
North Branch, MN 55056
(612) 674-7068
Admin Steven Mork.
Licensure Skilled care; Intermediate care. *Beds* SNF 67; ICF 68. *Certified* Medicaid; Medicare.
Owner Publicly owned.

North Mankato

Family House
2080 Haughton Ave, North Mankato, MN 56001
(507) 345-1652
Admin Paul Hagen.
Licensure Intermediate care for mentally retarded. *Beds* ICF/MR 6.
Owner Proprietary corp.
Admissions Requirements Minimum age 5.
Facilities Dining room; Activities room; Crafts room; Laundry room.
Activities Arts & crafts; Cards; Games; Reading groups; Prayer groups; Movies; Shopping trips; Dances/Social/Cultural gatherings.

Therese K Sexton Home—North
2080 Haughton Ave, North Mankato, MN 56001
(507) 345-8589
Admin Paul Hagen.
Licensure Intermediate care for mentally retarded. *Beds* ICF/MR 8.
Owner Proprietary corp.

Therese K Sexton Home—South
2050 Haughton Ave, North Mankato, MN 56001
(507) 345-8588
Admin Paul Hagen.
Licensure Intermediate care for mentally retarded. *Beds* ICF/MR 8.
Owner Proprietary corp.

North Saint Paul

North St Paul Care Center
2375 Skillman Ave E, North Saint Paul, MN 55109
(612) 777-7435, 770-1646 FAX
Admin Penelope Lee Heckman. *Dir of Nursing* Chris Malark. *Medical Dir* Thomas Altemeier.
Licensure Skilled care; Intermediate care; Retirement. *Beds* Swing beds SNF/ICF 47; Retirement 46. *Certified* Medicaid; Medicare.
Owner Proprietary corp.
Admissions Requirements Minimum age 18; Medical examination.
Staff RNs 2 (ft), 6 (pt); LPNs 1 (ft), 5 (pt); Nurses' aides 5 (ft), 19 (pt); Physical therapists 1 (pt); Speech therapists 1 (pt); Activities coordinators 1 (ft); Dietitians (consultant); Ophthalmologists (consultant);

Podiatrists (consultant); Audiologists (consultant); Occupational therapy assistants 1 (ft).
Facilities Dining room; Physical therapy room; Activities room; Crafts room; Laundry room; Barber/Beauty shop.
Activities Arts & crafts; Cards; Games; Reading groups; Prayer groups; Movies; Shopping trips; Dances/Social/Cultural gatherings; Intergenerational programs; Pet therapy.

Northfield

Laura Baker School
211 Oak St, Northfield, MN 55057
(507) 645-8866
Admin Gary F Gleason.
Licensure Supervised living. *Beds* Supervised living 73.
Owner Proprietary corp.

Minnesota Odd Fellows Home
815 Forest Ave, Northfield, MN 55057
(507) 645-6611
Admin Carlton Sather.
Medical Dir Patricia Vincent.
Licensure Skilled care; Alzheimer's care; Retirement. *Beds* SNF 120. *Certified* Medicaid; Medicare.
Owner Proprietary corp.
Admissions Requirements Medical examination.
Staff Physicians 1 (pt); RNs 6 (ft); LPNs 12 (ft); Nurses' aides 80 (pt); Physical therapists 1 (pt); Occupational therapists 2 (ft); Speech therapists 1 (pt); Dietitians 1 (pt); Ophthalmologists 1 (pt); Podiatrists 1 (pt); Dentists 1 (pt).
Affiliation Independent Order of Odd Fellows & Rebekahs.
Facilities Dining room; Physical therapy room; Activities room; Chapel; Crafts room; Laundry room; Barber/Beauty shop; Library.
Activities Arts & crafts; Cards; Games; Reading groups; Prayer groups; Movies; Shopping trips; Dances/Social/Cultural gatherings.

Northfield Hospital & HO Dilley Skilled Nursing Facility
801 W 1st St, Northfield, MN 55057
(507) 645-6661
Admin Ken Bank. *Dir of Nursing* Lois E Schonning RNC. *Medical Dir* Dr Robert Shannon.
Licensure Skilled care. *Beds* SNF 40. *Certified* Medicaid; Medicare.
Owner Nonprofit organization/foundation.
Admissions Requirements Medical examination; Physician's request.
Staff Physicians 16 (ft), 54 (pt); RNs 1 (ft), 2 (pt); LPNs 3 (ft), 7 (pt); Nurses' aides 6 (ft), 22 (pt); Physical therapists 4 (ft), 6 (pt); Occupational therapists 2 (ft), 3 (pt); Speech therapists 1 (pt); Activities coordinators 1 (ft); Dietitians 1 (ft); Ophthalmologists 2 (pt); Podiatrists 1 (pt); Audiologists 1 (pt).
Facilities Dining room; Physical therapy room; Activities room; Chapel; Barber/ Beauty shop.
Activities Arts & crafts; Cards; Games; Reading groups; Prayer groups; Movies; Shopping trips; Dances/Social/Cultural gatherings; Intergenerational programs; Pet therapy.

Northfield Retirement Center
900 Cannon Valley Dr, Northfield, MN 55057
(507) 645-9511
Admin Rev Gerhard J Nygaard. *Dir of Nursing* Corrine Hanson RN.
Licensure Intermediate care; Boarding care. *Beds* ICF 40; Boarding care 40.
Owner Proprietary corp.
Admissions Requirements Minimum age 18; Medical examination.

Staff RNs 1 (ft), 2 (pt); LPNs 4 (ft), 1 (pt); Nurses' aides 7 (ft), 18 (pt); Recreational therapists 1 (ft), 2 (pt); Activities coordinators 1 (ft); Dietitians 1 (pt).
Affiliation Lutheran.
Facilities Dining room; Activities room; Chapel; Crafts room; Laundry room; Barber/ Beauty shop; Library.
Activities Arts & crafts; Cards; Games; Reading groups; Prayer groups; Movies; Shopping trips; Dances/Social/Cultural gatherings.

Northome

Northome Nursing Home
PO Box 138, Northome, MN 56661
(218) 897-5235
Admin Paul Raygor. Dir of Nursing N Leseman RN. Medical Dir Dr G W Franklin.
Licensure Skilled care; Intermediate care for mentally retarded. Beds SNF 42; ICF/MR 16. Certified Medicaid; Medicare.
Owner Proprietary corp.
Admissions Requirements Minimum age 18; Medical examination; Physician's request.
Staff RNs 3 (ft), 1 (pt); LPNs 3 (ft), 1 (pt); Nurses' aides 12 (ft), 9 (pt); Physical therapists 1 (ft); Activities coordinators 1 (ft), 5 (pt).
Facilities Dining room; Physical therapy room; Activities room; Laundry room.
Activities Arts & crafts; Cards; Games; Reading groups; Prayer groups; Movies; Shopping trips.

Olivia

Olivia Healthcare Center
1003 W Maple, Olivia, MN 56277
(612) 523-1652
Admin David D Lamb. Dir of Nursing Susan Meyer RN. Medical Dir C A Anderson MD.
Licensure Skilled care. Beds SNF 94. Certified Medicaid; Medicare.
Owner Proprietary corp (Beverly Enterprises).
Staff Physicians 6 (pt); RNs 2 (ft), 1 (pt); LPNs 7 (ft), 5 (pt); Nurses' aides 21 (ft), 31 (pt); Physical therapists 1 (pt); Occupational therapists 1 (pt); Activities coordinators 1 (ft).
Facilities Dining room; Physical therapy room; Activities room; Crafts room; Laundry room; Barber/Beauty shop.
Activities Arts & crafts; Cards; Games; Reading groups; Prayer groups; Movies; Shopping trips; Dances/Social/Cultural gatherings; Reminiscence group.

Onamia

Mille Lacs Hospital & Home
200 N Elm, Onamia, MN 56359
(612) 532-3154, 532-3111 FAX
Admin Michael D Schafer. Dir of Nursing Kathryn E Mickus. Medical Dir Dennis Jacobson MD.
Licensure Skilled care; Intermediate care; Retirement. Beds Swing beds SNF/ICF 80; Retirement apts 16. Certified Medicaid; Medicare.
Owner Nonprofit organization/foundation.
Admissions Requirements Medical examination; Physician's request.
Staff Physicians 2 (ft); RNs 5 (ft), 1 (pt); LPNs 6 (ft), 2 (pt); Nurses' aides 30 (ft), 12 (pt); Physical therapists 1 (ft), 1 (pt); Activities coordinators 1 (ft); Dietitians (consultant).
Languages Chippewa.
Affiliation Roman Catholic.
Facilities Dining room; Physical therapy room; Activities room; Chapel; Crafts room; Barber/Beauty shop.

Activities Arts & crafts; Cards; Games; Reading groups; Prayer groups; Movies; Shopping trips; Dances/Social/Cultural gatherings; Intergenerational programs; Pet therapy.

Ortonville

Monarch Heights
501 Burdick Ave, Ortonville, MN 56278
(612) 839-6139
Admin Ernest Guillemette. Dir of Nursing Karen Russman RN.
Licensure Intermediate care for mentally retarded. Beds ICF/MR 12.
Owner Nonprofit organization/foundation.
Admissions Requirements Minimum age 18; Medical examination; Physician's request.
Staff Physicians 1 (pt); RNs 1 (pt); Physical therapists 1 (pt); Occupational therapists 1 (pt); Speech therapists 1 (pt); Dietitians 1 (pt); Podiatrists 1 (pt); Dentists 1 (pt); Direct care 12 (ft), 7 (pt).
Facilities Dining room; Activities room; Crafts room; Laundry room; Training kitchen.
Activities Arts & crafts; Cards; Games; Reading groups; Prayer groups; Movies; Shopping trips; Dances/Social/Cultural gatherings.

Northridge Residence
1075 Roy St, Ortonville, MN 56278
(612) 839-6113
Admin Daniel Olson.
Medical Dir Robert S Ross MD.
Licensure Skilled care. Beds SNF 74. Certified Medicaid; Medicare.
Owner Publicly owned.
Admissions Requirements Medical examination; Physician's request.
Staff Physicians 3 (pt); RNs 3 (ft), 2 (pt); LPNs 3 (ft), 4 (pt); Nurses' aides 20 (ft), 20 (pt); Physical therapists 1 (pt); Activities coordinators 4 (pt); Dietitians 1 (pt).
Facilities Dining room; Physical therapy room; Activities room; Chapel; Crafts room; Laundry room; Barber/Beauty shop.
Activities Arts & crafts; Cards; Games; Reading groups; Prayer groups; Movies; Shopping trips; Dances/Social/Cultural gatherings.

Osakis

Community Memorial Home
410 Main St SW, Osakis, MN 56360
(612) 859-2142
Admin David E Carlson. Dir of Nursing Rona Hanson RN. Medical Dir Paul E Van Gorp MD.
Licensure Skilled care. Beds SNF 62. Private Pay Patients 50%. Certified Medicaid; Medicare.
Owner Nonprofit organization/foundation.
Admissions Requirements Minimum age 18; Medical examination.
Staff RNs 1 (ft), 4 (pt); LPNs 2 (ft), 5 (pt); Nurses' aides 10 (ft), 25 (pt); Physical therapists 1 (pt); Recreational therapists 1 (ft), 1 (pt); Speech therapists 1 (pt); Activities coordinators 1 (ft); Dietitians 1 (pt).
Facilities Dining room; Physical therapy room; Activities room; Crafts room; Laundry room; Barber/Beauty shop; Library.
Activities Arts & crafts; Cards; Games; Reading groups; Prayer groups; Movies; Shopping trips; Dances/Social/Cultural gatherings; Intergenerational programs; Pet therapy.

REM Osakis Inc
405 Lake St, Osakis, MN 56360
(612) 859-4200
Admin Thomas Miller.

Licensure Intermediate care for mentally retarded. Beds ICF/MR 13.
Owner Proprietary corp.

Osseo

Berkshire Residence
501 2nd St SE, Osseo, MN 55369
(612) 425-3939, 424-2777 FAX
Admin Sonja L Johnson. Dir of Nursing Susanne Marks RN. Medical Dir Richard Williams MD.
Licensure Intermediate care; Alzheimer's care. Beds ICF 150. Private Pay Patients 40%. Certified Medicaid.
Owner Privately owned.
Admissions Requirements Medical examination; Physician's request.
Staff RNs 2 (ft), 7 (pt); LPNs 3 (ft), 21 (pt); Nurses' aides 5 (ft), 18 (pt); Physical therapists (contracted); Recreational therapists 3 (ft), 1 (pt); Occupational therapists (contracted); Speech therapists (contracted); Activities coordinators 1 (ft); Ophthalmologists (contracted); Podiatrists (contracted).
Facilities Dining room; Activities room; Chapel; Crafts room; Laundry room; Barber/ Beauty shop; Library.
Activities Arts & crafts; Cards; Games; Reading groups; Prayer groups; Movies; Shopping trips; Dances/Social/Cultural gatherings; Intergenerational programs; Pet therapy; Diners club; Choir; Art classes.

Osseo Health Care Center
525 2nd St SE, Osseo, MN 55369
(612) 425-2128
Admin Robert Dahl.
Licensure Skilled care. Beds SNF 137. Certified Medicaid; Medicare.
Owner Proprietary corp (Beverly Enterprises).

Ostrander

Ostrander Care Center
PO Box 36, Ostrander, MN 55961
(507) 657-2231
Admin George N Jensen.
Medical Dir Dr R Matson; Dr B Westra.
Licensure Skilled care. Beds SNF 57. Certified Medicaid; Medicare.
Owner Proprietary corp (Beverly Enterprises).
Admissions Requirements Medical examination; Physician's request.
Staff RNs 1 (ft), 5 (pt); LPNs 2 (ft), 5 (pt); Nurses' aides 9 (ft), 15 (pt); Activities coordinators 1 (ft); Dietitians 1 (pt).
Facilities Dining room; Activities room; Laundry room; Barber/Beauty shop.
Activities Arts & crafts; Cards; Games; Reading groups; Prayer groups; Movies; Shopping trips; Dances/Social/Cultural gatherings.

Owatonna

Cedarview Nursing Home
1409 S Cedar St, Owatonna, MN 55060
(507) 451-7240
Admin Greg M Johnson. Dir of Nursing Toni Anderson RN. Medical Dir A J Olson MD.
Licensure Skilled care. Beds SNF 108. Certified Medicaid; Medicare.
Owner Publicly owned.
Admissions Requirements Minimum age 18; Medical examination; Physician's request.
Staff Physicians 1 (pt); RNs 2 (ft), 2 (pt); LPNs 2 (ft), 12 (pt); Nurses' aides 10 (ft), 50 (pt); Physical therapists 1 (pt); Reality therapists 1 (pt); Recreational therapists 1 (pt); Speech therapists 1 (pt); Activities coordinators 1 (ft); Dietitians 1 (ft); Ophthalmologists 1 (pt); Podiatrists 1 (pt); Dentists 1 (pt).

Facilities Dining room; Physical therapy
room; Activities room; Chapel; Crafts room;
Laundry room; Barber/Beauty shop; Library;
Lobbies.
Activities Arts & crafts; Cards; Games;
Reading groups; Prayer groups; Movies;
Shopping trips; Dances/Social/Cultural
gatherings; Bingo; Fishing trips; Outings;
Picnics.

Owatonna Health Care Center
201 SW 18th St, Owatonna, MN 55060
(507) 451-6800
Admin Linda Long.
Licensure Skilled care. *Beds* SNF 110.
Certified Medicaid; Medicare.
Owner Proprietary corp (Beverly Enterprises).

Rainbow Residence
285 Cedardale Dr, Owatonna, MN 55060
(507) 451-5327
Admin James Karkhoff.
Licensure Intermediate care for mentally
retarded. *Beds* ICF/MR 16.
Owner Proprietary corp.

Safe Harbor
250 E Main St, Owatonna, MN 55060
(507) 455-2444
Admin Kirsten Skoglund Rollwitz.
Licensure Supervised living. *Beds* Supervised
living 11.
Owner Proprietary corp.

West Hills Lodge
545 Florence Ave, Owatonna, MN 55060
(507) 451-1172
Admin W H Taylor.
Licensure Supervised living. *Beds* Supervised
living 15.
Owner Proprietary corp.

Woodvale VI
592 Adams St, Owatonna, MN 55060
(507) 451-1296
Admin Ross Jacobson.
Licensure Intermediate care for mentally
retarded. *Beds* ICF/MR 15.
Owner Proprietary corp.
Admissions Requirements Minimum age 18;
Medical examination; Physician's request.
Staff Psychologists; Resident supervisors 9
(ft), 7 (pt).
Facilities Laundry room.
Activities Arts & crafts; Cards; Games;
Movies; Shopping trips; Dances/Social/
Cultural gatherings.

Park Rapids

Heartland Home
PO Box 214, 609 W 7th St, Park Rapids, MN
56470
(218) 732-4572
Admin Raylene Kimball.
Licensure Intermediate care for mentally
retarded. *Beds* ICF/MR 8.
Owner Proprietary corp.

Sunset Nursing Home
W 6th St, Park Rapids, MN 56470
(218) 732-3329
Admin Jon Tibbetts.
Licensure Skilled care. *Beds* SNF 130.
Certified Medicaid; Medicare.
Owner Publicly owned.
Admissions Requirements Medical
examination; Physician's request.
Facilities Dining room; Physical therapy
room; Activities room; Chapel; Crafts room;
Laundry room; Barber/Beauty shop.
Activities Arts & crafts; Cards; Games;
Reading groups; Prayer groups; Movies;
Dances/Social/Cultural gatherings.

Parkers Prairie

St Williams Nursing Home
Soo St, Parkers Prairie, MN 56361
(218) 328-4671
Admin Cyrilla Bitzan.
Licensure Intermediate care; Supervised
living. *Beds* ICF 70; Supervised living 24.
Owner Proprietary corp.

Paynesville

Paynesville Community Hospital/Koronis Manor
200 1st St W, Paynesville, MN 56362
(612) 243-3767, 243-7519 FAX
Admin William LaCroix. *Dir of Nursing*
Beverly Mueller. *Medical Dir* R J Lindeman
MD.
Licensure Skilled care; Retirement. *Beds* SNF
64. *Certified* Medicaid; Medicare.
Owner Publicly owned.
Admissions Requirements Physician's request.
Staff RNs 2 (ft), 4 (pt); LPNs 6 (ft), 3 (pt);
Nurses' aides 19 (ft), 13 (pt); Physical
therapists 1 (ft); Occupational therapists 1
(pt); Activities coordinators 1 (ft); Dietitians
1 (pt).
Facilities Dining room; Physical therapy
room; Activities room; Chapel; Barber/
Beauty shop.
Activities Arts & crafts; Cards; Games;
Movies; Shopping trips.

Paynesville Good Samaritan Home
311 Washburn E Ave, Paynesville, MN 56362
(612) 243-7451
Admin Elizabeth Crusoe.
Medical Dir Sandra Christle.
Licensure Boarding care. *Beds* Boarding care
46.
Owner Nonprofit corp (Evangelical Lutheran/
Good Samaritan Society).
Admissions Requirements Minimum age 21;
Medical examination.
Staff RNs 1 (ft), 1 (pt); LPNs 4 (pt); Nurses'
aides 3 (ft), 9 (pt); Recreational therapists;
Activities coordinators 1 (ft); Dietitians 1
(pt).
Affiliation Lutheran.
Facilities Dining room; Activities room;
Chapel; Crafts room; Laundry room; 3
lounges.
Activities Arts & crafts; Cards; Games;
Reading groups; Prayer groups; Movies;
Shopping trips; Dances/Social/Cultural
gatherings; Discussion groups; Study groups;
Resident council.

Pelican Rapids

Good Samaritan Center
119 N Broadway, Pelican Rapids, MN 56572
(218) 863-2401
Admin Greg Hayek. *Dir of Nursing* Estelle
Dellaneva. *Medical Dir* Owen Thompson
MD.
Licensure Intermediate care. *Beds* ICF 70.
Private Pay Patients 35%. *Certified*
Medicaid.
Owner Nonprofit corp (Evangelical Lutheran/
Good Samaritan Society).
Admissions Requirements Medical
examination; Physician's request.
Staff RNs 1 (ft), 3 (pt); LPNs 5 (ft), 3 (pt);
Nurses' aides 24 (ft), 12 (pt); Physical
therapists 1 (pt); Recreational therapists 1
(ft), 1 (pt); Activities coordinators 1 (ft);
Dietitians 1 (pt).
Affiliation Lutheran.
Facilities Dining room; Activities room;
Chapel; Crafts room; Laundry room; Barber/
Beauty shop; Dayroom.
Activities Arts & crafts; Cards; Games;
Reading groups; Prayer groups; Movies;
Shopping trips; Dances/Social/Cultural
gatherings; Intergenerational programs.

Pelican Valley Health Center
211 E Mill, Pelican Rapids, MN 56572
(218) 863-3111
Admin Craig M Christianson. *Dir of Nursing*
Maria Stokka. *Medical Dir* Owen Thompson
MD.
Licensure Skilled care. *Beds* SNF 46. *Private
Pay Patients* 48%. *Certified* Medicaid;
Medicare.
Owner Publicly owned.
Admissions Requirements Medical
examination.
Staff RNs 8 (ft), 4 (pt); LPNs 6 (ft), 4 (pt);
Nurses' aides 15 (ft), 15 (pt); Activities
coordinators.
Languages Norwegian, Swedish.
Affiliation Lutheran.
Facilities Dining room; Physical therapy
room; Activities room; Chapel; Crafts room;
Laundry room; Barber/Beauty shop.
Activities Arts & crafts; Cards; Games;
Reading groups; Prayer groups; Movies;
Shopping trips; Dances/Social/Cultural
gatherings.

Perham

Perham Memorial Hospital & Home
665 3rd St SW, Perham, MN 56573
(218) 346-4500
Admin Rick Failing. *Dir of Nursing* Marilyn
Oelfke. *Medical Dir* Dr Jeff Blickenstaff.
Licensure Skilled care. *Beds* SNF 102.
Certified Medicaid; Medicare.
Owner Publicly owned.
Admissions Requirements Medical
examination; Physician's request.
Staff Physicians 5 (ft); RNs 2 (ft), 3 (pt);
LPNs 11 (ft), 7 (pt); Nurses' aides 30 (ft), 21
(pt); Physical therapists 1 (pt); Occupational
therapists 1 (ft); Activities coordinators 1
(ft); Dietitians 1 (pt).
Facilities Dining room; Physical therapy
room; Activities room; Chapel; Crafts room;
Laundry room; Barber/Beauty shop.
Activities Arts & crafts; Cards; Games;
Reading groups; Prayer groups; Movies.

Pierz

St Marys Villa Nursing Home
1st Ave S & Faust St, Pierz, MN 56364
(612) 468-6405
Admin James B Birchem. *Dir of Nursing*
Jeneva Bellefeuille. *Medical Dir* Dr Michael
Neudecker.
Licensure Skilled care; Intermediate care. *Beds*
Swing beds SNF/ICF 101. *Private Pay
Patients* 20%. *Certified* Medicaid; Medicare.
Owner Nonprofit corp.
Admissions Requirements Medical
examination; Physician's request.
Staff RNs 5 (ft), 2 (pt); LPNs 5 (ft), 8 (pt);
Nurses' aides 19 (ft), 28 (pt); Activities
coordinators 1 (ft).
Affiliation Roman Catholic.
Facilities Dining room; Physical therapy
room; Activities room; Chapel; Crafts room;
Barber/Beauty shop; Physician's clinic.
Activities Arts & crafts; Cards; Games;
Reading groups; Prayer groups; Movies;
Shopping trips; Dances/Social/Cultural
gatherings; Intergenerational programs.

Pine City

Lakeside Medical Center
129 E 6th St, Pine City, MN 55063
(612) 629-2542
Admin Mary Blaufuss.
Medical Dir R F Mach MD.
Licensure Skilled care; Intermediate care. *Beds*
SNF 93; ICF 32. *Certified* Medicaid;
Medicare.
Owner Proprietary corp.

Admissions Requirements Minimum age 16; Medical examination.
Staff RNs 2 (ft), 4 (pt); LPNs 3 (ft), 9 (pt); Nurses' aides 17 (ft), 40 (pt); Physical therapists 1 (ft); Recreational therapists 1 (ft); Dietitians 1 (ft).
Facilities Dining room; Physical therapy room; Activities room; Chapel; Crafts room; Laundry room; Barber/Beauty shop.
Activities Arts & crafts; Reading groups; Movies; Dances/Social/Cultural gatherings; Reality orientation & remotivation.

Manor Inc
Rte 2, Pine City, MN 55063
(612) 629-6769
Admin James Anderson.
Licensure Supervised living. *Beds* Supervised living 30.
Owner Proprietary corp.

Pine Island

Pine Haven Care Center Inc
PO Box 768, 210 NW 3rd St, Pine Island, MN 55963
(507) 356-8304
Admin Sharon Brenny. *Dir of Nursing* JoAnne Judge-Dietz. *Medical Dir* Dr Allan Clark.
Licensure Skilled care. *Beds* SNF 74. *Private Pay Patients* 47%. *Certified* Medicaid; Medicare.
Owner Nonprofit corp.
Admissions Requirements Physician's request.
Staff RNs 1 (ft), 4 (pt); LPNs 2 (ft), 7 (pt); Nurses' aides 12 (ft), 30 (pt); Physical therapists; Activities coordinators 1 (ft); Dietitians.
Facilities Dining room; Physical therapy room; Activities room; Crafts room; Laundry room; Barber/Beauty shop.
Activities Arts & crafts; Cards; Games; Reading groups; Prayer groups; Movies; Shopping trips; Dances/Social/Cultural gatherings; Intergenerational programs; Pet therapy; Cooking; Exercises.

Pine River

Pine River Group Home
PO Box 96, Pine River, MN 56474
(218) 587-4888
Admin Bruce Winder.
Licensure Intermediate care for mentally retarded. *Beds* ICF/MR 11. *Certified* Medicaid.
Owner Proprietary corp.

Whispering Pines Good Samaritan Center
PO Box 29, Jefferson Ave & 4th St, Pine River, MN 56474
(218) 587-4423, 587-2671 FAX
Admin Jim Wolf. *Dir of Nursing* Judy Goldberg RN. *Medical Dir* Dr C R Pelzl.
Licensure Skilled care; Alzheimer's care. *Beds* SNF 113. *Private Pay Patients* 31%. *Certified* Medicaid; Medicare.
Owner Nonprofit corp (Evangelical Lutheran/ Good Samaritan Society).
Admissions Requirements Medical examination; Physician's request.
Staff Physicians (consultant); RNs 4 (ft), 8 (pt); LPNs 10 (ft), 5 (pt); Nurses' aides 40 (ft), 35 (pt); Physical therapists 1 (pt); Activities coordinators 1 (ft); Dietitians 1 (pt).
Languages Norwegian, Swedish.
Affiliation Lutheran.
Facilities Dining room; Physical therapy room; Activities room; Chapel; Crafts room; Laundry room; Barber/Beauty shop; Library.
Activities Arts & crafts; Cards; Games; Reading groups; Prayer groups; Movies; Shopping trips; Dances/Social/Cultural gatherings; Intergenerational programs; Pet therapy.

Pipestone

Good Samaritan Village
Rte 1, N Hiawatha, Pipestone, MN 56164
(507) 825-5428
Admin Bruce A Stratman. *Dir of Nursing* Karen Amdahl.
Licensure Intermediate care; Boarding care. *Beds* ICF 96; Boarding care 30.
Owner Nonprofit corp (Evangelical Lutheran/ Good Samaritan Society).
Admissions Requirements Medical examination.
Staff RNs; LPNs; Nurses' aides; Physical therapists; Occupational therapists; Activities coordinators; Dietitians; Chaplains; Art therapists; Music therapists.
Affiliation Lutheran.
Facilities Dining room; Physical therapy room; Activities room; Chapel; Crafts room; Laundry room; Barber/Beauty shop; Library; Covered patio; Art therapy room.
Activities Arts & crafts; Cards; Games; Reading groups; Prayer groups; Movies; Shopping trips; Dances/Social/Cultural gatherings; Art therapy; Music therapy; Exercise group; Van rides; Fishing; Birthday dinners.

Hiawatha Manor
107 5th Ave NE, Pipestone, MN 56164
(507) 825-5697
Admin Eldona Hillard, acting.
Medical Dir Ruth Kluis.
Licensure Intermediate care for mentally retarded. *Beds* ICF/MR 10.
Owner Proprietary corp.
Admissions Requirements Minimum age 18.
Staff RNs 1 (pt); Nurses' aides 9 (pt).
Facilities Dining room; Activities room; Laundry room.
Activities Arts & crafts; Cards; Games; Reading groups; Prayer groups; Movies; Shopping trips; Dances/Social/Cultural gatherings.

Pipestone County Medical Center
PO Box 370, 911 5th Ave SW, Pipestone, MN 56164
(507) 825-5811
Admin Allan J Christensen.
Medical Dir Dr R W Keyes.
Licensure Skilled care. *Beds* SNF 43. *Certified* Medicaid; Medicare.
Owner Publicly owned.
Admissions Requirements Medical examination.
Staff Physicians 9 (pt); RNs 2 (ft), 5 (pt); LPNs 2 (ft); Nurses' aides 7 (ft), 15 (pt); Physical therapists 1 (pt); Activities coordinators 1 (ft); Dietitians 1 (pt).
Facilities Dining room; Physical therapy room; Activities room; Chapel; Barber/ Beauty shop.
Activities Arts & crafts; Cards; Games; Movies; Dances/Social/Cultural gatherings.

Plainview

Hillcrest Nursing & Retirement Home
800 2nd Ave NW, Plainview, MN 55964
(507) 534-3191
Admin James W Pederson.
Medical Dir Kathy Martig.
Licensure Skilled care. *Beds* SNF 71. *Certified* Medicaid; Medicare.
Owner Publicly owned.
Admissions Requirements Minimum age 16; Medical examination; Physician's request.
Staff RNs 4 (ft), 4 (pt); LPNs 5 (ft), 4 (pt); Nurses' aides 20 (ft), 26 (pt); Activities coordinators 1 (ft), 2 (pt).
Facilities Dining room; Physical therapy room; Activities room; Chapel; Laundry room; Barber/Beauty shop.

Activities Arts & crafts; Cards; Games; Reading groups; Prayer groups; Movies; Shopping trips; Trips.

Plymouth

Hazelden Pioneer House
11505 36th Ave N, Plymouth, MN 55441
(612) 559-2022
Admin Harold Swift.
Licensure Supervised living. *Beds* Supervised living 67.
Owner Nonprofit corp.
Admissions Requirements Minimum age 14; Medical examination.
Facilities Dining room; Activities room; Laundry room; Library.
Activities Games; Movies; Dances/Social/ Cultural gatherings.

Journey House
18135 13th Ave N, Plymouth, MN 55442
(612) 476-6410
Admin Rachel L Feldman.
Licensure Supervised living. *Beds* Supervised living 6.
Owner Proprietary corp.

Anthony Louis Treatment Center
115 Forestview Ln, Plymouth, MN 55441
(612) 546-8008
Admin Jon D Benson.
Medical Dir Shar Benson.
Licensure Supervised living; Retirement. *Beds* Supervised living 15.
Owner Proprietary corp.
Admissions Requirements Minimum age 12.
Staff Physicians 1 (pt); RNs 1 (ft); Nurses' aides 6 (ft); Reality therapists 4 (ft); Recreational therapists 1 (ft); Dietitians 2 (ft).
Facilities Dining room; Activities room; Laundry room; Library.
Activities Games; YMCA/Softball; Football.

Mission Care Detox Center
3409 E Medicine Lake Blvd, Plymouth, MN 55441
(612) 559-1402
Admin Pat Murphy.
Licensure Supervised living. *Beds* Supervised living 22.
Owner Proprietary corp.

Mission Farms Nursing Home
3401 Medicine Lake Blvd, Plymouth, MN 55441
(612) 559-3123
Admin James M Pearson. *Dir of Nursing* Sandra Kaske RN. *Medical Dir* M M Millis MD.
Licensure Intermediate care; Boarding care. *Beds* ICF 72; Boarding care 32.
Owner Nonprofit corp.
Admissions Requirements Males only; Medical examination.
Staff RNs 3 (ft); LPNs 5 (ft), 2 (pt); Nurses' aides 14 (ft), 13 (pt); Recreational therapists 2 (ft), 1 (pt); Activities coordinators 1 (ft); Dietitians 1 (pt).
Languages Korean.
Facilities Dining room; Activities room; Chapel; Crafts room; Library.
Activities Arts & crafts; Cards; Games; Prayer groups; Movies; Shopping trips; Dances/ Social/Cultural gatherings; Special tours; Bowling; Pool; Circus; Ball games; Special music programs; Church services.

Outreach Plymouth Home East
11550 52nd Ave N, Plymouth, MN 55442
(612) 559-3015
Admin Eileen Harris.
Licensure Intermediate care for mentally retarded. *Beds* ICF/MR 6.
Owner Proprietary corp.

Outreach Plymouth Home West
2735 Olive Ln N, Plymouth, MN 55447
(612) 473-7182
Admin Eileen Harris.
Licensure Intermediate care for mentally retarded. *Beds* ICF/MR 6. *Certified* Medicaid; Medicare.
Owner Nonprofit corp.
Admissions Requirements Minimum age 21.
Staff RNs 1 (pt).
Facilities Dining room; Activities room; Laundry room.
Activities Arts & crafts; Cards; Games; Prayer groups; Movies; Shopping trips; Dances/ Social/Cultural gatherings; Golf; Swimming.

Preston

Fillmore Place
110 Fillmore Pl SE, Preston, MN 55965
(507) 765-3848
Admin LuWayne Ommen.
Medical Dir Betty Johnson.
Licensure Intermediate care for mentally retarded. *Beds* ICF/MR 16.
Owner Nonprofit corp.
Admissions Requirements Minimum age 16; Medical examination.
Staff Physicians 1 (pt); RNs 1 (ft); LPNs 3 (pt); Physical therapists 1 (pt); Speech therapists 1 (pt); Dietitians 1 (pt).
Facilities Activities room; Laundry room; 3 apartments.
Activities Arts & crafts; Cards; Games; Movies; Shopping trips; Dances/Social/ Cultural gatherings.

Preston Care Center
608 Winona St, Preston, MN 55965
(507) 765-3837
Admin James Framstad. *Dir of Nursing* Dianne Schmidt. *Medical Dir* Dr John Nehring.
Licensure Skilled care. *Beds* SNF 79. *Certified* Medicaid; Medicare; VA.
Owner Proprietary corp (Good Neighbor Services).
Admissions Requirements Medical examination.
Staff RNs 2 (ft), 2 (pt); LPNs 7 (ft), 2 (pt); Nurses' aides 23 (ft), 15 (pt); Physical therapists 1 (pt); Recreational therapists 1 (ft); Activities coordinators 1 (ft); Dietitians 1 (ft), 1 (pt).
Facilities Dining room; Physical therapy room; Activities room; Laundry room; Barber/Beauty shop.
Activities Arts & crafts; Cards; Games; Reading groups; Prayer groups; Movies; Shopping trips; Dances/Social/Cultural gatherings; Woodcrafts; Dining out; Picnics.

Princeton

Elim Home
101 7th Ave S, Princeton, MN 55371
(612) 389-1171
Admin Linda Letich, acting. *Dir of Nursing* Mark Thyen. *Medical Dir* Mike Metcalf MD.
Licensure Skilled care; Retirement. *Beds* SNF 140. *Certified* Medicaid; Medicare.
Owner Nonprofit organization/foundation.
Admissions Requirements Minimum age 16; Medical examination; Physician's request.
Staff RNs 2 (ft), 6 (pt); LPNs 4 (ft), 8 (pt); Nurses' aides 20 (ft), 40 (pt); Physical therapists 1 (pt); Recreational therapists 2 (ft), 1 (pt); Occupational therapists 1 (pt); Speech therapists 1 (pt); Activities coordinators 1 (ft); Dietitians 1 (ft); Ophthalmologists 1 (pt); Podiatrists 1 (pt); Chaplains 1 (pt).
Affiliation Evangelical Free Church.
Facilities Dining room; Physical therapy room; Activities room; Chapel; Crafts room; Laundry room; Barber/Beauty shop.
Activities Arts & crafts; Cards; Games; Reading groups; Prayer groups; Movies; Shopping trips; Dances/Social/Cultural gatherings.

Sahara House
407 LaGrande Ave S, Princeton, MN 55371
(612) 389-5703
Admin Jerry A Johnson.
Licensure Supervised living. *Beds* Supervised living 13.
Owner Nonprofit corp.
Admissions Requirements Minimum age 15; Males only; Medical examination; Physician's request.
Staff Reality therapists 3 (ft); Recreational therapists 1 (ft); Dietitians 2 (ft).
Facilities Dining room; Activities room; Laundry room.
Activities Cards; Games; Reading groups; Prayer groups; Movies; Shopping trips; Dances/Social/Cultural gatherings; AA/NA meetings.

Red Lake Falls

Hillcrest Nursing Home
PO Box 459, 311 Broadway Ave, Red Lake Falls, MN 56750
(218) 253-2157
Admin Janet Thompson. *Dir of Nursing* Sandra Boice.
Licensure Intermediate care. *Beds* ICF 74. *Private Pay Patients* 35-40%. *Certified* Medicaid.
Owner Nonprofit corp (Riverview Healthcare Association).
Admissions Requirements Medical examination; Physician's request.
Staff Physicians; RNs; LPNs; Nurses' aides; Physical therapists (consultant); Occupational therapists (consultant); Activities coordinators 1 (ft); Dietitians (consultant).
Facilities Dining room; Activities room; Chapel; Crafts room; Laundry room; Barber/ Beauty shop.
Activities Arts & crafts; Cards; Games; Reading groups; Prayer groups; Movies; Shopping trips; Dances/Social/Cultural gatherings.

Red Wing

Haven Health Center
213 Pioneer Rd, Red Wing, MN 55066
(612) 388-4752
Admin John Boughton.
Medical Dir Tom Witt MD.
Licensure Skilled care; Retirement. *Beds* SNF 85. *Certified* Medicaid; Medicare.
Owner Proprietary corp.
Admissions Requirements Minimum age 18; Medical examination.
Staff RNs 2 (ft), 2 (pt); LPNs 4 (ft), 7 (pt); Nurses' aides 12 (ft), 15 (pt); Physical therapists 1 (pt); Recreational therapists 1 (pt); Occupational therapists 1 (pt); Speech therapists 1 (pt); Activities coordinators 1 (ft); Dietitians 1 (pt).
Facilities Dining room; Physical therapy room; Activities room; Laundry room; Barber/Beauty shop.
Activities Arts & crafts; Cards; Games; Reading groups; Prayer groups; Movies; Shopping trips.

Red Wing Group Home
4911 W Hwy 61, Red Wing, MN 55066
(612) 388-9446
Admin Roy A Harley.
Licensure Intermediate care for mentally retarded. *Beds* ICF/MR 12.
Owner Proprietary corp.
Admissions Requirements Minimum age 16.
Staff Nurses' aides 12 (pt); Speech therapists 1 (pt).

Affiliation Lutheran.
Facilities Laundry room.
Activities Arts & crafts; Cards; Games; Movies; Shopping trips; Dances/Social/ Cultural gatherings; Special Olympics.

Red Wing Health Center
1400 W 4th St, Red Wing, MN 55066
(612) 388-2843
Admin Donna Van Loon.
Medical Dir Dr Charles Roth.
Licensure Skilled care; Intermediate care. *Beds* SNF 186; ICF 29. *Certified* Medicaid; Medicare.
Owner Proprietary corp.
Staff Physicians 10 (pt); RNs 5 (ft), 7 (pt); LPNs 10 (ft), 11 (pt); Nurses' aides 44 (ft), 86 (pt); Physical therapists 1 (ft); Occupational therapists 2 (ft), 3 (pt); Speech therapists 2 (ft), 2 (pt); Activities coordinators 1 (ft); Dietitians 1 (pt); Recreational staff 7 (ft).
Facilities Dining room; Physical therapy room; Activities room; Chapel; Crafts room; Laundry room; Barber/Beauty shop; Library; Child day care.
Activities Arts & crafts; Cards; Games; Reading groups; Prayer groups; Movies; Shopping trips; Dances/Social/Cultural gatherings; Adopt-a-grandparent.

REM—Park Heights
2606 Malmquist Ave, Red Wing, MN 55066
(612) 388-7158
Admin Douglas Miller.
Licensure Intermediate care for mentally retarded. *Beds* ICF/MR 16.
Owner Proprietary corp.

REM—Red Wing Inc
Box 62, 807 3rd St, Red Wing, MN 55066
(612) 388-5275
Admin Thomas Miller.
Licensure Intermediate care for mentally retarded. *Beds* ICF/MR 14.
Owner Proprietary corp.

Seminary Memorial Home
906 College Ave, Red Wing, MN 55066
(612) 388-1591
Admin Kyle Nordine. *Dir of Nursing* Judy Barfiend RN. *Medical Dir* Dr D R Bruns.
Licensure Skilled care; Retirement. *Beds* SNF 112.
Owner Proprietary corp.
Admissions Requirements Minimum age 16.
Staff RNs 4 (ft), 8 (pt); LPNs 11 (ft), 6 (pt); Nurses' aides 12 (ft), 33 (pt); Recreational therapists; Activities coordinators 1 (ft); Dietitians 1 (ft).
Affiliation Lutheran.
Facilities Dining room; Physical therapy room; Activities room; Chapel; Crafts room; Barber/Beauty shop; Library.
Activities Arts & crafts; Cards; Games; Reading groups; Prayer groups; Movies; Shopping trips; Dances/Social/Cultural gatherings.

Redwood Falls

REM Redwood Falls Inc A&B
PO Box 506, Redwood Falls, MN 56283
(507) 637-3541
Admin Dr Robert Miller.
Licensure Intermediate care for mentally retarded. *Beds* ICF/MR 132.
Owner Proprietary corp.
Admissions Requirements Minimum age 18.
Staff RNs; LPNs; Physical therapists; Physical therapists; Recreational therapists; Dietitians; Podiatrists.
Facilities Dining room; Laundry room; Barber/Beauty shop.
Activities Arts & crafts; Cards; Games; Movies; Shopping trips; Dances/Social/ Cultural gatherings.

Sunwood Care Center
200 S DeKalb St, Redwood Falls, MN 56283
(507) 637-5711
Admin Vernon Junker. *Dir of Nursing* Connie
Heffelfinger. *Medical Dir* Dr Dennis Nelson.
Licensure Skilled care. *Beds* SNF 92. *Private
Pay Patients* 30%. *Certified* Medicaid;
Medicare.
Owner Proprietary corp (Good Neighbor
Services).
Admissions Requirements Minimum age 16;
Medical examination; Physician's request.
Staff RNs; LPNs; Nurses' aides; Physical
therapists; Recreational therapists; Speech
therapists; Activities coordinators; Dietitians.
Facilities Dining room; Physical therapy
room; Activities room; Chapel; Crafts room;
Laundry room; Barber/Beauty shop.
Activities Arts & crafts; Cards; Games;
Reading groups; Prayer groups; Movies;
Shopping trips; Dances/Social/Cultural
gatherings.

Wood-Dale Home Inc
600 Sunrise Blvd, Redwood Falls, MN 56283
(507) 637-3587
Admin Alma J Little. *Dir of Nursing* Christy
Melzer RN. *Medical Dir* J B Flinn MD.
Licensure Skilled care. *Beds* SNF 60. *Certified*
Medicaid; Medicare.
Owner Proprietary corp.
Staff Physicians 5 (pt); RNs 2 (ft), 5 (pt);
LPNs 3 (ft), 5 (pt); Nurses' aides 12 (ft), 18
(pt); Physical therapists 1 (pt); Reality
therapists 1 (pt); Recreational therapists 1
(pt); Occupational therapists 1 (pt); Speech
therapists 1 (pt); Activities coordinators 2
(ft); Dietitians 1 (pt); Ophthalmologists 1
(pt); Podiatrists 1 (pt); Dentists 1 (pt).
Facilities Dining room; Physical therapy
room; Activities room; Crafts room; Laundry
room; Barber/Beauty shop.
Activities Arts & crafts; Cards; Games;
Reading groups; Prayer groups; Movies;
Shopping trips; Dances/Social/Cultural
gatherings; Seasonal sight-seeing trips.

Renville

Ren-Villa Nursing Home
205 SE Elm, Renville, MN 56284
(612) 329-8381
Admin Craig Doughty. *Dir of Nursing* Barbara
Forslund. *Medical Dir* Dr Mark Alquist.
Licensure Intermediate care. *Beds* ICF 76.
Private Pay Patients 50%. *Certified*
Medicaid.
Owner Publicly owned.
Admissions Requirements Medical
examination.
Staff RNs 2 (ft); LPNs 2 (ft), 9 (pt); Nurses'
aides 6 (ft), 35 (pt); Physical therapists
(consultant); Activities coordinators 1 (ft);
Dietitians (consultant).
Facilities Dining room; Physical therapy
room; Activities room; Crafts room; Laundry
room; Library; Resident's park.
Activities Arts & crafts; Cards; Games;
Reading groups; Prayer groups; Movies;
Shopping trips; Dances/Social/Cultural
gatherings; Intergenerational programs; Pet
therapy.

Revere

Revere Home
202 S Main, Revere, MN 56166
(507) 752-7182
Admin R David Reynolds.
Medical Dir Bev MaKarrall.
Licensure Boarding care. *Beds* Boarding care
22.
Owner Proprietary corp.
Admissions Requirements Minimum age 18.
Staff Nurses' aides; Activities coordinators;
Dietitians.

Facilities Dining room; Activities room;
Laundry room; Barber/Beauty shop.
Activities Arts & crafts; Cards; Games;
Reading groups; Movies; Shopping trips;
Bingo; Sight-seeing trips.

Richfield

Cotter Residence
6312 Portland Ave S, Richfield, MN 55423
(612) 861-3456
Admin Roberta Miller Rosenow.
Licensure Supervised living. *Beds* Supervised
living 6.
Owner Proprietary corp.

Four Seasons Care Center—Richfield
7727 Portland Ave S, Richfield, MN 55423
(612) 861-1691
Admin Robert R Hampton.
Medical Dir John Lamey MD.
Licensure Skilled care; Intermediate care. *Beds*
SNF 126; ICF 49. *Certified* Medicaid;
Medicare.
Owner Proprietary corp.
Admissions Requirements Medical
examination; Physician's request.
Staff RNs 8 (ft), 5 (pt); LPNs 6 (ft), 6 (pt);
Nurses' aides 36 (ft), 36 (pt); Physical
therapists 1 (ft); Occupational therapists 1
(ft); Speech therapists 1 (pt); Activities
coordinators 1 (ft); Dietitians 1 (pt);
Audiologists 1 (pt).
Facilities Dining room; Physical therapy
room; Activities room; Chapel; Crafts room;
Laundry room; Barber/Beauty shop.
Activities Arts & crafts; Cards; Games;
Reading groups; Prayer groups; Movies;
Shopping trips; Dances/Social/Cultural
gatherings; Sight-seeing outings.

Progress Valley II
308 E 78th St, Richfield, MN 55423
(612) 869-3223
Admin Mary Thorpe-Mease.
Licensure Supervised living. *Beds* ICF/MR
Supervised living 24.
Owner Proprietary corp.

Richfield Outreach Group Home
7425 4th Ave S, Richfield, MN 55423
(612) 866-2035
Admin Eileen Harris.
Licensure Intermediate care for mentally
retarded. *Beds* ICF/MR 6.
Owner Proprietary corp.

Richville

Shelton Group Home
Rte 1, Richville, MN 56576
(218) 758-2438
Admin Carol Shelton.
Licensure Intermediate care for mentally
retarded. *Beds* ICF/MR 8. *Certified*
Medicaid.
Owner Privately owned.

Robbinsdale

Crystal Lake Health Care Center
3815 W Broadway, Robbinsdale, MN 55422
(612) 588-4635
Admin Pam Guyer. *Dir of Nursing* Andrea
Sadowski. *Medical Dir* Dr Kephart.
Licensure Skilled care. *Beds* SNF 166.
Certified Medicaid; Medicare.
Owner Proprietary corp (Good Neighbor
Services).
Admissions Requirements Medical
examination; Physician's request.
Staff Physicians; RNs; LPNs; Nurses' aides;
Physical therapists; Reality therapists;
Recreational therapists; Occupational
therapists; Speech therapists; Activities
coordinators; Dietitians; Ophthalmologists;
Podiatrists; Dentists.

Facilities Dining room; Physical therapy
room; Activities room; Crafts room; Laundry
room; Barber/Beauty shop; Occupational
therapy room.
Activities Arts & crafts; Cards; Games;
Reading groups; Prayer groups; Movies;
Shopping trips; Dances/Social/Cultural
gatherings.

Erinkay Dungarvin XIII
3349 Chowen Ave N, Robbinsdale, MN 55422
(612) 529-7480
Admin Diane Madden.
Licensure Intermediate care for mentally
retarded. *Beds* ICF/MR 6.
Owner Proprietary corp.

Residential Alternatives IV
2759 France Ave N, Robbinsdale, MN 55422
(612) 521-0387
Admin Peter Jacobson.
Licensure Intermediate care for mentally
retarded. *Beds* ICF/MR 6.
Owner Proprietary corp.

Residential Alternatives VIII
3801 W Broadway, Robbinsdale, MN 55422
(612) 522-6363, 522-7556
Admin Peter Jacobson.
Licensure Intermediate care for mentally
retarded. *Beds* ICF/MR 9.
Owner Proprietary corp.
Admissions Requirements Minimum age 18;
Medical examination.
Staff LPNs 1 (pt); Dietitians 1 (pt).
Facilities Laundry room; 3 Separate apts-3
residents per apt.
Activities Routine social & domestic program.

Residential Alternatives IX
3807 W Broadway, Robbinsdale, MN 55422
(612) 521-9568
Admin Peter Jacobson.
Licensure Intermediate care for mentally
retarded. *Beds* ICF/MR 9.
Owner Proprietary corp.

Trevilla of Robbinsdale
3130 Grimes Ave N, Robbinsdale, MN 55422
(612) 588-0771, 588-2349 FAX
Admin Mark S Linz. *Dir of Nursing* Adeline
Stanoch. *Medical Dir* R Batemen MD.
Licensure Skilled care; Intermediate care for
mentally retarded. *Beds* SNF 132; ICF/MR
32. *Private Pay Patients* 5%. *Certified*
Medicaid; Medicare.
Owner Proprietary corp (Unicare).
Admissions Requirements Minimum age 18;
Medical examination; Physician's request.
Staff RNs 13 (ft), 6 (pt); LPNs 16 (ft), 5 (pt);
Nurses' aides 50 (ft), 30 (pt); Physical
therapists 1 (ft); Recreational therapists 8
(ft); Occupational therapists 1 (ft); Speech
therapists 1 (ft), 1 (pt); Dietitians 1 (pt).
Facilities Dining room; Physical therapy
room; Activities room; Crafts room; Barber/
Beauty shop; Library; Closed head injury
unit.
Activities Arts & crafts; Cards; Games;
Reading groups; Prayer groups; Movies;
Shopping trips; Dances/Social/Cultural
gatherings; Pet therapy; Ceramics; Camping.

Rochester

Bear Creek House
812 10th Ave SE, Rochester, MN 55904
(507) 288-0531
Admin Diane Sellner, acting.
Licensure Intermediate care for mentally
retarded. *Beds* ICF/MR 6.
Owner Proprietary corp.

Bethany Samaritan Heights
1530 11th Ave NW, Rochester, MN 55901
(507) 289-3336
Admin L E Bliese, acting.
Medical Dir Eric Tangelos; Diane Russell.

Licensure Skilled care; Retirement. *Beds* SNF 120. *Certified* Medicaid; Medicare.
Owner Nonprofit organization/foundation.
Admissions Requirements Minimum age 18.
Staff RNs 6 (ft), 3 (pt); LPNs 12 (ft), 6 (pt); Nurses' aides 24 (ft), 13 (pt); Activities coordinators 1 (ft).
Affiliation Lutheran.
Facilities Dining room; Physical therapy room; Activities room; Chapel; Laundry room; Barber/Beauty shop.
Activities Arts & crafts; Cards; Games; Reading groups; Prayer groups; Movies; Shopping trips; Dances/Social/Cultural gatherings.

Charter House Health Center
211 NW 2nd St, Rochester, MN 55901
(507) 286-8572
Admin Richard C Edwards.
Licensure Skilled care. *Beds* SNF 64. *Certified* Medicare.
Owner Nonprofit organization/foundation.

Crisis Receiving Unit
Box 1116, 2116 SE Campus Dr, Rochester, MN 55904
(507) 288-8750
Admin Robert Zabel.
Licensure Supervised living. *Beds* Supervised living 24.
Owner Proprietary corp.

Gables
604 5th St SW, Rochester, MN 55902
(507) 282-2500
Admin I Mary Keyes.
Licensure Supervised living. *Beds* Supervised living 30.
Owner Proprietary corp.

Guest House
PO Box 954, Rochester, MN 55901
(507) 288-4693
Admin Richard Frisch ACSW CCDP.
Medical Dir Russell F Smith MD CAC.
Licensure Supervised living. *Beds* Supervised living 43.
Owner Proprietary corp.
Staff Physicians 1 (ft); RNs 1 (ft); Physical therapists; Recreational therapists; Activities coordinators 1 (ft); Dietitians; Dentists.

Hiawatha Adult Home
2020 5th St SW, Rochester, MN 55902
(507) 289-7722
Admin Douglas Butler.
Licensure Intermediate care for mentally retarded. *Beds* ICF/MR 22.
Owner Proprietary corp.

Hiawatha Childrens Home
1820 Valkyrie Dr NW, Rochester, MN 55901
(507) 289-7222
Admin Douglas H Butler.
Licensure Intermediate care for mentally retarded. *Beds* ICF/MR 44.
Owner Proprietary corp.

Madonna Towers Inc
4001 19th Ave NW, Rochester, MN 55901
(507) 288-3911, 288-2494 FAX
Admin Alice J McHale. *Dir of Nursing* Ardell Murray. *Medical Dir* Guy Daugherty MD.
Licensure Skilled care; Retirement. *Beds* SNF 62; Retirement 140. *Private Pay Patients* 82%. *Certified* Medicaid; Medicare.
Owner Nonprofit corp (Missionary Oblates of Mary Immaculate).
Admissions Requirements Minimum age 62; Medical examination.
Staff Physicians 1 (pt); RNs 1 (ft), 9 (pt); LPNs 3 (ft), 6 (pt); Nurses' aides 8 (ft), 32 (pt); Activities coordinators 2 (ft).
Affiliation Roman Catholic.
Facilities Dining room; Activities room; Chapel; Crafts room; Laundry room; Barber/ Beauty shop; Library.

Activities Arts & crafts; Cards; Games; Reading groups; Prayer groups; Movies; Shopping trips; Dances/Social/Cultural gatherings.

Maple Manor Nursing Home
1875 19th St NW, Rochester, MN 55901
(507) 282-9449
Admin Patrick Blum.
Medical Dir Donna Manbeck.
Licensure Skilled care; Boarding care. *Beds* SNF 100; Boarding care 9. *Certified* Medicaid; Medicare.
Owner Proprietary corp.
Admissions Requirements Minimum age 16; Medical examination; Physician's request.
Staff RNs 4 (ft); LPNs 12 (ft); Nurses' aides 47 (ft); Physical therapists 1 (ft), 1 (pt); Activities coordinators 3 (ft); Dietitians 13 (ft).
Facilities Dining room; Physical therapy room; Activities room; Chapel; Crafts room; Laundry room; Barber/Beauty shop.
Activities Arts & crafts; Games; Prayer groups; Movies; Shopping trips; Dances/Social/ Cultural gatherings.

Meadow Park House
1605 8th Ave SE, Rochester, MN 55904
(507) 288-3893
Admin Diane Sellner, acting.
Licensure Intermediate care for mentally retarded. *Beds* ICF/MR 6.
Owner Proprietary corp.

Quarry Hill Treatment Program
2116 Campus Dr SE, Rochester, MN 55904
(507) 285-7050
Admin Barbara Peterson.
Licensure Supervised living. *Beds* Supervised living 22.
Owner Publicly owned.

REM Rochester Northwest
2509 55th St NW, Rochester, MN 55901
(507) 281-1105
Admin Thomas Miller.
Medical Dir Jack Priggen.
Licensure Intermediate care for mentally retarded. *Beds* ICF/MR 15.
Owner Proprietary corp.
Admissions Requirements Minimum age 16; Medical examination.
Staff RNs 1 (pt); Nurses' aides 10 (ft), 10 (pt); Activities coordinators 1 (pt); Dietitians.
Facilities Dining room; Activities room; Laundry room; 10 apartments.
Activities Arts & crafts; Cards; Games; Reading groups; Movies; Shopping trips; Dances/Social/Cultural gatherings.

REM Rochester Southeast
1631 19th Ave SE, Rochester, MN 55904
(507) 289-2696
Admin Tom Miller.
Licensure Intermediate care for mentally retarded. *Beds* ICF/MR 15.
Owner Proprietary corp.

REM Willow Creek A
1621 10th St SE, Rochester, MN 55904
(507) 281-4939
Admin Tom Miller.
Licensure Intermediate care for mentally retarded. *Beds* ICF/MR 15.
Owner Proprietary corp.

REM Willow Creek B
2206 11th Ave SE, Rochester, MN 55904
(507) 281-1148
Admin Tom Miller.
Licensure Intermediate care for mentally retarded. *Beds* ICF/MR 15.
Owner Proprietary corp.

Rochester Healthcare Center
2215 Hwy 52 N, Rochester, MN 55901
(507) 288-1818, 288-5502 FAX

Admin Joseph G Gubbels. *Dir of Nursing* Deb Miller. *Medical Dir* Dr Victoria Beckett.
Licensure Skilled care. *Beds* SNF 68. *Private Pay Patients* 20%. *Certified* Medicaid; Medicare.
Owner Proprietary corp (Beverly Enterprises).
Admissions Requirements Minimum age 18; Physician's request.
Staff Physicians 1 (pt); RNs 3 (ft), 2 (pt); LPNs 4 (ft), 2 (pt); Nurses' aides 20 (ft), 7 (pt); Physical therapists 1 (pt); Occupational therapists 1 (pt); Speech therapists 1 (pt); Activities coordinators 1 (ft), 1 (pt); Dietitians 1 (pt); Ophthalmologists 1 (pt); Podiatrists 1 (pt).
Facilities Dining room; Physical therapy room; Activities room; Laundry room; Barber/Beauty shop.
Activities Arts & crafts; Cards; Games; Reading groups; Prayer groups; Movies; Shopping trips; Dances/Social/Cultural gatherings; Intergenerational programs; Pet therapy.

Samaritan Bethany Home
PO Box 5947, 24 8th St NW, Rochester, MN 55903
(507) 289-4031, 289-6001 FAX
Admin John Boughton. *Dir of Nursing* Donna Bond. *Medical Dir* Peter Cross MD.
Licensure Skilled care; Alzheimer's care. *Beds* SNF 122. *Private Pay Patients* 44%. *Certified* Medicaid; Medicare.
Owner Nonprofit organization/foundation.
Admissions Requirements Minimum age 16; Medical examination; Physician's request.
Staff RNs; LPNs; Nurses' aides; Physical therapists; Occupational therapists; Speech therapists; Activities coordinators; Dietitians.
Facilities Dining room; Physical therapy room; Activities room; Chapel; Crafts room; Barber/Beauty shop.
Activities Arts & crafts; Cards; Games; Reading groups; Prayer groups; Movies; Shopping trips; Dances/Social/Cultural gatherings; Intergenerational programs.

Sixth Street House
805 6th St SE, Rochester, MN 55904
(507) 288-4138
Admin Diane Sellner, acting.
Licensure Intermediate care for mentally retarded. *Beds* ICF/MR 6.
Owner Proprietary corp.

Southside House
1416 4th St SE, Rochester, MN 55904
(507) 281-2523
Admin Diane Sellner, acting.
Licensure Intermediate care for mentally retarded. *Beds* ICF/MR 6.
Owner Nonprofit organization/foundation.
Admissions Requirements Minimum age 45; Medical examination.
Staff RNs 1 (ft); LPNs 2 (pt); Resident counselors 5 (ft), 2 (pt).
Languages Sign.
Facilities Dining room; Activities room; Laundry room.
Activities Arts & crafts; Movies; Shopping trips; Dances/Social/Cultural gatherings.

Woodside Convalescent Center
501 8th Ave SE, Rochester, MN 55904
(507) 288-6514
Admin Richard D Beadling.
Licensure Skilled care. *Beds* SNF 159. *Certified* Medicaid; Medicare.
Owner Proprietary corp (Hillhaven Corp).

Roseau

REM Roseau
208 2nd Ave NE, Roseau, MN 56751
(218) 463-1031
Admin David Petersen.
Licensure Intermediate care for mentally retarded. *Beds* ICF/MR 33.

Owner Proprietary corp.
Staff LPNs 2 (ft), 3 (pt); Nurses' aides 25 (ft), 26 (pt); Physical therapists 2 (pt); Activities coordinators 2 (pt); Dietitians 1 (pt).

Roseau Area Hospital
715 Delmore Dr, Roseau, MN 56751
(218) 463-2500
Admin David Hagen.
Licensure Skilled care; Intermediate care. *Beds* SNF 20; ICF 44. *Certified* Medicaid; Medicare.

Roseville

Dungarvin II Camara
3101 W Owasso Blvd, Roseville, MN 55112
(612) 483-8377
Admin Janice Carver.
Licensure Intermediate care for mentally retarded. *Beds* ICF/MR 6.
Owner Proprietary corp.
Admissions Requirements Medical examination; Physician's request.
Staff RNs 1 (pt).
Facilities Dining room; Laundry room.
Activities Arts & crafts; Cards; Games; Reading groups; Movies; Shopping trips; Dances/Social/Cultural gatherings.

Golden Age
1415 W County Rd B, Roseville, MN 55113
(612) 631-1616
Admin Pamela Schultz. *Dir of Nursing* Julie Stadler. *Medical Dir* Dr David Gilbertson.
Licensure Skilled care; Intermediate care; Board and care. *Beds* Swing beds SNF/ICF 133; Board and care 8. *Private Pay Patients* 20%. *Certified* Medicaid; Medicare.
Owner Proprietary corp (Good Neighbor Services).
Admissions Requirements Physician's request.
Staff Physicians; RNs; LPNs; Nurses' aides; Physical therapists; Recreational therapists; Occupational therapists; Speech therapists; Dietitians; Podiatrists; Audiologists.
Facilities Dining room; Physical therapy room; Activities room; Laundry room; Barber/Beauty shop.
Activities Arts & crafts; Cards; Games; Reading groups; Prayer groups; Movies; Shopping trips; Dances/Social/Cultural gatherings; Intergenerational programs; Pet therapy; Music therapy.

Lake Ridge Health Care Center
2727 N Victoria, Roseville, MN 55113
(612) 483-5431
Admin Greg Getchell.
Medical Dir Dr Timothy F Lane.
Licensure Skilled care. *Beds* SNF 240. *Certified* Medicaid; Medicare.
Owner Proprietary corp (Beverly Enterprises).
Admissions Requirements Minimum age 18; Medical examination; Physician's request.
Staff RNs 10 (ft), 35 (pt); LPNs 5 (ft), 7 (pt); Nurses' aides 34 (ft), 75 (pt); Physical therapists 1 (ft); Speech therapists 1 (pt); Activities coordinators 1 (ft); Dietitians 1 (pt); Podiatrists 1 (pt); Audiologists 1 (pt); Dentists 1 (pt).
Facilities Dining room; Physical therapy room; Activities room; Chapel; Crafts room; Barber/Beauty shop; Library; Dental office.
Activities Arts & crafts; Cards; Games; Reading groups; Prayer groups; Movies; Shopping trips; Dances/Social/Cultural gatherings; Exploration activities outside facility.

Rose of Sharon Manor
1000 Lovell, Roseville, MN 55113
(612) 484-3378
Admin Janet Eck. *Dir of Nursing* Laura Flohaug. *Medical Dir* Richard Burton MD.
Licensure Skilled care. *Beds* SNF 85. *Private Pay Patients* 20%. *Certified* Medicaid; Medicare.

Owner Proprietary corp (Unicare).
Admissions Requirements Minimum age 18; Medical examination; Physician's request.
Staff Physicians 1 (pt); RNs 3 (ft), 4 (pt); LPNs 3 (ft), 4 (pt); Nurses' aides 13 (ft), 32 (pt); Physical therapists 1 (pt); Recreational therapists 2 (ft); Occupational therapists 1 (pt); Speech therapists 1 (pt); Activities coordinators 1 (ft); Dietitians 1 (pt); Ophthalmologists 1 (pt); Podiatrists 1 (pt); Dentists 1 (pt); Optometrists 1 (pt).
Facilities Dining room; Physical therapy room; Activities room; Crafts room; Laundry room; Barber/Beauty shop; Occupational therapy room.
Activities Arts & crafts; Cards; Games; Reading groups; Prayer groups; Movies; Shopping trips; Dances/Social/Cultural gatherings; Intergenerational programs; Science hours.

Whitehouse Health Care Center
563 W County Rd B, Roseville, MN 55113
(612) 489-8851
Admin Leon Rotering. *Dir of Nursing* Shelly Wiggin. *Medical Dir* David Gilbertson DO.
Licensure Skilled care. *Beds* SNF 79. *Private Pay Patients* 25%. *Certified* Medicaid; Medicare.
Owner Proprietary corp (Good Neighbor Services).
Admissions Requirements Medical examination.
Staff RNs 5 (ft), 7 (pt); LPNs 3 (ft), 6 (pt); Nurses' aides 15 (ft), 36 (pt); Physical therapists 1 (ft), 3 (pt); Recreational therapists 1 (ft), 3 (pt); Occupational therapists 1 (pt); Speech therapists 1 (pt); Dietitians 1 (pt); Ophthalmologists 1 (pt); Podiatrists 1 (pt); Audiologists 1 (pt); Chaplains 1 (pt).
Facilities Dining room; Physical therapy room; Activities room; Laundry room; Barber/Beauty shop.
Activities Arts & crafts; Cards; Games; Reading groups; Prayer groups; Movies; Shopping trips; Dances/Social/Cultural gatherings; Intergenerational programs; Pet therapy.

Rush City

Hillcrest Health Care Center
650 Bremer Ave S, Rush City, MN 55069
(612) 358-4765
Admin Patricia A Behrendt. *Dir of Nursing* Sandy Olson RN. *Medical Dir* James M Giefer MD.
Licensure Skilled care; Intermediate care; Alzheimer's care. *Beds* SNF 63; ICF 2. *Certified* Medicaid; Medicare.
Owner Proprietary corp (Beverly Enterprises).
Admissions Requirements Medical examination; Physician's request.
Staff Physicians; RNs; LPNs; Nurses' aides; Physical therapists; Reality therapists; Recreational therapists; Occupational therapists; Speech therapists; Activities coordinators; Dietitians; Ophthalmologists; Podiatrists; Dentists.
Facilities Dining room; Physical therapy room; Activities room; Crafts room; Laundry room; Barber/Beauty shop; Library.
Activities Arts & crafts; Cards; Games; Reading groups; Prayer groups; Movies; Shopping trips; Dances/Social/Cultural gatherings.

Rushford

Good Shepherd Lutheran Home
PO Box 747, 800 Home, Rushford, MN 55971
(507) 864-7714
Admin Lauri Richert.
Medical Dir Dr John R Peterson.
Licensure Skilled care; Retirement. *Beds* SNF 98. *Certified* Medicaid; Medicare.

Owner Nonprofit corp.
Admissions Requirements Medical examination; Physician's request.
Staff Physicians 1 (pt); RNs; LPNs; Nurses' aides; Physical therapists; Activities coordinators; Dietitians.
Affiliation Lutheran.
Facilities Dining room; Physical therapy room; Activities room; Chapel; Crafts room; Laundry room; Barber/Beauty shop.
Activities Arts & crafts; Cards; Games; Reading groups; Prayer groups; Movies; Shopping trips; Dances/Social/Cultural gatherings.

Saint Anthony Village

St Anthony Health Center
3700 Foss Rd NE, Saint Anthony Village, MN 55421
(612) 788-9673
Admin Michael Milder.
Medical Dir Bernice Anderson.
Licensure Skilled care; Intermediate care. *Beds* SNF 128; ICF 26. *Certified* Medicaid; Medicare.
Owner Proprietary corp.
Staff Physicians; RNs; LPNs; Nurses' aides; Physical therapists; Recreational therapists; Occupational therapists; Speech therapists; Activities coordinators; Dietitians; Ophthalmologists.

Saint Charles

Whitewater Healthcare Center
525 Bluff Ave, Saint Charles, MN 55972
(507) 932-3283
Admin Faye Manee. *Dir of Nursing* Loretta Schillo. *Medical Dir* Richard Christiana MD.
Licensure Skilled care; Boarding care. *Beds* SNF 79; Boarding care 7. *Certified* Medicaid; Medicare.
Owner Proprietary corp (Beverly Enterprises).
Admissions Requirements Minimum age Adult; Medical examination; Physician's request.
Facilities Dining room; Physical therapy room; Activities room; Chapel; Crafts room; Laundry room; Barber/Beauty shop.
Activities Arts & crafts; Cards; Games; Reading groups; Prayer groups; Movies; Shopping trips; Dances/Social/Cultural gatherings.

Saint Cloud

Dans Boarding Care Home
1101 3rd St N, Saint Cloud, MN 56301
(612) 251-6567
Admin Doreen Murphy.
Licensure Boarding care. *Beds* Boarding care 12.
Owner Privately owned.
Admissions Requirements Minimum age 18; Males only; Medical examination.
Staff RNs; Nurses' aides; Dietitians.
Facilities Dining room; Activities room.
Activities Cards; Games; Movies; Shopping trips.

Opportunity Manor
861 17th Ave N, Saint Cloud, MN 56301
(612) 252-7349
Admin James Steiner.
Licensure Intermediate care for mentally retarded. *Beds* ICF/MR 12.
Owner Proprietary corp.

Opportunity Manor II
1311 13th Ave SE, Saint Cloud, MN 56301
(612) 255-0135
Admin James Steiner.
Licensure Intermediate care for mentally retarded. *Beds* ICF/MR 12.
Owner Proprietary corp.

REM—Fernwood Inc
1775 Roosevelt Rd, Saint Cloud, MN 56301
(612) 253-8134
Admin Juanita Hayes.
Licensure Intermediate care for mentally retarded. *Beds* ICF/MR 24.
Owner Proprietary corp.

REM St Cloud Inc
1506 33rd Ave N, Saint Cloud, MN 56301
(612) 252-8875
Admin Juanita Hayes.
Licensure Intermediate care for mentally retarded. *Beds* ICF/MR 15.
Owner Proprietary corp.

St Benedict's Center
1810 Minnesota Blvd SE, Saint Cloud, MN 56304
(612) 252-0010
Admin Sr Rita Budig, V Pres. *Dir of Nursing* Mark Thyen. *Medical Dir* Dr Hans Engman; Dr John Weitz.
Licensure Skilled care; Retirement; Alzheimer's care; Adult day care. *Beds* SNF 222; Retirement 67. *Private Pay Patients* 30%. *Certified* Medicaid; Medicare.
Owner Nonprofit organization/foundation.
Admissions Requirements Medical examination.
Staff RNs 8 (ft), 14 (pt); LPNs 18 (ft), 21 (pt); Nurses' aides 42 (ft), 94 (pt); Physical therapists (consultants); Dietitians.
Languages German.
Affiliation Roman Catholic.
Facilities Dining room; Physical therapy room; Activities room; Chapel; Crafts room; Laundry room; Barber/Beauty shop; Library; Respite care.
Activities Arts & crafts; Cards; Games; Reading groups; Prayer groups; Movies; Shopping trips; Dances/Social/Cultural gatherings; Intergenerational programs; Pet therapy.

St Cloud Manor
1717 Michigan Ave SE, Saint Cloud, MN 56301
(612) 251-9120
Admin Darwin Schwantes. *Dir of Nursing* Jon Hendrickson. *Medical Dir* Dr R L Thienes.
Licensure Skilled care. *Beds* SNF 108. *Certified* Medicaid; Medicare.
Owner Proprietary corp.
Admissions Requirements Minimum age 16; Medical examination; Physician's request.
Staff Physicians 9 (pt); RNs 5 (ft), 5 (pt); LPNs 5 (ft), 3 (pt); Nurses' aides 15 (ft), 46 (pt); Physical therapists 1 (pt); Reality therapists 1 (pt); Recreational therapists 1 (ft); Occupational therapists 1 (pt); Speech therapists 1 (pt); Activities coordinators 1 (ft), 1 (pt); Dietitians 1 (pt); Ophthalmologists 1 (pt); Podiatrists 1 (pt); Social workers 2 (ft).
Facilities Dining room; Physical therapy room; Activities room; Chapel; Crafts room; Laundry room; Barber/Beauty shop; Library.

St Elizabeth Home
PO Box 1801, Saint Cloud, MN 56302
(612) 252-8350
Admin Rev Richard Leisen.
Licensure Intermediate care for mentally retarded. *Beds* 14. *Certified* Medicaid.
Owner Nonprofit corp.

Saint James

Pleasant View Good Samaritan Center
1000 S 2nd St, Saint James, MN 56081
(507) 375-3286
Admin Rosalyn G Wielenga. *Dir of Nursing* Dorothy Christianson RN.
Licensure Intermediate care. *Beds* ICF 79.
Owner Nonprofit corp (Evangelical Lutheran/ Good Samaritan Society).
Admissions Requirements Minimum age 18.

Staff RNs 1 (ft), 1 (pt); LPNs 3 (ft), 3 (pt); Nurses' aides 9 (ft), 29 (pt); Activities coordinators 1 (ft).
Affiliation Lutheran.
Facilities Dining room; Activities room; Chapel; Crafts room; Laundry room; Barber/ Beauty shop; Library.
Activities Arts & crafts; Cards; Games; Reading groups; Prayer groups; Movies; Shopping trips.

Saint Louis Park

Greenwood Residence West
6019 W 39th St, Saint Louis Park, MN 55416
(612) 929-4681
Admin Norman Bollinger.
Medical Dir Dorothy Prickeril.
Licensure Intermediate care for mentally retarded. *Beds* ICF/MR 14.
Owner Proprietary corp.
Admissions Requirements Minimum age 18; Medical examination; Physician's request.
Staff RNs 1 (ft), 1 (pt); LPNs 2 (ft), 2 (pt); Nurses' aides 1 (ft), 1 (pt); Recreational therapists 1 (ft); Dietitians 1 (pt); 6 (pt).

Methodist Hospital Extended Care Facility
6500 Excelsior Blvd, Saint Louis Park, MN 55426
(612) 932-5325
Admin Sandra Toy. *Dir of Nursing* Linda Brixius RN. *Medical Dir* Hugh Edmondson MD.
Licensure Skilled care. *Beds* SNF 35. *Private Pay Patients* 0%. *Certified* Medicaid; Medicare.
Owner Nonprofit organization/foundation.
Admissions Requirements Minimum age 16; Medical examination; Physician's request.
Staff Physicians; RNs; LPNs; Nurses' aides; Activities coordinators.
Facilities Dining room; Activities room; Chapel.
Activities Cards; Movies.

Park Nursing & Convalescent Center
4415 W 36 1/2 St, Saint Louis Park, MN 55416
(612) 927-9717
Admin Vivian K Trettin.
Licensure Skilled care. *Beds* SNF 121. *Certified* Medicaid; Medicare.
Owner Proprietary corp (Unicare).

Park Plaza Healthcare Center
3201 Virginia Ave South, Saint Louis Park, MN 55426
(612) 935-0333
Admin Todd Carsen. *Dir of Nursing* Theresa Lang RN. *Medical Dir* Richard Bick MD.
Licensure Skilled care; Alzheimer's care. *Beds* SNF 300. *Certified* Medicaid; Medicare.
Owner Proprietary corp (Beverly Enterprises).
Admissions Requirements Medical examination; Physician's request.
Staff RNs; LPNs; Nurses' aides; Physical therapists; Recreational therapists; Occupational therapists; Speech therapists; Activities coordinators; Dietitians.
Languages Russian, Spanish.
Facilities Dining room; Physical therapy room; Activities room; Chapel; Barber/ Beauty shop.
Activities Arts & crafts; Cards; Games; Reading groups; Prayer groups; Movies; Shopping trips.

Summit House I
3029 Toledo Ave S, Saint Louis Park, MN 55416
(612) 925-5283
Admin Carol Robson.
Licensure Intermediate care for mentally retarded. *Beds* ICF/MR 6.
Owner Proprietary corp.

Summit House II
4600 Minnetonka Blvd, Saint Louis Park, MN 55416
(612) 926-5553
Admin Carol Robson. *Dir of Nursing* Scott Skobe RN. *Medical Dir* Leroy Geis MD.
Licensure Intermediate care for mentally retarded. *Beds* ICF/MR 6.
Owner Proprietary corp.
Staff RNs; Skilled counselors 14 (ft); Program directors 2 (ft).

Texas Terrace Convalescent Center
7900 W 28th St, Saint Louis Park, MN 55426
(612) 920-8380
Admin James C Platten. *Dir of Nursing* Linda Duos RN. *Medical Dir* Jesse Barron MD.
Licensure Skilled care; Alzheimer's care. *Beds* SNF 194. *Certified* Medicaid; Medicare.
Owner Proprietary corp (Unicare).
Admissions Requirements Minimum age 18; Medical examination; Physician's request.
Staff Physicians 1 (pt); Nurses' aides 60 (ft); Physical therapists 1 (ft); Recreational therapists 6 (ft); Occupational therapists 1 (ft); Speech therapists 1 (ft); Activities coordinators 1 (ft); Dietitians 1 (ft).
Languages Russian, Yiddish, Hebrew.
Facilities Dining room; Physical therapy room; Activities room; Chapel; Crafts room; Laundry room; Barber/Beauty shop; Library.
Activities Arts & crafts; Cards; Games; Reading groups; Prayer groups; Movies; Shopping trips; Dances/Social/Cultural gatherings.

Westwood Health Care Center
7500 W 22nd St, Saint Louis Park, MN 55426
(612) 546-4261
Admin Cheryl Stinski. *Dir of Nursing* Sandra Lamb RN. *Medical Dir* Dr Robert Sonntag.
Licensure Skilled care. *Beds* SNF 212. *Certified* Medicaid; Medicare.
Owner Proprietary corp.
Admissions Requirements Minimum age 16; Medical examination.
Staff Physicians 60 (pt); RNs 18 (ft), 7 (pt); LPNs 10 (ft), 6 (pt); Nurses' aides 40 (ft), 20 (pt); Physical therapists 1 (ft); Recreational therapists 2 (pt); Occupational therapists 1 (ft); Speech therapists 1 (pt); Activities coordinators 1 (ft); Dietitians 2 (ft); Ophthalmologists 1 (pt); Podiatrists 1 (pt); Audiologists 1 (pt).
Facilities Dining room; Physical therapy room; Activities room; Crafts room; Laundry room; Barber/Beauty shop; Library; Coffee shop; Smoking & nonsmoking lounges; Patios.
Activities Arts & crafts; Cards; Games; Reading groups; Prayer groups; Movies; Shopping trips; Dances/Social/Cultural gatherings; Intergenerational programs; Pet therapy.

Saint Paul

Aurora House
2134 Marshall Ave, Saint Paul, MN 55104
(612) 645-8622
Admin Terry Forss. *Dir of Nursing* Greg Cottle RN.
Licensure Intermediate care for mentally retarded. *Beds* ICF/MR 6.
Owner Proprietary corp.
Admissions Requirements Minimum age 18; Medical examination; Physician's request.
Staff RNs; Reality therapists 2 (ft), 8 (pt); Recreational therapists 1 (ft).
Facilities Dining room; Laundry room.
Activities Arts & crafts; Cards; Games; Reading groups; Movies; Shopping trips; Dances/Social/Cultural gatherings; Leisure services focus on treatment & education.

Bethel Care Center
420 Marshall Ave, Saint Paul, MN 55102
(612) 224-2368

Admin Ona Orth.
Licensure Skilled care. *Beds* SNF 149.
Certified Medicaid; Medicare.
Owner Proprietary corp.

Bethesda Lutheran Care Center
558 Capitol Blvd, Saint Paul, MN 55103
(612) 221-2347
Admin Ernie Gershone.
Licensure Skilled care. *Beds* SNF 138.
Certified Medicaid; Medicare.
Owner Nonprofit corp (Health East).
Affiliation Lutheran.

Board of Social Ministry
3881 Highland Ave, Saint Paul, MN 55110
(612) 426-5013
Admin Robert Armitage.
Licensure Skilled care; Intermediate care;
Alzheimer's care; Retirement. *Beds* 2100.
Certified Medicaid; Medicare.
Owner Nonprofit organization/foundation.
Admissions Requirements Medical
examination; Physician's request.
Languages Swedish, Norwegian, German.
Affiliation Lutheran.
Facilities Dining room; Physical therapy
room; Activities room; Chapel; Crafts room;
Laundry room; Barber/Beauty shop; Library.
Activities Arts & crafts; Games;
Reading groups; Prayer groups; Movies;
Shopping trips; Dances/Social/Cultural
gatherings.

Chez Nous—St Anthony Park
2248 Carter Ave, Saint Paul, MN 55108
(612) 644-2326
Admin Dan Kastrul.
Licensure Intermediate care for mentally
retarded. *Beds* ICF/MR 6.
Owner Proprietary corp.

Commonwealth Health Care Center
2237 Commonwealth Ave, Saint Paul, MN
55108
(612) 646-7486
Admin Patricia S Chevalier NHA. *Dir of
Nursing* Bonnie Carty RN. *Medical Dir*
Carolyn Johnson MD.
Licensure Skilled care; Closed Alzheimer's
unit. *Beds* SNF 108. *Private Pay Patients*
30%. *Certified* Medicaid; Medicare.
Owner Proprietary corp (Vantage Healthcare).
Admissions Requirements Minimum age 17;
Medical examination; Physician's request;
Recent history; TB test.
Staff Physicians; RNs; LPNs; Nurses' aides;
Physical therapists 1 (ft); Recreational
therapists; Occupational therapists 1 (ft);
Speech therapists; Dietitians;
Ophthalmologists; Podiatrists; Audiologists.
Facilities Dining room; Physical therapy
room; Activities room; Crafts room; Laundry
room; Barber/Beauty shop.
Activities Arts & crafts; Cards; Games;
Reading groups; Prayer groups; Movies;
Shopping trips; Dances/Social/Cultural
gatherings; Intergenerational programs; Pet
therapy.

Community Access—Edmund
1159 Edmund Ave, Saint Paul, MN 55105
(612) 641-0041
Admin Gerald Glomb.
Licensure Intermediate care for mentally
retarded. *Beds* ICF/MR 6.
Owner Proprietary corp.

Community Living Concepts
407 S McKnight, Saint Paul, MN 55119
(612) 739-3733
Admin Cynthia Lacoeur.
Licensure Intermediate care for mentally
retarded. *Beds* ICF/MR 6.
Owner Proprietary corp.

Dayton Boarding Care Home
740 Dayton Ave, Saint Paul, MN 55104
(612) 228-1051

Admin Stephen R Scalzo.
Licensure Boarding care. *Beds* Boarding care
26.
Owner Proprietary corp.

Dayton House of People Inc
565 Dayton Ave, Saint Paul, MN 55102
(612) 222-1009
Admin Mary Kay McJilton.
Licensure Supervised living. *Beds* Supervised
living 15.
Owner Proprietary corp.

Dungarvin III—Balbriggen
1270 E Larpenteur Ave, Saint Paul, MN
55109
(612) 776-2044
Admin Janice Carver.
Medical Dir Dr D Current.
Licensure Intermediate care for mentally
retarded. *Beds* ICF/MR 6.
Owner Proprietary corp.
Admissions Requirements Minimum age 18.
Facilities Dining room; Laundry room.
Activities Arts & crafts; Games; Movies;
Shopping trips; Dances/Social/Cultural
gatherings; Wide variety of activities as per
resident interest.

Episcopal Church Home of Minnesota
1879 Feronia Ave, Saint Paul, MN 55104
(612) 646-4061
Admin David Bredenberg.
Medical Dir Jack Beaird; Sharon Lewis.
Licensure Skilled care; Boarding care;
Retirement. *Beds* SNF 67; Boarding care 64;
Retirement 220. *Certified* Medicaid;
Medicare.
Owner Nonprofit organization/foundation.
Admissions Requirements Medical
examination.
Staff Physicians 1 (pt); RNs 7 (ft), 4 (pt);
LPNs 3 (ft), 2 (pt); Nurses' aides 17 (ft), 7
(pt); Physical therapists 1 (ft), 2 (pt);
Occupational therapists 1 (ft), 1 (pt); Speech
therapists 1 (pt); Activities coordinators 1
(ft); Dietitians 1 (pt); Ophthalmologists 1
(pt); Podiatrists 1 (pt).
Affiliation Episcopal.
Facilities Dining room; Activities room;
Chapel; Crafts room; Laundry room; Barber/
Beauty shop; Library.
Activities Arts & crafts; Cards; Games;
Reading groups; Prayer groups; Movies;
Shopping trips; Dances/Social/Cultural
gatherings.

Fairmount Community Access
1081 Fairmount Ave, Saint Paul, MN 55105
(612) 641-0041
Admin Gerald Glomb.
Licensure Intermediate care for mentally
retarded. *Beds* ICF/MR 6.
Owner Proprietary corp.

Familystyle Homes
398 Duke St, Saint Paul, MN 55102
(612) 222-6600
Admin Dr James Janecek.
Medical Dir James Janecek MD.
Licensure Boarding care. *Beds* ICF/MR
Boarding care 21.
Owner Proprietary corp.
Admissions Requirements Minimum age 18;
Medical examination; Physician's request.
Staff RNs 1 (ft); LPNs 2 (ft); Nurses' aides 3
(ft); Activities coordinators 1 (ft); Dietitians
1 (ft); Mental health counselors 4 (ft);
Mental health workers 15 (ft).
Facilities Dining room; Activities room;
Crafts room; Laundry room; Library; 23
Residential houses & duplexes.
Activities Arts & crafts; Cards; Games; Prayer
groups; Movies; Shopping trips; Dances/
Social/Cultural gatherings; Camping; Jogging.

Four Seasons Care Center—Capitol
445 Galtier Ave, Saint Paul, MN 55103
(612) 224-1848

Admin Gary D Dalzell.
Licensure Skilled care; Intermediate care. *Beds*
SNF 126; ICF 19. *Certified* Medicaid;
Medicare.
Owner Proprietary corp.

Four Seasons Care Center—Central
375 N Lexington Pkwy, Saint Paul, MN
55104
(612) 645-0577
Admin Frank Robinson. *Dir of Nursing* Kim
Vikstrom RN. *Medical Dir* Fred Webber
MD.
Licensure Skilled care; Intermediate care;
Alzheimer's care. *Beds* SNF 128; ICF 58.
Certified Medicaid; Medicare.
Owner Proprietary corp.
Admissions Requirements Minimum age 18;
Medical examination; Physician's request.
Staff Physicians 1 (ft); RNs 8 (ft), 7 (pt);
LPNs 9 (ft), 9 (pt); Nurses' aides 50 (ft), 60
(pt); Physical therapists 1 (ft); Occupational
therapists 1 (ft); Activities coordinators 1
(ft); Dietitians 1 (ft); Ophthalmologists 1
(pt); Podiatrists 1 (pt).
Facilities Dining room; Physical therapy
room; Activities room; Chapel; Laundry
room; Barber/Beauty shop; Library.
Activities Arts & crafts; Cards; Games;
Reading groups; Prayer groups; Movies;
Shopping trips; Dances/Social/Cultural
gatherings.

Frances Residence
1735 Arlington Ave E, Saint Paul, MN 55106
(612) 774-9014
Admin Jeffrey T Boston.
Medical Dir Jeffery T Boston.
Licensure Intermediate care for mentally
retarded. *Beds* ICF/MR 6.
Owner Proprietary corp.
Admissions Requirements Minimum age 18.
Staff RNs 1 (ft); LPNs 1 (pt); Physical
therapists 1 (pt); Activities coordinators 1
(pt).
Activities Community activities.

Greenwood Residence East
1609 Jackson St, Saint Paul, MN 55117
(612) 488-2561
Admin Norman Bollinger.
Medical Dir Deborah Dunn.
Licensure Intermediate care for mentally
retarded. *Beds* ICF/MR 16.
Owner Proprietary corp.
Admissions Requirements Minimum age 18;
Medical examination; Physician's request.
Staff RNs 1 (ft); LPNs 2 (ft), 2 (pt); Nurses'
aides 1 (ft), 2 (pt); Physical therapists 1 (pt);
Recreational therapists 1 (ft), 1 (pt).
Facilities Dining room; Physical therapy
room; Activities room; Crafts room; Laundry
room.
Activities Arts & crafts; Cards; Games;
Movies; Shopping trips; Dances/Social/
Cultural gatherings.

Guild Hall
286 Marshall Ave, Saint Paul, MN 55102
(612) 291-0067
Admin Grace Tangjerd Schmitt.
Licensure Supervised living. *Beds* Supervised
living 85.
Owner Proprietary corp.

Harmony Nursing Home
135 E Geranium Ave, Saint Paul, MN 55117
(612) 488-6658
Admin William McEachern.
Licensure Skilled care. *Beds* SNF 150.
Certified Medicaid; Medicare.
Owner Proprietary corp (King Care Centers
Inc).

Hayes Residence
1620 Randolph Ave, Saint Paul, MN 55105
(612) 690-4458
Admin Helen B Jennen. *Dir of Nursing* Fran
Nielsen, Health Supv.

Licensure Intermediate care. *Beds* ICF 40.
Private Pay Patients 10%.
Owner Proprietary corp.
Admissions Requirements Medical
examination; Physician's request.
Staff RNs 1 (ft); LPNs 3 (ft); Nurses' aides 4
(ft); Recreational therapists 1 (ft); Dietitians
1 (pt).
Facilities Dining room; Activities room;
Crafts room; Laundry room.
Activities Arts & crafts; Cards; Games;
Reading groups; Prayer groups; Movies;
Shopping trips; Dances/Social/Cultural
gatherings; Parties.

**Healtheast Transitional Community
Care—Bethesda**
559 Capitol Blvd, Saint Paul, MN 55103
(612) 221-2677
Admin Pauline Liukonen.
Licensure Nursing care. *Beds* Nursing care 34.
Owner Proprietary corp.

Hewitt House of People Inc
1593 Hewitt Ave, Saint Paul, MN 55104
(612) 645-9424
Admin Donald Bump.
Licensure Supervised living. *Beds* Supervised
living 22.
Owner Proprietary corp.

Highland Chateau Health Care Center
2319 W 7th St, Saint Paul, MN 55116
(612) 698-0793
Admin Doug Beardsley. *Dir of Nursing* Kathy
Riley. *Medical Dir* Wayne Thalhuber MD.
Licensure Skilled care; Alzheimer's care. *Beds*
SNF 111. *Certified* Medicaid; Medicare.
Owner Proprietary corp.
Admissions Requirements Minimum age 18;
Medical examination; Physician's request.
Staff RNs 8 (ft), 5 (pt); LPNs 7 (ft), 5 (pt);
Nurses' aides 28 (ft), 26 (pt); Physical
therapists 1 (ft); Recreational therapists 2
(ft); Activities coordinators 1 (ft); Dietitians
1 (pt).
Facilities Dining room; Physical therapy
room; Activities room; Laundry room;
Barber/Beauty shop.
Activities Arts & crafts; Cards; Games;
Reading groups; Prayer groups; Movies;
Shopping trips.

Hoikka House Inc
238 Pleasant Ave, Saint Paul, MN 55102
(612) 222-7491
Admin Rhoda E Miller.
Medical Dir Thomas Smith MD.
Licensure Boarding care for mentally ill. *Beds*
Boarding care for mentally ill 108.
Owner Proprietary corp.
Admissions Requirements Minimum age 18;
Medical examination; Physician's request.
Staff Physicians 2 (pt); RNs 2 (ft); LPNs 7
(ft); Recreational therapists 1 (ft); Activities
coordinators 2 (ft).
Facilities Dining room; Activities room;
Crafts room; Laundry room; 2 TV lounges; 2
Conference rooms; Exercise room.
Activities Arts & crafts; Cards; Games;
Reading groups; Movies; Shopping trips;
Dances/Social/Cultural gatherings.

Petra Howard House
700 E 8th St, Saint Paul, MN 55106
(612) 771-5575
Admin Mary Kay McJilton.
Licensure Supervised living. *Beds* Supervised
living 14.
Owner Proprietary corp.

Amy Johnson Residence
89 Virginia St, Saint Paul, MN 55102
(612) 227-0574
Admin Donetta Johnson.
Licensure Boarding care. *Beds* Boarding care
25.
Owner Proprietary corp.

Admissions Requirements Medical
examination.
Staff Nurses' aides 8 (pt); Activities
coordinators 2 (pt).
Facilities Dining room; Laundry room.
Activities Arts & crafts; Cards; Games;
Reading groups; Prayer groups; Movies;
Shopping trips; Dances/Social/Cultural
gatherings; Music; Resident council; Field
trips.

Langton Place
1910 W County Rd D, Saint Paul, MN 55112
(612) 631-6200
Admin Mark A Broman. *Dir of Nursing* Mary
Karpe. *Medical Dir* Dr Robert Blomberg.
Licensure Skilled care; Adult day care; Respite
care; Rehabilitation; Alzheimer's/Dementia
unit. *Beds* SNF 165. *Certified* Medicare.
Owner Nonprofit corp (Presbyterian Homes of
Minnesota).
Admissions Requirements Minimum age 55.
Staff Physicians 1 (pt); RNs 14 (ft), 17 (pt);
LPNs 5 (ft), 10 (pt); Nurses' aides 22 (ft), 47
(pt); Physical therapists 3 (ft); Recreational
therapists 2 (ft), 3 (pt); Occupational
therapists 3 (pt); Activities coordinators 1
(ft); Dietitians 1 (pt).
Affiliation Presbyterian.
Facilities Dining room; Physical therapy
room; Activities room; Chapel; Crafts room;
Laundry room; Barber/Beauty shop; Library.
Activities Arts & crafts; Cards; Games;
Reading groups; Prayer groups; Movies;
Shopping trips; Dances/Social/Cultural
gatherings; Intergenerational programs; Pet
therapy.

Little Sisters of the Poor
330 S Exchange St, Saint Paul, MN 55102
(612) 227-0336
Admin Sr Catherine Williamson. *Dir of
Nursing* Sr Bernadette McCarthy. *Medical
Dir* Dr Cecil Warren.
Licensure Skilled care; Intermediate care;
Retirement. *Beds* SNF 62; ICF 56;
Retirement apts 32. *Certified* Medicaid;
Medicare.
Owner Nonprofit corp (Little Sisters of the
Poor).
Admissions Requirements Minimum age 62;
Medical examination.
Staff Physicians; RNs; LPNs; Nurses' aides;
Physical therapists; Reality therapists;
Recreational therapists; Occupational
therapists; Speech therapists; Activities
coordinators; Dietitians; Podiatrists.
Languages French, Spanish.
Affiliation Roman Catholic.
Facilities Dining room; Physical therapy
room; Activities room; Chapel; Crafts room;
Laundry room; Barber/Beauty shop; Library.
Activities Arts & crafts; Cards; Games;
Reading groups; Prayer groups; Movies;
Shopping trips; Dances/Social/Cultural
gatherings; Intergenerational programs; Pet
therapy.

Lyngblomsten Care Center
1415 Almond Ave, Saint Paul, MN 55108
(612) 646-2941
Admin Evelyn Halverson.
Medical Dir Dr Donald Severson.
Licensure Skilled care. *Beds* SNF 256.
Certified Medicaid; Medicare.
Owner Nonprofit organization/foundation.
Admissions Requirements Medical
examination.
Staff Physical therapists 1 (ft), 1 (pt);
Occupational therapists 1 (ft); Activities
coordinators 1 (ft); Dietitians 3 (ft).
Affiliation Lutheran.
Facilities Dining room; Physical therapy
room; Activities room; Chapel; Crafts room;
Laundry room; Barber/Beauty shop; Library.

Activities Arts & crafts; Cards; Games;
Reading groups; Prayer groups; Movies;
Shopping trips; Dances/Social/Cultural
gatherings.

Lynnhurst Healthcare Center
471 Lynnhurst Ave W, Saint Paul, MN 55104
(612) 645-6453
Admin Neil Gulsvig.
Licensure Skilled care. *Beds* SNF 84. *Certified*
Medicaid; Medicare.
Owner Proprietary corp (Beverly Enterprises).

Mainstream
2096 Reaney Ave, Saint Paul, MN 55119
(612) 738-9248
Admin Donald Priebe.
Licensure Intermediate care for mentally
retarded. *Beds* ICF/MR 6.
Owner Proprietary corp.

Maplewood Care Center
1900 Sherren Ave E, Saint Paul, MN 55109
(612) 770-1365, 770-1646 FAX
Admin Angeline H Sewall. *Dir of Nursing*
Mary Beth Lacina. *Medical Dir* Dr James
Nolin.
Licensure Skilled care; Retirement. *Beds* SNF
176. *Certified* Medicaid; Medicare.
Owner Nonprofit organization/foundation
(Volunteers of America Care).
Admissions Requirements Minimum age 65;
Physician's request.
Staff RNs 16 (ft), 24 (pt); LPNs 6 (ft), 10 (pt);
Nurses' aides 65 (ft), 97 (pt); Physical
therapists 1 (ft); Reality therapists 4 (ft);
Recreational therapists 1 (ft); Occupational
therapists 1 (ft); Activities coordinators 1
(ft); Dietitians 1 (pt).
Facilities Dining room; Physical therapy
room; Activities room; Chapel; Crafts room;
Laundry room; Barber/Beauty shop.
Activities Arts & crafts; Cards; Games;
Reading groups; Prayer groups; Movies;
Shopping trips; Dances/Social/Cultural
gatherings; Intergenerational programs; Pet
therapy.

Midway Hospital Skilled Nursing Facility
1700 University Ave, Saint Paul, MN 55104
(612) 641-5740
Admin Pauline Liukonen.
Licensure Skilled care. *Beds* SNF 39.
Owner Proprietary corp.

Minnesota Jewish Group Home II—Tikvah
1778 Rome Ave, Saint Paul, MN 55103
(612) 690-1566
Admin Deborah Sheehan.
Licensure Intermediate care for mentally
retarded. *Beds* ICF/MR 6.
Owner Proprietary corp.
Affiliation Jewish.

Mounds Park Residence
908 Mound St, Saint Paul, MN 55106
(612) 776-7170
Admin Carole Hall.
Medical Dir Dr Paul Dyrdal.
Licensure Boarding care. *Beds* Boarding care
37.
Owner Proprietary corp.
Admissions Requirements Minimum age 18;
Medical examination.
Staff Physicians 3 (pt); LPNs 2 (ft), 1 (pt);
Nurses' aides 5 (ft), 1 (pt); Recreational
therapists 1 (ft), 1 (pt); Speech therapists 1
(ft); Activities coordinators 1 (ft), 1 (pt);
Dietitians 1 (pt); Ophthalmologists 1 (pt);
Podiatrists 1 (pt); Audiologists 1 (pt);
Dentists 1 (pt).
Facilities Dining room; Activities room;
Crafts room; Barber/Beauty shop; Library;
Lounges.
Activities Arts & crafts; Cards; Games;
Reading groups; Prayer groups; Movies;
Shopping trips; Dances/Social/Cultural
gatherings; Resident council.

Nekton Inc
296 N Snelling, Saint Paul, MN 55104
(612) 644-7680
Admin Stephen Kodluboy.
Licensure Intermediate care for mentally
retarded. *Beds* ICF/MR 6. *Certified*
Medicaid.
Owner Proprietary corp.
Admissions Requirements Medical
examination.
Staff RNs 1 (ft).
Facilities Regular community homes.
Activities Arts & crafts; Cards; Games;
Reading groups; Prayer groups; Movies;
Shopping trips; Dances/Social/Cultural
gatherings.

Nekton on Goodrich
917 Goodrich Ave, Saint Paul, MN 55105
(612) 221-0180
Admin Stephen Kodluboy.
Licensure Intermediate care for mentally
retarded. *Beds* ICF/MR 8.
Owner Proprietary corp.

Nekton on Mississippi
1866 Mississippi Blvd, Saint Paul, MN 55116
(612) 699-9348
Admin Stephen Kodluboy.
Licensure Intermediate care for mentally
retarded. *Beds* ICF/MR 6.
Owner Proprietary corp.

Nekton on Wheeler
148 Wheeler Ave S, Saint Paul, MN 55105
(612) 690-0120
Admin Stephen Kodluboy.
Licensure Intermediate care for mentally
retarded. *Beds* ICF/MR 6.
Owner Proprietary corp.

Nekton on Wyoming
445 E Wyoming, Saint Paul, MN 55107
(612) 291-8054
Admin Peter Sajevic.
Licensure Intermediate care for mentally
retarded. *Beds* ICF/MR 6.
Owner Proprietary corp.

New Connection Primary Treatment
73 Leech St, Saint Paul, MN 55102
(612) 224-4384
Admin William J Payne.
Licensure Supervised living. *Beds* Supervised
living 26.
Owner Proprietary corp.

New Directions
1143 Churchill Ave, Saint Paul, MN 55103
(612) 488-0397
Admin Jonathan Kigner.
Licensure Intermediate care for mentally
retarded. *Beds* ICF/MR 6.
Owner Proprietary corp.

New Foundations
796 Capitol Heights, Saint Paul, MN 55103
(612) 221-9880
Admin Tom Paul.
Licensure Supervised living. *Beds* Supervised
living 20.
Owner Proprietary corp.

Norhaven
1394 Jackson St, Saint Paul, MN 55117
(612) 488-0275
Admin Peter Sajevic.
Licensure Intermediate care for mentally
retarded. *Beds* ICF/MR 106.
Owner Proprietary corp.

Our House of Minnesota Inc 1
1846 Dayton Ave, Saint Paul, MN 55104
(612) 646-1104
Admin Pam Skillman.
Licensure Intermediate care for mentally
retarded. *Beds* ICF/MR 6.
Owner Proprietary corp.

Admissions Requirements Minimum age 18;
Medical examination; Physician's request.
Facilities Dining room; Laundry room.
Activities Arts & crafts; Cards; Games;
Reading groups; Prayer groups; Movies;
Shopping trips; Dances/Social/Cultural
gatherings; Adult education.

Our House of Minnesota Inc 2
1846 Portland Ave, Saint Paul, MN 55104
(612) 646-1104
Admin Pam Skillman.
Licensure Intermediate care for mentally
retarded. *Beds* ICF/MR 6.
Owner Proprietary corp.

Our Lady of Good Counsel
2076 St Anthony Ave, Saint Paul, MN 55104
(612) 646-2797
Admin Sr Mary Daniel. *Dir of Nursing* Sr
Mary Edwin OP. *Medical Dir* Dr Wayne H
Thalhuber; Dr LeRoy Geis.
Licensure Intermediate care. *Beds* ICF 40.
Private Pay Patients 0%.
Owner Nonprofit corp (Servants of Relief for
Incurable Cancer Inc).
Admissions Requirements Medical
examination; Physician's request; Incurable
cancer.
Staff RNs 3 (ft); LPNs 3 (ft); Nurses' aides 9
(ft).
Affiliation Roman Catholic.
Facilities Chapel; Barber/Beauty shop;
Library.
Activities Cards; Movies.

Parkway Manor Health Care Center
324 Johnson Pkwy, Saint Paul, MN 55106
(612) 774-9737
Admin Maureen Kehoe.
Licensure Skilled care; Intermediate care. *Beds*
SNF 276; ICF 16. *Certified* Medicaid;
Medicare.
Owner Proprietary corp (Beverly Enterprises).

People Inc—Dayton House
565 Dayton Avenue, Saint Paul, MN 55102
(612) 222-1009
Admin Mary Kay McJilton.
Licensure Intermediate care. *Beds* 15.
Owner Nonprofit corp.
Admissions Requirements Males only; Age 18-
65.
Staff Program directors 1 (ft); Chemical
dependency counselors 1 (ft); Daily basic
living coordinators 1 (ft); Chemical
dependency technicians 6 (pt).
Facilities Dining room; Physical therapy
room; Activities room; Laundry room;
Kitchen; Living room.
Activities Recreation events; Individual &
group counseling.

Peoples Child Care Residence
1611 Ames Ave, Saint Paul, MN 55106
(612) 774-5940
Admin Mary Kay McJilton.
Medical Dir Eunice A Davis MD.
Licensure Intermediate care for mentally
retarded. *Beds* ICF/MR 32.
Owner Proprietary corp.
Admissions Requirements Medical
examination.
Staff Physicians 1 (pt); RNs 2 (ft), 2 (pt);
LPNs 3 (ft), 1 (pt); Nurses' aides 6 (ft), 60
(pt); Physical therapists 1 (pt); Reality
therapists 6 (ft); Recreational therapists 1
(ft), 4 (pt); Occupational therapists 1 (pt);
Activities coordinators 1 (pt); Dietitians 1
(pt).
Facilities Physical therapy room; Activities
room; Crafts room; Laundry room; Barber/
Beauty shop.
Activities Arts & crafts; Games; Movies;
Shopping trips; Dances/Social/Cultural
gatherings.

Phoenix Residence Inc
135 Colorado St E, Saint Paul, MN 55107
(612) 227-7655
Admin Judy Douglas.
Medical Dir Judith Rikala.
Licensure Intermediate care for mentally
retarded; Retirement. *Beds* ICF/MR 51.
Owner Nonprofit corp.
Admissions Requirements Minimum age 18;
Medical examination; Physician's request.
Staff RNs 1 (ft), 2 (pt); LPNs 1 (ft), 4 (pt);
Nurses' aides 28 (ft), 32 (pt); Physical
therapists 2 (pt); Occupational therapists 1
(pt); Speech therapists 1 (pt); Activities
coordinators 1 (ft), 2 (pt); Dietitians 1 (pt);
Podiatrists 1 (pt); Dentists 1 (pt).
Facilities Dining room; Physical therapy
room; Activities room; Laundry room;
Library.
Activities Arts & crafts; Reading groups;
Movies; Shopping trips; Dances/Social/
Cultural gatherings; Bowling; Outings.

Pineview Residence
69 N Milton, Saint Paul, MN 55104
(612) 227-1333
Admin Joanne Chapman.
Licensure Boarding care. *Beds* Boarding care
22.
Owner Proprietary corp.
Admissions Requirements Minimum age 55;
Medical examination.
Staff Physicians; RNs; Nurses' aides;
Recreational therapists; Activities
coordinators; Dietitians.
Facilities Dining room; Activities room;
Crafts room; Laundry room; Barber/Beauty
shop.
Activities Arts & crafts; Cards; Games; Prayer
groups; Movies; Shopping trips; Dances/
Social/Cultural gatherings.

Pleasant Hill Care Center
200 Earl St, Saint Paul, MN 55106
(612) 224-3837
Admin Scott Batulis. *Dir of Nursing* Gloria
Wilkie. *Medical Dir* Dr Tom Altemeir.
Licensure Skilled care. *Beds* SNF 90. *Certified*
Medicaid; Medicare.
Owner Proprietary corp (Health East).
Facilities Dining room; Physical therapy
room; Activities room; Crafts room; Laundry
room; Barber/Beauty shop; Library; Patio.
Activities Arts & crafts; Cards; Games;
Reading groups; Prayer groups; Movies;
Shopping trips; Dances/Social/Cultural
gatherings.

Presbyterian Homes Johanna Shores
3220 Lake Johanna Blvd, Saint Paul, MN
55112
(612) 631-6000
Admin Fred Strandberg. *Dir of Nursing* Marj
Kuhl. *Medical Dir* R Blomberg MD.
Licensure Skilled care; Retirement;
Alzheimer's care. *Beds* 208.
Owner Nonprofit corp (Presbyterian Homes of
MN Inc).
Admissions Requirements Minimum age 65.
Staff Physicians 15 (pt); RNs 22 (ft), 18 (pt);
LPNs 9 (ft), 7 (pt); Nurses' aides 75 (ft);
Physical therapists 2 (ft), 2 (pt); Recreational
therapists 3 (pt); Occupational therapists 5
(pt); Speech therapists 1 (pt); Activities
coordinators 1 (ft); Ophthalmologists 1 (pt);
Podiatrists 1 (pt).
Affiliation Presbyterian.
Facilities Dining room; Physical therapy
room; Activities room; Chapel; Crafts room;
Laundry room; Barber/Beauty shop; Library;
Pool; Whirlpool; Handicapped gardens; 1
mile paved walkways; Lake front; Gazebo;
Woods & trails; Shuffleboard; Exercise
rooms; Private dining rooms; Sidewalk cafe;
Gift shop; Medical & dental clinic.

Activities Arts & crafts; Cards; Games;
Reading groups; Prayer groups; Movies;
Shopping trips; Dances/Social/Cultural
gatherings; Wellness program.

Quinlan Home
391 Pleasant Ave, Saint Paul, MN 55102
(612) 222-7200
Admin Laura Reynolds.
Licensure Boarding care. *Beds* Boarding care
26.
Owner Proprietary corp.
Admissions Requirements Minimum age 18;
Medical examination.
Staff Nurses' aides 5 (ft), 3 (pt); Activities
coordinators 1 (pt).
Facilities Dining room; Activities room;
Laundry room.
Activities Arts & crafts; Cards; Games;
Reading groups; Prayer groups; Movies;
Shopping trips; Dances/Social/Cultural
gatherings.

Ramsey Nursing Home
2000 White Bear Ave, Saint Paul, MN 55109
(612) 777-7486
Admin David J Berres. *Dir of Nursing* Karen
K Wierenga. *Medical Dir* Dr Robert L
Powers.
Licensure Skilled care. *Beds* SNF 180. *Private
Pay Patients* 18%. *Certified* Medicaid;
Medicare.
Owner Publicly owned.
Admissions Requirements Minimum age 18;
Medical examination; Physician's request.
Staff Physicians 1 (pt); RNs 4 (ft), 10 (pt);
LPNs 12 (pt); Nurses' aides 25 (ft), 64 (pt);
Physical therapists 2 (pt); Recreational
therapists 3 (ft), 3 (pt); Occupational
therapists 1 (ft); Speech therapists 1 (pt);
Activities coordinators 1 (ft); Dietitians 1
(ft); Podiatrists 1 (pt).
Facilities Dining room; Physical therapy
room; Activities room; Crafts room; Laundry
room; Barber/Beauty shop.
Activities Arts & crafts; Cards; Games;
Reading groups; Prayer groups; Movies;
Shopping trips; Dances/Social/Cultural
gatherings; Intergenerational programs.

Residence III
1968 Foxridge Rd, Saint Paul, MN 55119
(612) 735-9269
Admin Dennis M Holman.
Licensure Intermediate care for mentally
retarded. *Beds* ICF/MR 6.
Owner Proprietary corp.
Admissions Requirements Minimum age 15.
Facilities Dining room; Laundry room.

St Mary's Home
1925 Norfolk Ave, Saint Paul, MN 55116
(612) 698-5508, 698-7322 FAX
Admin Sr Bernice Ebner, Pres/CEO. *Dir of
Nursing* Phyllis Kirk. *Medical Dir* Dr
William Armstrong.
Licensure Skilled care; Alzheimer's care. *Beds*
SNF 140. *Private Pay Patients* 43%. *Certified*
Medicaid; Medicare.
Owner Nonprofit corp (Sacred Heart Corp).
Admissions Requirements Medical
examination; Physician's request.
Staff Physicians 42 (pt); RNs 5 (ft), 1 (pt);
LPNs 9 (ft), 2 (pt); Nurses' aides 27 (ft), 16
(pt); Physical therapists 1 (ft); Recreational
therapists 4 (ft); Occupational therapists 1
(ft), 1 (pt); Speech therapists 1 (ft);
Dietitians 1 (pt); Podiatrists 1 (pt);
Audiologists 1 (pt).
Languages German.
Affiliation Roman Catholic.
Facilities Dining room; Physical therapy
room; Activities room; Chapel; Crafts room;
Laundry room; Barber/Beauty shop; Library;
Auditorium; Occupational therapy room.

Activities Arts & crafts; Cards; Games;
Reading groups; Prayer groups; Movies;
Shopping trips; Dances/Social/Cultural
gatherings; Intergenerational programs; Pet
therapy.

St Paul's Church Home Inc
484 Ashland Ave, Saint Paul, MN 55102
(612) 227-8351, 227-3470 FAX
Admin Jerry L Hoganson. *Dir of Nursing* Kay
Wagers RN. *Medical Dir* Mario Garcia MD.
Licensure Skilled care; Intermediate care. *Beds*
SNF 105; ICF 23. *Private Pay Patients* 35%.
Certified Medicaid; Medicare.
Owner Nonprofit corp.
Admissions Requirements Minimum age 65;
Medical examination; Physician's request.
Staff RNs 5 (ft), 3 (pt); LPNs 5 (ft), 5 (pt);
Nurses' aides 40 (ft), 20 (pt); Physical
therapists 1 (pt); Recreational therapists 1
(ft); Occupational therapists 1 (ft); Speech
therapists 1 (pt); Activities coordinators 1
(ft); Dietitians 1 (pt).
Affiliation Church of Christ.
Facilities Dining room; Physical therapy
room; Activities room; Chapel; Crafts room;
Laundry room; Barber/Beauty shop; Library;
Solarium.
Activities Arts & crafts; Cards; Games;
Reading groups; Prayer groups; Movies;
Shopping trips; Dances/Social/Cultural
gatherings; Community outings; Resident
council; Family council.

Shalom Home
1554 Midway Pkwy, Saint Paul, MN 55108
(612) 646-6311
Admin Marshall Silberstein. *Dir of Nursing*
Ann Lutterman. *Medical Dir* Dr George
Battis.
Licensure Skilled care; Intermediate care;
Alzheimer's care. *Beds* SNF 274; ICF 28.
Certified Medicaid; Medicare.
Owner Nonprofit corp.
Admissions Requirements Minimum age 60;
Medical examination; Physician's request.
Languages Yiddish, Hebrew, German,
Russian.
Affiliation Jewish.
Facilities Dining room; Physical therapy
room; Activities room; Chapel; Barber/
Beauty shop; Library; Occupational therapy
room; Day care; In-house laundry; Special
care unit.
Activities Arts & crafts; Cards; Games;
Reading groups; Prayer groups; Movies;
Shopping trips; Dances/Social/Cultural
gatherings; Choir; Horticulture; Exercise;
Closed circuit TV network in-house.

Stevencroft
1436 Ashland Ave, Saint Paul, MN 55104
(612) 644-2514
Admin Sandra Sorensen.
Licensure Intermediate care for mentally
retarded. *Beds* ICF/MR 11.
Owner Proprietary corp.

Summit Manor Health Care Center
80 Western Ave N, Saint Paul, MN 55102
(612) 227-8988
Admin Joanne Volden.
Licensure Skilled care. *Beds* SNF 120.
Certified Medicaid; Medicare.
Owner Proprietary corp (Thro Co).
Admissions Requirements Minimum age 18;
Medical examination; Physician's request.
Staff RNs 10 (ft), 12 (pt); LPNs 5 (ft), 5 (pt);
Nurses' aides 25 (ft), 25 (pt); Physical
therapists 1 (ft); Recreational therapists 2
(ft); Occupational therapists 2 (ft); Speech
therapists 1 (pt); Activities coordinators 1
(ft); Ophthalmologists 1 (pt).
Facilities Dining room; Physical therapy
room; Activities room; Chapel; Laundry
room; Barber/Beauty shop.

Activities Arts & crafts; Cards; Games;
Reading groups; Prayer groups; Movies;
Shopping trips; Dances/Social/Cultural
gatherings.

Sur La Rue de Breen
1174 Breen St, Saint Paul, MN 55106
(612) 771-5399
Admin Peter Sajevic.
Licensure Intermediate care for mentally
retarded. *Beds* ICF/MR 6.
Owner Proprietary corp.

Sur La Rue de Wheelock Ridge
1561 Wheelock Ridge, Saint Paul, MN 55102
(612) 771-3162
Admin Peter Sajevic.
Licensure Intermediate care for mentally
retarded. *Beds* ICF/MR 6.
Owner Proprietary corp.

Team Center
54 W Exchange St, Saint Paul, MN 55102
(612) 291-2800
Admin Duwayne Johnson.
Licensure Supervised living; Supervised living
for chemical dependency. *Beds* Supervised
living 2; Supervised living for chemical
dependency 39.
Owner Proprietary corp.

Twin City Linnea Home
2040 W Como Ave, Saint Paul, MN 55108
(612) 646-2544
Admin Keith Johnson.
Licensure Boarding care. *Beds* Boarding care
73.
Owner Proprietary corp.

Twin Town Treatment Center
1706 University Ave, Saint Paul, MN 55104
(612) 645-3661
Admin Robert L Haven.
Medical Dir Jerry Schulz MD.
Licensure Supervised living. *Beds* Supervised
living 50.
Owner Proprietary corp.
Admissions Requirements Minimum age 15;
Medical examination.
Staff Physicians; RNs; LPNs; Nurses' aides;
Reality therapists; Dietitians; Chemical
dependency counselors 9 (ft).
Facilities Dining room; Group therapy rooms;
Lounges; Lecture room.
Activities YMCA; Aerobics; Relaxation
therapy.

United Hospital & Nursing Home
333 N Smith, Saint Paul, MN 55102
(612) 298-8888
Admin Thomas H Rockers.
Licensure Nursing care. *Beds* Nursing care 16.
Owner Proprietary corp.

Valor Hemingway
1365 Englewood Ave, Saint Paul, MN 55104
(612) 459-7747
Admin Eileen Harris.
Medical Dir Mary Ellen Hanson.
Licensure Intermediate care for mentally
retarded. *Beds* ICF/MR 6. *Certified*
Medicaid.
Owner Proprietary corp.
Admissions Requirements Minimum age 18;
Medical examination; Physician's request.
Staff RNs 1 (ft).
Facilities Dining room; Activities room.
Activities Arts & crafts; Cards; Games;
Movies; Shopping trips; Dances/Social/
Cultural gatherings.

Wilder Health Care Center
512 Humboldt Ave, Saint Paul, MN 55107
(612) 227-8091
Admin Robert Held.
Licensure Skilled care. *Beds* SNF 147.
Owner Proprietary corp.

Wilder Residence East
696 Dellwood Pl, Saint Paul, MN 55106
(612) 776-4107
Admin Ted A Schmidt.
Medical Dir Madeline Adcock.
Licensure Skilled care; Boarding care. *Beds*
SNF 65; Boarding care 43. *Certified*
Medicaid; Medicare.
Owner Proprietary corp.
Admissions Requirements Minimum age 60;
Medical examination; Physician's request.
Staff RNs 8 (ft); LPNs 12 (ft); Nurses' aides
98 (ft); Physical therapists 1 (pt);
Recreational therapists 1 (ft), 2 (pt);
Occupational therapists; Speech therapists;
Activities coordinators; Dietitians.
Facilities Dining room; Physical therapy
room; Activities room; Chapel; Crafts room;
Laundry room; Barber/Beauty shop; Library;
Solarium.
Activities Arts & crafts; Cards; Games;
Reading groups; Prayer groups; Movies;
Shopping trips; Dances/Social/Cultural
gatherings.

Wilder Residence West
514 Humboldt Ave, Saint Paul, MN 55107
(612) 227-6684
Admin Rick T Johnson. *Dir of Nursing*
Bonnie Peterson. *Medical Dir* Dr Patrick
Irvine.
Licensure Skilled care; Retirement;
Alzheimer's care. *Beds* SNF 50. *Certified*
Medicaid; Medicare.
Owner Nonprofit organization/foundation.
Admissions Requirements Minimum age 60.
Staff RNs 3 (ft), 4 (pt); LPNs 1 (ft), 3 (pt);
Nurses' aides 15 (ft), 10 (pt); Physical
therapists 1 (pt); Recreational therapists 1
(ft), 3 (pt); Occupational therapists 1 (pt);
Activities coordinators 1 (ft).
Facilities Dining room; Physical therapy
room; Activities room; Chapel; Crafts room;
Laundry room; Barber/Beauty shop; Library;
Gift shop.
Activities Arts & crafts; Cards; Games;
Reading groups; Prayer groups; Movies;
Shopping trips; Dances/Social/Cultural
gatherings; Happy hour; Outings;
Horticulture; Life review & enrichment.

Wilson Apartments
1975 Wilson Ave, Saint Paul, MN 55119
(612) 738-6603
Admin James Driscoll.
Licensure Intermediate care for mentally
retarded. *Beds* ICF/MR 15.
Owner Proprietary corp.

Saint Peter

Grandview Care Center
830 N Sunrise Dr, Saint Peter, MN 56082
(507) 931-9021
Admin Sharon Fisher. *Dir of Nursing* Mary
Rose Gag. *Medical Dir* Dr M Don
Olmanson.
Licensure Skilled care. *Beds* SNF 76. *Private
Pay Patients* 35%. *Certified* Medicaid;
Medicare.
Owner Proprietary corp (Good Neighbor
Services).
Admissions Requirements Minimum age 16.
Staff Physicians 8 (pt); RNs 2 (ft); LPNs 5
(ft); Nurses' aides 15 (ft); Physical therapists
1 (ft); Recreational therapists 1 (ft);
Occupational therapists 1 (pt); Speech
therapists 1 (pt); Activities coordinators 1
(ft); Dietitians 1 (pt); Ophthalmologists 1
(pt); Podiatrists 1 (pt); Audiologists 1 (pt).
Facilities Dining room; Physical therapy
room; Activities room; Crafts room; Laundry
room; Barber/Beauty shop; Library.
Activities Arts & crafts; Cards; Games;
Reading groups; Prayer groups; Movies;
Shopping trips; Dances/Social/Cultural
gatherings; Intergenerational programs.

Minnesota Supervised Living Facility
100 Freeman Dr, Saint Peter, MN 56082
(507) 931-7115
Admin Joseph Solien.
Licensure Supervised living. *Beds* Supervised
living 164.
Owner Publicly owned.

**St Peter Community Hospital & Health Care
Center**
618 W Broadway, Saint Peter, MN 56082
(507) 931-2200
Admin Jeanne Johnson CEO. *Dir of Nursing*
Kathy Peterson. *Medical Dir* M D
Olmanson MD.
Licensure Skilled care; Alzheimer's care. *Beds*
SNF 85. *Certified* Medicaid; Medicare.
Owner Nonprofit organization/foundation
(Health One Health Care).
Admissions Requirements Minimum age 16;
Medical examination.
Staff Physicians 7 (ft); RNs 5 (ft); LPNs 3 (ft),
11 (pt); Nurses' aides 8 (ft), 38 (pt); Physical
therapists 1 (ft); Occupational therapists 1
(ft); Speech therapists 1 (pt); Activities
coordinators 1 (ft), 2 (pt); Dietitians 1 (pt);
Podiatrists (consultants).
Facilities Dining room; Physical therapy
room; Activities room; Chapel; Crafts room;
Laundry room; Barber/Beauty shop.
Activities Arts & crafts; Cards; Games;
Reading groups; Prayer groups; Movies;
Shopping trips; Intergenerational programs;
Pet therapy.

St Peter Regional Treatment Center
100 Freeman Dr, Saint Peter, MN 56082
(507) 931-7115
Admin Joseph W Solien.
Licensure Intermediate care for mentally
retarded; Supervised living; Psychiatric
hospital. *Beds* ICF/MR 170; Supervised
living 204; Psychiatric hospital 234.

Sandstone

Pine County Group Home
206 Commercial, Sandstone, MN 55072
(612) 245-5362
Admin Bill Prepodnik.
Licensure Intermediate care for mentally
retarded. *Beds* ICF/MR 9.
Owner Proprietary corp.

Sandstone Area Nursing Home
317 Court Ave, Sandstone, MN 55072
(612) 245-2224
Admin James Blum.
Licensure Skilled care. *Beds* SNF 86. *Certified*
Medicaid; Medicare.
Owner Proprietary corp.

Sartell

Country Manor
520 1st NE, Sartell, MN 56377
(612) 253-1920
Admin Hollis Helgeson. *Dir of Nursing* Sue
Schwartz. *Medical Dir* Saint Cloud
Internists.
Licensure Skilled care; Retirement. *Beds* SNF
187; Retirement 180. *Private Pay Patients*
40%. *Certified* Medicaid; Medicare.
Owner Privately owned.
Admissions Requirements Medical
examination.
Staff RNs 10 (ft), 4 (pt); LPNs 15 (ft), 10 (pt);
Nurses' aides 40 (ft), 80 (pt); Physical
therapists 1 (ft); Recreational therapists 1
(ft); Occupational therapists 1 (ft); Activities
coordinators 1 (ft).
Facilities Dining room; Physical therapy
room; Activities room; Chapel; Crafts room;
Laundry room; Barber/Beauty shop; Library.

Activities Arts & crafts; Cards; Games;
Reading groups; Prayer groups; Movies;
Shopping trips; Dances/Social/Cultural
gatherings; Intergenerational programs.

Sauk Centre

Camphill Village Minnesota Inc
Rte 3 Box 249, Sauk Centre, MN 56378
(612) 732-6365
Licensure Supervised living. *Beds* Supervised
living 12.
Owner Proprietary corp.

Lakeview Childrens Home
Lincoln & W 2nd St, Sauk Centre, MN 56378
(612) 352-3081
Admin Joseph M Bartsh.
Licensure Supervised living facility. *Beds* 7.
Certified Medicaid.
Owner Proprietary corp.
Admissions Requirements Minimum age 3;
Medical examination.
Staff RNs 1 (pt); LPNs 1 (ft).
Facilities Dining room; Activities room;
Laundry room.
Activities Arts & crafts; Games; Movies;
Shopping trips; Dances/Social/Cultural
gatherings.

Pettit Childrens Home
401 Ash St, Sauk Centre, MN 56378
(612) 352-2844
Admin Cathy Marthaler.
Licensure Intermediate care for mentally
retarded. *Beds* ICF/MR 15.
Owner Privately owned.

REM—Sauk Centre Inc
205 6th St, Sauk Centre, MN 56378
(612) 352-3653
Admin Juanita Turner.
Licensure Intermediate care for mentally
retarded. *Beds* ICF/MR 7.
Owner Proprietary corp.
Admissions Requirements Minimum age 13;
Medical examination.
Staff RNs 1 (pt); LPNs 1 (pt); Activities
coordinators 1 (ft).
Facilities Dining room; Activities room;
Laundry room.
Activities Arts & crafts; Cards; Games;
Movies; Shopping trips; Dances/Social/
Cultural gatherings.

St Michaels Hospital & Nursing Home
425 N Elm St, Sauk Centre, MN 56378
(612) 352-2221
Admin Roy Provo.
Medical Dir A B Nietfeld; Gail Ostrom.
Licensure Skilled care. *Beds* SNF 60. *Certified*
Medicaid; Medicare.
Owner Publicly owned.
Admissions Requirements Physician's request.
Staff RNs; LPNs; Nurses' aides; Activities
coordinators.
Facilities Dining room; Physical therapy
room; Activities room; Chapel; Barber/
Beauty shop.
Activities Arts & crafts; Cards; Games;
Reading groups; Movies; Dances/Social/
Cultural gatherings.

Sauk Rapids

Good Shepherd Lutheran Home
1115 4th Ave N, Sauk Rapids, MN 56379
(612) 252-6525
Admin Thomas Bellefeuille.
Medical Dir Dr Vernon E Neils.
Licensure Skilled care. *Beds* SNF 174.
Certified Medicaid; Medicare.
Owner Proprietary corp.
Admissions Requirements Minimum age 16;
Medical examination; Physician's request.

Staff RNs 7 (ft), 7 (pt); LPNs 15 (ft), 9 (pt);
Nurses' aides 24 (ft), 39 (pt); Activities
coordinators 1 (ft).
Affiliation Lutheran.
Facilities Dining room; Physical therapy
room; Activities room; Chapel; Crafts room;
Laundry room; Barber/Beauty shop.
Activities Arts & crafts; Cards; Games;
Reading groups; Prayer groups; Movies;
Shopping trips; Dances/Social/Cultural
gatherings.

Granite Care Home
202 2nd Ave S, Sauk Rapids, MN 56379
(612) 251-4710
Admin Quinton W Hommerding.
Licensure Intermediate care for mentally
retarded. Beds ICF/MR 23.
Owner Proprietary corp.

Shakopee

Delphi
1411 E Shakopee Ave, Shakopee, MN 55379
(612) 445-1680
Admin Betsy Nelson.
Licensure Intermediate care for mentally
retarded. Beds ICF/MR 10.
Owner Proprietary corp.

Front Steps
1111 3rd Ave E, Shakopee, MN 55379
(612) 445-1273
Admin Jame Perron.
Licensure Intermediate care for mentally
retarded. Beds ICF/MR 15.
Owner Proprietary corp.

Shakopee Friendship Manor
1340 3rd Ave W, Shakopee, MN 55379
(612) 445-4155
Admin Timothy A Riffe. Dir of Nursing
Barbara Barry RN. Medical Dir R D
Pistulka MD.
Licensure Skilled care. Beds SNF 116.
Certified Medicaid; Medicare.
Owner Proprietary corp.
Admissions Requirements Minimum age 16;
Medical examination.
Facilities Dining room; Physical therapy
room; Activities room; Crafts room; Laundry
room; Barber/Beauty shop.
Activities Arts & crafts; Cards; Games;
Reading groups; Prayer groups; Movies;
Shopping trips; Dances/Social/Cultural
gatherings.

Sherburn

Friendship Haven I
Fox Lake Ave, Sherburn, MN 56171
(507) 764-3311
Admin Ruth Kirschmann.
Licensure Intermediate care for mentally
retarded. Beds ICF/MR 14.
Owner Proprietary corp.

Friendship Haven II
Fox Lake Ave, Sherburn, MN 56171
(507) 764-2421
Admin Ruth Kirschmann.
Licensure Intermediate care for mentally
retarded. Beds ICF/MR 6.
Owner Proprietary corp.

Shoreview

Lake Owasso Residence
210 Owasso Blvd N, Shoreview, MN 55126
(612) 484-2234
Admin Louis Speggen.
Licensure Intermediate care for mentally
retarded. Beds ICF/MR 64.
Owner Publicly owned.

Moores Haven Dungarvin VI
3490 N Victoria, Shoreview, MN 55126
(612) 482-8029
Admin Janice Carver.
Licensure Intermediate care for mentally
retarded. Beds ICF/MR 6.
Owner Proprietary corp.

Nekton on Hodgson Rd
5091 Hodgson Rd, Shoreview, MN 55112
(612) 483-4024
Admin Steve Kodluboy. Dir of Nursing Jean
Kube.
Licensure Intermediate care for mentally
retarded. Beds ICF/MR 6.
Owner Proprietary corp.
Facilities Ranch style home.
Activities Arts & crafts; Cards; Games;
Reading groups; Movies; Shopping trips;
Dances/Social/Cultural gatherings; Hiking;
Biking.

Residence I
935 Amble Rd, Shoreview, MN 55126
(612) 484-0985
Admin Dennis Holman.
Licensure Intermediate care for mentally
retarded. Beds ICF/MR 8.
Owner Proprietary corp.
Admissions Requirements Minimum age 18;
Medical examination; Physician's request
Mental retardation.
Staff RNs 1 (pt); Activities coordinators 2 (ft).
Facilities Dining room; Activities room.
Activities Cards; Games; Reading groups;
Prayer groups; Movies; Shopping trips;
Dances/Social/Cultural gatherings.

Residence II
925 Amble Rd, Shoreview, MN 55126
(612) 484-6718
Admin Dennis Holman.
Licensure Intermediate care for mentally
retarded. Beds ICF/MR 8.
Owner Proprietary corp.
Staff RNs 1 (pt); Activities coordinators 2 (ft).
Facilities Dining room; Activities room;
Laundry room.
Activities Cards; Games; Reading groups;
Prayer groups; Shopping trips; Dances/
Social/Cultural gatherings.

Slayton

Prairie View Inc
2220 27th St, Slayton, MN 56172
(507) 836-8955
Admin Louis R Nelson.
Medical Dir Kasey Lou Wagie.
Licensure Intermediate care for mentally
retarded. Beds ICF/MR 18.
Owner Privately owned.
Admissions Requirements Minimum age 18.
Staff Physicians 1 (pt); RNs 1 (ft), 1 (pt);
LPNs 4 (ft); Nurses' aides 13 (ft), 6 (pt);
Physical therapists 1 (pt); Recreational
therapists 1 (pt); Occupational therapists 1
(pt); Speech therapists 1 (pt); Activities
coordinators 1 (ft); Dietitians 1 (pt);
Ophthalmologists 1 (pt); Podiatrists 1 (pt);
Dentists 1 (pt).
Facilities Dining room; Laundry room; Living
rooms; Lounges; Kitchenettes.
Activities Arts & crafts; Cards; Games;
Reading groups; Prayer groups; Movies;
Shopping trips; Dances/Social/Cultural
gatherings; Weekly community outings.

Slayton Manor
2957 Redwood Ave S, Slayton, MN 56172
(507) 836-6135
Admin Wayman Fischgrabe. Dir of Nursing
Cheryl Gerth. Medical Dir Larry B Okerlund
MD.
Licensure Skilled care; Alzheimer's care. Beds
SNF 64. Certified Medicaid; Medicare.
Owner Proprietary corp (Beverly Enterprises).

Admissions Requirements Medical
examination; Physician's request.
Staff RNs 1 (ft), 3 (pt); LPNs 6 (ft); Nurses'
aides 16 (ft), 16 (pt); Physical therapists 1
(pt); Occupational therapists; Speech
therapists; Activities coordinators 1 (ft), 2
(pt); Dietitians; Social worker 1 (ft).
Facilities Dining room; Physical therapy
room; Activities room; Chapel; Crafts room;
Laundry room; Barber/Beauty shop; Library;
Whirlpool bath.
Activities Arts & crafts; Cards; Games;
Reading groups; Prayer groups; Movies;
Shopping trips; Dances/Social/Cultural
gatherings.

Sleepy Eye

Divine Providence Community Home
700 3rd Ave NW, Sleepy Eye, MN 56085
(507) 794-3011
Admin Sr Margaret Mary Schissler. Dir of
Nursing Sr Mary Lynn. Medical Dir Dr
Michael Ecker.
Licensure Intermediate care. Beds ICF 58.
Owner Proprietary corp.
Admissions Requirements Medical
examination; Physician's request.
Staff Physicians 3 (pt); RNs 2 (ft), 1 (pt);
LPNs 2 (ft), 4 (pt); Nurses' aides 14 (ft), 25
(pt); Activities coordinators 2 (ft), 1 (pt).
Affiliation Roman Catholic.
Facilities Dining room; Activities room;
Chapel; Crafts room; Barber/Beauty shop.
Activities Arts & crafts; Cards; Games;
Reading groups; Prayer groups; Movies;
Shopping trips; Dances/Social/Cultural
gatherings.

Sleepy Eye Care Center
1105 3rd Ave SW, Sleepy Eye, MN 56085
(507) 794-7995
Admin Del Begalka. Dir of Nursing Ethel
Roth. Medical Dir C M Galvin MD.
Licensure Skilled care; Retirement. Beds SNF
86. Certified Medicaid; Medicare.
Owner Nonprofit corp (Volunteers of America
Care).
Admissions Requirements Medical
examination; Physician's request.
Staff RNs 5 (ft); LPNs 3 (ft), 7 (pt); Nurses'
aides 20 (ft), 16 (pt); Physical therapists 2
(pt); Recreational therapists 1 (ft); Activities
coordinators 1 (ft); Dietitians 1 (ft).
Affiliation Volunteers of America.
Facilities Dining room; Physical therapy
room; Activities room; Chapel; Crafts room;
Laundry room; Barber/Beauty shop.
Activities Arts & crafts; Cards; Games;
Reading groups; Prayer groups; Shopping
trips; Dances/Social/Cultural gatherings.

South Saint Paul

Bryant Avenue Residence
1120 Bryant Ave, South Saint Paul, MN
55075
(612) 451-1344
Admin Anne Hendrickson.
Licensure Intermediate care for mentally
retarded. Beds ICF/MR 15.
Owner Proprietary corp.
Admissions Requirements Minimum age 18.
Staff RNs 1 (ft).
Facilities Dining room; Activities room;
Laundry room; Separate self-contained
apartment units.
Activities Arts & crafts; Cards; Games;
Reading groups; Movies; Shopping trips;
Dances/Social/Cultural gatherings.

Golden Oaks Nursing Home
1025 9th Ave S, South Saint Paul, MN 55075
(612) 455-6615
Admin Otto J Olson. Dir of Nursing Barbara
Dentinger RN. Medical Dir Mary Wangs
Ness MD.

Licensure Skilled care; Intermediate care. *Beds*
SNF 96; ICF 2. *Certified* Medicaid;
Medicare.
Owner Proprietary corp.
Admissions Requirements Minimum age 16;
Medical examination; Physician's request.
Staff RNs; LPNs; Nurses' aides; Activities
coordinators.
Facilities Dining room; Physical therapy
room; Activities room; Chapel; Crafts room;
Laundry room; Barber/Beauty shop; Library.
Activities Arts & crafts; Cards; Games;
Reading groups; Prayer groups; Movies;
Shopping trips; Dances/Social/Cultural
gatherings.

Maclare Residence
630 15th Ave N, South Saint Paul, MN 55075
(612) 457-4898
Admin James Driscoll.
Medical Dir Angela Pelequin.
Licensure Intermediate care for mentally
retarded. *Beds* 6. *Certified* Medicaid.
Owner Proprietary corp.
Admissions Requirements Minimum age 18;
Medical examination.
Staff RNs 1 (ft); LPNs 1 (pt).

Spruce Residence
1249 8th Ave N, South Saint Paul, MN 55075
(612) 455-0578
Admin James Driscoll.
Licensure Intermediate care for mentally
retarded. *Beds* ICF/MR 6.
Owner Proprietary corp.

Spicer

Group Living Home
256 N Lake Ave, Spicer, MN 56288
(612) 796-5881
Admin Sally Haag.
Licensure Supervised living. *Beds* Supervised
living 16.
Owner Privately owned.

Spring Grove

Tweeten Lutheran Health Care Center
125 5th Ave SE, Spring Grove, MN 55974
(507) 498-3211
Admin Robert J Schmidt. *Dir of Nursing* Jan
Kraabel RN. *Medical Dir* Glenn McCarty
DO.
Licensure Skilled care. *Beds* SNF 79. *Certified*
Medicaid; Medicare.
Owner Proprietary corp.
Admissions Requirements Medical
examination; Physician's request.
Staff Physicians 1 (ft); RNs 4 (ft), 6 (pt);
LPNs 3 (ft), 3 (pt); Nurses' aides 10 (ft), 29
(pt); Recreational therapists 1 (ft); Activities
coordinators 1 (ft), 1 (pt); Dietitians 1 (ft).
Affiliation Lutheran.
Facilities Dining room; Activities room;
Chapel; Crafts room; Laundry room; Barber/
Beauty shop.
Activities Arts & crafts; Cards; Games;
Reading groups; Prayer groups; Movies;
Shopping trips; Dances/Social/Cultural
gatherings.

Spring Park

Sage Crossing
4495 Shoreline Dr, Spring Park, MN 55384
(612) 471-8700
Admin Charles Vandeputte.
Licensure Supervised living. *Beds* Supervised
living 34.
Owner Proprietary corp.

Twin Birch Health Care Center
4527 Shoreline Dr, Spring Park, MN 55384
(612) 471-8411

Admin Mariann Kay Wiebusch. *Dir of
Nursing* Mark Wetsch. *Medical Dir* Dr Jerry
Petersen.
Licensure Skilled care; Retirement; Personal
assistance living; Alzheimer's care. *Beds*
SNF 192; Retirement 160; Personal
assistance living 30. *Private Pay Patients*
45%. *Certified* Medicaid; Medicare.
Owner Proprietary corp (Warren Ortenblad).
Admissions Requirements Minimum age 16;
Medical examination; Physician's request.
Staff Physicians; RNs; LPNs; Nurses' aides;
Physical therapists; Reality therapists;
Recreational therapists; Occupational
therapists; Speech therapists; Activities
coordinators; Dietitians; Ophthalmologists;
Podiatrists; Audiologists; Chaplains 1 (ft).
Facilities Dining room; Physical therapy
room; Activities room; Chapel; Crafts room;
Laundry room; Barber/Beauty shop; Library;
Ceramics area & kiln; Occupational therapy
room; Doctor's examination room.
Activities Arts & crafts; Cards; Games;
Reading groups; Prayer groups; Movies;
Shopping trips; Dances/Social/Cultural
gatherings.

Spring Valley

**Community Memorial Hospital & Community
Nursing Care**
800 Memorial Dr, Spring Valley, MN 55975
(507) 346-7381
Admin David Herder. *Dir of Nursing* Karyl
Tammel RN. *Medical Dir* Roger Morse MD.
Licensure Skilled care. *Beds* SNF 50. *Certified*
Medicaid; Medicare.
Owner Nonprofit organization/foundation.
Admissions Requirements Physician's request.
Staff RNs 1 (ft), 2 (pt); LPNs 1 (ft), 8 (pt);
Nurses' aides 8 (ft), 22 (pt); Physical
therapists 1 (ft); Activities coordinators 1
(ft), 1 (pt); Dietitians 1 (pt).
Facilities Dining room; Physical therapy
room; Activities room; Chapel; Crafts room;
Laundry room; Barber/Beauty shop.
Activities Arts & crafts; Cards; Games;
Reading groups; Prayer groups; Movies;
Shopping trips; Dances/Social/Cultural
gatherings; Intergenerational programs; Pet
therapy.

Springfield

St John Lutheran Home
PO Box 167, 710 E Walnut, Springfield, MN
56087
(507) 723-6251
Admin Randy D Snyder. *Dir of Nursing* Mary
S Krueger RN. *Medical Dir* Francis J Boyle
MD.
Licensure Skilled care; Intermediate care;
Board and care; Assisted living. *Beds* SNF
108; ICF 8; Board and care 23; Assisted
living 8. *Certified* Medicaid; Medicare.
Owner Nonprofit organization/foundation.
Admissions Requirements Medical
examination; Physician's request.
Staff RNs 4 (ft), 3 (pt); LPNs 9 (ft), 10 (pt);
Nurses' aides 26 (ft), 45 (pt); Physical
therapists 1 (ft); Recreational therapists 2
(ft), 4 (pt); Activities coordinators 1 (ft);
Dietitians 1 (ft).
Affiliation Lutheran.
Facilities Dining room; Physical therapy
room; Activities room; Chapel; Crafts room;
Barber/Beauty shop; Library; Child day care
center.
Activities Arts & crafts; Cards; Games;
Reading groups; Prayer groups; Movies;
Shopping trips; Dances/Social/Cultural
gatherings; Intergenerational programs; Pet
therapy.

Staples

United District Hospital & Home
401 Prairie Ave N, Staples, MN 56479
(218) 894-1515
Admin Tim Rice. *Dir of Nursing* Karen
Noetzelman. *Medical Dir* T J Lelwica MD.
Licensure Skilled care. *Beds* SNF 100.
Certified Medicaid; Medicare.
Owner Publicly owned.
Admissions Requirements Minimum age 16;
Medical examination; Physician's request.
Staff Physicians 4 (pt); RNs 4 (ft), 3 (pt);
LPNs 2 (ft), 13 (pt); Nurses' aides 13 (ft), 60
(pt); Physical therapists 2 (pt); Activities
coordinators 1 (ft); Dietitians 1 (ft).
Languages Finnish, Bohemian.
Facilities Dining room; Physical therapy
room; Activities room; Chapel; Crafts room;
Barber/Beauty shop; Library.
Activities Arts & crafts; Cards; Games;
Reading groups; Prayer groups; Movies;
Shopping trips; Dances/Social/Cultural
gatherings; Social services 32 hours per
week.

Starbuck

Minnewaska Lutheran Home
605 Main St, Starbuck, MN 56381
(612) 239-2217
Admin Bruce Prause. *Dir of Nursing* Andrea
Hilden. *Medical Dir* Dr Robert Bosl.
Licensure Skilled care; Intermediate care;
Board and care. *Beds* Swing beds SNF/ICF
60; Board and care 16. *Private Pay Patients*
59%.
Owner Nonprofit organization/foundation.
Admissions Requirements Minimum age 16;
Medical examination; Physician's request.
Staff RNs 3 (ft); LPNs 6 (ft), 2 (pt); Nurses'
aides 15 (ft), 15 (pt); Physical therapists 1
(ft); Activities coordinators 1 (ft); Dietitians
1 (pt).
Affiliation Lutheran.
Facilities Dining room; Activities room;
Chapel; Crafts room; Barber/Beauty shop.
Activities Arts & crafts; Cards; Games;
Reading groups; Prayer groups; Movies;
Shopping trips; Dances/Social/Cultural
gatherings.

Project New Hope—Starbuck
707 8th St E, Starbuck, MN 56381
(612) 763-6528
Admin Gerry Cascioli. *Dir of Nursing* Nancy
Scholl RN.
Licensure Intermediate care for mentally
retarded. *Beds* ICF/MR 6.
Owner Proprietary corp.
Admissions Requirements Minimum age 18;
Medical examination.
Staff RNs 1 (pt); LPNs 1 (pt).
Facilities Dining room.
Activities Arts & crafts; Cards; Games;
Reading groups; Movies; Shopping trips;
Dances/Social/Cultural gatherings.

Stewartville

Stewartville Nursing Home
120 4th St NE, Stewartville, MN 55976
(507) 533-4288
Admin Francis A Jensen. *Dir of Nursing* Ruth
Sherman RN. *Medical Dir* Craig D
Thauwald MD.
Licensure Skilled care; Retirement. *Beds* SNF
109. *Certified* Medicaid; Medicare.
Owner Publicly owned.
Admissions Requirements Medical
examination; Physician's request.
Staff RNs 4 (ft), 5 (pt); LPNs 4 (ft), 9 (pt);
Nurses' aides 16 (ft), 26 (pt); Physical
therapists 1 (pt); Reality therapists 1 (pt);
Recreational therapists 1 (ft), 2 (pt);
Activities coordinators 1 (ft); Dietitians 1
(pt).

Facilities Dining room; Physical therapy room; Activities room; Chapel; Crafts room; Laundry room; Barber/Beauty shop; Library.
Activities Arts & crafts; Cards; Games; Reading groups; Prayer groups; Movies; Shopping trips; Dances/Social/Cultural gatherings; Sight-seeing trips.

Stillwater

Greeley Healthcare Center
313 S Greeley St, Stillwater, MN 55082
(612) 439-5775
Admin Nancy Saatzer. *Dir of Nursing* Gail Geisenhoff. *Medical Dir* H V Pearson MD.
Licensure Skilled care; Alzheimer's care. *Beds* SNF 83. *Certified* Medicaid; Medicare.
Owner Proprietary corp (Beverly Enterprises).
Admissions Requirements Minimum age 16; Medical examination; Physician's request.
Staff RNs; LPNs; Nurses' aides; Physical therapists; Recreational therapists; Occupational therapists; Speech therapists; Dietitians; Social workers.
Facilities Physical therapy room.
Activities Arts & crafts; Cards; Games; Reading groups; Prayer groups; Movies; Shopping trips; Dances/Social/Cultural gatherings.

Jamestown
11550 Jasmine Trail N, Stillwater, MN 55082
(612) 429-5307
Admin Carol Frisch.
Licensure Supervised living. *Beds* Supervised living 28.
Owner Proprietary corp.

Linden Healthcare Center
105 W Linden St, Stillwater, MN 55082
(612) 439-5004
Admin David L Hagen. *Dir of Nursing* Gloria Bonse RN. *Medical Dir* James Hart MD.
Licensure Skilled care. *Beds* SNF 75. *Private Pay Patients* 30%. *Certified* Medicaid; Medicare.
Owner Proprietary corp (Beverly Enterprises).
Admissions Requirements Medical examination.
Staff Physicians 1 (pt); RNs 5 (ft); LPNs 6 (ft), 4 (pt); Nurses' aides 19 (ft), 10 (pt); Physical therapists (contracted); Occupational therapists 1 (pt); Speech therapists 1 (pt); Activities coordinators 2 (ft); Dietitians (consultant); Dietary technicians 1 (ft).
Facilities Dining room; Physical therapy room; Activities room; Laundry room; Barber/Beauty shop.
Activities Arts & crafts; Cards; Games; Reading groups; Prayer groups; Movies; Shopping trips; Dances/Social/Cultural gatherings; Intergenerational programs.

Nekton on Imperial Court
8050 Imperial Court, Stillwater, MN 55802
(612) 429-0079
Admin Peter Sajevic.
Licensure Intermediate care for mentally retarded. *Beds* ICF/MR 6. *Certified* Medicaid.
Owner Proprietary corp.

Stillwater Maple Manor Health Care Center
1119 N Owens St, Stillwater, MN 55082
(612) 439-7180
Admin Douglas Dolinsky.
Medical Dir Dr Paul Spilseth.
Licensure Skilled care. *Beds* SNF 132. *Certified* Medicaid; Medicare.
Owner Proprietary corp (Good Neighbor Services).
Staff RNs 17 (ft), 17 (pt); LPNs 10 (ft), 10 (pt); Nurses' aides 26 (ft), 60 (pt); Physical therapists 1 (ft); Recreational therapists 1 (ft); Occupational therapists 1 (pt); Speech

therapists 1 (ft); Activities coordinators 1 (ft); Dietitians 1 (ft); Ophthalmologists 1 (pt); Music therapists 1 (ft), 1 (pt).
Facilities Dining room; Physical therapy room; Activities room; Chapel; Crafts room; Laundry room; Barber/Beauty shop.
Activities Arts & crafts; Cards; Games; Reading groups; Prayer groups; Movies; Shopping trips; Dances/Social/Cultural gatherings.

Stillwater Residence
220 W Olive St, Stillwater, MN 55082
(612) 439-1601
Admin Laura L Reynolds.
Licensure Boarding care. *Beds* Boarding care 23.
Owner Proprietary corp.
Admissions Requirements Minimum age 18; Medical examination; Physician's request.
Staff RNs 1 (pt); LPNs 3 (pt); Nurses' aides 4 (ft), 5 (pt); Activities coordinators 1 (pt); Dietitians 1 (pt).
Facilities Dining room; Activities room; Crafts room; Laundry room.
Activities Arts & crafts; Cards; Games; Movies; Shopping trips; Dances/Social/Cultural gatherings; Resident council; AA meetings.

Thief River Falls

Crestview Home
101 S State Ave, Thief River Falls, MN 56701
(218) 681-3484
Admin Patricia Norberg.
Licensure Boarding care. *Beds* Boarding care 12.
Owner Privately owned.

Hansons Boarding Home
1023 N Dewey, Thief River Falls, MN 56701
(218) 681-4527
Admin Lyle D Hanson.
Licensure Intermediate care for mentally retarded. *Beds* ICF/MR 15.
Owner Proprietary corp.

Johnson's Riverside Boarding Home Inc
RR 4 Box 21, Thief River Falls, MN 56701
(218) 681-1278
Admin Paul Johnson. *Dir of Nursing* Irene Dosser. *Medical Dir* Irene Dosser.
Licensure Intermediate care for mentally retarded. *Beds* ICF/MR 15. *Private Pay Patients* 0%. *Certified* Medicaid.
Owner Proprietary corp.
Admissions Requirements Minimum age 18; Medical examination.
Staff RNs 1 (pt); Nurses' aides 10 (pt); Dietitians.
Facilities Dining room; Activities room; Laundry room.
Activities Arts & crafts; Cards; Games; Reading groups; Movies; Shopping trips; Dances/Social/Cultural gatherings; Fishing; Snowmobiling; Gardening; Pontoon rides; Picnics; Vacations.

Northern Lights Community Residence
324 E 10th St, Thief River Falls, MN 56701
(218) 681-4240
Admin Steve Levinson.
Licensure Supervised living. *Beds* Supervised living 15.
Owner Proprietary corp.

Northwest Medical Center
120 Labree Ave S, Thief River Falls, MN 56701
(218) 681-4240, 681-5614 FAX
Admin Jon D Braband COO. *Dir of Nursing* Marilyn Wigness RN. *Medical Dir* James Langland MD.
Licensure Skilled care. *Beds* SNF 90. *Private Pay Patients* 30%. *Certified* Medicaid; Medicare.

Owner Nonprofit corp (Northwest Medical Center).
Admissions Requirements Minimum age 21.
Staff Physical therapists; Dietitians; Ophthalmologists 1 (ft), 1 (pt).
Facilities Dining room; Physical therapy room; Activities room; Chapel; Crafts room; Laundry room.
Activities Arts & crafts; Cards; Games; Reading groups; Movies; Shopping trips.

Oakland Park Nursing Home
123 Baken St, Thief River Falls, MN 56701
(218) 681-1675
Admin Sherryll C Irvine.
Licensure Intermediate care. *Beds* ICF 75.
Owner Publicly owned.

Trident Halfway House
621 N Labree Ave, Thief River Falls, MN 56701
(218) 681-6187
Admin Jon Furuseth.
Licensure Supervised living. *Beds* Supervised living 9.
Owner Privately owned.

Valley Home
Hwy 32, S Arnold, Thief River Falls, MN 56701
(218) 681-3286
Admin Mildred Brekke.
Licensure Boarding care. *Beds* Boarding care 136.
Owner Proprietary corp.
Admissions Requirements Minimum age 62; Medical examination.
Staff LPNs 2 (ft); Nurses' aides 10 (ft), 3 (pt); Dietitians 1 (pt).
Languages Norwegian.
Activities Arts & crafts; Cards; Games; Reading groups; Prayer groups; Movies; Shopping trips; Dances/Social/Cultural gatherings.

Tower

Hearthside Homes
PO Box 700, Tower, MN 55790-0700
(218) 753-2430
Admin Ronald L Abrahamson.
Licensure Intermediate care for mentally retarded. *Beds* ICF/MR 32.
Owner Proprietary corp.
Admissions Requirements Minimum age 18; Medical examination.
Staff RNs 1 (ft); LPNs 1 (pt); Nurses' aides 4 (ft), 6 (pt); Recreational therapists 2 (ft).
Facilities Dining room; Crafts room.
Activities Arts & crafts; Cards; Games; Prayer groups; Movies; Shopping trips; Dances/Social/Cultural gatherings.

Tracy

Christian Manor Nursing Home
502 5th St E, Tracy, MN 56175
(507) 629-3331
Admin Rev Homer G Dobson. *Dir of Nursing* E Hewitt. *Medical Dir* K Chatterjee MD.
Licensure Skilled care. *Beds* SNF 67. *Private Pay Patients* 60%. *Certified* Medicaid; Medicare.
Owner Nonprofit organization/foundation.
Admissions Requirements Minimum age 19; Medical examination; Physician's request.
Staff Physicians 2 (pt); RNs 2 (ft), 1 (pt); LPNs 5 (ft), 2 (pt); Nurses' aides 14 (ft), 10 (pt); Activities coordinators 2 (ft), 2 (pt); Dietitians 1 (ft), 1 (pt).
Affiliation Church of Christ.
Facilities Dining room; Activities room; Chapel; Crafts room; Laundry room; Barber/Beauty shop.

Activities Arts & crafts; Cards; Games; Reading groups; Prayer groups; Movies; Dances/Social/Cultural gatherings; Intergenerational programs.

Tracy Nursing Home
487 2nd St, Tracy, MN 56175
(507) 629-4850
Admin Goldie Wilking. *Dir of Nursing* Pam Baumann.
Licensure Intermediate care; Board and care. *Beds* ICF 50; Board and care 8. *Private Pay Patients* 52%. *Certified* Medicaid.
Owner Nonprofit organization/foundation.
Admissions Requirements Physician's request.
Staff RNs 1 (ft), 2 (pt); LPNs 3 (ft); Nurses' aides 6 (ft), 16 (pt); Activities coordinators 1 (ft); Dietitians 1 (pt).
Facilities Dining room; Activities room; Chapel; Crafts room; Laundry room.
Activities Arts & crafts; Cards; Reading groups; Prayer groups; Movies; Shopping trips; Dances/Social/Cultural gatherings; Pastoral care.

Trimont

Trimont Nursing Home
303 Broadway S, Trimont, MN 56176
(507) 639-2381
Admin Norma Gates, acting. *Dir of Nursing* Kayla Krieger RN. *Medical Dir* Dr K L Reddy.
Licensure Skilled care. *Beds* SNF 41. *Certified* Medicaid; Medicare.
Owner Nonprofit corp (Health One Health Care).
Admissions Requirements Medical examination.
Staff RNs 1 (ft), 3 (pt); LPNs 2 (ft), 3 (pt); Nurses' aides 10 (ft), 11 (pt); Activities coordinators 1 (ft), 2 (pt); Dietitians 1 (pt).
Facilities Dining room; Activities room; Laundry room; Barber/Beauty shop; Library.
Activities Arts & crafts; Cards; Games; Reading groups; Prayer groups; Movies.

Truman

Lutheran Retirement Home of Southern Minnesota
400 N 4th Ave E, Truman, MN 56088
(507) 776-2031
Admin Rodney Dahlberg.
Medical Dir Dr M J Lester.
Licensure Skilled care. *Beds* SNF 113. *Certified* Medicaid; Medicare.
Owner Proprietary corp.
Admissions Requirements Minimum age 62; Medical examination; Physician's request.
Staff RNs 2 (ft), 4 (pt); LPNs 4 (ft), 5 (pt); Nurses' aides 21 (ft), 36 (pt); Activities coordinators 1 (ft); Dietitians 1 (pt); Rehabilitation aides 2 (ft), 1 (pt).
Affiliation Lutheran.
Facilities Dining room; Physical therapy room; Activities room; Chapel; Crafts room; Laundry room; Barber/Beauty shop; Library.
Activities Arts & crafts; Cards; Games; Reading groups; Prayer groups; Movies; Shopping trips; Dances/Social/Cultural gatherings.

Twin Valley

Lutheran Memorial Nursing Home
Hwy 32 N, Twin Valley, MN 56584
(218) 584-5181
Admin Dwight Fuglie.
Licensure Skilled care; Intermediate care. *Beds* SNF 40; ICF 64. *Certified* Medicaid; Medicare.
Owner Proprietary corp.
Affiliation Lutheran.

Lutheran Memorial Retirement Center
205 3rd St NW, Twin Valley, MN 56584
(218) 584-5181
Admin Dwight Fuglie.
Licensure Boarding care. *Beds* Boarding care 44.
Owner Proprietary corp.

Two Harbors

Caromin House Two Harbors
832 15th Ave, Two Harbors, MN 55616
(218) 834-5029
Admin Trudy Carlson.
Licensure Intermediate care for mentally retarded. *Beds* ICF/MR 6.
Owner Proprietary corp.

Lakeview Memorial Hospital
11th Ave & 4th St, Two Harbors, MN 55616
(218) 834-2211
Admin Michael E Walke.
Licensure Skilled care. *Beds* SNF 50. *Certified* Medicaid; Medicare.
Owner Nonprofit corp.

Sunrise Home
13th Ave & 4th St, Two Harbors, MN 55616
(218) 834-5574
Admin Jack L'Heureux.
Medical Dir Dr Eugene Rondeau.
Licensure Skilled care. *Beds* SNF 55. *Certified* Medicaid; Medicare.
Owner Publicly owned.
Admissions Requirements Minimum age 16; Medical examination; Physician's request.
Staff RNs 2 (ft), 2 (pt); LPNs 2 (ft), 5 (pt); Nurses' aides 14 (ft), 21 (pt); Physical therapists 1 (pt); Activities coordinators 1 (ft); Dietitians 1 (pt).
Facilities Dining room; Activities room; Crafts room; Laundry room; Barber/Beauty shop.
Activities Arts & crafts; Cards; Games; Reading groups; Prayer groups; Movies; Shopping trips; Dances/Social/Cultural gatherings.

Tyler

REM Tyler
303 Highland Ct, Tyler, MN 56178
(507) 247-5568
Admin Craig Miller.
Licensure Intermediate care for mentally retarded. *Beds* ICF/MR 15.
Owner Proprietary corp.

Al Vadheim Memorial Hospital
240 Willow St, Tyler, MN 56178
(507) 247-5521
Admin Pamela Gilchrist. *Dir of Nursing* Paula Hansen RN. *Medical Dir* Keith Carlson MD.
Licensure Skilled care. *Beds* SNF 43. *Certified* Medicaid; Medicare.
Owner Nonprofit corp.
Admissions Requirements Medical examination.
Staff RNs 1 (ft), 2 (pt); LPNs 3 (ft); Nurses' aides 8 (ft), 13 (pt); Physical therapists 1 (pt); Activities coordinators 1 (ft); Dietitians 1 (pt).
Facilities Dining room; Activities room; Barber/Beauty shop.
Activities Arts & crafts; Cards; Games; Movies; Bingo.

Ulen

Viking Manor Nursing Home
Ulen, MN 56585
(218) 596-8847
Admin Todd Kjos.
Licensure Intermediate care. *Beds* ICF 66.
Owner Publicly owned.

Victoria

Community Living Inc
PO Box 130, Victoria, MN 55386-0130
(612) 443-2048
Admin Jerry Gross.
Licensure Intermediate care for mentally retarded. *Beds* ICF/MR 42.
Owner Proprietary corp.
Admissions Requirements Minimum age 18; Medical examination; Physician's request.
Staff RNs 2 (ft).
Facilities Dining room; Activities room; Laundry room.
Activities Arts & crafts; Cards; Games; Reading groups; Movies; Shopping trips; Dances/Social/Cultural gatherings.

Virginia

Arrowhead Health Care Center
Box 971, 1201 8-1/2 St S, Virginia, MN 55792
(218) 741-4590
Admin Yvonne Michaud. *Dir of Nursing* Michelle King. *Medical Dir* Dr Matthew Weir.
Licensure Skilled care; Board & lodging. *Beds* SNF 110; Board & lodging 32. *Private Pay Patients* 15%. *Certified* Medicaid; Medicare.
Owner Privately owned (Philip K Schumacher).
Admissions Requirements Physician's request.
Staff RNs 8 (ft); LPNs 12 (ft); Nurses' aides 40 (ft); Physical therapists 1 (ft), 1 (pt); Occupational therapists 1 (ft); Speech therapists 1 (pt); Activities coordinators 1 (ft); Dietitians 1 (ft).
Facilities Dining room; Physical therapy room; Activities room; Crafts room; Laundry room; Barber/Beauty shop.
Activities Arts & crafts; Cards; Games; Reading groups; Prayer groups; Movies; Shopping trips; Dances/Social/Cultural gatherings; Intergenerational programs; Pet therapy.

Gethsemane Group Home
507 9th Ave S, Virginia, MN 55792
(218) 741-9437
Admin Sandra Johnson. *Dir of Nursing* Valborg Pepelnjak RN.
Licensure Intermediate care for mentally retarded. *Beds* ICF/MR 12.
Owner Proprietary corp.
Admissions Requirements Minimum age 18; Medical examination.
Staff RNs 1 (pt); Residential counselors 3 (ft), 5 (pt).
Affiliation Lutheran.
Facilities Dining room; Activities room; Crafts room; Laundry room.
Activities Arts & crafts; Cards; Games; Movies; Shopping trips; Dances/Social/Cultural gatherings.

Virginia Regional Medical Center & Nursing Home
901 9th St N, Virginia, MN 55792
(218) 741-3340
Admin Michael R Miller. *Dir of Nursing* Connie Devereux RN. *Medical Dir* Dr Donald Werner.
Licensure Skilled care; Intermediate care. *Beds* SNF 116. *Certified* Medicaid; Medicare.
Owner Publicly owned.
Admissions Requirements Minimum age 16; Medical examination; Physician's request.
Staff RNs; LPNs; Nurses' aides; Physical therapists; Activities coordinators; Dietitians.
Languages Finnish.
Facilities Dining room; Physical therapy room; Activities room; Chapel; Crafts room; Laundry room; Barber/Beauty shop; Library; Lounges; Atrium.

Activities Arts & crafts; Cards; Games; Reading groups; Prayer groups; Movies; Shopping trips; Dances/Social/Cultural gatherings.

Wabasha

River Valley Health Care Center
626 Shields Ave, Wabasha, MN 55981
(612) 565-4581
Admin Joseph L Ramnarine.
Medical Dir Max Bachhuber.
Licensure Skilled care. *Beds* SNF 115. *Certified* Medicaid; Medicare.
Owner Publicly owned.
Admissions Requirements Medical examination.
Staff RNs 6 (ft), 5 (pt); LPNs 6 (ft), 4 (pt); Nurses' aides 28 (ft), 16 (pt); Activities coordinators 1 (pt).

St Elizabeth Hospital
1200 5th Grant Blvd W, Wabasha, MN 55981
(612) 565-4531
Admin Tom Crowley.
Medical Dir Mary Tentis.
Licensure Skilled care; Boarding care. *Beds* SNF 42; Boarding care 10. *Certified* Medicaid; Medicare.
Owner Proprietary corp.
Admissions Requirements Minimum age; Medical examination; Physician's request.
Affiliation Roman Catholic.
Facilities Dining room; Physical therapy room; Chapel; Crafts room; Laundry room.
Activities Arts & crafts; Cards; Games; Reading groups; Prayer groups; Movies; Shopping trips; Dances/Social/Cultural gatherings.

Wabasso

Wabasso Healthcare Center
Maple & May Sts, Wabasso, MN 56293
(507) 342-5166
Admin Bradley Gauger. *Dir of Nursing* Carol Bratsch RN. *Medical Dir* David Dekert MD.
Licensure Skilled care. *Beds* SNF 50. *Certified* Medicaid; Medicare.
Owner Proprietary corp (Beverly Enterprises).
Admissions Requirements Minimum age 21; Medical examination; Physician's request.
Staff RNs 1 (ft), 1 (pt); LPNs 2 (ft), 4 (pt); Nurses' aides 10 (ft), 16 (pt); Activities coordinators 1 (ft).
Facilities Dining room; Physical therapy room; Activities room; Laundry room; Barber/Beauty shop.
Activities Arts & crafts; Cards; Games; Reading groups; Movies; Dances/Social/Cultural gatherings.

Waconia

Nightingale Nursing Home
232 S Elm St, Waconia, MN 55387
(612) 442-2546
Admin Muriel Maass. *Dir of Nursing* Ruth Goetze. *Medical Dir* Dr Joe Van Kirk.
Licensure Intermediate care; Boarding care. *Beds* ICF 33; Boarding care 4. *Certified* Medicaid.
Owner Nonprofit organization/foundation.
Admissions Requirements Minimum age 21; Medical examination; Physician's request.
Staff RNs 3 (ft), 2 (pt); LPNs 3 (ft), 1 (pt); Nurses' aides 8 (ft), 7 (pt); Activities coordinators 1 (ft); Dietitians 1 (pt).
Languages German.
Facilities Dining room; Activities room; Chapel; Laundry room.
Activities Arts & crafts; Cards; Games; Reading groups; Prayer groups; Movies; Shopping trips; Pet therapy; Religious services.

Waconia Healthcare Center
333 W 5th St, Waconia, MN 55387
(612) 442-5111
Admin Jim Duchene.
Licensure Skilled care. *Beds* SNF 100. *Certified* Medicaid; Medicare.
Owner Proprietary corp (Good Neighbor Services).

Wadena

Bell Hill Recovery Center
PO Box 206, Rte 2, Wadena, MN 56482
(218) 631-3610
Admin Audrey Schmitz.
Licensure Supervised living. *Beds* Supervised living 84.
Owner Proprietary corp.

Oakridge Home
Rte 1 Box 589, Wadena, MN 56482
(218) 631-4133
Admin Rodney Peltoma.
Licensure Intermediate care for mentally retarded. *Beds* ICF/MR 16.
Owner Proprietary corp.

Pembina Trail
Rte 1 Box 127, Wadena, MN 56482
(218) 631-1853
Admin Karen Crandall.
Medical Dir Karen Crandall.
Licensure Supervised living. *Beds* Supervised living 8.
Owner Proprietary corp.
Admissions Requirements Minimum age 18; Medical examination; Physician's request.
Activities Arts & crafts; Cards; Games; Reading groups; Prayer groups; Movies; Shopping trips; Dances/Social/Cultural gatherings.

Shady Lane Nursing Home
RR 2, Hwy 110 E, Wadena, MN 56482
(218) 631-1391
Admin Michael M Gibson. *Dir of Nursing* Jane Uselman. *Medical Dir* Leland Reichelt.
Licensure Skilled care. *Beds* SNF 115. *Private Pay Patients* 25%. *Certified* Medicaid.
Owner Publicly owned.
Admissions Requirements Minimum age 18.
Staff RNs 4 (ft); LPNs 7 (ft).
Facilities Dining room; Physical therapy room; Activities room; Chapel; Crafts room; Barber/Beauty shop.
Activities Arts & crafts; Cards; Games; Reading groups; Prayer groups; Movies; Shopping trips; Dances/Social/Cultural gatherings; Intergenerational programs.

Woodview Residential Services—Wadena
PO Box 573, Wadena, MN 56482
(218) 879-4536
Admin David Felske.
Licensure Supervised living. *Beds* Supervised living 13.
Owner Proprietary corp.

Waite Park

REM Waite Park Inc
46 9th Ave N, Waite Park, MN 56387
(612) 251-6142
Admin Juanita Hayes.
Licensure Intermediate care for mentally retarded. *Beds* ICF/MR 9.
Owner Proprietary corp.

St Francis Home
25 2nd St N, Waite Park, MN 56387
(612) 251-7630
Admin George Boswell.
Licensure Intermediate care for mentally retarded. *Beds* ICF/MR 6. *Certified* Medicaid; Medicare.
Owner Publicly owned.
Affiliation Roman Catholic.

Waite Park Nursing Home Inc
142 NW 1st St, Waite Park, MN 56387
(612) 252-9595
Admin Marlene Nyquist.
Medical Dir Dr Thienes.
Licensure Skilled care; Retirement. *Beds* SNF 74. *Certified* Medicaid; Medicare.
Owner Proprietary corp.
Admissions Requirements Medical examination; Physician's request.
Staff Physicians; RNs; LPNs; Nurses' aides; Physical therapists; Recreational therapists; Occupational therapists; Speech therapists; Activities coordinators; Dietitians; Ophthalmologists.
Languages German.
Facilities Dining room; Physical therapy room; Activities room; Laundry room; Barber/Beauty shop.
Activities Arts & crafts; Cards; Games; Reading groups; Prayer groups; Movies; Shopping trips; Dances/Social/Cultural gatherings.

Walker

Johnsons Long Lake Home
PO Box 687, Walker, MN 56484
(218) 547-1352
Admin Daniel L Krause.
Licensure Intermediate care for mentally retarded. *Beds* ICF/MR 6.
Owner Proprietary corp.

Woodrest Nursing Home
Box J, Walker, MN 56484
(218) 547-1855
Admin Shirley Ziegler.
Licensure Skilled care; Intermediate care. *Beds* SNF 60; ICF 6. *Certified* Medicaid; Medicare.
Owner Proprietary corp (Beverly Enterprises).

Wanamingo

Riverview Manor
Box 102A, RR 1, Wanamingo, MN 55983
(507) 824-2910
Admin Betty Malchow.
Licensure Intermediate care for mentally retarded. *Beds* ICF/MR 15.
Owner Proprietary corp.
Admissions Requirements Minimum age 18.
Staff Recreational therapists 1 (pt).
Facilities Dining room; Activities room; Laundry room.
Activities Arts & crafts; Cards; Games; Reading groups; Prayer groups; Movies; Shopping trips; Dances/Social/Cultural gatherings.

Warren

Good Samaritan Center
410 S McKinley St, Warren, MN 56762
(218) 745-5282
Admin Dwight Voigt.
Licensure Intermediate care for mentally retarded. *Beds* ICF/MR 102. *Certified* Medicaid.
Owner Nonprofit corp (Evangelical Lutheran/ Good Samaritan Society).

Warroad

Warroad Care Center
611 E Lake St, Warroad, MN 56763
(218) 386-1234
Admin Jeffry Stampohar.
Medical Dir Dr Michael Clark.
Licensure Skilled care. *Beds* SNF 49. *Certified* Medicaid; Medicare.
Owner Nonprofit corp.

Staff Physicians 2 (ft); RNs 4 (ft); LPNs 5 (ft);
Nurses' aides 25 (ft); Recreational therapists
2 (ft); Activities coordinators 1 (ft);
Dietitians 1 (ft); Audiologists 1 (pt); Dentists
1 (ft).
Facilities Dining room; Activities room;
Chapel; Laundry room; Barber/Beauty shop;
Library.
Activities Arts & crafts; Cards; Games;
Reading groups; Prayer groups; Movies;
Shopping trips; Dances/Social/Cultural
gatherings.

Waseca

Elm North Inc
Box 489, 104 22nd Ave NE, Waseca, MN
56093
(507) 835-1146
Admin Eugene L Miller.
Licensure Intermediate care for mentally
retarded. *Beds* ICF/MR 12.
Owner Proprietary corp.

Elm Residence
620 E Elm, Waseca, MN 56093
(507) 835-5430
Admin Eugene Miller.
Licensure Intermediate care for mentally
retarded. *Beds* ICF/MR 8.
Owner Proprietary corp.

Larry James Home
404 2nd St NE, Waseca, MN 56093
(507) 835-3580
Admin E L Miller. *Dir of Nursing* Maryl Scott
RN.
Licensure Intermediate care for mentally
retarded. *Beds* ICF/MR 8.
Owner Proprietary corp.
Admissions Requirements Minimum age 18;
Medical examination.
Staff RNs 2 (pt); LPNs 1 (pt).
Facilities Dining room; Activities room;
Laundry room.
Activities Arts & crafts; Games; Movies;
Shopping trips; Dances/Social/Cultural
gatherings.

Lakeshore Inn Nursing Home
108 8th St NW, Waseca, MN 56093
(507) 835-2800
Admin R P Madel Jr.
Licensure Skilled care. *Beds* SNF 94. *Certified*
Medicaid; Medicare.
Owner Proprietary corp.

Westside Boarding Care Home
914 8th Ave NW, Waseca, MN 56093
(507) 451-0832
Admin Margaret Striemer.
Licensure Boarding care. *Beds* Boarding care
13.
Owner Proprietary corp.

Watertown

Elim Home
PO Box 638, 409 Jefferson Ave SW,
Watertown, MN 55388
(612) 955-2691
Admin Trenton Carlson. *Dir of Nursing* Joy
Drawert. *Medical Dir* Dr D R Philip.
Licensure Skilled care; Retirement. *Beds* SNF
55. *Certified* Medicaid; Medicare.
Owner Proprietary corp.
Admissions Requirements Minimum age 18;
Medical examination; Physician's request.
Staff Physicians 3 (pt); RNs 1 (ft), 4 (pt);
LPNs 3 (ft), 5 (pt); Nurses' aides 10 (ft), 27
(pt); Physical therapists 1 (pt); Occupational
therapists 1 (pt); Activities coordinators 1
(ft); Dietitians 1 (pt).
Affiliation Evangelical Free Church.
Facilities Dining room; Physical therapy
room; Activities room; Crafts room; Laundry
room; Barber/Beauty shop; Outdoor patio.

Activities Arts & crafts; Cards; Games;
Reading groups; Prayer groups; Movies;
Shopping trips; One-on-one LEEP program.

Waterville

Hope Residences
Box 63, Paquin & Herbert, Waterville, MN
56096
(507) 362-8243
Admin Douglas Scharfe.
Licensure Intermediate care for mentally
retarded. *Beds* ICF/MR 14.
Owner Proprietary corp.
Admissions Requirements Minimum age 18.
Staff LPNs 1 (ft).
Facilities Dining room; Laundry room.
Activities Arts & crafts; Cards; Games;
Movies; Shopping trips; Dances/Social/
Cultural gatherings.

Le Sueur Residence
529 W Pacquin St, Waterville, MN 56096
(507) 362-8780
Admin Eugene Miller.
Licensure Intermediate care for mentally
retarded. *Beds* ICF/MR 10.
Owner Proprietary corp.

Waterville Care Center
205 1st St N, Waterville, MN 56096
(507) 362-4245
Admin Linda Nelson, acting. *Dir of Nursing*
Kathleen Nosbush. *Medical Dir* Dr Burton
Grimes.
Licensure Skilled care. *Beds* SNF 56. *Certified*
Medicaid; Medicare.
Owner Proprietary corp (Good Neighbor
Services).
Admissions Requirements Minimum age 16.
Staff RNs 1 (ft), 7 (pt); LPNs 5 (pt); Nurses'
aides 5 (ft), 20 (pt); Physical therapists 1
(pt); Recreational therapists 2 (pt);
Occupational therapists 1 (pt); Speech
therapists 1 (pt); Activities coordinators 1
(pt); Dietitians 1 (pt).
Facilities Dining room; Physical therapy
room; Activities room; Chapel; Laundry
room; Barber/Beauty shop.
Activities Arts & crafts; Cards; Games;
Movies; Shopping trips; Dances/Social/
Cultural gatherings.

Watkins

Hilltop Care Center
Rte 1 Box H, Watkins, MN 55389
(612) 764-2300
Admin Daniel Waage.
Medical Dir Dr Gardner.
Licensure Skilled care. *Beds* SNF 65. *Certified*
Medicaid; Medicare.
Owner Proprietary corp (Good Neighbor
Services).
Admissions Requirements Medical
examination; Physician's request.
Staff RNs 1 (ft), 3 (pt); LPNs 4 (ft), 4 (pt);
Nurses' aides 16 (ft), 15 (pt); Physical
therapists 1 (pt); Occupational therapists 1
(pt); Activities coordinators 1 (ft); Dietitians
1 (pt).
Facilities Dining room; Physical therapy
room; Activities room; Crafts room; Laundry
room; Barber/Beauty shop.
Activities Arts & crafts; Cards; Games;
Reading groups; Prayer groups; Movies;
Shopping trips; Dances/Social/Cultural
gatherings.

Waverly

New Beginnings at Waverly
Lake Waverly, Waverly, MN 55390
(612) 658-4811
Admin Clelland Gilchrist.

Licensure Supervised living. *Beds* Supervised
living 40.
Owner Proprietary corp.

Wayzata

Hammer Residence—Apartment & Annex
1909 E Wayzata Blvd, Wayzata, MN 55391
(612) 473-1261
Admin Roger A Deneen.
Licensure Intermediate care for mentally
retarded. *Beds* ICF/MR 21.
Owner Proprietary corp.

Hammer Residence—Gleason Lake Residence
16325 County Rd 15, Wayzata, MN 55391
(612) 473-1261
Admin Roger A Deneen.
Licensure Intermediate care for mentally
retarded. *Beds* ICF/MR 6.
Owner Proprietary corp.

Hillcrest Health Care Center
15409 Wayzata Blvd, Wayzata, MN 55391
(612) 473-5466
Admin Joanne Gilbertson.
Licensure Skilled care; Boarding care. *Beds*
SNF 155; Boarding care 60. *Certified*
Medicaid; Medicare.
Owner Proprietary corp (Beverly Enterprises).

Shadyway Group Home
522 Shadyway Rd, Wayzata, MN 55391
(612) 475-0089
Admin Dexter Andrews.
Licensure Intermediate care for mentally
retarded. *Beds* ICF/MR 6. *Private Pay
Patients* 0%.
Owner Nonprofit organization/foundation.
Admissions Requirements Minimum age 18;
Medical examination.
Languages Sign.
Facilities Dining room; Laundry room.
Activities Arts & crafts; Games; Movies;
Shopping trips; Dances/Social/Cultural
gatherings; Community integration.

Valor Aspen
1909 E Wayzata Blvd, Wayzata, MN 55391
(612) 722-3148
Admin Eileen L Harris.
Licensure Intermediate care for mentally
retarded. *Beds* ICF/MR 6.
Owner Proprietary corp.

Way Twelve Halfway House
645 E Wayzata Blvd, Wayzata, MN 55391
(612) 473-7371
Admin Karen Mattson.
Licensure Boarding care. *Beds* Boarding care
20.
Owner Nonprofit corp.
Admissions Requirements Minimum age 16-
25; Medical examination.
Facilities Laundry room.
Activities Arts & crafts; Games; Movies;
Shopping trips; Dances/Social/Cultural
gatherings; Individual & group therapy;
Lectures; Independent living skills.

Wells

Naeve Parkview Nursing Home
55 10th St SE, Wells, MN 56097
(507) 553-3115
Admin Cathrine A Hagen RN. *Dir of Nursing*
Jean Steinhauer RN. *Medical Dir* Dr
Kenneth Haycraft.
Licensure Skilled care. *Beds* SNF 61. *Certified*
Medicaid; Medicare.
Owner Privately owned.
Admissions Requirements Medical
examination; Physician's request.
Staff Physicians 3 (pt); RNs 2 (ft), 10 (pt);
LPNs 8 (pt); Nurses' aides 52 (pt); Physical
therapists 10 (pt); Activities coordinators 1
(ft), 1 (pt); Dietitians 1 (pt).
Languages German.

Facilities Dining room; Physical therapy room; Activities room; Chapel; Crafts room; Laundry room; Barber/Beauty shop.
Activities Arts & crafts; Cards; Games; Reading groups; Prayer groups; Movies; Shopping trips; Dances/Social/Cultural gatherings.

West Saint Paul

Dakota's Children Home
400 W Marie Ave, West Saint Paul, MN 55118
(612) 455-1286
Admin Kathleen Pine.
Licensure Intermediate care for mentally retarded. Beds ICF/MR 48.
Owner Proprietary corp.
Admissions Requirements Minimum age 3; Medical examination; Physician's request.
Staff RNs 2 (ft), 1 (pt); LPNs 1 (ft), 1 (pt); Recreational therapists 1 (ft); Occupational therapists 2 (ft); Activities coordinators 2 (ft); Dietitians 1 (ft).
Facilities Dining room; Activities room; Crafts room; Laundry room.
Activities Arts & crafts; Games; Reading groups; Movies; Shopping trips; Dances/Social/Cultural gatherings; Developmental programming.

Horizon Apartments
1094 Waterloo St, West Saint Paul, MN 55118
(612) 455-6285
Admin James R Driscoll.
Licensure Intermediate care for mentally retarded. Beds ICF/MR 15.
Owner Proprietary corp.

DCI—Thompson Avenue Group Home
219 E Thompson Ave, West Saint Paul, MN 55118
(612) 457-6006
Admin Kathleen Pine.
Licensure Intermediate care for mentally retarded. Beds ICF/MR 9.
Owner Proprietary corp.

Southview Acres Health Care Center
2000 Oakdale Ave, West Saint Paul, MN 55118
(612) 451-1821
Admin Edward Lemieux.
Licensure Skilled care. Beds SNF 262.
Certified Medicaid; Medicare.
Owner Proprietary corp.

Theodore I Residence
1312-1314 Livingston Ave, West Saint Paul, MN 55118
(612) 772-3578
Admin Patricia L Mitchell.
Licensure Supervised living. Beds Supervised living 10.
Owner Proprietary corp.

Westbrook

Westbrook Good Samaritan Center
149 1st Ave, Box 218, Westbrook, MN 56183
(507) 274-6155
Admin Gary Hofer.
Licensure Intermediate care. Beds ICF 49.
Owner Nonprofit corp (Evangelical Lutheran/ Good Samaritan Society).

Wheaton

Traverse County Nursing Home
PO Box 808, 303 7th St S, Wheaton, MN 56296
(612) 563-8124
Admin Gael A Coleman. Dir of Nursing Audrey Mitteness. Medical Dir James Poole MD.

Licensure Intermediate care. Beds ICF 64.
Private Pay Patients 35%. Certified Medicaid.
Owner Publicly owned.
Admissions Requirements Medical examination.
Staff RNs 3 (ft), 1 (pt); LPNs 3 (ft), 3 (pt); Nurses' aides 10 (ft), 26 (pt); Activities coordinators 1 (ft); Dietitians 1 (pt).
Facilities Dining room; Activities room; Chapel; Crafts room; Laundry room; Barber/ Beauty shop; Library; Rehabilitation.
Activities Arts & crafts; Cards; Games; Reading groups; Prayer groups; Movies; Shopping trips; Dances/Social/Cultural gatherings; Weekly rides.

White Bear Lake

Francis Residence II
2532 Oak Dr, White Bear Lake, MN 55110
(612) 774-9014
Admin Jeffrey Boston.
Licensure Supervised living. Beds Supervised living 6.
Owner Proprietary corp.

Northeast Residence I
4680 Bald Eagle Ave, White Bear Lake, MN 55110
(612) 426-1210
Admin Mary Jo Dolan.
Licensure Intermediate care for mentally retarded. Beds ICF/MR 9. Certified Medicaid.
Owner Proprietary corp.
Admissions Requirements Minimum age 16; Medical examination; Physician's request.
Facilities Dining room; Activities room; Crafts room; Laundry room.
Activities Arts & crafts; Movies; Shopping trips; Dances/Social/Cultural gatherings.

Northeast Residence II
1995 Oak Knoll Dr, White Bear Lake, MN 55110
(612) 426-4306
Admin Mary Jo Dolan.
Medical Dir Judy Zech.
Licensure Intermediate care for mentally retarded. Beds ICF/MR 6.
Owner Proprietary corp.
Admissions Requirements Minimum age 5; Medical examination.
Staff RNs 1 (pt).
Facilities Dining room; Activities room; Crafts room; Laundry room.
Activities Arts & crafts; Cards; Games; Movies; Shopping trips; Shopping trips; Dances/Social/Cultural gatherings; Swimming; Community gymnasium; Hayrides; Music.

White Bear Lake Care Center
1891 Florence St, White Bear Lake, MN 55110
(612) 426-1361
Admin Barbara DeLaHunt.
Medical Dir T Altemeier MD.
Licensure Skilled care. Beds SNF 201.
Certified Medicaid; Medicare.
Owner Proprietary corp (Health East).
Admissions Requirements Minimum age 18; Medical examination.
Staff RNs 7 (ft), 8 (pt); LPNs 13 (ft), 25 (pt); Nurses' aides 32 (ft), 68 (pt); Physical therapists 1 (ft); Recreational therapists 2 (ft); Occupational therapists 1 (ft); Speech therapists 1 (pt); Activities coordinators 1 (ft); Dietitians 1 (pt).
Facilities Dining room; Physical therapy room; Activities room; Crafts room; Laundry room; Barber/Beauty shop; Meditation room; Carpentry room.

Activities Arts & crafts; Cards; Games; Reading groups; Prayer groups; Movies; Shopping trips; Dances/Social/Cultural gatherings; Resident job program; Chaplain services.

Willmar

Alexander Home
901 Memorial Pkwy, Willmar, MN 56201
(612) 235-8315
Admin Kathryn Selseth-Kill. Dir of Nursing Linda Nelson RN. Medical Dir Dr Ronald Holmgren.
Licensure Intermediate care for mentally retarded. Beds ICF/MR 15.
Owner Proprietary corp.
Admissions Requirements Minimum age 18; Medical examination.
Staff Physicians 1 (pt); RNs 1 (pt); Activities coordinators 1 (ft).
Languages Spanish.
Facilities Dining room; Laundry room.
Activities Arts & crafts; Cards; Games; Reading groups; Movies; Shopping trips; Dances/Social/Cultural gatherings; Travel.

Ashwood Health Care Center
500 Russell St, Willmar, MN 56201
(612) 235-3181
Admin Dru Fischgrabe. Dir of Nursing Phyllis Meyer. Medical Dir Dr Michael T Anderson.
Licensure Skilled care; ICF/MI. Beds SNF 64; ICF/MI 35. Private Pay Patients 20%. Certified Medicaid; Medicare.
Owner Proprietary corp (Beverly Enterprises).
Admissions Requirements Minimum age 16; Medical examination; Physician's request.
Staff RNs 3 (ft); LPNs 7 (ft), 19 (pt); Nurses' aides 12 (ft), 15 (pt); Physical therapists 1 (ft); Occupational therapists 1 (ft); Speech therapists 1 (pt); Activities coordinators 1 (ft); Dietitians 1 (ft).
Facilities Dining room; Physical therapy room; Activities room; Crafts room; Laundry room; Barber/Beauty shop.
Activities Arts & crafts; Cards; Games; Reading groups; Prayer groups; Movies; Shopping trips; Dances/Social/Cultural gatherings; Intergenerational programs; Pet therapy.

Bethesda Heritage Center
1012 E 3rd St, Willmar, MN 56201
(612) 235-3924
Admin Anthony Ogdahl.
Licensure Intermediate care; Boarding care. Beds ICF 107; Boarding care 22.
Owner Nonprofit corp (Health One).

Bethesda Nursing Home—Pleasantview
901 E Willmar Ave, Willmar, MN 56201
(612) 235-9532
Admin Douglas Dewane.
Licensure Skilled care. Beds SNF 120.
Certified Medicaid; Medicare.
Owner Nonprofit corp (Health One).

Christian Nursing & Living Center
1801 Willmar Ave, Willmar, MN 56201
(612) 235-0050
Admin Dennis Kamstra. Dir of Nursing Renee Aro RN. Medical Dir Robert P Hodapp MD.
Licensure Skilled care; Retirement. Beds SNF 86. Certified Medicaid; Medicare.
Owner Proprietary corp.
Admissions Requirements Medical examination; Physician's request.
Staff Physicians 1 (pt); RNs 8 (ft); LPNs 11 (ft); Nurses' aides 5 (ft), 20 (pt); Physical therapists 1 (pt); Recreational therapists 3 (ft); Activities coordinators 1 (ft); Dietitians 1 (pt); Dentists 1 (pt).
Facilities Dining room; Physical therapy room; Activities room; Laundry room; Barber/Beauty shop; Library.

Activities Arts & crafts; Cards; Games;
Reading groups; Prayer groups; Movies;
Shopping trips; Dances/Social/Cultural
gatherings.

Friendship House
901 Memorial Pkwy, Willmar, MN 56201
(612) 235-8444
Admin Kathryn Selseth-Kill. *Dir of Nursing*
Linda Nelson RN. *Medical Dir* Ronald
Holmgren MD.
Licensure Intermediate care for mentally
retarded. *Beds* ICF/MR 15.
Owner Proprietary corp.
Admissions Requirements Minimum age 18;
Females only.
Staff Physicians 1 (pt); RNs 1 (pt); Activities
coordinators 1 (ft).
Facilities Dining room; Activities room;
Laundry room.
Activities Arts & crafts; Cards; Games;
Reading groups; Movies; Shopping trips;
Dances/Social/Cultural gatherings; Travel.

Heather Hill
901 Memorial Pkwy, Willmar, MN 56201
(612) 235-4373
Admin Kathryn Selseth-Kill. *Dir of Nursing*
Linda Nelson RN. *Medical Dir* Ronald
Holmgren MD.
Licensure Intermediate care for mentally
retarded. *Beds* ICF/MR 15.
Owner Proprietary corp.
Admissions Requirements Minimum age 18.
Staff Physicians 1 (pt); RNs 1 (pt); Activities
coordinators 1 (ft).
Facilities Dining room; Activities room;
Laundry room.
Activities Arts & crafts; Cards; Games;
Reading groups; Movies; Shopping trips;
Dances/Social/Cultural gatherings; Travel.

Kindlehope
1217 7th St SE, Willmar, MN 56201
(612) 235-2838
Admin David Meillier.
Medical Dir Dr Michael T Anderson.
Licensure Intermediate care for mentally
retarded. *Beds* ICF/MR 60.
Owner Proprietary corp.
Admissions Requirements Minimum age 16;
Medical examination; Physician's request.
Staff RNs 1 (pt); LPNs 2 (ft), 2 (pt); Nurses'
aides 9 (ft), 21 (pt); Recreational therapists 1
(ft); Dietitians 4 (ft); Social workers 4 (ft), 1
(pt).
Facilities Dining room; Laundry room.
Activities Arts & crafts; Cards; Games;
Movies; Shopping trips; Dances/Social/
Cultural gatherings; Trips to zoo; Dinner
theatre; Camping; Cross-country skiing.

Willmar Regional Treatment Center
PO Box 1128, Willmar, MN 56201
(612) 231-5100
Admin Gregory G Spartz, acting. *Dir of
Nursing* Dennis Butler RN. *Medical Dir*
Larry Olson MD.
Licensure Intermediate care for mentally
retarded. *Beds* ICF/MR 170.
Owner Publicly owned.

Windom

Sogge Good Samaritan Center
705 Sixth St, Windom, MN 56101
(507) 831-1788
Admin Wayne O Brodland. *Dir of Nursing*
Linda Dulaney RN. *Medical Dir* Dr James
Dokken.
Licensure Intermediate care; Retirement. *Beds*
ICF 93.
Owner Nonprofit corp (Evangelical Lutheran/
Good Samaritan Society).
Admissions Requirements Minimum age 16;
Medical examination; Physician's request.

Staff RNs 2 (ft), 5 (pt); LPNs 7 (pt); Nurses'
aides 11 (ft), 30 (pt); Activities coordinators
1 (ft).
Affiliation Lutheran.
Facilities Dining room; Physical therapy
room; Activities room; Crafts room; Laundry
room; Barber/Beauty shop.
Activities Arts & crafts; Cards; Games;
Reading groups; Prayer groups; Movies;
Shopping trips; Dances/Social/Cultural
gatherings.

Windom CRF
945 Prospect, Windom, MN 56101
(507) 831-3804
Admin D Bill Olson.
Licensure Intermediate care for mentally
retarded. *Beds* ICF/MR 12.
Owner Proprietary corp.
Admissions Requirements Minimum age 18;
Medical examination.
Staff Resident advisors 4 (ft), 5 (pt); Relief
staff 3 (pt).
Facilities Activities room; Laundry room.

Winnebago

Winnebago Adolescent Treatment
550 W Cleveland, Winnebago, MN 56098
(507) 893-4848
Admin James C Murphy.
Licensure Supervised living. *Beds* Supervised
living 24.
Owner Proprietary corp.

Winnebago Baptist Home
211 6th St NW, Winnebago, MN 56098
(507) 893-3171
Admin Phil England. *Dir of Nursing* Shirley
Ringler RN. *Medical Dir* Kirk Odden MD.
Licensure Skilled care; Intermediate care;
Board and care. *Beds* SNF 20; ICF 41;
Board and care 27. *Private Pay Patients*
52%. *Certified* Medicaid; Medicare.
Owner Nonprofit corp (American Baptist
Homes).
Admissions Requirements Minimum age 18;
Medical examination; Physician's request.
Staff RNs 1 (ft), 5 (pt); LPNs 1 (ft), 8 (pt);
Nurses' aides 9 (ft), 21 (pt); Activities
coordinators 1 (ft).
Affiliation Baptist.
Facilities Dining room; Activities room;
Crafts room; Laundry room; Barber/Beauty
shop.
Activities Arts & crafts; Cards; Games;
Reading groups; Prayer groups; Movies;
Shopping trips; Dances/Social/Cultural
gatherings; Intergenerational programs.

Winona

Broadway Residential Treatment Center
73 W Broadway, Winona, MN 55987
(507) 454-1046
Admin B Rowe Winnecoff.
Medical Dir Dr George Planausky.
Licensure Supervised living. *Beds* Supervised
living 9.
Owner Proprietary corp.

Community Memorial Hospital
855 Mankato Ave, Winona, MN 55987
(507) 454-3650
Admin Roger L Metz.
Licensure Skilled care. *Beds* SNF 104.
Certified Medicaid; Medicare.
Owner Proprietary corp.

St Annes Hospice
1347 W Broadway, Winona, MN 55987
(507) 454-3621
Admin Richard R Boyd.
Medical Dir Sidney O Hughes MD.

Licensure Skilled care; Intermediate care;
Boarding care; Adult day care. *Beds* SNF 97;
ICF 17; Boarding care 20. *Certified*
Medicaid; Medicare.
Owner Proprietary corp.
Admissions Requirements Minimum age 60;
Medical examination.
Staff RNs 4 (ft), 10 (pt); LPNs 4 (ft), 17 (pt);
Nurses' aides 24 (ft), 51 (pt); Physical
therapists 1 (pt); Activities coordinators 3
(ft); Dietitians 1 (pt).
Affiliation Roman Catholic.
Facilities Dining room; Physical therapy
room; Activities room; Chapel; Crafts room;
Laundry room; Barber/Beauty shop; Library;
Wheelchair van.
Activities Arts & crafts; Cards; Games;
Reading groups; Prayer groups; Movies;
Shopping trips; Dances/Social/Cultural
gatherings; Imaginary 3 day trips.

Sauer Memorial Home
1635 Service Dr, Winona, MN 55987
(507) 454-5540
Admin William H English.
Medical Dir Dr H J Andersen.
Licensure Skilled care; Retirement. *Beds* SNF
114. *Certified* Medicaid; Medicare.
Owner Proprietary corp.
Admissions Requirements Minimum age 16;
Medical examination.
Staff RNs 2 (ft), 3 (pt); LPNs 5 (ft), 7 (pt);
Nurses' aides 20 (ft), 27 (pt); Physical
therapists 1 (pt); Speech therapists 1 (pt);
Activities coordinators 2 (ft), 2 (pt).
Facilities Dining room; Physical therapy
room; Activities room; Chapel; Crafts room;
Laundry room; Barber/Beauty shop; Library.
Activities Arts & crafts; Cards; Games;
Reading groups; Prayer groups; Dances/
Social/Cultural gatherings.

377 Main Street
377 Main St, Winona, MN 55987
(507) 454-5909
Admin Sharon Kannenberg.
Licensure Supervised living. *Beds* Supervised
living 6.
Owner Proprietary corp.
Admissions Requirements Minimum age 18;
Medical examination; Physician's request.
Facilities Dining room; Laundry room; Living
room; Kitchen; Recreation room.
Activities Arts & crafts; Cards; Games;
Movies; Shopping trips; Dances/Social/
Cultural gatherings; Individualized skills
training; Community-based activities;
Recreation.

Two Fifty Two West Wabasha Street
252 W Wabasha St, Winona, MN 55987
(507) 454-5377
Admin Sharon Kannenberg.
Licensure Intermediate care for mentally
retarded. *Beds* ICF/MR 10.
Owner Proprietary corp.
Facilities Dining room; Activities room;
Laundry room; Living room; Kitchen.
Activities Arts & crafts; Cards; Games;
Movies; Shopping trips; Dances/Social/
Cultural gatherings; Skills training;
Community-based activities; Recreation.

Watkins Home
PO Box 127, 175 E Wabasha, Winona, MN
55987
(507) 454-4670
Admin Gary Baumgartner. *Dir of Nursing*
Mary Rohowetz RN. *Medical Dir* Andrew
Edin MD.
Licensure Skilled care; Intermediate care;
Board and care. *Beds* Swing beds SNF/ICF
105; Board and care 34. *Certified* Medicaid;
Medicare.
Owner Nonprofit organization/foundation.

Staff RNs 7 (ft), 2 (pt); LPNs 9 (ft), 11 (pt); Nurses' aides 16 (ft), 43 (pt); Recreational therapists 1 (ft); Occupational therapists 1 (ft); Speech therapists; Activities coordinators 1 (ft); Dietitians 1 (ft).
Facilities Dining room; Physical therapy room; Activities room; Laundry room; Barber/Beauty shop; Library.
Activities Arts & crafts; Cards; Games; Reading groups; Prayer groups; Movies; Shopping trips; Dances/Social/Cultural gatherings; Intergenerational programs; Pet therapy.

Winsted

Health One St Mary's
PO Box 750, 551 4th St N, Winsted, MN 55395
(612) 485-2151, 485-4241 FAX
Admin Joel V Nyquist. Dir of Nursing Thomas Wachlarowicz. Medical Dir Hal Wenngatz MD.
Licensure Skilled care; Alzheimer's unit. Beds SNF 95. Private Pay Patients 35%. Certified Medicaid; Medicare.
Owner Proprietary corp (Health One Corp).
Admissions Requirements Minimum age 18; Medical examination.
Staff RNs 4 (ft), 3 (pt); LPNs 4 (ft), 5 (pt); Nurses' aides 14 (ft), 22 (pt); Physical therapists 1 (ft); Recreational therapists 1 (ft); Occupational therapists 1 (ft); Activities coordinators 1 (ft); Dietitians 1 (ft).
Affiliation Roman Catholic.
Facilities Dining room; Physical therapy room; Activities room; Chapel; Crafts room; Laundry room; Barber/Beauty shop.
Activities Arts & crafts; Cards; Games; Reading groups; Prayer groups; Movies; Shopping trips; Dances/Social/Cultural gatherings; Pet therapy.

Winthrop

Winthrop Health Care Center
506 High St, Winthrop, MN 55396
(507) 647-5391
Admin John Rieke. Dir of Nursing Sandi Hjerm. Medical Dir Dean Bergerson MD.
Licensure Skilled care. Beds SNF 52. Private Pay Patients 40%. Certified Medicaid; Medicare.
Owner Proprietary corp (Good Neighbor Services).
Admissions Requirements Minimum age 18; Medical examination; Physician's request.
Staff Physicians 1 (pt); RNs 1 (ft), 3 (pt); LPNs 1 (ft), 5 (pt); Nurses' aides 7 (ft), 34 (pt); Physical therapists 3 (pt); Occupational therapists 1 (pt); Speech therapists 1 (pt); Activities coordinators 1 (ft); Dietitians 1 (pt).
Facilities Dining room; Physical therapy room; Activities room; Crafts room; Laundry room; Barber/Beauty shop; Dayroom lounge; Lobby; Patio; Van.
Activities Arts & crafts; Cards; Games; Reading groups; Prayer groups; Movies; Shopping trips; Dances/Social/Cultural gatherings; Intergenerational programs; Pet therapy; Church services; Trips to games and lunch; Fishing.

Woodbury

Jane Dickman Center
1665 Woodbury Dr, Woodbury, MN 55125
(612) 436-6623
Admin D E Johnson.
Licensure Intermediate care for mentally retarded. Beds ICF/MR 38.
Owner Proprietary corp.

Woodbury Health Care Center
7012 Carver Lake Rd, Woodbury, MN 55125
(612) 735-6000
Admin Dallas C Reese. Dir of Nursing Marion Johnson. Medical Dir Dr Kuhlenkamp.
Licensure Skilled care; Retirement. Beds SNF 212. Certified Medicaid; Medicare; VA.
Owner Proprietary corp.
Admissions Requirements Minimum age 16; Physician's request.
Staff Physicians 56 (pt); RNs 9 (ft), 20 (pt); LPNs 10 (ft), 9 (pt); Nurses' aides 36 (ft), 40 (pt); Physical therapists 1 (ft), 1 (pt); Recreational therapists 2 (ft); Occupational therapists 1 (ft); Speech therapists 1 (pt); Activities coordinators 1 (ft); Music therapists 2 (ft), 6 (pt); Chaplains 1 (ft).
Facilities Dining room; Physical therapy room; Activities room; Chapel; Crafts room; Laundry room; Barber/Beauty shop; Doctor's examination office.
Activities Arts & crafts; Cards; Games; Reading groups; Prayer groups; Movies; Shopping trips; Dances/Social/Cultural gatherings.

Woodstock

New Life Treatment Center
PO Box 38, Woodstock, MN 56186
(507) 777-4321
Admin Wes Van Essen. Dir of Nursing Pamela Talsma RN.
Licensure Supervised living. Beds Supervised living 18.
Owner Proprietary corp.
Admissions Requirements Minimum age 18.
Staff Physicians 1 (pt); RNs 1 (ft); LPNs 1 (ft); Nurses' aides 1 (ft); Dentists 1 (pt).
Facilities Dining room; Chapel; Laundry room.
Activities Movies.

Worthington

Fauskee Nursing Home Inc
965 McMillan St, Worthington, MN 56187
(507) 376-5312
Admin Betty Fauskee Atchison RN BA. Dir of Nursing Patricia Terhaar RN. Medical Dir Dr M W Plucker.
Licensure Skilled care; Intermediate care. Beds SNF 62; ICF 2. Certified Medicaid; Medicare.
Owner Proprietary corp.
Admissions Requirements Minimum age 18; Medical examination.
Staff RNs; LPNs; Nurses' aides; Recreational therapists; Activities coordinators; Dietitians.
Facilities Dining room; Activities room; Chapel; Crafts room; Laundry room; Barber/Beauty shop; Library.
Activities Arts & crafts; Cards; Games; Reading groups; Prayer groups; Movies; Dances/Social/Cultural gatherings; Hobby groups.

Lake Haven Nursing Home
1307 S Shore Dr, Worthington, MN 56187
(507) 376-3175
Admin Richard Atchison. Dir of Nursing Avis Torgrimson RN.
Licensure Intermediate care; Retirement. Beds ICF 88.
Owner Proprietary corp.
Admissions Requirements Medical examination; Physician's request.
Staff RNs 3 (ft), 1 (pt); LPNs 6 (ft), 4 (pt); Nurses' aides 25 (ft), 25 (pt); Recreational therapists 2 (ft), 1 (pt); Activities coordinators 1 (ft); 10 (ft), 20 (pt).
Facilities Dining room; Activities room; Laundry room; Barber/Beauty shop.
Activities Arts & crafts; Cards; Games; Reading groups; Prayer groups; Movies; Shopping trips; Dances/Social/Cultural gatherings.

McMillan Home
1205 Burlington Ave, Worthington, MN 56187
(507) 376-9555
Admin Donna Bruns.
Medical Dir Donna Bruns.
Licensure Intermediate care for mentally retarded; Retirement. Beds ICF/MR 8.
Owner Proprietary corp.
Admissions Requirements Minimum age 16.
Staff RNs 1 (pt); LPNs 1 (pt).
Facilities Dining room; Laundry room.
Activities Arts & crafts; Cards; Games; Movies; Shopping trips; Dances/Social/Cultural gatherings.

Project Independence Ridgewood
Box 23, 1381 Knollwood Dr, Worthington, MN 56187
(507) 376-6095
Admin Donna Bruns.
Licensure Intermediate care for mentally retarded. Beds ICF/MR 15.
Owner Proprietary corp.
Admissions Requirements Minimum age 16; Medical examination.
Staff RNs 1 (ft); LPNs 1 (ft), 1 (pt).
Facilities Dining room; Laundry room; Library; Living rooms.
Activities Arts & crafts; Cards; Games; Movies; Shopping trips; Dances/Social/Cultural gatherings; Daytime program outside facility.

Southwest Manor
921 7th Ave, Worthington, MN 56187
(507) 372-7278
Admin Donna Bruns.
Medical Dir Donna Bruns.
Licensure Supervised living. Beds Supervised living 6.
Owner Nonprofit organization/foundation.
Admissions Requirements Minimum age 18; Medical examination.
Staff RNs 1 (pt); LPNs 1 (pt).
Facilities Dining room; Laundry room.
Activities Arts & crafts; Cards; Games; Movies; Shopping trips; Dances/Social/Cultural gatherings.

Unity House
1224 4th Ave, Worthington, MN 56187
(507) 372-7671
Admin Allyson Ashley.
Licensure Supervised living. Beds Supervised living 12.
Owner Proprietary corp.
Admissions Requirements Minimum age 12; Medical examination; Mental illness; Chemical dependency.
Staff Physicians; Reality therapists 6 (ft); Activities coordinators.
Facilities Dining room; Crafts room; Laundry room.
Activities Arts & crafts; Cards; Games; Reading groups; Movies; Shopping trips; Dances/Social/Cultural gatherings.

Worthington Regional Hospital
1018 6th Ave, Worthington, MN 56187
(507) 372-2941
Admin David P Gehant.
Licensure Skilled care. Beds SNF 5. Certified Medicaid; Medicare.
Owner Nonprofit corp.

Zumbrota

Zumbrota Nursing Home
433 Mill St, Zumbrota, MN 55992
(507) 732-5139
Admin Jerry L Hoganson.
Medical Dir William Walter MD.
Licensure Skilled care; Boarding care. Beds SNF 65; Boarding care 6. Certified Medicaid; Medicare.
Owner Proprietary corp.

Staff RNs 2 (ft), 3 (pt); LPNs 1 (ft), 5 (pt); Nurses' aides 11 (ft), 26 (pt); Physical therapists 1 (pt); Activities coordinators 1 (ft), 2 (pt); Dietitians 1 (ft).

Facilities Dining room; Activities room; Chapel; Barber/Beauty shop.
Activities Arts & crafts; Cards; Games; Reading groups; Prayer groups; Movies; Shopping trips; Dances/Social/Cultural gatherings.

MISSISSIPPI

Aberdeen

Hillcrest Manor
PO Box 211, 505 Jackson St, Aberdeen, MS 39730
(601) 369-6431
Admin Dolores West. *Dir of Nursing* Sherrell Gill RN. *Medical Dir* Arthur Brown MD.
Licensure Skilled care; Intermediate care. *Beds* SNF 60; ICF 60. *Private Pay Patients* 15%. *Certified* Medicaid; Medicare.
Owner Proprietary corp.
Staff RNs 5 (ft); LPNs 6 (ft), 4 (pt); Nurses' aides 41 (ft), 4 (pt); Physical therapists 1 (ft); Activities coordinators 1 (ft); Dietitians 1 (ft).
Facilities Dining room; Physical therapy room; Activities room; Crafts room; Laundry room; Barber/Beauty shop.
Activities Arts & crafts; Games; Reading groups; Prayer groups; Movies; Pet therapy.

Monroe County Rest Home
Rte 2 Box 394, Aberdeen, MS 39730
(601) 369-4485
Admin Barbara Mabry.
Medical Dir Dr L R Murphree.
Licensure Personal care. *Beds* Personal care 12.
Owner Publicly owned.
Admissions Requirements Medical examination.
Staff Physicians; Nurses' aides 3 (ft); Activities coordinators 1 (ft).
Facilities Dining room; Activities room; Chapel; Laundry room; Barber/Beauty shop.
Activities Church groups provide most activities at this facility.

Ackerman

Choctaw County Nursing Home
148 W Cherry St, Ackerman, MS 39735
(601) 285-6235
Admin Robert B Hughes.
Medical Dir Dr Edward Pennington.
Licensure Skilled care; Intermediate care. *Beds* Swing beds SNF/ICF 60. *Certified* Medicaid.
Owner Publicly owned.
Admissions Requirements Medical examination; Physician's request.
Staff Physicians 4 (ft); RNs 2 (ft); LPNs 6 (ft), 2 (pt); Nurses' aides 14 (ft), 3 (pt); Activities coordinators 1 (ft); Dietitians 1 (ft); Social services 1 (ft).
Facilities Dining room; Activities room; Crafts room; Laundry room; Barber/Beauty shop; Porch; Lounge.
Activities Arts & crafts; Cards; Games; Reading groups; Prayer groups; Dances/Social/Cultural gatherings; Pet therapy; Outings.

Amory

Amory Manor Nursing Home
1215 S Boulevard, Amory, MS 38821
(601) 256-9344
Admin Kelly Faulkner.
Licensure Skilled care; Intermediate care. *Beds* SNF 60; ICF 60. *Certified* Medicaid.
Owner Proprietary corp (Beverly Enterprises).

Baldwyn

North Mississippi Nursing Home Inc—Baldwyn Nursing Facility
423 N 2nd St, Baldwyn, MS 38824
(601) 365-5276
Admin Durren L Westbrooke.
Licensure Skilled care; Intermediate care. *Beds* Swing beds SNF/ICF 36. *Certified* Medicaid.
Owner Proprietary corp.

Batesville

Batesville Manor Nursing Home
Rte 1 Drawer 553, Hospital Rd, Batesville, MS 38606
(601) 563-5636
Admin James McCauley.
Licensure Intermediate care. *Beds* ICF 120. *Certified* Medicaid.
Owner Proprietary corp (Beverly Enterprises).

Bay Saint Louis

Hotel Reed Nursing Center
400 N Beach Blvd, Bay Saint Louis, MS 39520
(601) 467-5462
Admin Ted Cain.
Licensure Skilled care; Intermediate care. *Beds* SNF 60; ICF 28. *Certified* Medicaid.
Owner Proprietary corp.

Bay Springs

Jasper County Nursing Home
PO Box 527, 6th St, Bay Springs, MS 39422
(601) 764-2101
Admin Jackie Belding.
Licensure Skilled care; Intermediate care. *Beds* SNF 43; ICF 24. *Certified* Medicaid.
Owner Publicly owned.

Belzoni

Humphreys County Memorial Hospital Intermediate Care Facility
500 CC Rd, Belzoni, MS 39038
(601) 247-3831
Admin Alvin Word III.
Licensure Skilled care; Intermediate care. *Beds* Swing beds SNF/ICF 7. *Certified* Medicaid; Medicare.

Humphreys County Nursing Home
PO Box 178, Belzoni, MS 39038-0178
(601) 247-1821
Admin Danny Kilpatrick.
Licensure Skilled care; Intermediate care. *Beds* Swing beds SNF/ICF 60. *Certified* Medicaid.
Owner Proprietary corp (National Heritage).

Biloxi

Kare Centre
2279 Atkinson Rd, Biloxi, MS 39531
(601) 388-1805, 388-5191 FAX
Admin Lucy Klueter. *Dir of Nursing* Evelyn Pierce. *Medical Dir* Dr Robert Middleton.
Licensure Skilled care; Intermediate care; Alzheimer's unit; Personal care; Retirement. *Beds* SNF 122; ICF 18; Retirement 100. *Certified* Medicaid; Medicare.
Owner Privately owned.
Admissions Requirements Medical examination.
Staff Physicians 2 (ft); RNs 4 (ft); LPNs 20 (ft), 7 (pt); Nurses' aides 60 (ft), 5 (pt); Physical therapists 2 (ft), 2 (pt); Recreational therapists 1 (ft); Occupational therapists 1 (ft); Speech therapists 1 (ft); Activities coordinators and staff 10 (ft); Dietitians and staff 20 (ft).
Facilities Dining room; Physical therapy room; Activities room; Crafts room; Laundry room; Barber/Beauty shop; Library.
Activities Arts & crafts; Cards; Games; Reading groups; Prayer groups; Movies; Shopping trips; Dances/Social/Cultural gatherings; Intergenerational programs; Pet therapy.

Booneville

Aletha Lodge Nursing Home Inc
PO Box 326, 200 Long St, Booneville, MS 38829
(601) 728-6234
Admin Lana Maxey.
Medical Dir Joseph Lewis Hurst MD.
Licensure Skilled care. *Beds* SNF 64. *Certified* Medicaid.
Owner Proprietary corp.
Admissions Requirements Medical examination; Physician's request.
Staff Physicians 1 (ft); RNs 1 (ft), 2 (pt); LPNs 6 (ft), 4 (pt); Nurses' aides 18 (ft), 3 (pt); Physical therapists 1 (ft); Speech therapists; Activities coordinators; Dietitians; Dentists.
Facilities Dining room; Activities room; Crafts room; Laundry room; Barber/Beauty shop; Library.
Activities Arts & crafts; Cards; Games; Reading groups; Prayer groups; Movies; Dances/Social/Cultural gatherings.

Brandon

Crossgate Manor Inc
355 Crossgate Blvd, Brandon, MS 39042
(601) 825-3192
Admin Margaret Higgins.
Licensure Skilled care; Intermediate care. *Beds*
Swing beds SNF/ICF 230. *Certified*
Medicaid.
Owner Proprietary corp (Beverly Enterprises).

Brookhaven

Brook Manor Nursing Center
Brookman Dr, Brookhaven, MS 39601
(601) 833-2881
Admin Carolyn Wilson.
Licensure Skilled care; Intermediate care. *Beds*
Swing beds SNF/ICF 58. *Certified* Medicaid.
Owner Proprietary corp (Beverly Enterprises).

Country Brook Living Center
525 Brookman Dr, Brookhaven, MS 39601
(601) 833-2330
Admin Barbara Pepper.
Licensure Skilled care; Intermediate care. *Beds*
Swing beds SNF/ICF 120. *Certified*
Medicaid.
Owner Proprietary corp (ARA Living
Centers).

Haven Hall Nursing Center
PO Box 848, 101 Mills St, Brookhaven, MS
39601
(601) 833-5608
Admin Cindy Freeman.
Licensure Intermediate care. *Beds* ICF 60.
Certified Medicaid.
Owner Proprietary corp.

Lincoln Residential Center
524 Brookman Dr, Brookhaven, MS 39601
(601) 833-1884
Admin Steve Haharan.
Medical Dir Jim Barnett MD.
Licensure Intermediate care for mentally
retarded. *Beds* ICF/MR 120. *Certified*
Medicaid.
Owner Proprietary corp.
Admissions Requirements Minimum age 18;
Medical examination.
Staff Physicians 1 (ft); RNs 1 (ft), 1 (pt);
LPNs 4 (ft), 5 (pt); Nurses' aides 54 (ft), 4
(pt); Physical therapists 1 (pt); Recreational
therapists 1 (ft); Occupational therapists 1
(ft); Speech therapists 1 (ft), 1 (pt); Activities
coordinators 1 (ft); Dietitians 1 (ft);
Ophthalmologists 1 (pt); Audiologists 1 (pt);
Dentists 1 (pt).
Facilities Dining room; Physical therapy
room; Activities room; Crafts room; Laundry
room; Barber/Beauty shop.
Activities Arts & crafts; Cards; Games;
Reading groups; Movies; Shopping trips;
Dances/Social/Cultural gatherings;
Vocational programs.

Silver Cross Home
PO Box 617, 303 N Jackson St, Brookhaven,
MS 39601
(601) 833-2361, 833-3115 FAX
Admin Gussie W Ashley. *Dir of Nursing* Sarah
A Rector. *Medical Dir* Dr David Strong.
Licensure Skilled care; Intermediate care. *Beds*
Swing beds SNF/ICF 60. *Private Pay
Patients* 52%. *Certified* Medicaid; Medicare.
Owner Nonprofit organization/foundation.
Admissions Requirements Physician's request.
Staff RNs 2 (ft), 2 (pt); LPNs 11 (ft), 3 (pt);
Nurses' aides 28 (ft), 4 (pt); Activities
coordinators 1 (ft).
Affiliation King's Daughters & Sons.
Facilities Dining room; Activities room;
Laundry room; Barber/Beauty shop; Sun
porch.
Activities Games; Prayer groups; Dances/
Social/Cultural gatherings.

Calhoun

Calhoun County Nursing Home
PO Box 110, Burke Rd, Calhoun, MS 38916
(601) 628-6651
Admin M B Martin.
Medical Dir Guy Farmer MD.
Licensure Skilled care; Intermediate care. *Beds*
Swing beds SNF/ICF 120. *Certified*
Medicaid.
Owner Publicly owned.
Admissions Requirements Medical
examination; Physician's request.
Staff RNs 3 (ft); LPNs 10 (ft), 3 (pt); Nurses'
aides 32 (ft), 6 (pt); Activities coordinators 1
(ft).
Facilities Dining room; Physical therapy
room; Activities room; Laundry room;
Barber/Beauty shop.
Activities Arts & crafts; Cards; Games;
Dances/Social/Cultural gatherings.

Canton

Canton Manor
PO Box 269, 1145 E Tisdale Ave, Canton, MS
39046
(601) 859-6712, 859-6713
Admin Robert R Dailey.
Medical Dir Clyde McLaurin MD.
Licensure Intermediate care for mentally
retarded. *Beds* ICF/MR 120. *Certified*
Medicaid.
Owner Proprietary corp (Unicare).
Admissions Requirements Minimum age 18;
Medical examination.
Staff Physicians 1 (ft); RNs 1 (ft); LPNs 10
(ft); Physical therapists 1 (ft); Recreational
therapists 1 (ft); Occupational therapists 1
(ft); Speech therapists 1 (ft); Activities
coordinators 1 (ft); Dietitians 1 (ft);
Ophthalmologists 1 (ft); Podiatrists 1 (ft).
Facilities Dining room; Physical therapy
room; Activities room; Crafts room; Laundry
room; Vocational training center.
Activities Arts & crafts; Cards; Games;
Movies; Shopping trips; Dances/Social/
Cultural gatherings.

Madison County Nursing Home
PO Box 281, 411 S Liberty St, Canton, MS
39046
(601) 948-6960
Admin Sidney L Whittington. *Dir of Nursing*
Joy Dilmore RN.
Licensure Skilled care. *Beds* SNF 60. *Certified*
Medicaid.
Owner Publicly owned.
Admissions Requirements Physician's request.
Staff RNs 1 (ft), 2 (pt); LPNs 8 (ft), 2 (pt);
Nurses' aides 13 (ft), 9 (pt); Physical
therapists 1 (ft); Activities coordinators 1
(ft); Dietitians 1 (ft).
Facilities Dining room; Activities room;
Laundry room; Barber/Beauty shop.
Activities Arts & crafts; Cards; Games;
Reading groups; Prayer groups; Bingo.

Carthage

Carthage Health Care Center Inc
PO Box 576, 1101 E Franklin St, Carthage,
MS 39051
(601) 267-4551
Admin Robert D Faulkner.
Licensure Skilled care; Intermediate care. *Beds*
Swing beds SNF/ICF 90. *Certified* Medicaid.
Owner Proprietary corp (Beverly Enterprises).

**Leake County Memorial Hospital & Skilled
Nursing Facility**
300 Ellis Ave, Carthage, MS 39051
(601) 267-4511
Admin Everett D Montgomery FACHE. *Dir of
Nursing* Deborah Chamblee RN. *Medical
Dir* James Mayfield MD.

Licensure Skilled care. *Beds* SNF 40. *Private
Pay Patients* 20%. *Certified* Medicaid.
Owner Publicly owned.
Admissions Requirements Medical
examination; Physician's request.
Staff Physicians 4 (ft); RNs 1 (ft), 1 (pt);
LPNs 4 (ft), 1 (pt); Nurses' aides 11 (ft), 4
(pt); Physical therapists 1 (pt); Activities
coordinators 1 (pt); Dietitians 1 (pt).
Facilities Dining room; Physical therapy
room; Activities room; Chapel; Crafts room;
Laundry room; Barber/Beauty shop; Library.
Activities Arts & crafts; Games; Movies.

Centreville

Centreville Health Care Center
PO Box 69, Lafayette St, Centreville, MS
39631
(601) 645-5253
Admin Evelyn Robbins.
Licensure Skilled care; Intermediate care. *Beds*
SNF 48; OP/ICF 48. *Certified* Medicaid.
Owner Proprietary corp (Beverly Enterprises).

Charleston

**Tallahatchie General Hospital—Extended Care
Facility**
PO Box F, 202 S Market St, Charleston, MS
38921
(601) 647-5535, 647-3677 FAX
Admin F W Ergle Jr. *Dir of Nursing* Peggy
Cole RN. *Medical Dir* Frank Hood MD,
Chief of Staff.
Licensure Skilled care; Hospital. *Beds* SNF
55; Hospital 25. *Certified* Medicaid.
Owner Publicly owned.
Staff RNs 1 (ft), 2 (pt); LPNs 7 (ft), 2 (pt);
Nurses' aides 16 (ft); Physical therapists 1
(pt); Activities coordinators 1 (ft); Dietitians
1 (ft), 1 (pt).
Facilities Dining room; Activities room;
Barber/Beauty shop.
Activities Arts & crafts; Cards; Games;
Reading groups; Prayer groups; Movies; Pet
therapy.

Clarksdale

Delta Manor
701 US Hwy 322 W, Clarksdale, MS 38614
(601) 627-2212
Admin Travis Cooper. *Dir of Nursing* Yvonne
Ashley. *Medical Dir* Dr P W Hill Jr.
Licensure Intermediate care for mentally
retarded. *Beds* ICF/MR 120. *Certified*
Medicaid.
Owner Proprietary corp (Unicare).
Admissions Requirements Minimum age 18;
Medical examination.
Staff Physicians 1 (pt); RNs 1 (ft); LPNs 7
(ft), 5 (pt); Physical therapists 1 (pt);
Recreational therapists 1 (ft); Occupational
therapists 1 (pt); Speech therapists 1 (pt);
Dietitians 7 (ft), 2 (pt); Ophthalmologists 1
(pt); Podiatrists 1 (pt); Dentists 1 (pt).
Facilities Dining room; Physical therapy
room; Activities room; Crafts room; Laundry
room; Barber/Beauty shop; Library.
Activities Arts & crafts; Cards; Games;
Reading groups; Movies; Shopping trips;
Dances/Social/Cultural gatherings.

Greenbough Nursing Center
340 DeSoto Ave Ext, Clarksdale, MS 38614
(601) 627-3486
Admin Dianne Sykes.
Licensure Skilled care; Intermediate care. *Beds*
SNF 34; ICF 32. *Certified* Medicaid.
Owner Proprietary corp (Beverly Enterprises).

River Oaks Convalescent Center
Box 1304, Clarksdale, MS 38614
(601) 627-2591
Admin Eva Ann Boschert.

Licensure Skilled care; Intermediate care. *Beds* SNF 60; ICF 60. *Certified* Medicaid.

Cleveland

Bolivar County Hospital—Long-Term Care Facility
Hwy 8 E, Cleveland, MS 38732
(601) 846-0061
Admin Noel Hart.
Medical Dir Dr S D Austin.
Licensure Skilled care. *Beds* SNF 34. *Certified* Medicaid.
Owner Publicly owned.
Admissions Requirements Medical examination.
Staff RNs 1 (ft); LPNs 5 (ft), 2 (pt); Nurses' aides 17 (ft), 3 (pt); Activities coordinators 1 (ft).
Facilities Dining room; Activities room; Barber/Beauty shop.
Activities Arts & crafts; Games; Prayer groups; Movies; Shopping trips; Dances/Social/Cultural gatherings.

Cleveland Health Care Center
Hwy 8 E, Cleveland, MS 38732
(601) 843-4014
Admin Albert Herndon Jr. *Dir of Nursing* Christine Lacy. *Medical Dir* Bennie Wright MD.
Licensure Skilled care; Intermediate care. *Beds* SNF 60; ICF 60. *Certified* Medicaid.
Owner Proprietary corp (Beverly Enterprises).
Admissions Requirements Medical examination; Physician's request.
Staff Physicians; RNs; LPNs; Nurses' aides; Speech therapists; Activities coordinators; Dietitians; Ophthalmologists.
Facilities Dining room; Activities room; Laundry room; Barber/Beauty shop; Library.
Activities Arts & crafts; Cards; Games; Reading groups; Prayer groups; Movies; Shopping trips; Dances/Social/Cultural gatherings.

Heritage Manor of Cleveland
PO Drawer 430, 200 Dr Martin L King Dr, Cleveland, MS 38732
(601) 843-5347
Admin Sharon W Sauerwein. *Dir of Nursing* Mary Ann Borganelli RN. *Medical Dir* John T Milam MD.
Licensure Skilled care. *Beds* SNF 75. *Private Pay Patients* 8%. *Certified* Medicaid.
Owner Proprietary corp (National Heritage Realty Inc).
Admissions Requirements Medical examination; Physician's request.
Staff RNs 2 (ft), 3 (pt); LPNs 6 (ft), 5 (pt); Nurses' aides 27 (ft), 7 (pt); Activities coordinators 1 (ft); Dietitians 1 (ft); Social services 1 (ft).
Facilities Dining room; Activities room; Laundry room; Barber/Beauty shop; Covered patio.
Activities Arts & crafts; Games; Reading groups; Prayer groups; Movies; Shopping trips; Dances/Social/Cultural gatherings; Intergenerational programs.

Clinton

Clinton Country Manor
1251 Pinehaven Rd, Clinton, MS 39056
(601) 924-0627
Admin Shirley Allen.
Medical Dir Dr Robert Estess.
Licensure Skilled care; Intermediate care. *Beds* SNF 60; ICF 60. *Certified* Medicaid.
Owner Proprietary corp.
Admissions Requirements Medical examination.

Staff Physicians 1 (ft), 5 (pt); RNs 2 (ft), 3 (pt); LPNs 8 (ft), 2 (pt); Nurses' aides 36 (ft), 12 (pt); Physical therapists 1 (pt); Activities coordinators 1 (ft); Podiatrists 1 (pt); Dentists 1 (pt).
Facilities Dining room; Activities room; Crafts room; Laundry room; Barber/Beauty shop.
Activities Arts & crafts; Cards; Games; Prayer groups; Movies; Shopping trips; Dances/Social/Cultural gatherings.

Heritage Manor of Clinton
101 W Northside Dr, Clinton, MS 39056
(601) 924-7043
Admin Mark S Clay. *Dir of Nursing* Kathryn S Eicke RN. *Medical Dir* Dr J S McIlwain.
Licensure Skilled care; Intermediate care. *Beds* Swing beds SNF/ICF 135. *Private Pay Patients* 23%. *Certified* Medicaid.
Owner Proprietary corp (National Heritage).
Admissions Requirements Medical examination; Physician's request.
Staff RNs 5 (ft), 1 (pt); LPNs 10 (ft), 2 (pt); Nurses' aides 63 (ft); Activities coordinators 1 (ft); Dietitians 1 (pt).
Facilities Dining room; Activities room; Crafts room; Laundry room; Barber/Beauty shop.
Activities Arts & crafts; Games; Reading groups; Prayer groups; Movies; Shopping trips; Dances/Social/Cultural gatherings.

Collins

Covington County Nursing Center
PO Box 1089, 1207 Old Hwy 49 S, Collins, MS 39428
(601) 765-8262
Admin Bronze Walker. *Dir of Nursing* Chris Kelly RN. *Medical Dir* Dr E P Reeves.
Licensure Skilled care; Intermediate care. *Beds* Swing beds SNF/ICF 60. *Certified* Medicaid.
Owner Proprietary corp (National Heritage).
Admissions Requirements Medical examination; Physician's request.
Staff Physicians 4 (pt); RNs 2 (ft), 3 (pt); LPNs 5 (ft), 4 (pt); Nurses' aides 18 (ft), 4 (pt); Physical therapists 1 (pt); Recreational therapists 1 (ft); Activities coordinators 1 (ft); Dietitians 1 (pt).
Facilities Dining room; Activities room; Crafts room; Laundry room; Barber/Beauty shop; Whirlpool; Living room; Lobby; Patio.
Activities Arts & crafts; Cards; Games; Reading groups; Prayer groups; Movies; Shopping trips; Dances/Social/Cultural gatherings.

Columbia

Cedars Intermediate Care Facility
PO Box 151, 511 S Main, Columbia, MS 39429
(601) 736-4747
Admin Jack Bradshaw. *Dir of Nursing* Vicky Burge RN. *Medical Dir* Dr Robert Herrington.
Licensure Intermediate care. *Beds* ICF 32. *Certified* Medicaid.
Owner Proprietary corp.
Admissions Requirements Medical examination.
Staff Physicians 1 (pt); RNs 1 (pt); LPNs 1 (ft), 2 (pt); Nurses' aides 10 (ft); Recreational therapists 1 (pt); Activities coordinators 1 (ft); Dietitians 1 (pt).
Facilities Dining room; Activities room; Laundry room.
Activities Arts & crafts; Cards; Games; Reading groups; Prayer groups; Movies; Shopping trips; Dances/Social/Cultural gatherings.

Heritage Manor of Columbia
PO Box 70, N Main St, Columbia, MS 39429
(601) 736-9557

Admin Anita Keller.
Licensure Skilled care; Intermediate care. *Beds* SNF 60; ICF 59. *Certified* Medicaid.
Owner Proprietary corp (National Heritage).

Myrtles Health Care Facility
1018 Alberta Ave, Columbia, MS 39429
(601) 736-8040
Admin Jeannette Crain.
Licensure Skilled care; Intermediate care. *Beds* Swing beds SNF/ICF 66. *Certified* Medicaid.
Owner Proprietary corp.

Columbus

Aurora Australis Lodge
310 N 20th St E, Columbus, MS 39701
(601) 327-8021
Admin Betty Meadows.
Licensure Skilled care; Intermediate care. *Beds* Swing beds SNF/ICF 120. *Certified* Medicaid.
Owner Proprietary corp.

Magnolia Manor Nursing Home
2002 5th St N, Columbus, MS 39701
(601) 328-1133
Admin Lowell D Scales.
Licensure Skilled care; Intermediate care. *Beds* Swing beds SNF/ICF 60. *Certified* Medicaid.
Owner Proprietary corp.
Staff RNs 2 (ft); LPNs 10 (ft), 1 (pt); Nurses' aides 20 (ft); Activities coordinators 1 (ft); Dietitians 1 (ft).
Facilities Dining room; Physical therapy room; Activities room; Crafts room; Laundry room; Barber/Beauty shop.
Activities Arts & crafts; Games; Shopping trips.

Corinth

Care Inn—Alcorn County
Jo Ann Dr, Corinth, MS 38834
(601) 287-8071
Admin Richard Atkins.
Licensure Skilled care; Intermediate care. *Beds* Swing beds SNF/ICF 120. *Certified* Medicaid.
Owner Proprietary corp.

Heritage Manor—Corinth
PO Box 1417, Alcorn Dr, Corinth, MS 38834
(601) 286-2286
Admin Mary F Mullen. *Dir of Nursing* Julia Potts. *Medical Dir* Dr William Jackson.
Licensure Skilled care; Intermediate care. *Beds* Swing beds SNF/ICF 95. *Certified* Medicaid.
Owner Proprietary corp (National Heritage Management).

Whitfield Nursing Home Inc
PO Box 1425, 2101 E Proper St, Corinth, MS 38834
(601) 286-3331
Admin Sarah J Whitfield. *Dir of Nursing* Joan Woolhouse RN, consultant.
Licensure Intermediate care. *Beds* ICF 44. *Private Pay Patients* 10%. *Certified* Medicaid.
Owner Proprietary corp.
Admissions Requirements Medical examination; Physician's request.
Staff RNs 1 (ft); LPNs 4 (ft), 2 (pt); Nurses' aides 7 (ft), 4 (pt); Activities coordinators 1 (ft); Dietitians 1 (pt); Social workers (consultant).
Facilities Dining room; Activities room; 30 private rooms.
Activities Arts & crafts; Games; Reading groups; Prayer groups; Movies; Shopping trips; Dances/Social/Cultural gatherings; Pet therapy; Exercise.

DeKalb

Kemper County Nursing Home
PO Box 577, Willow Ave, DeKalb, MS 39328
(601) 743-5888
Admin Patty C Nester. *Dir of Nursing* Debbie Myers RN. *Medical Dir* Jim Smith MD.
Licensure Skilled care; Intermediate care. *Beds* Swing beds SNF/ICF 60. *Private Pay Patients* 33%. *Certified* Medicaid.
Owner Proprietary corp (Edgar H Overstreet).
Admissions Requirements Physician's request.
Staff Physicians 2 (pt); RNs 2 (ft); LPNs 9 (ft); Nurses' aides 23 (ft); Physical therapists 1 (pt); Activities coordinators 1 (ft); Dietitians 1 (pt).
Facilities Dining room; Activities room; Chapel; Laundry room; Barber/Beauty shop; Library.
Activities Cards; Games; Reading groups; Prayer groups; Movies.

Duncan

Oak Grove Retirement Home
430 Oak Ave, Duncan, MS 38740
(601) 395-2577
Admin Charles E Smith. *Dir of Nursing* Bessie Smith. *Medical Dir* R T Hollingsworth MD.
Licensure Intermediate care. *Beds* ICF 59. *Private Pay Patients* 2%. *Certified* Medicaid.
Owner Proprietary corp.
Staff Physicians 1 (pt); RNs 2 (pt); LPNs 2 (ft), 2 (pt); Nurses' aides 9 (ft), 6 (pt); Activities coordinators 1 (ft); Dietitians 1 (pt); Podiatrists 1 (pt).
Facilities Dining room; Activities room; Laundry room; Barber/Beauty shop; Library.
Activities Arts & crafts; Cards; Games; Reading groups; Movies; Shopping trips; Dances/Social/Cultural gatherings.

Ellisville

Ellisville State School—Clover Circle ICF/MR
Hwy 11 S, Ellisville, MS 39437
(601) 477-9384, ext 294
Admin Danny Lamier.
Medical Dir E Mangaoang MD.
Licensure Intermediate care for mentally retarded. *Beds* ICF/MR 132. *Certified* Medicaid.
Owner Publicly owned.
Admissions Requirements Medical examination; Physician's request.
Staff Physicians 1 (ft), 2 (pt); RNs 3 (ft); LPNs 11 (ft); Nurses' aides 121 (ft); Physical therapists 1 (pt); Recreational therapists 3 (ft); Occupational therapists 1 (pt); Speech therapists 1 (ft), 1 (pt); Dietitians 1 (pt); Audiologists 1 (pt).
Facilities Dining room; Physical therapy room; Activities room; Chapel; Crafts room; Laundry room; Barber/Beauty shop.
Activities Arts & crafts; Cards; Games; Reading groups; Prayer groups; Movies; Shopping trips; Dances/Social/Cultural gatherings.

Ellisville State School—Hillside SNF/ICF
Hwy 11 S, Ellisville, MS 39437
(601) 477-9384
Admin Frank D Lamier.
Medical Dir Dr Rolando Estrella Vilar.
Licensure Skilled care; Intermediate care. *Beds* Swing beds SNF/ICF 88. *Certified* Medicaid.
Owner Publicly owned.
Admissions Requirements Minimum age 55; Medical examination; Physician's request.
Staff Physicians 1 (pt); RNs 3 (ft); LPNs 11 (ft); Nurses' aides 45 (ft); Physical therapists 1 (pt); Reality therapists 1 (pt); Occupational therapists 1 (pt); Speech therapists 1 (pt); Activities coordinators 1 (ft); Dietitians 1 (pt); Audiologists 2 (pt); Dentists 2 (pt).

Facilities Dining room; Physical therapy room; Activities room; Chapel; Crafts room; Laundry room; Barber/Beauty shop; Library.
Activities Arts & crafts; Cards; Games; Reading groups; Movies; Shopping trips; Dances/Social/Cultural gatherings.

Ellisville State School—Peacan Grove
Hwy 11 S, Ellisville, MS 39437
(601) 477-9384
Admin Leroy Stokley.
Medical Dir Evangelina Paulino MD.
Licensure Intermediate care for mentally retarded. *Beds* ICF/MR 217. *Certified* Medicaid.
Owner Publicly owned.
Staff Physicians 1 (pt); RNs 2 (ft); LPNs 13 (ft); Nurses' aides 157 (ft); Physical therapists 1 (pt); Recreational therapists 2 (ft); Occupational therapists 1 (pt); Speech therapists 1 (ft), 1 (pt); Activities coordinators 1 (ft); Dietitians 1 (pt); Dentists 3 (pt).
Facilities Dining room; Physical therapy room; Chapel; Laundry room; Barber/Beauty shop; Library.
Activities Arts & crafts; Cards; Games; Reading groups; Prayer groups; Movies; Shopping trips; Dances/Social/Cultural gatherings.

Jones County Nursing Home
Rte 4 Box 194, Ellisville, MS 39437
(601) 477-3334
Admin Charles T Smith.
Licensure Skilled care; Intermediate care. *Beds* Swing beds SNF/ICF 120. *Certified* Medicaid.
Owner Publicly owned.

Lakeview Skilled Nursing Home
Hwy 11 S, Ellisville State School, Ellisville, MS 39437
(601) 477-9384, ext 305
Admin Eliza Shows; Frank D Lamier.
Licensure Skilled care; Intermediate care for mentally retarded. *Beds* SNF 155; ICF/MR 50. *Certified* Medicaid.
Owner Publicly owned.

Eupora

Eupora Health Care Center Inc
200 Walnut St, Eupora, MS 39744
(601) 258-8293
Admin Gerald C Gary. *Dir of Nursing* Ruby Kimbrell. *Medical Dir* Dr Charles A Ozborn.
Licensure Skilled care; Intermediate care; Medicare. *Beds* SNF 35; ICF 45; Medicare 10. *Private Pay Patients* 10%. *Certified* Medicaid; Medicare.
Owner Proprietary corp (Beverly Enterprises).
Admissions Requirements Medical examination; Physician's request.
Staff Physicians 4 (pt); RNs 3 (ft), 5 (pt); LPNs 8 (ft), 5 (pt); Nurses' aides 30 (ft), 14 (pt); Physical therapists 1 (pt); Speech therapists 1 (pt); Activities coordinators 1 (ft); Dietitians 1 (pt).
Facilities Dining room; Physical therapy room; Activities room; Laundry room; Barber/Beauty shop; In-house voting precinct.
Activities Arts & crafts; Cards; Games; Reading groups; Prayer groups; Movies; Shopping trips; Dances/Social/Cultural gatherings.

Florence

Briar Hill Rest Home Inc
280 Gunter Rd, Florence, MS 39073
(601) 939-6371
Admin Barbara M Bridges. *Dir of Nursing* Lou Jones. *Medical Dir* Dr Terry K Brantley.

Licensure Skilled care; Intermediate care; Personal care. *Beds* Swing beds SNF/ICF 60; Personal care 4. *Private Pay Patients* 40%. *Certified* Medicaid.
Owner Proprietary corp.
Admissions Requirements Medical examination.
Staff Physicians 2 (pt); RNs 2 (ft), 2 (pt); LPNs 4 (ft), 2 (pt); Nurses' aides 17 (ft), 5 (pt); Activities coordinators 1 (ft); Dietitians 1 (ft).
Facilities Dining room; Activities room; Crafts room; Laundry room; Barber/Beauty shop.
Activities Arts & crafts; Cards; Games; Reading groups; Prayer groups; Movies; Dances/Social/Cultural gatherings; Pet therapy.

Forest

Lackey Convalescent Home
266 1st Ave, Forest, MS 39074
(601) 469-3951
Admin Virginia F Mangum. *Dir of Nursing* Martha Adcox RN.
Licensure Skilled care. *Beds* SNF 30.
Owner Publicly owned.
Admissions Requirements Medical examination; Physician's request.
Staff RNs 2 (ft), 3 (pt); LPNs 1 (ft), 1 (pt); Nurses' aides 10 (ft), 1 (pt); Physical therapists 1 (pt); Speech therapists 1 (pt); Activities coordinators 1 (ft); Dietitians 1 (ft).
Facilities Dining room; Activities room; Crafts room; Laundry room; Barber/Beauty shop.
Activities Arts & crafts; Cards; Games; Reading groups; Prayer groups; Movies; Dances/Social/Cultural gatherings.

Fulton

Daniel Nursing Home
PO Drawer 127, Hwy 25 S, Fulton, MS 38843
(601) 862-2165
Admin James C Holland.
Medical Dir Grayden Tubb MD.
Licensure Skilled care. *Beds* SNF 120. *Certified* Medicaid.
Owner Proprietary corp.
Admissions Requirements Medical examination; Physician's request.
Staff Physicians 1 (pt); RNs 2 (ft), 1 (pt); LPNs 12 (ft), 2 (pt); Nurses' aides 38 (ft), 3 (pt); Physical therapists 1 (pt); Activities coordinators 1 (ft); Dietitians 1 (pt); Dentists 1 (pt).
Facilities Dining room; Activities room; Laundry room; Barber/Beauty shop.
Activities Cards; Games; Reading groups; Prayer groups; Movies; Dances/Social/Cultural gatherings.

Greenville

Arnold Avenue Nursing Home
402 Arnold Ave, Greenville, MS 38701
(601) 332-0318
Admin D D Felts.
Licensure Skilled care; Intermediate care. *Beds* Swing beds SNF/ICF 60. *Certified* Medicaid.
Owner Proprietary corp.

Autumn Leaves Nursing Home Inc
PO Box 4042, 501 N Solomon St, Greenville, MS 38701
(601) 335-5863
Admin Joan Willis Horton.
Licensure Skilled care; Intermediate care. *Beds* Swing beds SNF/ICF 60. *Certified* Medicaid.
Owner Proprietary corp.

Greenville Convalescent Home Inc
1935 N Theobald Ext, Greenville, MS 38701
(601) 334-4501

Admin Alvin L Freeman. *Dir of Nursing* Betty Martin. *Medical Dir* Dr J Edward Hill.
Licensure Skilled care; Intermediate care. *Beds* Swing beds SNF/ICF 120. *Private Pay Patients* 1%. *Certified* Medicaid.
Owner Privately owned.
Staff RNs 2 (ft), 2 (pt); Activities coordinators 1 (ft).

Mississippi Extended Care of Greenville Inc
1221 E Union St, Greenville, MS 38701
(601) 335-5811
Admin J K Gresham.
Medical Dir Dr J Edward Hill.
Licensure Skilled care; Intermediate care. *Beds* Swing beds SNF/ICF 116. *Certified* Medicaid.
Owner Proprietary corp.
Admissions Requirements Minimum age 18; Medical examination; Physician's request.
Staff Physicians 14 (pt); RNs 2 (ft), 2 (pt); LPNs 10 (ft), 1 (pt); Nurses' aides 35 (ft), 10 (pt); Physical therapists 1 (pt); Reality therapists 1 (pt); Speech therapists 1 (pt); Activities coordinators 1 (ft); Dietitians 1 (ft); Dentists 1 (pt).
Facilities Dining room; Physical therapy room; Activities room; Crafts room; Laundry room; Barber/Beauty shop.
Activities Arts & crafts; Cards; Games; Prayer groups; Movies.

Greenwood

Golden Age Nursing Home
PO Box 853, Hwy 82 E, Greenwood, MS 38930
(601) 453-6323
Admin Alvin Loewenberg.
Licensure Skilled care; Intermediate care. *Beds* Swing beds SNF/ICF 180. *Certified* Medicaid.
Owner Nonprofit corp.

Heritage Manor of Greenwood
PO Box 1670, Hwy 82 By-Pass, Greenwood, MS 38930
(601) 453-9173
Admin Robert Greer.
Licensure Skilled care; Intermediate care. *Beds* SNF 40; ICF 70. *Certified* Medicaid.
Owner Proprietary corp (National Heritage).

Pemberton Manor Inc
PO Box 1958, W Claiborne Ext, Greenwood, MS 38930
(601) 453-8140
Admin Kathy B Buford. *Dir of Nursing* Willie B Young RN. *Medical Dir* J Edward Hill MD.
Licensure Skilled care; Intermediate care. *Beds* Swing beds SNF/ICF 120. *Certified* Medicaid.
Owner Proprietary corp.
Admissions Requirements Medical examination; Physician's request.
Staff Physicians 1 (pt); RNs 2 (ft), 9 (pt); LPNs 5 (ft), 16 (pt); Physical therapists 2 (pt); Speech therapists 2 (pt); Activities coordinators 2 (pt); Dietitians 1 (ft), 1 (pt).
Facilities Dining room; Activities room; Crafts room; Laundry room; Barber/Beauty shop.
Activities Arts & crafts; Cards; Games; Reading groups; Prayer groups; Movies; Shopping trips; Dances/Social/Cultural gatherings.

Grenada

Grandview Health Care Center
1950 Grandview Dr, Grenada, MS 38901
(601) 226-9554
Admin Elizabeth Herndon.
Licensure Skilled care; Intermediate care. *Beds* SNF 60; ICF 60. *Certified* Medicaid.
Owner Proprietary corp (Beverly Enterprises).

Heritage Manor of Grenada
1966 Hill Dr, Grenada, MS 38901
(601) 226-2442
Admin Joe Bannon.
Licensure Skilled care; Intermediate care. *Beds* Swing beds SNF/ICF 137. *Certified* Medicaid.
Owner Proprietary corp (National Heritage).

Gulfport

Britthaven of Gulfport
1530 Broad, Gulfport, MS 39501
(601) 864-6544
Admin Terri Reynolds.
Licensure Skilled care; Intermediate care. *Beds* SNF 60; ICF 60. *Certified* Medicaid; Medicare.
Owner Proprietary corp (Hillhaven Corp).

Tender Care Home
01512 Pass Rd, Gulfport, MS 39501
(601) 896-1302
Admin Aubrey F Dryden.
Licensure Personal care. *Beds* 8.
Owner Proprietary corp.

Hattiesburg

Conva-Rest Northgate—Warren Hall
298 Cahal St, Hattiesburg, MS 39401
(601) 582-9157
Admin Roy A Dumas.
Medical Dir Dr A J Carrol.
Licensure Skilled care; Alzheimer's care. *Beds* SNF 120. *Certified* Medicaid.
Owner Proprietary corp.
Admissions Requirements Medical examination; Physician's request.
Staff RNs 4 (ft); LPNs 13 (ft); Nurses' aides 30 (ft); Recreational therapists 1 (ft); Activities coordinators 1 (ft); Dietitians 1 (ft).
Facilities Dining room; Activities room; Crafts room; Laundry room; Barber/Beauty shop.
Activities Arts & crafts; Cards; Games; Reading groups; Prayer groups; Movies; Dances/Social/Cultural gatherings.

Conva-Rest Northgate—Monroe Hall
300 Cahal St, Hattiesburg, MS 39401
(601) 544-5300
Admin Lisa Bean.
Licensure Intermediate care. *Beds* ICF 100. *Certified* Medicaid.
Owner Proprietary corp.

Conva-Rest of Hattiesburg
Medical Blvd, Hattiesburg, MS 39401
(601) 264-3709
Admin Larry Fortenberry.
Licensure Skilled care. *Beds* SNF 192. *Certified* Medicaid.
Owner Proprietary corp.

For-Rest Convalescent Home
907 E Hardy St, Hattiesburg, MS 39401
(601) 584-7218
Admin Vera Mae Davis.
Licensure Personal care. *Beds* 7.
Owner Proprietary corp.

Hattiesburg Convalescent Center
514 Bay St, Hattiesburg, MS 39401
(601) 544-4230
Admin Jewell McMahan. *Dir of Nursing* Louise Rounsaville. *Medical Dir* Dr Clayton Cook.
Licensure Skilled care; Residential care; Alzheimer's care. *Beds* SNF 174; Residential care 50. *Private Pay Patients* 40%. *Certified* Medicaid; Medicare; VA.
Owner Proprietary corp.
Admissions Requirements Medical examination; Physician's request.

Staff RNs 20 (ft); LPNs 40 (ft); Nurses' aides 70 (ft); Physical therapists 2 (ft); Recreational therapists 1 (ft); Occupational therapists 1 (ft); Speech therapists 1 (ft); Activities coordinators 1 (ft); Dietitians 1 (ft); Ophthalmologists 1 (pt); Podiatrists 1 (pt).
Facilities Dining room; Physical therapy room; Activities room; Crafts room; Laundry room; Barber/Beauty shop.
Activities Arts & crafts; Cards; Games; Reading groups; Prayer groups; Movies; Shopping trips; Dances/Social/Cultural gatherings; Intergenerational programs; Pet therapy.

Hazlehurst

Pine Crest Guest Home
133 Pine St, Hazlehurst, MS 39083
(601) 894-1411
Admin Peggy Gaddy. *Dir of Nursing* Lucy Tomicich. *Medical Dir* Dr Fred McDonnell.
Licensure Skilled care; Intermediate care. *Beds* Swing beds SNF/ICF 120. *Certified* Medicaid.
Owner Proprietary corp.
Admissions Requirements Medical examination.
Staff Physicians 1 (pt); RNs 3 (ft), 1 (pt); LPNs 9 (ft), 3 (pt); Nurses' aides 31 (ft), 11 (pt); Physical therapists 2 (pt); Recreational therapists 1 (pt); Speech therapists 1 (pt); Activities coordinators 1 (ft); Dietitians 1 (ft), 1 (pt).
Facilities Dining room; Activities room; Crafts room; Laundry room; Barber/Beauty shop.
Activities Arts & crafts; Cards; Games; Reading groups; Prayer groups; Movies; Shopping trips; Dances/Social/Cultural gatherings.

Holly Springs

Heritage Manor of Holly Springs
PO Box 640, 960 E Salem Ave, Holly Springs, MS 38635
(601) 252-1141
Admin Jerry Beck. *Dir of Nursing* Geraldine Gholson RN. *Medical Dir* Marion Green MD.
Licensure Skilled care; Intermediate care. *Beds* Swing beds SNF/ICF 120. *Certified* Medicaid.
Owner Proprietary corp (National Heritage).
Staff RNs.

Houston

Floy Dyer Manor
Hwy 8 E, Houston, MS 38851
(601) 456-3701
Admin Ruth Rhodes.
Medical Dir Dr Edward Gore.
Licensure Skilled care; Intermediate care. *Beds* Swing beds SNF/ICF 66. *Certified* Medicaid.
Owner Proprietary corp.
Admissions Requirements Medical examination; Physician's request.
Staff RNs 2 (ft), 1 (pt); LPNs 4 (ft), 5 (pt); Nurses' aides 14 (ft), 2 (pt); Activities coordinators 1 (ft); Dietitians 1 (pt).
Facilities Dining room; Activities room; Barber/Beauty shop.
Activities Arts & crafts; Cards; Games; Movies; Shopping trips; Dances/Social/Cultural gatherings.

Indianola

Heritage Manor—Indianola
PO Box 669, 401 Hwy 82 W, Indianola, MS 38751
(601) 887-2682

Admin Eleta J Grimmett. *Dir of Nursing*
Linda Fike RN. *Medical Dir* Dr Joe Hull.
Licensure Skilled care; Intermediate care. *Beds*
Swing beds SNF/ICF 75. *Private Pay
Patients* 20%. *Certified* Medicaid.
Owner Proprietary corp (National Heritage).
Admissions Requirements Physician's request.
Staff Physicians 5 (pt); RNs 2 (ft), 2 (pt);
LPNs 7 (ft), 3 (pt); Nurses' aides 22 (ft), 7
(pt); Recreational therapists 1 (pt); Activities
coordinators 1 (ft); Dietitians 1 (ft), 1 (pt);
Podiatrists 1 (pt).
Facilities Dining room; Activities room;
Laundry room; Barber/Beauty shop.
Activities Arts & crafts; Cards; Games;
Reading groups; Prayer groups; Movies;
Shopping trips; Dances/Social/Cultural
gatherings; Intergenerational programs; Pet
therapy; Community involvement in Rock
and Roll Jamboree.

Iuka

Pickwick Manor Nursing Home
230 Kaki St, Iuka, MS 38852
(601) 423-9112
Admin James W Freeman Jr.
Medical Dir Dr Kelly Segars.
Licensure Skilled care; Intermediate care. *Beds*
Swing beds SNF/ICF 120. *Certified*
Medicaid.
Owner Proprietary corp (Beverly Enterprises).
Admissions Requirements Medical
examination; Physician's request.
Staff Physicians 6 (ft); RNs 2 (ft), 2 (pt);
LPNs 13 (ft); Nurses' aides 32 (ft), 10 (pt);
Physical therapists 1 (pt); Speech therapists
1 (pt); Activities coordinators 1 (ft);
Dietitians 1 (pt); Ophthalmologists 1 (pt);
Dentists 1 (pt).
Facilities Dining room; Activities room;
Chapel; Laundry room; Barber/Beauty shop.
Activities Arts & crafts; Games; Prayer groups;
Movies; Shopping trips; Dances/Social/
Cultural gatherings.

Jackson

Albermarle Health Care Center
3454 Albermarle Rd, Jackson, MS 39213
(601) 362-5394
Admin Debbie Spence.
Medical Dir Dr Aaron Shirley; Dr James
Anderson.
Licensure Skilled care; Intermediate care. *Beds*
SNF 59; ICF 60. *Certified* Medicaid;
Medicare.
Owner Proprietary corp (Beverly Enterprises).
Admissions Requirements Physician's request.
Staff RNs 6 (ft); LPNs 14 (ft); Nurses' aides
43 (ft); Activities coordinators 1 (ft);
Dietitians 1 (ft).
Facilities Dining room; Activities room;
Crafts room; Laundry room; Barber/Beauty
shop.
Activities Arts & crafts; Cards; Games;
Reading groups; Prayer groups; Movies;
Shopping trips; Dances/Social/Cultural
gatherings.

Alpha & Omega Personal Care
131 S Prentiss St, Jackson, MS 39203
(601) 354-0783
Admin Rev Myrtle McAllister.
Licensure Personal care. *Beds* Personal care
13.
Owner Nonprofit corp.

Ann's Personal Care Home
3137 James Hill St, Jackson, MS 39213
(601) 981-5963, 362-2182
Admin Ann Fleming Coleman.
Licensure Intermediate care for mentally
retarded. *Beds* ICF/MR 15.
Owner Privately owned.
Admissions Requirements Medical
examination; Physician's request.

Facilities Dining room; Activities room;
Laundry room.
Activities Cards; Prayer groups.

Armstrong's Personal Care Home I
129 Poindexter St, Jackson, MS 39203
(601) 355-7029
Admin Minnie Armstrong.
Licensure Personal care. *Beds* Personal care
24.
Owner Proprietary corp.

Armstrong's Personal Care Home II
227 Poindexter St, Jackson, MS 39203
(601) 355-0364
Admin Minnie Armstrong.
Licensure Personal care. *Beds* 10.
Owner Proprietary corp.

Belhaven Nursing Home
1004 North St, Jackson, MS 39202
(601) 355-0763
Admin Billie T Trussell. *Dir of Nursing* Eva
Patterson. *Medical Dir* Dr Calvin Ramsey.
Licensure Skilled care; Intermediate care. *Beds*
Swing beds SNF/ICF 60. *Certified* Medicaid.
Owner Proprietary corp.
Admissions Requirements Medical
examination.
Staff RNs 1 (ft), 3 (pt); LPNs 4 (ft), 4 (pt);
Nurses' aides 18 (ft), 2 (pt); Activities
coordinators 1 (ft); Dietitians 1 (ft).
Facilities Dining room; Activities room;
Crafts room; Laundry room; Barber/Beauty
shop.
Activities Arts & crafts; Cards; Games;
Movies; Shopping trips; Dances/Social/
Cultural gatherings; Intergenerational
programs; Pet therapy; Jets combo; Square
dancing.

Carter's Guest Home Inc
941 Cooper Rd, Jackson, MS 39212
(601) 372-6931
Admin Aline P Carter.
Licensure Skilled care; Intermediate care. *Beds*
Swing beds SNF/ICF 53. *Certified* Medicaid.
Owner Proprietary corp.

Coleman's Personal Care Home
917 Hunt St, Jackson, MS 39203
(601) 355-2420
Admin Theola Coleman.
Licensure Personal care. *Beds* Personal care 9.
Owner Proprietary corp.

Community Nursing Home
1129 Langley Ave, Jackson, MS 39204
(601) 355-0617
Admin Dillie Myrick. *Dir of Nursing* Blanche
Reed. *Medical Dir* Krooss.
Licensure Intermediate care. *Beds* ICF 60.
Certified Medicaid.
Owner Nonprofit corp.
Admissions Requirements Medical
examination; Physician's request.
Staff RNs 1 (ft); LPNs 5 (ft); Nurses' aides 18
(ft); Activities coordinators 1 (ft); Dietitians
1 (ft).
Facilities Dining room; Activities room;
Crafts room; Laundry room.
Activities Arts & crafts; Cards; Games; Prayer
groups; Movies; Shopping trips; Dances/
Social/Cultural gatherings.

Compere's Nursing Home Inc
865 North St, Jackson, MS 39202
(601) 948-6531
Admin Robert F Burkett.
Licensure Skilled care; Intermediate care. *Beds*
Swing beds SNF/ICF 60. *Certified* Medicaid.
Owner Proprietary corp.

Cottage Grove Nursing Home
1116 Forest Ave, Jackson, MS 39206-3216
(601) 366-6461
Admin Juadine Cleveland.

Licensure Intermediate care. *Beds* ICF 28.
Certified Medicaid.
Owner Proprietary corp.

Crawford's Nursing Home Inc
927 Cooper Rd, Jackson, MS 39212
(601) 372-8662
Admin Robert A Crawford.
Medical Dir Robert Lowe MD.
Licensure Intermediate care. *Beds* ICF 71.
Certified Medicaid.
Owner Proprietary corp.
Admissions Requirements Minimum age 21;
Medical examination; Physician's request.
Staff Physicians 2 (pt); RNs 1 (ft), 1 (pt);
LPNs 5 (ft), 1 (pt); Nurses' aides 30 (ft), 2
(pt); Physical therapists 1 (pt); Reality
therapists 1 (pt); Recreational therapists 1
(pt); Occupational therapists 1 (pt); Speech
therapists 1 (pt); Activities coordinators 1
(ft); Dietitians 1 (pt); Ophthalmologists 1
(pt); Podiatrists 1 (pt); Dentists 1 (pt).
Affiliation Baptist.
Facilities Dining room; Physical therapy
room; Activities room; Chapel; Crafts room;
Laundry room; Barber/Beauty shop.
Activities Arts & crafts; Cards; Games;
Reading groups; Prayer groups; Movies;
Shopping trips; Dances/Social/Cultural
gatherings; Trips.

Earle Street Personal Care Home
438 Earle St, Jackson, MS 39203
(601) 362-4032
Admin Izora Wells.
Licensure Personal care. *Beds* Personal care
11.
Owner Privately owned.
Admissions Requirements Minimum age 18;
Males only.
Facilities Dining room; Laundry room.
Activities Cards; Games; Dances/Social/
Cultural gatherings.

Hinds Residential Center
1480 Raymond Rd, Jackson, MS 39204
(601) 373-2472
Admin A D Buffington.
Licensure Personal care. *Beds* Personal care
46.
Owner Proprietary corp.
Admissions Requirements Medical
examination.
Staff Physicians 1 (pt); RNs 2 (ft); LPNs 5
(ft), 1 (pt); Nurses' aides 17 (ft), 1 (pt);
Physical therapists 1 (pt); Reality therapists
1 (pt); Recreational therapists 1 (ft); Speech
therapists 1 (pt); Activities coordinators 1
(ft); Dietitians 1 (pt); Ophthalmologists 1
(pt); Podiatrists 1 (pt); Audiologists 1 (pt);
Dentists 1 (pt).
Facilities Dining room; Activities room;
Barber/Beauty shop.
Activities Arts & crafts; Games; Reading
groups; Prayer groups; Movies.

Hunt Street Personal Care Home
933 Hunt St, Jackson, MS 39203
(601) 352-0046
Admin Mary A Henderson.
Licensure Personal care. *Beds* Personal care
11.
Owner Proprietary corp.

Inglewood Manor Nursing Home
1900 Chadwick Dr, Jackson, MS 39204
(601) 372-0231
Admin Sylvia Smith.
Licensure Skilled care; Intermediate care. *Beds*
Swing beds SNF/ICF 102. *Certified*
Medicaid.
Owner Proprietary corp (Beverly Enterprises).

Lakeland Health Care Center
3680 Lakeland Ln, Jackson, MS 39216
(601) 982-5505
Admin Mardie O Dixon.

Licensure Skilled care; Intermediate care. *Beds* SNF 69; ICF 36. *Certified* Medicaid.
Owner Proprietary corp (Beverly Enterprises).

Magnolia Nursing Home
3601 Peter Quinn, Jackson, MS 39213
(601) 366-1712
Admin Mildred Spell.
Licensure Intermediate care. *Beds* ICF 60. *Certified* Medicaid.
Owner Proprietary corp.

Manhattan Health Care Center
4540 Manhattan Rd, Jackson, MS 39206
(601) 982-7421
Admin Gwen Harper. *Dir of Nursing* Jean Bible CRNA. *Medical Dir* Hardy B Woodbridge MD.
Licensure Skilled care; Intermediate care. *Beds* Swing beds SNF/ICF 180. *Certified* Medicaid.
Owner Proprietary corp (Beverly Enterprises).
Admissions Requirements Medical examination.
Staff RNs 5 (ft), 2 (pt); LPNs 22 (ft), 3 (pt); Nurses' aides 60 (ft), 5 (pt); Activities coordinators 2 (ft); Dietitians 1 (ft).
Facilities Dining room; Activities room; Laundry room; Barber/Beauty shop.
Activities Arts & crafts; Games; Reading groups; Prayer groups; Movies; Shopping trips; Dances/Social/Cultural gatherings.

Mississippi Children's Rehabilitation Center
777 Lakeland Dr, Jackson, MS 39216
(601) 982-2911
Admin David Lightwine.
Medical Dir Marilyn Graves MD.
Licensure Intermediate care. *Beds* ICF 16. *Certified* Medicaid.
Owner Publicly owned.
Admissions Requirements Minimum age Birth; Physician's request.
Staff RNs 4 (ft), 1 (pt); LPNs 4 (ft); Nurses' aides 16 (ft); Physical therapists 3 (ft); Recreational therapists 2 (ft); Occupational therapists 2 (ft); Speech therapists 1 (ft); Dietitians 1 (pt).
Facilities Dining room; Physical therapy room; Activities room; Crafts room; Laundry room; Library; Outpatient physical therapy room; Classrooms.
Activities Arts & crafts; Games; Movies; Field trips.

Northside Haven
3125 W Northside Dr, Jackson, MS 39213
(601) 362-4050
Admin Bernice Johnson; Leola L Bracey, Asst.
Licensure Skilled care. *Beds* SNF 17. *Private Pay Patients* 90%.
Owner Nonprofit organization/foundation.
Staff Nurses' aides 3 (ft); Recreational therapists 1 (ft); Activities coordinators 1 (ft); Dietitians 1 (ft).

Pleasant Hills Health Center
1600 Raymond Rd, Jackson, MS 39204
(601) 371-1700
Admin Catherine Brinson. *Dir of Nursing* Peggy Gregory. *Medical Dir* William Gregory.
Licensure Skilled care; Intermediate care. *Beds* Swing beds SNF/ICF 60. *Certified* Medicaid.
Owner Proprietary corp.
Admissions Requirements Minimum age 78.
Staff Physicians 1 (pt); RNs 2 (ft); LPNs 5 (ft), 3 (pt); Nurses' aides 17 (ft), 3 (pt); Physical therapists 1 (pt); Activities coordinators 1 (ft), 1 (pt); Dietitians 1 (pt); Ophthalmologists 1 (pt).
Facilities Dining room; Physical therapy room; Activities room; Chapel; Laundry room; Barber/Beauty shop.
Activities Arts & crafts; Cards; Games; Reading groups; Prayer groups; Movies; Shopping trips; Dances/Social/Cultural gatherings.

Richmond's Boarding Home
852 Crawford St, Jackson, MS 39213
(601) 352-7694, 956-0056
Admin Rev R M Richmond Sr.
Licensure Personal care. *Beds* Personal care 14.
Owner Proprietary corp.

Spencer's Personal Care Home
532 Burns St, Jackson, MS 39203
(601) 355-4036
Admin Barbara Spencer.
Licensure Personal care. *Beds* Personal care 23.

Teat Personal Care Home
3227 Edwards Ave, Jackson, MS 39213
(601) 982-2872
Admin Eddie L Teat.
Licensure Personal care. *Beds* Personal care 13.
Owner Proprietary corp.

Wells Personal Care Home
2403 Rutledge, Jackson, MS 39213
(601) 362-4032
Admin Izora Wells.
Licensure Personal care. *Beds* Personal care 5.
Owner Proprietary corp.

Westhaven Personal Care Home
Rte 2 Box 170, Jackson, MS 39209
(601) 922-2363
Admin John Lea.
Licensure Personal care. *Beds* Personal care 32.
Owner Proprietary corp.

Kosciusko

Attala County Nursing Center
Hwy 12 W, Kosciusko, MS 39090
(601) 289-1200
Admin Myren Hughes.
Licensure Skilled care; Intermediate care. *Beds* Swing beds SNF/ICF 119. *Certified* Medicaid.
Owner Proprietary corp (National Heritage).

Laurel

Davison Rest Home Inc
PO Box 4476, Laurel, MS 39440
(601) 426-3201
Admin Geraldine Lorch.
Licensure Skilled care; Intermediate care. *Beds* Swing beds SNF/ICF 40. *Certified* Medicaid.
Owner Proprietary corp.

Hearthside Haven Inc
935 West Dr, Laurel, MS 39440
(601) 649-8006
Admin Brenda Leone.
Licensure Skilled care. *Beds* SNF 130. *Certified* Medicaid; Medicare.
Owner Proprietary corp.
Staff RNs 4 (ft); LPNs 14 (ft), 3 (pt); Nurses' aides 50 (ft), 15 (pt); Activities coordinators 1 (ft).
Facilities Dining room; Physical therapy room; Activities room; Chapel; Crafts room; Barber/Beauty shop.
Activities Arts & crafts; Games; Reading groups; Prayer groups; Movies; Shopping trips; Dances/Social/Cultural gatherings.

NuCare Convalescent Center
1036 West Dr, Laurel, MS 39440
(601) 425-3191
Admin Bobby Welborn. *Dir of Nursing* Bett Spann. *Medical Dir* James Waites MD.
Licensure Skilled care. *Beds* SNF 60. *Certified* Medicaid.
Owner Proprietary corp (Southeastern Health Care).
Admissions Requirements Medical examination; Physician's request.

Staff Physicians 4 (pt); RNs 1 (ft), 1 (pt); LPNs 7 (ft), 1 (pt); Nurses' aides 17 (ft), 5 (pt); Physical therapists 1 (pt); Recreational therapists 1 (pt); Occupational therapists 1 (pt); Speech therapists 1 (pt); Activities coordinators 1 (ft), 1 (pt); Dietitians 1 (pt); Ophthalmologists 1 (pt).
Facilities Dining room; Physical therapy room; Activities room; Laundry room; Barber/Beauty shop.
Activities Arts & crafts; Cards; Games; Reading groups; Movies; Shopping trips.

Leakesville

Greene County Hospital—Extended Care Facility
PO Box 39, Leakesville, MS 39451
(601) 394-2371
Admin Latricia Gornelson.
Licensure Skilled care; Intermediate care. *Beds* Swing beds SNF/ICF 26. *Certified* Medicaid.
Owner Publicly owned.

Melody Manor Convalescent Center
PO Box 640, Leakesville, MS 39451
(601) 394-2331
Admin Myrna Green.
Medical Dir Dr Alvaro Moreno.
Licensure Skilled care; Intermediate care. *Beds* Swing beds SNF/ICF 60. *Certified* Medicaid.
Owner Proprietary corp.
Admissions Requirements Medical examination; Physician's request.
Staff RNs 1 (ft), 1 (pt); LPNs 7 (ft), 1 (pt); Nurses' aides 16 (ft), 3 (pt); Activities coordinators 1 (ft), 1 (pt); Dietitians 1 (pt).
Facilities Dining room; Activities room; Crafts room; Laundry room; Barber/Beauty shop.
Activities Arts & crafts; Cards; Games; Reading groups; Prayer groups; Movies; Shopping trips.

Long Beach

South Mississippi Retardation Center
1170 W Railroad St, Long Beach, MS 39560
(601) 868-2923
Admin Pamela C Baker PhD. *Dir of Nursing* Gerry Braden RN. *Medical Dir* Pamela C Baker PhD.
Licensure Intermediate care for mentally retarded; Retirement; Transitional living. *Beds* ICF/MR 120; Transitional living cottages 15. *Certified* Medicaid.
Owner Publicly owned.
Staff Physicians 3 (pt); RNs 7 (ft); LPNs 9 (ft); Physical therapists 1 (pt); Recreational therapists 6 (ft); Occupational therapists 1 (pt); Speech therapists 2 (ft); Activities coordinators 1 (ft); Dietitians 1 (ft); Podiatrists 1 (pt); Dentists 1 (pt); Pharmacists.
Activities Arts & crafts; Cards; Games; Reading groups; Prayer groups; Movies; Shopping trips; Dances/Social/Cultural gatherings; Special Olympics.

Louisville

Tri-County Nursing Home Inc
PO Box 542, Louisville, MS 39339
(601) 773-8047
Admin Bruce Stone. *Dir of Nursing* Pamela D Thomas. *Medical Dir* Dewitt G Crawford MD.
Licensure Skilled care. *Beds* SNF 60. *Certified* Medicaid.
Owner Proprietary corp.
Admissions Requirements Medical examination; Physician's request.
Staff RNs 3 (ft), 2 (pt); LPNs 4 (ft), 4 (pt); Nurses' aides 13 (ft), 6 (pt).

Facilities Dining room; Activities room; Chapel; Crafts room; Laundry room; Barber/Beauty shop.
Activities Arts & crafts; Cards; Games; Reading groups; Prayer groups; Dances/Social/Cultural gatherings; Singing.

Winston County Nursing Home
PO Box 670, Hwy 14 E, Louisville, MS 39339
(601) 773-6211
Admin Dale Saulters.
Licensure Skilled care; Intermediate care. *Beds* ICF 44; Swing beds SNF/ICF 42. *Certified* Medicaid; Medicare.
Owner Publicly owned.

Lucedale

Glen Oaks Nursing Home
220 Glen Oaks Dr, Lucedale, MS 39452
(601) 947-2783
Admin Louise Parnell.
Licensure Skilled care; Intermediate care. *Beds* Swing beds SNF/ICF 60. *Certified* Medicaid.
Owner Proprietary corp.

Lumberton

Adventist Health Center
Rte 2 Box 79, Lumberton, MS 39455
(601) 794-8566
Admin Wayne Hayward.
Medical Dir Dr Thomas McFarland.
Licensure Skilled care; Intermediate care. *Beds* SNF 56; ICF 64. *Certified* Medicaid.
Owner Proprietary corp.
Admissions Requirements Medical examination.
Staff Physicians 3 (pt); RNs 3 (ft), 2 (pt); LPNs 11 (ft), 4 (pt); Nurses' aides 30 (ft), 24 (pt); Reality therapists 1 (ft), 1 (pt); Recreational therapists 2 (ft), 6 (pt); Activities coordinators 1 (ft); Dietitians 9 (ft), 4 (pt); Dentists 1 (pt).
Affiliation Seventh-Day Adventist.
Facilities Dining room; Physical therapy room; Activities room; Crafts room; Laundry room; Barber/Beauty shop.
Activities Arts & crafts; Games; Reading groups; Prayer groups; Movies; Shopping trips.

Madison

Willard F Bond Home
PO Box 720, 500 Old Canton Rd, Madison, MS 39110
(601) 856-8041
Admin Thomas Nichols.
Licensure Intermediate care. *Beds* ICF 60. *Certified* Medicaid.
Owner Proprietary corp.

Magee

Hillcrest Health Center Inc
1401 1st Ave NE, Magee, MS 39111
(601) 849-5443
Admin Mary Wilson.
Medical Dir Charles Pruitt Jr MD.
Licensure Skilled care; Intermediate care. *Beds* Swing beds SNF/ICF 120. *Certified* Medicaid.
Owner Proprietary corp.
Staff Physicians 6 (pt); RNs 1 (ft), 1 (pt); Physical therapists 1 (pt); Activities coordinators 1 (ft); Dietitians 1 (pt); Podiatrists 1 (pt).
Facilities Dining room; Activities room; Chapel; Laundry room; Barber/Beauty shop.
Activities Arts & crafts; Games; Reading groups; Prayer groups.

Marks

Quitman County Nursing Home
PO Box 330, 350 Getwell Dr, Marks, MS 39646
(601) 326-8031
Admin David W Fuller.
Medical Dir Dr Waller.
Licensure Intermediate care. *Beds* ICF 60. *Certified* Medicaid.
Owner Publicly owned.
Admissions Requirements Medical examination; Physician's request.
Staff Physicians 5 (pt); RNs 1 (ft); LPNs 5 (ft); Nurses' aides 9 (ft); Physical therapists 1 (pt); Recreational therapists 1 (ft); Speech therapists 1 (pt); Activities coordinators 1 (ft); Dietitians 1 (pt); Podiatrists 1 (pt).
Facilities Dining room; Physical therapy room; Activities room; Chapel; Crafts room; Laundry room; Barber/Beauty shop; Library.
Activities Arts & crafts; Cards; Games; Reading groups; Prayer groups; Movies; Shopping trips; Dances/Social/Cultural gatherings; Field trips; Picnics; Guest speakers.

McComb

McComb Extended Care & Nursing Home
501 S Locust St, McComb, MS 39648
(601) 684-8111
Admin Shirley Graham.
Licensure Skilled care; Intermediate care. *Beds* Swing beds SNF/ICF 145. *Certified* Medicaid.
Owner Proprietary corp (National Heritage).

Southwest Extended Care Center
415 Marion Ave, McComb, MS 39648
(601) 684-8700
Admin Ronald J Smith.
Licensure Skilled care; Intermediate care. *Beds* Swing beds SNF/ICF 120. *Certified* Medicaid.
Owner Proprietary corp (Beverly Enterprises).

Meadville

Meadville Nursing Home
Rte 2 Box 233, Meadville, MS 39643
(601) 384-5861
Admin Ellen B Harrigill. *Dir of Nursing* Dora Hester RN. *Medical Dir* E P Gabbert MD.
Licensure Skilled care; Intermediate care. *Beds* Swing beds SNF/ICF 60. *Certified* Medicaid.
Owner Proprietary corp (Southeastern Health Care Inc).
Admissions Requirements Medical examination; Physician's request.
Staff RNs 2 (ft); LPNs 8 (ft); Nurses' aides 20 (ft); Physical therapists 1 (pt); Recreational therapists 1 (pt); Speech therapists 1 (pt); Activities coordinators 1 (ft), 1 (pt); Dietitians 1 (pt).
Facilities Dining room; Activities room; Chapel; Crafts room; Laundry room; Barber/Beauty shop.
Activities Arts & crafts; Cards; Games; Reading groups; Prayer groups; Movies; Shopping trips.

Mendenhall

Conva-Rest of Mendenhall
925 Mangum Ave, Mendenhall, MS 39114
(601) 847-1311
Admin Carolyn Davis.
Licensure Skilled care; Intermediate care. *Beds* SNF 44; ICF 16. *Certified* Medicaid.
Owner Proprietary corp.

Meridian

Broadmoor Health Care Center Inc
4728 Hwy 39 N, Meridian, MS 39301
(601) 482-8151
Admin Jerry South.
Licensure Skilled care; Intermediate care. *Beds* SNF 60; ICF 60. *Certified* Medicaid.
Owner Proprietary corp (Beverly Enterprises).

King's Daughters & Sons Rest Home Inc
PO Box 3623, Hwy 39 N, Meridian, MS 39301
(601) 483-5256
Admin Johnnie Walters.
Licensure Intermediate care. *Beds* ICF 120.
Owner Nonprofit corp.
Affiliation King's Daughters & Sons.

Meridian Convalescent Home
517 33rd St, Meridian, MS 39301
(601) 483-3916
Admin Sue Ables.
Licensure Skilled care; Intermediate care. *Beds* Swing beds SNF/ICF 58. *Certified* Medicaid.
Owner Proprietary corp.

Meridian Nursing Center
3716 Hwy 39 N, Meridian, MS 39301
(601) 482-7164
Admin Robert Turcotte.
Licensure Skilled care; Intermediate care. *Beds* Swing beds SNF/ICF 60. *Certified* Medicaid.
Owner Proprietary corp (Meridian Healthcare).

Queen City Nursing Center
1201 28th Ave, Meridian, MS 39301
(601) 483-1467
Admin Michael W Howard.
Licensure Skilled care. *Beds* SNF 60. *Certified* Medicaid.
Owner Proprietary corp.

Reginald P White Intermediate & Skilled Care Facility
PO Box 4128, West Station, Meridian, MS 39301
(601) 482-6186
Admin Gerry Copeland.
Medical Dir James E Gracey.
Licensure Skilled care; Intermediate care. *Beds* SNF 119; ICF 96. *Certified* Medicaid.
Owner Publicly owned.
Staff Physicians 1 (ft); RNs 4 (ft); LPNs 13 (ft); Nurses' aides 57 (ft); Physical therapists 1 (pt); Activities coordinators 1 (ft); Dietitians 1 (pt); Dentists 1 (pt).
Facilities Dining room; Physical therapy room; Activities room; Laundry room; Barber/Beauty shop; Library.
Activities Arts & crafts; Cards; Games; Prayer groups; Movies; Shopping trips; Dances/Social/Cultural gatherings.

Monticello

Lawrence County Nursing Center Inc
PO Box 398, 700 S Jefferson St, Monticello, MS 39654
(601) 587-2593
Admin James Todd.
Licensure Skilled care. *Beds* SNF 60. *Certified* Medicaid.
Owner Proprietary corp (National Heritage).

Morton

Scott County Nursing & Personal Care Home
Old Hwy 80 E, Morton, MS 39117
(601) 732-6361
Admin Gary Pace.
Licensure Skilled care; Intermediate care; Personal care. *Beds* Swing beds SNF/ICF 110; Personal care 10. *Certified* Medicaid.
Owner Proprietary corp.

Moss Point

Gulf Coast Nursing Home of Moss Point Inc
4501 Jefferson Ave, Moss Point, MS 39563
(601) 762-7451
Admin John H Stinson.
Licensure Skilled care; Intermediate care. *Beds* SNF 35; ICF 49. *Certified* Medicaid.
Owner Proprietary corp.

Natchez

Adams County Nursing Center
587 John R Junkin Dr, Natchez, MS 39120
(601) 446-8426
Admin Kathy Conn.
Licensure Skilled care; Intermediate care. *Beds* Swing beds SNF/ICF 120. *Certified* Medicaid.
Owner Proprietary corp (National Heritage).

Glenburney Nursing Home
555 John R Junkin Dr, Natchez, MS 39120
(601) 442-4395
Admin Kathy Conn.
Medical Dir Teresa Loomis.
Licensure Skilled care. *Beds* SNF 96. *Certified* Medicaid.
Owner Proprietary corp (National Heritage).
Admissions Requirements Medical examination; Physician's request.
Staff RNs 2 (ft); LPNs 11 (ft), 1 (pt); Nurses' aides 31 (ft), 6 (pt); Activities coordinators 1 (ft); Dietitians 1 (ft).
Facilities Dining room; Laundry room; Barber/Beauty shop; Lobby.
Activities Arts & crafts; Games; Prayer groups; Movies; Shopping trips; Dances/Social/ Cultural gatherings.

Trace Haven Nursing Home
344 Arlington Ave, Natchez, MS 39120
(601) 442-4393
Admin Linda Crain.
Licensure Skilled care; Intermediate care. *Beds* Swing beds SNF/ICF 58. *Certified* Medicaid.
Owner Proprietary corp (National Heritage).

New Albany

Roselawn Retirement Home
118 S Glenfield Rd, New Albany, MS 38652
(601) 534-9506
Admin Ann H Thomas. *Dir of Nursing* Wanda Holcomb. *Medical Dir* Richard Russell MD.
Licensure Skilled care; Intermediate care. *Beds* Swing beds SNF/ICF 120. *Private Pay Patients* 6%. *Certified* Medicaid.
Owner Proprietary corp (Edgar H Overstreet).
Admissions Requirements Minimum age 18; Medical examination; Physician's request.
Staff Physicians 1 (pt); RNs 4 (ft), 1 (pt); LPNs 10 (ft), 2 (pt); Nurses' aides 36 (ft), 4 (pt); Physical therapists 1 (pt); Reality therapists 1 (pt); Recreational therapists 1 (pt); Occupational therapists 1 (pt); Speech therapists 1 (pt); Activities coordinators 1 (ft); Dietitians 1 (pt); Ophthalmologists 1 (pt); Podiatrists 1 (pt).
Facilities Dining room; Activities room; Chapel; Laundry room; Barber/Beauty shop.
Activities Arts & crafts; Cards; Games; Reading groups; Prayer groups; Movies; Dances/Social/Cultural gatherings.

Newton

Conva-Rest of Newton Inc
1009 S Main St, Newton, MS 39345
(601) 683-6601
Admin Marilyn M Rainer.
Medical Dir Dr Austin P Boggan.
Licensure Skilled care; Intermediate care; Alzheimer's care. *Beds* Swing beds SNF/ICF 120. *Certified* Medicaid.
Owner Proprietary corp.

Admissions Requirements Medical examination.
Staff Physicians 1 (ft), 5 (pt); RNs 4 (ft), 1 (pt); LPNs 10 (ft); Nurses' aides 35 (ft), 2 (pt); Physical therapists 1 (pt); Speech therapists 1 (pt); Activities coordinators 1 (ft); Dietitians 1 (ft), 1 (pt); Dentists 1 (pt); Social workers 1 (ft).
Facilities Dining room; Activities room; Crafts room; Laundry room; Barber/Beauty shop; Library; Dayroom; TV room; 2 patios.
Activities Arts & crafts; Cards; Games; Reading groups; Prayer groups; Movies; Shopping trips; Dances/Social/Cultural gatherings; Fishing trips; Coffee hour; Ladies tea; Bus rides.

Ocean Springs

Ocean Springs Nursing Center
1199 Ocean Springs Rd, Ocean Springs, MS 39564
(601) 875-9363
Admin Carol C Smith. *Dir of Nursing* Joy M David RN. *Medical Dir* William Striegel MD.
Licensure Skilled care; Personal care; Alzheimer's care. *Beds* SNF 73; Personal care 2. *Private Pay Patients* 40%. *Certified* Medicaid.
Owner Privately owned.
Admissions Requirements Medical examination; Physician's request.
Staff RNs 2 (ft), 2 (pt); LPNs 8 (ft), 2 (pt); Nurses' aides 26 (ft); Recreational therapists 1 (ft), 1 (pt); Activities coordinators 1 (ft), 1 (pt); Dietitians 1 (ft).
Facilities Dining room; Activities room; Laundry room; Barber/Beauty shop.
Activities Arts & crafts; Cards; Games; Reading groups; Prayer groups; Movies; Shopping trips; Pet therapy.

TLC Home for the Elderly
9009 Travis Ave, Ocean Springs, MS 39564
(601) 875-9525
Admin Marie H McMillan.
Licensure Personal care. *Beds* Personal care 11.

Okolona

Shearer Richardson Memorial Nursing Home
PO Box 419, Okolona, MS 38860
(601) 447-5463
Admin Brenda G Wise. *Dir of Nursing* Judy Boyles RN. *Medical Dir* Dr J H Shoemaker.
Licensure Skilled care; Intermediate care. *Beds* SNF 43; ICF 23. *Private Pay Patients* 17%. *Certified* Medicaid.
Owner Publicly owned.
Staff Physicians 2 (pt); RNs 2 (ft), 2 (pt); LPNs 8 (ft), 2 (pt); Nurses' aides 20 (ft), 2 (pt); Physical therapists 1 (pt); Activities coordinators 1 (ft); Dietitians.
Facilities Dining room; Activities room; Crafts room; Laundry room; Barber/Beauty shop.
Activities Arts & crafts; Cards; Games.

Oxford

Golden Years Retirement Center
606 Van Buren Ave, Oxford, MS 38655
(601) 234-4245
Admin Katie M Overstreet.
Licensure Intermediate care. *Beds* ICF 37. *Certified* Medicaid.
Owner Proprietary corp.

Gracelands Inc
1300 Belk St, Oxford, MS 38655
(601) 234-7821
Admin James D Braswell.
Medical Dir J O Gilmore MD.

Licensure Skilled care; Intermediate care. *Beds* Swing beds SNF/ICF 135. *Certified* Medicaid.
Owner Proprietary corp.
Admissions Requirements Minimum age 21; Medical examination; Physician's request.
Staff Physicians 8 (pt); RNs 3 (ft), 1 (pt); LPNs 15 (ft), 2 (pt); Nurses' aides 60 (ft), 10 (pt); Physical therapists 1 (pt); Activities coordinators 1 (ft), 1 (pt); Dietitians 2 (ft), 1 (pt); Dentists 1 (pt).
Facilities Dining room; Activities room; Chapel; Crafts room; Laundry room; Barber/ Beauty shop.
Activities Arts & crafts; Cards; Games; Movies.

North Mississippi Retardation Center—Wood Lane ICF/MR
PO Box 967, Hwy 7 By-Pass, Oxford, MS 38655
(601) 234-1476
Admin Marilyn McCluskey.
Licensure Intermediate care for mentally retarded. *Beds* ICF/MR 204. *Certified* Medicaid.
Owner Publicly owned.

North Mississippi Retardation Center—Woodlea Skilled Nursing Home
PO Box 967, Hwy 7 By-Pass, Oxford, MS 38655
(601) 234-1476
Admin Marilyn McCluskey.
Licensure Skilled care. *Beds* SNF 61. *Certified* Medicaid.
Owner Publicly owned.

Pascagoula

Jackson County Personal Care Home
21701 County Home Rd, Pascagoula, MS 39567
(601) 588-6227
Admin Norma Coleman.
Licensure Personal care. *Beds* Personal care 20.
Owner Publicly owned.

Plaza Nursing Center
4403 Hospital Rd, Pascagoula, MS 39567
(601) 762-8960
Admin Vic Price.
Licensure Skilled care; Intermediate care. *Beds* SNF 60; ICF 60. *Certified* Medicaid.
Owner Proprietary corp.

Singing River Hospital System—Extended Care Facility
2809 Denny Ave, Pascagoula, MS 39567
(601) 938-5000
Admin Robert L Lingle.
Licensure Skilled care. *Beds* 10. *Certified* Medicare.
Owner Publicly owned.

Pass Christian

Miramar Lodge Nursing Home
216 W Beach Blvd, Pass Christian, MS 39571
(601) 452-2416
Admin Verda J Reed.
Medical Dir C D Taylor Jr.
Licensure Skilled care; Intermediate care. *Beds* SNF 170; ICF 10. *Certified* Medicaid.
Owner Proprietary corp.
Admissions Requirements Medical examination; Physician's request.
Staff Physicians 5 (pt); RNs 3 (ft), 1 (pt); LPNs 18 (ft); Nurses' aides 76 (ft); Physical therapists 2 (pt); Reality therapists 1 (ft); Speech therapists 1 (pt); Activities coordinators 3 (ft); Dietitians 1 (ft); Audiologists 1 (pt).

Dixie White House Nursing Home Inc
PO Box 515, Menge Ave, Pass Christian, MS
 39571
(601) 452-4344
Admin Verna Cook.
Licensure Skilled care. *Beds* SNF 60. *Certified*
 Medicaid.
Owner Proprietary corp.

Petal

Conva-Rest of Petal
201 10th Ave, Petal, MS 39465
(601) 544-7441
Admin Roger Strickland.
Licensure Skilled care. *Beds* SNF 60. *Certified*
 Medicaid.
Owner Proprietary corp.

Philadelphia

Choctaw Residential Center
Rte 7 Box R-51, Philadelphia, MS 39350
(601) 656-2582
Admin Jimmy Wallace.
Licensure Skilled care. *Beds* 120. *Certified*
 Medicaid.

Neshoba County Nursing Home
PO Box 648, Hwy 19 S, Philadelphia, MS
 39350
(601) 656-3554
Admin Tommy L Dearing.
Medical Dir Mary Barrier.
Licensure Skilled care; Intermediate care. *Beds*
 SNF 75; ICF 5. *Certified* Medicaid.
Owner Publicly owned.
Admissions Requirements Medical
 examination; Physician's request.
Staff Physicians 6 (ft); RNs 6 (ft); LPNs 7 (ft),
 1 (pt); Nurses' aides 36 (ft), 2 (pt); Physical
 therapists 1 (ft); Dietitians 1 (ft).
Facilities Dining room; Physical therapy
 room; Activities room; Chapel; Crafts room;
 Laundry room; Barber/Beauty shop.
Activities Arts & crafts; Cards; Games;
 Reading groups; Prayer groups.

Picayune

Picayune Convalescent Center
PO Box 937, Picayune, MS 39466
(601) 798-1811
Admin Mena Andrews.
Licensure Skilled care; Intermediate care. *Beds*
 SNF 60; ICF 60. *Certified* Medicaid.
Owner Proprietary corp (National Heritage).

Pontotoc

Graceland's of Pontotoc
278 8th St, Pontotoc, MS 38863
(601) 489-6411
Admin Jane B Price. *Dir of Nursing* Mimi
 Hughes RN. *Medical Dir* James R Howard
 MD.
Licensure Skilled care; Intermediate care. *Beds*
 Swing beds SNF/ICF 60. *Certified* Medicaid.
Owner Proprietary corp.
Admissions Requirements Medical
 examination; Physician's request.
Staff RNs 1 (ft), 1 (pt); LPNs 7 (ft), 1 (pt);
 Nurses' aides 17 (ft), 3 (pt); Physical
 therapists 1 (pt); Activities coordinators 1
 (ft); Dietitians 1 (ft).
Facilities Dining room; Activities room;
 Laundry room; Barber/Beauty shop; Library.
Activities Arts & crafts; Cards; Games;
 Reading groups; Prayer groups; Movies;
 Shopping trips; Dances/Social/Cultural
 gatherings; Residents council; Cooking
 classes; Exercise classes.

**North Mississippi Medical Center—Pontotoc
Nursing Home**
176 S Main St, Pontotoc, MS 38863
(601) 489-5510
Admin William Currie. *Dir of Nursing*
 Dorothy Walls RN. *Medical Dir* John
 Patterson MD.
Licensure Skilled care; Intermediate care. *Beds*
 Swing beds SNF/ICF 44. *Private Pay
 Patients* 10%. *Certified* Medicaid; Medicare.
Owner Nonprofit corp (North Mississippi
 Health Services Inc).
Admissions Requirements Medical
 examination; Physician's request.
Staff Physicians 6 (ft); RNs 3 (ft); LPNs 6 (ft);
 Nurses' aides 9 (ft); Physical therapists
 (contracted); Activities coordinators 1 (ft);
 Dietitians 1 (ft).
Facilities Dining room; Physical therapy
 room; Activities room; Chapel; Crafts room;
 Laundry room; Barber/Beauty shop.
Activities Arts & crafts; Cards; Games;
 Reading groups; Prayer groups; Dances/
 Social/Cultural gatherings.

Sunshine Rest Home
Rte 6 Box 443, Pontotoc, MS 38863
(601) 489-1189
Admin James Westmoreland.
Licensure Intermediate care. *Beds* ICF 27.
 Certified Medicaid.
Owner Publicly owned.

Poplarville

Pearl River County Nursing Home
PO Box 392, W Moody St, Poplarville, MS
 39470
(601) 795-4543
Admin Dorthy C Bilbo.
Medical Dir Dr W F Stringer.
Licensure Skilled care; Intermediate care. *Beds*
 Swing beds SNF/ICF 60. *Certified* Medicaid.
Owner Publicly owned.
Staff Physicians 4 (ft); RNs 3 (ft); LPNs 6 (ft);
 Nurses' aides 10 (ft), 4 (pt); Physical
 therapists 1 (ft); Recreational therapists 1
 (pt); Speech therapists 1 (pt); Activities
 coordinators 2 (ft); Dietitians 2 (ft).
Facilities Dining room; Physical therapy
 room; Activities room; Chapel; Crafts room;
 Laundry room; Barber/Beauty shop.
Activities Arts & crafts; Games; Prayer groups;
 Movies; Shopping trips; Dances/Social/
 Cultural gatherings.

Prentiss

**Jefferson Davis County—Extended Care
Facility**
PO Box 1289, Berry St, Prentiss, MS 39474
(601) 792-4276
Admin Charles Smith.
Licensure Skilled care; Intermediate care. *Beds*
 Swing beds SNF/ICF 60. *Certified* Medicaid;
 Medicare.
Owner Publicly owned.

Quitman

Archuse Convalescent Center Inc
Hwy 511 E, Quitman, MS 39355
(601) 776-2141
Admin Mary Knight.
Medical Dir Walter Gunn MD.
Licensure Skilled care; Intermediate care. *Beds*
 Swing beds SNF/ICF 120. *Certified*
 Medicaid.
Owner Proprietary corp.
Admissions Requirements Medical
 examination; Physician's request.
Staff Physicians 5 (pt); RNs 3 (ft); LPNs 7
 (ft); Nurses' aides 27 (ft); Physical therapists
 1 (pt); Reality therapists 1 (pt); Recreational
 therapists 1 (pt); Occupational therapists 1

(pt); Speech therapists 1 (pt); Activities
 coordinators 1 (ft); Dietitians 1 (pt); Dentists
 1 (pt).
Facilities Dining room; Physical therapy
 room; Activities room; Crafts room; Laundry
 room; Barber/Beauty shop.
Activities Arts & crafts; Cards; Games;
 Reading groups; Prayer groups; Movies;
 Shopping trips; Dances/Social/Cultural
 gatherings.

Raleigh

Rolling Acres Retirement Center Inc
PO Box 128, Raleigh, MS 39153
(601) 782-4244
Admin Cleta Mullins.
Medical Dir Vance Baucum MD.
Licensure Skilled care; Intermediate care. *Beds*
 Swing beds SNF/ICF 120. *Certified*
 Medicaid.
Admissions Requirements Medical
 examination.
Staff Physicians 4 (pt); RNs 2 (ft); LPNs 10
 (ft); Nurses' aides 29 (ft), 13 (pt); Physical
 therapists 1 (pt); Activities coordinators 1
 (ft); Dietitians 2 (ft), 1 (pt); Podiatrists 1
 (pt); Dentists 2 (pt).
Facilities Dining room; Activities room;
 Crafts room; Laundry room; Barber/Beauty
 shop.
Activities Arts & crafts; Cards; Games;
 Reading groups; Prayer groups; Movies;
 Dances/Social/Cultural gatherings.

Ripley

Rest Haven Nursing Home
103 Cunningham Dr, Ripley, MS 38663
(601) 837-3062
Admin Mildred Murphree. *Dir of Nursing* Jay
 Spires. *Medical Dir* Thomas L Ketchum
 MD.
Licensure Skilled care; Intermediate care. *Beds*
 Swing beds SNF/ICF 60. *Certified* Medicaid.
Owner Proprietary corp.
Staff Physicians 7 (pt); RNs 2 (ft), 1 (pt);
 LPNs 6 (ft); Nurses' aides 11 (ft), 7 (pt);
 Dietitians 1 (pt).
Facilities Dining room; Physical therapy
 room; Activities room; Chapel; Crafts room;
 Laundry room; Barber/Beauty shop.
Activities Arts & crafts; Cards; Games;
 Reading groups; Prayer groups; Movies;
 Dances/Social/Cultural gatherings; Pet
 therapy.

Ripley Manor Nursing Home
PO Box 295, Ripley, MS 38663
(601) 837-3011
Admin Glen Canty.
Licensure Skilled care; Intermediate care. *Beds*
 Swing beds SNF/ICF 120.
Owner Proprietary corp (Beverly Enterprises).

Rolling Fork

Heritage Manor Rolling Fork
PO Box 279, 506 W Race St, Rolling Fork,
 MS 39159-0279
(601) 873-6218
Admin Mena Andrews. *Dir of Nursing*
 Annette Smith. *Medical Dir* Henry Lynch.
Licensure Skilled care; Intermediate care. *Beds*
 Swing beds SNF/ICF 60. *Private Pay
 Patients* 10%. *Certified* Medicaid.
Owner Proprietary corp (National Heritage).
Admissions Requirements Medical
 examination; Physician's request.
Staff Physicians 3 (pt); RNs 3 (ft), 1 (pt);
 LPNs 3 (ft), 6 (pt); Nurses' aides 22 (ft), 6
 (pt); Physical therapists 1 (pt); Occupational
 therapists 1 (pt); Speech therapists 1 (pt);
 Activities coordinators 1 (ft); Dietitians 1
 (pt); Podiatrists 1 (pt).

Facilities Dining room; Activities room; Crafts room; Laundry room; Barber/Beauty shop.
Activities Arts & crafts; Cards; Games; Reading groups; Prayer groups; Movies; Shopping trips; Dances/Social/Cultural gatherings; Intergenerational programs; Pet therapy.

Ruleville

Ruleville Health Center
800 Stansel Dr, Ruleville, MS 38771
(601) 756-4361, 756-2788 FAX
Admin Rosal Burden. *Dir of Nursing* Darlene Gerber. *Medical Dir* Bennie Wright MD.
Licensure Skilled care; Intermediate care. *Beds* SNF 45; ICF 45. *Certified* Medicaid; Medicare.
Owner Proprietary corp (Beverly Enterprises).
Admissions Requirements Minimum age 21; Medical examination; Physician's request.
Staff RNs; LPNs; Nurses' aides; Activities coordinators; Dietitians.
Facilities Dining room; Activities room; Laundry room; Barber/Beauty shop.
Activities Arts & crafts; Cards; Games; Reading groups; Prayer groups; Movies; Shopping trips; Dances/Social/Cultural gatherings; Intergenerational programs.

Sanatorium

Boswell Retardation Center—W L Jaquith ICF/MR
PO Box 128, Sanatorium, MS 39112
(601) 849-3321
Admin Bruce Womack. *Dir of Nursing* Patsy Burris RN. *Medical Dir* Paul D Cotten MD.
Licensure Intermediate care for mentally retarded. *Beds* ICF/MR 84. *Certified* Medicaid.
Owner Publicly owned.
Admissions Requirements Medical examination; Physician's request.
Staff Physicians 4 (pt); RNs 3 (ft); LPNs 8 (ft); Physical therapists 1 (pt); Recreational therapists 1 (ft); Occupational therapists 1 (pt); Speech therapists 1 (pt); Activities coordinators 1 (ft); Dietitians 1 (pt); Ophthalmologists 1 (pt).
Facilities Dining room; Physical therapy room; Activities room; Chapel; Barber/Beauty shop.
Activities Arts & crafts; Cards; Games; Movies; Shopping trips; Dances/Social/Cultural gatherings; Daily living skills; Horticultural therapy; Animal husbandry.

Sardis

North Panola Nursing Center
PO Box 160, Sardis, MS 38666
(601) 487-2720
Admin Robert R Clark NHA. *Dir of Nursing* Jackie Woods RN. *Medical Dir* H M Fairchild MD.
Licensure Skilled care. *Beds* SNF 54. *Private Pay Patients* 35%. *Certified* Medicaid.
Owner Publicly owned.
Admissions Requirements Medical examination; Physician's request.
Staff Physicians 3 (pt); RNs 1 (ft), 1 (pt); LPNs 6 (ft), 2 (pt); Nurses' aides 18 (ft), 6 (pt); Activities coordinators 1 (ft); Dietitians 1 (ft); Social workers 1 (ft).
Facilities Dining room; Physical therapy room; Activities room; Chapel; Crafts room; Laundry room; Barber/Beauty shop; Porch.
Activities Arts & crafts; Cards; Games; Reading groups; Prayer groups; Movies; Shopping trips.

Senatobia

Senatobia Convalescent Home
402 Getwell Dr, Senatobia, MS 38668
(601) 562-5664
Admin Denver Northrip.
Licensure Skilled care; Intermediate care. *Beds* Swing beds SNF/ICF 120. *Certified* Medicaid.
Owner Proprietary corp.

Shelby

Zion Grove Nursing Center
Church St, Shelby, MS 38774
(601) 398-5117
Admin Barbara Lenard. *Dir of Nursing* Louise Hicks RN. *Medical Dir* James Warrington MD.
Licensure Skilled care; Intermediate care. *Beds* Swing beds SNF/ICF 120. *Certified* Medicaid.
Owner Proprietary corp.
Admissions Requirements Medical examination; Physician's request.
Staff Physicians 1 (ft), 5 (pt); RNs 1 (ft), 3 (pt); LPNs 13 (ft); Nurses' aides 29 (ft), 9 (pt); Physical therapists 1 (pt); Speech therapists 1 (pt); Activities coordinators 1 (ft); Dietitians 1 (ft); Ophthalmologists 1 (pt).
Facilities Dining room; Physical therapy room; Activities room; Chapel; Crafts room; Laundry room; Barber/Beauty shop.
Activities Arts & crafts; Cards; Games; Reading groups; Prayer groups; Movies; Shopping trips; Dances/Social/Cultural gatherings.

Southaven

Southaven Health Care Center
1730 Dorchester Dr, Southaven, MS 38671
(601) 393-0050
Admin James Williams.
Licensure Skilled care; Intermediate care. *Beds* SNF 40; ICF 80. *Certified* Medicaid.
Owner Proprietary corp (Beverly Enterprises).

Starkville

Rolling Hills
PO Drawer 1566, 220 Womack St, Starkville, MS 39759
(601) 323-9183
Admin Ann Thompson.
Licensure Intermediate care for mentally retarded. *Beds* ICF/MR 120. *Certified* Medicaid.
Owner Proprietary corp (Unicare).

Starkville Manor Nursing Home
PO Box 1466, 1001 Hospital Rd, Starkville, MS 39759
(601) 323-6360
Admin Mark S Clay.
Medical Dir Vicki B Clay.
Licensure Skilled care; Intermediate care. *Beds* Swing beds SNF/ICF 119. *Certified* Medicaid.
Owner Proprietary corp (National Heritage).

Tupelo

Cedars Health Center
2800 W Main St, Tupelo, MS 38801
(601) 842-8555
Admin Paul Young.
Licensure Skilled care; Intermediate care. *Beds* SNF 60; ICF 60. *Certified* Medicaid.
Owner Nonprofit corp.

Lee Manor Nursing Home
1901 Briar Ridge Rd, Tupelo, MS 38801
(601) 844-0675
Admin Lewis Sewell.

Medical Dir Dr James L Brown.
Licensure Intermediate care. *Beds* ICF 120. *Certified* Medicaid.
Owner Proprietary corp (Beverly Enterprises).
Admissions Requirements Medical examination; Physician's request.
Staff Physicians 12 (pt); RNs 1 (ft); LPNs 8 (ft), 1 (pt); Nurses' aides 23 (ft); Physical therapists 1 (pt); Speech therapists 1 (pt); Activities coordinators 1 (ft), 1 (pt); Dietitians 1 (pt).
Facilities Dining room; Activities room; Chapel; Crafts room; Laundry room; Barber/Beauty shop; Library; Outside patio.
Activities Arts & crafts; Cards; Games; Reading groups; Prayer groups; Movies; Shopping trips; Dances/Social/Cultural gatherings; Cookouts; Picnics.

Tupelo Manor Nursing Home
646 Eason Blvd, Tupelo, MS 38801
(601) 842-2461
Admin Bass Douglas M.
Medical Dir James Brown MD.
Licensure Skilled care. *Beds* 120. *Certified* Medicaid.
Owner Proprietary corp (Beverly Enterprises).
Admissions Requirements Medical examination; Physician's request.
Activities Arts & crafts; Cards; Games; Reading groups; Prayer groups; Movies; Shopping trips.

Tylertown

Billdora
314 Enoch St, Tylertown, MS 39667
(601) 876-2173
Admin John K Gresham. *Dir of Nursing* Beverly Sumnall RN. *Medical Dir* Dr Ben Crawford.
Licensure Skilled care. *Beds* SNF 60. *Private Pay Patients* 10%. *Certified* Medicaid.
Owner Proprietary corp.
Admissions Requirements Medical examination.
Staff RNs 3 (ft); LPNs 8 (ft); Nurses' aides 18 (ft); Activities coordinators 1 (ft); Dietitians 1 (ft).
Facilities Dining room; Activities room; Laundry room.
Activities Arts & crafts; Games; Reading groups; Prayer groups.

Tylertown Extended Care Center
200 Medical Cir, Tylertown, MS 39667
(601) 876-2107
Admin Arline Beard.
Medical Dir Dr Ben Crawford.
Licensure Skilled care. *Beds* SNF 60. *Certified* Medicaid.
Owner Proprietary corp (Beverly Enterprises).
Admissions Requirements Medical examination; Physician's request.
Staff Physicians 8 (ft); RNs 2 (ft), 1 (pt); LPNs 6 (ft); Nurses' aides 22 (ft); Activities coordinators 1 (ft); Dietitians 1 (ft).
Facilities Dining room; Activities room; Laundry room; Barber/Beauty shop; Dayroom.
Activities Arts & crafts; Cards; Games; Reading groups; Prayer groups; Movies; Shopping trips; Dances/Social/Cultural gatherings.

Union

Hilltop Manor Inc
PO Box 266, County Line St, Union, MS 39365
(601) 774-8233
Admin Dewanda S Page. *Dir of Nursing* Glenda Barrett RN. *Medical Dir* A P Boggan MD.
Licensure Skilled care; Intermediate care. *Beds* Swing beds SNF/ICF 60. *Certified* Medicaid.
Owner Proprietary corp (National Heritage).

Staff Physicians 6 (pt); RNs 2 (ft), 2 (pt); LPNs 4 (ft), 4 (pt); Nurses' aides 16 (ft), 3 (pt); Physical therapists 1 (pt); Speech therapists 1 (pt); Activities coordinators 1 (ft), 1 (pt); Dietitians 1 (pt).
Facilities Dining room; Activities room; Laundry room; Barber/Beauty shop.
Activities Arts & crafts; Cards; Games; Reading groups; Prayer groups; Movies; Shopping trips; Dances/Social/Cultural gatherings.

Vicksburg

Mercy Extended Care Facility
100 McAuley Dr, Vicksburg, MS 39180
(601) 631-2131, 631-2124 FAX
Admin Carl E Barry. *Dir of Nursing* Jane Skinner. *Medical Dir* Joe M Ross Jr MD.
Licensure Skilled care. *Beds* SNF 31. *Private Pay Patients* 16%. *Certified* Medicare.
Owner Nonprofit organization/foundation.
Admissions Requirements Medical examination; Physician's request.
Staff Physicians 1 (pt); RNs 2 (ft), 1 (pt); LPNs; Nurses' aides; Physical therapists; Speech therapists; Activities coordinators; Dietitians.
Affiliation Roman Catholic.
Facilities Dining room; Activities room; Chapel; Crafts room; Barber/Beauty shop.
Activities Arts & crafts; Cards; Games; Reading groups; Prayer groups; Movies; Dances/Social/Cultural gatherings; Intergenerational programs; Pet therapy.

Shady Lawn Nursing Home Inc
23 Porter's Chapel Rd, Vicksburg, MS 39180
(601) 636-1448
Admin Jean Corbin.
Medical Dir Joe M Ross Jr MD.
Licensure Skilled care; Intermediate care. *Beds* Swing beds SNF/ICF 81. *Certified* Medicaid.
Owner Proprietary corp.
Admissions Requirements Medical examination.
Staff Physicians 1 (pt); RNs 2 (ft), 1 (pt); LPNs 8 (ft), 2 (pt); Nurses' aides 28 (ft), 2 (pt); Activities coordinators 1 (ft); Dietitians 1 (ft).
Facilities Dining room; Activities room; Chapel; Crafts room; Laundry room; Barber/ Beauty shop.
Activities Arts & crafts; Cards; Games; Reading groups; Prayer groups; Movies; Shopping trips; Dances/Social/Cultural gatherings.

Sydney House
900 Crawford St, Vicksburg, MS 39180
(601) 638-1514
Admin Mary Dell Greer. *Dir of Nursing* Mable L Cox RN. *Medical Dir* Lamar McMillin MD.
Licensure Intermediate care; Retirement; Alzheimer's care. *Beds* ICF 55. *Private Pay Patients* 100%.
Owner Privately owned (Integrated Health Services Inc).
Admissions Requirements Medical examination; Physician's request.
Staff RNs 1 (ft); LPNs 7 (ft), 1 (pt); Nurses' aides 23 (ft), 3 (pt); Activities coordinators 1 (ft); Dietitians 1 (pt).
Facilities Dining room; Activities room; Laundry room; Barber/Beauty shop.
Activities Arts & crafts; Cards; Games; Reading groups; Prayer groups; Movies; Shopping trips; Dances/Social/Cultural gatherings; Intergenerational programs; Pet therapy; Fishing trips.

Vicksburg Convalescent Home
1708 Cherry St, Vicksburg, MS 39180
(601) 638-3632
Admin Lola Snyder.
Medical Dir M E Hinman.

Licensure Skilled care; Intermediate care. *Beds* Swing beds SNF/ICF 100. *Certified* Medicaid.
Owner Proprietary corp.
Admissions Requirements Medical examination.
Staff RNs 2 (ft), 2 (pt); LPNs 11 (ft), 2 (pt); Nurses' aides 32 (ft), 5 (pt); Activities coordinators 1 (ft); Dietitians 1 (pt).
Facilities Dining room; Laundry room; Patio.
Activities Arts & crafts; Games; Prayer groups; Movies; Dances/Social/Cultural gatherings.

Vicksburg Trace Haven
40 Porter's Chapel Rd, Vicksburg, MS 39180
(601) 638-9211
Admin Eva Williams.
Licensure Skilled care; Intermediate care. *Beds* Swing beds SNF/ICF 120. *Certified* Medicaid.
Owner Proprietary corp (National Heritage).

Water Valley

Yalobusha County Nursing Home
PO Box 728, Hwy 7 S, Water Valley, MS 38965
(601) 473-1411
Admin Ted Whitley. *Dir of Nursing* Sue Logan RN. *Medical Dir* Dr Paul Odom.
Licensure Skilled care. *Beds* SNF 59. *Private Pay Patients* 34%. *Certified* Medicaid.
Owner Nonprofit organization/foundation.
Admissions Requirements Medical examination.
Staff Physicians 3 (ft); RNs 2 (ft), 3 (pt); LPNs 10 (ft), 7 (pt); Nurses' aides 29 (ft), 14 (pt); Reality therapists 1 (ft); Activities coordinators 1 (ft); Dietitians 1 (ft).
Facilities Dining room; Physical therapy room; Activities room; Chapel; Laundry room; Barber/Beauty shop; Library.
Activities Arts & crafts; Cards; Games; Prayer groups; Movies; Dances/Social/Cultural gatherings; Intergenerational programs; Pet therapy.

Waynesboro

Restful Acres Inc
1304 Walnut St, Waynesboro, MS 39267
(601) 735-9025
Admin Karen S Williams.
Licensure Skilled care; Intermediate care. *Beds* Swing beds SNF/ICF 60. *Certified* Medicaid.
Owner Proprietary corp.

West Point

Dugan Memorial Home
840 E Main St, West Point, MS 39773
(601) 494-3640
Admin Royce Fulgham. *Dir of Nursing* Barbara Simons. *Medical Dir* Dr T M Braddock.
Licensure Skilled care. *Beds* SNF 60.
Owner Proprietary corp.
Admissions Requirements Medical examination; Physician's request.
Staff Physicians 1 (ft); RNs 4 (ft), 2 (pt); LPNs 4 (ft), 3 (pt); Nurses' aides 26 (ft), 4 (pt); Activities coordinators 1 (ft).
Facilities Dining room; Activities room; Chapel; Laundry room; Barber/Beauty shop.
Activities Cards; Games; Reading groups; Prayer groups; Shopping trips; Dances/ Social/Cultural gatherings; Therapy (exercise & validation); Newsletter; Sight-seeing.

Hillhaven Convalescent Center—West Point
PO Box 817, West Point, MS 39773
(601) 494-6011
Admin Allen R Curtis.
Medical Dir William Billington DO.
Licensure Skilled care; Intermediate care. *Beds* Swing beds SNF/ICF 120. *Certified* Medicaid.

Owner Proprietary corp.
Admissions Requirements Minimum age 17; Medical examination; Physician's request.
Staff Physicians 1 (pt); RNs 5 (ft); LPNs 9 (ft), 4 (pt); Nurses' aides 40 (ft), 4 (pt); Physical therapists 1 (pt); Activities coordinators 1 (ft); Dietitians 1 (pt); Ophthalmologists 1 (pt); Podiatrists 1 (pt); Dentists 1 (pt).
Facilities Dining room; Activities room; Crafts room; Laundry room; Barber/Beauty shop.
Activities Arts & crafts; Cards; Games; Reading groups; Prayer groups; Movies; Shopping trips; Dances/Social/Cultural gatherings.

Whitfield

Hudspeth Center—Azalea Intermediate Care Facility
PO Box 127-B, Whitfield, MS 39193
(601) 939-8640
Admin Edwin C LeGrand III. *Dir of Nursing* Ladell Hamilton RN. *Medical Dir* Margaret Batson MD.
Licensure Intermediate care. *Beds* ICF 30. *Private Pay Patients* 0%. *Certified* Medicaid.
Owner Publicly owned.
Admissions Requirements Minimum age 5; Medical examination.
Staff Physicians 2 (ft), 1 (pt); RNs 1 (ft), 1 (pt); LPNs 3 (ft); Physical therapists 2 (pt); Recreational therapists 2 (ft); Occupational therapists 1 (pt); Speech therapists 1 (pt); Dietitians 1 (ft), 1 (pt); Ophthalmologists 1 (pt); Podiatrists 1 (pt).
Facilities Dining room; Physical therapy room; Activities room; Crafts room; Laundry room; Barber/Beauty shop; Library.
Activities Arts & crafts; Games; Movies; Shopping trips; Dances/Social/Cultural gatherings; Therapeutic self-help training.

Hudspeth Center—Rosewood Skilled Nursing
PO Box 127-B, Whitfield, MS 39193
(601) 939-8640
Admin Edwin C LeGrand III. *Dir of Nursing* Ladell Hamilton RN. *Medical Dir* Margaret Batson MD.
Licensure Skilled care. *Beds* SNF 55. *Private Pay Patients* 0%. *Certified* Medicaid.
Owner Publicly owned.
Admissions Requirements Minimum age 5; Medical examination.
Staff Physicians 2 (ft), 1 (pt); RNs 2 (ft), 1 (pt); LPNs 7 (ft), 1 (pt); Physical therapists 2 (pt); Recreational therapists 2 (ft); Occupational therapists 1 (pt); Speech therapists 1 (pt); Dietitians 1 (ft), 1 (pt); Ophthalmologists 1 (pt); Podiatrists 1 (pt).
Facilities Dining room; Physical therapy room; Activities room; Crafts room; Laundry room; Barber/Beauty shop; Library.
Activities Arts & crafts; Games; Movies; Shopping trips; Dances/Social/Cultural gatherings; Therapeutic self-help training activities.

Jaquith Nursing Home—Adams Inn
PO Box 7, Whitfield, MS 39193
(601) 939-1221, ext 364
Admin Robert E Brister. *Dir of Nursing* Sarah Pittman RN. *Medical Dir* Charles Sledge MD.
Licensure Intermediate care. *Beds* ICF 243. *Certified* Medicaid.
Owner Publicly owned.

Jaquith Nursing Home—Washington Inn
PO Box 7, Whitfield, MS 39193
(601) 939-1221, ext 364
Admin Robert E Brister. *Dir of Nursing* Sarah Pittman RN. *Medical Dir* Charles Sledge MD.
Licensure Skilled care. *Beds* SNF 134. *Certified* Medicaid.
Owner Publicly owned.

Wiggins

Azalea Gardens Nursing Center
530 Hall St, Wiggins, MS 39577
(601) 928-5281
Admin Jeanette Walker. *Dir of Nursing*
  Angela Woods RN. *Medical Dir* Dr Ger
  McHenry.
Licensure Skilled care; Intermediate care;
  Alzheimer's care. *Beds* SNF 97; ICF 40.
  Certified Medicaid.
Owner Privately owned.
Admissions Requirements Medical
  examination.
Staff Physical therapists 1 (pt); Occupational
  therapists 1 (pt); Speech therapists 1 (pt);
  Dietitians 1 (pt).
Facilities Dining room; Activities room;
  Crafts room; Laundry room; Barber/Beauty
  shop.
Activities Arts & crafts; Cards; Games;
  Reading groups; Prayer groups; Movies;
  Shopping trips; Dances/Social/Cultural
  gatherings; Pet therapy.

Winona

Winona Manor Nursing Home
PO Box 311, Hwy 82 W, Winona, MS 38967
(601) 283-1260
Admin Marvell Morgan.
Licensure Skilled care; Intermediate care. *Beds*
  Swing beds SNF/ICF 120. *Certified*
  Medicaid.
Owner Proprietary corp (National Heritage).

Yazoo City

Martha Coker Convalescent Home
401 E 9th St, Yazoo City, MS 39194
(601) 746-4621
Admin Anita S Boyd.
Medical Dir Dr Charles R Hogue.
Licensure Skilled care. *Beds* SNF 41.
Owner Nonprofit corp.
Admissions Requirements Medical
  examination.
Staff Physicians 6 (ft); RNs 1 (ft), 1 (pt);
  LPNs 3 (ft), 2 (pt); Nurses' aides 9 (ft), 3
  (pt); Physical therapists 1 (pt); Reality
  therapists 1 (pt); Recreational therapists 1
  (pt); Activities coordinators 1 (pt); Dietitians
  1 (ft), 1 (pt); Dentists 1 (pt).
Facilities Dining room; Physical therapy
  room; Activities room; Chapel; Crafts room;
  Laundry room; Barber/Beauty shop.
Activities Arts & crafts; Cards; Games;
  Reading groups; Prayer groups; Movies;
  Shopping trips; Dances/Social/Cultural
  gatherings.

Heritage Manor of Yazoo City
925 Calhoun Ave, Yazoo City, MS 39194
(601) 746-6651
Admin Bob Knott.
Licensure Skilled care; Intermediate care. *Beds*
  SNF 60; ICF 120. *Certified* Medicaid.
Owner Proprietary corp (National Heritage).

MISSOURI

Adrian

Adrian Manor Inc
PO Box 425, Adrian, MO 64720
(816) 297-2107
Admin Clarence B Price. *Dir of Nursing* Mary Harmon RN.
Licensure Skilled care. *Beds* SNF 60. *Private Pay Patients* 50%. *Certified* Medicaid.
Owner Nonprofit corp.
Admissions Requirements Medical examination.
Staff RNs 3 (ft); LPNs 5 (ft), 1 (pt); Nurses' aides 22 (ft), 5 (pt); Physical therapists 1 (pt); Occupational therapists 1 (pt); Speech therapists 1 (pt); Activities coordinators 1 (ft); Dietitians 1 (pt); Audiologists 1 (pt).
Facilities Dining room; Physical therapy room; Activities room; Chapel; Crafts room; Laundry room; Barber/Beauty shop.
Activities Arts & crafts; Cards; Games; Reading groups; Prayer groups; Movies; Intergenerational programs; Pet therapy.

Advance

Advance Nursing & Residential Care Center
PO Box 1339, Corner of Masters & Tiley, Advance, MO 63730
(314) 722-3440
Admin Glenda Cato.
Licensure Skilled care; Intermediate care. *Beds* Swing beds SNF/ICF 60. *Certified* Medicaid.
Owner Proprietary corp.

Albany

Colonial Manor of Albany
Hwy E 136, Box 244, Albany, MO 64402
(816) 726-5297
Admin Kathy Tompkins.
Licensure Intermediate care. *Beds* ICF 60. *Certified* Medicaid.
Owner Proprietary corp (Beverly Enterprises).

Anderson

McDonald County Nursing Center
PO Box 437, Anderson, MO 64831
(417) 845-3351
Admin Jeffrey A Ulin.
Licensure Skilled care; Intermediate care. *Beds* Swing beds SNF/ICF 100. *Certified* Medicaid.
Owner Proprietary corp (Beverly Enterprises).

Appleton City

Colonial Manor Nursing Home
600 N Ohio, Box 98, Appleton City, MO 64724
(816) 476-2128
Admin Howard P Ball.
Medical Dir Glen H Reed MD.
Licensure Intermediate care. *Beds* ICF 60. *Certified* Medicaid.

Owner Proprietary corp.
Staff LPNs 3 (ft); Nurses' aides 30 (ft); Activities coordinators 1 (ft).
Facilities Dining room; Physical therapy room; Activities room; Crafts room; Laundry room; Barber/Beauty shop.
Activities Arts & crafts; Games; Prayer groups; Movies; Shopping trips; Dances/Social/ Cultural gatherings; Bingo; Dominos; Bowling.

Arnold

Hillview Lodge Inc
1101 W Outer 21 Rd, Arnold, MO 63010
(314) 296-5141
Admin Frances Stiebel Weber. *Dir of Nursing* Martha Jones RN. *Medical Dir* Robert LaHue DO.
Licensure Intermediate care. *Beds* ICF 153. *Private Pay Patients* 35%. *Certified* Medicaid.
Owner Proprietary corp (Canadian International Health Service).
Admissions Requirements Minimum age 18; Medical examination; Physician's request.
Staff Physicians 2 (ft); RNs 1 (ft), 1 (pt); LPNs 1 (ft); Nurses' aides 50 (ft), 2 (pt); Physical therapists (contracted); Occupational therapists 1 (pt); Speech therapists 1 (pt); Activities coordinators 1 (ft); Dietitians (consultant); Ophthalmologists 1 (pt); Podiatrists 1 (pt).
Languages Italian.
Facilities Dining room; Physical therapy room; Activities room; Crafts room; Laundry room; Barber/Beauty shop.
Activities Arts & crafts; Cards; Games; Reading groups; Prayer groups; Movies; Dances/Social/Cultural gatherings; Pet therapy.

Woodland Manor Nursing Care
100 Woodland Ct, Arnold, MO 63010
(314) 296-1400
Admin John Foster.
Licensure Skilled care. *Beds* SNF 120. *Certified* Medicaid.
Owner Privately owned.

Ash Grove

Ash Grove Nursing Home Inc
400 Meadowview, Box 247, Ash Grove, MO 65604
(417) 672-2575
Admin Jimmy L Frieze. *Dir of Nursing* Wilma Gray RN.
Licensure Intermediate care. *Beds* ICF 60. *Certified* Medicaid.
Owner Proprietary corp.
Admissions Requirements Minimum age 18.
Staff RNs 1 (ft); LPNs 3 (ft), 4 (pt); Nurses' aides 16 (ft), 4 (pt); Activities coordinators 1 (ft).

Facilities Dining room; Physical therapy room; Activities room; Barber/Beauty shop.
Activities Arts & crafts; Games; Prayer groups; Movies.

Aurora

Aurora Nursing Center
1700 S Hudson, Aurora, MO 65605
(417) 678-2165, 678-2778 FAX
Admin Edward James Hitt. *Dir of Nursing* Melisa Teague RN. *Medical Dir* William P Hamilton MD.
Licensure Skilled care; Intermediate care; Retirement. *Beds* Swing beds SNF/ICF 127; Retirement 6. *Private Pay Patients* 15%. *Certified* Medicaid; Medicare.
Owner Proprietary corp (Aurora Enterprises Inc).
Admissions Requirements Minimum age 18; Physician's request.
Staff Physicians; RNs 4 (ft), 1 (pt); LPNs 7 (ft), 1 (pt); Nurses' aides 28 (ft); Physical therapists 2 (ft), 1 (pt); Recreational therapists 3 (ft); Occupational therapists 1 (pt); Speech therapists 1 (pt); Activities coordinators 1 (ft); Dietitians 1 (ft), 1 (pt).
Facilities Dining room; Physical therapy room; Activities room; Chapel; Laundry room; Barber/Beauty shop; Library.
Activities Arts & crafts; Cards; Games; Reading groups; Prayer groups; Movies; Shopping trips; Dances/Social/Cultural gatherings; Intergenerational programs; Pet therapy; Picnics; Fishing trips.

Ava

Crestview Healthcare
2001 S Jefferson St, Ava, MO 65608
(417) 683-4129
Admin Nancy J Kissee. *Dir of Nursing* Kristi McIntosh RN. *Medical Dir* M S Chern MD.
Licensure Skilled care. *Beds* SNF 120. *Certified* Medicaid; Medicare.
Owner Proprietary corp (Hillhaven Corp).
Staff Physicians 2 (pt); RNs; LPNs; Nurses' aides; Physical therapists 1 (pt); Speech therapists 1 (pt); Activities coordinators; Dietitians 1 (pt).
Facilities Dining room; Physical therapy room; Activities room; Chapel; Crafts room; Laundry room; Barber/Beauty shop; Library.
Activities Arts & crafts; Cards; Games; Reading groups; Prayer groups; Movies; Shopping trips.

Ballwin

Clayton House Health Care & Terrace
13995 E Clayton Rd, Ballwin, MO 63011
(314) 227-5070
Admin Robert Coleman. *Dir of Nursing* Robin Storey RN. *Medical Dir* James Sertl MD.

Licensure Skilled care; Intermediate care; Residential care; Alzheimer's care. *Beds* SNF 192; ICF 48; Residential care 42. *Certified* Medicaid; Medicare.
Owner Proprietary corp (Hillhaven Corp).
Admissions Requirements Medical examination.
Staff Physicians; RNs; LPNs; Nurses' aides; Physical therapists; Reality therapists; Recreational therapists; Occupational therapists; Speech therapists; Activities coordinators; Dietitians; Ophthalmologists.
Languages Spanish.
Facilities Dining room; Physical therapy room; Activities room; Chapel; Crafts room; Laundry room; Barber/Beauty shop; Library; Cocktail lounge; Private dining room; Atrium; Rotunda; Big-screen TV room.
Activities Arts & crafts; Cards; Games; Reading groups; Prayer groups; Movies; Shopping trips; Dances/Social/Cultural gatherings; Animal visits.

Clayton-on-the-Green Nursing Center
15197 Clayton Rd, Ballwin, MO 63011
(314) 394-7515
Admin Ethel Warshofsky.
Medical Dir Dr Virgil Fish.
Licensure Skilled care; Alzheimer's care. *Beds* SNF 180. *Certified* Medicaid; Medicare.
Owner Proprietary corp.
Admissions Requirements Minimum age 21; Medical examination; Physician's request.
Staff Physicians; RNs 5 (ft), 10 (pt); LPNs 3 (ft), 5 (pt); Nurses' aides 50 (ft); Physical therapists 1 (ft); Recreational therapists 2 (ft); Occupational therapists 1 (pt); Speech therapists 1 (pt); Activities coordinators 1 (ft); Dietitians 1 (pt); Ophthalmologists 1 (pt).
Facilities Dining room; Physical therapy room; Activities room; Chapel; Crafts room; Laundry room; Barber/Beauty shop.
Activities Arts & crafts; Cards; Games; Reading groups; Prayer groups; Movies; Shopping trips; Dances/Social/Cultural gatherings.

West County Care Center
PO Box 1407, 312 Solley Dr, Ballwin, MO 63011
(314) 227-1853
Admin Linda Starnes.
Medical Dir Donald C Walkenhorst DO.
Licensure Skilled care. *Beds* SNF 124. *Certified* Medicaid.
Owner Proprietary corp.
Admissions Requirements Minimum age 21.
Staff Physicians 1 (pt); RNs 4 (ft); LPNs 3 (ft), 2 (pt).
Facilities Dining room; Physical therapy room; Activities room; Crafts room; Laundry room; Barber/Beauty shop.
Activities Arts & crafts; Cards; Games; Reading groups; Prayer groups; Movies; Dances/Social/Cultural gatherings.

Bell City

Shetley Nursing Home
PO Box 123, N Walnut St, Bell City, MO 63735
(314) 733-4426
Admin Joyce Gilles.
Licensure Intermediate care. *Beds* 29.
Owner Proprietary corp.

Belleview

Belleview Valley Nursing Home Inc
HC Rte 63 Box 34, Belleview, MO 63623
(314) 697-5311
Admin Wilma Davis. *Dir of Nursing* Harriett Cramer.
Licensure Skilled care. *Beds* SNF 122. *Certified* Medicaid.
Owner Proprietary corp.

Admissions Requirements Medical examination.
Staff Physicians 3 (pt); RNs 1 (ft), 1 (pt); LPNs 5 (ft), 1 (pt); Nurses' aides 40 (ft), 15 (pt); Physical therapists 1 (pt); Reality therapists 1 (ft); Recreational therapists 1 (ft); Occupational therapists 1 (pt); Speech therapists 1 (pt); Activities coordinators 1 (ft); Dietitians 1 (pt).
Facilities Dining room; Physical therapy room; Activities room; Chapel; Crafts room; Laundry room; Barber/Beauty shop.
Activities Arts & crafts; Cards; Games; Reading groups; Prayer groups; Movies; Shopping trips; Dances/Social/Cultural gatherings.

Belton

Beautiful Savior Home
1003 S Cedar St, Belton, MO 64012
(816) 331-0781
Admin Mary Anderson. *Dir of Nursing* Georgia Spearman LPN. *Medical Dir* Ronald La Hue.
Licensure Intermediate care; Residential care; Retirement. *Beds* ICF 82; Residential care 40; Retirement units 47. *Certified* Medicaid.
Owner Nonprofit corp (Beautiful Savior Home Corp).
Admissions Requirements Medical examination.
Staff Physicians 4 (pt); RNs 1 (ft), 1 (pt); LPNs 7 (ft), 1 (pt); Nurses' aides 45 (ft), 2 (pt); Physical therapists 3 (pt); Reality therapists 1 (pt); Recreational therapists 1 (ft); Occupational therapists 1 (pt); Speech therapists 1 (pt); Activities coordinators 2 (ft); Dietitians 1 (ft), 1 (pt); Ophthalmologists 1 (pt); Podiatrists 1 (pt); Audiologists 1 (pt).
Languages Spanish, German, Italian.
Affiliation Lutheran.
Facilities Dining room; Physical therapy room; Activities room; Chapel; Crafts room; Laundry room; Barber/Beauty shop; Visiting lounges.
Activities Arts & crafts; Cards; Games; Reading groups; Prayer groups; Movies; Shopping trips; Dances/Social/Cultural gatherings; Intergenerational programs; Pet therapy.

Berkeley

Wood-Acre Inc
9732 Natural Bridge Rd, Berkeley, MO 63134
(314) 428-4725
Admin Michael Woodard.
Licensure Intermediate care. *Beds* ICF 24.
Owner Proprietary corp.

Bertrand

Bertrand Retirement Home Inc
603 W Hwy 62, Bertrand, MO 63823
(314) 471-6161
Admin Charlotte York.
Licensure Intermediate care. *Beds* ICF 40. *Certified* Medicaid.
Owner Proprietary corp.

Bethany

Bethany Care Center
PO Box 273, Bethany, MO 64424
(816) 425-2273
Admin T Waltemath-Teel.
Licensure Skilled care. *Beds* SNF 60. *Certified* Medicaid.
Owner Proprietary corp.

Crestview Home Inc
PO Box 430, Hwy 69 S, Bethany, MO 64424
(816) 425-3128

Admin Betty L Barratt. *Dir of Nursing* Carla Greene RN. *Medical Dir* G F Scamahorn DO.
Licensure Skilled care; Intermediate care. *Beds* Swing beds SNF/ICF 120. *Private Pay Patients* 58%. *Certified* Medicaid.
Owner Nonprofit corp.
Admissions Requirements Minimum age 16; Medical examination; Physician's request.
Staff RNs 3 (ft), 1 (pt); LPNs 10 (ft), 2 (pt); Nurses' aides 45 (ft), 2 (pt); Activities coordinators 1 (ft); Dietitians 10 (ft), 3 (pt).
Facilities Dining room; Physical therapy room; Activities room; Chapel; Crafts room; Laundry room; Barber/Beauty shop.
Activities Arts & crafts; Cards; Games; Reading groups; Prayer groups; Movies; Dances/Social/Cultural gatherings.

Birch Tree

Birch View Nursing Center
PO Box 180, Hwy 60 W, Birch Tree, MO 65438
(314) 292-3212
Admin Sharon L Bockman. *Dir of Nursing* Sarah Skinner RN. *Medical Dir* Jon W Roberts DO.
Licensure Skilled care. *Beds* SNF 90. *Certified* Medicaid; Medicare.
Owner Proprietary corp (Americare Corp).
Admissions Requirements Minimum age 18; Medical examination.
Staff Physicians 4 (pt); RNs 2 (ft); LPNs 9 (ft); Nurses' aides 35 (ft); Physical therapists 1 (pt); Occupational therapists 1 (pt); Speech therapists 1 (pt); Activities coordinators 1 (ft); Dietitians 1 (pt); Dentists 1 (pt).
Facilities Dining room; Activities room; Chapel; Crafts room; Laundry room; Barber/ Beauty shop.
Activities Arts & crafts; Cards; Games; Reading groups; Prayer groups; Movies; Shopping trips; Dances/Social/Cultural gatherings.

Bismarck

Colonial Retirement Center Inc
PO Box 727, 1162 Cedar St, Bismarck, MO 63624
(314) 734-2846
Admin Ronald L Conway. *Dir of Nursing* Carol Fear.
Licensure Intermediate care. *Beds* ICF 23. *Private Pay Patients* 30%.
Owner Proprietary corp.
Staff Physicians 1 (pt); RNs 1 (pt); LPNs 2 (ft); Nurses' aides 6 (ft), 3 (pt); Activities coordinators 1 (pt).
Facilities Dining room; Activities room; Laundry room.
Activities Arts & crafts; Cards; Games; Shopping trips; Pet therapy.

Black Jack

Garden Pointe Care Center Inc
11400 Mehl Ave, Black Jack, MO 63303
(314) 741-1166, 741-3721 FAX
Admin Barbara M Wagner. *Dir of Nursing* Margie Dodge RN. *Medical Dir* Edward Puro MD.
Licensure Skilled care; Intermediate care. *Beds* Swing beds SNF/ICF 150. *Private Pay Patients* 10%. *Certified* Medicaid.
Owner Proprietary corp.
Staff RNs 6 (ft), 4 (pt); LPNs 5 (ft), 5 (pt); Nurses' aides 32 (ft), 14 (pt); Physical therapists; Dietitians 1 (ft).

Bloomfield

Bloomfield Nursing Center
502 W Missouri, Bloomfield, MO 63825
(314) 568-2137

Admin Jacqueline McCollom. *Dir of Nursing* Diane Barnes RN. *Medical Dir* T W Henderson MD.
Licensure Skilled care. *Beds* SNF 60. *Private Pay Patients* 7%. *Certified* Medicaid.
Owner Proprietary corp (Beverly Enterprises).
Admissions Requirements Minimum age 18; Medical examination; Physician's request.
Staff RNs 1 (ft), 2 (pt); LPNs 3 (ft), 3 (pt); Nurses' aides 16 (ft), 16 (pt); Physical therapists 1 (ft); Recreational therapists (contracted); Occupational therapists (contracted); Speech therapists (contracted); Activities coordinators 1 (ft); Dietitians 1 (ft); Ophthalmologists (contracted); Podiatrists (contracted); Audiologists (contracted); Social services (consultant).
Languages By arrangement.
Facilities Dining room; Physical therapy room; Activities room; Crafts room; Laundry room; Barber/Beauty shop; Solarium; Enclosed patio; Meeting room/Chapel.
Activities Arts & crafts; Cards; Games; Reading groups; Prayer groups; Movies; Shopping trips; Dances/Social/Cultural gatherings; Intergenerational programs; Pet therapy; Daily exercise groups; Volunteer program.

Blue Springs

Blue Springs Care Center
930 E Duncan Rd, Blue Springs, MO 64015
(816) 229-6677
Admin Roberta Renicker.
Licensure Intermediate care. *Beds* ICF 120. *Certified* Medicaid.
Owner Proprietary corp.

Paseo Residential II
3433 Paseo, Blue Springs, MO 64109
(816) 921-3378
Admin Micaela Wilson. *Dir of Nursing* Elizabeth Channel. *Medical Dir* Scott MD.
Licensure Residential care. *Beds* Residential care 28. *Certified* Medicaid.
Owner Privately owned.
Admissions Requirements Minimum age 50; Medical examination.
Staff RNs 1 (pt); LPNs 1 (ft); Nurses' aides 4 (ft); Activities coordinators 1 (ft); Dietitians 1 (pt).
Facilities Dining room; Activities room; Laundry room.
Activities Arts & crafts; Cards; Games; Reading groups; Prayer groups; Movies; Shopping trips; Dances/Social/Cultural gatherings; Pet therapy.

St Mary's Manor
111 Mock Ave, Blue Springs, MO 64015
(816) 229-6817
Admin Michael S Levitt.
Licensure Skilled care; Intermediate care; Residential care. *Beds* Swing beds SNF/ICF 130; Residential care 57. *Certified* Medicaid; Medicare.
Owner Proprietary corp.

Bolivar

Citizens Memorial Healthcare Facility
1218 W Locust, Bolivar, MO 65613
(417) 326-7648
Admin Dennis W Owens. *Dir of Nursing* Margaret Martin RN. *Medical Dir* Dr Kieth Wright.
Licensure Skilled care; Retirement. *Beds* SNF 108; Retirement 6. *Certified* Medicaid.
Owner Nonprofit organization/foundation (Citizens Memorial Healthcare Foundation).
Admissions Requirements Minimum age 17; Medical examination; Physician's request.
Staff Physicians 1 (pt); RNs 2 (ft), 1 (pt); LPNs 8 (ft); Nurses' aides 50 (ft); Physical therapists 1 (ft); Reality therapists 1 (ft); Recreational therapists 1 (ft); Occupational

therapists 1 (pt); Speech therapists 1 (pt); Activities coordinators 1 (ft); Dietitians 1 (pt); Ophthalmologists 1 (pt); Podiatrists 1 (pt); Audiologists 1 (pt).
Facilities Dining room; Physical therapy room; Activities room; Crafts room; Laundry room; Barber/Beauty shop; Library.
Activities Arts & crafts; Games; Reading groups; Prayer groups; Movies; Shopping trips; Dances/Social/Cultural gatherings; Intergenerational programs; Pet therapy.

Bonne Terre

Bonne Terre Rest Home Inc
518 Grove, Bonne Terre, MO 63628
(314) 358-3400
Admin Thomas W McDowell.
Licensure Intermediate care. *Beds* ICF 27.
Owner Proprietary corp.

Boonville

Ashley Manor Care Center
Radio Hill Rd, Boonville, MO 65233
(816) 882-6584
Admin Mary Lou Hughes. *Dir of Nursing* Pam Morton LPN. *Medical Dir* Dennis Handley MD.
Licensure Intermediate care. *Beds* ICF 52. *Certified* Medicaid.
Owner Proprietary corp.
Admissions Requirements Minimum age Adult.
Staff Physicians 4 (ft); RNs 1 (pt); LPNs 5 (ft); Nurses' aides 20 (ft); Physical therapists 1 (pt); Occupational therapists 1 (pt); Speech therapists 1 (pt); Activities coordinators 1 (ft); Dietitians 1 (pt).
Facilities Dining room; Activities room; Laundry room; Barber/Beauty shop.
Activities Arts & crafts; Cards; Games; Reading groups; Prayer groups; Movies; Shopping trips; Dances/Social/Cultural gatherings.

Colonial Gardens Health Care Center
Hwy 5 W, Boonville, MO 65233
(816) 882-7007
Admin Ardell Myers. *Dir of Nursing* Janice DGraffenreid RN.
Licensure Skilled care; Intermediate care; Residential care. *Beds* SNF 60; ICF 19; Residential care 17. *Certified* Medicaid.
Owner Nonprofit organization/foundation.
Admissions Requirements Medical examination.
Staff Physicians 8 (pt); RNs 1 (ft), 1 (pt); LPNs 5 (ft), 1 (pt); Nurses' aides 20 (ft), 7 (pt); Physical therapists 1 (pt); Occupational therapists 1 (pt); Speech therapists 1 (pt); Activities coordinators 1 (ft); Dietitians 1 (pt); Ophthalmologists 1 (pt); Podiatrists 1 (pt); Dentists 1 (pt).
Facilities Dining room; Physical therapy room; Activities room; Chapel; Crafts room; Laundry room; Barber/Beauty shop.
Activities Arts & crafts; Cards; Games; Reading groups; Prayer groups; Movies; Dances/Social/Cultural gatherings.

Riverdell Health Care
1121 11th St, Boonville, MO 65233
(816) 882-7600
Admin Gary Nichols. *Dir of Nursing* Laurie Beach RN. *Medical Dir* T J Young DO.
Licensure Skilled care. *Beds* SNF 60. *Private Pay Patients* 10%. *Certified* Medicaid; Medicare.
Owner Privately owned.
Staff Physicians; RNs; LPNs; Nurses' aides; Activities coordinators; Dietitians; Podiatrists.
Facilities Dining room; Physical therapy room; Activities room; Laundry room; Barber/Beauty shop.

Activities Arts & crafts; Cards; Games; Reading groups; Prayer groups; Movies; Shopping trips.

Bowling Green

Moore & Pike County Nursing Home
400 S Saint Charles, Bowling Green, MO 63334
(314) 324-5281
Admin Martha E Moore.
Licensure Intermediate care. *Beds* ICF 68.
Owner Privately owned.

Sunset Nursing Home
Box 398, N Main Cross, Bowling Green, MO 63334
(314) 324-5191
Admin Judith A Barteau. *Dir of Nursing* Carley Lovell.
Licensure Intermediate care. *Beds* ICF 46. *Certified* Medicaid.
Owner Privately owned.
Admissions Requirements Minimum age 18; Medical examination.
Staff RNs 1 (pt); LPNs 4 (ft); Nurses' aides 15 (ft), 2 (pt); Activities coordinators 1 (ft); Maintenance, dietary, secretaries 5 (ft).
Facilities Dining room; Activities room; Crafts room; Laundry room; Barber/Beauty shop; Large yard; Fishing pond.
Activities Arts & crafts; Cards; Games; Reading groups; Prayer groups; Movies; Shopping trips; Dances/Social/Cultural gatherings; Intergenerational programs; Pet therapy; Community activities.

Branson

Rolling Hills Nursing Center
PO Box 1249, Hwy 248 W, Branson, MO 65616
(417) 334-6431
Admin Dan West. *Dir of Nursing* Nancy Howard RN. *Medical Dir* O K Broughton MD.
Licensure Skilled care. *Beds* SNF 100. *Private Pay Patients* 5%. *Certified* Medicaid; Medicare.
Owner Proprietary corp (Beverly Enterprises).
Admissions Requirements Minimum age 16; Physician's request.
Staff Physicians 6 (pt); RNs 3 (ft); LPNs 5 (ft), 2 (pt); Nurses' aides 24 (ft), 5 (pt); Physical therapists 2 (pt); Reality therapists 1 (pt); Recreational therapists 1 (pt); Occupational therapists 1 (pt); Speech therapists 1 (pt); Activities coordinators 1 (ft), 1 (pt); Dietitians 1 (pt); Ophthalmologists 1 (pt); Podiatrists 1 (pt); Audiologists 1 (pt).
Facilities Dining room; Physical therapy room; Activities room; Crafts room; Laundry room; Barber/Beauty shop; Covered patios.
Activities Arts & crafts; Cards; Games; Reading groups; Prayer groups; Movies; Shopping trips; Dances/Social/Cultural gatherings; Intergenerational programs; Pet therapy; Boat rides; Music shows.

Braymer

Golden Age Nursing Home District
Hwy 116 W, Braymer, MO 64624
(816) 645-2243
Admin Rita Cole. *Dir of Nursing* Lisa Paulsen. *Medical Dir* Lisa Paulsen.
Licensure Intermediate care; Alzheimer's care. *Beds* ICF 110. *Private Pay Patients* 40%. *Certified* Medicaid.
Owner Publicly owned.
Admissions Requirements Minimum age 21; Medical examination.

Staff RNs 1 (ft); LPNs 3 (ft); Nurses' aides 40 (ft), 6 (pt); Physical therapists 3 (ft); Activities coordinators 2 (ft); Dietitians 1 (ft).
Facilities Dining room; Physical therapy room; Activities room; Chapel; Laundry room; Barber/Beauty shop.
Activities Arts & crafts; Cards; Games; Reading groups; Prayer groups; Movies; Shopping trips; Dances/Social/Cultural gatherings; Intergenerational programs; Pet therapy.

Bridgeton

Bridgeton Nursing Center
12145 Bridgeton Square Dr, Bridgeton, MO 63044
(314) 298-7444
Admin Diane Meatheany.
Licensure Skilled care; Intermediate care. *Beds* Swing beds SNF/ICF 120. *Certified* Medicaid.
Owner Proprietary corp (Beverly Enterprises).

DePaul Health Center St Anne's Division
12303 DePaul Dr, Bridgeton, MO 63044
(314) 344-6000
Admin Frank A Petrich.
Medical Dir Frank R Mohs MD.
Licensure Skilled care; Intermediate care. *Beds* SNF 18; ICF 68. *Certified* Medicaid; Medicare.
Owner Nonprofit corp.
Admissions Requirements Medical examination; Physician's request.
Staff RNs 8 (ft), 12 (pt); LPNs 7 (ft), 3 (pt); Nurses' aides 26 (ft), 17 (pt); Ophthalmologists 1 (pt).
Affiliation Roman Catholic.
Facilities Dining room; Physical therapy room; Activities room; Chapel; Crafts room; Laundry room; Barber/Beauty shop; Library.
Activities Arts & crafts; Cards; Games; Reading groups; Prayer groups; Movies; Shopping trips; Dances/Social/Cultural gatherings.

Mark Twain Manor
11988 Mark Twain Ln, Bridgeton, MO 63044
(314) 291-8240
Admin Alfred J Jewson. *Dir of Nursing* Barbara Brown RN. *Medical Dir* Arnold Tepper MD.
Licensure Skilled care. *Beds* SNF 120. *Certified* Medicaid; Medicare.
Owner Proprietary corp.
Admissions Requirements Minimum age 18; Medical examination.
Staff RNs 4 (ft); LPNs 8 (ft), 2 (pt); Nurses' aides 35 (ft), 1 (pt); Activities coordinators 1 (ft), 2 (pt).
Facilities Dining room; Physical therapy room; Activities room; Crafts room; Laundry room; Barber/Beauty shop.
Activities Arts & crafts; Cards; Games; Reading groups; Prayer groups; Movies; Shopping trips; Dances/Social/Cultural gatherings.

Brookfield

Brookfield Nursing Center
315 Hunt, Brookfield, MO 64628
(816) 258-3367
Admin John P Hamilton.
Medical Dir Robert Smith MD.
Licensure Skilled care. *Beds* SNF 120. *Certified* Medicaid.
Owner Proprietary corp (Beverly Enterprises).
Admissions Requirements Medical examination; Physician's request.
Staff Physicians 3 (pt); RNs 4 (ft), 1 (pt); LPNs 6 (ft), 2 (pt); Nurses' aides 23 (ft), 4 (pt); Physical therapists 1 (pt); Recreational therapists 1 (pt); Occupational therapists 1 (pt); Speech therapists 1 (pt); Activities

coordinators 1 (ft); Dietitians 1 (pt); Ophthalmologists 1 (pt); Podiatrists 1 (pt); Audiologists 1 (pt); Dentists 1 (pt).
Facilities Dining room; Physical therapy room; Activities room; Chapel; Crafts room; Laundry room; Barber/Beauty shop.
Activities Arts & crafts; Cards; Games; Reading groups; Prayer groups; Movies; Shopping trips; Dances/Social/Cultural gatherings.

Maranatha Manor
620 West Ave, Brookfield, MO 64628
(816) 258-7708
Admin Janet Robinson; Betty Williams.
Licensure Intermediate care; Residential care. *Beds* ICF 27; Residential care 44.
Owner Proprietary corp.
Staff RNs 1 (ft), 1 (pt); LPNs 2 (ft); Nurses' aides 18 (ft); Physical therapists 1 (pt); Speech therapists 1 (pt); Activities coordinators 1 (pt); Dentists 1 (pt).
Facilities Dining room; Activities room; Laundry room; Barber/Beauty shop.
Activities Cards; Games; Prayer groups; Movies; Shopping trips.

McLarney Manor
PO Box 129, 116 E Pratt, Brookfield, MO 64628
(816) 258-7402
Admin Judith Lewis. *Dir of Nursing* Lisa Wilburn RN. *Medical Dir* B D Howell MD.
Licensure Skilled care; Intermediate care. *Beds* SNF 5; ICF 55. *Private Pay Patients* 40%. *Certified* Medicaid.
Owner Proprietary corp (Tiffany Care Centers).
Admissions Requirements Minimum age 21; Medical examination.
Staff Physicians 1 (ft); RNs 1 (ft), 2 (pt); LPNs 3 (ft), 3 (pt); Nurses' aides 12 (ft), 6 (pt); Physical therapists 1 (ft); Activities coordinators 1 (ft); Dietitians 1 (ft); Ophthalmologists 1 (pt); Podiatrists 1 (pt).
Facilities Dining room; Physical therapy room; Activities room; Crafts room; Laundry room; Barber/Beauty shop.
Activities Arts & crafts; Games; Reading groups; Prayer groups; Dances/Social/Cultural programs; Intergenerational programs.

Brunswick

Grand Chariton Manor Inc
RR 2, Box 11, 721 W Filmore, Brunswick, MO 65236
(816) 548-3182
Admin Sarah F Breshears.
Licensure Intermediate care. *Beds* ICF 60. *Certified* Medicaid.
Owner Proprietary corp.

Buffalo

Hickory Lane Care Center
PO Box 449, Hickory & Cooper Sts, Buffalo, MO 65622
(417) 345-2228
Admin Bruce Boehm Sr.
Licensure Skilled care. *Beds* SNF 120. *Certified* Medicaid; Medicare.
Owner Proprietary corp (Hillhaven Corp).

Butler

Heartland-Willow Lane Nursing Center
416 S High, Butler, MO 64730
(816) 679-6157
Admin Melba J Swope. *Dir of Nursing* Donna Short RN.
Licensure Skilled care. *Beds* SNF 100. *Certified* Medicaid; Medicare.
Owner Proprietary corp (Health Care & Retirement Corp).

Admissions Requirements Medical examination; Physician's request.
Staff RNs 3 (ft), 3 (pt); LPNs 17 (ft), 5 (pt); Nurses' aides 29 (ft), 3 (pt); Physical therapists 1 (pt); Reality therapists 1 (pt); Recreational therapists 1 (pt); Occupational therapists 1 (pt); Speech therapists 1 (pt); Activities coordinators 1 (ft); Dietitians 1 (ft), 1 (pt); Ophthalmologists 1 (pt).
Facilities Dining room; Physical therapy room; Activities room; Crafts room; Laundry room; Barber/Beauty shop.
Activities Arts & crafts; Cards; Games; Reading groups; Prayer groups; Movies; Shopping trips; Dances/Social/Cultural gatherings.

Medicalodge of Butler
Rte 4 Box 130, Butler, MO 64730
(816) 679-3179
Admin Patty Steinberg.
Licensure Intermediate care. *Beds* ICF 120. *Certified* Medicaid.
Owner Proprietary corp (Medicalodges Inc).

Cabool

Kabul Nursing Home Inc
PO Box H, 920 W Main, Cabool, MO 65689
(417) 962-3713
Admin Robert K Cameron.
Licensure Skilled care. *Beds* SNF 82. *Certified* Medicaid; Medicare.
Owner Nonprofit corp.

California

California Care Center
Rte 3 Box 87, California, MO 65018
(314) 796-3127
Admin Carolyn Cantrell. *Dir of Nursing* Jill Grisham RN. *Medical Dir* Richard Fulks MD.
Licensure Skilled care; Day care. *Beds* SNF 60. *Certified* Medicaid; Medicare.
Owner Proprietary corp (Healthcare Properties Inc).
Admissions Requirements Minimum age 18; Medical examination.
Staff Physicians 1 (pt); RNs 2 (ft); LPNs 4 (ft), 1 (pt); Nurses' aides 16 (ft), 12 (pt); Physical therapists 1 (pt); Recreational therapists 1 (pt); Occupational therapists 1 (pt); Speech therapists 1 (pt); Activities coordinators 1 (ft), 1 (pt); Dietitians 1 (ft), 1 (pt); Ophthalmologists 1 (pt); Podiatrists 1 (pt); Audiologists 1 (pt).
Languages Spanish.
Facilities Dining room; Physical therapy room; Activities room; Crafts room; Laundry room; Barber/Beauty shop; Library; Private and semi-private rooms; Nurse call system in baths; Garden patio; Enclosed courtyard.
Activities Arts & crafts; Cards; Games; Reading groups; Prayer groups; Movies; Shopping trips; Dances/Social/Cultural gatherings; Religious services; Entertainment; Family activities and entertainment.

Latham Care Center
109 N High, Box 19, California, MO 65018
(314) 796-3944
Admin Janice Claas. *Dir of Nursing* Barbara Peoples.
Licensure Intermediate care. *Beds* ICF 44. *Private Pay Patients* 90%.
Owner Proprietary corp.
Staff RNs 1 (pt); LPNs 3 (ft); Nurses' aides 18 (ft); Activities coordinators 1 (ft).
Facilities Dining room; Activities room; Crafts room; Laundry room; Barber/Beauty shop.
Activities Arts & crafts; Cards; Games; Reading groups; Prayer groups; Movies; Shopping trips; Intergenerational programs.

Camdenton

Camdenton Windsor Estates
Hwy 5 N, Camdenton, MO 65020
(314) 346-5654
Admin John Arth.
Licensure Skilled care. *Beds* SNF 60. *Certified* Medicaid; Medicare.
Owner Proprietary corp.

Mozark Health Resort
PO Box 1345, Camdenton, MO 65020
(314) 346-2445
Admin Joyce L Shaffer.
Medical Dir R R Porter DO.
Licensure Intermediate care. *Beds* ICF 32.
Owner Privately owned.
Admissions Requirements Minimum age 18.
Staff Physicians 1 (pt); RNs 1 (pt); LPNs 1 (pt); Nurses' aides 8 (pt); Recreational therapists 1 (pt).
Facilities Dining room; Activities room; Laundry room.
Activities Arts & crafts; Cards; Games; Reading groups; Movies; Shopping trips; Dances/Social/Cultural gatherings.

Cameron

Cameron Manor
801 Euclid, Cameron, MO 64429
(816) 632-7254
Admin Betty A Smith. *Dir of Nursing* Sally A Temple. *Medical Dir* E R Schmidt DO.
Licensure Intermediate care. *Beds* ICF 60. *Private Pay Patients* 50%. *Certified* Medicaid.
Owner Proprietary corp (Maxicare Inc).
Admissions Requirements Minimum age 17.
Staff LPNs 3 (ft); Nurses' aides 30 (ft); Physical therapists 1 (pt); Reality therapists 1 (pt); Occupational therapists 1 (pt); Speech therapists 1 (pt); Activities coordinators 1 (ft); Dietitians 1 (pt).
Facilities Dining room; Activities room; Barber/Beauty shop.
Activities Arts & crafts; Games; Reading groups; Prayer groups; Movies.

Indian Hills Nursing Home
1405 W Grand Ave, Cameron, MO 64429
(816) 632-2151
Admin Carmelita R Green. *Dir of Nursing* Steven J Pearl. *Medical Dir* E R Schmidt.
Licensure Skilled care. *Beds* SNF 84. *Private Pay Patients* 8%. *Certified* Medicaid; Medicare.
Owner Proprietary corp (Beverly Enterprises).
Admissions Requirements Minimum age 21; Medical examination.
Staff RNs 3 (ft); LPNs 3 (ft), 1 (pt); Nurses' aides 42 (ft), 5 (pt); Physical therapists (contracted); Occupational therapists 1 (ft); Activities coordinators 1 (ft); Dietitians 1 (ft).
Facilities Dining room; Physical therapy room; Activities room; Laundry room; Barber/Beauty shop; 2 dayrooms; Van.
Activities Arts & crafts; Cards; Games; Reading groups; Prayer groups; Movies; Shopping trips; Dances/Social/Cultural gatherings; Intergenerational programs; Pet therapy; Outings; Adopt-a-grandparent; Volunteer program.

Village
320 Little Brick Rd, Cameron, MO 64429
(816) 632-7611
Admin Ronnie Wilkinson.
Medical Dir Sue Coy.
Licensure Intermediate care; Residential care. *Beds* ICF 28; Residential care 25. *Certified* Medicaid.
Owner Proprietary corp.
Admissions Requirements Minimum age 21; Medical examination.

Staff Physicians 1 (pt); RNs 2 (ft); LPNs 2 (pt); Nurses' aides 9 (ft); Physical therapists 1 (pt); Reality therapists 1 (pt); Recreational therapists 1 (pt); Occupational therapists 1 (pt); Speech therapists 1 (pt); Activities coordinators 1 (ft).
Facilities Dining room; Physical therapy room; Activities room; Laundry room; Barber/Beauty shop.
Activities Cards; Games; Prayer groups.

Campbell

General Baptist Nursing Home
Rte 2 Box 650, Hwy 62 W, Campbell, MO 63933
(314) 246-2155
Admin Wanda Britt. *Dir of Nursing* Diana Burchell RN. *Medical Dir* Jerry Muse MD.
Licensure Intermediate care. *Beds* ICF 90. *Private Pay Patients* 41%. *Certified* Medicaid.
Owner Nonprofit corp.
Admissions Requirements Minimum age 18; Medical examination; Physician's request.
Staff RNs 1 (ft); LPNs 7 (ft), 3 (pt); Nurses' aides 35 (ft), 4 (pt); Physical therapists; Activities coordinators 2 (ft), 1 (pt); Dietitians.
Affiliation Baptist.
Facilities Dining room; Physical therapy room; Activities room; Chapel; Laundry room; Barber/Beauty shop; Resident's lounge.
Activities Arts & crafts; Cards; Games; Reading groups; Prayer groups; Movies; Shopping trips; Dances/Social/Cultural gatherings; Intergenerational programs.

Canton

Lewis County Nursing Home District
Rte 2, Canton, MO 63435
(314) 288-4454
Admin Patricia L Hardin-Cummings. *Dir of Nursing* Ella M Dochterman. *Medical Dir* Dr Buening.
Licensure Skilled care. *Beds* SNF 90. *Certified* Medicaid.
Owner Publicly owned.
Admissions Requirements Minimum age 16.
Staff RNs 4 (ft); LPNs 10 (ft); Nurses' aides 4 (ft); Recreational therapists 2 (ft); Activities coordinators 1 (ft), 1 (pt); Dietitians 1 (ft).
Facilities Dining room; Physical therapy room; Activities room; Laundry room; Barber/Beauty shop.
Activities Arts & crafts; Cards; Games; Reading groups; Prayer groups; Movies; Shopping trips; Dances/Social/Cultural gatherings.

Cape Girardeau

Cape Girardeau Care Center
2525 Boutin Dr, Cape Girardeau, MO 63701
(314) 334-5225
Admin Katherine M Lane. *Dir of Nursing* Helen Gwin. *Medical Dir* W W Hutton DO.
Licensure Intermediate care. *Beds* ICF 120. *Certified* Medicaid.
Owner Nonprofit corp.
Admissions Requirements Minimum age 19; Medical examination.
Staff RNs 1 (ft); LPNs 9 (ft); Nurses' aides 61 (ft); Activities coordinators 3 (ft); Dietitians.
Facilities Dining room; Physical therapy room; Laundry room; Barber/Beauty shop.
Activities Arts & crafts; Cards; Games; Reading groups; Prayer groups; Movies; Shopping trips; Dances/Social/Cultural gatherings.

Cape Girardeau Nursing Center
2852 Independence, Cape Girardeau, MO 63701
(314) 335-2086
Admin Dianne Walker. *Dir of Nursing* Patty Schmarje.
Licensure Skilled care. *Beds* SNF 120. *Certified* Medicaid; Medicare.
Owner Proprietary corp (Beverly Enterprises).
Admissions Requirements Medical examination; Physician's request.
Staff Physicians 26 (pt); RNs 6 (ft); LPNs 15 (ft); Nurses' aides 40 (ft); Physical therapists 1 (ft); Recreational therapists 1 (ft); Occupational therapists 1 (pt); Speech therapists 1 (pt); Activities coordinators 1 (ft); Dietitians 1 (ft); Ophthalmologists 1 (pt); Podiatrists 1 (pt); Dentists 1 (pt); Social workers 1 (ft).
Facilities Dining room; Physical therapy room; Activities room; Crafts room; Laundry room; Barber/Beauty shop; Library.
Activities Arts & crafts; Cards; Games; Reading groups; Prayer groups; Movies; Shopping trips; Dances/Social/Cultural gatherings.

Chateau Girardeau Health Center
3120 Independence St, Cape Girardeau, MO 63701
(314) 335-1281
Admin Barbara N Calvin. *Dir of Nursing* Phyllis T Watkins RN. *Medical Dir* Forest H Coulson MD.
Licensure Skilled care; Independent living; Assisted living. *Beds* SNF 60; Independent living apts 151; Assisted living apts 40. *Private Pay Patients* 87%. *Certified* Medicare.
Owner Nonprofit corp.
Admissions Requirements Minimum age 62; Medical examination.
Staff RNs 5 (ft); LPNs 3 (ft), 2 (pt); Nurses' aides 27 (ft), 3 (pt); Physical therapists; Activities coordinators 1 (ft), 1 (pt); Dietitians.
Facilities Dining room; Physical therapy room; Activities room; Crafts room; Laundry room; Barber/Beauty shop; Library; Free cable TV.
Activities Arts & crafts; Cards; Games; Reading groups; Prayer groups; Movies; Shopping trips; Dances/Social/Cultural gatherings; Intergenerational programs; Pet therapy; Outings; Residents council.

Lutheran Home
2825 Bloomfield Rd, Cape Girardeau, MO 63701
(314) 335-0158
Admin Janice T Unger.
Licensure Skilled care. *Beds* SNF 180. *Certified* Medicaid.
Owner Nonprofit corp.
Affiliation Lutheran.

Ratliff Nursing Home
717 N Spriggs, Cape Girardeau, MO 63701
(314) 335-5810
Admin Emmagene Ratliff.
Licensure Intermediate care. *Beds* ICF 17.
Owner Privately owned.

Carrollton

Carrollton Nursing Center
1502 N Jefferson, Carrollton, MO 64633
(816) 542-0156
Admin Loretta Stigall. *Dir of Nursing* Aimee Harris RN. *Medical Dir* Marvin E Ross DO.
Licensure Skilled care. *Beds* SNF 120. *Certified* Medicaid; Medicare.
Owner Proprietary corp (Lincoln Investments Inc).
Admissions Requirements Minimum age 18; Medical examination.

Staff Physicians 5 (pt); RNs 2 (ft), 2 (pt);
LPNs 11 (ft), 1 (pt); Nurses' aides 45 (ft), 5
(pt); Physical therapists 3 (pt); Recreational
therapists 1 (pt); Occupational therapists 1
(pt); Speech therapists 1 (pt); Activities
coordinators 2 (ft); Dietitians 1 (pt);
Podiatrists 1 (pt); Dentists 1 (pt).
Facilities Dining room; Physical therapy
room; Activities room; Chapel; Crafts room;
Laundry room; Barber/Beauty shop; 2
courtyards.
Activities Arts & crafts; Cards; Games;
Reading groups; Prayer groups; Movies;
Dances/Social/Cultural gatherings.

Lincoln Care Center
307 Grand, Carrollton, MO 64633
(816) 542-0588
Admin Jerry Wielborn. *Dir of Nursing* Carol
Hamblin.
Licensure Intermediate care. *Beds* ICF 63.
Private Pay Patients 70%.
Owner Proprietary corp.
Admissions Requirements Minimum age 17;
Medical examination.
Staff RNs 1 (pt); LPNs 1 (ft), 3 (pt); Nurses'
aides 14 (ft), 7 (pt); Activities coordinators 1
(ft); Dietitians 1 (pt).
Facilities Dining room; Activities room;
Laundry room; Barber/Beauty shop.
Activities Cards; Games; Prayer groups;
Movies.

Carthage

Maryetta's Rest Home
316 S Fulton, Carthage, MO 64836
(417) 358-6672
Admin Eldred F Gilbreath.
Licensure Intermediate care. *Beds* 17.
Owner Proprietary corp.

Regency Care Center of Carthage
1901 Buena Vista, Carthage, MO 64836
(417) 358-1937
Admin Donna Lane.
Licensure Skilled care; Intermediate care. *Beds*
Swing beds SNF/ICF 110. *Certified*
Medicaid; Medicare.
Owner Proprietary corp.

St Luke's Nursing Center
1220 E Fairview, Carthage, MO 64836
(417) 358-9084
Admin Sue Joslen.
Licensure Skilled care; Residential care. *Beds*
SNF 49; Residential care 31. *Certified*
Medicaid.
Owner Nonprofit corp.

Caruthersville

Caruthersville Nursing Center
500 Truman, Caruthersville, MO 63830
(314) 333-5150
Admin Connie D Marshall. *Dir of Nursing*
Judy Hollingsworth. *Medical Dir* Dr Sanan.
Licensure Skilled care; Intermediate care. *Beds*
Swing beds SNF/ICF 120. *Private Pay
Patients* 10%. *Certified* Medicaid; Medicare.
Owner Proprietary corp (Beverly Enterprises).
Admissions Requirements Minimum age 18.
Staff RNs 2 (ft), 2 (pt); LPNs 8 (ft), 6 (pt);
Nurses' aides 30 (ft), 20 (pt); Physical
therapists (consultant); Activities
coordinators 1 (ft).
Facilities Dining room; Physical therapy
room; Activities room; Crafts room; Laundry
room; Barber/Beauty shop.
Activities Arts & crafts; Cards; Games;
Reading groups; Prayer groups; Movies;
Shopping trips; Dances/Social/Cultural
gatherings.

Cassville

Barry County Care Center
PO Box 574, 1300 County Farm Rd,
Cassville, MO 65625
(417) 847-3386, 847-5449 FAX
Admin Reece Lancaster. *Dir of Nursing* Delris
Herrman. *Medical Dir* Dr James C Flanary.
Licensure Skilled care; Intermediate care;
Residential care. *Beds* SNF 40; ICF 8;
Residential care 22. *Private Pay Patients*
80%. *Certified* Medicaid.
Owner Proprietary corp.
Admissions Requirements Minimum age 18;
Medical examination; Physician's request.
Staff Physicians 1 (pt); RNs 1 (ft), 3 (pt);
LPNs 5 (ft); Nurses' aides 14 (ft), 2 (pt);
Physical therapists 1 (pt); Activities
coordinators 1 (ft); Dietitians 1 (pt).
Facilities Dining room; Physical therapy
room; Activities room; Laundry room;
Barber/Beauty shop.
Activities Arts & crafts; Cards; Games;
Reading groups; Prayer groups; Movies;
Shopping trips; Pet therapy.

Red Rose Inn
Rte 1 Box 289-A, Old Exeter Rd, Cassville,
MO 65625
(417) 847-2184
Admin Jane Prier. *Dir of Nursing* Kaye
Learned RN. *Medical Dir* Ricky Kime MD.
Licensure Skilled care; Intermediate care. *Beds*
Swing beds SNF/ICF 90. *Private Pay
Patients* 15%. *Certified* Medicaid.
Owner Proprietary corp (Rose Care Inc).
Facilities Dining room; Physical therapy
room; Laundry room; Barber/Beauty shop.
Activities Arts & crafts; Cards; Games;
Reading groups; Prayer groups; Movies;
Shopping trips; Dances/Social/Cultural
gatherings; Intergenerational programs; Pet
therapy.

Cedar Hill

Cedars Health Care Center
6400 The Cedars Court, Cedar Hill, MO
63016
(314) 942-2700
Admin Alice McCarthy.
Licensure Intermediate care. *Beds* ICF 120.
Certified Medicaid.
Owner Proprietary corp.

Centralia

Heritage Hall Nursing Center
750 E Hwy 22, Centralia, MO 65240
(314) 682-5551
Admin Rita Hampton.
Medical Dir Jamie Eryart.
Licensure Intermediate care. *Beds* ICF 60.
Certified Medicaid.
Owner Proprietary corp (Beverly Enterprises).
Admissions Requirements Minimum age 18;
Medical examination; Physician's request.
Staff RNs 1 (pt); LPNs 2 (ft), 2 (pt); Nurses'
aides 28 (ft), 6 (pt); Activities coordinators 1
(ft).
Facilities Dining room; Physical therapy
room; Activities room; Chapel; Crafts room;
Laundry room; Barber/Beauty shop.
Activities Arts & crafts; Cards; Games;
Reading groups; Prayer groups; Movies;
Dances/Social/Cultural gatherings.

Stuart House
117 S Hickman, Centralia, MO 65240
(314) 682-3204
Admin Alan Mashall.
Licensure Intermediate care. *Beds* ICF 27.
Owner Privately owned.

Chaffee

Chaffee Nursing Center
PO Box 68, Chaffee, MO 63740
(314) 887-3615
Admin William Van Pelt. *Dir of Nursing*
Shirley Gatewood RN. *Medical Dir* Dan
Frissell MD.
Licensure Skilled care. *Beds* SNF 60. *Private
Pay Patients* 18%. *Certified* Medicaid.
Owner Proprietary corp (Americare Systems
Inc).
Admissions Requirements Minimum age 21;
Medical examination; Physician's request.
Staff Physicians 1 (pt); RNs 2 (ft), 2 (pt);
LPNs 6 (ft), 2 (pt); Nurses' aides 20 (ft), 2
(pt); Physical therapists 1 (pt); Occupational
therapists 1 (pt); Speech therapists 1 (pt);
Activities coordinators 1 (ft); Dietitians 1
(pt); Ophthalmologists 1 (pt); Podiatrists 1
(pt); Audiologists 1 (pt).
Facilities Dining room; Physical therapy
room; Activities room; Chapel; Crafts room;
Laundry room; Barber/Beauty shop.
Activities Arts & crafts; Cards; Games;
Reading groups; Prayer groups; Movies;
Shopping trips; Dances/Social/Cultural
gatherings; Intergenerational programs; Pet
therapy.

Charleston

Charleston Manor
1220 E Marshall, Charleston, MO 63834
(314) 683-3721
Admin Floyd N McRoberts.
Medical Dir David Pfefferhoin; Beverly
Julian.
Licensure Skilled care. *Beds* SNF 120.
Certified Medicaid; Medicare.
Owner Proprietary corp (Americare Corp).
Admissions Requirements Minimum age 18;
Medical examination.
Staff Physicians 5 (pt); RNs 3 (ft); LPNs 12
(ft); Nurses' aides 53 (ft); Physical therapists
1 (pt); Recreational therapists 1 (pt);
Occupational therapists 1 (pt); Speech
therapists 1 (pt); Activities coordinators 2
(ft); Dietitians 1 (pt); Ophthalmologists 1
(pt); Podiatrists 1 (pt); Dentists 1 (pt).
Facilities Dining room; Physical therapy
room; Activities room; Laundry room;
Barber/Beauty shop.
Activities Arts & crafts; Cards; Games;
Reading groups; Prayer groups; Movies;
Shopping trips; Dances/Social/Cultural
gatherings.

Russell Retirement
200 E Commercial, Charleston, MO 63834
(314) 683-3353
Admin Dawn Fugate.
Licensure Residential care. *Beds* Residential
care 50. *Private Pay Patients* 90%.
Owner Privately owned.
Admissions Requirements Minimum age 50.
Staff Nurses' aides 5 (ft), 1 (pt).
Facilities Dining room; Activities room;
Barber/Beauty shop.
Activities Cards; Games; Movies.

Chesterfield

Chesterfield Manor Inc
14001 Olive Street Rd, Chesterfield, MO
63017
(314) 469-3500
Admin Ken Jessup.
Medical Dir Ted Vargas MD.
Licensure Skilled care. *Beds* SNF 136.
Certified Medicaid.
Admissions Requirements Medical
examination.
Staff RNs 2 (ft), 2 (pt); LPNs 2 (ft), 4 (pt);
Nurses' aides 10 (ft), 15 (pt); Physical
therapists 1 (pt); Speech therapists 1 (pt);

Activities coordinators 1 (ft); Dietitians 1 (ft); Ophthalmologists 1 (pt); Podiatrists 1 (pt); Dentists 1 (pt).
Facilities Dining room; Physical therapy room; Activities room; Chapel; Crafts room; Laundry room; Barber/Beauty shop.
Activities Arts & crafts; Cards; Games; Prayer groups; Movies.

Delmar Gardens of Chesterfield
14855 N Outer 40 Rd, Chesterfield, MO 63017
(314) 532-0150
Admin Henry Grossberg.
Licensure Skilled care. *Beds* SNF 240.
Certified Medicaid; Medicare.
Owner Proprietary corp.

Delmar Gardens West
13550 S Outer 40 Rd, Chesterfield, MO 63017
(314) 878-1330
Admin Barbara Grossberg.
Licensure Skilled care. *Beds* SNF 330.
Certified Medicaid; Medicare.
Owner Proprietary corp.

Friendship Village of West County
15201 Olive Street Rd, Chesterfield, MO 63017
(314) 532-1515
Admin Wes Sperr. *Dir of Nursing* Judy Thorp. *Medical Dir* Grant Izmirlian MD.
Licensure Skilled care; Retirement. *Beds* SNF 60. *Certified* Medicare.
Owner Nonprofit corp.
Admissions Requirements Minimum age 62.
Staff Physicians; RNs; LPNs; Nurses' aides; Physical therapists; Reality therapists; Recreational therapists; Occupational therapists; Speech therapists; Activities coordinators; Dietitians; Ophthalmologists; Podiatrists; Dentists.
Facilities Dining room; Physical therapy room; Activities room; Chapel; Crafts room; Laundry room; Barber/Beauty shop; Library.
Activities Arts & crafts; Cards; Games; Reading groups; Prayer groups; Movies; Shopping trips; Dances/Social/Cultural gatherings; Grandparents day; Residents council.

Jewish Center for Aged
13190 S Outer 40 Rd, Chesterfield, MO 63017
(314) 434-3330, 434-3330 ext 227
Admin Mary B Paspalas. *Dir of Nursing* Robin Storey. *Medical Dir* Ellen Binder MD.
Licensure Skilled care; Alzheimer's care. *Beds* SNF 276. *Private Pay Patients* 26%. *Certified* Medicaid; Medicare.
Owner Nonprofit organization/foundation.
Admissions Requirements Medical examination.
Staff Physicians 1 (ft), 1 (pt); RNs 7 (ft), 5 (pt); LPNs 9 (ft); Nurses' aides 52 (ft), 3 (pt); Physical therapists 1 (pt); Recreational therapists 1 (pt); Occupational therapists 1 (ft); Speech therapists 1 (pt); Activities coordinators 1 (ft); Ophthalmologists 1 (pt); Podiatrists 2 (pt).
Affiliation Jewish.
Facilities Dining room; Physical therapy room; Activities room; Chapel; Crafts room; Laundry room; Barber/Beauty shop; Library; Occupational therapy room; Speech therapy room; Dental; Podiatry; Medical exam room; Conference rooms; Gardens.
Activities Arts & crafts; Cards; Games; Reading groups; Prayer groups; Movies; Shopping trips; Dances/Social/Cultural gatherings; Intergenerational programs; Pet therapy; Music therapy.

Westchester House
550 White Rd, Chesterfield, MO 63017
(314) 469-1200

Admin Kevin Cantrell.
Medical Dir Dr Jamie Aquinaldo.
Licensure Skilled care. *Beds* SNF 159.
Owner Proprietary corp (National Heritage).
Admissions Requirements Minimum age 18.
Staff Physicians 1 (pt); RNs 6 (ft), 4 (pt); LPNs 3 (ft), 3 (pt); Nurses' aides 24 (ft), 22 (pt); Physical therapists 1 (pt); Activities coordinators 1 (ft), 1 (pt).
Facilities Dining room; Physical therapy room; Activities room; Crafts room; Laundry room; Barber/Beauty shop; Library.
Activities Arts & crafts; Cards; Games; Reading groups; Prayer groups; Movies; Shopping trips; Dances/Social/Cultural gatherings.

Chillicothe

Baptist Home, Chillicothe
Box 920, Chillicothe, MO 64601
(816) 646-6219
Admin Larry N Johnson. *Dir of Nursing* Martha Hague.
Licensure Intermediate care; Residential care. *Beds* ICF 16; Residential care 18.
Owner Nonprofit organization/foundation.
Admissions Requirements Minimum age 65; Medical examination.
Staff RNs; LPNs; Activities coordinators.
Affiliation Baptist.
Facilities Dining room; Physical therapy room; Activities room; Chapel; Laundry room; Barber/Beauty shop.
Activities Arts & crafts; Cards; Games; Reading groups; Prayer groups; Movies; Shopping trips; Dances/Social/Cultural gatherings.

Indian Hills Nursing Home Inc
2601 Fair St, Chillicothe, MO 64601
(816) 646-1230
Admin Tom Otke.
Licensure Intermediate care. *Beds* ICF 60. *Certified* Medicaid.
Owner Proprietary corp.
Staff RNs 1 (ft); LPNs 4 (ft), 2 (pt); Nurses' aides 21 (ft), 3 (pt); Physical therapists 1 (pt); Occupational therapists 1 (pt); Speech therapists 1 (pt); Activities coordinators 1 (ft); Dietitians 1 (pt); Audiologists 1 (pt).
Facilities Dining room; Physical therapy room; Activities room; Chapel; Crafts room; Laundry room; Barber/Beauty shop; Library.
Activities Arts & crafts; Cards; Games; Reading groups; Prayer groups; Movies; Shopping trips; Dances/Social/Cultural gatherings.

Jones-Darr
300 John F Kennedy Ave, Chillicothe, MO 64601
(816) 646-2808
Admin Trudy Grant. *Dir of Nursing* Karen Moore.
Licensure Intermediate care. *Beds* ICF 19. *Private Pay Patients* 2%.
Owner Privately owned.
Admissions Requirements Medical examination.
Staff RNs 1 (pt); LPNs 1 (ft), 2 (pt); Nurses' aides 3 (ft), 3 (pt).
Activities Arts & crafts; Games; Prayer groups; Pet therapy.

Livingston Manor Care Center
Hwy 36 E, Box 28, Chillicothe, MO 64601
(816) 646-5177
Admin Sharon Gamble. *Dir of Nursing* Nancy Gamble. *Medical Dir* Dr Sensenich DO.
Licensure Skilled care. *Beds* SNF 94. *Private Pay Patients* 30%. *Certified* Medicaid.
Owner Proprietary corp.
Admissions Requirements Minimum age 16; Medical examination.

Staff Physicians; RNs; LPNs; Nurses' aides; Physical therapists; Reality therapists; Recreational therapists; Occupational therapists; Speech therapists; Activities coordinators; Dietitians; Audiologists.
Facilities Dining room; Physical therapy room; Activities room; Crafts room; Laundry room; Barber/Beauty shop.
Activities Arts & crafts; Cards; Games; Reading groups; Prayer groups; Movies; Shopping trips; Dances/Social/Cultural gatherings; Pet therapy.

Morningside Center
1700 Morningside Dr, Chillicothe, MO 64601
(816) 646-0170
Admin Joan K Kimberling.
Licensure Intermediate care; Residential care. *Beds* ICF 60; Residential care 24. *Private Pay Patients* 25%. *Certified* Medicaid.
Owner Publicly owned.
Admissions Requirements Minimum age 17; Medical examination.
Staff RNs 2 (ft), 1 (pt); LPNs 5 (ft); Nurses' aides 12 (ft), 20 (pt); Recreational therapists (consultant); Activities coordinators 1 (ft); Dietitians (consultant); Social services (consultant).
Facilities Dining room; Physical therapy room; Activities room; Crafts room; Laundry room; Barber/Beauty shop.
Activities Arts & crafts; Cards; Games; Reading groups; Prayer groups; Movies; Shopping trips; Dances/Social/Cultural gatherings; Intergenerational programs; Pet therapy.

Suncrest Nursing Center
505 2nd St, Chillicothe, MO 64601
(816) 646-3476
Admin Retha Emerich. *Dir of Nursing* Linda Bush.
Licensure Intermediate care. *Beds* ICF 44. *Private Pay Patients* 50%.
Owner Privately owned.
Admissions Requirements Minimum age 18; Physician's request.
Staff RNs 1 (pt); LPNs 1 (ft), 1 (pt); Nurses' aides 15 (ft); Activities coordinators 1 (ft).
Facilities Dining room; Activities room; Crafts room; Laundry room; Vans for outings.
Activities Arts & crafts; Games; Movies; Shopping trips; Intergenerational programs.

Clarence

Clarence Nursing Home District
307 East St, Box 250, Clarence, MO 63437
(816) 699-2118
Admin Michael O'Neal. *Dir of Nursing* Carolyn Garnett. *Medical Dir* Dr D R Hull.
Licensure Intermediate care. *Beds* ICF 60. *Certified* Medicaid.
Owner Publicly owned.
Admissions Requirements Minimum age 17; Medical examination.
Staff Physicians 1 (pt); RNs 1 (pt); LPNs 3 (ft), 2 (pt); Nurses' aides 25 (ft), 9 (pt); Physical therapists 1 (ft), 1 (pt); Reality therapists 1 (ft); Recreational therapists 1 (ft); Occupational therapists 1 (pt); Speech therapists 1 (pt); Activities coordinators 1 (ft); Dietitians 1 (pt).
Facilities Dining room; Physical therapy room; Activities room; Crafts room; Laundry room; Barber/Beauty shop.
Activities Arts & crafts; Cards; Games; Reading groups; Prayer groups; Movies.

Clinton

Sycamore View Healthcare
1009 E Ohio, Clinton, MO 64735
(816) 885-5571

Admin Richard E Clark. *Dir of Nursing*
Wanda Kimble RN. *Medical Dir* Dr
Kenneth Scot.
Licensure Skilled care. *Beds* SNF 120.
Certified Medicaid; Medicare.
Owner Proprietary corp (Hillhaven Corp).
Admissions Requirements Minimum age 18;
Medical examination.
Staff RNs 2 (ft), 2 (pt); LPNs 8 (ft), 2 (pt);
Activities coordinators 1 (ft).
Facilities Dining room; Physical therapy
room; Activities room; Crafts room; Laundry
room; Barber/Beauty shop.
Activities Arts & crafts; Cards; Games;
Reading groups; Movies; Dances/Social/
Cultural gatherings.

Westwood Nursing Center
Harmon-Gaines Rd, Clinton, MO 64735
(816) 885-8196
Admin Melva Dean Hart.
Medical Dir R J Powell DO.
Licensure Skilled care. *Beds* SNF 100.
Certified Medicaid; Medicare.
Owner Proprietary corp (Beverly Enterprises).
Admissions Requirements Minimum age 21;
Physician's request.
Staff Physicians 1 (pt); RNs 2 (ft), 1 (pt);
LPNs 5 (ft), 3 (pt); Nurses' aides 27 (ft), 18
(pt); Physical therapists 2 (ft), 2 (pt);
Recreational therapists 1 (pt); Occupational
therapists 1 (pt); Speech therapists 1 (pt);
Activities coordinators 1 (pt); Dietitians 1
(pt); Dentists 1 (pt).
Facilities Dining room; Physical therapy
room; Activities room; Chapel; Crafts room;
Laundry room; Barber/Beauty shop.
Activities Arts & crafts; Cards; Games;
Reading groups; Prayer groups; Movies;
Dances/Social/Cultural gatherings.

Cole Camp

Good Samaritan Nursing Home
Rte 1 Box 28, Cole Camp, MO 65325
(816) 668-4515
Admin Donald D Wuebbold. *Dir of Nursing*
Pamela J Osburn RN. *Medical Dir* Aturo
Gonzalez DO.
Licensure Intermediate care. *Beds* ICF 60.
Certified Medicaid.
Owner Nonprofit corp.
Staff Physicians 1 (pt); RNs 1 (ft); LPNs 3
(ft), 3 (pt); Nurses' aides 23 (ft); Activities
coordinators 1 (ft).
Facilities Dining room; Physical therapy
room; Activities room; Chapel; Laundry
room; Barber/Beauty shop.
Activities Cards; Games; Reading groups;
Prayer groups; Movies; Pet therapy.

Columbia

Autumn Court Nursing Center
300 Portland St, Columbia, MO 65201
(314) 875-3033
Admin Glenda Hood. *Dir of Nursing* Caroline
Jackson RN.
Licensure Skilled care; Intermediate care. *Beds*
SNF 120. *Certified* Medicaid.
Owner Proprietary corp (Beverly Enterprises).
Admissions Requirements Minimum age 18;
Medical examination; Physician's request.
Staff RNs 3 (ft); LPNs 12 (ft); Nurses' aides
30 (ft); Reality therapists 1 (ft), 1 (pt);
Recreational therapists 1 (ft), 1 (pt);
Occupational therapists 1 (ft), 1 (pt); Speech
therapists 1 (pt); Activities coordinators 1
(ft); Dietitians 1 (pt); Ophthalmologists 1
(pt); Podiatrists 1 (pt).
Facilities Dining room; Physical therapy
room; Activities room; Chapel; Crafts room;
Laundry room; Barber/Beauty shop; Library.
Activities Arts & crafts; Cards; Games;
Reading groups; Prayer groups; Movies;
Shopping trips; Dances/Social/Cultural
gatherings.

Boone Retirement Center Inc
1623 Anthony St, Columbia, MO 65201
(314) 449-6105
Admin John Lloyd Jones. *Dir of Nursing*
Deana McDonald RN. *Medical Dir* Dr
Cathrine Van Vorn.
Licensure Skilled care; Alzheimer's care. *Beds*
SNF 122. *Private Pay Patients* 30%. *Certified*
Medicaid.
Owner Nonprofit corp.
Admissions Requirements Minimum age 21;
Medical examination; Physician's request.
Staff Physicians 1 (pt); RNs 4 (ft); LPNs 13
(ft); Nurses' aides 52 (ft), 4 (pt); Physical
therapists 1 (pt); Recreational therapists 3
(ft); Occupational therapists 1 (pt); Speech
therapists 1 (pt); Dietitians 1 (ft);
Ophthalmologists 1 (pt); Podiatrists 1 (pt).
Languages Vietnamese.
Facilities Dining room; Physical therapy
room; Activities room; Crafts room; Laundry
room; Barber/Beauty shop; Library; Lounges.
Activities Arts & crafts; Cards; Games; Prayer
groups; Movies; Shopping trips; Dances/
Social/Cultural gatherings; Intergenerational
programs; Pet therapy.

Candlelight Care Center
1201 Hunt Ave, Columbia, MO 65202
(314) 449-1448
Admin Richard E Clarke. *Dir of Nursing*
Connie Grone RN. *Medical Dir* Dr Kenneth
Weston.
Licensure Skilled care; Alzheimer's care. *Beds*
SNF 113. *Private Pay Patients* 40%. *Certified*
Medicaid; Medicare; VA.
Owner Proprietary corp (Hannovr Healthcare).
Admissions Requirements Minimum age 50;
Medical examination; Physician's request.
Staff RNs 5 (ft); LPNs 12 (ft); Nurses' aides
45 (ft), 5 (pt); Activities coordinators 1 (ft),
1 (pt).
Facilities Dining room; Physical therapy
room; Activities room; Barber/Beauty shop.
Activities Arts & crafts; Games; Reading
groups; Movies; Intergenerational programs;
Pet therapy.

Columbia House Healthcare
1801 Towne Dr, Columbia, MO 65202
(314) 474-6111, 474-0594 FAX
Admin John D Sullivan. *Dir of Nursing* Judy
Morgan RN-C. *Medical Dir* Jeffery Belden
MD.
Licensure Skilled care. *Beds* SNF 141. *Private
Pay Patients* 10%. *Certified* Medicaid;
Medicare.
Owner Proprietary corp (Hillhaven Corp).
Admissions Requirements Minimum age 18;
Medical examination.
Staff RNs 2 (ft), 1 (pt); LPNs 9 (ft), 1 (pt);
Nurses' aides 35 (ft), 10 (pt); Physical
therapists 1 (ft); Activities coordinators 2
(ft); Dietitians 1 (pt).
Facilities Dining room; Physical therapy
room; Activities room; Laundry room;
Barber/Beauty shop; Library.
Activities Cards; Games; Reading groups;
Prayer groups; Movies; Shopping trips;
Dances/Social/Cultural gatherings; Pet
therapy.

Columbia Manor Care Center
2012 Nifong, Columbia, MO 65201
(314) 449-1246
Admin Robert H Rogers. *Dir of Nursing*
Karen Harris. *Medical Dir* Dr Robert
Bynum.
Licensure Skilled care. *Beds* SNF 52.
Owner Privately owned.
Admissions Requirements Minimum age 16;
Medical examination.
Staff Physicians 1 (pt); RNs 2 (ft), 2 (pt);
LPNs 3 (ft), 1 (pt); Nurses' aides 15 (ft);
Physical therapists 1 (pt); Occupational
therapists; Speech therapists; Activities
coordinators; Dietitians.
Languages German.

Facilities Dining room; Activities room;
Crafts room; Laundry room; Barber/Beauty
shop; Library.
Activities Arts & crafts; Games; Reading
groups; Prayer groups; Movies; Shopping
trips; Pet therapy.

Lenoir Health Care Center
3300 New Haven Rd, Columbia, MO 65201
(314) 876-5800
Admin J Michael Pelzer. *Dir of Nursing*
Barbara J Reed RN. *Medical Dir* Georgia
Nolph MD.
Licensure Skilled care; Residential care;
Alzheimer's care; Independent living. *Beds*
SNF 92; Residential care 16; Alzheimer's
unit 17; Independent living units 128.
Owner Nonprofit organization/foundation
(National Benevolent Association).
Admissions Requirements Medical
examination.
Staff Physicians 1 (ft); RNs 3 (ft), 2 (pt);
LPNs 1 (ft); Nurses' aides 40 (ft); Physical
therapists 1 (pt); Activities coordinators 2
(ft); Dietitians 1 (ft).
Affiliation Disciples of Christ.
Facilities Dining room; Physical therapy
room; Activities room; Chapel; Crafts room;
Laundry room; Barber/Beauty shop; Library;
Child day care; Enclosed courtyard in
Alzheimer's wing.
Activities Arts & crafts; Cards; Games;
Reading groups; Prayer groups; Movies;
Shopping trips; Dances/Social/Cultural
gatherings; Intergenerational programs; Pet
therapy.

Concordia

Lutheran Good Shepherd Home & Nursing Home
3rd & West Sts, Concordia, MO 64020
(816) 463-2267
Admin Paul R Brackman.
Medical Dir Dr Robert LaHue.
Licensure Skilled care; Intermediate care;
Residential care. *Beds* SNF 120; ICF 28;
Residential care 78. *Certified* Medicaid;
Medicare.
Owner Nonprofit corp.
Staff Physicians 5 (pt); RNs 3 (ft); LPNs 1
(pt); Nurses' aides 12 (ft), 5 (pt); Physical
therapists 2 (pt); Occupational therapists 1
(pt); Speech therapists 1 (pt); Activities
coordinators 1 (ft); Dietitians 1 (ft); Dentists
1 (pt).
Affiliation Lutheran.
Facilities Dining room; Physical therapy
room; Activities room; Chapel; Crafts room;
Barber/Beauty shop.
Activities Arts & crafts; Cards; Games;
Reading groups; Movies.

Cool Valley

Bell Crest Inc
1301 S Florissant Rd, Cool Valley, MO 63121
(314) 521-6060
Admin Gayla Bentley.
Medical Dir Ranore Davison.
Licensure Intermediate care. *Beds* ICF 77.
Owner Proprietary corp.
Admissions Requirements Medical
examination.
Staff Physicians 1 (pt); RNs 1 (ft), 2 (pt);
LPNs 1 (ft); Nurses' aides 20 (ft), 10 (pt);
Physical therapists 1 (pt); Recreational
therapists 1 (ft); Occupational therapists 1
(pt); Speech therapists 1 (pt); Activities
coordinators 1 (ft); Dietitians 1 (pt);
Ophthalmologists 1 (pt).
Facilities Dining room; Activities room;
Crafts room; Laundry room; Barber/Beauty
shop; Van.
Activities Arts & crafts; Cards; Games;
Reading groups; Prayer groups; Shopping
trips; Dances/Social/Cultural gatherings.

Crane

Crane Health Care Center
127 NW Blvd, Crane, MO 65633
(417) 723-5281
Admin James S Dodds.
Licensure Skilled care; Intermediate care. *Beds* Swing beds SNF/ICF 120. *Certified* Medicaid; Medicare.
Owner Proprietary corp.

Creve Coeur

Evergreen Nursing Home & Rehabilitation Center Inc
12705 Olive Street Rd, Creve Coeur, MO 63141
(314) 434-8361
Admin Sherwin J Abrams.
Medical Dir Thomas Margulies.
Licensure Skilled care. *Beds* SNF 147. *Certified* Medicaid; Medicare.
Owner Proprietary corp.
Admissions Requirements Medical examination.
Facilities Dining room; Physical therapy room; Activities room; Chapel; Crafts room; Laundry room; Barber/Beauty shop; Library; Enclosed open air courtyard.
Activities Arts & crafts; Cards; Games; Reading groups; Prayer groups; Movies.

Fairview Gardens
850 Country Manor Ln, Box 12817, Creve Coeur, MO 63141
(314) 434-5900
Licensure Skilled care. *Beds* SNF 152. *Certified* Medicaid.
Owner Proprietary corp.

Cuba

Community Care Center of Cuba Inc
410 N Franklin, Cuba, MO 65453
(314) 885-2150
Admin Leigh Ann McGuirk. *Dir of Nursing* Joan Jolley. *Medical Dir* Dr G Riffel.
Licensure Skilled care. *Beds* SNF 65. *Certified* Medicaid; Medicare.
Owner Proprietary corp (Community Care Centers).
Admissions Requirements Minimum age 21; Medical examination.
Staff Physicians 1 (pt); RNs 2 (ft); LPNs 3 (ft), 5 (pt) 38 (ft); Physical therapists 1 (pt); Occupational therapists 1 (pt); Speech therapists 1 (pt); Activities coordinators 1 (ft); Dietitians 1 (pt); Ophthalmologists 1 (pt); Podiatrists 1 (pt); Dentists 1 (pt).
Facilities Dining room; Physical therapy room; Activities room; Chapel; Crafts room; Laundry room; Barber/Beauty shop.
Activities Arts & crafts; Cards; Games; Reading groups; Prayer groups; Movies; Shopping trips; Dances/Social/Cultural gatherings.

Des Peres

Des Peres Health Care
11692 Manchester Rd, Des Peres, MO 63131
(314) 966-3350
Admin Jennifer Gettman. *Dir of Nursing* Patricia Coleman RN. *Medical Dir* Varkey Phillip MD.
Licensure Skilled care. *Beds* SNF 143. *Private Pay Patients* 70%. *Certified* Medicaid; Medicare.
Owner Proprietary corp (Hillhaven Corp).
Admissions Requirements Minimum age 16; Physician's request.
Staff RNs 8 (ft), 1 (pt); LPNs 6 (ft), 1 (pt); Nurses' aides 60 (ft), 4 (pt); Physical therapists 1 (pt); Reality therapists 1 (pt); Recreational therapists 1 (ft); Occupational therapists 1 (pt); Speech therapists 1 (pt);

Activities coordinators 1 (ft), 1 (pt); Dietitians 1 (ft); Ophthalmologists 1 (pt); Podiatrists 1 (pt); Audiologists 1 (pt).
Facilities Dining room; Physical therapy room; Activities room; Barber/Beauty shop; Library.
Activities Arts & crafts; Cards; Games; Reading groups; Prayer groups; Movies; Shopping trips; Dances/Social/Cultural gatherings; Intergenerational programs; Pet therapy.

DeSoto

Burt Manor
Rte 1 Box 197A, DeSoto, MO 63020
(314) 586-2291
Admin Mary K Baisch. *Dir of Nursing* Monica Pashia RN. *Medical Dir* Michael K Blank MD.
Licensure Intermediate care. *Beds* ICF 61.
Owner Proprietary corp.
Admissions Requirements Minimum age 18; Medical examination; Physician's request.
Staff Physicians 2 (pt); RNs 1 (ft); LPNs 5 (ft); Nurses' aides 16 (ft), 10 (pt); Physical therapists; Occupational therapists; Speech therapists; Activities coordinators; Dietitians.
Facilities Dining room; Activities room; Barber/Beauty shop.
Activities Cards; Games; Prayer groups; Shopping trips; Dances/Social/Cultural gatherings.

Dexter

Crowley Ridge Care Center
PO Box 668, Hwy 60 W, Dexter, MO 63841
(314) 624-5557
Admin Karen Elliott.
Licensure Skilled care; Intermediate care. *Beds* Swing beds SNF/ICF 87. *Certified* Medicaid.
Owner Proprietary corp.

Dexter Nursing Center
PO Box 517, Dexter, MO 63841
(314) 624-7491
Admin Jacqueline McCollom.
Licensure Skilled care. *Beds* SNF 83. *Certified* Medicaid.
Owner Proprietary corp (Beverly Enterprises).

Sunshine Manor I
Star Rte Box 150-B, Dexter, MO 63841
(314) 568-2050
Admin Patsy Davis.
Licensure Intermediate care. *Beds* ICF 20. *Private Pay Patients* 0%. *Certified* Medicaid; Medicare.
Owner Privately owned.
Facilities Dining room; Activities room; Laundry room; Barber/Beauty shop; Private rooms.
Activities Games; Prayer groups; Movies; Shopping trips; Dances/Social/Cultural gatherings; Pet therapy.

Vintage Villa Nursing Center
PO Box 514, 228 E Market, Dexter, MO 63841
(314) 624-8908, 624-2239 FAX
Admin Linda McRoberts. *Dir of Nursing* Patty Stone RN. *Medical Dir* Tom Henderson MD.
Licensure Skilled care; Intermediate care; Medicare. *Beds* Swing beds SNF/ICF 60. *Private Pay Patients* 10%. *Certified* Medicaid; Medicare.
Owner Proprietary corp (Americare Systems Inc).
Admissions Requirements Minimum age 21; Medical examination; Physician's request.
Staff Physicians 4 (pt); RNs 1 (ft), 4 (pt); LPNs 14 (ft), 4 (pt); Nurses' aides 20 (ft), 6 (pt); Physical therapists 2 (ft); Occupational therapists 1 (pt); Speech therapists 1 (ft);

Activities coordinators 1 (ft); Dietitians 1 (ft); Ophthalmologists 4 (pt); Podiatrists 1 (pt); Administrators 1 (ft).
Facilities Dining room; Physical therapy room; Activities room; Laundry room; Barber/Beauty shop.
Activities Arts & crafts; Cards; Games; Reading groups; Prayer groups; Movies; Shopping trips; Dances/Social/Cultural gatherings; Pet therapy.

Doniphan

Doniphan Retirement Home
PO Box 130, Hwy 142 E, Doniphan, MO 63935
(314) 996-2191
Admin Robert W Adams. *Dir of Nursing* Cinthia Burns RN. *Medical Dir* Fred Caldwell MD.
Licensure Skilled care; Intermediate care. *Beds* SNF 60; ICF 30. *Private Pay Patients* 9%. *Certified* Medicaid; Medicare.
Owner Proprietary corp.
Admissions Requirements Medical examination; Physician's request.
Staff Physicians 3 (pt); RNs 3 (ft), 1 (pt); LPNs 6 (ft), 2 (pt); Physical therapists 1 (pt); Recreational therapists 1 (pt); Occupational therapists 1 (pt); Speech therapists 1 (pt); Activities coordinators 1 (ft); Dietitians (consultant).
Facilities Dining room; Physical therapy room; Laundry room; Barber/Beauty shop.
Activities Arts & crafts; Cards; Games; Reading groups; Movies; Intergenerational programs; Pet therapy.

East Prairie

East Prairie Nursing Center
PO Box 299, 21 Millar Rd, East Prairie, MO 63845
(314) 649-3551
Admin Karen J Elliott. *Dir of Nursing* JoAnne Alexander. *Medical Dir* Dr A L Weaver.
Licensure Skilled care; Intermediate care. *Beds* Swing beds SNF/ICF 70. *Private Pay Patients* 8%. *Certified* Medicaid.
Owner Proprietary corp.
Staff Physicians 1 (ft), 1 (pt); RNs 1 (ft), 3 (pt); LPNs 4 (ft), 3 (pt); Nurses' aides 20 (ft), 7 (pt); Physical therapists 1 (ft), 1 (pt); Reality therapists (consultant); Recreational therapists (consultant); Occupational therapists (consultant); Speech therapists (consultant); Activities coordinators 1 (ft); Dietitians 1 (ft); Ophthalmologists (consultant); Podiatrists (consultant); Audiologists (consultant).
Facilities Dining room; Physical therapy room; Activities room; Laundry room; Barber/Beauty shop; Dayroom.
Activities Arts & crafts; Cards; Games; Prayer groups; Movies; Shopping trips; Dances/Social/Cultural gatherings; Pet therapy; Fishing; Trips to park.

Edina

Knox County Nursing Home
Hwy 6 E, Edina, MO 63537
(816) 397-2282
Admin Gerald Foreman. *Dir of Nursing* Helen Karhoff LPN.
Licensure Intermediate care. *Beds* ICF 60. *Private Pay Patients* 50%. *Certified* Medicaid.
Owner Nonprofit organization/foundation.
Staff Physicians 1 (pt); RNs 1 (ft); LPNs 3 (ft), 2 (pt); Nurses' aides 8 (ft), 38 (pt); Physical therapists 1 (pt); Occupational therapists 1 (pt); Speech therapists 1 (pt); Activities coordinators 1 (pt); Dietitians 1 (ft).

Facilities Dining room; Activities room; Chapel; Crafts room; Laundry room; Barber/Beauty shop.
Activities Arts & crafts; Cards; Games; Reading groups; Prayer groups; Movies.

El Dorado Springs

Community Care Center
400 E Hospital Rd, El Dorado Springs, MO 64744
(417) 876-2531
Licensure Intermediate care. Beds ICF 120. Certified Medicaid.
Owner Proprietary corp (Beverly Enterprises).

Eldon

Eldon Health Care Center
Rte 1 Box 450, Eldon, MO 65026
(314) 392-3164
Admin Cathy S Brinker. Dir of Nursing Marion Hibdon RN. Medical Dir Robert Mason DO.
Licensure Skilled care. Beds SNF 60. Private Pay Patients 38%. Certified Medicaid; Medicare.
Owner Nonprofit organization/foundation (International Elderly Care).
Admissions Requirements Minimum age 16; Medical examination; Physician's request.
Staff RNs 1 (ft); LPNs 2 (ft), 1 (pt); Nurses' aides 11 (ft), 16 (pt); Activities coordinators 1 (ft).
Facilities Dining room; Physical therapy room; Laundry room; Barber/Beauty shop; Library; Living room; Solarium; Whirlpool bath.
Activities Arts & crafts; Cards; Games; Reading groups; Prayer groups; Movies; Shopping trips; Dances/Social/Cultural gatherings; Book & newspaper reading; Monthly birthday parties; Music programs; Special meals & holiday parties; Exercise group; Coffee group; Resident council; Active community auxiliary; Special pet visitor (dog).

Ellington

Brent B Tinnin Manor
E Polk Dr, Ellington, MO 63638
(314) 663-2545
Admin Mary Ann Wagy.
Licensure Skilled care; Intermediate care. Beds Swing beds SNF/ICF 60. Certified Medicaid; Medicare.
Owner Proprietary corp.

Ellisville

Westwinds Geriatric Center
16062 Manchester Rd, Ellisville, MO 63011
(314) 227-5000
Admin Ronald E Rogers.
Licensure Intermediate care. Beds 120. Certified Medicaid.
Owner Proprietary corp.

Elsberry

Elsberry Missouri Health Care Center
Rte 2 Box 26, Elsberry, MO 63343
(314) 898-2880
Admin George Stonebraker. Dir of Nursing Hazel Gladney.
Licensure Intermediate care. Beds ICF 60. Certified Medicaid.
Owner Nonprofit corp.
Admissions Requirements Minimum age 18; Medical examination.

Staff RNs 1 (pt); LPNs 3 (ft), 1 (pt); Nurses' aides 17 (ft), 7 (pt); Physical therapists 1 (pt); Occupational therapists 1 (pt); Speech therapists 1 (pt); Activities coordinators 1 (ft); Dietitians 1 (pt).
Facilities Dining room; Physical therapy room; Laundry room; Barber/Beauty shop.
Activities Arts & crafts; Cards; Games; Reading groups; Prayer groups; Movies; Shopping trips; Dances/Social/Cultural gatherings.

Eureka

Marymount Manor
PO Box 600, 313 Augustine Rd, Eureka, MO 63025
(314) 938-6770
Admin David Richardson; Kathi Kissinger. Dir of Nursing Thelma Gand RN. Medical Dir R Gavini MD.
Licensure Skilled care; Residential care. Beds SNF 146; Residential care 134. Certified Medicaid; Medicare.
Owner Privately owned.
Admissions Requirements Minimum age 21; Medical examination; Physician's request.
Staff Physicians 2 (pt); RNs 3 (ft), 3 (pt); LPNs 8 (ft), 4 (pt); Nurses' aides 48 (ft), 10 (pt); Physical therapists 1 (pt); Reality therapists 1 (pt); Occupational therapists 1 (pt); Speech therapists 1 (pt); Activities coordinators 3 (ft), 2 (pt); Dietitians 1 (pt); Ophthalmologists 1 (pt).
Facilities Dining room; Physical therapy room; Activities room; Crafts room; Laundry room; Barber/Beauty shop; Library; Visiting rooms.
Activities Arts & crafts; Cards; Games; Reading groups; Prayer groups; Movies; Shopping trips; Dances/Social/Cultural gatherings.

Price Memorial
PO Box 476, Forby Rd, Eureka, MO 63025
(314) 587-3200
Admin John Spilaosf.
Licensure Skilled care. Beds SNF 120. Certified Medicaid; Medicare.
Owner Nonprofit corp.

St Joseph's Hill Infirmary Inc
Saint Joseph's Rd, Eureka, MO 63025
(314) 938-5090
Admin Br Bernard Trosa.
Licensure Skilled care. Beds SNF 130.
Owner Nonprofit corp.
Affiliation Roman Catholic.

Excelsior Springs

Excelsior Springs Care Center
1410 Hospital Dr, Excelsior Springs, MO 64024
(816) 637-1010
Admin Mary Beth Johnson.
Medical Dir James Soeldner MD.
Licensure Skilled care. Beds SNF 120. Certified Medicaid.
Owner Proprietary corp (Beverly Enterprises).
Staff RNs 2 (ft), 2 (pt); LPNs 7 (ft), 2 (pt); Nurses' aides 35 (ft), 10 (pt); Activities coordinators 1 (ft), 1 (pt).
Facilities Dining room; Physical therapy room; Activities room; Barber/Beauty shop.
Activities Arts & crafts; Games; Reading groups; Prayer groups; Shopping trips; Dances/Social/Cultural gatherings.

Farmington

Bayless Boarding Home
PO Box 288, Rte 3, Farmington, MO 63640
(314) 756-2856
Admin Emma Lee Bayless.
Licensure Intermediate care. Beds ICF 4.
Owner Privately owned.

Admissions Requirements Males only.
Facilities Dining room; Activities room; Laundry room.
Activities Arts & crafts; Cards; Games; Movies; Shopping trips; Dances/Social/Cultural gatherings.

Camelot Nursing Center
705 Grand Canyon, Farmington, MO 63640
(314) 756-8911
Admin Barbara J Boyd. Dir of Nursing Linda King. Medical Dir Dr Robert Huckstep.
Licensure Skilled care. Beds SNF 90. Private Pay Patients 10%. Certified Medicaid; Medicare.
Owner Proprietary corp (Beverly Enterprises).
Admissions Requirements Medical examination; Physician's request.
Staff RNs 4 (ft), 1 (pt); LPNs 7 (ft), 3 (pt); Nurses' aides 33 (ft), 4 (pt); Physical therapists; Activities coordinators 1 (ft).
Facilities Dining room; Physical therapy room; Activities room; Laundry room; Barber/Beauty shop.
Activities Arts & crafts; Cards; Games; Reading groups; Prayer groups; Movies; Shopping trips; Dances/Social/Cultural gatherings; Intergenerational programs; Pet therapy.

Carriage Manor Care Center
PO Box 675, 508 N Washington, Farmington, MO 63640
(314) 756-5376
Admin Bruce Harris. Dir of Nursing Carol Hoffman.
Licensure Intermediate care; Retirement. Beds ICF 30; Retirement 4.
Owner Privately owned.
Admissions Requirements Medical examination.
Staff Physicians 1 (ft); RNs 1 (pt); LPNs 1 (ft), 1 (pt); Nurses' aides 10 (ft); Physical therapists 1 (pt); Activities coordinators 1 (ft); Dietitians 1 (ft).
Facilities Dining room; Laundry room; Library.
Activities Arts & crafts; Cards; Games; Pet therapy.

Thomas Dell Nursing Home & Manor Inc
PO Box 452, 773 Weber Rd, Farmington, MO 63640
(314) 756-6716
Admin Lester J Straughan; Janet Straughan.
Licensure Intermediate care; Residential care. Beds ICF 70; Residential care 22.
Owner Proprietary corp.

Easter's Home of Ruth Inc
401 S Henry, Farmington, MO 63640
(314) 756-4559
Admin Thomas W Straughan.
Licensure Intermediate care; Alzheimer's care. Beds ICF 42.
Owner Privately owned.
Admissions Requirements Minimum age 17.
Staff Physicians; RNs; LPNs; Nurses' aides; Physical therapists; Reality therapists; Recreational therapists; Occupational therapists; Speech therapists; Activities coordinators; Dietitians; Podiatrists.
Facilities Dining room; Activities room; Chapel; Crafts room; Laundry room; Barber/Beauty shop.
Activities Arts & crafts; Cards; Games; Reading groups; Prayer groups; Movies; Shopping trips; Dances/Social/Cultural gatherings; Intergenerational programs; Pet therapy.

Fleur de Lis
1108 W Liberty, Farmington, MO 63640
(314) 756-6658
Admin Pearl Underwood. Dir of Nursing Martha Young.
Licensure Intermediate care. Beds ICF 104. Certified Medicaid.

Owner Proprietary corp (Beverly Enterprises).
Admissions Requirements Minimum age 18;
  Medical examination; Physician's request.
Staff Physicians; RNs 1 (ft), 1 (pt); LPNs 6
  (ft), 1 (pt); Nurses' aides 26 (ft); Activities
  coordinators 1 (ft); Dietitians 1 (ft).
Facilities Dining room; Physical therapy
  room; Activities room; Crafts room; Laundry
  room; Barber/Beauty shop; Library.
Activities Arts & crafts; Cards; Games;
  Reading groups; Prayer groups; Movies;
  Shopping trips; Dances/Social/Cultural
  gatherings.

Maehill Care Center
783 Weber Rd, Farmington, MO 63640
(314) 756-8998
Admin Jane Coonce.
Licensure Skilled care; Intermediate care. *Beds*
  SNF 16; Swing beds SNF/ICF 2.
Owner Proprietary corp.

Presbyterian Manor at Farmington
500 Manor Court, Farmington, MO 63640
(314) 756-6768
Admin Rev Peter W F Adgie. *Dir of Nursing*
  Lana Jinkerson RN.
Licensure Skilled care; Residential care. *Beds*
  SNF 79; Residential care 60.
Owner Nonprofit corp.
Admissions Requirements Minimum age 65;
  Medical examination.
Staff Physicians 1 (pt); RNs 1 (ft), 1 (pt);
  LPNs 4 (ft), 2 (pt); Nurses' aides 37 (ft), 3
  (pt); Physical therapists 1 (pt); Occupational
  therapists 3 (pt); Activities coordinators 2
  (ft); Dietitians 1 (pt); Podiatrists 1 (pt);
  Dentists 1 (pt).
Affiliation Presbyterian.

Fayette

Phillips Home
303 S Main, Fayette, MO 65248
(816) 248-3333
Admin Lawrence Sapp Jr; Pegi Phillips-Sapp.
Licensure Intermediate care. *Beds* 30.
Owner Proprietary corp.

Southland Care Center
501 S Park, Fayette, MO 65248
(816) 248-3371
Admin Chris E Brown.
Licensure Skilled care; Intermediate care. *Beds*
  Swing beds SNF/ICF 60. *Certified* Medicaid.
Owner Privately owned.

Fenton

Cori Manor Nursing Home
560 Corisande Hill Rd, Fenton, MO 63026
(314) 343-2282, 343-2274 FAX
Admin Connie Radvin BSBA. *Dir of Nursing*
  Vera Eller RN. *Medical Dir* Robert Dorton
  MD.
Licensure Skilled care; Residential care;
  Alzheimer's care. *Beds* SNF 124; Residential
  care 22.
Owner Proprietary corp (Healthcare Corp).
Admissions Requirements Minimum age 17;
  Medical examination.
Staff Physicians 1 (ft); RNs 3 (ft); LPNs 5 (ft);
  Nurses' aides 45 (ft); Physical therapists 2
  (ft), 1 (pt); Occupational therapists 1 (pt);
  Speech therapists 1 (pt); Activities
  coordinators 2 (ft); Dietitians 1 (pt);
  Ophthalmologists 1 (pt); Podiatrists 1 (pt);
  Dentists 1 (pt).
Languages German, Spanish.
Facilities Dining room; Physical therapy
  room; Activities room; Crafts room; Laundry
  room; Barber/Beauty shop; Library; Living
  room.

Activities Arts & crafts; Cards; Games;
  Reading groups; Prayer groups; Movies;
  Shopping trips; Dances/Social/Cultural
  gatherings; Intergenerational programs; Pet
  therapy; Bowling; Church services.

Fieser Nursing Home
PO Box F, 404 Main, Fenton, MO 63026
(314) 343-4344
Admin Glen E Fieser. *Dir of Nursing* Gwen
  Stevens RN. *Medical Dir* R Kaza MD.
Licensure Intermediate care; Alzheimer's care.
  Beds ICF 60.
Owner Proprietary corp.
Admissions Requirements Medical
  examination.
Staff Physicians 1 (pt); RNs 3 (ft); LPNs 1
  (pt); Nurses' aides 18 (ft), 2 (pt); Physical
  therapists 1 (pt); Reality therapists 1 (pt);
  Recreational therapists 1 (pt); Occupational
  therapists 1 (pt); Speech therapists 1 (pt);
  Dietitians 1 (pt); Ophthalmologists 1 (pt);
  Podiatrists 1 (pt).
Facilities Dining room; Physical therapy
  room; Activities room; Crafts room; Laundry
  room; Barber/Beauty shop.
Activities Arts & crafts; Cards; Games;
  Reading groups; Prayer groups; Movies;
  Shopping trips; Dances/Social/Cultural
  gatherings.

Ferguson

Christian Old People's Home
800 Chambers Rd, Ferguson, MO 63135
(314) 522-8100
Admin Richard Klug. *Dir of Nursing* T
  Gestring RN. *Medical Dir* D Rosenberg
  MD.
Licensure Skilled care; Retirement. *Beds* SNF
  120. *Certified* Medicaid.
Admissions Requirements Minimum age 65.
Staff Physicians 4 (pt); RNs 5 (ft), 4 (pt);
  LPNs 4 (ft), 8 (pt); Nurses' aides 39 (ft), 19
  (pt); Physical therapists 2 (ft); Activities
  coordinators 3 (ft); Dietitians 1 (ft);
  Podiatrists 1 (pt); Dentists 1 (pt).
Facilities Dining room; Physical therapy
  room; Activities room; Chapel; Crafts room;
  Laundry room; Barber/Beauty shop; Library.
Activities Arts & crafts; Cards; Games;
  Reading groups; Prayer groups; Movies;
  Shopping trips; Dances/Social/Cultural
  gatherings.

Oak Knoll Nursing Home
37 N Clark, Ferguson, MO 63135
(314) 521-7419
Admin Eunice Schuerman. *Dir of Nursing* Ida
  Johnson. *Medical Dir* R A Latorpe MD.
Licensure Intermediate care; Alzheimer's care.
  Beds ICF 60.
Owner Proprietary corp.
Staff Physicians 1 (ft); RNs 2 (ft), 1 (pt);
  LPNs 1 (ft), 3 (pt); Dietitians 1 (ft).
Facilities Dining room; Activities room;
  Chapel; Crafts room; Laundry room; Barber/
  Beauty shop; Library.
Activities Arts & crafts; Cards; Games;
  Reading groups; Prayer groups; Movies;
  Shopping trips; Dances/Social/Cultural
  gatherings; Garden club.

Festus

Community Care Center of Festus
RR 1 Box 427, Festus, MO 63028
(314) 464-6220
Admin Connie D Marshall.
Licensure Skilled care. *Beds* SNF 81. *Certified*
  Medicaid.
Owner Proprietary corp.
Admissions Requirements Minimum age 18.
Staff Physicians; RNs; LPNs; Nurses' aides;
  Physical therapists; Speech therapists;
  Activities coordinators; Dietitians.

Facilities Dining room; Physical therapy
  room; Activities room; Laundry room;
  Barber/Beauty shop.
Activities Arts & crafts; Cards; Games;
  Reading groups; Prayer groups; Movies;
  Shopping trips; Dances/Social/Cultural
  gatherings.

Festus Manor
PO Box 548, Festus, MO 63028
(314) 937-9066
Admin Sharon Greco. *Dir of Nursing* Joanne
  Nash RN. *Medical Dir* Dr Moorthy.
Licensure Skilled care. *Beds* SNF 120.
  Certified Medicaid.
Owner Proprietary corp (Beverly Enterprises).
Admissions Requirements Minimum age 16.
Staff RNs 7 (ft); LPNs 8 (ft); Nurses' aides 55
  (ft), 6 (pt); Activities coordinators 1 (ft);
  Dietitians 1 (ft).
Facilities Dining room; Physical therapy
  room; Activities room; Crafts room; Laundry
  room; Barber/Beauty shop; Library.
Activities Arts & crafts; Cards; Games;
  Reading groups; Prayer groups; Movies;
  Shopping trips; Dances/Social/Cultural
  gatherings.

Jefferson Nursing Center
827 American Legion Dr, Festus, MO 63028
(314) 937-4644
Admin Maxine Boschert.
Licensure Skilled care. *Beds* SNF 90.
Owner Proprietary corp.

Flat River

Country Meadows Retirement Center
PO Box 545, 1301 Saint Joe Dr, Flat River,
  MO 63601
(314) 431-2889, 431-6411 FAX
Admin Margaret Parks. *Dir of Nursing* Sheila
  Skiles RN. *Medical Dir* Perry Bramhall DO.
Licensure Skilled care. *Beds* SNF 60. *Certified*
  Medicaid.
Owner Proprietary corp.
Admissions Requirements Medical
  examination.
Staff RNs 2 (ft), 1 (pt); LPNs 2 (ft), 1 (pt);
  Nurses' aides; Activities coordinators 1 (pt);
  Dietitians.
Facilities Dining room; Physical therapy
  room; Activities room; Laundry room;
  Barber/Beauty shop.
Activities Arts & crafts; Cards; Games;
  Reading groups; Prayer groups; Movies;
  Dances/Social/Cultural gatherings;
  Intergenerational programs; Pet therapy.

Desloge Health Care Center
PO Box AA, 801 Brim St, Flat River, MO
  63601
(314) 431-0223
Admin W Bruce Bible.
Medical Dir C W Chastain MD.
Licensure Skilled care. *Beds* SNF 120.
  Certified Medicaid; Medicare.
Owner Proprietary corp (National Health
  Corp).
Admissions Requirements Minimum age 18.
Staff Physicians 1 (pt); RNs 4 (ft); LPNs 14
  (ft), 6 (pt); Nurses' aides 30 (ft), 12 (pt);
  Physical therapists 2 (pt); Occupational
  therapists 1 (pt); Speech therapists 1 (pt);
  Activities coordinators 1 (ft); Dietitians 1
  (pt).
Facilities Dining room; Physical therapy
  room; Activities room; Crafts room; Laundry
  room; Barber/Beauty shop.
Activities Arts & crafts; Cards; Games;
  Reading groups; Prayer groups; Movies;
  Shopping trips; Dances/Social/Cultural
  gatherings.

Florissant

Americana Healthcare Center
1200 Graham Rd, Florissant, MO 63031
(314) 838-6555
Admin Anita Martinez. *Dir of Nursing* Sharon
McGauly. *Medical Dir* Stephen Hadzima.
Licensure Skilled care; Intermediate care. *Beds*
SNF 76; ICF 22. *Private Pay Patients* 80%.
Certified Medicaid; Medicare.
Owner Proprietary corp (Manor Care Inc).
Admissions Requirements Minimum age 18;
Medical examination.
Facilities Dining room; Physical therapy
room; Activities room; Chapel; Crafts room;
Laundry room; Barber/Beauty shop; Library;
Courtyards; Wheelchair accessible private
dining room.
Activities Arts & crafts; Cards; Games;
Reading groups; Prayer groups; Movies;
Shopping trips; Dances/Social/Cultural
gatherings; Intergenerational programs; Pet
therapy; Community service; Holiday
functions; Religious services.

Delmar Gardens North
4401 Parker Rd, Florissant, MO 63023
(314) 355-1516
Admin Catherine Bono. *Dir of Nursing* Linda
Moran. *Medical Dir* Barre Dandumidi.
Licensure Skilled care; Intermediate care. *Beds*
Swing beds SNF/ICF 180. *Certified*
Medicaid; Medicare.
Owner Proprietary corp.
Staff RNs; LPNs; Nurses' aides; Physical
therapists; Recreational therapists 3 (ft);
Occupational therapists; Speech therapists;
Dietitians; Podiatrists; Audiologists.

Florissant Nursing Center
615 Rancho Ln, Florissant, MO 63031
(314) 839-2150
Admin Natalie Colvis. *Dir of Nursing* Pat
Broemmel RN. *Medical Dir* Dr V Philip
MD.
Licensure Skilled care; Intermediate care. *Beds*
Swing beds SNF/ICF 120. *Certified*
Medicaid; Medicare.
Owner Proprietary corp (Beverly Enterprises).
Admissions Requirements Medical
examination.
Facilities Dining room; Physical therapy
room; Activities room; Crafts room; Barber/
Beauty shop.
Activities Arts & crafts; Cards; Games; Prayer
groups; Movies; Dances/Social/Cultural
gatherings; Intergenerational programs.

Fountainhead Manor
6768 N Hwy 67, Florissant, MO 63034
(314) 741-9101
Admin Judy Mincher.
Licensure Skilled care. *Beds* SNF 120.
Owner Privately owned.

Northgate Park Nursing Home
250 New Florissant Rd, Florissant, MO 63031
(314) 838-2211
Admin Yvonne Hopmann RN. *Dir of Nursing*
Carolyn Carroll. *Medical Dir* Joan Mass
MD.
Licensure Skilled care; Residential caree. *Beds*
SNF 180; Residential care 150. *Private Pay
Patients* 100%.
Owner Proprietary corp.
Staff Physicians 7 (pt); RNs 4 (ft), 6 (pt);
LPNs 6 (ft), 4 (pt); Nurses' aides 58 (ft), 17
(pt); Physical therapists 2 (pt); Occupational
therapists 1 (pt); Speech therapists 1 (pt);
Activities coordinators 1 (ft); Dietitians 1
(pt); Ophthalmologists 1 (pt); Podiatrists 1
(pt); Audiologists 1 (pt).
Facilities Dining room; Physical therapy
room; Activities room; Crafts room; Laundry
room; Barber/Beauty shop.

Activities Arts & crafts; Cards; Games;
Reading groups; Prayer groups; Movies;
Shopping trips; Dances/Social/Cultural
gatherings; Intergenerational programs; Pet
therapy.

St Sophia Geriatric Center
936 Charbonier Rd, Florissant, MO 63031
(314) 831-4800
Admin Edward Dering.
Licensure Skilled care. *Beds* SNF 240.
Certified Medicaid; Medicare.
Owner Proprietary corp.

Spanish Lake Nursing Center
13700 Old Halls Ferry, Florissant, MO 63033
(314) 355-6660
Admin David G Mixon. *Dir of Nursing*
Sharon Coulborn RN. *Medical Dir* Dr V
Philips.
Licensure Skilled care. *Beds* SNF 120.
Certified Medicaid.
Owner Proprietary corp (Beverly Enterprises).
Staff Physicians; RNs; LPNs; Nurses' aides;
Physical therapists; Occupational therapists;
Speech therapists; Activities coordinators;
Dietitians; Ophthalmologists; Podiatrists;
Dentists.
Languages Italian, German.
Facilities Dining room; Physical therapy
room; Activities room; Laundry room;
Barber/Beauty shop.
Activities Arts & crafts; Cards; Games;
Reading groups; Prayer groups; Movies;
Shopping trips; Dances/Social/Cultural
gatherings.

Forsyth

Plantation Hills Nursing Home
Rte 5 Box 458, Forsyth, MO 65653
(417) 546-3081
Admin Mary King Long DO. *Dir of Nursing*
Dixie Norton LPN. *Medical Dir* Mary King
Long DO.
Licensure Intermediate care. *Beds* ICF 67.
Private Pay Patients 100%.
Owner Proprietary corp.
Staff RNs 1 (pt); LPNs 2 (pt); Nurses' aides
22 (pt); Activities coordinators 1 (pt);
Dietitians 1 (pt).
Facilities Dining room; Laundry room;
Barber/Beauty shop; Physicians office.
Activities Arts & crafts; Cards; Games; Prayer
groups; Movies.

Fredericktown

Madison Memorial Hospital
College at Wood Ave, Box 431,
Fredericktown, MO 63645
(314) 783-3341
Admin Bill M Seek.
Medical Dir Arthur Newcomb MD.
Licensure Intermediate care. *Beds* 9.
Owner Publicly owned.
Staff Physicians 12 (ft); RNs 2 (ft); LPNs 4
(ft), 2 (pt); Nurses' aides 38 (ft); Physical
therapists 1 (ft); Speech therapists 1 (pt);
Activities coordinators 1 (ft); Dietitians 2
(ft).
Facilities Dining room; Physical therapy
room; Activities room; Chapel; Crafts room;
Laundry room; Barber/Beauty shop.
Activities Arts & crafts; Games; Reading
groups; Prayer groups; Movies; Dances/
Social/Cultural gatherings.

Ozark Nursing Home
700 S Main, Fredericktown, MO 63645
(314) 783-6333
Admin Frank Voertmann. *Dir of Nursing*
Wanda Grisson. *Medical Dir* Dr
Bentingannon.
Licensure Intermediate care. *Beds* ICF 42.
Private Pay Patients 70%.
Owner Privately owned.

Admissions Requirements Minimum age 40.
Staff RNs 1 (pt); LPNs 1 (ft), 1 (pt); Nurses'
aides 8 (ft), 2 (pt); Activities coordinators 1
(pt).
Facilities Dining room; Activities room;
Laundry room; Barber/Beauty shop.
Activities Arts & crafts; Cards; Games;
Reading groups; Prayer groups; Movies;
Shopping trips; Intergenerational programs;
Pet therapy.

Fulton

Fulton Manor Care Center
520 Manor Dr, Fulton, MO 65251
(314) 642-6834
Admin Catherine Woodson.
Medical Dir Dr George Grace.
Licensure Intermediate care. *Beds* ICF 52.
Owner Proprietary corp.
Admissions Requirements Minimum age Birth;
Medical examination; Physician's request.
Staff RNs 1 (pt); LPNs 3 (ft), 1 (pt); Nurses'
aides 10 (ft), 4 (pt); Activities coordinators 1
(pt).
Facilities Dining room; Activities room;
Laundry room.
Activities Arts & crafts; Cards; Games;
Reading groups; Prayer groups; Movies.

Fulton Presbyterian Manor
811 Center St, Fulton, MO 65251
(314) 642-6646
Admin Jane E Danie-Mitchell.
Licensure Intermediate care; Residential care.
Beds ICF 36; Residential care 41. *Certified*
Medicaid.
Owner Nonprofit corp.
Affiliation Presbyterian.

Heartland of Fulton
1510 Bluff St, Fulton, MO 65251
(314) 642-0202
Admin Martha Steward.
Licensure Skilled care; Intermediate care. *Beds*
Swing beds SNF/ICF 100. *Certified*
Medicaid; Medicare.
Owner Proprietary corp (Health Care
Retirement Corp).

Kingdom Nursing Home Association Inc
RR 6, 501 Collier Ln, Fulton, MO 65251
(314) 642-2022
Admin Pat Burton LPN. *Dir of Nursing* Sheila
Pattillo LPN.
Licensure Intermediate care. *Beds* ICF 28.
Certified Medicaid.
Owner Nonprofit corp.
Admissions Requirements Medical
examination.
Staff Physicians 5 (pt); RNs 1 (pt); LPNs 2
(ft), 2 (pt); Nurses' aides 6 (ft), 11 (pt);
Physical therapists 1 (pt); Reality therapists
1 (pt); Recreational therapists 1 (pt);
Occupational therapists 1 (pt); Speech
therapists 1 (pt); Activities coordinators 1
(pt); Dietitians 1 (pt); Ophthalmologists 1
(pt); Podiatrists 1 (pt); Dentists 1 (pt).
Facilities Dining room; Physical therapy
room; Activities room; Laundry room;
Barber/Beauty shop.
Activities Arts & crafts; Cards; Games;
Reading groups; Prayer groups; Movies;
Shopping trips; Dances/Social/Cultural
gatherings.

Modern Acre Home
Rte 2, Fulton, MO 65251
(314) 642-3160
Admin Sodonia Logan.
Licensure Intermediate care. *Beds* 22.
Owner Proprietary corp.

Sodonia's Home
222 E 6th, Fulton, MO 65251
(314) 642-3160
Admin Warren T Robinson.

Licensure Intermediate care. *Beds* 22.
Owner Proprietary corp.

Gainesville

Gainesville Health Care Center Inc
Box 628, Gainesville, MO 65655
(417) 679-4921
Admin Barbara Henegar.
Licensure Skilled care; Intermediate care. *Beds*
Swing beds SNF/ICF 90. *Certified* Medicaid;
Medicare.
Owner Proprietary corp.

Gallatin

Daviess County Nursing Home Corp
Hwy 6 W, Gallatin, MO 64640
(816) 663-3197
Admin Evelyn Morrissey. *Dir of Nursing*
Patricia A Roe.
Licensure Intermediate care. *Beds* ICF 97.
Private Pay Patients 60%. *Certified*
Medicaid.
Owner Nonprofit corp.
Admissions Requirements Medical
examination.
Staff RNs 1 (ft), 2 (pt); LPNs 5 (ft); Nurses'
aides 35 (ft), 8 (pt); Physical therapists 2 (ft),
1 (pt); Recreational therapists 1 (ft), 2 (pt);
Occupational therapists 1 (pt); Speech
therapists 1 (pt); Activities coordinators 1
(ft); Dietitians 1 (pt).
Facilities Dining room; Physical therapy
room; Activities room; Chapel; Crafts room;
Laundry room; Barber/Beauty shop; Library.
Activities Arts & crafts; Cards; Games;
Reading groups; Prayer groups; Movies;
Shopping trips; Dances/Social/Cultural
gatherings; Pet therapy.

Gallatin Sunrise Center
611 W Johnson, Gallatin, MO 64640
(816) 663-3301
Admin Everett S Boyd. *Dir of Nursing* Nancy
Kretzschmer.
Licensure Intermediate care; Alzheimer's care.
Beds ICF 18. *Private Pay Patients* 50%.
Owner Proprietary corp.
Staff Physicians 2 (ft); RNs 1 (ft); LPNs 2 (ft);
Nurses' aides 5 (ft); Activities coordinators 1
(ft); Dietitians 1 (ft).
Facilities Dining room; Activities room;
Crafts room; Laundry room; Barber/Beauty
shop.
Activities Arts & crafts; Cards; Games;
Reading groups; Movies; Pet therapy.

Gerald

Gerald Caring Center
PO Box 180, Hwy 50, Gerald, MO 63037
(314) 764-2135
Admin Jeffrey D Lincoln.
Licensure Skilled care. *Beds* SNF 60.
Owner Proprietary corp.

Gladstone

Kendallwood Trails Nursing Center Inc
2900 Kendallwood, Gladstone, MO 64119
(816) 453-1222
Admin William D Burford.
Licensure Skilled care. *Beds* SNF 290.
Certified Medicaid; Medicare.
Owner Proprietary corp.

Glasgow

Colonial Manor of Glasgow
100 Audsley Dr, Glasgow, MO 65254
(816) 338-2297
Admin Vici Littrell. *Dir of Nursing* Jan
Murdock. *Medical Dir* William Marshall
MD.

Licensure Intermediate care. *Beds* ICF 59.
Private Pay Patients 45%. *Certified*
Medicaid.
Owner Proprietary corp (Beverly Enterprises).
Admissions Requirements Medical
examination; Physician's request.
Staff LPNs 3 (ft), 1 (pt); Nurses' aides 17 (ft),
1 (pt); Activities coordinators 1 (ft);
Dietitians 1 (ft); Physical therapy aides 1
(ft).
Facilities Dining room; Physical therapy
room; Activities room; Chapel; Crafts room;
Laundry room; Barber/Beauty shop; Library.
Activities Arts & crafts; Cards; Games;
Reading groups; Prayer groups; Movies;
Shopping trips; Intergenerational programs.

Gower

Gower Convalescent Center Inc
Hwy 169 S, Gower, MO 64454
(816) 424-6483
Admin John Ronald Murawski. *Dir of Nursing*
Dorothy Kretzer RN.
Licensure Intermediate care; Retirement. *Beds*
ICF 74. *Certified* Medicaid.
Owner Nonprofit corp.
Admissions Requirements Minimum age 18.
Staff Physicians 2 (pt); RNs 1 (ft); LPNs 3
(ft); Nurses' aides 32 (ft); Physical therapists
1 (pt); Recreational therapists 2 (ft);
Occupational therapists 1 (pt); Speech
therapists 1 (pt); Activities coordinators 1
(ft); Dietitians 1 (pt); Podiatrists 1 (pt).
Facilities Dining room; Physical therapy
room; Activities room; Crafts room; Laundry
room; Barber/Beauty shop; Library.
Activities Arts & crafts; Cards; Games; Prayer
groups; Movies; Dances/Social/Cultural
gatherings.

Grandview

Grandview Manor Care Center
5301 E 125th St, Grandview, MO 64030
(816) 763-2855
Admin Vada Mae Eder RN MA. *Dir of
Nursing* Mary Bragulla.
Licensure Intermediate care. *Beds* ICF 102.
Owner Proprietary corp.
Staff RNs 1 (ft), 3 (pt); LPNs 4 (ft), 2 (pt);
Nurses' aides 20 (ft), 8 (pt); Physical
therapists 1 (pt); Reality therapists 1 (pt);
Recreational therapists 1 (pt); Occupational
therapists 1 (pt); Speech therapists 1 (pt);
Activities coordinators 1 (ft), 1 (pt);
Dietitians 1 (pt); Ophthalmologists 1 (pt).

Longview Nursing Center
6301 E 125th St, Grandview, MO 64030
(816) 765-7714
Admin Sam Fowler. *Dir of Nursing* Lynn
English. *Medical Dir* Dr Kirk Barnett.
Licensure Skilled care. *Beds* SNF 120. *Private
Pay Patients* 7%. *Certified* Medicaid;
Medicare.
Owner Proprietary corp (Beverly Enterprises).
Admissions Requirements Physician's request.
Staff RNs 4 (ft), 2 (pt); LPNs 6 (ft), 1 (pt);
Nurses' aides 20 (ft), 5 (pt); Physical
therapists; Activities coordinators 1 (ft), 1
(pt); Dietitians 1 (pt).
Facilities Dining room; Physical therapy
room; Activities room; Crafts room; Laundry
room; Barber/Beauty shop.
Activities Arts & crafts; Cards; Games;
Reading groups; Prayer groups; Movies;
Shopping trips; Dances/Social/Cultural
gatherings.

Villa Grandview
13111 Spring St, Grandview, MO 64030
(816) 761-4333
Admin Macaela Wilson.
Medical Dir Dr Kirk Barnett.
Licensure Intermediate care. *Beds* ICF 52.
Certified Medicaid.

Owner Proprietary corp (Life Care Centers of
America).
Admissions Requirements Medical
examination.
Staff Physicians 2 (pt); RNs 1 (pt); LPNs 3
(ft), 1 (pt); Nurses' aides 18 (ft), 5 (pt);
Physical therapists 3 (pt); Reality therapists
1 (pt); Occupational therapists 1 (pt); Speech
therapists 1 (pt); Activities coordinators 2
(pt); Dietitians 1 (pt); Podiatrists 1 (pt);
Dentists 1 (pt).
Facilities Dining room; Laundry room.
Activities Arts & crafts; Cards; Games; Prayer
groups.

Grant City

Worth County Convalescent Center
Rte 3 Box 100, 503 E 4th, Grant City, MO
64456
(816) 564-3304
Admin Mary Weaver. *Dir of Nursing* Marcia
Henry RN. *Medical Dir* Richard Swift DO.
Licensure Intermediate care. *Beds* ICF 60.
Private Pay Patients 75%. *Certified*
Medicaid.
Owner Nonprofit organization/foundation.
Admissions Requirements Medical
examination.
Staff Physicians 2 (ft); RNs 2 (ft), 1 (pt);
LPNs 4 (ft), 1 (pt); Nurses' aides 15 (ft), 8
(pt); Physical therapists; Occupational
therapists; Speech therapists 1 (pt); Activities
coordinators 1 (ft); Dietitians 1 (ft);
Audiologists 1 (pt).
Facilities Dining room; Physical therapy
room; Activities room; Chapel; Crafts room;
Laundry room; Barber/Beauty shop.
Activities Arts & crafts; Games; Reading
groups; Prayer groups; Movies; Shopping
trips; Pet therapy.

Greenfield

Dade County Nursing Home District
PO Box 51, 400 Broad St, Greenfield, MO
65661
(417) 637-5315
Admin Judy McGuire. *Dir of Nursing* Mary
Higgins LPN.
Licensure Intermediate care; Residential care.
Beds ICF 120; Residential care 24. *Private
Pay Patients* 45%. *Certified* Medicaid.
Owner Nonprofit organization/foundation.
Admissions Requirements Minimum age 18.
Staff RNs 2 (pt); LPNs 8 (ft), 3 (pt); Nurses'
aides 41 (ft); Physical therapists (consultant);
Occupational therapists (consultant);
Activities coordinators 1 (ft); Dietitians
(consultant); Physical therapy aides 2 (ft).
Facilities Dining room; Physical therapy
room; Activities room; Crafts room; Laundry
room; Barber/Beauty shop; Library.
Activities Arts & crafts; Games; Reading
groups; Prayer groups; Movies; Dances/
Social/Cultural gatherings.

Hallsville

Arah's Acres
Box J, Elizabeth St, Hallsville, MO 65255
(314) 696-2541
Admin Arah Kathryn Hubbard Grimes. *Dir of
Nursing* Mick Bryon RN.
Licensure Intermediate care. *Beds* ICF 18.
Owner Privately owned.
Admissions Requirements Medical
examination.
Staff RNs 1 (pt); LPNs 1 (ft), 1 (pt); Nurses'
aides 9 (ft); Activities coordinators 1 (ft), 1
(pt); Cooks 1 (pt); Housekeepers 1 (ft).
Facilities Dining room; Laundry room;
Barber/Beauty shop.
Activities Cards; Games; Prayer groups;
Shopping trips.

Hamilton

Hamilton Hill Crest Manor
Irwin & Colby Sts, Hamilton, MO 64644
(816) 583-2119
Admin Mark Garges.
Licensure Intermediate care. *Beds* ICF 90.
Certified Medicaid.
Owner Proprietary corp.
Staff Physicians 1 (ft); LPNs 4 (pt); Physical
therapists 2 (pt); Occupational therapists 2
(pt); Speech therapists 1 (pt); Activities
coordinators 1 (ft); Dietitians 1 (pt).
Facilities Dining room; Activities room;
Crafts room; Laundry room; Barber/Beauty
shop.
Activities Arts & crafts; Cards; Games;
Reading groups; Movies; Shopping trips;
Dances/Social/Cultural gatherings.

Hannibal

Beth-Haven Nursing Home
2500 Pleasant St, Hannibal, MO 63401
(314) 221-6000
Admin Paul Ewert.
Licensure Skilled care; Residential care. *Beds*
SNF 76; Residential care 44. *Certified*
Medicaid; Medicare.
Owner Nonprofit corp.

Luther Manor Retirement & Nursing Center
RFD 2, Hwy 61 N, Hannibal, MO 63401
(314) 221-5533
Admin Mary E Greening. *Dir of Nursing*
Gerry Higgins RN.
Licensure Intermediate care; Residential care;
Alzheimer's care. *Beds* ICF 60; Residential
care apts 18. *Private Pay Patients* 70%.
Certified Medicaid.
Owner Nonprofit corp.
Admissions Requirements Medical
examination.
Staff RNs 1 (ft); LPNs 6 (ft); Nurses' aides 21
(ft); Physical therapists 2 (ft); Occupational
therapists 2 (ft); Activities coordinators 1
(ft); Dietitians 1 (ft).
Affiliation Lutheran.
Facilities Dining room; Physical therapy
room; Activities room; Chapel; Crafts room;
Laundry room; Barber/Beauty shop; Library;
Solarium.
Activities Arts & crafts; Cards; Games;
Reading groups; Prayer groups; Movies;
Shopping trips; Dances/Social/Cultural
gatherings; Public buffets; Daily exercises.

Riverview Manor Inc
408 Rock, Hannibal, MO 63401
(314) 221-5910
Admin Phyllis Rupp.
Licensure Intermediate care. *Beds* ICF 39.
Owner Privately owned.

Becky Thatcher Nursing Home
711 Church St, Hannibal, MO 63401
(314) 221-4288
Admin Bill Callicott.
Licensure Intermediate care. *Beds* ICF 23.
Owner Privately owned.

Willow Care Center
Munger Ln, Hannibal, MO 63401
(314) 221-9122
Admin William McBride; David Wendler.
Medical Dir J H Walterscheid MD.
Licensure Skilled care. *Beds* SNF 120.
Certified Medicaid.
Owner Proprietary corp (Beverly Enterprises).
Admissions Requirements Medical
examination; Physician's request.
Facilities Dining room; Physical therapy
room; Activities room; Laundry room;
Barber/Beauty shop; Library.
Activities Arts & crafts; Cards; Games;
Reading groups; Prayer groups; Movies;
Dances/Social/Cultural gatherings.

Harrisonville

ABC Health Center
307 E South St, Harrisonville, MO 64701
(816) 884-3413
Admin Gary Holmes. *Dir of Nursing* Jo
Davis. *Medical Dir* Dr Wheeler.
Licensure Intermediate care. *Beds* ICF 60.
Private Pay Patients 35%. *Certified*
Medicaid.
Owner Proprietary corp (Horizon Healthcare
Corp).
Admissions Requirements Medical
examination.
Staff LPNs 4 (ft), 1 (pt); Nurses' aides 20 (ft);
Activities coordinators 1 (ft); Dietitians 1
(pt).
Facilities Dining room; Physical therapy
room; Activities room; Crafts room; Laundry
room; Barber/Beauty shop.
Activities Arts & crafts; Cards; Games;
Reading groups; Prayer groups; Movies;
Shopping trips; Dances/Social/Cultural
gatherings; Pet therapy.

Camden Health Center
2203 E Mechanic, Harrisonville, MO 64701
(816) 884-2622, 884-2170
Admin Rhonda Tieg.
Medical Dir Richard Price.
Licensure Intermediate care; Residential care.
Beds ICF 105; Residential care 15. *Certified*
Medicaid.
Owner Proprietary corp.
Admissions Requirements Minimum age 16;
Medical examination.
Staff RNs 1 (ft), 1 (pt); LPNs 3 (ft); Nurses'
aides 17 (ft); Recreational therapists 1 (ft);
Activities coordinators 1 (ft).
Facilities Dining room; Physical therapy
room; Activities room; Crafts room; Laundry
room; Barber/Beauty shop.
Activities Arts & crafts; Cards; Games; Prayer
groups; Movies; Shopping trips; Dances/
Social/Cultural gatherings.

Golden Years
2001 Jefferson Pkwy, Harrisonville, MO
64701
(816) 884-4731
Admin Kevin W Wood. *Dir of Nursing* Renee
Endicott RN. *Medical Dir* Richard C Price
MD.
Licensure Skilled care; Residential care. *Beds*
SNF 108; Residential care 24. *Private Pay
Patients* 60%. *Certified* Medicaid; Medicare.
Owner Proprietary corp.
Admissions Requirements Minimum age 40;
Medical examination.
Staff Physicians 4 (pt); RNs 2 (ft), 3 (pt);
LPNs 9 (ft); Nurses' aides 28 (ft); Physical
therapists 1 (pt); Recreational therapists 1
(ft); Occupational therapists 1 (pt); Speech
therapists 1 (pt); Activities coordinators 1
(ft); Dietitians 1 (ft).
Facilities Dining room; Physical therapy
room; Activities room; Laundry room;
Barber/Beauty shop.
Activities Arts & crafts; Cards; Games;
Reading groups; Prayer groups; Movies;
Shopping trips; Dances/Social/Cultural
gatherings; Intergenerational programs; Pet
therapy.

Pleasant View Rest Home
PO Box 423, Rte 2, 2001 County Home Rd,
Harrisonville, MO 64701
(816) 884-4731
Admin ALice C Reed.
Licensure Intermediate care. *Beds* 43.
Owner Proprietary corp.

Hayti

**Pemiscot Memorial Hospital Long-Term/
Skilled Care Unit**
PO Box 489, Hayti, MO 63851
(314) 359-1372, 359-2940 FAX
Admin Glenn D Haynes. *Dir of Nursing* Gearl
V Adams RN. *Medical Dir* Dr Charles
Craft.
Licensure Skilled care; Intermediate care;
Alzheimer's care. *Beds* SNF 23; ICF 60.
Private Pay Patients 12%. *Certified*
Medicaid; Medicare.
Owner Publicly owned.
Admissions Requirements Minimum age 18.
Staff Physicians 15 (ft); RNs 3 (ft), 2 (pt);
LPNs 8 (ft), 3 (pt); Nurses' aides 26 (ft), 5
(pt); Physical therapists 2 (pt); Reality
therapists 1 (ft); Recreational therapists 1
(ft); Occupational therapists 1 (pt); Speech
therapists 1 (pt); Activities coordinators 1
(ft); Dietitians 1 (ft); Ophthalmologists 1
(pt); Audiologists 1 (pt).
Facilities Dining room; Physical therapy
room; Activities room; Crafts room; Barber/
Beauty shop.
Activities Arts & crafts; Cards; Games;
Reading groups; Prayer groups; Movies;
Shopping trips; Dances/Social/Cultural
gatherings; Pet therapy.

Herculaneum

Westview Nursing Center
1333 Scenic Dr, Herculaneum, MO 63048
(314) 937-7333
Admin Elizabeth Shannon RN. *Dir of Nursing*
Tonya Milfeld BSN. *Medical Dir* Joseph
Elterman MD.
Licensure Skilled care; Alzheimer's care. *Beds*
SNF 136. *Certified* Medicaid; Medicare.
Owner Privately owned.
Staff RNs; LPNs; Nurses' aides; Physical
therapists 1 (pt); Occupational therapists 1
(pt); Activities coordinators; Dietitians 1
(pt); Ophthalmologists 1 (pt); Dentists 1 (pt);
Psychiatrists 3 (pt).
Facilities Dining room; Physical therapy
room; Activities room; Crafts room; Barber/
Beauty shop; Library.
Activities Arts & crafts; Cards; Games;
Reading groups; Prayer groups; Movies;
Shopping trips; Dances/Social/Cultural
gatherings.

Hermann

Frene Valley Geriatric & Rehabilitation Center
PO Box 292, 18th & Jefferson, Hermann, MO
65041
(314) 486-3193
Admin Ruth Lloyd. *Dir of Nursing* Mary
Steiner RN. *Medical Dir* George M
Workman MD.
Licensure Intermediate care. *Beds* ICF 60.
Private Pay Patients 66%. *Certified*
Medicaid.
Owner Proprietary corp (Frene Valley Corp).
Admissions Requirements Minimum age 18;
Medical examination.
Staff RNs 2 (ft), 1 (pt); LPNs 2 (ft), 1 (pt);
Nurses' aides 19 (ft), 5 (pt); Physical
therapists (consultant); Reality therapists
(consultant); Recreational therapists
(consultant); Occupational therapists
(consultant); Speech therapists (consultant);
Activities coordinators 1 (ft); Dietitians 1
(pt).
Languages German.
Facilities Dining room; Physical therapy
room; Activities room; Laundry room;
Barber/Beauty shop; Living room.

Activities Arts & crafts; Cards; Games; Reading groups; Prayer groups; Movies; Shopping trips; Dances/Social/Cultural gatherings; Intergenerational programs; Pet therapy.

Frene Valley Health Center
PO Box 157, 18th & Wein, Hermann, MO 65041
(314) 486-3155, 486-5631
Admin Gary E Lloyd.
Medical Dir G M Workman MD.
Licensure Intermediate care. *Beds* ICF 208. *Certified* Medicaid.
Owner Proprietary corp.
Admissions Requirements Minimum age 18; Medical examination.
Staff RNs 1 (ft); LPNs 3 (ft); Nurses' aides 16 (ft), 6 (pt); Activities coordinators 1 (ft).
Facilities Dining room; Physical therapy room; Activities room; Crafts room; Laundry room; Barber/Beauty shop.
Activities Arts & crafts; Games; Prayer groups; Movies; Shopping trips; Dances/Social/Cultural gatherings; Exercises; Church services.

Hermitage

Hermitage Park Regional Care Center
PO Box 325, Hermitage, MO 65668
(417) 745-2111, 759-7496
Admin Wayne Rainey Jr. *Dir of Nursing* Sue Johnson RN. *Medical Dir* Dr William Mathews.
Licensure Skilled care. *Beds* SNF 120. *Private Pay Patients* 32%. *Certified* Medicaid; Medicare; VA.
Owner Proprietary corp.
Admissions Requirements Minimum age 16; Medical examination; Physician's request.
Staff Physicians 1 (pt); RNs 1 (ft), 1 (pt); LPNs 10 (ft), 1 (pt); Physical therapists; Dietitians.
Facilities Dining room; Physical therapy room; Activities room; Laundry room; Barber/Beauty shop; Library.
Activities Arts & crafts; Cards; Reading groups; Prayer groups; Movies; Shopping trips; Dances/Social/Cultural gatherings; Intergenerational programs; Pet therapy; Volunteer program.

Higginsville

Higginsville Habilitation Center
Box 522, W 1st St, Higginsville, MO 64037
(816) 584-2142
Admin Bob Thompson.
Licensure Intermediate care for mentally retarded. *Beds* ICF/MR 310.

Meyer Care Center
PO Box 512, Truman Rd & 13 Hwy, Higginsville, MO 64037
(816) 584-4224
Admin Sue Fowler. *Dir of Nursing* Dorothy Bertrand RN. *Medical Dir* Marla Tobin MD.
Licensure Skilled care; Intermediate care; Residential care; Retirement. *Beds* SNF 24; ICF 60; Residential care 36; Retirement 185. *Private Pay Patients* 56%. *Certified* Medicaid.
Owner Nonprofit corp.
Admissions Requirements Minimum age 16; Medical examination.
Staff Physicians 5 (pt); RNs 2 (ft), 2 (pt); LPNs 2 (pt); Nurses' aides 55 (ft), 10 (pt); Physical therapists 1 (pt); Occupational therapists 1 (pt); Activities coordinators 1 (ft); Dietitians 1 (pt).
Facilities Dining room; Activities room; Chapel; Barber/Beauty shop.
Activities Arts & crafts; Cards; Games; Reading groups; Prayer groups; Movies; Shopping trips; Pet therapy.

Hillsboro

Castle Acres Nursing Home Inc
PO Box 308, Hillsboro, MO 63050
(314) 789-2882
Admin Mary E Ouhrabka.
Licensure Intermediate care. *Beds* ICF 29.
Owner Proprietary corp.

Cedar Grove Nursing Home
PO Box 367, Hillsboro, MO 63050
(314) 789-2481
Admin Charles D Williams. *Dir of Nursing* Pattie J Williams LPN. *Medical Dir* D M Carranza.
Licensure Intermediate care; Residential care. *Beds* ICF 48; Residential care 25.
Owner Proprietary corp (Extended Care Inc).
Admissions Requirements Minimum age 18; Medical examination.
Staff Physicians 1 (ft); LPNs 1 (ft); Nurses' aides 35 (ft); Activities coordinators 1 (ft); Dietitians 3 (ft); Podiatrists 1 (pt).
Facilities Dining room; Activities room; Laundry room; Barber/Beauty shop.
Activities Arts & crafts; Cards; Games; Reading groups; Prayer groups; Dances/Social/Cultural gatherings; Intergenerational programs; Pet therapy.

Holden

Holden Manor Care Center
2005 S Lexington, Holden, MO 64040
(816) 732-4138
Admin Nancy J Shields. *Dir of Nursing* Mary Hammond LPN. *Medical Dir* William Rhode DO.
Licensure Intermediate care. *Beds* ICF 52. *Private Pay Patients* 100%.
Owner Proprietary corp (C L Gerwick & Associates).
Admissions Requirements Medical examination.
Staff Physicians 1 (pt); RNs 1 (ft); LPNs 3 (ft); Nurses' aides 15 (ft); Physical therapists 1 (ft); Reality therapists 1 (pt); Recreational therapists 1 (pt); Occupational therapists 1 (pt); Speech therapists 1 (pt); Activities coordinators 1 (ft), 1 (pt); Dietitians 1 (ft); Podiatrists 1 (pt); Audiologists 1 (ft).
Facilities Dining room; Physical therapy room; Activities room; Chapel; Crafts room; Laundry room; Barber/Beauty shop; Library.
Activities Arts & crafts; Cards; Games; Reading groups; Prayer groups; Movies; Shopping trips; Dances/Social/Cultural gatherings; Intergenerational programs.

Houston

Houston House
PO Box 240, 1100 N Industrial Dr, Houston, MO 65483
(417) 967-2527
Admin Gary L Huff. *Dir of Nursing* Janet Wiseman RN. *Medical Dir* Dr Lynn Hauenstein.
Licensure Skilled care; Intermediate care. *Beds* Swing beds SNF/ICF 60. *Private Pay Patients* 15%. *Certified* Medicaid.
Owner Proprietary corp (Aurora Enterprises Inc).
Admissions Requirements Medical examination.
Staff Physicians 4 (pt); RNs 1 (ft), 4 (pt); LPNs 2 (ft), 4 (pt); Nurses' aides 20 (ft), 6 (pt); Physical therapists 1 (pt); Recreational therapists 2 (pt); Occupational therapists 1 (pt); Speech therapists 1 (pt); Activities coordinators 1 (pt); Dietitians 1 (pt); Podiatrists 1 (pt).
Languages German.
Facilities Dining room; Physical therapy room; Activities room; Crafts room; Laundry room; Barber/Beauty shop.

Activities Arts & crafts; Games; Reading groups; Prayer groups; Movies; Shopping trips; Dances/Social/Cultural gatherings; Adopt-a-grade program with local school.

Humansville

Big Spring Nursing Home
Rte 1 Box 28, Humansville, MO 65674
(417) 754-2450
Admin Norma Pitts. *Dir of Nursing* Darline Peebles. *Medical Dir* Dr Bill Mathews.
Licensure Intermediate care. *Beds* ICF 38. *Private Pay Patients* 50%. *Certified* Medicaid.
Owner Proprietary corp (American Eldercare Inc).
Admissions Requirements Minimum age 18; Medical examination.
Staff Physicians 5 (pt); RNs 1 (pt); LPNs 1 (ft), 2 (pt); Nurses' aides 9 (ft), 4 (pt); Recreational therapists 1 (pt).
Facilities Dining room; Activities room; Chapel; Crafts room; Laundry room.
Activities Arts & crafts; Cards; Games; Reading groups; Prayer groups; Movies; Sing-alongs; Outings; Lunch.

Northwood Hills Health Care Center
PO Box 187, N Arthur St, Humansville, MO 65674
(417) 754-2208
Admin Dennis Sloniker.
Licensure Skilled care; Intermediate care. *Beds* Swing beds SNF/ICF 120. *Certified* Medicaid.
Owner Proprietary corp (Beverly Enterprises).

Independence

Four Pines Retirement Home Inc
3713 Hardy, Independence, MO 64052
(816) 353-2737
Admin Evelyn Spangler.
Medical Dir Ron LaHue DO.
Licensure Intermediate care. *Beds* ICF 45.
Owner Proprietary corp.
Admissions Requirements Medical examination; Physician's request.
Staff RNs 1 (ft); LPNs 2 (ft), 1 (pt); Nurses' aides 13 (ft), 2 (pt); Activities coordinators 1 (pt); Dietitians 1 (pt).
Facilities Dining room; Physical therapy room; Activities room; Laundry room.
Activities Games; Reading groups; Prayer groups; Movies; Shopping trips.

General Baptist Nursing Home
419 N Hocker, Independence, MO 64050
(816) 252-4019
Admin Alberta Marshall, Charlotte Jennings.
Medical Dir Sharon Miles.
Licensure Intermediate care. *Beds* ICF 27.
Owner Nonprofit organization/foundation.
Staff Physicians 1 (pt); RNs 2 (pt); LPNs 2 (pt); Nurses' aides 13 (pt); Dietitians 1 (pt).
Affiliation Baptist.
Facilities Dining room; Chapel; Laundry room.
Activities Arts & crafts; Games; Reading groups; Prayer groups.

Independence Health Care Center
17451 E Medical Center Pkwy, Independence, MO 64050
(816) 373-7795
Admin Jean Zullig.
Medical Dir Keith Broughton DO.
Licensure Skilled care. *Beds* SNF 120. *Certified* Medicaid.
Owner Proprietary corp (Beverly Enterprises).
Staff Physicians 1 (pt); RNs 4 (ft), 1 (pt); LPNs 7 (ft), 2 (pt); Nurses' aides 40 (ft); Physical therapists 1 (pt); Occupational therapists 1 (pt); Speech therapists 1 (pt); Activities coordinators 1 (ft); Dietitians 1 (pt); Podiatrists 1 (pt); Dentists 1 (pt).

Facilities Dining room; Physical therapy room; Activities room; Crafts room; Laundry room; Barber/Beauty shop.
Activities Arts & crafts; Cards; Games; Reading groups; Prayer groups; Movies; Shopping trips; Dances/Social/Cultural gatherings.

Independence Manor Care Center
1600 S Kingshighway, Independence, MO 64050
(816) 833-4777
Admin Kim Collins.
Licensure Intermediate care. *Beds* ICF 102.
Owner Proprietary corp.
Admissions Requirements Medical examination; Physician's request.
Staff Physicians 1 (ft), 9 (pt); RNs 1 (ft), 1 (pt); LPNs 4 (ft), 3 (pt); Nurses' aides 22 (ft), 14 (pt); Physical therapists 1 (ft); Reality therapists 1 (ft), 1 (pt); Recreational therapists 1 (ft), 1 (pt); Occupational therapists 1 (pt); Speech therapists 1 (pt); Activities coordinators 1 (ft), 1 (pt); Dietitians 1 (pt); Ophthalmologists 1 (pt); Dentists 1 (pt).
Facilities Dining room; Physical therapy room; Activities room; Crafts room; Laundry room; Barber/Beauty shop.
Activities Arts & crafts; Cards; Games; Reading groups; Prayer groups; Movies; Out-to-lunch bunch; Classic cooks; Daily exercise.

Independence Regional Health Center—Extended Care
1509 W Truman Rd, Independence, MO 64050
(816) 836-8100
Admin Carole Ferguson. *Dir of Nursing* Teresa Halling RN. *Medical Dir* Dr Frank Lewis.
Licensure Skilled care. *Beds* SNF 72. *Certified* Medicare.
Owner Nonprofit organization/foundation.
Admissions Requirements Medical examination; Physician's request.
Staff RNs 9 (ft); LPNs 5 (ft), 4 (pt); Nurses' aides 20 (ft), 1 (pt); Physical therapists 2 (ft); Occupational therapists 3 (ft); Speech therapists 2 (ft); Activities coordinators 1 (pt); Dietitians 1 (ft); Social workers 1 (pt).
Languages Spanish.
Affiliation Reorganized Church of Jesus Christ of Latter-Day Saints.
Facilities Dining room; Physical therapy room; Activities room; Chapel; Crafts room; Laundry room.
Activities Arts & crafts; Cards; Games; Reading groups; Prayer groups; Movies.

Resthaven
1500 W Truman, Independence, MO 64050
(816) 254-3500
Admin W Kent Kirkwood.
Licensure Skilled care; Intermediate care. *Beds* Swing beds SNF/ICF 259. *Private Pay Patients* 50%. *Certified* Medicaid.
Owner Nonprofit corp.
Affiliation Latter Day Saints.

Windsor Estates Convalescent Center
10300 Truman Rd, Independence, MO 64052
(816) 836-1250
Admin Kathrine Sifers.
Medical Dir C M Cernech DO.
Licensure Skilled care. *Beds* SNF 89. *Certified* Medicaid; Medicare.
Owner Proprietary corp (Beverly Enterprises).
Admissions Requirements Minimum age 18.
Staff Physicians 1 (ft), 3 (pt); RNs 2 (ft), 1 (pt); LPNs 6 (ft), 2 (pt); Nurses' aides 34 (ft), 6 (pt); Physical therapists 1 (ft); Occupational therapists 1 (pt); Speech therapists 1 (pt); Activities coordinators 1 (ft); Dietitians 1 (pt); Podiatrists 1 (pt); Dentists 1 (pt).

Facilities Dining room; Physical therapy room; Activities room; Crafts room; Laundry room; Barber/Beauty shop.
Activities Arts & crafts; Games; Reading groups; Prayer groups; Movies; Dances/Social/Cultural gatherings.

Ironton

Baptist Home Inc
PO Box 87, Ironton, MO 63650
(314) 546-7429
Admin Edward C Goodwin. *Dir of Nursing* Retha Keller.
Licensure Intermediate care; Residential care; Alzheimer's care. *Beds* ICF 140; Residential care 74.
Owner Nonprofit corp.
Staff Physicians 3 (pt); RNs 5 (ft); LPNs 5 (ft); Nurses' aides 75 (ft); Physical therapists 2 (ft); Activities coordinators 5 (ft).
Affiliation Baptist.
Activities Arts & crafts; Cards; Games; Reading groups; Prayer groups; Movies; Shopping trips; Dances/Social/Cultural gatherings.

Jackson

Deal Nursing Home Inc
PO Box 371, 914 Cape Rd, Jackson, MO 63755
(314) 243-3121
Admin Billy Joe Thompson.
Licensure Intermediate care. *Beds* ICF 75.
Owner Proprietary corp.

Jackson Manor Nursing Home
710 Broadridge, Jackson, MO 63755
(314) 243-3101
Admin Rick Westphal.
Licensure Skilled care. *Beds* SNF 90. *Certified* Medicaid.
Owner Proprietary corp (Angell Group).

Jefferson City

Hillside Healthcare
1024 Adams, Jefferson City, MO 65101
(314) 635-8191
Admin Bruce Struble.
Licensure Skilled care. *Beds* SNF 120. *Certified* Medicaid; Medicare.
Owner Proprietary corp (Hillhaven Corp).

Jefferson City Manor Care Center
1720 Vieth Dr, Jefferson City, MO 65101
(314) 635-6193
Admin Carol Sims. *Dir of Nursing* Mary Chigwidden RN. *Medical Dir* Robert Tanner MD.
Licensure Skilled care. *Beds* SNF 102. *Certified* Medicaid; Medicare.
Owner Proprietary corp.
Staff RNs 2 (ft), 3 (pt); LPNs 8 (ft), 3 (pt); Nurses' aides 25 (ft), 15 (pt); Physical therapists 1 (ft), 2 (pt); Recreational therapists 1 (pt); Occupational therapists 1 (pt); Speech therapists 1 (pt); Activities coordinators 1 (ft), 1 (pt); Dietitians 1 (ft), 1 (pt).
Languages German.
Facilities Dining room; Physical therapy room; Laundry room; Barber/Beauty shop.
Activities Arts & crafts; Cards; Games; Reading groups; Prayer groups; Movies; Shopping trips; Dances/Social/Cultural gatherings; Pet therapy; Reality orientation.

Lincoln Nursing Center
3038 W Truman Blvd, Jefferson City, MO 65109
(314) 893-3404
Admin Donna Hurt. *Dir of Nursing* Mary Kellogg. *Medical Dir* James Allen.

Licensure Skilled care; Intermediate care. *Beds* Swing beds SNF/ICF 100. *Private Pay Patients* 29%. *Certified* Medicaid.
Owner Proprietary corp (Beverly Enterprises).
Admissions Requirements Medical examination.
Staff RNs 3 (ft); LPNs 6 (ft), 1 (pt); Nurses' aides 23 (ft), 6 (pt); Activities coordinators 1 (ft); CMTs 4 (ft), 1 (pt).
Facilities Dining room; Physical therapy room; Activities room; Laundry room; Barber/Beauty shop.
Activities Arts & crafts; Prayer groups; Movies.

St Joseph's Home for the Aged
1306 W Main St, Jefferson City, MO 65101
(314) 635-0166
Admin Sr M Bernardine Moors.
Licensure Intermediate care. *Beds* ICF 100.
Owner Nonprofit corp (Carmelite Sisters Divine Heart).

Southgate Nursing Center
PO Box 1014, 1207 Stadium Blvd, Jefferson City, MO 65102
(314) 635-3131
Admin Alex B Snavely.
Licensure Skilled care. *Beds* SNF 120. *Certified* Medicaid; Medicare.
Owner Proprietary corp (Beverly Enterprises).
Facilities Dining room; Physical therapy room; Activities room; Chapel; Crafts room; Laundry room; Barber/Beauty shop; Library.
Activities Arts & crafts; Cards; Games; Reading groups; Movies; Shopping trips; Pet therapy.

Villa Marie Skilled Nursing Facility
PO Box 1801, 1030 Edmonds St, Jefferson City, MO 65102
(314) 635-3381
Admin John J Driscoll. *Dir of Nursing* Jean M Decker. *Medical Dir* John I Matthews MD.
Licensure Skilled care; Alzheimer's care. *Beds* SNF 120. *Private Pay Patients* 50%. *Certified* Medicaid; Medicare.
Owner Nonprofit corp (SSM Health Care System).
Admissions Requirements Minimum age 21; Medical examination; Physician's request.
Staff Physicians 1 (ft); RNs 8 (ft), 3 (pt); LPNs 10 (ft), 4 (pt); Nurses' aides 42 (ft), 7 (pt); Physical therapists 1 (ft); Reality therapists 1 (ft); Recreational therapists 1 (ft); Occupational therapists 1 (ft); Speech therapists 1 (ft); Activities coordinators 1 (ft); Dietitians 1 (ft); Ophthalmologists; Podiatrists; Audiologists; Music therapists 1 (ft).
Facilities Dining room; Physical therapy room; Activities room; Chapel; Crafts room; Laundry room; Barber/Beauty shop; Library.
Activities Arts & crafts; Cards; Games; Reading groups; Prayer groups; Movies; Dances/Social/Cultural gatherings; Pet therapy; Music; Religious services.

Jonesburg

Jonesburg Caring Center Inc
PO Box 218, Cedar Ave & William Tell, Jonesburg, MO 63351
(314) 488-5400
Admin Dave Richardon. *Dir of Nursing* Kathy Wright. *Medical Dir* Costantino Carpio MD.
Licensure Skilled care. *Beds* SNF 60. *Certified* Medicaid.
Owner Proprietary corp.
Admissions Requirements Minimum age 18; Medical examination; Physician's request.
Staff Physicians 1 (pt); RNs 1 (pt); LPNs 1 (ft), 1 (pt); Nurses' aides 10 (ft), 1 (pt); Activities coordinators 1 (pt); Dietitians 1 (ft).

Facilities Dining room; Activities room; Laundry room.
Activities Arts & crafts; Cards; Games; Prayer groups; Movies; Shopping trips.

Joplin

Hope Manor
1402 Rex, Joplin, MO 64801
(417) 623-5551
Admin Pat Fenix.
Licensure Intermediate care. *Beds* ICF 24.
Owner Privately owned.
Admissions Requirements Minimum age 18; Medical examination.
Staff RNs 1 (pt); LPNs 1 (ft), 1 (pt); Nurses' aides 12 (ft).
Facilities Dining room; Activities room; Crafts room; Laundry room; Barber/Beauty shop.
Activities Arts & crafts; Games; Prayer groups.

Joplin Health Care Center
PO Box 2877, 2700 E 34th, Joplin, MO 64803
(417) 781-1737
Admin Tim Haynes. *Dir of Nursing* Jan Walker RN. *Medical Dir* O A Mehaffy MD.
Licensure Skilled care; Intermediate care. *Beds* Swing beds SNF/ICF 126. *Certified* Medicaid.
Owner Privately owned.
Staff RNs 4 (ft), 1 (pt); LPNs 10 (ft), 3 (pt); Nurses' aides 39 (ft), 6 (pt); Physical therapists 1 (pt); Occupational therapists 1 (pt); Speech therapists 1 (pt); Activities coordinators 1 (ft), 1 (pt).

Joplin House
2502 Moffet, Joplin, MO 64804
(417) 623-3264
Admin Janice Zacny. *Dir of Nursing* Lillian Jones RN. *Medical Dir* O A Mehaffy MD.
Licensure Skilled care; Intermediate care. *Beds* Swing beds SNF/ICF 120. *Private Pay Patients* 3%. *Certified* Medicaid; Medicare.
Owner Proprietary corp (Hillhaven Corp).
Admissions Requirements Medical examination; Physician's request.
Staff RNs; LPNs; Nurses' aides; Activities coordinators; Dietitians.
Facilities Dining room; Physical therapy room; Activities room; Laundry room; Barber/Beauty shop.
Activities Arts & crafts; Cards; Games; Reading groups; Prayer groups; Movies; Dances/Social/Cultural gatherings; Pet therapy.

Meadow View Nursing Center
1805 W 32nd St, Joplin, MO 64801
(417) 782-0114
Admin Jeffrey R Carter. *Dir of Nursing* Carol McGinn RN. *Medical Dir* Stephen Bazzano DO.
Licensure Skilled care. *Beds* SNF 120. *Certified* Medicaid; Medicare.
Owner Proprietary corp (Beverly Enterprises).
Admissions Requirements Minimum age 16; Medical examination; Physician's request.
Staff Physicians 1 (pt); RNs 3 (ft); LPNs 10 (ft), 2 (pt); Nurses' aides 41 (ft); Physical therapists 1 (pt); Occupational therapists 1 (pt); Speech therapists 1 (pt); Activities coordinators 1 (ft); Dietitians 1 (pt); Ophthalmologists 1 (pt); Podiatrists 1 (pt); Dentists 1 (pt).
Facilities Dining room; Physical therapy room; Activities room; Laundry room; Barber/Beauty shop; 3 Living rooms.
Activities Arts & crafts; Cards; Games; Reading groups; Prayer groups; Movies; Shopping trips; Dances/Social/Cultural gatherings.

Spring River Christian Village Inc
201 Northpark Ln, Box 1351, Joplin, MO 64801
(417) 623-4313

Admin Richard W Keller.
Licensure Skilled care; Intermediate care; Residential care. *Beds* Swing beds SNF/ICF 39; Residential care 53. *Certified* Medicaid.
Owner Nonprofit corp.

Tradition House Healthcare
PO Box 2039, 2810 Jackson, Joplin, MO 64803
(417) 624-2061
Admin Danetta Johnson.
Licensure Skilled care. *Beds* SNF 92. *Certified* Medicaid; Medicare.
Owner Proprietary corp (Hillhaven Corp).

Kahoka

Clark County Nursing Home
RR 2, Hwy 81 N, Kahoka, MO 63445-9506
(816) 727-3303
Admin Anne Conrad, Interim. *Dir of Nursing* Marilyn Day, temp.
Licensure Intermediate care. *Beds* ICF 120. *Private Pay Patients* 34%. *Certified* Medicaid.
Owner Publicly owned.
Admissions Requirements Physician's request.
Staff Physicians 2 (pt); RNs 2 (ft); LPNs 3 (ft), 4 (pt); Nurses' aides 22 (ft), 42 (pt); Physical therapists (consultant); Occupational therapists (consultant); Speech therapists (consultant); Activities coordinators 1 (pt); Dietitians 1 (ft).
Facilities Dining room; Physical therapy room; Activities room; Laundry room; Barber/Beauty shop; Fenced outside recreation area; Alarm system.
Activities Arts & crafts; Cards; Games; Reading groups; Prayer groups; Movies; Shopping trips.

Kansas City

Alpine North Nursing & Rehabilitation Center
4700 Cliffview Dr, Kansas City, MO 64150
(816) 741-5105, 746-1301 FAX
Admin Karen Leverich. *Dir of Nursing* Diana Hullinger. *Medical Dir* Dwight Cashier.
Licensure Skilled care. *Beds* SNF 186.
Owner Proprietary corp.
Staff RNs 5 (ft), 1 (pt); LPNs 9 (ft), 2 (pt); Nurses' aides 45 (ft); Physical therapists 1 (pt); Occupational therapists 1 (pt); Speech therapists 1 (pt); Activities coordinators 2 (ft); Dietitians 1 (ft); Ophthalmologists 1 (pt); Podiatrists 1 (pt); Audiologists 1 (pt).

Angels of Mercy Nursing Home
2836 Benton, Kansas City, MO 64128
(816) 924-5662
Admin Penny M Thompen. *Dir of Nursing* Leona Yillini LPN. *Medical Dir* Dr R L Williams.
Licensure Intermediate care. *Beds* ICF 34. *Private Pay Patients* 1%. *Certified* Medicaid.
Owner Privately owned.
Admissions Requirements Medical examination.
Staff Physicians 1 (pt); RNs 1 (pt); LPNs 1 (ft); Nurses' aides 9 (pt); Physical therapists 1 (ft); Activities coordinators 1 (pt); Dietitians 1 (ft).
Languages Spanish, German.
Facilities Dining room; Laundry room; Barber/Beauty shop.
Activities Arts & crafts; Cards; Games; Reading groups; Prayer groups; Movies; Pet therapy.

Armour Home
8100 Wornall Rd, Kansas City, MO 64114
(816) 363-1510
Admin R Larry Louthain. *Dir of Nursing* M Alice Mitchell. *Medical Dir* Dr Robert Lahue.

Licensure Skilled care; Residential care; Independent living. *Beds* SNF 34; Residential care 47; Independent living 24. *Certified* Medicaid; Medicare.
Owner Nonprofit corp.
Admissions Requirements Minimum age 65; Medical examination.
Staff Physicians 2 (pt); RNs 2 (ft); LPNs 7 (ft); Nurses' aides 12 (ft); Physical therapists 1 (pt); Activities coordinators 2 (ft); Dietitians 1 (pt); Ophthalmologists 1 (pt).
Facilities Dining room; Physical therapy room; Activities room; Chapel; Crafts room; Laundry room; Barber/Beauty shop; Library.
Activities Arts & crafts; Cards; Games; Reading groups; Prayer groups; Movies; Shopping trips; Dances/Social/Cultural gatherings.

Beacon Hill Nursing Home
2905 Campbell, Kansas City, MO 64109
(816) 531-6168
Admin Carole N Williams.
Medical Dir Leroy Williams DO.
Licensure Intermediate care. *Beds* ICF 37.
Owner Proprietary corp.
Admissions Requirements Minimum age 25; Medical examination.
Staff Physicians 1 (pt); RNs 1 (pt); LPNs 2 (ft); Nurses' aides 18 (ft); Activities coordinators 1 (pt).
Facilities Dining room; Laundry room.
Activities Arts & crafts; Cards; Games; Prayer groups; Movies; Dances/Social/Cultural gatherings.

Benton Care Center
622 Benton Blvd, Kansas City, MO 64124
(816) 241-5856
Admin Trish Carlopa. *Dir of Nursing* Ruth Stafford. *Medical Dir* Ray Baker MD; Harvey Munshaw MD.
Licensure Intermediate care. *Beds* ICF 46.
Owner Privately owned.
Staff Physicians 3 (ft); RNs 1 (ft); LPNs 3 (ft); Nurses' aides 25 (ft); Physical therapists 1 (ft); Occupational therapists 1 (ft); Activities coordinators 1 (ft); Dietitians 1 (ft); Ophthalmologists 1 (ft).
Facilities Activities room; Laundry room.
Activities Arts & crafts; Games; Reading groups; Movies.

Blue Hills Centre
12942 Wornall, Kansas City, MO 64145
(816) 941-0250
Admin Michael L Barnes. *Dir of Nursing* Linda Maniscalco. *Medical Dir* Dr Ron Lahve.
Licensure Skilled care; Alzheimer's care; Retirement. *Beds* SNF 183. *Certified* Medicaid; Medicare.
Owner Proprietary corp (Hillhaven Corp).
Staff Physicians 2 (ft); RNs 5 (ft); LPNs 10 (ft); Nurses' aides 80 (ft); Physical therapists 1 (ft); Recreational therapists 2 (ft); Occupational therapists 1 (ft); Speech therapists 1 (ft); Activities coordinators 1 (ft); Dietitians 1 (ft).
Facilities Dining room; Physical therapy room; Activities room; Chapel; Crafts room; Laundry room; Barber/Beauty shop; Library.
Activities Arts & crafts; Cards; Games; Reading groups; Prayer groups; Movies; Shopping trips; Dances/Social/Cultural gatherings.

Blue Ridge Nursing Home
7505 E 87th, Kansas City, MO 64138
(816) 761-6838
Admin Frank W Carroll. *Dir of Nursing* Bernadine Patel LPN.
Licensure Intermediate care; Alzheimer's care. *Beds* ICF 28.
Owner Proprietary corp.
Admissions Requirements Minimum age 18.

Facilities Dining room; Physical therapy room; Activities room; Crafts room; Laundry room; Barber/Beauty shop; Library.
Activities Arts & crafts; Cards; Games; Reading groups; Prayer groups; Movies; Shopping trips.

Brush Creek Manor
3918 Charlotte, Kansas City, MO 64110
(816) 931-0306
Admin Patricia A McCanless.
Licensure Intermediate care. *Beds* ICF 32.
Owner Proprietary corp.

Caldwell Manor Nursing Home
101 E 36th, Kansas City, MO 64111
(816) 753-6553
Admin James E Caldwell.
Licensure Intermediate care. *Beds* ICF 49.
Owner Publicly owned.

Carondelet Manor
621 Carondelet Dr, Kansas City, MO 64114
(816) 941-3370
Admin Dianne Doctor. *Dir of Nursing* Becky Long. *Medical Dir* Dr John Erwin.
Licensure Skilled care. *Beds* SNF 180. *Private Pay Patients* 70%. *Certified* Medicaid; Medicare.
Owner Nonprofit corp (Carondelet Long Term Care Facilities Inc).

Chippendale Nursing Home
3240 Norledge, Kansas City, MO 64123
(816) 231-1161
Admin Richard Ferling. *Dir of Nursing* Jenny Jeffries. *Medical Dir* R L Williams DO.
Licensure Intermediate care. *Beds* ICF 36.
Owner Publicly owned.
Admissions Requirements Minimum age 60; Medical examination.
Staff Physicians 3 (ft); RNs 1 (pt); LPNs 3 (ft); Nurses' aides 18 (ft), 4 (pt); Physical therapists 1 (pt); Reality therapists 1 (ft); Recreational therapists 1 (ft); Occupational therapists 1 (pt); Speech therapists 1 (pt); Activities coordinators 1 (ft); Ophthalmologists 1 (ft); Podiatrists 1 (ft).
Facilities Dining room; Activities room; Crafts room; Laundry room; Barber/Beauty shop.
Activities Arts & crafts; Cards; Games; Reading groups; Prayer groups; Movies; Shopping trips; Dances/Social/Cultural gatherings.

Clara Manor Nursing Home
3621 Warwick, Kansas City, MO 64111
(816) 756-1593
Admin John G Oliva.
Licensure Skilled care; Intermediate care. *Beds* Swing beds SNF/ICF 80. *Certified* Medicaid.
Owner Proprietary corp.

Cleveland Health Care Center
PO Box 5159, Kansas City, MO 64132
(816) 333-0700
Admin Laura Briggs MPA.
Medical Dir Dr Ron Lahue.
Licensure Skilled care; Residential care. *Beds* SNF 138; Residential care 12. *Certified* Medicaid; Medicare.
Owner Proprietary corp.
Admissions Requirements Minimum age 18.
Staff Physicians 1 (ft); RNs 3 (ft); LPNs 9 (ft); Nurses' aides 60 (ft); Physical therapists 1 (pt); Occupational therapists 1 (pt); Speech therapists 1 (pt); Activities coordinators 2 (ft); Dietitians 1 (ft); Ophthalmologists 1 (ft).
Facilities Dining room; Physical therapy room; Laundry room.
Activities Arts & crafts; Cards; Games; Reading groups; Prayer groups; Movies; Dances/Social/Cultural gatherings.

Colonial Nursing Home
100 E 36th, Kansas City, MO 64111
(816) 561-6373
Admin Ervin Ristau.

Medical Dir Sue Shanks.
Licensure Intermediate care. *Beds* ICF 51.
Owner Proprietary corp.
Admissions Requirements Minimum age 60; Medical examination.
Staff Physicians 6 (ft); RNs 1 (pt); LPNs 2 (ft); Nurses' aides 18 (ft), 4 (pt); Physical therapists 1 (pt); Reality therapists 1 (ft); Recreational therapists 1 (ft); Occupational therapists 1 (pt); Speech therapists 1 (pt); Activities coordinators 1 (ft); Ophthalmologists 1 (pt).
Facilities Dining room; Activities room; Crafts room; Laundry room; Barber/Beauty shop.
Activities Arts & crafts; Cards; Games; Reading groups; Prayer groups; Movies; Shopping trips; Dances/Social/Cultural gatherings.

Cosada Villa Nursing Center
8575 Cosada Dr, Kansas City, MO 64154
(816) 436-8575
Admin Tom Hudspeth.
Licensure Intermediate care; Residential care. *Beds* Swing beds SNF/ICF 180; Residential care 24. *Certified* Medicaid; Medicare.
Owner Proprietary corp.

ExPerius Health Care Inc
5331 Highland Ave, Kansas City, MO 64110
(816) 444-9164
Admin Edward R Garcia.
Licensure Intermediate care; Residential care. *Beds* ICF 100; Residential care 222. *Certified* Medicaid.
Owner Proprietary corp.
Affiliation Roman Catholic.

Gladstone Nursing Home
435 Gladstone Blvd, Kansas City, MO 64124
(816) 483-8164
Admin Kathryn Rush.
Medical Dir Dr Robert LaHue.
Licensure Intermediate care. *Beds* ICF 28.
Owner Proprietary corp.
Admissions Requirements Females only.
Staff Physicians 3 (ft); RNs 1 (pt); LPNs 1 (ft), 2 (pt); Physical therapists 1 (pt); Recreational therapists 1 (pt); Dietitians 1 (pt).
Facilities Activities room; Chapel; Crafts room; Laundry room.
Activities Arts & crafts; Cards; Games; Prayer groups; Movies.

Glennon Place
124-128 N Hardesty Ave, Kansas City, MO 64123
(816) 241-2020
Admin Judy Powell.
Licensure Skilled care; Residential care. *Beds* SNF 120; Residential care 46. *Certified* Medicaid.
Owner Proprietary corp (Beverly Enterprises).

Great Oaks Inc
115 E 83rd St, Kansas City, MO 64114
(816) 363-2900
Admin Marion V Pike.
Medical Dir Lydia Abercrombie.
Licensure Intermediate care. *Beds* ICF 12.
Owner Nonprofit corp.
Admissions Requirements Minimum age 18.
Staff RNs 3 (ft), 2 (pt); LPNs 3 (ft), 2 (pt); Nurses' aides 1 (ft); Activities coordinators 1 (ft); Dietitians 1 (ft), 4 (pt).
Affiliation Christian Science.
Facilities Dining room; Activities room; Laundry room; Barber/Beauty shop.
Activities Arts & crafts; Reading groups; Prayer groups; Movies; Singing.

Guardian Angel Nursing Home Inc
5234 NE Munger Ave, Kansas City, MO 64119
(816) 452-2654
Admin Barbara J Clark.

Licensure Intermediate care. *Beds* ICF 19.
Owner Proprietary corp.

Harvest Home Estates
3522 Walnut, Kansas City, MO 64111
(816) 561-9344
Admin Hazel Thompson.
Licensure Intermediate care. *Beds* 55.
Owner Proprietary corp.

Haven Manor Nursing Home
3526 Walnut St, Kansas City, MO 64111
(816) 931-9579
Admin Mary Bragulla.
Medical Dir Bob La Hue MD.
Licensure Intermediate care. *Beds* ICF 29.
Owner Proprietary corp.
Admissions Requirements Minimum age 29; Medical examination; Physician's request.
Staff Physicians 1 (ft); RNs 1 (pt); LPNs 1 (ft), 3 (pt); Nurses' aides 6 (ft), 6 (pt); Physical therapists 3 (pt); Reality therapists 1 (pt); Recreational therapists 1 (pt); Occupational therapists 1 (pt); Speech therapists 1 (pt); Activities coordinators 1 (pt); Ophthalmologists 1 (pt); Podiatrists 1 (pt); Dentists 1 (pt).
Facilities Dining room; Laundry room.
Activities Arts & crafts; Cards; Games; Reading groups; Prayer groups; Movies; Shopping trips; Dances/Social/Cultural gatherings.

Holmesdale Convalescent Center
8039 Holmes, Kansas City, MO 64131
(816) 363-6222
Admin Madeline Ryan. *Dir of Nursing* Mary Miller.
Licensure Skilled care. *Beds* SNF 100. *Certified* Medicare.
Owner Privately owned.
Staff RNs 4 (ft), 3 (pt); LPNs 2 (ft), 6 (pt); Nurses' aides 25 (ft); Physical therapists 1 (ft); Recreational therapists 1 (ft); Activities coordinators 1 (ft); Dietitians 1 (ft).
Facilities Dining room; Physical therapy room; Activities room; Laundry room; Barber/Beauty shop; 2 Solariums.
Activities Arts & crafts; Games; Reading groups; Prayer groups; Movies; Dances/Social/Cultural gatherings; Bingo; Happy hour; Birthday parties.

Hyde Park Nursing Home
401 E 36th St, Kansas City, MO 64109
(816) 931-6378
Admin Gloria Tillman.
Licensure Intermediate care. *Beds* ICF 45.
Owner Privately owned.

Jeanne Jugan Center
8745 James A Reed Rd, Kansas City, MO 64138
(816) 761-4744
Admin Sr Mary Rowley.
Licensure Skilled care; Intermediate care. *Beds* SNF 28; ICF 29.
Owner Nonprofit corp.

Midtown Manor Nursing Home
2700 Tracy, Kansas City, MO 64109
(816) 421-1272
Admin Claudia McDaniel.
Licensure Intermediate care. *Beds* ICF 55.
Owner Proprietary corp.

Mochel Manor
3400 Campbell, Kansas City, MO 64109
(816) 531-5746
Admin Eleanor Mochel. *Dir of Nursing* Mary Stroud. *Medical Dir* Dr Robert LaHue.
Licensure Intermediate care. *Beds* ICF 40.
Owner Proprietary corp.
Admissions Requirements Minimum age 18; Medical examination.
Staff RNs 1 (ft); LPNs 1 (ft), 1 (pt); Nurses' aides 15 (ft); Physical therapists; Activities coordinators 1 (ft); Dietitians 1 (pt).

Facilities Dining room; Crafts room; Laundry room.
Activities Arts & crafts; Cards; Games; Prayer groups; Movies; Dances/Social/Cultural gatherings; Pet therapy.

Myers Nursing & Convalescent Center
2315 Walrond, Kansas City, MO 64127
(816) 231-3180
Admin Agnes Dodd. *Dir of Nursing* Connie Harkness RN.
Licensure Intermediate care. *Beds* ICF 84. *Certified* Medicaid.
Owner Proprietary corp.
Staff RNs 1 (ft); LPNs 5 (ft); Activities coordinators 1 (ft); Dietitians 1 (ft).
Facilities Dining room; Activities room; Laundry room.
Activities Arts & crafts; Cards; Games; Reading groups; Prayer groups; Movies; Shopping trips; Dances/Social/Cultural gatherings; Outings.

George H Nettleton Home
5125 Swope Pkwy, Kansas City, MO 64130
(816) 924-5641
Admin Patricia Rodina MA. *Dir of Nursing* Jeanette Harris LPN. *Medical Dir* Robert Raich.
Licensure Intermediate care; Residential care; Alzheimer's care. *Beds* ICF 30; Residential care 43.
Owner Nonprofit corp.
Admissions Requirements Females only.
Staff Physicians 1 (pt); RNs 1 (pt); LPNs 2 (ft), 1 (pt); Nurses' aides 9 (ft), 15 (pt); Physical therapists 1 (pt); Reality therapists 1 (pt); Recreational therapists 1 (ft); Occupational therapists 1 (pt); Speech therapists 1 (pt); Dietitians 1 (pt); Ophthalmologists 1 (pt); Podiatrists 1 (pt); Social service 1 (pt).
Facilities Dining room; Activities room; Chapel; Laundry room; Barber/Beauty shop; Library; Sun room; Large parlor.
Activities Arts & crafts; Cards; Games; Reading groups; Prayer groups; Movies; Shopping trips; Dances/Social/Cultural gatherings.

New Mark Care Center
11221 N Oak Trafficway, Kansas City, MO 64155
(816) 734-4433
Admin D Martin Ebert.
Licensure Skilled care; Intermediate care; Residential care. *Beds* Swing beds SNF/ICF 120; Residential care 42. *Certified* Medicaid; Medicare.
Owner Proprietary corp.

Newberry Nursing Home
3215 Campbell, Kansas City, MO 64109
(816) 561-5282
Admin Paul Harper.
Medical Dir Dr Robert LaHue.
Licensure Intermediate care. *Beds* ICF 45.
Owner Proprietary corp.
Staff RNs 1 (pt); LPNs 1 (ft), 2 (pt); Nurses' aides 18 (ft), 2 (pt); Physical therapists 1 (pt); Recreational therapists 1 (ft).
Facilities Dining room; Activities room; Laundry room.
Activities Arts & crafts; Cards; Games; Reading groups; Prayer groups; Movies; Shopping trips; Dances/Social/Cultural gatherings.

Oak Park Manor & Residential Care Facility
PO Box 28401, 724 NE 79th Terrace, Kansas City, MO 64118
(816) 436-8940, 436-2940
Admin Paul Harper; Joseph Delanye.
Medical Dir Ruth Hershey.
Licensure Skilled care; Residential care. *Beds* SNF 120; Residential care 28. *Certified* Medicaid.
Owner Proprietary corp (Beverly Enterprises).

Admissions Requirements Minimum age 18.
Staff RNs 4 (ft); LPNs 7 (ft); Nurses' aides 50 (ft); Physical therapists 1 (ft); Recreational therapists 1 (ft).
Facilities Dining room; Physical therapy room; Activities room; Laundry room; Barber/Beauty shop.
Activities Arts & crafts; Games; Prayer groups; Movies; Shopping trips.

Oak Ridge Manor Nursing Home
512 Woodland, Kansas City, MO 64106
(816) 474-6869
Admin Beryl Pegues. *Dir of Nursing* Minnie Jones.
Licensure Intermediate care. *Beds* ICF 46.
Owner Proprietary corp.
Admissions Requirements Minimum age 18; Medical examination.
Staff Physicians 2 (pt); RNs 1 (pt); LPNs 1 (ft), 1 (pt); Nurses' aides 15 (ft), 3 (pt); Activities coordinators 1 (pt); Dietitians 1 (pt).
Facilities Dining room; Dayroom.
Activities Arts & crafts; Cards; Games; Dances/Social/Cultural gatherings.

Oakwood Manor
11515 Troost, Kansas City, MO 64131
(816) 942-6700
Admin Carla J Yach. *Dir of Nursing* Cynthia McQuinn. *Medical Dir* Chris Gena MD.
Licensure Skilled care; Intermediate care; Residential care. *Beds* Swing beds SNF/ICF 180; Residential care 30. *Private Pay Patients* 70%. *Certified* Medicaid; Medicare.
Owner Privately owned.
Admissions Requirements Minimum age 18; Medical examination.
Staff Physicians 1 (ft), 36 (pt); RNs 4 (ft), 1 (pt); LPNs 15 (ft), 2 (pt); Nurses' aides 45 (ft), 9 (pt); Physical therapists 1 (pt); Reality therapists 1 (ft); Speech therapists 1 (pt); Activities coordinators 1 (ft), 1 (pt); Dietitians 2 (pt); Ophthalmologists 1 (pt); Podiatrists 1 (pt).
Facilities Dining room; Physical therapy room; Activities room; Crafts room; Laundry room; Barber/Beauty shop; Library; Child day care.
Activities Arts & crafts; Cards; Games; Reading groups; Prayer groups; Movies; Shopping trips; Dances/Social/Cultural gatherings; Intergenerational programs; Pet therapy.

Our Lady of Mercy Home
918 E 9th St, Kansas City, MO 64106
(816) 842-6518
Admin Sr Mary Margaret Sneddon. *Dir of Nursing* Elsie Hunter RN.
Licensure Intermediate care; Residential care. *Beds* ICF 68; Residential care 85. *Certified* Medicaid.
Owner Nonprofit corp.
Admissions Requirements Females only; Medical examination; Physician's request.
Staff RNs 2 (ft), 2 (pt); LPNs 3 (ft); Nurses' aides 22 (ft); Recreational therapists 1 (ft), 3 (pt); Occupational therapists 1 (ft); Activities coordinators 1 (ft), 2 (pt); Dietitians 1 (pt).
Languages Spanish.
Affiliation Roman Catholic.
Facilities Dining room; Activities room; Chapel; Crafts room; Laundry room; Barber/Beauty shop; Library.
Activities Arts & crafts; Cards; Games; Prayer groups; Movies; Shopping trips; Dances/Social/Cultural gatherings.

Plaza Manor—A Geriatric & Convalescent Center
4330 Washington, Kansas City, MO 64111
(816) 753-6800
Admin David Gatewood.
Licensure Skilled care; Intermediate care. *Beds* Swing beds SNF/ICF 154. *Certified* Medicaid; Medicare.

Owner Proprietary corp.

River Heights Retirement Center Inc
PO Box 5159, Kansas City, MO 64132
(816) 882-2328
Admin Robert Clausen.
Licensure Residential care. *Beds* 120.
Owner Proprietary corp.

Roanoke Manor Nursing Home
3939 Wyandotte, Kansas City, MO 64111
(816) 753-6566
Admin Miriam J Zwiegel.
Licensure Intermediate care. *Beds* 43.
Owner Proprietary corp.

Senior Estates of Kansas City
2323 Swope Pkwy, Kansas City, MO 64130
(816) 924-0211
Admin Patricia L Stickler. *Dir of Nursing* Norma Anderson. *Medical Dir* Ron LaHue MD.
Licensure Skilled care; Residential care. *Beds* SNF 54; Residential care 14.
Owner Proprietary corp.
Admissions Requirements Minimum age 17; Medical examination; Physician's request.
Staff RNs 2 (ft); LPNs 7 (ft); Nurses' aides 23 (ft); Activities coordinators 1 (ft).
Activities Arts & crafts; Cards; Games; Reading groups; Prayer groups; Movies; Shopping trips; Dances/Social/Cultural gatherings; Camping.

Shalom Geriatric Center Inc
7801 Holmes, Kansas City, MO 64131
(816) 333-7800
Admin Melvyn Weissman. *Dir of Nursing* Marge Groves. *Medical Dir* Dr Harry Cohen.
Licensure Skilled care; Retirement; Alzheimer's care. *Beds* SNF 192. *Certified* Medicaid; Medicare.
Owner Nonprofit corp.
Admissions Requirements Minimum age 18; Medical examination; Physician's request.
Staff RNs 6 (ft), 3 (pt); LPNs 19 (ft), 10 (pt); Nurses' aides 54 (ft), 16 (pt); Physical therapists 1 (ft); Recreational therapists 1 (ft); Occupational therapists 1 (ft); Activities coordinators 1 (ft); Dietitians 1 (ft); Art therapists 1 (ft).
Affiliation Jewish.
Facilities Dining room; Physical therapy room; Activities room; Chapel; Crafts room; Laundry room; Barber/Beauty shop; Library.
Activities Arts & crafts; Cards; Games; Reading groups; Prayer groups; Movies; Dances/Social/Cultural gatherings.

South Park Care Center
904 E 68th St, Kansas City, MO 64131
(816) 333-5485
Admin Paul H Wilson.
Medical Dir Harold Keairnes MD.
Licensure Skilled care. *Beds* SNF 174. *Certified* Medicaid; Medicare.
Owner Proprietary corp (National Heritage).
Admissions Requirements Minimum age 18.
Staff Physicians 1 (ft); RNs 7 (ft); LPNs 21 (ft); Nurses' aides 59 (ft); Physical therapists 4 (ft); Reality therapists 1 (pt); Recreational therapists 1 (pt); Occupational therapists 1 (pt); Speech therapists 1 (pt); Activities coordinators 3 (ft); Dietitians 1 (pt).
Facilities Dining room; Physical therapy room; Activities room; Chapel; Crafts room; Laundry room; Barber/Beauty shop; Library.
Activities Arts & crafts; Cards; Games; Prayer groups; Movies; Shopping trips; Dances/Social/Cultural gatherings.

Swope Ridge Health Care Center
5900 Swope Pkwy, Kansas City, MO 64130
(816) 333-2700
Admin Charles Nigro.
Licensure Skilled care; Residential care. *Beds* SNF 60; Residential care 40. *Certified* Medicaid.

Owner Nonprofit corp.

Timberlake Care Center
12110 Homes, Kansas City, MO 64145
(816) 941-3006
Admin Cynthia Walters.
Licensure Skilled care; Intermediate care. *Beds* Swing beds SNF/ICF 88. *Certified* Medicaid.
Owner Proprietary corp.

Truman Medical Center East
7900 Lees Summit Rd, Kansas City, MO 64139
(816) 373-4415
Admin Clifford Browne Jr. *Dir of Nursing* Barbara Quirk RN. *Medical Dir* Jack Mulligan MD.
Licensure Skilled care; Intermediate care. *Beds* SNF 24; ICF 188. *Certified* Medicaid.
Owner Nonprofit organization/foundation.
Admissions Requirements Medical examination.
Staff Physicians 1 (ft); RNs 12 (ft); LPNs 29 (ft); Nurses' aides 83 (ft); Physical therapists 1 (ft); Recreational therapists 1 (ft); Occupational therapists 1 (ft); Speech therapists 1 (ft); Dietitians 1 (ft); Social workers 2 (ft).
Facilities Dining room; Physical therapy room; Activities room; Chapel; Crafts room; Laundry room; Barber/Beauty shop; Library.
Activities Arts & crafts; Cards; Games; Reading groups; Prayer groups; Movies; Shopping trips; Dances/Social/Cultural gatherings.

University Towers Medical Pavilion
615 E 6th St, Kansas City, MO 64106
(816) 283-1550
Admin Maria M Gemsky. *Dir of Nursing* Bonnie Mack RN. *Medical Dir* Elaine Joslyn DO.
Licensure Skilled care; Intermediate care. *Beds* SNF 6; ICF 44. *Private Pay Patients* 70%. *Certified* Medicaid; Medicare.
Owner Nonprofit corp.
Admissions Requirements Medical examination; Physician's request.
Staff Physicians 1 (ft); RNs 1 (ft), 3 (pt); LPNs 3 (ft), 1 (pt); Nurses' aides 20 (ft); Physical therapists 1 (pt); Activities coordinators 1 (ft); Dietitians 1 (pt); Podiatrists 1 (pt).
Facilities Dining room; Activities room; Crafts room; Laundry room; Barber/Beauty shop.
Activities Arts & crafts; Cards; Games; Reading groups; Prayer groups; Movies; Pet therapy; Church services; Mass; Community participation.

Wornall Health Care Center
12000 Wornall Rd, Kansas City, MO 64145
(816) 942-1676
Admin Charls Boudreaux Jr.
Licensure Skilled care. *Beds* SNF 240. *Certified* Medicaid; Medicare.
Owner Proprietary corp (Hillhaven Corp).

Kennett

Kennett Health Care Center
PO Box 696, Rte 1 S By-Pass, Kennett, MO 63857
(314) 888-1150
Admin Patty Webb. *Dir of Nursing* Para Lea White RN. *Medical Dir* Wothisak Soonattrakol MD.
Licensure Skilled care; Alzheimer's unit. *Beds* SNF 120; Alzheimer's unit 30. *Private Pay Patients* 18%. *Certified* Medicaid; Medicare.
Owner Proprietary corp (National Health Corp).
Staff Physicians 11 (pt); RNs 5 (ft); LPNs 18 (ft), 5 (pt); Nurses' aides 40 (ft), 9 (pt); Physical therapists 1 (pt); Speech therapists 1 (pt); Activities coordinators 1 (pt), 1 (pt); Dietitians 1 (pt); Ophthalmologists 1 (pt).

Facilities Dining room; Physical therapy room; Laundry room; Barber/Beauty shop; Activities/Crafts room.
Activities Arts & crafts; Cards; Games; Reading groups; Prayer groups; Dances/Social/Cultural gatherings; Pet therapy.

Kimberling City

Table Rock Health Care Center
Rte 3 Box 58-A, Table Rock Village, Kimberling City, MO 65686
(417) 739-2481
Admin Kevin D Cantrell.
Licensure Skilled care. *Beds* SNF 120. *Certified* Medicaid; Medicare.
Owner Proprietary corp.

King City

King City Manor
300 W Fairview, King City, MO 64463
(816) 535-4325
Admin Carolyn Stegeman. *Dir of Nursing* Bev Culver RN.
Licensure Intermediate care. *Beds* ICF 60. *Certified* Medicaid.
Owner Proprietary corp (Tiffany Care Centers).
Staff RNs 2 (ft); Nurses' aides 17 (ft), 4 (pt); Activities coordinators 1 (ft).
Facilities Dining room; Physical therapy room; Laundry room; Barber/Beauty shop; Library.
Activities Arts & crafts; Cards; Games; Reading groups; Prayer groups; Movies; Shopping trips; Dances/Social/Cultural gatherings.

Kirksville

Kirksville Manor Care Center Skilled Nursing Facility
1705 E LaHarpe, Kirksville, MO 63501
(816) 665-3774
Admin Robert Redman.
Medical Dir Nancy Bradley.
Licensure Skilled care. *Beds* SNF 132. *Certified* Medicaid; Medicare.
Owner Proprietary corp.
Admissions Requirements Minimum age 16; Medical examination; Physician's request.
Staff Physicians 3 (pt); RNs 4 (ft), 3 (pt); LPNs 14 (ft); Nurses' aides 35 (ft), 15 (pt); Physical therapists 2 (pt); Occupational therapists 1 (pt); Speech therapists 1 (pt); Activities coordinators 1 (ft); Dietitians 1 (pt); Ophthalmologists 1 (pt); Podiatrists 1 (pt); Dentists 1 (pt).
Facilities Dining room; Physical therapy room; Activities room; Chapel; Crafts room; Laundry room; Barber/Beauty shop; Library.
Activities Arts & crafts; Cards; Games; Reading groups; Prayer groups; Movies; Dances/Social/Cultural gatherings.

Twin Pines Adult Care Center
316 S Osteopathy, Kirksville, MO 63501
(816) 665-2887
Admin Marilyn Powell. *Dir of Nursing* Linda Conner RN. *Medical Dir* Harlene Harvey DO.
Licensure Skilled care; Adult day care; Alzheimer's care. *Beds* SNF 186; Adult day care 30. *Private Pay Patients* 25%. *Certified* Medicaid; Medicare.
Owner Nonprofit organization/foundation.
Admissions Requirements Minimum age 18; Medical examination; Physician's request.
Staff Physicians 1 (ft); RNs 4 (ft); LPNs.
Facilities Dining room; Physical therapy room; Activities room; Crafts room; Laundry room; Barber/Beauty shop.

Activities Arts & crafts; Cards; Games; Reading groups; Prayer groups; Movies; Shopping trips; Dances/Social/Cultural gatherings; Intergenerational programs; Pet therapy.

Kirkwood

Blind Girl's Home
221 W Washington Ave, Kirkwood, MO 63122
(314) 966-6033
Admin Colleen L Hill.
Medical Dir Dr Aaron Bernstein.
Licensure Intermediate care. *Beds* ICF 28.
Owner Nonprofit corp.
Admissions Requirements Minimum age 21; Females only; Medical examination; Physician's request.
Staff Physicians 1 (ft); RNs 1 (ft), 1 (pt); LPNs 3 (pt); Nurses' aides 5 (ft), 12 (pt); Recreational therapists 1 (pt); Activities coordinators 1 (pt); Dietitians 1 (ft).
Facilities Dining room; Physical therapy room; Activities room; Chapel; Laundry room; Barber/Beauty shop; Auditorium.
Activities Arts & crafts; Cards; Games; Reading groups; Shopping trips; Dances/Social/Cultural gatherings; Music programs.

Manor Grove Inc
711 S Kirkwood Rd, Kirkwood, MO 63122
(314) 965-0864
Admin Carolyn Ellerbusch.
Medical Dir Dr David Schoenwalder.
Licensure Skilled care. *Beds* SNF 107. *Certified* Medicaid.
Owner Nonprofit corp.
Staff Physicians 19 (pt); RNs 4 (ft), 8 (pt); LPNs 1 (ft), 3 (pt); Nurses' aides 20 (ft), 9 (pt); Physical therapists 1 (pt); Occupational therapists 1 (pt); Speech therapists 1 (pt); Activities coordinators 1 (ft); Ophthalmologists 1 (pt); Podiatrists 1 (pt); Audiologists 1 (pt); Dentists 1 (pt).
Facilities Dining room; Physical therapy room; Activities room; Crafts room; Laundry room; Barber/Beauty shop; Library.
Activities Arts & crafts; Cards; Games; Reading groups; Prayer groups; Movies; Shopping trips; Dances/Social/Cultural gatherings.

St Agnes Home
10341 Manchester Rd, Kirkwood, MO 63122
(314) 965-7616
Admin Sr M Damian.
Licensure Intermediate care; Retirement. *Beds* ICF 150; Retirement 88.
Owner Nonprofit organization/foundation.
Admissions Requirements Minimum age 65; Medical examination.
Staff RNs 2 (ft); LPNs 5 (ft), 1 (pt); Nurses' aides 40 (ft); Activities coordinators 2 (ft), 1 (pt); Dietitians 1 (pt).
Affiliation Roman Catholic.
Facilities Dining room; Physical therapy room; Activities room; Chapel; Crafts room; Laundry room; Barber/Beauty shop; Library; Medical and dental examination room.
Activities Arts & crafts; Cards; Games; Prayer groups; Movies; Shopping trips; Dances/Social/Cultural gatherings; Intergenerational programs; Pet therapy; Weekly happy hour.

La Belle

La Belle Manor
Hwy 6 W, La Belle, MO 63447
(816) 462-3234
Admin Eva J Coleman. *Dir of Nursing* Mrs Jerry Davidson. *Medical Dir* Dr Darrow.
Licensure Skilled care; Alzheimer's care. *Beds* SNF 92.
Owner Proprietary corp.
Admissions Requirements Minimum age 18.

Staff Physicians 3 (pt); RNs 2 (ft), 3 (pt); LPNs 4 (ft); Nurses' aides 25 (ft), 25 (pt); Physical therapists 3 (ft), 2 (pt); Recreational therapists 1 (ft); Occupational therapists; Speech therapists 1 (pt); Activities coordinators 1 (ft); Dietitians 1 (ft); Ophthalmologists 1 (pt); Podiatrists 1 (pt).
Facilities Dining room; Physical therapy room; Activities room; Chapel; Laundry room; Barber/Beauty shop.
Activities Arts & crafts; Cards; Games; Prayer groups; Movies; Shopping trips; Dances/Social/Cultural gatherings; Pet therapy.

Lamar

Lakeview Health Care Center
206 W 1st, Lamar, MO 64759
(417) 682-3315
Admin Doris Lilienkamp.
Licensure Skilled care. *Beds* SNF 123. *Certified* Medicaid; Medicare.
Owner Proprietary corp (Hillhaven Corp).

Lanagan

Cinnamon Hill Manor Inc
PO Box 219, Lanagan, MO 64847
(417) 436-2231
Admin Joetta Jenkins.
Licensure Intermediate care. *Beds* ICF 43.
Owner Proprietary corp.

LaPlata

LaPlata Nursing Home
Old Stagecoach Rd, LaPlata, MO 63549
(816) 332-4315
Admin Wanda L Smith. *Dir of Nursing* Arleen Tate RN. *Medical Dir* O L Woodward DO.
Licensure Intermediate care. *Beds* ICF 52. *Private Pay Patients* 50%. *Certified* Medicaid.
Owner Publicly owned.
Admissions Requirements Minimum age 21; Medical examination.
Staff RNs 1 (ft), 2 (pt); LPNs 2 (ft), 3 (pt); Nurses' aides 12 (ft), 13 (pt); Physical therapists 1 (ft); Occupational therapists 1 (pt); Speech therapists 1 (pt); Activities coordinators 1 (ft); Dietitians 1 (pt).
Facilities Dining room; Physical therapy room; Activities room; Crafts room; Laundry room.
Activities Arts & crafts; Cards; Games; Reading groups; Prayer groups; Movies; Shopping trips; Dances/Social/Cultural gatherings; Intergenerational programs; Pet therapy.

Lathrop

Lathrop Health Facility Inc
702 Center St, Box 285, Lathrop, MO 64465
(816) 528-4257
Admin Evelyn L Spiers.
Licensure Intermediate care. *Beds* ICF 84.
Owner Nonprofit corp.
Staff RNs 1 (ft), 2 (pt); LPNs 4 (ft), 1 (pt); Nurses' aides 28 (ft); Activities coordinators 1 (ft); Dietitians 6 (ft), 1 (pt).
Facilities Dining room; Activities room; Chapel; Laundry room; Barber/Beauty shop.
Activities Arts & crafts; Cards; Games; Reading groups; Prayer groups; Movies; Dances/Social/Cultural gatherings; Bus tours.

Laurie

Laurie Nursing Home/Laurie Knolls
PO Box 1068, State Rd O, Laurie, MO 65038
(314) 374-8263
Admin Sandy Carlson. *Dir of Nursing* Jewell Lichius RN. *Medical Dir* Dr H Petry.

Licensure Intermediate care; Residential care. *Beds* ICF 60; Residential care 36. *Private Pay Patients* 45%. *Certified* Medicaid.
Owner Publicly owned.
Admissions Requirements Medical examination.
Staff Physicians 3 (ft); RNs 1 (ft); LPNs 2 (ft), 1 (pt); Nurses' aides 35 (ft); Physical therapists 1 (pt); Speech therapists 1 (pt); Activities coordinators 1 (ft); Dietitians 1 (ft).
Facilities Dining room; Physical therapy room; Activities room; Laundry room; Barber/Beauty shop.
Activities Arts & crafts; Games; Reading groups; Prayer groups; Movies; Pet therapy.

Lawson

Graceland Manor
Rte 1 Box 460, Lawson, MO 64062
Admissions Requirements Medical examination.
Staff Nurses' aides 2 (ft).
Facilities Dining room; Activities room; Chapel; Laundry room.
Activities Arts & crafts; Games; Reading groups; Prayer groups; Shopping trips; Dances/Social/Cultural gatherings.

Smithview Manor Nursing Home
210 W 8th Terrace, Lawson, MO 64062
(816) 296-7412
Admin Genevie M Herndon.
Licensure Intermediate care. *Beds* ICF 60. *Certified* Medicaid.
Owner Proprietary corp.
Staff RNs 1 (pt); LPNs 3 (ft), 1 (pt); Nurses' aides 21 (ft), 4 (pt); Physical therapists 1 (pt); Occupational therapists 1 (pt); Speech therapists 1 (pt); Activities coordinators 1 (ft); Dietitians 1 (pt).
Facilities Dining room; Activities room; Laundry room; Barber/Beauty shop; TV room.
Activities Arts & crafts; Cards; Games; Reading groups; Prayer groups; Movies; Shopping trips; Dances/Social/Cultural gatherings; Musical entertainment.

Lebanon

Lebanon Care Center
PO Box K, Lebanon, MO 65536
(417) 532-9173
Admin Diana Gregory.
Licensure Skilled care. *Beds* SNF 180. *Certified* Medicaid; Medicare.
Owner Proprietary corp.

Lebanon Manor
175 Morton Rd, Lebanon, MO 65536
(417) 532-5351
Admin Shirley Henderson.
Licensure Intermediate care. *Beds* ICF 29.
Owner Proprietary corp.

Lee's Summit

John Knox Village Care Center
600 NW Pryor Rd, Lee's Summit, MO 64081
(816) 246-4343, ext 2400, 524-8400, ext 2344 FAX
Admin Mike Burke. *Dir of Nursing* Bernice Holtgrewe RN. *Medical Dir* John Murphy MD.
Licensure Skilled care; Retirement; Alzheimer's care. *Beds* SNF 420; Retirement 2000. *Private Pay Patients* 23%. *Certified* Medicaid; Medicare.
Owner Nonprofit corp.
Admissions Requirements Physician's request.
Staff Physicians 25 (pt); RNs 12 (ft), 3 (pt); LPNs 11 (ft), 12 (pt); Nurses' aides 159 (ft), 20 (pt); Physical therapists 1 (ft); Occupational therapists 1 (pt); Speech

therapists 1 (pt); Activities coordinators 5 (ft); Dietitians 1 (ft); Podiatrists 1 (pt); Audiologists 1 (pt).
Facilities Dining room; Physical therapy room; Activities room; Chapel; Crafts room; Laundry room; Barber/Beauty shop; Book cart; Respiratory therapy.
Activities Arts & crafts; Cards; Games; Reading groups; Prayer groups; Movies; Dances/Social/Cultural gatherings; Intergenerational programs; Pet therapy.

Lee's Summit Nursing Center
615 SW Oldham Pkwy, Lee's Summit, MO 64064
(816) 524-3328
Admin Roxann Bitzer. *Dir of Nursing* Sharon Byers. *Medical Dir* Dr Robert LaHue.
Licensure Skilled care. *Beds* SNF 120. *Certified* Medicaid.
Owner Proprietary corp (Beverly Enterprises).
Admissions Requirements Minimum age 21.
Staff Physicians 8 (pt); RNs 2 (ft), 2 (pt); LPNs 9 (ft), 3 (pt); Nurses' aides 36 (ft); Physical therapists 1 (pt); Recreational therapists 1 (ft); Occupational therapists 1 (pt); Speech therapists 1 (pt); Activities coordinators 1 (ft); Dietitians 1 (pt); Ophthalmologists 1 (pt); Podiatrists 1 (pt); Dentists 1 (pt); Psychologists 1 (pt); Certified dietary managers 1 (ft).
Facilities Dining room; Physical therapy room; Activities room; Crafts room; Laundry room; Barber/Beauty shop.
Activities Arts & crafts; Cards; Games; Reading groups; Prayer groups; Movies; Shopping trips; Dances/Social/Cultural gatherings.

White Ridge Health Center
1501 SW 3rd, Lee's Summit, MO 64063
(816) 525-6300
Admin Lee Thomas; Rick Summers.
Licensure Intermediate care; Residential care. *Beds* ICF 30; Residential care 30.
Owner Proprietary corp.

Lemay

Community Care Center of Lemay
9353 S Broadway, Lemay, MO 63125
(314) 631-0540
Admin Jeanne Price.
Medical Dir Lori Uroste.
Licensure Intermediate care; Alzheimer's care. *Beds* ICF 42.
Owner Privately owned.
Admissions Requirements Minimum age 60; Medical examination.
Staff Physicians 1 (pt); RNs 1 (pt); LPNs 3 (pt); Nurses' aides 15 (pt); Activities coordinators 1 (ft), 1 (pt); Dietitians 1 (ft).
Languages Italian.
Facilities Dining room; Activities room; Laundry room; Barber/Beauty shop.
Activities Arts & crafts; Cards; Games; Reading groups; Prayer groups; Movies; Shopping trips; Dances/Social/Cultural gatherings.

Lewistown

Prairie View Rest Home
Rte 2, Lewistown, MO 63452
(314) 497-2424
Admin Mildred L Huebotter. *Dir of Nursing* Janet Richardson. *Medical Dir* Gene Childress DO.
Licensure Intermediate care. *Beds* ICF 69.
Owner Nonprofit corp.
Admissions Requirements Minimum age 21.
Staff RNs 2 (pt); LPNs 3 (ft), 1 (pt); Nurses' aides 15 (ft); Occupational therapists 1 (ft), 1 (pt); Activities coordinators 2 (ft); Dietitians 1 (pt).

Facilities Dining room; Activities room; Crafts room; Laundry room; Barber/Beauty shop.
Activities Arts & crafts; Cards; Games; Prayer groups; Movies; Shopping trips; Dances/ Social/Cultural gatherings; Intergenerational programs; Pet therapy.

Lexington

Lafayette Manor Nursing Home
Hwy 13 S, Lexington, MO 64067
(816) 259-4697
Admin Harold T Ainsworth Jr. *Dir of Nursing* Connie McPherson RN. *Medical Dir* David Pullium DO.
Licensure Intermediate care; Alzheimer's care. *Beds* ICF 148. *Certified* Medicaid.
Owner Proprietary corp (Beverly Enterprises).
Admissions Requirements Minimum age 17; Medical examination.
Staff Physicians 6 (pt); RNs 1 (ft); LPNs 3 (ft); Nurses' aides 58 (ft), 4 (pt); Physical therapists 1 (pt); Occupational therapists 1 (pt); Speech therapists 1 (pt); Activities coordinators 1 (ft); Dietitians 1 (pt); Podiatrists 1 (pt); Dentists 1 (pt).
Facilities Dining room; Physical therapy room; Activities room; Chapel; Crafts room; Laundry room; Barber/Beauty shop.
Activities Arts & crafts; Games; Reading groups; Movies; Shopping trips; Dances/ Social/Cultural gatherings; Resident council.

Liberty

Heartland of Liberty
1200 W College, Liberty, MO 64068
(816) 781-3020
Admin John L Peterson. *Dir of Nursing* Pat Dixon RN. *Medical Dir* Dr John Owen.
Licensure Intermediate care. *Beds* ICF 140. *Certified* Medicaid.
Owner Proprietary corp (Health Care & Retirement Corp).
Admissions Requirements Minimum age 21; Medical examination; Physician's request.
Staff RNs 3 (ft); LPNs 10 (ft); Nurses' aides 43 (ft), 10 (pt); Recreational therapists 1 (ft), 1 (pt); Activities coordinators 1 (ft), 1 (pt); Dietitians 1 (pt); Social workers 1 (ft).
Languages Spanish.
Facilities Dining room; Physical therapy room; Activities room; Crafts room; Laundry room; Barber/Beauty shop; Library.
Activities Arts & crafts; Cards; Games; Reading groups; Prayer groups; Movies; Shopping trips; Dances/Social/Cultural gatherings; Intergenerational programs; Pet therapy.

Odd Fellows Home Association Inc
Rte 6 Box 194, Liberty, MO 64068
(816) 781-4880
Admin Helen Jo White.
Licensure Intermediate care; Residential care. *Beds* ICF 20; Residential care 15.
Owner Nonprofit corp.
Affiliation Independent Order of Odd Fellows & Rebekahs.

Pleasant Valley Manor Care Center
6814 Sobbie Rd, Liberty, MO 64068
(816) 781-5277
Admin Linda Gentry.
Medical Dir Dr Nancy Russell.
Licensure Intermediate care. *Beds* ICF 102.
Owner Proprietary corp.
Staff Physicians 2 (ft); RNs 1 (ft); LPNs 6 (ft), 1 (pt); Nurses' aides 22 (ft), 4 (pt); Physical therapists 3 (ft); Reality therapists 1 (ft); Recreational therapists 1 (ft); Occupational therapists 1 (ft); Activities coordinators 1 (ft); Dietitians 1 (ft); Podiatrists 1 (ft); Dentists 1 (ft).

Facilities Dining room; Physical therapy room; Activities room; Chapel; Laundry room; Barber/Beauty shop; Library.
Activities Arts & crafts; Games; Reading groups; Prayer groups; Movies; Shopping trips; Dances/Social/Cultural gatherings.

Licking

Texas County Missouri Health Care Center Inc
Rte 7 Box 40, Licking, MO 65542
(314) 674-2111
Admin Shelia Todaro.
Licensure Intermediate care. *Beds* ICF 60. *Certified* Medicaid.
Owner Nonprofit corp.

Lincoln

Lincoln Community Nursing Home
Rte 1 Box 302, Lincoln, MO 65338
(816) 547-3322
Admin Ruth Ann Hayes. *Dir of Nursing* Lorraine Schlesselman RN. *Medical Dir* D K Allcorn MD.
Licensure Intermediate care. *Beds* ICF 60. *Private Pay Patients* 55%. *Certified* Medicaid.
Owner Publicly owned.
Admissions Requirements Minimum age 17; Medical examination.
Staff RNs 1 (ft); LPNs 4 (ft); Nurses' aides 20 (ft), 5 (pt); Activities coordinators 1 (ft).
Facilities Dining room; Physical therapy room; Activities room; Chapel; Laundry room; Barber/Beauty shop.
Activities Arts & crafts; Games; Reading groups; Movies.

Linn

Green Meadows Health Care Inc
1 Green Meadows Ln, Linn, MO 65051
(314) 897-2218
Admin Weldon Curry. *Dir of Nursing* Dorathy Curry RN.
Licensure Skilled care; Intermediate care; Alzheimer's care. *Beds* Swing beds SNF/ICF 60. *Private Pay Patients* 50%. *Certified* Medicaid; Medicare.
Owner Proprietary corp.
Admissions Requirements Minimum age 21; Medical examination.
Staff Physicians 5 (pt); RNs 2 (ft); LPNs 4 (ft); Nurses' aides 9 (ft); Physical therapists 1 (ft); Activities coordinators 1 (ft); Dietitians 1 (ft); Ophthalmologists 1 (ft).
Facilities Dining room; Physical therapy room; Activities room; Chapel; Crafts room; Laundry room; Barber/Beauty shop; Library; Conversation room; Children's day care center; Secured outdoor areas.
Activities Arts & crafts; Cards; Games; Reading groups; Prayer groups; Movies; Shopping trips; Dances/Social/Cultural gatherings; Intergenerational programs.

Linn Manor Nursing Home
PO Box 499, Linn, MO 65051
(314) 897-9960
Admin Dorothy Curry; Weldon Curry.
Licensure Intermediate care. *Beds* ICF 41.
Owner Proprietary corp.

Lockwood

Good Shepherd Nursing Home & Residential Care Facility
200 W 12th, Box C, Lockwood, MO 65682
(417) 232-4571
Admin Mildred Shuster. *Dir of Nursing* Beth Paschall RN.
Licensure Intermediate care; Residential care. *Beds* ICF 66; Residential care 24. *Certified* Medicaid.
Owner Nonprofit corp.

Admissions Requirements Minimum age 14.
Staff Physicians 4 (pt); RNs 1 (ft); LPNs 3 (ft), 2 (pt); Nurses' aides 18 (ft), 6 (pt); Physical therapists 1 (pt); Recreational therapists 1 (ft); Occupational therapists 1 (pt); Activities coordinators 1 (ft); Dietitians 1 (ft).
Facilities Dining room; Activities room; Chapel; Laundry room; Barber/Beauty shop; Library.
Activities Arts & crafts; Cards; Games; Prayer groups; Movies.

Louisiana

Maple Grove Lodge Inc
PO Box 370, 2407 Kentucky, Louisiana, MO 63353
(314) 754-5456
Admin Joanne K Rucker. *Dir of Nursing* Darline Bange. *Medical Dir* L G Stuerman MD.
Licensure Intermediate care. *Beds* ICF 60. *Certified* Medicaid.
Owner Proprietary corp.
Admissions Requirements Minimum age 18; Medical examination.
Staff RNs 1 (pt); LPNs 3 (ft), 1 (pt); Nurses' aides 15 (ft), 3 (pt); Activities coordinators 1 (ft); Dietitians 1 (pt).
Facilities Dining room; Laundry room; Barber/Beauty shop.
Activities Arts & crafts; Prayer groups; Movies; Dances/Social/Cultural gatherings.

Smith-Barr Manor
2407 Georgia St, Box 470, Louisiana, MO 63353
(314) 754-6279
Admin Charles Ulry Jr. *Dir of Nursing* Karen Lynn RN. *Medical Dir* Larry Stuerman MD.
Licensure Skilled care. *Beds* SNF 71. *Certified* Medicaid; Medicare.
Admissions Requirements Minimum age 21.
Staff RNs 2 (ft), 1 (pt); LPNs 7 (ft), 1 (pt); Nurses' aides 23 (ft); Recreational therapists 1 (ft); Activities coordinators 1 (ft); Dietitians 1 (pt).
Facilities Dining room; Physical therapy room; Activities room; Laundry room; Barber/Beauty shop; Library.
Activities Arts & crafts; Games; Reading groups; Prayer groups; Movies; Dances/ Social/Cultural gatherings.

Lowry City

Truman Lake Manor
600 E 7th St, Box 188, Lowry City, MO 64763
(417) 644-2248
Admin Anna Gilles. *Dir of Nursing* Pat Jones. *Medical Dir* Dr Niko VanZanten.
Licensure Skilled care; Intermediate care. *Beds* Swing beds SNF/ICF 120. *Private Pay Patients* 25%. *Certified* Medicaid.
Owner Proprietary corp.
Admissions Requirements Minimum age 18; Medical examination.
Staff Physicians 8 (pt); RNs 2 (ft), 1 (pt); LPNs 7 (ft), 1 (pt); Nurses' aides 35 (ft), 1 (pt); Physical therapists 1 (pt); Occupational therapists 1 (pt); Activities coordinators 2 (ft); Dietitians 1 (ft), 1 (pt); Ophthalmologists 1 (pt); Audiologists 1 (pt); Dentists 1 (pt); Medical records staff 2 (ft), 1 (pt).
Facilities Dining room; Physical therapy room; Activities room; Crafts room; Laundry room; Barber/Beauty shop; Library.
Activities Arts & crafts; Cards; Games; Reading groups; Prayer groups; Movies; Shopping trips; Dances/Social/Cultural gatherings; Intergenerational programs; Pet therapy; Exercise groups.

Lutesville

Bond Nursing Care Center
Rte 2, Hwy 34 W, Lutesville, MO 63762
(314) 238-2614
Admin Gayle Spooler.
Licensure Skilled care; Intermediate care. *Beds*
  Swing beds SNF/ICF 120. *Certified*
  Medicaid.
Owner Proprietary corp.

Macon

Macon County Nursing Home District—Loch Haven
PO Box 187, Sunset Hills Dr, Macon, MO
  63552
(816) 385-3113
Admin Richard S Waller. *Dir of Nursing*
  Barbara Primm RN. *Medical Dir* Dr J E
  Campbell.
Licensure Skilled care; Intermediate care;
  Retirement. *Beds* SNF 60; ICF 120;
  Retirement apts 24. *Certified* Medicaid;
  Medicare.
Owner Publicly owned.
Admissions Requirements Minimum age 18.
Staff Physicians 1 (pt); RNs 5 (ft), 1 (pt);
  LPNs 10 (ft), 2 (pt); Nurses' aides 98 (ft);
  Physical therapists 1 (ft); Occupational
  therapists 1 (pt); Speech therapists 1 (pt);
  Activities coordinators 1 (ft), 2 (pt);
  Dietitians 1 (pt).
Languages Spanish, Italian.
Facilities Dining room; Physical therapy
  room; Activities room; Chapel; Crafts room;
  Laundry room; Barber/Beauty shop.
Activities Arts & crafts; Cards; Games;
  Reading groups; Prayer groups; Movies;
  Shopping trips; Dances/Social/Cultural
  gatherings; Music.

Macon Health Care Center
PO Box 465, Hwy 36 E, Macon, MO 63552
(816) 385-5797
Admin Kathlene Rowe. *Dir of Nursing*
  Tamyra Dowell. *Medical Dir* Joseph
  Quaranto MD.
Licensure Skilled care. *Beds* SNF 120. *Private
  Pay Patients* 35%. *Certified* Medicaid;
  Medicare; VA.
Owner Proprietary corp.
Admissions Requirements Minimum age 18;
  Medical examination.
Staff Physicians 9 (pt); RNs 2 (ft), 2 (pt);
  LPNs 9 (ft), 1 (pt); Nurses' aides 28 (ft), 8
  (pt); Physical therapists 1 (pt); Occupational
  therapists 1 (pt); Speech therapists 1 (pt);
  Activities coordinators 1 (ft), 1 (pt);
  Dietitians 1 (ft); Podiatrists 1 (pt).
Facilities Dining room; Physical therapy
  room; Activities room; Crafts room; Laundry
  room; Barber/Beauty shop.
Activities Arts & crafts; Cards; Games;
  Reading groups; Prayer groups; Movies;
  Shopping trips; Dances/Social/Cultural
  gatherings.

Madison

Wildwood Health Center
Rte 2, Madison, MO 65263
(816) 291-8636
Admin Margery Sue Waller. *Dir of Nursing*
  Judy Hollingsworth. *Medical Dir* Dr Robert
  Warbritton.
Licensure Intermediate care. *Beds* ICF 32.
Owner Privately owned.
Staff Physicians; RNs; LPNs; Nurses' aides;
  Activities coordinators; Dietitians.
Facilities Dining room; Activities room;
  Laundry room.
Activities Arts & crafts; Cards; Games;
  Reading groups; Prayer groups; Movies;
  Shopping trips; Dances/Social/Cultural
  gatherings.

Malden

Malden Nursing Center
PO Box 525, 1209 Stokelan Dr, Malden, MO
  63863
(314) 276-5115
Admin John Hisaw.
Licensure Skilled care; Intermediate care. *Beds*
  Swing beds SNF/ICF 60. *Certified* Medicaid.
Owner Proprietary corp.

Ridgeview Nursing
500 Barrett, Malden, MO 63863
(314) 276-3843
Admin Toni Robinson.
Medical Dir Tom Henderson.
Licensure Skilled care. *Beds* SNF 120.
  Certified Medicaid.
Owner Proprietary corp (Beverly Enterprises).
Admissions Requirements Minimum age 21.
Staff Physicians 5 (ft), 4 (pt); RNs 1 (ft), 2
  (pt); LPNs 5 (ft), 3 (pt); Nurses' aides 43
  (ft), 8 (pt); Physical therapists 2 (ft), 1 (pt);
  Recreational therapists 2 (ft); Occupational
  therapists 1 (pt); Speech therapists 1 (pt);
  Dietitians 1 (pt); Ophthalmologists 1 (pt);
  Dentists 1 (pt).
Facilities Dining room; Physical therapy
  room; Activities room; Laundry room;
  Barber/Beauty shop; Library.
Activities Arts & crafts; Cards; Games;
  Reading groups; Prayer groups; Movies;
  Shopping trips; Dances/Social/Cultural
  gatherings.

Manchester

Mari de Villa Retirement Center Inc
13900 Clayton Rd, Manchester, MO 63011
(314) 227-5347
Admin Joseph F Linneman.
Licensure Skilled care. *Beds* SNF 224.
Owner Proprietary corp.

Mansfield

Mansfield Nursing Home
Rte 1 Box 27, Mansfield, MO 65704
(417) 924-8116
Admin Michael D Baldus. *Dir of Nursing* Ann
  Orth LPN. *Medical Dir* Nestor G Dimayuga
  MD.
Licensure Intermediate care. *Beds* ICF 63.
  Private Pay Patients 20%. *Certified*
  Medicaid.
Owner Proprietary corp.
Admissions Requirements Minimum age 18;
  Medical examination.
Staff Physicians 1 (pt); RNs 1 (pt); LPNs 3
  (ft); Nurses' aides 24 (ft), 2 (pt); Activities
  coordinators 1 (ft); Dietitians 1 (pt); Medical
  technicians 3 (ft), 5 (pt).
Facilities Dining room; Physical therapy
  room; Activities room; Laundry room; Deck
  for outdoor parties.
Activities Arts & crafts; Cards; Games; Prayer
  groups; Movies; Shopping trips; Sunshine
  day; Wilder day; Ice cream socials; Fish day
  & fry; Tours.

Marceline

Marceline Healthcare
108 E Howell St, Marceline, MO 64658
(816) 376-3579
Admin Jeanne Morton. *Dir of Nursing* Ruth
  Baker RN.
Licensure Intermediate care. *Beds* ICF 80.
  Private Pay Patients 30%.
Owner Proprietary corp (Hillhaven Corp).

Pershing Regional Health Center
225 W Hayden, Marceline, MO 64658
(816) 376-3521, 258-5668 FAX

Admin Phil Hamilton Sr V Pres. *Dir of
  Nursing* Linda Haley RN, Unit Mgr.
  Medical Dir David Armin MD.
Licensure Skilled care; Intermediate care. *Beds*
  Swing beds SNF/ICF 40. *Private Pay
  Patients* 33%. *Certified* Medicaid; Medicare.
Owner Nonprofit corp (Pershing Memorial
  Hospital).
Admissions Requirements Minimum age 21;
  Physician's request.
Staff Physicians 2 (ft), 10 (pt); RNs 4 (ft), 2
  (pt); LPNs 4 (ft), 2 (pt); Nurses' aides 12
  (ft), 6 (pt); Physical therapists 1 (ft);
  Recreational therapists 1 (ft), 1 (pt);
  Occupational therapists 1 (pt); Speech
  therapists 1 (pt); Activities coordinators 1
  (ft); Dietitians 1 (ft); Ophthalmologists 1
  (pt); Podiatrists 1 (pt); Audiologists 1 (pt);
  Beauticians 1 (pt).
Facilities Dining room; Physical therapy
  room; Activities room; Chapel; Crafts room;
  Laundry room; Barber/Beauty shop; Library;
  2 physician clinics; X-ray department; Lab;
  Behavioral medicine unit.
Activities Arts & crafts; Cards; Games;
  Reading groups; Prayer groups; Movies;
  Shopping trips; Dances/Social/Cultural
  gatherings; Intergenerational programs; Pet
  therapy.

Pioneer Health Center
RR 1 Box 100, S Kansas Ave, Marceline, MO
  64658
(816) 376-2001
Admin Shirley White.
Medical Dir S P Galvez MD.
Licensure Skilled care. *Beds* SNF 84. *Certified*
  Medicaid; Medicare.
Owner Proprietary corp.
Admissions Requirements Minimum age 18;
  Medical examination; Physician's request.
Staff Physicians 1 (pt); RNs 2 (ft); LPNs 5
  (ft), 1 (pt); Nurses' aides 26 (ft), 7 (pt);
  Physical therapists 1 (pt); Occupational
  therapists 1 (pt); Speech therapists 1 (pt);
  Activities coordinators 1 (ft), 1 (pt);
  Dietitians 1 (pt); Podiatrists 1 (pt); Dentists
  1 (pt).
Facilities Dining room; Physical therapy
  room; Activities room; Laundry room;
  Barber/Beauty shop; Fire protection
  sprinkler; Individual room controlled heat;
  Central air conditioning; Cable television.
Activities Arts & crafts; Cards; Games;
  Movies; Shopping trips; Dances/Social/
  Cultural gatherings.

Marionville

Ozarks Methodist Manor
205 S College, Box C, Marionville, MO 65705
(417) 463-2573
Admin Beryl R Gourley. *Dir of Nursing* Pam
  Fite.
Licensure Intermediate care; Residential care.
  Beds ICF 78; Residential care 82.
Owner Nonprofit organization/foundation.
Admissions Requirements Minimum age 60;
  Medical examination.
Staff Physicians 1 (pt); RNs 2 (ft), 1 (pt);
  LPNs 7 (ft), 3 (pt); Nurses' aides 35 (ft), 33
  (pt); Physical therapists 5 (ft), 1 (pt);
  Dietitians 1 (ft); Ophthalmologists 1 (pt).
Affiliation Methodist.
Facilities Dining room; Physical therapy
  room; Activities room; Chapel; Crafts room;
  Laundry room; Barber/Beauty shop; Library.
Activities Arts & crafts; Cards; Games;
  Reading groups; Prayer groups; Movies;
  Shopping trips.

Marshall

Mar-Saline Manor Care Center
809 E Gordon, Marshall, MO 65340
(816) 886-2247

Admin Lydia A McGrath. *Dir of Nursing* Jane Coleman LPN.
Licensure Intermediate care. *Beds* ICF 92.
Owner Proprietary corp.
Admissions Requirements Medical examination.
Staff Physicians 1 (ft); RNs 1 (pt); LPNs 6 (ft); Physical therapists 1 (pt); Speech therapists 1 (pt); Activities coordinators 1 (ft); Dietitians 1 (pt); Podiatrists 1 (pt); Dentists 1 (pt).
Facilities Dining room; Activities room; Crafts room; Laundry room; Barber/Beauty shop.
Activities Arts & crafts; Cards; Games; Reading groups; Prayer groups; Movies; Shopping trips; Dances/Social/Cultural gatherings.

Marshall Habilitation Center
PO Box 190, Marshall, MO 65340
(816) 886-2202
Admin Wayne Crawford.
Licensure Intermediate care for mentally retarded. *Beds* ICF/MR 734.

Saline County Rest Home Inc
Rte 1 Box 206L, Marshall, MO 65340
(816) 886-9676
Admin Connie Breshears.
Licensure Intermediate care. *Beds* ICF 82.
Owner Nonprofit corp.

Marshfield

Webco Manor
1657 W Washington, Marshfield, MO 65706
(417) 468-5144
Admin Jo Walker. *Dir of Nursing* Laura Sullivan RN. *Medical Dir* Dr T M Macdonnell.
Licensure Skilled care; Residential care. *Beds* SNF 120; Residential care 24. *Private Pay Patients* 60%. *Certified* Medicaid.
Owner Nonprofit organization/foundation.
Staff Physicians 1 (pt); RNs 6 (ft); LPNs 12 (ft); Nurses' aides 60 (ft); Physical therapists 1 (pt); Recreational therapists 1 (pt); Occupational therapists 1 (pt); Speech therapists 1 (pt); Activities coordinators 1 (ft); Dietitians 1 (pt).
Facilities Dining room; Physical therapy room; Activities room; Chapel; Crafts room; Laundry room; Barber/Beauty shop; Library.
Activities Arts & crafts; Cards; Games; Reading groups; Prayer groups; Movies; Shopping trips; Intergenerational programs; Pet therapy.

White Oak Villa Nursing Home
PO Box 164, Marshfield, MO 65706
(417) 468-3701
Admin E Victor Perryman.
Licensure Intermediate care. *Beds* ICF 28.
Owner Privately owned.

Maryland Heights

Brookview Nursing Home Inc
2963 Doddridge, Maryland Heights, MO 63043
(314) 291-4557
Admin Gloria Lierman. *Dir of Nursing* Marilyn Kuebrich RN.
Licensure Skilled care. *Beds* SNF 116.
Owner Proprietary corp.
Facilities Dining room; Activities room; Crafts room; Barber/Beauty shop.
Activities Arts & crafts; Cards; Games; Reading groups; Prayer groups; Movies; Dances/Social/Cultural gatherings.

Forest Haven Care Center
3201 Parkwood Ln, Maryland Heights, MO 63043
(314) 291-1348
Admin Darlene Sredl.

Medical Dir Arnold S Tepper MD.
Licensure Skilled care. *Beds* SNF 120. *Certified* Medicaid.
Owner Proprietary corp.
Admissions Requirements Medical examination.
Staff Physicians 3 (pt); RNs 3 (ft), 4 (pt); LPNs 5 (ft), 1 (pt); Nurses' aides 36 (ft), 5 (pt); Physical therapists 1 (ft); Reality therapists 1 (pt); Recreational therapists 1 (pt); Occupational therapists 1 (pt); Speech therapists 1 (ft); Activities coordinators 1 (ft); Dietitians 1 (pt); Ophthalmologists 1 (pt); Podiatrists 1 (pt); Dentists 1 (pt).
Facilities Dining room; Physical therapy room; Activities room; Chapel; Crafts room; Laundry room; Barber/Beauty shop; Library.
Activities Arts & crafts; Games; Reading groups; Prayer groups; Movies; Shopping trips; Dances/Social/Cultural gatherings.

Maryville

Maryville Health Care Center
524 N Laura, Maryville, MO 64468
(816) 582-7447
Admin Shirley Talmadge. *Dir of Nursing* Phyllis Turner RN. *Medical Dir* Kanti Havaldar MD.
Licensure Skilled care; Intermediate care. *Beds* Swing beds SNF/ICF 108. *Private Pay Patients* 25%. *Certified* Medicaid; Medicare.
Owner Proprietary corp (Beverly Enterprises).
Admissions Requirements Minimum age 16; Medical examination; Physician's request.
Staff RNs 2 (ft), 1 (pt); LPNs 6 (ft), 1 (pt); Nurses' aides 38 (ft), 4 (pt); Physical therapists 1 (pt); Recreational therapists 1 (pt); Occupational therapists 1 (pt); Speech therapists 1 (pt); Activities coordinators 1 (ft); Dietitians 1 (ft).
Facilities Dining room; Physical therapy room; Activities room; Crafts room; Laundry room; Barber/Beauty shop.
Activities Arts & crafts; Cards; Games; Reading groups; Prayer groups; Movies; Shopping trips; Dances/Social/Cultural gatherings; Intergenerational programs; Pet therapy.

Nodaway Nursing Home Inc
Hwy 46 W, Maryville, MO 64468
(816) 562-2876
Admin Matthew C Clifton. *Dir of Nursing* Barbara Patton RN.
Licensure Skilled care; Residential care. *Beds* SNF 60; Residential care 30. *Private Pay Patients* 25%. *Certified* Medicaid.
Owner Proprietary corp (Tiffany Care Centers Inc).
Admissions Requirements Minimum age 21; Medical examination.
Staff RNs 1 (ft), 1 (pt); LPNs 5 (ft), 1 (pt); Nurses' aides 21 (ft), 2 (pt); Activities coordinators 1 (ft).
Facilities Dining room; Physical therapy room; Activities room; Crafts room; Laundry room; Barber/Beauty shop.
Activities Arts & crafts; Cards; Games; Reading groups; Prayer groups; Movies; Shopping trips; Dances/Social/Cultural gatherings.

Parkdale Manor
Route V & Munn Ave, Maryville, MO 64468
(816) 582-8161
Admin Wallis Ann Gray. *Dir of Nursing* Barbara J O'Connell RN.
Licensure Skilled care; Day care. *Beds* SNF 92. *Private Pay Patients* 100%.
Owner Proprietary corp.
Admissions Requirements Minimum age 16; Medical examination.
Staff RNs 3 (ft); LPNs 6 (ft), 1 (pt); Nurses' aides 20 (ft), 6 (pt); Physical therapists 1 (pt); Activities coordinators 1 (ft), 1 (pt); Dietitians 1 (pt).

Facilities Dining room; Physical therapy room; Activities room; Crafts room; Laundry room; Barber/Beauty shop; Library.
Activities Arts & crafts; Cards; Games; Reading groups; Prayer groups; Movies; Shopping trips; Dances/Social/Cultural gatherings; Intergenerational programs; Pet therapy; Exercise groups.

Matthews

Sells Rest Home Inc
Rte 1 Box 6A, Matthews, MO 63867
(314) 471-7861
Admin Annie Lee Sells.
Licensure Intermediate care. *Beds* ICF 94. *Certified* Medicaid.
Owner Proprietary corp.

Maysville

Sunset Home Inc
Hwy 33, Maysville, MO 64469
(816) 449-2158
Admin Roy Trussell.
Licensure Intermediate care. *Beds* ICF 119. *Certified* Medicaid.
Owner Nonprofit corp.
Staff RNs 1 (ft), 1 (pt); LPNs 2 (ft), 1 (pt); Activities coordinators 1 (ft), 1 (pt).

Memphis

Scotland County Nursing Home
RR 1 Box 52, Memphis, MO 63555
(816) 465-7221
Admin Gerald L Vice. *Dir of Nursing* Mary Ann Kerr RN.
Licensure Skilled care; Alzheimer's care. *Beds* SNF 120. *Certified* Medicaid.
Owner Publicly owned.
Staff Physicians 4 (pt); RNs 2 (ft), 3 (pt); LPNs 4 (ft), 4 (pt); Nurses' aides 40 (ft), 30 (pt); Physical therapists 2 (pt); Recreational therapists 2 (ft); Activities coordinators 1 (ft); Dietitians 1 (pt).
Activities Arts & crafts; Games; Movies; Shopping trips; Outings.

Mexico

Coldwell Nursing Home
RFD 2, Mexico, MO 65265
(314) 581-2752
Admin Frances Weber LPN. *Dir of Nursing* Helen McMellen. *Medical Dir* J E Taft DO.
Licensure Intermediate care. *Beds* ICF 64.
Owner Privately owned.
Admissions Requirements Minimum age 21; Medical examination.
Staff Physicians 1 (ft); RNs 1 (pt); LPNs 3 (ft); Nurses' aides 12 (ft), 1 (pt); Activities coordinators 1 (ft); Dietitians 1 (ft); Ophthalmologists 1 (pt).
Facilities Dining room; Activities room; Chapel; Crafts room; Laundry room; Barber/Beauty shop; Library.
Activities Arts & crafts; Cards; Games; Reading groups; Prayer groups; Movies; Dances/Social/Cultural gatherings.

King's Daughters Home
620 West Blvd, Mexico, MO 65265
(314) 581-1577
Admin Carol S Gilman. *Dir of Nursing* Judy Fletcher LPN.
Licensure Intermediate care. *Beds* ICF 30. *Private Pay Patients* 100%.
Owner Nonprofit organization/foundation.
Admissions Requirements Minimum age 65; Females only; Medical examination.
Staff RNs 1 (pt); LPNs 2 (ft), 3 (pt); Nurses' aides 8 (ft), 3 (pt); Activities coordinators 1 (pt).
Affiliation King's Daughters & Sons.

Facilities Dining room; Chapel; Laundry room; Barber/Beauty shop.
Activities Cards; Games; Prayer groups; Movies; Shopping trips; Intergenerational programs; Exercise class.

Mexico Manor Inc
219 E Bolivar, Mexico, MO 65265
(314) 581-0335
Admin Brenda Bowman.
Licensure Intermediate care. *Beds* ICF 31.
Owner Proprietary corp.
Admissions Requirements Minimum age 18; Medical examination.
Staff RNs 1 (pt); LPNs 2 (ft); Nurses' aides 18 (ft); Dentists 1 (ft).
Facilities Activities room; Laundry room.
Activities Games; Movies; Shopping trips.

Pine Oaks Nursing Center
Hwy 22 & Curtis Ave, Mexico, MO 65265
(314) 581-7261
Admin Fern Walker. *Dir of Nursing* Marty Wilsoncroft RN.
Licensure Skilled care. *Beds* SNF 164.
Certified Medicaid.
Owner Proprietary corp (Beverly Enterprises).
Admissions Requirements Medical examination.
Staff Physicians 1 (pt); RNs 3 (ft); LPNs; Nurses' aides 51 (ft); Physical therapists 1 (pt); Reality therapists 1 (pt); Recreational therapists 2 (ft); Occupational therapists 1 (pt); Speech therapists 1 (pt); Activities coordinators 1 (ft); Dietitians 1 (ft); Ophthalmologists 1 (pt); Podiatrists 1 (pt); Dentists 1 (pt).
Facilities Dining room; Physical therapy room; Activities room; Chapel; Crafts room; Laundry room; Barber/Beauty shop.
Activities Arts & crafts; Cards; Games; Reading groups; Prayer groups; Movies; Shopping trips; Dances/Social/Cultural gatherings.

Milan

Leewood Manor Nursing Home Inc
611 W 3rd, Milan, MO 63556
(816) 265-4433
Admin Ginger Dickson.
Licensure Intermediate care. *Beds* ICF 81.
Certified Medicaid.
Owner Proprietary corp.
Admissions Requirements Minimum age 17; Medical examination.
Staff RNs 1 (ft); LPNs 3 (ft); Nurses' aides 30 (ft); Physical therapists 1 (pt); Occupational therapists 1 (pt); Speech therapists 1 (pt); Activities coordinators 1 (ft); Dietitians 1 (pt).
Facilities Dining room; Laundry room; Barber/Beauty shop.
Activities Arts & crafts; Cards; Games; Movies; Shopping trips; Dances/Social/Cultural gatherings.

Milan Care Center Inc
Rte 3 Box 16, Milan, MO 63556
(816) 265-3168
Admin Michael E Malone.
Licensure Skilled care. *Beds* SNF 100.
Certified Medicaid; Medicare.
Owner Proprietary corp (Health Care & Retirement Corp).
Admissions Requirements Minimum age 16.
Staff Physicians 4 (pt); RNs 2 (ft), 1 (pt); LPNs 6 (ft); Nurses' aides 30 (ft), 10 (pt); Physical therapists 1 (pt); Occupational therapists 1 (pt); Speech therapists 1 (pt); Activities coordinators 1 (pt); Dietitians 1 (pt); Dentists 1 (pt).
Facilities Dining room; Physical therapy room; Activities room; Crafts room; Laundry room; Barber/Beauty shop.

Activities Arts & crafts; Cards; Games; Reading groups; Prayer groups; Movies; Shopping trips; Dances/Social/Cultural gatherings.

Miner

Miner Nursing & Residential Care Center
PO Box 430, Blodgett Rd, Miner, MO 63801
(314) 471-7683
Admin Janet S Housman.
Licensure Skilled care; Intermediate care; Residential care. *Beds* Swing beds SNF/ICF 60; Residential care 14. *Certified* Medicaid.
Owner Proprietary corp.

Mineral Point

Rainbow Springs Care Center
Rte 1 Box 666, Mineral Point, MO 63660
(314) 438-3398
Admin Donald H Bohr.
Licensure Intermediate care. *Beds* 15.
Owner Proprietary corp.

Moberly

Loma Linda Health Care
1600 E Rollins Box 126, Moberly, MO 65270
(816) 263-6887
Admin Leonard Fish.
Licensure Skilled care; Intermediate care. *Beds* Swing beds SNF/ICF 60. *Certified* Medicaid.
Owner Proprietary corp.

Maple Lawn Lodge
415 Woodland Ave, Moberly, MO 65270
(816) 263-5652
Admin Floyd Sims.
Licensure Intermediate care. *Beds* ICF 49.
Owner Proprietary corp.

Medigroup North Village Park Inc
2041 Silva Ln, Moberly, MO 65270
(816) 263-1894
Admin T Carol Wright.
Licensure Skilled care. *Beds* SNF 184.
Certified Medicaid; Medicare.
Owner Proprietary corp.

Moberly Caring Center
700 E Urbandale E, Moberly, MO 65270
(816) 263-9060
Admin Betty L Barrett.
Licensure Skilled care; Intermediate care. *Beds* Swing beds SNF/ICF 120. *Certified* Medicaid.
Owner Proprietary corp.

Mokane

Riverview Nursing Center
Rte 1, Mokane, MO 65059
(314) 676-3136
Admin S Jay Hitt.
Medical Dir Mel Hector.
Licensure Intermediate care. *Beds* ICF 60.
Certified Medicaid.
Owner Proprietary corp.
Admissions Requirements Medical examination.
Staff Physicians 1 (pt); RNs 2 (pt); LPNs 2 (ft), 2 (pt); Nurses' aides 17 (ft); Physical therapists 1 (pt); Reality therapists 1 (pt); Recreational therapists 2 (ft); Occupational therapists 1 (pt); Speech therapists 1 (pt); Activities coordinators 1 (pt); Dietitians 1 (pt); Dentists 1 (pt).
Facilities Dining room; Physical therapy room; Activities room; Laundry room; Barber/Beauty shop; Lounge.
Activities Arts & crafts; Cards; Games; Reading groups; Prayer groups; Movies; Shopping trips; Dances/Social/Cultural gatherings.

Monett

Camden Health Care Center
410 W Benton, Monett, MO 65708
(417) 235-6031
Admin Kerry D Soncrant.
Licensure Intermediate care. *Beds* ICF 120.
Certified Medicaid.
Owner Proprietary corp.

Fourth Street Care Center
910 4th St, Monett, MO 65708
(417) 235-7243
Admin Brosia Garner.
Licensure Intermediate care. *Beds* ICF 26.
Owner Privately owned.

Lacoba Homes Inc
PO Box 885, Hwy 60 E, Monett, MO 65708-0885
(417) 285-7954
Admin Marsha M Jones. *Dir of Nursing* Leslie Stringer-Bishoff. *Medical Dir* Sergio Cruz MD.
Licensure Intermediate care. *Beds* ICF 60.
Private Pay Patients 100%.
Owner Nonprofit corp.
Admissions Requirements Medical examination; Physician's request.
Staff RNs 2 (ft); Physical therapists.
Affiliation Baptist.
Facilities Dining room; Activities room; Laundry room; Barber/Beauty shop.
Activities Arts & crafts; Cards; Games; Reading groups; Prayer groups; Movies; Shopping trips; Pet therapy.

Monroe City

Monroe City Manor Care Center
Hwy 36 & Z Rd, Monroe City, MO 63456
(314) 735-4850
Admin Lillian M Edwards. *Dir of Nursing* Kathryn Burditt RN. *Medical Dir* Dr William E Rice.
Licensure Skilled care. *Beds* SNF 52. *Certified* Medicaid.
Owner Proprietary corp.
Admissions Requirements Medical examination; Physician's request.
Staff RNs 2 (ft); LPNs 4 (ft), 2 (pt); Nurses' aides 12 (ft), 13 (pt); Physical therapists; Activities coordinators 1 (ft), 1 (pt); Dietitians.
Facilities Dining room; Laundry room; Barber/Beauty shop; Whirlpool room.
Activities Arts & crafts; Cards; Games; Reading groups; Prayer groups; Movies; Shopping trips; Dances/Social/Cultural gatherings; Pet therapy; Bingo; Checkers; Pontoon rides; Morning exercise.

Montgomery City

Owens Home
100 S Wentz, Montgomery City, MO 63361
(314) 564-2207
Admin Sue Owens.
Licensure Residential care. *Beds* Residential care 14.
Owner Privately owned.
Staff RNs; Nurses' aides.
Facilities Dining room.
Activities Arts & crafts; Cards; Games.

Moscow Mills

Four Seasons Residential Care
PO Box 40, Moscow Mills, MO 63362
(314) 356-4231
Licensure Residential care; Group home. *Beds* Residential care 30; Group home 6.
Owner Privately owned.
Staff Physicians 1 (pt); RNs 1 (ft); LPNs 1 (ft); Nurses' aides 25 (ft); Activities coordinators 1 (ft), 1 (pt).

Facilities Dining room; Activities room; Laundry room; Barber/Beauty shop.
Activities Arts & crafts; Cards; Games; Shopping trips; Dances/Social/Cultural gatherings; Bowling.

Mound City

Tiffany Heights
1531 Nebraska, Mound City, MO 64470
(816) 442-3146
Admin Jennie Luna. *Dir of Nursing* Barbara Kunkel LPN.
Licensure Intermediate care. *Beds* ICF 60. *Private Pay Patients* 30%. *Certified* Medicaid.
Owner Proprietary corp (Tiffany Care Centers Inc).
Admissions Requirements Minimum age 21; Medical examination.
Staff Physicians 2 (pt); RNs 1 (pt); LPNs 2 (ft), 1 (pt); Nurses' aides 27 (ft); Physical therapists (consultant); Occupational therapists 1 (pt); Speech therapists 1 (pt); Activities coordinators 1 (ft); Dietitians (consultant).
Facilities Dining room; Physical therapy room; Activities room; Laundry room; Barber/Beauty shop.
Activities Arts & crafts; Cards; Games; Reading groups; Prayer groups; Movies; Shopping trips; Dances/Social/Cultural gatherings; Intergenerational programs; Pet therapy.

Mount Vernon

Lawrence County Nursing Home
PO Box 191, Carl Allen Dr, Mount Vernon, MO 65712
(417) 466-2183
Admin Kerry D Soncrant. *Dir of Nursing* Debbie Irwin RN. *Medical Dir* Dr Ron Williams DO.
Licensure Skilled care; Residential care. *Beds* SNF 120; Residential care 24. *Certified* Medicaid; Medicare.
Owner Publicly owned.
Admissions Requirements Minimum age 17; Medical examination; Physician's request.
Staff Physicians 1 (ft); RNs 4 (ft); LPNs 12 (ft); Nurses' aides 33 (ft); Physical therapists 1 (pt); Occupational therapists 1 (pt); Activities coordinators 2 (ft); Dietitians 1 (pt).
Facilities Dining room; Physical therapy room; Activities room; Crafts room; Laundry room; Barber/Beauty shop; Library.
Activities Arts & crafts; Cards; Games; Reading groups; Prayer groups; Movies; Shopping trips; Dances/Social/Cultural gatherings.

Mountain Grove

Heritage Manor of Mountain Grove
13th & Hovis, Mountain Grove, MO 65711
(417) 926-5128
Admin Kathleen Signaigo. *Dir of Nursing* Helen Beard RN. *Medical Dir* David Barbe MD.
Licensure Intermediate care. *Beds* ICF 120. *Certified* Medicaid.
Owner Proprietary corp (National Heritage).
Staff Physicians 1 (pt); RNs 2 (ft); LPNs 10 (ft), 1 (pt); Nurses' aides 43 (ft); Physical therapists 1 (pt); Speech therapists 1 (pt); Activities coordinators 1 (ft); Dietitians 1 (pt).
Facilities Dining room; Physical therapy room; Activities room; Crafts room; Laundry room; Barber/Beauty shop; Library.
Activities Arts & crafts; Cards; Games; Prayer groups; Shopping trips; Dances/Social/Cultural gatherings.

Neosho

Medicalodge of Neosho
400 Lyon Dr, Neosho, MO 64850
(417) 451-2544
Admin Theresa Theas. *Dir of Nursing* Frances Moebius RN. *Medical Dir* Edward Porter DO.
Licensure Skilled care; Intermediate care. *Beds* SNF 29; ICF 91. *Private Pay Patients* 10%. *Certified* Medicaid; Medicare.
Owner Proprietary corp (Medicalodges Inc).
Admissions Requirements Medical examination; Physician's request.
Staff RNs 2 (ft), 1 (pt); LPNs 15 (ft); Nurses' aides 34 (ft); Physical therapists 40 (ft); Activities coordinators 1 (ft); Dietitians 1 (ft).
Facilities Dining room; Physical therapy room; Activities room; Crafts room; Laundry room; Barber/Beauty shop.
Activities Arts & crafts; Cards; Games; Prayer groups; Movies; Dances/Social/Cultural gatherings; Pet therapy.

Neosho Senior Center
330 S Wood, Neosho, MO 64850
(417) 451-3600
Admin Barbara Johnson.
Licensure Intermediate care. *Beds* ICF 94. *Certified* Medicaid.
Owner Proprietary corp (Beverly Enterprises).

Nevada

Moore-Few Nursing Home
901 S Adams, Nevada, MO 64772
(417) 667-3355
Admin Elaine Schraml. *Dir of Nursing* Catherine Eaton RN. *Medical Dir* Warren C Lovinger MD.
Licensure Skilled care. *Beds* SNF 112. *Private Pay Patients* 39%. *Certified* Medicaid; Medicare.
Owner Publicly owned.
Admissions Requirements Medical examination; Physician's request.
Staff Physicians 1 (pt); RNs 2 (ft), 1 (pt); LPNs 9 (ft), 4 (pt); Nurses' aides 40 (ft), 8 (pt); Physical therapists 2 (pt); Occupational therapists 1 (pt); Speech therapists 1 (pt); Activities coordinators 1 (ft), 1 (pt); Dietitians 1 (pt); Ophthalmologists 1 (pt); Podiatrists 1 (pt); Audiologists 1 (pt); Dentists 1 (pt).
Facilities Dining room; Physical therapy room; Activities room; Chapel; Crafts room; Laundry room; Barber/Beauty shop; Library; Outside patio.
Activities Arts & crafts; Cards; Games; Reading groups; Prayer groups; Movies; Shopping trips; Dances/Social/Cultural gatherings; Adult basic education class.

Nevada Habilitation Center
PO Box 34, N Ash St, Nevada, MO 64772
(417) 667-7833
Admin Jim Jones.
Medical Dir John E Byrne MD.
Licensure Intermediate care for mentally retarded. *Beds* ICF/MR 383. *Certified* Medicaid.
Owner Publicly owned.
Staff Physicians 4 (ft); RNs 31 (ft); LPNs 29 (ft); Nurses' aides 424 (ft); Physical therapists 2 (ft); Recreational therapists 1 (ft); Occupational therapists 2 (ft); Speech therapists 4 (ft); Activities coordinators 1 (ft); Dietitians 2 (ft); Ophthalmologists 1 (ft); Podiatrists 1 (ft).
Facilities Dining room; Activities room; Chapel; Crafts room; Barber/Beauty shop; Library.
Activities Arts & crafts; Games; Movies; Shopping trips; Dances/Social/Cultural gatherings.

Nevada Manor
1210 W Ashland, Nevada, MO 64772
(417) 667-5064
Admin Virginia Nash.
Licensure Skilled care. *Beds* SNF 100. *Certified* Medicaid.
Owner Proprietary corp (Beverly Enterprises).

New Florence

New Florence Nursing Home Inc
Rte 1 Box 40, New Florence, MO 63363
(314) 835-2025
Admin Donald Spalding; Lauri Tiala. *Dir of Nursing* Janet Hall RN. *Medical Dir* George Workman MD.
Licensure Intermediate care; Residential care. *Beds* ICF 80; Residential care 40. *Certified* Medicaid.
Owner Nonprofit corp.
Admissions Requirements Minimum age 18.
Staff RNs 1 (ft); LPNs 1 (ft), 2 (pt); Nurses' aides 17 (ft), 7 (pt); Activities coordinators 1 (ft); Dietitians 1 (ft); Dentists 2 (pt).
Facilities Dining room; Physical therapy room; Activities room; Chapel; Crafts room; Laundry room; Barber/Beauty shop.
Activities Arts & crafts; Cards; Games; Reading groups; Prayer groups; Movies; Dances/Social/Cultural gatherings; Resident supper clubs.

New Haven

New Haven Care Center
201 W Hwy 100 Box 47, New Haven, MO 63068
(314) 237-2108
Admin Natalie Colvis.
Licensure Skilled care; Intermediate care. *Beds* Swing beds SNF/ICF 90. *Certified* Medicaid; Medicare.
Owner Proprietary corp (Beverly Enterprises).

New Madrid

New Madrid Nursing Center
1050 Dawson Rd, New Madrid, MO 63869
(314) 748-5622
Admin Jessie M Butler.
Medical Dir Dr Pattaropong.
Licensure Skilled care. *Beds* SNF 120. *Certified* Medicaid; Medicare.
Owner Proprietary corp (Beverly Enterprises).
Staff RNs 1 (ft), 1 (pt); LPNs 5 (ft), 1 (pt); Nurses' aides 22 (ft); Physical therapists 2 (ft); Activities coordinators 1 (ft); Dietitians 1 (ft); Dentists 1 (pt).
Facilities Dining room; Physical therapy room; Activities room; Laundry room; Barber/Beauty shop.
Activities Arts & crafts; Cards; Games; Reading groups; Prayer groups; Shopping trips; Dances/Social/Cultural gatherings.

Nixa

Nixa Park Care Center
PO Box 694, Nixa, MO 65714-0694
(417) 725-1777
Admin Leonard Ernstmann.
Licensure Skilled care; Intermediate care. *Beds* Swing beds SNF/ICF 60. *Certified* Medicaid; Medicare.
Owner Proprietary corp.

Normandy

Bell Manor Inc
3715 Saint Ann's Ln, Normandy, MO 63121
(314) 383-3353
Admin David Joe Bentley.
Licensure Intermediate care. *Beds* ICF 64.
Owner Proprietary corp.

Admissions Requirements Minimum age 18; Medical examination.
Staff Physicians 1 (pt); RNs 1 (ft), 1 (pt); LPNs 1 (pt); Nurses' aides 25 (ft), 5 (pt); Physical therapists 1 (pt); Occupational therapists 1 (pt); Speech therapists 1 (pt); Activities coordinators 1 (ft); Dietitians 1 (pt); Podiatrists 1 (pt); Dentists 1 (pt).
Facilities Dining room; Activities room; Crafts room; Laundry room; Barber/Beauty shop.
Activities Arts & crafts; Cards; Games; Reading groups; Prayer groups; Movies; Shopping trips; Dances/Social/Cultural gatherings.

Medigroup Castle Park
7301 St Charles Rock Rd, Normandy, MO 63133
(314) 726-5514
Admin Joann Will. *Dir of Nursing* Don A Ruffin. *Medical Dir* D Walkenhorst DO.
Licensure Skilled care. *Beds* SNF 116. *Certified* Medicaid.
Owner Proprietary corp.
Staff Physicians 1 (pt); RNs 2 (ft), 2 (pt); LPNs 8 (ft), 5 (pt); Nurses' aides 67 (ft); Physical therapists 2 (pt); Occupational therapists 2 (pt); Speech therapists 1 (pt); Activities coordinators 1 (ft); Dietitians 1 (ft).
Facilities Dining room; Physical therapy room; Activities room; Laundry room; Barber/Beauty shop.
Activities Arts & crafts; Cards; Games; Reading groups; Prayer groups; Movies; Shopping trips; Dances/Social/Cultural gatherings.

Normandy Nursing Center
7301 Saint Charles Rock Rd, Normandy, MO 63133
(314) 726-5514
Admin Joann Will.

Oak Grove

Oak Grove Health Care Center
21st & Mitchell Sts, Oak Grove, MO 64075
(816) 625-4118
Admin Connie Blowers. *Dir of Nursing* Darlene Burns RN. *Medical Dir* Stephan Griffith MD.
Licensure Skilled care; Alzheimer's care. *Beds* SNF 90. *Certified* Medicaid; Medicare.
Owner Proprietary corp (Angell Group).
Admissions Requirements Minimum age 17; Medical examination.
Staff Physicians 13 (pt); RNs 3 (ft), 1 (pt); LPNs 3 (ft), 1 (pt); Nurses' aides 33 (ft), 3 (pt); Physical therapists 3 (pt); Reality therapists 1 (pt); Recreational therapists 1 (pt); Occupational therapists 1 (pt); Speech therapists 1 (pt); Activities coordinators 1 (ft), 2 (pt); Dietitians 1 (pt); Ophthalmologists 1 (pt); Podiatrists 1 (pt); Dentists 1 (pt).
Facilities Dining room; Physical therapy room; Activities room; Crafts room; Laundry room; Barber/Beauty shop; Library.
Activities Arts & crafts; Cards; Games; Reading groups; Prayer groups; Movies; Shopping trips; Dances/Social/Cultural gatherings; Bowling; Spelling bees.

Odessa

New Haven Nursing Home
PO Box 37, 609 Golf St, Odessa, MO 64076
(816) 633-7539
Admin Denella Marlay. *Dir of Nursing* Ruth Theno RN.
Licensure Intermediate care. *Beds* ICF 60. *Certified* Medicaid.
Owner Proprietary corp (Beverly Enterprises).

Staff RNs 1 (ft); LPNs 4 (ft); Nurses' aides; Physical therapists; Speech therapists; Activities coordinators; Dietitians.
Facilities Dining room; Activities room; Laundry room; Barber/Beauty shop.
Activities Arts & crafts; Cards; Games; Reading groups; Prayer groups; Movies.

O'Fallon

Garden View Care Center
PO Box 9626, 700 Garden Path, O'Fallon, MO 63366
(314) 441-5432
Admin Suzanne Westhoff.
Licensure Skilled care. *Beds* SNF 120.
Owner Proprietary corp.

Oregon

Oregon Care Center
PO Box 532, 501 S Monroe, Oregon, MO 64473
(816) 446-3355
Admin Wava Duncan.
Licensure Intermediate care. *Beds* ICF 60.
Owner Proprietary corp (Tiffany Care Centers).
Staff Physicians 2 (ft); RNs 1 (pt); LPNs 1 (ft), 1 (pt); Nurses' aides 31 (ft), 12 (pt); Physical therapists 1 (pt); Occupational therapists 1 (pt); Speech therapists 1 (pt); Activities coordinators 2 (pt); Dietitians 1 (pt); Audiologists 1 (pt); Dentists 1 (pt).
Facilities Dining room; Physical therapy room; Activities room; Chapel; Crafts room; Laundry room; Barber/Beauty shop.
Activities Arts & crafts; Cards; Games; Prayer groups; Movies; Dances/Social/Cultural gatherings.

Pleasant Hill Nursing Home
Rte 1, Oregon, MO 64473
(816) 446-2281
Admin Dorothy Boehm.
Licensure Intermediate care. *Beds* 32.
Owner Proprietary corp.

Osage Beach

Osage Beach Health Care Center
PO Box 659, Lake Rd 54-29, Osage Beach, MO 65065
(314) 348-2225
Admin Robert W Lane. *Dir of Nursing* Georgia Hughes RN. *Medical Dir* Clemmons Haggerty DO.
Licensure Skilled care. *Beds* SNF 120. *Private Pay Patients* 23%. *Certified* Medicaid; Medicare.
Owner Proprietary corp (National Health Corp).
Admissions Requirements Minimum age 18; Medical examination.
Staff RNs 3 (ft); LPNs 11 (ft), 5 (pt); Nurses' aides 30 (ft), 3 (pt); Activities coordinators 2 (ft).
Facilities Dining room; Physical therapy room; Activities room; Laundry room; Barber/Beauty shop.
Activities Arts & crafts; Cards; Games; Reading groups; Prayer groups; Movies; Shopping trips; Dances/Social/Cultural gatherings; Intergenerational programs; Pet therapy.

Ozark Care Centers Inc
PO Box 278, Ozark Care Dr, Osage Beach, MO 65065
(314) 348-1711
Admin Katherine Fisch RN. *Dir of Nursing* Sue Dautenhahn RN. *Medical Dir* T W Garrison MD.
Licensure Skilled care; Intermediate care; Alzheimer's care. *Beds* Swing beds SNF/ICF 60. *Certified* Medicaid; Medicare.
Owner Proprietary corp.

Admissions Requirements Minimum age 17; Medical examination; Physician's request.
Staff Physicians; RNs 1 (ft), 1 (pt); LPNs 6 (ft); Nurses' aides 18 (ft), 2 (pt); Physical therapists; Occupational therapists; Speech therapists; Activities coordinators 1 (ft); Dietitians (consultant); Ophthalmologists; Podiatrists; Social workers (consultant).
Facilities Dining room; Physical therapy room; Activities room; Crafts room; Laundry room; Barber/Beauty shop; Child day care center.
Activities Arts & crafts; Cards; Games; Reading groups; Prayer groups; Movies; Shopping trips; Dances/Social/Cultural gatherings; Intergenerational programs; Pet therapy.

Owensville

Gasconade Manor Nursing & Care Center
PO Box 520, Hwy 19 & Springfield Rd, Owensville, MO 65066
(314) 437-4101, 437-4833
Admin Dale Grunewald. *Dir of Nursing* Donna Bond RN. *Medical Dir* Dr Robert LaHue.
Licensure Skilled care; Residential care. *Beds* SNF 60; Residential care 9. *Certified* Medicaid.
Owner Publicly owned.
Admissions Requirements Minimum age 16; Medical examination.
Staff RNs 2 (ft), 2 (pt); LPNs 3 (ft), 2 (pt); Nurses' aides 16 (ft), 6 (pt); Activities coordinators 1 (ft).
Facilities Dining room; Physical therapy room; Activities room; Laundry room; Barber/Beauty shop.
Activities Arts & crafts; Cards; Games; Prayer groups; Movies; Shopping trips; Dances/Social/Cultural gatherings.

Ozark

Ozark Nursing & Care Center
1106 N 3rd Ave, Ozark, MO 65721
(417) 485-7126
Admin John Harrison. *Dir of Nursing* Joeha Schnetzler RN. *Medical Dir* Randall Halley DO.
Licensure Skilled care. *Beds* SNF 120. *Certified* Medicaid; Medicare.
Owner Proprietary corp.
Admissions Requirements Medical examination.
Staff Physicians 2 (pt); RNs 1 (ft), 1 (pt); LPNs 9 (ft); Physical therapists 1 (pt); Occupational therapists 1 (pt); Speech therapists 1 (pt); Activities coordinators 1 (ft), 2 (pt); Dietitians 1 (pt); Ophthalmologists 1 (pt).
Facilities Dining room; Physical therapy room; Activities room; Crafts room; Laundry room; Barber/Beauty shop; Library; Century tub.
Activities Arts & crafts; Cards; Games; Reading groups; Prayer groups; Movies; Shopping trips; Dances/Social/Cultural gatherings.

Ozark Riverview Manor
PO Box 157, Ozark, MO 65721
(417) 485-6025
Admin Daniel L Serven.
Licensure Intermediate care. *Beds* ICF 56.
Owner Proprietary corp.

Pacific

Pacific Care Center Inc
105 S 6th, Pacific, MO 63069
(314) 257-4222
Admin Fay Davis.

Licensure Skilled care; Intermediate care. *Beds* Swing beds SNF/ICF 120. *Certified* Medicaid.
Owner Proprietary corp.

Palmyra

Maple Lawn Nursing Home
PO Box 232, Palmyra, MO 63461
(314) 769-2734
Admin James P Clark.
Licensure Skilled care; Intermediate care. *Beds* Swing beds SNF/ICF 120. *Certified* Medicaid; Medicare.
Owner Publicly owned.

Paris

Monroe Manor
200 South St, Paris, MO 65275
(816) 327-4125
Admin Norma Gritton. *Dir of Nursing* Joyce Riedesel LPN. *Medical Dir* Dr C R Warbritton.
Licensure Intermediate care. *Beds* ICF 120. *Certified* Medicaid.
Owner Publicly owned.
Staff RNs 1 (pt); LPNs 9 (ft); Nurses' aides 48 (ft); Physical therapists 1 (pt); Recreational therapists 4 (ft); Occupational therapists 1 (pt); Speech therapists 1 (pt); Activities coordinators 1 (ft); Dietitians 1 (pt).
Facilities Dining room; Physical therapy room; Activities room; Chapel; Crafts room; Laundry room; Barber/Beauty shop; Library.
Activities Arts & crafts; Cards; Games; Reading groups; Prayer groups; Movies; Shopping trips; Dances/Social/Cultural gatherings; Family meals.

Perry

Twain Haven Nursing Home
Hwy 154 E, Perry, MO 63342
(314) 565-2218
Admin Doris G Moore. *Dir of Nursing* Vickie Rouse.
Licensure Intermediate care. *Beds* ICF 50.
Owner Proprietary corp.
Staff Physicians 1 (pt); RNs 1 (pt); LPNs 2 (pt); Nurses' aides 20 (ft), 4 (pt); Activities coordinators 1 (ft).
Facilities Dining room; Activities room.
Activities Arts & crafts; Games; Reading groups; Prayer groups; Weekly church services; Exercises.

Perryville

American Care Center
430 N West St, Perryville, MO 63775
(314) 547-8383
Admin Norma Jean Steffens.
Licensure Skilled care. *Beds* 156. *Certified* Medicaid; Medicare.
Owner Nonprofit corp.

Perry County Nursing Home
Rte 2 Box 84, 800 Hwy 61, Perryville, MO 63775
(314) 547-6546
Admin Mary L King. *Dir of Nursing* Lola McDowell RN. *Medical Dir* Dr L Medrano.
Licensure Intermediate care. *Beds* ICF 123. *Private Pay Patients* 76%. *Certified* Medicaid.
Owner Nonprofit corp.
Admissions Requirements Minimum age 18; Medical examination.
Staff RNs 2 (ft), 4 (pt); LPNs 2 (ft), 1 (pt); Nurses' aides 50 (ft), 15 (pt); Physical therapists 2 (pt); Activities coordinators 1 (ft); Dietitians 1 (pt).
Languages German.

Facilities Dining room; Activities room; Chapel; Crafts room; Laundry room; Barber/ Beauty shop.
Activities Arts & crafts; Cards; Games; Prayer groups; Movies; Shopping trips.

Piedmont

Clark's Mountain Nursing Center
2100 Barnes, Piedmont, MO 63957
(314) 223-4297
Admin Vicki L McCrackin. *Dir of Nursing* Rhonda Payton RN.
Licensure Intermediate care. *Beds* ICF 90. *Certified* Medicaid.
Owner Proprietary corp (Beverly Enterprises).
Admissions Requirements Minimum age 18; Medical examination; Physician's request.
Staff Physicians 4 (pt); RNs 1 (ft); LPNs 6 (ft); Nurses' aides 31 (ft); Physical therapists 1 (pt); Occupational therapists 1 (pt); Speech therapists 1 (pt); Activities coordinators 1 (ft); Dietitians 1 (pt).
Facilities Dining room; Physical therapy room; Activities room; Laundry room; Barber/Beauty shop.
Activities Arts & crafts; Games; Reading groups; Prayer groups; Movies; Shopping trips.

Platte City

Platte City Caring Center
PO Box 823, 220 O'Rourke, Platte City, MO 64079
(816) 431-5222
Admin Philip Gardner.
Licensure Skilled care; Intermediate care. *Beds* Swing beds SNF/ICF 100. *Certified* Medicaid.
Owner Proprietary corp.

Plattsburg

Clinton Manor Inc
Hwy 116, Box 326, Plattsburg, MO 64477
(816) 539-2713
Admin Yvonne Breckenridge. *Dir of Nursing* Cheryl Routh. *Medical Dir* Dr L A Ozenberger.
Licensure Intermediate care. *Beds* ICF 64.
Owner Proprietary corp.
Admissions Requirements Medical examination; Physician's request.
Staff Physicians; RNs; LPNs; Nurses' aides; Recreational therapists; Activities coordinators.
Facilities Dining room; Activities room; Crafts room; Laundry room.
Activities Arts & crafts; Cards; Games; Reading groups; Prayer groups; Movies; Shopping trips.

Oakridge of Plattsburg
PO Box 247, E Clay Ave, Plattsburg, MO 64477
(816) 539-2128
Admin Gene Davidson. *Dir of Nursing* Judy Davidson RN.
Licensure Intermediate care. *Beds* ICF 60. *Private Pay Patients* 85%. *Certified* Medicaid.
Owner Nonprofit corp.
Staff Physicians 5 (pt); RNs 1 (ft); LPNs 3 (ft), 1 (pt); Nurses' aides 28 (ft); Activities coordinators 1 (ft); Dietitians 1 (pt).
Facilities Dining room; Activities room; Crafts room; Laundry room; Barber/Beauty shop.
Activities Arts & crafts; Cards; Games; Reading groups; Prayer groups; Movies; Dances/Social/Cultural gatherings; Pet therapy.

Point Lookout

Point Lookout Village Health Care Center
PO Box 528, Hwy V 20, Point Lookout, MO 65726
(417) 334-4105
Admin Gloria B Layton. *Dir of Nursing* Tammy E Sanders RN BSN. *Medical Dir* Charles A Spears MD.
Licensure Skilled care; Intermediate care. *Beds* Swing beds SNF/ICF 120. *Private Pay Patients* 45%. *Certified* Medicaid.
Owner Proprietary corp.
Staff RNs 4 (ft); LPNs 15 (ft), 2 (pt); Nurses' aides 37 (ft), 9 (pt); Physical therapists (consultant); Activities coordinators 2 (ft), 2 (pt); Dietitians (consultant).

Poplar Bluff

Assembly Nursing Home
203 N "B" St, Poplar Bluff, MO 63901
(314) 785-4559
Admin Brenda K Miller.
Licensure Intermediate care. *Beds* ICF 48.
Owner Proprietary corp.
Admissions Requirements Minimum age 18.
Staff RNs 1 (pt); LPNs 1 (ft), 1 (pt); Nurses' aides 13 (ft), 4 (pt); Activities coordinators 1 (ft), 1 (pt).
Facilities Dining room; Activities room; Laundry room; Barber/Beauty shop.
Activities Arts & crafts; Games; Prayer groups; Movies.

Bluff Nursing Center
2071 Barron Rd, Box 1066, Poplar Bluff, MO 63901
(314) 686-1147
Admin Betty Morris.
Medical Dir Barry B White MD.
Licensure Skilled care. *Beds* SNF 90. *Certified* Medicaid; Medicare.
Owner Proprietary corp (Beverly Enterprises).
Admissions Requirements Physician's request.
Staff Physicians 2 (ft); RNs 2 (ft), 1 (pt); LPNs 4 (ft), 4 (pt); Nurses' aides 36 (ft), 8 (pt); Physical therapists 1 (pt); Reality therapists 1 (pt); Recreational therapists 1 (pt); Occupational therapists 1 (pt); Speech therapists 1 (pt); Activities coordinators 1 (ft); Dietitians 1 (ft); Ophthalmologists 1 (pt); Podiatrists 1 (pt); Audiologists 1 (pt); Dentists 1 (pt).

Cedargate
PO Box 608, Hwy PP, Poplar Bluff, MO 63901
(314) 785-0188
Admin Ruth Warren. *Dir of Nursing* Ruth E Kanell RN. *Medical Dir* Fred Caldwell MD.
Licensure Skilled care. *Beds* SNF 108. *Private Pay Patients* 25%. *Certified* Medicaid; Medicare.
Owner Proprietary corp.
Admissions Requirements Minimum age 16.
Staff Physicians 25 (pt); RNs 3 (ft), 1 (pt); LPNs 10 (ft), 2 (pt); Nurses' aides 38 (ft), 6 (pt); Physical therapists (consultant); Recreational therapists 1 (pt); Occupational therapists 1 (pt); Speech therapists 1 (pt); Activities coordinators 1 (pt); Dietitians (consultant).
Facilities Dining room; Physical therapy room; Activities room; Crafts room; Laundry room; Barber/Beauty shop; Library.
Activities Arts & crafts; Cards; Games; Reading groups; Prayer groups; Movies; Shopping trips; Dances/Social/Cultural gatherings; Intergenerational programs.

Westwood Hills Health Care Center Inc
PO Box 1328, Hwy 67, Poplar Bluff, MO 63901
(314) 785-0851
Admin Michael Young BS MS. *Dir of Nursing* Janet Glass RN. *Medical Dir* Dr Ben Till.

Licensure Skilled care. *Beds* SNF 120.
Certified Medicaid; Medicare.
Owner Proprietary corp.
Admissions Requirements Physician's request.
Staff RNs 3 (ft); LPNs 10 (ft); Nurses' aides 25 (ft).
Facilities Dining room; Physical therapy room; Activities room; Laundry room; Barber/Beauty shop.
Activities Arts & crafts; Games; Prayer groups; Movies; Shopping trips; Dances/Social/Cultural gatherings.

Potosi

Moses Austin Group Care Home Inc
217 E Citadel, Potosi, MO 63664
(314) 438-3736
Admin Rick J Hurst.
Licensure Intermediate care for mentally retarded. *Beds* ICF/MR 9.
Owner Publicly owned.

Georgian Gardens
1 Georgian Gardens Dr, Potosi, MO 63664
(314) 438-6261
Admin Georgia Moebus.
Licensure Skilled care; Intermediate care. *Beds* Swing beds SNF/ICF 120. *Certified* Medicaid; Medicare.
Owner Proprietary corp.

Princeton

Princeton Care Center Inc
PO Box 147, Princeton, MO 64673
(816) 748-3228
Admin Karen Rockhold.
Licensure Intermediate care. *Beds* ICF 60. *Certified* Medicaid.
Owner Nonprofit corp.
Staff Physicians; RNs; LPNs; Nurses' aides; Physical therapists; Recreational therapists; Occupational therapists; Speech therapists; Activities coordinators; Dietitians; Audiologists; Dentists.
Facilities Dining room; Physical therapy room; Activities room; Laundry room; Barber/Beauty shop; Library.
Activities Arts & crafts; Cards; Games; Reading groups; Prayer groups; Movies; Shopping trips; Dances/Social/Cultural gatherings.

Puxico

Puxico Nursing Center
PO Box 218, Hwy 51 N, Puxico, MO 63960
(314) 222-3125
Admin Shirley Stewart. *Dir of Nursing* Elaine Lemons RN.
Licensure Intermediate care. *Beds* ICF 60. *Certified* Medicaid.
Owner Proprietary corp (Beverly Enterprises).
Admissions Requirements Medical examination; Physician's request.
Staff RNs; LPNs 4 (ft), 2 (pt); Nurses' aides; Physical therapists 1 (ft); Activities coordinators 1 (ft); Dietitians 1 (ft).
Facilities Dining room; Physical therapy room; Activities room; Laundry room; Barber/Beauty shop; Sitting room; TV room.
Activities Arts & crafts; Games; Prayer groups; Movies; Shopping trips; Dances/Social/Cultural gatherings.

Queen City

Schuyler County Nursing Home
Rte 1, Hwy 63 N, Queen City, MO 63561
(816) 766-2291
Admin Robert Seamster. *Dir of Nursing* Anna J March RN. *Medical Dir* Dr R E Minter.
Licensure Intermediate care; Alzheimer's care. *Beds* ICF 60. *Private Pay Patients* 40%. *Certified* Medicaid.

Owner Publicly owned.
Admissions Requirements Minimum age 17; Medical examination.
Staff Physicians 1 (pt); RNs 2 (ft); LPNs 2 (ft), 2 (pt); Nurses' aides 18 (ft), 13 (pt); Physical therapists 1 (pt); Occupational therapists 1 (pt); Speech therapists 1 (pt); Activities coordinators 1 (ft); Dietitians 1 (pt); Podiatrists 1 (pt).
Facilities Dining room; Physical therapy room; Activities room; Chapel; Crafts room; Laundry room; Barber/Beauty shop; Library.
Activities Games; Reading groups; Prayer groups; Movies; Intergenerational programs.

Raymore

Foxwood Springs Living Center
2500 W Foxwood Dr, Box 370, Raymore, MO 64083
(816) 331-3111
Admin Thomas R Williams. *Dir of Nursing* Sara Preiss RN. *Medical Dir* George K Landis MD.
Licensure Skilled care; Residential care; Retirement. *Beds* SNF 60; Residential care 62; Retirement 358. *Certified* Medicaid.
Owner Nonprofit corp (National Benevolent Association of Christian Homes).
Staff Physicians 4 (pt); RNs 4 (ft), 1 (pt); LPNs 5 (ft), 5 (pt); Nurses' aides 20 (ft), 10 (pt); Physical therapists 1 (pt); Activities coordinators 2 (ft), 1 (pt); Dietitians 2 (ft); Ophthalmologists 1 (pt); Dentists 1 (pt).
Affiliation Disciples of Christ.
Facilities Dining room; Physical therapy room; Activities room; Crafts room; Laundry room; Barber/Beauty shop; Library.
Activities Arts & crafts; Cards; Games; Reading groups; Prayer groups; Movies; Shopping trips; Dances/Social/Cultural gatherings.

Raytown

Bowen Health Center
6124 Raytown Rd, Raytown, MO 64133
(816) 358-8222
Admin Georgann Foster.
Licensure Intermediate care; Residential care. *Beds* ICF 92; Residential care 62. *Certified* Medicaid.
Owner Proprietary corp.

Park Place Care Center Inc
11901 Jessica Ln, Raytown, MO 64138
(816) 358-3535
Admin Robert D Steffen.
Medical Dir Doris Johnson.
Licensure Skilled care; Retirement. *Beds* SNF 120. *Certified* Medicaid.
Owner Proprietary corp.
Admissions Requirements Minimum age 18; Medical examination.
Staff Physicians; RNs; LPNs; Nurses' aides; Physical therapists 1 (pt); Reality therapists; Recreational therapists; Occupational therapists; Activities coordinators; Dietitians; Ophthalmologists; Podiatrists; Dentists.
Facilities Dining room; Physical therapy room; Activities room; Chapel; Crafts room; Laundry room; Barber/Beauty shop; Library.
Activities Arts & crafts; Cards; Games; Reading groups; Prayer groups; Movies.

Republic

Republic Park Care Center
901 E Hwy, Republic, MO 65738
Admin Robert A Foster.
Licensure Skilled care; Intermediate care. *Beds* Swing beds SNF/ICF 60. *Certified* Medicaid; Medicare.
Owner Proprietary corp.

Richland

Tri-County Nursing Home Inc
414 N Locust, Box 756, Richland, MO 65556
(314) 765-3243
Admin Dorothy J Setser.
Medical Dir Ruth P Zeigenbein.
Licensure Intermediate care. *Beds* ICF 86.
Owner Nonprofit corp.
Staff RNs 1 (pt); LPNs 4 (ft), 1 (pt); Nurses' aides 23 (ft), 2 (pt); Activities coordinators; CMTs 4 (ft), 1 (pt).

Richmond

Shirkey Leisure Acres
Rte 4 Box 44, Hwy 13 S, Richmond, MO 64085
(816) 776-5403
Admin Eugenia Swafford.
Medical Dir Dr Robert LaHue.
Licensure Intermediate care; Residential care. *Beds* ICF 141; Residential care 24. *Certified* Medicaid.
Owner Nonprofit corp.
Staff RNs 1 (ft); LPNs 4 (ft), 1 (pt); Nurses' aides 84 (ft); Physical therapists 1 (pt); Recreational therapists 1 (ft); Occupational therapists 1 (pt); Speech therapists 1 (pt); Activities coordinators 1 (ft), 1 (pt); Dietitians 1 (ft); Audiologists 1 (pt).
Facilities Dining room; Physical therapy room; Activities room; Chapel; Crafts room; Laundry room; Barber/Beauty shop; Library.
Activities Arts & crafts; Games; Reading groups; Prayer groups; Movies; Dances/Social/Cultural gatherings.

Rock Port

Pleasant View
Box B, Rock Port, MO 64482
(816) 744-6252
Admin Paul S Wheeler. *Dir of Nursing* Alene Trueblood LPN. *Medical Dir* Wallace Carpenter MD.
Licensure Intermediate care. *Beds* ICF 100. *Private Pay Patients* 55%. *Certified* Medicaid.
Owner Proprietary corp (Tiffany Care Centers Inc).
Admissions Requirements Minimum age 18; Medical examination; Physician's request.
Staff RNs (consultant); LPNs 3 (ft); Nurses' aides; Physical therapists (consultant); Occupational therapists (consultant); Speech therapists (consultant); Activities coordinators 1 (ft); Dietitians (consultant).
Facilities Dining room; Physical therapy room; Activities room; Crafts room; Laundry room; Barber/Beauty shop.
Activities Arts & crafts; Cards; Games; Reading groups; Movies; Shopping trips; Dances/Social/Cultural gatherings; Pet therapy; Volunteer program.

Rolla

Medigroup Heritage Park Inc
1200 McCutchen, Rolla, MO 65401
(314) 364-2311
Admin Christel Watson. *Dir of Nursing* Deborah Pelkie. *Medical Dir* Dr John James.
Licensure Skilled care; Intermediate care. *Beds* Swing beds SNF/ICF 120. *Certified* Medicaid; Medicare.
Owner Privately owned.
Facilities Dining room; Physical therapy room; Activities room; Barber/Beauty shop; Patio; Meditation room.
Activities Arts & crafts; Cards; Games; Prayer groups; Movies; Shopping trips; Dances/Social/Cultural gatherings.

Presbyterian Manor at Rolla
1200 Homelife Plaza, Rolla, MO 65401
(314) 364-7336
Admin Elinor Gent.
Licensure Skilled care; Residential care. *Beds*
SNF 30; Residential care 38. *Certified*
Medicaid.
Owner Nonprofit corp.
Admissions Requirements Minimum age 65;
Medical examination.
Staff RNs; LPNs; Nurses' aides 2 (pt);
Activities coordinators; Dietitians;
Podiatrists.
Affiliation Presbyterian.

Rolla Manor Care Center
1800 White Columns Dr, Rolla, MO 65401
(314) 364-7766
Admin Maria Oliver.
Licensure Skilled care. *Beds* SNF 102.
Certified Medicaid; Medicare.
Owner Proprietary corp.

Saint Charles

Charlevoix Nursing Center
1221 Boonslick Rd, Saint Charles, MO 63301
(314) 723-1600
Admin Carole J Coats.
Licensure Skilled care; Residential care. *Beds*
SNF 125; Residential care 17. *Certified*
Medicaid; Medicare.
Owner Proprietary corp (Hillhaven Corp).

Claywest House
2840 W Clay, Saint Charles, MO 63301
(314) 925-1500
Admin Sue Damrell. *Dir of Nursing* Judy
Strasser RN.
Licensure Skilled care; Alzheimer's care. *Beds*
SNF 180. *Certified* Medicaid; Medicare.
Owner Privately owned.
Admissions Requirements Minimum age 18;
Medical examination; Physician's request.
Staff Physicians; RNs; LPNs; Nurses' aides;
Physical therapists; Occupational therapists;
Speech therapists; Activities coordinators;
Dietitians; Ophthalmologists.
Facilities Dining room; Physical therapy
room; Activities room; Crafts room; Laundry
room; Barber/Beauty shop; Sun room;
Decks; Gazebos; Enclosed courtyard.
Activities Arts & crafts; Cards; Games;
Reading groups; Prayer groups; Movies;
Shopping trips; Dances/Social/Cultural
gatherings.

Jefferson Street Nursing Home
1014 Jefferson, Saint Charles, MO 63301
(314) 724-1565
Admin Linda Blewer Swindle. *Dir of Nursing*
Kaye Allen RN.
Licensure Intermediate care. *Beds* ICF 10.
Owner Proprietary corp.
Admissions Requirements Females only.
Staff RNs 1 (ft); Nurses' aides 3 (ft), 2 (pt).
Activities Arts & crafts; Cards; Games; Prayer
groups; Movies.

Parkside Meadows Inc
2150 Randolph St, Saint Charles, MO 63301
(314) 724-7800
Admin G Herbert Gessert. *Dir of Nursing*
Mary Bratcher RN. *Medical Dir* Gene Roxas
MD.
Licensure Intermediate care; Residential care;
Independent living. *Beds* ICF 60;
Residential care 15; Independent living
apartments 172. *Private Pay Patients* 60%.
Certified Medicaid.
Owner Nonprofit organization/foundation.
Admissions Requirements Medical
examination; Physician's request.
Staff RNs 3 (ft), 6 (pt); LPNs 2 (ft), 3 (pt);
Nurses' aides 31 (ft), 5 (pt); Activities
coordinators 1 (ft); Dietitians 1 (ft).
Affiliation United Church of Christ.

Facilities Dining room; Physical therapy
room; Activities room; Chapel; Crafts room;
Laundry room; Barber/Beauty shop.
Activities Arts & crafts; Cards; Games;
Reading groups; Prayer groups; Movies;
Shopping trips; Dances/Social/Cultural
gatherings; Intergenerational programs; Pet
therapy.

St Charles Health Care Center
PO Box 1230, 35 Sugar Maple Ln, Saint
Charles, MO 63301
(314) 946-8887
Admin Guy Crosson.
Licensure Skilled care. *Beds* SNF 120.
Certified Medicaid; Medicare.
Owner Proprietary corp.

St Joseph's Home
723 First Capitol Dr, Saint Charles, MO
63301
(314) 946-4140
Admin Sr Mary Rose.
Medical Dir Dr Brian Stuffelbam.
Licensure Intermediate care. *Beds* ICF 103.
Owner Nonprofit corp (Carmelite Sisters
Divine Heart).
Admissions Requirements Minimum age 65;
Medical examination.
Staff RNs 2 (ft), 1 (pt); LPNs 5 (ft); Nurses'
aides 25 (ft), 15 (pt); Physical therapists 1
(pt); Speech therapists 1 (pt); Activities
coordinators 3 (pt); Dietitians 1 (pt);
Podiatrists 1 (pt); Dentists 1 (pt).
Facilities Dining room; Physical therapy
room; Activities room; Chapel; Crafts room;
Laundry room; Barber/Beauty shop.
Activities Arts & crafts; Cards; Games;
Reading groups; Prayer groups; Movies;
Shopping trips; Dances/Social/Cultural
gatherings.

Saint Clair

St Clair Nursing Center
1035 Plaza Ct N, Saint Clair, MO 63077
(314) 629-2100
Admin Tim Nye. *Dir of Nursing* Shirley
Willard. *Medical Dir* Thomas Mitchell MD.
Licensure Skilled care; Alzheimer's care. *Beds*
SNF 60. *Private Pay Patients* 25%. *Certified*
Medicaid.
Owner Proprietary corp.
Admissions Requirements Minimum age 18;
Medical examination; Physician's request.
Staff RNs 2 (ft), 2 (pt); LPNs 4 (ft), 3 (pt);
Nurses' aides 12 (ft), 8 (pt); Activities
coordinators 1 (ft); Dietitians 1 (pt).
Facilities Dining room; Physical therapy
room; Activities room; Crafts room; Laundry
room; Barber/Beauty shop.
Activities Arts & crafts; Cards; Games;
Reading groups; Prayer groups; Movies;
Shopping trips; Pet therapy.

Saint Elizabeth

St Elizabeth Care Center
Rte 1 Box 22, Saint Elizabeth, MO 65075
(314) 493-2215
Admin Cathy Brinker. *Dir of Nursing*
Elizabeth Conley; Helen True LPN.
Licensure Intermediate care. *Beds* ICF 60.
Certified Medicaid.
Owner Proprietary corp.
Admissions Requirements Physician's request.
Staff Physicians 1 (pt); RNs 1 (pt); LPNs 4
(ft), 2 (pt); Nurses' aides 18 (ft), 8 (pt);
Physical therapists 1 (pt); Occupational
therapists 1 (pt); Speech therapists 1 (pt);
Activities coordinators 1 (ft); Dietitians 1
(pt).
Facilities Dining room; Physical therapy
room; Activities room; Laundry room;
Barber/Beauty shop.

Activities Arts & crafts; Games; Reading
groups; Prayer groups; Movies; Shopping
trips.

Saint James

St James Nursing Center
Rte 2 Box 69, Sidney St, Saint James, MO
65559
(314) 265-8921
Admin Mary Jo Hancock.
Licensure Skilled care. *Beds* SNF 90. *Certified*
Medicaid; Medicare.
Owner Proprietary corp (Beverly Enterprises).
Staff RNs 3 (ft); LPNs 8 (ft); Nurses' aides 60
(ft); Physical therapists 1 (ft); Reality
therapists 1 (ft); Recreational therapists 1
(ft); Occupational therapists 1 (ft); Speech
therapists 1 (ft); Activities coordinators 1
(ft); Dietitians 1 (ft); Podiatrists 1 (ft);
Audiologists 1 (ft); Dentists 1 (ft).
Facilities Dining room; Physical therapy
room; Activities room; Chapel; Crafts room;
Laundry room; Barber/Beauty shop.
Activities Arts & crafts; Cards; Games;
Reading groups; Prayer groups; Movies;
Shopping trips; Dances/Social/Cultural
gatherings.

Saint Joseph

Beverly Manor
1317 N 36th, Saint Joseph, MO 64506
(816) 233-8085
Admin Beverly Jean Cathcart.
Medical Dir Dr David Cathcart.
Licensure Skilled care. *Beds* SNF 120.
Certified Medicaid.
Owner Proprietary corp (Beverly Enterprises).
Admissions Requirements Minimum age 18;
Medical examination.
Staff Physicians; RNs; LPNs; Nurses' aides;
Physical therapists; Recreational therapists;
Occupational therapists; Speech therapists;
Activities coordinators; Dietitians;
Ophthalmologists; Podiatrists; Dentists.
Facilities Dining room; Physical therapy
room; Activities room; Crafts room; Laundry
room; Barber/Beauty shop; Library.
Activities Arts & crafts; Cards; Games;
Reading groups; Prayer groups; Movies;
Shopping trips; Dances/Social/Cultural
gatherings.

Carriage Square Health Care Center
4009 Gene Field Rd, Saint Joseph, MO
64506-1864
(816) 364-1526
Admin Clara L Lash. *Dir of Nursing* Alice
Latesky RN BSN. *Medical Dir* James
Conant MD.
Licensure Skilled care; Retirement;
Alzheimer's care. *Beds* SNF 120; Retirement
apts 16. *Private Pay Patients* 35%. *Certified*
Medicaid; Medicare; VA.
Owner Proprietary corp.
Admissions Requirements Minimum age 21;
Medical examination; Physician's request.
Staff Physicians; RNs 4 (ft); LPNs 13 (ft), 2
(pt); Nurses' aides 41 (ft), 2 (pt); Physical
therapists 2 (ft), 2 (pt); Recreational
therapists 1 (ft); Occupational therapists 1
(pt); Speech therapists 1 (pt); Activities
coordinators 1 (ft); Dietitians 1 (ft);
Podiatrists 2 (pt).
Facilities Dining room; Physical therapy
room; Activities room; Crafts room; Laundry
room; Barber/Beauty shop; Private and semi-
private rooms; Call light systems; Individual
temperature controls.
Activities Arts & crafts; Cards; Games;
Reading groups; Prayer groups; Movies;
Shopping trips; Dances/Social/Cultural
gatherings; Intergenerational programs; Pet
therapy.

Church Street Manor
611 N 11th, Saint Joseph, MO 64501
(816) 232-3740
Admin Veda Sollars.
Licensure Intermediate care. *Beds* ICF 15.
Owner Proprietary corp.

Citadel Health Care Pavilion
5026 Faraon St, Saint Joseph, MO 64506
(816) 279-1591
Admin Myrtle M Wright. *Dir of Nursing*
Donna Mullendore RN. *Medical Dir* James
Conant MD.
Licensure Skilled care. *Beds* SNF 100. *Private
Pay Patients* 35%. *Certified* Medicaid; VA.
Owner Privately owned.
Admissions Requirements Minimum age 18;
Medical examination; Physician's request.
Staff Physicians 1 (pt); RNs 4 (ft), 1 (pt);
LPNs 8 (ft), 1 (pt); Nurses' aides 40 (ft);
Physical therapists 1 (pt); Occupational
therapists 1 (pt); Speech therapists 1 (pt);
Activities coordinators 1 (ft); Dietitians 1
(pt).
Facilities Dining room; Physical therapy
room; Activities room; Chapel; Laundry
room; Barber/Beauty shop.
Activities Arts & crafts; Cards; Games; Prayer
groups; Movies; Dances/Social/Cultural
gatherings.

Heartland Centre
701 Faraon St, Saint Joseph, MO 64501
(816) 271-7376
Admin J William Crittenden. *Dir of Nursing*
Landis L Downing. *Medical Dir* Carlyn
Kline MD.
Licensure Skilled care; Intermediate care. *Beds*
SNF 46; ICF 104. *Certified* Medicaid;
Medicare.
Owner Nonprofit corp.
Admissions Requirements Medical
examination.
Staff RNs 7 (ft), 2 (pt); LPNs 12 (ft), 21 (pt);
Nurses' aides 29 (ft), 18 (pt); Physical
therapists 3 (ft), 3 (pt); Recreational
therapists 2 (ft); Occupational therapists 3
(ft), 1 (pt); Speech therapists 2 (ft), 1 (pt);
Dietitians 3 (pt); Podiatrists 1 (ft); Chaplains
1 (ft); Dentists 2 (pt).
Facilities Dining room; Physical therapy
room; Activities room; Chapel; Crafts room;
Laundry room; Barber/Beauty shop; Library.
Activities Arts & crafts; Cards; Games;
Reading groups; Prayer groups; Movies;
Shopping trips; Dances/Social/Cultural
gatherings.

St Joseph Convalescent Center Inc
811 N 9th, Box 283, Saint Joseph, MO 64501
(816) 233-5164
Admin Dorothy Blakesley.
Medical Dir Dr Donald Sklenar.
Licensure Intermediate care. *Beds* ICF 69.
Certified Medicaid.
Owner Proprietary corp.
Admissions Requirements Medical
examination.
Staff RNs 1 (ft); LPNs 7 (ft); Nurses' aides 27
(ft); Physical therapists 1 (ft), 1 (pt);
Occupational therapists 1 (pt); Speech
therapists 1 (pt); Activities coordinators 1
(ft).
Facilities Dining room; Activities room;
Chapel; Crafts room; Laundry room; Barber/
Beauty shop.
Activities Arts & crafts; Cards; Games;
Reading groups; Prayer groups; Dances/
Social/Cultural gatherings.

Saxton Riverside Care Center
1616 Weisenborn Rd, Saint Joseph, MO
64507
(816) 232-9874
Admin Edna Jessica Saxton.
Medical Dir Dr Sklenar; Dr Christ.

Licensure Intermediate care; Residential care.
Beds ICF 60; Residential care 100. *Certified*
Medicaid.
Owner Publicly owned.
Admissions Requirements Minimum age 18;
Medical examination; Physician's request.
Staff RNs 1 (ft), 1 (pt); LPNs 4 (ft), 1 (pt).
Facilities Dining room.

Tiffany Square Convalescent Center
3002 N 18th, Box 1308, Saint Joseph, MO
64505
(816) 364-4200
Admin S Marian Wilson. *Dir of Nursing* R
Kay Neil RN. *Medical Dir* David Cathcart
DO.
Licensure Intermediate care. *Beds* ICF 240.
Private Pay Patients 25%. *Certified*
Medicaid.
Owner Proprietary corp (Clinton Manor Inc).
Admissions Requirements Medical
examination.
Staff RNs 1 (ft), 4 (pt); LPNs 9 (ft), 4 (pt);
Nurses' aides 66 (ft), 5 (pt); Physical
therapists 1 (ft); Occupational therapists 1
(pt); Speech therapists 1 (pt); Activities
coordinators 1 (ft); Dietitians 1 (pt).
Facilities Dining room; Physical therapy
room; Activities room; Chapel; Laundry
room; Barber/Beauty shop.
Activities Arts & crafts; Games; Prayer groups;
Movies; Shopping trips; Dances/Social/
Cultural gatherings; Intergenerational
programs.

Saint Louis

Barry Alan Nursing Home
3326-38 Eminence Ave, Saint Louis, MO
63114
(314) 427-0988
Admin Deanna M Dotson. *Dir of Nursing*
Loretta Smith LPN.
Licensure Intermediate care. *Beds* ICF 34.
Owner Proprietary corp.
Admissions Requirements Minimum age 40;
Medical examination.
Staff Physicians 1 (pt); RNs 1 (pt); LPNs 1
(ft), 1 (pt); Nurses' aides 9 (ft), 5 (pt);
Recreational therapists 1 (pt); Occupational
therapists 1 (pt); Activities coordinators 1
(pt); Ophthalmologists 1 (pt).
Facilities Activities room; Crafts room.
Activities Arts & crafts; Cards; Games;
Reading groups; Prayer groups; Movies.

Auventine Retirement & Nursing Center
1 Arbor Terrace, Saint Louis, MO 63026
(314) 343-0016
Admin William Svejkosky.
Licensure Intermediate care; Residential care.
Beds ICF 20; Residential care 82.
Owner Privately owned.

Avalon Garden
4359 Taft Ave, Saint Louis, MO 63116
(314) 752-2022
Admin Giehl Rhee.
Medical Dir Seoung E Rhee MD.
Licensure Intermediate care. *Beds* ICF 64.
Owner Proprietary corp.
Admissions Requirements Minimum age 16;
Medical examination.
Staff Physicians 1 (ft); RNs 1 (ft); LPNs 2 (ft);
Nurses' aides 22 (ft), 4 (pt); Physical
therapists 1 (ft); Reality therapists 1 (ft);
Recreational therapists 1 (pt); Occupational
therapists 1 (pt); Speech therapists 1 (pt);
Activities coordinators 1 (pt); Dietitians 1
(pt); Podiatrists 1 (pt).
Facilities Dining room; Physical therapy
room; Activities room; Chapel; Crafts room;
Laundry room; Barber/Beauty shop.
Activities Arts & crafts; Cards; Games; Prayer
groups; Movies; Dances/Social/Cultural
gatherings.

Bernard West Pine Nursing Home Inc
4335 W Pine, Saint Louis, MO 63108
(314) 371-0200
Admin Roxanne Hinkle.
Medical Dir Miguel Abelcuda.
Licensure Skilled care. *Beds* SNF 141.
Certified Medicaid; Medicare.
Owner Proprietary corp.
Admissions Requirements Minimum age 18;
Medical examination; Physician's request.
Staff Physicians 16 (pt); RNs 2 (ft), 3 (pt);
LPNs 7 (ft), 1 (pt); Nurses' aides 37 (ft), 7
(pt); Physical therapists 2 (ft), 1 (pt);
Occupational therapists 1 (pt); Speech
therapists 1 (pt); Activities coordinators 1
(ft); Dietitians 1 (pt); Ophthalmologists 1
(pt); Podiatrists 1 (pt); Audiologists 1 (pt);
Dentists 1 (pt).
Facilities Dining room; Physical therapy
room; Activities room; Crafts room; Laundry
room; Barber/Beauty shop; Enclosed patios.
Activities Arts & crafts; Games; Reading
groups; Prayer groups; Dances/Social/
Cultural gatherings; Outings to area sights.

Bethesda-Dilworth Memorial Home
9645 Big Bend Rd, Saint Louis, MO 63122
(314) 968-5460
Admin Fletcher W Carter III. *Dir of Nursing*
Elaine McCluggage. *Medical Dir* Patrick
Majors MD.
Licensure Skilled care; Alzheimer's care. *Beds*
SNF 490. *Certified* Medicaid.
Owner Nonprofit corp.
Admissions Requirements Medical
examination.
Staff Physicians 1 (ft); RNs 33 (ft); LPNs 32
(ft); Nurses' aides 150 (ft); Physical
therapists 1 (ft); Recreational therapists 1
(ft); Occupational therapists 1 (ft); Activities
coordinators 1 (ft); Dietitians 1 (ft).
Facilities Dining room; Physical therapy
room; Activities room; Chapel; Crafts room;
Laundry room; Barber/Beauty shop; Library.
Activities Arts & crafts; Cards; Games;
Reading groups; Prayer groups; Movies;
Shopping trips; Dances/Social/Cultural
gatherings.

Bethesda Skilled Nursing Facility
3655 Vista Ave, Saint Louis, MO 63110
(314) 772-9200
Admin Connie Siffring.
Medical Dir B Dandamudi MD.
Licensure Skilled care. *Beds* 30. *Certified*
Medicare.
Owner Nonprofit corp.
Admissions Requirements Medical
examination; Physician's request.
Staff Physicians 1 (pt); RNs 2 (ft); LPNs 6
(ft); Nurses' aides 10 (ft); Physical therapists
3 (ft); Occupational therapists; Speech
therapists; Activities coordinators 1 (pt);
Dietitians 1 (ft); Podiatrists 1 (pt);
Audiologists 1 (pt).
Facilities Dining room; Physical therapy
room; Chapel.
Activities Arts & crafts; Cards; Games;
Reading groups; Prayer groups.

Birchway Health Care
4373 W Pine, Saint Louis, MO 63108
(314) 531-2644
Admin Ira Eaton; Sheila Eaton.
Medical Dir Varkey Philip MD.
Licensure Skilled care; Residential care. *Beds*
SNF 67; Residential care 9. *Certified*
Medicaid.
Owner Proprietary corp.
Admissions Requirements Medical
examination; Physician's request.
Facilities Dining room; Activities room;
Crafts room; Laundry room; Barber/Beauty
shop.
Activities Arts & crafts; Cards; Games; Prayer
groups; Shopping trips; Dances/Social/
Cultural gatherings.

Charles the First Medical Center Inc
5303 Bermuda Rd, Saint Louis, MO 63121
(314) 385-0910
Admin Charles L Twedell.
Licensure Skilled care. *Beds* SNF 52.
Owner Proprietary corp.

Charless Home
4431 S Broadway, Saint Louis, MO 63111
(314) 481-4840
Admin Joseph Berry, Exec Dir.
Medical Dir Dr Arnold Brody.
Licensure Intermediate care; Residential care;
Alzheimer's care. *Beds* ICF 40; Residential
care 68. *Private Pay Patients* 100%.
Owner Nonprofit organization/foundation.
Admissions Requirements Minimum age 55;
Females only.
Staff RNs 1 (pt); LPNs 4 (ft); Nurses' aides 15
(ft); Activities coordinators 1 (ft).
Languages German.
Facilities Dining room; Barber/Beauty shop;
Library.
Activities Arts & crafts; Cards; Games;
Reading groups; Prayer groups; Movies;
Shopping trips; Dances/Social/Cultural
gatherings; Tours.

Deaconess Manor
6220 Oakland Ave, Saint Louis, MO 63139
(314) 768-3500
Admin Alice L Walker.
Licensure Skilled care. *Beds* SNF 117.
Certified Medicaid; Medicare.
Owner Nonprofit corp.

Delhaven Manor
5460 Delmar Blvd, Saint Louis, MO 63112
(314) 361-2902, 361-2647 FAX
Admin Larry G Howdeshell. *Dir of Nursing*
Beatrice Hyde. *Medical Dir* Dr Conrado
Abinoja.
Licensure Skilled care; Intermediate care;
Retirement. *Beds* Swing beds SNF/ICF 156.
Certified Medicaid; Medicare.
Owner Proprietary corp (Health Facilities
Management Corp).
Admissions Requirements Medical
examination; Must qualify for ICF of SNF
placement; Chest X-ray.
Staff Physicians 3 (pt); RNs 6 (ft); LPNs 14
(ft), 3 (pt); Nurses' aides 65 (ft); Physical
therapists 1 (ft); Occupational therapists 1
(pt); Speech therapists 1 (pt); Activities
coordinators 1 (ft); Dietitians 1 (pt);
Podiatrists 1 (pt).
Facilities Dining room; Physical therapy
room; Activities room; Laundry room;
Barber/Beauty shop.
Activities Arts & crafts; Cards; Games;
Reading groups; Prayer groups; Movies;
Shopping trips; Dances/Social/Cultural
gatherings; Intergenerational programs; Pet
therapy; Bingo; Talent & fashion shows.

Delmar Gardens of South County Inc
5300 Butler Hill Rd, Saint Louis, MO 63128
(314) 842-0588
Admin Gabe Grossberg.
Licensure Skilled care; Intermediate care. *Beds*
Swing beds SNF/ICF 180. *Certified*
Medicaid; Medicare.
Owner Proprietary corp.

Edgewater Home Inc
5500 S Broadway, Saint Louis, MO 63111
(314) 832-5800
Admin James T Daake.
Medical Dir J Castro MD.
Licensure Skilled care. *Beds* SNF 151. *Private
Pay Patients* 100%.
Owner Privately owned.
Admissions Requirements Minimum age 21.
Staff RNs 3 (ft), 2 (pt); LPNs 9 (ft), 3 (pt);
Nurses' aides 80 (ft); Physical therapists 1
(ft), 1 (pt).

Facilities Dining room; Physical therapy
room; Activities room; Crafts room; Laundry
room; Barber/Beauty shop.
Activities Arts & crafts; Cards; Games;
Reading groups; Prayer groups; Movies;
Dances/Social/Cultural gatherings; Pet
therapy.

Fontaine Woods Nursing Home
9500 Bellefontaine Rd, Saint Louis, MO
63137
(314) 868-1400
Admin Gladys Sullivan.
Medical Dir Dr David Light.
Licensure Skilled care. *Beds* SNF 97.
Owner Proprietary corp.
Admissions Requirements Minimum age 50.
Staff RNs 2 (ft), 5 (pt); LPNs 2 (ft), 6 (pt);
Physical therapists 1 (pt); Activities
coordinators 2 (ft); Dietitians 1 (pt).
Facilities Dining room; Physical therapy
room; Activities room; Crafts room; Laundry
room; Barber/Beauty shop.
Activities Arts & crafts; Cards; Games;
Reading groups; Prayer groups; Movies;
Shopping trips; Dances/Social/Cultural
gatherings.

Frazier Nursing Home
4512 W Pine, Saint Louis, MO 63108
(314) 367-8516
Admin Deborah Frazier. *Dir of Nursing* Joan
Schmidt. *Medical Dir* Dr Nathan Kimelman.
Licensure Intermediate care. *Beds* ICF 36.
Owner Privately owned.
Admissions Requirements Medical
examination; Physician's request.
Staff Physicians 2 (pt); RNs 4 (pt); LPNs 2
(ft); Nurses' aides 12 (ft), 3 (pt);
Recreational therapists 2 (ft); Activities
coordinators 1 (ft); Dietitians 1 (pt);
Ophthalmologists 1 (pt).
Facilities Dining room; Activities room;
Crafts room; Laundry room; Barber/Beauty
shop; Library; Clubhouse available June-Oct.
Activities Arts & crafts; Cards; Games;
Reading groups; Prayer groups; Movies;
Shopping trips; Dances/Social/Cultural
gatherings; Van trips.

Friendship Village of South County
12503 Village Circle Dr, Saint Louis, MO
63127
(314) 842-6840
Admin Charles L Schott. *Dir of Nursing*
Dorcas Hall. *Medical Dir* Dr Robert
Morgan.
Licensure Skilled care; Retirement;
Alzheimer's care. *Beds* SNF 120; Retirement
apts & cottages 388. *Certified* Medicare.
Owner Nonprofit corp (Life Care Services
Corp).
Admissions Requirements Medical
examination.
Staff RNs 2 (ft), 1 (pt); LPNs 4 (ft), 3 (pt);
Nurses' aides 30 (ft), 2 (pt); Physical
therapists 1 (ft); Recreational therapists 1
(ft); Occupational therapists 1 (ft); Activities
coordinators 3 (ft); Dietitians (consultant).
Facilities Dining room; Physical therapy
room; Activities room; Chapel; Crafts room;
Laundry room; Barber/Beauty shop; Library;
Dentist's office; Doctor's examination room.
Activities Arts & crafts; Cards; Games;
Reading groups; Prayer groups; Movies;
Shopping trips; Dances/Social/Cultural
gatherings; Intergenerational programs; Pet
therapy.

Carrie Elligson Gietner Home Inc
5000 S Broadway, Saint Louis, MO 63111
(314) 752-0000
Admin Althea H Wilson. *Dir of Nursing*
Caroline Jones. *Medical Dir* Norman P
Knowlton MD.
Licensure Intermediate care; Residential care.
Beds ICF 75; Residential care 110. *Private
Pay Patients* 91%.

Owner Nonprofit corp.
Admissions Requirements Minimum age 69;
Medical examination.
Staff Physicians 1 (ft), 1 (pt); RNs 1 (ft), 1
(pt); LPNs 3 (ft), 1 (pt); Nurses' aides 35
(ft), 15 (pt); Physical therapists 2 (pt);
Occupational therapists 1 (pt); Speech
therapists 1 (pt); Activities coordinators 1
(ft); Dietitians 1 (ft); Ophthalmologists 1
(pt); Podiatrists 1 (pt).
Facilities Dining room; Activities room;
Chapel; Crafts room; Laundry room; Barber/
Beauty shop; Library; Grounds for strolling
and visiting.
Activities Arts & crafts; Cards; Games;
Reading groups; Prayer groups; Movies;
Shopping trips; Dances/Social/Cultural
gatherings; Intergenerational programs; Pet
therapy; Language club.

Good Samaritan Home
5200 S Broadway, Saint Louis, MO 63111-
2098
(314) 352-2400
Admin Charles Lockyear, Exec Dir. *Dir of
Nursing* Joan Furlong RN. *Medical Dir* Dr
Dale Terrell.
Licensure Intermediate care; Catered
residential living; Retirement; Alzheimer's
care. *Beds* ICF 86; Catered residential living
216. *Private Pay Patients* 100%.
Owner Nonprofit organization/foundation.
Admissions Requirements Minimum age 62;
Medical examination.
Staff Physicians 1 (ft); RNs 3 (ft); LPNs 4 (ft),
5 (pt); Nurses' aides 36 (ft), 50 (pt); Physical
therapists 1 (pt); Recreational therapists 2
(ft), 1 (pt); Ophthalmologists 1 (pt);
Podiatrists 1 (pt); CMTs 13 (ft), 3 (pt).
Affiliation United Church of Christ.
Facilities Dining room; Physical therapy
room; Activities room; Chapel; Crafts room;
Laundry room; Barber/Beauty shop; Library.
Activities Arts & crafts; Cards; Games; Prayer
groups; Movies; Shopping trips; Dances/
Social/Cultural gatherings; Intergenerational
programs; Pet therapy; Bingo; Trips to
community events; Parties; Religious
services.

Gravois Health Care Center
10954 Kennerly Rd, Saint Louis, MO 63128
(314) 843-4242
Admin Barbara M Wagner. *Dir of Nursing*
Rebecca Bernard RN.
Licensure Skilled care. *Beds* SNF 167.
Certified Medicare.
Owner Proprietary corp.
Admissions Requirements Minimum age 18.
Staff RNs 7 (ft), 2 (pt); LPNs 9 (ft), 1 (pt);
Nurses' aides 75 (ft), 1 (pt); Physical
therapists 1 (pt); Activities coordinators 1
(ft), 2 (pt).
Facilities Dining room; Physical therapy
room; Activities room; Crafts room; Laundry
room; Barber/Beauty shop.
Activities Arts & crafts; Cards; Games;
Reading groups; Prayer groups; Movies;
Dances/Social/Cultural gatherings.

Ferrier Harris Home for Aged
3636 Page Ave, Saint Louis, MO 63113
(314) 531-5549
Admin Bettye Dawson.
Medical Dir Dr Dunet F Belancourt.
Licensure Intermediate care. *Beds* ICF 30.
Owner Nonprofit corp.
Admissions Requirements Minimum age 45.
Staff Physicians 1 (pt); RNs 1 (pt); LPNs 2
(ft), 1 (pt).
Facilities Dining room; Physical therapy
room; Activities room; Chapel; Crafts room;
Laundry room; Barber/Beauty shop.
Activities Arts & crafts; Cards; Games;
Reading groups; Prayer groups; Shopping
trips; Dances/Social/Cultural gatherings.

Heritage of St Louis Inc
PO Box 5606, 4401 N Hanley, Saint Louis, MO 63121
(314) 521-6211
Admin Suzanne Westhoff. *Dir of Nursing* Sue Sullivan RN. *Medical Dir* David Rosenberg MD.
Licensure Skilled care. *Beds* SNF 120. *Certified* Medicaid.
Owner Proprietary corp.
Admissions Requirements Minimum age 65; Medical examination; Physician's request.
Staff Physicians 1 (ft), 1 (pt); RNs 2 (ft), 3 (pt); LPNs 4 (ft), 2 (pt); Nurses' aides 20 (ft), 10 (pt); Physical therapists 1 (pt); Reality therapists 1 (pt); Recreational therapists 1 (pt); Occupational therapists 1 (pt); Speech therapists 1 (pt); Activities coordinators 1 (ft), 1 (pt); Dietitians 1 (ft), 1 (pt).
Facilities Dining room; Physical therapy room; Activities room; Laundry room; Barber/Beauty shop.
Activities Arts & crafts; Cards; Games; Reading groups; Prayer groups; Movies.

Jerri's Benevolent Manor
730 Hodiamont, Saint Louis, MO 63112
(314)727-5219
Admin Laverne Haulcy.
Licensure Residential care. *Beds* Residential care 22.
Owner Proprietary corp.

Ranken Jordan Home for Convalescent Crippled Children
1064 Ladue Rd, Saint Louis, MO 63141
(314) 993-1207
Admin Johann L Ellerbrake. *Dir of Nursing* Ann A Young. *Medical Dir* Anthony J Rejent MD.
Licensure Skilled care. *Beds* SNF 26. *Certified* Medicaid.
Owner Nonprofit organization/foundation.

Katie Jane Memorial Home
6109 Bermuda Dr, Saint Louis, MO 63135-3208
(314) 456-3401
Admin Thomas A Daniels. *Dir of Nursing* Bonnie Hune. *Medical Dir* J O'Conner MD.
Licensure Intermediate care. *Beds* ICF 75.
Owner Proprietary corp.
Admissions Requirements Minimum age 21.
Staff Physicians 4 (pt); RNs 1 (pt); LPNs 3 (ft); Nurses' aides 16 (ft), 6 (pt); Activities coordinators 1 (ft); Dietary aides 3 (ft), 2 (pt).
Facilities Activities room; Laundry room.
Activities Arts & crafts; Cards; Games; Reading groups; Prayer groups; Dances/Social/Cultural gatherings.

Little Flower Nursing Home Inc
2500 S 18th St, Saint Louis, MO 63104
(314) 664-2267
Admin Ersie C Harris.
Medical Dir Leonard Piccione MD.
Licensure Intermediate care. *Beds* ICF 90. *Certified* Medicaid.
Owner Proprietary corp.
Staff Physicians 1 (ft), 6 (pt); RNs 3 (ft); LPNs 2 (ft), 2 (pt); Nurses' aides 21 (ft), 5 (pt); Physical therapists 1 (pt); Reality therapists 1 (pt); Recreational therapists 1 (ft); Occupational therapists 1 (pt); Speech therapists 1 (pt); Activities coordinators 1 (ft); Dietitians 1 (pt); Ophthalmologists 1 (pt); Audiologists 1 (pt); Dentists 1 (pt).
Facilities Dining room; Activities room; Chapel; Crafts room; Laundry room; Barber/Beauty shop.
Activities Arts & crafts; Cards; Games; Reading groups; Prayer groups; Movies; Shopping trips; Dances/Social/Cultural gatherings.

Little Sisters of the Poor
3225 N Florissant Ave, Saint Louis, MO 63107
(314) 421-6022
Admin Sr Marguerite McCarthy. *Dir of Nursing* Sr Carolyn RN BSN.
Licensure Intermediate care; HUD housing; Retirement. *Beds* ICF 112; HUD housing 68. *Certified* Medicaid.
Owner Nonprofit corp.
Admissions Requirements Minimum age 60; Medical examination.
Staff Physicians 8 (pt); RNs 3 (ft); LPNs 5 (ft), 3 (pt); Nurses' aides 60 (ft), 10 (pt); Physical therapists 1 (pt); Recreational therapists 1 (pt); Occupational therapists 1 (pt); Speech therapists 1 (pt); Activities coordinators 1 (pt); Dietitians 1 (pt); Ophthalmologists 2 (pt); Podiatrists 1 (pt); Dentists 2 (pt).
Affiliation Roman Catholic.
Facilities Dining room; Physical therapy room; Activities room; Chapel; Crafts room; Laundry room; Barber/Beauty shop; Library.
Activities Arts & crafts; Cards; Games; Reading groups; Prayer groups; Movies; Shopping trips; Dances/Social/Cultural gatherings.

Lutheran Altenheim Society of Missouri
1265 McLaren Ave, Saint Louis, MO 63147
(314) 388-2867
Admin E Willis Piehl.
Licensure Skilled care; Intermediate care; Residential care. *Beds* SNF 140; ICF 68; Residential care 78. *Certified* Medicaid.
Owner Nonprofit corp.
Affiliation Lutheran.

Lutheran Health Care Association
723 S Laclede Station Rd, Saint Louis, MO 63119
(314) 968-5570
Admin Patricia A Woodward NHA. *Dir of Nursing* Sharon Rullkoetter RN. *Medical Dir* Douglas Parashak MD.
Licensure Skilled care; Intermediate care; Residential care; Retirement. *Beds* Swing beds SNF/ICF 143. *Certified* Medicaid.
Owner Nonprofit organization/foundation.
Admissions Requirements Medical examination.
Staff Physicians 1 (pt); RNs 9 (ft), 5 (pt); LPNs 12 (ft), 2 (pt); Nurses' aides; Activities coordinators 1 (ft).
Affiliation Lutheran.
Facilities Dining room; Physical therapy room; Activities room; Chapel; Crafts room; Laundry room; Barber/Beauty shop.
Activities Arts & crafts; Cards; Games; Reading groups; Prayer groups; Movies; Shopping trips; Pet therapy.

Marquette Manor
3419 Gasconade, Saint Louis, MO 63118
(314) 351-7512
Admin Lawrence A Pulos.
Medical Dir Gerri Villaire.
Licensure Intermediate care; Residential care; Alzheimer's care. *Beds* ICF 126; Residential care 22. *Certified* Medicaid.
Owner Proprietary corp.
Admissions Requirements Medical examination.
Staff Physicians 1 (pt); RNs 1 (ft); LPNs 12 (ft); Nurses' aides 50 (ft); Physical therapists 1 (pt); Occupational therapists 1 (pt); Speech therapists 1 (pt); Activities coordinators 1 (ft); Dietitians 1 (pt); Ophthalmologists 1 (pt); Dentists 1 (pt).
Facilities Dining room; Physical therapy room; Activities room; Chapel; Barber/Beauty shop; Rooftop patio; Rose garden.
Activities Arts & crafts; Games; Reading groups; Prayer groups; Movies.

Mary Queen & Mother Center
7601 Watson Rd, Saint Louis, MO 63119
(314) 961-8485, 961-8489 FAX
Admin Sr Jeanne McGovern MS. *Dir of Nursing* Gail Marchesi RN. *Medical Dir* Rajendraprasad Dandamudi MD.
Licensure Skilled care. *Beds* SNF 220. *Private Pay Patients* 49%. *Certified* Medicaid; Medicare.
Owner Nonprofit corp.
Admissions Requirements Minimum age 62; Medical examination.
Staff Physicians 1 (pt); RNs 14 (ft), 6 (pt); LPNs 10 (ft), 6 (pt); Nurses' aides 96 (ft), 6 (pt); Physical therapists 1 (pt); Occupational therapists 1 (pt); Speech therapists 1 (pt); Activities coordinators 1 (ft); Dietitians 1 (ft); Ophthalmologists 1 (pt); Podiatrists 1 (pt); Dentists 1 (pt).
Affiliation Roman Catholic.
Facilities Dining room; Physical therapy room; Activities room; Chapel; Crafts room; Laundry room; Barber/Beauty shop.
Activities Arts & crafts; Cards; Games; Reading groups; Prayer groups; Movies; Dances/Social/Cultural gatherings; Intergenerational programs; Pet therapy.

Masonic Home of Missouri
5351 Delmar Blvd, Saint Louis, MO 63112
(314) 367-0100, 367-2206 FAX
Admin Harold S Pascal FAAMA.
Licensure Skilled care; Intermediate care; Residential care. *Beds* Swing beds SNF/ICF 276; Residential care 35. *Private Pay Patients* 100%.
Owner Nonprofit organization/foundation.
Staff RNs 3 (ft); LPNs 10 (ft); Nurses' aides 150 (ft); Recreational therapists 3 (ft); Activities coordinators 1 (ft); Dietitians 1 (ft).
Facilities Dining room; Physical therapy room; Activities room; Chapel; Crafts room; Laundry room; Barber/Beauty shop; Library.
Activities Arts & crafts; Cards; Games; Prayer groups; Movies; Shopping trips; Pet therapy.

Medicalodge of Halls Ferry
2115 Kappel Dr, Saint Louis, MO 63136
(314) 867-7474, 867-2292 FAX
Admin Dianne Mossberger. *Dir of Nursing* Cheri Malone. *Medical Dir* Dr Michael Spezia.
Licensure Skilled care; Intermediate care; Intermediate care for mentally retarded. *Beds* SNF 100; Swing beds ICF/ICF MR 48. *Private Pay Patients* 11%. *Certified* Medicaid; Medicare.
Owner Proprietary corp (Medicalodges Inc).
Admissions Requirements Minimum age 16; Medical examination; Physician's request.
Staff Physicians 6 (pt); RNs 1 (ft), 3 (pt); LPNs 6 (ft), 6 (pt); Nurses' aides 30 (ft), 8 (pt); Physical therapists 1 (ft), 1 (pt); Reality therapists 2 (ft), 1 (pt); Recreational therapists 1 (pt); Occupational therapists 1 (pt); Speech therapists 1 (pt); Activities coordinators 3 (ft); Dietitians 1 (pt); Ophthalmologists 1 (pt); Podiatrists 1 (pt); Audiologists 1 (pt).
Facilities Dining room; Physical therapy room; Activities room; Crafts room; Laundry room; Barber/Beauty shop.
Activities Arts & crafts; Cards; Games; Reading groups; Prayer groups; Movies; Shopping trips; Dances/Social/Cultural gatherings.

Memorial Home
3625 Magnolia, Saint Louis, MO 63110
(314) 771-2990
Admin Estelle M Vosen.
Licensure Intermediate care. *Beds* ICF 85.
Owner Proprietary corp.

Mercy Convalescent Center
3450 Russell, Saint Louis, MO 63104
(314) 664-1020

Admin Frank Manning.
Licensure Intermediate care. *Beds* ICF 254.
Certified Medicaid.
Owner Proprietary corp.

Mother of Good Counsel Home
6825 Natural Bridge, Saint Louis, MO 63121
(314) 383-4765
Admin Sr M Silvana Budde. *Dir of Nursing* Sr
M Christine Crowder. *Medical Dir* Dr
Walter Kutryb.
Licensure Skilled care. *Beds* SNF 110. *Private
Pay Patients* 78%.
Owner Nonprofit organization/foundation.
Admissions Requirements Females only.
Staff RNs 3 (ft), 3 (pt); LPNs 6 (ft), 3 (pt);
Nurses' aides 38 (ft), 18 (pt); Physical
therapists 1 (pt); Activities coordinators 1
(ft); Dietitians 1 (pt).
Languages German, Portuguese.
Affiliation Roman Catholic.
Facilities Dining room; Physical therapy
room; Activities room; Chapel; Crafts room;
Barber/Beauty shop; Library; Solariums.
Activities Arts & crafts; Cards; Games;
Reading groups; Prayer groups; Movies;
Intergenerational programs.

Northview Village
2415 N Kingshighway, Saint Louis, MO
63113
(314) 361-1300, 361-1492 FAX
Admin Marian Kling. *Dir of Nursing* Frances
Olomu. *Medical Dir* K J P N Moorthy.
Licensure Skilled care; Intermediate care. *Beds*
Swing beds SNF/ICF 121. *Certified*
Medicaid.
Owner Publicly owned.
Admissions Requirements Minimum age 18;
Medical examination; Physician's request.
Staff Physicians 4 (pt); RNs 6 (ft); LPNs 10
(ft); Nurses' aides 54 (ft), 3 (pt); Physical
therapists 1 (ft); Recreational therapists 1
(ft); Occupational therapists 1 (pt); Speech
therapists 1 (pt); Activities coordinators 1
(ft); Dietitians 1 (pt); Podiatrists 1 (pt).
Facilities Dining room; Physical therapy
room; Activities room; Chapel; Crafts room;
Laundry room; Barber/Beauty shop; Library.
Activities Arts & crafts; Cards; Games;
Reading groups; Prayer groups; Movies;
Shopping trips; Dances/Social/Cultural
gatherings; Intergenerational programs; Pet
therapy.

Oak Park
6637 Berthold, Saint Louis, MO 63139
(314) 781-3444
Admin Lily Landy. *Dir of Nursing* Sandra
Irby. *Medical Dir* Dr Abinoja.
Licensure Skilled care; Alzheimer's care. *Beds*
SNF 120. *Private Pay Patients* 50%. *Certified*
Medicaid.
Owner Privately owned.
Staff Physicians 3 (pt); RNs 2 (ft), 1 (pt);
LPNs 16 (ft); Nurses' aides 25 (ft); Physical
therapists 1 (pt); Recreational therapists 2
(ft), 1 (pt); Dietitians 1 (pt); Podiatrists 1
(pt); Audiologists 1 (pt).
Facilities Dining room; Physical therapy
room; Activities room; Crafts room; Laundry
room; Barber/Beauty shop.
Activities Arts & crafts; Cards; Games;
Reading groups; Prayer groups; Movies;
Shopping trips; Dances/Social/Cultural
gatherings; Intergenerational programs; Pet
therapy.

Parkside Towers
4960 Laclede Ave, Saint Louis, MO 63108
(314) 361-6240
Admin Libby S Routman. *Dir of Nursing* Sue
Hardin RN. *Medical Dir* Aaron Birenbaum
MD.
Licensure Skilled care. *Beds* SNF 166.
Certified Medicaid.

Owner Proprietary corp.
Staff RNs 3 (ft); LPNs 14 (ft); Nurses' aides
65 (ft), 3 (pt); Physical therapists 1 (ft);
Reality therapists 1 (ft).

Peace Haven Association
12630 Rott Rd, Saint Louis, MO 63127
(314) 965-3833
Admin Sondra Toner.
Licensure Skilled care. *Beds* SNF 28.
Owner Nonprofit corp.

**St Anthony's Medical Center—Rehabilitation
Center**
10010 Kennerly Rd, Saint Louis, MO 63128
(314) 525-1770, 525-1212 FAX
Admin Thomas P Long. *Dir of Nursing*
Christine Crouch RN. *Medical Dir*
Bartolome Kairuz MD.
Licensure Skilled care. *Beds* SNF 74. *Private
Pay Patients* 3%. *Certified* Medicaid;
Medicare.
Owner Nonprofit corp.
Admissions Requirements Medical
examination; Physician's request.
Staff RNs 12 (ft), 9 (pt); LPNs 6 (ft), 6 (pt);
Nurses' aides 23 (ft), 25 (pt); Physical
therapists 3 (ft); Recreational therapists 1
(ft); Occupational therapists 2 (ft); Speech
therapists 1 (ft); Dietitians 1 (ft).
Facilities Dining room; Physical therapy
room; Activities room; Chapel; Stroke
rehabilitation; Decubitis care; Orthopedic
rehabilitation.
Activities Arts & crafts; Cards; Games;
Reading groups; Prayer groups; Movies;
Dances/Social/Cultural gatherings.

St John's Mercy Skilled Nursing Center
615 S New Ballas Rd, Saint Louis, MO 63141
(314) 569-6000
Admin Virginia Moseley.
Licensure Skilled care. *Beds* SNF 120.
Owner Nonprofit corp.

St Louis Altenheim
5408 S Broadway, Saint Louis, MO 63111
(314) 353-7225
Admin Rose M Boehmer. *Dir of Nursing* Alice
M Catron RN. *Medical Dir* M Robert Hill
MD.
Licensure Intermediate care; Residential care.
Beds ICF 46; Residential care 108. *Private
Pay Patients* 100%.
Owner Nonprofit organization/foundation.
Admissions Requirements Minimum age 65;
Medical examination.
Staff Physicians 2 (pt); RNs 2 (ft), 1 (pt);
Nurses' aides 22 (ft); Physical therapists 1
(pt); Activities coordinators 1 (ft), 2 (pt).
Languages German.
Facilities Dining room; Physical therapy
room; Activities room; Chapel; Crafts room;
Laundry room; Barber/Beauty shop; Library.
Activities Arts & crafts; Cards; Games; Prayer
groups; Movies; Shopping trips; Dances/
Social/Cultural gatherings; Pet therapy.

St Louis Good Shepherd Homes Inc
9444 Midland Blvd, Saint Louis, MO 63114
(314) 427-8795
Admin Ed Anthonis Jr.
Licensure Intermediate care. *Beds* 34.
Owner Proprietary corp.

South Gate Care Center
5934 S Telegraph Rd, Saint Louis, MO 63129
(314) 846-2000
Admin C Michael Roth. *Dir of Nursing* Carla
Jurgensen.
Licensure Skilled care; Retirement. *Beds* SNF
180. *Certified* Medicaid.
Owner Nonprofit organization/foundation.
Admissions Requirements Medical
examination; Physician's request.
Staff Physicians 3 (ft); RNs 5 (ft), 8 (pt);
LPNs 10 (ft), 7 (pt); Nurses' aides 200 (ft),
50 (pt); Physical therapists 2 (ft);

Recreational therapists 1 (ft), 1 (pt);
Activities coordinators 1 (ft); Dietitians 1
(ft); Podiatrists 1 (pt).
Facilities Dining room; Physical therapy
room; Activities room; Crafts room; Laundry
room; Barber/Beauty shop; Library; Outdoor
gazebo.
Activities Arts & crafts; Cards; Games;
Reading groups; Prayer groups; Movies;
Shopping trips; Dances/Social/Cultural
gatherings.

Tower Village Inc
4518 Blair Ave, Saint Louis, MO 63107
(314) 534-4000
Admin Charles T Gooden. *Dir of Nursing*
Alfreda R Smith RN. *Medical Dir* Alphonso
Hillard MD.
Licensure Skilled care; Intermediate care;
Retirement. *Beds* Swing beds SNF/ICF 268;
Retirement 98. *Private Pay Patients* 1%.
Certified Medicaid; Medicare.
Owner Nonprofit corp.
Admissions Requirements Medical
examination.
Staff Physicians 6 (pt); RNs 5 (ft), 1 (pt);
LPNs 32 (ft); Nurses' aides 93 (ft); Physical
therapists 2 (pt); Recreational therapists 2
(pt); Occupational therapists 2 (pt); Speech
therapists 1 (pt); Activities coordinators 2
(ft); Dietitians 1 (ft); Ophthalmologists 2
(pt); Podiatrists 2 (pt).
Facilities Dining room; Physical therapy
room; Activities room; Chapel; Crafts room;
Laundry room; Barber/Beauty shop; Library.
Activities Arts & crafts; Cards; Games;
Reading groups; Prayer groups; Movies;
Shopping trips; Dances/Social/Cultural
gatherings; Pet therapy.

Harry S Truman Restorative Center
5700 Arsenal, Saint Louis, MO 63139
(314) 768-6600
Admin Shirley E Herr.
Licensure Skilled care; Intermediate care. *Beds*
Swing beds SNF/ICF 220. *Certified*
Medicaid; Medicare.
Owner Publicly owned.

Village North Health Center
11160 Village North Dr, Saint Louis, MO
63136
(314) 355-8010, 355-5613 FAX
Admin Dorothy Espenschied. *Dir of Nursing*
Barbara Brown RN. *Medical Dir* Stephen
Hadzima MD.
Licensure Skilled care; Independent living
apartments; Alzheimer's care. *Beds* SNF 60;
Independent living apts 213. *Private Pay
Patients* 75%. *Certified* Medicaid; Medicare.
Owner Nonprofit corp.
Admissions Requirements Minimum age 18;
Medical examination; Physician's request.
Staff Physicians 1 (pt); RNs 3 (ft), 2 (pt);
LPNs 8 (ft), 2 (pt); Nurses' aides 23 (ft), 6
(pt); Occupational therapists 1 (pt); Speech
therapists 1 (pt); Activities coordinators 1
(ft); Dietitians 1 (pt); Ophthalmologists 1
(pt); Podiatrists 1 (pt); Audiologists 1 (pt).
Facilities Dining room; Physical therapy
room; Activities room; Laundry room;
Barber/Beauty shop; Library.
Activities Arts & crafts; Cards; Games;
Reading groups; Prayer groups; Movies;
Shopping trips; Dances/Social/Cultural
gatherings; Intergenerational programs; Pet
therapy.

Saint Peters

St Peters Manor Care Center
150 Spencer Rd, Saint Peters, MO 63376
(314) 441-2750
Admin Donna L Morse.
Medical Dir Dr Martin Walsch.
Licensure Intermediate care. *Beds* ICF 102.
Owner Proprietary corp.

Admissions Requirements Medical
examination; Physician's request.
Staff RNs 2 (pt); LPNs 6 (ft); Physical
therapists 1 (pt); Occupational therapists 1
(pt); Speech therapists 1 (pt); Activities
coordinators 1 (ft), 1 (pt); Podiatrists 1 (pt).
Facilities Dining room; Barber/Beauty shop.
Activities Arts & crafts; Games; Reading
groups; Movies; Shopping trips; Dances/
Social/Cultural gatherings; Adopt-a-
grandparent program.

Sainte Genevieve

Riverview Manor Nursing Home
PO Box 151, N 4th St & Matthews Dr, Sainte
Genevieve, MO 63670
(314) 883-3454
Admin Martin F Radmer. *Dir of Nursing*
Betty Grobe. *Medical Dir* Dr Joseph F
Lutkewitte.
Licensure Intermediate care. *Beds* ICF 120.
Certified Medicaid.
Owner Publicly owned.
Admissions Requirements Minimum age 18;
Medical examination; Physician's request.
Staff Physicians 1 (pt); RNs 3 (ft); LPNs 2
(ft); Nurses' aides 49 (ft), 16 (pt);
Recreational therapists 2 (ft).
Facilities Dining room; Physical therapy
room; Activities room; Laundry room;
Barber/Beauty shop; Solarium.
Activities Arts & crafts; Cards; Games;
Reading groups; Prayer groups; Movies;
Shopping trips; Dances/Social/Cultural
gatherings.

Salem

Salem Care Center
PO Box 29, 1000 N Jackson, Salem, MO
65560
(314) 729-6649
Admin Gayle Roberts.
Licensure Skilled care. *Beds* SNF 60. *Certified*
Medicaid.
Owner Proprietary corp.

Seville Nursing Center
PO Box 746, Hwy 72, Salem, MO 65560
(314) 729-6141
Admin Mary Wilson.
Medical Dir James Bass MD.
Licensure Skilled care. *Beds* SNF 90. *Certified*
Medicaid; Medicare.
Owner Proprietary corp (Beverly Enterprises).
Admissions Requirements Minimum age 21.
Staff Physicians 1 (pt); RNs 2 (ft), 2 (pt);
LPNs 3 (ft), 3 (pt); Nurses' aides 20 (ft), 6
(pt); Physical therapists 2 (pt); Recreational
therapists 1 (pt); Occupational therapists 1
(pt); Speech therapists 1 (pt); Activities
coordinators 1 (ft); Dietitians 1 (pt);
Podiatrists 1 (pt); Dentists 1 (pt).
Facilities Dining room; Physical therapy
room; Activities room; Crafts room; Laundry
room; Barber/Beauty shop; Library.
Activities Arts & crafts; Cards; Games;
Reading groups; Prayer groups; Movies;
Shopping trips; Dances/Social/Cultural
gatherings; Outings.

Salisbury

Chariton Park
902 Manor Dr, Salisbury, MO 65281
(816) 388-6486, 388-6136 FAX
Admin Patricia Bell. *Dir of Nursing* Debbie
Windmiller LPN. *Medical Dir* Dr George
Quinn; Dr Donald Pressley.
Licensure Intermediate care; Residential care.
Beds ICF 80; Residential care 20. *Certified*
Medicaid.
Owner Proprietary corp.
Admissions Requirements Medical
examination; Physician's request.

Staff RNs; LPNs; Nurses' aides; Physical
therapists (consultant); Occupational
therapists (consultant); Speech therapists
(consultant); Activities coordinators;
Dietitians (consultant); Ophthalmologists
(consultant).
Facilities Dining room; Physical therapy
room; Laundry room; Barber/Beauty shop;
Library.
Activities Games; Reading groups; Prayer
groups; Movies; Dances/Social/Cultural
gatherings; Intergenerational programs.

Sarcoxie

Sarcoxie Nursing Center
PO Box 248, 16th & Miner St, Sarcoxie, MO
64862
(417) 548-3434
Admin Peggy R Frisinger. *Dir of Nursing* J
Mettlach RN. *Medical Dir* W Levanvo MD.
Licensure Skilled care; Intermediate care. *Beds*
Swing beds SNF/ICF 37. *Certified* Medicaid.
Owner Proprietary corp (Rose Care Inc).
Admissions Requirements Minimum age 18;
Medical examination.
Staff Physicians 1 (pt); RNs 1 (ft), 1 (pt);
LPNs 2 (ft), 3 (pt); Nurses' aides 10 (ft), 1
(pt); Physical therapists 1 (pt); Speech
therapists 1 (pt); Activities coordinators 1
(ft); Dietitians 1 (pt).
Facilities Dining room; Physical therapy
room; Activities room; Chapel; Laundry
room; Barber/Beauty shop; Library; Fire
sprinkler and alarm.
Activities Arts & crafts; Cards; Games;
Reading groups; Prayer groups; Movies;
Shopping trips; Pet therapy.

Savannah

La Verna Heights Retirement Center
PO Box 488, 104 E Park Ave, Savannah, MO
64485-0488
(816) 324-3179
Admin Sr M Magdalene Bergmann. *Dir of
Nursing* Pauline Youngblood LPN.
Licensure Intermediate care. *Beds* ICF 38.
Private Pay Patients 75%.
Owner Nonprofit corp.
Admissions Requirements Minimum age 55;
Females only; Medical examination.
Staff RNs; LPNs 2 (ft); Nurses' aides 16 (ft), 6
(pt); Activities coordinators 1 (ft); Dietitians
(consultant).
Languages German.
Affiliation Roman Catholic.
Facilities Dining room; Physical therapy
room; Activities room; Chapel; Laundry
room; Barber/Beauty shop; Library.
Activities Arts & crafts; Cards; Games;
Reading groups; Prayer groups; Movies;
Shopping trips; Dances/Social/Cultural
gatherings; Intergenerational programs.

La Verna Village Nursing Home Inc
PO Box 279, 904 Hall Ave, Savannah, MO
64485
(816) 324-3185
Admin Leon T Jennings.
Licensure Intermediate care. *Beds* ICF 120.
Certified Medicaid.
Owner Nonprofit corp.
Staff RNs 1 (ft), 2 (pt); LPNs 9 (ft); Nurses'
aides 58 (ft), 4 (pt); Activities coordinators 3
(ft).
Affiliation Roman Catholic.
Facilities Dining room; Activities room;
Chapel; Crafts room; Laundry room; Barber/
Beauty shop; Library.
Activities Arts & crafts; Cards; Games;
Reading groups; Prayer groups; Dances/
Social/Cultural gatherings.

Shady Lawn
RR 3 Box 209, Savannah, MO 64485
(816) 324-5991

Admin Brenda Elifrits. *Dir of Nursing* Barbara
Huff RN.
Licensure Intermediate care; Residential care.
Beds ICF 88; Residential care 30. *Certified*
Medicaid.
Owner Proprietary corp (Tiffany Care
Centers).
Admissions Requirements Minimum age 21;
Medical examination.
Staff Physicians 3 (pt); RNs 1 (ft); LPNs 4
(ft); Nurses' aides 30 (ft), 3 (pt); Physical
therapists 1 (ft), 1 (pt); Occupational
therapists 1 (pt); Speech therapists 1 (pt);
Activities coordinators 1 (ft), 1 (pt);
Dietitians 1 (ft), 1 (pt); Ophthalmologists 1
(pt); Podiatrists 1 (pt).
Facilities Dining room; Physical therapy
room; Activities room; Crafts room; Laundry
room; Barber/Beauty shop; Enclosed garden;
Courtyard.
Activities Arts & crafts; Cards; Games; Prayer
groups; Movies; Shopping trips; Dances/
Social/Cultural gatherings.

Sedalia

Brooking Park Geriatric Center
PO Box 1667, Sedalia, MO 65301
(816) 826-8803
Admin R H "Hank" Monsees.
Medical Dir Kenneth Azan MD.
Licensure Skilled care; Intermediate care;
Residential care. *Beds* SNF 60; ICF 138;
Residential care 42. *Certified* Medicaid;
Medicare.
Owner Proprietary corp.
Admissions Requirements Medical
examination.
Staff Physicians 1 (pt); RNs 4 (ft), 4 (pt);
LPNs 14 (ft), 2 (pt); Nurses' aides 60 (ft), 16
(pt); Physical therapists 1 (pt); Reality
therapists; Recreational therapists;
Occupational therapists 1 (pt); Speech
therapists 1 (pt); Activities coordinators 2
(ft); Dietitians 1 (ft); Chaplains; Social
workers.
Facilities Dining room; Physical therapy
room; Activities room; Crafts room; Barber/
Beauty shop; Library; Game room.
Activities Arts & crafts; Cards; Games;
Reading groups; Prayer groups; Movies;
Shopping trips; Dances/Social/Cultural
gatherings; Cooking; Exercise; Bingo; News
& views.

Buena Vista Home for the Aged
1609 E 9th St, Sedalia, MO 65301
(816) 826-5159
Admin Arlene M Benn.
Medical Dir Dr Donald Allcorn.
Licensure Intermediate care. *Beds* ICF 48.
Owner Nonprofit corp.
Staff Physicians 1 (ft); RNs 1 (ft); LPNs 3 (ft);
Nurses' aides 21 (ft); Physical therapists 1
(ft); Activities coordinators 1 (ft); Dietitians
3 (ft).
Facilities Dining room; Physical therapy
room; Activities room; Chapel; Laundry
room; Barber/Beauty shop.
Activities Arts & crafts; Cards; Games; Prayer
groups; Dances/Social/Cultural gatherings.

Fair View Nursing Home
1714 W 16th St, Sedalia, MO 65301
(816) 827-1594
Admin Constance Johnson Pope.
Licensure Intermediate care. *Beds* ICF 58.
Owner Proprietary corp.

Hawthorne House
1401 W 3rd St, Sedalia, MO 65301
(816) 827-4393
Admin Carole A Akery LPN. *Dir of Nursing* F
W Desnoyers LPN. *Medical Dir* B L
Boatright DO.
Licensure Intermediate care; Alzheimer's care.
Beds ICF 31. *Certified* Medicaid; Medicare.
Owner Privately owned.

Admissions Requirements Minimum age 18.
Staff Physicians 9 (pt); RNs 1 (pt); LPNs 2 (ft); Nurses' aides 12 (ft), 2 (pt); Physical therapists 1 (pt); Occupational therapists 1 (pt); Speech therapists 1 (pt); Activities coordinators 1 (pt); Dietitians 1 (pt); Podiatrists 1 (pt).
Facilities Dining room; Activities room; Crafts room; Laundry room; Barber/Beauty shop.
Activities Arts & crafts; Games; Reading groups; Prayer groups; Movies; Intergenerational programs; Pet therapy; Sunday services; Activities with scouts, 4-H club, and Lions club.

Rest Haven Convalescent & Rest Home
1800 S Ingram, Sedalia, MO 65301
(816) 827-0845
Admin Lee Stormer; John C Finley.
Licensure Intermediate care. *Beds* ICF 79. *Certified* Medicaid.
Owner Proprietary corp.

Truman Manor Nursing Home
PO Box 27, Sedalia, MO 65301
(816) 827-1750
Admin Martha Austin.
Licensure Intermediate care. *Beds* ICF 30.
Owner Proprietary corp.

Senath

Senath Nursing Home
Hwy 412 S, Drawer Q, Senath, MO 63876
(314) 738-2608
Admin George W Krone.
Licensure Skilled care. *Beds* SNF 120. *Certified* Medicaid.
Owner Proprietary corp.

Shawnee

Troost Avenue Nursing Home
8330 Grant Cir, Shawnee, MO 64104
(816) 931-1047
Admin Jerry Shaw; Wendy Morgan.
Licensure Intermediate care. *Beds* ICF 41.
Owner Proprietary corp.

Shelbina

Salt River Nursing Home
503 N Livingston, Box 529, Shelbina, MO 63468
(314) 588-4175
Admin C Von Snow.
Licensure Skilled care. *Beds* SNF 120. *Certified* Medicaid.
Owner Publicly owned.

Sikeston

SEMO Care Center
PO Box 302, 509 Ruth St, Sikeston, MO 63801
(314) 471-2565
Admin Gerry L Paylor.
Licensure Intermediate care. *Beds* ICF 82. *Certified* Medicaid.
Owner Proprietary corp.

Sikeston Convalescent Center
103 Kennedy Dr, Sikeston, MO 63801
(314) 471-6900
Admin Robert J Hodges. *Dir of Nursing* Marie Muench RN. *Medical Dir* M Critchlow MD.
Licensure Skilled care; Alzheimer's care. *Beds* SNF 120. *Certified* Medicaid.
Owner Proprietary corp.
Admissions Requirements Minimum age 17; Medical examination; Physician's request.
Staff Physicians 2 (pt); RNs 2 (ft), 1 (pt); LPNs 10 (ft); Physical therapists 1 (ft); Occupational therapists 1 (pt); Speech

therapists 1 (pt); Activities coordinators 1 (ft); Dietitians 1 (ft); Ophthalmologists 1 (pt); Podiatrists 1 (pt).
Facilities Dining room; Physical therapy room; Activities room; Chapel; Crafts room; Laundry room; Barber/Beauty shop.
Activities Arts & crafts; Cards; Games; Reading groups; Prayer groups; Movies; Shopping trips; Dances/Social/Cultural gatherings.

Sikeston Health Care Inc
Rte 3 Box 827, Sikeston, MO 63801
(314) 471-1174
Admin Janet Spitler.
Medical Dir A L Weaver.
Licensure Intermediate care. *Beds* ICF 100. *Certified* Medicaid.
Owner Proprietary corp.
Admissions Requirements Minimum age 21.
Staff Physicians 1 (pt); RNs 1 (ft), 1 (pt); LPNs 8 (ft), 3 (pt); Nurses' aides 37 (ft), 6 (pt); Physical therapists 1 (ft), 1 (pt); Occupational therapists 1 (pt); Speech therapists 1 (pt); Activities coordinators 1 (ft); Dietitians 1 (ft), 1 (pt); Dentists 1 (pt).
Facilities Dining room; Physical therapy room; Activities room; Crafts room; Laundry room; Barber/Beauty shop.
Activities Arts & crafts; Cards; Games; Prayer groups; Movies; Shopping trips; Dances/Social/Cultural gatherings.

Sikeston Nursing Center
628 N West St, Sikeston, MO 63801
(314) 471-7130
Admin Joyce Starling. *Dir of Nursing* Sherry McCoy. *Medical Dir* Dr Gordon Jones.
Licensure Skilled care; Intermediate care. *Beds* Swing bedsgs SNF/ICF 120. *Private Pay Patients* 2%. *Certified* Medicaid; Medicare.
Owner Proprietary corp (Beverly Enterprises).
Admissions Requirements Minimum age 21; Medical examination; Physician's request.
Staff Physicians 1 (ft), 1 (pt); RNs 1 (ft), 1 (pt); Physical therapists 1 (pt); Occupational therapists 1 (pt); Speech therapists 1 (pt); Activities coordinators 1 (ft); Dietitians 1 (pt).
Facilities Dining room; Physical therapy room; Activities room; Crafts room; Laundry room; Barber/Beauty shop; Library.
Activities Arts & crafts; Cards; Games; Reading groups; Prayer groups; Movies; Shopping trips; Dances/Social/Cultural gatherings; Pet therapy.

Silex

Rosedale Nursing Home
RR 1 Box 108, Silex, MO 63377
(314) 384-5213
Admin Mathias P Dasal.
Medical Dir Jose M A Navato MD.
Licensure Intermediate care; Residential care. *Beds* ICF 60; Residential care 11. *Certified* Medicaid.
Owner Proprietary corp.
Admissions Requirements Minimum age 16; Medical examination; Physician's request.
Staff RNs 1 (ft); LPNs 2 (ft), 1 (pt); Nurses' aides 7 (ft), 22 (pt); Activities coordinators 1 (ft).
Facilities Dining room; Physical therapy room; Activities room; Laundry room.
Activities Arts & crafts; Cards; Games; Reading groups; Prayer groups; Movies; Shopping trips; Dances/Social/Cultural gatherings.

Slater

Big Bend Retreat Inc
620 N Emerson, Slater, MO 65349
(816) 529-2237
Admin J P Butler Jr.

Licensure Intermediate care; Residential care. *Beds* ICF 60; Residential care 10.
Owner Proprietary corp.

Smithville

Smithville Convalescent Center
106 Hospital Dr, Box F, Smithville, MO 64089
(816) 532-0888
Admin Joyce Berry. *Dir of Nursing* Jan Clark RN.
Licensure Skilled care. *Beds* SNF 120. *Certified* Medicaid.
Owner Proprietary corp (Beverly Enterprises).
Staff Physicians 1 (pt); RNs 5 (ft); LPNs 12 (ft); Nurses' aides 45 (ft); Physical therapists 1 (pt); Reality therapists 1 (pt); Recreational therapists 2 (ft); Occupational therapists 1 (pt); Speech therapists 1 (pt); Activities coordinators 1 (ft); Dietitians 1 (pt); Ophthalmologists 1 (pt); Podiatrists 1 (pt).

Springfield

Americana Healthcare Center
2915 S Fremont, Springfield, MO 65804
(417) 883-4022
Admin Betty Luckie. *Dir of Nursing* Anne Moore RN. *Medical Dir* Judy Dasovich MD.
Licensure Skilled care; Intermediate care; Assisted living; Alzheimer's care. *Beds* SNF 186; ICF 40. *Private Pay Patients* 65%. *Certified* Medicare.
Owner Proprietary corp (Manor Care Inc).
Admissions Requirements Medical examination; Physician's request.
Staff Physicians 1 (pt); RNs 3 (ft), 1 (pt); LPNs 19 (ft), 3 (pt); Nurses' aides 76 (ft); Physical therapists 1 (pt); Reality therapists 1 (pt); Recreational therapists 1 (pt); Occupational therapists 1 (pt); Speech therapists 1 (pt); Activities coordinators 1 (ft), 1 (pt); Dietitians 1 (ft); Podiatrists 1 (pt).
Facilities Dining room; Physical therapy room; Activities room; Crafts room; Laundry room; Barber/Beauty shop; Library.
Activities Arts & crafts; Cards; Games; Reading groups; Prayer groups; Movies; Shopping trips; Dances/Social/Cultural gatherings; Intergenerational programs; Pet therapy; Family nights; Fishing; Sewing.

Cherry-Carecentre Inc
1330 Cherry, Springfield, MO 65802
(417) 862-3753
Admin John H Simmons. *Dir of Nursing* Kay Simmons.
Licensure Intermediate care; Residential care. *Beds* ICF 52; Residential care 10.
Owner Proprietary corp.
Admissions Requirements Minimum age 18; Medical examination.
Staff Physicians 1 (pt); RNs 1 (ft); LPNs 2 (ft), 6 (pt); Nurses' aides 3 (pt).
Languages French, Spanish, Tagalog.
Facilities Dining room; Laundry room.
Activities Prayer groups.

Foster's Nursing Home
1610 N Broadway, Springfield, MO 65803
(417) 866-3533
Admin Rose Deering. *Dir of Nursing* Cindy Foster RN. *Medical Dir* Efriam Reyes MD.
Licensure Skilled care. *Beds* SNF 100. *Certified* Medicaid.
Owner Proprietary corp.
Admissions Requirements Minimum age 16.
Staff Physicians 2 (pt); RNs 3 (ft); LPNs 7 (ft); Nurses' aides 56 (ft), 4 (pt); Physical therapists 1 (pt); Recreational therapists 1 (pt); Occupational therapists 1 (pt); Speech therapists 1 (pt); Activities coordinators 1 (ft); Dietitians 1 (pt).

Facilities Dining room; Laundry room; Barber/Beauty shop.
Activities Arts & crafts; Games; Reading groups; Prayer groups; Movies; Shopping trips; Dances/Social/Cultural gatherings.

Greene Haven
910 S West Ave, Springfield, MO 65802
(417) 865-8741
Admin Bernard A Olson. *Dir of Nursing* Gladys Grimes. *Medical Dir* William K Rosen.
Licensure Skilled care. *Beds* SNF 120. *Private Pay Patients* 24%. *Certified* Medicaid; Medicare.
Owner Nonprofit organization/foundation.
Admissions Requirements Physician's request.
Staff Physicians 1 (pt); RNs 2 (ft), 1 (pt); LPNs 11 (ft); Nurses' aides 38 (ft), 2 (pt); Physical therapists 1 (pt); Occupational therapists 1 (pt); Speech therapists 1 (pt); Activities coordinators 1 (ft); Dietitians 1 (pt); Ophthalmologists 1 (pt); Podiatrists 1 (pt).
Facilities Dining room; Physical therapy room; Activities room; Crafts room; Laundry room; Barber/Beauty shop.
Activities Arts & crafts; Games; Reading groups; Prayer groups; Movies; Shopping trips; Dances/Social/Cultural gatherings; Pet therapy; Music; Van rides; Ceramics.

Heritage Manor of Springfield
2323 W Grand, Springfield, MO 65802
(417) 862-7445
Admin Roy Miller. *Dir of Nursing* Charlotte Jenkins. *Medical Dir* Wayne Stine MD.
Licensure Intermediate care; Alzheimer's care. *Beds* ICF 100. *Private Pay Patients* 90%. *Certified* Medicaid.
Owner Proprietary corp (Health Care Capital).
Admissions Requirements Medical examination.
Staff Physicians 30 (pt); RNs 1 (ft), 1 (pt); LPNs 8 (ft), 2 (pt); Nurses' aides 32 (ft), 3 (pt); Physical therapists 1 (pt); Occupational therapists 1 (pt); Speech therapists 1 (pt); Activities coordinators 1 (ft), 1 (pt); Dietitians 1 (pt); Ophthalmologists 1 (pt); Podiatrists 1 (pt).
Facilities Dining room; Physical therapy room; Activities room; Crafts room; Laundry room; Barber/Beauty shop; Library service.
Activities Arts & crafts; Cards; Games; Reading groups; Prayer groups; Movies; Shopping trips; Dances/Social/Cultural gatherings; Pet therapy; Exercise groups.

Hillhaven Convalescent Center
1911 S National, Springfield, MO 65804
(417) 833-6520
Admin David R Devereaux.
Licensure Skilled care. *Beds* SNF 168. *Certified* Medicaid; Medicare.
Owner Proprietary corp (Hillhaven Corp).

Kimbrough Nursing Home
519 Cherry, Springfield, MO 65806
(417) 862-2109
Admin Jeanne Paris. *Dir of Nursing* Cheryl McCall.
Licensure Intermediate care. *Beds* ICF 66.
Owner Proprietary corp.
Admissions Requirements Medical examination.
Staff RNs; LPNs; Nurses' aides; Activities coordinators.
Activities Games; Prayer groups.

Maranatha Village
233 E Norton, Springfield, MO 65803
(417) 833-0016
Admin Raymond Junker.
Medical Dir K DeWayne Piker MD.
Licensure Skilled care; Residential care. *Beds* SNF 285; Residential care 10. *Certified* Medicaid.
Owner Nonprofit corp.

Staff Physicians 2 (pt); RNs 2 (ft); LPNs 8 (ft), 3 (pt); Nurses' aides 55 (ft), 7 (pt); Physical therapists 1 (pt); Occupational therapists 1 (pt); Activities coordinators 1 (ft); Dietitians 1 (ft); Dentists 1 (pt).
Affiliation Assembly of God.
Facilities Dining room; Physical therapy room; Activities room; Chapel; Crafts room; Laundry room; Barber/Beauty shop; Library.
Activities Arts & crafts; Games; Prayer groups; Shopping trips; Dances/Social/Cultural gatherings.

Mt Vernon Park Care Center
3403 W Mount Vernon, Springfield, MO 65802
(417) 864-5600, 864-6472 FAX
Admin Rick Westphal. *Dir of Nursing* Kathi Kessinger RN. *Medical Dir* Efraim Reyes MD.
Licensure Skilled care. *Beds* SNF 240. *Certified* Medicaid; Medicare.
Owner Privately owned.
Admissions Requirements Medical examination; Physician's request.
Staff Physicians 3 (ft); RNs 2 (ft); LPNs 7 (ft); Physical therapists 1 (ft); Recreational therapists 1 (ft); Occupational therapists 1 (pt); Speech therapists 1 (pt); Activities coordinators 1 (ft); Dietitians 1 (ft); Podiatrists 1 (pt).
Facilities Dining room; Physical therapy room; Activities room; Laundry room; Barber/Beauty shop; Pond.
Activities Arts & crafts; Cards; Games; Reading groups; Prayer groups; Movies; Shopping trips; Dances/Social/Cultural gatherings; Intergenerational programs; Pet therapy.

Primrose Place Health Care Center
1115 E Primrose St, Springfield, MO 65807
(417) 883-1546
Admin Sharon Warren. *Dir of Nursing* Leveta Longley RN. *Medical Dir* Wayne Stine MD.
Licensure Skilled care. *Beds* SNF 135.
Owner Nonprofit corp.
Admissions Requirements Minimum age 18; Medical examination; Physician's request.
Staff Physicians 1 (pt); RNs 4 (ft), 1 (pt); LPNs 16 (ft), 5 (pt); Nurses' aides 40 (ft), 5 (pt); Physical therapists 2 (pt); Reality therapists 1 (pt); Activities coordinators 1 (ft), 2 (pt); Dietitians 1 (ft), 1 (pt).
Facilities Dining room; Physical therapy room; Activities room; Crafts room; Laundry room; Barber/Beauty shop; Library; Senior walking course; Miniature golf course.
Activities Arts & crafts; Games; Reading groups; Movies; Shopping trips; Dances/Social/Cultural gatherings; Exercise groups.

St John's Mercy Villa
1100 E Montclair, Springfield, MO 65807
(417) 882-3992
Admin Donald Swafford RN BSN. *Dir of Nursing* Liz Tourville RN. *Medical Dir* W Timothy Wilson DO.
Licensure Skilled care; Respite care. *Beds* SNF 150. *Private Pay Patients* 100%.
Owner Nonprofit organization/foundation.
Admissions Requirements Minimum age 18; Medical examination; Physician's request.
Staff Physicians 1 (pt); RNs 5 (ft), 5 (pt); LPNs 4 (ft), 4 (pt); Nurses' aides 33 (ft), 30 (pt); Physical therapists (consultant); Reality therapists 1 (pt); Recreational therapists 1 (pt); Occupational therapists 1 (pt); Speech therapists 1 (pt); Activities coordinators 1 (ft); Dietitians 1 (pt).
Languages German, access to translators for other languages.
Affiliation Roman Catholic.
Facilities Dining room; Physical therapy room; Activities room; Chapel; Crafts room; Laundry room; Barber/Beauty shop; Library; Courtyard.

Activities Arts & crafts; Cards; Games; Prayer groups; Movies; Shopping trips; Dances/Social/Cultural gatherings; Intergenerational programs; Pet therapy; Daily mass.

Springfield Health Care Center
PO Box 3438 GS, 2800 S Fort, Springfield, MO 65808
(417) 882-0035
Admin Carolyn Smith. *Dir of Nursing* Virginia E Hicks RN. *Medical Dir* William Rosen MD.
Licensure Skilled care; Intermediate care. *Beds* SNF 36; ICF 84. *Private Pay Patients* 15-20%. *Certified* Medicaid; Medicare; VA.
Owner Privately owned (National Health Corp).
Admissions Requirements Minimum age 17; Medical examination; Physician's request.
Staff Physicians; RNs 4 (ft), 1 (pt); LPNs 8 (ft), 1 (pt); Nurses' aides 75 (ft), 3 (pt); Physical therapists 2 (pt); Occupational therapists 1 (pt); Speech therapists 1 (pt); Activities coordinators 1 (ft); Dietitians (consultant); Restorative aides 2 (ft).
Facilities Dining room; Physical therapy room; Activities room; Crafts room; Laundry room; Barber/Beauty shop.
Activities Arts & crafts; Games; Reading groups; Prayer groups; Movies; Dances/Social/Cultural gatherings; Intergenerational programs; Pet therapy.

Springfield Residential Center
2401 W Grand, Springfield, MO 65802
(417) 864-4545
Admin William A Kenny.
Licensure Skilled care; Intermediate care; Residential care. *Beds* Swing beds SNF/ICF 16; Residential care 138. *Certified* Medicaid.
Owner Proprietary corp.

Woodland Manor
1347 E Valley Water Mill Rd, Springfield, MO 65803
(417) 833-1220, 833-1525 FAX
Admin Rick Westphal. *Dir of Nursing* Debra Persing RN. *Medical Dir* Dennis Morrison DO.
Licensure Skilled care; Retirement. *Beds* SNF 180; Retirement apartments 24. *Private Pay Patients* 25%. *Certified* Medicaid.
Owner Privately owned (Healthcare Affiliates).
Admissions Requirements Minimum age 18; Medical examination.
Staff RNs 3 (ft); LPNs 17 (ft); Nurses' aides 48 (ft); Physical therapists 1 (pt); Occupational therapists 1 (pt); Speech therapists 1 (pt); Activities coordinators 3 (ft); Dietitians (consultant).
Facilities Dining room; Physical therapy room; Activities room; Chapel; Crafts room; Laundry room; Barber/Beauty shop; Library.
Activities Arts & crafts; Cards; Games; Reading groups; Prayer groups; Movies; Shopping trips; Dances/Social/Cultural gatherings; Intergenerational programs; Pet therapy.

Stanberry

Concerned Services Inc
PO Box 181, Stanberry, MO 64489
(816) 783-2955
Admin Neil Blair; Karen Blair. *Dir of Nursing* Carol Madden.
Licensure Intermediate care for mentally retarded. *Beds* ICF/MR 9. *Certified* Medicaid; Medicare.
Owner Proprietary corp.
Admissions Requirements Minimum age 16; Medical examination.
Facilities Dining room; Activities room; Laundry room.
Activities Arts & crafts; Cards; Games; Movies; Shopping trips; Dances/Social/Cultural gatherings.

Pine View Manor Inc
307 Pineview St, Stanberry, MO 64489
(816) 783-2118
Admin Robert L Adams. *Dir of Nursing* Betty
   Wilson. *Medical Dir* Dr A L Carlin.
Licensure Intermediate care. *Beds* ICF 80.
   Private Pay Patients 28%. *Certified*
   Medicaid.
Owner Nonprofit corp.
Admissions Requirements Physician's request.
Staff RNs 1 (ft); LPNs 6 (ft), 1 (pt); Nurses'
   aides 22 (ft), 5 (pt); Physical therapists;
   Activities coordinators 1 (ft); Dietitians 1
   (ft).
Affiliation Evangelical Lutheran.
Facilities Dining room; Physical therapy
   room; Activities room; Chapel; Crafts room;
   Laundry room; Barber/Beauty shop; Library;
   TV lounges.
Activities Arts & crafts; Cards; Games;
   Reading groups; Prayer groups; Movies;
   Shopping trips; Religious services.

Steele

River Oaks
PO Box 247, Hwy 164 & 61, Steele, MO
63877
(314) 695-2121
Admin Shirley H Davenport.
Licensure Skilled care. *Beds* SNF 90. *Certified*
   Medicaid; Medicare.
Owner Proprietary corp.
Admissions Requirements Minimum age 18;
   Medical examination.
Staff Physicians 3 (pt); RNs 4 (ft); LPNs 8
   (ft); Nurses' aides 30 (ft); Physical therapists
   1 (pt); Recreational therapists 1 (pt);
   Occupational therapists 1 (pt); Speech
   therapists 1 (pt); Activities coordinators 1
   (ft); Dietitians 1 (pt).
Facilities Dining room; Physical therapy
   room; Laundry room; Barber/Beauty shop.
Activities Arts & crafts; Cards; Games;
   Reading groups; Prayer groups; Movies;
   Shopping trips; Dances/Social/Cultural
   gatherings.

Steelville

Gibbs Care Center
Rte 2 Box 590, Steelville, MO 65565
(314) 775-5815
Admin Phillip C Marzluf. *Dir of Nursing*
   Mary Major. *Medical Dir* Mike Elders MD.
Licensure Intermediate care; Residential care.
   Beds ICF 60; Residential care 24. *Certified*
   Medicaid.
Owner Nonprofit corp.
Admissions Requirements Minimum age 21;
   Medical examination.
Staff RNs 1 (ft); LPNs 3 (ft), 1 (pt); Nurses'
   aides 24 (ft), 2 (pt); Activities coordinators 1
   (ft).
Facilities Dining room; Physical therapy
   room; Activities room; Chapel; Crafts room;
   Laundry room; Barber/Beauty shop; Library.
Activities Arts & crafts; Cards; Games; Prayer
   groups; Movies; Shopping trips.

Stockton

Stockton Nursing Home Inc
Drawer W, Owen Mill Rd, Stockton, MO
65785
(417) 276-5126
Admin Kevin Costello. *Dir of Nursing* Cleo
   Belsher. *Medical Dir* Steven Butcher DO.
Licensure Intermediate care. *Beds* ICF 120.
   Private Pay Patients 50%. *Certified*
   Medicaid.
Owner Nonprofit corp.
Admissions Requirements Minimum age 17;
   Medical examination; Physician's request.

Staff Physicians 2 (ft); RNs 1 (ft); LPNs 9 (ft),
2 (ft); Nurses' aides 40 (ft), 5 (pt); Physical
therapists 1 (ft); Occupational therapists 1
(pt); Speech therapists 1 (pt); Activities
coordinators 1 (ft), 1 (pt); Dietitians 1 (pt);
Ophthalmologists 1 (pt).
Facilities Dining room; Physical therapy
room; Activities room; Crafts room; Barber/
Beauty shop.
Activities Arts & crafts; Cards; Games; Prayer
groups; Movies; Shopping trips; Dances/
Social/Cultural gatherings; Intergenerational
programs; Pet therapy.

Stover

Golden Age Nursing Home
3rd & Mimosa Sts, Stover, MO 65078
(314) 377-4521
Admin Kathy McMillin. *Dir of Nursing* Melba
   Davis. *Medical Dir* Dr Arturo Gonzalez.
Licensure Intermediate care. *Beds* ICF 60.
   Private Pay Patients 48%. *Certified*
   Medicaid.
Owner Nonprofit organization/foundation.
Admissions Requirements Minimum age 21;
   Medical examination; Physician's request.
Staff Physicians 1 (pt); RNs 1 (pt); LPNs 5
   (ft); Nurses' aides 20 (ft), 4 (pt); Physical
   therapists 1 (ft), 1 (pt); Occupational
   therapists 1 (pt); Speech therapists 1 (pt);
   Activities coordinators 1 (ft); Dietitians 1
   (ft).
Languages German, Spanish.
Facilities Dining room; Physical therapy
   room; Activities room; Chapel; Laundry
   room; Barber/Beauty shop.
Activities Arts & crafts; Cards; Games;
   Reading groups; Prayer groups; Movies;
   Shopping trips; Pet therapy.

Sullivan

Sullivan Nursing Center
875 Dunsford Dr, Sullivan, MO 63080
(314) 468-3128
Admin Joyce Oberle.
Licensure Skilled care. *Beds* SNF 120.
   Certified Medicaid.
Owner Proprietary corp (Beverly Enterprises).

Sweet Springs

Sweet Springs Caring Center
518 E Marshall, Sweet Springs, MO 65351
(816) 335-6391
Admin Bobby F Reed Jr. *Dir of Nursing*
   Dorothy Bertrand RN.
Licensure Skilled care. *Beds* SNF 100.
   Certified Medicaid; Medicare.
Owner Proprietary corp.
Admissions Requirements Minimum age 17;
   Medical examination.
Staff RNs 2 (ft); LPNs 9 (ft), 1 (pt); Nurses'
   aides 21 (ft), 4 (pt); Activities coordinators 1
   (ft), 1 (pt); Dietitians 1 (pt).
Facilities Dining room; Activities room;
   Laundry room; Barber/Beauty shop.
Activities Arts & crafts; Cards; Games;
   Reading groups; Movies; Shopping trips;
   Dances/Social/Cultural gatherings; Bible
   study; Church; Exercise groups.

Thayer

Shady Oaks Health Care Center
PO Box 77, 715 Hwy 19, Thayer, MO 65791
(417) 264-7256
Admin Neta Clinton.
Licensure Skilled care; Residential care. *Beds*
   SNF 120; Residential care 35. *Certified*
   Medicaid; Medicare.
Owner Proprietary corp.

Tipton

Tipton Manor Inc
PO Box 599, 601 W Morgan St, Tipton, MO
65081
(816) 433-5574
Admin Charles W Albin. *Dir of Nursing*
   Natalie Potrament. *Medical Dir* C F
   Luebbert DO.
Licensure Intermediate care. *Beds* ICF 60.
   Private Pay Patients 35%. *Certified*
   Medicaid.
Owner Nonprofit corp.
Admissions Requirements Minimum age 18;
   Medical examination; Physician's request.
Staff RNs 1 (ft), 1 (pt); LPNs 3 (ft), 4 (pt);
   Nurses' aides 20 (ft), 10 (pt); Physical
   therapists 1 (pt); Recreational therapists 1
   (pt); Occupational therapists 1 (pt); Speech
   therapists 1 (pt); Activities coordinators 1
   (ft); Dietitians 1 (pt); Audiologists 1 (pt).
Facilities Dining room; Physical therapy
   room; Laundry room; Barber/Beauty shop.
Activities Arts & crafts; Cards; Games;
   Reading groups; Prayer groups; Movies;
   Dances/Social/Cultural gatherings;
   Intergenerational programs.

Trenton

Eastview Manor Care Center
1622 E 28th, Trenton, MO 64683
(816) 359-2251
Admin Mildred Linhart. *Dir of Nursing* Shelly
   Dunkin RN. *Medical Dir* A D Cross MD.
Licensure Intermediate care. *Beds* ICF 90.
   Private Pay Patients 60%. *Certified*
   Medicaid; VA.
Owner Proprietary corp.
Admissions Requirements Minimum age 21;
   Medical examination; Physician's request.
Staff RNs 1 (ft); LPNs 4 (ft), 3 (pt); Nurses'
   aides 38 (ft), 8 (pt); Physical therapists
   (consultant); Occupational therapists
   (consultant); Activities coordinators 1 (ft), 2
   (pt); Dietitians (consultant); Audiologists
   (consultant).
Facilities Dining room; Physical therapy
   room; Activities room; Barber/Beauty shop.
Activities Arts & crafts; Cards; Prayer groups;
   Movies.

**Sunnyview District Nursing Home of Grundy
County**
1311 E 28th, Box 657, Trenton, MO 64683
(816) 359-5647
Admin Tom Mason.
Licensure Skilled care; Residential care. *Beds*
   SNF 154; Residential care 30. *Certified*
   Medicaid.
Owner Publicly owned.
Admissions Requirements Minimum age 16.
Staff RNs 4 (ft); LPNs 7 (ft), 1 (pt); Nurses'
   aides 49 (ft), 16 (pt); Physical therapists 1
   (pt); Occupational therapists 1 (pt); Speech
   therapists 1 (pt); Activities coordinators 3
   (ft); Dietitians 1 (pt); Podiatrists 1 (pt);
   Social service directors 1 (pt).
Facilities Dining room; Physical therapy
   room; Chapel; Barber/Beauty shop; Living
   rooms; Lift van.
Activities Prayer groups; Movies; Sheltered
   workshop, Cooking classes.

Troy

Medicalodge of Troy
200 Thompson Rd, Troy, MO 63379
(314) 528-8446
Admin Joyce Hopkins.
Medical Dir Donald Mogerman DO.
Licensure Skilled care; Retirement. *Beds* SNF
   120. *Certified* Medicaid; Medicare.
Owner Proprietary corp (Medicalodges Inc).

Staff RNs 3 (ft); LPNs 10 (ft); Nurses' aides 60 (ft); Physical therapists 1 (ft), 1 (pt); Occupational therapists 1 (pt); Speech therapists 1 (pt); Activities coordinators 2 (ft); Dietitians 1 (pt).
Facilities Dining room; Physical therapy room; Activities room; Chapel; Crafts room; Laundry room; Barber/Beauty shop.
Activities Arts & crafts; Cards; Games; Reading groups; Prayer groups; Shopping trips; Dances/Social/Cultural gatherings.

Troy House Inc
350 Cap-au-Gris, Troy, MO 63379
(314) 528-4915
Admin Elery A Lockhart.
Licensure Residential care. *Beds* Residential care 9.
Owner Proprietary corp.

Tuscumbia

Miller County Nursing Home
Star Rte Box 20, Tuscumbia, MO 65082
(314) 369-2318
Admin Imogene Cornell. *Dir of Nursing* Fran Gilchrist RN. *Medical Dir* Charles Lady DO.
Licensure Intermediate care. *Beds* ICF 60. *Private Pay Patients* 50%. *Certified* Medicaid.
Owner Nonprofit organization/foundation.
Admissions Requirements Minimum age 18; Medical examination.
Staff Physicians 1 (pt); RNs 1 (ft); LPNs 3 (ft); Nurses' aides 32 (ft); Physical therapists 1 (ft), 1 (pt); Occupational therapists 1 (pt); Speech therapists 1 (pt); Activities coordinators 1 (ft); Dietitians 1 (pt); Ophthalmologists 1 (pt); Podiatrists 1 (pt).
Facilities Dining room; Physical therapy room; Activities room; Chapel; Crafts room; Laundry room; Barber/Beauty shop; Library.
Activities Arts & crafts; Cards; Games; Reading groups; Prayer groups; Movies; Dances/Social/Cultural gatherings; Intergenerational programs.

Union

Sunset Nursing & Retirement Home of Union
400 W Park Ave, Union, MO 63084
(314) 583-2252, 583-2252 FAX
Admin Ronald F Davis. *Dir of Nursing* Terrie L Owens RN. *Medical Dir* Donald L Baker MD.
Licensure Skilled care; Intermediate care; Alzheimer's care. *Beds* SNF 120; ICF 45. *Private Pay Patients* 40%. *Certified* Medicaid; Medicare.
Owner Proprietary corp (Sunset Nursing Homes).
Admissions Requirements Minimum age 19; Medical examination.
Staff Physicians 3 (pt); RNs 3 (ft), 1 (pt); LPNs 8 (ft), 1 (pt); Nurses' aides 60 (ft); Physical therapists 1 (pt); Reality therapists 5 (ft), 1 (pt); Activities coordinators 3 (ft), 1 (pt); Dietitians 1 (pt).
Languages Sign, German, Spanish.
Facilities Dining room; Physical therapy room; Activities room; Chapel; Crafts room; Laundry room; Barber/Beauty shop; Library; TV rooms; Outside patios; Covered porches.
Activities Arts & crafts; Cards; Games; Reading groups; Prayer groups; Movies; Shopping trips; Dances/Social/Cultural gatherings; Intergenerational programs; Pet therapy; Outings; Religious services.

Unionville

Putnam County Care Center
1814 Oak, Unionville, MO 63565
(816) 947-2492
Admin Nancy J Dory.

Medical Dir Mark O'Brien.
Licensure Intermediate care. *Beds* ICF 46. *Certified* Medicaid.
Owner Nonprofit organization/foundation.
Admissions Requirements Medical examination.
Staff Physicians; RNs; LPNs; Nurses' aides; Physical therapists; Occupational therapists; Speech therapists; Activities coordinators; Dietitians.
Facilities Dining room; Physical therapy room; Activities room; Barber/Beauty shop.
Activities Arts & crafts; Cards; Games; Prayer groups; Movies; Shopping trips.

University City

Delmar Gardens East Inc
894 Leland, University City, MO 63130
(314) 726-4767
Admin Michael T Checkett.
Licensure Skilled care. *Beds* SNF 128. *Certified* Medicaid; Medicare.
Owner Proprietary corp.

Valley Park

Cedarcroft Nursing Home
110 Highland Ave, Valley Park, MO 63088
(314) 225-5144
Admin Karen Brown. *Dir of Nursing* Mary Jo Maple RN. *Medical Dir* Conrad Abinoja MD.
Licensure Skilled care. *Beds* SNF 176. *Certified* Medicaid; Medicare.
Owner Proprietary corp.
Admissions Requirements Minimum age 21; Medical examination; Physician's request.
Staff Physicians 20 (pt); RNs 6 (ft), 2 (pt); LPNs 10 (ft); Nurses' aides 70 (ft); Physical therapists 1 (pt); Reality therapists 1 (pt); Recreational therapists 3 (ft); Occupational therapists 1 (pt); Speech therapists 1 (pt); Activities coordinators 1 (ft); Dietitians 2 (ft), 1 (pt); Ophthalmologists 1 (pt); Podiatrists 1 (pt); Dentists 1 (pt).
Facilities Dining room; Physical therapy room; Activities room; Chapel; Crafts room; Laundry room; Barber/Beauty shop; Library.
Activities Arts & crafts; Cards; Games; Prayer groups; Movies; Dances/Social/Cultural gatherings.

Van Buren

Riverways Manor
PO Box 118, Watercress Rd, Van Buren, MO 63965
(314) 323-4282, 323-8224 FAX
Admin Wilma Ball. *Dir of Nursing* Sandra Zimmer RN. *Medical Dir* Kurt Zimmer DO.
Licensure Skilled care. *Beds* SNF 60. *Private Pay Patients* 10%. *Certified* Medicaid; Medicare.
Owner Proprietary corp (Don C Bedell).
Staff Physicians; RNs; LPNs; Nurses' aides; Physical therapists; Recreational therapists; Occupational therapists; Activities coordinators; Dietitians; Podiatrists.
Facilities Dining room; Physical therapy room; Activities room; Crafts room; Laundry room; Barber/Beauty shop.
Activities Arts & crafts; Cards; Games; Reading groups; Prayer groups; Movies; Shopping trips.

Vandalia

Tri-County Nursing Home
601 N Galloway Rd, Vandalia, MO 63382
(314) 594-6468, 594-2510 FAX
Admin Shirley Whetstine. *Dir of Nursing* Carol Calvin RN. *Medical Dir* Rex D Carter DO.

Licensure Intermediate care; Alzheimer's care. *Beds* ICF 60. *Private Pay Patients* 50%. *Certified* Medicaid.
Owner Publicly owned.
Admissions Requirements Minimum age 16; Medical examination.
Staff Physicians 1 (ft), 1 (pt); LPNs 7 (ft), 5 (pt); Nurses' aides 25 (ft), 11 (pt); Physical therapists (consultant); Reality therapists 1 (pt); Occupational therapists 1 (pt); Speech therapists 1 (pt); Activities coordinators 2 (ft), 1 (pt); Dietitians (consultant); Podiatrists 1 (pt).
Facilities Dining room; Physical therapy room; Activities room; Chapel; Laundry room; Barber/Beauty shop.
Activities Arts & crafts; Cards; Games; Reading groups; Prayer groups; Movies; Shopping trips; Intergenerational programs; Quarterly family smorgasbord.

Versailles

Good Shepherd Nursing Home
PO Box 400, Fairground Rd, Versailles, MO 65084
(314) 378-5411
Admin Dolores Jones. *Dir of Nursing* Kathryn Nikkel. *Medical Dir* Ruth Kauffman.
Licensure Skilled care. *Beds* SNF 120. *Private Pay Patients* 50%. *Certified* Medicaid.
Owner Nonprofit organization/foundation (Good Shepherd Nursing Home District).
Admissions Requirements Minimum age 16.
Staff Physicians 4 (pt); RNs 3 (ft); LPNs 7 (ft), 2 (pt); Nurses' aides 50 (ft), 7 (pt); Physical therapists 1 (ft), 1 (pt); Activities coordinators 2 (ft); Dietitians 1 (ft), 1 (pt); Podiatrists 1 (ft).
Facilities Dining room; Physical therapy room; Activities room; Chapel; Laundry room; Barber/Beauty shop.
Activities Arts & crafts; Cards; Games; Reading groups; Prayer groups; Movies; Shopping trips; Dances/Social/Cultural gatherings; Intergenerational programs; Pet therapy.

Vienna

Maries Manor Nursing Home
PO Box 50AA, HCR 60, Vienna, MO 65582
(314) 422-3087
Admin Wayne Wheeler.
Licensure Skilled care; Intermediate care. *Beds* Swing beds SNF/ICF 108. *Certified* Medicaid; Medicare.
Owner Proprietary corp.

Warrensburg

Johnson County Care Center
122 E Market, Warrensburg, MO 64093
(816) 747-8101
Admin Valerie Whiteman.
Licensure Intermediate care. *Beds* ICF 87. *Certified* Medicaid.
Owner Proprietary corp.
Staff Physicians 1 (ft); RNs 1 (ft); LPNs 3 (ft), 2 (pt); Nurses' aides 30 (ft); Physical therapists 1 (ft); Recreational therapists 1 (ft); Occupational therapists 1 (pt); Speech therapists 1 (ft); Activities coordinators 1 (ft); Dietitians 1 (ft); Podiatrists 1 (pt); Audiologists 1 (pt); Dentists 1 (pt).
Facilities Dining room; Physical therapy room; Activities room; Laundry room; Barber/Beauty shop.
Activities Arts & crafts; Cards; Games; Prayer groups; Movies; Dances/Social/Cultural gatherings.

Pleasantview Care Center
Rte 2 Box 290, Hwy 50 E, Warrensburg, MO 64093
(816) 747-6457

Admin Ethel L Jackson. *Dir of Nursing* Ruby Horner LPN. *Medical Dir* Robert L La Hue DO.
Licensure Intermediate care; Residential care; Alzheimer's care. *Beds* ICF 41; Residential care 11. *Private Pay Patients* 10%.
Owner Proprietary corp.
Admissions Requirements Minimum age 18; Medical examination; Physician's request.
Staff RNs 1 (pt); LPNs 2 (ft), 1 (pt); Nurses' aides 15 (ft), 2 (pt); Activities coordinators 1 (ft).
Facilities Dining room; Activities room; Crafts room; Laundry room; Wander-guard door alarms.
Activities Arts & crafts; Cards; Games; Reading groups; Prayer groups; Movies; Shopping trips; Intergenerational programs; Pet therapy.

Ridge Crest Nursing Center
706 S Mitchell, Warrensburg, MO 64093
(816) 429-2177
Admin Kathy Loyd.
Licensure Skilled care. *Beds* SNF 120.
Certified Medicaid; Medicare.
Owner Proprietary corp (Beverly Enterprises).

Warrensburg Manor Care Center
400 Care Center Dr, Warrensburg, MO 64093
(816) 747-2216
Admin Valerie P Whiteman. *Dir of Nursing* Lawanah Gillette RN MSN. *Medical Dir* Dr A L Folkner.
Licensure Intermediate care. *Beds* ICF 92.
Private Pay Patients 100%.
Owner Proprietary corp.
Admissions Requirements Minimum age 20; Medical examination.
Staff RNs 1 (ft); LPNs 3 (ft), 2 (pt); Nurses' aides 15 (ft), 13 (pt); Physical therapists; Activities coordinators 1 (pt); Dietitians.
Facilities Dining room; Laundry room; Barber/Beauty shop.
Activities Arts & crafts; Games.

Warrenton

Fellowship Nursing Home Inc
PO Box 280, State Hwy AA, Warrenton, MO 63383
(314) 456-4183
Admin Charlotte M Fink.
Medical Dir Dr M Baig.
Licensure Skilled care. *Beds* SNF 120.
Certified Medicaid; Medicare.
Owner Proprietary corp.
Admissions Requirements Minimum age 18; Medical examination; Physician's request.
Staff Physicians 5 (pt); RNs 4 (ft), 3 (pt); LPNs 6 (ft), 4 (pt); Nurses' aides 70 (ft), 12 (pt); Physical therapists 1 (pt); Occupational therapists 1 (pt); Speech therapists 1 (pt); Activities coordinators 3 (ft); Dietitians 1 (pt); Podiatrists 1 (pt).
Facilities Dining room; Physical therapy room; Activities room; Laundry room; Barber/Beauty shop.
Activities Arts & crafts; Cards; Games; Reading groups; Prayer groups; Movies; Shopping trips; Dances/Social/Cultural gatherings.

Warsaw

Oakhaven Manor
PO Box 447, Warsaw, MO 65355
(816) 438-5135
Admin Glenda Foster.
Medical Dir Julie Fletcher.
Licensure Intermediate care. *Beds* ICF 35.
Owner Proprietary corp.
Admissions Requirements Minimum age 18.
Staff Physicians 3 (ft); RNs 2 (pt); LPNs 1 (ft); Nurses' aides 8 (ft); Physical therapists 1 (pt); Activities coordinators 1 (ft); Dietitians 1 (pt); CMTs 2 (ft), 1 (pt); Dentists 1 (pt).

Facilities Dining room; Barber/Beauty shop.
Activities Arts & crafts; Cards; Games; Prayer groups; Dances/Social/Cultural gatherings.

Washington

Cedarcrest Manor
324 W 5th St, Washington, MO 63090
(314) 239-7848, 239-5986 FAX
Admin Edward R Maschmann. *Dir of Nursing* Mary Ann Newbanks RN. *Medical Dir* David Brunworth MD.
Licensure Skilled care; Intermediate care; Intermediate care for mentally retarded; Alzheimer's care. *Beds* ICF/MR 5; Swing beds ICF & ICF/MR 184. *Private Pay Patients* 55%. *Certified* Medicaid; Medicare.
Owner Privately owned (North American Healthcare).
Admissions Requirements Minimum age 16; Medical examination; Physician's request.
Staff Physicians 2 (pt); RNs 6 (ft), 2 (pt); LPNs 15 (ft), 2 (pt); Nurses' aides 53 (ft), 16 (pt); Physical therapists 3 (ft), 1 (pt); Occupational therapists 1 (ft); Speech therapists 1 (ft); Activities coordinators 3 (ft); Dietitians 1 (pt); Ophthalmologists 1 (pt); Podiatrists 1 (pt); Audiologists 1 (pt).
Languages German, Spanish.
Facilities Dining room; Physical therapy room; Activities room; Chapel; Crafts room; Laundry room; Library; Yard.
Activities Arts & crafts; Cards; Games; Reading groups; Prayer groups; Movies; Shopping trips; Dances/Social/Cultural gatherings; Intergenerational programs; Pet therapy.

Waverly

Riverview Heights
PO Box 181, Thomas Dr, Waverly, MO 64096
(816) 493-2232
Admin Sheila Landis. *Dir of Nursing* Marla Dillon. *Medical Dir* Dr Gene McFadden.
Licensure Skilled care; Intermediate care; Intermediate care for mentally retarded. *Beds* Swing beds SNF/ICF, ICF/MR 60. *Private Pay Patients* 5%. *Certified* Medicaid.
Owner Proprietary corp (Beverly Enterprises).
Staff Physicians 2 (pt); RNs 1 (ft), 1 (pt); LPNs 4 (ft); Nurses' aides 20 (ft); Physical therapists 1 (pt); Reality therapists 1 (pt); Occupational therapists 1 (pt); Speech therapists 1 (pt); Activities coordinators 1 (ft); Dietitians 1 (pt); Podiatrists 1 (pt); Audiologists 1 (pt); Social service designees 1 (pt); Rehabilitation aides; Dentists 1 (pt).
Facilities Dining room; Laundry room; Barber/Beauty shop.
Activities Arts & crafts; Cards; Games; Reading groups; Prayer groups; Movies; Pet therapy.

Waynesville

Sunset Village of the Ozarks
Rte 2 Box 60, Waynesville, MO 65583
(314) 336-4322
Admin Elizabeth Opperman. *Dir of Nursing* Joy Petrich RN. *Medical Dir* C R Jenkins MD.
Licensure Skilled care; Retirement. *Beds* SNF 33. *Certified* Medicaid; Medicare.
Owner Nonprofit corp.
Admissions Requirements Minimum age 18; Medical examination; Physician's request.
Staff Physicians 1 (ft); RNs 2 (ft), 1 (pt); LPNs 4 (ft), 2 (pt); Nurses' aides 13 (ft); Physical therapists 1 (pt); Occupational therapists 1 (pt); Speech therapists 1 (pt); Activities coordinators 1 (ft); Dietitians 1 (pt); Ophthalmologists 1 (pt); Dentists 1 (pt); Pharmacists 1 (pt).

Facilities Dining room; Physical therapy room; Activities room; Chapel; Laundry room; Barber/Beauty shop; Library; Indoor pool; Workshop.
Activities Arts & crafts; Cards; Games; Prayer groups; Movies; Shopping trips; Dances/Social/Cultural gatherings; Tours.

Waynesville Nursing Center
700 Birch Ln, Waynesville, MO 65583
(314) 774-6456
Admin Anthony Erickson.
Licensure Skilled care. *Beds* SNF 120.
Certified Medicaid.
Owner Proprietary corp (Beverly Enterprises).

Webb City

Regency Care Center of Webb City
Rte 1 Box 100-C, Webb City, MO 64870
(417) 673-1933
Admin Cindy Pike.
Medical Dir Robert Ferguson MD.
Licensure Skilled care. *Beds* SNF 115.
Certified Medicaid; Medicare.
Owner Proprietary corp.
Admissions Requirements Minimum age 21; Medical examination.
Staff RNs 2 (ft); LPNs 14 (ft); Nurses' aides 48 (ft), 4 (pt); Physical therapists 1 (pt); Speech therapists 1 (pt); Activities coordinators 3 (ft); Dietitians 1 (pt).
Facilities Dining room; Physical therapy room; Activities room; Chapel; Crafts room; Laundry room; Barber/Beauty shop; Patio.
Activities Arts & crafts; Cards; Games; Reading groups; Prayer groups; Movies; Shopping trips; Dances/Social/Cultural gatherings; Adult basic education.

Wellsville

Gamma Road Lodge
250 Gamma Rd, Wellsville, MO 63384
(314) 684-2002
Admin V Fay Walden. *Dir of Nursing* Donna Butts RN. *Medical Dir* Dr Donald Shoup DO.
Licensure Skilled care; Intermediate care. *Beds* Swing beds SNF/ICF 120. *Private Pay Patients* 20%. *Certified* Medicaid; Medicare.
Owner Proprietary corp (Beverly Enterprises).
Admissions Requirements Minimum age 16; Medical examination; Physician's request.
Staff Physicians 3 (ft); RNs 4 (ft), 1 (pt); LPNs 12 (ft); Nurses' aides 41 (ft), 6 (pt); Physical therapists 1 (ft), 2 (pt); Recreational therapists 1 (ft); Occupational therapists 1 (pt); Speech therapists 1 (pt); Activities coordinators 1 (ft); Dietitians 1 (ft), 1 (pt); Ophthalmologists 1 (pt); Podiatrists 1 (pt).
Facilities Dining room; Physical therapy room; Activities room; Chapel; Crafts room; Laundry room; Barber/Beauty shop; Library; Living room.
Activities Arts & crafts; Cards; Games; Reading groups; Prayer groups; Movies; Shopping trips; Dances/Social/Cultural gatherings; Intergenerational programs; Pet therapy; Monthly birthday parties; Religious activities; Community activities.

Wentzville

Wentzvill Park Care Center
401 Mar Le Dr, Wentzville, MO 63385
(314) 327-5274
Admin Dave Walker.
Licensure Skilled care; Residential care. *Beds* SNF 196; Residential care 44. *Certified* Medicaid.
Owner Proprietary corp (Angell Group).

West Plains

Ozark Nursing Center
1410 Kentucky St, West Plains, MO 65775
(417) 256-7975
Admin Barbara Young.
Licensure Skilled care. *Beds* SNF 120.
Owner Proprietary corp (Beverly Enterprises).

West Plains Health Care Center
PO Box 497, 211 Davis Dr, West Plains, MO
65775
(417) 256-0798
Admin Mike Newton.
Licensure Skilled care; Intermediate care. *Beds*
Swing beds SNF/ICF 120. *Certified*
Medicaid; Medicare.
Owner Proprietary corp (National Health
Corp).

West Vue Home Inc
909 Kentucky St, West Plains, MO 65775
(417) 256-2152
Admin Warren Fletcher. *Dir of Nursing* Ruth
Fletcher RN. *Medical Dir* M L Fowler MD.
Licensure Skilled care; Retirement. *Beds* SNF
120. *Certified* Medicaid; Medicare.
Owner Nonprofit organization/foundation.
Admissions Requirements Medical
examination; Physician's request.
Staff Physicians 1 (pt); RNs 6 (ft); LPNs 10
(ft), 2 (pt); Nurses' aides 65 (ft); Physical
therapists 1 (pt); Occupational therapists 1
(pt); Speech therapists 1 (pt); Activities
coordinators 2 (ft); Dietitians 1 (pt);
Podiatrists 1 (pt); Dentists 1 (pt).
Affiliation Baptist.
Facilities Dining room; Physical therapy
room; Activities room; Crafts room; Laundry
room; Barber/Beauty shop.
Activities Arts & crafts; Cards; Games;
Reading groups; Prayer groups; Movies;
Shopping trips; Dances/Social/Cultural
gatherings; Adult education.

Willow Springs

**Willow Care Nursing Home & Willow West
Apartments**
PO Box 309, S Hwy 76, Willow Springs, MO
65793
(417) 469-3152
Admin Jack Whitaker. *Dir of Nursing* Barbara
Murphy RN. *Medical Dir* C F Smith MD.
Licensure Skilled care; Residential care. *Beds*
SNF 120; Residential care 24. *Certified*
Medicaid.
Owner Nonprofit corp.
Admissions Requirements Minimum age 16;
Medical examination; Physician's request.
Staff Physicians 6 (pt); RNs 6 (ft); LPNs 11
(ft); Nurses' aides 74 (ft); Physical therapists
1 (ft), 1 (pt); Occupational therapists 1 (pt);
Speech therapists 1 (ft); Activities
coordinators 1 (ft); Dietitians 1 (pt);
Podiatrists 1 (pt).
Facilities Dining room; Physical therapy
room; Activities room; Crafts room; Laundry
room; Barber/Beauty shop; Multipurpose
room.
Activities Arts & crafts; Cards; Games;
Reading groups; Prayer groups; Movies;
Shopping trips; Dances/Social/Cultural
gatherings.

Windsor

Windsor's Resthaven
206 E Jackson St, Windsor, MO 65360
(816) 647-3312
Admin Mary Dugger. *Dir of Nursing* Janet
Libby.
Licensure Intermediate care. *Beds* ICF 60.
Owner Proprietary corp.
Admissions Requirements Medical
examination.
Staff RNs 1 (ft); LPNs 3 (ft); Nurses' aides 35
(ft); Activities coordinators 1 (ft); Dietitians
1 (ft).
Facilities Dining room; Activities room;
Laundry room; Library.
Activities Arts & crafts; Cards; Games.

MONTANA

Anaconda

Community Nursing Home of Anaconda
615 Main St, Anaconda, MT 59711
(406) 563-8417
Admin Warren L Croston.
Licensure Skilled care; Intermediate care. *Beds* SNF 9; ICF 63. *Certified* Medicaid; Medicare.

Baker

Fallon County Medical Complex—Nursing Home
PO Box 820, 320 W Hospital Dr, Baker, MT 59313
(406) 778-3331
Admin Dan McLeod.
Licensure Skilled care. *Beds* SNF 32. *Certified* Medicaid; Medicare.

Big Sandy

Big Sandy Medical Center—Long Term Care
PO Box 530, 3 Montana Ave, Big Sandy, MT 59520
(406) 378-2188, 378-2180 FAX
Admin Harry Bold. *Dir of Nursing* Amber Beaudette. *Medical Dir* Michael S Curtiss MD.
Licensure Skilled care. *Beds* SNF 22. *Private Pay Patients* 50%. *Certified* Medicaid; Medicare.
Owner Publicly owned.
Staff Physicians 1 (pt); RNs 8 (ft); LPNs 2 (ft); Nurses' aides 12 (ft); Activities coordinators 1 (ft); Dietitians 4 (ft).
Facilities Dining room; Activities room; Crafts room; Laundry room; Barber/Beauty shop.
Activities Arts & crafts; Cards; Games; Reading groups; Prayer groups; Movies; Shopping trips; Dances/Social/Cultural gatherings.

Sande Convalescent Home
PO Box F, Big Sandy, MT 59520
(406) 378-2402
Admin David R Sande.
Medical Dir David R Sande.
Licensure Intermediate care. *Beds* ICF 29. *Certified* Medicaid.
Owner Proprietary corp.
Admissions Requirements Medical examination; Physician's request.
Staff RNs 1 (pt); LPNs 3 (ft), 1 (pt); Nurses' aides 4 (ft), 2 (pt); Recreational therapists 1 (pt); Activities coordinators 1 (pt); 3 (ft).
Facilities Dining room; Activities room; Laundry room.
Activities Arts & crafts; Cards; Games; Prayer groups; Movies; Shopping trips; Dances/Social/Cultural gatherings.

Big Timber

Pioneer Nursing Home
PO Box 787, Big Timber, MT 59011
(406) 932-4603
Admin Karen Herman.
Medical Dir Dr Thomas Ivey.
Licensure Skilled care; Intermediate care. *Beds* SNF 36; ICF 13. *Certified* Medicaid.
Owner Publicly owned.
Admissions Requirements Physician's request.
Staff RNs 1 (ft), 1 (pt); LPNs 3 (ft), 2 (pt); Nurses' aides 10 (ft), 9 (pt); Activities coordinators 1 (ft).
Facilities Dining room; Activities room; Laundry room.
Activities Arts & crafts; Cards; Games; Reading groups; Prayer groups; Movies; Shopping trips; Dances/Social/Cultural gatherings.

Bigfork

Lake View Care Center
PO Box 338, 1050 Grand Ave, Bigfork, MT 59911
(406) 837-5041, 837-5042
Admin Ed McCart.
Medical Dir Thomas Jenko MD.
Licensure Skilled care; Intermediate care. *Beds* SNF 70; ICF 13. *Certified* Medicaid; Medicare.
Owner Proprietary corp (Chartham Management).
Admissions Requirements Medical examination; Physician's request.
Staff Physicians 1 (pt); RNs 4 (ft), 3 (pt); LPNs 2 (ft), 3 (pt); Nurses' aides 17 (ft), 19 (pt); Physical therapists 1 (pt); Recreational therapists 1 (pt); Occupational therapists 1 (pt); Speech therapists 1 (pt); Activities coordinators 1 (pt); Dietitians 1 (pt); Ophthalmologists 1 (pt); Podiatrists 1 (pt); Dentists 1 (pt).
Facilities Dining room; Physical therapy room; Activities room; Crafts room; Laundry room; Barber/Beauty shop.
Activities Arts & crafts; Cards; Games; Reading groups; Prayer groups; Movies; Shopping trips; Dances/Social/Cultural gatherings.

Billings

Countryside Elderly Care
3320 Ravalli Pl, Billings, MT 59102
(406) 252-3734
Licensure Personal care. *Beds* Personal care 10.

Glendeen Nursing Home
4001 Rosebud Ln, Billings, MT 59101
(406) 252-6135
Admin Robert P Gilstrap.
Medical Dir Dr Ross Lemire.
Licensure Skilled care. *Beds* SNF 36. *Certified* Medicaid; Medicare.
Admissions Requirements Medical examination.

Parkview Convalescent Care
PO Box 31413, 600 S 27th St, Billings, MT 59107
(406) 259-8000
Licensure Skilled care; Intermediate care. *Beds* SNF 64; ICF 36. *Certified* Medicaid; Medicare.

St John's Lutheran Home
3940 Rimrock Rd, Billings, MT 59102
(406) 656-2710
Admin Steven F Olson.
Medical Dir Dr John Schaeffer.
Licensure Skilled care; Intermediate care; Adult day care. *Beds* SNF 103; ICF 73. *Certified* Medicaid; Medicare.
Admissions Requirements Medical examination; Physician's request.
Staff Physicians 1 (pt); RNs 7 (ft), 9 (pt); LPNs 11 (ft), 12 (pt); Nurses' aides 55 (ft), 1 (pt); Physical therapists 2 (pt); Dietitians 1 (pt).
Affiliation Lutheran.
Facilities Dining room; Physical therapy room; Activities room; Chapel; Laundry room; Barber/Beauty shop; Library.
Activities Arts & crafts; Cards; Games; Reading groups; Prayer groups; Movies; Shopping trips; Dances/Social/Cultural gatherings.

St John's Lutheran Home—Billings Heights
1415 Yellowstone River Rd, Billings, MT 59105
(406) 245-9330
Admin Marie Bousquet. *Dir of Nursing* Melody Hurst. *Medical Dir* Richard C Nelson.
Licensure Skilled care; Intermediate care. *Beds* SNF 43; ICF 16. *Private Pay Patients* 20%. *Certified* Medicaid; Medicare.
Owner Publicly owned.
Admissions Requirements Physician's request.
Staff RNs 3 (ft), 1 (pt); LPNs 4 (ft), 2 (pt); Nurses' aides 28 (ft), 3 (pt); Physical therapists; Activities coordinators 1 (ft), 1 (pt); Dietitians.
Affiliation Evangelical Lutheran.
Facilities Dining room; Physical therapy room; Activities room; Laundry room; Barber/Beauty shop.
Activities Arts & crafts; Cards; Games; Reading groups; Prayer groups; Movies; Shopping trips; Dances/Social/Cultural gatherings; Intergenerational programs; Pet therapy.

Valley Health Care Center
1807 24th St W, Billings, MT 59102
(406) 656-5010
Admin Joyce Fisher.
Licensure Skilled care. *Beds* SNF 130. *Certified* Medicaid; Medicare.

Western Manor Nursing Home
2115 Central Ave, Billings, MT 59102
(406) 656-6500
Admin Todd Hansen. *Dir of Nursing* Carolyn Grazley. *Medical Dir* Niel Sorenson MD.
Licensure Skilled care; Intermediate care. *Beds* SNF 24; ICF 134. *Private Pay Patients* 40%. *Certified* Medicaid; Medicare.
Owner Proprietary corp.
Admissions Requirements Medical examination; Physician's request.
Staff RNs 6 (ft), 6 (pt); LPNs 7 (ft), 2 (pt); Nurses' aides 35 (ft), 20 (pt); Physical therapists 1 (pt); Activities coordinators 2 (ft); Dietitians 1 (pt).
Facilities Dining room; Physical therapy room; Activities room; Crafts room; Laundry room; Barber/Beauty shop.
Activities Arts & crafts; Cards; Games; Reading groups; Prayer groups; Movies; Shopping trips; Dances/Social/Cultural gatherings; Intergenerational programs; Pet therapy.

Westpark Village Retirement Center
2351 Solomon Ave, Billings, MT 59102
(406) 652-4886
Licensure Personal care. *Beds* Personal care 50.

Boulder

Montana Developmental Center
PO Box 87, Boulder, MT 59632
(406) 225-3311, ext 241
Admin Richard L Heard. *Dir of Nursing* Margaret Keating RN. *Medical Dir* Dr Gilbert Preston.
Licensure Intermediate care for mentally retarded. *Beds* ICF/MR 251. *Certified* Medicaid.
Owner Privately owned.
Staff RNs 9 (ft); LPNs 18 (ft); Nurses' aides 166 (ft); Physical therapists 2 (ft); Recreational therapists 4 (ft); Occupational therapists 2 (ft); Speech therapists 3 (ft); Dietitians 1 (ft); Podiatrists 1 (ft).
Activities Arts & crafts; Cards; Games; Movies; Shopping trips; Dances/Social/Cultural gatherings; Trips; Special Olympics; Camping; Bowling.

Bozeman

Bozeman Care Center
321 N 5th, Bozeman, MT 59715
(406) 587-4404
Admin Sharon Armold. *Dir of Nursing* Janie McGrory. *Medical Dir* Dr C Kurtz.
Licensure Skilled care; Intermediate care. *Beds* SNF 89; ICF 5. *Certified* Medicaid; Medicare; VA.
Owner Proprietary corp (Health Marketing West).
Admissions Requirements Physician's request.
Facilities Dining room; Activities room; Crafts room; Laundry room; Barber/Beauty shop; Young adult head-injury extended-rehab unit.
Activities Arts & crafts; Cards; Games; Reading groups; Prayer groups; Movies; Shopping trips; Dances/Social/Cultural gatherings; Intergenerational programs; Pet therapy.

Gallatin County Rest Home
1221 W Durston Rd, Bozeman, MT 59715
(406) 585-1470
Admin Connie Wagner. *Dir of Nursing* Freda Reiser. *Medical Dir* Edward L King MD.
Licensure Skilled care. *Beds* SNF 56. *Certified* Medicaid; Medicare.
Owner Publicly owned.
Admissions Requirements Medical examination; Physician's request.

Staff RNs 4 (ft), 5 (pt); LPNs 1 (ft); Nurses' aides 9 (ft), 20 (pt); Activities coordinators 1 (ft); Dietitians 1 (ft).
Facilities Dining room; Physical therapy room; Activities room; Laundry room.
Activities Arts & crafts; Cards; Games; Reading groups; Prayer groups; Movies; Shopping trips; Dances/Social/Cultural gatherings.

Hamilton House
9420 Haggerty Ln, Bozeman, MT 59715
(406) 586-9459
Licensure Personal care. *Beds* Personal care 8.

Hillcrest Health Center
1201 Highland Blvd, Bozeman, MT 59715
(406) 587-4411
Admin Lotis L Thorsen.
Licensure Personal care. *Beds* Personal care 10.
Owner Nonprofit organization/foundation.
Admissions Requirements Minimum age 55; Medical examination.
Staff Nurses' aides 2 (ft), 4 (pt).
Facilities Dining room; Activities room; Chapel; Laundry room; Barber/Beauty shop; Library.
Activities Arts & crafts; Cards; Games; Reading groups; Prayer groups; Movies; Shopping trips; Dances/Social/Cultural gatherings.

King's Retirement Home
871 Bozeman Trail Rd, Bozeman, MT 59715
(406) 587-7763
Licensure Personal care. *Beds* Personal care 8.

Mountain View Care Center
15 W Lamme, Bozeman, MT 59715
(406) 587-2218
Admin Gary Kenner.
Medical Dir Dr Timothy Adams.
Licensure Skilled care. *Beds* SNF 60. *Certified* Medicaid; Medicare.
Admissions Requirements Minimum age 16; Medical examination; Physician's request.
Staff RNs 2 (ft), 1 (pt); LPNs 5 (ft), 5 (pt); Nurses' aides 30 (ft), 16 (pt); Recreational therapists 1 (ft); Activities coordinators 1 (ft).
Facilities Dining room; Physical therapy room; Activities room; Enclosed outside patio with area to garden.
Activities Arts & crafts; Cards; Games; Reading groups; Prayer groups; Movies; Dances/Social/Cultural gatherings; Special weekly painting sessions.

Broadus

Powder River Manor
PO Box 70, 104 N Trautman, Broadus, MT 59317
(406) 436-2646
Admin Verlin Buechler. *Dir of Nursing* Helen Viker. *Medical Dir* Dr Malcom Winter.
Licensure Skilled care; Alzheimer's care. *Beds* SNF 39. *Private Pay Patients* 43%. *Certified* Medicaid; Medicare.
Owner Publicly owned.
Admissions Requirements Medical examination; Physician's request.
Staff RNs 1 (ft), 4 (pt); LPNs 2 (pt); Nurses' aides 9 (ft), 8 (pt); Activities coordinators 1 (ft).
Facilities Dining room; Physical therapy room; Activities room; Crafts room; Laundry room; Barber/Beauty shop; Library.
Activities Arts & crafts; Cards; Games; Reading groups; Prayer groups; Movies; Shopping trips; Dances/Social/Cultural gatherings; Intergenerational programs; Pet therapy.

Browning

Blackfeet Nursing Home
PO Box 728, Browning, MT 59417
(406) 338-2686
Admin Fae Shelby.
Licensure Skilled care; Intermediate care. *Beds* SNF 29; ICF 20. *Certified* Medicaid.

Butte

Butte Convalescent Center
2400 Continental Dr, Butte, MT 59701
(406) 723-6556
Licensure Skilled care; Intermediate care. *Beds* SNF 40; ICF 60. *Certified* Medicaid; Medicare.
Owner Proprietary corp (Hillhaven Corp).

Butte Park Royal
3251 Nettie St, Butte, MT 59701
(406) 723-3225
Admin David J Murphy.
Medical Dir Dr Gilbert Preston.
Licensure Skilled care; Intermediate care. *Beds* SNF 33; ICF 153. *Certified* Medicaid; Medicare.
Admissions Requirements Medical examination; Physician's request.
Staff RNs 4 (ft), 2 (pt); LPNs 12 (ft), 7 (pt); Nurses' aides 67 (ft), 8 (pt); Physical therapists 1 (ft), 1 (pt); Recreational therapists 1 (ft); Occupational therapists 1 (pt); Activities coordinators 2 (ft).
Facilities Dining room; Physical therapy room; Activities room; Barber/Beauty shop; Library.
Activities Arts & crafts; Cards; Games; Prayer groups; Movies; Shopping trips; Dances/Social/Cultural gatherings.

Crest Nursing Home
3131 Amherst Ave, Butte, MT 59701
(406) 494-7035
Admin Colleen R Broderick.
Licensure Skilled care; Intermediate care. *Beds* SNF 43; ICF 60. *Certified* Medicaid; Medicare.
Admissions Requirements Minimum age 21; Medical examination; Physician's request.
Staff RNs; LPNs; Nurses' aides; Physical therapists; Activities coordinators; Dietitians.
Activities Arts & crafts; Cards; Games; Reading groups; Prayer groups; Movies; Shopping trips; Dances/Social/Cultural gatherings.

Chester

Liberty County Nursing Home
Monroe Ave, Chester, MT 59522
(406) 759-5181
Admin Richard O Brown. *Dir of Nursing* Ann Ruddick. *Medical Dir* Dr Richard S Buker Jr.
Licensure Skilled care. *Beds* SNF 40. *Certified* Medicaid; Medicare.
Owner Publicly owned.
Staff RNs 2 (ft); LPNs 4 (ft), 2 (pt); Nurses' aides 15 (ft), 8 (pt); Physical therapists 1 (pt); Activities coordinators 1 (pt); Dietitians 1 (pt); Dentists 1 (pt).
Facilities Dining room; Physical therapy room; Activities room; Chapel; Crafts room; Laundry room; Barber/Beauty shop; Library.
Activities Arts & crafts; Cards; Games; Reading groups; Prayer groups; Movies; Shopping trips; Dances/Social/Cultural gatherings.

Chinook

Sweet Memorial Nursing Home
PO Box 1149, Chinook, MT 59523
(406) 357-2549
Admin Norma Fraser.

Medical Dir James Begg MD.
Licensure Skilled care; Intermediate care. *Beds*
SNF 34; ICF 7. *Certified* Medicaid;
Medicare.
Admissions Requirements Physician's request.
Staff RNs 1 (ft), 1 (pt); LPNs 1 (ft), 4 (pt);
Nurses' aides 11 (ft), 4 (pt); Activities
coordinators 2 (pt).
Facilities Dining room; Activities room;
Laundry room; Barber/Beauty shop.
Activities Arts & crafts; Cards; Games;
Reading groups; Prayer groups; Movies;
Shopping trips; Dances/Social/Cultural
gatherings; Meals at senior citizen centers.

Choteau

Teton Medical Center—Nursing Home
PO Box 820, 915 4th St NW, Choteau, MT
59422
(406) 466-5763
Licensure Skilled care. *Beds* SNF 32. *Certified*
Medicaid; Medicare.

Teton Nursing Home
24 Main Ave N, Choteau, MT 59422
(406) 466-5338
Admin Arlene Wolbaum. *Dir of Nursing* Alice
Wentland RN. *Medical Dir* M A Johnson
MD.
Licensure Skilled care; Intermediate care. *Beds*
SNF 38; ICF 3. *Certified* Medicaid;
Medicare.
Owner Publicly owned.
Admissions Requirements Medical
examination.
Staff RNs 2 (ft), 4 (pt); LPNs 2 (pt); Nurses'
aides 11 (ft), 10 (pt); Activities coordinators
1 (ft), 1 (pt); Dietitians 1 (pt).
Facilities Dining room; Physical therapy
room; Activities room; Crafts room; Barber/
Beauty shop.
Activities Arts & crafts; Cards; Games;
Reading groups; Prayer groups; Movies;
Shopping trips; Dances/Social/Cultural
gatherings; Intergenerational programs; Pet
therapy.

Circle

McCone County Nursing Home
PO Box 48, Circle, MT 59215
(406) 485-3381
Admin Jamie M Tarbox NHA. *Dir of Nursing*
Sandra Rueb RN. *Medical Dir* N J Hastetter
MD.
Licensure Skilled care. *Beds* SNF 40. *Private
Pay Patients* 43%. *Certified* Medicaid;
Medicare; VA.
Owner Nonprofit organization/foundation.
Admissions Requirements Medical
examination; Physician's request.
Staff Physicians 1 (pt); RNs 2 (ft), 4 (pt);
LPNs 1 (ft), 1 (pt); Nurses' aides 6 (ft), 12
(pt); Activities coordinators 1 (ft); Dietitians
1 (pt); Mental health specialists 1 (pt).
Facilities Dining room; Physical therapy
room; Activities room; Crafts room; Laundry
room; Barber/Beauty shop; TV room.
Activities Arts & crafts; Cards; Games;
Reading groups; Prayer groups; Movies;
Shopping trips; Dances/Social/Cultural
gatherings; Group discussion.

Clancy

Hillbrook Nursing Home
Rte 2, Clancy, MT 59634
(406) 933-8311
Admin William Chapek. *Dir of Nursing*
Sharon Butler. *Medical Dir* Dr Harry Etter.
Licensure Skilled care; Intermediate care. *Beds*
Swing beds SNF/ICF 67. *Private Pay
Patients* 20%. *Certified* Medicaid; Medicare.
Owner Proprietary corp.
Admissions Requirements Physician's request.

Staff Physicians; RNs; LPNs; Nurses' aides;
Physical therapists; Reality therapists;
Recreational therapists; Occupational
therapists; Speech therapists; Activities
coordinators; Dietitians.
Facilities Dining room; Physical therapy
room; Activities room; Crafts room; Laundry
room; Barber/Beauty shop; Canteen; Garden;
Barbecue area.
Activities Arts & crafts; Cards; Games;
Reading groups; Prayer groups; Movies;
Shopping trips; Dances/Social/Cultural
gatherings; Intergenerational programs; Pet
therapy; Fishing.

Columbia Falls

Montana Veterans Home
PO Box 250, Columbia Falls, MT 59912
(406) 892-3256
Admin Michael Patrick Estenson. *Dir of
Nursing* Orlynda Goodman.
Licensure Skilled care; Intermediate care;
Retirement. *Beds* SNF 20; ICF 70. *Certified*
Medicaid; Medicare; VA.
Owner Privately owned.
Admissions Requirements Honorably
discharged veteran or spouse.
Staff Physicians 3 (pt); RNs 9 (ft); LPNs 8
(ft); Nurses' aides 28 (ft); Physical therapists
1 (pt); Activities coordinators 1 (ft);
Dietitians 1 (pt).
Facilities Dining room; Physical therapy
room; Activities room; Chapel; Crafts room;
Laundry room; Barber/Beauty shop; Library.
Activities Arts & crafts; Cards; Games;
Reading groups; Prayer groups; Movies;
Shopping trips; Dances/Social/Cultural
gatherings.

Columbus

Stillwater Convalescent Center
350 W Pike Ave, Columbus, MT 59019
(406) 322-5342
Admin Ronald I Borgman.
Medical Dir Dr Jack Exley.
Licensure Skilled care; Intermediate care. *Beds*
SNF 50; ICF 32. *Certified* Medicaid;
Medicare.
Staff Physicians 3 (pt); RNs 3 (ft), 3 (pt);
LPNs 5 (ft), 2 (pt); Nurses' aides 26 (ft), 6
(pt); Physical therapists 1 (pt); Speech
therapists 1 (pt); Activities coordinators 1
(ft); Dietitians 1 (pt).
Facilities Dining room; Physical therapy
room; Activities room; Crafts room; Laundry
room; Barber/Beauty shop.
Activities Arts & crafts; Cards; Games;
Reading groups; Prayer groups; Movies;
Shopping trips; Dances/Social/Cultural
gatherings.

Conrad

Pondera Medical Center—Extended & Long-Term Care
805 Sunset Blvd, Conrad, MT 59425
(406) 278-3211
Admin Esther Johnson.
Licensure Skilled care. *Beds* SNF 78. *Certified*
Medicaid; Medicare.
Owner Nonprofit corp (Lutheran Health
Systems).

Culbertson

Roosevelt Memorial Nursing Home
Box 419, Culbertson, MT 59218
(406) 787-6621, 787-6670 FAX
Admin Walter Busch. *Dir of Nursing* Dawn
Satrom RN. *Medical Dir* Dr John Mann.
Licensure Skilled care; Intermediate care. *Beds*
Swing beds SNF/ICF 40. *Private Pay
Patients* 50%. *Certified* Medicaid; Medicare.
Owner Nonprofit organization/foundation.

Admissions Requirements Physician's request.
Staff Physicians 1 (ft); RNs 5 (ft); LPNs 6 (ft);
Nurses' aides 15 (ft); Physical therapists 1
(ft), 1 (pt); Activities coordinators 1 (ft);
Dietitians 1 (ft).
Facilities Dining room; Physical therapy
room; Activities room; Chapel; Crafts room;
Laundry room; Barber/Beauty shop.
Activities Arts & crafts; Cards; Games;
Reading groups; Prayer groups; Movies;
Shopping trips; Dances/Social/Cultural
gatherings; Intergenerational programs; Pet
therapy.

Cut Bank

Glacier County Medical Center Nursing Hom
802 2nd St SE, Cut Bank, MT 59427
(406) 873-2251
Admin Mack Simpson.
Medical Dir Dr L Hemmer.
Licensure Skilled care. *Beds* SNF 39. *Certified*
Medicaid; Medicare.
Owner Privately owned.
Admissions Requirements Medical
examination.
Staff RNs 2 (ft), 1 (pt); LPNs 4 (ft); Nurses'
aides 12 (ft), 2 (pt); Activities coordinators 1
(ft); Dietitians 1 (pt).
Facilities Dining room; Physical therapy
room; Activities room; Chapel; Laundry
room; Barber/Beauty shop.
Activities Arts & crafts; Cards; Games; Prayer
groups; Movies; Shopping trips; Dances/
Social/Cultural gatherings.

Deer Lodge

Colonial Manor of Deer Lodge
1100 Texas Ave, Deer Lodge, MT 59722
(406) 846-1655
Admin Fern Knight.
Licensure Skilled care; Intermediate care. *Beds*
SNF 40; ICF 20. *Certified* Medicaid.
Owner Proprietary corp (Waverly Group).

Montana State Hospital—ICF
RFD 1, Galen, Deer Lodge, MT 59722
(406) 693-7000
Admin Joseph M Balkovatz.
Licensure Intermediate care. *Beds* ICF 185.
Certified Medicaid.

Powell County Memorial Hospital Long-Term Care Unit
1101 Texas Ave, Deer Lodge, MT 59722
(406) 846-2212
Admin Jon Frantsvog.
Medical Dir Peggy Madore.
Licensure Skilled care. *Beds* SNF 12. *Certified*
Medicaid; Medicare.
Owner Privately owned.
Admissions Requirements Medical
examination; Physician's request.
Staff RNs 5 (ft), 3 (pt); LPNs 4 (ft), 2 (pt);
Nurses' aides 5 (ft), 1 (pt); Physical
therapists 1 (pt); Activities coordinators 1
(pt).
Facilities Dining room; Physical therapy
room; Activities room; Barber/Beauty shop;
Library.
Activities Arts & crafts; Cards; Games;
Reading groups; Prayer groups; Movies;
Dances/Social/Cultural gatherings.

Dillon

Parkview Acres Convalescent Center
200 Oregon St, Dillon, MT 59725-3699
(406) 683-5105
Admin George Montrose.
Licensure Skilled care; Intermediate care. *Beds*
SNF 20; ICF 88. *Certified* Medicaid;
Medicare.
Owner Proprietary corp (Hillhaven Corp).

Ekalaka

Dahl Memorial Nursing Home
PO Box 46, Ekalaka, MT 59324
(406) 775-8730, 775-6289 FAX
Admin Paul K Longden. *Dir of Nursing* Rona Meyer. *Medical Dir* Darryl Espland DO.
Licensure Skilled care. *Beds* SNF 21. *Private Pay Patients* 45%. *Certified* Medicaid; Medicare.
Owner Nonprofit organization/foundation.
Admissions Requirements Medical examination.
Staff Physicians 1 (pt); RNs 2 (ft), 4 (pt); Nurses' aides 7 (ft), 2 (pt); Activities coordinators 1 (ft), 1 (pt); Dietitians 1 (pt).
Facilities Dining room; Activities room; Laundry room.
Activities Arts & crafts; Cards; Games; Reading groups; Prayer groups; Movies.

Ennis

Madison County Nursing Home—Ennis
PO Box 335, Ennis, MT 59729
(406) 682-7271
Admin J Page Puckett. *Dir of Nursing* Jeanne Bodine RN. *Medical Dir* Dr Gene C Wilkins.
Licensure Skilled care; Intermediate care. *Beds* SNF 20; ICF 20. *Certified* Medicaid.
Owner Publicly owned.
Admissions Requirements Medical examination; Physician's request.
Staff Physicians 2 (pt); RNs 2 (ft); LPNs 3 (ft), 1 (pt); Nurses' aides 10 (ft), 4 (pt); Activities coordinators 1 (ft); Dietitians 1 (ft); Dentists 1 (pt).
Facilities Dining room; Activities room; Laundry room; Barber/Beauty shop.
Activities Arts & crafts; Cards; Games; Reading groups; Prayer groups; Movies; Shopping trips; Dances/Social/Cultural gatherings; Exercise groups.

Eureka

Mountain View Manor Good Samaritan
PO Box 327, Eureka, MT 59917
(406) 296-2541
Admin Mark Bichler. *Dir of Nursing* Shirley Appleby RN. *Medical Dir* Dr Andy Ivy Jr.
Licensure Skilled care. *Beds* SNF 40. *Private Pay Patients* 13%. *Certified* Medicaid; Medicare.
Owner Nonprofit corp (Evangelical Lutheran/ Good Samaritan Society).
Admissions Requirements Medical examination.
Staff RNs 2 (ft), 5 (pt); LPNs 1 (ft), 4 (pt); Nurses' aides 8 (ft), 14 (pt); Physical therapists 1 (pt); Occupational therapists 1 (pt); Activities coordinators 1 (ft), 1 (pt); Dietitians 1 (pt); Social workers 1 (pt).
Affiliation Lutheran.
Facilities Dining room; Physical therapy room; Activities room; Chapel; Crafts room; Laundry room; Barber/Beauty shop; Fenced yard.
Activities Arts & crafts; Cards; Games; Reading groups; Prayer groups; Movies; Shopping trips; Dances/Social/Cultural gatherings; Intergenerational programs; Pet therapy; Day camping; Fishing; Rides; Parades; Ceramics; Devotions; Sing-alongs; Picnics; Rodeo; Ballgames.

Forsyth

Rosebud Health Care Center
383 N 17th St, Forsyth, MT 59327
(406) 356-2161, 356-2812 FAX
Admin Joyce Asay. *Dir of Nursing* Marilyn Kanta RN. *Medical Dir* J K Cope MD.

Licensure Skilled care; Intermediate care. *Beds* Swing beds SNF/ICF 55. *Certified* Medicaid; Medicare.
Owner Nonprofit organization/foundation.
Admissions Requirements Medical examination; Physician's request.
Staff Physicians 1 (ft); RNs 7 (ft); LPNs 2 (ft), 2 (pt); Nurses' aides 30 (ft), 10 (pt); Physical therapists (contracted); Recreational therapists; Activities coordinators 1 (ft), 1 (pt); Dietitians 1 (pt); Audiologists 1 (pt).
Facilities Dining room; Physical therapy room; Activities room; Laundry room; Barber/Beauty shop.
Activities Arts & crafts; Cards; Games; Reading groups; Prayer groups; Movies; Shopping trips; Dances/Social/Cultural gatherings.

Fort Benton

Chouteau County District Hospital & Nursing Home
1512 Saint Charles St, Fort Benton, MT 59442
(406) 622-3331
Admin Dale Polla. *Dir of Nursing* Pamela Cappis RN. *Medical Dir* W F Gertson MD.
Licensure Skilled care; Intermediate care. *Beds* Swing beds SNF/ICF 22. *Private Pay Patients* 50%. *Certified* Medicaid; Medicare.
Owner Publicly owned.
Admissions Requirements Physician's request.
Staff Physicians 1 (ft); RNs 3 (ft), 4 (pt); LPNs 2 (ft), 1 (pt); Nurses' aides 12 (ft), 4 (pt); Physical therapists 1 (pt); Recreational therapists 2 (pt); Activities coordinators 1 (pt).
Facilities Dining room; Physical therapy room; Activities room; Crafts room; Barber/ Beauty shop.
Activities Arts & crafts; Cards; Games; Reading groups; Prayer groups; Movies; Shopping trips.

Glasgow

Frances Mahon Deaconess Nursing Home
621 3rd St S, Glasgow, MT 59230
(406) 228-4351
Admin Kyle Hosptad.
Medical Dir Louise Johnston.
Licensure Skilled care. *Beds* SNF 6. *Certified* Medicaid; Medicare.

Valley View Home
1225 Perry Ln, Glasgow, MT 59230
(406) 228-2461
Admin Mary Newton.
Medical Dir Dr O'Dea.
Licensure Skilled care; Intermediate care. *Beds* SNF 50; ICF 42. *Certified* Medicaid; Medicare.
Staff RNs 1 (ft), 3 (pt); LPNs 4 (ft), 3 (pt); Nurses' aides 25 (ft), 8 (pt); Physical therapists 1 (pt); Activities coordinators 1 (ft); Dietitians 1 (ft).
Affiliation Lutheran.
Facilities Dining room; Activities room; Laundry room; Barber/Beauty shop.
Activities Arts & crafts; Cards; Games; Reading groups; Prayer groups; Movies; Shopping trips; Dances/Social/Cultural gatherings.

Glendive

Eastmont Human Services Center
700 E Little St, Glendive, MT 59330
(406) 365-6001
Admin Sylvia Y Hammer.
Medical Dir Sylvia Hammer; Patricia Holm; Ann Sveen.
Licensure Intermediate care for mentally retarded. *Beds* ICF/MR 55. *Certified* Medicaid.

Owner Publicly owned.
Admissions Requirements Court committed.
Staff RNs 2 (ft); LPNs 5 (ft); Recreational therapists 1 (ft); Speech therapists 1 (ft); Dietitians 1 (ft).
Languages Sign.
Facilities Dining room; Activities room; Crafts room.
Activities Arts & crafts; Games; Movies; Shopping trips; Dances/Social/Cultural gatherings.

Glendive Medical Center—Nursing Home
202 Prospect Dr, Glendive, MT 59330-1999
(406) 365-5692
Admin John Nordwick.
Medical Dir Dr N H Rausch.
Licensure Skilled care; Intermediate care. *Beds* SNF 30; ICF 45. *Certified* Medicaid; Medicare.
Admissions Requirements Minimum age 18; Medical examination; Physician's request.
Staff Physicians 6 (ft); RNs 3 (ft), 4 (pt); LPNs 3 (ft), 3 (pt); Nurses' aides 18 (ft), 18 (pt); Recreational therapists 1 (ft); Activities coordinators 1 (ft); Dietitians 1 (ft).
Facilities Dining room; Physical therapy room; Activities room; Chapel; Crafts room; Laundry room; Barber/Beauty shop.
Activities Arts & crafts; Cards; Games; Reading groups; Prayer groups; Movies; Shopping trips; Dances/Social/Cultural gatherings.

Great Falls

Cambridge Court
1109 6th Ave N, Great Falls, MT 59401
(406) 727-7151
Licensure Personal care. *Beds* Personal care 77.

Cascade County Convalescent Nursing Home
1130 17th Ave S, Great Falls, MT 59405
(406) 761-6467
Admin Donald E Pizzini. *Dir of Nursing* Doris Odegard. *Medical Dir* Dr John Hickes.
Licensure Skilled care; Alzheimer's care. *Beds* SNF 232. *Certified* Medicaid; Medicare.
Owner Publicly owned.
Admissions Requirements Medical examination; Physician's request.
Staff Physicians 1 (ft), 1 (pt); RNs 12 (ft), 11 (pt); LPNs 11 (ft), 9 (pt); Nurses' aides 80 (ft); Physical therapists 1 (ft); Activities coordinators 2 (ft); Dietitians 1 (pt); Pharmacists 2 (ft); Dentists 0 1 (pt).
Languages Spanish.
Facilities Dining room; Physical therapy room; Activities room; Chapel; Crafts room; Laundry room; Barber/Beauty shop; Library.
Activities Arts & crafts; Cards; Games; Reading groups; Prayer groups; Movies; Shopping trips; Dances/Social/Cultural gatherings.

Deaconess Skilled Nursing Center
2621 15th Ave S, Great Falls, MT 59405
(406) 791-1200, ext 5903
Admin Margaret Weedman.
Medical Dir Dr L L Howard.
Licensure Skilled care; Adult day care. *Beds* SNF 124; Adult day care. *Certified* Medicaid; Medicare.
Admissions Requirements Medical examination; Physician's request.
Facilities Dining room; Physical therapy room; Activities room; Chapel; Crafts room; Laundry room; Barber/Beauty shop; Library; Outside garden area; Enclosed sun porches; On-site doctor's office; Bus; Wheelchair van.
Activities Arts & crafts; Cards; Games; Reading groups; Prayer groups; Movies; Shopping trips; Dances/Social/Cultural gatherings.

Montana West Retirement Home Inc
1009 3rd Ave N, Great Falls, MT 59401
(406) 452-6302
Admin George B Eusterman Jr.
Medical Dir Mary Freeman.
Licensure Personal care. *Beds* Personal care 37.

Park Place Health Care Center
PO Box 5001, 15th Ave S & 32nd St, Great Falls, MT 59405-5001
(406) 761-4300
Admin Dale Zulauf.
Medical Dir Dorothy V Boettcher.
Licensure Skilled care; Intermediate care. *Beds* SNF 53; ICF 70. *Certified* Medicaid; Medicare.
Owner Proprietary corp (Hillhaven Corp).
Facilities Dining room; Physical therapy room; Activities room; Crafts room; Laundry room; Barber/Beauty shop; Library.
Activities Arts & crafts; Cards; Games; Reading groups; Prayer groups; Movies; Shopping trips; Dances/Social/Cultural gatherings.

Hamilton

Kahlwood Hospitality Home
492 Skalkaho Rd, Hamilton, MT 59840
(406) 363-2401
Licensure Personal care. *Beds* Personal care 6.

Valley View Estates Nursing Home
225 N 8th St, Hamilton, MT 59840
(406) 363-1144
Admin John B Muir.
Licensure Skilled care; Intermediate care. *Beds* SNF 59; ICF 39. *Certified* Medicaid; Medicare.

Hardin

Big Horn County Memorial Nursing Home
17 N Miles, Hardin, MT 59034
(406) 665-2310
Admin Michael N Sinclair.
Licensure Skilled care. *Beds* SNF 34. *Certified* Medicaid; Medicare.

Heritage Acres
200 N Mitchell Ave, Hardin, MT 59034
(406) 665-2802
Admin Jackie Suko. *Dir of Nursing* Bonnie Graber & Mary Hogan, acting directors. *Medical Dir* R R Whiting.
Licensure Skilled care; Retirement. *Beds* SNF 36; Retirement 20. *Private Pay Patients* 40%. *Certified* Medicaid; Medicare.
Owner Publicly owned.
Admissions Requirements Minimum age 18; Medical examination; Physician's request.
Staff RNs 3 (ft), 2 (pt); LPNs 3 (ft), 2 (pt); Nurses' aides 14 (ft), 10 (pt); Dietitians.
Languages Spanish, Native American languages.
Facilities Dining room; Activities room; Crafts room; Laundry room; Barber/Beauty shop; Library.
Activities Arts & crafts; Cards; Games; Prayer groups; Movies; Shopping trips; Dances/Social/Cultural gatherings; Intergenerational programs; Pet therapy; Bus rides.

Harlem

Harlem Rest Home
PO Box 279, 112 S Main, Harlem, MT 59526
(406) 353-2421
Admin A J Fuzesy.
Medical Dir K Fuzesy.
Licensure Intermediate care. *Beds* ICF 55. *Certified* Medicaid.
Owner Privately owned.
Staff RNs 2 (ft), 1 (pt); LPNs 1 (ft); Nurses' aides 12 (ft), 2 (pt); Activities coordinators 1 (ft).

Facilities Dining room; Activities room; Crafts room; Laundry room; Library.
Activities Arts & crafts; Cards; Games; Reading groups; Prayer groups; Movies; Shopping trips; Dances/Social/Cultural gatherings.

Harlowton

Wheatland Memorial Nursing Home
530 3rd St NW, Harlowton, MT 59036
(406) 632-4351
Admin Robert B Holmes.
Licensure Skilled care. *Beds* SNF 33. *Certified* Medicaid; Medicare.

Havre

Lutheran Home of the Good Shepherd
2229 5th Ave, Havre, MT 59501
(406) 265-2238
Admin Carol Ann Andrews. *Dir of Nursing* Claire Wendland RN. *Medical Dir* Dr Tom Booth.
Licensure Skilled care; Intermediate care. *Beds* Swing beds SNF/ICF 102. *Private Pay Patients* 40%. *Certified* Medicaid; Medicare.
Owner Nonprofit corp.
Admissions Requirements Medical examination; Physician's request.
Staff RNs 10 (ft), 3 (pt); LPNs 5 (ft), 1 (pt); Nurses' aides 25 (ft), 15 (pt); Recreational therapists 1 (ft), 3 (pt); Activities coordinators 1 (ft); Dietitians 1 (ft).
Affiliation Lutheran.
Facilities Dining room; Activities room; Chapel; Crafts room; Laundry room; Barber/Beauty shop.
Activities Arts & crafts; Cards; Games; Reading groups; Prayer groups; Movies; Shopping trips; Dances/Social/Cultural gatherings; Pet therapy.

Northern Montana Long Term Care
PO Box 1231, 30 13th St, Havre, MT 59501
(406) 265-2211
Licensure Skilled care. *Beds* SNF 22. *Certified* Medicaid; Medicare.

Helena

Big Sky Care Center
2475 Winne Ave, Helena, MT 59601
(406) 442-1350
Admin Page Puckett.
Licensure Skilled care; Intermediate care. *Beds* SNF 24; ICF 84. *Certified* Medicaid; Medicare.
Owner Proprietary corp (Hillhaven Corp).

Cedar Street Home
721 Cedar St, Helena, MT 59601
(406) 442-1676
Admin Janet Ford.
Medical Dir Elizabeth Henry.
Licensure Intermediate care. *Beds* 7. *Certified* Medicaid.

Cooney Convalescent Home
2555 Broadway, Helena, MT 59601
(406) 442-0572
Admin Joan Ashley RN BSN. *Dir of Nursing* Joan Lester RN. *Medical Dir* Martin Skinner MD.
Licensure Skilled care; Intermediate care. *Beds* SNF 70; ICF 6. *Private Pay Patients* 30%. *Certified* Medicaid; Medicare.
Owner Publicly owned.
Admissions Requirements Minimum age 65; Medical examination; Physician's request.
Staff RNs 2 (ft), 6 (pt); LPNs 4 (ft), 3 (pt); Nurses' aides 34 (ft), 7 (pt); Recreational therapists 1 (ft); Activities coordinators 2 (pt); Dietitians 1 (ft).

Facilities Dining room; Physical therapy room; Activities room; Crafts room; Laundry room; Barber/Beauty shop; Library; Summer garden; Patio; Gazebo.
Activities Arts & crafts; Cards; Games; Reading groups; Prayer groups; Movies; Shopping trips; Dances/Social/Cultural gatherings; Intergenerational programs; Pet therapy; Reality orientation; Exercise; Gardening; Religious services.

Helena Nursing Home Co
25 S Ewing, Helena, MT 59601
(406) 443-5880
Admin Gerald Hughes. *Dir of Nursing* Helen Tamol RN. *Medical Dir* David Jordan MD.
Licensure Skilled care; Intermediate care. *Beds* SNF 32; ICF 31. *Certified* Medicaid; Medicare.
Owner Privately owned.
Admissions Requirements Physician's request.
Staff Physicians 1 (pt); RNs 3 (ft), 2 (pt); LPNs 7 (ft); Nurses' aides 13 (ft), 1 (pt); Activities coordinators 1 (ft), 1 (pt); Dietitians 1 (pt); Kitchen staff 9 (ft).
Facilities Dining room; Physical therapy room; Activities room; Crafts room; Barber/Beauty shop.
Activities Arts & crafts; Cards; Games; Reading groups; Prayer groups; Movies; Shopping trips; Dances/Social/Cultural gatherings; Exercise.

Hot Springs

Hot Springs Convalescent Inc
Drawer U, Hot Springs, MT 59845
(406) 741-2992
Admin H Kent Ferguson.
Medical Dir Jacob V Lulack MD.
Licensure Skilled care; Intermediate care. *Beds* SNF 18; ICF 53. *Certified* Medicaid; Medicare.
Admissions Requirements Medical examination; Physician's request.
Staff RNs 4 (ft), 2 (pt); LPNs 1 (pt); Nurses' aides 9 (ft).
Facilities Dining room; Physical therapy room; Activities room; Laundry room; Barber/Beauty shop.
Activities Arts & crafts; Cards; Games; Reading groups; Prayer groups; Movies; Shopping trips; Dances/Social/Cultural gatherings.

Jordan

Garfield County Health Center Inc
PO Box 389, Jordan, MT 59337
(406) 557-2500
Admin James C Seibert. *Dir of Nursing* Rita Amundson.
Licensure Skilled care; Intermediate care; Personal care. *Beds* SNF 4; ICF/Personal care 14. *Certified* Medicaid; Medicare.
Owner Nonprofit corp.
Admissions Requirements Medical examination.
Staff RNs 2 (ft), 3 (pt); LPNs 2 (pt); Nurses' aides 2 (ft), 7 (pt); Activities coordinators 2 (pt); Dietitians (consultant); Physicians assistants 1 (ft), 1 (pt).
Facilities Dining room; Activities room; Laundry room.
Activities Arts & crafts; Cards; Games; Reading groups; Movies; Shopping trips; Church services; Singing; Playing musical instruments.

Kalispell

Brendan House Skilled Nursing Facility
350 Conway Dr, Kalispell, MT 59901
(406) 752-5460
Admin Karen E Black. *Dir of Nursing* Judy Leigh RN. *Medical Dir* Richard Wise MD.

Licensure Skilled care; Adult day care; Alzheimer's care. *Beds* SNF 80. *Certified* Medicaid; Medicare.
Owner Nonprofit organization/foundation.
Admissions Requirements Physician's request.
Staff Physicians 1 (ft); RNs 9 (ft); LPNs 6 (ft); Nurses' aides 27 (ft); Physical therapists 2 (ft); Occupational therapists 1 (ft); Speech therapists 1 (ft); Activities coordinators 2 (ft); Dietitians 1 (ft).
Activities Arts & crafts; Cards; Games; Reading groups; Prayer groups; Movies; Shopping trips; Dances/Social/Cultural gatherings.

Flathead County Care Center
1251 Willow Glen Dr, Kalispell, MT 59901
(406) 257-5575
Admin Marguerite Watne.
Medical Dir Anna Drew.
Licensure Skilled care. *Beds* SNF 54. *Certified* Medicaid; Medicare.
Admissions Requirements Physician's request.
Staff RNs 3 (ft), 3 (pt); LPNs 2 (ft); Nurses' aides 18 (ft), 5 (pt); Activities coordinators 1 (ft).
Facilities Dining room; Activities room; Crafts room; Laundry room; Library.
Activities Arts & crafts; Movies; Shopping trips; Church.

Friendship House Inc
606 2nd Ave W, Kalispell, MT 59901
(406) 257-8375
Licensure Personal care. *Beds* Personal care 20.

Immanuel Lutheran Home
Buffalo Hill, Kalispell, MT 59901
(406) 752-9622
Admin Lorraine Wagnild. *Dir of Nursing* Marge Keith. *Medical Dir* Dr Alfred V Swanberg.
Licensure Skilled care; Intermediate care; Retirement. *Beds* SNF 54; ICF 90. *Certified* Medicaid.
Owner Nonprofit corp.
Admissions Requirements Medical examination; Physician's request.
Staff RNs 7 (ft), 6 (pt); LPNs 9 (ft), 5 (pt); Nurses' aides 46 (ft), 22 (pt); Activities coordinators 3 (ft), 1 (pt); Dietitians 1 (ft).
Affiliation Lutheran.
Facilities Dining room; Activities room; Chapel; Crafts room; Laundry room; Barber/Beauty shop.
Activities Arts & crafts; Cards; Games; Reading groups; Prayer groups; Movies; Shopping trips; Dances/Social/Cultural gatherings; Educational groups with college teachers.

Laurel

Laurel Care Center
820 3rd Ave, Laurel, MT 59044
(406) 628-8251
Admin Phillip Gorby. *Dir of Nursing* Virla Kober.
Licensure Skilled care; Personal care; Adult day care. *Beds* SNF 50; Personal care 5; Adult day care. *Certified* Medicaid; Medicare; VA.
Owner Proprietary corp.
Admissions Requirements Minimum age 18.
Staff RNs 2 (ft), 1 (pt); LPNs 5 (ft), 2 (pt); Nurses' aides 20 (ft), 6 (pt); Activities coordinators 1 (ft), 1 (pt); Dietitians 1 (ft).
Facilities Dining room; Physical therapy room; Activities room; Chapel; Laundry room; Barber/Beauty shop.
Activities Arts & crafts; Cards; Games; Reading groups; Prayer groups; Movies; Shopping trips; Dances/Social/Cultural gatherings.

Winkel Personal Care Home
717-719 W 1st St, Laurel, MT 59044
(406) 628-2115
Licensure Personal care. *Beds* Personal care 7.

Lewistown

Central Montana Nursing Home
PO Box 580, 408 Wendell, Lewistown, MT 59457
(406) 538-7711
Admin Robert G Conrad. *Dir of Nursing* Phyllis Taylor RN.
Licensure Skilled care. *Beds* SNF 70. *Certified* Medicaid; Medicare.
Owner Nonprofit corp.
Admissions Requirements Minimum age 18; Medical examination; Physician's request.
Staff Physicians 11 (pt); RNs 5 (ft), 4 (pt); LPNs 3 (ft), 2 (pt); Nurses' aides 15 (ft), 26 (pt); Physical therapists 1 (pt); Activities coordinators 1 (ft), 1 (pt); Dietitians 1 (pt); Ophthalmologists 1 (pt); Dentists 1 (pt).
Facilities Dining room; Physical therapy room; Activities room; Chapel; Crafts room; Laundry room; Barber/Beauty shop; Library; Courtyard.
Activities Arts & crafts; Cards; Games; Reading groups; Prayer groups; Movies; Dances/Social/Cultural gatherings; Weekly restaurant outings.

Governor's House
316 8th Ave S, Lewistown, MT 59457
(406) 538-2468
Licensure Personal care. *Beds* Personal care 6.

Montana Center for the Aged
800 Casino Creek Dr, Lewistown, MT 59457
(406) 538-7451
Admin Gerald F Butcher. *Dir of Nursing* Day Brooks.
Licensure Intermediate care. *Beds* ICF 191. *Certified* Medicaid.
Owner Publicly owned.
Admissions Requirements Minimum age 55.
Staff RNs 6 (ft), 3 (pt); LPNs 3 (ft), 2 (pt); Nurses' aides 31 (ft), 5 (pt).
Facilities Dining room; Activities room; Laundry room; Barber/Beauty shop.
Activities Arts & crafts; Cards; Games; Prayer groups; Movies; Shopping trips; Dances/Social/Cultural gatherings.

Mountain View Personal Care & Retirement Home
RR 2 Box 2347, Lewistown, MT 59457
(406) 538-2731
Admin Terry R Zink.
Licensure Personal care; Retirement. *Beds* Personal care 32; Retirement home 16. *Private Pay Patients* 97%.
Owner Privately owned.
Admissions Requirements Minimum age 18; Medical examination.
Facilities Dining room; Laundry room.
Activities Arts & crafts; Cards; Games; Movies; Pet therapy.

Valle Vista Manor
402 Summit Ave, Lewistown, MT 59457
(406) 538-8775
Admin Bill McLain.
Medical Dir Dr Paul Gans.
Licensure Skilled care; Intermediate care. *Beds* SNF 31; ICF 70. *Certified* Medicaid; Medicare.
Staff RNs 5 (ft), 4 (pt); LPNs 5 (ft), 3 (pt); Nurses' aides 33 (ft), 16 (pt); Activities coordinators 1 (ft), 1 (pt); Dietitians 1 (pt); Dentists 1 (pt).
Facilities Dining room; Activities room; Chapel; Crafts room; Laundry room; Barber/Beauty shop.
Activities Arts & crafts; Cards; Games; Movies; Shopping trips; Dances/Social/Cultural gatherings.

Libby

Libby Care Center
308 E 3rd St, Libby, MT 59923
(406) 293-6285
Admin Joan Croucher. *Dir of Nursing* Synnove Balsiger. *Medical Dir* Roger Brus MD.
Licensure Skilled care; Intermediate care. *Beds* Swing beds SNF/ICF 38. *Private Pay Patients* 20%. *Certified* Medicaid; Medicare.
Owner Proprietary corp (National Heritage).
Admissions Requirements Medical examination.
Staff Physicians 1 (pt); RNs 5 (ft), 2 (pt); LPNs 5 (ft), 2 (pt); Nurses' aides 36 (ft), 12 (pt); Physical therapists 1 (pt); Activities coordinators 1 (ft), 2 (pt); Dietitians 1 (pt).
Facilities Dining room; Activities room; Chapel; Crafts room; Laundry room; Barber/Beauty shop; Library.
Activities Arts & crafts; Cards; Games; Reading groups; Prayer groups; Movies; Shopping trips; Dances/Social/Cultural gatherings; Pet therapy; Support group.

Livingston

Livingston Convalescent Center
510 S 14th St, Livingston, MT 59047
(406) 222-0672
Admin Judith A Melin.
Medical Dir Dr L M Baskett.
Licensure Skilled care; Intermediate care. *Beds* SNF 29; ICF 96. *Certified* Medicaid; Medicare.
Owner Proprietary corp (Hillhaven Corp).
Staff RNs 6 (ft); LPNs 7 (ft); Nurses' aides 30 (ft); Physical therapists 1 (ft); Reality therapists 1 (ft); Recreational therapists 1 (ft); Occupational therapists 1 (ft); Speech therapists 1 (ft); Activities coordinators 1 (ft); Dietitians 1 (ft); Dentists 1 (ft).
Facilities Dining room; Activities room; Laundry room; Barber/Beauty shop.
Activities Arts & crafts; Cards; Games; Reading groups; Prayer groups; Movies; Shopping trips; Dances/Social/Cultural gatherings.

New Frontier Personal Care & Retirement Center
121 S 3rd, Livingston, MT 59047
(406) 222-6102
Licensure Personal care. *Beds* Personal care 50.

Sessions Homestead
3185 A Park Rd, Rte 62, Livingston, MT 59047
(406) 222-2706
Licensure Personal care. *Beds* Personal care 10.

Malta

Good Samaritan Country Home
117 S 9th W, Malta, MT 59538
(406) 654-2535
Licensure Personal care. *Beds* Personal care 28.

Phillips County Good Samaritan Retirement Center
Box P, Malta, MT 59538
(406) 654-1190
Admin Henryka Shelton.
Medical Dir Michael Emond.
Licensure Skilled care; Intermediate care. *Beds* SNF 40; ICF 20. *Certified* Medicaid.
Owner Nonprofit corp (Evangelical Lutheran/ Good Samaritan Society).

Miles City

Custer County Rest Home
PO Box 130, Miles City, MT 59301
(406) 232-1035
Admin Milton E Benge.
Medical Dir Patricia Neiffer.
Licensure Skilled care; Intermediate care. *Beds*
SNF 40; ICF 81. *Certified* Medicaid;
Medicare.
Owner Publicly owned.
Admissions Requirements Physician's request.
Staff RNs 6 (ft), 5 (pt); LPNs 6 (ft), 4 (pt);
Nurses' aides 49 (ft), 4 (pt); Activities
coordinators 1 (ft); Dietitians 1 (ft).
Facilities Dining room; Physical therapy
room; Activities room; Chapel; Crafts room;
Laundry room; Barber/Beauty shop; Library.
Activities Arts & crafts; Cards; Games;
Reading groups; Prayer groups; Movies;
Shopping trips.

Friendship Villa Care Center
Rte 2 Box 3001, 1242 S Strevell, Miles City,
MT 59301
(406) 232-2687
Admin Charles J Blando. *Dir of Nursing*
Myrna Hillier. *Medical Dir* Dr
Campodonico.
Licensure Skilled care. *Beds* SNF 73. *Certified*
Medicaid; Medicare.
Owner Proprietary corp.
Admissions Requirements Medical
examination; Physician's request.
Staff RNs; LPNs; Nurses' aides; Physical
therapists; Activities coordinators.
Facilities Dining room; Physical therapy
room; Activities room; Chapel; Crafts room;
Laundry room; Barber/Beauty shop.
Activities Arts & crafts; Cards; Games;
Reading groups; Prayer groups; Movies;
Shopping trips; Dances/Social/Cultural
gatherings.

TLC Of Miles City Inc
2607 Main, Miles City, MT 59301
(406) 232-7988
Licensure Personal care. *Beds* Personal care 9.

Missoula

Community Nursing & Rehabilitation Facility
2651 South Ave W, Missoula, MT 59801
(406) 728-9162
Admin Danna J Miller. *Dir of Nursing* Sandra
Leischner RN. *Medical Dir* R Ratigan MD.
Licensure Skilled care; Retirement;
Alzheimer's care. *Beds* SNF 149. *Certified*
Medicaid; Medicare; VA.
Owner Privately owned.
Admissions Requirements Minimum age 16;
Medical examination; Physician's request.
Staff RNs 5 (ft), 6 (pt); LPNs 9 (ft), 7 (pt);
Nurses' aides 53 (ft), 17 (pt); Recreational
therapists 2 (ft); Activities coordinators 1
(ft); Dietitians 1 (pt).
Facilities Dining room; Physical therapy
room; Activities room; Crafts room; Laundry
room; Barber/Beauty shop; Library.
Activities Arts & crafts; Cards; Games;
Reading groups; Prayer groups; Movies;
Shopping trips; Dances/Social/Cultural
gatherings.

Flor Haven Home
433 S 3rd St W, Missoula, MT 59801
(406) 542-2598
Licensure Personal care. *Beds* Personal care
12.

Hawthorne House
1811 S 7th W, Missoula, MT 59801
(406) 543-4055
Licensure Personal care. *Beds* Personal care
35.

Heritage Hearth
1809 S 6th W, Missoula, MT 59801
(406) 543-3352
Licensure Personal care. *Beds* Personal care
11.

Hillside Manor
4720 23rd St, Missoula, MT 59803-1199
(406) 251-5100
Admin Connie Thisselle. *Dir of Nursing*
Joanne Verlanic-Scherger. *Medical Dir* T H
Roberts MD.
Licensure Skilled care; Adult day care;
Retirement. *Beds* SNF 102. *Certified*
Medicaid; Medicare.
Owner Privately owned.
Admissions Requirements Medical
examination; Physician's request.
Staff RNs 4 (ft), 6 (pt); LPNs 5 (ft), 5 (pt);
Nurses' aides 17 (ft), 12 (pt); Activities
coordinators 2 (ft), 1 (pt); Dietitians 1 (ft).
Facilities Dining room; Physical therapy
room; Activities room; Crafts room; Laundry
room; Barber/Beauty shop; Library.
Activities Arts & crafts; Cards; Games;
Reading groups; Prayer groups; Movies.

Maplewood Manor
1300 Speedway, Missoula, MT 59802
(406) 549-8127
Licensure Personal care. *Beds* Personal care
27.

Riverside Health Care Center
1301 E Broadway, Missoula, MT 59802
(406) 721-0680
Licensure Skilled care. *Beds* SNF 52. *Certified*
Medicaid; Medicare.

Royal Manor Care Center
3018 Rattlesnake Dr, Missoula, MT 59802
(406) 549-0988
Admin Gregory A Miller.
Medical Dir Mary Kloser.
Licensure Skilled care; Intermediate care. *Beds*
SNF 31; ICF 20. *Certified* Medicaid;
Medicare.
Owner Proprietary corp (Manor Care Inc).
Admissions Requirements Physician's request.
Staff RNs 2 (pt); LPNs 3 (ft), 1 (pt); Nurses'
aides 17 (ft), 4 (pt); Activities coordinators 1
(ft), 1 (pt); Dietitians 1 (pt).
Facilities Dining room; Laundry room.
Activities Arts & crafts; Cards; Games;
Reading groups; Prayer groups; Movies;
Shopping trips; Dances/Social/Cultural
gatherings.

Wayside Nursing Care Facility
2222 Rattlesnake, Missoula, MT 59802
(406) 549-6158
Admin Jo Waldbillig.
Medical Dir Dr D Hubbard.
Licensure Skilled care; Intermediate care. *Beds*
SNF 40; ICF 4. *Certified* Medicaid;
Medicare.
Admissions Requirements Physician's request.
Staff Physicians 1 (pt); RNs 2 (pt); LPNs 5
(ft); Nurses' aides 13 (ft), 6 (pt); Physical
therapists 1 (pt); Activities coordinators 1
(ft); Dietitians 1 (pt); Dentists 1 (pt).
Facilities Dining room; Activities room;
Crafts room; Laundry room; Barber/Beauty
shop.
Activities Arts & crafts; Cards; Games;
Reading groups; Prayer groups; Movies;
Shopping trips; Dances/Social/Cultural
gatherings.

Philipsburg

Granite County Memorial Nursing Home
Box 729, Philipsburg, MT 59858
(406) 859-3271
Admin Mike Kahoe. *Dir of Nursing* Margery
Metesh RN.
Licensure Skilled care. *Beds* SNF 13. *Certified*
Medicaid; Medicare.
Activities Arts & crafts; Cards; Games;
Reading groups; Prayer groups; Movies.

Plains

Clark Fork Valley Nursing Home
PO Box 768, Kruger Rd, Plains, MT 59859
(406) 826-3601
Admin Mike Billing.
Medical Dir Jacob Lulack MD.
Licensure Skilled care. *Beds* SNF 28. *Certified*
Medicaid; Medicare.
Staff Physicians 4 (ft); RNs 3 (ft), 4 (pt);
LPNs 3 (ft); Nurses' aides 7 (ft), 8 (pt);
Physical therapists 1 (pt); Activities
coordinators 1 (ft); Dietitians 1 (ft); Dentists
1 (pt).
Facilities Dining room; Physical therapy
room; Activities room; Crafts room; Laundry
room; Barber/Beauty shop.
Activities Arts & crafts; Games; Reading
groups; Prayer groups; Movies; Shopping
trips; Dances/Social/Cultural gatherings.

Plentywood

Sheridan Memorial Nursing Home
440 W Laurel Ave, Plentywood, MT 59254
(406) 765-1420
Admin Mark Rinehardt.
Medical Dir Dr Kirk Stoner.
Licensure Skilled care. *Beds* SNF 66. *Certified*
Medicaid; Medicare.
Admissions Requirements Medical
examination.
Staff Physicians 2 (ft); RNs 6 (pt); LPNs 2
(ft), 3 (pt); Nurses' aides 8 (ft), 28 (pt);
Occupational therapists 1 (pt); Activities
coordinators 1 (ft); Dietitians 1 (pt); Dentists
1 (pt).
Facilities Dining room; Physical therapy
room; Activities room; Crafts room; Laundry
room; Barber/Beauty shop.
Activities Arts & crafts; Games; Reading
groups; Prayer groups; Movies; Dances/
Social/Cultural gatherings.

Polson

St Joseph Convalescent Center
PO Box 1530, No 9 14th Ave W, Polson, MT
59860
(406) 883-4378
Admin William McDonald.
Licensure Skilled care; Intermediate care. *Beds*
SNF 50; ICF 62. *Certified* Medicaid;
Medicare.

Poplar

Poplar Community Hospital & Nursing Home
Box 38, Corner of H & Court, Poplar, MT
59255
(406) 768-3452
Admin Peggy Sage. *Dir of Nursing* Pam
Turnbaugh. *Medical Dir* Dr Craig
Nicholson.
Licensure Skilled care. *Beds* SNF 22. *Certified*
Medicaid; Medicare.
Owner Nonprofit organization/foundation.
Staff Physicians 6 (ft); RNs 8 (ft); LPNs 5 (ft);
Nurses' aides 20 (ft), 5 (pt); Physical
therapists 1 (pt); Activities coordinators 1
(ft); Dietitians 1 (pt).
Languages Sioux, Assiniboine.
Facilities Dining room; Activities room;
Crafts room; Barber/Beauty shop.
Activities Arts & crafts; Cards; Games;
Reading groups; Prayer groups; Movies;
Shopping trips; Dances/Social/Cultural
gatherings; Intergenerational programs; Pet
therapy; Adopt-a-grandparent.

Red Lodge

Carbon County Health Care Center
PO Box 430, 1 S Oaks, Red Lodge, MT 59068
(406) 446-2525
Admin Henry M Rae. *Dir of Nursing* Darlene Huseby RN. *Medical Dir* Dr James J Kane.
Licensure Skilled care; Intermediate care. *Beds* SNF 36; ICF 44. *Certified* Medicaid; Medicare.
Owner Proprietary corp (Hillhaven Corp).
Admissions Requirements Medical examination.
Staff RNs 5 (ft); LPNs 7 (ft); Nurses' aides 37 (ft).
Facilities Dining room; Physical therapy room; Activities room; Crafts room; Laundry room; Barber/Beauty shop.
Activities Arts & crafts; Cards; Games; Reading groups; Prayer groups; Movies; Dances/Social/Cultural gatherings.

Carbon County Memorial Nursing Home
PO Box 590, 600 W 21st St, Red Lodge, MT 59068
(406) 446-2346
Admin Milt Bedsaul, acting. *Dir of Nursing* Regina Bruner RN. *Medical Dir* David McLaughlin MD.
Licensure Skilled care. *Beds* SNF 30. *Private Pay Patients* 23%. *Certified* Medicaid; Medicare.
Owner Nonprofit organization/foundation (Lutheran Hospitals & Homes Society).
Admissions Requirements Physician's request.
Staff Physicians 2 (ft), 1 (pt); RNs 2 (ft), 1 (pt); LPNs 2 (ft), 4 (pt); Nurses' aides 9 (ft), 3 (pt); Physical therapists 1 (pt); Activities coordinators 1 (pt); Dietitians 1 (pt); Audiologists 1 (pt); Social services 1 (pt).
Affiliation Lutheran.
Facilities Dining room; Physical therapy room; Activities room; Barber/Beauty shop.
Activities Arts & crafts; Cards; Reading groups; Prayer groups; Dances/Social/Cultural gatherings; Cooking; Reminiscence.

Ronan

Happy Acres Home
919 Main St SW, Ronan, MT 59864
(406) 676-3934
Admin Judith A Frame.
Medical Dir Dr Jay L Ballhagen.
Licensure Intermediate care for mentally retarded. *Beds* ICF/MR 10. *Certified* Medicaid.
Owner Privately owned.
Admissions Requirements Minimum age 18; Females only; Medical examination.
Staff RNs; Nurses' aides 2 (ft), 4 (pt); Social workers 1 (pt).
Facilities Dining room; Activities room; Laundry room; Library.
Activities Arts & crafts; Cards; Games; Reading groups; Prayer groups; Shopping trips; Dances/Social/Cultural gatherings; Community activities.

St Luke Community Nursing Home
107 6th Ave SW, Ronan, MT 59864
(406) 676-2900
Admin James Oliverson.
Licensure Skilled care. *Beds* SNF 43. *Certified* Medicaid; Medicare.

West Side Rest Home
829 Main St SW, Ronan, MT 59864
(406) 676-5510
Admin Faye Abrahamson. *Dir of Nursing* Wendella Draper. *Medical Dir* Dr S T McDonald.
Licensure Intermediate care. *Beds* ICF 23. *Certified* Medicaid.
Owner Privately owned.
Admissions Requirements Physician's request.

Staff RNs 2 (ft); LPNs 3 (ft), 1 (pt); Nurses' aides 2 (ft), 6 (pt); Activities coordinators 1 (ft); Dietitians.
Languages Salish.
Facilities Dining room; Activities room; Crafts room; Laundry room; Library.
Activities Arts & crafts; Cards; Games; Reading groups; Prayer groups; Movies; Shopping trips; Dances/Social/Cultural gatherings; Pet therapy.

Roundup

Roundup Memorial Nursing Home
1202 3rd St W, Roundup, MT 59072
(406) 323-2302, 323-1170 FAX
Admin Fern E Mikkelson. *Dir of Nursing* Dorothy F Harper RN. *Medical Dir* Samuel V Boor MD.
Licensure Skilled care; Acute care. *Beds* SNF 37; Acute care 17. *Private Pay Patients* 40%. *Certified* Medicaid; Medicare.
Owner Publicly owned.
Admissions Requirements Medical examination; Physician's request.
Staff RNs 5 (ft), 1 (pt); LPNs 2 (ft), 2 (pt); Nurses' aides 14 (ft), 8 (pt); Physical therapists 1 (pt); Activities coordinators 1 (ft), 1 (pt); Dietitians 1 (pt).
Facilities Dining room; Physical therapy room; Activities room; Chapel; Laundry room; Barber/Beauty shop.
Activities Arts & crafts; Cards; Games; Reading groups; Prayer groups; Movies; Shopping trips; Dances/Social/Cultural gatherings.

Scobey

Daniels Memorial Nursing Home
PO Box 400, Scobey, MT 59263
(406) 487-2296
Admin Curtis Leibrand. *Dir of Nursing* Naomi Stentoft. *Medical Dir* Merle Fitz MD.
Licensure Skilled care; Adult day care. *Beds* SNF 45. *Certified* Medicaid; Medicare; VA.
Owner Nonprofit organization/foundation.
Admissions Requirements Physician's request.
Staff RNs; LPNs; Nurses' aides; Activities coordinators; Dietitians; Dentists.
Facilities Dining room; Activities room; Chapel; Crafts room; Laundry room; Barber/Beauty shop; Library.
Activities Arts & crafts; Cards; Games; Reading groups; Prayer groups; Movies; Shopping trips; Bingo; Cooking; Bus rides.

Shelby

Toole County Nursing Home
PO Box P, 640 Park Dr, Shelby, MT 59474
(406) 434-5536, 434-7253 FAX
Admin Warner Bartleson. *Dir of Nursing* Ann Fauque. *Medical Dir* Robert Stanchfield.
Licensure Skilled care; Intermediate care. *Beds* Swing beds SNF/ICF 53. *Private Pay Patients* 17%. *Certified* Medicaid; Medicare.
Owner Publicly owned.
Admissions Requirements Physician's request.
Staff Physicians; RNs; LPNs; Nurses' aides; Physical therapists; Occupational therapists; Activities coordinators; Dietitians; Audiologists.
Facilities Dining room; Physical therapy room; Activities room; Chapel; Crafts room; Laundry room; Barber/Beauty shop.
Activities Arts & crafts; Cards; Games; Reading groups; Prayer groups; Movies; Shopping trips; Dances/Social/Cultural gatherings; Intergenerational programs.

Sheridan

Madison County Nursing Home
326 Madison, Sheridan, MT 59749
(406) 842-5600
Admin Randall G Holom. *Dir of Nursing* Joan Andren RN. *Medical Dir* Sarah L Googe MD.
Licensure Intermediate care. *Beds* ICF 39. *Private Pay Patients* 41%. *Certified* Medicaid.
Owner Publicly owned.
Admissions Requirements Medical examination; Physician's request.
Staff RNs 2 (ft); LPNs 4 (ft), 3 (pt); Nurses' aides 13 (ft), 2 (pt); Physical therapists 1 (pt); Activities coordinators 3 (pt); Dietitians 1 (pt); Podiatrists 1 (pt); Audiologists 1 (pt); Dentists 2 (pt).
Facilities Dining room; Activities room; Laundry room; Barber/Beauty shop.
Activities Arts & crafts; Cards; Games; Reading groups; Prayer groups; Movies; Shopping trips; Dances/Social/Cultural gatherings; Intergenerational programs; Pet therapy; Family support groups.

Sidney

Richland Homes
Girard Rte Box 5001, Sidney, MT 59270
(406) 482-2120
Admin Donna Kay Jennings. *Dir of Nursing* Marolyn Fasig. *Medical Dir* Dr James Ashcraft.
Licensure Skilled care; Intermediate care. *Beds* SNF 49; ICF 36. *Private Pay Patients* 34%. *Certified* Medicaid; Medicare.
Owner Nonprofit organization/foundation.
Admissions Requirements Medical examination; Physician's request.
Staff RNs 4 (ft), 6 (pt); LPNs 3 (ft), 4 (pt); Nurses' aides 24 (ft), 20 (pt); Physical therapists (consultant); Occupational therapists 1 (pt); Speech therapists 1 (pt); Activities coordinators 1 (ft); Dietitians 1 (pt); Rehabilitation aides.
Facilities Dining room; Chapel; Laundry room; Barber/Beauty shop; Library.
Activities Arts & crafts; Cards; Games; Reading groups; Prayer groups; Movies; Shopping trips; Dances/Social/Cultural gatherings; Intergenerational programs; Pet therapy; Talking books.

Stevensville

North Valley Nursing Home
63 Main St, Stevensville, MT 59870
(406) 777-5411
Admin Nancy Summers. *Dir of Nursing* Tracey Davenport. *Medical Dir* Alan Rossi MD.
Licensure Skilled care; Intermediate care. *Beds* SNF 50; ICF 7. *Private Pay Patients* 30%. *Certified* Medicaid; Medicare.
Owner Proprietary corp.
Staff Physicians 5 (pt); RNs 2 (ft); LPNs 5 (ft), 4 (pt); Nurses' aides 17 (ft), 4 (pt); Activities coordinators 1 (ft).
Facilities Dining room; Activities room; Crafts room; Laundry room; Barber/Beauty shop.
Activities Arts & crafts; Cards; Games; Reading groups; Prayer groups; Movies; Shopping trips; Dances/Social/Cultural gatherings; Pet therapy.

Superior

Mineral County Nursing Home
PO Box 66, Brooklyn & Roosevelt, Superior, MT 59872
(406) 822-4841
Admin Robert E Smith.
Medical Dir James P Hoyne MD.

Licensure Skilled care. *Beds* SNF 20. *Certified* Medicaid; Medicare.
Admissions Requirements Medical examination; Physician's request.
Staff Physicians 3 (pt); RNs 7 (pt); LPNs 5 (pt); Nurses' aides 9 (pt); Physical therapists 1 (pt); Recreational therapists 1 (pt); Activities coordinators 1 (pt); Dietitians 1 (pt); Dentists 1 (pt).
Facilities Dining room; Physical therapy room; Activities room; Crafts room; Laundry room; Barber/Beauty shop.
Activities Arts & crafts; Cards; Games; Reading groups; Prayer groups; Movies; Shopping trips; Dances/Social/Cultural gatherings.

Terry

Prairie Community Nursing Home
Box 156, Terry, MT 59349
(406) 637-5511
Admin James Mantz. *Dir of Nursing* Carleen Gaub RN. *Medical Dir* Adele Lukaszewicz MD.
Licensure Skilled care; Intermediate care. *Beds* Swing beds SNF/ICF 16. *Private Pay Patients* 35%. *Certified* Medicaid; Medicare.
Owner Publicly owned.
Admissions Requirements Medical examination; Physician's request.
Staff Physicians 1 (ft); RNs 2 (ft), 5 (pt); Nurses' aides 3 (ft), 6 (pt); Activities coordinators 1 (pt).
Facilities Dining room; Activities room; Crafts room; Laundry room.
Activities Arts & crafts; Cards; Games; Reading groups; Prayer groups; Movies; Dances/Social/Cultural gatherings.

Townsend

Broadwater County Rest Home
PO Box 67, Townsend, MT 59644
(406) 266-3711
Admin Audrey A Solberg.
Licensure Personal care. *Beds* Personal care 16. *Certified* Medicaid.
Owner Publicly owned.
Admissions Requirements Minimum age 18; Medical examination; Physician's request.
Staff Nurses' aides 3 (ft), 3 (pt); Activities coordinators 1 (ft); Dietitians 1 (ft), 1 (pt).
Facilities Dining room; Activities room; Crafts room; Laundry room; Barber/Beauty shop.

Activities Arts & crafts; Cards; Games; Reading groups; Prayer groups; Movies; Shopping trips; Dances/Social/Cultural gatherings; Exercise groups; Singing; Music.

Broadwater Health Center Nursing Home
PO Box 519, 110 N Oak, Townsend, MT 59644
(406) 266-3186
Licensure Skilled care. *Beds* SNF 32. *Certified* Medicaid; Medicare.

Warm Springs

Warm Springs State Hospital
Bldg 219 Warm Springs Campus, Warm Springs, MT 59756
(406) 693-7000
Admin Richard Moore.
Licensure Intermediate care. *Beds* ICF 60. *Certified* Medicaid.

White Sulphur Springs

Mountainview Memorial Nursing Home
PO Box Q, White Sulphur Springs, MT 59645
(406) 547-3321
Admin Larry Putnam. *Dir of Nursing* Mary Hamel RN. *Medical Dir* Dr Pam Hiebert.
Licensure Skilled care. *Beds* SNF 31. *Certified* Medicaid; Medicare.
Owner Nonprofit corp.
Admissions Requirements Physician's request.
Staff RNs 6 (ft); LPNs 3 (ft); Nurses' aides 6 (ft), 2 (pt); Physical therapists 1 (pt); Activities coordinators 1 (ft); Dietitians 1 (pt).
Affiliation Lutheran.
Facilities Dining room; Physical therapy room; Laundry room.
Activities Arts & crafts; Cards; Games; Reading groups; Movies.

Whitefish

Colonial Manor of Whitefish
PO Box 1208, 1305E 7th St, Whitefish, MT 59937
(406) 862-3557
Admin Betty Elder.
Licensure Intermediate care. *Beds* ICF 60. *Certified* Medicaid.
Owner Proprietary corp (Waverly Group).

North Valley Hospital & Extended Care Center
6575 Hwy 93 S, Whitefish, MT 59937
(406) 862-2501
Admin Dale Jessup.
Licensure Skilled care; Intermediate care; Adult day care. *Beds* SNF 50; ICF 6. *Certified* Medicaid; Medicare.

Wibaux

Wibaux County Nursing Home
601 S Wibaux St, Wibaux, MT 59353
(406) 795-2429
Admin Bill O'Hara. *Dir of Nursing* Barbara Stockwell RN. *Medical Dir* Nancy Rausch MD.
Licensure Skilled care. *Beds* SNF 40. *Certified* Medicaid; Medicare.
Owner Nonprofit corp (Lutheran Health Systems).
Admissions Requirements Medical examination; Physician's request.
Staff RNs 2 (ft), 3 (pt); LPNs 2 (ft); Nurses' aides 5 (ft), 14 (pt); Activities coordinators 1 (ft).
Facilities Dining room; Activities room; Chapel; Crafts room; Laundry room; Barber/Beauty shop.
Activities Arts & crafts; Cards; Games; Reading groups; Movies.

Wolf Point

Faith Lutheran Home Inc
1000 6th Ave N, Wolf Point, MT 59201
(406) 653-1400
Admin Greg Sorum.
Medical Dir Elaine Keane.
Licensure Intermediate care; Retirement. *Beds* ICF 60. *Certified* Medicaid.
Owner Nonprofit corp.
Admissions Requirements Medical examination.
Staff RNs 1 (ft); LPNs 3 (ft), 3 (pt); Nurses' aides 10 (ft), 15 (pt); Activities coordinators 1 (ft).
Affiliation Lutheran.
Facilities Dining room; Physical therapy room; Activities room; Chapel; Crafts room; Laundry room; Barber/Beauty shop; Library.
Activities Arts & crafts; Cards; Games; Reading groups; Prayer groups; Movies; Shopping trips; Dances/Social/Cultural gatherings.

NEBRASKA

Adams

Gold Crest Retirement Center
PO Box 78, Adams, NE 68301
(402) 988-7115
Admin David Armstrong. *Dir of Nursing* Gay Miller RN. *Medical Dir* Dr Monroe Dowling.
Licensure Skilled care; Residential care; Health clinic. *Beds* SNF 52; Residential care 40. *Certified* Medicaid; Medicare.
Owner Nonprofit corp.
Admissions Requirements Medical examination; Physician's request.
Staff Physicians 1 (ft); RNs 5 (ft); LPNs 3 (ft); Nurses' aides 20 (ft); Physical therapists 1 (ft); Activities coordinators 2 (ft); Dietitians 1 (ft).
Languages German, Swedish, Danish.
Facilities Dining room; Physical therapy room; Activities room; Chapel; Crafts room; Laundry room; Barber/Beauty shop; Library.
Activities Arts & crafts; Cards; Games; Reading groups; Prayer groups; Movies; Shopping trips.

Ainsworth

Bethesda Care Center
143 N Fullerton St, Ainsworth, NE 69210-1515
(402) 387-2500
Admin Melanie Palmer. *Dir of Nursing* Diana Syfie RN. *Medical Dir* Dr F Shiffermiler.
Licensure Intermediate care. *Beds* ICF 47. *Certified* Medicaid.
Owner Nonprofit corp.
Admissions Requirements Medical examination; Physician's request.
Staff RNs 1 (ft), 1 (pt); LPNs 2 (ft), 2 (pt); Nurses' aides 12 (ft), 6 (pt); Physical therapists 1 (ft); Activities coordinators 1 (ft), 1 (pt).
Facilities Dining room; Activities room; Laundry room; Barber/Beauty shop.
Activities Arts & crafts; Cards; Games; Reading groups; Prayer groups; Shopping trips; Dances/Social/Cultural gatherings.

Albion

Wolf Memorial Good Samaritan Center
1222 S 7th St, Albion, NE 68620
(402) 395-5050
Admin David R Molin. *Dir of Nursing* Shirley Price. *Medical Dir* Dr Randy Kohl.
Licensure Intermediate care; Independent living. *Beds* ICF 62; Independent living units 13. *Private Pay Patients* 50%. *Certified* Medicaid.
Owner Nonprofit corp (Evangelical Lutheran/Good Samaritan Society).
Admissions Requirements Medical examination; Physician's request.

Staff RNs 2 (ft), 2 (pt); LPNs 7 (ft); Nurses' aides 13 (ft), 22 (pt); Physical therapists 2 (ft); Recreational therapists 1 (ft); Activities coordinators 1 (ft).
Affiliation Lutheran.
Facilities Dining room; Physical therapy room; Activities room; Chapel; Crafts room; Laundry room; Barber/Beauty shop.
Activities Arts & crafts; Games; Prayer groups; Movies; Dances/Social/Cultural gatherings; Intergenerational programs; Pet therapy.

Alliance

Good Samaritan Village
PO Box 970, 1016 E 6th, Alliance, NE 69301
(308) 762-5675
Admin Dan Guenther. *Dir of Nursing* Magdalene Greene RN.
Licensure Intermediate care. *Beds* ICF 105. *Private Pay Patients* 50%. *Certified* Medicaid.
Owner Nonprofit corp (Evangelical Lutheran/Good Samaritan Society).
Admissions Requirements Medical examination; Physician's request.
Staff RNs 2 (ft), 3 (pt); LPNs 4 (ft), 16 (pt); Nurses' aides 10 (ft), 36 (pt); Physical therapists (consultant); Activities coordinators 2 (ft), 2 (pt); Dietitians 1 (ft).
Languages Spanish.
Affiliation Lutheran.
Facilities Dining room; Physical therapy room; Activities room; Chapel; Laundry room; Barber/Beauty shop.
Activities Arts & crafts; Games; Reading groups; Prayer groups; Movies; Shopping trips; Dances/Social/Cultural gatherings; Intergenerational programs; Pet therapy.

St Joseph Gerontology Center
416 W 11th St, Alliance, NE 69301
(308) 762-2525
Admin Cheryl Mundt. *Dir of Nursing* Betty Leistritz RN. *Medical Dir* Dr John Ruffing.
Licensure Skilled care; Intermediate care. *Beds* 61. *Certified* Medicaid; Medicare.
Owner Proprietary corp.
Admissions Requirements Medical examination; Physician's request.
Staff RNs; LPNs; Nurses' aides; Activities coordinators.
Affiliation Roman Catholic.
Facilities Dining room; Activities room; Chapel; Crafts room; Laundry room; Barber/Beauty shop; Library; Hospitality room; Special dining room.
Activities Arts & crafts; Cards; Games; Reading groups; Prayer groups; Movies; Shopping trips; Dances/Social/Cultural gatherings; Birthday parties; News & exercise class.

Alma

Colonial Villa Good Samaritan Center
719 N Brown, Alma, NE 68920
(308) 928-2128
Admin Peggy Hodde. *Dir of Nursing* Vicki Bantam RN. *Medical Dir* Mary W Goessling.
Licensure Intermediate care. *Beds* ICF 60. *Certified* Medicaid.
Owner Nonprofit corp (Evangelical Lutheran/Good Samaritan Society).
Admissions Requirements Medical examination; Physician's request.
Staff RNs 1 (ft), 1 (pt); LPNs 5 (pt); Nurses' aides 10 (ft), 20 (pt); Physical therapists 1 (pt); Occupational therapists 1 (pt); Speech therapists 1 (pt); Activities coordinators 1 (ft); Dietitians 3 (ft), 4 (pt).
Affiliation Lutheran.
Facilities Dining room; Activities room; Chapel; Crafts room; Laundry room; Barber/Beauty shop.
Activities Arts & crafts; Cards; Games; Reading groups; Prayer groups; Movies; Shopping trips.

Arapahoe

C A Mues Memorial Good Samaritan Center
601 Main St, Arapahoe, NE 68922
(308) 962-5230
Admin Lawrence Eickhoff. *Dir of Nursing* Luella Bond RN.
Licensure Intermediate care; Alzheimer's care. *Beds* ICF 55. *Private Pay Patients* 60%. *Certified* Medicaid.
Owner Nonprofit corp (Evangelical Lutheran/Good Samaritan Society).
Admissions Requirements Medical examination; Physician's request.
Staff RNs 2 (ft); LPNs 3 (ft), 2 (pt); Nurses' aides 18 (ft), 8 (pt); Activities coordinators 1 (ft), 1 (pt); Dietitians 1 (pt).
Languages German.
Affiliation Lutheran.
Facilities Dining room; Physical therapy room; Activities room; Chapel; Crafts room; Laundry room; Barber/Beauty shop; Library; Prayer garden.
Activities Arts & crafts; Cards; Games; Reading groups; Prayer groups; Movies; Shopping trips; Dances/Social/Cultural gatherings; Intergenerational programs; Pet therapy.

Ashland

Bethesda Care Center
1700 Furnas St, Ashland, NE 68003
(402) 944-7031
Admin Shirley L Hemke. *Dir of Nursing* Betsy Lynch RN. *Medical Dir* Dr Dale Michels.
Licensure Intermediate care; Alzheimer's care. *Beds* ICF 101; Alzheimer's care 14. *Private Pay Patients* 56%. *Certified* Medicaid.
Owner Proprietary corp (Meritcare).

Staff RNs 1 (ft), 2 (pt); LPNs 5 (ft), 1 (pt); Nurses' aides 24 (ft), 6 (pt); Activities coordinators 2 (ft), 1 (pt).
Facilities Dining room; Physical therapy room; Activities room; Chapel; Crafts room; Laundry room; Barber/Beauty shop; Dayroom.
Activities Arts & crafts; Cards; Games; Reading groups; Prayer groups; Movies; Dances/Social/Cultural gatherings; Pet therapy.

Atkinson

Atkinson Good Samaritan Center
PO Box 699, 315 E Neeley St, Atkinson, NE 68713
(402) 925-2875
Admin Phyllis Langan. *Dir of Nursing* Sharon Spangler RN.
Licensure Intermediate care. *Beds* ICF 62. *Certified* Medicaid.
Owner Nonprofit corp (Evangelical Lutheran/ Good Samaritan Society).
Admissions Requirements Medical examination.
Staff RNs 2 (ft), 1 (pt); LPNs 1 (ft), 4 (pt); Nurses' aides 3 (ft), 18 (pt); Activities coordinators 1 (ft).
Affiliation Lutheran.
Facilities Dining room; Activities room; Chapel; Laundry room.
Activities Arts & crafts; Cards; Games; Reading groups; Prayer groups; Movies; Shopping trips; Dances/Social/Cultural gatherings.

Auburn

Nemaha County Good Samaritan Center
Rte 1 Box 4, Auburn, NE 68305-9799
(402) 274-3109
Admin Daniel H Guenther. *Dir of Nursing* Barbara Breazile RN.
Licensure Intermediate care. *Beds* ICF 114. *Certified* Medicaid.
Owner Nonprofit corp (Evangelical Lutheran/ Good Samaritan Society).
Affiliation Lutheran.

Aurora

Bethesda Care Center
PO Box 510, 610-616 13th St, Aurora, NE 68818
(402) 694-6905
Admin Diane Schlotman. *Dir of Nursing* Judith Trumble RN.
Licensure Intermediate care; Residential care. *Beds* ICF 45. *Certified* Medicaid.
Owner Nonprofit corp (MTC West Inc).
Admissions Requirements Physician's request.
Staff RNs; LPNs; Nurses' aides; Recreational therapists; Activities coordinators; Dietitians.
Languages German.
Facilities Dining room; Activities room; Laundry room; Barber/Beauty shop; Library.
Activities Arts & crafts; Cards; Games; Reading groups; Prayer groups; Movies; Shopping trips; Dances/Social/Cultural gatherings.

Hamilton Manor
1515 5th St, Aurora, NE 68818
(402) 694-2128
Admin Barry D Robertshaw. *Dir of Nursing* Robin B Sample RN.
Licensure Intermediate care. *Beds* ICF 109. *Certified* Medicaid.
Owner Publicly owned.

Axtell

Bethphage at Axtell
PO Box 67, Axtell, NE 68924
(308) 743-2401

Admin Sherri R Hansen. *Dir of Nursing* Linda Mattson RN.
Licensure Intermediate care for mentally retarded. *Beds* ICF/MR 182. *Certified* Medicaid.
Owner Nonprofit corp.
Admissions Requirements Medical examination; Physician's request.
Staff Physicians; RNs; LPNs; Nurses' aides; Physical therapists; Recreational therapists; Occupational therapists; Speech therapists; Activities coordinators; Dietitians; Podiatrists.
Languages Spanish.
Affiliation Lutheran.
Facilities Dining room; Physical therapy room; Activities room; Chapel; Crafts room; Laundry room; Barber/Beauty shop; Library; Classrooms; Swimming pool.
Activities Arts & crafts; Cards; Games; Reading groups; Movies; Shopping trips; Dances/Social/Cultural gatherings; Training; Swimming; Outdoor sports.

Battle Creek

Community Pride Care Center
RR 1 Box 54A, 901 S 4th St, Battle Creek, NE 68715
(402) 675-7845
Admin Fern J Salmen RN. *Dir of Nursing* Jacque A Hansen.
Licensure Intermediate care; Residential care. *Beds* ICF 44; Residential care 22. *Certified* Medicaid.
Owner Publicly owned.
Admissions Requirements Medical examination; Physician's request.
Staff RNs 1 (ft); LPNs 5 (ft); Nurses' aides 11 (ft), 8 (pt); Physical therapists (consultant); Reality therapists (consultant); Recreational therapists (consultant); Occupational therapists (consultant); Speech therapists (consultant); Activities coordinators 1 (ft); Dietitians 1 (ft); Audiologists (consultant).
Facilities Dining room; Physical therapy room; Activities room; Chapel; Crafts room; Laundry room; Barber/Beauty shop; Special care room for acutely ill or for isolation; Private and semi-private rooms with private baths equipped with handicapped-height toilets & hinged mirrors; Nurse call system; Sprinkler system; Smoke detectors; Solariums.
Activities Arts & crafts; Cards; Games; Reading groups; Prayer groups; Movies; Shopping trips; Dances/Social/Cultural gatherings; Intergenerational programs; Pet therapy; Community involvement.

Bayard

Chimney Rock Villa
PO Box A, Bayard, NE 69334
(308) 586-1142
Admin Lloyd Steel4. *Dir of Nursing* Diana Stevens RN.
Licensure Intermediate care; Alzheimer's care. *Beds* ICF 47. *Certified* Medicaid.
Owner Publicly owned.
Admissions Requirements Medical examination; Physician's request.
Staff RNs 1 (ft); LPNs 4 (ft); Nurses' aides 8 (ft), 8 (pt); Physical therapists 1 (pt); Occupational therapists 1 (pt); Activities coordinators 1 (ft); Dietitians 1 (ft).
Facilities Dining room; Activities room; Laundry room; Barber/Beauty shop; Library.
Activities Arts & crafts; Cards; Games; Reading groups; Prayer groups; Movies.

Beatrice

Beatrice Good Samaritan Center
1306 S 9th St, Beatrice, NE 68310
(402) 223-3304

Admin Marilou Luth.
Licensure Intermediate care; Health clinic. *Beds* ICF 130. *Certified* Medicaid.
Owner Nonprofit corp (Evangelical Lutheran/ Good Samaritan Society).
Affiliation Lutheran.

Beatrice Manor Care Center
1800 Irving St, Beatrice, NE 68310
(402) 223-2311
Admin Jeffrey Hoffman. *Dir of Nursing* Kathy Erickson RN.
Licensure Intermediate care. *Beds* ICF 84. *Certified* Medicaid.
Owner Proprietary corp.
Admissions Requirements Medical examination; Physician's request.
Staff LPNs 5 (ft); Nurses' aides 15 (ft), 10 (pt); Activities coordinators 1 (ft).
Facilities Dining room; Activities room; Laundry room; Barber/Beauty shop.
Activities Arts & crafts; Cards; Games; Reading groups; Prayer groups; Movies; Shopping trips; Dances/Social/Cultural gatherings.

Beaver City

Beaver City Manor
905 Floyd St, Beaver City, NE 68926
(308) 268-5111
Admin Thomas D Hardin. *Dir of Nursing* Janice Grummert RN.
Licensure Intermediate care; Health clinic. *Beds* ICF 53. *Certified* Medicaid.
Owner Publicly owned.

Beemer

Colonial Haven
RR 1, Beemer, NE 68716
(402) 528-3268
Admin Thomas J Schulte NHAP. *Dir of Nursing* Marion Brockmann RN.
Licensure Intermediate care; Alzheimer's care. *Beds* ICF 55. *Private Pay Patients* 67%. *Certified* Medicaid.
Owner Publicly owned.
Admissions Requirements Medical examination; Physician's request.
Staff Physicians 6 (pt); RNs 1 (ft), 3 (pt); LPNs 8 (pt); Nurses' aides 3 (ft), 22 (pt); Physical therapists 3 (pt); Occupational therapists 1 (pt); Speech therapists 2 (pt); Activities coordinators 2 (pt); Ophthalmologists 1 (pt); Podiatrists 1 (pt); Audiologists 2 (pt).
Languages German.
Facilities Dining room; Physical therapy room; Activities room; Chapel; Crafts room; Laundry room; Barber/Beauty shop.
Activities Arts & crafts; Cards; Games; Reading groups; Prayer groups; Movies; Shopping trips; Dances/Social/Cultural gatherings; Intergenerational programs; Pet therapy.

Bellevue

Hillcrest Care Center
1702 Hillcrest Dr, Bellevue, NE 68005
(402) 291-8500
Admin Jolene M Kemp. *Dir of Nursing* Joan Mitchell RN.
Licensure Intermediate care. *Beds* ICF 116. *Certified* Medicaid.
Owner Proprietary corp.
Admissions Requirements Medical examination; Physician's request.
Staff RNs 3 (ft); LPNs; Physical therapists; Reality therapists; Recreational therapists; Occupational therapists; Speech therapists; Activities coordinators; Dietitians; Ophthalmologists.

Facilities Dining room; Activities room;
Laundry room; Barber/Beauty shop.
Activities Arts & crafts; Cards; Games;
Reading groups; Prayer groups; Movies;
Shopping trips.

Bertrand

Bertrand Nursing Home
100 Minor Ave, Bertrand, NE 68927
(308) 472-3341
Admin Darlene M Hansen. *Dir of Nursing*
Sylvia Sattler RN.
Licensure Intermediate care. *Beds* ICF 52.
Certified Medicaid.
Owner Publicly owned.
Admissions Requirements Medical
examination; Physician's request.
Facilities Dining room; Activities room;
Chapel; Crafts room; Laundry room; Barber/
Beauty shop; Library.
Activities Arts & crafts; Cards; Games;
Reading groups; Prayer groups; Movies.

Blair

Crowell Memorial Home
245 S 22nd St, Blair, NE 68008
(402) 426-2177
Admin Patricia Williby. *Dir of Nursing*
Carolyn Sudyka. *Medical Dir* K C Bagby.
Licensure Skilled care; Retirement. *Beds* SNF
126; Retirement 8. *Private Pay Patients*
70%. *Certified* Medicaid.
Owner Nonprofit corp.
Admissions Requirements Medical
examination; Physician's request.
Staff RNs 3 (ft), 3 (pt); LPNs 4 (ft), 3 (pt);
Nurses' aides 41 (ft), 12 (pt); Activities
coordinators 3 (ft); Dietitians 1 (ft).
Affiliation Methodist.
Facilities Dining room; Activities room;
Chapel; Crafts room; Barber/Beauty shop.
Activities Arts & crafts; Cards; Games;
Reading groups; Prayer groups; Movies;
Shopping trips; Dances/Social/Cultural
gatherings; Intergenerational programs; Pet
therapy.

Good Shepherd Lutheran Home
2242 Wright St, Blair, NE 68008
(402) 426-3377
Admin Marlys Horky. *Dir of Nursing* Kathy
Cox RN.
Licensure Skilled care; Intermediate care;
Residential care. *Beds* 80. *Certified*
Medicaid.
Owner Nonprofit corp.
Admissions Requirements Medical
examination; Physician's request.
Staff RNs 3 (ft), 2 (pt); LPNs 5 (ft), 5 (pt);
Nurses' aides 20 (ft), 15 (pt); Physical
therapists 1 (pt); Speech therapists 1 (pt);
Dietitians 1 (pt).
Affiliation Lutheran.
Facilities Dining room; Activities room;
Chapel; Crafts room; Laundry room; Barber/
Beauty shop.
Activities Arts & crafts; Cards; Games;
Reading groups; Prayer groups; Movies;
Shopping trips; Dances/Social/Cultural
gatherings.

Bloomfield

Bloomfield Good Samaritan Center
300 N 2nd, Bloomfield, NE 68718
(402) 373-4506
Admin Paul LeRoy Nevin. *Dir of Nursing*
Dolores Broders RN. *Medical Dir* Dr D J
Nagengast.
Licensure Skilled care; Intermediate care. *Beds*
Swing beds SNF/ICF 75. *Private Pay
Patients* 35%. *Certified* Medicaid; VA.
Owner Nonprofit corp (Evangelical Lutheran/
Good Samaritan Society).

Admissions Requirements Medical
examination.
Staff RNs 3 (ft), 2 (pt); LPNs 3 (ft), 5 (pt);
Nurses' aides; Physical therapists;
Occupational therapists 1 (pt); Speech
therapists 1 (pt); Activities coordinators 1
(ft); Dietitians 1 (pt); Ophthalmologists 1
(pt); Podiatrists 1 (pt); Dentists 1 (pt).
Affiliation Lutheran.
Facilities Dining room; Physical therapy
room; Activities room; Chapel; Crafts room;
Laundry room; Barber/Beauty shop.
Activities Arts & crafts; Cards; Games;
Reading groups; Prayer groups; Movies;
Shopping trips; Dances/Social/Cultural
gatherings.

Blue Hill

Bethesda Care Center of Blue Hill
PO Box 156, 414 N Wilson, Blue Hill, NE
68930
(402) 756-2080
Admin Diann M Schmidt. *Dir of Nursing*
Debra Krueger RN. *Medical Dir* Frank
Kamm MD.
Licensure Intermediate care. *Beds* ICF 81.
Certified Medicaid.
Owner Nonprofit corp (MTC West Inc).
Admissions Requirements Medical
examination.
Staff RNs 1 (ft); LPNs 2 (ft), 1 (pt); Nurses'
aides 24 (ft), 9 (pt); Physical therapists 1
(pt); Occupational therapists 1 (pt); Speech
therapists 1 (pt); Recreational therapists 2
(ft); Activities coordinators 1 (ft); Dietitians
1 (pt); Podiatrists 1 (pt).
Facilities Dining room; Activities room;
Chapel; Crafts room; Barber/Beauty shop.
Activities Arts & crafts; Cards; Games;
Reading groups; Prayer groups; Movies;
Shopping trips; Baking; Recreational trips.

Bridgeport

Heritage of Bridgeport
5th & N Sts, Bridgeport, NE 69336
(308) 262-0725
Admin Robert Sutton. *Dir of Nursing* Evelyn
Rose RN.
Licensure Intermediate care; Residential care.
Beds ICF 61. *Certified* Medicaid.
Owner Proprietary corp.
Admissions Requirements Medical
examination.
Staff RNs 2 (ft); LPNs 2 (ft), 1 (pt); Nurses'
aides 12 (ft), 5 (pt); Reality therapists 1 (ft);
Activities coordinators 1 (ft).
Facilities Dining room; Activities room;
Barber/Beauty shop.
Activities Arts & crafts; Games; Prayer groups;
Movies; Shopping trips; Dances/Social/
Cultural gatherings.

Broken Bow

Sandhills Manor
E Hwy 2, Broken Bow, NE 68822
(308) 872-6421
Admin Clarine Dickinson. *Dir of Nursing*
Vickie R Shoemaker RN.
Licensure Intermediate care. *Beds* ICF 105.
Certified Medicaid.
Owner Proprietary corp (Beverly Enterprises).
Admissions Requirements Medical
examination; Physician's request.
Staff RNs; LPNs; Nurses' aides; Activities
coordinators.
Facilities Dining room; Physical therapy
room; Activities room; Chapel; Crafts room;
Laundry room; Barber/Beauty shop.
Activities Arts & crafts; Cards; Games;
Reading groups; Prayer groups; Movies;
Shopping trips; Dances/Social/Cultural
gatherings.

Butte

Butte Nursing Home
Box 49, Butte, NE 68722
(402) 775-2355
Admin Myron Armfield. *Dir of Nursing* Debra
Lee RN.
Licensure Intermediate care. *Beds* ICF 62.
Private Pay Patients 50%. *Certified*
Medicaid.
Owner Publicly owned.
Admissions Requirements Medical
examination.
Staff Physicians 2 (pt); RNs 2 (ft); LPNs 3
(ft); Nurses' aides 10 (ft), 15 (pt); Physical
therapists 1 (pt); Dietitians 1 (pt).
Facilities Dining room; Activities room;
Crafts room; Laundry room; Barber/Beauty
shop.
Activities Arts & crafts; Cards; Games;
Reading groups; Prayer groups; Movies;
Shopping trips.

Callaway

Callaway Good Samaritan Center
PO Box 398, W Kimball, Callaway, NE 68825
(308) 836-2267
Admin Juliane M Saxon. *Dir of Nursing*
JoAnn Farmer RN.
Licensure Intermediate care. *Beds* ICF 45.
Private Pay Patients 60%. *Certified*
Medicaid.
Owner Nonprofit corp (Evangelical Lutheran/
Good Samaritan Society).
Admissions Requirements Medical
examination.
Staff RNs 1 (ft), 2 (pt); LPNs 4 (ft), 2 (pt);
Nurses' aides 2 (ft), 6 (pt); Physical
therapists (consultant); Reality therapists
(consultant); Recreational therapists
(consultant); Occupational therapists
(consultant); Activities coordinators 1 (ft), 1
(pt); Dietitians (consultant);
Ophthalmologists (consultant); Podiatrists
(consultant); Audiologists (consultant).
Affiliation Lutheran.
Facilities Dining room; Physical therapy
room; Activities room; Chapel; Crafts room;
Laundry room; Barber/Beauty shop.
Activities Arts & crafts; Cards; Reading
groups; Prayer groups; Movies; Pet therapy;
Church services; Bible study.

Campbell

Grandview Manor
Broadstreet & Hwy 4, Campbell, NE 68932
(402) 756-8701
Admin Shirley L'Heureux. *Dir of Nursing*
Linda Waechter RN.
Licensure Intermediate care. *Beds* ICF 49.
Private Pay Patients 59%. *Certified*
Medicaid.
Owner Proprietary corp (Meritcare).
Admissions Requirements Medical
examination; Physician's request.
Staff Physicians; RNs; LPNs; Nurses' aides;
Activities coordinators.
Facilities Dining room; Activities room;
Chapel; Crafts room; Laundry room; Barber/
Beauty shop.
Activities Arts & crafts; Cards; Games;
Reading groups; Prayer groups; Movies;
Shopping trips; Dances/Social/Cultural
gatherings; Pet therapy; Music; Singing;
Records; Talking Books; Sunday church
services.

Central City

Bethesda Care Center
S 17th Ave, Central City, NE 68826-0259
(308) 946-3088
Admin Donice Woodworth. *Dir of Nursing*
Linda Wandfluh RN.

Licensure Intermediate care; Alzheimer's care. *Beds* ICF 72. *Certified* Medicaid.
Owner Nonprofit corp (MTC West Inc).
Admissions Requirements Physician's request.
Staff RNs 1 (ft), 2 (pt); LPNs 2 (ft), 1 (pt); Nurses' aides 8 (ft), 16 (pt); Physical therapists 1 (pt); Speech therapists 1 (pt); Activities coordinators 1 (ft), 1 (pt); Dietitians 1 (pt).
Facilities Dining room; Activities room; Chapel; Crafts room; Laundry room; Barber/ Beauty shop.
Activities Arts & crafts; Cards; Games; Reading groups; Prayer groups; Movies; Shopping trips; Dances/Social/Cultural gatherings; Picnics; Resident council; Alzheimer's support group.

Chadron

Crest View Manor
PO Box 861, 420 Gordon Ave, Chadron, NE 69337
(308) 432-3355
Admin Gwen Koinzan. *Dir of Nursing* Marilee Hawkins RN. *Medical Dir* R H Rasmussen MD.
Licensure Skilled care; Intermediate care. *Beds* 60. *Certified* Medicaid.
Owner Proprietary corp.
Staff RNs 2 (ft), 1 (pt); LPNs 6 (ft), 2 (pt); Nurses' aides 25 (ft), 5 (pt); Activities coordinators 1 (ft); Dietitians 1 (pt).
Facilities Dining room; Activities room; Chapel; Crafts room; Laundry room; Barber/ Beauty shop.
Activities Arts & crafts; Cards; Games; Reading groups; Prayer groups; Movies; Dances/Social/Cultural gatherings.

Chappell

Miller Memorial Nursing Home
589 Vincent Ave, Chappell, NE 69129
(308) 874-2292
Admin Patricia Livengood. *Dir of Nursing* Cynda T Baver RN.
Licensure Intermediate care; Residential care. *Beds* ICF 24; Residential care 12. *Certified* Medicaid.
Owner Publicly owned.
Admissions Requirements Medical examination; Physician's request.
Staff RNs 1 (ft); LPNs 2 (ft), 2 (pt); Nurses' aides 3 (ft), 10 (pt); Activities coordinators 1 (pt).
Facilities Dining room; Activities room; Crafts room; Laundry room; Barber/Beauty shop; Solarium.
Activities Arts & crafts; Cards; Games; Reading groups; Movies; Dances/Social/ Cultural gatherings.

Clarkson

Colonial Manor
PO Box J, W 3rd & Sunrise Dr, Clarkson, NE 68629
(402) 892-3494
Admin Judy Herink. *Dir of Nursing* Terri Ernesti RN. *Medical Dir* John R O'Neal MD.
Licensure Intermediate care. *Beds* ICF 60. *Private Pay Patients* 50%. *Certified* Medicaid.
Owner Proprietary corp (Beverly Enterprises).
Admissions Requirements Medical examination; Physician's request.
Staff RNs 1 (ft), 3 (pt); LPNs 3 (ft), 2 (pt); Nurses' aides 10 (ft), 11 (pt); Activities coordinators 1 (ft), 1 (pt); Dietitians 1 (ft); Podiatrists 1 (pt).
Languages Czech.
Facilities Dining room; Physical therapy room; Activities room; Chapel; Laundry room; Barber/Beauty shop.

Activities Arts & crafts; Cards; Games; Reading groups; Prayer groups; Movies; Dances/Social/Cultural gatherings; Intergenerational programs.

Coleridge

Park View Haven Nursing Home
PO Box 39, 325 N Madison, Coleridge, NE 68727
(402) 283-4224
Admin Deborah K Elofson. *Dir of Nursing* Cheri Hintz RN.
Licensure Skilled care; Intermediate care. *Beds* 67. *Certified* Medicaid; Medicare.
Owner Publicly owned.

Columbus

Columbus Manor
3918 27th St, Columbus, NE 68601
(402) 564-8014
Admin Teresa Wilcox. *Dir of Nursing* Patricia Peters RN.
Licensure Skilled care; Intermediate care. *Beds* 142. *Certified* Medicaid.
Owner Proprietary corp (Beverly Enterprises).

Val Morys Haven
1112 15th St, Columbus, NE 68601
(402) 564-3197
Admin Joe Hageman. *Dir of Nursing* Donna Wasco RN.
Licensure Intermediate care. *Beds* ICF 48. *Private Pay Patients* 60%. *Certified* Medicaid.
Owner Nonprofit organization/foundation.
Admissions Requirements Medical examination.
Staff RNs 2 (ft), 4 (pt); LPNs 4 (ft), 1 (pt); Nurses' aides 6 (ft), 17 (pt); Activities coordinators 1 (ft), 1 (pt).
Facilities Dining room; Activities room; Chapel; Crafts room; Laundry room.
Activities Arts & crafts; Games; Reading groups; Prayer groups; Intergenerational programs; Pet therapy.

Cozad

Southview Manor Care Center
318 W 18th, Cozad, NE 69130
(308) 784-3715
Admin Sandra Nichelson RN. *Dir of Nursing* Carolyn Greise RN. *Medical Dir* Dr R A Sitorius.
Licensure Skilled care; Intermediate care. *Beds* Swing beds SNF/ICF 90. *Certified* Medicaid; Medicare.
Owner Proprietary corp (Beverly Enterprises).
Admissions Requirements Medical examination; Physician's request.
Staff Physicians 6 (pt); RNs 3 (ft), 3 (pt); LPNs 8 (ft), 2 (pt); Nurses' aides 28 (ft), 8 (pt); Physical therapists 1 (pt); Recreational therapists 1 (pt); Occupational therapists 1 (pt); Speech therapists 1 (pt); Activities coordinators 1 (ft); Dietitians 1 (ft), 1 (pt); Podiatrists 1 (pt).
Facilities Dining room; Physical therapy room; Activities room; Chapel; Crafts room; Laundry room; Barber/Beauty shop; Lobby.
Activities Arts & crafts; Cards; Games; Reading groups; Prayer groups; Movies; Shopping trips; Dances/Social/Cultural gatherings; Intergenerational programs; Pet therapy.

Crawford

Ponderosa Villa
PO Box 526, Crawford, NE 69339-0526
(308) 665-1224
Admin Dixie G Moody. *Dir of Nursing* Kathy Owen RN.

Licensure Intermediate care. *Beds* ICF 55. *Certified* Medicaid.
Owner Publicly owned.
Admissions Requirements Medical examination; Physician's request.
Staff RNs 1 (ft), 3 (pt); LPNs 2 (ft), 2 (pt); Activities coordinators 1 (ft); Dietitians 1 (pt).
Facilities Dining room; Activities room; Chapel; Crafts room; Laundry room; Barber/ Beauty shop; Library.
Activities Arts & crafts; Cards; Games; Reading groups; Prayer groups; Movies; Shopping trips; Dances/Social/Cultural gatherings.

Creighton

Creighton Care Centre
Main St at Lundberg Dr, Creighton, NE 68729
(402) 358-3232
Admin Delberta Peterson. *Dir of Nursing* Vicky Potter RN.
Licensure Intermediate care. *Beds* ICF 50. *Certified* Medicaid.
Owner Proprietary corp.

Crete

Crete Manor
830 E 1st, Crete, NE 68333
(402) 826-4325
Admin John C Snyder. *Dir of Nursing* Jan Clark RN.
Licensure Intermediate care; Alzheimer's care. *Beds* ICF 96; Locked Alzheimer's unit 14. *Certified* Medicaid.
Owner Proprietary corp.
Admissions Requirements Medical examination.
Staff RNs 1 (ft), 1 (pt); LPNs 6 (ft); Nurses' aides 18 (ft), 20 (pt); Physical therapists 1 (pt); Occupational therapists 1 (pt); Speech therapists 1 (pt); Activities coordinators 1 (ft), 1 (pt); Dietitians 1 (pt).
Facilities Dining room; Chapel; Barber/Beauty shop; Library; Lounges.
Activities Arts & crafts; Cards; Games; Prayer groups; Movies; Dances/Social/Cultural gatherings.

Curtis

Sunset Haven Nursing Home
901 Howard St, Curtis, NE 69025
(308) 367-8388
Admin Mynette M Roblee. *Dir of Nursing* Marcia Seip RN.
Licensure Intermediate care. *Beds* ICF 49. *Certified* Medicaid.
Owner Nonprofit corp.
Admissions Requirements Medical examination.
Staff RNs 1 (pt); LPNs 1 (ft), 4 (pt); Nurses' aides 6 (ft), 6 (pt); Activities coordinators 1 (ft); Dietitians 1 (pt).
Facilities Dining room; Activities room; Chapel; Laundry room; Barber/Beauty shop.
Activities Arts & crafts; Cards; Games; Reading groups.

David City

David Place
PO Box 321, 260 S 10th, David City, NE 68632
(402) 367-3144
Admin Mary Lee High. *Dir of Nursing* Mary Steinberger RN. *Medical Dir* Gerald Luckey MD.
Licensure Skilled care; Intermediate care; Retirement; Alzheimer's care. *Beds* 96. *Certified* Medicaid; Medicare; VA.
Owner Proprietary corp.

Admissions Requirements Medical examination; Physician's request.
Staff RNs 20 (ft); LPNs 3 (ft); Nurses' aides 35 (ft); Activities coordinators 1 (ft).
Facilities Dining room; Physical therapy room; Activities room; Chapel; Crafts room; Laundry room; Barber/Beauty shop.
Activities Arts & crafts; Cards; Games; Reading groups; Prayer groups; Shopping trips; Dances/Social/Cultural gatherings.

St Joseph's Villa Inc
927 7th St, David City, NE 68632
(402) 367-3045
Admin Sr Esther Marie Miller. *Dir of Nursing* Sr Flora Jentgen RN BS. *Medical Dir* Dr Gerald Luckey.
Licensure Intermediate care. *Beds* ICF 65. *Private Pay Patients* 6%. *Certified* Medicaid.
Owner Nonprofit corp.
Admissions Requirements Minimum age 60; Medical examination.
Staff RNs 1 (ft), 1 (pt); LPNs 2 (ft), 2 (pt); Nurses' aides 17 (ft), 9 (pt); Physical therapists; Activities coordinators 1 (ft); Dietitians 1 (ft).
Languages Czech.
Affiliation Roman Catholic.
Facilities Dining room; Activities room; Chapel; Crafts room; Laundry room; Barber/Beauty shop; Library.
Activities Arts & crafts; Cards; Games; Prayer groups; Movies; Shopping trips; Dances/Social/Cultural gatherings; Intergenerational programs; Pet therapy.

Deshler

Parkview Haven Nursing Home
1203 4th St, Deshler, NE 68340
(402) 365-7237
Admin Harrietta Reynolds. *Dir of Nursing* Marjorie Bachenberg RN.
Licensure Intermediate care. *Beds* ICF 58. *Certified* Medicaid.
Owner Publicly owned.

Dodge

Parkview Home Inc
RR 2 Box 414, Dodge, NE 68633
(402) 693-2212
Admin Dwaine E Lauer. *Dir of Nursing* Donna Uher RN.
Licensure Intermediate care. *Beds* ICF 80. *Certified* Medicaid.
Owner Proprietary corp.
Admissions Requirements Medical examination; Physician's request.
Staff RNs 4 (ft), 3 (pt); LPNs 1 (ft), 2 (pt); Nurses' aides 11 (ft), 16 (pt); Reality therapists 4 (pt); Activities coordinators 1 (ft).
Facilities Dining room; Physical therapy room; Activities room; Chapel; Crafts room; Laundry room; Barber/Beauty shop; Library.
Activities Arts & crafts; Cards; Games; Reading groups; Prayer groups; Movies; Dances/Social/Cultural gatherings.

Edgar

Bethesda Care Center
Rte 1 Box 1183, 106 5th St, Edgar, NE 68935
(402) 224-5015
Admin Florence E Pridgen. *Dir of Nursing* Mary Ann Lang RN. *Medical Dir* Michael Sullivan MD.
Licensure Intermediate care. *Beds* ICF 54. *Private Pay Patients* 54%. *Certified* Medicaid.
Owner Proprietary corp (Meritcare Inc).
Admissions Requirements Medical examination; Physician's request.

Staff RNs 1 (ft), 2 (pt); LPNs 1 (ft), 3 (pt); Nurses' aides 10 (ft), 5 (pt); Activities coordinators 1 (ft); Dietitians 1 (pt).
Facilities Dining room; Chapel; Laundry room; Barber/Beauty shop.
Activities Arts & crafts; Games; Reading groups; Prayer groups; Movies; Shopping trips; Pet therapy.

Elkhorn

Elkhorn Manor
315 Hopper St, Elkhorn, NE 68022
(402) 289-2572
Admin Kenneth E Opp. *Dir of Nursing* Willene Strickland RN. *Medical Dir* Donald Darst MD.
Licensure Intermediate care. *Beds* ICF 132. *Certified* Medicaid.
Owner Proprietary corp.
Admissions Requirements Medical examination; Physician's request.
Staff RNs 4 (ft); LPNs 12 (ft); Nurses' aides 32 (ft); Recreational therapists 2 (ft); Occupational therapists 1 (pt); Activities coordinators 1 (ft); Dietitians 1 (ft).
Facilities Dining room; Activities room; Crafts room; Laundry room; Barber/Beauty shop.
Activities Arts & crafts; Cards; Games; Reading groups; Prayer groups; Movies; Shopping trips; Dances/Social/Cultural gatherings.

Elwood

Elwood Care Center
613 Smith St, Box 35, Elwood, NE 68937
(308) 785-3302
Admin D Maxine Misterek. *Dir of Nursing* Shelly Monter RN.
Licensure Intermediate care; Residential care; Health clinic. *Beds* ICF 51. *Certified* Medicaid.
Owner Publicly owned.
Admissions Requirements Minimum age 18; Medical examination.
Staff RNs 1 (ft), 1 (pt); LPNs 5 (ft), 1 (pt); Physical therapists 1 (pt); Activities coordinators 1 (pt); Dietitians 1 (pt).
Facilities Dining room; Activities room; Chapel; Crafts room; Laundry room; Barber/Beauty shop; Library.
Activities Arts & crafts; Cards; Games; Reading groups; Prayer groups; Movies.

Emerson

Heritage of Emerson
6th & NE, Emerson, NE 68733
(402) 695-2683
Admin Jeannia J Bottger. *Dir of Nursing* Vicki Summerfield RN.
Licensure Intermediate care. *Beds* ICF 63. *Certified* Medicaid.
Owner Proprietary corp.
Admissions Requirements Medical examination; Physician's request.
Staff Physicians 1 (ft); RNs; LPNs; Nurses' aides; Physical therapists; Activities coordinators; Dietitians.
Facilities Dining room; Physical therapy room; Activities room; Chapel; Crafts room; Laundry room; Barber/Beauty shop; Library.
Activities Arts & crafts; Cards; Games; Reading groups; Prayer groups; Movies; Shopping trips; Dances/Social/Cultural gatherings.

Exeter

Bethesda Care Center
425 S Empire Ave, Exeter, NE 68351
(402) 266-4501
Admin Christi Erickson. *Dir of Nursing* Marlene Gallup RN.

Licensure Intermediate care. *Beds* ICF 60. *Certified* Medicaid.
Owner Nonprofit corp (MTC West Inc).
Admissions Requirements Medical examination.
Staff RNs 1 (ft); LPNs 3 (ft), 1 (pt); Nurses' aides 14 (ft), 1 (pt); Physical therapists 1 (pt); Occupational therapists 1 (pt); Speech therapists 1 (pt); Activities coordinators 1 (ft), 1 (pt); Dietitians 1 (pt).
Facilities Dining room; Activities room; Chapel; Crafts room; Laundry room; Barber/Beauty shop; Living room setting with 45 inch TV & VCR; Screened porch & patio; Van used for resident transportation.
Activities Arts & crafts; Cards; Games; Reading groups; Prayer groups; Movies; Shopping trips; Dances/Social/Cultural gatherings; Bowling; Fishing; Ceramics.

Fairbury

Heritage Care Center
909 17th St, Fairbury, NE 68352
(402) 729-2289
Admin Michael G Steele. *Dir of Nursing* Janet F Steele RN.
Licensure Intermediate care. *Beds* ICF 96. *Certified* Medicaid.
Owner Proprietary corp.
Admissions Requirements Minimum age 18; Medical examination; Physician's request.
Staff RNs 2 (ft), 1 (pt); LPNs 2 (ft), 5 (pt); Nurses' aides 18 (ft), 17 (pt); Physical therapists; Activities coordinators 2 (ft); Dietitians.
Facilities Dining room; Physical therapy room; Activities room; Chapel; Crafts room; Laundry room; Barber/Beauty shop.
Activities Arts & crafts; Cards; Games; Reading groups; Prayer groups; Movies; Shopping trips; Dances/Social/Cultural gatherings; Pet therapy; Mother-daughter tea; Father-son barbecue.

Fairmont

Fairview Manor
PO Box 427, 255 F St, Fairmont, NE 68354
(402) 268-2271
Admin Richard Bauer. *Dir of Nursing* Charlotte M Hall RN.
Licensure Intermediate care. *Beds* ICF 54. *Private Pay Patients* 56%. *Certified* Medicaid.
Owner Publicly owned.
Admissions Requirements Medical examination; Physician's request.
Staff RNs 2 (ft), 1 (pt); LPNs 2 (ft), 4 (pt); Nurses' aides 10 (ft), 7 (pt); Activities coordinators 1 (ft); Dietitians 1 (ft).
Facilities Dining room; Physical therapy room; Activities room; Chapel; Laundry room; Barber/Beauty shop.
Activities Cards; Games; Reading groups; Prayer groups; Movies; Shopping trips; Dances/Social/Cultural gatherings; Pet therapy.

Falls City

Falls City Healthcare Center
28th & Towle St, Falls City, NE 68355
(402) 245-5252
Admin Kris Kubik. *Dir of Nursing* Emily Kelly RN. *Medical Dir* R L Burghart MD.
Licensure Intermediate care; Residential care. *Beds* ICF 85. *Certified* Medicaid.
Owner Proprietary corp.
Staff RNs; LPNs; Nurses' aides; Physical therapists; Recreational therapists; Occupational therapists; Speech therapists; Activities coordinators; Dietitians; Ophthalmologists; Podiatrists; Audiologists; Dentists.

Facilities Dining room; Physical therapy room; Activities room; Chapel; Crafts room; Laundry room; Barber/Beauty shop.
Activities Arts & crafts; Cards; Games; Reading groups; Prayer groups; Movies; Shopping trips; Dances/Social/Cultural gatherings.

Ketter Manor Inc
1010 E 21st St, Falls City, NE 68355
(402) 245-3700
Admin Vern B Ketter. *Dir of Nursing* Janet Bletscher RN.
Licensure Intermediate care. *Beds* ICF 61. *Certified* Medicaid.
Owner Proprietary corp.
Admissions Requirements Minimum age 30; Medical examination; Physician's request.
Staff RNs 1 (ft); LPNs 4 (ft); Activities coordinators 1 (ft); Dietitians 1 (ft).
Facilities Dining room; Laundry room; Barber/Beauty shop.
Activities Cards; Games; Prayer groups; Movies; Shopping trips.

Midland Villa
Rte 2, E 19th & Burton St, Falls City, NE 68355
(402) 245-4466
Admin Jo Ann Kalina. *Dir of Nursing* Joyce Backman. *Medical Dir* Dr David E Borg.
Licensure Skilled care; Alzheimer's care. *Beds* SNF 80. *Private Pay Patients* 60%. *Certified* Medicaid; Medicare.
Owner Privately owned.
Admissions Requirements Minimum age 18; Medical examination.
Staff Physicians; RNs 4 (ft), 4 (pt); LPNs 2 (ft), 4 (pt); Nurses' aides 20 (ft), 15 (pt); Physical therapists 1 (pt); Recreational therapists 1 (ft); Occupational therapists 1 (pt); Speech therapists 1 (pt); Activities coordinators; Dietitians; Ophthalmologists 1 (pt); Podiatrists.
Facilities Dining room; Activities room; Crafts room; Laundry room; Barber/Beauty shop.
Activities Arts & crafts; Cards; Games; Reading groups; Prayer groups; Movies; Shopping trips; Dances/Social/Cultural gatherings.

Firth

Lakeview Rest Home
Firth, NE 68358
(402) 791-5588
Admin Allen F Siebert. *Dir of Nursing* Joyce Helmink RN.
Licensure Intermediate care. *Beds* ICF 57. *Certified* Medicaid.
Owner Nonprofit corp.
Admissions Requirements Medical examination; Physician's request.
Staff Physicians 1 (pt); RNs 3 (pt); LPNs 1 (ft), 4 (pt); Nurses' aides 5 (ft), 13 (pt); Activities coordinators 1 (ft), 1 (pt); Dietitians 1 (pt).
Affiliation Reformed Church.
Facilities Dining room; Activities room; Chapel; Laundry room; Barber/Beauty shop.
Activities Cards; Games; Prayer groups; Movies; Shopping trips; Dances/Social/Cultural gatherings.

Franklin

Franklin Nursing Center
PO Box 167, W Hwy 136, Franklin, NE 68939
(308) 425-6262
Admin Dorothy Sweet. *Dir of Nursing* Dian Rogers RN. *Medical Dir* R A Houston MD.
Licensure Intermediate care. *Beds* ICF 72. *Certified* Medicaid.
Owner Proprietary corp (Beverly Enterprises).

Admissions Requirements Medical examination; Physician's request.
Staff RNs 1 (ft); LPNs 4 (ft); Nurses' aides 14 (ft), 8 (pt); Activities coordinators 1 (ft); Social service 1 (ft).
Facilities Dining room; Activities room; Chapel; Crafts room; Laundry room; Barber/Beauty shop.
Activities Arts & crafts; Cards; Games; Reading groups; Prayer groups; Movies; Shopping trips; Dances/Social/Cultural gatherings.

Fremont

Arbor Manor
2550 N Nye Ave, Fremont, NE 68025
(402) 727-1710
Admin Carolyn M Rabel. *Dir of Nursing* Theresa Ernesti RN.
Licensure Intermediate care. *Beds* ICF 151. *Certified* Medicaid.
Owner Proprietary corp.

Fremont Care Center Inc
2700 LaVerna St, Fremont, NE 68025
(402) 727-4900
Admin Jeffrey D Harmon. *Dir of Nursing* Deborah K Evert RN.
Licensure Intermediate care. *Beds* ICF 67. *Certified* Medicaid.
Owner Proprietary corp.

Friend

Friend Manor
905 2nd St, Friend, NE 68359
(402) 947-2541
Admin Leonard Torson.
Medical Dir Naomi Larka.
Licensure Intermediate care. *Beds* ICF 58. *Certified* Medicaid.
Owner Publicly owned.
Staff Physicians 1 (ft); RNs 3 (ft); LPNs 3 (ft), 1 (pt); Nurses' aides 10 (ft), 8 (pt); Physical therapists 1 (pt); Dietitians 1 (ft).

Fullerton

Fullerton Manor
202 N Esther, Fullerton, NE 68638
(308) 536-2225
Admin Mason Cash Benn. *Dir of Nursing* Norma J Willke RN.
Licensure Intermediate care; Alzheimer's care. *Beds* ICF 99. *Certified* Medicaid.
Owner Proprietary corp (Beverly Enterprises).
Admissions Requirements Minimum age 21; Medical examination; Physician's request.
Staff RNs 1 (ft); LPNs 4 (ft); Nurses' aides 18 (ft), 17 (pt); Activities coordinators 1 (ft), 1 (pt); Social services 1 (ft), 1 (pt).
Facilities Dining room; Activities room; Chapel; Laundry room; Barber/Beauty shop; Covered patio.
Activities Arts & crafts; Cards; Games; Prayer groups; Movies; Shopping trips; Dances/Social/Cultural gatherings; Swimming in city pool.

Geneva

Fillmore County Long-Term Care
1325 H St, Geneva, NE 68361
(402) 759-3167
Admin Larry G Warrelman.
Licensure Intermediate care. *Beds* 20. *Certified* Medicaid.
Owner Publicly owned.

Heritage of Geneva
501 N 13th St, Geneva, NE 68361
(402) 759-3194
Admin David Schlegel. *Dir of Nursing* Joyce Belau RN.

Licensure Intermediate care. *Beds* ICF 75. *Private Pay Patients* 60%. *Certified* Medicaid.
Owner Proprietary corp (Vetter Health Services).
Admissions Requirements Medical examination; Physician's request.
Staff RNs 1 (ft); LPNs 5 (ft); Nurses' aides 15 (ft), 10 (pt); Physical therapists; Activities coordinators 1 (ft), 1 (pt); Dietitians 1 (pt).
Facilities Dining room; Activities room; Laundry room; Barber/Beauty shop.
Activities Cards; Games; Reading groups; Prayer groups; Movies; Shopping trips; Dances/Social/Cultural gatherings; Pet therapy.

Genoa

Country View Care Village
PO Box 130, 606 Ewing Ave, Genoa, NE 68640
(402) 993-2279
Admin Nina M Wiese. *Dir of Nursing* Gail I Raitt. *Medical Dir* Abraham Rivera.
Licensure Intermediate care; Residential care. *Beds* ICF 40; Residential care 20. *Private Pay Patients* 57%. *Certified* Medicaid.
Owner Publicly owned.
Admissions Requirements Medical examination; Physician's request.
Staff Physicians 3 (pt); RNs 2 (ft), 1 (pt); LPNs 6 (pt); Nurses' aides 10 (ft), 12 (pt); Physical therapists 1 (pt); Reality therapists 1 (pt); Recreational therapists 1 (pt); Occupational therapists 1 (pt); Speech therapists 1 (pt); Activities coordinators 1 (pt); Dietitians 1 (pt); Podiatrists 1 (pt); Audiologists 1 (pt).
Languages Polish, Swedish.
Facilities Dining room; Physical therapy room; Activities room; Chapel; Laundry room; Barber/Beauty shop; Living room on each wing; Kitchenette (residential); Conference rooms.
Activities Arts & crafts; Cards; Games; Reading groups; Prayer groups; Movies; Shopping trips; Dances/Social/Cultural gatherings; Intergenerational programs; Pet therapy; Volunteer program.

Gering

Heritage Health Care Center
2025 21st St, Box 518, Gering, NE 69341
(308) 436-5007
Admin Charles K Gulley. *Dir of Nursing* Susan O'Connor RN. *Medical Dir* Dr Alan Johnson.
Licensure Skilled care; Intermediate care. *Beds* 101. *Certified* Medicaid; Medicare.
Owner Proprietary corp.
Admissions Requirements Medical examination; Physician's request.
Staff RNs 5 (ft), 2 (pt); LPNs 6 (ft), 2 (pt); Activities coordinators 1 (ft).
Languages Spanish translation available.
Facilities Dining room; Chapel; Laundry room; Barber/Beauty shop; Lounges; TV room.
Activities Arts & crafts; Cards; Games; Reading groups; Prayer groups; Movies; Shopping trips; Dances/Social/Cultural gatherings.

Northfield Villa Inc
2550 21st St, Gering, NE 69341
(308) 436-3101
Admin Floyd J Sauer. *Dir of Nursing* Jerene Lane RN.
Licensure Skilled care; Retirement; Alzheimer's care. *Beds* SNF 41.
Owner Nonprofit corp.
Staff RNs; LPNs; Nurses' aides; Physical therapists; Recreational therapists; Occupational therapists; Speech therapists; Activities coordinators; Dietitians; Dentists.

Facilities Dining room; Activities room; Chapel; Crafts room; Laundry room; Barber/Beauty shop; Library.
Activities Arts & crafts; Cards; Games; Prayer groups.

Gibbon

Good Samaritan Center
1011 7th, Gibbon, NE 68840
(308) 468-5353
Admin Margaret Krause. *Dir of Nursing* Janet Campbell RN.
Licensure Intermediate care; Health clinic. *Beds* ICF 47. *Certified* Medicaid.
Owner Nonprofit corp (Evangelical Lutheran/Good Samaritan Society).
Admissions Requirements Physician's request.
Staff RNs 1 (ft), 1 (pt); LPNs 4 (pt); Nurses' aides 21 (pt); Activities coordinators 1 (ft); Dietitians 1 (pt).
Languages Spanish.
Facilities Dining room; Activities room; Chapel; Crafts room; Laundry room; Barber/Beauty shop; Library.
Activities Arts & crafts; Cards; Games; Movies; Dances/Social/Cultural gatherings.

Gordon

Gordon Good Samaritan Center
500 E 10th St, Gordon, NE 69343
(308) 282-0806
Admin William Curry. *Dir of Nursing* Krissa Rucker RN.
Licensure Intermediate care; Basic care. *Beds* ICF 40; Basic care 10. *Certified* Medicaid.
Owner Nonprofit corp (Evangelical Lutheran/Good Samaritan Society).
Affiliation Lutheran.
Facilities Dining room; Physical therapy room; Activities room; Chapel; Laundry room; Barber/Beauty shop.
Activities Arts & crafts; Cards; Games; Reading groups; Movies; Shopping trips; Intergenerational programs.

Gothenburg

Slack Nursing Home
121 6th St, Gothenburg, NE 69138
(308) 537-7138
Admin Richard D Slack. *Dir of Nursing* Claudia L Gaibler.
Licensure Intermediate care. *Beds* ICF 71. *Certified* Medicaid.
Owner Proprietary corp.
Admissions Requirements Medical examination; Physician's request.
Staff Physicians 4 (pt); RNs 2 (ft); LPNs 3 (ft), 2 (pt); Nurses' aides 10 (ft), 12 (pt); Physical therapists 1 (pt); Recreational therapists 1 (pt); Occupational therapists 1 (pt); Speech therapists 1 (pt); Activities coordinators 1 (ft); Dietitians 1 (pt); Ophthalmologists 1 (pt); Podiatrists 1 (pt); Dentists 1 (pt).
Facilities Dining room; Activities room; Chapel; Crafts room; Laundry room; Barber/Beauty shop.
Activities Arts & crafts; Cards; Games; Reading groups; Prayer groups; Movies; Shopping trips; Dances/Social/Cultural gatherings.

Grand Island

Lakeview Nursing Center
1405 W Hwy 34, Grand Island, NE 68801
(308) 382-6397
Admin James R Falk. *Dir of Nursing* Kathy Morton RN. *Medical Dir* Donna Jorgensen.
Licensure Intermediate care. *Beds* ICF 97. *Certified* Medicaid.
Owner Proprietary corp (Beverly Enterprises).

Staff RNs 2 (ft), 1 (pt); LPNs 8 (ft), 2 (pt); Nurses' aides 25 (ft), 7 (pt); Physical therapists 1 (pt); Recreational therapists 1 (pt); Occupational therapists 1 (pt); Speech therapists 1 (pt); Activities coordinators 1 (ft); Dietitians 1 (ft).
Facilities Dining room; Physical therapy room; Activities room; Chapel; Crafts room; Laundry room; Barber/Beauty shop; Library; Private family dining area; Lakefront.
Activities Arts & crafts; Cards; Games; Reading groups; Prayer groups; Movies; Shopping trips; Dances/Social/Cultural gatherings.

Nebraska Veterans Home
Burkett Station, Grand Island, NE 68803
(308) 382-9420
Admin Richard L Terrell. *Dir of Nursing* Barbara Abernethy RN. *Medical Dir* Richard DeMay MD.
Licensure Skilled care; Intermediate care; Domiciliary care. *Beds* SNF 98; ICF 316; Domiciliary care 35.
Owner Publicly owned.
Staff Physicians 3 (ft); RNs 24 (ft); LPNs 23 (ft); Nurses' aides 170 (ft); Physical therapists (contracted); Recreational therapists 1 (pt); Occupational therapists 1 (pt); Speech therapists 1 (pt); Activities coordinators 1 (ft); Dietitians 1 (ft).
Facilities Dining room; Physical therapy room; Activities room; Chapel; Crafts room; Laundry room; Barber/Beauty shop; Library.
Activities Arts & crafts; Cards; Games; Reading groups; Prayer groups; Movies; Shopping trips; Dances/Social/Cultural gatherings; Pet therapy.

Park Place Nursing Center
610 N Darr, Grand Island, NE 68801
(308) 382-2635
Admin Geraldine Koepke. *Dir of Nursing* Kathy Anderson. *Medical Dir* D Wirth MD.
Licensure Skilled care. *Beds* SNF 97. *Private Pay Patients* 35%. *Certified* Medicaid.
Owner Proprietary corp (Beverly Enterprises).
Admissions Requirements Medical examination.
Staff RNs; LPNs; Nurses' aides; Physical therapists; Recreational therapists; Occupational therapists; Speech therapists; Activities coordinators; Dietitians; Podiatrists.
Facilities Dining room; Activities room; Chapel; Laundry room; Barber/Beauty shop; Library.
Activities Arts & crafts; Cards; Games; Reading groups; Prayer groups; Movies; Shopping trips; Dances/Social/Cultural gatherings; Intergenerational programs; Pet therapy.

Tiffany Square Care Center
3119 Faidley Ave, Grand Island, NE 68803
(308) 384-2333
Admin Jane Clifton. *Dir of Nursing* Jody Meyer RN.
Licensure Skilled care. *Beds* SNF 60.
Owner Proprietary corp.

Wedgewood
800 Stoeger Dr, Grand Island, NE 68803
(308) 382-5440
Admin Jill D Molzahn. *Dir of Nursing* Teri L McConnaho RN. *Medical Dir* Dean McGrath.
Licensure Skilled care; Intermediate care; Alzheimer's care; Residential care; Independent living. *Beds* Swing beds SNF/ICF 81; Residential care 46; Independent living 40.
Owner Proprietary corp.
Admissions Requirements Medical examination.
Staff RNs 3 (ft); LPNs 4 (ft), 2 (pt); Nurses' aides 34 (ft), 12 (pt); Physical therapists; Activities coordinators 1 (ft); Dietitians.

Languages German.
Facilities Dining room; Physical therapy room; Activities room; Crafts room; Laundry room; Barber/Beauty shop; Library; Alzheimer's wing.
Activities Arts & crafts; Cards; Games; Reading groups; Prayer groups; Movies; Shopping trips; Dances/Social/Cultural gatherings; Intergenerational programs; Pet therapy; Exercise.

Greeley

Greeley Care Home
PO Box 190, Greeley, NE 68842
(308) 428-5145
Admin Anne M Dugan. *Dir of Nursing* Lollie Dugan.
Licensure Intermediate care. *Beds* ICF 40. *Private Pay Patients* 85%. *Certified* Medicaid.
Owner Publicly owned.
Admissions Requirements Physician's request.
Staff RNs; LPNs; Nurses' aides; Physical therapists; Recreational therapists; Occupational therapists; Speech therapists; Activities coordinators; Dietitians.
Facilities Dining room; Physical therapy room; Activities room; Chapel; Crafts room; Laundry room; Barber/Beauty shop; Library.
Activities Arts & crafts; Cards; Games; Reading groups; Prayer groups; Movies; Dances/Social/Cultural gatherings; Intergenerational programs.

Gretna

Bethesda Care Center of Gretna
700 Hwy 6, Gretna, NE 68028
(402) 332-3446
Admin Francis E Hartwell. *Dir of Nursing* Mary Stewart RN.
Licensure Intermediate care; Alzheimer's care. *Beds* ICF 63. *Certified* Medicaid.
Owner Nonprofit corp (MTC West Inc).
Admissions Requirements Medical examination; Physician's request.
Staff RNs 3 (ft); LPNs 3 (ft); Nurses' aides 30 (ft); Physical therapists 1 (pt); Reality therapists 1 (pt); Recreational therapists 1 (pt); Occupational therapists 1 (pt); Speech therapists 1 (ft), 1 (pt); Activities coordinators 1 (ft); Dietitians.
Facilities Dining room; Activities room; Chapel; Crafts room; Laundry room; Barber/Beauty shop.
Activities Arts & crafts; Cards; Games; Reading groups; Prayer groups; Movies; Shopping trips; Dances/Social/Cultural gatherings.

Hartington

Hartington Nursing Center
401 W Darline St, Hartington, NE 68739
(402) 254-3905
Admin Elvera Lewis. *Dir of Nursing* Alice Uhling RN. *Medical Dir* Dr C J Vlach.
Licensure Skilled care; Intermediate care; Alzheimer's care. *Beds* 74. *Certified* Medicaid; Medicare.
Owner Proprietary corp (Beverly Enterprises).
Admissions Requirements Medical examination.
Staff Physicians 1 (pt); RNs 3 (ft), 2 (pt); LPNs 2 (ft), 1 (pt); Nurses' aides 13 (ft), 12 (pt); Activities coordinators 1 (ft), 1 (pt); Dietitians 1 (ft), 1 (pt).
Facilities Dining room; Physical therapy room; Activities room; Chapel; Crafts room; Laundry room; Barber/Beauty shop; Van with wheelchair lift.

Activities Arts & crafts; Cards; Games; Reading groups; Prayer groups; Movies; Shopping trips; Dances/Social/Cultural gatherings; Sightseeing trips; Fishing trips; Outdoor picnics; Dinner trips.

Harvard

Harvard Rest Haven
400 E 7th St, Harvard, NE 68944
(402) 772-7591
Admin Ronald E Crosby. *Dir of Nursing* Marge Young RN.
Licensure Intermediate care. *Beds* ICF 60. *Certified* Medicaid.
Owner Publicly owned.

Hastings

Good Samaritan Village—Perkins Pavilion
300 S 1st Ave, Hastings, NE 68901
(402) 463-3181
Admin Diane Berens. *Dir of Nursing* Cheryl Bliefernich RN. *Medical Dir* Dr Gerald Kuehn.
Licensure Skilled care; Intermediate care; Residential care; Health clinic. *Beds* SNF 59; ICF 102. *Certified* Medicaid; Medicare.
Owner Nonprofit corp (Evangelical Lutheran/ Good Samaritan Society).
Staff Physicians 1 (pt); RNs 6 (ft), 3 (pt); LPNs 5 (ft), 8 (pt); Nurses' aides 24 (ft), 35 (pt); Physical therapists 1 (pt); Recreational therapists 1 (ft); Occupational therapists 1 (pt); Speech therapists 1 (pt); Dietitians 1 (pt); Podiatrists 1 (pt); Dentists 1 (pt).
Affiliation Lutheran.
Facilities Dining room; Physical therapy room; Activities room; Chapel; Crafts room; Laundry room; Barber/Beauty shop; Library.
Activities Arts & crafts; Cards; Games; Reading groups; Prayer groups; Movies; Shopping trips; Dances/Social/Cultural gatherings.

Good Samaritan Village—Villa Grace
926 E "E" St, Box 2149, Hastings, NE 68902-2149
(402) 463-3181
Admin Donna Valentine. *Dir of Nursing* Judith Clark.
Licensure Intermediate care; Retirement; Alzheimer's care. *Beds* ICF 150. *Private Pay Patients* 35%. *Certified* Medicaid.
Owner Nonprofit corp (Evangelical Lutheran/ Good Samaritan Society).
Admissions Requirements Medical examination; Physician's request.
Staff RNs 2 (ft), 6 (pt); LPNs 3 (ft), 3 (pt); Nurses' aides 40 (ft), 33 (pt); Physical therapists (consultant); Occupational therapists (consultant); Speech therapists (consultant); Activities coordinators 2 (ft), 1 (pt); Dietitians 1 (pt).
Affiliation Lutheran.
Facilities Dining room; Physical therapy room; Activities room; Chapel; Crafts room; Barber/Beauty shop; Library; Senior center.
Activities Arts & crafts; Cards; Games; Reading groups; Prayer groups; Movies; Shopping trips; Dances/Social/Cultural gatherings; Intergenerational programs; Pet therapy.

Hastings Regional Center
PO Box 579, Hastings, NE 68901
(402) 463-2471
Admin Charles W Landgraf Jr.
Licensure Intermediate care; Intermediate care for mentally retarded. *Beds* 20.
Owner Publicly owned.

Hay Springs

Pioneer Manor Nursing Home
E Line Ave, Box 310, Hay Springs, NE 69347
(308) 638-4483

Admin Patsy A Bridge NHA. *Dir of Nursing* Marie Dreyer RN.
Licensure Intermediate care. *Beds* ICF 51. *Private Pay Patients* 75%. *Certified* Medicaid.
Owner Publicly owned.
Admissions Requirements Medical examination.
Staff Physicians 5 (pt); RNs 1 (ft), 1 (pt); LPNs 5 (ft), 2 (pt); Nurses' aides 14 (ft), 3 (pt); Physical therapists 1 (pt); Occupational therapists 1 (pt); Speech therapists 1 (pt); Activities coordinators 2 (ft); Dietitians 1 (pt); Ophthalmologists 1 (pt); Podiatrists 1 (pt); Audiologists 1 (pt).
Facilities Dining room; Activities room; Laundry room; Barber/Beauty shop.
Activities Arts & crafts; Cards; Games; Reading groups; Prayer groups; Movies; Shopping trips; Dances/Social/Cultural gatherings.

Hebron

Blue Valley Lutheran Home
4th & Park Ave, Hebron, NE 68370
(402) 768-6045
Admin LaVern L Poppe. *Dir of Nursing* Ruth Kripal RN.
Licensure Intermediate care. *Beds* ICF 178.
Owner Nonprofit corp.
Staff Physicians; RNs; LPNs; Nurses' aides; Physical therapists; Recreational therapists; Occupational therapists; Speech therapists; Activities coordinators; Dietitians.
Affiliation Lutheran.
Facilities Dining room; Activities room; Chapel; Crafts room; Laundry room; Barber/ Beauty shop.
Activities Arts & crafts; Cards; Games; Reading groups; Prayer groups; Movies; Shopping trips.

Holdrege

Christian Homes Inc
RFD 2 Box 24, Holdrege, NE 68949
(308) 995-4493
Admin Donald W Bakke. *Dir of Nursing* Linda Sughroue RN.
Licensure Intermediate care; Residential care; Health clinic. *Beds* ICF 82; Residential care 53. *Certified* Medicaid.
Owner Nonprofit corp (Christian Homes Inc).
Admissions Requirements Medical examination; Physician's request.
Staff RNs 3 (ft), 1 (pt); LPNs 6 (ft), 1 (pt); Nurses' aides 26 (ft), 15 (pt); Physical therapists 1 (ft); Activities coordinators 1 (ft), 1 (pt).
Affiliation Evangelical Free Church.
Facilities Dining room; Activities room; Crafts room; Laundry room; Barber/Beauty shop; Library.
Activities Arts & crafts; Games; Reading groups; Prayer groups; Movies; Shopping trips; Dances/Social/Cultural gatherings; Singing time; Exercise; Hayrides; Senior Olympics; Rhythm band.

M & S Anderson Health Care Unit
1319 10th Ave, Holdrege, NE 68949
(308) 995-8631
Admin James S McClure. *Dir of Nursing* Dorothy Patterson RN. *Medical Dir* W Reiner MD.
Licensure Skilled care; Intermediate care; Retirement. *Beds* 59. *Certified* Medicaid; Medicare.
Owner Nonprofit corp.
Admissions Requirements Medical examination.
Staff Physicians 1 (ft); RNs 4 (ft), 8 (pt); LPNs 3 (ft), 6 (pt); Nurses' aides 16 (ft), 9 (pt); Physical therapists 1 (pt); Speech therapists 1 (pt); Activities coordinators 1 (ft); Dietitians 1 (pt).

Affiliation Methodist.
Facilities Dining room; Physical therapy room; Activities room; Chapel; Crafts room; Laundry room; Barber/Beauty shop; Library; Gift shop.
Activities Arts & crafts; Cards; Games; Reading groups; Prayer groups; Movies; Shopping trips; Dances/Social/Cultural gatherings.

Hooper

Hooper Care Center
400 E Birchwood Dr, Hooper, NE 68031
(402) 654-3362
Admin Sally R Stecher. *Dir of Nursing* Terri Nilles RN.
Licensure Intermediate care. *Beds* ICF 64. *Certified* Medicaid.
Owner Proprietary corp.
Admissions Requirements Medical examination; Physician's request.
Staff RNs 1 (ft), 2 (pt); LPNs 3 (ft), 3 (pt); Nurses' aides 10 (ft), 13 (pt); Physical therapists 1 (ft); Recreational therapists 1 (ft); Activities coordinators 1 (ft), 1 (pt); Dietitians 1 (ft); Podiatrists 1 (ft).
Facilities Dining room; Physical therapy room; Activities room; Chapel; Laundry room; Barber/Beauty shop; Library.
Activities Arts & crafts; Cards; Games; Reading groups; Prayer groups; Movies; Shopping trips; Dances/Social/Cultural gatherings.

Humboldt

Colonial Acres Nursing Home
RR 2, Humboldt, NE 68376
(402) 862-3123
Admin John L Fischer. *Dir of Nursing* Carol Gimeson.
Licensure Intermediate care. *Beds* ICF 68. *Private Pay Patients* 60%. *Certified* Medicaid.
Owner Publicly owned.
Admissions Requirements Physician's request.
Staff RNs 1 (ft), 2 (pt); LPNs 2 (ft), 1 (pt); Nurses' aides 16 (ft), 6 (pt); Physical therapists 1 (pt); Recreational therapists 1 (pt); Speech therapists 1 (pt); Activities coordinators 1 (ft); Dietitians 1 (pt).
Activities Arts & crafts; Cards; Games; Reading groups; Prayer groups; Movies; Shopping trips; Dances/Social/Cultural gatherings; Pet therapy.

Imperial

Imperial Manor Nursing Home
933 Grant, Imperial, NE 69033
(308) 882-5333
Admin Lois Okerlund. *Dir of Nursing* Kate Langenfeld RN.
Licensure Intermediate care. *Beds* ICF 70. *Certified* Medicaid.
Owner Publicly owned.
Admissions Requirements Medical examination; Physician's request.
Staff RNs 1 (ft); LPNs 4 (ft); Nurses' aides 17 (ft), 4 (pt); Activities coordinators 2 (pt).
Facilities Dining room; Activities room; Chapel; Laundry room; Barber/Beauty shop.
Activities Cards; Games; Reading groups; Prayer groups; Movies; Shopping trips; Dances/Social/Cultural gatherings.

Kearney

Mother Hull Home Inc
125 E 23rd St, Kearney, NE 68847
(308) 234-2447
Admin Richard D Reuhle. *Dir of Nursing* Janet Asche RN. *Medical Dir* Sue Grubbs.
Licensure Intermediate care. *Beds* ICF 52. *Certified* Medicaid.

Owner Nonprofit corp.
Admissions Requirements Medical examination; Physician's request.
Staff RNs 1 (ft); LPNs 5 (ft), 5 (pt); Nurses' aides 9 (ft), 9 (pt); Physical therapists; Occupational therapists; Speech therapists; Activities coordinators 1 (ft); Dietitians 1 (ft).
Affiliation Women's Christian Temperance Union.
Facilities Dining room; Laundry room; Barber/Beauty shop; Resident lounge.
Activities Arts & crafts; Games; Reading groups; Prayer groups; Movies; Shopping trips.

Mt Carmel Home—Keens Memorial
412 W 18th St, Kearney, NE 68847
(308) 237-2287
Admin Sr Ann Mary Schmidt. *Dir of Nursing* Jacqueline R Severa RN.
Licensure Intermediate care. *Beds* ICF 76. *Certified* Medicaid.
Owner Nonprofit corp.
Admissions Requirements Medical examination.
Staff RNs 1 (ft); LPNs 4 (ft), 6 (pt); Nurses' aides 21 (ft), 11 (pt); Recreational therapists 1 (ft); Activities coordinators 1 (ft).
Affiliation Roman Catholic.
Facilities Dining room; Physical therapy room; Activities room; Chapel; Laundry room; Barber/Beauty shop; Family room.
Activities Cards; Games; Reading groups; Prayer groups; Movies.

St John's Center
3410 N Central Ave, Kearney, NE 68847
(308) 234-1888
Admin Harry A Carlsen. *Dir of Nursing* Barbara Kuticka. *Medical Dir* S McCammond MD.
Licensure Skilled care. *Beds* SNF 72. *Certified* Medicaid.
Owner Nonprofit corp (Evangelical Lutheran/ Good Samaritan Society).
Admissions Requirements Medical examination; Physician's request.
Staff Physicians 1 (ft); RNs 3 (ft); LPNs 8 (ft), 5 (pt); Nurses' aides 9 (ft), 5 (pt); Recreational therapists 1 (ft), 1 (pt); Activities coordinators 1 (ft); Dietitians 1 (pt).
Affiliation Lutheran.
Facilities Dining room; Physical therapy room; Activities room; Chapel; Crafts room; Laundry room; Barber/Beauty shop; Library.
Activities Arts & crafts; Games; Reading groups; Prayer groups; Movies; Shopping trips; Dances/Social/Cultural gatherings.

St Luke's Good Samaritan Village
2300 E 32nd St, Kearney, NE 68847-3999
(308) 237-3108
Admin Steve Chamley. *Dir of Nursing* Denise Green RN.
Licensure Intermediate care. *Beds* ICF 60. *Certified* Medicaid.
Owner Nonprofit corp (Evangelical Lutheran/ Good Samaritan Society).
Affiliation Lutheran.

Kenesaw

Haven Home
100 W Elm, Kenesaw, NE 68956
(402) 756-6411
Admin Linda Kothe. *Dir of Nursing* Marlys Brown RN.
Licensure Intermediate care. *Beds* ICF 87. *Private Pay Patients* 60%. *Certified* Medicaid.
Owner Proprietary corp (ARA Living Centers).

Staff RNs; LPNs; Nurses' aides; Physical therapists; Recreational therapists; Occupational therapists; Speech therapists; Activities coordinators; Dietitians; Podiatrists.
Facilities Dining room; Activities room; Crafts room; Laundry room; Barber/Beauty shop; Library.
Activities Arts & crafts; Cards; Games; Reading groups; Prayer groups; Movies; Shopping trips; Dances/Social/Cultural gatherings; Intergenerational programs; Pet therapy.

Kimball

Kimball County Manor
810 E 7th, Kimball, NE 69145
(308) 235-4693
Admin Earl L Baker. *Dir of Nursing* Joan Hilkemeier RN.
Licensure Intermediate care. *Beds* ICF 71. *Private Pay Patients* 45%. *Certified* Medicaid.
Owner Publicly owned.
Admissions Requirements Physician's request.
Staff Physicians 1 (pt); RNs 3 (ft), 2 (pt); LPNs 3 (ft), 3 (pt); Nurses' aides 12 (ft), 9 (pt); Physical therapists 1 (pt); Occupational therapists 1 (pt); Activities coordinators 1 (ft), 1 (pt); Dietitians 1 (pt).
Languages Spanish, German.
Facilities Dining room; Activities room; Chapel; Laundry room; Barber/Beauty shop.
Activities Arts & crafts; Cards; Reading groups; Prayer groups; Movies.

Laurel

Hillcrest Care Center
703 Cedar St, Laurel, NE 68745
(402) 256-3961
Admin Marcia Haisch. *Dir of Nursing* Marilyn White RN.
Licensure Intermediate care. *Beds* ICF 51. *Certified* Medicaid.
Owner Publicly owned.

Lewellen

Garden County Lewellen Nursing Home
Box E, Church St, Lewellen, NE 69147
(308) 778-5351
Admin Jody L Roberson. *Dir of Nursing* Ila Hanson RN.
Licensure Intermediate care; Alzheimer's care. *Beds* ICF 37. *Certified* Medicaid.
Owner Publicly owned.
Admissions Requirements Medical examination; Physician's request.
Staff Physicians 8 (pt); RNs 3 (ft); LPNs 2 (ft), 1 (pt); Nurses' aides 6 (ft); Physical therapists 1 (pt); Recreational therapists 1 (ft); Occupational therapists 1 (pt); Speech therapists 1 (pt); Activities coordinators 1 (ft); Dietitians 1 (pt); Audiologists 1 (pt).
Facilities Dining room; Activities room; Crafts room; Laundry room; Barber/Beauty shop; Library.
Activities Arts & crafts; Cards; Games; Reading groups; Prayer groups; Movies; Dances/Social/Cultural gatherings; Pet therapy.

Lexington

Westside Home Inc
1505 N Adams, Lexington, NE 68850
(308) 324-5531
Admin Susan M Appelt. *Dir of Nursing* Linda Mins RN.
Licensure Intermediate care. *Beds* ICF 124. *Certified* Medicaid.
Owner Proprietary corp.
Admissions Requirements Medical examination; Physician's request.

Staff RNs 1 (ft), 3 (pt); LPNs 4 (ft), 2 (pt); Nurses' aides 17 (ft), 10 (pt); Activities coordinators 1 (ft); Dietitians 1 (pt).
Facilities Dining room; Activities room; Chapel; Crafts room; Laundry room; Barber/Beauty shop.
Activities Arts & crafts; Cards; Games; Reading groups; Prayer groups; Movies; Shopping trips; Dances/Social/Cultural gatherings.

Lincoln

Gateway Manor Inc
225 N 56th St, Lincoln, NE 68504
(402) 464-6371
Admin Mary Lou Philippi. *Dir of Nursing* Beverly Anderson RN.
Licensure Intermediate care; Retirement. *Beds* ICF 18; Retirement 95. *Private Pay Patients* 80%. *Certified* Medicaid.
Owner Nonprofit organization/foundation.
Admissions Requirements Minimum age 62; Physician's request.
Staff RNs 3 (ft), 3 (pt); LPNs 1 (ft), 1 (pt); Nurses' aides 5 (ft), 3 (pt); Physical therapists (consultant); Activities coordinators 1 (pt); Dietitians (consultant); CSMs 6 (ft), 2 (pt).
Facilities Dining room; Activities room; Laundry room; Barber/Beauty shop; Library; Penthouse; Auditorium.
Activities Arts & crafts; Cards; Games; Reading groups; Prayer groups; Movies; Pet therapy.

Holmes Lake Manor
6101 Normal Blvd, Lincoln, NE 68506
(402) 489-7175
Admin Margaret E Cole. *Dir of Nursing* Dianne Lyon RN. *Medical Dir* Jon Hinrichs.
Licensure Skilled care; Intermediate care. *Beds* SNF 57; ICF 63. *Private Pay Patients* 100%.
Owner Proprietary corp.
Admissions Requirements Medical examination; Physician's request.
Staff Physicians; RNs 6 (ft), 3 (pt); LPNs 7 (ft); Physical therapists 1 (pt); Occupational therapists 1 (pt); Speech therapists 1 (pt); Activities coordinators 3 (ft), 1 (pt); Dietitians 1 (pt); Podiatrists 1 (pt).
Facilities Dining room; Physical therapy room; Activities room; Chapel; Laundry room; Barber/Beauty shop; Library.
Activities Arts & crafts; Cards; Games; Reading groups; Prayer groups; Movies; Shopping trips; Dances/Social/Cultural gatherings; Intergenerational programs; Pet therapy; Couples club; Diners delight; Special holiday events; Activities with outside friends.

Homestead Health Care Center
4735 S 54th St, Lincoln, NE 68516
(402) 488-0977, 488-1908 FAX
Admin Mary Morris. *Dir of Nursing* Shirley Bradsby RN. *Medical Dir* David Schneider.
Licensure Skilled care; Intermediate care. *Beds* SNF 36; ICF 111. *Private Pay Patients* 75%. *Certified* Medicaid; Medicare.
Owner Proprietary corp (Hillhaven Corp).
Admissions Requirements Medical examination.
Staff Physicians (consultant); RNs 6 (ft), 6 (pt); LPNs 6 (ft), 6 (pt); Nurses' aides 20 (ft), 60 (pt); Physical therapists (consultant); Activities coordinators 2 (ft); Dietitians 1 (ft).
Languages Spanish.
Facilities Dining room; Physical therapy room; Activities room; Chapel; Laundry room; Barber/Beauty shop.
Activities Arts & crafts; Cards; Games; Reading groups; Prayer groups; Movies; Shopping trips; Dances/Social/Cultural gatherings; Intergenerational programs; Pet therapy.

Lancaster Manor
1001 South St, Lincoln, NE 68502
(402) 471-7101
Admin Betty Harmon. *Dir of Nursing* Kathy Eslinger.
Licensure Skilled care; Intermediate care; Alzheimer's care. *Beds* SNF 60; ICF 240. *Certified* Medicaid.
Owner Publicly owned.
Admissions Requirements Minimum age 18; Medical examination.
Staff Physicians 1 (pt); RNs 12 (ft), 2 (pt); LPNs 14 (ft), 1 (pt); Nurses' aides 112 (ft), 14 (pt); Physical therapists 1 (ft), 2 (pt); Occupational therapists 1 (pt); Speech therapists 1 (pt); Activities coordinators 5 (ft); Dietitians 2 (ft); Ophthalmologists 1 (pt).
Facilities Dining room; Physical therapy room; Activities room; Chapel; Crafts room; Laundry room; Barber/Beauty shop; Library.
Activities Arts & crafts; Cards; Games; Reading groups; Prayer groups; Movies; Shopping trips; Dances/Social/Cultural gatherings.

Madonna Centers
5401 South St, Lincoln, NE 68506-2134
(402) 489-7102
Admin Marsha Halpern. *Dir of Nursing* Denise Linder. *Medical Dir* Dr George Wolcott.
Licensure Skilled care; Intermediate care; Alzheimer's care; Sub-acute care. *Beds* SNF 126; ICF 66. *Private Pay Patients* 40%. *Certified* Medicaid; Medicare.
Owner Nonprofit corp.
Admissions Requirements Medical examination; Physician's request.
Staff Physicians 1 (ft); RNs 41 (ft), 46 (pt); LPNs 53 (ft), 33 (pt); Nurses' aides 88 (ft), 95 (pt); Physical therapists 8 (ft), 2 (pt); Recreational therapists 4 (ft); Occupational therapists 7 (ft), 1 (pt); Speech therapists 4 (ft), 6 (pt); Dietitians 2 (ft), 1 (pt); Audiologists 2 (ft).
Affiliation Roman Catholic.
Facilities Dining room; Physical therapy room; Activities room; Chapel; Crafts room; Laundry room; Barber/Beauty shop; Library; Ventilator dependent care.
Activities Arts & crafts; Cards; Games; Reading groups; Prayer groups; Movies; Shopping trips; Dances/Social/Cultural gatherings; Intergenerational programs; Pet therapy.

Maplewood Care Center
4405 Normal Blvd, Lincoln, NE 68506
(402) 488-2355
Admin Stuart Lindeman. *Dir of Nursing* Marilyn Jackson RN. *Medical Dir* Dr D E Michels.
Licensure Skilled care; Intermediate care; Specialty respiratory care unit. *Beds* 120. *Certified* Medicaid; Medicare.
Owner Proprietary corp.
Admissions Requirements Medical examination; Physician's request.
Staff Physicians 5 (ft); RNs 9 (ft), 2 (pt); LPNs 15 (ft), 31 (pt); Nurses' aides 36 (ft); Physical therapists 1 (pt); Occupational therapists 1 (pt); Speech therapists 1 (pt); Activities coordinators 2 (ft); Dietitians 1 (ft).
Languages Spanish, German.
Facilities Dining room; Activities room; Crafts room; Laundry room; Barber/Beauty shop; Library.
Activities Arts & crafts; Cards; Games; Reading groups; Prayer groups; Movies; Shopping trips; Dances/Social/Cultural gatherings.

Milder Manor
1750 S 20th St, Lincoln, NE 68502
(402) 475-6791

Admin Anthony D Cates. *Dir of Nursing* Betty Otte RN.
Licensure Skilled care. *Beds* SNF 154. *Certified* Medicaid; Medicare.
Owner Proprietary corp.

Tabitha Nursing Home
4720 Randolph St, Lincoln, NE 68510
(402) 483-7671
Admin Robert E Moore Jr. *Dir of Nursing* Janet Vrtiska RN. *Medical Dir* James Carlson MD.
Licensure Skilled care; Intermediate care; Alzheimer's care. *Beds* SNF 109; ICF 127. *Certified* Medicaid; Medicare; VA.
Owner Nonprofit corp.
Admissions Requirements Medical examination; Physician's request.
Staff Physicians 1 (pt); RNs 27 (ft); RNs 24 (ft); Nurses' aides 57 (ft); Physical therapists 2 (ft); Occupational therapists 1 (ft); Speech therapists 1 (ft); Activities coordinators 5 (ft); Dietitians 2 (ft); Ophthalmologists 1 (pt).
Affiliation Lutheran.
Facilities Dining room; Physical therapy room; Activities room; Chapel; Crafts room; Laundry room; Barber/Beauty shop; Library.
Activities Arts & crafts; Cards; Games; Reading groups; Prayer groups; Movies; Shopping trips; Dances/Social/Cultural gatherings; Bingo; Parades; Fishing; Special meals; Trivia; Resident council.

Village Manor
3220 N 14th St, Lincoln, NE 68521
(402) 476-3274
Admin Todd D Vetter. *Dir of Nursing* Connie Allen RN.
Licensure Intermediate care. *Beds* ICF 75. *Certified* Medicaid.
Owner Proprietary corp.

Louisville

Louisville Care Center
RR 1 Box 191, Louisville, NE 68037
(402) 234-2125
Admin Jo Ann Mulligan. *Dir of Nursing* Barbara J Ross RN. *Medical Dir* Alan Wilsey MD.
Licensure Intermediate care. *Beds* ICF 55. *Private Pay Patients* 85%. *Certified* Medicaid.
Owner Publicly owned.
Admissions Requirements Medical examination; Physician's request.
Staff RNs 3 (ft), 2 (pt); LPNs 2 (pt); Nurses' aides 21 (ft); Activities coordinators 1 (ft), 1 (pt).
Facilities Dining room; Activities room; Laundry room; Barber/Beauty shop.
Activities Arts & crafts; Cards; Games; Reading groups; Prayer groups; Movies; Dances/Social/Cultural gatherings; Intergenerational programs; Pet therapy.

Loup City

Rose Lane Nursing Home
Rte 2 PO Box 46, Loup City, NE 68853
(308) 745-0303
Admin Terry C Warnke. *Dir of Nursing* Marilyn Jakob.
Licensure Intermediate care; Alzheimer's care. *Beds* ICF 77. *Certified* Medicaid.
Owner Publicly owned.
Admissions Requirements Medical examination.
Staff Physicians 1 (ft); RNs 1 (ft), 1 (pt); LPNs 2 (ft), 3 (pt); Nurses' aides 30 (ft), 9 (pt); Physical therapists 1 (ft), 1 (pt); Occupational therapists 1 (pt); Speech therapists 1 (pt); Activities coordinators 1 (ft); Dietitians 1 (ft); Ophthalmologists 1 (pt); Podiatrists 1 (pt); Audiologists 1 (pt).

Facilities Dining room; Physical therapy room; Activities room; Chapel; Crafts room; Laundry room; Barber/Beauty shop.
Activities Arts & crafts; Cards; Games; Reading groups; Prayer groups; Movies; Shopping trips; Dances/Social/Cultural gatherings; Pet therapy.

Lyons

Logan Valley Manor
RR 1 Box 48, Lyons, NE 68038
(402) 687-2121
Admin Tom Quick. *Dir of Nursing* Sandra Anderson RN.
Licensure Skilled care; Intermediate care. *Beds* 90. *Certified* Medicaid.
Owner Proprietary corp.
Admissions Requirements Medical examination.
Staff RNs 4 (ft), 2 (pt); LPNs 1 (ft), 2 (pt); Nurses' aides 16 (ft), 17 (pt); Activities coordinators 1 (ft), 1 (pt).
Facilities Dining room; Physical therapy room; Activities room; Chapel; Crafts room; Laundry room; Barber/Beauty shop.
Activities Arts & crafts; Cards; Games; Reading groups; Prayer groups; Movies; Shopping trips; Dances/Social/Cultural gatherings.

Macy

Carl T Curtis Health Education Center
Box 250, Macy, NE 68039
(402) 837-5381
Admin June Cook. *Dir of Nursing* June Cook. *Medical Dir* J E Nicolas MD.
Licensure Skilled care; Intermediate care. *Beds* 25. *Certified* Medicaid; Medicare.
Owner Nonprofit organization/foundation.
Admissions Requirements Medical examination.
Staff Physicians 3 (pt); RNs 6 (ft); LPNs 3 (pt); Nurses' aides 7 (ft); Physical therapists 1 (pt); Recreational therapists 1 (pt); Occupational therapists 1 (pt); Speech therapists 1 (pt); Activities coordinators 1 (ft); Dietitians 1 (ft); Ophthalmologists 1 (pt); Podiatrists 1 (pt); Dentists 1 (pt).
Languages Omaha, Winnebago.
Facilities Dining room; Physical therapy room; Activities room; Laundry room; Barber/Beauty shop.
Activities Arts & crafts; Cards; Games; Prayer groups; Movies; Shopping trips; Dances/Social/Cultural gatherings.

Madison

Countryside Home
RR 2 Box 3A, Madison, NE 68748
(402) 454-3373
Admin Lee A Jenkins. *Dir of Nursing* Ruth Pearson RN. *Medical Dir* Dr Biga.
Licensure Intermediate care. *Beds* ICF 72. *Private Pay Patients* 74%. *Certified* Medicaid.
Owner Publicly owned.
Admissions Requirements Medical examination; Physician's request.
Staff RNs 1 (ft), 2 (pt); LPNs 3 (ft), 6 (pt); Nurses' aides 6 (ft), 20 (pt); Activities coordinators 1 (ft), 1 (pt); Dietitians 1 (ft).
Facilities Dining room; Physical therapy room; Activities room; Chapel; Crafts room; Laundry room; Barber/Beauty shop.
Activities Arts & crafts; Cards; Games; Reading groups; Prayer groups; Movies; Shopping trips; Dances/Social/Cultural gatherings; Intergenerational programs; Pet therapy.

McCook

Hillcrest Nursing Home
309 W 7th St, McCook, NE 69001
(308) 345-4600
Admin C Don Harpst Jr. *Dir of Nursing*
Debra Jean Billiar. *Medical Dir* Joyce Hinze.
Licensure Intermediate care. *Beds* ICF 99.
Certified Medicaid; Medicare.
Owner Publicly owned.
Admissions Requirements Medical
examination; Physician's request.
Staff RNs 3 (ft), 1 (pt); LPNs 8 (ft), 3 (pt);
Nurses' aides 39 (ft), 9 (pt); Physical
therapists 1 (pt); Occupational therapists 1
(pt); Speech therapists 1 (pt); Dietitians 1
(pt); Ophthalmologists 1 (pt).
Facilities Dining room; Physical therapy
room; Activities room; Chapel; Crafts room;
Laundry room; Barber/Beauty shop.
Activities Arts & crafts; Cards; Games;
Reading groups; Prayer groups; Movies;
Shopping trips; Dances/Social/Cultural
gatherings.

Milford

Crestview Care Center
RR 1, 1100 W 1st St, Milford, NE 68405
(402) 761-2261
Admin Edith E Wymore RN. *Dir of Nursing*
Frances Prokop RN.
Licensure Intermediate care; Health clinic.
Beds ICF 66. *Certified* Medicaid.
Owner Proprietary corp.
Admissions Requirements Medical
examination.
Staff RNs 2 (ft); LPNs 2 (ft), 1 (pt); Nurses'
aides; Physical therapists; Activities
coordinators 1 (ft); Dietitians; Social
services.
Activities Arts & crafts; Cards; Games;
Reading groups; Prayer groups; Movies;
Shopping trips; Dances/Social/Cultural
gatherings.

Sunrise Country Manor
Rte 2 Box A, Milford, NE 68405
(402) 761-3230
Admin Kathy R Yates. *Dir of Nursing* Debra
Sutton RN.
Licensure Intermediate care; Domiciliary care.
Beds ICF 72. *Certified* Medicaid.
Owner Proprietary corp.

Minden

Bethany Home
515 W 1st St, Minden, NE 68959
(308) 832-1594
Admin Wesley K Anderson. *Dir of Nursing*
Marie J Johnson RN.
Licensure Intermediate care. *Beds* ICF 61.
Certified Medicaid.
Owner Nonprofit corp.

Mitchell

Western Nebraska Nursing Home
1508 22nd Ave, Mitchell, NE 69357
(308) 623-1212
Admin Clara Reisig Battin. *Dir of Nursing*
Dorothy Reisig RN.
Licensure Intermediate care. *Beds* ICF 50.
Certified Medicaid.
Owner Proprietary corp.
Admissions Requirements Medical
examination; Physician's request.
Staff RNs 1 (ft); LPNs 6 (ft); Nurses' aides 15
(ft); Physical therapists; Dietitians.
Facilities Dining room; Activities room;
Crafts room; Laundry room.
Activities Arts & crafts; Cards; Games;
Reading groups; Prayer groups; Movies;
Dances/Social/Cultural gatherings.

Nebraska City

Duff Memorial Nursing Home
13th St & 1st Corso, Nebraska City, NE
68410
(402) 873-3400
Admin Dolores Woodruff. *Dir of Nursing*
Bernadette Shanholtz RN.
Licensure Intermediate care. *Beds* ICF 63.
Certified Medicaid.
Owner Publicly owned.

Nebraska City Manor
1420 N 10th St, Nebraska City, NE 68410
(402) 873-3304
Admin Ann Miller. *Dir of Nursing* Patsy
Wademan RN. *Medical Dir* Portia Voelker.
Licensure Intermediate care; Residential care.
Beds ICF 118. *Certified* Medicaid.
Owner Proprietary corp.
Admissions Requirements Minimum age 18.
Staff RNs 2 (ft), 1 (pt); LPNs 6 (ft); Nurses'
aides 38 (ft), 5 (pt); Physical therapists 1 (ft);
Recreational therapists 1 (ft); Activities
coordinators 1 (ft), 2 (pt); Dietitians 1 (pt).
Facilities Dining room; Physical therapy
room; Activities room; Chapel; Crafts room;
Laundry room; Barber/Beauty shop; Library.
Activities Arts & crafts; Cards; Games;
Reading groups; Prayer groups; Movies;
Shopping trips; Dances/Social/Cultural
gatherings; Music; Puppet play; Family
gatherings.

Valley View Care Center
1800 14th St, Nebraska City, NE 68410
(402) 873-6650
Admin Lois Rakes. *Dir of Nursing* Nedra
Eiserman RN.
Licensure Intermediate care; Health clinic.
Beds ICF 74. *Certified* Medicaid.
Owner Proprietary corp.
Admissions Requirements Minimum age 16;
Medical examination.
Staff RNs 1 (ft), 3 (pt); LPNs 2 (ft), 1 (pt);
Nurses' aides 17 (ft), 5 (pt); Activities
coordinators 1 (ft), 1 (pt); Dentists 11 (ft).
Facilities Dining room; Activities room;
Laundry room; Barber/Beauty shop; Bathing
area.
Activities Arts & crafts; Cards; Games;
Reading groups; Prayer groups; Movies;
Shopping trips; Dances/Social/Cultural
gatherings.

Neligh

Neligh Nursing Center
1100 N 'T' St, Neligh, NE 68756
(402) 887-5428
Admin Patsy Uttecht. *Dir of Nursing* Shirley
Stearns RN.
Licensure Intermediate care. *Beds* ICF 99.
Certified Medicaid.
Owner Proprietary corp (Beverly Enterprises).

Nelson

Good Samaritan Center
PO Box 427, 150 W 8th, Nelson, NE 68961
(402) 225-2411
Admin Gloria Sigler. *Dir of Nursing* Chris
Stemper RN.
Licensure Intermediate care. *Beds* ICF 44.
Private Pay Patients 41%. *Certified*
Medicaid.
Owner Nonprofit corp (Evangelical Lutheran/
Good Samaritan Society).
Admissions Requirements Medical
examination; Physician's request.
Staff RNs 2 (ft), 4 (pt); LPNs 1 (pt); Nurses'
aides 14 (ft), 17 (pt); Physical therapists
(consultant); Recreational therapists
(consultant); Occupational therapists
(consultant); Speech therapists (consultant);
Activities coordinators 1 (pt); Dietitians
(consultant); Ophthalmologists (consultant);
Podiatrists (consultant); Audiologists
(consultant).
Affiliation Lutheran.
Facilities Dining room; Physical therapy
room; Activities room; Crafts room; Laundry
room; Barber/Beauty shop.
Activities Arts & crafts; Cards; Games;
Reading groups; Prayer groups; Movies;
Shopping trips; Dances/Social/Cultural
gatherings; Pet therapy.

Newman Grove

Mid Nebraska Lutheran Home
109 N 2nd St, Box 459, Newman Grove, NE
68758
(402) 447-6203
Admin Rose M Wissenburg. *Dir of Nursing*
Marilyn Nissen RN.
Licensure Intermediate care; Retirement. *Beds*
ICF 59; Retirement apts 6. *Private Pay
Patients* 66%. *Certified* Medicaid.
Owner Nonprofit corp.
Admissions Requirements Medical
examination; Physician's request.
Staff RNs 1 (ft), 3 (pt); LPNs 2 (ft), 4 (pt);
Nurses' aides 3 (ft), 17 (pt); Physical
therapists 1 (pt); Activities coordinators 1
(ft), 2 (pt); Dietitians 1 (pt); Restorative
aides 1 (ft), 1 (pt).
Affiliation Lutheran.
Facilities Dining room; Physical therapy
room; Activities room; Crafts room; Laundry
room; Barber/Beauty shop.
Activities Arts & crafts; Cards; Games;
Reading groups; Prayer groups; Movies;
Shopping trips; Dances/Social/Cultural
gatherings; Intergenerational programs; Pet
therapy; Woodworking.

Norfolk

Heritage of Bel Air
13th & Bel Air Rd, Norfolk, NE 68701
(402) 371-4991
Admin Linda Bomar. *Dir of Nursing* Sheryl
Kyriss RN.
Licensure Skilled care; Intermediate care. *Beds*
89. *Certified* Medicaid.
Owner Proprietary corp.
Staff RNs; LPNs 8 (ft), 2 (pt); Nurses' aides
20 (ft), 8 (pt); Physical therapists 1 (ft);
Recreational therapists; Occupational
therapists; Speech therapists; Activities
coordinators 1 (ft); Dietitians 1 (pt).
Facilities Dining room; Activities room;
Crafts room; Laundry room; Barber/Beauty
shop.
Activities Arts & crafts; Cards; Games;
Reading groups; Prayer groups; Movies;
Shopping trips; Dances/Social/Cultural
gatherings.

Nebraska Veterans Home Annex
Box 409, Norfolk, NE 68702
(402) 371-8468
Admin Duane J Hodge. *Dir of Nursing* Diana
Osborn RN. *Medical Dir* Dr Harold
Dahlheim.
Licensure Skilled care; Intermediate care. *Beds*
SNF 42; ICF 117. *Certified* Medicare.
Owner Publicly owned.
Admissions Requirements Disabled Veterans
or Veteran affiliation.
Staff Physicians 1 (ft) (& contracted); RNs 6
(ft), 2 (pt); LPNs 8 (ft), 3 (pt); Nurses' aides
48 (ft), 1 (pt); Physical therapists
(contracted); Reality therapists 1 (ft);
Recreational therapists 1 (ft); Occupational
therapists 1 (ft); Activities coordinators 1
(ft); Dietitians (contracted); Podiatrists
(contracted).
Facilities Dining room; Physical therapy
room; Activities room; Chapel; Crafts room;
Laundry room; Barber/Beauty shop; Library.

Activities Arts & crafts; Cards; Games;
Movies; Shopping trips; Dances/Social/
Cultural gatherings; Intergenerational
programs; Religious services.

Norfolk Nursing Center
1900 Vicki Ln, Norfolk, NE 68701
(402) 371-2303
Admin Patricia Montgomery. Dir of Nursing
Rachel Briggs RN.
Licensure Skilled care; Intermediate care;
Retirement. Beds 102. Certified Medicaid.
Owner Proprietary corp (Beverly Enterprises).
Admissions Requirements Medical
examination; Physician's request.
Staff RNs 3 (ft); LPNs 6 (ft); Nurses' aides 27
(ft), 3 (pt); Activities coordinators 1 (ft), 1
(pt).
Facilities Dining room; Physical therapy
room; Activities room; Chapel; Crafts room;
Laundry room; Barber/Beauty shop.
Activities Arts & crafts; Cards; Games;
Reading groups; Prayer groups; Movies;
Shopping trips; Dances/Social/Cultural
gatherings.

St Joseph's Nursing Home
401 N 18th St, Norfolk, NE 68701
(402) 371-9404
Admin Sr M Rita Hess. Dir of Nursing Sr
Maudie Hess RN.
Licensure Intermediate care. Beds ICF 74.
Certified Medicaid.
Owner Nonprofit corp.

North Bend

Birchwood Manor
1120 N Walnut, North Bend, NE 68649
(402) 652-3242
Admin Donald A Hruza. Dir of Nursing
Marilyn Heavican RN.
Licensure Intermediate care; Alzheimer's care.
Beds ICF 67. Certified Medicaid.
Owner Proprietary corp.
Admissions Requirements Minimum age 18;
Medical examination; Physician's request.
Staff Physicians 3 (pt); RNs 1 (ft), 2 (pt);
LPNs 5 (pt); Nurses' aides 20 (ft), 3 (pt);
Physical therapists 1 (pt); Occupational
therapists 1 (pt); Speech therapists 1 (pt);
Activities coordinators 1 (ft); Dietitians 1
(pt).
Languages Slavic, German.
Facilities Dining room; Physical therapy
room; Activities room; Chapel; Crafts room;
Laundry room; Barber/Beauty shop; Library.
Activities Arts & crafts; Cards; Games;
Reading groups; Prayer groups; Movies;
Shopping trips; Dances/Social/Cultural
gatherings.

North Platte

Centennial Park Retirement Village
Box 1605, 510 Centennial Cir, North Platte,
NE 69103
(308) 534-7000
Admin Ted Boese. Dir of Nursing Jaralyn
Martin RN.
Licensure Skilled care. Beds SNF 34. Certified
Medicare.
Owner Proprietary corp.

Linden Manor
420 W 4th St, North Platte, NE 69101
(308) 532-5774
Admin Karlene Rentschler. Dir of Nursing
Cynthia Wiese RN.
Licensure Skilled care; Intermediate care. Beds
100. Certified Medicaid.
Owner Proprietary corp.

Valley View Care Centre
2900 W "E" St, North Platte, NE 69101
(308) 534-2200

Admin Bernard Correll. Dir of Nursing Janelle
Hawks RN. Medical Dir Elayne Underwood.
Licensure Intermediate care. Beds ICF 112.
Certified Medicaid.
Owner Proprietary corp.
Admissions Requirements Medical
examination.
Staff RNs 1 (ft), 1 (pt); LPNs 4 (ft), 4 (pt);
Physical therapists 1 (pt); Occupational
therapists 1 (pt); Speech therapists 1 (pt);
Dietitians 1 (ft).
Facilities Dining room; Activities room;
Laundry room; Barber/Beauty shop.
Activities Arts & crafts; Cards; Games;
Reading groups; Prayer groups; Shopping
trips.

Oakland

Oakland Heights
207 S Engdahl, Oakland, NE 68045
(402) 685-5683
Admin Barbara C Andersen. Dir of Nursing
Vernelle Rasmus RN.
Licensure Intermediate care. Beds ICF 67.
Certified Medicaid.
Owner Publicly owned.
Admissions Requirements Medical
examination; Physician's request.
Staff RNs 1 (ft), 1 (pt); LPNs 1 (ft), 3 (pt);
Nurses' aides 9 (ft), 11 (pt); Activities
coordinators 2 (ft), 1 (pt).
Facilities Dining room; Activities room;
Chapel; Crafts room; Laundry room; Barber/
Beauty shop.
Activities Arts & crafts; Cards; Games;
Reading groups; Prayer groups; Movies;
Shopping trips; Dances/Social/Cultural
gatherings.

Ogallala

Indian Hills Manor
Rte 2 Box 35A, Ogallala, NE 69153
(308) 284-4068, 284-8381 FAX
Admin William McCarty. Dir of Nursing Ruth
Sagehorn. Medical Dir Dr Spencer.
Licensure Skilled care; Intermediate care. Beds
Swing beds SNF/ICF 81. Private Pay
Patients 55%. Certified Medicaid; Medicare.
Owner Proprietary corp (Platte Valley Care
Center).
Admissions Requirements Minimum age 21.
Staff Physicians 2 (pt); RNs 1 (ft), 3 (pt);
LPNs; Nurses' aides; Physical therapists 1
(pt); Occupational therapists 1 (pt); Speech
therapists 1 (pt); Activities coordinators 1
(ft), 1 (pt); Dietitians 1 (pt).
Facilities Dining room; Physical therapy
room; Activities room; Chapel; Crafts room;
Laundry room; Barber/Beauty shop; Van
with wheelchair lift; Family room; Patio.
Activities Arts & crafts; Cards; Games;
Reading groups; Prayer groups; Movies;
Shopping trips; Dances/Social/Cultural
gatherings; Intergenerational programs; Pet
therapy; Family support group; Spiritual
care; Volunteer program.

Omaha

Aksarben Manor
7410 Mercy Rd, Omaha, NE 68124
(402) 397-1220
Admin James Banark. Dir of Nursing Pat
Johnson RN. Medical Dir Thomas Cotton
MD.
Licensure Skilled care; Intermediate care. Beds
172. Certified Medicaid; Medicare.
Owner Proprietary corp (Hillhaven Corp).
Admissions Requirements Minimum age 18;
Medical examination.
Staff Physicians 1 (pt); RNs 5 (ft), 4 (pt);
LPNs 8 (ft), 2 (pt); Nurses' aides 36 (ft), 5
(pt); Physical therapists 1 (ft), 1 (pt);
Recreational therapists 1 (ft); Occupational

therapists 1 (pt); Speech therapists 1 (pt);
Ophthalmologists 1 (pt); Podiatrists 1 (pt);
Audiologists 1 (pt); Dentists 1 (pt).
Facilities Dining room; Physical therapy
room; Activities room; Chapel; Laundry
room; Barber/Beauty shop.
Activities Arts & crafts; Cards; Games; Prayer
groups; Movies; Shopping trips; Dances/
Social/Cultural gatherings.

Ambassador
1540 N 72nd St, Omaha, NE 68114
(402) 393-6500
Admin Kenneth Keller. Dir of Nursing Mary
Bollinger RN. Medical Dir Dr Jane F Potter.
Licensure Skilled care; Intermediate care. Beds
SNF 70; ICF 96. Certified Medicaid.
Owner Proprietary corp.
Admissions Requirements Medical
examination; Physician's request.
Staff Physicians; RNs; LPNs; Nurses' aides;
Physical therapists; Recreational therapists;
Occupational therapists; Speech therapists;
Activities coordinators; Dietitians;
Ophthalmologists; Podiatrists; Dentists.
Facilities Dining room; Chapel; Laundry
room; Barber/Beauty shop; Library.
Activities Arts & crafts; Cards; Games;
Reading groups; Prayer groups; Movies;
Shopping trips; Dances/Social/Cultural
gatherings.

Rose Blumkin Jewish Home
323 S 132nd St, Omaha, NE 68154
(402) 330-4272
Admin Eugene H Brandt. Dir of Nursing
Cherill Samson RN. Medical Dir Thomas B
Cotton MD.
Licensure Skilled care. Beds SNF 90. Private
Pay Patients 57%. Certified Medicaid;
Medicare.
Owner Nonprofit corp.
Admissions Requirements Minimum age 65;
Medical examination.
Staff Physicians; RNs 7 (ft), 3 (pt); LPNs 6
(ft), 3 (pt); Nurses' aides 17 (ft), 10 (pt);
Recreational therapists 1 (ft), 1 (pt);
Dietitians 1 (ft).
Affiliation Jewish.
Facilities Dining room; Physical therapy
room; Activities room; Chapel; Crafts room;
Laundry room; Barber/Beauty shop; Library;
Kosher kitchen.
Activities Arts & crafts; Cards; Games;
Movies; Shopping trips; Dances/Social/
Cultural gatherings; Pet therapy; Jewish
holiday observance; Participation in
community center activities.

Farwell Convalescent Center
13706 V St, Omaha, NE 68137
(806) 481-9027
Admin Cara Mirabella. Dir of Nursing Mary
Kay Hays. Medical Dir William T Green
MD.
Licensure Intermediate care; Retirement. Beds
94. Certified Medicaid.
Owner Publicly owned.
Staff LPNs 7 (ft); Nurses' aides 35 (ft), 2 (pt);
Activities coordinators 1 (ft).
Languages Spanish.
Facilities Dining room; Activities room;
Chapel; Laundry room; Barber/Beauty shop.
Activities Arts & crafts; Cards; Games; Prayer
groups; Movies; Shopping trips; Dances/
Social/Cultural gatherings.

Thomas Fitzgerald Veterans Home
156th & Maple, Omaha, NE 68164
(402) 595-2180
Admin Gerald N Rhone. Dir of Nursing Julie
Holling RN. Medical Dir Haskell Morris
MD.
Licensure Skilled care; Boarding home; Health
clinic; Alzheimer's care. Beds SNF 182;
Boarding home 10.
Owner Publicly owned.

Admissions Requirements Minimum age 50 for non-vets (widows & wives).
Staff Physicians 2 (pt); RNs 9 (pt); LPNs 14 (pt); Nurses' aides 42 (ft), 10 (pt); Physical therapists 1 (ft), 1 (pt); Recreational therapists 1 (ft); Occupational therapists 1 (ft); Activities coordinators 1 (ft); Dietitians 1 (pt).
Facilities Dining room; Physical therapy room; Activities room; Chapel; Crafts room; Laundry room; Barber/Beauty shop; Library; Kitchenette; Game room; Pavilion; Canteen; Pharmacy; Dental laboratory.
Activities Arts & crafts; Cards; Games; Reading groups; Prayer groups; Movies; Shopping trips; Dances/Social/Cultural gatherings; Bingo; Luncheons; Exercise programs; Horse races twice yearly; Riverboat cruise.

Florence Heights Village Nursing Center
3220 Scott St, Omaha, NE 68112
(402) 455-6636
Admin John Miller. *Dir of Nursing* Judy Merkel RN. *Medical Dir* Charles M Bressman MD.
Licensure Skilled care; Intermediate care. *Beds* 80. *Certified* Medicaid.
Owner Proprietary corp (Horizon Healthcare Corp).
Admissions Requirements Medical examination; Physician's request.
Staff RNs 3 (ft); LPNs 2 (ft), 2 (pt); Nurses' aides 20 (ft), 14 (pt); Physical therapists 1 (pt); Reality therapists 1 (pt); Recreational therapists 1 (pt); Activities coordinators 1 (ft); Dietitians 1 (pt); Dentists 1 (pt).
Facilities Dining room; Physical therapy room; Activities room; Chapel; Crafts room; Laundry room; Barber/Beauty shop; Library.
Activities Arts & crafts; Cards; Games; Prayer groups; Movies; Shopping trips.

Florence Home
7915 N 30th St, Omaha, NE 68112
(402) 457-4111
Admin Marian E Peterson. *Dir of Nursing* Kathy Nilssen RN. *Medical Dir* Charles McMinn MD.
Licensure Skilled care; Intermediate care; Retirement. *Beds* SNF 66; ICF 64; Retirement 80. *Private Pay Patients* 50%. *Certified* Medicaid.
Owner Nonprofit corp.
Admissions Requirements Minimum age 65; Medical examination; Physician's request.
Staff Physicians 1 (pt); RNs 3 (ft); LPNs 7 (ft); Nurses' aides 55 (ft), 4 (pt); Physical therapists (contracted); Speech therapists (contracted); Activities coordinators 1 (ft); Dietitians (contracted); Ophthalmologists (contracted); Audiologists (contracted); Social services directors; Activity assistants; Chaplains; Volunteer coordinators.
Facilities Dining room; Physical therapy room; Activities room; Chapel; Crafts room; Laundry room; Barber/Beauty shop; Library; Pharmacy; Cafeteria.
Activities Arts & crafts; Cards; Games; Reading groups; Prayer groups; Movies; Shopping trips; Intergenerational programs; Pet therapy; Woodworking; Community involvement.

Hallmark Care Center
5505 Grover St, Omaha, NE 68106
(402) 558-0225
Admin John W Hamilton. *Dir of Nursing* Nancy Dillon RN.
Licensure Intermediate care. *Beds* ICF 177. *Certified* Medicaid.
Owner Proprietary corp.

Lindenwood Nursing Home Inc
910 S 40th St, Omaha, NE 68105
(402) 342-2015
Admin Charlene Toland. *Dir of Nursing* Linda K Skala RN. *Medical Dir* Daniel Halm MD.

Licensure Intermediate care; Domiciliary care. *Beds* ICF 65. *Certified* Medicaid.
Owner Proprietary corp.
Staff RNs 1 (ft), 4 (pt); LPNs 5 (ft), 3 (pt); Nurses' aides 18 (ft), 15 (pt); Physical therapists 1 (pt); Recreational therapists 1 (ft); Occupational therapists 1 (pt); Activities coordinators 1 (ft); Dietitians 1 (ft); Podiatrists 1 (pt).
Facilities Dining room; Activities room; Crafts room; Laundry room; Barber/Beauty shop.
Activities Arts & crafts; Cards; Games; Reading groups; Prayer groups; Movies.

Lutheran Home
530 S 26th St, Omaha, NE 68105
(402) 346-3344
Admin Byron G Will. *Dir of Nursing* Linda F Lemons RN.
Licensure Skilled care; Intermediate care; Domiciliary care. *Beds* SNF 60; ICF 120. *Certified* Medicaid.
Owner Nonprofit corp.
Affiliation Lutheran.

Maple-Crest
2824 N 66th Ave, Omaha, NE 68104
(402) 551-2110
Admin Richard A Peterson. *Dir of Nursing* Lois Sweney RN. *Medical Dir* Lyle Nilson MD.
Licensure Skilled care; Intermediate care; Retirement. *Beds* SNF 61; ICF 123; Retirement apts 43. *Private Pay Patients* 47%. *Certified* Medicaid.
Owner Nonprofit corp (American Baptist Homes of the Midwest).
Admissions Requirements Medical examination; Physician's request.
Staff RNs 15 (ft), 2 (pt); LPNs 21 (ft), 4 (pt); Nurses' aides 55 (ft), 6 (pt); Physical therapists 1 (pt); Activities coordinators 2 (ft), 1 (pt); Dietitians 2 (pt).
Affiliation Baptist.
Facilities Dining room; Physical therapy room; Activities room; Chapel; Crafts room; Laundry room; Barber/Beauty shop; Library.
Activities Arts & crafts; Cards; Games; Reading groups; Prayer groups; Movies; Shopping trips; Intergenerational programs; Pet therapy.

Mercy Care Center
1870 S 75th St, Omaha, NE 68124
(402) 398-6800
Admin Joyce Gibbs.
Licensure Skilled care. *Beds* SNF 250. *Private Pay Patients* 50%. *Certified* Medicaid; Medicare.
Owner Nonprofit corp (Mercy Midlands).
Admissions Requirements Medical examination; Physician's request.
Staff Physicians 1 (ft); RNs 20 (ft), 20 (pt); LPNs 40 (ft), 40 (pt); Nurses' aides 60 (ft), 60 (pt); Physical therapists 2 (ft), 1 (pt); Recreational therapists 2 (ft); Occupational therapists 1 (ft); Speech therapists 1 (ft); Dietitians 1 (ft); Ophthalmologists 1 (pt); Podiatrists 1 (pt); Dentists 1 (pt); Social workers 2 (ft), 1 (pt); Pastoral care 1 (ft), 1 (pt); Admissions RNs 2 (ft), 1 (pt).
Facilities Dining room; Physical therapy room; Activities room; Chapel; Crafts room; Barber/Beauty shop.
Activities Arts & crafts; Cards; Games; Reading groups; Prayer groups; Movies; Shopping trips; Intergenerational programs; Pet therapy.

Millard Good Samaritan Center
12856 Deauville Dr, Omaha, NE 68137
(402) 895-2266, 895-6030 FAX
Admin Cara L Mirabelle. *Dir of Nursing* Peg Pearson RN. *Medical Dir* Dr Frederick Schwartz.

Licensure Skilled care; Intermediate care; Independent living apartments. *Beds* Swing beds SNF/ICF 113; Independent living apts 51. *Private Pay Patients* 55%. *Certified* Medicaid.
Owner Nonprofit corp (Evangelical Lutheran/ Good Samaritan Society).
Admissions Requirements Medical examination; Physician's request.
Staff RNs 4 (ft), 5 (pt); LPNs 3 (ft), 3 (pt); Nurses' aides 32 (ft), 29 (pt); Activities coordinators 2 (ft); Physical therapy aides 2 (ft).
Affiliation Lutheran.
Facilities Dining room; Physical therapy room; Activities room; Chapel; Barber/ Beauty shop; Multipurpose room.
Activities Arts & crafts; Cards; Games; Reading groups; Prayer groups; Movies; Shopping trips; Dances/Social/Cultural gatherings; Intergenerational programs; Pet therapy.

Montclair Nursing Center
2525 S 135th Ave, Omaha, NE 68144
(402) 333-2304
Admin Eileen J Corns. *Dir of Nursing* Dianna Averill RN. *Medical Dir* Donald J Darst.
Licensure Skilled care; Alzheimer's care. *Beds* SNF 179. *Certified* Medicaid; Medicare.
Owner Proprietary corp.
Admissions Requirements Medical examination; Physician's request.
Staff Physicians; RNs; LPNs; Nurses' aides; Physical therapists; Reality therapists; Occupational therapists; Speech therapists; Activities coordinators; Dietitians; Podiatrists; Dentists; Social workers.
Facilities Dining room; Physical therapy room; Activities room; Crafts room; Laundry room; Barber/Beauty shop; Library; Family room; Meeting space.
Activities Arts & crafts; Cards; Games; Reading groups; Prayer groups; Movies; Shopping trips; Dances/Social/Cultural gatherings; Fishing trips.

Northview Villa
2406 Fowler Ave, Omaha, NE 68111
(402) 457-4488
Admin Joyce McManus. *Dir of Nursing* Theresa B Wingett RN. *Medical Dir* William D Murphy MD.
Licensure Intermediate care. *Beds* ICF 60. *Certified* Medicaid.
Owner Proprietary corp.
Admissions Requirements Minimum age 19; Medical examination.
Staff Physicians; RNs; LPNs; Nurses' aides; Physical therapists; Reality therapists; Recreational therapists; Occupational therapists; Speech therapists; Activities coordinators; Dietitians; Ophthalmologists; Podiatrists; Audiologists; Dentists.
Facilities Dining room; Activities room.
Activities Arts & crafts; Cards; Games; Reading groups; Prayer groups; Movies; Shopping trips; Dances/Social/Cultural gatherings.

Oak Grove Manor
4809 Redman Ave, Omaha, NE 68104
(402) 455-5025
Admin Connie Disbrow. *Dir of Nursing* Donna Griggs RN.
Licensure Intermediate care. *Beds* ICF 129. *Certified* Medicaid.
Owner Proprietary corp (Beverly Enterprises).
Staff RNs 4 (ft), 2 (pt); LPNs 4 (ft), 4 (pt); Nurses' aides 21 (ft), 9 (pt); Activities coordinators 1 (ft), 1 (pt).
Facilities Dining room; Activities room; Crafts room; Laundry room; Barber/Beauty shop.
Activities Arts & crafts; Cards; Games; Reading groups; Prayer groups; Movies; Shopping trips; Dances/Social/Cultural gatherings.

Omaha Nursing Home Inc
4835 S 49th St, Omaha, NE 68117
(402) 733-7200
Admin Emelie Jonusas. *Dir of Nursing* Nancy
L Stephens RN.
Licensure Intermediate care. *Beds* ICF 83.
Certified Medicaid.
Owner Proprietary corp.

St Joseph Villa
2305 S 10th St, Omaha, NE 68108
(402) 345-5683
Admin Douglas C Umberger. *Dir of Nursing*
Linda Sather RN.
Licensure Skilled care. *Beds* SNF 180.
Certified Medicaid; Medicare.
Owner Proprietary corp.

Doctor Philip Sher Jewish Home
4801 N 52nd St, Omaha, NE 68104
(402) 451-7220
Admin Allan Greene.
Licensure Intermediate care. *Beds* ICF 80.
Certified Medicaid.
Owner Nonprofit corp.
Affiliation Jewish.

Skyline Manor & Skyline Villa
7300 Graceland Dr, Omaha, NE 68134
(402) 572-5750
Admin Nikki Ingram, acting. *Dir of Nursing*
Rita Bachtell RN. *Medical Dir* Dr Robert
Underriner.
Licensure Skilled care; Intermediate care;
Retirement. *Beds* SNF 56; ICF 48;
Retirement apts 430. *Private Pay Patients*
100%.
Owner Nonprofit corp.
Admissions Requirements Minimum age 62;
Medical examination.
Staff RNs; LPNs; Nurses' aides; Physical
therapists; Reality therapists; Recreational
therapists; Activities coordinators; Dietitians;
Podiatrists; Chaplains.
Facilities Dining room; Physical therapy
room; Activities room; Chapel; Crafts room;
Laundry room; Barber/Beauty shop; Library.
Activities Arts & crafts; Cards; Games;
Reading groups; Prayer groups; Movies;
Shopping trips; Dances/Social/Cultural
gatherings; Intergenerational programs; Pet
therapy.

Ville de Sante
6032 Ville de Sante Dr, Omaha, NE 68104
(402) 571-6770
Admin Donna Suing. *Dir of Nursing* Joan
Arnold RN.
Licensure Intermediate care. *Beds* ICF 128.
Certified Medicaid.
Owner Proprietary corp.
Admissions Requirements Minimum age 50;
Medical examination; Physician's request.
Staff RNs 3 (ft), 2 (pt); LPNs 4 (ft), 2 (pt);
Nurses' aides 25 (ft), 20 (pt); Activities
coordinators 1 (ft), 1 (pt).
Facilities Dining room; Activities room;
Chapel; Crafts room; Laundry room; Barber/
Beauty shop; Library.
Activities Arts & crafts; Cards; Games;
Reading groups; Prayer groups; Movies;
Shopping trips; Dances/Social/Cultural
gatherings.

Williams Care Manor
3525 Evans St, Omaha, NE 68111
(402) 451-5060
Admin Kinze M Williams. *Dir of Nursing*
Anna M Casey. *Medical Dir* Dr Alfred
Brody.
Licensure Intermediate care. *Beds* ICF 60.
Certified Medicaid.
Owner Proprietary corp.
Admissions Requirements Medical
examination; Physician's request.

Staff Physicians; RNs 2 (ft); LPNs 4 (ft), 2
(pt); Nurses' aides 20 (ft), 6 (pt); Physical
therapists; Recreational therapists;
Occupational therapists; Activities
coordinators; Dietitians; Podiatrists.
Facilities Dining room; Activities room;
Chapel; Crafts room; Laundry room; Barber/
Beauty shop.
Activities Arts & crafts; Cards; Games;
Reading groups; Prayer groups; Movies;
Shopping trips; Dances/Social/Cultural
gatherings.

O'Neill

O'Neill Nursing Center
Rte 1 Box 756, O'Neill, NE 68763
(402) 336-2384
Admin Evelyn Troshynski. *Dir of Nursing*
Kathryn M Grutsch RN.
Licensure Intermediate care. *Beds* ICF 72.
Certified Medicaid.
Owner Proprietary corp (Beverly Enterprises).
Staff RNs 2 (ft); LPNs 3 (ft); Nurses' aides 20
(ft), 5 (pt); Physical therapists 1 (pt);
Activities coordinators 1 (ft); Dietitians 1
(ft).
Facilities Dining room; Physical therapy
room; Activities room; Chapel; Crafts room;
Laundry room; Barber/Beauty shop.
Activities Arts & crafts; Cards; Games;
Reading groups; Prayer groups; Movies;
Shopping trips; Dances/Social/Cultural
gatherings.

Osceola

Osceola Good Samaritan Center
Rte 2 Box 1, 600 Center St, Osceola, NE
68651
(402) 747-2691
Admin Rollen Knapp. *Dir of Nursing* Gayle
Coffin RN.
Licensure Intermediate care. *Beds* ICF 61.
Certified Medicaid.
Owner Nonprofit corp (Evangelical Lutheran/
Good Samaritan Society).
Admissions Requirements Medical
examination; Physician's request.
Staff Physicians 2 (pt); RNs 2 (pt); LPNs 2
(ft), 6 (pt); Nurses' aides 9 (ft), 19 (pt);
Physical therapists 1 (pt); Activities
coordinators 1 (ft); Dietitians 1 (pt).
Facilities Dining room; Physical therapy
room; Activities room; Chapel; Crafts room;
Laundry room; Barber/Beauty shop.
Activities Arts & crafts; Cards; Games;
Reading groups; Prayer groups; Movies;
Shopping trips; Dances/Social/Cultural
gatherings; Community activities; Annual
special events; Annual bazaar.

Oxford

Walker Post Manor
PO Box 98, 404 W Derby, Oxford, NE 68967
(308) 824-3245
Admin Diane E Ross. *Dir of Nursing* Janet
Broeker RN. *Medical Dir* Roland R Morgan
MD.
Licensure Intermediate care. *Beds* ICF 59.
Certified Medicaid.
Owner Privately owned.
Facilities Dining room; Activities room;
Chapel; Crafts room; Laundry room; Barber/
Beauty shop.
Activities Arts & crafts; Cards; Games;
Reading groups; Prayer groups; Movies;
Shopping trips; Dances/Social/Cultural
gatherings.

Palmer

Coolidge Center
RR 2 Box 8, Palmer, NE 68864
(308) 894-2735

Admin Shirley Stratman. *Dir of Nursing*
Darlene Gee RN.
Licensure Intermediate care. *Beds* ICF 42.
Certified Medicaid.
Owner Proprietary corp.
Admissions Requirements Medical
examination.
Facilities Dining room; Activities room;
Laundry room; Barber/Beauty shop.
Activities Arts & crafts; Cards; Games;
Reading groups; Prayer groups; Movies;
Dances/Social/Cultural gatherings.

Papillion

Huntington Park Care Center
1507 Gold Coast Rd, Papillion, NE 68046
(402) 339-6010
Admin Susan E Anagnostou. *Dir of Nursing*
Louise Nazeck RN.
Licensure Intermediate care; Alzheimer's care.
Beds ICF 115. *Certified* Medicaid.
Owner Proprietary corp.
Admissions Requirements Minimum age 55;
Medical examination; Physician's request.
Staff Physicians 1 (pt); RNs 3 (ft), 1 (pt);
LPNs 6 (ft), 2 (pt); Nurses' aides 30 (ft), 20
(pt); Physical therapists 1 (pt); Recreational
therapists 1 (ft); Occupational therapists 1
(pt); Speech therapists 1 (pt); Activities
coordinators 1 (ft); Dietitians 1 (pt).
Facilities Dining room; Activities room;
Crafts room; Laundry room; Barber/Beauty
shop.
Activities Arts & crafts; Cards; Games;
Reading groups; Prayer groups; Movies;
Shopping trips; Dances/Social/Cultural
gatherings; Exercise; Discussion groups;
Alzheimer's therapy group.

Papillion Manor Inc
610 S Polk St, Papillion, NE 68046
(402) 339-7700
Admin Ruth Karcher.
Licensure Intermediate care. *Beds* ICF 83.
Owner Proprietary corp.
Admissions Requirements Medical
examination.
Staff RNs 3 (ft), 3 (pt); LPNs 3 (ft), 1 (pt);
Nurses' aides 15 (ft), 15 (pt); Activities
coordinators 1 (ft); Dietitians 1 (ft).
Facilities Dining room; Physical therapy
room; Activities room; Chapel; Laundry
room; Barber/Beauty shop.
Activities Arts & crafts; Cards; Games;
Reading groups; Prayer groups; Movies;
Shopping trips.

Pawnee City

Pawnee Manor
438 12th St, Pawnee City, NE 68420
(402) 852-2975
Admin Jenett Reed. *Dir of Nursing* Debra
Schultz RN.
Licensure Intermediate care. *Beds* ICF 66.
Certified Medicaid.
Owner Proprietary corp (ARA Living
Centers).
Staff RNs 1 (ft), 1 (pt); LPNs 3 (pt); Nurses'
aides 19 (pt); Activities coordinators 1 (ft).
Facilities Dining room; Activities room;
Chapel; Laundry room; Barber/Beauty shop.
Activities Arts & crafts; Cards; Games;
Reading groups; Prayer groups; Movies;
Shopping trips; Dances/Social/Cultural
gatherings; Banquets.

Pender

Pender Care Centre
200 Valley View Dr, Pender, NE 68047
(402) 385-3072
Admin Phyllis Hoy. *Dir of Nursing* Adeline
Shabram RN.

Licensure Intermediate care. *Beds* ICF 62. *Certified* Medicaid.
Owner Proprietary corp.
Admissions Requirements Minimum age 16; Medical examination; Physician's request.
Staff RNs 1 (ft), 2 (pt); LPNs 5 (pt); Nurses' aides 5 (ft), 19 (pt); Physical therapists 1 (pt); Activities coordinators 1 (ft); Dietitians 1 (pt); Ophthalmologists 1 (pt).
Facilities Dining room; Physical therapy room; Laundry room; Barber/Beauty shop.
Activities Arts & crafts; Cards; Games; Reading groups; Prayer groups; Movies; Shopping trips; Dances/Social/Cultural gatherings.

Pierce

Pierce Manor
515 E Main St, Pierce, NE 68767
(402) 329-6228
Admin Janet Zierke. *Dir of Nursing* Patricia Moeller RN. *Medical Dir* Laurrie Steele.
Licensure Intermediate care. *Beds* ICF 86. *Certified* Medicaid.
Owner Proprietary corp (ARA Living Centers).
Staff RNs 1 (ft); LPNs 1 (ft), 6 (pt); Nurses' aides 6 (ft), 26 (pt); Physical therapists 1 (pt); Occupational therapists 1 (pt); Speech therapists 1 (pt); Activities coordinators 1 (ft); Dietitians 1 (pt).
Facilities Dining room; Activities room; Chapel; Crafts room; Laundry room; Barber/Beauty shop; Library.
Activities Arts & crafts; Cards; Games; Reading groups; Prayer groups; Movies; Shopping trips; Dances/Social/Cultural gatherings; Awareness groups.

Plainview

Plainview Manor Inc
PO Box 219, 101 Harper, Plainview, NE 68769
(402) 582-3849
Admin Berkley E Holmstedt. *Dir of Nursing* Jeanne Tinkham RN.
Licensure Intermediate care. *Beds* ICF 60. *Certified* Medicaid.
Owner Proprietary corp.

Plattsmouth

Plattsmouth Manor
602 S 18th St, Plattsmouth, NE 68048
(402) 296-2800
Admin Judy Sealer. *Dir of Nursing* Marilyn Uhe RN.
Licensure Intermediate care. *Beds* ICF 123. *Certified* Medicaid.
Owner Proprietary corp (Beverly Enterprises).

Ponca

Elms Health Care
PO Box 628, Ponca, NE 68770
(402) 755-2233
Admin Jacqueline R Hatcher. *Dir of Nursing* Janis Morris RN. *Medical Dir* Carol Curry, Safety & Infection Control Dir.
Licensure Intermediate care. *Beds* ICF 53. *Private Pay Patients* 54%. *Certified* Medicaid.
Owner Proprietary corp.
Admissions Requirements Medical examination; Physician's request.
Staff Physicians 1 (ft); RNs 3 (ft); LPNs 2 (ft); Nurses' aides 22 (ft); Physical therapists 1 (ft); Recreational therapists 1 (ft); Activities coordinators 1 (ft); Dietitians 1 (ft); Ophthalmologists 1 (ft); Podiatrists 1 (ft); Audiologists 1 (ft).
Facilities Dining room; Activities room; Chapel; Crafts room; Laundry room; Barber/Beauty shop.

Activities Arts & crafts; Cards; Games; Reading groups; Prayer groups; Movies; Shopping trips; Dances/Social/Cultural gatherings; Intergenerational programs; Pet therapy.

Randolph

Colonial Manor of Randolph Inc
Box 1028, 811 S Main, Randolph, NE 68771
(402) 337-0444
Admin Roger E Johnson. *Dir of Nursing* Kathleen Keifer RN.
Licensure Intermediate care. *Beds* ICF 64. *Private Pay Patients* 50%. *Certified* Medicaid.
Owner Proprietary corp.
Staff RNs 1 (pt); LPNs 2 (ft), 1 (pt); Nurses' aides 12 (ft), 1 (pt); Physical therapists 1 (ft), 1 (pt); Occupational therapists 1 (pt); Activities coordinators 1 (ft), 1 (pt); Dietitians 1 (pt); Dentists 1 (pt).
Facilities Dining room; Chapel; Crafts room; Laundry room; Barber/Beauty shop.
Activities Arts & crafts; Cards; Games; Prayer groups; Movies; Shopping trips; Dances/Social/Cultural gatherings.

Ravenna

Ravenna Good Samaritan Center
411 W Genoa, Ravenna, NE 68869
(308) 452-3230
Admin Betty Critel. *Dir of Nursing* Teresa Coulter RN.
Licensure Intermediate care; Alzheimer's care. *Beds* ICF 83. *Certified* Medicaid.
Owner Nonprofit corp (Evangelical Lutheran/ Good Samaritan Society).
Admissions Requirements Minimum age 50; Medical examination; Physician's request.
Staff RNs 1 (ft), 2 (pt); LPNs 6 (ft); Nurses' aides 20 (ft), 5 (pt); Activities coordinators 1 (ft), 2 (pt); Dietitians 1 (ft).
Affiliation Lutheran.
Facilities Dining room; Physical therapy room; Activities room; Crafts room; Laundry room; Barber/Beauty shop; Library; Lounge area.
Activities Arts & crafts; Cards; Games; Reading groups; Prayer groups; Movies; Shopping trips; Dances/Social/Cultural gatherings; Hymn singing; Van trips.

Red Cloud

Heritage of Red Cloud
636 N Locust St, Red Cloud, NE 68970
(402) 746-3414
Admin Denise Georgi. *Dir of Nursing* Jennie Wentworth RN.
Licensure Intermediate care. *Beds* ICF 53. *Certified* Medicaid.
Owner Proprietary corp.

Saint Edward

Cloverlodge Care Center
Box B, 301 N 13th, Saint Edward, NE 68660
(402) 678-2294
Admin Helen A Zona. *Dir of Nursing* Catherine Bard RN. *Medical Dir* Deb Zarek.
Licensure Intermediate care; Domiciliary care. *Beds* ICF 65. *Certified* Medicaid.
Owner Proprietary corp.
Admissions Requirements Physician's request.
Staff RNs; LPNs; Nurses' aides; Physical therapists; Reality therapists; Recreational therapists; Occupational therapists; Speech therapists; Activities coordinators; Dietitians; Ophthalmologists; Podiatrists.
Facilities Dining room; Activities room; Chapel; Laundry room; Barber/Beauty shop.
Activities Arts & crafts; Cards; Games; Prayer groups; Movies; Shopping trips.

Saint Paul

Heritage Living Center
920 Jackson, Saint Paul, NE 68873
(308) 754-5430
Admin Kevin Sauberzweig. *Dir of Nursing* Kris Sauberzweig. *Medical Dir* Pat Swanson.
Licensure Intermediate care; Health clinic; Alzheimer's care. *Beds* ICF 74. *Certified* Medicaid.
Owner Proprietary corp.
Admissions Requirements Medical examination; Physician's request.
Staff LPNs; Nurses' aides; Activities coordinators.
Languages Polish, Czech.
Facilities Dining room; Laundry room; Barber/Beauty shop.
Activities Arts & crafts; Cards; Games; Prayer groups; Movies; Dances/Social/Cultural gatherings.

Sargent

Sargent Nursing Center
S Hwy 183, Box 480, Sargent, NE 68874
(308) 527-4201
Admin Diane Bremseth. *Dir of Nursing* Mary Harvey LPN.
Licensure Intermediate care; Domiciliary care. *Beds* ICF 44. *Certified* Medicaid.
Owner Proprietary corp (Beverly Enterprises).
Admissions Requirements Medical examination; Physician's request.
Staff RNs 1 (pt); LPNs 2 (ft), 1 (pt); Nurses' aides 7 (ft), 3 (pt); Activities coordinators 1 (ft); Dietary 3 (ft), 3 (pt); Social services 1 (pt).
Facilities Dining room; Activities room; Laundry room; Barber/Beauty shop; TV room.
Activities Arts & crafts; Cards; Games; Prayer groups; Movies; Shopping trips; Dances/ Social/Cultural gatherings; Group exercise; Current events; Bingo.

Schuyler

Schuyler Nursing Center
2023 Colfax Ave, Schuyler, NE 68661
(402) 352-3977
Admin Eric M Stewart. *Dir of Nursing* Verla Ann Wilson RN.
Licensure Intermediate care. *Beds* ICF 72. *Certified* Medicaid.
Owner Proprietary corp (Beverly Enterprises).
Admissions Requirements Medical examination.
Staff Physicians 5 (ft); RNs 2 (ft), 3 (pt); LPNs 3 (ft), 3 (pt); Nurses' aides 14 (ft), 10 (pt); Physical therapists 1 (pt); Speech therapists 1 (pt); Activities coordinators 1 (ft), 1 (pt); Dietitians 1 (pt); Podiatrists 1 (pt); Audiologists 1 (pt); Restorative aides 1 (ft), 1 (pt); Social services 1 (ft).
Facilities Dining room; Activities room; Chapel; Laundry room; Barber/Beauty shop; Library; TV; Card playing rooms.
Activities Arts & crafts; Cards; Games; Reading groups; Prayer groups; Movies; Dances/Social/Cultural gatherings; Intergenerational programs; Beauty groups.

Scottsbluff

Scottsbluff Nursing Center
111 W 36th St, Scottsbluff, NE 69361
(308) 635-2019
Admin Pamela Barbour. *Dir of Nursing* Connie Lungrin RN.
Licensure Intermediate care; Domiciliary care. *Beds* ICF 158. *Certified* Medicaid.
Owner Proprietary corp (Beverly Enterprises).

Western Nebraska Veterans Home
1102 W 42nd St, Scottsbluff, NE 69361
(308) 632-3381
Admin Robert C Brozek. *Dir of Nursing*
Davie Shutzer RN. *Medical Dir* Allen C
Landers MD; Kent T Lacey MD.
Licensure Skilled care; Domiciliary care. *Beds*
SNF 50; Domiciliary care 90. *Certified*
Medicare.
Owner Publicly owned.
Admissions Requirements Minimum age 50
for vets wife or widow; Medical
examination.
Staff Physicians 2 (pt); RNs 4 (ft), 2 (pt);
LPNs 8 (ft), 1 (pt); Nurses' aides 24 (ft), 7
(pt); Physical therapists 1 (pt); Occupational
therapists 1 (pt); Speech therapists 1 (pt);
Activities coordinators 1 (ft); Dietitians 1
(pt).
Facilities Dining room; Physical therapy
room; Chapel; Crafts room; Barber/Beauty
shop; Library.
Activities Arts & crafts; Cards; Games;
Reading groups; Prayer groups; Movies;
Shopping trips; Dances/Social/Cultural
gatherings; Intergenerational programs; Pet
therapy.

Scribner

Scribner Good Samaritan Center
815 Logan, Scribner, NE 68057
(402) 664-2527
Admin Clarence R Wegenast. *Dir of Nursing*
Marjorie Zieg RN.
Licensure Skilled care. *Beds* SNF 83. *Private
Pay Patients* 50%. *Certified* Medicaid.
Owner Nonprofit corp (Evangelical Lutheran/
Good Samaritan Society).
Admissions Requirements Medical
examination.
Staff RNs 5 (ft); LPNs 10 (ft); Nurses' aides
31 (ft); Physical therapists (consultant);
Activities coordinators 2 (ft); Dietitians
(consultant); Podiatrists (consultant).
Languages German.
Affiliation Evangelical Lutheran.
Facilities Dining room; Physical therapy
room; Activities room; Chapel; Crafts room;
Laundry room; Barber/Beauty shop.
Activities Arts & crafts; Cards; Games;
Reading groups; Prayer groups; Movies;
Shopping trips; Pet therapy.

Seward

Bethesda Care Center of Seward
624 Pinewood Ave, Seward, NE 68434-1099
(402) 643-4561
Admin Larry Lavelle. *Dir of Nursing* Janet
Staehr RN. *Medical Dir* Lori Wehrs.
Licensure Intermediate care. *Beds* ICF 56.
Certified Medicaid.
Owner Nonprofit corp (MTC West Inc).
Admissions Requirements Medical
examination.
Staff RNs 2 (ft), 1 (pt); LPNs 2 (ft), 2 (pt);
Nurses' aides 10 (ft), 13 (pt).
Facilities Dining room; Activities room;
Chapel; Laundry room; Barber/Beauty shop.
Activities Arts & crafts; Cards; Games;
Reading groups; Prayer groups; Movies;
Shopping trips; Dances/Social/Cultural
gatherings.

Anna Sundermann Home
446 Pinewood Ave, Seward, NE 68434
(402) 643-2902
Admin Ruth Ann Walter. *Dir of Nursing*
Rosalie Hurt.
Licensure Intermediate care; Alzheimer's unit;
Adult day care. *Beds* ICF 48; Alzheimer's
unit 12. *Private Pay Patients* 66%. *Certified*
Medicaid.
Owner Nonprofit corp.
Admissions Requirements Minimum age 55;
Medical examination.

Facilities Dining room; Activities room;
Chapel; Crafts room; Laundry room; Barber/
Beauty shop.
Activities Arts & crafts; Cards; Games;
Reading groups; Prayer groups; Movies;
Shopping trips; Dances/Social/Cultural
gatherings; Van service.

Sidney

Sidney Nursing Center
1435 Toledo St, Sidney, NE 69162
(308) 254-4756
Admin Doris Raasch. *Dir of Nursing* Jean
Lindfors RN.
Licensure Intermediate care. *Beds* ICF 58.
Certified Medicaid.
Owner Proprietary corp (Beverly Enterprises).
Admissions Requirements Medical
examination.
Staff RNs 1 (ft), 2 (pt); LPNs 3 (ft), 2 (pt);
Nurses' aides 11 (ft); Recreational therapists
1 (ft); Activities coordinators 1 (ft);
Dietitians 1 (ft).
Facilities Dining room; Physical therapy
room; Activities room; Crafts room; Laundry
room; Barber/Beauty shop; Library.
Activities Arts & crafts; Cards; Games;
Reading groups; Prayer groups; Movies;
Dances/Social/Cultural gatherings.

South Sioux City

Green Acres Care Center
3501 Dakota Ave, South Sioux City, NE
68776
(402) 494-4273
Admin Jerry Albright. *Dir of Nursing* Dorothy
Angerman RN.
Licensure Skilled care; Intermediate care. *Beds*
82. *Certified* Medicaid; Medicare.
Owner Proprietary corp.

Matney's Colonial Manor
3200 G St, South Sioux City, NE 68776
(402) 494-3043
Admin Edward H Matney. *Dir of Nursing*
Joanne Hannah RN.
Licensure Intermediate care. *Beds* ICF 88.
Certified Medicaid.
Owner Proprietary corp.

Spalding

Friendship Villa
PO Box 190, Spalding, NE 68665
(308) 497-2426
Admin Patrick Fairbanks. *Dir of Nursing* Peg
Fairbanks RN.
Licensure Intermediate care; Retirement. *Beds*
ICF 48. *Certified* Medicaid.
Owner Proprietary corp.
Admissions Requirements Medical
examination; Physician's request.
Staff RNs 1 (ft); LPNs 3 (ft); Nurses' aides 18
(ft); Physical therapists 1 (pt); Activities
coordinators 1 (pt); Dietitians 1 (pt); Social
service 1 (pt).
Facilities Dining room; Physical therapy
room; Activities room; Chapel; Crafts room;
Laundry room; Barber/Beauty shop.
Activities Arts & crafts; Games; Reading
groups; Movies; Shopping trips.

Stanton

Stanton Nursing Home
PO Box 407, 301 17th St, Stanton, NE 68779
(402) 439-2111
Admin William M Harris. *Dir of Nursing* Jean
Suehl RN. *Medical Dir* Dr Dozon.
Licensure Intermediate care; Alzheimer's ICF.
Beds ICF 76; Alzheimer's ICF 26. *Private
Pay Patients* 60%. *Certified* Medicaid.
Owner Publicly owned.

Admissions Requirements Medical
examination; Physician's request.
Staff Physicians 1 (pt); RNs 2 (ft), 2 (pt);
LPNs 3 (ft), 3 (pt); Nurses' aides 12 (ft), 12
(pt); Physical therapists 1 (pt); Occupational
therapists 1 (pt); Speech therapists 1 (pt);
Activities coordinators 1 (ft), 3 (pt);
Dietitians 1 (pt); Podiatrists 1 (pt);
Audiologists 1 (pt).
Facilities Dining room; Physical therapy
room; Activities room; Chapel; Crafts room;
Laundry room; Barber/Beauty shop.
Activities Arts & crafts; Cards; Games;
Reading groups; Prayer groups; Movies;
Shopping trips; Dances/Social/Cultural
gatherings; Intergenerational programs; Pet
therapy.

Stromsburg

Midwest Covenant Home
615 E 9th St, Stromsburg, NE 68666
(402) 764-2711
Admin Robert L Greenwall. *Dir of Nursing*
Grace Schulz RN.
Licensure Skilled care; Intermediate care;
Retirement. *Beds* SNF 64; ICF 40. *Certified*
Medicaid; Medicare.
Owner Nonprofit corp.
Staff RNs 3 (ft), 5 (pt); LPNs 4 (ft), 11 (pt);
Nurses' aides 9 (ft), 38 (pt); Physical
therapists 1 (pt); Speech therapists 1 (pt);
Activities coordinators 1 (ft), 2 (pt);
Dietitians 1 (pt).
Facilities Dining room; Physical therapy
room; Activities room; Chapel; Crafts room;
Laundry room; Barber/Beauty shop; Library.
Activities Arts & crafts; Cards; Games;
Reading groups; Prayer groups; Movies;
Shopping trips; Dances/Social/Cultural
gatherings.

Stuart

Parkside Manor
PO Box A, Main St, Stuart, NE 68780
(402) 924-3601
Admin Ruth Ann Walter. *Dir of Nursing* Kris
Cobb RN.
Licensure Intermediate care; Domiciliary care;
Health clinic. *Beds* ICF 55. *Certified*
Medicaid.
Owner Publicly owned.
Admissions Requirements Medical
examination; Physician's request.
Staff RNs 1 (ft); LPNs 4 (ft); Nurses' aides 10
(ft), 12 (pt); Physical therapists 1 (ft);
Activities coordinators 1 (ft); Dietitians 1
(ft); Ophthalmologists 1 (pt); Podiatrists 1
(pt); Dentists 1 (pt).
Facilities Dining room; Physical therapy
room; Activities room; Chapel; Crafts room;
Laundry room; Barber/Beauty shop.
Activities Arts & crafts; Cards; Games;
Reading groups; Prayer groups; Movies;
Shopping trips; Dances/Social/Cultural
gatherings.

Superior

Superior Good Samaritan Center
Rte 2 Box 6, 1710 Idaho, Superior, NE 68978
(402) 879-4791
Admin Douglas L Carpenter. *Dir of Nursing*
Carol Svoboda.
Licensure Intermediate care. *Beds* ICF 76.
Private Pay Patients 40%. *Certified*
Medicaid.
Owner Nonprofit corp (Evangelical Lutheran/
Good Samaritan Society).
Admissions Requirements Medical
examination; Physician's request.
Staff RNs; LPNs; Nurses' aides; Activities
coordinators.
Affiliation Lutheran.

Facilities Dining room; Physical therapy
room; Activities room; Chapel; Crafts room;
Laundry room; Barber/Beauty shop.
Activities Arts & crafts; Cards; Games;
Reading groups; Prayer groups; Movies;
Dances/Social/Cultural gatherings;
Intergenerational programs; Pet therapy.

Sutherland

Bethesda Care Center
333 Maple, Sutherland, NE 69165
(308) 386-4393
Admin Joan L Anderson. *Dir of Nursing* Joan
H Spurgin RN.
Licensure Intermediate care. *Beds* ICF 62.
Certified Medicaid.
Owner Nonprofit corp (MTC West Inc).
Admissions Requirements Medical
examination; Physician's request.
Staff RNs; LPNs; Nurses' aides; Activities
coordinators.
Facilities Dining room; Physical therapy
room; Activities room; Crafts room; Laundry
room; Barber/Beauty shop.
Activities Arts & crafts; Cards; Games;
Reading groups; Prayer groups; Movies;
Shopping trips; Dances/Social/Cultural
gatherings.

Sutton

Sutton Community Home
1106 N Saunders St, Box 543, Sutton, NE
68979-0543
(402) 773-5557
Admin Myrna J Ulmer. *Dir of Nursing* Elaine
Cook Yost RN.
Licensure Intermediate care. *Beds* ICF 46.
Certified Medicaid.
Owner Proprietary corp.
Staff RNs; LPNs; Nurses' aides; Physical
therapists; Occupational therapists; Activities
coordinators; Dietitians.
Facilities Dining room; Laundry room;
Barber/Beauty shop.
Activities Arts & crafts; Cards; Games;
Reading groups; Prayer groups; Movies;
Shopping trips.

Syracuse

Good Samaritan Center
1622 Walnut St, Syracuse, NE 68446
(402) 269-2251
Admin Thomas A Syverson. *Dir of Nursing*
Jacqueline Wooster RN.
Licensure Intermediate care. *Beds* ICF 113.
Certified Medicaid.
Owner Nonprofit corp (Evangelical Lutheran/
Good Samaritan Society).
Admissions Requirements Medical
examination; Physician's request.
Staff RNs 1 (ft), 3 (pt); LPNs 2 (ft), 4 (pt);
Nurses' aides 10 (ft), 48 (pt); Activities
coordinators 1 (ft); Dietitians 1 (pt).
Affiliation Lutheran.
Facilities Dining room; Physical therapy
room; Activities room; Chapel; Crafts room;
Laundry room; Barber/Beauty shop; Library.
Activities Arts & crafts; Cards; Games;
Reading groups; Prayer groups; Movies;
Dances/Social/Cultural gatherings.

Tecumseh

Maple Grove Home
Rte 2 Box 225, Tecumseh, NE 68450
(402) 335-2885
Admin Dorothy J Babel. *Dir of Nursing*
Ramona Boone RN. *Medical Dir* Dorothy
Zink.
Licensure Intermediate care. *Beds* ICF 29.
Private Pay Patients 50%. *Certified*
Medicaid.
Owner Nonprofit corp.

Staff Physicians; RNs; LPNs; Nurses' aides;
Activities coordinators.
Facilities Dining room; Activities room;
Chapel; Laundry room; Barber/Beauty shop.
Activities Arts & crafts; Cards; Games;
Reading groups; Prayer groups; Movies;
Intergenerational programs; Pet therapy.

Tecumseh Care Center
1133 N 3rd, Tecumseh, NE 68450
(402) 335-3357
Admin Robert Allen Graham. *Dir of Nursing*
Ellen L McMillan RN.
Licensure Intermediate care. *Beds* ICF 73.
Certified Medicaid.
Owner Proprietary corp.

Tekamah

Tekamah Nursing Center
823 M St, Tekamah, NE 68061
(402) 374-1414
Admin Lisa Teager. *Dir of Nursing* Mary Jo
Malone RN.
Licensure Intermediate care. *Beds* ICF 63.
Certified Medicaid.
Owner Proprietary corp (Beverly Enterprises).
Facilities Dining room; Activities room;
Chapel; Crafts room; Laundry room; Barber/
Beauty shop.

Tilden

Tilden Nursing Center
401 Park, Box 400, Tilden, NE 68781
(402) 368-5335
Admin Barbara Leapley. *Dir of Nursing*
Denise Humlicek RN.
Licensure Intermediate care. *Beds* ICF 51.
Certified Medicaid.
Owner Proprietary corp (Beverly Enterprises).
Admissions Requirements Medical
examination.
Staff RNs; LPNs; Nurses' aides; Activities
coordinators.
Facilities Dining room; Physical therapy
room; Activities room; Crafts room; Laundry
room; Barber/Beauty shop.
Activities Arts & crafts; Cards; Games;
Reading groups; Prayer groups; Movies;
Shopping trips; Dances/Social/Cultural
gatherings; Pet therapy.

Trenton

El Dorado Manor
Jct Hwys 25 & 34, Trenton, NE 69044
(308) 334-5241, 334-5242
Admin Virginia L McClure. *Dir of Nursing*
Bev Cathcart RN. *Medical Dir* John Satchel
DO.
Licensure Intermediate care; Residential care;
Day care. *Beds* ICF 52; Residential care 20;
Day care 2. *Private Pay Patients* 73%.
Certified Medicaid.
Owner Publicly owned.
Admissions Requirements Minimum age 35;
Medical examination; Physician's request.
Staff RNs 2 (ft); LPNs 5 (ft); Nurses' aides 14
(ft), 3 (pt); Physical therapists 1 (pt);
Activities coordinators 1 (ft).
Facilities Dining room; Physical therapy
room; Activities room; Chapel; Crafts room;
Laundry room; Barber/Beauty shop; Library.
Activities Arts & crafts; Cards; Games;
Reading groups; Prayer groups; Movies;
Shopping trips; Social hour; Style shows.

Utica

Bethesda Care Center
1350 Centennial Ave, Utica, NE 68456-0030
(402) 534-2041
Admin Alene E Dittmar. *Dir of Nursing*
Cynthia Rae Yound RN. *Medical Dir*
Donna D Tomes.

Licensure Intermediate care; Alzheimer's care.
Beds ICF 47. *Certified* Medicaid.
Owner Nonprofit corp (MTC West Inc).
Admissions Requirements Medical
examination.
Staff RNs 1 (ft), 2 (pt); LPNs 4 (pt); Nurses'
aides 10 (ft), 10 (pt); Recreational therapists
1 (pt); Activities coordinators 1 (ft).
Languages German.
Facilities Dining room; Physical therapy
room; Activities room; Chapel; Crafts room;
Laundry room; Barber/Beauty shop; Library.
Activities Arts & crafts; Cards; Games;
Reading groups; Prayer groups; Movies;
Shopping trips; Dances/Social/Cultural
gatherings.

Valentine

Pine View Good Samaritan Center
601 W 4th, Box 180, Valentine, NE 69201
(402) 376-1260
Admin James D Pierce. *Dir of Nursing* Nancy
Sinnett RN.
Licensure Intermediate care. *Beds* ICF 65.
Certified Medicaid.
Owner Nonprofit corp (Evangelical Lutheran/
Good Samaritan Society).
Admissions Requirements Medical
examination; Physician's request.
Staff RNs 2 (ft), 1 (pt).
Affiliation Lutheran.
Facilities Dining room; Physical therapy
room; Activities room; Chapel; Crafts room;
Laundry room; Barber/Beauty shop.
Activities Arts & crafts; Cards; Games; Prayer
groups; Movies; Shopping trips; Dances/
Social/Cultural gatherings.

Valley

Valhaven Nursing Center
300 W Meigs, Valley, NE 68064
(402) 359-2533
Admin Michael Ryan. *Dir of Nursing* Noreen
Barker RN.
Licensure Intermediate care. *Beds* ICF 60.
Certified Medicaid.
Owner Proprietary corp (Beverly Enterprises).

Verdigre

Alpine Village
706 James, Verdigre, NE 68783
(402) 668-2209
Admin Patricia McElhose. *Dir of Nursing*
Marcelene Vakoc RN.
Licensure Intermediate care; Retirement. *Beds*
ICF 70. *Certified* Medicaid.
Owner Publicly owned.
Admissions Requirements Medical
examination; Physician's request.
Staff Physicians; RNs 2 (ft), 1 (pt); LPNs 2
(ft), 1 (pt); Nurses' aides 15 (ft), 13 (pt);
Physical therapists 1 (ft), 1 (pt); Activities
coordinators 1 (ft), 2 (pt); Social workers 1
(ft); Physical therapy aides 2 (pt).
Facilities Dining room; Physical therapy
room; Activities room; Chapel; Crafts room;
Laundry room; Barber/Beauty shop;
Solarium with TV; Living room with TV;
Family room.
Activities Arts & crafts; Cards; Games;
Reading groups; Prayer groups; Movies;
Shopping trips; Dances/Social/Cultural
gatherings; Numerous clubs; Residents
council; Exercise groups; Music
entertainment.

Wahoo

Haven House
1145 Laurel St, Wahoo, NE 68066
(402) 443-3737

Admin Kevin Galligher. *Dir of Nursing* Johanna Cass RN. *Medical Dir* Dr Brian Elliot.
Licensure Skilled care; Intermediate care. *Beds* 75. *Certified* Medicaid.
Owner Proprietary corp.
Admissions Requirements Medical examination; Physician's request.
Languages Czech.
Facilities Dining room; Activities room; Laundry room; Barber/Beauty shop.
Activities Arts & crafts; Cards; Games; Reading groups; Prayer groups; Movies; Shopping trips; Dances/Social/Cultural gatherings.

Saunders County Care Center
PO Box 307, 844 W 9th St, Wahoo, NE 68066
(402) 443-4685
Admin Lorraine Syverson. *Dir of Nursing* Leann Jeppson RN.
Licensure Intermediate care. *Beds* ICF 75. *Certified* Medicaid.
Owner Nonprofit organization/foundation.
Admissions Requirements Medical examination.
Staff RNs 1 (ft), 3 (pt); LPNs 2 (ft), 4 (pt); Nurses' aides 16 (ft), 20 (pt); Physical therapists; Recreational therapists; Occupational therapists; Speech therapists; Activities coordinators 1 (ft), 1 (pt); Dietitians; Dentists.
Languages Czech, Swedish, German.
Facilities Dining room; Activities room; Chapel; Crafts room; Laundry room; Barber/Beauty shop.
Activities Arts & crafts; Cards; Games; Reading groups; Prayer groups; Movies; Shopping trips; Dances/Social/Cultural gatherings.

Wakefield

Wakefield Health Care Center
306 Ash St, Wakefield, NE 68784
(402) 287-2244
Admin W Russell Swigart Jr.
Licensure Intermediate care. *Beds* 65. *Certified* Medicaid.
Owner Publicly owned.

Wauneta

Heritage of Wauneta
PO Box 1204, 427 Legion St, Wauneta, NE 69045
(308) 394-5738
Admin Elaine W Hink. *Dir of Nursing* Donna Taylor RN.
Licensure Intermediate care. *Beds* ICF 44. *Certified* Medicaid.
Owner Proprietary corp (Vetter Health Services).
Admissions Requirements Medical examination.
Staff RNs 1 (ft); LPNs 4 (ft); Nurses' aides 9 (ft), 6 (pt); Physical therapists 1 (pt); Occupational therapists 1 (pt); Speech therapists 1 (pt); Activities coordinators 1 (pt); Dietitians 1 (pt); Ophthalmologists 1 (pt).
Facilities Dining room; Activities room; Chapel; Crafts room; Laundry room; Barber/Beauty shop.
Activities Arts & crafts; Cards; Games; Reading groups; Prayer groups; Movies; Shopping trips; Dances/Social/Cultural gatherings; Pet therapy; Outings; Family support; Community support.

Wausa

Wausa Nursing Center
PO Box L, Wausa, NE 68786
(402) 586-2216

Admin Sandra Leimer. *Dir of Nursing* Barbara Gillilan RN.
Licensure Intermediate care. *Beds* ICF 52. *Certified* Medicaid.
Owner Proprietary corp (Beverly Enterprises).
Staff RNs 1 (ft), 2 (pt); LPNs 1 (ft); Activities coordinators 1 (ft).
Facilities Dining room; Activities room; Crafts room; Laundry room; Barber/Beauty shop.
Activities Arts & crafts; Cards; Games; Reading groups; Prayer groups; Movies; Shopping trips; Dances/Social/Cultural gatherings.

Wayne

Wayne Care Centre
918 Main St, Wayne, NE 68787
(402) 375-1922
Admin Gil Haase. *Dir of Nursing* Carrol Baier RN.
Licensure Intermediate care. *Beds* ICF 94. *Certified* Medicaid.
Owner Proprietary corp.

West Point

West Point Living Center
Rte 3, Prospect Rd, West Point, NE 68788
(402) 372-2441
Admin Lauren A Lierman. *Dir of Nursing* Susan Reppert RN.
Licensure Intermediate care. *Beds* ICF 72. *Certified* Medicaid.
Owner Proprietary corp.
Admissions Requirements Medical examination.
Staff Physicians 5 (pt); RNs 4 (ft); LPNs 4 (pt); Nurses' aides 20 (pt); Physical therapists 1 (pt); Recreational therapists 1 (ft); Occupational therapists 1 (pt); Speech therapists 1 (pt); Activities coordinators 1 (ft); Dietitians 1 (pt); Dentists 1 (pt).
Facilities Dining room; Physical therapy room; Activities room; Laundry room; Barber/Beauty shop.
Activities Arts & crafts; Cards; Games; Reading groups; Prayer groups; Movies; Dances/Social/Cultural gatherings.

Wilber

Wilber Nursing Home
610 N Main, Wilber, NE 68465
(402) 821-2331
Admin Arthur Brown. *Dir of Nursing* Jo Vrtiska RN. *Medical Dir* Carmon Kubicek.
Licensure Intermediate care; Alzheimer's care. *Beds* ICF 120. *Certified* Medicaid.
Owner Publicly owned.
Admissions Requirements Medical examination; Physician's request.
Staff RNs 4 (ft), 2 (pt); LPNs 2 (ft), 2 (pt); Nurses' aides 34 (ft), 21 (pt); Activities coordinators 1 (ft), 1 (pt); Social service; Dietary supervisors 2 (ft).
Languages Czech.
Facilities Dining room; Physical therapy room; Activities room; Crafts room; Laundry room; Barber/Beauty shop; Recreation room; Fenced-in gazebo.
Activities Arts & crafts; Cards; Games; Reading groups; Prayer groups; Movies; Shopping trips; Dances/Social/Cultural gatherings; Summer outings.

Wisner

Wisner Manor
RR 1 Box 237, N 9th, Wisner, NE 68791
(402) 529-3286
Admin Elaine Kay Storovich. *Dir of Nursing* Erdine Moeller RN.
Licensure Intermediate care. *Beds* ICF 65. *Certified* Medicaid.

Owner Publicly owned.
Admissions Requirements Medical examination.
Staff RNs 1 (ft), 2 (pt); LPNs 1 (ft), 4 (pt); Nurses' aides 15 (pt); Physical therapists 1 (pt); Reality therapists 1 (pt); Recreational therapists 1 (ft); Activities coordinators 1 (ft); Dietitians 1 (pt); Dentists 1 (pt).
Facilities Dining room; Physical therapy room; Activities room; Chapel; Crafts room; Laundry room; Barber/Beauty shop; Library.
Activities Arts & crafts; Cards; Games; Reading groups; Prayer groups; Movies; Shopping trips; Dances/Social/Cultural gatherings; Fishing trips; Picnics; Fish fry.

Wood River

Western Hall County Good Samaritan Center
1401 East St, Box 517, Wood River, NE 68883-0517
(308) 583-2214
Admin Ken Marshall. *Dir of Nursing* Marian Hensley RN.
Licensure Intermediate care. *Beds* ICF 72. *Certified* Medicaid.
Owner Nonprofit corp (Evangelical Lutheran/ Good Samaritan Society).
Admissions Requirements Medical examination; Physician's request.
Staff RNs 1 (ft), 1 (pt); LPNs 1 (ft), 4 (pt); Nurses' aides 6 (ft), 12 (pt); Activities coordinators 1 (ft), 1 (pt); Dietitians 1 (ft).
Languages Spanish.
Facilities Dining room; Physical therapy room; Activities room; Chapel; Crafts room; Laundry room; Barber/Beauty shop; Library.
Activities Arts & crafts; Cards; Games; Reading groups; Prayer groups; Movies; Shopping trips; Dances/Social/Cultural gatherings; Daily services.

Wymore

Wymore Good Samaritan Center
105 E "D" St, Wymore, NE 68466
(402) 645-3354
Admin A Verle Ralston. *Dir of Nursing* Peggy Engle RN.
Licensure Intermediate care. *Beds* ICF 59. *Certified* Medicaid.
Owner Nonprofit corp (Evangelical Lutheran/ Good Samaritan Society).
Staff RNs 1 (ft); LPNs 1 (ft), 6 (pt); Nurses' aides 5 (ft), 20 (pt); Physical therapists 1 (ft), 1 (pt); Speech therapists 1 (pt); Activities coordinators 1 (ft), 1 (pt); Dietitians 1 (pt).
Affiliation Lutheran.
Facilities Dining room; Activities room; Chapel; Crafts room; Laundry room; Barber/Beauty shop; Library.
Activities Arts & crafts; Cards; Games; Reading groups; Prayer groups; Movies; Shopping trips; Dances/Social/Cultural gatherings; Therapeutic projects.

York

Hearthstone
2319 Lincoln Ave, York, NE 68467
(402) 362-4333
Admin Lyle Hight. *Dir of Nursing* Sue Lief RN.
Licensure Intermediate care. *Beds* ICF 170. *Certified* Medicaid.
Owner Nonprofit corp.
Staff Physicians 6 (ft); RNs 4 (ft), 4 (pt); LPNs 6 (ft), 6 (pt); Nurses' aides 36 (ft), 35 (pt); Physical therapists 1 (pt); Activities coordinators 1 (ft), 2 (pt); Dietitians 1 (pt); Dentists 1 (pt); Social services 1 (ft).

NEVADA

Boulder City

Boulder City Care Center
601 Adams Blvd, Boulder City, NV 89005
(702) 293-5151
Admin Susan J Grinsted.
Licensure Skilled care. *Beds* SNF 87. *Certified*
Medicaid; Medicare.
Owner Proprietary corp (Beverly Enterprises).

**Boulder City Hospital—Skilled Nursing
Facility**
901 Adams Blvd, Boulder City, NV 89005
(702) 293-4111
Admin Jack T Wood.
Licensure Skilled care. *Beds* SNF 10.

Caliente

Grover C Dils Medical Center
PO Box 38, Hwy 93 N, Caliente, NV 89008
(702) 726-3171
Admin Dorine Soper. *Dir of Nursing* Pam
Finley. *Medical Dir* Joseph Wilkin MD.
Licensure Skilled care. *Beds* SNF 14. *Certified*
Medicaid; Medicare.
Owner Publicly owned.
Staff Physicians 2 (pt); RNs 4 (ft), 2 (pt);
LPNs 4 (ft); Nurses' aides 7 (ft); Activities
coordinators 1 (ft); Dietitians 1 (pt).
Facilities Dining room; Activities room.
Activities Arts & crafts; Cards; Games; Prayer
groups.

Carson City

Carson Convalescent Center
2898 Hwy 50 E, Carson City, NV 89701
(702) 882-3301
Admin Gayle Cook.
Medical Dir William King MD.
Licensure Skilled care; Alzheimer's care. *Beds*
SNF 74. *Certified* Medicaid; Medicare.
Owner Proprietary corp (Hillhaven Corp).
Admissions Requirements Medical
examination.
Staff RNs 6 (ft), 6 (pt); LPNs 8 (ft), 8 (pt);
Nurses' aides 30 (ft), 10 (pt); Physical
therapists 3 (pt); Reality therapists 1 (pt);
Recreational therapists 1 (pt); Occupational
therapists 1 (pt); Speech therapists 1 (pt);
Activities coordinators 1 (ft); Dietitians 3
(pt); Ophthalmologists 1 (pt); Podiatrists 1
(pt); Dentists 1 (pt).
Facilities Dining room; Physical therapy
room; Activities room; Laundry room;
Barber/Beauty shop.
Activities Arts & crafts; Cards; Games;
Reading groups; Prayer groups; Movies;
Shopping trips; Dances/Social/Cultural
gatherings.

Eagle Valley Children's Home
Rte 1 Box 755, Carson City, NV 89702
(702) 882-1188

Admin Dianna Hoover. *Dir of Nursing* Tena
Howard RN. *Medical Dir* Thomas A Good
MD.
Licensure Intermediate care for mentally
retarded. *Beds* ICF/MR 15. *Certified*
Medicaid.
Owner Nonprofit organization/foundation.
Admissions Requirements Medical
examination; Physician's request.
Staff Physicians 1 (pt); RNs 1 (ft); LPNs 4
(ft), 13 (pt); Nurses' aides 15 (ft), 6 (pt);
Physical therapists 1 (pt); Recreational
therapists 1 (ft); Occupational therapists 1
(pt); Speech therapists 1 (ft); Dietitians 1
(ft).
Languages Spanish, German.
Facilities Dining room; Physical therapy
room; Activities room; Crafts room; Laundry
room; Library; Speech therapy room.
Activities Arts & crafts; Games; Reading
groups; Movies; Shopping trips; Dances/
Social/Cultural gatherings.

Sierra Convalescent Center
201 Koontz Ln, Carson City, NV 89701
(702) 883-3622
Admin Janey Mallow. *Dir of Nursing* Shirly
Paul RN.
Licensure Skilled care; Alzheimer's care. *Beds*
SNF 146. *Certified* Medicaid; Medicare.
Owner Proprietary corp (Beverly Enterprises).
Admissions Requirements Medical
examination; Physician's request.
Staff RNs; LPNs; Nurses' aides.
Facilities Dining room; Physical therapy
room; Activities room.
Activities Arts & crafts; Cards; Games;
Reading groups; Prayer groups; Movies;
Shopping trips; Dances/Social/Cultural
gatherings.

Elko

Ruby Mountains Manor
701 Walnut St, Elko, NV 89801
(702) 738-8051
Admin Larry Roberts. *Dir of Nursing* Judy
Saunders RN.
Licensure Skilled care. *Beds* SNF 76. *Certified*
Medicaid; Medicare.
Owner Proprietary corp.
Admissions Requirements Minimum age 21;
Medical examination; Physician's request.
Staff RNs; LPNs; Nurses' aides; Activities
coordinators; Dietitians.
Facilities Dining room; Physical therapy
room; Activities room; Chapel; Crafts room;
Laundry room; Barber/Beauty shop; Library.
Activities Arts & crafts; Cards; Games;
Reading groups; Prayer groups; Movies;
Shopping trips; Dances/Social/Cultural
gatherings.

Ely

White Pine Care Center
1500 Ave G, Ely, NV 89301
(702) 289-8801
Admin Russell D Fay.
Licensure Skilled care. *Beds* SNF 99. *Certified*
Medicaid; Medicare.
Staff Physicians 4 (pt); RNs 4 (ft), 1 (pt);
LPNs 10 (ft); Nurses' aides 32 (ft); Physical
therapists 1 (pt); Activities coordinators 1
(ft).
Facilities Dining room; Physical therapy
room; Activities room; Laundry room;
Barber/Beauty shop.
Activities Arts & crafts; Cards; Games; Prayer
groups; Movies; Birthday parties; Picnics.

Fallon

Fallon Convalescent Center
365 W "A" St, Fallon, NV 89406
(702) 423-6551
Admin Sandra Wright. *Dir of Nursing* Joan
McLaughlin. *Medical Dir* Dr Kurt Carlson.
Licensure Skilled care. *Beds* SNF 147.
Certified Medicaid; Medicare.
Owner Proprietary corp.
Admissions Requirements Medical
examination; Physician's request.
Staff Physicians 10 (ft); RNs 10 (ft); LPNs 14
(ft); Nurses' aides 50 (ft); Physical therapists
2 (ft); Recreational therapists 2 (ft); Speech
therapists 1 (ft); Activities coordinators 1
(ft); Dietitians 1 (ft); Dentists 1 (ft).
Facilities Dining room; Physical therapy
room; Activities room; Crafts room; Laundry
room; Barber/Beauty shop; Conference
room; Patios.
Activities Arts & crafts; Cards; Games;
Reading groups; Prayer groups; Movies;
Shopping trips; Dances/Social/Cultural
gatherings.

Gardnerville

Cottonwood Care Center
806 Tillman Ln, Gardnerville, NV 89410
(702) 265-3571
Admin Richard Barger MA. *Dir of Nursing*
Shirley Paul RN. *Medical Dir* Bruce
Armstrong MD.
Licensure Skilled care; Intermediate care. *Beds*
Swing beds SNF/ICF 125. *Private Pay
Patients* 30-35%. *Certified* Medicaid;
Medicare.
Owner Privately owned.
Admissions Requirements Medical
examination; Physician's request.
Staff Physicians 6 (pt); RNs 10 (ft); LPNs 15
(ft); Nurses' aides 42 (ft); Physical therapists
1 (pt); Recreational therapists 2 (ft);
Occupational therapists 1 (pt); Speech
therapists 1 (pt); Activities coordinators 2
(ft); Dietitians 1 (pt); Ophthalmologists 1
(pt).
Languages Spanish.

Facilities Dining room; Physical therapy room; Activities room; Crafts room; Laundry room; Barber/Beauty shop; Library; Van.
Activities Arts & crafts; Cards; Games; Prayer groups; Movies; Shopping trips; Dances/Social/Cultural gatherings; Intergenerational programs; Pet therapy; Bingo.

Hawthorne

Lefa L Seran Skilled Nursing Facility
PO Box 1510, 1st & A Sts, Hawthorne, NV 89415
(702) 945-2461
Admin Richard N Munger.
Licensure Skilled care. *Beds* SNF 20. *Certified* Medicaid; Medicare.

Henderson

Cosada Delmar Nursing Center of Green Valley
2501 Wigwam Pkwy, Henderson, NV 89014
(702) 361-6111
Admin Jackie Wilkerson.
Licensure Skilled care. *Beds* SNF 180. *Certified* Medicaid; Medicare.

Glen Halla Intermediate Care Facility
1745 Athol St, Henderson, NV 89015
(702) 565-8748
Admin Paul S Besser. *Dir of Nursing* Jeanne Heki RN.
Licensure Intermediate care. *Beds* ICF 48. *Certified* Medicaid.
Owner Proprietary corp.
Admissions Requirements Physician's request.
Staff Physicians 5 (ft), 1 (pt); RNs 2 (ft), 3 (pt); LPNs 4 (ft); Nurses' aides 9 (ft), 2 (pt); Recreational therapists 1 (ft); Activities coordinators 1 (ft); Dietitians 1 (ft).
Languages Spanish.
Facilities Dining room; Activities room; Crafts room; Laundry room; Barber/Beauty shop; Outdoor area.
Activities Arts & crafts; Cards; Games; Reading groups; Prayer groups; Movies; Shopping trips; Dances/Social/Cultural gatherings; Outings.

Henderson Convalescent Hospital
1180 E Lake Mead Dr, Henderson, NV 89105
(702) 565-8555
Admin Charles C Perry Jr. *Dir of Nursing* Helen Tyning RN. *Medical Dir* Al Waters MD.
Licensure Skilled care. *Beds* SNF 124. *Certified* Medicaid; Medicare.
Owner Proprietary corp (Americare Corp).
Admissions Requirements Medical examination; Physician's request.
Staff RNs 8 (ft), 2 (pt); LPNs 9 (ft), 3 (pt); Nurses' aides 44 (ft), 5 (pt); Physical therapists 1 (ft); Recreational therapists 1 (ft); Occupational therapists 1 (pt); Speech therapists 2 (pt); Activities coordinators 1 (ft), 2 (pt); Dietitians 1 (pt); Ophthalmologists 1 (pt); Podiatrists 2 (pt).
Languages Spanish, German, French, Italian, Polish.
Facilities Dining room; Physical therapy room; Activities room; Chapel; Crafts room; Laundry room; Barber/Beauty shop; Library.
Activities Arts & crafts; Cards; Games; Reading groups; Prayer groups; Movies; Shopping trips; Dances/Social/Cultural gatherings.

Las Vegas

Charleston Health Care Center
2035 W Charleston Blvd, Las Vegas, NV 89102
(702) 386-7980
Admin Dale A Moore. *Dir of Nursing* Elsie Turfley RN. *Medical Dir* Thomas Quam MD.

Licensure Skilled care; Intermediate care. *Beds* SNF 33; ICF 67. *Private Pay Patients* 31%. *Certified* Medicare.
Owner Proprietary corp.
Admissions Requirements Medical examination.
Staff RNs 7 (ft), 4 (pt); LPNs 6 (ft), 3 (pt); Nurses' aides 38 (ft), 14 (pt); Activities coordinators 2 (ft); Dietitians 1 (ft).
Facilities Dining room; Physical therapy room; Activities room; Crafts room; Laundry room; Barber/Beauty shop.
Activities Arts & crafts; Cards; Games; Prayer groups; Movies; Shopping trips; Intergenerational programs.

Desert Developmental Center
1300 S Jones Blvd, Las Vegas, NV 89158
(702) 486-6200
Admin Charlotte Crawford.
Licensure Intermediate care for mentally retarded. *Beds* ICF/MR 94. *Certified* Medicaid.

Desert Lane Care Center
660 Desert Ln, Las Vegas, NV 89106
(702) 382-5580
Admin Dale A Moore. *Dir of Nursing* JoAnn Good RN. *Medical Dir* Arthur Pitterman MD.
Licensure Skilled care. *Beds* SNF 208. *Certified* Medicaid; Medicare.
Owner Proprietary corp (Beverly Enterprises).
Admissions Requirements Medical examination; Physician's request.
Staff RNs 20 (ft), 2 (pt); LPNs 18 (ft), 1 (pt); Nurses' aides 73 (ft), 8 (pt); Dietitians 1 (pt); Dietary assistants 15 (ft), 4 (pt); Laundry 4 (ft); Office 8 (ft); Maintenance 3 (ft); Central supply 2 (ft); Medical records 4 (ft); Housekeeping 12 (ft); Social services 4 (ft); Activities 3 (ft).
Languages Tagalog, German.
Facilities Dining room; Physical therapy room; Activities room; Crafts room; Laundry room; Barber/Beauty shop.
Activities Arts & crafts; Cards; Games; Reading groups; Prayer groups; Movies; Shopping trips; Dances/Social/Cultural gatherings.

El Jen Convalescent Hospital
5538 W Duncan Dr, Las Vegas, NV 89130
(702) 645-2606
Admin James M Toomey.
Medical Dir LeRoy Wolever MD.
Licensure Skilled care. *Beds* SNF 104. *Certified* Medicaid; Medicare.
Staff Physicians 10 (pt); RNs 8 (ft), 1 (pt); LPNs 2 (ft), 1 (pt); Nurses' aides 45 (ft); Physical therapists 1 (pt); Reality therapists 1 (pt); Recreational therapists 1 (pt); Occupational therapists 1 (pt); Speech therapists 1 (pt); Activities coordinators 2 (ft); Dietitians 1 (ft), 1 (pt); Ophthalmologists 1 (pt); Podiatrists 1 (pt); Audiologists 1 (pt); Dentists 1 (pt); Social workers 1 (ft).
Facilities Dining room; Physical therapy room; Activities room; Crafts room; Laundry room; Barber/Beauty shop.
Activities Arts & crafts; Cards; Games; Reading groups; Prayer groups; Movies; Shopping trips; Dances/Social/Cultural gatherings.

El Jen Convalescent Hospital—Rehabilitation
5659 Duncan Dr, Las Vegas, NV 89130
(702) 645-1900
Admin James M Toomey.
Licensure Skilled care. *Beds* SNF 124. *Certified* Medicaid; Medicare.
Owner Proprietary corp (Hillhaven Corp).

Gaye Haven Intermediate Care Facility Inc
1813 Betty Ln, Las Vegas, NV 89115
(702) 452-8399
Admin Sandra V Manetas.

Medical Dir Amanda Blount DO.
Licensure Intermediate care. *Beds* ICF 20. *Certified* Medicaid.
Owner Proprietary corp; Privately owned.
Admissions Requirements Minimum age 20.
Staff Physicians 1 (pt); RNs 1 (pt); LPNs 5 (ft); Reality therapists 1 (ft); Recreational therapists 1 (ft); Activities coordinators 1 (ft), 1 (pt); Dietitians 1 (ft), 1 (pt).
Facilities Dining room; Activities room; Crafts room; Laundry room.
Activities Arts & crafts; Cards; Games; Movies; Shopping trips.

Las Vegas Convalescent Center
2832 Maryland Pkwy, Las Vegas, NV 89109
(702) 735-5848
Admin Patricia Morris.
Licensure Skilled care. *Beds* SNF 77. *Certified* Medicaid; Medicare.
Owner Proprietary corp (Hillhaven Corp).

Torrey Pines Care Center
1701 S Torrey Pines Dr, Las Vegas, NV 89102
(702) 871-0005
Admin Terry Granger.
Medical Dir Elizabeth Mongeau.
Licensure Skilled care; Intermediate care. *Beds* SNF 26; ICF 90. *Certified* Medicaid.
Owner Proprietary corp (Hillhaven Corp).
Staff RNs 6 (ft), 2 (pt); LPNs 10 (ft); Nurses' aides 34 (ft), 1 (pt); Activities coordinators 2 (ft); Dietitians 1 (ft).

Vegas Valley Convalescent Hospital
2945 Casa Vegas St, Las Vegas, NV 89109
(702) 735-7179
Admin Charles C Perry Jr.
Medical Dir Dr Robert Shreck.
Licensure Skilled care. *Beds* SNF 102. *Certified* Medicaid; Medicare.
Admissions Requirements Medical examination; Physician's request.
Staff RNs 10 (ft), 2 (pt); LPNs 15 (ft), 4 (pt); Nurses' aides 50 (ft), 5 (pt); Physical therapists 1 (pt); Occupational therapists 1 (pt); Activities coordinators 2 (pt); Dietitians 2 (pt).
Facilities Dining room; Physical therapy room; Activities room; Crafts room; Laundry room; Barber/Beauty shop.
Activities Arts & crafts; Cards; Games; Movies; Shopping trips; Dances/Social/Cultural gatherings.

Lovelock

Pershing General Hospital & Nursing Home
PO Box 661, Lovelock, NV 89419
(702) 273-2621
Admin Karen Holcher. *Dir of Nursing* Carma Krietler RN. *Medical Dir* S Sweeney.
Licensure Skilled care. *Beds* SNF 47. *Certified* Medicaid; Medicare.
Owner Nonprofit organization/foundation.
Admissions Requirements Physician's request; PASARR.
Staff Physicians 3 (ft); RNs 7 (ft); LPNs 2 (ft); Nurses' aides 19 (ft); Physical therapists 1 (pt); Recreational therapists 1 (pt); Occupational therapists 1 (pt); Speech therapists 1 (pt); Activities coordinators 1 (ft); Dietitians 1 (pt); Ophthalmologists 1 (pt); Podiatrists 1 (pt).
Languages Spanish.
Facilities Dining room; Physical therapy room; Activities room; Laundry room; Barber/Beauty shop; Private and semi-private rooms.
Activities Arts & crafts; Cards; Games; Reading groups; Prayer groups; Movies; Pet therapy; Luncheon outings.

North Las Vegas

North Las Vegas Care Center
3215 E Cheyenne Ave, North Las Vegas, NV 89030
(702) 649-7800
Admin Jacqueline S Lanter. *Dir of Nursing* Louise Hampton RN. *Medical Dir* Gary DesAuzo DO.
Licensure Skilled care. *Beds* SNF 182. *Certified* Medicaid; Medicare.
Owner Proprietary corp (Beverly Enterprises).
Admissions Requirements Medical examination.
Facilities Dining room; Physical therapy room; Activities room; Crafts room; Laundry room; Barber/Beauty shop; Outside patios.
Activities Arts & crafts; Cards; Games; Reading groups; Prayer groups; Movies; Shopping trips; Dances/Social/Cultural gatherings.

Reno

Manor Care Nursing Center
3101 Plumas, Reno, NV 89509
(702) 829-7220
Admin Jane Hirsch.
Licensure Skilled care. *Beds* SNF 120.

Physician's Hospital for Extended Care
2045 Silverada Blvd, Reno, NV 89512
(702) 359-3161
Admin Kathy L Wagner.
Licensure Skilled care. *Beds* SNF 97. *Certified* Medicaid; Medicare.

Reno Healthcare
1300 Mill St, Reno, NV 89502
(702) 786-1933
Admin Patricia Cornelson.
Licensure Skilled care. *Beds* SNF 119. *Certified* Medicaid; Medicare.
Owner Proprietary corp (Hillhaven Corp).

Riverside Hospital Skilled Care
2865 Idlewild Dr, Reno, NV 89509
(702) 329-0691
Admin Donna Santini. *Dir of Nursing* Harriet Beaman. *Medical Dir* Grant Anderson MD.
Licensure Skilled care. *Beds* SNF 182. *Certified* Medicaid; Medicare.
Owner Privately owned.
Admissions Requirements Physician's request.
Facilities Dining room; Physical therapy room; Activities room; Laundry room; Barber/Beauty shop.
Activities Arts & crafts; Cards; Games; Reading groups; Prayer groups; Movies; Shopping trips; Dances/Social/Cultural gatherings.

Sparks

Hearthstone of Northern Nevada
1950 Baring Blvd, Sparks, NV 89431
(702) 359-2244
Admin Dean Lillis.
Licensure Skilled care. *Beds* SNF 120. *Certified* Medicaid; Medicare.

Sierra Developmental Center
605 S 21st St, Sparks, NV 89431
(702) 359-6100
Admin David E Luke. *Dir of Nursing* Janice Young RN. *Medical Dir* Dr David Koroshec.
Licensure Intermediate care for mentally retarded. *Beds* ICF/MR 84. *Certified* Medicaid.
Owner Publicly owned.
Staff RNs 5 (ft); LPNs 6 (ft); Physical therapists 1 (ft); Recreational therapists 1 (ft); Occupational therapists 1 (ft); Speech therapists 1 (ft); Activities coordinators 1 (ft); Dietitians 1 (ft).
Languages Sign.

Sierra Health Care Center
1835 Oddie Blvd, Sparks, NV 89431
(702) 359-5420
Admin Tom W Morton.
Licensure Skilled care. *Beds* SNF 145. *Certified* Medicaid; Medicare.

Washoe Care Center
1375 Baring Blvd, Sparks, NV 89431
(702) 356-2707
Admin Jeanne M Stone. *Dir of Nursing* Genny Dixon RN. *Medical Dir* Dr J Forsythe.
Licensure Skilled care. *Beds* SNF 129. *Certified* Medicaid; Medicare.
Owner Proprietary corp.
Admissions Requirements Physician's request.
Staff Physicians 1 (ft); RNs 12 (ft); LPNs 10 (ft); Nurses' aides 30 (ft), 2 (pt); Physical therapists 1 (ft), 2 (pt); Speech therapists 1 (pt); Activities coordinators 1 (ft); Dietitians 1 (ft).
Facilities Dining room; Physical therapy room; Activities room; Laundry room; Barber/Beauty shop.
Activities Arts & crafts; Reading groups; Movies; Dances/Social/Cultural gatherings.

Tonopah

Nye Regional Medical Center
PO Box 391, 825 Erie Main, Tonopah, NV 89049
(702) 482-6233

Admin Richard L Kilburn. *Dir of Nursing* Elizabeth Deweese RN. *Medical Dir* Gerald Peterson DO.
Licensure Skilled care. *Beds* SNF 24. *Certified* Medicaid; Medicare.
Owner Publicly owned.
Admissions Requirements Physician's request.
Staff Physicians 1 (ft); RNs 3 (ft); LPNs 3 (ft); Nurses' aides 10 (ft); Activities coordinators 1 (ft); Dietitians 1 (pt).
Languages Spanish.
Facilities Dining room; Activities room; Crafts room; Laundry room.
Activities Arts & crafts; Cards; Games; Reading groups; Movies; Dances/Social/Cultural gatherings.

Winnemucca

Humboldt General Hospital
118 E Haskell St, Winnemucca, NV 89445
(702) 623-5222
Admin Joyce Neary RN PhD. *Dir of Nursing* Judy Albertson RN. *Medical Dir* Jeffrey W Lovett MD.
Licensure Skilled care. *Beds* SNF 14. *Private Pay Patients* 20%. *Certified* Medicaid; Medicare.
Owner Publicly owned.
Admissions Requirements Physician's request.
Staff Physicians 2 (ft); RNs 3 (ft); LPNs 4 (ft); Nurses' aides 8 (ft); Physical therapists 1 (pt); Recreational therapists 1 (pt); Occupational therapists 1 (pt); Activities coordinators 1 (pt); Dietitians 1 (pt); Ophthalmologists 1 (pt); Podiatrists 1 (pt); Audiologists 1 (pt); Dentists 1 (pt).
Languages Basque, Spanish.
Facilities Dining room; Activities room; Crafts room; Laundry room; Barber/Beauty shop; Library; Solarium.
Activities Arts & crafts; Cards; Games; Movies; Shopping trips; Dances/Social/Cultural gatherings; Intergenerational programs; Hospital auxiliary.

Yerington

South Lyon Community Hospital
PO Box 940, Surprise at Whitacre, Yerington, NV 89447
(702) 463-2301
Admin Grange E Eaves.
Licensure Skilled care. *Beds* SNF 30. *Certified* Medicaid; Medicare.

NEW HAMPSHIRE

Bedford

McKerley Health Care Bedford—Ridgewood
25 Ridgewood Rd, Bedford, NH 03102
(603) 623-8805
Admin John Metcalf. *Dir of Nursing* Margaret
 J Walker RN MBA. *Medical Dir* Rapheal
 Farra.
Licensure Alzheimer's care; Intermediate care.
 Beds ICF 150. *Private Pay Patients* 35%.
 Certified Medicaid.
Owner Proprietary corp (McKerley
 Management Services).
Staff RNs 15 (ft), 6 (pt); LPNs 8 (ft), 3 (pt);
 Nurses' aides 52 (ft), 12 (pt); Physical
 therapists 1 (pt); Occupational therapists 1
 (pt); Speech therapists 1 (pt); Activities
 coordinators 2 (ft), 1 (pt); Dietitians 1 (pt);
 Podiatrists 1 (pt).
Languages French.
Facilities Dining room; Physical therapy
 room; Activities room; Crafts room; Barber/
 Beauty shop; Library.
Activities Arts & crafts; Cards; Games;
 Reading groups; Prayer groups; Movies;
 Shopping trips; Dances/Social/Cultural
 gatherings; Intergenerational programs; Pet
 therapy; Sunshine group.

McKerley Health Care Center—Donald Street
480 Donald St, Bedford, NH 03102
(603) 627-4147
Admin Judith B Morton. *Dir of Nursing*
 Donna Guillemette. *Medical Dir* Dr William
 Heslin.
Licensure Intermediate care; Alzheimer's care.
 Beds ICF 102. *Private Pay Patients* 35%.
 Certified Medicaid.
Owner Proprietary corp (McKerley Health
 Care Inc).
Admissions Requirements Medical
 examination.
Staff RNs 6 (ft), 3 (pt); LPNs 8 (ft), 2 (pt);
 Nurses' aides 36 (ft), 4 (pt); Activities
 coordinators 2 (ft); Dietitians 1 (pt).
Languages French.
Facilities Dining room; Activities room;
 Chapel; Crafts room; Laundry room; Barber/
 Beauty shop.
Activities Arts & crafts; Cards; Games;
 Reading groups; Prayer groups; Movies;
 Shopping trips; Dances/Social/Cultural
 gatherings; Intergenerational programs; Pet
 therapy.

Berlin

Coos County Nursing Home
PO Box 416, Cates Hill Rd, Berlin, NH 03570
(603) 752-2343
Admin Paul Kaminski.
Licensure Intermediate care. *Beds* ICF 100.
 Certified Medicaid.

St Vincent de Paul Nursing Home
29 Providence Ave, Berlin, NH 03570
(603) 752-1820

Admin Sr Lorraine Boyer. *Dir of Nursing*
 Priscila Gazey RN. *Medical Dir* Dr Norman
 Couture.
Licensure Intermediate care. *Beds* ICF 80.
 Private Pay Patients 18%. *Certified*
 Medicaid.
Owner Nonprofit corp.
Admissions Requirements Minimum age 65;
 Physician's request.
Staff Physicians; RNs; LPNs; Nurses' aides;
 Physical therapists; Reality therapists;
 Recreational therapists; Occupational
 therapists; Speech therapists; Activities
 coordinators; Dietitians; Ophthalmologists;
 Podiatrists; Audiologists.
Languages French.
Facilities Dining room; Physical therapy
 room; Activities room; Chapel; Crafts room;
 Laundry room; Barber/Beauty shop; Library.
Activities Arts & crafts; Cards; Games;
 Reading groups; Prayer groups; Movies;
 Dances/Social/Cultural gatherings.

Boscawen

Merrimack County Nursing Home
RFD 14 Box 338, Boscawen, NH 03301
(603) 796-2165
Admin Howard Teaf.
Licensure Intermediate care. *Beds* ICF 312.
 Certified Medicaid.
Owner Publicly owned.

Center Ossipee

Ossipee Group Home
RR 1 Box 108, Moultonville Rd, Center
 Ossipee, NH 03814
(603) 539-4274
Admin Sandy Boothby RN.
Medical Dir Daniel Melville MD.
Licensure Intermediate care for mentally
 retarded. *Beds* ICF/MR 8. *Certified*
 Medicaid.
Owner Nonprofit organization/foundation.
Admissions Requirements Minimum age 21;
 Medical examination.
Staff Physicians 1 (pt); RNs 2 (ft); LPNs 4
 (pt); Physical therapists 1 (pt); Occupational
 therapists 1 (pt); Speech therapists 1 (pt);
 Program managers 6- 8 (ft), 2 (pt); Program
 coordinators 2 (ft).
Languages Sign.
Facilities Dining room; Physical therapy
 room; Activities room; Laundry room;
 Living room; Enclosed yard and patio.
Activities Arts & crafts; Cards; Games;
 Movies; Shopping trips; Dances/Social/
 Cultural gatherings; Beach trips.

Charleston

Charleston Group Home
RR 2 Box 60, Charleston, NH 03603
(603) 542-8706
Admin Kevin Cooney.

Licensure Intermediate care for mentally
 retarded. *Beds* ICF/MR 10. *Certified*
 Medicaid.

Chester

Jodoin Home
RFD 1, Box 45, Chester, NH 03036
(603) 483-5508
Admin Anita Jodoin.
Licensure Skilled care. *Beds* 4.

Chichester

King Road ICF
RFD 10 Box 938, Chichester, NH 03301
(603) 798-4745
Admin Timothy Sullivan.
Licensure Intermediate care for mentally
 retarded. *Beds* ICF/MR 6. *Certified*
 Medicaid.

Claremont

Beech Street ICF/MR
RFD 3 Box 305, 135 Beech St, Claremont,
 NH 03743
(603) 542-8706, 863-9160, 542-2729 FAX
Admin Kevin Cooney, Exec Dir; Sandra
 Harris, ICF/MR Svcs Dir. *Dir of Nursing*
 Kathleen Hemingway RN. *Medical Dir* Dr
 Timothy Wolfe.
Licensure Intermediate care for mentally
 retarded; Alzheimer's care. *Beds* ICF/MR 8.
 Private Pay Patients 0%. *Certified* Medicaid;
 Medicare.
Owner Nonprofit organization/foundation.
Staff Physicians 1 (pt); RNs 1 (pt); LPNs 1
 (ft), 1 (pt); Physical therapists (contracted);
 Occupational therapists (contracted); Speech
 therapists (contracted); Dietitians
 (contracted).
Activities Arts & crafts; Games; Reading
 groups; Prayer groups; Shopping trips;
 Dances/Social/Cultural gatherings;
 Community integration.

McKerley Health Care Center—Claremont
Hanover St Ext, Claremont, NH 03743
(603) 542-2606, (800) 722-0197
Admin Forrest McKerley. *Dir of Nursing*
 Louella Graham RN.
Licensure Intermediate care. *Beds* ICF 56.
Owner Proprietary corp (McKerley
 Management Services).
Admissions Requirements Medical
 examination; Physician's request.
Staff Physicians 4 (pt); RNs 12 (pt); LPNs 12
 (pt); Nurses' aides 14 (pt); Physical
 therapists 1 (pt); Occupational therapists 1
 (pt); Speech therapists 1 (pt); Activities
 coordinators 1 (pt); Dietitians 1 (pt);
 Ophthalmologists 1 (pt).

Facilities Dining room; Laundry room;
Barber/Beauty shop.
Activities Arts & crafts; Games; Prayer groups;
Movies; Dances/Social/Cultural gatherings;
Bingo.

Sullivan County Nursing Home
RFD 1, Claremont, NH 03743
(603) 542-9511
Admin Diane H Pappalardo. Dir of Nursing
Judith B Brogen RN. Medical Dir Richard
Hutchins MD.
Licensure Intermediate care; Retirement;
Alzheimer's care. Beds ICF 188. Certified
Medicaid.
Owner Publicly owned.
Admissions Requirements Medical
examination; Physician's request.
Staff Physicians 2 (pt); RNs 9 (ft), 3 (pt);
LPNs 5 (ft), 5 (pt); Nurses' aides 48 (ft), 20
(pt); Recreational therapists 1 (ft); Activities
coordinators 1 (ft); Dietitians 1 (pt); RPTAs
2 (ft); COTAs 1 (pt).
Languages French.
Facilities Dining room; Physical therapy
room; Activities room; Crafts room; Laundry
room; Barber/Beauty shop; Library;
Courtyard.
Activities Arts & crafts; Cards; Games;
Reading groups; Prayer groups; Movies;
Shopping trips; Dances/Social/Cultural
gatherings.

Concord

Havenwood-Heritage Heights
33 Christian Ave, Concord, NH 03301
(603) 224-5364
Admin Bruce T Edwards. Dir of Nursing
Frankie Pugh.
Licensure Skilled care; Intermediate care;
Retirement. Beds SNF 10; ICF 48;
Retirement 454. Private Pay Patients 80%.
Certified Medicaid; Medicare.
Owner Nonprofit corp.
Admissions Requirements Minimum age 62;
Medical examination.
Staff RNs 11 (ft), 5 (pt); LPNs 5 (ft), 1 (pt);
Nurses' aides 21 (ft), 7 (pt); Activities
coordinators 3 (ft); Dietitians 1 (ft); RNs
(consultant); LPNs (consultant); Nurses aides
(consultant).
Affiliation United Church of Christ.
Facilities Dining room; Physical therapy
room; Activities room; Chapel; Crafts room;
Laundry room; Barber/Beauty shop; Library.
Activities Arts & crafts; Cards; Games;
Reading groups; Prayer groups; Movies;
Shopping trips; Dances/Social/Cultural
gatherings.

McKerley Nursing Home
PO Box 2012, 20 Maitland St, Concord, NH
03301
(603) 224-6561
Admin Warren E Lapham. Dir of Nursing
Joyce Hubbard. Medical Dir Randy Hayes;
Gary Sobelson.
Licensure Intermediate care. Beds ICF 201.
Certified Medicaid.
Owner Proprietary corp (McKerley Health
Care Centers).
Staff RNs; LPNs; Nurses' aides; Recreational
therapists; Activities coordinators.
Facilities Dining room; Physical therapy
room; Activities room; Chapel; Crafts room;
Barber/Beauty shop; Library.
Activities Arts & crafts; Cards; Games;
Reading groups; Prayer groups; Movies;
Dances/Social/Cultural gatherings;
Intergenerational programs; Pet therapy.

New Hampshire Centennial Home for the Aged
96 Pleasant St, Concord, NH 03301
(603) 225-2021
Admin Arthur Bruemmer.
Licensure Home for aged; Life care. Beds 45.
Owner Nonprofit corp.

Admissions Requirements Minimum age 65;
Females only; Medical examination.
Facilities Dining room; Laundry room;
Barber/Beauty shop; Library.

New Hampshire Odd Fellows Home
200 Pleasant St, Concord, NH 03301
(603) 225-6644
Admin Leslie O Sherman. Dir of Nursing
Kathleen Nickerson. Medical Dir Louis E
Rosenthal MD; Daniel Eubank MD.
Licensure Intermediate care; Sheltered care;
Alzheimer's care; Retirement. Beds ICF 49;
Sheltered care 71. Private Pay Patients 50%.
Certified Medicaid.
Owner Nonprofit corp.
Admissions Requirements Medical
examination.
Staff RNs 5 (ft), 30 (pt); LPNs 3 (ft); Nurses'
aides 25 (ft), 10 (pt); Physical therapists
(contracted); Activities coordinators 1 (ft), 3
(pt); Dietitians.
Affiliation Independent Order of Odd Fellows
& Rebekahs.
Facilities Dining room; Physical therapy
room; Activities room; Crafts room; Laundry
room; Barber/Beauty shop; Library.
Activities Arts & crafts; Cards; Games;
Reading groups; Prayer groups; Movies;
Shopping trips; Dances/Social/Cultural
gatherings; Intergenerational programs; Pet
therapy; Pleasure trips.

Derry

McKerley Health Care Center—Derry
PO Box 1329, 8 Peabody Rd, Derry, NH
03038
(603) 434-1566
Admin Stephen Main.
Licensure Intermediate care. Beds ICF 100.
Owner Proprietary corp (McKerley
Management Services).

Derry Village

Birchwood Nursing Home
20 Chester Rd, Derry Village, NH 03103
(603) 432-3801
Admin Carol A Morrison.
Licensure Intermediate care. Beds ICF 52.
Certified Medicaid.

Dover

Dover House Healthcare
307 Plaza Dr, Dover, NH 03820
(603) 742-2676
Admin Kuder Kuann. Dir of Nursing Kate
Rockey. Medical Dir Vito Molori MD.
Licensure Skilled care; Intermediate care. Beds
Swing beds SNF/ICF 102. Certified
Medicaid; Medicare.
Owner Proprietary corp (Hillhaven Corp).
Admissions Requirements Medical
examination.
Staff RNs; LPNs; Nurses' aides; Physical
therapists; Recreational therapists; Activities
coordinators; Dietitians.
Facilities Dining room; Physical therapy
room; Activities room; Chapel; Crafts room;
Laundry room; Barber/Beauty shop; Library.
Activities Arts & crafts; Cards; Games;
Reading groups; Prayer groups; Movies;
Shopping trips; Dances/Social/Cultural
gatherings.

Riverside Rest Home
6th St Ext, Dover, NH 03820
(603) 742-1348
Admin Raymond F Bower. Dir of Nursing
Daralyn Stewart RN. Medical Dir Dr
Lawrence Sanders.
Licensure Intermediate care; Alzheimer's care;
Specialized ICF. Beds ICF 205; Alzheimer's
care 41; Specialized ICF 41. Private Pay
Patients 2%. Certified Medicaid.

Owner Nonprofit organization/foundation.
Admissions Requirements Medical
examination; Physician's request.
Staff Physicians 3 (pt); RNs 15 (ft), 8 (pt);
LPNs 6 (ft), 6 (pt); Nurses' aides 90 (ft), 20
(pt); Physical therapists (consultant);
Occupational therapists 1 (ft); Speech
therapists; Activities coordinators 1 (ft);
Dietitians 1 (pt); Ophthalmologists;
Podiatrists; Audiologists.
Languages French.
Facilities Dining room; Physical therapy
room; Activities room; Chapel; Crafts room;
Laundry room; Barber/Beauty shop.
Activities Arts & crafts; Cards; Games;
Reading groups; Prayer groups; Movies;
Shopping trips; Dances/Social/Cultural
gatherings; Intergenerational programs; Pet
therapy.

St Ann Home
195 Dover Point Rd, Dover, NH 03820
(603) 742-2612, 743-3055 FAX
Admin Sr Margaret Therese. Dir of Nursing Sr
Winifred Jordan. Medical Dir Dr Peter
Lampesis.
Licensure Intermediate care. Beds ICF 53.
Private Pay Patients 33%. Certified
Medicaid.
Owner Nonprofit organization/foundation.
Admissions Requirements Minimum age 65.
Staff Physicians 1 (pt); RNs 2 (ft), 4 (pt);
LPNs 7 (ft), 1 (pt); Nurses' aides 26 (ft), 9
(pt); Physical therapists 1 (pt); Recreational
therapists 2 (ft); Occupational therapists 1
(pt); Dietitians 1 (pt).
Facilities Dining room; Physical therapy
room; Activities room; Chapel; Laundry
room; Barber/Beauty shop.
Activities Arts & crafts; Cards; Games; Prayer
groups; Movies; Shopping trips.

Wentworth Home for the Aged
795 Central Ave, Dover, NH 03820
(603) 742-1915
Admin Mary Jane Allen.
Licensure Skilled care. Beds 36.

East Rochester

Highland Street
43 Highland St, East Rochester, NH 03867
(603) 332-2070
Admin Timothy Sullivan.
Licensure Intermediate care for mentally
retarded. Beds ICF/MR 6. Certified
Medicaid.

Epping

Rockingham County Nursing Home
PO Box 427, Epping, NH 03042
(603) 679-5335, 679-1843 FAX
Admin William F Sturtevant. Dir of Nursing
Joan Skinner. Medical Dir Karl Singer.
Licensure Intermediate care; Adult day health
care. Beds ICF 290. Certified Medicaid.
Owner Publicly owned.
Admissions Requirements Medical
examination.
Staff Physicians 4 (pt); RNs 34 (ft); LPNs 29
(ft); Nurses' aides 150 (ft); Physical
therapists 1 (ft), 1 (pt); Recreational
therapists 3 (ft); Occupational therapists 1
(ft); Speech therapists 1 (pt); Activities
coordinators 2 (ft); Dietitians 1 (ft);
Ophthalmologists 1 (pt); Podiatrists 1 (pt);
Audiologists 1 (pt).
Facilities Dining room; Physical therapy
room; Activities room; Chapel; Crafts room;
Laundry room; Barber/Beauty shop; Library;
Snack bar; Speech therapy room; Dental
office.
Activities Arts & crafts; Cards; Games;
Reading groups; Prayer groups; Movies;
Shopping trips; Dances/Social/Cultural
gatherings; Bingo; Cocktail parties; Picnics.

Epsom

Epsom Manor
RR 2 Box 107, Epsom, NH 03234
(603) 736-4772
Admin Lynn G Guenther. *Dir of Nursing*
Carole Dionne. *Medical Dir* Robert
Boynton.
Licensure Intermediate care; Retirement. *Beds*
ICF 108; Retirement 60. *Private Pay
Patients* 20%. *Certified* Medicaid.
Owner Proprietary corp (Lemire Enterprises).
Admissions Requirements Medical
examination.
Staff RNs; LPNs; Nurses' aides; Activities
coordinators 1 (ft); Dietitians 1 (pt).
Languages French.
Facilities Dining room; Activities room;
Laundry room; Barber/Beauty shop.
Activities Arts & crafts; Cards; Games;
Reading groups; Prayer groups; Movies; Pet
therapy.

Exeter

Eventide Home Inc
81 High St, Exeter, NH 03833
(603) 772-5743
Admin Sandra Cross. *Dir of Nursing* Eleese
Conroy.
Licensure Intermediate care. *Beds* ICF 19.
Certified Medicaid.
Owner Nonprofit corp.
Admissions Requirements Minimum age 65;
Females only; Medical examination.
Staff RNs 3 (ft), 3 (pt); LPNs 2 (pt); Nurses'
aides 3 (ft), 3 (pt); Activities coordinators 1
(pt); Dietitians 1 (pt).
Facilities Dining room; Activities room;
Barber/Beauty shop; Library.
Activities Arts & crafts; Cards; Games;
Reading groups; Shopping trips.

Exeter Healthcare Inc
131 Court St, Exeter, NH 03833
(603) 778-1668
Admin Frances Comeau.
Medical Dir Suzanne Robinson.
Licensure Skilled care; Intermediate care. *Beds*
SNF 100; ICF 15. *Certified* Medicaid;
Medicare.
Owner Nonprofit corp.
Admissions Requirements Medical
examination.
Staff RNs 7 (ft), 3 (pt); LPNs 9 (ft), 7 (pt);
Nurses' aides; Physical therapists 1 (ft);
Occupational therapists 1 (pt); Speech
therapists 1 (pt); Activities coordinators;
Dietitians; Ophthalmologists 1 (pt).
Facilities Dining room; Physical therapy
room; Activities room; Chapel; Crafts room;
Laundry room; Barber/Beauty shop; Library;
Family room for personal gatherings for such
occasions as birthdays & anniversaries.
Activities Arts & crafts; Cards; Games;
Reading groups; Prayer groups; Movies;
Shopping trips; Dances/Social/Cultural
gatherings; Monthly birthday parties; Weekly
teas; Dietary specials; Bingo; Cooking;
Canning.

Goodwin's of Exeter
8 Hampton Rd, Exeter, NH 03833
(603) 788-0531
Admin Maria L Horn.
Licensure Intermediate care. *Beds* ICF 81.
Certified Medicaid.

Franconia

McKerley Health Care Center—Franconia
148 Main St, Franconia, NH 03580
(603) 823-5502
Admin Priscilla Woodward. *Dir of Nursing*
Linda M Keller RN.
Licensure Intermediate care. *Beds* ICF 62.
Certified Medicaid.

Owner Proprietary corp (Beverly Enterprises).
Admissions Requirements Minimum age 18;
Physician's request.
Staff Physicians; RNs; LPNs; Nurses' aides;
Physical therapists; Occupational therapists;
Speech therapists; Activities coordinators;
Dietitians; Ophthalmologists.
Facilities Dining room; Physical therapy
room; Activities room; Laundry room;
Barber/Beauty shop.
Activities Arts & crafts; Games; Reading
groups; Prayer groups; Movies; Dances/
Social/Cultural gatherings.

Franklin

Mt Ridge Health Care Center Inc
244 Pleasant St, Franklin, NH 03235
(603) 934-2541
Admin Thomas P Matzke.
Licensure Intermediate care. *Beds* ICF 86.
Certified Medicaid.

Peabody Home
24 Peabody Pl, Franklin, NH 03235
(603) 934-3718
Admin Arthur W Swenson. *Dir of Nursing*
Ann Combs.
Licensure Intermediate care; Retirement. *Beds*
ICF 29; Retirement 20.
Owner Nonprofit organization/foundation.
Admissions Requirements Medical
examination; Physician's request.
Facilities Dining room; Activities room;
Crafts room; Laundry room; Barber/Beauty
shop; Library.
Activities Arts & crafts; Cards; Games;
Reading groups; Movies; Shopping trips;
Intergenerational programs; Pet therapy.

Sunny Knoll Retirement Home Inc
221 Victory Dr, Franklin, NH 03235
(603) 934-5447
Admin Donna Holden.
Medical Dir Donna Holden.
Licensure Sheltered care; Alzheimer's care.
Beds 35. *Certified* Medicare.
Owner Proprietary corp.
Admissions Requirements Medical
examination; Physician's request.
Staff Physicians; RNs; Nurses' aides;
Activities coordinators; Dietitians.
Facilities Dining room; Activities room;
Laundry room; Barber/Beauty shop; Library.
Activities Arts & crafts; Cards; Games;
Reading groups; Prayer groups; Movies;
Shopping trips; Dances/Social/Cultural
gatherings.

Fremont

Colonial Poplin Nursing Home
Rte 107, Main St, Fremont, NH 03044
(603) 895-3126
Admin Elizabeth E Goff.
Licensure Skilled care; Intermediate care. *Beds*
SNF 18; ICF 50.

Goffstown

Bel-Air Nursing Home
19 Center St, Goffstown, NH 03045
(603) 497-4871
Admin Ellen Mitchell.
Medical Dir Rota Krape.
Licensure Intermediate care. *Beds* ICF 32.
Certified Medicaid.
Owner Privately owned.
Staff RNs 2 (ft), 1 (pt); LPNs 1 (ft), 2 (pt);
Nurses' aides 7 (ft), 9 (pt); Recreational
therapists 1 (pt).
Languages French.
Facilities Dining room; Laundry room.
Activities Arts & crafts; Cards; Games; Prayer
groups; Movies.

Hillsborough County Nursing Home
400 Mast Rd, Goffstown, NH 03045
(603) 627-5540
Admin Robert Curran. *Dir of Nursing* Emily
Mercier RN. *Medical Dir* Marcel Dupuis
MD.
Licensure Intermediate care; Alzheimer's care.
Beds ICF 300. *Private Pay Patients* 0%.
Certified Medicaid.
Owner Publicly owned.
Admissions Requirements Medical
examination; Physician's request.
Staff Physicians 2 (pt); RNs 43 (ft); LPNs 9
(ft); Nurses' aides 126 (ft); Physical
therapists 1 (ft); Recreational therapists 6
(ft); Activities coordinators 1 (ft); Dietitians
1 (pt); Ophthalmologists 1 (pt); Podiatrists 1
(ft).
Languages French, Greek.
Facilities Dining room; Physical therapy
room; Activities room; Chapel; Crafts room;
Laundry room; Barber/Beauty shop; Library.
Activities Arts & crafts; Cards; Games;
Reading groups; Prayer groups; Movies;
Shopping trips; Dances/Social/Cultural
gatherings; Ceramics; Woodworking; Leather
working; Cooking.

Hampton

Seacoast Health Center Inc
22 Tuck Rd, Hampton, NH 03842
(603) 926-4551
Admin Daniel P Trahan.
Licensure Intermediate care. *Beds* ICF 107.
Certified Medicaid.
Owner Proprietary corp.
Admissions Requirements Physician's request.
Staff RNs 5 (ft); LPNs 10 (ft); Nurses' aides
20 (ft); Recreational therapists 2 (ft);
Activities coordinators 1 (ft); Dietitians 1
(ft).
Facilities Dining room; Activities room;
Crafts room; Laundry room; Barber/Beauty
shop; Gathering rooms.
Activities Arts & crafts; Cards; Games;
Reading groups; Prayer groups; Movies;
Shopping trips; Dances/Social/Cultural
gatherings.

Hanover

Hanover Terrace
Lyme Rd, Hanover, NH 03755
(603) 643-2854
Admin Jean A Raiche. *Dir of Nursing* Barbara
Bruno. *Medical Dir* Dr Joseph Grant.
Licensure Skilled care; Intermediate care;
Independent living. *Beds* SNF 26; ICF 74;
Independent living apartments 28. *Certified*
Medicaid; Medicare.
Owner Proprietary corp (Hillhaven Corp).
Staff Physicians 1 (pt); RNs 7 (ft), 1 (pt);
LPNs 6 (ft), 1 (pt); Nurses' aides 28 (ft);
Physical therapists 1 (pt); Occupational
therapists 1 (ft); Speech therapists 1 (pt);
Activities coordinators 1 (pt); Dietitians 1
(pt); Podiatrists 1 (pt); Audiologists 1 (pt);
Dentists 1 (pt); Social workers 1 (ft); Staff
coordinators 1 (ft).
Facilities Dining room; Physical therapy
room; Activities room; Chapel; Crafts room;
Laundry room; Barber/Beauty shop; Library.
Activities Arts & crafts; Cards; Games;
Reading groups; Movies; Shopping trips;
Dances/Social/Cultural gatherings.

Hillsborough

Hillsboro House Nursing Home
School St, Box 400, Hillsborough, NH 03244
(603) 464-5561
Admin David Irwin.
Licensure Intermediate care. *Beds* ICF 30.
Certified Medicaid.

Hudson

Fairview Nursing Home Inc
203 Lowell Rd, Hudson, NH 03051
(603) 882-5261
Admin Brian Courville.
Medical Dir Peter Hacker MD.
Licensure Intermediate care. *Beds* ICF 101.
Certified Medicaid.
Owner Proprietary corp (Courville
Management).
Admissions Requirements Minimum age 62;
Medical examination.
Staff RNs; LPNs; Nurses' aides; Physical
therapists; Reality therapists; Recreational
therapists; Occupational therapists; Speech
therapists; Activities coordinators; Dietitians.
Facilities Dining room; Physical therapy
room; Activities room; Chapel; Crafts room;
Laundry room; Barber/Beauty shop; Library.
Activities Arts & crafts; Cards; Games;
Reading groups; Prayer groups; Movies;
Shopping trips; Dances/Social/Cultural
gatherings.

Jaffrey

Monadnock Christian Nursing Home
PO Box 410, 5 Plantation Dr, Jaffrey, NH
03452
(603) 532-8762
Admin Joann Hall. *Dir of Nursing* Ursula
S1chribner RN.
Licensure Intermediate care; Alzheimer's care.
Beds ICF 51. *Certified* Medicaid.
Owner Nonprofit corp.
Admissions Requirements Medical
examination; Physician's request.
Staff RNs 6 (ft); LPNs 5 (ft); Nurses' aides 30
(ft); Activities coordinators 1 (ft); Dietitians
1 (pt).
Facilities Dining room; Activities room;
Chapel; Crafts room; Laundry room; Barber/
Beauty shop.
Activities Arts & crafts; Games; Reading
groups; Prayer groups; Movies; Shopping
trips; Dances/Social/Cultural gatherings;
Music; Bingo; Pets.

Keene

Cedarcrest Inc
91 Maple Ave, Keene, NH 03431
(603) 399-4446
Admin Sharon Kaiser RN BS NHA. *Dir of
Nursing* Sharon Kaiser RN. *Medical Dir*
Charles McMurphy MD.
Licensure Intermediate care for mentally
retarded. *Beds* ICF/MR 25. *Private Pay
Patients* 0%. *Certified* Medicaid.
Owner Nonprofit corp.
Admissions Requirements Minimum age birth
to 16 years; Medical examination; Severe or
profound multi-handicaps or physical
handicaps.
Staff Physicians 1 (pt); RNs 2 (ft), 6 (pt);
LPNs 2 (ft), 3 (pt); Nurses' aides 9 (ft), 13
(pt); Physical therapists 2 (pt); Occupational
therapists 1 (pt); Speech therapists 1 (pt);
Activities coordinators 1 (pt); Dietitians 1
(pt); Ophthalmologists 1 (pt); Audiologists 1
(pt); Psychologists 1 (pt); Teachers 5 (ft).
Facilities Dining room; Physical therapy
room; Activities room; Laundry room;
Library; Approved special education school.
Activities Arts & crafts; Movies; Shopping
trips.

McKerley Health Care Center
677 Court St, Keene, NH 03431
(603) 357-3800
Admin Malcolm Perry. *Dir of Nursing*
Meredith Howard RN. *Medical Dir* Dr
Walter Griffith.
Licensure Intermediate care. *Beds* ICF 100.
Private Pay Patients 32%. *Certified*
Medicaid.

Owner Proprietary corp (McKerley Health
Care Inc).
Admissions Requirements Medical
examination; Physician's request.
Staff RNs 5 (ft); LPNs 14 (ft), 4 (pt); Nurses'
aides 34 (ft), 16 (pt); Physical therapists
(consultant); Activities coordinators 2 (ft).
Facilities Dining room; Physical therapy
room; Activities room; Laundry room;
Barber/Beauty shop.
Activities Arts & crafts; Games; Reading
groups; Prayer groups; Movies; Shopping
trips; Dances/Social/Cultural gatherings;
Intergenerational programs; Pet therapy.

One-Eighty Court Nursing Home
180 Court St, Keene, NH 03431
(603) 352-7400
Admin Mary Lund.
Licensure Intermediate care. *Beds* ICF 15.
Owner Proprietary corp.
Staff RNs 3 (ft), 2 (pt); LPNs 2 (ft), 3 (pt);
Nurses' aides 4 (ft), 4 (pt).

Prospect Hill Home
361 Court St, Keene, NH 03431
(603) 352-0323
Admin Mary-Lou Hodgdon.
Licensure Skilled care. *Beds* 20.

Thirty-Nine Summer Nursing Home
39 Summer St, Keene, NH 03431
(603) 352-7117
Admin Earl Lund.
Licensure Intermediate care. *Beds* ICF 12.
Owner Proprietary corp.
Staff RNs 2 (ft), 3 (pt); LPNs 2 (ft), 2 (pt);
Nurses' aides 4 (ft), 4 (pt).

Westwood Healthcare Center
298 Main St, Keene, NH 03431
(603) 352-7311
Admin Jamie Pipher.
Licensure Intermediate care. *Beds* ICF 87.
Certified Medicaid.

Laconia

Belknap County Nursing Home
1152 N Main St, Laconia, NH 03246
(603) 524-4048
Admin Donald D Drouin Sr NHA. *Dir of
Nursing* Kathleen M Lord RN C. *Medical
Dir* Lawrence P Zyskowski MD.
Licensure Intermediate care. *Beds* ICF 85.
Certified Medicaid.
Owner Publicly owned.
Admissions Requirements Medical
examination; Physician's request.
Staff Physicians 1 (pt); RNs 21 (ft), 3 (pt);
LPNs 6 (ft), 2 (pt); Nurses' aides 46 (ft), 4
(pt); Physical therapists 1 (pt); Recreational
therapists 1 (pt); Occupational therapists 1
(pt); Speech therapists 1 (pt); Activities
coordinators 1 (ft), 3 (pt); Dietitians 1 (ft).
Languages French.
Facilities Dining room; Physical therapy
room; Activities room; Chapel; Crafts room;
Laundry room; Barber/Beauty shop; Outdoor
recreational area with level concrete
walkways, picnic tables, gazebo, stage, gas-
operated grill.
Activities Arts & crafts; Cards; Games;
Reading groups; Prayer groups; Movies;
Shopping trips; Dances/Social/Cultural
gatherings; Intergenerational programs; Pet
therapy; Cookouts.

McKerley Health Care Center—Laconia
175 Blueberry Ln, Laconia, NH 03246
(603) 524-3340
Admin Daniel Estee.
Licensure Intermediate care. *Beds* ICF 108.
Certified Medicaid.
Owner Proprietary corp (McKerley
Management Services).

St Francis Home
PO Box 1699, Court St, Laconia, NH 03246
(603) 524-0466
Admin Julieann R Fay. *Dir of Nursing* Claire
Falardeau RN. *Medical Dir* E C Squires
MD.
Licensure Intermediate care; Retirement. *Beds*
ICF 51. *Certified* Medicaid.
Owner Nonprofit corp.
Admissions Requirements Minimum age 65;
Medical examination.
Staff Physicians 1 (ft); RNs 4 (ft), 5 (pt);
LPNs 2 (ft), 1 (pt); Nurses' aides 21 (ft), 2
(pt); Physical therapists 1 (ft); Speech
therapists 1 (ft); Activities coordinators 1
(ft); Dietitians 1 (ft); Ophthalmologists 1
(ft); Dentists 1 (ft).
Languages French.
Affiliation Roman Catholic.
Facilities Dining room; Physical therapy
room; Activities room; Chapel; Laundry
room; Barber/Beauty shop; Lounge; Coffee
shop.
Activities Arts & crafts; Cards; Games;
Reading groups; Prayer groups; Movies;
Shopping trips; Dances/Social/Cultural
gatherings; Ceramics.

Taylor Home
435 Union Ave, Laconia, NH 03246
(603) 524-3409
Admin Howard Chandler.
Licensure Skilled care. *Beds* 42.

Lancaster

Country Village Health Care Center
24 N Main St, Lancaster, NH 03584
(603) 788-4735
Admin Kirt D Sampson. *Dir of Nursing* Ruth
Meek.
Licensure Intermediate care; Retirement. *Beds*
ICF 86. *Certified* Medicaid.
Owner Proprietary corp (McKerley
Management Services).
Admissions Requirements Medical
examination.
Staff Physicians 8 (pt); RNs 6 (ft), 4 (pt);
LPNs 2 (ft), 2 (pt); Nurses' aides 15 (ft), 10
(pt); Physical therapists 1 (pt); Occupational
therapists 1 (pt); Speech therapists 1 (pt);
Activities coordinators 1 (ft); Dietitians 1
(pt); Dentists 1 (pt).
Facilities Dining room; Physical therapy
room; Activities room; Chapel; Crafts room;
Laundry room; Barber/Beauty shop.
Activities Arts & crafts; Cards; Games;
Reading groups; Prayer groups; Movies;
Shopping trips; Dances/Social/Cultural
gatherings.

Lebanon

McKerley Health Care Center—Lebanon
Etna Rd 1, Box 131K, Lebanon, NH 03766
(603) 448-2234
Admin James P McKerley. *Dir of Nursing* Jo
West RN.
Licensure Intermediate care. *Beds* ICF 110.
Certified Medicare.
Owner Proprietary corp (Lemire Enterprises).
Admissions Requirements Physician's request.
Staff RNs 5 (ft); LPNs 13 (ft); Nurses' aides
50 (ft); Physical therapists 1 (pt);
Recreational therapists 2 (ft); Activities
coordinators 1 (ft); Dietitians 1 (pt).
Facilities Dining room; Physical therapy
room; Activities room; Barber/Beauty shop.
Activities Arts & crafts; Cards; Games;
Reading groups; Dances/Social/Cultural
gatherings.

Littleton

Oak Hill Residence
8 Oak Hill Ave, Littleton, NH 03561
(603) 444-5590
Admin Bryon & Rita Cascadden.
Beds 4.
Owner Privately owned.
Languages French.

Lyme

Orford Road Residence
PO Box 267, Rte 10, Lyme, NH 03768
(603) 795-4893
Admin Raymond Rusin, Dir. *Dir of Nursing*
Mary Lou Baker RN. *Medical Dir* Elaine
Himadi MD.
Licensure Intermediate care for mentally
retarded. *Beds* ICF/MR 10. *Certified*
Medicaid.
Owner Nonprofit corp (United Developmental
Services).
Admissions Requirements Minimum age 21;
Medical examination; Physician's request.
Staff Physicians 1 (pt); RNs 2 (ft); LPNs 2
(ft), 1 (pt); Nurses' aides 13 (ft), 1 (pt);
Physical therapists (consultant);
Occupational therapists (consultant); Speech
therapists (consultant); Activities
coordinators 1 (ft); Dietitians (consultant);
Therapy assistants; Developmental
specialists.
Facilities Dining room; Physical therapy
room; Activities room; Laundry room.
Activities Arts & crafts; Games; Reading
groups; Movies; Shopping trips; Dances/
Social/Cultural gatherings.

Manchester

Gale Home
133 Ash St, Manchester, NH 03104
(603) 622-6632
Admin Joan E Wright.
Medical Dir Dr Gregory White.
Licensure Intermediate care. *Beds* ICF 24.
Certified Medicaid.
Admissions Requirements Females only;
Medical examination.
Staff Physicians; RNs 2 (ft), 2 (pt); LPNs 2
(ft), 1 (pt); Nurses' aides 3 (ft), 5 (pt);
Physical therapists; Reality therapists;
Recreational therapists 1 (pt); Occupational
therapists; Speech therapists; Dietitians 3
(ft); Ophthalmologists; Dentists.
Facilities Dining room; Physical therapy
room; Activities room; Crafts room; Laundry
room; Barber/Beauty shop.
Activities Arts & crafts; Cards; Games; Prayer
groups; Movies; Shopping trips; Weekly
entertainment.

Hackett Hill Nursing Center
191 Hackett Hill Rd, Manchester, NH 03102
(603) 668-8161
Admin Alain Bernard.
Medical Dir Meg Welch.
Licensure Sheltered care; Alzheimer's care.
Beds Sheltered care 68.
Owner Proprietary corp (McKerley Health
Care Center).
Staff RNs 2 (ft), 5 (pt); LPNs 4 (ft), 6 (pt);
Nurses' aides 20 (ft), 16 (pt); Recreational
therapists 1 (ft); Activities coordinators 1
(ft); Dietitians 1 (ft).
Facilities Dining room; Activities room;
Crafts room; Laundry room; Barber/Beauty
shop; Library.
Activities Arts & crafts; Cards; Games;
Movies; Dances/Social/Cultural gatherings.

Hanover Hill Health Care Center
700 Hanover St, Manchester, NH 03104
(603) 627-3826
Admin Theodore Lee.

Licensure Skilled care; Intermediate care. *Beds*
SNF 118; ICF 6. *Certified* Medicaid;
Medicare.

Mammoth Nursing Home Inc
1 Mammoth Rd, Manchester, NH 03105
(603) 625-9891
Admin Susan Scagnellie.
Licensure Intermediate care. *Beds* ICF 55.
Certified Medicaid.
Owner Proprietary corp (Courville
Management).

Maple Leaf Health Care Center
198 Pearl St, Manchester, NH 03104
(603) 669-1660
Admin Rita Miville.
Licensure Skilled care; Intermediate care. *Beds*
SNF 102; ICF 12. *Certified* Medicaid.
Owner Proprietary corp (Lemire Enterprises).

Maple Leaf Nursing Home
593 Maple St, Manchester, NH 03104
(603) 669-1452
Admin Claire Lemire.
Licensure Intermediate care. *Beds* 63.
Certified Medicaid.

Masonic Home
813 Beech St, Manchester, NH 03104
(603) 669-7361
Admin Rene G Lemire. *Dir of Nursing* Toni
Gray RN DNS.
Licensure Skilled care; Sheltered care with
infirmary; Retirement. *Beds* 52.
Owner Nonprofit corp.
Admissions Requirements Medical
examination; Physician's request.
Staff RNs; LPNs; Nurses' aides; Activities
coordinators; Dietitians; Ophthalmologists.
Affiliation Masons.
Facilities Dining room; Activities room;
Chapel; Crafts room; Laundry room; Barber/
Beauty shop; Library.
Activities Arts & crafts; Cards; Games;
Reading groups; Prayer groups; Movies;
Shopping trips; Bus trips; Barbeques;
Birthday parties.

Mt Carmel Nursing Home
235 Myrtle St, Manchester, NH 03103
(603) 627-3811
Admin Sr Mark Louis. *Dir of Nursing* Sr
Joseph Jude RN. *Medical Dir* Dr Raphael
Farra.
Licensure Intermediate care; Alzheimer's care.
Beds ICF 120. *Private Pay Patients* 20%.
Certified Medicaid.
Owner Nonprofit organization/foundation.
Admissions Requirements Minimum age 65;
Medical examination; Physician's request.
Languages French.
Affiliation Roman Catholic.
Facilities Dining room; Physical therapy
room; Activities room; Chapel; Crafts room;
Laundry room; Barber/Beauty shop; Library.
Activities Arts & crafts; Cards; Games;
Reading groups; Prayer groups; Movies;
Shopping trips; Pet therapy.

Northwood Nursing Home
668 Amherst St, Manchester, NH 03104
(603) 625-6462
Admin Cynthia DuBois.
Licensure Intermediate care. *Beds* ICF 51.
Certified Medicaid.

St Teresa's Manor
519 Bridge St, Manchester, NH 03103
(603) 668-2373
Admin Mary Johnson.
Medical Dir Jonathan Jaffe.
Licensure Intermediate care. *Beds* ICF 51.
Certified Medicaid.

Villa Crest Inc
1276 Hanover St, Manchester, NH 03104
(603) 622-3262
Admin Susan D Lemire-Lacourse.

Licensure Intermediate care. *Beds* ICF 103.
Certified Medicaid.
Owner Proprietary corp (Lemire Enterprises).

Women's Aid Home
180 Pearl St, Manchester, NH 03104
(603) 669-6991
Admin Marjorie Huckabee.
Licensure Skilled care. *Beds* 39.

Meredith

Goldenview Health Care Center
Rte 104, RFD 3 Box 51, Meredith, NH 03253
(603) 279-8111
Admin Jeanne Sanders.
Licensure Intermediate care. *Beds* ICF 100.
Certified Medicaid.
Owner Proprietary corp (Lemire Enterprises).
Admissions Requirements Medical
examination; Physician's request.
Staff RNs; LPNs; Nurses' aides; Physical
therapists; Occupational therapists; Speech
therapists; Activities coordinators; Dietitians.
Facilities Dining room; Physical therapy
room; Activities room; Crafts room; Laundry
room; Barber/Beauty shop.
Activities Arts & crafts; Cards; Games;
Reading groups; Prayer groups; Movies;
Shopping trips; Dances/Social/Cultural
gatherings.

Milford

Crestwood Healthcare Center
18 Crosby St, Milford, NH 03055
(603) 673-7061
Admin Walter J Hozkiwicz.
Licensure Intermediate care. *Beds* ICF 82.
Certified Medicaid; VA.
Owner Proprietary corp (McKerley
Management Services).

Milford Nursing Home
41 Elm St, Milford, NH 03055
(603) 673-2907
Admin Dwight Sowerby.
Licensure Intermediate care. *Beds* ICF 55.
Certified Medicaid.
Owner Proprietary corp (McKerley
Management Services).

Milton

Kraus House
41 Old Wakefield Rd, Milton, NH 03851
(603) 652-9977
Admin Donna Kraus.
Licensure Skilled care. *Beds* 4.

Nashua

Courville at Nashua Inc
22 Hunt St, Nashua, NH 03060
(603) 889-5450
Admin Anitatine Andrade.
Medical Dir Dr John Posner.
Licensure Skilled care; Intermediate care. *Beds*
SNF 50; ICF 50.
Owner Proprietary corp (Courville
Management).
Admissions Requirements Physician's request.
Staff RNs 10 (ft); LPNs 14 (ft); Nurses' aides
26 (ft); Physical therapists 2 (pt);
Recreational therapists 1 (ft); Occupational
therapists 1 (pt); Speech therapists 1 (pt);
Activities coordinators 1 (ft); Dietitians 1
(ft); Dentists 1 (pt).
Facilities Dining room; Physical therapy
room; Activities room; Chapel; Crafts room;
Laundry room; Barber/Beauty shop; Library.
Activities Arts & crafts; Cards; Games;
Reading groups; Prayer groups; Movies;
Shopping trips; Dances/Social/Cultural
gatherings; Current events.

Greenbriar Terrace Healthcare
55 Harris Rd, Nashua, NH 03062
(603) 888-1573
Admin Arthur L O'Leary.
Licensure Skilled care; Intermediate care. *Beds* SNF 25; ICF 275. *Certified* Medicaid; Medicare.
Owner Proprietary corp (Hillhaven Corp).
Admissions Requirements Medical examination.
Languages French.
Facilities Dining room; Physical therapy room; Activities room; Chapel; Crafts room; Laundry room; Barber/Beauty shop; Library.
Activities Arts & crafts; Cards; Games; Reading groups; Prayer groups; Movies; Shopping trips; Dances/Social/Cultural gatherings.

Hunt Community
10 Allds St, Nashua, NH 03060
(603) 882-6511
Admin Christine C Hallock.
Medical Dir Barbara Carey.
Licensure Intermediate care; Independent living; Personal care. *Beds* ICF 40; Level V 75; Personal care 40.
Owner Nonprofit corp.
Admissions Requirements Minimum age 62; Medical examination.
Facilities Dining room; Physical therapy room; Activities room; Chapel; Crafts room; Laundry room; Barber/Beauty shop; Library.
Activities Arts & crafts; Cards; Games; Reading groups; Prayer groups; Movies; Shopping trips; Dances/Social/Cultural gatherings.

Nightingale Home
381 Main St, Nashua, NH 03060
(603) 882-1770
Admin Paul Donnelly.
Licensure Self care. *Beds* Self care 10.

Newport

Greenleaf Properties Inc
84 Pine St, Newport, NH 03773
(603) 863-1020
Admin Prey F Gadway. *Dir of Nursing* May Berner RN. *Medical Dir* Denis T Maryn MD.
Licensure Intermediate care. *Beds* ICF 51. *Certified* Medicaid.
Owner Proprietary corp.
Admissions Requirements Medical examination; Physician's request.
Staff RNs 1 (ft), 4 (pt); LPNs 4 (ft), 2 (pt); Nurses' aides 7 (ft), 16 (pt); Recreational therapists 1 (ft); Activities coordinators 1 (ft); Dietitians 1 (pt).
Facilities Dining room; Activities room; Laundry room; Barber/Beauty shop; Library.
Activities Arts & crafts; Cards; Games; Reading groups; Prayer groups; Movies; Shopping trips; Musical programs.

North Conway

Clipper Home of North Conway
1251 White Mountain Hwy, North Conway, NH 03860
(603) 356-7294
Admin Melinda Coons.
Licensure Intermediate care. *Beds* ICF 98. *Certified* Medicaid.

Merriman House
Memorial Hospital, Intervale Rd, North Conway, NH 03847
(603) 356-5461
Admin Gaye Ekberg RN. *Dir of Nursing* Gaye Ekberg RN. *Medical Dir* Miles Waltz MD.
Licensure Intermediate care; Alzheimer's care; Acute care and skilled care. *Beds* ICF 21. *Private Pay Patients* 50%. *Certified* Medicaid; Medicare.

Owner Nonprofit corp.
Staff Physicians; RNs 2 (ft), 1 (pt); LPNs 3 (ft); Nurses' aides 10 (ft), 2 (pt); Physical therapists 1 (ft); Occupational therapists 1 (pt); Speech therapists 1 (pt); Activities coordinators 1 (pt); Dietitians 1 (pt); Ophthalmologists; Podiatrists; Audiologists.
Facilities Dining room; Physical therapy room; Activities room; Chapel; Crafts room; Laundry room; Barber/Beauty shop; Sun porch; Yard.
Activities Arts & crafts; Cards; Games; Reading groups; Prayer groups; Movies; Shopping trips; Dances/Social/Cultural gatherings; Sight-seeing trips; Restaurant trips; Participation in community's senior center.

Ossipee

Mountain View Nursing Home
Rte 171, Ossipee, NH 03864
(603) 539-7511
Admin Gregory F Froton. *Dir of Nursing* Karen S Swinton RN. *Medical Dir* Gerald Bozuwa MD.
Licensure Intermediate care; Alzheimer's care. *Beds* ICF 103. *Certified* Medicaid.
Owner Publicly owned.
Admissions Requirements Medical examination; Physician's request.
Staff Physicians 1 (pt); RNs 9 (ft); LPNs 10 (ft); Nurses' aides 53 (ft); Physical therapists 1 (ft); Recreational therapists 4 (ft); Activities coordinators 1 (ft), 1 (pt).
Facilities Dining room; Physical therapy room; Activities room; Crafts room; Barber/Beauty shop; 26-bed Alzheimer's unit.
Activities Arts & crafts; Cards; Games; Prayer groups; Movies; Shopping trips; Dances/Social/Cultural gatherings.

Penacook

McKerley Harris Hill Nursing Home
30 Tremont St, Penacook, NH 03303
(603) 753-6551
Admin James P McKerley.
Licensure Intermediate care. *Beds* ICF 50. *Certified* Medicaid.
Owner Proprietary corp (McKerley Management Services).

Peterborough

Pheasant Wood Nursing Home
Pheasant Rd, Peterborough, NH 03458
(603) 924-7267
Admin Zofia Long.
Medical Dir Sylvia St John.
Licensure Intermediate care; Alzheimer's care. *Beds* ICF 101. *Certified* Medicaid.
Owner Proprietary corp.
Staff RNs 4 (ft), 3 (pt); LPNs 12 (ft), 4 (pt); Nurses' aides 35 (ft); Physical therapists 1 (ft); Activities coordinators 1 (ft); Dietitians 1 (ft).
Facilities Dining room; Physical therapy room; Activities room; Laundry room; Barber/Beauty shop.
Activities Arts & crafts; Cards; Games; Reading groups; Movies; Shopping trips; Dances/Social/Cultural gatherings.

Plymouth

Tamarack
PO Box 509, Old Ward Bridge Rd, Plymouth, NH 03247
(603) 536-4589
Admin David Stinson.
Licensure Intermediate care for mentally retarded. *Beds* ICF/MR 6. *Certified* Medicaid.

Portsmouth

Clipper Home of Portsmouth
188 Jones Ave, Portsmouth, NH 03801
(603) 431-2530
Admin Debra Hauser.
Licensure Intermediate care. *Beds* ICF 84. *Certified* Medicaid.

Edgewood Manor
928 South St, Portsmouth, NH 03801
(603) 436-0099
Admin Patricia M Ramsey. *Dir of Nursing* Sharon Plante RN. *Medical Dir* Dr Richard Altenborough.
Licensure Skilled care; Intermediate care. *Beds* SNF 106; ICF 50. *Certified* Medicaid; Medicare; VA.
Owner Proprietary corp.
Staff RNs; LPNs; Nurses' aides; Physical therapists; Recreational therapists; Occupational therapists; Speech therapists; Activities coordinators; Dietitians; Ophthalmologists.
Facilities Dining room; Physical therapy room; Activities room; Chapel; Crafts room; Laundry room; Barber/Beauty shop.
Activities Arts & crafts; Cards; Games; Reading groups; Prayer groups; Movies; Shopping trips; Dances/Social/Cultural gatherings.

Parrott Avenue Home
127 Parrott Ave, Portsmouth, NH 03801
(603) 436-2435
Admin Sharon J Christianson.
Medical Dir Richard Attenborough MD.
Licensure Sheltered care with nursing unit; Retirement. *Beds* Sheltered care with nursing unit 22.
Owner Nonprofit organization/foundation.
Admissions Requirements Medical examination; Physician's request.
Staff RNs 1 (ft), 2 (pt); LPNs 3 (pt); Nurses' aides 3 (ft), 4 (pt).
Facilities Dining room; Laundry room; Barber/Beauty shop; Library.
Activities Games; Shopping trips.

Mark H Wentworth Home
346 Pleasant St, Portsmouth, NH 03801
(603) 436-0169
Admin Donald E Reeves. *Dir of Nursing* Anne Levesque. *Medical Dir* Dr Richard Attenborough.
Licensure Sheltered care. *Beds* Sheltered care 75.
Owner Nonprofit corp.
Staff Physicians 1 (pt); RNs 2 (ft), 2 (pt); LPNs 4 (ft), 2 (pt); Nurses' aides 38 (ft), 6 (pt); Physical therapists; Reality therapists; Recreational therapists; Occupational therapists; Speech therapists; Activities coordinators; Dietitians; Ophthalmologists; Podiatrists; Dentists.

Rindge

Park Hill Manor Nursing Home
RR 1 Box 13, W Main St, Rindge, NH 03461-9801
Admin Edward MacLeod.
Licensure Intermediate care. *Beds* ICF 101. *Certified* Medicaid.
Owner Proprietary corp.

Rochester

Clipper Home of Rochester Inc
62 Rochester Hill Rd, Rochester, NH 03867
(603) 335-3955, 335-5841 FAX
Admin Frances B Copp. *Dir of Nursing* Anne Tremblay. *Medical Dir* Steven R Goldfarb.
Licensure Intermediate care. *Beds* ICF 72. *Private Pay Patients* 63%. *Certified* Medicaid.

Owner Proprietary corp (Clipper Home
Affiliates Inc).
Admissions Requirements Medical
examination.
Staff Physicians 1 (pt); RNs 3 (ft), 2 (pt);
LPNs 7 (ft), 9 (pt); Nurses' aides 14 (ft), 28
(pt); Activities coordinators 1 (ft), 1 (pt);
Dietitians 1 (ft).
Languages French.
Facilities Dining room; Laundry room;
Barber/Beauty shop; Library; Living rooms;
Central social/special event area.
Activities Games; Reading groups; Prayer
groups; Movies.

Gafney Home for the Aged
90 Wakefield St, Rochester, NH 03867
(603) 332-2705
Admin Laurie J Woodman.
Medical Dir Nancy Weeks.
Licensure Sheltered care; Retirement. *Beds*
Sheltered care 20.
Owner Nonprofit corp.
Admissions Requirements Minimum age 65;
Medical examination.
Staff RNs 2 (pt); LPNs 1 (ft); Nurses' aides 2
(pt).
Facilities Dining room; Laundry room;
Barber/Beauty shop; Library.
Activities Prayer groups.

Rochester Manor
Whitehall Rd, Rochester, NH 03867
(603) 332-7711
Admin Mary Flynn.
Licensure Intermediate care. *Beds* ICF 108.
Certified Medicaid; Medicare.

Rye

Webster at Rye
PO Box 530, 795 Washington St, Rye, NH
03870
(603) 964-8144
Admin Thomas Argue.
Licensure Intermediate care. *Beds* ICF 37.
Certified Medicaid.

Salem

Salemhaven Inc
23 Geremonty Dr, Salem, NH 03079
(603) 893-5586
Admin David Potvin.
Licensure Intermediate care. *Beds* ICF 100.
Certified Medicaid.
Owner Proprietary corp (Hillhaven Corp).

Warner

Austin Home Inc
White Plains Rd, Warner, NH 03278
(603) 456-3525
Admin Kathleen Y Fifield.
Medical Dir William Fifield; Kathleen Fifield,
Dorothea Young.
Licensure Sheltered care; Retirement;
Alzheimer's care. *Beds* Sheltered care 15.
Owner Privately owned.
Admissions Requirements Medical
examination.
Staff Nurses' aides.
Facilities Dining room; Laundry room;
Barber/Beauty shop; Library; Living room
with TV.
Activities Prayer groups; Shopping trips;
Dances/Social/Cultural gatherings; Church
functions; Fairs.

Pine Rock Farm
Denny Hill Rd, Box 266, Warner, NH 03278
(603) 456-3181
Admin Judith Waschsmuth.
Licensure Skilled care. *Beds* 15.

West Chesterfield

Bert Anne Annex
PO Box 144, West Chesterfield, NH 03466
(603) 256-6277
Admin Bertha Bergeron.
Licensure Skilled care. *Beds* 6.

Bert Anne Home for the Aged
PO Box 144, West Chesterfield, NH 03466
(603) 256-6277
Admin Bertha M Bergeron. *Dir of Nursing*
Gertrude Kung RN.
Licensure Sheltered care; Retirement;
Alzheimer's care. *Beds* Sheltered care 6.
Certified Medicare.
Owner Privately owned.
Admissions Requirements Minimum age 45.
Staff Physicians; RNs; Nurses' aides.
Languages German, French.
Facilities Dining room; Activities room;
Chapel; Crafts room; Laundry room; Barber/
Beauty shop.
Activities Cards; Games.

West Stewartstown

Coos County Nursing Hospital
PO Box 10, River Rd, West Stewartstown,
NH 03597
(603) 246-3321
Admin Jerilyn Pelch.
Medical Dir Joseph Capobianco MD.
Licensure Intermediate care. *Beds* ICF 101.
Certified Medicaid.
Owner Publicly owned.
Admissions Requirements Medical
examination; Physician's request.
Staff Physicians 4 (pt); RNs 5 (ft), 5 (pt);
LPNs 4 (ft), 2 (pt); Nurses' aides 29 (ft), 14
(pt); Physical therapists 1 (pt); Occupational
therapists 1 (pt); Speech therapists 1 (pt);
Activities coordinators 1 (ft); Dietitians 1
(pt).
Languages French.
Facilities Dining room; Physical therapy
room; Activities room; Chapel; Crafts room;
Laundry room; Barber/Beauty shop; Outside
patio with cookout facility; Picnic facilities;
Secure care system.
Activities Arts & crafts; Cards; Games;
Reading groups; Prayer groups; Movies;
Shopping trips; Dances/Social/Cultural
gatherings.

Westmoreland

Cheshire County Maplewood Nursing Home
River Rd, Westmoreland, NH 03467
(603) 399-4912, 399-7005 FAX
Admin Patrick F McManus. *Dir of Nursing*
Bonnie Carroll RN. *Medical Dir* Barry L
Stern MD.
Licensure Intermediate care; Alzheimer's care.
Beds ICF 150. *Private Pay Patients* 15%.
Certified Medicaid; Medicare.
Owner Publicly owned.
Admissions Requirements Minimum age 16;
Medical examination; Physician's request.
Staff Physicians 3 (pt); RNs 11 (ft), 6 (pt);
LPNs 9 (ft), 5 (pt); Nurses' aides 52 (ft), 23
(pt); Physical therapists 1 (pt); Occupational
therapists 1 (pt); Activities coordinators 1
(pt); Dietitians 1 (pt).

Facilities Dining room; Physical therapy
room; Activities room; Chapel; Crafts room;
Barber/Beauty shop; Gift shop.
Activities Arts & crafts; Cards; Games;
Reading groups; Prayer groups; Movies;
Shopping trips; Dances/Social/Cultural
gatherings; Intergenerational programs; Pet
therapy; Gourmet dining; Parties; Men's
club; Exercise groups; Cooking.

Whitefield

Morrison Nursing Home
2-6 Terrace St, Whitefield, NH 03598
(603) 837-2541
Admin Joyce A Willey. *Dir of Nursing*
Theresa Clothey. *Medical Dir* Jorge
deVillafane MD.
Licensure Intermediate care; Alzheimer's care.
Beds ICF 52. *Private Pay Patients* 33%.
Certified Medicaid.
Owner Nonprofit organization/foundation.
Admissions Requirements Minimum age 18;
Medical examination; Physician's request.
Staff Physicians 4 (pt); RNs 1 (ft), 2 (pt);
LPNs 4 (ft), 3 (pt); Nurses' aides 24 (ft), 6
(pt); Physical therapists 1 (pt); Speech
therapists 1 (pt); Activities coordinators 1
(ft); Dietitians 1 (pt); Ophthalmologists 1
(pt); Podiatrists 1 (pt).
Languages French.
Facilities Dining room; Activities room;
Crafts room; Barber/Beauty shop; Library.
Activities Arts & crafts; Cards; Games;
Reading groups; Prayer groups; Movies;
Dances/Social/Cultural gatherings;
Intergenerational programs; Pet therapy.

Winchester

Applewood Healthcare Center
Snow Rd, Winchester, NH 03470
(603) 239-6355
Admin Marcia Couitt.
Licensure Intermediate care. *Beds* ICF 70.
Certified Medicaid.

Wolfeboro

Clipper Home of Wolfeboro
Clark Rd, Wolfeboro, NH 03894
(603) 569-3950
Admin William E Gilmore.
Licensure Intermediate care. *Beds* ICF 98.
Certified Medicaid.

Woodsville

Grafton County Nursing Home
PO Box 267, Woodsville, NH 03785
(603) 787-6971, 787-2194 FAX
Admin William Siegmund. *Dir of Nursing*
Evelyn Bigelow RN.
Licensure Intermediate care. *Beds* ICF 135.
Certified Medicaid.
Owner Publicly owned.
Admissions Requirements Medical
examination; Physician's request.
Staff Physicians; RNs; LPNs; Nurses' aides;
Physical therapists; Occupational therapists;
Activities coordinators; Dietitians;
Podiatrists.
Facilities Dining room; Physical therapy
room; Activities room; Chapel; Crafts room;
Laundry room; Barber/Beauty shop; Library.
Activities Arts & crafts; Cards; Games;
Reading groups; Prayer groups; Movies;
Shopping trips; Dances/Social/Cultural
gatherings; Pet therapy.

NEW JERSEY

Absecon

Absecon Manor Nursing & Rehabilitation Center
1020 Pitney Ave, Absecon, NJ 08201
(609) 646-5400
Admin David Slutzker.
Licensure Long-term care; Residential care.
 Beds Long-term care 120; Residential care 60.

Allendale

Allendale Nursing Home
55 Harreton Rd, Allendale, NJ 07401
(201) 825-0660
Admin Hecter Giancarlo MD.
Licensure Skilled care; Intermediate care. *Beds* SNF 50; ICF 120. *Certified* Medicaid; Medicare.

Wiersma's Nursing Home
703 Franklin Trpk, Allendale, NJ 07401
(201) 327-3150
Admin Louis Wiersma, Pres.
Licensure Long-term care. *Beds* Long-term care 18.

Allenwood

Geraldine L Thompson Medical Home
Hospital Rd, Allenwood, NJ 08720
(201) 938-5250
Admin Diana Massaro-Jargowsky.
Medical Dir Dr James Cashman.
Licensure Skilled care. *Beds* SNF 73. *Certified* Medicaid.
Owner Publicly owned.
Admissions Requirements Minimum age 18.
Staff Physicians 2 (pt); RNs 5 (ft), 2 (pt); LPNs 3 (ft), 1 (pt); Nurses' aides 28 (ft), 6 (pt); Physical therapists 1 (pt); Recreational therapists 3 (ft); Activities coordinators 1 (ft); Dietitians 1 (pt); Podiatrists 1 (pt).
Facilities Dining room; Activities room; Chapel; Crafts room; Laundry room; Barber/ Beauty shop.
Activities Arts & crafts; Cards; Games; Reading groups; Prayer groups; Movies; Shopping trips; Dances/Social/Cultural gatherings; Video games; Community trips.

Andover

Andover Intermediate Care Center
Mulford Creamery, Andover, NJ 07821
(201) 383-6200
Admin Carla Icolari.
Medical Dir Dr Pavle Topalovic.
Licensure Intermediate care. *Beds* ICF 540. *Certified* Medicaid.
Admissions Requirements Physician's request.
Staff Physicians 1 (ft), 22 (pt); RNs 42 (ft), 21 (pt); LPNs 17 (ft), 10 (pt); Nurses' aides 142 (ft), 27 (pt); Physical therapists 1 (ft); Recreational therapists 10 (ft), 3 (pt); Speech

therapists 1 (pt); Activities coordinators 1 (ft); Dietitians 2 (ft); Podiatrists 3 (pt); Physical therapy assistants 4 (ft).
Facilities Dining room; Physical therapy room; Activities room; Chapel; Crafts room; Laundry room; Barber/Beauty shop; Swimming pool; Miniature golf course.
Activities Arts & crafts; Cards; Games; Reading groups; Prayer groups; Movies; Shopping trips; Dances/Social/Cultural gatherings; Plays; Validation-fantasy groups; Sensory retraining; Aerobics.

Atlantic City

Eastern Pines Convalescent Center
29 & 33 N Vermont Ave, Atlantic City, NJ 08401
(609) 344-8911
Admin William B Calvin.
Licensure Long-term care. *Beds* Long-term care 208. *Certified* Medicaid.

King David Care Center of Atlantic City
166 South Carolina Ave, Atlantic City, NJ 08401
(609) 344-2181, 347-7807 FAX
Admin Leonora P Dwyer LNHA. *Dir of Nursing* Carol McGovern BS RN CMA. *Medical Dir* Harry A Sweeney DO.
Licensure Skilled care; Intermediate care; Intermediate care for mentally retarded. *Beds* SNF 62; ICF 213; ICF/MR 45. *Private Pay Patients* 4%. *Certified* Medicaid; Medicare.
Owner Proprietary corp (Continental Health Affiliates Inc).
Admissions Requirements Minimum age 18; Medical examination; Physician's request.
Staff Physicians 1 (ft), 7 (pt); RNs 34 (ft), 7 (pt); LPNs 30 (ft); Nurses' aides 96 (ft), 10 (pt); Physical therapists 2 (ft); Recreational therapists 9 (ft), 2 (pt); Occupational therapists 1 (ft); Speech therapists 1 (ft), 1 (pt); Activities coordinators 1 (ft); Dietitians 2 (ft); Ophthalmologists 1 (pt); Podiatrists 1 (pt); Audiologists (by referral); Dentists 1 (pt).
Languages Spanish, Tagalog, Slovak, German, Russian.
Facilities Dining room; Physical therapy room; Activities room; Chapel; Crafts room; Laundry room; Barber/Beauty shop; Book mobile.
Activities Arts & crafts; Cards; Games; Reading groups; Prayer groups; Movies; Shopping trips; Dances/Social/Cultural gatherings; Intergenerational programs; Pet therapy.

Oceanside Convalescent & Rehabilitation Center
401 Boardwalk, Atlantic City, NJ 08401
(609) 348-0171
Admin Lee Anne Schwiers. *Dir of Nursing* Marietta Stewart. *Medical Dir* Harry Sweeney MD.

Licensure Long-term care. *Beds* Long-term care 104. *Certified* Medicaid; Medicare.
Owner Proprietary corp (Continental Health Affiliates).
Admissions Requirements Physician's request.
Staff Physicians 5 (pt); RNs 14 (ft), 5 (pt); LPNs 3 (ft), 1 (pt); Nurses' aides 33 (ft); Physical therapists 1 (ft) Occupational therapists 1 (pt); Speech therapists 1 (pt); Activities coordinators 1 (ft); Dietitians 1 (pt); Ophthalmologists 2 (pt); Podiatrists 1 (pt); Dentists 1 (pt).
Languages Spanish, Tagalog.
Facilities Dining room; Physical therapy room; Laundry room; TV lounge; Screened porch with ocean view.
Activities Arts & crafts; Cards; Games; Prayer groups; Movies; Shopping trips; Dances/ Social/Cultural gatherings; Boardwalk trips.

Westside Convalescent Center
2153 Venice Ave, Atlantic City, NJ 08401
(609) 348-2656
Admin Mary Wilson.
Licensure Long-term care. *Beds* Long-term care 30. *Certified* Medicaid.

Atlantic Highlands

Atlantic Highlands Nursing Home
8 Middletown Ave, Atlantic Highlands, NJ 07716
(201) 291-0600
Admin Gezor Kaszierer.
Licensure Long-term care. *Beds* Long-term care 155. *Certified* Medicaid; Medicare.

Barnegat

Barnegat Nursing Center
857 W Bay Ave, Barnegat, NJ 08005
(609) 698-1400
Admin Michael D Gentile. *Dir of Nursing* Natalie Lawless. *Medical Dir* Dr Philip Varner.
Licensure Skilled care. *Beds* SNF 120. *Certified* Medicaid; Medicare.
Owner Proprietary corp.
Admissions Requirements Minimum age 18; Medical examination; Physician's request.
Staff RNs 8 (ft), 3 (pt); LPNs 5 (ft), 1 (pt); Nurses' aides 25 (ft), 10 (pt); Physical therapists 1 (ft); Recreational therapists 1 (ft); Occupational therapists 1 (pt); Speech therapists 1 (pt); Activities coordinators 1 (ft); Dietitians 1 (pt).
Languages Italian, German.
Facilities Dining room; Physical therapy room; Activities room; Crafts room; Laundry room; Barber/Beauty shop.
Activities Arts & crafts; Cards; Games; Reading groups; Prayer groups; Movies; Shopping trips; Dances/Social/Cultural gatherings.

Bayville

Bayview Convalescent Center
Lakeside Blvd, Bayville, NJ 08721
(201) 269-0500, 269-6053 FAX
Admin Oscar Heller. *Dir of Nursing* Kim
   Servis. *Medical Dir* William Jones DO.
Licensure Skilled care; Intermediate care. *Beds*
   Swing beds SNF/ICF 323. *Certified*
   Medicaid; Medicare.
Owner Proprietary corp.
Admissions Requirements Minimum age 18;
   Physician's request.
Staff Physicians 3 (pt); RNs 11 (ft), 7 (pt);
   LPNs 13 (ft), 17 (pt); Nurses' aides 78 (ft),
   31 (pt); Physical therapists 1 (ft);
   Recreational therapists 7 (ft); Occupational
   therapists 1 (pt); Speech therapists 1 (pt);
   Activities coordinators 1 (ft); Dietitians 1
   (pt); Ophthalmologists 1 (pt); Podiatrists 1
   (pt); Dentists 1 (pt).
Facilities Dining room; Physical therapy
   room; Activities room; Crafts room; Laundry
   room; Barber/Beauty shop; Library; Outdoor
   barbecue.
Activities Arts & crafts; Cards; Games;
   Reading groups; Prayer groups; Movies;
   Shopping trips; Dances/Social/Cultural
   gatherings.

Belleville

Essex County Geriatric Center
520 Belleville, Belleville, NJ 07109
(201) 751-7200
Admin Marilyn Lamberti RN PhD LNHA.
   Dir of Nursing Elizabeth Johnson RN BA.
   Medical Dir Dr Russell Greco.
Licensure Long-term care. *Beds* Long-term
   care 216. *Private Pay Patients* 0%. *Certified*
   Medicaid.
Owner Publicly owned.
Admissions Requirements Minimum age 18;
   Medical examination; Medicaid approved.
Staff Physicians 1 (ft), 8 (pt); RNs 13 (ft), 8
   (pt); LPNs 47 (ft), 3 (pt); Nurses' aides 150
   (ft), 3 (pt); Recreational therapists 3 (ft);
   Speech therapists 1 (ft); Activities
   coordinators 1 (ft); Dietitians 1 (ft);
   Ophthalmologists (consultant); Podiatrists
   (consultant); Audiologists (consultant);
   Dentists 2 (ft); RNAs 2 (ft), 2 (pt).
Facilities Dining room; Physical therapy
   room; Activities room; Crafts room; Laundry
   room; Barber/Beauty shop; Dental clinic.
Activities Arts & crafts; Cards; Games;
   Reading groups; Prayer groups; Movies;
   Shopping trips; Dances/Social/Cultural
   gatherings; Intergenerational programs; Pet
   therapy; Religious services and programs.

Berkeley Heights

Berkeley Hall Nursing Home
311 Springfield Ave, Berkeley Heights, NJ
   07922
(201) 464-9260
Admin Noel W Swan.
Medical Dir Dr J J Aquino.
Licensure Long-term care. *Beds* Long-term
   care 67.
Admissions Requirements Medical
   examination.
Staff Physicians 10 (pt); RNs 6 (ft), 5 (pt);
   LPNs 8 (ft), 2 (pt); Nurses' aides 11 (ft), 8
   (pt); Physical therapists 1 (pt); Recreational
   therapists 1 (ft); Occupational therapists 1
   (pt); Speech therapists 1 (pt); Activities
   coordinators 1 (ft); Dietitians 1 (pt);
   Ophthalmologists 1 (pt); Podiatrists 1 (pt);
   Audiologists 1 (pt); Dentists 1 (pt).
Facilities Dining room; Physical therapy
   room; Activities room; Chapel; Crafts room;
   Laundry room; Barber/Beauty shop.

Activities Arts & crafts; Cards; Games;
   Reading groups; Prayer groups; Movies;
   Shopping trips; Dances/Social/Cultural
   gatherings.

Berkeley Heights Convalescent Center
35 Cottage St, Berkeley Heights, NJ 07922
(201) 464-0048
Admin Mihail Davidovich.
Medical Dir Dr Donald Kent.
Licensure Long-term care. *Beds* Long-term
   care 120. *Certified* Medicaid; Medicare.
Owner Proprietary corp.
Admissions Requirements Minimum age 60.
Staff Physicians 10 (pt); RNs 10 (ft); LPNs 15
   (ft); Nurses' aides 30 (ft); Recreational
   therapists 3 (ft); Dietitians 1 (ft).
Languages Russian.
Facilities Dining room; Physical therapy
   room; Activities room; Crafts room; Laundry
   room; Barber/Beauty shop; Library; Patio.
Activities Arts & crafts; Cards; Games;
   Reading groups; Prayer groups; Movies;
   Shopping trips; Dances/Social/Cultural
   gatherings.

Bernardsville

Fellowship Deaconry Inc
Old Army Rd, Shannon Lodge, Bernardsville,
   NJ 07924
(201) 766-0832
Admin Roy Gaida.
Licensure Long-term care; Residential care.
   Beds Long-term care 17; Residential care 57.
Owner Nonprofit corp.

Blackwood

Camden County Health Service Center
Lakeland, Blackwood, NJ 08012
(609) 757-8000
Admin Rose Simpson. *Dir of Nursing*
   Romayne Gallagher RN. *Medical Dir*
   William Hingston MD.
Licensure Skilled care; Intermediate care;
   Medical day care. *Beds* SNF 204; ICF 159;
   Medical day care 35. *Certified* Medicaid;
   Medicare.
Owner Publicly owned.
Admissions Requirements Minimum age 18;
   Medical examination; Physician's request.
Facilities Dining room; Physical therapy
   room; Activities room; Chapel; Crafts room;
   Barber/Beauty shop.
Activities Arts & crafts; Cards; Games;
   Reading groups; Prayer groups; Movies;
   Shopping trips; Dances/Social/Cultural
   gatherings.

Bloomfield

Hazelcrest Manor Nursing Home
60 Hazelwood Rd, Bloomfield, NJ 07003
(201) 743-2366
Admin Richard Del Vecchio Jr.
Medical Dir R Chhabria MD.
Licensure Long-term care. *Beds* Long-term
   care 18.
Admissions Requirements Physician's request.
Staff Physicians 2 (pt); RNs 1 (ft), 4 (pt);
   LPNs 3 (ft), 3 (pt); Nurses' aides 4 (ft), 3
   (pt); Recreational therapists 1 (pt); Activities
   coordinators 1 (pt); Dietitians 1 (pt);
   Ophthalmologists 1 (pt); Podiatrists 1 (pt);
   Audiologists 1 (pt); Dentists 1 (pt).
Facilities Dining room; Activities room;
   Laundry room.
Activities Arts & crafts; Cards; Games;
   Reading groups; Prayer groups.

Park Manor Nursing Home
23 Park Pl, Bloomfield, NJ 07003
(201) 743-7772
Admin Peter Peterson.
Licensure Long-term care. *Beds* Long-term
   care 61.

Parkview Nursing Home
15 Church St, Bloomfield, NJ 07003
(201) 748-4074
Admin Richard Del Vecchio Jr.
Licensure Intermediate care. *Beds* ICF 30.
   Certified Medicaid.

Boonton

Sarah Frances—Tally-Ho Manor
RD 1, Powerville Rd, Boonton, NJ 07005
(201) 334-2454
Admin Timothy D Doyle. *Dir of Nursing* Fran
   Benning RN.
Licensure Skilled care; Intermediate care;
   Residential care; Alzheimer's care. *Beds*
   SNF 22; ICF 41; Residential care 68.
Owner Proprietary corp.
Admissions Requirements Minimum age 18;
   Medical examination.
Staff Physicians 22 (pt); RNs 14 (ft); LPNs 3
   (ft); Nurses' aides 22 (ft); Physical therapists
   1 (pt); Recreational therapists 2 (pt);
   Activities coordinators 3 (ft); Dietitians 1
   (ft).
Languages Italian, Spanish, German.
Facilities Dining room; Activities room;
   Chapel; Crafts room; Laundry room; Barber/
   Beauty shop; Library.
Activities Arts & crafts; Cards; Games;
   Reading groups; Prayer groups; Movies;
   Shopping trips; Dances/Social/Cultural
   gatherings.

New Jersey Firemen's Home
565 Lathrop Ave, Boonton, NJ 07005
(201) 334-0024
Admin L George Hoth.
Licensure Long-term care; Residential care.
   Beds Long-term care 63; Residential care 39.
Admissions Requirements Medical
   examination.
Staff Physicians; RNs; LPNs; Nurses' aides;
   Activities coordinators.
Facilities Dining room; Activities room;
   Chapel; Laundry room; Barber/Beauty shop;
   Library.
Activities Arts & crafts; Cards; Games;
   Movies.

Bound Brook

Somerset Valley Nursing Home
1621 Rte 22, Bound Brook, NJ 08805
(201) 469-2000
Admin Don Van Dam MD.
Licensure Skilled care. *Beds* SNF 58. *Certified*
   Medicaid; Medicare.

Bricktown

Burnt Tavern Convalescent Center
1049 Burnt Tavern Rd, Bricktown, NJ 08723
(201) 840-3700
Admin Gordon Nedwed.
Licensure Long-term care. *Beds* Long-term
   care 180.
Owner Proprietary corp (HBA Management
   Inc).

Bridgeton

Bridgeton Nursing Center
99 Manheim Ave, Bridgeton, NJ 08302
(609) 455-2100
Admin Linda Tober.
Licensure Long-term care. *Beds* Long-term
   care 185. *Certified* Medicaid; Medicare.
Facilities Dining room; Physical therapy
   room; Activities room; Chapel; Laundry
   room; Barber/Beauty shop.
Activities Arts & crafts; Cards; Games;
   Reading groups; Prayer groups; Movies;
   Shopping trips; Dances/Social/Cultural
   gatherings.

Cumberland Manor
Rd 2, Cumberland Dr, Bridgeton, NJ 08302
(609) 455-8000
Admin Starret L Hill.
Licensure Long-term care. *Beds* Long-term care 196. *Certified* Medicaid.

Rainbow Nursing Center
RD 8 Box 318, Big Oak Rd, Bridgeton, NJ 08302
(609) 451-5000, 455-7371 FAX
Admin Janice Friday Brown. *Dir of Nursing* Linda Hinson RN. *Medical Dir* Stanley Leshner MD.
Licensure Skilled care; Intermediate care. *Beds* SNF 53; ICF 31. *Private Pay Patients* 30%. *Certified* Medicaid; Medicare.
Owner Proprietary corp (American Health Inc).
Admissions Requirements Minimum age 21.
Staff Physicians 4 (ft), 6 (pt); RNs 4 (ft), 6 (pt); LPNs 6 (ft), 7 (pt); Nurses' aides 28 (ft), 4 (pt); Physical therapists 1 (ft); Speech therapists 1 (pt); Activities coordinators 1 (ft), 1 (pt); Dietitians 1 (pt); Ophthalmologists 1 (pt); Podiatrists 1 (pt); Audiologists 1 (pt).
Facilities Dining room; Physical therapy room; Activities room; Crafts room; Laundry room; Barber/Beauty shop; Library books delivered; Fenced courtyard; Picnic pavilion with barbecue grills.
Activities Arts & crafts; Cards; Games; Reading groups; Prayer groups; Movies; Dances/Social/Cultural gatherings; Intergenerational programs; Pet therapy.

Bridgewater

Bridgeway Convalescent Center
270 Rte 28, Bridgewater, NJ 08807
(201) 722-7022
Admin Lucille A Link. *Dir of Nursing* Julie Murphy RN. *Medical Dir* Chik Chin MD.
Licensure Long-term care; Alzheimer's care. *Beds* Long-term care 120. *Certified* Medicaid; Medicare.
Owner Proprietary corp.
Staff RNs 2 (ft), 8 (pt); LPNs 7 (ft), 1 (pt); Nurses' aides 29 (ft), 10 (pt); Physical therapists 1 (pt); Recreational therapists 2 (ft), 2 (pt); Occupational therapists 1 (pt); Speech therapists 1 (pt); Dietitians 1 (ft).
Facilities Dining room; Physical therapy room; Activities room; Chapel; Crafts room; Laundry room; Barber/Beauty shop.
Activities Arts & crafts; Cards; Games; Reading groups; Prayer groups; Movies; Shopping trips; Dances/Social/Cultural gatherings.

Greenfield Convalescent Center
875 Rte 202-206 N, Bridgewater, NJ 08807
(201) 526-8600
Admin Timothy O'Leary.
Medical Dir Dr Brewster Miller.
Licensure Long-term care. *Beds* Long-term care 176. *Certified* Medicaid; Medicare.
Admissions Requirements Minimum age 18.
Facilities Dining room; Physical therapy room; Activities room; Chapel; Crafts room; Laundry room; Barber/Beauty shop; Library.
Activities Arts & crafts; Cards; Games; Reading groups; Prayer groups; Movies; Dances/Social/Cultural gatherings.

Burlington

Burlington Woods Convalescent Center
115 Sunset Rd, Burlington, NJ 08016
(609) 387-3620
Admin Martha Schneider.
Licensure Long-term care; Residential care. *Beds* Long-term care 180; Residential care 60. *Certified* Medicaid; Medicare.
Owner Proprietary corp (Geriatric & Medical Centers).

Masonic Home of New Jersey
Jacksonville Rd, Burlington, NJ 08016
(609) 386-0300
Admin T F Small III. *Dir of Nursing* Marjorie Powell RN. *Medical Dir* Jhin J Cynn MD.
Licensure Skilled care; Intermediate care; Residential health care; Alzheimer's care. *Beds* SNF 46; ICF 293; Residential health care 112. *Certified* Medicaid; Medicare.
Owner Nonprofit organization/foundation.
Admissions Requirements Medical examination.
Staff Physicians 1 (ft), 2 (pt); RNs 9 (ft), 11 (pt); LPNs 14 (ft), 21 (pt); Nurses' aides 88 (ft), 34 (pt); Physical therapists 1 (pt); Occupational therapists 1 (pt); Speech therapists 1 (pt); Activities coordinators 1 (ft); Dietitians 1 (ft); Ophthalmologists 1 (pt); Podiatrists 1 (pt); Dentists 1 (pt).
Affiliation Masons.
Facilities Dining room; Physical therapy room; Activities room; Chapel; Crafts room; Laundry room; Barber/Beauty shop; Library; Auditorium; Picnic pavilion; Gift shop.
Activities Arts & crafts; Cards; Games; Reading groups; Prayer groups; Movies; Shopping trips; Dances/Social/Cultural gatherings; Woodworking shop; Cultural exchange programs; Trips; Ceramics; Bell choir; Gardening.

Califon

Little Brook Nursing & Convalescent Center
PO Box 398, Sliker Rd, Califon, NJ 07830
(201) 832-2220
Admin Andrea Berry Shawn. *Dir of Nursing* Sue Sebatina RN. *Medical Dir* Raymond Byrd MD.
Licensure Long-term care. *Beds* Long-term care 30. *Certified* Medicaid; Medicare.
Owner Proprietary corp.
Staff Physicians; RNs; LPNs; Nurses' aides; Physical therapists; Reality therapists; Recreational therapists; Occupational therapists; Speech therapists; Activities coordinators; Dietitians; Podiatrists.
Facilities Dining room; Activities room; Crafts room; Laundry room.
Activities Arts & crafts; Cards; Games.

Camden

Mediplex Rehabilitation—Camden
2 Cooper Plaza, Camden, NJ 08103
(609) 342-7600, 541-4059 FAX
Admin Craig Koff LNHA. *Dir of Nursing* Sue McBride RN MSN. *Medical Dir* Dr Lucian Introcaso.
Licensure Skilled care; Intermediate care; Alzheimer's care. *Beds* SNF 60; ICF 60. *Private Pay Patients* 36%. *Certified* Medicaid; Medicare.
Owner Proprietary corp (Mediplex of New Jersey Inc).
Admissions Requirements Physician's request.
Staff Physicians 5 (ft); RNs 26 (ft), 22 (pt); LPNs 31 (ft), 7 (pt); Nurses' aides 37 (ft), 5 (pt); Physical therapists 11 (ft), 1 (pt); Recreational therapists 8 (ft); Occupational therapists 11 (ft), 2 (pt); Speech therapists 8 (ft); Dietitians 1 (ft).
Languages Spanish, interpreters available for others.
Facilities Dining room; Physical therapy room; Activities room; Crafts room; Laundry room; Barber/Beauty shop; Occupational therapy room; Speech language/Pathology room.
Activities Arts & crafts; Cards; Games; Reading groups; Prayer groups; Movies; Shopping trips; Dances/Social/Cultural gatherings; Intergenerational programs; Pet therapy.

Woodland Care Center
1105-1115 Linden St, Camden, NJ 08101
(609) 365-8500
Admin Ingrid R Blomgren.
Licensure Long-term care; Residential care. *Beds* Long-term care 120; Residential care 60.

Cape May Court House

Cape May Care Center
Rte 9, Shore Rd, Cape May Court House, NJ 08210
(609) 465-7633
Admin Susan Slaughter.
Medical Dir S Melita MD.
Licensure Skilled care. *Beds* SNF 116. *Certified* Medicaid; Medicare.
Admissions Requirements Minimum age 21.
Facilities Dining room; Physical therapy room; Activities room; Chapel; Crafts room; Laundry room; Barber/Beauty shop.
Activities Arts & crafts; Cards; Games; Reading groups; Prayer groups; Movies; Shopping trips; Dances/Social/Cultural gatherings; Casino trips.

Courthouse Convalescent Center
144 Magnolia Dr, Cape May Court House, NJ 08210
(609) 465-7171
Admin Karen K Bayer. *Dir of Nursing* G Cavagnaro RN. *Medical Dir* Robert G Beitman MD.
Licensure Long-term care. *Beds* Long-term care 120. *Certified* Medicaid; Medicare.
Owner Proprietary corp.
Admissions Requirements Minimum age 18; Physician's request.
Staff Physicians 6 (pt); RNs; LPNs 14 (ft), 3 (pt); Nurses' aides 42 (ft), 2 (pt); Physical therapists 1 (pt); Recreational therapists 2 (ft); Occupational therapists 1 (pt); Speech therapists 1 (pt); Dietitians 1 (pt); Ophthalmologists 1 (pt); Podiatrists 1 (pt); Dentists 1 (pt).
Languages Spanish.
Facilities Dining room; Physical therapy room; Activities room; Laundry room; Barber/Beauty shop.
Activities Arts & crafts; Cards; Games; Reading groups; Prayer groups; Movies; Dances/Social/Cultural gatherings; Lunches out; Trips to boardwalk.

Crest Haven
Rte 9, Garden State Pkwy, Cape May Court House, NJ 08210
(609) 465-7911
Admin Robert A Pastoria. *Dir of Nursing* Mary Lea Mills RN. *Medical Dir* Dr Clayton F Carr.
Licensure Long-term care. *Beds* Long-term care 140. *Certified* Medicaid.
Owner Proprietary corp (Vetter Health Services Inc).
Staff Physicians 1 (ft); RNs 15 (ft); LPNs 14 (ft); Nurses' aides 82 (ft); Recreational therapists 2 (ft); Activities coordinators 1 (ft); Dietitians 1 (pt); Dentists 1 (pt).
Facilities Dining room; Activities room; Barber/Beauty shop.
Activities Arts & crafts; Cards; Games; Reading groups; Prayer groups; Movies; Shopping trips; Dances/Social/Cultural gatherings.

Eastern Shore Nursing/Convalescent Center
RD 3 Box 232D, Cape May Court House, NJ 08210
(609) 465-2260
Admin Tamara W Moreland.
Licensure Long-term care. *Beds* Long-term care 120.

South Cape Nursing Home
Stites Ave, Cape May Court House, NJ 08210
(609) 465-5335

Admin Larry Powell.
Licensure Long-term care. *Beds* Long-term care 40. *Certified* Medicaid.

Carney's Point

Park View Nursing Center
5th & Park Ave, Carney's Point, NJ 08069
(609) 299-6800
Admin Georgia R Bradway.
Medical Dir A Auerbach DO.
Licensure Long-term care; Residential care. *Beds* Long-term care 180; Residential care 24. *Certified* Medicaid; Medicare.
Owner Proprietary corp.
Admissions Requirements Minimum age 18.
Staff Physicians 2 (pt); RNs 8 (ft), 13 (pt); LPNs 9 (ft), 5 (pt); Nurses' aides 43 (ft), 38 (pt); Physical therapists 1 (pt); Reality therapists 1 (ft); Recreational therapists 2 (ft), 1 (pt); Occupational therapists 1 (pt); Speech therapists 1 (pt); Activities coordinators 1 (ft); Dietitians 1 (pt); Ophthalmologists 1 (pt); Podiatrists 1 (pt); Dentists 1 (pt).
Languages Spanish, Italian, German.
Facilities Dining room; Physical therapy room; Activities room; Chapel; Crafts room; Laundry room; Barber/Beauty shop; Library.
Activities Arts & crafts; Cards; Games; Reading groups; Prayer groups; Movies; Shopping trips; Dances/Social/Cultural gatherings.

Southgate Health Care Center
307 Pennsville-Auburn Rd, Carneys Point, NJ 08069
(609) 299-8900, 299-7377 FAX
Admin Susan M Love. *Dir of Nursing* Eva Ceasar RN. *Medical Dir* Roberto Diaz MD.
Licensure Skilled care. *Beds* SNF 120. *Private Pay Patients* 30%. *Certified* Medicaid; Medicare.
Owner Proprietary corp.
Admissions Requirements Minimum age 16; Physician's request.
Staff Physicians (contracted); RNs 6 (ft); LPNs 9 (ft); Nurses' aides 45 (ft); Physical therapists (contracted); Recreational therapists 1 (ft), 1 (pt); Occupational therapists (contracted); Speech therapists (contracted); Activities coordinators 1 (ft); Dietitians (contracted); Podiatrists (contracted); Audiologists (contracted); Ancillary 25 (ft).
Facilities Dining room; Physical therapy room; Activities room; Chapel; Crafts room; Barber/Beauty shop; Library; Garden room; Patios.
Activities Arts & crafts; Cards; Games; Reading groups; Prayer groups; Movies; Shopping trips; Dances/Social/Cultural gatherings; Intergenerational programs; Pet therapy.

Cedar Grove

Cedar Grove Manor
398 Pompten Ave, Cedar Grove, NJ 07009
(201) 239-7600, 857-2701 FAX
Admin Marilyn Pomeroy. *Dir of Nursing* Christian Denosta. *Medical Dir* Terrence Aherne.
Licensure Skilled care; Intermediate care. *Beds* Swing beds SNF/ICF 180. *Private Pay Patients* 60%. *Certified* Medicaid; Medicare.
Owner Proprietary corp (Continental Health Affiliates).
Admissions Requirements Minimum age 50; Medical examination.
Staff Physicians 2 (pt); RNs 16 (ft), 3 (pt); LPNs 13 (ft), 8 (pt); Nurses' aides 73 (ft), 8 (pt); Physical therapists (contracted); Recreational therapists 3 (ft), 1 (pt); Occupational therapists 1 (pt); Speech

therapists 1 (pt); Dietitians 2 (pt); Ophthalmologists (contracted); Podiatrists (contracted); Audiologists (contracted).
Languages Italian, French, Spanish.
Facilities Dining room; Physical therapy room; Activities room; Crafts room; Barber/Beauty shop.
Activities Arts & crafts; Cards; Games; Reading groups; Prayer groups; Movies; Dances/Social/Cultural gatherings; Intergenerational programs; Pet therapy.

Hartwyck West Nursing Home
Pompton Ave & E Lindsley Rd, Cedar Grove, NJ 07009
(201) 256-7220
Admin Brenda Hackman. *Dir of Nursing* Amy Berkemyer RN. *Medical Dir* Daniel Burbank MD.
Licensure Skilled care; Alzheimer's care. *Beds* SNF 114. *Certified* Medicaid; Medicare.
Owner Nonprofit organization/foundation.
Admissions Requirements Physician's request.
Staff RNs; LPNs; Nurses' aides; Physical therapists; Recreational therapists; Occupational therapists; Speech therapists; Activities coordinators; Dietitians.
Facilities Dining room; Physical therapy room; Activities room; Chapel; Crafts room; Laundry room; Barber/Beauty shop; Library.
Activities Arts & crafts; Cards; Games; Reading groups; Prayer groups; Movies; Shopping trips.

Waterview
536 Ridge Rd, Cedar Grove, NJ 07009
(201) 239-9300
Admin Mark Wojak. *Dir of Nursing* Dorothy De Block RN. *Medical Dir* Alfred R Dardis MD.
Licensure Skilled care. *Beds* SNF 180. *Certified* Medicaid; Medicare.
Owner Proprietary corp (Multicare Management).
Admissions Requirements Minimum age 18.
Staff RNs 12 (ft); LPNs 8 (ft); Nurses' aides 45 (ft); Physical therapists; Recreational therapists 2 (ft); Occupational therapists; Activities coordinators 1 (ft); Dietitians 1 (ft); Podiatrists; Dentists.
Facilities Dining room; Physical therapy room; Activities room; Barber/Beauty shop; Library.
Activities Arts & crafts; Cards; Games; Reading groups; Prayer groups; Movies; Shopping trips; Dances/Social/Cultural gatherings.

Chatham

Garden Terrace Nursing Home
361 Main St, Chatham, NJ 07938
(201) 635-0899
Admin Peter R Flemming.
Licensure Long-term care. *Beds* Long-term care 34.

King James Care Center
415 Southern Blvd, Chatham, NJ 07928
(201) 822-1500
Admin Joseph J Desher. *Dir of Nursing* Beth Dolph RN. *Medical Dir* Joseph Fennelly MD.
Licensure Skilled care; Intermediate care. *Beds* SNF 50; ICF 57. *Private Pay Patients* 98%. *Certified* Medicare.
Owner Privately owned.
Admissions Requirements Minimum age 50; Medical examination; Physician's request.
Staff Physicians 4 (ft); RNs 4 (ft), 15 (pt); LPNs 3 (ft), 4 (pt); Nurses' aides 25 (ft), 23 (pt); Physical therapists 2 (pt); Recreational therapists 2 (ft); Dietitians 1 (ft).
Facilities Dining room; Physical therapy room; Activities room; Crafts room; Barber/Beauty shop; Library.

Activities Arts & crafts; Cards; Games; Reading groups; Movies; Shopping trips; Intergenerational programs; Pet therapy.

Cherry Hill

Cadbury Health Care Center
2150 Rte 38, Cherry Hill, NJ 08002
(609) 667-4550
Admin Kathryn N Dunlap. *Dir of Nursing* Marilyn Elliott RN. *Medical Dir* Joseph Termini MD.
Licensure Skilled care; Intermediate care; Retirement. *Beds* SNF 60; ICF 60. *Certified* Medicaid; Medicare.
Owner Nonprofit corp.
Admissions Requirements Minimum age 65.
Staff Physicians 4 (pt); RNs 10 (ft), 1 (pt); LPNs 4 (ft), 2 (pt); Nurses' aides 39 (ft), 12 (pt); Physical therapists 1 (pt); Recreational therapists F 1 (ft); Occupational therapists 1 (pt); Speech therapists 1 (pt); Activities coordinators 1 (ft); Dietitians 1 (ft); Ophthalmologists 1 (pt); Podiatrists 1 (pt); Dentists 1 (pt).
Affiliation Society of Friends.
Facilities Dining room; Physical therapy room; Activities room; Laundry room; Barber/Beauty shop; Library.
Activities Arts & crafts; Cards; Games; Reading groups; Prayer groups; Movies; Shopping trips; Dances/Social/Cultural gatherings.

Cherry Hill Convalescent Center
1399 Chapel Ave W, Cherry Hill, NJ 08002
(609) 663-9009
Admin Tiffany Tomasso.
Licensure Intermediate care for mentally retarded; Residential care. *Beds* ICF/MR 120; Residential care 30.

Jewish Geriatric Center
3025 W Chapel Ave, Cherry Hill, NJ 08034
(609) 667-3100
Admin Isadore Tennenberg.
Licensure Long-term care. *Beds* Long-term care 171. *Certified* Medicaid; Medicare.
Owner Nonprofit corp.
Affiliation Jewish.

Leader Nursing & Rehabilitation Center
1412 Marlton Pike, Cherry Hill, NJ 08034
(609) 428-6100, 429-2543 FAX
Admin Lyla Walsh. *Dir of Nursing* Carol Sellman RN. *Medical Dir* Frank Addugo MD.
Licensure Skilled care. *Beds* SNF 98. *Private Pay Patients* 60%. *Certified* Medicare.
Owner Proprietary corp (Manor Care Inc).
Staff Physicians 32 (pt); RNs 7 (ft), 5 (pt); LPNs 5 (ft), 3 (pt); Nurses' aides 31 (ft), 4 (pt); Physical therapists 1 (ft); Recreational therapists 1 (ft); Occupational therapists 1 (pt); Speech therapists 1 (pt); Dietitians 1 (pt); Ophthalmologists 1 (pt); Podiatrists 1 (pt); Dentists 1 (pt); Patient aides 6 (pt).
Facilities Dining room; Physical therapy room; Activities room; Laundry room; Barber/Beauty shop; Lounge areas; TV rooms.
Activities Arts & crafts; Cards; Games; Reading groups; Prayer groups; Movies; Shopping trips; Dances/Social/Cultural gatherings; Intergenerational programs.

Silver Court Nursing Center Inc
100 Arbor Ave, Cherry Hill, NJ 08034
(609) 795-3131
Admin Edward Rudow.
Medical Dir Dr R N Wells.
Licensure Long-term care; Residential care. *Beds* Long-term care 120; Residential care 82. *Certified* Medicaid.
Admissions Requirements Physician's request.
Staff Physicians 4 (pt); RNs 9 (ft), 4 (pt); LPNs 5 (ft), 3 (pt) 4 (ft); Nurses' aides 19 (ft), 11 (pt); Reality therapists 1 (pt);

Recreational therapists 2 (ft), 4 (pt);
Occupational therapists 1 (pt); Activities
coordinators 1 (ft).
Facilities Dining room; Activities room;
Crafts room; Laundry room.
Activities Arts & crafts; Cards; Games;
Reading groups; Prayer groups; Movies;
Shopping trips; Dances/Social/Cultural
gatherings.

Chester

Glenlora Nursing Home
Rte 24, Chester, NJ 07930
(201) 879-5055
Admin Ray C Walborn Jr.
Medical Dir Dr Alan Chanin.
Licensure Skilled care; Alzheimer's care. *Beds*
SNF 26.
Owner Privately owned.
Admissions Requirements Minimum age 16;
Medical examination; Physician's request.
Staff RNs 3 (ft), 5 (pt); LPNs 3 (ft); Nurses'
aides 10 (ft), 8 (pt); Physical therapists 1
(pt); Recreational therapists 1 (ft); Speech
therapists 1 (pt); Activities coordinators 1
(ft); Dietitians 1 (pt); Ophthalmologists 1
(pt).
Facilities Dining room; Activities room;
Crafts room; Laundry room; Barber/Beauty
shop; Library.
Activities Arts & crafts; Cards; Games;
Reading groups; Prayer groups; Movies;
Shopping trips; Dances/Social/Cultural
gatherings.

Cinnaminson

Cinnaminson Manor Nursing & Convalescent Center
1700 Wynwood Dr, Cinnaminson, NJ 08077
(609) 829-9000
Admin Barbara Kaddick.
Licensure Long-term care. *Beds* Long-term
care 104. *Certified* Medicare.
Owner Proprietary corp (Multicare
Management).
Staff RNs 8 (ft), 14 (pt); LPNs 1 (ft), 1 (pt);
Nurses' aides 36 (ft), 6 (pt); Physical
therapists 1 (ft); Recreational therapists 1
(ft); Occupational therapists 1 (pt); Speech
therapists 1 (pt); Activities coordinators 1
(ft); Dietitians 1 (pt).
Facilities Dining room; Physical therapy
room; Activities room; Crafts room; Laundry
room; Barber/Beauty shop; Library.
Activities Arts & crafts; Cards; Games;
Reading groups; Prayer groups; Movies;
Shopping trips; Dances/Social/Cultural
gatherings.

Clarksboro

Shady Lane Gloucester County Home
County House Rd & Shady Ln, Clarksboro,
NJ 08020
(609) 423-0020
Admin James G Sullivan PhD.
Medical Dir D B Weems Jr MD.
Licensure Intermediate care. *Beds* ICF 121.
Certified Medicaid.
Owner Publicly owned.
Admissions Requirements Minimum age 60;
Medical examination; Physician's request.
Staff Physicians 1 (pt); RNs 6 (ft), 1 (pt);
LPNs 13 (ft), 1 (pt); Nurses' aides 60 (ft), 6
(pt); Physical therapists 1 (pt); Recreational
therapists 3 (ft); Speech therapists 1 (pt);
Activities coordinators 1 (ft); Dietitians 1
(pt); Podiatrists 1 (pt); Dentists 1 (pt).
Facilities Dining room; Physical therapy
room; Activities room; Crafts room; Laundry
room; Barber/Beauty shop.
Activities Arts & crafts; Cards; Games;
Reading groups; Movies; Shopping trips;
Dances/Social/Cultural gatherings.

Cliffwood Beach

Cliffside Health Care Center
200 Center St, Cliffwood Beach, NJ 07735
(201) 566-8422
Admin Geraldine Crockett.
Medical Dir Dr H O Wiley.
Licensure Intermediate care. *Beds* ICF 108.
Certified Medicaid.
Owner Proprietary corp.
Admissions Requirements Medical
examination.
Staff RNs 3 (ft), 3 (pt); LPNs 6 (ft), 4 (pt);
Nurses' aides 27 (ft), 20 (pt); Recreational
therapists 1 (ft), 2 (pt); Activities
coordinators 1 (ft).
Facilities Dining room; Physical therapy
room; Activities room; Crafts room; Barber/
Beauty shop.
Activities Arts & crafts; Cards; Games;
Reading groups; Prayer groups; Movies;
Shopping trips; Dances/Social/Cultural
gatherings.

Clifton

Dolly Mount Nursing Home
20 Valley Rd, Clifton, NJ 07013
(201) 278-8781
Admin Carolyn Armando.
Licensure Long-term care. *Beds* Long-term
care 32. *Certified* Medicaid.

Columbia

Clover Rest Home
Washington & Green Sts, Columbia, NJ 07836
(201) 496-4307
Admin George Sandman.
Licensure Intermediate care; Residential care.
Beds ICF 30; Residential care 20. *Certified*
Medicaid.

Cranbury

Elms Nursing Home
65 N Main St, Cranbury, NJ 08512
(609) 395-0725
Admin Anita M Dietrick. *Dir of Nursing*
Kathleen Ellis RN. *Medical Dir* Syed S Ali
MD.
Licensure Intermediate care; Alzheimer's care.
Beds ICF 16. *Private Pay Patients* 50%.
Certified Medicaid.
Owner Privately owned.
Admissions Requirements Medical
examination.
Staff Physicians 1 (pt); RNs 1 (ft), 3 (pt);
LPNs 2 (ft), 4 (pt); Nurses' aides 3 (ft), 8
(pt); Physical therapists 1 (pt); Reality
therapists 1 (pt); Recreational therapists 1
(pt); Occupational therapists 1 (pt); Speech
therapists 1 (pt); Activities coordinators 1
(pt); Dietitians 1 (pt); Ophthalmologists 1
(pt); Podiatrists 1 (pt); Audiologists 1 (pt).
Languages Spanish.
Facilities Dining room; Activities room;
Laundry room.
Activities Arts & crafts; Cards; Games;
Reading groups; Prayer groups; Movies;
Shopping trips; Dances/Social/Cultural
gatherings; Pet therapy; Music therapy;
Exercise groups; Sunday church services;
Spiritual care.

Sunnyfield Nursing Home
Maplewood Ave RFD, Cranbury, NJ 08521
(609) 395-0641
Admin George E Conley. *Dir of Nursing*
Elizabeth Decrease RN.
Licensure Intermediate care. *Beds* ICF 28.
Certified Medicaid.
Owner Proprietary corp.
Admissions Requirements Minimum age 18;
Medical examination; Physician's request.

Staff Physicians 3 (pt); RNs 1 (ft), 6 (pt);
LPNs 2 (pt); Nurses' aides 6 (ft), 8 (pt);
Recreational therapists 1 (pt); Activities
coordinators 1 (pt); Dietitians 1 (pt).
Facilities Dining room; Activities room;
Crafts room.
Activities Arts & crafts; Cards; Games; Prayer
groups.

Cranford

Cranford Hall
600 Lincoln Park E, Cranford, NJ 07016
(201) 276-7100
Admin Maryanne Lyons. *Dir of Nursing*
Marie Wells RN. *Medical Dir* Virginia
Quintone MD.
Licensure Long-term care. *Beds* Long-term
care 120. *Certified* Medicaid.
Owner Privately owned.
Staff Physicians 9 (pt); RNs 9 (ft), 3 (pt);
LPNs 9 (ft), 3 (pt); Nurses' aides 40 (ft), 15
(pt); Physical therapists 1 (pt); Reality
therapists 1 (pt); Recreational therapists 1
(pt); Occupational therapists 1 (pt);
Activities coordinators 2 (ft), 2 (pt);
Dietitians 1 (ft); Ophthalmologists 1 (pt);
Podiatrists 1 (pt); Dentists 1 (pt).
Languages French, Spanish, Italian.
Facilities Dining room; Activities room;
Crafts room; Laundry room; Barber/Beauty
shop; 5 acres of grounds; Van with
wheelchair lift.
Activities Arts & crafts; Cards; Games;
Reading groups; Prayer groups; Movies;
Shopping trips; Dances/Social/Cultural
gatherings.

Cranford Health & Extended Care Center
205 Birchwood Ave, Cranford, NJ 07016
(201) 272-6660
Admin Edward Gorczynski. *Dir of Nursing*
Carole Mitchell. *Medical Dir* Dr Elim.
Licensure Skilled care. *Beds* SNF 188.
Certified Medicaid; Medicare.
Owner Proprietary corp.
Admissions Requirements Physician's request.
Staff RNs 18 (ft), 8 (pt); LPNs 12 (ft), 6 (pt);
Nurses' aides 45 (ft), 15 (pt); Recreational
therapists 4 (ft); Activities coordinators 1
(ft); Dietitians 1 (pt).
Facilities Dining room; Physical therapy
room; Activities room; Crafts room; Laundry
room; Barber/Beauty shop; Library.
Activities Arts & crafts; Cards; Games;
Reading groups; Prayer groups; Movies;
Shopping trips; Dances/Social/Cultural
gatherings.

Cresskill

Dunroven Nursing Home
221 County Rd, Cresskill, NJ 07626
(201) 567-9310, 567-9239 FAX
Admin Donald C DeVries. *Dir of Nursing*
Ruth Monahan RN. *Medical Dir* Harry
Roselle MD.
Licensure Skilled care; Intermediate care;
Retirement; Alzheimer's care. *Beds* Swing
beds SNF/ICF 100; Retirement 140. *Private
Pay Patients* 100%.
Owner Proprietary corp.
Admissions Requirements Minimum age 16;
Physician's request.
Staff Physicians 1 (pt); RNs 16 (ft); LPNs 12
(ft); Nurses' aides 39 (ft); Physical therapists
1 (pt); Recreational therapists 2 (ft), 2 (pt);
Occupational therapists 1 (pt); Speech
therapists 1 (pt); Activities coordinators 1
(ft); Dietitians 1 (pt); Ophthalmologists 1
(pt); Podiatrists 1 (pt).
Languages German, Spanish.
Facilities Dining room; Physical therapy
room; Activities room; Crafts room; Barber/
Beauty shop.

Activities Arts & crafts; Cards; Games; Reading groups; Prayer groups; Movies; Shopping trips; Dances/Social/Cultural gatherings; Intergenerational programs; Pet therapy; Remotivational therapy; Music therapy.

Deptford

Greenbriar—East Nursing Center
1511 Clements Bridge Rd, Deptford, NJ 08096
(609) 845-9400
Admin Craig Donaghy.
Medical Dir James G Kehler MD.
Licensure Long-term care. *Beds* Long-term care 240. *Certified* Medicaid; Medicare.
Staff Physicians; RNs; LPNs; Nurses' aides; Physical therapists; Speech therapists; Activities coordinators; Dietitians; Dentists.
Facilities Dining room; Physical therapy room; Activities room; Laundry room; Barber/Beauty shop; Library; TV rooms; Reading rooms; Lounge.
Activities Arts & crafts; Cards; Games; Prayer groups; Movies; Dances/Social/Cultural gatherings; Trips.

Dover

Dover Christian Nursing Home
66 N Sussex St, Dover, NJ 07801
(201) 361-5200
Admin George Cannata.
Licensure Long-term care; Residential care. *Beds* Long-term care 125; Residential care 50.

East Orange

Brookhaven Health Care Center
120 Parkend Pl, East Orange, NJ 07018
(201) 676-6221
Admin Richard D Lee.
Licensure Long-term care. *Beds* Long-term care 120.

East Orange Nursing Home
101 N Grove St, East Orange, NJ 07017
(201) 672-1700
Admin Joseph Cohen.
Licensure Long-term care. *Beds* Long-term care 195. *Certified* Medicaid; Medicare.

Garden State Health Care Center
140 Park Ave, East Orange, NJ 07017
(201) 677-1500
Admin Elliott Baruch.
Medical Dir Pasquale Cumpanile.
Licensure Long-term care. *Beds* Long-term care 228.
Staff Physical therapists 1 (pt); Speech therapists 1 (pt); Ophthalmologists 1 (pt); Podiatrists 1 (pt); Audiologists 1 (pt); Dentists 1 (pt); Psychologists 1 (pt).
Facilities Dining room; Physical therapy room; Activities room; Crafts room; Laundry room; Barber/Beauty shop.
Activities Arts & crafts; Cards; Games; Reading groups; Prayer groups; Movies.

Parkway Manor Health Center
480 N Walnut St, East Orange, NJ 07017
(201) 674-2700
Admin C Beth Kelly.
Licensure Long-term care. *Beds* Long-term care 180.

Eatontown

Eatontown Convalescent Center
139 Grant Ave, Eatontown, NJ 07724
(201) 542-4700
Admin Lois Sonnenberg. *Dir of Nursing* Edith Bonado RN. *Medical Dir* Roger Quinlan DO.

Licensure Long-term care. *Beds* Long-term care 108. *Certified* Medicaid; Medicare.
Owner Proprietary corp.
Admissions Requirements Minimum age 16; Medical examination; Physician's request.
Staff Physicians 1 (ft), 15 (pt); RNs 6 (ft), 3 (pt); LPNs 5 (ft), 4 (pt); Nurses' aides 34 (ft), 12 (pt); Recreational therapists 3 (ft); Activities coordinators 1 (ft); Dietitians 1 (ft).
Facilities Dining room; Activities room; Crafts room; Laundry room; Barber/Beauty shop.
Activities Arts & crafts; Cards; Games; Reading groups; Prayer groups; Movies; Shopping trips; Dances/Social/Cultural gatherings.

Edison

Birchwood Nursing & Convalescent Center
1350 Inman Ave, Edison, NJ 08820
(201) 754-7100
Admin Gerald J Roth MA LNHA. *Dir of Nursing* Marian Matlaga RN. *Medical Dir* Amarjit Saini MD.
Licensure Skilled care. *Beds* SNF 84. *Private Pay Patients* 55%. *Certified* Medicaid; Medicare.
Owner Proprietary corp.
Admissions Requirements Minimum age 18.
Staff RNs; LPNs; Nurses' aides; Activities coordinators; Dietitians.
Facilities Dining room; Physical therapy room; Activities room; Crafts room; Laundry room; Barber/Beauty shop; Library.
Activities Arts & crafts; Cards; Games; Reading groups; Prayer groups; Movies; Shopping trips; Dances/Social/Cultural gatherings; Pet therapy.

Edison Estates
465 Plainfield Ave, Edison, NJ 08817
(201) 985-1500
Admin Mildred Koslow.
Licensure Skilled care; Alzheimer's care. *Beds* SNF 348. *Certified* Medicaid.
Admissions Requirements Minimum age 65; Medical examination; Physician's request.
Staff Physicians 12 (pt); RNs 30 (ft), 3 (pt); LPNs 14 (ft), 7 (pt); Nurses' aides 108 (ft), 46 (pt); Physical therapists 5 (pt); Recreational therapists 6 (ft); Occupational therapists 2 (pt); Speech therapists 1 (pt); Activities coordinators 1 (ft); Dietitians 3 (ft); Podiatrists 1 (pt); Dentists 1 (pt); Social workers 2 (ft), 2 (pt).
Facilities Dining room; Physical therapy room; Activities room; Crafts room; Laundry room; Barber/Beauty shop; Library.
Activities Arts & crafts; Cards; Games; Reading groups; Prayer groups; Movies; Shopping trips; Dances/Social/Cultural gatherings.

Hartwyck at Oak Tree
2048 Oak Tree Rd, Edison, NJ 08820
(201) 906-2100, 321-7189 FAX
Admin David M Coluzzi. *Dir of Nursing* Agnes Romulo RN. *Medical Dir* Bruce Chodosh MD.
Licensure Skilled care; Ventilator care; Extended recovery/long-term care; Cognitive day care; Transitional living; Adult day care; Residential living. *Beds* SNF 120; Ventilator care 10; Extended recovery/long-term care 45. *Private Pay Patients* 48%. *Certified* Medicaid; Medicare.
Owner Nonprofit organization/foundation (Hartwyck Nursing Convalescent & Rehabilitation Center).
Facilities Dining room; Physical therapy room; Activities room; Chapel; Crafts room; Laundry room; Barber/Beauty shop.

Activities Arts & crafts; Cards; Games; Reading groups; Prayer groups; Movies; Shopping trips; Dances/Social/Cultural gatherings; Intergenerational programs; Pet therapy.

Elizabeth

Elizabeth Nursing Home
1048 Grove St, Elizabeth, NJ 07202
(201) 354-0002
Admin Zev Fishman.
Licensure Long-term care. *Beds* Long-term care 102. *Certified* Medicaid; Medicare.

Plaza Nursing & Convalescent Center
456 Rahway Ave, Elizabeth, NJ 07202
(201) 354-1300, 355-6886 FAX
Admin Nathan Fishman. *Dir of Nursing* Debra Forman RN. *Medical Dir* Robert Solomon MD.
Licensure Skilled care; Intermediate care. *Beds* Swing beds SNF/ICF 128. *Certified* Medicaid; Medicare.
Owner Proprietary corp.
Admissions Requirements Minimum age 60.
Staff Physicians 1 (pt); RNs 5 (ft), 5 (pt); LPNs 9 (ft), 5 (pt); Nurses' aides 22 (ft), 6 (pt); Physical therapists 1 (pt); Recreational therapists 2 (pt); Activities coordinators 1 (ft); Dietitians 1 (pt); Podiatrists 1 (pt).
Facilities Dining room; Physical therapy room; Activities room; Crafts room; Laundry room; Barber/Beauty shop; Patio; TV rooms.
Activities Arts & crafts; Cards; Games; Reading groups; Prayer groups; Movies; Dances/Social/Cultural gatherings; Book mobile.

Emerson

Emerson Convalescent Center
100 Kinderkamack Rd, Emerson, NJ 07630
(201) 265-3700
Admin Nathan Friedman.
Medical Dir J A Perez MD.
Licensure Long-term care. *Beds* Long-term care 150. *Certified* Medicaid.
Admissions Requirements Minimum age 50; Medical examination.
Staff RNs 12 (ft), 4 (pt); LPNs 8 (ft), 7 (pt); Nurses' aides 50 (ft), 7 (pt); Physical therapists 2 (pt); Recreational therapists 1 (ft); Occupational therapists 1 (pt); Speech therapists 1 (pt); Activities coordinators 1 (ft), 4 (pt); Dietitians 1 (pt); Ophthalmologists 1 (pt); Podiatrists 1 (pt); Dentists 1 (pt).
Facilities Dining room; Physical therapy room; Activities room; Crafts room; Laundry room; Barber/Beauty shop.
Activities Arts & crafts; Cards; Games; Reading groups; Prayer groups; Movies; Shopping trips; Dances/Social/Cultural gatherings; Current events; Bowling; Ceramics.

Englewood

Inglemoor Inc
333 Grand Ave, Englewood, NJ 07631
(201) 568-0900
Admin Doris Neibart. *Dir of Nursing* Rosemary Fernekees. *Medical Dir* Dr Robert Nutt.
Licensure Long-term care; Alzheimer's care. *Beds* Long-term care 62.
Owner Privately owned.
Staff RNs; LPNs; Nurses' aides; Physical therapists; Ophthalmologists.
Languages Spanish, Greek, Italian, Hebrew, Yiddish.
Facilities Dining room; Physical therapy room; Activities room; Chapel; Crafts room; Laundry room; Barber/Beauty shop; Library.

Activities Arts & crafts; Cards; Games; Reading groups; Prayer groups; Movies; Dances/Social/Cultural gatherings.

Englewood Cliffs

Cliff House
633 Palisade Ave, Englewood Cliffs, NJ 07632
(201) 567-2626
Admin Richard Heller.
Licensure Long-term care. *Beds* Long-term care 36. *Certified* Medicaid; Medicare.

Englishtown

Pine Brook Care Center
Pension Rd, Englishtown, NJ 07726
(201) 446-3600, 446-2153 FAX
Admin Gerald Friederwitzer. *Dir of Nursing* Bernardette Doody RNC. *Medical Dir* Jorge Rivero MD.
Licensure Skilled care; Intermediate care; Residential care. *Beds* Swing beds SNF/ICF 123; Residential care 60. *Private Pay Patients* 25%. *Certified* Medicaid; Medicare.
Owner Proprietary corp.
Admissions Requirements Medical examination.
Staff Physicians 5 (pt); RNs 6 (ft), 8 (pt); LPNs 3 (ft), 2 (pt); Nurses' aides 37 (ft), 9 (pt); Activities coordinators 1 (ft), 2 (pt); Dietitians 1 (pt).
Facilities Dining room; Physical therapy room; Activities room; Chapel; Crafts room; Laundry room; Barber/Beauty shop; Library; TV room (42" projection screen & VCR); Recreation room (42" projector screen & TV).
Activities Arts & crafts; Cards; Games; Reading groups; Prayer groups; Movies; Shopping trips; Dances/Social/Cultural gatherings.

Fair Lawn

Fair Lawn Manor Nursing Home
12-15 Saddle River Rd, Fair Lawn, NJ 07410
(201) 797-9522
Admin B Thelea Fudim.
Licensure Intermediate care. *Beds* ICF 161.

Flemington

Hunterdon Convalescent Center Inc
1 Leisure Ct, Flemington, NJ 08822
(201) 788-9292
Admin Wendy Brainard.
Licensure Long-term care. *Beds* Long-term care 150.

Forked River

Lacey Nursing & Rehabilitation Center
916 Lacey Rd, Forked River, NJ 08731
(609) 971-1400
Admin Paul Siedler.
Licensure Long-term care. *Beds* Long-term care 120.

Franklin Park

Franklin Convalescent Center
Rte 27 Lincoln Hwy, Franklin Park, NJ 08823
(201) 821-8000
Admin Mary Ann McCarty. *Dir of Nursing* Pat Buckelew. *Medical Dir* Dr Lee.
Licensure Skilled care. *Beds* SNF 180. *Certified* Medicaid; Medicare.
Owner Privately owned.
Admissions Requirements Medical examination.

Staff Physicians; RNs; LPNs; Nurses' aides; Physical therapists; Recreational therapists; Occupational therapists; Speech therapists; Activities coordinators; Dietitians; Ophthalmologists; Podiatrists; Dentists.
Facilities Dining room; Physical therapy room; Activities room; Crafts room; Laundry room; Barber/Beauty shop; Library.
Activities Arts & crafts; Cards; Games; Reading groups; Prayer groups; Movies; Shopping trips; Dances/Social/Cultural gatherings.

Freehold

Applewood Manor
689 W Main St, Freehold, NJ 07728
(201) 431-5200, 409-2446 FAX
Admin Michael A Del Sordo. *Dir of Nursing* Violeta Peters. *Medical Dir* Dr Howard Schoenfeld.
Licensure Skilled care; Intermediate care; Respite care; Alzheimer's care. *Beds* Swing beds SNF/ICF 121. *Private Pay Patients* 50%. *Certified* Medicaid; Medicare.
Owner Nonprofit organization/foundation.
Admissions Requirements Minimum age 18; Medical examination; Physician's request.
Staff Physicians 18 (pt); RNs 8 (ft); LPNs 8 (ft); Nurses' aides 25 (ft); Physical therapists 1 (pt); Recreational therapists 2 (ft), 1 (pt); Occupational therapists 1 (pt); Speech therapists 1 (pt); Activities coordinators 1 (ft); Dietitians 2 (pt); Ophthalmologists 1 (pt); Podiatrists 1 (pt); Audiologists 1 (pt).
Languages Spanish, Italian.
Facilities Dining room; Physical therapy room; Activities room; Laundry room; Barber/Beauty shop.
Activities Arts & crafts; Cards; Games; Reading groups; Prayer groups; Movies; Shopping trips; Dances/Social/Cultural gatherings; Intergenerational programs; Pet therapy.

John L Montgomery Medical Home
Dutch Lane Rd, Freehold, NJ 07728
(201) 431-7423
Admin Dora Z Kirby; Mary Jane Eddings, Asst; Diana Scotti, Exec Dir. *Dir of Nursing* Pat Ench. *Medical Dir* Ross E McRonald MD.
Licensure Skilled care; Intermediate care; Young adult care. *Beds* Swing beds SNF/ICF 260; Young adult care 30. *Private Pay Patients* 0%. *Certified* Medicaid.
Owner Publicly owned.
Admissions Requirements Minimum age 18; Medical examination; Physician's request.
Staff Physicians 2 (pt); RNs 19 (ft), 19 (pt); LPNs 11 (ft), 5 (pt); Nurses' aides 112 (ft), 8 (pt); Recreational therapists 9 (ft), 3 (pt); Activities coordinators 2 (ft); Dietitians 1 (ft), 1 (pt).
Facilities Dining room; Physical therapy room; Activities room; Chapel; Crafts room; Laundry room; Barber/Beauty shop; Library; 2 outdoor patios.
Activities Arts & crafts; Cards; Games; Reading groups; Prayer groups; Movies; Shopping trips; Dances/Social/Cultural gatherings; Intergenerational programs; Pet therapy.

Springview Nursing Home
3419 US Hwy 9, Freehold, NJ 07728
(201) 780-0660
Admin Benjamin Farber. *Dir of Nursing* Margaret Koury. *Medical Dir* Dr Schottlander.
Licensure Skilled care. *Beds* SNF 180. *Certified* Medicaid.
Owner Privately owned.
Admissions Requirements Minimum age 50; Medical examination.

Staff Physicians; RNs; LPNs; Nurses' aides; Physical therapists; Reality therapists; Recreational therapists; Occupational therapists; Speech therapists; Activities coordinators; Dietitians; Ophthalmologists; Podiatrists; Dentists.
Facilities Dining room; Physical therapy room; Activities room; Crafts room; Laundry room; Barber/Beauty shop; Library.
Activities Arts & crafts; Cards; Games; Reading groups; Prayer groups; Movies; Shopping trips; Dances/Social/Cultural gatherings.

Frenchtown

Valley View Manor Inc
Everittstown Rd, Frenchtown, NJ 08825
(201) 996-4112
Admin Lester Krosskove. *Dir of Nursing* Barbara Z Smith RN. *Medical Dir* Howard Jones MD.
Licensure Intermediate care. *Beds* ICF 45. *Private Pay Patients* 100%.
Owner Privately owned.
Admissions Requirements Minimum age 18.
Staff Physicians 9 (pt); RNs 2 (ft), 4 (pt); LPNs 3 (pt); Nurses' aides 4 (ft), 10 (pt); Activities coordinators 1 (ft); Dietitians 1 (pt); Podiatrists 1 (pt).
Facilities Dining room; Laundry room; Barber/Beauty shop.
Activities Arts & crafts; Games; Reading groups; Prayer groups; Movies; Shopping trips; Dances/Social/Cultural gatherings; Intergenerational programs; Pet therapy; Visits by religious groups.

Glen Gardner

Hunterdon Hills Nursing Home
Hill Rd, Glen Gardner, NJ 08826
(201) 537-2717
Admin Barry Scheier.
Medical Dir John McGowan.
Licensure Long-term care. *Beds* Long-term care 32. *Certified* Medicaid.
Owner Proprietary corp.
Admissions Requirements Physician's request.
Staff RNs 4 (ft); LPNs 1 (ft); Nurses' aides 10 (ft); Physical therapists 1 (pt); Reality therapists 1 (pt); Recreational therapists 1 (pt); Activities coordinators 1 (ft); Dietitians 1 (pt).
Facilities Dining room; Activities room; Laundry room.
Activities Arts & crafts; Cards; Games; Reading groups; Prayer groups; Movies; Shopping trips.

Green Brook

Greenbrook Nursing Home
303 Rock Ave, Green Brook, NJ 08812
(201) 968-5500
Admin Adrienne Mayernik. *Dir of Nursing* Joan Zdep RN. *Medical Dir* Dr James Foley.
Licensure Skilled care. *Beds* SNF 180. *Private Pay Patients* 30%. *Certified* Medicaid; Medicare.
Owner Nonprofit corp (Mega Care Inc).
Admissions Requirements Physician's request.
Staff RNs 12 (ft), 3 (pt); LPNs 12 (ft), 3 (pt); Nurses' aides 40 (ft), 17 (pt); Physical therapists 4 (pt); Recreational therapists 3 (ft), 1 (pt); Occupational therapists 2 (pt); Speech therapists 1 (pt); Activities coordinators 1 (ft); Dietitians 1 (pt); Ophthalmologists 1 (pt); Podiatrists 1 (pt).
Facilities Dining room; Physical therapy room; Activities room; Crafts room; Laundry room; Barber/Beauty shop; Library.

Activities Arts & crafts; Games; Prayer groups; Movies; Shopping trips; Dances/Social/Cultural gatherings; Intergenerational programs; Pet therapy; On-site child day care.

Guttenberg

Palisade Nursing Home
6819 Boulevard E, Guttenberg, NJ 07093
(201) 868-3600
Admin David Gross. *Dir of Nursing* Jeanette Bruen RN. *Medical Dir* Joseph Weisgras MD.
Licensure Skilled care. *Beds* SNF 106; Extra bed program 2. *Certified* Medicaid.
Owner Proprietary corp.
Staff Physicians 2 (ft); RNs 7 (ft), 4 (pt); LPNs 3 (ft); Nurses' aides 30 (ft); Physical therapists 1 (ft), 1 (pt); Reality therapists 1 (pt); Recreational therapists 2 (ft), 2 (pt); Occupational therapists 1 (pt); Speech therapists 1 (pt); Activities coordinators 1 (ft); Dietitians 1 (ft); Ophthalmologists 1 (pt); Podiatrists 1 (pt); Dentists 1 (pt).
Languages Spanish, Yiddish, Hebrew.
Facilities Dining room; Physical therapy room; Activities room; Chapel; Crafts room; Laundry room; Barber/Beauty shop; Library.
Activities Arts & crafts; Cards; Games; Reading groups; Prayer groups; Movies; Shopping trips; Dances/Social/Cultural gatherings.

Hackensack

Regent Care Center
50 Polifly Rd, Hackensack, NJ 07601
(201) 646-1166
Admin G Edward Davis.
Licensure Long-term care. *Beds* Long-term care 180.

Wellington Hall Nursing Home
301 Union St, Hackensack, NJ 07601
(201) 487-4900
Admin Bruce H London. *Dir of Nursing* Rosemary Raleigh RN. *Medical Dir* Arthur Chaney Jr MD.
Licensure Long-term care. *Beds* Long-term care 120. *Certified* Medicaid; Medicare.
Owner Privately owned.
Admissions Requirements Physician's request.
Staff RNs 4 (ft), 3 (pt); LPNs 3 (ft), 1 (pt); Nurses' aides 26 (ft), 20 (pt); Physical therapists 1 (ft); Occupational therapists 1 (pt); Speech therapists 1 (pt); Activities coordinators 2 (ft); Dietitians 1 (pt); Ophthalmologists 1 (pt); Dentists 1 (pt).
Facilities Dining room; Physical therapy room; Activities room; Chapel; Crafts room; Laundry room; Barber/Beauty shop; Library.
Activities Arts & crafts; Cards; Games; Reading groups; Prayer groups; Movies; Shopping trips; Dances/Social/Cultural gatherings.

Haddonfield

Haddonfield Presbyterian Home
132 Warwick Rd, Haddonfield, NJ 08033
(609) 429-5500
Admin Elizabeth A Gutekunst. *Dir of Nursing* Judith Slimm RN. *Medical Dir* Dr James Sobel.
Licensure Intermediate care; Residential care. *Beds* ICF 6; Residential care 59.
Owner Nonprofit organization/foundation.
Admissions Requirements Minimum age 62; Medical examination.
Staff Physicians 2 (pt); RNs 1 (ft), 2 (pt); LPNs 6 (pt); Nurses' aides 3 (ft), 3 (pt); Activities coordinators 1 (pt); Dietitians 1 (pt); Dentists 1 (pt).
Affiliation Presbyterian.

Facilities Dining room; Activities room; Chapel; Crafts room; Laundry room; Barber/Beauty shop; Library; Screened porches; Gazebo.
Activities Arts & crafts; Cards; Games; Reading groups; Prayer groups; Movies; Shopping trips; Dances/Social/Cultural gatherings.

Hamilton Square

King James Care Center of Mercer
1501 State Hwy 33, Hamilton Square, NJ 08690
(609) 586-1114
Admin Lori Gabriel. *Dir of Nursing* Jean Anderson RN. *Medical Dir* Albert Valenzuela MD.
Licensure Skilled care; Alzheimer's care. *Beds* SNF 120. *Private Pay Patients* 35%. *Certified* Medicaid; Medicare.
Owner Proprietary corp.
Admissions Requirements Minimum age 16; Medical examination.
Staff Physicians 8 (pt); RNs 6 (ft), 2 (pt); LPNs 4 (ft), 2 (pt); Nurses' aides 40 (ft), 4 (pt); Physical therapists 1 (pt); Reality therapists 1 (ft); Recreational therapists 1 (ft); Occupational therapists 1 (pt); Speech therapists 1 (pt); Activities coordinators 1 (ft); Dietitians 1 (ft), 1 (pt); Ophthalmologists 1 (pt); Podiatrists 1 (pt); Audiologists 1 (pt).
Languages Polish, Italian, Spanish.
Facilities Dining room; Physical therapy room; Activities room; Crafts room; Laundry room; Barber/Beauty shop; Library; Patio.
Activities Arts & crafts; Cards; Games; Reading groups; Prayer groups; Movies; Shopping trips; Dances/Social/Cultural gatherings; Intergenerational programs; Pet therapy.

University Nursing Center
1059 Edinburgh Rd, Hamilton Square, NJ 08690
(609) 588-0091
Admin David Gross. *Dir of Nursing* Barbara Collis. *Medical Dir* Joseph Singer.
Licensure Skilled care; Alzheimer's care. *Beds* SNF 180. *Private Pay Patients* 50%. *Certified* Medicaid; Medicare.
Owner Proprietary corp.
Admissions Requirements Minimum age 18.
Staff Physicians 1 (ft), 3 (pt); RNs 20 (ft), 5 (pt); LPNs 10 (ft), 5 (pt); Nurses' aides 60 (ft), 5 (pt); Physical therapists 1 (ft), 1 (pt); Reality therapists 2 (ft); Recreational therapists 4 (ft), 1 (pt); Occupational therapists 1 (pt); Speech therapists 1 (pt); Activities coordinators 1 (pt); Dietitians 2 (pt); Ophthalmologists 1 (pt); Podiatrists 1 (pt); Audiologists 1 (pt).
Languages Spanish, German, Hebrew, Yiddish.
Facilities Dining room; Physical therapy room; Activities room; Chapel; Crafts room; Laundry room; Barber/Beauty shop; Library.
Activities Arts & crafts; Cards; Games; Reading groups; Prayer groups; Movies; Shopping trips; Dances/Social/Cultural gatherings; Intergenerational programs; Pet therapy.

Hammonton

Greenbriar Nursing Center of Hammonton
43 N White Horse Pike, Hammonton, NJ 08037
(609) 567-3100
Admin Elizabeth M Hildenbrand.
Licensure Long-term care. *Beds* Long-term care 208.

Haskell

Lakeland Health Care Center
25 5th Ave, Haskell, NJ 07420
(201) 839-6000, 839-9153 FAX
Admin Chris Asmann-Finch LNHA. *Dir of Nursing* Carol Johnson RN. *Medical Dir* Ashok Gupta MD.
Licensure Skilled care; Intermediate care. *Beds* Swing beds SNF/ICF 201. *Certified* Medicaid; Medicare.
Owner Proprietary corp.
Admissions Requirements Minimum age 62.
Staff Physicians; RNs; LPNs; Nurses' aides; Physical therapists (contracted); Recreational therapists 5 (ft), 1 (pt); Occupational therapists (contracted); Speech therapists (contracted); Activities coordinators 1 (ft); Dietitians 1 (ft); Ophthalmologists (contracted); Podiatrists (contracted); Audiologists (contracted).
Languages Spanish, French, Polish.
Facilities Dining room; Physical therapy room; Activities room; Crafts room; Laundry room; Barber/Beauty shop; Patio.
Activities Arts & crafts; Cards; Games; Reading groups; Prayer groups; Movies; Shopping trips; Dances/Social/Cultural gatherings; Intergenerational programs; Pet therapy.

Wanaque Convalescent Center
1433 Ringwood Ave, Haskell, NJ 07420
(201) 839-2119
Admin Robert Mondrone.
Licensure Long-term care. *Beds* Long-term care 240.

Hazlet

Hazlet Manor Care Center
3325 Hwy 35, Hazlet, NJ 07730
(201) 264-5800
Admin Dr Hershel Gottlieb.
Licensure Long-term care; Residential care. *Beds* Long-term care 150; Residential care 12. *Certified* Medicaid; Medicare.

Arnold Walter Nursing Home
622 S Laurel Ave, Hazlet, NJ 07730
(201) 787-6300
Admin Benzion Schachter.
Licensure Long-term care. *Beds* Long-term care 132. *Certified* Medicaid; Medicare.

Hightstown

Applegarth Care Center
Applegarth Rd, Hightstown, NJ 08520
(609) 448-7036, 448-0914 FAX
Admin Harry C Veale. *Dir of Nursing* Joan T Dovgala RN. *Medical Dir* Dr Oscar Schimensky.
Licensure Intermediate care. *Beds* ICF 172. *Private Pay Patients* 40%. *Certified* Medicaid.
Owner Proprietary corp.
Admissions Requirements Minimum age 50.
Staff Physicians 10 (pt); RNs 7 (ft), 3 (pt); LPNs 11 (ft), 3 (pt); Nurses' aides 36 (ft), 12 (pt); Physical therapists (contracted); Occupational therapists 1 (pt); Speech therapists 1 (pt); Activities coordinators 1 (ft); Dietitians 1 (pt); Podiatrists 2 (pt).
Facilities Dining room; Activities room; Chapel; Laundry room; Barber/Beauty shop.
Activities Arts & crafts; Cards; Games; Movies; Shopping trips; Dances/Social/Cultural gatherings; Intergenerational programs; Pet therapy.

Sunlawn Nursing Home
576 Main St, Hightstown, NJ 08520
(609) 448-0528
Admin Eugene Callaghan.
Licensure Long-term care. *Beds* Long-term care 30.

Holmdel

Bayshore Health Care Center
715 N Beers St, Holmdel, NJ 07733
(201) 739-9000
Admin Jay S Solomon.
Licensure Long-term care. *Beds* Long-term care 120.

Garden State Manor
16 Van Brackle Rd, Holmdel, NJ 07733
(201) 264-3548
Admin Helen Dimitrow MD.
Medical Dir Dr Elias Lehaf.
Licensure Skilled care; Intermediate care. *Beds* SNF 2; ICF 25. *Certified* Medicaid.
Owner Proprietary corp.
Admissions Requirements Physician's request.
Staff Physicians 1 (pt); RNs 1 (ft), 2 (pt); LPNs 2 (ft), 2 (pt); Nurses' aides 17 (ft), 3 (pt); Activities coordinators 1 (pt); Dietitians 1 (pt); Ophthalmologists 1 (pt).
Facilities Dining room; Activities room.
Activities Arts & crafts; Games.

Holmdel Nursing Home
Rte 34, Holmdel, NJ 07733
(201) 946-4200
Admin Valerie A Kennedy.
Licensure Skilled care; Alzheimer's care. *Beds* SNF 41. *Certified* Medicaid; Medicare.
Owner Nonprofit corp.
Admissions Requirements Minimum age 21.
Staff Physicians; RNs; LPNs; Nurses' aides; Physical therapists; Reality therapists; Recreational therapists; Occupational therapists; Speech therapists; Activities coordinators; Dietitians; Ophthalmologists; Podiatrists; Dentists.
Facilities Dining room.
Activities Arts & crafts; Cards; Games; Reading groups; Prayer groups; Movies; Shopping trips; Dances/Social/Cultural gatherings; Parties.

Hope

Forest Manor Health Care Center
PO Box 283, State Park Rd, Hope, NJ 07844
(201) 459-4128, 459-4513 FAX
Admin I Joel Foreman LNHA.
Licensure Skilled care; Respite care; Alzheimer's care. *Beds* SNF 60. *Private Pay Patients* 98%. *Certified* Medicare.
Owner Proprietary corp.
Admissions Requirements Minimum age 16.
Staff RNs 7 (ft); LPNs 5 (ft); Nurses' aides 13 (ft); Physical therapists; Dietitians.
Languages German, Spanish.
Facilities Dining room; Activities room; Crafts room; Laundry room; Barber/Beauty shop; Library.
Activities Arts & crafts; Cards; Games; Reading groups; Prayer groups; Movies; Shopping trips; Dances/Social/Cultural gatherings; Intergenerational programs; Pet therapy.

Jackson

Bartley Manor Convalescent Center
20 Bartley Rd, Jackson, NJ 08527
(201) 370-4700, 370-4678 FAX
Admin Patricia De Muro LNHA. *Dir of Nursing* Doris Horenkamp. *Medical Dir* Dr Vincent De Muro.
Licensure Skilled care; Intermediate care. *Beds* Swing beds SNF/ICF 120. *Private Pay Patients* 42%. *Certified* Medicaid.
Owner Proprietary corp.
Admissions Requirements Must require 24-hour nursing supervision.
Staff Physicians; RNs; LPNs; Nurses' aides; Physical therapists; Recreational therapists; Occupational therapists; Speech therapists; Activities coordinators; Dietitians; Ophthalmologists; Podiatrists; Audiologists.
Facilities Dining room; Physical therapy room; Activities room; Laundry room; Barber/Beauty shop; Library; Dayrooms; Enclosed outside patios; Greenhouse; Wanderer alarm system.
Activities Arts & crafts; Cards; Games; Reading groups; Prayer groups; Movies; Shopping trips; Dances/Social/Cultural gatherings; Intergenerational programs; Pet therapy; Choral group.

Jackson Healthcare Center
1 Heritage Way, Jackson, NJ 08527
(201) 367-6600, 905-9641 FAX
Admin Janice Marchelle. *Dir of Nursing* Susan Friedman RN. *Medical Dir* Dr Edward Maron.
Licensure Skilled care. *Beds* SNF 186. *Private Pay Patients* 50%. *Certified* Medicaid; Medicare.
Owner Proprietary corp (Multicare Management Inc).
Admissions Requirements Minimum age 21.
Staff Physicians; RNs; LPNs; Nurses' aides; Physical therapists; Recreational therapists; Occupational therapists; Speech therapists; Activities coordinators; Dietitians; Podiatrists.
Languages Interpreters by request.
Facilities Dining room; Physical therapy room; Activities room; Chapel; Crafts room; Laundry room; Barber/Beauty shop; Library.
Activities Arts & crafts; Cards; Games; Prayer groups; Movies; Shopping trips; Dances/Social/Cultural gatherings; Intergenerational programs; Pet therapy.

Newmans Lakewood Nursing Home
12 Denmark Ln, Jackson, NJ 08527
(201) 363-2659
Admin Felice Newman.
Medical Dir Dr Harish Chander.
Licensure Intermediate care. *Beds* 44. *Certified* Medicaid.
Admissions Requirements Minimum age 35; Medical examination; Physician's request.
Staff Physicians 4 (pt); RNs 3 (ft); LPNs 3 (pt); Physical therapists 1 (pt); Reality therapists 1 (ft); Recreational therapists 1 (ft), 1 (pt); Occupational therapists 1 (pt); Speech therapists 1 (pt); Activities coordinators 1 (ft); Dietitians 1 (pt); Ophthalmologists 1 (pt); Podiatrists 1 (pt); Audiologists 1 (pt); Dentists 1 (pt).
Facilities Dining room; Activities room; Laundry room.
Activities Arts & crafts; Cards; Games; Reading groups; Prayer groups; Movies; Shopping trips.

Jamesburg

Monroe Village Health Care Center
117 Half Acre Rd, Jamesburg, NJ 08831
(201) 521-6400
Admin Christopher Csernus.
Licensure Long-term care. *Beds* Long-term care 60.

Jersey City

Harbor View Health Care Center
178-198 Ogden Ave, Jersey City, NJ 07306
(201) 963-1800
Admin Marilyn Gilbert.
Licensure Long-term care. *Beds* Long-term care 180.

Liberty House Nursing Home
620 Montgomery St, Jersey City, NJ 07302
(201) 435-0033
Admin Michael Katz.
Medical Dir J John DeGoia.
Licensure Long-term care. *Beds* Long-term care 180. *Certified* Medicaid; Medicare.

Staff Physicians; RNs; LPNs; Nurses' aides; Physical therapists; Recreational therapists; Occupational therapists; Speech therapists; Activities coordinators; Dietitians; Ophthalmologists; Podiatrists; Dentists.
Facilities Dining room; Physical therapy room; Activities room; Crafts room; Laundry room.
Activities Arts & crafts; Cards; Games; Reading groups; Prayer groups; Movies; Dances/Social/Cultural gatherings.

Berthold S Pollak Hospital
100 Clifton Pl, Jersey City, NJ 07304
(201) 432-1000
Admin Dorothea Stovekin. *Dir of Nursing* Maria Lapid RN. *Medical Dir* Francis T Molinari MD.
Licensure Skilled care. *Beds* SNF 460. *Certified* Medicaid.
Owner Publicly owned.
Admissions Requirements Minimum age 18; Physician's request.
Staff Physicians 6 (ft), 10 (pt); RNs 45 (ft), 5 (pt); LPNs 44 (ft), 3 (pt); Recreational therapists 8 (ft), 1 (pt); Activities coordinators 1 (ft); Dietitians 3 (ft).
Facilities Dining room; Physical therapy room; Activities room; Chapel; Crafts room; Laundry room; Barber/Beauty shop; Library.
Activities Arts & crafts; Cards; Games; Movies; Shopping trips; Dances/Social/Cultural gatherings; Bus trips; Bowling; Theater; Sport events.

Keansburg

Beachview Intermediate Care Facility
32 Laurel Ave, Keansburg, NJ 07734
(201) 787-8100
Admin Joseph Cappadona.
Licensure Intermediate care. *Beds* ICF 120. *Certified* Medicaid; Medicare.

Lakehurst

Manchester Manor Nursing Facility
101 State Hwy 70, Lakehurst, NJ 08733
(201) 657-1800
Admin Elizabeth Walstrom.
Licensure Long-term care. *Beds* Long-term care 180.
Owner Proprietary corp (HBA Management Inc).

Lakewood

Belle Reeve Health Care Center
485 River Ave, Lakewood, NJ 08701
(201) 364-7100
Admin Kerry Mulvihill.
Licensure Long-term care; Residential care. *Beds* Long-term care 180; Residential care 40.
Owner Proprietary corp.

Harrogate
400 Locust St, Lakewood, NJ 08701
(201) 905-7070
Admin Cynthia S Thorland.
Licensure Long-term care. *Beds* Long-term care 60.

Lakeview Manor Nursing Home
963 Ocean Ave, Lakewood, NJ 08701
(201) 367-7444, 367-7603 FAX
Admin Sharon Johnston BSW LNHA. *Dir of Nursing* Marilyn Meachem RN. *Medical Dir* Paul Moyer MD.
Licensure Skilled care; Intermediate care. *Beds* Swing beds SNF/ICF 120. *Private Pay Patients* 33%. *Certified* Medicaid; Medicare.
Owner Proprietary corp (Hospicomm).
Admissions Requirements Minimum age 18; Medical examination; Physician's request.

Staff RNs 4 (ft), 16 (pt); LPNs 6 (ft), 6 (pt); Nurses' aides 40 (ft), 6 (pt); Physical therapists 1 (pt); Recreational therapists 4 (ft); Occupational therapists 1 (pt); Speech therapists 1 (pt); Dietitians 1 (pt); Ophthalmologists (consultant); Podiatrists (consultant); Audiologists (consultant).
Languages Polish, Spanish, German.
Facilities Dining room; Physical therapy room; Activities room; Crafts room; Laundry room; Barber/Beauty shop; TV rooms.
Activities Arts & crafts; Cards; Games; Reading groups; Prayer groups; Movies; Shopping trips; Dances/Social/Cultural gatherings; Intergenerational programs; Pet therapy; Support groups; Gardening.

Leisure Chateau Care Center
962 River Ave, Lakewood, NJ 08701
(201) 370-8600
Admin Elizabeth E Miller. *Dir of Nursing* Jean Laverty. *Medical Dir* Dr Roseff.
Licensure Long-term care; Alzheimer's care. *Beds* Long-term care 242. *Certified* Medicaid; Medicare.
Owner Proprietary corp.
Staff RNs; LPNs; Nurses' aides; Physical therapists; Recreational therapists; Speech therapists; Activities coordinators; Dietitians.
Facilities Dining room; Physical therapy room; Activities room; Crafts room; Laundry room; Barber/Beauty shop.
Activities Arts & crafts; Cards; Games; Reading groups; Prayer groups; Movies; Shopping trips; Dances/Social/Cultural gatherings.

Leisure Park Health Center
1400 Rte 70, Lakewood, NJ 08701
(201) 370-0444
Admin Albert Bainger.
Licensure Long-term care. *Beds* Long-term care 60.

Medicenter of Lakewood
685 River Ave, Lakewood, NJ 08701
(201) 364-8300
Admin Gary Pizzichillo. *Dir of Nursing* Mrs Hennington. *Medical Dir* Dr James Meehan.
Licensure Long-term care; Alzheimer's care. *Beds* Long-term care 245.
Owner Proprietary corp (HBA Management Inc).
Admissions Requirements Minimum age 16.
Staff Physicians 1 (pt); RNs 15 (ft), 3 (pt); LPNs 15 (ft), 5 (pt); Nurses' aides 63 (ft), 5 (pt); Physical therapists 2 (ft); Recreational therapists 4 (ft); Occupational therapists 1 (ft); Speech therapists 1 (ft); Activities coordinators 1 (ft); Dietitians 1 (pt); Ophthalmologists 1 (pt); Podiatrists 1 (pt); Dentists 1 (pt).
Facilities Dining room; Physical therapy room; Activities room; Crafts room; Laundry room; Barber/Beauty shop; Rolling library.
Activities Arts & crafts; Cards; Games; Reading groups; Prayer groups; Movies; Shopping trips; Dances/Social/Cultural gatherings.

Ocean Convalescent Center
901 Monmouth Ave, Lakewood, NJ 08701
(201) 363-0151
Admin Andrew V Shawn. *Dir of Nursing* B Caruso. *Medical Dir* Dr Pineles.
Licensure Skilled care; Intermediate care. *Beds* Swing beds SNF/ICF 61. *Private Pay Patients* 10%. *Certified* Medicaid.
Owner Proprietary corp.
Admissions Requirements Minimum age 50; Medical examination.
Staff RNs 5 (ft); LPNs 2 (ft); Nurses' aides 22 (ft); Recreational therapists 1 (ft), 1 (pt).
Facilities Dining room; Activities room; Laundry room; Barber/Beauty shop.
Activities Arts & crafts; Games; Prayer groups; Movies; Pet therapy.

Pineland Nursing Home
Squankum Rd, Lakewood, NJ 08701
(201) 363-9507
Admin Lucie Zane.
Licensure Long-term care. *Beds* Long-term care 18. *Certified* Medicaid.
Owner Proprietary corp.

Summit Nursing Home
285 River Ave, Lakewood, NJ 08701
(201) 363-0400
Admin Lee Anne Schwiers RN LNHA. *Dir of Nursing* Rose Ann Woronkewycz BSN RN. *Medical Dir* Antonio E Marasca MD.
Licensure Skilled care; Intermediate care. *Beds* Swing beds SNF/ICF 180. *Certified* Medicaid; Medicare.
Owner Proprietary corp (Beverly Enterprises).
Staff RNs; LPNs; Nurses' aides; Recreational therapists; Activities coordinators.
Facilities Dining room; Physical therapy room; Activities room; Barber/Beauty shop.
Activities Arts & crafts; Cards; Games; Reading groups; Prayer groups; Movies; Dances/Social/Cultural gatherings; Pet therapy.

Lawrenceville

Lawrenceville Nursing Home
112 Franklyn Corner Rd, Lawrenceville, NJ 08648
(609) 896-1494
Admin Frank Puzio.
Medical Dir Dr S Goldsmith.
Licensure Skilled care; Alzheimer's care. *Beds* SNF 100. *Certified* Medicaid; Medicare.
Owner Proprietary corp.
Staff Physicians 1 (pt); RNs 12 (ft), 4 (pt); LPNs 4 (ft); Nurses' aides 36 (ft), 6 (pt); Physical therapists 1 (pt); Reality therapists 1 (ft); Recreational therapists 1 (ft); Occupational therapists 1 (pt); Speech therapists 1 (pt); Activities coordinators 1 (ft); Dietitians 1 (pt); Ophthalmologists 1 (pt); Podiatrists 1 (pt); Dentists 1 (pt).
Facilities Dining room; Physical therapy room; Activities room; Chapel; Crafts room; Laundry room; Barber/Beauty shop; Library.
Activities Arts & crafts; Cards; Games; Reading groups; Prayer groups; Movies; Shopping trips; Dances/Social/Cultural gatherings.

Lebanon

Union Forge Nursing Home
RD 1, 184 Cratetown Road, Lebanon, NJ 08833
(201) 236-2011
Admin Irene Pasternak. *Dir of Nursing* Cathy Bodine RN. *Medical Dir* Alan Kelsey MD.
Licensure Skilled care. *Beds* SNF 62.
Owner Proprietary corp.
Admissions Requirements Medical examination.
Facilities Dining room; Activities room; Laundry room; Barber/Beauty shop.
Activities Arts & crafts; Cards; Games; Reading groups; Prayer groups; Movies; Dances/Social/Cultural gatherings.

Lincoln Park

Lincoln Park Intermediate Care Center
499 Pinebrook Rd, Lincoln Park, NJ 07035
(201) 696-3300
Admin Jane K Bernheim. *Dir of Nursing* Virginia Rosso.
Licensure Skilled care. *Beds* SNF 544. *Private Pay Patients* 20%. *Certified* Medicaid; Medicare.
Owner Proprietary corp.
Admissions Requirements Medical examination; Physician's request.
Staff Dietitians 2 (ft), 1 (pt).

Facilities Dining room; Physical therapy room; Activities room; Chapel; Crafts room; Laundry room; Barber/Beauty shop; Library.
Activities Arts & crafts; Cards; Games; Reading groups; Prayer groups; Movies; Shopping trips; Dances/Social/Cultural gatherings; Intergenerational programs; Pet therapy.

Lincoln Park Nursing & Convalescent Home
521 Pinebrook Rd, Lincoln Park, NJ 07035
(201) 696-3300
Admin Karen Scienski. *Dir of Nursing* Gertrude O'Keefe.
Licensure Skilled care. *Beds* SNF 159. *Certified* Medicaid; Medicare.
Owner Proprietary corp.
Admissions Requirements Medical examination; Physician's request.
Facilities Dining room; Physical therapy room; Activities room; Chapel; Crafts room; Laundry room; Barber/Beauty shop; Library.
Activities Arts & crafts; Games; Reading groups; Prayer groups; Movies; Shopping trips; Dances/Social/Cultural gatherings.

Linden

Delaire Nursing & Convalescent Home
400 W Stimpson Ave, Linden, NJ 07036
(201) 862-3399
Admin Diana Czerepuszko.
Licensure Long-term care. *Beds* Long-term care 180.

Linwood

Linwood Convalescent Center
New Rd & Central Ave, Linwood, NJ 08221
(609) 927-6131
Admin Gary Hand.
Licensure Long-term care. *Beds* Long-term care 154. *Certified* Medicaid; Medicare.
Owner Proprietary corp.

Livingston

Inglemoor West Nursing Home
311 S Livingston Ave, Livingston, NJ 07039
(201) 994-0221
Admin Georgia S Eitzen RN. *Dir of Nursing* Eveline B Hirsch RN. *Medical Dir* George Kline Jr MD.
Licensure Skilled care; Intermediate care; Alzheimer's care. *Beds* Swing beds SNF/ICF 120.
Owner Proprietary corp.
Admissions Requirements Physician's request.
Staff RNs 15 (ft), 15 (pt); Nurses' aides 41 (ft), 9 (pt); Physical therapists 1 (pt); Occupational therapists 1 (pt); Speech therapists 1 (ft); Activities coordinators 2 (ft); Dietitians 1 (ft); Ophthalmologists 1 (pt); Podiatrists 1 (pt); Dentists 1 (pt).
Facilities Dining room; Physical therapy room; Activities room; Crafts room; Laundry room; Barber/Beauty shop; Library; Diet kitchen.
Activities Arts & crafts; Cards; Games; Reading groups; Prayer groups; Shopping trips; Dances/Social/Cultural gatherings; Lunches/Dinners.

Long Branch

Monmouth Convalescent Center
229 Bath Ave, Long Branch, NJ 07740
(201) 229-4300, 571-0165 FAX
Admin Deborah L Scheibe. *Dir of Nursing* Jo Williams RN. *Medical Dir* Dr Marshal Silver.
Licensure Skilled care; Intermediate care. *Beds* Swing beds SNF/ICF 113. *Certified* Medicaid; Medicare.
Owner Proprietary corp.

Admissions Requirements Minimum age 14; Medical examination; Physician's request.
Staff Physicians 15 (pt); RNs 4 (ft), 8 (pt); LPNs 6 (ft); Nurses' aides 18 (ft), 27 (pt); Physical therapists 1 (pt); Recreational therapists 1 (ft); Occupational therapists 1 (pt); Speech therapists 1 (pt); Activities coordinators 1 (ft).
Facilities Dining room; Physical therapy room; Activities room; Crafts room; Laundry room; Barber/Beauty shop.
Activities Arts & crafts; Cards; Games; Reading groups; Prayer groups; Movies; Shopping trips; Dances/Social/Cultural gatherings; Intergenerational programs; Pet therapy.

Westwood Hall Hebrew Home
281 Bath Ave, Long Branch, NJ 07740
(201) 222-5277
Admin Joanne E Escovar. *Dir of Nursing* Hazel A Prattis RN. *Medical Dir* Dr Alvin H Fried.
Licensure Skilled care; Intermediate care. *Beds* Swing beds SNF/ICF 84. *Certified* Medicaid; Medicare.
Owner Nonprofit corp.
Admissions Requirements Minimum age 55-60; Physician's request.
Staff RNs 3 (ft), 6 (pt); LPNs 5 (ft), 3 (pt); Nurses' aides 25 (ft), 14 (pt); Physical therapists 1 (pt); Activities coordinators 2 (ft); Dietitians 1 (pt).
Affiliation Jewish.
Facilities Physical therapy room; Activities room; Laundry room; Barber/Beauty shop.
Activities Arts & crafts; Cards; Games; Reading groups; Prayer groups; Movies; Dances/Social/Cultural gatherings; Intergenerational programs; Pet therapy.

Witmer House
75 Cooper Ave, Long Branch, NJ 07740
(201) 229-4352
Admin Mary Washington. *Dir of Nursing* Brenda Hodgkiss RN. *Medical Dir* Dr Herman Wiley.
Licensure Intermediate care; Residential care. *Beds* ICF 80; Residential care 34. *Certified* Medicaid.
Owner Proprietary corp.
Admissions Requirements Medical examination.
Staff Physicians 1 (pt); RNs 3 (ft), 3 (pt); LPNs 1 (ft), 4 (pt); Nurses' aides 8 (ft), 6 (pt); Activities coordinators 1 (ft), 1 (pt); Dietitians 1 (pt).
Languages English, Spanish, Tagalog.
Facilities Dining room; Activities room; Laundry room; Barber/Beauty shop.
Activities Arts & crafts; Cards; Games; Reading groups; Prayer groups; Movies; Shopping trips; Dances/Social/Cultural gatherings.

Madison

Pine Acres Nursing Home
51 Madison Ave, Madison, NJ 07940
(201) 377-2125
Admin Patricia Ledwith.
Licensure Long-term care. *Beds* Long-term care 102. *Certified* Medicaid; Medicare.
Owner Proprietary corp.

Royal Oaks
300 Madison Ave, Madison, NJ 07940
(201) 377-9762
Admin John Flemming.
Licensure Long-Term care. *Beds* 31.

Manahawkin

Manahawkin Convalescent Center
1121 Rte 72 W, Manahawkin, NJ 08050
(609) 597-8500
Admin Phyllis Bohnenberger.

Licensure Long-term care. *Beds* Long-term care 120.

Manasquan

Sunnyside Farms Nursing & Convalescent Home
Ramshorn Dr & Lakewood Rd, Manasquan, NJ 08736
(201) 528-9311
Admin Joseph Singer. *Dir of Nursing* Juliet Powell.
Licensure Skilled care; Personal care. *Beds* SNF 45; Personal care 12. *Private Pay Patients* 100%.
Owner Proprietary corp.
Admissions Requirements Physician's request.
Staff RNs 3 (ft), 4 (pt); LPNs 3 (pt); Nurses' aides 20 (ft), 5 (pt); Recreational therapists 1 (ft); Dietitians 1 (pt); Ophthalmologists 1 (pt); Podiatrists 1 (pt).
Facilities Dining room; Activities room; Barber/Beauty shop; Library.
Activities Arts & crafts; Cards; Games; Reading groups; Prayer groups; Movies; Shopping trips; Pet therapy.

Maple Shade

Rosewood Manor Nursing Center
Rte 38 & Mill Rd, Maple Shade, NJ 08052
(609) 779-1500
Admin G Dane Ewen.
Licensure Long-term care. *Beds* Long-term care 162. *Certified* Medicaid; Medicare.
Owner Proprietary corp.

Sterling Manor Nursing Center
794 N Forklanding Rd, Maple Shade, NJ 08052
(609) 779-9333
Admin Charles A Jackson. *Dir of Nursing* Bernadette Toner RN. *Medical Dir* Robert Warden DO.
Licensure Skilled care. *Beds* SNF 124. *Certified* Medicaid; Medicare.
Owner Proprietary corp.
Admissions Requirements Medical examination; Physician's request.
Staff Physicians 4 (ft); RNs 6 (ft), 2 (pt); LPNs 9 (ft), 3 (pt); Physical therapists 1 (ft), 1 (pt); Recreational therapists 3 (pt); Occupational therapists 1 (pt); Speech therapists 1 (pt); Dietitians 1 (pt); Ophthalmologists 1 (pt); Podiatrists 1 (pt).
Facilities Dining room; Physical therapy room; Activities room; Laundry room; Barber/Beauty shop.
Activities Arts & crafts; Cards; Games; Reading groups; Prayer groups; Movies; Dances/Social/Cultural gatherings.

Matawan

Emery Manor Nursing Home
Rte 34, Matawan, NJ 07747
(201) 566-6400
Admin Barbara A Fyfe. *Dir of Nursing* E Weigel. *Medical Dir* Dr A Kubal.
Licensure Skilled care. *Beds* SNF 100. *Certified* Medicaid; Medicare.
Owner Proprietary corp.
Staff Recreational therapists 1 (ft), 3 (pt); Activities coordinators 1 (ft).
Facilities Dining room; Physical therapy room; Activities room; Crafts room; Laundry room; Barber/Beauty shop.
Activities Arts & crafts; Cards; Games; Reading groups; Prayer groups; Movies; Shopping trips; Dances/Social/Cultural gatherings; Bowling; Happy hour.

Mt Pleasant Manor
38 Freneau Ave, Matawan, NJ 07747
(201) 566-4633
Admin Edward Gann Jr.

Licensure Long-term care. *Beds* Long-term care 27. *Certified* Medicaid.

Medford

Medford Convalescent & Nursing Center
185 Tuckerton Rd, Medford, NJ 08055
(609) 983-8500, 983-8965 FAX
Admin David F Graham LNHA. *Dir of Nursing* Maureen Cholette RN. *Medical Dir* Richard Molino MD.
Licensure Skilled care. *Beds* SNF 180. *Private Pay Patients* 28%. *Certified* Medicaid; Medicare.
Owner Proprietary corp.
Admissions Requirements Medical examination; Physician's request.
Staff Physicians 11 (pt); RNs 8 (ft), 10 (pt); LPNs 9 (ft), 5 (pt); Nurses' aides 49 (ft), 38 (pt); Physical therapists 1 (pt); Reality therapists 1 (pt); Recreational therapists 1 (pt); Occupational therapists 1 (pt); Speech therapists 1 (pt); Activities coordinators 3 (ft), 3 (pt); Dietitians 1 (pt); Ophthalmologists 1 (pt); Podiatrists 1 (pt); Audiologists 1 (pt).
Languages Italian, German.
Facilities Dining room; Physical therapy room; Activities room; Chapel; Barber/Beauty shop.
Activities Arts & crafts; Cards; Games; Reading groups; Prayer groups; Movies; Shopping trips; Dances/Social/Cultural gatherings; Pet therapy.

Medford Leas
PO Box 366, New Freedom Rd, Medford, NJ 08055
(609) 654-3000
Admin Lois Forrest. *Dir of Nursing* Kathleen Gentleman RN. *Medical Dir* Benjamin R Paradee MD.
Licensure Long-term care; Residential care; Alzheimer's care. *Beds* Long-term care 142; Residential care 99. *Certified* Medicare.
Owner Nonprofit corp.
Admissions Requirements Minimum age 65; Medical examination.
Staff Physicians 1 (ft), 3 (pt); RNs 12 (ft), 22 (pt); LPNs 3 (ft), 9 (pt); Nurses' aides 27 (ft), 41 (pt); Physical therapists 1 (pt); Activities coordinators 1 (ft); Dietitians 1 (pt); Dentists 1 (pt).
Affiliation Society of Friends.
Facilities Dining room; Physical therapy room; Activities room; Crafts room; Laundry room; Barber/Beauty shop; Library; Shuffleboard; Tennis; Greenhouse; Indoor pool; Putting green; Walking trails.
Activities Arts & crafts; Cards; Games; Reading groups; Movies; Shopping trips; Dances/Social/Cultural gatherings.

Mendham

Holly Manor Nursing Home
84 Cold Hill Rd, Mendham, NJ 07945
(201) 543-2500
Admin H Bradley Kate. *Dir of Nursing* Janice Fitzsimmons. *Medical Dir* Dr L Schlessinger.
Licensure Long-term care. *Beds* Long-term care 114. *Certified* Medicaid; Medicare.
Owner Proprietary corp.
Admissions Requirements Minimum age 16; Medical examination; Physician's request.
Staff Physicians 12 (pt); RNs 8 (ft), 7 (pt); LPNs 3 (ft), 2 (pt); Nurses' aides 40 (ft), 30 (pt); Physical therapists 1 (ft); Recreational therapists 2 (ft); Occupational therapists 1 (ft); Speech therapists 1 (ft); Activities coordinators 1 (ft); Dietitians 1 (ft).
Facilities Dining room; Physical therapy room; Laundry room; Barber/Beauty shop; 2 enclosed outdoor patios; Private & semi-private rooms.

Activities Arts & crafts; Cards; Games; Reading groups; Prayer groups; Movies; Shopping trips; Dances/Social/Cultural gatherings; Pet therapy; Gourmet dining.

Mercerville

Mercerville Nursing Center
2240 White Horse-Mercerville Rd, Mercerville, NJ 08619
(609) 586-7500
Admin Louise Wieliczky. *Dir of Nursing* Frances Grochala RN. *Medical Dir* Dr Robert Keene.
Licensure Skilled care; Alzheimer's care. *Beds* SNF 104. *Certified* Medicare.
Owner Proprietary corp (Multicare Management).
Admissions Requirements Minimum age 18; Medical examination.
Staff Physicians; RNs; LPNs; Nurses' aides; Physical therapists; Reality therapists; Recreational therapists; Occupational therapists; Speech therapists; Activities coordinators; Dietitians; Ophthalmologists; Dentists.
Languages Italian, Polish, Slavic, German.
Facilities Dining room; Physical therapy room; Activities room; Crafts room; Laundry room; Barber/Beauty shop; Library.
Activities Arts & crafts; Cards; Games; Reading groups; Prayer groups; Movies; Dances/Social/Cultural gatherings; Concerts; Luncheons; Planetarium shows.

Merchantville

Maple Lane Nursing Home
30 W Maple Ave, Merchantville, NJ 08109
(609) 662-4493
Admin Pat Clayton. *Dir of Nursing* Marilyn Scarpa. *Medical Dir* Abbas Husain MD.
Licensure Skilled care. *Beds* SNF 22. *Private Pay Patients* 100%.
Owner Privately owned.
Staff Physicians; RNs; LPNs; Nurses' aides; Physical therapists; Activities coordinators; Dietitians.
Facilities Activities room; Laundry room; Living room.
Activities Arts & crafts; Cards; Games; Reading groups; Prayer groups; Movies; Dances/Social/Cultural gatherings; Intergenerational programs; Music programs.

Middletown

Hilltop Private Nursing Home
Kings Hwy, Middletown, NJ 07748
(201) 671-0177
Admin Ethel Baskin RN.
Licensure Long-term care. *Beds* Long-term care 53. *Certified* Medicaid; Medicare.

Millville

Meridian Nursing Center—Millville
54 Sharp St, Millville, NJ 08332
(609) 327-2700
Admin Betty Betler.
Licensure Long-term care; Residential care. *Beds* Long-term care 120; Residential care 60.
Owner Proprietary corp (Meridian Healthcare).

Montclair

Cherry Nursing Home
111 Gates Ave, Montclair, NJ 07042
(201) 746-6999
Admin Vera Cherry. *Dir of Nursing* Ruth Hess. *Medical Dir* Dr Pande Josiforski.
Licensure Long-term care. *Beds* Long-term care 58. *Certified* Private.

Owner Proprietary corp.
Staff RNs; LPNs; Nurses' aides; Recreational therapists; Activities coordinators; Dietitians.
Facilities Dining room; Physical therapy room; Activities room; Chapel; Crafts room; Laundry room; Barber/Beauty shop.
Activities Arts & crafts; Cards; Games; Reading groups; Prayer groups; Movies; Shopping trips; Dances/Social/Cultural gatherings.

Clover Rest Nursing Home
16 Madison Ave, Montclair, NJ 07042
(201) 783-4501
Admin James Caron.
Licensure Long-term care. *Beds* Long-term care 24.
Owner Proprietary corp (Gericare Inc).

Little Nursing Home
71 Christopher St, Montclair, NJ 07042
(201) 744-5518
Admin R Cuminskey.
Licensure Long-term care. *Beds* Long-term care 25.

Madison
31 Madison Ave, Montclair, NJ 07042
(201) 783-4502, 783-5182 FAX
Admin Mary June Weber. *Dir of Nursing* Pat Mulligan. *Medical Dir* Dr De Julius.
Licensure Intermediate care. *Beds* ICF 21. *Private Pay Patients* 1%. *Certified* Medicaid.
Owner Privately owned (David Austin).
Staff Physicians 1 (ft); RNs 1 (ft); LPNs 2 (ft); Nurses' aides 8 (ft); Physical therapists 1 (ft); Occupational therapists 1 (ft); Speech therapists 1 (ft); Activities coordinators 1 (pt); Dietitians 1 (ft); Podiatrists 1 (ft); Social workers 1 (ft).
Activities Arts & crafts; Cards; Games; Reading groups; Prayer groups; Movies; Shopping trips; Dances/Social/Cultural gatherings; Intergenerational programs; Pet therapy; Happy Go Lucky Volunteer Club.

Montcalm Nursing Home
32 Pleasant Ave, Montclair, NJ 07042
(201) 744-4560
Admin Richard Ziegler.
Licensure Long-term care. *Beds* Long-term care 36.
Owner Proprietary corp (Gericare Inc).

Montclair Nursing Home
78 Midland Ave, Montclair, NJ 07042
(201) 783-4503, 783-5299 FAX
Admin Mary June Weber. *Dir of Nursing* Flo Shaffer.
Licensure Skilled care; Intermediate care. *Beds* Swing beds SNF/ICF 16.
Owner Proprietary corp (David Austin).
Admissions Requirements Minimum age 18.
Staff Physicians 1 (ft); RNs 1 (ft); LPNs 2 (ft); Nurses' aides 8 (ft); Physical therapists (contracted); Recreational therapists 1 (ft); Occupational therapists (contracted); Speech therapists (contracted); Activities coordinators (contracted); Dietitians (contracted); Podiatrists (contracted); Social workers 1 (ft).
Facilities Activities room.
Activities Arts & crafts; Cards; Games; Reading groups; Prayer groups; Movies; Shopping trips; Dances/Social/Cultural gatherings; Intergenerational programs; Pet therapy; Happy Go Lucky Volunteer Club.

St Vincent's Nursing Home
45 Elm St, Montclair, NJ 07042
(201) 746-4000
Admin Sr Alicia Mullins.
Licensure Intermediate care. *Beds* 135.
Affiliation Roman Catholic.

Van Dyk Manor
42 N Mountain Ave, Montclair, NJ 07042
(201) 783-9400, 746-1560 FAX

Admin Robert Brower. *Dir of Nursing* Sally Youngs. *Medical Dir* Dr Francis Mann.
Licensure Skilled care; Retirement; Alzheimer's care. *Beds* SNF 62; Retirement 3. *Private Pay Patients* 100%.
Owner Privately owned.
Staff RNs; LPNs; Nurses' aides; Physical therapists (contracted); Recreational therapists 1 (pt); Activities coordinators 1 (ft); Dietitians; Social services 1 (pt).
Languages French.
Facilities Dining room; Physical therapy room; Activities room; Chapel; Laundry room; Barber/Beauty shop; Wanderguard system.
Activities Arts & crafts; Cards; Games; Reading groups; Movies; Dances/Social/Cultural gatherings; Intergenerational programs; Pet therapy; Family nights; Dinner outings.

Moorestown

Greenleaf
28 E Main St, Moorestown, NJ 08057
(609) 235-4884
Admin Grace W Harrison. *Dir of Nursing* Eleanor Needs RN. *Medical Dir* Joseph Winston MD.
Licensure Skilled care; Retirement. *Beds* SNF 33; Retirement 26. *Private Pay Patients* 100%.
Owner Nonprofit corp.
Admissions Requirements Medical examination.
Staff Physicians 1 (pt); RNs 3 (ft), 8 (pt); LPNs 1 (ft), 2 (pt); Nurses' aides 9 (ft), 12 (pt); Physical therapists 1 (pt); Recreational therapists 1 (ft); Occupational therapists 1 (pt); Activities coordinators 1 (ft); Dietitians 1 (pt); Podiatrists 1 (pt).
Affiliation Society of Friends.
Facilities Dining room; Activities room; Crafts room; Laundry room; Barber/Beauty shop.
Activities Arts & crafts; Cards; Reading groups; Prayer groups; Movies; Shopping trips; Dances/Social/Cultural gatherings; Intergenerational programs.

Morgan

Carriage House Manor
Ernston Rd & Garden St Pkwy, Morgan, NJ 08879
(201) 721-8200
Admin Jane K Bernheim. *Dir of Nursing* Maxine Kaufman RN. *Medical Dir* Fernando Rodriguez MD.
Licensure Long-term care; Alzheimer's care. *Beds* Long-term care 220. *Certified* Medicaid; Medicare.
Owner Proprietary corp (Meritcare).
Admissions Requirements Minimum age 16; Medical examination; Physician's request.
Staff RNs 10 (ft), 5 (pt); LPNs 10 (ft), 5 (pt); Physical therapists 1 (ft); Reality therapists 5 (ft); Occupational therapists 1 (pt); Speech therapists 1 (pt); Activities coordinators 1 (ft); Dietitians 1 (pt); Ophthalmologists 1 (pt); Podiatrists 1 (pt); Dentists 1 (pt).
Languages Italian, German.
Facilities Dining room; Physical therapy room; Activities room; Chapel; Barber/Beauty shop.
Activities Arts & crafts; Cards; Games; Reading groups; Prayer groups; Movies; Shopping trips; Dances/Social/Cultural gatherings.

Morganville

Queen of Carmel Nursing Home
PO Box 203, Reids Hill Rd, Morganville, NJ 07751
(201) 946-4991

Admin Agnes Scheurich, acting. *Dir of Nursing* Patricia Bickauskas RN MSN. *Medical Dir* Anant S Kubal MD.
Licensure Skilled care. *Beds* SNF 31. *Private Pay Patients* 10%. *Certified* Medicaid.
Owner Proprietary corp.
Staff Physicians 1 (pt); RNs 2 (ft), 2 (pt); LPNs 2 (ft), 3 (pt); Nurses' aides 8 (ft), 3 (pt); Physical therapists 1 (pt); Recreational therapists 1 (pt); Activities coordinators 1 (pt); Dietitians 1 (pt); Ophthalmologists 1 (pt); Podiatrists 1 (pt); Audiologists 1 (pt).
Facilities Dining room.
Activities Arts & crafts; Cards; Games; Prayer groups; Movies; Shopping trips; Pet therapy.

Morris Plains

Morris View
PO Box 437, W Hanover Ave, Morris Plains, NJ 07950
(201) 285-2821
Admin John F Merrigan MPHA LNHA. *Dir of Nursing* Elizabeth Belz RN MSN. *Medical Dir* James H Wolf MD.
Licensure Skilled care. *Beds* SNF 422. *Private Pay Patients* 0%. *Certified* Medicaid.
Owner Publicly owned.
Staff Physicians 8 (pt); RNs 56 (ft), 27 (pt); LPNs 9 (ft), 8 (pt); Nurses' aides 175 (ft), 10 (pt); Physical therapists 5 (ft), 2 (pt); Reality therapists 1 (ft); Recreational therapists 10 (ft); Occupational therapists 1 (pt); Speech therapists 1 (pt); Activities coordinators 1 (ft); Dietitians 2 (pt); Ophthalmologists 1 (pt); Podiatrists 1 (pt); Audiologists 1 (pt).
Facilities Dining room; Physical therapy room; Activities room; Chapel; Crafts room; Laundry room; Barber/Beauty shop.
Activities Arts & crafts; Cards; Games; Reading groups; Prayer groups; Movies; Shopping trips; Dances/Social/Cultural gatherings; Intergenerational programs; Pet therapy.

Morristown

Morris Hills Multicare Center
77 Madison Ave, Morristown, NJ 07960
(201) 540-9800
Admin Christine Vogt. *Dir of Nursing* Connie Keller. *Medical Dir* Dr T Angelo.
Licensure Skilled care; Intermediate care. *Beds* SNF 138; ICF 166. *Certified* Medicaid; Medicare.
Owner Proprietary corp (Multicare Management).
Admissions Requirements Physician's request.
Staff Physicians; RNs; LPNs; Nurses' aides; Physical therapists; Recreational therapists; Speech therapists; Activities coordinators; Dietitians; Ophthalmologists; Podiatrists; Dentists.
Facilities Dining room; Physical therapy room; Activities room; Chapel; Laundry room; Barber/Beauty shop.
Activities Arts & crafts; Cards; Games; Reading groups; Prayer groups; Movies; Shopping trips; Dances/Social/Cultural gatherings.

Morristown Rehabilitation Center
66 Morris St, Morristown, NJ 07960
(201) 539-3000
Admin Lucy Grygorcewicz LNHA. *Dir of Nursing* Maria Marinelli RN. *Medical Dir* Bernard Grabelle MD.
Licensure Skilled care. *Beds* SNF 76. *Private Pay Patients* 10%. *Certified* Medicaid.
Owner Proprietary corp.
Admissions Requirements Minimum age 21; Medical examination; Physician's request.
Staff Physicians 1 (ft), 4 (pt); Recreational therapists 1 (ft), 2 (pt); Dietitians 1 (pt).

Facilities Dining room; Activities room; Crafts room.
Activities Arts & crafts; Cards; Games; Reading groups; Prayer groups; Movies; Dances/Social/Cultural gatherings; Intergenerational programs; Pet therapy.

Mount Holly

Mt Holly Center
62 Richmond Ave, Mount Holly, NJ 08060
(609) 267-8800, 267-3936 FAX
Admin Regina H Driesbach. *Dir of Nursing* Patricia Pyne RN. *Medical Dir* Claire L Jurkowski MD.
Licensure Skilled care; Intermediate care. *Beds* Swing beds SNF/ICF 120. *Private Pay Patients* 46%. *Certified* Medicaid; Medicare.
Owner Nonprofit corp.
Staff Physicians 27 (pt); RNs 7 (ft), 7 (pt); LPNs 6 (ft), 7 (pt); Nurses' aides 33 (ft), 27 (pt); Physical therapists 1 (pt); Recreational therapists 1 (ft), 1 (pt); Occupational therapists 1 (pt); Speech therapists 1 (pt); Activities coordinators 1 (ft); Dietitians 1 (pt); Ophthalmologists 9 (pt); Podiatrists 6 (pt); Orthopedic physicians (consultant); Surgeons (consultant); Internists (consultant); Dentists (consultant).
Facilities Dining room; Physical therapy room; Activities room; Crafts room; Laundry room; Barber/Beauty shop; Library; Dental/Podiatry exam room; Wheelchair van; 58 semi-private and 4 private rooms; Lounges.
Activities Arts & crafts; Cards; Games; Reading groups; Prayer groups; Movies; Shopping trips; Dances/Social/Cultural gatherings; Intergenerational programs; Pet therapy; Literary guild; Resident council; Outings.

Mount Laurel

Mt Laurel Convalescent Center
Church Rd, Mount Laurel, NJ 08057
(609) 235-7100
Admin John W Francks. *Dir of Nursing* Kathleen MacMillan. *Medical Dir* Dr Frank Pettinelli.
Licensure Long-term care. *Beds* Long-term care 280. *Certified* Medicaid; Medicare.
Owner Proprietary corp (Geriatric & Medical Centers).
Staff Physicians; RNs; LPNs; Nurses' aides; Physical therapists; Recreational therapists; Occupational therapists; Speech therapists; Activities coordinators; Dietitians; Ophthalmologists; Podiatrists; Dentists.
Facilities Dining room; Physical therapy room; Activities room; Crafts room; Laundry room; Barber/Beauty shop; Enclosed outdoor courtyard.
Activities Arts & crafts; Cards; Games; Reading groups; Prayer groups; Movies; Shopping trips; Dances/Social/Cultural gatherings.

Mountainside

Manor Care of Mountainside
1180 Rte 22 W, Mountainside, NJ 07092
(201) 654-0020
Admin Michael F Gabriel.
Licensure Long-term care; Residential care. *Beds* Long-term care 120; Residential care 30.

Navesink

King James Care Center of Middletown
PO Box R, 400 State Hwy 36, Navesink, NJ 07752
(201) 291-3400
Admin Herman Black.

Licensure Long-term care. *Beds* Long-term care 123. *Certified* Medicaid; Medicare.
Owner Nonprofit corp.

Neptune

Conv-A-Center
101 Walnut St & Hwy 33, Neptune, NJ 07753
(201) 774-3550
Admin Dean Charles Michals.
Licensure Long-term care. *Beds* Long-term care 100. *Certified* Medicaid; Medicare.
Owner Proprietary corp.

Grove Health Care Center
919 Green Grove Rd, Neptune, NJ 07753
(201) 922-3400
Admin A David Ornstein. *Dir of Nursing* Robette McEwan RN. *Medical Dir* Francis R Dynof MD.
Licensure Skilled care; Intermediate care. *Beds* Swing beds SNF/ICF 121. *Certified* Medicaid; Medicare.
Owner Nonprofit corp (Presbyterian Homes of New Jersey).
Admissions Requirements Minimum age 16; Medical examination; Physician's request.
Staff RNs; LPNs; Nurses' aides; Recreational therapists; Activities coordinators; Dietitians.
Affiliation Presbyterian.
Facilities Dining room; Physical therapy room; Activities room; Crafts room; Laundry room; Barber/Beauty shop.
Activities Arts & crafts; Cards; Games; Reading groups; Prayer groups; Movies; Shopping trips; Dances/Social/Cultural gatherings; Intergenerational programs; Pet therapy.

King Manor
2303 West Bangs Ave, Neptune, NJ 07753
(201) 774-3500
Admin Loreen Rahn.
Licensure Long-term care. *Beds* Long-term care 120.

Lodge
Rte 66, Neptune, NJ 07753
(201) 922-1900
Admin Ester Gold.
Medical Dir Dr Nathan Troum.
Licensure Intermediate care. *Beds* ICF 164. *Certified* Medicaid.
Owner Nonprofit corp (Presbyterian Homes of New Jersey).
Admissions Requirements Minimum age 16; Medical examination; Physician's request.
Staff Physicians 1 (pt); RNs 7 (ft); LPNs 5 (ft); Nurses' aides 51 (ft); Recreational therapists 3 (ft); Dietitians 2 (ft).
Affiliation Presbyterian.
Facilities Dining room; Physical therapy room; Activities room; Chapel; Crafts room; Laundry room; Barber/Beauty shop; Library.
Activities Arts & crafts; Cards; Games; Reading groups; Prayer groups; Movies; Shopping trips; Dances/Social/Cultural gatherings.

Medicenter of Neptune
2050 6th Ave, Neptune, NJ 07753
(201) 774-8300
Admin Mary Lou Browning.
Licensure Long-term care. *Beds* Long-term care 106. *Certified* Medicaid; Medicare.
Owner Proprietary corp.
Staff RNs 7 (ft), 7 (pt); LPNs 2 (ft), 4 (pt); Nurses' aides 33 (ft), 6 (pt); Physical therapists 1 (pt); Recreational therapists 2 (ft); Occupational therapists 1 (pt); Speech therapists 1 (pt); Activities coordinators 1 (ft); Dietitians 1 (pt).
Facilities Dining room; Physical therapy room; Activities room; Laundry room; Barber/Beauty shop; TV rooms.

Activities Arts & crafts; Cards; Games; Reading groups; Prayer groups; Movies; Shopping trips; Dances/Social/Cultural gatherings.

Neshanic

Foothill Acres Inc
Amwell Rd, Neshanic, NJ 08853
(201) 369-8711
Admin J R McGavisk. *Dir of Nursing* Maria DiMaria RN. *Medical Dir* H K Van Duyne MD.
Licensure Skilled care. *Beds* SNF 190. *Certified* Medicaid.
Owner Proprietary corp.
Admissions Requirements Minimum age 65.
Staff Physicians 1 (pt); RNs 12 (ft), 7 (pt); LPNs 5 (ft), 7 (pt); Nurses' aides 32 (ft), 40 (pt); Physical therapists 1 (pt); Activities coordinators 1 (ft); Dietitians 1 (ft).
Facilities Dining room; Physical therapy room; Activities room; Chapel; Laundry room; Barber/Beauty shop.
Activities Arts & crafts; Cards; Games; Reading groups; Prayer groups; Movies; Shopping trips; Dances/Social/Cultural gatherings.

New Brunswick

Francis E Parker Memorial Home
Easton Ave at Landing Ln, New Brunswick, NJ 08901
(201) 545-3110
Admin Robert M Piegari. *Dir of Nursing* Mrs Nunley.
Licensure Skilled care. *Beds* SNF 51.
Owner Nonprofit corp.
Staff RNs; LPNs; Nurses' aides; Reality therapists; Recreational therapists; Activities coordinators; Dietitians.
Facilities Dining room; Physical therapy room; Activities room; Laundry room; Barber/Beauty shop; Library.
Activities Arts & crafts; Cards; Games; Reading groups; Prayer groups; Movies; Shopping trips; Dances/Social/Cultural gatherings.

Rose Mountain Care Center
Rtes 1 & 18, New Brunswick, NJ 08901
(201) 828-2400
Admin Johnathan Rosenberg. *Dir of Nursing* Joanne Allen. *Medical Dir* William Allgair MD.
Licensure Skilled care; Intermediate care. *Beds* Swing beds SNF/ICF 112. *Private Pay Patients* 10%. *Certified* Medicaid.
Owner Proprietary corp.
Facilities Dining room; Physical therapy room; Activities room; Laundry room; Barber/Beauty shop.
Activities Arts & crafts; Cards; Games; Reading groups; Prayer groups; Movies; Shopping trips; Dances/Social/Cultural gatherings.

New Lisbon

Buttonwood Hospital of Burlington County
Pemberton-Browns Mills Rd, New Lisbon, NJ 08064
(609) 726-7000
Admin Lynn O'Connor. *Dir of Nursing* Dorothy Santoleri RN. *Medical Dir* Andrew Besen MD.
Licensure Long-term care; Psychiatric unit. *Beds* Long-term care 285; Psychiatric unit 30. *Certified* Medicaid.
Owner Nonprofit corp.
Admissions Requirements Physician's request.
Staff Physicians 2 (ft); RNs 33 (ft), 12 (pt); LPNs 33 (ft), 6 (pt); Nurses' aides 163 (ft), 35 (pt); Recreational therapists; Activities coordinators; Dietitians 1 (ft).

Facilities Dining room; Physical therapy room; Activities room; Chapel; Crafts room; Laundry room; Barber/Beauty shop; Library.
Activities Arts & crafts; Cards; Games; Reading groups; Prayer groups; Movies; Shopping trips; Dances/Social/Cultural gatherings.

New Milford

Woodcrest Center
800 River Rd, New Milford, NJ 07646
(201) 967-1700
Admin Robert M Hilsen. *Dir of Nursing* Gail Walsh RN. *Medical Dir* Bernard Greenspan DO.
Licensure Skilled care; Intermediate care. *Beds* Swing beds SNF/ICF 236. *Private Pay Patients* 55%. *Certified* Medicaid.
Owner Proprietary corp (Mediplex Corp).
Admissions Requirements Medical examination.
Staff Physicians 67 (pt) (attending); RNs 21 (ft); LPNs 8 (ft); Nurses' aides 82 (ft); Physical therapists (contracted); Recreational therapists 6 (ft); Occupational therapists (contracted); Speech therapists (contracted); Activities coordinators 1 (ft); Dietitians (contracted); Ophthalmologists (contracted); Podiatrists (contracted); Audiologists (contracted).
Languages Spanish, German, Polish, Italian, Tagalog.
Facilities Dining room; Physical therapy room; Activities room; Crafts room; Laundry room; Barber/Beauty shop; Dental clinic.
Activities Arts & crafts; Cards; Games; Reading groups; Prayer groups; Movies; Shopping trips; Dances/Social/Cultural gatherings.

New Providence

Glenside Nursing Home
144 Gales Dr, New Providence, NJ 07974
(201) 464-8600
Admin Brian Cumiskey. *Dir of Nursing* Ms Cochrane. *Medical Dir* Dr Pitoscia.
Licensure Long-term care; Alzheimer's care. *Beds* Long-term care 96. *Certified* Medicaid; Medicare.
Owner Proprietary corp (Health Care & Retirement Corp).
Staff Physicians 2 (ft), 32 (pt); RNs 12 (ft), 6 (pt); LPNs 3 (ft), 3 (pt); Nurses' aides 26 (ft), 5 (pt); Physical therapists 1 (pt); Recreational therapists 1 (ft); Occupational therapists 2 (pt); Activities coordinators 1 (ft), 1 (pt); Dietitians 1 (pt); Ophthalmologists 1 (pt); Dentists 1 (pt).
Facilities Dining room; Physical therapy room; Activities room; Crafts room; Laundry room.
Activities Arts & crafts; Cards; Games; Reading groups; Prayer groups; Movies; Shopping trips; Dances/Social/Cultural gatherings.

Newark

New Community Extended Care Facility
266 S Orange Ave, Newark, NJ 07103
(201) 624-2020
Admin Leroy Canady. *Dir of Nursing* Jacqueling Ragin. *Medical Dir* Paul A Kearney MD.
Licensure Long-term care. *Beds* Long-term care 180. *Certified* Medicaid.
Owner Nonprofit corp.
Admissions Requirements Medical examination; Physician's request.
Staff Physicians; RNs 10 (ft), 6 (pt); LPNs 12 (ft), 11 (pt); Nurses' aides 48 (ft), 33 (pt); Physical therapists 2 (pt); Recreational

therapists 4 (ft); Occupational therapists 1 (pt); Activities coordinators 1 (ft); Dietitians 1 (ft).
Languages Spanish.
Facilities Dining room; Physical therapy room; Activities room; Chapel; Laundry room; Barber/Beauty shop; Library.
Activities Arts & crafts; Cards; Games; Reading groups; Prayer groups; Movies; Shopping trips; Dances/Social/Cultural gatherings; Womens club.

Newark Health & Extended Care Facility
65 Jay St, Newark, NJ 07103
(201) 483-6800
Admin Samuel Paneth.
Licensure Long-term care. *Beds* Long-term care 420. *Certified* Medicaid; Medicare.
Owner Proprietary corp.

Newfield

Mater Dei Nursing Home
Rte 40, Upper Pittsgrove Twp, Newfield, NJ 08344
(609) 358-2061
Admin Sr Marie de Chantal Ray. *Dir of Nursing* Sr Laurence. *Medical Dir* Dr John Pastore.
Licensure Long-term care. *Beds* Long-term care 64. *Certified* Medicaid.
Owner Nonprofit corp (Diocese of Camden).
Staff Physicians 1 (pt); RNs 3 (ft), 10 (pt); LPNs 2 (ft), 2 (pt); Nurses' aides 25 (ft), 11 (pt); Physical therapists 1 (pt); Speech therapists 1 (pt); Activities coordinators 1 (ft), 1 (pt); Dietitians 1 (pt); Ophthalmologists 1 (pt); Dentists 1 (pt); Social services 1 (pt).
Affiliation Roman Catholic.
Facilities Dining room; Physical therapy room; Activities room; Chapel; Crafts room; Laundry room; Barber/Beauty shop; Library.
Activities Arts & crafts; Cards; Games; Reading groups; Prayer groups; Movies; Dances/Social/Cultural gatherings.

Newton

Barn Hill Convalescent Center
249 High St, Newton, NJ 07860
(201) 383-5600, 383-1397 FAX
Admin Richard Roberto. *Dir of Nursing* Sharon Havens RN. *Medical Dir* Joseph J Casella DO.
Licensure Skilled care; Intermediate care. *Beds* Swing beds SNF/ICF 120. *Certified* Medicaid; Medicare.
Owner Proprietary corp.
Admissions Requirements Minimum age 21; Medical examination; Physician's request.
Staff Physicians 1 (ft); RNs 6 (ft), 6 (pt); LPNs 6 (ft), 5 (pt); Nurses' aides 50 (ft), 19 (pt); Physical therapists 1 (pt); Reality therapists; Recreational therapists 1 (ft); Occupational therapists 1 (pt); Speech therapists 1 (pt); Activities coordinators 1 (ft); Dietitians 1 (pt); Podiatrists 1 (pt); Dentists 1 (pt).
Facilities Dining room; Physical therapy room; Activities room; Chapel; Crafts room; Laundry room; Barber/Beauty shop; Library.
Activities Arts & crafts; Cards; Games; Reading groups; Prayer groups; Movies; Shopping trips.

Newton Nursing Home
1 Summit Ave, Newton, NJ 07860
(201) 383-1450
Admin Michael Duffy. *Dir of Nursing* Joyce Faasse RN.
Licensure Skilled care. *Beds* SNF 36.
Owner Proprietary corp.
Admissions Requirements Medical examination; Physician's request.

Staff RNs 2 (ft), 2 (pt); LPNs 1 (ft); Nurses'
aides 9 (ft), 7 (pt); Recreational therapists 1
(ft); Dietitians 1 (pt).
Facilities Activities room.
Activities Arts & crafts; Cards; Games; Prayer
groups; Movies.

Sussex County Homestead
RD 3 Box 78, Newton, NJ 07860
(201) 948-5400
Admin Selma F Rooney. *Dir of Nursing* Janet
Donadio RN. *Medical Dir* D A Hannett
MD.
Licensure Long-term care. *Beds* Long-term
care 102. *Certified* Medicaid.
Owner Publicly owned.
Admissions Requirements Minimum age 18.
Facilities Dining room; Physical therapy
room; Activities room; Barber/Beauty shop.
Activities Arts & crafts; Cards; Games;
Movies; Shopping trips; Trips into
community.

North Bergen

Hudson View Care & Rehabilitation Center
9020 Wall St, North Bergen, NJ 07047
(201) 861-4040
Admin Linda DiNolfo. *Dir of Nursing* Patricia
DeRisi. *Medical Dir* Randolph A London
MD.
Licensure Skilled care; Alzheimer's care. *Beds*
SNF 273. *Private Pay Patients* 20%. *Certified*
Medicaid; Medicare.
Owner Proprietary corp (Health Care
Associates).
Admissions Requirements Minimum age 18;
Physician's request.
Staff Physicians 15 (pt); RNs 14 (ft), 5 (pt);
LPNs 16 (ft), 5 (pt); Nurses' aides 67 (ft), 37
(pt); Physical therapists 1 (pt); Reality
therapists 1 (ft); Recreational therapists 1
(ft); Occupational therapists 1 (pt); Speech
therapists 1 (pt); Activities coordinators 1
(ft); Dietitians 1 (ft); Ophthalmologists 2
(pt); Podiatrists 2 (pt); Audiologists 2 (pt).
Languages Spanish, Italian.
Facilities Dining room; Physical therapy
room; Activities room; Crafts room; Laundry
room; Barber/Beauty shop; Library;
Alzheimer's unit.
Activities Arts & crafts; Cards; Games;
Reading groups; Prayer groups; Movies;
Shopping trips; Dances/Social/Cultural
gatherings; Intergenerational programs; Pet
therapy.

North Cape May

Victoria Manor Nursing Center
3809 Bayshore Rd, North Cape May, NJ
08204
(609) 898-0677, 898-0104 FAX
Admin James L Dupes. *Dir of Nursing* Zenny
Sagun RN BSN. *Medical Dir* Robert A
Renza DO.
Licensure Skilled care; Residential care;
Retirement. *Beds* SNF 120; Residential care
20. *Retirement apartments* 50. *Private Pay
Patients* 40%. *Certified* Medicaid; Medicare.
Owner Privately owned.
Admissions Requirements Medical
examination; Physician's request.
Staff Physicians (contracted); RNs 6 (ft), 4
(pt); LPNs 7 (ft), 4 (pt); Nurses' aides 42
(ft), 7 (pt); Physical therapists (contracted);
Occupational therapists (contracted); Speech
therapists (contracted); Activities
coordinators 3 (ft); Dietitians;
Ophthalmologists (contracted); Podiatrists 1
(pt).
Facilities Dining room; Physical therapy
room; Activities room; Laundry room;
Barber/Beauty shop; Library; TV lounges;
Private dining rooms.

Activities Arts & crafts; Cards; Games;
Reading groups; Prayer groups; Movies;
Shopping trips; Dances/Social/Cultural
gatherings; Intergenerational programs; Pet
therapy.

Northfield

Meadowview Nursing Home
235 Dolphin Ave, Northfield, NJ 08225
(609) 645-5955
Admin Ramon W Lennie. *Dir of Nursing*
Shirley Woerner-Kallen. *Medical Dir* Samuel
Stetzer MD.
Licensure Skilled care. *Beds* SNF 180. *Private
Pay Patients* 5%. *Certified* Medicaid.
Owner Publicly owned.
Staff Physicians 3 (pt); RNs 17 (ft); LPNs 8
(ft); Nurses' aides 80 (ft); Physical therapists
1 (pt); Recreational therapists 3 (ft);
Occupational therapists 1 (pt); Speech
therapists 1 (pt); Activities coordinators 1
(ft); Dietitians 1 (pt); Ophthalmologists 1
(pt); Podiatrists 1 (pt); Audiologists 1 (pt);
Dentists 1 (pt).
Facilities Dining room; Physical therapy
room; Activities room; Chapel; Crafts room;
Laundry room; Barber/Beauty shop; Library.
Activities Arts & crafts; Cards; Games;
Reading groups; Prayer groups; Movies;
Shopping trips; Dances/Social/Cultural
gatherings; Intergenerational programs; Pet
therapy.

Oakland

Oakland Care Center
20 Breakneck Rd, Oakland, NJ 07436
(201) 337-3300, 337-6601 FAX
Admin Marie D Moore. *Dir of Nursing* Ruby
Young. *Medical Dir* Dr Bernard Schwam.
Licensure Skilled care; Intermediate care. *Beds*
Swing beds SNF/ICF 252. *Private Pay
Patients* 30%. *Certified* Medicaid; Medicare.
Owner Proprietary corp.
Admissions Requirements Minimum age 65.
Staff Physicians 10 (ft); RNs 30 (ft), 10 (pt);
LPNs 6 (ft), 5 (pt); Nurses' aides 75 (ft), 14
(pt); Physical therapists 1 (ft), 1 (pt); Reality
therapists 5 (ft); Recreational therapists 5
(ft); Occupational therapists 1 (ft); Speech
therapists 1 (ft); Activities coordinators 1
(ft); Dietitians 2 (ft); Ophthalmologists 1 (ft);
Podiatrists 2 (ft); Audiologists 1 (ft);
Rehabilitation nurses 1 (ft); Staff
development 1 (ft); Quality assurance 1 (ft).
Languages Spanish, Tagalog, Italian.
Facilities Dining room; Physical therapy
room; Activities room; Chapel; Crafts room;
Laundry room; Barber/Beauty shop; Library.
Activities Arts & crafts; Cards; Games;
Reading groups; Prayer groups; Movies;
Shopping trips; Dances/Social/Cultural
gatherings; Intergenerational programs; Pet
therapy; Outings.

Ocean Grove

Clara Swain Manor
63 Clark Ave, Ocean Grove, NJ 07756
(201) 775-0554
Admin John Dipasquale.
Medical Dir Y D Kong MD.
Licensure Long-term care; Residential care.
Beds Long-term care 68; Residential care 20.
Certified Medicaid.
Owner Proprietary corp.
Staff RNs 3 (ft), 2 (pt); LPNs 2 (ft), 4 (pt);
Nurses' aides 25 (ft), 8 (pt); Physical
therapists 1 (ft), 1 (pt); Activities
coordinators 2 (ft); Dietitians 1 (pt);
Podiatrists 1 (pt); Dentists 1 (pt).
Facilities Dining room; Activities room;
Crafts room; Laundry room; Barber/Beauty
shop.
Activities Arts & crafts; Games; Movies.

Ocean View

Lutheran Home at Ocean View
Rte 9, 184 Shore Rd, Ocean View, NJ 08230
(609) 624-3881
Admin Jeffrey Kissam.
Licensure Intermediate care; Residential care.
Beds ICF 120; Residential care 64. *Certified*
Medicaid.
Owner Nonprofit corp (Lutheran Social
Services).
Affiliation Lutheran.

Old Bridge

Summer Hill Nursing Home
111 Rte 516, Old Bridge, NJ 08857
(201) 254-8200
Admin Melvin Feingenbaum.
Licensure Long-term care. *Beds* Long-term
care 120. *Certified* Medicaid.
Owner Proprietary corp.

Old Tappan

Ingleside Nursing Home
1016 S Washington Ave, Old Tappan, NJ
07675
(201) 664-3144, 664-1298 FAX
Admin Doris Neibart. *Dir of Nursing* Peggy
Maurer. *Medical Dir* Dr Martin Pelavin.
Licensure Skilled care; Intermediate care;
Alzheimer's care. *Beds* Swing beds SNF/ICF
44. *Private Pay Patients* 100%.
Owner Privately owned.
Staff RNs 6 (ft), 5 (pt); LPNs 2 (ft), 1 (pt);
Nurses' aides 8 (ft), 13 (pt); Activities
coordinators 1 (pt); Dietitians 1 (ft).
Languages Greek, Spanish, Italian.
Facilities Dining room; Physical therapy
room; Activities room; Crafts room; Laundry
room; Barber/Beauty shop.
Activities Arts & crafts; Cards; Games;
Reading groups; Prayer groups; Movies;
Shopping trips; Dances/Social/Cultural
gatherings; Intergenerational programs; Pet
therapy.

Orange

White House Nursing Home
560 Berkeley Ave, Orange, NJ 07050
(201) 672-6500
Admin Eliezer M Grossman.
Medical Dir James Paolino MD.
Licensure Long-term care. *Beds* Long-term
care 176. *Certified* Medicaid.
Owner Proprietary corp.
Admissions Requirements Minimum age 18.
Staff RNs 8 (ft), 4 (pt); LPNs 12 (ft), 4 (pt);
Nurses' aides 62 (ft), 6 (pt); Recreational
therapists 3 (ft); Activities coordinators 1
(ft).
Languages Yiddish, Hebrew, Spanish,
Hungarian.
Facilities Dining room; Physical therapy
room; Activities room; Barber/Beauty shop;
Library.
Activities Arts & crafts; Cards; Games;
Reading groups; Prayer groups; Movies;
Shopping trips; Dances/Social/Cultural
gatherings.

Oxford

Warren Haven
306 RD, Oxford, NJ 07863
(201) 453-2131
Admin Jean S Sickles; Joyce W Free, Asst. *Dir
of Nursing* Carmine Quick RN. *Medical Dir*
Stanton S Sykes MD.
Licensure Skilled care. *Beds* SNF 180.
Certified Medicaid.
Owner Publicly owned.
Admissions Requirements Medical
examination; Physician's request.

Staff Physicians 10 (pt); RNs 11 (ft), 2 (pt); LPNs 10 (ft), 7 (pt); Nurses' aides 64 (ft), 4 (pt); Physical therapists 1 (pt); Recreational therapists 4 (pt); Occupational therapists 1 (pt); Speech therapists 1 (pt); Activities coordinators 1 (ft); Dietitians 1 (pt); Ophthalmologists 1 (pt); Podiatrists 1 (pt); Dentists 1 (pt).
Facilities Dining room; Physical therapy room; Activities room; Chapel; Crafts room; Laundry room; Barber/Beauty shop; Library.
Activities Arts & crafts; Cards; Games; Reading groups; Prayer groups; Movies; Shopping trips; Dances/Social/Cultural gatherings; Intergenerational programs.

Paramus

Dellridge Nursing Home
532 Fairview Ave, Paramus, NJ 07652
(201) 261-1589
Admin Patricia Volmer. *Dir of Nursing* Berniece Dufour RN. *Medical Dir* Alexander Haseldorn MD.
Licensure Skilled care; Alzheimer's care. *Beds* SNF 96. *Certified* Medicare.
Owner Proprietary corp.
Admissions Requirements Medical examination.
Staff Physicians 1 (pt); RNs 6 (ft), 14 (pt); LPNs 2 (ft), 6 (pt); Nurses' aides 23 (ft), 29 (pt); Physical therapists 1 (pt); Reality therapists 1 (pt); Recreational therapists 1 (ft), 1 (pt); Occupational therapists 1 (pt); Speech therapists 1 (pt); Activities coordinators 1 (ft); Dietitians 1 (pt); Ophthalmologists 1 (pt); Podiatrists 1 (pt); Dentists 1 (pt); Food service supervisors 1 (ft).
Facilities Dining room; Physical therapy room; Activities room; Crafts room; Barber/Beauty shop; Library.
Activities Arts & crafts; Cards; Games; Reading groups; Prayer groups; Movies; International days; Picnics; Family days.

New Jersey Home for Veterans at Paramus
PO Box 546, 1 Veterans Dr, Paramus, NJ 07653-0546
(201) 967-7676
Admin Joseph Loudermilk. *Dir of Nursing* T Wojekoski RN. *Medical Dir* A Lantin MD.
Licensure Intermediate care; Alzheimer's care. *Beds* ICF 142. *Certified* VA.
Owner Publicly owned.
Admissions Requirements Medical examination.
Staff Physicians 3 (ft); RNs 19 (ft); LPNs 5 (ft); Nurses' aides 62 (ft); Physical therapists 1 (ft); Recreational therapists 1 (ft); Occupational therapists 1 (ft); Speech therapists 1 (pt); Activities coordinators 1 (ft); Dietitians 2 (ft); Podiatrists 1 (ft); Audiologists 1 (pt).
Facilities Dining room; Physical therapy room; Activities room; Chapel; Crafts room; Laundry room; Barber/Beauty shop; Library.
Activities Cards; Games; Reading groups; Movies; Dances/Social/Cultural gatherings.

Paramus Health Care Center
593 Paramus Rd, Paramus, NJ 07652
(201) 444-1341
Admin Bruce Schur.
Licensure Long-term care. *Beds* Long-term care 35. *Certified* Medicaid.
Owner Proprietary corp.

Pine Rest Nursing Home
W 90 Ridgewood Ave, Paramus, NJ 07652
(201) 652-1950
Admin William Maloney.
Licensure Long-term care. *Beds* Long-term care 55.
Owner Proprietary corp.

Parsippany

Beverwyck Nursing Home
420 S Beverwyck Rd, Parsippany, NJ 07054
(201) 887-0156
Admin Blanche Bonifacio. *Dir of Nursing* Joyce Hanson. *Medical Dir* Dr Gilbert Mendel.
Licensure Skilled care; Intermediate care; Retirement. *Beds* Swing beds SNF/ICF 24. *Private Pay Patients* 100%.
Owner Proprietary corp.
Admissions Requirements Medical examination.
Staff Physicians 24 (pt); RNs 2 (ft); LPNs 2 (ft); Nurses' aides 7 (ft); Physical therapists 1 (pt); Recreational therapists 1 (pt); Activities coordinators 1 (ft); Dietitians 1 (pt); Ophthalmologists 1 (pt); Podiatrists 1 (pt); Audiologists 1 (pt).
Facilities Dining room; Activities room; Laundry room.
Activities Arts & crafts; Cards; Games; Reading groups; Prayer groups; Movies; Shopping trips; Dances/Social/Cultural gatherings; Intergenerational programs; Pet therapy.

Parsippany-Troy

Troy Hills House
200 Reynolds Ave, Parsippany-Troy, NJ 07050
(201) 887-8080
Admin Catherine Engler. *Dir of Nursing* C Chapman. *Medical Dir* Dr T Angelo.
Licensure Skilled care; Intermediate care. *Beds* SNF 31; ICF 97. *Certified* Medicaid; Medicare.
Owner Proprietary corp (Multicare Management).
Admissions Requirements Minimum age 18.
Staff Physicians 31 (pt); RNs; LPNs; Nurses' aides; Physical therapists; Recreational therapists; Occupational therapists; Speech therapists; Activities coordinators; Dietitians; Ophthalmologists; Dentists; Respiratory therapists.
Facilities Dining room; Physical therapy room; Activities room; Laundry room; Barber/Beauty shop; Library.
Activities Arts & crafts; Cards; Games; Reading groups; Prayer groups; Movies; Shopping trips; Dances/Social/Cultural gatherings.

Passaic

Chestnut Hill Convalescent Center
360 Chestnut St, Passaic, NJ 07055
(201) 777-7800
Admin Dr Richard Stefanacci. *Dir of Nursing* Kathryn Manger. *Medical Dir* Dr Paul DeMuro.
Licensure Skilled care; Intermediate care. *Beds* Swing beds SNF/ICF 94. *Private Pay Patients* 45%. *Certified* Medicaid; Medicare.
Owner Proprietary corp.
Admissions Requirements Medical examination; Physician's request.
Staff Physicians 1 (ft), 1 (pt); RNs 10 (ft), 3 (pt); LPNs 4 (ft), 2 (pt); Nurses' aides 40 (ft), 5 (pt); Physical therapists 1 (pt); Reality therapists 1 (pt); Recreational therapists 3 (ft); Occupational therapists (contracted); Speech therapists (contracted); Activities coordinators 1 (ft); Dietitians 1 (pt).
Languages Spanish, Polish.
Facilities Dining room; Physical therapy room; Activities room; Chapel; Crafts room; Barber/Beauty shop; Library.
Activities Arts & crafts; Cards; Games; Reading groups; Prayer groups; Movies; Dances/Social/Cultural gatherings.

Hamilton Plaza Nursing Center
56 Hamilton Ave, Passaic, NJ 07055
(201) 773-7070
Admin William Goldsmith. *Dir of Nursing* Kathleen Diciedue MSN. *Medical Dir* Dr Graber; Dr Lintz.
Licensure Skilled care. *Beds* SNF 120. *Certified* Medicaid; Medicare.
Owner Proprietary corp.
Admissions Requirements Minimum age 16; Medical examination.
Staff Physicians 7 (pt); RNs 6 (ft), 3 (pt); LPNs 3 (ft), 2 (pt); Nurses' aides 20 (ft), 19 (pt); Physical therapists 1 (ft), 2 (pt); Occupational therapists 1 (pt); Speech therapists 1 (pt); Dietitians 1 (pt); Ophthalmologists 1 (pt); Podiatrists 1 (pt); Dentists 1 (pt).
Languages Spanish, Polish, Russian, Italian.
Facilities Dining room; Physical therapy room; Activities room; Crafts room; Laundry room; Barber/Beauty shop; Library; TV & Occupational therapy room.
Activities Arts & crafts; Cards; Games; Reading groups; Prayer groups; Movies; Shopping trips; Dances/Social/Cultural gatherings; Pet therapy; Gourmet club; Picnics; Bingo.

Jefferson Manor Nursing Center
85 Columbia Ave, Passaic, NJ 07055
(201) 773-7070
Admin Patrick Meehan.
Licensure Skilled care; Intermediate care. *Beds* 88. *Certified* Medicaid.

Madison Manor Nursing Center
141 Madison St, Passaic, NJ 07055
(201) 773-0450
Admin Patrick Meehan.
Licensure Skilled care; Intermediate care. *Beds* 65. *Certified* Medicaid; Medicare.

Paterson

Preakness Hospital
PO Box V, Valley View Rd, Paterson, NJ 07509
(201) 904-5000
Admin Victor R Kattak. *Dir of Nursing* Elizabeth Palestis RN MS. *Medical Dir* Victor Abdy MD.
Licensure Skilled care; Intermediate care; Alzheimer's care. *Beds* Swing beds SNF/ICF 552. *Private Pay Patients* 1%. *Certified* Medicaid.
Owner Publicly owned.
Admissions Requirements Minimum age Medicaid; Medical examination; Physician's request.
Staff Physicians 1 (ft), 10 (pt); RNs 35 (ft), 15 (pt); LPNs 40 (ft), 10 (pt); Nurses' aides 180 (ft), 20 (pt); Physical therapists (consultant); Recreational therapists 10 (ft); Occupational therapists (consultant); Speech therapists (consultant); Dietitians 5 (ft); Ophthalmologists (consultant); Podiatrists (consultant); Audiologists (consultant).
Languages Spanish, Eastern & Western European languages, Asian, Island languages.
Facilities Dining room; Physical therapy room; Activities room; Chapel; Crafts room; Laundry room; Barber/Beauty shop; Library; Alzheimer's unit.
Activities Arts & crafts; Cards; Games; Reading groups; Prayer groups; Movies; Shopping trips; Dances/Social/Cultural gatherings; Intergenerational programs; Pet therapy; Community outpatient; Interdenominational services; Alzheimer's family support system.

White Birch Nursing Home
59 Birch St, Paterson, NJ 07505
(201) 942-8899
Admin Ernest Gianetti.
Medical Dir P Harami DO.

Licensure Long-term care. *Beds* Long-term care 42. *Certified* Medicaid; Medicare. *Owner* Proprietary corp.

Pennsauken

Cooper River Convalescent Center
5101 N Park Dr, Pennsauken, NJ 08109
(609) 665-9111
Admin Brian B Schoff, East; Beth Eichfeld, West. *Dir of Nursing* Diane Levan, East; Theresa Conley, West. *Medical Dir* Alex Makris.
Licensure Skilled care; Intermediate care. *Beds* Swing beds SNF/ICF 473. *Certified* Medicaid; Medicare.
Owner Proprietary corp (Geriatric & Medical Centers).
Staff Physicians; RNs; LPNs; Nurses' aides; Physical therapists; Recreational therapists; Occupational therapists; Speech therapists; Activities coordinators; Dietitians.
Facilities Dining room; Physical therapy room; Activities room; Crafts room; Laundry room; Barber/Beauty shop.
Activities Arts & crafts; Cards; Games; Reading groups; Prayer groups; Dances/Social/Cultural gatherings.

Perth Amboy

Amboy Care Center
Lindberg Ave, Perth Amboy, NJ 08861
(201) 826-0500
Admin Jonathan R Eigen. *Dir of Nursing* Marylee Zykorie. *Medical Dir* Dr Lupini.
Licensure Skilled care. *Beds* SNF 179. *Certified* Medicaid.
Owner Proprietary corp (Beverly Enterprises).
Languages Spanish.
Facilities Dining room; Physical therapy room; Activities room; Crafts room; Laundry room; Barber/Beauty shop.
Activities Arts & crafts; Cards; Games; Reading groups; Prayer groups; Movies; Shopping trips; Dances/Social/Cultural gatherings; Intergenerational programs; Pet therapy.

Perth Amboy Nursing Home
303 Elm St, Perth Amboy, NJ 08861
(201) 442-9540
Admin Berel D Tennenbaum. *Dir of Nursing* Marianne Pryga RN. *Medical Dir* Thaddius Balinski MD.
Licensure Long-term care. *Beds* Long-term care 250. *Certified* Medicaid; Medicare.
Owner Proprietary corp.
Admissions Requirements Minimum age 52; Medical examination; Physician's request.
Staff Physicians 8 (ft); RNs 54 (ft), 22 (pt); LPNs 73 (ft), 31 (pt); Nurses' aides 180 (ft), 73 (pt); Physical therapists 4 (ft), 2 (pt); Reality therapists 7 (ft); Recreational therapists 7 (ft); Occupational therapists 1 (ft); Speech therapists 1 (ft); Activities coordinators 1 (ft); Dietitians 1 (ft); Ophthalmologists 1 (ft); Podiatrists 1 (ft); Dentists 1 (ft).
Facilities Dining room; Physical therapy room; Activities room; Chapel; Crafts room; Laundry room; Barber/Beauty shop; Library.
Activities Arts & crafts; Cards; Games; Reading groups; Prayer groups; Movies; Shopping trips; Dances/Social/Cultural gatherings.

Phillipsburg

Care Center of Lopatcong
RFD School Ln, Phillipsburg, NJ 08865
(201) 859-0200
Admin Joan Longacre.

Licensure Long-term care. *Beds* Long-term care 150.
Owner Proprietary corp (Geriatric & Medical Centers).

Care Center of Phillipsburg
843 Wilbur Ave, Phillipsburg, NJ 08865
(201) 454-2627
Admin Mary Dombrowski-Tucker. *Dir of Nursing* Janet Kresge. *Medical Dir* Michael Raab MD.
Licensure Skilled care. *Beds* SNF 89. *Private Pay Patients* 30%. *Certified* Medicaid.
Owner Proprietary corp (Geriatric & Medical Centers Inc).
Admissions Requirements Minimum age 16; Medical examination.
Staff Physicians 11 (pt); RNs 6 (ft), 5 (pt); LPNs 5 (ft), 7 (pt); Nurses' aides 27 (ft), 4 (pt); Physical therapists 1 (pt); Recreational therapists 3 (ft); Occupational therapists 1 (pt); Speech therapists 1 (pt); Activities coordinators 1 (ft); Dietitians 1 (pt); Podiatrists 1 (pt).
Facilities Dining room; Activities room; Crafts room; Laundry room; Barber/Beauty shop; Library; TV rooms.
Activities Arts & crafts; Cards; Games; Reading groups; Prayer groups; Movies; Shopping trips; Dances/Social/Cultural gatherings; Intergenerational programs; Cooking groups.

Pine Brook

Hilltop Care Center
Hook Mountain Rd, Pine Brook, NJ 07058
(201) 227-1330
Admin Mary Jane Eicke. *Dir of Nursing* Essie Masci. *Medical Dir* Gilbert Mandel MD.
Licensure Skilled care; Alzheimer's care. *Beds* SNF 114. *Certified* Medicaid; Medicare.
Owner Proprietary corp (Continental Health Affiliates).
Admissions Requirements Medical examination.
Staff RNs 10 (ft), 4 (pt); LPNs 10 (ft), 3 (pt); Nurses' aides 40 (ft); Recreational therapists 2 (ft); Activities coordinators 1 (ft); Dietitians 1 (pt).
Facilities Dining room; Activities room; Crafts room; Barber/Beauty shop; Library.
Activities Arts & crafts; Cards; Games; Reading groups; Prayer groups; Dances/Social/Cultural gatherings.

Piscataway

Francis E Parker Memorial Home
1421 River Rd, Piscataway, NJ 08854
(201) 545-8330
Admin Robert Piegari. *Dir of Nursing* Mrs Fedor.
Licensure Skilled care. *Beds* SNF 60.
Owner Nonprofit corp.
Staff RNs; LPNs; Nurses' aides; Reality therapists; Recreational therapists; Activities coordinators; Dietitians.
Facilities Dining room; Physical therapy room; Activities room; Laundry room; Barber/Beauty shop; Library.
Activities Arts & crafts; Cards; Games; Reading groups; Prayer groups; Movies; Shopping trips; Dances/Social/Cultural gatherings.

Pittstown

Stone Arch Health Care Center
Rte 1 Box 37, Pittstown, NJ 08867
(201) 735-6600
Admin Nancy Goczalk Tofani. *Dir of Nursing* Brenda Demarest RN. *Medical Dir* Robert Pierce MD.

Licensure Long-term care; Retirement. *Beds* Long-term care 120. *Certified* Medicaid; Medicare.
Owner Proprietary corp.
Admissions Requirements Minimum age 18; Physician's request.
Staff RNs 6 (ft), 2 (pt); LPNs 4 (ft), 5 (pt); Nurses' aides 28 (ft), 16 (pt); Reality therapists 1 (pt); Recreational therapists 2 (ft), 2 (pt); Activities coordinators 1 (ft); Dietitians 7 (ft), 16 (pt); Social services 1 (pt).
Facilities Dining room; Physical therapy room; Activities room; Crafts room; Laundry room; Barber/Beauty shop; Patient lounge.
Activities Arts & crafts; Cards; Games; Reading groups; Prayer groups; Movies; Shopping trips; Dances/Social/Cultural gatherings; Bus rides; Theater; Excursions; Picnics.

Plainfield

Abbott Manor Convalescent Center
810 Central Ave, Plainfield, NJ 07060
(201) 757-0696, 757-7871 FAX
Admin Rachel Cobb. *Dir of Nursing* Maria Lapid RN. *Medical Dir* Joseph Robbins MD.
Licensure Skilled care. *Beds* SNF 35. *Private Pay Patients* 50%. *Certified* Medicaid.
Owner Proprietary corp.
Admissions Requirements Medical examination; Physician's request.
Staff RNs 1 (ft), 2 (pt); LPNs 5 (ft), 2 (pt); Physical therapists 1 (pt); Activities coordinators 1 (ft); Dietitians 1 (pt); Podiatrists 1 (pt).
Facilities Dining room; Activities room; Crafts room; Laundry room; Barber/Beauty shop; Library; Formal living room.
Activities Arts & crafts; Cards; Games; Reading groups; Prayer groups; Movies; Shopping trips; Dances/Social/Cultural gatherings; Intergenerational programs; Discussion; Outdoor activities; Volunteer group visits.

Hartwyck at Cedar Brook
1340 Park Ave, Plainfield, NJ 07060
(201) 754-3100
Admin Renee Lake. *Dir of Nursing* Sofia Caabay RN. *Medical Dir* Martin Sheehy MD.
Licensure Skilled care; Intermediate care; Alzheimer's day care. *Beds* Swing beds SNF/ICF 106; Alzheimer's day care 20. *Certified* Medicaid; Medicare.
Owner Nonprofit organization/foundation.
Admissions Requirements Medical examination.
Staff Physicians 1 (pt); RNs 6 (ft), 4 (pt); LPNs 6 (ft), 3 (pt); Nurses' aides 34 (ft), 15 (pt); Physical therapists 2 (ft), 2 (pt); Recreational therapists 1 (ft); Occupational therapists 1 (ft), 1 (pt); Activities coordinators 1 (ft).
Facilities Dining room; Physical therapy room; Activities room; Laundry room; Barber/Beauty shop; Outdoor courtyard.
Activities Arts & crafts; Cards; Games; Reading groups; Prayer groups; Movies; Shopping trips; Dances/Social/Cultural gatherings; Intergenerational programs; Pet therapy; Gardening; Cooking.

Robert Wood Johnson Jr Health Care
40-44 Norwood Ave, Plainfield, NJ 07060
(201) 769-1400, 769-1185 FAX
Admin Mary Ann Schachter. *Dir of Nursing* Karen Marsh. *Medical Dir* Dr Richard Sharrett.
Licensure Skilled care; Intermediate care. *Beds* SNF 60; ICF 60. *Certified* Medicaid; Medicare.
Owner Nonprofit corp (Presbyterian Homes of New Jersey).

Admissions Requirements Medical examination; Physician's request.
Staff RNs; LPNs; Nurses' aides; Physical therapists; Recreational therapists; Occupational therapists; Speech therapists; Activities coordinators; Dietitians.
Affiliation Presbyterian.
Facilities Dining room; Physical therapy room; Activities room; Crafts room; Laundry room; Barber/Beauty shop.
Activities Arts & crafts; Cards; Games; Reading groups; Prayer groups; Movies; Shopping trips; Dances/Social/Cultural gatherings; Intergenerational programs; Pet therapy.

Pleasantville

Green-Wood Health Care Center
John Henry Allen Ln & Church St, Pleasantville, NJ 08232
(609) 646-6900, 645-3799 FAX
Admin Olivia C Peters LNHA. *Dir of Nursing* Esther Boston RN. *Medical Dir* Jon Slotoroff DO.
Licensure Skilled care. *Beds* SNF 120. *Private Pay Patients* 20%. *Certified* Medicaid; Medicare.
Owner Proprietary corp.
Admissions Requirements Minimum age 18; Medical examination.
Staff Physicians 3 (ft), 12 (pt); RNs 12 (ft), 6 (pt); LPNs 15 (ft), 9 (pt); Nurses' aides 50 (ft), 20 (pt); Physical therapists 2 (ft), 1 (pt); Reality therapists 1 (ft); Recreational therapists 1 (ft), 1 (pt); Occupational therapists 1 (ft), 1 (pt); Speech therapists 1 (ft), 1 (pt); Activities coordinators 1 (pt); Dietitians 1 (ft), 1 (pt); Podiatrists 2 (ft); Audiologists 1 (ft); Respiratory 4 (pt).
Facilities Dining room; Physical therapy room; Activities room; Crafts room; Laundry room; Barber/Beauty shop.
Activities Arts & crafts; Cards; Games; Reading groups; Prayer groups; Movies; Shopping trips; Dances/Social/Cultural gatherings; Intergenerational programs; Pet therapy.

Our Lady's Residence
Glendale & Clematies, Pleasantville, NJ 08232
(609) 646-2450
Admin Sr Damiani Aurelia. *Dir of Nursing* Roberta Figiel RN. *Medical Dir* Francesco Pullia MD.
Licensure Skilled care; Alzheimer's care. *Beds* SNF 214. *Private Pay Patients* 40%. *Certified* Medicaid; Medicare.
Owner Nonprofit corp (Diocese of Camden).
Staff RNs 8 (ft), 16 (pt); LPNs 9 (ft), 6 (pt); Nurses' aides 66 (ft), 40 (pt); Physical therapists 2 (ft), 1 (pt); Reality therapists 1 (pt); Recreational therapists 1 (pt); Occupational therapists 1 (pt); Speech therapists 1 (pt); Activities coordinators 1 (ft); Dietitians 1 (pt); Ophthalmologists 2 (pt); Podiatrists 2 (pt); Audiologists 1 (pt).
Affiliation Roman Catholic.
Facilities Dining room; Physical therapy room; Activities room; Chapel; Crafts room; Laundry room; Barber/Beauty shop; TV/Music room.
Activities Arts & crafts; Cards; Games; Reading groups; Prayer groups; Movies; Shopping trips; Dances/Social/Cultural gatherings; Intergenerational programs; Pet therapy.

Point Pleasant

Claremont Care Center
1515 Hulse Rd, Point Pleasant, NJ 08742
(201) 295-9300, 295-0650 FAX
Admin Marion Penner RN FACHCA. *Dir of Nursing* Rosemarie Goodman RN BSN. *Medical Dir* Leon Dwulet MD.

Licensure Skilled care. *Beds* SNF 112. *Private Pay Patients* 55%. *Certified* Medicaid; Medicare.
Owner Proprietary corp (Genesis Health Ventures).
Admissions Requirements Physician's request.
Staff RNs 8 (ft), 2 (pt); LPNs 8 (ft), 4 (pt); Nurses' aides 29 (ft), 9 (pt); Physical therapists 1 (pt); Recreational therapists 2 (ft), 1 (pt); Occupational therapists 1 (pt); Speech therapists 1 (pt); Activities coordinators 1 (ft); Dietitians 1 (pt).
Facilities Dining room; Physical therapy room; Activities room; Crafts room; Laundry room; Barber/Beauty shop.
Activities Arts & crafts; Cards; Games; Reading groups; Prayer groups; Movies; Shopping trips; Dances/Social/Cultural gatherings; Intergenerational programs.

Point Pleasant Beach Nursing Home
703 Richmond Ave, Point Pleasant, NJ 08742
(201) 899-2525
Admin Marjorie Moret.
Licensure Intermediate care. *Beds* ICF 27. *Certified* Medicaid.
Owner Proprietary corp (Genesis Health Ventures).

Princeton

Princeton Nursing Home
35 Quarry St, Princeton, NJ 08540
(609) 924-9000
Admin William Bogner.
Licensure Long-term care. *Beds* Long-term care 119. *Certified* Medicaid; Medicare.
Owner Proprietary corp.

Rahway

Rahway Geriatrics Center Inc
1777 Lawrence St, Rahway, NJ 07065
(201) 499-7927
Admin Jeffrey S Schwartz.
Medical Dir Virginia Quintong MD.
Licensure Skilled care. *Beds* SNF 120. *Certified* Medicaid; Medicare.
Owner Nonprofit corp.
Admissions Requirements Minimum age 18; Medical examination; Physician's request.
Staff RNs 7 (ft); Nurses' aides 40 (ft); Physical therapists 1 (pt); Recreational therapists 3 (ft); Activities coordinators 1 (ft); Dietitians 1 (pt).
Languages French, Spanish.
Facilities Dining room; Physical therapy room; Activities room; Chapel; Crafts room; Laundry room; Barber/Beauty shop; Library.
Activities Arts & crafts; Cards; Games; Reading groups; Prayer groups; Movies; Shopping trips; Dances/Social/Cultural gatherings.

Raritan

Raritan Health & Extended Care Center
Rte 28, Raritan, NJ 08869
(201) 526-8950
Admin Michael Greenberg.
Licensure Long-term care. *Beds* Long-term care 128. *Certified* Medicaid; Medicare.
Owner Proprietary corp.

Red Bank

Red Bank Convalescent Center
100 Chapin Ave, Red Bank, NJ 07701
(201) 741-8811
Admin Ethelyn Leiblich. *Dir of Nursing* Wilma Radcliffe RN. *Medical Dir* Victor Siegel MD.
Licensure Long-term care; Respite care. *Beds* Long-term care 180. *Certified* Medicaid.
Owner Privately owned.

Admissions Requirements Minimum age 65; Medical examination.
Staff Physicians 13 (pt); RNs 6 (ft), 9 (pt); LPNs 1 (ft), 4 (pt); Nurses' aides 57 (ft), 20 (pt); Physical therapists 1 (pt); Speech therapists 1 (pt); Activities coordinators 1 (ft); Dietitians 1 (ft); Ophthalmologists 1 (pt); Podiatrists 1 (pt); Dentists 1 (pt); Social workers 1 (ft).
Languages Spanish, French, German.
Facilities Dining room; Physical therapy room; Activities room; Chapel; Crafts room; Laundry room; Barber/Beauty shop; Patio & picnic area.
Activities Arts & crafts; Cards; Games; Reading groups; Prayer groups; Movies; Dances/Social/Cultural gatherings; Pet therapy; Outings; Adopt-a-grandparent programs; Family support groups; Library visits.

Riverview Extended Care Residence
55 W Front St, Red Bank, NJ 07701
(201) 842-3800
Admin Donald E Lynch MPA LNHA. *Dir of Nursing* Eleanor Weigel RN. *Medical Dir* Victor Siegel MD.
Licensure Skilled care; Intermediate care. *Beds* SNF 52; ICF 52. *Private Pay Patients* 45%. *Certified* Medicaid; Medicare.
Owner Nonprofit corp.
Admissions Requirements Physician's request.
Staff Physical therapists; Speech therapists; Activities coordinators 2 (ft); Dietitians; Podiatrists.
Facilities Dining room; Physical therapy room; Activities room; Laundry room; Barber/Beauty shop; Dayroom on each unit.
Activities Arts & crafts; Cards; Games; Reading groups; Prayer groups; Movies; Shopping trips; Dances/Social/Cultural gatherings; Intergenerational programs; Pet therapy; Volunteer program offering gardening, music, plays.

Ridgewood

Ridgewood Home
330 Franklin Tpke, Ridgewood, NJ 07451
(201) 447-1900
Admin Robert Arnold LNHA. *Dir of Nursing* Judith McGuiness RN. *Medical Dir* Bernard Sklar MD.
Licensure Skilled care. *Beds* SNF 90. *Certified* Medicaid; Medicare.
Owner Proprietary corp.
Admissions Requirements Minimum age 18; Physician's request.
Activities Arts & crafts; Cards; Games; Reading groups; Prayer groups; Movies; Shopping trips; Dances/Social/Cultural gatherings; Intergenerational programs.

Van Dyk Nursing & Convalescent Home
304 S Van Dien Ave, Ridgewood, NJ 07450
(201) 445-8200
Admin William Van Dyk; Marvin Van Dyk. *Dir of Nursing* Ruth Husselman RNC. *Medical Dir* William Hopewell MD.
Licensure Skilled care. *Beds* SNF 93. *Private Pay Patients* 93%.
Owner Proprietary corp.
Admissions Requirements Minimum age 18.
Staff RNs 2 (ft), 10 (pt); LPNs 1 (ft), 8 (pt); Nurses' aides 33 (ft), 20 (pt); Physical therapists (consultant); Occupational therapists (consultant); Speech therapists (consultant); Activities coordinators 1 (ft), 1 (pt); Dietitians 1 (ft); Podiatrists 1 (pt).
Facilities Dining room; Activities room; Chapel; Crafts room; Laundry room; Barber/Beauty shop; Library.
Activities Arts & crafts; Cards; Games; Reading groups; Movies.

Riverside

Florence Nursing Home
PO Box 214, Riverside, NJ 08075
(609) 499-3224
Admin Paul Rosenthal.
Licensure Long-term care. *Beds* Long-term care 15.

Rochelle Park

Bristol Manor Health Care Center
96 Parkway, Rochelle Park, NJ 07662
(201) 845-0645
Admin Natalie Zanetich.
Licensure Long-term care; Residential care. *Beds* Long-term care 180; Residential care 150.

Rockleigh

Bergen County Intermediate Care Facility
35B Piermont Rd, Rockleigh, NJ 07647
(201) 784-9550
Admin Jeanette Seggebruch. *Dir of Nursing* Mary Gannon. *Medical Dir* Frank Mastrianno.
Licensure Intermediate care. *Beds* ICF 110. *Certified* Medicaid.
Owner Publicly owned.
Admissions Requirements Minimum age 65.
Staff Physicians 3 (pt); RNs 20 (ft); LPNs 5 (ft); Nurses' aides 54 (ft); Recreational therapists 1 (ft); Dietitians 1 (ft).
Facilities Dining room; Physical therapy room; Activities room; Chapel; Crafts room; Laundry room; Barber/Beauty shop; Library.
Activities Arts & crafts; Cards; Games; Reading groups; Prayer groups; Movies; Shopping trips; Dances/Social/Cultural gatherings; Intergenerational programs; Pet therapy.

Saddle Brook

Brook Wood Convalescent Home
30 Legregni St, Saddle Brook, NJ 07663
(201) 843-8411
Admin Frederick Soilson. *Dir of Nursing* Ann Barlas RN. *Medical Dir* Thomas Bellavia MD.
Licensure Skilled care; Alzheimer's care. *Beds* SNF 52. *Certified* Medicaid.
Owner Proprietary corp.
Admissions Requirements Minimum age 40.
Staff Physicians 6 (pt); RNs 3 (ft), 3 (pt); LPNs 6 (pt); Physical therapists 1 (pt); Activities coordinators 1 (ft), 1 (pt); Dietitians 1 (pt); Ophthalmologists 1 (pt); Podiatrists 1 (pt); Dentists 1 (pt).
Languages Spanish.
Facilities Dining room; Barber/Beauty shop.
Activities Arts & crafts; Cards; Games; Reading groups; Prayer groups; Movies; Bingo; Parties.

Saddle Brook Convalescent Home
15 Caldwell St, Saddle Brook, NJ 07663
(201) 843-7333
Admin Frederick Soilson.
Medical Dir Dr Bernard Ross.
Licensure Long-term care. *Beds* Long-term care 52. *Certified* Medicaid.
Owner Proprietary corp.
Staff RNs 2 (ft), 3 (pt); LPNs 5 (pt); Nurses' aides 9 (ft), 8 (pt); Physical therapists 1 (pt); Recreational therapists 1 (pt); Activities coordinators 1 (pt); Dietitians 1 (pt); Podiatrists 2 (pt); Dentists 2 (pt).
Facilities Dining room; Activities room; Laundry room; Barber/Beauty shop.
Activities Arts & crafts; Cards; Games; Reading groups; Prayer groups; Movies; Shopping trips; Dances/Social/Cultural gatherings.

Salem

Salem County Nursing & Convalescent Home
Rte 45, 438 Woodston Rd, Salem, NJ 08079
(609) 935-6677
Admin Lee Lanning.
Medical Dir John S Madara MD.
Licensure Skilled care. *Beds* SNF 110. *Certified* Medicaid; Medicare.
Owner Publicly owned.
Admissions Requirements Minimum age 18; Medical examination; Physician's request.
Staff Physicians 12 (pt); RNs 4 (ft), 4 (pt); LPNs 10 (ft), 2 (pt); Nurses' aides 49 (ft); Physical therapists 1 (ft); Recreational therapists 2 (ft); Occupational therapists 1 (pt); Speech therapists 1 (ft), 1 (pt); Dietitians 1 (pt); Ophthalmologists 3 (pt); Podiatrists 1 (pt); Dentists 1 (pt).
Facilities Dining room; Physical therapy room; Activities room; Crafts room; Laundry room; Barber/Beauty shop.
Activities Arts & crafts; Cards; Games; Reading groups; Prayer groups; Movies; Shopping trips; Dances/Social/Cultural gatherings.

Scotch Plains

Ashbrook Nursing Home
1610 Raritan Rd, Scotch Plains, NJ 08098
(201) 889-5500
Admin Daniel Moles.
Licensure Long-term care. *Beds* Long-term care 120. *Certified* Medicaid; Medicare.
Owner Proprietary corp.

Sewell

Gloucester Manor
Salina & Glassboro-Woodbury Rd, Sewell, NJ 08080
(609) 468-2500
Admin Christopher Gillies.
Medical Dir Robert Schwartz DO.
Licensure Long-term care. *Beds* Long-term care 226. *Certified* Medicaid; Medicare.
Owner Proprietary corp.
Staff Physicians 12 (ft); RNs 10 (ft), 4 (pt); LPNs 16 (ft), 3 (pt); Nurses' aides 70 (ft), 20 (pt); Physical therapists; Speech therapists; Activities coordinators; Dietitians; Ophthalmologists; Podiatrists; Dentists.
Facilities Dining room; Physical therapy room; Activities room; Laundry room; Barber/Beauty shop; Enclosed patio.
Activities Arts & crafts; Cards; Games; Reading groups; Prayer groups; Movies; Shopping trips; Dances/Social/Cultural gatherings.

Health Care Center at Washington
RR 1 Box 110A, Sewell, NJ 08080
(609) 582-3170, 582-3192 FAX
Admin L J Nogle. *Dir of Nursing* Sally Miller RN. *Medical Dir* Thomas A Cavalieri DO.
Licensure Skilled care; Alzheimer's care. *Beds* SNF 120. *Certified* Medicaid; Medicare.
Owner Nonprofit organization/foundation.
Admissions Requirements Minimum age 16; Physician's request.
Staff Physicians 11 (pt); RNs 6 (ft), 2 (pt); LPNs 14 (ft), 4 (pt); Nurses' aides 36 (ft), 9 (pt); Physical therapists 2 (pt); Activities coordinators 1 (ft), 3 (pt); Dietitians 1 (ft).
Facilities Dining room; Physical therapy room; Activities room; Laundry room; Barber/Beauty shop.
Activities Arts & crafts; Cards; Games; Prayer groups; Movies; Shopping trips; Dances/Social/Cultural gatherings; Pet therapy.

Shrewsbury

Shrewsbury Manor Nursing Home
515 Shrewsbury Ave, Shrewsbury, NJ 07704
(201) 741-2059
Admin Eleanor J Johnson.
Licensure Residential health care. *Beds* 35.

Somers Point

Ocean Point Health Care Center
555 Bay Ave, Somers Point, NJ 08244
(609) 927-9151
Admin Osman Lambiro.
Medical Dir Dr Stanley Edden.
Licensure Long-term care. *Beds* Long-term care 145. *Certified* Medicaid; Medicare.
Owner Nonprofit corp (Presbyterian Homes).
Facilities Dining room; Physical therapy room; Activities room; Chapel; Crafts room; Laundry room; Barber/Beauty shop; Library.
Activities Arts & crafts; Cards; Games; Reading groups; Prayer groups; Movies; Shopping trips; Dances/Social/Cultural gatherings.

Somerset

Central New Jersey Jewish Home for the Aged
380 DeMott Ln, Somerset, NJ 08857
(201) 873-2000, 873-2112 FAX
Admin Eliott V Solomon; Judy Tucker, Asst.
Medical Dir Lawrence Gross MD.
Licensure Skilled care; Intermediate care; Retirement. *Beds* Swing beds SNF/ICF 245; Retirement 100. *Private Pay Patients* 30%. *Certified* Medicaid.
Owner Nonprofit organization/foundation.
Admissions Requirements Minimum age 62; Medical examination.
Staff Physicians 6 (pt); RNs 22 (ft); LPNs 20 (ft); Nurses' aides 74 (ft); Physical therapists 1 (pt); Recreational therapists 4 (ft); Speech therapists 1 (pt); Activities coordinators 2 (pt); Dietitians 1 (ft), 1 (pt); Podiatrists 3 (pt).
Languages Yiddish.
Affiliation Jewish.
Facilities Dining room; Physical therapy room; Activities room; Chapel; Crafts room; Barber/Beauty shop; Library.
Activities Arts & crafts; Cards; Games; Reading groups; Prayer groups; Movies; Shopping trips; Dances/Social/Cultural gatherings; Intergenerational programs; Pet therapy.

King James Care Center of Somerset
1165 Easton Ave, Somerset, NJ 08873
(201) 246-4100
Admin Egon Scheil.
Licensure Long-term care. *Beds* Long-term care 180. *Certified* Medicaid; Medicare.
Owner Nonprofit corp.

Margaret McLaughlin McCarrick Care Center Inc
15 Dellwood Ln, Somerset, NJ 08873
(201) 545-4200
Admin Sr Raphaele Goebel, acting.
Licensure Long-term care. *Beds* Long-term care 120.

South Plainfield

Cedar Oaks Care Center Inc
1311 Durham Ave, South Plainfield, NJ 07080
(201) 287-9555, 287-8856 FAX
Admin Morris Wiesel. *Dir of Nursing* Nancy Bedner RN. *Medical Dir* Dr James Foley MD.
Licensure Skilled care; Intermediate care. *Beds* Swing beds SNF/ICF 120. *Private Pay Patients* 45%. *Certified* Medicaid; Medicare.
Owner Proprietary corp.

Admissions Requirements Minimum age 40; Medical examination; Physician's request.
Staff Physicians 1 (ft), 11 (pt); RNs 13 (ft), 2 (pt); LPNs 4 (ft), 2 (pt); Nurses' aides 39 (ft), 6 (pt); Physical therapists 1 (ft), 1 (pt); Recreational therapists 3 (ft); Occupational therapists 1 (ft); Speech therapists 1 (ft); Activities coordinators 1 (ft); Dietitians 1 (ft); Ophthalmologists 1 (pt); Podiatrists 1 (pt).
Facilities Dining room; Physical therapy room; Activities room; Chapel; Crafts room; Laundry room; Barber/Beauty shop.
Activities Arts & crafts; Cards; Games; Reading groups; Prayer groups; Movies; Shopping trips; Dances/Social/Cultural gatherings; Intergenerational programs; Pet therapy.

Stratford

Stratford Nursing & Convalescent Center
Laurel & Warwick Rds, Stratford, NJ 08084
(609) 784-2400
Admin Louis Neiman.
Licensure Long-term care. *Beds* Long-term care 104. *Certified* Medicaid; Medicare.
Owner Proprietary corp.

Succasunna

Merry Heart Nursing Home
200 Rte 10, Succasunna, NJ 07876
(201) 584-4000
Admin John P Kadimik; Hazel Kadimik. *Dir of Nursing* Muriel Shevac RN.
Licensure Skilled care. *Beds* SNF 61. *Certified* Medicaid; Medicare.
Owner Proprietary corp.
Admissions Requirements Medical examination; Physician's request.
Facilities Dining room; Activities room; Crafts room; Laundry room; Barber/Beauty shop; Library.
Activities Arts & crafts; Cards; Games; Reading groups; Prayer groups; Movies; Shopping trips; Dances/Social/Cultural gatherings; Variety; Music; Gourmet club; Residents council.

Summit

Cheshire Home
69 Division Ave, Summit, NJ 07901
(201) 966-1232
Admin Clara Corcoran LNHA. *Dir of Nursing* Ingrid Maclennan RN. *Medical Dir* Vincent Adamo MD.
Licensure Skilled care; Retirement. *Beds* SNF 35; Retirement 6. *Private Pay Patients* 0%. *Certified* Medicaid.
Owner Nonprofit corp.
Admissions Requirements Minimum age 18; Medical examination; Physically disabled.
Staff Physicians 2 (pt); RNs 2 (ft), 1 (pt); LPNs 5 (ft); Nurses' aides 16 (ft), 5 (pt); Physical therapists 1 (pt); Recreational therapists 1 (ft); Occupational therapists 1 (pt); Activities coordinators 1 (ft); Dietitians 1 (pt).
Facilities Dining room; Activities room; Crafts room; Laundry room; Library; Classroom.
Activities Arts & crafts; Cards; Games; Prayer groups; Movies; Shopping trips; Dances/Social/Cultural gatherings; Pet therapy; Educational; Vocational.

Teaneck

Teaneck Nursing Home
1104 Teaneck Rd, Teaneck, NJ 07660
(201) 833-2400
Admin Jeffrey D First. *Dir of Nursing* Toni Krug. *Medical Dir* Dr Harvey Gross.

Licensure Long-term care; Alzheimer's care. *Beds* Long-term care 107. *Certified* Medicaid; Medicare.
Owner Privately owned.
Admissions Requirements Minimum age 65.
Staff Physicians 1 (ft), 3 (pt); RNs 9 (ft), 2 (pt); LPNs 3 (ft), 7 (pt); Nurses' aides 25 (ft), 7 (pt); Physical therapists 1 (ft); Recreational therapists 2 (ft), 1 (pt); Speech therapists 1 (pt); Activities coordinators 1 (ft); Dietitians 1 (pt); Ophthalmologists 1 (pt); Podiatrists 1 (pt); Dentists 1 (pt).
Facilities Dining room; Physical therapy room; Activities room; Crafts room; Laundry room; Barber/Beauty shop; Library.
Activities Arts & crafts; Cards; Games; Reading groups; Prayer groups; Movies; Shopping trips; Dances/Social/Cultural gatherings.

Tenafly

County Manor
133 County Rd, Tenafly, NJ 07670
(201) 567-7800
Admin Ronald Pearl.
Licensure Long-term care. *Beds* Long-term care 64. *Certified* Medicare.
Staff Physicians; RNs; LPNs; Nurses' aides; Physical therapists; Recreational therapists; Occupational therapists; Speech therapists; Activities coordinators; Dietitians; Ophthalmologists; Podiatrists; Dentists.
Facilities Dining room; Physical therapy room; Activities room; Chapel; Crafts room; Laundry room; Barber/Beauty shop; Library.
Activities Arts & crafts; Cards; Games; Reading groups; Prayer groups; Movies.

Tinton Falls

Tinton Falls Conva-Center
524 Wardell Rd, Tinton Falls, NJ 07753
(201) 922-9330
Admin Jeffrey Satten. *Dir of Nursing* Arlene Pollack RN. *Medical Dir* Dr Marshal Silver.
Licensure Long-term care. *Beds* Long-term care 115. *Certified* Medicaid.
Owner Proprietary corp.
Admissions Requirements Medical examination.
Facilities Dining room; Activities room; Crafts room; Laundry room; Barber/Beauty shop; Library.
Activities Arts & crafts; Cards; Games; Prayer groups; Movies; Dances/Social/Cultural gatherings.

Toms River

Bey Lea Village
1351 Old Freehold Rd, Toms River, NJ 08753
(201) 240-0090, 505-1398 FAX
Admin Dorothea Miller RN. *Dir of Nursing* Linda S Mason RN. *Medical Dir* Henry Yo MD.
Licensure Skilled care; Residential care; Respite care. *Beds* SNF 120; Residential care 60. *Private Pay Patients* 46%. *Certified* Medicaid; Medicare.
Owner Privately owned (Hefson Enterprises Ltd Partnership).
Admissions Requirements Medical examination.
Staff Physicians 10 (pt); RNs 7 (ft), 8 (pt); LPNs 6 (ft), 8 (pt); Nurses' aides 36 (ft), 24 (pt); Physical therapists 1 (ft); Reality therapists 1 (ft); Recreational therapists 1 (ft); Occupational therapists 1 (pt); Speech therapists 1 (pt); Activities coordinators 1 (ft); Dietitians 1 (pt); Ophthalmologists 1 (pt); Podiatrists 1 (pt); Audiologists 1 (pt).
Languages Italian, Spanish, Filipino, German.

Facilities Dining room; Physical therapy room; Activities room; Laundry room; Barber/Beauty shop; Patio; Enclosed courtyards.
Activities Arts & crafts; Cards; Games; Reading groups; Prayer groups; Movies; Shopping trips; Dances/Social/Cultural gatherings; Intergenerational programs; Pet therapy; Family support groups.

Country Manor—Dover Inc
16 Whitesville Rd, Toms River, NJ 08753
(201) 341-1600
Admin Arnold Weiner. *Dir of Nursing* Jane Vega. *Medical Dir* Dr Jacob Goldstein.
Licensure Long-term care; Coma treatment; Alzheimer's care. *Beds* Long-term care 218; Coma treatment. *Certified* Medicaid; Medicare.
Owner Nonprofit corp.
Admissions Requirements Physician's request.
Staff Physicians 1 (ft), 20 (pt); RNs 16 (ft), 13 (pt); LPNs 17 (ft), 19 (pt); Nurses' aides 80 (ft), 48 (pt); Physical therapists 1 (ft); Reality therapists 5 (ft), 2 (pt); Recreational therapists 5 (ft); Occupational therapists 4 (pt); Speech therapists 1 (pt); Activities coordinators 1 (ft); Dietitians 1 (pt); Ophthalmologists 1 (pt); Podiatrists 1 (pt); Dentists 1 (pt).
Facilities Dining room; Physical therapy room; Activities room; Chapel; Crafts room; Barber/Beauty shop; Library; Occupational therapy room.
Activities Arts & crafts; Cards; Games; Reading groups; Prayer groups; Movies; Shopping trips; Dances/Social/Cultural gatherings; Wheelchair square dancing; Pet therapy; Greenhouse.

Green Acres Manor
1931 Lakewood Rd, Toms River, NJ 08755
(201) 286-2323
Admin Patricia Feerick-Nash. *Dir of Nursing* Jessica Quinn RN. *Medical Dir* Ruben Silva MD.
Licensure Skilled care; Intermediate care; Residential care. *Beds* Swing beds SNF/ICF 120; Residential care 60. *Certified* Medicaid; Medicare.
Owner Proprietary corp.
Admissions Requirements Minimum age 16; Medical examination.
Staff Physicians (contracted); RNs 8 (ft), 4 (pt); LPNs 10 (ft), 2 (pt); Nurses' aides 40 (ft), 10 (pt); Physical therapists 1 (pt); Recreational therapists 3 (ft), 1 (pt); Occupational therapists 1 (pt); Speech therapists 1 (pt); Activities coordinators 1 (ft); Dietitians 1 (pt); Ophthalmologists (contracted); Podiatrists (contracted); Audiologists (contracted).
Facilities Dining room; Physical therapy room; Activities room; Chapel; Crafts room; Laundry room; Barber/Beauty shop; Library.
Activities Arts & crafts; Cards; Games; Reading groups; Prayer groups; Movies; Shopping trips; Dances/Social/Cultural gatherings; Intergenerational programs; Pet therapy.

Holiday Care Center
4 Plaza Dr, Toms River, NJ 08757
(201) 240-0900
Admin David Clark Smith. *Dir of Nursing* Earla Finley RN. *Medical Dir* V Assanza MD.
Licensure Skilled care; Retirement. *Beds* SNF 180; Retirement 440. *Private Pay Patients* 45%. *Certified* Medicaid.
Owner Proprietary corp.
Admissions Requirements Minimum age 55; Medical examination; Physician's request.
Staff RNs 20 (ft); LPNs 30 (ft); Nurses' aides 60 (ft); Physical therapists 1 (ft); Recreational therapists 5 (ft); Occupational

therapists 2 (pt); Activities coordinators 1 (ft); Dietitians 1 (ft); Ophthalmologists 1 (pt); Podiatrists 1 (pt); Audiologists 1 (pt).
Languages Italian, Polish, Armenian.
Facilities Dining room; Physical therapy room; Activities room; Crafts room; Laundry room; Barber/Beauty shop.
Activities Arts & crafts; Cards; Games; Reading groups; Prayer groups; Movies; Shopping trips; Dances/Social/Cultural gatherings; Intergenerational programs; Pet therapy.

Toms River Convalescent Center
Hospital Dr, Toms River, NJ 08753
(201) 244-3100
Admin Jasper B Phelps.
Medical Dir Jeffrey Brustein MD.
Licensure Skilled care; Intermediate care. *Beds* 100. *Certified* Medicaid; Medicare.

Totowa Boro

Valley Rest Nursing Home
56 Bogert St, Totowa Boro, NJ 07512
(201) 942-2534
Admin Marion Henze. *Dir of Nursing* Michelle Fein. *Medical Dir* Dr Jan Barnes.
Licensure Skilled care. *Beds* SNF 32. *Private Pay Patients* 50%. *Certified* Medicaid.
Owner Proprietary corp.
Admissions Requirements Minimum age 65; Medical examination.
Staff Physicians 1 (pt); RNs 5 (ft), 2 (pt); LPNs 3 (ft), 2 (pt); Nurses' aides 12 (ft), 10 (pt); Physical therapists 1 (pt); Recreational therapists 1 (ft); Speech therapists 1 (pt); Activities coordinators 1 (ft); Dietitians 1 (pt); Ophthalmologists 1 (pt); Podiatrists 1 (pt).
Languages Italian, Spanish.
Facilities Dining room; Activities room; Laundry room.
Activities Arts & crafts; Cards; Games; Reading groups; Prayer groups; Movies; Shopping trips; Dances/Social/Cultural gatherings; Pet therapy.

Trenton

Ewing Nursing Home
1201 Parkway Ave, Trenton, NJ 08628
(609) 882-6900
Admin Vijaya Scrinivasan.
Licensure Long-term care. *Beds* Long-term care 102. *Certified* Medicaid; Medicare.
Owner Proprietary corp.

Mercer Convalescent Center
439 Bellevue Ave, Trenton, NJ 08618
(609) 396-2646
Admin Patricia Radke.
Medical Dir Dr Richard Gordon.
Licensure Long-term care. *Beds* Long-term care 100. *Certified* Medicaid; Medicare.
Owner Proprietary corp.
Staff Physicians 4 (pt); RNs 4 (ft), 4 (pt); LPNs 4 (ft), 6 (pt); Nurses' aides 50 (ft), 20 (pt); Physical therapists 1 (pt); Occupational therapists 1 (pt); Speech therapists 1 (pt); Activities coordinators 1 (ft); Dietitians 1 (pt); Ophthalmologists 1 (pt); Podiatrists 1 (pt); Audiologists 1 (pt); Dentists 1 (pt).
Facilities Dining room; Physical therapy room; Activities room; Crafts room; Laundry room; Barber/Beauty shop.
Activities Arts & crafts; Cards; Games; Reading groups; Prayer groups; Movies; Dances/Social/Cultural gatherings.

Mercer County Geriatric Center
2238 Hamilton Ave, Trenton, NJ 08619
(609) 588-5859
Admin Arthur Frisch.
Medical Dir A Strauss MD.
Licensure Long-term care. *Beds* Long-term care 240. *Certified* Medicaid.

Owner Publicly owned.
Staff Physicians 3 (ft), 1 (pt); RNs 15 (ft), 10 (pt); LPNs 30 (ft), 15 (pt); Nurses' aides 91 (ft), 28 (pt); Physical therapists 1 (pt); Recreational therapists 7 (ft); Occupational therapists 1 (pt); Speech therapists 1 (pt); Activities coordinators 1 (ft); Dietitians 1 (ft); Ophthalmologists 1 (ft); Podiatrists 1 (pt); Dentists 1 (pt).

Millhouse
325 Jersey St, Trenton, NJ 08611
(609) 394-3400, 396-5378 FAX
Admin Michael D Gentile. *Dir of Nursing* Lynn Taylor. *Medical Dir* Dr William Stanley.
Licensure Skilled care; Intermediate care; Residential care; Alzheimer's care. *Beds* SNF 60; ICF 120; Residential care 60. *Certified* Medicaid; Medicare.
Owner Proprietary corp (Seniors Management).
Admissions Requirements Minimum age 18; Medical examination; Physician's request.
Staff RNs 6 (ft); LPNs 20 (ft); Nurses' aides 65 (ft); Physical therapists 2 (ft); Recreational therapists 5 (ft); Occupational therapists 1 (ft); Speech therapists 1 (ft); Activities coordinators 1 (ft); Dietitians 1 (ft); Ophthalmologists 1 (ft); Podiatrists 1 (ft); Audiologists 1 (ft).
Languages Spanish.
Facilities Dining room; Physical therapy room; Activities room; Crafts room; Laundry room; Barber/Beauty shop; Library.
Activities Arts & crafts; Cards; Games; Reading groups; Prayer groups; Movies; Shopping trips; Dances/Social/Cultural gatherings; Intergenerational programs; Pet therapy.

Tuckerton

Seacrest Village Nursing Home
PO Box 1480, Center St, Tuckerton, NJ 08087
(609) 296-9292, 294-9464 FAX
Admin Karen A Scienski. *Dir of Nursing* Cathy Vakulchik RN. *Medical Dir* John J Kenny DO.
Licensure Skilled care. *Beds* SNF 120. *Certified* Medicaid; Medicare.
Owner Proprietary corp.
Admissions Requirements Medical examination; Physician's request.
Staff Physicians; RNs; LPNs; Nurses' aides; Physical therapists; Occupational therapists; Speech therapists; Activities coordinators; Dietitians; Podiatrists.
Facilities Dining room; Physical therapy room; Activities room; Laundry room; Barber/Beauty shop; Private and semi-private rooms.
Activities Arts & crafts; Cards; Games; Movies; Dances/Social/Cultural gatherings; Intergenerational programs; Pet therapy; Entertainment.

Union

Cornell Hall Convalescent Center
234 Chestnut St, Union, NJ 07083
(201) 687-7800, 687-1417 FAX
Admin Elizabeth J Bataille. *Dir of Nursing* Bette Goodrich. *Medical Dir* Joseph E McDonald MD.
Licensure Skilled care; Intermediate care; Residential care; Alzheimer's care. *Beds* Swing beds SNF/ICF 160; Residential care 20. *Private Pay Patients* 48-50%. *Certified* Medicaid; Medicare.
Owner Nonprofit organization/foundation.
Admissions Requirements Minimum age 18; Medical examination.
Staff Physicians 1 (pt); RNs 8 (ft), 12 (pt); LPNs 8 (ft), 8 (pt); Nurses' aides 54 (ft), 3 (pt); Physical therapists; Recreational therapists 3 (ft); Speech therapists; Activities

coordinators 1 (ft); Dietitians 1 (pt); Ophthalmologists (contracted); Podiatrists (contracted); Audiologists (contracted); Beauticians (contracted).
Languages Spanish, Polish, Italian.
Facilities Dining room; Activities room; Chapel; Crafts room; Laundry room; Barber/Beauty shop; Library; Physical therapy/speech therapy room; Kosher kitchen (on request); Greenhouse; Large screen TV.
Activities Arts & crafts; Cards; Games; Reading groups; Prayer groups; Movies; Shopping trips; Dances/Social/Cultural gatherings; Intergenerational programs; Pet therapy; Van rides; Picnics; Entertainers.

Vineland

Cumberland Convalescent Center Inc
1640 S Lincoln Ave, Vineland, NJ 08360
(609) 692-8080
Admin Josephine O Boyd.
Licensure Long-term care; Residential care. *Beds* Long-term care 180; Residential care 30.

Bishop McCarthy Residence
1045 E Chestnut Ave, Vineland, NJ 08360
(609) 692-2850, 794-8411 FAX
Admin Sr Mary Elvira Iacovone. *Dir of Nursing* Sr Lucia Maroor. *Medical Dir* Nicholas Marchione MD.
Licensure Skilled care. *Beds* SNF 147. *Private Pay Patients* 16%. *Certified* Medicaid; Medicare.
Owner Nonprofit organization/foundation (Diocese of Camden).
Admissions Requirements Medical examination; Physician's request.
Staff Physicians 9 (pt); RNs 4 (ft), 6 (pt); LPNs 11 (ft), 13 (pt); Nurses' aides 43 (ft), 25 (pt); Physical therapists 1 (pt); Occupational therapists 1 (pt); Speech therapists 1 (pt); Activities coordinators 2 (ft), 2 (pt); Dietitians 1 (pt); Audiologists 1 (pt).
Languages Spanish, Italian, Russian.
Affiliation Roman Catholic.
Facilities Dining room; Physical therapy room; Activities room; Chapel; Crafts room; Laundry room; Barber/Beauty shop; Library.
Activities Arts & crafts; Cards; Games; Prayer groups; Movies; Shopping trips; Dances/Social/Cultural gatherings; Intergenerational programs; Pet therapy.

Voorhees

Care Inn of Voorhees
2601 Evesham Rd, Voorhees, NJ 08043
(609) 596-1113
Admin Anita Calvo.
Licensure Skilled care; Intermediate care; Long-term care; Residential care. *Beds* Long-term care 240; Residential care 60. *Certified* Medicaid; Medicare.
Owner Proprietary corp.

Lakewood of Voorhees
1302 Laurel Oak Rd, Voorhees, NJ 08043
(609) 435-5996
Admin James Scalese. *Dir of Nursing* J Thornboro.
Licensure Skilled care; Intermediate care. *Beds* SNF 60; ICF 180. *Certified* Medicaid; Medicare.
Owner Proprietary corp (HBA Management Inc).
Staff Physicians 4 (pt); RNs 8 (ft), 4 (pt); LPNs 12 (ft), 5 (pt); Nurses' aides 90 (ft), 10 (pt); Physical therapists 1 (ft); Recreational therapists 4 (ft); Occupational therapists 1 (ft); Speech therapists 1 (ft); Activities coordinators 1 (ft); Dietitians 1 (ft); Ophthalmologists 1 (pt); Podiatrists 1 (pt); Dentists 1 (pt).
Languages Tagalog.

Facilities Dining room; Physical therapy room; Activities room; Crafts room; Barber/Beauty shop.
Activities Arts & crafts; Cards; Games; Reading groups; Prayer groups; Movies; Shopping trips; Dances/Social/Cultural gatherings.

Meridian Nursing Center—Voorhees
3001 Evesham Rd, Voorhees, NJ 08043
(609) 751-1600
Admin Linda Stevens.
Licensure Long-term care. *Beds* Long-term care 180.
Owner Proprietary corp (Meridian Healthcare).

Wall

Tower Lodge Nursing Home
1506 Gully Rd, Wall, NJ 07719
(201) 681-1400
Admin Santo F Tavormina LNHA. *Dir of Nursing* Elizabeth C Bruton RN. *Medical Dir* Dr Young Kong.
Licensure Skilled care; Intermediate care. *Beds* Swing beds SNF/ICF 60. *Private Pay Patients* 50%. *Certified* Medicaid; Medicare.
Owner Proprietary corp.
Admissions Requirements Medical examination; Physician's request.
Staff Physicians 1 (pt); RNs 2 (ft), 6 (pt); LPNs 3 (ft), 2 (pt); Nurses' aides 16 (ft), 5 (pt); Physical therapists 1 (pt); Activities coordinators 1 (ft), 1 (pt); Dietitians 1 (pt).
Facilities Dining room; Physical therapy room; Activities room; Crafts room; Laundry room; Visitors lounge.
Activities Arts & crafts; Cards; Games; Prayer groups; Movies; Shopping trips; Dances/Social/Cultural gatherings; Pet therapy.

Wayne

Alps Manor Nursing Home
1120 Alps Rd, Wayne, NJ 07470
(201) 684-2100
Admin Robert Guggenheim.
Medical Dir Paule Topalovic.
Licensure Long-term care. *Beds* Long-term care 197. *Certified* Medicaid.
Owner Proprietary corp.
Staff RNs 9 (ft), 4 (pt); LPNs 2 (ft), 1 (pt); Nurses' aides 38 (ft), 2 (pt); Recreational therapists 2 (ft), 1 (pt); Activities coordinators 1 (ft); Dietitians 1 (pt).
Facilities Dining room; Physical therapy room; Activities room; Laundry room; Barber/Beauty shop.
Activities Arts & crafts; Cards; Games; Reading groups; Prayer groups; Movies; Shopping trips; Dances/Social/Cultural gatherings; Picnics.

Lakeview Convalescent Center Inc
130 Terhune Dr, Wayne, NJ 07470
(201) 839-4500, 839-2729 FAX
Admin Richard F Grosso Jr. *Dir of Nursing* Margaret Nolan RN. *Medical Dir* Paul Krisa MD.
Licensure Skilled care. *Beds* SNF 120. *Private Pay Patients* 47%. *Certified* Medicaid; Medicare.
Owner Proprietary corp.
Admissions Requirements Minimum age 16; Physician's request.
Staff Physicians 16 (pt); RNs 7 (ft), 8 (pt); LPNs 3 (ft), 3 (pt); Nurses' aides 39 (ft), 9 (pt); Physical therapists 1 (ft); Recreational therapists 1 (ft), 3 (pt); Occupational therapists 1 (pt); Speech therapists 1 (pt); Activities coordinators 1 (ft); Dietitians 1 (ft).
Languages Italian, Spanish, Polish, Russian, Hebrew.

Facilities Dining room; Physical therapy room; Activities room; Laundry room; Barber/Beauty shop; TV lounges; Ventilator care.
Activities Arts & crafts; Cards; Games; Reading groups; Prayer groups; Movies; Shopping trips; Dances/Social/Cultural gatherings; Intergenerational programs; Pet therapy; Dancercise; Music therapy.

Llanfair House
1140 Black Oak Ridge Rd, Wayne, NJ 07470
(201) 835-7443
Admin Adrienne Mayernik.
Licensure Long-term care. *Beds* Long-term care 180. *Certified* Medicaid; Medicare.
Owner Proprietary corp.

North Jersey Nursing Center Restorative Care
PO Box 2039, Wayne, NJ 07474-2039
(201) 956-8007
Admin Isadore Zuckerman. *Dir of Nursing* Thoma Rubino. *Medical Dir* Robert Brabston MD.
Licensure Skilled care. *Beds* SNF 120. *Certified* Medicaid; Medicare.
Owner Privately owned.
Admissions Requirements Medical examination.
Staff Physicians 1 (pt); RNs 8 (ft); LPNs; Nurses' aides 16 (ft), 25 (pt); Physical therapists 1 (pt); Recreational therapists; Occupational therapists 1 (pt); Speech therapists; Activities coordinators; Dietitians; Ophthalmologists; Dentists.
Facilities Dining room; Physical therapy room; Activities room; Crafts room; Laundry room; Barber/Beauty shop.
Activities Arts & crafts; Cards; Games; Reading groups; Prayer groups; Movies; Shopping trips; Dances/Social/Cultural gatherings.

Oak Ridge Manor Nursing Center
261 Terhune Dr, Wayne, NJ 07470
(201) 835-3871
Admin Raef Marzella. *Dir of Nursing* Bridget Miller. *Medical Dir* Dr Seymour Schlossberg.
Licensure Skilled care; Intermediate care; Alzheimer's care. *Beds* SNF 60; ICF 60. *Private Pay Patients* 28%. *Certified* Medicaid; Medicare.
Owner Proprietary corp.
Admissions Requirements Physician's request.
Staff Physicians; RNs; LPNs; Nurses' aides; Physical therapists; Recreational therapists; Occupational therapists (contracted); Speech therapists (contracted); Activities coordinators; Dietitians; Ophthalmologists (contracted); Podiatrists (contracted); Audiologists (contracted).
Facilities Dining room; Physical therapy room; Activities room; Crafts room; Laundry room; Barber/Beauty shop; Library; Game rooms.
Activities Arts & crafts; Cards; Games; Reading groups; Prayer groups; Movies; Shopping trips; Dances/Social/Cultural gatherings; Intergenerational programs; Pet therapy; Ho-Ho-Hot Line; Santa's workshop; Alzheimer's support group.

Wayne Haven Nursing Home
493 Black Oak Ridge Rd, Wayne, NJ 07472
(201) 694-1842
Admin James Codiroli. *Dir of Nursing* Mary Zabriskie RN.
Licensure Long-term care; Residential care. *Beds* Long-term care 44; Residential care 34.
Owner Proprietary corp.
Admissions Requirements Minimum age 18.
Staff RNs 2 (ft), 2 (pt); LPNs 1 (ft), 1 (pt); Nurses' aides 16 (ft), 6 (pt); Activities coordinators 1 (ft); Dietitians 1 (pt).

Facilities Dining room; Activities room; Laundry room; Barber/Beauty shop.
Activities Arts & crafts; Cards; Games; Prayer groups; Movies.

West Caldwell

West Caldwell Care Center
165 Fairfield Ave, West Caldwell, NJ 07006
(201) 226-1100
Admin Bernadette Revicky.
Licensure Long-term care. *Beds* Long-term care 180.

West Deptford

Leader Nursing & Rehabilitation Center
550 Jessup Rd, West Deptford, NJ 08066
(609) 848-9551
Admin Terry Tressler.
Licensure Long-term care; Residential care. *Beds* Long-term care 120; Residential care 30.

West Milford

Milford Manor
69 Maple Rd, West Milford, NJ 07480
(201) 697-5640
Admin Margaret Gannon.
Medical Dir Dr Le.
Licensure Long-term care. *Beds* Long-term care 100.
Owner Proprietary corp.
Admissions Requirements Medical examination; Physician's request.
Staff Physicians; RNs; LPNs; Nurses' aides; Physical therapists; Reality therapists; Recreational therapists; Occupational therapists; Activities coordinators; Dietitians; Ophthalmologists; Podiatrists; Dentists.

West Orange

Daughters of Israel Pleasant Valley Home
1155 Pleasant Valley Way, West Orange, NJ 07052
(201) 731-5100, 736-7698 FAX
Admin Lawrence Gelfand. *Dir of Nursing* Mary Spielvogel. *Medical Dir* Dr Norman Gevirtz.
Licensure Skilled care; Retirement; Alzheimer's care. *Beds* SNF 287; Retirement 20. *Private Pay Patients* 23%. *Certified* Medicaid; Medicare.
Owner Nonprofit corp.
Admissions Requirements Minimum age 55; Medical examination.
Staff Physicians 1 (ft); RNs 18 (ft); LPNs 24 (ft); Nurses' aides 100 (ft); Physical therapists 1 (ft); Recreational therapists 6 (ft); Occupational therapists 1 (pt); Speech therapists 1 (pt); Activities coordinators 1 (ft); Dietitians 1 (ft), 1 (pt).
Languages Yiddish.
Affiliation Jewish.
Facilities Dining room; Physical therapy room; Activities room; Chapel; Crafts room; Laundry room; Barber/Beauty shop; Library; Kosher kitchen.
Activities Arts & crafts; Cards; Games; Reading groups; Prayer groups; Movies; Dances/Social/Cultural gatherings; Intergenerational programs; Pet therapy.

Theresa Grotta Center
20 Summit St, West Orange, NJ 07052
(201) 736-2000
Admin Harriet Gaidemak. *Dir of Nursing* Diane McEvoy. *Medical Dir* Dr S Jaslow.
Licensure Long-term care. *Beds* Long-term care 142. *Certified* Medicaid; Medicare.
Owner Nonprofit corp.
Admissions Requirements Minimum age 18; Medical examination.

Staff Physicians 6 (pt); RNs 12 (ft), 3 (pt); LPNs 5 (ft), 3 (pt); Nurses' aides 44 (ft); Physical therapists 7 (ft); Recreational therapists 3 (ft); Occupational therapists 3 (ft); Speech therapists 2 (ft); Activities coordinators 1 (ft); Dietitians 1 (ft).
Languages Spanish, Polish.
Facilities Dining room; Physical therapy room; Activities room; Crafts room; Laundry room; Barber/Beauty shop; Library.
Activities Arts & crafts; Cards; Games; Reading groups; Prayer groups; Movies; Shopping trips; Dances/Social/Cultural gatherings.

Northfield Manor
787 Northfield Ave, West Orange, NJ 07052
(201) 731-4500
Admin Jane Lough ACSW LNHA. *Dir of Nursing* Carol Drew RN. *Medical Dir* Dr Joseph Aaron.
Licensure Skilled care. *Beds* SNF 131. *Private Pay Patients* 90%. *Certified* Medicare.
Owner Proprietary corp (Continental Health Affiliates).
Admissions Requirements Minimum age 18; Medical examination; Physician's request.
Staff Physicians 1 (pt); RNs 7 (ft), 5 (pt); LPNs 9 (ft), 5 (pt); Nurses' aides 56 (ft), 10 (pt); Physical therapists 2 (pt); Reality therapists 2 (ft), 1 (pt); Recreational therapists 2 (ft), 1 (pt); Occupational therapists 1 (pt); Speech therapists 1 (pt); Activities coordinators 1 (ft); Dietitians 1 (pt); Ophthalmologists 1 (pt); Podiatrists 1 (pt); Dentists 1 (pt).
Facilities Dining room; Physical therapy room; Activities room; Crafts room; Laundry room; Barber/Beauty shop.
Activities Arts & crafts; Cards; Games; Reading groups; Prayer groups; Movies; Dances/Social/Cultural gatherings; Intergenerational programs; Pet therapy.

Westfield

Meridian Nursing Center—Westfield
1515 Lamberts Mill Rd, Westfield, NJ 07090
(201) 233-9700, 233-3577 FAX
Admin Linda Stevens RN LNHA. *Dir of Nursing* Kevin J O'Neill RNC CNA. *Medical Dir* Harold Wasserman MD.
Licensure Skilled care; Intermediate care. *Beds* SNF 59; ICF 164. *Certified* Medicaid; Medicare.
Owner Proprietary corp (Meridian Healthcare).
Staff Physicians 1 (ft); RNs 8 (ft), 15 (pt); LPNs 7 (ft), 9 (pt); Nurses' aides 63 (ft), 25 (pt); Physical therapists (consultant); Recreational therapists 4 (ft); Occupational therapists (consultant); Speech therapists (consultant); Activities coordinators 1 (ft); Dietitians 2 (ft); Ophthalmologists (consultant); Podiatrists (consultant); Audiologists (consultant).
Facilities Dining room; Physical therapy room; Activities room; Crafts room; Laundry room; Barber/Beauty shop; Library; Gift cart.
Activities Arts & crafts; Cards; Games; Reading groups; Prayer groups; Movies; Shopping trips; Dances/Social/Cultural gatherings; Intergenerational programs; Pet therapy; Support groups for family/residents; PRIDE program; Sensitivity program; Religious services; Bridge club; Bingo; Coffee hour; Sing-alongs; Exercise; Parties; Woodworking; Current issues; Plays; Music.

Westwood

Valley Nursing Home
300 Old Hook Rd, Westwood, NJ 07675
(201) 664-8888
Admin Dorothy Franklin RN.
Medical Dir H R Hoff MD.

Licensure Long-term care. *Beds* Long-term care 120.
Owner Proprietary corp.
Admissions Requirements Minimum age 17; Medical examination; Physician's request.
Staff RNs; LPNs; Nurses' aides; Physical therapists; Occupational therapists; Speech therapists; Activities coordinators; Dietitians; Ophthalmologists; Podiatrists; Audiologists; Dentists.
Facilities Dining room; Physical therapy room; Activities room; Chapel; Crafts room; Laundry room; Barber/Beauty shop; Library.
Activities Arts & crafts; Cards; Games; Reading groups; Prayer groups; Movies; Shopping trips; Dances/Social/Cultural gatherings.

Whippany

Crestwood Nursing Home
101 Whippany Rd, Whippany, NJ 07981
(201) 887-0311
Admin Joyce McKeag.
Licensure Long-term care. *Beds* Long-term care 75.
Owner Proprietary corp.

Whiting

Logan Manor
23 Schoolhouse Rd, Whiting, NJ 08759
(201) 849-4300
Admin Susan Wood.
Medical Dir Sundhiem; Virginia Zamorski MD.
Licensure Long-term care. *Beds* Long-term care 180. *Certified* Medicaid.
Owner Proprietary corp.
Staff Physicians; RNs; LPNs; Nurses' aides; Physical therapists; Recreational therapists; Speech therapists; Activities coordinators; Dietitians; Ophthalmologists; Podiatrists.
Facilities Dining room; Physical therapy room; Activities room; Crafts room; Laundry room; Barber/Beauty shop.
Activities Arts & crafts; Cards; Games; Prayer groups; Movies; Shopping trips; Dances/Social/Cultural gatherings.

Williamstown

Meadow View Nursing Center
1328 S Black Horse Pike, Williamstown, NJ 08094
(609) 875-0100, 629-4619 FAX
Admin Rudolph A Lucente NHA. *Dir of Nursing* Filsberta Parilla RN. *Medical Dir* Armando Montiel MD.
Licensure Skilled care; Ventilator/Respiratory care; Residential care; Alzheimer's care. *Beds* SNF 120; Ventilator/Respiratory care 30; Residential care 60. *Private Pay Patients* 40%. *Certified* Medicaid; Medicare.
Owner Proprietary corp.
Admissions Requirements Minimum age 16; Medical examination.
Staff Physicians 1 (pt); RNs 15 (ft), 5 (pt); LPNs 28 (ft), 10 (pt); Nurses' aides 56 (ft), 8 (pt); Physical therapists 1 (ft); Reality therapists 1 (ft); Recreational therapists 4 (ft); Occupational therapists 1 (pt); Speech therapists 1 (pt); Activities coordinators 1 (ft); Dietitians 1 (pt); Ophthalmologists 1 (pt); Podiatrists 2 (pt); Respiratory 12 (ft), 6 (pt).
Languages Spanish, Italian.
Facilities Dining room; Physical therapy room; Activities room; Chapel; Crafts room; Laundry room; Barber/Beauty shop.
Activities Arts & crafts; Cards; Games; Reading groups; Prayer groups; Movies; Shopping trips; Dances/Social/Cultural gatherings; Intergenerational programs; Pet therapy.

Woodbury

Greenbriar Nursing & Convalescent Center
190 N Evergreen Ave, Woodbury, NJ 08096
(609) 848-7400
Admin Edward J Zirbger III.
Licensure Intermediate care. *Beds* Long-term care 220. *Certified* Medicaid; Medicare.
Owner Proprietary corp.

Woodcliff Lake

Woodcliff Lake Manor Nursing Home
555 Chestnut Ridge Rd, Woodcliff Lake, NJ 07675
(201) 391-0900, 391-1644 FAX
Admin Don Van Dam MD LNHA. *Dir of Nursing* Geraldine Doll RN MS. *Medical Dir* Frank Mastrianno MD.
Licensure Skilled care; Intermediate care. *Beds* Swing beds SNF/ICF 104. *Private Pay Patients* 85%. *Certified* Medicaid; Medicare.
Owner Proprietary corp.
Admissions Requirements Minimum age 21.
Staff RNs; LPNs; Nurses' aides; Physical therapists (contracted); Recreational therapists; Occupational therapists (contracted); Activities coordinators; Dietitians; Ophthalmologists (contracted); Podiatrists (contracted); Audiologists (contracted).
Languages French.
Facilities Dining room; Physical therapy room; Activities room; Chapel; Crafts room; Laundry room; Barber/Beauty shop; Library.
Activities Arts & crafts; Cards; Games; Reading groups; Prayer groups; Movies; Dances/Social/Cultural gatherings; Intergenerational programs; Pet therapy.

Woodstown

Friends Home at Woodstown
PO Box 457, Friends Dr, Woodstown, NJ 08098
(609) 769-1500, 769-3783 FAX
Admin Robert L Hawthorne LNHA. *Dir of Nursing* Marie Allcorn RN. *Medical Dir* David Bauman MD.
Licensure Skilled care; Intermediate care; Residential care. *Beds* Swing beds SNF/ICF 60; Residential care 60. *Private Pay Patients* 80%. *Certified* Medicaid; Medicare.
Owner Nonprofit organization/foundation.
Admissions Requirements Minimum age 60; Medical examination.
Staff RNs 3 (ft), 7 (pt); LPNs 4 (ft), 3 (pt); Nurses' aides 21 (ft), 17 (pt); Physical therapists (consultant); Activities coordinators 1 (ft); Dietitians (consultant).
Affiliation Society of Friends.
Facilities Dining room; Physical therapy room; Activities room; Chapel; Crafts room; Laundry room; Barber/Beauty shop; Library.
Activities Arts & crafts; Cards; Games; Reading groups; Prayer groups; Movies; Shopping trips; Dances/Social/Cultural gatherings; Intergenerational programs; Pet therapy.

Wyckoff

Christian Health Care Center
301 Sicomac Ave, Wyckoff, NJ 07481
(201) 848-5200, 848-9758 FAX
Admin Robert Van Dyk. *Dir of Nursing* Susan Coppola. *Medical Dir* Robert J Oehrig MD.
Licensure Skilled care; Retirement; Alzheimer's care. *Beds* SNF 240; Retirement 40. *Private Pay Patients* 55%. *Certified* Medicaid.
Owner Nonprofit corp.
Admissions Requirements Minimum age 18; Medical examination.

Staff Physicians 1 (ft); RNs 12 (ft), 9 (pt); LPNs 9 (ft), 2 (pt); Nurses' aides 70 (ft), 55 (pt); Physical therapists; Recreational therapists 1 (ft); Activities coordinators 1 (ft); Dietitians 1 (ft), 2 (pt).
Languages Dutch, German, Spanish, French, Italian, Polish.

Facilities Dining room; Physical therapy room; Activities room; Chapel; Crafts room; Laundry room; Barber/Beauty shop; Library; Medical day care program; Gero-psychiatric program for Alzheimer's and other patients; Dual diagnosis day treatment program.

Activities Arts & crafts; Cards; Games; Reading groups; Prayer groups; Movies; Shopping trips; Dances/Social/Cultural gatherings; Intergenerational programs; Pet therapy.

NEW MEXICO

Alamogordo

Casa Arena Blanca
PO Box 1906, Alamogordo, NM 88310
(505) 434-4510
Admin Larry P Andrews.
Licensure Intermediate care. *Beds* ICF 96.
Certified Medicare.

Casa Arena Blanca Nursing Center
205 Moonglow, Alamogordo, NM 88301
(505) 434-4510
Admin Larry P Andrews.
Licensure Skilled care. *Beds* SNF 10. *Certified*
Medicare.

Betty Dare Good Samaritan Center
3101 N Florida, Alamogordo, NM 88310-9713
(505) 434-0033, 434-0034 FAX
Admin Jon Kosiak. *Dir of Nursing* Suzanne
Gauthier.
Licensure Intermediate care; Catered living.
Beds ICF 84; Catered living 6. *Private Pay*
Patients 25%. *Certified* Medicaid.
Owner Nonprofit corp (Evangelical Lutheran/
Good Samaritan Society).
Admissions Requirements Medical
examination; Physician's request.
Staff RNs 3 (ft); LPNs 3 (ft), 6 (pt); Nurses'
aides 23 (ft), 13 (pt); Physical therapists 1
(pt); Recreational therapists 2 (ft); Speech
therapists 1 (pt); Activities coordinators 1
(ft); Dietitians 1 (pt); Podiatrists 1 (pt);
Audiologists 1 (pt).
Languages Spanish.
Affiliation Evangelical Lutheran.
Facilities Dining room; Physical therapy
room; Activities room; Chapel; Crafts room;
Laundry room; Barber/Beauty shop; Library;
Resident lounges.
Activities Arts & crafts; Cards; Games;
Reading groups; Prayer groups; Movies;
Shopping trips; Dances/Social/Cultural
gatherings; Intergenerational programs; Pet
therapy; Adopt-a-grandparent.

Albuquerque

Albuquerque Manor Inc
500 Louisiana Blvd NE, Albuquerque, NM
87108
(505) 255-1717
Admin Danny K Prince.
Licensure Skilled care; Intermediate care. *Beds*
SNF 28; ICF 216. *Certified* Medicare.

ARCA Group Home—615 Louisiana
1515 4th St NW, Albuquerque, NM 87102
(505) 247-0321
Admin Cherie Hymes.
Licensure Intermediate care for mentally
retarded. *Beds* ICF/MR 8. *Certified*
Medicare.

ARCA Group Home—1120 Louisiana
1515 4th St NW, Albuquerque, NM 87102
(505) 247-0321
Admin Cherie Hymes.

Licensure Intermediate care for mentally
retarded. *Beds* ICF/MR 10. *Certified*
Medicare.

ARCA Group Home A Centro Familiar
1515 4th St NW, Albuquerque, NM 87102
(505) 247-0321
Admin Cherie Hymes.
Licensure Intermediate care for mentally
retarded. *Beds* ICF/MR 10. *Certified*
Medicare.

ARCA Group Home A Copper
1515 4th St NW, Albuquerque, NM 87102
(505) 247-0321
Admin Cherie Hymes.
Licensure Intermediate care for mentally
retarded. *Beds* ICF/MR 8. *Certified*
Medicare.

ARCA Group Home B Centro Familiar
1515 4th St NW, Albuquerque, NM 87102
(505) 247-0321
Admin Cherie Hymes.
Licensure Intermediate care for mentally
retarded. *Beds* ICF/MR 8. *Certified*
Medicare.

ARCA Group Home B Copper
1515 4th St NW, Albuquerque, NM 87102
(505) 247-0321
Admin Cherie Hymes.
Licensure Intermediate care for mentally
retarded. *Beds* ICF/MR 8. *Certified*
Medicare.

ARCA Group Home—Corrales
1515 4th St NW, Albuquerque, NM 87102
(505) 247-0321
Admin Cherie Hymes.
Licensure Intermediate care for mentally
retarded. *Beds* ICF/MR 4. *Certified*
Medicare.

ARCA Group Home Gibson 3
1515 4th St NW, 5609 Gibson SE,
Albuquerque, NM 87102
(505) 247-0321
Admin Cherie Hymes.
Medical Dir Vodra Cox.
Licensure Intermediate care for mentally
retarded. *Beds* ICF/MR 8. *Certified*
Medicaid.

ARCA Group Home Gibson 2
1515 4th St NW, 5605 Gibson SE,
Albuquerque, NM 87102
(505) 247-0321
Admin Cherie Hymes.
Medical Dir Vodra Cox.
Licensure Intermediate care for mentally
retarded. *Beds* ICF/MR 10. *Certified*
Medicaid.

ARCA Group Home—Gun Club
1515 4th St NW, Albuquerque, NM 87102
(505) 247-0321
Admin Cherie Hymes.

Licensure Intermediate care for mentally
retarded. *Beds* ICF/MR 8. *Certified*
Medicare.

ARCA Group Home—Trumbull
1515 4th St NW, Albuquerque, NM 87102
(505) 247-0321
Admin Cherie Hymes.
Licensure Intermediate care for mentally
retarded. *Beds* ICF/MR 5. *Certified*
Medicare.

Brushwood Care Center
1509 University Blvd NE, Albuquerque, NM
87102
(505) 243-2257
Admin Gary Purvines. *Dir of Nursing* Elisa
Gallegos RN. *Medical Dir* Donald Hedges
DO.
Licensure Intermediate care. *Beds* ICF 96.
Private Pay Patients 15%. *Certified*
Medicaid.
Owner Proprietary corp (National Heritage).
Admissions Requirements Medical
examination; Physician's request.
Staff RNs 2 (ft); LPNs 7 (ft), 4 (pt); Nurses'
aides 27 (ft), 9 (pt); Physical therapists
(contracted); Recreational therapists 1 (pt);
Occupational therapists 1 (pt); Speech
therapists 1 (pt); Activities coordinators 1
(ft); Dietitians 1 (ft).
Languages Spanish.
Facilities Dining room; Activities room;
Barber/Beauty shop.
Activities Arts & crafts; Cards; Games;
Reading groups; Prayer groups; Movies;
Shopping trips; Dances/Social/Cultural
gatherings; Intergenerational programs; Pet
therapy; Sing-alongs; Gardening club.

Casa Angelica
5629 Isleta Blvd SW, Albuquerque, NM 87105
(505) 877-5763
Admin Sr Stella Negri FDCC. *Dir of Nursing*
Sr Genevieve Aldeghi. *Medical Dir* Dr
William K Woodard.
Licensure Intermediate care for mentally
retarded. *Beds* ICF/MR 25.
Owner Nonprofit organization/foundation.
Admissions Requirements Minimum age 6
months; Medical examination; Physician's
request.
Staff Physicians 1 (pt); RNs 2 (ft); LPNs 2
(ft); Nurses' aides 10 (ft), 4 (pt); Physical
therapists; Activities coordinators 1 (pt);
Dietitians (consultant).
Affiliation Roman Catholic.
Facilities Dining room; Physical therapy
room; Activities room; Chapel; Laundry
room; Outdoor area.
Activities Games; Reading groups; Prayer
groups; Movies; Shopping trips;
Intergenerational programs; Pet therapy;
Outings.

El Centro Villa Nursing Center
1629 Bowe Ln SW, Albuquerque, NM 87108
(505) 877-2200
Admin Beverly A Vaughn.

Licensure Intermediate care. *Beds* ICF 62.
Certified Medicare.

**Horizon Healthcare Nursing
Center—Albuquerque**
236 High St NE, Albuquerque, NM 87102
(505) 881-4961
Admin Alan Oppenheim.
Medical Dir Don Hedges; John Jones.
Licensure Skilled care; Intermediate care. *Beds*
SNF 20; ICF 85.
Owner Proprietary corp.
Admissions Requirements Medical
examination; Physician's request.
Staff RNs 2 (ft); LPNs 7 (ft), 1 (pt); Nurses'
aides 25 (ft); Reality therapists 2 (ft);
Recreational therapists 3 (ft); Activities
coordinators 1 (ft); Dietitians 1 (pt).
Languages Spanish.
Facilities Dining room; Physical therapy
room; Activities room; Chapel; Crafts room;
Laundry room; Barber/Beauty shop; Library.
Activities Arts & crafts; Games; Movies;
Shopping trips; Dances/Social/Cultural
gatherings.

La Vida Llena Retirement Center
10501 Lagrima de Oro NE, Albuquerque, NM
87111
(505) 296-6700
Admin Leon F Adkins. *Dir of Nursing* Wendy
W Weslowski. *Medical Dir* Dr David Sears.
Licensure Skilled care; Intermediate care;
Retirement. *Beds* SNF 10; ICF 50;
Retirement 400. *Certified* Medicaid;
Medicare.
Owner Nonprofit organization/foundation.
Admissions Requirements Medical
examination; Physician's request.
Staff Physicians 1 (pt); RNs 5 (ft), 3 (pt);
LPNs 3 (ft), 3 (pt); Nurses' aides 16 (ft), 5
(pt); Physical therapists 1 (pt); Recreational
therapists 1 (ft); Occupational therapists 1
(pt); Speech therapists 1 (pt); Activities
coordinators 3 (ft); Dietitians (consultant);
Podiatrists 1 (pt).
Languages Spanish.
Facilities Dining room; Physical therapy
room; Activities room; Chapel; Crafts room;
Laundry room; Barber/Beauty shop; Library.
Activities Arts & crafts; Cards; Games;
Reading groups; Prayer groups; Movies;
Shopping trips; Intergenerational programs;
Pet therapy.

Ladera Health Care Center Inc
5901 Ouray Rd NW, Albuquerque, NM 87120
(505) 836-0023
Admin Julie A Hofland. *Dir of Nursing* Tracy
Vaughn.
Licensure Skilled care; Intermediate care. *Beds*
SNF 20; ICF 100. *Private Pay Patients* 4%.
Certified Medicaid; Medicare.
Owner Proprietary corp (Care Enterprises).
Admissions Requirements Medical
examination.
Staff RNs 4 (ft), 1 (pt); LPNs 8 (ft), 2 (pt);
Nurses' aides 40 (ft), 10 (pt); Physical
therapists 1 (ft); Activities coordinators 1
(ft), 1 (pt).
Languages Spanish.
Facilities Dining room; Physical therapy
room; Activities room; Laundry room;
Barber/Beauty shop.
Activities Arts & crafts; Cards; Games;
Reading groups; Prayer groups; Movies;
Shopping trips; Dances/Social/Cultural
gatherings; Intergenerational programs; Pet
therapy.

Las Palomas Health Care Center
8100 Palomas NE, Albuquerque, NM 87109
(505) 821-4200
Admin Lori Parrish.
Licensure Skilled care; Intermediate care. *Beds*
SNF 24; ICF 96. *Certified* Medicare.

**Manor Care Nursing Center of Northeast
Heights**
2216 Lester Dr NE, Albuquerque, NM 87112
(505) 296-4808
Admin Michael T Raso.
Medical Dir Dr Ed Sager.
Licensure Skilled care; Intermediate care. *Beds*
SNF 12; ICF 129. *Certified* Medicaid.
Owner Proprietary corp (Manor Care Inc).
Staff Physicians 1 (pt); RNs 9 (ft), 3 (pt);
LPNs 4 (ft), 4 (pt); Nurses' aides 46 (ft);
Physical therapists 1 (pt); Recreational
therapists 1 (pt); Activities coordinators 1
(ft); Dietitians 1 (ft); Dentists 1 (pt).
Facilities Dining room; Physical therapy
room; Activities room; Crafts room; Laundry
room; Barber/Beauty shop; Conference
room.
Activities Arts & crafts; Cards; Games;
Reading groups; Movies; Shopping trips;
Dances/Social/Cultural gatherings;
Community programs; Outings.

Manor Care of Camino Vista
7900 Constitution NE, Albuquerque, NM
87110
(505) 296-5565
Admin Nancy Colleen Owen.
Licensure Skilled care; Intermediate care. *Beds*
SNF 22; ICF 82. *Certified* Medicaid.
Owner Proprietary corp (Manor Care Inc).

Manor Care Sandia Nursing Center
5123 Juan Tabo NE, Albuquerque, NM 87111
(505) 292-3333
Admin Lynne Fisher Jones.
Licensure Skilled care; Intermediate care. *Beds*
SNF 24; ICF 124. *Certified* Medicare.

Manzano del Sol Good Samaritan Village
5201 Roma Ave NE, Albuquerque, NM 87108
(505) 262-2311
Admin Marilyn Goodsell.
Medical Dir Dr Jeff Bleakly.
Licensure Intermediate care; Retirement;
Alzheimer's care. *Beds* ICF 120. *Certified*
Medicaid.
Owner Nonprofit corp (Evangelical Lutheran/
Good Samaritan Society).
Admissions Requirements Medical
examination; Physician's request.
Languages Spanish.
Affiliation Lutheran.
Facilities Dining room; Physical therapy
room; Activities room; Chapel; Crafts room;
Laundry room; Barber/Beauty shop; Library.
Activities Arts & crafts; Cards; Games;
Reading groups; Prayer groups; Movies;
Shopping trips; Dances/Social/Cultural
gatherings.

Montebello on Academy
10500 Academy NE, Albuquerque, NM 87111
(505) 294-9944
Admin Susan Peyerl RN. *Dir of Nursing* Pat
Eckelman RN. *Medical Dir* Dr Marvin Call.
Licensure Skilled care; Intermediate care;
Personal care. *Beds* SNF 8; ICF 52; Personal
care 15. *Private Pay Patients* 100%. *Certified*
Medicare.
Owner Proprietary corp.
Admissions Requirements Medical
examination; Physician's request.
Staff Physicians 6 (pt); RNs 5 (ft); LPNs 2
(ft), 1 (pt); Nurses' aides 25 (ft), 5 (pt);
Physical therapists 1 (ft); Occupational
therapists 1 (ft); Speech therapists 1 (ft);
Activities coordinators 1 (ft), 1 (pt);
Dietitians 1 (pt); Social services 1 (ft).
Languages Spanish.
Facilities Dining room; Physical therapy
room; Activities room; Crafts room; Laundry
room; Barber/Beauty shop.
Activities Arts & crafts; Cards; Games;
Reading groups; Prayer groups; Movies;
Shopping trips; Dances/Social/Cultural
gatherings; Intergenerational programs; Pet
therapy; Museums; Zoos.

Pickard Presbyterian Convalescent Center
5900 Forest Hills NE, Albuquerque, NM
87109
(505) 822-6000
Admin Jean Hawk. *Dir of Nursing* Jan Cherry
RN. *Medical Dir* Louis Levin MD.
Licensure Skilled care; Intermediate care. *Beds*
SNF 30; ICF 90. *Private Pay Patients* 50%.
Certified Medicaid; Medicare.
Owner Nonprofit organization/foundation.
Admissions Requirements Medical
examination; Physician's request.
Staff Physicians 1 (pt); RNs 4 (ft), 1 (pt);
LPNs 11 (ft); Nurses' aides 48 (ft); Physical
therapists 1 (ft); Occupational therapists 1
(pt); Speech therapists 1 (pt); Activities
coordinators 2 (ft); Dietitians 1 (pt); Physical
therapy aides 2 (pt).
Languages Spanish.
Facilities Dining room; Physical therapy
room; Activities room; Chapel; Barber/
Beauty shop; Library; Large fenced areas;
Paved walking/wheelchair paths.
Activities Arts & crafts; Games; Reading
groups; Prayer groups; Movies; Shopping
trips; Dances/Social/Cultural gatherings;
Intergenerational programs.

St Francis Gardens
904 Las Lomas Rd NE, Albuquerque, NM
87102
(505) 842-1410
Admin Marcia Wegmann. *Dir of Nursing*
Virginia Mitchell RN CIC.
Licensure Intermediate care. *Beds* ICF 135.
Private Pay Patients 63%. *Certified*
Medicaid.
Owner Nonprofit corp (Sisters of Saint Francis
of Colorado Springs).
Admissions Requirements Minimum age 40;
Medical examination.
Staff Physicians 1 (pt); RNs 3 (ft), 2 (pt);
LPNs 5 (ft), 7 (pt); Nurses' aides 54 (ft), 10
(pt); Activities coordinators 2 (ft), 2 (pt);
Dietitians 1 (pt); Food service directors 1
(ft).
Languages Spanish.
Affiliation Roman Catholic.
Facilities Dining room; Activities room;
Chapel; Crafts room; Laundry room; Barber/
Beauty shop; Library; On-site child care
center.
Activities Arts & crafts; Cards; Games;
Reading groups; Prayer groups; Movies;
Shopping trips; Dances/Social/Cultural
gatherings; Intergenerational programs; Pet
therapy; Conversational Spanish; In-room
visits; Bingo; Exercise; Snack programs;
Current events; Baking; Religious activities;
Pastoral counseling.

St Joseph West Mesa Hospital
10501 Golf Course Rd NW, Albuquerque,
NM 87114
(505) 893-2000
Admin Michael L Brown.
Licensure Skilled care. *Beds* SNF 22. *Certified*
Medicare.

West Mesa Health Care Center
9150 McMahon Blvd NW, Albuquerque, NM
87114
(505) 898-7986
Admin Barbara Ann Cornier.
Licensure Intermediate care. *Beds* ICF 120.
Certified Medicare.

Alcalde

Santa Maria El Mirador Calle Quedo
PO Box 39, 1888 Calle Quedo, Alcalde, NM
87511
(505) 852-4244
Admin Mark Johnson.
Licensure Intermediate care for mentally
retarded. *Beds* ICF/MR 9.

Santa Maria El Mirador Group Home A
PO Box 39, Alcalde, NM 87511
(505) 852-4244
Admin Mark Johnson.
Licensure Intermediate care for mentally retarded. *Beds* ICF/MR 9. *Certified* Medicare.

Santa Maria El Mirador Group Home B
PO Box 39, Alcalde, NM 87511
(505) 852-4244
Admin Mark Johnson.
Licensure Intermediate care for mentally retarded. *Beds* ICF/MR 9. *Certified* Medicare.

Santa Maria El Mirador Group Home C
PO Box 39, Alcalde, NM 87511
(505) 852-4244
Admin Mark Johnson.
Licensure Intermediate care for mentally retarded. *Beds* ICF/MR 12. *Certified* Medicare.

Santa Maria El Mirador Sycamore
PO Box 39, 4007 Sycamore St, Alcalde, NM 87511
(505) 852-4244
Admin Mark Johnson.
Licensure Intermediate care for mentally retarded. *Beds* ICF/MR 9.

Santa Maria El Mirador Vista del Sur
PO Box 39, 1868 Vista del Sur, Alcalde, NM 87511
(505) 852-4244
Admin Mark Johnson.
Licensure Intermediate care for mentally retarded. *Beds* ICF/MR 9.

Artesia

Artesia General Hospital
702 N 13th St, Artesia, NM 88210
(505) 749-3333
Admin Joseph F Abrata Jr.
Licensure Skilled care; Intermediate care. *Beds* 38.

Artesia Good Samaritan Center
PO Box 620, 1402 Gilchrist, Artesia, NM 88210
(505) 746-9865
Admin Judith K Milner.
Medical Dir Shirley Sperling.
Licensure Intermediate care. *Beds* ICF 65. *Certified* Medicaid.
Owner Nonprofit corp (Evangelical Lutheran/ Good Samaritan Society).
Admissions Requirements Medical examination; Physician's request.
Staff RNs 2 (ft); LPNs 4 (ft), 8 (pt); Nurses' aides 5 (ft), 18 (pt); Reality therapists 1 (pt); Recreational therapists 1 (ft); Activities coordinators 1 (ft); Dietitians 1 (pt).
Facilities Dining room; Physical therapy room; Activities room; Chapel; Crafts room; Laundry room; Barber/Beauty shop.
Activities Arts & crafts; Cards; Games; Reading groups; Prayer groups; Movies; Shopping trips.

Aztec

Four Corners Good Samaritan Center
500 Care Ln, Aztec, NM 87410
(505) 334-9445
Admin Pat Kelly.
Licensure Intermediate care. *Beds* ICF 80; Apts 13 Child day care units 30. *Certified* Medicaid; VA.
Owner Nonprofit corp (Evangelical Lutheran/ Good Samaritan Society).
Staff RNs 4 (ft); LPNs 4 (ft), 3 (pt); Nurses' aides 23 (ft), 13 (pt); Physical therapists 1 (ft); Occupational therapists 1 (ft); Activities coordinators 1 (ft); Dietitians 1 (pt).
Affiliation Lutheran.

Facilities Dining room; Physical therapy room; Activities room; Chapel; Crafts room; Laundry room; Barber/Beauty shop.
Activities Arts & crafts; Cards; Games; Reading groups; Prayer groups; Movies; Shopping trips; Dances/Social/Cultural gatherings.

Belen

Belen Health Care Center
1831 Sosino Padilla Blvd, Belen, NM 87002
(505) 864-1600
Admin Kathleen Poutsch.
Licensure Intermediate care. *Beds* ICF 120. *Certified* Medicare.

Bloomfield

Hacienda de Salud—Bloomfield
400 W Blanco Blvd, Bloomfield, NM 87413
(505) 632-1823
Admin Tina M Steen.
Licensure Intermediate care. *Beds* ICF 90. *Certified* Medicare.

Carlsbad

CARC Fara—Lineberry
PO Box 1808, 902 W Cherry Ln, Carlsbad, NM 88221-1808
(505) 887-1570
Admin Bob Welch.
Licensure Intermediate care for mentally retarded. *Beds* ICF/MR 8. *Certified* Medicare.

CARC Fara—Scarborough
PO Box 1808, 902 W Cherry Ln, Carlsbad, NM 88221-1808
(505) 887-1570
Admin Bob Welch.
Licensure Intermediate care for mentally retarded. *Beds* ICF/MR 8. *Certified* Medicare.

CARC Fara—Spence Home
PO Box 1808, 902 W Cherry Ln, Carlsbad, NM 88221-1808
(505) 887-1570
Admin Bob Welch.
Licensure Intermediate care for mentally retarded. *Beds* ICF/MR 8. *Certified* Medicare.

CARC Fara—Washington Ranch 1
PO Box 1808, 902 W Cherry Ln, Carlsbad, NM 88221-1808
(505) 887-1570
Admin Bob Welch.
Licensure Intermediate care for mentally retarded. *Beds* ICF/MR 8. *Certified* Medicare.

CARC Fara—Washington Ranch 2
PO Box 1808, 902 W Cherry Ln, Carlsbad, NM 88221-1808
(505) 887-1570
Admin Bob Welch.
Licensure Intermediate care for mentally retarded. *Beds* ICF/MR 8. *Certified* Medicare.

Lakeview Christian Home of the Southwest Inc
1300 N Canal St, Carlsbad, NM 88220
(505) 887-0551
Admin Mark T Schinnerer. *Dir of Nursing* Debbie Landreth. *Medical Dir* Virgil McCollum.
Licensure Intermediate care; Retirement; Retirement. *Beds* ICF 120; Retirement 51. *Certified* Medicaid.
Owner Nonprofit corp.
Admissions Requirements Medical examination; Physician's request.

Staff RNs 8 (ft), 1 (pt); LPNs 6 (ft), 6 (pt); Nurses' aides 53 (ft), 6 (pt); Activities coordinators 1 (ft); Dietitians 1 (ft).
Affiliation Church of Christ.
Facilities Dining room; Activities room; Chapel; Crafts room; Laundry room; Barber/ Beauty shop; Library.
Activities Arts & crafts; Cards; Games; Reading groups; Prayer groups; Movies; Shopping trips; Dances/Social/Cultural gatherings.

Landsun Homes Inc
1900 Westridge Rd, Carlsbad, NM 88220
(505) 887-2894
Admin Daniel R York. *Dir of Nursing* Bobbie Moore RN. *Medical Dir* Ted E Hauser MD.
Licensure Intermediate care; Retirement. *Beds* ICF 67; Retirement 118. *Private Pay Patients* 50%. *Certified* Medicaid.
Owner Nonprofit organization/foundation.
Admissions Requirements Medical examination; Physician's request.
Staff Physicians 7 (pt); RNs 4 (ft); LPNs 7 (ft), 1 (pt); Nurses' aides 26 (ft), 12 (pt); Physical therapists 2 (pt); Reality therapists 1 (pt); Recreational therapists 1 (ft); Activities coordinators 1 (ft); Dietitians 1 (pt); Ophthalmologists 1 (pt); Podiatrists 1 (pt); Audiologists 1 (pt).
Languages Spanish.
Affiliation Methodist.
Facilities Dining room; Activities room; Chapel; Crafts room; Laundry room; Barber/ Beauty shop.
Activities Arts & crafts; Cards; Games; Reading groups; Prayer groups; Movies; Shopping trips; Dances/Social/Cultural gatherings.

Northgate Unit of Lakeview Christian Home of the Southwest Inc
1905 W Pierce, Carlsbad, NM 88220
(505) 885-3161
Admin JoAnna Knox. *Dir of Nursing* Iris Wisnoski RN. *Medical Dir* Virgil O McCollum MD.
Licensure Intermediate care. *Beds* ICF 112. *Certified* Medicaid.
Owner Nonprofit corp.
Admissions Requirements Medical examination.
Staff RNs 7 (ft); LPNs 4 (ft), 3 (pt); Nurses' aides; Physical therapists; Activities coordinators 1 (ft); Dietitians.
Affiliation Church of Christ.
Facilities Dining room; Physical therapy room; Chapel; Crafts room; Laundry room; Barber/Beauty shop; Private dining room.
Activities Arts & crafts; Games; Reading groups; Prayer groups; Movies; Shopping trips; Dances/Social/Cultural gatherings; Bible class; Resident council.

Carrizozo

New Horizons Developmental Center—Casa del Sol
PO Box 187, 804 E Ave, Carrizozo, NM 88301
(505) 648-2379
Admin Jenny Kelly.
Licensure Intermediate care for mentally retarded. *Beds* ICF/MR 4. *Certified* Medicare.

New Horizons Developmental Center—Casa Linda
PO Box 187, 804 E Ave, Carrizozo, NM 88301
(505) 648-2379
Admin Jenny Kelly.
Licensure Intermediate care for mentally retarded. *Beds* ICF/MR 15. *Certified* Medicare.

Clayton

Country Life Manor
PO Box 573, Clayton, NM 88415
(505) 374-2353
Admin James E Wagner.
Licensure Intermediate care. *Beds* ICF 54.
Certified Medicare.

Union County General Hospital
PO Box 489, 301 Harding St, Clayton, NM
88415
(505) 374-2585
Admin Doris Turgeon.
Licensure Skilled care; Intermediate care. *Beds*
Swing beds SNF/ICF 30.

Clovis

Americare Golden Age Nursing Center
1201 Norris St, Clovis, NM 88101
(505) 762-3754
Admin Betty Morris.
Medical Dir Mariellen Bonem.
Licensure Intermediate care. *Beds* ICF 59.
Certified Medicaid.
Owner Proprietary corp (Care Enterprises).
Admissions Requirements Medical
examination; Physician's request.
Facilities Dining room; Laundry room;
Barber/Beauty shop.
Activities Arts & crafts; Cards; Games; Prayer
groups; Movies; Shopping trips; Dances/
Social/Cultural gatherings.

High Plains Nursing Center
1400 W 21st St, Clovis, NM 88101
(505) 763-6695
Admin Juandell Dougherty.
Medical Dir Susie Small.
Licensure Intermediate care. *Beds* ICF 40.
Certified Medicaid.
Staff LPNs 6 (ft), 1 (pt); Nurses' aides 24 (ft);
Activities coordinators 1 (ft).
Facilities Dining room; Activities room;
Laundry room; Barber/Beauty shop.
Activities Arts & crafts; Cards; Games; Prayer
groups; Shopping trips; Dances/Social/
Cultural gatherings.

Retirement Ranch of Clovis
PO Box 1809, 2210 Mabry Dr, Clovis, NM
88101
(505) 762-4495
Admin William Michael Kesler.
Medical Dir Virginia Dickson.
Licensure Intermediate care; Retirement. *Beds*
ICF 102; Retirement apts 16. *Certified*
Medicaid.
Owner Nonprofit corp.
Admissions Requirements Medical
examination; Physician's request.
Staff RNs 1 (ft), 2 (pt); LPNs 9 (ft), 1 (pt);
Nurses' aides 43 (ft); Activities coordinators
1 (ft); Dietitians 1 (ft).
Languages Spanish.
Affiliation Presbyterian.
Facilities Dining room; Activities room;
Crafts room; Laundry room; Barber/Beauty
shop; Library.
Activities Arts & crafts; Cards; Games;
Reading groups; Prayer groups; Movies;
Shopping trips; Dances/Social/Cultural
gatherings.

Deming

Mimbres Memorial Nursing Home
900 W Ash St, Deming, NM 88030
(505) 546-2761
Admin Roy Rumbaugh. *Dir of Nursing* Helen
McGraw RN.
Licensure Intermediate care. *Beds* ICF 70.
Certified Medicaid.
Owner Publicly owned.
Admissions Requirements Minimum age 14.

Staff Physicians 10 (pt); RNs 4 (ft); LPNs 3
(ft), 2 (pt); Nurses' aides 22 (ft), 13 (pt);
Activities coordinators 1 (pt); Dietitians 1
(pt); Ophthalmologists 1 (pt).
Languages Spanish.
Facilities Dining room; Activities room;
Chapel; Crafts room; Laundry room; Barber/
Beauty shop.
Activities Arts & crafts; Cards; Games;
Reading groups; Prayer groups; Movies;
Shopping trips.

Espanola

Hacienda de Salud
720 Hacienda, Espanola, NM 87532
(505) 753-6769, 753-5098 FAX
Admin Mary Lou Martinez. *Dir of Nursing*
Cathleen O'Keefe.
Licensure Intermediate care. *Beds* ICF 120.
Private Pay Patients 1%. *Certified* Medicaid.
Owner Proprietary corp (Pilot Development).
Staff Physicians; RNs 3 (pt); LPNs 9 (pt);
Nurses' aides 42 (pt); Physical therapists
(contracted); Recreational therapists;
Occupational therapists (contracted); Speech
therapists 1 (pt); Activities coordinators 1
(ft), 1 (pt); Dietitians (contracted).
Languages Spanish.
Facilities Dining room; Physical therapy
room; Activities room; Laundry room;
Barber/Beauty shop; Library.
Activities Arts & crafts; Cards; Games;
Reading groups; Prayer groups; Movies;
Shopping trips; Dances/Social/Cultural
gatherings; Intergenerational programs; Pet
therapy.

Farmington

San Juan Manor
806 W Maple, Farmington, NM 87401
(505) 325-2910
Admin Ralph W Little. *Dir of Nursing* Kathy
Wright.
Licensure Intermediate care. *Beds* ICF 58.
Certified Medicaid.
Owner Proprietary corp (Hillhaven Corp).
Staff RNs 2 (ft); LPNs 4 (ft), 3 (pt); Nurses'
aides 16 (ft), 15 (pt); Activities coordinators
1 (ft).
Languages Navajo.
Facilities Dining room; Activities room;
Laundry room; Barber/Beauty shop; Lobby.
Activities Arts & crafts; Cards; Games;
Reading groups; Prayer groups; Movies;
Shopping trips; Dances/Social/Cultural
gatherings; Cultural events.

Fort Bayard

Fort Bayard Medical Center
PO Box 219, Fort Bayard, NM 88036
(505) 537-3302
Admin Linda Worley.
Medical Dir Larry Merrett MD.
Licensure Skilled care; Intermediate care. *Beds*
SNF 50; ICF 200. *Certified* Medicaid;
Medicare.
Admissions Requirements Medical
examination; Physician's request.
Staff Physicians 3 (ft); RNs 11 (ft); LPNs 18
(ft); Nurses' aides 109 (ft); Physical
therapists 1 (ft); Recreational therapists 1
(ft); Activities coordinators 1 (ft); Dietitians
1 (ft); Dentists 1 (pt).
Facilities Dining room; Physical therapy
room; Activities room; Crafts room; Barber/
Beauty shop; Library.
Activities Arts & crafts; Cards; Games;
Reading groups; Prayer groups; Movies;
Shopping trips.

Fort Stanton

Fort Stanton Hospital & Training School
PO Box 8, Fort Stanton, NM 88323
(505) 354-2211
Admin Ervin T Aldaz. *Dir of Nursing* Joel
Lacey RN. *Medical Dir* Roger A Beechie
MD.
Licensure Intermediate care for mentally
retarded. *Beds* ICF/MR 137. *Certified*
Medicaid; Medicare.
Owner Publicly owned.
Admissions Requirements Minimum age 14;
Medical examination; Physician's request;
Court commitment; Guardian request.
Staff Physicians 2 (ft); RNs 5 (ft); LPNs 7 (ft);
Nurses' aides 75 (ft); Physical therapists 1
(pt); Recreational therapists 3 (ft);
Occupational therapists 1 (pt); Speech
therapists 1 (ft); Activities coordinators 1
(ft); Dietitians 1 (ft); Podiatrists 1 (pt).
Languages Spanish.
Facilities Dining room; Physical therapy
room; Activities room; Chapel; Crafts room;
Laundry room; Barber/Beauty shop; Library;
Gymnasium; Swimming pool; Greenhouse;
Farm; Ceramics; Woodshops; Sheltered
workshop.
Activities Arts & crafts; Games; Reading
groups; Movies; Shopping trips; Dances/
Social/Cultural gatherings.

Fort Sumner

De Baca General Hospital
PO Box 349, 500 N 10th St, Fort Sumner,
NM 88119
(505) 355-2414
Admin Larry E Ellingson.
Licensure Skilled care; Intermediate care. *Beds*
Swing beds SNF/ICF 25.

Pecos Valley Care Center
PO Drawer L, 509 N 10th St, Fort Sumner,
NM 88119
(505) 355-2439
Admin Joyce Campbell.
Medical Dir E D Fikany MD.
Licensure Intermediate care. *Beds* ICF 44.
Certified Medicaid.
Owner Proprietary corp.
Admissions Requirements Medical
examination; Physician's request.
Staff RNs 1 (ft); LPNs 2 (ft), 3 (pt); Nurses'
aides 15 (ft), 2 (pt); Activities coordinators 1
(ft); Dietitians 1 (pt).
Facilities Dining room; Laundry room;
Barber/Beauty shop.
Activities Arts & crafts; Cards; Games;
Reading groups; Prayer groups; Shopping
trips; Dances/Social/Cultural gatherings;
Monthly birthday parties.

Gallup

Gallup Care Center
PO Box 1778, Gallup, NM 87301
(505) 722-2261
Admin Ben Aquilera.
Licensure Intermediate care. *Beds* ICF 100.
Certified Medicaid.
Owner Proprietary corp.

McKinley Manor
224 Nizhoni Blvd, Gallup, NM 87301
(505) 863-6348
Admin Glenda L Simpson.
Medical Dir Kevin Allen.
Licensure Intermediate care. *Beds* ICF 62.
Private Pay Patients 5%. *Certified* Medicaid.
Owner Proprietary corp (Horizon Health Care
Corp).
Admissions Requirements Minimum age 21;
Medical examination; Physician's request.
Staff Physicians 1 (pt); RNs 1 (ft); Physical
therapists 1 (ft); Activities coordinators 1
(ft); Dietitians 1 (ft); Podiatrists 1 (pt).

Languages Navajo, Spanish, Zuni.
Facilities Dining room; Laundry room;
Barber/Beauty shop; Native American
kitchen offered; Backyard.
Activities Arts & crafts; Cards; Games;
Reading groups; Prayer groups; Movies;
Shopping trips; Dances/Social/Cultural
gatherings; Intergenerational programs.

Rehoboth McKinley Christian Hospital
1901 Red Rock Dr, Gallup, NM 87301
(505) 863-6832
Admin David Conejo.
Licensure Skilled care; Intermediate care. *Beds*
SNF 8; Swing beds SNF/ICF 62.

Villa Guadalupe
1900 Mark Ave, Gallup, NM 87301
(505) 863-6894
Admin Sr Maria Christine Lynch. *Dir of
Nursing* Sr Paul Jones. *Medical Dir* Dr
Laura Hammons.
Licensure Skilled care. *Beds* SNF 42.
Owner Nonprofit organization/foundation
(Little Sisters of the Poor).
Admissions Requirements Minimum age 60;
Medical examination.
Staff Physicians 1 (pt); RNs 1 (ft); LPNs 2
(ft); Nurses' aides 6 (ft), 2 (pt); Dietitians 1
(pt).
Facilities Dining room; Physical therapy
room; Activities room; Chapel; Crafts room;
Laundry room; Barber/Beauty shop; Library.
Activities Arts & crafts; Cards; Games;
Reading groups; Prayer groups; Movies;
Shopping trips; Dances/Social/Cultural
gatherings; Intergenerational programs.

Grants

Grants Good Samaritan Center
840 Lobo Canyon Rd, Grants, NM 87020
(505) 287-8868, 287-5115 FAX
Admin Hendrick C Woesch. *Dir of Nursing*
Dave McCullough. *Medical Dir* Dr Ralph
Avedisian.
Licensure Intermediate care. *Beds* ICF 80.
Certified Medicaid.
Owner Nonprofit corp (Evangelical Lutheran/
Good Samaritan Society).
Admissions Requirements Medical
examination; Physician's request.
Staff RNs 1 (ft); LPNs 5 (ft), 2 (pt); Nurses'
aides 23 (ft), 13 (pt); Physical therapists 1
(ft); Activities coordinators 1 (ft); Dietitians.
Languages Navajo, Spanish.
Affiliation Lutheran.
Facilities Dining room; Activities room;
Chapel; Laundry room; Barber/Beauty shop.
Activities Arts & crafts; Cards; Games;
Reading groups; Prayer groups; Movies;
Shopping trips; Dances/Social/Cultural
gatherings; Intergenerational programs; Pet
therapy.

Hobbs

Hobbs Health Care Center
5715 Lovington Hwy, Hobbs, NM 88240
(505) 392-6845
Admin Dawn Chaney. *Dir of Nursing* Linda
Tackett RN. *Medical Dir* Dr Sam Kan
Kanala.
Licensure Skilled care; Intermediate care;
Alzheimer's care. *Beds* SNF 16; ICF 102.
Private Pay Patients 20%. *Certified*
Medicaid; Medicare.
Owner Proprietary corp (Horizon Healthcare
Corp).
Admissions Requirements Medical
examination; Physician's request.
Staff RNs 4 (ft), 1 (pt); LPNs 10 (ft), 6 (pt);
Nurses' aides 33 (ft), 14 (pt); Physical
therapists; Activities coordinators 1 (ft), 3
(pt); Dietitians 1 (ft).
Languages Spanish.

Facilities Dining room; Physical therapy
room; Activities room; Laundry room;
Barber/Beauty shop.
Activities Arts & crafts; Cards; Games; Prayer
groups; Movies; Shopping trips; Dances/
Social/Cultural gatherings; Pet therapy.

La Siesta Care Center
201 Bensing Rd, Hobbs, NM 88240
(505) 397-1113
Admin Eddie L Byrd.
Licensure Intermediate care. *Beds* ICF 55.
Certified Medicaid.
Staff RNs 1 (ft); LPNs 5 (ft); Nurses' aides 18
(ft); Physical therapists 1 (pt); Activities
coordinators 1 (pt); Dietitians 1 (pt).

Lea County Good Samaritan Village
1701 N Turner, Hobbs, NM 88240
(505) 393-3156
Admin Charles R Dingler.
Medical Dir Rita Wade.
Licensure Intermediate care. *Beds* ICF 108.
Certified Medicaid.
Owner Nonprofit corp (Evangelical Lutheran/
Good Samaritan Society).
Admissions Requirements Minimum age 18;
Medical examination; Physician's request.
Staff RNs 1 (ft), 1 (pt); LPNs 8 (ft), 2 (pt);
Nurses' aides 18 (ft), 5 (pt); Physical
therapists 1 (pt); Recreational therapists 2
(ft); Activities coordinators 2 (ft); Dietitians
1 (ft).
Facilities Dining room; Physical therapy
room; Activities room; Chapel; Crafts room;
Laundry room; Barber/Beauty shop; Library.
Activities Arts & crafts; Cards; Games;
Reading groups; Prayer groups; Movies;
Shopping trips; Dances/Social/Cultural
gatherings.

Las Cruces

Casa del Sol Senior Care Center
2905 E Missouri, Las Cruces, NM 88001
(505) 522-0404
Admin Jackie Dolliver.
Medical Dir Adex Cantu MD.
Licensure Intermediate care. *Beds* ICF 62.
Certified Medicaid.
Owner Proprietary corp (Hillhaven Corp).
Staff LPNs 5 (ft); Nurses' aides 8 (ft);
Activities coordinators 1 (ft).
Facilities Dining room; Physical therapy
room; Activities room; Crafts room; Laundry
room; Barber/Beauty shop; Library.
Activities Arts & crafts; Cards; Games;
Reading groups; Prayer groups; Movies;
Shopping trips; Dances/Social/Cultural
gatherings.

Las Cruces Nursing Center
2029 Sagecrest Ct, Las Cruces, NM 88001
(505) 522-7000
Admin Damacio R Marquez. *Dir of Nursing*
Judy De La O RN. *Medical Dir* Dr William
Austad.
Licensure Skilled care; Intermediate care;
Alzheimer's care. *Beds* SNF 24; ICF 96.
Certified Medicaid; Medicare.
Owner Privately owned.
Admissions Requirements Medical
examination; Physician's request.
Staff RNs; LPNs; Nurses' aides; Physical
therapists; Occupational therapists; Speech
therapists; Activities coordinators; Dietitians.
Languages Spanish.
Facilities Dining room; Physical therapy
room; Activities room; Laundry room;
Barber/Beauty shop; Library; Patio.
Activities Arts & crafts; Games; Reading
groups; Prayer groups; Movies; Shopping
trips; Dances/Social/Cultural gatherings; Pet
therapy.

Mountain Shadows Health Care Center
1005 Hill Rd, Las Cruces, NM 88005
(505) 523-4573

Admin Henry Wesley Handy.
Licensure Intermediate care. *Beds* ICF 83.
Certified Medicaid.
Owner Proprietary corp.

University Terrace Good Samaritan Village
3025 Terrace Dr, Las Cruces, NM 88001
(505) 522-1362
Admin William S Kubat.
Licensure Intermediate care. *Beds* ICF 62.
Certified Medicaid.
Admissions Requirements Medical
examination.
Staff RNs 4 (ft), 1 (pt); LPNs 4 (ft), 1 (pt);
Nurses' aides 23 (ft), 3 (pt); Activities
coordinators 1 (ft); Dietitians 1 (ft); Social
workers 1 (ft).
Affiliation Lutheran.
Facilities Dining room; Chapel; Crafts room;
Laundry room; Barber/Beauty shop; Library;
Swimming pool & jacuzzi.
Activities Arts & crafts; Cards; Games;
Reading groups; Prayer groups; Movies;
Shopping trips; Dances/Social/Cultural
gatherings; Sing-alongs; Birthday parties.

Las Vegas

Las Vegas Medical Center
PO Box 1388, Las Vegas, NM 87701
(505) 454-2100
Admin Pablo Hernandez.
Medical Dir Raymond Mathewson MD.
Licensure Intermediate care. *Beds* ICF 168.
Certified Medicaid; Medicare.
Admissions Requirements Minimum age 16;
Medical examination; Physician's request.
Staff Physicians 3 (ft); RNs 16 (ft); LPNs 21
(ft); Nurses' aides 119 (ft); Physical
therapists 1 (ft); Recreational therapists 1
(ft); Occupational therapists 1 (ft); Speech
therapists 2 (ft); Activities coordinators 6
(ft); Dietitians 2 (ft); Podiatrists 1 (pt);
Dentists 1 (ft).
Facilities Dining room; Physical therapy
room; Activities room; Crafts room; Barber/
Beauty shop.
Activities Arts & crafts; Cards; Games;
Reading groups; Prayer groups; Movies;
Shopping trips; Dances/Social/Cultural
gatherings.

Southwest Senior Care Inc
PO Box 999, 2301 Collins Dr, Las Vegas, NM
87701
(505) 425-9362
Admin Vaughn Gilbert.
Licensure Intermediate care. *Beds* ICF 102.
Certified Medicaid.
Owner Proprietary corp.

Lordsburg

Sunshine Haven
PO Box 340, W Railway Ave, Lordsburg, NM
88045
(505) 542-3539
Admin Rose Allen.
Medical Dir Lalitha Fernicola MD.
Licensure Intermediate care. *Beds* ICF 83.
Certified Medicaid.
Admissions Requirements Medical
examination.
Staff Physicians 1 (ft); RNs 1 (ft), 4 (pt);
LPNs 5 (ft); Nurses' aides 23 (ft), 1 (pt);
Physical therapists 1 (ft); Recreational
therapists 1 (ft), 1 (pt); Activities
coordinators 1 (ft); Dietitians 1 (ft);
Podiatrists 1 (pt).
Facilities Dining room; Physical therapy
room; Activities room; Crafts room; Laundry
room; Barber/Beauty shop.
Activities Arts & crafts; Cards; Games;
Reading groups; Prayer groups; Movies;
Dances/Social/Cultural gatherings.

Los Alamos

Sombrillo Intermediate Care Facility
1011 Sombrillo Ct, Los Alamos, NM 87544
(505) 662-4300
Admin Virginia Langston. *Dir of Nursing* Ann Wallace RN. *Medical Dir* Dr Maggie McCreery.
Licensure Intermediate care. *Beds* ICF 60. *Private Pay Patients* 50%. *Certified* Medicaid.
Owner Nonprofit organization/foundation.

Los Lunas

Los Lunas Hospital & Training School
PO Box 1269, Los Lunas, NM 87031
(505) 865-9611
Admin Carolyn Klintworth. *Dir of Nursing* Jean Babb RN. *Medical Dir* George Brown MD.
Licensure Intermediate care for mentally retarded. *Beds* ICF/MR 420. *Certified* Medicaid; Medicare.
Owner Publicly owned.
Admissions Requirements Physician's request.
Staff Physicians 4 (ft); RNs 19 (ft); LPNs 22 (ft); Nurses' aides 59 (ft); Physical therapists 2 (ft); Recreational therapists 12 (ft); Occupational therapists 2 (ft); Speech therapists 3 (ft); Dietitians 2 (ft); Podiatrists 1 (ft); Dentists 1 (ft).
Languages Spanish.
Facilities Dining room; Physical therapy room; Activities room; Chapel; Crafts room; Laundry room; Barber/Beauty shop; Library.
Activities Arts & crafts; Games; Reading groups; Prayer groups; Movies; Shopping trips; Dances/Social/Cultural gatherings.

Lovington

General Hospital
1600 N Main, Lovington, NM 88260
(505) 396-5611
Admin Nancy McIlwaine.
Licensure Skilled care; Intermediate care. *Beds* Swing beds SNF/ICF 28.

Lovington Good Samaritan Center
PO Box 1058, 1600 W Ave I, Lovington, NM 88260-1058
(505) 396-5212
Admin Mary Ellen Stroope.
Medical Dir Peggy Clayton.
Licensure Intermediate care. *Beds* ICF 62. *Certified* Medicaid.
Owner Nonprofit corp (Evangelical Lutheran/Good Samaritan Society).
Affiliation Lutheran.

New Laguna

Laguna Rainbow Nursing Center
PO Box 236, New Laguna, NM 87038
(505) 242-2227
Admin Talmage D Smith. *Dir of Nursing* Mary Kay Micheals RN. *Medical Dir* Judith Thierry MD.
Licensure Intermediate care; Retirement. *Beds* ICF 25; Retirement 40. *Private Pay Patients* 1%. *Certified* Medicaid.
Owner Nonprofit organization/foundation.
Admissions Requirements Medical examination; Physician's request.
Staff RNs 1 (ft); LPNs 3 (ft), 2 (pt); Nurses' aides 10 (ft), 4 (pt); Activities coordinators 1 (ft), 1 (pt); Dietitians 1 (ft).
Languages Laguna, Acoma.
Facilities Dining room; Physical therapy room; Activities room; Chapel; Crafts room; Laundry room; Barber/Beauty shop; Living room.
Activities Arts & crafts; Cards; Games; Prayer groups; Movies; Shopping trips; Dances/Social/Cultural gatherings; Pet therapy.

Portales

Roosevelt General Nursing Home
PO Drawer 60, 1700 S Ave O, Portales, NM 88130
(505) 356-4411
Admin Bernita Bradshaw. *Dir of Nursing* Kathy Lynch RN. *Medical Dir* Charles Lehman MD.
Licensure Intermediate care. *Beds* ICF 57. *Private Pay Patients* 43%. *Certified* Medicaid.
Owner Proprietary corp (Affiliated Medical Enterprises).
Admissions Requirements Minimum age 60; Medical examination; Physician's request.
Staff RNs 1 (ft); LPNs 4 (ft), 3 (pt); Nurses' aides 14 (ft), 12 (pt); Physical therapists 1 (pt); Recreational therapists 1 (ft); Activities coordinators 1 (ft), 1 (pt); Dietitians 1 (pt).
Facilities Dining room; Physical therapy room; Activities room; Crafts room; Barber/Beauty shop; Patio.
Activities Arts & crafts; Cards; Games; Reading groups; Prayer groups; Movies; Dances/Social/Cultural gatherings; Intergenerational programs; Pet therapy; Van rides; Musical programs.

Raton

Hacienda de Salud
1660 Hospital Dr, Raton, NM 87740
(505) 445-2734, 445-8451 FAX
Admin Dawn Mayhan. *Dir of Nursing* Alice Simmons. *Medical Dir* Byrch Williams MD.
Licensure Intermediate care; Residential care. *Beds* ICF 70; Residential care 10. *Private Pay Patients* 45%. *Certified* Medicaid; VA.
Owner Proprietary corp.
Admissions Requirements Medical examination; Physician's request.
Staff Physicians 1 (pt); RNs 4 (ft), 3 (pt); LPNs 5 (ft), 2 (pt); Nurses' aides 24 (ft), 8 (pt); Physical therapists 1 (pt); Recreational therapists 1 (ft); Activities coordinators 1 (ft); Dietitians 1 (pt).
Languages Spanish.
Facilities Dining room; Physical therapy room; Activities room; Chapel; Crafts room; Laundry room; Barber/Beauty shop.
Activities Arts & crafts; Cards; Games; Reading groups; Prayer groups; Movies; Shopping trips; Dances/Social/Cultural gatherings; Intergenerational programs; Pet therapy; Resident council; Family support group.

Miners Colfax Medical Center
200 Hospital Dr, Raton, NM 87740
(505) 445-3601
Admin John J Candelaria. *Dir of Nursing* Gloria Garcia. *Medical Dir* O T Bonnett MD.
Licensure Intermediate care; Sheltered care; Hospital swing beds. *Beds* ICF 27; Sheltered care 27; Hospital swing beds 38. *Certified* Medicaid; Miners Trust.
Owner Nonprofit organization/foundation.
Admissions Requirements Medical examination; Physician's request; Priority given to males.
Staff Physicians 5 (ft); RNs 2 (ft); LPNs 7 (ft), 1 (pt); Nurses' aides 7 (ft); Recreational therapists 1 (ft); Activities coordinators 1 (ft); Dietitians 1 (pt).
Languages Spanish, Italian, Slavic.
Facilities Dining room; Physical therapy room; Activities room; Chapel; Crafts room; Laundry room; Respiratory diagnostic; Black lung testing.
Activities Arts & crafts; Cards; Games; Reading groups; Prayer groups; Movies; Shopping trips; Dances/Social/Cultural gatherings; Monthly birthday parties; Ceramics; Picnics; Outings; Exercise.

Rio Rancho

Americare Rio Rancho Nursing Center
4210 Sabana Grande, Rio Rancho, NM 87124
(505) 892-6603
Admin Mariea L Smelser RN. *Dir of Nursing* Julie W Doering RN. *Medical Dir* William Anderson MD.
Licensure Skilled care; Intermediate care. *Beds* SNF 10; ICF 110. *Certified* Medicaid; Medicare.
Owner Proprietary corp (Care Enterprises).
Admissions Requirements Medical examination; Physician's request.
Staff RNs 4 (ft), 4 (pt); LPNs 9 (ft); Nurses' aides 50 (ft), 4 (pt); Physical therapists 1 (ft); Recreational therapists 1 (ft), 1 (pt); Occupational therapists (contracted); Speech therapists (contracted); Activities coordinators 1 (ft); Dietitians 1 (ft).
Languages Spanish.
Facilities Dining room; Physical therapy room; Activities room; Crafts room; Laundry room; Barber/Beauty shop.
Activities Arts & crafts; Cards; Games; Reading groups; Prayer groups; Movies; Shopping trips; Dances/Social/Cultural gatherings; Intergenerational programs; Pet therapy.

Roswell

Casa Maria Health Care Centre
1601 S Main, Roswell, NM 88201
(505) 623-6008
Admin Sr Loretta M Hall RN.
Medical Dir Charles Fenzi MD.
Licensure Intermediate care. *Beds* ICF 120. *Certified* Medicaid.
Owner Nonprofit organization/foundation.
Admissions Requirements Medical examination; Physician's request.
Staff Physicians; RNs 5 (ft); LPNs 12 (ft); Nurses' aides 48 (ft); Recreational therapists 2 (ft); Activities coordinators 1 (ft); Dietitians 1 (ft); Ophthalmologists 1 (ft); Podiatrists 1 (ft); Audiologists 1 (ft).
Languages Spanish, German, Greek, French.
Affiliation Roman Catholic.
Facilities Dining room; Physical therapy room; Activities room; Chapel; Crafts room; Laundry room; Barber/Beauty shop; Library.
Activities Arts & crafts; Cards; Games; Reading groups; Prayer groups; Movies; Dances/Social/Cultural gatherings; Intergenerational programs; Pet therapy.

Roswell Nursing Center
3200 Mission Arch, Roswell, NM 88201
(505) 624-2583
Admin Jerry Mayfield. *Dir of Nursing* Katricia Turner RN. *Medical Dir* Peter Rosario MD.
Licensure Skilled care; Intermediate care; Alzheimer's care. *Beds* SNF 24; ICF 96. *Private Pay Patients* 40%. *Certified* Medicaid; Medicare.
Owner Proprietary corp (Paradigm Management).
Admissions Requirements Physician's request.
Staff RNs 3 (ft), 3 (pt); LPNs 6 (ft), 4 (pt); Nurses' aides 45 (ft), 10 (pt); Physical therapists 1 (ft); Occupational therapists 1 (pt); Activities coordinators 1 (ft).
Languages Spanish.
Facilities Dining room; Physical therapy room; Activities room; Laundry room; Barber/Beauty shop.
Activities Arts & crafts; Cards; Games; Reading groups; Prayer groups; Movies; Shopping trips; Dances/Social/Cultural gatherings; Pet therapy.

Sunset Villa Nursing Home
1515 S Sunset, Roswell, NM 88201
(505) 623-7097
Admin Kay Rogers. *Dir of Nursing* J A Rogers RN. *Medical Dir* A Stoesser MD.

Licensure Intermediate care. *Beds* ICF 52. *Certified* Medicaid.
Owner Proprietary corp (Care Enterprises).
Admissions Requirements Medical examination; Physician's request.
Staff RNs 2 (ft), 20 (pt); LPNs 2 (ft), 2 (pt); Nurses' aides 17 (ft), 6 (pt).
Facilities Dining room; Activities room; Laundry room; Barber/Beauty shop.
Activities Arts & crafts; Cards; Games; Reading groups; Prayer groups; Movies; Shopping trips; Dances/Social/Cultural gatherings.

Ruidoso

Lincoln County Medical Center
PO Drawer 3 D/D HS, 211 Sudderth, Ruidoso, NM 88345
(505) 257-7381
Admin Steven G Keller.
Licensure Skilled care; Intermediate care. *Beds* Swing beds SNF/ICF 42.

Ruidoso Care Center
PO Box 2214, 5th & D Sts, Ruidoso, NM 88345
(505) 257-9071
Admin Gary Forvines.
Licensure Intermediate care. *Beds* ICF 83. *Certified* Medicaid.
Owner Proprietary corp.

Santa Fe

Casa Real
1650 Galisteo St, Santa Fe, NM 87501
(505) 984-8313
Admin Michael P Zimmerman.
Licensure Skilled care; Intermediate care. *Beds* SNF 16; ICF 80. *Certified* Medicare.

Granada de Santa Fe
313 Camino Alire, Santa Fe, NM 87501
(505) 983-7373
Admin Del Lewis.
Medical Dir Dr Matthew Kelly.
Licensure Intermediate care. *Beds* 45. *Certified* Medicaid.
Admissions Requirements Medical examination; Physician's request.
Staff Physicians 1 (pt); Speech therapists 1 (pt); Activities coordinators 1 (ft); Dietitians 1 (pt).
Facilities Dining room.
Activities Arts & crafts; Games; Prayer groups; Movies; Shopping trips.

Horizon Healthcare Nursing Center—Santa Fe
635 Harkle Rd, Santa Fe, NM 87501
(505) 982-2574
Admin Theresa Casarez.
Licensure Skilled care; Intermediate care. *Beds* SNF 22; ICF 98. *Certified* Medicaid; Medicare.
Owner Proprietary corp (Manor Care Inc).

La Residencia NC
PO Box 2327, 820 Paseo de Peralta, Santa Fe, NM 87504
(505) 983-2273
Admin John A Malley. *Dir of Nursing* Gary Thompson RN. *Medical Dir* Neal Devitt MD.
Licensure Intermediate care; Alzheimer's care. *Beds* ICF 135. *Private Pay Patients* 35%. *Certified* Medicaid.
Owner Nonprofit organization/foundation.
Admissions Requirements Minimum age 18; Medical examination; Physician's request.
Staff Physicians 1 (pt); RNs 5 (ft); LPNs 10 (ft), 1 (pt); Nurses' aides 41 (ft), 4 (pt); Physical therapists 1 (pt); Occupational therapists 1 (pt); Speech therapists 1 (pt); Activities coordinators 2 (ft); Dietitians 1 (ft); Podiatrists 1 (pt).
Languages Spanish.

Affiliation Presbyterian.
Facilities Dining room; Physical therapy room; Activities room; Chapel; Crafts room; Laundry room; Barber/Beauty shop; Library.
Activities Arts & crafts; Cards; Games; Reading groups; Prayer groups; Movies; Shopping trips; Dances/Social/Cultural gatherings; Intergenerational programs; Pet therapy; Music therapy.

Silver City

Gila Regional Medical Center
1313 E 32nd St, Silver City, NM 88061
(505) 388-1591
Admin Steve Jacobson.
Licensure Skilled care; Intermediate care. *Beds* Swing beds SNF/ICF 85.

Hacienda de Salud—Silver City
3514 Leslie Rd, Silver City, NM 88061
(505) 388-3127
Admin Mirian Schultz.
Licensure Intermediate care. *Beds* ICF 100. *Certified* Medicare.

Socorro

Socorro General Hospital
PO Box 1009, US Hwy 60 W, Socorro, NM 87801
Admin Jeffrey M Dye.
Licensure Skilled care; Intermediate care. *Beds* Swing beds SNF/ICF 38.

Socorro Good Samaritan Village
PO Box 1279, Hwy 60 W, Socorro, NM 87801
(505) 835-2724
Admin Sherry Friesen. *Dir of Nursing* Sandye Moye LPN.
Licensure Intermediate care. *Beds* ICF 62. *Private Pay Patients* 10%. *Certified* Medicaid.
Owner Nonprofit corp (Evangelical Lutheran/ Good Samaritan Society).
Admissions Requirements Medical examination.
Staff RNs; LPNs; Nurses' aides; Physical therapists; Activities coordinators; Dietitians.
Languages Spanish.
Affiliation Lutheran.
Facilities Dining room; Activities room; Crafts room; Laundry room; Barber/Beauty shop; Library; Chapel/Solarium; Life line units.
Activities Arts & crafts; Cards; Games; Prayer groups; Movies; Shopping trips; Dances/ Social/Cultural gatherings; Pet therapy.

Springer

Colfax General Hospital—Intermediate Care Facility
PO Box 458, 615 Prospect Ave, Springer, NM 87747
(505) 483-2443
Admin John Saint.
Licensure Intermediate care. *Beds* ICF 30. *Certified* Medicaid.

Taos

Plaza De Retiro Inc
414 Camino de la Placita, Taos, NM 87571
(505) 758-8248, 758-4150
Admin John W Himes. *Dir of Nursing* Michelle Kennedy. *Medical Dir* Michael Kaufman.
Licensure Intermediate care; Retirement. *Beds* ICF 12; Retirement units 52. *Private Pay Patients* 10%.
Owner Proprietary corp.
Admissions Requirements Minimum age 62.

Staff Physicians 1 (pt); RNs 1 (pt); LPNs 5 (ft); Nurses' aides 4 (ft); Physical therapists 1 (pt); Activities coordinators 1 (pt); Dietitians 1 (pt).
Languages Spanish.
Facilities Dining room; Physical therapy room; Activities room; Laundry room; Library.

Truth or Consequences

Buerra Vista Hospital
800 E 9th Ave, Truth or Consequences, NM 87901
(505) 894-2111
Admin Jim L Armstrong.
Licensure Skilled care; Intermediate care. *Beds* Swing beds SNF/ICF 34.

New Mexico Veterans Center
PO Box 927, 1400 S Broadway, Truth or Consequences, NM 87901
(505) 894-9081, 894-3596 FAX
Admin Marquita George MHA. *Dir of Nursing* Milledge Boyce. *Medical Dir* Mario Herrera MD.
Licensure Intermediate care; Alzheimer's care. *Beds* ICF 164. *Private Pay Patients* 25%. *Certified* Medicaid.
Admissions Requirements 90 days active duty in US Armed Services.
Staff Physicians 1 (ft); RNs 8 (ft); LPNs 12 (ft); Nurses' aides 55 (ft), 1 (pt); Physical therapists 1 (pt); Speech therapists 1 (pt); Activities coordinators 1 (ft); Dietitians 1 (pt).
Languages Spanish.
Facilities Dining room; Physical therapy room; Activities room; Crafts room; Laundry room; Barber/Beauty shop; Library; Swimming pool with natural hot mineral spring water; Child care facility.
Activities Arts & crafts; Cards; Games; Reading groups; Prayer groups; Movies; Dances/Social/Cultural gatherings; Intergenerational programs; Pet therapy.

Sierra Health Care Center
1400 N Silver, Truth or Consequences, NM 87901
(505) 894-7855
Admin L Neal Moore. *Dir of Nursing* Nancy Whitworth RN. *Medical Dir* Jim Malcolmson MD.
Licensure Intermediate care. *Beds* ICF 110. *Private Pay Patients* 27%. *Certified* Medicaid.
Owner Nonprofit corp.
Admissions Requirements Physician's request.
Staff Physicians 1 (ft), 3 (pt); RNs 3 (ft), 1 (pt); LPNs 7 (ft), 2 (pt); Nurses' aides 41 (ft), 2 (pt); Physical therapists 1 (ft); Speech therapists 1 (ft); Activities coordinators 1 (ft), 1 (pt); Dietitians 1 (ft); Podiatrists 1 (ft), 3 (pt).
Languages Spanish.
Facilities Dining room; Physical therapy room; Activities room; Chapel; Crafts room; Laundry room; Barber/Beauty shop; Library.
Activities Arts & crafts; Cards; Games; Prayer groups; Movies; Shopping trips; Dances/ Social/Cultural gatherings; Pet therapy.

Tucumcari

Dan C Trigg Memorial Hospital
PO Box 608, 301 E Miel De La Ladd, Tucumcari, NM 88401
(505) 461-0141
Admin Dan Noteware.
Licensure Skilled care; Intermediate care. *Beds* Swing beds SNF/ICF 50.

Van Ark Care Center
1005 S Monroe, Tucumcari, NM 88401
(505) 461-2570
Admin Troy Brigham.

Medical Dir Jean Anderson.
Licensure Intermediate care. *Beds* ICF 54.
　Certified Medicaid.
Owner Proprietary corp.
Admissions Requirements Medical
　examination; Physician's request.

Staff RNs 2 (ft), 1 (pt); LPNs 3 (ft); Nurses'
　aides 13 (ft), 4 (pt); Activities coordinators 1
　(ft); Dietitians 1 (ft).

Facilities Dining room; Activities room;
　Laundry room; Barber/Beauty shop.
Activities Arts & crafts; Cards; Games;
　Reading groups; Prayer groups; Movies;
　Shopping trips; Dances/Social/Cultural
　gatherings.

NEW YORK

Albany

Albany County Nursing Home
Albany-Shaker Rd, Albany, NY 12211
(518) 869-2231
Admin Robert J Lynch.
Medical Dir George Cuttita MD.
Licensure Skilled care. *Beds* 420. *Certified*
Medicaid; Medicare.
Owner Publicly owned.
Staff Physicians 2 (ft), 6 (pt); RNs 55 (ft);
LPNs 84 (ft); Physical therapists 5 (ft);
Occupational therapists 3 (ft); Speech
therapists 1 (ft); Activities coordinators 8
(ft); Dietitians 2 (ft); Ophthalmologists 2
(pt); Podiatrists 1 (pt); Audiologists 1 (ft);
Dentists 1 (pt).
Facilities Dining room; Physical therapy
room; Activities room; Crafts room; Laundry
room; Barber/Beauty shop.
Activities Arts & crafts; Cards; Games;
Reading groups; Prayer groups; Movies;
Shopping trips; Dances/Social/Cultural
gatherings.

Child's Nursing Home
25 Hackett Blvd, Albany, NY 12208
(518) 462-4211
Admin Robert Gilpatrick. *Dir of Nursing*
Joanne Breden RN. *Medical Dir* Dr David
Pankin.
Licensure Skilled care. *Beds* SNF 120.
Certified Medicaid; Medicare.
Owner Nonprofit corp.
Admissions Requirements Minimum age 16;
Medical examination; Physician's request.
Staff Physicians 1 (ft), 3 (pt); RNs 15 (ft), 4
(pt); LPNs 10 (ft), 6 (pt); Nurses' aides 55
(ft), 2 (pt); Physical therapists 1 (pt);
Recreational therapists 3 (ft), 2 (pt);
Occupational therapists 1 (pt); Speech
therapists 1 (pt); Activities coordinators 1
(ft); Dietitians 1 (pt); Podiatrists 2 (pt);
Audiologists 1 (pt); Dentists 1 (pt).
Affiliation Episcopal.
Facilities Dining room; Physical therapy
room; Activities room; Chapel; Crafts room;
Barber/Beauty shop; Visiting rooms.
Activities Arts & crafts; Games; Reading
groups; Prayer groups; Movies; Shopping
trips; Intergenerational programs; Pet
therapy; Nondenominational pastoral care.

Daughters of Sarah Nursing Home
Washington Ave & Rapp Rd, Albany, NY
12203
(518) 456-7831
Admin Stanley Poskanzer. *Dir of Nursing*
Mary Anne Murphy RN MA. *Medical Dir*
Mark Oldendorf MD.
Licensure Skilled care. *Beds* SNF 200.
Certified Medicaid; Medicare.
Owner Nonprofit organization/foundation.
Admissions Requirements Minimum age 16;
Physician's request.

Staff Physicians; RNs; LPNs; Nurses' aides;
Physical therapists; Occupational therapists;
Speech therapists; Activities coordinators;
Dietitians; Podiatrists; Audiologists;
Dentists; Optometric; Psychiatric.
Languages Yiddish.
Affiliation Jewish.
Facilities Dining room; Physical therapy
room; Activities room; Chapel; Crafts room;
Laundry room; Barber/Beauty shop; Library;
Private rooms; Kosher kitchen.
Activities Arts & crafts; Games; Reading
groups; Movies; Shopping trips;
Intergenerational programs; Pet therapy.

Eden Park Nursing Home
22 Holland Ave, Albany, NY 12209-1795
(518) 436-8441
Admin John Orlando. *Dir of Nursing* John
Greiner RN. *Medical Dir* James Pozniakas
MD.
Licensure Skilled care. *Beds* SNF 210. *Private
Pay Patients* 20%. *Certified* Medicaid;
Medicare.
Owner Proprietary corp (Eden Park Health
Services).
Admissions Requirements Minimum age 16.
Staff Physicians 6 (pt); RNs 24 (ft), 13 (pt);
LPNs 24 (ft), 10 (pt); Nurses' aides 80 (ft),
20 (pt); Physical therapists 2 (ft), 1 (pt);
Occupational therapists 1 (ft), 1 (pt); Speech
therapists 1 (pt); Activities coordinators 1
(ft); Dietitians 1 (ft); Ophthalmologists 1
(pt); Podiatrists 1 (pt); Dentists 1 (pt).
Facilities Dining room; Physical therapy
room; Activities room; Crafts room; Laundry
room; Barber/Beauty shop; Occupational
therapy room.
Activities Arts & crafts; Cards; Games; Prayer
groups; Movies; Shopping trips;
Intergenerational programs; Pet therapy;
Outside trips.

Ann Lee Home
Albany Shaker Rd, Albany, NY 12211
(518) 869-5331, 869-1713 FAX
Admin Thomas Coffey. *Dir of Nursing*
Marianne VanDerhydon. *Medical Dir*
Robert Yates.
Licensure Intermediate care. *Beds* ICF 175.
Private Pay Patients 8%. *Certified* Medicaid.
Owner Publicly owned.
Admissions Requirements Medical
examination.
Staff Physicians 12 (pt); RNs 8 (ft); LPNs 23
(ft); Nurses' aides 53 (ft); Physical therapists
1 (pt); Reality therapists 1 (ft); Recreational
therapists 1 (ft); Occupational therapists 1
(pt); Speech therapists 1 (pt); Activities
coordinators 1 (ft); Dietitians 1 (pt);
Ophthalmologists 1 (pt); Podiatrists 1 (pt);
Audiologists 1 (pt).
Facilities Dining room; Physical therapy
room; Activities room; Chapel; Crafts room;
Laundry room; Barber/Beauty shop.

Activities Arts & crafts; Cards; Games;
Reading groups; Prayer groups; Movies;
Shopping trips; Dances/Social/Cultural
gatherings; Intergenerational programs; Pet
therapy.

St Margarets House & Hospital for Babies
27 Hackett Blvd, Albany, NY 12208
(518) 465-2461
Admin Clinton Lewis.
Licensure Skilled care. *Beds* SNF 58. *Certified*
Medicaid.
Owner Nonprofit corp.

Teresian House Nursing Home Company Inc
Washington Ave Ext, Albany, NY 12203
(518) 456-2000
Admin Sr Joseph Mary. *Dir of Nursing*
Dorothy M Fitzgerald RN. *Medical Dir*
Francis R DeRossi MD.
Licensure Skilled care; Intermediate care. *Beds*
SNF 120; ICF 180. *Certified* Medicaid;
Medicare.
Owner Nonprofit corp.
Admissions Requirements Minimum age 65;
Medical examination.
Staff RNs 15 (ft), 13 (pt); LPNs 23 (ft), 11
(pt); Nurses' aides 118 (ft), 31 (pt); Physical
therapists 1 (ft), 1 (pt); Occupational
therapists 1 (ft); Activities coordinators 5
(ft); PT & OT aides 9 (ft).
Languages Spanish.
Affiliation Roman Catholic.
Facilities Dining room; Physical therapy
room; Activities room; Chapel; Crafts room;
Laundry room; Barber/Beauty shop; Library.
Activities Arts & crafts; Cards; Games;
Reading groups; Prayer groups; Movies;
Shopping trips; Dances/Social/Cultural
gatherings.

University Heights Nursing Home
325 Northern Blvd, Albany, NY 12204
(518) 449-1100
Admin Thomas Nicolla.
Licensure Skilled care. *Beds* SNF 200.
Certified Medicaid; Medicare.
Owner Proprietary corp.

Villa Mary Immaculate
301 Hackett Blvd, Albany, NY 12208
(518) 482-3363
Admin James A Reynolds. *Dir of Nursing*
Geneva Kittle RN. *Medical Dir* Nicholas
Vianna MD.
Licensure Skilled care. *Beds* SNF 160.
Certified Medicaid; Medicare.
Owner Nonprofit corp.
Admissions Requirements Minimum age 16;
Medical examination; Physician's request.
Staff Physicians 4 (pt); RNs 15 (ft), 12 (pt);
LPNs 12 (ft), 6 (pt); Nurses' aides 57 (ft), 14
(pt); Physical therapists 1 (pt); Occupational
therapists 1 (ft); Activities coordinators 1
(ft); Podiatrists 1 (pt).
Affiliation Roman Catholic.

Facilities Dining room; Physical therapy room; Activities room; Chapel; Crafts room; Laundry room; Barber/Beauty shop; Classrooms; 5 Courtyards; Solar corridor.
Activities Arts & crafts; Cards; Games; Reading groups; Prayer groups; Movies; Shopping trips; Pet therapy.

Westmere Convalescent Home
5 GippRd, Albany, NY 12203
(518) 456-8355
Admin Michael Levine.
Licensure Intermediate care. *Beds* 28.
Owner Proprietary corp.

Albion

Arnold Gregory Memorial Hospital Skilled Nursing Facility
243 S Main St, Albion, NY 14411
(716) 589-4422
Admin William P Gillick. *Dir of Nursing* Marion Gbrzinski RN. *Medical Dir* Diane L Arsenault MD.
Licensure Skilled care. *Beds* SNF 30. *Certified* Medicaid; Medicare.
Owner Nonprofit corp.
Admissions Requirements Medical examination; Physician's request.
Staff RNs 1 (ft), 1 (pt); LPNs 7 (ft), 5 (pt); Nurses' aides 7 (ft), 5 (pt); Physical therapists 2 (pt); Activities coordinators 1 (ft); Dietitians 1 (pt).
Facilities Dining room; Physical therapy room; Activities room; Crafts room; Laundry room; Barber/Beauty shop; Library.
Activities Arts & crafts; Cards; Games; Prayer groups; Movies; Shopping trips; Dances/Social/Cultural gatherings.

Orleans County Nursing Home
Rte 31, Albion, NY 14411
(716) 589-7004
Admin Stephen Heard.
Medical Dir Dr A Nassar.
Licensure Skilled care; Intermediate care. *Beds* SNF 95; ICF 37. *Certified* Medicaid; Medicare.
Owner Publicly owned.
Staff Physicians 3 (pt); RNs 8 (ft), 2 (pt); LPNs 11 (ft), 10 (pt); Nurses' aides 30 (ft), 36 (pt); Physical therapists 1 (pt); Speech therapists 1 (pt); Activities coordinators 1 (ft); Dietitians 1 (ft); Audiologists 1 (pt); Dentists 1 (pt).
Facilities Dining room; Physical therapy room; Activities room; Crafts room; Laundry room; Barber/Beauty shop.
Activities Arts & crafts; Cards; Games; Reading groups; Prayer groups; Movies; Shopping trips; Dances/Social/Cultural gatherings.

Alden

Erie County Home & Infirmary
11580 Walden Ave, Alden, NY 14004
(716) 937-9131
Admin James L Smith. *Dir of Nursing* Margaret Farley. *Medical Dir* Dr John T Gabbey.
Licensure Skilled care; Intermediate care. *Beds* SNF 513; ICF 125. *Certified* Medicaid; Medicare.
Owner Publicly owned.
Staff Physicians 1 (ft), 8 (pt); RNs 50 (ft), 7 (pt); LPNs 1 (ft), 18 (pt); Nurses' aides 261 (ft); Physical therapists 2 (ft), 2 (pt); Recreational therapists 7 (ft); Occupational therapists 2 (ft); Speech therapists 2 (ft); Activities coordinators 1 (ft); Dietitians 2 (ft); Physical therapy aides 4 (ft); Occupational therapy assistants 3 (ft); Dietary technicians 5 (ft).

Facilities Dining room; Physical therapy room; Activities room; Chapel; Crafts room; Laundry room; Barber/Beauty shop; Library; Candy shop; Boutique.
Activities Arts & crafts; Cards; Games; Reading groups; Prayer groups; Movies; Shopping trips; Dances/Social/Cultural gatherings.

Alexandria Bay

Edward John Noble Hospital of Alexandria Bay
19 Fuller St, Alexandria Bay, NY 13607
(315) 482-2511
Admin Joseph Kehoe. *Dir of Nursing* Willian Conner RN.
Licensure Skilled care. *Beds* SNF 22. *Certified* Medicaid; Medicare.
Owner Nonprofit corp.
Staff Physicians 1 (pt); RNs 1 (ft), 1 (pt); LPNs 7 (ft), 3 (pt); Nurses' aides 4 (ft), 2 (pt); Physical therapists 1 (pt); Occupational therapists 1 (pt); Activities coordinators 1 (ft), 1 (pt); Dietitians 1 (pt); Dentists 1 (pt).
Facilities Dining room; Barber/Beauty shop; Sun room.
Activities Arts & crafts; Cards; Games; Movies; Dances/Social/Cultural gatherings; Sing-alongs; Worship services; Island boat tours.

Allegany

Allegany Nursing Home
5th & Maple Ave, Allegany, NY 14706
(716) 373-2238
Admin Gerald Nye.
Licensure Skilled care. *Beds* SNF 37. *Certified* Medicaid; Medicare.
Owner Proprietary corp.
Admissions Requirements Medical examination.
Staff Physicians 1 (pt); RNs 2 (ft), 1 (pt); LPNs 3 (ft), 4 (pt); Nurses' aides 17 (ft), 6 (pt); Physical therapists 1 (pt); Activities coordinators 1 (ft); Dietitians 1 (pt); Podiatrists 1 (pt); Dentists 1 (pt).
Facilities Dining room; Physical therapy room; Activities room; Chapel; Crafts room; Laundry room; Barber/Beauty shop; Library.
Activities Arts & crafts; Cards; Games; Reading groups; Prayer groups; Movies; Shopping trips; Dances/Social/Cultural gatherings.

Amherst

Amherst Nursing & Convalescent Home
4459 Bailey Ave, Amherst, NY 14226
(716) 835-2543
Medical Dir Howard Lehman MD.
Licensure Skilled care. *Beds* SNF 83. *Certified* Medicaid; Medicare.
Owner Privately owned.
Admissions Requirements Minimum age 17; Medical examination; Physician's request.
Staff Physicians; RNs; LPNs; Nurses' aides; Physical therapists; Reality therapists; Recreational therapists; Occupational therapists; Speech therapists; Activities coordinators; Dietitians.
Facilities Dining room; Physical therapy room; Activities room; Crafts room; Laundry room; Barber/Beauty shop.
Activities Arts & crafts; Cards; Games; Reading groups; Prayer groups; Movies; Shopping trips; Dances/Social/Cultural gatherings.

Amityville

Broadlawn Manor Nursing Home
399 County Line Rd, Amityville, NY 11701
(516) 264-0222
Admin Patrick R Martone.

Licensure Skilled care; Intermediate care; Alzheimer's care. *Beds* SNF 200; ICF 120. *Certified* Medicaid; Medicare.
Owner Proprietary corp.
Staff Physicians; RNs; LPNs; Nurses' aides; Physical therapists; Recreational therapists; Occupational therapists; Speech therapists; Activities coordinators; Dietitians; Ophthalmologists; Podiatrists; Dentists.
Facilities Dining room; Physical therapy room; Activities room; Chapel; Crafts room; Laundry room; Barber/Beauty shop.
Activities Arts & crafts; Cards; Games; Prayer groups; Movies; Shopping trips; Dances/Social/Cultural gatherings.

Brunswick Nursing Home
366 Broadway, Amityville, NY 11701
(516) 789-7711, 789-7283 FAX
Admin John N Okwodu. *Dir of Nursing* Constance Griffith RN MPA. *Medical Dir* Louis A Ingrisano MD.
Licensure Skilled care. *Beds* SNF 94. *Certified* Medicaid; Medicare.
Owner Proprietary corp.
Admissions Requirements Minimum age 16.
Staff Physicians 1 (pt); RNs 8 (ft), 2 (pt); LPNs 8 (ft), 3 (pt); Nurses' aides 33 (ft), 10 (pt); Physical therapists 1 (pt); Recreational therapists 1 (pt); Occupational therapists 1 (pt); Speech therapists 1 (pt); Dietitians 1 (ft); Podiatrists 1 (pt); Audiologists 1 (pt).
Facilities Dining room; Physical therapy room; Activities room; Crafts room; Barber/Beauty shop.
Activities Arts & crafts; Games; Prayer groups; Movies; Shopping trips; Ethnic dinners; Picnics.

Amsterdam

Amsterdam Memorial Hospital Related Health Care Facility
Upper Market St, Amsterdam, NY 12010
(518) 842-3100, 842-0849 FAX
Admin Carmen C Paone. *Dir of Nursing* Fay Holt RN,. *Medical Dir* William C Blase MD.
Licensure Skilled care; Intermediate care. *Beds* SNF 120; ICF 40. *Private Pay Patients* 10%. *Certified* Medicaid; Medicare.
Owner Nonprofit corp.
Admissions Requirements Medical examination; Physician's request.
Staff RNs 7 (ft), 5 (pt); LPNs 16 (ft), 13 (pt); Nurses' aides 47 (ft), 26 (pt).
Facilities Dining room; Physical therapy room; Activities room; Crafts room; Barber/Beauty shop.
Activities Arts & crafts; Cards; Games; Reading groups; Prayer groups; Movies; Intergenerational programs; Pet therapy.

Montgomery County Infirmary
Sandy Dr, Amsterdam, NY 12010
(518) 843-3503
Admin Teresa M Blumberg. *Dir of Nursing* Janice Armer. *Medical Dir* Diamond, Achtyl & Weis Associates.
Licensure Skilled care. *Beds* SNF 120. *Private Pay Patients* 9%. *Certified* Medicaid; Medicare.
Owner Publicly owned.
Admissions Requirements Minimum age 18; Medical examination.
Staff Physicians (contracted); RNs 8 (ft), 5 (pt); LPNs 19 (ft), 4 (pt); Nurses' aides 46 (ft), 16 (pt); Physical therapists (contracted); Occupational therapists (contracted); Speech therapists (contracted); Activities coordinators 1 (ft); Dietitians (contracted); Nurse practitioners 1 (ft).
Facilities Dining room; Physical therapy room; Activities room; Chapel; Laundry room; Barber/Beauty shop; Solariums.

Activities Arts & crafts; Cards; Games; Reading groups; Prayer groups; Movies; Shopping trips; Dances/Social/Cultural gatherings; Intergenerational programs; Pet therapy.

Mt Loretto Nursing Home
RD 3, Swart Hill Rd, Amsterdam, NY 12010
(518) 842-6790
Admin Sr Patricia Anne CR.
Medical Dir Dr H A Rehman.
Licensure Skilled care. *Beds* SNF 82. *Private Pay Patients* 18%. *Certified* Medicaid; Medicare.
Owner Nonprofit corp.
Staff Physicians 1 (ft); RNs 5 (ft), 8 (pt); LPNs 9 (ft), 4 (pt); Nurses' aides 38 (ft), 14 (pt); Activities coordinators 1 (ft).
Affiliation Roman Catholic.
Facilities Dining room; Physical therapy room; Activities room; Chapel; Crafts room; Laundry room; Barber/Beauty shop; Sun porches; Outdoor patio.
Activities Arts & crafts; Games; Reading groups; Prayer groups; Movies; Shopping trips; Dances/Social/Cultural gatherings; Pet therapy; Summer outings.

Argyle

Pleasant Valley Infirmary
Rte 40, Argyle, NY 12809
(518) 638-8274, 638-6420 FAX
Admin Douglas E Cosey. *Dir of Nursing* Cynthia Canzeri-Labish RN. *Medical Dir* Michael J Lynch MD.
Licensure Skilled care; Intermediate care. *Beds* SNF 80; ICF 40. *Private Pay Patients* 10%. *Certified* Medicaid; Medicare.
Owner Publicly owned.
Admissions Requirements Medical examination; Physician's request.
Staff Physicians 2 (pt); RNs 10 (ft), 5 (pt); LPNs 8 (ft), 8 (pt); Nurses' aides 55 (ft), 8 (pt); Physical therapists 1 (pt); Occupational therapists 1 (pt); Speech therapists 1 (pt); Activities coordinators 1 (ft); Dietitians 1 (pt); Podiatrists 1 (pt); Nurse practitioners 1 (pt).
Facilities Dining room; Physical therapy room; Activities room; Crafts room; Laundry room; Barber/Beauty shop; Patio; Fenced-in yard with trees.
Activities Arts & crafts; Cards; Games; Reading groups; Prayer groups; Movies; Shopping trips; Dances/Social/Cultural gatherings; Intergenerational programs; Pet therapy.

Arverne

Lawrence Nursing Home Inc
350 Beach 54th St, Arverne, NY 11692
(718) 945-0400
Admin Benjamin Levine. *Dir of Nursing* Karen Thompson RN. *Medical Dir* Dr Tara Saiwi.
Licensure Skilled care. *Beds* SNF 200. *Certified* Medicaid; Medicare.
Owner Proprietary corp.
Staff RNs 9 (ft), 6 (pt); LPNs 23 (ft), 6 (pt); Nurses' aides 73 (ft), 15 (pt); Physical therapists 2 (pt); Occupational therapists 2 (pt); Speech therapists 1 (pt); Activities coordinators 1 (ft); Dietitians 1 (ft), 1 (pt).
Languages Spanish.
Facilities Dining room; Physical therapy room; Activities room; Crafts room; Laundry room; Barber/Beauty shop; Library.
Activities Arts & crafts; Cards; Games; Reading groups; Prayer groups; Movies; Shopping trips; Musical entertainment; Cultural & recreational trips.

Resort Health Related Facility
64-11 Beach Channel Dr, Arverne, NY 11692
(718) 945-0700, 945-5912 FAX

Admin Morris Tenenbaum. *Dir of Nursing* Leta Crawford. *Medical Dir* Tali Skoczylas.
Licensure Intermediate care; Alzheimer's care. *Beds* ICF 280. *Private Pay Patients* 2%. *Certified* Medicaid.
Owner Privately owned.
Admissions Requirements Minimum age 18; Medical examination; Physician's request.
Staff Physicians 5 (pt); RNs 8 (ft), 1 (pt); LPNs 13 (ft), 10 (pt); Nurses' aides 30 (ft), 15 (pt); Physical therapists 2 (pt); Recreational therapists 3 (ft), 1 (pt); Occupational therapists 2 (pt); Speech therapists 1 (pt); Activities coordinators 1 (ft); Dietitians 1 (pt), 3 (pt); Ophthalmologists 1 (pt); Podiatrists 1 (pt); Audiologists 1 (pt).
Languages Spanish, Yiddish, Hebrew, Polish.
Facilities Dining room; Physical therapy room; Activities room; Chapel; Crafts room; Laundry room; Barber/Beauty shop; Library; Private rooms available.
Activities Arts & crafts; Cards; Games; Reading groups; Prayer groups; Movies; Shopping trips; Dances/Social/Cultural gatherings; Intergenerational programs; Pet therapy; Baking; Discussion; Sing-alongs; Bingo; Resident council; Strolling musician; Religious services.

Resort Nursing Home
430 Beach 68th St, Arverne, NY 11692
(718) 474-5200
Admin Michael Tennebaum.
Licensure Skilled care. *Beds* SNF 280. *Certified* Medicaid; Medicare.
Owner Privately owned.

Astoria

Lyden Nursing Home
27-37 27th St, Astoria, NY 11102
(718) 932-4613
Admin Chaim Sieger.
Medical Dir Dr Murray Waksman.
Licensure Skilled care. *Beds* SNF 114. *Certified* Medicaid; Medicare.
Owner Privately owned.
Staff Physicians 4 (pt); RNs 7 (ft); LPNs 9 (ft), 3 (pt); Nurses' aides 24 (ft), 10 (pt); Physical therapists 1 (ft); Recreational therapists 1 (ft); Occupational therapists 1 (pt); Speech therapists 1 (pt); Activities coordinators 1 (ft); Dietitians 1 (ft); Ophthalmologists 1 (pt); Podiatrists 1 (pt); Dentists 1 (pt).
Affiliation Roman Catholic.
Facilities Dining room; Physical therapy room; Activities room; Crafts room; Laundry room; Barber/Beauty shop; Library.
Activities Arts & crafts; Cards; Games; Prayer groups; Movies; Dances/Social/Cultural gatherings; Ball game trips.

Auburn

Auburn Nursing Home
85 Thornton Ave, Auburn, NY 13021
(315) 253-7351
Admin Martha S MacKay. *Dir of Nursing* Monica W Moochler. *Medical Dir* Avanelle P Morgan MD.
Licensure Skilled care. *Beds* SNF 92. *Certified* Medicaid; Medicare.
Owner Nonprofit corp (Adventist Living Centers).
Admissions Requirements Minimum age 16; Physician's request; Must meet PRI classifications.
Staff Physicians 1 (pt); RNs 11 (ft), 7 (pt); LPNs 1 (ft), 4 (pt); Nurses' aides 42 (ft), 13 (pt); Physical therapists 1 (pt); Recreational therapists 12 (ft); Occupational therapists 1 (pt); Speech therapists 1 (pt); Activities coordinators 1 (ft); Dietitians 1 (pt).

Facilities Dining room; Activities room; Crafts room; Laundry room; Barber/Beauty shop.
Activities Arts & crafts; Cards; Games; Reading groups; Prayer groups; Movies; Shopping trips; Dances/Social/Cultural gatherings.

Cayuga County Nursing Home
PO Box 246, County House Rd, Auburn, NY 13021
(315) 253-7346, 253-7445 FAX
Admin Betty B Oropallo. *Dir of Nursing* Alice Amoia RN. *Medical Dir* Anthony J Graceffo MD.
Licensure Skilled care. *Beds* SNF 80. *Private Pay Patients* 8%. *Certified* Medicaid; Medicare.
Owner Publicly owned.
Admissions Requirements Minimum age 16.
Staff Physicians 1 (pt); RNs 9 (ft), 1 (pt); LPNs 12 (ft), 8 (pt); Nurses' aides 32 (ft), 15 (pt); Physical therapists 1 (pt); Occupational therapists 1 (pt); Speech therapists 1 (pt); Activities coordinators 1 (pt); Dietitians 1 (pt); Podiatrists 1 (pt); Audiologists 1 (pt); Dentists 1 (pt).
Languages Language bank available for French, Italian, Russian, Ukrainian, Japanese, German, Greek, Polish.
Facilities Dining room; Physical therapy room; Activities room; Chapel; Crafts room; Barber/Beauty shop; Gift shop.
Activities Arts & crafts; Cards; Games; Reading groups; Prayer groups; Movies; Shopping trips; Dances/Social/Cultural gatherings; Intergenerational programs; Pet therapy.

Mercy Health & Rehabilitation Center Nursing Home Company Inc
3 St Anthony St, Auburn, NY 13021
(315) 253-0351, 253-0351, ext 299 FAX
Admin Sr Mary Aquin. *Dir of Nursing* Rose Hogan RN. *Medical Dir* Robert Kalet DO.
Licensure Skilled care; Intermediate care. *Beds* SNF 252; ICF 45. *Certified* Medicaid; Medicare.
Owner Nonprofit corp.
Admissions Requirements Minimum age 16; Medical examination; Physician's request.
Staff Physicians; RNs; LPNs; Nurses' aides; Physical therapists; Recreational therapists; Occupational therapists; Dietitians.
Affiliation Roman Catholic.
Facilities Dining room; Physical therapy room; Activities room; Chapel; Crafts room; Laundry room; Barber/Beauty shop.
Activities Arts & crafts; Cards; Games; Reading groups; Prayer groups; Movies; Shopping trips; Dances/Social/Cultural gatherings.

Avon

Avon Nursing Home
Clinton St Ext, Avon, NY 14414
(716) 226-2225
Admin Richard Baker.
Licensure Skilled care. *Beds* SNF 40. *Certified* Medicaid; Medicare.
Owner Privately owned.

Baldwinsville

Syracuse Home Association
7740 Meigs Rd, Baldwinsville, NY 13027
(315) 638-2521
Admin Natalie Andreassi. *Dir of Nursing* Kathleen Donovan RN. *Medical Dir* John Pipas MD.
Licensure Intermediate care. *Beds* ICF 80. *Certified* Medicaid.
Owner Nonprofit corp.
Admissions Requirements Minimum age 65; Medical examination; Physician's request.

Staff Physicians 1 (pt); RNs 4 (ft), 6 (pt); LPNs 5 (ft), 2 (pt); Nurses' aides 11 (ft), 3 (pt); Physical therapists 1 (pt); Dietitians 1 (pt); Ophthalmologists 1 (pt).
Facilities Dining room; Physical therapy room; Activities room; Crafts room; Laundry room; Barber/Beauty shop; Library.
Activities Arts & crafts; Prayer groups; Movies; Shopping trips; Dances/Social/Cultural gatherings.

Ballston Spa

Saratoga County Infirmary/Health Related Facility
Ballston Ave, Ballston Spa, NY 12020
(518) 885-4315
Admin Lorraine A Frollo. *Dir of Nursing* Laura Benscoter RN. *Medical Dir* Stephen Strader MD.
Licensure Skilled care; Health related facility. *Beds* SNF 160; HRF 117. *Certified* Medicaid; Medicare.
Owner Publicly owned.
Admissions Requirements Physician's request.
Staff Physicians; RNs; LPNs; Nurses' aides; Physical therapists; Occupational therapists; Speech therapists; Activities coordinators; Dietitians; Ophthalmologists; Podiatrists; Dentists.
Facilities Dining room; Physical therapy room; Activities room; Crafts room; Laundry room; Barber/Beauty shop; Library.
Activities Arts & crafts; Cards; Games; Reading groups; Prayer groups; Movies; Shopping trips; Dances/Social/Cultural gatherings.

Batavia

Batavia Nursing Home Inc
257 State St, Batavia, NY 14020
(716) 343-1300
Admin David A Novak.
Licensure Skilled care. *Beds* SNF 62. *Certified* Medicaid; Medicare.
Owner Proprietary corp.

Genesee County Nursing Home
278 Bank St, Batavia, NY 14020
(716) 344-0584
Admin Michael Perry. *Dir of Nursing* Jean Zaso RN. *Medical Dir* Myron E Williams MD.
Licensure Skilled care; Intermediate care. *Beds* SNF 120; ICF 40. *Certified* Medicaid; Medicare.
Owner Publicly owned.
Admissions Requirements Minimum age 16.
Staff Physicians 2 (pt); RNs 14 (ft), 9 (pt); LPNs 7 (ft), 12 (pt); Nurses' aides 46 (ft), 59 (pt); Physical therapists 1 (pt); Occupational therapists 1 (pt); Speech therapists 1 (pt); Activities coordinators 1 (ft); Dietitians 1 (pt).
Facilities Dining room; Physical therapy room; Activities room; Chapel; Crafts room; Laundry room; Barber/Beauty shop; Library.
Activities Arts & crafts; Cards; Games; Reading groups; Prayer groups; Movies; Dances/Social/Cultural gatherings.

St Luke Manor of Batavia
17 Wiard St, Batavia, NY 14020
(716) 343-4288
Admin Elizabeth Van Valkenburg. *Dir of Nursing* Shari Neureuter RN. *Medical Dir* Myron E Williams Jr MD.
Licensure Skilled care. *Beds* SNF 20. *Certified* Medicaid; Medicare.
Owner Nonprofit corp (Catholic Charities).
Staff Physicians 3 (pt); RNs 2 (ft), 3 (pt); LPNs 2 (ft), 1 (pt); Nurses' aides 9 (ft), 3 (pt); Physical therapists 1 (pt); Activities coordinators 1 (pt); Dietitians 1 (pt); Podiatrists 1 (pt).
Affiliation Roman Catholic.

Facilities Dining room; Chapel.
Activities Arts & crafts; Cards; Games; Prayer groups; Movies; Pet therapy.

Bath

Steuben County Infirmary
County Rte 113, Bath, NY 14810
(607) 776-7651
Admin Terry A Rowe. *Dir of Nursing* Dorothea Anderson RN. *Medical Dir* Michelle L Mohr MD.
Licensure Skilled care. *Beds* SNF 105. *Private Pay Patients* 3%. *Certified* Medicaid; Medicare.
Owner Publicly owned.
Admissions Requirements Minimum age 21.
Staff Physicians 4 (pt); RNs 16 (ft); LPNs 9 (ft); Nurses' aides 62 (ft), 1 (pt); Activities coordinators 1 (ft); Dietitians 1 (pt); Ophthalmologists 1 (pt); Podiatrists 1 (pt); Dentists 1 (pt).
Facilities Dining room; Physical therapy room; Activities room; Chapel; Crafts room; Barber/Beauty shop; Library.
Activities Arts & crafts; Cards; Games; Reading groups; Prayer groups; Movies; Shopping trips; Dances/Social/Cultural gatherings.

Bay Shore

Sunrise Manor Nursing Home
1325 Brentwood Rd, Bay Shore, NY 11706
(516) 665-4960
Admin Desmond McManus. *Dir of Nursing* Ruth Wanzer. *Medical Dir* Dr George Raniolo.
Licensure Skilled care. *Beds* SNF 84. *Certified* Medicaid; Medicare.
Owner Privately owned.
Admissions Requirements Minimum age 16.
Staff RNs 5 (ft), 12 (pt); LPNs 5 (ft), 4 (pt); Nurses' aides 23 (ft), 13 (pt); Physical therapists 1 (pt); Recreational therapists 1 (ft), 3 (pt); Occupational therapists; Speech therapists; Activities coordinators 1 (ft), 2 (pt).
Facilities Dining room; Physical therapy room; Activities room; Barber/Beauty shop.
Activities Arts & crafts; Cards; Games; Reading groups; Prayer groups; Movies; Shopping trips; Dances/Social/Cultural gatherings.

Bayside

Ozanam Hall of Queens Nursing Home Inc
42-41 201st St, Bayside, NY 11361
(718) 423-2000
Admin Sr M Joseph Catherine. *Dir of Nursing* Sr Damian Ann RN. *Medical Dir* Dr Robert Caruso.
Licensure Skilled care; Intermediate care. *Beds* SNF 382; ICF 50. *Certified* Medicaid; Medicare.
Owner Nonprofit corp.
Admissions Requirements Minimum age 65; Medical examination.
Staff Physicians 2 (pt); RNs 32 (ft), 54 (pt); LPNs 8 (ft), 19 (pt); Nurses' aides 159 (ft), 87 (pt); Physical therapists 1 (ft), 2 (pt); Occupational therapists 1 (ft); Activities coordinators 1 (ft); Dietitians 2 (ft); Podiatrists 1 (pt).
Languages Spanish, Italian.
Affiliation Roman Catholic.
Facilities Dining room; Physical therapy room; Activities room; Chapel; Crafts room; Laundry room; Barber/Beauty shop.
Activities Arts & crafts; Cards; Games; Reading groups; Prayer groups; Movies; Shopping trips; Dances/Social/Cultural gatherings; Pet therapy.

St Mary's Hospital for Children
29-01 216th St, Bayside, NY 11360
(718) 990-8850, 423-6001 FAX
Admin Stuart C Kaplan. *Dir of Nursing* Jane McConville RN. *Medical Dir* Neil Lombardi MD.
Licensure Skilled care; Medical/Social day care. *Beds* SNF 95. *Certified* Medicaid.
Owner Nonprofit corp.
Admissions Requirements Minimum age 0-16 years; Medical examination; Physician's request; Handicapped & terminally ill children.
Staff RNs 17 (ft), 10 (pt); LPNs 6 (ft), 2 (pt); Nurses' aides 6 (ft), 2 (pt); Physical therapists 5 (ft); Recreational therapists 3 (ft), 5 (pt); Occupational therapists 3 (ft); Speech therapists 3 (ft); Activities coordinators 3 (ft), 5 (pt); Dietitians 1 (ft), 1 (pt).
Languages Spanish, French, Greek.
Affiliation Episcopal.
Facilities Dining room; Physical therapy room; Activities room; Chapel; Crafts room; Laundry room; Asthma, orthopedics, genetics, neurology, palliative care, and general pediatric programs.
Activities Arts & crafts; Games; Reading groups; Movies; Educational programs.

Beacon

Fishkill Health Related Center Inc
Dogwood Ln, Beacon, NY 12508
(914) 831-8704
Licensure Intermediate care. *Beds* ICF 160.
Owner Proprietary corp.

Binghamton

Elizabeth Church Manor
863 Front St, Binghamton, NY 13905
(607) 722-3463
Admin Ruth Davis.
Medical Dir Dr Oscar Astur.
Licensure Skilled care; Intermediate care. *Beds* SNF 56; ICF 49. *Certified* Medicaid; Medicare.
Owner Nonprofit corp.
Admissions Requirements Physician's request.
Staff Physicians 1 (pt); RNs 7 (ft), 8 (pt); LPNs 4 (ft), 3 (pt); Nurses' aides 18 (ft), 21 (pt); Physical therapists 1 (pt); Activities coordinators 1 (ft); Dietitians 1 (pt).
Affiliation Methodist.
Facilities Dining room; Physical therapy room; Activities room; Chapel; Crafts room; Laundry room; Barber/Beauty shop; Library.
Activities Arts & crafts; Cards; Games; Reading groups; Prayer groups; Movies; Shopping trips; Dances/Social/Cultural gatherings.

River Mede Manor
159-163 Front St, Binghamton, NY 13902
(607) 722-7225
Admin Elizabeth Slutzker.
Licensure Skilled care; Intermediate care. *Beds* SNF 309; ICF 47. *Certified* Medicaid; Medicare.
Owner Privately owned.

Boonville

Sunset Nursing Home Inc
Academy St, Boonville, NY 13309
(315) 942-4301
Admin Jerome Britton. *Dir of Nursing* Jeanne Gaetano RN. *Medical Dir* Robert Smith MD.
Licensure Skilled care; Alzheimer's care. *Beds* SNF 120. *Private Pay Patients* 35%. *Certified* Medicaid; Medicare.
Owner Proprietary corp.
Admissions Requirements Minimum age 16; Physician's request.

Staff Physicians 3 (pt); RNs 9 (ft), 3 (pt); LPNs 12 (ft), 6 (pt); Nurses' aides 47 (ft), 19 (pt); Physical therapists 1 (pt); Recreational therapists 3 (ft); Occupational therapists 1 (pt); Speech therapists 1 (pt); Activities coordinators 1 (ft); Dietitians 1 (ft), 1 (pt); Ophthalmologists 1 (pt); Podiatrists 1 (pt); Audiologists 1 (pt).
Languages Polish.
Facilities Dining room; Physical therapy room; Activities room; Chapel; Crafts room; Laundry room; Barber/Beauty shop; Library.
Activities Arts & crafts; Cards; Games; Reading groups; Prayer groups; Movies; Shopping trips; Dances/Social/Cultural gatherings; Intergenerational programs; Pet therapy.

Brentwood

Ross Nursing Home Inc
839 Suffolk Ave, Brentwood, NY 11717
(516) 273-4000
Admin Victor P Russo.
Licensure Skilled care. *Beds* SNF 135.
Certified Medicaid; Medicare.
Owner Privately owned.

Briarcliff Manor

Brandywine Nursing Home Inc
620 Sleepy Hollow Rd, Briarcliff Manor, NY 10510
(914) 941-5100
Admin P Roth.
Medical Dir Sidney Harvey MD; George Vogel MD.
Licensure Skilled care. *Beds* SNF 120.
Certified Medicaid; Medicare.
Owner Proprietary corp.
Admissions Requirements Minimum age 16.
Staff RNs 12 (ft), 5 (pt); LPNs 11 (ft), 4 (pt); Nurses' aides 50 (ft), 13 (pt); Physical therapists 2 (pt); Occupational therapists 1 (pt); Speech therapists 1 (pt); Activities coordinators 1 (ft); Dietitians 1 (pt).
Facilities Dining room; Physical therapy room; Activities room; Crafts room; Laundry room; Barber/Beauty shop; Library.
Activities Arts & crafts; Cards; Games; Reading groups; Prayer groups; Movies; Shopping trips; Dances/Social/Cultural gatherings.

Brockport

Cupola Nursing Home
122 West Ave, Brockport, NY 14420
(716) 637-4129
Admin Elizabeth Beihirch.
Licensure Skilled care. *Beds* SNF 87. *Certified* Medicaid; Medicare.
Owner Privately owned.

Bronx

Astor Gardens Nursing Home
2316 Bruner Ave, Bronx, NY 10469
(212) 882-6400
Admin Bruce Rowland. *Dir of Nursing* M Villanueva. *Medical Dir* Dr Michael DiGiacomo.
Licensure Skilled care. *Beds* SNF 175.
Certified Medicaid; Medicare.
Owner Privately owned.
Admissions Requirements Minimum age 16; Medical examination.
Staff Physicians 5 (pt); RNs 7 (ft); LPNs 14 (ft); Nurses' aides 55 (ft); Physical therapists 2 (pt); Occupational therapists 3 (ft); Speech therapists 1 (pt); Activities coordinators 1 (ft); Dietitians 1 (ft); Podiatrists; Audiologists.
Languages Spanish, Italian.

Facilities Dining room; Physical therapy room; Activities room; Crafts room; Laundry room; Barber/Beauty shop; Library; Garden.
Activities Arts & crafts; Cards; Games; Reading groups; Prayer groups; Movies; Shopping trips; Dances/Social/Cultural gatherings.

Bainbridge Nursing Home
3518 Bainbridge Ave, Bronx, NY 10467
(212) 655-1991
Admin Isaac Goldbrenner. *Dir of Nursing* Teresa Francis RN. *Medical Dir* Dr Jay Hershkowitz.
Licensure Skilled care. *Beds* SNF 200.
Certified Medicaid; Medicare.
Owner Privately owned.
Staff Physicians 7 (ft); RNs 10 (ft); LPNs 12 (ft); Nurses' aides 54 (ft); Physical therapists 1 (pt); Recreational therapists 3 (ft); Occupational therapists 1 (pt); Speech therapists 1 (pt); Activities coordinators 1 (ft); Dietitians 2 (ft); Ophthalmologists 1 (pt); Podiatrists 1 (pt); Dentists 1 (pt).
Languages Spanish, Yiddish, Hebrew.
Facilities Dining room; Physical therapy room; Activities room; Crafts room; Laundry room; Barber/Beauty shop; Dental office.
Activities Arts & crafts; Cards; Games; Reading groups; Prayer groups; Movies; Shopping trips; Dances/Social/Cultural gatherings; Ceramics; Bowling; Barbeques.

Baptist Home for the Aged
3260 Henry Hudson Pkwy, Bronx, NY 10463
(212) 549-1700
Licensure Intermediate care. *Beds* ICF 84.
Owner Nonprofit corp.

Bruckner Nursing Home
1010 Underhill Ave, Bronx, NY 10472
(212) 863-6700
Admin Abraham C Grossman. *Dir of Nursing* Irene Degnan RN. *Medical Dir* Ernst Smith MD.
Licensure Skilled care; Alzheimer's care. *Beds* SNF 200. *Certified* Medicaid; Medicare.
Owner Nonprofit corp.
Admissions Requirements Medical examination.
Staff Physicians; RNs; LPNs; Nurses' aides; Physical therapists; Recreational therapists; Occupational therapists; Speech therapists; Activities coordinators; Dietitians; Ophthalmologists; Podiatrists; Dentists.
Languages Spanish, Hebrew, Yiddish.
Facilities Dining room; Physical therapy room; Activities room; Crafts room; Laundry room; Barber/Beauty shop; Library.
Activities Arts & crafts; Cards; Games; Reading groups; Prayer groups; Movies; Shopping trips; Dances/Social/Cultural gatherings.

Concourse Nursing Home
1072 Grand Concourse, Bronx, NY 10456
(212) 681-4000
Admin Helen Neiman.
Licensure Skilled care. *Beds* SNF 240.
Certified Medicaid; Medicare.
Owner Privately owned.

Daughters of Jacob Nursing Home Company Inc
1160 Teller Ave, Bronx, NY 10456
(212) 293-1500
Admin Steven J Bernstein. *Dir of Nursing* Jeanne Ward RN. *Medical Dir* Sandra Selikson MD.
Licensure Skilled care; Intermediate care; Retirement. *Beds* SNF 347; ICF 168.
Certified Medicaid; Medicare.
Owner Nonprofit corp.
Admissions Requirements Minimum age 65; Medical examination.
Staff Physicians 7 (ft); RNs 54 (ft); LPNs 23 (ft); Nurses' aides 171 (ft); Physical therapists 4 (ft); Recreational therapists 7

(ft); Occupational therapists 2 (ft), 2 (pt); Speech therapists 1 (ft); Activities coordinators 2 (ft); Dietitians 4 (ft); Ophthalmologists 2 (ft); Podiatrists 2 (pt); Dentists 1 (pt).
Affiliation Jewish.
Facilities Dining room; Physical therapy room; Activities room; Chapel; Crafts room; Laundry room; Barber/Beauty shop; Library.
Activities Arts & crafts; Cards; Games; Reading groups; Prayer groups; Movies; Shopping trips; Dances/Social/Cultural gatherings; In-house TV station for resident program broadcasting.

East Haven Health Related Facility
2323-27 Eastchester Rd, Bronx, NY 10469
(212) 655-2848
Admin Joseph Brachfeld. *Dir of Nursing* Elaine Tucker RN. *Medical Dir* Dr Simon Liederman.
Licensure Intermediate care. *Beds* ICF 200.
Certified Medicaid.
Owner Privately owned.
Staff Physicians; RNs; LPNs; Nurses' aides; Physical therapists; Occupational therapists; Speech therapists; Activities coordinators; Dietitians; Ophthalmologists.
Facilities Dining room; Physical therapy room; Activities room; Chapel; Crafts room.
Activities Arts & crafts; Cards; Games; Prayer groups; Movies.

Eastchester Park Nursing Home
2700 Eastchester Rd, Bronx, NY 10469
(212) 231-5550
Admin May Preira. *Dir of Nursing* Lillian Burgess. *Medical Dir* Dr Hyman Blume.
Licensure Skilled care. *Beds* SNF 200.
Certified Medicaid; Medicare.
Owner Privately owned.
Admissions Requirements Medical examination.
Staff RNs 19 (ft); LPNs 21 (ft); Nurses' aides 52 (ft); Physical therapists 1 (pt); Recreational therapists 3 (ft); Occupational therapists 1 (pt); Speech therapists 1 (pt); Activities coordinators 1 (ft); Dietitians 2 (ft); Ophthalmologists 1 (pt); Podiatrists 1 (pt); Dentists 1 (pt).
Languages Spanish, French, Yiddish, Italian, German.
Facilities Dining room; Physical therapy room; Activities room; Chapel; Crafts room; Laundry room; Barber/Beauty shop; Library; 2 Outdoor sitting areas.
Activities Arts & crafts; Cards; Games; Reading groups; Prayer groups; Movies; Dances/Social/Cultural gatherings; Choral group; Adopt-a-grandchild program.

Fieldston Lodge Nursing Home
666 Kappock St, Bronx, NY 10463
(212) 549-1203, 549-1249 FAX
Admin Eugene G Battenfeld Jr CMACHCA. *Dir of Nursing* Irene McNear. *Medical Dir* Pourrat Monahemi MD.
Licensure Skilled care. *Beds* SNF 200. *Private Pay Patients* 5%. *Certified* Medicaid; Medicare.
Owner Privately owned (M Birnbaum, D Caruso).
Staff Physicians 1 (ft), 1 (pt); RNs 8 (ft), 4 (pt); LPNs 16 (ft), 8 (pt); Nurses' aides 25 (ft), 25 (pt); Physical therapists 1 (ft), 2 (pt); Recreational therapists 2 (ft), 1 (pt); Occupational therapists 2 (pt); Speech therapists 1 (pt); Activities coordinators 1 (ft); Dietitians 1 (ft); Ophthalmologists 1 (pt); Podiatrists 2 (pt); Audiologists 1 (pt).
Facilities Dining room; Physical therapy room; Activities room; Barber/Beauty shop; Library.
Activities Arts & crafts; Cards; Games; Reading groups; Prayer groups; Movies; Pet therapy.

Grand Manor Health Related Facility
700 White Plains Rd, Bronx, NY 10473
(212) 931-5033
Licensure Intermediate care. *Beds* ICF 240.
Owner Privately owned.

Hebrew Home for the Aged at Riverdale—Fairfield Division
3220 Henry Hudson Pkwy, Bronx, NY 10463
(212) 549-9400, 796-9031 FAX
Admin Marie Ferrara. *Dir of Nursing* Ralmetha Brooks. *Medical Dir* Jeffrey Gold MD.
Licensure Skilled care; Alzheimer's care. *Beds* SNF 167. *Private Pay Patients* 7%. *Certified* Medicaid; Medicare.
Owner Nonprofit corp.
Admissions Requirements Minimum age 65; Medical examination.
Staff Physicians 3 (pt); RNs 14 (ft), 3 (pt); LPNs 14 (ft); Nurses' aides 55 (ft), 20 (pt); Physical therapists 2 (ft), 2 (pt); Recreational therapists 3 (ft); Occupational therapists 2 (ft); Speech therapists 1 (pt); Activities coordinators 1 (ft); Dietitians 1 (ft); Ophthalmologists 1 (pt); Podiatrists 1 (pt); Audiologists 1 (pt).
Languages Russian, Spanish.
Affiliation Jewish.
Facilities Dining room; Physical therapy room; Activities room; Crafts room; Barber/Beauty shop; Library; Alzheimer's unit.
Activities Arts & crafts; Cards; Games; Reading groups; Movies; Shopping trips; Dances/Social/Cultural gatherings; Pet therapy; Sheltered workshop.

Hebrew Home for the Aged at Riverdale Inc
5901 Palisade Ave, Bronx, NY 10471
(212) 549-8700
Licensure Skilled care; Intermediate care. *Beds* SNF 220; ICF 216.
Owner Nonprofit corp.

Hebrew Hospital for the Chronic Sick
2200 Givan Ave, Bronx, NY 10475
(212) 379-5020
Admin Richard Shedlovsky.
Licensure Skilled care; Intermediate care. *Beds* SNF 400; ICF 80. *Certified* Medicaid; Medicare.
Owner Nonprofit corp.
Affiliation Jewish.

House of the Holy Comforter
2751 Grand Concourse, Bronx, NY 10468
(212) 867-8100
Admin Luba Mebert.
Licensure Skilled care. *Beds* 151. *Certified* Medicaid; Medicare.
Owner Nonprofit corp.

Jewish Home & Hospital for Aged—Bronx Division
100 W Kingsbridge Rd, Bronx, NY 10468
(212) 579-0500, 584-1009 FAX
Admin Kenneth Sherman. *Dir of Nursing* Margaret Harrington RN. *Medical Dir* Benjamin Kropsky MD.
Licensure Skilled care; Intermediate care; Alzheimer's emergency respite; Retirement. *Beds* SNF 544; ICF 107; Retirement 50. *Private Pay Patients* 5%. *Certified* Medicaid; Medicare.
Owner Nonprofit organization/foundation.
Admissions Requirements Minimum age 60; Medical examination.
Staff Physicians 11 (ft); RNs 134 (ft); LPNs 38 (ft); Nurses' aides 237 (ft); Physical therapists 8 (ft); Recreational therapists 10 (ft), 1 (pt); Occupational therapists 8 (ft); Speech therapists 1 (pt); Activities coordinators 2 (ft); Dietitians 10 (ft).
Languages Yiddish, Hebrew, Spanish, Polish, German.
Affiliation Jewish.

Facilities Dining room; Physical therapy room; Activities room; Chapel; Crafts room; Laundry room; Barber/Beauty shop; Library; Occupational therapy room; Boutique; Garden/Solarium; Coffee shop and cafeteria; Auditorium.
Activities Arts & crafts; Cards; Games; Reading groups; Prayer groups; Movies; Shopping trips; Dances/Social/Cultural gatherings; Intergenerational programs; Pet therapy.

Jeanne Jugan Residence
3200 Baychester Ave, Bronx, NY 10475
(212) 671-2120
Medical Dir Dr Giordano.
Licensure Skilled care; Intermediate care. *Beds* SNF 78; ICF 92.
Owner Nonprofit corp (Little Sisters of the Poor).
Admissions Requirements Minimum age 60; Medical examination.
Staff RNs 6 (ft), 10 (pt); LPNs 8 (ft), 6 (pt); Nurses' aides 28 (ft), 37 (pt); Occupational therapists 1 (pt); Speech therapists 1 (pt); Activities coordinators 1 (ft); Dietitians 1 (ft), 1 (pt).
Affiliation Roman Catholic.
Facilities Dining room; Physical therapy room; Activities room; Chapel; Crafts room; Laundry room; Barber/Beauty shop; Library; Occupational therapy room.
Activities Arts & crafts; Cards; Games; Reading groups; Prayer groups; Movies; Shopping trips; Dances/Social/Cultural gatherings.

Kings Harbor Care Center
2000 E Gunhill Rd, Bronx, NY 10469
(212) 320-0400
Licensure Skilled care. *Beds* SNF 360.
Owner Privately owned.

Kings Harbor Manor Facility
2355 Ely Ave, Bronx, NY 10469
(212) 320-0400
Licensure Intermediate care.
Owner Publicly owned.

Kings Terrace Nursing Home & Health Related Facility
2678 Kingsbridge Terr, Bronx, NY 10463
(212) 796-5800, 548-5982 FAX
Admin Lowell S Feldman. *Dir of Nursing* Mildred Tanner RN. *Medical Dir* Norman Spitzer MD.
Licensure Skilled care; Intermediate care. *Beds* SNF 120; ICF 120. *Private Pay Patients* 1%. *Certified* Medicaid; Medicare.
Owner Privately owned.
Admissions Requirements Minimum age 21; Medical examination; Physician's request.
Staff Physicians; RNs; LPNs; Nurses' aides; Physical therapists; Recreational therapists; Occupational therapists; Speech therapists; Activities coordinators; Dietitians; Ophthalmologists; Podiatrists; Audiologists.
Languages Spanish.
Facilities Dining room; Physical therapy room; Activities room; Crafts room; Laundry room; Barber/Beauty shop.
Activities Arts & crafts; Cards; Games; Reading groups; Prayer groups; Movies; Shopping trips; Dances/Social/Cultural gatherings; Intergenerational programs; Pet therapy.

Kingsbridge Heights Long-Term Home Health Care
3400 Cannon Pl, Bronx, NY 10463
(212) 796-8100
Admin Rose Boritzer.
Licensure Skilled care; Intermediate care; Home care. *Beds* SNF 200; ICF 120; Home care 200. *Certified* Medicaid; Medicare; VA.
Owner Proprietary corp.

Kingsbridge Heights Manor
3426 Cannon Pl, Bronx, NY 10463
(212) 796-8100
Admin Rose Boritzer. *Dir of Nursing* Charmaine Taylor. *Medical Dir* Leonard Essman MD.
Licensure Skilled care; Health care. *Beds* SNF 80; Health care 120. *Certified* Medicaid; Medicare.
Owner Privately owned.
Admissions Requirements Minimum age 18.
Staff Physicians 6 (pt); RNs 15 (ft); LPNs 50 (ft); Nurses' aides 180 (ft); Physical therapists 4 (ft); Recreational therapists 8 (ft); Occupational therapists 3 (pt); Speech therapists 2 (pt); Activities coordinators 2 (ft); Dietitians 5 (ft); Ophthalmologists 3 (pt); Podiatrists 2 (pt).
Languages Hebrew, Spanish, Italian.
Facilities Dining room; Physical therapy room; Activities room; Chapel; Crafts room; Laundry room; Barber/Beauty shop; Library.
Activities Arts & crafts; Games; Reading groups; Prayer groups; Movies; Shopping trips; Dances/Social/Cultural gatherings.

Laconia Nursing Home
1050 E 230th St, Bronx, NY 10466
(212) 654-5875, 881-0729 FAX
Admin Barry Braunstein. *Dir of Nursing* K Kannadin RN. *Medical Dir* Moshe Labi MD.
Licensure Skilled care. *Beds* SNF 240.
Certified Medicaid; Medicare.
Owner Proprietary corp.
Languages Spanish, Yiddish.
Facilities Dining room; Physical therapy room; Activities room; Crafts room; Laundry room; Barber/Beauty shop.
Activities Arts & crafts; Cards; Games; Reading groups; Prayer groups; Movies; Shopping trips; Dances/Social/Cultural gatherings; Pet therapy.

Loeb Center Montefiore Medical Center
111 E 210th St, Bronx, NY 10467
(212) 920-4696
Admin Harvey A Simon. *Dir of Nursing* Dora Adom RN. *Medical Dir* Dr Robert Kennedy.
Licensure Skilled care. *Beds* SNF 80. *Certified* Medicaid; Medicare.
Owner Nonprofit corp.
Admissions Requirements Physician's request.
Staff Physicians 4 (pt); RNs 34 (ft), 4 (pt); Nurses' aides 30 (ft); Physical therapists 3 (ft); Recreational therapists 1 (pt); Occupational therapists 2 (ft); Activities coordinators 1 (ft); Dietitians 1 (ft).
Facilities Dining room; Physical therapy room; Activities room; Laundry room; Library.
Activities Arts & crafts; Cards; Games; Reading groups; Prayer groups; Movies.

Methodist Church Home for the Aged
4499 Manhattan College Pkwy, Bronx, NY 10471
(212) 548-5100
Admin Margaret V Fishburne.
Medical Dir Dr Norman Spitzer.
Licensure Skilled care; Intermediate care. *Beds* SNF 80; ICF 33. *Certified* Medicaid; Medicare.
Owner Nonprofit corp.
Admissions Requirements Minimum age 62; Medical examination; Physician's request.
Staff Physicians 2 (pt); RNs 9 (ft), 7 (pt); LPNs 5 (ft), 6 (pt); Nurses' aides 31 (ft), 8 (pt); Physical therapists 1 (pt); Occupational therapists 1 (pt); Activities coordinators 2 (ft); Dietitians 1 (pt); Podiatrists 1 (pt); Dentists 1 (pt).
Affiliation Methodist.
Facilities Dining room; Physical therapy room; Activities room; Chapel; Crafts room; Barber/Beauty shop; Library; Lounges.

Activities Arts & crafts; Cards; Games; Reading groups; Prayer groups; Movies; Shopping trips; Dances/Social/Cultural gatherings.

Morningside House Nursing Home Company
1000 Pelham Pkwy S, Bronx, NY 10461
(212) 409-8200, 828-2697 FAX
Admin Cynthia J Wallace. *Dir of Nursing* Sylvia Williams. *Medical Dir* Michael Irwin MD.
Licensure Skilled care; Intermediate care. *Beds* SNF 242; ICF 144. *Private Pay Patients* 3%. *Certified* Medicaid; Medicare.
Owner Nonprofit corp.
Staff Physicians 1 (ft), 17 (pt); RNs 11 (ft), 8 (pt); LPNs 25 (ft), 7 (pt); Nurses' aides 135 (ft), 21 (pt); Physical therapists 1 (ft); Recreational therapists 3 (ft); Occupational therapists 1 (ft); Activities coordinators 1 (ft); Dietitians 1 (ft); Ophthalmologists 1 (pt); Podiatrists 2 (pt).

Morris Park Nursing Home
1235 Pelham Pkwy N, Bronx, NY 10469
(212) 231-4300
Admin M Berkowitz.
Medical Dir Dr Robert Lapin.
Licensure Skilled care. *Beds* SNF 191. *Certified* Medicaid; Medicare.
Owner Privately owned.
Admissions Requirements Medical examination; Physician's request.
Staff Physicians; RNs; LPNs; Nurses' aides; Physical therapists; Reality therapists; Recreational therapists; Occupational therapists; Speech therapists; Activities coordinators; Dietitians; Ophthalmologists; Podiatrists; Dentists.
Languages Italian.
Facilities Dining room; Physical therapy room; Activities room; Crafts room; Barber/Beauty shop; Library.
Activities Arts & crafts; Cards; Games; Reading groups; Prayer groups; Movies; Dances/Social/Cultural gatherings.

Mosholu Parkway Nursing Home
3356 Perry Ave, Bronx, NY 10467
(212) 655-3568
Admin Issac Shapiro.
Licensure Skilled care. *Beds* SNF 125. *Certified* Medicaid; Medicare.
Owner Privately owned.

Palisade Nursing Home Company Inc
5901 Palisade Ave, Bronx, NY 10471
(212) 549-8700
Licensure Skilled care; Intermediate care. *Beds* SNF 266; ICF 82.
Owner Nonprofit corp.

Parkview Nursing Home
6585 Broadway, Bronx, NY 10471
(212) 549-2200
Admin Joseph Leone. *Dir of Nursing* Shirley White. *Medical Dir* Argon Atal MD.
Licensure Skilled care. *Beds* SNF 200. *Certified* Medicaid; Medicare.
Owner Privately owned.
Admissions Requirements Minimum age 16; Medical examination; Physician's request.
Staff Physicians 8 (pt); RNs 5 (ft), 11 (pt); LPNs 17 (ft), 18 (pt); Nurses' aides 49 (ft), 52 (pt); Physical therapists 1 (pt); Occupational therapists 2 (pt); Speech therapists 1 (pt); Activities coordinators 3 (ft); Dietitians 2 (ft); Ophthalmologists 2 (pt); Podiatrists 1 (pt); Dentists 3 (pt).
Languages Spanish, Italian, Polish, Hebrew, Yiddish, French.
Facilities Dining room; Physical therapy room; Activities room; Crafts room; Laundry room; Barber/Beauty shop.

Activities Arts & crafts; Cards; Games; Reading groups; Prayer groups; Movies; Shopping trips; Dances/Social/Cultural gatherings; Dining out; Bowling competition with other home; Picnics.

Pelham Parkway Nursing Home
2401 Laconia Ave, Bronx, NY 10469
(212) 798-8600
Admin Lucy Saskin.
Licensure Skilled care. *Beds* SNF 200. *Certified* Medicaid; Medicare.
Owner Privately owned.

Providence Rest
3304 Waterbury Ave, Bronx, NY 10465
(212) 931-3000
Admin S Joanne.
Licensure Skilled care; Intermediate care. *Beds* SNF 149; ICF 51. *Certified* Medicaid; Medicare.
Owner Nonprofit corp (Catholic Charities-Arch of NY).

Riverdale Nursing Home
641 W 230th St, Bronx, NY 10463
(212) 796-4800, 796-4834 FAX
Admin Michael Kirshner. *Dir of Nursing* Margaret Tenzca. *Medical Dir* Dr Leslie Walter.
Licensure Skilled care; Alzheimer's care. *Beds* SNF 146. *Private Pay Patients* 10%. *Certified* Medicaid; Medicare.
Owner Proprietary corp (Riverdale Nursing Home).
Staff Physicians 12 (pt); RNs 6 (ft), 2 (pt); LPNs 12 (ft), 6 (pt); Nurses' aides 50 (ft), 25 (pt); Physical therapists 2 (ft); Recreational therapists 3 (ft), 1 (pt); Occupational therapists 2 (ft); Speech therapists 1 (pt); Activities coordinators 1 (ft); Dietitians 1 (ft), 1 (pt); Ophthalmologists 1 (pt); Podiatrists 1 (pt); Audiologists 1 (pt).
Languages Spanish, Haitian.
Facilities Dining room; Physical therapy room; Activities room; Laundry room; Barber/Beauty shop.
Activities Arts & crafts; Cards; Games; Reading groups; Prayer groups; Movies; Shopping trips; Dances/Social/Cultural gatherings; Intergenerational programs; Pet therapy.

Rofay Nursing Home
946 E 211th St, Bronx, NY 10469
(212) 882-1800, 547-9004 FAX
Admin Eugene Burger. *Dir of Nursing* E Rampino RN. *Medical Dir* M Teich MD.
Licensure Skilled care. *Beds* SNF 120. *Certified* Medicaid; Medicare.
Owner Privately owned.
Admissions Requirements Minimum age adult; Medical examination; Physician's request.
Staff Physicians; RNs; LPNs; Nurses' aides; Physical therapists; Reality therapists; Recreational therapists; Occupational therapists; Speech therapists; Activities coordinators; Dietitians; Ophthalmologists; Podiatrists; Dentists.
Facilities Dining room; Physical therapy room; Activities room; Chapel; Crafts room; Laundry room; Barber/Beauty shop; Library.
Activities Arts & crafts; Cards; Games; Reading groups; Prayer groups; Movies; Shopping trips; Dances/Social/Cultural gatherings.

Sacred Heart Home
3200 Baychester Ave, Bronx, NY 10475
(212) 671-2120
Licensure Intermediate care. *Beds* 44.
Owner Nonprofit corp.
Affiliation Roman Catholic.

St Patricks Home for the Aged & Infirm
66 Van Cortlandt Park S, Bronx, NY 10463
(212) 519-2800

Admin Sr M Patrick Michael. *Dir of Nursing* Sr M Veronica. *Medical Dir* Eusebius J Murphy MD.
Licensure Skilled care. *Beds* SNF 264. *Certified* Medicaid; Medicare.
Owner Nonprofit corp (Carmelite Sisters for the Aged & Infirm).
Admissions Requirements Minimum age 65; Medical examination.
Affiliation Roman Catholic.
Facilities Dining room; Physical therapy room; Activities room; Chapel; Crafts room; Laundry room; Barber/Beauty shop.
Activities Arts & crafts; Cards; Games; Prayer groups; Movies; Shopping trips; Dances/Social/Cultural gatherings.

Split Rock Nursing Home
3525 Baychester Ave, Bronx, NY 10466
(212) 798-8900
Admin Abe Zelmanowicz.
Licensure Skilled care. *Beds* SNF 240. *Certified* Medicaid; Medicare.
Owner Privately owned.

United Odd Fellow & Rebekah Home
1072 Havemeyer Ave, Bronx, NY 10462
(212) 863-6200
Admin Alexander D Sajdak.
Medical Dir Jack Wagner MD.
Licensure Skilled care; Intermediate care. *Beds* SNF 131; ICF 82. *Certified* Medicaid; Medicare.
Owner Nonprofit corp.
Admissions Requirements Medical examination.
Staff Physicians 1 (ft), 2 (pt); RNs 12 (ft), 3 (pt); LPNs 16 (ft), 3 (pt); Nurses' aides 46 (ft), 10 (pt); Physical therapists 1 (pt); Recreational therapists 1 (ft), 3 (pt); Occupational therapists 1 (pt); Speech therapists 1 (pt); Activities coordinators 1 (pt); Dietitians 1 (ft); Ophthalmologists 1 (pt); Podiatrists 1 (pt); Dentists 1 (pt).
Affiliation Independent Order of Odd Fellows & Rebekahs.
Facilities Dining room; Physical therapy room; Activities room; Chapel; Crafts room; Barber/Beauty shop.
Activities Arts & crafts; Cards; Games; Reading groups; Prayer groups; Movies; Shopping trips; Dances/Social/Cultural gatherings.

University Nursing Home
2505 Grand Ave, Bronx, NY 10468
(212) 295-1400
Admin Eva Spiegel.
Medical Dir Zoila Mahbee.
Licensure Skilled care. *Beds* SNF 46. *Certified* Medicaid; Medicare.
Owner Privately owned.

Wayne Health Related Facility/Skilled Nursing Facility
3530 Wayne Ave, Bronx, NY 10467
(212) 920-1500
Admin Alexander Hartman.
Medical Dir Dr J Hershkowitz.
Licensure Skilled care; Intermediate care. *Beds* SNF 80; ICF 160. *Certified* Medicaid; Medicare.
Owner Publicly owned.
Admissions Requirements Females only; Medical examination.
Staff Physicians 5 (pt); RNs 10 (ft), 5 (pt); LPNs 10 (ft), 5 (pt); Nurses' aides 30 (ft), 10 (pt); Physical therapists 1 (pt); Reality therapists 1 (pt); Recreational therapists 3 (ft); Occupational therapists 1 (pt); Speech therapists 1 (pt); Activities coordinators 2 (ft), 1 (pt); Dietitians 2 (ft); Ophthalmologists 1 (pt); Podiatrists 1 (pt).
Facilities Dining room; Physical therapy room; Activities room; Chapel; Crafts room; Laundry room; Barber/Beauty shop; Library.

Activities Arts & crafts; Cards; Games; Reading groups; Prayer groups; Movies; Shopping trips; Dances/Social/Cultural gatherings.

White Plains Nursing Home
3845 Carpenter Ave, Bronx, NY 10467
(212) 882-4464
Admin Barbara Seidner.
Licensure Skilled care. *Beds* SNF 240. *Certified* Medicaid; Medicare.
Owner Privately owned.
Admissions Requirements Medical examination; Physician's request.
Languages Spanish.
Facilities Dining room; Physical therapy room; Activities room; Laundry room; Barber/Beauty shop.
Activities Arts & crafts; Cards; Games; Prayer groups; Movies.

Williamsbridge Manor
1540 Tomlinson Ave, Bronx, NY 10461
(212) 892-6600, 931-1061 FAX
Admin David Paley. *Dir of Nursing* Juliann Cottral. *Medical Dir* Dr Ernst Smith.
Licensure Skilled care. *Beds* SNF 77. *Certified* Medicaid; Medicare.
Owner Privately owned (Abraham C Grossman).
Admissions Requirements Medical examination; Physician's request.
Staff Physicians 2 (pt); RNs; LPNs; Nurses' aides; Physical therapists 1 (pt); Occupational therapists 1 (pt); Speech therapists 1 (pt); Activities coordinators 1 (ft), 2 (pt); Dietitians 1 (ft); Ophthalmologists 1 (pt); Podiatrists 1 (pt); Audiologists 1 (pt).
Languages Spanish, Italian.
Facilities Dining room; Physical therapy room; Activities room; Laundry room; Barber/Beauty shop.
Activities Arts & crafts; Cards; Games; Reading groups; Prayer groups; Movies.

Workmen's Circle Home & Infirmary
3155 Grace Ave, Bronx, NY 10469
(212) 379-8100
Admin David Londin.
Medical Dir Dr Edward Isenberg.
Licensure Skilled care; Intermediate care. *Beds* SNF 308; ICF 190. *Certified* Medicaid; Medicare.
Owner Proprietary corp.
Staff Physicians 7 (ft), 21 (pt); RNs 36 (ft), 5 (pt); LPNs 38 (ft), 10 (pt); Nurses' aides 170 (ft), 45 (pt); Physical therapists 2 (ft); Recreational therapists 4 (ft), 10 (pt); Occupational therapists 1 (ft), 1 (pt); Speech therapists 1 (pt); Activities coordinators 1 (ft); Dietitians 3 (ft); Ophthalmologists 2 (pt); Podiatrists 2 (pt); Dentists 1 (pt).
Affiliation Jewish.
Facilities Dining room; Physical therapy room; Activities room; Chapel; Crafts room; Laundry room; Barber/Beauty shop; Library; Clinics; Pharmacy.
Activities Arts & crafts; Cards; Games; Reading groups; Prayer groups; Movies; Shopping trips; Dances/Social/Cultural gatherings; Plays.

Brooklyn

Aishel Avraham Residential Health Facility Inc
40 Heyward St, Brooklyn, NY 11211
(718) 858-6200
Admin David Steinberg.
Licensure Skilled care; Intermediate care. *Beds* SNF 160; ICF 40. *Certified* Medicaid; Medicare.
Owner Proprietary corp.
Affiliation Jewish.

Augustana Lutheran Home
1680 60th St, Brooklyn, NY 11204
(718) 232-2180

Admin Charles C Miller, Exec Dir. *Dir of Nursing* Norma Spero, Asst Exec Dir. *Medical Dir* Frank C Gulin MD.
Licensure Skilled care; Intermediate care; Alzheimer's care. *Beds* SNF 55; ICF 35. *Private Pay Patients* 10%. *Certified* Medicaid; Medicare.
Owner Nonprofit organization/foundation.
Admissions Requirements Medical examination.
Staff Physicians 3 (pt); RNs 8 (ft), 6 (pt); LPNs 4 (ft), 3 (pt); Nurses' aides 30 (ft), 10 (pt); Physical therapists 1 (pt); Recreational therapists 2 (pt); Occupational therapists 2 (pt); Speech therapists 1 (pt); Activities coordinators 1 (ft); Dietitians 1 (pt); Ophthalmologists 1 (pt); Podiatrists 1 (pt); Audiologists 1 (pt).
Languages Italian, Swedish, Norwegian, Spanish.
Affiliation Lutheran.
Facilities Dining room; Physical therapy room; Activities room; Chapel; Crafts room; Laundry room; Barber/Beauty shop; Sun parlors; Alzheimer's unit.
Activities Arts & crafts; Cards; Games; Prayer groups; Movies; Dances/Social/Cultural gatherings; Intergenerational programs.

Brooklyn Methodist Church Home
1485 Dumont Ave, Brooklyn, NY 11208
(718) 827-4500
Admin H Rober Phillips.
Medical Dir Dr Babu Jasty.
Licensure Skilled care. *Beds* SNF 120. *Certified* Medicaid; Medicare.
Owner Nonprofit corp.
Admissions Requirements Minimum age 21; Medical examination.
Staff Physicians 4 (pt); RNs 8 (ft), 14 (pt); LPNs 5 (ft), 3 (pt); Nurses' aides 45 (ft), 10 (pt); Physical therapists 1 (pt); Reality therapists 1 (pt); Recreational therapists 1 (pt); Occupational therapists 1 (pt); Speech therapists 1 (pt); Activities coordinators 1 (ft); Dietitians 1 (ft); Ophthalmologists 1 (pt); Podiatrists 1 (pt); Audiologists 1 (pt); Dentists 1 (pt).
Affiliation Methodist.
Facilities Dining room; Physical therapy room; Activities room; Chapel; Crafts room; Laundry room; Barber/Beauty shop; Library; Dayrooms.
Activities Arts & crafts; Cards; Games; Reading groups; Prayer groups; Movies; Shopping trips; Dances/Social/Cultural gatherings; Pet therapy.

Cabs Nursing Home Company Inc
270 Nostrand Ave, Brooklyn, NY 11205
(718) 638-0500
Admin David Wieder.
Medical Dir Dr Francisco Trilla.
Licensure Skilled care; Intermediate care. *Beds* SNF 95; ICF 62. *Certified* Medicaid; Medicare.
Owner Nonprofit corp.
Admissions Requirements Minimum age 18.
Staff RNs 8 (ft), 3 (pt); LPNs 11 (ft), 4 (pt); Nurses' aides 35 (ft), 25 (pt); Physical therapists 2 (pt); Recreational therapists 2 (ft); Occupational therapists 1 (pt); Speech therapists 1 (pt); Activities coordinators 1 (ft); Dietitians 1 (ft); Ophthalmologists 1 (pt); Podiatrists 1 (pt); Audiologists 1 (pt); Dentists 1 (pt).
Facilities Dining room; Physical therapy room; Activities room; Crafts room; Laundry room; Barber/Beauty shop.
Activities Arts & crafts; Cards; Games; Reading groups; Prayer groups; Movies; Shopping trips; Dances/Social/Cultural gatherings.

Carlton Nursing Home
405 Carlton Ave, Brooklyn, NY 11238
(718) 789-6262

Licensure Skilled care. *Beds* SNF 148. *Certified* Medicaid; Medicare.
Owner Privately owned.

Caton Park Nursing Home
1312 Caton Ave, Brooklyn, NY 11226
(718) 693-7000
Admin J Weiss.
Licensure Skilled care. *Beds* SNF 119. *Certified* Medicaid; Medicare.
Owner Privately owned.

Cobble Hill Nursing Home
380 Henry St, Brooklyn, NY 11201
(718) 855-6789, 852-5673 FAX
Admin Olga Lipschitz. *Dir of Nursing* Andree Mangicavallo. *Medical Dir* Dr Jamshid Hakim.
Licensure Skilled care. *Beds* SNF 520. *Private Pay Patients* 4%. *Certified* Medicaid; Medicare.
Owner Nonprofit corp.
Staff Physicians; RNs 38 (ft); LPNs 67 (ft); Nurses' aides 262 (ft); Physical therapists 5 (ft), 1 (pt); Recreational therapists 10 (ft); Occupational therapists 4 (ft); Speech therapists 1 (ft); Dietitians 5 (ft).
Facilities Dining room; Physical therapy room; Activities room; Laundry room; Barber/Beauty shop; Library.
Activities Arts & crafts; Cards; Games; Reading groups; Prayer groups; Movies; Shopping trips; Dances/Social/Cultural gatherings; Intergenerational programs; Pet therapy.

Concord Nursing Home Inc
300 Madison St, Brooklyn, NY 11216
(718) 636-7500
Admin James McPherson.
Licensure Skilled care; Intermediate care. *Beds* SNF 82; ICF 41. *Certified* Medicaid; Medicare.
Owner Nonprofit corp.

Crown Nursing Home
3457 Nostrand Ave, Brooklyn, NY 11229
(718) 615-1100
Admin Sally Gearhart; Martha Juliani, Admissions Dir. *Dir of Nursing* Advira Providence. *Medical Dir* Dr Jacob Dimant.
Licensure Skilled care; Alzheimer's care. *Beds* SNF 189. *Private Pay Patients* 35%. *Certified* Medicaid; Medicare.
Owner Proprietary corp.
Staff Physicians; RNs; LPNs; Nurses' aides; Physical therapists; Reality therapists; Recreational therapists; Occupational therapists; Speech therapists; Activities coordinators; Dietitians; Ophthalmologists; Podiatrists; Audiologists.
Languages Yiddish, Spanish, Italian.
Facilities Dining room; Physical therapy room; Activities room; Chapel; Crafts room; Laundry room; Barber/Beauty shop; Library.
Activities Arts & crafts; Cards; Games; Reading groups; Prayer groups; Movies; Shopping trips; Dances/Social/Cultural gatherings; Intergenerational programs; Pet therapy.

Dover Nursing Home
1919 Cortelyou Rd, Brooklyn, NY 11226
(718) 856-4646
Admin Morey Adler.
Licensure Skilled care. *Beds* SNF 41. *Certified* Medicaid; Medicare.
Owner Privately owned.

Flatbush Manor Care Center
2107 Ditmas Ave, Brooklyn, NY 11226
(718) 462-8100
Medical Dir Dr Maurice Dunst.
Licensure Skilled care; Intermediate care. *Beds* SNF 160; ICF 40.
Owner Privately owned.
Staff Physicians 5 (pt); RNs 14 (ft); LPNs 12 (ft); Nurses' aides 28 (ft); Physical therapists 2 (pt); Recreational therapists 5 (pt);

Occupational therapists 1 (pt); Speech therapists 1 (pt); Activities coordinators 1 (ft); Dietitians 2 (ft); Ophthalmologists 1 (pt); Podiatrists 1 (pt); Audiologists 1 (pt); Dentists 1 (pt); Psychiatrists 1 (pt); Urologists 1 (pt); Neurologists 1 (pt).
Facilities Dining room; Physical therapy room; Activities room; Chapel; Crafts room; Laundry room.
Activities Arts & crafts; Cards; Games; Prayer groups; Movies.

Marcus Garvey Nursing Company Inc
810-20 Saint Marks Ave, Brooklyn, NY 11213
(718) 467-7300
Admin Ruby Weston.
Medical Dir Pierre A Brutus.
Licensure Skilled care; Intermediate care. *Beds* SNF 240; ICF 55. *Certified* Medicaid; Medicare.
Owner Nonprofit corp.
Admissions Requirements Minimum age 40; Medical examination.
Staff RNs 13 (ft); LPNs 23 (ft), 7 (pt); Nurses' aides 84 (ft), 27 (pt); Physical therapists 1 (ft); Occupational therapists 1 (ft); Speech therapists 1 (pt); Activities coordinators 1 (ft); Dietitians 4 (ft); Podiatrists 1 (pt); Dentists 1 (pt).
Facilities Dining room; Physical therapy room; Activities room; Laundry room; Barber/Beauty shop.
Activities Arts & crafts; Cards; Games; Reading groups; Prayer groups; Movies; Shopping trips; Dances/Social/Cultural gatherings.

Greenpark Care Center
140 Saint Edwards St, Brooklyn, NY 11201
(718) 858-6400
Admin Simon Pelman.
Licensure Skilled care; Intermediate care. *Beds* SNF 120; ICF 280. *Certified* Medicaid; Medicare.
Owner Proprietary corp.

Haym Salomon Home for the Aged
2300 Cropsey Ave, Brooklyn, NY 11214
(718) 373-1700
Licensure Skilled care; Intermediate care. *Beds* SNF 165; ICF 55. *Certified* Medicaid; Medicare.
Owner Nonprofit corp.
Affiliation Jewish.

Holy Family Home for the Aged
1740 84th St, Brooklyn, NY 11214
(718) 232-3666
Licensure Skilled care; Intermediate care. *Beds* SNF 84; ICF 62. *Certified* Medicaid; Medicare.
Owner Nonprofit corp.
Affiliation Roman Catholic.

JHMCB Center for Nursing & Rehabilitation Inc
520 Prospect Pl, Brooklyn, NY 11238
(718) 636-1000
Admin George A Miller.
Medical Dir Benjamin Ross MD.
Licensure Skilled care; Alzheimer's care. *Beds* SNF 320. *Certified* Medicaid; Medicare.
Owner Nonprofit corp.
Admissions Requirements Minimum age 16; Physician's request.
Staff Physicians 1 (pt); RNs 54 (ft), 5 (pt); LPNs 27 (ft); Nurses' aides 150 (ft), 26 (pt); Physical therapists 2 (ft), 1 (pt); Recreational therapists 4 (ft), 1 (pt); Occupational therapists 3 (ft), 1 (pt); Speech therapists 1 (pt); Dietitians 2 (ft); Ophthalmologists 3 (pt); Dentists 1 (pt).
Languages French, Creole, Spanish.
Affiliation Jewish.
Facilities Dining room; Physical therapy room; Activities room; Chapel; Crafts room; Barber/Beauty shop; Library.

Activities Arts & crafts; Cards; Games; Reading groups; Prayer groups; Movies; Shopping trips; Dances/Social/Cultural gatherings; Trips to museums, parks, ball games, race track.

Lemberg Home & Geriatric Institute Inc
8629 Bay Pkwy, Brooklyn, NY 11214
(718) 266-0900
Admin Rose Clee.
Medical Dir Anthony Loucella MD.
Licensure Skilled care; Intermediate care. *Beds* SNF 20; ICF 25. *Certified* Medicaid; Medicare.
Owner Nonprofit corp.
Admissions Requirements Minimum age 65; Medical examination.
Staff Physicians; RNs 3 (ft), 2 (pt); LPNs 2 (ft), 2 (pt); Physical therapists 1 (pt); Recreational therapists 2 (pt); Occupational therapists 1 (pt); Speech therapists 1 (pt); Activities coordinators 1 (pt); Dietitians 1 (pt); Ophthalmologists 1 (pt); Podiatrists 1 (pt); Audiologists 1 (pt); Dentists 1 (pt).
Facilities Dining room; Physical therapy room; Activities room; Chapel; Laundry room; Library.
Activities Arts & crafts; Cards; Games; Reading groups; Prayer groups; Dances/Social/Cultural gatherings; Birthday parties; Holiday parties.

Linden Bay Care Center
2749 Linden Blvd, Brooklyn, NY 11208
(718) 277-5100, 647-2597 FAX
Admin Anthony A Summers PhD. *Dir of Nursing* Derine McLaughlin RN. *Medical Dir* Salvatore F Pisciotto DO MD.
Licensure Skilled care. *Beds* SNF 140. *Private Pay Patients* 4%. *Certified* Medicaid; Medicare.
Owner Privately owned.
Admissions Requirements Medical examination; Physician's request.
Staff RNs 11 (ft), 13 (pt); LPNs 15 (ft), 14 (pt); Nurses' aides 44 (ft), 31 (pt); Physical therapists 1 (ft); Recreational therapists 1 (ft); Occupational therapists 1 (ft); Speech therapists 1 (pt); Activities coordinators 1 (ft); Dietitians 1 (ft); Audiologists 1 (pt).
Languages Spanish, Italian, French, Yiddish.
Facilities Dining room; Physical therapy room; Activities room; Chapel; Crafts room; Laundry room; Library.
Activities Arts & crafts; Cards; Games; Prayer groups; Movies; Dances/Social/Cultural gatherings.

Madonna Residence Inc
1 Prospect Park W, Brooklyn, NY 11215
(718) 857-1200, 857-1666 FAX
Admin Sr Cecilia Regina Murphy. *Dir of Nursing* Theresa Geogheghan. *Medical Dir* Luciano Martinucci MD.
Licensure Skilled care; Intermediate care. *Beds* SNF 203; ICF 87. *Certified* Medicaid; Medicare.
Owner Nonprofit corp.
Admissions Requirements Minimum age 65; Medical examination.
Staff Physicians 50 (pt); RNs 15 (ft), 39 (pt); LPNs 14 (ft), 17 (pt); Nurses' aides; Physical therapists 2 (ft); Occupational therapists 1 (ft), 1 (pt); Speech therapists 1 (pt); Activities coordinators 1 (ft); Dietitians 2 (ft); Ophthalmologists 2 (pt); Podiatrists 1 (pt); Dentists 2 (pt); Social workers 4 (ft).
Languages Spanish, Italian, Polish, Haitian.
Affiliation Roman Catholic.
Facilities Dining room; Physical therapy room; Activities room; Chapel; Crafts room; Laundry room; Barber/Beauty shop; Library; Coffee shop; Gift shop; Occupational therapy room; Clinics.
Activities Arts & crafts; Cards; Games; Reading groups; Movies; Shopping trips; Dances/Social/Cultural gatherings; Pet therapy; Senior Olympics.

Menorah Home & Hospital for the Aged & Infirm
871 Bushwick Ave, Brooklyn, NY 11221
(718) 443-3000
Admin Shirley Windheim, Exec Dir; Jane Rosenthal, Adm. *Dir of Nursing* Enith Lacy RN. *Medical Dir* Max Kleinmann MD.
Licensure Skilled care; Intermediate care; Alzheimer's care. *Beds* SNF 233; ICF 40. *Certified* Medicaid; Medicare.
Owner Nonprofit corp.
Staff Physicians 3 (ft), 3 (pt); RNs 11 (ft), 5 (pt); LPNs 27 (ft), 12 (pt); Nurses' aides 132 (ft), 21 (pt); Reality therapists 1 (ft), 2 (pt); Recreational therapists 5 (ft), 4 (pt); Occupational therapists 2 (pt); Speech therapists 1 (pt); Activities coordinators 1 (pt); Dietitians 2 (pt).
Languages Yiddish, Italian, Spanish.
Affiliation Jewish.
Facilities Dining room; Physical therapy room; Activities room; Chapel; Crafts room; Laundry room; Barber/Beauty shop; Library; Occupational therapy; X-ray; Speech therapy room; Audiology.
Activities Arts & crafts; Cards; Games; Reading groups; Prayer groups; Movies; Shopping trips; Dances/Social/Cultural gatherings.

Menorah Nursing Home Inc
1516 Oriental Blvd, Brooklyn, NY 11235
(718) 646-4441
Admin Shirley Windheim. *Dir of Nursing* Suzanne Davis RN. *Medical Dir* Swaminathan Giridharan MD.
Licensure Skilled care; Intermediate care; Alzheimer's care. *Beds* SNF 180; ICF 73. *Certified* Medicaid; Medicare.
Owner Nonprofit corp.
Staff Physicians 3 (ft), 3 (pt); RNs 13 (ft), 6 (pt); LPNs 15 (ft), 8 (pt); Nurses' aides 106 (ft), 18 (pt); Physical therapists 1 (ft), 3 (pt); Recreational therapists 4 (ft), 4 (pt); Occupational therapists 1 (ft), 2 (pt); Speech therapists 1 (pt); Activities coordinators 1 (pt); Dietitians 1 (ft), 1 (pt).
Languages Yiddish, Hebrew, Italian, Russian.
Affiliation Jewish.
Facilities Dining room; Physical therapy room; Activities room; Chapel; Crafts room; Laundry room; Barber/Beauty shop; Library; Occupational therapy room; X-ray; Speech therapy room; Audiology.
Activities Arts & crafts; Cards; Games; Reading groups; Prayer groups; Movies; Shopping trips; Dances/Social/Cultural gatherings.

Metropolitan Jewish Geriatric Center
W 29th St & the Boardwalk, Brooklyn, NY 11224
(718) 266-5700, 449-1051 FAX
Admin Robert A Bloom. *Dir of Nursing* Leah Gilbert. *Medical Dir* Dr Lila Dogim.
Licensure Skilled care; Health related facility. *Beds* SNF 244; Health related facility 115. *Certified* Medicaid; Medicare.
Owner Nonprofit corp.
Admissions Requirements PRI submitted for review, evaluated by Central Intake.
Staff Physicians 6 (ft); RNs 18 (ft), 3 (pt); LPNs 29 (ft), 3 (pt); Nurses' aides 644 (ft), 4 (pt); Physical therapists 2 (ft), 1 (pt); Recreational therapists 2 (ft), 1 (pt); Occupational therapists 1 (pt); Speech therapists 1 (pt); Activities coordinators; Dietitians 2 (ft), 1 (pt); Ophthalmologists; Podiatrists; Audiologists 1 (pt).
Languages French, Spanish, Yiddish, Russian, Hungarian.
Affiliation Jewish.
Facilities Dining room; Physical therapy room; Activities room; Chapel; Crafts room; Laundry room; Barber/Beauty shop; Library; Boardwalk; Activity space.

Activities Arts & crafts; Cards; Games; Reading groups; Prayer groups; Movies; Shopping trips; Dances/Social/Cultural gatherings; Intergenerational programs; Pet therapy; Picnics; Religious services; Educational groups; Holiday reminiscence groups.

MJG Nursing Home
4915 10th Ave, Brooklyn, NY 11219
(718) 851-3710, 853-7024 FAX
Admin Judith W Bruce, Sr V Pres/CO. *Dir of Nursing* Barbara Young. *Medical Dir* Raymond Cecora MD.
Licensure Skilled care; Special care units; Alzheimer's care. *Beds* SNF 529. *Private Pay Patients* 3%. *Certified* Medicaid; Medicare.
Owner Nonprofit corp.
Admissions Requirements Minimum age 16.
Staff Physicians 9 (ft); RNs; LPNs; Nurses' aides; Physical therapists 6 (ft); Recreational therapists 8 (ft); Occupational therapists 4 (ft); Speech therapists 2 (ft); Dietitians 5 (ft); Ophthalmologists (consultant); Podiatrists (consultant); Audiologists 1 (pt); Pharmacists 4 (ft).
Languages Yiddish, Polish, Russian, Spanish, Italian, French, German, Hebrew, Filipino, Hungarian.
Affiliation Jewish.
Facilities Dining room; Physical therapy room; Activities room; Chapel; Crafts room; Barber/Beauty shop; Library; Specialty clinics; Diagnostic services; Pharmacy; Kosher kitchen.
Activities Arts & crafts; Cards; Games; Reading groups; Prayer groups; Movies; Shopping trips; Dances/Social/Cultural gatherings; Intergenerational programs; Pet therapy; Exercise groups.

New York Congregational Home for the Aged
123 Linden Blvd, Brooklyn, NY 11226
(718) 284-8256
Admin David F Fielding.
Medical Dir Dr Glenn Morris.
Licensure Skilled care; Intermediate care. *Beds* SNF 39; ICF 29. *Certified* Medicaid; Medicare.
Owner Nonprofit corp.
Affiliation Congregational.
Facilities Dining room; Physical therapy room; Activities room; Crafts room; Laundry room; Barber/Beauty shop; Library; Solarium garden.
Activities Arts & crafts; Cards; Games; Prayer groups; Movies; Dances/Social/Cultural gatherings.

Norwegian Christian Home & Health Center
1250-70 67th St, Brooklyn, NY 11219
(718) 232-2322
Licensure Skilled care; Intermediate care. *Beds* SNF 41; ICF 94. *Certified* Medicaid; Medicare.
Owner Nonprofit corp.

Oxford Nursing Home
144 S Oxford St, Brooklyn, NY 11217
(718) 638-0360
Admin Max Goldberg.
Licensure Skilled care. *Beds* SNF 235. *Certified* Medicaid; Medicare.
Owner Privately owned.

Palm Gardens Nursing Home
615 Ave C, Brooklyn, NY 11218
(718) 633-3300
Admin Israel Lefkowitz.
Licensure Skilled care. *Beds* SNF 240. *Certified* Medicaid; Medicare.
Owner Privately owned.

Palm Tree Nursing Home
5606 15th Ave, Brooklyn, NY 11219
(718) 851-1000
Admin Isaac Levy. *Dir of Nursing* Marie Micara RN. *Medical Dir* Dr George Jhagroo.

Licensure Skilled care; Alzheimer's care. *Beds* SNF 79. *Certified* Medicaid; Medicare.
Owner Privately owned.
Admissions Requirements Minimum age 65; Medical examination.
Staff Physicians 2 (ft); RNs 5 (ft); LPNs 7 (ft); Nurses' aides 11 (ft); Physical therapists 1 (ft); Occupational therapists 1 (pt); Speech therapists 1 (pt); Activities coordinators 1 (ft); Dietitians 2 (ft), 1 (pt); Ophthalmologists 1 (pt); Podiatrists 1 (pt); Dentists 1 (pt).
Facilities Dining room; Physical therapy room; Activities room; Crafts room; Laundry room; Barber/Beauty shop; Library; Dayroom.
Activities Arts & crafts; Cards; Games; Reading groups; Prayer groups; Movies; Shopping trips; Dances/Social/Cultural gatherings.

Parkshore Manor Health Care Center
1555 Rockaway Pkwy, Brooklyn, NY 11236
(718) 498-6400
Admin Lawrence Friedman. *Dir of Nursing* Frieda Siegal. *Medical Dir* Nazalin Varani MD.
Licensure Skilled care; Intermediate care; Alzheimer's care. *Beds* SNF 135; ICF 135. *Certified* Medicaid; Medicare.
Owner Privately owned.
Admissions Requirements Medical examination.
Staff Physicians; RNs; LPNs; Nurses' aides; Physical therapists; Reality therapists; Recreational therapists; Occupational therapists; Speech therapists; Activities coordinators; Dietitians; Ophthalmologists; Podiatrists; Dentists.
Languages Yiddish, Hebrew, Italian.
Facilities Dining room; Physical therapy room; Activities room; Chapel; Barber/Beauty shop; Library.
Activities Arts & crafts; Cards; Games; Reading groups; Prayer groups; Movies; Shopping trips; Dances/Social/Cultural gatherings.

Prospect Park Nursing Home Inc
1455 Coney Island Ave, Brooklyn, NY 11230
(718) 252-9800
Admin Shirley Kurzman. *Dir of Nursing* Evelyn Power RN. *Medical Dir* Lawrence Sher.
Licensure Skilled care; Alzheimer's care. *Beds* SNF 215. *Certified* Medicaid; Medicare.
Owner Nonprofit corp.
Admissions Requirements Minimum age 50; Medical examination.
Staff Physicians 2 (ft); RNs 7 (ft), 5 (pt); LPNs 21 (ft), 4 (pt); Nurses' aides 18 (ft), 12 (pt); Physical therapists 2 (ft), 1 (pt); Recreational therapists 1 (ft), 6 (pt); Occupational therapists 1 (pt); Speech therapists 1 (pt); Activities coordinators 1 (ft); Dietitians 3 (ft), 1 (pt); Ophthalmologists 2 (pt); Podiatrists 2 (pt); Dentists 1 (pt).
Languages Spanish, Yiddish, Hebrew, Russian, Italian, French, German, Hungarian.
Affiliation Jewish.
Facilities Dining room; Physical therapy room; Activities room; Crafts room; Laundry room; Barber/Beauty shop; Library; Dental office.
Activities Arts & crafts; Cards; Games; Reading groups; Prayer groups; Movies; Shopping trips; Dances/Social/Cultural gatherings.

River Manor Health Related Facility
630 E 104th St, Brooklyn, NY 11236
(718) 272-1050, 272-3160 FAX
Admin Stanley Farkas. *Dir of Nursing* Phyllis Payne RN. *Medical Dir* Michael Nichols MD.

Licensure Intermediate care; Retirement. *Beds* ICF 380. *Private Pay Patients* 2%. *Certified* Medicaid.
Owner Proprietary corp.
Admissions Requirements Medical examination; Physician's request.
Staff Physicians 2 (pt); RNs 6 (ft); LPNs 30 (ft); Nurses' aides 66 (ft); Physical therapists 1 (pt); Recreational therapists 4 (ft), 2 (pt); Occupational therapists 1 (pt); Speech therapists 1 (pt); Activities coordinators 1 (ft); Dietitians 3 (ft), 1 (pt); Ophthalmologists 1 (pt); Podiatrists 1 (pt); Audiologists 1 (pt).
Languages Yiddish, Hebrew, Spanish, Haitian, Chinese.
Facilities Dining room; Physical therapy room; Activities room; Laundry room; Barber/Beauty shop; Library; Kosher kitchen.
Activities Arts & crafts; Cards; Games; Reading groups; Prayer groups; Movies; Shopping trips; Dances/Social/Cultural gatherings; Intergenerational programs; Pet therapy.

Rutland Nursing Home Co Inc
585 Schenectady Ave, Brooklyn, NY 11203-1891
(718) 604-5000, 604-5221
Admin Harris Brodsky FACHE.
Medical Dir Morris Mienfeld MD.
Licensure Skilled care. *Beds* SNF 538. *Certified* Medicaid; Medicare.
Owner Nonprofit corp.
Staff Physicians; RNs; LPNs; Nurses' aides; Physical therapists; Reality therapists; Recreational therapists; Occupational therapists; Speech therapists; Activities coordinators; Dietitians; Ophthalmologists; Podiatrists; Audiologists; Dentists.
Affiliation Jewish.
Facilities Dining room; Physical therapy room; Activities room; Chapel; Crafts room; Laundry room; Barber/Beauty shop; Library.
Activities Arts & crafts; Cards; Games; Reading groups; Prayer groups; Movies; Shopping trips; Dances/Social/Cultural gatherings.

St John's Episcopal Homes for the Aged & the Blind
452 Herkimer St, Brooklyn, NY 11213
(718) 467-1885, 467-1945 FAX
Admin Thomas A Fiorilla. *Dir of Nursing* Cynthia Reid RN. *Medical Dir* Rasiklal Amin MD.
Licensure Skilled care; Intermediate care. *Beds* SNF 43; ICF 54. *Private Pay Patients* 3%. *Certified* Medicaid; Medicare.
Owner Nonprofit corp (Episcopal Health Services).
Admissions Requirements Minimum age 62 (blind), 60 (aged); PRI & Screen.
Staff Physicians 2 (pt); Physical therapists 2 (pt); Recreational therapists 2 (ft); Occupational therapists 1 (pt); Speech therapists 1 (pt); Activities coordinators 1 (ft); Dietitians 1 (ft); Ophthalmologists 1 (pt); Podiatrists 1 (pt).
Languages Spanish.
Affiliation Episcopal.
Facilities Dining room; Physical therapy room; Activities room; Chapel; Crafts room; Laundry room; Barber/Beauty shop.
Activities Arts & crafts; Cards; Games; Prayer groups; Movies; Dances/Social/Cultural gatherings; Pet therapy.

Samuel Schulman Institute
555 Rockaway Pkwy, Brooklyn, NY 11212
(718) 240-5101, 240-5101 FAX
Admin Marcel Baruch. *Dir of Nursing* Barbara Garrison RN. *Medical Dir* Evelyn P Dooley MD.
Licensure Skilled care; Alzheimer's care. *Beds* SNF 220. *Certified* Medicaid; Medicare.
Owner Nonprofit corp.

Admissions Requirements Minimum age 21; Medical examination; Physician's request.
Staff Physicians 5 (pt); RNs 50 (ft); LPNs 14 (ft); Nurses' aides 100 (ft); Physical therapists 4 (ft); Recreational therapists 6 (ft); Occupational therapists 2 (ft); Speech therapists 1 (pt); Dietitians 3 (ft); Audiologists 1 (pt).
Languages French, Italian, Spanish, Yiddish, Russian.
Facilities Dining room; Physical therapy room; Activities room; Chapel; Crafts room; Laundry room; Barber/Beauty shop; Library.
Activities Arts & crafts; Cards; Games; Reading groups; Prayer groups; Movies; Shopping trips; Dances/Social/Cultural gatherings; Intergenerational programs.

Samuel Schulman Institute for Nursing & Rehabilitation
555 Rockaway Pkwy, Brooklyn, NY 11212
(718) 240-5101, 240-5030 FAX
Admin Marcel Baruch. *Dir of Nursing* Barbara Garrison. *Medical Dir* E P Dooley MD.
Licensure Skilled care. *Beds* SNF 220. *Private Pay Patients* 5%. *Certified* Medicaid; Medicare.
Owner Nonprofit corp.
Admissions Requirements Medical examination; Physician's request.
Staff Physicians; RNs; LPNs; Nurses' aides; Physical therapists; Recreational therapists; Occupational therapists; Speech therapists; Activities coordinators; Dietitians; Ophthalmologists; Podiatrists; Audiologists.
Languages Spanish, Italian, Yiddish.
Facilities Dining room; Physical therapy room; Activities room; Chapel; Crafts room; Laundry room; Barber/Beauty shop; Library.
Activities Arts & crafts; Cards; Games; Reading groups; Prayer groups; Movies; Shopping trips; Dances/Social/Cultural gatherings; Intergenerational programs.

Sea-Crest Health Care Center
3035 W 24th St, Brooklyn, NY 11224
(718) 372-4500
Admin A L Urbach. *Dir of Nursing* Myra Levine RN. *Medical Dir* Dr Indravadan Shah.
Licensure Skilled care; Intermediate care. *Beds* SNF 231; ICF 89. *Certified* Medicaid; Medicare.
Owner Privately owned.
Admissions Requirements Minimum age 16; Medical examination; Physician's request.
Staff RNs 21 (ft), 15 (pt); LPNs 20 (ft), 16 (pt); Nurses' aides 86 (ft), 27 (pt); Recreational therapists 4 (ft); Activities coordinators 1 (ft); Dietitians 2 (ft); Social workers 4 (ft).
Languages Yiddish, Hebrew, Spanish, Italian.
Facilities Dining room; Physical therapy room; Activities room; Crafts room; Laundry room; Barber/Beauty shop; Library; Occupational therapy room; Speech therapy room.
Activities Arts & crafts; Cards; Games; Reading groups; Prayer groups; Movies; Dances/Social/Cultural gatherings; Barbeques; Outings.

Sephardic Home for the Aged Inc
2266 Cropsey Ave, Brooklyn, NY 11214
(718) 266-6100, 373-2825 FAX
Admin Herbert Freeman, Exec Dir. *Dir of Nursing* Josephine Mittelmark RN. *Medical Dir* Augusto Miyashiro MD.
Licensure Skilled care; Intermediate care. *Beds* SNF 184; ICF 87. *Private Pay Patients* 3%. *Certified* Medicaid; Medicare.
Owner Nonprofit organization/foundation.
Admissions Requirements Minimum age 65; Medical examination; Physician's request.
Staff Physicians 4 (ft); RNs 31 (ft); LPNs 18 (ft); Nurses' aides 98 (ft); Physical therapists 2 (ft), 1 (pt); Recreational therapists 4 (ft), 4 (pt); Occupational therapists 3 (ft); Speech

therapists 1 (pt); Dietitians 3 (ft); Ophthalmologists 1 (pt); Podiatrists 1 (pt); Audiologists 1 (pt).
Languages Spanish, Hebrew, Yiddish.
Affiliation Jewish.
Facilities Dining room; Physical therapy room; Activities room; Chapel; Crafts room; Laundry room; Barber/Beauty shop; Library.
Activities Arts & crafts; Cards; Games; Reading groups; Prayer groups; Movies; Shopping trips; Dances/Social/Cultural gatherings; Intergenerational programs.

Sheepshead Nursing Home
2840 Knapp St, Brooklyn, NY 11235
(718) 646-5700
Admin Theresa Holzer.
Licensure Skilled care. *Beds* SNF 200. *Certified* Medicaid; Medicare.
Owner Privately owned.

Shore View Nursing Home
2865 Brighton 3rd St, Brooklyn, NY 11235
(718) 891-4400
Admin Mr Eric Kalt. *Dir of Nursing* P Pyle RN. *Medical Dir* Dr I Shah.
Licensure Skilled care; Alzheimer's care. *Beds* SNF 320. *Certified* Medicaid; Medicare.
Owner Privately owned.
Admissions Requirements Medical examination; Physician's request.
Staff Physicians; RNs; LPNs; Nurses' aides; Physical therapists; Reality therapists; Recreational therapists; Occupational therapists; Speech therapists; Activities coordinators; Dietitians; Ophthalmologists; Podiatrists; Dentists.
Facilities Dining room; Physical therapy room; Activities room; Crafts room; Laundry room; Barber/Beauty shop; Library.
Activities Arts & crafts; Cards; Games; Reading groups; Prayer groups; Movies; Shopping trips; Dances/Social/Cultural gatherings.

Wartburg Lutheran Home for the Aging
2598 Fulton St, Brooklyn, NY 11207
(718) 498-2340
Admin Ronald B Stuckey. *Dir of Nursing* Mildred David. *Medical Dir* Dr S Y Gowd.
Licensure Skilled care; Intermediate care; Retirement. *Beds* SNF 102; ICF 123. *Certified* Medicaid; Medicare.
Owner Nonprofit corp.
Admissions Requirements Minimum age 18.
Staff Physicians 1 (pt); RNs 17 (ft); LPNs 32 (ft); Nurses' aides 78 (ft); Physical therapists 1 (ft); Recreational therapists 3 (ft), 1 (pt); Occupational therapists 1 (ft); Speech therapists 1 (pt); Activities coordinators 1 (ft); Dietitians 2 (ft), 1 (pt); Ophthalmologists 1 (pt); Podiatrists 1 (pt); Dentists 1 (pt).
Languages German, Spanish, Italian.
Affiliation Lutheran.
Facilities Dining room; Physical therapy room; Activities room; Chapel; Laundry room; Barber/Beauty shop; Library.
Activities Arts & crafts; Cards; Games; Reading groups; Prayer groups; Movies; Shopping trips; Dances/Social/Cultural gatherings.

Willoughby Nursing Home
949 Willoughby Ave, Brooklyn, NY 11221
(718) 443-1600
Admin Jerome Mann.
Licensure Skilled care. *Beds* SNF 161. *Certified* Medicaid; Medicare.
Owner Privately owned.

Buffalo

Rosa Coplon Jewish Home
10 Symphony Cir, Buffalo, NY 14201
(716) 885-3311, 885-3634 FAX

Admin David M Dunkelman. *Dir of Nursing* Jean Willis RN. *Medical Dir* Dr Stanley Pietrak.
Licensure Skilled care; Intermediate care. *Beds* SNF 111; ICF 55. *Private Pay Patients* 23%. *Certified* Medicaid; Medicare.
Owner Nonprofit corp.
Staff Physicians 1 (ft); RNs 5 (ft), 16 (pt); LPNs 13 (ft), 11 (pt); Nurses' aides 28 (ft), 35 (pt); Physical therapists 1 (ft); Recreational therapists 1 (ft); Occupational therapists 1 (ft); Speech therapists 1 (pt); Activities coordinators 1 (ft); Dietitians 1 (ft); Ophthalmologists 1 (pt); Podiatrists 1 (pt); Audiologists 1 (pt).
Languages Russian, German, Yiddish, Polish.
Affiliation Jewish.
Facilities Dining room; Physical therapy room; Activities room; Chapel; Crafts room; Laundry room; Barber/Beauty shop.
Activities Arts & crafts; Cards; Games; Reading groups; Prayer groups; Movies; Shopping trips; Dances/Social/Cultural gatherings; Intergenerational programs; Pet therapy.

Deaconess Skilled Nursing Facility
1001 Humboldt Pkwy, Buffalo, NY 14208
(716) 887-8002, 887-8050 FAX
Admin Marilyn J Gibbin. *Dir of Nursing* Joyce M Lienert RN. *Medical Dir* Dr Teresa Chau.
Licensure Skilled care. *Beds* SNF 162. *Private Pay Patients* 1%. *Certified* Medicaid; Medicare.
Owner Nonprofit corp.
Admissions Requirements Physician's request.
Staff Physicians 2 (pt); Physical therapists 1 (ft); Recreational therapists 2 (ft), 2 (pt); Occupational therapists 1 (pt); Speech therapists 1 (pt); Activities coordinators 1 (ft); Dietitians 1 (ft); Podiatrists 1 (pt); Audiologists 1 (pt); RNs, LPNs, Nurses aides 300 (ft).
Facilities Dining room; Physical therapy room; Activities room; Chapel; Crafts room; Laundry room; Barber/Beauty shop.
Activities Arts & crafts; Cards; Games; Reading groups; Prayer groups; Movies; Shopping trips; Dances/Social/Cultural gatherings; Intergenerational programs; Pet therapy.

Erie County Medical Center—Skilled Nursing Facility
462 Grider St, Buffalo, NY 14215
(716) 898-3583, 898-3342 FAX
Admin Randy K Gerlach. *Dir of Nursing* Karen Maricle RNMS. *Medical Dir* June Chang MD.
Licensure Skilled care. *Beds* SNF 120. *Private Pay Patients* 0%. *Certified* Medicaid; Medicare.
Owner Publicly owned.
Admissions Requirements Minimum age 16.
Staff Physicians 2 (pt); RNs 12 (ft), 1 (pt); LPNs 23 (ft), 1 (pt); Nurses' aides 46 (ft), 10 (pt); Physical therapists 2 (ft), 1 (pt); Recreational therapists 1 (pt); Occupational therapists 2 (ft), 1 (pt); Speech therapists (consultant); Dietitians 2 (ft); Ophthalmologists (consultant); Podiatrists (consultant); Audiologists (consultant).
Facilities Dining room; Physical therapy room; Chapel; Laundry room; Barber/Beauty shop; Activities/Crafts room.
Activities Arts & crafts; Cards; Games; Reading groups; Prayer groups; Movies; Dances/Social/Cultural gatherings.

Millard Fillmore Skilled Nursing Facility
3 Gates Cir, Buffalo, NY 14209
(716) 887-4833
Admin Joanne L Zink.
Medical Dir Dr Jack Freer.
Licensure Skilled care. *Beds* SNF 41. *Certified* Medicaid; Medicare.
Owner Nonprofit corp.

Admissions Requirements Minimum age 16.
Staff Physicians 2 (pt); RNs 7 (ft), 12 (pt);
LPNs 7 (ft), 10 (pt); Nurses' aides 20 (ft), 22
(pt); Physical therapists 1 (ft); Recreational
therapists 1 (pt); Occupational therapists 1
(pt); Speech therapists 1 (pt); Activities
coordinators 1 (ft); Dietitians 2 (pt);
Ophthalmologists 1 (pt); Podiatrists 1 (pt).
Languages Polish.
Facilities Dining room; Physical therapy
room; Activities room; Laundry room;
Barber/Beauty shop.
Activities Arts & crafts; Cards; Games;
Reading groups; Prayer groups; Movies;
Shopping trips; Dances/Social/Cultural
gatherings.

Georgian Court Nursing Home of Buffalo Inc
1040 Delaware Ave, Buffalo, NY 14209
(716) 886-7740
Admin C Menally.
Licensure Skilled care. *Beds* SNF 134.
Certified Medicaid; Medicare.
Owner Proprietary corp.

Hamlin Terrace Health Care Center
1014 Delaware Ave, Buffalo, NY 14209
(716) 882-8221
Admin Sharon Carlo. *Dir of Nursing* Joyce
Lienert RN. *Medical Dir* Dr Edwin
Lenahan.
Licensure Skilled care; Intermediate care. *Beds*
SNF 140; ICF 60. *Certified* Medicaid;
Medicare.
Owner Privately owned.
Admissions Requirements Minimum age 16;
Medical examination; Physician's request.
Staff Physicians 2 (pt); RNs 14 (ft); LPNs 19
(ft); Nurses' aides 70 (ft); Physical therapists
1 (pt); Occupational therapists 1 (ft), 1 (pt);
Speech therapists 1 (pt); Activities
coordinators 4 (ft); Dietitians 1 (ft);
Ophthalmologists 1 (pt); Podiatrists 1 (pt);
Dentists 1 (pt).
Facilities Dining room; Physical therapy
room; Activities room; Chapel; Crafts room;
Laundry room; Barber/Beauty shop; Library.
Activities Arts & crafts; Cards; Games;
Reading groups; Prayer groups; Movies;
Shopping trips; Dances/Social/Cultural
gatherings.

Manhattan Manor Nursing Home
300 Manhattan Ave, Buffalo, NY 14214
(716) 838-5460
Admin Lorraine Kramer. *Dir of Nursing* Jean
Bucholtz. *Medical Dir* Dr Painton.
Licensure Skilled care; Intermediate care. *Beds*
SNF 44; ICF 81. *Certified* Medicaid;
Medicare.
Owner Privately owned.
Admissions Requirements Minimum age 65;
Medical examination; Physician's request.
Staff RNs 3 (ft), 4 (pt); LPNs 2 (ft), 6 (pt);
Nurses' aides 29 (ft), 1 (pt); Physical
therapists 1 (pt); Occupational therapists 1
(pt); Speech therapists 1 (pt); Activities
coordinators 1 (ft); Dietitians 1 (ft);
Ophthalmologists 1 (pt); Podiatrists 1 (pt).
Languages German, Ukrainian, Polish,
Italian, Greek.
Facilities Dining room; Physical therapy
room; Activities room; Chapel; Crafts room;
Laundry room; Barber/Beauty shop; Library.
Activities Arts & crafts; Cards; Games;
Reading groups; Prayer groups; Movies;
Shopping trips; Dances/Social/Cultural
gatherings; Dinners.

Mercy Hospital—Skilled Nursing Facility
565 Abbott Rd, Buffalo, NY 14220
(716) 826-700, 827-2126 FAX
Admin Richard H Meyers. *Dir of Nursing*
Carol Nowinski. *Medical Dir* James Norton.
Licensure Skilled care; Retirement. *Beds* SNF
74; Retirement apts 32. *Private Pay Patients*
2%. *Certified* Medicaid; Medicare.
Owner Nonprofit corp.

Admissions Requirements Medical
examination; Physician's request.
Staff Physicians 1 (pt); RNs 8 (ft), 4 (pt);
LPNs 6 (ft), 5 (pt); Nurses' aides 26 (ft), 22
(pt); Physical therapists 1 (pt); Occupational
therapists 1 (pt); Speech therapists 1 (pt);
Activities coordinators 1 (ft), 1 (pt);
Dietitians 1 (pt).
Affiliation Roman Catholic.
Facilities Dining room; Physical therapy
room; Activities room; Chapel; Crafts room;
Laundry room; Barber/Beauty shop; Library.
Activities Arts & crafts; Cards; Games; Prayer
groups; Movies; Shopping trips.

**Nazareth Nursing Home & Health Related
Facility**
291 W North St, Buffalo, NY 14201
(716) 881-2323
Admin Austin J Barrett.
Medical Dir Donald M Wilson MD.
Licensure Skilled care; Intermediate care. *Beds*
SNF 95; ICF 30. *Certified* Medicaid;
Medicare.
Owner Nonprofit corp.
Admissions Requirements Minimum age 16;
Females only; Medical examination;
Physician's request.
Staff Physicians 1 (pt); RNs 5 (ft), 6 (pt);
LPNs 12 (ft), 7 (pt); Nurses' aides 40 (ft), 9
(pt); Physical therapists 2 (pt); Occupational
therapists 1 (pt); Speech therapists 1 (pt);
Activities coordinators 1 (ft); Dietitians 1
(pt); Ophthalmologists 2 (pt); Podiatrists 1
(pt); Dentists 1 (pt).
Affiliation Roman Catholic.
Facilities Dining room; Physical therapy
room; Activities room; Chapel; Crafts room;
Laundry room; Barber/Beauty shop; Library.
Activities Arts & crafts; Cards; Games;
Reading groups; Prayer groups; Movies;
Shopping trips; Dances/Social/Cultural
gatherings.

Niagara Lutheran Home Inc
64 Hager St, Buffalo, NY 14208
(716) 886-4377, 886-0036 FAX
Admin Donald L Broecker. *Dir of Nursing*
Rita Fenske. *Medical Dir* Donald M Wilson
MD.
Licensure Skilled care. *Beds* SNF 177.
Certified Medicaid; Medicare.
Owner Nonprofit corp.
Admissions Requirements Minimum age 21;
Medical examination; Physician's request.
Staff Physicians 1 (pt); RNs 17 (ft), 6 (pt);
LPNs 18 (ft), 5 (pt); Nurses' aides 46 (ft), 40
(pt); Physical therapists 1 (ft), 1 (pt);
Occupational therapists 1 (pt); Speech
therapists 1 (pt); Activities coordinators 3
(ft); Dietitians 1 (pt); Ophthalmologists 1
(pt); Podiatrists 1 (pt); Audiologists 1 (pt).
Affiliation Evangelical Lutheran.
Facilities Dining room; Physical therapy
room; Activities room; Chapel; Crafts room;
Laundry room; Barber/Beauty shop;
Occupational therapy room; Speech
pathology room; Treatment room; Sitting
rooms.
Activities Arts & crafts; Cards; Games;
Reading groups; Prayer groups; Movies;
Shopping trips; Dances/Social/Cultural
gatherings; Weekly church services;
Discussion groups; Holiday celebrations;
Picnics; Music; Volunteer program.

Ridge View Manor Nursing Home
300 Dorrance Ave, Buffalo, NY 14220-2795
(716) 825-4984, 825-0335 FAX
Admin Alice Breyer.
Medical Dir Dr Vincent Cotroneo.
Licensure Skilled care; Intermediate care. *Beds*
SNF 80; ICF 40. *Certified* Medicaid;
Medicare.
Owner Privately owned.
Admissions Requirements Minimum age 17;
Medical examination.

Staff Physicians 14 (pt); RNs 7 (ft), 3 (pt);
LPNs 12 (ft), 10 (pt); Nurses' aides 38 (ft),
35 (pt); Physical therapists 1 (pt);
Occupational therapists 1 (pt); Speech
therapists 1 (pt); Activities coordinators 2
(ft); Dietitians 1 (pt); Podiatrists 1 (pt);
Audiologists 1 (pt).
Facilities Dining room; Physical therapy
room; Activities room; Crafts room; Laundry
room; Barber/Beauty shop; Outdoor
walkways; Indoor atrium.
Activities Arts & crafts; Cards; Games;
Reading groups; Prayer groups; Movies;
Shopping trips; Dances/Social/Cultural
gatherings; Weekly cocktail parties;
Ceramics.

St Andrew's Presbyterian Manor
1205 Delaware Ave, Buffalo, NY 14209
(716) 885-3838
Licensure Skilled care. *Beds* SNF 91.
Owner Proprietary corp (Presbyterian Homes
of Western New York).

St Lukes Presbyterian Nursing Center
1175 Delaware Ave, Buffalo, NY 14209
(716) 885-6733
Admin Randy A Muenzner. *Dir of Nursing*
Mary Klink. *Medical Dir* Dr Matthew
O'Brien.
Licensure Skilled care; Intermediate care. *Beds*
SNF 80; ICF 40. *Certified* Medicaid;
Medicare.
Owner Nonprofit corp (Presbyterian Homes of
Western New York).
Admissions Requirements Minimum age 16.
Staff RNs; LPNs; Nurses' aides; Physical
therapists 1 (pt); Recreational therapists 2
(ft); Occupational therapists 1 (ft); Speech
therapists 1 (pt); Activities coordinators 1
(ft); Dietitians 1 (pt); Ophthalmologists 1
(pt); Podiatrists 1 (pt).
Affiliation Presbyterian.
Facilities Dining room; Physical therapy
room; Activities room; Chapel; Crafts room;
Laundry room; Barber/Beauty shop; Library.
Activities Arts & crafts; Cards; Games;
Reading groups; Prayer groups; Movies;
Shopping trips; Dances/Social/Cultural
gatherings.

**Sisters of Charity Hospital Skilled Nursing
Facility**
2157 Main St, Buffalo, NY 14214
(716) 862-2000
Admin Leonard Sicurella. *Dir of Nursing* Ruth
Balkin RN. *Medical Dir* Young Paik MD.
Licensure Skilled care. *Beds* SNF 80. *Certified*
Medicaid; Medicare.
Owner Nonprofit corp.
Admissions Requirements Minimum age 16;
Medical examination; Physician's request.
Staff Physicians 1 (pt); RNs 6 (ft), 6 (pt);
LPNs 16 (ft), 6 (pt); Nurses' aides 14 (ft), 14
(pt); Physical therapists 1 (ft), 1 (pt);
Recreational therapists 1 (ft), 1 (pt);
Occupational therapists 1 (ft), 1 (pt); Speech
therapists 1 (pt); Dietitians 1 (ft), 1 (pt);
Ophthalmologists 1 (pt); Podiatrists 1 (pt);
Dentists 1 (pt).
Languages Polish, Italian, Spanish.
Affiliation Roman Catholic.
Facilities Dining room; Physical therapy
room; Chapel; Crafts room; Laundry room;
Barber/Beauty shop.
Activities Arts & crafts; Cards; Games;
Reading groups; Prayer groups; Movies;
Shopping trips; Dances/Social/Cultural
gatherings; Sporting events.

24 Rhode Island Street Nursing Home
24 Rhode Island St, Buffalo, NY 14213
(716) 884-6500, 884-6116 FAX
Admin Darlene Jones Crispell. *Dir of Nursing*
Kathryn F Young. *Medical Dir* John A
Edwards MD.

Licensure Skilled care; Intermediate care; Retirement. *Beds* SNF 86; ICF 42; Retirement units 110. *Private Pay Patients* 27%. *Certified* Medicaid; Medicare.
Owner Nonprofit corp.
Admissions Requirements Minimum age 16; Medical examination.
Staff RNs 9 (ft), 3 (pt); LPNs 11 (ft), 7 (pt); Nurses' aides 30 (ft), 31 (pt); Physical therapists 2 (ft); Occupational therapists 1 (ft); Speech therapists 1 (ft); Activities coordinators 1 (ft); Dietitians 1 (ft); Activities aides 1 (ft), 2 (pt).
Affiliation Episcopal.
Facilities Dining room; Physical therapy room; Activities room; Chapel; Laundry room; Barber/Beauty shop; Child day care.
Activities Arts & crafts; Cards; Games; Prayer groups; Movies; Shopping trips; Dances/Social/Cultural gatherings; Intergenerational programs; Pet therapy; Exercise; Volunteer program.

Waterfront Health Care Center
200 7th St, Buffalo, NY 14201
(716) 847-2500
Admin Patricia W O'Connor. *Dir of Nursing* Maxine B Holder RN. *Medical Dir* Paul Katz MD.
Licensure Skilled care; Retirement; Alzheimer's care. *Beds* SNF 80; Retirement 50. *Private Pay Patients* 30%. *Certified* Medicaid; Medicare.
Owner Nonprofit corp.
Admissions Requirements Minimum age 16; Medical examination; Physician's request.
Staff Physicians 3 (pt); RNs 8 (ft), 10 (pt); LPNs 6 (ft), 15 (pt); Nurses' aides 22 (ft), 15 (pt); Physical therapists 1 (pt); Recreational therapists 2 (pt); Occupational therapists 1 (ft), 1 (pt); Speech therapists 1 (pt); Activities coordinators 1 (ft); Dietitians 1 (pt); Ophthalmologists 1 (pt); Podiatrists 1 (pt); Audiologists 1 (pt).
Languages Spanish.
Facilities Dining room; Physical therapy room; Activities room; Chapel; Crafts room; Laundry room; Barber/Beauty shop; Library.
Activities Arts & crafts; Cards; Games; Reading groups; Prayer groups; Movies; Shopping trips; Dances/Social/Cultural gatherings; Intergenerational programs; Pet therapy.

Cambridge

Mary McClellan Skilled Nursing Facility
1 Myrtle Ave, Cambridge, NY 12816
(518) 677-2611, 677-5145 FAX
Admin Peter W Acker. *Dir of Nursing* Katherine Runge RN. *Medical Dir* Newton Krumdieck MD.
Licensure Skilled care. *Beds* SNF 39. *Certified* Medicaid; Medicare.
Owner Nonprofit corp.
Admissions Requirements Minimum age 16; Medical examination; Physician's request.
Staff Physicians; RNs; LPNs; Nurses' aides; Physical therapists; Occupational therapists; Speech therapists; Activities coordinators; Dietitians; Ophthalmologists (consultant); Podiatrists; Audiologists.
Facilities Dining room; Physical therapy room; Chapel; Laundry room; Barber/Beauty shop.
Activities Arts & crafts; Cards; Games; Reading groups; Prayer groups; Movies; Dances/Social/Cultural gatherings.

Campbell Hall

Doanes Nursing Home
RD 2, Box 291, Campbell Hall, NY 10916
(914) 294-8154
Admin Joseph Cornetta. *Dir of Nursing* Judith Lyons. *Medical Dir* Dr Francis Imbarrato.

Licensure Skilled care; Intermediate care. *Beds* SNF 80; ICF 40. *Certified* Medicaid; Medicare.
Owner Privately owned.
Admissions Requirements Minimum age 16; Medical examination; Physician's request.
Staff Physicians; RNs; LPNs; Nurses' aides; Physical therapists; Reality therapists; Recreational therapists; Occupational therapists; Speech therapists; Activities coordinators; Dietitians; Ophthalmologists; Podiatrists; Dentists.
Facilities Dining room; Physical therapy room; Activities room; Chapel; Crafts room; Laundry room; Barber/Beauty shop.
Activities Arts & crafts; Cards; Games; Reading groups; Prayer groups; Movies; Dances/Social/Cultural gatherings.

Canandaigua

Elm Manor Nursing Home
210 N Main St, Canandaigua, NY 14424
(716) 394-3883
Admin James D Fuller. *Dir of Nursing* Cheri Fontaine RN. *Medical Dir* Dr William Forsyth.
Licensure Skilled care. *Beds* SNF 46. *Private Pay Patients* 55%. *Certified* Medicaid; Medicare.
Owner Privately owned (Robert Hurlbut).
Admissions Requirements Minimum age 16; Medical examination; Physician's request.
Staff Physicians 15 (pt); RNs 6 (ft), 1 (pt); LPNs 7 (ft), 3 (pt); Nurses' aides 25 (ft), 7 (pt); Physical therapists 1 (pt); Occupational therapists 1 (pt); Activities coordinators 1 (ft); Dietitians 1 (pt); Podiatrists 1 (pt); Audiologists 1 (pt).
Facilities Dining room; Activities room; Laundry room; Barber/Beauty shop.
Activities Arts & crafts; Cards; Games; Reading groups; Prayer groups; Movies; Shopping trips; Dances/Social/Cultural gatherings.

Ontario County Health Facility
RD 2, Canandaigua, NY 14424
(716) 394-2100
Admin Gerald B Cole.
Medical Dir Charles Bathrick MD.
Licensure Skilled care; Intermediate care. *Beds* SNF 48; ICF 50. *Certified* Medicaid; Medicare.
Owner Publicly owned.
Admissions Requirements Minimum age 18; Medical examination; Physician's request.
Staff Physicians 1 (pt); RNs 6 (ft), 3 (pt); LPNs 10 (ft), 1 (pt); Nurses' aides 30 (ft), 5 (pt); Physical therapists 1 (pt); Recreational therapists 1 (ft); Speech therapists 1 (pt); Activities coordinators 1 (ft), 1 (pt); Dietitians 1 (ft); Podiatrists 1 (pt); Audiologists 1 (pt); Dentists 1 (pt).
Facilities Dining room; Physical therapy room; Activities room; Crafts room; Laundry room; Barber/Beauty shop; Library.
Activities Arts & crafts; Cards; Games; Reading groups; Prayer groups; Movies; Shopping trips; Dances/Social/Cultural gatherings.

Thompson Nursing Home Inc
350 Parrish St, Canandaigua, NY 14424
(716) 396-6040, 396-6719 FAX
Admin Fred M Thomas. *Dir of Nursing* Susan M Sikes RN. *Medical Dir* George Allen MD.
Licensure Skilled care; Intermediate care; Adult day health care. *Beds* SNF 68; ICF 40. *Private Pay Patients* 31%. *Certified* Medicaid; Medicare.
Owner Nonprofit corp.
Admissions Requirements Minimum age 16; Medical examination; Physician's request.
Staff Physicians 1 (pt); RNs 5 (ft), 4 (pt); LPNs 11 (ft), 7 (pt); Nurses' aides 34 (ft), 19 (pt); Physical therapists 1 (pt); Reality

therapists 1 (pt); Recreational therapists 1 (ft), 1 (pt); Occupational therapists 2 (ft); Speech therapists 1 (pt); Activities coordinators 1 (ft); Dietitians 1 (ft), 1 (pt).
Facilities Dining room; Physical therapy room; Activities room; Chapel; Crafts room; Laundry room; Barber/Beauty shop.
Activities Arts & crafts; Cards; Games; Reading groups; Prayer groups; Movies; Shopping trips; Dances/Social/Cultural gatherings.

Canton

United Helpers Canton Nursing Home Inc
W Main St, Canton, NY 13617
(315) 386-4541
Admin Wheeler D Maynard Jr.
Licensure Skilled care; Intermediate care. *Beds* SNF 80; ICF 80. *Certified* Medicaid; Medicare.
Owner Nonprofit corp.

Carthage

Carthage Area Hospital
West Street Rd, Carthage, NY 13619
(315) 493-1000
Admin Jeffrey S Drop. *Dir of Nursing* Anthony H Doldo RN.
Licensure Skilled care. *Beds* SNF 30.
Owner Nonprofit corp.
Admissions Requirements Minimum age 16; Medical examination; Physician's request.
Staff Physicians 4 (ft); RNs 1 (ft), 2 (pt); LPNs 3 (ft), 3 (pt); Nurses' aides 8 (ft), 9 (pt); Physical therapists 1 (ft); Occupational therapists 1 (pt); Speech therapists 1 (pt); Activities coordinators 1 (pt); Dietitians 1 (pt); Podiatrists 1 (pt).
Languages Spanish.
Facilities Dining room; Physical therapy room; Laundry room; Barber/Beauty shop.
Activities Arts & crafts; Cards; Games; Reading groups; Prayer groups; Movies; Shopping trips; Dances/Social/Cultural gatherings; Pet therapy; Barbecues.

Greenbriar Nursing Home
West Street Rd, Carthage, NY 13619
(315) 493-3220
Admin James Sligar.
Licensure Skilled care. *Beds* SNF 40. *Certified* Medicaid; Medicare.
Owner Privately owned.

Castleton-on-Hudson

Resurrection Rest Home
Castleton-on-Hudson, NY 12033
(518) 732-7617
Admin S Therese.
Licensure Skilled care; Intermediate care. *Beds* 48. *Certified* Medicaid; Medicare.
Owner Nonprofit corp.

Catskill

Columbia-Greene Medical Center Long-Term Care Division
161 Jefferson Heights, Catskill, NY 12414
(518) 943-9380, 943-2000, ext 316 FAX
Admin Wesley I Hale. *Dir of Nursing* Barbara L White RN. *Medical Dir* Stanley Tomczyk MD.
Licensure Skilled care; Intermediate care. *Beds* SNF 80; ICF 40. *Certified* Medicaid; Medicare.
Owner Proprietary corp.
Admissions Requirements Minimum age 16; Medical examination; Physician's request.
Staff Physicians 8 (pt); RNs 12 (ft), 8 (pt); LPNs 10 (ft), 8 (pt); Nurses' aides 45 (ft), 10 (pt); Physical therapists 1 (pt); Reality therapists 2 (pt); Recreational therapists 2 (ft); Occupational therapists 1 (ft), 1 (pt);

Speech therapists 1 (pt); Activities coordinators 1 (ft); Dietitians 1 (ft); Podiatrists 1 (pt).
Facilities Dining room; Physical therapy room; Activities room; Crafts room; Laundry room; Barber/Beauty shop; Library.
Activities Arts & crafts; Cards; Games; Reading groups; Prayer groups; Movies; Shopping trips; Dances/Social/Cultural gatherings; Intergenerational programs; Pet therapy; Resident council; Limber up; Floor games; Music and art appreciation.

Eden Park Nursing Home
154 Jefferson Heights, Catskill, NY 12414
(518) 943-5151
Admin Patrick Cucinelli. *Dir of Nursing* Mary Ann Krier. *Medical Dir* Paul Snapper.
Licensure Skilled care; Intermediate care. *Beds* SNF 88; ICF 48. *Certified* Medicaid; Medicare.
Owner Proprietary corp (Eden Park Health Services).
Staff RNs 15 (ft); LPNs 15 (ft); Nurses' aides 55 (ft); Physical therapists 1 (ft); Recreational therapists 2 (ft); Occupational therapists 1 (ft); Activities coordinators 1 (ft).
Facilities Dining room; Physical therapy room; Activities room; Chapel; Crafts room; Laundry room; Barber/Beauty shop; Library.
Activities Arts & crafts; Cards; Games; Reading groups; Prayer groups; Movies; Shopping trips; Dances/Social/Cultural gatherings; Intergenerational programs; Pet therapy.

Center Moriches

Cedar Lodge Nursing Home
6 Frowein Rd, Center Moriches, NY 11934
(516) 878-4400
Admin Muriel Corcoran.
Licensure Skilled care. *Beds* SNF 100. *Certified* Medicaid; Medicare.
Owner Privately owned.

Cheektowaga

Garden Gate Manor
2365 Union Rd, Cheektowaga, NY 14227
(716) 668-8100
Admin Matthew J Hriczko. *Dir of Nursing* Barbara Ross. *Medical Dir* Dr Alan Smith.
Licensure Skilled care; Intermediate care. *Beds* SNF 120; ICF 40. *Certified* Medicaid; Medicare.
Owner Privately owned.
Admissions Requirements Medical examination.
Staff RNs; LPNs; Nurses' aides; Physical therapists; Recreational therapists; Occupational therapists; Speech therapists; Activities coordinators; Dietitians; Podiatrists; Audiologists.
Facilities Dining room; Physical therapy room; Activities room; Crafts room; Laundry room; Barber/Beauty shop; Roving library cart.
Activities Arts & crafts; Cards; Games; Reading groups; Prayer groups; Movies; Shopping trips; Dances/Social/Cultural gatherings; Intergenerational programs; Pet therapy; Church services.

Manor Oak Skilled Nursing Facilities Inc
3600 Harlem Rd, Cheektowaga, NY 14215
(716) 837-3880
Admin Randy Muenzner.
Licensure Skilled care. *Beds* SNF 158. *Certified* Medicaid; Medicare.
Owner Proprietary corp.

Chittenango

Stonehedge-Chittenango Nursing Home
331 Russell St, Chittenango, NY 13037
(315) 687-7255
Admin Gloria Coughlin.
Medical Dir Juaquin Solar MD.
Licensure Skilled care; Intermediate care. *Beds* SNF 40; ICF 40. *Certified* Medicaid; Medicare.
Owner Privately owned.
Admissions Requirements Medical examination; Physician's request.
Staff Physicians 1 (pt); RNs 3 (ft), 3 (pt); LPNs 4 (ft), 4 (pt); Nurses' aides 19 (ft), 15 (pt); Physical therapists 1 (pt); Activities coordinators 1 (ft); Dietitians 1 (pt); Dentists 1 (pt).
Facilities Dining room; Physical therapy room; Activities room; Laundry room; Barber/Beauty shop.
Activities Arts & crafts; Cards; Games; Reading groups; Prayer groups; Movies; Shopping trips; Dances/Social/Cultural gatherings.

Clarence

Brothers of Mercy Nursing & Rehabilitation Center
10570 Bergtold Rd, Clarence, NY 14031
(716) 759-6985
Admin Daniel J Kenny. *Dir of Nursing* Mildred Kody. *Medical Dir* Ferdinand A Paolini MD.
Licensure Skilled care; Intermediate care; Retirement. *Beds* SNF 200; ICF 40. *Certified* Medicaid; Medicare.
Owner Nonprofit corp.
Admissions Requirements Minimum age 16; Medical examination; Physician's request.
Staff Physicians 1 (ft), 1 (pt); RNs 38 (ft), 4 (pt); LPNs 25 (ft); Nurses' aides 122 (ft), 3 (pt); Physical therapists 9 (ft); Reality therapists 5 (ft); Recreational therapists 5 (ft); Occupational therapists 5 (ft), 3 (pt); Speech therapists 1 (ft), 1 (pt); Activities coordinators 1 (ft); Dietitians 3 (ft); Ophthalmologists 1 (pt); Podiatrists 1 (ft), 1 (pt).
Affiliation Roman Catholic.
Facilities Dining room; Physical therapy room; Activities room; Chapel; Crafts room; Laundry room; Barber/Beauty shop; Library; Gift shop; Occupational therapy clinic; Patios.
Activities Arts & crafts; Cards; Games; Reading groups; Prayer groups; Movies; Shopping trips; Dances/Social/Cultural gatherings; Walks; Birthday parties; Spouse program; Special meals.

Clifton Springs

Clifton Springs Hospital & Clinic Extended Care
2 Coulter Rd, Clifton Springs, NY 14432
(315) 462-9561
Admin M J Romeiser, acting.
Medical Dir Karen Miller.
Licensure Skilled care. *Beds* SNF 40. *Certified* Medicaid; Medicare.
Owner Nonprofit corp.
Admissions Requirements Medical examination.
Languages Spanish.
Facilities Dining room; Physical therapy room; Activities room; Chapel; Laundry room; Barber/Beauty shop.

Clinton

Martin Luther Nursing Home
110 Utica Rd, Clinton, NY 13323
(315) 853-5515, 853-4025 FAX
Admin Rev Hans J R Irmer. *Dir of Nursing* Elaine Cain RN. *Medical Dir* Gerald C Gant MD.
Licensure Skilled care; Intermediate care; Alzheimer's unit; Retirement; Independent living. *Beds* SNF 80; ICF 80; Retirement home 66; Independent living apts 139.
Private Pay Patients 23%. *Certified* Medicaid; Medicare.
Owner Nonprofit corp.
Admissions Requirements Minimum age 17.
Staff Physicians 2 (pt); RNs 10 (ft), 10 (pt); LPNs 10 (ft), 5 (pt); Nurses' aides 40 (ft), 15 (pt); Physical therapists; Occupational therapists (consultants); Speech therapists (consultant); Activities coordinators 3 (ft), 1 (pt); Dietitians (consultant); Podiatrists (consultant); Audiologists (consultant).
Languages Italian, Polish, French, German, Spanish.
Affiliation Lutheran.
Facilities Dining room; Physical therapy room; Activities room; Chapel; Crafts room; Laundry room; Barber/Beauty shop; Library.
Activities Arts & crafts; Cards; Games; Reading groups; Prayer groups; Movies; Shopping trips; Dances/Social/Cultural gatherings; Intergenerational programs; Pet therapy.

Cobleskill

Eden Park Health Services Inc
Parkway Dr, Cobleskill, NY 12043
(518) 234-3557
Admin David W Davis. *Dir of Nursing* Barbara Brooks. *Medical Dir* Dr Jacobus Vrolijk.
Licensure Skilled care; Intermediate care. *Beds* SNF 90; ICF 35. *Private Pay Patients* 9%. *Certified* Medicaid; Medicare.
Owner Proprietary corp (Eden Park Health Services Inc).
Admissions Requirements Minimum age 18; Medical examination; Physician's request.
Staff Physicians; RNs; LPNs; Nurses' aides; Physical therapists; Recreational therapists; Occupational therapists; Activities coordinators; Dietitians.
Facilities Dining room; Physical therapy room; Activities room; Crafts room; Laundry room; Barber/Beauty shop; Occupational therapy room.
Activities Arts & crafts; Cards; Games; Reading groups; Prayer groups; Movies; Shopping trips; Dances/Social/Cultural gatherings; Intergenerational programs; Pet therapy.

Cohoes

Capital Region Ford Nursing Home
421 W Columbia St, Cohoes, NY 12047
(518) 237-5630
Admin Sandra MacWilliam. *Dir of Nursing* Deborah Bolognino RN. *Medical Dir* Michael Wolff MD.
Licensure Skilled care. *Beds* SNF 80. *Private Pay Patients* 30%. *Certified* Medicaid; Medicare.
Owner Nonprofit organization/foundation.
Admissions Requirements Minimum age 19; Physician's request.
Staff Physicians 4 (pt); RNs 9 (ft), 5 (pt); LPNs 9 (ft), 4 (pt); Nurses' aides 26 (ft), 15 (pt); Physical therapists 1 (pt); Recreational therapists 2 (ft); Occupational therapists 1 (pt); Speech therapists 1 (pt); Dietitians 2 (ft).
Facilities Dining room; Physical therapy room; Activities room; Laundry room; Barber/Beauty shop.
Activities Arts & crafts; Cards; Games; Prayer groups; Movies; Shopping trips; Dances/Social/Cultural gatherings; Intergenerational programs; Pet therapy.

Commack

Rosalind & Joseph Gurwin Jewish Geriatric Center of Long Island
68 Hauppauge Rd, Commack, NY 11725
(516) 499-6500, 499-6581 FAX
Admin Herbert H Friedman. *Dir of Nursing* Florence Oldacre RN. *Medical Dir* Dr Richard Feinbloom.
Licensure Skilled care; Alzheimer's care; Retirement; Adult day care. *Beds* SNF 300. *Private Pay Patients* 10%. *Certified* Medicaid; Medicare.
Owner Nonprofit corp.
Admissions Requirements Minimum age 16; Medical examination.
Staff Physicians 4 (ft); RNs 32 (ft); LPNs 28 (ft); Nurses' aides 141 (ft); Physical therapists 3 (ft); Recreational therapists 5 (ft); Occupational therapists 3 (ft); Speech therapists 1 (pt); Activities coordinators 1 (ft); Dietitians 3 (ft); Ophthalmologists 2 (pt); Podiatrists 4 (pt); Audiologists 1 (pt).
Languages Yiddish, Spanish.
Affiliation Jewish.
Facilities Dining room; Physical therapy room; Activities room; Chapel; Crafts room; Laundry room; Barber/Beauty shop; Library; Kosher kitchen.
Activities Arts & crafts; Cards; Games; Reading groups; Prayer groups; Movies; Shopping trips; Dances/Social/Cultural gatherings; Intergenerational programs; Pet therapy.

Cooperstown

Meadows
RD 3, Cooperstown, NY 13326
(607) 547-2579
Admin Pamela Tritten. *Dir of Nursing* Eleanor Sosnowski. *Medical Dir* Donald Pollock MD.
Licensure Skilled care; Intermediate care. *Beds* SNF 136; ICF 38. *Certified* Medicaid; Medicare.
Owner Publicly owned.
Admissions Requirements Physician's request.
Staff Physicians 4 (pt); RNs; LPNs; Nurses' aides; Physical therapists 1 (pt); Occupational therapists 1 (ft), 1 (pt); Activities coordinators; Dietitians 1 (ft).
Facilities Dining room; Physical therapy room; Activities room; Chapel; Laundry room; Barber/Beauty shop.
Activities Arts & crafts; Cards; Reading groups; Prayer groups; Movies; Shopping trips.

Corning

Founders Pavilion
205 E 1st St, Corning, NY 14830
(607) 937-7500, 937-7346 FAX
Admin Linda L Patrick. *Dir of Nursing* Terry Taggart. *Medical Dir* Russell Woglom MD.
Licensure Skilled care. *Beds* SNF 120. *Private Pay Patients* 17%. *Certified* Medicaid; Medicare.
Owner Nonprofit corp.
Admissions Requirements Minimum age 16; Physician's request.
Staff RNs 15 (ft), 2 (pt); LPNs 15 (ft), 2 (pt); Nurses' aides 59 (ft), 5 (pt); Activities coordinators 1 (ft).
Facilities Dining room; Physical therapy room; Activities room; Laundry room; Barber/Beauty shop; Lounge.
Activities Arts & crafts; Cards; Games; Reading groups; Prayer groups; Movies; Shopping trips; Dances/Social/Cultural gatherings; Intergenerational programs; Talking books for the blind.

Cortland

Cortland Nursing Home
193 Clinton Ave, Cortland, NY 13045
(607) 756-9921
Admin Michael Sweeney. *Dir of Nursing* Diane Abdallah RN. *Medical Dir* Patrick Hayes MD.
Licensure Skilled care; Alzheimer's care. *Beds* SNF 80. *Certified* Medicaid; Medicare.
Owner Proprietary corp.
Admissions Requirements Minimum age 16; Medical examination.
Staff RNs 7 (ft), 3 (pt); LPNs 10 (ft), 2 (pt); Nurses' aides 40 (ft), 20 (pt); Physical therapists 1 (pt); Occupational therapists 1 (pt); Speech therapists 1 (pt); Activities coordinators 1 (ft), 1 (pt); Dietitians 1 (pt); Ophthalmologists 1 (pt); Podiatrists 1 (pt); Dentists 1 (pt).
Facilities Dining room; Physical therapy room; Activities room; Crafts room; Laundry room; Barber/Beauty shop; Library.
Activities Arts & crafts; Cards; Games; Reading groups; Prayer groups; Movies; Shopping trips; Dances/Social/Cultural gatherings.

New Medico Highgate Manor of Cortland
PO Box 5510, 28 Kellog Rd, Cortland, NY 13045
(607) 753-9631, (800) 642-2436 NY state, (800) 431-5021 outside state, (607) 756-2968 FAX
Admin Mitchell S Marsh. *Dir of Nursing* Sandra Russell RN. *Medical Dir* John E Eckel MD.
Licensure Skilled care; Intermediate care; Head trauma. *Beds* SNF 120; ICF 80. *Private Pay Patients* 25%. *Certified* Medicaid; Medicare.
Owner Proprietary corp (New Medico Associates).
Admissions Requirements Minimum age 16; Medical examination.
Staff Physicians 2 (ft), 12 (pt); RNs 25 (ft), 9 (pt); LPNs 35 (ft), 9 (pt); Nurses' aides 87 (ft), 35 (pt); Physical therapists 5 (ft); Recreational therapists 5 (ft); Occupational therapists 4 (ft); Speech therapists 6 (ft); Activities coordinators 1 (ft); Dietitians 1 (ft); Ophthalmologists 1 (pt); Podiatrists 1 (pt); Cognitive therapists 5 (ft).
Affiliation American Legion.
Facilities Dining room; Physical therapy room; Activities room; Chapel; Crafts room; Laundry room; Barber/Beauty shop; Library; Private dining rooms for residents to entertain; Patios.
Activities Arts & crafts; Cards; Games; Reading groups; Prayer groups; Movies; Shopping trips; Dances/Social/Cultural gatherings; Intergenerational programs; Pet therapy; One-on-one individual activities; Summer barbecues; Parties; Gardening.

Croton-on-Hudson

Sky View Haven Nursing Home
Albany Post Rd, Croton-on-Hudson, NY 10520
(914) 271-5336, 271-4455 FAX
Admin Kurt Oppenheim. *Dir of Nursing* Marianne Rattray RNM. *Medical Dir* Leonard Kaufman MD.
Licensure Skilled care; Intermediate care. *Beds* SNF 146; ICF 46. *Certified* Medicaid; Medicare.
Owner Proprietary corp.
Admissions Requirements Minimum age 16; Medical examination.
Staff Physicians (consultant); RNs 10 (ft), 5 (pt); LPNs 12 (ft), 10 (pt); Nurses' aides 75 (ft), 10 (pt); Physical therapists 2 (pt); Recreational therapists 4 (ft), 2 (pt); Occupational therapists 1 (pt); Speech therapists (consultant); Activities coordinators 1 (ft); Dietitians 1 (ft), 1 (pt); Ophthalmologists (consultant); Podiatrists (consultant); Audiologists (consultant).
Languages Spanish, Italian, German.
Facilities Dining room; Physical therapy room; Activities room; Crafts room; Laundry room; Barber/Beauty shop; Library; Large main living room.
Activities Arts & crafts; Cards; Games; Reading groups; Prayer groups; Movies; Shopping trips; Dances/Social/Cultural gatherings; Intergenerational programs; Pet therapy.

Cuba

Cuba Memorial Hospital Skilled Nursing Facility
140 W Main St, Cuba, NY 14727
(716) 968-2000, 968-2000 FAX
Admin Marc A Subject. *Dir of Nursing* Earletta Swift RN. *Medical Dir* Rajan Gulati MD.
Licensure Skilled care. *Beds* SNF 61. *Private Pay Patients* 8%. *Certified* Medicaid; Medicare.
Owner Nonprofit corp.
Admissions Requirements Minimum age 17; Medical examination; Physician's request.
Staff Physicians 3 (pt); RNs 4 (ft), 1 (pt); LPNs 9 (ft), 3 (pt); Nurses' aides 28 (ft), 6 (pt); Physical therapists 1 (pt); Speech therapists 1 (pt); Activities coordinators 1 (ft); Dietitians 1 (ft); Podiatrists 1 (pt); Audiologists 1 (pt); Activities aides 1 (ft).
Facilities Dining room; Physical therapy room; Activities room; Chapel; Crafts room; Laundry room; Barber/Beauty shop; Library.
Activities Arts & crafts; Cards; Games; Reading groups; Prayer groups; Movies; Shopping trips; Dances/Social/Cultural gatherings; Intergenerational programs; Pet therapy.

Delhi

Delaware County Home & Infirmary
Rd 1, Box 417, Delhi, NY 13753
(607) 746-2331
Admin Matthew Luger.
Medical Dir Fredrick Heinegg MD.
Licensure Skilled care; Intermediate care. *Beds* SNF 100; ICF 99. *Certified* Medicaid; Medicare.
Owner Publicly owned.
Admissions Requirements Minimum age 16; Medical examination.
Staff Physicians 3 (pt); RNs 18 (ft), 9 (pt); LPNs 35 (ft), 10 (pt); Nurses' aides 70 (ft), 40 (pt); Physical therapists 1 (ft); Occupational therapists 1 (ft); Speech therapists 1 (pt); Activities coordinators 1 (ft); Dietitians 1 (pt); Dentists 1 (pt).
Facilities Dining room; Physical therapy room; Activities room; Crafts room; Barber/Beauty shop.
Activities Arts & crafts; Cards; Games; Prayer groups; Movies; Shopping trips; Dances/Social/Cultural gatherings.

Delmar

Good Samaritan Nursing Home Company Inc
125 Rockefeller Rd, Delmar, NY 12054
(518) 439-8116
Admin Leon Bormann CNA. *Dir of Nursing* Diane Mager. *Medical Dir* Roger Drew MD.
Licensure Intermediate care. *Beds* ICF 100. *Private Pay Patients* 35%. *Certified* Medicaid.
Owner Nonprofit organization/foundation.
Admissions Requirements Medical examination; Physician's request.

Staff Physicians 2 (pt); RNs 5 (ft), 2 (pt); LPNs 6 (ft); Nurses' aides 30 (ft), 10 (pt); Physical therapists 1 (pt); Activities coordinators 1 (ft); Dietitians 1 (pt).
Affiliation Lutheran.
Facilities Dining room; Physical therapy room; Activities room; Chapel; Crafts room; Barber/Beauty shop.
Activities Arts & crafts; Cards; Games; Reading groups; Prayer groups; Movies; Shopping trips; Dances/Social/Cultural gatherings; Intergenerational programs; Pet therapy.

Dobbs Ferry

St Cabrini Nursing Home Inc
115 Broadway, Dobbs Ferry, NY 10522
(914) 693-6800, 693-8908 FAX
Admin William T Smith ACSW. *Dir of Nursing* Sr M Christopher Kurtz SC. *Medical Dir* Andrew Fader MD.
Licensure Skilled care; Alzheimer's care. *Beds* SNF 304. *Private Pay Patients* 10%. *Certified* Medicaid; Medicare.
Owner Nonprofit corp (Catholic Charities-Arch of New York).
Admissions Requirements Minimum age 65; Medical examination; PRI screening.
Staff Physicians 1 (ft), 11 (pt); RNs 35 (ft), 21 (pt); LPNs 15 (ft), 17 (pt); Nurses' aides 85 (ft), 10 (pt); Physical therapists 2 (ft), 1 (pt); Recreational therapists 2 (ft), 1 (pt); Occupational therapists 1 (ft); Speech therapists 1 (pt); Activities coordinators 1 (ft); Audiologists 1 (pt).
Languages Italian.
Affiliation Roman Catholic.
Facilities Dining room; Physical therapy room; Activities room; Chapel; Crafts room; Laundry room; Barber/Beauty shop.
Activities Arts & crafts; Cards; Games; Reading groups; Prayer groups; Movies; Shopping trips; Dances/Social/Cultural gatherings; Intergenerational programs; Pet therapy.

Dunkirk

Chautauqua County Home
Temple Rd, Dunkirk, NY 14048
(716) 366-6400
Admin Christopher L Carlson. *Dir of Nursing* Gail Riforgiat RN. *Medical Dir* Yi Yung Ting MD.
Licensure Skilled care; Intermediate care. *Beds* SNF 197; ICF 19. *Certified* Medicaid; Medicare.
Owner Publicly owned.
Admissions Requirements Minimum age 16; Medical examination; Physician's request.
Staff Physicians 1 (ft); RNs 9 (ft), 3 (pt); LPNs 23 (ft), 1 (pt); Nurses' aides 59 (ft), 20 (pt); Physical therapists 1 (pt); Occupational therapists 1 (pt); Speech therapists 1 (pt); Activities coordinators 1 (ft); Dietitians 1 (ft); Dentists 1 (pt).
Facilities Dining room; Physical therapy room; Activities room; Chapel; Crafts room; Laundry room; Barber/Beauty shop; Library.
Activities Arts & crafts; Cards; Games; Reading groups; Prayer groups; Movies; Shopping trips; Dances/Social/Cultural gatherings.

East Aurora

Aurora Park Health Care Center Inc
292 Main St, East Aurora, NY 14052
(716) 652-1560
Admin Neil Chur.
Licensure Skilled care; Intermediate care. *Beds* SNF 180; ICF 140. *Certified* Medicaid; Medicare.
Owner Proprietary corp.

East Islip

Little Flower Nursing Home & HRF
340 E Montauk Hwy, East Islip, NY 11730
(516) 581-6400
Admin Theresa M Santmann.
Licensure Skilled care; Intermediate care. *Beds* SNF 80; ICF 80. *Certified* Medicaid; Medicare.
Owner Privately owned.

East Syracuse

Sunnyside Nursing Home
7000 Collamer Rd, East Syracuse, NY 13057
(315) 656-7218
Admin Burnell Carney. *Dir of Nursing* Alice E Carney. *Medical Dir* Robert Weilt.
Licensure Skilled care; Retirement. *Beds* SNF 80; Retirement 20. *Private Pay Patients* 20%. *Certified* Medicaid; Medicare.
Owner Privately owned.
Admissions Requirements Medical examination; Physician's request.
Staff Physicians; RNs; LPNs; Nurses' aides; Physical therapists; Occupational therapists; Speech therapists; Activities coordinators; Dietitians; Podiatrists; Audiologists.
Facilities Dining room; Physical therapy room; Activities room; Crafts room; Laundry room; Barber/Beauty shop.
Activities Arts & crafts; Cards; Games; Movies; Shopping trips; Dances/Social/Cultural gatherings; Intergenerational programs; Pet therapy.

Eaton

Gerrit Smith Infirmary
River Rd, Box 111, Eaton, NY 13334-0111
(315) 684-3951
Admin William L Conole. *Dir of Nursing* Julie Hotaling. *Medical Dir* Robert Delorme.
Licensure Skilled care. *Beds* SNF 95. *Private Pay Patients* 3%. *Certified* Medicaid; Medicare.
Owner Publicly owned.
Admissions Requirements Minimum age 16; Medical examination; Physician's request.
Staff Physicians 2 (pt); RNs 8 (ft), 4 (pt); LPNs 14 (ft), 5 (pt); Nurses' aides 33 (ft), 20 (pt); Physical therapists 1 (pt); Recreational therapists 2 (ft); Occupational therapists 1 (pt); Speech therapists 1 (pt); Activities coordinators 1 (ft); Dietitians 1 (pt).
Languages Italian.
Facilities Dining room; Physical therapy room; Activities room; Laundry room; Barber/Beauty shop; Library.
Activities Arts & crafts; Cards; Games; Reading groups; Prayer groups; Movies; Shopping trips; Dances/Social/Cultural gatherings; Intergenerational programs; Pet therapy.

Eden

St George Nursing Home
2806 George St, Eden, NY 14057
(716) 992-3987
Admin Anthony St George Jr.
Licensure Skilled care. *Beds* SNF 40. *Certified* Medicaid; Medicare.
Owner Proprietary corp.

Edgemere

Rockaway Care Center
353 Beach 48th St, Edgemere, NY 11691
(718) 471-5000, 327-9214 FAX
Admin Michael Melnicke. *Dir of Nursing* Lillian Seabrook RN. *Medical Dir* Alexander Gardner MD.
Licensure Skilled care; Intermediate care. *Beds* SNF 80; ICF 135. *Private Pay Patients* 2%. *Certified* Medicaid; Medicare.

Owner Privately owned (Michael Melnicke).
Admissions Requirements Medical examination; Physician's request.
Staff Physicians; RNs; LPNs; Nurses' aides; Physical therapists; Reality therapists; Recreational therapists; Occupational therapists; Speech therapists; Activities coordinators; Dietitians; Ophthalmologists; Podiatrists; Audiologists.
Facilities Dining room; Physical therapy room; Activities room; Crafts room; Laundry room; Barber/Beauty shop; Library.
Activities Arts & crafts; Cards; Games; Reading groups; Prayer groups; Movies; Shopping trips; Dances/Social/Cultural gatherings; Pet therapy.

Elizabethtown

Horace Nye Home
Park St, Elizabethtown, NY 12932
(518) 873-6301, 873-6826 FAX
Admin Barbara A Feeley. *Dir of Nursing* Donna Garrison BSN. *Medical Dir* Dr Charles Moisan Jr.
Licensure Skilled care; Intermediate care. *Beds* SNF 60; ICF 40. *Private Pay Patients* 5%. *Certified* Medicaid; Medicare.
Owner Publicly owned.
Staff Physicians 1 (pt); RNs 9 (ft); LPNs 14 (ft); Nurses' aides 33 (ft), 20 (pt); Physical therapists 2 (pt); Occupational therapists 2 (pt); Speech therapists 1 (pt); Activities coordinators 1 (ft); Dietitians 1 (pt); Podiatrists 1 (pt); Audiologists 1 (pt).
Facilities Dining room; Physical therapy room; Activities room; Crafts room; Barber/Beauty shop.
Activities Arts & crafts; Games; Prayer groups; Movies; Shopping trips; Intergenerational programs.

Elmhurst

City Hospital at Elmhurst Public Home Infirmary
79-01 Broadway, Elmhurst, NY 11373
(718) 830-1515
Licensure Skilled care. *Beds* SNF 72.
Owner Publicly owned.

Elmira

Arnot-Ogden Memorial Hospital Skilled Nursing Unit
600 Roe Ave, Elmira, NY 14845
(607) 737-4305
Admin Sr Marie Michael Miller. *Dir of Nursing* Gaynelle Bowen. *Medical Dir* Otto Lederer MD.
Licensure Skilled care. *Beds* SNF 40. *Certified* Medicaid; Medicare.
Owner Nonprofit corp.
Admissions Requirements Minimum age 18.
Staff Physicians 1 (pt); RNs 5 (ft), 5 (pt); LPNs 2 (ft); Nurses' aides 22 (ft); Physical therapists 1 (pt); Recreational therapists 1 (pt); Occupational therapists 1 (pt); Speech therapists 1 (pt); Activities coordinators 1 (ft); Dietitians 1 (pt); Ophthalmologists 1 (pt); Podiatrists 1 (pt); Dentists 1 (pt).
Facilities Dining room; Physical therapy room; Activities room; Crafts room; Laundry room; Barber/Beauty shop; Library.
Activities Arts & crafts; Cards; Games; Reading groups; Prayer groups; Movies; Shopping trips.

Chemung County Health Center—Nursing Facility
Heritage Park, Elmira, NY 14901
(607) 737-2068
Admin Warren L Tessier.
Licensure Skilled care. *Beds* SNF 200. *Certified* Medicaid; Medicare.
Owner Publicly owned.

St Josephs Hospital—Skilled Nursing Facility
555 E Market St, Elmira, NY 14902
(607) 733-6541
Admin Sr Marie Michael Miller.
Medical Dir Dr A D Smith.
Licensure Skilled care. *Beds* SNF 31. *Certified* Medicaid; Medicare.
Owner Nonprofit corp.
Admissions Requirements Minimum age 16; Physician's request.
Activities Arts & crafts; Cards; Games; Reading groups; Prayer groups; Movies; Shopping trips.

Endicott

Sullivan Park Health Care Center Inc
Nantucket Dr, Endicott, NY 13760
(607) 754-2705
Admin Charles Yannett.
Licensure Skilled care; Intermediate care. *Beds* SNF 80; ICF 20. *Certified* Medicaid; Medicare.
Owner Proprietary corp.

Fairport

Crest Manor Nursing Home
6745 Pittsford-Palmyra Rd, Fairport, NY 14450
(716) 223-3633
Admin A John Bartholomew. *Dir of Nursing* Mary C Dryer.
Licensure Skilled care. *Beds* SNF 80. *Certified* Medicaid; Medicare.
Owner Privately owned.
Admissions Requirements Minimum age 16.
Staff RNs; LPNs; Nurses' aides.
Facilities Dining room; Physical therapy room; Activities room; Chapel; Crafts room; Laundry room; Barber/Beauty shop.
Activities Arts & crafts; Cards; Games; Reading groups; Prayer groups; Movies; Shopping trips.

Fairport Baptist Home
4646 Nine Mile Point Rd, Fairport, NY 14450
(716) 377-0350
Admin Alvin C Foster.
Licensure Skilled care; Intermediate care; Alzheimer's care. *Beds* SNF 102; ICF 94. *Certified* Medicaid; Medicare.
Owner Nonprofit corp.
Affiliation Baptist.
Facilities Dining room; Physical therapy room; Activities room; Chapel; Crafts room; Laundry room; Barber/Beauty shop; Library.

Far Rockaway

Bezalel Nursing Home Company
29-38 Far Rockaway Blvd, Far Rockaway, NY 11691
(718) 471-2600
Admin Solomon B Reifman. *Dir of Nursing* Rochelle Stern RN. *Medical Dir* Anthony Tavormina MD.
Licensure Skilled care; Intermediate care. *Beds* SNF 40; ICF 80. *Certified* Medicaid; Medicare.
Owner Nonprofit corp.
Admissions Requirements Minimum age 21; Medical examination.
Staff Physicians; RNs; LPNs; Nurses' aides; Physical therapists; Occupational therapists; Speech therapists; Activities coordinators; Dietitians.
Languages Spanish, Hebrew, Yiddish, Russian.
Affiliation Jewish.
Facilities Dining room; Physical therapy room; Activities room; Chapel; Laundry room; Barber/Beauty shop.

Activities Arts & crafts; Cards; Games; Reading groups; Prayer groups; Movies; Shopping trips; Dances/Social/Cultural gatherings; Birthday celebrations.

Brookhaven Beach Health Related Facility
250 Beach 17th St, Far Rockaway, NY 11691
(718) 471-7500
Admin Herbert Rothman.
Licensure Skilled care; Intermediate care. *Beds* SNF 118; ICF 180. *Certified* Medicaid; Medicare.
Owner Privately owned.

Far Rockaway Nursing Home
13-11 Virginia St, Far Rockaway, NY 11691
(718) 327-2909
Admin Aaron Feuereisen.
Licensure Skilled care. *Beds* SNF 100. *Certified* Medicaid; Medicare.
Owner Privately owned.

Haven Manor Nursing Home
1441 Gateway Blvd, Far Rockaway, NY 11691
(718) 471-1500
Admin Aron Cytryn. *Dir of Nursing* Ella Klug RN. *Medical Dir* Dr Marc S Kaufman.
Licensure Skilled care; Intermediate care; Alzheimer's care. *Beds* SNF 48; ICF 192. *Certified* Medicaid; Medicare.
Owner Privately owned.
Admissions Requirements Medical examination.
Staff Physicians; RNs; LPNs; Nurses' aides; Physical therapists; Reality therapists; Recreational therapists; Occupational therapists; Speech therapists; Activities coordinators; Dietitians; Ophthalmologists; Podiatrists; Dentists.
Languages Spanish, Yiddish, Hebrew, French.
Facilities Dining room; Physical therapy room; Activities room; Crafts room; Laundry room; Barber/Beauty shop; Library.
Activities Arts & crafts; Cards; Games; Reading groups; Prayer groups; Movies; Shopping trips; Dances/Social/Cultural gatherings.

Oceanview Nursing Home
315 Beach 9th St, Far Rockaway, NY 11691
(718) 471-6000
Admin Yehoshua Schachter. *Dir of Nursing* Ruby Norris RN. *Medical Dir* Dr E Gonzalez.
Licensure Skilled care. *Beds* SNF 102. *Certified* Medicaid; Medicare.
Owner Proprietary corp.
Admissions Requirements Minimum age 26; Medical examination; Physician's request.
Facilities Dining room; Physical therapy room; Activities room; Chapel; Crafts room; Laundry room; Barber/Beauty shop; Library.
Activities Arts & crafts; Cards; Games; Reading groups; Prayer groups; Movies; Dances/Social/Cultural gatherings.

Peninsula General Nursing Home
50-15 Beach Channel Dr, Far Rockaway, NY 11691
(718) 945-7100, ext 750, 634-4432 FAX
Admin Bernard Satin. *Dir of Nursing* Harlean Satin RN. *Medical Dir* Dr Jacob Milstein.
Licensure Skilled care; Alzheimer's care. *Beds* SNF 200. *Private Pay Patients* 5%. *Certified* Medicaid; Medicare.
Owner Nonprofit corp.
Admissions Requirements Minimum age 16.
Staff Physicians 5 (ft); RNs 28 (ft), 1 (pt); LPNs 25 (ft), 1 (pt); Nurses' aides 88 (ft); Physical therapists 8 (ft), 1 (pt); Recreational therapists 3 (ft), 1 (pt); Occupational therapists 5 (ft); Speech therapists 4 (ft); Activities coordinators 1 (ft); Dietitians 2 (ft); Podiatrists 2 (ft); Audiologists 1 (pt).
Languages Spanish, French, Yiddish, Haitian, Russian, Chinese, Indian dialects, Hebrew.

Facilities Dining room; Physical therapy room; Activities room; Chapel; Crafts room; Laundry room; Barber/Beauty shop; Library; Ground floor outdoor garden; Large second floor terrace; Adult day health care.
Activities Arts & crafts; Cards; Games; Reading groups; Prayer groups; Movies; Shopping trips; Dances/Social/Cultural gatherings; Resident council; Family council; Large print library; Art therapy; Sports; Barbecues.

Queens-Nassau Nursing Home
520 Beach 19th St, Far Rockaway, NY 11691
(718) 471-7202
Admin I Sherman. *Dir of Nursing* Barbara Porcano. *Medical Dir* Dr D Beer.
Licensure Skilled care. *Beds* SNF 200. *Certified* Medicaid; Medicare.
Owner Privately owned.
Facilities Dining room; Physical therapy room; Activities room; Laundry room; Barber/Beauty shop.
Activities Arts & crafts; Cards; Games; Reading groups; Prayer groups; Movies; Shopping trips; Dances/Social/Cultural gatherings.

St Johns Episcopal Hospital South Shore Division
17-11 Brookhaven Ave, Far Rockaway, NY 11691
(718) 917-3450
Licensure Skilled care. *Beds* SNF 163.
Owner Nonprofit corp.

Surfside Nursing Home
22-41 New Haven Ave, Far Rockaway, NY 11691
(718) 471-3400
Admin Dorothy Galasso. *Dir of Nursing* Gail Holtz.
Licensure Skilled care; Alzheimer's care. *Beds* SNF 175. *Certified* Medicaid; Medicare.
Owner Proprietary corp.
Staff Physicians; RNs; LPNs; Nurses' aides; Physical therapists; Recreational therapists; Occupational therapists; Speech therapists; Activities coordinators; Dietitians; Ophthalmologists; Podiatrists; Dentists.
Facilities Dining room; Physical therapy room; Activities room; Chapel; Crafts room; Barber/Beauty shop; Library.
Activities Arts & crafts; Cards; Games; Reading groups; Prayer groups; Movies.

West Lawrence Care Center
1410 Seagirt Blvd, Far Rockaway, NY 11691
(718) 471-7000
Admin Maurice H Radzik. *Dir of Nursing* Phyllis Siboney RN. *Medical Dir* Tara Saini MD.
Licensure Intermediate care. *Beds* ICF 210. *Certified* Medicaid.
Owner Proprietary corp.
Admissions Requirements Minimum age 60; Medical examination.
Staff Physicians 6 (pt); RNs 10 (ft), 1 (pt); LPNs 30 (ft); Nurses' aides 20 (ft); Physical therapists 2 (ft), 1 (pt); Recreational therapists 1 (ft), 1 (pt); Occupational therapists 2 (pt); Speech therapists 1 (pt); Activities coordinators 1 (ft); Dietitians 1 (ft), 1 (pt).
Languages Yiddish, Spanish, Haitian, French, Hebrew, Greek.
Facilities Dining room; Physical therapy room; Activities room; Chapel; Crafts room; Laundry room; Barber/Beauty shop; Library.
Activities Arts & crafts; Cards; Games; Reading groups; Prayer groups; Movies; Shopping trips; Dances/Social/Cultural gatherings.

Farmingdale

Daleview Nursing Home & Manor
274 & 530 Fulton St, Farmingdale, NY 11735
(516) 694-6242
Admin Paul J Dioguardi.
Medical Dir Armando Deschamps MD.
Licensure Skilled care; Intermediate care. *Beds*
SNF 86; ICF 56. *Certified* Medicaid;
Medicare.
Owner Privately owned.
Admissions Requirements Minimum age 16;
Physician's request.
Staff Physicians 17 (pt); RNs 5 (ft), 9 (pt);
LPNs 8 (ft), 6 (pt); Nurses' aides 25 (ft), 15
(pt); Physical therapists 1 (pt); Occupational
therapists 1 (pt); Speech therapists 1 (pt);
Activities coordinators 2 (ft), 2 (pt);
Dietitians 1 (ft); Ophthalmologists 3 (pt);
Podiatrists 1 (pt); Dentists 1 (pt).
Facilities Dining room; Physical therapy
room; Activities room; Laundry room;
Barber/Beauty shop.
Activities Arts & crafts; Cards; Games;
Reading groups; Prayer groups; Movies;
Shopping trips; Dances/Social/Cultural
gatherings; Musical entertainment.

Flushing

Cliffside Nursing Home
119-19 Graham Ct, Flushing, NY 11354
(718) 886-0700
Admin Jack Deutsch. *Dir of Nursing* Diane
Reeder RN. *Medical Dir* Gerald Kreitman
MD.
Licensure Skilled care; Alzheimer's care. *Beds*
SNF 220. *Certified* Medicaid; Medicare.
Owner Privately owned.
Admissions Requirements Physician's request.
Staff Physicians 1 (pt); RNs 10 (ft), 5 (pt);
LPNs 22 (ft), 12 (pt); Nurses' aides 65 (ft),
35 (pt); Physical therapists 1 (pt);
Recreational therapists 2 (ft), 2 (pt);
Occupational therapists 2 (pt); Speech
therapists 1 (pt); Activities coordinators 1
(ft), 1 (pt); Dietitians 2 (ft).
Languages Yiddish, Hebrew, Spanish,
Russian, German, Hungarian, French.
Facilities Dining room; Physical therapy
room; Activities room; Barber/Beauty shop;
Library; Outside sitting area.
Activities Arts & crafts; Cards; Games;
Reading groups; Prayer groups; Movies;
Dances/Social/Cultural gatherings;
Discussion groups; Cooking; Baking.

**College Nursing Home—Waterview Nursing
Care Center**
119-15 27th Ave, Flushing, NY 11354
(718) 461-5000
Licensure Skilled care. *Beds* SNF 200.

Flushing Manor Care Center
139-66 35th Ave, Flushing, NY 11354
(718) 961-5300, 961-8715 FAX
Admin Herb Eisen. *Dir of Nursing* Vivienne
Smith RN. *Medical Dir* William Benenson
MD.
Licensure Skilled care; Intermediate care. *Beds*
SNF 178; ICF 100. *Private Pay Patients*
18%. *Certified* Medicaid; Medicare.
Owner Privately owned (Esther Benenson
EdD).
Admissions Requirements Medical
examination; Physician's request.
Staff Physicians 43 (pt); RNs 15 (ft), 5 (pt);
LPNs 28 (ft), 7 (pt); Nurses' aides 98 (ft), 20
(pt); Physical therapists 2 (ft), 1 (pt);
Recreational therapists 1 (ft); Occupational
therapists 1 (ft), 3 (pt); Speech therapists 1
(pt); Activities coordinators 3 (ft); Dietitians
2 (ft), 1 (pt); Ophthalmologists 1 (pt);
Podiatrists 2 (pt); Audiologists 1 (pt).
Languages Spanish, Italian, Slavic, Korean,
Yiddish.

Facilities Dining room; Physical therapy
room; Activities room; Chapel; Crafts room;
Laundry room; Barber/Beauty shop; Library;
Outdoor patios.
Activities Arts & crafts; Cards; Games;
Reading groups; Prayer groups; Movies;
Shopping trips; Dances/Social/Cultural
gatherings; Pet therapy; Trips; Special
events.

Flushing Manor Nursing Home Inc
35-15 Parsons Blvd, Flushing, NY 11354
(718) 961-3500, 461-1784 FAX
Admin Esther Benenson. *Dir of Nursing* Mary
Frey RN. *Medical Dir* William Benenson
MD.
Licensure Skilled care. *Beds* SNF 227. *Private
Pay Patients* 18%. *Certified* Medicaid;
Medicare.
Owner Privately owned (Esther Benenson
EdD).
Admissions Requirements Medical
examination; Physician's request.
Staff Physicians 43 (pt); RNs 13 (ft), 5 (pt);
LPNs 16 (ft), 8 (pt); Nurses' aides 60 (ft), 25
(pt); Physical therapists 2 (ft), 2 (pt);
Recreational therapists 1 (ft); Occupational
therapists 1 (ft), 3 (pt); Speech therapists 1
(pt); Activities coordinators 2 (ft), 2 (pt);
Dietitians 2 (ft), 1 (pt); Ophthalmologists 1
(pt); Podiatrists 2 (pt); Audiologists 1 (pt).
Languages Spanish, Korean, Italian, Yiddish,
Russian, Chinese.
Facilities Dining room; Physical therapy
room; Activities room; Chapel; Crafts room;
Laundry room; Barber/Beauty shop; Library.
Activities Arts & crafts; Cards; Games;
Reading groups; Prayer groups; Movies;
Shopping trips; Dances/Social/Cultural
gatherings; Intergenerational programs; Pet
therapy; Trips; Special events.

Franklin Nursing Home
142-27 Franklin Ave, Flushing, NY 11355
(718) 463-8200
Admin Sylvia R Stern LNHA. *Dir of Nursing*
LaVerne Mullin RN. *Medical Dir* Dr
Anthony Crusco.
Licensure Skilled care. *Beds* SNF 320.
Certified Medicaid; Medicare.
Owner Privately owned.
Admissions Requirements Minimum age 16;
PRI.
Staff Physicians; RNs; LPNs; Nurses' aides;
Physical therapists; Recreational therapists;
Occupational therapists; Speech therapists;
Activities coordinators; Dietitians;
Ophthalmologists; Podiatrists; Social
workers.
Languages Yiddish, Spanish, Korean, Chinese.
Facilities Dining room; Physical therapy
room; Activities room; Crafts room; Barber/
Beauty shop; Kosher kitchen.
Activities Arts & crafts; Cards; Games;
Reading groups; Prayer groups; Movies;
Trips.

Long Island Nursing Home
144-61 38th Ave, Flushing, NY 11354
(718) 939-7500, 886-2559 FAX
Admin Phyllis Schindler. *Dir of Nursing*
Marilyn DeCesare. *Medical Dir* Dr Abraham
Khaski.
Licensure Skilled care. *Beds* SNF 200. *Private
Pay Patients* 17%. *Certified* Medicaid;
Medicare.
Owner Privately owned.
Admissions Requirements Minimum age 25;
Medical examination; Physician's request.
Staff Physicians 5 (pt); RNs 13 (ft); LPNs 21
(ft); Nurses' aides 118 (ft); Physical
therapists 2 (pt); Recreational therapists 5
(ft); Occupational therapists 2 (pt); Speech
therapists 1 (pt); Activities coordinators 1
(ft); Dietitians 2 (ft); Ophthalmologists 1
(pt); Podiatrists 1 (pt); Audiologists 1 (pt).
Languages Spanish, Korean, Tagalog, Chinese,
Greek.

Facilities Dining room; Physical therapy
room; Activities room; Chapel; Crafts room;
Barber/Beauty shop; Library.
Activities Arts & crafts; Cards; Games;
Reading groups; Prayer groups; Movies;
Shopping trips; Dances/Social/Cultural
gatherings; Intergenerational programs; Pet
therapy; Glee club; Family council; Resident
council.

Meadow Park Nursing Home
78-10 164th St, Flushing, NY 11366
(718) 591-8300, 591-0400 FAX
Admin Jeffrey Sicklick. *Dir of Nursing* Jeanne
Ostendorf. *Medical Dir* Dr Morton Kurtz;
Dr Raymond Elias.
Licensure Skilled care. *Beds* SNF 143.
Certified Medicaid; Medicare.
Owner Proprietary corp.
Admissions Requirements Minimum age 21;
Medical examination; PRI admission
criteria.
Staff Physicians 6 (pt); RNs 11 (ft); LPNs 20
(ft); Nurses' aides 36 (ft), 20 (pt); Physical
therapists 2 (pt); Occupational therapists 1
(pt); Speech therapists 1 (pt); Activities
coordinators 1 (pt); Dietitians 1 (ft);
Ophthalmologists 1 (pt); Podiatrists 1 (pt).
Facilities Dining room; Physical therapy
room; Activities room.
Activities Arts & crafts; Cards; Games;
Reading groups; Prayer groups; Movies;
Dances/Social/Cultural gatherings;
Intergenerational programs.

Rego Park Nursing Home
111-26 Corona Ave, Flushing, NY 11368
(718) 592-6400, 592-6555 FAX
Admin Arnold Klein. *Dir of Nursing* Ann
Morawski. *Medical Dir* Dr Peter Barra.
Licensure Skilled care. *Beds* SNF 200. *Private
Pay Patients* 15%. *Certified* Medicaid;
Medicare.
Owner Proprietary corp.
Admissions Requirements Medical
examination.
Staff Physicians 5 (pt); RNs 10 (ft); LPNs 17
(ft); Nurses' aides 78 (ft); Physical therapists
1 (pt); Recreational therapists 3 (ft);
Occupational therapists 1 (ft); Speech
therapists 1 (ft); Dietitians 2 (ft);
Ophthalmologists 1 (pt); Podiatrists 1 (pt);
Audiologists 1 (pt).
Languages Spanish, Yiddish, Hebrew,
Russian.
Affiliation Jewish.
Facilities Dining room; Physical therapy
room; Activities room; Chapel; Crafts room;
Laundry room; Barber/Beauty shop.
Activities Arts & crafts; Cards; Games;
Reading groups; Prayer groups; Movies;
Shopping trips; Dances/Social/Cultural
gatherings; Intergenerational programs;
Dance therapy; Barbecues; Family activities.

Waterview Nursing Care Center
119-15 27th Ave, Flushing, NY 11354
(718) 461-5000
Admin Larry I Slatky. *Dir of Nursing* Delores
Belizaire. *Medical Dir* Dr Chenna Reddy.
Licensure Skilled care; Alzheimer's care. *Beds*
SNF 200. *Certified* Medicaid; Medicare.
Owner Privately owned.
Staff Physicians 1 (pt); RNs 12 (ft), 2 (pt);
LPNs 20 (ft), 8 (pt); Nurses' aides 80 (ft), 30
(pt); Physical therapists 1 (pt); Recreational
therapists 4 (ft); Occupational therapists 1
(pt); Speech therapists 1 (pt); Activities
coordinators 1 (ft); Dietitians 2 (ft), 2 (pt);
Ophthalmologists 1 (pt); Podiatrists 1 (pt);
Dentists 1 (pt).
Languages Hebrew, Yiddish, Polish, Italian,
Indian, Spanish.
Facilities Dining room; Physical therapy
room; Activities room; Chapel; Crafts room;
Laundry room; Barber/Beauty shop; Library.

Activities Arts & crafts; Cards; Games; Reading groups; Prayer groups; Movies; Shopping trips; Dances/Social/Cultural gatherings.

Woodcrest Nursing Home
119-09 26th Ave, Flushing, NY 11354
(718) 762-6100, 463-5343 FAX
Admin Josef Hirsch. *Dir of Nursing* Elma Gonzales. *Medical Dir* Gerald Kreitman.
Licensure Skilled care. *Beds* SNF 200. *Private Pay Patients* 5%. *Certified* Medicaid; Medicare.
Owner Privately owned.
Admissions Requirements Minimum age 21; Medical examination.
Staff Physicians 6 (pt); RNs 13 (ft), 7 (pt); LPNs 16 (ft), 5 (pt); Nurses' aides 43 (ft), 24 (pt); Physical therapists 2 (ft), 1 (pt); Recreational therapists 2 (ft), 1 (pt); Occupational therapists 2 (pt); Speech therapists 1 (pt); Activities coordinators 1 (ft); Dietitians 1 (ft); Ophthalmologists 1 (pt); Podiatrists 2 (pt); Audiologists 1 (pt).
Languages Spanish, Yiddish, Hebrew, Hungarian.
Facilities Dining room; Physical therapy room; Activities room; Crafts room; Laundry room; Barber/Beauty shop; Library.
Activities Arts & crafts; Cards; Games; Reading groups; Prayer groups; Movies; Dances/Social/Cultural gatherings; Intergenerational programs; Pet therapy.

Forest Hills

Fairview Nursing Home
69-70 Grand Central Pkwy, Forest Hills, NY 11375
(718) 263-4600
Admin Abraham N Klein. *Dir of Nursing* Stephanie Manor. *Medical Dir* Dr Elias.
Licensure Skilled care. *Beds* SNF 200. *Certified* Medicaid; Medicare.
Owner Privately owned.
Staff Physicians 5 (pt); RNs 10 (ft), 3 (pt); LPNs 15 (ft), 10 (pt); Nurses' aides 55 (ft), 20 (pt); Physical therapists 1 (ft); Recreational therapists 1 (ft), 3 (pt); Occupational therapists 1 (ft); Speech therapists 1 (pt); Activities coordinators 1 (ft); Dietitians 2 (ft); Ophthalmologists 1 (pt); Podiatrists 1 (pt); Dentists 1 (pt).
Languages French, Spanish, German, Polish, Yiddish, Hebrew.
Facilities Dining room; Physical therapy room; Activities room; Chapel; Crafts room; Laundry room; Barber/Beauty shop; Library.
Activities Arts & crafts; Cards; Games; Reading groups; Prayer groups; Movies; Dances/Social/Cultural gatherings; Trips to cultural events.

Forest Hills Nursing Home
71-44 Yellowstone Blvd, Forest Hills, NY 11375
(718) 544-4300
Admin Cathrine Powers.
Licensure Skilled care. *Beds* SNF 100. *Certified* Medicaid; Medicare.
Owner Privately owned.

Forest View Nursing Home
71-20 110th St, Forest Hills, NY 11375
(718) 793-3200
Admin Joseph L Bloch.
Medical Dir Hiralal Patel.
Licensure Skilled care. *Beds* SNF 159. *Certified* Medicaid; Medicare.
Owner Privately owned.
Admissions Requirements Medical examination; Physician's request.
Staff Physicians 6 (pt); RNs 4 (ft), 3 (pt); LPNs 18 (ft), 12 (pt); Nurses' aides 43 (ft), 28 (pt); Physical therapists 1 (ft), 1 (pt); Recreational therapists 1 (ft), 3 (pt);

Occupational therapists 1 (pt); Speech therapists 1 (pt); Activities coordinators 1 (ft); Dietitians 1 (ft).
Facilities Dining room; Physical therapy room; Activities room; Laundry room; Barber/Beauty shop; Library.
Activities Arts & crafts; Cards; Games; Reading groups; Movies; Dances/Social/ Cultural gatherings; Barbeques; Trips to museums & race track.

Fort Edward

Fort Hudson Nursing Home Inc
Upper Broadway, Fort Edward, NY 12828
(518) 747-2811
Admin Dorothy S Kubricky. *Dir of Nursing* Donna Wassel RN. *Medical Dir* Philip J Gara Jr MD.
Licensure Skilled care; Intermediate care. *Beds* SNF 80; ICF 80. *Certified* Medicaid; Medicare.
Owner Nonprofit corp.
Admissions Requirements Minimum age 16; Medical examination.
Staff Physicians 1 (pt); RNs 9 (ft), 6 (pt); LPNs 15 (ft), 10 (pt); Nurses' aides 34 (ft), 23 (pt); Physical therapists 1 (pt); Occupational therapists 1 (pt); Speech therapists 1 (pt); Activities coordinators 1 (ft); Dietitians 1 (pt).
Facilities Dining room; Physical therapy room; Activities room; Crafts room; Laundry room; Barber/Beauty shop; Movie/Theater room; Quiet room.
Activities Arts & crafts; Cards; Games; Reading groups; Prayer groups; Movies; Shopping trips; Dances/Social/Cultural gatherings.

Franklin Square

Franklin Park Nursing Home
135 Franklin Ave, Franklin Square, NY 11010
(516) 488-1600
Admin Clifford Schein.
Medical Dir Dr Harold Langs.
Licensure Skilled care. *Beds* SNF 150. *Certified* Medicaid; Medicare.
Owner Privately owned.
Admissions Requirements Minimum age 17; Medical examination.

Freeport

South Shore Nursing Home Inc
275 W Merrick Rd, Freeport, NY 11520
(516) 623-4000
Admin Marylynne Geraghty. *Dir of Nursing* R Donges RN. *Medical Dir* T Walker MD.
Licensure Skilled care. *Beds* SNF 100. *Certified* Medicaid; Medicare.
Owner Proprietary corp.
Admissions Requirements Minimum age 16.
Staff RNs 13 (ft); LPNs 12 (ft); Nurses' aides 46 (ft); Physical therapists 1 (pt); Occupational therapists 1 (pt); Activities coordinators 1 (ft); Dietitians 1 (pt).
Facilities Dining room; Physical therapy room; Activities room; Laundry room; Barber/Beauty shop.
Activities Arts & crafts; Cards; Games; Reading groups; Prayer groups; Movies; Shopping trips; Dances/Social/Cultural gatherings.

Fulton

Andrew Michaud Nursing Home
450 S 4th St, Fulton, NY 13069
(315) 592-9521
Admin Fred Blackwood.
Licensure Skilled care. *Beds* SNF 89. *Certified* Medicaid; Medicare.
Owner Publicly owned.

Gasport

United Church Colony Homes Inc
4540 Lincoln Dr, Gasport, NY 14067
(716) 772-2631
Admin Joan M McAndrew. *Dir of Nursing* Linda J Baehr RN. *Medical Dir* B Eun Lee MD.
Licensure Skilled care; Retirement; Alzheimer's care. *Beds* SNF 83; Retirement 193. *Private Pay Patients* 24%. *Certified* Medicaid; Medicare.
Owner Nonprofit corp (United Church Home Society).
Admissions Requirements Minimum age 16; Physician's request.
Staff Physicians 2 (pt); RNs 3 (ft), 5 (pt); LPNs 9 (ft), 9 (pt); Nurses' aides 30 (ft), 16 (pt); Physical therapists 3 (pt); Occupational therapists 1 (pt); Speech therapists (consultant); Activities coordinators 1 (ft); Dietitians 1 (ft); Podiatrists 1 (pt); Audiologists 1 (pt).
Affiliation United Church of Christ.
Facilities Dining room; Physical therapy room; Activities room; Chapel; Crafts room; Laundry room; Barber/Beauty shop; Library; Alzheimer's.
Activities Arts & crafts; Cards; Games; Reading groups; Prayer groups; Movies; Shopping trips; Dances/Social/Cultural gatherings; Pet therapy; Balloon volleyball tournaments.

Geneseo

Livingston County Skilled Nursing Facility
4223 Lakeville Rd, Geneseo, NY 14454
(716) 243-3340
Admin Wayne Lux. *Dir of Nursing* Jane Hill. *Medical Dir* Dr Sweeney.
Licensure Skilled care. *Beds* SNF 126. *Private Pay Patients* 8%. *Certified* Medicaid; Medicare.
Owner Publicly owned.
Admissions Requirements Minimum age 16; Medical examination; Physician's request.
Staff Physicians 2 (pt); RNs 12 (ft), 1 (pt); LPNs 17 (ft), 2 (pt); Nurses' aides 50 (ft), 12 (pt); Physical therapists 2 (ft); Activities coordinators 1 (ft); Dietitians 1 (pt); Podiatrists 1 (pt); Audiologists 1 (pt).
Facilities Dining room; Physical therapy room; Activities room; Chapel; Laundry room; Barber/Beauty shop.
Activities Arts & crafts; Cards; Games; Reading groups; Prayer groups; Movies; Shopping trips; Dances/Social/Cultural gatherings; Intergenerational programs; Pet therapy.

Geneva

Geneva General Hospital Nursing Home Company Inc & Progressive Care Unit
196-198 North St, Geneva, NY 14456
(315) 789-4222
Admin James Dooley.
Licensure Skilled care; Intermediate care. *Beds* SNF 109; ICF 34. *Certified* Medicaid; Medicare.
Owner Nonprofit corp.

Gerry

Heritage Village Health Center
Rte 60 Box 351, Gerry, NY 14740
(716) 985-4612
Admin Vivian J DiNardo. *Dir of Nursing* Lois Favro RN.
Licensure Skilled care; Intermediate care; Retirement. *Beds* SNF 80; ICF 40; Retirement 200. *Private Pay Patients* 30%. *Certified* Medicaid; Medicare.
Owner Nonprofit corp.

Admissions Requirements Minimum age 16; Medical examination; Physician's request.
Staff RNs 6 (ft), 5 (pt); LPNs 11 (ft), 7 (pt); Nurses' aides 30 (ft), 22 (pt); Physical therapists (contracted); Speech therapists (contracted); Activities coordinators 1 (ft); Dietitians 1 (ft).
Affiliation Free Methodist.
Facilities Dining room; Physical therapy room; Activities room; Chapel; Crafts room.
Activities Arts & crafts; Games; Reading groups; Prayer groups; Movies; Shopping trips; Dances/Social/Cultural gatherings; Intergenerational programs; Pet therapy.

Getzville

Beechwood Residence
2235 Millersport Hwy, Getzville, NY 14068
(716) 688-8822
Licensure Intermediate care. *Beds* 157.
Owner Nonprofit corp.
Affiliation Methodist.

Niagara Frontier Nursing Home Company Inc
100 Stahl Rd, Getzville, NY 14068
(716) 688-8822
Admin Arthur Shade.
Licensure Skilled care; Intermediate care. *Beds* SNF 120. *Certified* Medicaid; Medicare.
Owner Nonprofit corp.

Glen Cove

Forest Manor Health Related Facility Inc
6 Medical Plaza, Glen Cove, NY 11542
(516) 671-9010, 259-9370 FAX
Admin Joan Baier. *Dir of Nursing* Patricia Arrigan RN. *Medical Dir* Dr Kurzwiel.
Licensure Intermediate care. *Beds* ICF 148. *Certified* Medicaid.
Owner Privately owned.
Staff Physicians (consultant); RNs (consultant); LPNs; Nurses' aides; Physical therapists; Recreational therapists; Occupational therapists; Speech therapists; Activities coordinators; Dietitians; Ophthalmologists (consultant); Podiatrists (consultant); Audiologists (consultant).
Facilities Dining room; Activities room; Crafts room; Laundry room; Barber/Beauty shop; Library.
Activities Arts & crafts; Cards; Games; Reading groups; Prayer groups; Movies; Shopping trips; Dances/Social/Cultural gatherings.

Glengariff Health Care Center
Dosoris Ln, Glen Cove, NY 11542
(516) 676-1100
Admin Kenneth Winston. *Dir of Nursing* Joan Kelly RN. *Medical Dir* Ferdinand Kann MD.
Licensure Skilled care; Intermediate care. *Beds* SNF 202; ICF 60. *Certified* Medicaid; Medicare.
Owner Proprietary corp.
Admissions Requirements Minimum age 16; Medical examination; Physician's request.
Staff Physicians 4 (pt); RNs 15 (ft), 5 (pt); LPNs 20 (ft), 5 (pt); Nurses' aides 60 (ft), 15 (pt); Physical therapists 1 (pt); Recreational therapists 4 (ft); Occupational therapists 1 (pt); Speech therapists 1 (pt); Activities coordinators 1 (ft); Dietitians 2 (pt); Ophthalmologists 1 (pt); Podiatrists 1 (pt); Dentists 1 (pt).
Facilities Dining room; Physical therapy room; Activities room; Crafts room; Laundry room; Barber/Beauty shop; Library.
Activities Arts & crafts; Cards; Games; Reading groups; Prayer groups; Movies; Shopping trips; Dances/Social/Cultural gatherings.

Montclair Nursing Home
2 Medical Plaza, Glen Cove, NY 11542
(516) 671-0858
Admin Joseph Kane.
Medical Dir Gabriella Wasserman.
Licensure Skilled care. *Beds* SNF 102. *Certified* Medicaid; Medicare.
Owner Privately owned.
Staff RNs 8 (ft), 4 (pt); LPNs 5 (ft), 4 (pt); Nurses' aides 30 (ft), 11 (pt).
Facilities Dining room; Activities room; Barber/Beauty shop.
Activities Arts & crafts; Cards; Games; Reading groups; Prayer groups; Movies; Shopping trips; Dances/Social/Cultural gatherings.

Glen Oaks

New Glen Oaks Nursing Home
260-01 79th Ave, Glen Oaks, NY 11004
(718) 343-0770, 343-0773 FAX
Admin Mark O Larsen. *Dir of Nursing* Patricia Cavaliere RN. *Medical Dir* John J Rawlings MD.
Licensure Skilled care; Alzheimer's care. *Beds* SNF 60. *Private Pay Patients* 20-25%. *Certified* Medicaid; Medicare.
Owner Privately owned.
Staff Physicians; RNs; LPNs; Nurses' aides; Physical therapists; Recreational therapists; Occupational therapists; Speech therapists; Activities coordinators; Dietitians; Ophthalmologists; Podiatrists; Audiologists.
Facilities Dining room; Physical therapy room; Activities room; Chapel; Crafts room; Barber/Beauty shop; Conference room; Kosher kitchen.
Activities Arts & crafts; Games; Prayer groups; Movies; Shopping trips; Dances/Social/Cultural gatherings; Pet therapy; Trips to beaches, Rockefeller Center, etc; Religious services; Therapeutic recreation.

Glens Falls

Eden Park Nursing Home & Health Related Facility
170 Warren St, Glens Falls, NY 12801
(518) 793-5163
Admin Lloyd F Cote. *Dir of Nursing* Susan Bartholomew RN. *Medical Dir* Robert Evans DO.
Licensure Skilled care; Intermediate care. *Beds* SNF 80; ICF 36. *Private Pay Patients* 23%. *Certified* Medicaid; Medicare.
Owner Proprietary corp (Eden Park Health Services Inc).
Admissions Requirements Minimum age 16; Medical examination; Physician's request.
Staff Physicians 5 (pt); RNs 8 (ft), 8 (pt); LPNs 7 (ft), 12 (pt); Nurses' aides 39 (ft), 18 (pt); Physical therapists 1 (pt); Occupational therapists 1 (pt); Speech therapists 1 (pt); Activities coordinators 1 (ft); Dietitians 1 (pt); Podiatrists 1 (pt); Audiologists 1 (pt); RPAs 1 (pt).
Facilities Dining room; Physical therapy room; Activities room; Crafts room; Barber/Beauty shop; Library; Wheelchair garden.
Activities Arts & crafts; Games; Reading groups; Prayer groups; Movies; Shopping trips; Dances/Social/Cultural gatherings; Pet therapy; Music; Drama programs.

Hallmark Nursing Centre Inc
152 Sherman Ave, Glens Falls, NY 12801
(518) 583-4225
Admin Kathryn A Costello. *Dir of Nursing* Pamela Stanton RN. *Medical Dir* Dr Thomas Kandora.
Licensure Skilled care. *Beds* SNF 80. *Private Pay Patients* 32%. *Certified* Medicaid; Medicare.
Owner Proprietary corp (Hallmark Nursing Centre Inc).
Admissions Requirements PRI/screen.

Staff Physicians 2 (pt); RNs 4 (ft), 7 (pt); LPNs 6 (ft), 1 (pt); Nurses' aides 17 (ft), 15 (pt); Physical therapists 1 (ft); Recreational therapists 1 (ft); Occupational therapists (consultant); Speech therapists (consultant); Activities coordinators 1 (pt); Dietitians (consultant); Podiatrists (consultant); Audiologists (consultant).
Facilities Dining room; Physical therapy room; Activities room; Laundry room; Barber/Beauty shop.
Activities Arts & crafts; Cards; Games; Reading groups; Prayer groups; Movies; Shopping trips; Dances/Social/Cultural gatherings; Intergenerational programs.

Gloversville

Fulton County Infirmary
RR 1 Box 292, Gloversville, NY 12078
(518) 725-8631
Admin Cynthia Dodge. *Dir of Nursing* Shirley Wands RN. *Medical Dir* R Curtis Mills MD.
Licensure Skilled care; Intermediate care. *Beds* SNF 134; ICF 42. *Certified* Medicaid; Medicare.
Owner Publicly owned.
Admissions Requirements Minimum age 16; Medical examination.
Staff Physicians 5 (pt); RNs 16 (ft); LPNs 20 (ft), 2 (pt); Nurses' aides 60 (ft), 35 (pt); Physical therapists 1 (ft); Recreational therapists 1 (pt); Occupational therapists 1 (ft); Speech therapists 1 (pt); Activities coordinators 1 (ft); Dietitians 1 (pt); Ophthalmologists 1 (pt); Podiatrists 1 (pt); Dentists, Respiratory therapists 2 (pt).
Facilities Dining room; Physical therapy room; Activities room; Crafts room; Laundry room; Barber/Beauty shop; Occupational therapy room.
Activities Arts & crafts; Cards; Games; Reading groups; Prayer groups; Movies; Shopping trips; Dances/Social/Cultural gatherings; Intergenerational programs; Pet therapy; Community involvement; Resident volunteer services; Travel club; Gardening; Baking.

Gloversville Extended Care & Nursing Home Co Inc
99 E State St, Gloversville, NY 12078
(518) 725-8611
Admin Daniel Governanti. *Dir of Nursing* Julia Ferrara RN.
Licensure Skilled care. *Beds* SNF 84. *Certified* Medicaid; Medicare.
Owner Nonprofit corp.
Admissions Requirements Minimum age 16; Physician's request.
Staff Physicians; RNs; LPNs; Nurses' aides; Physical therapists; Activities coordinators; Dietitians.
Facilities Dining room; Physical therapy room; Activities room; Laundry room; Barber/Beauty shop.
Activities Arts & crafts; Cards; Games; Reading groups; Prayer groups; Movies; Dances/Social/Cultural gatherings.

Goshen

Arden Hill Life Care Center
Harriman Dr, Goshen, NY 10924
(914) 294-9797
Licensure Skilled care; Intermediate care. *Beds* SNF 80; ICF 40.
Owner Nonprofit corp.

Orange County Home & Infirmary
Quarry Rd, Goshen, NY 10924
(914) 294-7971
Admin John Watson.
Licensure Skilled care; Intermediate care. *Beds* SNF 380; ICF 120. *Certified* Medicaid; Medicare.
Owner Publicly owned.

Gouverneur

Kinney Nursing Home
57 W Barney St, Gouverneur, NY 13642
(315) 287-1400
Admin Byron Quinton.
Licensure Skilled care. *Beds* SNF 40. *Certified* Medicaid; Medicare.
Owner Nonprofit corp.
Staff RNs; LPNs; Nurses' aides; Physical therapists; Activities coordinators; Dietitians.
Facilities Dining room; Physical therapy room; Activities room; Crafts room; Laundry room; Barber/Beauty shop.
Activities Arts & crafts; Cards; Games; Reading groups; Prayer groups; Movies; Shopping trips; Dances/Social/Cultural gatherings.

Gowanda

Gowanda Nursing Home
100 Miller St, Gowanda, NY 14070
(716) 532-5700, 532-5703 FAX
Admin Colin C Hart. *Dir of Nursing* Felicia L Williams RN. *Medical Dir* C Frederick Kurtz MD.
Licensure Skilled care; Intermediate care. *Beds* SNF 80; ICF 40. *Private Pay Patients* 23%. *Certified* Medicaid; Medicare.
Owner Privately owned.
Admissions Requirements Minimum age 16; Medical examination; Physician's request.
Staff RNs 6 (ft), 4 (pt); LPNs 4 (ft), 6 (pt); Nurses' aides 30 (ft), 25 (pt); Physical therapists 1 (pt); Occupational therapists 1 (pt); Speech therapists 1 (pt); Activities coordinators 1 (ft), 2 (pt).
Languages Polish, Spanish.
Facilities Dining room; Physical therapy room; Activities room; Crafts room; Laundry room; Barber/Beauty shop; Quiet room; Treatment room.
Activities Arts & crafts; Cards; Games; Reading groups; Prayer groups; Movies; Shopping trips; Pet therapy; Ceramics.

Grand Island

Grand Island Manor Nursing Home
PO Box 826, Grand Island, NY 14072
(716) 773-5900
Admin Sam W Ware Jr.
Medical Dir Ida Levine MD.
Licensure Skilled care. *Beds* SNF 80. *Certified* Medicaid; Medicare.
Owner Privately owned.
Admissions Requirements Minimum age 16.
Staff Physicians 1 (pt); RNs 5 (ft), 5 (pt); LPNs 10 (ft), 4 (pt); Nurses' aides 16 (ft), 24 (pt); Physical therapists 1 (pt); Recreational therapists 1 (ft), 1 (pt); Occupational therapists 1 (pt); Speech therapists 1 (pt); Dietitians 1 (pt); Ophthalmologists 1 (pt); Podiatrists 1 (pt); Audiologists 1 (pt); Dentists 1 (pt).
Facilities Dining room; Physical therapy room; Activities room; Crafts room; Laundry room; Barber/Beauty shop.
Activities Arts & crafts; Cards; Games; Reading groups; Prayer groups; Movies; Shopping trips; Dances/Social/Cultural gatherings.

Granville

Indian River Nursing Home & Health Related Facility Inc
17 Madison St, Granville, NY 12832-1299
(518) 642-2710, 642-1318 FAX
Admin Daniel L Morris. *Dir of Nursing* Mary Anne Raley RN. *Medical Dir* John E Glennon.
Licensure Skilled care; Intermediate care; Retirement. *Beds* SNF 40; ICF 40; Retirement 20-60. *Private Pay Patients* 23%. *Certified* Medicaid; Medicare; VA.
Owner Proprietary corp.
Admissions Requirements Minimum age 18; Medical examination.
Staff Physicians; RNs; LPNs; Nurses' aides; Physical therapists; Activities coordinators; Dietitians; Podiatrists.
Facilities Dining room; Physical therapy room; Activities room; Crafts room; Barber/Beauty shop.
Activities Arts & crafts; Cards; Games; Reading groups; Prayer groups; Movies; Shopping trips; Pet therapy.

Great Neck

Grace Plaza of Great Neck Inc
15 Saint Pauls Pl, Great Neck, NY 11021
(516) 466-3001
Admin Celia Strow. *Dir of Nursing* Jo Wolfson. *Medical Dir* Lester Corn MD.
Licensure Skilled care; Intermediate care. *Beds* SNF 165; ICF 49. *Certified* Medicaid; Medicare.
Owner Proprietary corp.
Admissions Requirements Minimum age 16; Medical examination; Physician's request.
Staff RNs 20 (ft), 10 (pt); LPNs 20 (ft), 12 (pt); Nurses' aides 85 (ft), 30 (pt); Physical therapists 1 (pt); Recreational therapists 4 (ft), 2 (pt); Occupational therapists 1 (pt); Speech therapists 1 (pt); Activities coordinators 1 (ft); Dietitians 2 (ft).
Facilities Dining room; Physical therapy room; Activities room; Crafts room; Laundry room; Barber/Beauty shop.
Activities Arts & crafts; Cards; Games; Reading groups; Prayer groups; Movies; Dances/Social/Cultural gatherings.

Wedgewood Nursing Home
199 Community Dr, Great Neck, NY 11021
(516) 365-9229, 365-3562 FAX
Admin Jay Cherlin. *Dir of Nursing* Rita Berger. *Medical Dir* Dr Nathan Stein.
Licensure Skilled care. *Beds* SNF 200. *Certified* Medicaid; Medicare.
Owner Privately owned.
Facilities Dining room; Physical therapy room; Activities room; Crafts room; Laundry room; Barber/Beauty shop.
Activities Arts & crafts; Cards; Games; Reading groups; Prayer groups; Movies; Shopping trips; Dances/Social/Cultural gatherings; Intergenerational programs; Pet therapy.

Greenhurst

Fenton Park Health Related Facility
Rte 430, Greenhurst, NY 14742
(716) 483-5000
Admin Frederick J Landy. *Dir of Nursing* Donna Johnson RN. *Medical Dir* Dr Charles Sinatra.
Licensure Intermediate care; Alzheimer's care. *Beds* ICF 100. *Private Pay Patients* 30%. *Certified* Medicaid.
Owner Privately owned.
Admissions Requirements Minimum age 18; Medical examination; Physician's request.
Staff Physicians 1 (pt); RNs 3 (ft), 2 (pt); LPNs 8 (ft), 5 (pt); Nurses' aides 19 (ft), 8 (pt); Physical therapists 1 (pt); Recreational therapists 1 (ft); Occupational therapists 1 (pt); Speech therapists 1 (pt); Activities coordinators 1 (ft); Dietitians 1 (ft); Ophthalmologists 1 (pt); Podiatrists 1 (pt); Dentists 1 (pt); Social workers; Medical records; Business office; Maintenance supervisors; Housekeeping; Laundry supervisors.
Languages Swedish.

Facilities Dining room; Physical therapy room; Activities room; Chapel; Crafts room; Laundry room; Barber/Beauty shop; Library; Atrium room; TV lounges; Lake access; Picnic areas; Courtyards.
Activities Arts & crafts; Cards; Games; Reading groups; Prayer groups; Movies; Shopping trips; Dances/Social/Cultural gatherings; Intergenerational programs; Pet therapy; Baking club; Bake sales; Exercise programs; Reality orientation; Music therapy; Field trips; Rummage sales.

Greenport

San Simeon by the Sound—Skilled Nursing Facility
North Rd, Greenport, NY 11944
(516) 477-2110
Admin Arthur Loeffler.
Licensure Skilled care; Intermediate care. *Beds* SNF 91; ICF 59. *Certified* Medicaid; Medicare.
Owner Nonprofit corp.

Groton

Groton Residential Care Facility
120 Sykes St, Groton, NY 13073
(607) 898-5876
Admin Sharon M Pepper, Exec Dir. *Dir of Nursing* Virginia Casey RN. *Medical Dir* David Newman MD.
Licensure Skilled care; Intermediate care. *Beds* SNF 40; ICF 40. *Private Pay Patients* 10%. *Certified* Medicaid; Medicare.
Owner Nonprofit corp.
Admissions Requirements Minimum age 16.
Staff Physicians 1 (pt); RNs 5 (ft), 2 (pt); LPNs 7 (ft); Nurses' aides 21 (ft), 16 (pt); Physical therapists (consultant); Occupational therapists 1 (pt); Speech therapists 1 (pt); Activities coordinators 1 (ft); Dietitians (consultant); Podiatrists 1 (pt).
Facilities Dining room; Physical therapy room; Activities room; Laundry room; Barber/Beauty shop.
Activities Arts & crafts; Cards; Games; Prayer groups; Movies; Shopping trips; Dances/Social/Cultural gatherings; Intergenerational programs.

Guilderland Center

Guilderland Center Nursing Home Inc
127 Main St, Guilderland Center, NY 12085
(518) 861-5141
Admin James Reed & Hazel Reed.
Licensure Skilled care. *Beds* SNF 127. *Certified* Medicaid; Medicare.
Owner Proprietary corp.

Hamburg

Autumn View Manor
S 4650 Southwestern Blvd, Hamburg, NY 14075
(716) 648-2450
Admin Suzette Wilson.
Medical Dir Douglas Moffat.
Licensure Skilled care; Intermediate care. *Beds* SNF 122; ICF 38. *Certified* Medicaid; Medicare.
Owner Privately owned.
Admissions Requirements Minimum age 18; Physician's request.
Staff RNs 20 (ft); LPNs 25 (ft); Nurses' aides 80 (ft); Physical therapists 1 (ft); Recreational therapists 2 (ft), 1 (pt); Occupational therapists 1 (ft); Speech therapists 1 (ft); Activities coordinators 1 (ft); Dietitians 1 (ft); Ophthalmologists 1 (ft); Podiatrists 1 (ft); Dentists 1 (pt); Social workers; Business office personnel; Housekeeping; Laundry; Dietary.

Facilities Dining room; Physical therapy room; Activities room; Crafts room; Laundry room; Barber/Beauty shop.
Activities Arts & crafts; Cards; Games; Reading groups; Prayer groups; Movies; Shopping trips; Dances/Social/Cultural gatherings; Religious services.

Hamburg Health Care Center
5775 Maelou Dr, Hamburg, NY 14075
(716) 648-2820, 648-2980 FAX
Admin Margaret Mary Wagner. *Dir of Nursing* Mary E Gerstner RN. *Medical Dir* Eric Goodwin MD.
Licensure Skilled care; Health related. *Beds* SNF 120; Health related 40.
Owner Privately owned (Robert M Chur).
Admissions Requirements Minimum age 16; Medical examination; Physician's request.
Staff Physicians; RNs; LPNs; Nurses' aides; Physical therapists; Occupational therapists; Speech therapists; Activities coordinators; Dietitians.
Facilities Dining room; Physical therapy room; Activities room; Chapel; Crafts room; Laundry room; Barber/Beauty shop; Occupational therapy room; Speech therapy room; Large front porch.
Activities Arts & crafts; Cards; Games; Reading groups; Prayer groups; Movies; Shopping trips; Dances/Social/Cultural gatherings; Intergenerational programs; Pet therapy; Current events; Cooking; Gardening; Exercise groups; Residents council; Community outings; Ceramics; Ecumenical worship services; Reminiscence groups.

Hamilton

Community Memorial Hospital Inc—Nursing Home Unit
150 Broad St, Hamilton, NY 13346
(315) 824-1100
Admin David Felton.
Licensure Skilled care. *Beds* SNF 40. *Certified* Medicaid; Medicare.
Owner Nonprofit corp.

Harris

Community General Hospital of Sullivan County
PO Box 800, Bushville Rd, Harris, NY 12742
(914) 794-3300
Admin Barbara Hallenbeck. *Dir of Nursing* Mary Ann Burlingame. *Medical Dir* Dr Alan Greenbaum.
Licensure Skilled care. *Beds* SNF 40. *Certified* Medicaid; Medicare.
Owner Nonprofit corp.
Admissions Requirements Medical examination.
Staff Physicians 60 (pt); RNs 5 (ft); LPNs 6 (ft), 1 (pt); Nurses' aides 13 (ft), 1 (pt); Physical therapists 1 (pt); Occupational therapists 1 (pt); Speech therapists 1 (pt); Activities coordinators 1 (ft); Dietitians 1 (pt); Podiatrists 1 (pt).
Facilities Dining room; Physical therapy room; Activities room; Chapel; Crafts room.
Activities Arts & crafts; Cards; Games; Prayer groups; Movies; Shopping trips; Dances/Social/Cultural gatherings.

Hastings on Hudson

Andrus Retirement Community
185 Old Broadway, Hastings on Hudson, NY 10706
(914) 478-3700, 478-3541 FAX
Admin James J Lindes. *Dir of Nursing* Jeanne Brimigion WSN. *Medical Dir* James J Jones MD.

Licensure Skilled care; Intermediate care; Elder care; Alzheimer's care; Retirement. *Beds* SNF 52; ICF/Elder care 195.
Owner Nonprofit corp (Sardna Foundation).
Admissions Requirements Minimum age 65; Medical examination; Independent in all activities of daily living.
Staff Physicians 3 (pt); RNs 7 (ft), 5 (pt); LPNs 5 (ft), 5 (pt); Nurses' aides 16 (ft), 18 (pt); Physical therapists 2 (pt); Recreational therapists 2 (ft); Occupational therapists (consultant); Speech therapists (consultant); Activities coordinators 2 (ft), 1 (pt); Dietitians 2 (ft); Podiatrists (contracted); Audiologists (contracted); Opticians (consultant); Psychiatrists.
Languages Spanish, German, other languages by request.
Facilities Dining room; Physical therapy room; Activities room; Crafts room; Laundry room; Barber/Beauty shop; Library; Card room; Auditorium; Music room; Gardens; Private rooms with private baths.
Activities Arts & crafts; Cards; Games; Reading groups; Prayer groups; Movies; Shopping trips; Dances/Social/Cultural gatherings; Intergenerational programs; Pet therapy; Educational programs.

Haverstraw

Riverside Nursing Home
87 S Rte 9W, Haverstraw, NY 10927
(914) 429-5381
Admin Sarah Muschel.
Licensure Skilled care. *Beds* SNF 100. *Certified* Medicaid; Medicare.
Owner Privately owned.

Hawthorne

Rosary Hill Home
600 Linda Ave, Hawthorne, NY 10532
(914) 769-0114
Licensure Skilled care. *Beds* SNF 72.
Owner Nonprofit corp (Catholic Charities-Arch of New York).

Ruth Taylor Geriatric & Rehabilitation Institute/Westchester County Medical Center
25 Bradhurst Ave, Hawthorne, NY 10532
(914) 285-7762, 285-1578 FAX
Admin J Raymond Diehl Jr. *Dir of Nursing* Patricia Cassidy. *Medical Dir* Steven R Gambert MD.
Licensure Skilled care; Intermediate care; Dementia unit; Alzheimer's care. *Beds* SNF 275; ICF 125. *Certified* Medicaid; Medicare.
Owner Publicly owned.
Admissions Requirements Medical examination.
Staff Physicians 8 (ft), 2 (pt); RNs 30 (ft); LPNs 70 (ft); Nurses' aides 150 (ft); Physical therapists 1 (ft); Recreational therapists 1 (ft), 1 (pt); Occupational therapists 2 (ft); Speech therapists 1 (ft); Activities coordinators 1 (ft); Dietitians 4 (ft); Podiatrists 1 (pt); Audiologists 1 (ft).
Facilities Dining room; Physical therapy room; Activities room; Chapel; Crafts room; Laundry room; Barber/Beauty shop; Occupational therapy room; Coffee shop; Lawn and picnic areas; Physical therapy gym; Auditorium.
Activities Arts & crafts; Cards; Games; Reading groups; Prayer groups; Movies; Shopping trips; Dances/Social/Cultural gatherings; Intergenerational programs; Pet therapy; Resident incentive work programs; RSVP.

Hempstead

Hempstead Park Nursing Home
800 Front St, Hempstead, NY 11554
(516) 560-1446, 560-1301 FAX

Admin David Fridkin. *Dir of Nursing* Gail Baxter. *Medical Dir* K L Tio MD.
Licensure Skilled care; Alzheimer's care. *Beds* SNF 240. *Private Pay Patients* 30%. *Certified* Medicaid; Medicare.
Owner Privately owned.
Admissions Requirements Medical examination; Physician's request.
Staff Physicians 35 (ft); RNs 19 (ft); LPNs 24 (ft); Nurses' aides 109 (ft); Physical therapists 2 (ft); Occupational therapists 1 (ft); Speech therapists 1 (pt); Activities coordinators 1 (ft); Dietitians 2 (ft); Ophthalmologists 3 (ft); Podiatrists 3 (ft); Audiologists 1 (ft).
Languages Spanish, Chinese, Polish, Italian.
Facilities Dining room; Physical therapy room; Activities room; Chapel; Crafts room; Laundry room; Barber/Beauty shop; Outside patio.
Activities Arts & crafts; Cards; Games; Reading groups; Prayer groups; Movies; Dances/Social/Cultural gatherings; Pet therapy; Exercise programs; Alzheimer's support group.

Mayfair Nursing Home
100 Baldwin Rd, Hempstead, NY 11550
(516) 538-7171
Admin John Ryan.
Licensure Skilled care. *Beds* SNF 200. *Certified* Medicaid; Medicare.
Owner Privately owned.

Herkimer

Folts Home
104 N Washington St, Herkimer, NY 13350
(315) 866-6964
Admin Virginia Sheehan.
Medical Dir Stephen P Martell MD.
Licensure Skilled care; Intermediate care. *Beds* SNF 79; ICF 45. *Certified* Medicaid; Medicare.
Owner Nonprofit corp.
Admissions Requirements Minimum age 16; Medical examination.
Staff RNs 10 (ft); LPNs 19 (ft), 6 (pt); Nurses' aides 58 (ft); Physical therapists; Occupational therapists; Activities coordinators; Dietitians; Podiatrists; Dentists.
Affiliation Methodist.
Facilities Dining room; Physical therapy room; Activities room; Chapel; Crafts room; Laundry room; Barber/Beauty shop.
Activities Arts & crafts; Cards; Games; Reading groups; Prayer groups; Movies; Shopping trips; Dances/Social/Cultural gatherings.

Valley Health Services Inc
690 W German St, Herkimer, NY 13350
(315) 866-3330
Admin Carmen C Paone. *Dir of Nursing* Charlotte Szarjeko. *Medical Dir* Dr Richard Trimble.
Licensure Skilled care. *Beds* SNF 128. *Certified* Medicaid; Medicare.
Owner Nonprofit corp.
Admissions Requirements Physician's request.
Staff RNs 11 (ft), 4 (pt); LPNs 24 (ft), 14 (pt); Nurses' aides 31 (ft), 32 (pt); Physical therapists 1 (ft); Recreational therapists 1 (ft); Occupational therapists 1 (ft); Activities coordinators 1 (ft).
Facilities Dining room; Physical therapy room; Crafts room; Barber/Beauty shop.
Activities Arts & crafts; Cards; Games; Reading groups; Prayer groups; Movies; Shopping trips; Dances/Social/Cultural gatherings.

Highland

Hudson Valley Nursing Center
Rte 44/55, Vineyard Ave, Highland, NY
12528
(914) 691-7201
Admin Alan Porter.
Licensure Skilled care; Intermediate care. *Beds*
SNF 120; ICF 70. *Certified* Medicaid;
Medicare.
Owner Privately owned.

Hollis

Hollis Park Manor Nursing Home
191-06 Hillside Ave, Hollis, NY 11423
(718) 479-1010, 464-8245 FAX
Admin Marianne Giacalone. *Dir of Nursing*
Yvonne Grant RN. *Medical Dir* John
Coman MD.
Licensure Skilled care. *Beds* SNF 80. *Private
Pay Patients* 30%. *Certified* Medicaid;
Medicare.
Owner Privately owned.
Admissions Requirements Minimum age 16;
Medical examination.
Staff Physicians 8 (pt); RNs 4 (ft), 2 (pt);
LPNs 9 (ft), 4 (pt); Physical therapists 1 (pt);
Recreational therapists 1 (ft); Occupational
therapists 1 (pt); Speech therapists 1 (pt);
Dietitians 1 (pt); Ophthalmologists 1 (pt);
Podiatrists 1 (pt); Audiologists 1 (pt);
Recreational therapy assistants 1 (pt).
Facilities Dining room; Physical therapy
room; Activities room; Laundry room;
Barber/Beauty shop; Patio; Roof garden;
Dental office; Private, semi-private, and club
room units.
Activities Arts & crafts; Cards; Games;
Reading groups; Prayer groups; Movies;
Dances/Social/Cultural gatherings; Pet
therapy.

Holliswood Care Center Inc
195-44 Woodhull Ave, Hollis, NY 11423
(718) 740-3500
Admin Hal Schifter.
Licensure Skilled care; Intermediate care. *Beds*
SNF 116; ICF 200. *Certified* Medicaid;
Medicare.
Owner Proprietary corp.

Holmes

Kent Nursing Home
RR 1 Box 85, Holmes, NY 12531
(914) 878-3241, 878-4218 FAX
Admin Joan Kean. *Dir of Nursing* Judith A
Robins. *Medical Dir* Dr Pines.
Licensure Skilled care. *Beds* SNF 160. *Private
Pay Patients* 10%. *Certified* Medicaid;
Medicare.
Owner Privately owned.
Admissions Requirements Minimum age 16.
Staff Physicians 12 (pt); RNs 9 (ft), 3 (pt);
LPNs 7 (ft), 7 (pt); Nurses' aides 29 (ft), 20
(pt); Physical therapists 1 (ft); Recreational
therapists 1 (ft), 2 (pt); Occupational
therapists 1 (pt); Speech therapists 1 (pt);
Activities coordinators 1 (ft); Dietitians 1
(pt); Podiatrists 2 (pt); Audiologists 1 (pt).
Facilities Dining room; Physical therapy
room; Activities room; Crafts room; Laundry
room; Barber/Beauty shop.
Activities Arts & crafts; Cards; Games;
Reading groups; Prayer groups; Movies;
Dances/Social/Cultural gatherings; Pet
therapy.

Hoosick Falls

Hoosick Falls Health Center
21 Danforth St, Hoosick Falls, NY 12090
(518) 686-4371

Admin Leslie Beadle. *Dir of Nursing* Mildred
C Lewis RN. *Medical Dir* Dr Newton
Krumdieck.
Licensure Skilled care. *Beds* SNF 41. *Certified*
Medicaid; Medicare.
Owner Nonprofit corp.
Staff RNs 2 (ft), 4 (pt); LPNs 4 (ft); Nurses'
aides 11 (ft), 8 (pt); Physical therapists 1
(pt); Occupational therapists 1 (pt); Speech
therapists 1 (pt); Activities coordinators 1
(ft); Dietitians 1 (pt); Physical therapy aides
1 (ft).
Facilities Dining room; Physical therapy
room; Activities room; Laundry room;
Barber/Beauty shop.
Activities Arts & crafts; Games; Reading
groups; Prayer groups; Movies; Shopping
trips; Dances/Social/Cultural gatherings.

Hornell

Hornell Nursing Home & HRF
434 Monroe Ave, Hornell, NY 14843
(607) 324-7740
Admin James Bicker.
Licensure Skilled care; Intermediate care. *Beds*
SNF 60; ICF 54. *Certified* Medicaid;
Medicare.
Owner Privately owned.

Horseheads

**Bethany Nursing Home & Health Related
Facility Inc**
751 Watkins Rd, Horseheads, NY 14845
(607) 739-8711
Admin Sharon M Pepper. *Dir of Nursing*
Stephanie Mitchell RN. *Medical Dir* Dr
Joseph Calderone.
Licensure Skilled care; Retirement. *Beds* SNF
80. *Certified* Medicaid; Medicare.
Owner Nonprofit corp.
Admissions Requirements Minimum age 16;
Physician's request.
Staff RNs 12 (ft), 3 (pt); LPNs 16 (ft), 2 (pt);
Nurses' aides 47 (ft), 4 (pt); Activities
coordinators 1 (ft), 1 (pt); Dietitians 1 (ft);
Social workers 1 (ft), 1 (pt).
Affiliation Methodist.
Facilities Dining room; Physical therapy
room; Activities room; Crafts room; Laundry
room; Barber/Beauty shop; Library.
Activities Arts & crafts; Cards; Games;
Reading groups; Prayer groups; Movies;
Shopping trips; Dances/Social/Cultural
gatherings.

Elcor Health Home
110 Colonial Dr, Horseheads, NY 14845
(607) 739-0304
Admin Richard Poes.
Medical Dir Dr John Roemmelt.
Licensure Skilled care. *Beds* SNF 105.
Certified Medicaid; Medicare.
Owner Privately owned.
Staff RNs 3 (ft), 9 (pt); LPNs 10 (ft), 5 (pt);
Nurses' aides 46 (ft), 21 (pt); Activities
coordinators 1 (ft).
Facilities Dining room; Physical therapy
room; Activities room; Crafts room; Laundry
room; Barber/Beauty shop; Dental room.
Activities Arts & crafts; Cards; Games;
Reading groups; Prayer groups; Movies;
Shopping trips; Dances/Social/Cultural
gatherings.

**Elcor's Marriott Manor Health Related
Facility**
108 Colonial Dr, Horseheads, NY 14845
(607) 739-0304
Admin Richard Poes.
Medical Dir John Roemmelt MD.
Licensure Intermediate care. *Beds* ICF 120.
Certified Medicaid.
Owner Privately owned.
Admissions Requirements Medical
examination.

Staff Physicians 1 (pt); RNs 2 (ft), 2 (pt);
LPNs 6 (ft), 8 (pt); Nurses' aides 17 (ft), 13
(pt); Activities coordinators 2 (ft), 1 (pt);
Dietitians 1 (pt).
Facilities Dining room; Physical therapy
room; Activities room; Crafts room; Laundry
room; Barber/Beauty shop; Library.
Activities Arts & crafts; Cards; Games;
Reading groups; Prayer groups; Movies;
Shopping trips; Dances/Social/Cultural
gatherings.

Houghton

Houghton Nursing Care Center Inc
PO Box G-12, RD 1, Houghton, NY 14744
(716) 567-2207
Admin Harold McIntire.
Medical Dir Storer Emmett MD.
Licensure Skilled care; Intermediate care. *Beds*
SNF 40; ICF 40. *Certified* Medicaid;
Medicare.
Owner Proprietary corp.
Admissions Requirements Minimum age 16;
Medical examination.
Staff Physicians 3 (pt); RNs 5 (ft), 3 (pt);
LPNs 4 (ft), 6 (pt); Nurses' aides 28 (ft), 15
(pt); Activities coordinators 1 (ft), 1 (pt);
Dietitians 1 (ft).
Facilities Dining room; Physical therapy
room; Activities room; Crafts room; Laundry
room; Barber/Beauty shop; Library.
Activities Arts & crafts; Cards; Games;
Reading groups; Prayer groups; Movies;
Shopping trips.

Hudson

Eden Park Nursing Home
30 Prospect Ave, Hudson, NY 12534
(518) 828-9439
Admin Michael A Palmieri.
Medical Dir Dr Rosewall Shaw.
Licensure Skilled care. *Beds* SNF 78. *Certified*
Medicaid; Medicare.
Owner Proprietary corp (Eden Park Health
Services Inc).
Admissions Requirements Minimum age 16;
Medical examination; Physician's request.
Staff Physicians 1 (pt); Physical therapists 1
(ft); Occupational therapists 1 (pt); Speech
therapists 1 (pt); Activities coordinators 1
(ft), 1 (pt); Dietitians 1 (pt);
Ophthalmologists 1 (pt); Podiatrists 1 (pt);
Audiologists 1 (pt); Dentists 1 (pt).
Facilities Dining room; Physical therapy
room; Activities room; Crafts room; Laundry
room; Barber/Beauty shop.
Activities Arts & crafts; Cards; Games;
Reading groups; Prayer groups; Movies;
Shopping trips; Dances/Social/Cultural
gatherings.

Firemen's Home of the State of New York
Harry-Howard Ave, Hudson, NY 12534
(518) 828-7695
Admin David C Gluck. *Dir of Nursing* Susan
Neer RN.
Licensure Skilled care; Intermediate care. *Beds*
SNF 90; ICF 50.
Owner Nonprofit corp.
Admissions Requirements Must be volunteer
firefighter.
Staff RNs 25 (ft), 4 (pt); LPNs 5 (ft), 1 (pt);
Nurses' aides 32 (ft), 6 (pt); Physical
therapists 1 (pt); Recreational therapists 1
(ft), 1 (pt); Occupational therapists 1 (pt);
Activities coordinators 1 (pt); Dietitians 1
(pt); Ophthalmologists 1 (pt).
Affiliation Volunteer Firefighting Service.
Facilities Dining room; Physical therapy
room; Activities room; Chapel; Crafts room;
Laundry room; Barber/Beauty shop; Library;
TV room.

Activities Arts & crafts; Cards; Games; Reading groups; Prayer groups; Movies; Shopping trips; Dances/Social/Cultural gatherings; Parades; Trips; Conventions.

Huntington

Carillon House Nursing Home
830 Park Ave, Huntington, NY 11743
(516) 271-5800
Admin Joseph F Carillo II.
Licensure Skilled care; Intermediate care. *Beds* SNF 237; ICF 85. *Certified* Medicaid; Medicare.
Owner Privately owned.

Hilaire Farm Nursing Home
Hilaire Dr, Huntington, NY 11743
(516) 427-0254
Admin Michael M Gottsegen.
Licensure Skilled care. *Beds* SNF 76. *Certified* Medicaid; Medicare.
Owner Privately owned.

Huntington Station

Birchwood Nursing Home
78 Birchwood Dr, Huntington Station, NY 11746
(516) 423-3673
Admin Dr Timothy P Steffens. *Dir of Nursing* Monna Rockefeller RN. *Medical Dir* Dr Frederick R Long.
Licensure Skilled care; Intermediate care; Retirement. *Beds* SNF 120; ICF 75. *Certified* Medicaid; Medicare.
Owner Privately owned.
Admissions Requirements Minimum age 18; Medical examination; Physician's request.
Staff Physicians 32 (pt); RNs 3 (ft), 13 (pt); LPNs 8 (ft), 24 (pt); Nurses' aides 52 (ft), 34 (pt); Physical therapists 2 (ft); Recreational therapists 3 (ft); Occupational therapists 1 (pt); Speech therapists 1 (pt); Activities coordinators 1 (ft); Dietitians 1 (ft); Ophthalmologists 1 (pt); Podiatrists 1 (pt).
Facilities Dining room; Physical therapy room; Activities room; Chapel; Crafts room; Laundry room; Barber/Beauty shop; Library.
Activities Arts & crafts; Cards; Games; Reading groups; Prayer groups; Movies; Shopping trips; Dances/Social/Cultural gatherings.

Hyde Park

Victory Lake Nursing Center
101 N Quaker Ln, Hyde Park, NY 12538
(914) 229-9177
Admin George H Pelote.
Licensure Skilled care. *Beds* SNF 120. *Certified* Medicaid; Medicare.
Owner Nonprofit corp.
Admissions Requirements Minimum age 16; Medical examination; Physician's request.
Staff Physicians 1 (ft), 8 (pt); RNs 16 (ft), 6 (pt); LPNs 12 (ft), 8 (pt); Nurses' aides 46 (ft), 12 (pt); Physical therapists 1 (pt); Reality therapists 2 (ft); Recreational therapists 2 (ft); Occupational therapists 1 (pt); Speech therapists 1 (pt); Activities coordinators 1 (ft); Dietitians 2 (ft); Ophthalmologists 1 (pt); Podiatrists 1 (pt); Audiologists 1 (pt); Dentists 1 (pt).
Facilities Dining room; Physical therapy room; Activities room; Chapel; Crafts room; Laundry room; Barber/Beauty shop; Library.
Activities Arts & crafts; Cards; Games; Reading groups; Prayer groups; Movies; Shopping trips; Dances/Social/Cultural gatherings.

Ilion

Mohawk Valley Nursing Home Inc
295 W Main St, Ilion, NY 13357
(315) 895-7474
Admin Marjorie Dolch.
Medical Dir Richard Brown DO.
Licensure Skilled care. *Beds* SNF 120. *Certified* Medicaid; Medicare.
Owner Nonprofit corp.
Admissions Requirements Minimum age 16; Medical examination; Physician's request.
Staff RNs 7 (ft), 9 (pt); LPNs 13 (ft), 13 (pt); Nurses' aides 49 (ft), 50 (pt); Physical therapists 1 (ft), 1 (pt); Occupational therapists 1 (ft); Activities coordinators 1 (ft); Dentists 1 (pt).
Facilities Dining room; Activities room; Chapel; Crafts room; Barber/Beauty shop.
Activities Arts & crafts; Cards; Games; Reading groups; Prayer groups; Movies; Dances/Social/Cultural gatherings.

Irving

Lake Shore Hospital Inc HRF
845 Rtes 5 & 20, Irving, NY 14081
(716) 549-0620
Admin Ivan Tarnopoll. *Dir of Nursing* Starlene Luther RN. *Medical Dir* Russell J Joy DO.
Licensure Intermediate care. *Beds* ICF 80. *Certified* Medicaid.
Owner Nonprofit corp.
Admissions Requirements Minimum age 16; Physician's request.
Staff Physicians 1 (pt); RNs 1 (ft), 1 (pt); LPNs 6 (ft), 5 (pt); Nurses' aides 12 (ft), 13 (pt); Physical therapists 1 (pt); Recreational therapists 1 (ft), 2 (pt); Occupational therapists 1 (ft), 5 (pt); Dietitians 1 (ft).
Facilities Dining room; Physical therapy room; Activities room; Crafts room; Barber/Beauty shop.
Activities Arts & crafts; Cards; Games; Reading groups; Prayer groups; Movies; Shopping trips; Dances/Social/Cultural gatherings; Cooking.

Lake Shore Nursing Home Inc
801 Rtes 5 & 20, Irving, NY 14081
(716) 934-4531
Licensure Skilled care. *Beds* SNF 40.
Owner Proprietary corp.

Island Park

Bayview Nursing Home
1 Long Beach Rd, Island Park, NY 11558
(516) 432-0300
Admin Richard Lap.
Licensure Skilled care. *Beds* SNF 185. *Certified* Medicaid; Medicare.
Owner Nonprofit corp.

Ithaca

Lakeside Nursing Home Inc
1229 Trumansburg Rd, Ithaca, NY 14850
(607) 273-8072
Admin Jeffery Earle. *Dir of Nursing* Mary Ellen Schreher. *Medical Dir* Jerry Hersh MD.
Licensure Skilled care; Intermediate care. *Beds* SNF 160; ICF 100. *Certified* Medicaid; Medicare.
Owner Proprietary corp.
Admissions Requirements Minimum age 16; Medical examination; Physician's request.
Staff Physicians 1 (pt); RNs 20 (ft), 10 (pt); LPNs 10 (ft), 5 (pt); Nurses' aides 100 (ft), 20 (pt); Physical therapists 1 (ft); Recreational therapists 2 (ft), 1 (pt); Occupational therapists 1 (pt); Speech

therapists 1 (pt); Activities coordinators 1 (ft); Dietitians 1 (ft); Ophthalmologists 1 (pt); Podiatrists 1 (pt); Dentists 1 (pt).
Facilities Dining room; Physical therapy room; Activities room; Chapel; Crafts room; Laundry room; Barber/Beauty shop; Library.
Activities Arts & crafts; Cards; Games; Reading groups; Prayer groups; Movies; Shopping trips; Dances/Social/Cultural gatherings.

Oak Hill Manor Nursing Home
602 Hudson St, Ithaca, NY 14850
(607) 272-8282
Admin Eugene Battaglini.
Medical Dir Thomas Mosher MD.
Licensure Skilled care. *Beds* SNF 60. *Certified* Medicaid; Medicare.
Owner Nonprofit corp.
Admissions Requirements Minimum age 16.
Staff RNs 6 (ft), 4 (pt); LPNs 3 (ft), 4 (pt); Nurses' aides 25 (ft), 7 (pt); Physical therapists 1 (pt); Recreational therapists 1 (ft), 1 (pt); Speech therapists 1 (pt); Dietitians 1 (pt).
Facilities Dining room; Physical therapy room; Activities room; Laundry room; Barber/Beauty shop.
Activities Arts & crafts; Cards; Games; Reading groups; Prayer groups; Movies; Shopping trips; Dances/Social/Cultural gatherings.

Reconstruction Home Inc
318 S Albany St, Ithaca, NY 14850
(607) 273-4166
Admin Jerome Lutherhouse.
Licensure Skilled care. *Beds* SNF 80. *Certified* Medicaid; Medicare.
Owner Nonprofit corp.

Jamaica

Chapin Home for the Aging
165-01 Chapin Pkwy, Jamaica, NY 11432
(718) 739-2523, 739-4797 FAX
Admin Janet M Unger. *Dir of Nursing* Evelyn McPherson RN. *Medical Dir* John J Rawlings MD.
Licensure Skilled care; Health related facility. *Beds* SNF 49; Health related facility 29. *Private Pay Patients* 13%. *Certified* Medicaid; Medicare.
Owner Nonprofit corp.
Admissions Requirements Medical examination.
Staff Physicians 4 (pt); RNs 4 (ft), 2 (pt); LPNs 6 (ft), 4 (pt); Nurses' aides 22 (ft), 2 (pt); Physical therapists 1 (pt); Occupational therapists 1 (pt); Speech therapists 1 (pt); Activities coordinators 1 (ft); Dietitians 1 (pt); Podiatrists 1 (pt).
Languages Chinese, French, Spanish, Greek, Italian, German, Tagalog.
Facilities Dining room; Physical therapy room; Activities room; Chapel; Crafts room; Laundry room; Barber/Beauty shop; Library; General store.
Activities Arts & crafts; Cards; Games; Reading groups; Prayer groups; Movies; Shopping trips; Intergenerational programs; Pet therapy; Piano music.

Highland Care Center
91-31 175th St, Jamaica, NY 11432
(718) 657-6363
Admin Chiam Kaminetsky.
Licensure Skilled care; Intermediate care. *Beds* SNF 120; ICF 200. *Certified* Medicaid; Medicare.
Owner Privately owned.

Jamaica Hospital Nursing Home Company Inc
90-28 Van Wyck Expwy, Jamaica, NY 11418
(718) 291-5300
Admin Joseph S Kane. *Dir of Nursing* Ann Bonadio. *Medical Dir* Charles Huey MD.

Licensure Skilled care; Alzheimer's care. *Beds* SNF 200. *Certified* Medicaid; Medicare. *Owner* Nonprofit corp.
Staff Physicians 5 (pt); RNs 20 (ft); LPNs 17 (ft); Nurses' aides; Physical therapists 2 (ft), 1 (pt); Recreational therapists 1 (ft); Occupational therapists 2 (ft); Speech therapists 1 (pt); Activities coordinators 1 (ft); Dietitians 1 (ft); Ophthalmologists 1 (pt); Podiatrists 1 (pt); Dentists 1 (pt).
Facilities Dining room; Physical therapy room; Activities room; Laundry room; Barber/Beauty shop; Library.
Activities Arts & crafts; Cards; Games; Reading groups; Movies; Shopping trips; Dances/Social/Cultural gatherings.

Monsignor Fitzpatrick Pavilion for Skilled Nursing Care
152-11 89th Ave, Jamaica, NY 11432
(718) 291-4300, ext 2870, 291-4300, ext 2898 FAX
Admin Gregory R Bradley. *Dir of Nursing* Eileen Finkle. *Medical Dir* Dr Robert Caruso.
Licensure Skilled care. *Beds* SNF 105. *Certified* Medicaid; Medicare.
Owner Nonprofit corp (Catholic Medical Center of Brooklyn & Queens).
Staff Physicians; RNs; LPNs; Nurses' aides; Physical therapists; Recreational therapists; Occupational therapists; Speech therapists; Activities coordinators; Dietitians; Ophthalmologists; Podiatrists; Audiologists.
Affiliation Roman Catholic.
Facilities Dining room; Physical therapy room; Activities room; Chapel; Crafts room; Barber/Beauty shop; Library.
Activities Arts & crafts; Cards; Games; Reading groups; Prayer groups; Movies; Shopping trips; Dances/Social/Cultural gatherings; Intergenerational programs; Pet therapy.

Margaret Tietz Center for Nursing Care Inc
164-11 Chapin Pkwy, Jamaica, NY 11432
(718) 523-6400
Admin Kenneth M Brown. *Dir of Nursing* Carol McNally. *Medical Dir* Gail Lowenstein MD.
Licensure Skilled care; Intermediate care; Alzheimer's care. *Beds* SNF 120; ICF 80. *Certified* Medicaid; Medicare.
Owner Nonprofit corp.
Admissions Requirements Minimum age 18; Medical examination; Physician's request.
Staff Physicians 1 (ft), 5 (pt); Physical therapists 2 (pt); Recreational therapists 2 (ft), 2 (pt); Occupational therapists 2 (ft); Speech therapists 1 (pt); Activities coordinators 1 (ft); Dietitians 1 (ft), 1 (pt); Ophthalmologists 1 (pt); Podiatrists 1 (pt); Dentists 1 (pt).
Facilities Dining room; Physical therapy room; Activities room; Chapel; Crafts room; Laundry room; Barber/Beauty shop; Library; Garden; Terraces on each floor.
Activities Arts & crafts; Cards; Games; Reading groups; Prayer groups; Movies; Shopping trips; Dances/Social/Cultural gatherings.

Jamaica Estates

Hillside Manor Health Related Facility
182-15 Hillside Ave, Jamaica Estates, NY 11432
(718) 291-8200
Admin Bengt Barbaccia.
Licensure Skilled care; Intermediate care. *Beds* SNF 205; ICF 195. *Certified* Medicaid; Medicare.
Owner Privately owned.

Jamestown

Fenton Park Nursing Home
150 Prather Ave, Jamestown, NY 14701
(716) 488-1921
Admin Charlotte M Albano. *Dir of Nursing* Joan Kuell RN. *Medical Dir* Charles Sinatra MD.
Licensure Skilled care. *Beds* SNF 200. *Certified* Medicaid; Medicare.
Owner Privately owned.
Admissions Requirements Physician's request.
Staff Physicians; RNs; LPNs; Nurses' aides; Physical therapists; Recreational therapists; Occupational therapists; Speech therapists; Activities coordinators; Dietitians; Ophthalmologists; Podiatrists; Dentists.
Facilities Dining room; Physical therapy room; Activities room; Crafts room; Laundry room; Barber/Beauty shop.
Activities Arts & crafts; Cards; Games; Reading groups; Prayer groups; Movies; Shopping trips; Dances/Social/Cultural gatherings.

Lutheran Retirement Home
715 Falconer St, Jamestown, NY 14701
(716) 665-4905
Admin Floyd Addison.
Medical Dir John D Voltmann MD.
Licensure Skilled care; Intermediate care. *Beds* SNF 124; ICF 128. *Certified* Medicaid; Medicare.
Owner Nonprofit corp.
Staff RNs 12 (ft); LPNs 16 (ft); Nurses' aides 65 (ft); Physical therapists 1 (pt); Recreational therapists 4 (ft), 1 (pt); Occupational therapists 1 (pt); Speech therapists 1 (pt); Activities coordinators 1 (ft); Dietitians 3 (ft), 1 (pt); Podiatrists 1 (pt); Dentists 1 (pt).
Affiliation Lutheran.
Facilities Dining room; Physical therapy room; Activities room; Chapel; Laundry room; Barber/Beauty shop.
Activities Arts & crafts; Cards; Games; Reading groups; Prayer groups; Movies; Shopping trips; Dances/Social/Cultural gatherings.

Manor Oak Skilled Nursing Facilities Inc
423 Baker St, Jamestown, NY 14701
(716) 484-9181
Admin Francis Stolte; James E Bottomley, Asst. *Dir of Nursing* Valerie Czajka RN. *Medical Dir* Dr Alina T Wiecha.
Licensure Skilled care. *Beds* SNF 104. *Certified* Medicaid; Medicare.
Owner Proprietary corp.
Admissions Requirements Minimum age 16; Physician's request.
Staff RNs 10 (ft); LPNs 14 (ft); Nurses' aides 47 (ft); Physical therapists 1 (ft); Occupational therapists 1 (pt); Dietitians 1 (pt).
Facilities Dining room; Physical therapy room; Activities room; Crafts room; Barber/ Beauty shop.
Activities Arts & crafts; Cards; Games; Reading groups; Movies; Shopping trips; Dances/Social/Cultural gatherings; Pet therapy; Music therapy; Rehabilitation program.

Johnson City

James G Johnston Memorial Nursing Home
285 Deyo Hill Rd, Johnson City, NY 13790
(607) 798-1001
Licensure Skilled care; Intermediate care. *Beds* SNF 40; ICF 40.
Owner Proprietary corp.

Susquehanna Nursing Home & Health Related Facility
282 Riverside Dr, Johnson City, NY 13790
(607) 729-9206, 797-3229 FAX

Admin Paul J Sadlon. *Dir of Nursing* Doris L Render RN. *Medical Dir* Dr Vincent I Maddi.
Licensure Skilled care; Intermediate care; Retirement; Adult day care; Alzheimer's care. *Beds* SNF 120; ICF 40; Retirement apts 24; Adult day care 20. *Private Pay Patients* 50%. *Certified* Medicaid; Medicare.
Owner Privately owned.
Admissions Requirements Medical examination.
Staff RNs; LPNs; Nurses' aides; Physical therapists; Recreational therapists; Occupational therapists; Speech therapists; Activities coordinators; Dietitians; Podiatrists; Audiologists.
Facilities Dining room; Physical therapy room; Activities room; Crafts room; Barber/ Beauty shop; Adult day care.
Activities Arts & crafts; Cards; Games; Reading groups; Prayer groups; Movies; Shopping trips; Dances/Social/Cultural gatherings; Intergenerational programs; Pet therapy.

Wilson Hospital Skilled Nursing Facility
33-57 Harrison St, Johnson City, NY 13790
(607) 770-6289
Admin Alan Kopman.
Medical Dir Louis R Borelli MD.
Licensure Skilled care. *Beds* SNF 100. *Certified* Medicaid; Medicare.
Owner Nonprofit corp.
Admissions Requirements Minimum age 16; Medical examination; Physician's request.
Staff RNs 15 (ft), 8 (pt); LPNs 13 (ft), 7 (pt); Nurses' aides 24 (ft), 14 (pt); Physical therapists 3 (ft), 3 (pt); Occupational therapists 2 (ft); Speech therapists 1 (ft); Activities coordinators 2 (ft); Dietitians 1 (pt); Audiologists 1 (ft); Dentists 1 (pt).
Facilities Dining room; Physical therapy room; Laundry room; Barber/Beauty shop.
Activities Arts & crafts; Games; Reading groups; Prayer groups; Movies; Shopping trips; Dances/Social/Cultural gatherings.

Johnstown

Wells Nursing Home Inc
201 W Madison Ave, Johnstown, NY 12095
(518) 762-4546
Admin Joyce Brower. *Dir of Nursing* Nita Bell RN. *Medical Dir* Vincent Leonti MD.
Licensure Skilled care. *Beds* SNF 60. *Certified* Medicaid; Medicare.
Owner Nonprofit corp.
Admissions Requirements Medical examination; Physician's request.
Staff Physicians 2 (pt); RNs 4 (ft), 3 (pt); LPNs 2 (ft), 2 (pt); Nurses' aides 18 (ft), 20 (pt); Physical therapists 1 (ft); Activities coordinators 1 (ft), 1 (pt); Dietitians 1 (pt).
Facilities Dining room; Physical therapy room; Activities room; Crafts room; Laundry room; Barber/Beauty shop.
Activities Arts & crafts; Cards; Games; Reading groups; Prayer groups; Movies; Shopping trips; Dances/Social/Cultural gatherings.

Kenmore

Abbey Nursing Home
2865 Elmwood Ave, Kenmore, NY 14217
(716) 876-5900
Admin Frances Larson.
Medical Dir Dr C T Yu.
Licensure Skilled care. *Beds* SNF 79. *Certified* Medicaid; Medicare.
Owner Proprietary corp.
Admissions Requirements Minimum age 60; Medical examination.
Staff Physicians 5 (pt); RNs 4 (ft), 8 (pt); LPNs 5 (ft), 4 (pt); Nurses' aides 21 (ft), 20 (pt); Physical therapists 1 (pt); Recreational therapists 1 (ft); Occupational therapists 1

(pt); Speech therapists 1 (pt); Activities
coordinators 1 (ft); Dietitians 1 (ft);
Podiatrists 1 (pt); Audiologists 1 (pt);
Dentists 1 (pt).
Facilities Dining room; Physical therapy
room; Activities room; Laundry room.
Activities Arts & crafts; Cards; Games;
Reading groups; Prayer groups; Movies;
Dances/Social/Cultural gatherings; Picnics.

Kenmore Mercy Hospital Skilled Nursing Facility
2950 Elmwood Ave, Kenmore, NY 14217
(716) 879-6101
Admin Francis J Redding, Dir; Shari Borner,
Asst Dir. *Dir of Nursing* Jacqueline M
Pellien RN. *Medical Dir* Dr Joseph C
Tutton.
Licensure Skilled care. *Beds* SNF 80. *Certified*
Medicaid; Medicare.
Owner Nonprofit corp.
Admissions Requirements Medical
examination.
Staff Physicians 1 (ft); RNs 8 (ft), 7 (pt);
LPNs 10 (ft), 9 (pt); Physical therapists 4
(pt); Occupational therapists 1 (pt); Speech
therapists 1 (pt); Activities coordinators 1
(ft); Dietitians 1 (pt); Podiatrists 1 (pt);
Dentists 1 (pt).
Affiliation Roman Catholic.
Facilities Dining room; Physical therapy
room; Activities room; Chapel; Barber/
Beauty shop.
Activities Arts & crafts; Games; Prayer groups;
Movies; Dances/Social/Cultural gatherings;
Baking; Sing-alongs; Exercise class; Music
therapy; Field trips.

Schofield Residence
3333 Elmwood Ave, Kenmore, NY 14217
(716) 874-1566
Admin Edward Gray.
Licensure Skilled care; Intermediate care. *Beds*
SNF 80; ICF 40. *Certified* Medicaid;
Medicare.
Owner Nonprofit corp.

Kings Park

St Johnland Nursing Home Inc
395 Sunken Meadow Rd, Kings Park, NY
11754
(516) 269-5800, 269-5876 FAX
Admin Joan R Wood. *Dir of Nursing* Doris
Bierhanzl. *Medical Dir* Thomas J Morley.
Licensure Skilled care; Intermediate care;
Adult day health care; Alzheimer's care.
Beds SNF 160; ICF 40; Adult day health
care 40. *Certified* Medicaid; Medicare.
Owner Nonprofit corp.
Admissions Requirements Medical
examination; Physician's request.
Languages Italian, German.
Facilities Dining room; Physical therapy
room; Activities room; Chapel; Crafts room;
Laundry room; Barber/Beauty shop; Library.
Activities Arts & crafts; Cards; Games;
Reading groups; Prayer groups; Movies;
Shopping trips; Dances/Social/Cultural
gatherings; Intergenerational programs; Pet
therapy.

Kingston

Albany Avenue Nursing Home
166 Albany Ave, Kingston, NY 12401
(914) 338-1780
Admin Charlotte Shuler. *Dir of Nursing*
Elnora McSpirit RN. *Medical Dir* Johannes
Weltin MD.
Licensure Skilled care. *Beds* SNF 22. *Private
Pay Patients* 100%.
Owner Proprietary corp.
Admissions Requirements Minimum age 21.
Staff RNs 5 (ft), 9 (pt); LPNs 3 (ft), 5 (pt);
Nurses' aides 4 (ft), 8 (pt); Activities
coordinators 1 (ft).

Facilities Activities room; Laundry room.
Activities Arts & crafts; Cards; Games;
Reading groups; Prayer groups; Movies;
Music.

Hutton Nursing Home
346 Washington Ave, Kingston, NY 12401
(914) 331-6327, 331-0247 FAX
Admin Paula A Anderson, acting. *Dir of
Nursing* Vincent S Mogavero, Acting.
Medical Dir Chester Robbins MD.
Licensure Skilled care. *Beds* SNF 80. *Certified*
Medicaid; Medicare.
Owner Privately owned (Charles A Glessing).
Admissions Requirements Minimum age 16;
Medical examination; Physician's request.
Staff RNs 5 (ft), 6 (pt); LPNs 8 (ft), 4 (pt);
Nurses' aides 33 (ft), 12 (pt); Physical
therapists 1 (ft); Occupational therapists 1
(ft); Activities coordinators 1 (ft); Dietitians
1 (pt).
Facilities Dining room; Physical therapy
room; Activities room; Crafts room; Barber/
Beauty shop.
Activities Arts & crafts; Cards; Games;
Reading groups; Prayer groups; Movies;
Shopping trips; Dances/Social/Cultural
gatherings; Intergenerational programs; Pet
therapy.

Ulster County Infirmary & Annex
Golden Hill Dr, Kingston, NY 12401
(914) 339-4540, 339-3709
Admin Elnora McSpirit.
Medical Dir Dr Arthur Carr.
Licensure Skilled care; Intermediate care. *Beds*
SNF 200; ICF 80. *Certified* Medicaid;
Medicare.
Owner Publicly owned.
Staff Physicians 7 (pt); RNs 28 (ft); LPNs 24
(ft); Nurses' aides 106 (ft); Physical
therapists 1 (pt); Occupational therapists 1
(pt); Activities coordinators 2 (ft); Dietitians
1 (ft); Dentists 1 (pt).
Facilities Dining room; Physical therapy
room; Activities room; Chapel; Crafts room;
Laundry room; Barber/Beauty shop; Library.
Activities Arts & crafts; Cards; Games;
Reading groups; Prayer groups; Movies;
Shopping trips; Dances/Social/Cultural
gatherings.

Lake Placid

Placid Memorial Hospital Inc
Church St, Lake Placid, NY 12946
(518) 523-3311
Beds 15.
Owner Nonprofit corp.

Uihlein Mercy Center
420 Old Military Rd, Lake Placid, NY 12946
(518) 523-2464
Admin Sr Mary Camillus RSM. *Dir of Nursing*
Joan Hasley. *Medical Dir* H Douglas Wilson
MD.
Licensure Skilled care; Alzheimer's care. *Beds*
SNF 156. *Private Pay Patients* 21%. *Certified*
Medicaid; Medicare.
Owner Nonprofit corp.
Admissions Requirements Minimum age 16;
Medical examination; Physician's request.
Staff Physicians 1 (ft), 3 (pt); RNs 9 (ft), 8
(pt); LPNs 11 (ft), 8 (pt); Nurses' aides 60
(ft), 20 (pt); Physical therapists 2 (pt);
Recreational therapists 1 (ft); Occupational
therapists 1 (pt); Speech therapists 1 (pt);
Activities coordinators 1 (ft); Dietitians 1
(ft); Ophthalmologists 1 (pt); Podiatrists 1
(pt); Audiologists 1 (pt).
Affiliation Roman Catholic.
Facilities Dining room; Physical therapy
room; Activities room; Chapel; Crafts room;
Laundry room; Barber/Beauty shop; Library.
Activities Arts & crafts; Cards; Games; Prayer
groups; Movies; Shopping trips; Dances/
Social/Cultural gatherings; Intergenerational
programs; Pet therapy.

Lancaster

Furgala Nursing Home
1818 Como Park Blvd, Lancaster, NY 14086
(716) 683-6165
Admin Chester J Furgala. *Dir of Nursing*
Caroline P Furgala RN BS. *Medical Dir* Dr
Pedro Joven.
Licensure Skilled care. *Beds* SNF 89. *Private
Pay Patients* 50%. *Certified* Medicaid;
Medicare.
Owner Privately owned.
Admissions Requirements Minimum age 18;
Medical examination; Physician's request.
Staff RNs 9 (ft); LPNs 6 (ft), 2 (pt); Nurses'
aides 50 (ft), 5 (pt); Physical therapists 1
(pt); Reality therapists 1 (pt); Recreational
therapists 1 (ft); Occupational therapists 1
(ft); Speech therapists 1 (pt); Activities
coordinators; Dietitians 1 (pt);
Ophthalmologists 1 (pt); Podiatrists 1 (pt);
Audiologists 1 (pt).
Languages Polish, Italian.
Facilities Dining room; Physical therapy
room; Activities room; Chapel; Crafts room;
Laundry room; Barber/Beauty shop; 2
Courtyards.
Activities Arts & crafts; Cards; Games;
Reading groups; Prayer groups; Movies;
Shopping trips; Dances/Social/Cultural
gatherings; Intergenerational programs; Pet
therapy.

Latham

Our Lady of Hope Residence—Little Sisters of the Poor
1 Jeanne Jugan Ln, Latham, NY 12110
(518) 785-4551
Admin M Mary Vincent.
Licensure Skilled care; Intermediate care. *Beds*
SNF 80; ICF 97. *Certified* Medicaid;
Medicare.
Owner Nonprofit corp (Little Sisters of the
Poor).
Affiliation Roman Catholic.

Leroy

Leroy Village Green Nursing Home & Health Related Facility Inc
10 Munson St, Leroy, NY 14482
(716) 768-2561
Admin Robert Harrington.
Medical Dir Nayan Kumar MD.
Licensure Skilled care; Intermediate care. *Beds*
SNF 80; ICF 60. *Certified* Medicaid;
Medicare.
Owner Proprietary corp.
Admissions Requirements Minimum age 16.
Staff Physicians 1 (pt); RNs 12 (ft); LPNs 13
(ft); Nurses' aides 46 (ft); Physical therapists
1 (pt); Occupational therapists 1 (pt); Speech
therapists 1 (pt); Activities coordinators 1
(ft); Dietitians 1 (pt); Ophthalmologists 1
(pt); Dentists 1 (pt).
Facilities Dining room; Physical therapy
room; Activities room; Laundry room;
Barber/Beauty shop.
Activities Arts & crafts; Cards; Games;
Reading groups; Prayer groups; Movies;
Dances/Social/Cultural gatherings.

Lewiston

Fairchild Manor Nursing Home
765 Fairchild Pl, Lewiston, NY 14092
(716) 754-4322
Admin Henry M Sloma.
Medical Dir Anthony B Schiam MD.
Licensure Skilled care. *Beds* SNF 100.
Certified Medicaid; Medicare.
Owner Privately owned.
Staff Physicians 17 (pt); RNs 6 (ft), 5 (pt);
LPNs 12 (ft), 13 (pt); Nurses' aides 31 (ft),
22 (pt); Physical therapists 1 (pt); Speech

therapists 1 (pt); Activities coordinators 1 (ft); Dietitians 1 (ft), 1 (pt); Ophthalmologists 1 (pt); Podiatrists 1 (pt); Audiologists 1 (pt); Dentists 1 (pt).
Facilities Dining room; Physical therapy room; Activities room; Crafts room; Barber/Beauty shop; Library.
Activities Arts & crafts; Cards; Games; Reading groups; Prayer groups; Movies; Shopping trips; Dances/Social/Cultural gatherings.

Liberty

Sullivan County Home & Infirmary
PO Box 231, Liberty, NY 12754-0231
(914) 292-8640, 794-3459 FAX
Admin George H Lane. *Dir of Nursing* Albert Hauser. *Medical Dir* Arthur Riesenberg MD.
Licensure Skilled care; Intermediate care; Adult day care. *Beds* SNF 120; ICF 40.
Private Pay Patients 1%. *Certified* Medicaid; Medicare.
Owner Publicly owned.
Admissions Requirements Minimum age 16; Medical examination.
Staff Physicians 1 (ft), 1 (pt); RNs 15 (ft); LPNs 11 (ft); Nurses' aides 34 (ft); Physical therapists 1 (pt); Occupational therapists 1 (pt); Speech therapists 1 (pt); Dietitians 1 (ft); Ophthalmologists 1 (pt); Podiatrists 1 (pt); Audiologists 1 (pt); Reality therapists; Recreational therapists 1 (ft).
Facilities Dining room; Physical therapy room; Activities room; Chapel; Crafts room; Laundry room; Barber/Beauty shop; Library.
Activities Arts & crafts; Cards; Games; Prayer groups; Movies; Shopping trips; Dances/Social/Cultural gatherings; Intergenerational programs; Pet therapy.

Walnut Mountain Nursing Home
Lake St, Liberty, NY 12754
(914) 292-4200
Admin John J Rada.
Medical Dir Walter Dobushak MD.
Licensure Skilled care; Intermediate care. *Beds* SNF 104; ICF 74. *Certified* Medicaid; Medicare.
Owner Privately owned.
Admissions Requirements Minimum age 16; Medical examination; Physician's request.
Staff RNs; LPNs; Nurses' aides; Physical therapists; Occupational therapists; Speech therapists; Activities coordinators; Dietitians; Ophthalmologists; Podiatrists; Dentists.
Facilities Dining room; Physical therapy room; Activities room; Chapel; Crafts room; Barber/Beauty shop.
Activities Arts & crafts; Cards; Games; Reading groups; Movies.

Little Falls

Little Falls Hospital
140 Burwell St, Little Falls, NY 13365
(315) 823-1000
Admin David S Armstrong Jr. *Dir of Nursing* Regina Guiney RN. *Medical Dir* Dr Douglas Haas.
Licensure Skilled care; Acute care. *Beds* SNF 34; Acute care 100. *Private Pay Patients* 15%. *Certified* Medicaid; Medicare.
Owner Nonprofit corp.
Admissions Requirements Minimum age 16; Medical examination; Physician's request.
Staff Physicians 20 (ft); RNs 3 (ft), 3 (pt); LPNs 5 (ft), 2 (pt); Nurses' aides 12 (ft), 9 (pt); Physical therapists 3 (pt); Reality therapists 1 (pt); Occupational therapists 1 (pt); Speech therapists 1 (pt); Activities coordinators 1 (ft); Dietitians 1 (pt); Ophthalmologists 1 (pt); Podiatrists 1 (pt); Dentists 1 (ft).
Languages Italian, Polish, Slovak, Spanish.

Facilities Dining room; Physical therapy room; Activities room; Chapel; Crafts room; Laundry room; Barber/Beauty shop; Library.
Activities Arts & crafts; Cards; Games; Reading groups; Prayer groups; Movies; Shopping trips; Dances/Social/Cultural gatherings; Intergenerational programs; Pet therapy; Resident council; Programs with other nursing homes.

Van Allen Nursing Home
755 E Monroe St, Little Falls, NY 13365
(315) 823-0973
Admin William Van Allen.
Medical Dir Dr Oscar Stivala.
Licensure Skilled care; Intermediate care. *Beds* SNF 42; ICF 38. *Certified* Medicaid; Medicare.
Owner Privately owned.
Admissions Requirements Physician's request.
Staff Physicians 7 (pt); RNs 6 (ft), 6 (pt); LPNs 5 (ft), 6 (pt); Activities coordinators 1 (ft).
Facilities Dining room; Physical therapy room; Activities room; Chapel; Laundry room; Barber/Beauty shop.
Activities Arts & crafts; Cards; Games; Reading groups; Prayer groups; Movies; Shopping trips; Dances/Social/Cultural gatherings.

Little Neck

Little Neck Nursing Home
260-19 Nassau Blvd, Little Neck, NY 11362
(718) 423-6400, 428-0737 FAX
Admin Frank Misiano. *Dir of Nursing* Phyllis Hunte RN. *Medical Dir* Louis Orens MD.
Licensure Skilled care. *Beds* SNF 120. *Private Pay Patients* 17%. *Certified* Medicaid; Medicare.
Owner Proprietary corp.
Admissions Requirements Minimum age 16; Medical examination; Physician's request.
Staff Physicians; RNs; LPNs; Nurses' aides; Physical therapists; Recreational therapists; Occupational therapists; Speech therapists; Activities coordinators; Dietitians; Ophthalmologists; Podiatrists; Audiologists.
Facilities Dining room; Physical therapy room; Activities room; Laundry room; Barber/Beauty shop.
Activities Arts & crafts; Cards; Games; Reading groups; Prayer groups; Movies; Dances/Social/Cultural gatherings; Pet therapy.

Liverpool

Birchwood Health Care Center Inc
4800 Bear Rd, Liverpool, NY 13088
(315) 457-9946
Admin Robert M Chur. *Dir of Nursing* Marty Coburn. *Medical Dir* David Wrisley MD.
Licensure Skilled care; Intermediate care. *Beds* SNF 120; ICF 40.
Owner Proprietary corp.
Admissions Requirements Minimum age 16; Medical examination; Physician's request.
Staff Physicians 1 (pt); RNs 9 (ft), 7 (pt); LPNs 20 (ft), 18 (pt); Nurses' aides 54 (ft), 40 (pt); Physical therapists 3 (pt); Occupational therapists 1 (ft); Speech therapists 1 (pt); Activities coordinators 1 (ft); Dietitians 2 (pt).
Facilities Dining room; Physical therapy room; Activities room; Chapel; Crafts room; Laundry room; Barber/Beauty shop; Occupational therapy room; Speech therapy room; Large front porch.
Activities Arts & crafts; Cards; Games; Reading groups; Prayer groups; Movies; Shopping trips; Dances/Social/Cultural gatherings; Current events; Cooking; Gardening; Exercise groups; Resident

council; Community outings; Ceramics; Ecumenical worship services; Reminiscence groups.

Livingston

Adventist Nursing Home Inc
Rte 9 Box 95, Livingston, NY 12541
(518) 851-3041
Admin Joseph H Newcomb.
Medical Dir Joseph Fusco MD.
Licensure Skilled care; Intermediate care; Retirement. *Beds* SNF 80; ICF 40. *Certified* Medicaid; Medicare.
Owner Nonprofit corp (Adventist Health Systems-USA).
Admissions Requirements Minimum age 18; Medical examination.
Staff RNs 21 (ft); LPNs 13 (ft); Nurses' aides 80 (ft); Physical therapists 1 (ft); Recreational therapists 1 (ft); Occupational therapists 1 (pt); Speech therapists 1 (pt); Activities coordinators 1 (ft); Dietitians 1 (pt); Ophthalmologists 1 (pt); Podiatrists 1 (pt); Physical therapy aides 2 (ft), 1 (pt); Dentists 1 (pt).
Affiliation Seventh-Day Adventist.
Facilities Dining room; Physical therapy room; Activities room; Crafts room; Barber/Beauty shop.
Activities Arts & crafts; Cards; Games; Reading groups; Prayer groups; Movies; Shopping trips; Dances/Social/Cultural gatherings; Day care center 2 days per week.

Livonia

Conesus Lake Nursing Home
Rte 15, Livonia, NY 14487
(716) 346-3001
Admin Gail West.
Licensure Skilled care. *Beds* SNF 48. *Certified* Medicaid; Medicare.
Owner Privately owned.

Lockport

Briody Nursing Home
909 Lincoln Ave, Lockport, NY 14094
(716) 434-6361
Admin Joan Briody.
Medical Dir Berjenda Goupta MD.
Licensure Skilled care. *Beds* SNF 82. *Certified* Medicaid; Medicare.
Owner Privately owned.
Admissions Requirements Minimum age 16.
Staff Physicians 1 (pt); RNs 5 (ft), 6 (pt); LPNs 6 (ft), 7 (pt); Nurses' aides 45 (ft), 15 (pt); Occupational therapists 1 (pt); Speech therapists 1 (pt); Activities coordinators 2 (ft); Dietitians 1 (pt); Ophthalmologists 1 (pt); Podiatrists 1 (pt).
Activities Arts & crafts; Cards; Games; Reading groups; Prayer groups; Movies; Shopping trips; Dances/Social/Cultural gatherings.

Mt View Health Facility
5465 Upper Mountain Rd, Lockport, NY 14094
(716) 439-6003
Admin Richard Majlea.
Licensure Skilled care. *Beds* SNF 172. *Certified* Medicaid; Medicare.
Owner Publicly owned.

Odd Fellow & Rebekah Nursing Home Inc
104 Old Niagara Rd, Lockport, NY 14094
(716) 434-6324
Admin Bonnie Cunningham.
Licensure Skilled care; Intermediate care. *Beds* SNF 40; ICF 80. *Certified* Medicaid; Medicare.
Owner Nonprofit corp.
Affiliation Independent Order of Odd Fellows & Rebekahs.

St Clare Manor
543 Locust St, Lockport, NY 14094
(716) 434-4718
Admin Sr Mary Christopher. *Dir of Nursing* Marjorie Hicks. *Medical Dir* William C Stein MD.
Licensure Skilled care. *Beds* SNF 28. *Private Pay Patients* 22%. *Certified* Medicaid; Medicare.
Owner Nonprofit corp (Catholic Charities).
Admissions Requirements Minimum age 16; Medical examination; Physician's request.
Staff Physicians 4 (pt); RNs 1 (ft), 3 (pt); LPNs 3 (ft), 2 (pt); Nurses' aides 9 (ft), 6 (pt); Physical therapists 1 (pt); Recreational therapists 1 (pt); Dietitians 1 (ft).
Languages Polish, Italian.
Affiliation Roman Catholic.
Facilities Dining room; Physical therapy room; Activities room; Chapel; Laundry room; Barber/Beauty shop.
Activities Arts & crafts; Cards; Games; Reading groups; Prayer groups; Movies; Shopping trips; Pet therapy.

Long Beach

Long Beach Grandell Company
645 W Broadway, Long Beach, NY 11561
(516) 889-1100
Admin Vernon Rossner.
Licensure Skilled care; Intermediate care. *Beds* SNF 54; ICF 224. *Certified* Medicaid; Medicare.
Owner Privately owned.

Long Beach Memorial Nursing Home Inc
375 E Bay Dr, Long Beach, NY 11561
(516) 432-8000
Admin Douglas L Melzer. *Dir of Nursing* Catherine C Cox RN. *Medical Dir* Munagala J Reddy MD.
Licensure Skilled care; Intermediate care. *Beds* SNF 150; ICF 50. *Certified* Medicaid; Medicare.
Owner Nonprofit corp.
Admissions Requirements Medical examination; Physician's request.
Staff Physicians 1 (ft); RNs 18 (ft), 15 (pt); LPNs 20 (ft), 13 (pt); Nurses' aides 51 (ft), 19 (pt); Physical therapists 1 (ft); Recreational therapists 1 (ft); Occupational therapists 2 (ft); Speech therapists 1 (pt); Activities coordinators 3 (ft); Dietitians 2 (ft); Ophthalmologists 1 (pt); Podiatrists 1 (pt).
Facilities Dining room; Physical therapy room; Activities room; Crafts room; Laundry room; Barber/Beauty shop; Occupational therapy room.
Activities Arts & crafts; Cards; Games; Reading groups; Prayer groups; Shopping trips; Dances/Social/Cultural gatherings; Dinner trips; Sports trips.

Long Island Tides Nursing Home
640 W Broadway, Long Beach, NY 11561
(516) 431-4400
Admin Jay Cherlin. *Dir of Nursing* Rochelle Stern. *Medical Dir* Dr R Tizes.
Licensure Skilled care. *Beds* SNF 182. *Certified* Medicaid; Medicare.
Owner Privately owned.
Admissions Requirements Physician's request.
Languages Spanish, Italian, German.
Facilities Dining room; Physical therapy room; Activities room; Chapel; Crafts room; Laundry room; Barber/Beauty shop.
Activities Arts & crafts; Cards; Games; Reading groups; Prayer groups; Movies; Shopping trips; Dances/Social/Cultural gatherings; Intergenerational programs; Pet therapy.

Lowville

Lewis County Residential Health Care Facility
7785 N State St, Lowville, NY 13367
(315) 376-5200
Admin Steven Goold. *Dir of Nursing* Margaret Shunk RN. *Medical Dir* Howard Meny MD.
Licensure Skilled care; Intermediate care. *Beds* SNF 98; ICF 40. *Private Pay Patients* 10%. *Certified* Medicaid; Medicare.
Owner Publicly owned.
Admissions Requirements Minimum age 16; Medical examination; Physician's request.
Staff Physicians 8 (ft); RNs 8 (ft), 2 (pt); LPNs 10 (ft), 5 (pt); Nurses' aides 30 (ft), 24 (pt); Physical therapists 3 (ft); Recreational therapists 4 (pt); Activities coordinators 1 (ft); Dietitians 1 (ft).
Facilities Dining room; Physical therapy room; Activities room; Chapel; Crafts room; Laundry room; Barber/Beauty shop.
Activities Arts & crafts; Cards; Games; Reading groups; Prayer groups; Movies; Shopping trips; Dances/Social/Cultural gatherings; Intergenerational programs; Pet therapy.

Lynbrook

East Rockaway Nursing Home
243 Atlantic Ave, Lynbrook, NY 11563
(516) 599-2744
Admin Robert J Keon. *Dir of Nursing* Millie Caldwell. *Medical Dir* Francis Gomez MD.
Licensure Skilled care. *Beds* SNF 100. *Private Pay Patients* 20%. *Certified* Medicaid; Medicare.
Owner Privately owned.
Staff RNs; LPNs; Nurses' aides; Physical therapists; Recreational therapists; Occupational therapists; Activities coordinators; Dietitians.
Activities Arts & crafts; Cards; Games; Prayer groups; Movies; Dances/Social/Cultural gatherings; Pet therapy.

Lyons

Wayne County Nursing Home & Health Related Facility
7376 Rte 31, Lyons, NY 14489
(315) 946-4817
Admin John F Demske. *Dir of Nursing* Helene Scribner. *Medical Dir* Dr David Blaszok.
Licensure Skilled care; Intermediate care. *Beds* SNF 150; ICF 40. *Private Pay Patients* 6%. *Certified* Medicaid; Medicare.
Owner Publicly owned.
Admissions Requirements Minimum age 16.
Staff Physicians 1 (pt); RNs 6 (ft), 1 (pt); LPNs 19 (ft), 7 (pt); Nurses' aides 75 (ft), 27 (pt); Occupational therapists 1 (pt); Speech therapists 1 (pt); Activities coordinators; Dietitians 1 (ft); Ophthalmologists 1 (pt); Podiatrists 1 (pt).
Facilities Dining room; Physical therapy room; Activities room; Crafts room; Laundry room; Barber/Beauty shop; Library.
Activities Arts & crafts; Cards; Games; Reading groups; Prayer groups; Movies; Shopping trips; Dances/Social/Cultural gatherings; Pet therapy.

Machias

Cattaraugus County Home & Infirmary
Rte 16, Machias, NY 14101
(716) 353-8516
Admin Margaret Mary Wagner.
Licensure Skilled care; Intermediate care. *Beds* SNF 79; ICF 36. *Certified* Medicaid; Medicare.
Owner Publicly owned.

Malone

Franklin County Nursing Home
Rte 30, Finney Blvd, Malone, NY 12953
(518) 483-3300, 483-6785 FAX
Admin Edna M Connors.
Medical Dir Jonathan Lowell MD.
Licensure Skilled care. *Beds* SNF 80. *Private Pay Patients* 10%. *Certified* Medicaid; Medicare.
Owner Publicly owned.
Admissions Requirements Minimum age 16; Physician's request.
Staff Physicians 3 (pt); RNs 6 (ft), 3 (pt); LPNs 7 (ft), 7 (pt); Nurses' aides 33 (ft), 18 (pt); Activities coordinators 1 (ft).
Facilities Dining room; Physical therapy room; Activities room; Crafts room; Laundry room; Barber/Beauty shop.
Activities Arts & crafts; Cards; Games; Reading groups; Prayer groups; Movies; Shopping trips; Dances/Social/Cultural gatherings.

Alice Hyde Nursing Home
115 Park St, Malone, NY 12953
(518) 483-3000
Admin Arthur Lelio. *Dir of Nursing* Florence King RN. *Medical Dir* Dr John T St Mary.
Licensure Skilled care. *Beds* SNF 75. *Certified* Medicaid; Medicare.
Owner Nonprofit corp.
Admissions Requirements Physician's request.
Staff Physicians; RNs; LPNs; Nurses' aides; Physical therapists; Activities coordinators; Dietitians.
Facilities Dining room; Activities room; Crafts room; Barber/Beauty shop; Library.
Activities Arts & crafts; Cards; Games; Reading groups; Prayer groups; Movies; Shopping trips.

Mamaroneck

Sarah R Neuman Nursing Home
845 Palmer Ave, Mamaroneck, NY 10543
(914) 698-6005, 698-6857 FAX
Admin Marianne Keevins. *Dir of Nursing* Barbara Lambert RN. *Medical Dir* E Bevon Miele MD.
Licensure Skilled care; Intermediate care. *Beds* SNF 180; ICF 90. *Private Pay Patients* 55%. *Certified* Medicaid; Medicare.
Owner Privately owned.
Admissions Requirements Medical examination.
Staff Physicians 5 (pt); RNs 10 (ft), 7 (pt); LPNs 12 (ft), 5 (pt); Nurses' aides 70 (ft), 15 (pt); Physical therapists 1 (ft); Occupational therapists 1 (pt); Speech therapists 1 (pt); Activities coordinators 2 (ft); Dietitians 2 (ft).
Languages Spanish, Italian.
Facilities Dining room; Physical therapy room; Activities room; Crafts room; Laundry room; Barber/Beauty shop; Patio; Garden; Card/TV rooms.
Activities Arts & crafts; Cards; Games; Reading groups; Prayer groups; Movies; Shopping trips; Dances/Social/Cultural gatherings; Outings to Radio City and dinner theater; Yearly play by staff and residents.

Margaretville

Margaretville Memorial Hospital Nursing Home
Rte 28, Margaretville, NY 12455
(914) 586-2631
Admin Joseph Kehoe.
Licensure Skilled care. *Beds* SNF 31. *Certified* Medicaid; Medicare.
Owner Nonprofit corp.

Maryknoll

Maryknoll Nursing Home Inc
Maryknoll Sister Center, Maryknoll, NY
10545
(914) 941-9230
Licensure Skilled care. *Beds* SNF 60.
Owner Nonprofit corp.

Maspeth

Midway Nursing Home
69-95 Queens Midtown Expwy, Maspeth, NY
11378
(718) 429-2200, 898-7582 FAX
Admin Arthur Boden. *Dir of Nursing* Elaine K
Shapiro RN. *Medical Dir* Samuel Feig MD.
Licensure Skilled care. *Beds* SNF 200.
Certified Medicaid; Medicare.
Owner Privately owned.
Admissions Requirements Physician's request.
Facilities Dining room; Physical therapy
room; Activities room; Barber/Beauty shop;
Kosher kitchen.
Activities Arts & crafts; Cards; Games;
Reading groups; Prayer groups; Movies;
Dances/Social/Cultural gatherings;
Intergenerational programs; Pet therapy.

Massapequa

Park View Nursing Home Inc
5353 Merrick Rd, Massapequa, NY 11758
(516) 798-1800
Admin Owen Kaye.
Licensure Skilled care. *Beds* SNF 164.
Certified Medicaid; Medicare.
Owner Proprietary corp.

Massena

Highland Nursing Home Inc
Rte 2 Highland Rd, Massena, NY 13662
(315) 769-9956
Admin Edward J Kaneb.
Medical Dir Dr S Goswami.
Licensure Skilled care. *Beds* SNF 140.
Certified Medicaid; Medicare.
Owner Proprietary corp.
Admissions Requirements Minimum age 16;
Physician's request.
Staff Physicians 20 (pt); RNs 6 (ft), 4 (pt);
LPNs 16 (ft), 4 (pt); Nurses' aides 45 (ft), 25
(pt); Physical therapists 1 (ft); Occupational
therapists 1 (pt); Speech therapists 1 (pt);
Activities coordinators 1 (ft); Dietitians 1
(pt).
Facilities Dining room; Physical therapy
room; Activities room; Chapel; Crafts room;
Laundry room; Barber/Beauty shop.
Activities Arts & crafts; Cards; Games;
Reading groups; Prayer groups; Movies;
Shopping trips; Dances/Social/Cultural
gatherings.

**St Regis Nursing Home & Health Related
Facility Inc**
Saint Regis Blvd, Massena, NY 13662
(315) 769-2494
Admin John Bogosian.
Medical Dir Henry Dobies MD.
Licensure Skilled care; Intermediate care. *Beds*
SNF 44; ICF 108. *Certified* Medicaid;
Medicare.
Owner Nonprofit corp.
Admissions Requirements Physician's request.
Staff RNs 13 (ft); LPNs 15 (ft); Nurses' aides
53 (ft), 2 (pt); Physical therapists 1 (pt);
Recreational therapists 1 (pt); Occupational
therapists 1 (pt); Speech therapists 1 (pt);
Activities coordinators 2 (ft); Dietitians 1
(ft).
Facilities Dining room; Physical therapy
room; Activities room; Crafts room; Laundry
room; Barber/Beauty shop.

Activities Arts & crafts; Cards; Games;
Reading groups; Prayer groups; Movies;
Shopping trips; Dances/Social/Cultural
gatherings.

Medina

**Medina Memorial Hospital Skilled Nursing
Facility**
500 Ohio St, Medina, NY 14103
(716) 798-2000, 798-5079 FAX
Admin James H Wesp. *Dir of Nursing* Kathy
Frerichs. *Medical Dir* Harvey Blanchet.
Licensure Skilled care. *Beds* SNF 30. *Private
Pay Patients* 20%. *Certified* Medicaid;
Medicare.
Owner Nonprofit corp.
Admissions Requirements Medical
examination.
Staff Physicians; RNs; LPNs; Nurses' aides;
Physical therapists; Speech therapists;
Activities coordinators; Dietitians.
Facilities Dining room; Activities room;
Barber/Beauty shop.
Activities Arts & crafts; Games; Reading
groups; Prayer groups; Movies.

Orchard Manor Inc
600 Bates Rd, Medina, NY 14103
(716) 798-4100
Admin Thomas Morien. *Dir of Nursing*
Patricia Dool RN. *Medical Dir* Harvey J
Blanchet Jr MD.
Licensure Skilled care; Intermediate care. *Beds*
SNF 64; ICF 56. *Private Pay Patients* 30%.
Certified Medicaid; Medicare.
Owner Nonprofit organization/foundation.
Admissions Requirements Minimum age 16;
Medical examination; Physician's request.
Staff Physicians 3 (pt); RNs 7 (ft), 6 (pt);
LPNs 14 (ft), 7 (pt); Nurses' aides 30 (ft), 30
(pt); Physical therapists 1 (pt); Recreational
therapists 1 (pt); Occupational therapists 1
(pt); Speech therapists 1 (pt); Activities
coordinators 2 (ft); Dietitians 1 (pt);
Ophthalmologists 1 (pt); Podiatrists 1 (pt);
Audiologists 1 (pt); Social workers 1 (pt);
Dentists 1 (pt).
Facilities Dining room; Physical therapy
room; Activities room; Chapel; Crafts room;
Laundry room; Barber/Beauty shop; Library;
Outdoor courtyard.
Activities Arts & crafts; Cards; Games;
Reading groups; Movies; Shopping trips;
Dances/Social/Cultural gatherings; Pet
therapy; Resident and family parties; Family
support group.

Middle Island

Crest Hall Health Related Facility
Oakcrest Ave & Church Lane, Middle Island,
NY 11953
(516) 924-8830
Admin Dwight T Worthy. *Dir of Nursing*
Elizabeth Frattuna. *Medical Dir* Mark
Steinberg MD.
Licensure Intermediate care. *Beds* ICF 120.
Certified Medicaid.
Owner Privately owned.
Admissions Requirements Minimum age 18;
Physician's request.
Staff Physicians 1 (ft); RNs 1 (ft); LPNs 20
(ft); Nurses' aides 20 (ft), 7 (pt); Physical
therapists 1 (ft); Reality therapists 4 (pt);
Recreational therapists 1 (ft), 4 (pt);
Occupational therapists 1 (ft); Speech
therapists 1 (ft); Activities coordinators 1 (ft);
Ophthalmologists 1 (ft); Podiatrists 2 (ft).
Facilities Dining room; Physical therapy
room; Activities room; Crafts room; Laundry
room; Barber/Beauty shop.
Activities Arts & crafts; Cards; Games;
Reading groups; Prayer groups; Movies;
Shopping trips; Dances/Social/Cultural
gatherings.

Oak Hollow Nursing Center
Church Ln & Oak Crest Ave, Middle Island,
NY 11953
(516) 924-8820
Admin Joan Portnoy. *Dir of Nursing*
Constance Nadig. *Medical Dir* Dr Robert
Mullaney.
Licensure Skilled care. *Beds* SNF 164.
Certified Medicaid; Medicare.
Owner Privately owned.
Admissions Requirements Minimum age 18;
Medical examination.
Staff RNs 8 (ft), 9 (pt); LPNs 17 (ft), 10 (pt);
Nurses' aides 46 (ft), 24 (pt); Physical
therapists 1 (pt); Occupational therapists 1
(pt); Speech therapists 1 (pt); Activities
coordinators 1 (ft); Dietitians 1 (pt);
Ophthalmologists 2 (pt); Podiatrists 1 (pt).
Facilities Dining room; Physical therapy
room; Activities room; Crafts room; Laundry
room; Barber/Beauty shop; Book cart.
Activities Arts & crafts; Cards; Games;
Reading groups; Prayer groups; Movies;
Shopping trips; Dances/Social/Cultural
gatherings; Special events.

Middle Village

Dry Harbor Nursing Home
61-35 Dry Harbor Rd, Middle Village, NY
11379
(718) 446-3600, 779-3969 FAX
Admin Samuel Lieberman. *Dir of Nursing*
Anna Marie Verbil. *Medical Dir* Martin
Feierman MD.
Licensure Skilled care; Intermediate care;
Alzheimer's care. *Beds* SNF 160; ICF 200.
Certified Medicaid; Medicare.
Owner Proprietary corp.
Admissions Requirements Medical
examination.
Staff Physicians 1 (ft), 5 (pt); RNs 8 (ft);
LPNs 25 (ft); Nurses' aides 80 (ft); Physical
therapists 3 (ft); Recreational therapists 1
(ft); Occupational therapists 1 (ft); Speech
therapists 1 (ft); Activities coordinators 7
(ft); Dietitians 2 (ft); Ophthalmologists 1
(pt); Podiatrists 1 (pt); Audiologists 1 (pt);
Dentists 1 (pt).
Languages Spanish, Hebrew, Russian.
Facilities Dining room; Physical therapy
room; Activities room; Crafts room; Laundry
room; Barber/Beauty shop; Library.
Activities Arts & crafts; Cards; Games;
Reading groups; Prayer groups; Movies;
Shopping trips; Dances/Social/Cultural
gatherings; Intergenerational programs; Pet
therapy; Alzheimer's residents group;
Alzheimer's family support group.

Middletown

Middletown Park Manor Health Facility
105 Dunning Rd, Middletown, NY 10940
(914) 343-0801, 343-1838 FAX
Admin Audrey E Martin. *Dir of Nursing*
Margaret McKenna. *Medical Dir* Dr Samuel
Mills.
Licensure Skilled care; Intermediate care. *Beds*
SNF 85; ICF 45. *Certified* Medicaid;
Medicare.
Owner Privately owned.
Admissions Requirements Medical
examination; Physician's request.
Staff RNs; LPNs; Nurses' aides; Physical
therapists; Recreational therapists;
Occupational therapists; Speech therapists;
Activities coordinators; Dietitians.
Facilities Dining room; Physical therapy
room; Activities room; Crafts room; Laundry
room; Barber/Beauty shop.
Activities Arts & crafts; Cards; Games;
Reading groups; Prayer groups; Movies;
Shopping trips; Dances/Social/Cultural
gatherings; Intergenerational programs; Pet
therapy.

St Teresas Nursing Home Inc
120 Highland Ave, Middletown, NY 10940
(914) 342-1033
Admin Sr Mary Grace. *Dir of Nursing* Sr Mary Ann RN. *Medical Dir* Samuel Mills MD.
Licensure Skilled care. *Beds* SNF 92. *Certified* Medicaid; Medicare.
Owner Nonprofit corp (Catholic Charities-Arch of NY).
Admissions Requirements Minimum age 65; Medical examination; Physician's request.
Staff Physicians 1 (pt); RNs 12 (ft), 2 (pt); LPNs 4 (ft); Nurses' aides 49 (ft), 4 (pt); Physical therapists 2 (pt); Recreational therapists 1 (ft), 2 (pt); Occupational therapists 1 (pt); Speech therapists 1 (pt); Activities coordinators 1 (ft); Dietitians 1 (pt); Ophthalmologists 1 (pt); Podiatrists 1 (pt).
Languages Spanish.
Affiliation Roman Catholic.
Facilities Dining room; Physical therapy room; Activities room; Chapel; Crafts room; Laundry room; Barber/Beauty shop; Library.
Activities Arts & crafts; Cards; Games; Reading groups; Prayer groups; Movies; Shopping trips.

Millbrook

Dutchess County Health Care Facility
Oak Summit Rd, Millbrook, NY 12545
(914) 677-3925
Licensure Skilled care. *Beds* SNF 62. *Certified* Medicaid; Medicare.
Owner Publicly owned.
Admissions Requirements Minimum age 16; Medical examination; Physician's request.
Facilities Dining room; Physical therapy room; Activities room; Crafts room; Laundry room; Barber/Beauty shop; Library.
Activities Arts & crafts; Cards; Games; Reading groups; Prayer groups; Movies; Shopping trips; Dances/Social/Cultural gatherings.

Minoa

Hallmark Nursing Centre Inc
217 East Ave, Minoa, NY 13116
(315) 656-7277
Admin Raymond Klocek.
Medical Dir David Saunders MD.
Licensure Skilled care. *Beds* SNF 82. *Certified* Medicaid; Medicare.
Owner Proprietary corp.
Staff Physicians 5 (pt); RNs 7 (ft), 3 (pt); LPNs 10 (ft), 4 (pt); Nurses' aides 30 (ft), 19 (pt); Physical therapists 1 (pt); Recreational therapists 1 (ft); Occupational therapists 1 (pt); Speech therapists 1 (pt); Activities coordinators 1 (ft); Dietitians 1 (pt); Ophthalmologists 1 (pt); Podiatrists 1 (pt); Dentists 1 (pt).
Facilities Dining room; Physical therapy room; Activities room; Chapel; Crafts room; Laundry room; Barber/Beauty shop; Library.
Activities Arts & crafts; Cards; Games; Reading groups; Prayer groups; Movies; Shopping trips; Dances/Social/Cultural gatherings.

Mohegan Lake

Marrs Nursing Home
3550 Lexington Ave, Mohegan Lake, NY 10547
(914) 528-2000
Admin Paula C Ress. *Dir of Nursing* Constance Daniels RN. *Medical Dir* Dr John Vesce.
Licensure Skilled care. *Beds* SNF 120. *Certified* Medicaid; Medicare.
Owner Privately owned.

Admissions Requirements Minimum age 16; Medical examination.
Staff Physicians; RNs; LPNs; Nurses' aides; Physical therapists; Recreational therapists; Occupational therapists; Speech therapists; Activities coordinators; Dietitians; Ophthalmologists; Podiatrists; Dentists.
Languages Italian, Spanish.
Facilities Dining room; Physical therapy room; Activities room; Crafts room; Laundry room; Barber/Beauty shop.
Activities Arts & crafts; Games; Reading groups; Prayer groups; Movies; Dances/Social/Cultural gatherings; Music therapy.

Monsey

Northern Metropolitan Residential Health Care Facility Inc
225 Maple Ave, Monsey, NY 10952
(914) 352-9000
Admin Donna Mack. *Dir of Nursing* Toby Lewis. *Medical Dir* Stanley Greenbaum MD.
Licensure Skilled care; Adult day care. *Beds* SNF 120. *Private Pay Patients* 10%. *Certified* Medicaid; Medicare.
Owner Nonprofit corp.
Admissions Requirements Minimum age 16; Medical examination.
Staff Physicians 9 (pt); RNs 10 (ft), 9 (pt); LPNs 8 (ft), 2 (pt); Nurses' aides 45 (ft), 10 (pt); Physical therapists 1 (pt); Recreational therapists 2 (ft); Occupational therapists 1 (pt); Speech therapists 1 (pt); Activities coordinators 1 (ft); Dietitians 1 (ft).
Languages Yiddish.
Facilities Dining room; Physical therapy room; Activities room; Chapel; Crafts room; Laundry room; Barber/Beauty shop; Library.
Activities Arts & crafts; Cards; Games; Reading groups; Prayer groups; Movies; Shopping trips; Dances/Social/Cultural gatherings; Intergenerational programs; Pet therapy.

Montgomery

Montgomery Nursing Home
Albany Post Rd, Montgomery, NY 12549
(914) 457-3155
Admin Matthew Marciano.
Medical Dir Dr Sung J Sohn.
Licensure Skilled care. *Beds* SNF 100. *Certified* Medicaid; Medicare.
Owner Privately owned.
Admissions Requirements Medical examination.
Staff RNs 3 (ft), 8 (pt); LPNs 5 (ft), 10 (pt); Nurses' aides 33 (ft), 17 (pt); Physical therapists 1 (pt); Recreational therapists 1 (pt); Occupational therapists 1 (pt); Speech therapists 1 (pt); Activities coordinators 1 (ft); Dietitians 1 (ft); Ophthalmologists 1 (pt); Podiatrists 1 (pt); Audiologists 1 (pt); Dentists.
Facilities Dining room; Physical therapy room; Activities room; Chapel; Crafts room; Laundry room; Barber/Beauty shop.
Activities Arts & crafts; Cards; Games; Reading groups; Prayer groups; Movies; Shopping trips; Dances/Social/Cultural gatherings.

Montour Falls

Schuyler Hospital Skilled Nursing Facility
Montour-Townsend Rd, Montour Falls, NY 14865
(607) 535-7121, 535-9097 FAX
Admin Barbara C Chapman. *Dir of Nursing* Elizabeth Hoffmeier RN. *Medical Dir* William F Tague MD.
Licensure Skilled care. *Beds* SNF 120. *Private Pay Patients* 14%. *Certified* Medicaid; Medicare.
Owner Nonprofit corp.

Admissions Requirements Minimum age 16; Medical examination.
Staff Physicians 9 (pt); RNs 9 (ft), 2 (pt); LPNs 10 (ft), 9 (pt); Nurses' aides 32 (ft), 33 (pt); Physical therapists 1 (pt); Occupational therapists 1 (pt); Speech therapists 1 (pt); Activities coordinators 1 (ft); Dietitians 1 (ft); Ophthalmologists 1 (pt); Podiatrists 1 (pt); Audiologists 1 (pt).
Facilities Dining room; Physical therapy room; Activities room; Chapel; Crafts room; Laundry room; Barber/Beauty shop; Library cart; Gift cart.
Activities Arts & crafts; Cards; Games; Reading groups; Prayer groups; Movies; Shopping trips; Dances/Social/Cultural gatherings.

Moravia

Howd Nursing Home
PO Box 1079, 7 Keeler Ave, Moravia, NY 13118
(315) 497-0440, 497-0494 FAX
Admin William T Cifaratta. *Dir of Nursing* Laura McLaughlin. *Medical Dir* Philip Robinson MD.
Licensure Skilled care. *Beds* SNF 40. *Private Pay Patients* 38%. *Certified* Medicaid; Medicare.
Owner Privately owned.
Admissions Requirements Minimum age 16; Medical examination; Physician's request.
Staff RNs 4 (ft); Nurses' aides 4 (ft); LPNs 22 (ft); Physical therapists 1 (pt); Recreational therapists 1 (pt); Occupational therapists 1 (pt); Speech therapists 1 (pt); Activities coordinators 1 (pt); Dietitians 1 (pt); Podiatrists 1 (pt); Audiologists 1 (pt).
Facilities Dining room; Physical therapy room; Activities room; Crafts room; Laundry room; Barber/Beauty shop.
Activities Arts & crafts; Cards; Games; Reading groups; Prayer groups; Movies; Dances/Social/Cultural gatherings; Intergenerational programs; Pet therapy.

Mount Kisco

Swiss Home Health Related Facility
53 Mountain Ave, Mount Kisco, NY 10549
(914) 666-4657
Medical Dir J L Stewart.
Licensure Intermediate care. *Beds* ICF 28. *Certified* Medicaid.
Owner Nonprofit corp.
Admissions Requirements Medical examination.
Staff RNs 1 (ft), 2 (pt); LPNs 3 (ft), 3 (pt); Nurses' aides 3 (ft), 2 (pt); Recreational therapists 1 (pt); Activities coordinators 1 (pt); Dietitians 1 (pt).
Facilities Dining room; Activities room; Laundry room; Barber/Beauty shop; Library.
Activities Arts & crafts; Cards; Games; Prayer groups; Movies; Shopping trips; Dances/Social/Cultural gatherings.

Mount Morris

Livingston County Health Related Facility—Skilled Nursing Facility
County Campus, Bldg No 1, Mount Morris, NY 14510
(716) 658-2881
Admin Linda M Hewitt. *Dir of Nursing* Irene Megliore RN. *Medical Dir* Dr Jeffrey Hanson.
Licensure Skilled care; Intermediate care; Adult day health care. *Beds* SNF 42; ICF 142; Adult day health care 15. *Private Pay Patients* 5-10%. *Certified* Medicaid; Medicare.
Owner Publicly owned.
Admissions Requirements Minimum age 18; Medical examination.

Staff Physicians 2 (pt); RNs 12 (ft), 1 (pt); LPNs 21 (ft), 2 (pt); Nurses' aides 43 (ft); Physical therapists 2 (pt); Occupational therapists 1 (pt); Speech therapists 1 (pt); Activities coordinators 1 (ft); Dietitians 1 (pt); Podiatrists 1 (pt); Audiologists 1 (pt); Activities aides 4 (ft), 1 (pt).
Facilities Dining room; Physical therapy room; Activities room; Chapel; Crafts room; Laundry room; Barber/Beauty shop; Auditorium; Library-on-wheels.
Activities Arts & crafts; Cards; Games; Reading groups; Prayer groups; Movies; Shopping trips; Dances/Social/Cultural gatherings; Intergenerational programs; Pet therapy.

Mount Vernon

Shalom Nursing Home
10 Claremont Ave, Mount Vernon, NY 10550
(914) 699-1600
Admin Howard Wolf.
Licensure Skilled care. *Beds* SNF 240. *Certified* Medicaid; Medicare.
Owner Nonprofit corp.

Wartburg Home of the Evangelical Lutheran Church
Bradley Ave, Mount Vernon, NY 10710
(914) 699-0800, 699-2874 FAX
Admin Mary Frances Barrett. *Dir of Nursing* JoAnne Stola. *Medical Dir* Debabrata Dutta MD.
Licensure Skilled care; Intermediate care; Adult home; Independent living; Adult day care; Domiciliary care. *Beds* SNF 80; ICF 48; Adult home 84; Independent living cottages 31. *Private Pay Patients* 30%. *Certified* Medicaid; Medicare.
Owner Nonprofit organization/foundation.
Admissions Requirements Minimum age 16; Medical examination; Physician's request.
Staff Physicians; RNs 28 (ft); Nurses' aides 57 (ft); Physical therapists 1 (ft); Occupational therapists; Speech therapists; Activities coordinators; Dietitians; Chaplains 1 (ft).
Affiliation Lutheran.
Facilities Dining room; Physical therapy room; Activities room; Chapel; Crafts room; Laundry room; Barber/Beauty shop; Library; Gardens; TV circuit.
Activities Arts & crafts; Games; Reading groups; Prayer groups; Movies; Shopping trips; Dances/Social/Cultural gatherings; Intergenerational programs; Pet therapy; Excursions; Festivals for the needy; Church services.

Nanuet

Elmwood Manor Nursing Home Inc
199 N Middletown Rd, Nanuet, NY 10954
(914) 623-3904
Admin Daniel Harfenist.
Licensure Skilled care. *Beds* SNF 228. *Certified* Medicaid; Medicare.
Owner Proprietary corp.

Neponsit

Neponsit Health Care Center
149-25 Rockaway Beach Blvd, Neponsit, NY 11694
(718) 474-1900, 474-1995 FAX
Admin Moshe G Bain. *Dir of Nursing* Christine McGrath RN. *Medical Dir* Estella Gonzales MD.
Licensure Intermediate care. *Beds* ICF 231. *Private Pay Patients* 2%. *Certified* Medicaid.
Owner Publicly owned.
Admissions Requirements Minimum age 17; Medical examination; Physician's request.
Staff Physicians 1 (ft), 1 (pt); RNs 33 (ft); LPNs 11 (ft); Nurses' aides 57 (ft); Physical therapists 1 (pt); Recreational therapists 2

(ft), 1 (pt); Occupational therapists 1 (pt); Activities coordinators 1 (ft); Dietitians 1 (ft); Ophthalmologists 1 (pt); Podiatrists 1 (pt); Audiologists 1 (pt).
Languages Spanish, Hebrew, Italian, Russian, Polish.
Facilities Dining room; Physical therapy room; Activities room; Chapel; Crafts room; Laundry room; Barber/Beauty shop; Library; Game room; Social hall; Theater; Boutique.
Activities Arts & crafts; Cards; Games; Reading groups; Prayer groups; Movies; Shopping trips; Dances/Social/Cultural gatherings; Intergenerational programs; Pet therapy.

Nesconset

Nesconset Nursing Center
100 Southern Blvd, Nesconset, NY 11767
(516) 361-8800
Licensure Skilled care; Intermediate care. *Beds* SNF 180; ICF 60.
Owner Proprietary corp.

New Berlin

Chase Memorial Nursing Home Co Inc
1 Terrace Heights, New Berlin, NY 13411
(607) 847-6117
Admin Merritt C Meyers.
Licensure Skilled care. *Beds* SNF 80. *Certified* Medicaid; Medicare.
Owner Nonprofit corp.

New City

Friedwald House
475 New Hempstead Rd, New City, NY 10956
(914) 354-7000
Admin Stephen J Epstein. *Dir of Nursing* Janet Allen RN. *Medical Dir* Vincent Garofalo MD.
Licensure Intermediate care. *Beds* ICF 180. *Certified* Medicaid.
Owner Privately owned.
Admissions Requirements Minimum age 16; Medical examination; Physician's request.
Staff Physicians 1 (ft), 9 (pt); RNs 10 (ft); LPNs 6 (ft); Nurses' aides 20 (ft), 5 (pt); Physical therapists 1 (ft); Recreational therapists 2 (ft); Occupational therapists 1 (pt); Speech therapists 1 (pt); Activities coordinators 1 (ft); Dietitians 1 (ft); Ophthalmologists 1 (pt); Podiatrists 1 (pt); Dentists 1 (pt).
Languages Yiddish, Hebrew, Italian.
Facilities Dining room; Physical therapy room; Activities room; Chapel; Crafts room; Laundry room; Barber/Beauty shop; Library.
Activities Arts & crafts; Cards; Games; Reading groups; Prayer groups; Movies; Shopping trips; Dances/Social/Cultural gatherings.

New Hartford

Presbyterian Home for Central New York
PO Box 1144, Middle Settlement Rd, New Hartford, NY 13413-1144
(315) 797-7500, 792-9503 FAX
Admin Raymond L Garrett, Exec Dir. *Dir of Nursing* Lucy F Viti. *Medical Dir* William F Krause MD.
Licensure Skilled care; Intermediate care; Respite care; Adult day care. *Beds* SNF 162; ICF 80. *Certified* Medicaid; Medicare.
Owner Nonprofit corp.
Admissions Requirements Minimum age 16; Medical examination.
Staff RNs 19 (ft), 12 (pt); LPNs 26 (ft), 4 (pt); Nurses' aides 96 (ft), 22 (pt); Physical therapists 1 (pt); Occupational therapists 1

(pt); Speech therapists 1 (pt); Activities coordinators 1 (ft); Dietitians 1 (ft); Audiologists 1 (pt).
Affiliation Presbyterian.
Facilities Dining room; Physical therapy room; Activities room; Chapel; Crafts room; Laundry room; Barber/Beauty shop; Library.
Activities Arts & crafts; Cards; Games; Reading groups; Prayer groups; Movies; Shopping trips; Dances/Social/Cultural gatherings; Walk groups; Grooming groups.

Charles T Sitrin Nursing Home Company Inc
PO Box 1000, Tilden Ave, New Hartford, NY 13413
(315) 797-3114
Admin Richard A Wilson. *Dir of Nursing* Patricia A Barr. *Medical Dir* Irving Cramer MD.
Licensure Skilled care; Intermediate care; Day care. *Beds* SNF 71; ICF 40; Day care 20. *Certified* Medicaid; Medicare.
Owner Nonprofit corp.
Admissions Requirements Minimum age 16; Medical examination.
Staff Physicians 2 (pt); RNs 9 (ft), 6 (pt); LPNs 9 (ft), 7 (pt); Nurses' aides 32 (ft), 27 (pt); Physical therapists 1 (pt); Recreational therapists 1 (ft), 1 (pt); Occupational therapists 1 (pt); Speech therapists 1 (pt); Dietitians 2 (pt); Ophthalmologists 1 (pt).
Affiliation Jewish.
Facilities Dining room; Physical therapy room; Activities room; Chapel; Crafts room; Laundry room; Barber/Beauty shop; Library.
Activities Arts & crafts; Cards; Games; Reading groups; Prayer groups; Movies; Shopping trips; Dances/Social/Cultural gatherings.

New Hyde Park

Parker Jewish Geriatric Institute
271-11 76th Ave, New Hyde Park, NY 11042
(718) 343-2100, (516) 437-0090, (718) 470-6850 FAX
Admin David Glaser. *Dir of Nursing* Ethel Mitty RN EdD. *Medical Dir* Conn Foley MD.
Licensure Skilled care; Alzheimer's respite center; Adult day care. *Beds* SNF 527. *Private Pay Patients* 3%. *Certified* Medicaid; Medicare.
Owner Nonprofit corp.
Admissions Requirements Minimum age 18; Medical examination.
Staff Physicians 5 (ft), 12 (pt); LPNs 51 (ft), 10 (pt); Nurses' aides 250 (ft), 86 (pt); Physical therapists 15 (ft), 2 (pt); Recreational therapists 5 (ft), 4 (pt); Occupational therapists 10 (ft); Speech therapists 1 (ft), 1 (pt); Activities coordinators 1 (ft); Dietitians 6 (ft), 5 (pt); Ophthalmologists 1 (pt); Podiatrists 4 (pt); Audiologists 1 (ft); RNs, HNs, AHNs 108 (ft), 16 (pt).
Languages Yiddish, Hebrew, Spanish, Italian.
Affiliation Jewish.
Facilities Dining room; Physical therapy room; Activities room; Chapel; Crafts room; Laundry room; Barber/Beauty shop; Library; Work activities center; Diagnostic and treatment center; In- and out-patient rehabilitation facilities.
Activities Arts & crafts; Cards; Games; Reading groups; Prayer groups; Movies; Shopping trips; Dances/Social/Cultural gatherings; Intergenerational programs; Pet therapy.

New Paltz

New Paltz Nursing Home
1 Jansen Rd, New Paltz, NY 12561
(914) 255-0830
Admin Norton Blue.

Licensure Skilled care. *Beds* SNF 79. *Certified*
Medicaid; Medicare.
Owner Privately owned.

New Rochelle

Bayberry Nursing Home
40 Keogh Ln, New Rochelle, NY 10805
(914) 636-3947
Admin Leonard Russ. *Dir of Nursing* Carole
Coviello RN. *Medical Dir* A V Clement.
Licensure Skilled care. *Beds* SNF 60. *Certified*
Medicaid; Medicare.
Owner Privately owned.
Staff Physicians 15 (pt); RNs 6 (ft), 10 (pt);
LPNs 2 (ft), 6 (pt); Nurses' aides 19 (ft), 8
(pt); Physical therapists 1 (pt); Reality
therapists 1 (pt); Recreational therapists 2
(pt); Occupational therapists 1 (pt);
Activities coordinators 1 (ft); Dietitians 1
(pt); Ophthalmologists 1 (pt); Podiatrists 1
(pt); Dentists 1 (pt).
Languages Italian, German, French, Spanish.
Facilities Dining room; Physical therapy
room; Activities room; Chapel; Crafts room;
Laundry room; Barber/Beauty shop; Library.
Activities Arts & crafts; Cards; Games;
Reading groups; Prayer groups; Movies;
Shopping trips; Dances/Social/Cultural
gatherings; Exercise sessions.

Dumont Masonic Home
676 Pelham Rd, New Rochelle, NY 10805
(914) 632-9600
Licensure Skilled care; Intermediate care. *Beds*
SNF 120; ICF 70.
Owner Nonprofit corp.

German Masonic Home Corp
676 Pelham Rd, New Rochelle, NY 10805
(914) 632-9600
Admin Pearl Sherman.
Licensure Skilled care. *Beds* 120. *Certified*
Medicaid; Medicare.
Owner Nonprofit corp.
Affiliation Masons.

Howe Avenue Nursing Home Inc
16 Guion Pl, New Rochelle, NY 10802
(914) 632-5000
Admin Carol Ann Zeidler RN. *Dir of Nursing*
Audrey Berkeley RN. *Medical Dir* Richard P
Barone MD.
Licensure Skilled care. *Beds* SNF 150. *Private
Pay Patients* 10%. *Certified* Medicaid;
Medicare.
Owner Nonprofit corp.
Admissions Requirements Minimum age 16.
Staff Physicians 1 (pt); RNs 28 (ft), 3 (pt);
LPNs 17 (ft); Nurses' aides 66 (ft); Physical
therapists 3 (ft); Recreational therapists 3
(ft); Occupational therapists 2 (ft); Speech
therapists (consultants); Dietitians 1 (ft);
Ophthalmologists (consultants); Podiatrists
(consultants); Audiologists (consultants).
Languages Spanish, French, German, Italian,
Hungarian.
Facilities Dining room; Physical therapy
room; Activities room; Crafts room; Laundry
room; Barber/Beauty shop.
Activities Arts & crafts; Cards; Games;
Reading groups; Prayer groups; Movies;
Shopping trips; Dances/Social/Cultural
gatherings; Pottery.

New Rochelle Nursing Home
31 Lockwood Ave, New Rochelle, NY 10801
(914) 576-0600
Admin Gilbert Preira. *Dir of Nursing* M
Vlymen RN. *Medical Dir* Dr J Kaltchthaler.
Licensure Skilled care; Adult day care; Long-
term care. *Beds* SNF 160; Adult day care
50; Long-term care 75. *Certified* Medicaid;
Medicare.
Owner Privately owned.
Admissions Requirements Minimum age 45;
Medical examination; Physician's request.

Staff Physicians 1 (pt); RNs 12 (ft), 10 (pt);
LPNs 12 (ft), 12 (pt); Nurses' aides 40 (ft),
40 (pt); Physical therapists 1 (ft);
Recreational therapists 3 (ft), 2 (pt);
Occupational therapists 1 (pt); Speech
therapists 1 (pt); Activities coordinators 1
(ft); Dietitians 1 (ft).
Languages Spanish, French, Italian.
Facilities Dining room; Physical therapy
room; Activities room; Crafts room; Laundry
room; Barber/Beauty shop.
Activities Arts & crafts; Cards; Games;
Reading groups; Prayer groups; Movies;
Shopping trips; Dances/Social/Cultural
gatherings.

United Hebrew Geriatric Center
60 Willow Dr, New Rochelle, NY 10805
(914) 632-2804
Admin Saunders T Preiss, Exec V Pres-CEO.
Dir of Nursing Patricia McCormack RN.
Medical Dir Frank A Napolitano MD.
Licensure Skilled care; Intermediate care;
Retirement; Alzheimer's care. *Beds* SNF
166; ICF 104; Retirement 155. *Private Pay
Patients* 10%. *Certified* Medicaid; Medicare.
Owner Nonprofit organization/foundation.
Admissions Requirements Medical
examination.
Staff Physicians 7 (ft); RNs 40 (ft), 20 (pt);
LPNs 22 (ft), 9 (pt); Nurses' aides 91 (ft), 21
(pt); Physical therapists 1 (ft); Recreational
therapists 5 (ft), 1 (pt); Occupational
therapists 2 (ft); Dietitians 2 (ft); Activities
director and assistant 2 (ft); Dentists 1 (pt).
Affiliation Jewish.
Facilities Dining room; Physical therapy
room; Activities room; Chapel; Crafts room;
Laundry room; Barber/Beauty shop; Library;
Kosher kitchen; Garden; Outdoor recreation
area.
Activities Arts & crafts; Cards; Games;
Reading groups; Prayer groups; Movies;
Dances/Social/Cultural gatherings;
Intergenerational programs; Current events;
Gardening; Sing-alongs; Cooking; Men's
club; Women's club.

Woodland Nursing Home Corp
490 Pelham Rd, New Rochelle, NY 10805
(914) 636-2800
Admin Irene Ross. *Dir of Nursing* Bernadette
Costagliola. *Medical Dir* Alan Jaffe.
Licensure Skilled care. *Beds* SNF 182.
Certified Medicaid; Medicare.
Owner Proprietary corp.
Admissions Requirements Medical
examination; Physician's request.
Staff Physicians 21 (pt); RNs 14 (ft); LPNs 29
(ft); Nurses' aides 93 (ft); Physical therapists
2 (pt); Occupational therapists 1 (pt); Speech
therapists 1 (pt); Activities coordinators 1
(ft); Dietitians 1 (pt); Ophthalmologists 1
(pt); Podiatrists 1 (pt); Dentists 1 (pt).
Languages Italian, Spanish.
Facilities Dining room; Physical therapy
room; Activities room; Laundry room;
Barber/Beauty shop; Library.
Activities Arts & crafts; Cards; Games;
Reading groups; Prayer groups; Movies;
Dances/Social/Cultural gatherings.

New York

American Nursing Home
62 Ave B, New York, NY 10009
(212) 677-4161
Admin Moses Unger.
Medical Dir Joseph J Kelter.
Licensure Skilled care. *Beds* SNF 240.
Certified Medicaid; Medicare.
Owner Privately owned.

Amsterdam Nursing Home Corp
1060 Amsterdam Ave, New York, NY 10025
(212) 316-7711
Admin James Davis. *Dir of Nursing* Flor
Domingo. *Medical Dir* Dr Sandra Selikson.

Licensure Skilled care; Intermediate care. *Beds*
SNF 135; ICF 168. *Private Pay Patients*
15%. *Certified* Medicaid; Medicare.
Owner Nonprofit corp.
Staff Physicians 5 (pt); Physical therapists 2
(ft); Recreational therapists 4 (ft);
Occupational therapists 1 (ft), 1 (pt); Speech
therapists 1 (pt); Activities coordinators 1
(ft); Dietitians; Podiatrists 2 (pt).

Beth Abraham Hospital
612 Allerton Ave, New York, NY 10467
(212) 920-5881, 920-2632 FAX
Admin Cecelia C Zuckerman. *Dir of Nursing*
Miriam Somer. *Medical Dir* Dr Walter
Schwartz.
Licensure Skilled care. *Beds* SNF 520. *Private
Pay Patients* 5%. *Certified* Medicaid;
Medicare.
Owner Nonprofit organization/foundation.
Admissions Requirements Minimum age 16;
Physician's request; PRI & screen.
Staff Physicians 6 (ft), 2 (pt); RNs 111 (ft), 40
(pt); LPNs 23 (ft), 1 (pt); Nurses' aides 237
(ft), 37 (pt); Physical therapists 8 (ft);
Recreational therapists 6 (ft); Occupational
therapists 7 (ft); Speech therapists 3 (ft);
Activities coordinators 1 (ft); Dietitians 8
(ft), 1 (pt).
Languages Spanish, Yiddish, Hebrew,
Russian, Italian.
Affiliation Jewish.
Facilities Dining room; Physical therapy
room; Activities room; Chapel; Crafts room;
Laundry room; Barber/Beauty shop; Library;
Occupational therapy room.
Activities Arts & crafts; Cards; Games;
Reading groups; Prayer groups; Movies;
Shopping trips; Dances/Social/Cultural
gatherings; Intergenerational programs; Pet
therapy; Music therapy.

Bialystoker Home & Infirmary for the Aged
228 E Broadway, New York, NY 10002
(212) 475-7755
Medical Dir Dr Albert Khaski.
Licensure Skilled care; Intermediate care. *Beds*
SNF 73; ICF 22. *Certified* Medicaid;
Medicare.
Owner Nonprofit corp.
Admissions Requirements Minimum age 65;
Medical examination.
Affiliation Jewish.
Facilities Dining room; Physical therapy
room; Activities room; Chapel; Crafts room;
Laundry room; Barber/Beauty shop; Library.
Activities Arts & crafts; Prayer groups;
Movies.

**Coler Memorial Hospital Skilled Nursing
Facility**
Roosevelt Island, New York, NY 10044
(212) 848-6000
Licensure Skilled care. *Beds* SNF 775.
Certified Medicaid; Medicare.
Owner Proprietary corp (New York Health
Corp).

Terence Cardinal Cooke Health Care Center
1249 5th Ave, New York, NY 10029
(212) 360-3600, 289-2739 FAX
Admin John F Keane, Pres. *Dir of Nursing*
Eula T Diggs. *Medical Dir* Gerhard Treser
MD.
Licensure Skilled care; Intermediate care for
mentally retarded; Specialty hospital; SNF
for AIDS patients. *Beds* SNF 237; ICF/MR
100; Specialty hospital 50; SNF for AIDS
patients 44. *Certified* Medicaid; Medicare.
Owner Nonprofit corp.
Admissions Requirements Medical
examination; Physician's request.
Affiliation Roman Catholic.
Facilities Dining room; Physical therapy
room; Activities room; Chapel; Crafts room;
Laundry room; Barber/Beauty shop; Library.

Activities Arts & crafts; Cards; Games; Reading groups; Prayer groups; Movies; Shopping trips; Dances/Social/Cultural gatherings.

Dewitt Nursing Home
211 E 79th St, New York, NY 10021
(212) 879-1600, 988-6298 FAX
Admin Marilyn Lichtman; Michael A Hotz. Dir of Nursing Sonia Bogosian. Medical Dir Dr Miodrag Ristich.
Licensure Skilled care. Beds SNF 499. Private Pay Patients 14%. Certified Medicaid; Medicare.
Owner Privately owned.
Admissions Requirements Minimum age 16; Medical examination; Physician's request.
Staff RNs 62 (ft), 1 (pt); LPNs 45 (ft), 3 (pt); Nurses' aides 249 (ft), 4 (pt); Physical therapists 1 (ft), 2 (pt); Reality therapists 1 (ft); Recreational therapists 3 (ft); Occupational therapists 1 (ft), 1 (pt); Speech therapists 1 (pt); Activities coordinators 1 (ft); Dietitians 3 (ft), 1 (pt).
Languages 23 languages.
Facilities Dining room; Physical therapy room; Activities room; Chapel; Crafts room; Laundry room; Barber/Beauty shop; Library; OT; Speech; Dental.
Activities Arts & crafts; Cards; Games; Reading groups; Prayer groups; Movies; Shopping trips; Dances/Social/Cultural gatherings; Intergenerational programs; Pet therapy.

Fort Tryon Nursing Home
801 W 190th St, New York, NY 10040
(212) 923-2530
Admin Israel Sherman.
Medical Dir Dr Ben W Aberman.
Licensure Skilled care. Beds SNF 205. Certified Medicaid; Medicare.
Owner Privately owned.
Staff RNs 15 (ft), 8 (pt); LPNs 6 (ft), 16 (pt); Nurses' aides 52 (ft), 27 (pt); Physical therapists 3 (pt); Occupational therapists 1 (pt); Speech therapists 1 (pt); Activities coordinators 1 (ft); Dietitians 1 (ft); Ophthalmologists 1 (pt); Podiatrists 1 (pt); Audiologists 1 (pt); Dentists 1 (pt).
Affiliation Jewish.
Facilities Dining room; Physical therapy room; Activities room; Chapel; Crafts room; Barber/Beauty shop.
Activities Arts & crafts; Cards; Games; Movies; Dances/Social/Cultural gatherings; Birthday parties; Masquerades.

Goldwater Memorial Hospital
Franklin D Roosevelt Island, New York, NY 10044
(212) 750-6800
Admin I Bernard Hirsch. Dir of Nursing Howard Garrison RN. Medical Dir Mathew H M Lee MD.
Licensure Skilled care. Beds SNF 412. Certified Medicaid; Medicare.
Owner Proprietary corp (New York Health Corp).
Admissions Requirements Minimum age 18; Medical examination.
Staff Physicians 5 (ft), 4 (pt); RNs 65 (ft); LPNs 50 (ft); Nurses' aides 169 (ft); Physical therapists 23 (ft); Reality therapists 5 (ft); Recreational therapists 13 (ft), 2 (pt); Occupational therapists 17 (ft); Speech therapists 7 (ft); Dietitians 3 (ft); Ophthalmologists 2 (pt); Podiatrists 3 (ft); Dentists 2 (pt).
Facilities Dining room; Physical therapy room; Activities room; Chapel; Crafts room; Laundry room; Barber/Beauty shop; Library; Occupational therapy room; Speech therapy room; Audiology center; Language bank.
Activities Arts & crafts; Cards; Games; Reading groups; Prayer groups; Movies; Shopping trips; Dances/Social/Cultural gatherings; Creative writing; Music groups.

Greater Harlem Nursing Home Company Inc
30 W 138th St, New York, NY 10037
(212) 690-7400, 862-7834 FAX
Admin Sybil Williams. Dir of Nursing Flossie Kendrick RN. Medical Dir Karel Kennedy MD.
Licensure Skilled care. Beds SNF 200. Certified Medicaid; Medicare.
Owner Nonprofit corp.
Admissions Requirements Minimum age 17; Physician's request.
Staff Physicians 4 (pt); RNs 15 (ft); LPNs 16 (ft); Nurses' aides 90 (ft); Physical therapists 2 (ft); Recreational therapists 4 (ft); Occupational therapists 1 (ft); Speech therapists 1 (pt); Dietitians 1 (ft), 1 (pt); Audiologists 1 (pt).
Languages Spanish.
Facilities Dining room; Physical therapy room; Activities room; Crafts room; Laundry room; Barber/Beauty shop.
Activities Arts & crafts; Cards; Games; Movies; Dances/Social/Cultural gatherings; Intergenerational programs; Pet therapy.

Hebrew Home for the Aged at Riverdale
5901 Palisade Ave, New York, NY 10471
(212) 549-8700
Admin Jacob Reingold. Dir of Nursing Jeanette Seggebruch. Medical Dir Harrison G Bloom MD.
Licensure Skilled care; Intermediate care; Retirement; Alzheimer's care. Beds SNF 486; ICF 298. Certified Medicaid; Medicare.
Owner Nonprofit corp.
Admissions Requirements Medical examination.
Staff Physicians 8 (ft), 2 (pt); RNs 60 (ft), 10 (pt); LPNs 36 (ft), 8 (pt); Nurses' aides 217 (ft); Physical therapists 2 (ft), 2 (pt); Occupational therapists 2 (ft), 1 (pt); Speech therapists 1 (ft); Activities coordinators 7 (ft), 14 (pt); Dietitians 5 (ft); Ophthalmologists 4 (pt); Podiatrists 4 (pt); Dentists 3 (pt).
Languages Yiddish, Hebrew.
Affiliation Jewish.
Facilities Dining room; Physical therapy room; Activities room; Chapel; Crafts room; Laundry room; Barber/Beauty shop; Occupational therapy room; Laboratory; Pharmacy; Radiology; Audiology suite.
Activities Arts & crafts; Cards; Games; Reading groups; Prayer groups; Movies; Shopping trips; Dances/Social/Cultural gatherings.

Home of the Sages of Israel
25 Bialystoker Pl, New York, NY 10002
(212) 673-8500, 353-9471 FAX
Admin Hersh Fluss. Dir of Nursing Rebecca Miladu. Medical Dir Dr Albert Khaski.
Licensure Skilled care. Beds SNF 58. Certified Medicaid; Medicare.
Owner Nonprofit organization/foundation.
Admissions Requirements Minimum age 62; Medical examination.
Staff Physicians 3 (pt); RNs 6 (ft), 2 (pt); LPNs 6 (ft), 1 (pt); Nurses' aides 16 (ft), 1 (pt); Physical therapists 1 (pt); Recreational therapists 1 (ft), 1 (pt); Occupational therapists 1 (pt); Speech therapists 1 (pt); Dietitians 1 (pt); Ophthalmologists 1 (pt); Podiatrists 1 (pt).
Languages Yiddish.
Facilities Dining room; Physical therapy room; Activities room; Chapel; Crafts room; Laundry room; Library.
Activities Arts & crafts; Cards; Games; Reading groups; Prayer groups; Movies.

Isabella Geriatric Center
515 Audubon Ave, New York, NY 10040
(212) 781-9800, 923-0927 FAX
Admin Thomas F Coughlin. Dir of Nursing Hope Miller. Medical Dir Arthur J Lennon MD.

Licensure Skilled care; Intermediate care; Home health care; Retirement; Alzheimer's care. Beds SNF 355; ICF 197; Home health care 100; Retirement 85. Private Pay Patients 12%. Certified Medicaid; Medicare.
Owner Nonprofit corp.
Admissions Requirements Minimum age 55; Medical examination.
Staff Physicians; RNs; LPNs; Nurses' aides; Physical therapists; Recreational therapists; Occupational therapists; Speech therapists; Activities coordinators; Dietitians; Ophthalmologists; Podiatrists.
Languages French, German, Yiddish.
Facilities Dining room; Physical therapy room; Activities room; Chapel; Crafts room; Laundry room; Barber/Beauty shop; Library.
Activities Arts & crafts; Cards; Games; Reading groups; Prayer groups; Movies; Shopping trips; Dances/Social/Cultural gatherings; Intergenerational programs; Pet therapy; Therapeutic recreation; Volunteer program; Community services program.

Jewish Home & Hospital for Aged—Manhattan Division
120 W 106th St, New York, NY 10025
(212) 870-5000, 870-4895 FAX
Admin Helene Meyers. Dir of Nursing Ellen Shulman RN. Medical Dir Richard Neufeld MD; Leslie Libow MD, Chief of Staff.
Licensure Skilled care; Intermediate care; Retirement; Alzheimer's emergency respite. Beds SNF 476; ICF 38; Retirement 50. Private Pay Patients 19%. Certified Medicaid; Medicare.
Owner Nonprofit corp.
Admissions Requirements Minimum age 60; Medical examination.
Staff Physicians 7 (ft), 50 (pt); RNs 76 (ft); LPNs 29 (ft); Nurses' aides 227 (ft); Physical therapists 3 (ft), 4 (pt); Recreational therapists 8 (ft); Occupational therapists 3 (ft); Activities coordinators 1 (ft); Dietitians 5 (ft); Ophthalmologists 3 (ft); Podiatrists 1 (pt); Dentists 2 (ft); Nursing supervisors 11 (ft); Occupational therapy assistants 2 (ft); Speech pathologists 1 (pt).
Languages Spanish, Yiddish, Hebrew, Russian, German, Polish.
Affiliation Jewish.
Facilities Physical therapy room; Chapel; Crafts room; Barber/Beauty shop; Library; Garden/Solarium; Occupational therapy room; Coffee shop; Cafeteria; Auditorium; Boutique.
Activities Arts & crafts; Cards; Games; Reading groups; Prayer groups; Movies; Shopping trips; Dances/Social/Cultural gatherings; Intergenerational programs; Pet therapy.

Kateri Residence
150 Riverside Dr, New York, NY 10024
(212) 595-4410
Admin James D Cameron. Dir of Nursing Margaret Taylor RN. Medical Dir Anthony Lechich MD.
Licensure Skilled care. Beds SNF 520. Certified Medicaid; Medicare.
Owner Nonprofit corp (Catholic Charities-Arch of NY).
Admissions Requirements Minimum age 65; Medical examination; Physician's request.
Staff Physicians 9 (pt); RNs 41 (ft); LPNs 85 (ft); Nurses' aides 232 (ft); Physical therapists 2 (ft); Recreational therapists 6 (ft); Occupational therapists 1 (ft); Speech therapists 1 (ft); Activities coordinators 1 (ft); Dietitians 70 (ft); Ophthalmologists 1 (pt); Podiatrists 1 (pt); Dentists 1 (pt); Social workers 5 (ft), 2 (pt).
Languages Spanish, Yiddish, Hebrew.
Affiliation Roman Catholic.
Facilities Dining room; Physical therapy room; Activities room; Chapel; Crafts room; Laundry room; Barber/Beauty shop; Library.

Activities Arts & crafts; Cards; Games; Reading groups; Prayer groups; Movies; Shopping trips; Dances/Social/Cultural gatherings.

New Gouverneur Hospital Skilled Nursing Facility
227 Madison St, New York, NY 10002
(212) 374-4000
Admin Alan H Rosenblut.
Licensure Skilled care. *Beds* SNF 210. *Certified* Medicaid; Medicare.
Owner Publicly owned.

Florence Nightingale Nursing Home
1760 3rd Ave, New York, NY 10029
(212) 410-8700, 410-8797 FAX
Admin William J Pascocello. *Dir of Nursing* Margaret Lutz. *Medical Dir* Mitchel Kaplan MD; Mitchell Wolfson MD.
Licensure Skilled care. *Beds* SNF 561. *Private Pay Patients* 10%. *Certified* Medicaid; Medicare.
Owner Privately owned.
Admissions Requirements Medical examination; Physician's request.
Staff Physicians 4 (pt); RNs 10 (ft), 2 (pt); LPNs 42 (ft), 9 (pt); Nurses' aides 175 (ft), 44 (pt); Physical therapists 2 (ft), 4 (pt); Recreational therapists 5 (ft), 3 (pt); Occupational therapists 2 (ft), 1 (pt); Speech therapists 1 (pt); Activities coordinators 1 (ft); Dietitians 4 (ft); Ophthalmologists 1 (pt); Podiatrists 2 (pt); Audiologists 1 (pt); Dentists 1 (pt); Psychiatrists 3 (pt).
Languages Numerous languages available.
Activities Arts & crafts; Cards; Games; Reading groups; Prayer groups; Movies; Shopping trips; Dances/Social/Cultural gatherings; Intergenerational programs; Pet therapy; Religious services.

St Roses Home
71 Jackson St, New York, NY 10002
(212) 677-8132
Admin Sr M Rosaria OP. *Dir of Nursing* Sr M Rosalie RN. *Medical Dir* Arthur Larkin MD.
Licensure Skilled care. *Beds* SNF 60.
Owner Nonprofit corp.
Admissions Requirements St Rose's Home application completed and signed by physician; Copy of patient's pathology report or CAT scan.
Staff RNs 5 (ft); LPNs 4 (ft); Nurses' aides 5 (ft); Activities coordinators 1 (ft); Dietitians 1 (ft); Ophthalmologists 1 (ft).
Languages Spanish.
Facilities Activities room; Chapel; Laundry room.
Activities Arts & crafts; Cards; Games; Prayer groups; Movies.

Frances Schervier Home & Hospital
2975 Independence Ave, New York, NY 10463
(212) 548-1700, 601-3384 FAX
Admin Patricia A Krasnausky. *Dir of Nursing* Deborah D Lynch RN. *Medical Dir* Jeffrey N Nichols MD.
Licensure Skilled care; Intermediate care; Retirement. *Beds* SNF 284; ICF 80; Retirement apts 153. *Private Pay Patients* 17%. *Certified* Medicaid; Medicare.
Owner Nonprofit corp (Franciscan Sisters of the Poor Health Systems Inc).
Admissions Requirements Minimum age 65; Medical examination.
Staff Physicians 1 (ft), 46 (pt); RNs 46 (ft), 2 (pt); LPNs 23 (ft), 2 (pt); Nurses' aides 105 (ft), 38 (pt); Physical therapists 4 (ft); Recreational therapists 2 (ft); Occupational therapists 2 (ft); Speech therapists 1 (pt); Activities coordinators 2 (ft), 1 (pt); Dietitians 4 (ft); Ophthalmologists 2 (pt); Podiatrists 2 (pt); Audiologists 1 (pt); Registry 7 (pt); Per Diem 7 (pt).
Languages Spanish, French, German, Sign.

Affiliation Roman Catholic.
Facilities Dining room; Physical therapy room; Activities room; Chapel; Crafts room; Laundry room; Barber/Beauty shop; Library; Recreation hall.
Activities Arts & crafts; Cards; Games; Reading groups; Prayer groups; Movies; Shopping trips; Dances/Social/Cultural gatherings; Intergenerational programs; Pet therapy.

Village Nursing Home Inc
607 Hudson St, New York, NY 10014
(212) 255-3003, 645-9209 FAX
Admin Abraham L Seiman. *Dir of Nursing* Phyllis Downer. *Medical Dir* Stephen Wener MD.
Licensure Skilled care; Alzheimer's care. *Beds* SNF 200. *Certified* Medicaid; Medicare.
Owner Nonprofit corp.
Staff Physicians 1 (ft), 5 (pt); Physical therapists 2 (ft); Recreational therapists 3 (ft), 2 (pt); Occupational therapists 2 (ft); Speech therapists 1 (pt); Dietitians 4 (ft); Ophthalmologists (consultant); Podiatrists (consultant); Audiologists.
Languages Spanish, Chinese.
Activities Arts & crafts; Games; Reading groups; Prayer groups; Movies; Dances/Social/Cultural gatherings; Intergenerational programs; Alzheimer's program.

Mary Manning Walsh Nursing Home Company Inc
1339 York Ave, New York, NY 10021
(212) 628-2800
Admin Sr M Kevin Patricia.
Licensure Skilled care; Intermediate care. *Beds* SNF 328; ICF 34. *Certified* Medicaid; Medicare.
Owner Nonprofit corp (Catholic Charities-Arch of NY).

Newark

Newark Manor Nursing Home
222 W Pearl St, Newark, NY 14513
(315) 331-4690
Admin Janis Sharrow.
Licensure Skilled care. *Beds* SNF 60. *Certified* Medicaid; Medicare.
Owner Privately owned.

Newark-Wayne Community Hospital Inc—Skilled Nursing Facility
Box 111, Driving Park Ave, Newark, NY 14530
(315) 332-2022
Admin Sylvia Courtney. *Dir of Nursing* Sandra Schuck. *Medical Dir* Gerald Duffner MD.
Licensure Skilled care. *Beds* SNF 84. *Private Pay Patients* 15%. *Certified* Medicaid; Medicare.
Owner Nonprofit organization/foundation.
Admissions Requirements Minimum age 16; Physician's request.
Staff Physicians 14 (pt); RNs 4 (ft), 5 (pt); LPNs 9 (ft), 5 (pt); Nurses' aides 23 (ft), 23 (pt); Physical therapists 2 (ft); Occupational therapists 1 (ft); Speech therapists 1 (ft), 1 (pt); Activities coordinators 1 (ft); Dietitians 1 (ft); Podiatrists 1 (pt); Audiologists 1 (pt).
Languages Dutch, Spanish, German.
Facilities Dining room; Physical therapy room; Activities room; Laundry room; Barber/Beauty shop.
Activities Arts & crafts; Cards; Games; Reading groups; Prayer groups; Movies; Shopping trips; Dances/Social/Cultural gatherings; Intergenerational programs; Pet therapy; Family dinners.

Newburgh

Sylcox Nursing Home & Health Related Facility
56 Meadow Hill Rd, Newburgh, NY 12550
(914) 564-1700
Admin Edward Sylcox Sr.
Licensure Skilled care; Intermediate care. *Beds* SNF 120; ICF 40. *Certified* Medicaid; Medicare.
Owner Privately owned.

Newfane

Newfane Health Facility
2709 Transit Rd, Newfane, NY 14108
(716) 778-7111
Admin Joan M McAndrew. *Dir of Nursing* Donna Haley RN. *Medical Dir* Dr Walter Altbach.
Licensure Skilled care; Intermediate care. *Beds* SNF 124; ICF 51. *Certified* Medicaid; Medicare.
Owner Privately owned.
Admissions Requirements Medical examination; Physician's request.
Staff Physicians 1 (pt); RNs 10 (ft), 6 (pt); LPNs 10 (ft), 9 (pt); Nurses' aides 29 (ft), 48 (pt); Physical therapists 1 (pt); Occupational therapists 2 (pt); Speech therapists 1 (pt); Activities coordinators 1 (ft); Dietitians 1 (pt); Podiatrists 1 (pt).
Facilities Dining room; Physical therapy room; Activities room; Crafts room; Laundry room; Barber/Beauty shop; Library.
Activities Arts & crafts; Cards; Games; Reading groups; Prayer groups; Movies; Shopping trips; Dances/Social/Cultural gatherings.

Niagara Falls

Mt St Mary's Long-Term Care Facility Inc
2600 Main St, Niagara Falls, NY 14305
(716) 285-9155, 285-4558 FAX
Admin Casimier T Czamara. *Dir of Nursing* Sharon Hewner. *Medical Dir* Christian Kivi MD.
Licensure Skilled care. *Beds* SNF 129. *Certified* Medicaid; Medicare.
Owner Nonprofit corp.
Staff RNs; LPNs; Nurses' aides; Physical therapists; Activities coordinators; Dietitians.
Affiliation Roman Catholic.
Facilities Dining room; Physical therapy room; Activities room; Laundry room; Barber/Beauty shop.
Activities Arts & crafts; Cards; Games; Reading groups; Prayer groups; Movies; Shopping trips; Dances/Social/Cultural gatherings; Intergenerational programs; Pet therapy.

Niagara Falls Memorial Nursing Home Company Inc
621 10th St, Niagara Falls, NY 14302
(716) 278-4578
Admin John Ferguson. *Dir of Nursing* J Salerno. *Medical Dir* William Henderson MD.
Licensure Skilled care. *Beds* SNF 120. *Certified* Medicaid; Medicare.
Owner Nonprofit corp.
Admissions Requirements Physician's request.
Staff Physicians 124 (ft); RNs 11 (ft); LPNs 13 (ft), 9 (pt); Nurses' aides 44 (ft), 20 (pt); Physical therapists 1 (ft); Recreational therapists 1 (ft); Occupational therapists 1 (ft); Speech therapists 1 (pt); Activities coordinators 2 (ft); Dietitians 1 (ft), 1 (pt); Ophthalmologists 1 (pt); Dentists 1 (pt).
Facilities Dining room; Activities room; Crafts room; Laundry room; Barber/Beauty shop.

Activities Arts & crafts; Cards; Games;
Reading groups; Prayer groups; Movies;
Shopping trips; Dances/Social/Cultural
gatherings.

Niagara Geriatric Center
822 Cedar Ave, Niagara Falls, NY 14301
(716) 282-1207
Admin James G Marrione.
Medical Dir William Sullivan.
Licensure Intermediate care. *Beds* ICF 160.
Certified Medicaid.
Owner Privately owned.
Admissions Requirements Minimum age 16;
Medical examination.
Staff RNs 2 (ft), 3 (pt); LPNs 8 (ft), 10 (pt);
Nurses' aides 11 (ft), 16 (pt); Activities
coordinators 1 (ft); Dietitians 1 (ft), 1 (pt).
Languages Polish, Italian, Sign.
Facilities Dining room; Activities room;
Laundry room; Barber/Beauty shop; Library.
Activities Arts & crafts; Cards; Games;
Reading groups; Prayer groups; Movies;
Shopping trips; Dances/Social/Cultural
gatherings; Field trips; Fishing.

St Mary's Manor
515 6th St, Niagara Falls, NY 14301
(716) 285-3236
Admin Sr M Joseph Clare.
Medical Dir Melvin B Dyster MD.
Licensure Skilled care. *Beds* SNF 119.
Certified Medicaid; Medicare.
Owner Nonprofit corp (Catholic Charities of
Buffalo).
Admissions Requirements Minimum age 17;
Medical examination; Physician's request.
Staff RNs 10 (ft), 6 (pt); LPNs 13 (ft), 4 (pt);
Nurses' aides 49 (ft), 16 (pt); Physical
therapists 2 (pt); Occupational therapists 1
(pt); Speech therapists 1 (pt); Activities
coordinators 2 (ft); Dietitians 1 (ft); Dentists
1 (pt).
Facilities Dining room; Physical therapy
room; Activities room; Chapel; Crafts room;
Laundry room; Barber/Beauty shop.
Activities Arts & crafts; Cards; Games;
Reading groups; Prayer groups; Movies;
Shopping trips; Dances/Social/Cultural
gatherings.

North Bellmore

Belair Nursing Home
2478 Jerusalem Ave, North Bellmore, NY
11710
(516) 826-1160
Admin Mildred Greenberg.
Licensure Skilled care. *Beds* SNF 102.
Certified Medicaid; Medicare.
Owner Privately owned.

North Creek

Adirondack Tri-County Nursing Home Inc
PO Box 500, Ski Bowl Rd, North Creek, NY
12853
(518) 251-2447
Admin Roger K Brown. *Dir of Nursing* Linda
Smith RN. *Medical Dir* John Rugge MD.
Licensure Skilled care; Adult day care. *Beds*
SNF 60. *Private Pay Patients* 14%. *Certified*
Medicaid; Medicare.
Owner Nonprofit corp.
Admissions Requirements Medical
examination; Physician's request.
Staff RNs 3 (ft), 4 (pt); LPNs 3 (ft), 9 (pt);
Nurses' aides 8 (ft), 22 (pt); Physical
therapists 1 (pt); Speech therapists 1 (pt);
Activities coordinators 1 (ft).
Facilities Dining room; Physical therapy
room; Activities room; Crafts room; Laundry
room; Barber/Beauty shop.
Activities Arts & crafts; Cards; Games;
Reading groups; Prayer groups; Movies;
Shopping trips; Pet therapy.

North Hornell

Mercycare
Bethesda Dr, North Hornell, NY 14843
Licensure Skilled care. *Beds* SNF 55.
Owner Nonprofit corp.

North Tonawanda

**Degraff Memorial Hospital—Skilled Nursing
Facility**
445 Tremont St, North Tonawanda, NY
14120
(716) 694-4500
Admin Randy K Gerlach. *Dir of Nursing* Jean
Spezio RN. *Medical Dir* Dr Ralph Berg.
Licensure Skilled care. *Beds* SNF 44. *Private
Pay Patients* 5%. *Certified* Medicaid;
Medicare.
Owner Nonprofit corp.
Admissions Requirements Minimum age 16;
Medical examination; Physician's request.
Staff RNs 5 (ft), 5 (pt); LPNs 8 (ft), 5 (pt);
Nurses' aides 12 (ft), 22 (pt); Physical
therapists 1 (pt); Activities coordinators 2
(pt); Dietitians 1 (pt).
Facilities Dining room; Physical therapy
room; Barber/Beauty shop; Library; Multi-
purpose room.
Activities Arts & crafts; Cards; Games; Prayer
groups; Movies; Shopping trips; Dances/
Social/Cultural gatherings; Intergenerational
programs; Pet therapy.

Northgate Manor
7264 Nash Rd, North Tonawanda, NY 14120
(716) 694-7700
Admin Anna M Bojarczuk-Foy. *Dir of Nursing*
Patricia Fitzpatrick. *Medical Dir* Richard
Carlson MD.
Licensure Skilled care; Intermediate care. *Beds*
SNF 168; ICF 38. *Certified* Medicaid;
Medicare.
Owner Privately owned.
Admissions Requirements Minimum age 16;
Medical examination; Physician's request.
Staff RNs 7 (ft), 8 (pt); LPNs 20 (ft), 21 (pt);
Nurses' aides 68 (ft), 15 (pt); Occupational
therapists 1 (ft), 1 (pt); Activities
coordinators 3 (ft); Dietitians 1 (ft).
Facilities Dining room; Physical therapy
room; Activities room; Laundry room;
Barber/Beauty shop; Occupational therapy
room.
Activities Arts & crafts; Cards; Games;
Reading groups; Prayer groups; Movies;
Shopping trips; Dances/Social/Cultural
gatherings; Intergenerational programs.

Norwich

**Chenango Memorial Hospital—Skilled Nursing
Facility**
179 N Broad St, Norwich, NY 13815
(607) 335-4111, 334-2024 FAX
Admin Dorothy C Zegarelli. *Dir of Nursing*
Michelle Perras RN. *Medical Dir* Paul F
MacLeod MD.
Licensure Skilled care. *Beds* SNF 54. *Private
Pay Patients* 12%. *Certified* Medicaid;
Medicare.
Owner Nonprofit corp.
Admissions Requirements Minimum age 19.
Staff Physicians 8 (pt); RNs 5 (ft), 5 (pt);
LPNs 5 (ft), 2 (pt); Nurses' aides 15 (ft), 18
(pt); Physical therapists 3 (pt); Occupational
therapists 1 (pt); Speech therapists 1 (pt);
Activities coordinators 1 (ft); Dietitians 1
(ft), 1 (pt); Ophthalmologists 2 (pt);
Podiatrists 2 (pt); Audiologists 1 (pt); Social
services 1 (ft), 1 (pt).
Facilities Dining room; Physical therapy
room; Activities room; Chapel; Crafts room;
Laundry room; Barber/Beauty shop; Library.

Activities Arts & crafts; Cards; Games;
Reading groups; Prayer groups; Movies;
Shopping trips; Dances/Social/Cultural
gatherings; Intergenerational programs; Pet
therapy.

Valley View Manor Nursing Home
Park St, Norwich, NY 13815
(607) 334-9931
Admin Stephanie J Benner. *Dir of Nursing*
Maureen Laughren RN. *Medical Dir* Dr
Robert Frank.
Licensure Skilled care. *Beds* SNF 82. *Certified*
Medicaid; Medicare.
Owner Privately owned.
Staff RNs 10 (ft), 4 (pt); LPNs 9 (ft), 4 (pt);
Nurses' aides 35 (ft), 16 (pt); Physical
therapists 1 (pt); Occupational therapists 1
(pt); Speech therapists 1 (pt); Activities
coordinators 2 (ft); Dietitians 1 (pt).
Facilities Dining room; Barber/Beauty shop.
Activities Arts & crafts; Cards; Games;
Reading groups; Prayer groups; Movies;
Shopping trips; Dances/Social/Cultural
gatherings; Pet therapy.

Oceanside

Nassau Nursing Home
2914 Lincoln Ave, Oceanside, NY 11572
(516) 536-2300, 763-2531 FAX
Admin Cheryl Fredsall LNHA. *Dir of Nursing*
Ruth West RN. *Medical Dir* Adam
Rafalowicz MD.
Licensure Skilled care. *Beds* SNF 100. *Private
Pay Patients* 25%. *Certified* Medicaid;
Medicare.
Owner Privately owned.
Admissions Requirements Minimum age 21;
Medical examination; Physician's request.
Staff Physicians; RNs; LPNs; Nurses' aides;
Physical therapists; Recreational therapists;
Occupational therapists; Speech therapists;
Activities coordinators; Dietitians;
Ophthalmologists; Podiatrists; Dentists.
Facilities Dining room; Physical therapy
room; Activities room; Barber/Beauty shop;
Kosher kitchen.
Activities Arts & crafts; Games; Reading
groups; Prayer groups; Movies; Shopping
trips; Dances/Social/Cultural gatherings;
Intergenerational programs; Pet therapy;
Fitness; Discussions.

Ogdensburg

**A Barton Hepburn Hospital Skilled Nursing
Facility**
214 King St, Ogdensburg, NY 13669
(315) 393-3600
Admin Donald C Lewis. *Dir of Nursing* Sr
Mary Brennan. *Medical Dir* Mark Chalom
MD.
Licensure Skilled care. *Beds* SNF 29. *Certified*
Medicaid; Medicare.
Owner Nonprofit corp.
Admissions Requirements Minimum age 16;
Medical examination; Physician's request.
Staff Physicians 8 (ft); RNs 1 (ft); LPNs 3 (ft),
3 (pt); Nurses' aides 11 (ft), 6 (pt); Physical
therapists 1 (ft); Occupational therapists 1
(ft); Activities coordinators 1 (ft); Dietitians
1 (ft).
Affiliation Roman Catholic.
Facilities Dining room.
Activities Arts & crafts; Cards; Games;
Reading groups; Prayer groups; Movies;
Shopping trips; Dances/Social/Cultural
gatherings.

St Josephs Home
420 Lafayette St, Ogdensburg, NY 13669
(315) 393-3780
Admin William O'Reilly. *Dir of Nursing*
Barbara Colbert. *Medical Dir* Dr Michael
Schuler.

Licensure Skilled care. *Beds* SNF 82. *Private Pay Patients* 33%. *Certified* Medicaid; Medicare.
Owner Nonprofit corp.
Admissions Requirements Minimum age 16; Medical examination.
Staff RNs; LPNs; Nurses' aides; Activities coordinators 1 (ft).
Affiliation Roman Catholic.
Facilities Dining room; Physical therapy room; Activities room; Chapel; Laundry room; Barber/Beauty shop.
Activities Cards; Games; Reading groups; Prayer groups; Movies; Dances/Social/ Cultural gatherings.

United Helpers Cedars Nursing Home Inc
RD 4, Riverside Dr, Ogdensburg, NY 13669
(315) 393-4810
Admin Cynthia L Barlow.
Medical Dir Mark Chalom MD.
Licensure Skilled care. *Beds* SNF 82. *Certified* Medicaid; Medicare.
Owner Nonprofit corp.
Admissions Requirements Minimum age 16; Medical examination; Physician's request.
Staff Physicians 1 (pt); RNs 8 (ft), 5 (pt); LPNs 6 (ft), 3 (pt); Nurses' aides 22 (ft), 15 (pt); Physical therapists 1 (pt); Occupational therapists 1 (pt); Activities coordinators 1 (ft); Dietitians 1 (pt).
Facilities Dining room; Physical therapy room; Laundry room; Barber/Beauty shop.
Activities Arts & crafts; Cards; Games; Prayer groups; Movies; Shopping trips; Dances/ Social/Cultural gatherings.

United Helpers Nursing Home Inc
Riverside Dr, Ogdensburg, NY 13669
(315) 393-0730
Admin Robert Russell.
Licensure Skilled care; Intermediate care. *Beds* SNF 40; ICF 80. *Certified* Medicaid; Medicare.
Owner Nonprofit corp.

Olean

Cattaraugus County Public Nursing Home
2245 W State St, Olean, NY 14760
(716) 373-1910
Admin Maureen Mooney-Myers. *Dir of Nursing* Patricia K Drake RN. *Medical Dir* Duncan C Wormer MD.
Licensure Skilled care. *Beds* SNF 120. *Certified* Medicaid; Medicare.
Owner Publicly owned.
Admissions Requirements Minimum age 16; Medical examination; Physician's request.
Staff Physicians 45 (pt); RNs 7 (ft), 10 (pt); LPNs 16 (ft), 9 (pt); Nurses' aides 44 (ft), 21 (pt); Physical therapists 1 (ft); Occupational therapists 1 (pt); Speech therapists 1 (pt); Activities coordinators 1 (ft); Dietitians 1 (pt); Podiatrists 1 (pt); Dentists 1 (pt).
Facilities Dining room; Physical therapy room; Activities room; Chapel; Crafts room; Laundry room; Barber/Beauty shop; Library; Atrium; Patient lounges.
Activities Arts & crafts; Cards; Games; Reading groups; Prayer groups; Movies; Shopping trips; Dances/Social/Cultural gatherings; Cooking; Trading post; Gardening; Makeup; Bowling; Resident council; Baking services.

St Josephs Manor
W State St, Olean, NY 14760
(716) 372-7810
Admin Margaret McIntire. *Dir of Nursing* Michael Paar. *Medical Dir* Dr Ben M L Hwang.
Licensure Skilled care. *Beds* SNF 22. *Certified* Medicaid; Medicare.
Owner Nonprofit corp (Catholic Charities of Buffalo).
Admissions Requirements Minimum age 21; Physician's request.

Staff RNs 2 (ft), 3 (pt); LPNs 3 (ft), 2 (pt); Nurses' aides 8 (ft), 8 (pt); Physical therapists 1 (pt); Activities coordinators 1 (pt); Dietitians 1 (pt).
Affiliation Roman Catholic.
Facilities Dining room; Activities room; Chapel; Crafts room; Laundry room.
Activities Arts & crafts; Games; Reading groups; Prayer groups; Movies.

Oneida

Oneida City Hospital—Extended Care Facility
221 Broad St, Oneida, NY 13421
(315) 363-6000
Admin Christine D Giamporcaro. *Dir of Nursing* Gail Hood. *Medical Dir* Waldo Zeun MD.
Licensure Skilled care; Intermediate care. *Beds* SNF 77; ICF 31. *Certified* Medicaid; Medicare.
Owner Publicly owned.
Admissions Requirements Minimum age 16; Medical examination; Physician's request.
Staff RNs 10 (ft), 4 (pt); LPNs 15 (ft), 12 (pt); Nurses' aides 45 (ft), 29 (pt); Physical therapists 4 (ft); Activities coordinators 1 (ft); Dietitians 1 (ft) Social workers 1 (ft).
Facilities Dining room; Physical therapy room; Activities room; Crafts room; Laundry room; Barber/Beauty shop.
Activities Arts & crafts; Cards; Games; Reading groups; Prayer groups; Movies; Shopping trips; Dances/Social/Cultural gatherings.

Oneonta

Aurelia Osborn Fox Memorial Hospital
1 Norton Ave, Oneonta, NY 13820
(607) 432-2000
Admin Gary M Smith. *Dir of Nursing* Raenell K Birdsall. *Medical Dir* Mohammed Egal.
Licensure Skilled care; Intermediate care. *Beds* SNF 85; ICF 45. *Certified* Medicaid; Medicare.
Owner Nonprofit corp.
Admissions Requirements Minimum age 17; Physician's request.
Staff Physicians 1 (pt); RNs 7 (ft), 6 (pt); LPNs 9 (ft), 12 (pt); Nurses' aides 30 (ft), 24 (pt); Physical therapists 1 (pt); Speech therapists 1 (pt); Activities coordinators 1 (ft), 2 (pt); Dietitians 1 (ft).
Facilities Dining room; Physical therapy room; Activities room; Crafts room; Laundry room; Barber/Beauty shop; Library.
Activities Arts & crafts; Cards; Games; Reading groups; Prayer groups; Movies; Shopping trips; Dances/Social/Cultural gatherings; Outings.

Oneonta-Richmond Inc
330 Chestnut St, Oneonta, NY 13820
(607) 432-8500, 432-1061 FAX
Admin Walter J Owens. *Dir of Nursing* Carrie Post RN. *Medical Dir* Reade Sisson MD.
Licensure Skilled care. *Beds* SNF 80. *Private Pay Patients* 38%. *Certified* Medicaid; Medicare.
Owner Proprietary corp (Residence Nursing Homes).
Admissions Requirements Minimum age 18; Physician's request.
Staff Physicians 2 (pt); RNs 7 (ft), 6 (pt); LPNs 12 (ft), 15 (pt); Nurses' aides 25 (ft), 30 (pt); Physical therapists 1 (pt); Occupational therapists 1 (pt); Speech therapists 1 (pt); Activities coordinators 1 (ft); Dietitians 1 (pt); Podiatrists 1 (pt); Audiologists 1 (pt).
Facilities Dining room; Physical therapy room; Activities room; Crafts room; Barber/ Beauty shop.
Activities Arts & crafts; Cards; Games; Reading groups; Prayer groups; Movies; Shopping trips; Pet therapy; Dining out.

Orchard Park

Orchard Park Health Care Center Inc
6060 Armor Rd, Orchard Park, NY 14127
(716) 662-4433
Admin Mary Tribuzzi. *Dir of Nursing* Ann Cornish. *Medical Dir* Dr James Norton.
Licensure Skilled care; Intermediate care. *Beds* SNF 86; ICF 80. *Certified* Medicaid; Medicare.
Owner Proprietary corp.
Admissions Requirements Minimum age 16; Medical examination; Physician's request.
Staff Physicians; RNs; LPNs; Nurses' aides; Physical therapists; Recreational therapists; Occupational therapists; Speech therapists; Activities coordinators; Dietitians; Ophthalmologists; Podiatrists; Audiologists; Social workers.
Facilities Dining room; Physical therapy room; Activities room; Crafts room; Laundry room; Barber/Beauty shop.
Activities Arts & crafts; Cards; Games; Reading groups; Prayer groups; Movies; Shopping trips; Dances/Social/Cultural gatherings; Van rides; Senior Olympics.

Oriskany

Eastern Star Home & Infirmary
Utica St, Oriskany, NY 13424
(315) 736-9311
Admin Unamae Ferguson. *Dir of Nursing* Karen Wentrick. *Medical Dir* Dr A Jabhon.
Licensure Skilled care; Intermediate care; Alzheimer's care; Retirement. *Beds* SNF 54; ICF 28. *Certified* Medicaid; Medicare.
Owner Nonprofit corp.
Admissions Requirements Medical examination; Physician's request.
Staff Physicians; RNs; LPNs; Nurses' aides; Physical therapists; Recreational therapists; Occupational therapists; Activities coordinators; Dietitians; Ophthalmologists.
Affiliation Order of Eastern Star.
Facilities Dining room; Physical therapy room; Activities room; Chapel; Crafts room; Laundry room; Barber/Beauty shop; Library.
Activities Arts & crafts; Cards; Games; Reading groups; Prayer groups; Movies; Shopping trips; Dances/Social/Cultural gatherings; Chapter meetings; Luncheon & dinner outings; Picnics.

Ossining

Asthmatic Childrens Foundation of New York Inc
Spring Valley Rd, Ossining, NY 10562
(914) 762-2110
Admin Raphael Cubisino. *Dir of Nursing* John Greenwood RN. *Medical Dir* Dr Armond V Mascia.
Licensure Skilled care. *Beds* SNF 36. *Certified* Medicaid.
Owner Nonprofit organization/foundation.
Admissions Requirements Minimum age 5.
Staff Physicians; RNs; Nurses' aides; Activities coordinators; Dietitians; Dentists.
Facilities Dining room; Activities room; Crafts room; Laundry room; Library; Gym.
Activities Arts & crafts; Games; Reading groups; Prayer groups; Movies; Shopping trips; Dances/Social/Cultural gatherings.

Bethel Methodist Home
19 Narragansett Ave, Ossining, NY 10562
(914) 941-7300
Admin Janet M Beard.
Licensure Health related; Retirement. *Beds* Health related; Retirement 112. *Certified* Medicaid; Medicare.
Owner Nonprofit corp.
Staff Physicians; RNs; LPNs; Nurses' aides; Physical therapists; Recreational therapists; Occupational therapists; Speech therapists; Dietitians.

Languages Spanish.
Affiliation Methodist.
Facilities Dining room; Physical therapy room; Activities room; Chapel; Crafts room; Laundry room; Barber/Beauty shop; Library; Swimming pool at retirement facility.
Activities Arts & crafts; Cards; Games; Reading groups; Movies; Dances/Social/Cultural gatherings.

Bethel Nursing Home Company Inc
17 Narragansett Ave, Ossining, NY 10562
(914) 941-7300
Admin Janet M Beard.
Licensure Skilled care. *Beds* SNF 78.
Owner Nonprofit corp.

Briar Crest Nursing Home
31 Overton Rd, Ossining, NY 10562
(914) 941-4047
Admin Jacqueline M Quarto. *Dir of Nursing* Jeannette Gibson RN. *Medical Dir* Michael Giatzis MD.
Licensure Skilled care Alzheimer's care. *Beds* SNF 86. *Certified* Medicaid; Medicare.
Owner Proprietary corp.
Admissions Requirements Minimum age 18.
Staff RNs 8 (ft), 4 (pt); LPNs 8 (ft), 4 (pt); Nurses' aides 43 (ft), 6 (pt); Physical therapists 2 (pt); Recreational therapists 2 (ft), 5 (pt); Occupational therapists 1 (pt); Activities coordinators 1 (ft); Dietitians 1 (pt).
Languages Spanish.
Activities Arts & crafts; Cards; Games; Reading groups; Prayer groups; Movies; Dances/Social/Cultural gatherings; Intergenerational programs; Pet therapy; Barbecues; Picnics; Alzheimer's program.

Cedar Manor Nursing Home
PO Box 928, Cedar Ln, Ossining, NY 10562
(914) 762-1600
Admin Jean Wetstine. *Dir of Nursing* Susan Brown. *Medical Dir* Stuart Pines MD.
Licensure Skilled care. *Beds* SNF 153. *Private Pay Patients* 25%. *Certified* Medicaid; Medicare.
Owner Privately owned.
Admissions Requirements Minimum age 21; Physician's request.
Staff RNs; LPNs; Nurses' aides; Physical therapists; Occupational therapists; Speech therapists; Activities coordinators; Dietitians; Ophthalmologists; Podiatrists; Audiologists.
Languages Spanish.
Facilities Dining room; Physical therapy room; Activities room; Crafts room; Laundry room; Barber/Beauty shop.
Activities Arts & crafts; Cards; Games; Reading groups; Prayer groups; Movies; Dances/Social/Cultural gatherings.

Victoria Home for Retired Men & Women
N Malcolm St, Ossining, NY 10562
(914) 941-2450
Admin Madeline Callahan. *Dir of Nursing* Patricia Draper. *Medical Dir* Dr E Argenziano.
Licensure Intermediate care. *Beds* ICF 49. *Certified* Medicaid.
Owner Nonprofit corp.
Admissions Requirements Medical examination.
Staff Physicians 1 (pt); RNs 1 (ft), 1 (pt); LPNs 2 (ft), 5 (pt); Nurses' aides 5 (ft), 4 (pt); Physical therapists 1 (pt); Activities coordinators 1 (pt); Dietitians 1 (pt); Social services 1 (pt).
Facilities Dining room; Activities room; Laundry room; Barber/Beauty shop; Library; Living rooms.
Activities Arts & crafts; Cards; Games; Reading groups; Prayer groups; Movies; Shopping trips.

Oswego

Harr-Wood Nursing Home
17 Sunrise Dr, Oswego, NY 13126
(315) 342-4790
Admin Martin D Miller.
Licensure Skilled care. *Beds* SNF 120. *Certified* Medicaid; Medicare.
Owner Privately owned.

Hillcrest Nursing Home
132 Ellen St, Oswego, NY 13126
(315) 342-2440
Admin Stanley J Wojciechowski. *Dir of Nursing* Joyce Boronkay RN. *Medical Dir* Roger Cook MD.
Licensure Skilled care; Intermediate care. *Beds* SNF 80; ICF 40. *Certified* Medicaid; Medicare.
Owner Privately owned.
Staff Physicians 6 (pt); RNs 7 (ft), 3 (pt); LPNs 11 (ft), 4 (pt); Nurses' aides 38 (ft), 4 (pt); Physical therapists 1 (pt); Speech therapists 1 (pt); Activities coordinators 1 (ft); Dietitians 1 (ft); Ophthalmologists 1 (pt).
Languages Polish, Italian, Hindi.
Facilities Dining room; Physical therapy room; Activities room; Chapel; Crafts room; Laundry room; Barber/Beauty shop.
Activities Arts & crafts; Cards; Games; Reading groups; Prayer groups; Movies.

Oswego Hospital Extended Care Facility
110 W 6th St, Oswego, NY 13126
(315) 349-5506
Admin Corte J Spencer. *Dir of Nursing* Gail Greenwood RN. *Medical Dir* Bipin Parekh MD.
Licensure Skilled care. *Beds* SNF 38. *Private Pay Patients* 5%. *Certified* Medicaid; Medicare.
Owner Nonprofit organization/foundation.
Admissions Requirements Minimum age 16; Medical examination.
Staff Physicians 8 (pt); RNs 2 (ft), 1 (pt); LPNs 6 (ft), 2 (pt); Nurses' aides 12 (ft), 12 (pt); Physical therapists 1 (ft); Speech therapists 1 (pt); Activities coordinators 1 (ft); Dietitians 1 (pt); Ophthalmologists 1 (pt); Podiatrists 1 (pt).
Facilities Dining room; Physical therapy room; Activities room; Chapel; Barber/Beauty shop; Library; Dental office.
Activities Arts & crafts; Cards; Games; Prayer groups; Movies; Dances/Social/Cultural gatherings; Pet therapy; Trips to farm.

Pontiac Nursing Home
E River Rd, Oswego, NY 13126
(315) 343-1800
Admin John Vivenzio.
Licensure Skilled care. *Beds* SNF 80. *Certified* Medicaid; Medicare.
Owner Privately owned.

St Luke Nursing Home Company Inc
RD 4, East River Rd, Oswego, NY 13126
(315) 342-3166
Admin Francis A Boyce.
Medical Dir Dr David D O'Brien Jr.
Licensure Intermediate care. *Beds* ICF 120. *Certified* Medicaid.
Owner Nonprofit corp.
Admissions Requirements Minimum age 16; Medical examination.
Staff RNs 4 (ft), 2 (pt); LPNs 10 (ft), 9 (pt); Nurses' aides 22 (ft), 18 (pt); Physical therapists 1 (pt); Speech therapists 1 (pt); Activities coordinators 2 (ft); Dietitians 1 (pt).
Languages Polish.
Affiliation Roman Catholic.
Facilities Dining room; Physical therapy room; Activities room; Crafts room; Barber/Beauty shop; Library.

Activities Arts & crafts; Cards; Games; Reading groups; Prayer groups; Movies; Shopping trips; Dances/Social/Cultural gatherings.

Owego

Riverview Manor Nursing Home
510 5th Ave, Owego, NY 13827
(607) 687-2594
Admin Paul J Prybylski. *Dir of Nursing* Birdie Abrams RN. *Medical Dir* Keith A Nichols MD.
Licensure Skilled care. *Beds* SNF 77. *Private Pay Patients* 50%. *Certified* Medicaid; Medicare.
Owner Privately owned (Larry M Ramsay).
Admissions Requirements Minimum age 16; Medical examination; Physician's request.
Staff Physicians 14 (pt); RNs 7 (ft), 5 (pt); LPNs 4 (ft), 2 (pt); Nurses' aides 30 (ft), 21 (pt); Physical therapists 1 (pt); Reality therapists 1 (pt); Recreational therapists 1 (pt); Occupational therapists 1 (pt); Speech therapists 1 (pt); Activities coordinators 1 (ft), 1 (pt); Dietitians 1 (pt); Ophthalmologists 1 (pt); Podiatrists 1 (pt); Audiologists 1 (pt).
Facilities Dining room; Physical therapy room; Activities room; Crafts room; Laundry room; Barber/Beauty shop; Library.
Activities Arts & crafts; Cards; Games; Reading groups; Prayer groups; Movies; Shopping trips; Dances/Social/Cultural gatherings; Pet therapy.

Oxford

New York State Veterans Home
Rte 220, E River Rd, Oxford, NY 13830
(607) 843-6991
Admin Mary J Brown. *Dir of Nursing* Shirley Panlauskas RN. *Medical Dir* Raymond Vickers MD.
Licensure Skilled care; Intermediate care. *Beds* SNF 124; ICF 118. *Certified* Medicaid; Medicare.
Owner Publicly owned.
Admissions Requirements Medical examination; Physician's request.
Staff Physicians 1 (ft), 2 (pt); RNs 20 (ft); LPNs 39 (ft); Nurses' aides 74 (ft); Physical therapists 1 (ft); Recreational therapists 4 (ft); Occupational therapists 1 (ft); Speech therapists 1 (pt); Dietitians 1 (ft); Ophthalmologists 1 (pt); Dentists 1 (pt).
Facilities Dining room; Physical therapy room; Activities room; Chapel; Crafts room; Barber/Beauty shop; Library.
Activities Arts & crafts; Cards; Games; Reading groups; Prayer groups; Movies; Shopping trips; Dances/Social/Cultural gatherings; Pet therapy program twice monthly.

Painted Post

Three Rivers Health Care Center Inc
101 Creekside Dr, Painted Post, NY 14870
(607) 936-4108
Licensure Skilled care; Intermediate care. *Beds* SNF 80; ICF 40.
Owner Proprietary corp.

Palatine Bridge

Palatine Nursing Home
Upper Lafayette St, Palatine Bridge, NY 13428
(518) 673-5212
Admin Laverne A Bouton III.
Medical Dir Dr Benjamin Button.
Licensure Skilled care. *Beds* SNF 50.
Owner Privately owned.

Staff Physicians 1 (pt); RNs 4 (ft), 2 (pt); LPNs 5 (ft), 1 (pt); Nurses' aides 18 (ft), 9 (pt); Physical therapists 1 (pt); Reality therapists 2 (ft); Recreational therapists 1 (ft); Occupational therapists 1 (pt); Speech therapists 1 (pt); Activities coordinators 1 (ft); Dietitians 1 (pt); Podiatrists 1 (pt); Audiologists 1 (pt); Dentists 1 (pt).
Facilities Dining room; Physical therapy room; Activities room; Chapel; Laundry room; Barber/Beauty shop.
Activities Arts & crafts; Cards; Games; Reading groups; Prayer groups; Movies; Shopping trips.

Patchogue

Patchogue Nursing Center
25 Schoenfeld Blvd, Patchogue, NY 11772
(516) 289-7700
Admin Paul C Maggio. *Dir of Nursing* Joy Uhrie RN. *Medical Dir* Hasmukh Patel MD.
Licensure Skilled care. *Beds* SNF 120. *Certified* Medicaid; Medicare.
Owner Privately owned.
Staff Physicians 1 (pt); RNs 10 (ft), 1 (pt); LPNs 12 (ft); Nurses' aides 70 (ft); Physical therapists 1 (pt); Recreational therapists 2 (ft), 2 (pt); Occupational therapists 1 (pt); Speech therapists 1 (pt); Activities coordinators 1 (ft); Dietitians 1 (pt); Podiatrists 1 (pt); Audiologists 1 (pt); Dentists 1 (pt).
Facilities Dining room; Physical therapy room; Activities room; Crafts room; Laundry room; Barber/Beauty shop; Dental treatment room.
Activities Arts & crafts; Cards; Games; Prayer groups; Movies; Shopping trips; Dances/ Social/Cultural gatherings.

Pawling

Lovely Hill Nursing Home
Rte 22 & S Reservoir Rd, Pawling, NY 12564
(914) 855-5700
Admin Clayton M Harbby. *Dir of Nursing* Mary E Fay. *Medical Dir* Jeffrey Carr MD.
Licensure Skilled care; Intermediate care. *Beds* SNF 80; ICF 40. *Certified* Medicaid; Medicare.
Owner Privately owned.
Admissions Requirements Minimum age 16; Medical examination.
Staff Physicians; RNs; LPNs; Nurses' aides; Physical therapists; Recreational therapists; Occupational therapists; Speech therapists; Activities coordinators; Dietitians; Ophthalmologists; Podiatrists; Dentists.
Facilities Dining room; Physical therapy room; Activities room; Chapel; Crafts room; Barber/Beauty shop; Library.
Activities Arts & crafts; Cards; Games; Reading groups; Prayer groups; Movies; Shopping trips; Dances/Social/Cultural gatherings.

Peekskill

Cortlandt Nursing Care Center Inc
110 Oregon Rd, Peekskill, NY 10566
(914) 739-9150
Admin Joel Garson. *Dir of Nursing* Kathleen Tangorra RN. *Medical Dir* Steven Rockes MD.
Licensure Skilled care; Intermediate care; Alzheimer's care. *Beds* SNF 40; ICF 80. *Certified* Medicaid; Medicare.
Owner Proprietary corp.
Staff RNs 7 (ft), 1 (pt); LPNs 9 (ft), 1 (pt); Nurses' aides 25 (ft), 15 (pt); Physical therapists 1 (pt); Recreational therapists 1 (ft); Occupational therapists 1 (pt); Speech therapists 1 (pt); Activities coordinators 3 (ft); Dietitians 1 (ft); Social workers 1 (ft).

Languages Italian, Spanish, Yiddish, Hebrew, German.
Facilities Dining room; Physical therapy room; Activities room; Crafts room; Laundry room; Barber/Beauty shop; 5 balconies on patient floors; Enclosed outdoor courtyard; 5 acres of grounds.
Activities Arts & crafts; Cards; Games; Reading groups; Prayer groups; Movies; Shopping trips; Dances/Social/Cultural gatherings; Intergenerational programs; Pet therapy.

Field Home—Holy Comforter
Catherine St, Peekskill, NY 10566
(914) 739-2244
Licensure Skilled care; Intermediate care. *Beds* SNF 150; ICF 50.
Owner Nonprofit corp.

Westledge Nursing Home
2100 E Main St, Peekskill, NY 10566
(914) 737-8400
Admin Grace Kinsey Katz. *Dir of Nursing* Mrs A Bobay. *Medical Dir* Stuart L Pines MD.
Licensure Skilled care. *Beds* SNF 100. *Certified* Medicaid; Medicare.
Owner Privately owned.
Admissions Requirements Medical examination; Physician's request.
Staff RNs 7 (ft), 6 (pt); LPNs 8 (ft), 7 (pt); Nurses' aides 39 (ft), 13 (pt); Physical therapists 1 (pt); Activities coordinators 2 (ft); Dietitians 1 (ft), 1 (pt).
Facilities Dining room; Physical therapy room; Activities room; Laundry room; Barber/Beauty shop; Library; Dayrooms; Patios; Lounges.
Activities Arts & crafts; Games; Prayer groups; Movies; Dances/Social/Cultural gatherings; Resident council; Music; Dance; Holiday programs.

Penfield

Penfield Nursing Home
1700 Penfield Rd, Penfield, NY 14526
(716) 586-7433
Admin Diedre L Murphy.
Medical Dir Kenneth S Thomson MD.
Licensure Skilled care; Alzheimer's care. *Beds* SNF 48. *Certified* Medicaid; Medicare.
Owner Privately owned.
Admissions Requirements Minimum age 16; Medical examination.
Staff Physicians 1 (pt); RNs 2 (ft), 6 (pt); LPNs 2 (ft), 5 (pt); Nurses' aides 12 (ft), 14 (pt); Physical therapists 1 (pt); Occupational therapists 1 (pt); Activities coordinators 1 (ft); Dietitians 1 (pt); Ophthalmologists 1 (pt); Podiatrists 1 (pt); Dentists 1 (pt); Social workers 2 (pt); Rehabilitation aides 1 (ft).
Facilities Dining room; Physical therapy room; Activities room; Laundry room; Barber/Beauty shop; Living room/TV room; Patio.
Activities Arts & crafts; Cards; Games; Reading groups; Prayer groups; Movies; Shopping trips; Dances/Social/Cultural gatherings; Field trips; Performances.

Penn Yan

Penn Yan Manor Nursing Home Inc
655 N Liberty St, Penn Yan, NY 14527
(315) 536-2311
Admin Noreen B Curtis. *Dir of Nursing* Ruth B Dorrough RN. *Medical Dir* Dr Norman W Lindenmuth.
Licensure Skilled care. *Beds* SNF 46. *Certified* Medicaid; Medicare.
Owner Nonprofit corp.
Admissions Requirements Minimum age 16; Medical examination; Physician's request.

Staff Physicians 1 (pt); RNs 3 (ft), 1 (pt); LPNs 4 (ft), 4 (pt); Nurses' aides 21 (ft), 16 (pt); Physical therapists 1 (pt); Occupational therapists 1 (pt); Speech therapists 1 (pt); Activities coordinators 1 (pt); Dietitians 1 (pt); Ophthalmologists 1 (pt); Podiatrists 1 (pt); Dentists 1 (pt); Maintenance; Housekeeping; Office.
Facilities Dining room; Physical therapy room; Activities room; Chapel; Crafts room; Laundry room; Barber/Beauty shop; Library.
Activities Arts & crafts; Cards; Games; Reading groups; Prayer groups; Movies; Dances/Social/Cultural gatherings.

Soldiers & Sailors Memorial Hospital Health Related Facility
418 N Main St, Penn Yan, NY 14527
(315) 536-4431
Admin James Krembs.
Licensure Skilled care; Intermediate care. *Beds* SNF 40; ICF 40. *Certified* Medicaid; Medicare.
Owner Nonprofit corp.

Philmont

Pine Haven Home
Rte 217, Philmont, NY 12565
(518) 672-7263
Admin Alice M Blaauw RN. *Dir of Nursing* Nancy DeLaurentis RN. *Medical Dir* Irma Waldo MD.
Licensure Skilled care; Intermediate care; Alzheimer's care. *Beds* SNF 80; ICF 40. *Private Pay Patients* 15%. *Certified* Medicaid; Medicare.
Owner Publicly owned.
Admissions Requirements Minimum age 18; Medical examination; Columbia County resident.
Staff Physicians 6 (pt); RNs 13 (ft), 6 (pt); LPNs 7 (ft), 8 (pt); Nurses' aides 40 (ft), 21 (pt); Physical therapists 1 (pt); Occupational therapists 1 (pt); Speech therapists 1 (pt); Activities coordinators 1 (ft); Dietitians 1 (pt).
Facilities Dining room; Physical therapy room; Activities room; Chapel; Crafts room; Laundry room; Barber/Beauty shop; Alzheimer's.
Activities Arts & crafts; Cards; Games; Prayer groups; Movies; Shopping trips; Dances/ Social/Cultural gatherings; Pet therapy.

Plainview

Central Island Nursing Home
825 Old Country Rd, Plainview, NY 11803
(516) 433-0600, 433-0615 FAX
Admin Martha Sweet FACHCA. *Dir of Nursing* Ann Bowker RN. *Medical Dir* Donald Orofino MD.
Licensure Skilled care. *Beds* SNF 202. *Certified* Medicaid; Medicare.
Owner Proprietary corp.
Facilities Dining room; Physical therapy room; Activities room; Chapel; Crafts room; Laundry room; Barber/Beauty shop; Library; Patio; Atrium.
Activities Arts & crafts; Games; Reading groups; Prayer groups; Movies; Dances/ Social/Cultural gatherings; Choral group; Rhythm band; Discussion group; Garden club; Bowling; Knitting club; Boutique; Outside entertainment; Outside trips.

Plattsburgh

Champlain Valley Physicians Hospital Medical Center—Skilled Nursing Facility
100 Beekman St, Plattsburgh, NY 12901
(518) 561-2000
Admin Neil H Gruber.

Licensure Skilled care. *Beds* SNF 54. *Certified* Medicaid; Medicare.
Owner Nonprofit corp.

Clinton County Nursing Home
3 Flynn Ave, Plattsburgh, NY 12901
(518) 563-0950
Admin Barbara A Thompson. *Dir of Nursing* Elizabeth Brown RN. *Medical Dir* Dr William LaDue.
Licensure Skilled care; Intermediate care. *Beds* SNF 55; ICF 25. *Certified* Medicaid; Medicare.
Owner Publicly owned.
Admissions Requirements Minimum age 16; Medical examination; Physician's request.
Staff Physicians 1 (pt); RNs 6 (ft), 7 (pt); LPNs 8 (ft), 7 (pt); Nurses' aides 20 (ft), 22 (pt); Physical therapists 1 (pt) Recreational therapists 1 (ft); Speech therapists 1 (pt); Activities coordinators 2 (pt); Dietitians 1 (pt).
Facilities Dining room; Physical therapy room; Activities room; Laundry room; Barber/Beauty shop; Central courtyard-patio.
Activities Games; Prayer groups; Movies; Shopping trips; Dances/Social/Cultural gatherings; Monthly theme culminating in a special event.

Meadowbrook Nursing Home
80 N Prospect Ave, Plattsburgh, NY 12901
(518) 563-5440
Admin Hobbie Hyatt.
Licensure Skilled care; Intermediate care. *Beds* SNF 80; ICF 40. *Certified* Medicaid; Medicare.
Owner Privately owned.

Sacred Heart Home Inc
8 Mickle St, Plattsburgh, NY 12901
(518) 563-3261
Admin William J Dooley. *Dir of Nursing* Sr Caroline M Stoltz RN. *Medical Dir* John P Dickard MD.
Licensure Skilled care. *Beds* SNF 89. *Certified* Medicaid; Medicare.
Owner Nonprofit corp.
Admissions Requirements Minimum age 21.
Staff Physicians 1 (pt); RNs 9 (ft), 6 (pt); LPNs 6 (ft), 5 (pt); Nurses' aides 33 (ft), 31 (pt); Activities coordinators 1 (ft); Dietitians 1 (ft).
Affiliation Roman Catholic.
Facilities Dining room; Physical therapy room; Activities room; Chapel; Crafts room; Laundry room; Barber/Beauty shop; Library.
Activities Arts & crafts; Cards; Games; Reading groups; Prayer groups; Movies; Shopping trips; Lovely lady/Handsome gent contest; Spelling contest; Bingo.

Pomona

Summit Park Hospital—Rockland County Infirmary
Sanatorium Rd, Pomona, NY 10970
(914) 354-0200, 354-1283 FAX
Admin Richard J Maloney MPH. *Dir of Nursing* Frances Shewell RN. *Medical Dir* Martin M Myles MD.
Licensure Skilled care. *Beds* SNF 300. *Private Pay Patients* 1%. *Certified* Medicaid; Medicare.
Owner Publicly owned.
Facilities Dining room; Physical therapy room; Activities room; Chapel; Crafts room; Laundry room; Barber/Beauty shop; Library.
Activities Arts & crafts; Cards; Games; Reading groups; Prayer groups; Movies; Shopping trips; Dances/Social/Cultural gatherings; Intergenerational programs; Pet therapy.

Port Chester

King Street Home Inc
787 King St, Port Chester, NY 10573
(914) 937-5800
Admin Yale Wilner.
Licensure Skilled care; Intermediate care. *Beds* SNF 80; ICF 40. *Certified* Medicaid; Medicare.
Owner Proprietary corp.
Admissions Requirements Minimum age 55; Medical examination; Physician's request.
Staff Physicians; RNs; Nurses' aides; Physical therapists; Recreational therapists; Occupational therapists; Speech therapists; Activities coordinators; Dietitians; Ophthalmologists; Podiatrists; Dentists.
Facilities Dining room; Physical therapy room; Activities room; Chapel; Crafts room; Laundry room; Barber/Beauty shop; Library; 10 acres; 8 outdoor terraces; Outdoor walks.
Activities Arts & crafts; Cards; Games; Reading groups; Prayer groups; Movies; Shopping trips; Dances/Social/Cultural gatherings.

Port Chester Nursing Home
1000 High St, Port Chester, NY 10573
(914) 937-1200
Medical Dir Joseph Silberstein MD.
Licensure Skilled care. *Beds* SNF 160. *Certified* Medicaid; Medicare.
Owner Nonprofit corp.
Staff Physicians 1 (pt); RNs 8 (ft); LPNs 11 (ft); Nurses' aides 41 (ft); Physical therapists 1 (pt); Occupational therapists 1 (pt); Speech therapists 1 (pt); Activities coordinators 3 (ft).
Affiliation Jewish.
Facilities Dining room; Physical therapy room; Activities room; Laundry room; Barber/Beauty shop; Library.
Activities Arts & crafts; Cards; Games; Reading groups; Prayer groups; Movies; Shopping trips.

United Hospital
406 Boston Post Rd, Port Chester, NY 10573
(914) 939-7000
Licensure Skilled care. *Beds* SNF 40.
Owner Nonprofit corp.

Port Jefferson

Port Jefferson Health Care Facility
Dark Hollow Rd, Port Jefferson, NY 11777
(516) 473-5400, 473-7182 FAX
Admin Donna Solomon MPA. *Dir of Nursing* Joan Greve RNC. *Medical Dir* Jerome Feldstein MD.
Licensure Skilled care. *Beds* SNF 120. *Private Pay Patients* 30%. *Certified* Medicaid; Medicare.
Owner Proprietary corp (Michael Miness).
Admissions Requirements Medical examination; Physician's request.
Staff Physicians 1 (pt); RNs; LPNs; Nurses' aides; Physical therapists 1 (pt); Recreational therapists 2 (ft); Occupational therapists 1 (pt); Speech therapists 1 (pt); Activities coordinators 1 (ft); Dietitians 1 (pt); Podiatrists 1 (pt); Audiologists 1 (pt); Optometrists 1 (pt); Beauticians 1 (pt).
Languages Interpreters available.
Facilities Dining room; Physical therapy room; Activities room; Chapel; Laundry room; Barber/Beauty shop; Resident lounge; Patio; Elevated deck; Gazebo; Picnic grounds.
Activities Arts & crafts; Cards; Games; Reading groups; Prayer groups; Movies; Shopping trips; Dances/Social/Cultural gatherings; Intergenerational programs; Pet therapy; Summer barbeques; Luncheons; Visiting library; Recreational therapy.

Sunrest Health Facilities Inc
125 E Oakland Ave, Port Jefferson, NY 11777
(516) 928-2000
Admin Paul Dioguardi.
Licensure Skilled care; Intermediate care. *Beds* SNF 141; ICF 69. *Certified* Medicaid; Medicare.
Owner Proprietary corp.

Port Jefferson Station

Woodhaven Nursing Home
1360 Rte 112, Port Jefferson Station, NY 11776
(516) 473-7100, 473-7118 FAX
Admin Eurydice Loucopoulos.
Licensure Skilled care; Retirement. *Beds* SNF 143; Retirement 353. *Certified* Medicaid; Medicare.
Owner Proprietary corp.
Staff Physicians; RNs; LPNs; Nurses' aides; Physical therapists; Reality therapists; Recreational therapists; Occupational therapists; Speech therapists; Activities coordinators; Dietitians; Ophthalmologists; Podiatrists; Audiologists.
Languages Spanish, Greek, Hebrew.
Facilities Dining room; Physical therapy room; Activities room; Crafts room; Laundry room; Barber/Beauty shop; Library.
Activities Arts & crafts; Cards; Games; Reading groups; Prayer groups; Movies; Dances/Social/Cultural gatherings; Intergenerational programs; Pet therapy; Family support group.

Port Washington

Sands Point Nursing Home
1440 Port Washington Blvd, Port Washington, NY 11050
(516) 767-2320
Admin Chana Zlotnick.
Medical Dir Dr J Rawlings.
Licensure Skilled care. *Beds* SNF 130. *Certified* Medicaid; Medicare.
Owner Privately owned.
Admissions Requirements Medical examination; Physician's request.
Staff RNs 5 (ft), 9 (pt); LPNs 13 (ft), 5 (pt); Nurses' aides 41 (ft), 13 (pt); Activities coordinators 1 (ft); Dietitians 1 (pt).
Facilities Dining room; Physical therapy room; Activities room; Laundry room; Barber/Beauty shop; Library.
Activities Arts & crafts; Cards; Games; Reading groups; Prayer groups; Movies; Shopping trips; Dances/Social/Cultural gatherings; Nursery group visits; Bible study.

Potsdam

Potsdam Nursing Home
Cottage Grove, Potsdam, NY 13676
(315) 265-6330
Admin Norma Secours.
Licensure Skilled care. *Beds* SNF 80. *Certified* Medicaid; Medicare.
Owner Nonprofit corp.

Poughkeepsie

Eden Park Nursing Home
100 Franklin St, Poughkeepsie, NY 12601
(914) 454-4100
Licensure Skilled care; Intermediate care. *Beds* 120. *Certified* Medicaid; Medicare.
Owner Proprietary corp (Eden Park Health Services Inc).

Purdys

Salem Hills Nursing Care Center
Rte 22 Box 66, Purdys, NY 10578
(914) 277-3626

Admin Martha M Habermann. *Dir of Nursing* Patricia S Power RN. *Medical Dir* Charles Block MD.
Licensure Skilled care; Intermediate care. *Beds* SNF 63; ICF 63. *Certified* Medicaid; Medicare.
Owner Privately owned.
Admissions Requirements Minimum age 16; Meet the criteria for SNF/ICF.
Staff RNs; LPNs; Nurses' aides; Physical therapists; Speech therapists; Activities coordinators; Dietitians.
Facilities Dining room; Physical therapy room; Activities room; Laundry room; Barber/Beauty shop.
Activities Arts & crafts; Cards; Games; Reading groups; Prayer groups; Movies; Pet therapy.

Purdys Station

Waterview Hills Nursing Center Inc
Box 257, Old Rte 22, Purdys Station, NY 10578
(914) 277-3691
Admin Barry F Reisler. *Dir of Nursing* Patricia Mackin RN. *Medical Dir* Dhimant Pandya MD.
Licensure Skilled care; Alzheimer's care. *Beds* SNF 130. *Certified* Medicaid; Medicare.
Owner Proprietary corp.
Admissions Requirements Minimum age 21; Medical examination.
Staff RNs; LPNs; Nurses' aides; Physical therapists; Occupational therapists; Speech therapists; Activities coordinators; Dietitians.
Facilities Dining room; Physical therapy room; Activities room; Crafts room; Laundry room; Barber/Beauty shop; Library; Century tub; Kitchenettes; Garden room; Treatment rooms.
Activities Arts & crafts; Cards; Games; Reading groups; Prayer groups; Movies; Dances/Social/Cultural gatherings; Art therapy; Pet therapy; Horticulture groups.

Queens Village

Queen of Peace Residence
110-30 221st St, Queens Village, NY 11429
(718) 464-1800
Admin Christine de la Trinite.
Licensure Skilled care; Intermediate care. *Beds* SNF 70; ICF 85. *Certified* Medicaid; Medicare.
Owner Nonprofit corp.

Windsor Park Nursing Home
212-40 Hillside Ave, Queens Village, NY 11427
(718) 468-0800
Admin Elizabeth Rothchild. *Dir of Nursing* Vna Johnson RN. *Medical Dir* Michael Sheehtman MD.
Licensure Skilled care. *Beds* SNF 70. *Certified* Medicaid; Medicare.
Owner Proprietary corp.
Admissions Requirements Minimum age 80; Medical examination; Physician's request.
Staff Physicians; RNs; LPNs; Nurses' aides; Physical therapists; Reality therapists; Recreational therapists; Occupational therapists; Speech therapists; Activities coordinators; Dietitians; Ophthalmologists; Podiatrists; Dentists.
Facilities Dining room; Physical therapy room; Activities room; Chapel; Crafts room; Laundry room; Barber/Beauty shop; Library.
Activities Arts & crafts; Cards; Games; Prayer groups; Movies; Shopping trips; Dances/Social/Cultural gatherings; Field trips.

Queensbury

Westmount Health Facility
RR 5 Box 240, Gurney Ln, Queensbury, NY 12804
(518) 761-6540
Admin Margaret A Stuerzebecher. *Dir of Nursing* Carolyn E Hohenstein. *Medical Dir* John E Cunningham Jr MD.
Licensure Skilled care. *Beds* SNF 80. *Private Pay Patients* 5%. *Certified* Medicaid; Medicare.
Owner Publicly owned.
Admissions Requirements Minimum age 16; Medical examination; Physician's request.
Staff Physicians 3 (ft); RNs 9 (ft); LPNs 9 (ft); Nurses' aides 39 (ft); Activities coordinators 1 (ft).
Facilities Dining room; Physical therapy room; Activities room; Laundry room; Barber/Beauty shop.
Activities Arts & crafts; Cards; Games; Reading groups; Prayer groups; Movies; Shopping trips; Dances/Social/Cultural gatherings; Intergenerational programs; Pet therapy.

Rego Park

Van Doren Nursing Home
59-20 Van Doren St, Rego Park, NY 11368
(718) 592-9200, 592-9780 FAX
Admin Robert Oppenheimer LNHA MSW. *Dir of Nursing* Teresa Flowe RN. *Medical Dir* Dr Constantin Anagnostopoulos.
Licensure Skilled care. *Beds* SNF 200. *Private Pay Patients* 10%. *Certified* Medicaid; Medicare.
Owner Privately owned.
Admissions Requirements Minimum age 40.
Staff Physical therapists (consultant); Recreational therapists 1 (ft); Occupational therapists (consultant); Speech therapists (consultant); Activities coordinators 1 (ft); Dietitians 2 (ft); Ophthalmologists (consultant); Podiatrists (consultant); Audiologists (consultant).
Languages Russian, Spanish, Hebrew, French.
Facilities Dining room; Physical therapy room; Activities room; Laundry room; Barber/Beauty shop.
Activities Arts & crafts; Games; Reading groups; Prayer groups; Movies; Dances/Social/Cultural gatherings; Resident group therapy program; Family group therapy program.

Rensselaer

Rosewood Gardens
Rd 2, Rtes 4 & 40, Rensselaer, NY 12144
(518) 286-1621
Admin Beverly R Benno. *Dir of Nursing* Shirley Sheridan. *Medical Dir* A Farol MD.
Licensure Skilled care; Intermediate care. *Beds* SNF 40; ICF 40. *Certified* Medicaid; Medicare.
Owner Proprietary corp.
Staff RNs; LPNs; Nurses' aides; Physical therapists; Recreational therapists; Occupational therapists; Speech therapists; Activities coordinators; Dietitians; Ophthalmologists.

Rhinebeck

Baptist Home of Brooklyn New York
PO Box 129, Rhinebeck, NY 12572
(914) 876-2071, 876-2197 FAX
Admin Douglas P MacKechnie CSW LNHA. *Dir of Nursing* Mary DeWitt RN. *Medical Dir* Leon Krakower MD.
Licensure Skilled care; Intermediate care. *Beds* SNF 80; ICF 40. *Private Pay Patients* 21%. *Certified* Medicaid; Medicare.
Owner Nonprofit corp.

Admissions Requirements Medical examination; Physician's request.
Staff Physicians 3 (pt); RNs 4 (ft), 17 (pt); LPNs 7 (ft), 6 (pt); Nurses' aides 37 (ft), 31 (pt); Physical therapists 1 (pt); Recreational therapists 1 (ft); Occupational therapists 1 (pt); Speech therapists 1 (pt); Dietitians 1 (pt); Ophthalmologists 1 (pt); Podiatrists 1 (pt); Audiologists 1 (pt); Beauticians 2 (pt).
Affiliation Baptist.
Facilities Dining room; Physical therapy room; Activities room; Chapel; Crafts room; Laundry room; Barber/Beauty shop; Library; Coffee shop; Private rooms.
Activities Arts & crafts; Cards; Games; Reading groups; Prayer groups; Movies; Shopping trips; Intergenerational gatherings; Intergenerational programs; Pet therapy.

Ferncliff Nursing Home Co Inc
PO Box 386, River Rd, Rhinebeck, NY 12572
(914) 876-2011
Admin Sr Robert Walsh.
Medical Dir George Verrilli MD.
Licensure Skilled care; Intermediate care; Alzheimer's care. *Beds* SNF 240; ICF 80. *Certified* Medicaid; Medicare.
Owner Nonprofit corp.
Admissions Requirements Medical examination.
Staff Physicians 8 (pt); RNs 14 (ft), 12 (pt); LPNs 18 (ft), 20 (pt); Nurses' aides 104 (ft), 49 (pt); Physical therapists 1 (ft); Occupational therapists 1 (pt); Speech therapists 1 (pt); Activities coordinators 1 (ft); Dietitians 1 (ft); Ophthalmologists 1 (pt); Podiatrists 1 (pt); Dentists 4 (pt).
Affiliation Roman Catholic.
Facilities Dining room; Physical therapy room; Activities room; Chapel; Crafts room; Laundry room; Barber/Beauty shop; Library; Lounge; Gift shop.
Activities Arts & crafts; Cards; Games; Reading groups; Movies; Shopping trips; Dances/Social/Cultural gatherings; Grooming; Cooking.

Northern Dutchess Hospital
Springbrook Ave, Rhinebeck, NY 12572
(914) 876-3001
Admin Michael C Mazzarella. *Dir of Nursing* Laura Tilipko RN. *Medical Dir* William G Thompson MD.
Licensure Skilled care; Retirement. *Beds* SNF 50. *Certified* Medicaid; Medicare.
Owner Nonprofit corp.
Staff RNs 3 (ft), 3 (pt); LPNs 4 (ft), 3 (pt); Nurses' aides 19 (ft), 10 (pt); Physical therapists 1 (pt); Recreational therapists 1 (ft), 2 (pt); Occupational therapists 1 (pt); Speech therapists 1 (pt); Activities coordinators 1 (ft); Dietitians 1 (pt); Ophthalmologists 1 (pt); Podiatrists 1 (pt); Dentists 1 (pt).
Facilities Dining room; Physical therapy room; Activities room; Chapel; Crafts room; Barber/Beauty shop.
Activities Arts & crafts; Cards; Games; Reading groups; Prayer groups; Movies; Shopping trips; Dances/Social/Cultural gatherings.

Riverhead

Central Suffolk Hospital Skilled Nursing Facility
1300 Roanoke Ave, Riverhead, NY 11901
Licensure Skilled care. *Beds* SNF 60.
Owner Nonprofit corp.

Riverhead Nursing Home & Health Related Facility
1146 Woodcrest Ave, Riverhead, NY 11901
(516) 727-7744
Admin Madeline C Butler. *Dir of Nursing* Mrs Zepmeisel RN. *Medical Dir* I F Frankel MD.

Licensure Skilled care; Intermediate care. *Beds* SNF 121; ICF 60. *Certified* Medicaid; Medicare.
Owner Privately owned.
Admissions Requirements Medical examination; Physician's request.
Staff RNs; LPNs; Nurses' aides; Physical therapists; Reality therapists; Occupational therapists; Speech therapists; Activities coordinators; Dietitians.
Languages Polish.
Facilities Dining room; Physical therapy room; Activities room; Chapel; Crafts room; Laundry room; Barber/Beauty shop; Library.
Activities Arts & crafts; Cards; Games; Reading groups; Movies; Shopping trips; Dances/Social/Cultural gatherings; Bingo; Resident council; Food service committee; Welcoming committee.

Rochester

Aberdeen Nursing Home
1290 Lake Ave, Rochester, NY 14613
(716) 254-1593
Admin Joseph B Dilal III. *Dir of Nursing* Rose Samentello RN.
Licensure Skilled care. *Beds* SNF 98. *Certified* Medicaid; Medicare.
Owner Proprietary corp.
Admissions Requirements Minimum age 18; Physician's request.
Staff RNs; LPNs; Nurses' aides; Physical therapists; Recreational therapists; Speech therapists; Activities coordinators; Dietitians; Ophthalmologists.
Facilities Dining room; Physical therapy room; Activities room; Laundry room; Barber/Beauty shop; Library.
Activities Arts & crafts; Cards; Games; Reading groups; Prayer groups; Movies; Shopping trips; Dances/Social/Cultural gatherings.

Alaimo Nursing Home
1140 Norton St, Rochester, NY 14621
(716) 467-2100
Admin Claudia Spindelman.
Medical Dir Caroline Christ.
Licensure Skilled care; Alzheimer's care. *Beds* 42. *Certified* Medicaid; Medicare.
Owner Proprietary corp.
Staff Physicians; RNs; LPNs; Nurses' aides; Physical therapists; Recreational therapists; Speech therapists; Activities coordinators; Dietitians; Ophthalmologists.
Facilities Dining room; Laundry room.
Activities Arts & crafts; Cards; Games; Reading groups; Prayer groups; Movies; Shopping trips; Dances/Social/Cultural gatherings.

Baird Nursing Home
2150 Saint Paul St, Rochester, NY 14621
(716) 342-5540
Admin Stephen T Heard. *Dir of Nursing* Dorothy Wasson RN. *Medical Dir* Dr John Burkhardt.
Licensure Skilled care. *Beds* SNF 28. *Private Pay Patients* 100%.
Owner Privately owned.
Admissions Requirements Minimum age 16.
Staff Physicians 7 (pt); RNs 2 (ft), 2 (pt); LPNs 2 (ft), 3 (pt); Nurses' aides 6 (ft), 10 (pt); Physical therapists 1 (pt); Occupational therapists 1 (pt); Speech therapists 1 (pt); Activities coordinators 1 (ft); Dietitians 1 (pt); Ophthalmologists 1 (pt); Podiatrists 1 (pt); Audiologists 1 (pt).
Facilities Dining room; Physical therapy room; Activities room; Crafts room; Laundry room; Barber/Beauty shop.
Activities Arts & crafts; Cards; Games; Reading groups; Prayer groups; Movies; Shopping trips; Dances/Social/Cultural gatherings; Intergenerational programs; Pet therapy.

Beechwood Sanitarium
900 Culver Rd, Rochester, NY 14609
(716) 288-3335
Admin Herbert Chambery. *Dir of Nursing* Hattie Knisely. *Medical Dir* Louis Siegel.
Licensure Skilled care. *Beds* SNF 80. *Private Pay Patients* 64%. *Certified* Medicaid; Medicare.
Owner Privately owned.
Admissions Requirements Medical examination; Physician's request.
Staff RNs 4 (ft), 4 (pt); LPNs 11 (ft), 2 (pt); Nurses' aides 27 (ft), 8 (pt); Physical therapists (consultant); Occupational therapists (consultant); Speech therapists (consultant); Activities coordinators 1 (ft); Dietitians (consultant); Ophthalmologists (consultant); Podiatrists (consultant); Audiologists (consultant); Occupational therapy aides; Physical therapy aides.
Facilities Dining room; Physical therapy room; Activities room; Crafts room; Laundry room; Barber/Beauty shop; Library.
Activities Arts & crafts; Cards; Games; Reading groups; Shopping trips; Dances/Social/Cultural gatherings.

Blossom Health Care Center
989 Blossom Rd, Rochester, NY 14610
(716) 482-3500
Admin Barbara Kitanik. *Dir of Nursing* Elizabeth De Mara. *Medical Dir* Ernest T Anderson MD.
Licensure Skilled care; Alzheimer's care. *Beds* SNF 80. *Private Pay Patients* 50%. *Certified* Medicaid; Medicare.
Owner Privately owned.
Admissions Requirements Physician's request; Code required assessment forms.
Staff Physicians 4 (pt); RNs 9 (ft), 6 (pt); LPNs 7 (ft), 2 (pt); Nurses' aides 34 (ft), 8 (pt); Physical therapists 1 (pt); Occupational therapists 1 (pt); Speech therapists 2 (pt); Activities coordinators 1 (ft); Dietitians 1 (pt).
Facilities Dining room; Physical therapy room; Activities room; Barber/Beauty shop; Wanderguard system.
Activities Arts & crafts; Cards; Games; Reading groups; Prayer groups; Movies; Shopping trips; Dances/Social/Cultural gatherings; Pet therapy; Rehabilitation programs.

Brae Loch Manor
1290 Lake Ave, Rochester, NY 14613
(716) 254-1593
Licensure Skilled care. *Beds* SNF 98.
Owner Proprietary corp.

Brightonian
1919 Elmwood Ave, Rochester, NY 14620
(716) 271-8700
Admin Stephen Sclamo. *Dir of Nursing* Dolores Westcott RN. *Medical Dir* Ernest T Anderson MD.
Licensure Skilled care. *Beds* SNF 54. *Certified* Medicaid; Medicare.
Owner Proprietary corp.
Admissions Requirements Minimum age 16; Medical examination; Physician's request.
Staff Physicians 1 (ft); RNs 4 (ft), 7 (pt); LPNs 3 (ft), 2 (pt); Nurses' aides 22 (ft); Physical therapists 1 (pt); Occupational therapists 1 (pt); Speech therapists 1 (pt); Activities coordinators 2 (ft); Dietitians 1 (ft), 1 (pt); Podiatrists 1 (pt); Audiologists 1 (pt).
Facilities Dining room; Physical therapy room; Activities room; Crafts room; Laundry room; Barber/Beauty shop; Greenhouse.
Activities Arts & crafts; Cards; Games; Reading groups; Prayer groups; Movies; Shopping trips; Dances/Social/Cultural gatherings; Pet therapy; Cruise trips; Beach tours; Bus trips.

Episcopal Church Home
505 Mount Hope Ave, Rochester, NY 14620
(716) 546-8400, 325-6553 FAX
Admin Loren J Ranaletta. *Dir of Nursing* Karen Ekiert RN. *Medical Dir* Dr Patricia Bomba.
Licensure Skilled care; Health related. *Beds* SNF 80; Health related 62. *Certified* Medicaid; Medicare.
Owner Nonprofit corp.
Admissions Requirements Minimum age 65; Medical examination; Physician's request; Pre-admission medical form.
Staff RNs 9 (ft), 4 (pt); LPNs 9 (ft), 4 (pt); Nurses' aides 41 (ft), 11 (pt); Physical therapists; Activities coordinators 2 (ft), 1 (pt); Dietitians.
Facilities Dining room; Physical therapy room; Activities room; Chapel; Crafts room; Barber/Beauty shop; Library.
Activities Arts & crafts; Cards; Games; Reading groups; Prayer groups; Movies; Shopping trips; Dances/Social/Cultural gatherings; Pet therapy; Exercise; Music.

Genesee Hospital Extended Care Facility
224 Alexander St, Rochester, NY 14607
(716) 263-6000
Admin John D Hellems. *Dir of Nursing* Shirley Reber RN. *Medical Dir* Neal McNabb MD.
Licensure Skilled care. *Beds* SNF 40. *Certified* Medicaid; Medicare.
Owner Nonprofit corp.
Admissions Requirements Medical examination; Physician's request.
Staff Physicians 30 (ft); RNs 4 (ft), 1 (pt); LPNs 4 (ft), 1 (pt); Nurses' aides 17 (ft), 3 (pt); Physical therapists 1 (ft); Activities coordinators 1 (pt); Dietitians 1 (ft).
Languages Italian, Spanish.
Facilities Dining room; Physical therapy room; Activities room; Chapel; Laundry room; Barber/Beauty shop.
Activities Arts & crafts; Games; Reading groups; Prayer groups; Movies; Music therapy; Broadcasting within facility; Pet visitations.

Goodman Gardens Nursing Home Company Inc
8 N Goodman St, Rochester, NY 14607-1555
(716) 473-1970, 244-1773 FAX
Admin Chester F Nedvesky. *Dir of Nursing* Susan Reynolds. *Medical Dir* Donald G Symer MD.
Licensure Skilled care. *Beds* SNF 152. *Private Pay Patients* 56%. *Certified* Medicaid; Medicare.
Owner Nonprofit corp.
Admissions Requirements Minimum age 65; Medical examination.
Staff Physicians (contracted); RNs 3 (ft), 3 (pt); LPNs 18 (ft), 18 (pt); Nurses' aides 49 (ft), 10 (pt); Physical therapists; Recreational therapists 2 (ft), 3 (pt); Activities coordinators 1 (ft).
Facilities Dining room; Physical therapy room; Activities room; Chapel; Crafts room; Laundry room; Barber/Beauty shop; Library.
Activities Arts & crafts; Games; Reading groups; Prayer groups; Movies; Shopping trips; Pet therapy.

Hamilton Manor Nursing Home
1172 Long Pond Rd, Rochester, NY 14626
(716) 225-0450
Admin Morris F Richardson. *Dir of Nursing* Pheebe Dutille RN. *Medical Dir* Russell Barton MD.
Licensure Skilled care. *Beds* SNF 40. *Certified* Medicaid; Medicare.
Owner Privately owned.
Staff RNs 2 (ft), 2 (pt); LPNs 2 (ft), 5 (pt); Nurses' aides 10 (ft), 11 (pt); Physical therapists 1 (pt); Occupational therapists 1

(pt); Speech therapists 1 (pt); Activities coordinators 1 (pt); Ophthalmologists; Podiatrists 1 (pt).
Facilities Dining room; Activities room; Crafts room; Laundry room; Barber/Beauty shop.
Activities Arts & crafts; Cards; Games; Reading groups; Prayer groups; Movies; Shopping trips.

Hurlbut Nursing Home
1177 E Henrietta Rd, Rochester, NY 14623
(716) 424-4770
Admin Vincent F Distefano.
Medical Dir Kenneth Nudo MD.
Licensure Skilled care. *Beds* SNF 160. *Certified* Medicaid; Medicare.
Owner Privately owned.
Staff Physicians; RNs; LPNs.
Facilities Dining room; Physical therapy room; Activities room; Chapel; Crafts room; Laundry room; Barber/Beauty shop; Library.
Activities Arts & crafts; Cards; Games; Reading groups; Prayer groups.

Jewish Home of Rochester
2021 Winton Rd S, Rochester, NY 14618
(716) 427-7760, 427-2207 FAX
Admin Arnold S Gissin. *Dir of Nursing* Mercelle Grant RN. *Medical Dir* Bernard Shore MD.
Licensure Skilled care; Intermediate care; Alzheimer's care. *Beds* SNF 188; ICF 174. *Private Pay Patients* 15-20%. *Certified* Medicaid; Medicare.
Owner Nonprofit corp.
Admissions Requirements Minimum age 65 (with exceptions).
Staff Physicians 1 (ft), 5 (pt); RNs 22 (ft); Nurses' aides 113 (ft); Physical therapists 2 (ft), 1 (pt); Recreational therapists 5 (ft); Occupational therapists 1 (ft); Speech therapists 1 (pt); Dietitians 1 (ft); Ophthalmologists 1 (pt); Podiatrists 1 (pt); Audiologists 1 (pt).
Affiliation Jewish.
Facilities Dining room; Physical therapy room; Activities room; Chapel; Crafts room; Barber/Beauty shop; Library.
Activities Arts & crafts; Cards; Games; Reading groups; Prayer groups; Movies; Shopping trips; Dances/Social/Cultural gatherings; Intergenerational programs; Pet therapy.

Kirkhaven
254 Alexander St, Rochester, NY 14607
(716) 461-1991, 461-9833 FAX
Admin Philip B Price. *Dir of Nursing* Norma Hopkins RN (Acting). *Medical Dir* John A Jurik MD.
Licensure Skilled care; Intermediate care; Alzheimer's care. *Beds* SNF 114; ICF 33. *Private Pay Patients* 40%. *Certified* Medicaid; Medicare.
Owner Nonprofit organization/foundation.
Admissions Requirements Medical examination; Physician's request.
Staff Physicians 3 (pt); RNs 11 (ft), 12 (pt); LPNs 8 (ft), 13 (pt); Nurses' aides 34 (ft), 42 (pt); Physical therapists (consultant); Recreational therapists 1 (ft), 1 (pt); Occupational therapists 1 (ft); Speech therapists (consultant); Activities coordinators 2 (ft), 1 (pt); Dietitians 1 (ft); Podiatrists (consultant); Audiologists (consultant); Dentists (consultant); Psychiatrists (consultant).
Affiliation Presbyterian.
Facilities Dining room; Physical therapy room; Barber/Beauty shop.
Activities Arts & crafts; Cards; Games; Movies; Shopping trips; Dances/Social/Cultural gatherings; Intergenerational programs; Pet therapy.

Lakeshore Nursing Home
425 Beach Ave, Rochester, NY 14612
(716) 663-0930
Admin Claude B Flack. *Dir of Nursing* Cheryl O'Brien RN.
Licensure Skilled care; Alzheimer's care. *Beds* SNF 229. *Certified* Medicaid; Medicare.
Owner Privately owned.
Admissions Requirements Minimum age 16; Medical examination; Physician's request.
Staff Physicians; RNs; LPNs; Nurses' aides; Physical therapists; Recreational therapists; Occupational therapists; Speech therapists; Activities coordinators; Dietitians; Audiologists; Dentists; Clerks.
Facilities Dining room; Physical therapy room; Activities room; Crafts room; Laundry room; Barber/Beauty shop; Library.
Activities Arts & crafts; Cards; Games; Reading groups; Prayer groups; Movies.

Latta Road Nursing Home
2100 Latta Rd, Rochester, NY 14612
(716) 225-0910
Admin Eleanor Richardson.
Licensure Skilled care. *Beds* SNF 40. *Certified* Medicaid; Medicare.
Owner Privately owned.

Latta Road Nursing Home A
2102 Latta Rd, Rochester, NY 14612
(716) 225-0920
Admin Daniel E Richardson.
Licensure Skilled care. *Beds* SNF 40. *Certified* Medicaid; Medicare.
Owner Privately owned.

Monroe Community Hospital
435 E Henrietta Rd, Rochester, NY 14603
(716) 473-4080
Admin J Raymond Diehl Jr.
Medical Dir Anthony J Izzo MD, Acting.
Licensure Skilled care; Intermediate care. *Beds* SNF 354; ICF 212. *Certified* Medicaid; Medicare.
Owner Publicly owned.
Staff Physicians 19 (ft), 75 (pt); RNs 83 (ft), 22 (pt); LPNs 135 (ft), 16 (pt); Nurses' aides 131 (ft), 17 (pt); Physical therapists 11 (ft); Recreational therapists 9 (ft); Occupational therapists 5 (ft); Speech therapists 1 (ft); Activities coordinators 1 (ft); Dietitians 4 (ft); Ophthalmologists 3 (pt); Podiatrists 1 (pt); Dentists 1 (ft).
Facilities Dining room; Physical therapy room; Activities room; Chapel; Crafts room; Laundry room; Barber/Beauty shop; Library.
Activities Arts & crafts; Cards; Games; Reading groups; Prayer groups; Movies; Shopping trips; Dances/Social/Cultural gatherings.

Norlock Manor
1140 Norton St, Rochester, NY 14621
(716) 467-2100
Licensure Skilled care. *Beds* SNF 42.
Owner Publicly owned.

Nortonian Nursing Home
1335 Portland Ave, Rochester, NY 14621
(716) 544-4000
Admin John Hansen.
Licensure Skilled care. *Beds* SNF 120. *Certified* Medicaid; Medicare.
Owner Privately owned.

Park Hope Nursing Home
1556 Mount Hope Ave, Rochester, NY 14620
(716) 473-2444
Admin Kathryn S Brady.
Licensure Skilled care. *Beds* SNF 120. *Certified* Medicaid; Medicare.
Owner Proprietary corp.

Park Ridge Nursing Home
1555 Long Pond Rd, Rochester, NY 14626
(716) 225-7150
Admin Frank R Tripodi.
Medical Dir Nathaniel J Hurst MD.

Licensure Skilled care. *Beds* SNF 120. *Certified* Medicaid; Medicare.
Owner Nonprofit corp.
Admissions Requirements Minimum age 16; Medical examination; Physician's request.
Staff RNs; LPNs; Nurses' aides; Physical therapists; Recreational therapists 1 (ft); Occupational therapists 1 (ft); Speech therapists 1 (pt); Activities coordinators 1 (pt); Dietitians 1 (ft); Podiatrists 1 (pt).
Facilities Dining room; Physical therapy room; Activities room; Crafts room; Laundry room; Barber/Beauty shop.
Activities Arts & crafts; Cards; Games; Reading groups; Prayer groups; Movies; Shopping trips; Dances/Social/Cultural gatherings; Gift cart; Gardening; Mom & tots visit.

Pinnacle Nursing Home
1175 Monroe Ave, Rochester, NY 14620
(716) 442-0450, 442-2417 FAX
Admin Charles T Greenblott. *Dir of Nursing* Janet Sexton. *Medical Dir* Ronald Vukman MD.
Licensure Skilled care. *Beds* SNF 161. *Certified* Medicaid; Medicare.
Owner Proprietary corp.
Admissions Requirements Minimum age 21; Medical examination.
Staff Physicians 2 (pt); RNs 10 (ft), 8 (pt); LPNs 12 (ft), 8 (pt); Nurses' aides 30 (ft), 30 (pt); Physical therapists 1 (pt); Occupational therapists 1 (pt); Speech therapists 1 (pt); Activities coordinators 1 (pt); Dietitians 1 (pt); Ophthalmologists 1 (pt); Audiologists 1 (pt).
Facilities Dining room; Physical therapy room; Activities room; Crafts room; Laundry room; Barber/Beauty shop; Library.
Activities Arts & crafts; Cards; Games; Reading groups; Prayer groups; Movies; Shopping trips; Dances/Social/Cultural gatherings; Intergenerational programs; Pet therapy.

Rochester Friendly Home
3156 East Ave, Rochester, NY 14618
(716) 381-1600
Admin James E Tewhirst.
Licensure Skilled care; Intermediate care; Retirement; Alzheimer's care. *Beds* SNF 80; ICF 124. *Certified* Medicaid; Medicare.
Owner Nonprofit corp.
Admissions Requirements Minimum age 55; Medical examination; Physician's request.
Staff Physicians 3 (pt); RNs 6 (ft), 19 (pt); LPNs 8 (ft), 22 (pt); Nurses' aides 40 (ft), 42 (pt); Physical therapists 2 (ft); Occupational therapists 1 (pt); Speech therapists 1 (pt); Activities coordinators 1 (ft); Dietitians 1 (ft); Ophthalmologists 1 (pt); Podiatrists 1 (pt); Dentists 1 (pt); Medical directors 1 (pt); Assistant directors of nursing 1 (ft); Social workers 3 (pt); Pharmacists 1 (pt); Volunteer coordinators 1 (pt); Directors of nursing 1 (ft).
Facilities Dining room; Physical therapy room; Activities room; Crafts room; Laundry room; Barber/Beauty shop; Library.
Activities Arts & crafts; Cards; Games; Reading groups; Movies; Shopping trips; Dances/Social/Cultural gatherings.

St John's Nursing Home Inc & Home for the Aging
150 Highland Ave, Rochester, NY 14620
(716) 271-5413
Admin Vincent Parks.
Medical Dir R Paul Miller MD.
Licensure Skilled care; Intermediate care. *Beds* SNF 230; ICF 241. *Certified* Medicaid; Medicare.
Owner Nonprofit corp.
Admissions Requirements Medical examination.

Staff Physicians 3 (ft), 2 (pt); RNs 23 (ft), 14 (pt); LPNs 29 (ft), 16 (pt); Nurses' aides 109 (ft), 24 (pt); Physical therapists 4 (ft); Recreational therapists 4 (ft); Occupational therapists 3 (ft); Speech therapists 2 (ft), 1 (pt); Activities coordinators 1 (ft); Dietitians 2 (ft), 1 (pt); Ophthalmologists 1 (pt); Podiatrists 1 (pt); Dentists 1 (pt).
Facilities Dining room; Physical therapy room; Activities room; Chapel; Crafts room; Laundry room; Barber/Beauty shop; Library.
Activities Arts & crafts; Cards; Games; Reading groups; Prayer groups; Movies; Shopping trips; Dances/Social/Cultural gatherings; Performing arts troupe of residents; Sunshine olympics; Recreational outings.

Sainte Ann's Home—The Heritage
1500 Portland Ave, Rochester, NY 14621
(716) 342-1700, 342-9585 FAX
Admin Sr Marie Michelle Peartree, Pres.
Medical Dir James B Wood MD, V Pres.
Licensure Skilled care; Health related facility; Alzheimer's care. *Beds* SNF 354; Health related facility 237. *Private Pay Patients* 62%.
Owner Nonprofit corp.
Staff Physicians 3 (ft); RNs 25 (ft); LPNs 25 (ft); Nurses' aides 125 (ft); Physical therapists 2 (ft); Recreational therapists 5 (ft); Occupational therapists 1 (ft); Dietitians 4 (ft).
Languages Italian, Spanish.
Activities Arts & crafts; Cards; Games; Reading groups; Prayer groups; Movies; Shopping trips; Dances/Social/Cultural gatherings; Intergenerational programs; Pet therapy; Pastoral care.

Strong Memorial Hospital Skilled Nursing Facility
601 Elmwood Ave, Rochester, NY 14642
(716) 275-2644
Admin Fran Carlin-Rogers. *Dir of Nursing* Margaret Smith RN. *Medical Dir* A Izzo MD.
Licensure Skilled care. *Beds* SNF 40. *Certified* Medicaid; Medicare.
Owner Nonprofit corp.
Admissions Requirements Physician's request.
Staff Physicians 1 (pt); RNs; LPNs; Physical therapists 1 (ft); Recreational therapists 1 (ft); Occupational therapists 1 (pt); Speech therapists 1 (pt); Dietitians 1 (pt); Podiatrists 1 (pt).
Facilities Dining room; Physical therapy room; Activities room; Chapel; Laundry room; Use of all hospital facilities.
Activities Arts & crafts; Group & individual activities.

Wesley-on-East Ltd
630 East Ave, Rochester, NY 14607-2194
(716) 473-1970, 244-1773 FAX
Admin Jon R Zemans. *Dir of Nursing* Susan Reynolds. *Medical Dir* Donald G Symer MD.
Licensure Intermediate care. *Beds* ICF 95. *Private Pay Patients* 56%. *Certified* Medicaid.
Owner Nonprofit organization/foundation.
Admissions Requirements Minimum age 65; Medical examination.
Staff Physicians (contracted); RNs 3 (ft), 3 (pt); LPNs 18 (ft), 18 (pt); Nurses' aides 49 (ft), 10 (pt); Recreational therapists 2 (ft), 3 (pt); Activities coordinators 1 (ft).
Facilities Dining room; Activities room; Chapel; Crafts room; Laundry room; Barber/Beauty shop; Library.
Activities Arts & crafts; Cards; Games; Reading groups; Prayer groups; Movies; Shopping trips; Dances/Social/Cultural gatherings; Intergenerational programs; Pet therapy.

Westgate Nursing Home
525 Beahan Rd, Rochester, NY 14624
(716) 247-7880
Admin David Giunta. *Dir of Nursing* AGnes Gaulin.
Licensure Skilled care. *Beds* SNF 124. *Certified* Medicaid; Medicare.
Owner Privately owned.
Admissions Requirements Minimum age 16; Medical examination; Physician's request.
Staff RNs; LPNs; Nurses' aides; Physical therapists; Reality therapists; Recreational therapists; Occupational therapists; Activities coordinators; Dietitians; Ophthalmologists; Dentists.
Facilities Dining room; Physical therapy room; Activities room; Chapel; Crafts room; Laundry room; Barber/Beauty shop; Library.
Activities Arts & crafts; Cards; Games; Reading groups; Prayer groups; Movies; Shopping trips; Dances/Social/Cultural gatherings; Wheelchair accesible van.

Woodside Manor Nursing Home Inc
2425 Clinton Ave S, Rochester, NY 14618
(716) 461-0370
Admin Margaret Gallagher.
Licensure Skilled care. *Beds* SNF 44. *Certified* Medicaid; Medicare.
Owner Proprietary corp.

Rockaway Park

Ocean Promenade Health Related Facility
140 Beach 113th St, Rockaway Park, NY 11694
(718) 945-6350
Licensure Intermediate care. *Beds* ICF 120.
Owner Proprietary corp.

Park Nursing Home
128 Beach 115th St, Rockaway Park, NY 11694
(718) 474-6400
Admin Ralph Newman.
Licensure Skilled care. *Beds* SNF 196. *Certified* Medicaid; Medicare.
Owner Privately owned.

Promenade Nursing Home
140 Beach 114th St, Rockaway Park, NY 11694
(718) 945-4600
Admin Moses Vogel. *Dir of Nursing* Jodee Berkowitz RN. *Medical Dir* Reuben Tizes MD.
Licensure Skilled care. *Beds* SNF 240. *Certified* Medicaid; Medicare.
Owner Privately owned.
Admissions Requirements Medical examination; Physician's request.
Staff Physicians 4 (pt); RNs 8 (ft), 4 (pt); LPNs 21 (ft), 6 (pt); Nurses' aides 77 (ft), 12 (pt); Physical therapists 1 (ft); Occupational therapists 1 (ft); Speech therapists 1 (pt); Activities coordinators 1 (ft); Dietitians 1 (ft); Ophthalmologists 2 (ft).
Languages Yiddish, Hebrew, Italian, French.
Facilities Dining room; Physical therapy room; Activities room; Chapel; Crafts room; Laundry room; Barber/Beauty shop; Library.
Activities Arts & crafts; Cards; Games; Reading groups; Prayer groups; Movies; Shopping trips; Dances/Social/Cultural gatherings.

Rockville Centre

Rockville Nursing Center Inc
41 Maine Ave, Rockville Centre, NY 11570
(516) 536-7730, 536-4108 FAX
Admin Siegmundo Hirsch PhD. *Dir of Nursing* Bernardine Faverzani. *Medical Dir* Oscar Devera.
Licensure Skilled care. *Beds* SNF 158. *Private Pay Patients* 30%. *Certified* Medicaid; Medicare.

Owner Proprietary corp.
Admissions Requirements Minimum age 16; Physician's request.
Staff RNs 12 (ft), 5 (pt); LPNs 14 (ft), 2 (pt); Nurses' aides 47 (ft), 22 (pt); Physical therapists 1 (pt); Recreational therapists 2 (ft); Speech therapists 1 (pt); Activities coordinators 1 (ft); Dietitians 1 (ft), 1 (pt); Ophthalmologists 1 (pt); Podiatrists 1 (pt); Audiologists 1 (pt); Dentists 1 (pt).
Languages Spanish, German, Hebrew, Yiddish, Italian, French, Creole.
Facilities Dining room; Physical therapy room; Activities room; Crafts room; Laundry room; Barber/Beauty shop.
Activities Arts & crafts; Cards; Games; Reading groups; Prayer groups; Movies; Dances/Social/Cultural gatherings; Excursions.

Rockville Residence Manor
50 Maine Ave, Rockville Centre, NY 11570
(516) 536-8000
Licensure Intermediate care. *Beds* ICF 66.
Owner Privately owned.

Rome

Health Related Facility & Nursing Home Company of Rome Inc
800 W Chestnut St, Rome, NY 13440
(315) 339-3210
Admin H Priscilla Emmans. *Dir of Nursing* Mary Marlar. *Medical Dir* Dr S V Ramineni.
Licensure Intermediate care. *Beds* ICF 100.
Owner Nonprofit corp.
Admissions Requirements Minimum age; Medical examination; Physician's request.
Staff Physicians 1 (pt); RNs 3 (ft), 4 (pt); LPNs 2 (ft), 5 (pt); Nurses' aides 12 (ft), 20 (pt); Physical therapists 1 (pt); Occupational therapists 1 (pt); Speech therapists 1 (pt); Activities coordinators 1 (ft), 1 (pt); Dietitians 1 (pt).
Facilities Dining room; Physical therapy room; Activities room; Laundry room; Barber/Beauty shop.
Activities Arts & crafts; Cards; Games; Prayer groups; Movies; Shopping trips; Dances/Social/Cultural gatherings.

Rome & Murphy Memorial Hospital Skilled Nursing Facility
1500 N James St, Rome, NY 13440
(315) 338-7000
Admin Kent Longnecker.
Medical Dir Dr Neville Harper.
Licensure Skilled care. *Beds* SNF 40. *Certified* Medicaid; Medicare.
Owner Publicly owned.
Admissions Requirements Minimum age 16; Medical examination; Physician's request.
Staff Physicians 1 (pt); RNs 2 (ft), 1 (pt); LPNs 3 (ft), 3 (pt); Nurses' aides 15 (ft); Physical therapists 1 (pt); Occupational therapists 1 (pt); Activities coordinators 1 (ft); Dietitians 1 (pt); Ophthalmologists 1 (pt).
Languages Italian, Polish, Spanish.
Facilities Dining room; Physical therapy room; Activities room; Chapel; Crafts room; Laundry room; Barber/Beauty shop.
Activities Arts & crafts; Cards; Games; Reading groups; Prayer groups; Movies; Shopping trips; Dances/Social/Cultural gatherings; Picnics.

Rome-Parkway Inc
950 Floyd Ave, Rome, NY 13440
(315) 336-5400
Admin Joseph Corradino. *Dir of Nursing* Karen Smith RN. *Medical Dir* Dr Gary Wakeman.
Licensure Skilled care. *Beds* SNF 80.
Owner Proprietary corp.
Admissions Requirements Minimum age 21; Medical examination; Physician's request.

Staff Physicians 1 (pt); RNs 6 (ft), 2 (pt);
LPNs 9 (ft), 6 (pt); Nurses' aides 28 (ft), 25
(pt); Physical therapists 2 (ft), 1 (pt);
Recreational therapists 2 (ft); Occupational
therapists 1 (ft), 1 (pt); Speech therapists 1
(pt); Dietitians 1 (ft), 1 (pt).
Facilities Dining room; Physical therapy
room; Activities room; Crafts room; Laundry
room; Barber/Beauty shop.
Activities Arts & crafts; Cards; Games;
Reading groups; Prayer groups; Movies;
Shopping trips; Dances/Social/Cultural
gatherings.

Betsy Ross Health Related Facility
Elsie St-Cedarbrook Ln, Rome, NY 13440
(315) 339-2220
Licensure Intermediate care. *Beds* ICF 120.
Owner Privately owned.

Stonehedge Nursing Home
801 N James St, Rome, NY 13440
(315) 337-0550
Admin Brian Jordan.
Medical Dir Dr James J DiCastro.
Licensure Skilled care. *Beds* SNF 160.
Certified Medicaid; Medicare.
Owner Privately owned.
Admissions Requirements Minimum age 16.
Staff RNs 9 (ft), 4 (pt); LPNs 18 (ft), 10 (pt);
Nurses' aides 70 (ft), 35 (pt); Physical
therapists 1 (pt); Reality therapists 1 (ft);
Recreational therapists 1 (ft); Occupational
therapists 1 (pt); Speech therapists 1 (pt);
Activities coordinators 1 (ft); Dietitians 2
(ft), 6 (pt); Dentists 1 (pt).
Facilities Dining room; Physical therapy
room; Activities room; Chapel; Crafts room;
Laundry room; Barber/Beauty shop.
Activities Arts & crafts; Cards; Games;
Reading groups; Prayer groups; Movies;
Shopping trips; Dances/Social/Cultural
gatherings.

Roscoe

**Roscoe Community Nursing Home Company
Inc**
Rockland Rd, Roscoe, NY 12776
(607) 498-4121
Admin Richard D Sherman.
Medical Dir Alan Fried MD.
Licensure Skilled care. *Beds* SNF 85. *Certified*
Medicaid; Medicare.
Owner Nonprofit corp.
Admissions Requirements Minimum age 16;
Medical examination; Physician's request.
Staff Physicians 2 (pt); RNs 6 (ft), 4 (pt);
LPNs 6 (ft), 1 (pt); Nurses' aides 50 (ft), 2
(pt); Physical therapists 1 (pt); Occupational
therapists 1 (pt); Speech therapists 1 (pt);
Activities coordinators 1 (ft); Dietitians 1
(pt); Ophthalmologists 1 (pt).
Facilities Dining room; Physical therapy
room; Activities room; Crafts room; Laundry
room; Barber/Beauty shop; Library.
Activities Arts & crafts; Cards; Games;
Reading groups; Prayer groups; Movies;
Shopping trips; Dances/Social/Cultural
gatherings.

Roslyn Heights

Sunharbor Manor
255 Warner Ave, Roslyn Heights, NY 11577
(516) 621-5400
Admin Clifford R Osinoff.
Medical Dir Dr J Cohen.
Licensure Skilled care; Intermediate care. *Beds*
SNF 212; ICF 54. *Private Pay Patients* 45%.
Certified Medicaid; Medicare.
Owner Privately owned.
Admissions Requirements Minimum age 16.
Facilities Dining room; Physical therapy
room; Activities room; Chapel; Crafts room;
Laundry room; Barber/Beauty shop; Library.

Activities Arts & crafts; Cards; Games;
Reading groups; Prayer groups; Movies;
Intergenerational programs; Pet therapy.

Rouses Point

Cedar Hedge Nursing Home
260 Lake St, Rouses Point, NY 12979
(518) 297-5190
Admin William H Pollock. *Dir of Nursing*
Dawn L Pollock RN.
Licensure Skilled care. *Beds* SNF 60. *Certified*
Medicaid; Medicare.
Owner Privately owned.
Admissions Requirements Minimum age 18;
Medical examination; Physician's request.
Staff Physicians 1 (pt); RNs 4 (ft), 2 (pt);
LPNs 5 (ft), 2 (pt); Nurses' aides 24 (ft), 6
(pt); Physical therapists 1 (pt); Speech
therapists 1 (pt); Activities coordinators 1
(ft); Dietitians 1 (pt); Podiatrists 1 (pt);
Dentists 1 (pt).
Languages French.
Facilities Dining room; Physical therapy
room; Activities room; Laundry room;
Barber/Beauty shop; Leisure areas.
Activities Arts & crafts; Cards; Games;
Reading groups; Prayer groups; Movies;
Shopping trips; Dances/Social/Cultural
gatherings.

Rye

Osborn
101 Theall Rd, Rye, NY 10580
(914) 967-4100
Admin Mark Zwerger. *Dir of Nursing* Carole
Edelman RN. *Medical Dir* John DuBois
MD.
Licensure Skilled care; Intermediate care. *Beds*
SNF 70; ICF 109. *Private Pay Patients* 50%.
Owner Nonprofit corp.
Admissions Requirements Minimum age 65;
Medical examination.
Staff Physicians 4 (pt); RNs; LPNs; Nurses'
aides; Physical therapists 1 (ft); Occupational
therapists (consultant); Speech therapists
(consultant); Dietitians 1 (ft);
Ophthalmologists 1 (pt); Podiatrists 1 (pt);
Audiologists (consultant); Activities
coordinators & aides 5 (ft).
Languages Italian, Spanish.
Facilities Dining room; Physical therapy
room; Activities room; Chapel; Crafts room;
Laundry room; Barber/Beauty shop; Library;
Theater; Solarium.
Activities Arts & crafts; Cards; Games;
Reading groups; Prayer groups; Movies;
Shopping trips; Dances/Social/Cultural
gatherings; Intergenerational programs; Pet
therapy.

Saint James

St James Nursing Home Skilled Facility
275 Moriches Rd, Saint James, NY 11780
(516) 862-8000, 862-8000, ext 44 FAX
Admin Hal James Schifter. *Dir of Nursing* B
R Foray RN MS. *Medical Dir* R Anthony
Martino MD.
Licensure Skilled care. *Beds* SNF 230. *Private
Pay Patients* 25%. *Certified* Medicaid;
Medicare.
Owner Privately owned.
Admissions Requirements Physician's request.
Staff Physicians 1 (pt); RNs 14 (ft), 8 (pt);
LPNs 20 (ft), 10 (pt); Nurses' aides 71 (ft),
31 (pt); Physical therapists 2 (ft), 2 (pt);
Recreational therapists 3 (ft); Activities 1 (pt);
Occupational therapists 1 (ft), 1 (pt); Speech
therapists 1 (pt); Activities coordinators 1
(ft); Dietitians 2 (ft), 1 (pt);
Ophthalmologists 1 (pt); Podiatrists 1 (pt);
Audiologists 1 (pt).
Languages Spanish, Italian, French, German.

Facilities Dining room; Physical therapy
room; Activities room; Chapel; Crafts room;
Laundry room; Barber/Beauty shop; Library.
Activities Arts & crafts; Cards; Games;
Reading groups; Prayer groups; Movies;
Shopping trips; Dances/Social/Cultural
gatherings; Intergenerational programs; Pet
therapy; Religious services; Community
visits.

St James Plaza Health Related Facility
273 Moriches Rd, Saint James, NY 11780
(516) 862-8990, ext 292
Admin Robert A Baffa. *Dir of Nursing* Ann
McHugh. *Medical Dir* Anthony Martino
MD.
Licensure Intermediate care. *Beds* ICF 250.
Private Pay Patients 12%. *Certified*
Medicaid.
Owner Proprietary corp.
Admissions Requirements Minimum age 16;
Medical examination; Physician's request.
Staff Physicians 1 (pt); RNs 7 (ft), 3 (pt);
LPNs 15 (ft), 3 (pt); Nurses' aides 42 (ft), 7
(pt); Physical therapists 1 (ft), 2 (pt);
Recreational therapists 2 (ft), 3 (pt);
Occupational therapists 1 (pt); Speech
therapists 1 (pt); Activities coordinators 1
(ft); Dietitians 1 (pt); Ophthalmologists 6
(pt); Podiatrists 5 (pt); Audiologists 1 (pt);
Social workers 2 (ft); Assistants 1 (pt).
Facilities Dining room; Physical therapy
room; Activities room; Chapel; Crafts room;
Laundry room; Barber/Beauty shop; Library.
Activities Arts & crafts; Cards; Games;
Reading groups; Prayer groups; Movies;
Shopping trips; Dances/Social/Cultural
gatherings; Intergenerational programs; Pet
therapy.

Salamanca

Salamanca Nursing Home Inc
451 Broad St, Salamanca, NY 14779
(716) 945-1800
Admin Doris Ann Brown.
Medical Dir Dr Paul Sum.
Licensure Skilled care; Intermediate care. *Beds*
SNF 80; ICF 40. *Certified* Medicaid;
Medicare.
Owner Proprietary corp.
Admissions Requirements Minimum age 16;
Medical examination; Physician's request.
Staff Physicians 13 (pt); RNs 6 (ft), 4 (pt);
LPNs 5 (ft), 12 (pt); Nurses' aides 32 (ft), 17
(pt); Physical therapists 1 (pt); Recreational
therapists 2 (ft); Occupational therapists 1
(pt); Speech therapists 1 (pt); Activities
coordinators 2 (ft); Dietitians 1 (ft);
Podiatrists 1 (pt); Dentists 1 (pt).
Facilities Dining room; Physical therapy
room; Activities room; Laundry room;
Barber/Beauty shop; Library.
Activities Arts & crafts; Cards; Games;
Reading groups; Prayer groups; Movies;
Shopping trips; Dances/Social/Cultural
gatherings.

Saratoga Springs

Saratoga Hospital Nursing Home
211 Church St, Saratoga Springs, NY 12866
(518) 584-6000, 583-8496 FAX
Admin James E Shoemaker.
Medical Dir Dr Warren Letts.
Licensure Skilled care. *Beds* SNF 72. *Private
Pay Patients* 15%. *Certified* Medicaid;
Medicare.
Owner Nonprofit corp.
Admissions Requirements Minimum age 16;
Medical examination; Physician's request.
Staff RNs; LPNs; Nurses' aides; Physical
therapists; Speech therapists; Activities
coordinators; Dietitians; Podiatrists;
Dentists.
Languages Languages by arrangement.

Facilities Dining room; Physical therapy room; Activities room; Chapel; Crafts room; Laundry room; Barber/Beauty shop; Library.
Activities Arts & crafts; Cards; Games; Reading groups; Movies; Shopping trips; Dances/Social/Cultural gatherings; Intergenerational programs; Pet therapy.

Wesley Health Care Center Inc
Lawrence St, Saratoga Springs, NY 12866
(518) 587-3600
Admin Ralph J Barron Jr.
Medical Dir Fred A Phillips Jr MD.
Licensure Skilled care; Intermediate care; Alzheimer's care. *Beds* SNF 194; ICF 70. *Certified* Medicaid; Medicare.
Owner Nonprofit corp.
Admissions Requirements Minimum age 16; Medical examination; Physician's request.
Affiliation Methodist.
Facilities Dining room; Physical therapy room; Activities room; Chapel; Crafts room; Laundry room; Barber/Beauty shop; Library.
Activities Arts & crafts; Cards; Games; Reading groups; Prayer groups; Movies; Shopping trips; Dances/Social/Cultural gatherings.

Sayville

Good Samaritan Nursing Home
101 Elm St, Sayville, NY 11782
(516) 567-6600
Admin Kenneth B Knutsen. *Dir of Nursing* Susan Bowes RN. *Medical Dir* John Canning MD.
Licensure Skilled care; Alzheimer's care. *Beds* SNF 100. *Certified* Medicaid; Medicare.
Owner Nonprofit corp.
Staff RNs 6 (ft), 7 (pt); LPNs 4 (ft), 6 (pt); Nurses' aides 30 (ft), 20 (pt); Physical therapists 1 (pt); Recreational therapists 1 (ft), 4 (pt); Occupational therapists 1 (pt); Activities coordinators 1 (ft); Dietitians 1 (ft).
Languages Italian.
Affiliation Roman Catholic.
Facilities Dining room; Physical therapy room; Activities room; Chapel; Crafts room; Barber/Beauty shop.
Activities Arts & crafts; Cards; Games; Reading groups; Prayer groups; Movies; Dances/Social/Cultural gatherings; Pet visits; Special meals.

Scarsdale

Sprain Brook Manor Nursing Home
77 Jackson Ave, Scarsdale, NY 10583
(914) 472-3200
Admin Henry Book. *Dir of Nursing* Linda Murray RN. *Medical Dir* John F Salimbene MD.
Licensure Skilled care. *Beds* SNF 121. *Certified* Medicaid; Medicare.
Owner Privately owned.
Staff RNs 20 (ft); LPNs 5 (ft); Nurses' aides 50 (ft); Physical therapists; Recreational therapists 2 (ft); Occupational therapists 1 (pt); Speech therapists 1 (pt); Activities coordinators 1 (ft); Dietitians 1 (ft); Ophthalmologists; Podiatrists; Dentists.
Languages Spanish, Italian, Yiddish, Hebrew, German, Portuguese.
Activities Arts & crafts; Cards; Games; Reading groups; Prayer groups; Movies; Shopping trips; Dances/Social/Cultural gatherings.

Schenectady

Hallmark Nursing Centre
526 Altamont Ave, Schenectady, NY 12303
(518) 346-6121
Admin Raymond Klocek. *Dir of Nursing* Patricia Jenner. *Medical Dir* Gary Dunkerley MD.
Licensure Skilled care; Alzheimer's care. *Beds* SNF 224. *Private Pay Patients* 25%. *Certified* Medicaid; Medicare.
Owner Proprietary corp.
Admissions Requirements Minimum age 16; Medical examination; Physician's request.
Staff Physicians 14 (pt); RNs 13 (ft), 11 (pt); LPNs 15 (ft), 12 (pt); Nurses' aides 85 (ft), 30 (pt); Physical therapists 3 (pt); Recreational therapists 1 (ft), 4 (pt); Occupational therapists 2 (ft), 1 (pt); Speech therapists 1 (pt); Activities coordinators 1 (ft); Dietitians 1 (ft), 1 (pt); Ophthalmologists 1 (pt); Podiatrists 1 (pt); Audiologists 1 (pt).
Languages Spanish, Polish, Italian.
Facilities Dining room; Physical therapy room; Activities room; Chapel; Crafts room; Laundry room; Barber/Beauty shop; Library.
Activities Arts & crafts; Cards; Games; Reading groups; Prayer groups; Movies; Shopping trips; Dances/Social/Cultural gatherings; Intergenerational programs; Pet therapy.

Kingsway Arms Nursing Center Inc
Kings Rd, Schenectady, NY 12304
(518) 393-4117
Admin Robert DeAngelis.
Licensure Skilled care; Intermediate care. *Beds* SNF 131; ICF 29. *Certified* Medicaid; Medicare.
Owner Proprietary corp.

Silver Haven Nursing Home
1940 Hamburg St, Schenectady, NY 12304
(518) 370-5051
Admin Jean E Duket. *Dir of Nursing* Dorothy Kenny RN. *Medical Dir* A J Arony MD.
Licensure Skilled care. *Beds* SNF 86. *Certified* Medicaid; Medicare.
Owner Privately owned.
Staff Physicians 3 (pt); RNs 7 (ft), 8 (pt); LPNs 5 (ft), 11 (pt); Nurses' aides 28 (ft), 16 (pt); Activities coordinators 1 (ft); Physical therapy assistants 1 (ft).
Facilities Dining room; Physical therapy room; Barber/Beauty shop.
Activities Arts & crafts; Cards; Games; Reading groups; Prayer groups; Movies; Shopping trips; Dances/Social/Cultural gatherings; Pet therapy.

Scotia

Baptist Retirement Center
297 N Ballston Ave, Scotia, NY 12302
(518) 370-4700
Admin Timothy W Bartos. *Dir of Nursing* Jeffrey J Holmstrom. *Medical Dir* Robert J Halbig MD.
Licensure Skilled care; Intermediate care; Alzheimer's care. *Beds* SNF 100; ICF 80. *Certified* Medicaid; Medicare.
Owner Nonprofit corp.
Admissions Requirements Minimum age 16; Medical examination.
Staff RNs 12 (ft), 24 (pt); LPNs 15 (ft), 21 (pt); Nurses' aides 44 (ft), 40 (pt); Physical therapists 1 (ft); Occupational therapists 1 (ft); Activities coordinators 1 (ft); Dietitians 1 (pt).
Affiliation Baptist.
Facilities Dining room; Physical therapy room; Activities room; Chapel; Crafts room; Laundry room; Barber/Beauty shop; Library; Occupational therapy room.
Activities Arts & crafts; Cards; Games; Reading groups; Prayer groups; Movies; Shopping trips; Dances/Social/Cultural gatherings.

Glendale Nursing Home
RD 1, Hetcheltown Rd, Scotia, NY 12302
(518) 384-3601

Admin John T McGrath. *Dir of Nursing* Anne O'Brien RN. *Medical Dir* Jung-Wen Chen MD.
Licensure Skilled care; Intermediate care. *Beds* SNF 378; ICF 150. *Certified* Medicaid; Medicare.
Owner Publicly owned.
Staff Physicians 1 (ft), 5 (pt); RNs 45 (ft), 25 (pt); LPNs 38 (ft), 8 (pt); Nurses' aides 181 (ft), 5 (pt); Physical therapists 1 (ft); Recreational therapists 5 (ft); Occupational therapists 2 (pt); Speech therapists 1 (pt); Activities coordinators 1 (ft); Dietitians 1 (ft); Ophthalmologists 1 (pt); Podiatrists 1 (pt); Dentists 1 (pt).
Facilities Dining room; Physical therapy room; Activities room; Chapel; Crafts room; Laundry room; Barber/Beauty shop; Bookmobile.
Activities Arts & crafts; Cards; Games; Reading groups; Prayer groups; Movies; Shopping trips; Dances/Social/Cultural gatherings; Picnics.

Sidney

Hospital Skilled Nursing Facility
Pearl St, Sidney, NY 13838
(607) 563-3512
Admin Betty J Ebert. *Dir of Nursing* Helen Dassance. *Medical Dir* A Maxwell Steinbach.
Licensure Skilled care. *Beds* SNF 30. *Private Pay Patients* 10%. *Certified* Medicaid; Medicare.
Owner Publicly owned.
Admissions Requirements Minimum age 16; Medical examination; Physician's request.
Staff Physicians 15 (pt); Physical therapists 1 (pt); Occupational therapists 1 (pt); Speech therapists 1 (pt); Activities coordinators 1 (pt); Dietitians 1 (pt); Podiatrists 1 (pt); RNs, LPNs, Nurses aides 23 (ft), 1 (pt); Dentists 1 (pt).
Facilities Dining room; Physical therapy room; Activities room; Chapel; Crafts room; Barber/Beauty shop; Patio.
Activities Arts & crafts; Cards; Games; Reading groups; Prayer groups; Movies; Dances/Social/Cultural gatherings; Pet therapy.

Smithtown

Lutheran Center for the Aging
Rte 25A, Smithtown, NY 11787
(516) 724-2200, 724-2219 FAX
Admin John T Digilio Jr. *Dir of Nursing* Elizabeth Dowling RN. *Medical Dir* Yang Sieng Lu MD, Acting.
Licensure Skilled care; Intermediate care; Alzheimer's care. *Beds* SNF 293; ICF 60. *Certified* Medicaid; Medicare.
Owner Nonprofit corp (Wartburg Lutheran Services).
Admissions Requirements Minimum age 18; Medical examination; Physician's request.
Staff Physicians; RNs; LPNs; Nurses' aides; Physical therapists; Recreational therapists; Occupational therapists; Speech therapists; Activities coordinators; Dietitians.
Languages Italian, Spanish, German.
Affiliation Lutheran.
Facilities Dining room; Physical therapy room; Activities room; Crafts room; Laundry room; Barber/Beauty shop; Library.
Activities Arts & crafts; Cards; Games; Reading groups; Prayer groups; Movies; Shopping trips; Dances/Social/Cultural gatherings; Intergenerational programs; Pet therapy.

Sodus

Blossom View Nursing Home
6884 Maple Ave, Sodus, NY 14551
(315) 483-9118

Admin Donna M Brown.
Medical Dir John L Ghertner MD.
Licensure Skilled care. *Beds* SNF 60. *Certified* Medicaid; Medicare.
Owner Proprietary corp.
Facilities Dining room; Physical therapy room; Activities room; Barber/Beauty shop.
Activities Arts & crafts; Games; Reading groups; Prayer groups; Shopping trips; Dances/Social/Cultural gatherings.

Somers

Somers Manor Nursing Home Inc
PO Box 445, Rte 100, Somers, NY 10589
(914) 232-5101
Admin Janice C Depp. *Dir of Nursing* Mary Joy Bloomer RN. *Medical Dir* James L Koo MD.
Licensure Skilled care; Intermediate care. *Beds* SNF 123; ICF 101. *Certified* Medicaid; Medicare.
Owner Proprietary corp.
Admissions Requirements Minimum age 17; Medical examination; Physician's request.
Staff RNs; LPNs; Nurses' aides; Physical therapists 2 (pt); Occupational therapists 1 (pt); Activities coordinators 1 (ft); Dietitians 1 (ft).
Facilities Dining room; Physical therapy room; Activities room; Crafts room; Laundry room; Barber/Beauty shop.
Activities Arts & crafts; Cards; Games; Reading groups; Prayer groups; Movies; Shopping trips; Dances/Social/Cultural gatherings.

Southampton

Southampton Nursing Home Inc
330 Meeting House Ln, Southampton, NY 11968
(516) 283-2134
Admin Maureen O Mahoney. *Dir of Nursing* Margaret Schultz. *Medical Dir* Dean Monaco MD.
Licensure Skilled care. *Beds* SNF 62. *Certified* Medicaid; Medicare.
Owner Nonprofit corp.
Admissions Requirements Minimum age 16.
Staff Activities coordinators 2 (ft); Dietitians 1 (ft).
Facilities Dining room; Physical therapy room; Activities room; Crafts room; Barber/Beauty shop; Library.
Activities Arts & crafts; Cards; Games; Reading groups; Prayer groups; Movies; Dances/Social/Cultural gatherings.

Spencerport

Wedgewood Nursing Home
5 Church St, Spencerport, NY 14559
(716) 352-4810
Admin Wendy F Matthews. *Dir of Nursing* Denise Quattrone. *Medical Dir* Paul Rapoza MD.
Licensure Skilled care. *Beds* SNF 29. *Certified* Medicaid; Medicare.
Owner Privately owned.
Admissions Requirements Minimum age 14; Physician's request.
Staff RNs 2 (ft), 5 (pt); LPNs 1 (ft), 8 (pt); Nurses' aides 2 (ft), 24 (pt); Physical therapists 1 (pt); Occupational therapists 1 (pt); Speech therapists 1 (pt); Activities coordinators 1 (pt); Dietitians 1 (pt); Podiatrists 1 (pt); Audiologists 1 (pt).
Facilities Dining room; Activities room; Crafts room; Laundry room; Barber/Beauty shop; Library.
Activities Arts & crafts; Games; Prayer groups; Movies; Shopping trips; Pet therapy.

Spring Valley

Hillcrest Nursing Home
661 N Main St, Spring Valley, NY 10977
(914) 356-0567, 352-2704 FAX
Admin Harry Satin. *Dir of Nursing* Federica Guerrero RN. *Medical Dir* Fletcher Johnson MD.
Licensure Skilled care. *Beds* SNF 200. *Private Pay Patients* 1%. *Certified* Medicaid; Medicare.
Owner Proprietary corp.
Admissions Requirements Medical examination; Physician's request.
Staff RNs 30 (ft); Nurses' aides 73 (ft), 8 (pt); Physical therapists 1 (pt); Recreational therapists 5 (ft), 1 (pt); Occupational therapists 1 (pt); Speech therapists 1 (pt); Activities coordinators 1 (ft); Dietitians 1 (ft); Podiatrists 2 (pt).
Facilities Dining room; Physical therapy room; Activities room; Crafts room; Laundry room; Barber/Beauty shop.
Activities Arts & crafts; Cards; Games; Reading groups; Prayer groups; Movies; Shopping trips; Dances/Social/Cultural gatherings; Intergenerational programs; Pet therapy; Horse races; Bowling.

Springville

Jennie B Richmond Chaffee Nursing Home Company Inc
222 E Main St, Springville, NY 14141
(716) 592-2871
Admin Roger Ford. *Dir of Nursing* Wade Stearns RN.
Licensure Skilled care; Intermediate care. *Beds* SNF 40; ICF 40. *Certified* Medicaid; Medicare.
Owner Nonprofit corp.
Admissions Requirements Medical examination.
Staff RNs 3 (ft), 4 (pt); LPNs 8 (ft), 10 (pt); Nurses' aides 13 (ft), 24 (pt); Physical therapists 2 (ft), 2 (pt); Recreational therapists 2 (ft), 1 (pt); Occupational therapists 2 (ft); Speech therapists 1 (pt); Dietitians 2 (ft).
Facilities Dining room; Physical therapy room; Activities room; Laundry room; Barber/Beauty shop.
Activities Arts & crafts; Cards; Games; Reading groups; Prayer groups; Movies; Dances/Social/Cultural gatherings.

Fiddlers Green Manor Nursing Home
168 W Main St, Springville, NY 14141
(716) 592-4781
Admin Thomas DuPont.
Medical Dir Mary Eileen Beland.
Licensure Skilled care; Alzheimer's care. *Beds* SNF 82. *Certified* Medicaid; Medicare.
Owner Privately owned.
Admissions Requirements Medical examination.
Staff Physicians 5 (pt); RNs 4 (ft), 9 (pt); LPNs 8 (ft), 4 (pt); Nurses' aides 24 (ft), 28 (pt); Occupational therapists 1 (ft), 1 (pt); Speech therapists 1 (pt); Activities coordinators 1 (ft), 1 (pt); Ophthalmologists 1 (pt).
Facilities Dining room; Physical therapy room; Activities room; Laundry room; Barber/Beauty shop.
Activities Arts & crafts; Games; Prayer groups; Movies; Shopping trips.

Staatsburg

Hyde Park Nursing Home
Rte 9 & Anderson School Rd, Staatsburg, NY 12580
(914) 889-4500
Admin Raphael Yenowitz. *Dir of Nursing* Patricia McDermott RN. *Medical Dir* Pinaki Ray MD.

Licensure Skilled care. *Beds* SNF 120. *Certified* Medicaid; Medicare.
Owner Privately owned.
Staff Physicians 5 (pt); RNs 18 (ft), 8 (pt); LPNs 12 (ft), 6 (pt); Nurses' aides 40 (ft), 15 (pt); Physical therapists 1 (pt); Recreational therapists 1 (ft); Occupational therapists 1 (ft); Speech therapists 1 (pt); Activities coordinators 1 (ft); Dietitians 1 (ft); Ophthalmologists 1 (pt); Dentists 1 (pt).
Facilities Dining room; Physical therapy room; Activities room; Crafts room; Laundry room; Barber/Beauty shop; Library.
Activities Arts & crafts; Games; Reading groups; Prayer groups; Movies; Shopping trips; Dances/Social/Cultural gatherings.

Stamford

Community Skilled Nursing Facility
Harper St, Stamford, NY 12167
(607) 652-7521
Admin Pamela Tritten. *Dir of Nursing* June Egan RN. *Medical Dir* Glen Joshpe MD.
Licensure Skilled care. *Beds* SNF 53. *Private Pay Patients* 25%. *Certified* Medicaid; Medicare.
Owner Nonprofit corp.
Admissions Requirements Minimum age 16.
Staff RNs 5 (ft), 4 (pt); LPNs 4 (ft), 6 (pt); Nurses' aides 20 (ft), 8 (pt); Activities coordinators 1 (ft), 1 (pt); Dietitians 1 (ft).
Facilities Dining room; Physical therapy room; Activities room; Barber/Beauty shop.
Activities Arts & crafts; Cards; Reading groups; Movies.

Staten Island

Carmel Richmond Nursing Home Inc
88 Old Town Rd, Staten Island, NY 10304
(718) 979-5000
Licensure Skilled care; Intermediate care. *Beds* SNF 270; ICF 30. *Certified* Medicaid; Medicare.
Owner Nonprofit corp (Catholic Charities-Arch of NY).

Clove Lakes Nursing Home & Health Related Facility
25 Fanning St, Staten Island, NY 10314
(718) 761-2100
Admin Nicholas Demisay. *Dir of Nursing* Anna Fredericksen RN. *Medical Dir* Jacob Dimant MD.
Licensure Skilled care; Intermediate care; Alzheimer's care. *Beds* SNF 326; ICF 250. *Certified* Medicaid; Medicare.
Owner Privately owned.
Admissions Requirements Minimum age 16; Medical examination; Physician's request.
Staff Physicians 1 (pt); RNs 26 (ft), 7 (pt); LPNs 43 (ft), 11 (pt); Nurses' aides 145 (ft), 13 (pt); Physical therapists 3 (pt); Recreational therapists 9 (ft), 5 (pt); Occupational therapists 2 (ft), 2 (pt); Speech therapists 1 (pt); Activities coordinators 1 (ft); Dietitians 8 (ft).
Languages French, German, Italian, Spanish, Sign.
Facilities Dining room; Physical therapy room; Activities room; Chapel; Crafts room; Laundry room; Barber/Beauty shop; Library; Greenhouse.
Activities Arts & crafts; Cards; Games; Reading groups; Prayer groups; Movies; Shopping trips; Dances/Social/Cultural gatherings; Horticultural program.

Eger Lutheran Homes
120 Meisner Ave, Staten Island, NY 10306
(718) 979-1800, 667-6950 FAX
Admin Paul K Jensen. *Dir of Nursing* Maureen Dugan. *Medical Dir* Jonathan Musher MD.

Licensure Skilled care; Intermediate care; Alzheimer's care. *Beds* SNF 336; ICF 42. *Private Pay Patients* 9%. *Certified* Medicaid; Medicare.
Owner Nonprofit corp.
Admissions Requirements Minimum age 16; Medical examination; Physician's request.
Staff Physicians 1 (pt); RNs 3 (ft), 25 (pt); LPNs 19 (ft), 26 (pt); Nurses' aides 119 (ft), 131 (pt); Physical therapists 1 (ft); Recreational therapists 3 (ft); Occupational therapists 1 (ft); Activities coordinators 1 (ft); Dietitians 1 (ft).
Affiliation Lutheran.
Facilities Dining room; Physical therapy room; Activities room; Chapel; Crafts room; Laundry room; Barber/Beauty shop; Library.
Activities Arts & crafts; Cards; Games; Prayer groups; Movies; Shopping trips; Dances/ Social/Cultural gatherings; Pet therapy.

Golden Gate Health Care Center
191 Bradley Ave, Staten Island, NY 10314
(718) 698-8800, 698-5536 FAX
Admin Alan Chopp. *Dir of Nursing* Christine Tacardon RN. *Medical Dir* Dr Morton Kleiner.
Licensure Skilled care; Intermediate care. *Beds* SNF 118; ICF 120. *Certified* Medicaid; Medicare.
Owner Privately owned.
Admissions Requirements Minimum age 21.
Staff Physicians 3 (ft), 11 (pt); RNs 16 (ft), 11 (pt); LPNs 14 (ft), 10 (pt); Nurses' aides 60 (ft), 2 (pt); Physical therapists 1 (ft); Recreational therapists 1 (ft); Occupational therapists 1 (ft); Speech therapists 1 (pt); Activities coordinators 1 (ft); Dietitians 3 (ft); Ophthalmologists 1 (pt); Podiatrists 1 (pt); Audiologists 1 (pt).
Facilities Dining room; Physical therapy room; Activities room; Crafts room; Laundry room; Barber/Beauty shop; Library.
Activities Arts & crafts; Cards; Games; Reading groups; Prayer groups; Movies; Shopping trips; Dances/Social/Cultural gatherings; Intergenerational programs; Pet therapy; Garden; Covered patio.

Lily Pond Nursing Home
150 Lily Pond Ave, Staten Island, NY 10305
(718) 981-5300
Admin Miriam Rozenberg. *Dir of Nursing* D Hepkins RN.
Licensure Skilled care. *Beds* SNF 35. *Certified* Medicaid; Medicare.
Owner Privately owned.
Admissions Requirements Minimum age 62; Medical examination; Physician's request.
Staff Physicians 2 (pt); RNs 1 (ft), 3 (pt); LPNs 3 (ft), 2 (pt); Nurses' aides 10 (ft), 3 (pt); Physical therapists 1 (pt); Recreational therapists 1 (ft), 3 (pt); Occupational therapists 1 (pt); Speech therapists 1 (pt); Activities coordinators 1 (ft), 3 (pt); Dietitians 1 (pt); Ophthalmologists 1 (pt); Podiatrists 1 (pt); Dentists 1 (pt); Pharmacists 1 (pt).
Languages Italian, Spanish.
Facilities Dining room; Physical therapy room; Activities room; Crafts room; Laundry room; Barber/Beauty shop.
Activities Arts & crafts; Cards; Games; Prayer groups; Movies; Dances/Social/Cultural gatherings; Outings to the circus; Plays.

New Brighton Manor Care Center
200 Lafayette Ave, Staten Island, NY 10301
(718) 448-9000
Admin Joshuah Levy.
Licensure Skilled care; Intermediate care. *Beds* SNF 80; ICF 220. *Certified* Medicaid; Medicare.
Owner Privately owned.

New Vanderbilt Nursing Home
135 Vanderbilt Ave, Staten Island, NY 10304
(718) 447-0701

Admin Henry A Schon. *Dir of Nursing* Josephine Choe. *Medical Dir* Dr Howard Guterman.
Licensure Skilled care; Alzheimer's care. *Beds* SNF 320. *Certified* Medicaid; Medicare.
Owner Privately owned.
Admissions Requirements Minimum age 35; Medical examination.
Staff Physicians 5 (pt); RNs 26 (ft), 6 (pt); LPNs 22 (ft), 8 (pt); Nurses' aides 80 (ft), 20 (pt); Physical therapists 2 (ft), 1 (pt); Recreational therapists 4 (ft), 3 (pt); Occupational therapists 1 (ft); Speech therapists 1 (pt); Activities coordinators 1 (ft); Dietitians 4 (ft); Ophthalmologists 2 (pt); Podiatrists 1 (pt); Dentists 1 (pt).
Languages Italian, Spanish.
Facilities Dining room; Physical therapy room; Activities room; Crafts room; Laundry room; Barber/Beauty shop.
Activities Arts & crafts; Cards; Games; Reading groups; Prayer groups; Movies; Dances/Social/Cultural gatherings.

Sea View Hospital & Home
460 Brielle Ave, Staten Island, NY 10314
(718) 390-8181
Admin Michael Cantatore.
Licensure Skilled care. *Beds* SNF 304. *Certified* Medicaid; Medicare.
Owner Proprietary corp (New York Health Corp).

Silver Lake Nursing Home
275 Castleton Ave, Staten Island, NY 10301
(718) 447-7800
Admin Otto Weingarten.
Medical Dir Dr Barbara Malach.
Licensure Skilled care. *Beds* SNF 278. *Certified* Medicaid; Medicare.
Owner Privately owned.
Admissions Requirements Minimum age 18; Medical examination; Physician's request.
Staff Physicians; RNs; LPNs; Nurses' aides; Physical therapists; Reality therapists; Recreational therapists; Occupational therapists; Speech therapists; Activities coordinators; Dietitians; Ophthalmologists; Podiatrists; Dentists.
Languages Hebrew, Yiddish, Italian, Spanish, Chinese.
Facilities Dining room; Physical therapy room; Activities room; Chapel; Crafts room; Barber/Beauty shop; Library.
Activities Arts & crafts; Cards; Games; Reading groups; Prayer groups; Movies; Shopping trips; Dances/Social/Cultural gatherings.

Verrazano Nursing Home
100 Castleton Ave, Staten Island, NY 10301
(718) 273-1300
Admin Israel Weingarten.
Medical Dir L Sasso MD.
Licensure Skilled care. *Beds* SNF 120. *Certified* Medicaid; Medicare.
Owner Privately owned.
Admissions Requirements Minimum age 16; Medical examination; Physician's request.
Staff Physicians 3 (pt); RNs 4 (ft), 4 (pt); LPNs 9 (ft), 6 (pt); Nurses' aides 26 (ft), 4 (pt); Physical therapists 1 (pt); Recreational therapists 1 (ft), 2 (pt); Occupational therapists 1 (pt); Speech therapists 1 (pt); Activities coordinators 1 (ft); Dietitians 1 (ft), 1 (pt); Ophthalmologists 1 (pt); Dentists 1 (pt).
Languages Spanish, Italian, Yiddish, Hebrew, Hungarian.
Facilities Dining room; Physical therapy room; Activities room; Barber/Beauty shop.
Activities Arts & crafts; Cards; Games; Reading groups; Prayer groups; Movies; Shopping trips; Dances/Social/Cultural gatherings.

Suffern

Ramapo Manor Nursing Center Inc
Cragmere Rd, Suffern, NY 10901
(914) 357-1230
Admin Robert Heyman. *Dir of Nursing* Ruth Avrin BSN. *Medical Dir* George Cox MD.
Licensure Skilled care; Intermediate care; Alzheimer's care. *Beds* SNF 122; ICF 41. *Private Pay Patients* 20%. *Certified* Medicaid; Medicare; VA.
Owner Privately owned.
Admissions Requirements Minimum age 16; Medical examination.
Staff RNs 28 (ft); LPNs 8 (ft); Nurses' aides 75 (ft); Physical therapists 1 (pt); Recreational therapists 3 (ft), 2 (pt); Occupational therapists 1 (pt); Speech therapists 1 (pt); Activities coordinators 1 (ft); Dietitians 1 (ft); Orderlies 1 (ft).
Languages French, Spanish, Russian, Hebrew, Yiddish, Italian, Portuguese.
Facilities Dining room; Activities room; Crafts room; Barber/Beauty shop; Library; Gift shop; Laundry; Dialysis care; Decubitis care.
Activities Arts & crafts; Cards; Games; Reading groups; Prayer groups; Movies; Shopping trips; Dances/Social/Cultural gatherings; Intergenerational programs; Music therapy; Stroke group; Resident chorus.

Syracuse

Castle Rest Nursing Home
116 E Castle St, Syracuse, NY 13205
(315) 475-1641
Admin Thomas Fahey.
Licensure Skilled care. *Beds* SNF 140. *Certified* Medicaid; Medicare.
Owner Privately owned.
Admissions Requirements Minimum age 65.
Facilities Dining room; Physical therapy room; Activities room; Crafts room; Barber/Beauty shop; Library.
Activities Arts & crafts; Cards; Games; Reading groups; Prayer groups; Movies; Shopping trips; Dances/Social/Cultural gatherings; Picnics; Fishing trips; Luncheon outings.

Community General Hospital of Greater Syracuse Nursing Home Unit
Broad Rd, Syracuse, NY 13215
(315) 492-5011, 492-5329 FAX
Admin Adella S Fowler. *Dir of Nursing* Lucy J Hill. *Medical Dir* J T Barry MD.
Licensure Skilled care. *Beds* SNF 50. *Private Pay Patients* 7%. *Certified* Medicaid; Medicare.
Owner Nonprofit corp.
Admissions Requirements Physician's request.
Languages Interpreter available.
Facilities Dining room; Physical therapy room; Activities room; Chapel; Laundry room; Barber/Beauty services provided.
Activities Arts & crafts; Cards; Games; Reading groups; Prayer groups; Movies; Dances/Social/Cultural gatherings; Pet therapy; Trips to state fair, dinner, zoo; Religious services.

Hill Haven Nursing Home
4001 E Genesee St, Syracuse, NY 13214
(315) 446-8310
Admin Gladys Stanton.
Licensure Skilled care. *Beds* SNF 121. *Certified* Medicaid; Medicare.
Owner Privately owned.

James Square Health & Rehabilitation Centre
918 James St, Syracuse, NY 13203
(315) 474-1561
Admin Mark Squire. *Dir of Nursing* Joan Roen Beck RN. *Medical Dir* Helmam J Rubinson MD.

Licensure Skilled care; Intermediate care. *Beds* SNF 415; ICF 40. *Certified* Medicaid; Medicare.
Owner Proprietary corp.
Staff Physicians 7 (ft); RNs 30 (ft), 15 (pt); LPNs 55 (ft), 23 (pt); Nurses' aides 180 (ft), 55 (pt); Physical therapists 2 (ft), 1 (pt); Reality therapists 1 (ft); Recreational therapists 7 (ft); Occupational therapists 2 (ft); Speech therapists 1 (ft); Activities coordinators 1 (ft); Dietitians 3 (ft); Volunteer coordinators 1 (ft).
Languages Italian, Polish.
Facilities Dining room; Physical therapy room; Activities room; Crafts room; Laundry room; Barber/Beauty shop; Library; Ventilator-dependent program.
Activities Arts & crafts; Cards; Games; Reading groups; Prayer groups; Movies; Shopping trips; Dances/Social/Cultural gatherings; Intergenerational programs; Pet therapy.

Jewish Home of Central New York
4101 E Genesee St, Syracuse, NY 13214
(315) 446-9111, 446-0255 FAX
Admin Harvey N Finkelstein; Mary Ellen Bloodgood, Asst Exec Dir. *Dir of Nursing* Dorothy Sokolowski. *Medical Dir* Dr Albert Tripodi.
Licensure Skilled care; Intermediate care; Adult day care. *Beds* SNF 145; ICF 6. *Private Pay Patients* 12%. *Certified* Medicaid; Medicare.
Owner Nonprofit corp.
Admissions Requirements Medical examination; Physician's request.
Staff RNs 13 (ft); LPNs 19 (ft); Nurses' aides 66 (ft); Activities coordinators 1 (ft); Dietitians 1 (ft).
Affiliation Jewish.
Facilities Dining room; Physical therapy room; Activities room; Chapel; Crafts room; Laundry room; Barber/Beauty shop.
Activities Arts & crafts; Cards; Games; Reading groups; Prayer groups; Movies; Shopping trips; Dances/Social/Cultural gatherings; Intergenerational programs; Pet therapy.

Loretto Geriatric Center
700 E Brighton Ave, Syracuse, NY 13205
(315) 469-5561
Admin Patrick M Deptula MS.
Medical Dir Frank Brand MD.
Licensure Skilled care; Intermediate care; Retirement. *Beds* SNF 240; ICF 280. *Certified* Medicaid; Medicare.
Owner Nonprofit corp.
Admissions Requirements Minimum age 62.
Staff Physicians 1 (ft); RNs 29 (ft), 12 (pt); LPNs 41 (ft), 15 (pt); Nurses' aides 113 (ft), 49 (pt); Physical therapists 2 (ft); Recreational therapists 7 (ft); Occupational therapists 1 (ft); Speech therapists 1 (pt); Activities coordinators 1 (ft); Dietitians 1 (ft); Ophthalmologists 1 (pt); Podiatrists 2 (pt); Dentists 1 (pt).
Facilities Dining room; Physical therapy room; Activities room; Chapel; Crafts room; Laundry room; Barber/Beauty shop; Library.
Activities Arts & crafts; Cards; Games; Reading groups; Prayer groups; Movies; Shopping trips; Dances/Social/Cultural gatherings.

Plaza Nursing Home Company Inc
614 S Crouse Ave, Syracuse, NY 13210
(315) 474-4431, 471-3851 FAX
Admin Edward A Leone. *Dir of Nursing* Esther LeVine RN. *Medical Dir* Leo Jivoff MD.
Licensure Skilled care; Sub-acute care; Enriched housing; Retirement; Alzheimer's care. *Beds* SNF 242; Enriched housing 40. *Private Pay Patients* 15%. *Certified* Medicaid; Medicare.
Owner Nonprofit corp.

Admissions Requirements Minimum age 16; Physician's request.
Staff Physicians 4 (pt); RNs 28 (ft); LPNs 27 (ft); Nurses' aides 89 (ft); Physical therapists 4 (ft); Recreational therapists 3 (ft); Occupational therapists 4 (ft); Speech therapists 1 (pt); Activities coordinators 1 (ft); Dietitians 1 (pt); Podiatrists 1 (pt); Audiologists 1 (pt); Horticultural therapists 1 (pt); Dentists 1 (pt).
Facilities Dining room; Physical therapy room; Activities room; Chapel; Crafts room; Laundry room; Barber/Beauty shop; Occupational therapy room; Alzheimer's unit; Dementia unit.
Activities Arts & crafts; Cards; Games; Reading groups; Prayer groups; Movies; Shopping trips; Dances/Social/Cultural gatherings; Intergenerational programs; Pet therapy.

St Camillus Residential Health Care Facility
813 Fay Rd, Syracuse, NY 13219
(315) 488-2951
Admin Robert Mack.
Medical Dir Dr John O'Brien.
Licensure Skilled care; Intermediate care. *Beds* SNF 130; ICF 120. *Certified* Medicaid; Medicare.
Owner Nonprofit corp.
Admissions Requirements Physician's request.
Staff Physicians 1 (ft), 9 (pt); RNs 18 (ft), 5 (pt); LPNs 17 (ft), 10 (pt); Nurses' aides 45 (ft), 20 (pt); Physical therapists 8 (ft); Recreational therapists 6 (ft); Occupational therapists 3 (ft); Speech therapists 6 (ft), 1 (pt); Activities coordinators 1 (ft); Dietitians 3 (ft); Podiatrists 2 (pt); Audiologists 1 (ft); Dentists 5 (pt).
Affiliation Roman Catholic.
Facilities Dining room; Physical therapy room; Activities room; Chapel; Crafts room; Laundry room; Barber/Beauty shop; Library.
Activities Arts & crafts; Cards; Games; Reading groups; Prayer groups; Movies; Shopping trips; Dances/Social/Cultural gatherings.

Van Duyn Home & Hospital
W Seneca Tpke, Syracuse, NY 13215
(315) 469-5511
Admin Raymond J Schumacher. *Dir of Nursing* Shirley Lewis. *Medical Dir* Arthur H Dube MD.
Licensure Skilled care; Intermediate care. *Beds* SNF 418; ICF 108. *Private Pay Patients* 11%. *Certified* Medicaid; Medicare.
Owner Publicly owned.
Admissions Requirements Physician's request.
Staff Physicians 1 (ft), 17 (pt); Physical therapists 2 (ft); Recreational therapists 7 (ft); Occupational therapists 2 (ft); Speech therapists (contracted); Activities coordinators 1 (ft); Dietitians 1 (ft); Ophthalmologists 2 (pt); Podiatrists 2 (pt); Audiologists (contracted); Radiology technicians 1 (ft), 1 (pt); Dentists 2 (pt); Social services 7 (ft); Inhalation therapists 1 (ft).
Facilities Dining room; Physical therapy room; Activities room; Chapel; Crafts room; Laundry room; Barber/Beauty shop; Library; Occupational therapy room; Pharmacy; Clinic; Inhalation therapy room.
Activities Arts & crafts; Cards; Games; Reading groups; Prayer groups; Movies; Shopping trips; Dances/Social/Cultural gatherings; Intergenerational programs; Pet therapy; Aerobics; Wheelchair volleyball.

Tarrytown

Tarrytown Hall Nursing Home
Wood Ct, Tarrytown, NY 10591
(914) 631-2600
Admin Leslie Kaye.

Licensure Skilled care; Intermediate care. *Beds* SNF 80; ICF 40. *Certified* Medicaid; Medicare.
Owner Privately owned.

Ticonderoga

Moses-Ludington Nursing Home Company Inc
Wicker St, Ticonderoga, NY 12883
(518) 585-6771
Admin Margaret Haroff. *Dir of Nursing* Regina Muscatello RN. *Medical Dir* Michael Beehner MD.
Licensure Skilled care. *Beds* SNF 40. *Certified* Medicaid; Medicare.
Owner Nonprofit corp.
Staff Physicians 1 (ft); RNs 5 (ft), 1 (pt); LPNs 4 (ft); Nurses' aides 14 (ft), 10 (pt); Physical therapists 1 (pt); Recreational therapists 2 (ft); Activities coordinators 1 (ft); Dietitians 1 (pt); Dentists 1 (pt).
Facilities Dining room; Physical therapy room; Activities room; Barber/Beauty shop.
Activities Arts & crafts; Cards; Games; Reading groups; Prayer groups; Movies; Shopping trips; Dances/Social/Cultural gatherings; Cooking club.

Tonawanda

Sheridan Manor Nursing Home Inc
2799 Sheridan Dr, Tonawanda, NY 14150
(716) 837-4466, 837-3606 FAX
Admin Dennis W Johnson. *Dir of Nursing* Maureen Wagner RN. *Medical Dir* Dr Harry Rubenstein.
Licensure Skilled care. *Beds* SNF 100. *Private Pay Patients* 50%. *Certified* Medicaid; Medicare.
Owner Proprietary corp.
Admissions Requirements Minimum age 18; Medical examination; Physician's request.
Staff RNs 5 (ft), 3 (pt); LPNs 10 (ft), 5 (pt); Nurses' aides 42 (ft), 18 (pt); Physical therapists 1 (pt); Recreational therapists 1 (ft), 3 (pt); Occupational therapists 1 (pt); Speech therapists 1 (pt); Dietitians 1 (pt); Podiatrists 1 (pt).
Facilities Dining room; Physical therapy room; Activities room; Laundry room; Barber/Beauty shop.
Activities Arts & crafts; Cards; Games; Reading groups; Prayer groups; Movies; Shopping trips; Dances/Social/Cultural gatherings; Intergenerational programs; Pet therapy.

Troy

James A Eddy Memorial Geriatric Center
2256 Burdett Ave, Troy, NY 12180
(518) 274-9890
Admin Peter G Young. *Dir of Nursing* Gayleen Kelsey. *Medical Dir* Arsenio Agopovich MD.
Licensure Skilled care; Intermediate care; Retirement; Alzheimer's care. *Beds* SNF 30; ICF 30. *Certified* Medicaid; Medicare.
Owner Nonprofit corp.
Admissions Requirements Minimum age 16; Medical examination.
Staff RNs 4 (ft), 4 (pt); LPNs 3 (ft), 6 (pt); Nurses' aides 12 (ft), 19 (pt); Physical therapists 1 (pt); Occupational therapists 1 (pt); Activities coordinators 1 (ft).
Facilities Dining room; Physical therapy room; Activities room; Laundry room; Barber/Beauty shop; Library.
Activities Arts & crafts; Cards; Games; Reading groups; Prayer groups; Movies; Shopping trips; Dances/Social/Cultural gatherings; Baking clubs; Men's clubs; Gardening; Stimulation program.

Eden Park Health Services Inc
2417 15th St, Troy, NY 12180
(518) 272-0404
Admin Eugene Evans.
Licensure Skilled care. *Beds* SNF 130.
Certified Medicaid; Medicare.
Owner Proprietary corp (Eden Park Health
Services Inc).

Hallmark Nursing Centre
49 Marvin Ave, Troy, NY 12180
(518) 273-6646
Admin Patricia M Morse. *Dir of Nursing*
Mary Beth Ryan. *Medical Dir* Dr Myron
Fribush.
Licensure Skilled care. *Beds* SNF 80. *Private
Pay Patients* 39%. *Certified* Medicaid;
Medicare.
Owner Proprietary corp.
Admissions Requirements Minimum age 16.
Staff Physicians; RNs; LPNs; Nurses' aides;
Physical therapists; Occupational therapists;
Speech therapists; Activities coordinators;
Dietitians; Podiatrists.
Facilities Dining room; Physical therapy
room; Activities room; Barber/Beauty shop.
Activities Arts & crafts; Cards; Games;
Reading groups; Prayer groups; Movies;
Dances/Social/Cultural gatherings;
Intergenerational programs; Pet therapy.

Highgate Manor of Rensselaer
100 New Turnpike Rd, Troy, NY 12182
(518) 235-1410
Admin Gregory J Zucco. *Dir of Nursing* Mary
Calabrese RN. *Medical Dir* Antonio Farol
MD; Lucilo Roman MD.
Licensure Skilled care; Intermediate care. *Beds*
SNF 80; ICF 40. *Certified* Medicaid;
Medicare.
Owner Proprietary corp (New Medico
Associates).
Admissions Requirements Minimum age 16;
Medical examination; Physician's request.
Staff Physicians 1 (ft), 2 (pt); RNs 14 (ft), 4
(pt); LPNs 14 (ft), 17 (pt); Nurses' aides 38
(ft), 32 (pt); Physical therapists 4 (ft);
Recreational therapists 4 (ft); Occupational
therapists 4 (ft); Speech therapists 4 (ft);
Activities coordinators 1 (ft); Dietitians 1
(ft).
Facilities Dining room; Physical therapy
room; Activities room; Crafts room; Barber/
Beauty shop; Dayroom.
Activities Arts & crafts; Cards; Games;
Reading groups; Prayer groups; Movies;
Shopping trips; Dances/Social/Cultural
gatherings.

Leisure Arms Health Related Facility
2405 15th St, Troy, NY 12180
(518) 271-7665
Admin Rebecca Smith. *Dir of Nursing*
Barbara Asadorian. *Medical Dir* Dr Myron
Fribush.
Licensure Intermediate care. *Beds* ICF 88.
Private Pay Patients 10%. *Certified*
Medicaid.
Owner Proprietary corp (Eden Park Health
Services).
Admissions Requirements Minimum age 16;
Medical examination.
Staff RNs 2 (ft); LPNs 4 (ft), 7 (pt); Nurses'
aides 12 (ft), 7 (pt); Activities coordinators 1
(ft); Dietitians 1 (pt).
Facilities Dining room; Activities room;
Laundry room; Barber/Beauty shop.
Activities Arts & crafts; Cards; Games; Prayer
groups; Movies; Shopping trips; Dances/
Social/Cultural gatherings; Intergenerational
programs.

Van Rensselaer Manor
133 Bloomingrove Dr, Troy, NY 12181
(518) 283-2000
Admin Bob Beaudion.

Licensure Skilled care; Intermediate care. *Beds*
SNF 232; ICF 130. *Certified* Medicaid;
Medicare.
Owner Publicly owned.

Tupper Lake

Mercy Healthcare Center
114 Wawbeek Ave, Tupper Lake, NY 12986
(518) 359-3355
Admin Sr Mary Paschal Hill RSM.
Medical Dir H Douglas Wilson MD.
Licensure Skilled care. *Beds* SNF 54. *Certified*
Medicaid; Medicare.
Owner Nonprofit corp.
Admissions Requirements Minimum age 16.
Staff Physicians 4 (pt); RNs 3 (ft), 4 (pt);
LPNs 4 (ft), 2 (pt); Nurses' aides 26 (ft), 10
(pt); Physical therapists 1 (pt); Activities
coordinators 1 (pt); Dietitians 1 (pt);
Ophthalmologists 1 (pt).
Languages French.
Affiliation Roman Catholic.
Facilities Dining room; Physical therapy
room; Activities room; Chapel; Laundry
room; Barber/Beauty shop.
Activities Arts & crafts; Cards; Games; Prayer
groups; Movies; Shopping trips; Dances/
Social/Cultural gatherings.

Uniondale

A Holly Patterson Geriatric Center
875 Jerusalem Ave, Uniondale, NY 11553-
3098
(516) 566-5700
Admin William J St George. *Dir of Nursing*
Holly Ledowski RN.
Licensure Skilled care; Alzheimer's unit. *Beds*
SNF 889. *Certified* Medicaid; Medicare.
Owner Publicly owned.
Admissions Requirements County resident;
Medicaid eligible.
Staff Physicians 2 (ft), 17 (pt); RNs; LPNs;
Nurses' aides; Physical therapists 4 (ft);
Recreational therapists 14 (ft); Occupational
therapists 1 (ft), 1 (pt); Speech therapists 1
(ft); Activities coordinators 1 (ft); Dietitians
6 (ft); Ophthalmologists 2 (pt); Podiatrists 2
(pt); Audiologists 2 (pt).
Languages By request.
Facilities Dining room; Physical therapy
room; Activities room; Chapel; Crafts room;
Laundry room; Barber/Beauty shop; Library;
Auditorium.
Activities Arts & crafts; Cards; Games;
Reading groups; Prayer groups; Movies;
Shopping trips; Dances/Social/Cultural
gatherings; Intergenerational programs; Pet
therapy.

Utica

Allen-Calder Skilled Nursing Facility
PO Box 479, Utica, NY 13503
(315) 798-6093
Admin Grace Steppello RN BPS. *Dir of
Nursing* Kathleen Galindo RN MPS.
Medical Dir Guy Wilcox MD.
Licensure Skilled care. *Beds* SNF 76. *Certified*
Medicaid; Medicare.
Owner Nonprofit corp.
Admissions Requirements Minimum age 16;
Medical examination; Physician's request.
Staff RNs 5 (ft), 7 (pt); LPNs 8 (ft), 8 (pt);
Nurses' aides 20 (ft), 29 (pt); Physical
therapists 7 (ft); Recreational therapists 1
(ft), 1 (pt); Occupational therapists;
Dietitians 1 (ft); COTAs 1 (pt); Staff
developers 1 (ft).
Languages Language bank available.
Facilities Dining room; Physical therapy
room; Chapel; Laundry room; Barber/Beauty
shop; Dayroom/Activity room.

Activities Arts & crafts; Cards; Games;
Reading groups; Movies;
Shopping trips; Dances/Social/Cultural
gatherings; Intergenerational programs; Pet
therapy.

Broadacres
Walker Rd, Utica, NY 13502
(315) 798-9200
Admin Richard DuRose.
Medical Dir Dr Jeanne F Arnold.
Licensure Skilled care. *Beds* SNF 168.
Certified Medicaid; Medicare.
Owner Publicly owned.
Staff Physicians 17 (pt); RNs 16 (ft), 7 (pt);
LPNs 34 (ft), 7 (pt); Nurses' aides 93 (ft), 36
(pt); Physical therapists 1 (pt); Occupational
therapists 1 (pt); Speech therapists 1 (pt);
Activities coordinators 1 (ft); Dietitians 1
(pt); Podiatrists; Dentists 1 (pt).
Facilities Dining room; Physical therapy
room; Activities room; Crafts room; Laundry
room; Barber/Beauty shop; Library.
Activities Arts & crafts; Cards; Games;
Reading groups; Prayer groups; Movies;
Shopping trips; Dances/Social/Cultural
gatherings.

Eden Park Nursing Home & HRF
1800 E Butterfield Ave, Utica, NY 13501
(315) 797-3570
Admin Clara Mae Durant.
Medical Dir Esther Johnston MD.
Licensure Skilled care; Intermediate care. *Beds*
SNF 80; ICF 37. *Certified* Medicaid;
Medicare.
Owner Proprietary corp (Eden Park Health
Services Inc).
Admissions Requirements Minimum age 16;
Medical examination; Physician's request.
Staff Physicians 17 (pt); RNs 9 (ft), 4 (pt);
LPNs 13 (ft), 6 (pt); Nurses' aides 44 (ft), 15
(pt); Physical therapists 1 (ft); Occupational
therapists 1 (pt); Speech therapists 1 (pt);
Activities coordinators 1 (ft); Dietitians 1
(pt); Podiatrists 1 (pt); Dentists 1 (pt).
Facilities Dining room; Physical therapy
room; Activities room; Crafts room; Laundry
room; Barber/Beauty shop.
Activities Arts & crafts; Cards; Games;
Reading groups; Prayer groups; Movies;
Shopping trips; Dances/Social/Cultural
gatherings.

Faxton Sunset St Luke's Home
1657 Sunset Ave, Utica, NY 13502
(315) 797-7392, 797-1402 FAX
Admin Ronald T Cerow. *Dir of Nursing*
Johann Varieur RN. *Medical Dir* Joseph C
Booth MD.
Licensure Skilled care; Intermediate care. *Beds*
SNF 59; ICF 140. *Private Pay Patients* 25%.
Certified Medicaid; Medicare.
Owner Nonprofit corp.
Admissions Requirements Minimum age 16;
Medical examination; Physician's request.
Staff RNs 6 (ft), 7 (pt); LPNs 18 (ft), 14 (pt);
Nurses' aides 40 (ft), 34 (pt); Physical
therapists; Activities coordinators 1 (ft);
Dietitians 1 (ft).
Facilities Dining room; Physical therapy
room; Activities room; Crafts room; Laundry
room; Barber/Beauty shop; Library; Resident
lounges.
Activities Arts & crafts; Cards; Games;
Reading groups; Prayer groups; Movies;
Shopping trips; Dances/Social/Cultural
gatherings; Intergenerational programs; Pet
therapy; Horse racing; Camping; Opera.

Genesee Nursing Home
1634 Genesee St, Utica, NY 13502
(315) 724-2151
Admin Stephen A Ross. *Dir of Nursing* Ada
Buffington RN.
Licensure Skilled care. *Beds* SNF 100.
Certified Medicaid; Medicare.
Owner Privately owned.

Admissions Requirements Minimum age 18; Medical examination.
Staff Physicians 2 (ft); RNs 5 (ft), 3 (pt); LPNs 8 (ft), 5 (pt); Nurses' aides 40 (ft), 10 (pt); Physical therapists 2 (ft); Reality therapists 1 (ft); Recreational therapists 3 (ft); Occupational therapists 1 (ft); Activities coordinators 1 (ft); Dietitians 1 (ft); Ophthalmologists 1 (pt); Dentists 1 (pt).
Languages French.
Facilities Physical therapy room; Activities room; Crafts room; Laundry room; Barber/Beauty shop.
Activities Arts & crafts; Games; Reading groups; Prayer groups; Movies; Shopping trips.

Masonic Home & Health Facility
2150 Bleecker St, Utica, NY 13501-1788
(315) 798-4833, 798-4901 FAX
Admin Richard M Dowe. *Dir of Nursing* Bernadette Millett RN. *Medical Dir* Edward B Bradley MD.
Licensure Skilled care; Intermediate care; Domiciliary care; Independent living. *Beds* SNF 259; ICF 129; Domiciliary care 55; Independent living apts 14. *Certified* Medicaid; Medicare.
Owner Nonprofit organization/foundation.
Admissions Requirements Minimum age 65; Medical examination.
Staff Physicians 2 (ft); RNs 32 (ft), 15 (pt); LPNs 47 (ft), 6 (pt); Nurses' aides 131 (ft), 27 (pt); Physical therapists 1 (ft); Occupational therapists 1 (ft); Speech therapists 1 (ft); Activities coordinators 1 (ft); Dietitians 1 (ft); Ophthalmologists 1 (pt); Podiatrists 1 (pt); Audiologists 1 (pt).
Affiliation Masons.
Facilities Dining room; Physical therapy room; Activities room; Chapel; Crafts room; Laundry room; Barber/Beauty shop; Library.
Activities Arts & crafts; Cards; Games; Reading groups; Prayer groups; Movies; Shopping trips; Dances/Social/Cultural gatherings; Pet therapy.

St Joseph Nursing Home Company of Utica
2535 Genesee St, Utica, NY 13501
(315) 797-1230
Admin Sr M Zavier.
Medical Dir Theodore C Mehalic MD.
Licensure Skilled care. *Beds* SNF 120. *Certified* Medicaid; Medicare.
Owner Nonprofit corp.
Staff RNs 7 (ft), 11 (pt); LPNs 13 (ft), 5 (pt); Nurses' aides 50 (ft), 32 (pt); Physical therapists 1 (pt); Occupational therapists 1 (pt); Activities coordinators 1 (ft); Dietitians 1 (pt).
Facilities Dining room; Physical therapy room; Activities room; Chapel; Laundry room; Barber/Beauty shop; Occupational therapy room; Library cart.
Activities Arts & crafts; Cards; Games; Reading groups; Prayer groups; Movies; Shopping trips; Pen pal club with 7th & 8th graders; Weekly pre-nursery school activity weekly; Fund raising.

Valatie

Barnwell Nursing Home
Church St, Valatie, NY 12184
(518) 758-6222, 758-9829 FAX
Admin Greta M Hutchinson. *Dir of Nursing* Katharine Logan RN. *Medical Dir* Dr Carl Whitbeck.
Licensure Skilled care; Intermediate care. *Beds* SNF 152; ICF 76. *Certified* Medicaid; Medicare.
Owner Proprietary corp.
Admissions Requirements Medical examination; Physician's request.
Staff RNs; LPNs; Nurses' aides; Physical therapists; Recreational therapists; Occupational therapists; Speech therapists

(consultant); Activities coordinators; Dietitians (consultant); Podiatrists (consultant); Audiologists (consultant).
Facilities Dining room; Physical therapy room; Activities room; Chapel; Crafts room; Laundry room; Barber/Beauty shop; Library; Greenhouse; Gazebo; Wheelchair lift equipped bus.
Activities Arts & crafts; Cards; Games; Reading groups; Prayer groups; Movies; Shopping trips; Dances/Social/Cultural gatherings; Intergenerational programs; Pet therapy.

Valley Cottage

Nyack Manor Nursing Home
Christian Herald Rd, Valley Cottage, NY 10989
(914) 268-6861
Admin Herbert A Rothman.
Medical Dir Norman Rubinstein MD.
Licensure Skilled care. *Beds* SNF 160. *Certified* Medicaid; Medicare.
Owner Privately owned.

Tolstoy Foundation Nursing Home Company Inc
Lake Rd, Valley Cottage, NY 10989
(914) 268-6813
Admin Vladimir Grigoriev.
Licensure Skilled care. *Beds* SNF 96. *Certified* Medicaid; Medicare.
Owner Nonprofit corp.
Admissions Requirements Minimum age 65; Medical examination.
Staff Physicians 1 (pt); RNs 12 (ft); LPNs 4 (ft); Nurses' aides 40 (ft); Physical therapists 1 (pt); Reality therapists 1 (pt); Occupational therapists 1 (pt); Speech therapists 1 (pt); Activities coordinators 1 (ft); Dietitians 1 (pt); Ophthalmologists 2 (pt); Podiatrists 2 (pt); Dentists 1 (pt).
Facilities Dining room; Physical therapy room; Activities room; Chapel; Laundry room; Barber/Beauty shop; Library.
Activities Arts & crafts; Cards; Games; Reading groups; Prayer groups; Movies; Shopping trips.

Vestal

Vestal Nursing Center
860 Old Vestal Rd, Vestal, NY 13850
(607) 754-4105
Admin Denise B Johnson. *Dir of Nursing* Carol Scurry. *Medical Dir* Edmund Goldenberg, HRF; Duncan Sze-Tu, SNF.
Licensure Skilled care; Intermediate care. *Beds* SNF 120; ICF 60. *Certified* Medicaid; Medicare.
Owner Proprietary corp.

Willow Point Nursing Home
3700 Old Vestal Rd, Vestal, NY 13850
(607) 798-8000, 770-8740 FAX
Admin Gregory R Brown, Acting. *Dir of Nursing* Donna Angelo RN. *Medical Dir* F Keith Kennedy MD.
Licensure Skilled care; Intermediate care; Alzheimer's care. *Beds* SNF 263; ICF 120. *Private Pay Patients* 1%. *Certified* Medicaid; Medicare.
Owner Publicly owned.
Admissions Requirements Minimum age 16; Physician's request.
Staff Physicians 1 (pt); RNs 14 (ft); LPNs 20 (ft), 11 (pt); Nurses' aides 124 (ft), 68 (pt); Physical therapists 1 (ft); Reality therapists 1 (ft); Recreational therapists 1 (ft); Occupational therapists 1 (ft); Speech therapists 1 (pt); Dietitians 2 (pt); Ophthalmologists 1 (pt); Podiatrists 1 (pt); Audiologists 1 (pt); Activities aides 4 (ft); Physical therapy aides 2 (ft), 1 (pt); Occupational therapy aides 1 (pt); Volunteer coordinators 1 (pt); Senior activities aides 1

(ft); In-service directors 1 (ft); Dentists 1 (pt); Social work supervisors 1 (ft); Social work assistants 3 (ft), 1 (pt).
Facilities Dining room; Physical therapy room; Activities room; Chapel; Crafts room; Laundry room; Barber/Beauty shop; Library.
Activities Arts & crafts; Cards; Games; Reading groups; Prayer groups; Movies; Shopping trips; Dances/Social/Cultural gatherings; Intergenerational programs; Pet therapy.

Wappingers Falls

Central Dutchess Nursing Home Inc
37 Mesier Ave, Wappingers Falls, NY 12590
(914) 297-3793
Admin Everett Alexander. *Dir of Nursing* Marguerite Ippolito. *Medical Dir* Thomas Robinson.
Licensure Skilled care. *Beds* SNF 62. *Private Pay Patients* 26%. *Certified* Medicaid; Medicare.
Owner Proprietary corp.
Admissions Requirements Medical examination.
Staff RNs 9 (ft), 12 (pt); LPNs 1 (ft), 4 (pt); Nurses' aides 17 (ft), 16 (pt); Physical therapists 1 (pt); Occupational therapists 1 (pt); Speech therapists 1 (pt); Activities coordinators 1 (ft), 1 (pt); Dietitians 1 (pt); Ophthalmologists; Podiatrists; Audiologists.
Facilities Dining room; Physical therapy room; Activities room; Laundry room; Barber/Beauty shop.
Activities Arts & crafts; Cards; Games; Reading groups; Prayer groups; Movies; Shopping trips; Dances/Social/Cultural gatherings; Intergenerational programs; Pet therapy; Family participation.

Warsaw

East Side Nursing Home
62 Prospect St, Warsaw, NY 14569
(716) 786-8151
Admin Sophia Hayes.
Medical Dir Dr J Thomas Reagan.
Licensure Skilled care. *Beds* SNF 80. *Certified* Medicaid; Medicare.
Owner Privately owned.
Staff Physicians 10 (pt); RNs 6 (ft), 5 (pt); LPNs 9 (ft), 6 (pt); Nurses' aides 30 (ft), 21 (pt); Physical therapists 1 (pt); Occupational therapists 1 (pt); Speech therapists 1 (pt); Activities coordinators 1 (ft); Dietitians 1 (pt); Ophthalmologists 1 (pt).
Facilities Dining room; Physical therapy room; Laundry room; Barber/Beauty shop.
Activities Arts & crafts; Games; Prayer groups; Movies; Dances/Social/Cultural gatherings.

Manor Oak Skilled Nursing Facilities Inc
283 N Main St, Warsaw, NY 14569
(716) 786-2211
Admin Peter Young.
Medical Dir Frederich Downs MD.
Licensure Skilled care. *Beds* SNF 100. *Certified* Medicaid; Medicare.
Owner Proprietary corp.
Admissions Requirements Minimum age 16; Medical examination; Physician's request.
Staff RNs 5 (ft); LPNs 8 (ft), 7 (pt); Nurses' aides 31 (ft), 40 (pt); Physical therapists 1 (ft); Speech therapists 1 (pt); Activities coordinators 1 (ft); Dietitians 1 (ft); Ophthalmologists 1 (pt); Podiatrists 1 (pt); Audiologists 1 (pt); Dentists 1 (pt).
Facilities Dining room; Physical therapy room; Activities room; Crafts room; Laundry room; Barber/Beauty shop.
Activities Arts & crafts; Cards; Games; Reading groups; Prayer groups; Movies; Shopping trips; Dances/Social/Cultural gatherings; Adopt-a-grandparent; Fitness classes; Special dinners; Trips to parks, zoo, racetrack, & restaurants.

Wyoming County Community Hospital Skilled Nursing Facility
400 N Main St, Warsaw, NY 14569
(716) 786-2233, 786-8139 FAX
Admin William E Holt. *Dir of Nursing* Joanne Whaley, Asst. *Medical Dir* Douglas Mayhle MD.
Licensure Skilled care. *Beds* SNF 72. *Private Pay Patients* 5%. *Certified* Medicaid; Medicare.
Owner Publicly owned.
Admissions Requirements Medical examination.
Staff Physicians 11 (pt); RNs 6 (ft), 4 (pt); LPNs 12 (ft), 8 (pt); Nurses' aides 26 (ft), 16 (pt); Physical therapists 1 (ft); Recreational therapists 1 (ft); Occupational therapists 1 (pt); Speech therapists 1 (pt); Activities coordinators 1 (ft), 1 (pt); Dietitians 4 (ft), 1 (pt); Ophthalmologists 1 (pt); Podiatrists 1 (pt); Audiologists 1 (pt); Dentists 2 (pt).
Facilities Dining room; Physical therapy room; Activities room; Chapel; Crafts room; Laundry room; Barber/Beauty shop; Library; Occupational therapy room.
Activities Arts & crafts; Cards; Games; Reading groups; Prayer groups; Movies; Shopping trips; Dances/Social/Cultural gatherings; Intergenerational programs; Pet therapy; Gardening; Community functions.

Waterloo

Seneca Nursing Home & HRF
200 Douglas Dr, Waterloo, NY 13165
(315) 539-9202
Admin Warren Elston. *Dir of Nursing* Mary Lou Maguire RN.
Licensure Skilled care; Intermediate care; Adult day health care. *Beds* SNF 80; ICF 40; Adult day health care 10. *Certified* Medicaid; Medicare.
Owner Privately owned.
Admissions Requirements Physician's request.
Staff RNs; LPNs; Nurses' aides; Physical therapists; Occupational therapists; Activities coordinators; Dietitians; Ophthalmologists.
Facilities Dining room; Physical therapy room; Activities room; Chapel; Crafts room; Laundry room; Barber/Beauty shop; Library.
Activities Arts & crafts; Cards; Games; Reading groups; Prayer groups; Movies; Shopping trips; Dances/Social/Cultural gatherings.

Taylor-Brown Memorial Hospital Nursing Home
369 E Main St, Waterloo, NY 13165
(315) 539-9204
Licensure Skilled care. *Beds* SNF 53.
Owner Nonprofit corp.

Watertown

Madonna Home of Mercy Hospital of Watertown
218 Stone St, Watertown, NY 13601
(315) 782-7400
Admin Sharon M Harris. *Dir of Nursing* Susan Kellogg RN BA. *Medical Dir* Collins Kellogg MD.
Licensure Skilled care; Intermediate care. *Beds* SNF 204; ICF 48. *Private Pay Patients* 10%. *Certified* Medicaid; Medicare.
Owner Nonprofit corp.
Admissions Requirements Minimum age 16; Medical examination; Physician's request.
Staff Physicians 1 (pt); RNs 9 (ft); LPNs 30 (ft); Nurses' aides 70 (ft); Recreational therapists 1 (pt); Occupational therapists 1 (pt); Speech therapists 1 (ft); Activities coordinators 1 (ft), 1 (pt); Dietitians 1 (pt); Podiatrists 1 (pt).
Languages Volunteer interpreters as required.
Affiliation Roman Catholic.

Facilities Activities room; Chapel; Crafts room; Laundry room; Barber/Beauty shop; Van for handicapped.
Activities Arts & crafts; Cards; Games; Reading groups; Prayer groups; Movies; Shopping trips; Dances/Social/Cultural gatherings; Intergenerational programs; Pet therapy.

Mercy Hospital Health Related Facility
218 Stone St, Watertown, NY 13601
(315) 782-7400
Licensure Intermediate care. *Beds* ICF 58.
Owner Nonprofit corp.

Samaritan-Keep Nursing Home Inc
133 Pratt St, Watertown, NY 13601
(315) 785-4400
Admin Gordon Paul Jeffery II. *Dir of Nursing* Pamela Puccia RN. *Medical Dir* William Heady MD.
Licensure Skilled care; Intermediate care; Adult day care; Retirement. *Beds* SNF 196; ICF 76; Adult day care 45; Retirement 124. *Certified* Medicaid; Medicare; VA.
Owner Nonprofit corp.
Admissions Requirements Minimum age 16; Medical examination; Physician's request.
Staff Physicians 1 (ft); RNs 14 (ft), 6 (pt); LPNs 27 (ft), 13 (pt); Nurses' aides 81 (ft), 33 (pt); Physical therapists 1 (pt); Occupational therapists 2 (ft); Speech therapists 1 (ft); Activities coordinators 1 (ft); Dietitians 1 (ft); Ophthalmologists 1 (ft); Podiatrists 1 (ft); Dentists 1 (pt).
Languages Greek, Spanish, Italian.
Facilities Dining room; Physical therapy room; Activities room; Chapel; Crafts room; Laundry room; Barber/Beauty shop; Library.
Activities Arts & crafts; Cards; Games; Reading groups; Prayer groups; Movies; Shopping trips; Dances/Social/Cultural gatherings; Intergenerational programs; Pet therapy.

Waterville

Harding Nursing Home
220 Tower St, Waterville, NY 13480
(315) 841-4156, 841-8856 FAX
Admin Louise S Harding. *Dir of Nursing* Mary L Fanning RN. *Medical Dir* Robert Delorme MD.
Licensure Skilled care; Intermediate care. *Beds* SNF 62; ICF 30. *Certified* Medicaid; Medicare.
Owner Privately owned.
Admissions Requirements Minimum age 21; Medical examination.
Staff Physicians 3 (pt); RNs 6 (ft), 4 (pt); LPNs 6 (ft), 6 (pt); Nurses' aides 44 (ft), 6 (pt); Physical therapists 1 (pt); Activities coordinators 1 (ft); Dietitians 1 (pt); Ophthalmologists 1 (pt); Podiatrists 1 (pt).
Facilities Dining room; Physical therapy room; Activities room; Crafts room; Laundry room; Barber/Beauty shop; Library.
Activities Arts & crafts; Cards; Games; Reading groups; Prayer groups; Movies; Shopping trips; Dances/Social/Cultural gatherings; Intergenerational programs; Pet therapy; Senior citizen men's club; Religious services.

Waverly

Tioga General Hospital Health Related Facility
32 Ithica St, Waverly, NY 14892
(607) 565-2861
Licensure Intermediate care. *Beds* ICF 51.
Owner Nonprofit corp.

Tioga Nursing Home Inc
37 N Chemung St, Waverly, NY 14892
(607) 565-2861
Admin Fred Kauffman.

Licensure Skilled care. *Beds* SNF 80. *Certified* Medicaid; Medicare.
Owner Nonprofit corp.

Webster

Hill Haven Nursing Home of Rochester County
1550 Empire Blvd, Webster, NY 14580
(716) 671-4300, 671-2263 FAX
Admin Robert Goldstein. *Dir of Nursing* Dr Carl Oshrain. *Medical Dir* Zsolt de Papp MD.
Licensure Skilled care; Intermediate care; Alzheimer's care. *Beds* SNF 187; ICF 168. *Certified* Medicaid; Medicare.
Owner Privately owned.
Admissions Requirements Minimum age 17; Medical examination; Physician's request.
Staff Physicians 3 (pt); RNs 18 (ft), 20 (pt); LPNs 34 (ft), 11 (pt); Nurses' aides 108 (ft), 33 (pt); Physical therapists 1 (ft); Occupational therapists 1 (pt); Speech therapists 1 (pt); Activities coordinators 1 (ft); Dietitians 1 (ft); Ophthalmologists 1 (pt); Podiatrists 1 (pt); Audiologists 1 (pt).
Facilities Dining room; Physical therapy room; Activities room; Crafts room; Laundry room; Barber/Beauty shop; Library.
Activities Arts & crafts; Cards; Games; Reading groups; Prayer groups; Movies; Shopping trips; Dances/Social/Cultural gatherings; Intergenerational programs; Pet therapy; Garden club; Recreational therapy.

Maplewood Nursing Home Inc
100 Daniel Dr, Webster, NY 14580
(716) 872-1800
Admin James H Chambery. *Dir of Nursing* Judith A Chambery. *Medical Dir* Stephan Cohen.
Licensure Skilled care. *Beds* SNF 72. *Certified* Medicaid; Medicare.
Owner Proprietary corp.
Admissions Requirements Medical examination; Physician's request; Financial disclosure.
Staff Physicians 1 (pt); RNs 25 (ft), 4 (pt); LPNs 8 (ft), 3 (pt); Nurses' aides 60 (ft), 30 (pt); Physical therapists 1 (pt); Occupational therapists 1 (pt); Speech therapists 1 (pt); Activities coordinators 1 (ft), 1 (pt); Dietitians 1 (pt); Ophthalmologists 1 (pt).
Facilities Dining room; Physical therapy room; Activities room; Crafts room; Barber/Beauty shop; Wheelchair bus.
Activities Arts & crafts; Cards; Games; Prayer groups; Movies; Shopping trips; Dances/Social/Cultural gatherings.

Wellsville

Wellsville Highland Inc
160 Seneca St, Wellsville, NY 14895
(716) 593-3750
Admin Beverly R Rahr.
Medical Dir Dr Coch.
Licensure Skilled care. *Beds* SNF 80. *Certified* Medicaid; Medicare.
Owner Proprietary corp.
Admissions Requirements Minimum age 21.
Staff Physicians; RNs 7 (ft); LPNs 9 (ft), 5 (pt); Nurses' aides 22 (ft), 21 (pt); Physical therapists 1 (pt); Occupational therapists; Speech therapists; Activities coordinators 1 (ft), 1 (pt); Dietitians 1 (pt); Ophthalmologists; Podiatrists.
Facilities Dining room; Physical therapy room; Activities room; Crafts room; Laundry room; Barber/Beauty shop.
Activities Arts & crafts; Cards; Games; Reading groups; Prayer groups; Movies.

Wellsville Manor Nursing Home
Rte 417, 4100 Bolivar Rd, Wellsville, NY 14895
(716) 593-4400

Licensure Skilled care; Intermediate care. *Beds*
SNF 80; ICF 40.
Owner Publicly owned.

West Babylon

Berkshire Nursing Center
10 Berkshire Rd, West Babylon, NY 11704
(516) 587-0600
Admin Stuart Goldberg.
Licensure Skilled care. *Beds* SNF 175.
Certified Medicaid; Medicare.
Owner Proprietary corp.

East Neck Nursing Center
132 Great East Neck Rd, West Babylon, NY
11707
(516) 422-4800
Licensure Skilled care; Intermediate care. *Beds*
SNF 240; ICF 60.
Owner Proprietary corp.

West Islip

Consolation Nursing Home Inc
111 Beach Dr, West Islip, NY 11795
(516) 587-1600, 587-5954 FAX
Admin Sr Audrey Harsen OP. *Dir of Nursing*
Nancy Toto RN. *Medical Dir* Dr Martin D
Podgainy.
Licensure Skilled care; Intermediate care. *Beds*
SNF 199; ICF 51. *Private Pay Patients* 15%.
Certified Medicaid; Medicare.
Owner Nonprofit corp.
Admissions Requirements Minimum age 65;
Medical examination; Physician's request.
Staff Physicians 1 (pt); RNs 10 (ft), 5 (pt);
LPNs 15 (ft), 10 (pt); Nurses' aides 95 (ft),
15 (pt); Physical therapists 1 (ft);
Recreational therapists 5 (ft), 1 (pt);
Occupational therapists 1 (ft); Speech
therapists 1 (pt); Activities coordinators 1
(ft); Dietitians 1 (ft), 1 (pt).
Languages Spanish, Italian.
Affiliation Roman Catholic.
Facilities Dining room; Physical therapy
room; Activities room; Chapel; Crafts room;
Barber/Beauty shop; Library; Auditorium; 10
dayrooms; 2 courtyards; Outdoor pavilion.
Activities Arts & crafts; Cards; Games;
Reading groups; Prayer groups; Movies;
Shopping trips; Dances/Social/Cultural
gatherings; Pet therapy.

West Seneca

Seneca Manor
2987 Seneca St, West Seneca, NY 14224
(716) 828-0500
Admin Matthew J Hriczko. *Dir of Nursing*
Carol Nowinski. *Medical Dir* Dr Herle.
Licensure Skilled care; Intermediate care. *Beds*
SNF 120; ICF 40. Certified Medicaid;
Medicare.
Owner Privately owned.
Admissions Requirements Minimum age 16.
Staff Physicians; RNs; LPNs; Nurses' aides;
Physical therapists 1 (pt); Occupational
therapists 1 (pt); Speech therapists 1 (pt);
Activities coordinators 2 (ft); Dietitians 1
(pt); Ophthalmologists 1 (pt); Podiatrists 1
(pt); Dentists 1 (pt).
Facilities Dining room; Physical therapy
room; Activities room; Crafts room; Laundry
room; Barber/Beauty shop.
Activities Arts & crafts; Cards; Games;
Reading groups; Prayer groups; Movies;
Shopping trips; Dances/Social/Cultural
gatherings.

Westfield

Westfield Health Care Center Inc
26 Cass St, Westfield, NY 14787
(716) 326-4646

Admin James E Pratt. *Dir of Nursing* Deborah
Mackmer. *Medical Dir* Robert Berke.
Licensure Skilled care; Intermediate care. *Beds*
SNF 80; ICF 40. Certified Medicaid;
Medicare.
Owner Proprietary corp.
Admissions Requirements Minimum age 17;
Physician's request.
Facilities Dining room; Physical therapy
room; Activities room; Chapel; Laundry
room; Barber/Beauty shop.
Activities Arts & crafts; Cards; Games;
Reading groups; Prayer groups; Movies;
Shopping trips; Dances/Social/Cultural
gatherings.

White Plains

**Nathan Miller Center for Nursing Care
Inc—White Plains Center Division**
220 W Post Rd, White Plains, NY 10606
(914) 686-8880
Admin Lorraine Goldman MPS. *Dir of
Nursing* Cecile Hughes RN BS. *Medical Dir*
Gerald Blandford MD.
Licensure Skilled care; Alzheimer's care. *Beds*
SNF 88. Certified Medicaid; Medicare.
Owner Nonprofit corp (Nathan Miller Center
for Nursing Care Inc).
Admissions Requirements Patient review
instrument (PRI).
Staff Physicians 1 (ft), 3 (pt); RNs 7 (ft), 2
(pt); LPNs 9 (ft), 7 (pt); Nurses' aides 50
(ft), 1 (pt); Physical therapists 1 (pt);
Occupational therapists 1 (pt); Speech
therapists 1 (pt); Activities coordinators 2
(ft); Dietitians 2 (pt).
Languages Spanish.
Facilities Dining room; Activities room;
Laundry room; Barber/Beauty shop; Park.
Activities Arts & crafts; Cards; Games; Prayer
groups; Movies; Dances/Social/Cultural
gatherings; Pet therapy.

**Nathan Miller Center for Nursing Care
Inc—Nathan Miller Center Division**
37 DeKalb Ave, White Plains, NY 10605
(914) 686-8880
Admin Dulcy B Miller MSAM. *Dir of Nursing*
Annabel LoMedico RN. *Medical Dir* Gerald
Blandford MD.
Licensure Skilled care; Respite care;
Alzheimer's care. *Beds* SNF 64; Respite care
1. Certified Medicaid; Medicare.
Owner Nonprofit corp (Nathan Miller Center
for Nursing Care Inc).
Admissions Requirements Patient review
instrument (PRI).
Staff Physicians 1 (ft), 1 (pt); RNs 5 (ft), 2
(pt); LPNs 4 (ft), 6 (pt); Nurses' aides 33
(ft); Physical therapists 1 (pt); Occupational
therapists 1 (pt); Activities coordinators 1
(ft), 1 (pt); Dietitians 1 (pt).
Languages Spanish.
Facilities Dining room; Activities room;
Laundry room; Barber/Beauty shop.
Activities Arts & crafts; Cards; Games; Prayer
groups; Movies; Dances/Social/Cultural
gatherings; Pet therapy.

Tibbits Health Related Facility
12 Tibbits Ave, White Plains, NY 10606
(914) 428-0910
Admin James Marmon. *Dir of Nursing* Janet
Yuscak RN. *Medical Dir* Dr Frederick
Saunders.
Licensure Skilled care; Intermediate care;
Alzheimer's care. *Beds* SNF 102; ICF 128.
Certified Medicaid; Medicare.
Owner Privately owned.
Staff RNs 11 (ft), 5 (pt); LPNs 14 (ft), 13 (pt);
Nurses' aides 37 (ft), 22 (pt); Physical
therapists 1 (ft); Occupational therapists 1
(pt); Speech therapists 1 (pt); Activities
coordinators 4 (ft); Dietitians 1 (ft).
Affiliation Roman Catholic.

Facilities Dining room; Physical therapy
room; Activities room; Chapel; Barber/
Beauty shop; Library.
Activities Arts & crafts; Cards; Games;
Reading groups; Prayer groups; Movies;
Shopping trips; Dances/Social/Cultural
gatherings.

White Plains Center for Nursing Care
220 W Post Rd, White Plains, NY 10606
(914) 946-8005
Licensure Skilled care. *Beds* SNF 88.
Owner Nonprofit corp.

Whitestone

Bridge View Nursing Home
143-10 20th Ave, Whitestone, NY 11357
(718) 961-1212
Admin Henry Jacoby.
Medical Dir Alexander Sebo MD.
Licensure Skilled care. *Beds* SNF 200.
Certified Medicaid; Medicare.
Owner Privately owned.
Admissions Requirements Medical
examination; Physician's request.
Staff Physicians 3 (pt); RNs 4 (ft); LPNs 15
(ft); Nurses' aides 34 (ft); Physical therapists
1 (ft); Recreational therapists 3 (ft);
Occupational therapists 1 (pt); Speech
therapists 1 (pt); Dietitians 1 (ft);
Ophthalmologists 1 (pt); Podiatrists 1 (pt);
Audiologists 1 (pt); Dentists 1 (pt).

Clearview Nursing Home
157-15 19th Ave, Whitestone, NY 11357
(718) 746-0400
Admin Raymond Small.
Licensure Skilled care. *Beds* SNF 179.
Certified Medicaid; Medicare.
Owner Proprietary corp.

Williamsville

Amherst Presbyterian Nursing Center
200 Bassett Rd, Williamsville, NY 14221
(716) 689-6681
Admin Daniel A Goupil. *Dir of Nursing*
Carmen A Lippert RN. *Medical Dir* Paul R
Katz MD.
Licensure Skilled care; Intermediate care;
Rehabilitation. *Beds* SNF 120; ICF 80.
Private Pay Patients 30%. Certified
Medicaid; Medicare.
Owner Nonprofit corp (Presbyterian Homes of
Western New York Inc).
Admissions Requirements Minimum age 16;
Medical examination.
Staff Physicians 4 (pt); RNs 12 (ft), 12 (pt);
LPNs 25 (ft), 10 (pt); Nurses' aides 54 (ft),
18 (pt); Physical therapists 1 (ft), 5 (pt);
Occupational therapists 1 (pt); Speech
therapists 1 (pt); Activities coordinators 1
(ft); Dietitians 1 (pt).
Affiliation Presbyterian.
Facilities Dining room; Physical therapy
room; Activities room; Chapel; Crafts room;
Laundry room; Barber/Beauty shop; Library.
Activities Arts & crafts; Cards; Games;
Reading groups; Prayer groups; Movies;
Shopping trips; Dances/Social/Cultural
gatherings; Intergenerational programs; Pet
therapy.

Heathwood Health Care Center Inc
815 Hopkins Rd, Williamsville, NY 14221
(716) 688-0111
Admin Barbara Bernardis. *Dir of Nursing*
Joan Wells. *Medical Dir* Dr Ida Levine.
Licensure Skilled care; Intermediate care. *Beds*
SNF 120; ICF 40. Certified Medicaid;
Medicare.
Owner Publicly owned.
Admissions Requirements Minimum age 16;
Medical examination; Physician's request.

Staff Physicians 1 (pt); RNs 8 (ft), 14 (pt); LPNs 22 (ft), 16 (pt); Nurses' aides 42 (ft), 34 (pt); Physical therapists 2 (pt); Occupational therapists 3 (pt); Speech therapists 1 (pt); Activities coordinators 1 (ft); Dietitians 2 (ft).
Facilities Dining room; Physical therapy room; Activities room; Chapel; Crafts room; Laundry room; Barber/Beauty shop; Occupational therapy room; Speech therapy room; Large front porch.
Activities Arts & crafts; Cards; Games; Reading groups; Prayer groups; Movies; Shopping trips; Dances/Social/Cultural gatherings; Current events; Cooking; Gardening; Exercise groups; Resident council; Ceramics; Community outings; Reminiscense groups; Ecumenical worship services.

St Francis Home of Williamsville
147 Reist St, Williamsville, NY 14221
(716) 633-5400
Admin Daniel Kenny.
Licensure Skilled care; Intermediate care. *Beds* SNF 103; ICF 39. *Certified* Medicaid; Medicare.
Owner Nonprofit corp (Catholic Charities of Buffalo).

Williamsville Suburban Nursing Home
193 S Union Rd, Williamsville, NY 14221
(716) 632-6152
Licensure Skilled care. *Beds* SNF 80.
Owner Nonprofit corp.

Williamsville View Manor
165 S Union Rd, Williamsville, NY 14221
(716) 633-9610
Admin Sam W Ware Jr. *Dir of Nursing* Louise Theriault RN. *Medical Dir* Joseph Gentile MD.
Licensure Intermediate care; Retirement. *Beds* ICF 140. *Certified* Medicaid.
Owner Privately owned.
Admissions Requirements Minimum age 16.
Staff RNs 4 (ft), 4 (pt); LPNs 6 (ft), 24 (pt); Nurses' aides 16 (ft), 40 (pt); Physical therapists 1 (pt); Recreational therapists 1 (ft); Occupational therapists 1 (pt); Activities coordinators 1 (ft); Dietitians 1 (ft).
Facilities Dining room; Physical therapy room; Activities room; Chapel; Crafts room; Laundry room; Barber/Beauty shop; Library.
Activities Arts & crafts; Cards; Games; Reading groups; Prayer groups; Movies; Shopping trips; Dances/Social/Cultural gatherings; Special dinners.

Woodbury

United Presbyterian Home at Syosset Inc
378 Syosset-Woodbury Rd, Woodbury, NY 11797
(516) 921-3900
Admin Alfred S Heim. *Dir of Nursing* Mr Trousdell MD.
Licensure Skilled care; Intermediate care. *Beds* SNF 352; ICF 250. *Certified* Medicaid; Medicare.
Owner Nonprofit corp.
Admissions Requirements Minimum age 16; Medical examination.
Staff Physicians 6 (ft); RNs 50 (ft); LPNs 60 (ft); Dietitians; Rehabilitation therapists.
Facilities Dining room; Physical therapy room; Activities room; Chapel; Crafts room; Laundry room; Barber/Beauty shop; Library; Game room; Music room; Bank branch; Long-term home health care; United lifeline; Personal emergency response system.
Activities Arts & crafts; Cards; Games; Reading groups; Movies; Shopping trips; Dances/Social/Cultural gatherings; May festival; Candlelight dinner; Variety shows; Barbeques; Community outreach programs.

Woodbury Health Related Facility
8565 Jericho Tpke, Woodbury, NY 11797
(516) 367-3400
Admin Mitchell B Teller.
Medical Dir Kathleen Gill.
Licensure Intermediate care. *Beds* ICF 100. *Certified* Medicaid; Medicare.
Owner Privately owned.
Admissions Requirements Medical examination; Physician's request.
Staff RNs; LPNs; Nurses' aides; Physical therapists; Recreational therapists; Dietitians.
Facilities Dining room; Physical therapy room; Activities room; Crafts room; Barber/Beauty shop; Library; 11 acres with pond.
Activities Arts & crafts; Cards; Games; Reading groups; Prayer groups; Movies; Shopping trips; Dances/Social/Cultural gatherings.

Woodbury Nursing Home
8533 Jericho Tpke, Woodbury, NY 11797
(516) 692-4100
Admin Maxwell White.
Licensure Skilled care. *Beds* SNF 123. *Certified* Medicaid; Medicare.
Owner Privately owned.

Woodmere

Woodmere Health Care Center Inc
130 Irving Pl, Woodmere, NY 11598
(516) 374-9300
Admin Miriam Feldman.
Medical Dir Dr Harold Langs.
Licensure Skilled care. *Beds* SNF 186. *Certified* Medicaid; Medicare.
Owner Proprietary corp.
Admissions Requirements Minimum age 18.
Staff Physicians; RNs; LPNs; Nurses' aides; Physical therapists; Reality therapists; Recreational therapists; Occupational therapists; Speech therapists; Activities coordinators; Dietitians; Ophthalmologists; Podiatrists; Audiologists; Dentists; Nursing care coordinators.
Facilities Dining room; Physical therapy room; Activities room; Crafts room; Laundry room; Barber/Beauty shop; Library.
Activities Arts & crafts; Cards; Games; Reading groups; Prayer groups; Movies; Shopping trips; Dances/Social/Cultural gatherings; Various outdoor trips; Picnics.

Woodmere Health Related Facility
121 Franklin Pl, Woodmere, NY 11598
(516) 374-9300
Licensure Intermediate care. *Beds* ICF 150.
Owner Proprietary corp.

Yaphank

Yaphank Infirmary
14 Yaphank Ave, Yaphank, NY 11980-9741
(516) 282-1419
Admin Kenneth E Gaul. *Dir of Nursing* G Biondo, Acting. *Medical Dir* Dr Damianos.
Licensure Skilled care. *Beds* SNF 215. *Private Pay Patients* 35%. *Certified* Medicaid; Medicare.
Owner Publicly owned.
Admissions Requirements Physician's request.
Staff Physicians 1 (ft), 2 (pt); RNs 17 (ft); LPNs 65 (ft); Nurses' aides 131 (ft); Physical therapists 1 (ft), 1 (pt); Recreational therapists 7 (ft), 1 (pt); Occupational therapists 1 (pt); Speech therapists 1 (pt); Activities coordinators 1 (ft); Dietitians 1 (ft); Podiatrists 1 (pt).
Facilities Dining room; Physical therapy room; Activities room; Crafts room; Barber/Beauty shop.

Activities Games; Reading groups; Prayer groups; Movies; Dances/Social/Cultural gatherings; Pet therapy; Art.

Yonkers

Home for Aged Blind
75 Stratton St S, Yonkers, NY 10701
(914) 963-4661, 963-4765 FAX
Admin Arthur R Marlowe. *Dir of Nursing* Ethel Autorino. *Medical Dir* Dr Arthur Berman.
Licensure Skilled care; Intermediate care; Alzheimer's care; Medical day care. *Beds* SNF 153; ICF 41. *Private Pay Patients* 5%. *Certified* Medicaid; Medicare.
Owner Nonprofit corp.
Admissions Requirements Minimum age 65; Medical examination.
Facilities Dining room; Physical therapy room; Activities room; Chapel; Crafts room; Barber/Beauty shop; Alzheimer's unit.
Activities Arts & crafts; Games; Reading groups; Dances/Social/Cultural gatherings; Pet therapy.

Hudson View Nursing Home Inc
65 Ashburton Ave, Yonkers, NY 10701
(914) 963-4000
Admin Scott Sandford.
Licensure Skilled care. *Beds* SNF 300. *Certified* Medicaid; Medicare.
Owner Proprietary corp.

New Sans Souci Nursing Home
115 Park Ave, Yonkers, NY 10703
(914) 423-9800
Admin Marilyn Mittman. *Dir of Nursing* J DiScenza RN. *Medical Dir* Dr Reddy.
Licensure Skilled care. *Beds* SNF 120. *Certified* Medicaid; Medicare.
Owner Privately owned.
Staff Physicians 1 (pt); RNs 10 (ft), 9 (pt); LPNs 12 (ft), 5 (pt); Nurses' aides 30 (ft), 21 (pt); Physical therapists 2 (pt); Recreational therapists 1 (ft), 2 (pt); Occupational therapists 1 (pt); Speech therapists 1 (pt); Dietitians 1 (pt).
Facilities Dining room; Physical therapy room; Activities room; Crafts room; Barber/Beauty shop.
Activities Arts & crafts; Cards; Games; Reading groups; Prayer groups; Movies; Dances/Social/Cultural gatherings; Boat trips; Barbeques.

St Josephs Hospital Nursing Home of Yonkers New York Inc
127 S Broadway, Yonkers, NY 10701
(914) 965-6700
Admin Dennis J Verzi. *Dir of Nursing* Rosalie Schiel RN. *Medical Dir* Dr Thomas Kalchthaler.
Licensure Skilled care; Intermediate care; Alzheimer's care. *Beds* SNF 160; ICF 40. *Certified* Medicaid; Medicare.
Owner Nonprofit corp.
Admissions Requirements Minimum age 16; Medical examination; Physician's request.
Staff Physicians 3 (ft); RNs 33 (ft); LPNs 34 (ft); Nurses' aides 91 (ft); Physical therapists 1 (ft); Reality therapists 1 (ft); Recreational therapists 3 (ft); Occupational therapists 2 (ft); Activities coordinators 1 (ft); Dietitians 2 (ft).
Languages Spanish, Portuguese, Arabic, Italian, Russian, German, French.
Affiliation Roman Catholic.
Facilities Dining room; Physical therapy room; Activities room; Chapel; Barber/Beauty shop; Non-occupant day program for adults; Long-term home health care program.
Activities Arts & crafts; Cards; Games; Reading groups; Prayer groups; Movies; Dances/Social/Cultural gatherings.

NORTH CAROLINA

Ahoskie

Guardian Care of Ahoskie
604 Stokes St E, Ahoskie, NC 27910
(919) 332-2126
Admin Yvonne F Jernigan. *Dir of Nursing*
Rebecca E Cartern RN.
Licensure Intermediate care. *Beds* ICF 131.
Certified Medicaid.
Owner Proprietary corp (Hillhaven Corp).
Admissions Requirements Medical
examination.
Staff RNs 2 (ft), 1 (pt); LPNs 11 (ft), 4 (pt);
Nurses' aides 30 (ft), 12 (pt); Activities
coordinators 1 (ft); Dietitians 1 (ft).
Facilities Dining room; Activities room;
Crafts room; Laundry room; Barber/Beauty
shop.
Activities Arts & crafts; Games; Reading
groups; Prayer groups; Movies; Shopping
trips; Dances/Social/Cultural gatherings.

Albemarle

Britthaven of Piedmont
PO Box 1250, 33426 Old Salisbury Rd,
Albemarle, NC 28002
(704) 983-1195, 983-1353 FAX
Admin Paula T Smith. *Dir of Nursing* Sharon
M Scheble. *Medical Dir* Dr Eric M Johnsen.
Licensure Skilled care; Intermediate care. *Beds*
SNF 60; ICF 60. *Private Pay Patients* 15%.
Certified Medicaid; Medicare.
Owner Proprietary corp (Britthaven Inc).
Admissions Requirements Minimum age 18;
Medical examination.
Facilities Dining room; Physical therapy
room; Activities room; Crafts room; Laundry
room; Barber/Beauty shop.
Activities Arts & crafts; Cards; Games;
Reading groups; Prayer groups; Movies;
Shopping trips; Dances/Social/Cultural
gatherings.

Lutheran Nursing Homes Inc—Albemarle Unit
Rte 1 Box 204, 24724 Hwy, Albemarle, NC
28001
(704) 982-8191
Admin Jon D Lawson. *Dir of Nursing* Ethel
Plyler. *Medical Dir* Thomas F Kelley MD.
Licensure Skilled care; Intermediate care;
Home for aged. *Beds* SNF 54; ICF 22;
Home for aged 12. *Certified* Medicaid;
Medicare.
Owner Nonprofit corp (North Carolina
Lutheran Homes).
Admissions Requirements Minimum age 60;
Medical examination; Physician's request.
Staff Physicians; RNs; LPNs; Nurses' aides;
Activities coordinators; Dietitians; Dentists.
Affiliation Lutheran.
Facilities Dining room; Physical therapy
room; Activities room; Chapel; Crafts room;
Laundry room; Barber/Beauty shop; Library;
Living room; Sitting room.

Activities Arts & crafts; Cards; Games;
Reading groups; Prayer groups; Movies;
Shopping trips; Dances/Social/Cultural
gatherings.

Stanly Manor
PO Box 38, 625 Bethany Church Rd,
Albemarle, NC 28002
(704) 982-0770
Admin Jack Musker. *Dir of Nursing* Alice
McKeon. *Medical Dir* Paul Pastorini MD.
Licensure Skilled care; Home for Aged. *Beds*
SNF 30; ICF 30; Home for aged 20.
Certified Medicaid; Medicare.
Owner Nonprofit organization/foundation.
Admissions Requirements Minimum age 18;
Medical examination; Physician's request.
Staff RNs 4 (ft); LPNs 7 (ft); Nurses' aides 25
(ft); Recreational therapists 1 (ft); Dietitians
1 (pt).
Facilities Dining room; Physical therapy
room; Activities room; Laundry room;
Barber/Beauty shop.
Activities Arts & crafts; Cards; Games;
Reading groups; Prayer groups; Movies;
Shopping trips; Intergenerational programs;
Pet therapy.

Asheboro

Brian Center Nursing Care—Asheboro
230 E Presnell St, Asheboro, NC 27203
(919) 629-1447
Admin Vincent E Hoskyns.
Medical Dir Ken Gobel MD.
Licensure Skilled care; Intermediate care. *Beds*
SNF 158; ICF 80. *Certified* Medicaid;
Medicare.
Owner Proprietary corp (Brian Center
Management Corp).
Admissions Requirements Minimum age 18.
Staff Physicians 22 (pt); RNs 10 (ft), 4 (pt);
LPNs 20 (ft), 10 (pt); Nurses' aides 65 (ft),
15 (pt); Physical therapists 2 (pt); Speech
therapists 1 (pt); Activities coordinators 3
(ft); Dietitians 1 (pt); Ophthalmologists 3
(pt); Podiatrists 1 (pt); Audiologists 1 (pt);
Dentists 1 (pt).
Facilities Dining room; Physical therapy
room; Activities room; Crafts room; Laundry
room; Barber/Beauty shop; Library.
Activities Arts & crafts; Cards; Games; Prayer
groups; Movies; Shopping trips; Dances/
Social/Cultural gatherings.

Clapp's Convalescent Nursing Home Inc
Rte 10 Box 357, Hwy 42E, Asheboro, NC
27203
(919) 625-2074
Admin George Donald Clapp.
Licensure Skilled care. *Beds* SNF 26. *Certified*
Medicare.

Meadowbrook Manor of Asheboro
400 US 220 Bypass Connector, Asheboro, NC
27203
(919) 672-5450
Admin Joanne W Moffitt.

Licensure Skilled care; Intermediate care;
Home for aged. *Beds* SNF 50; ICF 50;
Home for aged 20. *Certified* Medicaid;
Medicare.

Asheville

Aston Park Health Care Center Inc
380 Brevard Rd, Asheville, NC 28806
(704) 253-4437
Admin Martha M Smart. *Dir of Nursing*
Louise R Carter. *Medical Dir* Kenneth
Kubitschek MD.
Licensure Skilled care; Intermediate care. *Beds*
SNF 63; ICF 57. *Private Pay Patients* 40%.
Certified Medicaid; Medicare.
Owner Nonprofit organization/foundation.
Admissions Requirements Minimum age 18;
Medical examination.
Staff RNs 4 (ft); LPNs 15 (ft); Nurses' aides
63 (ft); Physical therapists 1 (pt);
Recreational therapists 1 (pt); Occupational
therapists 1 (pt); Speech therapists 1 (pt);
Activities coordinators 1 (ft); Dietitians 1
(ft); Ophthalmologists 1 (pt); Podiatrists 1
(pt); Audiologists 1 (pt).
Facilities Dining room; Physical therapy
room; Activities room; Crafts room; Laundry
room; Barber/Beauty shop; Library;
Dayroom.
Activities Arts & crafts; Cards; Games;
Reading groups; Prayer groups; Movies;
Shopping trips; Dances/Social/Cultural
gatherings; Intergenerational programs; Pet
therapy.

Autumnfield of Asheville
141 Hillside, Asheville, NC 28801
(704) 253-4000
Admin Gilen R Meibaum. *Dir of Nursing*
Alesia Swann; Jenny Clark RN. *Medical Dir*
Dave Khatri MD.
Licensure Intermediate care; Home for aged;
Alzheimer's care. *Beds* ICF 18; Home for
aged 25. *Certified* Medicaid.
Owner Proprietary corp (OMG Inc).
Admissions Requirements Minimum age 21;
Medical examination; Physician's request.
Staff RNs 1 (pt); LPNs 2 (ft), 5 (pt); Nurses'
aides 14 (ft), 2 (pt); Activities coordinators 1
(ft); Dietitians 1 (ft); Ophthalmologists 1
(pt); Podiatrists 1 (pt).
Facilities Dining room; Activities room.
Activities Bingo; Cookouts; Car shows;
Educational encouragement.

Biltmore Manor Inc
PO Box 15073, 14 All Souls Crescent,
Asheville, NC 28813
(704) 274-2336
Admin Robert C Brady.
Licensure Skilled care; Intermediate care;
Home for aged. *Beds* SNF 53; ICF 26;
Home for aged 21. *Certified* Medicaid;
Medicare.

Brentwood Hills Nursing Center
500 Beaverdam Rd, Asheville, NC 28804
(704) 254-8833
Admin Wayne Adams.
Medical Dir Mary Burgess.
Licensure Skilled care; Retirement;
Alzheimer's care. *Beds* SNF 77. *Certified*
Medicaid; Medicare.
Owner Proprietary corp (Beverly Enterprises).
Admissions Requirements Minimum age 21.
Staff Physicians 1 (ft); RNs 5 (ft); LPNs 15
(ft); Nurses' aides 15 (ft); Physical therapists
2 (ft); Recreational therapists 1 (ft);
Occupational therapists 1 (pt); Speech
therapists 1 (pt); Activities coordinators 1
(ft); Dietitians 1 (ft); Ophthalmologists 1
(pt); Podiatrists 1 (pt).
Facilities Dining room; Physical therapy
room; Activities room; Crafts room; Laundry
room; Barber/Beauty shop.
Activities Arts & crafts; Cards; Games;
Reading groups; Prayer groups; Movies;
Shopping trips; Dances/Social/Cultural
gatherings.

Brian Center Health & Retirement—Asheville
67 Mountainbrook Rd, Asheville, NC 28805
(704) 258-8787
Admin Deborah Jo Koch.
Medical Dir Dr Ricard Olson.
Licensure Skilled care; Intermediate care;
Home for aged. *Beds* SNF 42; ICF 18;
Home for aged 12. *Certified* Medicaid;
Medicare.
Owner Proprietary corp (Brian Center
Management Corp).
Admissions Requirements Minimum age 21;
Physician's request.
Staff Physicians 16 (pt); RNs 3 (ft), 1 (pt);
LPNs 5 (ft), 2 (pt); Nurses' aides 23 (ft), 6
(pt); Physical therapists 1 (pt); Speech
therapists 1 (pt); Activities coordinators 1
(ft), 1 (pt); Dietitians 1 (ft);
Ophthalmologists 1 (pt); Dentists.
Facilities Dining room; Physical therapy
room; Laundry room; Barber/Beauty shop.
Activities Arts & crafts; Cards; Games;
Reading groups; Prayer groups; Movies;
Shopping trips; Dances/Social/Cultural
gatherings; Supper club; Exercise class.

Brooks-Howell Home
29 Spears Ave, Asheville, NC 28801
(704) 253-6712
Admin Vivian T McGraw.
Licensure Skilled care; Intermediate care. *Beds*
SNF 40; ICF 18.
Affiliation Methodist.
Facilities Dining room; Physical therapy
room; Activities room; Chapel; Crafts room;
Laundry room; Barber/Beauty shop; Library.
Activities Arts & crafts; Cards; Games;
Reading groups; Prayer groups; Movies;
Shopping trips; Dances/Social/Cultural
gatherings.

Deerfield Episcopal Retirement Community Inc
1617 Hendersonville Rd, Asheville, NC 28803
(704) 274-1531
Admin Richard Weimann, Exec Dir. *Dir of
Nursing* Nyla Sailer. *Medical Dir* Dr Fuller
Shuford.
Licensure Skilled care; Home for aged;
Retirement. *Beds* SNF 31; Home for aged 8;
Retirement 85.
Owner Nonprofit organization/foundation.
Admissions Requirements Minimum age 62;
Medical examination.
Staff RNs 3 (ft), 5 (pt); LPNs 5 (ft), 2 (pt);
Nurses' aides 18 (ft), 12 (pt); Activities
coordinators 1 (ft), 1 (pt).
Affiliation Episcopal.
Facilities Dining room; Activities room;
Chapel; Laundry room; Barber/Beauty shop;
Library.

Activities Arts & crafts; Cards; Games;
Reading groups; Prayer groups; Movies;
Shopping trips; Dances/Social/Cultural
gatherings.

Green Tree Ridge
PO Box 5621, 70 Sweeten Creek Rd,
Asheville, NC 28813
(704) 274-7646
Admin James D Sawyer. *Dir of Nursing* Fran
Mills. *Medical Dir* Margaret A Noel MD.
Licensure Skilled care; Intermediate care;
Home for aged. *Beds* SNF 40; ICF 20;
Home for aged 40. *Certified* Medicaid;
Medicare; VA.
Owner Nonprofit corp.
Admissions Requirements Minimum age 18;
Medical examination.
Staff Physicians 2 (pt); RNs 6 (ft), 5 (pt);
LPNs 12 (ft), 4 (pt); Nurses' aides 34 (ft), 7
(pt); Physical therapists 1 (pt); Occupational
therapists 1 (pt); Speech therapists 1 (pt);
Activities coordinators 2 (ft); Dietitians 10
(ft), 6 (pt).
Facilities Dining room; Physical therapy
room; Activities room; Chapel; Crafts room;
Laundry room; Barber/Beauty shop; Private
dining room.
Activities Arts & crafts; Cards; Games;
Reading groups; Prayer groups; Movies;
Dances/Social/Cultural gatherings;
Intergenerational programs; Pet therapy;
Music therapy.

Hillhaven Rehabilitation & Convalescent Center
91 Victoria Rd, Asheville, NC 28801
(704) 255-0076
Admin Glenn T Pierce. *Dir of Nursing* Susan
Latta RN. *Medical Dir* Robert Reynolds
MD.
Licensure Skilled care; Intermediate care. *Beds*
SNF 60; ICF 60. *Certified* Medicaid;
Medicare.
Owner Proprietary corp (Hillhaven Corp).
Admissions Requirements Minimum age 18;
Medical examination; Physician's request.
Staff RNs; LPNs; Nurses' aides; Physical
therapists; Recreational therapists;
Occupational therapists; Speech therapists.
Facilities Dining room; Physical therapy
room; Activities room; Barber/Beauty shop.
Activities Arts & crafts; Cards; Games;
Reading groups; Prayer groups; Movies;
Shopping trips; Dances/Social/Cultural
gatherings.

St Joseph's Hospital Restorative Care
428 Biltmore Ave, Asheville, NC 28801
(704) 255-3100
Admin Dick Hattan.
Licensure Skilled care. *Beds* SNF 30. *Certified*
Medicaid; Medicare.

Victoria Health Care Center
455 Victoria Rd, Asheville, NC 28801
(704) 252-0099
Admin Debra G Koontz.
Medical Dir John Kelly MD.
Licensure Skilled care; Intermediate care. *Beds*
SNF 60; ICF 60. *Certified* Medicaid;
Medicare.
Owner Proprietary corp (Waverly Group).
Admissions Requirements Medical
examination; Physician's request.
Staff RNs 5 (ft); LPNs 12 (ft); Physical
therapists 3 (ft); Recreational therapists 1
(ft); Speech therapists 1 (pt); Activities
coordinators 1 (ft); Dietitians 1 (ft); Dentists
1 (pt).
Facilities Dining room; Physical therapy
room; Activities room; Laundry room;
Barber/Beauty shop.
Activities Arts & crafts; Cards; Games;
Reading groups; Movies; Dances/Social/
Cultural gatherings.

Banner Elk

Life Care Center
Rte 1 Box 143, Banner Elk, NC 28604
(704) 898-5136, 898-8426 FAX
Admin Gerald A Woods. *Dir of Nursing*
Donna Rau RN. *Medical Dir* Cathy Messick
MD.
Licensure Skilled care; Intermediate care. *Beds*
SNF 60; ICF 60. *Private Pay Patients* 13%.
Certified Medicaid; Medicare.
Owner Proprietary corp (Life Care Centers of
America).
Admissions Requirements Minimum age 18;
Medical examination; Physician's request.
Staff Physicians 4 (pt); RNs 7 (ft), 1 (pt);
LPNs 20 (ft), 2 (pt); Nurses' aides 36 (ft), 6
(pt); Physical therapists 1 (ft); Speech
therapists 1 (pt); Activities coordinators 2
(ft); Dietitians 1 (ft); Ophthalmologists 1
(pt); Podiatrists 1 (pt).
Facilities Dining room; Physical therapy
room; Activities room; Laundry room;
Barber/Beauty shop.
Activities Arts & crafts; Cards; Games;
Reading groups; Prayer groups; Movies.

Barco

Sentara Nursing Center
Rte 168 Box 226, Barco, NC 27917
(919) 453-8072, 453-3725 FAX
Admin Joyce T Butler. *Dir of Nursing* Betty J
Andrews. *Medical Dir* Dr Martz.
Licensure Skilled care; Intermediate care;
Home for aged. *Beds* SNF 25; ICF 50;
Home for aged 25. *Private Pay Patients* 22%.
Certified Medicaid; Medicare.
Owner Nonprofit corp (Sentara Life Care
Corp).
Admissions Requirements Minimum age 18;
Medical examination.
Staff RNs 3 (ft), 3 (pt); LPNs 8 (ft), 6 (pt);
Nurses' aides 20 (ft), 16 (pt); Physical
therapists (contracted); Activities
coordinators 1 (ft); Dietitians 1 (ft);
Podiatrists (consultant).
Facilities Dining room; Physical therapy
room; Activities room; Crafts room; Barber/
Beauty shop; Individual heating/air
conditioning; Individual TV and telephone
hook-ups; Emergency generators; Door
alarms; Nurse's call system.
Activities Arts & crafts; Cards; Games;
Reading groups; Prayer groups; Movies;
Shopping trips; Dances/Social/Cultural
gatherings; Intergenerational programs; Pet
therapy; Family & community participation.

Biscoe

Autumn Care of Biscoe
PO Box 708, Lambert Rd, Biscoe, NC 27209
(919) 428-2117
Admin Betty C Davis.
Medical Dir Dr C N Eckerson.
Licensure Skilled care. *Beds* SNF 57. *Certified*
Medicaid; Medicare.
Owner Proprietary corp (Autumn Corp).
Admissions Requirements Medical
examination.
Staff RNs 2 (ft), 1 (pt); LPNs 6 (ft), 1 (pt);
Nurses' aides 14 (ft), 4 (pt); Activities
coordinators 1 (ft); Dietitians 1 (ft).
Facilities Dining room; Activities room;
Chapel; Crafts room; Barber/Beauty shop.
Activities Arts & crafts; Games; Prayer groups;
Movies; Dances/Social/Cultural gatherings.

Black Mountain

Black Mountain Center
Old Hwy 70, Black Mountain, NC 28711
(704) 669-3100
Admin Dr Jack St Clair.
Medical Dir Dr Rasheeda Ahsanuddin.

Licensure Intermediate care for mentally retarded. *Beds* ICF/MR 120. *Certified* Medicaid.
Owner Publicly owned.
Admissions Requirements Medical examination.
Staff Physicians 2 (ft); RNs 11 (ft); LPNs 4 (ft); Nurses' aides 99 (ft); Physical therapists 1 (ft); Recreational therapists 3 (ft); Occupational therapists 1 (ft); Speech therapists 2 (ft); Dietitians 2 (ft).
Facilities Dining room; Physical therapy room; Activities room; Chapel; Laundry room; Barber/Beauty shop; Library.
Activities Arts & crafts; Cards; Games; Reading groups; Prayer groups; Movies; Shopping trips; Dances/Social/Cultural gatherings; Individual training in self-help; Community living; Vocational skills.

Highland Farms Inc
200 Tabernacle Rd, Black Mountain, NC 28711
(704) 669-6473
Admin Sheila L Morse.
Licensure Skilled care; Home for Aged. *Beds* SNF 60; Home for Aged 30. *Certified* Medicaid; Medicare.

Blowing Rock

Blowing Rock Hospital—SNF/ICF
PO Box 148, Chestnut Dr, Blowing Rock, NC 28605
(704) 295-3136
Admin James P White. *Dir of Nursing* Venn A Long. *Medical Dir* Charles Davant Jr MD.
Licensure Skilled care; Intermediate care. *Beds* SNF 66; ICF 6. *Certified* Medicaid; Medicare; VA.
Owner Nonprofit corp.
Admissions Requirements Medical examination; Physician's request.
Staff Physical therapists 2 (pt); Activities coordinators 1 (ft), 1 (pt).
Facilities Dining room; Physical therapy room; Activities room; Chapel; Crafts room; Laundry room; Barber/Beauty shop.
Activities Arts & crafts; Cards; Games; Reading groups; Prayer groups; Movies; Shopping trips; Dances/Social/Cultural gatherings; Ceramics; Exercise.

Boone

Watauga Nursing Care Center
PO Box 2150, 535-A Elizabeth Dr, Boone, NC 28607
(704) 264-6720
Admin Valerie J Keck Boughman. *Dir of Nursing* Chris Ferguson RN. *Medical Dir* Mark R Harter MD.
Licensure Skilled care; Intermediate care. *Beds* SNF 50; ICF 54. *Private Pay Patients* 23%. *Certified* Medicaid; Medicare.
Owner Proprietary corp (Angell Care Inc).
Admissions Requirements Minimum age 16; Physician's request.
Staff Physicians 15 (pt); RNs 7 (ft), 2 (pt); LPNs 6 (ft), 3 (pt); Nurses' aides 47 (ft), 12 (pt); Physical therapists 1 (ft); Occupational therapists 1 (pt); Speech therapists 1 (pt); Activities coordinators 1 (ft); Dietitians 1 (pt); Ophthalmologists 1 (pt); Podiatrists 1 (pt).
Facilities Dining room; Physical therapy room; Activities room; Crafts room; Barber/Beauty shop; Covered patio.
Activities Arts & crafts; Cards; Games; Reading groups; Prayer groups; Movies; Shopping trips; Intergenerational programs; Pet therapy.

Bostic

Haven in the Hills Inc
Rte 2 Box 582, Bostic, NC 28018
(704) 245-2998
Admin Jane Held; Ted Hunt. *Dir of Nursing* Wanda Robinson.
Licensure Intermediate care; Rest home. *Beds* ICF 22; Rest home 28. *Private Pay Patients* 35-40%.
Owner Proprietary corp.
Admissions Requirements Medical examination; Physician's request.
Staff Physicians 2 (pt); RNs 3 (pt); LPNs 2 (pt); Activities coordinators 1 (pt); Dietitians 1 (pt).
Facilities Dining room; Activities room; Chapel; Laundry room; Barber/Beauty shop.
Activities Games; Prayer groups; Movies; Dances/Social/Cultural gatherings.

Brevard

Brian Center Health & Retirement—Brevard
PO Box 1096, 531 Country Club Rd, Brevard, NC 28712
(704) 884-2031
Admin Patricia F Woody.
Licensure Skilled care; Intermediate care; Home for aged. *Beds* SNF 66; ICF 41; Home for aged 33. *Certified* Medicaid; Medicare.
Owner Proprietary corp (Brian Center Management Corp).

Bryson City

Mountain View Manor Nursing Center
PO Drawer Y, Bryson City, NC 28713
(704) 488-2101
Admin W Kenneth Smith. *Dir of Nursing* Patricia Manning. *Medical Dir* K M Mathiesen.
Licensure Skilled care; Intermediate care. *Beds* SNF 41; ICF 79. *Private Pay Patients* 18%. *Certified* Medicaid; Medicare.
Owner Proprietary corp (Southeastern Health Facilities Inc).
Admissions Requirements Medical examination.
Staff RNs 6 (ft); LPNs 10 (ft); Nurses' aides 49 (ft); Activities coordinators 1 (ft); Dietitians 1 (ft).
Activities Arts & crafts; Cards; Games; Prayer groups; Movies; Shopping trips; Intergenerational programs; Pet therapy; Field trips.

Burgaw

Guardian Care of Burgaw
PO Box 874, Hwy 117-A S, Burgaw, NC 28425
(919) 259-2149
Admin Bridget S Becher.
Licensure Intermediate care. *Beds* ICF 72. *Certified* Medicaid.
Owner Proprietary corp (Hillhaven Corp).
Admissions Requirements Medical examination.
Staff Physicians 4 (pt); RNs 1 (ft), 2 (pt); LPNs 6 (ft), 4 (pt); Nurses' aides 16 (ft), 7 (pt); Activities coordinators 1 (ft); Dietitians 1 (ft); Podiatrists 2 (pt); Dentists 2 (pt).
Facilities Dining room; Activities room; Laundry room; Barber/Beauty shop.
Activities Arts & crafts; Cards; Games; Prayer groups; Movies; Shopping trips.

Huntington Health Care & Retirement Center
PO Box 1436, 311 S Campbell St, Burgaw, NC 28425
(919) 259-6007
Admin Keith Avant.

Licensure Skilled care; Intermediate care; Home for Aged. *Beds* SNF 17; ICF 51; Home for Aged 20.

Pender Memorial Hospital—Skilled Nursing Facility
PO Box 835, 507 Freemont St, Burgaw, NC 28425
(919) 259-5451
Admin Cameron Highsmith. *Dir of Nursing* Kevin Ballance RN. *Medical Dir* Dr Michael Rallis.
Licensure Skilled care. *Beds* SNF 23. *Private Pay Patients* 10%. *Certified* Medicaid; Medicare.
Owner Nonprofit organization/foundation.
Staff Physicians 7 (ft); Physical therapists 1 (ft); Speech therapists 1 (pt); Activities coordinators 1 (ft); Dietitians 1 (ft).
Facilities Dining room; Physical therapy room; Activities room; Chapel; Laundry room.
Activities Arts & crafts; Games; Reading groups; Prayer groups; Dances/Social/Cultural gatherings.

Burlington

Alamance Memorial Hospital Skilled Nursing Division
PO Box 202, Burlington, NC 27216
(919) 229-2600
Admin Robert E Byrd. *Dir of Nursing* Joan Severa RN. *Medical Dir* Robert A Watson MD.
Licensure Skilled care. *Beds* SNF 81. *Private Pay Patients* 15%. *Certified* Medicaid; Medicare.
Owner Nonprofit corp.
Admissions Requirements Medical examination; Physician's request.
Staff Physicians 35 (pt); RNs 9 (ft), 2 (pt); LPNs 6 (ft), 1 (pt); Nurses' aides 26 (ft), 11 (pt); Physical therapists 1 (ft); Occupational therapists 1 (pt); Speech therapists 1 (pt); Activities coordinators 2 (ft), 1 (pt); Dietitians 1 (ft); Ophthalmologists 2 (pt); Podiatrists 2 (pt).
Facilities Dining room; Physical therapy room; Activities room; Crafts room; Barber/Beauty shop; Library.
Activities Arts & crafts; Cards; Games; Reading groups; Prayer groups; Movies; Intergenerational programs; Pet therapy; Hymn singing.

Central Piedmont Nursing Center
323 Baldwin Rd, Burlington, NC 27217
(919) 229-5571
Admin Jeanne K Hutcheson. *Dir of Nursing* Annette T Frye. *Medical Dir* Meindert Niemeyer MD.
Licensure Skilled care; Intermediate care; Retirement; Alzheimer's care. *Beds* SNF 60; ICF 100; Retirement apts 54; 20-bed secure Alzheimer's unit. *Private Pay Patients* 50%. *Certified* Medicaid; Medicare.
Owner Proprietary corp (White Oak Manor Inc).
Admissions Requirements Minimum age 18; Medical examination; Physician's request.
Staff Physicians 1 (pt); RNs 4 (ft); LPNs 13 (ft), 6 (pt); Nurses' aides 55 (ft), 15 (pt); Physical therapists 3 (pt); Occupational therapists 2 (pt); Speech therapists 1 (pt); Activities coordinators 1 (ft), 3 (pt); Dietitians 1 (ft); Podiatrists 1 (ft).
Facilities Dining room; Physical therapy room; Activities room; Crafts room; Laundry room; Barber/Beauty shop.
Activities Arts & crafts; Cards; Games; Reading groups; Prayer groups; Movies; Shopping trips; Dances/Social/Cultural gatherings; Intergenerational programs; Pet therapy; Painting & ceramics classes.

Twin Lakes Center
100 Wade Coble Dr, Burlington, NC 27215
(919) 538-1400
Admin Rev Warren A Tyler. *Dir of Nursing*
Judith A Holsinger. *Medical Dir* Dr
Meindert Niemeyer.
Licensure Skilled care; Intermediate care;
Assisted living; Independent living. *Beds*
SNF 36; ICF 37; Assisted living 30;
Independent living units 109. *Private Pay
Patients* 70%. *Certified* Medicaid; Medicare.
Owner Nonprofit organization/foundation.
Admissions Requirements Physician's request.
Staff Physicians 1 (pt); RNs 7 (ft), 4 (pt);
LPNs 7 (ft), 3 (pt); Nurses' aides 26 (ft), 11
(pt); Physical therapists 1 (pt); Reality
therapists 1 (pt); Occupational therapists 1
(pt); Speech therapists 1 (pt); Activities
coordinators 2 (ft); Dietitians 1 (pt);
Ophthalmologists 1 (pt); Podiatrists 1 (pt);
Audiologists 1 (pt).
Affiliation Lutheran.
Facilities Dining room; Physical therapy
room; Activities room; Chapel; Crafts room;
Laundry room; Barber/Beauty shop; Library.
Activities Arts & crafts; Cards; Games;
Reading groups; Prayer groups; Movies;
Shopping trips; Dances/Social/Cultural
gatherings; Intergenerational programs; Pet
therapy.

Burnsville

Yancey Nursing Center
320 Pensacola Rd, Burnsville, NC 28714
(704) 682-9759
Admin Juanita C Fickling.
Licensure Skilled care; Intermediate care. *Beds*
SNF 60; ICF 20.

Butner

Murdoch Center
C St, Butner, NC 27509
(919) 575-7734
Admin J Michael Hennike.
Licensure Intermediate care for mentally
retarded. *Beds* 394. *Certified* Medicaid.

John Umstead Hospital—ICF
12th St, Butner, NC 27509
(919) 575-7211, 575-7013 FAX
Admin B Gene Barrett, Hosp Dir. *Dir of
Nursing* Patricia L Christian PhD. *Medical
Dir* P J Irigaray MD.
Licensure Intermediate care; Psychiatric
hospital. *Beds* ICF 32; Psychiatric hospital
698. *Certified* Medicaid; Medicare.
Owner Publicly owned.
Admissions Requirements Minimum age 5;
Medical examination; Psychiatric evaluation.
Staff Physicians 1 (ft); RNs 2 (ft); LPNs 2 (ft);
Nurses' aides 9 (ft); Physical therapists 1 (ft);
Recreational therapists 1 (ft); Occupational
therapists 1 (ft); Speech therapists 1 (pt);
Activities coordinators 1 (ft); Dietitians 1
(ft); Ophthalmologists 2 (pt).
Facilities Dining room; Physical therapy
room; Chapel; Laundry room; Barber/Beauty
shop; Library.
Activities Arts & crafts; Games; Shopping
trips; Dances/Social/Cultural gatherings;
Chaplaincy program.

Candler

Pisgah Manor Health Care Center
PO Box 1000, Holcombe Cove Rd, Candler,
NC 28715
(704) 667-9851
Admin David L Kidder.
Medical Dir Dr Everett Smith.
Licensure Intermediate care. *Beds* ICF 118.
Certified Medicaid.
Admissions Requirements Minimum age 18;
Medical examination; Physician's request.

Staff Physicians 1 (pt); RNs 1 (ft), 1 (pt);
LPNs 9 (ft), 7 (pt); Nurses' aides 12 (ft), 53
(pt); Activities coordinators 1 (ft), 4 (pt);
Dietitians 1 (pt).
Affiliation Seventh-Day Adventist.
Facilities Dining room; Activities room;
Crafts room; Laundry room; Barber/Beauty
shop; Library; TV room.
Activities Arts & crafts; Cards; Games;
Reading groups; Prayer groups; Movies;
Shopping trips; Dances/Social/Cultural
gatherings.

Canton

Canton Health Care Center
PO Box 1398, 27 N Main St, Canton, NC
28716
(704) 648-3551, 648-0201 FAX
Admin Rita D Van Nuys. *Dir of Nursing*
Carolyn Shelton RN. *Medical Dir* Dr George
Freeman.
Licensure Skilled care; Intermediate care. *Beds*
SNF 74; ICF 40. *Private Pay Patients* 15%.
Certified Medicaid; Medicare.
Owner Proprietary corp (National Health
Corp).
Admissions Requirements Minimum age 21;
Medical examination; Physician's request.
Staff Physicians 1 (pt); RNs 4 (ft), 5 (pt);
LPNs 12 (ft), 11 (pt); Nurses' aides 46 (ft), 3
(pt); Physical therapists (contracted);
Occupational therapists 1 (pt); Speech
therapists 1 (pt); Activities coordinators 2
(ft); Dietitians 1 (pt); Ophthalmologists 1
(pt); Podiatrists 1 (pt).
Facilities Dining room; Physical therapy
room; Activities room; Laundry room;
Barber/Beauty shop.
Activities Arts & crafts; Cards; Games;
Reading groups; Prayer groups; Movies;
Shopping trips; Dances/Social/Cultural
gatherings; Intergenerational programs; Pet
therapy.

Silver Bluff
Box 102, NC 110 Rte 5, Canton, NC 28716
(704) 648-2044
Admin Jean K Longley.
Licensure Intermediate care; Home for Aged.
Beds ICF 35; Home for Aged 85.

Chapel Hill

Britthaven of Chapel Hill
1716 Legion Rd, Chapel Hill, NC 27514
(919) 929-7146
Admin Linda D Freeman.
Licensure Intermediate care. *Beds* ICF 58.
Certified Medicaid.
Owner Proprietary corp (Hillhaven Corp).

Carol Woods
750 Weaver Dairy Rd, Chapel Hill, NC 27514
(919) 968-4511
Admin John A Diffey.
Medical Dir Robert J Sullivan.
Licensure Skilled care; Home for aged. *Beds*
SNF 30; Home for aged 30. *Certified*
Medicare.
Owner Nonprofit corp.
Admissions Requirements Minimum age 65;
Medical examination; Physician's request.
Staff Physicians 1 (pt); RNs 6 (ft), 10 (pt);
LPNs 6 (ft), 10 (pt); Nurses' aides 15 (ft), 10
(pt); Physical therapists 1 (pt); Recreational
therapists 1 (ft); Occupational therapists 1
(pt); Speech therapists 1 (pt); Dietitians 1
(ft); Ophthalmologists 1 (pt); Dentists 1 (pt).
Facilities Dining room; Physical therapy
room; Activities room; Crafts room; Laundry
room; Barber/Beauty shop; Library.
Activities Arts & crafts; Cards; Games;
Reading groups; Shopping trips; Dances/
Social/Cultural gatherings.

Hillhaven Convalescent Center of Chapel Hill
1602 E Franklin St, Chapel Hill, NC 27514
(919) 967-1418
Admin Sharon Luquire.
Medical Dir Dr Glen Pickard.
Licensure Skilled care; Intermediate care. *Beds*
SNF 60; ICF 60. *Certified* Medicaid;
Medicare.
Owner Proprietary corp (Hillhaven Corp).
Admissions Requirements Medical
examination.
Staff RNs 5 (ft), 2 (pt); LPNs 8 (ft), 5 (pt);
Nurses' aides 33 (ft), 6 (pt); Physical
therapists 2 (ft); Recreational therapists 1
(ft); Occupational therapists 1 (pt); Speech
therapists 1 (pt); Activities coordinators 1
(pt); Dietitians 1 (ft).
Facilities Dining room; Physical therapy
room; Activities room; Laundry room;
Barber/Beauty shop.
Activities Arts & crafts; Cards; Games;
Reading groups; Prayer groups; Movies;
Shopping trips; Dances/Social/Cultural
gatherings.

Charlotte

Beverly Manor of Charlotte
2616 E 5th St, Charlotte, NC 28204
(704) 333-5165
Admin Paul T Babinski. *Dir of Nursing*
Martha Edwards RN. *Medical Dir* Alex
Sanchez MD.
Licensure Skilled care; Intermediate care. *Beds*
SNF 88; ICF 32. *Certified* Medicaid;
Medicare.
Owner Proprietary corp (Beverly Enterprises).
Admissions Requirements Medical
examination.
Staff Physicians 4 (pt); RNs 6 (ft); LPNs 11
(ft); Nurses' aides 75 (ft), 5 (pt); Physical
therapists 1 (pt); Occupational therapists 1
(pt); Speech therapists 1 (pt); Activities
coordinators 1 (ft); Dietitians 1 (pt);
Ophthalmologists 1 (pt); Podiatrists 1 (pt);
Dentists 1 (pt).
Facilities Dining room; Physical therapy
room; Activities room; Crafts room; Laundry
room; Barber/Beauty shop; Library; Enclosed
courtyard with front porch.
Activities Arts & crafts; Cards; Games;
Reading groups; Prayer groups; Movies;
Shopping trips; Dances/Social/Cultural
gatherings; Bingo; Exercise; Resident council.

Brian Center Health & Retirement—Charlotte
5939 Reddman Rd, Charlotte, NC 28212
(704) 563-6862
Admin Vickie W Ledford.
Licensure Skilled care; Intermediate care. *Beds*
SNF 90; ICF 30. *Certified* Medicaid;
Medicare.
Owner Proprietary corp (Brian Center
Management Corp).

Brian Center Nursing Care—Shamrock
2727 Shamrock Dr, Charlotte, NC 28205
(704) 563-0886
Admin Fred A Newhart.
Licensure Skilled care; Intermediate care. *Beds*
SNF 40; ICF 60.
Owner Proprietary corp (Brian Center
Management Corp).

Britthaven of Charlotte
2623 Cranbrook Ln, Charlotte, NC 28207
(704) 332-1161
Admin Paul J Minton Jr.
Medical Dir Russell Long MD.
Licensure Skilled care; Intermediate care;
Home for Aged. *Beds* SNF 56; ICF 52;
Home for Aged 25. *Certified* Medicaid;
Medicare.
Owner Proprietary corp (Hillhaven Corp).
Admissions Requirements Minimum age 18;
Medical examination; Physician's request.

Staff RNs 8 (ft), 2 (pt); LPNs 10 (ft), 4 (pt); Nurses' aides 42 (ft), 10 (pt); Physical therapists 1 (ft); Activities coordinators 1 (ft).
Facilities Dining room; Physical therapy room; Activities room; Crafts room; Laundry room; Barber/Beauty shop.
Activities Arts & crafts; Cards; Games; Reading groups; Prayer groups; Movies; Shopping trips; Dances/Social/Cultural gatherings.

Hawthorne Nursing Center
333 Hawthorne Ln, Charlotte, NC 28204
(704) 372-1270
Admin James F Leach.
Medical Dir Donald Goodman MD.
Licensure Skilled care. *Beds* SNF 142. *Certified* Medicaid; Medicare.
Owner Proprietary corp (National Heritage).
Admissions Requirements Physician's request.
Staff RNs 7 (ft), 4 (pt); LPNs 12 (ft), 6 (pt); Nurses' aides 40 (ft), 10 (pt); Physical therapists 1 (ft); Speech therapists 2 (pt); Activities coordinators 2 (ft); Dietitians 1 (pt).
Facilities Dining room; Physical therapy room; Activities room; Chapel; Laundry room; Barber/Beauty shop.
Activities Arts & crafts; Cards; Games; Reading groups; Prayer groups; Movies; Shopping trips; Dances/Social/Cultural gatherings.

Hillcrest Manor Nursing Home
2435 Sharon Rd, Charlotte, NC 28211
(704) 366-1511
Admin William B O'Neal Jr.
Medical Dir Dr Charles L Stuckey.
Licensure Intermediate care. *Beds* ICF 24.
Admissions Requirements Medical examination.
Staff RNs 1 (ft), 2 (pt); LPNs 6 (ft); Nurses' aides 6 (ft); Activities coordinators 1 (pt); Dietitians 1 (pt).

Hospitality Care Center of Charlotte
4801 Randolph Rd, Charlotte, NC 28211
(704) 364-8363
Admin John L Hankins Jr.
Licensure Skilled care; Intermediate care. *Beds* SNF 62; ICF 38. *Certified* Medicaid; Medicare.
Owner Proprietary corp (Beverly Enterprises).

Mecklenburg Autistic Group Homes Inc
3201 Park Rd, Charlotte, NC 28209
(704) 527-5366
Admin J Michael Dyson.
Medical Dir Dr Joal Fischer.
Licensure Intermediate care for mentally retarded. *Beds* 10. *Certified* Medicaid.
Owner Nonprofit corp.
Admissions Requirements Minimum age 18; Medical examination.
Staff Physicians 1 (pt); RNs 1 (pt); Nurses' aides 5 (ft); Speech therapists 1 (pt); Dietitians 1 (pt).
Facilities Dining room; Activities room; Crafts room; Laundry room.
Activities Arts & crafts; Cards; Games; Reading groups; Movies; Shopping trips; Dances/Social/Cultural gatherings.

Providence Convalescent Residence
300 Providence Rd, Charlotte, NC 28207
(704) 334-1671
Admin William S Bradley Jr.
Medical Dir Dr Henry Stuckey.
Licensure Skilled care; Home for aged. *Beds* SNF 133; Home for aged 17. *Certified* Medicaid; Medicare.
Owner Proprietary corp (Beverly Enterprises).
Admissions Requirements Minimum age 55; Medical examination; Physician's request.
Staff Physicians 26 (pt); RNs 9 (ft), 2 (pt); LPNs 10 (ft), 2 (pt); Nurses' aides 46 (ft), 16 (pt); Physical therapists 2 (pt); Speech

therapists 1 (pt); Activities coordinators 1 (ft); Dietitians 1 (pt); Podiatrists 1 (pt); Dentists 1 (pt).
Facilities Dining room; Physical therapy room; Activities room; Chapel; Crafts room; Laundry room; Barber/Beauty shop.
Activities Arts & crafts; Games; Reading groups; Movies; Shopping trips; Dances/Social/Cultural gatherings.

Sharon Towers
5100 Sharon Rd, Charlotte, NC 28210
(704) 553-1670
Admin Paul A Craig Jr. *Dir of Nursing* Betty W Mauney RN. *Medical Dir* Dr Jack Hobson.
Licensure Skilled care; Home for Aged. *Beds* SNF 96; Home for Aged 8.
Owner Nonprofit corp.
Admissions Requirements Minimum age 65; Medical examination; Physician's request.
Staff RNs 16 (ft), 6 (pt); LPNs 12 (ft), 4 (pt); Nurses' aides 30 (ft), 18 (pt); Activities coordinators 1 (ft); Dietitians 1 (ft).
Affiliation Presbyterian.
Facilities Dining room; Physical therapy room; Activities room; Chapel; Crafts room; Laundry room; Barber/Beauty shop; Library; Pool table area; Sewing room; Art room.
Activities Arts & crafts; Cards; Games; Reading groups; Prayer groups; Movies; Shopping trips; Dances/Social/Cultural gatherings; Exercise classes.

Sharon Village
PO Box 220130, 4009 Craig Ave, Charlotte, NC 28222
(704) 365-2620
Admin Ted P Jones.
Licensure Skilled care; Intermediate care. *Beds* SNF 60; ICF 120. *Certified* Medicaid; Medicare.

Southminster
8919 Park Rd, Charlotte, NC 28210
(704) 551-6800
Admin James Sherwood.
Licensure Skilled care; Intermediate care; Home for Aged. *Beds* SNF 30; ICF 30; Home for Aged 20.

Wesley Nursing Center—Asbury Care Center—Epworth Place
3600 Shamrock Dr, Charlotte, NC 28215
(704) 537-9731
Admin Raymond O Hall.
Licensure Skilled care; Intermediate care; Home for Aged. *Beds* SNF 289; ICF 100; Home for Aged 133. *Certified* Medicaid; Medicare.

Wesleyan Nursing Home Inc
2623 Cranbrook Ln, Charlotte, NC 28207
(704) 332-1161
Admin Carolyn Sherrill.
Medical Dir Russell Long MD.
Licensure Skilled care; Intermediate care; Home for aged; Retirement. *Beds* SNF 56; ICF 52; Home for aged 25; Retirement 30. *Certified* Medicaid; Medicare.
Admissions Requirements Minimum age 18; Medical examination; Physician's request.
Staff RNs 7 (ft), 2 (pt); LPNs 8 (ft), 3 (pt); Nurses' aides 40 (ft), 13 (pt); Physical therapists; Occupational therapists; Speech therapists; Activities coordinators 2 (ft), 1 (pt); Dietitians; Podiatrists; Dentists.
Facilities Dining room; Physical therapy room; Activities room; Crafts room; Laundry room; Barber/Beauty shop.
Activities Arts & crafts; Cards; Games; Reading groups; Prayer groups; Movies; Shopping trips; Dances/Social/Cultural gatherings.

Wessel's Nursing Home
515 Templeton Ave, Charlotte, NC 28203
(704) 333-9045
Admin Linda J Howard.

Medical Dir W Tyson Bennett MD.
Licensure Skilled care. *Beds* SNF 26. *Certified* Medicaid; Medicare.
Owner Proprietary corp.
Admissions Requirements Medical examination; Physician's request.
Staff Physicians 2 (pt); RNs 1 (ft), 1 (pt); LPNs 3 (ft); Nurses' aides 7 (ft), 4 (pt); Physical therapists 1 (pt); Activities coordinators 1 (ft); Dietitians 1 (pt); Ophthalmologists 1 (pt); Podiatrists; Dentists 1 (pt).
Facilities Activities room; Laundry room.
Activities Arts & crafts; Games; Reading groups; Prayer groups; Movies.

Cherryville

Carolina Care Center
PO Box 580, Hwy 274 N, Cherryville, NC 28021
(704) 435-4161
Admin Judy B Beam.
Medical Dir Marjorie Humphrey.
Licensure Skilled care; Intermediate care; Home for Aged. *Beds* SNF 21; ICF 86; Home for Aged 12. *Certified* Medicaid; Medicare.
Owner Privately owned.
Admissions Requirements Medical examination.
Staff RNs 6 (ft), 1 (pt); LPNs 7 (ft), 1 (pt); Nurses' aides 31 (ft), 2 (pt); Activities coordinators 1 (ft); Dietitians 1 (ft).
Facilities Dining room; Activities room; Crafts room; Laundry room; Barber/Beauty shop.
Activities Arts & crafts; Cards; Games; Prayer groups; Movies; Shopping trips; Dances/Social/Cultural gatherings.

Meadowbrook Manor of Cherryville
PO Box 610, 700 Self St, Cherryville, NC 28021
(704) 435-6029
Admin Winnie Jo Brock. *Dir of Nursing* Krista Baxter. *Medical Dir* Dr M E Agner.
Licensure Intermediate care; Rest home. *Beds* ICF 54; Rest home 57. *Private Pay Patients* 12%. *Certified* Medicaid.
Owner Proprietary corp (Angell Group).
Admissions Requirements Minimum age 18; Medical examination.
Staff Physicians (contracted); RNs 2 (ft); LPNs 5 (ft), 2 (pt); Nurses' aides 20 (ft), 10 (pt); Physical therapists (contracted); Recreational therapists (contracted); Occupational therapists (contracted); Speech therapists (contracted); Activities coordinators 1 (ft); Dietitians (contracted); Ophthalmologists (contracted); Podiatrists (contracted); Audiologists (contracted).
Facilities Dining room; Physical therapy room; Activities room; Chapel; Crafts room; Laundry room; Barber/Beauty shop.
Activities Arts & crafts; Cards; Games; Reading groups; Prayer groups; Movies; Shopping trips; Dances/Social/Cultural gatherings; Pet therapy.

Clemmons

Bluementhal Jewish Home
PO Box 38, 7870 Fair Oaks Dr, Clemmons, NC 27012
(919) 766-6401
Admin Donald J Morris. *Dir of Nursing* Patsy Petree RN. *Medical Dir* William C Sugg MD.
Licensure Skilled care; Intermediate care; Home for Aged; Alzheimer's care. *Beds* SNF 90; ICF 44; Home for Aged 46. *Certified* Medicaid; Medicare.
Owner Nonprofit organization/foundation.
Admissions Requirements Minimum age 65; Medical examination; Physician's request.

Staff Physicians 3 (pt); RNs 18 (ft); LPNs 10 (ft); Nurses' aides 46 (ft), 10 (pt); Physical therapists 1 (pt); Recreational therapists 3 (ft); Occupational therapists 2 (pt); Speech therapists 1 (pt); Activities coordinators 1 (ft); Dietitians 1 (ft), 1 (pt); Ophthalmologists 3 (pt); Podiatrists 1 (pt); Dentists 1 (pt); Social workers 2 (ft).
Languages Yiddish, Hebrew, German.
Affiliation Jewish.
Facilities Dining room; Physical therapy room; Activities room; Chapel; Crafts room; Barber/Beauty shop; Library; Gardens; Large terrace; Wooded area.
Activities Arts & crafts; Cards; Games; Reading groups; Prayer groups; Movies; Shopping trips; Dances/Social/Cultural gatherings; Religious services & celebrations; Discussion groups; Holidays; Concert & lecture series; Volunteer programs; Resident council.

Meadowbrook Manor
PO Box 249, Hwy 158, Clemmons, NC 27012
(919) 766-9158
Admin C Jean Small. *Dir of Nursing* Maureen Huey. *Medical Dir* Dr Robert Eberle.
Licensure Skilled care; Intermediate care; Retirement. *Beds* SNF 60; ICF 60; Retirement 185. *Private Pay Patients* 40%. *Certified* Medicaid; Medicare; VA.
Owner Proprietary corp (Angell Group).
Admissions Requirements Minimum age 18; Medical examination; Physician's request.
Staff RNs 5 (ft), 2 (pt); LPNs 16 (ft), 4 (pt); Nurses' aides 60 (ft), 15 (pt); Physical therapists (contracted); Recreational therapists 1 (ft), 1 (pt); Occupational therapists (contracted); Speech therapists (contracted); Activities coordinators 1 (ft), 1 (pt); Dietitians 1 (ft); Ophthalmologists (contracted); Podiatrists (contracted); Dentists (contracted).
Languages Spanish, Italian.
Facilities Dining room; Physical therapy room; Activities room; Crafts room; Laundry room; Barber/Beauty shop; Library; Private dining room.
Activities Arts & crafts; Games; Reading groups; Movies; Dances/Social/Cultural gatherings; Intergenerational programs; Pet therapy.

Clinton

Mary Gran Nursing Center
PO Box 379, Clinton, NC 28328
(919) 592-7981
Admin Jeffrey Wilson. *Dir of Nursing* Janice Lindsay. *Medical Dir* Latham Peak.
Licensure Skilled care; Intermediate care; Alzheimer's care. *Beds* SNF 120; ICF 62. *Private Pay Patients* 20%. *Certified* Medicaid; Medicare.
Owner Proprietary corp.
Admissions Requirements Medical examination; Physician's request.
Staff RNs 15 (ft), 5 (pt); LPNs 15 (ft), 5 (pt); Nurses' aides 45 (ft), 15 (pt).
Facilities Dining room; Activities room; Chapel; Laundry room; Barber/Beauty shop.
Activities Arts & crafts; Cards; Games; Reading groups; Prayer groups; Movies; Shopping trips.

Sampson County Memorial Hospital—Skilled Nursing Facility
PO Box 258, Clinton, NC 28328
(919) 592-8511
Admin Lee Pridgen.
Licensure Skilled care. *Beds* SNF 30. *Certified* Medicaid; Medicare.

Clyde

Britthaven of Clyde
PO Box 459, Clyde, NC 28721
(704) 627-2789
Admin Robin J Suddreth.
Medical Dir Dr E B Goodwin Jr.
Licensure Intermediate care. *Beds* ICF 50. *Certified* Medicaid.
Owner Proprietary corp (Britthaven Inc).
Admissions Requirements Medical examination.
Staff LPNs 5 (ft); Nurses' aides 17 (ft); Activities coordinators 1 (ft).
Facilities Dining room; Activities room; Laundry room; Barber/Beauty shop.
Activities Arts & crafts; Games; Reading groups; Prayer groups; Movies; Dances/Social/Cultural gatherings.

Concord

Cabarrus Nursing Center
PO Box 748, 515 Lake Concord Rd, Concord, NC 28026-0748
(704) 786-9151
Admin Rebecca A Pullin. *Dir of Nursing* Melania Eaves RN. *Medical Dir* Dr Robert E Hammonds.
Licensure Skilled care; Intermediate care. *Beds* SNF 88; ICF 32. *Certified* Medicaid; Medicare.
Admissions Requirements Medical examination; Physician's request.
Staff RNs 5 (ft), 4 (pt); LPNs 7 (ft), 2 (pt); Nurses' aides 31 (ft), 21 (pt); Physical therapists 1 (pt); Activities coordinators 1 (ft); Dietitians 1 (ft); Ophthalmologists 1 (ft); Dentists 1 (ft).
Facilities Dining room; Physical therapy room; Activities room; Chapel; Crafts room; Laundry room; Barber/Beauty shop; Reading room; TV room.
Activities Arts & crafts; Cards; Games; Reading groups; Prayer groups; Movies; Shopping trips; Dances/Social/Cultural gatherings.

Concord Nursing Center
PO Box 748, 430 Brookwood Ave NE, Concord, NC 28025-0748
(704) 788-4115
Admin Shirley S Rogers LNHA. *Dir of Nursing* Melanie Talbert RN. *Medical Dir* E M Tomlin MD.
Licensure Skilled care. *Beds* SNF 120. *Certified* Medicaid; Medicare.
Owner Privately owned (Nancy F Taylor).
Admissions Requirements Medical examination; Physician's request.
Staff Physicians 1 (ft); RNs 7 (ft); LPNs 9 (ft); Nurses' aides 25 (ft); Physical therapists 1 (ft); Speech therapists 1 (ft); Activities coordinators 1 (ft); Dietitians 1 (ft); Ophthalmologists 1 (ft); Podiatrists 1 (ft).
Facilities Dining room; Physical therapy room; Activities room; Chapel; Crafts room; Laundry room; Barber/Beauty shop.
Activities Arts & crafts; Games; Prayer groups; Movies; Shopping trips; Pet therapy.

Five Oaks Nursing Center Inc
PO Box 384, 413 Winecoff School Rd, Concord, NC 28026-0384
(704) 788-2131, 788-2131, ext 206
Admin Dorothy M Critz LNHA. *Dir of Nursing* Marie Alexander RN. *Medical Dir* Vincent Keipper MD.
Licensure Skilled care; Intermediate care. *Beds* SNF 87; ICF 48. *Private Pay Patients* 40%. *Certified* Medicaid; Medicare.
Owner Privately owned.
Admissions Requirements Medical examination; Physician's request.
Staff Physicians 8 (pt); RNs 5 (ft), 3 (pt); LPNs 9 (ft), 4 (pt); Nurses' aides 48 (ft), 17 (pt); Physical therapists 2 (pt); Reality

therapists 1 (pt); Recreational therapists 1 (ft); Occupational therapists 1 (pt); Speech therapists 1 (pt); Activities coordinators 1 (ft); Dietitians 1 (ft); Podiatrists 1 (pt).
Facilities Dining room; Physical therapy room; Activities room; Crafts room; Laundry room; Barber/Beauty shop; Library.
Activities Arts & crafts; Cards; Games; Reading groups; Prayer groups; Movies; Shopping trips; Dances/Social/Cultural gatherings; Intergenerational programs; Pet therapy.

Odell Nursing Center
2339 Odell School Rd, Concord, NC 28025
(704) 782-9770
Admin Sherry S Johnson. *Dir of Nursing* Sandra Freeze RN.
Licensure Skilled care; Intermediate care. *Beds* SNF 23; ICF 24. *Certified* Medicaid; Medicare.
Owner Proprietary corp.
Admissions Requirements Medical examination; Physician's request.
Staff Physicians 1 (pt); RNs 2 (ft), 1 (pt); LPNs 4 (ft), 2 (pt); Nurses' aides 10 (ft), 4 (pt); Physical therapists 2 (pt); Recreational therapists 1 (ft); Occupational therapists 1 (pt); Speech therapists 1 (pt); Activities coordinators 1 (ft); Dietitians 1 (ft); Ophthalmologists 1 (pt).
Facilities Dining room; Physical therapy room; Activities room; Chapel; Crafts room; Laundry room; Barber/Beauty shop.
Activities Arts & crafts; Cards; Games; Reading groups; Prayer groups; Movies.

Piedmont Residential Developmental Center
PO Box 909, Concord, NC 28025
(704) 788-2304
Admin Paul Caldwell.
Licensure Intermediate care for mentally retarded. *Beds* 10. *Certified* Medicaid.

Danbury

Stokes-Reynolds Memorial Hospital—SNF
PO Box 10, Danbury, NC 27016
(919) 593-2831
Admin Sandra D Priddy.
Medical Dir Dr Renato Zarate.
Licensure Skilled care. *Beds* SNF 40. *Certified* Medicaid; Medicare.
Owner Nonprofit corp.
Staff Physicians 5 (pt); RNs 1 (ft); LPNs 8 (ft); Nurses' aides 22 (ft); Physical therapists 1 (ft); Activities coordinators 1 (ft); Dietitians 1 (ft); Dentists 1 (ft).

Davidson

Pines at Davidson
PO Box 118, 400 Avinger Ln, Davidson, NC 28036
(704) 896-1100
Admin E L Muller.
Licensure Skilled care; Intermediate care; Home of Aged. *Beds* SNF 20; ICF 20; Home of Aged 20.

Denton

Mountain Vista Health Park
Rte 1 Box 591, Jackson Hill Rd, Denton, NC 27239
(704) 869-2181
Admin Edwin L Ware. *Dir of Nursing* Kathy McDonald RN. *Medical Dir* Drs FH & FC Mangundayao.
Licensure Skilled care; Intermediate care; Home for Aged. *Beds* SNF 24; ICF 36; Home for Aged 60. *Certified* Medicaid; Medicare.
Owner Proprietary corp (Tullock Management).
Admissions Requirements Minimum age 18; Medical examination; Physician's request.

Staff RNs 4 (ft), 1 (pt); LPNs 7 (ft), 1 (pt); Nurses' aides 23 (ft), 6 (pt); Activities coordinators 2 (ft).
Facilities Dining room; Physical therapy room; Activities room; Chapel; Crafts room; Laundry room; Barber/Beauty shop.
Activities Arts & crafts; Cards; Games; Reading groups; Prayer groups; Movies; Shopping trips; Dances/Social/Cultural gatherings.

Drexel

Autumn Care of Drexel
PO Box 1278, 307 Oakland Ave, Drexel, NC 28619
(704) 433-6180
Admin Mary G Taychert. *Dir of Nursing* Frances Burns RN. *Medical Dir* C J Dellinger MD.
Licensure Skilled care; Intermediate care; Home for aged. *Beds* SNF 50; ICF 50; Home for aged 20. *Certified* Medicaid; Medicare.
Owner Proprietary corp (Autumn Corp).
Admissions Requirements Minimum age 21; Medical examination; Physician's request.
Staff Physicians; RNs 8 (ft), 6 (pt); LPNs 7 (ft), 5 (pt); Nurses' aides 45 (ft); Physical therapists 1 (pt); Speech therapists 1 (pt); Activities coordinators 1 (ft), 3 (pt); Dietitians 1 (pt).
Facilities Dining room; Physical therapy room; Activities room; Chapel; Crafts room; Laundry room; Barber/Beauty shop.
Activities Arts & crafts; Cards; Games; Reading groups; Prayer groups; Movies; Dances/Social/Cultural gatherings.

Dunn

Charles Parrish Memorial Nursing Center
PO Box 1707, 201 N Ellis Ave, Dunn, NC 28334
(919) 892-4021
Admin Joy N Strickland.
Medical Dir L R Doffermyre MD.
Licensure Skilled care; Intermediate care. *Beds* SNF 63; ICF 39. *Certified* Medicaid; Medicare.
Admissions Requirements Medical examination.
Staff RNs 6 (ft); LPNs 9 (ft), 2 (pt); Nurses' aides 36 (ft), 5 (pt); Physical therapists 1 (ft).
Facilities Dining room; Laundry room.
Activities Arts & crafts; Cards; Games; Reading groups; Prayer groups; Movies; Dances/Social/Cultural gatherings; Exercise classes.

Durham

Greenery Rehabilitation Center
3100 Erwin Rd, Durham, NC 27705
(919) 383-1546
Admin Soultana Rouses. *Dir of Nursing* Gwen Cobb RN. *Medical Dir* Arnett Coleman MD.
Licensure Skilled care; Intermediate care. *Beds* SNF 112; ICF 13. *Certified* Medicaid; Medicare.
Owner Proprietary corp (Greenery Rehab Grp).
Admissions Requirements Medical examination; Physician's request.
Staff RNs 10 (ft), 3 (pt); LPNs 20 (ft), 2 (pt); Nurses' aides 60 (ft), 8 (pt); Recreational therapists 1 (ft); Activities coordinators 1 (ft); Dietitians 1 (ft).
Facilities Dining room; Physical therapy room; Activities room; Chapel; Crafts room; Laundry room; Barber/Beauty shop.
Activities Arts & crafts; Cards; Games; Reading groups; Prayer groups; Movies; Shopping trips; Dances/Social/Cultural gatherings; Local activities.

Hillcrest Convalescent Center Inc
PO Box 2657, 01417 W Pettigrew St, Durham, NC 27705
(919) 286-7705
Admin J R Garrett Jr.
Medical Dir Lewis M McKee MD.
Licensure Skilled care. *Beds* SNF 120. *Certified* Medicaid; Medicare.
Admissions Requirements Medical examination; Physician's request.
Staff RNs 5 (ft), 2 (pt); LPNs 10 (ft), 5 (pt); Nurses' aides 37 (ft), 10 (pt); Physical therapists 1 (ft), 1 (pt); Reality therapists 1 (pt); Recreational therapists 2 (pt); Occupational therapists 1 (pt); Speech therapists 1 (pt); Activities coordinators 1 (ft); Dietitians 1 (ft), 1 (pt); Ophthalmologists 1 (pt); Podiatrists 1 (pt); Audiologists 1 (pt); Dentists 1 (pt).
Facilities Dining room; Physical therapy room; Activities room; Chapel; Crafts room; Laundry room; Barber/Beauty shop; Library.
Activities Arts & crafts; Cards; Games; Reading groups; Prayer groups; Movies; Shopping trips; Dances/Social/Cultural gatherings; Current events; Music appreciation.

Hillhaven LaSalle Nursing Center
411 S LaSalle St, Durham, NC 27705
(919) 383-5521
Admin Paula Kish. *Dir of Nursing* Royallette Mayfield. *Medical Dir* Mark Currie MD.
Licensure Skilled care; Intermediate care. *Beds* SNF 46; ICF 80. *Private Pay Patients* 3%. *Certified* Medicaid; Medicare.
Owner Proprietary corp (Hillhaven Corp).
Admissions Requirements Minimum age 18; Medical examination; Physician's request.
Staff RNs; LPNs; Nurses' aides 3 (ft); Physical therapists 1 (ft); Recreational therapists 1 (ft); Activities coordinators.
Facilities Dining room; Physical therapy room; Activities room; Chapel; Crafts room; Laundry room; Barber/Beauty shop.
Activities Arts & crafts; Games; Reading groups; Prayer groups; Movies; Shopping trips; Dances/Social/Cultural gatherings; Pet therapy; Educational classes.

Hillhaven Orange Nursing Center
Rte 1 Box 155, Mount Sinai Rd, Durham, NC 27705
(919) 489-2361
Admin Virginia L Smith.
Medical Dir Dr Byron Cole.
Licensure Skilled care; Intermediate care. *Beds* SNF 41; ICF 74. *Certified* Medicaid; Medicare.
Owner Proprietary corp (Hillhaven Corp).
Admissions Requirements Medical examination.
Staff Physicians 1 (ft); RNs 5 (ft); LPNs 12 (ft), 4 (pt); Nurses' aides 40 (ft), 15 (pt); Physical therapists 1 (pt); Reality therapists 1 (pt); Recreational therapists 1 (ft), 1 (pt); Speech therapists 1 (pt); Activities coordinators 1 (ft); Dietitians 1 (ft); Ophthalmologists; Podiatrists; Audiologists; Dentists.
Facilities Dining room; Physical therapy room; Activities room; Barber/Beauty shop.
Activities Arts & crafts; Cards; Games; Reading groups; Prayer groups; Movies; Shopping trips; Dances/Social/Cultural gatherings.

Hillhaven Rehabilitation & Convalescent Center
1515 W Pettigrew St, Durham, NC 27705
(919) 286-0751
Admin Christine Coley. *Dir of Nursing* Jacqueline Roberts. *Medical Dir* Richard Bruch.
Licensure Skilled care; Alzheimer's care. *Beds* SNF 107. *Certified* Medicaid; Medicare.
Owner Proprietary corp (Hillhaven Corp).
Admissions Requirements Physician's request.

Staff RNs; LPNs; Nurses' aides 21 (ft), 7 (pt); Physical therapists 1 (ft), 2 (pt); Recreational therapists 1 (pt); Speech therapists; Activities coordinators 1 (ft); Dietitians 1 (ft).
Facilities Dining room; Physical therapy room; Activities room; Chapel; Crafts room; Laundry room; Barber/Beauty shop.
Activities Arts & crafts; Cards; Games; Reading groups; Prayer groups; Movies; Shopping trips; Dances/Social/Cultural gatherings.

Hillhaven Rose Manor Convalescent Center
4230 N Roxboro Rd, Durham, NC 27704
(919) 477-9805
Admin Mary Lynn Williams. *Dir of Nursing* Lois Finestone. *Medical Dir* Donald Neish MD.
Licensure Skilled care; Intermediate care; Alzheimer's care. *Beds* SNF 58; ICF 69. *Certified* Medicaid; Medicare.
Owner Proprietary corp (Hillhaven Corp).
Admissions Requirements Medical examination; Physician's request.
Staff RNs; LPNs; Nurses' aides; Physical therapists; Recreational therapists; Occupational therapists; Speech therapists; Activities coordinators; Dietitians; Ophthalmologists; Dentists.
Facilities Dining room; Physical therapy room; Activities room; Chapel; Crafts room; Laundry room; Barber/Beauty shop.
Activities Arts & crafts; Games; Reading groups; Prayer groups; Movies; Dances/Social/Cultural gatherings.

Methodist Retirement Homes Inc
2616 Erwin Rd, Durham, NC 27705
(919) 383-2567
Admin Michele Joiner.
Medical Dir Dr Donald Neish.
Licensure Skilled care; Intermediate care. *Beds* SNF 31; ICF 94. *Certified* Medicaid; Medicare.
Owner Proprietary corp (Pinnacle Care Corp).
Admissions Requirements Medical examination.
Staff Physicians 1 (pt); RNs 10 (ft), 3 (pt); LPNs 21 (ft), 7 (pt); Nurses' aides 51 (ft), 13 (pt); Physical therapists 2 (pt); Recreational therapists 4 (ft); Speech therapists 1 (pt); Activities coordinators 1 (ft), 1 (pt); Dietitians 1 (ft); Dentists 1 (pt).
Affiliation Methodist.
Facilities Dining room; Physical therapy room; Activities room; Chapel; Crafts room; Laundry room; Barber/Beauty shop; Library; Store operated by patients.
Activities Arts & crafts; Cards; Games; Reading groups; Prayer groups; Movies; Shopping trips; Dances/Social/Cultural gatherings; Music & singing; Talent shows; Horticulture; Science; Community service projects; Exercise groups; Cooking.

Eden

Brian Center Health & Retirement—Eden
226 N Oakland Ave, Eden, NC 27288
(919) 623-1750
Admin Helen S Myers.
Licensure Skilled care; Intermediate care; Home for Aged. *Beds* SNF 72; ICF 40; Home for Aged 20. *Certified* Medicaid; Medicare.

Morehead Memorial Nursing Center
117 E Kings Hwy, Eden, NC 27288
(919) 623-9711
Admin Robert A Enders. *Dir of Nursing* Vicki P Lantrip. *Medical Dir* Dr Paul Fiore.
Licensure Skilled care. *Beds* SNF 41. *Private Pay Patients* 15%. *Certified* Medicaid; Medicare.
Owner Nonprofit organization/foundation.
Admissions Requirements Minimum age 18; Medical examination.

Staff RNs 4 (ft); LPNs 4 (ft), 2 (pt); Nurses' aides 14 (ft), 7 (pt); Recreational therapists 1 (pt); Activities coordinators 1 (ft).
Facilities Dining room; Physical therapy room; Activities room; Barber/Beauty shop.
Activities Arts & crafts; Cards; Games; Reading groups; Prayer groups; Movies; Shopping trips; Dances/Social/Cultural gatherings.

Edenton

Britthaven of Edenton
PO Box 566, Paradise Rd, Edenton, NC 27932
(919) 482-7481
Admin Craig Miller. *Dir of Nursing* DeAnna Darnell RN. *Medical Dir* Archie Walker MD; James Slade MD.
Licensure Skilled care; Intermediate care; Home for aged. *Beds* SNF 32; ICF 98; Home for aged 30. *Certified* Medicaid; Medicare; VA.
Owner Proprietary corp (Britthaven Inc).
Admissions Requirements Minimum age 18; Medical examination.
Staff RNs 5 (ft), 3 (pt); LPNs 12 (ft), 6 (pt); Nurses' aides 37 (ft), 15 (pt); Activities coordinators 1 (ft), 1 (pt); Dietitians 1 (ft); Dentists 1 (pt).
Facilities Dining room; Physical therapy room; Activities room; Crafts room; Laundry room; Barber/Beauty shop.
Activities Arts & crafts; Cards; Games; Reading groups; Prayer groups; Movies; Shopping trips; Dances/Social/Cultural gatherings.

Chowan Hospital Inc—Skilled Nursing Facility
PO Box 629, Virginia Rd, Edenton, NC 27932
(919) 482-8451, 482-2965 FAX
Admin Marvin A Bryan. *Dir of Nursing* Judy A Peele RN. *Medical Dir* Lance Potocki MD.
Licensure Skilled care. *Beds* SNF 40. *Certified* Medicaid; Medicare.
Owner Nonprofit organization/foundation.
Staff Physicians 1 (ft); RNs 5 (ft); LPNs 6 (ft), 2 (pt); Nurses' aides 12 (ft), 4 (pt); Physical therapists 1 (ft); Activities coordinators 1 (ft); Dietitians 1 (ft).
Facilities Dining room; Physical therapy room; Activities room; Crafts room; Barber/Beauty shop.
Activities Arts & crafts; Cards; Games; Reading groups; Prayer groups; Movies; Dances/Social/Cultural gatherings; Pet therapy.

Elizabeth City

Guardian Care of Elizabeth City
901 S Halstead Blvd, Elizabeth City, NC 27909
(919) 338-0137
Admin Mary Ann Crocker. *Dir of Nursing* Sarah Hall RN. *Medical Dir* Dr William Wassink.
Licensure Skilled care; Intermediate care; Alzheimer's care. *Beds* SNF 31; ICF 89. *Certified* Medicaid; Medicare.
Owner Proprietary corp (Hillhaven Corp).
Admissions Requirements Minimum age 21; Medical examination.
Staff RNs 2 (ft), 5 (pt); LPNs 6 (ft), 5 (pt); Nurses' aides 45 (ft), 7 (pt); Recreational therapists 1 (ft); Activities coordinators 1 (pt); Dietitians 1 (pt).
Facilities Dining room; Physical therapy room; Activities room; Chapel; Crafts room; Laundry room; Barber/Beauty shop.
Activities Arts & crafts; Cards; Games; Reading groups; Prayer groups; Movies; Shopping trips; Dances/Social/Cultural gatherings.

W R Winslow Memorial Home Inc
1700 W Ehringhaus St, Elizabeth City, NC 27909
(919) 338-3975
Admin David L Fardulis. *Dir of Nursing* Jane Meyer RN. *Medical Dir* S Michael Sutton MD.
Licensure Skilled care; Intermediate care; Retirement. *Beds* SNF 34; ICF 87; Retirement 9. *Certified* Medicaid; Medicare.
Owner Nonprofit organization/foundation.
Admissions Requirements Medical examination.
Facilities Dining room; Physical therapy room; Activities room; Chapel; Crafts room; Laundry room; Barber/Beauty shop; Library.
Activities Arts & crafts; Games; Reading groups; Prayer groups; Movies; Shopping trips; Dances/Social/Cultural gatherings.

Elizabethtown

Elizabethtown Nursing Center Inc
PO Box 1447, 208 Mercer Rd, Elizabethtown, NC 28337
(919) 862-8181
Admin Janet R Tennant. *Dir of Nursing* Barbara Nobles RN.
Licensure Skilled care; Intermediate care. *Beds* SNF 52; ICF 32. *Certified* Medicaid; Medicare.
Owner Privately owned.
Admissions Requirements Medical examination; Physician's request.
Staff RNs 3 (ft), 4 (pt); LPNs 5 (ft), 6 (pt); Nurses' aides 26 (ft), 10 (pt); Activities coordinators 1 (ft), 1 (pt).
Facilities Dining room; Activities room; Crafts room; Laundry room; Barber/Beauty shop.
Activities Arts & crafts; Games; Prayer groups; Movies; Shopping trips; Dances/Social/Cultural gatherings.

Elkin

Hugh Chatham Memorial Hospital—SNF
Parkwood Dr, Elkin, NC 28621
(919) 835-3722
Admin William S Clark.
Licensure Skilled care. *Beds* SNF 79. *Certified* Medicaid; Medicare.

Guardian Care of Elkin
560 Johnson Ridge Rd, Elkin, NC 28621
(919) 835-7802
Admin Marilyn Gardner. *Dir of Nursing* Verona Coe. *Medical Dir* Dr Hal Stuart.
Licensure Skilled care; Intermediate care. *Beds* SNF 50; ICF 50. *Certified* Medicaid; Medicare.
Owner Proprietary corp (Hillhaven Corp).
Admissions Requirements Medical examination; Physician's request.
Staff RNs; LPNs; Nurses' aides; Physical therapists; Occupational therapists; Speech therapists; Activities coordinators; Dietitians.
Facilities Dining room; Physical therapy room; Activities room; Crafts room; Laundry room; Barber/Beauty shop.
Activities Arts & crafts; Cards; Games; Reading groups; Prayer groups; Movies; Shopping trips; Dances/Social/Cultural gatherings; Intergenerational programs; Adopt-a-resident; "Ho-Ho" Hotline.

Enfield

Convalescent Care of Enfield Inc
PO Box 456, 208 Cary St,, Enfield, NC 27823
(919) 445-2111
Admin Donald L Williams.
Medical Dir Dr Alton Anderson.
Licensure Skilled care. *Beds* SNF 63. *Certified* Medicaid; Medicare.

Admissions Requirements Medical examination; Physician's request.
Staff Physicians 3 (pt); RNs 6 (ft), 1 (pt); LPNs 5 (ft); Nurses' aides 21 (ft), 3 (pt); Physical therapists 1 (pt); Reality therapists 1 (pt); Recreational therapists 1 (ft); Occupational therapists 1 (pt); Speech therapists 1 (pt); Activities coordinators 1 (ft); Dietitians 1 (ft), 1 (pt); Ophthalmologists 1 (pt); Podiatrists 1 (pt); Dentists 1 (pt).
Facilities Dining room; Physical therapy room; Activities room; Laundry room; Barber/Beauty shop.
Activities Arts & crafts; Cards; Games; Reading groups; Prayer groups; Movies; Shopping trips.

Falcon

Golden Years Nursing Home
PO Box 40, 214 NW St, Falcon, NC 28342
(919) 892-6048
Admin Wilma Honeycutt Johnson. *Dir of Nursing* Jane Slate RN. *Medical Dir* Dr Andrew G Misulia.
Licensure Intermediate care. *Beds* ICF 58. *Certified* Medicaid.
Owner Proprietary corp.
Admissions Requirements Minimum age 55.
Staff Physicians 1 (ft); RNs 2 (ft); LPNs 4 (ft), 4 (pt); Nurses' aides 15 (ft), 7 (pt); Activities coordinators 1 (ft); Dietitians 1 (pt).
Facilities Dining room; Physical therapy room; Activities room; Laundry room; Barber/Beauty shop.
Activities Arts & crafts; Games; Reading groups; Prayer groups; Movies.

Farmville

Guardian Care of Farmville
Rte 1 Box 96, Farmville, NC 27828
(919) 753-5547
Admin Alawoise S Flanagan.
Licensure Intermediate care. *Beds* ICF 56. *Certified* Medicaid.
Owner Proprietary corp (Hillhaven Corp).

Fayetteville

Americas Health Care of Fayetteville
707 Murchison Rd, Fayetteville, NC 28301
(919) 483-3400
Admin Mildred Hunt.
Medical Dir Mildred P Hunt.
Licensure Skilled care; Intermediate care; Home for aged. *Beds* SNF 70; ICF 58; Home for aged 40. *Certified* Medicaid; Medicare.
Owner Proprietary corp.
Admissions Requirements Medical examination.
Staff RNs 8 (ft); LPNs 14 (ft); Nurses' aides 32 (ft); Activities coordinators.
Facilities Dining room; Activities room; Crafts room; Laundry room; Barber/Beauty shop.
Activities Arts & crafts; Cards; Games; Reading groups; Prayer groups; Movies; Shopping trips; Dances/Social/Cultural gatherings.

Bethesda Health Care Facility
Rte 1 Box 118-A, Fayetteville, NC 28301
(919) 323-3223, 323-5379 FAX
Admin Barbara S Broome. *Dir of Nursing* Joyce Housand. *Medical Dir* Christian F Siewers MD.
Licensure Skilled care; Intermediate care. *Beds* SNF 16; ICF 44. *Private Pay Patients* 25%. *Certified* Medicaid; Medicare.
Owner Proprietary corp.
Admissions Requirements Medical examination; Physician's request.

Staff Physicians 3 (pt); RNs 2 (ft), 2 (pt); LPNs 6 (ft), 3 (pt); Nurses' aides 25 (ft), 2 (pt); Physical therapists 1 (pt); Reality therapists 1 (ft); Recreational therapists 1 (ft); Occupational therapists 1 (pt); Speech therapists 1 (pt); Activities coordinators 1 (ft); Dietitians 1 (pt); Ophthalmologists (consultant); Podiatrists (consultant); Audiologists (consultant).
Facilities Dining room; Physical therapy room; Activities room; Chapel; Crafts room; Laundry room; Barber/Beauty shop.
Activities Arts & crafts; Cards; Games; Reading groups; Prayer groups; Movies; Shopping trips; Dances/Social/Cultural gatherings; Intergenerational programs; Pet therapy.

Highland House of Fayetteville Inc
PO Box 35887, 1700 Pamalee Dr, Fayetteville, NC 28303
(919) 488-2295
Admin Allyson M Wherren.
Licensure Intermediate care; Home for aged. *Beds* ICF 62; Home for aged 37. *Certified* Medicaid.
Admissions Requirements Minimum age 18; Medical examination.
Staff RNs 1 (ft); LPNs 7 (ft); Nurses' aides 28 (ft); Physical therapists 2 (ft); Speech therapists 1 (pt); Activities coordinators 2 (ft), 1 (pt); Podiatrists 1 (pt); Dentists 1 (pt).
Facilities Dining room; Activities room; Chapel; Crafts room; Laundry room; Barber/ Beauty shop.
Activities Arts & crafts; Cards; Games; Reading groups; Prayer groups; Movies; Shopping trips; Dances/Social/Cultural gatherings.

Rest Haven Nursing Home
1769 Dunn Rd, Fayetteville, NC 28301
(919) 483-5027, 483-2880 FAX
Admin Charlotte C Fitch. *Dir of Nursing* Resa Edge. *Medical Dir* Brian Fleming MD.
Licensure Intermediate care. *Beds* ICF 46. *Private Pay Patients* 10%. *Certified* Medicaid.
Owner Privately owned.
Admissions Requirements Medical examination; Physician's request.
Staff RNs 1 (ft); LPNs 3 (ft), 4 (pt); Nurses' aides 11 (ft), 7 (pt); Activities coordinators 1 (ft).
Facilities Dining room; Activities room; Crafts room; Laundry room; Barber/Beauty shop.
Activities Arts & crafts; Games; Reading groups; Prayer groups; Movies.

Whispering Pines Nursing Home
523 Country Club Dr, Fayetteville, NC 28301
(919) 488-0711
Admin Jeanne A Novello.
Licensure Intermediate care; Home for aged. *Beds* ICF 58; Home for aged 1. *Certified* Medicaid.
Admissions Requirements Medical examination; Physician's request.
Staff Physicians 9 (pt); RNs 1 (ft), 1 (pt); LPNs 3 (ft), 4 (pt); Nurses' aides 17 (ft), 6 (pt); Physical therapists 1 (pt); Recreational therapists 1 (ft); Dietitians 1 (pt).
Facilities Activities room; Barber/Beauty shop; Library.
Activities Arts & crafts; Cards; Games; Reading groups; Prayer groups; Movies; Shopping trips; Dances/Social/Cultural gatherings.

Fletcher

Fletcher Living Center
PO Box 5339, Howard Gap Rd, Fletcher, NC 28732
(704) 684-4857
Admin Connie Hayward.

Licensure Skilled care. *Beds* SNF 50. *Certified* Medicaid; Medicare.

Franklin

Britthaven of Franklin
245 Old Murphy Rd, Franklin, NC 28734
(704) 524-7806
Admin Toni Lovingood.
Licensure Skilled care; Intermediate care. *Beds* SNF 60; ICF 93. *Certified* Medicaid; Medicare.

Fuquay-Varina

Kinton Nursing Home Inc
PO Box 519, 415 Sunset Dr, Fuquay-Varina, NC 27592
(919) 552-5609
Admin Ruth C Kinton. *Dir of Nursing* Karen Reid.
Licensure Intermediate care; Home for aged. *Beds* ICF 49; Home for aged 31. *Certified* Medicaid.
Owner Privately owned.
Admissions Requirements Medical examination.
Staff RNs 2 (ft); LPNs 4 (ft), 5 (pt); Nurses' aides 20 (ft), 5 (pt); Activities coordinators 2 (ft), 1 (pt); Dietitians 7 (ft), 1 (pt).
Facilities Dining room; Activities room; Laundry room; Barber/Beauty shop.
Activities Arts & crafts; Games; Movies; Shopping trips.

Southern Wake Short-Term Skilled Nursing Facility
400 Ransom St, Fuquay-Varina, NC 27526
(919) 552-2206
Admin William J Mountford Jr. *Dir of Nursing* Mary Faucette. *Medical Dir* Cyril Allen MD.
Licensure Skilled care. *Beds* SNF 16. *Private Pay Patients* 10%. *Certified* Medicaid; Medicare.
Owner Publicly owned (Wake Medical Center).
Admissions Requirements Minimum age 18; Medical examination; Physician's request.
Staff RNs 1 (ft), 1 (pt); LPNs 3 (ft), 2 (pt); Nurses' aides 4 (ft), 3 (pt); Physical therapists 1 (pt); Activities coordinators 1 (pt); Dietitians.
Facilities Dining room; Activities room.
Activities Arts & crafts; Games; Reading groups; Prayer groups; Movies; Dances/ Social/Cultural gatherings; Pet therapy.

Gastonia

Autumnfield Inc of Lowell
398 Wilkinson Blvd, Gastonia, NC 28054
(704) 824-4316
Admin Sally A Skaggs.
Medical Dir Dr W H Hammond Jr.
Licensure Skilled care. *Beds* SNF 50. *Certified* Medicaid; Medicare.
Admissions Requirements Minimum age 18.
Staff RNs 3 (ft), 1 (pt); LPNs 3 (ft), 2 (pt); Nurses' aides 15 (ft), 3 (pt); Physical therapists; Speech therapists; Activities coordinators 1 (ft); Dietitians 1 (ft); Ophthalmologists; Podiatrists; Dentists.
Facilities Dining room; Activities room; Barber/Beauty shop.
Activities Arts & crafts; Cards; Games; Reading groups; Prayer groups; Movies; Shopping trips; Dances/Social/Cultural gatherings.

Brian Center Nursing Care—Gastonia Inc
969 Cox Rd, Gastonia, NC 28054
(704) 866-8596
Admin Doris Powell.
Medical Dir Dr James S Forrester.

Licensure Skilled care; Intermediate care. *Beds* SNF 120; ICF 42. *Certified* Medicaid; Medicare.
Owner Proprietary corp (Brian Center Management Corp).
Staff RNs 8 (ft), 1 (pt); LPNs 9 (ft), 7 (pt); Nurses' aides 41 (ft), 10 (pt); Physical therapists 1 (pt); Activities coordinators 1 (ft); Dietitians 2 (ft).
Facilities Dining room; Physical therapy room; Activities room; Laundry room; Barber/Beauty shop.
Activities Arts & crafts; Games; Reading groups; Prayer groups; Movies; Dances/ Social/Cultural gatherings.

Covenant Village Inc
1351 Robinwood Rd, Gastonia, NC 28054
(704) 867-2319
Admin Thomas P Hauer.
Medical Dir Dr Thomason.
Licensure Skilled care; Intermediate care. *Beds* SNF 36; ICF 4.
Owner Nonprofit corp.
Admissions Requirements Minimum age 65; Medical examination; Physician's request.
Staff RNs 7 (ft); LPNs 3 (ft); Nurses' aides 20 (ft); Physical therapists; Activities coordinators 1 (ft); Dietitians 1 (ft).
Affiliation Presbyterian.
Facilities Dining room; Activities room; Chapel; Crafts room; Laundry room; Barber/ Beauty shop; Library.
Activities Arts & crafts; Cards; Games; Reading groups; Prayer groups; Movies; Shopping trips; Dances/Social/Cultural gatherings.

Gaston Memorial Hospital Extended Care Service
2525 Court Dr, Gastonia, NC 28053
(704) 866-2000
Admin Wayne Shovelin.
Licensure Skilled care. *Beds* SNF 17. *Certified* Medicaid; Medicare.

Hillhaven Health Care of Gastonia
416 N Highland St, Gastonia, NC 28052
(704) 864-0371
Admin Kathy F Putnam. *Dir of Nursing* Gena H Avery.
Licensure Skilled care; Intermediate care. *Beds* SNF 61; ICF 57. *Certified* Medicaid; Medicare.
Owner Proprietary corp (Hillhaven Corp).
Admissions Requirements Minimum age 18; Medical examination.
Staff RNs 7 (ft), 2 (pt); LPNs 11 (ft), 2 (pt); Nurses' aides 47 (ft), 3 (pt); Activities coordinators 1 (ft); Dietitians 1 (ft), 1 (pt); Social workers 1 (ft), 1 (pt).
Facilities Dining room; Physical therapy room; Activities room; Crafts room; Laundry room; Barber/Beauty shop.
Activities Arts & crafts; Cards; Games; Reading groups; Prayer groups; Movies; Shopping trips; Dances/Social/Cultural gatherings.

Meadowbrook Manor of Gastonia
960 X-Ray Dr, Gastonia, NC 28054
(704) 861-0981
Admin Sharon D Stiles.
Licensure Skilled care; Intermediate care. *Beds* SNF 60; ICF 60. *Certified* Medicaid; Medicare.
Owner Proprietary corp (Tullock Management).

Goldsboro

Britthaven of Goldsboro
2401 Wayne Memorial Dr, Goldsboro, NC 27530
(919) 736-2121
Admin William T McConnell Jr.

Licensure Skilled care; Intermediate care. *Beds* SNF 111; ICF 53. *Certified* Medicaid; Medicare.
Owner Proprietary corp (Britthaven Inc).

Caswell Annex
Hwy 581, Goldsboro, NC 27530
(919) 731-3470
Admin Richard Zaharia.
Licensure Intermediate care for mentally retarded. *Beds* 100. *Certified* Medicaid.

Cherry Hospital—ICF
Caller Box 8000, Hwy 581, Goldsboro, NC 27530
(919) 731-3200
Admin J Field Montgomery, Jr.
Licensure Intermediate care. *Beds* ICF 66. *Certified* Medicaid.

Guardian Care of Goldsboro
501 Forest Hill Dr, Goldsboro, NC 27534
(919) 735-4427
Admin Catherine T Hollowell. *Dir of Nursing* Sandy Levasseur. *Medical Dir* Dr H D Tyndall.
Licensure Skilled care. *Beds* SNF 49. *Private Pay Patients* 100%.
Owner Proprietary corp (Hillhaven Corp).
Staff RNs 4 (pt); LPNs 4 (ft), 2 (pt); Nurses' aides 14 (ft), 6 (pt); Activities coordinators 1 (ft).
Facilities Dining room; Chapel; Laundry room; Barber/Beauty shop.
Activities Arts & crafts; Games; Movies; Pet therapy.

Howell's Child Care Center—Walnut Creek
Rte 9 Box 246, Goldsboro, NC 27530
(919) 778-3524
Admin Valentine H Gray.
Licensure Intermediate care. *Beds* 37. *Certified* Medicaid.

O'Berry Center—Skilled Nursing Facility
PO Box 247, Goldsboro, NC 27530
(919) 731-3545
Admin Dr Jerry H Lyall. *Dir of Nursing* Linda Fish, Nurs Coord. *Medical Dir* James Hughs MD.
Licensure Skilled care; Retirement. *Beds* SNF 34. *Certified* Medicaid; Medicare.
Owner Publicly owned.
Admissions Requirements Minimum age 7.
Staff Physicians; RNs; LPNs; Nurses' aides; Physical therapists; Recreational therapists; Occupational therapists; Speech therapists; Activities coordinators.
Facilities Dining room; Physical therapy room; Activities room; Chapel; Crafts room; Laundry room; Barber/Beauty shop; Library; Training areas.
Activities Arts & crafts; Prayer groups; Movies; Shopping trips; Dances/Social/Cultural gatherings; Developmental skills for severely/profoundly MR with multiple handicaps.

Graham

Hillhaven of Alamance Inc
779 Woody Dr, Graham, NC 27253
(919) 228-8394
Admin Wayne D Powers. *Dir of Nursing* Dorothy Coleman. *Medical Dir* Clinton Crissman.
Licensure Intermediate care. *Beds* ICF 120. *Private Pay Patients* 15%. *Certified* Medicaid.
Owner Proprietary corp (Hillhaven Corp).
Admissions Requirements Medical examination; Physician's request.
Staff RNs 3 (ft); LPNs 8 (ft); Nurses' aides 30 (ft); Activities coordinators 1 (ft), 1 (pt); Dietitians 1 (ft).
Facilities Dining room; Physical therapy room; Activities room; Crafts room; Laundry room; Barber/Beauty shop.

Activities Arts & crafts; Cards; Games; Reading groups; Prayer groups; Movies; Shopping trips.

Granite Falls

Camelot Manor Nursing Care Facility Inc
PO Box 448, 100 Sunset St, Granite Falls, NC 28630
(704) 396-2380
Admin Judith E Henry.
Licensure Skilled care; Intermediate care. *Beds* SNF 60; ICF 60. *Certified* Medicaid; Medicare.

Grantsboro

Bayboro Health Care Center & Britthaven of Pamlico
Rte 1 Box 171, Grantsboro, NC 28529
(919) 745-5005
Admin Max Hodges.
Licensure Skilled care; Intermediate care; Home for Aged. *Beds* SNF 33; ICF 33; Home for Aged 34. *Certified* Medicaid; Medicare.

Greensboro

Americas Healthcare of Greensboro
PO Box 20946, 603 S Benbow Rd, Greensboro, NC 27420
(919) 275-9941
Admin Donald Bjorlin. *Dir of Nursing* Maggie Surgeon-Talley RN. *Medical Dir* J D Trader MD.
Licensure Skilled care. *Beds* SNF 100. *Private Pay Patients* 5%. *Certified* Medicaid; Medicare.
Owner Proprietary corp.
Admissions Requirements Physician's request.
Facilities Dining room; Physical therapy room; Activities room; Laundry room; Barber/Beauty shop.
Activities Arts & crafts; Cards; Games; Reading groups; Prayer groups; Movies; Shopping trips; Dances/Social/Cultural gatherings.

Evergreens Inc—Greensboro
4007 W Wendover Ave, Greensboro, NC 27407
(919) 292-8620
Admin Dennis W Streets, MPH Exec Dir. *Dir of Nursing* Gladys McNew RN. *Medical Dir* William B Herring MD.
Licensure Skilled care; Intermediate care; Home for aged & disabled (rest home); Adult day health program. *Beds* SNF 94; ICF 172; Rest home 94; Adult day health program 25. *Certified* Medicaid; Medicare.
Owner Nonprofit corp (The Evergreens Inc).
Admissions Requirements Minimum age 21; Medical examination; Physician's request.
Staff Physicians 1 (pt); RNs 16 (ft); LPNs 11 (ft), 3 (pt); Nurses' aides 137 (ft), 4 (pt); Physical therapists 2 (pt); Recreational therapists 3 (ft), 3 (pt); Speech therapists 1 (pt); Dietitians 2 (ft), 2 (pt).
Facilities Dining room; Physical therapy room; Activities room; Chapel; Crafts room; Laundry room; Barber/Beauty shop; Library.
Activities Arts & crafts; Cards; Games; Reading groups; Prayer groups; Movies; Shopping trips; Dances/Social/Cultural gatherings; Grooming; Music; Pet program; Community exchange program; Exercise; Bowling; Swimming.

Friends Homes Inc
925 New Garden Rd, Greensboro, NC 27410
(919) 292-8187, 854-9137 FAX
Admin Wilson M Sheldon Jr. *Dir of Nursing* Patricia Kivett. *Medical Dir* Dr Robert Thacker.

Licensure Skilled care; Intermediate care; Home for aged; Independent living. *Beds* SNF 32; ICF 37; Home for aged 55; Independent living 180. *Private Pay Patients* 80%. *Certified* Medicaid; Medicare.
Owner Nonprofit corp.
Admissions Requirements Minimum age 60; Medical examination.
Staff RNs 10 (ft); LPNs 6 (ft), 3 (pt); Nurses' aides 47 (ft), 11 (pt); Physical therapists 1 (ft); Reality therapists 1 (ft); Recreational therapists 2 (ft); Occupational therapists 1 (ft); Activities coordinators 1 (ft); Dietitians 2 (ft).
Affiliation Society of Friends.
Facilities Dining room; Physical therapy room; Activities room; Crafts room; Laundry room; Barber/Beauty shop; Library; Guest room; Exercise bikes.
Activities Arts & crafts; Cards; Games; Reading groups; Prayer groups; Movies; Shopping trips; Dances/Social/Cultural gatherings; Intergenerational programs; Pet therapy; Exercise classes; Alzheimer's support group.

Greensboro Health Care Center
1201 Carolina St, Greensboro, NC 27401
(919) 275-0751
Admin Timothy W Lane.
Medical Dir Dr William McKeown.
Licensure Skilled care; Intermediate care. *Beds* SNF 35; ICF 70. *Certified* Medicaid; Medicare.
Owner Proprietary corp (Beverly Enterprises).
Facilities Dining room; Physical therapy room; Activities room; Crafts room; Laundry room; Barber/Beauty shop.
Activities Arts & crafts; Games; Movies; Shopping trips.

Healthhaven Nursing Center
801 Greenhaven Dr, Greensboro, NC 27406
(919) 292-8371
Admin Garry W McCluskey.
Licensure Skilled care; Intermediate care. *Beds* SNF 60; ICF 60. *Certified* Medicaid; Medicare.
Owner Proprietary corp (Angell Group).

Clarence Johnson Care Center
PO Box 16668, 512 Pisgah Church Rd, Greensboro, NC 27416-0668
(919) 272-6725
Admin Mary Ruth McDuffie. *Dir of Nursing* Essie P Haynes.
Licensure Intermediate care; Alzheimer's care. *Beds* ICF 29.
Owner Privately owned.
Admissions Requirements Minimum age 18; Medical examination; Physician's request.
Staff Physicians 1 (pt); RNs 1 (ft), 2 (pt); LPNs 1 (ft), 5 (pt); Nurses' aides 5 (ft), 6 (pt); Recreational therapists 1 (pt); Speech therapists 1 (ft); Dietitians 1 (ft).
Facilities Dining room; Activities room; Crafts room; Laundry room; Living room.
Activities Arts & crafts; Cards; Games; Reading groups; Prayer groups; Movies; Shopping trips; Dances/Social/Cultural gatherings.

Masonic & Eastern Star Home of North Carolina Inc
700 S Holden Rd, Greensboro, NC 27420
(919) 299-0031
Admin Tommy L Jones. *Dir of Nursing* Rebecca Burton RN.
Licensure Skilled care; Intermediate care. *Beds* SNF 32; ICF 56.
Admissions Requirements Minimum age 60; Medical examination.
Staff Physicians 1 (pt); RNs 10 (ft), 3 (pt); LPNs 4 (ft), 1 (pt); Nurses' aides 28 (ft), 13 (pt); Physical therapists 2 (pt); Recreational therapists 1 (ft); Activities coordinators 1 (ft); Dentists 1 (pt); Dermatologists 1 (pt).
Affiliation Masons.

Facilities Dining room; Physical therapy room; Activities room; Chapel; Crafts room; Laundry room; Barber/Beauty shop; Library.
Activities Arts & crafts; Games; Prayer groups; Movies; Shopping trips; Dances/Social/Cultural gatherings.

L Richardson Memorial Hospital—Skilled Nursing Facility
PO Drawer 16167, 2401 Southside Blvd, Greensboro, NC 27406
(919) 275-9741, 271-6992 FAX
Admin J C Coleman, Pres. *Dir of Nursing* Sarah Graham RN, VP Pt Care Svcs. *Medical Dir* Jerome Spruil MD.
Licensure Skilled care; Acute care. *Beds* SNF 57; Acute care 67. *Private Pay Patients* 15%. *Certified* Medicaid; Medicare.
Owner Nonprofit organization/foundation.
Admissions Requirements Medical examination; Physician's request.
Staff Physicians 1 (pt); RNs 4 (ft), 1 (pt); LPNs 6 (ft), 1 (pt); Nurses' aides 21 (ft); Physical therapists 1 (pt); Recreational therapists 1 (ft); Speech therapists (contracted); Activities coordinators 1 (ft); Dietitians 1 (pt); Ophthalmologists 1 (pt); Podiatrists 2 (pt); Audiologists (contracted); Social services directors 1 (ft).
Facilities Dining room; Physical therapy room; Activities room; Chapel; Crafts room.
Activities Arts & crafts; Cards; Games; Reading groups; Prayer groups; Movies; Shopping trips; Intergenerational programs; Puppet therapy.

Starmount Villa
109 S Holden Rd, Greensboro, NC 27407
(919) 292-5390
Admin Julia George.
Medical Dir William D McKeown.
Licensure Skilled care; Intermediate care. *Beds* SNF 62; ICF 64. *Certified* Medicaid; Medicare.
Owner Proprietary corp (Mercy Health Initiatives).
Staff RNs 4 (ft), 1 (pt); LPNs 15 (ft), 4 (pt); Nurses' aides 30 (ft), 6 (pt); Physical therapists 1 (pt); Reality therapists 1 (pt); Speech therapists 1 (pt); Activities coordinators 2 (ft); Dietitians 1 (ft); Ophthalmologists; Podiatrists.
Facilities Dining room; Physical therapy room; Activities room; Chapel; Crafts room; Laundry room; Barber/Beauty shop; Library.
Activities Arts & crafts; Cards; Games; Reading groups; Prayer groups; Movies; Shopping trips; Dances/Social/Cultural gatherings.

Greenville

Americas Health Care
Rte 1 Box 21, Greenville, NC 27834
(919) 758-7100, 758-1485 FAX
Admin Laurie Ann Hillis. *Dir of Nursing* Deloris Roberson. *Medical Dir* Dr Dixon.
Licensure Skilled care; Intermediate care. *Beds* SNF 51; ICF 69. *Certified* Medicaid; Medicare.
Owner Proprietary corp (Hillhaven Corp).
Admissions Requirements Minimum age 18; Medical examination; Physician's request.
Staff Physicians 21 (pt); RNs 6 (ft), 2 (pt); LPNs 7 (ft), 4 (pt); Nurses' aides 28 (ft), 19 (pt); Physical therapists 2 (pt); Speech therapists 1 (pt); Activities coordinators 1 (ft), 1 (pt); Dietitians 1 (pt); Social workers 1 (ft).
Facilities Dining room; Physical therapy room; Activities room; Crafts room; Laundry room; Barber/Beauty shop; Library.
Activities Arts & crafts; Cards; Games; Reading groups; Prayer groups; Movies; Shopping trips; Dances/Social/Cultural gatherings; Intergenerational programs; Pet therapy.

Greenville Villa
PO Box 5046, 127 Moye Blvd, Greenville, NC 27835
(919) 758-4121
Admin Hal Garland.
Licensure Skilled care; Intermediate care. *Beds* SNF 65; ICF 87. *Certified* Medicaid; Medicare.
Owner Proprietary corp (Beverly Enterprises).

Hamlet

Britthaven of Hamlet
PO Box 1489, Hwy 177 S, Hamlet, NC 28345
(919) 582-0021
Admin Melton W Mullinix Jr.
Licensure Skilled care; Intermediate care; Home for Aged. *Beds* SNF 40; ICF 25; Home for Aged 10. *Certified* Medicaid; Medicare.

Henderson

Guardian Care of Henderson
PO Box 1616, 280 S Beckford Dr, Henderson, NC 27536
(919) 438-6141
Admin Helen O Brame.
Licensure Intermediate care. *Beds* ICF 80. *Certified* Medicaid.
Owner Proprietary corp (Hillhaven Corp).

Pine Haven Convalescent Center of Henderson Inc
PO Box 1098, 1245 Park Ave, Henderson, NC 27536
(919) 492-1088
Admin Susan D Pegram.
Licensure Intermediate care; Home for aged. *Beds* ICF 52; Home for aged 23. *Certified* Medicaid.

Hendersonville

Carolina Village Inc
600 Carolina Village Rd, Hendersonville, NC 28739
(704) 692-6275
Admin Doley S Bell Jr.
Licensure Skilled care. *Beds* SNF 58. *Certified* Medicaid; Medicare.

Hendersonville Retirement Center
200 Heritage Dr, Hendersonville, NC 28739
(704) 693-5849
Admin Gary D Catlett.
Licensure Skilled care; Intermediate care; Home for Aged. *Beds* SNF 10; ICF 64; Home for Aged 46. *Certified* Medicaid; Medicare.

Lakewood Manor Nursing Center
1510 Hebron St, Hendersonville, NC 28739
(704) 693-8461
Admin R Lee Crabill Jr.
Licensure Skilled care; Intermediate care. *Beds* SNF 30; ICF 120. *Certified* Medicaid; Medicare.
Owner Proprietary corp (Beverly Enterprises).

Margaret R Pardee Memorial Hospital
715 Fleming St, Hendersonville, NC 28739
(704) 693-6522, 692-3681 FAX
Admin Frank J Aaron. *Dir of Nursing* Sandy Smith RN.
Licensure Skilled care. *Beds* SNF 40. *Private Pay Patients* 10%. *Certified* Medicaid; Medicare.
Owner Publicly owned.
Staff Physicians 87 (ft); RNs 3 (ft), 4 (pt); LPNs 5 (ft), 3 (pt); Nurses' aides 12 (ft), 4 (pt); Physical therapists 2 (ft); Occupational therapists 1 (pt); Speech therapists 1 (pt); Activities coordinators 1 (ft); Dietitians 1 (ft); Ophthalmologists 3 (ft).

Facilities Activities room; Barber/Beauty shop.
Activities Arts & crafts; Cards; Games; Prayer groups; Movies; Dances/Social/Cultural gatherings.

Hertford

Brian Center Nursing Care—Hertford
Rte 2 Box 2, Hertford, NC 27944
(919) 426-5391
Admin J M Crawford.
Licensure Skilled care; Intermediate care. *Beds* SNF 39; ICF 39. *Certified* Medicaid; Medicare.
Owner Proprietary corp (Brian Center Management Corp).

Hickory

Brian Center Health & Retirement—Hickory East
Rte 11 Box 355, Hickory, NC 28602
(704) 322-3343
Admin Billie S Hudson.
Licensure Skilled care; Intermediate care; Home for aged. *Beds* SNF 67; ICF 43; Home for aged 40. *Certified* Medicaid; Medicare.
Owner Proprietary corp (Brian Center Management Corp).

Brian Center Nursing Care—Hickory
220 13th Ave Pl NW, Hickory, NC 28601
(704) 328-5646, 328-6189 FAX
Admin William C Parke. *Dir of Nursing* Rebecca Wilson. *Medical Dir* Dr John K Earl.
Licensure Skilled care; Intermediate care. *Beds* SNF 63; ICF 41. *Private Pay Patients* 26%. *Certified* Medicaid; Medicare.
Owner Proprietary corp (Brian Center Management Corp).
Admissions Requirements Minimum age 18; Medical examination.
Staff Physicians (contracted); RNs 2 (ft), 5 (pt); LPNs 5 (ft), 8 (pt); Nurses' aides 26 (ft), 23 (pt); Physical therapists (contracted); Occupational therapists (contracted); Speech therapists (contracted); Activities coordinators 1 (ft); Dietitians 1 (ft); Ophthalmologists (contracted); Podiatrists (contracted).
Facilities Dining room; Physical therapy room; Activities room; Crafts room; Laundry room; Barber/Beauty shop.
Activities Arts & crafts; Cards; Games; Reading groups; Prayer groups; Movies; Shopping trips; Dances/Social/Cultural gatherings; Intergenerational programs; Pet therapy; Seasonal holiday parties; Community events.

Lutheran Nursing Homes Inc—Hickory Unit
PO Box 9147, 1265 21st St NE, Hickory, NC 28602
(704) 328-2006
Admin Rev Floyd Addison Jr. *Dir of Nursing* Irene Everett RN. *Medical Dir* Dr George Tolhurst.
Licensure Skilled care; Intermediate care; Home for aged; Alzheimer's care. *Beds* SNF 48; ICF 56; Home for aged 36. *Certified* Medicaid; Medicare.
Owner Nonprofit corp (North Carolina Lutheran Homes).
Staff RNs 8 (ft), 2 (pt); LPNs 8 (ft); Nurses' aides 17 (ft), 8 (pt); Activities coordinators 1 (ft).
Affiliation Lutheran.
Facilities Dining room; Activities room; Chapel; Crafts room; Laundry room; Barber/Beauty shop; Library; Dayroom.
Activities Arts & crafts; Cards; Games; Reading groups; Prayer groups; Movies; Shopping trips; Dances/Social/Cultural gatherings.

Pellcare—Hickory
1125 10th St Blvd NW, Hickory, NC 28601
(704) 322-6995
Admin Connie L Wright. *Dir of Nursing*
Christopher N Propst RN. *Medical Dir* John
K Earl MD.
Licensure Skilled care; Intermediate care;
Alzheimer's care. *Beds* SNF 60; ICF 60.
Certified Medicaid; Medicare.
Owner Proprietary corp.
Admissions Requirements Minimum age 18;
Medical examination; Physician's request.
Staff Physicians 1 (ft); RNs 3 (ft), 4 (pt);
LPNs 8 (ft), 2 (pt); Nurses' aides 38 (ft), 12
(pt); Physical therapists 1 (ft); Occupational
therapists 1 (pt); Speech therapists 1 (pt);
Activities coordinators 2 (ft); Dietitians 1
(pt); Ophthalmologists 1 (pt); Dentists 1 (pt).
Facilities Dining room; Physical therapy
room; Activities room; Crafts room; Laundry
room; Barber/Beauty shop.
Activities Arts & crafts; Games; Prayer groups;
Movies; Shopping trips; Dances/Social/
Cultural gatherings; Birthday parties; Special
church services at Easter, Thanksgiving, &
Christmas.

High Point

Evergreens—High Point
206 Greensboro Rd, High Point, NC 27260
(919) 886-4121
Admin Felton B Wooten. *Dir of Nursing*
Martha Hayworth. *Medical Dir* Dr Eldora
Terrell.
Licensure Skilled care; Intermediate care; Rest
home. *Beds* SNF 27; ICF 66; Rest home 27.
Certified Medicaid; Medicare.
Owner Nonprofit corp.
Admissions Requirements Minimum age 21;
Medical examination; Physician's request.
Staff Physicians 1 (pt); RNs 5 (ft); LPNs 11
(ft); Nurses' aides 40 (ft), 10 (pt);
Recreational therapists 1 (ft); Dietitians 1
(pt).
Facilities Dining room; Physical therapy
room; Activities room; Chapel; Crafts room;
Laundry room; Barber/Beauty shop; Library.
Activities Arts & crafts; Games; Reading
groups; Prayer groups; Movies; Dances/
Social/Cultural gatherings; Pet therapy.

High Point Care Center
3830 N Main St, High Point, NC 27260
(919) 869-3752
Admin Mark C Johnson. *Dir of Nursing*
Esther Sykes RN. *Medical Dir* Bansi P Shah
MD.
Licensure Skilled care; Intermediate care. *Beds*
SNF 42; ICF 58. *Certified* Medicaid;
Medicare.
Owner Proprietary corp.
Admissions Requirements Medical
examination.
Staff Physicians 2 (pt); RNs 3 (ft), 1 (pt);
LPNs 6 (ft), 2 (pt); Nurses' aides 27 (ft), 20
(pt); Activities coordinators 1 (ft); Dietitians
1 (ft).
Facilities Dining room; Activities room;
Chapel; Crafts room; Laundry room; Barber/
Beauty shop.
Activities Arts & crafts; Cards; Games;
Reading groups; Prayer groups; Movies;
Shopping trips.

Maryfield Nursing Home
1315 Greensboro Rd, High Point, NC 27260
(919) 886-2444
Admin Sr Lucy Hennessy. *Dir of Nursing*
Marge Myers RN. *Medical Dir* W H Flythe
MD.
Licensure Skilled care; Intermediate care;
Retirement. *Beds* SNF 111; ICF 4. *Certified*
Medicaid; Medicare.
Owner Nonprofit corp.
Admissions Requirements Medical
examination; Physician's request.

Staff Physicians 1 (pt); RNs 9 (ft), 6 (pt);
LPNs 6 (ft), 3 (pt); Nurses' aides 40 (ft), 10
(pt); Physical therapists 1 (pt); Recreational
therapists 2 (ft); Speech therapists 1 (pt);
Activities coordinators 1 (ft); Dietitians 1
(pt); Ophthalmologists 1 (pt).
Affiliation Roman Catholic.
Facilities Dining room; Physical therapy
room; Activities room; Chapel; Crafts room;
Laundry room; Barber/Beauty shop; Library.
Activities Arts & crafts; Cards; Games;
Reading groups; Prayer groups; Movies;
Shopping trips; Dances/Social/Cultural
gatherings; Picnics; Fishing trips; Trips to
zoo.

Medical Park Nursing Center
707 N Elm St, High Point, NC 27262
(919) 885-0141
Admin David C Huff.
Medical Dir Sam T Bickley MD.
Licensure Skilled care; Intermediate care. *Beds*
SNF 93; ICF 106. *Certified* Medicaid;
Medicare.
Admissions Requirements Medical
examination; Physician's request.
Staff Physicians 4 (pt); RNs 20 (ft); LPNs 30
(ft); Nurses' aides 60 (ft); Physical therapists
2 (ft); Reality therapists 2 (ft); Recreational
therapists 3 (ft); Speech therapists 1 (ft);
Activities coordinators 1 (ft); Dietitians 1
(ft); Podiatrists 1 (pt); Dentists 1 (pt).
Facilities Dining room; Physical therapy
room; Activities room; Crafts room; Laundry
room; Barber/Beauty shop.
Activities Arts & crafts; Cards; Games;
Reading groups; Prayer groups; Movies;
Shopping trips; Dances/Social/Cultural
gatherings.

Presbyterian Home of High Point
201 Greensboro Rd, Box 500, High Point, NC
27260-3434
(919) 883-9111
Admin Betty Hayes. *Dir of Nursing* Patsy
Peterson RN. *Medical Dir* Dr Lyle Smith;
Dr Don Douglass.
Licensure Skilled care; Intermediate care;
Home for aged; Independent living. *Beds*
SNF 74; ICF 10; Home for aged 69;
Independent living 145. *Private Pay Patients*
91%. *Certified* Medicaid; Medicare.
Owner Nonprofit organization/foundation.
Admissions Requirements Minimum age 62;
Medical examination.
Staff Physicians 1 (pt); RNs 10 (ft), 12 (pt);
LPNs 3 (ft), 3 (pt); Nurses' aides 42 (ft), 24
(pt); Physical therapists 1 (pt); Recreational
therapists 1 (pt); Activities coordinators 3
(ft); Dietitians 1 (ft); Podiatrists 1 (pt).
Affiliation Presbyterian.
Activities Arts & crafts; Cards; Games;
Reading groups; Prayer groups; Movies;
Shopping trips; Dances/Social/Cultural
gatherings; Pet therapy.

Wesleyan Arms Inc
1901 N Centennial St, High Point, NC 27260
(919) 884-2222
Admin Gregory B Ledbetter. *Dir of Nursing*
Malvia Keller. *Medical Dir* Alton A Reeder
MD.
Licensure Skilled care; Intermediate care;
Domiciliary care; Independent living;
Apartments. *Beds* SNF 50; ICF 79;
Domiciliary care 38; Independent living 33;
Apts 193. *Private Pay Patients* 40%.
Certified Medicaid; Medicare.
Owner Nonprofit corp.
Admissions Requirements Medical
examination.
Staff Physicians; RNs; LPNs; Nurses' aides;
Physical therapists; Activities coordinators;
Dietitians (contracted); Ophthalmologists
(contracted); Podiatrists (contracted); Social
workers.
Affiliation First Wesleyan Church.

Facilities Dining room; Physical therapy
room; Activities room; Chapel; Crafts room;
Barber/Beauty shop; Library.
Activities Arts & crafts; Games; Reading
groups; Prayer groups; Movies; Shopping
trips; Dances/Social/Cultural gatherings;
Intergenerational programs; Pet therapy.

Huntersville

Huntersville Oaks Nursing Home
13001 Old Statesville Rd, Huntersville, NC
28078
(704) 875-7400
Admin Richard V Delinger. *Dir of Nursing*
Doris Smith. *Medical Dir* David Scott Moss
MD.
Licensure Skilled care; Intermediate care;
Alzheimer's care. *Beds* SNF 147; ICF 142.
Certified Medicaid; Medicare.
Owner Nonprofit corp.
Facilities Dining room; Physical therapy
room; Activities room; Chapel; Crafts room;
Laundry room; Barber/Beauty shop.
Activities Arts & crafts; Games; Reading
groups; Prayer groups; Movies; Shopping
trips.

Jacksonville

Britthaven of Jacksonville
225 White St, Jacksonville, NC 28540
(919) 353-7222
Admin Troy C Hefner.
Medical Dir Dr Wesley Murfin.
Licensure Skilled care; Intermediate care;
Home for aged. *Beds* SNF 69; ICF 113;
Home for aged 14. *Certified* Medicaid;
Medicare.
Owner Proprietary corp (Britthaven Inc).
Admissions Requirements Minimum age 18;
Medical examination; Physician's request.
Staff RNs 9 (ft), 4 (pt); LPNs 25 (ft), 6 (pt);
Nurses' aides 75 (ft), 40 (pt); Activities
coordinators 2 (ft); Dietitians 1 (ft);
Ophthalmologists 1 (pt); Podiatrists 1 (pt);
Dentists 1 (pt).
Facilities Dining room; Activities room;
Chapel; Crafts room; Laundry room; Barber/
Beauty shop; Library.
Activities Arts & crafts; Cards; Games; Prayer
groups; Movies; Shopping trips; Dances/
Social/Cultural gatherings.

Britthaven of Onslow
PO Box 5021, 1839 Onslow Dr, Jacksonville,
NC 28540
(919) 455-3610
Admin Cary Corley.
Medical Dir Dr Gregory Streeter.
Licensure Skilled care. *Beds* SNF 80. *Certified*
Medicaid; Medicare.
Owner Proprietary corp (Britthaven Inc).
Admissions Requirements Minimum age 18;
Medical examination.
Staff Physicians 2 (ft); RNs 3 (ft), 4 (pt);
LPNs 8 (ft), 1 (pt); Nurses' aides 25 (ft), 32
(pt); Physical therapists 1 (pt); Speech
therapists 1 (pt); Activities coordinators 1
(ft); Dietitians 1 (ft); Ophthalmologists 1
(pt); Dentists 1 (pt).
Facilities Dining room; Physical therapy
room; Activities room; Crafts room; Laundry
room; Barber/Beauty shop.
Activities Arts & crafts; Cards; Games;
Reading groups; Prayer groups; Movies;
Shopping trips; Dances/Social/Cultural
gatherings; Picnics.

Jefferson

Emerald Health Care of Ashe
Hwy 221 S, Jefferson, NC 28640
(919) 246-5581
Admin Frances L Messer.

Licensure Skilled care; Intermediate care;
Home for Aged. *Beds* SNF 60; ICF 60;
Home for Aged 30.

Kenansville

Duplin General Hospital—Skilled Nursing Facility
PO Box 278, N Main St, Kenansville, NC
28349
(919) 296-0941
Admin Richard E Harrell.
Licensure Skilled care. *Beds* SNF 20. *Certified*
Medicaid; Medicare.

Guardian Care of Kenansville
PO Box 478, Beasley St, Kenansville, NC
28349
(919) 296-1561
Admin Elizabeth Kinsley. *Dir of Nursing* Elsie
Pitts RN. *Medical Dir* Corazon Ngo MD.
Licensure Skilled care; Intermediate care. *Beds*
SNF 28; ICF 64. *Certified* Medicaid;
Medicare.
Owner Proprietary corp (Hillhaven Corp).
Admissions Requirements Physician's request.
Staff Physicians 8 (ft); RNs 5 (ft), 2 (pt);
LPNs 3 (ft), 1 (pt); Nurses' aides 27 (ft), 5
(pt); Speech therapists 1 (ft); Activities
coordinators 1 (ft); Dietitians 1 (ft); Social
workers 1 (ft).
Facilities Dining room; Physical therapy
room; Activities room; Laundry room;
Barber/Beauty shop.
Activities Arts & crafts; Games; Prayer groups;
Movies; Dances/Social/Cultural gatherings;
Music performances; Birthday parties;
Special parties.

Kernersville

Britthaven of Kernersville
731 Piney Grove Rd, Kernersville, NC 27284
(919) 996-4038
Admin William E Wood.
Medical Dir Dr Wesley Phillips.
Licensure Intermediate care. *Beds* ICF 60.
Certified Medicaid.
Owner Proprietary corp (Hillhaven Corp).
Admissions Requirements Minimum age 18;
Medical examination.
Staff RNs 2 (ft); LPNs 6 (ft); Nurses' aides 25
(ft), 10 (pt); Recreational therapists 1 (pt);
Activities coordinators 1 (ft).
Facilities Dining room; Activities room;
Laundry room; Barber/Beauty shop.
Activities Arts & crafts; Cards; Games;
Reading groups; Prayer groups; Movies;
Shopping trips; Dances/Social/Cultural
gatherings.

Oakwood Knoll Nursing Center Inc
2680 Hwy 66 S, Kernersville, NC 27284
(919) 869-4114
Admin Rachel Gordon. *Dir of Nursing* Gay
Wyche. *Medical Dir* Sam Bickley MD.
Licensure Intermediate care. *Beds* ICF 32.
Certified Medicaid.
Owner Privately owned.
Admissions Requirements Medical
examination.
Staff Physicians 1 (ft); RNs 1 (ft); LPNs 3 (ft);
Nurses' aides 5 (ft), 8 (pt); Speech therapists
1 (ft); Activities coordinators 1 (ft);
Dietitians 1 (ft); Social workers 1 (ft).
Facilities Dining room; Activities room;
Crafts room; Laundry room; Barber/Beauty
shop.
Activities Arts & crafts; Games; Reading
groups; Prayer groups; Movies; Shopping
trips; Dances/Social/Cultural gatherings.

Kings Mountain

Kings Mountain Convalescent Center
PO Box 578, 716 Sipes St, Kings Mountain,
NC 28086
(704) 739-8132, 739-8133 FAX
Admin Karen Greene Radford. *Dir of Nursing*
Joan H Bradley. *Medical Dir* Dr Joseph Lee
III.
Licensure Skilled care; Intermediate care. *Beds*
SNF 62; ICF 62. *Certified* Medicaid;
Medicare.
Owner Proprietary corp (White Oak Manor
Inc).
Staff Physicians 1 (pt); RNs 5 (ft), 2 (pt);
LPNs 9 (ft), 5 (pt); Nurses' aides 39 (ft), 3
(pt); Physical therapists 1 (pt); Speech
therapists 1 (pt); Activities coordinators 2
(ft), 1 (pt); Dietitians 1 (pt).
Facilities Dining room; Physical therapy
room; Activities room; Crafts room; Laundry
room; Barber/Beauty shop.
Activities Arts & crafts; Cards; Games;
Reading groups; Prayer groups; Movies;
Shopping trips; Dances/Social/Cultural
gatherings; Pet therapy.

Kings Mountain Hospital—Skilled Nursing Facility
PO Box 339, 706 W King St, Kings Mountain,
NC 28086
(704) 739-3601
Admin Huitt Reep.
Licensure Skilled care. *Beds* SNF 10. *Certified*
Medicaid; Medicare.

Kinston

Britthaven of Kinston
PO Box 3527, 317 Rhodes Ave, Kinston, NC
28501
(919) 523-0082
Admin Dean Picot.
Licensure Skilled care; Intermediate care. *Beds*
SNF 125; ICF 57. *Certified* Medicaid;
Medicare.
Owner Proprietary corp (Britthaven Inc).

Caswell Center
2415 W Vernon Ave, Kinston, NC 28501
(919) 559-5222
Admin Jimmie S Woodall. *Dir of Nursing*
Janet Roberts. *Medical Dir* Dr K S Salameh.
Licensure Intermediate care for mentally
retarded; Care for mentally retarded
(regular). *Beds* ICF/MR 752; Care for
mentally retarded (regular) 159. *Private Pay
Patients* 2%. *Certified* Medicaid.
Owner Publicly owned.
Admissions Requirements Minimum age 8.
Staff Physicians 9 (ft); RNs 40 (ft); LPNs 60
(ft); Physical therapists 9 (ft); Reality
therapists 5 (ft); Recreational therapists 5
(ft); Occupational therapists 5 (ft); Speech
therapists 4 (ft); Dietitians 12 (ft).
Languages Sign.
Facilities Dining room; Physical therapy
room; Activities room; Chapel; Crafts room;
Laundry room; Barber/Beauty shop; Library.
Activities Arts & crafts; Games; Reading
groups; Prayer groups; Movies; Shopping
trips; Dances/Social/Cultural gatherings;
Intergenerational programs; Pet therapy.

Guardian Care of Kinston
PO Box 1438, Cunningham Rd, Kinston, NC
28503
(919) 527-5146
Admin Charles E Sharpe Jr. *Dir of Nursing*
Jennifer Adams.
Licensure Intermediate care. *Beds* ICF 114.
Certified Medicaid.
Owner Proprietary corp (Hillhaven Corp).
Admissions Requirements Minimum age 18;
Medical examination; Physician's request.

Staff RNs 3 (ft), 1 (pt); LPNs 7 (ft), 4 (pt);
Nurses' aides 34 (ft), 9 (pt); Speech
therapists 1 (pt); Activities coordinators 1
(ft); Dietitians 1 (ft).
Facilities Dining room; Physical therapy
room; Activities room; Crafts room; Laundry
room; Barber/Beauty shop.
Activities Arts & crafts; Cards; Games;
Reading groups; Prayer groups; Movies;
Shopping trips; Dances/Social/Cultural
gatherings.

Lenoir Memorial Hospital Inc
PO Drawer 1678, 100 Airport Rd, Kinston,
NC 28501
(919) 522-7818
Admin Jim R Hobbs. *Dir of Nursing* Sue
Taylor. *Medical Dir* Samuel Gilmore MD.
Licensure Skilled care. *Beds* SNF 26. *Certified*
Medicaid; Medicare.
Owner Nonprofit organization/foundation.
Staff Physicians 65 (ft); RNs 168 (ft), 2 (pt);
LPNs 52 (ft); Nurses' aides 78 (ft), 13 (pt);
Physical therapists 6 (ft); Activities
coordinators 1 (ft); Dietitians 2 (ft);
Ophthalmologists 4 (ft).
Facilities Dining room; Physical therapy
room; Activities room; Crafts room.
Activities Arts & crafts; Cards; Games.

LaGrange

Howell's Child Care Center Inc/Bear Creek
100 Howell Dr, LaGrange, NC 28551
(919) 778-3067
Admin Tina Howell.
Medical Dir Janice M Boyd.
Licensure Intermediate care for mentally
retarded. *Beds* ICF/MR 120. *Certified*
Medicaid.
Owner Nonprofit corp.
Staff Physicians 1 (pt); RNs 8 (ft), 4 (pt);
LPNs 8 (ft), 2 (pt); Nurses' aides 161 (ft), 40
(pt); Physical therapists 1 (ft); Recreational
therapists 4 (ft); Occupational therapists 1
(ft); Speech therapists 1 (ft); Dietitians 1 (ft).
Facilities Dining room; Physical therapy
room; Activities room; Chapel; Barber/
Beauty shop.

Lake Waccamaw

Lake Waccamaw Convalescent Center
PO Box 196, Cameron St, Lake Waccamaw,
NC 28450
(919) 646-3144
Admin Margaret E Marley. *Dir of Nursing*
Sherry Grainger. *Medical Dir* John Munroe
MD.
Licensure Skilled care; Intermediate care;
Home for aged. *Beds* SNF 60; ICF 67;
Home for aged 15. *Certified* Medicaid;
Medicare.
Owner Proprietary corp.
Admissions Requirements Medical
examination; Physician's request.
Staff RNs 5 (ft); LPNs 10 (ft), 1 (pt); Physical
therapists 1 (ft); Activities coordinators 2
(ft); Ophthalmologists 1 (pt); Ward clerks 3
(ft); Dentists 1 (pt).
Facilities Dining room; Physical therapy
room; Activities room; Chapel; Crafts room;
Laundry room; Barber/Beauty shop.
Activities Arts & crafts; Games; Reading
groups; Prayer groups; Movies; Shopping
trips; Dances/Social/Cultural gatherings.

Laurinburg

Century Care of Laurinburg Inc
Rte 3 Box 95, Hasty Rd, Laurinburg, NC
28352
(919) 276-8400
Admin Noah Kinlaw Duncan.
Licensure Intermediate care. *Beds* ICF 74.
Certified Medicaid.

Edwin Morgan Center Scotland Memorial Hospital—SNF
517 Peden St, Laurinburg, NC 28352
(919) 276-0016
Admin Bob Haley.
Licensure Skilled care. *Beds* SNF 40. *Certified* Medicaid; Medicare.

Scotia Village
2200 Elm Ave, Laurinburg, NC 28352
(919) 277-2000
Admin G W Pleasants III.
Licensure Skilled care; Home for Aged. *Beds* SNF 20; Home for Aged 20.

Lenoir

Meadowbrook Manor of Lenoir
322 Nu-Way Cir, Lenoir, NC 28645
(704) 758-7326
Admin Dorothy A Durand.
Licensure Skilled care; Intermediate care. *Beds* SNF 88; ICF 32. *Certified* Medicaid; Medicare.
Owner Proprietary corp (Brian Center Management Corp).

Lexington

Brian Center Nursing Care—Lexington
Rte 1 Box 1876, Lexington, NC 27292
(704) 249-7521
Admin Laird C Leeder Jr. *Dir of Nursing* Diane Roseberry. *Medical Dir* Michael Garrison MD.
Licensure Skilled care. *Beds* SNF 56. *Certified* Medicaid; Medicare.
Owner Proprietary corp (Brian Center Management Corp).
Admissions Requirements Medical examination; Physician's request.
Staff Physicians 1 (pt); RNs 3 (ft), 4 (pt); LPNs; Nurses' aides 21 (ft), 2 (pt); Activities coordinators 2 (pt); Dietitians 1 (ft).
Facilities Dining room; Activities room; Laundry room; Barber/Beauty shop.
Activities Arts & crafts; Cards; Games; Reading groups; Prayer groups; Movies; Shopping trips.

Buena Vista Nursing
PO Box 419, Everhart Rd, Lexington, NC 27293
(704) 246-6644
Admin Thurman L Fritts. *Dir of Nursing* Lillian B Fritts.
Licensure Intermediate care. *Beds* ICF 43. *Certified* Medicaid.
Owner Privately owned.
Admissions Requirements Medical examination; Physician's request.
Staff RNs 2 (ft), 1 (pt); LPNs 4 (ft), 1 (pt); Nurses' aides 14 (ft), 2 (pt); Activities coordinators 1 (ft), 1 (pt).
Facilities Dining room; Activities room; Chapel; Crafts room; Laundry room; Barber/Beauty shop.
Activities Arts & crafts; Cards; Games; Reading groups; Prayer groups; Movies; Shopping trips.

Centerclair Inc
Rte 20 Box 711, Younts Rd, Lexington, NC 27292
(704) 249-7057, 246-4709 FAX
Admin Geneva F Williams. *Dir of Nursing* Olga James RN. *Medical Dir* Gerald P Briggs MD.
Licensure Intermediate care. *Beds* ICF 60. *Private Pay Patients* 46%. *Certified* Medicaid.
Owner Privately owned.
Admissions Requirements Medical examination.
Staff RNs 3 (ft); LPNs 2 (ft), 1 (pt); Nurses' aides 12 (ft), 9 (pt); Physical therapists (contracted); Occupational therapists

(contracted); Speech therapists (contracted); Activities coordinators 1 (ft); Dietitians (contracted); Podiatrists (quarterly); Social services 1 (ft).
Facilities Dining room; Activities room; Laundry room; Barber/Beauty shop; Courtyard; Sun porch; Child day care center.
Activities Arts & crafts; Games; Reading groups; Prayer groups; Movies; Shopping trips; Dances/Social/Cultural gatherings; Intergenerational programs; Dining out; Trips to fair, zoo, circus.

Golden Age Inc
Rte 22 Box 2470, Cowplace Rd, Lexington, NC 27292
(704) 956-1132
Admin Samuel E McBride.
Licensure Skilled care; Home for aged. *Beds* SNF 50; Home for aged 14. *Certified* Medicaid; Medicare.

Lillington

Adams & Kinton Nursing Home
PO Box 789, Hwy 421, Lillington, NC 27546
(919) 893-5142
Admin John H Kinton Jr.
Licensure Skilled care; Intermediate care; Home for aged. *Beds* SNF 40; ICF 89; Home for aged 108. *Certified* Medicaid; Medicare.

Lincolnton

Brian Center Health & Retirement—Lincolnton
PO Box 249, 816 S Aspen St, Lincolnton, NC 28093
(704) 735-8065
Admin Lynda Price.
Licensure Skilled care; Intermediate care; Home for Aged. *Beds* SNF 36; ICF 18; Home for Aged 43. *Certified* Medicaid; Medicare.

Lincoln County Hospital Inc
PO Box 677, Lincolnton, NC 28092
(704) 735-3071
Admin Kenneth C Wehunt.
Licensure Skilled care. *Beds* SNF 9.

Lincoln Nursing Center
1410 E Gaston St, Lincolnton, NC 28093-0898
(704) 732-1138
Admin Susie H Martin.
Licensure Skilled care; Intermediate care; Home for aged. *Beds* SNF 60; ICF 50; Home for aged 10. *Certified* Medicaid; Medicare.
Owner Proprietary corp (Hillhaven Corp).

Louisburg

Louisburg Nursing Center
PO Box 629, 202 Smoke Tree Way, Louisburg, NC 27549
(919) 496-2188
Admin Eva McDougal. *Dir of Nursing* Vivian Barnes. *Medical Dir* Dr Paul E Kile.
Licensure Intermediate care. *Beds* ICF 92. *Private Pay Patients* 10%. *Certified* Medicaid.
Owner Proprietary corp (Triad Medical Services Inc.
Admissions Requirements Medical examination; Physician's request.
Staff RNs 1 (ft), 1 (pt); LPNs 8 (ft), 6 (pt); Nurses' aides 32 (ft), 8 (pt); Activities coordinators 1 (ft).
Facilities Dining room; Physical therapy room; Activities room; Barber/Beauty shop.
Activities Arts & crafts; Games; Reading groups; Prayer groups; Movies.

Lumberton

Kingsdale Manor
PO Box 1675, 1555 Willis Ave, Lumberton, NC 28358
(919) 739-6048
Admin Larris Mullins. *Dir of Nursing* Rudine Smith. *Medical Dir* Dr Charles R Beasley.
Licensure Skilled care; Intermediate care. *Beds* SNF 31; ICF 94. *Private Pay Patients* 1%. *Certified* Medicaid; Medicare.
Owner Proprietary corp (Beverly Enterprises).
Admissions Requirements Medical examination; Physician's request.
Staff Physicians 1 (ft); RNs 3 (ft), 4 (pt); LPNs 8 (ft), 3 (pt); Nurses' aides 42 (ft), 7 (pt); Physical therapists 1 (pt); Activities coordinators 1 (ft); Dietitians 1 (ft).
Facilities Dining room; Physical therapy room; Activities room; Laundry room; Barber/Beauty shop.
Activities Arts & crafts; Games; Reading groups; Prayer groups; Movies; Shopping trips; Dances/Social/Cultural gatherings.

North Carolina Cancer Institute—Skilled Nursing Facility
Hwy 711, Lumberton, NC 28358
(919) 739-2821
Admin Kenneth Jackson. *Dir of Nursing* Peggy Hughes RN. *Medical Dir* W C Hedgpeth MD.
Licensure Skilled care. *Beds* SNF 52. *Certified* Medicaid; Medicare.
Owner Nonprofit corp.
Admissions Requirements Physician's request.
Staff Physicians 1 (ft); RNs 5 (ft); LPNs 5 (ft), 1 (pt); Nurses' aides 22 (ft), 2 (pt); Activities coordinators 1 (pt); Dietitians 1 (pt).
Facilities Dining room; Activities room; Chapel; Crafts room; Laundry room; Barber/Beauty shop.
Activities Arts & crafts; Cards; Games; Prayer groups.

Southeastern General Hospital Long-Term Care Facility
1150 Pine Run Dr, Lumberton, NC 28358
(919) 671-5703
Admin John C Eckert. *Dir of Nursing* Julie D Rikard. *Medical Dir* George S Nettles MD.
Licensure Skilled care; Intermediate care; Alzheimer's care; Alzheimer's day care. *Beds* SNF 60; ICF 55; Alzheimer's care 15; Alzheimer's day care 10. *Certified* Medicaid; Medicare.
Owner Nonprofit corp.
Staff Physicians 1 (ft); RNs 9 (ft); LPNs 17 (ft); Nurses' aides 45 (ft); Physical therapists 1 (pt); Recreational therapists 1 (ft); Occupational therapists 1 (pt); Speech therapists 1 (pt); Activities coordinators 1 (ft); Dietitians 1 (pt); Ophthalmologists 1 (pt); Podiatrists 1 (pt).

Wesley Pines
100 Wesley Pines Rd, Lumberton, NC 28358
(919) 738-9691
Admin Rev Paul G Bunn. *Dir of Nursing* Kathy Freeman. *Medical Dir* Ben Hardin.
Licensure Skilled care; Intermediate care; Home for aged; Independent living. *Beds* SNF 36; ICF 23; Home for aged 44; Independent living 50. *Private Pay Patients* 75%. *Certified* Medicaid; Medicare.
Owner Nonprofit organization/foundation.
Admissions Requirements Minimum age 62; Medical examination.
Staff Physicians 1 (pt); RNs 2 (ft), 4 (pt); LPNs 5 (ft); Nurses' aides 14 (ft), 10 (pt); Physical therapists 2 (pt); Speech therapists 1 (pt); Activities coordinators 1 (ft); Dietitians 1 (pt); Podiatrists 1 (pt).
Languages French, Swahili.
Affiliation Methodist.

Facilities Dining room; Physical therapy room; Activities room; Chapel; Crafts room; Laundry room; Barber/Beauty shop; Library; Family rooms.
Activities Arts & crafts; Cards; Games; Prayer groups; Shopping trips; Dances/Social/Cultural gatherings; Worship.

Madison

Britthaven of Madison
Rte 2 Box 886, Madison, NC 27025
(919) 548-9658, 548-1299 FAX
Admin Jeffreys B Barrett LNHA. *Dir of Nursing* Carol Ann Shreve RN. *Medical Dir* C W Joyce MD.
Licensure Skilled care; Intermediate care. *Beds* SNF 22; ICF 78. *Private Pay Patients* 5%. *Certified* Medicaid; Medicare.
Owner Proprietary corp (Britthaven Inc).
Admissions Requirements Medical examination.
Staff Physicians 4 (ft); RNs 7 (ft), 3 (pt); LPNs 7 (ft), 2 (pt); Nurses' aides 40 (ft), 6 (pt); Activities coordinators 1 (ft).
Facilities Dining room; Activities room; Crafts room; Laundry room; Barber/Beauty shop; Courtyard.
Activities Arts & crafts; Cards; Games; Reading groups; Prayer groups; Intergenerational programs; Pet therapy; Adult education/GED.

Marion

Autumn Care of Marion
PO Box 339, 610 Airport Rd, Marion, NC 28752
(704) 652-6701
Admin Ronnie V Rawls.
Medical Dir Dr Michael McCall.
Licensure Skilled care; Intermediate care; Home for aged. *Beds* SNF 50; ICF 30; Home for aged 15. *Certified* Medicaid; Medicare.
Owner Proprietary corp (Autumn Corp).
Admissions Requirements Minimum age 21; Medical examination.
Staff Physicians 8 (pt); RNs 7 (ft), 5 (pt); LPNs 6 (ft), 3 (pt); Nurses' aides 35 (ft), 15 (pt); Physical therapists 2 (pt); Speech therapists 1 (pt); Activities coordinators 1 (ft); Dietitians 1 (pt); Ophthalmologists 1 (pt); Podiatrists 1 (pt); Dentists 1 (pt).
Facilities Dining room; Physical therapy room; Activities room; Crafts room; Laundry room; Barber/Beauty shop.
Activities Arts & crafts; Cards; Games; Reading groups; Prayer groups; Movies; Shopping trips; Dances/Social/Cultural gatherings.

Mars Hill

Madison Manor Nursing Center
50 Manor Rd, Mars Hill, NC 28754
(704) 689-5200
Admin Mary J Lance. *Dir of Nursing* Cindy Kraksh. *Medical Dir* Dr Otis Duck.
Licensure Skilled care; Intermediate care. *Beds* SNF 51; ICF 49. *Certified* Medicaid; Medicare; VA.
Owner Proprietary corp (Mercy Health Initiatives).
Admissions Requirements Minimum age 18.
Staff Physicians 3 (pt); RNs 3 (ft), 2 (pt); LPNs 12 (ft), 3 (pt); Nurses' aides 32 (ft), 3 (pt); Physical therapists 2 (ft); Occupational therapists 1 (pt); Speech therapists 1 (pt); Activities coordinators 1 (ft), 1 (pt); Ophthalmologists 1 (pt); Social workers 1 (ft), 1 (pt).
Facilities Dining room; Physical therapy room; Activities room; Laundry room; Barber/Beauty shop; Courtyard.

Activities Arts & crafts; Cards; Games; Reading groups; Prayer groups; Movies; Dances/Social/Cultural gatherings; Exercise; Cooking; Singing; Music therapy; Sensory stimulation; Worship service; Gardening.

Marshville

Autumn Care of Marshville
PO Box 608, 311 W Pheifer St, Marshville, NC 28103
(704) 624-6643
Admin Patricia A Troxell.
Licensure Skilled care; Intermediate care; Home for Aged. *Beds* SNF 40; ICF 40; Home for Aged 20. *Certified* Medicaid; Medicare.

Matthews

Plantation Estates Medical Facility
701 Plantation Estates Dr, Matthews, NC 28105
(704) 845-5900
Admin Julie A Cunningham.
Licensure Skilled care; Home for Aged. *Beds* SNF 60; Home for Aged 44.

Mebane

Presbyterian Home of Hawfields Inc
2502 S NC 119, Mebane, NC 27302
(919) 578-4701
Admin Max Kernedle; Marvin E Yount Jr, Exec Dir. *Dir of Nursing* Lamont Morrisey MD. *Medical Dir* Eugene Wade MD.
Licensure Intermediate care; Rest home; Independent living. *Beds* ICF 68; Rest home 48; Independent living 4. *Certified* Medicaid.
Owner Nonprofit organization/foundation.
Admissions Requirements Medical examination; Physician's request.
Staff Physicians 3 (pt); RNs 2 (ft), 1 (pt); LPNs 7 (ft), 5 (pt); Nurses' aides 22 (ft), 18 (pt); Physical therapists (contracted); Occupational therapists 1 (pt); Speech therapists 1 (pt); Activities coordinators 2 (ft); Dietitians 1 (pt); Ophthalmologists 1 (pt); Podiatrists 1 (pt).
Affiliation Presbyterian.
Facilities Dining room; Physical therapy room; Activities room; Crafts room; Laundry room; Barber/Beauty shop.
Activities Arts & crafts; Cards; Games; Reading groups; Prayer groups; Shopping trips; Pet therapy.

Mocksville

Autumn Care of Mocksville
PO Box 527, 1007 Howard St, Mocksville, NC 27028
(704) 634-3535, 634-1269 FAX
Admin Kenneth M Edwards. *Dir of Nursing* Darcille D Cosby. *Medical Dir* Dr George Kimberly.
Licensure Skilled care; Intermediate care; Home for aged. *Beds* SNF 35; ICF 42; Home for aged 8. *Private Pay Patients* 22%. *Certified* Medicaid; Medicare.
Owner Proprietary corp (Autumn Corp).
Admissions Requirements Minimum age 18; Medical examination; Physician's request.
Staff RNs 3 (ft), 1 (pt); LPNs 10 (ft), 2 (pt); Nurses' aides 33 (ft), 7 (pt); Recreational therapists 1 (ft); Dietitians 1 (pt).
Facilities Dining room; Physical therapy room; Activities room; Crafts room; Laundry room; Barber/Beauty shop.
Activities Arts & crafts; Games; Prayer groups; Dances/Social/Cultural gatherings; Intergenerational programs.

Monroe

Guardian Care of Monroe
PO Box 1189, 1212 Sunset Dr E, Monroe, NC 28110
(704) 283-8548, 289-6681 FAX
Admin Jane C Pendergrass. *Dir of Nursing* Mary Lou Ward. *Medical Dir* Dr B W Springs.
Licensure Skilled care; Intermediate care; Home for aged. *Beds* SNF 33; ICF 114; Home for aged 27. *Certified* Medicaid; Medicare.
Owner Proprietary corp (Hillhaven Corp).
Admissions Requirements Minimum age per state req to retirement sec; Medical examination; Physician's request.
Staff Physicians 14 (ft); RNs 3 (ft), 2 (pt); LPNs 13 (ft), 4 (pt); Nurses' aides 54 (ft), 4 (pt); Physical therapists (contracted); Speech therapists (contracted); Activities coordinators 2 (ft), 1 (pt); Dietitians 1 (pt); Podiatrists (contracted); Dentists (contracted).
Facilities Dining room; Physical therapy room; Activities room; Crafts room; Laundry room; Barber/Beauty shop.
Activities Arts & crafts; Games; Reading groups; Prayer groups; Movies; Shopping trips; Dances/Social/Cultural gatherings; Pet therapy.

Union Memorial Hospital—SNF/ICF
PO Box 5003, 600 Hospital Dr, Monroe, NC 28110
(704) 283-2111
Admin J Larry Bishop. *Dir of Nursing* Carol Williams RN.
Licensure Skilled care; Intermediate care; Alzheimer's care. *Beds* SNF 34; ICF 32. *Certified* Medicaid; Medicare.
Owner Nonprofit corp.
Admissions Requirements Medical examination.
Staff RNs 6 (ft), 1 (pt); LPNs 6 (ft), 2 (pt); Nurses' aides 29 (ft), 6 (pt); Physical therapists 1 (ft); Speech therapists; Activities coordinators 1 (ft); Dietitians 1 (ft); Social service 1 (ft); Ward secretaries 1 (ft).
Facilities Dining room; Physical therapy room; Activities room; Crafts room; Laundry room; Barber/Beauty shop.
Activities Arts & crafts; Games; Prayer groups; Movies; Exercise.

Mooresville

Brian Center Health & Retirement
752 E Center Ave, Mooresville, NC 28115
(704) 663-3448, 664-7463 FAX
Admin Patsy B Sherrill. *Dir of Nursing* Tess Gunther. *Medical Dir* William W Skeen MD.
Licensure Skilled care; Intermediate care; Home for aged. *Beds* SNF 55; ICF 76; Home for aged 20. *Certified* Medicaid; Medicare.
Owner Proprietary corp (Brian Center Management Corp).
Admissions Requirements Medical examination; Physician's request.
Staff RNs; LPNs; Nurses' aides; Physical therapists (contracted); Activities coordinators; Dietitians.
Facilities Dining room; Physical therapy room; Activities room; Laundry room; Barber/Beauty shop.
Activities Arts & crafts; Games; Prayer groups; I Make a Difference program.

Meridian Nursing Center—Mooresville
550 Glenwood Dr, Mooresville, NC 28115
(704) 664-7494
Admin Joseph Townsend.

Licensure Skilled care; Intermediate care; Home for Aged. *Beds* SNF 35; ICF 35; Home for Aged 30. *Certified* Medicaid; Medicare.
Owner Proprietary corp (Meridian Healthcare).

Morehead City

Harborview Health Care Center
812 Shepard St, Morehead City, NC 28557
(919) 726-6855
Admin Doris B Jernigan; Kaye R Jernigan, Asst Admin. *Dir of Nursing* Bonnie Higgins. *Medical Dir* William M Brady MD.
Licensure Skilled care; Intermediate care; Home for aged. *Beds* SNF 20; ICF 42; Home for aged 13. *Certified* Medicaid; Medicare.
Owner Privately owned.
Admissions Requirements Physician's request.
Staff RNs; LPNs; Nurses' aides; Recreational therapists; Activities coordinators; Dietitians.
Facilities Dining room; Activities room; Chapel; Crafts room; Laundry room; Barber/Beauty shop; Library.
Activities Arts & crafts; Cards; Games; Reading groups; Prayer groups; Movies; Shopping trips; Dances/Social/Cultural gatherings; Intergenerational programs; Pet therapy.

Morehead Nursing Center
Penny Ln, Morehead City, NC 28557
(919) 726-0031
Admin Beverly Jorgenson. *Dir of Nursing* Kathy Glussman RN. *Medical Dir* Dr Donald Reece.
Licensure Skilled care; Intermediate care. *Beds* SNF 31; ICF 61. *Certified* Medicaid; Medicare.
Owner Proprietary corp (Angell Care).
Admissions Requirements Medical examination; Physician's request.
Staff RNs 3 (ft), 1 (pt); LPNs 7 (ft), 5 (pt); Nurses' aides 32 (ft), 3 (pt); Physical therapists 1 (pt); Occupational therapists 1 (pt); Speech therapists 1 (pt); Activities coordinators 1 (ft); Dietitians 1 (ft).
Languages German.
Facilities Dining room; Physical therapy room; Activities room; Crafts room; Laundry room; Barber/Beauty shop.
Activities Arts & crafts; Cards; Games; Movies; Dances/Social/Cultural gatherings.

Morganton

Britthaven of Morganton
107 Magnolia Dr, Morganton, NC 28655
(704) 437-8760
Admin R P Carothers.
Licensure Skilled care; Intermediate care. *Beds* SNF 31; ICF 60. *Certified* Medicaid; Medicare.
Owner Proprietary corp (Britthaven Inc).

Broughton Hospital—Intermediate Care Facility
1000 S Sterling St, Morganton, NC 28655
(704) 433-2324
Admin Dr Arthur J Robarge. *Dir of Nursing* Juanita Long RN. *Medical Dir* Dr Ludwik Tramer.
Licensure Intermediate care. *Beds* ICF 50. *Certified* Medicaid.
Owner Publicly owned.
Admissions Requirements Psychiatric determination according to NC law.
Staff RNs 156 (ft); LPNs 54 (ft); Physical therapists 1 (ft); Recreational therapists 19 (ft); Occupational therapists 12 (ft); Speech therapists 2 (ft); Activities coordinators 1 (ft); Dietitians 4 (ft).
Facilities Dining room; Physical therapy room; Activities room; Chapel; Crafts room; Laundry room; Barber/Beauty shop; Library.

Foothills ICF/MR Group Home
309 E View St, Morganton, NC 28655
(704) 433-6488
Admin Janie Cloer.
Licensure Intermediate care; Intermediate care for mentally retarded. *Beds* 5. *Certified* Medicaid.

Meadowbrook Manor of Sparta
PO Box 207, Morganton, NC 28655
(919) 372-2441
Admin Nancy N Hipps.
Licensure Skilled care; Intermediate care; Home for Aged. *Beds* SNF 20; ICF 40; Home for Aged 32. *Certified* Medicaid; Medicare.

Pinnacle Care Center
109 Foothills Dr, Morganton, NC 28655
(704) 433-7160
Admin Amy G Hughes.
Medical Dir Dr Luther Clontz.
Licensure Skilled care; Intermediate care. *Beds* SNF 70; ICF 50. *Certified* Medicaid; Medicare; VA.
Owner Proprietary corp (Pinnacle Care Corp).
Admissions Requirements Minimum age 18.
Staff Physicians 1 (pt); RNs 5 (ft), 1 (pt); LPNs 14 (ft), 4 (pt); Nurses' aides 45 (ft), 9 (pt); Physical therapists 1 (ft), 1 (pt); Recreational therapists 1 (pt); Occupational therapists 1 (pt); Speech therapists 1 (pt); Activities coordinators 2 (ft); Dietitians 1 (pt); Ophthalmologists 1 (pt); Rehabilitation aides 2 (ft).
Facilities Dining room; Physical therapy room; Activities room; Crafts room; Laundry room; Barber/Beauty shop.
Activities Arts & crafts; Cards; Games; Reading groups; Prayer groups; Movies; Shopping trips; Dances/Social/Cultural gatherings.

Western Carolina Center
200 Enola Rd, Morganton, NC 28655
(704) 433-2711
Admin J Iverson Riddle. *Dir of Nursing* Helen C Wilson RN. *Medical Dir* Luther H Clontz MD.
Licensure Intermediate care for mentally retarded. *Beds* ICF/MR 498. *Certified* Medicaid.
Owner Publicly owned.
Staff Physicians 7 (ft), 1 (pt); RNs 38 (ft); LPNs 31 (ft), 3 (pt); Physical therapists 2 (ft); Recreational therapists 10 (ft); Occupational therapists 6 (ft); Speech therapists 9 (ft); Dietitians 3 (ft); Podiatrists 2 (ft).
Facilities Dining room; Physical therapy room; Chapel; Crafts room; Laundry room; Barber/Beauty shop; Library.

Mount Airy

Northern Surry Skilled Nursing Facility
PO Box 1101, Mount Airy, NC 27030
(919) 789-9541
Admin John K Lockhart FACHE. *Dir of Nursing* Barbara B Starling RN.
Licensure Skilled care. *Beds* SNF 13. *Private Pay Patients* 10%. *Certified* Medicaid; Medicare.
Owner Publicly owned.
Admissions Requirements Medical examination; Physician's request.
Facilities Dining room; Physical therapy room; Activities room; Chapel; Crafts room; Laundry room; Library.
Activities Arts & crafts; Cards; Games; Reading groups; Prayer groups; Movies; Pet therapy.

Surry Community Nursing Center
942 Allred Mill Rd, Mount Airy, NC 27030
(919) 789-5076

Admin Rebecca M Phillips. *Dir of Nursing* Wanda Jackson. *Medical Dir* J Gillum Burke MD.
Licensure Skilled care; Intermediate care. *Beds* SNF 60; ICF 60. *Certified* Medicaid; Medicare.
Owner Proprietary corp (Beverly Enterprises).
Admissions Requirements Minimum age 18; Medical examination; Physician's request.
Staff RNs 1 (ft), 9 (pt); LPNs 4 (ft), 9 (pt); Nurses' aides 30 (ft), 6 (pt); Physical therapists 1 (ft); Recreational therapists 1 (ft); Speech therapists 1 (ft); Activities coordinators 1 (ft); Dietitians 1 (ft); Ophthalmologists 1 (ft); Podiatrists 1 (ft); Dentists 1 (ft).
Facilities Dining room; Physical therapy room; Activities room; Crafts room; Laundry room; Barber/Beauty shop; Library.
Activities Arts & crafts; Cards; Games; Reading groups; Prayer groups; Movies; Shopping trips; Dances/Social/Cultural gatherings.

Mount Olive

Medical Park Nursing Center
PO Box 569, Smith Chapel Rd, Mount Olive, NC 28365
(919) 658-9522
Admin M J Goff NHA. *Dir of Nursing* Marie Abrams RN. *Medical Dir* Hervy B Kornegay MD.
Licensure Skilled care; Intermediate care; Rest home. *Beds* SNF 75; ICF 75; Rest home 1. *Private Pay Patients* 25%. *Certified* Medicaid; Medicare.
Owner Proprietary corp (Angell Care Inc).
Admissions Requirements Minimum age 18; Medical examination; Physician's request.
Staff Physicians 5 (pt); RNs 4 (ft), 2 (pt); LPNs 10 (ft), 4 (pt); Nurses' aides 59 (ft), 16 (pt); Physical therapists 1 (ft); Recreational therapists 1 (pt); Speech therapists 1 (pt); Activities coordinators 1 (ft); Dietitians 1 (ft); Dentists 1 (pt).
Facilities Dining room; Physical therapy room; Activities room; Chapel; Crafts room; Laundry room; Barber/Beauty shop.
Activities Arts & crafts; Games; Reading groups; Prayer groups; Movies; Shopping trips.

Murphy

Murphy Medical Center
2002 US Hwy 64 E, Murphy, NC 28906
(704) 837-8161, 837-8161, ext 281 FAX
Admin Mike Stevenson; Toni Lovingood, Asst. *Dir of Nursing* Joan Archambault RN. *Medical Dir* Mike Wootten MD.
Licensure Skilled care; Intermediate care. *Beds* SNF 28; ICF 92. *Certified* Medicaid; Medicare.
Owner Nonprofit organization/foundation.
Admissions Requirements Physician's request.
Staff Physicians 17 (ft); Physical therapists 1 (ft); Activities coordinators 1 (ft); Dietitians 1 (ft); Ophthalmologists 1 (ft).
Facilities Dining room; Physical therapy room; Activities room; Chapel; Crafts room; Laundry room; Barber/Beauty shop.
Activities Arts & crafts; Games; Reading groups; Prayer groups; Movies; Shopping trips; Picnics; Outdoor activities.

Nags Head

Britthaven of Outer Banks
430 W Health Center Dr, Nags Head, NC 27959
(919) 441-3116
Admin Richard L Blackmon. *Dir of Nursing* Deborah Porter. *Medical Dir* Keith Carmack.

Licensure Skilled care; Intermediate care; Home for aged. *Beds* SNF 32; ICF 64; Home for aged 24. *Private Pay Patients* 20%. *Certified* Medicaid; Medicare.
Owner Proprietary corp (Britthaven Inc).
Admissions Requirements Medical examination; Physician's request.
Staff Physicians 1 (pt); RNs; LPNs; Nurses' aides; Physical therapists 1 (pt); Recreational therapists 1 (ft); Speech therapists 1 (pt); Activities coordinators 1 (ft); Dietitians 1 (pt); Podiatrists 1 (pt).
Facilities Dining room; Physical therapy room; Activities room; Laundry room; Barber/Beauty shop.
Activities Arts & crafts; Cards; Games; Reading groups; Prayer groups; Movies; Shopping trips; Dances/Social/Cultural gatherings; Intergenerational programs; Pet therapy.

Nebo

McDowell Nursing Center
Rte 3 Box 270, Nebo, NC 28761
(704) 652-3032
Admin Juanita C Fickling.
Licensure Skilled care; Intermediate care. *Beds* SNF 34; ICF 66. *Certified* Medicaid; Medicare.
Staff Physicians 2 (pt); RNs 5 (ft), 1 (pt); LPNs 9 (ft), 1 (pt); Nurses' aides 43 (ft); Physical therapists 1 (pt); Activities coordinators 2 (ft); Dietitians 1 (pt); Podiatrists 1 (pt); Dentists 1 (pt).
Facilities Dining room; Activities room; Crafts room; Laundry room; Barber/Beauty shop.
Activities Arts & crafts; Cards; Games; Reading groups; Prayer groups; Movies; Shopping trips; Dances/Social/Cultural gatherings.

New Bern

Britthaven of New Bern
2600 Old Cherry Point Rd, New Bern, NC 28560
(919) 637-4730, 637-9678 FAX
Admin Frances Hall. *Dir of Nursing* Lillian Helms RN. *Medical Dir* E Rodney Hornbake MD.
Licensure Skilled care; Intermediate care; Home for aged; Alzheimer's care. *Beds* Swing beds SNF/ICF 60; Home for aged 13; Alzheimer's care 30. *Private Pay Patients* 40%. *Certified* Medicaid; Medicare; VA.
Owner Proprietary corp (Britthaven Inc).
Admissions Requirements Minimum age 18; Medical examination.
Staff RNs 3 (ft), 5 (pt); LPNs 13 (ft), 7 (pt); Nurses' aides 52 (ft), 6 (pt); Physical therapists; Activities coordinators 2 (ft); Dietitians.
Facilities Dining room; Activities room; Laundry room; Barber/Beauty shop; 2 patios.
Activities Arts & crafts; Games; Reading groups; Prayer groups; Movies; Shopping trips; Dances/Social/Cultural gatherings; Intergenerational programs; Pet therapy; Music; Sing-alongs; Church.

Guardian Care of New Bern
836 Hospital Dr, New Bern, NC 28560
(919) 638-6001
Admin Jean M Corley.
Licensure Intermediate care. *Beds* ICF 116. *Certified* Medicaid.
Owner Proprietary corp (Hillhaven Corp).

Howell's Child Care Center Inc (Riverbend)
PO Box 2159, New Bern, NC 28561
(919) 638-6519
Admin Joseph A Howell.
Medical Dir Dr Ron May.

Licensure Intermediate care for mentally retarded. *Beds* 125. *Certified* Medicaid.
Owner Nonprofit corp.
Admissions Requirements Minimum age Birth.
Staff Physicians 1 (ft), 4 (pt); RNs; Nurses' aides 157 (ft); Physical therapists 1 (ft); Recreational therapists 1 (ft); Occupational therapists 1 (ft); Speech therapists 1 (ft); Activities coordinators 1 (ft); Dietitians 1 (ft).
Facilities Dining room; Physical therapy room; Activities room; Chapel; Crafts room; Laundry room; Barber/Beauty shop; Classrooms; Gymnasium; Swimming pool; Water therapy room.
Activities Arts & crafts; Cards; Games; Movies; Shopping trips; Dances/Social/Cultural gatherings.

Newton

J W Abernethy Center—United Church Retirement Homes Inc
100 Leonard Ave, Newton, NC 28658
(704) 464-8260
Admin Rev Van D Grimes. *Dir of Nursing* W Larry Sink. *Medical Dir* Dr William Long.
Licensure Skilled care; Intermediate care; Home for aged; Independent living. *Beds* SNF 31; ICF 67; Home for aged 33; Independent living 90. *Certified* Medicaid; Medicare.
Owner Nonprofit corp.
Admissions Requirements Minimum age 62; Medical examination.
Staff Physicians 4 (pt); RNs 7 (ft), 3 (pt); LPNs 10 (ft), 3 (pt); Nurses' aides 32 (ft), 13 (pt); Physical therapists 1 (ft); Recreational therapists 1 (ft); Activities coordinators 1 (ft); Dietitians 1 (ft).
Affiliation Church of Christ.
Facilities Dining room; Physical therapy room; Activities room; Chapel; Crafts room; Laundry room; Barber/Beauty shop; Library.
Activities Arts & crafts; Cards; Games; Reading groups; Prayer groups; Movies; Shopping trips; Dances/Social/Cultural gatherings; Personalized activities & programs.

Oxford

Americas Health Care of Oxford
Prospect Ave, Oxford, NC 27565
(919) 693-1531
Admin Ron Burrell.
Medical Dir Joy W Moss.
Licensure Skilled care; Intermediate care; Home for aged. *Beds* SNF 20; ICF 140; Home for aged 20. *Certified* Medicaid; Medicare.
Owner Privately owned.
Admissions Requirements Medical examination.
Staff RNs 1 (ft); LPNs 9 (ft), 4 (pt); Nurses' aides 42 (ft); Activities coordinators 1 (ft); Dietitians 1 (ft).
Facilities Dining room; Physical therapy room; Activities room; Crafts room; Laundry room; Barber/Beauty shop.
Activities Arts & crafts; Cards; Games; Reading groups; Prayer groups; Movies; Dances/Social/Cultural gatherings; Music.

Granville County Group Home
Rte 3 Box 193, Oxford, NC 27565
(919) 693-4610
Admin Ruth E Gierisch.
Licensure Intermediate care for mentally retarded. *Beds* 5. *Certified* Medicaid.

Pinehurst

Manor Care of Pinehurst
PO Box 1667, Hwy 211 & Rattlesnake Tr, Pinehurst, NC 28374
(919) 295-1781
Admin Jacqueline R Rio. *Dir of Nursing* Willavene Bradham RN. *Medical Dir* Ward Patrick MD.
Licensure Skilled care; Intermediate care. *Beds* SNF 59; ICF 61. *Certified* Medicaid; Medicare; VA.
Owner Proprietary corp (Manor Care Inc).
Admissions Requirements Minimum age 18; Medical examination; Physician's request.
Staff Physicians 1 (pt); RNs 7 (ft), 4 (pt); LPNs 9 (ft), 4 (pt); Nurses' aides 35 (ft), 11 (pt); Physical therapists 1 (ft); Recreational therapists 1 (ft); Activities coordinators 1 (ft); Dietitians 1 (ft); Chaplains 1 (pt).
Facilities Dining room; Physical therapy room; Activities room; Chapel; Crafts room; Laundry room; Barber/Beauty shop.
Activities Arts & crafts; Cards; Games; Reading groups; Prayer groups; Movies; Shopping trips; Dances/Social/Cultural gatherings.

Pinehurst Nursing Center
PO Box 1179, Hwy 5 S, Pinehurst, NC 28374
(919) 295-6158
Admin David S Fralin.
Medical Dir Dr F Owens.
Licensure Intermediate care; Home for aged. *Beds* ICF 64; Home for aged 17. *Certified* Medicaid.
Staff RNs 1 (ft); LPNs 5 (ft), 6 (pt); Nurses' aides 25 (ft), 4 (pt); Activities coordinators 1 (ft).
Facilities Dining room; Activities room; Chapel; Laundry room; Barber/Beauty shop; Library.
Activities Arts & crafts; Cards; Games; Movies.

Pleasant Garden

Clapp's Nursing Center Inc
PO Box 249, 4558 Pleasant Garden Rd, Pleasant Garden, NC 27313
(919) 674-2252
Admin Riley W Clapp. *Dir of Nursing* Tonie Bryant. *Medical Dir* Dr Wilson O Elkins.
Licensure Skilled care; Home for aged. *Beds* SNF 28; Home for aged 19. *Private Pay Patients* 80%. *Certified* Medicaid; Medicare.
Owner Proprietary corp.
Admissions Requirements Minimum age 18; Medical examination; Physician's request.
Staff Physicians 1 (pt); RNs 4 (ft), 4 (pt); LPNs 3 (ft), 2 (pt); Nurses' aides 18 (ft), 6 (pt); Physical therapists 1 (pt); Speech therapists 1 (pt); Activities coordinators 1 (ft); Dietitians 1 (pt).
Facilities Dining room; Activities room; Chapel; Crafts room; Laundry room; Barber/Beauty shop; Library.
Activities Arts & crafts; Cards; Games; Reading groups; Prayer groups; Movies; Dances/Social/Cultural gatherings; Pet therapy.

Plymouth

Plumblee Nursing Center
Hwy 64, 7 Medical Plaza, Plymouth, NC 27962
(919) 793-2100
Admin Billy Cuthrell.
Licensure Skilled care; Intermediate care; Home for Aged. *Beds* SNF 23; ICF 41; Home for Aged 26. *Certified* Medicaid; Medicare.

Raeford

Autumn Care of Raeford
PO Box 10, 1206 N Fulton St, Raeford, NC 28376-0010
(919) 875-4280, 875-5375 FAX
Admin Michael A Ianucilli. *Dir of Nursing* Denise Conn RN. *Medical Dir* W Ward Patrick MD.
Licensure Skilled care; Intermediate care; Home for aged. *Beds* SNF 24; ICF 38; Home for the aged 6. *Private Pay Patients* 14%. *Certified* Medicaid; Medicare.
Owner Proprietary corp (Autumn Corp).
Admissions Requirements Minimum age 18; Medical examination; Physician's request.
Staff RNs 2 (ft), 4 (pt); LPNs 6 (ft), 6 (pt); Nurses' aides 24 (ft), 5 (pt); Activities coordinators 1 (ft).
Facilities Dining room; Physical therapy room; Activities room; Laundry room; Barber/Beauty shop; Library; Country store.
Activities Arts & crafts; Cards; Games; Reading groups; Prayer groups; Movies; Dances/Social/Cultural gatherings; Intergenerational programs; GED instruction.

Raleigh

Blue Ridge Manor
3830 Blue Ridge Rd, Raleigh, NC 27612
(919) 781-4900
Admin Rachel A Brantley.
Licensure Skilled care; Intermediate care. *Beds* SNF 40; ICF 98. *Certified* Medicaid; Medicare.

Brian Center Nursing Care—Raleigh
3000 Holston Ln, Raleigh, NC 27610
(919) 828-3904
Admin Peter D Falk.
Licensure Skilled care; Intermediate care. *Beds* SNF 84; ICF 41. *Certified* Medicaid; Medicare.
Owner Proprietary corp (Brian Center Management Corp).

Britthaven of Raleigh
3609 Bond St, Raleigh, NC 27604
(919) 231-8113, 833-0543 FAX
Admin Joe Doby. *Dir of Nursing* Cheryl Leibowitz. *Medical Dir* Dr Joseph Mangano.
Licensure Skilled care; Home for aged. *Beds* SNF 94; ICF 26; Home for aged 6. *Certified* Medicaid; Medicare.
Owner Proprietary corp (Britthaven Inc).
Facilities Dining room; Physical therapy room; Activities room; Crafts room; Laundry room; Barber/Beauty shop.

Glenwood Hills Intermediate Care Facility
3910 Blue Ridge Rd, Raleigh, NC 27612
(919) 787-4747
Admin Rachel Brantley.
Licensure Intermediate care. *Beds* 30. *Certified* Medicaid.

Hillhaven Convalescent Center
616 Wade Ave, Raleigh, NC 27605
(919) 828-6251
Admin Dennis Redmond. *Dir of Nursing* Sallie Rascoe RN.
Licensure Skilled care; Intermediate care; Alzheimer's care. *Beds* SNF 116; ICF 58. *Certified* Medicaid; Medicare.
Owner Proprietary corp (Hillhaven Corp).
Staff RNs 9 (ft), 17 (pt); LPNs 8 (ft), 14 (pt); Nurses' aides 59 (ft), 6 (pt); Physical therapists 1 (ft); Occupational therapists 1 (ft); Speech therapists 1 (ft); Activities coordinators 2 (ft); Dietitians 2 (ft).
Facilities Dining room; Physical therapy room; Activities room; Crafts room; Laundry room; Barber/Beauty shop.

Activities Arts & crafts; Cards; Games; Reading groups; Prayer groups; Movies; Shopping trips; Dances/Social/Cultural gatherings.

Hillhaven Sunnybrook Convalescent Center
25 Sunnybrook Rd, Raleigh, NC 27610
(919) 828-0747
Admin Linda Roberts.
Licensure Skilled care; Intermediate care. *Beds* SNF 51; ICF 75. *Certified* Medicaid; Medicare.
Owner Proprietary corp (Hillhaven Corp).

Mayview Convalescent Center
513 E Whitaker Mill Rd, Raleigh, NC 27608
(919) 828-2348
Admin Travis H Tomlinson Jr.
Medical Dir Dr James S Parsons.
Licensure Skilled care. *Beds* SNF 139. *Certified* Medicaid; Medicare.
Admissions Requirements Physician's request.
Facilities Dining room; Physical therapy room; Activities room; Crafts room; Laundry room; Barber/Beauty shop.
Activities Arts & crafts; Cards; Games; Reading groups; Prayer groups; Movies; Dances/Social/Cultural gatherings.

Stewart Health Center
1500 Sawmill Rd, Raleigh, NC 27615
(919) 848-7000
Admin Kyle W Dilday. *Dir of Nursing* Louise Mauney RN. *Medical Dir* Dr Wells Edmundson.
Licensure Skilled care; Intermediate care; Home for aged; Alzheimer's care. *Beds* SNF 36; ICF 36; Home for aged 81.
Owner Nonprofit corp.
Admissions Requirements Minimum age 18; Medical examination; Physician's request.
Staff Physicians 2 (pt); RNs 14 (ft), 6 (pt); LPNs 26 (ft), 11 (pt); Nurses' aides 58 (ft), 21 (pt); Physical therapists 1 (ft), 2 (pt); Reality therapists 1 (ft); Recreational therapists 1 (ft); Occupational therapists 1 (pt); Speech therapists 1 (pt); Activities coordinators 1 (ft); Dietitians 1 (ft); Ophthalmologists 1 (pt); Podiatrists 1 (pt); Dentists 1 (pt).
Facilities Dining room; Physical therapy room; Activities room; Chapel; Crafts room; Laundry room; Barber/Beauty shop; Library; Pool rooms; Swimming pool.
Activities Arts & crafts; Cards; Games; Reading groups; Prayer groups; Movies; Shopping trips; Dances/Social/Cultural gatherings.

Reidsville

Maplewood Nursing Center
543 Maple Ave, Reidsville, NC 27320
(919) 342-1382
Admin Susan E Meyer. *Dir of Nursing* Linda Smith. *Medical Dir* Dr George Lothian.
Licensure Skilled care; Intermediate care. *Beds* SNF 44; ICF 66. *Certified* Medicaid; Medicare.
Owner Proprietary corp (Beverly Enterprises).
Admissions Requirements Minimum age 18; Medical examination; Physician's request.
Staff Physicians 1 (pt); RNs 8 (ft), 1 (pt); LPNs 4 (ft); Nurses' aides 40 (ft), 20 (pt); Physical therapists 1 (pt); Speech therapists 1 (pt); Activities coordinators 2 (ft); Dietitians 1 (pt); Ophthalmologists 1 (pt); Podiatrists 1 (pt); Dentists 1 (pt).
Facilities Dining room; Physical therapy room; Activities room; Crafts room; Laundry room; Barber/Beauty shop.
Activities Arts & crafts; Reading groups; Prayer groups; Shopping trips; Dances/Social/Cultural gatherings.

Annie Penn Memorial Hospital—Skilled Nursing Facility
618 S Main St, Reidsville, NC 27320
(919) 349-8461
Admin Susan F Wheless.
Licensure Skilled care. *Beds* SNF 42. *Certified* Medicaid; Medicare.

Rich Square

Roanoke Valley Nursing Home
N Main St, Box 560, Rich Square, NC 27869
(919) 539-4161
Admin James T Johnson. *Dir of Nursing* Peggy A Futrell.
Licensure Intermediate care; Retirement. *Beds* ICF 69. *Certified* Medicaid.
Owner Privately owned.
Admissions Requirements Medical examination.
Staff RNs 2 (ft); LPNs 5 (ft); Nurses' aides 29 (ft); Activities coordinators 1 (ft); Dietitians 1 (ft).
Facilities Dining room; Physical therapy room; Activities room; Chapel; Crafts room; Laundry room; Barber/Beauty shop.
Activities Arts & crafts; Cards; Games; Prayer groups; Dances/Social/Cultural gatherings.

Roanoke Rapids

Guardian Care of Roanoke Rapids
305 14th St, Roanoke Rapids, NC 27870
(919) 537-6181
Admin Joan D Garvey. *Dir of Nursing* Judy Glisan. *Medical Dir* Dr William Brown.
Licensure Intermediate care. *Beds* ICF 110. *Certified* Medicaid.
Owner Proprietary corp (Hillhaven Corp).
Admissions Requirements Medical examination.
Staff RNs 5 (ft), 2 (pt); LPNs 8 (ft), 3 (pt); Nurses' aides 40 (ft), 10 (pt); Recreational therapists 1 (ft); Activities coordinators 1 (ft); Dietitians 1 (ft).
Facilities Dining room; Activities room; Chapel; Crafts room; Laundry room; Barber/Beauty shop.
Activities Arts & crafts; Cards; Games; Reading groups; Prayer groups; Movies; Shopping trips; Dances/Social/Cultural gatherings.

Rockingham

Country Villa
PO Box 1237, 804 Long Dr, Rockingham, NC 28379
(919) 997-4493, 997-4050 FAX
Admin Cynthia R Tolman. *Dir of Nursing* Mary B Ratliff RN. *Medical Dir* Dr Hugh Queen.
Licensure Intermediate care. *Beds* ICF 120. *Private Pay Patients* 10%. *Certified* Medicaid.
Owner Proprietary corp (Hillhaven Corp).
Admissions Requirements Medical examination; Physician's request.
Staff Physicians; RNs 3 (ft); LPNs 10 (ft), 4 (pt); Nurses' aides 42 (ft); Activities coordinators 2 (ft); Ophthalmologists (consultant); Podiatrists (consultant); Dentists (consultant); Psychologists (consultant).
Facilities Dining room; Laundry room; Barber/Beauty shop.
Activities Arts & crafts; Cards; Games; Reading groups; Prayer groups; Movies; Shopping trips; Dances/Social/Cultural gatherings; Intergenerational programs.

Richmond Memorial Hospital
925 Long Dr, Rockingham, NC 28379
(919) 997-2561
Admin James M Iseman.
Licensure Skilled care. *Beds* SNF 45.

Rocky Mount

Carrolton of Nash County Inc
PO Box 8495, 3195 Hunter Hill Rd, Rocky Mount, NC 27804
(919) 443-0867
Admin Robert Vernon Jr.
Licensure Skilled care; Intermediate care; Home for aged. *Beds* SNF 50; ICF 31; Home for aged 9. *Certified* Medicaid; Medicare.

Guardian Care of Rocky Mt
160 Winstead Ave, Rocky Mount, NC 27804
(919) 443-7666
Admin Louis Milite.
Medical Dir Lewis Thorp MD.
Licensure Skilled care; Intermediate care. *Beds* SNF 20; ICF 98. *Certified* Medicaid; Medicare.
Owner Proprietary corp (Hillhaven Corp).
Admissions Requirements Minimum age 18; Medical examination; Physician's request.
Staff RNs; LPNs; Nurses' aides; Recreational therapists; Speech therapists; Activities coordinators.
Facilities Dining room; Activities room; Chapel; Crafts room; Laundry room; Barber/Beauty shop.
Activities Arts & crafts; Cards; Games; Reading groups; Prayer groups; Movies; Dances/Social/Cultural gatherings.

Westgate Nursing Center
2221 Raleigh Rd, Rocky Mount, NC 27803
(919) 442-4156
Admin Carrol S Roberson.
Licensure Skilled care; Intermediate care; Home for aged. *Beds* SNF 40; ICF 60; Home for aged 15. *Certified* Medicaid; Medicare.

Roxboro

Person County Memorial Hospital—SNF
Reginald L Harris Annex, 615 Ridge Rd, Roxboro, NC 27573
(919) 599-2121
Admin S Grant Boone Jr.
Licensure Skilled care. *Beds* SNF 23. *Certified* Medicaid; Medicare.

Roxboro Nursing Center
901 Ridge Rd, Roxboro, NC 27573
(919) 599-0106
Admin Kendall S Oliver. *Dir of Nursing* Vivian Barnes. *Medical Dir* Dr Thomas D Long.
Licensure Skilled care; Intermediate care; Rest home. *Beds* SNF 20; ICF 107; Rest home 5. *Private Pay Patients* 15%. *Certified* Medicaid; Medicare.
Owner Proprietary corp (Triad Medical Services Inc).
Admissions Requirements Minimum age 18; Medical examination; Physician's request.
Staff Physicians 6 (pt); RNs 1 (ft), 4 (pt); LPNs 9 (ft), 8 (pt); Nurses' aides 45 (ft), 10 (pt); Physical therapists (contracted); Reality therapists 2 (ft); Recreational therapists 2 (ft); Occupational therapists (contracted); Speech therapists (contracted); Activities coordinators 1 (ft); Dietitians (consultant); Ophthalmologists (consultant); Podiatrists (consultant); Audiologists (contracted).
Facilities Dining room; Physical therapy room; Activities room; Crafts room; Laundry room; Barber/Beauty shop; Library.
Activities Arts & crafts; Cards; Games; Reading groups; Prayer groups; Movies; Shopping trips; Dances/Social/Cultural gatherings; Pet therapy.

Rutherfordton

Rutherford County Convalescent Center
Rte 2 Box 39-A, Oscar Justice Rd, Rutherfordton, NC 28139
(704) 286-9001, 286-9002 FAX
Admin Brenda S Price. *Dir of Nursing* Barbara Perry RN. *Medical Dir* Landis P Mitchell MD.
Licensure Skilled care; Alzheimer's care. *Beds* SNF 50. *Private Pay Patients* 20%. *Certified* Medicaid; Medicare.
Owner Proprietary corp (White Oak Manor Inc).
Admissions Requirements Medical examination; Physician's request.
Staff Physicians 1 (ft); RNs 4 (ft); LPNs 7 (ft); Nurses' aides 20 (ft), 4 (pt); Physical therapists 1 (pt); Speech therapists 1 (ft); Activities coordinators 1 (ft), 1 (pt); Dietitians 1 (pt); Podiatrists 1 (pt).
Facilities Dining room; Activities room; Crafts room; Laundry room; Barber/Beauty shop.
Activities Arts & crafts; Cards; Games; Reading groups; Prayer groups; Movies; Shopping trips; Pet therapy; Family nights.

Woodlands Skilled Nursing Center
125 Tryon Rd, Rutherfordton, NC 28139
(704) 287-2169, 286-3873 FAX
Admin Sally A Skaggs. *Dir of Nursing* Jane Wright. *Medical Dir* Bobby F England; Joe B Godfrey.
Licensure Skilled care; Intermediate care. *Beds* SNF 108; ICF 42. *Private Pay Patients* 20%. *Certified* Medicaid; Medicare.
Owner Nonprofit corp.
Admissions Requirements Medical examination; Physician's request.
Staff Physicians 2 (pt); RNs 9 (ft), 1 (pt); LPNs 12 (ft), 3 (pt); Nurses' aides 42 (ft), 32 (pt); Physical therapists 1 (ft), 1 (pt); Recreational therapists 1 (ft); Speech therapists 1 (pt); Activities coordinators 1 (ft); Dietitians 1 (pt); Ophthalmologists 1 (pt); Dentists 1 (pt).
Facilities Dining room; Physical therapy room; Activities room; Laundry room; Barber/Beauty shop; Dayrooms; Kitchen; Offices.
Activities Arts & crafts; Games; Reading groups; Prayer groups; Movies; Shopping trips; Dances/Social/Cultural gatherings; Pet therapy.

Salisbury

Autumn Care of Salisbury
PO Drawer 1789, 1505 Bringle Ferry Rd, Salisbury, NC 28145
(704) 637-5885
Admin Deborah A Sheffield.
Licensure Skilled care; Intermediate care; Home for Aged. *Beds* SNF 30; ICF 47; Home for Aged 20. *Certified* Medicaid; Medicare.

Brian Center Nursing Care—Salisbury
635 Statesville Blvd, Salisbury, NC 28144
(704) 633-7390
Admin Larry M Parrish.
Licensure Skilled care; Intermediate care. *Beds* SNF 116; ICF 69. *Certified* Medicaid; Medicare.
Owner Proprietary corp (Brian Center Management Corp).

JoLene's Nursing Home Inc
PO Box 2167, 615 W Innes St, Salisbury, NC 28144
(704) 633-2781
Admin Cherrathee Y Hager.
Licensure Skilled care; Home for aged. *Beds* SNF 41; Home for aged 25. *Certified* Medicaid; Medicare.

Lutheran Nursing Homes Inc—Salisbury Unit
820 Klumac Rd, Salisbury, NC 28144
(704) 637-3784
Admin William Beilfuss. *Dir of Nursing* Donna Stepanian RN. *Medical Dir* Cecil Farrington MD.
Licensure Skilled care; Intermediate care; Rest home. *Beds* SNF 60; ICF 25; Rest home 25. *Certified* Medicaid; Medicare.
Owner Nonprofit corp (NC Lutheran Homes).
Admissions Requirements Minimum age 60; Medical examination.
Staff RNs 10 (ft), 8 (pt); LPNs 9 (ft), 6 (pt); Nurses' aides; Physical therapists; Activities coordinators; Dietitians.
Affiliation Lutheran.
Facilities Dining room; Physical therapy room; Activities room; Chapel; Crafts room; Laundry room; Barber/Beauty shop; Library.
Activities Arts & crafts; Cards; Games; Reading groups; Prayer groups; Movies; Shopping trips; Dances/Social/Cultural gatherings; Church services; Bible study.

Meridian Nursing Center—Salisbury
710 Julian Rd, Salisbury, NC 28144
(704) 636-5812
Admin Jack Musker.
Licensure Skilled care; Intermediate care; Home for Aged. *Beds* SNF 50; ICF 50; Home for Aged 20. *Certified* Medicaid; Medicare.
Owner Proprietary corp (Meridian Healthcare).

Saluda

Autumn Care of Saluda
PO Box 488, Esseola Cir, Saluda, NC 28773
(704) 749-2261
Admin William D Adams. *Dir of Nursing* Ursi Ward. *Medical Dir* Brad Epstein.
Licensure Intermediate care. *Beds* ICF 59. *Certified* Medicaid.
Owner Proprietary corp (Autumn Corp).
Staff Physicians 3 (ft); RNs 2 (ft); LPNs 5 (ft); Nurses' aides 20 (ft), 5 (pt); Activities coordinators 1 (ft); Dietitians 1 (ft); Podiatrists 1 (pt).
Facilities Dining room; Activities room; Laundry room; Barber/Beauty shop.
Activities Arts & crafts; Cards; Games; Reading groups; Prayer groups; Dances/Social/Cultural gatherings; Pet therapy.

Sanford

Convalescent Center of Lee County Inc
PO Box 1346, 714 Westover Dr, Sanford, NC 27330
(919) 775-5404
Admin Ethel L McLean. *Dir of Nursing* Ethel McLean. *Medical Dir* John Dotterer.
Licensure Skilled care; Intermediate care. *Beds* SNF 26; ICF 74. *Certified* Medicaid; Medicare.
Owner Proprietary corp.
Staff RNs 2 (ft), 2 (pt); LPNs 10 (ft), 3 (pt); Nurses' aides 40 (ft), 11 (pt); Activities coordinators 2 (ft); Social workers 1 (ft).

Convalescent Center of Sanford Inc
4000 Farrell Rd, Sanford, NC 27330
(919) 775-7207
Admin Jean Godwin. *Dir of Nursing* Joyce F Smith RN. *Medical Dir* John F Blue MD.
Licensure Skilled care; Intermediate care. *Beds* SNF 55; ICF 46. *Certified* Medicaid; Medicare.
Owner Proprietary corp.
Admissions Requirements Minimum age 18; Medical examination.
Staff Physicians 8 (pt); RNs 3 (ft), 1 (pt); LPNs 11 (ft); Nurses' aides 43 (ft), 4 (pt); Physical therapists 1 (pt); Occupational

therapists 1 (pt); Speech therapists 1 (pt); Activities coordinators 2 (ft); Dietitians 1 (pt); Ophthalmologists 1 (pt); Dentists 1 (pt).
Facilities Dining room; Laundry room; Barber/Beauty shop.
Activities Arts & crafts; Games; Reading groups; Prayer groups; Movies; Shopping trips; Dances/Social/Cultural gatherings.

Scotland Neck

Guardian Care of Scotland Neck
1400 Junior High School Rd, Scotland Neck, NC 27874
(919) 826-5146
Admin Laura Lineback. *Dir of Nursing* Peggy Wright RN. *Medical Dir* Dr G V Bynum, consultant.
Licensure Intermediate care. *Beds* ICF 62. *Private Pay Patients* 9%. *Certified* Medicaid.
Owner Proprietary corp (Hillhaven Corp).
Admissions Requirements Minimum age 18; Medical examination; Physician's request.
Staff Physicians 1 (ft); RNs 1 (ft); LPNs 4 (ft), 4 (pt); Nurses' aides 20 (ft), 3 (pt); Physical therapists (contracted); Activities coordinators 1 (ft); Dietitians (contracted); Food service supervisors 1 (ft).
Facilities Dining room; Activities room; Laundry room; Barber/Beauty shop; Front porch with rockers.
Activities Arts & crafts; Cards; Games; Prayer groups; Movies; Dances/Social/Cultural gatherings.

Sea Level

Sailors' Snug Harbor
PO Box 150, Hwy 70 E, Sea Level, NC 28570
(919) 225-4411
Admin Thomas A Katsanis. *Dir of Nursing* Cathy Gilgo. *Medical Dir* Dr Roy Genz.
Licensure Skilled care; Intermediate care; Retirement. *Beds* SNF 22; ICF 20; Retirement 80. *Private Pay Patients* 100%.
Owner Nonprofit corp.
Admissions Requirements Medical examination.
Staff RNs 4 (ft), 1 (pt); LPNs 6 (ft); Nurses' aides 16 (ft), 3 (pt); Recreational therapists 4 (ft); Dietitians 1 (ft).
Facilities Dining room; Physical therapy room; Activities room; Chapel; Crafts room; Laundry room; Barber/Beauty shop; Library.
Activities Arts & crafts; Cards; Games; Prayer groups; Movies; Shopping trips; Dances/Social/Cultural gatherings.

Sea Level Hospital—SNF/ICF
Hwy 70 E, Sea Level, NC 28577
(919) 225-4611
Admin Beatrice Vaughan.
Medical Dir Jean D Long.
Licensure Skilled care; Intermediate care; Retirement. *Beds* SNF 24; ICF 30. *Certified* Medicaid; Medicare.
Owner Nonprofit corp.
Staff Physicians 3 (ft); RNs; LPNs; Nurses' aides; Physical therapists 1 (pt); Speech therapists 1 (pt); Activities coordinators 1 (ft); Dietitians 1 (pt).
Facilities Dining room; Physical therapy room; Activities room; Chapel; Crafts room; Laundry room; Barber/Beauty shop.
Activities Arts & crafts; Games; Prayer groups; Movies; Shopping trips; Dances/Social/Cultural gatherings.

Shelby

Cleveland Memorial Hospital—Skilled Nursing Facility
201 Grover St, Shelby, NC 28150
(704) 487-3000
Admin C Curtis Copenhaver.

Licensure Skilled care. *Beds* SNF 29. *Certified* Medicaid; Medicare.

Meadowbrook Manor of Shelby
PO Box 2287, 1101 N Morgan St, Shelby, NC 28150
(704) 482-5396
Admin John W Strawcutter. *Dir of Nursing* Deborah Wheeling. *Medical Dir* R A Jones MD.
Licensure Skilled care; Intermediate care. *Beds* SNF 35; ICF 65. *Private Pay Patients* 20%. *Certified* Medicaid; Medicare.
Owner Proprietary corp (Angell Group).
Admissions Requirements Medical examination; Physician's request.
Staff RNs; LPNs; Nurses' aides; Recreational therapists; Speech therapists; Activities coordinators.
Facilities Dining room; Physical therapy room; Activities room; Laundry room; Barber/Beauty shop.
Activities Arts & crafts; Cards; Games; Reading groups; Prayer groups; Dances/Social/Cultural gatherings.

Shelby Convalescent Center
PO Box 790, 401 N Morgan St, Shelby, NC 28150
(704) 482-7326
Admin Gwen H Butler.
Medical Dir Dr Richard Maybin.
Licensure Skilled care; Intermediate care. *Beds* SNF 60; ICF 100. *Certified* Medicaid; Medicare.
Admissions Requirements Medical examination; Physician's request.
Staff RNs 5 (ft), 1 (pt); LPNs 14 (ft), 5 (pt); Nurses' aides 52 (ft), 18 (pt); Physical therapists 1 (ft); Activities coordinators 1 (ft); Dietitians 1 (pt).
Facilities Dining room; Physical therapy room; Activities room; Crafts room; Laundry room; Barber/Beauty shop; Resident lounge.
Activities Arts & crafts; Games; Reading groups; Prayer groups; Movies; Shopping trips; Dances/Social/Cultural gatherings; Birthday parties; Exercise class.

Siler City

Meadowbrook Manor of Siler City
900 W Dolphin St, Siler City, NC 27344
(919) 663-3431
Admin Christine P Caviness. *Dir of Nursing* Linda Emerson RN. *Medical Dir* John Dykers MD.
Licensure Skilled care; Intermediate care; Home for aged. *Beds* SNF 98; ICF 52; Home for aged 10. *Certified* Medicaid; Medicare.
Owner Proprietary corp (Brian Center Management Corp).
Admissions Requirements Medical examination; Physician's request.
Staff Physicians 1 (pt); RNs 6 (ft), 4 (pt); LPNs 5 (ft), 6 (pt); Nurses' aides 44 (ft), 15 (pt); Physical therapists 2 (ft); Speech therapists 1 (pt); Activities coordinators 2 (ft); Dietitians 1 (pt); Social workers; Certified food service 2 (ft).
Facilities Dining room; Physical therapy room; Activities room; Chapel; Crafts room; Laundry room; Barber/Beauty shop; Library; Family room.
Activities Arts & crafts; Cards; Games; Reading groups; Prayer groups; Movies; Shopping trips; Dances/Social/Cultural gatherings; Education; Current events; Therapy groups; Resident council.

Smithfield

Britthaven of Smithfield
PO Box 2390, 411 Barbour Rd, Smithfield, NC 27577
(919) 934-6017

Admin Mike Kelly.
Licensure Skilled care; Intermediate care; Home for Aged. *Beds* SNF 64; ICF 56; Home for Aged 60. *Certified* Medicaid; Medicare.
Owner Proprietary corp (Britthaven Inc).

Johnston County Memorial Nursing Center Inc
PO Box 1940, 902 Berkshire Rd, Smithfield, NC 27577
(919) 934-3171
Admin David F Arnn. *Dir of Nursing* Dianne Shirley RN. *Medical Dir* Woodrow Batten MD.
Licensure Skilled care; Intermediate care. *Beds* SNF 84; ICF 36. *Private Pay Patients* 12%. *Certified* Medicaid; Medicare.
Owner Privately owned.
Admissions Requirements Medical examination; Physician's request.
Staff Physicians 12 (pt); RNs 7 (ft), 1 (pt); LPNs 13 (ft), 1 (pt); Nurses' aides; Physical therapists 1 (pt); Recreational therapists 1 (pt); Occupational therapists 1 (pt); Speech therapists 1 (pt); Activities coordinators; Dietitians 1 (pt).
Facilities Dining room; Physical therapy room; Activities room; Crafts room; Laundry room; Barber/Beauty shop.
Activities Arts & crafts; Cards; Games; Prayer groups; Movies.

Snow Hill

Britthaven of Snow Hill
PO Box 157, 1304 SE 2nd St, Snow Hill, NC 28580
(919) 747-8126, 747-8851 FAX
Admin Linda J Fields. *Dir of Nursing* Margaret Bryant. *Medical Dir* Dr Mark Dumas.
Licensure Intermediate care; Home for aged. *Beds* ICF 75; Home for aged 7. *Certified* Medicaid.
Owner Proprietary corp (Britthaven Inc).
Admissions Requirements Medical examination; Physician's request.
Staff RNs 1 (ft), 2 (pt); LPNs 4 (ft), 12 (pt); Nurses' aides 20 (ft), 10 (pt); Activities coordinators 1 (ft); Dietitians 1 (ft).
Facilities Dining room; Activities room; Laundry room; Barber/Beauty shop.
Activities Arts & crafts; Cards; Games; Reading groups; Prayer groups; Movies; Shopping trips; Dances/Social/Cultural gatherings; Pet therapy.

Southern Pines

Penick Memorial Home
PO Box 2001, E Rhode Island Ave Ext, Southern Pines, NC 28387
(919) 692-0300
Admin Philip S Brown. *Dir of Nursing* Sylvia F Andrews. *Medical Dir* Donald K Wallace.
Licensure Skilled care; Intermediate care; Residential care. *Beds* SNF 33; ICF 13; Residential care 175. *Private Pay Patients* 75%. *Certified* Medicaid; Medicare.
Owner Nonprofit corp.
Admissions Requirements Minimum age 60; Medical examination.
Staff Physicians 1 (pt); RNs 6 (ft), 2 (pt); LPNs 7 (ft), 3 (pt); Nurses' aides 30 (ft), 10 (pt); Physical therapists 1 (ft); Activities coordinators 1 (ft); Dietitians 1 (pt).
Facilities Dining room; Physical therapy room; Activities room; Chapel; Crafts room; Laundry room; Barber/Beauty shop; Library.
Activities Arts & crafts; Cards; Games; Reading groups; Prayer groups; Movies; Shopping trips; Dances/Social/Cultural gatherings.

St Joseph of the Pines Inc
590 Central Dr, Southern Pines, NC 28387
(919) 692-2212, 692-5323 FAX

Admin George Kecatos. *Dir of Nursing* Cathy Wright BSN. *Medical Dir* Donald Wallace MD.
Licensure Skilled care; Independent living; Adult day care. *Beds* SNF 86; Independent living 12. *Certified* Medicaid; Medicare.
Owner Nonprofit organization/foundation.
Admissions Requirements Minimum age 18.
Affiliation Roman Catholic.
Facilities Dining room; Activities room; Chapel; Barber/Beauty shop; Library.
Activities Arts & crafts; Games; Reading groups; Shopping trips; Pet therapy.

Southport

Ocean Trail Convalescent Home Inc
430 Fodale Ave, Southport, NC 28461
(919) 457-9581
Admin Sue Brown.
Medical Dir Dr Gene A Wallin.
Licensure Intermediate care; Home for aged. *Beds* ICF 64; Home for aged 42. *Certified* Medicaid.
Owner Privately owned.
Admissions Requirements Medical examination.
Staff Physicians 7 (ft); RNs 1 (pt); LPNs 8 (ft); Nurses' aides 30 (ft); Reality therapists 1 (ft); Recreational therapists 1 (ft); Dietitians 1 (ft).
Facilities Dining room; Activities room; Laundry room; Barber/Beauty shop.
Activities Arts & crafts; Cards; Games; Reading groups; Prayer groups; Movies; Shopping trips; Dances/Social/Cultural gatherings; Exercise classes; VCR; Activities for visual & hearing impaired available.

Spencer

Spencer Nursing Home
PO Box 5, 1404 S Salisbury Ave, Spencer, NC 28159
(704) 633-3892
Admin Patricia W Walton.
Licensure Skilled care; Intermediate care. *Beds* SNF 30; ICF 40. *Certified* Medicaid; Medicare.

Spruce Pines

Brian Center Health & Retirement—Spruce Pine
218 Laurel Creek Crt, Spruce Pines, NC 28777
(704) 765-7312
Admin Ted W Goins Jr.
Licensure Skilled care; Intermediate care; Home for Aged. *Beds* SNF 33; ICF 44; Home for Aged 40. *Certified* Medicaid; Medicare.

Stanley

Stanley Total Living Center Inc
514 Old Mount Holly Rd, Stanley, NC 28164
(704) 263-1986
Admin Barbara Rhyne.
Licensure Skilled care; Intermediate care; Home for Aged. *Beds* SNF 18; ICF 18; Home for Aged 24. *Certified* Medicaid; Medicare.

Statesville

Brian Center of Health & Retirement
520 Valley St, Statesville, NC 28677
(704) 873-0517
Admin Isaac Kuhn.
Licensure Skilled care; Intermediate care; Home for aged. *Beds* SNF 87; ICF 60; Home for aged 20. *Certified* Medicaid; Medicare.

Owner Proprietary corp (Brian Center Management Corp).

Iredell Memorial Hospital
PO Box 1400, Brookdale Dr & Harness Rd, Statesville, NC 28677
(919) 552-2206
Admin Arnold Nunnery.
Licensure Skilled care. *Beds* SNF 16.

Stokesdale

Countryside Manor
7700 US 158 E, Stokesdale, NC 27357
(919) 643-6301
Admin Cynthia (Cindy) L King. *Dir of Nursing* Sylvia Tyndall. *Medical Dir* Dr David M Kaplan.
Licensure Intermediate care; Retirement; Alzheimer's care. *Beds* ICF 60; Retirement 50. *Private Pay Patients* 48%. *Certified* Medicaid.
Owner Privately owned.
Admissions Requirements Medical examination.
Staff Physicians 2 (pt); RNs 3 (ft); LPNs 2 (ft), 3 (pt); Nurses' aides 18 (ft), 9 (pt); Physical therapists 1 (pt); Occupational therapists 1 (pt); Speech therapists 1 (pt); Activities coordinators 1 (ft); Ophthalmologists 1 (pt); Podiatrists 1 (pt); Audiologists 1 (pt).
Facilities Dining room; Activities room; Crafts room; Laundry room; Barber/Beauty shop; Library; Alzheimer's & dementia unit.
Activities Arts & crafts; Cards; Games; Prayer groups; Movies; Shopping trips; Dances/ Social/Cultural gatherings; Intergenerational programs; Pet therapy.

Sylva

Mt Trace Nursing Center
50 Mt Trace Rd, Sylva, NC 28779
(704) 586-9130, 586-4499 FAX
Admin Isaac S Coe. *Dir of Nursing* Martha Chovan. *Medical Dir* Frank Betchart MD.
Licensure Skilled care; Intermediate care. *Beds* SNF 30; ICF 30. *Private Pay Patients* 40%. *Certified* Medicaid; Medicare.
Owner Nonprofit organization/foundation.
Admissions Requirements Medical examination.
Facilities Dining room; Physical therapy room; Activities room; Chapel; Barber/ Beauty shop.
Activities Arts & crafts; Cards; Games; Reading groups; Prayer groups.

Skyland Care Center Inc
21 Skyland Dr, Sylva, NC 28779
(704) 586-8935
Admin James L Hayes.
Medical Dir E H Henning MD.
Licensure Intermediate care. *Beds* ICF 94. *Certified* Medicaid.
Admissions Requirements Minimum age 18.
Staff RNs 1 (ft); LPNs 9 (ft); Nurses' aides 22 (ft); Recreational therapists 1 (ft); Activities coordinators 1 (ft); Dietitians 1 (pt); Dentists 1 (pt).
Facilities Dining room; Activities room; Laundry room; Barber/Beauty shop.
Activities Arts & crafts; Games; Reading groups; Prayer groups; Movies; Shopping trips.

Tarboro

Albemarle
200 Trade St, Tarboro, NC 27886
(919) 823-2646
Admin Charles H Harrell. *Dir of Nursing* E Ayscue. *Medical Dir* Dr John Brooks.

Licensure Skilled care; Intermediate care; Retirement; Home for aged. *Beds* Swing beds SNF/ICF 30; Retirement apts 150; Home for aged 10. *Certified* Medicaid; Medicare.
Owner Nonprofit organization/foundation.
Admissions Requirements Minimum age 65; Medical examination; Physician's request.
Staff RNs; LPNs; Nurses' aides; Recreational therapists; Dietitians.
Facilities Dining room; Physical therapy room; Activities room; Chapel; Crafts room; Laundry room; Barber/Beauty shop; Library; Auditorium.
Activities Arts & crafts; Cards; Games; Reading groups; Movies; Shopping trips.

Beverly Health Care Center
PO Box 7008, 1000 Western Blvd, Tarboro, NC 27886
(919) 823-0401
Admin Effie Webb.
Medical Dir Dr L M Cutchin.
Licensure Skilled care; Intermediate care. *Beds* SNF 62; ICF 97. *Certified* Medicaid; Medicare.
Owner Proprietary corp (Mercy Health Initiatives).
Admissions Requirements Medical examination.
Staff Physicians 10 (ft); RNs 6 (ft), 1 (pt); LPNs 11 (ft), 5 (pt); Nurses' aides 56 (ft), 15 (pt); Physical therapists 1 (pt); Speech therapists 1 (pt); Activities coordinators 2 (ft); Dietitians 1 (ft); Ophthalmologists 1 (pt); Podiatrists 1 (pt); Dentists 1 (pt).
Facilities Dining room; Physical therapy room; Activities room; Chapel; Crafts room; Laundry room; Barber/Beauty shop.
Activities Arts & crafts; Cards; Games; Reading groups; Prayer groups; Movies; Shopping trips; Dances/Social/Cultural gatherings; Adult basic education class.

Westgate Nursing Center of Tarboro
PO Box 7035, 911 Western Blvd, Tarboro, NC 27886
(919) 823-2041, 823-4306 FAX
Admin C Saunders Roberson Jr. *Dir of Nursing* Helen Ezzelle RN.
Licensure Skilled care; Intermediate care; Home for aged. *Beds* SNF 60; ICF 58; Home for aged 10. *Private Pay Patients* 2%. *Certified* Medicaid.
Owner Proprietary corp (Carrolton Management Co).
Admissions Requirements Medical examination; Physician's request.
Facilities Dining room; Activities room; Crafts room; Laundry room; Barber/Beauty shop.
Activities Arts & crafts; Games; Prayer groups; Movies; Shopping trips.

Taylorsville

Emerald Health & Progressive Alzheimers Enhancement Center
PO Box 218, Hwy 16 S, Taylorsville, NC 28681
(704) 632-8146
Admin Sandra P Loftin.
Licensure Skilled care; Intermediate care. *Beds* SNF 63; ICF 60. *Certified* Medicaid; Medicare.

Thomasville

Britthaven of Davidson
706 Pineywood Rd, Thomasville, NC 27360
(919) 475-9116
Admin Su M James.
Medical Dir Dr Harold C Burchel.
Licensure Skilled care; Intermediate care. *Beds* SNF 60; ICF 52. *Certified* Medicaid; Medicare.
Owner Proprietary corp (Hillhaven Inc).

Admissions Requirements Medical
examination; Physician's request.
Staff Physicians 1 (pt); RNs 4 (ft), 5 (pt);
LPNs 6 (ft), 4 (pt); Nurses' aides 60 (ft);
Physical therapists 1 (ft); Speech therapists 1
(pt); Activities coordinators 1 (ft); Dietitians
1 (ft); Ophthalmologists 1 (pt); Podiatrists 1
(pt).
Facilities Dining room; Physical therapy
room; Activities room; Chapel; Crafts room;
Laundry room; Barber/Beauty shop.
Activities Arts & crafts; Cards; Games;
Reading groups; Prayer groups; Movies;
Dances/Social/Cultural gatherings.

Liberty House Nursing Home
1028 Blair St, Thomasville, NC 27360
(919) 472-7771
Admin Howard Staples. *Dir of Nursing*
Maldia Hart. *Medical Dir* Dr Thomas
Futrell.
Licensure Skilled care; Intermediate care. *Beds*
SNF 61; ICF 59. *Certified* Medicaid;
Medicare.
Owner Proprietary corp (Beverly Enterprises).
Admissions Requirements Minimum age 18;
Medical examination; Physician's request.
Facilities Dining room; Physical therapy
room; Activities room; Chapel; Crafts room;
Laundry room; Barber/Beauty shop.
Activities Arts & crafts; Cards; Games;
Reading groups; Prayer groups; Movies;
Shopping trips; Dances/Social/Cultural
gatherings.

Piedmont Retirement Center
100 Hedrick Dr, Thomasville, NC 27360
(919) 472-2017
Admin D Russell Myers Jr. *Dir of Nursing*
Judy M Harrelson RN. *Medical Dir* James E
Hunter MD.
Licensure Skilled care; Intermediate care for
mentally retarded; Retirement living. *Beds*
SNF 24; ICF/MR 72; Retirement living 84.
Private Pay Patients 100%.
Owner Nonprofit corp.
Admissions Requirements Minimum age 62;
Medical examination.
Staff RNs; LPNs; Nurses' aides; Activities
coordinators; Dietitians.
Affiliation United Church of Christ.
Facilities Dining room; Activities room;
Crafts room; Laundry room; Barber/Beauty
shop.
Activities Arts & crafts; Games; Prayer groups;
Movies; Shopping trips; Dances/Social/
Cultural gatherings; Intergenerational
programs; Pet therapy.

Troy

**Montgomery Memorial Hospital—Skilled
Nursing Facility**
520 Allen St, Troy, NC 27371
(919) 572-1301
Admin Edgar Hayworth.
Licensure Skilled care. *Beds* SNF 21. *Certified*
Medicaid; Medicare.

Tryon

White Oak Terrace
200 Oak St, Tryon, NC 28782
(704) 859-9161
Admin Doris G Cole.
Licensure Skilled care; Home for aged. *Beds*
SNF 60; Home for aged 30. *Certified*
Medicaid; Medicare.
Facilities Dining room; Physical therapy
room; Activities room; Crafts room; Laundry
room; Barber/Beauty shop.
Activities Arts & crafts; Cards; Games;
Reading groups; Prayer groups; Movies;
Shopping trips; Dances/Social/Cultural
gatherings.

Wadesboro

Anson County Hospital—SNF
500 Morven Rd, Wadesboro, NC 28170
(704) 694-5131
Admin Joseph R Tucker. *Dir of Nursing* Beth
Swink RN.
Licensure Skilled care. *Beds* SNF 45. *Certified*
Medicaid; Medicare.
Owner Publicly owned.
Admissions Requirements Medical
examination; Physician's request.
Staff Physicians; RNs; LPNs; Nurses' aides;
Physical therapists; Activities coordinators;
Dietitians.
Languages Spanish.
Facilities Dining room; Activities room;
Laundry room; Barber/Beauty shop.
Activities Arts & crafts; Cards; Games;
Reading groups; Prayer groups; Movies;
Dances/Social/Cultural gatherings.

Wadesboro Nursing Home Inc
PO Box 658, 2000 Country Club Rd,
Wadesboro, NC 28170
(704) 694-4106
Admin Violet U Lee. *Dir of Nursing* Elaine P
Cooke RN.
Licensure Intermediate care; Home for aged.
Beds ICF 66; Home for aged 53. *Certified*
Medicaid.
Owner Proprietary corp.
Admissions Requirements Medical
examination; Physician's request.
Staff RNs 1 (ft); LPNs 8 (ft), 1 (pt); Activities
coordinators 1 (ft); Dietitians 1 (pt).
Facilities Dining room; Activities room;
Laundry room; Barber/Beauty shop.
Activities Arts & crafts; Cards; Games;
Reading groups; Prayer groups; Shopping
trips; Dances/Social/Cultural gatherings.

Walnut Cove

Guardian Care of Walnut Cove
PO Box 158, 508 Windmill St, Walnut Cove,
NC 27052
(919) 591-4353
Admin Joan H Smith.
Medical Dir H W Hollingsworth MD.
Licensure Skilled care; Intermediate care;
Home for aged. *Beds* SNF 60; ICF 30;
Home for aged 14. *Certified* Medicaid;
Medicare.
Owner Proprietary corp (Hillhaven Corp).
Admissions Requirements Medical
examination.
Staff Physicians 3 (pt); RNs 4 (ft), 7 (pt);
LPNs 3 (ft), 3 (pt); Nurses' aides 20 (ft), 9
(pt); Physical therapists 1 (ft), 1 (pt);
Occupational therapists 1 (pt); Speech
therapists 1 (pt); Activities coordinators 1
(ft); Dietitians 1 (ft), 1 (pt); Podiatrists 1
(pt); Dentists 1 (pt).
Facilities Dining room; Physical therapy
room; Activities room; Chapel; Laundry
room; Barber/Beauty shop.
Activities Arts & crafts; Cards; Games;
Reading groups; Prayer groups; Movies;
Shopping trips; Dances/Social/Cultural
gatherings; Therapeutic activities relating to
exercise/strengthening.

Warrenton

Warren Hills Personal Care & Nursing Facility
PO Box 618, W Ridgeway St Extension,
Warrenton, NC 27589
(919) 257-2011
Admin Vicky Newman.
Licensure Skilled care; Intermediate care;
Home for Aged. *Beds* SNF 48; ICF 52;
Home for Aged 60. *Certified* Medicaid;
Medicare.

Warsaw

Meadowbrook Manor of Duplin
PO Box 667, Warsaw, NC 28398
(919) 293-3144, 293-3146 FAX
Admin Lydia McBride. *Dir of Nursing* Erna
Walker. *Medical Dir* Dr Kornegay.
Licensure Skilled care; Intermediate care;
Retirement. *Beds* SNF 10; ICF 40;
Retirement 60. *Private Pay Patients* 15%.
Certified Medicaid; Medicare.
Owner Proprietary corp (Angell Care Inc).
Admissions Requirements Medical
examination.
Staff RNs 1 (ft), 5 (pt); LPNs 4 (ft), 1 (pt);
Nurses' aides 28 (ft), 12 (pt); Physical
therapists 1 (pt); Recreational therapists 1
(ft), 1 (pt); Occupational therapists 1 (pt);
Speech therapists 1 (pt); Dietitians 1 (ft).
Facilities Dining room; Physical therapy
room; Activities room; Crafts room; Laundry
room; Barber/Beauty shop.
Activities Arts & crafts; Cards; Games;
Reading groups; Prayer groups; Movies;
Shopping trips; Dances/Social/Cultural
gatherings; Intergenerational programs; Pet
therapy; Community support.

Washington

Britthaven of Washington
120 Washington St, Washington, NC 27889
(919) 946-7141
Admin Dan Cotten.
Medical Dir Dr Frank Sheldon.
Licensure Skilled care. *Beds* SNF 60. *Certified*
Medicaid; Medicare.
Owner Proprietary corp (Britthaven Inc).
Admissions Requirements Medical
examination.
Staff Physicians 15 (pt); RNs 4 (ft), 3 (pt);
LPNs 9 (ft), 4 (pt); Nurses' aides 40 (ft), 8
(pt); Physical therapists 1 (pt); Speech
therapists 1 (pt); Activities coordinators 1
(ft); Dietitians 1 (pt); Podiatrists 1 (pt);
Dentists 1 (pt).
Facilities Dining room; Activities room;
Crafts room; Laundry room; Barber/Beauty
shop.
Activities Arts & crafts; Cards; Games;
Reading groups; Prayer groups; Movies;
Shopping trips; Dances/Social/Cultural
gatherings.

Ridgewood Manor Inc
PO Box 1868, 1604 Highland Dr, Washington,
NC 27889
(919) 946-9570
Admin Shirley Robinson.
Medical Dir Dr Ray G Silverthorne.
Licensure Skilled care; Intermediate care. *Beds*
SNF 96; ICF 24. *Certified* Medicaid;
Medicare.
Owner Proprietary corp.
Admissions Requirements Minimum age 21;
Medical examination; Physician's request.
Staff Physicians 2 (pt); RNs 14 (ft), 4 (pt);
LPNs 10 (ft), 5 (pt); Nurses' aides 80 (ft), 12
(pt); Physical therapists 1 (pt); Recreational
therapists 1 (ft); Speech therapists 1 (pt);
Activities coordinators 2 (pt); Dietitians 1
(ft), 1 (pt); Podiatrists 1 (pt).
Languages Spanish.
Facilities Dining room; Physical therapy
room; Activities room; Chapel; Crafts room;
Laundry room; Barber/Beauty shop; Library.
Activities Arts & crafts; Cards; Games;
Reading groups; Prayer groups; Movies;
Shopping trips; Dances/Social/Cultural
gatherings.

Waynesville

Autumn Care of Waynesville
PO Box 783, Timberlane Rd, Waynesville, NC
28786
(704) 456-7381

Admin Christine S Henson.
Medical Dir Dr James B Milling.
Licensure Skilled care. *Beds* SNF 56. *Certified* Medicaid; Medicare.
Owner Proprietary corp (Autumn Corp).
Admissions Requirements Medical examination; Physician's request.
Staff Physicians 5 (pt); RNs 4 (ft); LPNs 5 (ft), 3 (pt); Nurses' aides 15 (ft), 3 (pt); Physical therapists 1 (ft); Recreational therapists 1 (ft); Speech therapists 1 (pt); Activities coordinators 1 (ft); Dietitians 1 (ft), 1 (pt); Audiologists 1 (pt); Dentists 1 (pt).
Facilities Dining room; Activities room; Crafts room; Laundry room; Barber/Beauty shop.
Activities Arts & crafts; Games; Reading groups; Prayer groups; Movies; Dances/Social/Cultural gatherings.

Whiteville

Century Care Center Inc
PO Box 1217, 316 W Burkhead St, Whiteville, NC 28472
(919) 642-7139
Admin O Wade Avant Jr.
Medical Dir Dr F M Carroll.
Licensure Skilled care; Intermediate care. *Beds* SNF 32; ICF 74. *Certified* Medicaid; Medicare.
Admissions Requirements Minimum age 18.
Staff Physicians 1 (pt); RNs 10 (ft), 2 (pt); LPNs 6 (ft), 1 (pt); Nurses' aides 40 (ft), 2 (pt); Physical therapists 1 (pt); Speech therapists 1 (pt); Activities coordinators 1 (ft); Dietitians 1 (pt); Ophthalmologists 1 (pt); Dentists 1 (pt).

Wilkesboro

Britthaven of Wilkesboro Inc
1016 Fletcher St, Wilkesboro, NC 28697
(919) 667-9261
Admin R Philip Hill.
Licensure Skilled care; Intermediate care. *Beds* SNF 98; ICF 58. *Certified* Medicaid; Medicare.
Owner Proprietary corp (Britthaven Inc).
Admissions Requirements Medical examination.
Staff Physicians 5 (ft); RNs 4 (ft), 2 (pt); LPNs 9 (ft), 10 (pt); Nurses' aides 39 (ft), 30 (pt); Physical therapists 1 (ft); Speech therapists 1 (ft); Activities coordinators 2 (ft); Dietitians 1 (ft); Podiatrists 1 (pt); Dentists 1 (pt).
Facilities Dining room; Physical therapy room; Activities room; Laundry room; Barber/Beauty shop; Library.
Activities Arts & crafts; Games; Prayer groups; Movies; Shopping trips; Dances/Social/Cultural gatherings.

Vespers Nursing Home
1000 College St, Wilkesboro, NC 28697
(919) 838-4141, 838-0539 FAX
Admin Grace M Nye. *Dir of Nursing* Jane Sowder RN. *Medical Dir* Larry S Kilby MD.
Licensure Skilled care; Intermediate care. *Beds* SNF 66; ICF 54. *Private Pay Patients* 15%. *Certified* Medicaid; Medicare.
Owner Proprietary corp (Pruitt Corp).
Admissions Requirements Medical examination.
Staff Physicians (contracted); RNs 7 (ft), 6 (pt); LPNs 4 (ft), 6 (pt); Nurses' aides 28 (ft), 11 (pt); Physical therapists 1 (pt); Occupational therapists (contracted); Speech therapists (contracted); Activities coordinators 1 (ft); Dietitians 1 (ft); Ophthalmologists (contracted); Podiatrists (contracted); Audiologists (contracted).

Facilities Dining room; Physical therapy room; Activities room; Chapel; Crafts room; Laundry room; Barber/Beauty shop; Lounges.
Activities Arts & crafts; Cards; Games; Reading groups; Prayer groups; Movies; Shopping trips; Dances/Social/Cultural gatherings; Intergenerational programs; Pet therapy; Community involvement; Family/resident/staff programs.

Williamston

Albemarle Villa
PO Box 1068, 119 Gatlin St, Williamston, NC 27892
(919) 792-1616
Admin Alvin J Woodring.
Licensure Skilled care; Intermediate care. *Beds* SNF 36; ICF 88. *Certified* Medicaid; Medicare.
Owner Proprietary corp (Beverly Enterprises).

Wilmington

Bowden Nursing Home
221 Summer Rest Rd, Wilmington, NC 28403
(919) 256-3733
Admin Edwin L Ware. *Dir of Nursing* Eileen Pratesi RN. *Medical Dir* James J Pence MD.
Licensure Intermediate care. *Beds* ICF 80. *Certified* Medicaid.
Owner Proprietary corp.
Admissions Requirements Medical examination; Physician's request.
Staff RNs 4 (ft); LPNs 6 (ft), 1 (pt); Nurses' aides 32 (ft); Activities coordinators 1 (ft), 1 (pt); Dietitians 1 (pt).
Facilities Dining room; Laundry room; Barber/Beauty shop.
Activities Arts & crafts; Games; Reading groups; Prayer groups; Movies; Dances/Social/Cultural gatherings.

Britthaven of Wilmington
5429 Oleander Dr, Wilmington, NC 28403
(919) 791-3451, 791-5231 FAX
Admin Maureen M Murphy. *Dir of Nursing* Alysia Walker RN. *Medical Dir* James Pence MD.
Licensure Skilled care. *Beds* SNF 50. *Private Pay Patients* 5%. *Certified* Medicaid; Medicare.
Owner Proprietary corp (Britthaven Inc).
Admissions Requirements Minimum age 18; Medical examination; Physician's request.
Staff RNs; LPNs; Nurses' aides; Physical therapists; Activities coordinators; Dietitians (consultant).
Facilities Dining room; Laundry room.
Activities Arts & crafts; Games; Reading groups; Prayer groups; Movies; Shopping trips; Dances/Social/Cultural gatherings; Pet therapy.

Cornelia Nixon Davis Health Care Center
1011 Porter's Neck Rd, Wilmington, NC 28405
(919) 686-7195
Admin John Paluck Jr.
Licensure Skilled care; Intermediate care. *Beds* SNF 155; ICF 44. *Certified* Medicaid; Medicare.

Hillhaven Rehabilitation & Convalescent Center
2006 S 16th St, Wilmington, NC 28401
(919) 763-6271
Admin Faye M Kennedy.
Medical Dir H L Armistead Jr MD.
Licensure Skilled care; Intermediate care. *Beds* SNF 56; ICF 44. *Certified* Medicaid; Medicare.
Owner Proprietary corp (Hillhaven Corp).
Admissions Requirements Medical examination; Physician's request.

Staff RNs 6 (ft), 3 (pt); LPNs 4 (ft), 3 (pt); Nurses' aides 26 (ft), 6 (pt); Physical therapists 2 (ft); Recreational therapists 1 (ft), 1 (pt); Dietitians 1 (ft).
Facilities Dining room; Physical therapy room; Activities room; Crafts room; Laundry room; Barber/Beauty shop.
Activities Arts & crafts; Cards; Games; Reading groups; Prayer groups; Movies; Shopping trips; Dances/Social/Cultural gatherings.

Pinnacle Care Center
820 Wellington Ave, Wilmington, NC 28401
(919) 343-0425
Admin David Tripp. *Dir of Nursing* Susan Bowes RN. *Medical Dir* Dr Richard Haines.
Licensure Skilled care; Intermediate care; Retirement/assisted living. *Beds* SNF 60; ICF 60; Retirement/assisted living 30. *Private Pay Patients* 15%. *Certified* Medicaid; Medicare.
Owner Proprietary corp (Pinnacle Care Corp).
Staff Physicians 1 (ft), 25 (pt); RNs 6 (ft), 5 (pt); LPNs 15 (ft), 8 (pt); Nurses' aides 53 (ft), 3 (pt); Physical therapists 3 (ft); Recreational therapists 1 (ft); Occupational therapists 3 (ft); Speech therapists 2 (ft); Activities coordinators 1 (ft); Podiatrists 1 (ft), 1 (pt); Dentists 1 (ft); Occupational therapy aides; Occupational therapy assistants; Physical therapy aides 2 (pt); Physical therapy assistants 2 (pt).
Languages French, German.
Facilities Dining room; Physical therapy room; Activities room; Laundry room; Barber/Beauty shop; Library.
Activities Arts & crafts; Cards; Games; Prayer groups; Movies; Shopping trips; Dances/Social/Cultural gatherings; Intergenerational programs; Pet therapy; Pediatric therapies.

Wilson

Britthaven of Wilson
403 Crestview Ave, Wilson, NC 27893
(919) 237-0724
Admin E B Coggin; Pat Horne AIT. *Dir of Nursing* Judy Heerschap. *Medical Dir* Dr Lawrence Krabill.
Licensure Skilled care. *Beds* SNF 46. *Private Pay Patients* 100%.
Owner Proprietary corp (Britthaven Inc).
Admissions Requirements Medical examination; Physician's request.
Staff Physicians 1 (pt); RNs 3 (ft), 2 (pt); LPNs 2 (ft), 6 (pt); Nurses' aides 15 (ft), 4 (pt); Physical therapists 1 (pt); Occupational therapists 1 (pt); Speech therapists 1 (pt); Activities coordinators 1 (ft); Dietitians 1 (pt); Podiatrists 1 (pt).
Facilities Dining room; Activities room; Crafts room; Laundry room; Barber/Beauty shop.
Activities Arts & crafts; Games; Prayer groups; Movies; Shopping trips; Dances/Social/Cultural gatherings; Intergenerational programs; Pet therapy.

North Carolina Special Care Center
1000 Ward Blvd, Wilson, NC 27893
(919) 399-2100
Admin Richard S Yell. *Dir of Nursing* Dale Hilburn. *Medical Dir* Marsha O Edmundson MD.
Licensure Skilled care; Intermediate care. *Beds* SNF 109; ICF 99. *Certified* Medicaid; Medicare.
Staff Physicians; RNs; LPNs; Nurses' aides; Physical therapists; Recreational therapists; Activities coordinators; Dietitians; Podiatrists.
Facilities Dining room; Physical therapy room; Activities room; Chapel; Crafts room; Laundry room; Barber/Beauty shop; Library.

Activities Arts & crafts; Cards; Games; Reading groups; Prayer groups; Movies; Shopping trips; Dances/Social/Cultural gatherings; Intergenerational programs.

Westwood Manor Nursing Center
PO Box 7156, 1804 Forest Hills Rd W, Wilson, NC 27895
(919) 237-8161
Admin Valdeko Kreil. *Dir of Nursing* Myrtle Necci RN. *Medical Dir* John McCain MD.
Licensure Skilled care; Intermediate care; Alzheimer's care. *Beds* SNF 60; ICF 50. *Certified* Medicaid; Medicare; VA.
Owner Proprietary corp (Beverly Enterprises).
Admissions Requirements Medical examination; Physician's request.
Staff RNs 6 (ft), 4 (pt); LPNs 9 (ft), 6 (pt); Nurses' aides 28 (ft), 18 (pt); Recreational therapists 1 (ft); Speech therapists 1 (ft); Dietitians 1 (ft); Social workers 1 (ft).
Facilities Dining room; Physical therapy room; Activities room; Laundry room; Barber/Beauty shop; Family room with fireplace.
Activities Arts & crafts; Cards; Games; Prayer groups; Movies; Shopping trips; Dances/Social/Cultural gatherings; RO; Current events; Exercise; Education classes.

Winston-Salem

Baptist Retirement Homes of North Carolina Inc
1199 Hayes Forest Dr, Winston-Salem, NC 27106
(919) 788-2441
Admin Jackson S Hoyle. *Dir of Nursing* Kathy Siegle. *Medical Dir* Dr Norman Adair.
Licensure Skilled care; Intermediate care; Home for aged. *Beds* SNF 25; ICF 60; Home for aged 36. *Certified* Medicaid; Medicare.
Owner Proprietary corp.
Admissions Requirements Minimum age 65; Medical examination; Physician's request.
Staff Physicians 3 (pt); RNs 7 (ft); LPNs 12 (ft), 5 (pt); Nurses' aides 40 (ft), 12 (pt); Physical therapists 1 (pt); Reality therapists 1 (pt); Recreational therapists 3 (ft), 1 (pt); Occupational therapists 1 (pt); Speech therapists 1 (pt); Activities coordinators 1 (ft); Dietitians 1 (ft); Ophthalmologists 1 (pt); Podiatrists 1 (pt); Dentists 1 (pt).
Affiliation Baptist.
Facilities Dining room; Activities room; Chapel; Crafts room; Laundry room; Barber/Beauty shop; Library.
Activities Arts & crafts; Cards; Games; Reading groups; Prayer groups; Movies; Shopping trips; Dances/Social/Cultural gatherings.

Knollwood Hall
5755 Shattalon Dr, Winston-Salem, NC 27105
(919) 767-2750
Admin Steven E Prater.
Licensure Skilled care; Intermediate care. *Beds* SNF 100; ICF 100. *Certified* Medicaid; Medicare.
Owner Proprietary corp (Regency Health Care Centers).
Facilities Dining room; Physical therapy room; Activities room; Crafts room; Barber/Beauty shop.
Activities Arts & crafts; Cards; Games; Reading groups; Prayer groups; Movies; Shopping trips; Dances/Social/Cultural gatherings.

Moravian Home Inc
5401 Indiana Ave, Winston-Salem, NC 27106
(919) 767-8130
Admin Lonnie Hoffpauir.

Medical Dir Clementine Shaw.
Licensure Skilled care; Intermediate care; Home for aged. *Beds* SNF 20; ICF 64; Home for aged 82.
Admissions Requirements Minimum age 65.
Affiliation Moravian.
Facilities Dining room; Activities room; Chapel; Crafts room; Laundry room; Barber/Beauty shop; Library.

Oaks at Forsyth
901 Bethesda Rd, Winston-Salem, NC 27103
(919) 768-2211
Admin Allen R Curtis.
Licensure Skilled care; Intermediate care. *Beds* SNF 95; ICF 56. *Certified* Medicaid; Medicare.

Pellcare Corp
5350 Old Walkertown Rd, Winston-Salem, NC 27106-2050
(919) 595-2166, 595-6543 FAX
Admin Robert N Schappell. *Dir of Nursing* Ann Corns RN. *Medical Dir* Dr R Jacinto.
Licensure Skilled care; Intermediate care. *Beds* SNF 60; ICF 157. *Private Pay Patients* 1%. *Certified* Medicaid; Medicare.
Owner Proprietary corp (Joe Pell).
Admissions Requirements Minimum age 18; Medical examination.
Staff Physicians 1 (ft); RNs 6 (ft), 5 (pt); LPNs 14 (ft), 8 (pt); Nurses' aides 77 (ft), 5 (pt); Physical therapists (contracted); Occupational therapists 1 (ft); Speech therapists 1 (ft); Activities coordinators 1 (ft); Dietitians 1 (ft); Podiatrists 1 (ft); Audiologists 1 (ft).
Facilities Dining room; Physical therapy room; Activities room; Chapel; Crafts room; Laundry room; Barber/Beauty shop.
Activities Arts & crafts; Cards; Games; Reading groups; Prayer groups; Movies; Shopping trips; Pet therapy.

Silas Creek Manor
3350 Silas Creek Pkwy, Winston-Salem, NC 27103
(919) 765-0550
Admin Rae McMillan. *Dir of Nursing* Maureen Huey RN. *Medical Dir* Dr Story.
Licensure Skilled care; Intermediate care. *Beds* SNF 69; ICF 30. *Certified* Medicaid; Medicare.
Owner Proprietary corp (Hillhaven Corp).
Admissions Requirements Medical examination; Physician's request.
Staff RNs 8 (ft), 4 (pt); LPNs 5 (ft), 5 (pt); Nurses' aides 32 (ft), 5 (pt); Physical therapists; Occupational therapists; Speech therapists; Activities coordinators; Dietitians.
Facilities Dining room; Physical therapy room; Activities room; Crafts room; Laundry room; Barber/Beauty shop.
Activities Arts & crafts; Cards; Games; Reading groups; Prayer groups; Movies; Shopping trips; Dances/Social/Cultural gatherings.

Triad Rehabilitation Center
5581 University Pkwy, Winston-Salem, NC 27105
(919) 767-2815
Admin Annie L Tilley. *Dir of Nursing* Beulah Wade RN. *Medical Dir* Dr James Minick.
Licensure Skilled care. *Beds* SNF 40. *Certified* Medicaid; Medicare.
Owner Proprietary corp (Brian Center Management Corp).
Admissions Requirements Medical examination.

Staff Physicians 2 (pt); RNs 2 (ft), 2 (pt); LPNs 3 (ft), 6 (pt); Nurses' aides; Activities coordinators 1 (pt); Dietitians 1 (ft).
Facilities Dining room; Activities room; Laundry room; Barber/Beauty shop.
Activities Arts & crafts; Cards; Games; Reading groups; Prayer groups; Movies; Patient, families, staff picnics; Cookouts.

Triad United Methodist Home
1240 Arbor Rd, Winston-Salem, NC 27104-1197
(919) 724-7921
Admin Susan D Holmes.
Licensure Skilled care; Intermediate care; Home for Aged. *Beds* SNF 24; ICF 36; Home for Aged 29.

Winston-Salem Convalescent Center
1900 W 1st St, Winston-Salem, NC 27104-4240
(919) 724-2821
Admin Philip E Denton.
Medical Dir Lloyd J Story MD.
Licensure Skilled care; Intermediate care. *Beds* SNF 114; ICF 116. *Certified* Medicaid; Medicare.
Owner Proprietary corp (Hillhaven Corp).
Admissions Requirements Minimum age 18; Medical examination; Physician's request.
Staff RNs; LPNs; Nurses' aides; Physical therapists; Activities coordinators; Dietitians.
Facilities Dining room; Physical therapy room; Activities room; Crafts room; Laundry room; Barber/Beauty shop; Dayrooms.
Activities Arts & crafts; Cards; Games; Reading groups; Prayer groups; Movies; Shopping trips; Dances/Social/Cultural gatherings; Regular special events; Birthday parties.

Yadkinville

Hoots Memorial Hospital
PO Box 68, 625 W Main St, Yadkinville, NC 27055
(919) 679-2041
Admin George Repa.
Licensure Skilled care. *Beds* SNF 10.

Yadkin Nursing Care Center
PO Box 879, 903 W Main St, Yadkinville, NC 27055
(919) 679-8852
Admin Nolan G Brown.
Medical Dir Sam J Crawley MD.
Licensure Skilled care; Intermediate care. *Beds* SNF 63; ICF 84. *Certified* Medicaid; Medicare.
Owner Proprietary corp (Angell Group).
Admissions Requirements Medical examination; Physician's request.
Staff Physicians 5 (pt); RNs 3 (ft); LPNs 9 (ft); Nurses' aides 22 (ft); Physical therapists 1 (pt); Reality therapists 1 (pt); Recreational therapists 2 (ft), 1 (pt); Occupational therapists 1 (pt); Activities coordinators 2 (ft), 1 (pt); Dietitians 1 (ft), 1 (pt); Ophthalmologists 1 (pt); Podiatrists 1 (pt); Dentists 1 (pt).
Facilities Dining room; Physical therapy room; Activities room; Chapel; Crafts room; Laundry room; Barber/Beauty shop; Library.
Activities Arts & crafts; Cards; Games; Reading groups; Prayer groups; Movies; Shopping trips; Dances/Social/Cultural gatherings.

Yanceyville

**Brian Center Health &
Retirement—Yanceyville**
PO Box M, Main St N, Yanceyville, NC
   27379
(919) 694-5916
Admin Gilen M Norwood.
Licensure Skilled care; Intermediate care;
   Home for Aged. *Beds* SNF 48; ICF 29;
   Home for Aged 20. *Certified* Medicaid;
   Medicare.

Zebulon

Guardian Care of Zebulon
509 W Gannon Ave, Zebulon, NC 27597
(919) 269-9621
Admin Karen S Sparrow.
Licensure Skilled care. *Beds* SNF 60. *Certified*
   Medicaid; Medicare.
Owner Proprietary corp (Hillhaven Corp).

NORTH DAKOTA

Aneta

Aneta Good Samaritan Center
PO Box 287, Aneta, ND 58212
(701) 326-4234
Admin Jane M Strommen. *Dir of Nursing* Karla Messner. *Medical Dir* Jonathan Berg MD.
Licensure Intermediate care. *Beds* ICF 51. *Private Pay Patients* 50%. *Certified* Medicare.
Owner Nonprofit corp (Evangelical Lutheran/ Good Samaritan Society).
Admissions Requirements Medical examination.
Staff Physicians 1 (pt); RNs 1 (ft); LPNs 1 (ft), 4 (pt); Nurses' aides 3 (ft), 15 (pt); Activities coordinators 1 (pt).
Facilities Dining room; Activities room; Laundry room; Barber/Beauty shop.
Activities Arts & crafts; Cards; Games; Reading groups; Prayer groups; Movies; Shopping trips; Dances/Social/Cultural gatherings; Intergenerational programs; Pet therapy.

Arthur

Arthur Good Samaritan Center
Box 16, Arthur, ND 58006
(701) 967-8316
Admin Rev Ben Doughty. *Dir of Nursing* Emily Idso. *Medical Dir* Laurel Maker.
Licensure Intermediate care. *Beds* ICF 96. *Certified* Medicaid.
Admissions Requirements Medical examination; Physician's request.
Staff RNs 1 (ft), 5 (pt); LPNs 2 (pt); Nurses' aides 20 (ft), 5 (pt); Activities coordinators 2 (ft), 2 (pt).
Affiliation Lutheran.
Facilities Dining room; Activities room; Chapel; Crafts room; Laundry room; Barber/ Beauty shop; Library.
Activities Arts & crafts; Cards; Games; Reading groups; Prayer groups; Movies; Shopping trips; Dances/Social/Cultural gatherings.

Ashley

Ashley Medical Center
612 Center Ave N, Ashley, ND 58413
(701) 288-3433, 288-3433 FAX
Admin Leo Geiger. *Dir of Nursing* Faye Salzer. *Medical Dir* Gordon Roget MD.
Licensure Skilled care; Retirement. *Beds* SNF 44; Retirement apts 8. *Private Pay Patients* 30%. *Certified* Medicaid; Medicare.
Owner Nonprofit corp.
Admissions Requirements Medical examination; Physician's request.
Staff Physicians 2 (ft); RNs 2 (ft), 3 (pt); LPNs 2 (ft), 1 (pt); Nurses' aides 17 (ft), 4 (pt); Physical therapists 1 (pt); Activities coordinators 1 (ft), 1 (pt); Dietitians.
Languages German.

Facilities Dining room; Physical therapy room; Activities room; Chapel; Crafts room; Laundry room; Barber/Beauty shop; Library.
Activities Arts & crafts; Games; Reading groups; Prayer groups; Movies.

Beulah

Beulah Community Nursing Home
106 4th St NW, Beulah, ND 58523
(701) 873-4322
Admin David Almen. *Dir of Nursing* Loretta Greni.
Licensure Skilled care. *Beds* SNF 70. *Certified* Medicaid; Medicare.

Bismarck

Baptist Home Inc
1100 Boulevard Ave, Bismarck, ND 58501
(701) 223-3040
Admin Alvin Haas. *Dir of Nursing* Judy Barondeau RN.
Licensure Skilled care; Basic care; Residential care; Alzheimer's care. *Beds* SNF 124; Basic care 26; Residential care 50. *Private Pay Patients* 40%. *Certified* Medicaid; Medicare.
Owner Nonprofit corp.
Admissions Requirements Physician's request.
Staff RNs 8 (ft); LPNs 8 (ft); Nurses' aides 80 (ft); Recreational therapists 1 (ft); Dietitians 1 (ft).
Languages German.
Facilities Dining room; Physical therapy room; Activities room; Chapel; Crafts room; Laundry room; Barber/Beauty shop; Library.
Activities Arts & crafts; Cards; Games; Reading groups; Prayer groups; Movies; Shopping trips; Intergenerational programs.

Missouri Slope Lutheran Care Center
2425 Hillview Ave, Bismarck, ND 58501
(701) 223-9407
Admin Robert Thompson. *Dir of Nursing* Anita Wilkens RN BS. *Medical Dir* Dr Steven Miller.
Licensure Skilled care; Retirement; Alzheimer's care. *Beds* SNF 223; Retirement apts 13. *Certified* Medicaid; Medicare.
Owner Nonprofit corp.
Admissions Requirements Medical examination; Physician's request.
Staff RNs 18 (ft), 9 (pt); LPNs 7 (ft), 3 (pt); Nurses' aides 81 (ft), 20 (pt); Physical therapists 1 (pt); Recreational therapists 5 (ft); Speech therapists 1 (pt); Activities coordinators 1 (ft); Dietitians 1 (ft).
Languages German, Norwegian.
Affiliation Lutheran.
Facilities Dining room; Physical therapy room; Activities room; Chapel; Crafts room; Laundry room; Barber/Beauty shop; Library.
Activities Arts & crafts; Cards; Games; Reading groups; Prayer groups; Movies; Shopping trips; Dances/Social/Cultural gatherings.

St Vincent's Nursing Home
1021 26th St N, Bismarck, ND 58501
(701) 223-6888
Admin Keith Gendreau. *Dir of Nursing* Mary Ann Steffan. *Medical Dir* Dr Rudolfo Carriedo.
Licensure Skilled care. *Beds* SNF 97. *Certified* Medicaid; Medicare.
Admissions Requirements Medical examination; Physician's request.
Staff Physicians 8 (pt); RNs 10 (ft), 6 (pt); LPNs 10 (ft), 6 (pt); Nurses' aides 70 (ft), 16 (pt); Physical therapists 1 (pt); Recreational therapists 4 (ft), 1 (pt); Occupational therapists 1 (pt); Speech therapists 1 (pt); Activities coordinators 1 (pt); Dietitians 1 (pt); Ophthalmologists 1 (pt); Podiatrists 1 (pt); Dentists 1 (pt).
Affiliation Roman Catholic.
Facilities Dining room; Physical therapy room; Activities room; Chapel; Crafts room; Laundry room; Barber/Beauty shop; Library.
Activities Arts & crafts; Cards; Games; Reading groups; Prayer groups; Movies; Shopping trips; Dances/Social/Cultural gatherings; Senior Olympics.

Bottineau

Bottineau Good Samaritan Center
725 E 10th, Bottineau, ND 58318
(701) 228-3796
Admin Richard Hunt. *Dir of Nursing* Barbara Knoepfle.
Licensure Intermediate care. *Beds* ICF 81. *Certified* Medicaid.
Owner Nonprofit corp (Evangelical Lutheran/ Good Samaritan Society).

St Andrew's Nursing Home
316 Ohmer St, Bottineau, ND 58318
(701) 228-2255
Admin Keith Korman. *Dir of Nursing* Gwen Wall RN. *Medical Dir* K W Kihle MD.
Licensure Skilled care; Retirement. *Beds* SNF 26. *Certified* Medicaid; Medicare.
Owner Nonprofit corp.
Affiliation Roman Catholic.
Facilities Dining room; Physical therapy room; Activities room; Chapel; Crafts room; Laundry room; Barber/Beauty shop.
Activities Arts & crafts; Cards; Games; Reading groups; Prayer groups; Movies; Shopping trips; Dances/Social/Cultural gatherings.

Bowman

Sunset Care Corporation
802 NW Dover, Bowman, ND 58623
(701) 523-3214
Admin Tony Hanson. *Dir of Nursing* Naomi Kraiger RN. *Medical Dir* Robert Thom MD.

Licensure Skilled care; Retirement; Alzheimer's care; Basic care; Independent living. *Beds* SNF 63; Basic care 7; Independent living 16. *Certified* Medicaid; Medicare.
Owner Nonprofit corp.
Admissions Requirements Medical examination; Physician's request.
Staff RNs 6 (ft), 5 (pt); LPNs 2 (ft), 6 (pt); Nurses' aides 30 (ft), 10 (pt); Activities coordinators 1 (ft), 2 (pt).
Affiliation Lutheran.
Facilities Dining room; Physical therapy room; Activities room; Chapel; Crafts room; Laundry room; Barber/Beauty shop; Day care.
Activities Arts & crafts; Cards; Games; Reading groups; Prayer groups; Movies; Shopping trips; Dances/Social/Cultural gatherings.

Cando

Resthaven Healthcare Center
701 11th St, Box 579, Cando, ND 58324
(701) 968-3351
Admin Jeanne Stout. *Dir of Nursing* Eileen M Heardt RN. *Medical Dir* G H Hitts MD; P W Marsh MD.
Licensure Skilled care. *Beds* SNF 74. *Certified* Medicaid; Medicare.
Owner Proprietary corp.
Admissions Requirements Medical examination.
Staff RNs 1 (ft), 10 (pt); LPNs 5 (pt); Nurses' aides 17 (ft), 14 (pt); Physical therapists 1 (pt); Activities coordinators 1 (ft), 2 (pt); Dietitians 1 (pt).
Facilities Dining room; Physical therapy room; Activities room; Chapel; Crafts room; Laundry room; Barber/Beauty shop.
Activities Arts & crafts; Games; Reading groups; Prayer groups; Movies; Shopping trips; Dances/Social/Cultural gatherings.

Carrington

Carrington Health Center—SNF
800 N 4th, Carrington, ND 58421
(701) 652-3141
Admin Duane Jerde. *Dir of Nursing* Doran Walth.
Licensure Skilled care. *Beds* SNF 40. *Certified* Medicaid; Medicare.
Owner Nonprofit corp.
Staff Physicians 3 (ft); RNs 1 (ft), 2 (pt); LPNs 2 (ft), 5 (pt); Nurses' aides 6 (ft), 10 (pt); Physical therapists 1 (ft); Activities coordinators 2 (ft); Dietitians 1 (pt).
Affiliation Roman Catholic.
Facilities Dining room; Physical therapy room; Activities room; Chapel; Crafts room; Laundry room; Barber/Beauty shop.
Activities Arts & crafts; Cards; Games; Reading groups; Prayer groups; Movies; Shopping trips; Dances/Social/Cultural gatherings.

Golden Acres Manor
No 1 E Main St, Carrington, ND 58421
(701) 652-3117
Admin Allan Metzger. *Dir of Nursing* Sheila Tuhy.
Licensure Skilled care. *Beds* SNF 60. *Certified* Medicaid; Medicare.

Cavalier

Pembina County Memorial Nursing Home
Hwy 5, Box M, Cavalier, ND 58220
(701) 265-8461, 265-8752 FAX
Admin Brad Solberg. *Dir of Nursing* Pat Robbins. *Medical Dir* E J Larson MD.

Licensure Skilled care; Congregate housing. *Beds* SNF 60; Congregate housing 20. *Private Pay Patients* 65%. *Certified* Medicaid; Medicare.
Owner Nonprofit organization/foundation (Lutheran Health Systems).
Admissions Requirements Medical examination; Physician's request.
Staff RNs 2 (ft), 2 (pt); LPNs 4 (ft), 4 (pt); Nurses' aides 22 (ft), 16 (pt); Physical therapists 1 (pt); Activities coordinators 1 (ft), 1 (pt); Dietitians 1 (pt).
Affiliation Lutheran.
Facilities Dining room; Physical therapy room; Activities room; Crafts room; Barber/Beauty shop.
Activities Arts & crafts; Cards; Games; Reading groups; Prayer groups; Movies; Dances/Social/Cultural gatherings; Intergenerational programs.

Cooperstown

Griggs County Nursing Home
Box 728, Cooperstown, ND 58425
(701) 797-3212
Admin Joan Bachman. *Dir of Nursing* Tom O'Keefe RN BSN. *Medical Dir* Patty Pepper DO.
Licensure Skilled care. *Beds* SNF 50. *Private Pay Patients* 40%. *Certified* Medicaid; Medicare.
Owner Nonprofit corp.
Admissions Requirements Medical examination.
Staff RNs 1 (ft), 2 (pt); LPNs 2 (ft), 6 (pt); Nurses' aides 10 (ft), 17 (pt); Physical therapists 1 (pt); Activities coordinators 1 (ft); Dietitians 1 (pt).
Facilities Dining room; Physical therapy room; Activities room; Laundry room; Barber/Beauty shop.
Activities Arts & crafts; Cards; Games; Reading groups; Prayer groups; Movies; Shopping trips; Dances/Social/Cultural gatherings.

Crosby

Crosby Good Samaritan Center
704 SE 4th, Box 187, Crosby, ND 58730
(701) 965-6086
Admin Valerie Eide. *Dir of Nursing* Deborah Melby.
Licensure Intermediate care. *Beds* ICF 81. *Certified* Medicaid.

Devils Lake

Devils Lake Good Samaritan Center
302 7th Ave, Devils Lake, ND 58301
(701) 662-7525
Admin Reuben Schnaidt. *Dir of Nursing* Donna Rook.
Licensure Intermediate care; Alzheimer's care. *Beds* ICF 84. *Certified* Medicaid.
Owner Nonprofit corp (Evangelical Lutheran/Good Samaritan Society).
Admissions Requirements Medical examination.
Staff RNs 1 (ft); LPNs 4 (ft), 10 (pt); Nurses' aides 8 (ft), 20 (pt); Physical therapists 1 (pt); Activities coordinators 1 (ft); Dietitians 1 (pt).
Facilities Dining room; Activities room; Chapel; Laundry room; Barber/Beauty shop; Dayrooms.
Activities Arts & crafts; Cards; Games; Reading groups; Movies; Shopping trips; Dances/Social/Cultural gatherings.

Lake Region Lutheran Home
E 14th Ave, Devils Lake, ND 58301
(701) 662-4905
Admin Al Holte. *Dir of Nursing* Ann Hunt. *Medical Dir* Dr D A Rada.

Licensure Skilled care. *Beds* SNF 108. *Private Pay Patients* 45%. *Certified* Medicaid; Medicare.
Owner Nonprofit organization/foundation.
Admissions Requirements Medical examination.
Staff Physicians 1 (ft), 6 (pt); RNs 8 (ft), 2 (pt); Nurses' aides 55 (ft), 10 (pt); Physical therapists 1 (pt); Recreational therapists 2 (ft), 1 (pt); Activities coordinators 1 (ft); Dietitians 1 (ft).
Affiliation Lutheran.
Facilities Dining room; Physical therapy room; Activities room; Chapel; Crafts room; Laundry room; Barber/Beauty shop; Library.
Activities Arts & crafts; Cards; Games; Reading groups; Prayer groups; Movies; Shopping trips; Pet therapy.

Dickinson

Dickinson Nursing Center
851 4th Ave E, Dickinson, ND 58601
(701) 225-5138
Admin Larry Potter. *Dir of Nursing* Joan Brew. *Medical Dir* Dr. Laslo Kolta.
Licensure Skilled care; Intermediate care. *Beds* SNF 110; ICF 75. *Certified* Medicaid; Medicare.
Owner Proprietary corp (Beverly Enterprises).
Admissions Requirements Medical examination; Physician's request.
Staff RNs 6 (ft), 5 (pt); LPNs 5 (ft), 6 (pt); Nurses' aides 40 (ft), 38 (pt); Activities coordinators 1 (ft).
Facilities Dining room; Physical therapy room; Activities room; Chapel; Crafts room; Laundry room; Barber/Beauty shop.
Activities Arts & crafts; Cards; Games; Reading groups; Prayer groups; Movies; Shopping trips; Dances/Social/Cultural gatherings.

St Luke's Home
242 W 10th St, Dickinson, ND 58601
(701) 225-6026, 225-0568 FAX
Admin Lyle D Brudvig. *Dir of Nursing* Judith Hicks RN. *Medical Dir* Dennis Wolf MD.
Licensure Skilled care; Adult day care. *Beds* SNF 83. *Private Pay Patients* 55%. *Certified* Medicaid; Medicare.
Owner Nonprofit organization/foundation.
Admissions Requirements Medical examination; Physician's request.
Staff Physicians 1 (pt); RNs 3 (ft), 4 (pt); LPNs 4 (ft), 4 (pt); Nurses' aides 35 (ft), 20 (pt); Physical therapists (contracted); Reality therapists 1 (pt); Recreational therapists 2 (ft), 3 (pt); Activities coordinators 1 (ft); Dietitians (contracted); Physical therapy aides 1 (ft), 2 (pt).
Affiliation Lutheran.
Facilities Dining room; Physical therapy room; Activities room; Chapel; Crafts room; Laundry room; Barber/Beauty shop; Library.
Activities Arts & crafts; Cards; Games; Reading groups; Prayer groups; Movies; Shopping trips; Dances/Social/Cultural gatherings; Intergenerational programs; Pet therapy.

Dunseith

Dunseith Community Nursing Home
15 1st St NE, Box 669, Dunseith, ND 58329
(701) 244-5495
Admin Cliff Tuttle. *Dir of Nursing* Sandra Waagen. *Medical Dir* Dr Dave Crozier.
Licensure Skilled care. *Beds* SNF 40. *Certified* Medicaid; Medicare.
Admissions Requirements Medical examination.
Staff Physicians 2 (pt); RNs 2 (ft), 1 (pt); LPNs 3 (ft), 2 (pt); Nurses' aides 9 (ft), 2 (pt); Physical therapists 1 (pt); Activities coordinators 1 (ft), 1 (pt); Dietitians 1 (pt).

Facilities Dining room; Physical therapy room; Activities room; Crafts room; Laundry room; Barber/Beauty shop.
Activities Arts & crafts; Cards; Games; Reading groups; Prayer groups; Movies; Shopping trips; Dances/Social/Cultural gatherings.

Elgin

Jacobson Memorial Hospital Care Center
PO Box 367, 601 East St N, Elgin, ND 58533
(701) 584-2792, 584-3348 FAX
Admin Jacqueline Seibel. Dir of Nursing Phyllis Ketterling RN. Medical Dir S K Patel MD.
Licensure Skilled care; Intermediate care; Acute care. Beds Swing beds SNF/ICF 25; Acute care 25. Private Pay Patients 28%. Certified Medicaid; Medicare.
Owner Nonprofit corp.
Admissions Requirements Physician's request.
Staff Physicians 2 (ft); RNs 1 (ft), 3 (pt); LPNs 1 (ft), 3 (pt); Nurses' aides 4 (ft), 12 (pt); Physical therapists 1 (pt); Activities coordinators 1 (ft), 1 (pt); Dietitians 1 (pt).
Languages German.
Facilities Dining room; Physical therapy room; Activities room; Chapel; Crafts room; Barber/Beauty shop.
Activities Arts & crafts; Cards; Games; Reading groups; Prayer groups; Movies; Dances/Social/Cultural gatherings; Intergenerational programs.

Ellendale

Ellendale Nursing Center
Hwy 281 N, Ellendale, ND 58436
(701) 349-3312
Admin John Schiermeister. Dir of Nursing Elva Miller RN. Medical Dir Brian Bonte MD.
Licensure Skilled care. Beds SNF 84. Private Pay Patients 9%. Certified Medicaid; Medicare.
Owner Nonprofit corp (BHS Long Term Care Inc).
Admissions Requirements Medical examination; Physician's request.
Staff Physicians 1 (pt); RNs 5 (ft), 3 (pt); LPNs 2 (ft), 1 (pt); Nurses' aides 22 (ft), 17 (pt); Physical therapists 1 (pt); Activities coordinators 1 (ft); Dietitians 1 (pt).
Languages German.
Facilities Dining room; Physical therapy room; Activities room; Chapel; Crafts room; Barber/Beauty shop.
Activities Arts & crafts; Cards; Games; Reading groups; Prayer groups; Movies; Shopping trips; Dances/Social/Cultural gatherings.

Enderlin

Enderlin Hillcrest Manor Ltd
110 Hillcrest Dr, Enderlin, ND 58027
(701) 437-3544
Admin Mark A Bertilrud. Dir of Nursing Alana Cavett. Medical Dir Dr James Buhr.
Licensure Intermediate care. Beds ICF 62. Certified Medicaid.
Owner Nonprofit corp (Lutheran Health Systems).
Admissions Requirements Medical examination; Physician's request.
Staff RNs 1 (ft), 1 (pt); LPNs 1 (ft), 5 (pt); Nurses' aides 3 (ft), 17 (pt); Activities coordinators 1 (ft).
Affiliation Lutheran.
Facilities Dining room; Activities room; Crafts room; Laundry room; Barber/Beauty shop.

Activities Arts & crafts; Cards; Games; Reading groups; Prayer groups; Movies; Shopping trips; Dances/Social/Cultural gatherings.

Fargo

Americana Healthcare Center
1315 S University Dr, Fargo, ND 58103
(701) 237-3030
Admin Arline Payne. Dir of Nursing Marie Braaten. Medical Dir Dr J Talbot.
Licensure Skilled care. Beds 104. Certified Medicaid; Medicare.
Owner Proprietary corp (Manor Care Inc).
Admissions Requirements Medical examination; Physician's request.
Staff RNs; LPNs; Nurses' aides; Physical therapists; Occupational therapists; Speech therapists; Activities coordinators.
Facilities Dining room; Physical therapy room; Activities room; Crafts room; Laundry room; Barber/Beauty shop; Library.
Activities Arts & crafts; Cards; Games; Reading groups; Prayer groups; Movies; Shopping trips; Dances/Social/Cultural gatherings.

Bethany Homes
201 S University Dr, Fargo, ND 58102
(701) 237-0720
Admin John Thompson. Dir of Nursing Sandy Savageau SNF; Gl Gunderson ICF. Medical Dir G J Kavanaugh MD.
Licensure Skilled care; Intermediate care; Retirement; Alzheimer's care. Beds SNF 96; ICF 96; Retirement 158. Certified Medicaid; Medicare.
Owner Nonprofit corp.
Staff Physicians 1 (ft); RNs 7 (ft), 8 (pt); LPNs 8 (ft), 8 (pt); Nurses' aides 38 (ft), 62 (pt); Physical therapists 1 (pt); Reality therapists 2 (ft); Occupational therapists 1 (pt); Speech therapists 1 (pt); Activities coordinators 1 (ft); Dietitians 2 (ft).
Facilities Dining room; Physical therapy room; Activities room; Chapel; Crafts room; Laundry room; Barber/Beauty shop; Library; Coffee shop.
Activities Arts & crafts; Cards; Games; Reading groups; Prayer groups; Movies; Shopping trips; Dances/Social/Cultural gatherings.

Elim Home
3534 S University Dr, Fargo, ND 58104
(701) 237-4392
Admin Steve N Karnes. Dir of Nursing Rita Rice. Medical Dir Dr Henry Wiers.
Licensure Skilled care; Alzheimer's care. Beds SNF 128. Private Pay Patients 50%. Certified Medicaid; Medicare.
Owner Nonprofit organization/foundation.
Admissions Requirements Minimum age 18; Medical examination; Physician's request.
Staff RNs 7 (ft), 8 (pt); LPNs 3 (ft), 2 (pt); Nurses' aides 30 (ft), 40 (pt); Recreational therapists 1 (ft), 3 (pt); Activities coordinators 1 (ft).
Affiliation Evangelical Free Church.
Facilities Dining room; Physical therapy room; Activities room; Chapel; Laundry room; Barber/Beauty shop; Library.
Activities Arts & crafts; Cards; Games; Reading groups; Prayer groups; Movies; Shopping trips; Dances/Social/Cultural gatherings; Intergenerational programs; Pet therapy.

Fargo Nursing Home
1351 Broadway, Fargo, ND 58102
(701) 235-7597
Admin Paul DeVoe. Dir of Nursing Pam Richardt. Medical Dir Janelle Sanda/Edith Jamieson.
Licensure Skilled care; Alzheimer's care. Beds SNF 102. Certified Medicaid; Medicare.

Owner Nonprofit corp (Lutheran Health Systems).
Admissions Requirements Medical examination; Physician's request.
Staff RNs 2 (ft), 6 (pt); LPNs 7 (ft), 3 (pt); Nurses' aides 32 (ft), 30 (pt); Activities coordinators 1 (ft); Dietitians 1 (pt).
Facilities Dining room; Physical therapy room; Activities room; Chapel; Crafts room; Laundry room; Barber/Beauty shop.
Activities Arts & crafts; Cards; Games; Reading groups; Prayer groups; Movies; Shopping trips; Dances/Social/Cultural gatherings.

Villa Maria Healthcare Ltd
3102 S University Dr, Fargo, ND 58103
(701) 293-7750
Admin Nancy Tedros. Dir of Nursing Judy Moffett. Medical Dir Richard Linsmeier.
Licensure Skilled care; Alzheimer's care. Beds SNF 132. Private Pay Patients 35%. Certified Medicaid; Medicare.
Owner Nonprofit organization/foundation (Lutheran Health Systems).
Admissions Requirements Medical examination.
Staff RNs 3 (ft), 1 (pt); LPNs 7 (ft), 3 (pt); Nurses' aides 30 (ft), 35 (pt); Recreational therapists 1 (ft); Occupational therapists 2 (pt); Activities coordinators 1 (ft); Dietitians 1 (pt).
Facilities Dining room; Physical therapy room; Activities room; Chapel; Crafts room; Laundry room; Barber/Beauty shop; Library.
Activities Arts & crafts; Cards; Games; Reading groups; Prayer groups; Movies; Shopping trips; Dances/Social/Cultural gatherings; Intergenerational programs; Pet therapy.

Forman

Sargent Manor Health Care Center
525 5th St, Box 69, Forman, ND 58032
(701) 724-6211
Admin DeDe Cookson. Dir of Nursing Annette Stevens. Medical Dir Dr Matt Kidd.
Licensure Intermediate care. Beds ICF 62. Private Pay Patients 50%. Certified Medicaid.
Owner Privately owned.
Admissions Requirements Medical examination.
Staff RNs 1 (ft); LPNs 6 (pt); Nurses' aides 16 (pt); Activities coordinators 1 (ft), 1 (pt); Dietitians; Social workers.
Facilities Dining room; Physical therapy room; Activities room; Chapel; Crafts room; Laundry room; Barber/Beauty shop; Library.
Activities Arts & crafts; Cards; Games; Reading groups; Prayer groups; Movies; Shopping trips; Dances/Social/Cultural gatherings.

Garrison

Garrison Memorial Hospital—ICF
407 3rd Ave SE, Box 39, Garrison, ND 58540
(701) 463-2275
Admin Sr Madonna Wagendorf. Dir of Nursing Rosalie Yahnke RN. Medical Dir John T Boyle MD.
Licensure Intermediate care. Beds ICF 24. Certified Medicaid.
Admissions Requirements Medical examination.
Staff Physicians 1 (pt); RNs 3 (pt); LPNs 1 (ft), 6 (pt); Nurses' aides 3 (ft), 6 (pt); Physical therapists 1 (pt); Activities coordinators 1 (ft); Dietitians 1 (pt); Dentists 1 (pt).
Affiliation Roman Catholic.
Facilities Dining room; Physical therapy room; Activities room; Chapel; Crafts room; Laundry room; Barber/Beauty shop.

Activities Arts & crafts; Cards; Games; Prayer groups; Movies; Shopping trips; Dances/ Social/Cultural gatherings.

Garrison Nursing Center
Box 219, Garrison, ND 58540
(701) 463-2226
Admin Mark Siebold. *Dir of Nursing* Lorna Olson RN. *Medical Dir* Greg Culver MD.
Licensure Skilled care; Intermediate care. *Beds* Swing beds SNF/ICF 71. *Private Pay Patients* 15%. *Certified* Medicaid; Medicare.
Owner Nonprofit organization/foundation (Benedictine Healthcare).
Admissions Requirements Medical examination.
Staff RNs; LPNs; Nurses' aides; Activities coordinators.
Affiliation Roman Catholic.
Facilities Dining room; Physical therapy room; Activities room; Chapel; Crafts room; Laundry room; Barber/Beauty shop.
Activities Arts & crafts; Cards; Games; Reading groups; Movies; Dances/Social/ Cultural gatherings; Intergenerational programs.

Glen Ullin

Marian Manor Nursing Home
Box 528, 604 Ash Ave E, Glen Ullin, ND 58631
(701) 348-3107
Admin Rodney Auer. *Dir of Nursing* Barbara Ding RN. *Medical Dir* Dr George Hsu.
Licensure Skilled care; Alzheimer's care. *Beds* SNF 86. *Private Pay Patients* 54%. *Certified* Medicaid; Medicare.
Owner Nonprofit organization/foundation.
Admissions Requirements Medical examination; Physician's request.
Staff RNs 4 (ft), 4 (pt); LPNs 3 (ft), 10 (pt); Nurses' aides 15 (ft), 41 (pt); Recreational therapists 1 (ft); Activities coordinators 1 (ft); Dietitians 1 (pt).
Languages German.
Facilities Dining room; Physical therapy room; Activities room; Chapel; Crafts room; Laundry room; Barber/Beauty shop.
Activities Arts & crafts; Cards; Games; Reading groups; Prayer groups; Movies; Dances/Social/Cultural gatherings; Pet therapy.

Grafton

Lutheran Sunset Home
333 Eastern Ave, Grafton, ND 58237
(701) 352-1901
Admin Rodney Alme. *Dir of Nursing* Adele Momerak.
Licensure Skilled care. *Beds* SNF 119. *Certified* Medicaid; Medicare.
Affiliation Lutheran.

Grand Forks

Valley Memorial Home—Almonte
1023 Almonte Ave, Grand Forks, ND 58201
(701) 772-4815
Admin James Opdahl. *Dir of Nursing* Betty Kappedel. *Medical Dir* Keith Vandergon MD.
Licensure Intermediate care; Retirement; Alzheimer's care; Basic care. *Beds* ICF 118; Basic care 68. *Certified* Medicaid.
Owner Nonprofit corp.
Admissions Requirements Medical examination.
Staff Physicians 1 (pt); RNs 2 (ft), 9 (pt); LPNs 1 (ft), 10 (pt); Nurses' aides 16 (ft), 49 (pt); Physical therapists 2 (pt); Activities coordinators 1 (ft), 5 (pt); Dietitians 1 (pt); Chaplains 1 (ft).
Affiliation Lutheran.

Facilities Dining room; Physical therapy room; Activities room; Chapel; Crafts room; Laundry room; Barber/Beauty shop.
Activities Arts & crafts; Cards; Games; Reading groups; Movies; Shopping trips; Dances/Social/Cultural gatherings.

Valley Memorial Home—Medical Park
2900 14th Ave S, Grand Forks, ND 58201
(701) 780-5500
Admin James Opdahl. *Dir of Nursing* Bruce Johnson. *Medical Dir* Keith Vandergon MD.
Licensure Skilled care; Retirement. *Beds* SNF 160. *Certified* Medicaid; Medicare.
Owner Nonprofit corp.
Admissions Requirements Medical examination.
Staff Physicians 1 (pt); RNs 7 (ft), 2 (pt); LPNs 10 (ft), 23 (pt); Nurses' aides 51 (ft), 75 (pt); Physical therapists 1 (ft), 5 (pt); Occupational therapists 1 (ft); Activities coordinators 1 (ft), 3 (pt); Dietitians 1 (ft); Chaplains 1 (ft).
Affiliation Lutheran.
Facilities Dining room; Physical therapy room; Activities room; Chapel; Crafts room; Laundry room; Barber/Beauty shop.
Activities Arts & crafts; Cards; Games; Reading groups; Prayer groups; Movies; Shopping trips; Dances/Social/Cultural gatherings.

Hankinson

St Gerard's Nursing Home
613 1st Ave SW, Box 279, Hankinson, ND 58041
(701) 242-7891
Admin Gene Hoefs. *Dir of Nursing* Sr Marilyn.
Licensure Skilled care. *Beds* 23. *Certified* Medicaid; Medicare.

Harvey

St Aloisius Medical Center
325 E Brewster St, Harvey, ND 58341
(701) 324-4651, 324-4651 FAX
Admin Ron Volk. *Dir of Nursing* Alyce Heer, Acute; David Simon, LTC. *Medical Dir* Charles Nyhus MD.
Licensure Skilled care; Intermediate care. *Beds* Swing beds SNF/ICF 116. *Certified* Medicaid; Medicare.
Owner Nonprofit corp (SMP Health Corp).
Admissions Requirements Medical examination; Physician's request.
Staff RNs 5 (ft), 3 (pt); LPNs 5 (ft), 6 (pt); Nurses' aides 45 (ft), 20 (pt); Physical therapists 1 (ft); Recreational therapists 2 (ft), 2 (pt).
Affiliation Roman Catholic.
Facilities Dining room; Physical therapy room; Activities room; Chapel; Laundry room; Barber/Beauty shop.
Activities Arts & crafts; Cards; Games; Prayer groups; Movies; Dances/Social/Cultural gatherings.

Hatton

Tri-County Retirement & Nursing Home
930 Dakota Ave, Hatton, ND 58240
(701) 543-3102
Admin Thomas Klotz. *Dir of Nursing* Marcia Wilson. *Medical Dir* Dr D J Hlavinka.
Licensure Skilled care. *Beds* SNF 60. *Certified* Medicaid; Medicare.
Owner Nonprofit organization/foundation.
Staff RNs 6 (ft); LPNs 2 (ft); Nurses' aides 35 (ft); Physical therapists 1 (ft); Activities coordinators 3 (ft); Dietitians 1 (ft).
Languages Norwegian.
Affiliation Lutheran.

Facilities Dining room; Physical therapy room; Activities room; Chapel; Crafts room; Laundry room; Barber/Beauty shop.
Activities Arts & crafts; Cards; Games; Reading groups; Movies; Birthday parties.

Hettinger

Hillcrest Care Center
RR 2 Box 126, Hettinger, ND 58639
(701) 567-2401, 567-4648 FAX
Admin Bob Owens. *Dir of Nursing* Jean Pagel. *Medical Dir* Dr Joe Mattson.
Licensure Skilled care. *Beds* SNF 88. *Private Pay Patients* 40%. *Certified* Medicaid; Medicare; VA.
Owner Proprietary corp (Lantis Enterprises).
Admissions Requirements Physician's request.
Staff RNs 12 (ft); LPNs 9 (ft); Nurses' aides 40 (ft); Physical therapists 1 (ft); Activities coordinators 1 (ft); Dietitians 1 (ft); Ophthalmologists 1 (ft).
Facilities Dining room; Physical therapy room; Activities room; Crafts room; Barber/ Beauty shop.
Activities Arts & crafts; Cards; Games; Reading groups; Prayer groups; Movies; Shopping trips; Dances/Social/Cultural gatherings; Intergenerational programs.

Hillsboro

Hillsboro Community Nursing Home
PO Box 609, 320 1st Ave SE, Hillsboro, ND 58045
(701) 436-5755
Admin Bruce Bowersox. *Dir of Nursing* Harriet Gibbons. *Medical Dir* Richard E Martin MD.
Licensure Skilled care; Alzheimer's care. *Beds* SNF 50. *Private Pay Patients* 50%. *Certified* Medicaid; Medicare.
Owner Nonprofit organization/foundation.
Admissions Requirements Minimum age 18; Physician's request.
Staff RNs 3 (ft), 3 (pt); LPNs 1 (ft), 2 (pt); Nurses' aides 20 (ft), 13 (pt); Physical therapists 1 (pt); Speech therapists 1 (pt); Activities coordinators 3 (pt); Dietitians 1 (pt).
Languages Norwegian.
Facilities Dining room; Physical therapy room; Activities room; Chapel; Crafts room; Laundry room; Barber/Beauty shop.
Activities Arts & crafts; Cards; Games; Reading groups; Movies; Dances/Social/ Cultural gatherings; Intergenerational programs.

Jamestown

Central Dakota Nursing Home
501 19th St NE, Jamestown, ND 58401
(701) 252-5660
Admin Alex C Schweitzer. *Dir of Nursing* Shelley Barth. *Medical Dir* William Stewart MD.
Licensure Skilled care; Retirement; Alzheimer's care. *Beds* SNF 100. *Certified* Medicaid; Medicare.
Owner Nonprofit corp (Lutheran Health Systems).
Staff RNs 5 (ft), 5 (pt); LPNs 2 (ft), 2 (pt); Nurses' aides 20 (ft), 34 (pt); Physical therapists 1 (ft); Recreational therapists 1 (ft), 1 (pt); Occupational therapists 1 (ft); Activities coordinators 1 (ft); Social workers 1 (ft).
Facilities Dining room; Physical therapy room; Activities room; Chapel; Crafts room; Laundry room; Barber/Beauty shop.
Activities Arts & crafts; Cards; Games; Reading groups; Prayer groups; Movies; Shopping trips; Dances/Social/Cultural gatherings; Aerobics; Work therapy; Bingo.

Hi-Acres Manor Nursing Center
1300 2nd Pl NE, Jamestown, ND 58401
(701) 252-5881, 252-7765 FAX
Admin Gary M Riffe. *Dir of Nursing* Sharlene LaQua RN. *Medical Dir* Scott Rowe MD.
Licensure Skilled care; Intermediate care; Retirement. *Beds* SNF 116; ICF 26; Retirement 10. *Private Pay Patients* 35-40%. *Certified* Medicaid; Medicare; VA.
Owner Proprietary corp.
Admissions Requirements Medical examination.
Staff RNs 6 (ft), 7 (pt); LPNs 13 (ft), 7 (pt); Nurses' aides 50 (ft), 36 (pt); Physical therapists (contracted); Recreational therapists 1 (pt); Activities coordinators 2 (ft), 3 (pt); Dietitians 1 (ft).
Facilities Dining room; Physical therapy room; Activities room; Chapel; Crafts room; Laundry room; Barber/Beauty shop.
Activities Arts & crafts; Games; Reading groups; Prayer groups; Movies; Shopping trips; Dances/Social/Cultural gatherings.

Kenmare

Kenmare Community Hospital
PO Box 337, Kenmare, ND 58746
(701) 385-4296, 385-4341 FAX
Admin Ella Gutzke. *Dir of Nursing* Connie Schmit.
Licensure Skilled care; Acute care. *Beds* SNF 12; Acute care 24. *Private Pay Patients* 25%. *Certified* Medicaid; Medicare.
Owner Nonprofit organization/foundation.
Admissions Requirements Physician's request.
Staff Physicians (contracted); RNs 1 (ft), 8 (pt); LPNs 2 (ft), 4 (pt); Nurses' aides 5 (ft), 10 (pt); Physical therapists 1 (pt); Activities coordinators 1 (ft), 1 (pt); Dietitians 1 (pt).
Languages German, Norwegian, Swedish.
Facilities Dining room; Physical therapy room; Activities room; Crafts room; Laundry room; Barber/Beauty shop.
Activities Arts & crafts; Cards; Games; Reading groups; Prayer groups; Movies; Shopping trips; Dances/Social/Cultural gatherings; Pet therapy; Ethnic dinners.

Killdeer

Hill Top Home of Comfort Inc
201 Hill Top Dr, Killdeer, ND 58640
(701) 764-5682
Admin John DeVries. *Dir of Nursing* Linda Wallace. *Medical Dir* Dr James Baumgartner.
Licensure Skilled care; Basic care. *Beds* SNF 40; Basic care 24. *Private Pay Patients* 60%. *Certified* Medicaid; Medicare.
Owner Nonprofit organization/foundation.
Admissions Requirements Medical examination.
Staff RNs 3 (ft); LPNs 5 (ft); Nurses' aides 20 (ft), 10 (pt); Physical therapists 1 (pt); Activities coordinators 1 (ft), 2 (pt); Dietitians 1 (pt).
Facilities Dining room; Physical therapy room; Activities room; Crafts room; Laundry room; Barber/Beauty shop; Library.
Activities Arts & crafts; Cards; Games; Reading groups; Prayer groups; Movies; Intergenerational programs.

La Moure

La Moure Healthcare Manor
Box 627, La Moure, ND 58458
(701) 883-5363
Admin Adele Spicer. *Dir of Nursing* Elaine Chase. *Medical Dir* Dr Paul Vangerud.
Licensure Intermediate care. *Beds* ICF 60. *Private Pay Patients* 38%. *Certified* Medicaid.
Owner Nonprofit organization/foundation (Benedictine Healthcare).

Admissions Requirements Medical examination; Physician's request.
Staff RNs 2 (ft), 1 (pt); LPNs 2 (ft), 2 (pt); Nurses' aides 15 (ft), 8 (pt); Activities coordinators 2 (ft), 1 (pt).
Languages German.
Affiliation Roman Catholic.
Facilities Dining room; Physical therapy room; Activities room; Crafts room; Laundry room; Barber/Beauty shop.
Activities Arts & crafts; Cards; Games; Reading groups; Prayer groups; Movies; Shopping trips; Dances/Social/Cultural gatherings; Intergenerational programs; Pet therapy.

Langdon

Maple Manor Nursing Home
Hwy 5 W, Box 549, Langdon, ND 58249
(701) 256-2987
Admin Charles Shortridge. *Dir of Nursing* Gail Melland RN. *Medical Dir* N J Kaluzniak MD.
Licensure Skilled care. *Beds* SNF 63. *Certified* Medicaid; Medicare.
Owner Proprietary corp.
Admissions Requirements Minimum age 21; Medical examination; Physician's request.
Staff Physicians 2 (pt); RNs 1 (ft), 7 (pt); LPNs 1 (ft), 3 (pt); Nurses' aides 14 (ft), 25 (pt); Physical therapists 1 (pt); Activities coordinators 1 (ft), 1 (pt); Dietitians 1 (ft), 1 (pt).
Facilities Dining room; Activities room; Chapel; Crafts room; Laundry room; Barber/Beauty shop.
Activities Arts & crafts; Cards; Games; Reading groups; Prayer groups; Movies; Shopping trips; Dances/Social/Cultural gatherings.

Larimore

Larimore Good Samaritan Center
501 E Front St, Larimore, ND 58251
(701) 343-6244
Admin Betty Bloomquist. *Dir of Nursing* Ione Lucas. *Medical Dir* Dr Jon Rice.
Licensure Intermediate care. *Beds* ICF 68. *Certified* Medicaid.
Owner Nonprofit corp (Evangelical Lutheran/ Good Samaritan Society).
Admissions Requirements Medical examination; Physician's request.
Staff Physicians 1 (pt); RNs 1 (ft), 3 (pt); LPNs 3 (ft), 5 (pt); Nurses' aides 10 (ft), 12 (pt); Physical therapists 1 (pt); Activities coordinators 1 (ft), 1 (pt); Dietitians 1 (ft).
Affiliation Lutheran.
Facilities Dining room; Physical therapy room; Activities room; Crafts room; Laundry room; Barber/Beauty shop.
Activities Arts & crafts; Cards; Games; Reading groups; Prayer groups; Movies; Shopping trips; Dances/Social/Cultural gatherings; Picnics; Manicures; Hiking; Worship service; Mind bending; Outings & fieldtrips; Music appreciation; Resident volunteer program.

Lisbon

Community Memorial Nursing Home
905 Main, Box 353, Lisbon, ND 58054
(701) 683-5241
Admin Wendell Rawlings. *Dir of Nursing* Betty Nelson RN. *Medical Dir* A K Lewis MD.
Licensure Skilled care. *Beds* 45. *Certified* Medicaid; Medicare.
Owner Nonprofit corp (Lutheran Health Systems).
Admissions Requirements Medical examination; Physician's request.

Staff Physicians 4 (pt); RNs 3 (pt); LPNs 2 (ft), 9 (pt); Nurses' aides 10 (ft), 21 (pt); Physical therapists 1 (ft); Activities coordinators 1 (ft); Dietitians 1 (ft); Social workers 1 (ft).
Facilities Dining room; Physical therapy room; Activities room; Chapel; Crafts room; Barber/Beauty shop; Library.
Activities Arts & crafts; Cards; Games; Reading groups; Prayer groups; Movies; Shopping trips; Dances/Social/Cultural gatherings.

Parkside Lutheran Home
Prospect St, Box 153, Lisbon, ND 58054
(701) 683-5239
Admin Arlys Carter. *Dir of Nursing* Claudia Dupree.
Licensure Intermediate care. *Beds* ICF 40. *Certified* Medicaid.
Affiliation Lutheran.

Mandan

Dacotah Alpha
1007 18th St NW, Mandan, ND 58554
(701) 663-0376
Admin Dorothy Fisher. *Dir of Nursing* Carol Nagel RN. *Medical Dir* Paul Knudson MD.
Licensure Intermediate care. *Beds* ICF 9. *Private Pay Patients* 0%. *Certified* Medicaid.
Owner Nonprofit corp.
Admissions Requirements Minimum age 18; Medical examination; Physician's request; Physically disabled and traumatic brain injured.
Staff Physicians 1 (pt); RNs 1 (ft); LPNs 3 (ft); Nurses' aides 7 (ft); Physical therapists (contracted); Reality therapists 1 (pt); Recreational therapists 1 (pt); Occupational therapists 1 (pt); Speech therapists 1 (pt); Activities coordinators 1 (pt); Dietitians (contracted).
Facilities Dining room; Physical therapy room; Activities room; Crafts room; Laundry room.
Activities Arts & crafts; Cards; Games; Reading groups; Movies; Shopping trips; Dances/Social/Cultural gatherings; Independent living skills; Cognitive retraining.

Mandan Villa
201 14th St NW, Mandan, ND 58554
(701) 663-4267
Admin Layne Gross. *Dir of Nursing* Lila Kalvoda. *Medical Dir* Arthur Van Vranken MD.
Licensure Skilled care; Intermediate care; Alzheimer's care. *Beds* SNF 92; ICF 28. *Certified* Medicaid; Medicare.
Owner Proprietary corp (Beverly Enterprises).
Admissions Requirements Medical examination.
Staff RNs 7 (ft); LPNs 8 (ft); Nurses' aides 20 (ft), 15 (pt); Physical therapists 1 (pt); Activities coordinators 3 (ft), 2 (pt); Dietitians 1 (pt).
Facilities Dining room; Physical therapy room; Activities room; Crafts room; Laundry room; Barber/Beauty shop.
Activities Arts & crafts; Cards; Games; Reading groups; Prayer groups; Movies; Shopping trips; Dances/Social/Cultural gatherings.

Mayville

Luther Memorial Home
750 Main St E, Mayville, ND 58257
(701) 786-2172
Admin Brett Ulrich. *Dir of Nursing* Margaret Dahl.
Licensure Skilled care; Intermediate care. *Beds* SNF 69; ICF 30. *Certified* Medicaid; Medicare.
Affiliation Lutheran.

McVille

Friendship Healthcare Center
Nyhus St, McVille, ND 58254
(701) 322-4314
Admin Mark Johnson. *Dir of Nursing* Marcia
Wilson.
Licensure Skilled care. *Beds* SNF 52. *Certified*
Medicaid; Medicare.

Minot

Americana Healthcare Center
600 S Main, Minot, ND 58701
(701) 852-1255
Admin Deborah Barnes. *Dir of Nursing* Mary
Kraljic. *Medical Dir* Dr Richard Larson.
Licensure Skilled care. *Beds* 106. *Certified*
Medicaid; Medicare.
Owner Proprietary corp (Manor Care Inc).
Admissions Requirements Medical
examination.
Staff RNs 7 (ft), 5 (pt); LPNs 4 (ft), 2 (pt);
Nurses' aides 30 (ft), 22 (pt); Physical
therapists 1 (ft); Recreational therapists;
Occupational therapists 1 (pt); Speech
therapists 1 (pt); Activities coordinators 1
(ft); Dietitians 1 (pt).
Facilities Dining room; Physical therapy
room; Activities room; Chapel; Crafts room;
Laundry room; Barber/Beauty shop.
Activities Arts & crafts; Cards; Games;
Reading groups; Prayer groups; Movies;
Shopping trips; Dances/Social/Cultural
gatherings.

Trinity Nursing Home
305 8th Ave SE, Minot, ND 58701
(701) 857-5000
Admin Terry G Hoff. *Dir of Nursing* Margaret
Smothers RN.
Licensure Skilled care; Intermediate care;
Retirement; Alzheimer's care. *Beds* SNF
204; ICF 121. *Certified* Medicaid; Medicare.
Owner Nonprofit corp.
Admissions Requirements Medical
examination; Physician's request.
Staff Physicians 1 (pt); RNs 13 (ft), 12 (pt);
LPNs 17 (ft), 15 (pt); Nurses' aides 67 (ft),
65 (pt); Physical therapists 1 (ft);
Recreational therapists 7 (ft); Occupational
therapists 1 (pt); Speech therapists 1 (pt);
Activities coordinators 1 (ft); Dietitians 1
(ft); Ophthalmologists 1 (pt).
Languages Norwegian.
Facilities Dining room; Physical therapy
room; Activities room; Chapel; Crafts room;
Laundry room; Barber/Beauty shop; Sewing
room.
Activities Arts & crafts; Cards; Games;
Reading groups; Prayer groups; Movies;
Shopping trips; Dances/Social/Cultural
gatherings.

Mohall

North Central Good Samaritan Center
602 E Main St, Mohall, ND 58761
(701) 756-6831
Admin Paul Schroeder. *Dir of Nursing* Cindy
Strand.
Licensure Intermediate care. *Beds* ICF 59.
Certified Medicaid.
Owner Nonprofit corp (Evangelical Lutheran/
Good Samaritan Society).

Mott

Mott Good Samaritan Nursing Center
401 Millionaire Ave, Mott, ND 58646
(701) 824-3222
Admin Mildred Waddell. *Dir of Nursing*
Kathryn Greff.
Licensure Intermediate care. *Beds* ICF 60.
Certified Medicaid.

Owner Nonprofit corp (Evangelical Lutheran/
Good Samaritan Society).
Admissions Requirements Medical
examination.
Affiliation Lutheran.
Facilities Dining room; Activities room;
Chapel; Crafts room; Laundry room; Barber/
Beauty shop; Library.
Activities Arts & crafts; Cards; Games;
Reading groups; Prayer groups; Movies;
Shopping trips; Dances/Social/Cultural
gatherings.

Napoleon

Logan County Home for the Aged
311 E 4th, Napoleon, ND 58561
(701) 754-2602
Admin Kyle Engelhardt. *Dir of Nursing*
Shirley Regner.
Licensure Intermediate care. *Beds* ICF 44.
Certified Medicaid.
Staff RNs 3 (pt); LPNs 2 (pt); Nurses' aides 5
(ft), 7 (pt); Activities coordinators 1 (ft);
Dietitians 1 (pt).
Facilities Dining room; Activities room;
Chapel; Crafts room; Laundry room; Barber/
Beauty shop.
Activities Arts & crafts; Cards; Games;
Reading groups; Prayer groups; Movies;
Shopping trips; Dances/Social/Cultural
gatherings.

New Rockford

Lutheran Home of the Good Shepherd
1226 1st Ave N, New Rockford, ND 58536
(701) 947-2944
Admin Tim Burchill. *Dir of Nursing* Kathryn
Jenrick. *Medical Dir* Dr E J Schwinghamer.
Licensure Skilled care; Intermediate care. *Beds*
SNF 58; ICF 28. *Certified* Medicaid;
Medicare.
Admissions Requirements Medical
examination.
Affiliation Lutheran.
Facilities Dining room; Activities room;
Crafts room; Laundry room; Barber/Beauty
shop.
Activities Arts & crafts; Cards; Games;
Reading groups; Prayer groups; Movies;
Shopping trips; Dances/Social/Cultural
gatherings.

New Salem

Elm Crest Manor
100 Elm Ave, Box 396, New Salem, ND
58563
(701) 843-7526
Admin Gary Kreidt. *Dir of Nursing* Laverne
Lottes RN. *Medical Dir* Steve Miller MD.
Licensure Intermediate care. *Beds* ICF 60.
Private Pay Patients 50%. *Certified*
Medicaid.
Owner Nonprofit corp.
Admissions Requirements Medical
examination.
Staff RNs 2 (ft), 3 (pt); LPNs 3 (ft), 2 (pt);
Nurses' aides 8 (ft), 15 (pt); Activities
coordinators 1 (ft).
Affiliation United Church of Christ.
Facilities Dining room; Physical therapy
room; Activities room; Chapel; Crafts room;
Laundry room; Barber/Beauty shop.
Activities Arts & crafts; Cards; Games; Prayer
groups; Movies; Shopping trips; Dances/
Social/Cultural gatherings; Pet therapy.

New Town

New Town Nursing Home
Box 399, New Town, ND 58763
(701) 627-4711

Admin Lorraine Quie. *Dir of Nursing* Brenda
Carnicas RN. *Medical Dir* Herbert J Wilson
MD.
Licensure Skilled care; Intermediate care. *Beds*
Swing beds SNF/ICF 67. *Private Pay
Patients* 26%. *Certified* Medicaid; Medicare.
Owner Nonprofit corp (Evangelical Lutheran/
Good Samaritan Society).
Admissions Requirements Medical
examination; Physician's request.
Staff Physicians; RNs; LPNs; Nurses' aides;
Physical therapists; Occupational therapists;
Activities coordinators; Dietitians.
Affiliation Lutheran.
Facilities Dining room; Physical therapy
room; Activities room; Chapel; Crafts room;
Laundry room; Barber/Beauty shop.
Activities Cards; Games; Reading groups;
Prayer groups; Movies; Shopping trips;
Dances/Social/Cultural gatherings.

Northwood

**Northwood Deaconess Hospital & Home
Association**
PO Box 190, 4 N Park St, Northwood, ND
58267
(701) 587-6060, 587-6009 FAX
Admin Larry Feickert. *Dir of Nursing* Carla
Sletten RN. *Medical Dir* Dr Jonathon Berg.
Licensure Skilled care; Intermediate care;
Retirement. *Beds* SNF 51; ICF 39;
Retirement 28. *Certified* Medicaid;
Medicare.
Owner Nonprofit organization/foundation.
Admissions Requirements Medical
examination.
Staff RNs 5 (ft), 3 (pt); LPNs 5 (ft), 8 (pt);
Nurses' aides 18 (ft), 42 (pt); Physical
therapists 2 (pt); Recreational therapists 1
(ft), 3 (pt); Activities coordinators 1 (ft).
Affiliation Lutheran.
Facilities Dining room; Physical therapy
room; Activities room; Chapel; Crafts room;
Laundry room; Barber/Beauty shop; Library.
Activities Arts & crafts; Cards; Games;
Reading groups; Prayer groups; Movies;
Shopping trips; Dances/Social/Cultural
gatherings; Intergenerational programs; Pet
therapy.

Oakes

Oakes Manor Good Samaritan Center
213 N 9th, Oakes, ND 58474
(701) 742-3274
Admin Marlyn Tande. *Dir of Nursing* Marilyn
Folkestad. *Medical Dir* Dr Rup Nagala.
Licensure Intermediate care. *Beds* ICF 142.
Private Pay Patients 40%. *Certified*
Medicaid.
Owner Nonprofit corp (Evangelical Lutheran/
Good Samaritan Society).
Admissions Requirements Medical
examination.
Staff RNs 2 (ft), 6 (pt); LPNs 2 (ft), 6 (pt);
Nurses' aides 20 (ft), 30 (pt); Activities
coordinators 1 (ft); Dietitians 1 (pt).
Affiliation Lutheran.
Facilities Dining room; Physical therapy
room; Activities room; Crafts room; Laundry
room; Barber/Beauty shop.
Activities Arts & crafts; Cards; Games;
Reading groups; Prayer groups; Shopping
trips; Dances/Social/Cultural gatherings;
Intergenerational programs; Pet therapy.

Osnabrock

Good Samaritan Center
HCR 1 Box 4, Osnabrock, ND 58269
(701) 496-3131
Admin Rob Kretzinger. *Dir of Nursing* Joanne
Samuelson. *Medical Dir* Dr Warren Jensen.

Licensure Intermediate care. *Beds* ICF 41.
Private Pay Patients 53%. *Certified*
Medicaid.
Owner Nonprofit corp (Evangelical Lutheran/
Good Samaritan Society).
Admissions Requirements Medical
examination; Physician's request.
Staff RNs 2 (ft), 1 (pt); LPNs 2 (ft), 3 (pt);
Nurses' aides 2 (ft), 14 (pt); Activities
coordinators 1 (ft).
Affiliation Lutheran.
Facilities Dining room; Physical therapy
room; Activities room; Laundry room;
Barber/Beauty shop; Family room.
Activities Arts & crafts; Cards; Games;
Reading groups; Prayer groups; Movies;
Shopping trips; Dances/Social/Cultural
gatherings; Intergenerational programs.

Park River

Park River Good Samaritan Center
301 S Hwy 12, Box 659, Park River, ND
58270
(701) 284-7115
Admin Jerome Swanson. *Dir of Nursing* Grace
Rhodes. *Medical Dir* Dr M J Lewis.
Licensure Skilled care; Retirement. *Beds* SNF
80. *Certified* Medicaid; Medicare.
Owner Nonprofit corp (Evangelical Lutheran/
Good Samaritan Society).
Admissions Requirements Medical
examination.
Staff RNs 6 (ft); LPNs 4 (ft), 4 (pt); Nurses'
aides 2 (ft), 1 (pt); Nurses' aides 8 (ft), 18
(pt); Physical therapists 2 (pt); Activities
coordinators 1 (ft).
Facilities Dining room; Physical therapy
room; Activities room; Laundry room;
Barber/Beauty shop; Non-denominational
chapel; Crafts room; Library room.
Activities Arts & crafts; Cards; Games;
Reading groups; Prayer groups; Movies;
Shopping trips; Dances/Social/Cultural
gatherings.

Parshall

Rock View Good Samaritan Center
Parshall, ND 58770
(701) 862-3138
Admin Mary Brendle. *Dir of Nursing* Rebecca
Rortvedt.
Licensure Intermediate care. *Beds* ICF 60.
Certified Medicaid.
Owner Nonprofit corp (Evangelical Lutheran/
Good Samaritan Society).

Rolette

Presentation Care Center—Rolette
304 John St, Rolette, ND 58366
(701) 246-3786
Admin Michael Baumgartner. *Dir of Nursing*
Peggy McDougall.
Licensure Skilled care; Intermediate care. *Beds*
Swing beds SNF/ICF 48. *Certified* Medicare.

Rolla

Rolla Community Hospital—SNF
213 3rd St NE, Rolla, ND 58367
(701) 477-3161
Admin Michael Baumgartner.
Medical Dir Arnold Overland.
Licensure Skilled care; Intermediate care. *Beds*
SNF 26; ICF 22. *Certified* Medicaid;
Medicare.
Owner Publicly owned.
Staff RNs 2 (ft), 1 (pt); LPNs 4 (ft), 3 (pt);
Nurses' aides 15 (ft), 7 (pt); Physical
therapists 1 (ft); Occupational therapists 1
(ft); Activities coordinators 1 (ft), 1 (pt).
Facilities Dining room; Physical therapy
room; Activities room; Chapel; Crafts room;
Laundry room; Barber/Beauty shop; Library.

Activities Arts & crafts; Cards; Games;
Reading groups; Prayer groups; Movies;
Shopping trips; Dances/Social/Cultural
gatherings.

Rugby

Good Samaritan
PO Box 197, Rugby, ND 58368-9998
(701) 776-5261
Admin Charles Schulz. *Dir of Nursing* Lavona
Gebhardt. *Medical Dir* Dr Lee Potter.
Licensure Skilled care; Intermediate care. *Beds*
SNF 74; ICF 30. *Certified* Medicaid;
Medicare.
Affiliation Lutheran.
Facilities Dining room; Activities room;
Chapel; Crafts room; Laundry room; Barber/
Beauty shop; Library; Family room.
Activities Arts & crafts; Cards; Games;
Reading groups; Prayer groups; Movies;
Shopping trips; Dances/Social/Cultural
gatherings.

Harold S Haaland Home
1025 3rd Ave S, Rugby, ND 58368
(701) 776-6839
Admin Chuck Schultz.
Medical Dir Kay Hovland.
Licensure Basic/custodial; Retirement;
Alzheimer's care. *Beds* Basic/custodial 80.
Certified Medicaid; Medicare.
Owner Nonprofit organization/foundation.
Admissions Requirements Medical
examination; Physician's request.
Staff Physicians (consultants) 12 (ft); RNs 1
(ft); LPNs 2 (ft), 3 (pt); Nurses' aides 3 (ft),
6 (pt); Dietitians 1 (pt).
Languages Norwegian German, French.
Facilities Dining room; Activities room;
Chapel; Crafts room; Laundry room; Barber/
Beauty shop; Library; Greenhouse;
Carpenter shop; Exercise course.
Activities Arts & crafts; Cards; Games;
Reading groups; Prayer groups; Movies;
Shopping trips; Dances/Social/Cultural
gatherings; Bus trips; Bingo; Exercises;
Cooking; Baking; Fishing; Gardening;
Recitals.

Stanley

Mountrail Bethel Home
Box 700, Stanley, ND 58784
(701) 628-2442
Admin Fern Wittmayer. *Dir of Nursing* Judith
Skaar. *Medical Dir* Dr Dietmar Bennett.
Licensure Skilled care. *Beds* Swing beds SNF/
ICF 57. *Private Pay Patients* 48%. *Certified*
Medicaid; Medicare.
Owner Nonprofit organization/foundation.
Admissions Requirements Medical
examination.
Staff RNs 1 (ft), 2 (pt); LPNs 3 (ft), 1 (pt);
Nurses' aides 15 (ft), 18 (pt); Recreational
therapists 1 (ft), 1 (pt); Activities
coordinators 1 (ft), 1 (pt); Dietitians
(consultant).
Affiliation Evangelical Lutheran.
Facilities Dining room; Physical therapy
room; Activities room; Chapel; Crafts room;
Laundry room; Barber/Beauty shop; Library;
Family visitation room.
Activities Arts & crafts; Cards; Games;
Reading groups; Prayer groups; Movies;
Shopping trips; Dances/Social/Cultural
gatherings; Intergenerational programs; Pet
therapy.

Steele

Golden Manor Inc
215 4th St NW, Steele, ND 58482
(701) 475-2251
Admin Mark A Pederson. *Dir of Nursing* Alice
Olson RN. *Medical Dir* Ron Tello MD.

Licensure Intermediate care. *Beds* ICF 42.
Private Pay Patients 60%. *Certified*
Medicaid.
Owner Nonprofit corp.
Admissions Requirements Medical
examination.
Staff RNs 4 (pt); LPNs 2 (pt); Nurses' aides 5
(ft), 8 (pt); Physical therapists 1 (ft), 1 (pt);
Recreational therapists 1 (pt); Activities
coordinators 1 (ft), 3 (pt).
Facilities Dining room; Activities room;
Crafts room; Barber/Beauty shop.
Activities Arts & crafts; Cards; Games;
Reading groups; Prayer groups; Movies;
Shopping trips; Dances/Social/Cultural
gatherings.

Strasburg

Strasburg Nursing Home
Rte 1 Box 220, Strasburg, ND 58573
(701) 336-2651
Admin Andrew J Reis. *Dir of Nursing* Judy
Reierson. *Medical Dir* H P Janssen MD.
Licensure Skilled care. *Beds* SNF 80. *Certified*
Medicaid; Medicare.
Owner Nonprofit corp.
Admissions Requirements Medical
examination; Physician's request.
Staff RNs 5 (ft), 4 (pt); LPNs 2 (ft), 2 (pt);
Nurses' aides 16 (ft), 13 (pt); Activities
coordinators 1 (ft); Dietitians 1 (pt).
Languages German.
Facilities Dining room; Physical therapy
room; Activities room; Chapel; Laundry
room; Barber/Beauty shop.
Activities Arts & crafts; Cards; Games;
Reading groups; Prayer groups; Movies.

Tioga

Tioga Community Nursing Home
810 N Welo St, Tioga, ND 58852
(701) 664-3313
Admin Lowell D Herfindahl. *Dir of Nursing*
Shelly Anderson. *Medical Dir* Dr Mukesh U
Patel.
Licensure Skilled care. *Beds* SNF 30. *Certified*
Medicaid; Medicare.
Owner Nonprofit corp.
Admissions Requirements Medical
examination; Physician's request.
Staff Physicians 2 (pt); RNs 1 (ft), 3 (pt);
LPNs 3 (ft), 10 (pt); Nurses' aides 5 (ft), 11
(pt); Physical therapists 1 (pt); Activities
coordinators 1 (pt); Dietitians 1 (pt).
Facilities Dining room; Activities room;
Chapel; Crafts room; Barber/Beauty shop.
Activities Arts & crafts; Cards; Games;
Reading groups; Prayer groups; Movies;
Shopping trips; Dances/Social/Cultural
gatherings.

Underwood

Prairieview Homes Inc
83 Lincoln Ave, Box 10, Underwood, ND
58576
(701) 442-3222
Admin Randal Albrecht. *Dir of Nursing*
Coleen Schulz. *Medical Dir* Dr John T
Boyle.
Licensure Skilled care. *Beds* SNF 64. *Certified*
Medicaid; Medicare.
Owner Proprietary corp.
Admissions Requirements Medical
examination; Physician's request.
Staff RNs 2 (ft), 8 (pt); LPNs 3 (pt); Nurses'
aides 3 (ft), 23 (pt); Activities coordinators 1
(ft), 1 (pt).
Facilities Dining room; Physical therapy
room; Activities room; Chapel; Laundry
room; Barber/Beauty shop.
Activities Arts & crafts; Cards; Games;
Reading groups; Prayer groups; Movies.

Valley City

Sheyenne Care Center
979 Central Ave N, Valley City, ND 58072
(701) 845-2320, 845-8222 ICF
Admin James Tourville. *Dir of Nursing*
  Marlene Deschamp SNF; Kathy Lindemann
  ICF. *Medical Dir* Dr R E Wiisanen.
Licensure Skilled care; Intermediate care. *Beds*
  SNF 78; ICF 92. *Certified* Medicaid;
  Medicare.
Owner Nonprofit corp (Lutheran Health
  Systems).
Admissions Requirements Medical
  examination; Physician's request.
Facilities Dining room; Physical therapy
  room; Activities room; Chapel; Crafts room;
  Laundry room; Barber/Beauty shop.
Activities Arts & crafts; Cards; Games; Prayer
  groups; Movies; Shopping trips; Dances/
  Social/Cultural gatherings.

Velva

Souris Valley Care Center
Hwy 41 S, Velva, ND 58790
(701) 338-2072
Admin James Sewick. *Dir of Nursing* DeMaris
  Fitzpatrick.
Licensure Intermediate care. *Beds* ICF 48.
Owner Nonprofit corp.
Admissions Requirements Minimum age 55;
  Medical examination; Physician's request.
Staff RNs 2 (pt); LPNs 7 (pt); Nurses' aides
  25 (pt); Activities coordinators 1 (pt).
Affiliation Lutheran.
Facilities Dining room; Physical therapy
  room; Activities room; Chapel; Crafts room;
  Laundry room; Barber/Beauty shop; Library.
Activities Arts & crafts; Cards; Games;
  Reading groups; Prayer groups; Movies;
  Shopping trips; Dances/Social/Cultural
  gatherings.

Wahpeton

Wahpeton Health Care Center
1307 N 7th St, Wahpeton, ND 58075
(701) 642-6667
Admin Kathy Hoeft. *Dir of Nursing* Theresa
  Rick. *Medical Dir* Evelyn Aguila.
Licensure Skilled care; Intermediate care. *Beds*
  SNF 109; ICF 89. *Private Pay Patients* 40%.
  Certified Medicaid; Medicare.
Owner Nonprofit organization/foundation
  (Benedictine Healthcare).
Admissions Requirements Physician's request.
Staff Physicians 15 (ft); RNs 10 (ft); LPNs 25
  (ft); Nurses' aides 70 (ft); Physical therapists
  1 (pt); Occupational therapists 1 (pt); Speech
  therapists 1 (pt); Activities coordinators 1
  (ft); Dietitians 1 (ft).
Facilities Dining room; Physical therapy
  room; Activities room; Crafts room; Laundry
  room; Barber/Beauty shop.

Activities Arts & crafts; Cards; Games;
  Reading groups; Prayer groups; Movies;
  Shopping trips; Dances/Social/Cultural
  gatherings; Intergenerational programs; Pet
  therapy.

Walhalla

Pembilier Nursing Center
Box 467, 500 Delano, Walhalla, ND 58282
(701) 549-3310
Admin Tim Miller. *Dir of Nursing* Carol
  Anderson. *Medical Dir* Dr Warren Jensen.
Licensure Skilled care. *Beds* SNF 60. *Private
  Pay Patients* 50%. *Certified* Medicaid;
  Medicare.
Owner Nonprofit organization/foundation.
Admissions Requirements Medical
  examination; Physician's request.
Staff Physicians 3 (pt); RNs 2 (ft), 2 (pt);
  LPNs 3 (ft), 3 (pt); Nurses' aides 20 (ft), 14
  (pt); Physical therapists 2 (pt); Activities
  coordinators 1 (ft), 2 (pt); Dietitians 1 (pt).
Facilities Dining room; Physical therapy
  room; Activities room; Chapel; Crafts room;
  Laundry room; Barber/Beauty shop.
Activities Arts & crafts; Cards; Games;
  Reading groups; Prayer groups; Movies;
  Shopping trips.

Watford City

Good Shepherd Home
709 4th Ave NE, Box 564, Watford City, ND
  58854
(701) 842-2331
Admin Nyla J Dahl. *Dir of Nursing* Rebecca
  Heringer. *Medical Dir* G D Ebel MD.
Licensure Skilled care; Retirement. *Beds* SNF
  49; Retirement apts 7. *Private Pay Patients*
  60%. *Certified* Medicaid; Medicare.
Owner Nonprofit organization/foundation.
Admissions Requirements Medical
  examination; Physician's request.
Staff Physicians 2 (pt); RNs 2 (ft), 3 (pt);
  LPNs 1 (ft), 6 (pt); Nurses' aides 5 (ft), 20
  (pt); Physical therapists 1 (pt); Activities
  coordinators 1 (ft), 1 (pt); Dietitians 1 (pt);
  Ophthalmologists 1 (pt).
Languages Norwegian.
Affiliation Evangelical Lutheran.
Facilities Dining room; Physical therapy
  room; Activities room; Chapel; Crafts room;
  Laundry room; Barber/Beauty shop; Library.
Activities Arts & crafts; Cards; Games;
  Reading groups; Prayer groups; Movies;
  Shopping trips; Dances/Social/Cultural
  gatherings; Intergenerational programs; Pet
  therapy.

Westhope

Westhope Home
PO Box 366, 201 3rd St E, Westhope, ND
  58793
(701) 245-6477
Admin Darwin M Lee. *Dir of Nursing* Jeanive
  Solheim. *Medical Dir* Dr Kenneth Kihle.
Licensure Skilled care; Intermediate care. *Beds*
  Swing beds SNF/ICF 59. *Private Pay
  Patients* 60%. *Certified* Medicaid; Medicare.
Owner Nonprofit organization/foundation.
Admissions Requirements Minimum age 16;
  Medical examination; Physician's request.
Staff Physicians 4 (pt); RNs 5 (ft), 1 (pt);
  LPNs 3 (ft), 1 (pt); Nurses' aides 15 (ft), 13
  (pt); Physical therapists 1 (pt); Activities
  coordinators 1 (ft); Dietitians 1 (pt).
Affiliation Lutheran.
Facilities Dining room; Physical therapy
  room; Activities room; Chapel; Crafts room;
  Laundry room; Barber/Beauty shop; Bus;
  Park; Clinic.
Activities Arts & crafts; Cards; Games;
  Reading groups; Prayer groups; Movies;
  Shopping trips; Dances/Social/Cultural
  gatherings; Intergenerational programs; Pet
  therapy; Bus outings.

Williston

Bethel Lutheran Home
PO Box 1828, 1515 2nd Ave W, Williston,
  ND 58802-1828
(701) 572-6766
Admin Wayne L Hansen. *Dir of Nursing* Opal
  Smith.
Licensure Skilled care; Intermediate care. *Beds*
  SNF 118; ICF 61. *Certified* Medicaid;
  Medicare.

Wishek

Wishek Home for the Aged
400 S 4th, Box 187, Wishek, ND 58495
(701) 452-2333
Admin Harvey Schanzenbach. *Dir of Nursing*
  Ramona Dewald. *Medical Dir* Dr Kosiak.
Licensure Skilled care; Retirement. *Beds* SNF
  95. *Certified* Medicaid; Medicare.
Owner Nonprofit corp.
Admissions Requirements Medical
  examination; Physician's request.
Staff Physicians 2 (pt); RNs 3 (ft); LPNs 5
  (ft), 3 (pt); Nurses' aides 20 (ft), 10 (pt);
  Physical therapists 2 (pt); Dietitians 1 (ft).
Languages German.
Affiliation Church of Christ.
Facilities Dining room; Physical therapy
  room; Activities room; Chapel; Crafts room;
  Laundry room; Barber/Beauty shop; Library.
Activities Arts & crafts; Cards; Games;
  Reading groups; Prayer groups; Movies;
  Shopping trips; Dances/Social/Cultural
  gatherings.

OHIO

Adena

McGraw Nursing Home
Rte 2, 73841 Pleasant Grove, Adena, OH 43901
(614) 546-3013
Licensure Intermediate care. *Beds* ICF 43. *Certified* Medicaid.
Owner Proprietary corp.

Reynolds Nursing Home Inc
Rte 1, Adena, OH 43901
(614) 546-3620
Licensure Intermediate care. *Beds* ICF 50. *Certified* Medicaid.
Owner Proprietary corp.

Akron

Dee-Maret Nursing Home
1140 S Hawkins Ave, Akron, OH 44320
(216) 836-2310
Licensure Nursing home. *Beds* 13.
Owner Proprietary corp.

Ellet Manor
2755 Ellet Ave, Akron, OH 44312
(216) 733-3623
Admin Mariann Riley. *Dir of Nursing* Lisa Cohen RN. *Medical Dir* George Tabakov MD.
Licensure Intermediate care; Alzheimer's care. *Beds* ICF 16. *Certified* Medicaid.
Owner Proprietary corp.
Admissions Requirements Medical examination.
Staff LPNs 3 (ft), 1 (pt); Nurses' aides 6 (ft), 3 (pt); Recreational therapists 1 (pt); Activities coordinators 1 (ft); Dietitians 1 (pt); Podiatrists 1 (pt).
Facilities Dining room; Activities room; Crafts room; Laundry room.
Activities Arts & crafts; Cards; Games; Reading groups; Prayer groups; Movies; Shopping trips; Dances/Social/Cultural gatherings.

Frederick Boulevard Group Home
1445 Frederick Blvd, Akron, OH 44320
(216) 836-4244
Licensure Intermediate care for mentally retarded. *Beds* ICF/MR 10. *Certified* Medicaid.
Owner Proprietary corp.

Greenlawn Avenue Group Home
1588 Greenlawn Ave, Akron, OH 44301
(216) 773-6282
Licensure Intermediate care for mentally retarded. *Beds* ICF/MR 22. *Certified* Medicaid.
Owner Proprietary corp.

Healthaven Nursing Home
615 Latham Ln, Akron, OH 44319
(216) 644-3914
Medical Dir Dr John M Kim.
Licensure Intermediate care. *Beds* ICF 56. *Certified* Medicaid.

Owner Proprietary corp.
Admissions Requirements Minimum age 60; Medical examination.
Staff Physicians 1 (ft); RNs 1 (ft), 1 (pt); LPNs 6 (ft), 4 (pt); Nurses' aides 16 (ft), 9 (pt); Activities coordinators 1 (pt); Dietitians 1 (pt).
Affiliation Methodist.
Facilities Dining room; Activities room; Crafts room; Laundry room; Library.
Activities Arts & crafts; Cards; Games; Prayer groups; Movies; Shopping trips.

Hillhaven Convalescent Center
145 Olive St, Akron, OH 44310
(216) 762-0901
Admin A Wayne Davis. *Dir of Nursing* Lois Douglas RN. *Medical Dir* Walter R Hoffman DO.
Licensure Skilled care; Intermediate care. *Beds* SNF 30; ICF 144. *Certified* Medicaid; Medicare.
Owner Proprietary corp (Hillhaven Corp).
Admissions Requirements Medical examination; Physician's request.
Staff Physicians 40 (pt); RNs 6 (ft), 3 (pt); LPNs 10 (ft), 15 (pt); Nurses' aides 48 (ft), 9 (pt); Physical therapists 1 (ft); Recreational therapists 1 (ft); Occupational therapists 1 (pt); Speech therapists 1 (pt); Activities coordinators 2 (ft); Dietitians 1 (pt); Ophthalmologists 1 (pt); Podiatrists 1 (pt); Dentists 1 (pt).
Facilities Dining room; Physical therapy room; Activities room; Chapel; Crafts room; Laundry room; Barber/Beauty shop.
Activities Arts & crafts; Cards; Games; Reading groups; Prayer groups; Movies; Shopping trips.

Little Forest Medical Center
797 E Market St, Akron, OH 44305
(216) 434-4514
Licensure Skilled care; Intermediate care. *Beds* Swing beds SNF/ICF 256. *Certified* Medicaid; Medicare.
Owner Proprietary corp.

Lorantffy Care Center Inc
2631 Copley Rd, Akron, OH 44321
(216) 666-1313, 666-2611
Admin Rev Tibor Domotor. *Dir of Nursing* Clara Brown RN. *Medical Dir* Arpad Batizy MD.
Licensure Skilled care; Intermediate care; Rest home. *Beds* ICF 74; ICF 12; Rest home 15. *Certified* Medicaid; Medicare.
Owner Proprietary corp.
Admissions Requirements Medical examination.
Staff Physicians; RNs; LPNs; Nurses' aides; Physical therapists; Speech therapists; Activities coordinators; Dietitians.
Languages Hungarian.
Affiliation Christian Reformed Hungarian Church.
Facilities Dining room; Physical therapy room; Activities room; Chapel; Crafts room; Laundry room; Barber/Beauty shop.

Activities Arts & crafts; Cards; Games; Prayer groups; Movies; Dances/Social/Cultural gatherings; Church services.

Manor Care Nursing Center of Akron
1211 W Market St, Akron, OH 44313
(216) 867-8530
Admin Pat Tyler. *Dir of Nursing* Mary Ann Webb RN. *Medical Dir* Dr Stephen Cochran.
Licensure Skilled care; Intermediate care; Hyperalimentation and dialysis care. *Beds* SNF 36; ICF 73. *Private Pay Patients* 90%. *Certified* Medicare.
Owner Proprietary corp (Manor Care).
Admissions Requirements Minimum age 16; Medical examination; Physician's request.
Staff Physicians 1 (ft); RNs 8 (ft), 4 (pt); LPNs 13 (ft), 10 (pt); Nurses' aides 30 (ft), 12 (pt); Physical therapists 1 (ft); Recreational therapists 1 (ft); Occupational therapists 1 (ft); Speech therapists 1 (ft); Activities coordinators 1 (ft); Dietitians 1 (ft); Ophthalmologists 1 (ft); Podiatrists 1 (ft); Audiologists 1 (ft).
Languages Sign.
Facilities Dining room; Physical therapy room; Activities room; Crafts room; Laundry room; Barber/Beauty shop; Library.
Activities Arts & crafts; Cards; Games; Reading groups; Prayer groups; Movies; Shopping trips; Dances/Social/Cultural gatherings; Intergenerational programs; Pet therapy; Outside trips; Family participation.

MARS—Springfield Group Home
3568 E Waterloo Rd, Akron, OH 44312
(216) 628-5885
Licensure Intermediate care for mentally retarded. *Beds* ICF/MR 8. *Certified* Medicaid.
Owner Proprietary corp.

Middlebury Manor Nursing & Convalescent Home
974 E Market St, Akron, OH 44305
(216) 659-6167
Licensure Skilled care; Intermediate care. *Beds* Swing beds SNF/ICF 150. *Certified* Medicaid; Medicare.
Owner Nonprofit corp.

Ridgewood Place
3558 Ridgewood Rd, Akron, OH 44313
(216) 666-3776
Admin John Durkin. *Dir of Nursing* Laura Debord RN. *Medical Dir* Dr Dale Dodd.
Licensure Skilled care; Intermediate care. *Beds* SNF 48; Swing beds SNF/ICF 139. *Private Pay Patients* 21%. *Certified* Medicaid; Medicare.
Owner Proprietary corp.
Admissions Requirements Medical examination; Physician's request.
Staff Physicians 1 (ft); RNs 6 (ft); LPNs 23 (ft); Nurses' aides 43 (ft), 18 (pt); Physical therapists 2 (ft); Occupational therapists 1 (pt); Speech therapists 1 (pt); Activities coordinators 2 (ft); Dietitians 1 (ft).

Languages Greek, Hungarian.
Facilities Dining room; Physical therapy room; Activities room; Laundry room; Barber/Beauty shop.
Activities Arts & crafts; Games; Reading groups; Prayer groups; Movies; Shopping trips; Dances/Social/Cultural gatherings; Pet therapy.

Rockynol Retirement Community
1596 Newcastle Cir, Akron, OH 44313
(216) 867-2150
Admin Thomas Miller; Mary Cochran. *Dir of Nursing* Rose Scaduto. *Medical Dir* Steve Cochran MD.
Licensure Skilled care; Intermediate care; Rest home; Retirement. *Beds* Swing beds SNF/ICF 72; Rest home 34; Retirement 138. *Private Pay Patients* 38%. *Certified* Medicaid; Medicare.
Owner Nonprofit corp (Ohio Presbyterian Retirement Service).
Admissions Requirements Minimum age 60.
Staff Physicians (consultant); RNs 6 (ft), 8 (pt); LPNs 5 (ft), 11 (pt); Nurses' aides 26 (ft), 10 (pt); Physical therapists (contracted); Occupational therapists (contracted); Speech therapists (contracted); Activities coordinators 3 (ft); Dietitians 1 (ft); Ophthalmologists (contracted); Podiatrists (contracted); Audiologists (contracted).
Affiliation Presbyterian.
Facilities Dining room; Physical therapy room; Activities room; Chapel; Crafts room; Barber/Beauty shop; Library; Laundry services provided.
Activities Arts & crafts; Cards; Games; Reading groups; Prayer groups; Movies; Shopping trips; Dances/Social/Cultural gatherings; Intergenerational programs; Pet therapy; Baking; Special lunches; Special Alzheimer activities.

St Edward Home
3131 Smith Rd, Akron, OH 44313
(216) 666-1183
Admin John J Hennelly. *Dir of Nursing* Donna Bender RN.
Licensure Intermediate care; Alzheimer's care. *Beds* ICF 100. *Certified* Medicaid.
Owner Proprietary corp.
Admissions Requirements Medical examination.
Staff RNs 4 (ft), 8 (pt); LPNs 2 (ft), 4 (pt); Nurses' aides 28 (ft), 19 (pt); Activities coordinators 1 (ft); Dietitians 1 (ft).
Affiliation Roman Catholic.
Facilities Dining room; Physical therapy room; Activities room; Chapel; Crafts room; Laundry room; Secluded walkway with terraces; Picnic pavilion.
Activities Arts & crafts; Cards; Games; Reading groups; Prayer groups; Movies; Shopping trips; Dances/Social/Cultural gatherings; Religious services.

Edwin Shaw Hospital
1621 Flickinger Rd, Akron, OH 44312
(216) 784-1271
Licensure Skilled care; Intermediate care. *Beds* SNF 43; ICF 18. *Certified* Medicaid; Medicare.
Owner Publicly owned.

Sumner Home for the Aged
80 W Center St, 604, Akron, OH 44308
(216) 762-9341
Admin Christine Hunter. *Dir of Nursing* Marie Fatur.
Licensure Skilled care; Intermediate care; Rest home. *Beds* Swing beds SNF/ICF 30; Rest home 70.
Owner Proprietary corp.
Admissions Requirements Minimum age 65; Medical examination.

Staff RNs 1 (ft), 2 (pt); LPNs 6 (ft), 6 (pt); Nurses' aides 1 (ft), 6 (pt); Physical therapists; Recreational therapists 1 (ft); Activities coordinators 1 (ft); Dietitians; Ophthalmologists; Dentists.
Facilities Dining room; Physical therapy room; Activities room; Chapel; Crafts room; Laundry room; Barber/Beauty shop; Library.
Activities Arts & crafts; Cards; Games; Reading groups; Prayer groups; Movies; Shopping trips; Dances/Social/Cultural gatherings.

Valley View Nursing Home
721 Hickory St, Akron, OH 44303
(216) 762-6486
Admin James Wilson. *Dir of Nursing* Linda Postich. *Medical Dir* Dr John McFadden.
Licensure Skilled care; Intermediate care. *Beds* Swing beds SNF/ICF 234. *Certified* Medicaid; Medicare.
Owner Proprietary corp (Beverly Enterprises).
Admissions Requirements Minimum age 14; Medical examination.
Staff Physicians; RNs; LPNs; Nurses' aides; Physical therapists; Occupational therapists; Speech therapists; Activities coordinators; Dietitians; Ophthalmologists; Podiatrists.
Facilities Dining room; Physical therapy room; Activities room; Laundry room; Barber/Beauty shop.
Activities Arts & crafts; Cards; Games; Reading groups; Prayer groups; Movies; Shopping trips; Dances/Social/Cultural gatherings.

Wyant Woods Care Center
200 Wyant Rd, Akron, OH 44313
(216) 836-7953, 836-6806 FAX
Admin James P Howell. *Dir of Nursing* Karen Kemerer RN. *Medical Dir* Judith Gooding MD.
Licensure Intermediate care; Alzheimer's living center. *Beds* ICF 200. *Certified* Medicaid.
Owner Proprietary corp (Horizon Healthcare Corp).
Admissions Requirements Medical examination.
Staff Physicians 12 (ft); RNs 6 (ft); LPNs 22 (ft); Nurses' aides 64 (ft), 16 (pt); Physical therapists 1 (ft), 1 (pt); Recreational therapists 2 (ft); Occupational therapists 2 (ft), 1 (pt); Speech therapists 1 (ft), 1 (pt); Activities coordinators 2 (ft); Dietitians 1 (ft); Ophthalmologists 1 (pt); Podiatrists 1 (ft); Audiologists 1 (ft).
Facilities Dining room; Physical therapy room; Activities room; Crafts room; Laundry room; Barber/Beauty shop; Enclosed patio; Lounge.
Activities Arts & crafts; Cards; Games; Reading groups; Prayer groups; Movies; Shopping trips; Dances/Social/Cultural gatherings; Intergenerational programs; Pet therapy; Monthly meal with a theme; Church services.

Albany

Russell Nursing Home
101 Washington St, Albany, OH 45710
(614) 698-3631
Admin Helen Kaylor.
Medical Dir Marie McVey.
Licensure Intermediate care. *Beds* ICF 25. *Certified* Medicaid.
Owner Proprietary corp.
Admissions Requirements Minimum age 21; Medical examination; Physician's request.
Staff Physicians; RNs; LPNs; Nurses' aides; Physical therapists; Reality therapists; Activities coordinators; Dietitians; Ophthalmologists; Podiatrists.
Facilities Dining room; Physical therapy room; Activities room; Chapel; Crafts room; Laundry room; Library.

Activities Arts & crafts; Cards; Games; Reading groups; Prayer groups; Shopping trips; Dances/Social/Cultural gatherings.

Alliance

Alliance Nursing Home Inc
11677 N Rockhill Rd, Alliance, OH 44601
(216) 821-0071
Licensure Intermediate care; Intermediate care for mentally retarded. *Beds* ICF 45; ICF/MR 30. *Certified* Medicaid.
Owner Proprietary corp.

Bel-Air Care Center
2350 S Cherry St, Alliance, OH 44601
(216) 821-3939, 821-9402 FAX
Admin David E Childs Jr. *Dir of Nursing* Catherine DeMuth. *Medical Dir* Michael McGrady MD.
Licensure Intermediate care; Assisted living. *Beds* ICF 54; Assisted living 16. *Private Pay Patients* 65%. *Certified* Medicaid.
Owner Privately owned.
Admissions Requirements Minimum age 60; Medical examination.
Staff RNs 1 (ft), 1 (pt); LPNs 5 (ft), 5 (pt); Nurses' aides 12 (ft), 10 (pt); Physical therapists 1 (pt); Activities coordinators 2 (ft), 1 (pt); Dietitians 1 (pt).
Facilities Dining room; Laundry room; Barber/Beauty shop; Library.
Activities Arts & crafts; Cards; Games; Reading groups; Prayer groups; Movies; Shopping trips; Dances/Social/Cultural gatherings; Pet therapy.

Blossom Nursing Center
11750 Klinger Ave, Alliance, OH 44601
(216) 823-8263
Admin Michele L Yarde. *Dir of Nursing* Thelma Yoho RN. *Medical Dir* Dr Michael McGrady.
Licensure Skilled care; Intermediate care. *Beds* SNF 50; ICF 50. *Certified* Medicaid; Medicare.
Owner Proprietary corp (Altercare Inc).
Admissions Requirements Medical examination; Physician's request.
Staff RNs 10 (pt); LPNs 7 (pt); Nurses' aides 15 (ft), 30 (pt); Physical therapists 1 (pt); Speech therapists 1 (pt); Activities coordinators 1 (ft), 1 (pt); Dietitians 1 (pt); Ophthalmologists 1 (pt).
Facilities Dining room; Physical therapy room; Activities room; Crafts room; Laundry room; Barber/Beauty shop; Lounges; Outside patios.
Activities Arts & crafts; Cards; Games; Prayer groups; Movies; Shopping trips; Dances/Social/Cultural gatherings; Bingo; Bowling; Lunch outings.

Canterbury Villa of Alliance
1785 Freshley Ave, Alliance, OH 44601
(216) 821-4000
Admin James C Egli. *Dir of Nursing* Beverly Lockhart. *Medical Dir* Donald Carter MD.
Licensure Skilled care; Intermediate care; Alzheimer's care. *Beds* Swing beds SNF/ICF 100. *Certified* Medicaid; Medicare.
Owner Proprietary corp (Canterbury Care Centers).
Admissions Requirements Medical examination; Physician's request.
Staff Physicians 3 (pt); RNs 4 (ft), 3 (pt); LPNs 5 (ft), 3 (pt); Nurses' aides 20 (ft), 10 (pt); Physical therapists 1 (pt); Occupational therapists 1 (pt); Speech therapists 1 (pt); Activities coordinators 1 (ft), 2 (pt); Dietitians 1 (pt); Ophthalmologists 1 (pt); Podiatrists 1 (pt); Dentists 1 (pt).
Facilities Dining room; Physical therapy room; Activities room; Chapel; Laundry room; Barber/Beauty shop; Library.

Activities Arts & crafts; Cards; Games; Reading groups; Prayer groups; Movies; Shopping trips; Dances/Social/Cultural gatherings.

Health Center
145 E College St, Alliance, OH 44601
(216) 823-9104
Admin Joseph R Ketchaver. *Dir of Nursing* Betty Starkweather RN; Gloria Woods RN. *Medical Dir* Dr Anthony Lee.
Licensure Intermediate care; Intermediate care for mentally retarded. *Beds* ICF 58; ICF/MR 20. *Certified* Medicaid.
Owner Proprietary corp.
Admissions Requirements Medical examination; Physician's request.
Staff Physicians; RNs; LPNs; Nurses' aides; Physical therapists; Occupational therapists; Speech therapists; Activities coordinators; Dietitians; Ophthalmologists; Podiatrists; Dentists.
Facilities Dining room; Physical therapy room; Activities room; Laundry room; Barber/Beauty shop.
Activities Arts & crafts; Cards; Games; Prayer groups; Movies; Shopping trips.

McCrea Manor Nursing Center
2040 McCrea St, Alliance, OH 44601
(216) 823-9005, (614) 457-0584, 823-9407 FAX
Admin James C Egli. *Dir of Nursing* Kathy Hardesty. *Medical Dir* Dr Duane Kuentz.
Licensure Skilled care; Intermediate care. *Beds* SNF 24; ICF 76. *Private Pay Patients* 32%. *Certified* Medicaid; Medicare.
Owner Proprietary corp (Paradigm Management Group).
Admissions Requirements Medical examination; Physician's request.
Facilities Dining room; Physical therapy room; Activities room; Chapel; Crafts room; Laundry room.
Activities Arts & crafts; Cards; Games; Reading groups; Prayer groups; Movies; Shopping trips; Dances/Social/Cultural gatherings; Pet therapy.

Ro-Ker Nursing Home
1495 Freshley Ave, Alliance, OH 44601
(216) 823-1097
Admin E Maureen Ledhy. *Dir of Nursing* Iris Baddeley LPN.
Licensure Intermediate care. *Beds* ICF 78. *Certified* Medicaid.
Owner Proprietary corp (Horizon Healthcare Corp).
Admissions Requirements Medical examination.
Staff RNs; LPNs; Nurses' aides; Activities coordinators.
Facilities Dining room; Laundry room; Barber/Beauty shop.
Activities Arts & crafts; Cards; Games; Reading groups; Prayer groups; Movies; Shopping trips.

Rose Lawn Geriatric Center
11999 Klinger Ave NE, Alliance, OH 44601
(216) 823-0618
Licensure Skilled care; Intermediate care; Rest home. *Beds* Swing beds SNF/ICF 16; Rest home 13.
Owner Proprietary corp.

Sun Valley Nursing Center Inc
1850 Electric Blvd, Alliance, OH 44601
(216) 823-4287
Licensure Intermediate care. *Beds* ICF 37. *Certified* Medicaid.
Owner Proprietary corp.

Amelia

Sunrise Manor & Convalescent Center Inc
PO Box 3434, State Rte 132, Amelia, OH 45102
(513) 797-5144
Admin Florel Meeker. *Dir of Nursing* Patricia Jones.
Licensure Intermediate care. *Beds* ICF 52. *Certified* Medicaid.
Owner Proprietary corp.
Admissions Requirements Medical examination.
Staff Physicians 8 (ft); RNs 1 (ft); LPNs 8 (ft); Nurses' aides 20 (ft); Physical therapists 1 (ft); Dietitians 1 (ft).
Facilities Dining room; Physical therapy room; Activities room; Chapel; Crafts room; Laundry room.
Activities Arts & crafts; Cards; Games; Reading groups; Prayer groups; Movies; Shopping trips; Dances/Social/Cultural gatherings.

Amherst

Amherst Manor
175 N Lake Dr, Amherst, OH 44001
(216) 988-4415
Licensure Intermediate care. *Beds* ICF 102. *Certified* Medicaid.
Owner Proprietary corp.

Andover

Miller Memorial Health Care Center
486 S Main St, Andover, OH 44003
(216) 293-5416, 293-7428 FAX
Admin Edward Fabian LNHA. *Dir of Nursing* Shirley French RN. *Medical Dir* Randall Tharp DO.
Licensure Skilled care; Alzheimer's care. *Beds* SNF 200. *Private Pay Patients* 30%. *Certified* Medicaid; Medicare.
Owner Proprietary corp.
Admissions Requirements Medical examination.
Staff Physicians 2 (ft).
Facilities Dining room; Physical therapy room; Activities room; Chapel; Crafts room; Laundry room; Barber/Beauty shop; Library; Occupational therapy room; Speech therapy room; Alzheimer's unit.
Activities Arts & crafts; Cards; Games; Reading groups; Prayer groups; Movies; Shopping trips; Dances/Social/Cultural gatherings; Intergenerational programs; Pet therapy.

Apple Creek

Apple Creek Developmental Center
2532 S Apple Creek Rd, Apple Creek, OH 44606
(216) 698-2411
Licensure Intermediate care for mentally retarded. *Beds* ICF/MR 316. *Certified* Medicaid.
Owner Publicly owned.

Archbold

Fairlawn Haven
E Lutz Rd, Archbold, OH 43502
(419) 445-3075
Medical Dir Robert A Ebersole.
Licensure Intermediate care. *Beds* ICF 100. *Certified* Medicaid.
Owner Proprietary corp.
Admissions Requirements Minimum age; Medical examination.
Staff RNs 2 (ft), 10 (pt); LPNs 4 (ft), 5 (pt); Nurses' aides 24 (ft), 34 (pt); Physical therapists 1 (pt); Activities coordinators 1 (ft), 2 (pt); Dietitians 1 (pt); Podiatrists 1 (pt); Dentists 1 (pt).

Affiliation Mennonite.
Facilities Dining room; Physical therapy room; Activities room; Crafts room; Laundry room; Barber/Beauty shop; Library.
Activities Arts & crafts; Cards; Games; Reading groups; Prayer groups; Movies; Shopping trips; Dances/Social/Cultural gatherings.

Arlington

Arlington Good Samaritan Center
PO Box 200, State Rte 103, Arlington, OH 45814
(419) 365-5115
Licensure Intermediate care. *Beds* ICF 50. *Certified* Medicaid.
Owner Nonprofit corp (Evangelical Lutheran/ Good Samaritan Society).

Ashland

Ashland Manor
20 Amberwood Pkwy, Ashland, OH 44805
(419) 289-3859, 281-6357 FAX
Admin Dan Ihrig. *Dir of Nursing* Gail Goodson. *Medical Dir* Michael Stencel.
Licensure Skilled care; Intermediate care. *Beds* Swing beds SNF/ICF 100. *Certified* Medicaid; Medicare.
Owner Proprietary corp (Landover Properties Ltd).
Admissions Requirements Minimum age 16; Medical examination; Physician's request.
Staff Physicians 12 (ft); RNs 6 (ft), 2 (pt); LPNs 5 (ft), 2 (pt); Nurses' aides 32 (ft), 22 (pt); Physical therapists 1 (pt); Occupational therapists 1 (pt); Speech therapists 1 (pt); Activities coordinators 1 (ft), 1 (pt); Dietitians (consultant); Ophthalmologists 1 (pt); Podiatrists 1 (pt); Audiologists 1 (pt).
Facilities Dining room; Physical therapy room; Activities room; Barber/Beauty shop.
Activities Arts & crafts; Cards; Games; Prayer groups; Movies; Shopping trips; Dances/ Social/Cultural gatherings; Intergenerational programs; Pet therapy.

Brethren Care Inc
2000 Center St, Ashland, OH 44805
(419) 289-1585
Admin Darrel Barnes. *Dir of Nursing* Regina Smeltzer RN. *Medical Dir* Dr Charles Slagle.
Licensure Intermediate care; Retirement. *Beds* ICF 91. *Certified* Medicaid.
Owner Proprietary corp.
Admissions Requirements Medical examination; Physician's request.
Staff RNs 1 (ft), 6 (pt); LPNs 4 (ft), 6 (pt); Nurses' aides 17 (ft), 38 (pt); Activities coordinators 1 (ft), 1 (pt).
Affiliation Church of the Brethren.
Facilities Dining room; Activities room; Laundry room; Barber/Beauty shop; Conference room.
Activities Cards; Games; Reading groups; Prayer groups; Movies.

Good Shepherd Home for the Aged
622 S Center St, Ashland, OH 44805
(419) 289-3523
Licensure Skilled care; Intermediate care. *Beds* Swing beds SNF/ICF 130. *Certified* Medicaid; Medicare.
Owner Proprietary corp.

Griffeth Nursing Home
1251 Wooster Rd, Ashland, OH 44805
(419) 322-9595
Licensure Intermediate care. *Beds* ICF 50. *Certified* Medicaid.
Owner Proprietary corp.
Admissions Requirements Medical examination; Physician's request.

Staff RNs 1 (pt); LPNs 3 (ft), 4 (pt); Nurses'
aides 10 (ft), 4 (pt); Recreational therapists 2
(ft), 1 (pt); Activities coordinators 1 (ft);
Dietitians 1 (pt).
Facilities Dining room; Activities room;
Crafts room; Laundry room.
Activities Arts & crafts; Cards; Games;
Reading groups; Prayer groups; Movies;
Shopping trips; Dances/Social/Cultural
gatherings.

Ashtabula

Ashtabula Medicare Nursing Center
2217 West Ave, Ashtabula, OH 44004
(216) 964-8446
Licensure Skilled care; Intermediate care. *Beds*
Swing beds SNF/ICF 207. *Certified*
Medicaid; Medicare.
Owner Proprietary corp.

Country Club Center III
925 E 26th St, Ashtabula, OH 44004
(216) 992-0022, 992-7423 FAX
Admin John Gresock. *Dir of Nursing* Diane
Slone. *Medical Dir* Dr S K Choi.
Licensure Skilled care; Intermediate care;
Retirement. *Beds* Swing beds SNF/ICF 65.
Private Pay Patients 40%. *Certified*
Medicaid; Medicare.
Owner Proprietary corp (J E Holland
Associates).
Admissions Requirements Medical
examination; Physician's request.
Staff Physicians 5 (pt); RNs 2 (ft), 3 (pt);
LPNs 5 (ft), 5 (pt); Nurses' aides 17 (ft), 12
(pt); Physical therapists 3 (pt); Occupational
therapists 1 (pt); Activities coordinators 1
(ft), 1 (pt); Dietitians 1 (pt); Podiatrists 1
(pt); Audiologists 1 (pt).
Facilities Dining room; Physical therapy
room; Activities room; Chapel; Crafts room;
Laundry room; Barber/Beauty shop.
Activities Arts & crafts; Cards; Games;
Reading groups; Prayer groups; Movies;
Shopping trips; Dances/Social/Cultural
gatherings; Pet therapy.

Smith Home for Aged Women
4533 Park Ave, Ashtabula, OH 44004
(216) 992-9441
Admin Leonard Kroner.
Medical Dir Dr Hassain.
Licensure Intermediate care; Rest home. *Beds*
ICF 12; Rest home 18.
Owner Proprietary corp.
Admissions Requirements Minimum age 65;
Females only; Medical examination.
Staff Physicians 1 (pt); RNs 3 (pt); LPNs 3
(pt); Nurses' aides 9 (pt).
Facilities Dining room; Activities room;
Chapel; Crafts room; Laundry room; Barber/
Beauty shop; Library.
Activities Cards; Games; Prayer groups;
Shopping trips.

Athens

Kimes Convalescent Center
Albany Rd, Athens, OH 45701
(614) 593-3391
Admin Mrs Harold R Kimes.
Medical Dir W Baumgaertel MD.
Licensure Skilled care; Intermediate care. *Beds*
Swing beds SNF/ICF 61.
Owner Proprietary corp.
Admissions Requirements Medical
examination.
Staff Physicians 7 (pt); RNs 2 (ft); LPNs 8
(ft); Nurses' aides 18 (ft), 5 (pt); Physical
therapists 1 (pt); Speech therapists 1 (pt);
Ophthalmologists 1 (pt); Dentists 1 (pt).
Facilities Dining room; Chapel; Laundry
room; Barber/Beauty shop; Library.
Activities Cards; Games; Reading groups;
Senior citizen band appearances; Religious
services by 5 groups.

Aurora

Anna Maria of Aurora Inc
889 N Aurora Rd, Aurora, OH 44202
(216) 562-6171
Admin George J Norton. *Dir of Nursing*
Marlene Peoples RN. *Medical Dir* Willard E
Stoner MD.
Licensure Skilled care; Intermediate care; Rest
home; Alzheimer's care. *Beds* Swing beds
SNF/ICF 127; Rest home 25. *Certified*
Medicare.
Owner Proprietary corp.
Admissions Requirements Medical
examination; Physician's request.
Facilities Dining room; Physical therapy
room; Activities room; Chapel; Crafts room;
Laundry room; Barber/Beauty shop; Library.
Activities Arts & crafts; Cards; Games;
Reading groups; Prayer groups; Movies;
Shopping trips; Dances/Social/Cultural
gatherings.

Austintown

Austin Woods Nursing Center
4780 Kirk Rd, Austintown, OH 44515
(216) 792-7681
Admin Norman Reuven.
Medical Dir Dr Wilkens.
Licensure Skilled care; Intermediate care. *Beds*
Swing beds SNF/ICF 230. *Certified*
Medicaid; Medicare.
Owner Proprietary corp.
Admissions Requirements Minimum age 18.
Staff Physicians; RNs; LPNs; Nurses' aides;
Physical therapists; Recreational therapists;
Speech therapists; Activities coordinators;
Dietitians; Podiatrists; Dentists.
Facilities Dining room; Physical therapy
room; Activities room; Chapel; Crafts room;
Laundry room; Barber/Beauty shop; Library;
Auditorium.
Activities Arts & crafts; Cards; Games;
Reading groups; Prayer groups; Movies;
Shopping trips; Dances/Social/Cultural
gatherings.

Gateways to Better Living Inc
153 Javit Ct, Austintown, OH 44515
(216) 797-0010
Admin Janet Watts. *Dir of Nursing* Linda
McLaughlin RN. *Medical Dir* Dr E
Kornhauser.
Licensure Intermediate care for mentally
retarded. *Beds* ICF/MR 32. *Certified*
Medicaid.
Owner Publicly owned.
Staff RNs 2 (ft); LPNs 6 (ft); Nurses' aides 35
(ft); Recreational therapists 1 (ft); Speech
therapists 2 (ft); Activities coordinators 1
(ft); Dietitians 2 (ft).

Avon

Avon Oaks Nursing Home
37800 French Creek Rd, Avon, OH 44011
(216) 934-5204, 871-2710, 934-4757 FAX
Admin Joan E Reidy CFACHCA. *Dir of
Nursing* Laura Englehart RN. *Medical Dir*
Itri Eren MD.
Licensure Skilled care; Intermediate care;
Alzheimer's care. *Beds* SNF 16; ICF 89.
Private Pay Patients 40%. *Certified*
Medicaid; Medicare.
Owner Proprietary corp.
Admissions Requirements Medical
examination.
Staff Physicians 6 (pt); RNs 6 (ft), 2 (pt);
LPNs 11 (ft), 6 (pt); Nurses' aides 31 (ft), 10
(pt); Physical therapists 1 (pt); Reality
therapists 1 (pt); Occupational therapists 1
(pt); Speech therapists 1 (pt); Activities
coordinators 2 (ft), 1 (pt); Dietitians 1 (pt);
Ophthalmologists 1 (pt); Podiatrists 1 (pt);
Audiologists 1 (pt).
Languages Spanish, Hungarian.

Facilities Dining room; Physical therapy
room; Activities room; Crafts room; Laundry
room; Barber/Beauty shop; Library; Kitchen
for cooking class; Child care center;
Alzheimer's unit.
Activities Arts & crafts; Cards; Games;
Reading groups; Prayer groups; Movies;
Shopping trips; Dances/Social/Cultural
gatherings; Intergenerational programs; Pet
therapy; Cooking class.

Good Samaritan Nursing Home Inc
32900 Detroit Rd, Avon, OH 44011
(216) 937-6201 Lorain, 327-4619 Elyria, 835-
3737 Cleveland, 835-3740 FAX
Admin Gail Bash; Charlotte Lazzaro. *Dir of
Nursing* Sharon Kratt RN. *Medical Dir* Dr
Mourad Fanous.
Licensure Skilled care; Intermediate care;
Alzheimer's care. *Beds* SNF 24; ICF 188.
Private Pay Patients 30%. *Certified*
Medicaid; Medicare.
Owner Proprietary corp.
Admissions Requirements Medical
examination; Physician's request.
Staff Physicians 8 (pt); RNs 11 (ft); LPNs 38
(ft); Nurses' aides 82 (ft), 15 (pt); Physical
therapists 1 (pt); Occupational therapists 1
(pt); Speech therapists 2 (pt); Activities
coordinators 2 (ft); Dietitians 1 (ft);
Ophthalmologists 1 (pt); Podiatrists 1 (pt);
Audiologists 2 (pt).
Languages Spanish.
Facilities Dining room; Physical therapy
room; Activities room; Chapel; Crafts room;
Laundry room; Barber/Beauty shop; Library.
Activities Arts & crafts; Cards; Games;
Reading groups; Prayer groups; Movies;
Shopping trips; Dances/Social/Cultural
gatherings; Intergenerational programs; Pet
therapy.

Bainbridge

Maple View Manor Nursing Home
PO Box 613, 430 S Maple St, Bainbridge, OH
45612
(614) 634-3301
Admin Sherry Zimmerman. *Dir of Nursing*
Brenda Elliott. *Medical Dir* Dr Dirk
Juschka.
Licensure Intermediate care. *Beds* ICF 20.
Private Pay Patients 15%. *Certified*
Medicaid.
Owner Proprietary corp.
Facilities Dining room; Laundry room.
Activities Arts & crafts; Cards; Games;
Reading groups; Shopping trips.

Baltic

Baltic Country Manor
130 Buena Vista St, Baltic, OH 43804
(216) 897-4311
Admin Mark J Morley. *Dir of Nursing*
Barbara Sparr. *Medical Dir* Dr Maurice
Stutzman.
Licensure Skilled care; Intermediate care;
Alzheimer's care. *Beds* SNF 8; ICF 92.
Certified Medicaid; Medicare.
Owner Proprietary corp (Canterbury Care
Centers).
Admissions Requirements Minimum age 18;
Medical examination.
Staff Physicians 1 (ft), 1 (pt); RNs 4 (ft), 1
(pt); LPNs 8 (ft), 2 (pt); Nurses' aides 15
(ft), 13 (pt); Physical therapists 3 (pt);
Recreational therapists 1 (ft); Speech
therapists 1 (pt); Activities coordinators 1
(ft); Dietitians 2 (pt); Ophthalmologists 1
(pt).
Languages Pennsylvania Dutch.
Facilities Dining room; Physical therapy
room; Activities room; Laundry room;
Barber/Beauty shop; Outdoor patio.

Activities Arts & crafts; Cards; Prayer groups; Movies; Shopping trips; Dances/Social/Cultural gatherings; Picnics; Community choirs and quartet.

Baltimore

Gaulden Manor
225 Hansberger Ave, Baltimore, OH 43105
(614) 862-8093
Admin April Cross. *Dir of Nursing* Dana Keller. *Medical Dir* Dr Anna Whetstone.
Licensure Intermediate care. *Beds* ICF 45. *Private Pay Patients* 50%. *Certified* Medicaid.
Owner Proprietary corp (Alpha Homes Inc).
Admissions Requirements Medical examination.
Staff Physicians 1 (pt); RNs 1 (ft), 2 (pt); LPNs 4 (ft), 1 (pt); Nurses' aides 12 (ft), 8 (pt); Activities coordinators 1 (ft); Dietitians 1 (pt); Ophthalmologists 1 (pt); Podiatrists 1 (pt).
Languages Polish.
Facilities Dining room; Activities room; Crafts room; Laundry room; Barber/Beauty shop.
Activities Arts & crafts; Cards; Games; Reading groups; Prayer groups; Movies; Shopping trips; Dances/Social/Cultural gatherings; Intergenerational programs; Pet therapy.

Barberton

Barberton Citizens Hospital
155 5th St NE, Barberton, OH 44203
(216) 745-1611
Licensure Skilled care; Intermediate care. *Beds* Swing beds SNF/ICF 21. *Certified* Medicaid; Medicare.
Owner Proprietary corp.

Manor Care Nursing Center
85 3rd St SE, Barberton, OH 44203
(216) 753-5005, 753-5009 FAX
Admin LeRoy J Wilson NHA. *Dir of Nursing* Zonia Miller RN. *Medical Dir* Robert Littlejohn MD.
Licensure Skilled care; Intermediate care. *Beds* SNF 31; ICF 89. *Certified* Medicaid; Medicare.
Owner Proprietary corp (Manor Care Inc).
Admissions Requirements Minimum age 21; Medical examination; Physician's request.
Staff Physicians 2 (pt); RNs 5 (ft), 2 (pt); LPNs 10 (ft), 10 (pt); Nurses' aides 30 (ft), 14 (pt); Physical therapists 1 (ft), 1 (pt); Occupational therapists 1 (pt); Speech therapists 1 (pt); Activities coordinators 2 (ft); Dietitians 1 (pt); Ophthalmologists 1 (pt); Podiatrists 1 (pt); Audiologists 1 (pt); Medical records; Social services (consultant).
Facilities Dining room; Physical therapy room; Activities room; Crafts room; Laundry room; Barber/Beauty shop; Library; TV lounge.
Activities Arts & crafts; Cards; Games; Reading groups; Prayer groups; Movies; Shopping trips; Dances/Social/Cultural gatherings; Intergenerational programs; Pet therapy; Bowling leagues.

Pleasant View Health Care Center
401 Snyder Ave, Barberton, OH 44203
(216) 745-6028, 745-7923 FAX
Admin Kenneth Morris. *Dir of Nursing* Dianne Boyle. *Medical Dir* Phillip N Gilcrest MD.
Licensure Skilled care. *Beds* SNF 48. *Private Pay Patients* 50%. *Certified* Medicaid; Medicare.
Owner Proprietary corp.
Admissions Requirements Minimum age 18; Medical examination; Physician's request.

Staff Physicians 3 (pt); RNs 2 (ft), 3 (pt); LPNs 3 (ft), 2 (pt); Nurses' aides 15 (ft), 5 (pt); Physical therapists (consultant); Reality therapists (consultant); Recreational therapists (consultant); Occupational therapists (consultant); Speech therapists (consultant); Activities coordinators (consultant); Dietitians (consultant).
Facilities Dining room; Physical therapy room; Laundry room; Barber/Beauty shop.
Activities Games; Prayer groups; Movies; Dances/Social/Cultural gatherings.

Toth's Rest Home
42 1st St SE, Barberton, OH 44203
(216) 745-5786
Licensure Rest home. *Beds* 9.
Owner Proprietary corp.

Barnesville

Barnesville Health Care Center
400 Carrie Ave, Barnesville, OH 43713
(614) 425-3648
Licensure Intermediate care. *Beds* ICF 100. *Certified* Medicaid.
Owner Proprietary corp.

Barnesville Home
320 E Main St, Barnesville, OH 43713
(614) 425-1565
Licensure Intermediate care for mentally retarded. *Beds* ICF/MR 10. *Certified* Medicaid.
Owner Nonprofit corp (Alternative Residences Two Inc).

Wiley Avenue Home
608 Wiley Ave, Barnesville, OH 43713
(614) 425-2395
Licensure Intermediate care for mentally retarded. *Beds* ICF/MR 8. *Certified* Medicaid.
Owner Nonprofit corp (Alternative Residences Two Inc).

Batavia

Batavia Nursing & Convalescent Inn
4000 Golden Age Dr, Batavia, OH 45103
(513) 732-6500
Medical Dir Dr Jonathan Head.
Licensure Skilled care; Intermediate care. *Beds* Swing beds SNF/ICF 216. *Certified* Medicaid; Medicare.
Owner Proprietary corp.
Admissions Requirements Medical examination.
Facilities Dining room; Physical therapy room; Activities room; Crafts room; Laundry room; Barber/Beauty shop; Library.
Activities Arts & crafts; Cards; Games; Reading groups; Movies; Shopping trips; Dances/Social/Cultural gatherings.

Batavia Nursing Home Inc
Box 93, S 4th St, Batavia, OH 45103
(513) 732-1535
Licensure Intermediate care. *Beds* ICF 34. *Certified* Medicaid.
Owner Proprietary corp.

Bay Village

Bradley Road Nursing Home
605 Bradley Rd, Bay Village, OH 44140
(216) 871-3474
Admin John T ONeill LNHA. *Dir of Nursing* Iva Neel BSN RN. *Medical Dir* James E Mulligan MD.
Licensure Skilled care; Alzheimer's care. *Beds* SNF 109. *Certified* Medicare.
Owner Privately owned.
Admissions Requirements Minimum age 50.
Staff Physicians 30 (pt); RNs 9 (ft), 2 (pt); LPNs 14 (ft), 1 (pt); Nurses' aides 50 (ft); Physical therapists 1 (pt); Occupational

therapists 1 (pt); Speech therapists 1 (pt); Activities coordinators 1 (pt); Dietitians 1 (pt); Ophthalmologists 1 (pt); Podiatrists 1 (pt); Audiologists 1 (pt).
Facilities Dining room; Physical therapy room; Activities room; Crafts room; Laundry room; Barber/Beauty shop; Library; Private rooms; Alzheimer's unit.
Activities Arts & crafts; Games; Prayer groups; Movies; Dances/Social/Cultural gatherings; Intergenerational programs; Pet therapy.

Beachwood

Beach Haven Health Care Center
23900 Chagrin Blvd, Beachwood, OH 44122
(216) 464-1000, 464-3099 FAX
Admin Sam Zimerman. *Dir of Nursing* Nancy Davidson RN. *Medical Dir* Dusan Naunovich MD.
Licensure Skilled care; Intermediate care. *Beds* Swing beds SNF/ICF 210. *Private Pay Patients* 1%. *Certified* Medicaid; Medicare.
Owner Proprietary corp.
Admissions Requirements Minimum age 18; Medical examination.
Staff Physicians; RNs 11 (ft), 4 (pt); LPNs 20 (ft), 13 (pt); Nurses' aides 71 (ft), 14 (pt); Physical therapists 1 (ft); Speech therapists 1 (ft); Activities coordinators 3 (ft); Dietitians 2 (ft), 1 (pt); Ophthalmologists (consultant); Podiatrists (consultant); Audiologists (consultant).
Languages Polish, Russian, Yiddish.
Facilities Dining room; Physical therapy room; Activities room; Crafts room; Laundry room; Barber/Beauty shop; Library.
Activities Arts & crafts; Cards; Games; Reading groups; Prayer groups; Movies; Shopping trips; Dances/Social/Cultural gatherings; Zoo visits with small animals.

Menorah Park Center for the Aging
27100 Cedar Rd, Beachwood, OH 44122
(216) 831-6500, 831-5492 FAX
Admin Steven Raichilson. *Dir of Nursing* Dolly Bheemaswarroop RN. *Medical Dir* Julius Fishman MD.
Licensure Skilled care; Intermediate care; Alzheimer's care. *Beds* Swing beds SNF/ICF 352. *Private Pay Patients* 35%. *Certified* Medicaid; Medicare.
Owner Nonprofit organization/foundation.
Admissions Requirements Minimum age 65; Medical examination.
Staff Physicians 1 (ft), 21 (pt); RNs 19 (ft), 18 (pt); LPNs 28 (ft), 37 (pt); Nurses' aides 125 (ft), 12 (pt); Physical therapists 1 (ft), 1 (pt); Recreational therapists 5 (ft), 3 (pt); Occupational therapists 2 (pt); Speech therapists 1 (pt); Activities coordinators 1 (ft); Dietitians 1 (ft), 2 (pt); Ophthalmologists 1 (pt); Podiatrists 1 (pt); Audiologists 1 (pt); Dentists 1 (pt).
Facilities Dining room; Physical therapy room; Activities room; Chapel; Crafts room; Laundry room; Barber/Beauty shop; Library; Alzheimer's unit.
Activities Arts & crafts; Cards; Games; Reading groups; Prayer groups; Movies; Shopping trips; Dances/Social/Cultural gatherings; Intergenerational programs; Pet therapy; Horticultural therapy; Music therapy; Art therapy.

Villa Santa Anna Home for the Aged Inc
25000 Chagrin Blvd, Beachwood, OH 44122-5665
(216) 464-9250, 464-9253 FAX
Admin Sr Mary Elisabeth Ann Rechka VSC FACHCA. *Dir of Nursing* Deborah Lawson RN. *Medical Dir* Sylvia Marshall MD.
Licensure Intermediate care. *Beds* ICF 68. *Private Pay Patients* 23%. *Certified* Medicaid.
Owner Nonprofit organization/foundation.

Admissions Requirements Minimum age 65; Medical examination.
Staff Physicians 10 (pt); RNs 1 (ft), 3 (pt); LPNs 4 (ft), 4 (pt); Nurses' aides 15 (ft), 4 (pt); Physical therapists 2 (pt); Reality therapists 1 (pt); Activities coordinators 4 (pt); Dietitians 1 (pt); Ophthalmologists 1 (pt); Podiatrists 2 (pt); Chaplains 2 (pt).
Languages Slovak, Italian, Spanish, Polish.
Affiliation Roman Catholic.
Facilities Dining room; Physical therapy room; Activities room; Chapel; Crafts room; Laundry room; Barber/Beauty shop; Library; TV room.
Activities Arts & crafts; Games; Prayer groups; Movies; Shopping trips; Dances/Social/Cultural gatherings; Intergenerational programs; Pet therapy; Liturgy.

Beaver

Pineview Manor Inc
4136 Germany Rd, Beaver, OH 45613
(614) 226-3074
Admin Linda Fisher. *Dir of Nursing* Sherry Leach RN.
Licensure Intermediate care. *Beds* ICF 50. *Certified* Medicaid.
Owner Proprietary corp.
Staff Physicians 1 (pt); RNs 1 (pt); LPNs 4 (ft), 1 (pt); Nurses' aides 30 (ft), 5 (pt); Recreational therapists 1 (ft); Activities coordinators 1 (ft); Dietitians 1 (pt); Ophthalmologists 1 (pt).
Facilities Dining room; Activities room; Laundry room.
Activities Arts & crafts; Cards; Games; Prayer groups; Movies; Shopping trips; Dances/Social/Cultural gatherings.

Bedford

Oak Park Health Care Inc
24613 Broadway Ave, Bedford, OH 44146
(216) 439-1448, 232-2541 FAX
Admin Carol A Borgione. *Dir of Nursing* Laurie Ripley. *Medical Dir* Lelio Franceseschini MD.
Licensure Skilled care; Intermediate care. *Beds* Swing beds SNF/ICF 150. *Private Pay Patients* 40%. *Certified* Medicaid; Medicare.
Owner Proprietary corp.
Staff Physicians 1 (ft); RNs 4 (ft), 8 (pt); LPNs 12 (ft), 8 (pt); Nurses' aides 60 (ft), 13 (pt); Physical therapists 1 (pt); Occupational therapists 2 (pt); Speech therapists 2 (pt); Activities coordinators 2 (ft); Dietitians 1 (pt); Podiatrists 6 (pt).
Facilities Dining room; Physical therapy room; Activities room; Crafts room; Laundry room; Barber/Beauty shop.
Activities Arts & crafts; Cards; Games; Reading groups; Prayer groups; Movies; Dances/Social/Cultural gatherings; Intergenerational programs.

Bellaire

Country Club Retirement Center IV
55801 Conno-Mara Dr, Bellaire, OH 43906
(614) 676-2300
Licensure Skilled care; Intermediate care; Rest home. *Beds* SNF 10; ICF 52; Rest home 13. *Certified* Medicaid; Medicare.
Owner Proprietary corp.

Bellbrook

Carriage by the Lake Nursing Center
1957 N Lakeman Dr, Bellbrook, OH 45305
(513) 848-8421
Admin Gary P Davis. *Dir of Nursing* Sheila Daugherty. *Medical Dir* Dr Charles Moody.
Licensure Skilled care; Intermediate care. *Beds* Swing beds SNF/ICF 78. *Certified* Medicaid; Medicare.

Owner Proprietary corp (Health Care Management Corp).
Admissions Requirements Medical examination.
Staff RNs 5 (ft), 4 (pt); LPNs 3 (ft), 3 (pt); Nurses' aides 20 (ft), 15 (pt); Physical therapists 1 (pt); Occupational therapists 1 (pt); Speech therapists 1 (pt); Activities coordinators 1 (ft); Dietitians 1 (pt); Ophthalmologists 1 (pt); Podiatrists 1 (pt).
Facilities Dining room; Physical therapy room; Activities room; Crafts room; Laundry room; Barber/Beauty shop.
Activities Arts & crafts; Cards; Games; Reading groups; Prayer groups; Movies; Dances/Social/Cultural gatherings; Intergenerational programs; Pet therapy.

Bellefontaine

Heartland of Bellefontaine
221 N School St, Bellefontaine, OH 43311
(513) 599-5123
Admin Charles George.
Medical Dir Dr David Eubanks.
Licensure Skilled care; Intermediate care; Rest home. *Beds* Swing beds SNF/ICF 75; Rest home 25. *Certified* Medicaid; Medicare.
Owner Proprietary corp (Health Care and Retirement Corp).
Admissions Requirements Minimum age 40; Medical examination.
Staff Physicians; RNs; LPNs; Nurses' aides; Physical therapists; Occupational therapists; Speech therapists; Activities coordinators; Dietitians; Ophthalmologists; Podiatrists.
Facilities Dining room; Physical therapy room; Activities room; Laundry room; Barber/Beauty shop.
Activities Arts & crafts; Cards; Games; Reading groups; Prayer groups; Movies; Shopping trips; Dances/Social/Cultural gatherings.

Logan County Home
3023 County Rd 91, Bellefontaine, OH 43311
(513) 592-2901
Admin Sue Crawfis. *Dir of Nursing* Sue Allen. *Medical Dir* Dr A Roldan.
Licensure Intermediate care. *Beds* ICF 95. *Certified* Medicaid.
Owner Publicly owned.
Admissions Requirements Medical examination.
Staff Physicians 1 (pt); RNs 2 (ft), 2 (pt); LPNs 7 (ft), 3 (pt); Nurses' aides 21 (ft), 18 (pt); Activities coordinators 1 (ft), 1 (pt).
Facilities Dining room; Crafts room; Barber/Beauty shop; Library.
Activities Arts & crafts; Cards; Games; Reading groups; Prayer groups; Movies; Shopping trips; Dances/Social/Cultural gatherings.

Bellevue

Bellevue Nursing Home
One Aldrick Sq, Bellevue, OH 44811
(419) 483-6225
Licensure Intermediate care. *Beds* ICF 23. *Certified* Medicaid.
Owner Proprietary corp.

Bellville

Overlook Villa Care Center
4910 Algire Rd, Bellville, OH 44813
(419) 886-3922
Admin Donald De Vaux. *Dir of Nursing* Myrna Simons. *Medical Dir* Dr David Clymer.
Licensure Intermediate care. *Beds* ICF 27. *Certified* Medicaid.
Owner Proprietary corp (Long Term Care Management Services).

Admissions Requirements Medical examination.
Staff Physicians 1 (pt); RNs 1 (ft); LPNs 1 (ft), 3 (pt); Nurses' aides 6 (ft); Activities coordinators 1 (ft); Dietitians 1 (ft).
Facilities Dining room; Activities room; Crafts room; Laundry room; Barber/Beauty shop.
Activities Arts & crafts; Cards; Games; Reading groups; Prayer groups; Movies; Shopping trips; Dances/Social/Cultural gatherings.

Belmont

Bell Nursing Home Inc
42350 National Rd, Belmont, OH 43718
(614) 782-1561
Admin Michael G Maistros. *Dir of Nursing* Rose Pittenger. *Medical Dir* Dr Matt Kirkland.
Licensure Skilled care; Intermediate care. *Beds* Swing beds SNF/ICF 52. *Certified* Medicaid; Medicare.
Owner Proprietary corp.
Staff Physicians; RNs; LPNs; Nurses' aides; Physical therapists; Occupational therapists; Activities coordinators; Dietitians; Ophthalmologists; Dentists.
Facilities Dining room; Physical therapy room; Activities room; Chapel; Laundry room; Barber/Beauty shop.

Berea

Aristocrat Berea
255 Front St, Berea, OH 44017
(216) 243-4000
Admin Michael Coury.
Licensure Skilled care; Intermediate care. *Beds* SNF 31; ICF 54. *Certified* Medicaid; Medicare.
Owner Proprietary corp.

Berea North Quality Care Nursing Center
49 Sheldon Rd, Berea, OH 44017
(216) 234-0454
Licensure Nursing home. *Beds* Nursing home 50.
Owner Proprietary corp.

Berea Quality Care Nursing Center
570 N Rocky River Dr, Berea, OH 44017
(216) 234-2294
Admin Mr C E Rogerson. *Dir of Nursing* Kathy Lazroff LPN. *Medical Dir* William Bond MD.
Licensure Intermediate care; Retirement. *Beds* ICF 50. *Certified* Medicaid.
Owner Proprietary corp (Northwestern Service Corp).
Admissions Requirements Medical examination.
Staff Physicians 1 (ft); RNs 1 (pt); LPNs 6 (ft); Nurses' aides 19 (ft), 2 (pt); Physical therapists 1 (ft); Activities coordinators 2 (ft); Dietitians 1 (ft); Ophthalmologists 1 (pt); Dentists 1 (pt).
Facilities Dining room; Physical therapy room; Activities room; Chapel; Laundry room; Barber/Beauty shop; Living room.
Activities Arts & crafts; Cards; Games; Prayer groups; Movies; Van outings.

Bethel

Morris Nursing Home
322 S Charity St, Bethel, OH 45106
(513) 734-7401
Licensure Intermediate care. *Beds* ICF 18. *Certified* Medicaid.
Owner Proprietary corp.

Bethesda

Star Nursing Home
40060 National Rd, Bethesda, OH 43719
(614) 782-1944, 782-1543 FAX
Admin Tino Agostini. *Dir of Nursing* Deborah Karcher. *Medical Dir* Dr Phillip Murray.
Licensure Intermediate care. *Beds* ICF 50. *Certified* Medicaid.
Owner Proprietary corp.
Staff Physicians 1 (ft); Physical therapists 1 (pt); Activities coordinators 1 (ft); Dietitians 1 (pt); Podiatrists 1 (pt); Audiologists 1 (pt).
Facilities Activities room; Laundry room; Barber/Beauty shop.
Activities Arts & crafts; Games; Reading groups; Movies; Shopping trips; Pet therapy.

Bidwell

Buckeye Community Services—Bidwell Home
Rte 1 Box 576, Bidwell, OH 45614
(614) 286-5039
Licensure Intermediate care for mentally retarded. *Beds* ICF/MR 5. *Certified* Medicaid.
Owner Proprietary corp.

Scenic Hills Nursing Center
RR 2, Bidwell, OH 45614
(614) 466-7150
Licensure Skilled care; Intermediate care. *Beds* Swing beds SNF/ICF 100. *Certified* Medicaid; Medicare.
Owner Proprietary corp (Health Care Management).

Blanchester

Blanchester Care Center
839 E Cherry St, Blanchester, OH 45107
(513) 783-4911, 783-4573 FAX
Admin Joetta Meyer. *Dir of Nursing* Paulette Powers RN. *Medical Dir* Bruce Staley MD.
Licensure Skilled care; Intermediate care; Alzheimer's care. *Beds* Swing beds SNF/ICF 50. *Private Pay Patients* 36%. *Certified* Medicaid; Medicare.
Owner Proprietary corp (Arbor Health Care Corp).
Admissions Requirements Medical examination; Physician's request.
Staff Physicians 7 (pt); RNs 2 (ft), 2 (pt); LPNs 5 (ft), 2 (pt); Nurses' aides 17 (ft), 3 (pt); Physical therapists 1 (pt); Occupational therapists 1 (pt); Speech therapists 1 (pt); Activities coordinators 1 (ft); Dietitians 1 (pt); Ophthalmologists 1 (pt); Podiatrists 1 (pt); Audiologists 1 (pt).
Facilities Dining room; Physical therapy room; Activities room; Laundry room; Barber/Beauty shop; Enclosed garden with fence, walkways, and benches.
Activities Cards; Games; Reading groups; Prayer groups; Movies; Shopping trips; Dances/Social/Cultural gatherings; Intergenerational programs; Pet therapy; Junior high school volunteer program; Adopt-a-grandparent.

Continental Manor Nursing & Rehabilitation Center
820 E Center St, Blanchester, OH 45107
(513) 783-4949, 783-4940 FAX
Admin Nancy Hamann. *Dir of Nursing* Fabiola Galvis RN BSN. *Medical Dir* Dr Thomas Neville.
Licensure Skilled care; Intermediate care. *Beds* Swing beds SNF/ICF 74. *Certified* Medicaid; Medicare.
Owner Proprietary corp.
Admissions Requirements Medical examination; Physician's request.
Staff Physicians 7 (ft); RNs 6 (ft); LPNs 9 (ft), 3 (pt); Nurses' aides 28 (ft), 4 (pt); Physical therapists 1 (ft); Speech therapists 1 (pt);

Activities coordinators 2 (ft); Dietitians 1 (pt); Ophthalmologists 1 (pt); Podiatrists 1 (pt).
Languages Spanish.
Facilities Dining room; Physical therapy room; Activities room; Laundry room; Barber/Beauty shop.
Activities Arts & crafts; Cards; Games; Reading groups; Prayer groups; Movies.

Bloomville

Bloomville Nursing Care Center
22 Clinton St, Bloomville, OH 44818
(419) 983-2021
Admin Christopher P Widman. *Dir of Nursing* Marlene Siefert. *Medical Dir* Dr Felton.
Licensure Intermediate care. *Beds* ICF 30. *Certified* Medicaid.
Owner Proprietary corp.
Staff Physicians 1 (ft); RNs 1 (ft), 5 (pt); LPNs 1 (ft); Nurses' aides 8 (ft), 6 (pt); Activities coordinators 1 (ft); Dietitians 1 (pt).
Facilities Dining room; Activities room; Chapel; Crafts room; Laundry room.
Activities Arts & crafts; Cards; Games; Reading groups; Prayer groups; Movies; Shopping trips; Dances/Social/Cultural gatherings; Pet therapy.

Blue Ash

Blue Ash Nursing & Convalescent Home Inc
4900 Cooper Rd, Blue Ash, OH 45242
(513) 793-3362
Licensure Skilled care; Intermediate care. *Beds* Swing beds SNF/ICF 114. *Certified* Medicaid; Medicare.
Owner Proprietary corp.

Bluffton

Mennonite Memorial Home
410 W Elm St, Bluffton, OH 45817
(419) 358-1015
Admin Paul I Dyck. *Dir of Nursing* Mary Weaver. *Medical Dir* O Lugibihl MD.
Licensure Intermediate care; Alzheimer's care; Retirement. *Beds* ICF 92. *Certified* Medicaid.
Owner Nonprofit corp.
Admissions Requirements Minimum age 62.
Staff RNs 6 (ft), 3 (pt); LPNs 4 (ft), 4 (pt); Nurses' aides 22 (ft), 29 (pt); Occupational therapists 2 (ft); Activities coordinators 1 (ft); Social workers 1 (ft).
Affiliation Mennonite.
Facilities Dining room; Activities room; Chapel; Crafts room; Laundry room; Barber/Beauty shop; Library.
Activities Arts & crafts; Games; Reading groups; Prayer groups; Movies; Shopping trips; Dances/Social/Cultural gatherings.

Richland Manor Nursing Home
7400 Swaney Rd, Bluffton, OH 45817
(419) 643-3161, 643-4511
Licensure Skilled care; Intermediate care. *Beds* Swing beds SNF/ICF 104. *Certified* Medicaid; Medicare.
Owner Proprietary corp.

Boardman

Gateways to Better Living No 8
1132 Western Reserve Rd, Boardman, OH 44514
(216) 744-5221
Licensure Intermediate care for mentally retarded. *Beds* ICF/MR 8. *Certified* Medicaid.
Owner Proprietary corp.

Ron Joy Nursing Home
830 Boardman-Canfield Rd, Boardman, OH 44512
(216) 758-8106
Admin Felix Savon. *Dir of Nursing* Karen J Radney RN. *Medical Dir* Paul Ho MD.
Licensure Skilled care; Intermediate care; Retirement. *Beds* Swing beds SNF/ICF 87; Retirement 60. *Private Pay Patients* 50%. *Certified* Medicaid.
Owner Proprietary corp.
Admissions Requirements Medical examination.
Staff RNs 4 (ft), 1 (pt); LPNs 7 (ft), 3 (pt); Nurses' aides 22 (ft), 4 (pt); Physical therapists 1 (pt); Occupational therapists 1 (pt); Speech therapists 1 (pt); Activities coordinators 1 (ft); Dietitians 1 (pt); Ophthalmologists 1 (pt); Podiatrists 1 (pt).
Languages Greek, Italian.
Facilities Dining room; Physical therapy room; Activities room; Crafts room; Laundry room; Barber/Beauty shop.
Activities Arts & crafts; Cards; Games; Reading groups; Prayer groups; Movies; Dances/Social/Cultural gatherings.

Westwood Rehabilitation Medical Center
7148 West Blvd, Boardman, OH 44512
(216) 726-9061
Admin William Heckman. *Dir of Nursing* Patricia A Holmes RN. *Medical Dir* Anthony Pannozzo MD.
Licensure Skilled care; Intermediate care; Alzheimer's care. *Beds* Swing beds SNF/ICF 149. *Certified* Medicaid; Medicare.
Owner Proprietary corp.
Admissions Requirements Medical examination; Physician's request.
Staff Physicians 1 (ft), 3 (pt); RNs 7 (ft), 1 (pt); LPNs 24 (ft), 6 (pt); Nurses' aides; Physical therapists 1 (ft), 1 (pt); Occupational therapists 1 (pt); Speech therapists 1 (pt); Activities coordinators 3 (ft); Dietitians 1 (ft), 1 (pt); Ophthalmologists 1 (pt); Podiatrists 1 (pt); Psychologists 1 (pt); Rehab nurses 1 (ft); Rehab nurses aides 2 (ft), 1 (pt); Dentists 1 (pt).
Facilities Dining room; Physical therapy room; Activities room; Crafts room; Laundry room; Barber/Beauty shop.
Activities Arts & crafts; Cards; Games; Reading groups; Prayer groups; Movies; Shopping trips; Dances/Social/Cultural gatherings.

Bowerston

Bowerston Health Care Center
9076 Cumberland Rd, Bowerston, OH 44695
(614) 269-8393
Admin Chet Bradeen. *Dir of Nursing* Phyllis Warren Supv. *Medical Dir* Isam Tabbah MD.
Licensure Intermediate care. *Beds* ICF 25. *Certified* Medicaid; Medicare.
Owner Privately owned.
Admissions Requirements Medical examination; Physician's request.
Staff Physicians; RNs; LPNs; Nurses' aides; Activities coordinators; Dietitians; Ophthalmologists; Podiatrists; Audiologists; Administrative assistants.
Facilities Dining room.
Activities Arts & crafts; Cards; Games; Reading groups; Prayer groups; Movies; Shopping trips; Dances/Social/Cultural gatherings; Intergenerational programs.

Sunnyslope Nursing Home
102 Boyce Dr, Bowerston, OH 44695
(614) 269-8001
Admin Glenn W Roth. *Dir of Nursing* Wandalee Brannon LPN.

Licensure Skilled care; Intermediate care; Retirement; Alzheimer's care. *Beds* Swing beds SNF/ICF 48.
Owner Proprietary corp.
Admissions Requirements Medical examination.
Staff LPNs 6 (ft), 1 (pt); Nurses' aides 11 (ft), 6 (pt); Activities coordinators 1 (ft); Dietitians 1 (ft).
Facilities Dining room; Laundry room; Barber/Beauty shop; Library.
Activities Cards; Games; Reading groups; Prayer groups; Movies; Shopping trips; Picnics; Van rides.

Bowling Green

Bowling Green Manor
1021 Poe Rd, Bowling Green, OH 43402
(419) 352-4694
Admin Rhoda Terlizzi.
Medical Dir Thomas W Watson MD.
Licensure Skilled care; Intermediate care. *Beds* Swing beds SNF/ICF 100. *Certified* Medicaid; Medicare.
Owner Proprietary corp (HCF Inc).
Admissions Requirements Medical examination.
Staff Physicians 1 (ft); RNs 5 (ft); LPNs 10 (ft), 1 (pt); Nurses' aides 36 (ft); Physical therapists 1 (pt); Reality therapists 1 (ft); Recreational therapists 1 (ft); Speech therapists 1 (pt); Activities coordinators 1 (ft), 1 (pt); Dietitians 1 (ft).
Facilities Dining room; Physical therapy room; Activities room; Crafts room; Laundry room; Barber/Beauty shop.
Activities Arts & crafts; Cards; Games; Reading groups; Prayer groups; Movies; Shopping trips; Dances/Social/Cultural gatherings.

Community Nursing Home
850 W Poe Rd, Bowling Green, OH 43402
(419) 352-7558, 352-8637 FAX
Admin Mel Beal. *Dir of Nursing* Karen Bell RN. *Medical Dir* Marjorie Conrad MD.
Licensure Skilled care; Intermediate care. *Beds* SNF 25; ICF 75. *Private Pay Patients* 27%. *Certified* Medicaid; Medicare.
Owner Proprietary corp (Beverly Enterprises).
Admissions Requirements Minimum age 18; Medical examination.
Staff RNs 8 (ft), 2 (pt); LPNs 6 (ft), 1 (pt); Nurses' aides 35 (ft), 17 (pt); Physical therapists 1 (pt); Occupational therapists 1 (pt); Speech therapists 1 (pt); Activities coordinators 1 (ft); Dietitians 1 (pt); Podiatrists 1 (pt).
Facilities Dining room; Physical therapy room; Activities room; Crafts room; Laundry room; Barber/Beauty shop.
Activities Arts & crafts; Cards; Games; Shopping trips.

Wood County Nursing Home
11080 E Gypsy Ln, Bowling Green, OH 43402
(419) 353-8411
Admin Martin Jan. *Dir of Nursing* Carolyn Frum RN. *Medical Dir* Thomas Wojciechowski MD.
Licensure Skilled care; Intermediate care. *Beds* Swing beds SNF/ICF 127. *Private Pay Patients* 35%. *Certified* Medicaid; Medicare.
Owner Publicly owned.
Admissions Requirements Physician's request.
Staff Physicians 7 (pt); RNs 5 (ft), 2 (pt); LPNs 8 (ft), 2 (pt); Nurses' aides 24 (ft), 28 (pt); Physical therapists 1 (pt); Reality therapists 1 (pt); Occupational therapists 1 (pt); Speech therapists 1 (pt); Activities coordinators 1 (ft); Dietitians 1 (pt); Podiatrists 1 (pt); Audiologists 1 (pt).
Facilities Dining room; Physical therapy room; Activities room; Chapel; Crafts room; Laundry room; Barber/Beauty shop; Mobile library.

Activities Arts & crafts; Cards; Games; Reading groups; Prayer groups; Movies; Shopping trips; Dances/Social/Cultural gatherings; Intergenerational programs; Pet therapy.

Wooster Nursing Home
PO Box 1102, 416 W Wooster St, Bowling Green, OH 43402
(419) 352-6414
Admin Ernest R Tebeau. *Dir of Nursing* Robin L Coger LPN. *Medical Dir* Mohammad Sidiq MD.
Licensure Intermediate care. *Beds* ICF 21. *Private Pay Patients* 10%. *Certified* Medicaid.
Owner Proprietary corp (Rapids Nursing Homes Inc).
Staff Physicians 1 (pt); RNs 1 (pt); LPNs 2 (ft), 2 (pt); Nurses' aides 6 (ft), 4 (pt); Physical therapists (contracted); Occupational therapists (contracted); Speech therapists (contracted); Activities coordinators 1 (ft), 1 (pt); Dietitians 1 (pt); Ophthalmologists (contracted); Podiatrists 1 (pt); Audiologists (contracted); Dentists (contracted).
Facilities Dining room.
Activities Arts & crafts; Cards; Games; Reading groups; Movies; Pet therapy.

Bradford

Bradford Living Care Center
325 S Miami, Bradford, OH 45308
(513) 448-2259
Admin Jonathan Trimble. *Dir of Nursing* Marcia Conley LPN. *Medical Dir* Dr Girouard.
Licensure Intermediate care. *Beds* ICF 17. *Certified* Medicaid.
Owner Nonprofit corp.
Admissions Requirements Medical examination.
Staff Physicians; RNs; LPNs; Nurses' aides; Activities coordinators; Dietitians.
Facilities Dining room; Laundry room; Barber/Beauty shop.
Activities Arts & crafts; Cards; Games; Reading groups; Prayer groups; Shopping trips; Beauty shop.

Sunny Acres Nursing Home
325 S Miami St, Bradford, OH 45308
(513) 473-3017
Licensure Intermediate care. *Beds* ICF 16. *Certified* Medicaid.
Owner Nonprofit corp.

Bratenahl

Bolton Convalescent Home
13802 Lakeshore Blvd, Bratenahl, OH 44110
(216) 451-3334
Admin Deborah Leffel. *Dir of Nursing* Michael Voytko LPN. *Medical Dir* Dr Ashok Patil.
Licensure Intermediate care. *Beds* ICF 16. *Certified* Medicaid.
Owner Proprietary corp (RTG Nursing Homes Inc).
Admissions Requirements Minimum age 21; Medical examination; Physician's request.
Staff Physicians 1 (pt); RNs 1 (pt); LPNs 2 (ft), 1 (pt); Nurses' aides 4 (ft), 3 (pt); Speech therapists 1 (pt); Activities coordinators 1 (pt); Dietitians 1 (pt); Ophthalmologists 1 (pt).
Facilities Dining room; Laundry room.
Activities Arts & crafts; Cards; Games; Reading groups; Prayer groups; Outings.

Brecksville

Haven Hill Home
4400 Oakes Rd Cottage 1, Brecksville, OH 44141
(216) 842-0388
Admin Joyce A Swaisgood.
Medical Dir Dr Barry Brooks.
Licensure Intermediate care for mentally retarded. *Beds* ICF/MR 13. *Certified* Medicaid.
Owner Proprietary corp.
Admissions Requirements Minimum age 18; Medical examination.
Staff RNs 4 (pt); LPNs 3 (ft), 2 (pt); Nurses' aides 4 (ft), 4 (pt); Recreational therapists 1 (pt).
Facilities Dining room; Activities room; Laundry room.
Activities Arts & crafts; Games; Movies; Shopping trips; Dances/Social/Cultural gatherings.

Brewster

Brewster Parke Convalescent Center
264 Mohican St, Brewster, OH 44613
(216) 767-4179, 832-2171
Admin Cheryl Childs. *Dir of Nursing* Marlene Church. *Medical Dir* B W Cruz MD.
Licensure Intermediate care; Retirement. *Beds* ICF 51; Retirement 56. *Private Pay Patients* 60%. *Certified* Medicaid.
Owner Proprietary corp.
Admissions Requirements Minimum age 55.
Staff Physicians 1 (pt); RNs 1 (ft), 1 (pt); LPNs 4 (ft), 2 (pt); Nurses' aides 9 (ft), 7 (pt); Physical therapists 1 (ft); Reality therapists 1 (pt); Activities coordinators 2 (ft); Dietitians 1 (ft); Ophthalmologists 1 (pt); Podiatrists 1 (pt); Dentists 1 (pt).
Facilities Dining room; Activities room; Chapel; Laundry room; Barber/Beauty shop; Library; Gazebo; Gardens; On-site medical clinic.
Activities Arts & crafts; Cards; Games; Reading groups; Prayer groups; Movies; Shopping trips; Dances/Social/Cultural gatherings.

Bridgeport

Heartland-Lansing Nursing Center
300 Commercial Dr, Bridgeport, OH 43912
(614) 635-4600
Admin Mark H Forman NHA. *Dir of Nursing* Carol Wagner RN LPN. *Medical Dir* Fausto Lazo MD.
Licensure Skilled care; Intermediate care. *Beds* SNF 51; ICF 49. *Private Pay Patients* 20%. *Certified* Medicaid; Medicare.
Owner Proprietary corp (Health Care and Retirement Corp).
Facilities Dining room; Physical therapy room; Activities room; Laundry room; Barber/Beauty shop; Library; Family dining area; Semi-private rooms.
Activities Arts & crafts; Cards; Games; Reading groups; Prayer groups; Movies; Shopping trips; Intergenerational programs; Guest relations program.

Broadview Heights

Broadview Developmental Center
9543 Broadview Rd, Broadview Heights, OH 44147
(216) 526-5000
Admin Purcell Taylor Jr Ed D.
Medical Dir Chu Ho Chung MD.
Licensure Intermediate care for mentally retarded. *Beds* ICF/MR 192. *Certified* Medicaid.
Owner Publicly owned.
Admissions Requirements Medical examination.

Staff Physicians 2 (ft); RNs 5 (ft), 2 (pt);
LPNs 7 (ft); Nurses' aides 180 (ft), 10 (pt);
Physical therapists 1 (ft), 3 (pt); Recreational
therapists 12 (ft), 1 (pt); Occupational
therapists 1 (ft), 1 (pt); Speech therapists 1
(ft); Dietitians 1 (ft); Ophthalmologists 1 (ft);
Podiatrists 1 (pt).
Facilities Dining room; Physical therapy
room; Activities room; Chapel; Crafts room;
Laundry room; Barber/Beauty shop; Library;
Residential units; Pre-vocational classrooms;
Gymnasium; Swimming pool; Bowling alley.
Activities Arts & crafts; Games; Reading
groups; Prayer groups; Movies; Shopping
trips; Dances/Social/Cultural gatherings.

Phoenix Residential Centers Inc
9571 Broadview Rd, Broadview Heights, OH
44147
(216) 582-1085
Licensure Intermediate care for mentally
retarded. *Beds* ICF/MR 65. *Certified*
Medicaid.
Owner Proprietary corp.

Royalview Manor
2801 E Royalton Rd, Broadview Heights, OH
44147
(216) 526-4770
Admin Donna Wilson NHA. *Dir of Nursing*
Cindy Hochstetler. *Medical Dir* Dr
Juguilion.
Licensure Skilled care; Intermediate care. *Beds*
SNF 12; ICF 147. *Certified* Medicaid;
Medicare.
Owner Proprietary corp.
Staff Physicians 12 (pt); RNs 5 (ft), 5 (pt);
LPNs 15 (ft), 9 (pt); Nurses' aides 52 (ft), 13
(pt); Physical therapists 1 (pt); Occupational
therapists 1 (pt); Speech therapists 1 (pt);
Activities coordinators 2 (ft); Dietitians 1
(ft), 1 (pt); Ophthalmologists 1 (pt);
Podiatrists 1 (pt); Audiologists 1 (pt);
Dentists 1 (pt).
Facilities Dining room; Physical therapy
room; Activities room; Crafts room; Laundry
room; Barber/Beauty shop; Library.
Activities Arts & crafts; Cards; Games; Prayer
groups; Movies.

Brook Park

Lamp
6034 Engle Rd, Brook Park, OH 44142
(216) 433-4446
Licensure Intermediate care. *Beds* ICF 34.
Owner Proprietary corp.

Brookville

Brookhaven Nursing & Care Center
770 Albert Rd, Box 280, Brookville, OH
45309
(513) 833-2133
Admin Ruby J Ferrier.
Medical Dir Vinton Young MD.
Licensure Skilled care; Intermediate care. *Beds*
Swing beds SNF/ICF 100. *Certified*
Medicaid; Medicare.
Owner Proprietary corp (Health Care
Management).
Admissions Requirements Medical
examination.
Staff Physicians 8 (pt); RNs 4 (ft), 4 (pt);
LPNs 4 (ft), 3 (pt) 2 (ft), 1 (pt); Nurses'
aides 27 (ft), 19 (pt); Physical therapists 2
(pt); Occupational therapists 1 (pt); Speech
therapists 1 (pt); Activities coordinators 1
(ft), 1 (pt); Dietitians 1 (pt);
Ophthalmologists 1 (pt); Podiatrists 1 (pt);
Audiologists 1 (pt); Dentists 1 (pt).
Facilities Dining room; Physical therapy
room; Activities room; Chapel; Crafts room;
Laundry room; Barber/Beauty shop; Library.

Activities Arts & crafts; Cards; Games;
Reading groups; Prayer groups; Movies;
Shopping trips; Dances/Social/Cultural
gatherings.

Brunswick

Pearlview Extended Care & Nursing Center
4426 Homestead Dr, Brunswick, OH 44212
(216) 225-9121
Admin Basil Gaitanoros. *Dir of Nursing* Ellen
Raley RN. *Medical Dir* Dr T Gaitanoros.
Licensure Skilled care; Intermediate care. *Beds*
SNF 36; ICF 91. *Certified* Medicaid;
Medicare.
Owner Proprietary corp.
Admissions Requirements Minimum age 62.
Staff Physicians 4 (pt); RNs 6 (ft), 6 (pt);
LPNs 4 (ft), 6 (pt); Nurses' aides 34 (ft), 34
(pt); Physical therapists 1 (pt); Speech
therapists 1 (pt); Activities coordinators 1
(ft); Dietitians 1 (pt); Ophthalmologists 1
(pt); Podiatrists 1 (pt); Dentists 1 (pt).
Facilities Dining room; Physical therapy
room; Activities room; Chapel; Crafts room;
Laundry room; Barber/Beauty shop.
Activities Arts & crafts; Cards; Games;
Movies; Dances/Social/Cultural gatherings;
Patio & bake sales.

Willowood Nursing Home Inc
PO Box 810, 1186 Hadcock Rd, Brunswick,
OH 44212-0810
(216) 225-3156, 273-4876 FAX
Admin Patrick M Pozderac; Denise T
Pozderac. *Dir of Nursing* Estella Brualdi.
Medical Dir Dr Neil F Grabenstetter.
Licensure Skilled care; Intermediate care;
Intermediate care for mentally retarded.
Beds SNF 25; ICF 75; ICF/MR 96. *Private
Pay Patients* 8%. *Certified* Medicaid;
Medicare.
Owner Proprietary corp.
Admissions Requirements Medical
examination.
Staff Physicians 2 (pt); RNs 6 (ft), 6 (pt);
LPNs 24 (ft), 14 (pt); Nurses' aides 85 (ft),
35 (pt); Physical therapists 2 (pt);
Recreational therapists 1 (ft); Occupational
therapists 2 (pt); Speech therapists 1 (pt);
Activities coordinators 2 (ft); Dietitians 1
(ft); Ophthalmologists 1 (pt); Podiatrists 1
(pt).
Facilities Dining room; Physical therapy
room; Activities room; Chapel; Crafts room;
Laundry room; Barber/Beauty shop.
Activities Arts & crafts; Cards; Games;
Reading groups; Prayer groups; Movies;
Shopping trips; Dances/Social/Cultural
gatherings; Intergenerational programs; Pet
therapy.

Bryan

Bryan Nursing Care Center
PO Box 647, 1104 Wesley Ave, Bryan, OH
43506
(419) 636-5071
Admin Patrick M O'Neill. *Dir of Nursing*
Carol Childress RN. *Medical Dir* R K
Meyer MD.
Licensure Intermediate care. *Beds* ICF 189.
Private Pay Patients 50%. *Certified*
Medicaid.
Owner Proprietary corp (Bryan Nursing Home
Inc).
Admissions Requirements Medical
examination; Physician's request.
Staff RNs 4 (ft), 4 (pt); LPNs 20 (ft), 10 (pt);
Nurses' aides 40 (ft), 20 (pt); Physical
therapists (contracted); Activities
coordinators 2 (ft); Dietitians 1 (ft).
Facilities Dining room; Physical therapy
room; Activities room; Crafts room; Laundry
room; Barber/Beauty shop; Library; Private
and semi-private rooms.

Activities Arts & crafts; Cards; Games; Prayer
groups; Movies; Dances/Social/Cultural
gatherings; Intergenerational programs; Pet
therapy.

Cardinal Drive Home
1211 Cardinal Dr, Bryan, OH 43506
(419) 636-2369
Licensure Intermediate care for mentally
retarded. *Beds* ICF/MR 8. *Certified*
Medicaid.
Owner Proprietary corp.

Williams County Hillside Nursing Home
9876 RR 3 & Rd 16, Bryan, OH 43506
(419) 636-4508
Admin Marcia J Hauer. *Dir of Nursing* Donna
Batterson RN. *Medical Dir* R W Dilworth
MD.
Licensure Intermediate care. *Beds* ICF 71.
Private Pay Patients 35%.
Owner Publicly owned.
Staff RNs 1 (ft), 7 (pt); LPNs 2 (ft), 6 (pt);
Nurses' aides 24 (ft), 11 (pt); Activities
coordinators 1 (ft).

Bucyrus

Heartland of Bucyrus
PO Box 764, 1170 W Mansfield, Bucyrus, OH
44820
(419) 562-9907
Admin Ann Stover-Wyatt. *Dir of Nursing* Jo
Ellen Fitch RN. *Medical Dir* Ralph Lyon
DO.
Licensure Skilled care; Intermediate care. *Beds*
SNF 100; ICF 100. *Certified* Medicaid;
Medicare.
Owner Proprietary corp (Health Care and
Retirement Corp).
Admissions Requirements Medical
examination; Physician's request.
Staff RNs 4 (ft), 1 (pt); LPNs 8 (ft), 2 (pt);
Nurses' aides 29 (ft), 6 (pt); Recreational
therapists 1 (ft); Speech therapists 1 (ft);
Activities coordinators 1 (ft); Dietitians 1
(ft); Ophthalmologists 1 (ft); Podiatrists 1
(ft).
Facilities Dining room; Physical therapy
room; Activities room; Laundry room;
Barber/Beauty shop; Glassed-in porch;
Gazebo.
Activities Arts & crafts; Cards; Games;
Reading groups; Prayer groups; Movies;
Shopping trips; Dances/Social/Cultural
gatherings; Intergenerational programs; Pet
therapy; Annual bridal show; Annual football
kick-off/Hog roast.

Maplecrest Home
717 Rogers St, Bucyrus, OH 44820
(419) 562-4988
Licensure Rest home. *Beds* Rest home 25.
Owner Proprietary corp.

Oakwood Manor
1929 Whetstone St, Bucyrus, OH 44820
(419) 562-7644
Admin Catherine M Carter. *Dir of Nursing*
Jan Strouse. *Medical Dir* Dr Skinner.
Licensure Skilled care; Intermediate care;
Alzheimer's care. *Beds* Swing beds SNF/ICF
100. *Certified* Medicaid; Medicare.
Owner Proprietary corp.
Staff Physicians 1 (pt); RNs 5 (ft); LPNs 15
(ft), 5 (pt); Nurses' aides 40 (ft), 10 (pt);
Physical therapists 1 (ft), 1 (pt); Reality
therapists 1 (ft); Recreational therapists 1
(ft); Occupational therapists 1 (ft); Speech
therapists 1 (pt); Activities coordinators 1
(ft); Dietitians 1 (pt); Ophthalmologists 2
(pt); Podiatrists 1 (pt); Dentists 1 (pt).
Facilities Dining room; Physical therapy
room; Activities room; Crafts room; Laundry
room; Barber/Beauty shop.

Activities Arts & crafts; Cards; Games; Reading groups; Prayer groups; Movies; Shopping trips; Dances/Social/Cultural gatherings.

Westfall Nursing Home
320 E Warren St, Bucyrus, OH 44820
(419) 562-6986
Licensure Intermediate care. *Beds* ICF 17.
Owner Proprietary corp.

Cadiz

Alternative Residences Two Inc— Cadiz Home
215 Burton Ave, Cadiz, OH 43907
(614) 942-4931
Admin Bob Connell.
Medical Dir Janet Ruckman.
Licensure Intermediate care for mentally retarded. *Beds* ICF/MR 10. *Certified* Medicaid.
Owner Proprietary corp.
Staff Physicians 1 (pt); RNs 1 (pt); LPNs 1 (ft), 3 (pt); Physical therapists 1 (pt); Occupational therapists 1 (pt); Speech therapists 1 (pt); Dietitians 1 (pt); Ophthalmologists 1 (pt); Podiatrists 1 (pt); Dentists 1 (pt).

Carriage Inn of Cadiz Inc
259 Jamison Ave, Cadiz, OH 43907
(614) 942-8084
Licensure Skilled care; Intermediate care. *Beds* SNF 13; ICF 127. *Certified* Medicaid; Medicare.
Owner Proprietary corp.

Caldwell

Summit Acres Nursing Home
Rte 1 Box 140, Caldwell, OH 43724
(614) 732-2364
Admin Donald J Crock. *Dir of Nursing* Nancy Morris. *Medical Dir* Dr Fredrick Cox.
Licensure Skilled care; Intermediate care. *Beds* SNF 11; ICF 139. *Certified* Medicaid; Medicare.
Owner Proprietary corp.
Staff Physicians 3 (pt); RNs 9 (ft), 1 (pt); LPNs 16 (ft), 2 (pt); Nurses' aides 52 (ft), 7 (pt); Physical therapists 1 (pt); Recreational therapists 2 (pt); Speech therapists 1 (pt); Activities coordinators 4 (ft); Dietitians 1 (pt); Ophthalmologists 1 (pt); Podiatrists 1 (pt); Dentists 1 (pt).
Facilities Dining room; Physical therapy room; Activities room; Chapel; Crafts room; Laundry room; Barber/Beauty shop; Library.
Activities Arts & crafts; Cards; Games; Reading groups; Prayer groups; Movies; Shopping trips; Dances/Social/Cultural gatherings.

Summit Acres Nursing Home Inc—Home B
Rte 1 Box 140, Caldwell, OH 43724
(614) 732-2364
Admin Donald J Crock. *Dir of Nursing* Nancy Morris. *Medical Dir* Dr Cox.
Licensure Skilled care; Intermediate care. *Beds* SNF 11; ICF 139. *Certified* Medicaid; Medicare.
Owner Proprietary corp.
Staff Physicians 2 (pt); RNs 8 (ft), 2 (pt); LPNs 13 (ft), 4 (pt); Nurses' aides 52 (ft), 2 (pt); Physical therapists 1 (pt); Recreational therapists 2 (pt); Speech therapists 1 (pt); Activities coordinators 4 (ft); Dietitians & Aides 11 (pt); Ophthalmologists 1 (pt).
Facilities Dining room; Physical therapy room; Activities room; Chapel; Laundry room; Barber/Beauty shop; Library.
Activities Arts & crafts; Cards; Games; Reading groups; Prayer groups; Movies; Shopping trips; Dances/Social/Cultural gatherings.

Cambridge

Cambridge Health Care Center
1471 Wills Creek Valley Dr, Cambridge, OH 43725
(614) 439-4437, 439-3169 FAX
Admin Betty Bell. *Dir of Nursing* Marilyn Moorehead. *Medical Dir* Thomas Swan MD.
Licensure Skilled care; Intermediate care; Alzheimer's care. *Beds* SNF 49; ICF 110. *Private Pay Patients* 30%. *Certified* Medicaid; Medicare.
Owner Proprietary corp.
Admissions Requirements Medical examination.
Staff Physicians 1 (pt); RNs 9 (ft), 4 (pt); LPNs 28 (ft), 10 (pt); Nurses' aides 52 (ft), 20 (pt); Physical therapists 1 (pt); Reality therapists 1 (pt); Recreational therapists 3 (ft); Speech therapists 1 (pt); Activities coordinators 1 (ft); Dietitians 1 (pt).
Facilities Dining room; Physical therapy room; Activities room; Chapel; Crafts room; Laundry room; Barber/Beauty shop; Library.
Activities Arts & crafts; Cards; Games; Reading groups; Prayer groups; Movies; Shopping trips; Dances/Social/Cultural gatherings; Intergenerational programs; Pet therapy.

Red Carpet Health Care Center
PO Box 1489, 8420 Georgetown Rd, Cambridge, OH 43725
(614) 439-4401, 432-3529 FAX
Admin Vernon Beynon. *Dir of Nursing* Helen Correa. *Medical Dir* Dr Raj Tripathi.
Licensure Intermediate care; Rest home. *Beds* ICF 78; Rest home 84. *Certified* Medicaid.
Owner Proprietary corp.
Admissions Requirements Medical examination.
Staff Physicians; RNs; LPNs; Nurses' aides; Physical therapists; Activities coordinators; Dietitians.
Facilities Dining room; Activities room; Crafts room; Barber/Beauty shop.
Activities Arts & crafts; Cards; Games; Movies; Shopping trips; Dances/Social/Cultural gatherings; Church services.

Canal Fulton

Alternative Residences Two Inc—346 Waterside Home
346 Waterside St, Canal Fulton, OH 44614
(216) 854-3237
Licensure Intermediate care for mentally retarded. *Beds* ICF/MR 8. *Certified* Medicaid.
Owner Proprietary corp.

Chapel Hill Home
12200 Strausser St NW, Canal Fulton, OH 44614
(216) 854-4177
Admin Gloria J Prose.
Medical Dir Paula Mellot.
Licensure Skilled care; Alzheimer's care; Retirement. *Beds* SNF 126. *Private Pay Patients* 60%. *Certified* Medicaid; Medicare.
Owner Nonprofit corp (United Church Homes).
Admissions Requirements Medical examination.
Staff Physicians 3 (pt); RNs 15 (ft), 5 (pt); LPNs 17 (ft), 4 (pt); Nurses' aides 50 (ft), 35 (pt); Physical therapists 2 (ft); Occupational therapists 1 (ft); Activities coordinators 1 (ft); Dietitians 1 (ft); Podiatrists 1 (pt).
Facilities Dining room; Physical therapy room; Activities room; Chapel; Crafts room; Laundry room; Barber/Beauty shop; Library; Alzheimer's unit.
Activities Arts & crafts; Cards; Games; Reading groups; Prayer groups; Movies; Shopping trips; Dances/Social/Cultural gatherings.

Echoing Ridge Residential Center
643 Beverly Ave, Canal Fulton, OH 44614
(216) 854-6621
Admin William T Hall. *Dir of Nursing* Margaret Reed. *Medical Dir* Dr David Sassano.
Licensure Intermediate care for mentally retarded; Apartment living. *Beds* ICF/MR 50; Apts 20. *Private Pay Patients* 2%. *Certified* Medicaid.
Owner Nonprofit corp (Echoing Hills Village).
Admissions Requirements Minimum age 18; Medical examination.
Staff Physicians 1 (pt); RNs 2 (ft), 2 (pt); LPNs 7 (ft), 7 (pt); Nurses' aides 27 (ft), 5 (pt); Physical therapists 3 (pt); Reality therapists 2 (ft); Recreational therapists 3 (pt); Occupational therapists 2 (pt); Speech therapists 1 (ft); Activities coordinators 1 (pt); Dietitians 1 (pt); Ophthalmologists 1 (pt); Podiatrists 1 (pt); Audiologists 1 (pt).
Languages Spanish, Sign.
Facilities Dining room; Physical therapy room; Activities room; Laundry room; Library; Pool room.
Activities Arts & crafts; Games; Reading groups; Prayer groups; Movies; Shopping trips; Training groups.

Gaslite Villa Convalescent Center Inc
7055 High Mill Ave NW, Canal Fulton, OH 44614
(216) 854-4545
Admin Corita C Maxson. *Dir of Nursing* Susan E Diamond. *Medical Dir* Patrick D McFeely MD.
Licensure Intermediate care; Retirement. *Beds* ICF 98. *Certified* Medicaid.
Owner Proprietary corp.
Admissions Requirements Minimum age 55; Medical examination.
Staff Physicians 1 (ft); RNs 2 (ft), 1 (pt); LPNs 4 (ft), 4 (pt); Nurses' aides 29 (ft), 9 (pt); Physical therapists 1 (pt); Activities coordinators 1 (ft); Dietitians 1 (pt); Ophthalmologists 1 (pt).
Facilities Dining room; Activities room; Chapel; Crafts room; Laundry room; Barber/Beauty shop.
Activities Arts & crafts; Cards; Games; Prayer groups; Movies; Shopping trips; Dances/Social/Cultural gatherings; Religious services; Bus trips; Baking.

Peterson Enterprises Inc—352 Waterside Home
352 Waterside St, Canal Fulton, OH 44614
(216) 854-2934
Licensure Intermediate care for mentally retarded. *Beds* ICF/MR 8. *Certified* Medicaid.
Owner Proprietary corp.

Canal Winchester

Winchester Place I & II
36 Lehman Dr, Canal Winchester, OH 43110
(614) 837-9666
Admin Stephen C Wise. *Dir of Nursing* Carol Meyer. *Medical Dir* Dr Gail Burrien.
Licensure Skilled care; Intermediate care; Alzheimer's care. *Beds* SNF 10; ICF 191. *Certified* Medicaid; Medicare.
Owner Proprietary corp (Hillhaven Corp).
Admissions Requirements Medical examination.
Staff Physicians 2 (ft), 4 (pt); RNs 8 (ft), 2 (pt); LPNs 10 (ft), 2 (pt); Nurses' aides 75 (ft), 4 (pt); Physical therapists 1 (ft); Occupational therapists 1 (ft); Speech therapists 1 (ft); Activities coordinators 1 (ft); Dietitians 1 (ft); Ophthalmologists 1 (ft); Podiatrists 1 (pt); Dentists 1 (pt).
Facilities Dining room; Physical therapy room; Activities room; Crafts room; Laundry room; Barber/Beauty shop; Library; Multi-purpose room.

Activities Arts & crafts; Cards; Games;
Reading groups; Prayer groups; Movies;
Shopping trips; Dances/Social/Cultural
gatherings.

Canton

Arbors at Canton
2714 13th St NW, Canton, OH 44708
(216) 456-2842
Admin Tom Strobl. *Dir of Nursing* Beth
Strean RN. *Medical Dir* Rochelle Broome
MD.
Licensure Skilled care; Intermediate care. *Beds*
SNF 32; ICF 95. *Private Pay Patients* 25%.
Certified Medicaid; Medicare.
Owner Proprietary corp (Arbor Health Care).
Admissions Requirements Minimum age 18;
Medical examination; Physician's request.
Staff Physicians 3 (pt); RNs 8 (ft), 4 (pt);
LPNs 5 (ft), 11 (pt); Nurses' aides 50 (ft), 4
(pt); Physical therapists 1 (ft); Reality
therapists 1 (ft); Recreational therapists 1
(ft); Occupational therapists 1 (pt); Speech
therapists 1 (ft), 1 (pt); Activities
coordinators 1 (ft); Dietitians 1 (pt);
Ophthalmologists 1 (pt); Podiatrists 1 (pt);
Audiologists 1 (pt); Respiratory therapists 1
(ft), 3 (pt).
Facilities Dining room; Physical therapy
room; Activities room; Crafts room; Laundry
room; Barber/Beauty shop; Respiratory
therapy unit.
Activities Arts & crafts; Cards; Games;
Reading groups; Prayer groups; Movies;
Shopping trips; Dances/Social/Cultural
gatherings; Intergenerational programs; Pet
therapy.

Autumn Villa Care Center
1612 Harrisburg Rd NE, Canton, OH 44705
(216) 453-6886
Admin D Ferrebee. *Dir of Nursing* Sally
Bredenberg. *Medical Dir* J Vrabel DO.
Licensure Intermediate care. *Beds* ICF 50.
Private Pay Patients 1%. *Certified* Medicaid.
Owner Proprietary corp (Longterm Care
Management).
Admissions Requirements Minimum age 18;
Medical examination; Physician's request.
Staff Physicians; RNs; LPNs; Nurses' aides;
Physical therapists; Speech therapists;
Activities coordinators; Dietitians;
Ophthalmologists; Podiatrists; Audiologists.
Facilities Dining room; Activities room;
Crafts room; Laundry room; Barber/Beauty
shop; Fenced yard.
Activities Arts & crafts; Cards; Games;
Reading groups; Prayer groups; Movies;
Shopping trips; Dances/Social/Cultural
gatherings; Pet therapy; Summer cookouts.

Baker-Sumser Health Care Center
836 34th St, Canton, OH 44709
(216) 492-7131
Medical Dir Dr Aziz Alasyali.
Licensure Intermediate care; Rest home. *Beds*
ICF 100; Rest home 75. *Certified* Medicaid.
Owner Proprietary corp.
Admissions Requirements Minimum age 55;
Medical examination; Physician's request.
Staff RNs 2 (ft), 8 (pt); LPNs 3 (ft), 3 (pt);
Nurses' aides 18 (ft), 29 (pt); Activities
coordinators 1 (ft); Dietitians 1 (ft).
Facilities Dining room; Physical therapy
room; Activities room; Chapel; Crafts room;
Laundry room; Barber/Beauty shop; Library;
Community rooms.
Activities Arts & crafts; Cards; Games; Prayer
groups; Movies; Shopping trips; Dances/
Social/Cultural gatherings.

Bethany Nursing Home
626 34th St NW, Canton, OH 44709
(216) 492-7171
Admin John F Baum. *Dir of Nursing* Mildred
Downerd RN. *Medical Dir* Elizabeth E
Baum MD.

Licensure Skilled care; Intermediate care. *Beds*
Swing beds SNF/ICF 32.
Owner Proprietary corp.
Admissions Requirements Minimum age 18;
Medical examination; Physician's request.
Staff Physicians 1 (ft); RNs 4 (ft); LPNs 3 (ft);
Nurses' aides 12 (ft), 16 (pt); Activities
coordinators 1 (pt); Dietitians 1 (pt).
Facilities Dining room; Activities room;
Laundry room; Barber/Beauty shop.
Activities Arts & crafts; Cards; Games;
Reading groups; Prayer groups; Movies;
Shopping trips; Musical programs; Sing-
alongs; Social activities; Teas & dinners.

Canton Christian Home
2550 Cleveland Ave N, Canton, OH 44709
(216) 456-0004
Admin Paul E Wiener. *Dir of Nursing* Judith
A Workinger RN. *Medical Dir* A J Gilbert
MD.
Licensure Intermediate care; Retirement. *Beds*
ICF 75. *Private Pay Patients* 70%. *Certified*
Medicaid.
Owner Nonprofit corp.
Admissions Requirements Minimum age 62;
Medical examination.
Staff Physicians 1 (ft); RNs 7 (ft), 3 (pt);
LPNs 9 (ft), 3 (pt); Nurses' aides 37 (ft), 5
(pt); Activities coordinators 2 (ft); Dietitians
1 (ft); Chaplains 1 (pt).
Affiliation Church of Christ.
Facilities Dining room; Physical therapy
room; Activities room; Chapel; Crafts room;
Laundry room; Barber/Beauty shop; Library;
Patio; Shuffleboard courts; Putting green;
Gift shop.
Activities Arts & crafts; Cards; Games;
Reading groups; Prayer groups; Movies;
Shopping trips; Dances/Social/Cultural
gatherings; Intergenerational programs; Pet
therapy; Monthly banking trips.

Canton Health Care Center
1223 N Market Ave, Canton, OH 44714
(216) 454-2152
Admin Michele Joiner. *Dir of Nursing* Nancy
Allen.
Licensure Intermediate care; Intermediate care
for mentally retarded. *Beds* ICF 35; ICF/MR
165. *Certified* Medicaid.
Owner Proprietary corp (American Health
Care Centers).
Admissions Requirements Minimum age 18;
Medical examination; Physician's request.
Staff RNs 8 (ft), 2 (pt); LPNs 34 (ft), 1 (pt);
Nurses' aides 58 (ft), 19 (pt); Physical
therapists; Recreational therapists;
Occupational therapists; Speech therapists;
Activities coordinators 2 (ft); Dietitians;
Ophthalmologists; Podiatrists; Social service
workers 3 (ft).
Facilities Dining room; Physical therapy
room; Activities room; Crafts room; Laundry
room; Barber/Beauty shop.
Activities Arts & crafts; Cards; Games;
Reading groups; Prayer groups; Movies;
Shopping trips; Dances/Social/Cultural
gatherings.

Canton Regency Health Care Center
4515 22nd St NW, Canton, OH 44708
(216) 477-7664
Admin John L Prose. *Dir of Nursing* Janet
Rose. *Medical Dir* Carl Simmers.
Licensure Skilled care; Intermediate care;
Retirement. *Beds* SNF 12; ICF 38;
Retirement apts 148. *Private Pay Patients*
75%. *Certified* Medicare.
Owner Proprietary corp (Congregate Housing
Partnership).
Admissions Requirements Medical
examination; Physician's request.
Staff RNs 5 (ft); LPNs 5 (ft), 4 (pt); Nurses'
aides 5 (ft), 20 (pt).
Facilities Dining room; Physical therapy
room; Activities room; Crafts room; Laundry
room; Barber/Beauty shop; Library.

Activities Arts & crafts; Cards; Games; Prayer
groups; Movies; Shopping trips.

Colonial Nursing Center
1528 N Market Ave, Canton, OH 44714-2683
(216) 453-8456
Admin Esther R Chapman. *Dir of Nursing*
Dorothy Klingelsmith RN. *Medical Dir*
Sandra Beichler DO.
Licensure Intermediate care. *Beds* ICF 70.
Certified Medicaid.
Owner Proprietary corp (American Health
Care Centers).
Admissions Requirements Minimum age 40;
Medical examination.
Staff Physicians 2 (pt); RNs 4 (ft), 1 (pt);
LPNs 9 (ft), 3 (pt); Nurses' aides 26 (ft), 6
(pt); Physical therapists 1 (pt); Occupational
therapists 1 (pt); Speech therapists 1 (pt);
Activities coordinators 1 (ft); Dietitians 1
(pt); Ophthalmologists 1 (pt); Podiatrists 1
(pt).
Facilities Dining room; Activities room;
Laundry room.
Activities Arts & crafts; Cards; Games;
Reading groups; Prayer groups; Movies;
Shopping trips; Dances/Social/Cultural
gatherings; Pet therapy.

Cormon Health Care
1435 Market Ave N, Canton, OH 44714
(216) 453-0831
Admin Kelly Engler. *Dir of Nursing* Farakana
As-Samad RN.
Licensure Intermediate care. *Beds* ICF 35.
Certified Medicaid.
Owner Proprietary corp (Altercare Inc).
Admissions Requirements Medical
examination; Physician's request.
Staff RNs 1 (ft); LPNs 4 (ft), 2 (pt); Nurses'
aides 10 (ft); Activities coordinators 1 (ft);
Dietitians 1 (pt); Ophthalmologists 1 (pt);
Podiatrists 1 (pt).
Facilities Dining room; Activities room.
Activities Arts & crafts; Cards; Games; Prayer
groups; Movies; Pet therapy.

House of Loreto
2812 Harvard Ave NW, Canton, OH 44709
(216) 453-8137
Licensure Skilled care; Intermediate care. *Beds*
Swing beds SNF/ICF 98.
Owner Proprietary corp.

Jean Carol's Nursing Home Inc
1432 E Tuscarawas St, Canton, OH 44707
(216) 453-2196
Admin Judith K Bendick. *Dir of Nursing* Ina
Jones LPN. *Medical Dir* Saroj Kothari MD.
Licensure Intermediate care. *Beds* ICF 50.
Certified Medicaid.
Owner Proprietary corp.
Admissions Requirements Minimum age 18;
Medical examination.
Staff Physicians 1 (pt); RNs 2 (pt); LPNs 3
(ft), 2 (pt); Nurses' aides 26 (ft); Activities
coordinators 1 (ft); Dietitians 1 (pt);
Psychologists 1 (pt); QMRPs 1 (pt).
Facilities Dining room; Activities room;
Crafts room; Laundry room; Barber/Beauty
shop.
Activities Arts & crafts; Cards; Games;
Reading groups; Prayer groups; Movies;
Shopping trips; Dances/Social/Cultural
gatherings; In-house fashion shows; Talking
books; Exercise to music program; Coffee/
social hour; Community outings.

Manor Care Nursing Center
5005 Higbee Ave NW, Canton, OH 44718
(216) 492-7835
Admin Patricia Tyler. *Dir of Nursing*
Jacqueline Hibbard. *Medical Dir* Dr Daniel
Cannone.
Licensure Skilled care; Intermediate care. *Beds*
SNF 44; ICF 103. *Certified* Medicaid;
Medicare.
Owner Proprietary corp (Manor Care).

Admissions Requirements Medical
examination; Chest X-Ray.
Staff RNs; LPNs; Nurses' aides; Recreational
therapists; Activities coordinators.
Facilities Dining room; Physical therapy
room; Activities room; Laundry room;
Barber/Beauty shop.
Activities Arts & crafts; Cards; Games;
Reading groups; Prayer groups; Movies;
Shopping trips; Dances/Social/Cultural
gatherings.

McKinley Life Care Centre
800 Market Ave N, Canton, OH 44702
(216) 456-1014
Admin Robert R Jones. *Dir of Nursing* Carol
Richards. *Medical Dir* John Jenerette MD.
Licensure Skilled care; Intermediate care;
Independent living; Assisted living;
Alzheimer's care. *Beds* Swing beds SNF/ICF
166; Independent living 24; Assisted living
23. *Certified* Medicaid; Medicare.
Owner Proprietary corp.
Admissions Requirements Minimum age 60.
Staff Physicians 2 (pt); RNs 12 (ft); LPNs 31
(ft); Nurses' aides 90 (ft); Physical therapists
1 (pt); Occupational therapists 1 (pt); Speech
therapists 1 (pt); Activities coordinators 4
(ft); Dietitians 1 (pt); Ophthalmologists 1
(pt); Podiatrists 1 (pt); Audiologists 1 (pt).
Facilities Dining room; Physical therapy
room; Activities room; Crafts room; Laundry
room; Barber/Beauty shop; Library;
Courtyard/Atrium.
Activities Arts & crafts; Cards; Games;
Reading groups; Prayer groups; Movies;
Shopping trips; Dances/Social/Cultural
gatherings; Intergenerational programs.

Park View Manor Inc
1223 Market Ave N, Canton, OH 44714
(216) 833-8352
Medical Dir Dr H J Gashash.
Licensure Intermediate care. *Beds* ICF 23.
Certified Medicaid.
Owner Proprietary corp.
Admissions Requirements Females only.
Staff Physicians 1 (pt); LPNs 2 (ft), 2 (pt);
Nurses' aides 6 (ft), 3 (pt); Activities
coordinators 1 (pt); Dietitians 1 (pt);
Ophthalmologists 1 (pt); Podiatrists 1 (pt);
Dentists 1 (pt).
Facilities Dining room; Activities room;
Crafts room.
Activities Arts & crafts; Cards; Games;
Reading groups; Prayer groups; Movies;
Shopping trips; Dances/Social/Cultural
gatherings.

Smith Nursing Home Inc
2330 Penn Pl NE, Canton, OH 44704-2298
(216) 456-9070
Admin Abraham Smith; Olar M Smith. *Dir of
Nursing* Arlene Logan. *Medical Dir* Joseph
Vrabel.
Licensure Intermediate care. *Beds* ICF 50.
Private Pay Patients 8%. *Certified* Medicaid.
Owner Proprietary corp.
Admissions Requirements Medical
examination.
Staff Physicians 1 (ft); RNs 2 (ft); LPNs 6 (ft);
Nurses' aides 20 (ft); Physical therapists 1
(ft); Reality therapists 1 (ft); Recreational
therapists 1 (ft); Occupational therapists 1
(ft); Speech therapists 1 (ft); Activities
coordinators 1 (ft); Dietitians 2 (ft);
Ophthalmologists 1 (ft); Podiatrists 1 (ft);
Audiologists 1 (ft).
Facilities Dining room; Physical therapy
room; Activities room; Chapel; Crafts room;
Laundry room; Barber/Beauty shop; Lounge/
Reading room.
Activities Arts & crafts; Cards; Games;
Reading groups; Prayer groups; Movies;
Shopping trips; Dances/Social/Cultural
gatherings; Intergenerational programs;
Religious programs.

Twin-M Nursing Home
1722 Homedale Ave NW, Canton, OH 44708
(216) 454-6508
Admin Deborah Leffel. *Dir of Nursing* Gert
Curran.
Licensure Skilled care; Intermediate care. *Beds*
Swing beds SNF/ICF 23.
Owner Proprietary corp (American Health
Care Centers).
Admissions Requirements Medical
examination; Physician's request.
Staff RNs 2 (ft), 1 (pt); LPNs 2 (ft); Nurses'
aides 5 (ft), 8 (pt); Activities coordinators 1
(ft); Social services 1 (pt).
Facilities Dining room; Activities room;
Laundry room.
Activities Cards; Games; Reading groups;
Prayer groups; Movies; Shopping trips;
Dances/Social/Cultural gatherings.

White Oak Convalescent Home
3516 White Oak Dr SW, Canton, OH 44710
(216) 452-3035
Licensure Intermediate care. *Beds* ICF 40.
Certified Medicaid.
Owner Proprietary corp.

Carey

Carey Nursing Home
127 Brayton St, Carey, OH 43316
(419) 396-7488
Admin Donald L Lynch. *Dir of Nursing* Pat
England. *Medical Dir* Dr William Kose.
Licensure Intermediate care; Retirement. *Beds*
ICF 16. *Certified* Medicaid.
Owner Proprietary corp.
Admissions Requirements Medical
examination.
Staff Physicians 1 (pt); LPNs 4 (ft); Nurses'
aides 3 (ft), 3 (pt); Activities coordinators 1
(ft); Dietitians 1 (pt); Podiatrists 1 (pt).
Facilities Dining room; Activities room;
Laundry room.
Activities Arts & crafts; Cards; Games;
Reading groups; Prayer groups; Movies;
Shopping trips; Picnics.

Indian Trail Care Center Inc
821 E Findlay St, Carey, OH 43316
(419) 396-6344
Admin Donald L Lynch. *Dir of Nursing* Patti
Lynch. *Medical Dir* Dr William Kose.
Licensure Intermediate care; Residential care.
Beds ICF 51; Residential care 8. *Certified*
Medicaid.
Owner Proprietary corp.
Admissions Requirements Medical
examination.
Staff Physicians 1 (pt); RNs 1 (pt); LPNs 6
(ft); Nurses' aides 18 (ft), 8 (pt); Activities
coordinators 1 (ft); Dietitians 1 (pt).
Facilities Dining room; Activities room;
Crafts room; Laundry room; Barber/Beauty
shop; Library.
Activities Arts & crafts; Cards; Games;
Reading groups; Prayer groups; Movies;
Shopping trips; Dances/Social/Cultural
gatherings; Intergenerational programs.

Carlisle

Carlisle Manor Health Care Inc
730 Hillcrest Dr, Carlisle, OH 45005
(513) 746-2662
Licensure Intermediate care. *Beds* ICF 48.
Certified Medicaid.
Owner Proprietary corp.

Fairview Home
624 Fairview Dr, Carlisle, OH 45005
(513) 746-4201
Licensure Intermediate care for mentally
retarded. *Beds* ICF/MR 14. *Certified*
Medicaid.
Owner Proprietary corp.

Carrollton

Atwood Nursing Center
PO Box 397, 347 Steubenville Rd SE,
Carrollton, OH 44615
(216) 223-1536
Medical Dir T J Atchison MD.
Licensure Intermediate care. *Beds* ICF 17.
Certified Medicaid.
Owner Proprietary corp.
Admissions Requirements Minimum age 18.
Staff Physicians 1 (pt); RNs 1 (ft), 2 (pt);
LPNs 2 (ft), 1 (pt); Nurses' aides 8 (ft), 8
(pt); Physical therapists 1 (pt); Reality
therapists 1 (ft); Recreational therapists 1
(ft); Occupational therapists 1 (pt); Speech
therapists 1 (pt); Activities coordinators 1
(ft); Dietitians 1 (ft); Podiatrists 1 (pt);
Dentists 1 (pt).
Facilities Dining room; Activities room;
Crafts room; Laundry room.
Activities Arts & crafts; Cards; Games;
Reading groups; Prayer groups; Movies;
Shopping trips; Dances/Social/Cultural
gatherings.

Carroll Health Care Center Inc
648 Long St, Carrollton, OH 44615
(216) 627-5501
Admin Alan Miller. *Dir of Nursing* Cheryl
Grimes RN. *Medical Dir* Donald Wingard
DO.
Licensure Skilled care; Intermediate care. *Beds*
SNF 50; ICF 101. *Certified* Medicaid;
Medicare.
Owner Proprietary corp.
Admissions Requirements Minimum age 18.
Staff Physicians 4 (pt); RNs 5 (ft), 3 (pt);
LPNs 11 (ft), 4 (pt); Nurses' aides 30 (ft), 30
(pt); Physical therapists 2 (ft); Reality
therapists 1 (pt); Recreational therapists 1
(pt); Occupational therapists 1 (pt); Speech
therapists 1 (pt); Activities coordinators 2
(ft); Dietitians 1 (ft), 1 (pt); Podiatrists 1
(pt); Audiologists 1 (pt).
Facilities Dining room; Physical therapy
room; Activities room; Chapel; Crafts room;
Laundry room; Barber/Beauty shop; Library.
Activities Arts & crafts; Cards; Games;
Reading groups; Prayer groups; Movies;
Shopping trips; Dances/Social/Cultural
gatherings; Pet therapy.

Carrollton House
520 S Lisbon St, Carrollton, OH 44615
(216) 627-7552
Licensure Intermediate care for mentally
retarded. *Beds* ICF/MR 10. *Certified*
Medicaid.
Owner Nonprofit corp (Alternative Residences
Two Inc).

Celina

Celina Manor
1001 Myers Rd, Celina, OH 45822
(419) 586-6645
Admin Glenn V Propst. *Dir of Nursing*
Marianne Roether. *Medical Dir* Donald R
Fox MD.
Licensure Skilled care; Intermediate care. *Beds*
Swing beds SNF/ICF 101. *Certified*
Medicaid; Medicare.
Owner Proprietary corp (HCF Inc).
Admissions Requirements Medical
examination.
Staff Physicians; RNs 6 (ft), 3 (pt); LPNs 7
(ft), 4 (pt); Nurses' aides 32 (ft), 20 (pt);
Physical therapists 1 (ft); Activities
coordinators 1 (ft), 1 (pt); Dietitians 1 (ft).
Facilities Dining room; Physical therapy
room; Activities room; Chapel; Laundry
room; Barber/Beauty shop; Library; Patios.
Activities Arts & crafts; Games; Movies;
Dances/Social/Cultural gatherings; Field
trips.

Hometown Nursing Home of Celina
PO Box 109, Celina, OH 45822
(419) 586-3016
Admin Jerry Robertson.
Medical Dir Phillip Masser; Betty Patton.
Licensure Intermediate care. *Beds* ICF 50.
  Certified Medicaid.
Owner Proprietary corp.
Admissions Requirements Medical
  examination; Physician's request.
Staff Physicians 1 (pt); RNs 1 (ft), 3 (pt);
  LPNs 4 (ft), 2 (pt); Nurses' aides 10 (ft), 22
  (pt); Physical therapists 1 (pt); Activities
  coordinators 1 (ft); Dietitians 1 (pt);
  Ophthalmologists 1 (pt); Social service
  workers; Dentists 1 (pt).
Facilities Dining room; Activities room;
  Laundry room; Barber/Beauty shop.
Activities Arts & crafts; Cards; Games; Prayer
  groups; Movies; Shopping trips; Dances/
  Social/Cultural gatherings; Bingo.

Mud Pike Home
PO Box 137, 4784 Mud Pike, Celina, OH
  45822
(513) 586-2369
Admin Garry B Mosier BA QMRP. *Dir of
  Nursing* Ruth Hanna RN.
Licensure Intermediate care for mentally
  retarded. *Beds* ICF/MR 8. *Certified*
  Medicaid.
Owner Proprietary corp.
Admissions Requirements Minimum age 18;
  Medical examination.
Staff Physicians 1 (pt); RNs 1 (pt);
  Occupational therapists 1 (pt); Activities
  coordinators 1 (ft); Dietitians 1 (pt);
  Podiatrists 1 (pt); Habilitation specialists 1
  (ft).
Facilities Dining room; Activities room;
  Laundry room.
Activities Games; Movies; Shopping trips;
  Dances/Social/Cultural gatherings.

Centerburg

Canterbury Villa of Centerburg
80 Miller St, Centerburg, OH 43011
(614) 625-6873
Admin Susan Mehr. *Dir of Nursing* Laura
  Segraves. *Medical Dir* Dr Posada.
Licensure Intermediate care. *Beds* ICF 50.
  Certified Medicaid.
Owner Proprietary corp (Horizon Healthcare
  Corp).
Admissions Requirements Medical
  examination.
Staff RNs 1 (pt); LPNs 4 (ft), 2 (pt); Nurses'
  aides 15 (ft); Activities coordinators 1 (ft);
  Dietitians 2 (ft); Ophthalmologists 1 (pt).
Facilities Dining room; Activities room;
  Crafts room; Laundry room.
Activities Arts & crafts; Cards; Games;
  Reading groups; Prayer groups; Movies;
  Shopping trips; Dances/Social/Cultural
  gatherings.

Centerburg Nursing Center
PO Box 418, Fairview Ave, Centerburg, OH
  43011
(614) 625-5774
Medical Dir Hernando Posado MD.
Licensure Skilled care; Intermediate care. *Beds*
  Swing beds SNF/ICF 83. *Certified* Medicaid;
  Medicare.
Owner Proprietary corp (Health Care and
  Retirement Corp).
Staff Physicians 1 (pt); RNs 2 (ft), 3 (pt);
  LPNs 14 (ft), 5 (pt); Nurses' aides 30 (ft);
  Physical therapists 1 (pt); Occupational
  therapists 1 (pt); Speech therapists 1 (pt);
  Activities coordinators 1 (ft); Dietitians 1
  (pt); Podiatrists 1 (pt); Dentists 1 (pt).

Facilities Dining room; Laundry room;
  Barber/Beauty shop.
Activities Arts & crafts; Cards; Games;
  Reading groups; Prayer groups; Movies;
  Shopping trips; Dances/Social/Cultural
  gatherings.

Harrod Nursing Home
26 N Hartford Ave, Centerburg, OH 43011
(614) 625-5049
Licensure Nursing home. *Beds* 28.
Owner Proprietary corp.

Morning View Care Center
4531 Columbus Rd, Centerburg, OH 43011
(614) 625-5401, 625-3567 FAX
Admin Teri James. *Dir of Nursing* Dianne
  Tracey.
Licensure Intermediate care. *Beds* ICF 34.
  Certified Medicaid.
Owner Proprietary corp.
Staff Physicians; RNs; LPNs; Nurses' aides;
  Physical therapists; Activities coordinators;
  Dietitians; Podiatrists.
Facilities Dining room; Activities room;
  Crafts room; Laundry room; Barber/Beauty
  shop; Library.
Activities Arts & crafts; Cards; Games;
  Reading groups; Prayer groups; Movies;
  Shopping trips; Intergenerational programs;
  Pet therapy; Adopt-a-grandparent program.

Centerville

**Alternative Residences Inc—McEwen Road
Home**
8265 McEwen Rd, Centerville, OH 45459
Licensure Intermediate care for mentally
  retarded. *Beds* ICF/MR 10. *Certified*
  Medicaid.
Owner Proprietary corp.

Chagrin Falls

Hamlet Manor
150 Cleveland St, Chagrin Falls, OH 44022
(216) 247-4200, 247-4153 FAX
Admin Jack Wilson. *Dir of Nursing* JoAnne
  Bergole RN. *Medical Dir* Ralph Wieland
  MD FACP.
Licensure Intermediate care; Retirement;
  Assisted living. *Beds* ICF 98; Retirement
  apartments 144; Assisted living 100. *Private
  Pay Patients* 100%.
Owner Proprietary corp (Beverly Enterprises).
Admissions Requirements Physician's request.
Staff Physicians 10 (pt); RNs 6 (ft); LPNs 7
  (ft), 2 (pt); Nurses' aides 31 (ft); Physical
  therapists 3 (pt); Recreational therapists 1
  (pt); Occupational therapists 1 (pt); Speech
  therapists 1 (pt); Activities coordinators 2
  (ft); Dietitians 1 (pt); Podiatrists 1 (pt);
  Audiologists 1 (pt).
Facilities Dining room; Physical therapy
  room; Activities room; Crafts room; Laundry
  room; Barber/Beauty shop; Library.
Activities Arts & crafts; Cards; Games;
  Reading groups; Prayer groups; Movies;
  Shopping trips; Dances/Social/Cultural
  gatherings; Intergenerational programs; Pet
  therapy.

Chardon

Heather Hill Inc
PO Box 309, 12340 Bass Lake Rd, Chardon,
  OH 44024
(216) 942-6424
Admin Robert G Hare. *Dir of Nursing* Shirley
  French RN. *Medical Dir* Martha Hackett
  MD.
Licensure Skilled care; Intermediate care;
  Alzheimer's care; Rest home. *Beds* Swing
  beds SNF/ICF 152; Rest home 32. *Certified*
  Medicaid; Medicare.
Owner Nonprofit corp.

Admissions Requirements Minimum age 18;
  Medical examination.
Staff Physicians; RNs; LPNs; Nurses' aides;
  Physical therapists; Occupational therapists;
  Speech therapists; Activities coordinators;
  Dietitians; Ophthalmologists; Podiatrists.
Facilities Dining room; Physical therapy
  room; Activities room; Chapel; Crafts room;
  Laundry room; Barber/Beauty shop; Library;
  Occupational therapy rooms.
Activities Arts & crafts; Cards; Games;
  Reading groups; Prayer groups; Movies;
  Shopping trips; Dances/Social/Cultural
  gatherings.

Rehabilitation Hospital at Heather Hill
12340 Bass Lake Rd, Chardon, OH 44024
(216) 285-4040, 951-5445, (800) 423-2972
Admin Linus Vaikus.

Chesterland

Maple Nursing Home
13417 Rockhaven Rd, Chesterland, OH 44026
(216) 286-6180
Admin Vera Light. *Dir of Nursing* Nancy
  Batteiger LPN. *Medical Dir* Dr William
  Larrick.
Licensure Intermediate care. *Beds* ICF 21.
  Certified Medicaid; Medicare.
Owner Proprietary corp.
Admissions Requirements Medical
  examination.
Staff Physicians 1 (ft); RNs 1 (pt); LPNs 2
  (ft), 1 (pt); Nurses' aides 5 (ft), 3 (pt);
  Activities coordinators 1 (ft); Dietitians 1
  (pt); Podiatrists 1 (pt).
Facilities Dining room; Dayroom.
Activities Arts & crafts; Games; Pet therapy.

Metzenbaum Residence
8132 Cedar Rd, Chesterland, OH 44026
(216) 729-9409
Licensure Intermediate care for mentally
  retarded. *Beds* ICF/MR 40. *Certified*
  Medicaid.
Owner Publicly owned.

Chesterville

Morrow Manor Inc
PO Box 44, State Rtes 95 & 314, Chesterville,
  OH 43317
(419) 768-2401
Admin Darlene K Kunze.
Medical Dir Edward D Blackburn; Alice A
  Cole.
Licensure Intermediate care. *Beds* ICF 50.
  Certified Medicaid.
Owner Proprietary corp.
Admissions Requirements Minimum age 18;
  Medical examination.
Staff RNs 1 (ft), 1 (pt); LPNs 5 (ft); Nurses'
  aides 16 (ft), 2 (pt); Activities coordinators 1
  (ft).
Facilities Dining room; Laundry room;
  Barber/Beauty shop.
Activities Arts & crafts; Cards; Games;
  Reading groups; Prayer groups; Movies;
  Shopping trips; Dances/Social/Cultural
  gatherings.

Cheviot

Hillebrand Nursing Center
4307 Bridgetown Rd, Cheviot, OH 45211
(513) 574-4550
Medical Dir Dr Gene Simon.
Licensure Skilled care; Intermediate care. *Beds*
  SNF 52; ICF 58. *Certified* Medicaid;
  Medicare.
Owner Proprietary corp.
Staff Physicians; RNs 6 (ft), 12 (pt); LPNs 2
  (ft), 10 (pt); Nurses' aides 25 (ft), 28 (pt);
  Physical therapists 2 (ft); Recreational

therapists 2 (ft), 1 (pt); Speech therapists 1 (ft); Activities coordinators 2 (ft); Dietitians 1 (pt); Podiatrists 1 (pt).
Facilities Dining room; Physical therapy room; Activities room; Chapel; Barber/Beauty shop; Library.
Activities Arts & crafts; Cards; Games; Reading groups; Prayer groups; Movies; Dances/Social/Cultural gatherings.

Chillicothe

Heartland of Chillicothe
1058 Columbus St, Chillicothe, OH 45601
(614) 773-5000
Admin Laura L Minner. *Dir of Nursing* Kathy Corcoran RN. *Medical Dir* Daniel Colopy MD.
Licensure Skilled care; Intermediate care. *Beds* Swing beds SNF/ICF 101. *Certified* Medicaid; Medicare.
Owner Proprietary corp (Health Care and Retirement Corp).
Admissions Requirements Medical examination.
Staff Physicians 1 (pt); RNs; LPNs; Nurses' aides; Activities coordinators; Social workers 1 (ft); Restorative CNAs 1 (ft).
Facilities Dining room; Physical therapy room; Activities room; Laundry room; Barber/Beauty shop.
Activities Arts & crafts; Cards; Games; Reading groups; Prayer groups; Movies; Shopping trips; Dances/Social/Cultural gatherings.

Marietta Place Nursing Home
60 Marietta Rd, Chillicothe, OH 45601
(614) 772-5900
Licensure Skilled care; Intermediate care. *Beds* SNF 8; ICF 93. *Certified* Medicaid; Medicare.
Owner Proprietary corp (Hillhaven Corp).
Admissions Requirements Medical examination; Physician's request.
Staff RNs 12 (ft); LPNs 4 (ft); Nurses' aides 30 (ft), 2 (pt); Physical therapists 1 (pt); Speech therapists 1 (pt); Activities coordinators 1 (ft), 1 (pt); Dietitians 1 (pt); Ophthalmologists; Podiatrists; Dentists.
Facilities Dining room; Activities room; Laundry room; Barber/Beauty shop; Library.
Activities Arts & crafts; Cards; Games; Reading groups; Prayer groups; Movies; Shopping trips; Dances/Social/Cultural gatherings.

Westmoreland Place
230 Cherry St, Chillicothe, OH 45601
(614) 773-6470
Admin Jerry Kuyoth. *Dir of Nursing* Lois Dudley. *Medical Dir* Dr John Seidensticker.
Licensure Skilled care; Intermediate care. *Beds* SNF 50; ICF 100. *Private Pay Patients* 33%. *Certified* Medicaid; Medicare.
Owner Proprietary corp (Nursing Care Management).
Admissions Requirements Medical examination; Physician's request.
Staff RNs 9 (ft), 1 (pt); LPNs 18 (ft), 3 (pt); Nurses' aides 70 (ft); Physical therapists 1 (pt); Occupational therapists 1 (pt); Speech therapists 1 (pt); Activities coordinators 1 (ft); Dietitians 1 (pt); Ophthalmologists 1 (pt); Podiatrists 1 (pt); Audiologists 1 (pt); Community outreach coordinators 1 (pt).
Facilities Dining room; Physical therapy room; Activities room; Chapel; Crafts room; Laundry room; Barber/Beauty shop.
Activities Arts & crafts; Games; Prayer groups; Movies; Dances/Social/Cultural gatherings; Intergenerational programs; Pet therapy.

Cincinnati

Aaron Convalescent Home
21 W Columbia Ave, Cincinnati, OH 45215
(513) 554-1141
Licensure Intermediate care. *Beds* ICF 142. *Certified* Medicaid.
Owner Proprietary corp.

Able Manor Nursing Home
2927 Douglas Terrace, Cincinnati, OH 45212
(513) 531-6676
Licensure Intermediate care. *Beds* ICF 33. *Certified* Medicaid.
Owner Proprietary corp.

Alaska Nursing Home
3584 Alaska Ave, Cincinnati, OH 45229
(513) 281-7782
Licensure Intermediate care. *Beds* ICF 43. *Certified* Medicaid.
Owner Proprietary corp.

Alois Alzheimer Center
70 Damon Rd, Cincinnati, OH 45218
(513) 825-2255, 825-2998 FAX
Admin Mitchell J Durant PhD. *Dir of Nursing* Dianne Torgersen BSN RNC. *Medical Dir* Dr Stuart A Zakem.
Licensure Skilled care; Intermediate care; Day care; Respite care; Alzheimer's care. *Beds* Swing beds SNF/ICF 82. *Private Pay Patients* 100%.
Owner Proprietary corp (Crystalwood Inc).
Admissions Requirements Medical examination; Alzheimer patients.
Staff Physicians 1 (ft), 4 (pt); RNs 3 (ft), 4 (pt); LPNs 6 (ft), 4 (pt); Nurses' aides 26 (ft), 14 (pt); Physical therapists 1 (pt); Activities coordinators 1 (ft); Dietitians 1 (pt); Podiatrists 1 (pt).
Facilities Dining room; Physical therapy room; Activities room; Chapel; Crafts room; Laundry room; Barber/Beauty shop; Library.
Activities Arts & crafts; Cards; Games; Reading groups; Prayer groups; Movies; Shopping trips; Dances/Social/Cultural gatherings; Intergenerational programs; Pet therapy; Gardening; Music therapy; Outings; One-on-one activities.

Ambassador North
5501 Verulam St, Cincinnati, OH 45213
(513) 531-3654
Licensure Skilled care; Intermediate care. *Beds* Swing beds SNF/ICF 50. *Certified* Medicaid; Medicare.
Owner Proprietary corp.

Ambassador South
3030 Carpathia, Cincinnati, OH 45213
(513) 631-1310
Licensure Skilled care; Intermediate care. *Beds* Swing beds SNF/ICF 50. *Certified* Medicaid; Medicare.
Owner Proprietary corp.

Amber Health Care Center
PO Box 5099, Cincinnati, OH 45205
(614) 252-4893, 252-2535
Admin Larry Rosenberg. *Dir of Nursing* Judith M Tracey RNC. *Medical Dir* E Harris.
Licensure Intermediate care. *Beds* ICF 133. *Certified* Medicaid.
Owner Proprietary corp.
Admissions Requirements Medical examination; Physician's request.
Staff Physicians 6 (pt); RNs 8 (ft) 13C 14 (ft); Nurses' aides 42 (ft); Physical therapists 2 (pt); Recreational therapists 3 (ft); Occupational therapists 1 (pt); Speech therapists 1 (pt); Activities coordinators 1 (ft); Dietitians 1 (pt); Ophthalmologists 1 (pt); Podiatrists 1 (pt); Dentists 1 (pt); Social services 1 (ft); Optometrists 1 (pt); Medical records 2 (ft); QMRPs 1 (pt); Psychologists 1 (pt).

Facilities Dining room; Physical therapy room; Activities room; Crafts room; Laundry room; Barber/Beauty shop; Library; 5 TV lounges.
Activities Arts & crafts; Cards; Games; Reading groups; Prayer groups; Movies; Shopping trips; Dances/Social/Cultural gatherings; Discussion groups; Exercise class.

Arcadia Manor
5500 Verulam Ave, Cincinnati, OH 45213
(513) 631-0003
Licensure Skilled care; Intermediate care. *Beds* Swing beds SNF/ICF 121. *Certified* Medicaid; Medicare.
Owner Proprietary corp.

Archbishop Leibold Home
476 Riddle Rd, Cincinnati, OH 45220
(513) 281-8001
Admin Sr Andrea Munarriz.
Medical Dir Sr Mildred Ryan.
Licensure Intermediate care; Rest home. *Beds* ICF 75; Rest home 50. *Certified* Medicaid.
Owner Proprietary corp.
Affiliation Roman Catholic.
Facilities Dining room; Physical therapy room; Activities room; Chapel; Crafts room; Laundry room; Barber/Beauty shop; Library.
Activities Arts & crafts; Cards; Games; Reading groups; Prayer groups; Movies; Shopping trips; Dances/Social/Cultural gatherings.

Beechknoll Convalescent Center
6550 Hamilton Ave, Cincinnati, OH 45224
(513) 522-5516
Admin Mark Wellinghoff. *Dir of Nursing* Wilma McGlasson RNC. *Medical Dir* Richard Longshore MD.
Licensure Skilled care; Intermediate care; Retirement; Alzheimer's care. *Beds* SNF 20; Swing beds SNF/ICF 80. *Certified* Medicare.
Owner Proprietary corp.
Admissions Requirements Minimum age 16; Medical examination.
Staff Physicians 1 (pt); RNs 8 (ft), 9 (pt); LPNs 9 (ft), 9 (pt); Nurses' aides 37 (ft), 23 (pt); Activities coordinators 4 (ft); Dentists 1 (pt).
Facilities Dining room; Physical therapy room; Activities room; Crafts room; Laundry room; Barber/Beauty shop; Library.
Activities Arts & crafts; Cards; Games; Reading groups; Prayer groups; Movies; Shopping trips; Dances/Social/Cultural gatherings.

Beechknoll Terrace Retirement Center
6552 Hamilton Ave, Cincinnati, OH 45224
(513) 522-5516
Licensure Rest home. *Beds* Rest home 104.
Owner Proprietary corp.

Beechwood Home
2140 Pogue Ave, Cincinnati, OH 45208
(513) 321-9294
Licensure Skilled care; Intermediate care. *Beds* Swing beds SNF/ICF 70. *Certified* Medicaid; Medicare.
Owner Proprietary corp.

Bethesda Scarlet Oaks
440 Lafayette Ave, Cincinnati, OH 45220
(513) 861-0400, 221-4209 FAX
Admin Richard A Fratianne CFACHCA. *Dir of Nursing* Jan Boblenz RNC. *Medical Dir* John Spaccarelli MD.
Licensure Intermediate care; Retirement. *Beds* ICF 70. *Private Pay Patients* 100%.
Owner Nonprofit organization/foundation.
Admissions Requirements Medical examination.
Staff Physicians 2 (pt); RNs 5 (ft), 3 (pt); LPNs 4 (ft), 1 (pt); Nurses' aides 20 (ft), 9 (pt); Physical therapists 1 (pt); Occupational therapists (consultant); Speech therapists (consultant); Activities coordinators 1 (ft), 1

(pt); Dietitians 1 (pt); Ophthalmologists (consultant); Podiatrists 2 (pt); Audiologists (consultant).
Affiliation United Methodist.
Facilities Dining room; Physical therapy room; Activities room; Chapel; Crafts room; Laundry room; Barber/Beauty shop; Library.
Activities Arts & crafts; Cards; Games; Reading groups; Prayer groups; Movies; Shopping trips; Dances/Social/Cultural gatherings; Intergenerational programs; Pet therapy.

Brookwood Retirement Community
12100 Reed Hartman Hwy, Cincinnati, OH 45241
(513) 530-9555
Licensure Skilled care; Intermediate care; Rest home. *Beds* Swing beds SNF/ICF 65; Rest home 87.
Owner Proprietary corp.

Byrnes Convalescent Center Inc
2203 Fulton Ave, Cincinnati, OH 45206
(513) 751-1752
Admin Ron Jimmar.
Medical Dir Kyu H Kim; Denise Tartaglia.
Licensure Intermediate care. *Beds* ICF 64. *Certified* Medicaid.
Owner Proprietary corp.
Staff RNs 1 (ft), 1 (pt); LPNs 7 (ft), 3 (pt); Nurses' aides 10 (ft), 8 (pt); Activities coordinators 1 (ft), 1 (pt); Dietitians 1 (ft).
Facilities Dining room; Activities room; Crafts room; Barber/Beauty shop.
Activities Arts & crafts; Cards; Games; Reading groups; Prayer groups; Movies; Dances/Social/Cultural gatherings.

Camargo Manor Nursing Home
7625 Camargo Rd, Cincinnati, OH 45243
(513) 561-6210
Admin Franklin Nathan. *Dir of Nursing* Peggy Kelch RN. *Medical Dir* Nolan Weinberg MD.
Licensure Skilled care; Intermediate care; Retirement. *Beds* Swing beds SNF/ICF 53.
Owner Proprietary corp.
Admissions Requirements Medical examination.
Staff RNs; LPNs; Nurses' aides; Physical therapists; Recreational therapists; Occupational therapists; Activities coordinators; Dietitians; Ophthalmologists; Podiatrists.
Facilities Dining room; Activities room; Laundry room; Barber/Beauty shop.
Activities Arts & crafts; Cards; Games; Reading groups; Prayer groups; Movies; Shopping trips; Dances/Social/Cultural gatherings; Therapy groups.

Christian Care of Cincinnati Inc
1067 Compton Rd, Cincinnati, OH 45231
(513) 522-5553
Admin Barbara Craig RN MGS. *Dir of Nursing* B Craig RN; V Shields LPN, Asst. *Medical Dir* Dr Shields.
Licensure Intermediate care. *Beds* ICF 33. *Private Pay Patients* 1%. *Certified* Medicaid.
Owner Proprietary corp.
Admissions Requirements Minimum age 21; Medical examination; Physician's request.
Staff RNs 1 (pt); LPNs 2 (ft), 4 (pt); Nurses' aides 10 (ft), 11 (pt); Physical therapists 1 (pt); Activities coordinators 1 (ft).
Facilities Dining room; Laundry room.
Activities Arts & crafts; Games; Reading groups; Prayer groups; Pet therapy.

Clifton Care Center Inc
625 Probasco Ave, Cincinnati, OH 45220
(513) 281-2464
Licensure Skilled care; Intermediate care. *Beds* SNF 32; ICF 110. *Certified* Medicaid; Medicare.
Owner Proprietary corp.

Clifton Villa
515 Melish Ave, Cincinnati, OH 45229
(513) 961-2853
Admin Mona Jo Trowbridge. *Dir of Nursing* Holly Ziegenhardt. *Medical Dir* Dr Kyu Kim.
Licensure Intermediate care; Rest home; Alzheimer's care. *Beds* ICF 100; Rest home 50. *Certified* Medicaid.
Owner Proprietary corp.
Admissions Requirements Physician's request.
Staff Physicians; RNs; LPNs; Nurses' aides; Physical therapists; Recreational therapists; Activities coordinators; Dietitians.
Facilities Dining room; Physical therapy room; Activities room; Crafts room; Laundry room; Barber/Beauty shop; Library.
Activities Arts & crafts; Cards; Games; Reading groups; Prayer groups; Movies; Dances/Social/Cultural gatherings; Pet therapy.

Clovernook Inc
7025 Clovernook Ave, Cincinnati, OH 45231
(513) 522-2033, 522-4122 FAX
Admin Franklin Nathan. *Dir of Nursing* Johanna Donovan. *Medical Dir* Kevin Budke MD; Janson Becker MD.
Licensure Skilled care; Intermediate care. *Beds* SNF 25; ICF 137. *Certified* Medicaid; Medicare.
Owner Proprietary corp.
Admissions Requirements Medical examination; Physician's request.
Staff Physicians 2 (pt).
Facilities Dining room; Physical therapy room; Activities room; Crafts room; Laundry room; Barber/Beauty shop.
Activities Arts & crafts; Cards; Games; Reading groups; Prayer groups; Movies; Pet therapy.

Cottingham Retirement Community
3995 Cottingham Dr, Cincinnati, OH 45241
(513) 563-3600
Admin William C Wexler. *Dir of Nursing* Margie Berryman. *Medical Dir* Steven Grendel MD.
Licensure Skilled care; Intermediate care; Retirement. *Beds* SNF 60; ICF 95; Retirement community 122. *Private Pay Patients* 99%. *Certified* Medicare.
Owner Proprietary corp.
Admissions Requirements Medical examination.
Staff Physicians 3 (pt); RNs 4 (ft), 4 (pt); LPNs 3 (ft), 7 (pt); Nurses' aides 19 (ft), 15 (pt); Physical therapists 1 (pt); Reality therapists 1 (pt); Recreational therapists 1 (pt); Occupational therapists 1 (pt); Speech therapists 1 (pt); Activities coordinators 3 (ft); Dietitians 1 (ft); Ophthalmologists 1 (pt); Podiatrists 1 (pt); Audiologists 1 (pt).
Facilities Dining room; Physical therapy room; Activities room; Chapel; Crafts room; Laundry room; Barber/Beauty shop; Library; Swimming pool.
Activities Arts & crafts; Cards; Games; Reading groups; Prayer groups; Movies; Shopping trips; Dances/Social/Cultural gatherings; Intergenerational programs; Pet therapy.

Crestview Nursing Home
2420 Harrison Ave, Cincinnati, OH 45211
(513) 481-1100
Admin Ron Jimmar. *Dir of Nursing* Beth Merritt. *Medical Dir* Dr Luid Quiroga.
Licensure Skilled care; Intermediate care. *Beds* Swing beds SNF/ICF 140. *Certified* Medicaid; Medicare.
Owner Proprietary corp (Parke Care Inc).
Admissions Requirements Medical examination.
Staff RNs; LPNs; Nurses' aides; Physical therapists; Speech therapists; Activities coordinators; Dietitians.

Facilities Dining room; Activities room; Barber/Beauty shop.
Activities Arts & crafts; Cards; Games; Reading groups; Prayer groups; Movies; Shopping trips; Dances/Social/Cultural gatherings; Bowling.

Daly Parks Geriatric Center
6300 Daly Rd, Cincinnati, OH 45224
(513) 542-6800
Admin Beth Dobrozsi. *Dir of Nursing* Janet Leach. *Medical Dir* Dr James Fidelholtz.
Licensure Skilled care; Intermediate care. *Beds* Swing beds SNF/ICF 132. *Private Pay Patients* 30%. *Certified* Medicaid; Medicare.
Owner Proprietary corp (Parke Care Inc).
Admissions Requirements Medical examination.
Staff Physicians; RNs; LPNs; Nurses' aides; Physical therapists; Reality therapists; Recreational therapists; Occupational therapists; Speech therapists; Activities coordinators; Dietitians; Ophthalmologists; Podiatrists.
Facilities Dining room; Physical therapy room; Activities room; Crafts room; Barber/Beauty shop.
Activities Arts & crafts; Cards; Games; Reading groups; Prayer groups; Movies; Shopping trips; Dances/Social/Cultural gatherings; Intergenerational programs; Pet therapy; Remotivation; Music therapy; Behavioral rehabilitation; Mobility training.

Deer Parke Nursing Home
6922 Ohio Ave, Cincinnati, OH 45236
(513) 793-2090, 793-4840 FAX
Admin Patricia Troehler. *Dir of Nursing* Elaine Nolan. *Medical Dir* Stephen Berg.
Licensure Skilled care; Intermediate care. *Beds* Swing beds SNF/ICF 136. *Private Pay Patients* 45%. *Certified* Medicaid; Medicare.
Owner Proprietary corp (Parke Care Inc).
Admissions Requirements Medical examination; Physician's request.
Staff RNs 9 (ft); LPNs 13 (ft); Nurses' aides 38 (ft); Physical therapists 1 (pt); Recreational therapists 1 (pt); Occupational therapists 1 (pt); Activities coordinators 3 (ft); Dietitians 1 (ft).
Facilities Dining room; Activities room; Laundry room; Barber/Beauty shop.
Activities Movies; Pet therapy.

Daniel Drake Memorial Hospital
151 W Galbraith Rd, Cincinnati, OH 45216
(513) 761-3440
Admin Jan C Taylor.
Medical Dir Walter E Matern; Marie Moore.
Licensure Skilled care; Intermediate care. *Beds* Swing beds SNF/ICF 244. *Certified* Medicaid; Medicare.
Owner Publicly owned.
Admissions Requirements Medical examination.
Staff Physicians 9 (ft), 41 (pt); RNs 87 (ft); LPNs 82 (ft); Nurses' aides 145 (ft); Physical therapists 6 (ft); Recreational therapists 8 (ft); Occupational therapists 6 (ft); Speech therapists 3 (ft); Dietitians 3 (ft); Ophthalmologists 2 (pt); Podiatrists 1 (pt); Dentists 1 (pt).
Facilities Dining room; Physical therapy room; Activities room; Chapel; Crafts room; Laundry room; Barber/Beauty shop; Library; Occupational therapy room; Speech therapy room; Audiology test room; Auditorium; Patient lounge.
Activities Arts & crafts; Cards; Games; Reading groups; Prayer groups; Movies; Shopping trips; Dances/Social/Cultural gatherings; Outings.

East Galbraith Health Care Center & Nursing Home
3889 E Galbraith Rd, Cincinnati, OH 45236
(513) 793-5220

Admin Brenda Henderson Waugh. *Dir of Nursing* Amy Alexander; Sharon Strunk. *Medical Dir* Loraine Glaser MD; Stuart Zakem MD.
Licensure Skilled care; Intermediate care. *Beds* Swing beds SNF/ICF 236. *Private Pay Patients* 85%. *Certified* Medicaid; Medicare.
Owner Proprietary corp.
Admissions Requirements Minimum age Adult; Medical examination.
Staff Physicians 1 (pt); RNs 5 (ft), 2 (pt); LPNs 14 (ft), 4 (pt); Nurses' aides 25 (ft), 4 (pt); Physical therapists 1 (ft); Recreational therapists 4 (ft); Occupational therapists 1 (ft); Speech therapists 1 (ft); Activities coordinators 1 (ft); Dietitians 1 (ft); Ophthalmologists 1 (pt); Podiatrists 1 (pt); Audiologists 1 (pt).
Facilities Dining room; Physical therapy room; Activities room; Crafts room; Barber/Beauty shop; Multi-purpose rooms.
Activities Arts & crafts; Cards; Games; Reading groups; Prayer groups; Movies; Shopping trips; Dances/Social/Cultural gatherings; Intergenerational programs; Pet therapy.

Eastgate Health Care Center
4400 Glen Este-Withamsville Rd, Cincinnati, OH 45245
(513) 752-3710
Licensure Skilled care; Intermediate care; Rest home. *Beds* SNF 50; Swing beds SNF/ICF 50; Rest home 102. *Certified* Medicare.
Owner Proprietary corp.

Elite Nursing Home
PO Box 6276, Cincinnati, OH 45206
(513) 221-3900
Licensure Intermediate care. *Beds* ICF 50. *Certified* Medicaid.
Owner Proprietary corp.

Empress Convalescent Home 1
2321 Upland Pl, Cincinnati, OH 45206
(513) 281-7700
Admin Hugo G Eichelberg. *Dir of Nursing* M Compuber RN. *Medical Dir* Lenzy G Southall MD.
Licensure Intermediate care. *Beds* ICF 45. *Certified* Medicaid.
Owner Proprietary corp.
Admissions Requirements Medical examination.
Staff Physicians 4 (pt); RNs 5 (ft); LPNs 2 (ft) 11 (ft), 3 (pt); Physical therapists 1 (pt); Activities coordinators 1 (ft); Dietitians 1 (pt); Ophthalmologists 1 (pt); Podiatrists 1 (pt); Dentists 1 (pt).
Languages German.
Facilities Dining room; Activities room; Chapel; Crafts room; Laundry room; Library.
Activities Arts & crafts; Cards; Games; Reading groups; Prayer groups; Movies; Shopping trips; Dances/Social/Cultural gatherings; Picnics; Outings.

Empress Convalescent Home 2
2327 Upland Pl, Cincinnati, OH 45206
(513) 281-7700
Admin Hugo G Eichelberg. *Dir of Nursing* M Capuber RN. *Medical Dir* Dr Lenzy Southall.
Licensure Intermediate care. *Beds* ICF 25. *Certified* Medicaid.
Owner Proprietary corp.
Admissions Requirements Females only; Medical examination; Physician's request.
Staff Physicians 4 (pt); RNs 1 (ft); LPNs 4 (ft), 2 (pt); Nurses' aides 8 (ft), 3 (pt); Physical therapists; Reality therapists; Speech therapists; Activities coordinators 1 (ft); Dietitians 1 (pt); Ophthalmologists 1 (pt); Podiatrists 1 (pt); Dentists 1 (pt).
Languages German.

Facilities Dining room; Activities room; Chapel; Crafts room; Laundry room.
Activities Arts & crafts; Cards; Games; Reading groups; Prayer groups; Movies; Dances/Social/Cultural gatherings; Picnics; Outings.

Fairview Nursing Home
1804 Kinney Ave, Cincinnati, OH 45207
(513) 221-0433
Licensure Skilled care; Intermediate care. *Beds* Swing beds SNF/ICF 50. *Certified* Medicaid; Medicare.
Owner Proprietary corp.

Forestview Nursing Home
610 Forest Ave, Cincinnati, OH 45229
(513) 751-1602
Licensure Intermediate care. *Beds* ICF 28. *Certified* Medicaid.
Owner Proprietary corp.

Gardenview Nursing Home
3544 Washington Ave, Cincinnati, OH 45229
(513) 751-2241
Licensure Skilled care; Intermediate care. *Beds* Swing beds SNF/ICF 45. *Certified* Medicaid; Medicare.
Owner Proprietary corp.

Glen Manor
6969 Glenmeadow Ln, Cincinnati, OH 45237
(513) 351-7007
Admin Ann E Clabaugh. *Dir of Nursing* Mary Basnight RN. *Medical Dir* Stanley Wacksman MD.
Licensure Skilled care; Intermediate care; Alzheimer's care. *Beds* Swing beds SNF/ICF 118. *Certified* Medicaid; Medicare.
Owner Proprietary corp.
Admissions Requirements Minimum age 65; Medical examination.
Staff Physicians 1 (pt); RNs 8 (ft), 5 (pt); LPNs 12 (ft), 5 (pt); Nurses' aides 34 (ft), 7 (pt); Physical therapists 1 (pt); Recreational therapists 2 (ft); Occupational therapists 1 (ft), 1 (pt); Speech therapists 1 (pt); Activities coordinators 1 (ft); Dietitians 1 (pt); Ophthalmologists 1 (pt).
Affiliation Jewish.
Facilities Dining room; Physical therapy room; Activities room; Chapel; Crafts room; Laundry room; Barber/Beauty shop; Library.
Activities Arts & crafts; Cards; Games; Reading groups; Movies; Shopping trips; Dances/Social/Cultural gatherings.

Glen Orchard Home
7851 Glen Orchard, Cincinnati, OH 45237
(513) 821-7628
Admin David C Horn LISW QMRP. *Dir of Nursing* Pam Bell RN. *Medical Dir* Charles Dillard MD.
Licensure Intermediate care for mentally retarded. *Beds* ICF/MR 10. *Private Pay Patients* 0%. *Certified* Medicaid.
Owner Nonprofit corp (Peterson Enterprises Inc).
Admissions Requirements Minimum age 18.
Staff Physicians 1 (pt); RNs 1 (ft); LPNs 2 (pt); Speech therapists 1 (pt); Dietitians 1 (pt).
Facilities Dining room; Activities room; Laundry room.
Activities Arts & crafts; Cards; Games; Reading groups; Movies; Shopping trips; Dances/Social/Cultural gatherings.

Glen Parke
548 Glenwood Ave, Cincinnati, OH 45229
(513) 961-8881
Admin Helen E Martin. *Dir of Nursing* Laurie Westermeyer RN. *Medical Dir* Dr Mediodia.
Licensure Intermediate care; Intermediate care for mentally retarded. *Beds* ICF 105; ICF/MR 50. *Certified* Medicaid.
Owner Proprietary corp.

Staff Physicians 4 (pt); RNs 7 (ft); LPNs 17 (ft); Nurses' aides 60 (ft); Physical therapists 2 (pt); Recreational therapists 4 (ft), 1 (pt); Occupational therapists 2 (ft); Speech therapists 1 (pt); Activities coordinators 2 (ft); Dietitians 1 (ft); Ophthalmologists 1 (pt); Podiatrists 1 (pt); Dentists 1 (pt).
Facilities Dining room; Physical therapy room; Activities room; Crafts room; Barber/Beauty shop.
Activities Arts & crafts; Cards; Games; Reading groups; Prayer groups; Movies; Shopping trips; Dances/Social/Cultural gatherings.

Gold Crest Nursing Home
3663 Reading Rd, Cincinnati, OH 45229
(513) 861-1036
Admin Vandadean R Fulton.
Medical Dir Dr Morris Plotnick.
Licensure Intermediate care. *Beds* ICF 50. *Certified* Medicaid.
Owner Proprietary corp.
Admissions Requirements Medical examination.
Staff Physicians; RNs; LPNs; Nurses' aides; Activities coordinators; Dietitians; Ophthalmologists; Dentists.
Facilities Dining room; Activities room; Crafts room; Laundry room.
Activities Arts & crafts; Cards; Games; Reading groups; Prayer groups; Movies; Shopping trips; Dances/Social/Cultural gatherings; National Nursing Home Week.

Golden Age Retirement Home
3635 Reading Rd, Cincinnati, OH 45229
(513) 281-1922
Admin Henrietta DePuccio. *Dir of Nursing* Marie Willingham. *Medical Dir* Morris Plotnick MD.
Licensure Skilled care; Intermediate care. *Beds* Swing beds SNF/ICF 50. *Certified* Medicaid; Medicare.
Owner Proprietary corp.
Admissions Requirements Medical examination; Physician's request.
Staff Physicians; RNs; LPNs; Nurses' aides; Physical therapists; Reality therapists; Recreational therapists; Speech therapists; Activities coordinators; Dietitians.
Facilities Dining room; Physical therapy room; Laundry room.
Activities Arts & crafts; Cards; Games; Reading groups; Prayer groups; Movies; Shopping trips; Dances/Social/Cultural gatherings.

Grace Manor Nursing Home
2409 Grandview Ave, Cincinnati, OH 45206
(513) 281-8900
Admin Hugo G Eichelberg. *Dir of Nursing* Debbie Eckart. *Medical Dir* Lenzy G Southall MD.
Licensure Intermediate care. *Beds* ICF 30. *Certified* Medicaid.
Owner Proprietary corp.
Admissions Requirements Females only; Medical examination.
Staff Physicians 5 (pt); RNs 1 (ft); LPNs 4 (ft); Nurses' aides 9 (ft); Physical therapists 1 (pt); Reality therapists 1 (pt); Recreational therapists 1 (pt); Speech therapists; Activities coordinators 1 (ft); Dietitians 1 (pt); Ophthalmologists 1 (pt); Podiatrists 1 (pt).
Languages German.
Facilities Dining room; Activities room; Crafts room; Laundry room.
Activities Arts & crafts; Cards; Games; Reading groups; Prayer groups; Movies; Dances/Social/Cultural gatherings.

Hamilton County Eastern Star Home Inc
1630 W North Bend Rd, Cincinnati, OH 45224
(513) 542-6464

Licensure Skilled care; Intermediate care; Rest home. *Beds* Swing beds SNF/ICF 44; Rest home 26.
Owner Proprietary corp.
Affiliation Order of Eastern Star.

Harrison House Inc
2171 Harrison Ave, Cincinnati, OH 45211
(513) 662-5800, 662-5803 FAX
Admin Patricia Gault. *Dir of Nursing* Joyce Barnes. *Medical Dir* George Shields MD.
Licensure Skilled care; Intermediate care. *Beds* SNF 45; ICF 56. *Private Pay Patients* 14%. *Certified* Medicaid; Medicare.
Owner Proprietary corp.
Admissions Requirements Minimum age 21; Medical examination.
Staff Physicians 1 (pt); RNs 5 (ft), 4 (pt); LPNs 13 (ft), 4 (pt); Nurses' aides 22 (ft), 18 (pt); Physical therapists 1 (pt); Occupational therapists 1 (pt); Speech therapists 1 (pt); Activities coordinators 1 (ft); Dietitians 1 (pt); Ophthalmologists 1 (pt); Podiatrists 1 (pt).
Facilities Dining room; Physical therapy room; Activities room; Chapel; Crafts room; Laundry room; Barber/Beauty shop; Library; Courtyard.
Activities Arts & crafts; Cards; Games; Reading groups; Prayer groups; Movies; Dances/Social/Cultural gatherings; Pet therapy; Church services; Birthday parties; Wheelchair bowling.

Hillside Nursing Home
3539 Eden Ave, Cincinnati, OH 45229
(513) 861-1482
Admin Thomas F Grimes Jr LNHA. *Dir of Nursing* Kathleen Zucker RN. *Medical Dir* George Shields MD.
Licensure Intermediate care. *Beds* ICF 67. *Private Pay Patients* 1%. *Certified* Medicaid.
Owner Proprietary corp (Kind Health Services).
Staff Physicians 1 (pt); RNs 2 (ft), 3 (pt); LPNs 12 (ft); Nurses' aides 26 (ft); Physical therapists 1 (pt); Recreational therapists 1 (ft); Activities coordinators 1 (ft); Dietitians 1 (ft); Ophthalmologists 1 (pt); Podiatrists 1 (pt); Audiologists 1 (pt).
Facilities Dining room; Activities room; Crafts room; Laundry room.
Activities Arts & crafts; Cards; Games; Reading groups; Prayer groups; Movies; Shopping trips; Dances/Social/Cultural gatherings; Intergenerational programs; Pet therapy; Discussion groups.

Hilltop Nursing Home
2586 LaFeuille Ave, Cincinnati, OH 45211
(513) 662-3149
Admin Frances R Glaser. *Dir of Nursing* Mary Nau. *Medical Dir* Manual Mediodia MD.
Licensure Skilled care; Intermediate care; Retirement; Alzheimer's care. *Beds* SNF 24; ICF 30. *Certified* Medicare.
Owner Proprietary corp.
Admissions Requirements Minimum age 40; Females only.
Staff RNs 4 (ft), 1 (pt); LPNs 9 (ft), 4 (pt); Nurses' aides 22 (ft), 6 (pt); Physical therapists 1 (pt); Recreational therapists 1 (ft), 1 (pt); Activities coordinators 1 (ft); Dietitians 1 (ft); Music therapists 1 (ft).
Facilities Dining room; Physical therapy room; Activities room; Chapel; Crafts room; Barber/Beauty shop; Library.
Activities Arts & crafts; Cards; Games; Reading groups; Prayer groups; Movies; Shopping trips; Dances/Social/Cultural gatherings; Music therapy.

Hillview Nursing Home
2025 Wyoming Ave, Cincinnati, OH 45205
(513) 251-2557, 251-2648 FAX
Admin Sara Zuchowicki. *Dir of Nursing* Patricia Waldman. *Medical Dir* George Shields MD.

Licensure Skilled care; Intermediate care. *Beds* SNF 70; ICF 30. *Certified* Medicaid; Medicare.
Owner Proprietary corp.
Staff Physicians 1 (pt); RNs 4 (ft), 1 (pt); LPNs 11 (ft), 3 (pt); Nurses' aides 38 (ft); Physical therapists 1 (pt); Recreational therapists 2 (pt); Occupational therapists 1 (pt); Speech therapists 1 (pt); Activities coordinators 1 (ft); Dietitians 1 (pt); Podiatrists 1 (pt); Audiologists 1 (pt).
Languages German, Russian.
Facilities Dining room; Physical therapy room; Laundry room; Barber/Beauty shop.
Activities Arts & crafts; Cards; Games; Reading groups; Prayer groups; Movies; Dances/Social/Cultural gatherings; Pet therapy.

Judson Village
2373 Harrison Ave, Cincinnati, OH 45211
(513) 662-5880, 662-4180 FAX
Admin James Piepenbrink. *Dir of Nursing* Suzanne Murphy. *Medical Dir* William Rudemiller.
Licensure Intermediate care; Assisted living; Retirement. *Beds* ICF 50; Assisted living 50; Retirement units 20. *Private Pay Patients* 80%. *Certified* Medicaid.
Owner Nonprofit corp.
Admissions Requirements Minimum age 65; Medical examination.
Staff RNs 2 (ft), 9 (pt); LPNs 6 (ft), 4 (pt); Nurses' aides 18 (ft), 15 (pt); Physical therapists; Activities coordinators 1 (ft), 3 (pt); Dietitians.
Affiliation Baptist.
Facilities Dining room; Chapel; Laundry room; Barber/Beauty shop; Library.
Activities Arts & crafts; Cards; Games; Reading groups; Prayer groups; Movies; Shopping trips; Dances/Social/Cultural gatherings; Intergenerational programs; Pet therapy; Religious services.

Kenwood Terrace Nursing Center Inc
8440 Montgomery Rd, Cincinnati, OH 45236
(513) 793-2255
Admin Ann Glass Block.
Medical Dir Dr Robert Burt.
Licensure Skilled care; Intermediate care. *Beds* SNF 38; ICF 70. *Certified* Medicaid; Medicare.
Owner Proprietary corp.
Staff RNs; LPNs; Nurses' aides; Physical therapists; Reality therapists; Recreational therapists; Occupational therapists; Speech therapists; Activities coordinators; Dietitians; Ophthalmologists.
Facilities Dining room; Physical therapy room; Activities room; Barber/Beauty shop.
Activities Arts & crafts; Cards; Games; Reading groups; Prayer groups; Movies; Shopping trips; Dances/Social/Cultural gatherings.

Marjorie P Lee Home for the Aged
3550 Shaw Ave, Cincinnati, OH 45208
(513) 871-2090
Admin Adrienne Walsh.
Medical Dir Donald Nunlist Young; Suzanne Murphy.
Licensure Intermediate care; Rest home; Alzheimer's care. *Beds* ICF 72; Rest home 50. *Certified* Medicaid.
Owner Proprietary corp.
Admissions Requirements Medical examination; Physician's request.
Staff Physicians 5 (pt); RNs 3 (ft), 1 (pt); LPNs 10 (ft), 2 (pt); Nurses' aides 27 (ft), 10 (pt); Physical therapists 1 (pt); Activities coordinators 3 (ft); Dietitians 1 (ft); Ophthalmologists 1 (pt); Dentists 1 (pt).
Affiliation Episcopal.
Facilities Dining room; Physical therapy room; Activities room; Chapel; Crafts room; Laundry room; Barber/Beauty shop; Library; Corner store; Game area.

Activities Arts & crafts; Cards; Games; Reading groups; Prayer groups; Movies; Shopping trips; Dances/Social/Cultural gatherings.

Lincoln Avenue & Crawford's Home
1346 Lincoln Ave, Cincinnati, OH 45206
(513) 861-2044, 559-1494
Licensure Intermediate care. *Beds* ICF 100. *Certified* Medicaid.
Owner Proprietary corp.

Llanfair Terrace
1701 Llanfair Ave, Cincinnati, OH 45224
(513) 681-4230
Licensure Skilled care; Intermediate care; Rest home. *Beds* Swing beds SNF/ICF 75; Rest home 25. *Certified* Medicaid; Medicare.
Owner Nonprofit corp (Ohio Presbyterian Homes).

Madison Nursing Home
PO Box 27166, 6845 Indian Hill Rd, Cincinnati, OH 45227-0166
(513) 271-0429
Licensure Intermediate care. *Beds* ICF 27. *Certified* Medicaid.
Owner Proprietary corp.

Manor Care Nursing Home
2250 Banning Rd, Cincinnati, OH 45239
(513) 591-0400
Licensure Skilled care; Intermediate care. *Beds* SNF 55; ICF 96. *Certified* Medicaid; Medicare.
Owner Proprietary corp (Manor Care Inc).

Manor Care of Woodside Nursing Center
5970 Kenwood Rd, Cincinnati, OH 45243
(513) 561-4111
Medical Dir Jack Rhodes MD.
Licensure Skilled care; Intermediate care. *Beds* SNF 13; Swing beds SNF/ICF 143. *Certified* Medicare.
Owner Proprietary corp.
Staff Physicians 1 (pt); RNs 11 (ft), 5 (pt); LPNs 14 (ft), 4 (pt); Nurses' aides 54 (ft), 27 (pt); Physical therapists 1 (ft); Occupational therapists 1 (pt); Speech therapists 1 (pt); Activities coordinators 2 (pt); Dietitians 1 (ft); Ophthalmologists 1 (pt); Podiatrists 1 (pt); Audiologists 1 (pt); Dentists 1 (pt).
Facilities Dining room; Physical therapy room; Activities room; Laundry room; Barber/Beauty shop.
Activities Arts & crafts; Cards; Games; Reading groups; Prayer groups; Movies; Shopping trips; Dances/Social/Cultural gatherings.

Maple Knoll Village
11100 Springfield Pike, Cincinnati, OH 45246
(513) 785-2400
Licensure Skilled care; Intermediate care. *Beds* SNF 114; ICF 60. *Certified* Medicaid; Medicare.
Owner Proprietary corp.

George A Martin Gerontology Center
3603 Washington Ave, Cincinnati, OH 45229
(513) 961-0144
Medical Dir John Falk MD.
Licensure Intermediate care. *Beds* ICF 25. *Certified* Medicaid.
Owner Proprietary corp.
Admissions Requirements Minimum age 21; Medical examination; Physician's request.
Staff Physicians; RNs; LPNs; Nurses' aides; Physical therapists; Reality therapists; Recreational therapists; Occupational therapists; Speech therapists; Activities coordinators; Dietitians; Ophthalmologists; Dentists.
Facilities Dining room; Activities room; Laundry room.
Activities Arts & crafts; Cards; Games; Reading groups; Prayer groups; Movies; Shopping trips; Dances/Social/Cultural gatherings.

Meadowbrook Care Center
8211 Weller Rd, Cincinnati, OH 45242
(513) 489-2444
Licensure Skilled care; Intermediate care. *Beds* Swing beds SNF/ICF 156. *Certified* Medicaid; Medicare.
Owner Proprietary corp.

Montgomery Care Center Inc
7777 Cooper Rd, Cincinnati, OH 45242
(513) 793-5092
Admin Michael J Bradford.
Medical Dir S Berg; I Morgan.
Licensure Skilled care; Intermediate care. *Beds* SNF 28; ICF 74. *Certified* Medicaid; Medicare.
Owner Proprietary corp.
Staff RNs; LPNs; Nurses' aides; Physical therapists; Recreational therapists; Occupational therapists; Speech therapists; Activities coordinators.
Facilities Dining room; Physical therapy room; Activities room; Chapel; Laundry room; Barber/Beauty shop.
Activities Arts & crafts; Cards; Games; Reading groups; Prayer groups; Movies; Dances/Social/Cultural gatherings; Dining out; Ethnic & special theme dinners.

Mt Healthy Christian Home
8097 Hamilton Ave, Cincinnati, OH 45231
(513) 931-5000
Admin J Donald Sams. *Dir of Nursing* Arlene Windhorst. *Medical Dir* Dr Janice Singerman; Dr Stephen Berg.
Licensure Skilled care; Intermediate care; Rest home. *Beds* Swing beds SNF/ICF 64; Rest home 32. *Certified* Medicaid.
Owner Proprietary corp.
Admissions Requirements Minimum age 62; Medical examination.
Staff Physicians 2 (pt); RNs 3 (ft), 5 (pt); LPNs 9 (ft), 3 (pt); Nurses' aides 34 (ft), 4 (pt); Physical therapists 1 (pt); Recreational therapists 1 (pt); Activities coordinators 1 (ft); Dietitians 1 (pt); Ophthalmologists 1 (pt).
Languages German.
Affiliation Church of Christ.
Facilities Dining room; Physical therapy room; Activities room; Chapel; Crafts room; Laundry room; Barber/Beauty shop; Library; Multipurpose room.
Activities Arts & crafts; Cards; Games; Reading groups; Prayer groups; Movies; Shopping trips.

Mt Washington Care Center
6900 Beechmont Ave, Cincinnati, OH 45230
(513) 231-4561
Admin Daniel J Suer. *Dir of Nursing* Janet Boblenz. *Medical Dir* Dr Tom Popa; Dr Art Gendelmen.
Licensure Skilled care; Intermediate care. *Beds* SNF 18; ICF 118. *Certified* Medicaid; Medicare.
Owner Proprietary corp.
Staff Physicians 1 (pt); RNs 6 (ft); LPNs 30 (ft); Physical therapists 1 (pt); Reality therapists 1 (pt); Recreational therapists 1 (pt); Occupational therapists 1 (pt); Speech therapists 1 (pt); Activities coordinators 3 (ft); Dietitians 1 (pt); Ophthalmologists 1 (pt); Podiatrists 1 (pt); Dentists 1 (pt).
Facilities Dining room; Physical therapy room; Activities room; Chapel; Crafts room; Laundry room; Barber/Beauty shop; Library.
Activities Arts & crafts; Cards; Games; Reading groups; Prayer groups; Movies; Shopping trips; Dances/Social/Cultural gatherings; Outpatient physical therapy.

Oak Pavilion Nursing Center
510 Oak St, Cincinnati, OH 45219
(513) 751-0880
Admin Mavis Phipps. *Dir of Nursing* Margaret Bradshaw. *Medical Dir* Dr Edmund Rothfeld.

Licensure Skilled care; Intermediate care. *Beds* SNF 50; ICF 100. *Private Pay Patients* 2%. *Certified* Medicaid; Medicare.
Owner Proprietary corp (Health Care & Retirement Corp).
Admissions Requirements Minimum age 21.
Staff RNs 10 (ft); LPNs 20 (ft), 5 (pt); Nurses' aides 60 (ft), 10 (pt); Physical therapists; Activities coordinators 2 (ft); Dietitians 1 (ft).
Facilities Dining room; Physical therapy room; Activities room; Laundry room; Barber/Beauty shop.
Activities Arts & crafts; Cards; Games; Reading groups; Prayer groups; Movies; Shopping trips; Dances/Social/Cultural gatherings; Intergenerational programs; Pet therapy.

Oakview Nursing Home
618 Forest Ave, Cincinnati, OH 45229
(513) 751-2062
Licensure Intermediate care. *Beds* ICF 27. *Certified* Medicaid.
Owner Proprietary corp (Buckeye Family and Nursing Home).

Ohio House
1620 Miramar, Cincinnati, OH 45237
(513) 761-6843
Licensure Intermediate care for mentally retarded. *Beds* ICF/MR 7. *Certified* Medicaid.
Owner Proprietary corp.

Orthodox Jewish Home for the Aged
1171 Towne St, Cincinnati, OH 45216
(513) 242-1360
Admin Leonard Sternberg ACSW. *Dir of Nursing* Leah Satzber. *Medical Dir* Dr Walter Schur.
Licensure Skilled care; Intermediate care; Alzheimer's care. *Beds* Swing beds SNF/ICF 172. *Certified* Medicaid; Medicare.
Owner Proprietary corp.
Admissions Requirements Minimum age 65; Medical examination.
Staff RNs; LPNs; Nurses' aides; Physical therapists; Reality therapists; Recreational therapists; Activities coordinators; Podiatrists.
Affiliation Jewish.
Facilities Dining room; Physical therapy room; Activities room; Chapel; Crafts room; Laundry room; Barber/Beauty shop; Library.
Activities Arts & crafts; Cards; Games; Reading groups; Prayer groups; Movies; Shopping trips; Dances/Social/Cultural gatherings.

Pavilion
7025 Clovernook Ave, Cincinnati, OH 45231
(513) 522-2033
Licensure Rest home. *Beds* Rest home 38.
Owner Proprietary corp.

Pavilion at Camargo Manor
7625 Camargo Rd, Cincinnati, OH 45243
(513) 561-6210
Licensure Rest home. *Beds* Rest home 83.
Owner Proprietary corp.

Peterson Enterprises Inc—Ridgeway Home
710 Ridgeway Ave, Cincinnati, OH 45229
(513) 861-0068
Licensure Intermediate care for mentally retarded. *Beds* ICF/MR 10. *Certified* Medicaid.
Owner Proprietary corp.

Peterson Ridge Home
4894 Ridge Ave, Cincinnati, OH 45209
(513) 631-9204
Admin David C Horn. *Dir of Nursing* Pam Bell RN. *Medical Dir* Dr Charles Dillard.
Licensure Intermediate care for mentally retarded. *Beds* ICF/MR 10. *Private Pay Patients* 0%. *Certified* Medicaid.
Owner Nonprofit corp (Peterson Enterprises).

Admissions Requirements Minimum age 18.
Staff Physicians 1 (pt); RNs 1 (pt); LPNs 2 (pt); Nurses' aides 5 (ft), 4 (pt); Physical therapists 1 (pt); Occupational therapists 1 (pt); Speech therapists 1 (pt); Dietitians 1 (pt); Ophthalmologists 1 (pt); Podiatrists 1 (pt); Audiologists 1 (pt).
Facilities Dining room; Activities room; Laundry room.
Activities Arts & crafts; Cards; Games; Movies; Shopping trips.

Price Hill Nursing Home
584 Elberon Ave, Cincinnati, OH 45205
(513) 251-0367
Admin Larry Rosenberg. *Dir of Nursing* Teresa Di Tullio. *Medical Dir* Morris Plotnick MD.
Licensure Skilled care; Intermediate care. *Beds* Swing beds SNF/ICF 50. *Certified* Medicaid; Medicare.
Owner Proprietary corp.
Admissions Requirements Minimum age 18; Medical examination.
Staff Physicians 6 (pt); RNs 4 (ft); LPNs 6 (ft), 3 (pt); Nurses' aides 14 (ft), 2 (pt); Physical therapists 1 (pt); Occupational therapists 1 (pt); Speech therapists 1 (pt); Activities coordinators 1 (ft), 1 (pt); Dietitians 1 (pt); Ophthalmologists 1 (pt); Podiatrists 1 (pt); Audiologists 1 (pt).
Facilities Dining room; Physical therapy room; Laundry room; Barber/Beauty shop.
Activities Arts & crafts; Cards; Games; Reading groups; Prayer groups; Movies; Shopping trips; Dances/Social/Cultural gatherings; Intergenerational programs; Pet therapy.

Purcell Center
448 Purcell Ave, Cincinnati, OH 45205
(513) 251-4193
Licensure Intermediate care for mentally retarded. *Beds* ICF/MR 8. *Certified* Medicaid.
Owner Proprietary corp.

Queen City Nursing Home
400 Forest Ave, Cincinnati, OH 45229
(513) 961-6452
Licensure Intermediate living. *Beds* ICF 37. *Certified* Medicaid.
Owner Proprietary corp.

Red Haven Nursing Home Inc
751 Greenwood Ave, Cincinnati, OH 45229
(513) 751-1157
Licensure Intermediate care. *Beds* ICF 31. *Certified* Medicaid.
Owner Proprietary corp.

Restview Nursing Home
3550 Washington Ave, Cincinnati, OH 45229
(513) 751-1308
Licensure Intermediate care. *Beds* ICF 44. *Certified* Medicaid.
Owner Proprietary corp.

Riverview Home
5999 Bender Rd, Cincinnati, OH 45233
(513) 922-1440
Licensure Skilled care; Intermediate care; Rest home. *Beds* Swing beds SNF/ICF 100; Rest home 50. *Certified* Medicaid; Medicare.
Owner Nonprofit corp (United Church Homes).

St Clare Retirement Community
100 Compton Rd, Cincinnati, OH 45215
(513) 761-9036
Admin Michael D Atwood. *Dir of Nursing* Patricia Morford. *Medical Dir* Richard G Klopp MD.
Licensure Skilled care; Intermediate care; Rest home; Independent living. *Beds* Swing beds SNF/ICF 110; Rest home 50; Independent living apts 11. *Private Pay Patients* 95%.
Owner Nonprofit corp (Franciscan Sisters).

Admissions Requirements Medical examination; Physician's request.
Staff Physicians 1 (pt); RNs 2 (ft), 5 (pt); LPNs 10 (ft), 17 (pt); Nurses' aides 24 (ft), 20 (pt); Physical therapists 1 (ft); Occupational therapists 1 (ft); Speech therapists 1 (pt); Activities coordinators 1 (ft); Dietitians 1 (pt); Podiatrists 1 (pt); Dentists 1 (pt); Hostesses-aides (rest home) 3 (ft), 7 (pt).
Languages German.
Affiliation Roman Catholic.
Facilities Dining room; Physical therapy room; Activities room; Chapel; Crafts room; Laundry room; Barber/Beauty shop; Library; Indoor swimming pool & whirlpool.
Activities Arts & crafts; Cards; Games; Reading groups; Prayer groups; Movies; Shopping trips; Dances/Social/Cultural gatherings; Intergenerational programs; Pet therapy.

St Joseph Infant Home
10722 Wyscarver Rd, Cincinnati, OH 45241
(513) 563-2520
Licensure Intermediate care for mentally retarded. *Beds* ICF/MR 32. *Certified* Medicaid.
Owner Proprietary corp.

St Luke Center
3901 Brotherton Rd, Cincinnati, OH 45209
(513) 272-0600, 271-8886 FAX
Admin Julianna Greer. *Dir of Nursing* Jackie Wurth. *Medical Dir* Frank Perrino.
Licensure Skilled care; Intermediate care. *Beds* Swing beds SNF/ICF 150. *Certified* Medicaid; Medicare.
Owner Nonprofit organization/foundation (Episcopal Retirement Homes Inc).
Staff RNs 7 (ft), 3 (pt); LPNs 11 (ft), 7 (pt); Nurses' aides 58 (ft), 6 (pt); Physical therapists (consultants); Occupational therapists 1 (pt); Speech therapists 1 (pt); Activities coordinators 1 (ft); Dietitians 1 (pt); Ophthalmologists 1 (pt); Podiatrists 1 (pt).
Affiliation Episcopal.
Activities Arts & crafts; Cards; Games; Reading groups; Prayer groups; Movies; Shopping trips; Dances/Social/Cultural gatherings; Pet therapy.

St Margaret Hall
1960 Madison Rd, Cincinnati, OH 45206
(513) 751-5880
Licensure Skilled care; Intermediate care; Rest home. *Beds* Swing beds SNF/ICF 99; Rest home 45.
Owner Proprietary corp.

St Theresa Home
6760 Belkenton Ave, Cincinnati, OH 45236
(513) 891-1090, 891-1094
Admin Sr Brenda Hilger.
Medical Dir Sandra Frommeyer.
Licensure Skilled care; Intermediate care; Rest home. *Beds* Swing beds SNF/ICF 37; Rest home 63. *Certified* Medicaid.
Owner Nonprofit corp.
Admissions Requirements Medical examination.
Staff RNs 1 (ft); LPNs 6 (ft); Nurses' aides 18 (ft), 20 (pt); Activities coordinators 2 (ft); Dietitians 1 (ft).
Affiliation Roman Catholic.
Facilities Dining room; Activities room; Chapel; Crafts room; Laundry room; Barber/Beauty shop.
Activities Arts & crafts; Cards; Games; Reading groups; Prayer groups; Movies; Shopping trips; Dances/Social/Cultural gatherings.

Salem Park Nursing Home
6128 Salem Rd, Cincinnati, OH 45230
(513) 231-8292

Admin Barbara Wolf. *Dir of Nursing* Helen Bishop RNC. *Medical Dir* John Cardosi MD.
Licensure Skilled care; Intermediate care. *Beds* Swing beds SNF/ICF 107. *Certified* Medicaid; Medicare.
Owner Proprietary corp (Parke Care Inc).
Staff RNs 8 (ft), 7 (pt); LPNs 3 (ft), 2 (pt); Nurses' aides 25 (ft), 20 (pt); Physical therapists 1 (pt); Occupational therapists 1 (pt); Speech therapists 1 (pt); Activities coordinators 1 (ft); Dietitians 2 (pt); Ophthalmologists 1 (pt); Podiatrists 1 (pt); Dentists 1 (pt).
Facilities Dining room; Physical therapy room; Activities room; Crafts room; Laundry room; Barber/Beauty shop.
Activities Arts & crafts; Cards; Games; Reading groups; Prayer groups; Movies; Shopping trips; Dances/Social/Cultural gatherings; Dinners; Exercises; Current events; Happy hour; Parties.

Summit Nursing & Convalescent Home Inc
2586 La Feuille Ave, Cincinnati, OH 45211
(513) 662-2444
Admin Frances R Glaser. *Dir of Nursing* Mary Noll. *Medical Dir* Manuel Mediodia MD.
Licensure Skilled care; Intermediate care; Alzheimer's care. *Beds* SNF 50; ICF 115. *Certified* Medicaid; Medicare.
Owner Proprietary corp.
Admissions Requirements Minimum age 40; Medical examination.
Facilities Dining room; Physical therapy room; Activities room; Chapel; Crafts room; Laundry room; Barber/Beauty shop; Library.
Activities Arts & crafts; Cards; Games; Reading groups; Prayer groups; Movies; Shopping trips; Dances/Social/Cultural gatherings; Outside recreational sports.

Terrace at Westside
1859 Grand Ave, Cincinnati, OH 45214
(513) 921-4181
Licensure Rest home. *Beds* Rest home 41.
Owner Proprietary corp.

Three Rivers Convalescent Center
7800 Jandaracres Dr, Cincinnati, OH 45211
(513) 941-0787
Admin David P Walsh. *Dir of Nursing* Dorothy Daughters. *Medical Dir* Dr George Shields.
Licensure Skilled care; Intermediate care; Alzheimer's care. *Beds* Swing beds SNF/ICF 160. *Certified* Medicaid; Medicare.
Owner Proprietary corp.
Admissions Requirements Minimum age Geriatric; Medical examination; Physician's request.
Staff Physicians 1 (pt); RNs 10 (ft), 2 (pt); LPNs 19 (ft), 4 (pt); Nurses' aides 45 (ft), 10 (pt); Physical therapists 1 (pt); Recreational therapists 3 (ft); Speech therapists 1 (pt); Activities coordinators 1 (ft); Dietitians 1 (pt); Ophthalmologists 1 (pt); Podiatrists 1 (pt); Dentists 1 (pt).
Languages Italian, German.
Facilities Dining room; Physical therapy room; Activities room; Chapel; Crafts room; Laundry room; Barber/Beauty shop; Library.
Activities Arts & crafts; Cards; Games; Reading groups; Prayer groups; Movies; Shopping trips; Dances/Social/Cultural gatherings.

Twin Towers
5343 Hamilton Ave, Cincinnati, OH 45224
(513) 853-2000
Admin Joseph R Graham. *Dir of Nursing* Marlene Drake RN. *Medical Dir* Kenneth A Frederick MD.
Licensure Intermediate care; Rest home. *Beds* ICF 136; Rest home 40. *Private Pay Patients* 60%. *Certified* Medicaid.
Owner Nonprofit organization/foundation.

Admissions Requirements Minimum age 62; Medical examination.
Staff RNs 10 (ft); LPNs 25 (ft); Nurses' aides 55 (ft); Activities coordinators 1 (ft); Dietitians 1 (ft).
Affiliation United Methodist.
Facilities Dining room; Physical therapy room; Activities room; Chapel; Crafts room; Laundry room; Barber/Beauty shop; Library; Swimming pool.
Activities Arts & crafts; Cards; Games; Reading groups; Prayer groups; Movies; Shopping trips; Dances/Social/Cultural gatherings; Intergenerational programs; Pet therapy.

Valley House
3731 Isabella Ave, Cincinnati, OH 45209
(513) 631-3423
Licensure Intermediate care for mentally retarded. *Beds* ICF/MR 7.
Owner Proprietary corp.

Washington Nursing Home
3615 Washington Ave, Cincinnati, OH 45229
(513) 751-5223
Licensure Skilled care; Intermediate care. *Beds* Swing beds SNF/ICF 55. *Certified* Medicaid; Medicare.
Owner Proprietary corp.
Staff Physicians; RNs; LPNs; Nurses' aides; Physical therapists; Activities coordinators; Dietitians; Ophthalmologists.
Facilities Dining room; Activities room.
Activities Arts & crafts; Cards; Games; Reading groups; Prayer groups; Movies; Shopping trips; Dances/Social/Cultural gatherings.

Wesley Hall Inc
315 Lilienthal St, Cincinnati, OH 45204
(513) 471-8667
Medical Dir Dr George Shields.
Licensure Intermediate care. *Beds* ICF 128. *Certified* Medicaid.
Owner Proprietary corp.
Staff Physicians 1 (pt); RNs 5 (ft); LPNs 15 (ft); Nurses' aides 56 (ft); Physical therapists 2 (ft); Occupational therapists 1 (pt); Activities coordinators 3 (ft); Dietitians 19 (ft); Podiatrists 1 (pt).
Affiliation Methodist.
Facilities Dining room; Physical therapy room; Activities room; Chapel; Crafts room; Laundry room; Barber/Beauty shop.
Activities Arts & crafts; Cards; Games; Prayer groups; Dances/Social/Cultural gatherings.

West Hills Nursing Home Inc
2841 Harrison Ave, Cincinnati, OH 45211
(513) 481-4555
Licensure Intermediate care. *Beds* ICF 46. *Certified* Medicaid.
Owner Proprietary corp.

West Park Villa Health Care Center
2950 W Park Dr, Cincinnati, OH 45238
(513) 451-8900
Licensure Skilled care; Intermediate care. *Beds* Swing beds SNF/ICF 100. *Certified* Medicaid; Medicare.
Owner Nonprofit corp.

West Side Health Care Center
1857 Grand Ave, Cincinnati, OH 45214
(513) 921-4130
Licensure Intermediate care. *Beds* ICF 75. *Certified* Medicaid.
Owner Proprietary corp.

Western Hills Care Center Inc
6210 Cleves Warsaw Rd, Cincinnati, OH 45238
(513) 941-0099
Licensure Skilled care; Intermediate care. *Beds* SNF 26; Swing beds SNF/ICF 94. *Certified* Medicare.
Owner Proprietary corp.

Windsor Park Nursing Home Inc
2245 Park Ave, Cincinnati, OH 45206
(513) 861-9275
Licensure Intermediate care. *Beds* ICF 49.
Certified Medicaid.
Owner Proprietary corp.

Zion Nursing Home Inc
3610 Washington Ave, Cincinnati, OH 45229
(513) 221-2775
Licensure Intermediate care. *Beds* ICF 50.
Certified Medicaid.
Owner Proprietary corp.

Circleville

Americare—Circleville
1155 Atwater Ave, Circleville, OH 43113
(614) 477-1695
Admin John Mills. *Dir of Nursing* Marge
Little. *Medical Dir* Dr Bolender.
Licensure Skilled care; Intermediate care. *Beds*
SNF 20; ICF 80. *Private Pay Patients* 25%.
Certified Medicaid; Medicare.
Owner Proprietary corp (Care Enterprises).
Admissions Requirements Medical
examination; Physician's request.
Staff Physicians; RNs; LPNs; Nurses' aides;
Physical therapists; Occupational therapists;
Speech therapists; Activities coordinators;
Dietitians; Ophthalmologists; Podiatrists;
Audiologists.
Facilities Dining room; Physical therapy
room; Activities room; Crafts room; Laundry
room; Barber/Beauty shop; Library.
Activities Arts & crafts; Cards; Games;
Reading groups; Prayer groups; Movies;
Shopping trips.

Brown Memorial Home Inc
158 E Mound St, Circleville, OH 43113
(614) 474-6238
Admin James E Kraus. *Dir of Nursing* John
Fox. *Medical Dir* Dr Andrew Smith.
Licensure Intermediate care. *Beds* ICF 35.
Certified Medicaid.
Owner Nonprofit organization/foundation.
Admissions Requirements Medical
examination.
Staff RNs 1 (ft), 1 (pt); LPNs 4 (ft), 2 (pt);
Nurses' aides 19 (ft), 6 (pt); Activities
coordinators 1 (ft); Dietitians 1 (pt).
Facilities Dining room; Activities room;
Chapel; Laundry room; Barber/Beauty shop;
Visitor's parlor.
Activities Arts & crafts; Cards; Games; Prayer
groups; Movies; Shopping trips; Pet therapy.

Logan Elm Health Care Center
370 Tarlton Rd, Circleville, OH 43113
(614) 474-3121
Admin Thomas Kauffman. *Dir of Nursing*
Esther Boyer. *Medical Dir* Andrew Smith
MD.
Licensure Skilled care; Intermediate care. *Beds*
SNF 27; ICF 74. *Certified* Medicaid;
Medicare.
Owner Proprietary corp (Nursing Care
Management of America).
Admissions Requirements Minimum age
Adult; Medical examination.
Staff Physicians 1 (pt); RNs 5 (ft), 1 (pt);
LPNs 8 (ft), 6 (pt); Nurses' aides 36 (ft), 9
(pt); Physical therapists (contracted);
Occupational therapists 1 (pt); Speech
therapists 1 (pt); Activities coordinators 1
(ft); Dietitians 1 (pt); Ophthalmologists 1
(pt); Podiatrists 1 (pt); Audiologists 1 (pt);
Respiratory therapists.
Facilities Dining room; Physical therapy
room; Activities room; Crafts room; Laundry
room; Barber/Beauty shop; Ventilator-heavy
care program.
Activities Arts & crafts; Cards; Games;
Reading groups; Prayer groups; Movies;
Shopping trips; Dances/Social/Cultural
gatherings; Pet therapy.

Pickaway Manor Care Center
391 Clark Dr, Circleville, OH 43113
(614) 474-6036
Admin Charles P Bradley. *Dir of Nursing*
Virginia Davis. *Medical Dir* Carlos Alvarez
MD.
Licensure Skilled care; Intermediate care. *Beds*
Swing beds SNF/ICF 100. *Certified*
Medicaid; Medicare.
Owner Proprietary corp (National Heritage).
Admissions Requirements Medical
examination; Physician's request.
Staff RNs 8 (ft), 5 (pt); LPNs 9 (ft), 2 (pt);
Nurses' aides 27 (ft); Physical therapists 1
(pt); Reality therapists 1 (ft); Recreational
therapists 1 (ft); Occupational therapists 1
(pt); Speech therapists 1 (pt); Activities
coordinators 1 (ft); Dietitians 1 (pt);
Ophthalmologists 1 (pt); Podiatrists 1 (pt).
Facilities Dining room; Physical therapy
room; Activities room; Crafts room; Laundry
room; Barber/Beauty shop.
Activities Arts & crafts; Cards; Games;
Reading groups; Prayer groups; Movies;
Shopping trips; Dances/Social/Cultural
gatherings.

Clarksburg

Walnut Manor Care Center
PO Box 158, 11017 Main St, Clarksburg, OH
43115
(614) 993-4201
Admin Eric Gustafson. *Dir of Nursing* Jodi
Calhoun. *Medical Dir* Dr Lane.
Licensure Intermediate care. *Beds* ICF 22.
Certified Medicaid.
Owner Proprietary corp (A & D Hicks).
Staff Physicians 1 (pt); RNs 1 (pt); LPNs 3
(ft); Nurses' aides 6 (ft), 1 (pt); Physical
therapists; Recreational therapists 1 (pt);
Activities coordinators 1 (ft); Dietitians 1
(pt); Ophthalmologists 1 (pt); Podiatrists 1
(pt).

Cleveland

Algart Health Care Inc
8902 Detroit Ave, Cleveland, OH 44102
(216) 631-1550, 631-2343 FAX
Admin Gary Klein. *Dir of Nursing* Evelyn
Schlegel. *Medical Dir* Dr Nanovich.
Licensure Intermediate care; Retirement. *Beds*
ICF 54. *Private Pay Patients* 4%. *Certified*
Medicaid.
Owner Proprietary corp.
Staff RNs 3 (ft); LPNs 4 (ft); Nurses' aides 25
(ft); Dietitians 1 (ft).
Languages Spanish.
Facilities Dining room; Physical therapy
room; Activities room; Laundry room.
Activities Arts & crafts; Games; Reading
groups; Prayer groups; Movies; Shopping
trips; Pet therapy.

Baldwin Manor Nursing Home Inc
2437 Baldwin Rd, Cleveland, OH 44104
(216) 229-4800
Admin David Newman. *Dir of Nursing* Julie
Gross RN. *Medical Dir* A Aronshteyn MD.
Licensure Skilled care; Intermediate care. *Beds*
Swing beds SNF/ICF 50. *Certified* Medicaid;
Medicare.
Owner Proprietary corp.
Admissions Requirements Medical
examination.
Staff Physicians 1 (pt); RNs 2 (ft); LPNs 3
(ft); Nurses' aides 16 (ft), 1 (pt); Physical
therapists 1 (ft); Occupational therapists 1
(ft), 1 (pt); Speech therapists 1 (pt);
Activities coordinators 1 (ft); Dietitians 1
(pt); Ophthalmologists 1 (pt); Podiatrists 1
(pt); Dentists 1 (pt).
Facilities Dining room; Physical therapy
room; Activities room; Chapel; Crafts room;
Laundry room; Library.

Activities Arts & crafts; Cards; Games;
Reading groups; Prayer groups; Movies;
Shopping trips.

Eliza Bryant Center
7201 Wade Park Ave, Cleveland, OH 44103
(216) 361-6141
Admin Shirley Hrovatt; Ronald Winbush,
Exec Dir.
Licensure Intermediate care. *Beds* ICF 100.
Certified Medicaid.
Owner Proprietary corp.
Staff Physicians 4 (pt); RNs 4 (pt); LPNs 12
(ft); Nurses' aides 25 (ft); Physical therapists
1 (pt); Activities coordinators 1 (ft), 1 (pt);
Dietitians 1 (pt); Ophthalmologists 1 (pt);
Social workers 1 (ft).
Facilities Dining room; Physical therapy
room; Activities room; Crafts room; Laundry
room; Barber/Beauty shop; Library.
Activities Arts & crafts; Cards; Games;
Reading groups; Prayer groups; Movies;
Shopping trips; Dances/Social/Cultural
gatherings.

Carnegie Care Center
8800 Carnegie Ave, Cleveland, OH 44106
(216) 229-3300
Licensure Intermediate care. *Beds* ICF 220.
Certified Medicaid.
Owner Proprietary corp.

Cleveland Golden Age Nursing Home
928 E 152nd St, Cleveland, OH 44110
(216) 761-3000
Licensure Intermediate care. *Beds* ICF 100.
Certified Medicaid.
Owner Proprietary corp.

Communicare Nursing Center
2415 E 55th St, Cleveland, OH 44104
(216) 391-7100, 391-7104 FAX
Admin Jeffrey S Singleton. *Dir of Nursing*
Madge Stewart. *Medical Dir* Dr Richard
King.
Licensure Intermediate care. *Beds* ICF 155.
Private Pay Patients 0%. *Certified* Medicaid.
Owner Proprietary corp (CommuniCare Inc).
Admissions Requirements Medical
examination.
Staff Physicians (consultant); RNs 3 (ft), 6
(pt); LPNs 7 (ft), 18 (pt); Nurses' aides 42
(ft), 16 (pt); Physical therapists (consultant);
Occupational therapists (consultant); Speech
therapists (consultant); Activities
coordinators 3 (ft); Dietitians 1 (ft);
Ophthalmologists (consultant); Podiatrists
(consultant).
Facilities Dining room; Physical therapy
room.
Activities Arts & crafts; Cards; Games;
Reading groups; Prayer groups; Movies;
Shopping trips; Dances/Social/Cultural
gatherings.

Concord Manor Nursing Home
1877 E 82nd St, Cleveland, OH 44103
(216) 791-0727
Medical Dir Dr Navnvich.
Licensure Intermediate care. *Beds* ICF 34.
Certified Medicaid.
Owner Proprietary corp.
Admissions Requirements Medical
examination; Physician's request.
Staff Physicians 1 (pt); RNs 1 (pt); LPNs 2
(ft), 2 (pt); Nurses' aides 11 (ft); Activities
coordinators 1 (pt); Dietitians 1 (pt);
Ophthalmologists 1 (pt); Podiatrists 1 (pt);
Dentists 1 (pt).
Facilities Dining room; Activities room;
Laundry room.
Activities Arts & crafts; Cards; Games; Prayer
groups; Movies; Shopping trips.

Country Estate
PO Box 40175, Cleveland, OH 44140-0175
(216) 871-2261

Licensure Intermediate care. *Beds* ICF 44.
Certified Medicaid.
Owner Proprietary corp.

Crestmont Nursing Home Inc
12709 Bellaire Rd, Cleveland, OH 44135
(216) 941-4545
Licensure Intermediate care. *Beds* ICF 28.
Certified Medicaid.
Owner Proprietary corp.

Cuyahoga County Nursing Home
3305 Franklin Blvd, Cleveland, OH 44113
(216) 961-4344
Admin Henny L Morehouse. *Dir of Nursing*
Alicia Tupaz RN. *Medical Dir* Yalcin
Dincman MD.
Licensure Intermediate care. *Beds* ICF 177.
Private Pay Patients 2%. *Certified* Medicaid.
Owner Publicly owned.
Admissions Requirements Minimum age 21.
Staff Physicians 5 (pt); RNs 15 (ft), 1 (pt);
LPNs 15 (ft), 1 (pt); Nurses' aides 76 (ft), 6
(pt); Physical therapists 1 (pt); Recreational
therapists 3 (ft); Occupational therapists 2
(ft), 1 (pt); Activities coordinators 1 (ft);
Dietitians 1 (pt); Podiatrists 1 (pt).
Languages Spanish.
Facilities Dining room; Physical therapy
room; Activities room; Crafts room; Laundry
room; Barber/Beauty shop; Library;
Occupational therapy room.
Activities Arts & crafts; Games; Reading
groups; Prayer groups; Movies; Shopping
trips; Dances/Social/Cultural gatherings; Pet
therapy; Gardening; Concerts; Athletic
events.

Euclid Manor Nursing Home
17322 Euclid Ave, Cleveland, OH 44118
(216) 486-2280, 486-8536 FAX
Admin Marvin Neuman NHA. *Dir of Nursing*
Carolyn Price RNC. *Medical Dir* Nachman
Kacen MD.
Licensure Skilled care; Intermediate care. *Beds*
Swing beds SNF/ICF 174. *Private Pay
Patients* 10%. *Certified* Medicaid; Medicare.
Owner Proprietary corp.
Admissions Requirements Medical
examination.
Staff Physicians; RNs; LPNs; Nurses' aides;
Physical therapists; Reality therapists;
Occupational therapists; Speech therapists;
Activities coordinators; Dietitians;
Ophthalmologists; Podiatrists; Audiologists.
Facilities Dining room; Physical therapy
room; Activities room; Crafts room; Laundry
room.
Activities Arts & crafts; Cards; Games;
Reading groups; Prayer groups; Movies;
Shopping trips; Dances/Social/Cultural
gatherings; Pet therapy.

Forest Hills Nursing Home
736 Lakeview Rd, Cleveland, OH 44143
(216) 268-3800, 268-3814 FAX
Admin Barry Lieberman. *Dir of Nursing* Sue
Oravecz. *Medical Dir* Dr Patawaran.
Licensure Skilled care; Intermediate care. *Beds*
SNF 28; ICF 199. *Private Pay Patients* 1%.
Certified Medicaid; Medicare.
Owner Proprietary corp.
Admissions Requirements Medical
examination.
Staff Physicians 5 (pt); RNs 10 (ft); LPNs 30
(ft); Nurses' aides 75 (ft); Physical therapists
1 (pt); Recreational therapists 3 (ft); Speech
therapists 1 (ft); Activities coordinators 1
(ft); Dietitians 1 (ft); Ophthalmologists 1
(pt); Podiatrists 2 (pt); Audiologists 1 (pt).
Facilities Dining room; Physical therapy
room; Activities room; Barber/Beauty shop;
Private rooms.
Activities Arts & crafts; Cards; Games;
Reading groups; Prayer groups; Movies;
Shopping trips; Dances/Social/Cultural
gatherings; Intergenerational programs; Pet
therapy.

Franklin Plaza
3600 Franklin Blvd, Cleveland, OH 44113
(216) 651-1600, 651-8330 FAX
Admin Edith Ruck. *Dir of Nursing* Carole
Staul. *Medical Dir* Dr Jarawal Jephtak.
Licensure Skilled care; Intermediate care. *Beds*
SNF 72; ICF 155. *Certified* Medicaid;
Medicare.
Owner Proprietary corp.
Admissions Requirements Medical
examination.
Staff Physicians 35 (ft); RNs 12 (ft); LPNs 33
(ft); Nurses' aides 70 (ft); Physical therapists
1 (ft); Recreational therapists 3 (ft);
Occupational therapists 1 (ft); Speech
therapists 1 (ft); Activities coordinators 1
(ft); Dietitians 1 (ft); Ophthalmologists 1 (ft);
Podiatrists 1 (ft).
Languages Hungarian.
Facilities Dining room; Physical therapy
room; Activities room; Laundry room;
Barber/Beauty shop.
Activities Arts & crafts; Cards; Games;
Reading groups; Prayer groups; Movies;
Shopping trips; Dances/Social/Cultural
gatherings; Pet therapy.

Geri-Care Inc
2438 Mapleside Rd, Cleveland, OH 44104
(216) 229-9600
Admin David Neuman. *Dir of Nursing* Julie
Gross RN. *Medical Dir* A Aronshteyn MD.
Licensure Skilled care; Intermediate care. *Beds*
ICF Swing beds SNF/ICF 36. *Certified*
Medicaid.
Owner Proprietary corp.
Admissions Requirements Medical
examination.
Staff Physicians 1 (pt); RNs 2 (pt); LPNs 4
(ft), 1 (pt); Nurses' aides 10 (ft); Physical
therapists 1 (pt); Occupational therapists 1
(pt); Speech therapists 1 (pt); Activities
coordinators 1 (ft); Dietitians 1 (pt);
Ophthalmologists 1 (pt); Podiatrists 1 (pt);
Dentists 1 (pt).
Facilities Dining room; Physical therapy
room; Activities room; Crafts room; Laundry
room; Library.
Activities Arts & crafts; Cards; Games;
Reading groups; Prayer groups; Movies;
Shopping trips.

Inner City Nursing Home Inc
9014 Cedar Ave, Cleveland, OH 44106
(216) 795-1363
Admin Ethel L Pye.
Medical Dir Billy Brown MD.
Licensure Intermediate care. *Beds* ICF 50.
Certified Medicaid.
Owner Proprietary corp.
Admissions Requirements Minimum age 18;
Medical examination.
Staff Physicians; RNs; LPNs; Nurses' aides;
Activities coordinators; Dietitians;
Ophthalmologists; Dentists.
Facilities Dining room; Laundry room;
Barber/Beauty shop.
Activities Arts & crafts; Games; Reading
groups; Prayer groups; Dances/Social/
Cultural gatherings.

Eliza Jennings Home
10603 Detroit Ave, Cleveland, OH 44102
(216) 226-0282
Licensure Rest home. *Beds* Rest home 58.
Owner Proprietary corp.

Lake Shore Nursing Center
16101 Lake Shore Blvd, Cleveland, OH 44110
(216) 486-2300
Admin Michael A Scocos. *Dir of Nursing* Beth
Conklin RN. *Medical Dir* William L George.
Licensure Skilled care; Intermediate care. *Beds*
SNF 20; ICF 182. *Certified* Medicaid;
Medicare.
Owner Proprietary corp (Manor Care).
Admissions Requirements Medical
examination.

Staff Physicians 3 (pt); RNs 6 (ft), 6 (pt);
LPNs 21 (ft), 16 (pt); Nurses' aides 40 (ft),
20 (pt); Physical therapists 1 (ft);
Recreational therapists 1 (ft); Occupational
therapists 1 (pt); Speech therapists 1 (pt);
Activities coordinators 1 (pt); Dietitians 1
(ft); Ophthalmologists 1 (ft); Podiatrists 1
(pt); Dentists 1 (pt).
Languages Slavic, Croatian, Italian, German,
Lithuanian.
Facilities Dining room; Physical therapy
room; Activities room; Crafts room; Laundry
room; Barber/Beauty shop; Library.
Activities Arts & crafts; Cards; Games;
Reading groups; Prayer groups; Movies;
Shopping trips; Dances/Social/Cultural
gatherings.

Laub Pavilion of Cleveland Ohio
10603 Detroit Ave, Cleveland, OH 44102
(216) 226-0282
Licensure Intermediate care. *Beds* ICF 131.
Certified Medicaid.
Owner Proprietary corp.

Little Sisters of the Poor—Home for the Aged
4291 Richmond Rd, Cleveland, OH 44122
(216) 464-1222
Admin Sr Marguerite. *Dir of Nursing* Sr
Bernadette. *Medical Dir* Dr Yalcin
Dinceman.
Licensure Intermediate care; Rest home;
Assisted living. *Beds* ICF 99; Rest home 41;
Assisted living 16. *Certified* Medicaid.
Owner Nonprofit corp (Little Sisters of the
Poor).
Admissions Requirements Medical
examination.
Staff RNs 5 (ft), 11 (pt); LPNs 7 (ft), 6 (pt);
Nurses' aides 36 (ft), 11 (pt); Physical
therapists 1 (pt); Activities coordinators 1
(ft).
Affiliation Roman Catholic.
Facilities Dining room; Physical therapy
room; Activities room; Chapel; Crafts room;
Laundry room; Barber/Beauty shop; Library.
Activities Arts & crafts; Cards; Games;
Reading groups; Prayer groups; Movies;
Shopping trips; Dances/Social/Cultural
gatherings; Social service counseling.

Madonna Hall
1906 E 82nd St, Cleveland, OH 44103
(216) 421-5660
Admin Howard B Bram.
Medical Dir Pamala Murphy MD.
Licensure Intermediate care. *Beds* ICF 99.
Certified Medicaid.
Owner Proprietary corp.
Admissions Requirements Minimum age 60;
Medical examination.
Staff RNs 1 (ft), 1 (pt); LPNs 6 (ft), 4 (pt);
Nurses' aides 23 (ft); Activities coordinators
2 (ft).
Affiliation Roman Catholic.
Facilities Dining room; Physical therapy
room; Activities room; Chapel; Crafts room;
Laundry room.
Activities Arts & crafts; Cards; Games;
Movies; Shopping trips; Dances/Social/
Cultural gatherings.

Manor Care Nursing Center of Rocky River
4102 Rocky River Dr, Cleveland, OH 44135
(216) 251-3300
Admin Thomas A Armagno.
Medical Dir Javier Clemente MD.
Licensure Skilled care; Intermediate care. *Beds*
SNF 29; ICF 181. *Certified* Medicaid;
Medicare.
Owner Proprietary corp (Manor Care).
Admissions Requirements Medical
examination.
Staff Physicians 2 (pt); RNs 8 (ft), 9 (pt);
LPNs 13 (ft), 11 (pt); Nurses' aides 50 (ft),
32 (pt); Physical therapists 1 (ft), 3 (pt);
Reality therapists 1 (ft); Recreational
therapists 1 (ft); Occupational therapists 2

(ft), 1 (pt); Speech therapists 1 (pt);
Activities coordinators 1 (ft); Dietitians 1
(pt); Ophthalmologists 1 (pt); Podiatrists 1
(pt); Audiologists 1 (pt); Dentists 1 (pt).
Facilities Dining room; Physical therapy
room; Activities room; Chapel; Crafts room;
Laundry room; Barber/Beauty shop; Library;
Patio.
Activities Arts & crafts; Cards; Games;
Reading groups; Prayer groups; Movies;
Shopping trips; Dances/Social/Cultural
gatherings; Field trips.

Marietta Manor
694 E 109th St, Cleveland, OH 44108
(216) 851-7100
Medical Dir Dr Naunovich.
Licensure Intermediate care. *Beds* ICF 17.
Certified Medicaid.
Owner Proprietary corp.
Admissions Requirements Females only.
Staff Physicians 1 (ft); RNs 1 (ft); LPNs 4 (ft),
2 (pt); Nurses' aides 8 (ft), 2 (pt); Activities
coordinators 1 (ft); Dietitians 1 (ft);
Podiatrists 1 (ft); Dentists 1 (ft).
Affiliation Presbyterian.
Facilities Dining room; Activities room;
Laundry room.
Activities Arts & crafts; Games; Prayer groups;
Shopping trips.

Mary Louise Nursing Home
670 Lakeview Rd, Cleveland, OH 44108
(216) 541-9474
Licensure Intermediate care. *Beds* ICF 11.
Certified Medicaid.
Owner Proprietary corp.

Medi-Care Nursing Home
18220 Euclid Ave, Cleveland, OH 44112
(216) 486-6300
Admin Cynthia D Lowenkamp. *Dir of Nursing*
Judith Levert RN. *Medical Dir* Leonard
Lewin MD.
Licensure Skilled care; Intermediate care;
Alzheimer's care. *Beds* Swing beds SNF/ICF
50. *Private Pay Patients* 10%. *Certified*
Medicaid; Medicare.
Owner Proprietary corp.
Admissions Requirements Minimum age 18;
Medical examination.
Staff Physicians; RNs; LPNs; Nurses' aides;
Physical therapists; Recreational therapists;
Occupational therapists; Speech therapists;
Activities coordinators; Dietitians;
Ophthalmologists; Podiatrists; Audiologists.
Facilities Dining room; Physical therapy
room; Activities room; Laundry room.
Activities Arts & crafts; Cards; Games;
Reading groups; Prayer groups; Movies;
Shopping trips; Dances/Social/Cultural
gatherings; Intergenerational programs; Pet
therapy; Theme day celebrations.

Mt Pleasant Nursing Home
10406 Kinsman Rd, Cleveland, OH 44104
(216) 271-0073
Medical Dir Dr Naunovich.
Licensure Intermediate care. *Beds* ICF 33.
Certified Medicaid.
Owner Proprietary corp.
Staff Physicians 1 (ft); RNs 1 (ft); LPNs 5 (ft),
4 (pt); Nurses' aides 10 (ft), 5 (pt); Activities
coordinators 1 (ft); Dietitians 1 (ft);
Podiatrists 1 (ft); Dentists 1 (ft).
Affiliation Presbyterian.
Facilities Dining room; Activities room;
Laundry room.
Activities Arts & crafts; Cards; Games; Prayer
groups; Shopping trips.

Overlook House
2187 Overlook Rd, Cleveland, OH 44106
(216) 795-3550
Licensure Skilled care; Intermediate care. *Beds*
Swing beds SNF/ICF 33.
Owner Proprietary corp.
Affiliation Christian Science.

Facilities Dining room; Activities room;
Chapel; Laundry room; Barber/Beauty shop;
Library.
Activities Reading groups; Prayer groups;
Movies; Dances/Social/Cultural gatherings.

Prospect Manor
PO Box 1985, Cleveland, OH 44106
(216) 361-6655
Licensure Intermediate care. *Beds* ICF 48.
Certified Medicaid.
Owner Proprietary corp.

Rae Ann Nursing Center
18223 Rockland Ave, Cleveland, OH 44135
(216) 267-5445
Licensure Intermediate care for mentally
retarded. *Beds* ICF/MR 30. *Certified*
Medicaid.
Owner Proprietary corp.

**Rose Park Convalescent & Rehabilitation
Center**
18810 Harvard Ave, Cleveland, OH 44122
(216) 752-3600
Licensure Intermediate care. *Beds* ICF 209.
Certified Medicaid.
Owner Proprietary corp.

St Alexis Hospital Skilled Nursing Facility
5163 Broadway, Cleveland, OH 44127
(216) 429-8460, 429-8748 FAX
Admin James Charles. *Dir of Nursing* D H
Metzger RN. *Medical Dir* T J Maximin MD.
Licensure Skilled care. *Beds* SNF 35. *Private
Pay Patients* 2%. *Certified* Medicaid;
Medicare.
Owner Proprietary corp.
Admissions Requirements Physician's request;
No children.
Staff Physicians 1 (ft), 20 (pt); RNs 8 (ft), 5
(pt); LPNs 6 (ft), 6 (pt); Nurses' aides 4 (ft),
11 (pt); Physical therapists 1 (ft), 1 (pt);
Recreational therapists 1 (ft); Occupational
therapists 1 (ft); Speech therapists 1 (pt);
Dietitians 1 (pt); Ophthalmologists 1 (pt);
Podiatrists 1 (pt); Audiologists 1 (pt).
Languages Polish, Slavic, Language bank.
Affiliation Roman Catholic.
Facilities Dining room; Physical therapy
room; Activities room; Chapel; Crafts room;
Barber/Beauty shop; Library.
Activities Arts & crafts; Cards; Games; Prayer
groups; Movies; Pet therapy.

Singleton Health Care Center
1867 E 82nd St, Cleveland, OH 44103
(216) 231-8467
Licensure Intermediate care. *Beds* ICF 50.
Certified Medicaid.
Owner Proprietary corp.

Slovene Home for the Aged
18621 Neff Rd, Cleveland, OH 44119
(216) 486-0268
Licensure Skilled care; Intermediate care. *Beds*
Swing beds SNF/ICF 150. *Certified*
Medicaid; Medicare.
Owner Proprietary corp.

Stella Maris
1320 Washington Ave, Cleveland, OH 44113
(216) 781-0550
Licensure Skilled care; Intermediate care. *Beds*
Swing beds SNF/ICF 17.
Owner Proprietary corp.

Sunset Nursing Home
1802 Crawford Rd, Cleveland, OH 44106
(216) 795-5710
Admin Ms M Dinkes.
Medical Dir Ms Mosby.
Licensure Intermediate care. *Beds* ICF 15.
Certified Medicaid.
Owner Proprietary corp.
Admissions Requirements Females only.
Staff Physicians 1 (pt); RNs 1 (ft); LPNs 2
(ft), 2 (pt); Nurses' aides 9 (ft), 2 (pt);
Physical therapists 1 (pt); Reality therapists

1 (pt); Recreational therapists 1 (pt);
Occupational therapists 1 (pt); Speech
therapists 1 (pt); Activities coordinators 1
(pt); Dietitians 1 (pt); Ophthalmologists 1
(pt); Podiatrists 1 (pt); Dentists 1 (pt).
Facilities Dining room; Crafts room.
Activities Arts & crafts; Games; Prayer groups.

**United Cerebral Palsy Association Home of
Cuyahoga County**
2803 Martin Luther King Jr Dr, Cleveland,
OH 44104
(216) 721-1620
Admin Patricia Hurley. *Dir of Nursing*
Marleen Gross RN. *Medical Dir* Virgene
Nowacek MD.
Licensure Intermediate care for mentally
retarded. *Beds* ICF/MR 10.
Owner Proprietary corp.
Admissions Requirements Minimum age 18;
Medical examination.
Staff Physicians 1 (pt); RNs 2 (pt); Nurses'
aides 4 (ft), 5 (pt); Physical therapists 1 (pt);
Recreational therapists 1 (pt); Occupational
therapists 1 (pt); Speech therapists 1 (pt);
Activities coordinators 1 (pt); Dietitians 1
(pt).
Languages Sign.
Facilities Activities room; Laundry room;
Each apartment has dining room, kitchen,
bedroom, & bathroom.
Activities Arts & crafts; Cards; Games;
Reading groups; Movies; Shopping trips;
Dances/Social/Cultural gatherings.

University Manor Health Care Center Inc
2186 Ambleside Rd, Cleveland, OH 44106
(216) 721-1400
Licensure Intermediate care. *Beds* ICF 208.
Certified Medicaid.
Owner Proprietary corp.

Villa Care Center
4835 Broadview Rd, Cleveland, OH 44134
(216) 749-4939
Admin Mary Lou Fleck LSW LNHA. *Dir of
Nursing* Kathy Zabak RN. *Medical Dir* M T
Sheth MD.
Licensure Intermediate care. *Beds* ICF 50.
Certified Medicaid.
Owner Proprietary corp.
Admissions Requirements Medical
examination.
Staff Physicians 3 (pt); RNs 4 (ft), 1 (pt);
LPNs 3 (pt); Nurses' aides 16 (ft), 5 (pt);
Activities coordinators 2 (ft); Dietitians 1
(pt); Ophthalmologists (consultant);
Podiatrists (consultant); Audiologists
(consultant).
Languages Polish, Slovak.
Facilities Dining room; Activities room;
Crafts room.
Activities Arts & crafts; Cards; Games;
Reading groups; Prayer groups; Movies;
Shopping trips; Dances/Social/Cultural
gatherings; Intergenerational programs; Pet
therapy.

Margaret Wagner House
2373 Euclid Hgts Blvd, Cleveland, OH 44106
(216) 795-5450
Medical Dir George Gelehrter MD.
Licensure Skilled care; Intermediate care. *Beds*
Swing beds SNF/ICF 184. *Certified*
Medicaid; Medicare.
Owner Proprietary corp.
Admissions Requirements Minimum age 60;
Medical examination; Physician's request.
Staff Physicians; RNs; LPNs; Nurses' aides;
Physical therapists; Reality therapists;
Recreational therapists; Occupational
therapists; Activities coordinators; Dietitians.
Facilities Dining room; Physical therapy
room; Activities room; Chapel; Crafts room;
Laundry room; Barber/Beauty shop; Dentist
& podiatrist offices.

Activities Arts & crafts; Cards; Games; Reading groups; Prayer groups; Movies; Shopping trips; Dances/Social/Cultural gatherings.

Westpark Healthcare Campus—Aristocrat West
4387 W 150th St, Cleveland, OH 44135
(216) 252-7730, 252-6826 FAX
Admin Daniel Zawadzki. *Dir of Nursing* Rose Marie Uberstein. *Medical Dir* Dr J Cua.
Licensure Skilled care; Intermediate care; Alzheimer's care. *Beds* SNF 124; ICF 124; Alzheimer's care unit 50. *Certified* Medicaid; Medicare.
Owner Privately owned.
Admissions Requirements Minimum age 14; Medical examination.
Staff RNs; LPNs; Nurses' aides; Physical therapists; Reality therapists; Recreational therapists; Occupational therapists; Speech therapists; Activities coordinators; Dietitians; Ophthalmologists; Podiatrists; Audiologists.
Languages Spanish, Slavic.
Facilities Dining room; Physical therapy room; Activities room; Crafts room; Laundry room; Barber/Beauty shop; Library.
Activities Arts & crafts; Cards; Games; Reading groups; Prayer groups; Movies; Shopping trips; Dances/Social/Cultural gatherings; Intergenerational programs; Pet therapy.

Cleveland Heights

Judson Park
1801 Chestnut Hills Dr, Cleveland Heights, OH 44106
(216) 721-1234
Admin Cynthia H Dunn.
Medical Dir Diane McCarty.
Licensure Intermediate care; Alzheimer's care; Retirement. *Beds* ICF 93. *Certified* Medicaid.
Owner Proprietary corp.
Admissions Requirements Minimum age 62; Medical examination.
Staff Physicians 1 (pt); RNs 16 (ft); LPNs 12 (ft), 2 (pt); Nurses' aides 46 (ft), 8 (pt); Physical therapists 3 (pt); Reality therapists 1 (pt); Recreational therapists 3 (ft), 3 (pt); Occupational therapists 1 (ft); Speech therapists 1 (pt); Activities coordinators 3 (ft); Dietitians 2 (ft); Ophthalmologists 1 (pt); Podiatrists 1 (pt); Dentists 1 (pt).
Facilities Dining room; Physical therapy room; Activities room; Chapel; Crafts room; Laundry room; Barber/Beauty shop; Library.
Activities Arts & crafts; Games; Reading groups; Prayer groups; Movies; Shopping trips; Dances/Social/Cultural gatherings.

Montefiore Home
3151 Mayfield Rd, Cleveland Heights, OH 44118
(216) 371-5500
Admin Edward W Vinocur. *Dir of Nursing* Eliza Popovsky. *Medical Dir* Morton Rosenthal MD.
Licensure Skilled care; Intermediate care; Alzheimer's care. *Beds* Swing beds SNF/ICF 174. *Private Pay Patients* 30%. *Certified* Medicaid; Medicare.
Owner Nonprofit organization/foundation.
Admissions Requirements Minimum age 65; Medical examination.
Staff Physicians 4 (pt); RNs 12 (ft); LPNs 39 (ft); Nurses' aides 69 (ft); Physical therapists 2 (ft), 1 (pt); Recreational therapists 5 (ft); Occupational therapists 1 (pt); Speech therapists 1 (pt); Activities coordinators 1 (ft); Dietitians 1 (pt); Ophthalmologists 1 (pt); Podiatrists 1 (pt); Audiologists 1 (pt).
Affiliation Jewish.

Facilities Dining room; Physical therapy room; Activities room; Chapel; Crafts room; Barber/Beauty shop; Library; Alzheimer's unit.
Activities Arts & crafts; Cards; Games; Reading groups; Movies; Shopping trips; Dances/Social/Cultural gatherings; Intergenerational programs; Pet therapy.

PVA No 1 Inc—Overlook House
2528 Overlook Dr, Cleveland Heights, OH 44106
(216) 932-4850
Licensure Intermediate care for mentally retarded. *Beds* ICF/MR 8. *Certified* Medicaid.
Owner Proprietary corp.

Rose Nursing Home
2435 W St James Pkwy, Cleveland Heights, OH 44106
(216) 229-2984
Admin Robert Gelender. *Dir of Nursing* Evelyn Brock.
Licensure Skilled care; Intermediate care. *Beds* Swing beds SNF/ICF 22.
Owner Proprietary corp.
Admissions Requirements Medical examination.
Staff LPNs 3 (ft); Nurses' aides 5 (ft); Dietitians 1 (ft); Ophthalmologists 1 (ft).
Facilities Laundry room.

Whitecliff Manor
12504 Cedar Rd, Cleveland Heights, OH 44106
(216) 371-3600
Licensure Skilled care; Intermediate care. *Beds* Swing beds SNF/ICF 131. *Certified* Medicaid; Medicare.
Owner Proprietary corp.

Cleves

Miami Haven
5485 State Rte 128, Cleves, OH 45002
(513) 353-2900
Admin Bertha B Hobbs NHA. *Dir of Nursing* Bertha B Hobbs RN.
Licensure Intermediate care. *Beds* ICF 29. *Certified* Medicaid.
Owner Proprietary corp.
Admissions Requirements Medical examination.
Staff RNs 2; LPNs 6; Nurses' aides 20; Activities coordinators; Dietitians.
Languages Spanish, Japanese, Latin.
Facilities Dining room; Activities room; Crafts room; Laundry room; Library.
Activities Arts & crafts; Cards; Games; Reading groups; Prayer groups; Movies; Shopping trips; Dances/Social/Cultural gatherings.

Clinton

Rafferty's Nursing Home
7055 S Cleveland-Massillon Rd, Clinton, OH 44216
(216) 882-6371
Admin Alvet A McNamer. *Dir of Nursing* Debbie Harper. *Medical Dir* Dr Gilcrest.
Licensure Intermediate care. *Beds* ICF 30. *Certified* Medicaid.
Owner Privately owned.
Staff Physicians; RNs; LPNs; Nurses' aides; Physical therapists; Recreational therapists; Occupational therapists; Speech therapists; Activities coordinators; Dietitians; Ophthalmologists; Podiatrists; Audiologists.
Facilities Dining room; Crafts room; Laundry room; Library.
Activities Arts & crafts; Cards; Games; Reading groups; Prayer groups; Movies; Shopping trips; Intergenerational programs; Pet therapy.

Cloverdale

Paradise Oaks Quality Care Nursing Center
PO Box 98, Main St, Cloverdale, OH 45827
(419) 488-3911
Admin Randall L Cox.
Medical Dir Rosalie Wright.
Licensure Skilled care; Intermediate care. *Beds* SNF 50; ICF 50. *Certified* Medicaid; Medicare.
Owner Proprietary corp (Northwestern Service Corp).
Admissions Requirements Medical examination.
Staff Physicians; RNs; LPNs; Nurses' aides.
Facilities Dining room; Physical therapy room; Activities room; Chapel; Crafts room; Laundry room; Barber/Beauty shop.
Activities Arts & crafts; Cards; Games; Reading groups; Prayer groups; Movies; Shopping trips.

Clyde

Buckeye Nursing Home
234 W Buckeye St, Clyde, OH 43410
(419) 547-0711
Admin Larry F Tebeau.
Licensure Intermediate care. *Beds* ICF 25. *Certified* Medicaid.
Owner Proprietary corp.
Admissions Requirements Medical examination.
Staff RNs 2 (pt); LPNs 9 (ft), 2 (pt); Nurses' aides 12 (ft), 4 (pt); Recreational therapists 1 (pt); Activities coordinators 1 (pt); Dietitians 1 (pt).
Facilities Dining room; Activities room; Laundry room; Barber/Beauty shop.
Activities Arts & crafts; Cards; Games; Reading groups; Prayer groups; Movies; Shopping trips; Dances/Social/Cultural gatherings.

Hospitality Nursing Home
167 E Forest St, Clyde, OH 43410
(419) 547-0764
Licensure Intermediate care. *Beds* ICF 21. *Certified* Medicaid.
Owner Proprietary corp.

Woodsview Nursing Center
700 Helen St, Clyde, OH 43410
(419) 547-9595
Admin William D Hilliard NHA. *Dir of Nursing* Emily Smathers RN. *Medical Dir* Francis Aona MD.
Licensure Skilled care; Intermediate care; Assisted living. *Beds* SNF 20; ICF 80; Assisted living 40. *Private Pay Patients* 50%. *Certified* Medicaid.
Owner Proprietary corp (Arbor Health Care).

Coldwater

Briarwood Manor
830 W Main St, Coldwater, OH 45828
(419) 678-2311
Admin Brenda Hebden.
Medical Dir Rosemary Schmit.
Licensure Skilled care; Intermediate care. *Beds* Swing beds SNF/ICF 100. *Certified* Medicaid; Medicare.
Owner Proprietary corp (HCF Inc).
Admissions Requirements Medical examination; Physician's request.
Staff Physicians 2 (pt); RNs 5 (ft), 9 (pt); LPNs 6 (ft), 1 (pt); Nurses' aides 33 (ft), 38 (pt); Physical therapists 2 (pt); Speech therapists 1 (pt); Activities coordinators 1 (ft); Dietitians 1 (ft); Ophthalmologists 1 (pt).
Facilities Dining room; Physical therapy room; Activities room; Chapel; Laundry room; Barber/Beauty shop.

Activities Arts & crafts; Cards; Games; Reading groups; Prayer groups; Movies; Shopping trips; Dances/Social/Cultural gatherings; Gardening.

Columbia Station

Villa Camillus
10515 E River Rd, Columbia Station, OH 44028
(216) 236-5091
Admin Bruce Schirhart.
Medical Dir V R Mankad MD.
Licensure Skilled care. *Beds* SNF 50. *Certified* Medicare.
Owner Proprietary corp.
Admissions Requirements Minimum age 18; Females only; Medical examination.
Staff Physicians 1 (pt); RNs 1 (ft), 4 (pt); LPNs 1 (ft), 4 (pt); Nurses' aides 21 (pt); Physical therapists 1 (pt); Recreational therapists 1 (pt); Speech therapists 1 (pt); Activities coordinators 1 (pt); Dietitians 1 (pt); Ophthalmologists 1 (pt); Podiatrists 1 (pt).
Facilities Dining room; Physical therapy room; Activities room; Chapel; Crafts room; Laundry room; Barber/Beauty shop; Library.
Activities Arts & crafts; Cards; Games; Prayer groups; Movies; Dances/Social/Cultural gatherings.

Columbiana

Windsor Manor
550 E Park Ave, c/o Parkside HCO, Columbiana, OH 44408
(216) 424-7203
Admin Sally A Beil NHA. *Dir of Nursing* Maureen Bezon RN. *Medical Dir* Dr William Stevenson.
Licensure Skilled care; Intermediate care. *Beds* Swing beds SNF/ICF 50. *Certified* Medicaid; Medicare.
Owner Proprietary corp.
Admissions Requirements Medical examination.
Staff Physicians 1 (pt); RNs 1 (ft), 3 (pt); LPNs 4 (ft), 10 (pt); Nurses' aides 20 (ft), 6 (pt); Physical therapists 1 (pt); Occupational therapists 1 (pt); Speech therapists 1 (pt); Activities coordinators 1 (pt); Dietitians 1 (pt); Podiatrists 1 (pt); Dentists 1 (pt).
Facilities Dining room; Physical therapy room; Activities room; Crafts room; Laundry room; Barber/Beauty shop.
Activities Arts & crafts; Cards; Games; Reading groups; Prayer groups; Movies; Shopping trips; Dances/Social/Cultural gatherings; Fashion shows.

Columbus

ADD—1167 Neil
1167 Neil Ave, Columbus, OH 43201
(614) 291-7005
Licensure Intermediate care for mentally retarded. *Beds* ICF/MR 7. *Certified* Medicaid.
Owner Proprietary corp.

ADD—Hampstead
2357-2359 Hampstead Dr, Columbus, OH 43229
(614) 486-4361
Licensure Intermediate care for mentally retarded. *Beds* ICF/MR 9. *Certified* Medicaid.
Owner Proprietary corp.

ADD—Ida
1382/84 Ida Ave, Columbus, OH 43212
(614) 481-0327
Licensure Intermediate care for mentally retarded. *Beds* ICF/MR 8. *Certified* Medicaid.
Owner Proprietary corp.

ADD—Indianola
3257 Indianola Ave, Columbus, OH 43202
(614) 262-4088
Licensure Intermediate care for mentally retarded. *Beds* ICF/MR 6. *Certified* Medicaid.
Owner Proprietary corp.

ADD—Kimberly
3860 Kimberly Pkwy N, Columbus, OH 43232
(614) 863-8580
Licensure Intermediate care for mentally retarded. *Beds* ICF/MR 6. *Certified* Medicaid.
Owner Proprietary corp.

ADD—Lane Avenue
190 E Lane Ave, Columbus, OH 43201
(614) 291-9841
Licensure Intermediate care for mentally retarded. *Beds* ICF/MR 12. *Certified* Medicaid.
Owner Proprietary corp.

ADD—Maize Road
4171 Maize Rd, Columbus, OH 43224
(614) 268-5934
Licensure Intermediate care for mentally retarded. *Beds* ICF/MR 6. *Certified* Medicaid.
Owner Proprietary corp.

ADD—Teakwood
2433-2435 Teakwood Dr, Columbus, OH 43229
(614) 888-1077
Licensure Intermediate care for mentally retarded. *Beds* ICF/MR 8. *Certified* Medicaid.
Owner Proprietary corp.

ADD—1299 Neil
1299 Neil Ave, Columbus, OH 43201
(614) 421-7497
Licensure Intermediate care for mentally retarded. *Beds* ICF/MR 8. *Certified* Medicaid.
Owner Proprietary corp.

ADD—Whittier
318-20 E Whittier St, Columbus, OH 43206
(614) 443-6798
Licensure Intermediate care for mentally retarded. *Beds* ICF/MR 6. *Certified* Medicaid.
Owner Proprietary corp.

Alternative Residences Inc
1818 Sullivant Ave, Columbus, OH 43223
(614) 486-5923
Admin Vince Pettinelli.
Medical Dir Rhonda Cullumber.
Licensure Intermediate care for mentally retarded. *Beds* ICF/MR 12. *Private Pay Patients* 0%. *Certified* Medicaid.
Owner Proprietary corp (Alternative Residences Inc).
Staff Physicians 1 (ft); RNs 1 (ft); LPNs 2 (pt); Physical therapists 1 (ft); Occupational therapists 1 (ft); Speech therapists 1 (pt); Dietitians 1 (ft); Ophthalmologists 1 (ft); Podiatrists 1 (ft); Audiologists 1 (ft); Psychiatrists 1 (ft).
Facilities Dining room; Activities room; Crafts room; Laundry room.
Activities Arts & crafts; Cards; Games; Movies; Shopping trips; Dances/Social/Cultural gatherings.

Alternative Residences Inc—C & W Home
500 E Columbus St, Columbus, OH 43206
(614) 444-0976
Admin Vince Pettinelli. *Dir of Nursing* Rhonda Cullumber.
Licensure Intermediate care for mentally retarded. *Beds* ICF/MR 12. *Private Pay Patients* 0%. *Certified* Medicaid.
Owner Proprietary corp.

Admissions Requirements Medical examination.
Staff LPNs 1 (ft), 1 (pt); Dietitians.
Facilities Dining room; Laundry room.

Alternative Residences Inc—1834 Home
1834 Sullivant Ave, Columbus, OH 43223
(614) 486-5923
Licensure Intermediate care for mentally retarded. *Beds* ICF/MR 12. *Certified* Medicaid.
Owner Proprietary corp.

Alternative Residences Inc—James Road Home
97 S James Rd, Columbus, OH 43213
(614) 486-5923
Licensure Intermediate care for mentally retarded. *Beds* ICF/MR 8. *Certified* Medicaid.
Owner Proprietary corp.

Alternative Residences Inc—Norcross Home
5587 Norcross Rd, Columbus, OH 43229
(614) 486-5923
Licensure Intermediate care for mentally retarded. *Beds* ICF/MR 6. *Certified* Medicaid.
Owner Proprietary corp.

Alternative Residences Inc—Saville Row Home
2674 Saville Row, Columbus, OH 43224
(614) 486-5923
Licensure Intermediate care for mentally retarded. *Beds* ICF/MR 8. *Certified* Medicaid.
Owner Proprietary corp.

Alum Crest Nursing Home
1599 Alum Creek Dr, Columbus, OH 43207
(614) 445-8261, 443-0486 FAX
Admin Carl Holbrook. *Dir of Nursing* Michael Cindrich RN. *Medical Dir* Gail W Burrier MD.
Licensure Skilled care; Intermediate care. *Beds* SNF 64; ICF 211. *Private Pay Patients* 15%. *Certified* Medicaid; Medicare.
Owner Publicly owned.
Staff Physicians 1 (ft), 4 (pt); RNs 12 (ft), 4 (pt); LPNs 34 (ft), 6 (pt); Nurses' aides 127 (ft), 20 (pt); Physical therapists 1 (ft), 1 (pt); Recreational therapists 1 (ft); Occupational therapists 1 (ft), 1 (pt); Speech therapists 1 (ft), 1 (pt); Activities coordinators 4 (ft), 1 (pt); Dietitians 1 (ft); Ophthalmologists 1 (pt); Podiatrists 1 (pt); Audiologists 1 (pt).
Facilities Dining room; Physical therapy room; Activities room; Chapel; Crafts room; Laundry room; Barber/Beauty shop; Library.
Activities Arts & crafts; Cards; Games; Reading groups; Prayer groups; Movies; Shopping trips; Dances/Social/Cultural gatherings; Intergenerational programs; Pet therapy.

Alvis House Mental Retardation Unit
624 S Ohio Ave, Columbus, OH 43205
(614) 252-6196
Admin Denise M Robinson. *Dir of Nursing* Mary Waterfield RN. *Medical Dir* Beth O Tranen DO.
Licensure Intermediate care for mentally retarded. *Beds* ICF/MR 15. *Certified* Medicaid.
Owner Nonprofit corp.
Admissions Requirements Minimum age 18; Males only; Medical examination.
Staff Physicians 1 (pt); RNs 1 (ft); LPNs 2 (pt); Nurses' aides 8 (ft), 5 (pt); Occupational therapists 1 (pt); Speech therapists 1 (pt); Activities coordinators 1 (ft); Dietitians 1 (pt); Podiatrists 1 (pt).
Facilities Dining room; Activities room; Laundry room; TV lounge; Upstairs lounge.
Activities Arts & crafts; Cards; Games; Movies; Shopping trips; Housekeeping; Laundry; Cooking; Money management.

Americare Columbus Nursing Center
1700 Heinzerling Dr, Columbus, OH 43223
(614) 274-4222
Admin Carol J Keene. *Dir of Nursing* Bonnie
Phillips RN. *Medical Dir* Dr Michael
Downy.
Licensure Skilled care; Intermediate care;
Alzheimer's care. *Beds* SNF 22; ICF 78.
Certified Medicaid; Medicare.
Owner Proprietary corp (Care Enterprises).
Admissions Requirements Medical
examination; Physician's request.
Staff Physicians 1 (pt); RNs 4 (ft), 1 (pt);
LPNs 6 (ft), 1 (pt); Nurses' aides;
Physical therapists 1 (ft); Activities coordinators 2
(ft), 1 (pt); Dietitians 1 (ft), 1 (pt).
Facilities Dining room; Physical therapy
room; Activities room; Crafts room; Laundry
room; Barber/Beauty shop; Private dining
room; Rehabilitation dining room;
Physician's exam rooms; Dental chair.
Activities Arts & crafts; Cards; Games;
Reading groups; Prayer groups; Movies;
Shopping trips; Dances/Social/Cultural
gatherings; Exercises; Cooking club.

Arlington Court Nursing Home
1605 NW Professional Plaza, Columbus, OH
43220
(614) 451-5677
Admin James D Herron. *Dir of Nursing*
Barbara Rattan RN. *Medical Dir* Michael
Moftah MD.
Licensure Skilled care; Intermediate care. *Beds*
Swing beds SNF/ICF 120.
Owner Proprietary corp.
Staff RNs 4 (ft), 6 (pt); LPNs 3 (ft), 7 (pt);
Nurses' aides 15 (ft), 15 (pt); Physical
therapists 1 (pt); Recreational therapists 1
(ft); Activities coordinators 1 (ft); Dietitians
1 (pt).
Facilities Dining room; Physical therapy
room; Activities room; Chapel; Crafts room;
Barber/Beauty shop; Library.
Activities Arts & crafts; Cards; Games;
Reading groups; Prayer groups; Movies;
Dances/Social/Cultural gatherings.

Bescare Nursing Home
1288 Bryden Rd, Columbus, OH 43205
(614) 258-6371
Admin H Thomas Wilson. *Dir of Nursing*
Arteen Glenn. *Medical Dir* Dr Sergio
Payuyo.
Licensure Intermediate care. *Beds* ICF 17.
Certified Medicaid.
Owner Proprietary corp.
Staff Physicians 1 (pt); LPNs 3 (ft); Nurses'
aides 3 (ft), 2 (pt); Activities coordinators 1
(ft).
Facilities Dining room; Activities room;
Crafts room; Laundry room.
Activities Arts & crafts; Cards; Games; Prayer
groups; Movies; Shopping trips.

Bon-Ing Inc
173 Woodland Ave, Columbus, OH 43203
(614) 253-8451
Licensure Rest home. *Beds* Rest home 24.
Owner Proprietary corp.

Bryden Manor Nursing Home
1138 Bryden Rd, Columbus, OH 43205
(614) 252-4727
Licensure Intermediate care. *Beds* ICF 34.
Certified Medicaid.
Owner Proprietary corp.

Capitol South Care Center
1169 Bryden Rd, Columbus, OH 43205
(614) 258-6623
Licensure Skilled care; Intermediate care. *Beds*
Swing beds SNF/ICF 147. *Certified*
Medicaid; Medicare.
Owner Proprietary corp.

Central Ohio Rehabilitation Center
1331 Edgehill Rd, Columbus, OH 43212
(614) 294-5181

Licensure Intermediate care for mentally
retarded. *Beds* ICF/MR 23. *Certified*
Medicaid.
Owner Proprietary corp.

Christian Home for the Aged
PO Box 03605, 1454 Eastwood Ave,
Columbus, OH 43203
(614) 258-2769
Licensure Intermediate care. *Beds* 14.
Certified Medicaid.
Owner Proprietary corp.

Clearview Convalescent Center
2120 E 5th Ave, Columbus, OH 43219
(614) 258-8437
Licensure Skilled care; Intermediate care. *Beds*
SNF 19; ICF 74. *Certified* Medicaid;
Medicare.
Owner Proprietary corp (Health Resources
Development).

Columbus Center for Human Services Inc
600 Industrial Mile Rd, Columbus, OH 43228
(614) 278-9362
Licensure Intermediate care for mentally
retarded. *Beds* ICF/MR 70. *Certified*
Medicaid.
Owner Proprietary corp.

Columbus Quality Care Nursing Center
4301 Clime Rd N, Columbus, OH 43228
(614) 276-4400
Admin Wayne Davis. *Dir of Nursing* Joyce
Mueller RN. *Medical Dir* William Maher
DO.
Licensure Skilled care; Intermediate care. *Beds*
Swing beds SNF/ICF 100. *Private Pay
Patients* 45%. *Certified* Medicaid; Medicare.
Owner Proprietary corp (Northwestern Service
Corp).
Staff Physicians 1 (pt); RNs 3 (ft); LPNs 12
(pt); Nurses' aides 29 (ft), 9 (pt); Physical
therapists 1 (pt); Recreational therapists 1
(ft); Occupational therapists 1 (pt); Speech
therapists 1 (pt); Activities coordinators 1
(ft); Dietitians 1 (pt); Ophthalmologists 1
(pt); Podiatrists 1 (pt); Audiologists 1 (pt).
Languages Spanish.
Facilities Dining room; Physical therapy
room; Activities room; Crafts room; Laundry
room; Barber/Beauty shop.
Activities Arts & crafts; Cards; Games;
Reading groups; Prayer groups; Movies;
Shopping trips; Dances/Social/Cultural
gatherings; Intergenerational programs; Pet
therapy.

East Broad Manor
1243 E Broad St, Columbus, OH 43205
(614) 252-3836
Admin Edward J Powell. *Dir of Nursing* Jane
C Belt RN. *Medical Dir* William Conway
MD.
Licensure Intermediate care. *Beds* ICF 29.
Certified Medicaid.
Owner Proprietary corp.
Admissions Requirements Minimum age 18;
Females only; Medical examination.
Staff Physicians 1 (pt); RNs 1 (ft); LPNs 3
(ft), 5 (pt); Nurses' aides 7 (ft), 3 (pt);
Physical therapists 1 (pt); Speech therapists
1 (pt); Activities coordinators 1 (ft);
Dietitians 1 (pt); Ophthalmologists 1 (pt);
Podiatrists 1 (pt); Dentists 1 (pt).
Facilities Dining room; Activities room.
Activities Arts & crafts; Cards; Games; Prayer
groups; Movies; Shopping trips; Dances/
Social/Cultural gatherings; Camping trips.

Eastland Care Center
2425 Kimberly Pkwy E, Columbus, OH 43232
(614) 868-9306
Admin Richard M Tobin. *Dir of Nursing*
Carolyn C Vacca RN. *Medical Dir* Richard
N McCarty MD.
Licensure Skilled care; Intermediate care. *Beds*
Swing beds SNF/ICF 100. *Certified*
Medicaid; Medicare.

Owner Nonprofit corp (Volunteers of America
Care).
Admissions Requirements Medical
examination; Physician's request.
Staff Physicians 1 (pt); RNs 4 (ft), 2 (pt);
LPNs 7 (ft), 4 (pt); Nurses' aides 28 (ft), 11
(pt); Physical therapists 1 (pt); Occupational
therapists 1 (pt); Speech therapists 1 (pt);
Activities coordinators 2 (ft); Dietitians 1
(pt); Ophthalmologists 1 (pt); Podiatrists 1
(pt); Dentists 1 (pt).
Facilities Dining room; Physical therapy
room; Activities room; Chapel; Crafts room;
Laundry room; Barber/Beauty shop; Patio;
Front living room.
Activities Arts & crafts; Cards; Games;
Reading groups; Prayer groups; Movies;
Shopping trips; Dances/Social/Cultural
gatherings.

First Community Village Healthcare Center
1801 Riverside Dr, Columbus, OH 43212
(614) 486-9511, 486-7315 FAX
Admin Nancy Billings LNHA. *Dir of Nursing*
Jean Leyde RN. *Medical Dir* Steven
Lichtblau MD.
Licensure Skilled care; Intermediate care;
Retirement; Alzheimer's care. *Beds* Swing
beds SNF/ICF 175; Retirement 275-300.
Private Pay Patients 18%. *Certified*
Medicaid; Medicare.
Owner Nonprofit corp.
Staff Physicians 4 (pt); RNs 9 (ft), 10 (pt);
LPNs 10 (ft), 5 (pt); Nurses' aides 48 (ft), 11
(pt); Physical therapists 1 (ft), 1 (pt);
Occupational therapists 1 (pt); Speech
therapists 1 (pt); Activities coordinators 3
(ft); Dietitians 1 (ft); Ophthalmologists 1
(pt); Podiatrists 1 (pt); Audiologists 1 (pt);
Art therapists 1 (ft).
Affiliation First Community Church.
Facilities 2 wheelchair gardens; Visiting
parlors.
Activities Arts & crafts; Cards; Games;
Reading groups; Prayer groups; Movies;
Shopping trips; Dances/Social/Cultural
gatherings; Intergenerational programs; Pet
therapy; Vespers; Sing-alongs.

Franklin Woods Health Care Center
2770 Clime Rd, Columbus, OH 43223
(614) 276-8222
Admin Mary Ellen Thornton. *Dir of Nursing*
Amanda Ross RN. *Medical Dir* Raymond
Pongonis DO.
Licensure Skilled care; Intermediate care. *Beds*
SNF 32; ICF 68. *Private Pay Patients* 10%.
Certified Medicaid; Medicare.
Owner Proprietary corp.

Friendship Village Health Center
5800 Forest Hills Blvd, Columbus, OH 43231
(614) 890-8282, 890-8287 FAX
Admin Tamie Kondoff; Tim Dowd, Exec Dir.
Dir of Nursing Colleen Sigman. *Medical Dir*
John B Krupko MD.
Licensure Skilled care; Intermediate care;
Retirement. *Beds* Swing beds SNF/ICF 90;
Retirement 350. *Private Pay Patients* 8%.
Certified Medicaid; Medicare.
Owner Nonprofit corp.
Admissions Requirements Physician's request.
Staff Physicians 1 (pt); RNs 8 (ft), 4 (pt);
LPNs 9 (ft), 2 (pt); Nurses' aides 35 (ft), 12
(pt); Physical therapists 1 (ft); Occupational
therapists 1 (pt); Speech therapists 1 (pt);
Activities coordinators 1 (ft); Dietitians 1
(pt); Ophthalmologists 1 (pt).
Facilities Dining room; Physical therapy
room; Activities room; Crafts room; Laundry
room; Barber/Beauty shop; Library.
Activities Arts & crafts; Cards; Games;
Reading groups; Prayer groups; Movies;
Shopping trips; Dances/Social/Cultural
gatherings; Intergenerational programs; Pet
therapy.

Genesis
4133 Karl Rd, Columbus, OH 43224
(614) 263-5971
Licensure Intermediate care for mentally
retarded. *Beds* ICF/MR 24. *Certified*
Medicaid.
Owner Proprietary corp.

Heartland—Thurber Village
920 Thurber Dr W, Columbus, OH 43215
(614) 464-2275
Admin Brenda Ferguson Stabile. *Dir of
Nursing* Donna Taylor Stevenson. *Medical
Dir* Raymond Pongonis DO.
Licensure Skilled care; Intermediate care. *Beds*
Swing beds SNF/ICF 148. *Certified*
Medicaid; Medicare.
Owner Proprietary corp (Health Care and
Retirement Corp).
Admissions Requirements Medical
examination; Physician's request.
Staff Physicians 2 (ft); RNs 5 (ft); LPNs 12
(ft), 1 (pt); Physical therapists 1 (ft);
Occupational therapists 1 (pt); Speech
therapists 1 (pt); Activities coordinators 1
(ft); Dietitians 1 (pt); Ophthalmologists 1
(pt); Podiatrists 1 (pt); Dentists 1 (pt).
Facilities Dining room; Physical therapy
room; Activities room; Laundry room;
Barber/Beauty shop; General store.
Activities Arts & crafts; Cards; Games;
Reading groups; Prayer groups; Movies;
Shopping trips; Dances/Social/Cultural
gatherings.

Heinzerling Developmental Center
1755 Heinzerling Dr, Columbus, OH 43223
(614) 272-2000
Licensure Intermediate care for mentally
retarded. *Beds* ICF/MR 104. *Certified*
Medicaid.
Owner Proprietary corp.
Admissions Requirements Minimum age 21.

Heinzerling Memorial Foundation
1800 Heinzerling Dr, Columbus, OH 43223
(614) 272-8888
Licensure Intermediate care for mentally
retarded. *Beds* ICF/MR 104. *Certified*
Medicaid.
Owner Proprietary corp.

**Heritage House-Columbus Jewish Home for
the Aged**
1151 College Ave, Columbus, OH 43209
(614) 237-7417
Licensure Skilled care; Intermediate care. *Beds*
Swing beds SNF/ICF 146. *Certified*
Medicaid; Medicare.
Owner Proprietary corp.
Affiliation Jewish.

Kimberly Woods
2434-2460 Kimberly Woods Dr, Columbus,
OH 43232
(614) 866-0103
Licensure Intermediate care for mentally
retarded. *Beds* ICF/MR 16. *Certified*
Medicaid.
Owner Proprietary corp.

Lutheran Senior City Inc
935 N Cassady Ave, Columbus, OH 43219
(614) 252-4987, 252-7236 FAX
Admin Rebecca S Menter; Robert C
Mendenhall. *Dir of Nursing* Elizabeth A
Feeney RN. *Medical Dir* Patrick Dineen
MD.
Licensure Skilled care; Intermediate care; Rest
home; Assisted living; Independent living;
Respite care; Alzheimer's care. *Beds* Swing
beds SNF/ICF 136; Rest home 25; Assisted
living 74; Independent living 47. *Certified*
Medicaid; Medicare.
Owner Nonprofit corp.
Admissions Requirements Minimum age 65;
Medical examination.

Staff Physicians 6 (pt); RNs 14 (ft), 5 (pt);
LPNs 14 (ft), 4 (pt); Nurses' aides 64 (ft), 4
(pt); Physical therapists 1 (ft); Recreational
therapists 1 (ft); Occupational therapists 4
(ft); Activities coordinators 1 (ft); Dietitians
1 (ft); Podiatrists 2 (pt).
Affiliation Lutheran.
Facilities Dining room; Physical therapy
room; Activities room; Chapel; Crafts room;
Laundry room; Barber/Beauty shop; Library;
Private & semi-private rooms.
Activities Arts & crafts; Cards; Games;
Reading groups; Prayer groups; Movies;
Shopping trips; Dances/Social/Cultural
gatherings; Gardening; Ceramics;
Woodworking; Exercise classes; Outings.

Mayfair Village Nursing Care Center
3000 Bethel Rd, Columbus, OH 43220
(614) 889-6320
Admin Sharon L Reynolds.
Medical Dir Charles Twul MD.
Licensure Skilled care; Intermediate care. *Beds*
Swing beds SNF/ICF 100. *Certified*
Medicaid; Medicare.
Owner Proprietary corp (National Heritage).
Admissions Requirements Minimum age 18;
Medical examination; Physician's request.
Staff Physicians 1 (pt); RNs 6 (ft), 13 (pt);
LPNs 4 (ft); Nurses' aides 26 (ft), 12 (pt);
Physical therapists 1 (pt); Reality therapists
1 (ft); Recreational therapists 1 (ft);
Occupational therapists 1 (pt); Speech
therapists 1 (pt); Dietitians 1 (pt);
Ophthalmologists 1 (pt); Podiatrists 1 (pt);
Audiologists 1 (pt); Dentists 1 (pt).
Facilities Dining room; Physical therapy
room; Activities room; Crafts room; Laundry
room; Barber/Beauty shop; Library.
Activities Arts & crafts; Cards; Games;
Reading groups; Prayer groups; Movies;
Shopping trips; Dances/Social/Cultural
gatherings.

Minerva Park Nursing Home
5460 Cleveland Ave, Columbus, OH 43231-
7612
(614) 882-2490, 882-6767 FAX
Admin JoAnn Rasmussen; Ann Clark, Asst.
Dir of Nursing Sherree Barkey. *Medical Dir*
Dr H T Villavecer.
Licensure Intermediate care. *Beds* ICF 101.
Private Pay Patients 25%. *Certified*
Medicaid.
Owner Proprietary corp (Hillhaven Corp).
Admissions Requirements Medical
examination; Physician's request.
Staff Physicians 9 (ft); RNs 7 (ft); LPNs 6 (ft);
Nurses' aides 30 (ft), 10 (pt); Physical
therapists 1 (ft); Reality therapists 1 (ft);
Recreational therapists 2 (ft); Occupational
therapists 2 (ft); Speech therapists 1 (ft);
Activities coordinators 2 (ft); Dietitians 1
(ft); Podiatrists 1 (ft).
Facilities Dining room; Physical therapy
room; Activities room; Crafts room; Laundry
room; Barber/Beauty shop; Library; Lounge;
Porch.
Activities Arts & crafts; Cards; Games;
Reading groups; Prayer groups; Movies;
Shopping trips; Dances/Social/Cultural
gatherings; Intergenerational programs; Pet
therapy; Breakfast and dinner cooking club.

Mohun Hall Infirmary
Saint Mary of the Springs, Columbus, OH
43219
(614) 253-8517
Admin Sr Barbara Jean Welker OP. *Dir of
Nursing* Sue Moxley. *Medical Dir* Dr Robert
Hershfield.
Licensure Skilled care; Intermediate care;
Retirement. *Beds* SNF 25; ICF 45;
Retirement 75.
Owner Nonprofit corp.
Admissions Requirements Females only;
Physician's request; Must be a member of
Dominican Sisters.

Staff RNs; LPNs; Nurses' aides; Physical
therapists; Recreational therapists; Activities
coordinators; Dietitians; Podiatrists.
Facilities Dining room; Physical therapy
room; Activities room; Chapel; Laundry
room; Barber/Beauty shop; Library.
Activities Cards; Games; Prayer groups;
Movies; Shopping trips.

Northland Terrace
5700 Karl Rd, Columbus, OH 43229
(614) 846-5420, 846-7613 FAX
Admin Sharon L Reynolds. *Dir of Nursing*
Sue Longhenry RN. *Medical Dir* Stephen D
Shell MD.
Licensure Skilled care; Intermediate care; Care
for ventilator-dependent adults/children.
Beds SNF 104; ICF 156. *Private Pay
Patients* 13%. *Certified* Medicaid; Medicare.
Owner Proprietary corp.
Admissions Requirements Minimum age 2
months; Medical examination.
Staff RNs 19 (ft), 15 (pt); LPNs 45 (ft), 11
(pt); Nurses' aides 75 (ft), 12 (pt); Physical
therapists 1 (ft); Occupational therapists 1
(ft); Speech therapists 1 (pt); Activities
coordinators 1 (ft); Dietitians 1 (ft);
Ophthalmologists 1 (pt).
Facilities Dining room; Physical therapy
room; Activities room; Laundry room;
Barber/Beauty shop; Library.
Activities Arts & crafts; Cards; Games;
Reading groups; Prayer groups; Movies;
Shopping trips; Dances/Social/Cultural
gatherings; Intergenerational programs; Pet
therapy.

**Margaret Clark Oakfield Convalescent Center
of Columbus**
500 N Nelson Rd, Columbus, OH 43219
(614) 252-5244
Admin Harriett A White.
Medical Dir Marina Pilic.
Licensure Intermediate care; Retirement;
Alzheimer's care. *Beds* ICF 152. *Certified*
Medicaid.
Owner Proprietary corp.
Admissions Requirements Medical
examination; Physician's request.
Staff Physicians 6 (pt); RNs 6 (ft), 5 (pt);
LPNs 10 (ft), 1 (pt); Nurses' aides 37 (ft), 3
(pt); Reality therapists 2 (ft), 1 (pt);
Recreational therapists 2 (ft); Activities
coordinators 2 (ft), 1 (pt).
Facilities Dining room; Activities room;
Laundry room; Barber/Beauty shop.
Activities Arts & crafts; Cards; Games;
Reading groups; Prayer groups; Movies;
Shopping trips; Dances/Social/Cultural
gatherings.

Parkwood Nursing Home
32 Parkwood Ave, Columbus, OH 43203
(614) 258-3088
Admin Edward J Powell. *Dir of Nursing* Jane
C Belt RN. *Medical Dir* William F Conway
MD.
Licensure Intermediate care. *Beds* ICF 25.
Private Pay Patients 1%. *Certified* Medicaid.
Owner Proprietary corp.
Admissions Requirements Minimum age 18;
Females only.
Staff Physicians 1 (pt); RNs 1 (ft); LPNs 2
(ft), 3 (pt); Nurses' aides 7 (ft), 4 (pt);
Physical therapists 1 (pt); Occupational
therapists 1 (pt); Speech therapists 1 (pt);
Activities coordinators 1 (ft); Dietitians 1
(pt); Ophthalmologists 1 (pt); Podiatrists 1
(pt).
Facilities Dining room; Activities room.
Activities Arts & crafts; Cards; Games; Prayer
groups; Movies; Shopping trips; Dances/
Social/Cultural gatherings; Pet therapy.

Patterson Health Center Inc
71 Woodland Ave, Columbus, OH 43203
(614) 258-7424
Admin Esther R Chapman.

Licensure Intermediate care. *Beds* ICF 43. *Certified* Medicaid.
Owner Proprietary corp (Omnilife Systems Inc).

Isabelle Ridgway Nursing Center
1520 Hawthorne Ave, Columbus, OH 43203
(614) 252-4931
Admin Russell Boyce. *Dir of Nursing* Donna Angelo. *Medical Dir* George Barnett Jr MD.
Licensure Skilled care; Intermediate care. *Beds* Swing beds SNF/ICF 100. *Certified* Medicaid; Medicare.
Owner Proprietary corp.
Admissions Requirements Minimum age 21; Medical examination; Physician's request.
Staff Physicians 5 (pt); RNs 3 (ft); LPNs 14 (ft); Physical therapists 1 (pt); Occupational therapists 1 (pt); Speech therapists 1 (pt); Activities coordinators 1 (ft); Dietitians 1 (pt); Ophthalmologists 1 (pt); Podiatrists 1 (pt); Dentists 1 (pt).
Facilities Dining room; Physical therapy room; Activities room; Chapel; Laundry room; Barber/Beauty shop; Senior activity room.
Activities Arts & crafts; Games; Reading groups; Prayer groups; Movies; Shopping trips; Dances/Social/Cultural gatherings; One-on-one companion programs.

Riverside United Methodist Hospital's Extended Care Unit
3535 Olentangy River Rd, Columbus, OH 43214
(614) 261-5000
Admin Erie Chapman III. *Dir of Nursing* Claudia Wilder. *Medical Dir* Dr John Burkhart.
Licensure Skilled care. *Beds* SNF 48. *Certified* Medicare.
Owner Nonprofit corp.
Admissions Requirements Minimum age 16; Physician's request.
Staff Physicians 1 (pt); RNs 18 (ft), 6 (pt); LPNs 6 (ft), 1 (pt); Nurses' aides 8 (ft); Physical therapists 15 (ft); Occupational therapists 5 (ft); Speech therapists 4 (ft); Activities coordinators 1 (ft); Dietitians 1 (ft); Ophthalmologists; Podiatrists; Dentists.
Affiliation Methodist.
Facilities Dining room; Physical therapy room; Activities room; Chapel; Barber/Beauty shop; Library.
Activities Arts & crafts; Cards; Games; Reading groups; Movies; Holiday parties.

Rosegate Care Center
1850 Crown Park Ct, Columbus, OH 43235
(614) 459-7293
Admin Michael Anthony LNHA. *Dir of Nursing* Joyce Beecroft RN. *Medical Dir* Link Murphy MD.
Licensure Intermediate care. *Beds* ICF 100. *Private Pay Patients* 60%. *Certified* Medicaid.
Owner Proprietary corp (National Heritage).
Admissions Requirements Medical examination.
Staff Physicians 3 (pt); RNs 9 (ft), 9 (pt); LPNs 6 (ft), 3 (pt); Nurses' aides 44 (ft); Physical therapists 1 (pt); Occupational therapists 1 (pt); Speech therapists 1 (pt); Activities coordinators 1 (ft); Dietitians 1 (pt); Ophthalmologists 1 (pt); Podiatrists 1 (pt).
Facilities Dining room; Physical therapy room; Activities room; Laundry room; Barber/Beauty shop; Cafe.
Activities Arts & crafts; Cards; Games; Reading groups; Prayer groups; Movies; Shopping trips; Dances/Social/Cultural gatherings; Intergenerational programs; Pet therapy.

St Luke Convalescent Center—Central
44 S Souder Ave, Columbus, OH 43222
(614) 228-5900
Admin J M Boyd.
Medical Dir John Raabe MD.
Licensure Intermediate care. *Beds* ICF 120. *Certified* Medicaid.
Owner Proprietary corp (Arbor Health Care).
Facilities Dining room; Physical therapy room; Activities room; Chapel; Crafts room; Laundry room; Barber/Beauty shop; Library.
Activities Arts & crafts; Cards; Games; Reading groups; Prayer groups; Movies; Shopping trips; Dances/Social/Cultural gatherings.

St Luke Convalescent Center—East
5500 E Broad St, Columbus, OH 43213
(614) 868-0888
Admin William A Wershing. *Dir of Nursing* Sandra Hirsch RN. *Medical Dir* John P Hanyak MD.
Licensure Intermediate care; Alzheimer's care. *Beds* ICF 100. *Certified* Medicaid.
Owner Proprietary corp.
Admissions Requirements Medical examination; Physician's request.
Staff Physicians 1 (ft); RNs 7 (ft); LPNs 6 (ft); Nurses' aides 30 (ft); Activities coordinators 1 (ft).
Facilities Dining room; Physical therapy room; Activities room; Barber/Beauty shop; Solariums.
Activities Arts & crafts; Cards; Games; Reading groups; Movies; Dances/Social/Cultural gatherings.

St Raphaels Home for the Aged
1550 Roxbury Rd, Columbus, OH 43212
(614) 486-0436
Admin Sr Maureen Hughes.
Medical Dir Haushong Ma'ani MD.
Licensure Skilled care; Intermediate care. *Beds* Swing beds SNF/ICF 78. *Certified* Medicaid; Medicare.
Owner Proprietary corp.
Admissions Requirements Medical examination.
Staff Physicians 1 (pt); RNs 6 (ft); LPNs 4 (ft); Physical therapists 1 (pt); Occupational therapists 1 (pt); Speech therapists 1 (pt); Activities coordinators 1 (ft), 1 (pt); Dietitians 1 (pt); Ophthalmologists 1 (pt); Dentists 1 (pt).
Affiliation Roman Catholic.
Facilities Dining room; Physical therapy room; Activities room; Chapel; Crafts room; Laundry room; Barber/Beauty shop; Library.
Activities Arts & crafts; Cards; Games; Reading groups; Prayer groups; Movies; Shopping trips; Dances/Social/Cultural gatherings; Pet therapy.

St Rita's Home for the Aged Inc
880 Greenlawn Ave, Columbus, OH 43223
(614) 443-9433
Admin Sr M Veronica. *Dir of Nursing* Phyllis Wright RN. *Medical Dir* Mina Mokhtari MD.
Licensure Skilled care; Intermediate care. *Beds* Swing beds SNF/ICF 100. *Certified* Medicaid; Medicare.
Owner Proprietary corp.
Admissions Requirements Minimum age 65; Medical examination; Physician's request.
Staff Physicians 1 (ft); RNs 6 (ft), 1 (pt); LPNs 10 (ft), 3 (pt); Nurses' aides 47 (ft), 8 (pt); Physical therapists 1 (ft); Occupational therapists 1 (pt); Activities coordinators 2 (ft); Dietitians 1 (pt); Ophthalmologists 1 (pt); Podiatrists 1 (pt); Dentists 1 (pt); Food service managers 1 (ft).
Affiliation Roman Catholic.
Facilities Dining room; Physical therapy room; Activities room; Chapel; Crafts room; Laundry room; Barber/Beauty shop; Library; Ancillary services room.

Activities Arts & crafts; Cards; Games; Reading groups; Movies; Shopping trips; Dances/Social/Cultural gatherings; Cooking; Music therapy; One-on-one projects; Bowling.

Shasta Home
3273 Shasta Dr, Columbus, OH 43229
(614) 890-6370
Admin Nancy West. *Dir of Nursing* Mary Berry RN.
Licensure Intermediate care for mentally retarded. *Beds* ICF/MR 11. *Certified* Medicaid.
Owner Proprietary corp.
Admissions Requirements Minimum age 21; Medical examination; Physician's request.
Staff LPNs 2 (ft), 2 (pt); Physical therapists 1 (pt); Occupational therapists 1 (pt); Speech therapists 1 (pt); Dietitians 1 (pt); Ophthalmologists 1 (pt); Podiatrists 1 (pt).
Facilities Dining room; Laundry room.
Activities Arts & crafts; Cards; Games; Movies; Shopping trips; Dances/Social/Cultural gatherings; Sheltered workshop; Employment.

Wahroonga Home
3660 Westerville Rd, Columbus, OH 43224
(614) 471-1515
Licensure Intermediate care for mentally retarded. *Beds* ICF/MR 13. *Certified* Medicaid.
Owner Proprietary corp.

Wecare Health Facility
740 Canonby Pl, Columbus, OH 43223
(614) 224-5738
Admin Darl Reynolds. *Dir of Nursing* Debbie McDaniel BSN RN. *Medical Dir* Gerald Lane DO.
Licensure Intermediate care. *Beds* ICF 101. *Certified* Medicaid.
Owner Proprietary corp.
Admissions Requirements Minimum age 21; Medical examination; Physician's request.
Staff Physicians 1 (pt); RNs 4 (ft); LPNs 9 (ft), 1 (pt); Nurses' aides 40 (ft); Physical therapists 1 (pt); Recreational therapists 4 (ft), 1 (pt); Occupational therapists 1 (pt); Speech therapists 1 (pt); Activities coordinators 1 (ft); Dietitians 2 (pt); Podiatrists 1 (pt); Audiologists 1 (pt); Dentists 1 (pt).
Facilities Dining room; Physical therapy room; Activities room; Crafts room; Laundry room; Barber/Beauty shop.
Activities Arts & crafts; Cards; Games; Reading groups; Prayer groups; Movies; Shopping trips; Dances/Social/Cultural gatherings; Intergenerational programs.

Wesley Glen Inc
5155 N High St, Columbus, OH 43214
(614) 888-7492
Admin Wesley Clarke. *Dir of Nursing* Dorothy Pfefferle. *Medical Dir* Ronald C Van Buren MD.
Licensure Skilled care; Intermediate care; Retirement; Alzheimer's care. *Beds* Swing beds SNF/ICF 83. *Private Pay Patients* 77%. *Certified* Medicaid; Medicare.
Owner Nonprofit organization/foundation.
Admissions Requirements Minimum age 65; Medical examination; Physician's request.
Staff Physicians 1 (pt); RNs 5 (ft), 3 (pt); LPNs 3 (ft), 2 (pt); Nurses' aides 37 (ft), 10 (pt); Physical therapists 1 (pt); Speech therapists 1 (pt); Activities coordinators 2 (ft); Dietitians 1 (ft); Podiatrists 1 (pt); Dentists 1 (pt).
Affiliation Methodist.
Facilities Dining room; Physical therapy room; Activities room; Chapel; Crafts room; Laundry room; Barber/Beauty shop; Library; Alzheimer's unit.

Activities Arts & crafts; Cards; Games; Reading groups; Prayer groups; Movies; Shopping trips; Dances/Social/Cultural gatherings.

Westminster-Thurber Retirement Community
645-717 Neil Ave, Columbus, OH 43215
(614) 228-8888, 228-8002 FAX
Admin Patricia B Mullins. *Dir of Nursing* Laurelyn Hutchinson. *Medical Dir* Roy L Donnerberg MD.
Licensure Skilled care; Intermediate care; Rest home; Independent living; Alzheimer's care. *Beds* Swing beds SNF/ICF 92; Rest home 52; Independent living units 203. *Private Pay Patients* 65%. *Certified* Medicaid; Medicare.
Owner Nonprofit organization/foundation (Ohio Presbyterian Retirement Services).
Admissions Requirements Minimum age 60; Medical examination.
Staff Physicians (consultant); RNs 10 (ft), 9 (pt); LPNs 8 (ft), 7 (pt); Nurses' aides 51 (ft), 4 (pt); Physical therapists 1 (ft); Recreational therapists 3 (ft); Occupational therapists (consultant); Speech therapists (consultant); Activities coordinators 1 (ft); Dietitians (consultant); Ophthalmologists (consultant); Podiatrists (consultant).
Affiliation Presbyterian.
Facilities Dining room; Physical therapy room; Activities room; Chapel; Crafts room; Laundry room; Barber/Beauty shop; Library; Alzheimer's unit.
Activities Arts & crafts; Cards; Games; Reading groups; Prayer groups; Movies; Shopping trips; Dances/Social/Cultural gatherings; Intergenerational programs; Pet therapy.

Whetstone Convalescent Center
3700 Olentangy River Rd, Columbus, OH 43214
(614) 457-1100, 457-1100, ext 140 FAX
Admin Mary Ann Evans; Warren J Harris, Exec Dir. *Dir of Nursing* Mary P Monahan. *Medical Dir* Dr William T Paul.
Licensure Skilled care; Intermediate care. *Beds* Swing beds SNF/ICF 200. *Certified* Medicaid; Medicare.
Owner Nonprofit corp (Episcopal Retirement Homes Inc).
Admissions Requirements Medical examination; Physician's request.
Staff Physicians 1 (pt); RNs 23 (ft), 3 (pt); LPNs 14 (ft), 2 (pt); Nurses' aides 70 (ft), 16 (pt); Physical therapists 1 (ft), 1 (pt); Occupational therapists (consultant); Speech therapists (consultant); Activities coordinators 1 (ft); Dietitians 1 (pt); Food service managers 3 (ft); Respiratory therapists (consultant); Psychologists (consultant) 1 (ft).
Affiliation Episcopal.
Facilities Dining room; Physical therapy room; Activities room; Chapel; Crafts room; Laundry room; Barber/Beauty shop; Library; Social services conference room; 6 lounges; Courtyard.
Activities Arts & crafts; Cards; Games; Reading groups; Prayer groups; Movies; Shopping trips; Dances/Social/Cultural gatherings; Intergenerational programs; Pet therapy; Continuing education; Music appreciation; Ceramics; Current events; One-on-one exercise; Pastoral counseling; Religious activities.

Willow Brook Christian Home
55 Lazelle Rd, Columbus, OH 43235
(614) 885-3300
Admin Larry Harris. *Dir of Nursing* Margaret Dronsfield.
Licensure Intermediate care. *Beds* ICF 50. *Private Pay Patients* 40%. *Certified* Medicaid.
Owner Nonprofit corp.
Admissions Requirements Medical examination.

Staff Physicians 8 (pt); RNs 3 (ft), 3 (pt); LPNs 1 (ft), 2 (pt); Nurses' aides 8 (ft), 15 (pt); Physical therapists 1 (pt); Speech therapists 1 (pt); Activities coordinators 1 (ft), 1 (pt); Dietitians 1 (pt); Podiatrists 1 (pt).
Affiliation Church of Christ.
Facilities Dining room; Physical therapy room; Activities room; Chapel; Crafts room; Barber/Beauty shop.
Activities Arts & crafts; Cards; Games; Reading groups; Prayer groups; Movies; Shopping trips; Dances/Social/Cultural gatherings.

Woodland Manor
81 Woodland Ave, Columbus, OH 43203
(614) 258-8688
Admin Edward J Powell. *Dir of Nursing* Jane Belt RN. *Medical Dir* William F Conway MD.
Licensure Intermediate care. *Beds* ICF 29. *Certified* Medicaid.
Owner Proprietary corp.
Admissions Requirements Minimum age 18.
Staff Physicians 1 (pt); RNs 1 (ft); LPNs 3 (ft), 5 (pt); Nurses' aides 3 (ft), 3 (pt); Physical therapists 1 (pt); Speech therapists 1 (pt); Activities coordinators 1 (ft); Dietitians 1 (pt); Ophthalmologists 1 (pt); Podiatrists 1 (pt); Dentists 1 (pt).
Facilities Dining room; Activities room; Laundry room.
Activities Arts & crafts; Cards; Games; Prayer groups; Movies; Shopping trips; Dances/Social/Cultural gatherings.

Woodward House
340 Derrer Rd, Columbus, OH 43204
(614) 274-7000
Licensure Intermediate care for mentally retarded. *Beds* ICF/MR 8. *Certified* Medicaid.
Owner Proprietary corp.

Yorkshire Health Care Center
1425 Yorkland Rd, Columbus, OH 43232
(614) 861-6666, 861-6750 FAX
Admin Fran Richardson. *Dir of Nursing* Margaret Louthen RN. *Medical Dir* S L Richardson MD.
Licensure Skilled care; Intermediate care. *Beds* SNF 50; ICF 150. *Private Pay Patients* 20%. *Certified* Medicaid; Medicare.
Owner Proprietary corp (Beverly Enterprises).
Admissions Requirements Minimum age 18; Medical examination; Physician's request.
Staff Physicians 1 (pt); RNs 28 (ft); LPNs 12 (ft); Nurses' aides 70 (ft), 20 (pt); Physical therapists 1 (pt); Occupational therapists 1 (pt); Speech therapists 1 (ft); Activities coordinators 3 (ft); Dietitians 1 (pt); Ophthalmologists 1 (pt); Podiatrists 1 (pt); Dentists 1 (pt).
Facilities Dining room; Physical therapy room; Activities room; Crafts room; Laundry room; Barber/Beauty shop.
Activities Arts & crafts; Cards; Games; Reading groups; Prayer groups; Movies; Shopping trips; Dances/Social/Cultural gatherings.

Conneaut

Inn-Conneaut Health Center
22 Parrish Rd, Conneaut, OH 44030
(216) 599-7911
Admin Richard D Van Allen.
Medical Dir William Anderson Jr MD.
Licensure Skilled care; Intermediate care. *Beds* Swing beds SNF/ICF 100. *Certified* Medicaid; Medicare.
Owner Proprietary corp.
Admissions Requirements Minimum age 21; Medical examination.
Staff Physicians 8 (pt); RNs 6 (ft), 4 (pt); LPNs 5 (ft), 3 (pt); Nurses' aides 27 (ft), 5 (pt); Physical therapists 1 (pt); Reality

therapists 1 (pt); Recreational therapists 1 (ft); Occupational therapists 1 (pt); Speech therapists 1 (pt); Activities coordinators 1 (ft); Dietitians 1 (pt); Podiatrists 2 (pt); Dentists 1 (pt).
Facilities Dining room; Physical therapy room; Activities room; Crafts room; Laundry room; Barber/Beauty shop; Library.
Activities Arts & crafts; Cards; Games; Reading groups; Prayer groups; Movies; Shopping trips; Dances/Social/Cultural gatherings.

Convoy

Convoy Care Center
127 Mentzer Dr, Convoy, OH 45832
(419) 749-2194
Admin Peg Zeis. *Dir of Nursing* Sharon Geyer RN. *Medical Dir* Joel Knerr MD.
Licensure Intermediate care. *Beds* ICF 50. *Private Pay Patients* 60%. *Certified* Medicaid.
Owner Proprietary corp.
Admissions Requirements Medical examination; Physician's request.
Staff RNs 1 (ft), 3 (pt); LPNs 3 (ft), 2 (pt); Nurses' aides 13 (ft), 10 (pt); Physical therapists 1 (pt); Occupational therapists 1 (pt); Speech therapists 1 (pt); Activities coordinators 1 (ft); Dietitians 1 (pt); Podiatrists 1 (pt); Audiologists 1 (pt).
Facilities Dining room; Physical therapy room; Activities room; Crafts room; Laundry room; Barber/Beauty shop; Library.
Activities Arts & crafts; Cards; Games; Reading groups; Prayer groups; Movies; Shopping trips; Dances/Social/Cultural gatherings; Intergenerational programs; Pet therapy.

Coolville

Arcadia Nursing Center
PO Box A, E Main St, Coolville, OH 45723
(614) 667-3156
Admin Kevin R Ruffing. *Dir of Nursing* Robin Wright. *Medical Dir* Dr Sprague.
Licensure Skilled care; Intermediate care. *Beds* Swing beds SNF/ICF 75. *Certified* Medicaid; Medicare.
Owner Proprietary corp (Health Care Management).
Facilities Dining room; Physical therapy room; Activities room; Crafts room; Laundry room; Barber/Beauty shop.
Activities Arts & crafts; Cards; Games; Reading groups; Prayer groups; Movies; Shopping trips; Dances/Social/Cultural gatherings; Intergenerational programs; Pet therapy.

Cortland

Cortland Quality Care Nursing Center
369 N High St, Cortland, OH 44410
(216) 638-4915, 638-4128 FAX
Admin Cynthia M Woodford. *Dir of Nursing* Yvette Kimbler RN. *Medical Dir* Edward R Urban DO.
Licensure Skilled care; Intermediate care; Alzheimer's care. *Beds* Swing beds SNF/ICF 50. *Private Pay Patients* 100%.
Owner Proprietary corp (Northwestern Service Corp).
Admissions Requirements Physician's request.
Staff Physicians 3 (ft); RNs 1 (ft), 3 (pt); LPNs 2 (ft), 1 (pt); Nurses' aides 10 (ft), 12 (pt); Speech therapists 1 (pt); Activities coordinators 1 (ft), 1 (pt); Dietitians 1 (ft), 1 (pt); Podiatrists 2 (pt).
Facilities Dining room; Physical therapy room; Activities room; Crafts room; Laundry room; Barber/Beauty shop.

Activities Arts & crafts; Cards; Games; Reading groups; Prayer groups; Movies; Shopping trips; Dances/Social/Cultural gatherings; Intergenerational programs; Pet therapy.

Faber Nursing Home
4250 Sodom-Hutchings Rd NE, Cortland, OH 44410
(216) 637-7906
Admin Lynn Meyers. *Dir of Nursing* Martha Richards LPN. *Medical Dir* Dr John W Dowswell.
Licensure Intermediate care. *Beds* ICF 38. *Certified* Medicaid.
Owner Proprietary corp.
Staff Physicians 1 (ft), 3 (pt); RNs 1 (pt); LPNs 3 (ft), 4 (pt); Nurses' aides 11 (ft), 4 (pt); Speech therapists 1 (pt); Activities coordinators 1 (ft); Dietitians 1 (pt); Ophthalmologists 1 (pt); Podiatrists 1 (pt); Dentists 1 (pt).

Coshocton

Coshocton County Home
3201 CR 16, Coshocton, OH 43812
(614) 622-2074
Medical Dir G W Stelzner MD.
Licensure Skilled care; Intermediate care. *Beds* Swing beds SNF/ICF 74. *Certified* Medicaid.
Owner Publicly owned.
Admissions Requirements Minimum age 18; Medical examination.
Staff RNs 2 (ft), 1 (pt); LPNs 8 (ft), 2 (pt); Nurses' aides 15 (ft), 3 (pt); Activities coordinators 2 (ft).
Facilities Dining room; Physical therapy room; Activities room; Chapel; Crafts room; Laundry room; Barber/Beauty shop; TV lounges.
Activities Arts & crafts; Cards; Games; Reading groups; Prayer groups; Movies; Shopping trips; Dances/Social/Cultural gatherings.

Coshocton County Memorial Hospital
PO Box 330, 1460 Orange St, Coshocton, OH 43812
(614) 622-6411
Licensure Skilled care; Intermediate care. *Beds* Swing beds SNF/ICF 61. *Certified* Medicaid; Medicare.
Owner Nonprofit corp.

Coshocton Health Care Center
100 S Whitewoman St, Coshocton, OH 43812
(614) 622-1220
Admin Wayne E Derr. *Dir of Nursing* Kaye Burch RN.
Licensure Intermediate care; Alzheimer's care. *Beds* ICF 110. *Certified* Medicaid.
Owner Proprietary corp.
Admissions Requirements Minimum age 18; Medical examination; Physician's request.
Staff RNs 6 (ft), 7 (pt); LPNs 4 (ft), 3 (pt); Nurses' aides 23 (ft), 14 (pt); Activities coordinators 2 (ft), 2 (pt); Dietitians 1 (pt); Dentists 1 (pt).
Languages French, Spanish, German.
Facilities Dining room; Physical therapy room; Activities room; Chapel; Crafts room; Laundry room; Barber/Beauty shop; Library; 2 Private lounges; Whirlpool room.
Activities Arts & crafts; Cards; Games; Reading groups; Prayer groups; Movies; Shopping trips; Dances/Social/Cultural gatherings.

Jacob's Dwelling
25645 TR 36, Coshocton, OH 43812
(614) 824-3635
Licensure Intermediate care. *Beds* ICF 24. *Certified* Medicaid.
Owner Proprietary corp.

Covington

Covington Care Center
75 Mote Dr, Covington, OH 45318
(513) 473-2075, 473-2963 FAX
Admin J Michael Williams. *Dir of Nursing* Karin Collins RN. *Medical Dir* Dr Alka Shah.
Licensure Skilled care; Intermediate care. *Beds* Swing beds SNF/ICF 106. *Private Pay Patients* 40%. *Certified* Medicaid; Medicare.
Owner Nonprofit organization/foundation.
Admissions Requirements Medical examination.
Staff RNs; LPNs; Nurses' aides; Physical therapists; Dietitians.
Facilities Dining room; Physical therapy room; Activities room; Crafts room; Laundry room; Barber/Beauty shop; Library.
Activities Arts & crafts; Cards; Games; Reading groups; Prayer groups; Movies; Shopping trips; Dances/Social/Cultural gatherings; Intergenerational programs; Pet therapy.

Crestline

Crestline Nursing Home Inc
327 W Main St, Crestline, OH 43351
(419) 683-3255
Admin Cindy Weatherholtz LNHA. *Dir of Nursing* Anna Saxton. *Medical Dir* Chi H Yang MD.
Licensure Skilled care; Residential care; Alzheimer's care. *Beds* SNF 30; Residential care 14. *Private Pay Patients* 100%.
Owner Proprietary corp.
Admissions Requirements Medical examination; Physician's request.
Staff RNs 2 (ft), 1 (pt); LPNs 2 (ft), 1 (pt); Nurses' aides 2 (ft), 1 (pt); Physical therapists (consultant); Reality therapists (consultant); Recreational therapists 1 (ft), 1 (pt); Occupational therapists (consultant); Speech therapists (consultant); Activities coordinators 1 (ft), 1 (pt); Dietitians 1 (ft), 1 (pt); Ophthalmologists (consultant); Podiatrists; Audiologists (consultant).
Facilities Dining room; Activities room; Crafts room; Laundry room; Barber/Beauty shop; Private rooms; Outdoor recreation area.
Activities Arts & crafts; Cards; Games; Reading groups; Prayer groups; Movies; Shopping trips; Dances/Social/Cultural gatherings; Intergenerational programs; Pet therapy; Parties; Baby day; Annual friends family picnic.

Cridersville

Cridersville Nursing Home
603 E Main St, Cridersville, OH 45806
(419) 645-4468
Admin Wilma A Springer. *Dir of Nursing* Melinda Smith RN. *Medical Dir* Evelyn M Steere MD.
Licensure Intermediate care. *Beds* ICF 50. *Certified* Medicaid.
Owner Proprietary corp.
Admissions Requirements Medical examination; Physician's request.
Facilities Dining room; Activities room; Chapel; Crafts room; Laundry room; Barber/Beauty shop; Library.
Activities Arts & crafts; Cards; Games; Reading groups; Prayer groups; Movies; Shopping trips.

Crooksville

Ketcham's Nursing Home
RR 2, 14063 State Rte 37 E, Crooksville, OH 43731
(614) 342-2877

Licensure Intermediate care. *Beds* ICF 30. *Certified* Medicaid.
Owner Proprietary corp.

Cuyahoga Falls

Bethel Rest Home
2107 4th St, Cuyahoga Falls, OH 44221
(216) 928-5757
Licensure Rest home. *Beds* 18.
Owner Proprietary corp.

Cuyahoga Falls Country Place
2728 Bailey Rd, Cuyahoga Falls, OH 44221
(216) 929-4231
Medical Dir Walter R Hoffman DO.
Licensure Skilled care; Intermediate care. *Beds* SNF 27; Swing beds SNF/ICF 80. *Certified* Medicare.
Owner Proprietary corp.
Admissions Requirements Minimum age 21; Medical examination; Physician's request.
Staff Physicians 3 (pt); RNs 2 (ft), 10 (pt); LPNs 9 (ft), 3 (pt); Nurses' aides 29 (ft), 10 (pt); Physical therapists 1 (ft), 1 (pt); Recreational therapists 1 (ft); Speech therapists 1 (pt); Activities coordinators 1 (ft); Dietitians 1 (ft), 1 (pt); Ophthalmologists 1 (pt); Podiatrists 1 (pt); Dentists 1 (pt).
Facilities Dining room; Physical therapy room; Activities room; Crafts room; Laundry room; Barber/Beauty shop; Library.
Activities Arts & crafts; Cards; Games; Reading groups; Prayer groups; Movies; Shopping trips; Dances/Social/Cultural gatherings.

Fowler House
1770 2nd St, Cuyahoga Falls, OH 44223
(216) 920-1447
Licensure Intermediate care for mentally retarded. *Beds* ICF/MR 12. *Certified* Medicaid.
Owner Proprietary corp.

Twin Pines Retreat
PO Box 1688, 456 Seasons Rd, Cuyahoga Falls, OH 44224
(216) 688-5553
Licensure Intermediate care. *Beds* ICF 50. *Certified* Medicaid.
Owner Proprietary corp.

Dalton

Shady Lawn Home
15028 Old Lincolnway W, Dalton, OH 44618
(216) 828-2278
Medical Dir Dr Robert Cananne.
Licensure Skilled care; Intermediate care. *Beds* Swing beds SNF/ICF 160. *Certified* Medicaid; Medicare.
Owner Proprietary corp.
Admissions Requirements Medical examination.
Staff Physicians; RNs; LPNs; Nurses' aides; Physical therapists; Reality therapists; Recreational therapists; Speech therapists; Activities coordinators; Dietitians; Podiatrists; Dentists.
Facilities Dining room; Physical therapy room; Activities room; Crafts room; Laundry room; Barber/Beauty shop.
Activities Arts & crafts; Cards; Games; Reading groups; Prayer groups; Movies; Dances/Social/Cultural gatherings.

Danville

Morning View Care Center
25326 Snively Rd, Danville, OH 43014
(614) 599-6357, 599-5692 FAX
Admin Dixie Waite. *Dir of Nursing* Nancy George RN; Judy Mille RD. *Medical Dir* Dr John Tidyman.

Licensure Intermediate care. *Beds* ICF 42. *Private Pay Patients* 30%. *Certified* Medicaid.
Owner Proprietary corp.
Admissions Requirements Medical examination.
Staff RNs 4 (ft); LPNs 3 (ft), 2 (pt); Nurses' aides 12 (ft), 6 (pt); Activities coordinators 1 (ft); Dietitians 1 (pt).
Facilities Dining room; Activities room; Laundry room; Barber/Beauty shop; Library; 2 sitting rooms; Garden room.
Activities Arts & crafts; Cards; Games; Reading groups; Prayer groups; Movies; Shopping trips; Dances/Social/Cultural gatherings; Intergenerational programs; Pet therapy; Exercise groups.

Dayton

Alta Nursing Home Inc
PO Box 1336, 20 Livingston Ave, Dayton, OH 45401
(513) 253-4673, 258-8496 FAX
Admin Sol Augenbraun. *Dir of Nursing* Illa Rucker RN. *Medical Dir* James Nagle MD.
Licensure Skilled care; Intermediate care. *Beds* SNF 50; ICF 50. *Private Pay Patients* 28%. *Certified* Medicaid; Medicare.
Owner Proprietary corp.
Admissions Requirements Medical examination; Physician's request.
Staff Physicians 3 (ft); RNs 4 (ft); LPNs 9 (ft); Nurses' aides 35 (ft); Physical therapists 1 (ft); Reality therapists 1 (ft); Recreational therapists 1 (ft); Occupational therapists 2 (ft); Activities coordinators 1 (ft); Dietitians 1 (ft); Podiatrists 1 (ft).
Facilities Dining room; Physical therapy room; Activities room; Crafts room; Laundry room.
Activities Arts & crafts; Cards; Games; Reading groups; Prayer groups; Movies; Shopping trips; Dances/Social/Cultural gatherings; Intergenerational programs; Pet therapy.

Alternative Residences Inc—Regency Ridge Home
283 Regency Ridge, Dayton, OH 45459
(513) 228-2200
Licensure Intermediate care for mentally retarded. *Beds* ICF/MR 12. *Certified* Medicaid.
Owner Proprietary corp.

Barnett's Stilhaven Nursing Home
201 Central Ave, Dayton, OH 45406
(513) 223-2835
Admin Joe Barnett.
Medical Dir Vivek Agarwal MD.
Licensure Intermediate care; Retirement. *Beds* ICF 50. *Certified* Medicaid.
Owner Proprietary corp.
Admissions Requirements Minimum age 18; Medical examination.
Staff Physicians 1 (pt); RNs 1 (pt); LPNs 5 (ft), 2 (pt); Nurses' aides 20 (ft), 5 (pt); Activities coordinators 2 (ft), 2 (pt); Dietitians 1 (pt).
Facilities Dining room; Activities room; Chapel; Crafts room; Laundry room; Barber/Beauty shop; Enclosed patio with partial covered roof.
Activities Arts & crafts; Cards; Games; Reading groups; Prayer groups; Movies; Shopping trips; Dances/Social/Cultural gatherings.

Bethany Lutheran Village
6451 Far Hills Ave, Dayton, OH 45459
(513) 433-2110
Admin Donald E Claggett. *Dir of Nursing* Mary Jo Gunn RN. *Medical Dir* Fernando N Perez MD.
Licensure Skilled care; Intermediate care; Retirement. *Beds* Swing beds SNF/ICF 232. *Certified* Medicaid; Medicare.

Owner Proprietary corp.
Admissions Requirements Minimum age 60; Medical examination.
Staff RNs 13 (ft), 5 (pt); LPNs 9 (ft), 3 (pt); Nurses' aides 52 (ft), 22 (pt); Activities coordinators 1 (ft); Dietitians 1 (ft).
Affiliation Lutheran.
Facilities Dining room; Physical therapy room; Activities room; Chapel; Crafts room; Barber/Beauty shop; Library; Laundry done in-house.
Activities Arts & crafts; Cards; Games; Reading groups; Prayer groups; Movies; Shopping trips; Dances/Social/Cultural gatherings.

Catalpa Manor
3650 Klepinger Rd, Dayton, OH 45416
(513) 278-0663
Admin Florence Julian.
Medical Dir Dr Sugumaran.
Licensure Skilled care; Intermediate care. *Beds* Swing beds SNF/ICF 201. *Certified* Medicaid; Medicare.
Owner Proprietary corp (Unicare).
Admissions Requirements Medical examination.
Staff Physicians 20 (pt); RNs 6 (ft), 4 (pt); LPNs 15 (ft), 2 (pt); Nurses' aides 47 (ft), 24 (pt); Physical therapists 1 (pt); Speech therapists 1 (pt); Activities coordinators 3 (ft); Dietitians 1 (ft); Ophthalmologists 1 (pt); Podiatrists 1 (pt); Dentists 1 (pt); Rehabilitation aides 1 (ft).
Languages German.
Facilities Dining room; Physical therapy room; Activities room; Crafts room; Laundry room; Barber/Beauty shop.
Activities Arts & crafts; Cards; Games; Reading groups; Prayer groups; Movies; Shopping trips; Dances/Social/Cultural gatherings.

Crestview Nursing Home II
4381 Tonawanda Trail, Dayton, OH 45430
(513) 426-5033
Admin Esther L Hofferbert. *Dir of Nursing* Kay Llacera RN. *Medical Dir* Douglas Romer MD.
Licensure Skilled care; Intermediate care. *Beds* Swing beds SNF/ICF 102. *Certified* Medicaid; Medicare.
Owner Proprietary corp.
Admissions Requirements Medical examination.
Staff Physicians 2 (pt); RNs 5 (ft), 9 (pt); LPNs 1 (ft), 2 (pt); Nurses' aides 46 (ft), 5 (pt); Physical therapists 1 (pt); Recreational therapists 1 (pt); Speech therapists 1 (pt); Activities coordinators 1 (ft); Dietitians 1 (pt); Ophthalmologists 1 (pt); Podiatrists 1 (pt); Dentists 1 (pt).
Facilities Dining room; Physical therapy room; Activities room; Barber/Beauty shop.
Activities Arts & crafts; Cards; Games; Reading groups; Prayer groups; Dances/Social/Cultural gatherings; Bingo; Outings; Bowling; Religious services; Bible study; Special dinners; Exercise; Ceramics; Poetry group.

Dayton Health Care Center
652 Superior Ave, Dayton, OH 45407
(513) 228-7216
Licensure Intermediate care. *Beds* ICF 38. *Certified* Medicaid.
Owner Proprietary corp (Buckeye Family and Nursing Home).

Dayton Mental Health Center—Building 64
2611 Wayne Ave, Dayton, OH 45420
(513) 258-0440
Licensure Intermediate care for mentally retarded. *Beds* ICF/MR 20. *Certified* Medicaid.
Owner Publicly owned.

Eastview Manor Nursing Home
519 McLain St, Dayton, OH 45403
(513) 222-0823
Licensure Intermediate care. *Beds* ICF 24. *Certified* Medicaid.
Owner Proprietary corp (Buckeye Family and Nursing Home).

Echoing Valley Residential Home
7040 Union School House Rd, Dayton, OH 45424
(513) 237-7881, 237-0803 FAX
Admin Dan Swanson. *Dir of Nursing* Marlene Leonard RN. *Medical Dir* Vivek Agarwal.
Licensure Intermediate care for mentally retarded. *Beds* ICF/MR 36. *Private Pay Patients* 0%. *Certified* Medicaid.
Owner Nonprofit corp (Echoing Hills Village Inc).
Admissions Requirements Medical examination.
Staff Physicians 1 (pt); RNs 2 (ft), 1 (pt); LPNs 4 (ft), 2 (pt); Nurses' aides 26 (ft), 1 (pt); Physical therapists 1 (pt); Occupational therapists 1 (pt); Speech therapists 2 (pt); Activities coordinators 1 (ft); Dietitians 1 (pt); Podiatrists 1 (pt); Audiologists 1 (pt).
Facilities Dining room; Physical therapy room; Activities room; Crafts room; Laundry room.
Activities Arts & crafts; Cards; Games; Reading groups; Prayer groups; Movies; Shopping trips; Dances/Social/Cultural gatherings.

Echoing Woods Residential Home
5455 Salem Bend Dr, Dayton, OH 45426
(513) 854-5151
Admin Kent Dyer.
Medical Dir Phyllis Lane.
Licensure Intermediate care for mentally retarded. *Beds* ICF/MR 36. *Certified* Medicaid.
Owner Proprietary corp.
Admissions Requirements Minimum age 18; Medical examination; Physician's request.
Staff Physicians 1 (pt); LPNs 3 (ft), 3 (pt); Recreational therapists 1 (ft); Occupational therapists 1 (pt); Speech therapists 1 (pt); Dietitians 1 (pt); Ophthalmologists 1 (pt); Podiatrists 1 (pt).
Facilities Dining room; Physical therapy room; Activities room; Crafts room; Laundry room.
Activities Arts & crafts; Cards; Games; Reading groups; Prayer groups; Movies; Shopping trips; Dances/Social/Cultural gatherings.

Friendship Village
5790 Denlinger Rd, Dayton, OH 45426
(513) 837-5581
Licensure Skilled care. *Beds* SNF 97. *Certified* Medicare.
Owner Proprietary corp.

Glenn Haven Nursing Home
5205 N Main, Dayton, OH 45415
(513) 275-0791
Admin Deborah Hardy. *Dir of Nursing* Linda Lancione. *Medical Dir* V Agarwal MD.
Licensure Intermediate care. *Beds* ICF 34. *Private Pay Patients* 20%. *Certified* Medicaid.
Owner Privately owned.
Admissions Requirements Medical examination; Physician's request.
Staff RNs 1 (pt); LPNs 4 (ft), 3 (pt); Nurses' aides 13 (ft), 2 (pt); Activities coordinators 1 (ft); Dietitians 1 (pt).
Facilities Dining room; Activities room; Laundry room; Barber/Beauty shop.
Activities Arts & crafts; Cards; Games; Reading groups; Prayer groups; Movies; Shopping trips; Dances/Social/Cultural gatherings; Intergenerational programs; Pet therapy.

Grafton Oaks Nursing Center
405 Grafton Ave, Dayton, OH 45406
(513) 276-4040
Admin Helen Hamilton. *Dir of Nursing* Pat Kendrick RN. *Medical Dir* James Nagle MD.
Licensure Skilled care; Intermediate care. *Beds* Swing beds SNF/ICF 100. *Certified* Medicaid; Medicare.
Owner Proprietary corp.
Admissions Requirements Minimum age 18.
Staff Physicians 1 (ft), 1 (pt); RNs 1 (pt); LPNs 4 (ft); Nurses' aides 12 (ft), 2 (pt); Activities coordinators 1 (ft); Dietitians 1 (pt); Ophthalmologists 1 (pt); Social workers.
Facilities Dining room; Physical therapy room; Activities room; Crafts room; Laundry room; Barber/Beauty shop.
Activities Arts & crafts; Cards; Games; Reading groups; Prayer groups; Movies; Shopping trips; Dances/Social/Cultural gatherings; Intergenerational programs; Pet therapy.

Grandview Health Care Center
923 W Grand Ave, Dayton, OH 45407
(513) 278-6597
Medical Dir Dr O'Samkari.
Licensure Intermediate care. *Beds* ICF 24. *Certified* Medicaid.
Owner Proprietary corp (Buckeye Family and Nursing Home).
Admissions Requirements Females only; Medical examination.
Staff Physicians 2 (pt); RNs 1 (ft), 2 (pt); LPNs 3 (ft); Nurses' aides 8 (ft), 2 (pt); Physical therapists 1 (pt); Reality therapists 1 (pt); Recreational therapists 1 (pt); Activities coordinators 1 (ft); Dietitians 1 (pt); Ophthalmologists 1 (pt); Podiatrists 1 (pt); Audiologists 1 (pt); Dentists 1 (pt).
Facilities Dining room; Activities room; Laundry room.
Activities Arts & crafts; Cards; Games; Reading groups; Prayer groups; Movies; Shopping trips; Dances/Social/Cultural gatherings.

Heartland—Beavercreek
1974 N Fairfield Rd, Dayton, OH 45432
(513) 429-1106
Licensure Skilled care; Intermediate care. *Beds* Swing beds SNF/ICF 100. *Certified* Medicaid; Medicare.
Owner Proprietary corp (Health Care and Retirement Corp).

Hester Memorial Nursing Home
322 Park Dr, Dayton, OH 45410
(513) 223-5453
Admin Jim McPherson.
Medical Dir Dr James B Nogle.
Licensure Intermediate care. *Beds* ICF 45. *Certified* Medicaid.
Owner Proprietary corp.
Admissions Requirements Medical examination.
Affiliation Church of God.
Facilities Dining room; Activities room; Laundry room.
Activities Arts & crafts; Cards; Games; Reading groups; Prayer groups; Movies; Shopping trips; Dances/Social/Cultural gatherings.

Hickory Creek Nursing Center Inc
3421 Pinnacle Rd, Dayton, OH 45418
(513) 268-3488
Admin Joyce McGonigal. *Dir of Nursing* Patricia Yeary RN. *Medical Dir* Julia Lucente MD.
Licensure Skilled care; Intermediate care. *Beds* Swing beds SNF/ICF 150. *Private Pay Patients* 20%. *Certified* Medicaid; Medicare.
Owner Proprietary corp (Health Care Management Corp).
Admissions Requirements Minimum age 18; Medical examination.

Staff Physicians 4 (pt); RNs 9 (ft), 4 (pt); LPNs 15 (ft), 6 (pt); Nurses' aides 59 (ft), 10 (pt); Physical therapists 1 (pt); Occupational therapists 1 (pt); Speech therapists 1 (pt); Activities coordinators 2 (ft); Dietitians 1 (pt); Ophthalmologists 1 (pt); Podiatrists 1 (pt); Audiologists 1 (pt).
Facilities Dining room; Physical therapy room; Activities room; Crafts room; Laundry room; Barber/Beauty shop.
Activities Arts & crafts; Cards; Games; Reading groups; Prayer groups; Movies; Shopping trips; Dances/Social/Cultural gatherings; Intergenerational programs; Pet therapy.

Hill Top House Nursing Home Inc
437 Blackwood Ave, Dayton, OH 45403
(513) 253-8944
Licensure Skilled care; Intermediate care. *Beds* Swing beds SNF/ICF 63.
Owner Proprietary corp.

Jewish Home for Aged
4911 Covenant House Dr, Dayton, OH 45426
(513) 837-2651
Licensure Skilled care; Intermediate care. *Beds* Swing beds SNF/ICF 46. *Certified* Medicaid; Medicare.
Owner Proprietary corp.
Affiliation Jewish.
Facilities Dining room; Physical therapy room; Activities room; Chapel; Crafts room; Barber/Beauty shop.
Activities Arts & crafts; Cards; Games; Reading groups; Movies; Shopping trips; Dances/Social/Cultural gatherings.

King Tree Center
26055 Emery Rd No A, Dayton, OH 44128
(513) 278-0723
Admin Donald C Leine. *Dir of Nursing* Darlene Hartley RN. *Medical Dir* R Chunduri MD.
Licensure Skilled care; Intermediate care. *Beds* SNF 50; ICF 150. *Certified* Medicaid; Medicare.
Owner Proprietary corp.
Admissions Requirements Minimum age 16; Medical examination; Physician's request.
Staff Physicians 20 (pt); RNs 16 (ft); LPNs 10 (ft), 4 (pt); Nurses' aides 67 (ft); Physical therapists 1 (ft); Occupational therapists 1 (pt); Speech therapists 1 (pt); Activities coordinators 3 (ft); Dietitians 1 (pt); Ophthalmologists 1 (pt); Dentists 1 (pt).
Facilities Dining room; Physical therapy room; Activities room; Chapel; Crafts room; Laundry room; Barber/Beauty shop; Library.
Activities Arts & crafts; Cards; Games; Reading groups; Prayer groups; Movies; Shopping trips; Dances/Social/Cultural gatherings.

Linden Health Care Center
42 Linden Ave, Dayton, OH 45403
(513) 252-4711
Licensure Intermediate care. *Beds* ICF 25. *Certified* Medicaid.
Owner Proprietary corp.
Admissions Requirements Medical examination.
Staff Physicians 1 (pt); RNs 1 (pt); LPNs 2 (ft), 3 (pt); Nurses' aides 7 (ft), 3 (pt); Activities coordinators 1 (ft); Dietitians 1 (pt); Ophthalmologists 1 (pt); Podiatrists 1 (pt); Dentists 1 (pt).
Facilities Dining room; Laundry room.
Activities Arts & crafts; Cards; Games; Prayer groups; Movies; Shopping trips.

Mapleview Manor
1033 Grand Ave, Dayton, OH 45407
(513) 277-1281
Licensure Intermediate care for mentally retarded. *Beds* ICF/MR 22. *Certified* Medicaid.

Owner Proprietary corp (Buckeye Family and Nursing Home).

Maria-Joseph Center
4830 Salem Ave, Dayton, OH 45416
(513) 278-2692, 278-9016 FAX
Admin Bonnie G Langdon. *Dir of Nursing* Penny S Kenley RN. *Medical Dir* Mark J Weis MD; Pani Akuthota, Rehab.
Licensure Skilled care; Intermediate care; Independent living; Alzheimer's care. *Beds* SNF 124; ICF 260; Independent living 56. *Private Pay Patients* 60%. *Certified* Medicaid; Medicare.
Owner Nonprofit organization/foundation.
Admissions Requirements Medical examination.
Staff Physicians 1 (ft), 3 (pt); RNs 27 (ft), 11 (pt); LPNs 40 (ft), 6 (pt); Nurses' aides 114 (ft), 25 (pt); Physical therapists 1 (ft); Occupational therapists 1 (ft); Speech therapists 2 (pt); Activities coordinators 7 (ft), 3 (pt); Dietitians 1 (ft), 2 (pt); Ophthalmologists 1 (pt); Podiatrists 1 (pt); Audiologists 1 (pt).
Affiliation Roman Catholic.
Facilities Dining room; Physical therapy room; Activities room; Chapel; Crafts room; Laundry room; Barber/Beauty shop; Library.
Activities Arts & crafts; Cards; Games; Reading groups; Prayer groups; Movies; Shopping trips; Dances/Social/Cultural gatherings; Intergenerational programs; Pet therapy; Lifeline program.

McGills Nursing Home—South
15 Arnold Pl, Dayton, OH 45407
(513) 274-2447
Licensure Intermediate care. *Beds* ICF 30. *Certified* Medicaid.
Owner Proprietary corp.

Mercy Siena Woods
235 W Orchard Springs Dr, Dayton, OH 45415
(513) 278-8211, 278-9528 FAX
Admin Susan Hayes. *Dir of Nursing* Cheryl Bombok RN. *Medical Dir* Ramamohau Chunduri MD.
Licensure Intermediate care. *Beds* ICF 99. *Private Pay Patients* 49%. *Certified* Medicaid.
Owner Nonprofit organization/foundation (Sisters of Mercy).
Admissions Requirements Medical examination; Physician's request.
Staff RNs 7 (ft), 8 (pt); LPNs 2 (ft), 3 (pt); Nurses' aides 30 (ft), 15 (pt); Physical therapists 1 (pt); Occupational therapists 1 (pt); Activities coordinators 1 (ft); Dietitians 1 (pt); Podiatrists 1 (pt).
Facilities Dining room; Physical therapy room; Activities room; Chapel; Crafts room; Laundry room; Barber/Beauty shop; Library; Auditorium.
Activities Arts & crafts; Games; Reading groups; Prayer groups; Movies; Shopping trips; Dances/Social/Cultural gatherings; Intergenerational programs; Pet therapy; Sensory therapy.

Oakview Manor
34 Arnold Pl, Dayton, OH 45407
(513) 275-3711
Licensure Intermediate care for mentally retarded. *Beds* ICF/MR 19. *Certified* Medicaid.
Owner Proprietary corp.

Parkview Manor
250 Park Dr, Dayton, OH 45410
(513) 224-7906
Admin James Lauricella Jr. *Dir of Nursing* Judy McCullough RN. *Medical Dir* James Nagle MD.
Licensure Intermediate care; Rest home. *Beds* ICF 51; Rest home 14. *Certified* Medicaid.
Owner Proprietary corp.

Admissions Requirements Physician's request.
Staff RNs 1 (ft); LPNs 3 (ft), 2 (pt); Nurses'
aides 21 (ft), 5 (pt); Physical therapists 1
(pt); Activities coordinators 1 (pt); Dietitians
1 (pt).
Facilities Dining room; Activities room;
Laundry room; Barber/Beauty shop.
Activities Arts & crafts; Games; Reading
groups; Prayer groups; Movies; Shopping
trips; Exercise.

Rust-McGills Nursing Center
15 Arnold Pl, Dayton, OH 45407-2199
(513) 456-3640
Admin Flossie E McGill.
Medical Dir Flossie E McGill.
Licensure Skilled care; Intermediate care;
Retirement. *Beds* ICF 13; Swing beds SNF/
ICF 10.
Owner Proprietary corp.
Staff RNs 1 (pt); LPNs 3 (ft); Nurses' aides 8
(ft); Activities coordinators 1 (pt); Dietitians
1 (pt); Ophthalmologists 1 (pt); Dentists 1
(pt).
Facilities Dining room; Activities room;
Crafts room; Laundry room; Barber/Beauty
shop.
Activities Arts & crafts; Cards; Games;
Reading groups; Prayer groups; Shopping
trips.

Schulze Nursing Home
PO Box 557, 409 Forest Ave, Dayton, OH
45405
(513) 228-7143
Admin Robert Huff.
Medical Dir Lynne J Huff; Gary Collier.
Licensure Intermediate care; Alzheimer's care.
Beds ICF 35. *Certified* Medicaid.
Owner Proprietary corp.
Admissions Requirements Females only.
Staff RNs; LPNs; Nurses' aides; Activities
coordinators.
Facilities Dining room; Barber/Beauty shop.
Activities Arts & crafts; Cards; Games;
Reading groups; Prayer groups; Movies;
Shopping trips; Dances/Social/Cultural
gatherings.

Mary Scott Nursing Center
3109 Campus Dr, Dayton, OH 45406
(513) 278-0761
Medical Dir Dr Robert McConnell.
Licensure Intermediate care. *Beds* ICF 130.
Certified Medicaid.
Owner Proprietary corp (Health Care
Management).
Admissions Requirements Medical
examination.
Staff Physicians 1 (pt); RNs 4 (ft), 1 (pt);
LPNs 12 (ft), 1 (pt); Nurses' aides 40 (ft), 6
(pt); Activities coordinators 1 (ft); Dietitians
1 (ft).
Facilities Dining room; Physical therapy
room; Activities room; Crafts room; Laundry
room; Barber/Beauty shop; Library.
Activities Arts & crafts; Cards; Games;
Reading groups; Prayer groups; Movies;
Shopping trips; Dances/Social/Cultural
gatherings.

Stillwater Health Center
8100 N Main St, Dayton, OH 45415
(513) 890-0646
Admin Benton Wahl. *Dir of Nursing* Janet
Zykoski. *Medical Dir* Ceferino Cata MD.
Licensure Intermediate care; Intermediate care
for mentally retarded. *Beds* ICF 140; ICF/
MR 34. *Certified* Medicaid.
Owner Publicly owned.
Admissions Requirements Minimum age 0-18;
Medical examination.
Staff Physicians 1 (pt); RNs 4 (ft), 1 (pt);
LPNs 3 (ft); Nurses' aides 15 (ft), 9 (pt);
Physical therapists 1 (pt); Recreational
therapists 1 (ft); Occupational therapists 1
(pt); Speech therapists 2 (pt); Activities
coordinators 1 (ft); Dietitians 1 (ft).

Facilities Dining room; Physical therapy
room; Activities room; Laundry room.
Activities Arts & crafts; Cards; Games;
Reading groups; Prayer groups; Movies;
Shopping trips; Dances/Social/Cultural
gatherings; Exercise groups; Daily outside
activities.

Trinity Home
3218 Indian Ripple Rd, Dayton, OH 45440
(513) 426-8481
Dir of Nursing Charlotte Lynch RN. *Medical
Dir* Sherry Stanley MD.
Licensure Skilled care; Intermediate care; Rest
home. *Beds* Swing beds SNF/ICF 72; Rest
home 36. *Certified* Medicaid; Medicare.
Owner Nonprofit corp (United Church
Homes).
Admissions Requirements Minimum age 65;
Medical examination.
Staff Physicians; RNs; LPNs; Nurses' aides;
Physical therapists; Occupational therapists;
Speech therapists; Activities coordinators;
Dietitians.
Affiliation Church of Christ.
Facilities Dining room; Physical therapy
room; Activities room; Chapel; Crafts room;
Laundry room; Barber/Beauty shop; Library.
Activities Arts & crafts; Cards; Games;
Reading groups; Prayer groups; Movies;
Shopping trips; Dances/Social/Cultural
gatherings; Seasonal programs.

Washington Manor Nursing Center
7300 McEwen Rd, Dayton, OH 45459
(513) 433-3441
Licensure Skilled care; Intermediate care;
Retirement. *Beds* Swing beds SNF/ICF 178.
Certified Medicaid; Medicare.
Owner Proprietary corp.
Admissions Requirements Medical
examination; Physician's request.
Staff Physicians; RNs; LPNs; Nurses' aides;
Physical therapists; Occupational therapists;
Speech therapists; Activities coordinators;
Dietitians; Ophthalmologists; Dentists.
Facilities Dining room; Physical therapy
room; Activities room; Chapel; Crafts room;
Laundry room; Barber/Beauty shop; 2
lounges.
Activities Arts & crafts; Cards; Games; Prayer
groups; Movies; Dances/Social/Cultural
gatherings; Exercises; Bingo; Current events;
Music.

Widows Home of Dayton
50 S Findlay St, Dayton, OH 45403
(513) 252-1661, 252-7280
Admin Harvey S Klein Jr. *Dir of Nursing*
Dorothy Creekmore.
Licensure Skilled care; Intermediate care; Rest
home. *Beds* Swing beds SNF/ICF 14; Rest
home 30.
Owner Proprietary corp.
Admissions Requirements Minimum age 65;
Females only; Medical examination.
Staff LPNs 3 (ft), 3 (pt); Nurses' aides 8 (ft), 9
(pt); Dietitians 1 (pt).
Facilities Dining room; Activities room;
Chapel; Crafts room; Laundry room; Barber/
Beauty shop; Library.
Activities Arts & crafts; Cards; Games; Prayer
groups; Shopping trips; Dances/Social/
Cultural gatherings.

Yale Manor Nursing Home
35 Yale Ave, Dayton, OH 45406
(513) 276-5237
Licensure Intermediate care for mentally
retarded. *Beds* ICF/MR 42. *Certified*
Medicaid.
Owner Proprietary corp (Buckeye Family and
Nursing Home).

Deer Park

East Galbraith Nursing Home
3875 E Galbraith Rd, Deer Park, OH 45236
(513) 793-5220
Admin Frank Nathan. *Dir of Nursing* Sharon
Strunk RN. *Medical Dir* Dr Stuart Zakem.
Licensure Skilled care; Intermediate care. *Beds*
Swing beds SNF/ICF 91. *Certified* Medicaid;
Medicare.
Owner Proprietary corp.
Staff Physicians 1 (pt); RNs 2 (ft), 1 (pt);
LPNs 6 (ft), 2 (pt); Nurses' aides 15 (ft), 4
(pt); Physical therapists 1 (ft), 1 (pt);
Occupational therapists 1 (pt); Speech
therapists 1 (pt); Activities coordinators 3
(ft); Dietitians 1 (pt); Ophthalmologists 1
(pt); Podiatrists 1 (pt); Dentists 1 (pt).
Facilities Dining room; Physical therapy
room; Activities room; Chapel; Crafts room;
Laundry room; Barber/Beauty shop;
Multipurpose rooms.
Activities Arts & crafts; Cards; Games;
Reading groups; Prayer groups; Movies;
Shopping trips; Dances/Social/Cultural
gatherings.

Defiance

Defiance Health Care Center
1701 S Jefferson Ave, Defiance, OH 43512
(419) 782-7879
Admin M Wendy Hockley. *Dir of Nursing*
Lori Corressel. *Medical Dir* Dr William
Busteed.
Licensure Skilled care; Intermediate care. *Beds*
Swing beds SNF/ICF 51. *Private Pay
Patients* 35%. *Certified* Medicaid; Medicare.
Owner Proprietary corp (Health Resources
Development).
Admissions Requirements Minimum age 18;
Medical examination.
Staff Physicians 1 (pt); RNs 1 (pt); LPNs 4
(ft), 6 (pt); Nurses' aides 13 (ft), 13 (pt);
Physical therapists 1 (pt); Reality therapists
1 (ft); Recreational therapists 1 (pt);
Occupational therapists 1 (pt); Speech
therapists 1 (pt); Activities coordinators 1
(ft); Dietitians 1 (pt); Ophthalmologists 1
(pt); Podiatrists 1 (pt).
Facilities Dining room; Physical therapy
room; Activities room; Chapel; Crafts room;
Laundry room; Barber/Beauty shop; Library;
Gazebo.
Activities Arts & crafts; Cards; Games;
Reading groups; Prayer groups; Movies;
Shopping trips; Dances/Social/Cultural
gatherings; Van outings.

Glenwood Care Center
301 Glenwood Dr, Defiance, OH 43512
(419) 598-8383
Admin M Wendy Hockley. *Dir of Nursing*
Connie Bayless LPN. *Medical Dir* Dr Harry
Doyle.
Licensure Intermediate care; Alzheimer's care.
Beds ICF 50. *Private Pay Patients* 36%.
Certified Medicaid.
Owner Proprietary corp.
Admissions Requirements Minimum age 18;
Medical examination.
Staff Physicians 1 (pt); RNs 1 (pt); LPNs 5
(ft), 4 (pt); Nurses' aides 10 (ft), 12 (pt);
Physical therapists 1 (pt); Reality therapists
1 (pt); Recreational therapists 1 (ft);
Occupational therapists 1 (pt); Speech
therapists 1 (pt); Activities coordinators 1
(ft); Dietitians 1 (pt); Ophthalmologists 1
(pt); Podiatrists 1 (pt).
Facilities Dining room; Activities room;
Crafts room; Laundry room; Barber/Beauty
shop; Library.
Activities Arts & crafts; Cards; Games;
Reading groups; Prayer groups; Movies;
Shopping trips; Dances/Social/Cultural
gatherings; Intergenerational programs; Pet
therapy.

Leisure Oaks Convalescent Center
214 Harding St, Defiance, OH 43512
(419) 784-1014
Medical Dir John Forester Jr MD.
Licensure Skilled care; Intermediate care. *Beds* SNF 25; ICF 68. *Certified* Medicaid; Medicare.
Owner Nonprofit corp (Volunteers of America Care).
Admissions Requirements Medical examination; Physician's request.
Staff RNs 3 (ft), 8 (pt); LPNs 2 (ft), 8 (pt); Nurses' aides 20 (ft), 20 (pt); Physical therapists 1 (pt); Speech therapists 1 (pt); Activities coordinators 1 (pt); Dietitians 1 (pt); Podiatrists 1 (pt); Audiologists 1 (pt); Dentists 1 (pt).
Affiliation Volunteers of America.
Facilities Dining room; Physical therapy room; Activities room; Chapel; Crafts room; Laundry room; Barber/Beauty shop; Library.
Activities Arts & crafts; Cards; Games; Reading groups; Prayer groups; Movies; Shopping trips; Dances/Social/Cultural gatherings; Pet therapy.

Twin Rivers Nursing Care Center
395 Harding St, Defiance, OH 43512
(419) 784-1450
Medical Dir Dr John Fauster.
Licensure Skilled care; Intermediate care. *Beds* Swing beds SNF/ICF 100. *Certified* Medicaid; Medicare.
Owner Proprietary corp.
Admissions Requirements Medical examination.
Staff Physicians 1 (pt); RNs 2 (ft), 3 (pt); LPNs 2 (ft), 11 (pt); Nurses' aides 15 (ft), 29 (pt); Physical therapists 1 (pt); Speech therapists 1 (pt); Activities coordinators 1 (ft), 1 (pt); Dietitians 1 (ft); Podiatrists 1 (pt); Dentists 1 (pt).
Facilities Dining room; Physical therapy room; Activities room; Laundry room; Barber/Beauty shop; Library.
Activities Arts & crafts; Cards; Games; Reading groups; Movies; Shopping trips; Dances/Social/Cultural gatherings.

Delaware

Delaware Court Inc
4 New Market Dr, Delaware, OH 43015
(614) 369-6400
Licensure Skilled care; Intermediate care; Rest home. *Beds* Swing beds SNF/ICF 75; Rest home 25. *Certified* Medicaid; Medicare.
Owner Proprietary corp.

Delaware Park Care Center
2270 Warrensburg Rd, Delaware, OH 43015
(614) 369-9614
Admin W Robert Huffman. *Dir of Nursing* Rosanna Crim RN. *Medical Dir* Robert Gnade MD.
Licensure Skilled care; Intermediate care. *Beds* Swing beds SNF/ICF 117. *Certified* Medicaid; Medicare.
Owner Proprietary corp (Arbor Health Care).
Admissions Requirements Medical examination.
Staff Physicians; RNs; LPNs; Nurses' aides; Physical therapists; Recreational therapists; Occupational therapists; Speech therapists; Activities coordinators; Ophthalmologists.
Facilities Dining room; Physical therapy room; Activities room; Laundry room; Barber/Beauty shop; Private dining room; Rehab dining room.
Activities Arts & crafts; Cards; Games; Reading groups; Prayer groups; Movies; Shopping trips; Dances/Social/Cultural gatherings.

Evergreen Manor
36 Griswold Dr, Delaware, OH 43015
(614) 362-6031

Admin Merry Linn. *Dir of Nursing* Sharon Dendinger. *Medical Dir* Dr Shivashanker.
Licensure Intermediate care. *Beds* ICF 34. *Private Pay Patients* 5%. *Certified* Medicaid.
Owner Proprietary corp (Alpha Nursing Homes Inc).
Admissions Requirements Medical examination; Physician's request.
Staff LPNs 5 (ft); Nurses' aides 10 (ft); Activities coordinators 1 (ft).
Facilities Dining room; Activities room; Laundry room.
Activities Arts & crafts; Cards; Games; Movies; Shopping trips; Dances/Social/Cultural gatherings; Pet therapy; Religious services.

Sarah Moore Home Inc
47 E William St, Delaware, OH 43015
(614) 362-9641
Licensure Intermediate care. *Beds* ICF 32. *Certified* Medicaid.
Owner Proprietary corp.

Sunny Vee Nursing Home Inc
54 W Lincoln Ave, Delaware, OH 43015
(614) 363-1587
Licensure Skilled care; Intermediate care. *Beds* Swing beds SNF/ICF 56. *Certified* Medicaid; Medicare.
Owner Proprietary corp.

Wintersong Village of Delaware
478 S Sandusky St, Delaware, OH 43015
(614) 369-8741
Admin Michael L Daffin.
Medical Dir Linda Hinos.
Licensure Intermediate care. *Beds* ICF 50. *Certified* Medicaid.
Owner Proprietary corp.
Staff Physicians; RNs; LPNs; Nurses' aides; Activities coordinators; Dietitians.
Facilities Dining room; Activities room; Laundry room; Barber/Beauty shop.
Activities Arts & crafts; Cards; Games; Reading groups; Movies; Dances/Social/Cultural gatherings.

Delphos

Sarah Jane Chambers Geriatric Center
328 W 2nd, Delphos, OH 45833
(419) 695-1921
Admin Virginia Christen. *Dir of Nursing* Esther Miller RN. *Medical Dir* Walter W Wolery MD.
Licensure Intermediate care. *Beds* ICF 50. *Private Pay Patients* 60%. *Certified* Medicaid.
Owner Proprietary corp (Arnold C Dienstberger Foundation Inc).
Admissions Requirements Minimum age 18.
Staff RNs 10 (pt); LPNs 3 (pt); Nurses' aides 8 (ft), 23 (pt); Activities coordinators 1 (ft), 1 (pt); Dietitians 3 (ft), 7 (pt).
Facilities Dining room; Activities room; Laundry room; Barber/Beauty shop.
Activities Arts & crafts; Cards; Games; Reading groups; Prayer groups; Movies.

Delphos Memorial Home
PO Box 334, 1425 E Fifth St, Delphos, OH 45833
(419) 695-2871, 692-4242
Admin Virginia Christen. *Dir of Nursing* Sharon Gengler RN. *Medical Dir* Walter W Wolery MD.
Licensure Intermediate care. *Beds* ICF 100. *Certified* Medicaid.
Owner Nonprofit organization/foundation.
Admissions Requirements Minimum age 18.
Staff RNs 4 (ft), 9 (pt); LPNs 2 (ft), 7 (pt); Nurses' aides 25 (ft), 26 (pt); Activities coordinators 1 (ft), 3 (pt).
Facilities Dining room; Activities room; Laundry room; Barber/Beauty shop.
Activities Arts & crafts; Cards; Games; Reading groups; Prayer groups; Movies.

Dennison

Charity Nursing Facility
509 Grant St, Dennison, OH 44621
(216) 339-4544
Licensure Intermediate care. *Beds* ICF 18. *Certified* Medicaid.
Owner Proprietary corp.

Deshler

Oak Grove Nursing Home Inc
620 E Water St, Deshler, OH 43516
(419) 278-6921
Admin Sally Hurles. *Dir of Nursing* Sue Stover RN. *Medical Dir* Mikal Moga DO.
Licensure Intermediate care; Retirement. *Beds* ICF 66; Retirement 5. *Private Pay Patients* 35%. *Certified* Medicaid.
Owner Proprietary corp (Northwestern Service Corp).
Admissions Requirements Minimum age 16.
Staff RNs 1 (ft), 1 (pt); LPNs 6 (ft), 4 (pt); Nurses' aides 11 (ft), 19 (pt); Activities coordinators 1 (ft), 1 (pt); Dietitians 1 (pt).
Facilities Dining room; Activities room; Chapel; Crafts room; Laundry room; Barber/Beauty shop; Library; 4 outside covered patios.
Activities Arts & crafts; Cards; Games; Reading groups; Prayer groups; Movies; Shopping trips; Intergenerational programs; Pet therapy; Van rides.

Dover

Country Club Center
860 Iron Ave, Dover, OH 44622
(216) 343-5568
Admin Richard L Morris. *Dir of Nursing* Constance Ivan RN. *Medical Dir* Dr Phillip Doughten.
Licensure Skilled care; Intermediate care; Independent living. *Beds* Swing beds SNF/ICF 72; Independent living apts 36. *Certified* Medicaid; Medicare.
Owner Proprietary corp.
Admissions Requirements Minimum age 55.
Staff RNs 3 (ft), 2 (pt); LPNs 5 (ft), 4 (pt); Nurses' aides 20 (ft), 7 (pt); Recreational therapists 1 (ft); Activities coordinators 1 (ft); Dietitians 1 (pt).
Facilities Dining room; Physical therapy room; Activities room; Crafts room; Laundry room; Barber/Beauty shop.
Activities Arts & crafts; Cards; Games; Reading groups; Prayer groups; Movies; Shopping trips; Dances/Social/Cultural gatherings; Intergenerational programs; Pet therapy.

Hennis Care Centre
1720 Cross St, Dover, OH 44622
(216) 364-8849
Licensure Intermediate care; Rest home. *Beds* ICF 103; Rest home 50. *Certified* Medicaid.
Owner Proprietary corp.

Horizons of Tuscarawas & Carroll Counties Inc
417 N Tuscarawas Ave, Dover, OH 44622
(216) 364-5415
Admin Janet E Watts.
Medical Dir Brenda Gallion.
Licensure Intermediate care for mentally retarded. *Beds* ICF/MR 12. *Certified* Medicaid.
Owner Nonprofit corp.
Admissions Requirements Minimum age 18; Medical examination.
Staff RNs 1 (pt); LPNs 3 (pt); Nurses' aides 5 (ft), 25 (pt); Physical therapists 1 (pt); Recreational therapists 1 (pt); Occupational therapists 1 (pt); Speech therapists 1 (pt); Activities coordinators 1 (ft); Dietitians 1 (pt); Podiatrists 1 (pt).

Facilities Dining room; Activities room; Laundry room.
Activities Arts & crafts; Cards; Games; Reading groups; Prayer groups; Movies; Shopping trips; Dances/Social/Cultural gatherings; Dining out.

New Dawn Health Care & Retirement Center
865 E Iron Ave, Dover, OH 44622
(216) 343-5521
Admin Dan Hershberger. *Dir of Nursing* Mildred Weston RN. *Medical Dir* Dr Paul McFadden.
Licensure Intermediate care; Rest home. *Beds* ICF 101; Rest home 56. *Certified* Medicaid.
Owner Proprietary corp.
Admissions Requirements Medical examination.
Staff Physicians 1 (pt); RNs 2 (ft), 8 (pt); LPNs 1 (ft), 5 (pt); Nurses' aides 6 (ft), 42 (pt); Activities coordinators 1 (ft), 1 (pt); Medical records 1 (pt).
Facilities Dining room; Physical therapy room; Activities room; Chapel; Crafts room; Laundry room; Barber/Beauty shop; In-service room.
Activities Arts & crafts; Cards; Games; Reading groups; Prayer groups; Movies; Shopping trips; Dances/Social/Cultural gatherings.

Park Village Health Care Center
1525 Crater Ave, Dover, OH 44622
(216) 364-4436
Admin Robert O'Donnell.
Licensure Intermediate care. *Beds* ICF 100. *Certified* Medicaid.
Owner Proprietary corp.
Admissions Requirements Minimum age 18; Physician's request.
Facilities Dining room; Activities room; Crafts room; Laundry room; Barber/Beauty shop.
Activities Arts & crafts; Cards; Games; Reading groups; Prayer groups; Movies; Shopping trips; Dances/Social/Cultural gatherings.

Doylestown

Doylestown Health Care Center
95 Black Dr, Doylestown, OH 44230
(216) 658-2061
Admin Richard E Nace. *Dir of Nursing* Victoria Overton. *Medical Dir* Phillip N Gilcrest MD.
Licensure Skilled care; Intermediate care. *Beds* Swing beds SNF/ICF 100. *Certified* Medicaid; Medicare.
Owner Proprietary corp.
Staff Physicians; RNs; LPNs; Nurses' aides; Physical therapists; Occupational therapists; Speech therapists; Activities coordinators; Dietitians; Podiatrists; Audiologists.
Facilities Dining room; Physical therapy room; Activities room; Chapel; Crafts room; Laundry room; Barber/Beauty shop; Library.
Activities Arts & crafts; Cards; Games; Reading groups; Prayer groups; Movies; Shopping trips; Dances/Social/Cultural gatherings; Intergenerational programs; Pet therapy.

Sara Lee Nursing Home Inc
140 Wall Rd, Doylestown, OH 44230
(216) 336-3600
Admin Roger Myers. *Dir of Nursing* Amy Steele. *Medical Dir* P L Gilcrest MD.
Licensure Intermediate care. *Beds* ICF 48. *Private Pay Patients* 20%. *Certified* Medicaid.
Owner Proprietary corp.
Admissions Requirements Minimum age 18.
Staff Physicians; RNs; LPNs; Nurses' aides; Physical therapists; Speech therapists; Activities coordinators; Dietitians; Podiatrists; Audiologists.

Facilities Dining room; Activities room; Crafts room; Laundry room; Barber/Beauty shop.
Activities Arts & crafts; Cards; Games; Reading groups; Prayer groups; Movies; Shopping trips; Intergenerational programs; Pet therapy.

Dublin

Friendship Village of Dublin Health Center
6000 Riverside Dr, Dublin, OH 43017
(614) 764-1600
Licensure Skilled care; Intermediate care. *Beds* Swing beds SNF/ICF 60. *Certified* Medicaid; Medicare.
Owner Proprietary corp.

East Cleveland

Ambassador Nursing Center
1835 Belmore Rd, East Cleveland, OH 44112
(216) 268-3611, 761-1322 FAX
Admin Robert F Geyer. *Dir of Nursing* Carolyn Jackson BSN. *Medical Dir* Basil Waldbaum MD.
Licensure Skilled care; Intermediate care. *Beds* SNF 54; ICF 100. *Certified* Medicaid; Medicare.
Owner Proprietary corp (Care Services Assoc).
Admissions Requirements Medical examination.
Staff Physicians 5 (pt); RNs 2 (ft), 10 (pt); LPNs 18 (ft), 12 (pt); Nurses' aides 50 (ft), 15 (pt); Physical therapists; Occupational therapists 1 (pt); Speech therapists 1 (pt); Activities coordinators 1 (ft); Dietitians 2 (pt).
Facilities Dining room; Physical therapy room; Activities room; Crafts room; Laundry room; Barber/Beauty shop.
Activities Arts & crafts; Cards; Games; Reading groups; Prayer groups; Movies; Shopping trips; Dances/Social/Cultural gatherings.

Eastern Star Home of Cuyahoga County
2114 Noble Rd, East Cleveland, OH 44112
(216) 761-0170
Licensure Intermediate care. *Beds* ICF 81. *Certified* Medicaid.
Owner Proprietary corp.
Affiliation Order of Eastern Star.

A M McGregor Home
14900 Terrace Rd, East Cleveland, OH 44112
(216) 851-8200
Admin Carol A Marks CFACHCA. *Dir of Nursing* Shirley A Baker RNC. *Medical Dir* Richard Christie MD.
Licensure Intermediate care; Rest home. *Beds* ICF 70; Rest home 30. *Private Pay Patients* 4%.
Owner Nonprofit organization/foundation.
Admissions Requirements Minimum age 65; Medical examination.
Staff Physicians; RNs; LPNs; Nurses' aides; Physical therapists; Recreational therapists; Occupational therapists; Speech therapists; Activities coordinators; Dietitians; Ophthalmologists; Podiatrists; Audiologists.
Facilities Dining room; Physical therapy room; Activities room; Chapel; Crafts room; Laundry room; Barber/Beauty shop; Library.
Activities Arts & crafts; Cards; Games; Reading groups; Prayer groups; Movies; Shopping trips; Dances/Social/Cultural gatherings; Intergenerational programs; Pet therapy.

East Liverpool

Robert E Boyce Pavilion
425 W 5th St, East Liverpool, OH 43920
(216) 385-7200

Admin Melvin Creely. *Dir of Nursing* Sandra Bonitatibus BSN CNA. *Medical Dir* Dr Janis Lauva.
Licensure Skilled care. *Beds* SNF 20. *Private Pay Patients* 0%. *Certified* Medicaid; Medicare.
Owner Proprietary corp.
Admissions Requirements Minimum age 18.
Staff Physicians 10 (ft); RNs 4 (ft), 3 (pt); LPNs 1 (ft), 4 (pt); Nurses' aides 8 (ft), 2 (pt); Physical therapists 1 (ft); Recreational therapists 1 (ft); Occupational therapists 1 (ft); Speech therapists 1 (ft); Activities coordinators 1 (ft); Dietitians 1 (ft); Ophthalmologists 1 (pt); Podiatrists 1 (pt).
Facilities Dining room; Physical therapy room; Activities room.
Activities Arts & crafts; Cards; Games; Reading groups; Prayer groups; Pet therapy.

Convalescent Center 2
701 Armstrong Ln, East Liverpool, OH 43920
(216) 385-5212
Admin Geraldine Adkins. *Dir of Nursing* Joan Covert RN. *Medical Dir* Dr William Horger.
Licensure Intermediate care. *Beds* ICF 50.
Owner Proprietary corp.

East Liverpool Convalescent Center
709 Armstrong Ln, East Liverpool, OH 43920
(216) 385-3600
Licensure Intermediate care. *Beds* ICF 60. *Certified* Medicaid.
Owner Proprietary corp.

East Liverpool Extended Care Center
430 W 5th St, East Liverpool, OH 43920
(216) 385-0516
Admin Peter Visnic. *Dir of Nursing* Dorothy White RN. *Medical Dir* Janis Lauva MD.
Licensure Intermediate care. *Beds* ICF 50. *Private Pay Patients* 45%. *Certified* Medicaid.
Owner Proprietary corp.
Admissions Requirements Minimum age 14; Medical examination; Physician's request.
Staff Physicians 1 (pt); RNs 3 (ft), 2 (pt); LPNs 4 (ft); Nurses' aides 16 (ft), 6 (pt); Physical therapists 1 (pt); Occupational therapists 1 (pt); Speech therapists 1 (pt); Activities coordinators 1 (ft); Dietitians 1 (pt).
Facilities Dining room; Physical therapy room; Activities room; Laundry room; Barber/Beauty shop; TV lounges; Patio.
Activities Arts & crafts; Cards; Games; Reading groups; Prayer groups; Movies.

Nentwick Convalescent Home Inc
500 Selfridge St, East Liverpool, OH 43920
(216) 386-5594
Medical Dir Dr William Sarger.
Licensure Intermediate care. *Beds* ICF 100. *Certified* Medicaid.
Owner Proprietary corp.
Admissions Requirements Medical examination.
Staff Physicians 1 (pt); RNs 6 (ft); LPNs 4 (ft); Nurses' aides 35 (ft), 4 (pt); Physical therapists 1 (pt); Occupational therapists 1 (pt); Speech therapists 1 (pt); Activities coordinators 3 (ft); Dietitians 1 (pt); Podiatrists 1 (pt); Audiologists 1 (pt); Dentists 1 (pt).
Facilities Dining room; Physical therapy room; Activities room; Chapel; Crafts room; Laundry room; Barber/Beauty shop; Library; Courtyard; Whirlpool baths.
Activities Arts & crafts; Cards; Games; Reading groups; Prayer groups; Movies; Shopping trips; Dances/Social/Cultural gatherings; Ceramics; Newspaper; Leathercraft; Exercise groups; Resident council; Resident dietary support group.

Ross Nursing Home
945 Ambrose Ave, East Liverpool, OH 43920
(216) 385-6623

Medical Dir Dr William Horger.
Licensure Intermediate care. *Beds* ICF 50.
  Certified Medicaid.
Owner Proprietary corp.
Admissions Requirements Medical
  examination; Physician's request.
Staff Physicians 1 (ft), 3 (pt); RNs 1 (ft), 1
  (pt); LPNs 7 (ft); Nurses' aides 20 (ft), 6
  (pt); Recreational therapists 1 (ft); Activities
  coordinators 1 (ft); Dietitians 2 (pt).
Facilities Dining room; Activities room;
  Laundry room.
Activities Arts & crafts; Games; Prayer groups;
  Shopping trips.

Eaton

Governor Harris Homestead
310 N Cherry St, Eaton, OH 45320
(513) 456-5120
Admin Randall Blough. *Dir of Nursing* Linda
  Blough. *Medical Dir* Mark Vosler DO.
Licensure Intermediate care. *Beds* ICF 27.
  Certified Medicaid.
Owner Proprietary corp.
Admissions Requirements Minimum age 60;
  Medical examination; Physician's request.
Staff RNs 1 (pt); LPNs 4 (ft), 2 (pt); Nurses'
  aides 9 (ft), 3 (pt); Activities coordinators 2
  (pt).
Facilities Dining room; Barber/Beauty shop.
Activities Arts & crafts; Cards; Games;
  Reading groups; Prayer groups; Movies;
  Shopping trips; Dances/Social/Cultural
  gatherings; Pets.

Heartland of Eaton
515 S Maple St Ext, Eaton, OH 45320
(513) 456-5537
Admin David Gray.
Medical Dir Richard Siehl DO.
Licensure Skilled care; Intermediate care;
  Alzheimer's care. *Beds* Swing beds SNF/ICF
  100. *Certified* Medicaid; Medicare.
Owner Proprietary corp (Health Care and
  Retirement Corp).
Admissions Requirements Minimum age 35;
  Medical examination; Physician's request.
Staff Physicians 1 (pt); RNs 3 (ft), 3 (pt);
  LPNs 3 (ft), 8 (pt); Nurses' aides 29 (ft), 11
  (pt); Physical therapists 1 (pt); Occupational
  therapists 1 (pt); Speech therapists 1 (pt);
  Activities coordinators 2 (pt); Dietitians 1
  (ft).
Facilities Dining room; Physical therapy
  room; Activities room; Barber/Beauty shop.
Activities Arts & crafts; Cards; Games;
  Reading groups; Shopping trips; Dances/
  Social/Cultural gatherings; Fair; Pork
  festival; Picnics; Rock 'n roll jamboree;
  Flower arranging; Bible study; Worship
  services.

Oak Lawn Manor
120 N Cherry St, Eaton, OH 45320
(513) 456-7167
Licensure Intermediate care. *Beds* ICF 34.
  Certified Medicaid.
Owner Proprietary corp.
Staff RNs 1 (pt); LPNs 3 (ft), 3 (pt); Nurses'
  aides 6 (ft), 4 (pt); Activities coordinators 1
  (pt).
Facilities Dining room; Activities room;
  Crafts room; Laundry room.
Activities Arts & crafts; Cards; Games;
  Reading groups; Prayer groups; Movies;
  Shopping trips; Dances/Social/Cultural
  gatherings.

Edgerton

Park View Nursing Center
US Rte 6 W, Edgerton, OH 43517
(419) 298-2321
Medical Dir Dr R Meyer.

Licensure Skilled care; Intermediate care. *Beds*
  SNF 25; ICF 75. *Certified* Medicaid;
  Medicare.
Owner Proprietary corp.
Admissions Requirements Medical
  examination.
Staff RNs 3 (ft), 1 (pt); LPNs 3 (ft), 6 (pt);
  Nurses' aides 24 (ft), 2 (pt); Physical
  therapists 1 (pt); Activities coordinators 2
  (ft); Dietitians 1 (pt); Podiatrists 1 (pt).
Facilities Dining room; Physical therapy
  room; Activities room; Laundry room;
  Barber/Beauty shop.
Activities Arts & crafts; Cards; Games;
  Reading groups; Prayer groups; Movies;
  Shopping trips; Dances/Social/Cultural
  gatherings.

Elyria

Elyria United Methodist Home
807 West Ave, Elyria, OH 44035
(216) 323-3395
Admin Roger W Turnau. *Dir of Nursing* Mary
  Tompos. *Medical Dir* Roger L Baldoza MD.
Licensure Skilled care; Intermediate care;
  Retirement. *Beds* Swing beds SNF/ICF 209.
  Certified Medicaid; Medicare.
Owner Nonprofit organization/foundation.
Admissions Requirements Minimum age 65;
  Medical examination.
Staff Physicians 6 (pt); RNs 7 (ft), 7 (pt);
  LPNs 27 (ft), 19 (pt); Nurses' aides 80 (ft),
  14 (pt); Physical therapists 1 (pt);
  Recreational therapists 1 (pt); Occupational
  therapists 1 (pt); Speech therapists 1 (pt);
  Activities coordinators 3 (ft); Dietitians 1
  (ft); Ophthalmologists 1 (pt); Dentists 1 (pt).
Affiliation Methodist.
Facilities Dining room; Physical therapy
  room; Activities room; Chapel; Crafts room;
  Laundry room; Barber/Beauty shop; Library;
  Kitchen/Lounge; Store.
Activities Arts & crafts; Cards; Games;
  Reading groups; Prayer groups; Movies;
  Shopping trips; Dances/Social/Cultural
  gatherings; Support groups; Cooking &
  baking; Mens club.

J Ferry Nursing Home
1015 Middle Ave, Elyria, OH 44035
(216) 323-2892
Admin Nancy A Comer. *Dir of Nursing*
  Bernadene Ulichney. *Medical Dir* Dr
  Viswanth.
Licensure Intermediate care. *Beds* ICF 26.
  Certified Medicaid.
Owner Proprietary corp (Altercare Inc).
Admissions Requirements Physician's request.
Staff Physicians 3 (pt); RNs 1 (pt); LPNs 4
  (ft), 1 (pt); Nurses' aides 12 (ft); Physical
  therapists; Activities coordinators 1 (pt);
  Activities coordinators 1 (pt); Dietitians.
Facilities Dining room.
Activities Arts & crafts; Cards; Games; Prayer
  groups; Movies; Pet therapy.

Ohio Residential Services Inc—Elyria
1243, 1267, 1271 East Ave, Elyria, OH 44035
(216) 322-0720
Licensure Intermediate care for mentally
  retarded. *Beds* ICF/MR 20. *Certified*
  Medicaid.
Owner Proprietary corp.

Palm Crest East Nursing Home
1251 East Ave, Elyria, OH 44035
(216) 322-0726, 322-2810 FAX
Admin Barbara Chadwick. *Dir of Nursing*
  Anna Marie Harrison. *Medical Dir* T C Lin
  MD.
Licensure Intermediate care; Intermediate care
  for mentally retarded. *Beds* ICF 30; ICF/MR
  20. *Private Pay Patients* 1%. *Certified*
  Medicaid.
Owner Proprietary corp.
Admissions Requirements Medical
  examination; Physician's request.

Staff RNs 1 (ft), 1 (pt); LPNs 3 (ft), 3 (pt);
  Nurses' aides 12 (ft), 12 (pt); Activities
  coordinators 1 (ft); Dietitians (consultant);
  Podiatrists (consultant).
Facilities Dining room; Activities room.
Activities Arts & crafts; Cards; Games;
  Reading groups; Prayer groups; Movies;
  Shopping trips; Dances/Social/Cultural
  gatherings; Intergenerational programs; Pet
  therapy; Outside activities.

Palm Crest Nursing Home
221 West Ave, Elyria, OH 44035
(216) 322-2525
Admin Barbara Chadwick. *Dir of Nursing*
  Anna Marie Harrison. *Medical Dir* T C Lin
  MD.
Licensure Intermediate care. *Beds* ICF 50.
  Private Pay Patients 0%. *Certified* Medicaid.
Owner Proprietary corp.
Admissions Requirements Medical
  examination; Physician's request.
Staff LPNs 5 (ft), 2 (pt); Nurses' aides 12 (ft),
  5 (pt); Activities coordinators (consultant);
  Dietitians 1 (ft); Podiatrists (consultant).
Facilities Dining room; Activities room.
Activities Arts & crafts; Cards; Games;
  Reading groups; Prayer groups; Movies;
  Shopping trips; Dances/Social/Cultural
  gatherings; Intergenerational programs; Pet
  therapy; Outside activities.

Englewood

Englewood Manor Inc
20 Union Blvd, Englewood, OH 45322
(513) 836-5143
Admin James A Lauricella. *Dir of Nursing*
  Geneva Brunk RN. *Medical Dir* Willard C
  Clark MD.
Licensure Skilled care; Intermediate care. *Beds*
  Swing beds SNF/ICF 80. *Private Pay*
  Patients 36%. *Certified* Medicaid; Medicare.
Owner Proprietary corp.
Admissions Requirements Medical
  examination.
Staff Physicians 1 (pt); RNs 2 (ft), 1 (pt);
  LPNs 8 (ft), 2 (pt); Nurses' aides 37 (ft);
  Physical therapists 1 (pt); Speech therapists
  1 (pt); Activities coordinators 2 (ft);
  Dietitians 1 (pt); Podiatrists 1 (pt).
Facilities Dining room; Physical therapy
  room; Activities room; Crafts room; Laundry
  room; Barber/Beauty shop; Library.
Activities Arts & crafts; Cards; Games;
  Reading groups; Prayer groups; Movies;
  Shopping trips; Intergenerational programs;
  Pet therapy.

Grace Brethren Village
1010 Taywood Rd, Englewood, OH 45322
(513) 836-4011
Admin Joseph Lefkovitz NHA. *Dir of Nursing*
  Pam Jones RN.
Licensure Intermediate care; Retirement
  living. *Beds* ICF 50; Retirement living 76.
  Private Pay Patients 100%.
Owner Nonprofit corp.
Admissions Requirements Minimum age 65;
Staff RNs 2 (ft), 1 (pt); LPNs 3 (ft), 3 (pt);
  Nurses' aides 8 (ft), 9 (pt); Activities
  coordinators 1 (ft); Dietitians 1 (pt).
Facilities Dining room; Activities room;
  Chapel; Crafts room; Barber/Beauty shop;
  Library.
Activities Arts & crafts; Cards; Games; Prayer
  groups; Movies; Dances/Social/Cultural
  gatherings.

Euclid

Brae View Manor Health Care Facility
20611 Euclid Ave, Euclid, OH 44117
(800) 872-2937, (216) 486-9300, 486-2603
  FAX
Admin Lisa A Arbuckle. *Dir of Nursing* Terry
  Blazak. *Medical Dir* Dr Terrance Isakov.

Licensure Skilled care; Intermediate care. *Beds* SNF 69; ICF 161. *Certified* Medicaid; Medicare.
Owner Proprietary corp.
Admissions Requirements Minimum age 45.
Staff Physicians 5 (ft); RNs 4 (ft), 2 (pt); LPNs 8 (ft), 5 (pt); Nurses' aides 35 (ft), 8 (pt); Physical therapists 1 (ft); Recreational therapists 1 (ft); Occupational therapists 1 (ft), 1 (pt); Speech therapists 1 (pt); Activities coordinators 1 (ft); Dietitians 1 (ft); Ophthalmologists 1 (pt); Podiatrists 1 (pt); Audiologists 1 (pt).
Facilities Dining room; Physical therapy room; Activities room; Crafts room; Laundry room; Barber/Beauty shop.
Activities Arts & crafts; Cards; Games; Prayer groups; Movies; Shopping trips; Dances/ Social/Cultural gatherings.

Cuy-La Home
1691 Hillandale Dr, Euclid, OH 44132
(216) 731-2690
Licensure Intermediate care. *Beds* ICF 33. *Certified* Medicaid.
Owner Proprietary corp.

Euclid General Hospital
E 185th St & Lake Erie, Euclid, OH 44119
(216) 531-9000
Licensure Skilled care. *Beds* SNF 24. *Certified* Medicare.

Indian Hills Nursing Center
1500 E 191st St, Euclid, OH 44117
(216) 486-8880
Licensure Skilled care; Intermediate care. *Beds* Swing beds SNF/ICF 100. *Certified* Medicaid; Medicare.
Owner Proprietary corp.

Mt St Joseph
21800 Chardon Rd, Euclid, OH 44117
(216) 531-7426
Licensure Skilled care; Intermediate care. *Beds* Swing beds SNF/ICF 100. *Certified* Medicaid; Medicare.
Owner Proprietary corp.

Rose-Mary, The Grasselli Rehabilitation & Education Center
19350 Euclid Ave, Euclid, OH 44117
(216) 481-4823
Licensure Intermediate care for mentally retarded. *Beds* ICF/MR 40. *Certified* Medicaid.
Owner Proprietary corp.

Fairborn

Christel Manor Nursing Home
789 Stoneybrook Trail, Fairborn, OH 45324
(513) 878-0262
Licensure Intermediate care. *Beds* ICF 100. *Certified* Medicaid.
Owner Proprietary corp.

Fairborn Family Care Home
25 N Maple Ave, Fairborn, OH 45324
(513) 376-3996
Licensure Intermediate care for mentally retarded. *Beds* ICF/MR 8. *Certified* Medicaid.
Owner Proprietary corp.

Heritage Inn Nursing Home
201 W Dayton Dr, Fairborn, OH 45324
(513) 878-6153
Licensure Intermediate care. *Beds* ICF 34. *Certified* Medicaid.
Owner Proprietary corp.

Villa Fairborn
829 Fairfield-Yellow Springs Rd, Fairborn, OH 45324
(513) 878-7046, 878-2874 FAX
Admin Amy E Salser LSW NHA. *Dir of Nursing* Joan M Pigg RN BSN. *Medical Dir* Cleanne Cass DO.

Licensure Skilled care; Intermediate care. *Beds* SNF 8; ICF 108. *Private Pay Patients* 25-35%. *Certified* Medicaid; Medicare; VA.
Owner Proprietary corp (Villa Health Care Management Inc).
Admissions Requirements Medical examination; Physician's request.
Staff RNs 2 (ft), 8 (pt); LPNs 8 (ft), 2 (pt); Nurses' aides 33 (ft), 6 (pt); Physical therapists; Occupational therapists 1 (pt); Speech therapists 1 (pt); Activities coordinators 2 (ft); Dietitians 1 (pt); Ophthalmologists; Podiatrists 1 (pt); Audiologists.
Facilities Dining room; Physical therapy room; Activities room; Chapel; Crafts room; Laundry room; Barber/Beauty shop; Library; Lounges.
Activities Arts & crafts; Cards; Games; Reading groups; Prayer groups; Movies; Shopping trips; Dances/Social/Cultural gatherings; Intergenerational programs; Pet therapy; Weekly visits by churches.

Fairfield

Camelot Lake
5099 Camelot Dr, Fairfield, OH 45214
(513) 829-8922
Licensure Intermediate care for mentally retarded. *Beds* ICF/MR 36. *Certified* Medicaid.
Owner Proprietary corp.

Community Multicare Center
908 Symmes Rd, Fairfield, OH 45014
(513) 868-6500
Medical Dir Kurt Landel MD.
Licensure Skilled care; Intermediate care. *Beds* SNF 50; ICF 51. *Certified* Medicaid; Medicare.
Owner Proprietary corp.
Staff Physicians 1 (pt); Physical therapists 1 (ft), 1 (pt); Occupational therapists 2 (pt); Speech therapists 1 (pt); Activities coordinators 1 (ft); Dietitians 1 (ft).
Facilities Dining room; Physical therapy room; Activities room; Laundry room; Barber/Beauty shop.
Activities Arts & crafts; Cards; Games; Reading groups; Prayer groups; Movies; Shopping trips; Dances/Social/Cultural gatherings.

Crestwood Care Center Inc
6200 Pleasant Ave, Fairfield, OH 45014
(513) 829-5349
Admin Mildred P Wilson, Sr Mary Antonita. *Dir of Nursing* Verna Eilers RN. *Medical Dir* Howard Hunter MD.
Licensure Skilled care; Intermediate care. *Beds* Swing beds SNF/ICF 60. *Certified* Medicaid; Medicare.
Owner Proprietary corp.
Admissions Requirements Minimum age 50; Physician's request.
Staff Physicians 6 (pt); RNs 3 (ft), 2 (pt); LPNs 7 (ft), 1 (pt); Nurses' aides 17 (ft), 2 (pt); Activities coordinators 1 (ft), 1 (pt); Dietitians 1 (pt).
Facilities Dining room; Activities room; Barber/Beauty shop; Library.
Activities Arts & crafts; Cards; Games; Reading groups; Prayer groups; Movies; Shopping trips; Dances/Social/Cultural gatherings; Dining out; Bingo; Yard sales; Charity fairs.

Fairfield Center
350 Kolb Dr, Fairfield, OH 45014
(513) 874-0423
Licensure Intermediate care for mentally retarded. *Beds* ICF/MR 119. *Certified* Medicaid.
Owner Publicly owned.

Tri-County Extended Care Center
5200 Camelot Dr, Fairfield, OH 45014
(513) 829-8100
Admin Barry A Kohn. *Dir of Nursing* Mary Morris RN. *Medical Dir* Elmer Wahl MD.
Licensure Skilled care; Intermediate care. *Beds* SNF 217; ICF 41. *Certified* Medicaid; Medicare.
Owner Proprietary corp.
Admissions Requirements Medical examination.
Staff RNs 9 (ft), 4 (pt); LPNs 33 (ft), 5 (pt); Nurses' aides 130 (ft), 4 (pt); Physical therapists 1 (ft); Recreational therapists 3 (ft); Occupational therapists 1 (pt); Speech therapists 1 (pt); Activities coordinators 1 (ft); Dietitians 1 (pt); Ophthalmologists 1 (pt); Podiatrists 1 (pt); Dentists 1 (pt).
Facilities Dining room; Physical therapy room; Activities room; Chapel; Crafts room; Laundry room; Barber/Beauty shop.
Activities Arts & crafts; Cards; Games; Reading groups; Prayer groups; Movies; Dances/Social/Cultural gatherings.

Woodridge
3801 Woodridge Blvd, Fairfield, OH 45014
(513) 874-9933
Licensure Skilled care; Intermediate care; Rest home. *Beds* Swing beds SNF/ICF 59; Rest home 30.
Owner Proprietary corp.

Fairlawn

Arbors at Fairlawn
575 S Cleveland-Massillon Rd, Fairlawn, OH 44313
(216) 666-5866
Licensure Skilled care; Rest home. *Beds* SNF 75; Rest home 85. *Certified* Medicaid; Medicare.
Owner Proprietary corp.

Felicity

Longworth Manor
305 W Main St, Felicity, OH 45120
(513) 876-3261, 876-3360
Admin Sharon Arnett. *Dir of Nursing* Helen Seal. *Medical Dir* Blair Chick MD.
Licensure Intermediate care for mentally retarded. *Beds* ICF/MR 30. *Certified* Medicaid.
Owner Proprietary corp.
Admissions Requirements Minimum age 18.
Staff Physicians 1 (pt); RNs 1 (ft); LPNs 3 (ft), 3 (pt); Nurses' aides 9 (ft), 14 (pt); Physical therapists 1 (pt); Occupational therapists 1 (pt); Speech therapists 1 (pt); Activities coordinators 1 (ft); Dietitians 1 (pt); Ophthalmologists 1 (pt); Podiatrists 1 (pt); Dentists 1 (pt).
Facilities Dining room; Activities room; Crafts room; Laundry room.
Activities Arts & crafts; Cards; Games; Movies; Shopping trips; Dances/Social/ Cultural gatherings.

Findlay

Blanchard Valley Residential Center
1700 E Sandusky St, Findlay, OH 45840
(419) 422-6386
Licensure Intermediate care for mentally retarded. *Beds* ICF/MR 31. *Certified* Medicaid.
Owner Publicly owned.

Fox Run Manor
PO Box 944, 2101 Greendale Blvd, Findlay, OH 45839-0944
(419) 424-0832, 424-0833 FAX
Admin Amy P Dauterman. *Dir of Nursing* Linda Hartman. *Medical Dir* Dr Lisa Knor.

Licensure Skilled care; Intermediate care. *Beds* Swing beds SNF/ICF 100. *Certified* Medicaid; Medicare.
Owner Proprietary corp (HCF Inc).
Admissions Requirements Medical examination; Physician's request.
Staff Physicians (consultant); RNs 7 (ft), 1 (pt); LPNs 8 (ft), 4 (pt); Nurses' aides 30 (ft), 20 (pt); Physical therapists 1 (pt); Reality therapists 1 (pt); Recreational therapists 1 (pt); Occupational therapists 1 (pt); Speech therapists 1 (pt); Activities coordinators 1 (ft), 1 (pt); Dietitians 1 (ft); Ophthalmologists 1 (pt); Podiatrists 1 (pt).
Facilities Dining room; Physical therapy room; Activities room; Crafts room; Laundry room; Barber/Beauty shop; Library.
Activities Arts & crafts; Cards; Games; Reading groups; Prayer groups; Movies; Shopping trips; Dances/Social/Cultural gatherings; Intergenerational programs; Pet therapy.

Heritage Manor
2820 Greenacre Dr, Findlay, OH 45840
(419) 424-1808
Admin L Don Manley.
Medical Dir William Kose; Susan Hackworth.
Licensure Skilled care; Intermediate care; Retirement. *Beds* SNF 126; ICF 24. *Certified* Medicaid; Medicare.
Owner Proprietary corp.
Staff RNs 7 (ft); LPNs 6 (ft); Nurses' aides 30 (ft), 17 (pt); Physical therapists 1 (ft); Reality therapists 1 (ft); Recreational therapists 1 (ft); Occupational therapists 1 (pt); Speech therapists 1 (pt); Activities coordinators 2 (ft); Dietitians 1 (pt).
Facilities Dining room; Physical therapy room; Activities room; Barber/Beauty shop.
Activities Arts & crafts; Cards; Games; Reading groups; Prayer groups; Movies; Shopping trips; Dances/Social/Cultural gatherings.

Manley's Manor Nursing Home Inc
1918 N Main St, Findlay, OH 45840
Licensure Nursing home. *Beds* 50.
Owner Proprietary corp.

Marlesta No 1
401 Infirmary Rd, Findlay, OH 45840
(419) 423-9183
Admin Gail Fisher. *Dir of Nursing* Jill Combs. *Medical Dir* Dr Blake, Dr Elderbrock, Dr Miller.
Licensure Intermediate care. *Beds* ICF 40. *Certified* Medicaid.
Owner Proprietary corp.
Admissions Requirements Medical examination.
Staff RNs 1 (pt); LPNs 4 (ft), 2 (pt); Nurses' aides 13 (ft), 3 (pt); Activities coordinators 1 (ft).
Facilities Dining room; Activities room; Laundry room.
Activities Arts & crafts; Cards; Games; Reading groups; Prayer groups; Movies; Dances/Social/Cultural gatherings.

Marlesta No 2
401 Infirmary Rd, Findlay, OH 45840
(419) 422-3978
Admin Gail Fisher. *Dir of Nursing* Diane Radabaugh. *Medical Dir* Dr Blake, Dr Elderbrock, Dr Miller.
Licensure Intermediate care. *Beds* ICF 60. *Certified* Medicaid.
Owner Proprietary corp.
Admissions Requirements Medical examination.
Staff RNs 1 (pt); LPNs 4 (ft), 4 (pt); Nurses' aides 13 (ft), 3 (pt); Activities coordinators 1 (ft).
Facilities Dining room; Activities room; Laundry room; Barber/Beauty shop; Examination room.

Activities Arts & crafts; Cards; Games; Reading groups; Prayer groups; Movies; Dances/Social/Cultural gatherings.

Judson Palmer Home
2911 N Main St, Findlay, OH 45840
(419) 422-9656
Admin Arlo Rader.
Medical Dir Dr Gary Hirshfeld.
Licensure Rest home. *Beds* Rest home 17. *Private Pay Patients* 0%.
Owner Nonprofit organization/foundation.
Admissions Requirements Minimum age 55; Females only; Medical examination.
Staff RNs 1 (ft); Nurses' aides 3 (ft), 7 (pt); Dietitians 2 (ft).
Facilities Dining room; Laundry room; Barber/Beauty shop.
Activities Games; Pet therapy.

Winebrenner Extended Care Facility
425 Frazer St, Findlay, OH 45840
(419) 424-9591
Medical Dir C L Samuelson MD.
Licensure Intermediate care. *Beds* ICF 150. *Certified* Medicaid.
Owner Proprietary corp.
Admissions Requirements Medical examination.
Staff Physicians 1 (pt); RNs 4 (ft), 6 (pt); LPNs 9 (ft), 6 (pt); Physical therapists 1 (pt); Activities coordinators 2 (ft); Dietitians 1 (ft).
Affiliation Church of God.
Facilities Dining room; Chapel; Laundry room; Barber/Beauty shop; Solarium; Gift shop.
Activities Arts & crafts; Games; Reading groups; Prayer groups; Movies; Shopping trips.

Winebrenner Haven
425 Frazer St, Findlay, OH 45840
(419) 424-9591
Medical Dir C L Samuelson MD.
Licensure Intermediate care. *Beds* ICF 24. *Certified* Medicaid.
Owner Proprietary corp.
Admissions Requirements Medical examination.
Staff Physicians 1 (pt); LPNs 3 (ft), 2 (pt); Nurses' aides 2 (pt); Activities coordinators 1 (ft).
Affiliation Church of God.
Facilities Dining room; Activities room; Chapel; Laundry room; Barber/Beauty shop; Library.
Activities Arts & crafts; Cards; Games; Reading groups; Prayer groups; Movies; Shopping trips.

Flushing

Hillview Nursing Home
E High St, Box 44, Flushing, OH 43977
(614) 968-3113
Medical Dir Dr Modi.
Licensure Intermediate care. *Beds* ICF 23. *Certified* Medicaid.
Owner Proprietary corp.
Admissions Requirements Medical examination.
Staff Physicians 1 (ft); RNs 1 (ft); LPNs 2 (ft), 3 (pt); Nurses' aides 4 (ft), 4 (pt); Dietitians 1 (pt).
Facilities Dining room; Laundry room.
Activities Arts & crafts; Cards; Games; Prayer groups.

Fostoria

Edgewood Manor of Fostoria
25 Christopher Dr, Fostoria, OH 44830
(419) 435-8112
Admin Diana L Ruffing. *Dir of Nursing* Imogene Garbe RN. *Medical Dir* Dr Randolph Gibbs.

Licensure Skilled care; Intermediate care; Rest home. *Beds* Swing beds SNF/ICF 85; Rest home 17. *Private Pay Patients* 50%. *Certified* Medicaid; Medicare.
Owner Proprietary corp (Cloverleaf Enterprises).
Admissions Requirements Medical examination.
Staff RNs; LPNs; Nurses' aides; Activities coordinators; Dietitians.
Facilities Dining room; Activities room; Crafts room; Laundry room; Barber/Beauty shop.
Activities Arts & crafts; Cards; Games; Reading groups; Prayer groups; Movies; Shopping trips; Dances/Social/Cultural gatherings; Intergenerational programs; Pet therapy.

Good Shepherd Home
PO Box G, 725 Columbus Ave, Fostoria, OH 44830
(419) 435-1801
Licensure Intermediate care. *Beds* ICF 100. *Certified* Medicaid.
Owner Proprietary corp.
Admissions Requirements Medical examination.
Staff RNs 3 (ft), 2 (pt); LPNs 10 (ft), 3 (pt); Nurses' aides 38 (ft), 17 (pt); Physical therapists 1 (pt); Recreational therapists 2 (ft); Speech therapists 1 (pt); Activities coordinators 1 (ft).
Affiliation Church of the Brethren.

Fowler

Meadowbrook Manor of Hartford
3090 Five Point-Hartford Rd, Fowler, OH 44418
(216) 772-5253
Admin John Patrick.
Medical Dir Laurie Horig.
Licensure Intermediate care. *Beds* ICF 54. *Certified* Medicaid.
Owner Proprietary corp.
Admissions Requirements Physician's request.
Staff RNs 4 (ft); LPNs 3 (ft), 6 (pt); Nurses' aides 15 (ft), 10 (pt).
Facilities Dining room; Activities room; Laundry room; Barber/Beauty shop.
Activities Arts & crafts; Cards; Games; Reading groups; Prayer groups; Movies; Shopping trips; Dances/Social/Cultural gatherings.

Frankfort

Valley View Manor
3363 Ragged Ridge Rd, Frankfort, OH 45628
(614) 998-2948
Admin Sylvester Sutherland. *Dir of Nursing* Kathy Weaver. *Medical Dir* Dr Dava B Mehta.
Licensure Intermediate care. *Beds* ICF 44. *Private Pay Patients* 28%. *Certified* Medicaid.
Owner Privately owned.
Admissions Requirements Medical examination.
Staff Physicians 2 (ft); RNs 1 (ft); LPNs 5 (ft); Nurses' aides 10 (ft); Recreational therapists 1 (ft); Activities coordinators 1 (ft); Dietitians 1 (ft).
Facilities Dining room; Activities room; Crafts room; Laundry room; Barber/Beauty shop; Library.
Activities Arts & crafts; Cards; Games; Reading groups; Movies; Shopping trips; Dances/Social/Cultural gatherings.

Franklin

Carlisle Manor
730 Hillcrest Ave, Franklin, OH 45005
(513) 746-2662

Admin Terri L Dickey.
Medical Dir Scott Zollett MD.
Licensure Intermediate care. Beds 48.
  Certified Medicaid.
Owner Proprietary corp.
Staff Physicians 4 (ft); RNs 3 (ft); LPNs 5 (ft);
  Nurses' aides 9 (ft), 2 (pt); Physical
  therapists 1 (pt); Occupational therapists 1
  (pt); Activities coordinators 1 (ft); Dietitians
  1 (pt); Ophthalmologists 1 (pt); Podiatrists 1
  (pt); Dentists 1 (pt).
Facilities Dining room; Activities room;
  Laundry room.
Activities Arts & crafts; Cards; Games;
  Reading groups; Prayer groups; Movies;
  Shopping trips; Dances/Social/Cultural
  gatherings.

Franklin Nursing Home
422 Mission Ln, Franklin, OH 45005
(513) 746-3943
Admin Mildred R Gilliam. Dir of Nursing
  Judith Beachler RN. Medical Dir Scott
  Swope DO.
Licensure Skilled care; Intermediate care. Beds
  Swing beds SNF/ICF 99. Private Pay
  Patients 23%. Certified Medicaid; Medicare.
Owner Privately owned.
Admissions Requirements Minimum age 18;
  Medical examination.
Staff Physicians 2 (pt); RNs 5 (ft); LPNs 14
  (ft); Nurses' aides 40 (ft), 3 (pt); Physical
  therapists 1 (pt); Occupational therapists 1
  (pt); Speech therapists 1 (pt); Activities
  coordinators 2 (ft); Dietitians 1 (pt);
  Ophthalmologists 1 (pt); Podiatrists 2 (pt).
Facilities Dining room; Physical therapy
  room; Activities room; Laundry room;
  Barber/Beauty shop; Patient lounges; Formal
  living room.
Activities Arts & crafts; Cards; Games;
  Reading groups; Prayer groups; Movies;
  Shopping trips; Dances/Social/Cultural
  gatherings.

Zartman Nursing Home
120 S Main St, Franklin, OH 45005
(513) 746-9588
Licensure Skilled care; Intermediate care. Beds
  Swing beds SNF/ICF 10.
Owner Proprietary corp.

Franklin Furnace

Fountainhead Nursing Home
PO Box 36, Old Rte 52, Franklin Furnace,
  OH 45629
(614) 354-9151
Licensure Intermediate care. Beds ICF 30.
  Certified Medicaid.
Owner Proprietary corp.

Fredericktown

Hillcrest Nursing Center
RD 3, 1765 Painter Rd, Fredericktown, OH
  43019
(419) 886-3931, 886-4357 FAX
Admin Joan Levering. Dir of Nursing Linda
  Lamson RN. Medical Dir Dr A H
  Neyestani.
Licensure Skilled care; Intermediate care. Beds
  Swing beds SNF/ICF 50. Private Pay
  Patients 40%. Certified Medicaid; Medicare.
Owner Proprietary corp (Levering
  Management).
Admissions Requirements Medical
  examination.
Staff RNs 1 (ft), 2 (pt); LPNs 6 (ft), 1 (pt);
  Nurses' aides 19 (ft); Physical therapists 1
  (pt); Occupational therapists 1 (pt); Speech
  therapists 1 (pt); Activities coordinators 2
  (ft); Dietitians 1 (pt); Podiatrists 1 (pt).
Facilities Dining room; Activities room;
  Crafts room; Laundry room; Barber/Beauty
  shop.

Activities Arts & crafts; Cards; Games;
  Reading groups; Movies;
  Shopping trips; Dances/Social/Cultural
  gatherings; Intergenerational programs; Pet
  therapy; Family participation; Lunch trips.

Fremont

Bethesda Care Center
600 N Brush St, Fremont, OH 43420
(419) 334-9521
Admin Steven L Rankin. Dir of Nursing Vicki
  Cline. Medical Dir Daniel Kelterhouse.
Licensure Skilled care. Beds SNF 108. Private
  Pay Patients 62%. Certified Medicaid;
  Medicare.
Owner Nonprofit organization/foundation
  (Volunteers of America Care).
Admissions Requirements Physician's request.
Staff Physicians 1 (ft), 10 (pt); RNs 5 (ft), 2
  (pt); LPNs 11 (ft), 13 (pt); Nurses' aides 39
  (ft), 15 (pt); Physical therapists 1 (ft);
  Occupational therapists 1 (ft); Speech
  therapists 1 (ft); Activities coordinators 1
  (ft); Dietitians 1 (ft); Ophthalmologists 1 (ft);
  Podiatrists 1 (ft).
Languages German.
Affiliation Volunteers of America.
Facilities Dining room; Physical therapy
  room; Activities room; Chapel; Laundry
  room; Barber/Beauty shop; Library.
Activities Arts & crafts; Cards; Games; Prayer
  groups; Movies; Shopping trips;
  Intergenerational programs; Pet therapy;
  Family involvement; Community
  involvement.

Countryside Continuing Care Center
1865 Countryside Dr, Fremont, OH 43420
(419) 334-2602
Admin Gregory T Storer.
Medical Dir Michael J Hazlett MD.
Licensure Skilled care; Intermediate care. Beds
  Swing beds SNF/ICF 119. Certified
  Medicaid; Medicare.
Owner Publicly owned.
Admissions Requirements Medical
  examination; Physician's request.
Staff Physicians 1 (pt); RNs 3 (ft), 4 (pt);
  LPNs 8 (ft), 4 (pt); Nurses' aides 31 (ft), 31
  (pt); Physical therapists 1 (pt); Occupational
  therapists 1 (pt); Speech therapists 1 (ft), 1
  (pt); Dietitians 1 (pt); Ophthalmologists 1
  (pt); Dentists 1 (pt).
Facilities Dining room; Physical therapy
  room; Activities room; Chapel; Crafts room;
  Laundry room; Barber/Beauty shop.
Activities Arts & crafts; Cards; Games; Prayer
  groups; Movies; Shopping trips; Dances/
  Social/Cultural gatherings.

Fremont Quality Care Nursing Center
825 June St, Fremont, OH 43420
(419) 332-0357
Admin Gene A Geaslen. Dir of Nursing Peggy
  Snyder RN. Medical Dir David A Wassil
  DO.
Licensure Intermediate care. Beds ICF 100.
  Private Pay Patients 25%. Certified
  Medicaid.
Owner Proprietary corp (Northwestern Service
  Corp).
Admissions Requirements Medical
  examination.
Staff Physicians 1 (pt); RNs 1 (ft), 1 (pt);
  Activities coordinators 1 (ft), 2 (pt);
  Dietitians 1 (pt); Podiatrists 1 (pt).
Facilities Dining room; Laundry room;
  Barber/Beauty shop; Wheelchair van.
Activities Arts & crafts; Cards; Games; Prayer
  groups; Movies; Shopping trips; Dances/
  Social/Cultural gatherings; Intergenerational
  programs; Pet therapy.

Parkview Care Center
PO Box 1108, 1406 Oak Harbor Rd, Fremont,
  OH 43420
(419) 332-2589

Admin James L Oedy. Dir of Nursing Martha
  J McCoy. Medical Dir David T DeFrance
  MD.
Licensure Intermediate care; Retirement. Beds
  ICF 50; Retirement 16. Private Pay Patients
  75-80%. Certified Medicaid.
Owner Proprietary corp.
Admissions Requirements Minimum age 65;
  Medical examination.
Staff Physicians 1 (ft); RNs 1 (pt); LPNs 6
  (ft); Nurses' aides 30 (ft); Activities
  coordinators 2 (pt); Dietitians 1 (pt).
Facilities Dining room; Activities room;
  Chapel; Crafts room; Laundry room; Barber/
  Beauty shop.
Activities Arts & crafts; Cards; Games; Prayer
  groups; Movies; Shopping trips; Dances/
  Social/Cultural gatherings.

Fulton

Morning View Care Center 2
PO Box 38, 101 Main St, Fulton, OH 43321
(419) 864-6941
Admin Teri James. Dir of Nursing Marsha
  Tschop RN. Medical Dir Daniel Dalhausen
  MD.
Licensure Intermediate care for mentally
  retarded. Beds ICF/MR 65. Private Pay
  Patients 0%. Certified Medicaid.
Owner Proprietary corp (Morning View Care
  Center).
Admissions Requirements Medical
  examination; Physician's request.
Staff Physicians 1 (pt); RNs 1 (ft); LPNs 9
  (ft); Physical therapists 1 (pt); Occupational
  therapists 1 (pt); Speech therapists 1 (pt);
  Activities coordinators 2 (ft); Dietitians 1
  (pt); Ophthalmologists 1 (pt); Podiatrists 1
  (pt); Audiologists 1 (pt); Habilitation
  technicians 40 (ft), 10 (pt).
Facilities Dining room; Laundry room;
  Barber/Beauty shop.
Activities Arts & crafts; Cards; Games;
  Reading groups; Movies; Shopping trips;
  Dances/Social/Cultural gatherings.

Furnace

New Dawn Convalescent Center
PO Box 36, Furnace, OH 45505
(513) 324-5709, 324-5700
Medical Dir Dr Kneisley.
Licensure Intermediate care. Beds 21.
  Certified Medicaid.
Owner Nonprofit corp.
Admissions Requirements Females only.
Staff RNs 1 (pt); LPNs 4 (ft); Nurses' aides 10
  (ft); Activities coordinators 1 (ft).
Affiliation Swedenborgian.

Gahanna

Bon-Ing Inc
121 James Rd, Gahanna, OH 43230
(614) 475-7222, 475-7311 FAX
Admin Jennie E Ingram. Dir of Nursing Vera
  Leonard RN.
Licensure Intermediate care; Alzheimer's care.
  Beds ICF 100. Certified Medicaid.
Owner Proprietary corp.
Admissions Requirements Medical
  examination.
Staff Physicians; RNs 2 (ft), 1 (pt); LPNs 3
  (ft), 4 (pt); Nurses' aides 25 (ft); Physical
  therapists (consultant); Occupational
  therapists (consultant); Speech therapists
  (consultant); Activities coordinators 1 (ft);
  Dietitians 1 (pt); Social workers 1 (ft).
Facilities Dining room; Physical therapy
  room; Activities room; Chapel; Laundry
  room; Barber/Beauty shop; Semi-private
  rooms with half baths.
Activities Arts & crafts; Cards; Games;
  Reading groups; Prayer groups; Movies;
  Shopping trips; Dances/Social/Cultural

gatherings; Intergenerational programs; Pet therapy; Church services; Bible study; Dining with family or friends.

Galion

Atwood Manor Nursing Center
347 W Atwood St, Galion, OH 44833
(419) 468-1893
Admin Merry Linn. *Dir of Nursing* Linda Reed. *Medical Dir* Dale C Angerman MD.
Licensure Intermediate care. *Beds* ICF 50. *Private Pay Patients* 37%. *Certified* Medicaid.
Owner Proprietary corp.
Admissions Requirements Medical examination.
Staff Physicians 1 (ft); RNs 1 (pt); LPNs 6 (ft), 1 (pt); Nurses' aides 12 (ft), 13 (pt); Physical therapists 1 (pt); Activities coordinators 1 (ft); Dietitians 1 (ft); Podiatrists 1 (pt).
Facilities Dining room; Activities room; Chapel; Crafts room; Laundry room; Barber/Beauty shop; Library.
Activities Arts & crafts; Cards; Games; Reading groups; Prayer groups; Movies; Shopping trips; Dances/Social/Cultural gatherings; Pet therapy.

Rosewood Manor
935 Rosewood Dr, Galion, OH 44833
(419) 468-7544, 468-5884 FAX
Admin Stephen Nemeth. *Dir of Nursing* Eileen Miller. *Medical Dir* Dale Angerman MD.
Licensure Skilled care; Intermediate care; Alzheimer's care. *Beds* SNF 12; ICF 78. *Private Pay Patients* 35%. *Certified* Medicaid; Medicare.
Owner Proprietary corp (Horizon Healthcare Corp).
Admissions Requirements Medical examination; Physician's request.
Staff Physicians 10 (pt); RNs 4 (ft), 2 (pt); LPNs 1 (ft), 7 (pt); Nurses' aides 2 (ft), 40 (pt); Physical therapists 2 (pt); Recreational therapists 1 (ft); Occupational therapists 1 (pt); Speech therapists 1 (pt); Activities coordinators 1 (ft), 1 (pt); Dietitians 1 (pt); Ophthalmologists 1 (pt); Podiatrists 1 (pt); Audiologists 1 (pt).
Facilities Dining room; Physical therapy room; Activities room; Chapel; Crafts room; Laundry room; Barber/Beauty shop; Library.
Activities Arts & crafts; Cards; Games; Reading groups; Prayer groups; Movies; Shopping trips; Dances/Social/Cultural gatherings; Pet therapy; Reality orientation & grooming group for Alzheimer's patients.

Village Care
925 Wagner Ave, Galion, OH 44833
(419) 468-1090
Admin Helen J Lundon.
Medical Dir Dr William Mantley; Dr Warren Sawyer.
Licensure Skilled care; Intermediate care. *Beds* Swing beds SNF/ICF 58. *Certified* Medicaid; Medicare.
Owner Proprietary corp.
Admissions Requirements Medical examination.
Staff Physicians 2 (pt); RNs 8 (ft), 4 (pt); LPNs 3 (ft), 9 (pt); Nurses' aides 11 (ft), 22 (pt); Physical therapists 1 (pt); Reality therapists 1 (pt); Recreational therapists 1 (pt); Occupational therapists 1 (pt); Speech therapists 1 (pt); Activities coordinators 1 (ft), 1 (pt); Dietitians 1 (ft), 1 (pt); Ophthalmologists 1 (pt); Podiatrists 1 (pt); Audiologists 1 (pt); Dentists 1 (pt).
Facilities Dining room; Physical therapy room; Activities room; Crafts room; Laundry room; Barber/Beauty shop; Library; Greenhouse.

Activities Arts & crafts; Cards; Games; Reading groups; Prayer groups; Movies; Shopping trips; Dances/Social/Cultural gatherings.

Gallipolis

Alternative Residence Two Inc—Middleton Estates
Rte 1, Gallipolis, OH 45631
446-2283
Licensure Intermediate care for mentally retarded. *Beds* ICF/MR 35. *Certified* Medicaid.
Owner Proprietary corp.

Buckeye Community Services—Transitional Facility
PO Box 906, Gallipolis, OH 45631
(614) 286-5039
Licensure Intermediate care for mentally retarded. *Beds* ICF/MR 8. *Certified* Medicaid.
Owner Proprietary corp.

Gallipolis Development Center
2500 Ohio Ave, Gallipolis, OH 45631
(614) 446-1642
Licensure Intermediate care for mentally retarded. *Beds* ICF/MR 320. *Certified* Medicaid.
Owner Publicly owned.

Pinecrest Care Center
555 Jackson Pike Rd, Gallipolis, OH 45631
(614) 446-7112
Medical Dir Dr Balusamy Subbiah.
Licensure Skilled care; Intermediate care. *Beds* Swing beds SNF/ICF 116. *Certified* Medicaid; Medicare.
Owner Proprietary corp.
Admissions Requirements Physician's request.
Facilities Dining room; Physical therapy room; Activities room; Laundry room; Barber/Beauty shop.
Activities Arts & crafts; Games; Reading groups; Prayer groups; Movies; Shopping trips.

Garfield Heights

Jennings Hall Inc
10204 Granger Rd, Garfield Heights, OH 44125
(216) 581-2900
Admin Sr Mary Loretta. *Dir of Nursing* Judith Skimin. *Medical Dir* Dr Ikram Syed.
Licensure Intermediate care. *Beds* ICF 100. *Private Pay Patients* 38%. *Certified* Medicaid.
Owner Nonprofit corp.
Admissions Requirements Medical examination; Physician's request.
Staff Physicians 7 (ft); RNs 6 (ft); LPNs 11 (ft); Nurses' aides 39 (ft); Physical therapists 2 (ft); Recreational therapists 1 (ft); Activities coordinators 2 (ft); Dietitians 1 (ft); Podiatrists 1 (ft).
Languages Slavic.
Affiliation Roman Catholic.
Facilities Dining room; Physical therapy room; Activities room; Chapel; Crafts room; Laundry room; Barber/Beauty shop; Library.
Activities Arts & crafts; Cards; Games; Reading groups; Prayer groups; Movies; Dances/Social/Cultural gatherings; Pet therapy.

Geneva

Con Lea Nursing Home
388 S Broadway, Geneva, OH 44041
(216) 466-3512
Admin Paul Wadowick LSW NHA. *Dir of Nursing* Carol Saylor RN.
Licensure Intermediate care. *Beds* ICF 42. *Certified* Medicaid.

Owner Proprietary corp.
Admissions Requirements Females only; Medical examination.
Staff RNs 1 (ft), 1 (pt); LPNs 2 (ft), 4 (pt); Nurses' aides 11 (ft), 4 (pt); Activities coordinators 1 (ft).
Facilities Dining room.
Activities Arts & crafts; Cards; Games; Reading groups; Prayer groups; Movies; Shopping trips; Dances/Social/Cultural gatherings.

Esther Marie Nursing Center
60 West St, Geneva, OH 44141
(216) 466-1181
Admin Gerri Harris MA LNHA. *Dir of Nursing* Jackie Sullivan LPN. *Medical Dir* M Meshgin Poosh MD.
Licensure Intermediate care. *Beds* ICF 50. *Private Pay Patients* 45%. *Certified* Medicaid.
Owner Proprietary corp.
Admissions Requirements Medical examination.
Languages Spanish, Russian, German, Polish, Hungarian.
Facilities Dining room; Activities room; Laundry room; Barber/Beauty shop.
Activities Arts & crafts; Cards; Games; Reading groups; Prayer groups; Movies; Shopping trips; Dances/Social/Cultural gatherings; Pet therapy.

Geneva Health Care
840 Sherman St, Geneva, OH 44041
(216) 466-4881
Admin Donna Colvui. *Dir of Nursing* M Kerestman RN. *Medical Dir* Cheng-Nan Huang MD.
Licensure Skilled care; Intermediate care. *Beds* Swing beds SNF/ICF 106. *Certified* Medicaid; Medicare.
Owner Proprietary corp.
Admissions Requirements Minimum age 16; Medical examination; Physician's request.
Staff RNs; LPNs; Nurses' aides; Physical therapists; Speech therapists; Activities coordinators; Dietitians; Ophthalmologists.
Facilities Dining room; Physical therapy room; Activities room; Crafts room; Laundry room; Barber/Beauty shop.
Activities Arts & crafts; Cards; Games; Reading groups; Prayer groups; Movies; Shopping trips; Dances/Social/Cultural gatherings.

Grand Manner Inc
PO Box 207, Geneva, OH 44041
(216) 466-3942
Medical Dir Miroslav Kavur DO.
Licensure Intermediate care. *Beds* ICF 16. *Certified* Medicaid.
Owner Proprietary corp.
Admissions Requirements Minimum age 25; Medical examination; Physician's request.
Staff RNs 1 (pt); LPNs 4 (ft), 1 (pt); Nurses' aides 8 (ft); Activities coordinators 1 (ft).
Facilities Dining room; Laundry room.
Activities Arts & crafts; Cards; Games; Prayer groups; Shopping trips.

Lakeland Nursing Home
3142 S County Line, Geneva, OH 44041
(216) 466-1678
Admin James F Clark. *Dir of Nursing* Sherry L DeGroodt RN. *Medical Dir* John Popovic MD.
Licensure Intermediate care for mentally retarded. *Beds* ICF/MR 25. *Private Pay Patients* 0%. *Certified* Medicaid.
Owner Proprietary corp.
Admissions Requirements Minimum age 18; Females only; Medical examination; Psychological examination.
Staff Physicians 1 (ft); RNs 1 (ft); LPNs 2 (ft); Nurses' aides 12 (ft), 2 (pt); Physical therapists 1 (pt); Occupational therapists (consultant); Speech therapists (consultant);

Activities coordinators 1 (ft), 1 (pt);
Dietitians 1 (pt); Ophthalmologists 1 (pt);
Podiatrists 1 (pt); Audiologists (consultant);
QMRPs 1 (ft), 1 (pt).
Facilities Dining room; Laundry room;
Activitis/Crafts room; Specialty treatment
areas; Semi-private rooms.
Activities Arts & crafts; Cards; Games;
Reading groups; Movies; Shopping trips;
Dances/Social/Cultural gatherings;
Discussion groups; Independent living skills.

Manor Home
PO Box 640, 246 N Broadway, Geneva, OH
44041
(216) 466-1808
Admin Gary A Toth.
Medical Dir Ron Newsome.
Licensure Intermediate care for mentally
retarded. *Beds* ICF/MR 50. *Certified*
Medicaid.
Owner Proprietary corp.
Admissions Requirements Minimum age 18;
Males only.
Staff RNs 1 (ft); LPNs 6 (ft), 1 (pt); Nurses'
aides 39 (ft), 2 (pt); Physical therapists 1
(pt); Recreational therapists 4 (pt);
Occupational therapists 1 (pt); Speech
therapists 1 (pt); Activities coordinators 1
(ft); Dietitians 1 (pt); Ophthalmologists 1
(pt); Podiatrists 1 (pt); Dentists 1 (pt).
Facilities Dining room; Physical therapy
room; Activities room; Crafts room; Laundry
room; Barber/Beauty shop; Library.
Activities Arts & crafts; Cards; Games;
Reading groups; Prayer groups; Movies;
Shopping trips; Dances/Social/Cultural
gatherings.

Rae-Ann Geneva
PO Box 653, 839 W Main St, Geneva, OH
44041
(216) 466-5733
Licensure Intermediate care. *Beds* ICF 84.
Certified Medicaid.
Owner Proprietary corp.

Genoa

Genoa Care Center
300 Cherry St, Genoa, OH 43430
(419) 855-7755
Admin William J McClellan. *Dir of Nursing*
Jane Tank RN BSN. *Medical Dir* Dr Mark
Nadaud; Mitcheal Bowen DO.
Licensure Skilled care; Intermediate care. *Beds*
Swing beds SNF/ICF 100. *Certified*
Medicaid; Medicare.
Owner Proprietary corp.
Admissions Requirements Medical
examination; Physician's request.
Staff RNs; LPNs; Nurses' aides; Physical
therapists; Occupational therapists; Speech
therapists; Activities coordinators; Dietitians.
Facilities Dining room; Physical therapy
room; Activities room; Crafts room; Laundry
room; Barber/Beauty shop; 2 lounges.
Activities Arts & crafts; Cards; Games;
Reading groups; Prayer groups; Movies;
Shopping trips; Dances/Social/Cultural
gatherings.

Georgetown

Georgetown Nursing Home Inc
312 W State St, Georgetown, OH 45121
(513) 378-6616
Admin Connie Fenton.
Medical Dir Dr James Kaya.
Licensure Intermediate care. *Beds* ICF 33.
Certified Medicaid.
Owner Proprietary corp.
Admissions Requirements Medical
examination.
Staff RNs 1 (pt); LPNs 3 (ft), 3 (pt); Nurses'
aides 10 (ft), 1 (pt); Activities coordinators 1
(ft).

Facilities Dining room; Activities room;
Laundry room; Barber/Beauty shop.
Activities Arts & crafts; Cards; Games;
Reading groups; Prayer groups; Movies;
Shopping trips; Dances/Social/Cultural
gatherings.

Meadow Wood Nursing Home Inc
61 Stephens Ave, Georgetown, OH 45121
(513) 378-3727
Admin Jack Crout.
Medical Dir Leslie Hampton MD.
Licensure Skilled care; Intermediate care. *Beds*
Swing beds SNF/ICF 53. *Certified* Medicaid;
Medicare.
Owner Proprietary corp.
Admissions Requirements Medical
examination.
Staff Physicians 6 (pt); RNs 2 (ft), 2 (pt);
LPNs 4 (ft), 3 (pt); Nurses' aides 11 (ft), 18
(pt); Physical therapists 1 (pt); Speech
therapists 1 (pt) Activities coordinators 1
(pt); Dietitians 1 (pt); Podiatrists 1 (pt);
Audiologists 1 (pt); Dentists 1 (pt).
Facilities Dining room; Physical therapy
room; Activities room.
Activities Arts & crafts; Cards; Games;
Movies; Dances/Social/Cultural gatherings.

Villa Georgetown
8065 Dr Faul Rd, Georgetown, OH 45121
(513) 378-4178
Licensure Skilled care; Intermediate care. *Beds*
Swing beds SNF/ICF 100. *Certified*
Medicaid; Medicare.
Owner Proprietary corp (Community Care
Centers).

Gibsonburg

Gibsonburg Health Care Center
355 Windsor Ln, Gibsonburg, OH 43431
(419) 637-2104
Licensure Skilled care; Intermediate care; Rest
home. *Beds* Swing beds SNF/ICF 88; Rest
home 12. *Certified* Medicaid; Medicare.
Owner Proprietary corp.

Glendale

St Mary's Memorial Home
469 Albion Ave, Glendale, OH 45246
(513) 771-2170
Licensure Skilled care; Intermediate care. *Beds*
Swing beds SNF/ICF 21.
Owner Proprietary corp.

Grand Rapids

Rapids Nursing Home
PO Box 256, 24201 W 3rd St, Grand Rapids,
OH 43522
(419) 832-5195
Licensure Intermediate care. *Beds* ICF 25.
Certified Medicaid.
Owner Proprietary corp.
Admissions Requirements Medical
examination.
Staff RNs 1 (ft), 1 (pt); LPNs 2 (ft), 2 (pt);
Nurses' aides 8 (ft), 2 (pt); Activities
coordinators 1 (ft); Dietitians 1 (pt).
Facilities Dining room; Crafts room; Laundry
room; Barber/Beauty shop.
Activities Arts & crafts; Cards; Games; Prayer
groups; Movies; Shopping trips; Dances/
Social/Cultural gatherings.

Green Springs

Elmwood Nursing Home
430 N Broadway St, Green Springs, OH
44836
(419) 639-2581
Admin Kathy Luhring LNHA. *Dir of Nursing*
Judith Harrah. *Medical Dir* Cheryl Gray
MD.

Licensure Intermediate care; Retirement;
Alzheimer's care. *Beds* ICF 16; Retirement
15. *Private Pay Patients* 50%. *Certified*
Medicaid.
Owner Proprietary corp.
Admissions Requirements Minimum age 18;
Medical examination; Physician's request.
Staff Physicians 1 (pt); RNs 2 (pt); LPNs 3
(ft), 2 (pt); Nurses' aides 10 (ft), 5 (pt);
Physical therapists 1 (pt); Reality therapists
2 (pt); Recreational therapists 1 (pt);
Occupational therapists 1 (pt); Speech
therapists 1 (pt); Activities coordinators 2
(ft); Dietitians 1 (pt); Ophthalmologists 1
(pt); Podiatrists 1 (pt); Audiologists 1 (pt).
Facilities Dining room; Activities room;
Crafts room; Laundry room; Barber/Beauty
shop.
Activities Arts & crafts; Cards; Games;
Reading groups; Prayer groups; Movies;
Shopping trips; Dances/Social/Cultural
gatherings; Intergenerational programs; Pet
therapy; Community social events.

**St Francis Rehabilitation Hospital & Nursing
Home**
401 N Boadway St, Green Springs, OH 44836
(419) 639-2626
Admin Sr Michael Marie Wiesen. *Dir of
Nursing* Cathy Benninghoff RN. *Medical Dir*
Robert Gosling MD.
Licensure Skilled care; Intermediate care. *Beds*
SNF 40; ICF 70. *Certified* Medicaid;
Medicare.
Owner Proprietary corp.
Admissions Requirements Minimum age 13;
Physician's request.
Staff Physicians 29 (pt); RNs; LPNs; Nurses'
aides; Physical therapists 15 (ft);
Recreational therapists 5 (ft); Occupational
therapists 8 (ft); Speech therapists 3 (ft);
Dietitians 2 (ft); Ophthalmologists 1 (pt);
Podiatrists 1 (pt); Dentists 1 (pt).
Affiliation Roman Catholic.
Facilities Dining room; Physical therapy
room; Activities room; Chapel; Laundry
room; Barber/Beauty shop; Occupational
therapy room; Cafeteria; Student dormitory;
Medical building; Bus; Van; Meeting rooms;
Laboratory.
Activities Arts & crafts; Cards; Games;
Reading groups; Prayer groups; Movies;
Shopping trips; Dances/Social/Cultural
gatherings; Camping; Swimming; Fishing.

Greenfield

Edgewood Manor of Greenfield Inc
850 Nellie St, Greenfield, OH 45123
(513) 981-2165
Admin Dan M McCuen. *Dir of Nursing* Kay
Robinson RN. *Medical Dir* Dr Onusko MD.
Licensure Skilled care; Intermediate care. *Beds*
Swing beds SNF/ICF 63. *Private Pay
Patients* 30%. *Certified* Medicaid; Medicare;
VA.
Owner Proprietary corp (Edgewood Manor
Corp).
Admissions Requirements Medical
examination; Physician's request.
Staff Physicians 5 (pt); RNs 3 (ft); LPNs 6
(ft); Nurses' aides 20 (ft); Physical therapists
(contracted); Reality therapists (contracted);
Recreational therapists (contracted);
Occupational therapists (contracted); Speech
therapists (contracted); Activities
coordinators 1 (ft); Dietitians (contracted).
Facilities Dining room; Physical therapy
room; Activities room; Laundry room;
Barber/Beauty shop.
Activities Arts & crafts; Cards; Games;
Reading groups; Prayer groups; Movies;
Shopping trips; Dances/Social/Cultural
gatherings; Intergenerational programs; Pet
therapy.

Leigh Lane Care Center
238 S Washington St, Greenfield, OH 45123
(513) 981-3349
Admin Connie Fenton. *Dir of Nursing* Janet Williams. *Medical Dir* Dr Daxa Mehta.
Licensure Intermediate care. *Beds* ICF 22. *Private Pay Patients* 0%. *Certified* Medicaid; Medicare.
Owner Proprietary corp.
Admissions Requirements Physician's request.
Facilities Dining room; Laundry room.
Activities Arts & crafts; Cards; Games; Movies; Shopping trips.

Greenville

Brethren's Home
750 Chestnut St, Greenville, OH 45331
(513) 547-8000
Admin Robert D Cain Jr.
Medical Dir Alvan Thuma MD.
Licensure Skilled care; Intermediate care; Rest home; Retirement. *Beds* SNF 160; ICF 112; Rest home 162; Retirement 250. *Certified* Medicaid; Medicare.
Owner Nonprofit corp.
Admissions Requirements Minimum age 65; Medical examination.
Affiliation Church of the Brethren.
Facilities Dining room; Physical therapy room; Activities room; Chapel; Crafts room; Laundry room; Barber/Beauty shop; Library.
Activities Arts & crafts; Cards; Games; Reading groups; Prayer groups; Movies; Shopping trips; Dances/Social/Cultural gatherings.

Gade Nursing Home Inc
405 Chestnut St, Greenville, OH 45331
(513) 548-1993
Admin Tim Gade. *Dir of Nursing* Robin Haney. *Medical Dir* Dr Alvin Heise.
Licensure Skilled care; Intermediate care. *Beds* Swing beds SNF/ICF 51. *Certified* Medicaid; Medicare.
Owner Proprietary corp.
Admissions Requirements Medical examination; Physician's request.
Staff Physicians 1 (ft), 8 (pt); RNs 1 (ft), 1 (pt); LPNs 3 (ft), 2 (pt); Nurses' aides 10 (ft), 6 (pt); Physical therapists 1 (pt); Occupational therapists 1 (pt); Speech therapists 1 (pt); Activities coordinators 2 (ft); Dietitians 1 (pt).
Facilities Dining room; Physical therapy room; Activities room; Laundry room; Barber/Beauty shop.
Activities Arts & crafts; Games; Reading groups; Movies; Shopping trips.

Gade Nursing Home Inc 1
208 Sweitzer St, Greenville, OH 45331
(513) 548-1993
Admin Tim Gade. *Dir of Nursing* Robin Haney. *Medical Dir* Dr Alvin Heise.
Licensure Intermediate care. *Beds* ICF 19. *Certified* Medicaid.
Owner Proprietary corp.
Admissions Requirements Medical examination; Physician's request.
Staff Physicians 1 (ft), 3 (pt); LPNs 2 (ft), 2 (pt); Nurses' aides 2 (ft), 4 (pt); Activities coordinators 1 (ft).
Facilities Dining room; Laundry room; Library.
Activities Arts & crafts; Games; Reading groups; Movies; Shopping trips.

Heartland of Greenville
130 Marion Dr, Greenville, OH 45331
(513) 548-3141, 548-3140 FAX
Admin Brenda Graf DuPuy. *Dir of Nursing* Glenna Allen. *Medical Dir* Dr Margaret Hensel.
Licensure Skilled care; Intermediate care. *Beds* Swing beds SNF/ICF 70. *Certified* Medicaid; Medicare.

Owner Proprietary corp (Health Care and Retirement Corp).
Admissions Requirements Medical examination.
Staff Physicians; RNs; LPNs; Nurses' aides; Physical therapists; Recreational therapists; Speech therapists; Activities coordinators; Dietitians; Ophthalmologists; Podiatrists.
Facilities Dining room; Physical therapy room; Activities room; Crafts room; Laundry room; Barber/Beauty shop.
Activities Arts & crafts; Cards; Games; Reading groups; Prayer groups; Movies; Shopping trips; Dances/Social/Cultural gatherings; Intergenerational programs; Pet therapy.

Rest Haven Nursing Home Inc
1096 N Ohio St, Greenville, OH 45331
(513) 548-1138
Admin Elma L Moss. *Dir of Nursing* LaRose Boyer RN. *Medical Dir* Dr Alvin Heise.
Licensure Skilled care; Intermediate care. *Beds* Swing beds SNF/ICF 68. *Certified* Medicaid; Medicare.
Owner Proprietary corp.
Admissions Requirements Minimum age 20; Medical examination.
Staff RNs 4 (ft), 3 (pt); LPNs 4 (ft), 3 (pt); Nurses' aides 24 (ft), 14 (pt); Physical therapists 1 (pt); Speech therapists 1 (pt); Activities coordinators 1 (ft); Dietitians 1 (pt); Social services 1 (ft).
Facilities Dining room; Physical therapy room; Chapel; Laundry room; Barber/Beauty shop.
Activities Arts & crafts; Cards; Games; Prayer groups; Shopping trips; Dances/Social/Cultural gatherings; Outings to fairs, parades.

Grove City

Monterey Nursing Inn
3929 Hoover Rd, Grove City, OH 43123
(614) 875-7700
Licensure Skilled care; Intermediate care. *Beds* Swing beds SNF/ICF 200. *Certified* Medicaid; Medicare.
Owner Proprietary corp (Beverly Enterprises).

Hamden

Huston Nursing Home
Rte 1, Hamden, OH 45634
(614) 384-3485, 384-2676
Admin Marjorie Huston. *Dir of Nursing* Linda Burns. *Medical Dir* Dr Doug Jones.
Licensure Skilled care; Intermediate care. *Beds* Swing beds SNF/ICF 80. *Certified* Medicaid; Medicare.
Owner Privately owned.
Admissions Requirements Physician's request.
Staff Physicians; RNs; LPNs; Nurses' aides; Physical therapists; Reality therapists; Recreational therapists; Occupational therapists; Speech therapists; Activities coordinators; Dietitians; Ophthalmologists.
Facilities Dining room; Physical therapy room; Activities room; Laundry room; Barber/Beauty shop.
Activities Arts & crafts; Cards; Games; Reading groups; Prayer groups; Movies; Shopping trips; Dances/Social/Cultural gatherings.

Hamilton

Butler County Care Facility
1800 Princeton Rd, Hamilton, OH 45011
(513) 867-5930
Licensure Intermediate care. *Beds* ICF 121. *Certified* Medicaid.
Owner Publicly owned.

Center Haven Health Center
422 N 2nd St, Hamilton, OH 45011
(513) 868-9600
Admin Shirley Trieschman. *Dir of Nursing* Jo Ann Miranda. *Medical Dir* Erich Ringel MD.
Licensure Intermediate care. *Beds* ICF 29. *Certified* Medicaid.
Owner Proprietary corp (Omni-Life Systems Inc).
Admissions Requirements Physician's request.
Staff RNs 2 (pt); LPNs 3 (ft), 4 (pt); Nurses' aides 11 (ft), 2 (pt); Physical therapists (contracted); Reality therapists (contracted); Recreational therapists 1 (ft); Occupational therapists (contracted); Speech therapists (contracted); Dietitians 1 (pt); Podiatrists (contracted).
Facilities Dining room; Activities room; Laundry room.
Activities Arts & crafts; Cards; Games; Reading groups; Prayer groups; Movies; Shopping trips; Dances/Social/Cultural gatherings; Intergenerational programs; Pet therapy.

Glenward Health Care Center
3472 Hamilton-Mason Rd, Hamilton, OH 45011
(513) 863-3100
Admin Glyndon Powell. *Dir of Nursing* Susan Castor RN. *Medical Dir* Edward P Drohan MD.
Licensure Skilled care; Intermediate care. *Beds* SNF 22; ICF 95. *Certified* Medicaid; Medicare.
Owner Proprietary corp.
Admissions Requirements Minimum age 18.
Staff Physicians 11 (pt); RNs 8 (ft), 3 (pt); LPNs 13 (ft), 3 (pt); Nurses' aides 44 (ft), 3 (pt); Physical therapists 2 (pt); Occupational therapists 1 (pt); Speech therapists 1 (pt); Activities coordinators 2 (ft); Dietitians 1 (pt); Ophthalmologists 1 (pt); Podiatrists 1 (pt); Dentists 1 (pt).
Facilities Dining room; Physical therapy room; Activities room; Crafts room; Laundry room; Barber/Beauty shop.
Activities Arts & crafts; Cards; Games; Reading groups; Prayer groups; Movies; Shopping trips; Dances/Social/Cultural gatherings.

Golden Years Nursing Home
2436 Old Oxford Rd, Hamilton, OH 45013
(513) 893-0471
Medical Dir Harry Davin MD.
Licensure Intermediate care. *Beds* ICF 50. *Certified* Medicaid.
Owner Proprietary corp.
Staff RNs 2 (pt); LPNs 3 (ft), 3 (pt); Nurses' aides 9 (ft), 5 (pt); Activities coordinators 1 (ft); Dietitians 1 (pt).
Facilities Dining room; Laundry room; Barber/Beauty shop.
Activities Arts & crafts; Cards; Games; Dances/Social/Cultural gatherings.

Greenwood Manor Nursing Home
925 Greenwood Ave, Hamilton, OH 45011
(513) 867-8334
Admin M O'Reilly.
Medical Dir Dr E Ringel.
Licensure Intermediate care. *Beds* ICF 27. *Certified* Medicaid.
Owner Proprietary corp.
Admissions Requirements Medical examination.
Staff Physicians; LPNs; Nurses' aides; Physical therapists; Recreational therapists; Occupational therapists; Speech therapists; Activities coordinators; Dietitians; Podiatrists; Dentists.
Facilities Dining room; Activities room; Laundry room.
Activities Arts & crafts; Cards; Games; Shopping trips.

Helton Health Center
422 N 2nd St, Hamilton, OH 45011
(513) 868-8842
Admin Stephen P Plouck. *Dir of Nursing*
Joann Miranda. *Medical Dir* Dr Erich
Ringel.
Licensure Intermediate care. *Beds* ICF 24.
Certified Medicaid.
Owner Proprietary corp (Omnilife Systems
Inc).
Admissions Requirements Medical
examination; Physician's request.
Staff Physicians 3 (pt); RNs 1 (ft); LPNs 4
(ft); Nurses' aides 6 (ft); Physical therapists 1
(pt); Activities coordinators 1 (pt); Dietitians
1 (pt); Ophthalmologists 1 (pt); Dentists 1
(pt).
Facilities Dining room; Activities room;
Laundry room.
Activities Arts & crafts; Cards; Games;
Reading groups; Prayer groups.

Hillandale Health Care
4195 Hamilton-Mason Rd, Hamilton, OH
45011
(513) 868-2266
Licensure Skilled care; Intermediate care. *Beds*
Swing beds SNF/ICF 12.
Owner Proprietary corp.

Parkway Nursing Home
4070 Hamilton-Mason Rd, Hamilton, OH
45011
(513) 868-3300, 868-3318, 868-3326
Admin Beth Braunecker.
Medical Dir Marlene Kunz.
Licensure Intermediate care; Alzheimer's care.
Beds ICF 77. *Certified* Medicaid.
Owner Proprietary corp (Parke Care Inc).
Staff RNs 1 (ft); LPNs 7 (ft), 2 (pt); Nurses'
aides 15 (ft), 5 (pt); Activities coordinators 1
(ft); Social workers 1 (ft).
Facilities Dining room; Activities room;
Laundry room.
Activities Arts & crafts; Cards; Games;
Reading groups; Prayer groups; Movies;
Shopping trips; Dances/Social/Cultural
gatherings; Church; Cooking classes; Senior
Olympics; Performers; Birthday parties.

Powell's Convalescent Home
2923 Hamilton-Mason Rd, Hamilton, OH
45011
(513) 863-0360
Licensure Skilled care; Intermediate care. *Beds*
SNF 31; ICF 67. *Certified* Medicaid;
Medicare.
Owner Proprietary corp.

Schroder Manor Retirement Community
1302 Millville Ave, Hamilton, OH 45013
(513) 867-1300
Admin Sr M Pascaline Colling SFP. *Dir of
Nursing* Marian LoBuono RN. *Medical Dir*
Warren Daudistel MD.
Licensure Skilled care; Intermediate care;
Alzheimer's and related diseases unit;
Retirement. *Beds* SNF 85; ICF 88;
Alzheimer's and related diseases unit 13.
Certified Medicare.
Owner Nonprofit corp (Franciscan Health
System).
Admissions Requirements Medical
examination.
Staff Physicians 1 (pt); RNs 3 (ft); LPNs 3
(ft); Nurses' aides; Physical therapists 1 (pt);
Reality therapists 1 (ft); Occupational
therapists 1 (pt); Speech therapists; Activities
coordinators 1 (ft); Dietitians 1 (ft);
Podiatrists 2 (pt); Audiologists 1 (pt).
Facilities Dining room; Physical therapy
room; Activities room; Chapel; Crafts room;
Laundry room; Barber/Beauty shop; Library.
Activities Arts & crafts; Cards; Games;
Reading groups; Prayer groups; Movies;
Shopping trips; Dances/Social/Cultural
gatherings; Intergenerational programs; Pet
therapy.

Sunnybreeze Nursing Home Inc
350 Hancock Ave, Hamilton, OH 45011
(513) 863-4218
Admin Mildred Ross. *Dir of Nursing* Patty
Yeary. *Medical Dir* Harry Davin MD.
Licensure Skilled care; Intermediate care;
Retirement. *Beds* Swing beds SNF/ICF 81.
Owner Proprietary corp.
Admissions Requirements Medical
examination; Physician's request.
Staff Physicians 6 (pt); RNs 1 (ft), 2 (pt);
LPNs 8 (ft), 4 (pt); Nurses' aides 25 (ft), 14
(pt); Physical therapists 1 (pt); Reality
therapists 1 (pt); Recreational therapists 1
(pt); Occupational therapists 1 (pt); Speech
therapists 1 (pt); Activities coordinators 1
(ft), 1 (pt); Dietitians 1 (pt);
Ophthalmologists 1 (pt); Podiatrists 1 (pt);
Dentists 1 (pt).
Facilities Dining room; Activities room;
Laundry room; Barber/Beauty shop.
Activities Arts & crafts; Cards; Games;
Reading groups; Movies; Shopping trips;
Dances/Social/Cultural gatherings.

Westhaven Nursing Home
215 N "C" St, Hamilton, OH 45013
(513) 863-5511
Admin J Gentry.
Medical Dir Dr E Ringel.
Licensure Intermediate care. *Beds* ICF 23.
Certified Medicaid.
Owner Proprietary corp (Buckeye Family and
Nursing Home).
Admissions Requirements Females only;
Medical examination.
Staff Physicians; LPNs; Nurses' aides;
Recreational therapists; Occupational
therapists; Speech therapists; Activities
coordinators; Dietitians; Podiatrists;
Dentists.
Facilities Dining room; Activities room;
Laundry room.
Activities Cards; Games; Shopping trips.

Westover Retirement Community
855 Stahlheber Rd, Hamilton, OH 45013
(513) 895-9539
Admin Fred Voelkel; Jeffrey P Thurman, Pres.
Dir of Nursing Marion Meier. *Medical Dir*
Daniel Niehaus MD.
Licensure Intermediate care; Independent
living. *Beds* ICF 46; Independent living 140.
Private Pay Patients 100%.
Owner Nonprofit organization/foundation.
Admissions Requirements Minimum age 65;
Medical examination.
Staff Physicians; RNs 8 (ft), 4 (pt); LPNs 2
(pt); Nurses' aides 26 (ft), 10 (pt); Physical
therapists 1 (pt); Recreational therapists 2
(ft); Activities coordinators 1 (ft); Dietitians
1 (pt).
Facilities Dining room; Physical therapy
room; Activities room; Chapel; Crafts room;
Laundry room; Barber/Beauty shop; Library;
Pre-school; 2 25-passenger buses; Van.
Activities Arts & crafts; Cards; Games;
Reading groups; Movies; Shopping trips;
Intergenerational programs; Pet therapy;
Outings.

Hartville

Hartville Health Care Center Inc
1420 Smith Kramer Rd, Hartville, OH 44632
(216) 877-2666
Admin James Alexander. *Dir of Nursing*
Gertrude Stilts RN.
Licensure Intermediate care. *Beds* ICF 66.
Certified Medicaid.
Owner Privately owned.
Admissions Requirements Minimum age 60.
Facilities Dining room; Activities room;
Laundry room; Barber/Beauty shop; Library.
Activities Arts & crafts; Cards; Games;
Reading groups; Prayer groups; Movies;
Dances/Social/Cultural gatherings.

Hartville Meadows
844 Sunnyside SW, Hartville, OH 44632
(216) 877-3694
Licensure Intermediate care for mentally
retarded. *Beds* ICF/MR 32. *Certified*
Medicaid.
Owner Proprietary corp.

Hayesville

Wintersong Village of Hayesville
82 S Mechanic St, Hayesville, OH 44838
(419) 368-4381
Admin Robert H Rice. *Dir of Nursing* Jessie
Van Auker RN; Pat Abrams.
Licensure Intermediate care. *Beds* ICF 22.
Certified Medicaid.
Owner Proprietary corp.
Admissions Requirements Medical
examination; Physician's request.
Staff Physicians 2 (ft); RNs 1 (ft); LPNs 3 (ft);
Nurses' aides 9 (ft); Activities coordinators 1
(ft); Dietitians 1 (pt).
Facilities Dining room; Activities room;
Crafts room; Laundry room.
Activities Arts & crafts; Cards; Games;
Reading groups; Movies; Shopping trips;
Dances/Social/Cultural gatherings.

Heath

AnMac Home III
1723 Watson Rd, Heath, OH 43056
Licensure Intermediate care for mentally
retarded. *Beds* ICF/MR 12. *Certified*
Medicaid.
Owner Proprietary corp.

Hicksville

Fountain Manor Nursing Home
401 Fountain St, Hicksville, OH 43526
(419) 542-7795
Admin Earl E Brinsrield. *Dir of Nursing* Irene
Dalton RN. *Medical Dir* Laverne Miller
MD.
Licensure Skilled care; Intermediate care. *Beds*
Swing beds SNF/ICF 64. *Certified* Medicaid;
Medicare.
Owner Proprietary corp.
Admissions Requirements Minimum age 18;
Medical examination; Physician's request.
Staff Physicians 3 (pt); RNs 2 (ft), 1 (pt);
LPNs 6 (ft), 5 (pt); Nurses' aides 15 (ft), 7
(pt); Physical therapists 1 (pt); Speech
therapists 1 (pt); Activities coordinators 1
(ft), 1 (pt); Dietitians 1 (pt);
Ophthalmologists 1 (pt).
Facilities Dining room; Activities room;
Crafts room; Laundry room; Barber/Beauty
shop.
Activities Arts & crafts; Cards; Games;
Reading groups; Prayer groups; Movies;
Shopping trips; Dances/Social/Cultural
gatherings.

Hilliard

Arbors at Hilliard
5471 Scioto Darby Rd, Hilliard, OH 43026
(614) 876-7356
Admin Jan S Goldhardt. *Dir of Nursing* Lynn
Temple RN. *Medical Dir* Michael Kirwin
MD.
Licensure Intermediate care. *Beds* ICF 122.
Certified Medicare.
Owner Proprietary corp (Arbor Health Care).
Admissions Requirements Medical
examination.
Staff RNs 3 (ft), 8 (pt); LPNs 5 (ft), 1 (pt);
Nurses' aides 28 (ft), 8 (pt); Activities
coordinators 1 (ft).
Facilities Dining room; Physical therapy
room; Activities room; Crafts room; Laundry
room; Barber/Beauty shop.

Activities Arts & crafts; Cards; Games; Prayer groups; Movies; Shopping trips; Dances/Social/Cultural gatherings.

Glenmont
4599 Avery Rd, Hilliard, OH 43026
(614) 876-0084
Licensure Skilled care; Intermediate care. *Beds* Swing beds SNF/ICF 37.
Owner Proprietary corp.

Hillsboro

Alternative Residences Three Inc—Hillsboro Home
133 Willetsville Pike, Hillsboro, OH 45133
Licensure Intermediate care for mentally retarded. *Beds* ICF/MR 12. *Certified* Medicaid.
Owner Proprietary corp.

Alternative Residences Three Inc—Taylor Home
116 Taylor Dr, Hillsboro, OH 45133
Licensure Intermediate care for mentally retarded. *Beds* ICF/MR 12. *Certified* Medicaid.
Owner Proprietary corp.

Alternative Residences Three Inc—Willetsville Home
131 Willetsville Pike, Hillsboro, OH 45133
Licensure Intermediate care for mentally retarded. *Beds* ICF/MR 12.
Owner Proprietary corp.

Heartland of Hillsboro
1141 Northview Dr, Hillsboro, OH 45133
(513) 393-5766
Licensure Skilled care; Intermediate care. *Beds* Swing beds SNF/ICF 100. *Certified* Medicaid; Medicare.
Owner Proprietary corp (Health Care and Retirement Corp).

Oakland Nursing Center
175 Chillicothe Ave, Hillsboro, OH 45133
(513) 393-1925
Admin George Oney.
Licensure Intermediate care. *Beds* ICF 101. *Certified* Medicaid.
Owner Proprietary corp.
Admissions Requirements Medical examination; Physician's request.
Staff RNs 3 (ft), 1 (pt); LPNs 5 (ft), 7 (pt); Nurses' aides 27 (ft), 13 (pt); Activities coordinators 3 (ft), 2 (pt); Dietitians 1 (pt).
Facilities Dining room; Physical therapy room; Activities room; Laundry room; Barber/Beauty shop.
Activities Arts & crafts; Cards; Games; Reading groups; Prayer groups; Movies; Shopping trips; Dances/Social/Cultural gatherings.

Holgate

Holgate Quality Care Nursing Center
400 Joe E Brown Ave, Holgate, OH 43527
(419) 264-2911
Admin Donald C Leine. *Dir of Nursing* Elaine Klemens RN. *Medical Dir* William Richter MD.
Licensure Intermediate care. *Beds* ICF 51. *Private Pay Patients* 50%. *Certified* Medicaid.
Owner Proprietary corp (Northwestern Service Corp).
Admissions Requirements Minimum age 30; Medical examination; Physician's request.
Staff RNs 1 (ft), 1 (pt); LPNs 4 (ft), 1 (pt); Nurses' aides 19 (ft); Dietitians 1 (pt).
Languages Spanish.
Facilities Dining room; Physical therapy room; Activities room; Chapel; Crafts room; Barber/Beauty shop.

Activities Arts & crafts; Cards; Games; Reading groups; Prayer groups; Movies; Shopping trips; Dances/Social/Cultural gatherings; Intergenerational programs; Pet therapy.

Holland

Spring Meadows Extended Care Facility
1125 Clarion Ave, Holland, OH 43528
(419) 866-6124, 866-0155 FAX
Admin John H Stone. *Dir of Nursing* Jennie Matura RN. *Medical Dir* Karim Zafar MD.
Licensure Intermediate care. *Beds* ICF 100. *Private Pay Patients* 60%. *Certified* Medicaid.
Owner Proprietary corp.
Staff RNs 5 (ft); LPNs 12 (ft), 6 (pt); Nurses' aides 43 (ft), 10 (pt); Recreational therapists 2 (ft); Activities coordinators 1 (ft); Dietitians 1 (pt); Podiatrists 1 (pt).
Facilities Dining room; Physical therapy room; Activities room; Chapel; Crafts room; Laundry room; Barber/Beauty shop.
Activities Arts & crafts; Cards; Games; Reading groups; Prayer groups; Movies; Shopping trips; Dances/Social/Cultural gatherings; Intergenerational programs; Pet therapy.

Huber Heights

Spring Creek Nursing Center
5440 Charlesgate Rd, Huber Heights, OH 45424
(513) 236-6707
Licensure Skilled care; Intermediate care. *Beds* Swing beds SNF/ICF 100. *Certified* Medicaid; Medicare.
Owner Proprietary corp (Health Care Management).

Hudson

Hudson Elms Inc
597 E Streetsboro Rd, Hudson, OH 44236
(216) 650-0436
Licensure Intermediate care; Retirement. *Beds* ICF 50. *Certified* Medicaid.
Owner Proprietary corp.

Huntsburg

Blossom Hill Nursing Home
12496 Princeton Rd, Huntsburg, OH 44046
(216) 635-5567
Licensure Intermediate care. *Beds* ICF 86. *Certified* Medicaid.
Owner Proprietary corp.

Huron

Erie County Care Facility
3916 E Perkins Ave, Huron, OH 44839
(419) 627-8733, 627-8735 FAX
Admin William J Hart. *Dir of Nursing* Mary J Slusher RN. *Medical Dir* Sidhaiyan Aiyappasamy MD.
Licensure Intermediate care. *Beds* ICF 160. *Private Pay Patients* 3%. *Certified* Medicaid.
Owner Publicly owned.
Admissions Requirements Medical examination.
Staff Physicians 1 (ft), 14 (pt); RNs 4 (ft), 2 (pt); LPNs 20 (ft), 6 (pt); Nurses' aides 51 (ft), 15 (pt); Physical therapists 1 (pt); Occupational therapists 1 (pt); Speech therapists 1 (pt); Activities coordinators 1 (ft); Dietitians 1 (pt); Ophthalmologists 1 (pt); Podiatrists 2 (pt); Audiologists 1 (pt).
Facilities Dining room; Physical therapy room; Activities room; Chapel; Crafts room; Laundry room; Barber/Beauty shop; Library; Hydro-therapy pool.

Activities Arts & crafts; Cards; Games; Reading groups; Prayer groups; Movies; Shopping trips; Dances/Social/Cultural gatherings; Intergenerational programs; Pet therapy.

Huron Health Care Center
1920 W Cleveland Rd, Huron, OH 44839
(419) 433-4990
Licensure Intermediate care. *Beds* ICF 100. *Certified* Medicaid.
Owner Proprietary corp.

Indian Lake

Heartland of Indian Lake
1442 St Rte 33 W, Indian Lake, OH 43331
(513) 843-4929
Admin Charles T George.
Medical Dir Sue Evans.
Licensure Skilled care; Intermediate care; Intermediate care for mentally retarded. *Beds* SNF 50; ICF 78; ICF/MR 18. *Certified* Medicaid; Medicare.
Owner Proprietary corp.
Admissions Requirements Minimum age 18; Medical examination; Physician's request.
Staff Physicians 1 (pt); RNs 5 (ft), 1 (pt); LPNs 14 (ft), 2 (pt); Nurses' aides 61 (ft), 4 (pt); Physical therapists 1 (ft); Recreational therapists 1 (ft); Occupational therapists 1 (ft); Speech therapists 1 (ft); Dietitians 1 (pt); Ophthalmologists 1 (pt); Podiatrists 1 (pt).
Facilities Dining room; Physical therapy room; Activities room; Barber/Beauty shop.
Activities Arts & crafts; Cards; Games; Reading groups; Movies; Shopping trips; Dances/Social/Cultural gatherings.

Ironton

Bryant Health Center Inc
5th & Clinton Sts, Ironton, OH 45638
(614) 532-6188
Licensure Intermediate care. *Beds* ICF 93. *Certified* Medicaid.
Owner Proprietary corp.

Jo-Lin Health Center Inc
1050 Clinton St, Ironton, OH 45638
(614) 532-6096
Licensure Skilled care; Intermediate care. *Beds* Swing beds SNF/ICF 159. *Certified* Medicaid; Medicare.
Owner Proprietary corp.

Sunset Nursing Center
813 1/2 Marion Pike, Ironton, OH 45638
(614) 532-0449
Medical Dir Dr A B Payne.
Licensure Intermediate care. *Beds* ICF 50. *Certified* Medicaid.
Owner Proprietary corp.
Facilities Dining room; Physical therapy room; Activities room; Chapel; Crafts room; Laundry room; Barber/Beauty shop; Library.
Activities Arts & crafts; Cards; Games; Reading groups; Prayer groups; Movies; Shopping trips; Dances/Social/Cultural gatherings.

Jackson

Buckeye Community Services—South Street Home
6 South St, Jackson, OH 45640
(614) 286-5039
Licensure Intermediate care for mentally retarded. *Beds* ICF/MR 8. *Certified* Medicaid.
Owner Proprietary corp.

Four Winds Nursing Facility
215 Seth Ave, Jackson, OH 45640
(614) 286-7551

Licensure Skilled care; Intermediate care. *Beds* Swing beds SNF/ICF 100. *Certified* Medicaid; Medicare.
Owner Proprietary corp.

Heartland of Jackson
8668 State Rte 93, Jackson, OH 45640
(614) 286-5026, 286-6975 FAX
Admin Nancy F Raines. *Dir of Nursing* Gail Rawlins. *Medical Dir* Louis Jindra.
Licensure Skilled care; Intermediate care; Alzheimer's care. *Beds* SNF 28; ICF 72. *Private Pay Patients* 12%. *Certified* Medicaid; Medicare.
Owner Proprietary corp (Health Care and Retirement Corp).
Admissions Requirements Medical examination.
Staff Physicians 3 (pt); RNs 4 (ft); LPNs 9 (ft); Nurses' aides 35 (ft); Physical therapists 1 (ft); Occupational therapists 1 (ft); Speech therapists 1 (ft); Activities coordinators 1 (ft); Dietitians 1 (ft); Ophthalmologists 1 (ft); Podiatrists 1 (ft); Dentists 1 (ft).
Facilities Dining room; Physical therapy room; Activities room; Laundry room; Barber/Beauty shop; Outdoor shelterhouse.
Activities Arts & crafts; Cards; Games; Reading groups; Prayer groups; Movies; Shopping trips; Dances/Social/Cultural gatherings; Intergenerational programs; Pet therapy.

Jamestown

Heathergreen II Inc
4960 US Rte 35 E, Jamestown, OH 45335
(513) 675-3311
Licensure Skilled care; Intermediate care. *Beds* Swing beds SNF/ICF 101. *Certified* Medicaid; Medicare.
Owner Proprietary corp.

Jamestown Family Care Home
4333 Waynesville-Jamestown Rd, Jamestown, OH 45335
(513) 376-3996
Licensure Intermediate care for mentally retarded. *Beds* ICF/MR 8. *Certified* Medicaid.
Owner Proprietary corp.

Jefferson

Jefferson Geriatric Center
222 E Beech St, Jefferson, OH 44047
(216) 576-0060
Licensure Skilled care; Intermediate care. *Beds* Swing beds SNF/ICF 100. *Certified* Medicaid; Medicare.
Owner Proprietary corp.

Johnstown

Northview Nursing Home
267 N Main St, Johnstown, OH 43031
(614) 967-7896
Medical Dir Robert Young MD.
Licensure Intermediate care. *Beds* ICF 36. *Certified* Medicaid.
Owner Proprietary corp.
Staff Physicians 2 (pt); RNs 1 (ft), 2 (pt); LPNs 1 (ft), 3 (pt); Nurses' aides 8 (ft), 5 (pt); Activities coordinators 1 (ft); Dietitians 1 (pt); Ophthalmologists 1 (pt); Podiatrists 1 (pt); Dentists 1 (pt).
Facilities Dining room; Activities room; Chapel; Crafts room; Laundry room; Barber/Beauty shop.
Activities Arts & crafts; Cards; Games; Reading groups; Prayer groups; Movies; Dances/Social/Cultural gatherings.

Kensington

East Carroll Nursing Home
7233 Apollo Rd NE, Kensington, OH 44427
(216) 223-1536
Admin Jean Miller. *Dir of Nursing* Lois Slentz LPN. *Medical Dir* Donald Wingard DO.
Licensure Intermediate care for mentally retarded. *Beds* ICF/MR 26. *Certified* Medicaid.
Owner Proprietary corp.
Admissions Requirements Medical examination.
Staff LPNs; Nurses' aides; Activities coordinators.
Facilities Dining room; Activities room; Crafts room; Laundry room.
Activities Arts & crafts; Cards; Games; Reading groups; Movies; Shopping trips; Dances/Social/Cultural gatherings; Sunday school.

Kent

Independence—Vine
923 Vine St, Kent, OH 44240
(216) 296-2851
Licensure Intermediate care for mentally retarded. *Beds* ICF/MR 8. *Certified* Medicaid.
Owner Proprietary corp.

Kent Quality Care
1290 Fairchild Ave, Kent, OH 44240
(216) 678-4912, 678-2489 FAX
Admin Richard J Chasko. *Dir of Nursing* Pat Harriger RN. *Medical Dir* James Mottice MD.
Licensure Intermediate care; Alzheimer's care. *Beds* ICF 100. *Private Pay Patients* 45%. *Certified* Medicaid.
Owner Proprietary corp (Northwestern Service Corp).
Staff Physicians 1 (ft); RNs 2 (ft), 2 (pt); LPNs 6 (ft), 8 (pt); Nurses' aides 30 (ft), 23 (pt); Physical therapists 1 (ft); Recreational therapists 1 (ft); Occupational therapists 1 (ft); Speech therapists 1 (ft); Activities coordinators 1 (ft); Dietitians 1 (ft); Ophthalmologists 1 (ft); Podiatrists 1 (ft); Audiologists 1 (ft).
Facilities Dining room; Physical therapy room; Activities room; Chapel; Crafts room; Laundry room; Barber/Beauty shop; Library.
Activities Arts & crafts; Cards; Games; Reading groups; Prayer groups; Movies; Shopping trips; Dances/Social/Cultural gatherings; Intergenerational programs; Pet therapy.

Kenton

Corinthian
PO Box 218, 320 N Wayne St, Kenton, OH 43326
(419) 673-1295
Medical Dir Dr J Sanders.
Licensure Skilled care; Intermediate care. *Beds* Swing beds SNF/ICF 82. *Certified* Medicaid; Medicare.
Owner Proprietary corp.
Admissions Requirements Minimum age 18; Medical examination; Physician's request.
Staff Physicians 10 (pt); RNs 3 (ft), 1 (pt); LPNs 3 (ft), 6 (pt); Nurses' aides 21 (ft), 13 (pt); Physical therapists 1 (pt); Reality therapists 1 (pt); Recreational therapists 1 (pt); Occupational therapists 1 (pt); Speech therapists 1 (pt); Activities coordinators 1 (ft), 2 (pt); Dietitians 1 (pt); Ophthalmologists 1 (pt); Podiatrists 1 (pt); Dentists 1 (pt).
Languages Sign.
Facilities Dining room; Activities room; Crafts room; Laundry room; Barber/Beauty shop; Library.

Activities Arts & crafts; Cards; Games; Reading groups; Prayer groups; Movies; Shopping trips; Dances/Social/Cultural gatherings; Van outings.

Green Acres Nursing Home Inc
117 Cemetery Rd, Kenton, OH 43326
(419) 674-4197
Admin Doris A Baldwin. *Dir of Nursing* Sandra E Kahler RN. *Medical Dir* Dr Jim Sanders.
Licensure Intermediate care. *Beds* ICF 101. *Certified* Medicaid.
Owner Privately owned.
Admissions Requirements Medical examination.
Staff RNs 1 (ft), 1 (pt); LPNs 8 (ft), 1 (pt); Nurses' aides 25 (ft), 16 (pt); Physical therapists 1 (pt); Activities coordinators 2 (ft), 1 (pt); Dietitians 1 (ft).
Facilities Dining room; Activities room; Laundry room; Barber/Beauty shop.
Activities Arts & crafts; Cards; Games; Reading groups; Prayer groups; Movies; Shopping trips; Dances/Social/Cultural gatherings; Kitchen corner.

Hardin County Home
12846 State Rte 309, Kenton, OH 43326
(419) 673-5251
Licensure Intermediate care. *Beds* ICF 51. *Certified* Medicaid.
Owner Publicly owned.

Lovin' Care Center
911 W Pattison Ave, Kenton, OH 43326
(419) 675-6193, 675-3168
Admin Cindy Weatherholtz.
Medical Dir Susan Jarvis.
Licensure Intermediate care. *Beds* ICF 50. *Certified* Medicaid.
Owner Proprietary corp.
Staff Physicians 1 (pt); RNs 1 (ft); LPNs 3 (ft), 2 (pt); Activities coordinators 1 (ft); Dietitians 1 (ft).
Facilities Dining room; Activities room; Laundry room; Barber/Beauty shop.
Activities Arts & crafts; Cards; Games; Reading groups; Prayer groups; Movies; Shopping trips; Dances/Social/Cultural gatherings.

Kettering

Heartland of Kettering
3313 Wilmington Pike, Kettering, OH 45429
(513) 298-8084
Admin William G Shannon. *Dir of Nursing* Cal Kogut RN.
Licensure Skilled care; Intermediate care. *Beds* Swing beds SNF/ICF 100. *Certified* Medicaid; Medicare.
Owner Proprietary corp (Health Care and Retirement Corp).
Admissions Requirements Minimum age 55; Medical examination.
Staff RNs 6 (ft); LPNs 7 (ft); Nurses' aides 65 (ft); Physical therapists 3 (pt); Occupational therapists 1 (pt); Speech therapists 1 (pt); Activities coordinators 1 (ft); Dietitians 1 (ft); Ophthalmologists 1 (pt); Dentists 1 (pt); Social workers 1 (ft).
Facilities Dining room; Physical therapy room; Activities room; Laundry room; Barber/Beauty shop; 5 Lounges (4 with TVs); 2 large porches/patios.
Activities Arts & crafts; Cards; Games; Prayer groups; Movies; Dances/Social/Cultural gatherings; Lunches out & other outings in facility bus.

Kettering Convalescent Center
1150 W Dorothy Ln, Kettering, OH 45409
(513) 293-1152
Admin Richard H Steiner. *Dir of Nursing* Kathy Edwards RN. *Medical Dir* Yevette Pelfry MD.

Licensure Skilled care. *Beds* SNF 168. *Private Pay Patients* 30%. *Certified* Medicaid; Medicare.
Owner Nonprofit organization/foundation (Volunteers of America Health Services).
Admissions Requirements Medical examination; Physician's request.
Staff RNs 10 (ft), 13 (pt); LPNs 3 (ft), 12 (pt); Nurses' aides 50 (ft), 47 (pt); Physical therapists 2 (ft); Recreational therapists 3 (pt); Activities coordinators 1 (ft).
Affiliation Volunteers of America.
Facilities Dining room; Physical therapy room; Activities room; Chapel; Laundry room; Barber/Beauty shop.
Activities Arts & crafts; Cards; Games; Reading groups; Prayer groups; Movies; Shopping trips; Dances/Social/Cultural gatherings.

Kimbolton

Bell Nursing Home
PO Box 51, Main St, Kimbolton, OH 43749
(614) 432-7717
Admin James Romig. *Dir of Nursing* Laura Saltz RN. *Medical Dir* Janet Brockwell MD.
Licensure Intermediate care. *Beds* ICF 50. *Private Pay Patients* 16%. *Certified* Medicaid.
Owner Proprietary corp.
Staff Physicians 2 (pt); RNs 1 (ft); LPNs 6 (ft), 1 (pt); Nurses' aides 18 (ft); Physical therapists 1 (pt); Activities coordinators 1 (ft); Dietitians 1 (pt); Podiatrists 1 (pt).
Facilities Dining room; Activities room; Laundry room.
Activities Arts & crafts; Cards; Games; Reading groups; Prayer groups; Movies; Shopping trips; Dances/Social/Cultural gatherings.

Kingston

Gospel Light Nursing Home
PO Box 238, 3rd St, Kingston, OH 45644
(614) 642-2503
Admin Helen M Davis. *Dir of Nursing* Nina Williams. *Medical Dir* Michael Geron MD.
Licensure Intermediate care. *Beds* ICF 50. *Certified* Medicaid.
Owner Proprietary corp.
Staff Physicians 1 (ft), 1 (pt); RNs 1 (ft); LPNs 4 (ft); Nurses' aides 25 (ft); Recreational therapists 1 (ft); Activities coordinators 1 (ft); Dietitians 1 (pt); Podiatrists 1 (ft).
Facilities Dining room; Physical therapy room; Activities room; Crafts room; Laundry room.
Activities Arts & crafts; Cards; Reading groups; Prayer groups; Movies; Shopping trips; Dances/Social/Cultural gatherings; Intergenerational programs; Pet therapy.

Kingsville

Ashtabula County Nursing Home
Dibble Rd, Kingsville, OH 44048
(216) 224-2161
Admin Carolyn Constiner.
Medical Dir Pat Hunter.
Licensure Intermediate care. *Beds* ICF 310. *Certified* Medicaid.
Owner Publicly owned.
Admissions Requirements Minimum age 18.
Staff Physicians 2 (pt); RNs 14 (ft), 2 (pt); LPNs 28 (ft); Nurses' aides 98 (ft), 6 (pt); Physical therapists 1 (pt); Recreational therapists 5 (ft); Speech therapists 1 (pt); Activities coordinators 1 (ft); Dietitians 1 (pt); Ophthalmologists 1 (pt); Podiatrists 1 (pt).
Facilities Dining room; Physical therapy room; Activities room; Chapel; Crafts room; Laundry room; Barber/Beauty shop; Library.

Activities Arts & crafts; Cards; Games; Reading groups; Prayer groups; Movies; Shopping trips; Dances/Social/Cultural gatherings.

Kinsman

Boyd's Kinsman
PO Box 315, Rte 5, Kinsman, OH 44428
(216) 876-5581
Admin Paula L Ruley. *Dir of Nursing* Carlene Jones.
Licensure Intermediate care for mentally retarded. *Beds* ICF/MR 47. *Certified* Medicaid.
Owner Proprietary corp.
Admissions Requirements Minimum age 18.
Staff RNs 1 (ft), 2 (pt); LPNs 2 (pt); Nurses' aides 2 (ft), 7 (pt); Speech therapists 1 (pt); Activities coordinators 1 (ft).
Facilities Dining room; Activities room; Crafts room; Laundry room; Library.
Activities Arts & crafts; Cards; Games; Movies; Shopping trips; Dances/Social/Cultural gatherings; Church; Bowling.

Kirkersville

Pine Kirk Nursing Home
205 E Main St, Box 64, Kirkersville, OH 43033
(614) 927-3209
Admin Karen Rosser. *Dir of Nursing* Beverly Bradley. *Medical Dir* Dr J I Fast DO.
Licensure Intermediate care. *Beds* ICF 39. *Certified* Medicare.
Owner Proprietary corp.
Admissions Requirements Medical examination; Physician's request.
Staff Physicians 1 (ft); RNs 2 (ft); LPNs 4 (ft); Nurses' aides 9 (ft); Activities coordinators 1 (ft); Dietitians 1 (ft); Ophthalmologists 1 (ft).
Facilities Dining room; Laundry room.
Activities Arts & crafts; Cards; Games; Reading groups; Prayer groups; Movies; Shopping trips; Dances/Social/Cultural gatherings.

Kirtland

Western Reserve Convalescent Homes
9769 Chillicothe Rd, Kirtland, OH 44094
(216) 946-7858
Admin William E Rabe.
Medical Dir Donald Patchin MD.
Licensure Skilled care; Intermediate care. *Beds* SNF 20; ICF 130. *Certified* Medicaid; Medicare.
Owner Proprietary corp (Beverly Enterprises).
Admissions Requirements Minimum age 18; Medical examination; Physician's request.
Staff Physicians 5 (pt); RNs 5 (ft), 2 (pt); LPNs 5 (ft), 5 (pt); Nurses' aides 40 (ft); Physical therapists 2 (ft); Occupational therapists 1 (pt); Speech therapists 1 (ft); Activities coordinators 1 (ft), 1 (pt); Dietitians 1 (ft); Ophthalmologists 1 (pt); Podiatrists 1 (pt); Audiologists 1 (pt); Dentists 1 (pt).
Facilities Dining room; Physical therapy room; Activities room; Chapel; Crafts room; Laundry room; Barber/Beauty shop; Library.
Activities Arts & crafts; Cards; Games; Reading groups; Prayer groups; Movies; Shopping trips; Dances/Social/Cultural gatherings.

Western Reserve Extended Care
9685 Chillicothe Rd, Kirtland, OH 44094
(216) 951-7272
Admin Frances C Horton. *Dir of Nursing* Donna Higgins. *Medical Dir* Armin Green MD.
Licensure Skilled care; Intermediate care. *Beds* SNF 24; ICF 28. *Certified* Medicare.
Owner Proprietary corp (Beverly Enterprises).

Admissions Requirements Minimum age 18; Medical examination; Physician's request.
Staff RNs 8 (ft), 3 (pt); LPNs 10 (ft); Nurses' aides 13 (ft), 1 (pt); Physical therapists 1 (ft); Recreational therapists 1 (ft); Activities coordinators 1 (ft); Dietitians 1 (ft); Podiatrists 1 (pt).
Facilities Dining room; Physical therapy room; Activities room; Laundry room; Barber/Beauty shop; Library.
Activities Arts & crafts; Cards; Games; Prayer groups; Movies; Dances/Social/Cultural gatherings.

Lake Milton

Edgewater Quality Care Nursing Center
1930 Craig Dr, Lake Milton, OH 44429
(216) 744-7353
Admin Michael J Anthony.
Medical Dir Diane Prentice.
Licensure Intermediate care. *Beds* ICF 75. *Certified* Medicaid.
Owner Proprietary corp (Northwestern Service Corp).
Admissions Requirements Medical examination.
Staff RNs 1 (ft), 1 (pt); LPNs 8 (ft); Nurses' aides 14 (ft), 8 (pt); Activities coordinators 1 (ft), 1 (pt); Dietitians 1 (ft).
Facilities Dining room; Activities room; Laundry room; Barber/Beauty shop.
Activities Arts & crafts; Cards; Games; Reading groups; Prayer groups; Movies; Shopping trips.

Lakeview

Heartland of Indian Lake Nursing Center
14480 State Rte 366, Lakeview, OH 43331
(513) 843-4929
Licensure Intermediate care; Intermediate care for mentally retarded. *Beds* ICF 82; ICF/MR 18. *Certified* Medicaid.
Owner Proprietary corp (Health Care and Retirement Corp).

Heartland of Indian Lake Rehabilitation Center
14442 State Rte 33 W, Lakeview, OH 43331
(513) 843-4929
Licensure Skilled care; Intermediate care. *Beds* SNF 25; ICF 25. *Certified* Medicaid; Medicare.
Owner Proprietary corp (Health Care and Retirement Corp).

Lakewood

Aristocrat Lakewood
13900 Detroit Ave, Lakewood, OH 44107
(216) 228-7650
Admin Timothy M Coury. *Dir of Nursing* Nancy Smitley. *Medical Dir* Dr James Tsai.
Licensure Skilled care; Intermediate care. *Beds* Swing beds SNF/ICF 132. *Certified* Medicaid; Medicare.
Owner Proprietary corp.
Admissions Requirements Minimum age 18; Medical examination; Physician's request.
Staff Physicians; RNs; LPNs; Nurses' aides; Physical therapists; Recreational therapists; Occupational therapists; Speech therapists; Activities coordinators; Dietitians; Ophthalmologists; Podiatrists; Dentists.
Facilities Dining room; Physical therapy room; Activities room; Crafts room; Laundry room; Barber/Beauty shop; Library.
Activities Arts & crafts; Cards; Games; Reading groups; Prayer groups; Movies; Shopping trips; Dances/Social/Cultural gatherings.

Crestmont Nursing Home North Inc
13330 Detroit Ave, Lakewood, OH 44107
(216) 228-9550

Licensure Skilled care; Intermediate care; Rest home. *Beds* Swing beds SNF/ICF 73; Rest home 19. *Certified* Medicaid.
Owner Proprietary corp.

Wright Nursing Center
13315 Detroit Ave, Lakewood, OH 44107
(216) 226-3858
Licensure Intermediate care. *Beds* ICF 50.
Certified Medicaid.
Owner Proprietary corp.

Lancaster

Americare—Homestead Nursing & Rehabilitation Center
1900 E Main St, Lancaster, OH 43130
(614) 653-8630
Admin Andrea Korody. *Dir of Nursing* Sandy O'Brien. *Medical Dir* Dr John Lloyd; Dr Robert Sprouse.
Licensure Skilled care; Intermediate care; Alzheimer's care. *Beds* SNF 28; ICF 74. *Certified* Medicaid; Medicare.
Owner Proprietary corp (Care Enterprises).
Admissions Requirements Medical examination.
Staff Physicians 2 (pt); RNs 8 (ft); LPNs 6 (ft), 1 (pt); Nurses' aides 55 (ft), 4 (pt); Physical therapists 1 (pt); Activities coordinators 1 (ft), 1 (pt).
Languages Hungarian.
Facilities Dining room; Physical therapy room; Activities room; Crafts room; Laundry room; Barber/Beauty shop.
Activities Arts & crafts; Cards; Games; Reading groups; Prayer groups; Movies; Shopping trips; Dances/Social/Cultural gatherings.

Americare—Lancaster Nursing & Rehabilitation Center
PO Box 786, Lancaster, OH 43130
(614) 654-0641
Medical Dir Dr John Bowling.
Licensure Skilled care; Intermediate care. *Beds* SNF 20; ICF 80. *Certified* Medicaid; Medicare.
Owner Proprietary corp (Care Enterprises).
Staff Physicians 1 (pt); RNs 5 (ft), 3 (pt); LPNs 5 (ft), 2 (pt); Nurses' aides 29 (ft), 18 (pt); Physical therapists 2 (pt); Occupational therapists 1 (pt); Speech therapists 1 (pt); Activities coordinators 1 (ft); Dietitians 1 (pt); Podiatrists 1 (pt).
Facilities Dining room; Physical therapy room; Activities room; Crafts room; Laundry room; Barber/Beauty shop.
Activities Arts & crafts; Cards; Games; Reading groups; Prayer groups; Movies; Shopping trips; Dances/Social/Cultural gatherings.

Crestview Manor Nursing Home I
925 Becks Knob Rd, Lancaster, OH 43130
(614) 654-2634
Admin Winfield S Eckert; Cathy L Eckert. *Dir of Nursing* Betty Dunn RN. *Medical Dir* Richard E Hartle MD.
Licensure Skilled care; Intermediate care. *Beds* Swing beds SNF/ICF 101. *Private Pay Patients* 35%. *Certified* Medicaid; Medicare.
Owner Proprietary corp (Crestview Manor Nursing Home Inc).
Admissions Requirements Minimum age 18; Medical examination.
Staff Physicians 3 (pt); RNs 5 (ft), 4 (pt); LPNs 5 (ft), 5 (pt); Nurses' aides 53 (ft), 4 (pt); Physical therapists 1 (pt); Reality therapists 2 (ft); Recreational therapists 1 (pt); Occupational therapists 1 (pt); Speech therapists 1 (pt); Activities coordinators 1 (pt); Dietitians 1 (pt); Podiatrists 1 (pt); Audiologists 1 (pt); Dentists 1 (pt).
Facilities Dining room; Physical therapy room; Activities room; Crafts room; Laundry room; Barber/Beauty shop.

Activities Arts & crafts; Cards; Games; Reading groups; Prayer groups; Movies; Shopping trips; Dances/Social/Cultural gatherings; Intergenerational programs; Pet therapy.

Crestview Manor Nursing Home II
957 Becks Knob Rd, Lancaster, OH 43130
(614) 654-2634
Admin Winfield S Eckert; Cathy L Eckert. *Dir of Nursing* W Chris Bailey RN. *Medical Dir* Richard E Hartle MD.
Licensure Skilled care; Intermediate care. *Beds* Swing beds SNF/ICF 101. *Private Pay Patients* 40%. *Certified* Medicaid; Medicare.
Owner Proprietary corp (Crestview Manor Nursing Home Inc).
Admissions Requirements Minimum age 18; Medical examination.
Staff Physicians 3 (pt); RNs 4 (ft), 3 (pt); LPNs 8 (ft), 3 (pt); Nurses' aides 52 (ft), 4 (pt); Physical therapists 1 (pt); Reality therapists 2 (ft); Recreational therapists 1 (pt); Occupational therapists 1 (pt); Speech therapists 1 (pt); Activities coordinators 1 (pt); Dietitians 1 (pt); Podiatrists 1 (pt); Audiologists 1 (pt); Dentists 1 (pt).
Facilities Dining room; Physical therapy room; Activities room; Chapel; Crafts room; Laundry room; Barber/Beauty shop.
Activities Arts & crafts; Cards; Games; Reading groups; Prayer groups; Movies; Shopping trips; Dances/Social/Cultural gatherings; Intergenerational programs; Pet therapy.

Crites Nursing Home 2
1318 E Main St, Lancaster, OH 43130
(614) 653-3431
Admin Randall Crites. *Dir of Nursing* Shirley Tipple RN. *Medical Dir* Galen Durose DO.
Licensure Intermediate care; Retirement. *Beds* ICF 60. *Certified* Medicaid.
Owner Privately owned.
Staff RNs 2 (ft), 5 (pt); LPNs 8 (ft), 6 (pt); Nurses' aides 20 (ft), 8 (pt); Activities coordinators 2 (ft), 2 (pt); Dietitians 1 (ft).
Facilities Dining room; Activities room; Crafts room; Laundry room.
Activities Arts & crafts; Cards; Games; Reading groups; Movies; Shopping trips; Dances/Social/Cultural gatherings.

Johnston Nursing Home
1246 E Main St, Lancaster, OH 43130
(614) 653-1410
Admin Randall Crites. *Dir of Nursing* Linda Godenschwager. *Medical Dir* Galen G Durose DO.
Licensure Intermediate care. *Beds* ICF 30. *Certified* Medicaid.
Owner Privately owned.
Staff RNs 2 (ft), 2 (pt); LPNs 8 (ft), 4 (pt); Nurses' aides 12 (ft), 6 (pt); Activities coordinators 1 (ft), 2 (pt); Dietitians 1 (ft).
Facilities Dining room; Activities room; Crafts room; Laundry room.
Activities Arts & crafts; Cards; Games; Reading groups; Movies; Shopping trips.

Valley View Nursing Home
5185 Lithopolis Rd, Lancaster, OH 43130
(614) 687-0566
Admin William T Ray. *Dir of Nursing* S Kay Johnson. *Medical Dir* Ralph R Romaker MD.
Licensure Intermediate care. *Beds* ICF 25. *Private Pay Patients* 35%. *Certified* Medicaid.
Owner Privately owned.
Admissions Requirements Minimum age 21; Medical examination.
Staff Physicians 1 (pt); RNs 2 (ft), 3 (pt); LPNs 1 (pt); Nurses' aides 6 (ft), 8 (pt); Activities coordinators 1 (pt); Dietitians 1 (pt).

Facilities Dining room; Activities room; Laundry room.
Activities Arts & crafts; Cards; Games; Movies; Shopping trips; Dances/Social/Cultural gatherings; Pet therapy.

Laurelville

Wintersong Village of Laurelville
PO Box 128, 16128 Pike St, Laurelville, OH 43135
(614) 332-3221
Admin Michael Daffin.
Medical Dir Joyce Hoover.
Licensure Intermediate care. *Beds* ICF 18. *Certified* Medicaid.
Owner Proprietary corp.
Admissions Requirements Medical examination.
Staff Physicians 2 (pt); RNs 2 (pt); LPNs 2 (ft), 1 (pt); Nurses' aides 7 (ft), 3 (pt); Recreational therapists 1 (pt); Activities coordinators 1 (pt); Dietitians 1 (pt); Ophthalmologists.
Facilities Dining room; Activities room; Laundry room; Barber/Beauty shop.
Activities Arts & crafts; Cards; Games; Reading groups; Prayer groups; Movies; Shopping trips.

Lebanon

Cedars of Lebanon
102 W Silver St, Lebanon, OH 45036
(513) 932-0300
Licensure Intermediate care. *Beds* ICF 45. *Certified* Medicaid.
Owner Proprietary corp.

Lebanon Country Manor
700 Monroe Rd, Lebanon, OH 45036
(513) 932-0105
Admin Gwen Schlesinger. *Dir of Nursing* Patricia Spaulding. *Medical Dir* Charles Horsley.
Licensure Intermediate care. *Beds* ICF 100. *Certified* Medicaid.
Owner Proprietary corp (Hillhaven Corp).
Admissions Requirements Medical examination.
Staff Physicians; RNs; LPNs; Nurses' aides; Physical therapists; Reality therapists; Occupational therapists; Speech therapists; Activities coordinators; Dietitians; Podiatrists; Audiologists.
Facilities Dining room; Physical therapy room; Activities room; Crafts room; Laundry room; Barber/Beauty shop; Library.
Activities Arts & crafts; Cards; Games; Reading groups; Prayer groups; Movies; Shopping trips; Dances/Social/Cultural gatherings; Intergenerational programs; Pet therapy.

Lebanon Health Care Center
115 Oregonia Rd, Lebanon, OH 45036
(513) 932-1121
Licensure Skilled care; Intermediate care. *Beds* SNF 44; ICF 56. *Certified* Medicaid; Medicare.
Owner Proprietary corp.

Lebanon Nursing Home
220 S Mechanic St, Lebanon, OH 45036
(513) 932-4861
Admin Bernard Moskowitz. *Dir of Nursing* Sue Tate. *Medical Dir* Dr Ralph Young.
Licensure Intermediate care; Alzheimer's care. *Beds* ICF 36. *Certified* Medicaid.
Owner Proprietary corp (Health Care Opportunities).
Admissions Requirements Medical examination.

Staff Physicians 1 (ft); RNs 1 (pt); LPNs 4 (ft), 3 (pt); Nurses' aides 14 (ft), 4 (pt); Activities coordinators 2 (ft); Dietitians 1 (pt); Ophthalmologists 1 (pt); Podiatrists 1 (pt).
Facilities Dining room; Garden.
Activities Arts & crafts; Cards; Games; Reading groups; Prayer groups; Movies; Shopping trips; Dances/Social/Cultural gatherings; Intergenerational programs; Pet therapy.

Otterbein-Lebanon Home
585 N State Rte 741, Lebanon, OH 45036
(513) 932-2020, 932-4860, ext 4545 FAX
Admin Charles W Peckham Jr. *Dir of Nursing* Louann Mayers RN. *Medical Dir* Dr James Barry.
Licensure Skilled care; Intermediate care. *Beds* SNF 134; ICF 222. *Private Pay Patients* 66%. *Certified* Medicaid; Medicare.
Owner Nonprofit organization/foundation (Otterbein Homes, Inc).
Admissions Requirements Minimum age 62; Medical examination.
Staff Physicians 1 (ft), 1 (pt); RNs 30 (ft), 7 (pt); LPNs 23 (ft), 2 (pt); Nurses' aides 92 (ft), 4 (pt); Physical therapists 1 (ft); Recreational therapists 1 (ft); Occupational therapists 1 (ft); Speech therapists 1 (pt); Activities coordinators 3 (ft), 2 (pt); Dietitians 1 (pt); Ophthalmologists 1 (pt); Podiatrists 1 (pt); Audiologists 1 (pt).
Affiliation Methodist.
Facilities Dining room; Physical therapy room; Activities room; Chapel; Crafts room; Laundry room; Barber/Beauty shop; Library.
Activities Arts & crafts; Cards; Games; Reading groups; Prayer groups; Movies; Shopping trips; Dances/Social/Cultural gatherings; Intergenerational programs; Pet therapy.

Lexington

Griffeth Nursing Home Inc
RR 7, Vanderbilt Rd, Lexington, OH 44904
(419) 756-3623
Licensure Intermediate care. *Beds* ICF 50. *Certified* Medicaid.
Owner Proprietary corp.
Admissions Requirements Medical examination; Physician's request.
Staff RNs 1 (pt); LPNs 3 (ft), 4 (pt); Nurses' aides 10 (ft), 4 (pt); Recreational therapists 2 (ft), 1 (pt); Activities coordinators 1 (ft); Dietitians 1 (ft).
Facilities Dining room; Activities room; Crafts room; Laundry room.
Activities Arts & crafts; Cards; Games; Reading groups; Prayer groups; Movies; Shopping trips; Dances/Social/Cultural gatherings.

Lexington Court Care Center
250 Delaware, Lexington, OH 44904
(419) 884-2000
Licensure Intermediate care. *Beds* ICF 100. *Certified* Medicaid.
Owner Proprietary corp.

Lima

Allen County Inn
3125 Ada Rd, Lima, OH 45801
(419) 228-2346
Admin Jerome J O'Neal. *Dir of Nursing* Nancy Sidey. *Medical Dir* Dwight Becker MD.
Licensure Intermediate care. *Beds* ICF 134. *Certified* Medicaid.
Owner Publicly owned.
Admissions Requirements Medical examination; Physician's request.

Staff Physicians 1 (pt); RNs 3 (ft), 1 (pt); LPNs 7 (ft), 4 (pt); Nurses' aides 22 (ft), 3 (pt); Activities coordinators 1 (ft); Dietitians 1 (pt).
Facilities Dining room; Activities room; Chapel; Crafts room; Laundry room; Barber/Beauty shop; Library.
Activities Arts & crafts; Cards; Games; Reading groups; Prayer groups; Movies; Shopping trips; Dances/Social/Cultural gatherings.

Mary Ann Brown Residential Facility
2450 Mandolin Dr, Lima, OH 45801
(419) 229-3200
Licensure Intermediate care for mentally retarded. *Beds* ICF/MR 32. *Certified* Medicaid.

Columbia Nursing Home
651 Columbia Dr, Lima, OH 45805
(419) 227-2443
Admin Patricia Ann Parton. *Dir of Nursing* Iris Jay RN. *Medical Dir* Dr James Bowlus.
Licensure Skilled care; Intermediate care. *Beds* Swing beds SNF/ICF 50. *Certified* Medicaid; Medicare.
Owner Proprietary corp (Beverly Enterprises).
Admissions Requirements Medical examination; Physician's request.
Staff Physicians 1 (pt); RNs 5 (ft), 3 (pt); LPNs 3 (pt); Nurses' aides 13 (ft), 5 (pt); Physical therapists 1 (pt); Recreational therapists 1 (pt); Occupational therapists 1 (pt); Speech therapists 1 (pt); Activities coordinators; Dietitians 1 (pt); Podiatrists 1 (pt).
Facilities Dining room; Laundry room; Barber/Beauty shop.
Activities Arts & crafts; Cards; Games; Reading groups; Prayer groups; Movies; Shopping trips; Dances/Social/Cultural gatherings.

Lima Convalescent Home
1650 Allentown Rd, Lima, OH 45805
(419) 224-9741
Licensure Skilled care; Intermediate care. *Beds* Swing beds SNF/ICF 100.
Owner Proprietary corp.

Lima Manor
750 Brower Rd, Lima, OH 45801
(419) 227-2611
Admin Joyce A Emrick. *Dir of Nursing* Mary Davis. *Medical Dir* J S Sanoy MD.
Licensure Skilled care; Intermediate care. *Beds* Swing beds SNF/ICF 100. *Certified* Medicaid; Medicare.
Owner Proprietary corp (HCF Inc).
Admissions Requirements Medical examination; Physician's request.
Staff RNs 6 (ft), 6 (pt); RNs 8 (ft), 6 (pt); LPNs 2 (ft); Nurses' aides 46 (ft), 20 (pt); Physical therapists 2 (pt); Occupational therapists 1 (pt); Speech therapists 1 (pt); Activities coordinators 1 (ft); Dietitians 1 (ft).
Facilities Dining room; Physical therapy room; Activities room; Chapel; Crafts room; Laundry room; Barber/Beauty shop.
Activities Arts & crafts; Cards; Games; Reading groups; Prayer groups; Movies; Shopping trips; Dances/Social/Cultural gatherings.

Lost Creek Care Center
804 S Mumaugh Rd, Lima, OH 45804
(419) 225-9040
Admin Albert C Parton Jr. *Dir of Nursing* Jean Lewis RN. *Medical Dir* Melvin Monroe MD.
Licensure Skilled care; Intermediate care. *Beds* Swing beds SNF/ICF 100. *Private Pay Patients* 40%. *Certified* Medicaid; Medicare; VA.
Owner Nonprofit corp (Volunteers of America Care).

Admissions Requirements Medical examination; Physician's request.
Staff Physicians 30 (pt); RNs 10 (pt); LPNs 10 (pt); Nurses' aides 72 (pt); Physical therapists 1 (pt); Recreational therapists 1 (pt); Occupational therapists 1 (pt); Speech therapists 1 (pt); Activities coordinators 1 (pt); Dietitians 1 (pt); Ophthalmologists 1 (pt); Podiatrists 1 (pt).
Facilities Dining room; Physical therapy room; Activities room; Chapel; Crafts room; Laundry room; Barber/Beauty shop; Library.
Activities Arts & crafts; Cards; Games; Reading groups; Prayer groups; Movies; Shopping trips; Dances/Social/Cultural gatherings; Intergenerational programs; Pet therapy.

Oaks Convalescent Center
599 S Shawnee St, Lima, OH 45804
(419) 227-2154
Admin Mary Ellen Thornton. *Dir of Nursing* Ginny Rainsburg RN. *Medical Dir* Dr Thompson.
Licensure Skilled care; Intermediate care. *Beds* SNF 19; ICF 81. *Certified* Medicaid; Medicare.
Owner Proprietary corp (Beverly Enterprises).
Admissions Requirements Minimum age 18; Medical examination; Physician's request.
Staff RNs 4 (ft), 4 (pt); LPNs 7 (ft), 3 (pt); Nurses' aides 30 (ft), 18 (pt); Activities coordinators 1 (ft); Dietitians 1 (ft).
Facilities Dining room; Physical therapy room; Activities room; Crafts room; Laundry room; Barber/Beauty shop.
Activities Arts & crafts; Cards; Games; Reading groups; Prayer groups; Movies; Shopping trips; Dances/Social/Cultural gatherings.

Shawnee Manor
2535 Fort Amanda Rd, Lima, OH 45804
(419) 999-2055
Licensure Skilled care; Intermediate care. *Beds* Swing beds SNF/ICF 150. *Certified* Medicaid; Medicare.
Owner Proprietary corp (HCF Inc).

Springview Manor
883 W Spring St, Lima, OH 45805
(419) 227-3661
Licensure Intermediate care. *Beds* ICF 43. *Certified* Medicaid.
Owner Proprietary corp.
Staff Physicians 1 (ft), 1 (pt); RNs 3 (ft), 1 (pt); LPNs 3 (ft); Nurses' aides 15 (ft), 2 (pt); Physical therapists 1 (ft); Recreational therapists 1 (ft); Occupational therapists 1 (ft); Speech therapists 1 (ft); Activities coordinators 1 (ft); Dietitians 1 (ft); Podiatrists 1 (ft).
Facilities Dining room; Physical therapy room; Activities room; Crafts room; Laundry room; Barber/Beauty shop; Library.
Activities Arts & crafts; Cards; Games; Reading groups; Prayer groups; Movies; Shopping trips; Dances/Social/Cultural gatherings.

Lincoln Heights

Brown's Nursing Home
1153 Lindy St, Lincoln Heights, OH 45215
(513) 733-4240
Licensure Intermediate care. *Beds* ICF 70. *Certified* Medicaid.
Owner Proprietary corp.

Lisbon

Opportunity Homes Inc
7891 State Rte 45, Lisbon, OH 44432
(216) 424-1411
Admin Mary Jane Jones. *Dir of Nursing* Marilyn Robb. *Medical Dir* William Stevenson.

Licensure Intermediate care for mentally retarded. *Beds* ICF/MR 22. *Certified* Medicaid.
Owner Proprietary corp.
Admissions Requirements Medical examination.
Staff LPNs 6 (ft), 1 (pt); Nurses' aides 6 (ft), 11 (pt); Activities coordinators 1 (pt); Dietitians 1 (ft); Social services 2 (ft); QMRPs 2 (ft); Therapy aides 3 (ft).
Facilities Dining room; Physical therapy room; Activities room; Crafts room; Laundry room.
Activities Arts & crafts; Games; Movies; Shopping trips; Dances/Social/Cultural gatherings; Pet therapy; Special Olympics; Community awareness.

Pleasant View Nursing Home
7451 Pleasant View Dr, Lisbon, OH 44432
(216) 424-3721
Admin Iva G Myers.
Medical Dir Dr Walter Dombroski.
Licensure Intermediate care. *Beds* ICF 50. *Certified* Medicaid.
Owner Proprietary corp.
Staff RNs 1 (pt); LPNs 3 (ft), 4 (pt); Nurses' aides 12 (ft), 7 (pt); Activities coordinators 1 (ft).
Facilities Dining room; Activities room; Crafts room; Laundry room.
Activities Arts & crafts; Cards; Games; Reading groups; Prayer groups; Movies; Shopping trips; Dances/Social/Cultural gatherings.

Sunrise Homes Inc
PO Boyx 479, Lisbon, OH 44432
Licensure Intermediate care for mentally retarded. *Beds* ICF/MR 24. *Certified* Medicaid.
Owner Proprietary corp.

Lodi

SHC Hastings House
210 Bank St, Lodi, OH 44254
(216) 948-3930
Licensure Intermediate care for mentally retarded. *Beds* ICF/MR 8. *Certified* Medicaid.
Owner Proprietary corp.

Logan

Arcadia Acres
20017 State Rte 93 S, Logan, OH 43138
(614) 385-2461
Licensure Intermediate care. *Beds* ICF 50. *Certified* Medicaid.
Owner Proprietary corp.

Buckeye Community Services—Culver Street Home
30 N Culver St, Logan, OH 43138
(614) 286-5039
Licensure Intermediate care for mentally retarded. *Beds* ICF/MR 8. *Certified* Medicaid.
Owner Proprietary corp.

Buckeye Community Services—Hunter Street Home
412 W Hunter St, Logan, OH 43138
(614) 286-5039
Admin Pamela S Pauley. *Dir of Nursing* Jennifer VanSickle RN.
Licensure Intermediate care for mentally retarded. *Beds* ICF/MR 5. *Certified* Medicaid.
Owner Nonprofit corp.
Admissions Requirements Minimum age Legal adult; Males only.
Staff RNs 1 (pt); LPNs 3 (pt); Physical therapists 1 (pt); Occupational therapists 1 (pt); Speech therapists 1 (pt); Activities coordinators 1 (pt).

Activities Arts & crafts; Cards; Games; Reading groups; Movies; Shopping trips; Dances/Social/Cultural gatherings.

Buckeye Community Services—Walnut Street Home
823 Walnut-Dowler Rd, Logan, OH 43138
(614) 286-5039
Licensure Intermediate care for mentally retarded. *Beds* ICF/MR 10. *Certified* Medicaid.
Owner Proprietary corp.

Hocking Valley Community Hospital
PO Box 966, Logan, OH 43138-0966
(614) 385-5631
Licensure Skilled care; Intermediate care. *Beds* SNF 30; ICF 30. *Certified* Medicaid; Medicare.
Owner Publicly owned.

Logan Health Care Center
300 Arlington Ave, Logan, OH 43138
(614) 385-2155
Admin Raymond L Sill. *Dir of Nursing* JoAnne Conkle RN. *Medical Dir* Dr Teresa Ouilan.
Licensure Skilled care; Intermediate care. *Beds* SNF 16; ICF 143. *Certified* Medicaid; Medicare.
Owner Proprietary corp (Hillhaven Corp).
Admissions Requirements Medical examination; Physician's request.
Staff RNs; LPNs; Nurses' aides; Activities coordinators; Dietitians.
Facilities Dining room; Physical therapy room; Activities room; Crafts room; Laundry room; Barber/Beauty shop.
Activities Arts & crafts; Cards; Games; Reading groups; Prayer groups; Movies; Shopping trips; Dances/Social/Cultural gatherings; Intergenerational programs; Pet therapy.

London

Madison Elms
218 Elm St, London, OH 43140
(614) 852-3100
Admin Gary Brand. *Dir of Nursing* Sharon Ellis RN. *Medical Dir* William T Bacon MD.
Licensure Skilled care; Intermediate care. *Beds* Swing beds SNF/ICF 100. *Certified* Medicaid; Medicare.
Owner Proprietary corp (Arbor Health Care).
Admissions Requirements Medical examination.
Staff RNs 5 (ft), 1 (pt); LPNs 4 (ft), 1 (pt); Nurses' aides 26 (ft), 3 (pt); Physical therapists 1 (ft); Occupational therapists 1 (ft); Speech therapists 1 (ft); Activities coordinators 1 (ft); Dietitians 1 (pt); Ophthalmologists; Dentists.
Facilities Dining room; Physical therapy room; Chapel; Laundry room; Barber/Beauty shop.
Activities Arts & crafts; Cards; Games; Reading groups; Prayer groups; Movies; Shopping trips; Dances/Social/Cultural gatherings.

Lorain

Anchor Lodge Nursing Home Inc
3756 W Erie Ave, Lorain, OH 44053
(216) 244-2019
Admin Marenia G Davis.
Medical Dir Dr I A Eren.
Licensure Intermediate care; Retirement; Alzheimer's care. *Beds* ICF 103. *Certified* Medicaid.
Owner Proprietary corp.
Admissions Requirements Medical examination.

Staff RNs 2 (ft), 2 (pt); LPNs 6 (ft), 8 (pt); Nurses' aides 28 (ft), 12 (pt); Physical therapists 1 (ft), 1 (pt); Recreational therapists 1 (ft); Activities coordinators 1 (ft); Dietitians 1 (ft); Ophthalmologists 1 (ft); Podiatrists 1 (ft); Dentists 1 (ft).
Languages Spanish, Hungarian.
Facilities Dining room; Physical therapy room; Activities room; Crafts room; Laundry room; Barber/Beauty shop; Library.
Activities Arts & crafts; Cards; Games; Reading groups; Prayer groups; Movies; Shopping trips; Dances/Social/Cultural gatherings.

Autumn Aegis Nursing Home
3905 Oberlin Ave, Lorain, OH 44053
(216) 282-6768
Licensure Intermediate care. *Beds* ICF 100. *Certified* Medicaid.
Owner Proprietary corp.

Lorain Manor Nursing Home
1882 E 32nd St, Lorain, OH 44055
(216) 277-8173
Licensure Intermediate care. *Beds* ICF 76. *Certified* Medicaid.
Owner Proprietary corp.

Meister Road Homes
4609 Meister Rd, Lorain, OH 44052
(216) 282-3074
Admin Dr Ellen L Payner. *Dir of Nursing* Patricia Paul RN.
Licensure Intermediate care for mentally retarded. *Beds* ICF/MR 18. *Certified* Medicaid.
Owner Publicly owned.
Admissions Requirements Minimum age 7.
Staff RNs 2 (ft); LPNs 2 (ft), 4 (pt); Nurses' aides 8 (ft), 20 (pt); Recreational therapists 1 (ft); Dietitians 1 (ft).
Facilities Dining room; Laundry room.
Activities Arts & crafts; Games; Reading groups; Movies; Shopping trips; Dances/Social/Cultural gatherings; County ARC activities; School & community functions.

Oak Hills Nursing Center
3650 Beavercrest Dr, Lorain, OH 44053
(216) 282-9171, 282-9730 FAX
Admin Gary L Plasschaert MHA. *Dir of Nursing* JoAnn Buck. *Medical Dir* Dr John Gray.
Licensure Skilled care; Intermediate care. *Beds* Swing beds SNF/ICF 100. *Private Pay Patients* 20%. *Certified* Medicaid; Medicare.
Owner Proprietary corp (Unicare).
Admissions Requirements Medical examination; Physician's request.
Staff Physicians 1 (pt); RNs 3 (ft), 1 (pt); LPNs 5 (ft), 2 (pt); Nurses' aides 40 (ft), 10 (pt); Physical therapists 1 (pt); Occupational therapists 1 (pt); Speech therapists 1 (pt); Activities coordinators 1 (pt); Dietitians 1 (pt); Ophthalmologists 1 (pt); Podiatrists 1 (pt); Audiologists 1 (pt).
Facilities Dining room; Physical therapy room; Activities room; Crafts room; Laundry room; Barber/Beauty shop.
Activities Arts & crafts; Cards; Games; Reading groups; Prayer groups; Movies; Shopping trips; Dances/Social/Cultural gatherings; Intergenerational programs; Pet therapy; Outside trips.

Ohio Extended Care Center
3364 Kolbe Rd, Lorain, OH 44053
(216) 282-2244
Licensure Skilled care; Intermediate care. *Beds* SNF 23; ICF 180. *Certified* Medicaid; Medicare.
Owner Proprietary corp.

Loudonville

Colonial Manor Health Care Center
747 S Mount Vernon Ave, Loudonville, OH 44842
(419) 994-4191, 994-4193 FAX
Admin Linda Snowbarger. *Dir of Nursing* Patricia Shireman. *Medical Dir* Dr Jon Cooperrider.
Licensure Intermediate care; Alzheimer's care. *Beds* ICF 80. *Certified* Medicaid.
Owner Proprietary corp (Nationwide Management).
Admissions Requirements Minimum age 18.
Staff RNs 3 (ft), 4 (pt); LPNs 5 (ft), 9 (pt); Nurses' aides 24 (ft), 9 (pt); Recreational therapists 1 (ft); Activities coordinators 2 (ft); Dietitians 1 (pt).
Facilities Dining room; Physical therapy room; Activities room; Crafts room; Laundry room; Barber/Beauty shop.
Activities Arts & crafts; Cards; Games; Reading groups; Prayer groups; Movies; Shopping trips; Pet therapy.

Colonial Manor Health Care Center Inc II
630 E Washington St, Loudonville, OH 44842
(419) 994-3148
Admin Linda S Snowbarger. *Dir of Nursing* Lynn Morgan. *Medical Dir* Dr J H Cooperrider MD.
Licensure Intermediate care for mentally retarded. *Beds* ICF/MR 32. *Private Pay Patients* 0%. *Certified* Medicaid.
Owner Privately owned (Linda & Jack Snowbarger).
Admissions Requirements Minimum age 15; Medical examination; Physician's request.
Staff Physicians (consultant); RNs 1 (ft); LPNs 4 (ft), 2 (pt); Nurses' aides 12 (ft), 6 (pt); Physical therapists (consultant); Recreational therapists 3 (ft), 1 (pt); Occupational therapists (consultant); Speech therapists (consultant); Dietitians 1 (ft); Ophthalmologists (consultant); Podiatrists (consultant); Audiologists (consultant).
Facilities Dining room; Activities room; Laundry room; Barber/Beauty shop.
Activities Arts & crafts; Games; Movies; Shopping trips; Dances/Social/Cultural gatherings; Family visits.

Loudonville Nursing Home Inc
205 N Water, Loudonville, OH 44842
(419) 994-4250
Admin Marlen Radbill. *Dir of Nursing* John McMullen. *Medical Dir* A C Kuttothara.
Licensure Intermediate care. *Beds* ICF 25. *Private Pay Patients* 30%. *Certified* Medicaid.
Owner Privately owned.
Admissions Requirements Medical examination.
Staff Physicians 1 (pt); RNs 1 (pt); LPNs 2 (ft), 2 (pt); Nurses' aides 6 (ft), 4 (pt); Activities coordinators 1 (ft); Dietitians 1 (pt).
Facilities Dining room; Activities room; Chapel; Crafts room; Laundry room; Barber/Beauty shop; Patio/Dining area.
Activities Arts & crafts; Cards; Games; Reading groups; Prayer groups; Movies; Shopping trips; Dances/Social/Cultural gatherings; Intergenerational programs; Pet therapy.

Louisville

Mapleview Care Center Inc
4466 Lynnhaven Ave NE, Louisville, OH 44641
(216) 875-5060
Licensure Intermediate care. *Beds* ICF 50. *Certified* Medicaid.
Owner Proprietary corp.

Marcelle Home
7121 W Saint Francis St, Louisville, OH 44641
(216) 875-4224
Licensure Intermediate care. *Beds* ICF 50. *Certified* Medicaid.
Owner Proprietary corp (Altercare Inc).

Miller Care Center Inc
11701 Louisville St NE, Louisville, OH 44641
(216) 875-8444
Licensure Intermediate care. *Beds* ICF 50. *Certified* Medicaid.
Owner Proprietary corp.

Joseph T Nist Geriatric Nursing Home
7770 Columbus Rd NE, Louisville, OH 44641
(216) 875-1436
Admin John E Reiser. *Dir of Nursing* Donna Craig RN. *Medical Dir* Eugene Pogorelec DO.
Licensure Skilled care; Intermediate care. *Beds* Swing beds SNF/ICF 248. *Certified* Medicaid; Medicare.
Owner Publicly owned.
Admissions Requirements Medical examination.
Staff RNs 8 (ft), 4 (pt); LPNs 18 (ft), 12 (pt); Nurses' aides 70 (ft), 30 (pt); Activities coordinators 2 (ft).
Facilities Dining room; Physical therapy room; Activities room; Crafts room; Laundry room; Barber/Beauty shop; Library.
Activities Arts & crafts; Cards; Games; Reading groups; Prayer groups; Movies; Shopping trips; Dances/Social/Cultural gatherings.

St Joseph Hospice
2308 Reno Dr, Louisville, OH 44641
(216) 875-5562
Admin Sr Monica Bellinger. *Dir of Nursing* Marilyn May. *Medical Dir* Dr Joseph Kolp.
Licensure Intermediate care. *Beds* ICF 100. *Certified* Medicaid.
Owner Proprietary corp.
Admissions Requirements Minimum age 60; Medical examination; Physician's request.
Staff Physicians 4 (ft), 10 (pt); RNs 6 (ft), 10 (pt); LPNs 5 (ft), 5 (pt); Nurses' aides 20 (ft), 29 (pt); Activities coordinators 1 (ft), 2 (pt); Physical therapist aides 2 (ft).
Affiliation Roman Catholic.
Facilities Dining room; Activities room; Chapel; Crafts room; Laundry room; Barber/Beauty shop.
Activities Arts & crafts; Cards; Games; Reading groups; Prayer groups; Movies; Shopping trips; Dances/Social/Cultural gatherings.

Molly Stark Hospital
7900 Columbus Rd, Louisville, OH 44641
(216) 875-5531
Admin Donald T McKenna. *Dir of Nursing* Roberta Wolf RN. *Medical Dir* Eugene Pogorelec.
Licensure Skilled care; Intermediate care; Intermediate care for mentally retarded. *Beds* ICF/MR 50; Swing beds SNF/ICF 30. *Certified* Medicaid; Medicare.
Owner Publicly owned.
Admissions Requirements Physician's request.
Staff Physicians 4 (pt); RNs 9 (ft), 9 (pt); LPNs 24 (ft), 9 (pt); Nurses' aides 50 (ft), 9 (pt); Physical therapists 1 (pt); Recreational therapists 1 (ft); Occupational therapists 1 (pt); Speech therapists 1 (pt); Activities coordinators 1 (ft); Dietitians 1 (ft); Ophthalmologists 1 (pt); Dentists 3 (pt).
Facilities Dining room; Physical therapy room; Activities room; Chapel; Crafts room; Laundry room; Barber/Beauty shop.
Activities Arts & crafts; Cards; Games; Reading groups; Prayer groups; Movies; Shopping trips; Dances/Social/Cultural gatherings.

Loveland

Loveland Health Care
501 N 2nd St, Loveland, OH 45140
(513) 683-0010, 683-1936 FAX
Admin Bernie Neuer LNHA. *Dir of Nursing* Nancy Jackson RN. *Medical Dir* William Blake Selnick DO.
Licensure Skilled care; Intermediate care. *Beds* Swing beds SNF/ICF 109. *Private Pay Patients* 15%. *Certified* Medicaid; Medicare.
Owner Proprietary corp.
Admissions Requirements Minimum age 18; Medical examination.
Staff RNs 6 (ft); LPNs 13 (ft); Nurses' aides 48 (ft); Physical therapists 1 (ft); Activities coordinators 2 (ft); Dietitians 1 (ft).
Facilities Dining room; Physical therapy room; Activities room; Chapel; Crafts room; Laundry room; Barber/Beauty shop; Library.
Activities Arts & crafts; Cards; Games; Reading groups; Prayer groups; Movies; Shopping trips; Dances/Social/Cultural gatherings; Intergenerational programs; Pet therapy.

Lucasville

Edgewood Manor of Lucasville Inc
PO Box 789, Lucasville, OH 45648
(614) 259-5536
Licensure Skilled care; Intermediate care; Intermediate care for mentally retarded. *Beds* SNF 26; ICF 74; ICF/MR 65. *Certified* Medicaid; Medicare.
Owner Proprietary corp.

Madeira

Madeira Nursing Inc
6940 Stiegler Ln, Madeira, OH 45243
(513) 561-6400
Admin Lisa G Weber.
Medical Dir David S Norris MD.
Licensure Skilled care; Intermediate care. *Beds* SNF 33; ICF 65. *Certified* Medicaid; Medicare.
Owner Proprietary corp.
Admissions Requirements Minimum age 18; Medical examination.
Staff RNs 5 (ft), 2 (pt); LPNs 5 (ft), 1 (pt); Nurses' aides 30 (ft), 2 (pt); Physical therapists 1 (pt); Speech therapists 1 (pt); Activities coordinators 1 (ft); Dietitians 1 (pt); Ophthalmologists 1 (pt); Podiatrists 1 (pt); Dentists 1 (pt).
Facilities Dining room; Activities room; Barber/Beauty shop.
Activities Arts & crafts; Cards; Games; Reading groups; Prayer groups; Movies; Dances/Social/Cultural gatherings.

Madison

Broadfield Manor Nursing & Convalescent Home
7927 Middle Ridge Rd, Madison, OH 44057
(216) 466-3702
Admin Torild Barbins.
Medical Dir Janis Zemzars MD.
Licensure Skilled care; Intermediate care; Intermediate care for mentally retarded. *Beds* ICF/MR 49; Swing beds SNF/ICF 93. *Certified* Medicaid; Medicare.
Owner Proprietary corp.
Admissions Requirements Medical examination.
Staff Physicians 4 (pt); Physical therapists 1 (pt); Occupational therapists 1 (pt); Speech therapists 1 (pt); Activities coordinators 2 (ft); Dietitians 1 (pt); Podiatrists 1 (pt); Dentists 1 (pt).
Facilities Dining room; Physical therapy room; Activities room; Crafts room; Laundry room; Barber/Beauty shop.

Activities Arts & crafts; Cards; Games; Reading groups; Prayer groups; Movies; Shopping trips; Dances/Social/Cultural gatherings; Organ music at mealtime 3 times a week.

Gables Nursing Home
PO Box 272, 731 Lake St, Madison, OH 44057
(216) 428-1519
Licensure Intermediate care for mentally retarded. *Beds* ICF/MR 20. *Certified* Medicaid.
Owner Proprietary corp.

Inn-Madison Health Center
6831 Chapel Rd, Madison, OH 44057
(216) 428-5103
Admin R D Van Allen. *Dir of Nursing* Cori Dye RN. *Medical Dir* Dr M Rezai.
Licensure Skilled care; Intermediate care; Alzheimer's care. *Beds* Swing beds SNF/ICF 120. *Private Pay Patients* 2%. *Certified* Medicaid; Medicare.
Owner Proprietary corp.
Admissions Requirements Minimum age 16; Medical examination; Physician's request.
Staff Physicians 4 (ft); RNs 6 (ft), 3 (pt); LPNs 21 (ft); Nurses' aides 28 (ft), 4 (pt); Physical therapists (consultant); Reality therapists 1 (ft); Recreational therapists 1 (ft); Occupational therapists (consultant); Speech therapists (consultant); Activities coordinators 1 (ft); Dietitians (consultant); Ophthalmologists (consultant); Podiatrists (consultant); Audiologists (consultant); Dentists (consultant).
Facilities Dining room; Physical therapy room; Activities room; Chapel; Crafts room; Laundry room; Barber/Beauty shop; Library.
Activities Arts & crafts; Cards; Games; Reading groups; Prayer groups; Movies; Shopping trips; Dances/Social/Cultural gatherings; Intergenerational programs; Pet therapy; Music therapy; Remotivation techniques; Reality orientation.

Madison Health Care
7600 S Ridge Rd, Madison, OH 44057
(216) 428-1492, 951-9299
Admin Dale Rumburg. *Dir of Nursing* Ogla Dennison. *Medical Dir* Dr Moses Moschkovich.
Licensure Skilled care; Intermediate care; Retirement; Alzheimer's care. *Beds* SNF 113; ICF 17; Retirement 5. *Private Pay Patients* 15%. *Certified* Medicaid; Medicare.
Owner Proprietary corp.
Admissions Requirements Medical examination.
Staff Physicians 2 (pt); RNs 5 (ft), 1 (pt); LPNs 10 (ft), 2 (pt); Nurses' aides 40 (ft), 10 (pt); Physical therapists 1 (pt); Speech therapists 1 (pt); Activities coordinators 2 (ft); Dietitians 1 (pt); Ophthalmologists 1 (pt); Podiatrists 1 (pt); Audiologists 1 (pt).
Facilities Dining room; Physical therapy room; Activities room; Crafts room; Laundry room; Barber/Beauty shop; Library.
Activities Arts & crafts; Cards; Games; Prayer groups; Movies; Shopping trips; Picnics; Festivals; Ball games.

Madison Village Nursing Home
148 E Main St, Madison, OH 44057
(216) 428-6969
Licensure Intermediate care for mentally retarded. *Beds* ICF/MR 8. *Certified* Medicaid.
Owner Proprietary corp.

Stewart Lodge
7774 Warner Rd, Madison, OH 44057
(216) 428-7121
Licensure Intermediate care for mentally retarded. *Beds* ICF/MR 54. *Certified* Medicaid.
Owner Proprietary corp.

Malta

Parmiter Nursing Home
800 N Main St, Malta, OH 43758
(614) 962-4861
Admin Evelyn J Reynolds. *Dir of Nursing* Phyllis Keaton RN. *Medical Dir* Robinson Kirkpatrick.
Licensure Intermediate care. *Beds* ICF 30. *Private Pay Patients* 5%. *Certified* Medicaid.
Owner Proprietary corp.
Admissions Requirements Minimum age 18; Medical examination.
Staff RNs; LPNs; Nurses' aides; Activities coordinators; Dietitians; Podiatrists; Social services.
Facilities Dining room; Activities room; Laundry room.
Activities Arts & crafts; Cards; Games; Reading groups; Prayer groups; Movies; Shopping trips; Dances/Social/Cultural gatherings; Intergenerational programs; Pet therapy; Country rides.

Mansfield

Chenita Nursing Home
111 S Diamond St, Mansfield, OH 44903
(419) 524-4149
Admin Anthony L Wheaton. *Dir of Nursing* Jessie Van Aucker. *Medical Dir* Gordon F Morkel MD.
Licensure Intermediate care. *Beds* ICF 50. *Private Pay Patients* 10%. *Certified* Medicaid.
Owner Proprietary corp.
Admissions Requirements Minimum age 16; Medical examination.
Staff Physicians 1 (pt); RNs 2 (ft); LPNs 4 (ft), 1 (pt); Nurses' aides 14 (ft); Physical therapists 1 (pt); Reality therapists 1 (pt); Recreational therapists 1 (ft); Occupational therapists 1 (pt); Speech therapists 1 (pt); Activities coordinators 1 (ft); Dietitians 1 (pt); Ophthalmologists 1 (pt); Podiatrists 1 (pt); Audiologists 1 (pt).
Facilities Dining room; Physical therapy room; Activities room; Crafts room; Laundry room; Library.
Activities Arts & crafts; Cards; Games; Reading groups; Prayer groups; Movies; Shopping trips; Dances/Social/Cultural gatherings.

Chenita Nursing Home No 1
245 W 4th St, Mansfield, OH 44902
(419) 524-2335
Admin Anthony L Wheaton. *Dir of Nursing* Jessie Van Aucker. *Medical Dir* Gordon F Morkel.
Licensure Intermediate care. *Beds* ICF 13. *Private Pay Patients* 0%. *Certified* Medicaid.
Owner Proprietary corp.
Admissions Requirements Minimum age 16; Medical examination.
Staff LPNs 3 (ft); Nurses' aides 3 (ft), 2 (pt); Activities coordinators 1 (ft); Dietitians 1 (pt).
Facilities Dining room; Activities room; Crafts room; Laundry room.
Activities Arts & crafts; Cards; Games; Reading groups; Movies; Shopping trips; Dances/Social/Cultural gatherings.

Cherry Hill Home
786 Ferndale Rd, Mansfield, OH 44905
(419) 526-3447
Licensure Intermediate care for mentally retarded. *Beds* ICF/MR 8. *Certified* Medicaid.
Owner Publicly owned.

Crestwood Care Center, Mansfield
Rock Rd, Mansfield, OH 44903
(419) 347-1266

Licensure Skilled care; Intermediate care. *Beds* ICF 20; Swing beds SNF/ICF 5.
Owner Proprietary corp.

Geriatric Center—Mansfield Memorial Homes
PO Box 966, 50 Blymyer Ave, Mansfield, OH 44901
(419) 524-4178
Medical Dir Charles G Young MD.
Licensure Skilled care; Intermediate care. *Beds* SNF 18; ICF 81. *Certified* Medicaid; Medicare.
Owner Proprietary corp.
Admissions Requirements Minimum age; Medical examination; Physician's request.
Staff RNs 7 (ft), 8 (pt); LPNs 5 (ft), 7 (pt); Nurses' aides 25 (ft), 15 (pt); Physical therapists 1 (ft); Reality therapists 1 (ft); Recreational therapists 1 (ft); Occupational therapists 1 (ft), 1 (pt); Speech therapists 1 (pt); Activities coordinators 1 (ft); Dietitians 1 (pt).
Facilities Dining room; Physical therapy room; Activities room; Chapel; Crafts room; Laundry room; Barber/Beauty shop; Library.
Activities Arts & crafts; Cards; Games; Reading groups; Prayer groups; Movies; Shopping trips; Dances/Social/Cultural gatherings; Occupational therapy; Speech therapy.

Glendale Home
624 Glendale Blvd, Mansfield, OH 44907
(419) 756-8914
Licensure Intermediate care for mentally retarded. *Beds* ICF/MR 12. *Certified* Medicaid.
Owner Publicly owned.

Mifflin Care Center
1600 Crider Rd, Mansfield, OH 44903
(419) 589-7611, 589-3476 FAX
Admin Dr James A McCaulley. *Dir of Nursing* Diane Wasiniak. *Medical Dir* Dr Beddard.
Licensure Skilled care; Intermediate care. *Beds* Swing beds SNF/ICF 100. *Private Pay Patients* 50%. *Certified* Medicaid; Medicare.
Owner Proprietary corp.
Admissions Requirements Medical examination; Physician's request.
Staff Physicians 1 (pt); RNs 4 (ft), 2 (pt); LPNs 6 (ft), 5 (pt); Nurses' aides 28 (ft), 2 (pt); Physical therapists 1 (pt); Occupational therapists 1 (pt); Speech therapists 1 (pt); Activities coordinators 1 (ft); Dietitians 1 (pt); Ophthalmologists 1 (pt); Podiatrists 1 (pt); Audiologists 1 (pt); Dietary & housekeeping 25 (ft).
Facilities Dining room; Physical therapy room; Activities room; Crafts room; Laundry room; Barber/Beauty shop; Theater; 4 private rooms; 16 private suites; 40 semi-private rooms; Individual heating & air conditioning controls.
Activities Arts & crafts; Cards; Games; Reading groups; Movies; Shopping trips; Dances/Social/Cultural gatherings; Performances by different groups.

Rosemont Nursing Home
1159 Wyandotte Ave, Mansfield, OH 44906
(419) 747-2666
Licensure Intermediate care. *Beds* ICF 24. *Certified* Medicaid.
Owner Proprietary corp.

Sturges Convalescent Home
81 Sturges Ave, Mansfield, OH 44902
(419) 522-3651
Licensure Intermediate care. *Beds* ICF 29. *Certified* Medicaid.
Owner Proprietary corp.

Twin Oaks
73 Madison Rd, Mansfield, OH 44905
(419) 526-0124, 522-8816 FAX
Admin Anthony L Wheaton. *Dir of Nursing* Nina Wright. *Medical Dir* Dr P K Athmaram.

Licensure Intermediate care for mentally retarded. *Beds* ICF/MR 32. *Private Pay Patients* 3%. *Certified* Medicaid.
Owner Proprietary corp.
Admissions Requirements Minimum age 16; Medical examination.
Staff Physicians 1 (pt); RNs 1 (ft); LPNs 6 (ft); Nurses' aides 14 (ft); Physical therapists 1 (pt); Recreational therapists 2 (ft); Occupational therapists 1 (pt); Speech therapists 1 (pt); Activities coordinators 1 (ft); Dietitians 1 (pt); Ophthalmologists 1 (pt); Podiatrists 1 (pt); Dentists 1 (pt).
Facilities Dining room; Physical therapy room; Activities room; Crafts room; Laundry room; Library.
Activities Arts & crafts; Cards; Games; Reading groups; Prayer groups; Movies; Shopping trips; Dances/Social/Cultural gatherings.

Watts Home
140 Home Ave, Mansfield, OH 44903
(419) 526-0120
Licensure Intermediate care for mentally retarded. *Beds* ICF/MR 5. *Certified* Medicaid.
Owner Publicly owned.

Winchester Terrace
70 Winchester Rd, Mansfield, OH 44907
(419) 756-4747
Admin Linn Dunn. *Dir of Nursing* Geri Sullivan RN. *Medical Dir* Donald Beddard MD.
Licensure Skilled care. *Beds* SNF 63. *Private Pay Patients* 100%.
Owner Proprietary corp (Levering Management).
Admissions Requirements Medical examination.
Staff RNs 4 (ft); LPNs 6 (ft); Nurses' aides 25 (ft), 3 (pt); Activities coordinators 1 (ft).
Facilities Dining room; Activities room; Crafts room; Laundry room; Barber/Beauty shop.
Activities Arts & crafts; Cards; Games; Prayer groups; Movies; Shopping trips; Dances/Social/Cultural gatherings.

Woodlawn Nursing Home
535 Lexington Ave, Mansfield, OH 44907
(419) 756-7111
Admin Michael Rau. *Dir of Nursing* Cathy Wiltanger. *Medical Dir* Dr Beddard.
Licensure Skilled care; Intermediate care; Rest home. *Beds* SNF 126; ICF 29; Rest home 9. *Certified* Medicaid; Medicare.
Owner Proprietary corp.
Staff RNs 8 (ft), 4 (pt); LPNs 10 (ft), 5 (pt); Nurses' aides 45 (ft), 15 (pt); Recreational therapists 2 (pt); Activities coordinators 1 (ft); Dietitians 1 (pt).
Facilities Dining room; Activities room; Crafts room; Laundry room; Barber/Beauty shop.
Activities Arts & crafts; Cards; Games; Reading groups; Prayer groups; Movies; Shopping trips; Dances/Social/Cultural gatherings; Intergenerational programs; Pet therapy.

Mantua

Hattie Larlham Foundation
9772 Diagonal Rd, Mantua, OH 44255
(216) 274-2272
Medical Dir Mary Marsick MD.
Licensure Intermediate care for mentally retarded. *Beds* ICF/MR 130. *Certified* Medicaid.
Owner Nonprofit organization/foundation.
Admissions Requirements Medical examination.
Staff Physicians 1 (ft); RNs 9 (ft); LPNs 17 (ft); Nurses' aides 94 (ft); Physical therapists 3 (ft); Recreational therapists 1 (ft);

Occupational therapists 4 (ft); Speech therapists 1 (ft); Dietitians 1 (ft); Audiologists 1 (pt); Dentists 1 (pt).
Facilities Physical therapy room; Activities room; Chapel; Laundry room.

Maple Heights

Maple Care Center
16231 Broadway Ave, Maple Heights, OH 44137
(216) 641-3712
Medical Dir M Reddy MD.
Licensure Skilled care; Intermediate care. *Beds* Swing beds SNF/ICF 100.
Owner Proprietary corp.
Admissions Requirements Medical examination.
Staff RNs 3 (ft); LPNs 6 (ft); Nurses' aides 28 (ft); Physical therapists 1 (pt); Activities coordinators 1 (ft), 1 (pt).
Facilities Dining room; Physical therapy room; Activities room; Chapel; Crafts room; Library; Occupational therapy room; Exam room; Shampoo room; Patio.
Activities Arts & crafts; Cards; Games; Reading groups; Prayer groups; Movies; Dances/Social/Cultural gatherings; Entertainment and shows.

Pedone Nursing Center
19900 Clare Ave, Maple Heights, OH 44137
(216) 662-3343, 662-1887 FAX
Admin Esther Zaidman RN. *Dir of Nursing* Chris Gazdik. *Medical Dir* Dr Nachman Kacen.
Licensure Skilled care; Intermediate care; Retirement. *Beds* Swing beds SNF/ICF 116; Retirement 80. *Certified* Medicaid; Medicare.
Owner Proprietary corp.
Admissions Requirements Medical examination.
Staff Physicians; RNs; LPNs; Nurses' aides; Physical therapists; Speech therapists; Activities coordinators; Dietitians; Podiatrists; Audiologists.
Facilities Dining room; Physical therapy room; Activities room; Chapel; Crafts room; Laundry room; Barber/Beauty shop; Enclosed garden.
Activities Arts & crafts; Cards; Games; Reading groups; Prayer groups; Movies; Shopping trips; Dances/Social/Cultural gatherings; Intergenerational programs; Pet therapy.

Marietta

Marie Antoinette Pavilion
355 Putnam Ave, Marietta, OH 45750
(614) 373-4369
Admin H A Kolshorn.
Medical Dir C Dehmlow MD.
Licensure Intermediate care; Retirement; Alzheimer's care. *Beds* ICF 50. *Certified* Medicaid.
Owner Proprietary corp.
Admissions Requirements Medical examination.
Staff Physicians 1 (pt); RNs 2 (ft); LPNs 11 (ft), 4 (pt); Nurses' aides 18 (ft), 4 (pt); Physical therapists 2 (pt); Occupational therapists 1 (pt); Speech therapists 1 (pt); Activities coordinators 2 (ft), 1 (pt); Dietitians 1 (pt); Ophthalmologists 1 (pt); Podiatrists 1 (pt); Dentists 1 (pt).
Languages German, French, Arabic.
Facilities Dining room; Activities room; Crafts room; Laundry room; Barber/Beauty shop; Library.
Activities Arts & crafts; Cards; Games; Reading groups; Prayer groups; Movies; Shopping trips; Dances/Social/Cultural gatherings.

Arbors at Marietta
400 7th St, Marietta, OH 45750
(614) 373-3597
Licensure Skilled care; Intermediate care; Rest home. *Beds* SNF 23; ICF 119; Rest home 32. *Certified* Medicaid; Medicare.
Owner Proprietary corp (Arbor Health Care).

Heartland of Marietta
Rte 60, Devola, Marietta, OH 45750
(614) 373-8920
Licensure Intermediate care. *Beds* ICF 101. *Certified* Medicaid.
Owner Proprietary corp (Health Care and Retirement Corp).

Marietta Convalescent Center
117 Barlett St, Marietta, OH 45750
(614) 373-1867
Admin Donna J Barker. *Dir of Nursing* Lillie Varner RN. *Medical Dir* Kenneth E Bennett MD.
Licensure Skilled care; Intermediate care. *Beds* Swing beds SNF/ICF 120. *Certified* Medicaid.
Owner Proprietary corp.
Admissions Requirements Medical examination; Physician's request.
Staff Physicians 1 (ft), 10 (pt); RNs 6 (ft), 3 (pt); LPNs 9 (ft), 5 (pt); Nurses' aides 30 (ft), 5 (pt); Physical therapists 1 (pt); Activities coordinators 2 (ft), 2 (pt); Dietitians 1 (pt); Ophthalmologists 1 (pt); Podiatrists 1 (pt).
Facilities Dining room; Activities room; Chapel; Crafts room; Laundry room; Barber/ Beauty shop; 2 lounges.
Activities Arts & crafts; Games; Reading groups; Prayer groups; Movies; Shopping trips; Dances/Social/Cultural gatherings.

Marion

Americare—Marion
524 James Way, Marion, OH 43302
(614) 389-6306, 389-2240 FAX
Admin Mark J Morley. *Dir of Nursing* Jo Walters. *Medical Dir* Dr Ronald Landefeld.
Licensure Skilled care; Intermediate care. *Beds* SNF 25; ICF 75. *Private Pay Patients* 45%. *Certified* Medicaid; Medicare.
Owner Proprietary corp (Care Enterprises).
Staff RNs 5 (ft); LPNs 8 (ft); Nurses' aides 20 (ft); Activities coordinators 1 (ft).
Activities Arts & crafts; Cards; Games; Reading groups; Prayer groups; Movies; Shopping trips; Dances/Social/Cultural gatherings; Intergenerational programs; Pet therapy.

Community Nursing Center
175 Community Dr, Marion, OH 43302
(614) 387-7537
Admin Michael J Rau. *Dir of Nursing* Carol Buchanan.
Licensure Skilled care; Intermediate care; Retirement; Alzheimer's care. *Beds* SNF 8; ICF 101. *Certified* Medicaid; Medicare.
Owner Proprietary corp (Hillhaven Corp).
Admissions Requirements Minimum age 18; Medical examination.
Staff RNs 4 (ft), 1 (pt); LPNs 7 (ft), 2 (pt); Nurses' aides 35 (ft), 15 (pt); Physical therapists 1 (pt); Recreational therapists 1 (ft); Occupational therapists 1 (pt); Speech therapists 1 (pt); Activities coordinators 2 (ft); Dietitians 1 (pt).
Facilities Dining room; Physical therapy room; Activities room; Crafts room; Laundry room; Barber/Beauty shop.
Activities Arts & crafts; Cards; Games; Reading groups; Prayer groups; Movies; Shopping trips; Dances/Social/Cultural gatherings.

Hillside Nursing Home
333 N Prospect, Marion, OH 43302
(614) 382-5042

Admin James L Baack. *Dir of Nursing* Colleen Place. *Medical Dir* Richard Chen MD.
Licensure Intermediate care; Adult foster care; Retirement. *Beds* ICF 24; Adult foster care 16. *Private Pay Patients* 15%. *Certified* Medicaid.
Owner Proprietary corp (Buckeye Family of Nursing Homes).
Admissions Requirements Medical examination.
Staff Physicians 1 (pt); RNs 1 (pt); LPNs 3 (ft), 2 (pt); Nurses' aides 9 (ft), 4 (pt); Activities coordinators 1 (ft); Dietitians 1 (pt); Ophthalmologists 1 (pt); Podiatrists 1 (pt).
Facilities Dining room; Laundry room.
Activities Arts & crafts; Cards; Games; Prayer groups; Movies; Shopping trips; Dances/ Social/Cultural gatherings; Occasional functions off-site.

Maplewood Nursing Center Inc
409 Bellefontaine Ave, Marion, OH 43302
(614) 383-2126
Medical Dir Dr Warren Sawyer.
Licensure Skilled care; Intermediate care. *Beds* Swing beds SNF/ICF 50. *Certified* Medicaid; Medicare.
Owner Proprietary corp.
Admissions Requirements Minimum age 21.
Staff Physicians 1 (pt); RNs 5 (ft); LPNs 4 (ft); Nurses' aides 25 (ft); Physical therapists 1 (ft); Occupational therapists 1 (pt); Speech therapists 1 (pt); Activities coordinators 1 (ft); Dietitians 1 (pt); Ophthalmologists 1 (pt); Podiatrists 1 (pt); Dentists 1 (pt).
Facilities Dining room; Physical therapy room; Activities room; Chapel; Laundry room; Barber/Beauty shop.
Activities Arts & crafts; Cards; Prayer groups; Movies.

Marion County Home—Eastlawn Manor
1422 Mt Vernon Ave, Marion, OH 43302
(614) 389-4624
Admin Larry M Marburger.
Medical Dir Dr Ronald Landefeld.
Licensure Skilled care; Intermediate care. *Beds* SNF 26; ICF 113. *Certified* Medicaid; Medicare.
Owner Publicly owned.
Admissions Requirements Physician's request.
Staff RNs 9 (ft), 3 (pt); LPNs 12 (ft), 6 (pt); Nurses' aides 41 (ft), 12 (pt); Physical therapists 4 (ft); Activities coordinators 2 (ft), 1 (pt).
Facilities Dining room; Physical therapy room; Activities room; Chapel; Crafts room; Laundry room; Barber/Beauty shop; Library.
Activities Arts & crafts; Cards; Games; Reading groups; Prayer groups; Movies; Shopping trips; Dances/Social/Cultural gatherings.

Marion Manor Nursing Home Inc
195 Executive Dr, Marion, OH 43302
(614) 387-9545
Licensure Skilled care; Intermediate care. *Beds* SNF 25; ICF 75. *Certified* Medicaid; Medicare.
Owner Proprietary corp.

Morning View Care Center
677 Marion-Cardington Rd W, Box 656, Marion, OH 43302
(614) 389-1214, 389-2074 FAX
Admin Dixie Waite. *Dir of Nursing* Debbie Radebaugh. *Medical Dir* Dr Ronald Landefeld.
Licensure Intermediate care. *Beds* ICF 30. *Private Pay Patients* 10%. *Certified* Medicaid.
Owner Proprietary corp (Dearth Management).
Admissions Requirements Medical examination.
Staff RNs; LPNs; Nurses' aides; Activities coordinators; Dietitians; Ophthalmologists.

Facilities Dining room; Laundry room; Barber/Beauty shop; Library.
Activities Arts & crafts; Cards; Games; Reading groups; Prayer groups; Movies; Shopping trips; Dances/Social/Cultural gatherings; Pet therapy.

Martins Ferry

East Ohio Regional Hospital Long-Term Care Unit
90 N 4th St, Martins Ferry, OH 43935
(614) 633-1100
Admin Angelo Calbone. *Dir of Nursing* J Loccisano RN. *Medical Dir* Dr F W Cook.
Licensure Skilled care; Intermediate care. *Beds* Swing beds SNF/ICF 75. *Certified* Medicaid; Medicare.
Owner Proprietary corp.
Admissions Requirements Medical examination; Physician's request.
Staff RNs; LPNs; Nurses' aides; Physical therapists; Activities coordinators; Dietitians.
Facilities Dining room; Physical therapy room; Activities room; Chapel; Crafts room; Barber/Beauty shop.
Activities Arts & crafts; Cards; Games; Reading groups; Prayer groups; Movies; Shopping trips; Dances/Social/Cultural gatherings.

Valley View Nursing Home
56143 Colerain Pike, Martins Ferry, OH 43935
(614) 633-9637
Admin Alice L Callarik. *Dir of Nursing* Kathleen Wolf RN. *Medical Dir* Dr Burke.
Licensure Intermediate care. *Beds* ICF 25. *Private Pay Patients* 12%. *Certified* Medicaid.
Owner Privately owned.
Admissions Requirements Minimum age 18; Medical examination; Physician's request.
Staff Physicians 1 (ft); RNs 1 (ft); LPNs 6 (ft); Nurses' aides 9 (ft); Physical therapists 1 (ft); Activities coordinators 1 (ft); Dietitians 1 (ft); Podiatrists 1 (ft).
Facilities Dining room; Activities room; Laundry room.
Activities Arts & crafts; Cards; Games; Prayer groups; Movies; Shopping trips; Dances/ Social/Cultural gatherings.

Marysville

Heartland of Marysville
755 Plum St, Marysville, OH 43040
(513) 644-8836
Licensure Skilled care; Intermediate care. *Beds* Swing beds SNF/ICF 100. *Certified* Medicaid; Medicare.
Owner Proprietary corp (Health Care and Retirement Corp).

Milcrest Nursing Center
730 Milcrest Dr, Marysville, OH 43040
(513) 642-1026
Admin Donna Crawford. *Dir of Nursing* Maxine Gregg. *Medical Dir* Malcolm MacIvor MD.
Licensure Skilled care; Intermediate care. *Beds* ICF/MR Swing beds SNF/ICF 50. *Certified* Medicaid; Medicare.
Owner Proprietary corp.
Admissions Requirements Minimum age 40.
Staff RNs 2 (ft), 1 (pt); LPNs 3 (ft), 3 (pt); Nurses' aides 16 (ft), 3 (pt); Physical therapists 1 (pt); Recreational therapists 1 (ft), 1 (pt); Activities coordinators 1 (pt); Dietitians 1 (pt); Podiatrists 1 (pt).
Facilities Dining room; Physical therapy room; Laundry room; Barber/Beauty shop.
Activities Arts & crafts; Cards; Games; Reading groups; Prayer groups; Movies; Shopping trips; Dances/Social/Cultural

gatherings; Current events; Adopt-a-grandparent program; Children's hour; Pet visiting; Out-to-lunch group.

Union Manor
18000 State Rte 4, Marysville, OH 43040
(513) 642-3893
Licensure Intermediate care. *Beds* ICF 114. *Certified* Medicaid.
Owner Publicly owned.

Mason

Altercare of Mason
5640 Cox-Smith Rd, Mason, OH 45040
(513) 398-2881, 398-2881 FAX
Admin Thomas G Cunningham. *Dir of Nursing* Jenny Koeblen RN. *Medical Dir* Martin Lehenbaur MD.
Licensure Intermediate care. *Beds* ICF 50. *Private Pay Patients* 20%. *Certified* Medicaid.
Owner Proprietary corp.
Admissions Requirements Minimum age 40; Medical examination; Physician's request.
Staff Physicians 5 (pt); RNs 1 (ft); LPNs 5 (ft); Nurses' aides 15 (ft), 2 (pt); Physical therapists 1 (pt); Recreational therapists 2 (pt); Activities coordinators 2 (pt); Dietitians 1 (pt).
Facilities Dining room; Activities room; Laundry room.
Activities Arts & crafts; Cards; Games; Reading groups; Prayer groups; Movies; Shopping trips; Dances/Social/Cultural gatherings; Intergenerational programs; Pet therapy.

Massillon

Alternative Residences Two Inc—19th Street Home
115 19th St SE, Massillon, OH 44646
(216) 833-6542
Licensure Intermediate care for mentally retarded. *Beds* ICF/MR 8. *Certified* Medicaid.
Owner Proprietary corp.

Alternative Residences Two Inc—Tremont Avenue Home
1865 Tremont Ave SE, Massillon, OH 44646
(216) 833-5564
Licensure Intermediate care for mentally retarded. *Beds* ICF/MR 8. *Certified* Medicaid.
Owner Proprietary corp.

AnMac Home V
1608 Forest Ave SE, Massillon, OH 44646
(216) 832-2789
Licensure Intermediate care for mentally retarded. *Beds* ICF/MR 10. *Certified* Medicaid.
Owner Proprietary corp.

AnMac Home VI
1620 Forest Ave SE, Massillon, OH 44646
(216) 832-2797
Licensure Intermediate care for mentally retarded. *Beds* ICF/MR 10. *Certified* Medicaid.
Owner Proprietary corp.

Eventide Nursing Home
200 Stewart Ave NW, Massillon, OH 44646
(216) 477-4686
Licensure Skilled care; Intermediate care. *Beds* Swing beds SNF/ICF 14.
Owner Proprietary corp.

Hanover House Inc
435 Avis Ave, Massillon, OH 44646
(216) 837-1741, 837-1747 FAX
Admin Amy J Francis. *Dir of Nursing* Judy Dinkins RN. *Medical Dir* M Kamel MD.

Licensure Skilled care; Intermediate care. *Beds* SNF 49; ICF 151. *Private Pay Patients* 48%. *Certified* Medicaid; Medicare.
Owner Proprietary corp (Emery Medical Management).
Admissions Requirements Minimum age 16.
Staff Physicians 4 (pt); RNs 7 (ft), 6 (pt); LPNs 18 (ft), 9 (pt); Nurses' aides 65 (ft), 5 (pt); Physical therapists 1 (ft), 2 (pt); Occupational therapists 1 (pt); Speech therapists 1 (pt); Activities coordinators 1 (ft), 2 (pt); Dietitians 1 (ft), 1 (pt).
Facilities Dining room; Physical therapy room; Activities room; Chapel; Crafts room; Laundry room; Barber/Beauty shop.
Activities Arts & crafts; Cards; Games; Reading groups; Prayer groups; Movies; Shopping trips; Dances/Social/Cultural gatherings; Pet therapy.

Hospitality House
205 Rohr Ave NW, Massillon, OH 44646
(216) 837-2100
Medical Dir Dr Wayne Lutzke.
Licensure Intermediate care. *Beds* ICF 28. *Certified* Medicaid.
Owner Proprietary corp.
Admissions Requirements Minimum age 60; Medical examination.
Staff RNs 1 (pt); LPNs 3 (ft), 4 (pt); Nurses' aides 5 (ft), 10 (pt); Activities coordinators 1 (pt).
Facilities Dining room; Activities room; Crafts room; Laundry room; Barber/Beauty shop.
Activities Arts & crafts; Cards; Games; Movies; Shopping trips.

Meadow Wind Health Care Center Inc
300 23rd St NE, Massillon, OH 44646
(216) 833-2026
Licensure Skilled care; Intermediate care. *Beds* Swing beds SNF/ICF 100. *Certified* Medicaid; Medicare.
Owner Proprietary corp.

Rose Lane Health Center
5425 High Mill Ave NW, Massillon, OH 44646
(216) 833-3174
Admin Dennis Potts. *Dir of Nursing* Carole Zay RN. *Medical Dir* Donald Zimmerman MD.
Licensure Skilled care; Intermediate care. *Beds* SNF 25; ICF 162. *Private Pay Patients* 20-25%. *Certified* Medicaid; Medicare.
Owner Proprietary corp.
Admissions Requirements Minimum age 16; Medical examination; Physician's request.
Staff Physicians 28 (pt); RNs 10 (ft), 4 (pt); LPNs 20 (ft), 10 (pt); Nurses' aides 60 (ft), 35 (pt); Physical therapists 1 (ft), 1 (pt); Recreational therapists 3 (ft); Occupational therapists 1 (pt); Speech therapists (contracted); Activities coordinators 1 (ft); Dietitians 1 (ft); Ophthalmologists (contracted); Podiatrists (contracted); Audiologists (contracted).
Facilities Dining room; Physical therapy room; Activities room; Chapel; Crafts room; Laundry room; Barber/Beauty shop; Multi-purpose areas.
Activities Arts & crafts; Cards; Games; Reading groups; Prayer groups; Movies; Shopping trips; Dances/Social/Cultural gatherings; Quilting; Gardening; Fishing; Religious services.

Shalem Rest
906 16th St SE, Massillon, OH 44646
(216) 832-0403
Medical Dir A Alasyali MD.
Licensure Intermediate care. *Beds* ICF 19. *Certified* Medicaid.
Owner Proprietary corp.
Admissions Requirements Minimum age; Medical examination.

Staff Physicians; RNs; LPNs; Nurses' aides; Physical therapists; Reality therapists; Recreational therapists; Occupational therapists; Speech therapists; Activities coordinators; Dietitians; Ophthalmologists; Podiatrists; Audiologists; Dentists.
Facilities Dining room; Activities room; Crafts room; Laundry room.
Activities Arts & crafts; Cards; Games; Reading groups; Prayer groups; Movies; Dances/Social/Cultural gatherings.

Walnut Hills Pavilion
1236 Huron Rd SE, Massillon, OH 44646
(216) 832-5252
Admin Abraham Smith. *Dir of Nursing* Sally Bredenberg. *Medical Dir* Dr Joseph Urabel DO.
Licensure Intermediate care. *Beds* ICF 23. *Certified* Medicaid.
Owner Proprietary corp.
Admissions Requirements Minimum age 18; Medical examination.
Staff Physicians; LPNs 3 (ft), 4 (pt); Nurses' aides 8 (ft), 2 (pt); Activities coordinators 1 (ft); Dietitians 2 (ft), 2 (pt).
Facilities Dining room; Activities room; Crafts room; Laundry room.
Activities Arts & crafts; Cards; Games; Reading groups; Prayer groups; Shopping trips; Breakfast outings.

Masury

O'Brien Memorial Nursing Home
563 Brookfield Ave SE, Masury, OH 44438
(216) 448-2557, 448-2558, 448-0100 FAX
Admin Sr Mary Carl Kotheimer MSN LNHA. *Dir of Nursing* Mary Helen Sandor RN. *Medical Dir* Samuel J Pipes DO.
Licensure Skilled care; Intermediate care. *Beds* Swing beds SNF/ICF 159. *Private Pay Patients* 12%. *Certified* Medicaid; Medicare.
Owner Proprietary corp (Windsor House Inc).
Admissions Requirements Medical examination; Physician's request.
Staff Physicians 1 (pt); RNs 5 (ft), 6 (pt); LPNs 22 (ft), 4 (pt); Nurses' aides 61 (ft), 11 (pt); Physical therapists 1 (pt); Occupational therapists 1 (pt); Speech therapists 1 (pt); Activities coordinators 1 (ft); Dietitians 1 (pt); Ophthalmologists 1 (pt); Podiatrists 1 (pt); Audiologists 1 (pt); Dentists (consultant).
Facilities Dining room; Physical therapy room; Activities room; Laundry room; Barber/Beauty shop; Library; Living room.
Activities Arts & crafts; Cards; Games; Reading groups; Prayer groups; Movies; Shopping trips; Dances/Social/Cultural gatherings.

Orange Village Care Center
8055 Addison Rd SE, Masury, OH 44460
(216) 448-2547
Admin Arnold C Yost Jr. *Dir of Nursing* Dorothy Tomorie. *Medical Dir* Dr Pat DiTommaso.
Licensure Intermediate care; Intermediate care for mentally retarded. *Beds* ICF 76; ICF/MR 40. *Private Pay Patients* 7%. *Certified* Medicaid.
Owner Proprietary corp (American Health Care Centers).
Admissions Requirements Minimum age 6; Medical examination; Physician's request.
Staff Physicians 1 (pt); RNs 3 (ft), 2 (pt); LPNs 13 (ft), 4 (pt); Nurses' aides 40 (ft), 22 (pt); Physical therapists 1 (pt); Occupational therapists 1 (pt); Speech therapists 1 (pt); Activities coordinators 5 (ft); Dietitians 1 (pt); Ophthalmologists 1 (pt); Podiatrists 1 (pt); Audiologists 1 (pt).
Facilities Dining room; Physical therapy room; Activities room; Crafts room; Barber/Beauty shop.

Activities Arts & crafts; Cards; Games; Prayer groups; Movies; Shopping trips; Dances/Social/Cultural gatherings; Sight-seeing; Educational and pleasure outings.

Maumee

Garden Family Care Home
6660 Garden Rd, Maumee, OH 43537
(419) 866-1434
Licensure Intermediate care for mentally retarded. *Beds* ICF/MR 5.
Owner Proprietary corp.

Lucas County Children Services—Extended Care Unit
2500 River Rd, Maumee, OH 43537
(419) 893-4861
Admin Faith E Marcinek. *Dir of Nursing* Debra Osborn.
Licensure Intermediate care for mentally retarded. *Beds* ICF/MR 32. *Certified* Medicaid.
Owner Publicly owned.
Admissions Requirements Medical examination.
Staff Physicians 1 (pt); RNs 3 (ft), 1 (pt); LPNs 4 (ft), 4 (pt); Nurses' aides 8 (ft), 23 (pt); Physical therapists 2 (pt); Recreational therapists 1 (ft); Occupational therapists 2 (pt); Speech therapists 1 (pt); Dietitians 1 (pt); Program managers 3 (ft), 3 (pt).
Facilities Dining room; Physical therapy room; Activities room; Crafts room; Laundry room.
Activities Arts & crafts; Games; Movies; Shopping trips.

Elizabeth Scott Memorial Care Center
2720 Albon Rd, Maumee, OH 43537
(419) 865-3002
Admin Philip E Witker. *Dir of Nursing* Nancy Johnson RN.
Licensure Intermediate care; Retirement. *Beds* ICF 50. *Certified* Medicaid.
Owner Proprietary corp.
Admissions Requirements Medical examination; Physician's request.
Staff RNs 6 (ft); LPNs 2 (ft); Nurses' aides 28 (ft); Activities coordinators 1 (ft); Dietitians 1 (pt).
Facilities Dining room; Activities room; Crafts room; Laundry room; Barber/Beauty shop.
Activities Arts & crafts; Cards; Games; Reading groups; Prayer groups; Movies; Shopping trips; Dances/Social/Cultural gatherings.

Sunshine Children's Home
7223 Maumee-Western Rd, Maumee, OH 43537
(419) 865-0251
Licensure Intermediate care for mentally retarded. *Beds* ICF/MR 80. *Certified* Medicaid.
Owner Proprietary corp.

Mayfield Heights

Manor Care Nursing Center of Mayfield Heights
6757 Mayfield Rd, Mayfield Heights, OH 44124
(216) 473-0090
Admin Sally B Hahn. *Dir of Nursing* Jane E Bibb RN. *Medical Dir* T Isakov MD.
Licensure Skilled care; Intermediate care. *Beds* SNF 77; ICF 13. *Certified* Medicare.
Owner Proprietary corp (Manor Care Inc).
Admissions Requirements Minimum age 18.
Staff Physicians 1 (pt); RNs 11 (ft), 9 (pt); LPNs 10 (ft), 8 (pt); Nurses' aides 32 (ft), 16 (pt); Physical therapists 2 (ft), 1 (pt); Recreational therapists 2 (ft); Occupational

therapists 1 (pt); Speech therapists 1 (pt); Dietitians 1 (pt); Ophthalmologists 1 (pt); Dentists 1 (pt).
Facilities Dining room; Physical therapy room; Activities room; Laundry room; Barber/Beauty shop; Shopping cart.
Activities Arts & crafts; Cards; Games; Reading groups; Prayer groups; Movies; Shopping trips; Dances/Social/Cultural gatherings; Exercise group.

McArthur

Twin Maples Nursing Home Inc
Rte 1, McArthur, OH 45651
(614) 596-5955
Medical Dir Dr Susan Crapes.
Licensure Intermediate care. *Beds* ICF 42. *Certified* Medicaid.
Owner Proprietary corp.
Admissions Requirements Medical examination; Physician's request.
Staff RNs 3 (pt); LPNs 4 (ft), 3 (pt); Nurses' aides 11 (ft), 4 (pt); Physical therapists 1 (pt); Activities coordinators 1 (ft), 1 (pt); Dietitians 1 (pt); Podiatrists 1 (pt); Dentists 1 (pt).
Facilities Dining room; Activities room; Laundry room.
Activities Cards; Games; Reading groups; Shopping trips.

McConnelsville

Mark Rest Center—CareServe
4114 N State Rte 376 NW, McConnelsville, OH 43756-9702
(614) 962-3761, 962-2122, 962-4979 FAX
Admin David D Bankes NHA. *Dir of Nursing* Harriet Huck RN. *Medical Dir* John Shaner MD.
Licensure Skilled care; Intermediate care; Alzheimer's care. *Beds* Swing beds SNF/ICF 151. *Private Pay Patients* 20%. *Certified* Medicaid; Medicare.
Owner Nonprofit organization/foundation.
Admissions Requirements Minimum age 18; Medical examination; Physician's request.
Staff Physicians 4 (pt); RNs 10 (ft), 2 (pt); LPNs 16 (ft), 9 (pt); Nurses' aides 44 (ft), 23 (pt); Physical therapists 2 (pt); Occupational therapists 1 (pt); Speech therapists 1 (pt); Activities coordinators 1 (ft); Dietitians 1 (pt); Ophthalmologists (consultant); Podiatrists 1 (pt); Audiologists (consultant).
Facilities Dining room; Physical therapy room; Activities room; Crafts room; Laundry room; Barber/Beauty shop; Library; 7 lounges, 4 with TV; Outside patios.
Activities Arts & crafts; Cards; Games; Reading groups; Prayer groups; Movies; Shopping trips; Dances/Social/Cultural gatherings; Intergenerational programs; Pet therapy.

Morgan County Care Center
856 Riverside Dr, McConnelsville, OH 43756
(614) 942-5303
Licensure Intermediate care. *Beds* ICF 50. *Certified* Medicaid.
Owner Proprietary corp (Community Care Centers).

McDermott

Rendezvous Medi-Home
Rte 2 Box 135, McDermott, OH 45652
(614) 858-4546
Licensure Intermediate care. *Beds* ICF 46. *Certified* Medicaid.
Owner Proprietary corp.

Rest Haven Nursing Home
Baker St, McDermott, OH 45652
(614) 259-2838

Licensure Intermediate care. *Beds* ICF 23. *Certified* Medicaid.
Owner Proprietary corp.

Medina

Care House
809 E Washington St, Medina, OH 44256
(216) 725-4123
Licensure Rest home. *Beds* Rest home 50.
Owner Proprietary corp.
Admissions Requirements Medical examination.
Facilities Dining room; Activities room; Crafts room; Barber/Beauty shop; Library.
Activities Arts & crafts; Cards; Games; Reading groups; Prayer groups; Movies; Shopping trips.

Eckfield Rest Home Inc
1530 Remsen Rd, Medina, OH 44256
(216) 239-1717
Licensure Rest home. *Beds* Rest home 22.
Owner Proprietary corp.

Evergreen Care Center
555 Springbrook Dr, Medina, OH 44256
(216) 725-3393
Licensure Skilled care; Intermediate care. *Beds* SNF 16; ICF 104. *Certified* Medicaid; Medicare.
Owner Proprietary corp (Beverly Enterprises).

Ohio Pythian Sisters Home of Medina
550 Miner Dr, Medina, OH 44256
(216) 725-1550
Admin Irvin S Bayer. *Dir of Nursing* Martha Grannis RN. *Medical Dir* Dr Irene Leszkiewicz.
Licensure Intermediate care. *Beds* ICF 50. *Certified* Medicaid.
Owner Nonprofit corp.
Admissions Requirements Minimum age 65; Medical examination; Physician's request.
Staff Physicians 1 (pt); RNs 1 (ft), 1 (pt); LPNs 5 (ft), 2 (pt); Nurses' aides 19 (ft), 4 (pt); Activities coordinators 1 (ft); Dietitians 1 (pt).
Facilities Dining room; Activities room; Crafts room; Laundry room; Barber/Beauty shop.
Activities Arts & crafts; Cards; Games; Reading groups; Prayer groups; Movies; Shopping trips.

Paradise Village
PO Box 481, 4281 Paradise Rd, Medina, OH 44256
(216) 723-2100
Admin Eugene G Glick. *Dir of Nursing* Shirley Adkins. *Medical Dir* Dr Marc Williams.
Licensure Intermediate care for mentally retarded. *Beds* ICF/MR 24. *Private Pay Patients* 0%. *Certified* Medicaid.
Owner Privately owned.
Admissions Requirements Minimum age 16; Medical examination.
Staff Physicians (contracted); RNs 1 (pt); LPNs 3 (pt); Physical therapists (contracted); Occupational therapists (contracted); Speech therapists (contracted); Activities coordinators 1 (pt); Dietitians (contracted); Podiatrists (contracted); Audiologists (contracted); Development aides 12 (ft), 13 (pt).
Facilities Dining room; Laundry room.
Activities Arts & crafts; Cards; Games; Movies; Shopping trips; Active treatment.

Sophia Huntington Parker Home
635 N Huntington St, Medina, OH 44256
(216) 722-4672
Admin Irvin S Bayer. *Dir of Nursing* Martha Grannis RN. *Medical Dir* Dr Irene Leszkiewicz.
Licensure Skilled care; Intermediate care. *Beds* Swing beds SNF/ICF 34.

Owner Nonprofit corp.
Admissions Requirements Minimum age 62; Females only; Medical examination; Physician's request.
Staff Physicians 1 (pt); RNs 1 (pt); LPNs 3 (ft), 4 (pt); Nurses' aides 9 (ft), 6 (pt); Activities coordinators 1 (ft); Dietitians 1 (pt).
Affiliation Knights of Pythias.
Facilities Dining room; Activities room; Chapel; Crafts room; Laundry room; Barber/Beauty shop.
Activities Arts & crafts; Cards; Games; Reading groups; Prayer groups; Movies; Shopping trips.

Samaritan Care Center
806 E Washington St, Medina, OH 44256
(216) 725-4123
Admin Gary L DeHass.
Licensure Skilled care; Intermediate care; Rest home. *Beds* Swing beds SNF/ICF 49; Rest home 81.
Owner Proprietary corp.
Admissions Requirements Medical examination.
Facilities Dining room; Physical therapy room; Activities room; Barber/Beauty shop.
Activities Arts & crafts; Cards; Games; Reading groups; Prayer groups; Movies.

Shangri-La Rest Home Inc
2400 Columbia Rd, Medina, OH 44256
(216) 483-3131, 225-9171, 336-4747
Admin Linda L Ferguson RN MSN NHA. *Dir of Nursing* Pat Reynolds RN MEd. *Medical Dir* Judith F Gooding MD.
Licensure Skilled care; Intermediate care; Rest home. *Beds* Swing beds SNF/ICF 200; Rest home 38. *Certified* Medicaid; Medicare.
Owner Proprietary corp.
Staff Physicians 1 (pt); RNs 7 (ft); LPNs 19 (ft); Nurses' aides 64 (ft), 24 (pt); Physical therapists 1 (pt); Speech therapists 1 (pt); Activities coordinators 1 (ft); Dietitians 1 (pt); Ophthalmologists 1 (pt); Dentists 1 (pt).
Facilities Dining room; Physical therapy room; Activities room; Crafts room; Laundry room; Barber/Beauty shop.
Activities Arts & crafts; Cards; Games; Prayer groups; Movies; Dances/Social/Cultural gatherings.

SHC Lafayette Road Home
202 W Lafayette Rd, Medina, OH 44256
(216) 723-1880
Admin Eugene G Glick. *Dir of Nursing* Shirley Adkins. *Medical Dir* Dr Marc Williams.
Licensure Intermediate care for mentally retarded. *Beds* ICF/MR 8. *Private Pay Patients* 0%. *Certified* Medicaid.
Owner Nonprofit organization/foundation.
Admissions Requirements Minimum age 16; Medical examination.
Staff Physicians (contracted); RNs 1 (pt); LPNs 3 (pt); Physical therapists (contracted); Occupational therapists (contracted); Speech therapists (contracted); Activities coordinators 1 (pt); Dietitians (contracted); Podiatrists (contracted); Audiologists (contracted); Development aides 2 (ft), 3 (pt).
Facilities Dining room; Laundry room.
Activities Arts & crafts; Cards; Games; Movies; Shopping trips; Dances/Social/Cultural gatherings; Active treatment.

Mentor

Greenlawn Nursing Home
9901 Johnnycake Ridge Rd, Mentor, OH 44060
(216) 357-7900
Licensure Intermediate care; Alzheimer's care. *Beds* ICF 71. *Certified* Medicaid.
Owner Proprietary corp (Altercare Inc).

Admissions Requirements Medical examination.
Staff Physicians 1 (pt); RNs 1 (ft), 2 (pt); LPNs 6 (ft), 3 (pt); Nurses' aides 25 (ft); Activities coordinators 1 (ft), 2 (pt); Dietitians 1 (pt); Ophthalmologists 1 (pt).
Facilities Dining room; Activities room; Laundry room; Barber/Beauty shop.
Activities Arts & crafts; Cards; Games; Reading groups; Prayer groups; Movies; Shopping trips.

Heartland of Mentor Nursing Center
8300 Center St, Mentor, OH 44060
(216) 256-1496
Licensure Skilled care; Intermediate care; Rest home. *Beds* Swing beds SNF/ICF 100; Rest home 60. *Certified* Medicaid; Medicare.
Owner Proprietary corp (Health Care and Retirement Corp).

Lake County Adult Residential Center
8211 Deepwood Blvd, Mentor, OH 44060
(216) 255-7411
Licensure Intermediate care for mentally retarded. *Beds* ICF/MR 64. *Certified* Medicaid.
Owner Publicly owned.

Lake County Child Development Center
8121 Deepwood Blvd, Mentor, OH 44060
(216) 255-7411
Licensure Intermediate care for mentally retarded. *Beds* ICF/MR 26. *Certified* Medicaid.
Owner Publicly owned.

Mentor Way Villa Nursing Home
8903 Mentor Ave & Shady Lane, Mentor, OH 44060
(216) 255-9309
Admin Lenore Finerman. *Dir of Nursing* Kathy Taylor. *Medical Dir* Dr Edwin Basquinez.
Licensure Intermediate care. *Beds* ICF 79. *Private Pay Patients* 5%. *Certified* Medicaid.
Owner Proprietary corp (Southworth Odonnell Inc).
Staff RNs; LPNs; Nurses' aides; Dietitians.
Facilities Activities room; Laundry room.
Activities Arts & crafts; Cards; Games; Reading groups; Prayer groups; Movies; Shopping trips; Dances/Social/Cultural gatherings; Intergenerational programs; Pet therapy.

Miamisburg

Friendly Nursing Home Inc
542 E Linden Ave, Miamisburg, OH 45342
(513) 866-4051
Licensure Intermediate care. *Beds* ICF 36. *Certified* Medicaid.
Owner Proprietary corp.

Heartland of Oak Ridge
450 Oak Ridge Blvd, Miamisburg, OH 45342
(513) 866-8885
Licensure Skilled care; Intermediate care; Rest home. *Beds* Swing beds SNF/ICF 100; Rest home 60. *Certified* Medicaid; Medicare.
Owner Proprietary corp (Health Care and Retirement Corp).

Miami Christel Manor Inc
1120 S Dunaway St, Miamisburg, OH 45342
(513) 866-9089, 866-6907 FAX
Admin Patsy VanDyke. *Dir of Nursing* Kathleen Yowler. *Medical Dir* Jo Yvette Pelfrey MD.
Licensure Intermediate care. *Beds* ICF 101. *Private Pay Patients* 25%. *Certified* Medicaid.
Owner Privately owned.
Admissions Requirements Medical examination; Must need ICF long-term care.

Staff Physicians 10 (pt); RNs 8 (ft); LPNs 14 (ft); Nurses' aides 43 (ft); Physical therapists 1 (pt); Recreational therapists 1 (pt); Occupational therapists 1 (pt); Speech therapists 1 (pt); Activities coordinators 1 (ft), 2 (pt); Dietitians 1 (pt); Ophthalmologists 1 (pt); Podiatrists 1 (pt); Audiologists 1 (pt).
Facilities Dining room; Physical therapy room; Activities room; Chapel; Laundry room; Barber/Beauty shop; Goldfish pond; 2 patios.
Activities Arts & crafts; Cards; Games; Reading groups; Prayer groups; Movies; Shopping trips; Dances/Social/Cultural gatherings; Intergenerational programs; Pet therapy; One-on-one activities.

Middleburg Heights

Southwest Health Care Center
7250 Old Oak Blvd, Middleburg Heights, OH 44130
(216) 243-7888
Licensure Skilled care; Intermediate care; Rest home. *Beds* Swing beds SNF/ICF 90; Rest home 10.
Owner Proprietary corp.

Middlefield

Briar Hill Nursing Home
PO Box 277, Middlefield, OH 44062
(216) 632-5241
Licensure Intermediate care. *Beds* ICF 39. *Certified* Medicaid.
Owner Nonprofit corp.

Middletown

Colonial Manor
508 S Main St, Middletown, OH 45044
(513) 423-3882
Admin Bob Sisson.
Medical Dir Dr Jeff Zollett.
Licensure Skilled care; Intermediate care; Retirement. *Beds* Swing beds SNF/ICF 29.
Owner Proprietary corp.
Admissions Requirements Minimum age 18; Medical examination; Physician's request.
Staff RNs 1 (ft); LPNs 4 (ft), 3 (pt); Nurses' aides 12 (ft), 4 (pt); Physical therapists 1 (pt); Recreational therapists 1 (ft); Occupational therapists 1 (pt); Speech therapists 1 (pt); Activities coordinators 1 (ft); Dietitians 1 (pt); Ophthalmologists 1 (pt); Podiatrists 1 (pt); Dentists 1 (pt).
Facilities Dining room; Laundry room.
Activities Arts & crafts; Cards; Games; Reading groups; Prayer groups; Movies; Shopping trips; Dances/Social/Cultural gatherings.

Doty House of Middletown Inc
4710 Timber Trail Dr, Middletown, OH 45044
(513) 423-9496
Licensure Intermediate care for mentally retarded. *Beds* ICF/MR 20. *Certified* Medicaid.
Owner Proprietary corp.

Garden Manor Extended Care Center Inc
PO Box 850, 6898 Hamilton-Middletown Rd, Middletown, OH 45042
(513) 424-5321
Medical Dir Jeffery Zollett MD.
Licensure Skilled care; Intermediate care. *Beds* SNF 182; ICF 59. *Certified* Medicaid; Medicare.
Owner Proprietary corp.

Middletown Health Care Center
3100 S Main St, Middletown, OH 45042
(513) 423-9621

Licensure Intermediate care for mentally retarded. *Beds* ICF/MR 24. *Certified* Medicaid.
Owner Proprietary corp (Buckeye Family and Nursing Home).

Barbara Park Convalescent Center
751 Kensington St, Middletown, OH 45042
(513) 424-3874
Admin Larry N Steele. *Dir of Nursing* Judith A Fadden.
Licensure Skilled care; Intermediate care. *Beds* Swing beds SNF/ICF 208. *Certified* Medicaid; Medicare.
Owner Proprietary corp (Parke Care Inc).
Staff RNs 7 (ft); LPNs 23 (ft); Nurses' aides 87 (ft); Physical therapists 1 (pt); Occupational therapists 1 (pt); Speech therapists 1 (pt); Activities coordinators 3 (ft); Dietitians 1 (pt); Ophthalmologists 1 (pt).
Facilities Dining room; Physical therapy room; Activities room; Chapel; Crafts room; Laundry room; Barber/Beauty shop.
Activities Arts & crafts; Cards; Games; Reading groups; Prayer groups; Movies; Shopping trips; Dances/Social/Cultural gatherings.

Willow Knoll Nursing Center
4400 Vannest Ave, Middletown, OH 45042
(513) 422-5600
Admin Cheryl L Withrow LNHA. *Dir of Nursing* Patricia Watson RN. *Medical Dir* Jeffrey Jarrett MD.
Licensure Skilled care. *Beds* SNF 100. *Certified* Medicaid; Medicare.
Owner Nonprofit corp.
Admissions Requirements Medical examination.
Facilities Dining room; Physical therapy room; Activities room; Laundry room; Barber/Beauty shop.
Activities Arts & crafts; Cards; Games; Prayer groups; Movies; Shopping trips; Dances/Social/Cultural gatherings; Pet therapy.

Milan

Canterbury Villa of Milan
185 S Main St, Milan, OH 44846
(419) 499-2576
Medical Dir R L Blackann DO.
Licensure Intermediate care. *Beds* ICF 96. *Certified* Medicaid.
Owner Proprietary corp.
Admissions Requirements Medical examination; Physician's request.
Staff RNs 1 (ft), 2 (pt); LPNs 8 (ft), 5 (pt); Nurses' aides 25 (ft), 13 (pt); Activities coordinators 1 (ft); Dietitians 1 (pt); Social workers.
Facilities Dining room; Barber/Beauty shop.
Activities Arts & crafts; Games; Prayer groups; Movies; Shopping trips.

Milford

Clermont Nursing & Convalescent Center
934 State Rte 28, Milford, OH 45150
(513) 831-1770
Licensure Skilled care; Intermediate care. *Beds* Swing beds SNF/ICF 208. *Certified* Medicaid; Medicare.
Owner Proprietary corp.

SEM Haven Health Care Center
225 Cleveland Ave, Milford, OH 45150
(513) 248-1270
Admin Alice D Lamping. *Dir of Nursing* Helen Canfield RN BSN. *Medical Dir* Jonathon Head MD.
Licensure Skilled care; Intermediate care; Rest home. *Beds* Swing beds SNF/ICF 100; Rest home 46. *Private Pay Patients* 55%. *Certified* Medicaid; Medicare.
Owner Nonprofit corp.

Admissions Requirements Medical
examination.
Staff Physicians 1 (pt); RNs 7 (ft), 5 (pt);
LPNs 9 (ft), 5 (pt); Nurses' aides 27 (ft), 21
(pt); Physical therapists 1 (pt); Occupational
therapists 1 (pt); Speech therapists 1 (pt);
Activities coordinators 2 (ft), 1 (pt);
Dietitians 1 (ft); Podiatrists 1 (pt); Dentists
1 (pt); Medical records clerks 1 (ft); Social
workers MSW 1 (ft).
Facilities Dining room; Physical therapy
room; Activities room; Chapel; Crafts room;
Laundry room; Barber/Beauty shop;
Lounges; Classroom.
Activities Arts & crafts; Cards; Games;
Reading groups; Prayer groups; Movies;
Shopping trips; Dances/Social/Cultural
gatherings; Intergenerational programs; Pet
therapy.

Millersburg

Altercare of Millersburg
4678 State Rte 83, Rte 3, Millersburg, OH
44654
(216) 674-4444
Licensure Skilled care; Intermediate care. *Beds*
SNF 24; ICF 76. *Certified* Medicaid;
Medicare.
Owner Proprietary corp (Altercare Inc).

AnMac IV Group Home
5650 T R 332 Star Rte, Millersburg, OH
44654
(216) 674-2281
Licensure Intermediate care for mentally
retarded. *Beds* ICF/MR 10. *Certified*
Medicaid.
Owner Proprietary corp.

Fairview Castle Nursing Home
W Jackson St, Millersburg, OH 44654
(216) 674-3791
Licensure Intermediate care. *Beds* ICF 34.
Certified Medicaid.
Owner Proprietary corp.

Overlook Castle Nursing Home
Hebron St, Millersburg, OH 44654
(216) 674-5036
Licensure Intermediate care for mentally
retarded. *Beds* ICF/MR 35. *Certified*
Medicaid.
Owner Proprietary corp.

Scenic View Nursing Home
Twp Rd 334, Millersburg, OH 44654
(216) 674-8010
Licensure Intermediate care for mentally
retarded. *Beds* ICF/MR 164. *Certified*
Medicaid.
Owner Proprietary corp.

Sunset View
RR 5, Millersburg, OH 44654
(216) 674-4871
Licensure Intermediate care for mentally
retarded. *Beds* ICF/MR 75. *Certified*
Medicaid.
Owner Proprietary corp.

Terrace View Castle Nursing Home
Hebron St, Millersburg, OH 44654
(216) 674-8444
Licensure Intermediate care for mentally
retarded. *Beds* ICF/MR 180. *Certified*
Medicaid.
Owner Proprietary corp.

Valley View Castle Nursing Home
RFD 1, Millersburg, OH 44654
(216) 674-2781
Licensure Intermediate care. *Beds* ICF 42.
Certified Medicaid.
Owner Proprietary corp.

Mineral Ridge

Glenn View Manor
3379 Main St, Mineral Ridge, OH 44440
(216) 652-9901, 743-2242
Admin Richard J Chasko. *Dir of Nursing*
Nancy Gray. *Medical Dir* Dr J Enyeart.
Licensure Intermediate care; Alzheimer's care.
Beds ICF 216. *Certified* Medicaid.
Owner Proprietary corp.
Admissions Requirements Minimum age 50.
Staff Physicians 2 (ft); RNs 12 (ft); LPNs 21
(ft); Nurses' aides 73 (ft); Physical therapists
1 (ft); Occupational therapists 1 (ft);
Activities coordinators 3 (ft); Dietitians 1
(ft); Ophthalmologists 1 (ft); Podiatrists 1
(ft).
Facilities Dining room; Physical therapy
room; Activities room; Chapel; Crafts room;
Laundry room; Barber/Beauty shop; Library;
Pool; Sun room; Gift shop; Putting green.
Activities Arts & crafts; Games; Reading
groups; Prayer groups; Movies; Shopping
trips; Dances/Social/Cultural gatherings.

Youngstown Developmental Center
4891 E County Line Rd, Mineral Ridge, OH
44440
(216) 544-2231
Licensure Intermediate care for mentally
retarded. *Beds* ICF/MR 117. *Certified*
Medicaid.
Owner Publicly owned.

Minerva

Great Trail Care Center
400 Carolyn Ct, Minerva, OH 44657
(216) 868-4104
Admin Patrick D Martell. *Dir of Nursing*
Donna Wey RN. *Medical Dir* Dr Robert
Hinks.
Licensure Skilled care; Intermediate care;
Alzheimer's care. *Beds* SNF 25; ICF 75.
Certified Medicaid; Medicare.
Owner Proprietary corp.
Admissions Requirements Medical
examination.
Staff RNs 2 (ft), 4 (pt); LPNs 2 (ft), 5 (pt);
Nurses' aides 15 (ft), 14 (pt); Physical
therapists; Reality therapists; Recreational
therapists; Occupational therapists; Speech
therapists; Activities coordinators; Dietitians;
Ophthalmologists; Podiatrists; Dentists.
Facilities Dining room; Physical therapy
room; Activities room; Crafts room; Laundry
room; Barber/Beauty shop; Library.
Activities Arts & crafts; Cards; Games;
Reading groups; Prayer groups; Movies;
Shopping trips; Dances/Social/Cultural
gatherings.

Minerva Convalescent Center Inc
1035 E Lincoln Way, Minerva, OH 44657
(216) 868-4147
Admin Michael A Martell. *Dir of Nursing*
Marcella Drakulich RN. *Medical Dir* Dr
Robert Hines.
Licensure Intermediate care. *Beds* ICF 57.
Private Pay Patients 20%. *Certified*
Medicaid.
Owner Proprietary corp.
Admissions Requirements Medical
examination.
Staff Physicians 1 (ft); RNs 1 (ft), 1 (pt);
LPNs 3 (ft), 3 (pt); Nurses' aides 15 (ft), 5
(pt); Activities coordinators 1 (pt).
Facilities Dining room; Laundry room;
Barber/Beauty shop.
Activities Arts & crafts; Games; Prayer groups;
Movies; Dances/Social/Cultural gatherings;
Intergenerational programs; Pet therapy.

Minster

Heritage Manor Nursing Center
24 N Hamilton St, Minster, OH 45865
(419) 628-2396
Admin Donald J Crock.
Medical Dir Joseph Steurnagel MC.
Licensure Skilled care; Intermediate care for
mentally retarded; Rest home. *Beds* SNF 75;
ICF/MR 34; Rest home 10. *Certified*
Medicaid; Medicare.
Owner Proprietary corp (Health Care
Management).
Admissions Requirements Medical
examination; Physician's request.
Staff RNs 7 (ft), 7 (pt); LPNs 8 (ft), 1 (pt);
Nurses' aides 31 (ft), 31 (pt); Physical
therapists 2 (pt); Occupational therapists 1
(pt); Speech therapists 1 (pt); Activities
coordinators 2 (ft); Dietitians 1 (pt).
Facilities Dining room; Physical therapy
room; Activities room; Chapel; Laundry
room; Barber/Beauty shop.
Activities Arts & crafts; Cards; Games; Prayer
groups; Movies; Shopping trips; Dances/
Social/Cultural gatherings; Remotivation.

Monclova

Monclova Care Center
9831 Garden Rd, Monclova, OH 43542
(419) 865-6241
Licensure Intermediate care. *Beds* ICF 100.
Certified Medicaid.
Owner Proprietary corp.

Villa West
10005 Garden Rd, Monclova, OH 43542
(419) 865-1248
Admin Ken Terhune. *Dir of Nursing* Margie
Davis.
Licensure Intermediate care. *Beds* ICF 100.
Private Pay Patients 15%. *Certified*
Medicaid.
Owner Proprietary corp.
Admissions Requirements Minimum age 18;
Medical examination.
Staff Physicians 1 (pt); RNs 4 (ft); LPNs 8
(ft); Nurses' aides 27 (ft); Physical therapists
1 (pt); Recreational therapists 1 (pt);
Activities coordinators 6 (ft); Dietitians 1
(pt); Ophthalmologists 1 (pt); Podiatrists 1
(pt).
Languages Spanish.
Facilities Dining room; Activities room;
Crafts room; Laundry room; Barber/Beauty
shop; Library.
Activities Arts & crafts; Cards; Games;
Reading groups; Prayer groups; Movies;
Shopping trips; Dances/Social/Cultural
gatherings; Pet therapy.

Monroe

Mt Pleasant Village
225 Britton Lane, Monroe, OH 45050
(513) 539-7391
Admin Mariellen Sutton; David A Loop, Exec
Dir. *Dir of Nursing* Charlene Himes.
Medical Dir Dr Gordon F Smith.
Licensure Skilled care; Intermediate care;
Alzheimer's care; Retirement. *Beds* SNF 71;
ICF 28. *Certified* Medicaid; Medicare.
Owner Nonprofit corp (Ohio Presbyterian
Homes).
Admissions Requirements Minimum age 60;
Medical examination.
Staff Physicians 2 (ft); RNs 7 (ft), 3 (pt);
LPNs 10 (ft), 5 (pt); Nurses' aides 18 (ft), 9
(pt); Physical therapists 2 (ft); Recreational
therapists 1 (ft); Occupational therapists 1
(ft); Speech therapists 1 (ft); Activities
coordinators 3 (ft); Dietitians 1 (ft);
Ophthalmologists 1 (ft); Podiatrists 1 (ft);
Dentists 1 (ft).
Affiliation Presbyterian.

Facilities Dining room; Physical therapy room; Activities room; Chapel; Crafts room; Laundry room; Barber/Beauty shop; Library; Child day care center; Special care unit.
Activities Arts & crafts; Cards; Games; Reading groups; Prayer groups; Movies; Shopping trips; Dances/Social/Cultural gatherings.

Montgomery

Meadowbrook Living Center
8211 Weller Rd, Montgomery, OH 45242
(513) 489-2444
Admin Rebecca Scripture Pater. *Dir of Nursing* Cecilia Bunker RNC. *Medical Dir* Paul Gendelman MD.
Licensure Skilled care; Intermediate care; Alzheimer's care. *Beds* Swing beds SNF/ICF 156. *Certified* Medicaid; Medicare.
Owner Nonprofit corp (Adventist Living Centers).
Admissions Requirements Medical examination.
Staff Physicians 2 (pt); RNs 12 (ft), 9 (pt); LPNs 7 (ft), 5 (pt); Nurses' aides 60 (ft), 26 (pt); Physical therapists 1 (pt); Reality therapists 1 (pt); Recreational therapists 1 (pt); Occupational therapists 1 (pt); Speech therapists 1 (pt); Activities coordinators 2 (ft); Dietitians 1 (pt); Ophthalmologists 1 (pt); Podiatrists 1 (pt); Dentists 1 (pt); Social services 1 (ft); Treatment nurses 1 (ft); In-services 1 (ft).
Languages Spanish, French, German, Russian.
Affiliation Seventh-Day Adventist.
Facilities Dining room; Physical therapy room; Activities room; Barber/Beauty shop.
Activities Arts & crafts; Cards; Games; Reading groups; Prayer groups; Movies; Shopping trips; Dances/Social/Cultural gatherings; Intergenerational programs; Pet therapy.

Montpelier

Evergreen Manor Nursing Home
924 Robinair Way, Montpelier, OH 43543
(419) 485-3416
Admin Iris Shook. *Dir of Nursing* Bettylu Redden RN. *Medical Dir* Clarence A Bell MD.
Licensure Skilled care; Intermediate care; Alzheimer's care. *Beds* Swing beds SNF/ICF 50. *Private Pay Patients* 30%. *Certified* Medicaid; Medicare.
Owner Proprietary corp (American Health Care Corp).
Admissions Requirements Medical examination; Physician's request.
Staff Physicians 6 (pt); RNs 4 (ft), 2 (pt); LPNs 4 (ft), 1 (pt); Nurses' aides 17 (ft); Physical therapists; Occupational therapists (consultant); Speech therapists (consultant); Activities coordinators 1 (ft); Dietitians; Podiatrists (consultant).
Facilities Dining room; Physical therapy room; Activities room; Crafts room; Laundry room; Barber/Beauty shop.
Activities Arts & crafts; Cards; Games; Reading groups; Prayer groups; Movies; Dances/Social/Cultural gatherings; Intergenerational programs; Pet therapy.

Evergreen North Nursing Home
PO Box 109, Rte 20, Montpelier, OH 43543
(419) 924-2898
Admin Iris Shook.
Medical Dir Clarence Bell MD.
Licensure Intermediate care. *Beds* ICF 23. *Certified* Medicaid.
Owner Proprietary corp (American Health Care Centers).
Staff Physicians; RNs; LPNs 4 (ft), 2 (pt); Nurses' aides 6 (ft), 3 (pt); Activities coordinators 1 (ft); Dietitians.

Facilities Dining room; Crafts room; Laundry room.
Activities Arts & crafts; Cards; Games; Reading groups; Prayer groups; Shopping trips; Dances/Social/Cultural gatherings.

Morrow

Pine Crest Nursing Center
463 E Pike St, Morrow, OH 45152
(513) 899-2801
Admin Freda Kilburn. *Dir of Nursing* Mary Mave RN. *Medical Dir* Carl Durning MD.
Licensure Intermediate care; Residential care. *Beds* ICF 50. *Certified* Medicaid.
Owner Proprietary corp (Congregate Living of America).
Admissions Requirements Physician's request.
Staff Physicians 3 (ft); RNs 4 (ft); LPNs 8 (ft); Nurses' aides 25 (ft); Activities coordinators 1 (ft); Dietitians 1 (ft).
Facilities Dining room; Activities room; Crafts room; Laundry room; Barber/Beauty shop.
Activities Arts & crafts; Cards; Games; Reading groups; Prayer groups; Movies; Shopping trips; Dances/Social/Cultural gatherings; Pet therapy.

Mount Gilead

Morrow County Extended Care Facility
651 W Marion Rd, Mount Gilead, OH 43338
(419) 946-5015
Admin Randal M Arnett. *Dir of Nursing* Terry Weber RN. *Medical Dir* John P Stone MD.
Licensure Skilled care; Intermediate care. *Beds* Swing beds SNF/ICF 10. *Certified* Medicaid; Medicare.
Owner Publicly owned.
Admissions Requirements Medical examination; Physician's request.
Staff Physicians; RNs; LPNs; Nurses' aides; Physical therapists; Speech therapists; Activities coordinators; Dietitians; Ophthalmologists; Podiatrists.
Facilities Dining room; Physical therapy room; Activities room; Chapel; Barber/Beauty shop; Library.
Activities Arts & crafts; Cards; Games; Reading groups; Movies; Dances/Social/Cultural gatherings; BirtHday/Holiday parties; Family events.

Woodside Village Care Center Ltd
841 W Marion Rd, Mount Gilead, OH 43338
(419) 947-2015
Licensure Intermediate care. *Beds* ICF 100. *Certified* Medicaid.
Owner Proprietary corp.

Mount Orab

Mt Orab Nursing Care Center
PO Box 416, Farley Lane, Mount Orab, OH 45154
(513) 444-2588
Admin George Balz. *Dir of Nursing* Patricia Swanson. *Medical Dir* Dr Gene Conway.
Licensure Intermediate care. *Beds* ICF 22. *Private Pay Patients* 1%. *Certified* Medicaid.
Owner Proprietary corp.
Admissions Requirements Medical examination; Physician's request.
Staff RNs 1 (pt); LPNs 3 (ft), 5 (pt); Nurses' aides 6 (ft), 3 (pt); Physical therapists 1 (pt); Occupational therapists 1 (pt); Activities coordinators 1 (ft); Dietitians 1 (ft); Podiatrists 1 (pt).

Facilities Dining room; Activities room; Laundry room.
Activities Arts & crafts; Cards; Games; Reading groups; Prayer groups; Movies; Shopping trips; Dances/Social/Cultural gatherings; Intergenerational programs; Pet therapy.

Mount Saint Joseph

Mother Margaret Hall
Delhi Pike, Mount Saint Joseph, OH 45051
(513) 244-4692
Admin Sr Agnes Celestia.
Medical Dir Ronald Gall MD.
Licensure Intermediate care. *Beds* ICF 132. *Certified* Medicaid.
Owner Proprietary corp.
Admissions Requirements Medical examination; Physician's request.
Staff Physicians 2 (pt); Physical therapists 2 (pt); Recreational therapists 1 (ft); Occupational therapists 1 (pt); Speech therapists 1 (pt); Activities coordinators 1 (ft); Dietitians 1 (ft), 1 (pt); Podiatrists 1 (pt); Dentists 1 (pt).
Affiliation Roman Catholic.
Facilities Dining room; Physical therapy room; Activities room; Chapel; Crafts room; Laundry room; Barber/Beauty shop; Library; Speech therapy room.
Activities Arts & crafts; Cards; Games; Reading groups; Prayer groups; Movies; Shopping trips; Dances/Social/Cultural gatherings.

Mount Vernon

Hannah Browning Home
7 E Sugar St, Mount Vernon, OH 43050
(614) 392-7111
Medical Dir Kay Hall.
Licensure Rest home. *Beds* Rest home 9.
Owner Proprietary corp.
Admissions Requirements Females only; Medical examination.
Staff Nurses' aides.
Facilities Dining room; Laundry room.

Country Club Center II
1350 Yauger Rd, Mount Vernon, OH 43050
(614) 397-2350
Admin Tanya Ressing. *Dir of Nursing* Kristina R Leiter RN. *Medical Dir* Dr W Elder.
Licensure Skilled care; Intermediate care; Retirement; Alzheimer's care. *Beds* Swing beds SNF/ICF 76. *Certified* Medicaid; Medicare.
Owner Proprietary corp (JE Holland Associates).
Admissions Requirements Medical examination; Physician's request.
Staff Physicians 1 (pt); RNs 6 (ft); LPNs 9 (ft); Physical therapists 1 (ft); Reality therapists 1 (ft); Recreational therapists 1 (ft); Occupational therapists 1 (ft); Speech therapists 1 (ft); Activities coordinators 1 (ft), 2 (pt); Dietitians 1 (ft); Ophthalmologists 1 (ft); Podiatrists 1 (ft); Dentists 1 (ft).
Facilities Dining room; Physical therapy room; Activities room; Chapel; Crafts room; Laundry room; Barber/Beauty shop; Library.
Activities Arts & crafts; Cards; Games; Reading groups; Prayer groups; Movies; Shopping trips; Dances/Social/Cultural gatherings; Choral group travels to other facilities; Out-to-lunch bunch.

Country Court
1076 Coshocton Ave, Mount Vernon, OH 43050
(614) 397-4125
Licensure Skilled care; Intermediate care. *Beds* Swing beds SNF/ICF 122. *Certified* Medicaid; Medicare.
Owner Proprietary corp.

Mt Vernon Nursing Home
PO Box 790, 414 Wooster Rd, Mount Vernon, OH 43050
(614) 397-9626
Licensure Intermediate care. *Beds* ICF 44. *Certified* Medicaid.
Owner Proprietary corp (Longterm Care Management).

Northside Manor Living Center
PO Box 1069, 13 Avalon Rd, Mount Vernon, OH 43050
(614) 397-3200
Admin Lee Mitchell. *Dir of Nursing* Helen Dove. *Medical Dir* Glenn A Iben MD.
Licensure Skilled care; Intermediate care. *Beds* SNF 50; ICF 59. *Certified* Medicaid; Medicare.
Owner Nonprofit corp (Adventist Living Centers).
Staff Physicians 1 (pt); RNs 5 (ft), 2 (pt); LPNs 5 (ft), 3 (pt); Nurses' aides 23 (ft), 20 (pt); Physical therapists 1 (pt); Reality therapists 1 (ft); Occupational therapists 1 (pt); Speech therapists 1 (pt); Activities coordinators 1 (ft), 1 (pt); Dietitians 1 (pt); Ophthalmologists 1 (pt); Podiatrists 1 (pt); Audiologists 1 (pt).
Affiliation Seventh-Day Adventist.
Facilities Dining room; Physical therapy room; Activities room; Laundry room; Barber/Beauty shop.
Activities Arts & crafts; Cards; Games; Reading groups; Prayer groups; Movies; Shopping trips; Dances/Social/Cultural gatherings; Intergenerational programs; Pet therapy.

Ohio Eastern Star Home
1451 Gambier Rd, Mount Vernon, OH 43050
(614) 397-1706
Admin Andrew Beyers. *Dir of Nursing* Louise LaBenne RN. *Medical Dir* Henry Lapp MD.
Licensure Skilled care; Intermediate care; Retirement. *Beds* Swing beds SNF/ICF 86.
Owner Proprietary corp.
Staff Physicians 1 (pt); RNs 3 (ft), 2 (pt); LPNs 2 (ft), 2 (pt); Nurses' aides 19 (ft), 7 (pt); Activities coordinators 1 (ft), 1 (pt).
Affiliation Order of Eastern Star.
Activities Arts & crafts; Cards; Games; Reading groups; Prayer groups; Movies; Shopping trips; Dances/Social/Cultural gatherings; Field trips.

Rose Garden Nursing Home
303 N Main St, Mount Vernon, OH 43050
(614) 393-2046
Admin Eleanor Burke.
Medical Dir Carol Hanger.
Licensure Intermediate care; Alzheimer's care. *Beds* ICF 30. *Certified* Medicaid.
Owner Privately owned.
Admissions Requirements Medical examination; Physician's request.
Staff RNs 1 (ft); LPNs 4 (ft); Nurses' aides 10 (ft); Activities coordinators 1 (ft); Dietitians 1 (ft).
Facilities Dining room; Activities room; Laundry room.
Activities Arts & crafts; Cards; Games; Prayer groups; Movies; Shopping trips; Daily exercise.

Napoleon

Filling Memorial Home of Mercy
Rte 5, Napoleon, OH 43545
(419) 592-6451
Admin Paul E Oehrtman. *Dir of Nursing* Carol A Nachtrab.
Licensure Intermediate care for mentally retarded. *Beds* ICF/MR 53. *Certified* Medicaid.
Owner Proprietary corp.
Admissions Requirements Medical examination.

Staff RNs 3 (ft), 2 (pt); LPNs 2 (ft), 7 (pt); Recreational therapists 2 (ft); Occupational therapists 2 (ft); Activities coordinators 1 (ft); Dietitians 1 (pt).
Affiliation Lutheran.
Facilities Dining room; Physical therapy room; Activities room; Chapel; Laundry room.
Activities Arts & crafts; Games; Movies; Shopping trips; Dances/Social/Cultural gatherings.

Henry County Residential Home
340 E Clinton St, Napoleon, OH 43545
(419) 592-0238
Licensure Intermediate care for mentally retarded. *Beds* ICF/MR 8. *Certified* Medicaid.
Owner Proprietary corp.

Lutheran Home
1036 S Perry St, Napoleon, OH 43545
(419) 592-1688, 599-4791 FAX
Admin Melvin F Zehnder. *Dir of Nursing* Mary Osborn RN. *Medical Dir* William Richter, MD.
Licensure Intermediate care; Retirement. *Beds* ICF 100; Retirement. *Private Pay Patients* 65%. *Certified* Medicaid.
Owner Nonprofit organization/foundation.
Admissions Requirements Minimum age 65; Medical examination.
Staff RNs 3 (ft); LPNs 6 (ft), 5 (pt); Nurses' aides 29 (ft), 19 (pt); Physical therapists 1 (pt); Speech therapists 1 (pt); Activities coordinators 2 (ft), 1 (pt); Dietitians 1 (pt).
Languages German, Spanish.
Affiliation Lutheran.
Facilities Dining room; Activities room; Chapel; Crafts room; Laundry room; Barber/Beauty shop; Library; Solariums.
Activities Arts & crafts; Cards; Games; Reading groups; Prayer groups; Movies; Shopping trips; Dances/Social/Cultural gatherings; Intergenerational programs; Pet therapy; Music; Current events; German club.

Northcrest Nursing Home
RD 6, Northcrest Dr, Napoleon, OH 43545
(419) 599-4070
Admin Mary Anne Moomaw. *Dir of Nursing* Colleen Wiley. *Medical Dir* Dr Busteed.
Licensure Skilled care; Intermediate care. *Beds* SNF 16; ICF 84. *Certified* Medicaid; Medicare.
Owner Proprietary corp (Beverly Enterprises).
Admissions Requirements Minimum age 12; Medical examination; Physician's request.
Staff RNs 2 (ft); LPNs 15 (ft); Nurses' aides 86 (ft); Physical therapists 1 (pt); Speech therapists 1 (pt); Activities coordinators 1 (ft); Dietitians 1 (pt); Ophthalmologists 1 (pt); Podiatrists 1 (pt).
Facilities Dining room; Physical therapy room; Activities room; Laundry room; Barber/Beauty shop.
Activities Arts & crafts; Cards; Games; Reading groups; Prayer groups; Movies; Shopping trips; Dances/Social/Cultural gatherings.

Navarre

Country Lawn Nursing Home
RR 3, 10608 Navarre Rd SW, Navarre, OH 44662
(216) 767-3455
Licensure Intermediate care. *Beds* ICF 131. *Certified* Medicaid.
Owner Proprietary corp (Altercare Inc).

Lodge Nursing Home
23 Ohio St, Navarre, OH 44662
(216) 879-5930
Licensure Intermediate care. *Beds* ICF 30. *Certified* Medicaid.
Owner Proprietary corp.

Navarre Community Health Center
517 Park St, Navarre, OH 44662
(216) 879-2765
Admin Gregory R Colaner. *Dir of Nursing* Jeannie Janson RN. *Medical Dir* Eugene Pogorelec DO.
Licensure Skilled care; Intermediate care. *Beds* SNF 23; ICF 55. *Certified* Medicaid; Medicare.
Owner Proprietary corp (Altercare Inc).
Admissions Requirements Medical examination.
Staff Physicians; RNs; LPNs; Nurses' aides; Physical therapists; Recreational therapists; Occupational therapists; Speech therapists; Activities coordinators; Dietitians; Ophthalmologists; Podiatrists; Audiologists.
Facilities Dining room; Physical therapy room; Activities room; Chapel; Crafts room; Laundry room; Barber/Beauty shop; Library.
Activities Arts & crafts; Cards; Games; Reading groups; Prayer groups; Movies; Shopping trips.

New Boston

Heritage Square New Boston
3304 Rhodes Ave, New Boston, OH 45662
(614) 456-8245
Licensure Rest home. *Beds* Rest home 116.
Owner Proprietary corp.

New Bremen

Lone Pine Nursing Home Inc
403 N Main St, New Bremen, OH 45869
(419) 629-2793
Medical Dir Dr Harbard.
Licensure Intermediate care. *Beds* ICF 19. *Certified* Medicaid.
Owner Proprietary corp.
Admissions Requirements Medical examination.
Staff RNs 1 (ft); LPNs 2 (ft), 1 (pt); Nurses' aides 10 (ft), 2 (pt); Recreational therapists 1 (pt); Activities coordinators 1 (ft); Ophthalmologists 1 (pt); Podiatrists 1 (pt); Dentists 1 (pt).
Facilities Dining room; Activities room; Laundry room.
Activities Arts & crafts; Cards; Games; Reading groups; Prayer groups; Movies; Shopping trips; Dances/Social/Cultural gatherings.

New Carlisle

Belle Manor Nursing Home
107-111 N Pike St, New Carlisle, OH 45344
(513) 845-3561
Admin Sanford R Gerber. *Dir of Nursing* Janet Addeo. *Medical Dir* Thomas Honningford DO.
Licensure Skilled care; Intermediate care. *Beds* Swing beds SNF/ICF 123. *Certified* Medicaid; Medicare.
Owner Proprietary corp.
Admissions Requirements Medical examination.
Staff Physicians 1 (pt); RNs 6 (ft), 2 (pt); LPNs 4 (ft), 3 (pt); Nurses' aides 40 (ft), 12 (pt); Physical therapists 2 (ft); Reality therapists 1 (pt); Recreational therapists 1 (ft); Occupational therapists 1 (pt); Speech therapists 1 (pt); Activities coordinators 1 (ft); Dietitians 1 (pt); Ophthalmologists 1 (pt); Podiatrists 1 (pt); Dentists 1 (pt).
Facilities Dining room; Physical therapy room; Activities room; Chapel; Crafts room; Laundry room; Barber/Beauty shop; Library.
Activities Arts & crafts; Cards; Games; Reading groups; Prayer groups; Movies; Shopping trips; Dances/Social/Cultural gatherings.

ОН ОН

Dayview Care Center
1885 N Dayton-Lakeview Rd, New Carlisle,
OH 45344
(513) 845-8219
Admin Jim Snyder. *Dir of Nursing* Glen
Gibbons. *Medical Dir* Stuart Edmiston.
Licensure Intermediate care; Retirement. *Beds*
ICF 50. *Private Pay Patients* 22%. *Certified*
Medicaid.
Owner Nonprofit organization/foundation.
Admissions Requirements Medical
examination.
Staff RNs 3 (ft), 1 (pt); LPNs 3 (ft), 2 (pt);
Nurses' aides 14 (ft), 6 (pt); Activities
coordinators 1 (ft), 1 (pt).
Affiliation Missionary Church.
Facilities Dining room; Activities room;
Laundry room; Barber/Beauty shop.
Activities Arts & crafts; Cards; Games;
Reading groups; Prayer groups; Shopping
trips; Dances/Social/Cultural gatherings; Pet
therapy.

New Concord

New Concord Nursing Center
75 Fox Creek Rd, New Concord, OH 43762
(614) 826-7640
Admin Mark S Richards. *Dir of Nursing*
Georgia Shepard. *Medical Dir* Carl Spragg
MD.
Licensure Intermediate care. *Beds* ICF 50.
Private Pay Patients 10%. *Certified*
Medicaid.
Owner Proprietary corp.
Admissions Requirements Minimum age 45;
Medical examination.
Staff RNs 1 (ft), 1 (pt); LPNs 3 (ft), 4 (pt);
Nurses' aides 14 (ft), 12 (pt); Activities
coordinators 1 (ft); Dietitians 1 (pt).
Facilities Dining room; Activities room;
Laundry room; Barber/Beauty shop;
Solarium.
Activities Arts & crafts; Cards; Games;
Reading groups; Prayer groups; Movies;
Coffee hour; Current events.

New Lebanon

Canterbury Care Center
101 Mills Pl, New Lebanon, OH 45345
(513) 687-1311, 687-3659 FAX
Admin Wretha M Haines. *Dir of Nursing*
Brenda D Osborn RN C BSN. *Medical Dir*
Michael O Phillips MD.
Licensure Intermediate care. *Beds* ICF 100.
Private Pay Patients 25%. *Certified*
Medicaid.
Owner Privately owned.
Admissions Requirements Medical
examination.
Staff Physicians 1 (ft); RNs 5 (ft), 3 (pt);
LPNs 5 (ft), 13 (pt); Nurses' aides 25 (ft), 29
(pt); Physical therapists 1 (pt); Speech
therapists 1 (pt); Activities coordinators 1
(ft); Dietitians 1 (pt); Ophthalmologists 1
(pt); Podiatrists 1 (pt); Audiologists 1 (pt).
Facilities Dining room; Physical therapy
room; Activities room; Crafts room; Laundry
room; Barber/Beauty shop.
Activities Arts & crafts; Games; Reading
groups; Prayer groups; Movies; Shopping
trips; Dances/Social/Cultural gatherings;
Intergenerational programs; Pet therapy;
Church services.

New Lexington

**Americare—New Lexington Nursing &
Rehabilitation Center**
920 S Main St, New Lexington, OH 43764
(614) 342-5161
Admin Robert C Wells. *Dir of Nursing* Debra
D Wilson. *Medical Dir* Dr Ralph E
Herendeen.

Licensure Skilled care; Intermediate care. *Beds*
SNF 20; ICF 80. *Certified* Medicaid;
Medicare.
Owner Proprietary corp (Care Enterprises).

New London

Firelands Nursing Center
204 W Main St, New London, OH 44851
(419) 929-1563
Admin Paul Kocsis. *Dir of Nursing* Ann
Holland. *Medical Dir* Dr Erlenbach.
Licensure Skilled care; Intermediate care;
Alzheimer's care. *Beds* Swing beds SNF/ICF
50. *Certified* Medicaid; Medicare.
Owner Proprietary corp (Health Care
Management).
Admissions Requirements Medical
examination; Physician's request.
Staff Physicians 7 (pt); RNs 3 (ft); LPNs 3
(ft), 2 (pt); Nurses' aides 15 (ft), 5 (pt);
Physical therapists 1 (pt); Occupational
therapists 1 (pt); Speech therapists 1 (pt);
Activities coordinators 1 (ft); Dietitians 1
(ft), 1 (pt); Ophthalmologists 1 (pt);
Podiatrists 1 (pt); Dentists 1 (pt).
Facilities Dining room; Physical therapy
room; Activities room; Laundry room;
Barber/Beauty shop.
Activities Arts & crafts; Cards; Games;
Reading groups; Prayer groups; Movies;
Shopping trips; Dances/Social/Cultural
gatherings; Outings; Cheese socials; Ice
cream socials.

New Paris

Heartland of Cedar Springs
7739 Rte 40, New Paris, OH 45347
(513) 437-2311
Admin James V Kyle. *Dir of Nursing* Susan
Melzer RN. *Medical Dir* Jeung W Ahn MD.
Licensure Intermediate care for mentally
retarded. *Beds* ICF/MR 66. *Certified*
Medicaid.
Owner Proprietary corp (National Heritage).
Admissions Requirements Minimum age 45;
Medical examination.
Staff Physicians 1 (pt); RNs 4 (ft), 2 (pt);
LPNs 4 (ft); Nurses' aides 39 (ft), 4 (pt);
Physical therapists 1 (pt); Reality therapists
1 (pt); Recreational therapists 1 (pt);
Occupational therapists 1 (pt); Speech
therapists 1 (pt); Activities coordinators 1
(ft); Dietitians 1 (pt); Ophthalmologists 1
(pt); Podiatrists 1 (pt); Dentists 1 (pt);
QMRPs 4 (ft).
Facilities Dining room; Physical therapy
room; Activities room; Crafts room; Laundry
room; Barber/Beauty shop.
Activities Arts & crafts; Cards; Games;
Reading groups; Prayer groups; Movies;
Shopping trips; Dances/Social/Cultural
gatherings; Exercise groups; Boy/Girl Scouts;
Swimming; Bowling.

New Philadelphia

Kaderly Home
1416 Kaderly NW, New Philadelphia, OH
44663
(216) 343-6322
Licensure Intermediate care for mentally
retarded. *Beds* ICF/MR 12. *Certified*
Medicaid.
Owner Proprietary corp.

South Broadway Nursing Home Inc
245-251 S Broadway, New Philadelphia, OH
44663
(216) 339-2151
Admin Gloria Sentz.
Medical Dir Joan Butler.
Licensure Intermediate care. *Beds* ICF 49.
Certified Medicaid.
Owner Proprietary corp.

Admissions Requirements Medical
examination; Physician's request.
Staff Physicians; RNs; LPNs; Nurses' aides;
Activities coordinators; Dietitians.
Facilities Dining room; Activities room;
Laundry room.
Activities Arts & crafts; Cards; Games;
Reading groups; Prayer groups; Shopping
trips.

Valley Manor Nursing Home
Rte 4 Box 4348, New Philadelphia, OH 44663
(216) 339-3595
Admin Shirley G Hebb. *Dir of Nursing* Rita
Goth.
Licensure Skilled care; Intermediate care. *Beds*
Swing beds SNF/ICF 219. *Certified*
Medicaid; Medicare.
Owner Proprietary corp.
Admissions Requirements Minimum age 16;
Medical examination.
Staff RNs 10 (ft); LPNs 20 (ft); Nurses' aides
160 (ft); Activities coordinators 1 (ft);
Dietitians 1 (ft).
Facilities Dining room; Physical therapy
room; Activities room; Crafts room; Laundry
room; Barber/Beauty shop.
Activities Arts & crafts; Cards; Games;
Reading groups; Prayer groups; Movies;
Shopping trips; Dances/Social/Cultural
gatherings.

New Richmond

Dobbins Nursing Home Inc
400 Main St, New Richmond, OH 45157
(513) 553-4139
Admin Patricia Meeker.
Medical Dir John Wehby MD.
Licensure Intermediate care. *Beds* ICF 22.
Certified Medicaid.
Owner Proprietary corp.
Admissions Requirements Females only.
Staff RNs 1 (pt); LPNs 3 (ft), 2 (pt); Nurses'
aides 12 (ft); Physical therapists 1 (pt);
Recreational therapists 1 (pt); Activities
coordinators 1 (ft); Dietitians 1 (pt);
Podiatrists 1 (pt); Dentists 1 (pt).
Facilities Dining room; Activities room;
Crafts room; Laundry room; Barber/Beauty
shop.
Activities Arts & crafts; Cards; Games;
Reading groups; Prayer groups; Movies;
Shopping trips; Dances/Social/Cultural
gatherings; Fund raisers.

Newark

AnMac Home I
1960 Reddington Rd, Newark, OH 43055
(614) 522-2936
Licensure Intermediate care for mentally
retarded. *Beds* ICF/MR 12. *Certified*
Medicaid.
Owner Proprietary corp.

AnMac Home II
1968 Reddington Rd, Newark, OH 43055
(614) 522-6065
Licensure Intermediate care for mentally
retarded. *Beds* ICF/MR 12. *Certified*
Medicaid.
Owner Proprietary corp.

Arlington Nursing Home Inc
98 S 30th St, Newark, OH 43055
(614) 344-0303
Admin Roy Hodges.
Medical Dir Dr T T Mills.
Licensure Skilled care; Intermediate care. *Beds*
Swing beds SNF/ICF 200. *Certified*
Medicaid; Medicare.
Owner Proprietary corp.
Staff Physicians; RNs; LPNs; Nurses' aides;
Physical therapists; Reality therapists;
Recreational therapists; Occupational

therapists; Speech therapists; Activities coordinators; Dietitians; Ophthalmologists; Podiatrists; Dentists.
Facilities Dining room; Physical therapy room; Activities room; Crafts room; Laundry room; Barber/Beauty shop; Library; Hydrotherapy room; Occupational therapy room.
Activities Arts & crafts; Cards; Games; Reading groups; Prayer groups; Movies; Shopping trips; Dances/Social/Cultural gatherings.

Athena Manor
17 Forry St, Newark, OH 43055
(614) 349-8175
Admin April Cross. *Dir of Nursing* Sue Miller. *Medical Dir* Dr Donald Adams.
Licensure Intermediate care; Retirement. *Beds* ICF 48; Retirement apts 10. *Certified* Medicaid.
Owner Proprietary corp (Alpha Corp).
Admissions Requirements Medical examination.
Staff Physicians 1 (pt); RNs 1 (ft), 1 (pt); LPNs 3 (ft), 3 (pt); Nurses' aides 12 (ft), 8 (pt); Activities coordinators 1 (ft); Dietitians 1 (pt); Podiatrists 1 (pt).
Facilities Dining room; Activities room; Crafts room; Laundry room; Barber/Beauty shop.
Activities Arts & crafts; Cards; Games; Reading groups; Prayer groups; Movies; Shopping trips; Dances/Social/Cultural gatherings; Intergenerational programs; Pet therapy; Dining out.

Fairview Manor Nursing Home Inc
12883 Technicglas Rd, Newark, OH 43055
(614) 984-4262
Admin Pansy Pickenpaugh.
Medical Dir Victor Whitacre MD.
Licensure Skilled care; Intermediate care. *Beds* Swing beds SNF/ICF 76. *Certified* Medicaid; Medicare.
Owner Proprietary corp.
Admissions Requirements Minimum age 18.
Staff Physicians 3 (pt); RNs 4 (ft), 3 (pt); LPNs 6 (ft), 3 (pt); Nurses' aides 22 (ft), 7 (pt); Physical therapists 1 (pt); Activities coordinators 1 (ft); Dietitians 1 (ft); Rehabilitation aides 1 (ft).
Facilities Dining room; Activities room; Crafts room; Laundry room; Barber/Beauty shop; Library; TV lounges.
Activities Arts & crafts; Cards; Games; Reading groups; Prayer groups; Movies; Shopping trips; Dances/Social/Cultural gatherings.

Heath Nursing & Convalescent Center
717 S 30th St, Newark, OH 43056
(614) 522-1171
Licensure Skilled care; Intermediate care. *Beds* Swing beds SNF/ICF 216. *Certified* Medicaid; Medicare.
Owner Proprietary corp.

LPN Geriatric Nursing Center
1450 W Main St, Newark, OH 43055
(614) 344-9465
Admin Sara F Johnson. *Dir of Nursing* Opal Yost RN. *Medical Dir* Patty E Whisman MD.
Licensure Skilled care; Intermediate care; Retirement; Alzheimer's care. *Beds* Swing beds SNF/ICF 101. *Certified* Medicaid; Medicare.
Owner Proprietary corp.
Admissions Requirements Medical examination.
Staff Physicians 22 (pt); RNs 4 (ft), 2 (pt); LPNs 4 (ft), 4 (pt); Nurses' aides 18 (ft), 18 (pt); Physical therapists 2 (pt); Reality therapists 1 (pt); Recreational therapists 1 (pt); Occupational therapists 1 (pt); Speech therapists 1 (pt); Activities coordinators 1 (ft), 1 (pt); Dietitians 1 (pt);

Ophthalmologists 1 (pt); Podiatrists 1 (pt); Dentists 1 (pt); Social services 1 (pt); Pastoral services 1 (pt).
Facilities Dining room; Physical therapy room; Activities room; Chapel; Crafts room; Laundry room; Barber/Beauty shop; Library.
Activities Arts & crafts; Cards; Games; Reading groups; Prayer groups; Movies; Shopping trips; Dances/Social/Cultural gatherings; Bingo; Dancercise; Pet therapy; Grandparent program; Political participation; Community services; Fishing trips; Special therapies; Outings.

LPN Health Care Facility
151 Price Rd, Newark, OH 43055
(614) 366-2321
Medical Dir Charles F Sinsabaugh MD.
Licensure Skilled care; Intermediate care; Retirement. *Beds* Swing beds SNF/ICF 101. *Certified* Medicaid; Medicare.
Owner Proprietary corp.
Admissions Requirements Minimum age 55; Physician's request.
Staff RNs 8 (ft), 2 (pt); LPNs 9 (ft), 3 (pt); Nurses' aides 26 (ft), 8 (pt); Physical therapists 2 (ft); Speech therapists 1 (pt); Activities coordinators 1 (ft); Dietitians 1 (pt).
Facilities Dining room; Physical therapy room; Activities room; Chapel; Laundry room; Barber/Beauty shop.
Activities Arts & crafts; Cards; Games; Prayer groups; Movies; Shopping trips; Dances/Social/Cultural gatherings.

Newark Healthcare Centre
75 & 85 McMillen Dr, Newark, OH 43055
(614) 344-0357
Admin Paul L Massa. *Dir of Nursing* Lucinda Swank RN. *Medical Dir* Fred N Karaffa MD.
Licensure Skilled care; Intermediate care; Retirement; Alzheimer's care. *Beds* SNF 22; ICF 278. *Certified* Medicaid; Medicare.
Owner Proprietary corp (Hillhaven Corp).
Admissions Requirements Minimum age 18; Physician's request.
Staff Physicians 1 (pt); RNs 25 (ft); LPNs 25 (ft); Nurses' aides 80 (ft), 30 (pt); Physical therapists 1 (ft), 1 (pt); Occupational therapists 1 (ft), 1 (pt); Speech therapists 1 (pt); Activities coordinators 1 (ft); Dietitians 1 (pt); Ophthalmologists 1 (pt); Podiatrists 1 (pt).
Facilities Dining room; Physical therapy room; Activities room; Chapel; Crafts room; Laundry room; Barber/Beauty shop.
Activities Arts & crafts; Cards; Games; Reading groups; Prayer groups; Movies; Shopping trips; Dances/Social/Cultural gatherings.

Newbury

Holly Hill Nursing Home
10190 Fairmount Rd, Newbury, OH 44065
(216) 564-9101, 338-8220, 338-5778 FAX
Admin George H Ohman. *Dir of Nursing* Judy Hall. *Medical Dir* Dr Al Evans.
Licensure Intermediate care. *Beds* ICF 75. *Private Pay Patients* 45%. *Certified* Medicaid.
Owner Privately owned.
Admissions Requirements Medical examination.
Staff Physicians; RNs 3 (ft), 2 (pt); LPNs 2 (ft), 4 (pt); Nurses' aides 15 (ft), 20 (pt); Physical therapists; Speech therapists; Activities coordinators 1 (ft); Dietitians 1 (pt); Podiatrists; Dentists 1 (pt).
Facilities Dining room; Activities room; Crafts room; Laundry room; Barber/Beauty shop; Library; Private physicians exam room; Private and semi-private rooms; Patio and garden area; Living room with fireplace; Solarium.

Activities Arts & crafts; Cards; Games; Reading groups; Prayer groups; Dances/Social/Cultural gatherings; Intergenerational programs; Pet therapy.

Newcomerstown

Riverside Manor Nursing & Rehabilitation Center
1100 E State Rd, Newcomerstown, OH 43832
(614) 498-5165, 498-8064 FAX
Admin Stanley H Richards. *Dir of Nursing* Judy Mizer RN. *Medical Dir* Terry Overholser DO.
Licensure Skilled care; Intermediate care; Residential care; Alzheimer's care. *Beds* Swing beds SNF/ICF 100; Residential care 25. *Private Pay Patients* 25%. *Certified* Medicaid; Medicare.
Owner Proprietary corp.
Admissions Requirements Medical examination; Physician's request.
Staff RNs 7 (ft), 4 (pt); LPNs 6 (ft), 3 (pt); Nurses' aides 36 (ft), 20 (pt); Physical therapists 1 (ft); Activities coordinators 1 (ft).
Facilities Dining room; Physical therapy room; Activities room; Crafts room; Laundry room; Barber/Beauty shop.
Activities Arts & crafts; Cards; Games; Reading groups; Prayer groups; Movies; Shopping trips; Dances/Social/Cultural gatherings; Intergenerational programs.

Newton Falls

Charles Court Health Care Center
PO Box 208, 150 Charles Court, Newton Falls, OH 44444
(216) 872-1987, 872-5040 FAX
Admin Suzanne L Poppelreuter.
Medical Dir Julio Cuesta.
Licensure Intermediate care. *Beds* ICF 25. *Certified* Medicaid.
Owner Proprietary corp.
Admissions Requirements Females only.
Staff RNs 1 (pt); LPNs 4 (ft); Nurses' aides 6 (ft), 5 (pt).
Facilities Dining room; Activities room; Laundry room.
Activities Arts & crafts; Cards; Games; Reading groups; Prayer groups; Movies; Shopping trips; Dances/Social/Cultural gatherings.

Laurie Ann Nursing Home
2200 Milton Blvd, Newton Falls, OH 44444
(216) 872-1990
Licensure Intermediate care. *Beds* ICF 50. *Certified* Medicaid.
Owner Proprietary corp.

Niles

Autumn Hills Care Center Inc
2565 Niles-Vienna Rd, Niles, OH 44446
(216) 652-2053
Licensure Skilled care; Intermediate care; Rest home. *Beds* Swing beds SNF/ICF 82; Rest home 18. *Certified* Medicaid; Medicare.
Owner Proprietary corp.

Shepherd of the Valley Nursing Home
1500 McKinley Ave, Niles, OH 44446
(216) 544-0771
Admin Donald Kacmar. *Dir of Nursing* Susan Bendel RN. *Medical Dir* Mary Beth Williams.
Licensure Skilled care; Intermediate care; Alzheimer's care; Retirement. *Beds* SNF 100; ICF 40. *Certified* Medicaid; Medicare.
Owner Proprietary corp.
Admissions Requirements Medical examination; Physician's request.
Staff RNs 3 (ft), 10 (pt); LPNs 10 (ft), 8 (pt); Nurses' aides 42 (ft), 35 (pt); Activities coordinators 1 (ft), 1 (pt); Dietitians 1 (ft).

Affiliation Lutheran.
Activities Arts & crafts; Games; Reading groups; Prayer groups; Movies; Shopping trips.

North Baltimore

Blakely Care Center
600 Sterling Dr, North Baltimore, OH 45872
(419) 257-2421
Admin Thomas Blakely. *Dir of Nursing* Douglas Blakely.
Licensure Skilled care; Intermediate care. *Beds* Swing beds SNF/ICF 53. *Certified* Medicaid; Medicare.
Owner Proprietary corp.
Admissions Requirements Medical examination.
Staff Physicians 3 (pt); RNs 2 (ft), 1 (pt); LPNs 5 (ft), 5 (pt); Nurses' aides 14 (ft), 16 (pt); Physical therapists 1 (pt); Reality therapists 3 (pt); Recreational therapists 1 (pt); Occupational therapists 1 (pt); Speech therapists 1 (pt); Activities coordinators 2 (ft); Dietitians 1 (pt); Ophthalmologists 1 (pt); Podiatrists 1 (pt); Dentists 1 (pt).
Facilities Dining room; Activities room; Laundry room; Barber/Beauty shop.
Activities Arts & crafts; Cards; Games; Reading groups; Prayer groups; Movies; Shopping trips; Dances/Social/Cultural gatherings.

North Canton

St Luke Lutheran Home
220 Applegrove St NE, North Canton, OH 44720
(216) 499-8341
Admin Rev Luther W Lautenschlager. *Dir of Nursing* Linda J Scherger RN MSN. *Medical Dir* Dr James Elliott.
Licensure Skilled care; Rest home; Alzheimer's care. *Beds* SNF 202; Rest home 32. *Private Pay Patients* 30%. *Certified* Medicaid; Medicare.
Owner Nonprofit organization/foundation.
Admissions Requirements Minimum age Retirement age; Medical examination.
Staff Physicians 1 (pt); RNs 6 (ft), 17 (pt); LPNs 28 (ft), 9 (pt); Nurses' aides 80 (ft), 38 (pt); Physical therapists 1 (pt); Occupational therapists 1 (pt); Speech therapists 1 (pt); Activities coordinators 1 (ft); Dietitians 1 (ft); Ophthalmologists 1 (pt); Podiatrists 1 (pt); Audiologists 1 (pt).
Affiliation Lutheran.
Facilities Dining room; Physical therapy room; Activities room; Chapel; Crafts room; Laundry room; Barber/Beauty shop.
Activities Arts & crafts; Cards; Games; Reading groups; Prayer groups; Movies; Shopping trips.

Windsor Medical Center Inc
1454 Easton St NW, North Canton, OH 44720
(216) 499-8300
Licensure Skilled care; Intermediate care; Retirement; Alzheimer's care. *Beds* Swing beds SNF/ICF 41.
Owner Proprietary corp.
Facilities Dining room; Physical therapy room; Activities room; Chapel; Crafts room; Laundry room; Barber/Beauty shop; Library.
Activities Arts & crafts; Cards; Games; Reading groups; Prayer groups; Movies; Shopping trips; Dances/Social/Cultural gatherings; Special events.

North Lima

Diamondhead Extended Care Center 2
9184 Market St, North Lima, OH 44452
(216) 758-5743

Admin Jacqueline O Diamond. *Dir of Nursing* Patricia Hatala RN. *Medical Dir* Anthony Dominic DO.
Licensure Intermediate care. *Beds* ICF 106. *Certified* Medicaid.
Owner Privately owned.
Admissions Requirements Medical examination.
Staff RNs 5 (ft), 3 (pt); LPNs 8 (ft), 5 (pt); Nurses' aides 37 (ft), 12 (pt); Physical therapists 1 (ft); Speech therapists 3 (pt); Activities coordinators 2 (ft); Dietitians 1 (ft); Ophthalmologists 1 (pt).
Languages Spanish, Italian, Slavic.
Facilities Dining room; Physical therapy room; Activities room; Crafts room; Laundry room; Barber/Beauty shop; Patio with gliders, picnic tables & umbrellas.
Activities Arts & crafts; Cards; Games; Prayer groups; Movies; Shopping trips; Dances/Social/Cultural gatherings; Bingo; Sing-alongs; Exercise programs; Ice cream on wheels.

Mar Lima Inc—Diamondhead Extended Care Center 1
9174 Market St, North Lima, OH 44452
(216) 758-8321
Admin William L Magourias. *Dir of Nursing* Bonita M Maher RN. *Medical Dir* Gary W Stucke DO.
Licensure Intermediate care; Intermediate care for mentally retarded. *Beds* ICF 101; ICF/MR 29. *Private Pay Patients* 1%. *Certified* Medicaid.
Owner Proprietary corp.
Admissions Requirements Medical examination; Physician's request.
Staff Physicians 3 (pt); RNs 8 (ft), 3 (pt); LPNs 11 (ft), 2 (pt); Nurses' aides 50 (ft), 20 (pt); Physical therapists 2 (pt); Occupational therapists 1 (pt); Speech therapists 1 (pt); Activities coordinators 2 (ft); Dietitians 1 (pt); Ophthalmologists 1 (pt); Podiatrists 1 (pt); Audiologists 1 (pt).
Facilities Dining room; Physical therapy room; Activities room; Laundry room; Barber/Beauty shop; Programming rooms.
Activities Arts & crafts; Cards; Games; Reading groups; Prayer groups; Movies; Shopping trips; Dances/Social/Cultural gatherings; Outside activities.

Rolling Acres Care Center
RR 1, 9625 Market St Ext, North Lima, OH 44452
(216) 549-3939, 549-3939 FAX
Admin Edward G Martell; Sally Krier Grim. *Dir of Nursing* Suzanne Gurelea RN. *Medical Dir* Joseph Mersol MD.
Licensure Skilled care; Intermediate care. *Beds* SNF 29; ICF 101. *Private Pay Patients* 10%. *Certified* Medicaid; Medicare.
Owner Proprietary corp (Medi Management Inc).
Admissions Requirements Medical examination; Physician's request.
Staff Physicians 1 (pt); RNs 3 (ft), 2 (pt); LPNs 12 (ft), 2 (pt); Nurses' aides 34 (ft), 5 (pt); Physical therapists 1 (pt); Reality therapists 1 (pt); Recreational therapists 2 (ft); Occupational therapists 1 (pt); Speech therapists 1 (pt); Activities coordinators 1 (ft); Dietitians 1 (pt); Ophthalmologists 1 (pt); Podiatrists 1 (pt); Audiologists 1 (pt).
Languages French.
Facilities Dining room; Physical therapy room; Activities room; Crafts room; Laundry room; Barber/Beauty shop.
Activities Arts & crafts; Cards; Games; Reading groups; Prayer groups; Movies; Shopping trips; Dances/Social/Cultural gatherings; Intergenerational programs; Pet therapy.

North Olmsted

Manor Care Nursing Center
23225 Lorain Rd, North Olmsted, OH 44070
(216) 779-6900
Admin Joanne Ryder. *Dir of Nursing* Delice Feretti. *Medical Dir* Klaus Neumann MD.
Licensure Skilled care; Intermediate care. *Beds* SNF 55; ICF 143. *Certified* Medicaid; Medicare.
Owner Proprietary corp (Manor Care).
Admissions Requirements Medical examination.
Staff Physical therapists 1 (pt); Recreational therapists 1 (pt); Occupational therapists 1 (pt); Speech therapists 1 (pt); Activities coordinators 1 (pt); Dietitians 1 (pt); Ophthalmologists 1 (pt); Podiatrists 1 (pt); Dentists 1 (pt).
Facilities Dining room; Physical therapy room; Activities room; Crafts room; Barber/Beauty shop; Library.
Activities Arts & crafts; Cards; Games; Reading groups; Prayer groups; Movies; Shopping trips; Dances/Social/Cultural gatherings.

Olmsted Manor Skilled Nursing Center
27500 Mill Rd, North Olmsted, OH 44070
(216) 777-8444, 777-5796 FAX
Admin Deborah L Lontor. *Dir of Nursing* Margaret Reichley. *Medical Dir* Dr Charles Pavluk.
Licensure Skilled care; Intermediate care; Alzheimer's care. *Beds* Swing beds SNF/ICF 99. *Private Pay Patients* 50%. *Certified* Medicaid; Medicare.
Owner Proprietary corp.
Staff Physicians 3 (ft); RNs 15 (ft); LPNs 20 (ft); Nurses' aides 45 (ft); Physical therapists 1 (ft); Reality therapists 1 (ft); Recreational therapists 2 (ft); Occupational therapists 1 (ft); Speech therapists 1 (ft); Activities coordinators 1 (ft); Dietitians 1 (ft); Ophthalmologists 1 (ft); Podiatrists 1 (ft); Audiologists 1 (ft).
Languages Hungarian, German, Spanish, Italian, Japanese, Polish.
Facilities Dining room; Physical therapy room; Activities room; Crafts room; Laundry room; Barber/Beauty shop; Library; Common living centers; Gift shop; Alzheimer's unit.
Activities Arts & crafts; Cards; Games; Reading groups; Prayer groups; Movies; Shopping trips; Dances/Social/Cultural gatherings; Intergenerational programs; Pet therapy; Outings.

North Randall

Suburban Pavilion Inc
20265 Emery Rd, North Randall, OH 44128
(216) 475-8880
Medical Dir Alan Kravitz MD.
Licensure Skilled care; Intermediate care. *Beds* SNF 36; ICF 62. *Certified* Medicaid; Medicare.
Owner Proprietary corp.
Admissions Requirements Medical examination; Physician's request.
Staff RNs 7 (ft), 2 (pt); LPNs 10 (ft), 2 (pt); Nurses' aides 35 (ft), 5 (pt); Physical therapists 1 (ft); Recreational therapists 1 (ft); Occupational therapists 1 (pt); Speech therapists 1 (ft); Activities coordinators 1 (ft); Dietitians 1 (pt); Podiatrists 1 (pt); Audiologists 1 (pt); Dentists 1 (pt).
Facilities Dining room; Physical therapy room; Activities room; Crafts room; Barber/Beauty shop.
Activities Arts & crafts; Cards; Games; Reading groups; Prayer groups; Movies; Dances/Social/Cultural gatherings.

North Ridgeville

Altercare of North Ridgeville
35990 Westminster Ave, North Ridgeville, OH 44039
(216) 327-8511, 327-8798 FAX
Admin Nancy A Comer. *Dir of Nursing* Bernadene Ulichney. *Medical Dir* David Brill DO.
Licensure Skilled care; Intermediate care; Residential care. *Beds* SNF 24; ICF 76; Residential care 64. *Certified* Medicaid; Medicare.
Owner Proprietary corp (Altercare Inc).
Admissions Requirements Medical examination; Physician's request.
Staff Physicians 8 (pt); RNs 5 (ft); LPNs 10 (ft); Nurses' aides 40 (ft); Physical therapists 1 (ft); Recreational therapists 2 (ft); Occupational therapists 1 (ft); Speech therapists 1 (ft); Activities coordinators 2 (ft); Dietitians 1 (pt); Ophthalmologists 1 (pt); Podiatrists 1 (pt); Audiologists 1 (pt).
Activities Arts & crafts; Cards; Games; Reading groups; Prayer groups; Movies; Shopping trips; Dances/Social/Cultural gatherings; Intergenerational programs; Pet therapy.

Center Ridge Nursing Home
38600 Center Ridge Rd, North Ridgeville, OH 44039
(216) 327-1295, 327-2510 FAX
Admin John T O'Neill LNHA. *Dir of Nursing* Barbara McGrady RN. *Medical Dir* Rudy Moc MD.
Licensure Skilled care; Intermediate care. *Beds* Swing beds SNF/ICF 100. *Private Pay Patients* 50%. *Certified* Medicaid; Medicare.
Owner Privately owned.
Staff Physicians 12 (pt); RNs 6 (pt); LPNs 15 (pt); Nurses' aides 25 (pt); Physical therapists 1 (pt); Occupational therapists 1 (pt); Speech therapists 1 (pt); Activities coordinators 1 (ft), 1 (pt); Dietitians 1 (pt); Ophthalmologists 1 (pt); Podiatrists 1 (pt); Audiologists 1 (pt).
Facilities Dining room; Physical therapy room; Activities room; Crafts room; Laundry room; Barber/Beauty shop.
Activities Arts & crafts; Cards; Games; Reading groups; Prayer groups; Movies; Shopping trips; Dances/Social/Cultural gatherings; Intergenerational programs; Pet therapy.

Holly Terrace Nursing Home
32415 Center Ridge Rd, North Ridgeville, OH 44039
(216) 327-8382
Admin Ruth M Jackson. *Dir of Nursing* Patricia Cook RN NHA. *Medical Dir* Firas Atassi MD.
Licensure Intermediate care. *Beds* ICF 18. *Certified* Medicaid.
Owner Privately owned.
Admissions Requirements Medical examination.
Staff Physicians 1 (pt); RNs 1 (ft), 2 (pt); LPNs 4 (ft), 2 (pt); Nurses' aides 5 (ft), 4 (pt); Activities coordinators 1 (ft), 1 (pt); Dietitians 1 (pt); Ophthalmologists 1 (pt); Social workers 1 (pt).
Facilities Dining room; Activities room; Laundry room; Sitting room; Large porch.
Activities Arts & crafts; Cards; Games; Reading groups; Prayer groups.

North Royalton

Mt Royal Villa
13900 Bennett Rd, North Royalton, OH 44133
(216) 237-7966
Licensure Skilled care; Intermediate care; Rest home. *Beds* Swing beds SNF/ICF 43; Rest home 63.

Owner Proprietary corp.

Northeast Care Center Inc—Alpha
PO Box 33399, 12627 York Rd, North Royalton, OH 44133
(216) 582-3300
Licensure Intermediate care for mentally retarded. *Beds* ICF/MR 48. *Certified* Medicaid.
Owner Proprietary corp.

Patrician Inc
9001 W 130th St, North Royalton, OH 44133
(216) 237-3104
Licensure Skilled care; Intermediate care. *Beds* SNF 77; ICF 148. *Certified* Medicaid; Medicare.
Owner Proprietary corp.
Staff Physicians 1 (pt); RNs 11 (ft), 11 (pt); LPNs 11 (ft), 11 (pt); Nurses' aides 56 (ft), 32 (pt); Physical therapists 1 (ft); Reality therapists 1 (ft); Recreational therapists 1 (ft); Occupational therapists 1 (pt); Speech therapists 1 (pt); Activities coordinators 3 (ft); Dietitians 1 (pt); Ophthalmologists 1 (pt); Podiatrists 1 (pt); Dentists 1 (pt).
Facilities Dining room; Physical therapy room; Activities room; Chapel; Crafts room; Barber/Beauty shop; Library.
Activities Arts & crafts; Cards; Games; Reading groups; Prayer groups; Movies; Dances/Social/Cultural gatherings.

Northfield

Western Reserve Psychiatric Center
PO Box 305, 1756 Sagamore Rd, Northfield, OH 44067
(216) 467-3131
Licensure Intermediate care for mentally retarded. *Beds* ICF/MR 60. *Certified* Medicaid.
Owner Proprietary corp.

Norton

Ideal Nursing Home
5671 Wooster Rd W, Norton, OH 44203
(216) 825-2525
Admin Deborah Leffel. *Dir of Nursing* Trudi Baker LPN. *Medical Dir* Dr P Gilcrest.
Licensure Intermediate care. *Beds* ICF 20. *Private Pay Patients* 0%. *Certified* Medicaid.
Owner Proprietary corp (RTG Nursing Homes Inc).
Admissions Requirements Females only; Medical examination.
Staff Physicians (consultant); RNs (consultant); LPNs 2 (ft), 4 (pt); Nurses' aides 6 (ft), 2 (pt); Activities coordinators 1 (pt); Dietitians (consultant); Podiatrists (consultant); Social service 1 (pt).
Facilities Laundry room.
Activities Games; Reading groups; Prayer groups; Shopping trips; Dances/Social/Cultural gatherings; Intergenerational programs.

Norwalk

Gaymont Nursing Center
66 Norwood Ave, Norwalk, OH 44857
(419) 668-8258
Admin William C. Dotson.
Medical Dir Warren Sawyer MD.
Licensure Skilled care; Intermediate care; Retirement. *Beds* Swing beds SNF/ICF 100. *Certified* Medicaid; Medicare.
Owner Privately owned.
Admissions Requirements Medical examination; Physician's request.
Staff Physicians; RNs; LPNs; Nurses' aides; Physical therapists; Occupational therapists; Speech therapists; Activities coordinators; Dietitians; Ophthalmologists.

Facilities Dining room; Physical therapy room; Activities room; Chapel; Crafts room; Laundry room; Barber/Beauty shop.
Activities Arts & crafts; Games; Reading groups; Prayer groups; Movies; Shopping trips; Dances/Social/Cultural gatherings.

Norwalk Memorial Home
272 Benedict Ave, Norwalk, OH 44857
(419) 668-8101
Admin Richard C Westhofen. *Dir of Nursing* Sharen Hochsedler RN. *Medical Dir* Harold D Erlenbach MD.
Licensure Skilled care; Intermediate care. *Beds* Swing beds SNF/ICF 50. *Certified* Medicaid; Medicare.
Owner Nonprofit corp.
Admissions Requirements Medical examination; Physician's request.
Staff RNs 1 (ft), 1 (pt); LPNs 1 (ft), 7 (pt); Nurses' aides 9 (ft), 13 (pt); Activities coordinators 1 (pt); Housekeeping 3 (ft), 2 (pt).
Facilities Dining room; Physical therapy room; Activities room; Crafts room; Laundry room; Barber/Beauty shop.
Activities Arts & crafts; Cards; Games; Reading groups; Prayer groups; Movies; Shopping trips; Dances/Social/Cultural gatherings.

Twilight Gardens Home Inc
196 W Main St, Norwalk, OH 44857
(419) 668-2086
Admin Carol Starkey.
Medical Dir Ronald D Winland.
Licensure Skilled care; Intermediate care. *Beds* Swing beds SNF/ICF 100. *Certified* Medicaid; Medicare.
Owner Proprietary corp.
Admissions Requirements Medical examination; Physician's request.
Staff RNs 2 (ft), 1 (pt); LPNs 9 (ft), 12 (pt); Nurses' aides 36 (ft), 11 (pt); Physical therapists; Recreational therapists; Occupational therapists; Speech therapists; Activities coordinators 1 (ft); Dietitians; Podiatrists; Ophthalmologists; Dentists.
Facilities Dining room; Physical therapy room; Activities room; Crafts room; Laundry room; Barber/Beauty shop; Library; Sun room; Meditation room; TV room.
Activities Arts & crafts; Cards; Games; Reading groups; Prayer groups; Movies; Shopping trips; Dances/Social/Cultural gatherings.

Norwood

Victory Park Nursing Home
1578 Sherman Ave, Norwood, OH 45212
(513) 351-0153
Admin Herb Seidner. *Dir of Nursing* Pam Connelly. *Medical Dir* Dr Manuel Mediodia Jr.
Licensure Skilled care; Intermediate care; Independent living; Alzheimer's care. *Beds* SNF 56; ICF 46; Independent living 11. *Certified* Medicaid; Medicare.
Owner Privately owned.
Admissions Requirements Medical examination; Physician's request.
Staff Physicians; RNs; LPNs; Nurses' aides; Activities coordinators; Dietitians; Ophthalmologists.
Facilities Dining room; Activities room; Chapel; Laundry room; Barber/Beauty shop; TV room.
Activities Arts & crafts; Cards; Games; Reading groups; Prayer groups; Movies; Dances/Social/Cultural gatherings.

Oak Harbor

Ottawa County Riverview Nursing Home
8180 W State Rte 163, Oak Harbor, OH 43449
(419) 898-2851, 898-0944
Admin John Moore CFACHCA. *Dir of Nursing* Lois Karshuk RN. *Medical Dir* Robert W Minick MD.
Licensure Skilled care; Intermediate care; Adult day care. *Beds* Swing beds SNF/ICF 166. *Private Pay Patients* 41%. *Certified* Medicaid; Medicare.
Owner Publicly owned.
Admissions Requirements Medical examination; Physician's request.
Staff Physicians 8 (pt); RNs 9 (ft), 9 (pt); LPNs 7 (ft), 14 (pt); Nurses' aides 52 (ft), 27 (pt); Physical therapists 2 (pt); Recreational therapists 1 (ft); Occupational therapists 1 (pt); Speech therapists 1 (pt); Activities coordinators 1 (ft), 2 (pt); Dietitians 1 (pt); Ophthalmologists 1 (pt); Podiatrists 1 (pt); Audiologists 1 (pt).
Languages Spanish.
Facilities Dining room; Activities room; Crafts room; Barber/Beauty shop.
Activities Arts & crafts; Cards; Games; Reading groups; Prayer groups; Movies; Shopping trips; Dances/Social/Cultural gatherings; Intergenerational programs; Pet therapy; Birthday parties; Wine & cheese parties; Bingo; Picnics; "Make your own sundae" parties.

Oak Hill

Davis Home for the Aged
315 Washington St, Oak Hill, OH 45656
(614) 682-7585
Admin Theresa Stout.
Licensure Rest home. *Beds* Rest home 32.
Owner Nonprofit organization/foundation.
Admissions Requirements Minimum age 50; Females only; Medical examination.
Staff LPNs 1 (ft).
Facilities Dining room; Laundry room; Barber/Beauty shop.
Activities Arts & crafts; Cards; Reading groups; Shopping trips; Bible study; Visiting groups.

Oberlin

Carter's Nursing Home
PO Box 276, 284 E Lorain St, Oberlin, OH 44074
(216) 774-7202
Admin Wanda L Carter. *Dir of Nursing* Dorothy Stephens.
Licensure Intermediate care. *Beds* ICF 50. *Certified* Medicaid.
Owner Proprietary corp.
Admissions Requirements Medical examination.
Staff Physicians 5 (ft); RNs 1 (ft), 1 (pt); LPNs 4 (ft), 2 (pt); Nurses' aides 9 (ft), 4 (pt); Activities coordinators 1 (ft), 1 (pt); Dietitians 1 (pt); Ophthalmologists 1 (pt).
Facilities Dining room; Activities room; Crafts room; Laundry room.
Activities Arts & crafts; Cards; Games; Prayer groups; Shopping trips; Dances/Social/Cultural gatherings.

Tressie's Nursing Home
277 N Professor St, Oberlin, OH 44074
(216) 774-1255
Admin Don H Wessell NHA. *Dir of Nursing* Debbie Carver RN. *Medical Dir* Feite Hofman MD.
Licensure Intermediate care; Retirement. *Beds* ICF 19; Retirement 1. *Private Pay Patients* 42%. *Certified* Medicaid.
Owner Proprietary corp.
Admissions Requirements Males only.

Staff RNs 1 (ft); LPNs 2 (ft), 5 (pt); Nurses' aides 5 (ft), 5 (pt); Activities coordinators 1 (pt).
Facilities Dining room; Activities room; Laundry room.
Activities Arts & crafts; Cards; Games; Reading groups; Prayer groups; Movies; Shopping trips; Dances/Social/Cultural gatherings; Pet therapy.

Welcome Nursing Home Inc
54 E Hamilton St, Oberlin, OH 44074
(216) 775-1491
Admin Don H Wessell NHA. *Dir of Nursing* Theo M Wessell RN NHA. *Medical Dir* Feite Hofman MD.
Licensure Skilled care; Intermediate care; Retirement. *Beds* Swing beds SNF/ICF 53; Retirement 3. *Private Pay Patients* 53%. *Certified* Medicaid; Medicare.
Owner Proprietary corp.
Admissions Requirements Minimum age 18; Medical examination; Physician's request.
Staff RNs 3 (ft), 3 (pt); LPNs 6 (ft), 4 (pt); Nurses' aides 12 (ft), 10 (pt); Physical therapists 1 (pt); Activities coordinators 1 (ft); Dietitians 1 (pt).
Facilities Dining room; Physical therapy room; Activities room; Barber/Beauty shop; Library.
Activities Arts & crafts; Cards; Games; Reading groups; Prayer groups; Movies; Shopping trips; Dances/Social/Cultural gatherings; Intergenerational programs; Pet therapy.

Will-O-Lee Nursing Home 1
PO Box 149, Rte 58 N, Oberlin, OH 44074
(216) 775-3639
Admin William McKinney. *Dir of Nursing* John Jonesco.
Licensure Intermediate care. *Beds* ICF 45. *Certified* Medicaid.
Owner Proprietary corp.
Admissions Requirements Medical examination.
Staff Physicians 1 (pt); RNs 2 (ft), 2 (pt); LPNs 9 (ft); Nurses' aides 17 (ft); Activities coordinators 1 (ft); Dietitians 1 (ft); Ophthalmologists 1 (pt); Activities aides 3 (ft).
Facilities Dining room; Activities room; Chapel; Laundry room.
Activities Arts & crafts; Cards; Games; Reading groups; Prayer groups; Movies; Shopping trips; Dances/Social/Cultural gatherings.

Will-O-Lee Nursing Home 2
PO Box 149, 345 N Professor St, Oberlin, OH 44074
(216) 775-3639
Medical Dir George Hoover.
Licensure Intermediate care for mentally retarded. *Beds* ICF/MR 25. *Certified* Medicaid.
Owner Proprietary corp.
Admissions Requirements Medical examination.
Staff Physicians 2 (pt); RNs 1 (ft), 1 (pt); LPNs 10 (ft); Nurses' aides 9 (ft); Recreational therapists 1 (ft); Activities coordinators 1 (ft); Dietitians 1 (ft); Podiatrists 1 (pt); Dentists 1 (pt).
Facilities Dining room; Activities room; Crafts room; Laundry room.
Activities Arts & crafts; Cards; Games; Reading groups; Prayer groups; Movies; Shopping trips; Dances/Social/Cultural gatherings.

Oregon

Americare Oregon Nursing & Rehabilitation Center
904 Isaac Sts Dr, Oregon, OH 43616
(419) 691-2483
Admin Joyce Arend.

Medical Dir Marty Agha.
Licensure Skilled care; Intermediate care. *Beds* SNF 24; ICF 76. *Certified* Medicaid; Medicare.
Owner Proprietary corp (Care Enterprises).
Admissions Requirements Medical examination; Physician's request.
Staff RNs; LPNs; Nurses' aides; Recreational therapists; Activities coordinators; Dietitians.
Facilities Dining room; Physical therapy room; Activities room; Crafts room; Laundry room; Barber/Beauty shop.
Activities Arts & crafts; Cards; Games; Reading groups; Prayer groups; Movies; Shopping trips; Dances/Social/Cultural gatherings; Happy hour.

Little Sisters of the Poor
4900 Navarre Ave, Oregon, OH 43616
(419) 698-4331, 698-8601 FAX
Admin Sr Rose Marie Mayock. *Dir of Nursing* Sr Martha Lieb RN. *Medical Dir* Frank Abbati MD.
Licensure Intermediate care; Rest home; Assisted living. *Beds* ICF 96; Rest home 40; Assisted living 20. *Private Pay Patients* 20%. *Certified* Medicaid.
Owner Nonprofit organization/foundation (Little Sisters of the Poor).
Admissions Requirements Minimum age 60; Medical examination.
Staff Physicians 5 (pt); RNs 2 (ft), 2 (pt); LPNs 8 (ft), 5 (pt); Nurses' aides 31 (ft), 17 (pt); Physical therapists 1 (pt); Activities coordinators 1 (ft); Dietitians 1 (pt); Podiatrists 1 (pt).
Affiliation Roman Catholic.
Facilities Dining room; Physical therapy room; Activities room; Chapel; Crafts room; Laundry room; Barber/Beauty shop; Library.
Activities Arts & crafts; Cards; Games; Reading groups; Prayer groups; Movies; Shopping trips; Dances/Social/Cultural gatherings.

Manor Care Nursing Center
3953 Navarre Ave, Oregon, OH 43616
(419) 698-4521
Licensure Skilled care; Intermediate care. *Beds* SNF 20; ICF 90. *Certified* Medicaid; Medicare.
Owner Proprietary corp (Manor Care).

Orrville

Brenn-Field Nursing Center
1980 Lynn Dr, Orrville, OH 44667
(216) 683-4075
Admin Richard Brenneman. *Dir of Nursing* Dorothy Brenneman.
Licensure Intermediate care; Retirement. *Beds* ICF 100. *Certified* Medicaid.
Owner Proprietary corp.
Admissions Requirements Medical examination.
Staff RNs 2 (ft), 3 (pt); LPNs 6 (ft), 5 (pt); Nurses' aides 15 (ft), 25 (pt); Physical therapists 1 (pt); Recreational therapists 1 (pt); Activities coordinators 1 (ft); Dietitians 1 (ft).
Languages Italian.
Facilities Dining room; Physical therapy room; Activities room; Crafts room; Laundry room; Barber/Beauty shop; Library.
Activities Arts & crafts; Cards; Games; Reading groups; Prayer groups; Movies; Shopping trips.

Orwell

Village Square Nursing Center
PO Box 99, 7787 Staley Rd, Orwell, OH 44076
(216) 437-6611
Admin Mary Brown. *Dir of Nursing* Darlene Peterson RN. *Medical Dir* Dr L A Loria.

Licensure Intermediate care. *Beds* ICF 50. *Certified* Medicaid.
Owner Proprietary corp (Horizon Healthcare Corp).
Admissions Requirements Medical examination.
Staff RNs; LPNs; Nurses' aides; Physical therapists; Activities coordinators; Dietitians; Ophthalmologists; Podiatrists.
Facilities Dining room; Activities room; Crafts room; Laundry room.
Activities Arts & crafts; Cards; Games; Reading groups; Prayer groups; Movies; Shopping trips; Dances/Social/Cultural gatherings.

Ottawa

Alternative Residences Inc—Ottawa Home
8076 Rd 13-G, Ottawa, OH 45875
(419) 523-4981
Licensure Intermediate care for mentally retarded. *Beds* ICF/MR 10. *Certified* Medicaid.
Owner Proprietary corp.

Alternative Residences Inc—Putnam Home
8088 Rd 13-G, Ottawa, OH 45875
(419) 523-4790
Licensure Intermediate care for mentally retarded. *Beds* ICF/MR 10. *Certified* Medicaid.
Owner Proprietary corp.

Calvary Manor Nursing Home
RR 4, 575 Glandorf Rd, Ottawa, OH 45875
(419) 538-6529
Admin Larry Schroeder. *Dir of Nursing* Mildred Brickner. *Medical Dir* Dr Ogle.
Licensure Intermediate care. *Beds* ICF 78. *Private Pay Patients* 33%. *Certified* Medicaid.
Owner Proprietary corp.
Admissions Requirements Medical examination.
Staff RNs 6 (ft), 5 (pt); LPNs 6 (ft), 4 (pt); Nurses' aides 12 (ft), 17 (pt); Recreational therapists 1 (ft), 2 (pt); Activities coordinators 1 (ft); Dietitians 1 (pt).
Languages Spanish.
Facilities Dining room; Physical therapy room; Activities room; Chapel; Laundry room; Barber/Beauty shop.
Activities Arts & crafts; Cards; Games; Reading groups; Prayer groups; Movies; Shopping trips; Dances/Social/Cultural gatherings; Intergenerational programs; Pet therapy.

Hometown Nursing Home of Ottawa
PO Box 254, Ottawa, OH 45875
(419) 523-4370
Medical Dir Dr James Overmier.
Licensure Intermediate care. *Beds* ICF 50. *Certified* Medicaid.
Owner Proprietary corp.
Admissions Requirements Minimum age 18; Medical examination.
Staff RNs 3 (ft); LPNs 1 (ft), 4 (pt); Nurses' aides 8 (ft), 14 (pt); Physical therapists 1 (pt); Reality therapists 1 (pt); Recreational therapists 1 (pt); Occupational therapists 1 (pt); Speech therapists 1 (pt); Activities coordinators 1 (ft), 1 (pt); Dietitians 1 (pt); Ophthalmologists 1 (pt); Podiatrists 1 (pt); Audiologists 1 (pt); Dentists 1 (pt).
Facilities Dining room; Activities room; Chapel; Crafts room; Laundry room; Barber/Beauty shop; Library.
Activities Arts & crafts; Cards; Games; Reading groups; Prayer groups; Movies; Shopping trips; Dances/Social/Cultural gatherings.

Putnam Acres Care Center
RR 1, Rd 5-H, Ottawa, OH 45875
(419) 523-4092

Admin Anita S Warden. *Dir of Nursing* Natalie Saloum RN. *Medical Dir* James Overmier MD.
Licensure Intermediate care; Alzheimer's care. *Beds* ICF 88. *Certified* Medicaid.
Owner Publicly owned.
Admissions Requirements Minimum age 16.
Staff Physicians 1 (pt); RNs 4 (ft), 3 (pt); LPNs 2 (ft), 5 (pt); Nurses' aides 23 (ft), 17 (pt); Physical therapists 1 (pt); Occupational therapists 1 (pt); Speech therapists 1 (pt); Activities coordinators 2 (ft); Dietitians 1 (pt); Ophthalmologists 1 (pt); Podiatrists 1 (pt); Dentists 1 (pt).
Facilities Dining room; Physical therapy room; Activities room; Chapel; Crafts room; Laundry room; Barber/Beauty shop; Library.
Activities Arts & crafts; Cards; Games; Reading groups; Prayer groups; Movies; Shopping trips; Dances/Social/Cultural gatherings.

Oxford

Oxford View Nursing Center
6099 Fairfield Rd, Oxford, OH 45056
(513) 523-6353, 863-5038 FAX
Admin Mark E Johnson. *Dir of Nursing* Jan Kirkpatrick RN. *Medical Dir* Dr Terry Hunt.
Licensure Skilled care; Intermediate care. *Beds* SNF 30; ICF 118. *Private Pay Patients* 37%. *Certified* Medicaid; Medicare.
Owner Proprietary corp.
Admissions Requirements Minimum age over 65 preferred.
Staff RNs 3 (ft), 3 (pt); LPNs 15 (ft), 10 (pt); Nurses' aides 15 (ft), 50 (pt); Physical therapists 1 (pt); Occupational therapists 1 (pt); Speech therapists 1 (pt); Activities coordinators 3 (ft); Dietitians 2 (pt).
Facilities Dining room; Physical therapy room; Activities room; Laundry room; Barber/Beauty shop.
Activities Arts & crafts; Cards; Games; Reading groups; Prayer groups; Movies; Shopping trips; Dances/Social/Cultural gatherings; Intergenerational programs; Pet therapy; Exercise groups; Weekly bus outings; Music appreciation; Adopt-a-grandparent.

Painesville

Cerri's Painesville Nursing Home
252 W Jackson St, Painesville, OH 44077
(216) 354-5300
Admin Lenore Finerman. *Dir of Nursing* Sharon Schultz. *Medical Dir* Dr Stabler.
Licensure Intermediate care. *Beds* ICF 18. *Certified* Medicaid.
Owner Proprietary corp.
Admissions Requirements Minimum age 20; Females only; Medical examination; Physician's request.
Staff RNs 1 (pt); LPNs 6 (ft); Nurses' aides 15 (ft); Dietitians 1 (ft).
Facilities Dining room; Crafts room; Laundry room; Yard; Patio; Garden.
Activities Arts & crafts; Cards; Games; Reading groups; Prayer groups; Movies; Shopping trips; Dances/Social/Cultural gatherings; Camping.

Homestead I
164 Liberty St, Painesville, OH 44077
(216) 953-0791
Licensure Skilled care; Intermediate care. *Beds* Swing beds SNF/ICF 53. *Certified* Medicaid; Medicare.
Owner Proprietary corp.

Homestead II
60 Wood St, Painesville, OH 44077
(216) 352-0788, 951-0964

Admin Myra Shinas. *Dir of Nursing* Elaine Gallovic RN. *Medical Dir* Dr Robert Whitehouse.
Licensure Skilled care; Intermediate care. *Beds* Swing beds SNF/ICF 52. *Certified* Medicaid; Medicare.
Owner Proprietary corp (Multi-Care Inc).
Staff Physicians 6 (pt); RNs 3 (ft), 1 (pt); LPNs 4 (ft), 3 (pt); Nurses' aides 21 (ft), 6 (pt); Physical therapists 1 (pt); Speech therapists 1 (pt); Activities coordinators 1 (ft); Dietitians 1 (pt); Ophthalmologists 1 (pt); Podiatrists 1 (pt); Dentists 1 (pt).
Facilities Dining room; Physical therapy room; Activities room; Crafts room; Laundry room; Barber/Beauty shop.
Activities Arts & crafts; Cards; Games; Reading groups; Prayer groups; Movies; Shopping trips; Dances/Social/Cultural gatherings.

Ivy House
308 S State St, Painesville, OH 44077
(216) 354-2131
Admin Marie Swaim.
Medical Dir Dr F Veroni.
Licensure Intermediate care. *Beds* ICF 50. *Certified* Medicaid.
Owner Proprietary corp.
Admissions Requirements Minimum age 60; Medical examination.
Staff Physicians 1 (pt); RNs 1 (ft); LPNs 4 (ft); Recreational therapists 1 (ft), 1 (pt); Activities coordinators 1 (ft), 1 (pt); Dietitians 1 (pt).
Facilities Dining room; Activities room; Chapel; Crafts room; Laundry room; Barber/Beauty shop; Library.
Activities Arts & crafts; Cards; Games; Reading groups; Prayer groups; Movies; Shopping trips; Dances/Social/Cultural gatherings.

Pandora

Hilty Memorial Home
5570 State Rte 12, Pandora, OH 45877
(419) 384-3218
Admin Carolyn Skinker Wetzel. *Dir of Nursing* Noralu Kahle. *Medical Dir* Dr Oliver Lugibihl.
Licensure Intermediate care. *Beds* ICF 61. *Private Pay Patients* 55%. *Certified* Medicaid.
Owner Nonprofit organization/foundation (Missionary Church, East Central District).
Admissions Requirements Medical examination.
Staff RNs; LPNs; Nurses' aides; Physical therapists; Dietitians; Intergenerational activities coordinators 1 (ft).
Facilities Dining room; Activities room; Chapel; Laundry room; Barber/Beauty shop; Child day care center; Child care observatory.
Activities Arts & crafts; Cards; Games; Reading groups; Prayer groups; Movies; Shopping trips; Intergenerational programs; Pet therapy.

Parma

Broadview Nursing Home
5520 Broadview Rd, Parma, OH 44134
(216) 749-4010
Licensure Skilled care; Intermediate care. *Beds* Swing beds SNF/ICF 218. *Certified* Medicaid; Medicare.
Owner Proprietary corp.

Holy Family Home
6707 State Rd, Parma, OH 44134
(216) 885-3100
Admin Sr M Denise. *Dir of Nursing* Sr M Luke. *Medical Dir* Dr O Mazanec.
Licensure Skilled care. *Beds* SNF 50. *Private Pay Patients* 0%.

Owner Proprietary corp.
Admissions Requirements Physician's request; Terminal cancer; Unable to pay for care; No mental condition.
Staff Physicians 1 (pt); RNs 3 (ft); LPNs 5 (ft), 1 (pt); Nurses' aides 9 (ft), 7 (pt); Dietitians 1 (pt); Podiatrists 1 (pt); Dentists 1 (pt).
Facilities Activities room; Chapel; Crafts room; Laundry room; Barber/Beauty shop; Library.
Activities Arts & crafts; Movies.

Mt Alverna Home Annex Inc
6765 State Rd, Parma, OH 44134
(216) 843-7800
Licensure Skilled care; Intermediate care. *Beds* Swing beds SNF/ICF 50.
Owner Proprietary corp.

Mt Alverna Home Inc
6765 State Rd, Parma, OH 44134
(216) 843-7800, 843-7107 FAX
Admin Robert J Sherrin. *Dir of Nursing* Carolyn Lehman MSN RN. *Medical Dir* T J Maximin MD.
Licensure Intermediate care; Alzheimer's care. *Beds* ICF 203. *Certified* Medicaid.
Owner Nonprofit corp (Franciscan Sisters).
Admissions Requirements Medical examination.
Staff Physicians 5 (pt); RNs 9 (ft), 7 (pt); LPNs 9 (ft), 7 (pt); Nurses' aides 45 (ft), 18 (pt); Physical therapists 3 (pt); Occupational therapists 1 (pt); Activities coordinators 2 (ft), 1 (pt); Dietitians 1 (pt); Podiatrists 1 (pt).
Affiliation Roman Catholic.
Facilities Dining room; Physical therapy room; Activities room; Chapel; Crafts room; Laundry room; Barber/Beauty shop; Library.
Activities Arts & crafts; Cards; Games; Reading groups; Prayer groups; Movies; Shopping trips; Dances/Social/Cultural gatherings; Intergenerational programs; Pet therapy.

Nelson Broadview Nursing Home
5520 Broadview Rd, Parma, OH 44134
(216) 749-4010
Licensure Intermediate care. *Beds* 27. *Certified* Medicaid.
Owner Proprietary corp.

Parma Care Center
5553 Broadview Rd, Parma, OH 44134
(216) 661-6800, 661-6763 FAX
Admin Louis Schonfeld. *Dir of Nursing* Linda Dreese RN. *Medical Dir* Dr J Go.
Licensure Skilled care; Intermediate care; Assisted living. *Beds* Swing beds SNF/ICF 70; Assisted living 30. *Private Pay Patients* 40%. *Certified* Medicaid; Medicare.
Owner Proprietary corp.
Admissions Requirements Medical examination.
Staff Physicians 5 (pt); RNs 1 (ft), 2 (pt); LPNs 7 (ft), 3 (pt); Nurses' aides 38 (ft), 5 (pt); Physical therapists 1 (pt); Occupational therapists 1 (pt); Speech therapists 1 (pt); Activities coordinators 3 (ft); Dietitians 1 (pt); Ophthalmologists 1 (pt); Podiatrists 3 (pt); Audiologists 1 (pt).
Facilities Dining room; Physical therapy room; Activities room; Chapel; Crafts room; Laundry room; Barber/Beauty shop; Occupational therapy room; Speech therapy room; Private and semi-private rooms; Lounges with large screen TVs.
Activities Arts & crafts; Cards; Games; Prayer groups; Movies; Shopping trips; Dances/ Social/Cultural gatherings; Pet therapy; Trips to park, amusement centers, tourist areas.

Pleasantview Nursing Home
7377 Ridge Rd, Parma, OH 44129
(216) 845-0200
Medical Dir Dr T Burney.

Licensure Skilled care; Intermediate care. *Beds* SNF 40; ICF 147. *Certified* Medicaid; Medicare.
Owner Proprietary corp.
Admissions Requirements Medical examination.
Staff RNs 7 (ft), 5 (pt); LPNs 11 (ft), 12 (pt); Nurses' aides 43 (ft), 35 (pt); Physical therapists 1 (ft), 1 (pt); Recreational therapists 1 (ft); Speech therapists 1 (pt); Activities coordinators 1 (pt); Dietitians 1 (pt); Ophthalmologists 2 (pt); Dentists 1 (pt).
Facilities Dining room; Physical therapy room; Activities room; Chapel; Crafts room; Laundry room; Barber/Beauty shop; Library.
Activities Arts & crafts; Games; Reading groups; Prayer groups; Movies; Dances/ Social/Cultural gatherings.

Parma Heights

Aristocrat South
6455 Pearl Rd, Parma Heights, OH 44130
(216) 888-5900
Admin Tom Coury.
Licensure Skilled care; Intermediate care; Intermediate care for mentally retarded; Retirement. *Beds* SNF 37; ICF 123; ICF/ MR 39. *Certified* Medicaid; Medicare.
Owner Proprietary corp.
Admissions Requirements Minimum age 15; Medical examination.
Staff RNs; LPNs; Nurses' aides; Physical therapists; Reality therapists; Occupational therapists; Speech therapists; Activities coordinators; Dietitians; Ophthalmologists; Podiatrists.
Facilities Dining room; Physical therapy room; Activities room; Crafts room; Laundry room; Barber/Beauty shop; Library.
Activities Arts & crafts; Cards; Games; Reading groups; Prayer groups; Dances/ Social/Cultural gatherings.

Paulding

Hometown Nursing Home of Paulding
RR 2, Box 1241, Paulding, OH 45879
(419) 399-4940
Admin Patricia Parton. *Dir of Nursing* Linda Eifrid RN. *Medical Dir* David Fanney DO.
Licensure Intermediate care. *Beds* ICF 50. *Private Pay Patients* 40%. *Certified* Medicaid.
Owner Proprietary corp.
Admissions Requirements Medical examination; Physician's request.
Staff RNs 2 (ft), 2 (pt); LPNs 1 (ft), 5 (pt); Nurses' aides 8 (ft), 15 (pt); Activities coordinators 1 (ft), 1 (pt); Dietitians 1 (pt).
Languages Spanish.
Facilities Dining room; Activities room; Laundry room; Barber/Beauty shop.
Activities Arts & crafts; Cards; Games; Reading groups; Prayer groups; Movies; Psychosocial group; Room-bound visits.

Payne

Dallas Lamb Foundation Home
PO Box 56, 650 N Main, Payne, OH 45880
(419) 263-2334
Licensure Intermediate care. *Beds* ICF 50. *Certified* Medicaid.
Owner Proprietary corp.

Peebles

Hillcrest Nursing Home
3564 Lawshe Rd, Peebles, OH 45660
(513) 386-2522
Admin Oscar Jarnicki. *Dir of Nursing* Connie Fenton RN. *Medical Dir* Dr K Lim.
Licensure Intermediate care; Intermediate care for mentally retarded. *Beds* ICF 30; ICF/MR 20. *Certified* Medicaid.

Owner Proprietary corp (Congregate Living of America).
Staff RNs 2 (ft); LPNs 6 (ft), 3 (pt); Nurses' aides 25 (ft); Recreational therapists 1 (ft); Dietitians 1 (pt).
Facilities Dining room; Activities room; Crafts room; Laundry room; Barber/Beauty shop; Library.
Activities Arts & crafts; Cards; Games; Reading groups; Prayer groups; Movies; Shopping trips; Dances/Social/Cultural gatherings.

Pemberville

Portage Valley Inc
20311 Pemberville Rd, Pemberville, OH 43450
(419) 833-7000
Admin Brian R Tansey. *Dir of Nursing* Elsie Street RN. *Medical Dir* Gustave Link MD.
Licensure Skilled care; Intermediate care. *Beds* Swing beds SNF/ICF 100. *Certified* Medicaid; Medicare.
Owner Proprietary corp.
Admissions Requirements Medical examination; Physician's request.
Staff Physicians 1 (pt); RNs 3 (ft), 3 (pt); LPNs 6 (ft), 8 (pt); Nurses' aides 18 (ft), 28 (pt); Activities coordinators 1 (ft); Dietitians 1 (ft).
Affiliation Methodist.
Facilities Dining room; Physical therapy room; Activities room; Laundry room; Barber/Beauty shop.
Activities Arts & crafts; Cards; Games; Reading groups; Prayer groups; Movies; Shopping trips; Dances/Social/Cultural gatherings.

Peninsula

Wayside Farm Inc
4557 Quick Rd, Peninsula, OH 44264
(216) 923-7828
Licensure Intermediate care for mentally retarded. *Beds* ICF/MR 95. *Certified* Medicaid.
Owner Proprietary corp.

Perry

Perry Ridge Nursing Home Inc
5051 S Ridge Rd, Perry, OH 44081
(216) 259-4300
Licensure Intermediate care. *Beds* ICF 39. *Certified* Medicaid.
Owner Proprietary corp.

Perrysburg

Belmont Nursing Center
28546 Starbright Blvd, Perrysburg, OH 43551
(419) 666-0935
Admin Judith A Bishop. *Dir of Nursing* Janice Knaggs RN. *Medical Dir* Bruce Vogel DO.
Licensure Skilled care; Intermediate care. *Beds* Swing beds SNF/ICF 100. *Certified* Medicaid; Medicare.
Owner Proprietary corp (Shive Nursing Centers).
Admissions Requirements Medical examination.
Staff RNs; LPNs; Nurses' aides; Recreational therapists 1 (ft); Dietitians 1 (ft).
Facilities Dining room; Physical therapy room; Activities room; Crafts room; Barber/ Beauty shop; Library; Central living room.
Activities Arts & crafts; Cards; Games; Reading groups; Prayer groups; Movies; Shopping trips; Dances/Social/Cultural gatherings; Intergenerational programs; Pet therapy.

Heartland of Perrysburg
10540 Fremont Pike, Perrysburg, OH 43551
(419) 874-3578
Admin Jean Wolfe.
Medical Dir S R Torres MD.
Licensure Skilled care; Alzheimer's care. *Beds*
SNF 131. *Certified* Medicare.
Owner Proprietary corp (Health Care and
Retirement Corp).
Staff RNs 6 (ft), 9 (pt); LPNs 12 (ft), 3 (pt);
Nurses' aides 34 (ft), 21 (pt); Physical
therapists 1 (ft); Recreational therapists 1
(ft); Speech therapists 1 (ft); Activities
coordinators 1 (ft); Dietitians 1 (ft);
Ophthalmologists 1 (pt); Podiatrists 1 (pt);
Dentists 1 (pt).
Facilities Dining room; Physical therapy
room; Activities room; Crafts room; Laundry
room; Barber/Beauty shop.
Activities Arts & crafts; Cards; Games;
Reading groups; Prayer groups; Movies;
Shopping trips; Dances/Social/Cultural
gatherings.

Pickerington

Echo Manor Extended Care Center
10270 Blacklick Eastern Rd NW,
Pickerington, OH 43147
(614) 864-1718
Licensure Skilled care; Intermediate care. *Beds*
Swing beds SNF/ICF 100. *Certified*
Medicaid; Medicare.
Owner Proprietary corp.

Pickerington Health Care Center
1300 N Hill Rd, Pickerington, OH 43147
(614) 863-1858
Licensure Skilled care; Intermediate care. *Beds*
Swing beds SNF/ICF 100. *Certified*
Medicaid; Medicare.
Owner Proprietary corp.

Piketon

Casey Nursing Home
2386 Wakefield Mound Rd, Piketon, OH
45661
(614) 289-2137
Admin Erma Jewett.
Medical Dir K A Wilkinson MD.
Licensure Intermediate care. *Beds* ICF 38.
Certified Medicaid.
Owner Proprietary corp.
Admissions Requirements Medical
examination; Physician's request.
Staff RNs 1 (pt); LPNs 4 (ft), 1 (pt); Nurses'
aides 9 (ft); Recreational therapists 1 (ft);
Activities coordinators 1 (ft).
Facilities Dining room; Activities room;
Crafts room; Laundry room.
Activities Arts & crafts; Games; Reading
groups; Prayer groups; Movies; Shopping
trips; Dances/Social/Cultural gatherings.

Piketon Nursing Center
300 Overlook Dr, Piketon, OH 45661
(614) 289-4074
Admin Don De Vaux. *Dir of Nursing* Sandy
Osborne. *Medical Dir* Kenneth Wilkinson.
Licensure Intermediate care. *Beds* ICF 25.
Private Pay Patients 1%. *Certified* Medicare.
Owner Proprietary corp (LTC Management).
Admissions Requirements Medical
examination.
Staff Physicians 1 (ft); RNs 1 (ft); LPNs 4 (ft);
Nurses' aides 10 (ft); Reality therapists 1
(ft); Activities coordinators 1 (ft); Dietitians
1 (ft); Podiatrists 1 (ft).
Facilities Dining room; Activities room;
Laundry room.
Activities Arts & crafts; Cards; Games;
Reading groups; Prayer groups; Movies;
Shopping trips; Dances/Social/Cultural
gatherings; Pet therapy.

Pleasant Hill Convalescent Center
PO Box 334, 7143 US Rte 23, Piketon, OH
45661
(614) 289-2394
Licensure Skilled care; Intermediate care. *Beds*
Swing beds SNF/ICF 201. *Certified*
Medicaid; Medicare.
Owner Proprietary corp.

Riverside Manor
214 Main St, Piketon, OH 45661
(614) 289-2129
Licensure Intermediate care. *Beds* ICF 25.
Certified Medicaid.
Owner Proprietary corp.

Piqua

Heartland of Piqua
275 Kienle Dr, Piqua, OH 45356
(513) 773-9346
Licensure Skilled care; Intermediate care. *Beds*
Swing beds SNF/ICF 100. *Certified*
Medicaid; Medicare.
Owner Proprietary corp (Health Care and
Retirement Corp).

Piqua Manor
W High St, Piqua, OH 45356
(513) 773-0040
Medical Dir Jack P Steinhilben MD.
Licensure Skilled care; Intermediate care. *Beds*
Swing beds SNF/ICF 100. *Certified*
Medicaid; Medicare.
Owner Proprietary corp (HCF Inc).
Admissions Requirements Medical
examination; Physician's request.
Staff RNs 2 (ft), 5 (pt); LPNs 7 (ft), 5 (pt);
Nurses' aides 13 (ft), 20 (pt); Physical
therapists 1 (ft); Activities coordinators 2
(ft).
Facilities Dining room; Physical therapy
room; Activities room; Crafts room; Laundry
room; Barber/Beauty shop.
Activities Arts & crafts; Cards; Games;
Reading groups; Prayer groups; Movies;
Shopping trips; Dances/Social/Cultural
gatherings.

The Plains

**Buckeye Community Services—Childrens
Transitional Facility**
33 Hartman Rd, The Plains, OH 45780
(614) 286-5039
Licensure Intermediate care for mentally
retarded. *Beds* ICF/MR 10. *Certified*
Medicaid.
Owner Proprietary corp.

Hickory Creek of Athens
51 E 4th St, The Plains, OH 45780
(614) 797-4561
Admin David Lucid. *Dir of Nursing* Carol
McQuate RN. *Medical Dir* Edward A
Sprague MD.
Licensure Skilled care; Intermediate care. *Beds*
Swing beds SNF/ICF 132. *Certified*
Medicaid; Medicare.
Owner Proprietary corp (Health Care
Management).
Admissions Requirements Medical
examination; Physician's request.
Staff Physicians 9 (ft); RNs 7 (ft), 3 (pt);
LPNs 12 (ft), 5 (pt); Nurses' aides 46 (ft), 16
(pt); Physical therapists 1 (pt); Occupational
therapists 1 (pt); Speech therapists 1 (pt);
Activities coordinators 1 (ft); Dietitians 1
(ft); Ophthalmologists 1 (pt); Podiatrists 1
(pt); Dentists 2 (pt); Psychologists 1 (pt).
Facilities Dining room; Physical therapy
room; Activities room; Laundry room;
Barber/Beauty shop.
Activities Arts & crafts; Cards; Games;
Reading groups; Prayer groups; Shopping
trips; Dances/Social/Cultural gatherings.

Pomeroy

Americare Pomeroy
36759 Rocksprings Rd, Pomeroy, OH 45769
(614) 992-6606
Admin William J Bias. *Dir of Nursing* LaRue
Hill. *Medical Dir* Wilma Mansfield MD.
Licensure Skilled care; Intermediate care. *Beds*
SNF 20; ICF 80. *Private Pay Patients* 7%.
Certified Medicaid; Medicare.
Owner Proprietary corp (Care Enterprises).
Admissions Requirements Physician's request.
Staff RNs; LPNs; Nurses' aides; Physical
therapists; Occupational therapists; Speech
therapists; Activities coordinators; Dietitians.
Facilities Dining room; Physical therapy
room; Activities room; Crafts room; Laundry
room; Barber/Beauty shop.
Activities Arts & crafts; Cards; Games;
Reading groups; Prayer groups; Movies;
Shopping trips; Dances/Social/Cultural
gatherings; Pet therapy.

Veterans Memorial Hospital SNF/ICF Facility
115 1/2 E Memorial Dr, Pomeroy, OH 45769
(614) 992-2104
Licensure Skilled care; Intermediate care. *Beds*
Swing beds SNF/ICF 35. *Certified* Medicaid;
Medicare.
Owner Proprietary corp.

Port Clinton

Edgewood Manor Nursing Center
1330 S Fulton St, Port Clinton, OH 43452
(419) 734-5506
Medical Dir R W Minick MD.
Licensure Skilled care; Intermediate care. *Beds*
Swing beds SNF/ICF 100. *Certified*
Medicaid; Medicare.
Owner Proprietary corp (Shive Nursing
Centers).
Admissions Requirements Medical
examination.
Staff Physicians 7 (pt); RNs 6 (ft); LPNs 3
(ft), 6 (pt); Nurses' aides 44 (ft); Physical
therapists; Recreational therapists;
Occupational therapists; Speech therapists;
Activities coordinators 1 (ft); Dietitians 1
(pt); Podiatrists 1 (pt); Audiologists;
Dentists.
Facilities Dining room; Physical therapy
room; Activities room; Chapel; Laundry
room; Barber/Beauty shop; Library; Living
room.
Activities Arts & crafts; Cards; Games; Prayer
groups; Movies; Shopping trips; Dances/
Social/Cultural gatherings; Exercises.

Portage

Portage Group Homes—Nichols
355 W Main St, Portage, OH 43451
(419) 352-5115
Admin Gregory A Bair.
Medical Dir Judy Yackee.
Licensure Intermediate care for mentally
retarded. *Beds* ICF/MR 9. *Certified*
Medicaid.
Owner Publicly owned.
Admissions Requirements Minimum age 18.
Staff Physicians 1 (pt); RNs 3 (ft); LPNs 2
(ft); Nurses' aides 10 (ft); Recreational
therapists 1 (pt); Occupational therapists 1
(pt); Speech therapists 1 (pt); Activities
coordinators 1 (pt); Dietitians 1 (pt).
Activities Arts & crafts; Cards; Games;
Reading groups; Prayer groups; Movies;
Shopping trips; Dances/Social/Cultural
gatherings.

Portage Group Homes—Restle
353 W Main St, Portage, OH 43451
(419) 686-6031
Admin Gregory A Bair.
Medical Dir Judy Yackee.

Licensure Intermediate care for mentally retarded. *Beds* ICF/MR 8. *Certified* Medicaid.
Owner Publicly owned.
Admissions Requirements Minimum age 18.
Staff Physicians 1 (pt); RNs 3 (ft); LPNs 2 (ft); Nurses' aides 10 (ft); Recreational therapists 1 (pt); Occupational therapists 1 (pt); Speech therapists 1 (pt); Activities coordinators 1 (pt); Dietitians 1 (pt).
Activities Arts & crafts; Cards; Games; Reading groups; Prayer groups; Movies; Shopping trips; Dances/Social/Cultural gatherings.

Portage Group Homes—Werner
351 W Main St, Portage, OH 43451
(419) 686-6951
Admin Gregory A Bair.
Medical Dir Judy Yackee.
Licensure Intermediate care for mentally retarded. *Beds* ICF/MR 10. *Certified* Medicaid.
Owner Publicly owned.
Admissions Requirements Minimum age 18.
Staff Physicians 1 (pt); RNs 3 (ft); LPNs 2 (ft); Nurses' aides 10 (ft); Recreational therapists 1 (pt); Occupational therapists 1 (pt); Speech therapists 1 (pt); Activities coordinators 1 (pt); Dietitians 1 (pt).
Activities Arts & crafts; Cards; Games; Reading groups; Prayer groups; Movies; Shopping trips; Dances/Social/Cultural gatherings.

Portsmouth

Flannery's Health Care Center
605 Front St, Portsmouth, OH 45662
(614) 353-5535
Admin Karen Bryan. *Dir of Nursing* Barbara Rowe.
Licensure Intermediate care. *Beds* ICF 29. *Certified* Medicaid.
Owner Proprietary corp.
Admissions Requirements Minimum age 21; Medical examination; Physician's request.
Staff Physicians 2 (pt); RNs 1 (ft); LPNs 6 (ft); Nurses' aides 14 (ft); Activities coordinators 1 (ft).
Facilities Dining room; Physical therapy room; Activities room; Crafts room; Laundry room; Barber/Beauty shop; Library.
Activities Arts & crafts; Cards; Games; Reading groups; Prayer groups; Shopping trips; Dances/Social/Cultural gatherings.

Golden Years Convalescent Center
PO Box 1148, 2125 Royce St, Portsmouth, OH 45662
(614) 354-6635
Admin Wanda Bennington. *Dir of Nursing* Beverly Logan RN. *Medical Dir* Miller Toombs MD.
Licensure Skilled care; Intermediate care; Alzheimer's care. *Beds* SNF 26; ICF 74. *Certified* Medicaid; Medicare.
Owner Proprietary corp.
Admissions Requirements Medical examination.
Staff Physicians 10 (pt); RNs 7 (ft); LPNs 18 (ft); Nurses' aides 65 (ft), 2 (pt); Physical therapists 1 (pt); Occupational therapists 1 (ft), 1 (pt); Speech therapists 1 (pt); Activities coordinators 1 (ft); Dietitians 1 (pt); Ophthalmologists 2 (pt); Podiatrists 2 (pt); Audiologists 1 (pt).
Facilities Dining room; Physical therapy room; Activities room; Chapel; Crafts room; Laundry room; Barber/Beauty shop; Library.
Activities Arts & crafts; Cards; Games; Reading groups; Prayer groups; Movies; Shopping trips; Dances/Social/Cultural gatherings; Pet therapy.

Heartland of Portsmouth
Rte 6 Box 10, Feurt Hill Rd, Portsmouth, OH 45662
(614) 354-4505
Admin Jeffrey C Hunter. *Dir of Nursing* Lois Zuhars RN. *Medical Dir* Aaron Adams DO.
Licensure Skilled care; Intermediate care. *Beds* Swing beds SNF/ICF 100. *Certified* Medicaid; Medicare.
Owner Proprietary corp (Health Care and Retirement Corp).
Staff RNs 3 (ft), 2 (pt); LPNs 8 (ft), 2 (pt); Nurses' aides 30 (ft), 15 (pt); Physical therapists 1 (ft); Activities coordinators 1 (ft); Dietitians 1 (ft).
Facilities Dining room; Physical therapy room; Activities room; Laundry room; Barber/Beauty shop.
Activities Arts & crafts; Cards; Games; Reading groups; Prayer groups; Movies; Shopping trips; Dances/Social/Cultural gatherings.

Hill View Health Care Facility
1610 28th St, Portsmouth, OH 45662
(614) 354-3135
Admin John E Zinsmeister NHA; Calvin Rodeheffer, Exec Dir. *Dir of Nursing* Marijo Pyles. *Medical Dir* Thomas K Swope DO.
Licensure Skilled care; Intermediate care; Retirement. *Beds* Swing beds SNF/ICF 55; Retirement 300. *Private Pay Patients* 80%. *Certified* Medicaid; Medicare.
Owner Nonprofit corp.
Admissions Requirements Medical examination; Physician's request.
Staff Physicians 10 (pt); RNs 2 (ft), 4 (pt); LPNs 5 (ft), 6 (pt); Nurses' aides 21 (ft), 4 (pt); Physical therapists 1 (pt); Occupational therapists 1 (pt); Speech therapists 1 (pt); Activities coordinators 2 (ft), 1 (pt); Dietitians 2 (ft); Ophthalmologists 1 (pt); Podiatrists 1 (pt); Audiologists 1 (pt).
Affiliation United Methodist.
Facilities Dining room; Physical therapy room; Activities room; Crafts room; Laundry room; Barber/Beauty shop; Library; Multi-purpose room.
Activities Arts & crafts; Cards; Games; Reading groups; Prayer groups; Movies; Shopping trips; Dances/Social/Cultural gatherings.

Hilltop Nursing Home
1319 Spring St, Portsmouth, OH 45662
(614) 354-6619
Licensure Intermediate care. *Beds* ICF 25. *Certified* Medicaid.
Owner Proprietary corp.

Scioto Memorial Convalescent Center
727 8th St, Portsmouth, OH 45662
(614) 354-8631
Licensure Skilled care; Intermediate care. *Beds* SNF 12; ICF 88. *Certified* Medicaid; Medicare.
Owner Proprietary corp.

Ravenna

Altercare of Ravenna
245 New Milford Rd, Ravenna, OH 44266
(216) 296-6415
Admin Ann Marie Riley NHA. *Dir of Nursing* Gertrude Stilts RN. *Medical Dir* Scott Smith MD.
Licensure Skilled care; Intermediate care. *Beds* SNF 24; ICF 75. *Certified* Medicaid; Medicare.
Owner Proprietary corp (Altercare Inc).
Admissions Requirements Medical examination.
Staff Physicians 6 (pt); RNs 4 (ft), 1 (pt); LPNs 5 (ft), 3 (pt); Nurses' aides 35 (ft), 8 (pt); Physical therapists 2 (pt); Recreational therapists 1 (ft), 1 (pt); Occupational therapists 2 (pt); Speech therapists 1 (pt);

Activities coordinators 1 (ft); Dietitians 1 (pt); Ophthalmologists 1 (pt); Podiatrists 1 (pt); Audiologists 1 (pt); Dentists 1 (pt).
Facilities Dining room; Physical therapy room; Laundry room; Barber/Beauty shop.
Activities Arts & crafts; Cards; Games; Prayer groups; Movies; Dances/Social/Cultural gatherings; Pet therapy.

Independence—Highland
130 E Highland Ave, Ravenna, OH 44266
(216) 296-2851
Licensure Intermediate care for mentally retarded. *Beds* ICF/MR 9. *Certified* Medicaid.
Owner Proprietary corp.

Independence—Meridian
168 N Meridian St, Ravenna, OH 44266
(216) 296-2851
Licensure Intermediate care for mentally retarded. *Beds* ICF/MR 8. *Certified* Medicaid.
Owner Proprietary corp.

Independence—Washington
4771 Washington Ave, Ravenna, OH 44266
(216) 296-2851
Licensure Intermediate care for mentally retarded. *Beds* ICF/MR 8. *Certified* Medicaid.
Owner Proprietary corp.

Longmeadow Care Center
565 Bryn Mawr, Ravenna, OH 44266
(216) 297-5781
Admin Mary Ellen Thornton. *Dir of Nursing* Patricia Gregory RN. *Medical Dir* Louis Castaldi MD.
Licensure Skilled care; Intermediate care. *Beds* Swing beds SNF/ICF 120. *Certified* Medicaid; Medicare.
Owner Proprietary corp (Beverly Enterprises).
Admissions Requirements Minimum age 18.
Staff RNs 6 (ft), 3 (pt); LPNs 5 (ft), 5 (pt); Nurses' aides 35 (ft), 15 (pt); Activities coordinators 1 (ft), 1 (pt).
Facilities Dining room; Physical therapy room; Activities room; Crafts room; Laundry room; Barber/Beauty shop.
Activities Arts & crafts; Cards; Games; Reading groups; Prayer groups; Movies; Shopping trips; Dances/Social/Cultural gatherings.

Portage County Nursing Home
7988 Infirmary Rd, Ravenna, OH 44266
(216) 296-9977
Medical Dir Albert Tsai MD.
Licensure Intermediate care. *Beds* ICF 99. *Certified* Medicaid.
Owner Publicly owned.
Admissions Requirements Medical examination.
Staff Physicians 1 (pt); RNs 4 (ft); LPNs 5 (ft), 5 (pt); Nurses' aides 21 (ft), 14 (pt); Physical therapists 1 (pt); Activities coordinators 1 (ft); Dietitians 1 (pt); Ophthalmologists 1 (pt); Podiatrists 1 (pt); Dentists 1 (pt).
Facilities Dining room; Physical therapy room; Activities room; Chapel; Crafts room; Barber/Beauty shop.
Activities Arts & crafts; Cards; Games; Reading groups; Prayer groups; Movies; Shopping trips; Dances/Social/Cultural gatherings.

Reading

Aaron Convalescent Home
21 W Columbia St, Reading, OH 45215
(513) 554-1141
Admin Patricia E Vogel. *Dir of Nursing* Rae M Smith. *Medical Dir* George Shields MD.
Licensure Intermediate care. *Beds* 142. *Certified* Medicaid.
Owner Proprietary corp.

Staff Physicians; RNs; LPNs; Nurses' aides; Physical therapists; Speech therapists; Activities coordinators; Dietitians; Ophthalmologists.
Facilities Dining room; Physical therapy room; Activities room; Chapel; Crafts room; Laundry room; Barber/Beauty shop.
Activities Arts & crafts; Cards; Games; Reading groups; Prayer groups; Movies; Shopping trips; Dances/Social/Cultural gatherings.

Richfield

Pine Valley Nursing Center
PO Box 383, Richfield, OH 44286
(216) 659-6166
Admin Dr Sheth.
Licensure Skilled care; Intermediate care. *Beds* Swing beds SNF/ICF 95. *Certified* Medicaid; Medicare.
Owner Proprietary corp.
Admissions Requirements Minimum age 14; Medical examination.
Staff Physicians 4 (pt); RNs 4 (ft), 3 (pt); LPNs 10 (ft), 1 (pt); Nurses' aides 30 (ft), 17 (pt); Physical therapists 1 (pt); Activities coordinators 1 (ft); Dietitians 1 (pt).
Facilities Dining room; Activities room; Laundry room; Barber/Beauty shop.
Activities Arts & crafts; Cards; Games; Prayer groups; Movies; Shopping trips; Dances/Social/Cultural gatherings.

Ripley

Ohio Valley Manor Convalescent Center
5280 State Rtes 62-68, Ripley, OH 45167
(513) 392-4318
Admin George W Balz. *Dir of Nursing* Connie Pollard RN. *Medical Dir* Gene Conway MD.
Licensure Skilled care; Intermediate care. *Beds* Swing beds SNF/ICF 100. *Certified* Medicaid; Medicare.
Owner Proprietary corp.
Admissions Requirements Medical examination; Physician's request.
Staff Physicians 5 (pt); RNs 6 (ft), 3 (pt); LPNs 10 (ft), 7 (pt); Nurses' aides 34 (ft), 20 (pt); Physical therapists 1 (ft), 1 (pt); Occupational therapists 1 (ft); Speech therapists 1 (pt); Activities coordinators 1 (ft); Dietitians 1 (pt); Ophthalmologists 1 (pt); Podiatrists 1 (pt); Dentists 1 (pt).
Facilities Dining room; Physical therapy room; Activities room; Laundry room; Barber/Beauty shop; Library.
Activities Arts & crafts; Cards; Games; Reading groups; Prayer groups; Movies; Shopping trips; Dances/Social/Cultural gatherings.

Rittman

Americare Rittman Nursing & Rehabilitation Center
275 E Sunset Dr, Rittman, OH 44270
(216) 927-2060
Admin Laura A Matthews. *Dir of Nursing* Dianna Carderas RN. *Medical Dir* Dr Knapic.
Licensure Skilled care; Intermediate care. *Beds* SNF 18; ICF 82. *Certified* Medicaid; Medicare.
Owner Proprietary corp (Care Enterprises).
Staff Physical therapists; Speech therapists; Activities coordinators; Dietitians; Ophthalmologists; Dentists.

Apostolic Christian Home Inc
10680 Steiner Rd, Rittman, OH 44270
(216) 927-1010
Licensure Intermediate care. *Beds* ICF 75. *Certified* Medicaid.
Owner Proprietary corp.
Affiliation Apostolic Christian.

Rock Creek

Char-Lotte Nursing Home Inc
Rte 45 Box 177, Rock Creek, OH 44084
(216) 563-5547
Licensure Skilled care; Intermediate care. *Beds* 119. *Certified* Medicaid; Medicare.
Owner Proprietary corp.

Rockford

Colonial Nursing Home
611 S Main St, Rockford, OH 45882
(419) 363-2193
Licensure Intermediate care for mentally retarded. *Beds* ICF/MR 34. *Certified* Medicaid.
Owner Proprietary corp.

Shane Hill Nursing Home Inc
Rte 3, Rockford, OH 45882
(419) 363-2620
Admin John L Smith. *Dir of Nursing* Sue Barna. *Medical Dir* Dr R D Bradrick; Dr Philip Masser.
Licensure Intermediate care. *Beds* ICF 100. *Certified* Medicaid.
Owner Proprietary corp.
Admissions Requirements Medical examination; Physician's request.
Staff Physicians 6 (pt); RNs 5 (ft), 2 (pt); LPNs 9 (ft), 5 (pt); Nurses' aides 35 (ft), 5 (pt); Physical therapists 1 (pt); Recreational therapists 2 (ft), 1 (pt); Speech therapists 1 (pt); Activities coordinators 1 (ft); Dietitians 1 (pt); Ophthalmologists 1 (pt).
Facilities Dining room; Physical therapy room; Activities room; Chapel; Crafts room; Laundry room; Barber/Beauty shop; Library.
Activities Arts & crafts; Cards; Games; Reading groups; Prayer groups; Movies; Dances/Social/Cultural gatherings.

Rocky River

Welsh Home for the Aged
22199 Center Ridge Rd, Rocky River, OH 44116
(216) 331-0420
Licensure Intermediate care. *Beds* ICF 34. *Certified* Medicaid.
Owner Proprietary corp.

Sabina

Autumn Years Nursing Center
580 E Washington Ave, Sabina, OH 45169
(513) 584-4440
Licensure Intermediate care. *Beds* ICF 50. *Certified* Medicaid.
Owner Proprietary corp.

Deiber Nursing Home Inc
91 E Elm St, Sabina, OH 45169-1330
(614) 773-2104
Licensure Intermediate care. *Beds* 33. *Certified* Medicaid.
Owner Proprietary corp.

Eden Manor Nursing Home
273 S Howard St, Sabina, OH 45169
(513) 584-4313
Licensure Intermediate care. *Beds* 30. *Certified* Medicaid.
Owner Proprietary corp.

Saint Clairsville

Belmont County Oakview Nursing Home
45240 National Rd, Saint Clairsville, OH 43950
(614) 695-4925
Licensure Intermediate care. *Beds* ICF 71.
Owner Publicly owned.

Belmont Habilitation Center
68401 Hammond Rd, Saint Clairsville, OH 43950
Licensure Intermediate care for mentally retarded. *Beds* ICF/MR 85. *Certified* Medicaid.
Owner Nonprofit corp (Alternative Residences Two Inc).

Forest Hill, A Zandex Retirement Community
100 Reservoir Rd, Saint Clairsville, OH 43950
(614) 695-7233, 695-2499 FAX
Admin Susan McLeod Crozier. *Dir of Nursing* Dorothy Douglas RN. *Medical Dir* Dr George Cholak.
Licensure Skilled care; Intermediate care; Residential care; Rest home. *Beds* Swing beds SNF/ICF 79; Residential care 38; Rest home 30. *Private Pay Patients* 40%. *Certified* Medicaid; Medicare.
Owner Proprietary corp.
Admissions Requirements Medical examination.
Staff Physicians; RNs; LPNs; Nurses' aides; Physical therapists; Occupational therapists; Speech therapists; Activities coordinators; Dietitians; Podiatrists.
Languages Polish, German.
Facilities Dining room; Physical therapy room; Activities room; Chapel; Crafts room; Laundry room; Barber/Beauty shop; Library.
Activities Arts & crafts; Cards; Games; Reading groups; Prayer groups; Movies; Shopping trips; Dances/Social/Cultural gatherings; Intergenerational programs; Pet therapy; Exercise; Grooming; Cooking.

Woodland Acres Nursing Home Inc
RD 4, Cresent Rd, Saint Clairsville, OH 43950
(614) 695-0800
Licensure Nursing home. *Beds* Nursing home 16.
Owner Proprietary corp.

Saint Marys

Valley Nursing Home
1140 Knoxville Rd, Saint Marys, OH 45885
(419) 394-3308
Admin Reah Buchanan. *Dir of Nursing* Barb Overman RN. *Medical Dir* Dr Robert Gill.
Licensure Skilled care; Intermediate care. *Beds* SNF 24; ICF 76. *Private Pay Patients* 50%. *Certified* Medicaid; Medicare.
Owner Proprietary corp (Beverly Enterprises).
Staff Physicians 1 (pt); Physical therapists 1 (pt); Dietitians.
Facilities Dining room; Activities room; Laundry room; Barber/Beauty shop.
Activities Arts & crafts; Cards; Games; Prayer groups; Movies; Shopping trips.

Salem

Mary Fletcher Health Care Center
767 Benton Rd, Salem, OH 44460
(216) 332-0391
Licensure Intermediate care. *Beds* ICF 23. *Certified* Medicaid.
Owner Proprietary corp.

Hutton Nursing Center I
2511 Bentley Dr, Salem, OH 44460
(216) 337-9503, 337-7063 FAX
Admin Grace Banez RNC BSN LNHA. *Dir of Nursing* Sally Stamp RN. *Medical Dir* Dr W F Stevenson.
Licensure Intermediate care. *Beds* ICF 100. *Private Pay Patients* 10-15%. *Certified* Medicaid.
Owner Proprietary corp (American Health Care Centers).
Admissions Requirements Medical examination; Physician's request.

Staff Physicians 1 (ft); RNs 2 (ft), 4 (pt); LPNs 9 (ft), 4 (pt); Nurses' aides 25 (ft), 19 (pt); Physical therapists 1 (pt); Occupational therapists 1 (pt); Speech therapists 1 (pt); Activities coordinators 2 (ft); Dietitians 1 (pt); Ophthalmologists 1 (pt); Podiatrists 1 (pt).
Facilities Dining room; Activities room; Laundry room; Barber/Beauty shop; Library.
Activities Arts & crafts; Games; Prayer groups; Movies; Shopping trips; Dances/Social/Cultural gatherings; Intergenerational programs; Pet therapy.

Hutton Nursing Center II
250 Continental Dr, Salem, OH 44460
(216) 337-9503, 337-9506 FAX
Admin Darlene Hutton. *Dir of Nursing* Carol Hohen.
Licensure Intermediate care. *Beds* ICF 100. *Certified* Medicare.
Owner Proprietary corp (American Health Care Centers).
Admissions Requirements Females only; Medical examination.
Staff Physicians 1 (pt); RNs 5 (ft), 1 (pt); LPNs 7 (ft), 1 (pt); Nurses' aides 23 (ft), 11 (pt); Physical therapists 1 (pt); Occupational therapists 1 (pt); Speech therapists 1 (pt); Activities coordinators 1 (ft), 2 (pt); Dietitians 1 (pt); Ophthalmologists 1 (pt); Podiatrists 1 (pt).
Facilities Dining room; Activities room; Chapel; Laundry room; Barber/Beauty shop; Library.
Activities Arts & crafts; Games; Prayer groups; Movies; Shopping trips; Dances/Social/Cultural gatherings; Intergenerational programs; Pet therapy.

Hutton Nursing Center III
230 Continental Dr, Salem, OH 44460
(216) 337-9503, 337-9505 FAX
Admin Grace Banez RNC BSN LNHA. *Dir of Nursing* Lori Perry.
Licensure Intermediate care. *Beds* ICF 50. *Private Pay Patients* 30%. *Certified* Medicaid.
Owner Proprietary corp (American Health Care Centers).
Admissions Requirements Medical examination; Physician's request.
Staff Physicians 1 (ft); RNs 2 (ft), 2 (pt); LPNs 4 (ft), 2 (pt); Nurses' aides 14 (ft), 9 (pt); Physical therapists 1 (pt); Occupational therapists 1 (pt); Speech therapists 1 (pt); Activities coordinators 2 (pt); Dietitians 1 (pt); Ophthalmologists 1 (pt); Podiatrists 1 (pt).
Facilities Dining room; Activities room; Chapel; Laundry room; Barber/Beauty shop; Library.
Activities Arts & crafts; Games; Prayer groups; Movies; Shopping trips; Dances/Social/Cultural gatherings; Intergenerational programs; Pet therapy.

Salem Community Hospital
1995 E State St, Salem, OH 44460
(216) 332-7396
Licensure Skilled care. *Beds* SNF 15. *Certified* Medicare.
Owner Proprietary corp.

Salem Convalescent Center
1985 E Pershing St, Salem, OH 44460
(216) 332-1588
Admin Duane Herron. *Dir of Nursing* Jacquelyn McKeorsig RN. *Medical Dir* W F Stevenson MD.
Licensure Intermediate care; Rest home. *Beds* ICF 90; Rest home 14. *Certified* Medicaid.
Owner Privately owned.
Admissions Requirements Medical examination; Physician's request.
Staff RNs 4 (ft), 2 (pt); LPNs 6 (ft), 5 (pt); Nurses' aides 26 (ft), 10 (pt); Activities coordinators 2 (ft), 1 (pt).

Facilities Dining room; Activities room; Chapel; Crafts room; Laundry room; Barber/Beauty shop.
Activities Arts & crafts; Cards; Games; Reading groups; Prayer groups; Movies; Shopping trips; Dances/Social/Cultural gatherings; Picnics; Outings to parks; Country rides.

Valley Road Nursing Home
451 Valley Rd, Salem, OH 44460
(216) 537-4621
Admin Mariann Riley. *Dir of Nursing* Janet Holmes RN.
Licensure Intermediate care; Alzheimer's care. *Beds* ICF 44. *Certified* Medicaid.
Owner Proprietary corp.
Admissions Requirements Minimum age 18.
Staff RNs 1 (ft); LPNs 4 (ft), 1 (pt); Nurses' aides 7 (ft), 4 (pt); Recreational therapists 1 (pt); Activities coordinators 1 (ft).
Facilities Dining room; Activities room; Laundry room.
Activities Arts & crafts; Cards; Games; Prayer groups; Movies; Shopping trips; Dances/Social/Cultural gatherings.

Sandusky

Classic Care South
3423 S Columbus Ave, Sandusky, OH 44870
(419) 625-6534
Admin Gloria Fidler. *Dir of Nursing* Jeannie VanCouwenbergh RN.
Licensure Intermediate care. *Beds* ICF 34. *Certified* Medicaid.
Owner Proprietary corp (Health Resources Development).
Staff Physicians 1 (pt); RNs 1 (ft); LPNs 4 (ft), 2 (pt); Nurses' aides 11 (ft), 5 (pt); Recreational therapists 1 (pt); Dietitians 1 (ft).
Facilities Dining room; Activities room; Laundry room.
Activities Arts & crafts; Cards; Games; Reading groups; Prayer groups; Movies; Shopping trips; Dances/Social/Cultural gatherings.

Classic Center
620 W Strub Rd, Sandusky, OH 44870
(419) 626-5373
Medical Dir D B Cuthbertson MD.
Licensure Intermediate care. *Beds* ICF 50. *Certified* Medicaid.
Owner Proprietary corp (Health Resources Development).
Admissions Requirements Medical examination; Physician's request.
Staff Physicians 1 (ft), 4 (pt); RNs 2 (ft), 1 (pt); LPNs 3 (ft), 3 (pt); Nurses' aides 10 (ft), 7 (pt); Physical therapists 1 (pt); Reality therapists 1 (pt); Recreational therapists 1 (ft); Occupational therapists 1 (pt); Speech therapists 1 (pt); Activities coordinators 1 (ft); Dietitians 1 (pt); Ophthalmologists 1 (pt); Podiatrists 2 (pt); Audiologists 1 (pt); Dentists 1 (pt).
Facilities Dining room; Activities room; Chapel; Laundry room; Barber/Beauty shop; Library.
Activities Arts & crafts; Cards; Games; Reading groups; Prayer groups; Movies; Shopping trips; Dances/Social/Cultural gatherings; Outings.

Hospitality Care Center 1
531 Wayne St, Sandusky, OH 44870
(419) 625-4449
Licensure Intermediate care. *Beds* ICF 23. *Certified* Medicaid.
Owner Proprietary corp.

Hospitality Care Center 2
403 E Adams St, Sandusky, OH 44870
(419) 626-5444
Admin E Maureen Leahy.
Medical Dir Liz Wobser.

Licensure Intermediate care. *Beds* ICF 26. *Certified* Medicaid.
Owner Proprietary corp.
Admissions Requirements Minimum age 18.
Staff Physicians 1 (pt); LPNs 2 (ft); Nurses' aides 9 (ft); Activities coordinators 1 (ft); Dietitians 1 (pt); Ophthalmologists 1 (pt).
Facilities Dining room; Laundry room.
Activities Arts & crafts; Cards; Games; Reading groups; Prayer groups; Movies; Shopping trips; Dances/Social/Cultural gatherings.

Lutheran Memorial Home
795 Bardshar Rd, Sandusky, OH 44870
(419) 625-4046
Admin Frances Landis. *Dir of Nursing* Evelyn Moore. *Medical Dir* Dean J Reichenbach MD.
Licensure Skilled care; Intermediate care. *Beds* Swing beds SNF/ICF 50.
Owner Nonprofit corp.
Admissions Requirements Medical examination.
Staff Physicians 1 (ft); RNs 1 (ft); LPNs 4 (ft), 8 (pt); Nurses' aides 14 (ft), 13 (pt); Activities coordinators 1 (ft); Dietitians 1 (pt).
Affiliation Lutheran.
Facilities Dining room; Physical therapy room; Activities room; Chapel; Crafts room; Laundry room; Barber/Beauty shop.
Activities Arts & crafts; Cards; Games; Reading groups; Prayer groups; Movies; Shopping trips; Dances/Social/Cultural gatherings; Intergenerational programs; Pet therapy; Dining out.

St Ann Skilled Nursing Center
1912 Hayes Ave, Sandusky, OH 44870
(419) 626-8450
Admin Sr Nancy Linenkugel. *Dir of Nursing* Arlene Fleming RN. *Medical Dir* Sidhaiyan Aiyappasamy MD.
Licensure Skilled care. *Beds* SNF 46. *Certified* Medicaid; Medicare.
Owner Nonprofit organization/foundation.
Staff Physicians; RNs 4 (ft), 4 (pt); LPNs 5 (ft), 8 (pt); Physical therapists; Occupational therapists; Speech therapists; Activities coordinators; Dietitians; Ophthalmologists; Podiatrists; Dentists; Social service 1 (pt); Psychology services; Hearing services.
Affiliation Roman Catholic.
Facilities Dining room; Physical therapy room; Activities room; Chapel; Crafts room.
Activities Arts & crafts; Cards; Games; Movies; Intergenerational programs; Pet therapy.

Sandusky Nursing Home Inc
232 Jackson St, Sandusky, OH 44870
(419) 626-6688
Medical Dir W P Skirball MD.
Licensure Intermediate care; Intermediate care for mentally retarded. *Beds* ICF 70; ICF/MR 68. *Certified* Medicaid.
Owner Proprietary corp.
Staff Physicians 3 (pt); RNs 1 (ft), 2 (pt); LPNs 9 (ft), 3 (pt); Nurses' aides 30 (ft); Physical therapists 1 (pt); Recreational therapists 1 (ft); Occupational therapists 1 (pt); Speech therapists 1 (pt); Activities coordinators 1 (pt); Dietitians 1 (pt); Ophthalmologists 1 (pt); Podiatrists 1 (pt); Audiologists 1 (pt); Dentists 1 (pt).
Facilities Dining room; Physical therapy room; Activities room; Crafts room; Laundry room; Barber/Beauty shop; Library.
Activities Arts & crafts; Cards; Games; Prayer groups; Movies; Shopping trips; Dances/Social/Cultural gatherings.

Secrest-Giffin Care Facility
Columbus Ave, Sandusky, OH 44870
(419) 625-2454

Licensure Intermediate care. *Beds* ICF 342.
 Certified Medicaid.
Owner Publicly owned.

True Light Inc
507 Wayne St, Sandusky, OH 44870
(419) 627-9955
Admin William J Hunt.
Medical Dir Sidhaiyan Aiyappasamy MD.
Licensure Intermediate care. *Beds* ICF 50.
 Certified Medicaid.
Owner Proprietary corp.
Admissions Requirements Medical
 examination.
Staff Physicians 1 (pt); RNs 1 (pt); LPNs 6
 (ft), 2 (pt); Nurses' aides 12 (ft), 6 (pt);
 Physical therapists 1 (pt); Occupational
 therapists 1 (pt); Speech therapists 1 (pt);
 Activities coordinators 1 (ft); Dietitians 1
 (pt); Ophthalmologists 1 (pt); Podiatrists 1
 (pt); Audiologists 1 (pt); Dentists 1 (pt).
Facilities Dining room; Activities room;
 Crafts room; Laundry room.
Activities Arts & crafts; Cards; Games;
 Reading groups; Prayer groups; Movies;
 Shopping trips; Dances/Social/Cultural
 gatherings.

Sebring

Crandall Medical Center
800 S 15th St, Sebring, OH 44672
(216) 938-6126
Admin Geraldine Sposato. *Dir of Nursing*
 Janice Saunier. *Medical Dir* George H
 Davies MD.
Licensure Skilled care; Intermediate care. *Beds*
 Swing beds SNF/ICF 198. *Private Pay
 Patients* 47%. *Certified* Medicaid; Medicare.
Owner Nonprofit organization/foundation.
Admissions Requirements Minimum age 18.
Staff Physicians 2 (pt); RNs 7 (ft), 11 (pt);
 LPNs 20 (ft), 7 (pt); Nurses' aides 65 (ft), 24
 (pt); Physical therapists 1 (ft), 1 (pt);
 Occupational therapists 1 (pt); Speech
 therapists 1 (pt); Activities coordinators 2
 (ft); Dietitians 1 (pt); Ophthalmologists 1
 (pt); Podiatrists 1 (pt); Audiologists 1 (pt).
Affiliation Methodist.
Facilities Dining room; Physical therapy
 room; Activities room; Chapel; Crafts room;
 Laundry room; Barber/Beauty shop; Library;
 Private rooms.
Activities Arts & crafts; Cards; Games;
 Reading groups; Prayer groups; Movies;
 Shopping trips; Dances/Social/Cultural
 gatherings; Intergenerational programs; Pet
 therapy.

Seville

Canterbury Villa of Seville
76 High St, Seville, OH 44273
(216) 769-2015
Licensure Skilled care; Intermediate care. *Beds*
 Swing beds SNF/ICF 100. *Certified*
 Medicaid; Medicare.
Owner Proprietary corp.

Shadyside

Shadyside Care Center
60583 State Rte 7, Shadyside, OH 43947
(614) 676-8381, 676-3979 FAX
Admin Karen L Palmer, Asst. *Dir of Nursing*
 Joni Ann Fox RN. *Medical Dir* Theron R
 Rolston MD.
Licensure Intermediate care. *Beds* ICF 100.
 Private Pay Patients 17%. *Certified*
 Medicaid.
Owner Proprietary corp (Zandex Inc).
Admissions Requirements Medical
 examination; Physician's request.
Staff Physicians 7 (pt); RNs 4 (ft), 3 (pt);
 LPNs 7 (ft), 3 (pt); Nurses' aides 40 (ft), 20
 (pt); Physical therapists 1 (pt); Recreational

therapists 1 (ft); Occupational therapists 1
 (pt); Speech therapists 1 (pt); Activities
 coordinators 1 (ft); Dietitians 1 (pt);
 Podiatrists 1 (pt); Audiologists 1 (pt).
Facilities Dining room; Physical therapy
 room; Activities room; Chapel; Crafts room;
 Laundry room; Barber/Beauty shop; Living
 room; 2 sitting rooms.
Activities Arts & crafts; Cards; Games;
 Reading groups; Prayer groups; Movies;
 Shopping trips; Dances/Social/Cultural
 gatherings; Intergenerational programs; Pet
 therapy.

Shelby

Crestwood Care Center
225 W Main St, Shelby, OH 44875
(419) 347-1266
Licensure Skilled care; Intermediate care. *Beds*
 Swing beds SNF/ICF 127. *Certified*
 Medicaid; Medicare.
Owner Proprietary corp.

Heritage Care Center
100 Rogers Ln, Shelby, OH 44875
(419) 347-1313
Admin Stephen Nemeth. *Dir of Nursing* F
 Renee Reber RN.
Licensure Skilled care; Intermediate care. *Beds*
 Swing beds SNF/ICF 50. *Certified* Medicaid;
 Medicare.
Owner Proprietary corp (Horizon Healthcare
 Corp).
Admissions Requirements Medical
 examination.
Staff RNs 2 (ft), 2 (pt); LPNs 3 (ft), 1 (pt);
 Nurses' aides 12 (ft); Physical therapists 1
 (pt); Activities coordinators 1 (ft); Dietitians
 1 (ft).
Facilities Dining room; Activities room;
 Laundry room; Barber/Beauty shop.
Activities Arts & crafts; Cards; Games;
 Reading groups; Prayer groups; Movies;
 Shopping trips; Dances/Social/Cultural
 gatherings; Daily exercises.

Sidney

Alternative Residences Inc—Sidney Home
877 Park St, Sidney, OH 45365
(513) 228-2200
Licensure Intermediate care for mentally
 retarded. *Beds* ICF/MR 10. *Certified*
 Medicaid.
Owner Proprietary corp (Alternative
 Residences Inc).

Fair Haven Shelby County Home
2901 Fair Rd, Sidney, OH 45365
(513) 492-6900
Admin Bill S Stine NHA; Evelyn J Stine LSW
 LPN RAC Asst Admin. *Dir of Nursing* F
 Barbara Ward RN. *Medical Dir* George J
 Schroer MD.
Licensure Intermediate care; Rest home. *Beds*
 ICF 125; Rest home 20. *Certified* Medicaid.
Owner Publicly owned.
Admissions Requirements Minimum age 18;
 Medical examination; County resident.
Staff Physicians 1 (pt); RNs 6 (ft), 4 (pt);
 LPNs 10 (ft), 2 (pt); Nurses' aides 41 (ft), 16
 (pt); Activities coordinators 3 (ft); Dietitians
 1 (pt); Podiatrists 1 (pt); Administrative
 assistants; Chaplains 1 (pt); Dietetic
 technicians.
Facilities Dining room; Activities room;
 Chapel; Crafts room; Laundry room; Barber/
 Beauty shop; Library; Independent lounges
 for TV and visitation; Activity center
 kitchen.
Activities Arts & crafts; Cards; Games;
 Reading groups; Prayer groups; Movies;
 Shopping trips; Dances/Social/Cultural
 gatherings; Intergenerational programs; Pet
 therapy; Church services.

Franklin Nursing Center of Sidney
510 Buckeye St, Sidney, OH 45365
(513) 492-3171
Licensure Intermediate care. *Beds* ICF 51.
 Certified Medicaid.
Owner Proprietary corp.

Dorothy Love Retirement Community
3003 W Cisco Rd, Sidney, OH 45365
(513) 498-2391
Admin Paul T Schultz. *Dir of Nursing* Ethel
 Feathers. *Medical Dir* Dr Robert Miller.
Licensure Skilled care; Intermediate care;
 Congregate care; Alzheimer's care; Housing.
 Beds Swing beds SNF/ICF 96; Congregate
 care 39; Housing 101. *Private Pay Patients*
 58%. *Certified* Medicaid; Medicare.
Owner Nonprofit corp (Ohio Presbyterian
 Retirement Services).
Admissions Requirements Minimum age 55;
 Medical examination.
Staff RNs; LPNs; Nurses' aides; Physical
 therapists; Reality therapists; Recreational
 therapists; Occupational therapists; Speech
 therapists; Activities coordinators;
 Podiatrists; Audiologists.
Affiliation Presbyterian.
Facilities Dining room; Physical therapy
 room; Activities room; Chapel; Crafts room;
 Laundry room; Barber/Beauty shop; Library;
 Greenhouse; Fish ponds.
Activities Arts & crafts; Cards; Games;
 Reading groups; Prayer groups; Movies;
 Shopping trips; Dances/Social/Cultural
 gatherings; Volunteer program; Shuffleboard;
 Current events; Horseshoes; Fishing;
 Gardening.

Sunny Acres Care Center
705 Fulton St, Sidney, OH 45365
(513) 492-9591
Licensure Skilled care; Intermediate care. *Beds*
 Swing beds SNF/ICF 60. *Certified* Medicaid;
 Medicare.
Owner Proprietary corp.

Solon

Aurora Road Home
36440 Aurora Rd, Solon, OH 44139
(216) 248-0588
Licensure Intermediate care for mentally
 retarded. *Beds* ICF/MR 10. *Certified*
 Medicaid.
Owner Proprietary corp.

Somerville

Woodland Manor Nursing Home
4166 Somerville Rd, Somerville, OH 45064
(513) 523-4449 & 523-7486
Admin Dora Webb.
Medical Dir Gayneil Browning.
Licensure Intermediate care. *Beds* ICF 50.
 Certified Medicaid.
Owner Privately owned.
Admissions Requirements Medical
 examination.
Staff Physicians 8 (pt); RNs 1 (ft), 1 (pt);
 LPNs 3 (ft), 2 (pt); Nurses' aides 16 (ft), 1
 (pt); Activities coordinators 2 (pt); Dietitians
 1 (pt).
Facilities Dining room; Physical therapy
 room; Activities room; Laundry room.
Activities Arts & crafts; Cards; Games;
 Reading groups; Prayer groups; Movies;
 Shopping trips; Dances/Social/Cultural
 gatherings.

South Point

Heartland of Riverview
Rte 4 Box 312, South Point, OH 45680
(614) 894-3287
Admin O David Bevins. *Dir of Nursing*
 Frances Conley. *Medical Dir* Randall
 McCallister MD.

Licensure Skilled care; Intermediate care. *Beds* SNF 24; ICF 76. *Private Pay Patients* 15%. *Certified* Medicaid; Medicare.
Owner Proprietary corp (Healthcare & Retirement Corp).
Admissions Requirements Medical examination; Physician's request.
Staff Physicians 1 (ft), 1 (pt); RNs 4 (ft), 1 (pt); LPNs 12 (ft), 1 (pt); Nurses' aides 41 (ft), 7 (pt); Physical therapists 1 (ft); Speech therapists 1 (pt); Activities coordinators 1 (ft), 1 (pt); Dietitians 1 (ft).
Facilities Dining room; Physical therapy room; Activities room; Laundry room; Barber/Beauty shop.
Activities Arts & crafts; Cards; Games; Prayer groups; Movies; Shopping trips; Intergenerational programs; Pet therapy.

Pulley Care Center
Rte 4 Box 349A, South Point, OH 45680
(614) 894-3476
Licensure Skilled care; Intermediate care. *Beds* Swing beds SNF/ICF 100. *Certified* Medicaid; Medicare.
Owner Proprietary corp.

Pulley Nursing Home
RFD 2, Box 44, South Point, OH 45680
(614) 894-3442
Licensure Intermediate care. *Beds* ICF 35. *Certified* Medicaid.
Owner Proprietary corp.

South Vienna

Sharonview Nursing Home
Box 447, South Vienna, OH 45369
(513) 568-4342
Admin Susan K Rodabaugh.
Medical Dir Michael McKee; Janna Brown.
Licensure Intermediate care; Intermediate care for mentally retarded; Alzheimer's care. *Beds* ICF 30; ICF/MR 20. *Certified* Medicaid.
Owner Proprietary corp.
Admissions Requirements Minimum age 18; Medical examination.
Staff Physicians 2 (pt); RNs 2 (ft), 2 (pt); LPNs 4 (ft), 5 (pt); Nurses' aides 12 (ft), 10 (pt); Physical therapists 1 (pt); Reality therapists 1 (pt); Recreational therapists 1 (pt); Occupational therapists 1 (pt); Speech therapists 2 (pt); Activities coordinators 2 (ft); Dietitians 1 (pt); Ophthalmologists 1 (pt); Podiatrists 1 (pt); Dentists 1 (pt).
Facilities Dining room; Activities room; Crafts room; Laundry room; Barber/Beauty shop; Habilitation room; Programming room.
Activities Arts & crafts; Cards; Games; Reading groups; Prayer groups; Movies; Shopping trips; Dances/Social/Cultural gatherings; Ceramics.

Spencerville

Roselawn Manor Nursing Home
420 E 4th St, Spencerville, OH 45887
(419) 647-6022
Admin Sean G Cleary NHA. *Dir of Nursing* Elsie Wein. *Medical Dir* W T Wright MD.
Licensure Intermediate care. *Beds* ICF 100. *Certified* Medicaid.
Owner Proprietary corp (HCF Inc).
Staff Physicians 1 (pt); RNs 4 (ft); LPNs 10 (ft), 2 (pt); Nurses' aides 40 (ft), 10 (pt); Physical therapists 1 (pt); Activities coordinators 1 (ft); Dietitians 1 (ft); Ophthalmologists 1 (pt); Podiatrists 1 (pt).
Facilities Dining room; Activities room; Crafts room; Laundry room; Barber/Beauty shop.
Activities Arts & crafts; Cards; Games; Reading groups; Prayer groups; Movies; Shopping trips; Dances/Social/Cultural gatherings.

Springdale

Peterson Enterprises Inc—Springdale Home
1165 Walnut St, Springdale, OH 45246
(513) 861-0068
Licensure Intermediate care for mentally retarded. *Beds* ICF/MR 10. *Certified* Medicaid.
Owner Proprietary corp.

Springfield

Applin Nursing Home
237 W Pleasant St, Springfield, OH 45506
Licensure Intermediate care. *Beds* 22. *Certified* Medicaid.
Owner Nonprofit corp.

Clark Memorial Home
106 Kewbury Rd, Springfield, OH 45504
(513) 399-4262
Licensure Rest home. *Beds* Rest home 20.
Owner Proprietary corp.

Columbia House
436 W Columbia St, Springfield, OH 45504
(513) 323-4077
Admin Joyce Thiem. *Dir of Nursing* C Stonerock. *Medical Dir* S H Siddigi.
Licensure Intermediate care for mentally retarded. *Beds* ICF/MR 8. *Private Pay Patients* 0%. *Certified* Medicaid.
Owner Proprietary corp.
Admissions Requirements Minimum age 18; Males only; Medical examination.
Staff RNs 2 (pt); LPNs 1 (pt); Dietitians.
Facilities Dining room; Activities room; Laundry room.
Activities Arts & crafts; Cards; Games; Movies; Shopping trips; Dances/Social/Cultural gatherings.

Eaglewood Village—Care Center
2000 Villa Rd, Springfield, OH 45503
(513) 399-7195, 399-1474 FAX
Admin Beth Siman. *Dir of Nursing* Mariann Ciul RN. *Medical Dir* Helen Jones MD.
Licensure Skilled care; Intermediate care; Retirement. *Beds* Swing beds SNF/ICF 50; Retirement apts 80. *Private Pay Patients* 40%. *Certified* Medicaid; Medicare.
Owner Proprietary corp.
Staff RNs 5 (ft); LPNs 2 (ft), 1 (pt); Nurses' aides 13 (ft), 9 (pt); Physical therapists (consultant); Occupational therapists (consultant); Speech therapists (consultant); Activities coordinators 1 (ft); Dietitians 1 (pt); Ophthalmologists (consultant); Podiatrists (consultant); Audiologists (consultant).
Facilities Dining room; Physical therapy room; Activities room; Laundry room; Barber/Beauty shop.
Activities Arts & crafts; Cards; Games; Reading groups; Prayer groups; Movies; Shopping trips; Dances/Social/Cultural gatherings; Intergenerational programs; Pet therapy.

Good Shepherd Village
422 N Burnett Rd, Springfield, OH 45503
(513) 322-1911
Licensure Skilled care; Intermediate care. *Beds* Swing beds SNF/ICF 81.
Owner Proprietary corp.

Health Center at Oakwood Village
1500 Villa Rd, Springfield, OH 45503
(513) 390-9000, 390-9333 FAX
Admin Mary Young. *Dir of Nursing* Sharlene Newman. *Medical Dir* Mark Roberto MD.
Licensure Intermediate care; Rest home; Independent living. *Beds* ICF 50; Rest home 52; Independent living 180. *Private Pay Patients* 100%.
Owner Nonprofit corp (Mercy Health System).
Admissions Requirements Minimum age 62; Medical examination; Physician's request.

Staff Physicians (contracted); RNs; LPNs; Nurses' aides; Physical therapists (contracted); Occupational therapists (contracted); Speech therapists (contracted); Activities coordinators; Dietitians (contracted); Podiatrists (contracted).
Affiliation Roman Catholic.
Facilities Dining room; Activities room; Chapel; Crafts room; Laundry room; Barber/Beauty shop; Library.
Activities Arts & crafts; Cards; Games; Reading groups; Prayer groups; Movies; Dances/Social/Cultural gatherings; Intergenerational programs; Pet therapy.

Heartland of Springfield
2615 Derr Rd, Springfield, OH 45503
(513) 390-0005
Admin Ann C Levy. *Dir of Nursing* Sue Hartley RN. *Medical Dir* Barry Paxton MD.
Licensure Skilled care; Intermediate care. *Beds* Swing beds SNF/ICF 100. *Certified* Medicaid; Medicare.
Owner Proprietary corp (Health Care and Retirement Corp).
Admissions Requirements Minimum age 55.
Staff Physicians; RNs; LPNs; Nurses' aides; Physical therapists; Recreational therapists; Occupational therapists; Speech therapists; Activities coordinators; Dietitians; Ophthalmologists; Podiatrists; Dentists.
Facilities Dining room; Physical therapy room; Activities room; Laundry room; Barber/Beauty shop; Library.
Activities Arts & crafts; Cards; Games; Reading groups; Prayer groups; Movies; Shopping trips; Dances/Social/Cultural gatherings.

K W Hess Ohio Pythian Home of Springfield Ohio
901 W High St, Springfield, OH 45506
(513) 322-1941
Licensure Intermediate care. *Beds* ICF 98. *Certified* Medicaid.
Owner Proprietary corp.
Affiliation Knights of Pythias.

Hope House Manor Inc
2317 E Home Rd, Springfield, OH 45503
(513) 399-9217
Admin Chuck Komp. *Dir of Nursing* Joyce Rutherford-Donner. *Medical Dir* Dr Vemana.
Licensure Skilled care; Intermediate care. *Beds* Swing beds SNF/ICF 100. *Certified* Medicaid; Medicare; VA.
Owner Proprietary corp.
Admissions Requirements Minimum age 10; Medical examination.
Staff Physicians 1 (ft); RNs 9 (ft), 4 (pt); LPNs 5 (ft), 3 (pt); Nurses' aides 28 (ft), 19 (pt); Physical therapists 1 (pt); Occupational therapists 1 (pt); Speech therapists 1 (pt); Activities coordinators 3 (ft), 1 (pt); Dietitians 2 (pt); Ophthalmologists 1 (pt); Podiatrists 1 (pt); Dentists 1 (pt); Social workers 1 (ft).
Facilities Dining room; Physical therapy room; Activities room; Crafts room; Laundry room; Barber/Beauty shop; Social services; Central lounge; 2 small lounges on each wing.
Activities Arts & crafts; Cards; Games; Reading groups; Prayer groups; Movies; Shopping trips; Dances/Social/Cultural gatherings.

Max-Uhl Nursing Home
1365 1/2 Seminole Ave, Springfield, OH 45506
(513) 323-0321
Licensure Intermediate care. *Beds* ICF 15. *Certified* Medicaid.
Owner Proprietary corp.

F F Mueller Residential Center
2535 Kenton St, Springfield, OH 45505
(513) 323-9125
Admin Dr Michael J O'Neill, Res Svcs Dir.
Dir of Nursing Jenny Wallace.
Licensure Intermediate care for mentally
retarded; Retirement. *Beds* ICF/MR 72.
Certified Medicaid.
Owner Publicly owned.
Admissions Requirements Medical
examination.
Staff RNs 7 (ft), 5 (pt); LPNs 5 (pt);
Recreational therapists 2 (ft), 8 (pt);
Activities coordinators 1 (ft); Dietitians 1
(pt).
Languages Sign, Blissymbolics.
Facilities Dining room; Activities room;
Laundry room; Cottage style living.
Activities Arts & crafts; Cards; Games;
Movies; Shopping trips; Dances/Social/
Cultural gatherings; Sheltered workshop;
Special Olympics; Softball; Basketball;
Swimming.

New Horizon Nursing Home
1157 Driscoll Ave, Springfield, OH 45506
(513) 324-1831
Licensure Intermediate care. *Beds* ICF 24.
Certified Medicaid.
Owner Proprietary corp.

Odd Fellows Home of Ohio
404 E McCreight Ave, Springfield, OH 45503
(513) 399-8311
Admin Joseph Kramer. *Dir of Nursing* Lorene
Simms RN. *Medical Dir* Metin Ercan MD.
Licensure Intermediate care; Rest home;
Independent living. *Beds* ICF 100; Rest
home 37; Independent living 29. *Certified*
Medicaid.
Owner Nonprofit corp.
Admissions Requirements Medical
examination.
Staff Physicians 1 (pt); RNs 5 (ft), 2 (pt);
LPNs 7 (ft); Nurses' aides 33 (ft); Activities
coordinators 1 (ft); Dietitians 1 (pt);
Ophthalmologists 1 (pt).
Affiliation Independent Order of Odd Fellows
& Rebekahs.
Facilities Dining room; Physical therapy
room; Activities room; Chapel; Crafts room;
Laundry room; Barber/Beauty shop; Library.
Activities Arts & crafts; Cards; Games;
Reading groups; Prayer groups; Movies;
Shopping trips; Dances/Social/Cultural
gatherings.

Ohio Masonic Home
PO Box 120, 2655 W National Rd,
Springfield, OH 45501
(513) 325-1531
Admin Thomas D Scott. *Dir of Nursing*
Duane Szymanski. *Medical Dir* William C
Fippin MD.
Licensure Skilled care; Intermediate care;
Alzheimer's care; Retirement. *Beds* Swing
beds SNF/ICF 436.
Owner Proprietary corp.
Admissions Requirements Medical
examination.
Staff Physicians 1 (ft); RNs 22 (ft), 11 (pt);
LPNs 10 (ft), 2 (pt); Nurses' aides 149 (ft),
28 (pt); Physical therapists 1 (ft); Activities
coordinators 1 (ft); Dietitians 1 (ft);
Ophthalmologists 1 (pt); Dentists 1 (pt).
Affiliation Masons.
Facilities Dining room; Physical therapy
room; Activities room; Chapel; Crafts room;
Laundry room; Barber/Beauty shop; Library.
Activities Arts & crafts; Cards; Games;
Reading groups; Movies; Shopping trips;
Dances/Social/Cultural gatherings.

Pillars Health Care
336 W Columbia St, Springfield, OH 45504
(513) 323-9104

Admin Jerry Goodman. *Dir of Nursing*
Margaret Stephens. *Medical Dir* Mark
Roberto.
Licensure Intermediate care. *Beds* ICF 46.
Certified Medicaid.
Owner Proprietary corp.
Staff RNs; LPNs; Nurses' aides; Activities
coordinators; Dietitians.
Facilities Dining room; Activities room;
Laundry room; Barber/Beauty shop.
Activities Arts & crafts; Cards; Games;
Reading groups; Prayer groups; Movies;
Shopping trips; Dances/Social/Cultural
gatherings.

Ridgewood Nursing Center
1600 Saint Paris Pike, Springfield, OH 45504
(513) 399-8131, 399-5906 FAX
Admin R Philip Murray. *Dir of Nursing*
Diane Wilson RN. *Medical Dir* Cleanne
Cass MD.
Licensure Skilled care; Intermediate care. *Beds*
Swing beds SNF/ICF 50. *Private Pay*
Patients 30%. *Certified* Medicaid; Medicare.
Owner Proprietary corp (Unicare).
Admissions Requirements Medical
examination.
Staff Physicians 1 (pt); RNs 2 (ft), 2 (pt);
LPNs 2 (ft), 3 (pt); Nurses' aides 12 (ft), 7
(pt); Physical therapists 1 (pt); Occupational
therapists 1 (pt); Speech therapists 1 (pt);
Activities coordinators 1 (pt); Dietitians 1
(pt); Ophthalmologists 1 (pt); Podiatrists 1
(pt); Audiologists 1 (pt).
Languages Spanish.
Facilities Dining room; Activities room;
Laundry room; Barber/Beauty shop; Library.
Activities Arts & crafts; Cards; Games;
Reading groups; Prayer groups; Movies;
Intergenerational programs; Adopt-a-
grandparent.

St John's Center
100 W McCreight Ave, Springfield, OH 45504
(513) 399-9910
Admin Marianne S Wildermuth. *Dir of*
Nursing Ruth Stadler RN. *Medical Dir* Sally
A Abbott MD.
Licensure Skilled care; Intermediate care;
Alzheimer's unit; Adult day care. *Beds* SNF
50; ICF 100. *Private Pay Patients* 25%.
Certified Medicaid; Medicare.
Owner Nonprofit organization/foundation.
Admissions Requirements Medical
examination.
Staff Physicians 1 (pt); RNs 13 (ft), 6 (pt);
LPNs 19 (ft), 11 (pt); Nurses' aides 46 (ft),
41 (pt); Physical therapists 2 (ft);
Occupational therapists 2 (ft); Activities
coordinators 1 (ft); Dietitians 1 (ft);
Pharmacists 1 (ft); RT staff 7 (ft); Volunteer
coordinators 1 (ft); Chaplains 1 (pt);
Respiratory therapists.
Affiliation Roman Catholic.
Facilities Dining room; Physical therapy
room; Activities room; Chapel; Crafts room;
Laundry room; Barber/Beauty shop; Dental
office; Pharmacy; Occupational therapy
room.
Activities Arts & crafts; Cards; Games;
Reading groups; Prayer groups; Movies;
Shopping trips; Dances/Social/Cultural
gatherings; Intergenerational programs; Pet
therapy.

Seminole Villa Care Center
1365 Seminole Ave, Springfield, OH 45506
(513) 323-1471
Admin Janet R Pavkov. *Dir of Nursing* Eva
Knipp. *Medical Dir* S Delaveris.
Licensure Intermediate care for mentally
retarded. *Beds* ICF/MR 34. *Certified*
Medicaid.
Owner Proprietary corp (American Health
Care Centers).
Admissions Requirements Minimum age 35.

Staff Physicians 3 (pt); RNs 2 (ft), 2 (pt);
LPNs 3 (ft), 3 (pt); Nurses' aides 10 (ft), 9
(pt); Physical therapists 1 (pt); Occupational
therapists 1 (ft), 1 (pt); Speech therapists 1
(pt); Activities coordinators 1 (ft), 1 (pt);
Dietitians 2 (pt); Ophthalmologists 1 (pt);
Podiatrists 1 (pt); Dentists 1 (pt);
Psychologists 1 (pt); Psychiatrists 1 (pt);
Social workers 1 (ft), 1 (pt).
Facilities Dining room; Activities room;
Crafts room; Laundry room; Resident
kitchen.
Activities Arts & crafts; Cards; Games;
Reading groups; Prayer groups; Movies;
Shopping trips; Dances/Social/Cultural
gatherings; Sewing; Cooking; Hospitality
group; Gardening.

Springview Center
3130 E Main St, Springfield, OH 45505
(513) 325-9263
Licensure Intermediate care for mentally
retarded. *Beds* ICF/MR 90. *Certified*
Medicaid.
Owner Publicly owned.

Sunnyland Villa
1365 1/2 Seminole, Springfield, OH 45506
(513) 322-3436, 322-2470 FAX
Admin Charles E Komp. *Dir of Nursing* Mary
Anne Grewe RN. *Medical Dir* Sira Vemana
MD.
Licensure Skilled care; Intermediate care. *Beds*
Swing beds SNF/ICF 100. *Private Pay*
Patients 10%. *Certified* Medicaid; Medicare.
Owner Proprietary corp (American Health
Care Corp).
Admissions Requirements Medical
examination; Physician's request.
Staff Physicians 1 (ft); RNs 4 (ft), 1 (pt);
LPNs 7 (ft), 2 (pt); Nurses' aides 32 (ft), 22
(pt); Physical therapists 1 (pt); Reality
therapists 1 (pt); Recreational therapists 1
(pt); Occupational therapists 1 (pt); Speech
therapists 1 (pt); Activities coordinators 2
(ft); Dietitians 2 (pt); Ophthalmologists 1
(pt); Podiatrists 1 (pt); Audiologists 1 (pt).
Facilities Dining room; Physical therapy
room; Activities room; Crafts room; Laundry
room; Barber/Beauty shop.
Activities Arts & crafts; Cards; Games;
Reading groups; Prayer groups; Movies;
Shopping trips; Dances/Social/Cultural
gatherings; Intergenerational programs; Pet
therapy; Trips to zoo, fair; Elderly United.

Villa Springfield
701 Villa Rd, Springfield, OH 45503
(513) 399-5551
Admin Evelyn L Winland. *Dir of Nursing*
Barbara Blake RN. *Medical Dir* Dr M
Erean.
Licensure Intermediate care. *Beds* ICF 86.
Private Pay Patients 10%. *Certified*
Medicaid.
Owner Proprietary corp.
Admissions Requirements Minimum age 21;
Medical examination; Physician's request.
Staff Physicians; RNs 3 (ft), 2 (pt); LPNs 4
(ft), 3 (pt); Nurses' aides 30 (ft), 3 (pt);
Physical therapists 1 (pt); Occupational
therapists 1 (pt); Speech therapists 1 (pt);
Activities coordinators 1 (ft), 1 (pt);
Dietitians 1 (pt); Podiatrists 1 (pt);
Audiologists 1 (pt); Dentists 1 (pt).
Facilities Dining room; Physical therapy
room; Activities room; Crafts room; Laundry
room; Barber/Beauty shop.
Activities Arts & crafts; Cards; Games;
Reading groups; Prayer groups; Movies;
Shopping trips; Dances/Social/Cultural
gatherings; Intergenerational programs; Pet
therapy.

Steubenville

Carriage Inn of Steubenville Inc
3102 Saint Charles Dr, Steubenville, OH 43952
(614) 264-7161
Admin Robert J Sherrin.
Medical Dir Anthony V Scurti MD.
Licensure Skilled care; Intermediate care. *Beds* SNF 60; ICF 60. *Certified* Medicaid; Medicare.
Owner Proprietary corp.
Admissions Requirements Physician's request.
Staff Physicians 1 (pt); RNs 5 (ft), 4 (pt); LPNs 1 (ft), 9 (pt); Nurses' aides 12 (ft), 18 (pt); Physical therapists 1 (ft); Recreational therapists 1 (pt); Occupational therapists; Speech therapists; Activities coordinators 1 (pt); Dietitians; Podiatrists; Audiologists; Dentists.
Facilities Dining room; Physical therapy room; Activities room; Chapel; Crafts room; Laundry room; Barber/Beauty shop.
Activities Arts & crafts; Cards; Games; Prayer groups; Movies; Shopping trips; Dances/Social/Cultural gatherings.

LaBelle View Nursing Center
1336 Maryland Ave, Steubenville, OH 43952
(614) 282-4581, 282-4583 FAX
Admin Elizabeth A Miller. *Dir of Nursing* Constance I Miller. *Medical Dir* Augusto P Fojas MD.
Licensure Intermediate care. *Beds* ICF 101. *Private Pay Patients* 3%. *Certified* Medicaid; Medicare.
Owner Proprietary corp (American Health Care Centers).
Admissions Requirements Minimum age 18; Medical examination; Physician's request.
Staff Physicians 4 (pt); RNs 4 (pt); LPNs 12 (ft), 5 (pt); Nurses' aides; Physical therapists 1 (pt); Reality therapists 1 (pt); Speech therapists 1 (pt); Activities coordinators 2 (ft); Dietitians 1 (ft), 1 (pt); Ophthalmologists 1 (pt); Podiatrists 1 (pt); Audiologists 1 (pt).
Languages Italian.
Facilities Dining room; Activities room; Crafts room; Laundry room; Barber/Beauty shop; TV room; Wheelchair van; Dental office; X-ray department; Lab.
Activities Arts & crafts; Cards; Games; Reading groups; Prayer groups; Movies; Shopping trips; Dances/Social/Cultural gatherings; Intergenerational programs; Pet therapy; Reality orientation; Community involvement; Volunteer program.

Lancia Convalescent Center
717 N 6th St, Steubenville, OH 43952
(614) 282-3605
Medical Dir John P Smarella MD.
Licensure Intermediate care. *Beds* ICF 50. *Certified* Medicaid.
Owner Proprietary corp.
Admissions Requirements Medical examination.
Staff Physicians 1 (pt); RNs 1 (ft); LPNs 5 (pt); Nurses' aides 12 (ft), 6 (pt); Physical therapists 1 (pt); Speech therapists 1 (pt); Activities coordinators 1 (ft); Dietitians 1 (pt); Podiatrists 1 (pt); Dentists 1 (pt).
Facilities Dining room; Physical therapy room; Laundry room; Barber/Beauty shop.
Activities Arts & crafts; Cards; Games; Prayer groups; Shopping trips.

Lancia Country Club Manor
575 Lovers Ln, Steubenville, OH 43952
(614) 266-6118
Licensure Skilled care; Intermediate care. *Beds* Swing beds SNF/ICF 50.
Owner Proprietary corp.

Lancia Villa Royale Nursing Home
1852 Sinclair Ave, Steubenville, OH 43952
(614) 264-7101

Admin James J Bolger. *Dir of Nursing* Mary Ann Lee RN. *Medical Dir* J P Smarrella MD.
Licensure Skilled care; Intermediate care. *Beds* Swing beds SNF/ICF 100. *Certified* Medicaid; Medicare.
Owner Proprietary corp.
Admissions Requirements Medical examination; Physician's request.
Staff Physicians 6 (pt); RNs 5 (ft); LPNs 12 (ft); Nurses' aides 34 (ft), 10 (pt); Physical therapists 2 (ft), 1 (pt); Speech therapists 1 (pt); Activities coordinators 2 (ft); Dietitians 2 (pt); Ophthalmologists 2 (pt).
Facilities Dining room; Physical therapy room; Activities room; Chapel; Crafts room; Laundry room; Barber/Beauty shop.
Activities Arts & crafts; Cards; Games; Reading groups; Prayer groups; Movies; Shopping trips; Dances/Social/Cultural gatherings; Sports events.

Riverview Nursing Home
925 N 4th St, Steubenville, OH 43952
(614) 282-4158
Admin Joseph C Pino. *Dir of Nursing* Jaye W Bennett LPN. *Medical Dir* Karen M Gross MD.
Licensure Intermediate care. *Beds* ICF 44. *Private Pay Patients* 20%. *Certified* Medicaid.
Owner Proprietary corp.
Staff Physicians 1 (pt); RNs 1 (pt); LPNs 4 (ft), 2 (pt); Nurses' aides 14 (ft), 3 (pt); Physical therapists (consultant); Reality therapists 1 (pt); Occupational therapists 1 (pt); Speech therapists 1 (pt); Activities coordinators 1 (ft); Dietitians (consultant); Ophthalmologists 1 (pt); Podiatrists 1 (pt); Audiologists 1 (pt); Social services 1 (ft).
Facilities Dining room; Activities room; Barber/Beauty shop.
Activities Arts & crafts; Cards; Games; Reading groups; Prayer groups; Movies; Shopping trips; Dances/Social/Cultural gatherings; Pet therapy; Religious services.

Shaffer Plaza
256 John Scott Hwy, Steubenville, OH 43952
(614) 264-3259
Admin Rick Pfannenschmidt.
Medical Dir Mary Jane Johnston.
Licensure Intermediate care for mentally retarded. *Beds* ICF/MR 33. *Certified* Medicaid.
Owner Publicly owned.
Admissions Requirements Minimum age 18; Medical examination.
Staff Physicians 1 (pt); RNs 1 (pt); LPNs 3 (ft), 3 (pt); Nurses' aides 12 (ft), 11 (pt); Physical therapists 1 (pt); Recreational therapists 1 (ft); Occupational therapists 1 (pt); Speech therapists 1 (pt); Dietitians 1 (pt); Ophthalmologists 1 (pt); Podiatrists 1 (pt); Dentists 1 (pt).
Facilities Dining room; Physical therapy room; Activities room; Crafts room; Laundry room.
Activities Arts & crafts; Cards; Games; Movies; Shopping trips; Dances/Social/Cultural gatherings; Swimming; Bowling; Sheltered workshop.

Stow

MARS—Ellsworth Home
4223 Ellsworth Rd, Stow, OH 44224
(216) 929-6506
Licensure Intermediate care for mentally retarded. *Beds* ICF/MR 4. *Certified* Medicaid.
Owner Proprietary corp.

MARS—Lakeview Home
3455 Lakeview Blvd, Stow, OH 44224
(216) 864-8464

Admin Sherry Gedeon. *Dir of Nursing* Dorothy Collins. *Medical Dir* Dr Robert Norman.
Licensure Intermediate care for mentally retarded. *Beds* ICF/MR 4. *Private Pay Patients* 0%. *Certified* Medicaid.
Owner Nonprofit organization/foundation (Metro Akron Residential Services).
Admissions Requirements Must be referred by county.
Staff Physicians (contracted); RNs 1 (pt); LPNs 1 (pt); Physical therapists (contracted); Recreational therapists (contracted); Occupational therapists (contracted); Speech therapists (contracted); Dietitians (contracted); Audiologists (contracted).
Facilities Dining room; Activities room; Crafts room; Laundry room; Library.
Activities Arts & crafts; Cards; Games; Movies; Shopping trips; Dances/Social/Cultural gatherings.

Stow—Glen Health Care Center
4285 Kent Rd, Stow, OH 44224
(216) 686-2545
Admin Arnold Levine. *Dir of Nursing* Judy Worron RN. *Medical Dir* Atul Goswami MD.
Licensure Intermediate care; Residential care. *Beds* ICF 100; Residential care 75. *Private Pay Patients* 50%. *Certified* Medicaid.
Owner Proprietary corp.
Admissions Requirements Medical examination; Physician's request.
Staff Physicians 1 (pt); RNs 6 (ft); LPNs 13 (ft); Nurses' aides 60 (ft); Physical therapists 1 (pt); Occupational therapists 1 (pt); Speech therapists 1 (pt); Activities coordinators 1 (pt); Dietitians 1 (pt); Ophthalmologists 1 (pt); Podiatrists 1 (pt); Audiologists 1 (pt).
Facilities Dining room; Physical therapy room; Activities room; Chapel; Laundry room; Barber/Beauty shop.
Activities Arts & crafts; Cards; Games; Reading groups; Prayer groups; Movies; Shopping trips; Dances/Social/Cultural gatherings; Pet therapy.

Strongsville

Altenheim
15653 Pearl Rd, Strongsville, OH 44136
(216) 238-3361
Admin Shawn Litten. *Dir of Nursing* Michael Hoffner BSN. *Medical Dir* William D Smucker.
Licensure Skilled care; Retirement. *Beds* SNF 100. *Private Pay Patients* 50%. *Certified* Medicaid; Medicare.
Owner Nonprofit organization/foundation.
Admissions Requirements Medical examination.
Staff Physicians 1 (ft); RNs 6 (ft); LPNs 15 (ft); Nurses' aides 45 (ft); Physical therapists 1 (pt); Speech therapists 1 (pt); Activities coordinators 1 (ft), 2 (pt); Dietitians 1 (ft), 1 (pt); Ophthalmologists 1 (pt); Podiatrists 1 (pt).
Languages German, Hungarian, Polish.
Facilities Dining room; Physical therapy room; Activities room; Chapel; Crafts room; Laundry room; Barber/Beauty shop; Library.
Activities Arts & crafts; Cards; Games; Reading groups; Prayer groups; Movies; Shopping trips; Dances/Social/Cultural gatherings.

Struthers

Maplecrest Nursing & Home for the Aged
400 Sexton St, Struthers, OH 44471
(216) 755-1466
Medical Dir Dr Jeffery Resch.
Licensure Skilled care; Intermediate care. *Beds* ICF 13; Swing beds SNF/ICF 35.
Owner Proprietary corp.

Admissions Requirements Medical examination.
Staff Physicians 1 (pt); RNs 2 (ft), 1 (pt); LPNs 2 (ft), 1 (pt); Nurses' aides 13 (ft), 2 (pt); Physical therapists 1 (pt); Occupational therapists 1 (pt); Speech therapists 1 (pt); Dietitians 1 (pt); Podiatrists 1 (pt).
Facilities Dining room; Physical therapy room; Activities room; Laundry room; Barber/Beauty shop.
Activities Games; Prayer groups; Dances/ Social/Cultural gatherings.

Sunbury

Morning View Care Center III
14961 N Old CCC Hwy, Sunbury, OH 43074
(614) 965-3984
Admin Bonnie Coulter. *Dir of Nursing* Sandra Bright. *Medical Dir* Dr Charles Marti.
Licensure Skilled care; Intermediate care. *Beds* swing beds SNF/ICF 50. *Certified* Medicaid; Medicare.
Owner Proprietary corp (Morning View Care Centers).
Admissions Requirements Medical examination; Physician's request.
Staff Physicians 1 (pt); RNs 2 (ft), 1 (pt); LPNs 3 (ft), 2 (pt); Nurses' aides 12 (ft), 7 (pt); Physical therapists 1 (pt); Occupational therapists 1 (pt); Speech therapists 1 (pt); Activities coordinators 1 (ft); Dietitians 1 (pt); Ophthalmologists 1 (pt); Podiatrists 1 (pt); Audiologists 1 (pt).
Facilities Dining room; Activities room; Crafts room; Laundry room; Barber/Beauty shop.
Activities Arts & crafts; Cards; Games; Reading groups; Prayer groups; Movies; Shopping trips; Dances/Social/Cultural gatherings; Pet therapy.

Sunbury Nursing Home
144 N Columbus St, Sunbury, OH 43074
(614) 965-4915
Admin JoAnne Colfack. *Dir of Nursing* Sherry Gallion. *Medical Dir* Dr Charles Marti.
Licensure Intermediate care. *Beds* ICF 30. *Private Pay Patients* 20%. *Certified* Medicaid; Medicare.
Owner Privately owned (Morning View Care Centers).
Staff RNs 1 (ft); LPNs 5 (ft), 1 (pt); Nurses' aides 7 (ft), 3 (pt); Physical therapists 1 (pt); Activities coordinators 1 (ft); Dietitians 1 (pt); Podiatrists 1 (pt).
Facilities Dining room; Activities room; Crafts room; Laundry room; Barber/Beauty shop.
Activities Arts & crafts; Cards; Games; Reading groups; Prayer groups; Movies; Shopping trips; Dances/Social/Cultural gatherings; Pet therapy.

Swanton

Maple Tree Inn Inc
401 W Airpost Hwy, Swanton, OH 43558
(419) 825-1111
Admin Susan Bender. *Dir of Nursing* Linda Rufenacht. *Medical Dir* Dr Philip Lepkowski.
Licensure Intermediate care; Alzheimer's care. *Beds* ICF 51. *Certified* Medicaid.
Owner Privately owned.
Admissions Requirements Medical examination.
Staff RNs 1 (ft), 4 (pt); LPNs 1 (ft), 4 (pt); Nurses' aides 6 (ft), 10 (pt); Physical therapists; Occupational therapists; Speech therapists; Activities coordinators 1 (ft); Dietitians 1 (pt); Ophthalmologists; Podiatrists; Dentists.

Facilities Dining room; Activities room; Laundry room.
Activities Arts & crafts; Cards; Games; Reading groups; Prayer groups; Movies; Shopping trips; Dances/Social/Cultural gatherings; Individual programs for Alzheimer's Disease.

Swanton Health Care & Retirement Center
214 S Munson Rd, Swanton, OH 43558
(419) 825-1145
Licensure Intermediate care. *Beds* ICF 48. *Certified* Medicaid.
Owner Proprietary corp.

Sylvania

Briarfield Inc
5757 Whiteford Rd, Sylvania, OH 43560
(419) 882-1875
Admin Joseph H Giauque; Daniel J Giauque. *Dir of Nursing* Diana Waugh RN. *Medical Dir* Dr A M Quinto.
Licensure Intermediate care. *Beds* ICF 109. *Certified* Medicaid.
Owner Proprietary corp.
Admissions Requirements Medical examination.
Staff Physicians 1 (pt); RNs 7 (ft), 1 (pt); LPNs 10 (ft); Nurses' aides 43 (ft); Reality therapists 1 (ft); Activities coordinators 2 (ft); Dietitians 1 (pt).
Facilities Dining room; Activities room; Crafts room; Laundry room; Barber/Beauty shop.
Activities Arts & crafts; Cards; Games; Reading groups; Prayer groups; Movies; Shopping trips; Dances/Social/Cultural gatherings; Outings; Camping; Volunteering at a facility for severely retarded children.

Lake Park Nursing Care Center
5100 Harroun Rd, Sylvania, OH 43560
(419) 885-1444
Admin Georgia A Poplar FACHCA.
Medical Dir R E Scherbarth MD.
Licensure Skilled care. *Beds* SNF 131. *Certified* Medicare.
Owner Nonprofit corp.
Admissions Requirements Minimum age 3 months; Physician's request.
Staff Physicians 1 (ft); RNs 15 (ft), 10 (pt); LPNs 16 (ft), 9 (pt); Nurses' aides 40 (ft), 40 (pt); Physical therapists 10 (ft); Recreational therapists 2 (ft), 1 (pt); Occupational therapists 4 (ft), 2 (pt); Speech therapists 3 (ft), 3 (pt); Dietitians 1 (ft), 1 (pt); Podiatrists 2 (pt); Dental hygienists 1 (pt); MSWs 2 (ft).
Languages Polish, Hungarian, Spanish.
Affiliation Methodist.
Facilities Dining room; Physical therapy room; Activities room; Chapel; Crafts room; Barber/Beauty shop; Library.
Activities Arts & crafts; Cards; Games; Reading groups; Prayer groups; Movies; Shopping trips; Dances/Social/Cultural gatherings.

Tallmadge

Colonial Gardens Inc
563 Colony Park, Tallmadge, OH 44278
(216) 630-9780
Admin Richard S Kesic. *Dir of Nursing* Holly Kuemerle RN. *Medical Dir* Carl J Mader MD.
Licensure Skilled care; Intermediate care. *Beds* SNF 47; ICF 143. *Certified* Medicaid; Medicare.
Owner Proprietary corp (American Health Care Centers).
Admissions Requirements Minimum age 18.
Staff Physicians 30 (pt); RNs 3 (ft), 6 (pt); LPNs 17 (ft); Nurses' aides 33 (ft), 33 (pt); Physical therapists 1 (pt); Occupational therapists 1 (pt); Speech therapists 1 (pt);

Activities coordinators 2 (ft), 4 (pt); Dietitians 1 (ft); Ophthalmologists 1 (pt); Podiatrists 1 (pt).
Facilities Dining room; Physical therapy room; Activities room; Crafts room; Laundry room; Barber/Beauty shop.
Activities Arts & crafts; Cards; Games; Reading groups; Prayer groups; Movies; Shopping trips; Dances/Social/Cultural gatherings.

Cooper Nursing Home No 2
340 Southwest Ave, Tallmadge, OH 44278
(216) 633-4723
Admin Robert L Zucker.
Medical Dir Dr Stuart Goldstein.
Licensure Intermediate care. *Beds* ICF 31. *Certified* Medicaid.
Owner Proprietary corp.
Admissions Requirements Minimum age 21; Females only; Medical examination; Physician's request.
Staff Physicians 1 (pt); RNs 1 (pt); LPNs 5 (ft), 1 (pt); Nurses' aides 11 (ft), 4 (pt); Reality therapists 1 (pt); Activities coordinators 1 (ft); Dietitians 1 (pt); Ophthalmologists 1 (pt); Podiatrists 1 (pt); Dentists 1 (pt).
Facilities Dining room; Activities room; Laundry room; Kitchen; Lounge areas.
Activities Arts & crafts; Games; Prayer groups; Dances/Social/Cultural gatherings.

Summit County Home
1134 North Ave, Tallmadge, OH 44278
(216) 688-8600
Admin Leah J Bryan. *Dir of Nursing* Anne Richardson RN. *Medical Dir* Judith Gooding MD.
Licensure Intermediate care. *Beds* ICF 120. *Certified* Medicaid.
Owner Proprietary corp (Crown Care Inc).
Admissions Requirements Medical examination; Physician's request.
Staff RNs 5 (ft), 4 (pt); LPNs 10 (ft), 10 (pt); Nurses' aides 50 (ft), 11 (pt); Physical therapists 1 (ft); Occupational therapists 1 (ft); Activities coordinators 1 (ft); Dietitians 1 (ft).
Facilities Dining room; Physical therapy room; Activities room; Laundry room; Barber/Beauty shop.
Activities Arts & crafts; Cards; Games; Reading groups; Prayer groups; Movies; Shopping trips; Dances/Social/Cultural gatherings.

Thornville

Heartland-Fairfield
7820 Pleasantville Rd, Thornville, OH 43076
(614) 536-7381
Admin Carl M L Holbrook.
Medical Dir Dr Robert Sprouse.
Licensure Skilled care; Intermediate care; Intermediate care for mentally retarded. *Beds* ICF/MR 36; Swing beds SNF/ICF 150. *Certified* Medicaid; Medicare.
Owner Proprietary corp (Health Care and Retirement Corp).
Admissions Requirements Medical examination; Physician's request.
Staff Physicians 2 (pt); RNs 10 (ft); LPNs 25 (ft), 2 (pt); Nurses' aides 90 (ft), 20 (pt); Physical therapists 2 (pt); Recreational therapists 2 (ft); Occupational therapists 1 (pt); Speech therapists 1 (pt); Activities coordinators 1 (ft); Dietitians 1 (pt); Ophthalmologists 1 (pt); Podiatrists 1 (pt); Audiologists 1 (pt); Dentists 2 (pt).
Facilities Dining room; Physical therapy room; Activities room; Crafts room; Laundry room; Barber/Beauty shop.
Activities Arts & crafts; Cards; Games; Reading groups; Prayer groups; Movies; Shopping trips; Dances/Social/Cultural gatherings.

Tiffin

Alta Mira Nursing Home
1344 W Seneca Ave, Tiffin, OH 44883
(419) 447-7373
Admin Marilyn J Smith-McCoy. *Dir of Nursing* Mary Traxler LPN. *Medical Dir* G R Korrapati MD.
Licensure Intermediate care. *Beds* ICF 40. *Private Pay Patients* 50%. *Certified* Medicaid.
Owner Proprietary corp.
Staff RNs 2 (pt); LPNs 4 (ft), 3 (pt); Nurses' aides 10 (ft), 8 (pt); Activities coordinators 1 (ft).
Activities Arts & crafts; Cards; Games; Prayer groups; Movies; Pet therapy; Music.

Autumnwood Care Center
670 E State Rte 18, Tiffin, OH 44883
(419) 447-7151
Licensure Skilled care; Intermediate care. *Beds* SNF 25; ICF 125. *Certified* Medicaid; Medicare.
Owner Nonprofit corp (Volunteers of America Care).

Riverfront Manor Inc
2320 W County Rd 6, Tiffin, OH 44883
(419) 447-4662
Admin Christopher P Widman. *Dir of Nursing* Ann Seitz. *Medical Dir* Dr Korrapati.
Licensure Intermediate care. *Beds* ICF 44. *Certified* Medicaid.
Owner Proprietary corp (Cloverleaf Healthcare).
Staff Physicians 1 (ft); RNs 2 (pt); LPNs 4 (ft), 2 (pt); Nurses' aides 12 (ft), 6 (pt); Activities coordinators 1 (ft); Dietitians 1 (pt).
Facilities Dining room; Activities room; Chapel; Crafts room; Laundry room; Barber/Beauty shop; Private & semi-private rooms.
Activities Arts & crafts; Cards; Games; Reading groups; Prayer groups; Movies; Shopping trips; Dances/Social/Cultural gatherings; Pet therapy.

St Francis Home
182 Saint Francis Ave, Tiffin, OH 44883
(419) 447-2723
Admin Angelo Vivino. *Dir of Nursing* Deborh Maloy RN. *Medical Dir* Anthony Lupica MD.
Licensure Skilled care; Intermediate care; Rest home; Residential care. *Beds* Swing beds SNF/ICF 81; Rest home 36; Residential care 33. *Private Pay Patients* 75%. *Certified* Medicaid.
Owner Nonprofit organization/foundation.
Admissions Requirements Minimum age 70.
Staff Physicians; RNs; LPNs; Nurses' aides; Reality therapists; Recreational therapists; Activities coordinators; Dietitians; Podiatrists.
Affiliation Roman Catholic.
Facilities Dining room; Physical therapy room; Activities room; Chapel; Crafts room; Laundry room; Barber/Beauty shop; Library.
Activities Arts & crafts; Cards; Games; Prayer groups; Movies; Shopping trips; Dances/Social/Cultural gatherings.

South Washington Street Nursing Home
248 S Washington St, Tiffin, OH 44883
(419) 447-0773
Licensure Intermediate care. *Beds* ICF 25. *Certified* Medicaid.
Owner Proprietary corp.

Tiffin Developmental Center
600 N River Rd, Tiffin, OH 44883
(419) 447-1450
Admin Jerry D Johnson. *Dir of Nursing* Joyce Millar. *Medical Dir* Dr Krishnaiah Garlapati.
Licensure Intermediate care for mentally retarded. *Beds* ICF/MR 220. *Certified* Medicaid.
Owner Publicly owned.

Toledo

Americare—Toledo Nursing & Rehabilitation Center
2051 Collingwood Blvd, Toledo, OH 43620
(419) 243-5191
Medical Dir Dr Antonio Paat.
Licensure Skilled care; Intermediate care. *Beds* SNF 28; ICF 146. *Certified* Medicaid; Medicare.
Owner Proprietary corp (Care Enterprises).
Admissions Requirements Medical examination.
Staff RNs 6 (ft), 6 (pt); LPNs 9 (ft), 16 (pt); Nurses' aides 38 (ft), 26 (pt); Activities coordinators 1 (ft).
Facilities Dining room; Physical therapy room; Activities room; Chapel; Laundry room; Barber/Beauty shop; Patio.
Activities Arts & crafts; Cards; Games; Prayer groups; Movies; Shopping trips; Dances/Social/Cultural gatherings.

Arbors at Toledo
2900 Cherry St, Toledo, OH 43608
(419) 242-7458, 242-2428 FAX
Admin Robert D Brooks. *Dir of Nursing* Elaine Hetherwick. *Medical Dir* Dr Samuel Karr.
Licensure Skilled care; Intermediate care; Sub-acute extensive care. *Beds* SNF 46; ICF 54; Sub-acute extensive care unit 22. *Private Pay Patients* 20%. *Certified* Medicaid; Medicare.
Owner Proprietary corp (Arbor Health Care Co).
Admissions Requirements Medical examination.
Staff RNs 4 (ft), 3 (pt); LPNs 5 (ft), 2 (pt); Nurses' aides 33 (ft), 5 (pt); Physical therapists (contracted); Activities coordinators 1 (ft); Dietitians.
Facilities Dining room; Physical therapy room; Activities room; Crafts room; Laundry room; Barber/Beauty shop.
Activities Arts & crafts; Games; Prayer groups; Movies; Dances/Social/Cultural gatherings; Intergenerational programs; Pet therapy.

Ashland Avenue Nursing Home
2283 Ashland Ave, Toledo, OH 43620
(419) 241-6457
Licensure Intermediate care. *Beds* ICF 50. *Certified* Medicaid.
Owner Proprietary corp.
Admissions Requirements Minimum age 18; Medical examination; Physician's request.
Staff RNs 1 (pt); LPNs 3 (ft), 5 (pt); Nurses' aides 9 (ft), 11 (pt); Activities coordinators 1 (ft); Dietitians 1 (ft); Audiologists 1 (ft).
Facilities Dining room; Activities room; Chapel; Crafts room; Laundry room; Barber/Beauty shop; Library.
Activities Arts & crafts; Cards; Games; Reading groups; Prayer groups; Movies; Shopping trips; Dances/Social/Cultural gatherings.

Autumnwood of Sylvania
4111 Holland Sylvania Rd, Toledo, OH 43623
(419) 882-2087, 885-1422 FAX
Admin William L Stewart CFACHCA. *Dir of Nursing* Sally Klein RN. *Medical Dir* R Rocchi MD.
Licensure Intermediate care. *Beds* ICF 99. *Private Pay Patients* 35%. *Certified* Medicaid.
Owner Proprietary corp (Health Enterprises).
Admissions Requirements Medical examination.
Staff RNs 4 (ft), 4 (pt); LPNs 8 (ft), 6 (pt); Nurses' aides 30 (ft), 22 (pt); Recreational therapists 1 (ft), 1 (pt).
Facilities Dining room; Activities room; Laundry room; Barber/Beauty shop.
Activities Arts & crafts; Cards; Games; Reading groups; Prayer groups; Movies; Dances/Social/Cultural gatherings; Intergenerational programs; Pet therapy.

Bancroft Family Care Home
5415 W Bancroft St, Toledo, OH 43615
(419) 536-0032
Licensure Intermediate care for mentally retarded. *Beds* ICF/MR 6. *Certified* Medicaid.
Owner Proprietary corp.

Byrnebrook Nursing Home
1011 N Byrne Rd, Toledo, OH 43607
(419) 531-5321
Admin Cynthia M Allen. *Dir of Nursing* Barb Seiling RN. *Medical Dir* Dr Dan Williams.
Licensure Skilled care; Intermediate care. *Beds* SNF 18; ICF 55. *Certified* Medicaid; Medicare.
Owner Proprietary corp.
Admissions Requirements Medical examination; Physician's request.
Staff Physicians 33 (ft); RNs 4 (ft), 2 (pt); LPNs 9 (ft), 4 (pt); Nurses' aides 23 (ft), 8 (pt); Reality therapists 1 (pt); Activities coordinators 1 (ft), 1 (pt).
Languages Polish.
Facilities Dining room; Physical therapy room; Activities room; Crafts room; Laundry room; Barber/Beauty shop.
Activities Arts & crafts; Cards; Games; Reading groups; Prayer groups; Movies; Dances/Social/Cultural gatherings.

Collingwood Nursing Home
1835 Collingwood Blvd, Toledo, OH 43624
(419) 255-0333
Licensure Intermediate care. *Beds* ICF 34. *Certified* Medicaid.
Owner Proprietary corp.

Darlington House
2735 Darlington Rd, Toledo, OH 43606
(419) 531-4465
Admin Aaron B Handler. *Dir of Nursing* H JoAnne Schwartzberg. *Medical Dir* Eli C Abramson MD.
Licensure Skilled care; Intermediate care; Retirement; Alzheimer's care. *Beds* Swing beds SNF/ICF 125. *Certified* Medicaid; Medicare.
Owner Nonprofit corp.
Admissions Requirements Minimum age 65; Medical examination.
Staff Physicians 2 (pt); RNs 12 (ft); LPNs 14 (ft), 4 (pt); Nurses' aides 45 (ft); Physical therapists 2 (pt); Recreational therapists 1 (pt); Occupational therapists 1 (pt); Speech therapists 2 (pt); Activities coordinators 1 (ft), 7 (pt); Dietitians 1 (ft); Ophthalmologists 1 (pt).
Affiliation Jewish.
Facilities Dining room; Physical therapy room; Activities room; Chapel; Crafts room; Laundry room; Barber/Beauty shop; Library; Little theater; Garden.
Activities Arts & crafts; Cards; Games; Reading groups; Movies; Shopping trips; Dances/Social/Cultural gatherings; Baking; Singing; Classical music.

Edgewood Nursing Home
4848 Dorr, Toledo, OH 43615
(419) 531-2037
Admin Bruce E Alexander. *Dir of Nursing* Barbara Falzone. *Medical Dir* Dr R Rocchi.
Licensure Intermediate care. *Beds* ICF 48. *Private Pay Patients* 100%.
Owner Privately owned.
Admissions Requirements Medical examination.
Staff Physicians 1 (ft); LPNs 4 (ft); Nurses' aides 13 (ft), 2 (pt); Activities coordinators 1 (ft); Podiatrists 1 (pt).

Facilities Dining room; Laundry room;
Barber/Beauty shop; Fenced-in backyard
with patio, swing, lawn furniture, picnic
benches, flower gardens; Screened porch;
Lounge with cable TV.
Activities Arts & crafts; Cards; Games;
Movies; Bookmobile.

Fairview Manor Nursing Center
4420 South St, Toledo, OH 43615
(419) 531-4201
Admin Bennett Balmer. *Dir of Nursing*
Barbara Kozek RN. *Medical Dir* Dr
Margaret Miller.
Licensure Skilled care; Intermediate care. *Beds*
Swing beds SNF/ICF 137. *Certified*
Medicaid; Medicare.
Owner Proprietary corp (Shive Nursing
Centers).
Staff Physicians 45 (ft); Physical therapists 1
(pt).
Facilities Dining room; Physical therapy
room; Activities room; Chapel; Crafts room;
Laundry room; Barber/Beauty shop; Library.
Activities Arts & crafts; Games; Reading
groups; Prayer groups; Movies; Shopping
trips; Dances/Social/Cultural gatherings;
Parties.

Glanzman Colonial Nursing Center
3121 Glanzman Rd, Toledo, OH 43614
(419) 385-6616, 385-5590 FAX
Admin Barbara Noland. *Dir of Nursing* Linda
Romer. *Medical Dir* Fredrick Hiss.
Licensure Skilled care; Intermediate care. *Beds*
Swing beds SNF/ICF 94. *Private Pay
Patients* 49%. *Certified* Medicaid; Medicare.
Owner Proprietary corp (Paradigm
Enterprises).
Admissions Requirements Physician's request.
Staff RNs 4 (ft), 1 (pt); LPNs 8 (ft), 4 (pt);
Nurses' aides 25 (ft), 10 (pt); Activities
coordinators 1 (ft), 1 (pt); Dietitians 1 (pt).
Facilities Dining room; Activities room;
Laundry room; Barber/Beauty shop; Library.
Activities Arts & crafts; Cards; Games;
Reading groups; Prayer groups; Movies;
Shopping trips; Pet therapy.

Golden Haven Nursing Home
2901 Tremainsville Rd, Toledo, OH 43613
(419) 472-2183
Admin Jeffery L Cohen; Dora Cohen.
Medical Dir Dr Margaret Miller.
Licensure Skilled care; Intermediate care;
Retirement. *Beds* SNF 54; ICF 40. *Certified*
Medicaid; Medicare.
Owner Proprietary corp.
Admissions Requirements Minimum age 18.
Staff RNs 2 (ft); LPNs 10 (ft); Nurses' aides
25 (ft); Activities coordinators 1 (ft);
Dietitians 1 (pt).
Languages Spanish, German, Polish.
Facilities Dining room; Activities room;
Laundry room; Barber/Beauty shop; Library;
Screened porch; Patio.
Activities Arts & crafts; Cards; Games;
Reading groups; Prayer groups; Movies;
Dances/Social/Cultural gatherings.

Heartland—Holly Glen
4293 Monroe St, Toledo, OH 43606
(419) 474-6021
Licensure Skilled care; Intermediate care. *Beds*
Swing beds SNF/ICF 100.
Owner Proprietary corp (Health Care and
Retirement Corp).

Hospitality Care Center Toledo
3225 Glanzman Rd, Toledo, OH 43614
(419) 382-5694
Licensure Intermediate care. *Beds* ICF 26.
Certified Medicaid.
Owner Proprietary corp.

Imperial Manor
4816 Dorr St, Toledo, OH 43615
(419) 536-7656

Admin Marie S Houston. *Dir of Nursing*
Louise Grubbs. *Medical Dir* Youseff
Hazamah MD.
Licensure Intermediate care. *Beds* ICF 30.
Certified Medicaid.
Owner Privately owned.
Staff RNs; LPNs; Nurses' aides; Activities
coordinators; Dietitians.
Facilities Dining room; Activities room;
Laundry room; Barber/Beauty shop.
Activities Arts & crafts; Cards; Games; Prayer
groups.

Josina Lott Foundation Residential Center
120 S Holland-Sylvania Rd, Toledo, OH
43615
(419) 866-9013
Licensure Intermediate care for mentally
retarded. *Beds* ICF/MR 32. *Certified*
Medicaid.
Owner Nonprofit organization/foundation.

Lutheran Old Folks Home
2411 Seaman St, Toledo, OH 43605
(419) 693-0751
Medical Dir William Winslow MD.
Licensure Intermediate care; Rest home. *Beds*
ICF 235; Rest home 8. *Certified* Medicaid.
Owner Proprietary corp.
Admissions Requirements Minimum age 65;
Medical examination.
Languages German, Spanish.
Affiliation Lutheran.
Facilities Dining room; Physical therapy
room; Activities room; Chapel; Crafts room;
Laundry room; Barber/Beauty shop; Library;
Resident bakery; Auditorium; Picnic grove;
Shelter.
Activities Arts & crafts; Cards; Games;
Reading groups; Prayer groups; Movies;
Shopping trips; Dances/Social/Cultural
gatherings; Discussion groups; Couples club;
Association for residents' children.

Marks Nursing Home
2109 Collingwood Blvd, Toledo, OH 43620
(419) 246-6082
Licensure Intermediate care. *Beds* ICF 31.
Certified Medicaid.
Owner Proprietary corp.

Mielke's Nursing Home
2007 Terrace View W, Toledo, OH 43607
(419) 826-4891
Admin Helen Brown.
Medical Dir Clara Mausser LPN.
Licensure Intermediate care. *Beds* 12.
Certified Medicaid.
Owner Proprietary corp.
Staff Physicians 2 (pt); RNs 1 (pt); LPNs 1
(ft), 2 (pt); Nurses' aides 4 (ft), 6 (pt);
Physical therapists 1 (pt); Recreational
therapists 1 (pt); Activities coordinators 1
(pt); Dietitians 1 (pt); Podiatrists 1 (pt).
Facilities Dining room; Activities room;
Laundry room.
Activities Arts & crafts; Cards; Games;
Reading groups; Prayer groups; Shopping
trips; Barber & beauty services available;
Various religious services Sunday afternoon
& Wednesday evening.

Northwest Ohio Development Center
1101 S Detroit Ave, Toledo, OH 43614
(419) 385-0231
Admin Warren Karmol. *Dir of Nursing* Rae J
Rehfeldt RN.
Licensure Intermediate care for mentally
retarded. *Beds* ICF/MR 170. *Certified*
Medicaid.
Owner Publicly owned.
Staff Physicians 10 (pt); RNs 6 (ft); LPNs 10
(ft); Nurses' aides 100 (ft), 60 (pt);
Recreational therapists 3 (ft), 2 (pt);
Occupational therapists 1 (ft); Speech
therapists 3 (ft); Activities coordinators 1
(ft).

Activities Arts & crafts; Cards; Games;
Reading groups; Prayer groups; Movies;
Shopping trips; Dances/Social/Cultural
gatherings.

Riverside Convalescent Home
1819 Summit St, Toledo, OH 43611
(419) 729-0860
Admin Opal Evanoff RN. *Dir of Nursing* Opal
Evanoff RN. *Medical Dir* R O Naturdad
MD.
Licensure Intermediate care. *Beds* ICF 10.
Certified Medicaid.
Owner Privately owned.
Admissions Requirements Medical
examination; Physician's request.
Staff Physicians; RNs; LPNs; Nurses' aides;
Recreational therapists; Activities
coordinators; Podiatrists.
Facilities Dining room; Activities room;
Crafts room; Laundry room.
Activities Arts & crafts; Cards; Games;
Movies; Pet therapy.

Robinwood Care Center Inc
1011 N Byrne, Toledo, OH 43607
(419) 242-3702
Medical Dir Isador Binzer MD.
Licensure Intermediate care. *Beds* ICF 20.
Certified Medicaid.
Owner Proprietary corp.
Staff Physicians 1 (ft), 4 (pt); RNs 1 (pt);
LPNs 2 (ft), 1 (pt); Nurses' aides 7 (ft), 2
(pt); Dietitians 1 (ft); Podiatrists 1 (pt).
Facilities Dining room; Laundry room.
Activities Arts & crafts; Cards; Games.

Seagate Nursing Home
2803 117th St, Toledo, OH 43611
(419) 726-9820
Licensure Intermediate care. *Beds* ICF 19.
Certified Medicaid.
Owner Proprietary corp.

Sunset House
4020 Indian Rd, Toledo, OH 43606
(419) 536-4645
Licensure Intermediate care; Rest home. *Beds*
ICF 44; Rest home 36. *Certified* Medicaid.
Owner Proprietary corp.

Toledo Mental Health Center
930 S Detroit Ave, Toledo, OH 43699
(419) 381-1881, ext 684
Admin Juanita H Price. *Dir of Nursing* Jan
Beauerson RN. *Medical Dir* Bahdam Maryle
MD.
Licensure Intermediate care for mentally
retarded. *Beds* ICF/MR 24. *Certified*
Medicaid.
Owner Publicly owned.
Admissions Requirements Minimum age 18.
Staff Physicians; RNs; LPNs; Nurses' aides;
Physical therapists; Reality therapists;
Recreational therapists; Occupational
therapists; Speech therapists; Activities
coordinators; Dietitians; Ophthalmologists;
Dentists.
Facilities Dining room; Physical therapy
room; Activities room; Chapel; Crafts room;
Laundry room; Barber/Beauty shop; Library.
Activities Arts & crafts; Cards; Games;
Reading groups; Prayer groups; Movies;
Shopping trips; Dances/Social/Cultural
gatherings.

Villa North Nursing Home
4645 Lewis Ave, Toledo, OH 43612
(419) 478-5131
Licensure Skilled care; Intermediate care. *Beds*
Swing beds SNF/ICF 250. *Certified*
Medicaid; Medicare.
Owner Proprietary corp.

Waterford Commons
955 Gardenlake Pkwy, Toledo, OH 43614
(419) 382-2200, 382-2200, ext 366 FAX
Admin Aileen K Frost. *Dir of Nursing* Fran
Darmofal. *Medical Dir* Dr Mark Zilkowski.

Licensure Skilled care; Assisted living. *Beds*
SNF 75; Assisted living 26. *Certified*
Medicaid; Medicare.
Owner Proprietary corp (Integrated Health
Services Inc).
Admissions Requirements Medical
examination.
Staff Physicians 1 (pt); RNs; LPNs; Nurses'
aides; Physical therapists; Recreational
therapists; Occupational therapists; Speech
therapists 3 (ft); Activities coordinators 2
(ft); Dietitians 1 (pt); Podiatrists 1 (pt).
Facilities Dining room; Physical therapy
room; Activities room; Laundry room;
Barber/Beauty shop; Library; Greenhouse;
Ice cream/Gift shop.
Activities Arts & crafts; Cards; Games;
Reading groups; Prayer groups; Movies;
Shopping trips; Dances/Social/Cultural
gatherings; Intergenerational programs; Pet
therapy.

Wunderley Nursing Home
2205 Parkwood Ave, Toledo, OH 43620
(419) 244-8208
Licensure Intermediate care. *Beds* ICF 29.
Certified Medicaid.
Owner Proprietary corp.

Zeigler Collingwood Home
3242 Collingwood Blvd, Toledo, OH 43610
(419) 244-5787
Licensure Intermediate care for mentally
retarded. *Beds* ICF/MR 8. *Certified*
Medicaid.
Owner Proprietary corp.

Troy

Dettmer Hospital/Koester ECF
3130 N Dixie Hwy, Troy, OH 45373
(513) 332-7500, 332-7672 FAX
Admin Jonathan B Trimble LNHA. *Dir of
Nursing* Carla Shirley RN. *Medical Dir*
Robert Gierard MD.
Licensure Skilled care; Intermediate care. *Beds*
Swing beds SNF/ICF 50. *Private Pay
Patients* 32%. *Certified* Medicaid; Medicare.
Owner Nonprofit organization/foundation.
Admissions Requirements Minimum age 18;
Medical examination; Physician's request.
Staff Physicians 1 (pt); RNs 6 (ft); LPNs 6
(ft), 3 (pt); Nurses' aides 26 (ft); Physical
therapists 1 (pt); Recreational therapists 1
(pt); Occupational therapists 1 (pt); Speech
therapists 1 (pt); Activities coordinators 1
(ft); Dietitians 1 (ft); Ophthalmologists 1
(pt); Podiatrists 1 (pt).
Facilities Dining room; Physical therapy
room; Activities room; Chapel; Crafts room;
Laundry room; Barber/Beauty shop; Library.
Activities Arts & crafts; Cards; Games;
Reading groups; Prayer groups; Movies;
Shopping trips; Dances/Social/Cultural
gatherings; Intergenerational programs; Pet
therapy.

Highland View Nursing Home
500 Crescent Dr, Troy, OH 45373
(513) 335-7161
Licensure Skilled care; Intermediate care. *Beds*
Swing beds SNF/ICF 61.
Owner Proprietary corp.

Johnson Nursing Home
845 N Harrison St, Troy, OH 45373
(513) 335-2125
Licensure Skilled care; Intermediate care. *Beds*
Swing beds SNF/ICF 18.
Owner Proprietary corp.

Miami Health Care Center
3232 N County Rd 25A, Troy, OH 45373
(513) 339-5946
Medical Dir Mark J Peters MD.
Licensure Intermediate care. *Beds* ICF 150.
Certified Medicaid.
Owner Proprietary corp.

Staff Physicians 30 (pt); RNs 5 (ft), 5 (pt);
LPNs 9 (ft), 9 (pt); Nurses' aides 25 (ft), 11
(pt); Physical therapists; Recreational
therapists 3 (ft); Speech therapists; Activities
coordinators 1 (ft); Dietitians 1 (pt);
Ophthalmologists; Podiatrists; Dentists.
Facilities Dining room; Physical therapy
room; Activities room; Chapel; Crafts room;
Laundry room; Barber/Beauty shop; Library.
Activities Arts & crafts; Cards; Games;
Reading groups; Prayer groups; Movies;
Shopping trips; Dances/Social/Cultural
gatherings; Dinners; Theater; Special outings.

Villa Convalescent Center Inc
512 Crescent Dr, Troy, OH 45373
(513) 335-7161
Licensure Skilled care; Intermediate care. *Beds*
SNF 26; ICF 169. *Certified* Medicaid;
Medicare.
Owner Proprietary corp.

Uhrichsville

Dove Nursing Facility
Rte 1, Newport County Rd 28, Uhrichsville,
OH 44683
(614) 339-4544
Licensure Intermediate care. *Beds* ICF 32.
Certified Medicaid.
Owner Proprietary corp.

Rohrigs Nursing Home No 1
449-451 E 4th St, Uhrichsville, OH 44683
(614) 922-2610
Admin Margaret Rohrig LPN NHA.
Licensure Intermediate care. *Beds* ICF 14.
Certified Medicaid.
Owner Privately owned.
Admissions Requirements Medical
examination; Physician's request.
Staff RNs 1 (ft), 1 (pt); LPNs 2 (ft); Nurses'
aides 7 (ft), 1 (pt); Activities coordinators 2
(ft); Dietitians 1 (ft), 1 (pt); SSDs 2 (ft).
Facilities Dining room; Activities room;
Chapel; Crafts room; Laundry room.
Activities Arts & crafts; Cards; Games;
Reading groups; Prayer groups; Shopping
trips; Dances/Social/Cultural gatherings;
Outings.

Twin City Health Care Center Inc
200 Spanson Dr, Uhrichsville, OH 44683
(614) 922-2208
Admin Richard D McCloy. *Dir of Nursing*
Carole McCloy. *Medical Dir* Dr James Scott.
Licensure Intermediate care; Rest home. *Beds*
ICF 67; Rest home 29. *Certified* Medicaid.
Owner Proprietary corp.
Admissions Requirements Minimum age 18.
Staff RNs 4 (ft); LPNs 4 (ft); Nurses' aides 19
(ft); Activities coordinators 1 (ft), 1 (pt);
Dietitians 1 (pt).
Facilities Dining room; Physical therapy
room; Activities room; Crafts room; Laundry
room; Barber/Beauty shop.
Activities Arts & crafts; Cards; Games;
Reading groups; Movies; Shopping trips;
Dances/Social/Cultural gatherings.

Union City

Crotinger Nursing Home
907 Central Ave, Union City, OH 45390
(513) 968-5284, 968-3571
Admin Kim T Nye. *Dir of Nursing* Sue
Livingston. *Medical Dir* Dr C R Chambers.
Licensure Intermediate care. *Beds* ICF 50.
Certified Medicaid.
Owner Proprietary corp.
Staff RNs 1 (ft), 1 (pt); LPNs 3 (ft), 2 (pt);
Nurses' aides 29 (ft), 3 (pt); Activities
coordinators 1 (ft).

Facilities Activities room; Laundry room.
Activities Arts & crafts; Cards; Games;
Reading groups; Prayer groups; Movies;
Shopping trips; Dances/Social/Cultural
gatherings.

Union City Christel Manor
400 Gade Ave, Union City, OH 45390
(513) 968-6265
Licensure Intermediate care for mentally
retarded. *Beds* ICF/MR 50. *Certified*
Medicaid.
Owner Proprietary corp.

Upper Sandusky

**Fairhaven Retirement & Health Care
Community**
850 Marseilles Ave, Upper Sandusky, OH
43351
(419) 294-4973
Admin Gary E Ulrich. *Dir of Nursing* Lynn
Altvater RN. *Medical Dir* Thomas Thornton
MD.
Licensure Skilled care; Intermediate care;
Alzheimer's care; Retirement. *Beds* SNF
100; ICF 50. *Certified* Medicaid; Medicare.
Owner Nonprofit corp (United Church
Homes).
Admissions Requirements Minimum age 65.
Staff Physicians 1 (pt); RNs 16 (ft), 8 (pt);
LPNs 7 (ft), 4 (pt); Nurses' aides 44 (ft), 33
(pt); Physical therapists 1 (pt); Recreational
therapists 1 (ft), 1 (pt); Activities
coordinators 2 (ft), 2 (pt); Dietitians 1 (pt).
Affiliation Church of Christ.
Facilities Dining room; Physical therapy
room; Activities room; Chapel; Crafts room;
Laundry room; Barber/Beauty shop; Library.
Activities Arts & crafts; Cards; Games;
Reading groups; Prayer groups; Movies;
Shopping trips; Dances/Social/Cultural
gatherings.

Sunny Villa Care Center
342 S 8th, Upper Sandusky, OH 43351
(419) 294-3482
Admin Bernard D Fegan. *Dir of Nursing*
Paula Hurley LPN. *Medical Dir* Dr N J
Zohoury.
Licensure Intermediate care. *Beds* ICF 321.
Private Pay Patients 25%. *Certified*
Medicaid; Medicare.
Owner Proprietary corp (H & P Management
Inc).
Admissions Requirements Medical
examination; Physician's request.
Staff RNs; LPNs; Nurses' aides; Physical
therapists (contracted); Activities
coordinators; Dietitians (contracted).
Facilities Dining room; Activities room;
Laundry room.
Activities Arts & crafts; Cards; Games;
Reading groups; Movies; Shopping trips;
Dances/Social/Cultural gatherings; Pet
therapy.

Wyandot County Home
7830 N State Hwy 199, Upper Sandusky, OH
43351
(419) 294-1714
Admin Joseph D Jolliff. *Dir of Nursing* Jean
Aller.
Licensure Intermediate care. *Beds* ICF 100.
Certified Medicaid.
Owner Publicly owned.
Staff RNs; LPNs; Nurses' aides; Recreational
therapists; Activities coordinators.
Facilities Dining room; Activities room;
Chapel; Crafts room; Laundry room; Barber/
Beauty shop.
Activities Arts & crafts; Cards; Games;
Reading groups; Movies; Shopping trips;
Dances/Social/Cultural gatherings.

Wyandot Manor
800 Mission Dr, Upper Sandusky, OH 43351
(419) 294-3803

Admin Ann Stover-Wyatt. *Dir of Nursing*
Nancy Crisler. *Medical Dir* Dr William
Kose.
Licensure Skilled care; Intermediate care. *Beds*
Swing beds SNF/ICF 100. *Certified*
Medicaid; Medicare.
Owner Proprietary corp (HCF Inc).
Admissions Requirements Medical
examination; Physician's request.
Staff Physicians 1 (ft), 5 (pt); RNs 5 (ft), 1
(pt); LPNs 4 (ft), 1 (pt); Nurses' aides 30
(ft), 4 (pt); Physical therapists 1 (pt);
Recreational therapists 2 (ft), 1 (pt);
Occupational therapists 1 (pt); Speech
therapists 1 (pt); Activities coordinators 1
(ft); Dietitians 1 (ft); Ophthalmologists 1
(pt); Podiatrists 1 (pt); Dentists 1 (pt).
Facilities Dining room; Physical therapy
room; Activities room; Laundry room;
Barber/Beauty shop; Library; 3 lounges.
Activities Arts & crafts; Cards; Games; Prayer
groups; Movies; Shopping trips; Dances/
Social/Cultural gatherings; Bingo; Church
groups; Welcome new residents; Birthdays;
Cooking; Bingo; Gardening.

Urbana

Champaign County Residential Services Inc
400 N Oakland, Urbana, OH 43078
(513) 653-4076
Admin Than Johnson.
Medical Dir Mark Schlater.
Licensure Intermediate care for mentally
retarded. *Beds* ICF/MR 10. *Certified*
Medicaid.
Owner Proprietary corp.
Admissions Requirements Minimum age 18;
Medical examination.
Staff LPNs 1 (ft); Occupational therapists 1
(pt); Activities coordinators 1 (ft).
Facilities Dining room; Activities room;
Laundry room.
Activities Arts & crafts; Cards; Games;
Reading groups; Movies; Shopping trips;
Dances/Social/Cultural gatherings; Camping;
Special Olympics.

Champaign Nursing Home
PO Box 149, 2380 S Rte 68, Urbana, OH
43078
(513) 653-5291
Admin Dale R Long. *Dir of Nursing* Marty
Castle RN BS. *Medical Dir* Jae J Koh MD.
Licensure Skilled care; Intermediate care;
Intermediate care for mentally retarded.
Beds ICF/MR 20; Swing beds SNF/ICF 130.
Private Pay Patients 15%. *Certified*
Medicaid; Medicare.
Owner Publicly owned.
Staff Physicians 1 (pt); RNs 9 (ft), 1 (pt);
LPNs 10 (ft), 4 (pt); Nurses' aides 66 (ft), 5
(pt); Physical therapists 1 (pt); Recreational
therapists 1 (ft), 1 (pt); Occupational
therapists 1 (ft), 1 (pt); Speech therapists 2 (pt);
Activities coordinators 1 (ft); Dietitians 1
(pt); Ophthalmologists 1 (pt); Podiatrists 1
(pt); Audiologists 1 (pt).
Facilities Dining room; Physical therapy
room; Activities room; Chapel; Crafts room;
Laundry room; Barber/Beauty shop; Library.
Activities Arts & crafts; Cards; Games;
Reading groups; Prayer groups; Movies;
Shopping trips; Dances/Social/Cultural
gatherings; Intergenerational programs; Pet
therapy.

Heartland of Urbana
741 E Water St, Urbana, OH 43078
(513) 652-1381
Admin Daniel Higgins.
Medical Dir Dr Barry Paxton.
Licensure Skilled care; Intermediate care. *Beds*
Swing beds SNF/ICF 100. *Certified*
Medicaid; Medicare.
Owner Proprietary corp (Health Care and
Retirement Corp).

Admissions Requirements Minimum age 14;
Medical examination; Physician's request.
Staff RNs 5 (ft), 2 (pt); LPNs 6 (ft), 2 (pt);
Nurses' aides 31 (ft), 18 (pt); Physical
therapists 1 (pt); Occupational therapists 1
(pt); Speech therapists 1 (pt); Activities
coordinators 1 (ft), 1 (pt); Dietitians 1 (ft).
Facilities Dining room; Physical therapy
room; Activities room; Crafts room; Laundry
room; Barber/Beauty shop; Library.
Activities Arts & crafts; Cards; Games;
Reading groups; Prayer groups; Movies;
Shopping trips; Dances/Social/Cultural
gatherings.

McAuley Center
906 Scioto St, Urbana, OH 43078
(513) 653-5432
Licensure Skilled care; Intermediate care. *Beds*
Swing beds SNF/ICF 100. *Certified*
Medicaid; Medicare.
Owner Proprietary corp.

Scioto Street Home
334 Scioto St, Urbana, OH 43078
(513) 652-1194
Licensure Intermediate care for mentally
retarded. *Beds* ICF/MR 8. *Certified*
Medicaid.
Owner Nonprofit corp (Champaign County
Residential Services).

Utica

Utica Nursing Home
PO Box 618, 233 N Main St, Utica, OH
43080
(614) 892-3414
Admin Karen A Rosser. *Dir of Nursing* Mary
C Wilson. *Medical Dir* Dr Hernando
Posada.
Licensure Intermediate care. *Beds* ICF 35.
Certified Medicaid.
Owner Proprietary corp.
Admissions Requirements Medical
examination.
Staff Physicians 1 (pt); RNs 2 (ft), 1 (pt);
LPNs 2 (ft), 1 (pt); Nurses' aides 5 (ft), 8
(pt); Activities coordinators 1 (ft).
Facilities Dining room; Activities room;
Laundry room.
Activities Arts & crafts; Cards; Games; Prayer
groups; Shopping trips; Church.

Van Wert

Hillcrest Nursing Home
308 S Washington St, Van Wert, OH 45891
(419) 238-0975
Licensure Intermediate care. *Beds* ICF 25.
Certified Medicaid.
Owner Proprietary corp.

Van Wert Manor
160 Fox Rd, Van Wert, OH 45891
(419) 238-6655
Admin Laurie Weigt NHA. *Dir of Nursing*
Diane Stevenson RN. *Medical Dir* M J
Osborn DO.
Licensure Skilled care; Intermediate care. *Beds*
Swing beds SNF/ICF 100. *Private Pay
Patients* 25%. *Certified* Medicaid; Medicare.
Owner Proprietary corp (HCF Inc).
Admissions Requirements Medical
examination; Physician's request.
Staff Physicians 1 (pt); RNs 4 (ft), 3 (pt);
LPNs 11 (ft), 2 (pt); Nurses' aides 47 (ft);
Physical therapists 1 (pt); Occupational
therapists 1 (pt); Speech therapists 1 (pt);
Activities coordinators 1 (ft), 1 (pt);
Dietitians 1 (pt); Ophthalmologists 1 (pt);
Podiatrists 1 (pt); Audiologists 1 (pt).
Languages Sign.
Facilities Dining room; Physical therapy
room; Activities room; Chapel; Crafts room;
Laundry room; Barber/Beauty shop; Library;
Outside patios; Florida room; Porch swings.

Activities Arts & crafts; Cards; Games;
Reading groups; Prayer groups; Movies;
Shopping trips; Dances/Social/Cultural
gatherings; Intergenerational programs; Pet
therapy; County fair.

Vancrest
RR 4, Van Wert, OH 45891
(419) 238-4646
Admin Thelma L Thompson. *Dir of Nursing*
Ann Warnecke RN. *Medical Dir* A C Diller
MD.
Licensure Skilled care; Intermediate care. *Beds*
Swing beds SNF/ICF 50. *Certified* Medicaid;
Medicare.
Owner Proprietary corp.
Staff Physicians 2 (pt); RNs 1 (ft), 3 (pt);
LPNs 1 (ft), 5 (pt); Nurses' aides 22 (ft), 14
(pt); Physical therapists 1 (pt); Activities
coordinators 1 (ft); Dietitians 1 (pt);
Ophthalmologists 1 (pt).
Facilities Dining room; Physical therapy
room; Activities room; Crafts room; Laundry
room; Barber/Beauty shop.
Activities Arts & crafts; Cards; Games;
Reading groups; Movies; Dances/Social/
Cultural gatherings.

Vandalia

Franklin Nursing Center of Vandalia
208 N Cassell Rd, Vandalia, OH 45377
(513) 898-4202
Licensure Intermediate care. *Beds* ICF 161.
Certified Medicaid.
Owner Proprietary corp.

Vermilion

Riverview Nursing Home
5472 Liberty St, Vermilion, OH 44089
(216) 967-6614
Admin C York.
Licensure Intermediate care. *Beds* 19.
Certified Medicaid.
Owner Proprietary corp.
Admissions Requirements Medical
examination; Physician's request.
Staff RNs 1 (pt); LPNs 2 (ft), 4 (pt); Nurses'
aides 9 (ft), 2 (pt); Reality therapists 1 (pt);
Activities coordinators 1 (ft); Dietitians 1
(ft); Podiatrists 1 (ft).
Facilities Dining room; Activities room;
Crafts room; Laundry room; Barber/Beauty
shop.
Activities Arts & crafts; Cards; Games;
Reading groups; Prayer groups; Movies;
Shopping trips.

Vermilion Manor Nursing Home
4210 Telegraph Ln, Vermilion, OH 44089
(216) 967-1800
Licensure Skilled care; Intermediate care. *Beds*
Swing beds SNF/ICF 100. *Certified*
Medicaid; Medicare.
Owner Proprietary corp (HCF Inc).

Versailles

Versailles Healthcare Center
200 Marker Rd, Versailles, OH 45380
(513) 526-5570
Admin Marilyn Barga. *Dir of Nursing* Shirley
Rockhold RN. *Medical Dir* Dr C W Platt.
Licensure Skilled care. *Beds* SNF 50. *Certified*
Medicaid.
Owner Proprietary corp (Community Care
Centers).
Staff RNs 3 (ft); LPNs 2 (ft), 3 (pt); Nurses'
aides 11 (ft), 15 (pt); Activities coordinators
1 (ft); Dietitians 1 (pt); Ophthalmologists 1
(pt).
Facilities Dining room; Activities room;
Chapel; Crafts room; Laundry room; Barber/
Beauty shop.

Activities Arts & crafts; Cards; Games; Reading groups; Prayer groups; Movies; Shopping trips; Dances/Social/Cultural gatherings.

Wadsworth

Magnolia Care Center
365 Johnson Rd, Wadsworth, OH 44281
(216) 335-1558
Admin Kevin J Sabo. *Dir of Nursing* Peg Barber RN. *Medical Dir* William Knapic MD.
Licensure Skilled care; Intermediate care. *Beds* Swing beds SNF/ICF 109. *Certified* Medicaid; Medicare.
Owner Proprietary corp (Beverly Enterprises).
Admissions Requirements Minimum age 18.
Staff Physicians; RNs; LPNs; Nurses' aides; Physical therapists; Speech therapists; Activities coordinators; Dietitians; Ophthalmologists; Podiatrists; Dentists.
Facilities Dining room; Physical therapy room; Activities room; Chapel; Crafts room; Laundry room; Barber/Beauty shop.
Activities Arts & crafts; Cards; Games; Reading groups; Prayer groups; Movies; Shopping trips; Dances/Social/Cultural gatherings.

Society for Handicapped Citizens of Medina County Inc
165 2nd St, Wadsworth, OH 44281
(216) 725-7041
Licensure Intermediate care for mentally retarded. *Beds* ICF/MR 7. *Certified* Medicaid.
Owner Proprietary corp.

Wadsworth Health Care Center Inc
147 Garfield St, Wadsworth, OH 44281
(216) 335-2555
Licensure Skilled care; Intermediate care. *Beds* Swing beds SNF/ICF 112. *Certified* Medicaid; Medicare.
Owner Proprietary corp.

Walnut Creek

Walnut Hills Nursing Home Inc
4748 Olde Pump St, Walnut Creek, OH 44687
(216) 852-2457
Admin David A Miller.
Licensure Intermediate care; Retirement. *Beds* ICF 102. *Certified* Medicaid.
Owner Proprietary corp.
Staff Physicians; RNs; LPNs; Nurses' aides; Activities coordinators.
Languages Pennsylvania Dutch.
Facilities Dining room; Activities room; Crafts room; Laundry room; Barber/Beauty shop; Library.
Activities Arts & crafts; Cards; Games; Reading groups; Prayer groups; Movies; Shopping trips; Dances/Social/Cultural gatherings.

Walnut Hills Rest Home
4770 Olde Pump St, Walnut Creek, OH 44687
(216) 852-2457
Licensure Rest home. *Beds* Rest home 80.
Owner Proprietary corp.

Wapakoneta

Auglaize Acres
Rte 4, Wapakoneta, OH 45895
(419) 738-3816, 738-3819
Admin Alice Dewese. *Dir of Nursing* Marie Perrin RN. *Medical Dir* Robert J Herman MD.
Licensure Intermediate care. *Beds* ICF 142. *Certified* Medicaid.
Owner Publicly owned.
Admissions Requirements Minimum age 18; Medical examination.

Staff RNs 3 (ft), 8 (pt); LPNs 12 (ft), 3 (pt); Nurses' aides 31 (ft), 12 (pt); Activities coordinators 3 (ft).
Facilities Dining room; Physical therapy room; Activities room; Chapel; Crafts room; Laundry room; Barber/Beauty shop; Solariums.
Activities Arts & crafts; Cards; Games; Reading groups; Prayer groups; Movies; Shopping trips; Dances/Social/Cultural gatherings.

Wapakoneta Manor
RR 4, Rte 501, Wapakoneta, OH 45895
(419) 738-3711
Admin Iva DeWitt Hoblet.
Medical Dir Charlotte E Newland.
Licensure Skilled care; Intermediate care. *Beds* Swing beds SNF/ICF 100. *Certified* Medicaid; Medicare.
Owner Proprietary corp (HCF Inc).
Staff Physicians 4 (pt); RNs 2 (ft), 3 (pt); LPNs 6 (ft), 6 (pt); Nurses' aides 29 (ft), 17 (pt); Physical therapists 1 (pt); Occupational therapists 1 (pt); Speech therapists 1 (pt); Activities coordinators 1 (pt); Dietitians 1 (ft), 1 (pt); Ophthalmologists 1 (pt); Podiatrists 1 (pt); Dentists 1 (pt).
Facilities Dining room; Physical therapy room; Activities room; Laundry room; Barber/Beauty shop; Library.
Activities Arts & crafts; Games; Reading groups; Prayer groups; Movies; Dances/Social/Cultural gatherings.

Warren

Albert's Nursing & Residential Facility
PO Box 2357, Warren, OH 44484-0357
(216) 369-2137
Medical Dir Dr Frank Guarnieri.
Licensure Intermediate care for mentally retarded. *Beds* ICF/MR 32. *Certified* Medicaid.
Owner Proprietary corp.
Staff Physicians 1 (pt); RNs 1 (pt); LPNs 4 (ft), 1 (pt); Nurses' aides 32 (ft), 8 (pt); Physical therapists 1 (pt); Occupational therapists 1 (pt); Speech therapists 1 (pt); Activities coordinators 1 (ft); Dietitians 1 (pt); Ophthalmologists 1 (pt); Podiatrists 1 (pt); Audiologists 1 (pt); Dentists 1 (pt).
Activities Arts & crafts; Cards; Games; Reading groups; Prayer groups; Movies; Shopping trips; Dances/Social/Cultural gatherings.

Albert's Nursing Home
PO Box 2357, 2035 Van Wye SE, Warren, OH 44484-0357
(216) 369-2534, 369-2642 FAX
Admin Helen Albert. *Dir of Nursing* Arlene Jobe RN. *Medical Dir* Jagdish Patel MD.
Licensure Skilled care; Intermediate care; Intermediate care for mentally retarded. *Beds* ICF/MR 28; Swing beds SNF/ICF 21. *Private Pay Patients* 1%. *Certified* Medicaid; Medicare.
Owner Privately owned.
Admissions Requirements Medical examination; Physician's request.
Staff Physicians 3 (pt); RNs 1 (ft), 3 (pt); LPNs 4 (ft); Nurses' aides 26 (ft), 5 (pt); Physical therapists 1 (pt); Occupational therapists 1 (pt); Speech therapists 1 (pt); Activities coordinators 2 (pt); Dietitians 1 (pt); Podiatrists 1 (pt); Audiologists 1 (pt); Physical therapy aides 1 (pt); Occupational therapy aides 1 (pt).
Facilities Dining room; Physical therapy room; Activities room; Laundry room.
Activities Arts & crafts; Cards; Games; Reading groups; Prayer groups; Movies; Shopping trips; Dances/Social/Cultural gatherings; Pet therapy.

Community Skilled Nursing Centre of Warren
1320 Mahoning Ave NW, Warren, OH 44483
(216) 373-1160
Admin Charles E Hogan.
Medical Dir Dr J N Cavalier.
Licensure Skilled care; Intermediate care; Alzheimer's care. *Beds* Swing beds SNF/ICF 160. *Certified* Medicaid; Medicare.
Owner Proprietary corp.
Admissions Requirements Medical examination; Physician's request.
Staff Physicians 2 (ft); RNs 9 (ft), 7 (pt); LPNs 17 (ft), 6 (pt); Nurses' aides 86 (ft), 3 (pt); Physical therapists 1 (ft); Reality therapists 1 (pt); Occupational therapists 1 (ft); Speech therapists 1 (pt); Activities coordinators 2 (ft); Dietitians 1 (ft); Ophthalmologists 1 (pt).
Facilities Dining room; Physical therapy room; Activities room; Chapel; Crafts room; Laundry room; Barber/Beauty shop.
Activities Arts & crafts; Cards; Games; Reading groups; Prayer groups; Movies; Shopping trips; Dances/Social/Cultural gatherings.

Gillette Nursing Home
3310 Elm Rd, Warren, OH 44483
(216) 372-1960
Medical Dir Dr List.
Licensure Intermediate care. *Beds* ICF 100. *Certified* Medicaid.
Owner Proprietary corp.
Admissions Requirements Medical examination; Physician's request.
Staff Physicians 1 (pt); RNs 1 (pt); LPNs 5 (ft); Nurses' aides 9 (ft); Activities coordinators 1 (pt); Dietitians 1 (pt); Podiatrists 1 (pt).

Gillette's The Country Place
2473 North Rd NE, Warren, OH 44483
(216) 372-2251
Admin Bruce E Maher. *Dir of Nursing* Dolores Lehman RN. *Medical Dir* Walter I Droba MD.
Licensure Skilled care; Intermediate care. *Beds* Swing beds SNF/ICF 222. *Certified* Medicaid; Medicare.
Owner Proprietary corp (Horizon Healthcare Corp).
Admissions Requirements Medical examination.
Staff Physicians 6 (pt); RNs 5 (ft), 2 (pt); LPNs 24 (ft), 1 (pt); Nurses' aides 70 (ft), 5 (pt); Physical therapists 1 (pt); Occupational therapists 1 (pt); Speech therapists 1 (pt); Activities coordinators 1 (ft); Dietitians 1 (pt); Ophthalmologists 1 (pt); Podiatrists 1 (pt); Dentists 1 (pt); Social service coordinators 2 (pt).
Languages Greek.
Facilities Dining room; Physical therapy room; Laundry room; Barber/Beauty shop.
Activities Arts & crafts; Cards; Games; Reading groups; Prayer groups; Movies; Shopping trips; Dances/Social/Cultural gatherings; Breakfast & lunch outings; Baking; Gardening; Personal grooming.

Imperial Skilled Care Center
4121 Tod Ave NW, Warren, OH 44485
(216) 898-4033
Admin Betty Gowdy. *Dir of Nursing* Ann Kolmorgen RN. *Medical Dir* Walter Droba MD.
Licensure Skilled care; Intermediate care. *Beds* SNF 28; ICF 93. *Private Pay Patients* 4%. *Certified* Medicaid; Medicare.
Owner Proprietary corp.
Admissions Requirements Medical examination; Physician's request.
Staff Physicians 3 (pt); RNs 3 (ft), 4 (pt); LPNs 6 (ft), 5 (pt); Nurses' aides 26 (ft), 17 (pt); Physical therapists 1 (ft); Occupational therapists 1 (ft); Speech therapists 1 (ft);

Activities coordinators 2 (ft); Dietitians 1 (ft); Ophthalmologists 1 (pt); Podiatrists 1 (pt); Audiologists 1 (pt).
Facilities Dining room; Physical therapy room; Activities room; Crafts room; Laundry room; Barber/Beauty shop.
Activities Arts & crafts; Cards; Games; Reading groups; Prayer groups; Movies; Shopping trips; Dances/Social/Cultural gatherings.

Ridge Crest Care Center
1926 Ridge Ave SE, Warren, OH 44484
(216) 369-4672, 369-6486 FAX
Admin Richard W Porter. *Dir of Nursing* Jane Banning-Lucarell. *Medical Dir* Julio Cuesta.
Licensure Skilled care; Intermediate care; Alzheimer's care. *Beds* SNF 8; ICF 56. *Private Pay Patients* 19%. *Certified* Medicaid.
Owner Proprietary corp (Horizon Health Care Corp).
Admissions Requirements Medical examination.
Staff Physicians (contracted); RNs 2 (ft), 1 (pt); LPNs 10 (ft), 2 (pt); Nurses' aides 32 (ft), 8 (pt); Physical therapists 2 (pt); Reality therapists (contracted); Recreational therapists (contracted); Occupational therapists 2 (pt); Speech therapists 3 (pt); Activities coordinators 2 (ft); Dietitians 1 (pt); Ophthalmologists (contracted); Podiatrists (contracted); Audiologists (contracted).
Facilities Dining room; Physical therapy room; Activities room; Laundry room; Barber/Beauty shop; 36-bed Alzheimer's unit with large enclosed courtyard.
Activities Arts & crafts; Cards; Games; Reading groups; Prayer groups; Movies; Shopping trips; Dances/Social/Cultural gatherings; Intergenerational programs; Pet therapy.

Washington Square Nursing Center
202 Washington St NW, Warren, OH 44483
(216) 399-8997, 393-5889 FAX
Admin Bruce Maher. *Dir of Nursing* D Rae Lehman RN. *Medical Dir* Dr Pollis; Dr McGuire.
Licensure Intermediate care; Alzheimer's care. *Beds* ICF 100. *Certified* Medicaid.
Owner Proprietary corp (Horizon Healthcare Corp).
Admissions Requirements Medical examination.
Staff RNs 4 (ft), 1 (pt); LPNs 7 (ft), 2 (pt); Nurses' aides 15 (ft), 10 (pt); Physical therapists 1 (pt); Occupational therapists 1 (pt); Speech therapists 1 (pt); Activities coordinators 1 (ft); Dietitians 1 (pt); Ophthalmologists 1 (pt); Podiatrists 1 (pt).
Facilities Dining room; Physical therapy room; Activities room; Crafts room; Laundry room; Barber/Beauty shop.
Activities Arts & crafts; Cards; Games; Prayer groups; Movies; Shopping trips; Dances/Social/Cultural gatherings; Intergenerational programs.

Warrensville

Cuyahoga County Hospital—Sunny Acres
4310 Richmond Rd, Warrensville, OH 44122
(216) 464-9500
Admin W J Wilson.
Medical Dir William G Ansley MD.
Licensure Skilled care. *Beds* SNF 320. *Certified* Medicaid; Medicare.
Owner Publicly owned.
Admissions Requirements Minimum age 15.
Staff Physicians 9 (ft); RNs 75 (ft), 20 (pt); LPNs 19 (ft), 3 (pt); Nurses' aides 158 (ft); Physical therapists 4 (ft), 1 (pt); Recreational therapists 1 (ft); Occupational therapists 3 (ft); Activities coordinators 1 (ft); Dietitians 2 (ft); Dentists 1 (pt).

Facilities Dining room; Physical therapy room; Activities room; Chapel; Crafts room; Laundry room; Barber/Beauty shop; Library.
Activities Arts & crafts; Cards; Games; Reading groups; Prayer groups; Movies; Shopping trips; Special entertainment.

Warrensville Heights

Warrensville Center
4325 Green Rd, Warrensville Heights, OH 44128
Licensure Intermediate care for mentally retarded. *Beds* 261. *Certified* Medicaid.
Owner Publicly owned.

Warsaw

Echoing Hills Residential Center
36272 CR 79, Warsaw, OH 43844
(614) 327-2311
Medical Dir Jerold Meyer MD.
Licensure Intermediate care for mentally retarded. *Beds* ICF/MR 50. *Certified* Medicaid.
Owner Nonprofit corp.
Admissions Requirements Minimum age 18; Medical examination.
Staff Physicians 1 (pt); RNs 5 (ft); LPNs 5 (ft), 2 (pt); Nurses' aides 40 (ft), 1 (pt); Physical therapists 1 (pt); Occupational therapists 1 (pt); Speech therapists 1 (pt); Activities coordinators 1 (ft); Dietitians 1 (pt); Ophthalmologists 1 (pt); Podiatrists 1 (pt); Dentists 1 (pt).
Facilities Dining room; Physical therapy room; Activities room; Laundry room; Library.
Activities Arts & crafts; Prayer groups; Movies; Shopping trips; Dances/Social/Cultural gatherings; Camping; Travel.

Washington Court House

Auburn Manor
375 Glenn Ave, Washington Court House, OH 43160
(614) 335-0204
Admin Theresa Haynes. *Dir of Nursing* Marsha Snyder RN. *Medical Dir* Dr Robert Heiny.
Licensure Skilled care; Intermediate care. *Beds* Swing beds SNF/ICF 99. *Private Pay Patients* 30%. *Certified* Medicaid; Medicare.
Owner Proprietary corp (Trinity Living Centers).
Admissions Requirements Medical examination; Physician's request.
Staff RNs; LPNs; Nurses' aides; Physical therapists; Activities coordinators; Dietitians.
Facilities Dining room; Physical therapy room; Activities room; Chapel; Crafts room; Laundry room; Barber/Beauty shop.
Activities Cards; Games; Reading groups; Prayer groups; Movies; Dances/Social/Cultural gatherings; Pet therapy.

Case Convalescent Center
726 Rawling St, Washington Court House, OH 43160
(614) 335-7143
Licensure Skilled care; Intermediate care. *Beds* Swing beds SNF/ICF 144. *Certified* Medicaid; Medicare.
Owner Proprietary corp.

Court House Manor
250 Glenn Ave, Washington Court House, OH 43160
(614) 335-9290, 335-9337 FAX
Admin Laura S Pride NHA. *Dir of Nursing* Cindy Le Master RN. *Medical Dir* Ralph Gebhart MD.
Licensure Skilled care; Intermediate care; Alzheimer's care. *Beds* Swing beds SNF/ICF 100. *Private Pay Patients* 20%. *Certified* Medicaid; Medicare.

Owner Proprietary corp (HCF Inc).
Admissions Requirements Medical examination.
Staff Physicians 1 (pt); RNs 4 (ft); LPNs 10 (ft), 6 (pt); Nurses' aides 28 (ft), 19 (pt); Physical therapists 1 (pt); Speech therapists 1 (pt); Activities coordinators 1 (ft), 1 (pt); Dietitians 1 (ft); Podiatrists 1 (pt); Audiologists 1 (pt).
Facilities Dining room; Physical therapy room; Activities room; Laundry room; Barber/Beauty shop.
Activities Arts & crafts; Cards; Games; Reading groups; Prayer groups; Movies; Shopping trips; Dances/Social/Cultural gatherings; Intergenerational programs; Pet therapy.

Green Acres Nursing Home
6674 Stafford Rd, Washington Court House, OH 43160
(614) 335-2511
Licensure Intermediate care. *Beds* ICF 25. *Certified* Medicaid.
Owner Proprietary corp.
Admissions Requirements Medical examination; Physician's request.
Staff Physicians 1 (ft); RNs 1 (pt); LPNs 3 (ft); Nurses' aides 7 (ft); Physical therapists 1 (ft); Activities coordinators 1 (ft); Dietitians 1 (ft); Dentists 1 (pt).
Facilities Dining room; Laundry room.
Activities Arts & crafts; Cards; Games; Prayer groups; Shopping trips.

Quiet Acres
1771 Palmer Rd, Washington Court House, OH 43160
(614) 335-6391
Admin Pierre Sweeney. *Dir of Nursing* Cynthia Stoncrock. *Medical Dir* Robert U Anderson MD.
Licensure Intermediate care. *Beds* ICF 50. *Certified* Medicaid.
Owner Privately owned.
Staff RNs 1 (ft); LPNs 3 (ft), 3 (pt); Nurses' aides 10 (ft), 6 (pt); Activities coordinators 1 (ft); Dietitians 1 (pt).
Facilities Dining room; Activities room; Laundry room; Barber/Beauty shop.
Activities Arts & crafts; Cards; Games; Reading groups; Prayer groups; Movies; Shopping trips.

Wintersong Village of Washington Court House Inc
719 Rawling St, Washington Court House, OH 43160
(614) 335-1380
Medical Dir Dr Hugh Payton.
Licensure Intermediate care. *Beds* ICF 50. *Certified* Medicaid.
Owner Proprietary corp.
Staff Physicians 5 (pt); RNs 1 (ft), 1 (pt); LPNs 4 (ft); Nurses' aides 10 (ft), 6 (pt); Activities coordinators 1 (ft); Dietitians 1 (pt); Podiatrists 1 (pt).
Facilities Dining room; Activities room; Laundry room.
Activities Arts & crafts; Cards; Games; Reading groups; Prayer groups; Shopping trips.

Waterville

Browning Care Center
8885 Browning Rd, Waterville, OH 43566
(419) 878-8523
Licensure Skilled care; Intermediate care. *Beds* Swing beds SNF/ICF 149. *Certified* Medicaid; Medicare.
Owner Nonprofit corp (Health Care and Retirement Corp).

Hillcrest Care Center
564 S River Rd, Box 19, Waterville, OH 43566
(419) 878-0118

Admin William J Krech II. *Dir of Nursing*
Debbie Anello RN BSN.
Licensure Intermediate care; Retirement. *Beds*
ICF 100. *Certified* Medicaid.
Owner Proprietary corp (Columbia Corp).
Admissions Requirements Medical
examination.
Staff RNs 8 (ft), 2 (pt); LPNs 10 (ft), 2 (pt);
Nurses' aides 34 (ft), 16 (pt); Physical
therapists 1 (pt); Reality therapists 1 (ft);
Recreational therapists 1 (ft); Occupational
therapists 1 (pt); Speech therapists 1 (pt);
Dietitians 1 (pt).
Languages Sign.
Facilities Dining room; Physical therapy
room; Activities room; Crafts room; Laundry
room; Barber/Beauty shop.
Activities Arts & crafts; Cards; Games;
Reading groups; Prayer groups; Movies;
Shopping trips; Dances/Social/Cultural
gatherings.

Wauseon

Detwiler Manor
604 S Shoop Ave, Wauseon, OH 43567
(419) 337-9250
Admin Spence Tiffany. *Dir of Nursing* Carol
Hayes. *Medical Dir* Ben H Reed MD.
Licensure Intermediate care. *Beds* ICF 71.
Private Pay Patients 30%. *Certified*
Medicaid.
Owner Publicly owned.
Admissions Requirements Medical
examination; Physician's request.
Staff RNs 3 (ft), 1 (pt); LPNs 6 (ft); Nurses'
aides 14 (ft), 9 (pt); Activities coordinators 1
(ft), 2 (pt); Dietitians 1 (pt).
Facilities Dining room; Activities room;
Chapel; Laundry room; Barber/Beauty shop.
Activities Arts & crafts; Cards; Games;
Movies; Shopping trips; Dances/Social/
Cultural gatherings; Intergenerational
programs; Pet therapy.

Fulton County Family Care Home
410 N Fulton St, Wauseon, OH 43567
(419) 337-7346
Licensure Intermediate care for mentally
retarded. *Beds* ICF/MR 6. *Certified*
Medicaid.
Owner Publicly owned.

Heartland of Wauseon
303 W Leggett St, Box 1, Wauseon, OH 43567
(419) 337-3050
Licensure Skilled care; Intermediate care. *Beds*
SNF 12; ICF 41. *Certified* Medicaid;
Medicare.
Owner Proprietary corp (Health Care and
Retirement Corp).

Waverly

**Buckeye Community Services—Grandview
Avenue Homes**
207 Grandview Ave, Waverly, OH 45690
(614) 286-5039
Licensure Intermediate care for mentally
retarded. *Beds* ICF/MR 8. *Certified*
Medicaid.
Owner Proprietary corp.

Gayhart's Nursing Home
119 Valley View Dr, Waverly, OH 45690
(614) 289-4024
Licensure Intermediate care. *Beds* ICF 30.
Certified Medicaid.
Owner Proprietary corp.

Mullins Nursing Home
444 Cherry St, Waverly, OH 45690
(614) 289-4360
Licensure Intermediate care. *Beds* ICF 32.
Certified Medicaid.
Owner Proprietary corp.

Waynesville

Heffner's Ivy Cottage Nursing Home
RR 3, 5596 Elbon Rd, Waynesville, OH
45068
(513) 932-3950
Admin Phyllis D Arnold.
Licensure Intermediate care. *Beds* ICF 25.
Certified Medicaid.
Owner Proprietary corp.
Admissions Requirements Minimum age 18;
Medical examination.
Staff RNs 1 (pt); LPNs 2 (ft), 1 (pt); Nurses'
aides 5 (ft), 1 (pt); Activities coordinators 1
(pt).
Facilities Dining room; Activities room.
Activities Arts & crafts; Games; Movies;
Shopping trips; Dances/Social/Cultural
gatherings.

Quaker Heights Nursing Home
514 W High St, Box 677, Waynesville, OH
45068
(513) 897-6050
Medical Dir John Murphy III.
Licensure Intermediate care. *Beds* ICF 98.
Certified Medicaid.
Owner Proprietary corp.
Admissions Requirements Medical
examination.
Staff Physicians 6 (pt); RNs 7 (ft); LPNs 9
(ft); Nurses' aides 37 (ft); Physical therapists
1 (pt); Activities coordinators 2 (ft);
Dietitians 1 (ft); Dentists 1 (ft).
Affiliation Society of Friends.
Facilities Dining room; Physical therapy
room; Activities room; Crafts room; Laundry
room; Barber/Beauty shop.
Activities Arts & crafts; Cards; Games;
Reading groups; Prayer groups; Movies;
Dances/Social/Cultural gatherings.

Wellington

Elms Nursing Home
136 S Main St, Wellington, OH 44090
(216) 647-2414
Admin Janet A Ohman; Ralph S Keller. *Dir of
Nursing* Mary Hartmann RN. *Medical Dir*
Dr Leonard Nagle.
Licensure Intermediate care. *Beds* ICF 74.
Private Pay Patients 40%. *Certified*
Medicaid.
Owner Proprietary corp.
Admissions Requirements Minimum age 65.
Staff Physicians 7 (pt); RNs 2 (ft), 2 (pt);
LPNs 5 (ft), 6 (pt); Nurses' aides 20 (ft), 12
(pt); Activities coordinators 1 (ft), 1 (pt);
Dietitians (consultant); Ophthalmologists
(consultant); Podiatrists (consultant);
Physical therapy aides 1 (pt); Dentists
(consultant).
Facilities Dining room; Activities room;
Laundry room; Barber/Beauty shop.
Activities Arts & crafts; Cards; Games;
Reading groups; Prayer groups; Movies;
Dances/Social/Cultural gatherings;
Intergenerational programs; Pet therapy;
Monthly birthday parties; Special occasion/
holiday parties; Non-denominational Sunday
services.

Weber Health Care Center Inc
214 Herrick Ave E, Wellington, OH 44090
(216) 647-2088
Licensure Intermediate care; Intermediate care
for mentally retarded. *Beds* ICF 29; ICF/MR
40. *Certified* Medicaid.
Owner Proprietary corp.

**Wellington Estates Inc—Hartford-Salem
Manor**
124-126 Forest St, Box 386, Wellington, OH
44090
(216) 647-2088

Licensure Intermediate care for mentally
retarded. *Beds* ICF/MR 10. *Certified*
Medicaid.
Owner Proprietary corp.

Wellington Manor
PO Box 393, 116 Prospect St, Wellington, OH
44090
(216) 647-3910
Admin Kay Justice. *Dir of Nursing* Kay
Justice. *Medical Dir* Jess Belza MD.
Licensure Intermediate care. *Beds* ICF 17.
Private Pay Patients 1%. *Certified* Medicaid.
Owner Proprietary corp.
Admissions Requirements Medical
examination; TB test results.
Staff Physicians 1 (ft); RNs 1 (ft); LPNs 3 (ft),
1 (pt); Nurses' aides 7 (ft), 6 (pt);
Recreational therapists 1 (ft); Activities
coordinators 1 (ft), 1 (pt); Dietitians 1 (pt);
Podiatrists 1 (pt).
Facilities Dining room; Activities room;
Laundry room.
Activities Arts & crafts; Cards; Games;
Reading groups; Prayer groups; Movies;
Shopping trips; Dances/Social/Cultural
gatherings.

Wellston

Edgewood Manor of Wellston Inc
405 N Park Ave, Wellston, OH 45692
(614) 384-2880
Medical Dir Dr A R Hambrick.
Licensure Intermediate care. *Beds* ICF 50.
Certified Medicaid.
Owner Proprietary corp.
Admissions Requirements Medical
examination.
Staff Physicians 1 (pt); RNs 1 (pt); LPNs 6
(ft); Nurses' aides 12 (ft), 1 (pt);
Recreational therapists 1 (ft); Activities
coordinators 1 (ft); Podiatrists 1 (pt);
Audiologists 1 (pt); Dentists 1 (pt).
Facilities Dining room; Activities room;
Crafts room; Laundry room; Barber/Beauty
shop.
Activities Arts & crafts; Cards; Games;
Reading groups; Prayer groups; Movies;
Shopping trips; Dances/Social/Cultural
gatherings.

Jenkins Memorial Nursing Home
142 Jenkins Memorial Rd, Wellston, OH
45692
(614) 384-2119
Licensure Skilled care; Intermediate care. *Beds*
Swing beds SNF/ICF 43. *Certified* Medicaid;
Medicare.
Owner Proprietary corp.

Wellsville

Mansion Health Care Center
1037 Main St, Wellsville, OH 43968
(216) 532-2085
Licensure Intermediate care. *Beds* ICF 21.
Certified Medicaid.
Owner Proprietary corp.

West Carrollton

Alternative Residences Inc—Indian Trail
400 Indian Trail, West Carrollton, OH 45449
(513) 228-2200
Licensure Intermediate care for mentally
retarded. *Beds* ICF/MR 8. *Certified*
Medicaid.
Owner Proprietary corp.

Elm Creek Nursing Center
115 Elmwood Cir, West Carrollton, OH 45449
(513) 866-3814, 866-4320 FAX
Admin Sherlie S Baker. *Dir of Nursing* Darcie
Connolly-Hart RN. *Medical Dir* C Y Rhee
MD.

Licensure Skilled care; Intermediate care. *Beds* Swing beds SNF/ICF 100. *Private Pay Patients* 30%. *Certified* Medicaid; Medicare.
Owner Proprietary corp (Health Care Management Corp).
Admissions Requirements Minimum age 16; Medical examination; Physician's request.
Staff Physicians 1 (pt); RNs 5 (ft), 1 (pt); LPNs 8 (ft), 1 (pt); Nurses' aides 30 (ft), 3 (pt); Physical therapists 1 (pt); Recreational therapists 1 (ft); Occupational therapists 1 (pt); Speech therapists 1 (pt); Activities coordinators 2 (ft); Dietitians 1 (ft), 1 (pt); Ophthalmologists 1 (pt); Podiatrists 1 (pt); Audiologists 1 (pt); Restorative aides 1 (ft).
Facilities Dining room; Physical therapy room; Activities room; Crafts room; Laundry room; Barber/Beauty shop; 3 lounges; Private and semi-private rooms.
Activities Arts & crafts; Cards; Games; Prayer groups; Movies; Shopping trips; Dances/ Social/Cultural gatherings; Intergenerational programs; Pet therapy.

West Chester

Bonnie's Nursing Home Inc
9018 Cincinnati-Columbus Rd, West Chester, OH 45069
(513) 777-6363
Licensure Skilled care; Intermediate care. *Beds* Swing beds SNF/ICF 40.
Owner Proprietary corp.

Willows Nursing Home
9117 Cincinnati-Columbus Rd, West Chester, OH 45069
(513) 777-6164
Licensure Skilled care; Intermediate care. *Beds* Swing beds SNF/ICF 105. *Certified* Medicaid; Medicare.
Owner Proprietary corp.

West Jefferson

Hampton Court
375 W Main St, West Jefferson, OH 43162
(614) 879-7661
Licensure Skilled care; Intermediate care. *Beds* Swing beds SNF/ICF 50. *Certified* Medicaid; Medicare.
Owner Proprietary corp (Arbor Health Care).

West Lafayette

Dewhurst
PO Box 28, 22000 Orchard St, West Lafayette, OH 43845
(614) 545-6366
Licensure Intermediate care for mentally retarded. *Beds* ICF/MR 32. *Certified* Medicaid.
Owner Proprietary corp.

Edgerton Manor
22059 Orchard St, West Lafayette, OH 43845
(614) 545-6366
Admin Renee Guilliams.
Medical Dir W R Agricola MD.
Licensure Intermediate care for mentally retarded. *Beds* ICF/MR 15. *Certified* Medicaid.
Owner Proprietary corp.
Admissions Requirements Minimum age 4; Medical examination.
Staff Physicians 1 (pt); RNs 1 (ft); LPNs 4 (ft), 1 (pt); Nurses' aides 9 (ft), 3 (pt); Physical therapists 1 (pt); Recreational therapists 1 (ft); Occupational therapists 1 (pt); Speech therapists 1 (pt); Activities coordinators 1 (pt); Dietitians 2 (ft); Ophthalmologists 1 (pt); Podiatrists 1 (pt); Audiologists 1 (pt); Dentists 1 (pt).

Facilities Dining room; Activities room; Crafts room; Laundry room; Library.
Activities Arts & crafts; Cards; Games; Reading groups; Movies; Shopping trips; Dances/Social/Cultural gatherings.

Guilliams Family Home
220 S Kirk, West Lafayette, OH 43845
(614) 545-9058
Admin Renee Guilliams.
Medical Dir W R Agricola MD.
Licensure Intermediate care for mentally retarded. *Beds* ICF/MR 5. *Certified* Medicaid.
Owner Nonprofit corp.
Admissions Requirements Minimum age 16; Females only; Medical examination.
Staff Physicians 1 (pt); RNs 1 (pt); LPNs 1 (ft); Nurses' aides 3 (ft), 1 (pt); Physical therapists 1 (pt); Recreational therapists 1 (pt); Occupational therapists 1 (pt); Speech therapists 1 (pt); Activities coordinators 1 (pt); Ophthalmologists 1 (pt); Podiatrists 1 (pt); Audiologists 1 (pt); Dentists 1 (pt).
Facilities Dining room; Activities room; Crafts room; Laundry room.
Activities Arts & crafts; Cards; Games; Reading groups; Movies; Shopping trips; Dances/Social/Cultural gatherings.

Rose Lawn
PO Box 28, 21990 Orchard St, West Lafayette, OH 43845
(614) 545-6366
Admin Renee Guilliams.
Medical Dir W R Agricola MD.
Licensure Intermediate care for mentally retarded. *Beds* ICF/MR 30. *Certified* Medicaid.
Owner Proprietary corp.
Admissions Requirements Minimum age 4; Medical examination.
Staff Physicians 1 (pt); RNs 1 (ft), 1 (pt); LPNs 5 (ft), 1 (pt); Nurses' aides 13 (ft), 4 (pt); Physical therapists 1 (pt); Reality therapists 1 (pt); Occupational therapists 1 (pt); Speech therapists 1 (pt); Activities coordinators 1 (ft); Dietitians 4 (ft), 1 (pt); Ophthalmologists 1 (pt); Podiatrists 1 (pt); Audiologists 1 (pt); Dentists 1 (pt); Mental health technicians; Behavior modification specialists; Social workers; Special education teachers; QMRPs.
Facilities Dining room; Activities room; Crafts room; Laundry room; Library; Program areas.
Activities Arts & crafts; Cards; Games; Reading groups; Movies; Shopping trips; Dances/Social/Cultural gatherings.

West Lafayette Care Center
620 E Main St, West Lafayette, OH 43845
(614) 545-6355
Admin Atwood J Cool. *Dir of Nursing* D Ruth Cheney RN.
Licensure Intermediate care. *Beds* ICF 96. *Certified* Medicaid.
Owner Proprietary corp (Regency Health Care Centers).
Admissions Requirements Medical examination; Physician's request.
Staff RNs; LPNs; Nurses' aides; Physical therapists; Occupational therapists; Activities coordinators; Dietitians.
Facilities Dining room; Physical therapy room; Activities room; Crafts room; Laundry room; Barber/Beauty shop.
Activities Arts & crafts; Cards; Games; Reading groups; Prayer groups; Shopping trips.

West Liberty

Green Hills Center
6557 US 68 S, West Liberty, OH 43357
(513) 465-5065

Admin Kathy Boling. *Dir of Nursing* Lorraine Botkin RN BSN. *Medical Dir* Grant Varian MD.
Licensure Skilled care; Intermediate care; Alzheimer's unit; Adult day care; Apartment living. *Beds* Swing beds SNF/ICF 105; Apartment living 40. *Private Pay Patients* 34%. *Certified* Medicaid; Medicare.
Owner Nonprofit organization/foundation.
Admissions Requirements Medical examination; Physician's request.
Staff RNs 8 (ft), 9 (pt); LPNs 5 (ft), 6 (pt); Nurses' aides 28 (ft), 12 (pt); Physical therapists 1 (pt); Occupational therapists 1 (pt); Speech therapists 1 (pt); Activities coordinators 1 (pt); Dietitians 1 (pt); Podiatrists 1 (pt); Dentists 1 (pt).
Facilities Dining room; Physical therapy room; Activities room; Chapel; Crafts room; Laundry room; Barber/Beauty shop; Library; Speech therapy room; Soda Shoppe; Child day care; Adult day care center.
Activities Arts & crafts; Cards; Games; Reading groups; Prayer groups; Movies; Shopping trips; Dances/Social/Cultural gatherings; Intergenerational programs; Pet therapy.

West Union

Adams County Manor
10856 State Rte 41, West Union, OH 45693
(513) 544-2205
Admin Glenda Walton; Rosalie Hughes.
Medical Dir Gary Greenlee MD.
Licensure Intermediate care. *Beds* ICF 40. *Certified* Medicaid.
Owner Proprietary corp.
Staff RNs 2 (pt); LPNs 4 (ft), 2 (pt); Nurses' aides 11 (ft), 5 (pt); Recreational therapists 2 (pt); Activities coordinators 1 (ft); Dietitians 3 (pt).
Facilities Dining room; Activities room; Crafts room; Laundry room.
Activities Arts & crafts; Cards; Games; Reading groups; Prayer groups; Shopping trips; Dances/Social/Cultural gatherings.

Eagle Creek Nursing Center
141 Spruce Ln, West Union, OH 45693
(513) 544-5531, 544-5157 FAX
Admin Greg Stout. *Dir of Nursing* Juanita Wilson. *Medical Dir* Dale Mathias MD.
Licensure Skilled care; Intermediate care. *Beds* Swing beds SNF/ICF 100. *Private Pay Patients* 11%. *Certified* Medicaid; Medicare; VA.
Owner Proprietary corp (Health Care Management Corp).
Admissions Requirements Medical examination.
Staff Physicians 4 (pt); RNs 4 (ft), 2 (pt); LPNs 11 (ft), 4 (pt); Nurses' aides 41 (ft), 9 (pt); Physical therapists 1 (pt); Occupational therapists 2 (pt); Speech therapists 2 (pt); Activities coordinators 1 (ft); Dietitians 1 (ft), 1 (pt); Ophthalmologists 1 (pt); Podiatrists 1 (pt); Audiologists 1 (pt).
Facilities Dining room; Activities room; Crafts room; Laundry room; Barber/Beauty shop.
Activities Arts & crafts; Games; Reading groups; Prayer groups; Movies; Shopping trips; Dances/Social/Cultural gatherings; Intergenerational programs.

Revmont Nursing Home
7980 State Rte 125, West Union, OH 45693
(513) 544-2923
Admin Connie Fenton. *Dir of Nursing* Betty Brodt. *Medical Dir* Dr F Stevens.
Licensure Intermediate care. *Beds* ICF 16. *Private Pay Patients* 5%.
Owner Privately owned.
Admissions Requirements Minimum age 80; Females only.

Staff Physicians; RNs; LPNs; Nurses' aides; Activities coordinators; Dietitians.
Facilities Dining room; Activities room; Crafts room; Laundry room.
Activities Arts & crafts; Cards; Games; Reading groups; Prayer groups; Movies; Pet therapy.

West Unity

Egly Drive Family Home
101 Egly Dr, West Unity, OH 43570
(419) 924-2806
Licensure Intermediate care for mentally retarded. *Beds* ICF/MR 8. *Certified* Medicaid.
Owner Proprietary corp.

Westchester

Bonnie's Nursing Home
PO Box 363, 9018 Cincinnati-Columbus Rd, Westchester, OH 45069
(513) 777-6363
Admin Greg Carson.
Medical Dir Sandra Gilbert.
Licensure Intermediate care. *Beds* ICF 40.
Owner Proprietary corp.
Admissions Requirements Medical examination.
Staff LPNs; Nurses' aides; Activities coordinators; Dietitians.
Facilities Dining room; Activities room; Laundry room; Barber/Beauty shop.
Activities Arts & crafts; Cards; Games; Movies; Dances/Social/Cultural gatherings.

Westerville

Columbus Colony for the Elderly Care Inc
1150 Colony Dr, Westerville, OH 43081
(614) 891-5055
Admin Willliam L Stewart.
Medical Dir H T Villavacer MD.
Licensure Skilled care; Intermediate care. *Beds* Swing beds SNF/ICF 100. *Certified* Medicaid; Medicare.
Owner Proprietary corp.
Staff Physicians 1 (pt); RNs 5 (ft), 3 (pt); LPNs 5 (ft), 5 (pt); Nurses' aides 23 (ft), 23 (pt); Recreational therapists 1 (ft), 1 (pt); Activities coordinators 1 (ft).
Facilities Dining room; Physical therapy room; Activities room; Crafts room; Laundry room; Barber/Beauty shop.
Activities Arts & crafts; Cards; Games; Reading groups; Prayer groups; Movies; Shopping trips; Dances/Social/Cultural gatherings; Outings; Special meals.

Edgewood Manor of Westerville
140 N State St, Westerville, OH 43081
(614) 882-4055
Admin John H Law. *Dir of Nursing* Kathy Dettore. *Medical Dir* H T Villavacer MD.
Licensure Intermediate care. *Beds* ICF 70. *Certified* Medicaid.
Owner Proprietary corp.
Admissions Requirements Medical examination.
Staff Physicians 1 (ft); RNs 3 (ft), 3 (pt); LPNs 3 (ft), 5 (pt); Nurses' aides 14 (ft), 4 (pt); Physical therapists 1 (pt); Recreational therapists 1 (pt); Occupational therapists 1 (pt); Speech therapists 1 (pt); Activities coordinators 1 (ft), 1 (pt); Dietitians 1 (pt); Ophthalmologists 1 (pt); Dentists 1 (pt).
Facilities Dining room; Activities room; Crafts room; Laundry room; Barber/Beauty shop.
Activities Arts & crafts; Cards; Games; Reading groups; Prayer groups; Movies; Shopping trips; Dances/Social/Cultural gatherings.

Mann Nursing Home
25 W Home St, Westerville, OH 43081
(614) 882-2565
Admin Linda J Reash. *Dir of Nursing* Shirlee Tarfford RN. *Medical Dir* John Bohlen MD.
Licensure Intermediate care. *Beds* ICF 184. *Certified* Medicaid.
Owner Proprietary corp (Altercare Inc).
Admissions Requirements Medical examination.
Staff Physicians 1 (ft), 11 (pt); RNs 5 (ft), 4 (pt); LPNs 20 (ft), 20 (pt); Physical therapists 1 (pt); Reality therapists 1 (pt); Recreational therapists 1 (pt); Occupational therapists 1 (pt); Activities coordinators 1 (ft); Dietitians 1 (pt).
Facilities Dining room; Activities room; Crafts room; Laundry room; Barber/Beauty shop.
Activities Arts & crafts; Cards; Games; Reading groups; Prayer groups; Movies; Shopping trips; Dances/Social/Cultural gatherings.

Manor Care of Westerville Nursing Center
140 County Line Rd, Westerville, OH 43081
(614) 882-1511
Admin Robert Morris.
Medical Dir H T Villanecer MD; Patricia Custard MD.
Licensure Skilled care; Intermediate care; Alzheimer's care. *Beds* SNF 30; ICF 150. *Certified* Medicaid; Medicare.
Owner Proprietary corp (Manor Care).
Admissions Requirements Minimum age 18.
Staff RNs; LPNs; Nurses' aides; Physical therapists 1 (ft); Occupational therapists 1 (pt); Speech therapists 1 (pt); Activities coordinators 2 (ft); Dietitians 1 (ft); Ophthalmologists 1 (pt).
Facilities Dining room; Physical therapy room; Activities room; Barber/Beauty shop.
Activities Arts & crafts; Cards; Games; Reading groups; Prayer groups; Movies; Shopping trips; Dances/Social/Cultural gatherings.

Village at Westerville Nursing Center
1060 Eastwind Rd, Westerville, OH 43081
(614) 895-1038
Licensure Skilled care; Intermediate care. *Beds* SNF 24; ICF 76. *Certified* Medicaid; Medicare.
Owner Proprietary corp (Health Care and Retirement Corp).

Westlake

Dover Nursing Home
28305 Detroit Rd, Westlake, OH 44145
(216) 871-0500
Licensure Skilled care; Intermediate care. *Beds* Swing beds SNF/ICF 100. *Certified* Medicaid; Medicare.
Owner Proprietary corp.

Lutheran Home
2116 Dover Center Rd, Westlake, OH 44145
(216) 871-0090
Admin Mary J Zukie. *Dir of Nursing* Marjorie Gray RN. *Medical Dir* Carlos A Maldonado MD.
Licensure Skilled care; Intermediate care; Retirement. *Beds* Swing beds SNF/ICF 222; Retirement 12. *Certified* Medicaid; Medicare.
Owner Nonprofit organization/foundation.
Admissions Requirements Minimum age 65; Medical examination.
Staff Physicians 6 (pt); RNs; LPNs; Nurses' aides; Physical therapists 2 (pt); Occupational therapists 1 (pt); Activities coordinators 2 (pt); Dietitians 1 (pt); Podiatrists 1 (pt).
Affiliation Lutheran.
Facilities Dining room; Physical therapy room; Activities room; Chapel; Crafts room; Laundry room; Barber/Beauty shop.
Activities Arts & crafts; Cards; Games; Reading groups; Prayer groups; Movies; Dances/Social/Cultural gatherings; Intergenerational programs; Pet therapy.

Oakridge Home
26520 Center Ridge Rd, Westlake, OH 44145
(216) 871-3030
Admin Bryan Newmyer.
Medical Dir James L Rush MD.
Licensure Skilled care; Intermediate care. *Beds* Swing beds SNF/ICF 119. *Certified* Medicaid; Medicare.
Owner Nonprofit corp.
Admissions Requirements Medical examination.
Staff RNs 4 (ft), 6 (pt); LPNs 6 (ft), 5 (pt); Nurses' aides 33 (ft), 23 (pt); Physical therapists 1 (ft); Speech therapists 1 (pt); Activities coordinators 1 (ft); Dietitians 1 (pt).
Facilities Dining room; Physical therapy room; Activities room; Crafts room; Laundry room; Barber/Beauty shop.
Activities Arts & crafts; Cards; Games; Reading groups; Prayer groups; Movies; Shopping trips; Dances/Social/Cultural gatherings; Religious services; Resident suggested activities.

Rae-Ann Suburban
29505 Detroit Rd, Westlake, OH 44145
(216) 871-5181
Licensure Intermediate care. *Beds* ICF 54. *Certified* Medicaid.
Owner Proprietary corp.

Westbay Manor I
27601 Westchester Pkwy, Westlake, OH 44145
(216) 871-5900, 871-3180 FAX
Admin Elizabeth T Benson NHA. *Dir of Nursing* Carol Clancy RN. *Medical Dir* Robert Wagar MD.
Licensure Skilled care; Intermediate care. *Beds* SNF 12; ICF 141. *Private Pay Patients* 20%. *Certified* Medicaid; Medicare.
Owner Proprietary corp (Associated Health Care).
Admissions Requirements Medical examination.
Staff Physicians 1 (pt); RNs 8 (ft), 8 (pt); LPNs 11 (ft), 19 (pt); Nurses' aides 30 (ft), 32 (pt); Physical therapists 1 (ft); Recreational therapists 1 (ft), 2 (pt); Occupational therapists 1 (ft), 1 (pt) (consultant); Speech therapists 1 (pt); Activities coordinators 1 (ft); Dietitians 1 (pt); Podiatrists 1 (pt); Audiologists (consultant); Opticians 1 (pt).
Facilities Dining room; Physical therapy room; Activities room; Crafts room; Laundry room; Barber/Beauty shop; Library.
Activities Arts & crafts; Cards; Games; Reading groups; Prayer groups; Movies; Dances/Social/Cultural gatherings; Intergenerational programs; Pet therapy; Religious services.

Westbay Manor II
27601 Westchester Pkwy, Westlake, OH 44145
(216) 871-5900, 871-3180 FAX
Admin Elizabeth T Benson NHA. *Dir of Nursing* Ruth Toth RNC. *Medical Dir* Robert Wagar MD.
Licensure Skilled care; Intermediate care. *Beds* SNF 10; ICF 96. *Private Pay Patients* 90%. *Certified* Medicare.
Owner Proprietary corp (Associated Health Care).
Admissions Requirements Medical examination.
Staff Physicians 1 (pt); RNs 3 (ft), 3 (pt); LPNs 8 (ft), 13 (pt); Nurses' aides 24 (ft), 19 (pt); Physical therapists 1 (ft); Recreational therapists 2 (ft), 2 (pt); Occupational therapists (consultants); Speech therapists 1

(pt); Activities coordinators 1 (ft); Dietitians 1 (pt); Podiatrists 1 (pt); Audiologists (consultant); Opticians 1 (pt).
Facilities Dining room; Physical therapy room; Activities room; Crafts room; Laundry room; Barber/Beauty shop; Library.
Activities Arts & crafts; Cards; Games; Reading groups; Prayer groups; Movies; Dances/Social/Cultural gatherings; Intergenerational programs; Pet therapy; Visits by clergy; Religious services.

Wheelersburg

Best Care Nursing Facility
2159 Dogwood Ridge Rd, Wheelersburg, OH 45694
(614) 574-2558
Medical Dir W L Herrmann MD.
Licensure Skilled care; Intermediate care. *Beds* SNF 20; ICF 131. *Certified* Medicaid; Medicare.
Owner Proprietary corp.
Admissions Requirements Medical examination; Physician's request.
Staff Physicians; RNs; LPNs; Nurses' aides; Physical therapists; Reality therapists; Recreational therapists; Occupational therapists; Speech therapists; Activities coordinators 2 (ft), 2 (pt); Dietitians; Ophthalmologists; Podiatrists; Audiologists; Dentists.
Facilities Dining room; Physical therapy room; Activities room; Chapel; Crafts room; Laundry room; Barber/Beauty shop; Library.
Activities Arts & crafts; Cards; Games; Reading groups; Prayer groups; Movies; Shopping trips; Dances/Social/Cultural gatherings.

Greenbriar Convalescent Center
PO Box 29, 1242 Crescent Dr, Wheelersburg, OH 45694
(614) 574-8441
Licensure Skilled care; Intermediate care. *Beds* Swing beds SNF/ICF 151. *Certified* Medicaid; Medicare.
Owner Proprietary corp.

Whitehouse

Bittersweet Home
12660 Archbold-Whitehouse Rd, Whitehouse, OH 43571
(419) 875-6986
Admin Elizabeth Ruth Kay. *Dir of Nursing* Joan Koch.
Licensure Intermediate care for mentally retarded. *Beds* ICF/MR 20. *Private Pay Patients* 0%. *Certified* Medicaid.
Owner Nonprofit corp.
Admissions Requirements Minimum age 18.
Staff RNs 1 (ft); LPNs 1 (pt); Speech therapists 1 (pt); Activities coordinators 2 (ft); Dietitians 1 (pt).
Languages Sign.
Facilities Dining room; Activities room; Crafts room; Library; Farm; Woods; Swimming pool; Walking trails.
Activities Arts & crafts; Games; Movies; Shopping trips; Dances/Social/Cultural gatherings; Intergenerational programs; Pet therapy; Biking; Hiking; Handball; Choir.

Whitehouse Country Manor
11239 Waterville St, Whitehouse, OH 43571
(419) 877-5338
Admin Carol Husing. *Dir of Nursing* Catherine Dotson RN. *Medical Dir* Terry D Roode DO.
Licensure Intermediate care. *Beds* ICF 100. *Certified* Medicaid.
Owner Proprietary corp (Hillhaven Corp).
Admissions Requirements Medical examination.

Staff Physicians 1 (ft); RNs 2 (ft), 5 (pt); LPNs 5 (ft), 9 (pt); Nurses' aides 24 (ft), 26 (pt); Physical therapists 1 (pt); Reality therapists 7 (ft); Occupational therapists 1 (pt); Speech therapists 1 (pt); Activities coordinators 1 (ft), 1 (pt); Dietitians 1 (pt); Ophthalmologists 1 (pt); Podiatrists 1 (pt); Social workers 1 (ft).
Facilities Dining room; Activities room; Crafts room; Laundry room; Barber/Beauty shop.
Activities Arts & crafts; Cards; Games; Reading groups; Prayer groups; Movies; Dances/Social/Cultural gatherings; Discussion groups; Reality orientation; Birthday parties; Resident council; Eat-ins; Music; Grooming; Outings.

Wickliffe

Wickliffe Country Place
1919 Bishop Rd, Wickliffe, OH 44092
(216) 944-9400
Admin Bartlett T Bell.
Medical Dir David M Berzon MD.
Licensure Skilled care; Intermediate care. *Beds* SNF 37; Swing beds SNF/ICF 152. *Certified* Medicare.
Owner Proprietary corp.
Admissions Requirements Minimum age 15; Medical examination; Physician's request.
Staff Physicians 5 (pt); RNs 5 (ft), 6 (pt); Physical therapists 1 (ft); Reality therapists 1 (pt); Recreational therapists 2 (ft); Occupational therapists 1 (pt); Speech therapists 1 (pt); Activities coordinators 1 (ft); Dietitians 1 (ft); Ophthalmologists 1 (pt); Podiatrists 1 (pt); Dentists 1 (pt).
Facilities Dining room; Physical therapy room; Activities room; Crafts room; Laundry room; Barber/Beauty shop; Library.
Activities Arts & crafts; Cards; Games; Reading groups; Prayer groups; Movies; Shopping trips; Dances/Social/Cultural gatherings.

Willard

Hillside Acres
370 E Howard St, Willard, OH 44890
(419) 935-0148
Licensure Skilled care; Intermediate care; Retirement; Alzheimer's care. *Beds* Swing beds SNF/ICF 135. *Certified* Medicaid; Medicare.
Owner Proprietary corp.
Staff Physicians; RNs; LPNs; Nurses' aides; Physical therapists; Occupational therapists; Speech therapists; Activities coordinators; Dietitians; Ophthalmologists.
Facilities Dining room; Activities room; Chapel; Crafts room; Laundry room; Barber/Beauty shop.
Activities Arts & crafts; Cards; Games; Reading groups; Prayer groups; Movies; Shopping trips; Dances/Social/Cultural gatherings.

Willard Quality Care Nursing Center
725 Wessor Ave, Willard, OH 44890
(419) 935-6511
Admin Tamara Thornton. *Dir of Nursing* Sheryl L Long RN. *Medical Dir* Dr John Russo.
Licensure Skilled care; Intermediate care. *Beds* Swing beds SNF/ICF 51. *Certified* Medicaid; Medicare.
Owner Proprietary corp (Northwestern Service Corp).
Admissions Requirements Medical examination.
Staff Physicians 2 (ft), 4 (pt); RNs 1 (ft), 2 (pt); LPNs 3 (ft), 4 (pt); Nurses' aides 10 (ft), 10 (pt); Physical therapists 1 (pt); Activities coordinators 1 (ft); Dietitians 1 (ft); Ophthalmologists 1 (pt); Dentists 1 (pt).
Languages Spanish.

Facilities Dining room; Activities room; Crafts room; Laundry room; Barber/Beauty shop; Library.
Activities Arts & crafts; Cards; Games; Reading groups; Prayer groups; Movies; Shopping trips; Dances/Social/Cultural gatherings; Pet therapy.

Williamsburg

Locust Ridge Nursing Home Inc
12745 Elm Corner Rd, Williamsburg, OH 45176
(513) 444-2920, (800) 543-9074 FAX
Admin Howard L Meeker. *Dir of Nursing* Cheryl Phillips RN. *Medical Dir* Deborah Maham MD.
Licensure Skilled care; Intermediate care. *Beds* SNF 16; ICF 85. *Private Pay Patients* 25%. *Certified* Medicaid; Medicare.
Owner Proprietary corp.
Staff Physicians 9 (pt); RNs 4 (ft), 4 (pt); LPNs 13 (ft), 3 (pt); Nurses' aides 46 (ft), 3 (pt); Physical therapists 1 (ft); Activities coordinators 3 (ft); Dietitians 1 (ft).
Activities Arts & crafts; Cards; Games; Reading groups; Prayer groups; Movies; Dances/Social/Cultural gatherings; Evening outings; Zoo trips.

Williston

Luther Home of Mercy
5810 N Main St, Williston, OH 43468
(419) 836-7741
Admin Rev Donald L Wukotich. *Dir of Nursing* Dolores Schimming RN. *Medical Dir* Albert Perras MD.
Licensure Intermediate care for mentally retarded. *Beds* ICF/MR 129. *Certified* Medicaid.
Owner Proprietary corp.
Staff Physicians 1 (pt); RNs 2 (ft), 8 (pt); LPNs 12 (ft), 10 (pt); Nurses' aides 99 (ft), 29 (pt); Physical therapists 1 (pt); Recreational therapists 4 (ft); Occupational therapists 1 (pt); Speech therapists 1 (pt); Activities coordinators 1 (ft); Dietitians 1 (ft); Podiatrists 1 (ft).
Affiliation Lutheran.
Facilities Dining room; Physical therapy room; Activities room; Chapel; Crafts room.
Activities Arts & crafts; Cards; Games; Reading groups; Prayer groups; Movies; Shopping trips; Dances/Social/Cultural gatherings.

Willoughby

Fairmount Health Center of Breckenridge Village
36855 Ridge Rd, Willoughby, OH 44094
(216) 942-4342
Admin Philip Braisted. *Dir of Nursing* Gail Kahoun RN. *Medical Dir* Ian Glass MD.
Licensure Skilled care; Intermediate care; Retirement. *Beds* SNF 50; ICF 50; Retirement 758. *Private Pay Patients* 60%. *Certified* Medicaid; Medicare.
Owner Nonprofit corp (Ohio Presbyterian Retirement Services).
Admissions Requirements Minimum age 60; Medical examination.
Staff Physicians 1 (pt); RNs 5 (ft), 2 (pt); LPNs 9 (ft), 3 (pt); Nurses' aides 34 (ft), 9 (pt); Physical therapists 1 (pt); Occupational therapists 1 (pt); Speech therapists 1 (pt); Activities coordinators 1 (ft), 2 (pt); Dietitians 1 (pt); Ophthalmologists; Podiatrists; Audiologists; Chaplains 1 (pt).
Affiliation Presbyterian.
Facilities Dining room; Physical therapy room; Activities room; Laundry room; Barber/Beauty shop; Community plaza.

Activities Arts & crafts; Cards; Games;
Reading groups; Prayer groups; Movies;
Dances/Social/Cultural gatherings;
Intergenerational programs; Pet therapy;
Fitness programs; Educational classes.

Manor Care Willoughby
37603 Euclid Ave, Willoughby, OH 44094
(216) 951-5551, 951-8426 FAX
Admin Myra Knouff LNHA. *Dir of Nursing*
Shirley Craig RNC. *Medical Dir* Edwin V
Basquinez MD.
Licensure Skilled care; Intermediate care;
Alzheimer's care. *Beds* Swing beds SNF/ICF
131. *Certified* Medicaid; Medicare.
Owner Proprietary corp (Manor Healthcare
Corp).
Staff Physicians.
Facilities Dining room; Physical therapy
room; Activities room; Crafts room; Laundry
room; Barber/Beauty shop.
Activities Arts & crafts; Cards; Games;
Reading groups; Prayer groups; Movies;
Shopping trips; Intergenerational programs;
Pet therapy.

Wilmington

Senior Health Care Inc
PO Box 109, 201 E Locust St, Wilmington,
OH 45177
(513) 364-2695
Admin Ruth Reynolds NHA. *Dir of Nursing*
Zelma Johnson.
Licensure Intermediate care. *Beds* ICF 18.
Private Pay Patients 2%. *Certified* Medicaid.
Owner Proprietary corp (Alpha Nursing
Homes Inc).
Admissions Requirements Minimum age 16;
Medical examination; Physician's request.
Staff RNs 1 (ft); LPNs 1 (ft), 4 (pt); Nurses'
aides 5 (ft), 3 (pt); Activities coordinators 1
(ft); Dietitians 1 (pt).
Facilities Dining room; Activities room;
Laundry room.
Activities Arts & crafts; Cards; Games;
Reading groups; Prayer groups; Movies;
Shopping trips; Family participation;
Visitations by church groups.

Wilmington Extended Care Facility
75 Hale St, Wilmington, OH 45177
(513) 382-1621
Licensure Skilled care; Intermediate care. *Beds*
Swing beds SNF/ICF 104. *Certified*
Medicaid; Medicare.
Owner Proprietary corp.

Windsor

Town Hall Estates Windsor Inc
Rtes 322 & 534, Windsor, OH 44099
(216) 272-5600, 272-5600 FAX
Admin Donald E Stair. *Dir of Nursing* Nancy
Filipek. *Medical Dir* Douglas Burchette.
Licensure Intermediate care; Retirement;
Alzheimer's care. *Beds* ICF 99; Retirement
4. *Private Pay Patients* 30%. *Certified*
Medicaid.
Owner Nonprofit corp (American Religious
Town Hall Meeting Inc).
Admissions Requirements Minimum age 55;
Medical examination; Physician's request.
Staff Physicians 3 (pt); RNs 3 (ft), 1 (pt);
LPNs 7 (ft), 1 (pt); Recreational therapists 1
(ft); Activities coordinators 1 (ft); Dietitians
1 (pt); Podiatrists 1 (pt).
Facilities Dining room; Activities room;
Chapel; Laundry room; Barber/Beauty shop.
Activities Arts & crafts; Cards; Games;
Reading groups; Prayer groups; Movies;
Shopping trips; Dances/Social/Cultural
gatherings; Intergenerational programs; Pet
therapy.

Wintersville

Dixon Health Care Center
135 Reichart Ave, Wintersville, OH 43952
(614) 264-1155
Admin Phyllis Lovejoy. *Dir of Nursing* Janis
Rauch. *Medical Dir* Elvira B Acosta.
Licensure Skilled care; Intermediate care. *Beds*
Swing beds SNF/ICF 100. *Private Pay
Patients* 20%. *Certified* Medicaid; Medicare.
Owner Proprietary corp (American Health
Care Centers).
Admissions Requirements Medical
examination.
Staff Physicians 13 (ft); RNs 4 (ft), 5 (pt);
LPNs 11 (ft), 3 (pt); Nurses' aides 24 (ft);
Physical therapists 1 (ft); Occupational
therapists 1 (pt); Speech therapists 1 (pt);
Activities coordinators 2 (ft); Dietitians 1
(ft), 1 (pt); Podiatrists 1 (ft).
Facilities Dining room; Physical therapy
room; Activities room; Crafts room; Laundry
room; Barber/Beauty shop; Library.
Activities Arts & crafts; Cards; Games;
Reading groups; Prayer groups; Movies;
Shopping trips; Dances/Social/Cultural
gatherings; Pet therapy.

Forester Nursing Home Inc
524 Canton Rd, Wintersville, OH 43952
(614) 264-7788
Admin Ruth Eddy.
Medical Dir Carolyn Kennedy.
Licensure Skilled care; Intermediate care. *Beds*
Swing beds SNF/ICF 50.
Owner Proprietary corp.
Admissions Requirements Minimum age 30;
Medical examination; Physician's request.
Staff RNs 3 (ft), 1 (pt); LPNs 1 (ft), 3 (pt);
Nurses' aides 18 (ft), 5 (pt); Physical
therapists 1 (pt); Speech therapists 1 (pt);
Ophthalmologists 1 (pt); Podiatrists 2 (pt);
Dentists 1 (pt).
Facilities Dining room; Activities room;
Chapel; Crafts room; Laundry room; Barber/
Beauty shop.
Activities Arts & crafts; Cards; Games; Prayer
groups; Movies; Shopping trips; Vegetable
gardening.

Woodsfield

Americare—Woodsfield
Airport Rd, Woodsfield, OH 43793
(614) 472-1678
Admin Christine Morton. *Dir of Nursing*
Cindy Headley RN. *Medical Dir* Michelle
Urban MD.
Licensure Skilled care; Intermediate care. *Beds*
SNF 20; ICF 80. *Private Pay Patients* 23%.
Certified Medicaid; Medicare.
Owner Proprietary corp (Care Enterprises).
Admissions Requirements Medical
examination.
Staff Physicians; RNs; LPNs; Nurses' aides;
Physical therapists; Activities coordinators;
Dietitians; Ophthalmologists.
Facilities Dining room; Physical therapy
room; Activities room; Laundry room;
Barber/Beauty shop; Library.
Activities Arts & crafts; Cards; Games;
Reading groups; Prayer groups; Movies;
Shopping trips; Dances/Social/Cultural
gatherings.

Monroe County Care Center
47045 Moore Ridge Rd, Woodsfield, OH
43793
(614) 472-0144
Admin R C Wells. *Dir of Nursing* J
Pickenpaugh. *Medical Dir* M Urban.
Licensure Intermediate care; Retirement. *Beds*
ICF 49. *Certified* Medicaid; Medicare.
Owner Publicly owned.
Admissions Requirements Physician's request.

Staff Physicians 2 (pt); RNs 1 (ft); LPNs 8
(ft); Nurses' aides 30 (ft); Physical therapists;
Occupational therapists; Activities
coordinators 1 (ft); Dietitians 1 (pt);
Podiatrists 1 (pt).
Facilities Dining room; Physical therapy
room; Activities room; Chapel; Crafts room;
Laundry room; Barber/Beauty shop; Library.
Activities Arts & crafts; Cards; Games;
Reading groups; Prayer groups; Movies;
Shopping trips; Dances/Social/Cultural
gatherings; Intergenerational programs; Pet
therapy.

Woodstock

Fountain Park Nursing Home Inc
1649 Park Rd, Woodstock, OH 43084
(513) 826-3351
Admin Katherine B Engle.
Medical Dir Linda Strietenberger.
Licensure Skilled care; Intermediate care;
Alzheimer's care. *Beds* Swing beds SNF/ICF
51. *Certified* Medicaid; Medicare.
Owner Proprietary corp.
Staff Physicians 1 (ft); RNs 5 (ft); LPNs 6 (ft);
Nurses' aides 14 (ft); Recreational therapists
1 (ft); Activities coordinators 1 (ft).
Facilities Dining room; Physical therapy
room; Activities room; Chapel; Crafts room;
Laundry room; Barber/Beauty shop.
Activities Arts & crafts; Cards; Games;
Reading groups; Prayer groups; Movies;
Shopping trips; Dances/Social/Cultural
gatherings.

Wooster

Glendora Nursing Home
1552 N Honeytown Rd, Wooster, OH 44691
(216) 264-0912, 263-4321 FAX
Admin Robert Trivanovich. *Dir of Nursing*
Ruth Haston LPN. *Medical Dir* Dr Charles
Milligan.
Licensure Intermediate care. *Beds* ICF 36.
Private Pay Patients 15%. *Certified*
Medicaid.
Owner Proprietary corp.
Admissions Requirements Medical
examination.
Staff RNs 1 (pt); LPNs 5 (ft), 1 (pt); Nurses'
aides 10 (ft), 2 (pt); Activities coordinators 1
(ft); Dietitians 1 (ft).
Facilities Dining room; Activities room;
Laundry room; Barber/Beauty shop.
Activities Arts & crafts; Cards; Games;
Reading groups; Prayer groups; Movies; Pet
therapy.

Gruter Foundation Inc
3071 N Elyria Rd, Wooster, OH 44691
(216) 264-2446
Licensure Skilled care; Intermediate care. *Beds*
ICF 14; Swing beds SNF/ICF 226.
Owner Proprietary corp.

Horn Nursing Home Inc
230 N Market St, Wooster, OH 44691
(216) 262-2951
Admin Christopher Shook. *Dir of Nursing* B J
Stuart.
Licensure Intermediate care; Retirement. *Beds*
ICF 78. *Certified* Medicaid.
Owner Proprietary corp.
Admissions Requirements Medical
examination; Physician's request.
Staff RNs 3 (ft), 3 (pt); LPNs 4 (ft), 7 (pt);
Nurses' aides 21 (ft), 20 (pt); Physical
therapists 1 (pt); Activities coordinators 1
(ft); Dietitians 1 (pt).
Facilities Dining room; Physical therapy
room; Activities room; Chapel; Laundry
room; Barber/Beauty shop; Library.
Activities Arts & crafts; Cards; Games;
Reading groups; Prayer groups; Movies;
Shopping trips; Dances/Social/Cultural
gatherings; Spell down; Book reviews.

Smithville Western Care Center
4110 Smithville Western Rd, Wooster, OH 44691
(216) 345-6050
Admin James M Horn. *Dir of Nursing* Nancy Guldin RN. *Medical Dir* John Robinson MD.
Licensure Skilled care; Intermediate care; Retirement. *Beds* Swing beds SNF/ICF 135. *Certified* Medicaid; Medicare.
Owner Proprietary corp.
Admissions Requirements Medical examination; Physician's request.
Staff Physicians 1 (pt); RNs 3 (ft), 8 (pt); LPNs 8 (ft), 14 (pt); Nurses' aides 23 (ft), 43 (pt); Physical therapists 1 (pt); Occupational therapists 1 (pt); Speech therapists 1 (pt); Activities coordinators 2 (ft); Dietitians 1 (pt); Ophthalmologists 1 (pt); Podiatrists 1 (pt); Dentists 1 (pt); Social service workers 1 (ft); Chaplains 1 (pt).
Facilities Dining room; Physical therapy room; Activities room; Chapel; Crafts room; Laundry room; Barber/Beauty shop; Private lounge.
Activities Arts & crafts; Cards; Games; Reading groups; Prayer groups; Movies; Group outings.

Wayne County Care Center
876 Geyer Chapel Rd, Wooster, OH 44691
(216) 262-1786
Admin Dorothy J Barnes. *Dir of Nursing* Judith Potts. *Medical Dir* James Bay.
Licensure Intermediate care; Assisted living. *Beds* ICF 50; Assisted living 50. *Certified* Medicaid.
Owner Publicly owned.
Admissions Requirements Minimum age 18; Medical examination; Physician's request.
Staff LPNs; Nurses' aides; Activities coordinators; Dietitians; Chaplains.
Facilities Dining room; Activities room; Chapel; Crafts room; Laundry room; Barber/Beauty shop; Country store.
Activities Arts & crafts; Cards; Games; Reading groups; Prayer groups; Movies; Shopping trips; Dances/Social/Cultural gatherings; Pet therapy; Bell choir; Choral groups.

Wayne Manor Rest Home
4138 Swanson Blvd, Wooster, OH 44691
(216) 345-9007
Licensure Rest home. *Beds* Rest home 18.
Owner Proprietary corp.

West View Manor
1715 Mechanicsburg Rd, Wooster, OH 44691
(216) 264-8640
Admin Rev Gale D Crumrine. *Dir of Nursing* Marcella Lee RN.
Licensure Intermediate care; Rest home. *Beds* ICF 93; Rest home 46. *Certified* Medicaid.
Owner Proprietary corp.
Admissions Requirements Minimum age 62; Medical examination.
Staff RNs; LPNs; Nurses' aides; Activities coordinators.
Affiliation Church of the Brethren.
Facilities Dining room; Physical therapy room; Activities room; Chapel; Laundry room; Barber/Beauty shop.
Activities Arts & crafts; Cards; Games; Prayer groups; Movies; Bible study.

Worthington

Norworth Convalescent Center
6830 High St, Worthington, OH 43085
(614) 888-4553
Licensure Skilled care; Intermediate care. *Beds* Swing beds SNF/ICF 150. *Certified* Medicaid; Medicare.
Owner Proprietary corp.

Worthington Christian Village
165 Highbluffs Blvd, Worthington, OH 43085
(614) 846-6076
Licensure Skilled care; Intermediate care. *Beds* Swing beds SNF/ICF 50. *Certified* Medicaid; Medicare.
Owner Proprietary corp.

Worthington Nursing & Convalescent Center
1030 High St, Worthington, OH 43085
(614) 885-0408
Licensure Skilled care; Intermediate care. *Beds* Swing beds SNF/ICF 100. *Certified* Medicaid; Medicare.
Owner Proprietary corp.

Xenia

Greene Oaks Health Center
164 Office Park Dr, Xenia, OH 45385
(513) 376-8217
Licensure Skilled care; Intermediate care. *Beds* Swing beds SNF/ICF 60. *Certified* Medicaid; Medicare.
Owner Proprietary corp.

Greenewood Manor
711 Dayton-Xenia Rd, Xenia, OH 45385
(513) 376-7550
Admin Darinda Jessup. *Dir of Nursing* Caralee Reis. *Medical Dir* Dr R D Hendrickson.
Licensure Skilled care; Intermediate care. *Beds* Swing beds SNF/ICF 100. *Private Pay Patients* 6%. *Certified* Medicaid; Medicare.
Owner Publicly owned.
Admissions Requirements Medical examination.
Staff Physicians 6 (pt); RNs 3 (ft), 1 (pt); LPNs 8 (ft), 4 (pt); Nurses' aides 34 (ft), 30 (pt); Physical therapists 1 (ft); Occupational therapists 1 (pt); Speech therapists 1 (pt); Activities coordinators 1 (ft); Dietitians 1 (ft); Podiatrists 1 (pt).
Facilities Dining room; Physical therapy room; Activities room; Chapel; Crafts room; Laundry room; Barber/Beauty shop; Library.
Activities Arts & crafts; Cards; Games; Reading groups; Prayer groups; Movies; Shopping trips; Dances/Social/Cultural gatherings; Pet therapy.

Heathergreene Inc
126 Wilson Dr, Xenia, OH 45385
(513) 376-2121
Admin Julie White. *Dir of Nursing* Oreida Schroeder. *Medical Dir* Dr Eugene Schmitt.
Licensure Skilled care; Intermediate care. *Beds* Swing beds SNF/ICF 100. *Private Pay Patients* 35%. *Certified* Medicaid; Medicare.
Owner Proprietary corp.
Admissions Requirements Medical examination; Physician's request.
Staff Physicians; RNs; LPNs; Nurses' aides; Physical therapists; Occupational therapists; Speech therapists; Activities coordinators; Dietitians; Ophthalmologists; Podiatrists; Audiologists.
Facilities Dining room; Physical therapy room; Activities room; Chapel; Crafts room; Laundry room; Barber/Beauty shop.
Activities Arts & crafts; Cards; Games; Reading groups; Prayer groups; Movies; Shopping trips; Dances/Social/Cultural gatherings; Intergenerational programs; Pet therapy.

Hospitality Home East
1301 Monroe Dr, Xenia, OH 45385
(513) 372-4495
Licensure Skilled care; Intermediate care. *Beds* Swing beds SNF/ICF 100. *Certified* Medicaid; Medicare.
Owner Proprietary corp (Hannover Healthcare).

Hospitality Home West
1384 Monroe Dr, Xenia, OH 45385
(513) 372-8081
Licensure Skilled care; Intermediate care. *Beds* Swing beds SNF/ICF 90. *Certified* Medicaid; Medicare.
Owner Proprietary corp (Hannover Healthcare).

Toward Independence Inc
46 S Detroit St, Xenia, OH 45315
(513) 376-3996
Admin Bethanne K Cliffe. *Dir of Nursing* Lesley Davis LPN. *Medical Dir* Fred Stockwell MD.
Licensure Intermediate care for mentally retarded. *Beds* ICF/MR 3 8-bed group homes. *Certified* Medicaid.
Owner Nonprofit corp.
Admissions Requirements Minimum age 18; Medical examination.
Staff Physicians 2 (pt); RNs 1 (pt); LPNs 1 (ft), 5 (pt); Physical therapists 1 (pt); Occupational therapists 1 (pt); Speech therapists 1 (pt); Dietitians 1 (pt); Ophthalmologists 1 (pt); Podiatrists 1 (pt); Dentists 1 (pt).
Languages Sign.
Activities Movies; Shopping trips; Dances/Social/Cultural gatherings.

Xenia Family Care Home
83 W 3rd St, Xenia, OH 45385
(513) 376-3996
Licensure Intermediate care for mentally retarded. *Beds* ICF/MR 8. *Certified* Medicaid.
Owner Proprietary corp.

Yellow Springs

Friends Care Center
150 E Herman St, Yellow Springs, OH 45387
(513) 767-7363, 767-2333 FAX
Admin David L Colburn LNHA. *Dir of Nursing* Esther Hofferbert RN LNHA. *Medical Dir* Carl Hyde MD.
Licensure Skilled care; Alzheimer's care. *Beds* SNF 66. *Private Pay Patients* 30%. *Certified* Medicaid; Medicare.
Owner Nonprofit organization/foundation.
Staff Physicians 3 (pt); RNs 8 (ft), 2 (pt); LPNs 5 (ft), 2 (pt); Nurses' aides 26 (ft), 16 (pt); Physical therapists 1 (pt); Occupational therapists 1 (pt); Speech therapists 1 (pt); Activities coordinators 1 (ft), 2 (pt); Dietitians 1 (pt); Podiatrists 1 (pt).
Facilities Dining room; Physical therapy room; Activities room; Crafts room; Laundry room; Barber/Beauty shop; Multi-purpose room; Greenhouse.
Activities Arts & crafts; Cards; Games; Reading groups; Prayer groups; Movies; Shopping trips; Dances/Social/Cultural gatherings.

Yorkville

Ford-Hull-Mar
212 4th St, Yorkville, OH 43971
(614) 859-6496
Admin Hazel A Marinsnick. *Dir of Nursing* Judy Fowler RN. *Medical Dir* Dr Mejia.
Licensure Intermediate care; Alzheimer's care. *Beds* ICF 21. *Certified* Medicaid.
Owner Proprietary corp.
Admissions Requirements Minimum age 18; Medical examination; Physician's request.
Staff Physicians 1 (ft); RNs 1 (ft); LPNs 3 (ft), 1 (pt); Nurses' aides 3 (ft), 2 (pt); Physical therapists 1 (pt); Recreational therapists 1 (pt); Activities coordinators 2 (pt); Dietitians 1 (ft); Ophthalmologists 1 (pt); Dentists 1 (pt).
Facilities Dining room; Activities room; Chapel; Crafts room; Laundry room; Library.

Activities Arts & crafts; Cards; Games; Reading groups; Prayer groups; Movies; Shopping trips; Dances/Social/Cultural gatherings.

Youngstown

Alcoholic Clinic of Youngstown
2151 Rush Blvd, Youngstown, OH 44507
(216) 744-1181
Licensure Alcoholic nursing home. *Beds* Alcoholic nursing home 34.
Owner Proprietary corp.

Ashley Place Health Care Inc
PO Box 4240, 5291 Ashley Cir, Youngstown, OH 44515
(216) 793-3010, 799-8082 FAX
Admin Patricia Andrews. *Dir of Nursing* Bonnie Newton RN. *Medical Dir* Dr M El Hayek.
Licensure Skilled care; Intermediate care; Pediatric care; Sub-acute care. *Beds* SNF 41; ICF 53; Pediatric 14. *Certified* Medicaid; Medicare.
Owner Proprietary corp.
Admissions Requirements Medical examination; Physician's request.
Staff RNs 3 (ft), 12 (pt); LPNs 27 (ft), 25 (pt); Nurses' aides 12 (ft), 26 (pt); Physical therapists (contracted); Occupational therapists (contracted); Speech therapists (contracted); Activities coordinators 3 (ft); Dietitians (contracted); Ophthalmologists (contracted); Podiatrists (contracted); Audiologists (contracted).
Facilities Dining room; Physical therapy room; Activities room; Chapel; Crafts room; Laundry room; Barber/Beauty shop; Library.
Activities Arts & crafts; Cards; Games; Reading groups; Prayer groups; Movies; Dances/Social/Cultural gatherings; Intergenerational programs; Pet therapy.

Assumption Nursing Home
550 W Chalmers Ave, Youngstown, OH 44511
(216) 743-1186
Admin William B Smaltz. *Dir of Nursing* Sr Mary Edwin Spisak. *Medical Dir* Dr Nicholas Garritano.
Licensure Intermediate care. *Beds* ICF 126. *Private Pay Patients* 50%. *Certified* Medicaid.
Owner Nonprofit corp.
Admissions Requirements Minimum age 18; Medical examination; Physician's request.
Staff RNs 7 (ft), 12 (pt); LPNs 7 (ft); Nurses' aides 47 (ft), 6 (pt); Physical therapists 1 (pt); Recreational therapists 1 (ft); Speech therapists 1 (pt); Activities coordinators 1 (ft); Dietitians 1 (ft); Ophthalmologists 1 (pt); Podiatrists 1 (pt); Audiologists 1 (pt).
Affiliation Roman Catholic.
Facilities Dining room; Physical therapy room; Activities room; Chapel; Crafts room; Laundry room; Barber/Beauty shop; Library.
Activities Arts & crafts; Cards; Games; Reading groups; Movies; Shopping trips; Dances/Social/Cultural gatherings; Rosary; Spiritual care.

Camelot Arms Care Center
2958 Canfield Rd, Youngstown, OH 44511
(216) 792-5511
Admin Frederick F Mattix Jr.
Medical Dir Sally Marx.
Licensure Intermediate care. *Beds* ICF 100. *Certified* Medicaid.
Owner Proprietary corp (American Health Care Centers).
Admissions Requirements Medical examination.
Staff Physicians 1 (ft), 4 (pt); RNs 4 (ft), 1 (pt); LPNs 6 (ft), 4 (pt); Nurses' aides 15 (ft), 20 (pt); Physical therapists 1 (ft), 1 (pt);

Speech therapists 1 (ft); Activities coordinators 1 (ft), 1 (pt); Dietitians 2 (ft); Ophthalmologists 1 (ft); Dentists 1 (pt).
Languages Spanish, Italian, Swahili.
Facilities Dining room; Physical therapy room; Activities room; Laundry room; Barber/Beauty shop.
Activities Arts & crafts; Cards; Games; Reading groups; Prayer groups; Movies; Shopping trips; Dances/Social/Cultural gatherings.

Colonial Manor
196 Colonial Dr, Youngstown, OH 44505
(216) 759-3790
Admin Richard L Macaluso. *Dir of Nursing* Mary Agnes Turkiewicz RN. *Medical Dir* Brian Gordon MD.
Licensure Skilled care; Intermediate care. *Beds* Swing beds SNF/ICF 100. *Certified* Medicaid; Medicare.
Owner Proprietary corp (Horizon Healthcare Corp).
Staff Physicians 2 (pt); RNs 3 (ft), 6 (pt); LPNs 6 (ft), 5 (pt); Nurses' aides 24 (ft), 10 (pt); Physical therapists 1 (ft); Reality therapists 1 (ft); Recreational therapists 1 (pt); Occupational therapists 1 (pt); Speech therapists 1 (pt); Activities coordinators 1 (ft); Dietitians 1 (pt); Ophthalmologists 1 (pt); Podiatrists 1 (pt).
Facilities Dining room; Physical therapy room; Activities room; Chapel; Crafts room; Laundry room; Barber/Beauty shop.
Activities Arts & crafts; Cards; Games; Reading groups; Prayer groups; Movies; Shopping trips; Dances/Social/Cultural gatherings; Exercise program.

Covington House Inc
264 Broadway St, Youngstown, OH 44504
(216) 744-2151
Licensure Intermediate care. *Beds* ICF 28. *Certified* Medicaid.
Owner Proprietary corp.

Danridge Nursing Home
1825 Oak Hill Ave, Youngstown, OH 44507
(216) 746-5157
Admin Ezell Armour.
Medical Dir Lorie Mickel.
Licensure Intermediate care. *Beds* ICF 32. *Certified* Medicaid.
Owner Privately owned.
Admissions Requirements Medical examination.
Staff Physicians 1 (ft); RNs 1 (ft); LPNs 3 (ft), 3 (pt); Nurses' aides 6 (ft), 2 (pt); Activities coordinators 1 (ft); Dietitians 1 (ft); Ophthalmologists 1 (ft).
Facilities Dining room; Activities room; Laundry room.
Activities Arts & crafts; Games; Movies; Shopping trips; Dances/Social/Cultural gatherings.

Gateways to Better Living 1
1406 5th Ave, Youngstown, OH 44504
(216) 746-3039
Licensure Intermediate care for mentally retarded. *Beds* ICF/MR 10. *Certified* Medicaid.
Owner Publicly owned.
Admissions Requirements Minimum age 14.
Staff Physicians 1 (pt); RNs 1 (pt); LPNs 1 (pt); Recreational therapists 1 (pt); Speech therapists 1 (pt); Activities coordinators 1 (pt); Dietitians 1 (pt); Audiologists 1 (pt).
Facilities Dining room.
Activities Arts & crafts; Cards; Games; Reading groups; Movies; Shopping trips; Dances/Social/Cultural gatherings.

Gateways to Better Living 3
2601 Donald Ave, Youngstown, OH 44509
(216) 792-2854

Licensure Intermediate care for mentally retarded; Alzheimer's care; Retirement. *Beds* ICF/MR 10. *Certified* Medicaid.
Owner Proprietary corp.
Admissions Requirements Minimum age 14.
Staff Physicians 1 (pt); RNs 1 (pt); LPNs 1 (pt); Recreational therapists 1 (pt); Speech therapists 1 (pt); Activities coordinators 1 (pt); Dietitians 1 (pt); Audiologists 1 (pt).
Facilities Dining room; Library.
Activities Arts & crafts; Cards; Games; Reading groups; Movies; Shopping trips; Dances/Social/Cultural gatherings.

Gateways to Better Living 4
1398 S Canfield-Niles Rd, Youngstown, OH 44515
(216) 793-8980
Licensure Intermediate care for mentally retarded. *Beds* ICF/MR 10. *Certified* Medicaid.
Owner Proprietary corp.

Gateways to Better Living 5
750 Early Rd, Youngstown, OH 44505
(216) 744-5221
Licensure Intermediate care for mentally retarded. *Beds* ICF/MR 10. *Certified* Medicaid.
Owner Proprietary corp.

Gateways to Better Living 9
660 Early Rd, Youngstown, OH 44505
(216) 792-2854
Licensure Intermediate care for mentally retarded. *Beds* ICF/MR 11. *Certified* Medicaid.
Owner Publicly owned.

Gateways to Better Living 10
335 Wilcox Rd, Youngstown, OH 44515
(216) 793-3554
Licensure Intermediate care for mentally retarded. *Beds* ICF/MR 10. *Certified* Medicaid.
Owner Proprietary corp.

Gateways to Better Living 16
359 Redondo Rd, Youngstown, OH 44504
(216) 792-2854
Admin Dennis Allen. *Dir of Nursing* Karen Potts RN. *Medical Dir* Edgar Kornhauser DO.
Licensure Intermediate care for mentally retarded. *Beds* ICF/MR 8. *Certified* Medicaid.
Owner Nonprofit corp.
Admissions Requirements Minimum age 14; Females only; Medical examination.
Staff Physicians 1 (pt); RNs 1 (pt); LPNs 1 (pt); Nurses' aides 4 (ft), 2 (pt); Recreational therapists 1 (pt); Speech therapists 1 (pt); Activities coordinators 1 (pt); Dietitians 1 (pt); Ophthalmologists 1 (pt); Podiatrists 1 (pt); Dentists 1 (pt); Medical specialists; Social services; Counselors; Psychologists.
Facilities Dining room; Activities room; Crafts room; Laundry room.
Activities Arts & crafts; Games; Movies; Shopping trips; Dances/Social/Cultural gatherings; Habilitation services; Therapeutic services; Recreation/leisure time activities.

Heritage Manor, Jewish Home for Aged
517 Gypsy Lane, Box 449, Youngstown, OH 44501
(216) 746-1076
Admin Gary Weiss. *Dir of Nursing* Helen Schreiner. *Medical Dir* William D Loeser.
Licensure Skilled care; Intermediate care; Alzheimer's care. *Beds* Swing beds SNF/ICF 72. *Certified* Medicaid; Medicare.
Owner Proprietary corp.
Admissions Requirements Physician's request.
Staff Physicians 2 (pt); RNs 5 (ft), 3 (pt); LPNs 3 (ft), 1 (pt); Nurses' aides 21 (ft), 1 (pt); Recreational therapists 1 (ft), 2 (pt); Occupational therapists 1 (pt); Speech

therapists 1 (pt); Activities coordinators 1 (pt); Dietitians 1 (pt); Ophthalmologists 1 (pt).
Languages German, Yiddish, Hebrew, Russian, Hungarian.
Affiliation Jewish.
Facilities Dining room; Physical therapy room; Activities room; Chapel; Crafts room; Laundry room; Barber/Beauty shop.
Activities Arts & crafts; Cards; Games; Reading groups; Movies; Shopping trips; Dances/Social/Cultural gatherings.

Little Forest Rehabilitation Center
5665 South Ave, Youngstown, OH 44512
(216) 782-1173, 782-1176 FAX
Admin Vincent Lisi. *Dir of Nursing* Catharine Morrison RN. *Medical Dir* Joseph Mersol MD.
Licensure Skilled care; Intermediate care. *Beds* SNF 23; ICF 198. *Certified* Medicaid; Medicare.
Owner Proprietary corp (Horizon Healthcare Corp).
Facilities Dining room; Physical therapy room; Activities room; Chapel; Crafts room; Laundry room; Barber/Beauty shop.
Activities Arts & crafts; Cards; Games; Reading groups; Prayer groups; Movies; Shopping trips; Dances/Social/Cultural gatherings; Intergenerational programs; Pet therapy.

Manor House Inc
259 Park Ave, Youngstown, OH 44504
(216) 746-0043
Admin Mary Ann Robb. *Dir of Nursing* Diane Wylie. *Medical Dir* Dr Ronald Fasline.
Licensure Intermediate care for mentally retarded. *Certified* Medicaid.
Owner Proprietary corp.
Admissions Requirements Minimum age 30; Medical examination.
Staff Physicians 1 (pt); RNs 1 (pt); LPNs 3 (ft), 3 (pt); Nurses' aides 5 (ft); Activities coordinators 1 (ft); Dietitians 1 (pt).
Facilities Dining room; Activities room; Laundry room.
Activities Arts & crafts; Cards; Games; Reading groups; Prayer groups; Movies; Shopping trips; Dances/Social/Cultural gatherings.

Meridian Arms Living Center
650 S Meridian Rd, Youngstown, OH 44509
(216) 792-7799
Admin Roy Wright. *Dir of Nursing* Sue Reeder. *Medical Dir* M El Hayer MD.
Licensure Skilled care; Independent living/Assisted living. *Beds* SNF 50; Independent living/Assisted living 50. *Certified* Medicaid; Medicare.
Owner Proprietary corp (American Health Care Centers).
Facilities Dining room; Physical therapy room; Activities room; Crafts room; Laundry room; Barber/Beauty shop; Library; Private patios; Cable TV; Individual heating & cooling controls; Jacuzzi; Courtyard.
Activities Arts & crafts; Cards; Games; Reading groups; Prayer groups; Movies; Shopping trips; Dances/Social/Cultural gatherings; Intergenerational programs; Pet therapy.

North Manor Center
115 Illinois Ave, Youngstown, OH 44505
(216) 744-0188
Admin Edward J Fabian. *Dir of Nursing* Carrie Bender. *Medical Dir* Karapenini Prasad MD.
Licensure Intermediate care; Retirement. *Beds* ICF 100. *Certified* Medicaid.
Owner Proprietary corp.
Admissions Requirements Minimum age 40; Medical examination.

Staff RNs 2 (ft); LPNs 10 (ft); Nurses' aides 32 (ft); Recreational therapists 1 (ft); Speech therapists 1 (pt); Activities coordinators 2 (ft); Dietitians 1 (pt); Ophthalmologists 1 (pt).
Facilities Dining room; Activities room; Crafts room; Laundry room; Barber/Beauty shop; Library.
Activities Arts & crafts; Cards; Games; Reading groups; Prayer groups; Movies; Shopping trips; Dances/Social/Cultural gatherings.

Northside Nursing Home
480 Lora Ave, Youngstown, OH 44504
(216) 743-5235
Licensure Intermediate care. *Beds* ICF 31. *Certified* Medicaid.
Owner Proprietary corp.

Omni Manor
3245 Vestal Rd, Youngstown, OH 44509
(216) 793-5648
Licensure Skilled care; Intermediate care. *Beds* SNF 50; ICF 159. *Certified* Medicaid; Medicare.
Owner Proprietary corp.

Paisley House
1408 Mahoning Ave, Youngstown, OH 44509
(216) 799-9431
Admin Jane Evans. *Dir of Nursing* Vera Sulick RN. *Medical Dir* Kevin Nash MD.
Licensure Assisted care. *Beds* Assisted care 21. *Private Pay Patients* 90-100%.
Owner Nonprofit corp.
Admissions Requirements Minimum age 72; Females only; Must be alert and ambulatory.
Staff Physicians 1 (pt); RNs 1 (ft), 5 (pt); LPNs 4 (pt); Nurses' aides 3 (ft), 3 (pt); Activities coordinators 2 (pt); Podiatrists 1 (pt).
Facilities Dining room; Activities room; Crafts room; Barber/Beauty shop; Library; Private rooms; Elevator to all floors.
Activities Arts & crafts; Cards; Games; Prayer groups; Movies; Dances/Social/Cultural gatherings; Intergenerational programs; Pet therapy; Rides.

Park Vista Unit, Ohio Presbyterian Home
1216 Fifth Ave, Youngstown, OH 44504
(216) 746-2944
Admin David F Johnson, Exec Dir. *Dir of Nursing* Shirley Armour RNC. *Medical Dir* James L Smeltzer MD.
Licensure Skilled care; Intermediate care; Rest home; Alzheimer's care. *Beds* Swing beds SNF/ICF 98; Rest home 54. *Certified* Medicaid; Medicare.
Owner Nonprofit corp (Ohio Presbyterian Homes).
Admissions Requirements Minimum age 65; Medical examination.
Staff Physicians 2 (pt); RNs 11 (ft), 7 (pt); LPNs 9 (ft), 11 (pt); Nurses' aides 41 (ft), 7 (pt); Physical therapists 1 (pt); Speech therapists 1 (pt); Activities coordinators 1 (ft); Dietitians 1 (pt); Ophthalmologists 1 (pt); Dentists 1 (pt).
Affiliation Presbyterian.
Facilities Dining room; Physical therapy room; Activities room; Chapel; Crafts room; Laundry room; Barber/Beauty shop; Library.
Activities Arts & crafts; Cards; Games; Reading groups; Prayer groups; Movies; Shopping trips; Dances/Social/Cultural gatherings; Trips to local entertainment; Sight-seeing.

Ridgewood Nursing Center Inc
1012 Glenwood Ave, Youngstown, OH 44502
Licensure Intermediate care. *Beds* 38. *Certified* Medicaid.
Owner Proprietary corp.

Sleigh Bell Residence
461 S Canfield-Niles Rd, Youngstown, OH 44515
(216) 799-9791
Admin Carl L Casale.
Licensure Intermediate care; Retirement; Alzheimer's care. *Beds* ICF 98. *Certified* Medicaid.
Owner Proprietary corp.
Staff RNs 8 (ft); LPNs 10 (ft); Nurses' aides 60 (ft), 20 (pt); Physical therapists 1 (pt); Activities coordinators 1 (ft), 1 (pt); Dietitians & aides 10 (ft).
Facilities Dining room; Physical therapy room; Activities room; Crafts room; Barber/Beauty shop.
Activities Arts & crafts; Cards; Games; Reading groups; Prayer groups; Movies; Shopping trips; Dances/Social/Cultural gatherings; Picnics; Shopping trips.

Windsor Nursing Home
1735 Belmont Ave, Youngstown, OH 44504
(216) 743-1393
Admin Robert Kay. *Dir of Nursing* Gerry House. *Medical Dir* Joseph Mersol MD.
Licensure Skilled care; Intermediate care. *Beds* Swing beds SNF/ICF 109. *Private Pay Patients* 5%. *Certified* Medicaid; Medicare.
Owner Proprietary corp.
Admissions Requirements Medical examination; Physician's request.
Staff Physicians; RNs 5 (ft), 3 (pt); LPNs 13 (ft), 2 (pt); Nurses' aides 46 (ft), 6 (pt); Physical therapists; Occupational therapists; Speech therapists; Activities coordinators 2 (ft); Dietitians; Ophthalmologists; Podiatrists; Audiologists.
Facilities Dining room; Physical therapy room; Activities room; Crafts room; Laundry room; Barber/Beauty shop.
Activities Arts & crafts; Cards; Games; Reading groups; Prayer groups; Movies; Shopping trips; Dances/Social/Cultural gatherings.

Zanesville

Cedar Hill Care Center
1136 Adair Ave, Zanesville, OH 43701
(614) 454-6823
Licensure Skilled care; Intermediate care. *Beds* Swing beds SNF/ICF 108. *Certified* Medicaid; Medicare.
Owner Proprietary corp.

Drake Nursing Home
750 Findley Ave, Zanesville, OH 43701
(614) 452-3449
Admin Philip Drake.
Medical Dir Carolee Frank.
Licensure Intermediate care. *Beds* ICF 30. *Certified* Medicaid.
Owner Proprietary corp.
Admissions Requirements Medical examination.
Staff Physicians 1 (pt); RNs 1 (ft); LPNs 2 (ft), 4 (pt); Nurses' aides 4 (ft), 5 (pt); Activities coordinators 1 (pt); Dietitians 1 (pt).
Facilities Dining room; Activities room.
Activities Arts & crafts; Cards; Games; Reading groups; Prayer groups.

Good Samaritan Hospital
800 Forest Ave, Zanesville, OH 43701
(614) 454-5000
Admin Daniel Rissing. *Dir of Nursing* Ed Fell RN. *Medical Dir* Robert Thompson MD.
Licensure Skilled care. *Beds* SNF 18. *Certified* Medicare.
Owner Nonprofit corp.
Admissions Requirements Physician's request.
Staff RNs 2 (ft), 4 (pt); LPNs 5 (ft), 7 (pt); Nurses' aides 2 (ft), 3 (pt); Physical therapists 1 (pt); Occupational therapists 1 (pt); Speech therapists 1 (pt); Activities coordinators 1 (pt); Dietitians 1 (pt).

Affiliation Roman Catholic.
Facilities Dining room; Physical therapy room; Activities room; Chapel; Laundry room; Barber/Beauty shop; Library.
Activities Arts & crafts; Cards; Games; Reading groups; Prayer groups; Movies; Dances/Social/Cultural gatherings; Orientation group.

Ohio District Council Nursing Home
3125 E Pike, Zanesville, OH 43701
(614) 452-4351
Medical Dir Dr Eugene Capocasale.
Licensure Skilled care; Intermediate care. *Beds* Swing beds SNF/ICF 100. *Certified* Medicaid; Medicare.
Owner Proprietary corp.
Admissions Requirements Medical examination; Physician's request.
Staff Physicians 1 (ft); RNs 3 (ft), 2 (pt); LPNs 13 (ft); Physical therapists 1 (pt); Reality therapists 2 (ft); Recreational therapists 2 (ft); Occupational therapists; Speech therapists; Activities coordinators 2 (ft); Dietitians; Ophthalmologists; Podiatrists; Audiologists; Dentists.
Facilities Dining room; Physical therapy room; Activities room; Chapel; Crafts room; Laundry room; Barber/Beauty shop; Library.
Activities Arts & crafts; Cards; Games; Prayer groups; Movies; Shopping trips; Dances/ Social/Cultural gatherings.

Helen Purcell Home
1854 Norwood Blvd, Zanesville, OH 43701
(614) 453-1745
Licensure Skilled care; Intermediate care; Rest home. *Beds* Swing beds SNF/ICF 36; Rest home 38. *Private Pay Patients* 100%.
Owner Nonprofit organization/foundation.

Admissions Requirements Minimum age 65; Females only; Medical examination; Physician's request.
Staff Physicians 1 (pt); RNs 2 (ft), 3 (pt); LPNs 5 (ft), 4 (pt); Nurses' aides 18 (ft), 15 (pt); Activities coordinators 1 (ft), 1 (pt); Dietitians 1 (pt); Podiatrists 1 (pt); Dentists 1 (pt).
Facilities Dining room; Activities room; Laundry room; Barber/Beauty shop; Library; Private rooms.
Activities Arts & crafts; Cards; Games; Reading groups; Prayer groups; Movies; Shopping trips; Dances/Social/Cultural gatherings; Pet therapy.

Sunny View
2991 Maple Ave, Zanesville, OH 43701
(614) 454-4663
Admin Roger E Drake. *Dir of Nursing* Lisa Feldner RN. *Medical Dir* Joe Booth MD.
Licensure Skilled care; Intermediate care; Adult day care program. *Beds* Swing beds SNF/ICF 100.
Owner Proprietary corp.
Staff Physicians 1 (ft); RNs 1 (ft), 3 (pt); LPNs 5 (ft), 3 (pt); Nurses' aides 22 (ft), 5 (pt); Activities coordinators 2 (ft); Dietitians 1 (pt).
Facilities Dining room; Activities room; Laundry room; Barber/Beauty shop; Garden; Patios.
Activities Arts & crafts; Cards; Games; Prayer groups; Movies; Shopping trips.

Willow Haven Nursing Home
PO Box 2038, 1122 Taylor St, Zanesville, OH 43701
(614) 454-9747
Medical Dir Dr David Klein.

Licensure Intermediate care. *Beds* ICF 100. *Certified* Medicaid.
Owner Proprietary corp.
Admissions Requirements Minimum age 18; Medical examination.
Staff RNs 3 (ft), 3 (pt); LPNs 6 (ft), 1 (pt); Nurses' aides 38 (ft), 15 (pt); Physical therapists 1 (pt); Reality therapists 2 (ft); Recreational therapists 2 (ft); Dietitians 1 (ft).
Facilities Dining room; Physical therapy room; Activities room; Crafts room; Laundry room; Barber/Beauty shop; Library.
Activities Arts & crafts; Cards; Games; Reading groups; Prayer groups; Dances/ Social/Cultural gatherings.

Winterhouse
PO Box 2627, 1856 Adams Ln, Zanesville, OH 43701
(614) 454-9769
Medical Dir Thomas P Forrestal MD.
Licensure Skilled care; Intermediate care. *Beds* Swing beds SNF/ICF 101. *Certified* Medicaid; Medicare.
Owner Proprietary corp (Arbor Health Care).
Staff Physicians 1 (pt); RNs 4 (ft), 3 (pt); LPNs 6 (ft), 1 (pt); Nurses' aides 41 (ft), 8 (pt); Activities coordinators 3 (ft); Dietitians 11 (ft).
Facilities Dining room; Activities room; Crafts room; Laundry room; Barber/Beauty shop.
Activities Arts & crafts; Cards; Games; Reading groups; Prayer groups; Movies; Shopping trips; Dances/Social/Cultural gatherings.

OKLAHOMA

Ada

Ada Retirement & Care Center
PO Box 1185, 931 N Country Club Rd, Ada, OK 74820
(405) 332-3631
Admin Gussie J Corvin.
Licensure Intermediate care. *Beds* ICF 85.
Certified Medicaid.

Ballard Nursing Center
210 W 5th, Ada, OK 74820
(405) 436-1414
Admin Gary Reed.
Licensure Intermediate care. *Beds* ICF 73.
Certified Medicaid.

Jan Frances Care Center
815 N Country Club Rd, Ada, OK 74820
(405) 332-5328
Admin Henry Malone.
Medical Dir Dr Martin Stokes.
Licensure Intermediate care. *Beds* ICF 120.
Certified Medicaid.
Owner Proprietary corp (Beverly Enterprises).
Admissions Requirements Minimum age 18; Physician's request.
Staff Physicians 6 (ft); RNs 1 (ft); LPNs 6 (ft), 4 (pt); Nurses' aides 25 (ft), 25 (pt); Physical therapists 1 (ft), 1 (pt); Reality therapists 1 (ft); Activities coordinators 1 (ft); Dietitians 1 (ft).
Facilities Dining room; Physical therapy room; Activities room; Chapel; Crafts room; Laundry room; Barber/Beauty shop.
Activities Arts & crafts; Cards; Games; Reading groups; Prayer groups; Movies; Shopping trips; Dances/Social/Cultural gatherings.

McCall's Chapel School Inc
Rte 7 Box 232, Ada, OK 74820
(405) 436-0373
Admin Eileen Lindsay.
Medical Dir George K Stephens MD.
Licensure Intermediate care for mentally retarded; Retirement; Room & board. *Beds* ICF/MR 98; Room & board 60. *Certified* Medicaid.
Owner Nonprofit corp.
Admissions Requirements Minimum age 14; Medical examination.
Staff LPNs; Nurses' aides; Recreational therapists.
Facilities Dining room; Activities room; Crafts room; Laundry room; Barber/Beauty shop; Library; Gym; Classrooms.
Activities Arts & crafts; Games; Reading groups; Prayer groups; Movies; Shopping trips; Dances/Social/Cultural gatherings.

Allen

Woodland Hills Nursing Center
200 N Easton, Allen, OK 74825
(405) 857-2472
Admin Fay Rinehart.

Licensure Intermediate care. *Beds* ICF 49.
Certified Medicaid.

Altus

Altus House Nursing Home
1059 E Pecan, Altus, OK 73521
(405) 482-8342
Admin Nina D Gilliland.
Licensure Intermediate care. *Beds* ICF 90.
Certified Medicaid.
Owner Proprietary corp (Amity Care).
Admissions Requirements Medical examination.
Staff RNs 1 (ft); LPNs 3 (ft); Nurses' aides 23 (ft), 2 (pt); Activities coordinators 1 (ft); Dietitians 1 (pt).
Facilities Dining room; Activities room; Crafts room; Barber/Beauty shop.
Activities Arts & crafts; Games; Reading groups; Prayer groups; Dances/Social/Cultural gatherings.

English Village Manor Inc
1515 Canterbury, Altus, OK 73521
(405) 477-1133
Admin Patsy I Banks Cope.
Licensure Intermediate care. *Beds* ICF 128.
Certified Medicaid.

Jackson County Memorial Hospital
1200 E Pecan, Altus, OK 73521
(405) 481-4781, ext 500, 482-4501 FAX
Admin William G Wilson, Pres/CEO. *Dir of Nursing* Susan Walliser RN, VP Pt Care Svcs. *Medical Dir* J H Lee COS.
Licensure Skilled care; Adult day care; Respite care. *Beds* SNF 25. *Private Pay Patients* 1%.
Certified Medicaid; Medicare.
Owner Publicly owned.
Admissions Requirements Medical examination; Physician's request.
Staff RNs 2 (ft); LPNs 6 (ft); Nurses' aides 6 (ft), 2 (pt); Physical therapists 2 (ft); Occupational therapists 1 (ft); Speech therapists 1 (ft); Activities coordinators 1 (pt); Dietitians 2 (ft).
Facilities Whirlpool room.
Activities Arts & crafts; Cards; Games.

Park Lane Manor Inc
PO Box 659, 702 N Park Ln, Altus, OK 73521
(405) 482-8800
Admin Jan B Winters.
Licensure Intermediate care. *Beds* 55.
Certified Medicaid.

Alva

Beadles Rest Home
916 Noble, Alva, OK 73717
(405) 327-1274
Admin Emma Jordon.
Licensure Intermediate care. *Beds* ICF 64.
Certified Medicaid.
Admissions Requirements Medical examination; Physician's request.

Staff RNs 2 (ft); LPNs 2 (ft), 1 (pt); Nurses' aides 16 (ft); Activities coordinators 1 (ft); Dietitians 1 (pt).
Facilities Dining room; Activities room; Library.
Activities Arts & crafts; Cards; Games; Reading groups; Prayer groups; Movies; Shopping trips; Special days each month.

Share Medical Center
730 Share Dr, Alva, OK 73717
(405) 327-2800, 327-2032 FAX
Admin Charley Jane Gaskill. *Dir of Nursing* Madeline Nighswonger. *Medical Dir* Kirt Bierig MD.
Licensure Intermediate care; Alzheimer's care. *Beds* ICF 80. *Private Pay Patients* 60%. *Certified* Medicaid.
Owner Nonprofit organization/foundation.
Admissions Requirements Medical examination; Physician's request.
Staff RNs 1 (pt); LPNs 4 (ft), 1 (pt); Nurses' aides 35 (ft); Physical therapists 1 (pt); Recreational therapists 1 (pt); Speech therapists 1 (pt); Activities coordinators 1 (ft); Dietitians 1 (ft).
Languages Spanish.
Facilities Dining room; Physical therapy room; Activities room; Crafts room; Laundry room; Barber/Beauty shop; Library; Special care unit.
Activities Arts & crafts; Cards; Games; Reading groups; Movies; Shopping trips; Intergenerational programs; Pet therapy; AD support group.

Anadarko

Galilean Center
201 W Kansas, Anadarko, OK 73005
(405) 247-6611
Admin Liz Johns.
Licensure Intermediate care; Intermediate care for mentally retarded. *Beds* ICF 12; ICF/MR 212. *Certified* Medicaid.

Silver Crest Manor Inc
300 W Washington, Anadarko, OK 73005
(405) 247-3347
Admin Wanda Silvers.
Licensure Intermediate care. *Beds* ICF 92.
Certified Medicaid.

Antlers

Antlers Nursing Home
507 E Main, Antlers, OK 74523
(405) 298-3294
Admin Sue Fuller.
Licensure Intermediate care. *Beds* ICF 133.
Certified Medicaid.

Ardmore

Ardmore Memorial Convalescent Home
1037 15th NW, Ardmore, OK 73401
(405) 223-8304

Admin Eugene Lutts.
Licensure Intermediate care. *Beds* ICF 56.
Certified Medicaid.

Elmbrook Home
1811 9th NW, Ardmore, OK 73401
(405) 223-3303
Licensure Intermediate care. *Beds* ICF 120.
Certified Medicaid.

Lakeland Manor Inc
604 Lake Murray Dr, Ardmore, OK 73401
(405) 223-4501
Admin Michael Stringer.
Licensure Intermediate care. *Beds* ICF 62.
Certified Medicaid.

Lu-Ken Manor
832 Isabel SW, Ardmore, OK 73401
(405) 343-2295
Admin James A Kenaga.
Licensure Intermediate care. *Beds* ICF 104.
Certified Medicaid.

Silver Star Nursing Home
111 13th NW, Ardmore, OK 73401
(405) 223-4803
Admin Nema Scott Davis. *Dir of Nursing*
Marian Ross LPN.
Licensure Intermediate care. *Beds* ICF 76.
Certified Medicaid.
Owner Privately owned.
Admissions Requirements Medical
examination; Physician's request.
Staff LPNs 4 (ft); Nurses' aides 10 (ft);
Activities coordinators 1 (ft); Dietitians 1
(ft).
Facilities Dining room; Crafts room; Laundry
room; Barber/Beauty shop; Lobby.
Activities Arts & crafts; Cards; Games;
Reading groups; Prayer groups; Movies;
Shopping trips; Dances/Social/Cultural
gatherings; Bingo; Cooking class; Exercise.

Woodview Home
1630 3rd NE, Ardmore, OK 73401
(405) 226-5454
Admin Kenneth Walker. *Dir of Nursing*
Geraldean Toti RN.
Licensure Intermediate care; Alzheimer's care.
Beds ICF 49. *Private Pay Patients* 30%.
Certified Medicaid.
Owner Proprietary corp.
Admissions Requirements Medical
examination; Physician's request.
Staff RNs 1 (ft); LPNs 3 (ft); Nurses' aides 15
(ft); Physical therapists 1 (ft); Speech
therapists 1 (pt); Activities coordinators 1
(ft); Dietitians 1 (pt).
Facilities Dining room; Physical therapy
room; Activities room; Crafts room; Laundry
room; Barber/Beauty shop; Garden room.
Activities Arts & crafts; Cards; Games;
Reading groups; Prayer groups; Movies;
Shopping trips; Dances/Social/Cultural
gatherings; Intergenerational programs.

Arkoma

Medi-Home of Arkoma
PO Box 410, Arkoma, OK 74901
(918) 875-3107
Admin Sherman H Babb. *Dir of Nursing*
Cerise Travis RN.
Licensure Intermediate care. *Beds* ICF 56.
Certified Medicaid.
Owner Proprietary corp.
Admissions Requirements Medical
examination; Physician's request.
Staff RNs 1 (ft); LPNs 4 (ft); Nurses' aides 8
(ft); Activities coordinators 1 (ft); Dietitians
1 (ft).
Facilities Dining room; Chapel; Laundry
room; Barber/Beauty shop.
Activities Arts & crafts; Cards; Games;
Reading groups; Prayer groups; Movies.

Atoka

Atoka Care Center
PO Box 708, 323 W 6th, Atoka, OK 74525
(405) 889-3373
Admin Patricia Woods.
Medical Dir Edna Sheffield.
Licensure Intermediate care. *Beds* ICF 96.
Certified Medicaid.
Admissions Requirements Medical
examination; Physician's request.

Atoka Colonial Manor Inc
100 Virginia St, Atoka, OK 74525
(405) 889-7341
Admin Johnny Faulkenberry.
Licensure Intermediate care. *Beds* ICF 96.
Certified Medicaid.

Plantation Manor Inc
505 E "B" St, Atoka, OK 74525
(405) 889-2517
Admin Judith R Miller.
Licensure Intermediate care. *Beds* ICF 85.
Certified Medicaid.
Admissions Requirements Minimum age 19;
Medical examination; Physician's request.
Staff RNs 1 (pt); LPNs 2 (ft); Nurses' aides 23
(ft); Activities coordinators 1 (ft); Dietitians
1 (pt).
Facilities Dining room; Physical therapy
room; Activities room; Crafts room; Laundry
room.
Activities Arts & crafts; Cards; Games;
Reading groups; Shopping trips; Dances/
Social/Cultural gatherings.

Barnsdall

Barnsdall Nursing Home
411 S 4th, Barnsdall, OK 74002
(918) 847-2572
Admin June Miller. *Dir of Nursing* Marjorie
Schneider LPN.
Licensure Intermediate care. *Beds* ICF 40.
Certified Medicaid.
Owner Privately owned.
Admissions Requirements Medical
examination.
Staff Physicians 1 (ft), 1 (pt); RNs 1 (pt);
LPNs 3 (ft), 1 (pt); Nurses' aides 12 (ft), 10
(pt); Activities coordinators 1 (ft); Dietitians
1 (ft).
Facilities Dining room; Activities room;
Laundry room; Barber/Beauty shop.
Activities Arts & crafts; Cards; Games;
Reading groups; Prayer groups; Movies;
Shopping trips; Dances/Social/Cultural
gatherings.

Bartlesville

Heritage Manor
3434 Kentucky Pl, Bartlesville, OK 74006
(918) 333-9545
Admin PauLa Bakke. *Dir of Nursing* Saundra
Deaton. *Medical Dir* Dr Supak.
Licensure Intermediate care; Retirement. *Beds*
ICF 126; Retirement 35. *Private Pay
Patients* 75%. *Certified* Medicaid.
Owner Proprietary corp (Hillhaven Corp).
Admissions Requirements Medical
examination; Physician's request.
Staff RNs; LPNs; Nurses' aides; Recreational
therapists; Activities coordinators; Dietitians.
Facilities Dining room; Activities room;
Laundry room; Barber/Beauty shop.
Activities Arts & crafts; Cards; Games;
Reading groups; Prayer groups; Movies; Pet
therapy.

Beaver

Beaver County Nursing Home
200 E 8th, Beaver, OK 73932
(405) 625-4571

Admin LaVern Melton.
Licensure Intermediate care. *Beds* ICF 62.
Certified Medicaid.

Beggs

Beggs Nursing Center
306 E 7th, Beggs, OK 74421
(918) 267-3362
Admin Judy McKee.
Licensure Intermediate care. *Beds* ICF 50.
Certified Medicaid.

Bethany

Bethany Village Health Care Center
6900 NW 39th Expwy, Bethany, OK 73008
(405) 495-6110
Admin Jan Probst. *Dir of Nursing* Jana
Gourley RN. *Medical Dir* John Pittman
MD.
Licensure Intermediate care; Alzheimer's care.
Beds ICF 161. *Certified* Medicaid.
Owner Proprietary corp (Convalescent
Services).
Admissions Requirements Minimum age 45;
Medical examination.
Staff RNs 3 (ft); LPNs 12 (ft); Nurses' aides
37 (ft); Physical therapists 1 (pt);
Recreational therapists 1 (ft); Speech
therapists 1 (pt); Activities coordinators 1
(ft); Dietitians 1 (pt).
Facilities Dining room; Physical therapy
room; Activities room; Chapel; Crafts room;
Laundry room; Barber/Beauty shop; Library.
Activities Arts & crafts; Cards; Games;
Reading groups; Prayer groups; Movies;
Shopping trips; Dances/Social/Cultural
gatherings.

Children's Convalescent Center
6800 NW 39th Expressway, Bethany, OK
73008
(405) 789-6711
Admin Albert Gray.
Licensure Skilled care. *Beds* SNF 82.

Evening Star Nursing Home
6912 NW 23rd, Bethany, OK 73008
(405) 789-8491
Admin Glenda Kouba. *Dir of Nursing* Sherry
Bonnett LPN.
Licensure Intermediate care; Alzheimer's care.
Beds ICF 55. *Private Pay Patients* 10%.
Certified Medicaid.
Owner Proprietary corp (ARA Living
Centers).
Admissions Requirements Medical
examination.
Staff RNs 1 (pt); LPNs 1 (ft); Nurses' aides 13
(ft); Activities coordinators 1 (ft).
Facilities Dining room; Activities room;
Crafts room; Laundry room; Barber/Beauty
shop; Alzheimer's unit.
Activities Arts & crafts; Games; Prayer groups;
Movies; Shopping trips; Dances/Social/
Cultural gatherings; Intergenerational
programs.

Putnam City Convalescent Center
7000 NW 32nd, Bethany, OK 73008
(405) 789-7242
Admin Mike Utter.
Licensure Intermediate care. *Beds* ICF 161.
Certified Medicaid.

Western Oaks Health Care Center
2200 N Flamingo, Bethany, OK 73008
(405) 787-2844
Admin David Shelby. *Dir of Nursing* Mary
Heron. *Medical Dir* Dr Leon Gilbert.
Licensure Skilled care; Intermediate care. *Beds*
SNF 17; ICF 218. *Private Pay Patients* 45%.
Certified Medicaid; Medicare.
Owner Proprietary corp (Care Givers Inc).
Admissions Requirements Medical
examination; Physician's request.

Staff RNs 5 (ft); LPNs 10 (ft); Nurses' aides 60 (ft); Physical therapists 1 (ft); Occupational therapists 1 (ft); Speech therapists 1 (ft); Dietitians 1 (ft).
Facilities Dining room; Physical therapy room; Activities room; Crafts room; Laundry room; Barber/Beauty shop; Library.
Activities Arts & crafts; Cards; Games; Reading groups; Prayer groups; Movies; Shopping trips; Pet therapy.

Billings

Billings Fairchild Center Inc
Hwy 15, Box 278, Billings, OK 74630
(405) 725-3533
Admin Albert Hardin.
Licensure Intermediate care; Intermediate care for mentally retarded. *Beds* ICF 10; ICF/MR 144. *Certified* Medicaid.

Binger

Binger Nursing Home
PO Box R, Hwy 281 N, Binger, OK 73009
(405) 656-2302
Admin Vicki Borden. *Dir of Nursing* Thelda Smart RN. *Medical Dir* Troy Harden.
Licensure Intermediate care. *Beds* ICF 50. *Private Pay Patients* 33%. *Certified* Medicaid.
Owner Privately owned (MMRS Properties of Oklahoma).
Admissions Requirements Medical examination; Physician's request.
Staff Physicians; RNs; LPNs; Nurses' aides; Activities coordinators; Dietitians.
Facilities Dining room; Physical therapy room; Activities room; Laundry room; Barber/Beauty shop.
Activities Arts & crafts; Games; Prayer groups; Movies; Intergenerational programs.

Bixby

Bixby Manor Nursing Home
15600 S Memorial Dr, Bixby, OK 74008
(918) 366-4491
Admin Yvonne Roberts.
Medical Dir Dana Quay.
Licensure Intermediate care. *Beds* ICF 102. *Certified* Medicaid.
Owner Proprietary corp.
Admissions Requirements Minimum age 18; Medical examination.
Staff Physicians 1 (pt); RNs 1 (pt); LPNs 5 (ft); Nurses' aides 32 (ft); Physical therapists 1 (pt); Speech therapists 1 (pt); Activities coordinators 1 (ft), 1 (pt); Dietitians 1 (pt); Ophthalmologists 1 (pt).
Languages Spanish.
Facilities Dining room; Physical therapy room; Activities room; Crafts room; Laundry room; Barber/Beauty shop.
Activities Arts & crafts; Cards; Games; Prayer groups; Movies; Shopping trips; Dances/ Social/Cultural gatherings.

Blackwell

Blackwell Nursing Home Inc
1200 W Coolidge, Blackwell, OK 74631
(405) 363-1624
Admin Gwen Barnes.
Licensure Intermediate care. *Beds* ICF 71. *Certified* Medicaid.

Hillcrest Manor
1110 S 6th, Blackwell, OK 74631
(405) 363-3244
Admin LaVersa Holder Johnson.
Licensure Intermediate care. *Beds* ICF 137. *Certified* Medicaid.

Blanchard

Senior Village Nursing Home
PO Box 649, 1100 N Madison, Blanchard, OK 73010
(405) 485-3314
Admin Bob Simmons.
Licensure Intermediate care. *Beds* ICF 50.
Certified Medicaid.

Boise City

Cimarron Nursing Home
100 E Ellis, Boise City, OK 73933
(405) 544-2501
Admin Barbara Jo Wardlaw. *Dir of Nursing* Mary Van Leer LPN.
Licensure Intermediate care. *Beds* 44.
Certified Medicaid.
Owner Publicly owned.
Admissions Requirements Medical examination.
Staff RNs 1 (pt); LPNs 3 (ft); Nurses' aides 6 (ft), 11 (pt); Activities coordinators 1 (ft); Dietitians 1 (pt).
Languages Spanish.
Facilities Dining room; Activities room; Barber/Beauty shop.
Activities Arts & crafts; Cards; Games; Reading groups; Prayer groups; Movies; Shopping trips.

Boley

Boley Intermediate Care Facility
Hwy 62, Boley, OK 74829
(918) 667-3311
Admin John B Bruner.
Licensure Intermediate care. *Beds* ICF 25.
Certified Medicaid.

Bristow

Rainbow Health Care Center
PO Box 1219, 111 E Washington, Bristow, OK 74010
(918) 367-2246
Admin Phoebe M Blackwell. *Dir of Nursing* Vinita Bishop.
Licensure Intermediate care. *Beds* ICF 106.
Private Pay Patients 25%. *Certified* Medicaid.
Owner Proprietary corp.
Admissions Requirements Minimum age 18; Medical examination.
Staff RNs 1 (pt); LPNs 4 (ft), 3 (pt); Nurses' aides 22 (ft), 8 (pt); Dietitians 1 (pt).
Facilities Dining room; Activities room; Crafts room; Laundry room; Barber/Beauty shop.
Activities Arts & crafts; Cards; Games; Reading groups; Prayer groups; Movies.

Broken Arrow

Broken Arrow Nursing Home Inc
425 N Date, Broken Arrow, OK 74012
(918) 251-5343
Admin Tommy Cooper.
Licensure Intermediate care. *Beds* ICF 81.
Certified Medicaid.

Franciscan Villa
17110 E 51st St S, Broken Arrow, OK 74012
(918) 355-1596
Admin Irene Hulsey.
Medical Dir Dr Keven Steichen; C Mark Teter.
Licensure Intermediate care; Retirement. *Beds* ICF 60. *Certified* Medicaid.
Owner Nonprofit corp.
Admissions Requirements Minimum age 65; Medical examination.

Staff Physicians 2 (ft); RNs 3 (ft); LPNs 3 (ft); Nurses' aides 27 (ft); Physical therapists 1 (ft); Activities coordinators 3 (ft); Dietitians 1 (ft); Ophthalmologists 1 (ft).
Affiliation Roman Catholic.
Facilities Dining room; Physical therapy room; Activities room; Chapel; Crafts room; Laundry room; Barber/Beauty shop; Library; Solarium; Patio.
Activities Arts & crafts; Cards; Games; Reading groups; Prayer groups; Movies; Shopping trips; Dances/Social/Cultural gatherings.

Gateway Foundation Inc
1217 E College, Broken Arrow, OK 74012
(918) 251-2676
Admin Beaulah Cline. *Dir of Nursing* Dorothy Terebesy RN.
Licensure Intermediate care for mentally retarded; Group homes. *Beds* ICF/MR 68; Group homes 52. *Certified* Medicaid.
Owner Nonprofit corp.
Admissions Requirements Minimum age 18; Medical examination.
Staff RNs 1 (ft); LPNs 3 (ft); Nurses' aides 85 (ft); Physical therapists 1 (ft), 1 (pt); Recreational therapists 1 (ft); Occupational therapists 1 (ft); Speech therapists 1 (pt); Activities coordinators 3 (ft); Dietitians 1 (ft); Ophthalmologists 1 (pt); Podiatrists 1 (pt); Dentists 1 (pt).
Facilities Dining room; Physical therapy room; Activities room; Chapel; Crafts room; Laundry room; Barber/Beauty shop; Library; Indoor gym; Solar roof pool; Educational facilities.
Activities Arts & crafts; Cards; Games; Reading groups; Prayer groups; Movies; Shopping trips; Dances/Social/Cultural gatherings; Sheltered workshop.

Gateway Foundation Inc II
1217 E College, Broken Arrow, OK 74012
(918) 251-2676
Admin Beulah Cline.
Licensure Intermediate care for mentally retarded. *Beds* ICF/MR 16.

Helen Raney Nursing Home Inc
700 S Ash, Broken Arrow, OK 74012
(918) 251-5384
Admin Reba Raney.
Licensure Intermediate care. *Beds* ICF 52.
Certified Medicaid.

Senior Citizens Nursing Home
1300 E College, Broken Arrow, OK 74012
(918) 251-1571
Admin Leonard Brill.
Licensure Intermediate care. *Beds* 89.
Certified Medicaid.

Tidings of Peace Nursing Center
1709 S Main, Broken Arrow, OK 74012
(918) 251-2626
Admin Judith L Blaylock. *Dir of Nursing* Gwen Droessler.
Licensure Intermediate care. *Beds* ICF 80.
Private Pay Patients 25%. *Certified* Medicaid; Medicare.
Owner Privately owned.
Admissions Requirements Medical examination; Physician's request.
Staff Physicians 4 (pt); LPNs 5 (ft); Nurses' aides 20 (ft), 4 (pt); Physical therapists 1 (pt); Recreational therapists 1 (pt); Activities coordinators 1 (ft); Dietitians 1 (pt).
Facilities Dining room; Laundry room; Barber/Beauty shop.
Activities Arts & crafts; Cards; Games; Reading groups; Prayer groups; Movies; Shopping trips; Dances/Social/Cultural gatherings; Intergenerational programs; Pet therapy.

Broken Bow

Broken Bow Nursing Home
805 N Bock St, Broken Bow, OK 74728
(405) 584-6433
Admin Lois Hutchison.
Licensure Intermediate care. *Beds* ICF 95.
 Certified Medicaid.

McCurtain Manor Nursing Center
PO Box 880, 1201 Dierks, Broken Bow, OK
 74728
(405) 584-9158
Admin Rose Strange. *Dir of Nursing* Linda
 Johnson RN.
Licensure Intermediate care. *Beds* ICF 60.
 Certified Medicaid.
Owner Nonprofit corp (Heartway Corp).
Admissions Requirements Medical
 examination; Physician's request.
Staff Physicians 1 (pt); RNs 1 (ft); LPNs 3
 (ft), 3 (pt); Nurses' aides 11 (ft), 6 (pt);
 Dietitians 1 (pt).
Languages Choctaw Indian.
Facilities Dining room; Laundry room;
 Barber/Beauty shop.
Activities Arts & crafts; Cards; Games; Prayer
 groups; Movies.

Buffalo

Western Nursing Home
111 Walnut Dr, Buffalo, OK 73834
(405) 735-2415
Admin Debra Thompson. *Dir of Nursing*
 Niodene McLaughlin.
Licensure Intermediate care. *Beds* ICF 76.
 Certified Medicaid.
Owner Proprietary corp (Amity Care).
Facilities Dining room; Activities room;
 Crafts room; Laundry room; Barber/Beauty
 shop.
Activities Arts & crafts; Games; Reading
 groups; Prayer groups; Movies; Shopping
 trips; Dances/Social/Cultural gatherings.

Caddo

Caddo Nursing Home
PO Box 168, 200 S McPherson, Caddo, OK
 74729
(405) 367-2264, 367-2265
Admin Hatsene Milligan. *Dir of Nursing*
 Roxie Atherton RN.
Licensure Intermediate care. *Beds* ICF 34.
 Private Pay Patients 35%. *Certified*
 Medicaid.
Owner Publicly owned.
Admissions Requirements Medical
 examination.
Staff RNs 1 (ft); LPNs 3 (ft), 1 (pt); Nurses'
 aides 9 (ft), 3 (pt); Physical therapists
 (consultant); Activities coordinators 1 (ft).
Facilities Dining room; Activities room;
 Crafts room; Laundry room; Barber/Beauty
 shop.
Activities Arts & crafts; Games; Reading
 groups; Prayer groups; Movies; Shopping
 trips; Dances/Social/Cultural gatherings.

Calera

Calera Manor Nursing Home
Access & Blue Ave, Calera, OK 74730
(405) 434-5727
Admin Gerald Buchanan.
Medical Dir Rao Sureddi MD.
Licensure Intermediate care. *Beds* ICF 50.
 Certified Medicaid; Medicare.
Owner Privately owned.
Admissions Requirements Medical
 examination; Physician's request.
Staff RNs 1 (pt); LPNs 2 (ft), 1 (pt); Nurses'
 aides 10 (ft), 1 (pt); Activities coordinators 1
 (ft); Dietitians 1 (pt); Medication aides 4 (ft);
 Office managers 1 (ft).

Facilities Dining room; Physical therapy
 room; Activities room; Laundry room.
Activities Arts & crafts; Cards; Games; Prayer
 groups; Shopping trips; Dances/Social/
 Cultural gatherings.

Carmen

Carmen Home
N Grand St, Box 158, Carmen, OK 73726
(405) 987-2577
Admin Rev J M Lemmon.
Medical Dir Betty Oakley.
Licensure Intermediate care. *Beds* ICF 65.
 Certified Medicaid.
Admissions Requirements Medical
 examination; Physician's request.
Staff RNs 1 (ft); LPNs 3 (ft), 1 (pt); Nurses'
 aides 11 (ft), 10 (pt); Physical therapists 1
 (pt); Recreational therapists 1 (pt); Activities
 coordinators 1 (ft); Dietitians 1 (pt); Dentists
 1 (pt).
Affiliation Pentecostal Holiness.
Facilities Dining room; Activities room;
 Chapel; Crafts room; Laundry room; Barber/
 Beauty shop.
Activities Arts & crafts; Cards; Games; Prayer
 groups; Dances/Social/Cultural gatherings.

Carnegie

Carnegie Nursing Home
225 N Broadway, Carnegie, OK 73015
(405) 654-1439
Admin Lloyd Hilburn.
Licensure Intermediate care. *Beds* ICF 100.
 Certified Medicaid.

Catoosa

Rolling Hills Care Center Inc
801 N 193rd East Ave, Catoosa, OK 74015
(918) 266-5500
Admin Karen Steitz.
Licensure Skilled care. *Beds* SNF 105.

Chandler

Chandler Hillcrest Manor Inc
PO Box 429, Chandler, OK 74834
(405) 258-1131
Admin Judith Austin Cox.
Licensure Intermediate care. *Beds* ICF 52.
 Certified Medicaid.

Pioneer Estate
2nd & Steel, Chandler, OK 74834
(405) 258-1375
Admin Peggy Inskeep.
Medical Dir Doris McCorkle.
Licensure Intermediate care. *Beds* ICF 49.
 Certified Medicaid.
Admissions Requirements Medical
 examination.
Staff RNs 1 (pt); LPNs 3 (ft); Nurses' aides 12
 (ft), 4 (pt); Physical therapists 1 (pt);
 Activities coordinators 1 (ft); Dietitians 1
 (pt).
Facilities Dining room; Activities room;
 Chapel; Crafts room; Laundry room; Barber/
 Beauty shop.
Activities Arts & crafts; Cards; Games;
 Reading groups; Prayer groups; Movies;
 Shopping trips.

Checotah

Cedars Manor Inc
1001 W Gentry, Checotah, OK 74426
(918) 473-2247
Admin Betty Kelsoe. *Dir of Nursing* Dorothy
 Stokes. *Medical Dir* Dr John F Rice.
Licensure Intermediate care. *Beds* ICF 76.
 Certified Medicaid.
Owner Proprietary corp.
Admissions Requirements Physician's request.

Staff Physicians; RNs; LPNs; Nurses' aides;
 Physical therapists; Speech therapists;
 Activities coordinators; Dietitians; Dentists.
Facilities Dining room; Physical therapy
 room; Activities room; Crafts room; Laundry
 room; Barber/Beauty shop.
Activities Arts & crafts; Cards; Games;
 Reading groups; Prayer groups; Movies;
 Shopping trips; Dances/Social/Cultural
 gatherings.

Checotah Manor Inc
PO Box 429, 112 SE 1st St, Checotah, OK
 74432
(918) 473-2251
Admin Deborah Kelsoe. *Dir of Nursing* Jan
 Rogers. *Medical Dir* Dr John Rice.
Licensure Intermediate care. *Beds* ICF 82.
 Private Pay Patients 10%. *Certified*
 Medicaid.
Owner Proprietary corp.
Admissions Requirements Medical
 examination; Physician's request.
Staff Physicians 1 (pt); RNs 1 (ft); LPNs 5
 (ft), 2 (pt); Nurses' aides; Physical therapists;
 Speech therapists 1 (pt); Activities
 coordinators 1 (ft), 1 (pt); Dietitians 1 (pt);
 Ophthalmologists 1 (pt); Podiatrists 1 (pt).
Facilities Dining room; Activities room;
 Laundry room; Barber/Beauty shop.
Activities Arts & crafts; Cards; Games;
 Reading groups; Prayer groups; Movies;
 Shopping trips; Dances/Social/Cultural
 gatherings; Pet therapy.

Odd Fellows Rest Home
211 North Ave, Checotah, OK 74426
(918) 473-5814
Admin Willie M Harris.
Licensure Intermediate care. *Beds* 28.
 Certified Medicaid.
Affiliation Independent Order of Odd Fellows
 & Rebekahs.

Chelsea

Colonial Manor
PO Box 69, 401 Redbud Ln, Chelsea, OK
 74016
(918) 789-3215
Admin Mary Ann Sartin. *Dir of Nursing*
 Wanda Robinson RN. *Medical Dir* Dr
 William Purick.
Licensure Intermediate care. *Beds* ICF 60.
 Private Pay Patients 15%. *Certified*
 Medicaid.
Owner Proprietary corp (Medi-Plex II Inc).
Admissions Requirements Medical
 examination.
Staff RNs 1 (ft); LPNs; Nurses' aides; Physical
 therapists (contracted); Activities
 coordinators 1 (pt); Dietitians 1 (pt).
Facilities Dining room; Physical therapy
 room; Activities room; Chapel; Crafts room;
 Laundry room; Barber/Beauty shop.
Activities Arts & crafts; Games; Reading
 groups; Prayer groups; Movies; Shopping
 trips; Dances/Social/Cultural gatherings.

Cherokee

Cherokee Manor
1100 Memorial Dr, Cherokee, OK 73728
(405) 596-2941
Admin Oliver C Harris. *Dir of Nursing* Jane
 Summers. *Medical Dir* Dr Dean Vaughan.
Licensure Intermediate care; Retirement. *Beds*
 ICF 54; Retirement 12. *Private Pay Patients*
 70%. *Certified* Medicaid.
Owner Proprietary corp.
Admissions Requirements Minimum age
 Adult; Physician's request.
Staff Physicians; RNs; LPNs; Nurses' aides;
 Physical therapists; Activities coordinators;
 Dietitians.

Facilities Dining room; Physical therapy
room; Activities room; Chapel; Crafts room;
Laundry room; Barber/Beauty shop.
Activities Arts & crafts; Cards; Games;
Reading groups; Prayer groups; Movies;
Shopping trips; Dances/Social/Cultural
gatherings.

Cheyenne

Cheyenne Convalescent Home
PO Box 510, 301 S Don Cearlock, Cheyenne,
OK 73628
(405) 497-3328
Admin Lucille Dykes. *Dir of Nursing* Judy
Denney. *Medical Dir* F K Buster MD.
Licensure Intermediate care. *Beds* ICF 36.
Private Pay Patients 30%. *Certified*
Medicaid.
Owner Proprietary corp (Joe Bauermeister).
Admissions Requirements Medical
examination.
Staff RNs 1 (pt); LPNs 2 (ft), 1 (pt); Nurses'
aides 8 (ft), 3 (pt); Activities coordinators 1
(ft); Dietitians 1 (pt).
Facilities Dining room; Activities room;
Crafts room; Laundry room; Barber/Beauty
shop; Whirlpool bath.
Activities Arts & crafts; Cards; Games; Prayer
groups; Movies; Shopping trips; Dances/
Social/Cultural gatherings; Intergenerational
programs.

Chickasha

Chickasha Nursing Center Inc
2700 S 9th, Chickasha, OK 73018
(405) 224-3593
Admin Linda Martin.
Licensure Intermediate care. *Beds* ICF 60.
Certified Medicaid.

Christian Care Retirement Village
Box 580, Chickasha, OK 73023
(405) 224-0909
Admin Carl R Phelps.
Licensure Skilled care. *Beds* SNF 104.

Community Care Center
2027 Idaho Ave, Chickasha, OK 73018
(405) 224-1513
Admin David Greiner.
Licensure Intermediate care. *Beds* ICF 58.
Certified Medicaid.
Owner Proprietary corp (Amity Care).

Convalescent Center of Grady County
PO Box 928, Chickasha, OK 73023
(405) 224-6456
Admin Claudia Hansbro.
Licensure Intermediate care. *Beds* ICF 100.
Certified Medicaid.
Owner Proprietary corp (Amity Care).

Shanoan Springs Residence Inc
PO Box 949, 12th & Montana, Chickasha, OK
73018
(405) 224-1397
Admin Paula F McCathern. *Dir of Nursing*
Marita Douglas. *Medical Dir* Burton B
McDougal MD.
Licensure Intermediate care. *Beds* ICF 82.
Private Pay Patients 40%. *Certified*
Medicaid; Medicare.
Admissions Requirements Medical
examination; Physician's request.
Staff Physicians 1 (ft); RNs 1 (ft); LPNs 7 (ft);
Recreational therapists 1 (ft); Activities
coordinators 1 (ft); Dietitians 1 (ft).
Facilities Dining room; Activities room;
Chapel; Crafts room; Laundry room; Barber/
Beauty shop.
Activities Arts & crafts; Cards; Games;
Reading groups; Movies; Shopping trips;
Dances/Social/Cultural gatherings; Pet
therapy.

Chouteau

Chouteau Nursing Center
113 E Jones Ave, Chouteau, OK 74337
(918) 476-8918
Admin Norma Redmond.
Licensure Intermediate care. *Beds* ICF 55.
Certified Medicaid.
Owner Proprietary corp (Beverly Enterprises).

Claremore

Claremore Nursing Home Inc
1500 N Sioux, Claremore, OK 74017
(918) 341-4857
Admin Sam Lessley. *Dir of Nursing* Gloria
Hewling RN.
Licensure Intermediate care. *Beds* ICF 72.
Certified Medicaid.
Owner Proprietary corp.
Admissions Requirements Physician's request.
Staff RNs 1 (ft), 1 (pt); LPNs 3 (ft), 1 (pt);
Nurses' aides 26 (ft); Activities coordinators
1 (ft), 1 (pt).
Facilities Dining room; Activities room;
Crafts room; Laundry room; Barber/Beauty
shop; Library.
Activities Arts & crafts; Cards; Games;
Reading groups; Prayer groups; Movies;
Shopping trips; Dances/Social/Cultural
gatherings.

Claremore Regional Medical Center SNF
1202 N Muskogee, Claremore, OK 74017
(918) 341-2556
Admin John K Barto Jr.
Licensure Skilled care. *Beds* SNF 12.

Wood Manor Inc
630 N Dorothy, Claremore, OK 74017
(918) 341-4365
Admin Tony Shoemaker.
Licensure Intermediate care. *Beds* ICF 129.
Certified Medicaid.
Admissions Requirements Medical
examination; Physician's request.
Staff RNs 1 (ft); LPNs 4 (ft); Nurses' aides 37
(ft); Physical therapists 1 (pt); Speech
therapists 1 (pt); Dietitians 1 (pt).
Facilities Dining room; Crafts room; Laundry
room; Barber/Beauty shop.
Activities Arts & crafts; Cards; Games;
Reading groups; Prayer groups; Shopping
trips; Dances/Social/Cultural gatherings.

Cleveland

Cleveland Manor Nursing Home
PO Box 198, Cleveland, OK 74020
(918) 358-3135
Admin K R Bob May. *Dir of Nursing* Edris P
Cooper LPN.
Licensure Intermediate care; Alzheimer's care.
Beds ICF 50. *Certified* Medicaid.
Owner Privately owned.
Admissions Requirements Medical
examination; Physician's request.
Staff Physicians 5 (ft); RNs 1 (ft); LPNs 4 (ft);
Nurses' aides 16 (ft), 3 (pt); Activities
coordinators 1 (ft); Dietitians 1 (ft); Dentists
1 (pt).
Facilities Dining room; Laundry room;
Barber/Beauty shop.
Activities Arts & crafts; Cards; Games;
Reading groups; Prayer groups; Shopping
trips; Dances/Social/Cultural gatherings.

Clinton

Highland Park Manor
2400 Modelle, Clinton, OK 73601
(405) 323-1110
Admin Joan Wolfe.
Licensure Intermediate care. *Beds* ICF 100.
Certified Medicaid.

Prairie View Manor
3200 Hayes, Clinton, OK 73601
(405) 323-0990
Admin Janice Raab.
Licensure Skilled care. *Beds* SNF 60.

United Methodist Health Care Center
2316 Modelle, Clinton, OK 73601
(405) 323-0912
Admin Michael R Sewell. *Dir of Nursing* Judy
Unruh RN.
Licensure Intermediate care; Retirement. *Beds*
ICF 101. *Certified* Medicaid.
Owner Nonprofit corp.
Admissions Requirements Medical
examination; Physician's request.
Staff RNs 1 (ft); LPNs 7 (ft); Nurses' aides 40
(ft), 10 (pt); Physical therapists 1 (ft);
Recreational therapists 2 (ft); Activities
coordinators 1 (ft); Dietitians 1 (ft).
Affiliation Methodist.
Facilities Dining room; Physical therapy
room; Activities room; Chapel; Crafts room;
Laundry room; Barber/Beauty shop; Library.
Activities Arts & crafts; Cards; Games;
Reading groups; Prayer groups.

Coalgate

Ruth Wilson Hurley Manor
25 N Covington, Coalgate, OK 74538
(405) 927-2000
Admin Steven Lynch. *Dir of Nursing* Susan
Lorey RN. *Medical Dir* Wallace Byrd MD.
Licensure Intermediate care. *Beds* ICF 75.
Private Pay Patients 40%. *Certified*
Medicaid.
Owner Nonprofit corp.
Admissions Requirements Minimum age 14;
Medical examination; Physician's request.
Staff RNs 1 (ft); LPNs 3 (ft), 2 (pt); Nurses'
aides 24 (ft), 7 (pt); Activities coordinators 1
(ft), 1 (pt).
Languages American Indian.
Facilities Dining room; Activities room;
Chapel; Crafts room; Laundry room; Barber/
Beauty shop.
Activities Arts & crafts; Cards; Games; Prayer
groups; Movies; Dances/Social/Cultural
gatherings; Intergenerational programs;
Exercise.

Colbert

Southern Pointe
PO Box 847, Colbert, OK 74733
(405) 296-4500
Admin Billie Brown. *Dir of Nursing* Celeste
Justus.
Licensure Intermediate care. *Beds* ICF 65.
Private Pay Patients 25%. *Certified*
Medicaid.
Owner Privately owned (Kathy Chappell).
Admissions Requirements Medical
examination; Physician's request.
Staff RNs 1 (ft), 1 (pt); LPNs 4 (ft), 1 (pt);
Nurses' aides 16 (ft), 3 (pt); Recreational
therapists 1 (ft); Activities coordinators 1
(ft); Dietitians 1 (ft).
Facilities Dining room; Physical therapy
room; Activities room; Crafts room; Laundry
room; Barber/Beauty shop.
Activities Arts & crafts; Cards; Games;
Reading groups; Prayer groups; Movies;
Shopping trips; Dances/Social/Cultural
gatherings; Intergenerational programs; Pet
therapy.

Collinsville

Collinsville Manor Nursing Home
PO Box 279, 2300 W Broadway, Collinsville,
OK 74021
(918) 371-2545, 272-5991 FAX
Admin Jacquelyn Hudson. *Dir of Nursing*
Helen Cullison RN.

Licensure Intermediate care; Alzheimer's care. *Beds* ICF 100. *Private Pay Patients* 45%. *Certified* Medicaid.
Owner Proprietary corp (Sequoyah Investments Inc).
Admissions Requirements Medical examination.
Staff RNs 2 (ft), 1 (pt); LPNs 3 (ft); Nurses' aides 23 (ft), 3 (pt); Activities coordinators 1 (ft); Dietitians 1 (ft).
Languages German.
Facilities Dining room; Activities room; Crafts room; Laundry room; Barber/Beauty shop; Covered veranda.
Activities Arts & crafts; Cards; Games; Reading groups; Prayer groups; Movies; Shopping trips; Dances/Social/Cultural gatherings; Intergenerational programs; Pet therapy; Volunteer program; Monthly birthday parties.

Comanche

B & B Nursing Home
701 S 9th, Comanche, OK 73529
(405) 439-5569
Admin Rhonda Rusler.
Licensure Intermediate care; Alzheimer's care. *Beds* ICF 90. *Certified* Medicaid.
Owner Privately owned.
Admissions Requirements Medical examination; Physician's request.
Staff Physicians; RNs; LPNs; Nurses' aides; Physical therapists; Activities coordinators; Dietitians.
Facilities Dining room; Physical therapy room; Activities room; Crafts room; Laundry room; Barber/Beauty shop.
Activities Arts & crafts; Cards; Games; Reading groups; Prayer groups; Movies; Shopping trips; Dances/Social/Cultural gatherings.

Meridian Nursing Home Inc
PO Box 126, Comanche, OK 73529
(405) 439-2398
Admin Coweta Bishop.
Licensure Intermediate care. *Beds* ICF 50. *Certified* Medicaid.
Admissions Requirements Medical examination; Physician's request.
Staff Physicians 1 (pt); RNs 1 (ft); LPNs 6 (ft); Nurses' aides 11 (ft); Physical therapists 1 (ft); Recreational therapists 1 (ft); Activities coordinators 1 (ft); Dietitians 4 (ft); Social workers 1 (ft).
Facilities Dining room; Physical therapy room; Activities room; Crafts room; Laundry room; Barber/Beauty shop; Library.
Activities Cards; Games; Reading groups; Prayer groups; Shopping trips; Community plays; Seasonal parties.

Commerce

Eastwood Manor
Hwy 66 & 6th St, Commerce, OK 74339
(918) 675-4455
Admin Helen F Gering.
Licensure Intermediate care. *Beds* ICF 53. *Certified* Medicaid.

Cordell

Cordell Care Center
1420 N Crider Rd, Cordell, OK 73632
(405) 832-3871
Admin Frank D Loveless.
Licensure Skilled care. *Beds* SNF 80.

Cordell Christian Home
1400 N College, Cordell, OK 73632
(405) 832-3371
Admin Lowell Donley. *Dir of Nursing* Denice Church RN.

Licensure Intermediate care. *Beds* ICF 110. *Private Pay Patients* 60%. *Certified* Medicaid.
Owner Nonprofit corp.
Admissions Requirements Minimum age 62; Medical examination; Physician's request.
Staff RNs 1 (ft); LPNs 5 (ft), 2 (pt); Nurses' aides 40 (ft), 6 (pt); Activities coordinators 1 (ft); Dietitians (contracted).
Affiliation Church of Christ.
Facilities Dining room; Activities room; Crafts room; Laundry room; Barber/Beauty shop; Gazebo; Courtyard.
Activities Arts & crafts; Cards; Games; Prayer groups; Movies; Shopping trips; Dances/Social/Cultural gatherings; Community trips.

Corn

Corn Heritage Village
106 W Adams, Corn, OK 73024
(405) 343-2295
Admin Jerry Unruh. *Dir of Nursing* Judy Unruh.
Licensure Intermediate care; Retirement. *Beds* ICF 104; Retirement 16. *Private Pay Patients* 70%. *Certified* Medicaid.
Owner Nonprofit organization/foundation.
Admissions Requirements Medical examination.
Staff RNs 1 (ft); LPNs 4 (ft), 1 (pt); Nurses' aides 15 (ft); Activities coordinators 1 (ft); Dietitians 1 (pt).
Languages German.
Affiliation Mennonite.
Facilities Dining room; Physical therapy room; Activities room; Chapel; Crafts room; Laundry room; Barber/Beauty shop; Conference room.
Activities Arts & crafts; Cards; Games; Shopping trips.

Coweta

Coweta Manor
Coweta, OK 74429
(918) 251-6075
Admin Stella Maria Walker.
Licensure Intermediate care. *Beds* ICF 100. *Certified* Medicaid.

Crescent

Crescent Care Center
E Sanderson, Crescent, OK 73028
(405) 969-2680
Admin Elsie Hall.
Licensure Intermediate care. *Beds* ICF 47. *Certified* Medicaid.
Owner Proprietary corp (ARA Living Centers).

Cushing

Colonial Plaza Nursing Home Inc
1405 E Moses, Cushing, OK 74023
(918) 225-2220
Admin Marilyn Edgerwood.
Licensure Intermediate care. *Beds* ICF 67. *Certified* Medicaid.

Cushing Regional Hospital
1027 E Cherry, Cushing, OK 74023
(918) 225-2915
Admin Jerald D Goodner.
Licensure Skilled care. *Beds* SNF 17.

Rest Haven Nursing Home
310 N Central, Cushing, OK 74023
(918) 225-1477
Admin Russell E Myers Jr. *Dir of Nursing* Agnes Rowland.
Licensure Intermediate care. *Beds* ICF 55. *Certified* Medicaid.
Owner Privately owned.

Admissions Requirements Medical examination; Physician's request.
Staff RNs; LPNs; Nurses' aides; Activities coordinators; Dietitians.
Facilities Dining room; Activities room; Laundry room; Barber/Beauty shop.
Activities Arts & crafts; Cards; Games; Shopping trips.

Cyril

Cyril Nursing Home
410 S 4th St, Cyril, OK 73029
(405) 464-2426, 464-2705 FAX
Admin Anna M McClung. *Dir of Nursing* Vicki Walker. *Medical Dir* J Cunningham DO.
Licensure Intermediate care. *Beds* ICF 80. *Private Pay Patients* 33%. *Certified* Medicaid; Medicare.
Owner Proprietary corp (Texas Health Enterprises Inc).
Admissions Requirements Medical examination; Physician's request.
Staff Physicians 1 (pt); RNs 1 (pt); LPNs 6 (ft); Nurses' aides 19 (ft), 5 (pt); Recreational therapists 1 (pt); Activities coordinators 1 (ft); Dietitians 1 (ft); Ophthalmologists 1 (pt).
Languages Spanish.
Facilities Dining room; Activities room; Chapel; Crafts room; Laundry room; Barber/Beauty shop; Patio.
Activities Arts & crafts; Cards; Games; Reading groups; Prayer groups; Movies; Dances/Social/Cultural gatherings; Intergenerational programs; Pet therapy.

Davis

Burford Manor
505 S 7th, Davis, OK 73030
(405) 369-2653
Admin Bill M Burford. *Dir of Nursing* Nancy Smith.
Licensure Intermediate care. *Beds* ICF 73. *Private Pay Patients* 25%. *Certified* Medicaid.
Owner Privately owned.
Admissions Requirements Medical examination; Physician's request.
Staff RNs; LPNs 4 (ft); Nurses' aides 18 (ft), 6 (pt); Activities coordinators 1 (ft), 1 (pt); Dietitians 1 (ft).
Facilities Dining room; Crafts room; Laundry room; Barber/Beauty shop.
Activities Arts & crafts; Cards; Games; Reading groups; Prayer groups; Movies.

Del City

Del City Cerebral Palsy Center
3317 SE 18th St, Del City, OK 73115
(405) 677-2421
Admin Gene Lister.
Licensure Intermediate care for mentally retarded. *Beds* ICF/MR 16.

Evergreen Nursing Home
400 S Scott, Del City, OK 73115
(405) 677-3349
Admin Charles M Holthaus. *Dir of Nursing* Lorretta Gautt LPN. *Medical Dir* Tracy Skolnick DO.
Licensure Intermediate care. *Beds* ICF 61. *Certified* Medicaid.
Owner Proprietary corp (Amity Care).
Admissions Requirements Minimum age 18; Medical examination.
Staff Physicians 1 (pt); RNs 1 (pt); LPNs 3 (ft); Nurses' aides 13 (ft); Physical therapists 1 (pt); Reality therapists 1 (pt); Recreational therapists 1 (pt); Activities coordinators 2 (ft); Dietitians 1 (pt); Ophthalmologists 1 (pt); Dentists 1 (pt).

Facilities Dining room; Activities room; Crafts room; Laundry room; Barber/Beauty shop; Library.
Activities Arts & crafts; Cards; Games; Reading groups; Prayer groups; Movies; Shopping trips; Dances/Social/Cultural gatherings.

Dewey

Forrest Manor Nursing Home
1410 N Choctaw, Dewey, OK 74029
(918) 534-3355
Admin Beth Smith.
Licensure Intermediate care. *Beds* ICF 116.
Certified Medicaid.
Owner Proprietary corp (Beverly Enterprises).
Staff RNs; LPNs; Nurses' aides; Physical therapists; Activities coordinators; Dietitians; Dentists.
Facilities Dining room; Physical therapy room; Activities room; Crafts room; Laundry room; Barber/Beauty shop.
Activities Arts & crafts; Cards; Games; Shopping trips; Dances/Social/Cultural gatherings.

Medicalodge of Dewey
Box 520 Rte 1, Dewey, OK 74029
(918) 534-2848
Admin Ellen Williams.
Licensure Intermediate care. *Beds* ICF 62.
Certified Medicaid.
Owner Proprietary corp (Medicalodges Inc).

Drumright

Drumright Nursing Home
Pine & Bristow, Drumright, OK 74030
(918) 352-3249
Admin Marie Cooper.
Licensure Intermediate care. *Beds* ICF 133.
Certified Medicaid.

Duncan

Duncan Care Center
700 Palm, Duncan, OK 73537
(405) 255-9000
Admin Carol Putman. *Dir of Nursing* Billie Wheeler.
Licensure Intermediate care; Alzheimer's care. *Beds* ICF 160; Alzheimer's care 40. *Private Pay Patients* 60%. *Certified* Medicaid.
Owner Proprietary corp (ARA Living Centers).
Admissions Requirements Medical examination; Physician's request.
Staff RNs; LPNs; Nurses' aides; Physical therapists; Speech therapists; Activities coordinators; Dietitians.
Facilities Dining room; Activities room; Crafts room; Laundry room; Barber/Beauty shop; Library; Sun room; Outdoor patio.
Activities Arts & crafts; Cards; Games; Prayer groups; Movies; Shopping trips; Dances/Social/Cultural gatherings; Pet therapy.

Duncan Regional Hospital SNF
PO Box 2000, 1407 Whisenant Dr, Duncan, OK 73533
(405) 252-5300
Admin David J Robertson.
Licensure Skilled care. *Beds* SNF 12.

Kanakuk Nursing Home
N Hwy 81, Duncan, OK 73533
(405) 255-4600
Admin Dr Jack Gregston.
Licensure Intermediate care. *Beds* ICF 94.
Certified Medicaid.

Kenya Village Nursing Home
1205 S 4th, Duncan, OK 73533
(405) 252-3955
Admin Rev Worth McGee.

Licensure Intermediate care. *Beds* ICF 31.
Certified Medicaid.
Admissions Requirements Minimum age 18; Medical examination.
Staff RNs 1 (pt); LPNs 2 (ft); Nurses' aides 6 (ft), 3 (pt); Physical therapists 1 (pt); Recreational therapists 1 (ft); Activities coordinators 1 (ft); Dietitians 1 (pt).
Facilities Dining room; Physical therapy room; Laundry room; Barber/Beauty shop.
Activities Arts & crafts; Cards; Games; Reading groups; Prayer groups; Shopping trips.

Lahey's Nursing Home
PO Box 1664, Duncan, OK 73534-1664
(405) 255-6378
Admin Donald J Legner.
Medical Dir David Fisher MD.
Licensure Intermediate care. *Beds* ICF 47.
Certified Medicaid.
Admissions Requirements Medical examination.
Staff RNs 1 (ft); LPNs 3 (ft); Nurses' aides 15 (ft), 4 (pt); Physical therapists 1 (pt); Activities coordinators 1 (ft), 1 (pt); Dietitians 1 (pt); Dentists 1 (pt).
Facilities Dining room; Physical therapy room; Activities room; Crafts room; Laundry room; Barber/Beauty shop.
Activities Arts & crafts; Cards; Games; Reading groups; Prayer groups; Movies; Shopping trips; Dances/Social/Cultural gatherings.

Durant

Bryan County Manor
1401 N Washington, Durant, OK 74701
(405) 924-1263
Admin Elise Stumpff.
Licensure Intermediate care. *Beds* ICF 65.
Certified Medicaid.

Four Seasons Nursing Center of Durant
1212 Four Seasons Dr, Durant, OK 74701
(405) 924-5300
Admin Phillip K Stumpff.
Licensure Intermediate care. *Beds* ICF 122.
Certified Medicaid.

King's Daughters & Sons Nursing Home
1223 Baltimore, Durant, OK 74701
(405) 924-0496
Admin Bonnie A Bates.
Licensure Intermediate care. *Beds* ICF 65.
Certified Medicaid.
Staff RNs; LPNs; Nurses' aides.
Affiliation King's Daughters & Sons.
Facilities Dining room; Physical therapy room; Activities room; Chapel; Crafts room; Laundry room; Barber/Beauty shop.
Activities Arts & crafts; Cards; Games; Prayer groups.

Oak Ridge Manor
1100 Oak Ridge, Durant, OK 74701
(405) 924-3244
Admin Erik J Stumpff. *Dir of Nursing* Patricia Henderson RN.
Licensure Intermediate care. *Beds* ICF 84.
Certified Medicaid.
Admissions Requirements Minimum age 18; Medical examination; Physician's request.
Staff RNs 1 (ft); LPNs 2 (ft); Nurses' aides 24 (ft); Reality therapists 1 (pt); Recreational therapists 1 (pt); Activities coordinators 1 (ft); Dietitians 2 (pt).
Facilities Dining room; Physical therapy room; Activities room; Chapel; Crafts room; Laundry room; Barber/Beauty shop; Library.
Activities Arts & crafts; Cards; Games; Reading groups; Prayer groups; Movies; Shopping trips; Dances/Social/Cultural gatherings.

Edmond

Bryant Nursing Center
1100 E 9th, Edmond, OK 73034
(405) 341-5617
Admin John Westphal.
Licensure Skilled care; Intermediate care. *Beds* SNF 40; ICF 60.

Edmond Nursing Center
39 SE 33rd St, Edmond, OK 73034
(405) 341-5555
Admin Pam Kovacs.
Medical Dir Loretta Slates.
Licensure Intermediate care. *Beds* ICF 109.
Certified Medicaid.
Owner Proprietary corp (ARA Living Centers).
Staff LPNs 5 (ft), 3 (pt); Nurses' aides 20 (ft), 9 (pt); Activities coordinators 2 (ft), 2 (pt); Dietitians 3 (ft), 5 (pt).

Oklahoma Christian Home
906 N Blvd, Edmond, OK 73034
(405) 341-0810
Admin Charles Hattendorf. *Dir of Nursing* Jessie Shields RN. *Medical Dir* Dr Brian Levy.
Licensure Intermediate care; Personal care; Independent housing; Alzheimer's care. *Beds* ICF 60; Personal care 50; Independent housing 60. *Private Pay Patients* 60%. *Certified* Medicaid.
Owner Nonprofit organization/foundation (National Benevolent Association of Christian Homes).
Admissions Requirements Minimum age 62; Medical examination.
Staff RNs 5 (ft); LPNs 5 (ft); Nurses' aides 25 (ft); Reality therapists; Activities coordinators 1 (ft); Dietitians 2 (ft).
Affiliation Disciples of Christ.
Facilities Dining room; Physical therapy room; Activities room; Chapel; Crafts room; Laundry room; Barber/Beauty shop; Library.
Activities Arts & crafts; Cards; Games; Reading groups; Movies; Shopping trips; Dances/Social/Cultural gatherings; Intergenerational programs; Pet therapy; Bible study; Devotions.

Timberlane Manor
PO Box 2017, 2520 S Rankin, Edmond, OK 73013
(405) 341-1433
Admin Linda Smith. *Dir of Nursing* Cathy Williams.
Licensure Intermediate care. *Beds* ICF 100.
Certified Medicaid.
Owner Proprietary corp (Amity Care).
Admissions Requirements Medical examination; Physician's request.
Staff RNs; LPNs; Nurses' aides; Activities coordinators; Dietitians.
Facilities Dining room; Physical therapy room; Activities room; Crafts room; Laundry room; Town Square (Ice cream parlor; General store; Bakery ; Barber shop; Beauty shop; Chapel; Library).
Activities Arts & crafts; Cards; Games; Reading groups; Prayer groups; Movies; Shopping trips; Dances/Social/Cultural gatherings; Intergenerational programs; Pet therapy.

El Reno

El Reno Nursing Center
PO Box 1399, 1901 Parkview Dr, El Reno, OK 73036
(405) 262-2833
Admin Linda Jones.
Licensure Intermediate care. *Beds* ICF 121.
Certified Medicaid.
Admissions Requirements Medical examination; Physician's request.

Staff RNs 3 (ft); LPNs 3 (ft); Nurses' aides 23 (ft), 2 (pt); Activities coordinators 1 (ft); Dietitians 1 (ft).
Facilities Dining room; Activities room; Crafts room; Laundry room; Barber/Beauty shop; Library.
Activities Arts & crafts; Cards; Games; Reading groups; Prayer groups; Movies; Shopping trips; Dances/Social/Cultural gatherings.

Sunset Estates of El Reno Inc
2100 Townsend Dr, El Reno, OK 73036
(405) 262-3323
Admin Rita J Harris.
Licensure Intermediate care. *Beds* ICF 66.
Certified Medicaid.

Elk City

Elk City Nursing Centre
Box 629, 301 N Garrett, Elk City, OK 73644
(405) 225-2811
Admin Sheila Smith. *Dir of Nursing* Jo Carole Kitchel. *Medical Dir* Dr Gill; Dr Perkins.
Licensure Intermediate care. *Beds* ICF 112.
Private Pay Patients 50%. *Certified* Medicaid.
Owner Proprietary corp (Southwest Health Care).
Admissions Requirements Medical examination.
Staff RNs; LPNs; Nurses' aides; Physical therapists; Activities coordinators; Dietitians.
Facilities Dining room; Activities room; Crafts room; Laundry room; Barber/Beauty shop.
Activities Arts & crafts; Cards; Games; Prayer groups; Movies; Shopping trips; Dances/ Social/Cultural gatherings; Intergenerational programs; Pet therapy.

Enid

Bass Memorial Baptist Hospital
600 S Monroe, Enid, OK 73701
(405) 233-2300
Admin W Eugene Baxter.
Licensure Skilled care. *Beds* SNF 15.

East View Nursing Center
410 N 30th, Enid, OK 73701
(405) 237-1973
Admin Pat Lewis. *Dir of Nursing* Barbara Owings. *Medical Dir* Larry Ensz DO.
Licensure Intermediate care. *Beds* ICF 102.
Private Pay Patients 50%. *Certified* Medicaid.
Owner Proprietary corp (Amity Care).
Staff RNs 2 (ft); LPNs 4 (ft), 2 (pt); Nurses' aides 30 (ft); Activities coordinators 1 (ft).
Facilities Dining room; Physical therapy room; Activities room; Chapel; Laundry room; Barber/Beauty shop.
Activities Arts & crafts; Cards; Games; Reading groups; Prayer groups; Movies; Shopping trips; Dances/Social/Cultural gatherings; Intergenerational programs; Pet therapy; Holiday events; Halloween night for children from community.

Enid Memorial Hospital SNF
401 S 3rd, Enid, OK 73701
(405) 234-3371
Admin Shirley Haskins.
Licensure Skilled care. *Beds* SNF 10.

Enid State School
2600 E Willow, Enid, OK 73701
(405) 237-1027
Admin Ray Nelson.
Licensure Intermediate care for mentally retarded. *Beds* ICF/MR 401.

Greenbrier Nursing Home
1121 E Owen Garriott, Enid, OK 73701
(405) 233-0121
Admin Dortha Schmitz.

Licensure Intermediate care. *Beds* 52.
Certified Medicaid.

Highland Park Manor
1410 W Willow Rd, Enid, OK 73701
(405) 234-2526
Admin Marcia Brunsvold.
Licensure Intermediate care. *Beds* ICF 110.
Certified Medicaid.

Kenwood Manor
502 W Pine, Enid, OK 73701
(405) 233-2722
Admin William D Jones. *Dir of Nursing* Janie Davis LPN.
Licensure Intermediate care. *Beds* ICF 45.
Private Pay Patients 33%. *Certified* Medicaid.
Owner Proprietary corp (Enid Memorial Hospital Corp).
Admissions Requirements Physician's request.
Staff RNs 1 (pt); LPNs 3 (ft); Nurses' aides 12 (ft), 4 (pt); Physical therapists 1 (ft), 1 (pt); Activities coordinators 1 (ft); Dietitians 1 (pt).
Languages Spanish.
Facilities Dining room; Activities room; Crafts room; Laundry room; Barber/Beauty shop; Whirlpool baths.
Activities Arts & crafts; Cards; Games; Reading groups; Prayer groups; Movies; Dances/Social/Cultural gatherings; Intergenerational programs.

Living Center
1409 N 17th, Enid, OK 73701
(405) 234-1411
Admin Betty J Harris.
Medical Dir Dr Stafford.
Licensure Intermediate care. *Beds* ICF 50.
Facilities Dining room; Physical therapy room; Activities room; Chapel; Crafts room; Laundry room; Barber/Beauty shop; Library.
Activities Arts & crafts; Cards; Games; Reading groups; Prayer groups; Movies; Shopping trips; Dances/Social/Cultural gatherings.

Methodist Home of Enid Inc
PO Box 10489, 301 S Oakwood Rd, Enid, OK 73702
(405) 237-6164
Admin Dwight Martin. *Dir of Nursing* Barbara Lund RN.
Licensure Skilled care; Intermediate care. *Beds* SNF 30; ICF 99. *Certified* Medicaid.
Owner Nonprofit corp.
Affiliation Methodist.

Pekrul Manor
313 E Oxford, Enid, OK 73701
(405) 237-3871
Admin Virgil Pekrul.
Licensure Intermediate care. *Beds* ICF 50.
Certified Medicaid.

St Mary's Hospital Skilled Nursing Facility
PO Box 232, Enid, OK 73702
(405) 233-6100, 233-3982 FAX
Admin Mary T Brasseaux. *Dir of Nursing* Carolyn Williams. *Medical Dir* Daniel Washburn MD.
Licensure Skilled care. *Beds* SNF 14. *Certified* Medicare.
Owner Proprietary corp.
Admissions Requirements Physician's request.
Staff RNs 2 (ft), 2 (pt); LPNs 3 (pt); Nurses' aides 6 (ft), 1 (pt); Physical therapists 1 (ft); Recreational therapists 1 (pt); Occupational therapists 1 (pt); Speech therapists (contracted); Activities coordinators 1 (pt); Dietitians 1 (pt).
Facilities Dining room; Activities room.
Activities Arts & crafts; Games; Movies.

Sunnyside Center
1824 S Van Buren, Enid, OK 73701
(405) 233-6422
Admin Carroll Young.

Medical Dir Jaspal Chawla MD.
Licensure Intermediate care for mentally retarded. *Beds* ICF/MR 112. *Certified* Medicaid.
Staff LPNs 4 (ft), 1 (pt); Nurses' aides 38 (ft); Physical therapists 1 (ft); Activities coordinators 1 (ft); Dietitians 1 (pt).
Facilities Dining room; Physical therapy room; Activities room; Crafts room; Laundry room; Barber/Beauty shop.
Activities Arts & crafts; Cards; Games; Reading groups; Prayer groups; Movies; Shopping trips; Dances/Social/Cultural gatherings; Special Olympics.

Erick

Erick Nursing Home
112 S Magnolia, Erick, OK 73645
(405) 526-3088
Admin Jim Dykes.
Licensure Intermediate care. *Beds* ICF 31.
Certified Medicaid.

Eufaula

Eufaula Manor
107 McKinley, Eufaula, OK 74432
(918) 689-3211
Admin Bonnie Brockman. *Dir of Nursing* Dolores Spirlock RN.
Licensure Intermediate care. *Beds* ICF 80.
Certified Medicaid.
Facilities Dining room; Activities room; Laundry room; Barber/Beauty shop.
Activities Arts & crafts; Cards; Games; Reading groups; Prayer groups; Movies; Shopping trips; Dances/Social/Cultural gatherings.

Friendly Manor Nursing Home Company
6th & Woodland, Eufaula, OK 74432
(918) 689-2508
Admin James Nixon. *Dir of Nursing* Barbara Smith RN. *Medical Dir* Norma L Sneed MD.
Licensure Intermediate care. *Beds* ICF 70.
Certified Medicaid.
Owner Proprietary corp.
Admissions Requirements Minimum age 16; Medical examination; Physician's request.
Staff Physicians 5 (pt); RNs 1 (ft); LPNs 4 (ft); Nurses' aides 22 (ft), 1 (pt); Physical therapists 1 (pt); Recreational therapists 1 (ft); Occupational therapists 1 (pt); Speech therapists 1 (pt); Activities coordinators 1 (ft); Dietitians 1 (pt).
Facilities Dining room; Physical therapy room; Activities room; Chapel; Crafts room; Laundry room; Barber/Beauty shop; Library.
Activities Arts & crafts; Cards; Games; Reading groups; Prayer groups; Movies; Shopping trips; Dances/Social/Cultural gatherings.

Fairfax

Fairfax Nursing Home
401 S 8th, Fairfax, OK 74637
(918) 642-3234
Admin Kathryn Lee.
Licensure Intermediate care. *Beds* ICF 50.
Certified Medicaid.

Fairland

Fairland Nursing Home
12 E Conner, Fairland, OK 74343
(918) 676-3685
Admin Jane A Wooley. *Dir of Nursing* Allyne Hunter.
Licensure Intermediate care. *Beds* ICF 29.
Certified Medicaid.
Owner Proprietary corp.
Admissions Requirements Physician's request.

Staff Physicians; RNs; LPNs; Nurses' aides;
Activities coordinators; Dietitians;
Ophthalmologists; Podiatrists.
Facilities Dining room; Activities room;
Crafts room; Laundry room; Barber/Beauty
shop.
Activities Arts & crafts; Cards; Games; Prayer
groups; Movies; Dances/Social/Cultural
gatherings.

Fairview

**Fairview Fellowship Home for Senior Citizens
Inc**
605 E State Rd, Fairview, OK 73737
(405) 227-3784
Admin Dwight D Martin. *Dir of Nursing*
Johnie Skalicky RN.
Licensure Intermediate care; Retirement. *Beds*
ICF 100. *Certified* Medicaid.
Owner Nonprofit corp.
Admissions Requirements Medical
examination.
Staff RNs 2 (ft), 1 (pt); LPNs 4 (ft), 4 (pt);
Nurses' aides 20 (ft), 18 (pt); Physical
therapists 1 (pt).
Facilities Dining room; Physical therapy
room; Activities room; Chapel; Crafts room;
Laundry room; Barber/Beauty shop.
Activities Arts & crafts; Games; Reading
groups; Movies; Shopping trips.

Fort Gibson

Fort Gibson Nursing Home
205 E Popular, Fort Gibson, OK 74434
(918) 478-2456
Admin Jerry Morgan.
Licensure Intermediate care. *Beds* ICF 48.
Certified Medicaid.

Frederick

Memorial Nursing Center
317 E Josephine, Frederick, OK 73542
(405) 639-2622
Admin Charles L Chittum Jr. *Dir of Nursing*
Linda Melton RN. *Medical Dir* Dr Gerald
Martin.
Licensure Intermediate care. *Beds* ICF 25.
Private Pay Patients 84%. *Certified*
Medicaid; Medicare.
Owner Publicly owned.
Admissions Requirements Medical
examination; Physician's request.
Staff RNs 1 (ft), 1 (pt); LPNs 2 (ft); Nurses'
aides 10 (ft), 2 (pt); Activities coordinators 1
(ft); Dietitians 1 (ft); CMAs 4 (ft).
Languages Spanish.
Facilities Dining room; Activities room;
Barber/Beauty shop.
Activities Arts & crafts; Games; Reading
groups; Prayer groups; Movies; Dances/
Social/Cultural gatherings; Intergenerational
programs.

Pioneer Manor
313 E Lucille, Frederick, OK 73542
(405) 335-5591
Admin Timothy Pickert. *Dir of Nursing*
Barbara Roden LPN.
Licensure Intermediate care. *Beds* ICF 110.
Owner Proprietary corp.
Admissions Requirements Physician's request.
Staff RNs; LPNs; Nurses' aides; Activities
coordinators.
Facilities Dining room; Physical therapy
room; Activities room; Crafts room; Laundry
room; Barber/Beauty shop.
Activities Arts & crafts; Cards; Games;
Reading groups; Prayer groups; Shopping
trips; Dances/Social/Cultural gatherings.

Garber

Garber Nursing Home
209 E Garber Rd, Garber, OK 73738
(405) 863-2297
Admin Donna Mungon.
Licensure Intermediate care. *Beds* ICF 57.
Certified Medicaid.

Geary

Geary Community Nursing Home
PO Box 47, 1104 N Galena, Geary, OK 73040
(405) 884-5440
Admin John D Mackey. *Dir of Nursing* Betty
Austin.
Licensure Intermediate care. *Beds* ICF 67.
Private Pay Patients 67%. *Certified*
Medicaid.
Owner Nonprofit organization/foundation.
Admissions Requirements Medical
examination; Physician's request.
Staff RNs 1 (ft); LPNs 2 (ft), 2 (pt); Nurses'
aides 20 (ft), 10 (pt); Physical therapists 1
(pt); Activities coordinators 2 (ft); Dietitians
5 (ft), 3 (pt).
Facilities Dining room; Activities room;
Crafts room; Laundry room; Barber/Beauty
shop.
Activities Arts & crafts; Games; Music groups;
Church groups.

Glenpool

Glenpool Health Care Center
1700 E 141st, Glenpool, OK 74033
(918) 291-4230
Admin Glenda Thomas. *Dir of Nursing* Lee
Stern. *Medical Dir* Dr Scott Mays.
Licensure Intermediate care. *Beds* ICF 100.
Private Pay Patients 40%. *Certified*
Medicaid.
Owner Proprietary corp.
Admissions Requirements Medical
examination.
Staff RNs 1 (ft); LPNs 5 (ft), 3 (pt); Nurses'
aides; Activities coordinators.
Facilities Dining room; Activities room;
Laundry room; Barber/Beauty shop.
Activities Arts & crafts; Cards; Games;
Reading groups; Prayer groups; Shopping
trips; Dances/Social/Cultural gatherings.

Grandfield

Colonial Village
900 Westfield, Grandfield, OK 73546
(405) 479-5244
Admin Dorothy Haney.
Licensure Intermediate care. *Beds* ICF 40.
Certified Medicaid.

Grove

Betty Ann Nursing Home
1202 S Main, Grove, OK 74344
(918) 786-2275
Admin Randy Jobe.
Licensure Intermediate care. *Beds* ICF 60.
Certified Medicaid.
Staff RNs 1 (pt); LPNs 3 (ft); Nurses' aides 20
(ft); Activities coordinators 1 (ft); Dietitians
1 (pt).
Facilities Dining room; Physical therapy
room; Activities room; Chapel; Crafts room;
Laundry room; Barber/Beauty shop; Library.
Activities Arts & crafts; Cards; Games;
Reading groups; Prayer groups; Movies;
Shopping trips; Dances/Social/Cultural
gatherings.

Grand Lake Manor
PO Box 1029, Grove, OK 74344
(918) 786-2276
Admin Gary Dominguez. *Dir of Nursing* Alice
Wolf LPN.

Licensure Intermediate care. *Beds* ICF 100.
Certified Medicaid.
Admissions Requirements Medical
examination.
Staff RNs 1 (pt); LPNs 5 (ft), 1 (pt); Nurses'
aides 18 (ft), 3 (pt); Physical therapists 1
(pt); Activities coordinators 1 (ft); Dietitians
1 (pt).
Facilities Dining room; Physical therapy
room; Laundry room; Barber/Beauty shop.
Activities Arts & crafts; Games; Movies;
Shopping trips; Dances/Social/Cultural
gatherings.

Guthrie

Cole's Rest Haven Nursing Home
1310 E Oklahoma, Guthrie, OK 73044
(405) 282-1686
Admin John Chambers.
Medical Dir Lenora Chambers.
Licensure Intermediate care. *Beds* ICF 50.
Certified Medicaid.
Owner Proprietary corp.
Admissions Requirements Minimum age 16.
Staff RNs; LPNs; Nurses' aides; Activities
coordinators; Dietitians.
Facilities Dining room; Activities room;
Laundry room; Barber/Beauty shop; Activity
bus.
Activities Arts & crafts; Cards; Games;
Reading groups; Prayer groups; Movies;
Shopping trips; Dances/Social/Cultural
gatherings.

Colonial Estates
PO Box 977, Guthrie, OK 73044
(405) 282-3630
Admin Arlene Smith. *Dir of Nursing* Janell
Miller.
Licensure Intermediate care. *Beds* ICF 85.
Certified Medicare.
Owner Proprietary corp.
Facilities Dining room; Activities room;
Chapel.
Activities Arts & crafts; Cards; Games.

Golden Age Nursing Home of Guthrie Inc
419 E Oklahoma, Guthrie, OK 73044
(405) 282-0144
Admin Clara Duehning.
Licensure Intermediate care. *Beds* ICF 94.
Certified Medicaid.
Staff RNs 1 (ft), 2 (pt); LPNs 3 (ft), 2 (pt);
Nurses' aides 35 (ft), 5 (pt); Dietitians 1 (pt).
Facilities Dining room; Physical therapy
room; Barber/Beauty shop.
Activities Arts & crafts; Games; Shopping
trips.

Guthrie Retirement & Care Center
405 N 20th, Guthrie, OK 73044
(405) 282-1515
Admin Mishell Blevins Garver.
Licensure Intermediate care. *Beds* ICF 100.
Certified Medicaid.

Westview Living Center
PO Box 977, 1900 W Harrison, Guthrie, OK
73044
(405) 282-0205
Admin Shirley Dunham.
Licensure Intermediate care for mentally
retarded. *Beds* ICF/MR 51. *Certified*
Medicaid.

Guymon

**Dr W F & Mada Dunaway Manor Nursing
Home of Guymon Inc**
PO Box 831, 1401 N Lelia, Guymon, OK
73942
(405) 338-3186
Admin Virgil L Pekrul Jr. *Dir of Nursing* Elisa
Padilla RN. *Medical Dir* Ruth Wadley MD.
Licensure Intermediate care; Alzheimer's care.
Beds ICF 77. *Certified* Medicaid.

Owner Nonprofit corp.
Admissions Requirements Physician's request.
Staff RNs 1 (ft); LPNs 2 (ft); Nurses' aides 30 (ft); Reality therapists; Recreational therapists; Activities coordinators 1 (ft), 1 (pt); Dietitians.
Languages Spanish.
Affiliation Methodist.
Facilities Dining room; Physical therapy room; Activities room; Chapel; Crafts room; Laundry room; Barber/Beauty shop; Library; Garden; Large patio.
Activities Arts & crafts; Cards; Games; Reading groups; Prayer groups; Movies; Shopping trips; Dances/Social/Cultural gatherings; Music groups.

Harrah

Harrah Nursing Center Inc
2400 White's Meadow Dr, Harrah, OK 73045
(405) 454-6255
Admin Ellen Sue Kanady.
Licensure Skilled care. *Beds* SNF 60.

Summit Ridge Retirement Center
18501 NE 63rd St, Harrah, OK 73045
(405) 454-2431
Admin Paul G Proctor Jr.
Licensure Intermediate care. *Beds* ICF 16.

Hartshorne

Twin City Nursing Home
310 S 11th, Hartshorne, OK 74547
(918) 297-2414
Admin Frances Mordecai.
Licensure Intermediate care. *Beds* ICF 55. *Certified* Medicaid.

Haskell

Haskell Shamrock Care Center
PO Box 1319, Hwy 64 & Ash, Haskell, OK 74436
(918) 482-3310
Admin Janisue Langford. *Dir of Nursing* Carol Cooper.
Licensure Intermediate care. *Beds* ICF 58. *Private Pay Patients* 22%. *Certified* Medicare.
Owner Proprietary corp (Shamrock Health Management Corp).
Admissions Requirements Medical examination; Physician's request.
Staff RNs 1 (pt); LPNs 2 (ft), 2 (pt); Nurses' aides 9 (ft), 5 (pt); Activities coordinators 1 (ft).
Facilities Dining room; Activities room; Crafts room; Laundry room; Barber/Beauty shop.
Activities Arts & crafts; Cards; Games; Reading groups; Prayer groups; Movies; Shopping trips.

Healdton

Healdton Nursing Home
406 E Main, Healdton, OK 73438
(405) 229-0737
Admin Rosie Foster.
Licensure Intermediate care. *Beds* ICF 51. *Certified* Medicaid.
Owner Proprietary corp (ARA Living Centers).

Heavener

Heavener Nursing Home
Rte 1 Box 1000, Heavener, OK 74937
(918) 653-2464
Admin Carolyn Yandell. *Dir of Nursing* Ginger Lockhart RN. *Medical Dir* M G Kemp MD.

Licensure Intermediate care. *Beds* ICF 41. *Private Pay Patients* 25%. *Certified* Medicaid.
Owner Proprietary corp.
Admissions Requirements Medical examination; Physician's request.
Staff RNs 1 (ft); LPNs 2 (ft), 1 (pt); Nurses' aides 10 (ft), 3 (pt); Activities coordinators 1 (ft); Dietitians 1 (pt).
Facilities Dining room; Activities room; Laundry room.
Activities Arts & crafts; Cards; Games; Movies; Shopping trips.

Vista Nursing Home Inc
114 W 2nd St, Heavener, OK 74937
(918) 653-2472
Admin Mary E Foresee. *Dir of Nursing* Marcella Williams.
Licensure Intermediate care. *Beds* ICF 51. *Private Pay Patients* 4%. *Certified* Medicaid.
Owner Proprietary corp.
Admissions Requirements Physician's request.
Staff RNs 1 (ft); LPNs 5 (ft); Nurses' aides 12 (ft), 4 (pt); Activities coordinators 1 (ft); Dietitians; Office secretaries 1 (ft); Cooks & dietary aides 4 (ft); Food service supervisors 1 (ft); Administrative 1 (ft); Housekeeping 1 (ft), 1 (pt); Laundry 1 (ft), 1 (pt); Maintenance 1 (ft), 1 (pt).
Facilities Dining room; Activities room; Laundry room; Barber/Beauty shop.
Activities Arts & crafts; Cards; Games; Reading groups; Prayer groups; Movies; Shopping trips; Exercise.

Helena

Helena Care Center
200 W 3rd, Helena, OK 73741
(405) 852-3286
Admin Ernest Johnson.
Medical Dir Dr Gaylon Crawford.
Licensure Intermediate care. *Beds* ICF 50. *Certified* Medicaid.
Admissions Requirements Medical examination; Physician's request.
Staff Physicians 1 (pt); RNs 1 (pt); LPNs 1 (ft); Nurses' aides 12 (ft), 3 (pt); Physical therapists 2 (pt); Reality therapists 1 (pt); Recreational therapists 1 (pt); Activities coordinators 1 (ft), 1 (pt); Dietitians 1 (pt); Dentists 1 (pt).
Facilities Dining room; Physical therapy room; Activities room; Crafts room; Laundry room; Barber/Beauty shop.
Activities Arts & crafts; Cards; Games; Reading groups; Prayer groups; Movies; Shopping trips; Church services.

Hennessey

Hennessey Care Center
705 E 3rd, Hennessey, OK 73742
(405) 853-6027
Admin Gail Tilson. *Dir of Nursing* Neva Hale RN.
Licensure Intermediate care; Vacation/Respite care. *Beds* ICF 50; Vacation/Respite care 8. *Private Pay Patients* 50%. *Certified* Medicaid.
Owner Proprietary corp (ARA Living Centers).
Admissions Requirements Physician's request.
Staff RNs 1 (ft); LPNs 1 (ft); Nurses' aides 12 (ft); Activities coordinators 1 (ft); Dietitians 1 (ft).
Languages Spanish.
Facilities Dining room; Laundry room; Barber/Beauty shop.
Activities Arts & crafts; Cards; Games; Reading groups; Prayer groups; Movies; Dances/Social/Cultural gatherings; Intergenerational programs; Pet therapy; Remotivation; Nail care; Family interaction; Social group interaction.

Henryetta

Bono Nursing Home
212 N Antes, Henryetta, OK 74437
(918) 652-8797
Admin Toni Johnson. *Dir of Nursing* Kathy Cox RN. *Medical Dir* Ted Lewis MD.
Licensure Intermediate care. *Beds* ICF 53. *Private Pay Patients* 20%. *Certified* Medicaid.
Owner Privately owned.
Admissions Requirements Medical examination.
Staff Physicians 1 (pt); RNs 2 (ft), 1 (pt); LPNs 2 (ft), 1 (pt); Nurses' aides 10 (ft), 10 (pt); Recreational therapists 1 (ft); Activities coordinators 1 (ft), 1 (pt); Dietitians 1 (pt).
Facilities Dining room; Activities room; Crafts room; Laundry room; Barber/Beauty shop.
Activities Arts & crafts; Cards; Games; Reading groups; Prayer groups; Movies; Shopping trips; Dances/Social/Cultural gatherings; Pet therapy.

Fountain View Manor
107 E Barclay, Box 520, Henryetta, OK 74437
(918) 652-7021
Admin Opal Molet.
Licensure Intermediate care. *Beds* ICF 140. *Certified* Medicaid.

Lake Drive Nursing Home Inc
600 Lake Rd, Henryetta, OK 74437
(918) 652-8101
Admin June Duncan.
Licensure Intermediate care for mentally retarded. *Beds* ICF/MR 60. *Certified* Medicaid.

Hinton

Red Rock Manor Inc
PO Box 279, 501 W Main, Hinton, OK 73047
(405) 542-6677
Admin Glenda Sue Boling.
Licensure Intermediate care. *Beds* ICF 40. *Certified* Medicaid.
Admissions Requirements Medical examination; Physician's request.
Staff Physicians 1 (ft); RNs 1 (pt); LPNs 1 (ft), 2 (pt); Nurses' aides 16 (ft); Physical therapists 1 (pt); Reality therapists 1 (pt); Recreational therapists 1 (ft); Activities coordinators 1 (ft); Dietitians 1 (pt); Podiatrists 1 (pt); Dentists 1 (pt).
Facilities Dining room; Activities room; Laundry room; Barber/Beauty shop.
Activities Arts & crafts; Cards; Games; Reading groups; Prayer groups; Shopping trips.

Hobart

B & K Nursing Center
101 S Main, Hobart, OK 73651
(405) 726-3394
Admin Lorin Winters. *Dir of Nursing* Ethelyn Ragsdale. *Medical Dir* Dr Michael Kreiger.
Licensure Intermediate care. *Beds* ICF 50. *Certified* Medicaid.
Owner Proprietary corp.
Admissions Requirements Medical examination; Physician's request.
Staff Physicians 1 (pt); RNs 1 (pt); LPNs 2 (ft), 1 (pt); Nurses' aides 25 (ft), 7 (pt); Physical therapists 1 (pt); Reality therapists 1 (pt); Recreational therapists 1 (ft), 1 (pt); Occupational therapists 1 (ft), 1 (pt); Speech therapists 1 (pt); Activities coordinators 1 (ft), 1 (pt); Dietitians 1 (pt); Ophthalmologists 1 (pt); Podiatrists 1 (pt); Audiologists 1 (pt).
Facilities Dining room; Physical therapy room; Activities room; Laundry room; Barber/Beauty shop; Library.

Activities Arts & crafts; Cards; Games; Reading groups; Prayer groups; Movies; Shopping trips; Dances/Social/Cultural gatherings; Intergenerational programs; Pet therapy.

Hobart Good Samaritan Center
PO Box 680, 709 N Lowe, Hobart, OK 73651
(405) 726-3381
Admin Maria Hierstein.
Licensure Intermediate care. *Beds* ICF 60. *Certified* Medicaid.
Owner Nonprofit corp (Evangelical Lutheran/ Good Samaritan Society).

Hobart Good Samaritan Home
PO Box 680, 330 N Randlett, Hobart, OK 73651
(405) 726-5596
Admin Teresa Healy.
Medical Dir Margaret Medrano.
Licensure Intermediate care. *Beds* ICF 28. *Certified* Medicaid.
Owner Nonprofit corp (Evangelical Lutheran/ Good Samaritan Society).
Admissions Requirements Medical examination; Physician's request.
Staff RNs 1 (pt); LPNs 2 (ft); Nurses' aides 12 (ft); Activities coordinators 1 (ft).
Affiliation Lutheran.
Facilities Dining room; Physical therapy room; Activities room; Chapel; Laundry room; Barber/Beauty shop.
Activities Arts & crafts; Cards; Games; Reading groups; Prayer groups; Movies; Shopping trips.

Holdenville

Boyce Manor Inc
1600 E Hwy St, Holdenville, OK 74848
(405) 379-3560
Admin Naomi L Boyce.
Medical Dir T E Trow MD.
Licensure Intermediate care. *Beds* ICF 125. *Certified* Medicaid.
Admissions Requirements Minimum age 17; Medical examination; Physician's request.
Staff Physicians 1 (pt); RNs 1 (ft); LPNs 11 (ft); Nurses' aides 35 (ft); Physical therapists 1 (ft); Reality therapists 1 (ft); Recreational therapists 1 (ft); Speech therapists 1 (pt); Activities coordinators 1 (pt); Dietitians 1 (pt); Dentists 1 (pt).

Heritage Village Nursing Home
Rte 1 Box 54, Holdenville, OK 74848
(405) 379-6671
Admin Gerrol Adkins.
Licensure Skilled care. *Beds* SNF 60.

Holdenville Nursing Home
515 S Chestnut, Holdenville, OK 74848
(405) 379-2126
Admin Charles Simmons.
Medical Dir Ruth White.
Licensure Intermediate care. *Beds* ICF 51. *Certified* Medicaid.
Admissions Requirements Minimum age 18; Medical examination.
Staff Physicians; RNs; LPNs; Nurses' aides; Physical therapists; Activities coordinators; Dietitians.
Facilities Dining room; Crafts room; Laundry room; Barber/Beauty shop.
Activities Arts & crafts; Games; Prayer groups; Shopping trips; Dances/Social/Cultural gatherings.

Hollis

Colonial Manor I
400 E Sycamore, Hollis, OK 73550
(405) 688-2223
Admin Pat Hair.
Licensure Intermediate care. *Beds* ICF 69. *Certified* Medicaid.

Colonial Manor II
120 W Versa, Hollis, OK 73550
(405) 688-2828
Admin Bill R Hair.
Licensure Intermediate care. *Beds* ICF 92. *Certified* Medicaid.

Hominy

Hominy Nursing Home
700 N Katy, Box 577, Hominy, OK 74035
(918) 885-4746
Admin Robert Chandler. *Dir of Nursing* Carol Passmore LPN.
Licensure Intermediate care. *Beds* ICF 63. *Certified* Medicaid.
Admissions Requirements Medical examination; Physician's request.
Staff LPNs 2 (ft), 1 (pt); Nurses' aides 15 (ft); Activities coordinators 1 (pt); Dietitians 1 (pt).
Facilities Dining room; Activities room; Chapel; Crafts room; Laundry room; Barber/ Beauty shop.
Activities Arts & crafts; Cards; Games; Prayer groups; Shopping trips; Dances/Social/ Cultural gatherings.

Hugo

Hugo Golden Age Home
1200 W Finley, Hugo, OK 74743
(405) 326-8383
Admin Steven D Thomas.
Licensure Intermediate care. *Beds* ICF 100. *Certified* Medicaid.

Hugo Manor Nursing Home
601 N Broadway, Hugo, OK 74743
(405) 326-6278
Admin Kathlen Hammond.
Licensure Intermediate care. *Beds* ICF 80. *Certified* Medicaid.
Admissions Requirements Medical examination.
Staff Physicians 1 (pt); RNs 1 (pt); LPNs 2 (ft); Activities coordinators 1 (ft); Dietitians 1 (pt); Dentists 1 (pt).
Facilities Dining room; Physical therapy room; Activities room; Crafts room; Laundry room; Barber/Beauty shop.
Activities Arts & crafts; Cards; Games; Reading groups; Prayer groups; Movies; Shopping trips; Dances/Social/Cultural gatherings.

Rose Haven Health Care Center
PO Box 387, Hugo, OK 74743
(405) 326-3677
Admin Florence E Harrison RN. *Dir of Nursing* James Rhoden. *Medical Dir* James Grimaud DO.
Licensure Intermediate care. *Beds* ICF 40. *Private Pay Patients* 3%. *Certified* Medicaid; Medicare.
Owner Privately owned.
Admissions Requirements Medical examination; Physician's request.
Staff Physicians 1 (pt); RNs 1 (pt); LPNs 5 (ft); Nurses' aides 10 (ft); Physical therapists 1 (ft); Activities coordinators 1 (ft); Dietitians 1 (pt).
Facilities Dining room; Physical therapy room; Activities room; Chapel; Crafts room; Laundry room; Barber/Beauty shop; Library; TV room; Private lobby.
Activities Arts & crafts; Cards; Games; Reading groups; Prayer groups; Movies; Shopping trips; Dances/Social/Cultural gatherings; Intergenerational programs; Pet therapy.

Hydro

Maple Lawn Manor
800 Arapaho, Hydro, OK 73048
(405) 663-2455

Admin Roy D Dick EdD. *Dir of Nursing* Elsie Cox RN. *Medical Dir* Ralph Buller MD.
Licensure Intermediate care. *Beds* ICF 60. *Private Pay Patients* 60%. *Certified* Medicaid; Medicare.
Owner Nonprofit organization/foundation.
Staff RNs 2 (pt); LPNs 3 (ft), 1 (pt); Nurses' aides 13 (ft), 6 (pt); Activities coordinators 1 (ft); Dietitians 1 (ft).
Affiliation Mennonite.
Facilities Dining room; Activities room; Chapel; Laundry room; Barber/Beauty shop.
Activities Arts & crafts; Cards; Games; Shopping trips; Intergenerational programs.

Idabel

Hill Nursing Home
808 NW 1st, Idabel, OK 74745
(405) 286-5398
Admin Gladys Hill.
Licensure Intermediate care. *Beds* ICF 51. *Certified* Medicaid.

Memorial Heights Nursing Center
PO Box 839, 1305 SE Adams, Idabel, OK 74745
(405) 286-3366
Admin Brenda Hunter. *Dir of Nursing* Betty Volker. *Medical Dir* Dr Jon T Maxwell.
Licensure Intermediate care; Retirement. *Beds* ICF 118; Retirement 22. *Certified* Medicaid.
Owner Nonprofit corp (Heartway Corp).
Admissions Requirements Medical examination.
Staff RNs 1 (ft), 1 (pt); LPNs 5 (ft); Nurses' aides 40 (ft), 10 (pt); Activities coordinators 1 (ft); Dietitians 1 (pt); Physical therapy aides 1 (ft); Social service directors 1 (ft).
Facilities Dining room; Physical therapy room; Activities room; Laundry room; Barber/Beauty shop; Glassed-in front foyer; Patio.
Activities Arts & crafts; Cards; Games; Reading groups; Prayer groups; Movies; Shopping trips; Dances/Social/Cultural gatherings; Intergenerational programs; Pet therapy; Music therapy.

Oak Grove Manor Inc
PO Box 299, Idabel, OK 74745
(405) 286-2537
Admin Julie K Bivin RN. *Dir of Nursing* Faye Pugh RN. *Medical Dir* T D Howard MD.
Licensure Intermediate care. *Beds* ICF 96. *Private Pay Patients* 20%. *Certified* Medicaid.
Owner Proprietary corp.
Admissions Requirements Physician's request.
Staff Physicians 1 (pt); RNs 2 (ft); LPNs 3 (ft), 2 (pt); Nurses' aides 30 (ft), 3 (pt); Physical therapists 1 (pt); Reality therapists 1 (pt); Recreational therapists 1 (pt); Occupational therapists 1 (pt); Speech therapists 1 (pt); Activities coordinators 2 (ft); Dietitians 1 (ft); Ophthalmologists 1 (pt); Podiatrists 1 (pt); Dentists 1 (pt).
Facilities Dining room; Activities room; Crafts room; Laundry room; Barber/Beauty shop; Lounges; Whirlpool baths; Patio sitting area; Medical examination room; Wheelchair van; Covered deck with swing.
Activities Arts & crafts; Cards; Games; Reading groups; Prayer groups; Movies; Shopping trips; Dances/Social/Cultural gatherings.

Jay

Guinn Nursing Home 1
N Main, Jay, OK 74346
(918) 253-4500
Admin Danny Guinn.
Licensure Intermediate care. *Beds* ICF 48. *Certified* Medicaid.

Guinn Nursing Home 2
E Monroe, Box 409, Jay, OK 74346
(918) 253-4226
Admin Charles Guinn.
Licensure Intermediate care. *Beds* ICF 50.
Certified Medicaid.

Jenks

Ambassador Manor South
PO Box 970, 711 N 5th St, Jenks, OK 74037
(918) 299-8508
Admin Patricia Schmitt. *Dir of Nursing* Olive
Burke. *Medical Dir* Nancy Turpin.
Licensure Intermediate care; Alzheimer's care.
Beds ICF 85. *Private Pay Patients* 33%.
Certified Medicaid.
Owner Proprietary corp (JoAnne O Posey).
Admissions Requirements Medical
examination; Physician's request.
Staff RNs 1 (ft); LPNs 4 (ft), 2 (pt); Nurses'
aides 25 (ft); Physical therapists 1 (pt);
Activities coordinators 1 (ft); Dietitians 1
(pt); Podiatrists 1 (pt).
Facilities Dining room; Activities room;
Crafts room; Laundry room; Barber/Beauty
shop.
Activities Arts & crafts; Cards; Games;
Reading groups; Prayer groups; Movies;
Shopping trips; Dances/Social/Cultural
gatherings; Intergenerational programs; Pet
therapy.

Riverside Nursing Home Inc
601 N 5th, Jenks, OK 74037
(918) 299-9444
Admin Lucy J Northcutt.
Medical Dir Barbara Sutterfield.
Licensure Intermediate care. *Beds* ICF 102.
Certified Medicaid.
Owner Proprietary corp.
Admissions Requirements Medical
examination; Physician's request.
Staff RNs 1 (ft); LPNs 6 (ft); Nurses' aides 31
(ft); Recreational therapists 1 (pt);
Occupational therapists 1 (pt); Activities
coordinators 1 (ft); Dietitians 1 (ft).
Facilities Dining room; Physical therapy
room; Activities room; Crafts room; Laundry
room; Barber/Beauty shop.
Activities Arts & crafts; Cards; Games;
Reading groups; Prayer groups; Movies;
Shopping trips; Dances/Social/Cultural
gatherings.

Jones

Oak Hills Nursing Home
1100 W Georgia, Jones, OK 73049
(405) 399-2294
Admin Phyllis Murry.
Licensure Intermediate care. *Beds* ICF 160.
Certified Medicaid.

Kingfisher

Cimarron Nursing Center
905 Beall Rd, Kingfisher, OK 73750
(405) 375-6857
Admin Terry Petitt. *Dir of Nursing* Ellie Le
Doux.
Licensure Skilled care; Retirement. *Beds* SNF
82. *Private Pay Patients* 85%. *Certified*
Medicaid.
Owner Proprietary corp (JiCo Inc).
Facilities Dining room; Physical therapy
room; Activities room; Chapel; Crafts room;
Laundry room; Barber/Beauty shop; Library.
Activities Arts & crafts; Cards; Games;
Reading groups; Prayer groups; Dances/
Social/Cultural gatherings.

First Shamrock Care Center
PO Box 1227, Kingfisher, OK 73750
(405) 375-3157
Admin Wanda D Willms.

Licensure Intermediate care. *Beds* ICF 55.
Certified Medicaid.

Second Shamrock Care Center
PO Box 1228, Kingfisher, OK 73750
(405) 375-3106
Admin Delores Armstrong. *Dir of Nursing*
Donna H Treece LPN.
Licensure Intermediate care; Alzheimer's care.
Beds ICF 48. *Certified* Medicaid.
Owner Proprietary corp.
Admissions Requirements Medical
examination.
Staff RNs; LPNs; Nurses' aides; Activities
coordinators; Dietitians.
Languages Spanish.
Facilities Dining room; Activities room;
Crafts room; Laundry room; Barber/Beauty
shop.
Activities Arts & crafts; Cards; Games;
Reading groups; Prayer groups; Movies;
Shopping trips; Dances/Social/Cultural
gatherings; Monthly birthday parties.

Kingston

Texoma Manor Inc
Rte B Box 83, Kingston, OK 73439
(405) 564-2351
Admin Stacia Goodwin.
Licensure Intermediate care. *Beds* ICF 60.
Certified Medicaid.

Konawa

New Horizon Home
PO Box 217, 500 E Main, Konawa, OK 74849
(405) 925-3645, 925-2343 FAX
Admin Robert Chandler. *Dir of Nursing* Linda
Willmore LPN. *Medical Dir* Martin Stokes
MD.
Licensure Intermediate care; Intermediate care
for mentally retarded. *Beds* ICF 35; ICF/MR
173. *Certified* Medicaid.
Owner Proprietary corp (Oklahoma Nursing
Homes Ltd).
Admissions Requirements Minimum age 18;
Medical examination.
Staff Physicians 1 (pt); RNs 1 (ft); LPNs 7
(ft), 2 (pt); Nurses' aides 59 (ft); Physical
therapists; Reality therapists 1 (ft);
Recreational therapists 1 (ft); Activities
coordinators 5 (ft); Dietitians 1 (pt);
Ophthalmologists 1 (pt); Podiatrists 1 (pt);
Dentists 1 (pt).
Facilities Dining room; Physical therapy
room; Activities room; Crafts room; Laundry
room; Barber/Beauty shop.
Activities Arts & crafts; Cards; Games;
Reading groups; Prayer groups; Movies;
Shopping trips; Dances/Social/Cultural
gatherings.

Lawton

Arlington Manor
1202 Arlington, Lawton, OK 73501
(405) 353-3373
Admin W W Greb. *Dir of Nursing* Marion
Kribbs LPN. *Medical Dir* Brent Smith MD.
Licensure Intermediate care. *Beds* ICF 54.
Certified Medicaid.
Owner Proprietary corp.
Admissions Requirements Physician's request.
Staff Physicians 1 (pt); RNs 1 (ft); LPNs 5 (ft);
Nurses' aides 10 (ft); Physical therapists 1
(ft); Recreational therapists 1 (pt); Activities
coordinators 1 (ft); Dietitians 1 (ft).
Facilities Dining room; Physical therapy
room; Activities room; Chapel; Crafts room;
Laundry room; Barber/Beauty shop.
Activities Arts & crafts; Cards; Games;
Reading groups; Prayer groups; Movies;
Dances/Social/Cultural gatherings; Pet
therapy.

Cedar Crest Manor
1700 Fort Sill Blvd, Lawton, OK 73501
(405) 355-1616
Admin Don W Greb. *Dir of Nursing* Sandy
Pappan RN.
Licensure Skilled care; Intermediate care;
Alzheimer's care. *Beds* Swing beds SNF/ICF
95. *Certified* Medicaid; Medicare.
Owner Proprietary corp.
Admissions Requirements Medical
examination; Physician's request.
Staff Physicians 12 (pt); RNs 1 (ft), 1 (pt);
LPNs 7 (ft), 2 (pt); Nurses' aides 36 (ft), 5
(pt); Physical therapists 1 (ft); Recreational
therapists 1 (pt); Activities coordinators 1
(ft), 1 (pt); Dietitians 1 (ft);
Ophthalmologists 1 (pt); Podiatrists 1 (pt);
Dentists.
Facilities Dining room; Physical therapy
room; Activities room; Chapel; Crafts room;
Laundry room; Barber/Beauty shop; Library.
Activities Arts & crafts; Cards; Games;
Reading groups; Prayer groups; Movies;
Shopping trips; Dances/Social/Cultural
gatherings.

Lawton Heights Nursing Center
1301 NW Andrews, Lawton, OK 73507-3599
(405) 355-5720
Admin David H Dennis. *Dir of Nursing*
Marilyn Anthony RN. *Medical Dir* Dr Stan
Jackson.
Licensure Intermediate care. *Beds* ICF 96.
Private Pay Patients 50%. *Certified*
Medicaid.
Owner Proprietary corp.
Admissions Requirements Minimum age 5;
Medical examination; Physician's request.
Staff Physicians 1 (pt); RNs 1 (ft); LPNs 9
(ft); Nurses' aides 29 (ft), 5 (pt); Physical
therapists 1 (pt); Activities coordinators 1
(ft), 2 (pt); Dietitians 1 (pt).
Facilities Dining room; Physical therapy
room; Activities room; Crafts room; Laundry
room; Barber/Beauty shop.
Activities Arts & crafts; Cards; Games;
Reading groups; Prayer groups; Movies;
Shopping trips; Dances/Social/Cultural
gatherings; Intergenerational programs; Pet
therapy.

McMahon-Tomlinson Nursing Center
3126 Arlington, Lawton, OK 73505
(405) 357-3240
Admin Floyd Sanders.
Licensure Intermediate care. *Beds* ICF 118.
Certified Medicaid.
Owner Publicly owned.
Staff RNs 1 (ft); LPNs 13 (ft); Nurses' aides
45 (ft); Recreational therapists 1 (ft);
Activities coordinators 1 (ft).
Facilities Dining room; Physical therapy
room; Activities room; Chapel; Laundry
room; Barber/Beauty shop; Library.
Activities Arts & crafts; Cards; Games;
Reading groups; Prayer groups; Movies;
Shopping trips; Dances/Social/Cultural
gatherings.

**Southwestern Medical Center Skilled Nursing
Facility**
5602 SW Lee Blvd, Lawton, OK 73505
(405) 531-4700
Admin Eva Miller. *Dir of Nursing* Joan L
Harwell. *Medical Dir* Dr Jack Hash.
Licensure Skilled care. *Beds* SNF 8. *Private
Pay Patients* 2%. *Certified* Medicare.
Admissions Requirements Physician's request.
Staff RNs 2 (ft); LPNs 4 (ft), 2 (pt);
Nurses' aides 3 (ft); Physical therapists 3 (ft);
Speech therapists 1 (pt); Activities
coordinators 1 (ft); Dietitians 1 (ft).
Facilities Dining room; Physical therapy
room; Activities room; Chapel; Crafts room.
Activities Arts & crafts; Cards; Games;
Reading groups; Movies.

Western Hills Health Care Center
PO Box 6130, Lawton, OK 73506
(405) 353-3653
Admin Betty L Houston.
Medical Dir Thomas Leckman.
Licensure Skilled care; Intermediate care. *Beds*
SNF 16; ICF 135. *Certified* Medicaid.
Admissions Requirements Minimum age 21;
Medical examination; Physician's request.
Staff RNs 1 (pt); LPNs 6 (ft), 2 (pt); Nurses'
aides 48 (ft); Physical therapists 1 (ft), 1 (pt);
Reality therapists 1 (pt); Speech therapists 1
(pt); Activities coordinators 1 (ft); Dietitians
1 (pt).
Activities Arts & crafts; Cards; Games;
Reading groups; Prayer groups; Movies;
Shopping trips; Dances/Social/Cultural
gatherings; Grandfriends program; Visiting
pets program; Residents advisory council.

Willow Park Health Care Center
7019 NW Cache Rd, Lawton, OK 73505
(405) 536-1279
Admin Patricia Scott-Dye.
Licensure Skilled care; Intermediate care. *Beds*
SNF 41; ICF 110.

Woodland Care Center
7403 W Gore, Lawton, OK 73505
(405) 536-7401
Admin Phyllis Bowers.
Licensure Intermediate care. *Beds* ICF 100.
Certified Medicaid.

Lexington

Lexington Nursing Home
632 SE 3rd, Lexington, OK 73051
(405) 527-6531
Admin Bonnie R Hackney.
Licensure Intermediate care. *Beds* ICF 60.
Certified Medicaid.
Admissions Requirements Medical
examination.
Staff RNs; LPNs; Nurses' aides; Physical
therapists; Reality therapists; Recreational
therapists; Activities coordinators; Dietitians.
Facilities Dining room; Activities room;
Crafts room; Laundry room; Barber/Beauty
shop.
Activities Arts & crafts; Cards; Games;
Reading groups; Prayer groups; Movies;
Shopping trips; Dances/Social/Cultural
gatherings.

Sunset Manor of Lexington
2nd & Broadway, Lexington, OK 73701
(405) 527-6519
Admin Vickie L Gee.
Medical Dir Michaele Cole.
Licensure Intermediate care. *Beds* ICF 101.
Certified Medicaid.
Owner Proprietary corp.
Admissions Requirements Medical
examination.
Staff RNs 1 (ft), 1 (pt); LPNs 4 (ft), 1 (pt);
Nurses' aides 26 (ft), 3 (pt); Physical
therapists 1 (ft); Activities coordinators 1
(ft); Dietitians 1 (pt).
Facilities Dining room; Activities room;
Crafts room; Laundry room; Barber/Beauty
shop.
Activities Arts & crafts; Cards; Games;
Reading groups; Prayer groups; Movies;
Shopping trips; Dances/Social/Cultural
gatherings.

Lindsay

Washita Valley Nursing Center
Rte 4 Box 3, Hwy 19 W, Lindsay, OK 73052
(405) 756-4334
Admin Jean Fortenberry.
Licensure Intermediate care. *Beds* ICF 106.
Certified Medicaid.
Owner Proprietary corp (ARA Living
Centers).

Staff LPNs 4 (ft); Nurses' aides 28 (ft);
Activities coordinators 1 (ft).
Facilities Dining room; Physical therapy
room; Activities room; Crafts room; Barber/
Beauty shop; Library.
Activities Arts & crafts; Cards; Games;
Shopping trips; Dances/Social/Cultural
gatherings.

Locust Grove

Parkhill East Nursing Home
PO Box 517, Locust Grove, OK 74352
(918) 479-8411
Admin Sandra Lynn Overstreet.
Licensure Intermediate care. *Beds* ICF 50.
Certified Medicaid.

Parkhill South Nursing Home
PO Box 578, Locust Grove, OK 74352
(918) 479-5784
Admin Helen McKinnney.
Licensure Intermediate care. *Beds* ICF 54.
Certified Medicaid.

Madill

Brookside Manor Nursing Home
PO Box 848, Hwy 99 S, Madill, OK 73446
(405) 795-2100
Admin Alberta Stumpff. *Dir of Nursing*
Phyllis J Williams RN. *Beds* ICF 140.
Licensure Intermediate care. *Beds* ICF 140.
Certified Medicaid.
Owner Privately owned.
Admissions Requirements Physician's request.
Staff Physicians; RNs 1 (ft); LPNs 5 (ft);
Physical therapists 1 (ft); Activities
coordinators 2 (ft); Dietitians 1 (ft).
Facilities Dining room; Activities room;
Chapel; Crafts room; Laundry room; Barber/
Beauty shop.
Activities Arts & crafts; Cards; Games;
Reading groups; Prayer groups; Dominoes;
Bingo.

Mangum

Mangum Nursing Center
320 Carey, Mangum, OK 73554
(405) 782-3346
Admin Judith Tidmore.
Medical Dir R Kay Staton LPN.
Licensure Intermediate care. *Beds* ICF 140.
Certified Medicaid.
Owner Proprietary corp (Amity Care).
Admissions Requirements Minimum age 18;
Physician's request.
Staff RNs 1 (ft); LPNs 4 (pt); Nurses' aides 49
(pt); Physical therapists 1 (ft); Speech
therapists 1 (ft).
Facilities Dining room; Physical therapy
room; Activities room; Laundry room.
Activities Arts & crafts; Cards; Games;
Reading groups; Prayer groups; Movies;
Shopping trips; Dances/Social/Cultural
gatherings.

Mannford

Cimarron Pointe Care Center
PO Box 1300, 404 E Cimarron, Mannford,
OK 74044
(918) 865-7701, 865-7792 FAX
Admin Janice Meredith. *Dir of Nursing*
Katherine Masterson RN. *Medical Dir*
Michael Elmen DO.
Licensure Intermediate care. *Beds* ICF 75.
Private Pay Patients 48%.
Owner Proprietary corp.

Marietta

Lake Country Manor
401 Medical Circle Dr, Marietta, OK 73448
(405) 276-3318

Admin Virginia Howard.
Medical Dir Joni Harrison.
Licensure Intermediate care; Alzheimer's care.
Beds ICF 62. *Certified* Medicaid.
Owner Privately owned.
Admissions Requirements Physician's request.
Staff RNs 1 (pt); LPNs 3 (ft), 1 (pt); Nurses'
aides 20 (ft), 2 (pt); Activities coordinators 1
(ft); Dietitians 6 (ft), 1 (pt).
Facilities Dining room; Activities room;
Chapel; Crafts room; Laundry room; Barber/
Beauty shop; Library.
Activities Arts & crafts; Cards; Games;
Reading groups; Prayer groups; Movies;
Shopping trips; Dances/Social/Cultural
gatherings.

Marlow

Gregston Nursing Home
711 S Broadway, Marlow, OK 73055
(405) 658-2319
Admin J Lynn Gregston.
Medical Dir Charlotte Loughridge.
Licensure Intermediate care. *Beds* ICF 86.
Certified Medicaid.
Staff Physicians 1 (ft); RNs 1 (pt); LPNs 3
(ft), 1 (pt); Nurses' aides 16 (ft); Physical
therapists 1 (pt); Recreational therapists 1
(ft); Activities coordinators 1 (ft); Dietitians
1 (ft), 1 (pt); Dentists 2 (pt).
Facilities Dining room; Physical therapy
room; Activities room; Chapel; Crafts room;
Laundry room; Barber/Beauty shop; Library.
Activities Arts & crafts; Cards; Games;
Reading groups; Prayer groups; Shopping
trips; Singing groups; Band groups; Bingo;
Quilting.

Marlow Manor
PO Box 148, 702 S 9th, Marlow, OK 73055
(405) 658-5468
Admin Linda Curtis.
Medical Dir Dr W K Walker.
Licensure Intermediate care. *Beds* ICF 69.
Certified Medicaid.
Owner Proprietary corp (ARA Living
Centers).
Admissions Requirements Medical
examination.
Staff RNs 1 (pt); LPNs 2 (ft), 5 (pt); Nurses'
aides 45 (ft); Physical therapists 1 (pt);
Recreational therapists 1 (ft); Activities
coordinators 1 (ft); Dietitians 1 (pt); Dentists
1 (pt).
Facilities Dining room; Activities room;
Crafts room; Laundry room; Barber/Beauty
shop.
Activities Arts & crafts; Cards; Games;
Reading groups; Prayer groups.

Maud

Sunset Estates of Maud
409 W King, Maud, OK 74854
(405) 374-2207
Admin Jeff Van Arnam. *Dir of Nursing*
Farrelee Dean.
Licensure Intermediate care; Alzheimer's care.
Beds ICF 62. *Certified* Medicaid.
Owner Proprietary corp (Beverly Enterprises).
Admissions Requirements Minimum age 18;
Medical examination; Physician's request.
Staff Physicians; RNs; LPNs; Nurses' aides;
Physical therapists; Recreational therapists;
Activities coordinators; Dietitians.
Facilities Dining room; Physical therapy
room; Activities room; Crafts room; Laundry
room; Barber/Beauty shop.
Activities Arts & crafts; Cards; Games;
Reading groups; Prayer groups; Movies;
Shopping trips; Dances/Social/Cultural
gatherings.

Maysville

McCaskill Nursing Home
903 Parkview Dr, Maysville, OK 73057
(405) 867-4412
Admin Vanice Burditt.
Licensure Intermediate care. *Beds* ICF 58.
Certified Medicaid.

McAlester

Blevins Retirement & Care Center
1220 E Electric, McAlester, OK 74501
(918) 423-9095
Admin Charles H Blevins.
Medical Dir Donna Guthrie.
Licensure Intermediate care. *Beds* ICF 55.
Certified Medicaid.
Admissions Requirements Medical
examination.
Staff RNs 1 (ft); LPNs 3 (ft); Nurses' aides 15
(ft); Dietitians 1 (ft).
Facilities Dining room; Activities room;
Chapel; Crafts room; Laundry room; Barber/
Beauty shop.
Activities Arts & crafts; Cards; Games; Prayer
groups; Movies; Shopping trips; Dances/
Social/Cultural gatherings.

Colonial Lodge Nursing Home
614 W Harrison, McAlester, OK 74501
(918) 423-6011
Admin Mary M Klein.
Licensure Intermediate care. *Beds* ICF 80.
Certified Medicaid.
Owner Proprietary corp (Manor Care Inc).

Colonial Park Nursing Home
1600 N "D" St, McAlester, OK 74501
(918) 423-0330
Admin Carol Bullett.
Medical Dir William Gupton MD.
Licensure Intermediate care. *Beds* 55.
Certified Medicaid.
Owner Proprietary corp (Manor Care Inc).
Admissions Requirements Medical
examination; Physician's request.
Staff RNs 1 (pt); LPNs 2 (ft), 4 (pt); Nurses'
aides 14 (ft), 4 (pt); Activities coordinators 1
(ft); Dietitians 1 (pt); Dentists 1 (pt).
Facilities Dining room; Activities room;
Crafts room; Laundry room; Barber/Beauty
shop.
Activities Arts & crafts; Cards; Games;
Reading groups; Prayer groups; Movies;
Shopping trips; Dances/Social/Cultural
gatherings.

Heritage Hills
PO Box 1166, 411 N West St, McAlester, OK
74501
(918) 423-2920
Admin Davis Waynetta Gailey.
Medical Dir Debbie Fassino.
Licensure Intermediate care. *Beds* ICF 56.
Certified Medicaid.
Owner Privately owned.
Admissions Requirements Physician's request.
Staff Physicians; RNs 1 (ft); LPNs 3 (ft), 4
(pt); Nurses' aides 7 (ft), 4 (pt); Dietitians 1
(pt).
Facilities Dining room; Activities room;
Crafts room; Laundry room; Barber/Beauty
shop.
Activities Arts & crafts; Cards; Games;
Reading groups; Prayer groups; Movies;
Shopping trips; Dances/Social/Cultural
gatherings.

McAlester Regional Hospital
1 Clark Bass Blvd, McAlester, OK 74501
(918) 426-1800, ext 7008
Admin Ed Majors. *Dir of Nursing* Cyndi Lang
RN. *Medical Dir* Dr Larry Lewis.
Licensure Skilled care. *Beds* SNF 24. *Certified*
Medicare.
Owner Proprietary corp.

Staff RNs 2 (ft); LPNs 4 (ft), 1 (pt); Nurses'
aides 3 (ft), 1 (pt); Physical therapists 2 (ft);
Activities coordinators 1 (ft); Dietitians 2
(ft).
Facilities Activities room.
Activities Arts & crafts; Cards; Games; Prayer
groups; Movies; Singing; Guest speakers.

Mitchell Manor Convalescent Home Inc
315 W Electric, McAlester, OK 74501
(918) 423-4661
Admin Oleta Mitchell. *Dir of Nursing*
Margaret Haile RN.
Licensure Intermediate care. *Beds* ICF 100.
Certified Medicaid.
Owner Proprietary corp.
Admissions Requirements Physician's request.
Staff RNs; LPNs; Nurses' aides; Activities
coordinators; Dietitians.
Facilities Dining room; Physical therapy
room; Activities room; Chapel; Crafts room;
Laundry room; Barber/Beauty shop; Library.
Activities Arts & crafts; Cards; Games;
Reading groups; Prayer groups; Movies;
Shopping trips; Dances/Social/Cultural
gatherings.

Regency House Convalescent Center
615 E Morris, McAlester, OK 74501
(918) 426-0850
Admin Margaret Cravins. *Dir of Nursing*
Shirley Sennett.
Licensure Intermediate care. *Beds* ICF 63.
Certified Medicaid.
Owner Proprietary corp (ARA Living
Centers).
Admissions Requirements Minimum age 25;
Physician's request.
Staff RNs 1 (ft); LPNs 3 (ft) 3 (ft); Nurses'
aides 14 (ft); Recreational therapists 1 (ft);
Activities coordinators 1 (ft); Dietitians 1
(ft); Social service; Beauticians; Barbers.
Languages Choctaw.
Facilities Dining room; Physical therapy
room; Activities room; Crafts room; Laundry
room; Barber/Beauty shop.
Activities Arts & crafts; Cards; Games;
Reading groups; Prayer groups; Movies;
Shopping trips; Dances/Social/Cultural
gatherings.

McLoud

McLoud Nursing Center Inc
Box 250, McLoud, OK 74851-9998
(405) 964-2961
Admin Cynthia Jones.
Licensure Skilled care. *Beds* SNF 60.

Medford

Medford Nursing Home
616 S Front St, Medford, OK 73759
(405) 395-2105
Admin Opal M Stocker. *Dir of Nursing* Lora
Ramsey RN.
Licensure Intermediate care. *Beds* ICF 84.
Certified Medicaid; Medicare.
Owner Privately owned.
Facilities Dining room; Activities room;
Laundry room; Barber/Beauty shop.
Activities Arts & crafts; Cards; Games;
Reading groups; Prayer groups; Movies;
Shopping trips.

Miami

Baptist Regional Health Center SNF
200 "B" SW, Miami, OK 74354
(918) 542-6611, ext 410
Admin Adonna Lowe. *Dir of Nursing* Janice
Mullen RN. *Medical Dir* Clark Osborn MD.
Licensure Skilled care. *Beds* SNF 15. *Private
Pay Patients* 1%. *Certified* Medicare.
Owner Nonprofit corp (Baptist Healthcare
Inc).

Admissions Requirements Minimum age 18;
Physician's request.
Staff Physicians 1 (ft), 4 (pt); RNs 1 (ft), 1
(pt); LPNs 3 (ft), 2 (pt); Nurses' aides 2 (ft),
3 (pt); Physical therapists; Dietitians.
Facilities Dining room; Physical therapy
room; Activities room; Chapel; Crafts room;
Laundry room; Barber/Beauty shop.
Activities Arts & crafts; Cards; Games;
Movies.

Care Nursing Home
130 W Steve Owens, Miami, OK 74354
(918) 542-9324
Admin Pattie Henson.
Medical Dir Berta Carder.
Licensure Intermediate care. *Beds* ICF 58.
Certified Medicaid.
Owner Proprietary corp (Health Enterprises of
America).
Admissions Requirements Medical
examination; Physician's request.
Staff RNs; LPNs; Nurses' aides; Activities
coordinators; Dietitians.
Facilities Dining room; Activities room;
Crafts room; Laundry room; Barber/Beauty
shop.
Activities Arts & crafts; Cards; Games; Prayer
groups; Shopping trips; Dances/Social/
Cultural gatherings; Church groups.

Heritage House
1410 E Steve Owens, Miami, OK 74354
(918) 542-8407
Admin Sue Quapaw.
Licensure Intermediate care. *Beds* ICF 100.
Certified Medicaid.
Staff RNs 1 (pt); LPNs 5 (ft); Nurses' aides 20
(ft); Physical therapists 1 (pt); Speech
therapists 1 (pt); Activities coordinators 1
(ft); Dietitians 1 (pt).
Facilities Dining room; Activities room;
Laundry room; Barber/Beauty shop.
Activities Arts & crafts; Games; Prayer groups;
Shopping trips; Dances/Social/Cultural
gatherings; Daily exercise class.

Miami Nursing Center
PO Box 1268, 1100 E St NE, Miami, OK
74355
(918) 542-3335
Admin Bobbye J Davis. *Dir of Nursing* Jane
Peters RN.
Licensure Intermediate care. *Beds* ICF 82.
Private Pay Patients 42%. *Certified*
Medicaid.
Owner Privately owned.
Staff RNs 1 (ft); LPNs 5 (ft); Nurses' aides 40
(ft), 5 (pt); Recreational therapists 2 (ft);
Activities coordinators 1 (ft); Dietitians 1
(ft).

Midwest City

Colonial Manor Nursing Home
8016 SE 15th, Midwest City, OK 73110
(405) 737-5685
Admin Linda Smith.
Medical Dir Mary Ann Bell.
Licensure Intermediate care. *Beds* ICF 100.
Certified Medicaid.
Owner Proprietary corp.
Admissions Requirements Medical
examination; Physician's request.
Staff Physicians 1 (ft); LPNs 4 (ft), 1 (pt);
Nurses' aides 40 (ft), 10 (pt); Activities
coordinators 1 (ft); Dietitians 1 (ft).
Facilities Dining room; Physical therapy
room; Activities room; Crafts room; Laundry
room; Barber/Beauty shop.
Activities Arts & crafts; Cards; Games;
Reading groups; Prayer groups; Movies;
Shopping trips; Dances/Social/Cultural
gatherings.

Four Seasons Nursing Center of Midwest City
2900 Parklawn Dr, Midwest City, OK 73110
(405) 737-6601

Admin Mary Ellen Mislan.
Licensure Skilled care; Intermediate care. *Beds* SNF 24; ICF 92.

Wood Crest Nursing Center
1401 Crosby Blvd, Midwest City, OK 73110
(918) 733-1794, 737-9062 FAX
Admin Linda Hardison. *Dir of Nursing* Pam Kerr RN. *Medical Dir* Michael Rosenfeld MD.
Licensure Intermediate care. *Beds* ICF 170. *Private Pay Patients* 10%. *Certified* Medicaid.
Owner Proprietary corp.
Admissions Requirements Minimum age 18; Physician's request.
Staff Physicians 2 (ft); RNs 1 (ft); LPNs 9 (ft); Nurses' aides 60 (ft); Physical therapists (contracted); Recreational therapists 1 (ft); Activities coordinators 1 (ft); Dietitians 1 (ft); Podiatrists (contracted).
Languages Spanish.
Facilities Dining room; Activities room; Laundry room; Barber/Beauty shop; Whirlpools; Lab; X-ray facilities.
Activities Arts & crafts; Games; Reading groups; Prayer groups; Movies; Shopping trips; Dances/Social/Cultural gatherings.

Moore

East Moore Nursing Center
320 N Eastern, Moore, OK 73160
(405) 794-0224
Admin Lewisa Andrew.
Licensure Skilled care. *Beds* SNF 100.

Hillcrest Nursing Center
2120 N Broadway, Moore, OK 73160
(405) 794-4429
Admin Mary Stacy.
Medical Dir Perry Taaca MD.
Licensure Intermediate care. *Beds* ICF 154. *Certified* Medicaid.
Owner Nonprofit corp (Adventist Living Centers).
Admissions Requirements Medical examination; Physician's request.
Staff RNs 1 (ft); LPNs 5 (ft); Nurses' aides 48 (ft); Physical therapists 1 (pt); Activities coordinators 1 (ft); Dietitians 1 (ft).
Facilities Dining room; Activities room; Crafts room; Laundry room; Barber/Beauty shop; Library.
Activities Arts & crafts; Cards; Games; Reading groups; Prayer groups; Movies; Shopping trips; Dances/Social/Cultural gatherings.

Mooreland

Mooreland Golden Age Nursing Home
PO Box 338, Mooreland, OK 73852
(405) 994-5570
Admin James H Cooper. *Dir of Nursing* Anita Miller.
Licensure Intermediate care. *Beds* ICF 52. *Private Pay Patients* 37%. *Certified* Medicaid; Medicare.
Owner Publicly owned.
Admissions Requirements Physician's request.
Staff Physicians 1 (pt); RNs 1 (ft); LPNs 6 (ft); Nurses' aides 20 (ft), 2 (pt); Physical therapists 1 (pt); Activities coordinators 1 (ft), 1 (pt); Dietitians 1 (pt).
Languages Spanish.
Facilities Dining room; Activities room; Laundry room; Barber/Beauty shop.
Activities Arts & crafts; Cards; Games; Movies; Dances/Social/Cultural gatherings.

Mountain View

Autumn Splendor Health Care
PO Box 206, 320 N 7th, Mountain View, OK 73062
(405) 347-2120

Admin Peggy Hines.
Medical Dir J B Tolbert MD.
Licensure Intermediate care. *Beds* ICF 32. *Certified* Medicaid.
Admissions Requirements Medical examination; Physician's request.
Staff RNs 1 (pt); LPNs 3 (ft), 2 (pt); Nurses' aides 14 (ft), 3 (pt); Activities coordinators 1 (ft); Dietitians 1 (pt).
Facilities Dining room; Activities room; Crafts room; Laundry room.
Activities Arts & crafts; Cards; Games; Reading groups; Prayer groups; Movies; Shopping trips; Dances/Social/Cultural gatherings.

Muldrow

Muldrow Nursing Home
NW Corner Ironwood & SE 9th, Muldrow, OK 74948
(918) 427-3441
Admin Christy Pointer.
Licensure Intermediate care. *Beds* ICF 75. *Certified* Medicaid.

Muskogee

Adult Living Center East
602 N "M", Muskogee, OK 74401
(918) 682-9232
Admin Thresia Conrad.
Licensure Intermediate care. *Beds* ICF 58. *Certified* Medicaid.
Staff Physicians 1 (pt); RNs 1 (pt); LPNs 2 (ft); Nurses' aides 20 (ft); Activities coordinators 1 (pt); Dietitians 1 (pt); Dentists 1 (pt).
Facilities Dining room; Laundry room; Barber/Beauty shop.
Activities Arts & crafts; Cards; Games; Reading groups; Prayer groups; Shopping trips; Dances/Social/Cultural gatherings.

Azalea Park Manor
4717 W Okmulgee, Muskogee, OK 74401
(918) 683-2914
Admin Leann Pardue. *Dir of Nursing* Connie Rinehart RN.
Licensure Intermediate care; Alzheimer's care. *Beds* ICF 105. *Certified* Medicaid.
Owner Proprietary corp (Amity Care Corp).
Staff RNs 1 (ft); LPNs 3 (ft); Nurses' aides 8 (ft), 1 (pt); Activities coordinators 1 (ft); Dietitians 1 (pt).
Facilities Dining room; Physical therapy room; Activities room; Crafts room; Laundry room; Barber/Beauty shop.
Activities Arts & crafts; Cards; Games; Reading groups; Prayer groups; Movies; Shopping trips; Dances/Social/Cultural gatherings.

Broadway Manor
1622 E Broadway, Muskogee, OK 74401
(918) 683-2851
Admin Michael T Scott.
Licensure Intermediate care. *Beds* ICF 95. *Certified* Medicaid.

Eastgate Village Retirement Center
3500 Haskell Blvd, Muskogee, OK 74403
(918) 682-3191
Admin Sam D Scott.
Licensure Intermediate care. *Beds* ICF 100. *Private Pay Patients* 60%. *Certified* Medicaid.
Owner Proprietary corp.
Staff Physicians 1 (pt); RNs 1 (ft); LPNs 7 (ft); Nurses' aides 47 (ft); Physical therapists 1 (pt); Recreational therapists 1 (ft); Activities coordinators 1 (ft); Dietitians 1 (pt); Ophthalmologists 1 (pt); Podiatrists 1 (pt); Audiologists 1 (pt).

Activities Arts & crafts; Cards; Games; Reading groups; Prayer groups; Movies; Shopping trips; Dances/Social/Cultural gatherings.

Heritage Nursing Home Inc
3317 Denver, Muskogee, OK 74401
(918) 683-3227
Admin Patricia LeGrant. *Dir of Nursing* Judy Tinker RN.
Licensure Intermediate care. *Beds* ICF 119. *Certified* Medicaid.
Owner Privately owned.
Staff Physicians; RNs; LPNs; Nurses' aides; Activities coordinators; Dietitians; Administrators; Office managers; Laundry; Maintenance; Housekeeping personnel.

McIntosh Nursing Home Inc
PO Box 679, 2100 W Fondulac, Muskogee, OK 74401
(918) 682-1970
Admin Johnnie C McIntosh; Margaret S Anderson. *Dir of Nursing* Annetta Davison RN.
Licensure Intermediate care; Alzheimer's care. *Beds* ICF 64. *Certified* Medicaid; Medicare.
Owner Proprietary corp.
Admissions Requirements Medical examination; Physician's request.
Staff Physicians 1 (pt); RNs 1 (pt); LPNs 5 (ft); Nurses' aides 25 (ft), 3 (pt); Reality therapists 1 (ft); Recreational therapists 1 (ft); Occupational therapists 1 (pt); Speech therapists 1 (ft); Activities coordinators 1 (pt); Dietitians 1 (pt); Ophthalmologists 1 (pt); Podiatrists 1 (pt).
Facilities Dining room; Physical therapy room; Activities room; Crafts room; Laundry room; Barber/Beauty shop; Library.
Activities Arts & crafts; Cards; Games; Reading groups; Prayer groups; Movies; Shopping trips; Dances/Social/Cultural gatherings; Intergenerational programs; Pet therapy.

Park Boulevard
841 N 38th St, Muskogee, OK 74401
(918) 683-8070
Admin Jerry L Franks.
Medical Dir Lu Harrison.
Licensure Intermediate care; Alzheimer's care. *Beds* ICF 90. *Certified* Medicaid.
Owner Privately owned.
Admissions Requirements Medical examination; Physician's request.
Staff RNs; LPNs; Nurses' aides; Activities coordinators.
Facilities Dining room; Physical therapy room; Activities room; Crafts room; Laundry room; Barber/Beauty shop; Library.
Activities Arts & crafts; Cards; Games; Prayer groups; Movies; Shopping trips; Dances/Social/Cultural gatherings; Exercise classes.

Pleasant Valley Health Care Center
1120 Illinois, Muskogee, OK 74401
(918) 682-5391
Admin Louis Nevitt. *Dir of Nursing* Velma Trussell RN.
Licensure Intermediate care. *Beds* ICF 71. *Certified* Medicaid.
Staff RNs 1 (ft), 1 (pt); LPNs 3 (ft), 2 (pt); Nurses' aides 18 (ft); Reality therapists 1 (ft); Recreational therapists 1 (ft); Activities coordinators 1 (ft); Dietitians 1 (ft); Podiatrists 1 (ft); Dentists 1 (ft).
Facilities Dining room; Activities room; Chapel; Laundry room; Barber/Beauty shop.
Activities Arts & crafts; Cards; Games; Reading groups; Prayer groups; Movies; Shopping trips; Dances/Social/Cultural gatherings.

Tower Hill Nursing Home
PO Box 1310, 424 Tower Hill Dr, Muskogee, OK 74401
(918) 683-2983

Admin William E Brock.
Licensure Intermediate care. *Beds* ICF 48.
   Certified Medicaid.

York Manor
500 S York, Muskogee, OK 74403
(918) 682-6724
Admin John H Fish.
Licensure Intermediate care. *Beds* ICF 60.
   Certified Medicaid.
Owner Nonprofit corp (Heartway Corp).
Admissions Requirements Physician's request.
Staff RNs 1 (ft); LPNs 4 (ft); Nurses' aides 22
   (ft); Activities coordinators 1 (ft); Dietitians
   1 (pt).
Facilities Dining room; Activities room;
   Laundry room; Barber/Beauty shop.
Activities Arts & crafts; Cards; Games;
   Reading groups; Prayer groups; Shopping
   trips; Dances/Social/Cultural gatherings.

Mustang

Mustang Nursing Home
400 N Clear Springs Rd, Mustang, OK 73064
(405) 376-3020
Admin Charlotte Gibbs.
Licensure Skilled care. *Beds* SNF 70.

Newkirk

Newkirk Nursing Center Inc
PO Box 427, Newkirk, OK 74647
(405) 362-3277
Admin Stacy Merrifield. *Dir of Nursing* Mary
   L Wilson RN. *Medical Dir* Mark Palmer
   MD.
Licensure Intermediate care; Alzheimer's care.
   Beds ICF 43. *Private Pay Patients* 20%.
   Certified Medicaid; Medicare.
Owner Privately owned.
Admissions Requirements Medical
   examination; Physician's request.
Staff Physicians; RNs; LPNs; Nurses' aides;
   Physical therapists; Recreational therapists;
   Activities coordinators; Dietitians;
   Ophthalmologists.
Facilities Dining room; Physical therapy
   room; Activities room; Chapel; Crafts room;
   Laundry room; Barber/Beauty shop.
Activities Arts & crafts; Cards; Games;
   Reading groups; Prayer groups; Movies;
   Shopping trips; Dances/Social/Cultural
   gatherings; Intergenerational programs; Pet
   therapy.

Norman

Cedar Creek Living Center
600 SW 24th Ave, Norman, OK 73069
(405) 321-1111
Admin Delbert Gilman.
Licensure Skilled care. *Beds* SNF 89.

Four Seasons Nursing Center of Norman
1210 W Robinson, Norman, OK 73069
(405) 321-8824
Admin Lori Hitchcock RN. *Dir of Nursing*
   Edith Jones RN.
Licensure Skilled care; Intermediate care. *Beds*
   SNF 62; ICF 56. *Certified* Medicare.
Owner Proprietary corp (Manor Care Inc).
Staff Physicians; RNs; LPNs; Nurses' aides;
   Physical therapists; Reality therapists;
   Recreational therapists; Occupational
   therapists; Speech therapists; Activities
   coordinators; Dietitians.

Holiday Heights Nursing Home
301 E Dale, Norman, OK 73069
(405) 321-7932
Admin Kay Simmons.
Licensure Intermediate care. *Beds* ICF 51.
   Certified Medicaid.

Morningside Nursing Home
512 N Interstate Rd, Norman, OK 73072
(405) 321-7483
Admin Bob Simmons Jr.
Licensure Intermediate care. *Beds* ICF 52.
   Certified Medicaid.

River Oaks Estates Nursing Center
201 48th Ave SW, Norman, OK 73072
(405) 366-8800
Admin Bill Shawn.
Licensure Skilled care. *Beds* SNF 120.

Rosewood Manor Living Center
501 E Robinson, Norman, OK 73071
(405) 321-6666
Admin Charlene Bartlett.
Licensure Intermediate care. *Beds* ICF 200.
   Certified Medicaid.
Owner Nonprofit corp (Adventist Living
   Centers).

Nowata

Hays House Nursing Home
300 S Mississippi, Nowata, OK 74048
(918) 273-2002
Admin Walter C Deane.
Licensure Intermediate care for mentally
   retarded. *Beds* ICF/MR 112. *Certified*
   Medicaid.
Admissions Requirements Medical
   examination.
Staff RNs 1 (ft); LPNs 2 (ft), 1 (pt); Nurses'
   aides 28 (ft), 4 (pt); Recreational therapists 6
   (ft); Activities coordinators 1 (ft); Dietitians
   1 (ft), 1 (pt).
Facilities Dining room; Activities room;
   Crafts room; Laundry room; Barber/Beauty
   shop.
Activities Arts & crafts; Cards; Games;
   Reading groups; Prayer groups; Movies;
   Shopping trips; Dances/Social/Cultural
   gatherings.

Nowata Nursing Home
436 S Joe, Nowata, OK 74048
(918) 273-2236
Admin Kathryn Smith.
Licensure Intermediate care. *Beds* ICF 50.
   Certified Medicaid.

Osage Nursing Home
822 W Osage, Nowata, OK 74048
(918) 273-2012
Admin Louise Deane. *Dir of Nursing* Rubye
   Martin.
Licensure Intermediate care. *Beds* ICF 50.
   Private Pay Patients 20%. *Certified*
   Medicaid.
Owner Privately owned.
Admissions Requirements Medical
   examination.
Staff Physicians 3 (ft); RNs (consultant); LPNs
   5 (ft); Nurses' aides 20 (ft); Activities
   coordinators 1 (ft); Dietitians (consultant);
   Podiatrists 1 (ft).
Facilities Dining room; Activities room;
   Chapel; Crafts room; Laundry room; Barber/
   Beauty shop.
Activities Arts & crafts; Cards; Games;
   Reading groups; Prayer groups; Movies;
   Shopping trips; Dances/Social/Cultural
   gatherings; Intergenerational programs; Pet
   therapy.

Okarche

Center of Family Love
PO Box 245, 6th & Texas, Okarche, OK
   73762
(405) 263-4658
Admin Anna Carter. *Dir of Nursing* Vicki
   Cain LPN.
Licensure Intermediate care for mentally
   retarded. *Beds* ICF/MR 54. *Certified*
   Medicaid; Medicare.

Owner Nonprofit corp.
Admissions Requirements Minimum age 18;
   Medical examination.
Staff RNs; LPNs; Nurses' aides; Recreational
   therapists; Speech therapists; Activities
   coordinators; Dietitians.
Facilities Dining room; Physical therapy
   room; Activities room; Crafts room; Laundry
   room; Barber/Beauty shop; Occupational
   therapy room; Home economics room.
Activities Arts & crafts; Games; Prayer groups;
   Movies; Shopping trips; Dances/Social/
   Cultural gatherings; Music.

Okeene

Buchanan Nursing Home of Okeene Inc
PO Box 492, Okeene, OK 73763
(405) 822-4441
Admin Mildred Buchanan.
Licensure Intermediate care. *Beds* ICF 119.
   Certified Medicaid.

Okemah

Colonial Park Nursing Home Inc
PO Box 27, Okemah, OK 74859
(918) 623-1936
Admin James R Smart.
Licensure Skilled care. *Beds* SNF 60.

Okemah Pioneer Nursing Home Inc
PO Box 27, Okemah, OK 74859
(918) 623-1126
Admin James Robert Smart.
Medical Dir Florence Holdaway.
Licensure Intermediate care. *Beds* ICF 76.
   Certified Medicaid.
Owner Proprietary corp.
Admissions Requirements Medical
   examination.
Staff RNs 1 (ft); LPNs 3 (ft); Nurses' aides 16
   (ft); Physical therapists 1 (ft); Occupational
   therapists 1 (ft); Activities coordinators 1
   (ft); Dietitians 1 (ft).
Facilities Dining room; Activities room;
   Laundry room; Barber/Beauty shop.
Activities Arts & crafts; Cards; Games;
   Reading groups; Prayer groups; Movies;
   Shopping trips; Dances/Social/Cultural
   gatherings.

Oklahoma City

All American Health Care
1913 NE 50th St, Oklahoma City, OK 73111
(405) 427-5414
Admin Krizzo M Meadows. *Dir of Nursing*
   Marion Bolar RN. *Medical Dir* Dr Perry
   Tacca.
Licensure Intermediate care. *Beds* ICF 107.
   Certified Medicaid.
Owner Privately owned.
Facilities Dining room; Physical therapy
   room; Activities room; Chapel; Crafts room;
   Laundry room; Barber/Beauty shop; Family
   room; Sun room.
Activities Arts & crafts; Cards; Games;
   Reading groups; Prayer groups; Movies;
   Shopping trips; Dances/Social/Cultural
   gatherings; Intergenerational programs; Pet
   therapy.

Alvira Heights Manor
1215 NE 34th, Oklahoma City, OK 73111
(405) 424-4009
Admin Shirley Bauermeister. *Dir of Nursing*
   June Rhoten LPN.
Licensure Intermediate care. *Beds* ICF 72.
   Private Pay Patients 2%. *Certified* Medicaid.
Owner Privately owned.
Staff Physicians; RNs; LPNs; Nurses' aides;
   Physical therapists; Activities coordinators;
   Dietitians; Podiatrists.
Languages Spanish.

Facilities Dining room; Activities room; Crafts room; Laundry room.
Activities Arts & crafts; Cards; Games; Reading groups; Prayer groups; Shopping trips; Religious activities and visitations by church groups; Visitations by school groups.

Bellevue Nursing Center
6500 N Portland Ave, Oklahoma City, OK 73116
(405) 843-5796
Admin Norman L Thompson. *Dir of Nursing* Vivian Doerr RN. *Medical Dir* Dr John DeVore.
Licensure Skilled care; Adult day care. *Beds* SNF 220. *Private Pay Patients* 100%.
Owner Privately owned.
Admissions Requirements Medical examination.
Staff Physicians 1 (pt); RNs 7 (ft); LPNs 8 (ft); Nurses' aides 70 (ft); Physical therapists 1 (pt); Occupational therapists 1 (pt); Speech therapists 1 (pt); Activities coordinators 2 (ft); Dietitians 1 (pt); Ophthalmologists 1 (pt); Podiatrists 2 (pt).
Facilities Dining room; Physical therapy room; Activities room; Chapel; Crafts room; Laundry room; Barber/Beauty shop; Library.
Activities Arts & crafts; Cards; Games; Reading groups; Prayer groups; Movies; Shopping trips; Dances/Social/Cultural gatherings; Intergenerational programs; Pet therapy.

Canterbury Health Center
1400 NW 122nd, Oklahoma City, OK 73114
(405) 755-8952
Admin Marilyn Smotherman. *Dir of Nursing* Linda LaForge. *Medical Dir* Jeffrey Steinbauer MD.
Licensure Skilled care; Intermediate care; Assisted living. *Beds* SNF 60; ICF 60; Assisted living 60. *Certified* Medicaid.
Owner Nonprofit organization/foundation.
Admissions Requirements Medical examination; Physician's request.
Languages Spanish.
Affiliation Episcopal.
Facilities Dining room; Physical therapy room; Activities room; Chapel; Crafts room; Laundry room; Barber/Beauty shop; Library.
Activities Arts & crafts; Cards; Games; Reading groups; Prayer groups; Movies; Shopping trips; Dances/Social/Cultural gatherings; Intergenerational programs; Pet therapy.

Central Oklahoma Christian Home
6312 N Portland, Oklahoma City, OK 73112
(405) 946-6932
Admin Royce W Dunn. *Dir of Nursing* Gohla Lowery RN.
Licensure Intermediate care. *Beds* ICF 148. *Certified* Medicaid.
Owner Nonprofit corp.
Admissions Requirements Medical examination.
Staff RNs 1 (ft); LPNs 9 (ft); Nurses' aides 37 (ft); Physical therapists 1 (ft); Occupational therapists 1 (ft); Activities coordinators 1 (ft).
Affiliation Church of Christ.
Facilities Dining room; Physical therapy room; Activities room; Chapel; Crafts room; Laundry room; Barber/Beauty shop.
Activities Arts & crafts; Cards; Games; Prayer groups; Movies; Shopping trips; Religious services; Music therapy.

Convalescent Center of Oklahoma City
3233 NW 10th, Oklahoma City, OK 73107
(405) 943-8366
Admin Claudia M Hansbro.
Licensure Intermediate care. *Beds* ICF 142. *Certified* Medicaid.
Owner Proprietary corp (Amity Care).

Edwards Redeemer Nursing Center
1530 NE Grand Blvd, Oklahoma City, OK 73117
(405) 424-2273
Admin Kaylene Bass. *Dir of Nursing* Laura Wright LPN. *Medical Dir* Michael Rosenfeld MD.
Licensure Intermediate care; Alzheimer's care. *Beds* ICF 96. *Private Pay Patients* 25%. *Certified* Medicaid.
Owner Proprietary corp.
Admissions Requirements Minimum age 18; Physician's request.
Staff RNs 1 (pt); LPNs 6 (ft); Nurses' aides 50 (ft); Physical therapists (contracted); Occupational therapists (contracted); Speech therapists (contracted); Activities coordinators 1 (ft); Dietitians 1 (pt); Ophthalmologists (contracted); Podiatrists (contracted).
Facilities Dining room; Activities room; Crafts room; Laundry room; Barber/Beauty shop.
Activities Arts & crafts; Cards; Games; Reading groups; Prayer groups; Movies; Shopping trips; Dances/Social/Cultural gatherings; Intergenerational programs; Pet therapy.

Fairview Manor Nursing Center
3233 NW 10th St, Oklahoma City, OK 73107
(405) 943-8366
Admin Claudia Hansbro. *Dir of Nursing* Rae Roberts.
Licensure Intermediate care. *Beds* ICF 142. *Certified* Medicaid.
Owner Proprietary corp (Amity Care).
Admissions Requirements Medical examination; Physician's request.
Staff Physicians 1 (ft); RNs 1 (ft); LPNs 5 (ft), 2 (pt); Nurses' aides 33 (ft); Activities coordinators 1 (ft); Dietitians 1 (ft).
Languages Spanish, Vietnamese.
Facilities Dining room; Activities room; Crafts room; Laundry room; Barber/Beauty shop; Library; Lobby area; 2 sitting rooms.
Activities Arts & crafts; Cards; Games; Reading groups; Prayer groups; Movies; Shopping trips; Dances/Social/Cultural gatherings; Dances; Concerts; Church groups; Family council; Resident council.

Four Seasons Nursing Center of Northwest Oklahoma City
5301 N Brookline Rd, Oklahoma City, OK 73112
(405) 946-3351
Admin Lola Whitlock.
Medical Dir Rita Lophem.
Licensure Skilled care. *Beds* SNF 136. *Certified* Medicare.
Owner Proprietary corp (Manor Care Inc).
Admissions Requirements Medical examination.
Facilities Dining room; Physical therapy room; Activities room; Laundry room; Barber/Beauty shop.
Activities Arts & crafts; Cards; Games; Reading groups; Prayer groups; Movies; Shopping trips; Dances/Social/Cultural gatherings.

Four Seasons Nursing Center of Southwest Oklahoma City
5600 S Walker, Oklahoma City, OK 73109
(405) 632-7771
Admin Paula Matlock.
Licensure Skilled care; Intermediate care. *Beds* SNF 26; ICF 94. *Certified* Medicaid.
Owner Proprietary corp (Manor Care Inc).

Four Seasons Nursing Center of Warr Acres
6501 N MacArthur, Oklahoma City, OK 73132
(405) 721-5444
Admin Chiquita Henderson.

Licensure Skilled care; Intermediate care. *Beds* SNF 45; ICF 58. *Certified* Medicaid.
Owner Proprietary corp (Manor Care Inc).

Four Seasons Nursing Center of Windsor Hills
2416 N Ann Arbor, Oklahoma City, OK 73127
(405) 942-8566
Admin Sharon Ollenburger.
Licensure Skilled care; Intermediate care. *Beds* SNF 18; ICF 94. *Certified* Medicaid.
Owner Proprietary corp (Manor Care Inc).

Ghana Village Nursing Home
3000 NE 17th, Oklahoma City, OK 73121
(405) 427-8364
Admin Rose Greer.
Licensure Intermediate care. *Beds* ICF 44. *Certified* Medicaid.
Owner Proprietary corp.
Admissions Requirements Physician's request.
Facilities Dining room; Activities room; Crafts room; Laundry room.
Activities Arts & crafts; Cards; Games; Reading groups; Prayer groups; Shopping trips; Field trips; Attending sporting events.

Hefner Village Nursing Center
5701 W Britton Rd, Oklahoma City, OK 73132
(405) 722-1010
Admin Barbara Baker.
Licensure Intermediate care. *Beds* ICF 173. *Certified* Medicaid.
Admissions Requirements Medical examination; Physician's request.
Staff RNs 2 (ft), 1 (pt); LPNs 7 (ft), 1 (pt); Nurses' aides 40 (ft); Physical therapists 1 (ft); Activities coordinators 3 (ft); Dietitians 1 (ft).
Facilities Dining room; Physical therapy room; Activities room; Crafts room; Laundry room; Barber/Beauty shop.
Activities Arts & crafts; Cards; Games; Reading groups; Prayer groups; Movies; Shopping trips; Dances/Social/Cultural gatherings.

Hillcrest Health Center Skilled Nursing Facility
2129 SW 59th, Oklahoma City, OK 73119
(405) 680-2210
Admin Wanda Lewellen. *Dir of Nursing* Mike O'Connell RN. *Medical Dir* Kim King DO.
Licensure Skilled care. *Beds* SNF 14. *Certified* Medicare.
Owner Nonprofit organization/foundation.
Admissions Requirements Medical examination.
Staff Physicians; RNs 2 (ft), 1 (pt); LPNs 2 (ft), 2 (pt); Nurses' aides 4 (ft), 2 (pt); Physical therapists; Speech therapists; Activities coordinators; Dietitians.
Languages Spanish.
Facilities Dining room; Activities room.
Activities Arts & crafts; Cards; Games.

Lackey Manor Nursing Home
9700 Mashburn Blvd, Oklahoma City, OK 73162
(405) 721-2466, 722-8039 FAX
Admin Josephine H Kelly. *Dir of Nursing* Wanda DuShane. *Medical Dir* Elwood Herndon MD.
Licensure Intermediate care; Retirement; Alzheimer's care. *Beds* ICF 121; Retirement 293. *Private Pay Patients* 80%. *Certified* Medicaid.
Owner Nonprofit corp (Baptist General Convention of OK).
Admissions Requirements Medical examination; Physician's request.
Staff RNs 1 (ft); LPNs 7 (ft), 1 (pt); Physical therapists 1 (ft); Occupational therapists 1 (ft); Activities coordinators 1 (ft); Dietitians 1 (ft).
Affiliation Baptist.

Facilities Dining room; Activities room;
Chapel; Crafts room; Laundry room; Barber/
Beauty shop; Library.
Activities Arts & crafts; Games; Reading
groups; Prayer groups; Movies; Church
services.

Morning Star Nursing Home
3804 N Barr, Oklahoma City, OK 73122
(405) 787-0522
Admin Pat Faris.
Licensure Intermediate care. *Beds* 55.
Certified Medicaid.
Owner Proprietary corp (ARA Living
Centers).
Admissions Requirements Minimum age 18;
Medical examination; Physician's request.
Staff Physicians 11 (pt); RNs 1 (pt); LPNs 6
(ft), 1 (pt); Nurses' aides 11 (ft); Activities
coordinators 1 (ft); Dietitians 1 (pt).
Facilities Dining room; Activities room;
Laundry room; Barber/Beauty shop.
Activities Arts & crafts; Cards; Games;
Reading groups; Prayer groups; Movies;
Shopping trips; Dances/Social/Cultural
gatherings.

Northwest Nursing Center
2801 NW 61st, Oklahoma City, OK 73112
(405) 842-6601
Admin Bette Jo Trigg.
Medical Dir Hugh A Stout MD.
Licensure Intermediate care. *Beds* ICF 100.
Certified Medicaid.
Admissions Requirements Medical
examination; Physician's request.
Staff RNs 3 (ft); LPNs 4 (ft), 1 (pt); Physical
therapists 1 (ft); Activities coordinators 1
(ft).
Facilities Dining room; Physical therapy
room; Activities room; Laundry room;
Barber/Beauty shop.
Activities Arts & crafts; Cards; Games;
Reading groups; Prayer groups; Movies;
Shopping trips; Dances/Social/Cultural
gatherings.

Oklahoma County Home
7401 NE 23rd, Oklahoma City, OK 73141
(405) 427-2426
Admin Mary Thomas.
Licensure Intermediate care. *Beds* 84.
Certified Medicaid.

Park Manor Nursing Home
1214 N Broadway Dr, Oklahoma City, OK
73103
(405) 235-7488
Admin Keith Long.
Medical Dir Perry Taaca MD.
Licensure Intermediate care. *Beds* ICF 120.
Certified Medicaid.
Admissions Requirements Minimum age 18;
Medical examination; Physician's request.
Staff RNs 1 (pt); LPNs 4 (ft), 3 (pt); Nurses'
aides 22 (ft); Physical therapists 1 (pt);
Occupational therapists 1 (pt); Speech
therapists 1 (pt); Activities coordinators 1
(ft); Dietitians 1 (pt); Ophthalmologists 1
(pt); Podiatrists 1 (pt); Audiologists 1 (pt);
Dentists 1 (pt).
Facilities Dining room; Physical therapy
room; Activities room; Chapel; Crafts room;
Laundry room; Barber/Beauty shop; 2
indoor patios.
Activities Arts & crafts; Cards; Games;
Reading groups; Prayer groups; Movies;
Shopping trips; Dances/Social/Cultural
gatherings.

Portland Health Care Facility
3718 N Portland, Oklahoma City, OK 73112
(405) 942-1014
Admin Charlene Allen.
Medical Dir Mayuri Shah MD.
Licensure Intermediate care. *Beds* ICF 29.
Certified Medicaid.

Staff RNs 1 (ft), 1 (pt); LPNs 1 (pt); Nurses'
aides 16 (ft); Reality therapists 1 (ft);
Recreational therapists 1 (ft); Activities
coordinators 1 (ft); Dietitians 1 (ft).
Facilities Dining room; Activities room;
Crafts room; Laundry room; Barber/Beauty
shop.
Activities Arts & crafts; Cards; Games;
Reading groups; Prayer groups; Movies;
Shopping trips; Dances/Social/Cultural
gatherings.

St Ann's Home
3825 NW 19th, Oklahoma City, OK 73107
(405) 942-8607
Admin Joy Ecker.
Licensure Intermediate care. *Beds* ICF 82.
Certified Medicaid.
Owner Nonprofit organization/foundation.
Admissions Requirements Medical
examination.
Staff Physicians; RNs; LPNs; Nurses' aides;
Physical therapists; Recreational therapists;
Speech therapists; Activities coordinators;
Dietitians; Ophthalmologists.
Affiliation Roman Catholic.
Facilities Dining room; Physical therapy
room; Activities room; Chapel; Crafts room;
Laundry room; Barber/Beauty shop.
Activities Arts & crafts; Cards; Games;
Reading groups; Prayer groups; Movies;
Shopping trips; Dances/Social/Cultural
gatherings; Singing; Parties; Outings.

Shady View Nursing Home
1163 E Madison, Oklahoma City, OK 73111
(405) 424-1486
Admin Jim Cummins.
Licensure Intermediate care. *Beds* ICF 70.
Certified Medicaid.

Skyview Nursing Center
2200 Coltrane Rd, Oklahoma City, OK 73121
(405) 427-1322
Admin Judy Sullivan Crane. *Dir of Nursing*
Estelle Bugg RN. *Medical Dir* Dr G E
Finley.
Licensure Intermediate care. *Beds* ICF 60.
Private Pay Patients 10%. *Certified*
Medicaid.
Owner Privately owned.
Staff Physicians; RNs 1 (ft); LPNs 4 (ft), 1
(pt); Nurses' aides 15 (ft), 2 (pt); Physical
therapists; Recreational therapists 1 (ft);
Activities coordinators 1 (ft); Dietitians 1
(pt).
Facilities Dining room; Activities room;
Laundry room; Barber/Beauty shop; Yard.
Activities Arts & crafts; Cards; Games;
Reading groups; Prayer groups; Movies;
Shopping trips; Intergenerational programs.

South Park Health Care Center
5725 S Ross, Oklahoma City, OK 73109
(405) 685-4791
Admin Connie Bailey.
Licensure Skilled care; Intermediate care. *Beds*
SNF 106; ICF 248.

Southern Oaks Manor
301 SW 74th, Oklahoma City, OK 73139
(405) 634-0573
Admin Jack Murdock.
Licensure Intermediate care. *Beds* ICF 105.
Certified Medicaid.

Southwestern Convalescent Manor
5512 S Western, Oklahoma City, OK 73109
(405) 632-2318
Admin Bettye Jeffers.
Medical Dir Roger Lienke MD.
Licensure Intermediate care. *Beds* ICF 59.
Certified Medicaid.
Admissions Requirements Minimum age 21.
Staff RNs 1 (pt); LPNs 4 (ft); Nurses' aides 16
(ft); Activities coordinators 1 (ft).

Facilities Dining room; Activities room;
Laundry room; Barber/Beauty shop.
Activities Arts & crafts; Games; Prayer groups;
Movies; Shopping trips.

Terrace Gardens Nursing Center
1921 NE 21st, Oklahoma City, OK 73111
(405) 424-1449
Admin Betty L Heiliger. *Dir of Nursing* Paula
Ford RN.
Licensure Intermediate care. *Beds* ICF 105.
Certified Medicaid.
Owner Privately owned.
Admissions Requirements Medical
examination; Physician's request.
Staff RNs 1 (ft); LPNs 8 (ft); Nurses' aides 35
(ft); Physical therapists; Activities
coordinators 1 (ft); Dietitians 1 (ft);
Podiatrists (consultant); Physical therapy
aides 1 (ft).
Facilities Dining room; Activities room;
Laundry room; Barber/Beauty shop.
Activities Arts & crafts; Cards; Games;
Reading groups; Prayer groups; Movies;
Dances/Social/Cultural gatherings.

Walnut Creek Nursing Home
2400 SW 55th, Oklahoma City, OK 73119
(405) 681-5381
Admin Darlene Orman.
Licensure Intermediate care. *Beds* ICF 120.
Certified Medicaid.
Owner Proprietary corp (Amity Care).

Westlake Nursing Center
13500 Brandon Pl, Oklahoma City, OK 73142
(405) 720-0010
Admin Shelley Jean Claro.
Licensure Skilled care. *Beds* SNF 100.

Wilshire Nursing Home
505 E Wilshire Blvd, Oklahoma City, OK
73114
(405) 478-0531
Admin Nita Yeager. *Dir of Nursing* Mary
Hunter.
Licensure Intermediate care. *Beds* ICF 56.
Certified Medicaid.
Owner Proprietary corp (Amity Care).

Woodside Nursing Center
1900 N 36th, Oklahoma City, OK 73136
(405) 427-6533
Admin Gayla J Collins.
Licensure Intermediate care. *Beds* ICF 137.
Certified Medicaid.

Okmulgee

Highland Park Manor
1307 E Walnut, Okmulgee, OK 74447
(918) 756-5611
Admin Donna Thomas. *Dir of Nursing* Robyn
Barnett RN. *Medical Dir* R D Miller MD.
Licensure Intermediate care. *Beds* ICF 100.
Private Pay Patients 25%. *Certified*
Medicaid.
Owner Proprietary corp (Northeastern Health
Care Inc).
Admissions Requirements Medical
examination; Physician's request.
Staff Physicians 14 (pt); RNs 1 (ft); LPNs 7
(ft), 2 (pt); Nurses' aides 31 (ft), 4 (pt);
Physical therapists 1 (pt); Recreational
therapists 1 (ft); Speech therapists 1 (pt);
Activities coordinators 1 (ft); Dietitians 1
(pt).
Facilities Dining room; Physical therapy
room; Activities room; Chapel; Crafts room;
Laundry room; Barber/Beauty shop.
Activities Arts & crafts; Cards; Games;
Reading groups; Prayer groups; Movies;
Shopping trips; Dances/Social/Cultural
gatherings; Intergenerational programs; Pet
therapy.

Leisure Manor
1535 E 6th, Okmulgee, OK 74447
(918) 756-3355
Admin Beverly Walker.
Licensure Intermediate care. *Beds* ICF 63.
Certified Medicaid.

Okmulgee Terrace Nursing Home Inc
PO Box 1299, 1st & Miami, Okmulgee, OK 74447
(918) 756-3556
Admin Ramona Williamson.
Licensure Intermediate care for mentally retarded. *Beds* ICF/MR 63. *Certified* Medicaid.

Rebold Manor
1701 E 6th, Okmulgee, OK 74447
(918) 756-1967
Admin Bob Barnard.
Licensure Intermediate care. *Beds* ICF 114.
Certified Medicaid.

Owasso

Evergreen Care Center
12600 E 73rd St N, Owasso, OK 74055
(918) 272-8007, 272-8007 ext 302 FAX
Admin Katherine Mullens. *Dir of Nursing* Flo Whitlock RN. *Medical Dir* Ambrose Solano MD.
Licensure Intermediate care; Retirement. *Beds* ICF 120; Retirement 300. *Private Pay Patients* 74%. *Certified* Medicaid.
Owner Nonprofit organization/foundation (Baptist General Convention of Oklahoma).
Admissions Requirements Medical examination; Physician's request.
Staff RNs 1 (ft); LPNs 4 (ft), 2 (pt); Nurses' aides 21 (ft), 3 (pt); Physical therapists (consultant); Activities coordinators 1 (ft), 1 (pt); Dietitians (consultant); Physical therapy aides 1 (ft); Certified dietary managers 1 (ft); CMAs 10 (ft).
Languages Spanish, Yiddish, Italian, German.
Affiliation Baptist.
Facilities Dining room; Activities room; Crafts room; Laundry room; Barber/Beauty shop; Library.
Activities Arts & crafts; Games; Reading groups; Movies; Dances/Social/Cultural gatherings; Intergenerational programs; Exercise; Story hour; Sing-a-longs; Parties; Visiting bands.

Pauls Valley

Colonial Nursing & Retirement Center
PO Box 267, 105 Washington, Pauls Valley, OK 73075
(405) 238-5528
Admin Theodora G Presgrove. *Dir of Nursing* Virginia Sue Martin.
Licensure Intermediate care. *Beds* ICF 109.
Private Pay Patients 30%. *Certified* Medicaid.
Owner Proprietary corp.

Pauls Valley State School
PO Box 609, US Hwy 77, 5 miles S, Pauls Valley, OK 73075
(405) 238-6401
Admin Thomas E Evans PhD.
Licensure Intermediate care for mentally retarded. *Beds* ICF/MR 417.

Pawhuska

Pawhuska Nursing Home
Box 959, Pawhuska, OK 74056
(918) 287-3940
Admin DeAnn Hudson.
Licensure Intermediate care. *Beds* ICF 80.
Certified Medicaid.
Staff RNs 1 (pt); LPNs 2 (ft), 1 (pt); Dietitians 1 (pt).

Facilities Dining room; Crafts room; Laundry room; Barber/Beauty shop.
Activities Arts & crafts; Cards; Games; Prayer groups; Shopping trips.

Pawnee

Pawnee Care Center
PO Box 190, 800 9th St, Pawnee, OK 74058
(918) 762-2515
Admin Mary Hurt. *Dir of Nursing* Susan Buckner.
Licensure Intermediate care. *Beds* ICF 52.
Private Pay Patients 30%. *Certified* Medicaid.
Owner Proprietary corp (ARA Living Centers).
Admissions Requirements Minimum age 18; Physician's request.
Staff RNs 1 (pt); LPNs 2 (ft), 1 (pt); Nurses' aides 20 (ft), 5 (pt); Activities coordinators 1 (ft), 1 (pt).
Facilities Dining room; Physical therapy room; Activities room; Crafts room; Laundry room; Barber/Beauty shop.
Activities Arts & crafts; Cards; Games; Prayer groups; Movies; Shopping trips; Dances/ Social/Cultural gatherings; Intergenerational programs.

Perry

Perry Green Valley Nursing Center
1103 Birch St, Perry, OK 73077
(405) 336-2285
Admin Anita Schwandt.
Licensure Intermediate care. *Beds* ICF 82.
Certified Medicaid.

Perry Nursing Home
410 15th St, Perry, OK 73077
(405) 336-4461
Admin Kathleen William.
Licensure Intermediate care. *Beds* ICF 51.
Certified Medicaid.

Picher

Leigh Manor
2nd & Frances, Picher, OK 74360
(918) 673-1660
Admin John Edwards.
Licensure Intermediate care. *Beds* ICF 30.
Certified Medicaid.

Pocola

Medi-Branch Nursing Center
PO Box 150, Intersection of Home & Pryor, Pocola, OK 74902
(918) 436-2228
Admin Phillip M Green.
Licensure Skilled care. *Beds* SNF 90.

Ponca City

Highland Nursing Center
1401 W Highland, Ponca City, OK 74601
(405) 765-4454
Admin Joe M Nimmo.
Licensure Intermediate care. *Beds* ICF 97.
Certified Medicaid.

Ponca City Nursing Home
1400 N Waverly, Ponca City, OK 74601
(405) 762-6668
Admin Wesley E Nimmo.
Medical Dir Grace Paige.
Licensure Intermediate care; Retirement. *Beds* ICF 143. *Certified* Medicaid.
Owner Privately owned.
Staff Physicians; RNs; LPNs; Nurses' aides; Physical therapists; Recreational therapists; Occupational therapists; Activities coordinators; Dietitians.

Facilities Dining room; Physical therapy room; Activities room; Chapel; Crafts room; Laundry room; Barber/Beauty shop; Library.
Activities Arts & crafts; Cards; Games; Reading groups; Prayer groups; Movies; Shopping trips; Dances/Social/Cultural gatherings.

Shawn Manor Nursing Home
2024 Turner Rd, Ponca City, OK 74601
(405) 765-3364
Admin Pauline Bivin. *Dir of Nursing* Carolyn Sissons RN.
Licensure Intermediate care. *Beds* ICF 86.
Certified Medicaid.
Owner Proprietary corp.
Staff RNs 1 (ft); LPNs 4 (ft); Nurses' aides 30 (ft); Activities coordinators 1 (ft), 1 (pt).
Facilities Dining room; Activities room; Chapel; Crafts room; Laundry room; Barber/ Beauty shop.
Activities Arts & crafts; Cards; Games; Reading groups; Prayer groups; Movies.

Westminster Village Inc
1601 Academy Rd, Ponca City, OK 74604
(405) 762-6641
Admin James E Rosenbaum FACHE, CEO. *Dir of Nursing* Helen S Beck RN. *Medical Dir* Dean Hinz MD.
Licensure Intermediate care; Residential care; Retirement. *Beds* ICF 18; Residential care 20; Retirement apts 50. *Private Pay Patients* 100%.
Owner Nonprofit corp (CSJ Health Systems).
Admissions Requirements Minimum age 55; Medical examination; Physician's request.
Staff Physicians 1 (pt); RNs 1 (ft); LPNs 4 (ft); Nurses' aides 14 (ft); Physical therapists 1 (pt); Activities coordinators 1 (ft); Dietitians 1 (pt); Pharmacists 1 (pt).
Affiliation Roman Catholic.
Facilities Dining room; Physical therapy room; Activities room; Chapel; Crafts room; Laundry room; Barber/Beauty shop; Library.
Activities Arts & crafts; Cards; Games; Reading groups; Prayer groups; Movies; Shopping trips; Dances/Social/Cultural gatherings; Intergenerational programs; Pet therapy.

Poteau

Eastern Oklahoma Skilled Nursing Facility
105 Wall, Poteau, OK 74953
(918) 647-8161
Admin Brenda Hunter. *Dir of Nursing* Pam Henderson RN. *Medical Dir* M Kemp MD.
Licensure Skilled care. *Beds* SNF 8. *Certified* Medicare.
Owner Nonprofit organization/foundation.
Admissions Requirements Physician's request.
Staff Physicians 12 (ft), 4 (pt); RNs 2 (ft), 1 (pt); LPNs 2 (ft), 2 (pt); Nurses' aides 1 (pt); Physical therapists 1 (ft); Speech therapists 1 (pt); Activities coordinators 1 (ft); Dietitians 1 (pt); Podiatrists 1 (pt); Dentists 1 (pt).
Facilities Dining room; Activities room; Library.
Activities Arts & crafts; Cards; Games; Reading groups; Prayer groups; Movies.

LeFlore Nursing Home
410 Carter St, Poteau, OK 74953
(918) 647-4194
Admin Don Farmer. *Dir of Nursing* Toni Fry RN.
Licensure Intermediate care. *Beds* ICF 63.
Certified Medicaid.
Owner Proprietary corp.
Staff RNs; LPNs; Nurses' aides; Activities coordinators; Dietitians.
Facilities Dining room; Physical therapy room; Activities room; Laundry room.
Activities Arts & crafts; Cards; Games; Reading groups; Prayer groups; Movies; Shopping trips; Dances/Social/Cultural gatherings.

Poteau Nursing Home
1212 Reynolds, Poteau, OK 74953
(918) 647-4247
Admin Arthur Wayne Hoffman.
Licensure Intermediate care. *Beds* 81.
  Certified Medicaid.

Prague

Parkland Manor
1400 D Ave, Prague, OK 74864
(405) 567-2201
Admin Dorothea Thomas.
Licensure Intermediate care. *Beds* ICF 58.
  Certified Medicaid.

Pryor

Colonial Terrace Care Center Inc
1320 NE 1st Pl, Pryor, OK 74361
(918) 825-5311
Admin Linda Moore.
Licensure Intermediate care. *Beds* ICF 75.
  Certified Medicaid.

Grand Valley Hospital
PO Box 278, Pryor, OK 74362
(918) 825-1600, 825-1600, ext 390 FAX
Admin Joel W Tate. *Dir of Nursing* Barbara
  Hodges RN.
Licensure Skilled care. *Beds* SNF 6.
Owner Nonprofit organization/foundation.

Shady Rest Care Center Inc
210 S Adair, Pryor, OK 74361
(918) 825-4455
Admin Glenda J Thomas.
Medical Dir Mary Lou Estes.
Licensure Intermediate care; Retirement. *Beds*
  ICF 65. *Certified* Medicaid.
Owner Proprietary corp.
Admissions Requirements Medical
  examination.
Staff RNs 1 (pt); LPNs 2 (ft), 2 (pt); Nurses'
  aides 18 (ft); Activities coordinators 1 (ft);
  Dietitians 1 (pt).
Facilities Dining room; Chapel; Laundry
  room; Barber/Beauty shop.
Activities Arts & crafts; Cards; Games;
  Reading groups; Prayer groups; Movies;
  Shopping trips; Dances/Social/Cultural
  gatherings.

Purcell

Broadlawn Manor
915-1017 N 7th, Purcell, OK 73080
(405) 527-2122
Admin Louise Deane.
Medical Dir Dr John Rollins.
Licensure Intermediate care. *Beds* 69.
  Certified Medicaid.
Admissions Requirements Minimum age 29;
  Medical examination.
Staff Physicians; RNs; LPNs; Nurses' aides;
  Reality therapists; Recreational therapists;
  Activities coordinators; Dietitians; Dentists.
Facilities Dining room; Activities room;
  Crafts room; Laundry room; Barber/Beauty
  shop; Library.
Activities Arts & crafts; Cards; Games;
  Reading groups; Prayer groups; Movies;
  Shopping trips; Dances/Social/Cultural
  gatherings; Easter egg hunt.

Purcell Nursing Home
801 N 6th, Purcell, OK 73080
(405) 527-7543
Admin Kenneth Greener.
Licensure Intermediate care. *Beds* ICF 105.
  Certified Medicaid.
Owner Proprietary corp (Amity Care).
Staff Physicians 1 (ft); RNs 1 (pt); LPNs 4
  (ft); Nurses' aides 30 (ft), 5 (pt);
  Recreational therapists 1 (ft); Occupational
  therapists 1 (pt); Activities coordinators 1
  (ft); Dietitians 6 (ft).

Facilities Dining room; Physical therapy
  room; Activities room; Crafts room; Laundry
  room; Barber/Beauty shop.
Activities Arts & crafts; Cards; Games;
  Reading groups; Prayer groups; Movies;
  Shopping trips; Dances/Social/Cultural
  gatherings.

Quapaw

Quapaw Nursing Home
PO Box 825, 407 Whitebird, Quapaw, OK
  74363
(918) 674-2233
Admin John Paul Waldon. *Dir of Nursing*
  Shirley Reed. *Medical Dir* Merrill Thomas
  DO.
Licensure Intermediate care; Alzheimer's care.
  Beds ICF 66. *Certified* Medicaid.
Owner Privately owned.
Admissions Requirements Physician's request.
Staff RNs 2 (pt); LPNs 5 (ft); Nurses' aides 19
  (ft); Activities coordinators 1 (ft), 1 (pt);
  Dietitians 1 (pt); Social services 1 (ft).
Facilities Dining room; Activities room;
  Crafts room; Laundry room; Barber/Beauty
  shop; Whirlpool room; Day care.
Activities Arts & crafts; Games; Reading
  groups; Prayer groups; Movies; Shopping
  trips; Dances/Social/Cultural gatherings;
  Church services.

Quinton

Quinton Nursing Home Inc
PO Box 359, 1209 W Main, Quinton, OK
  74561
(918) 469-2655, 469-2600
Admin Emmett Daniel.
Licensure Intermediate care. *Beds* ICF 78.
  Certified Medicaid.
Staff Physicians 1 (ft), 1 (pt); RNs 1 (pt);
  LPNs 5 (ft); Nurses' aides 16 (ft); Activities
  coordinators 1 (ft); Dietitians 1 (pt);
  Podiatrists 1 (pt); Dentists 2 (pt).
Facilities Dining room; Activities room;
  Crafts room; Laundry room; Barber/Beauty
  shop.
Activities Arts & crafts; Cards; Games;
  Reading groups; Shopping trips; Dances/
  Social/Cultural gatherings.

Ringling

Ringling Nursing Home
PO Box 750, 2nd & H Sts, Ringling, OK
  73456
(405) 662-2262
Admin Shelia V Stone.
Licensure Intermediate care. *Beds* ICF 50.
  Certified Medicaid.
Owner Proprietary corp (ARA Living
  Centers).

Roland

Sequoyah East
Rte 1 Box 393A, Roland, OK 74954
(918) 427-7401
Admin Danette Vessell. *Dir of Nursing* Bonnie
  Wilson. *Medical Dir* Dr Bert Corley.
Licensure Intermediate care. *Beds* ICF 60.
  Private Pay Patients 50%.
Owner Proprietary corp (Sequoyah House
  Inc).
Staff LPNs 4 (ft); Nurses' aides 8 (ft), 8 (pt);
  Activities coordinators 1 (ft); Dietitians.

Ryan

Ryan Nursing Home Inc
702 Lee St, Ryan, OK 73565
(405) 757-2517
Admin Jimmy L Thorn.
Medical Dir Sharon Howe.

Licensure Intermediate care. *Beds* ICF 69.
  Certified Medicaid.
Owner Proprietary corp.
Admissions Requirements Medical
  examination.
Staff Physicians; RNs; LPNs; Nurses' aides;
  Physical therapists; Recreational therapists;
  Activities coordinators; Dietitians.
Facilities Dining room; Physical therapy
  room; Activities room; Chapel; Crafts room;
  Laundry room; Barber/Beauty shop; Library.
Activities Arts & crafts; Cards; Games;
  Reading groups; Prayer groups; Movies;
  Shopping trips; Dances/Social/Cultural
  gatherings.

Salina

Parkhill North Nursing Home
Hwys 20 & 82, Salina, OK 74365
(918) 434-5600
Admin Jeanan Hobbs.
Licensure Intermediate care. *Beds* ICF 53.
  Certified Medicaid.

Sallisaw

Sequoyah Manor
PO Box 427, 615 E Redwood, Sallisaw, OK
  74955
(918) 775-4881
Admin Laveta Kyle.
Licensure Intermediate care. *Beds* ICF 161.
  Certified Medicaid.

Sand Springs

Oak Dale Manor
1025 N Adams, Sand Springs, OK 74063
(918) 245-5908
Admin Thomas A Connery.
Licensure Intermediate care. *Beds* ICF 207.
  Certified Medicaid.

Sapulpa

North Side Nursing Home
PO Box 1110, 102 E Line, Sapulpa, OK
  74066
(918) 224-0833
Admin Nellie Blair. *Dir of Nursing* Charlene
  Hopkins LPN. *Medical Dir* Dr Gerald
  Zumwaltman.
Licensure Intermediate care. *Beds* ICF 33.
Owner Privately owned.
Admissions Requirements Medical
  examination; Physician's request.
Staff Physicians; RNs; LPNs; Nurses' aides;
  Physical therapists; Recreational therapists;
  Activities coordinators; Dietitians;
  Ophthalmologists; Podiatrists.
Facilities Dining room; Physical therapy
  room; Activities room; Crafts room; Laundry
  room; Barber/Beauty shop; Library.
Activities Arts & crafts; Cards; Games;
  Reading groups; Prayer groups; Movies;
  Shopping trips; Dances/Social/Cultural
  gatherings; Intergenerational programs; Pet
  therapy.

Pleasant Manor Nursing Home
310 W Taft, Sapulpa, OK 74066
(918) 224-6012
Admin Erma J Brumley. *Dir of Nursing* Edna
  Sells RN. *Medical Dir* Philip Joseph MD.
Licensure Intermediate care. *Beds* ICF 142.
  Private Pay Patients 25%. *Certified*
  Medicaid.
Owner Proprietary corp (Medi-Plex II).
Admissions Requirements Minimum age 65;
  Medical examination; Physician's request.
Staff RNs; LPNs; Nurses' aides; Activities
  coordinators; Ophthalmologists.
Facilities Dining room; Physical therapy
  room; Activities room; Chapel; Crafts room;
  Laundry room; Barber/Beauty shop.

Activities Arts & crafts; Cards; Games; Reading groups; Prayer groups; Movies; Shopping trips; Dances/Social/Cultural gatherings; Intergenerational programs; Pet therapy.

Ranch Terrace
1310 E Cleveland, Sapulpa, OK 74066
(918) 224-2578
Admin L D Lawson. *Dir of Nursing* Teresa Morgan.
Licensure Intermediate care. *Beds* ICF 85. *Private Pay Patients* 30%. *Certified* Medicaid.
Owner Privately owned.
Admissions Requirements Medical examination; Physician's request.
Staff Physicians 1 (pt); RNs 1 (ft); LPNs 4 (ft); Nurses' aides 21 (ft); Physical therapists 1 (pt); Activities coordinators 1 (ft); Dietitians 1 (pt).
Activities Arts & crafts; Cards; Games; Reading groups; Prayer groups; Movies.

Sapulpa Nursing Center Inc
PO Box 1108, 1701 S Main, Sapulpa, OK 74066
(918) 224-5790
Admin Claire Barber.
Licensure Intermediate care. *Beds* ICF 57. *Certified* Medicaid.
Staff Physicians 2 (pt); RNs 1 (pt); LPNs 2 (ft); Nurses' aides 28 (ft); Physical therapists 1 (pt); Activities coordinators 1 (ft); Dietitians 1 (pt); Dentists 1 (pt).
Facilities Dining room; Physical therapy room; Activities room; Crafts room; Laundry room; Barber/Beauty shop.
Activities Arts & crafts; Cards; Games; Prayer groups; Shopping trips.

Sayre

Hensley Nursing Home Inc
PO Box 465, Hwy 152, Sayre, OK 73662
(405) 928-2494
Admin Dale Hensley. *Dir of Nursing* Dave Huddleston.
Licensure Intermediate care. *Beds* ICF 67. *Private Pay Patients* 30%. *Certified* Medicaid.
Owner Proprietary corp.
Staff RNs 1 (pt); LPNs 4 (ft); Nurses' aides 25 (ft), 6 (pt); Activities coordinators 1 (ft), 1 (pt); Dietitians 1 (ft), 1 (pt).

Seiling

Seiling Nursing Center
Rte 1 E, Seiling, OK 73663
(405) 922-4433
Admin Jeneva Helterbrake.
Licensure Intermediate care. *Beds* ICF 31. *Certified* Medicaid.

Seminole

Seminole Estates Nursing Center Inc
1200 Hwy 9 E, Seminole, OK 74868
(405) 382-1127
Admin Auttis Johnson.
Licensure Skilled care. *Beds* SNF 60.

Seminole Pioneer Nursing Home Inc
1705 State St, Seminole, OK 74868
(405) 382-1270
Admin Marchetta Black.
Medical Dir Auttis Johnson.
Licensure Intermediate care. *Beds* ICF 146. *Certified* Medicaid.

Shattuck

Convalescent Center of Shattuck
201 N Alfalfa, Box 189, Shattuck, OK 73858
(405) 938-2501

Admin Karen Bittman.
Licensure Intermediate care. *Beds* ICF 60. *Certified* Medicaid.
Owner Proprietary corp (Amity Care).
Admissions Requirements Minimum age 18; Medical examination.
Staff RNs 1 (pt); LPNs 2 (ft), 1 (pt); Nurses' aides 13 (ft), 2 (pt); Physical therapists 1 (pt); Recreational therapists 1 (pt); Activities coordinators 1 (pt); Dietitians 1 (pt).
Facilities Dining room; Activities room; Crafts room; Laundry room; Barber/Beauty shop.
Activities Arts & crafts; Cards; Games; Prayer groups; Movies; Shopping trips; Dances/Social/Cultural gatherings.

Newman Memorial Hospital SNF
905-919 S Main, Shattuck, OK 73858
(405) 938-2551
Admin Walter E Shain.
Licensure Skilled care. *Beds* SNF 20.

Shawnee

Golden Rule Home Inc
PO Box 1853, W Hardesty Rd, Shawnee, OK 74802-1853
(405) 273-7106
Admin Charles R Smith.
Licensure Intermediate care. *Beds* ICF 31. *Certified* Medicaid.

Independence Manor
909 E Independence, Shawnee, OK 74801
(405) 273-7156
Admin Jimmy E Rose.
Licensure Intermediate care. *Beds* ICF 100. *Certified* Medicaid.

Parkview Nursing Home Inc
1100 E Edwards, Shawnee, OK 74801
(405) 273-4835
Admin Betty Louise Scott.
Licensure Intermediate care. *Beds* ICF 78. *Certified* Medicaid.

Shawnee Care Center
1202 W Gilmore, Shawnee, OK 74801
(405) 273-8043
Admin Dennis P Widowski.
Licensure Intermediate care. *Beds* ICF 114. *Certified* Medicaid.
Owner Proprietary corp (Beverly Enterprises).

Shawnee Colonial Estates Nursing Home Inc
535 W Federal, Shawnee, OK 74801
(405) 273-1826
Admin Cindy Jones. *Dir of Nursing* Betty Wood RN.
Licensure Intermediate care. *Beds* ICF 160. *Certified* Medicaid.
Owner Proprietary corp.
Admissions Requirements Minimum age 18; Medical examination.
Staff RNs 2 (ft); LPNs 7 (ft); Nurses' aides 60 (ft), 20 (pt); Activities coordinators 1 (ft); Social services 1 (ft).
Facilities Dining room; Physical therapy room; Activities room; Crafts room; Laundry room; Barber/Beauty shop.
Activities Arts & crafts; Cards; Games; Reading groups; Prayer groups; Movies; Dances/Social/Cultural gatherings; Current events.

Shawnee Sunset Estates
1402 E Independence, Shawnee, OK 74801
(405) 275-1574, 273-5091 FAX
Admin William R Stewart. *Dir of Nursing* Lloyd Tucker.
Licensure Intermediate care. *Beds* ICF 72. *Private Pay Patients* 35%. *Certified* Medicaid.
Owner Privately owned.

Staff RNs 1 (ft); LPNs 5 (ft); Nurses' aides 27 (ft), 2 (pt); Physical therapists 1 (ft), 1 (pt); Recreational therapists 1 (pt); Activities coordinators 1 (ft); Dietitians 1 (pt).
Activities Arts & crafts; Cards; Games; Prayer groups; Movies; Shopping trips; Dances/Social/Cultural gatherings.

Skiatook

Skiatook Nursing Home
PO Box 218, Skiatook, OK 74070
(918) 396-2149
Admin Evelyn Reed.
Licensure Intermediate care. *Beds* ICF 70. *Certified* Medicaid.

Snyder

Ayers Nursing Home
801 B St, Snyder, OK 73566
(405) 569-2258
Admin Pat Ayers.
Licensure Intermediate care. *Beds* ICF 87. *Certified* Medicaid.

Spiro

Spiro Nursing Home
401 S Main, Spiro, OK 74959
(918) 962-2308
Admin Gary McClure.
Licensure Intermediate care. *Beds* ICF 95. *Certified* Medicaid.

Stigler

Stigler
114 NE 3rd, Stigler, OK 74462
(918) 967-2389
Admin Georgetta L Duvall. *Dir of Nursing* Janet Pearce. *Medical Dir* Georgetta L Duvall; Mozell Heflin.
Licensure Intermediate care. *Beds* ICF 100. *Certified* Medicaid.
Owner Privately owned.
Staff Physicians 4 (ft), 2 (pt); RNs 1 (ft); LPNs 5 (ft); Nurses' aides 35 (ft); Activities coordinators 1 (ft); Dietitians 1 (ft).
Facilities Dining room; Activities room; Crafts room; Laundry room; Barber/Beauty shop.
Activities Arts & crafts; Cards; Games; Reading groups; Prayer groups; Movies; Shopping trips; Dances/Social/Cultural gatherings; Intergenerational programs; Pet therapy.

Stillwater

Hearthstone Resident Care Center
PO Box 1629, 3014 S Main, Stillwater, OK 74076
(405) 372-9526
Admin Tandy Sammer.
Licensure Intermediate care for mentally retarded. *Beds* ICF/MR 91. *Certified* Medicaid.

Stillwater Nursing Home Inc
1215 W 10th St, Stillwater, OK 74074
(405) 372-1000
Licensure Intermediate care. *Beds* ICF 112. *Certified* Medicaid.
Owner Proprietary corp (Amity Care).
Staff RNs 1 (ft), 1 (pt); LPNs 3 (ft); Physical therapists 1 (pt); Activities coordinators 1 (ft); Dietitians 1 (pt); Dentists 1 (pt).

Stillwater Rosewood Care Center
PO Box 2437, 1601 S Main, Stillwater, OK 74076
(405) 377-4000
Admin Donna Price.
Medical Dir Dr Sid Williams.

Licensure Intermediate care. *Beds* ICF 104.
Certified Medicaid.
Staff Physicians 3 (pt); RNs 2 (pt); LPNs 3
(ft), 3 (pt); Activities coordinators 2 (ft);
Dietitians 1 (pt).
Facilities Dining room; Physical therapy
room; Activities room; Crafts room; Laundry
room; Barber/Beauty shop.
Activities Arts & crafts; Cards; Games; Prayer
groups; Movies; Shopping trips; Dances/
Social/Cultural gatherings; Remotivation.

Westhaven Nursing Home Inc
1215 S Western, Stillwater, OK 74074
(405) 743-1140
Admin Wendy Lott.
Medical Dir Betty Foster.
Licensure Intermediate care; Alzheimer's care.
Beds ICF 125. *Certified* Medicaid.
Facilities Dining room; Activities room;
Laundry room; Barber/Beauty shop.
Activities Arts & crafts; Cards; Games;
Reading groups; Prayer groups; Movies;
Shopping trips; Dances/Social/Cultural
gatherings.

Stilwell

Stilwell Nursing Home
PO Box 651, 422 W Locust, Stilwell, OK
74960
(918) 696-7715
Admin Fredna Latta.
Licensure Intermediate care. *Beds* ICF 104.
Certified Medicaid.

Stonewall

Stonegate Nursing Center
6th & Collins, Stonewall, OK 74868
(405) 265-4247
Admin Betty Hilton.
Medical Dir Jeannie Ables.
Licensure Intermediate care. *Beds* ICF 53.
Certified Medicaid.
Owner Privately owned.
Admissions Requirements Minimum age 18;
Physician's request.
Staff Physicians 1 (pt); RNs 1 (pt); Nurses'
aides 20 (ft); Physical therapists 1 (pt);
Activities coordinators 1 (ft); Dietitians 1
(pt).
Facilities Dining room; Activities room;
Crafts room; Laundry room; Barber/Beauty
shop.
Activities Arts & crafts; Cards; Games;
Reading groups; Prayer groups; Movies;
Shopping trips; Dances/Social/Cultural
gatherings.

Stratford

Grand Place
PO Box 670, Stratford, OK 74872
(405) 928-3374
Admin Marcus McClanahan.
Licensure Intermediate care. *Beds* ICF 101.
Certified Medicaid.

Stratford Nursing Center
PO Box 636, Stratford, OK 74872
(405) 759-2268
Admin Dolores Tucker. *Dir of Nursing* Mary
Alinger RN. *Medical Dir* Dr M L Stokes.
Licensure Intermediate care. *Beds* ICF 106.
Private Pay Patients 10%. *Certified*
Medicaid.
Owner Proprietary corp.
Admissions Requirements Medical
examination; Physician's request.
Staff RNs 1 (ft); LPNs 4 (ft), 1 (pt); Nurses'
aides 25 (ft), 5 (pt); Physical therapists 1 (ft),
1 (pt); Activities coordinators 1 (ft);
Dietitians 1 (pt).
Facilities Dining room; Physical therapy
room; Activities room; Crafts room; Laundry
room; Barber/Beauty shop.

Activities Arts & crafts; Cards; Games;
Reading groups; Prayer groups; Movies;
Shopping trips; Dances/Social/Cultural
gatherings.

Stroud

Stroud Health Care Center
416 N 7th Ave, Stroud, OK 74079
(918) 968-2507
Admin Debbie J Keim.
Licensure Intermediate care. *Beds* ICF 50.
Certified Medicaid.

Stroud Shamrock Care Center
721 W Olive, Stroud, OK 74079
(918) 968-2075
Admin Dennis Davis.
Licensure Intermediate care. *Beds* ICF 58.
Certified Medicaid.

Sulphur

Artesian Home
1415 W 15th, Sulphur, OK 73086
(405) 622-2030
Admin Robert H Walker.
Licensure Intermediate care. *Beds* ICF 62.
Certified Medicaid.

Callaway Nursing Home
1300 W Lindsay, Sulphur, OK 73086
(405) 622-2416
Admin Rosalina S Jewell.
Licensure Intermediate care. *Beds* ICF 86.
Certified Medicaid.

Tahlequah

Davis Nursing Home
1201 N Vinita Ave, Tahlequah, OK 74464
(918) 456-6181
Admin Veraman Davis.
Licensure Intermediate care. *Beds* ICF 139.
Certified Medicaid.

Go Ye Village Med-Center
1200 W 4th St, Tahlequah, OK 74464
(918) 456-1631
Admin James Richardson. *Dir of Nursing*
Frann Thompson LPN. *Medical Dir* John F
Porter DO.
Licensure Intermediate care; Alzheimer's care;
Retirement. *Beds* ICF 32.
Owner Nonprofit corp.
Admissions Requirements Minimum age 55;
Medical examination; Physician's request.
Staff Physicians 1 (ft); RNs 1 (ft), 1 (pt);
LPNs 4 (ft), 2 (pt); Nurses' aides 15 (ft), 5
(pt); Physical therapists 1 (pt); Reality
therapists 1 (pt); Occupational therapists 1
(pt); Activities coordinators 1 (ft); Dietitians
1 (pt); Chaplains 2 (ft).
Facilities Dining room; Physical therapy
room; Activities room; Chapel; Crafts room;
Laundry room; Barber/Beauty shop; Library;
Store.
Activities Arts & crafts; Cards; Games;
Reading groups; Prayer groups; Movies;
Shopping trips; Dances/Social/Cultural
gatherings.

Tahlequah Nursing Home
614 E Cherry, Tahlequah, OK 74464
(918) 456-2573
Admin Billie Davis.
Licensure Intermediate care. *Beds* ICF 125.
Certified Medicaid.

Ward Manor Inc
PO Box 1415, Tahlequah, OK 74465
(918) 456-3456
Admin Ataloa L Trammel.
Licensure Intermediate care. *Beds* ICF 45.
Certified Medicaid.

Talihina

Talihina Manor Nursing Home
1st & Emmertt, Talihina, OK 74571
(918) 567-2279
Admin Estelle M Yancey.
Licensure Intermediate care. *Beds* ICF 69.
Certified Medicaid.

Tecumseh

Sunset Estates
201 W Walnut, Tecumseh, OK 74873
(405) 598-2167
Admin Ken Prator.
Medical Dir Robert Zumwalt MD.
Licensure Intermediate care. *Beds* ICF 100.
Certified Medicaid.
Admissions Requirements Minimum age 18;
Physician's request.
Staff RNs 1 (ft); LPNs 6 (ft), 2 (pt); Nurses'
aides 39 (ft); Physical therapists 1 (pt);
Activities coordinators 1 (ft); Dietitians 1
(pt).
Facilities Dining room; Physical therapy
room; Activities room; Crafts room; Laundry
room; Barber/Beauty shop.
Activities Arts & crafts; Cards; Games; Prayer
groups; Movies; Shopping trips; Dances/
Social/Cultural gatherings.

Temple

Temple Manor Nursing Home
PO Box 528, Temple, OK 73568-0528
(405) 342-6411
Admin Lois Powell.
Licensure Intermediate care. *Beds* ICF 48.
Certified Medicaid.

Thomas

Thomas Nursing Center
PO Box 38, 601 E Frisco, Thomas, OK 73669
(405) 661-2171
Admin Charleen Jantz; Betty Palesano, Asst.
Dir of Nursing Evelyn Shephard RN.
Licensure Intermediate care. *Beds* ICF 60.
Private Pay Patients 70%. *Certified*
Medicaid.
Owner Nonprofit corp.
Staff Physicians 2 (ft), 1 (pt); RNs 1 (ft);
LPNs 4 (ft); Nurses' aides; Speech therapists
1 (pt); Activities coordinators 1 (ft), 1 (pt);
Dietitians 1 (ft); Restorative therapists 1 (ft).
Facilities Dining room; Physical therapy
room; Activities room; Chapel; Laundry
room; Barber/Beauty shop.
Activities Arts & crafts; Cards; Games;
Reading groups; Prayer groups; Movies;
Shopping trips; Dances/Social/Cultural
gatherings; Pet therapy; Church group
activities.

Tishomingo

Hillcrest Nursing Home
1200 E Main, Tishomingo, OK 73460
(405) 371-2636
Admin Frank Harris.
Licensure Intermediate care. *Beds* ICF 50.
Certified Medicaid.

Lawn View Nursing Home
Box 127, 607 S Byrd, Tishomingo, OK 73460
(405) 371-2317
Admin Vearlene Burchett. *Dir of Nursing*
Wilma Davis RN. *Medical Dir* Pat Bell MD.
Licensure Intermediate care. *Beds* ICF 60.
Private Pay Patients 15%. *Certified*
Medicaid; Medicare.
Owner Proprietary corp (Red River
Management).
Admissions Requirements Minimum age 18;
Medical examination.

Staff Physicians 3 (ft); RNs 1 (ft); LPNs 4 (ft); Nurses' aides 25 (ft); Physical therapists 1 (ft); Recreational therapists 1 (ft); Activities coordinators 1 (ft); Dietitians 1 (ft).
Facilities Dining room; Physical therapy room; Activities room; Crafts room; Laundry room; Barber/Beauty shop; Library.
Activities Arts & crafts; Cards; Games; Reading groups; Prayer groups; Movies; Shopping trips; Dances/Social/Cultural gatherings; Intergenerational programs; Pet therapy.

Tonkawa

Willow Haven
1301 N 5th, Tonkawa, OK 74653
(405) 628-2525, 628-3517 FAX
Admin Patricia Scott. *Dir of Nursing* Sharon Davis.
Licensure Intermediate care. *Beds* ICF 49. *Private Pay Patients* 48%. *Certified* Medicaid.
Owner Proprietary corp (Medi-Plex II).
Admissions Requirements Medical examination; Physician's request.
Staff RNs 1 (ft); LPNs 2 (ft); Nurses' aides 15 (ft), 1 (pt); Activities coordinators 1 (ft); Dietitians 1 (pt).
Facilities Dining room; Activities room; Crafts room; Laundry room; Barber/Beauty shop.
Activities Arts & crafts; Cards; Games; Reading groups; Prayer groups; Dances/Social/Cultural gatherings; Pet therapy.

Tulsa

Ambassador Manor Nursing Center Inc
1340 E 61st St, Tulsa, OK 74136
(918) 743-8978
Admin Sharon Convey.
Medical Dir Marla McMillian.
Licensure Intermediate care; Alzheimer's care. *Beds* ICF 142. *Certified* Medicaid.
Owner Proprietary corp.
Admissions Requirements Minimum age 55; Medical examination.
Staff Physicians 1 (ft); RNs 2 (ft); LPNs 8 (ft); Nurses' aides 40 (ft); Physical therapists 1 (ft); Recreational therapists 1 (ft); Activities coordinators 1 (ft); Dietitians 1 (ft); Ophthalmologists 1 (ft); Dentists 1 (ft).
Facilities Dining room; Physical therapy room; Activities room; Chapel; Crafts room; Laundry room; Barber/Beauty shop; Library.
Activities Arts & crafts; Cards; Games; Reading groups; Prayer groups; Movies; Shopping trips; Dances/Social/Cultural gatherings; Opera; Ballet; Concerts.

Black's Nursing Home
3601 N Columbia, Tulsa, OK 74110
(918) 583-1509
Admin Mary Henderson.
Licensure Intermediate care. *Beds* ICF 54. *Certified* Medicaid.
Admissions Requirements Minimum age 18; Medical examination; Physician's request.
Staff Physicians 1 (pt); LPNs 3 (ft); Nurses' aides 14 (ft), 2 (pt); Dietitians 1 (pt).
Facilities Dining room; Laundry room; Barber/Beauty shop.
Activities Arts & crafts; Cards; Games; Reading groups; Prayer groups; Movies; Shopping trips; Dances/Social/Cultural gatherings.

Chamor Nursing Center
2550 E 36th N, Tulsa, OK 74110
(918) 425-7548
Admin Terri G Firth.
Licensure Intermediate care. *Beds* ICF 100. *Certified* Medicaid.

Colonial Manor Nursing Home
1815 E Skelly Dr, Tulsa, OK 74105
(918) 743-7838
Admin Robert H Gary.
Licensure Intermediate care. *Beds* ICF 120. *Certified* Medicaid.

Convalescent Center Inc
3333 E 28th, Tulsa, OK 74114
(918) 747-8008
Admin Robert H Gary.
Licensure Intermediate care. *Beds* ICF 56. *Certified* Medicaid.

Doctors' Hospital SNF
2323 Harvard, Tulsa, OK 74114
(918) 744-4000
Admin Harvey Shapiro.
Licensure Skilled care. *Beds* SNF 14.

Four Seasons Nursing Center
2425 S Memorial, Tulsa, OK 74129
(918) 628-0932
Admin Sandra Downing. *Dir of Nursing* Wilma Frailey RN. *Medical Dir* Dr James C King.
Licensure Skilled care; Intermediate care. *Beds* Swing beds SNF/ICF 118. *Certified* Medicaid.
Owner Proprietary corp.
Admissions Requirements Medical examination; Physician's request.
Staff RNs 1 (ft); Nurses' aides 42 (ft).
Facilities Dining room; Physical therapy room; Activities room; Laundry room; Barber/Beauty shop.
Activities Arts & crafts; Cards; Games; Movies; Shopping trips; Dances/Social/Cultural gatherings.

Georgian Court Nursing Home
2552 E 21st, Tulsa, OK 74114
(918) 742-7319
Admin Barbara Hardin.
Medical Dir Dr G Bryant Boyd.
Licensure Skilled care. *Beds* SNF 48.
Owner Proprietary corp (Health Care & Retirement corp).
Admissions Requirements Physician's request.
Staff Physicians 1 (pt); RNs 1 (ft), 1 (pt); LPNs 5 (ft), 4 (pt); Nurses' aides 12 (ft), 7 (pt); Physical therapists 1 (pt); Activities coordinators 1 (ft); Dietitians 1 (pt); Podiatrists 1 (pt); Dentists 1 (pt).
Facilities Dining room; Laundry room; Barber/Beauty shop.
Activities Arts & crafts; Cards; Games; Reading groups; Movies; Shopping trips; Dances/Social/Cultural gatherings.

Hillcrest Medical Center SNF
1120 S Utica, Tulsa, OK 74104
(918) 584-1351
Admin Claudia McKenzie.
Licensure Skilled care. *Beds* SNF 20.

Homestead Nursing Home
1021 Charles Page Blvd, Tulsa, OK 74127
(918) 587-4189, 582-9508 FAX
Admin Joy Pat Wilkerson. *Dir of Nursing* Virginia Coleman. *Medical Dir* Virginia Coleman.
Licensure Intermediate care. *Beds* ICF 53. *Certified* Medicaid.
Owner Proprietary corp.
Admissions Requirements Minimum age 16; Medical examination; Physician's request.
Staff RNs 1 (pt); LPNs 3 (ft), 1 (pt); Nurses' aides 17 (ft), 1 (pt); Reality therapists 1 (ft); Activities coordinators 1 (ft); Dietitians 1 (pt); Ophthalmologists 1 (pt); Podiatrists 1 (pt).
Facilities Dining room; Laundry room; Barber/Beauty shop.
Activities Arts & crafts; Cards; Games; Reading groups; Prayer groups; Movies; Dances/Social/Cultural gatherings.

Leisure Village Nursing Center
2154 S 85th E Ave, Tulsa, OK 74129
(918) 622-4747
Admin Beverly Champion.
Licensure Intermediate care. *Beds* ICF 117. *Certified* Medicaid.

Mayfair Nursing Home
7707 S Memorial Dr, Tulsa, OK 74133
(918) 250-8571
Admin John Read Pearson.
Licensure Skilled care; Alzheimer's care. *Beds* SNF 100.
Owner Proprietary corp (Hillhaven Corp).
Admissions Requirements Medical examination; Physician's request.
Staff RNs; LPNs; Nurses' aides.
Facilities Dining room; Physical therapy room; Activities room; Crafts room; Barber/Beauty shop; Library.
Activities Arts & crafts; Cards; Games; Reading groups; Prayer groups; Movies; Shopping trips; Dances/Social/Cultural gatherings; Wine & cheese; Ceramics; Cooking.

Oklahoma Methodist Home for the Aged
4134 E 31st St, Tulsa, OK 74135
(918) 743-2565
Admin Charles H Richardson. *Dir of Nursing* Vivian Adair RN. *Medical Dir* Dr Price Kraft.
Licensure Intermediate care; Retirement. *Beds* ICF 100; Retirement 200. *Private Pay Patients* 20%. *Certified* Medicaid.
Owner Nonprofit corp.
Admissions Requirements Minimum age 60; Medical examination.
Staff RNs 4 (ft), 1 (pt); LPNs 12 (ft); Nurses' aides 44 (ft); Physical therapists 1 (ft), 1 (pt); Activities coordinators 2 (ft); Dietitians 1 (pt).
Affiliation United Methodist.
Facilities Dining room; Physical therapy room; Activities room; Chapel; Crafts room; Laundry room; Barber/Beauty shop; Library; Dental office.
Activities Arts & crafts; Games; Prayer groups; Movies; Shopping trips; Dances/Social/Cultural gatherings; Intergenerational programs.

Park Terrace Convalescent Center
5115 E 51st, Tulsa, OK 74135
(918) 627-5961
Admin John Fish.
Licensure Skilled care; Intermediate care. *Beds* SNF 8; ICF 118.
Admissions Requirements Medical examination.
Staff RNs; LPNs; Nurses' aides; Recreational therapists; Activities coordinators.
Facilities Dining room; Activities room; Crafts room; Laundry room; Barber/Beauty shop.
Activities Arts & crafts; Cards; Games; Reading groups; Movies; Shopping trips.

Regency Park Manor Health Care Center
3910 Park Rd, Tulsa, OK 74115
(918) 425-1355
Admin Florence Alexander.
Licensure Intermediate care. *Beds* ICF 105. *Certified* Medicaid.
Owner Proprietary corp (ARA Living Centers).

Rest Haven Nursing Home
1944 N Iroquois, Tulsa, OK 74106
(918) 583-1509
Admin Mary F Henderson.
Medical Dir Dr Angelo Dagessandro.
Licensure Intermediate care. *Beds* ICF 131. *Certified* Medicaid.
Admissions Requirements Minimum age 21; Medical examination; Physician's request.

Staff Physicians 3 (pt); RNs 2 (pt); LPNs 3 (ft); Nurses' aides 23 (ft); Physical therapists 1 (pt); Reality therapists 1 (ft); Recreational therapists 1 (pt); Activities coordinators 1 (ft); Dietitians 1 (pt).
Facilities Dining room; Physical therapy room; Activities room; Chapel; Laundry room; Barber/Beauty shop.
Activities Arts & crafts; Games; Reading groups; Prayer groups; Movies; Shopping trips; Dances/Social/Cultural gatherings.

St Francis Hospital SNF
6161 S Yale, Tulsa, OK 74136
(918) 494-1305
Admin Sr Mary Blandine.
Licensure Skilled care. *Beds* SNF 30.

St John Medical Center
1923 S Utica Ave, Tulsa, OK 74104
(918) 744-2312
Admin Sr M Therese Gottschalk. *Dir of Nursing* Margaret Weigel. *Medical Dir* Dr R Goen.
Licensure Skilled care. *Beds* SNF 30. *Private Pay Patients* 10%. *Certified* Medicare.
Owner Nonprofit organization/foundation.
Admissions Requirements Physician's request.
Staff Physicians; RNs; LPNs; Nurses' aides; Physical therapists; Recreational therapists; Occupational therapists; Speech therapists; Dietitians; Ophthalmologists; Podiatrists.
Affiliation Roman Catholic.
Facilities Dining room; Physical therapy room; Activities room; Chapel; Barber/Beauty shop; Library; Dayroom.
Activities Arts & crafts; Cards; Games; Prayer groups; Movies; Dances/Social/Cultural gatherings; Singing.

St Simeon's Episcopal Home Inc
3701 N Cincinnati, Tulsa, OK 74106
(918) 425-3583
Admin Jerry D Pinson.
Licensure Intermediate care. *Beds* ICF 25. *Certified* Medicaid.
Affiliation Episcopal.

Sherwood Manor Nursing Home
2415 W Skelly Dr, Tulsa, OK 74107
(918) 446-4284, 446-1152 FAX
Admin Patsy Hulsey. *Dir of Nursing* Sandy Hendryx. *Medical Dir* Terrence Williams.
Licensure Intermediate care. *Beds* ICF 102. *Private Pay Patients* 20%. *Certified* Medicaid.
Owner Proprietary corp.
Admissions Requirements Medical examination; Physician's request.
Staff RNs 1 (ft); LPNs 6 (ft), 1 (pt); Nurses' aides 30 (ft); Activities coordinators 1 (ft); Dietitians.
Facilities Dining room; Activities room; Laundry room; Barber/Beauty shop.
Activities Arts & crafts; Cards; Games; Reading groups; Prayer groups; Movies; Shopping trips; Dances/Social/Cultural gatherings; Intergenerational programs.

Skyline Terrace Nursing Center
6202 E 61st, Tulsa, OK 74136
(918) 494-8830, 494-8837 FAX
Admin Carl Lyons. *Dir of Nursing* Linda Coyle RN BSN. *Medical Dir* Arthur Hale MD.
Licensure Skilled care; Alzheimer's unit; Respite care. *Beds* SNF 209; Alzheimer's unit 30. *Private Pay Patients* 95%. *Certified* Medicare.
Owner Proprietary corp.
Admissions Requirements Medical examination; Physician's request.
Staff Physicians 1 (pt); RNs 8 (ft); LPNs 4 (ft); Nurses' aides 40 (ft); Physical therapists 1 (ft); Reality therapists 1 (pt); Recreational therapists 2 (ft); Occupational therapists 1

(pt); Speech therapists 1 (pt); Activities coordinators 1 (ft); Dietitians 1 (pt); Podiatrists 1 (pt); Audiologists 1 (pt).
Facilities Dining room; Physical therapy room; Activities room; Chapel; Crafts room; Laundry room; Barber/Beauty shop; Library; Rehabilitation head injury; Ventilator care.
Activities Arts & crafts; Cards; Games; Reading groups; Prayer groups; Movies; Shopping trips; Dances/Social/Cultural gatherings; Intergenerational programs; Pet therapy.

Southern Hills Nursing Center
5170 S Vandalia, Tulsa, OK 74135
(918) 496-3963
Admin Julia Galvin.
Licensure Intermediate care. *Beds* ICF 118. *Certified* Medicaid.

Tulsa Christian Home Inc
6201 E 36th St, Tulsa, OK 74135
(918) 622-3430
Admin Arlene VanHooser. *Dir of Nursing* Charline Dyer RN. *Medical Dir* Robert Mahaffey MD.
Licensure Intermediate care; Retirement. *Beds* ICF 100; Retirement 11. *Private Pay Patients* 40%. *Certified* Medicaid.
Owner Nonprofit corp.
Admissions Requirements Medical examination; Physician's request.
Staff Physicians 1 (pt); RNs 3 (ft); LPNs 7 (ft); Nurses' aides 38 (ft), 3 (pt); Physical therapists 1 (pt); Reality therapists 1 (ft); Activities coordinators 1 (ft); Dietitians 1 (pt).
Affiliation Church of Christ.
Facilities Dining room; Activities room; Crafts room; Laundry room; Barber/Beauty shop; Library.
Activities Arts & crafts; Cards; Games; Reading groups; Prayer groups; Movies; Shopping trips; Pet therapy.

Tulsa Jewish Community Retirement & Health Care Center Inc
2025 E 71st St, Tulsa, OK 74136
(918) 496-8333
Admin Seth D Levy. *Dir of Nursing* Elyse Kester.
Licensure Intermediate care; Retirement; Alzheimer's care. *Beds* ICF 40; Retirement apts 61. *Private Pay Patients* 100%.
Owner Nonprofit organization/foundation.
Admissions Requirements Medical examination; Physician's request.
Staff RNs 1 (ft), 1 (pt); LPNs 5 (ft), 1 (pt); Nurses' aides 18 (ft), 3 (pt); Activities coordinators 1 (ft), 2 (pt); Dietitians 1 (ft).
Languages German, Yiddish.
Affiliation Jewish.
Facilities Dining room; Physical therapy room; Activities room; Crafts room; Laundry room; Barber/Beauty shop; Library.
Activities Arts & crafts; Games; Reading groups; Movies; Dances/Social/Cultural gatherings; Intergenerational programs; Pet therapy; Music; Exercise.

Tulsa Nursing Center
10912 E 14th St, Tulsa, OK 74128
(918) 438-2440
Admin Coleene Bland.
Licensure Intermediate care. *Beds* ICF 177. *Certified* Medicaid.

University Village Inc
855 S Lewis, Tulsa, OK 74136
(918) 299-2661
Admin Barbara J Clark.
Medical Dir Dr Edward Slothour.
Licensure Skilled care. *Beds* SNF 70.
Admissions Requirements Medical examination.

Staff Physicians 1 (ft); RNs 5 (ft), 1 (pt); LPNs 3 (ft), 2 (pt); Nurses' aides 24 (ft), 6 (pt); Physical therapists 1 (pt); Activities coordinators 1 (ft); Dietitians 1 (ft).
Affiliation Oral Roberts Ministries.
Facilities Dining room; Physical therapy room; Activities room; Chapel; Crafts room; Laundry room; Barber/Beauty shop; Library.
Activities Arts & crafts; Cards; Games; Reading groups; Prayer groups; Movies; Shopping trips; Dances/Social/Cultural gatherings.

Woodland Park Home
5707 S Memorial Dr, Tulsa, OK 74145
(918) 252-2521
Admin Ed Rucker.
Licensure Intermediate care for mentally retarded. *Beds* ICF/MR 101. *Certified* Medicaid.

Tuttle

Tuttle Nursing Center
108 S 12th, Tuttle, OK 73089
(405) 381-3363
Admin Joyce Ferris.
Licensure Intermediate care. *Beds* ICF 52. *Certified* Medicaid.

Valliant

Valliant Nursing Center Inc
300 N Dalton, Valliant, OK 74764
(405) 933-7803
Admin Phillip Gilbert. *Dir of Nursing* Irene Farris RN.
Licensure Intermediate care. *Beds* ICF 65. *Certified* Medicaid.
Owner Proprietary corp.
Admissions Requirements Medical examination.
Staff RNs 1 (ft); LPNs 3 (ft), 1 (pt); Nurses' aides 26 (ft); Activities coordinators 1 (ft).
Facilities Dining room; Laundry room; Barber/Beauty shop.
Activities Arts & crafts; Games; Prayer groups; Movies; Dances/Social/Cultural gatherings.

Vian

Vian Nursing Home
Thornton St, Vian, OK 74962
(918) 773-5258
Admin Billy E Fullbright.
Licensure Intermediate care. *Beds* ICF 119. *Certified* Medicaid.

Vici

Town of Vici Nursing Home
PO Box 119, 619 Speck, Vici, OK 73859
(405) 995-4216
Admin Jean Eagon. *Dir of Nursing* Karen Shaw.
Licensure Intermediate care. *Beds* ICF 61. *Private Pay Patients* 58%. *Certified* Medicaid.
Owner Publicly owned.
Admissions Requirements Medical examination; Physician's request.
Staff RNs; LPNs; Nurses' aides; Physical therapists; Activities coordinators; Dietitians.
Facilities Dining room; Activities room; Laundry room; Barber/Beauty shop; Sun room/Atrium.
Activities Arts & crafts; Cards; Games; Reading groups; Prayer groups; Movies; Dances/Social/Cultural gatherings; Intergenerational programs; Pet therapy.

Vinita

Autumn Nursing Centers Inc 1
240 N Scraper, Vinita, OK 74301
(918) 256-7861

Admin Kunigunda M Lodes. *Dir of Nursing* Nancy Stanley RN.
Licensure Intermediate care. *Beds* ICF 62. *Certified* Medicaid.
Owner Privately owned.
Admissions Requirements Medical examination.
Staff RNs 1 (ft); LPNs 1 (ft), 2 (pt); Nurses' aides 9 (ft), 6 (pt); Activities coordinators 1 (ft); Dietitians 1 (ft), 1 (pt).
Facilities Dining room; Laundry room; Barber/Beauty shop.
Activities Arts & crafts; Cards; Games; Reading groups; Prayer groups; Movies; Shopping trips; Dances/Social/Cultural gatherings; Trips to park.

Autumn Nursing Centers Inc 2
1200 W Canadian, Vinita, OK 74301
(918) 256-6366
Admin Wathena S Cusick.
Licensure Intermediate care. *Beds* ICF 133. *Certified* Medicaid.

Home of Hope Inc
PO Box 903, Vinita, OK 74301
(918) 256-7825
Admin Dale Dunston; Charlotte McComb, Exec Dir. *Dir of Nursing* Wanda Hintz.
Licensure Intermediate care for mentally retarded. *Beds* ICF/MR 94. *Certified* Medicaid; Medicare.
Owner Nonprofit corp.
Admissions Requirements Minimum age 18; Medical examination; Physician's request.
Staff Physicians; RNs 1 (pt); LPNs 5 (ft); Nurses' aides 41 (ft); Physical therapists 1 (pt); Recreational therapists 1 (ft); Occupational therapists 1 (ft); Speech therapists 1 (ft); Activities coordinators 1 (ft); Dietitians 1 (ft); Podiatrists 1 (pt); Audiologists 1 (pt).
Facilities Dining room; Physical therapy room; Activities room; Crafts room; Laundry room; Barber/Beauty shop.
Activities Arts & crafts; Games; Reading groups; Movies; Shopping trips; Dances/Social/Cultural gatherings; Pet therapy.

Wagoner

Ross Nursing Home 1 Inc
205 N Lincoln, Wagoner, OK 74467
(918) 485-2203
Admin Dawna Barnes.
Licensure Intermediate care. *Beds* ICF 87. *Certified* Medicaid.

Ross Nursing Home 2 Inc
109 S Harrill, Wagoner, OK 74467
(918) 485-3972
Admin Leona Limon. *Dir of Nursing* Teresa Rains. *Medical Dir* Dr Robert Johnson.
Licensure Intermediate care. *Beds* ICF 54. *Private Pay Patients* 20%. *Certified* Medicaid.
Owner Proprietary corp (Ross Nursing Home Inc).
Admissions Requirements Physician's request.
Staff RNs; LPNs; Nurses' aides; Physical therapists; Speech therapists; Activities coordinators; Dietitians.
Facilities Dining room; Laundry room; Barber/Beauty shop.
Activities Arts & crafts; Cards; Games; Reading groups; Prayer groups; Movies; Shopping trips; Dances/Social/Cultural gatherings; Pet therapy; Adopt-a-grandparent program.

Wakita

Community Health Center
500 Cherokee St, Wakita, OK 73771
(405) 594-2292
Admin Vicki Lunday.
Medical Dir Steven P Treat DO.

Licensure Intermediate care. *Beds* ICF 47. *Certified* Medicaid.
Owner Nonprofit corp.
Staff Physicians 1 (ft), 1 (pt); RNs 5 (ft), 4 (pt); LPNs 2 (ft); Nurses' aides 27 (ft); Physical therapists 1 (pt); Activities coordinators 1 (ft); Dietitians 1 (ft); Dentists 1 (ft).
Facilities Dining room; Physical therapy room; Activities room; Chapel; Crafts room; Laundry room; Barber/Beauty shop; Library; Sun room.
Activities Arts & crafts; Cards; Games; Reading groups; Prayer groups; Movies; Shopping trips; Dances/Social/Cultural gatherings.

Walters

Parkview Manor
PO Box 246, 600 E California, Walters, OK 73752
(405) 875-3376
Admin Hazel Piatt.
Licensure Intermediate care. *Beds* ICF 54. *Certified* Medicaid.

Warner

Countryside Estates Inc
Hwy 64 E, Box 629, Warner, OK 74469
(918) 463-5143
Admin Margie Burris.
Licensure Intermediate care. *Beds* ICF 111. *Certified* Medicaid.
Staff Physicians 1 (pt); RNs 1 (pt); LPNs 5 (ft); Nurses' aides 27 (ft); Physical therapists 1 (pt); Activities coordinators 1 (ft); Dietitians 1 (pt).
Facilities Dining room; Laundry room; Barber/Beauty shop; TV area.
Activities Arts & crafts; Cards; Games; Prayer groups; Shopping trips; Dances/Social/ Cultural gatherings.

Watonga

Sunset Estates of Watonga Inc
816 Nash Blvd, Watonga, OK 73772
(405) 623-7249
Admin Michael Aebischer. *Dir of Nursing* Regina Stinson RN.
Licensure Intermediate care. *Beds* ICF 75. *Certified* Medicaid.
Staff Physicians 4 (pt); RNs 1 (ft); LPNs 3 (pt); Nurses' aides 19 (ft), 3 (pt); Activities coordinators 1 (ft); Dietitians 1 (pt).
Facilities Dining room; Activities room; Crafts room; Laundry room; Barber/Beauty shop.
Activities Arts & crafts; Cards; Games; Reading groups; Prayer groups; Movies; Shopping trips; Dances/Social/Cultural gatherings.

Waurika

Wood Nursing & Convalescent Center
PO Box 390, Waurika, OK 73573
(405) 228-2249
Admin Vickie Wood.
Licensure Intermediate care. *Beds* ICF 83. *Certified* Medicaid.

Waynoka

Waynoka Nursing Center
Rte 2 Box 50, Waynoka, OK 73860
(405) 824-5661
Admin Betty J Harris. *Dir of Nursing* Becky Kath LPN.
Licensure Intermediate care. *Beds* ICF 40. *Certified* Medicaid.
Owner Proprietary corp.
Admissions Requirements Physician's request.

Staff Physicians; RNs; LPNs; Nurses' aides; Dietitians.
Languages Spanish.
Facilities Dining room; Activities room; Laundry room; Barber/Beauty shop; Whirlpool tub.
Activities Arts & crafts; Cards; Games; Reading groups; Prayer groups; Movies; Shopping trips; Dances/Social/Cultural gatherings.

Weatherford

Little Bird Nursing Home Inc
801 N Washington, Weatherford, OK 73096
(405) 772-3993
Admin Lola Little Bird.
Licensure Intermediate care. *Beds* ICF 81. *Certified* Medicaid.

Weatherford Nursing Center
1001 N 7th, Weatherford, OK 73096
(405) 772-3368
Admin Vonda R Carroll. *Dir of Nursing* Iris Ainsworth.
Licensure Intermediate care. *Beds* ICF 52. *Certified* Medicaid.
Owner Proprietary corp.
Admissions Requirements Medical examination.
Staff RNs 1 (pt); LPNs 3 (ft); Nurses' aides 8 (ft); Activities coordinators 1 (ft), 1 (pt); Dietitians 1 (pt); CMAs 3 (ft), 2 (pt).
Facilities Dining room; Laundry room; Barber/Beauty shop.
Activities Arts & crafts; Cards; Games; Reading groups; Prayer groups; Movies; Shopping trips; Dances/Social/Cultural gatherings; Volunteer church activities.

Weleetka

Adkins Nursing Home
300 W 9th, Weleetka, OK 74880
(405) 786-2244
Admin Donna Simmons.
Licensure Intermediate care. *Beds* ICF 60. *Certified* Medicaid.

Adkins-Weleetka Nursing Home
122 E 10th, Weleetka, OK 74880
(405) 786-2401
Admin Gerrol Adkins.
Licensure Intermediate care for mentally retarded. *Beds* ICF/MR 56. *Certified* Medicaid.

Westville

Westville Nursing Home
308 Williams St, Westville, OK 74965
(918) 723-5476
Admin Sadie Blackwood.
Licensure Intermediate care. *Beds* ICF 79. *Certified* Medicaid.

Wetumka

Pioneer Nursing Home of Hughes County Inc
620 S Alabama, Wetumka, OK 74883
(405) 452-3271
Admin Cindy Hayes. *Dir of Nursing* Jane Gustin LPN.
Licensure Intermediate care for mentally retarded. *Beds* ICF/MR 50. *Certified* Medicaid.
Staff Physicians; RNs; LPNs; Nurses' aides; Physical therapists; Activities coordinators; Dietitians; Ophthalmologists; Dentists.
Facilities Dining room; Activities room; Crafts room; Laundry room; Barber/Beauty shop.
Activities Arts & crafts; Games; Reading groups; Prayer groups; Shopping trips; Dances/Social/Cultural gatherings.

Wetumka Nursing Home Inc
700 N Main, Wetumka, OK 74883
(405) 452-5126
Admin Loretta Goodin. *Dir of Nursing*
Pauline Jacobs LPN. *Medical Dir* Dr Wade
Warren.
Licensure Intermediate care. *Beds* ICF 50.
Certified Medicare.
Owner Proprietary corp.
Admissions Requirements Physician's request.
Staff RNs 1 (ft); LPNs 3 (ft), 1 (pt); Nurses'
aides 10 (ft); Dietitians 1 (pt).
Facilities Dining room; Physical therapy
room; Activities room; Chapel; Crafts room;
Laundry room; Barber/Beauty shop; Library.
Activities Arts & crafts; Cards; Games;
Reading groups; Prayer groups; Shopping
trips; Dances/Social/Cultural gatherings.

Wewoka

Elmwood Manor Inc
300 S Seminole, Wewoka, OK 74884
(405) 257-6621
Admin John Grimes.
Licensure Intermediate care. *Beds* ICF 47.
Certified Medicaid.

Oakridge Nursing Home
7th & Compton, Wewoka, OK 74884
(405) 257-5800
Admin Kay Parsons.
Licensure Intermediate care for mentally
retarded. *Beds* ICF/MR 160. *Certified*
Medicaid.
Staff Physicians 1 (pt); RNs 1 (ft); LPNs 6
(ft); Nurses' aides 30 (ft); Recreational
therapists 1 (ft); Activities coordinators 4
(ft); Dietitians 1 (ft).

Wewoka Nursing Home Inc
200 E 4th, Wewoka, OK 74884
(405) 257-3393
Admin Virginia Concicao.
Licensure Intermediate care. *Beds* ICF 57.
Certified Medicaid.

Wilburton

Latimer Nursing Home
PO Box 508, 108 SW 9th, Wilburton, OK
74578
(918) 465-2255
Admin Rita Raeger.
Licensure Intermediate care. *Beds* ICF 48.
Certified Medicaid.

Ranchwood Lodge Home
900 W Ranchwood Dr, Wilburton, OK 74578
(918) 465-2314
Admin Rosie Foster.
Medical Dir Liz Hawthorne.
Licensure Intermediate care. *Beds* ICF 55.
Certified Medicaid.
Owner Proprietary corp (ARA Living
Centers).
Admissions Requirements Medical
examination; Physician's request.
Staff Physicians; RNs; LPNs; Nurses' aides;
Physical therapists; Reality therapists;
Recreational therapists; Occupational
therapists; Activities coordinators; Dietitians;
Podiatrists; Audiologists; Dentists.

Facilities Dining room; Activities room;
Chapel; Crafts room; Laundry room; Barber/
Beauty shop.
Activities Arts & crafts; Cards; Games; Prayer
groups; Movies; Shopping trips; Dances/
Social/Cultural gatherings.

Wilburton Nursing Home Inc
200 NE 1st, Box 607, Wilburton, OK 74578
(918) 465-2221
Admin Barbara Webb. *Dir of Nursing*
Deborah Morgan LPN.
Licensure Intermediate care. *Beds* ICF 38.
Certified Medicaid.
Admissions Requirements Medical
examination.
Staff Physicians 1 (pt); RNs 1 (pt); LPNs 2
(ft); Nurses' aides 11 (ft); Reality therapists
1 (ft); Recreational therapists 1 (ft);
Activities coordinators 1 (ft); Dietitians 1
(pt); Ophthalmologists 1 (pt); Podiatrists 1
(pt); Dentists 1 (pt).
Facilities Dining room; Activities room;
Chapel; Crafts room; Laundry room; Barber/
Beauty shop; Library.
Activities Arts & crafts; Cards; Games; Prayer
groups; Movies; Shopping trips; Dances/
Social/Cultural gatherings.

Wilson

Wilson Nursing Center
406 E Main, Wilson, OK 73463
(405) 668-2337
Admin Linda Curtis.
Medical Dir Nadine Goode.
Licensure Intermediate care. *Beds* ICF 60.
Certified Medicaid.
Owner Proprietary corp (ARA Living
Centers).
Admissions Requirements Medical
examination; Physician's request.
Staff RNs; LPNs; Nurses' aides; Reality
therapists; Recreational therapists; Activities
coordinators; Dietitians 1 (pt).
Facilities Dining room; Activities room;
Crafts room; Laundry room; Barber/Beauty
shop.
Activities Arts & crafts; Games; Reading
groups; Prayer groups; Movies; Shopping
trips; Dances/Social/Cultural gatherings;
Family nights; Exercise group.

Woodward

**Colonial Manor Nursing Home of Woodward
Inc**
2608 Reardon Rd, Woodward, OK 73801
(405) 254-3456
Admin Kenneth Morrison.
Licensure Intermediate care. *Beds* ICF 50.
Certified Medicaid.

Woodward Nursing Center
PO Box 587, 429 Downs Ave, Woodward, OK
73801
(405) 256-6448
Admin Ileta M Allen.
Licensure Intermediate care. *Beds* ICF 80.
Certified Medicaid.
Owner Proprietary corp (Amity Care).

Wynnewood

Colonial Convalescent Home Inc
810 E California, Wynnewood, OK 73098
(405) 665-2330
Admin Nancy R Scott.
Licensure Intermediate care. *Beds* ICF 79.
Certified Medicaid.

Yale

Yale Nursing Home
E Chicago & H Sts, Yale, OK 74085
(918) 387-2412
Admin Zoletta Kinney.
Licensure Intermediate care. *Beds* ICF 50.
Certified Medicaid.
Staff RNs 1 (pt); LPNs 2 (ft); Nurses' aides 26
(ft); Physical therapists 1 (pt); Activities
coordinators 1 (ft); Dietitians 1 (pt); Dentists
1 (pt).
Facilities Dining room; Physical therapy
room; Activities room; Chapel; Crafts room;
Laundry room; Barber/Beauty shop.
Activities Arts & crafts; Cards; Games; Prayer
groups; Shopping trips; Dances/Social/
Cultural gatherings.

Yukon

Cottonwood Manor Nursing Home
300 Walnut, Yukon, OK 73099
(405) 354-2563
Admin John Propps.
Licensure Intermediate care for mentally
retarded. *Beds* ICF/MR 130. *Certified*
Medicaid.

Ranchwood Nursing Center
2730 N Mustang Rd, Yukon, OK 73099
(405) 354-2022
Admin Carol Valerius.
Licensure Skilled care. *Beds* SNF 120.

Spanish Cove
1401 S Cornwell, Yukon, OK 73099
(405) 354-1901
Admin Joe Hendras.
Licensure Skilled care. *Beds* SNF 29.

Yukon Convalescent Home
1110 Cornwell, Yukon, OK 73099
(405) 354-5373
Admin Gregory Brown.
Medical Dir Dianne Lee.
Licensure Intermediate care. *Beds* ICF 69.
Certified Medicaid.
Owner Proprietary corp (ARA Living
Centers).
Admissions Requirements Medical
examination.
Staff Physicians 1 (ft); RNs 1 (pt); LPNs 6
(ft); Nurses' aides 17 (ft), 1 (pt); Physical
therapists 1 (pt); Occupational therapists 1
(pt); Activities coordinators 2 (ft); Dietitians
1 (pt); Podiatrists 1 (pt).
Facilities Dining room; Activities room;
Crafts room; Laundry room; Barber/Beauty
shop.
Activities Arts & crafts; Cards; Games;
Reading groups; Prayer groups; Movies;
Shopping trips; Dances/Social/Cultural
gatherings.

OREGON

Albany

Albany Care Center
805 19th Ave SE, Albany, OR 97321
(503) 926-4741
Admin Kent Van Winckel. *Dir of Nursing*
Donna Selig. *Medical Dir* Dr Lear.
Licensure Intermediate care. *Beds* ICF 92.
Certified Medicaid.
Owner Proprietary corp (Beverly Enterprises).
Admissions Requirements Medical
examination; Physician's request.
Staff RNs 8 (ft), 5 (pt); LPNs 6 (ft), 5 (pt);
Nurses' aides 40 (ft), 15 (pt); Physical
therapists 1 (pt); Recreational therapists 1
(pt); Occupational therapists; Activities
coordinators 1 (ft); Dietitians 1 (ft);
Ophthalmologists; Podiatrists; Dentists.
Facilities Dining room; Physical therapy
room; Activities room; Barber/Beauty shop.
Activities Arts & crafts; Games; Prayer groups;
Shopping trips.

Linn Care Center
1023 W 6th Ave, Albany, OR 97321
(503) 926-8664
Admin Keith Eitemiller. *Dir of Nursing* Carol
Mara. *Medical Dir* Benjamin Bonnlander;
Daniel Mulkey.
Licensure Skilled care; Intermediate care;
Alzheimer's care. *Beds* SNF 24; ICF 82.
Certified Medicaid; Medicare.
Owner Proprietary corp (Beverly Enterprises).
Admissions Requirements Medical
examination; Physician's request.
Staff RNs 7 (ft); Nurses' aides 27 (ft); Physical
therapists 1 (pt); Recreational therapists 3
(pt); Occupational therapists 1 (pt); Speech
therapists 1 (pt); Activities coordinators 1
(ft); Dietitians 1 (pt).
Facilities Dining room; Physical therapy
room; Activities room; Crafts room; Laundry
room; Barber/Beauty shop; TV room.
Activities Arts & crafts; Games; Reading
groups; Prayer groups; Movies; Shopping
trips.

Mennonite Home
5353 Columbus St SE, Albany, OR 97321
(503) 928-7232
Admin Karl Birky. *Dir of Nursing* Helen
McGovern RN. *Medical Dir* Donald Kerr
MD.
Licensure Intermediate care; Retirement. *Beds*
ICF 95. *Certified* Medicaid.
Owner Nonprofit corp.
Admissions Requirements Medical
examination; Physician's request.
Staff RNs 5 (ft), 7 (pt); LPNs 2 (ft), 2 (pt);
Nurses' aides 36 (ft), 22 (pt); Physical
therapists 1 (ft); Activities coordinators 1
(ft); Dietitians 1 (ft).
Affiliation Mennonite.
Facilities Dining room; Activities room;
Crafts room; Laundry room; Barber/Beauty
shop; Library.

Activities Arts & crafts; Games; Reading
groups; Prayer groups; Movies; Shopping
trips; Dances/Social/Cultural gatherings.

Ashland

Linda Vista Care Center
135 Maple St, Ashland, OR 97520
(503) 482-2341
Admin John Anderson.
Medical Dir Jerome Nitzberg MD.
Licensure Intermediate care. *Beds* ICF 67.
Certified Medicaid.
Owner Proprietary corp (Care Center Inc).
Facilities Dining room; Physical therapy
room; Activities room; Crafts room; Laundry
room; Barber/Beauty shop.
Activities Arts & crafts; Cards; Games;
Reading groups; Prayer groups; Movies;
Shopping trips; Dances/Social/Cultural
gatherings.

Astoria

Clatsop Care & Rehabilitation Center
646 16th St, Astoria, OR 97103
(503) 325-0313
Admin Kenneth M Taylor. *Dir of Nursing*
Jean Still. *Medical Dir* Paul Voeller MD.
Licensure Skilled care; Intermediate care;
Retirement. *Beds* SNF 18; ICF 12. *Certified*
Medicaid; Medicare.
Owner Nonprofit organization/foundation.
Admissions Requirements Minimum age 18;
Medical examination; Physician's request.
Staff Physicians 1 (pt); RNs 4 (ft), 1 (pt);
LPNs 3 (ft), 1 (pt); Nurses' aides 16 (ft), 7
(pt); Physical therapists 1 (pt); Occupational
therapists 1 (pt); Speech therapists 1 (pt);
Activities coordinators 1 (ft); Dietitians 1
(pt); Ophthalmologists 1 (pt).
Facilities Dining room; Physical therapy
room; Chapel; Laundry room; Barber/Beauty
shop.
Activities Arts & crafts; Cards; Games;
Reading groups; Shopping trips; Dances/
Social/Cultural gatherings.

Crestview Care Center
263 W Exchange, Astoria, OR 97103
(503) 325-1753
Admin Rob Washbond.
Licensure Intermediate care; Day/Respite care.
Beds ICF 82; Day/Respite care 8. *Certified*
Medicaid.

Baker

L & M Cedar Manor Home
4000 Cedar St, Baker, OR 97814
(503) 523-6333
Admin Richard K Stagg.
Licensure Intermediate care. *Beds* ICF 54.
Certified Medicaid.
Admissions Requirements Physician's request.

Staff RNs 1 (ft), 1 (pt); LPNs 4 (ft), 1 (pt);
Nurses' aides 25 (ft), 5 (pt); Activities
coordinators 1 (ft); Dietitians 1 (pt).
Facilities Dining room; Activities room;
Laundry room; Barber/Beauty shop; Library.
Activities Arts & crafts; Cards; Games;
Reading groups; Movies; Shopping trips;
Dances/Social/Cultural gatherings.

St Elizabeth Health Care Center
3985 Midway Dr, Baker, OR 97814
(503) 523-4452
Admin Michael R Reeve. *Dir of Nursing*
Leslie Lindsey RN. *Medical Dir* Steve
Delashmutt MD.
Licensure Intermediate care; Alzheimer's care.
Beds ICF 80. *Private Pay Patients* 47%.
Certified Medicaid.
Owner Nonprofit corp (Sisters of St Francis of
Philadelphia).
Admissions Requirements Physician's request.
Staff RNs 1 (ft), 3 (pt); LPNs 3 (ft), 1 (pt);
Nurses' aides 29 (ft), 6 (pt); Activities
coordinators 2 (ft); Housekeeping 5 (ft);
Pastoral care 1 (pt).
Affiliation Roman Catholic.
Facilities Dining room; Physical therapy
room; Activities room; Chapel; Crafts room;
Laundry room; Barber/Beauty shop; Library;
TV room; Solarium; Courtyard; Smoking
room.
Activities Arts & crafts; Cards; Games;
Reading groups; Prayer groups; Movies;
Shopping trips; Dances/Social/Cultural
gatherings; Pet therapy.

Bandon

Oceanview Care Center
2790 Beach Loop Rd, Bandon, OR 97411
(503) 347-4424
Admin Sharon Duerst. *Dir of Nursing* Carolyn
Schwindt RN.
Licensure Intermediate care. *Beds* ICF 37.
Certified Medicaid.
Owner Privately owned.
Admissions Requirements Medical
examination; Physician's request.
Staff Physicians; RNs 2 (ft), 1 (pt); LPNs;
Nurses' aides 19 (ft); Activities coordinators
1 (ft); Dietitians.
Facilities Dining room; Activities room;
Crafts room; Laundry room; Barber/Beauty
shop; Library.
Activities Arts & crafts; Cards; Games;
Reading groups; Prayer groups; Movies;
Shopping trips; Dances/Social/Cultural
gatherings; Pool; Bowling.

Beaverton

Hyland Hills Care Center
11850 SW Allen Blvd, Beaverton, OR 97005
(503) 646-7164
Admin John Evans.

Licensure Intermediate care; Respite care.
Beds ICF 104; Respite care 15. *Certified* Medicaid.
Owner Proprietary corp (Hillhaven Corp).

Maryville Nursing Home
14645 SW Farmington Rd, Beaverton, OR 97007
(503) 643-8626
Admin Sr Theresa Margaret Yettick.
Medical Dir Donald R Alson MD.
Licensure Skilled care; Intermediate care. *Beds* SNF 2; ICF 135. *Certified* Medicaid; Medicare.
Staff RNs 10 (ft); LPNs 3 (ft); Nurses' aides 36 (ft); Physical therapists 2 (pt); Recreational therapists 2 (ft); Activities coordinators 1 (ft); Dietitians 1 (pt); Ophthalmologists 1 (pt); Podiatrists 1 (pt); Dentists 1 (pt).
Affiliation Roman Catholic.
Facilities Dining room; Physical therapy room; Activities room; Chapel; Crafts room; Laundry room; Barber/Beauty shop; Library; Lounge.
Activities Arts & crafts; Cards; Games; Prayer groups; Movies; Dances/Social/Cultural gatherings; Sing-alongs.

Bend

Bachelor Butte Nursing Home
119 SE Wilson, Bend, OR 97702
(503) 382-7161
Admin Gary Arnett. *Dir of Nursing* Linda Campbell RN. *Medical Dir* Paul Johnson MD.
Licensure Intermediate care. *Beds* ICF 87. *Certified* Medicaid.
Owner Proprietary corp.
Admissions Requirements Medical examination.
Staff Physicians 1 (pt); RNs 6 (ft); LPNs 5 (ft); Nurses' aides 30 (ft); Physical therapists 1 (pt); Recreational therapists 1 (ft); Occupational therapists 1 (pt); Speech therapists 1 (pt); Activities coordinators 1 (ft); Dietitians 1 (ft); Ophthalmologists 1 (pt); Podiatrists 1 (pt); Dentists 1 (pt).
Facilities Dining room; Activities room; Crafts room; Laundry room; Barber/Beauty shop.
Activities Arts & crafts; Cards; Games; Reading groups; Prayer groups; Movies; Shopping trips; Exercise classes.

Central Oregon Health Care Center
1876 NE Hwy 20, Bend, OR 97701
(503) 382-5531
Admin Tim Eide.
Licensure Skilled care; Intermediate care; Day care. *Beds* SNF 34; ICF 66; Day care 10. *Certified* Medicaid; Medicare.

Harmony House Nursing Home
95 E Xerxes St, Bend, OR 97701
(503) 382-0479
Admin Frank Martynowicz.
Licensure Intermediate care. *Beds* ICF 40.

Brookings

Curry Good Samaritan Center
PO Box 1217, 1 Park Ave, Brookings, OR 97415
(503) 469-3111
Admin Rosemary Rosengren.
Licensure Skilled care; Intermediate care; Day care. *Beds* SNF 20; ICF 51; Day care 7. *Certified* Medicaid; Medicare.
Owner Nonprofit corp (Evangelical Lutheran/Good Samaritan Society).

Burns

Burns Nursing Home
348 W Adams, Burns, OR 97720
(503) 573-6888
Admin Karen R Dinsmore. *Dir of Nursing* Marilynn Scheen RN.
Licensure Intermediate care; Residential care; Alzheimer's care. *Beds* ICF 40; Residential care 9. *Private Pay Patients* 35%. *Certified* Medicaid.
Owner Privately owned.
Admissions Requirements Physician's request.
Staff RNs 3 (ft); LPNs 1 (pt); Nurses' aides 10 (ft), 5 (pt); Recreational therapists 1 (ft); Activities coordinators 1 (ft); Dietitians 1 (pt).
Languages Spanish, Basque.
Facilities Dining room; Activities room; Crafts room; Laundry room.
Activities Arts & crafts; Cards; Games; Reading groups; Prayer groups; Movies; Shopping trips; Dances/Social/Cultural gatherings; Pet therapy.

Canby

Canby Care Center
390 NW 2nd Ave, Canby, OR 97013
(503) 266-5541
Admin Miriam Larson. *Dir of Nursing* Erna Virene. *Medical Dir* Dr Lynn Kadwell.
Licensure Intermediate care. *Beds* ICF 48. *Certified* Medicaid.
Owner Proprietary corp.
Admissions Requirements Physician's request.
Staff RNs 1 (ft), 3 (pt); LPNs 3 (ft), 2 (pt); Nurses' aides 16 (ft), 10 (pt); Activities coordinators 1 (ft).
Facilities Dining room; Laundry room.
Activities Arts & crafts; Games; Reading groups; Prayer groups; Movies; Shopping trips; Dances/Social/Cultural gatherings; Intergenerational programs; Pet therapy.

Elmhurst Nursing Home
1105 S Elm St, Canby, OR 97013
(503) 266-1131
Admin Dale Stephens. *Dir of Nursing* Debbie Bly. *Medical Dir* Daniel Hughson.
Licensure Intermediate care; Alzheimer's care. *Beds* ICF 43. *Private Pay Patients* 40%. *Certified* Medicaid.
Owner Proprietary corp.
Admissions Requirements Minimum age 16.
Staff RNs 2 (ft); LPNs 1 (ft), 1 (pt); Nurses' aides 15 (ft), 10 (pt); Recreational therapists 1 (pt); Occupational therapists 1 (pt); Dietitians 1 (pt); Podiatrists 1 (pt).
Languages Spanish.
Facilities Dining room; Activities room; Crafts room; Laundry room; Barber/Beauty shop.
Activities Arts & crafts; Cards; Games; Reading groups; Prayer groups; Movies; Shopping trips; Pet therapy.

Central Point

Central Point Care Center
155 S 1st St, Central Point, OR 97502
(503) 664-3355
Admin DoriLee Eastman. *Dir of Nursing* Shirley Ross RN. *Medical Dir* Mike Robinson DO.
Licensure Intermediate care. *Beds* ICF 33. *Certified* Medicaid.
Owner Privately owned.
Admissions Requirements Physician's request.
Staff Physicians 1 (ft); RNs 2 (ft); LPNs 4 (ft); Nurses' aides 11 (ft), 5 (pt); Physical therapists 1 (ft); Activities coordinators 1 (ft); Dietitians 1 (ft); Ophthalmologists 1 (ft); Podiatrists 1 (ft).
Facilities Dining room.
Activities Arts & crafts; Cards; Games; Reading groups; Shopping trips; Dances/Social/Cultural gatherings.

Colton

Colton Care Center
29872 S Hult Rd, Colton, OR 97017
(503) 824-3311
Admin Betty Rabourn.
Licensure Intermediate care. *Beds* ICF 35. *Certified* Medicaid.

Coos Bay

Hearthside Care Center
2625 Coos Bay Blvd, Coos Bay, OR 97420
(503) 267-2161
Admin Donald Chance. *Dir of Nursing* Pearl E Derrick. *Medical Dir* Dr Wayne Murray.
Licensure Intermediate care. *Beds* ICF 92. *Certified* Medicaid.
Owner Proprietary corp (National Heritage).
Admissions Requirements Physician's request.
Staff RNs 4 (ft); LPNs 5 (ft); Nurses' aides 35 (ft); Physical therapists 1 (ft); Activities coordinators 1 (ft).
Facilities Dining room; Physical therapy room; Activities room; Crafts room; Laundry room; Barber/Beauty shop; Library.
Activities Arts & crafts; Cards; Games; Reading groups; Prayer groups; Movies; Shopping trips; Dances/Social/Cultural gatherings.

Life Care Center of Coos Bay
2890 Ocean Blvd, Coos Bay, OR 97420
(503) 267-5433
Admin Patrick Burke. *Dir of Nursing* Nadine Wilkes. *Medical Dir* Charles Holloway.
Licensure Skilled care; Intermediate care; Respite care; Alzheimer's care. *Beds* SNF 18; ICF 96. *Private Pay Patients* 30%. *Certified* Medicaid; Medicare.
Owner Proprietary corp (Life Care Centers of America).
Admissions Requirements Medical examination; Physician's request.
Staff Physicians 1 (pt); RNs 5 (ft), 2 (pt); LPNs 4 (ft), 2 (pt); Nurses' aides 40 (ft), 5 (pt); Physical therapists 1 (pt); Speech therapists 1 (pt); Activities coordinators 2 (ft); Dietitians 1 (ft); Podiatrists 1 (pt).
Languages Spanish.
Facilities Dining room; Physical therapy room; Activities room; Chapel; Crafts room; Laundry room; Barber/Beauty shop; Library.
Activities Arts & crafts; Cards; Games; Reading groups; Prayer groups; Movies; Shopping trips; Dances/Social/Cultural gatherings; Intergenerational programs; Pet therapy.

Coquille

Coquille Care Center
HC 83 Box 5610, Coquille, OR 97423
(503) 396-2302
Admin Debra B Dalton RN. *Dir of Nursing* Debra B Dalton RN.
Licensure Intermediate care. *Beds* ICF 37. *Certified* Medicaid.
Owner Privately owned.
Admissions Requirements Medical examination; Physician's request.
Staff RNs 3 (ft), 1 (pt); LPNs 1 (ft); Nurses' aides 13 (ft), 4 (pt); Activities coordinators 1 (ft).
Facilities Dining room; Activities room; Crafts room; Laundry room.
Activities Arts & crafts; Cards; Games; Reading groups; Prayer groups; Movies; Shopping trips; Cooking club; Picnics; Van outings.

Cornelius

Good Shepherd Lutheran Home
Rte 4 Box 96, Cornelius, OR 97113
(503) 357-6191
Admin Ron Drews.
Medical Dir Otto Loehden MD.
Licensure Intermediate care for mentally retarded. *Beds* ICF/MR 87. *Certified* Medicaid.
Admissions Requirements Medical examination.
Staff RNs 3 (ft), 1 (pt); LPNs 4 (ft), 2 (pt); Physical therapists 1 (pt); Recreational therapists 1 (pt); Occupational therapists 1 (ft), 1 (pt); Speech therapists 1 (ft), 1 (pt); Dietitians 1 (pt).
Affiliation Lutheran.
Facilities Dining room; Activities room; Chapel; Crafts room; Laundry room; Library.
Activities Arts & crafts; Cards; Games; Reading groups; Movies; Shopping trips; Dances/Social/Cultural gatherings.

Corvallis

Corvallis Care Center
980 NW Spruce St, Corvallis, OR 97330
(503) 757-0151
Admin Kara Pierson.
Medical Dir James W Gulick MD.
Licensure Skilled care; Intermediate care. *Beds* SNF 18; ICF 68. *Certified* Medicaid; Medicare.
Owner Proprietary corp (Beverly Enterprises).
Staff RNs 8 (ft); LPNs 3 (ft); Nurses' aides 30 (ft), 4 (pt); Physical therapists 1 (pt); Occupational therapists 1 (pt); Speech therapists 1 (pt); Activities coordinators 1 (ft); Dietitians 1 (pt); Podiatrists 1 (pt); Audiologists 1 (pt).
Facilities Dining room; Activities room; Laundry room; Barber/Beauty shop.
Activities Arts & crafts; Cards; Reading groups; Prayer groups; Movies; Shopping trips; Dances/Social/Cultural gatherings; Music.

Corvallis Manor
160 NE Conifer Ave, Corvallis, OR 97330
(503) 757-1651
Admin Merlin Hart.
Medical Dir Dr Norman Castillo.
Licensure Skilled care; Intermediate care. *Beds* SNF 27; ICF 99. *Certified* Medicaid; Medicare.
Admissions Requirements Physician's request.
Staff Physicians 1 (pt); RNs 6 (ft), 5 (pt); LPNs 2 (ft), 1 (pt); Nurses' aides 30 (ft), 20 (pt); Physical therapists 1 (pt); Occupational therapists 1 (ft), 1 (pt); Speech therapists 1 (pt); Activities coordinators 1 (ft), 1 (pt); Dietitians 1 (pt).
Facilities Dining room; Physical therapy room; Activities room; Laundry room; Barber/Beauty shop; Library.
Activities Arts & crafts; Cards; Games; Reading groups; Prayer groups; Movies; Shopping trips; Dances/Social/Cultural gatherings.

Heart of the Valley Center
2700 NW Harrison Blvd, Corvallis, OR 97330
(503) 757-1763
Admin Dennis L Russell. *Dir of Nursing* Marla Wimer. *Medical Dir* Dr James Gallant.
Licensure Intermediate care; Retirement; Alzheimer's care. *Beds* ICF 79. *Certified* Medicaid.
Owner Proprietary corp.
Staff RNs 6 (ft); LPNs 6 (ft); Nurses' aides 25 (ft); Recreational therapists 1 (ft); Activities coordinators 2 (ft).

Facilities Dining room; Physical therapy room; Activities room; Crafts room; Laundry room; Barber/Beauty shop; Library; Resident & guest lounges; Companion motel room.
Activities Arts & crafts; Cards; Games; Reading groups; Prayer groups; Movies; Shopping trips.

Cottage Grove

Coast Fork Nursing Center
515 Grant St, Cottage Grove, OR 97424
(503) 942-5528
Admin Jane F Boren RN. *Dir of Nursing* Mary Anne McMurren RN. *Medical Dir* Michael Thompson MD.
Licensure Skilled care; Intermediate care; Alzheimer's care. *Beds* SNF 27; ICF 53. *Private Pay Patients* 20%. *Certified* Medicaid; Medicare.
Owner Proprietary corp (Prestige Care Inc).
Admissions Requirements Medical examination.
Languages Spanish.
Facilities Dining room; Physical therapy room; Activities room; Crafts room; Laundry room; Barber/Beauty shop; Library; Ventilator unit.
Activities Arts & crafts; Cards; Games; Reading groups; Prayer groups; Movies; Shopping trips; Dances/Social/Cultural gatherings; Intergenerational programs; Pet therapy; Sensory stimulation; Reality orientation.

Cottage Grove Hospital Skilled Nursing Facility
1340 Birch Ave, Cottage Grove, OR 97424
(503) 942-0511
Admin John L Hoopes. *Dir of Nursing* Judy Spangler RN.
Licensure Skilled care. *Beds* SNF 39. *Certified* Medicaid.
Owner Nonprofit corp.
Admissions Requirements Medical examination; Physician's request.
Staff Physicians 19 (ft); RNs 2 (ft); LPNs 2 (ft), 2 (pt); Nurses' aides 2 (ft), 12 (pt); Physical therapists 1 (ft), 1 (pt); Activities coordinators 1 (ft); Dietitians 1 (ft); Ophthalmologists 1 (ft); Dentists 1 (ft).
Facilities Dining room; Physical therapy room; Activities room; Laundry room.
Activities Arts & crafts; Cards; Games; Reading groups; Prayer groups; Movies; Shopping trips; Dances/Social/Cultural gatherings.

Creswell

Creswell Care Center
525 S 2nd St, Creswell, OR 97426
(503) 895-3333
Admin Constance Johnson.
Licensure Skilled care; Intermediate care; Day care; Respite care. *Beds* SNF 20; ICF 37; Day care 10; Respite care 4. *Certified* Medicaid; Medicare.
Owner Proprietary corp.
Admissions Requirements Medical examination; Physician's request.
Facilities Dining room; Physical therapy room; Activities room; Crafts room; Laundry room; Barber/Beauty shop; Library.
Activities Arts & crafts; Cards; Games; Reading groups; Prayer groups; Movies; Shopping trips; Dances/Social/Cultural gatherings.

Dallas

Birch Street Manor
862 SW Birch St, Dallas, OR 97338
(503) 623-8131
Admin Ralph L Jull. *Dir of Nursing* Debra Wynia. *Medical Dir* Robert McQueen MD.

Licensure Intermediate care. *Beds* ICF 44. *Private Pay Patients* 25%. *Certified* Medicaid.
Owner Privately owned.
Admissions Requirements Medical examination; Physician's request.
Staff RNs 2 (ft); LPNs 2 (ft), 1 (pt); Nurses' aides 15 (ft), 2 (pt); Physical therapists 1 (pt); Recreational therapists 2 (pt); Activities coordinators 1 (pt).
Facilities Dining room; Activities room; Crafts room; Laundry room; Barber/Beauty shop; Library.
Activities Arts & crafts; Cards; Games; Reading groups; Prayer groups; Movies; Pet therapy.

Dallas Nursing Home
348 W Ellendale, Dallas, OR 97338
(503) 623-5581
Admin Jerry W Barkman. *Dir of Nursing* Shirley Kolb RN. *Medical Dir* Tom Flaming DO.
Licensure Skilled care; Intermediate care; Retirement; Alzheimer's care. *Beds* SNF 16; ICF 101; Retirement 73. *Private Pay Patients* 48%. *Certified* Medicaid; Medicare.
Owner Nonprofit organization/foundation.
Admissions Requirements Physician's request; No pediatrics.
Staff Physicians 1 (pt); RNs 5 (ft); LPNs 4 (ft); Nurses' aides 90 (ft); Physical therapists; Activities coordinators 2 (ft); Dietitians.
Languages Spanish, German.
Affiliation Mennonite.
Facilities Dining room; Physical therapy room; Activities room; Chapel; Laundry room; Barber/Beauty shop.
Activities Arts & crafts; Cards; Games; Reading groups; Prayer groups; Movies; Shopping trips; Dances/Social/Cultural gatherings; Intergenerational programs; Pet therapy.

The Dalles

Columbia Basin Nursing Home
1015 Webber Rd, The Dalles, OR 97058
(503) 296-2156
Admin Betty L Meyer. *Dir of Nursing* Nancy Hammel RN. *Medical Dir* Thomas Hodge MD.
Licensure Skilled care; Intermediate care. *Beds* SNF 14; ICF 106. *Certified* Medicaid; Medicare.
Owner Nonprofit organization/foundation.
Admissions Requirements Medical examination; Physician's request.
Staff RNs 8 (ft); LPNs 7 (ft); Nurses' aides 35 (ft); Physical therapists 1 (ft); Speech therapists 1 (pt); Activities coordinators 1 (ft); Dietitians 1 (ft); Ophthalmologists 1 (pt); Podiatrists 1 (pt); Dentists 1 (pt).
Facilities Dining room; Physical therapy room; Activities room; Crafts room; Laundry room; Barber/Beauty shop; Store.
Activities Arts & crafts; Games; Reading groups; Prayer groups; Movies; Shopping trips; Dances/Social/Cultural gatherings; Bus trips; Gourmet cooking class.

Valley Vista Care Center
PO Box 6, 1023 W 25th Ave, The Dalles, OR 97058
(503) 298-5158
Admin Marla Shelby, Prov.
Licensure Skilled care; Intermediate care. *Beds* SNF 6; ICF 77. *Certified* Medicaid; Medicare.
Admissions Requirements Medical examination; Physician's request.
Facilities Dining room; Physical therapy room; Activities room; Crafts room; Laundry room; Barber/Beauty shop.

Activities Arts & crafts; Cards; Games;
Reading groups; Prayer groups; Movies;
Shopping trips; Dances/Social/Cultural
gatherings; Community activities.

Enterprise

Wallowa County Memorial Hospital
401 E 1st St, Enterprise, OR 97828
(503) 426-3111
Admin Ron Bender, Prov.
Medical Dir Barbara Biamont.
Licensure Intermediate care. Beds ICF 32.
Certified Medicaid.
Owner Publicly owned.
Staff RNs 2 (ft); LPNs 2 (ft); Nurses' aides 8
(ft); Recreational therapists.

Eugene

Cascade Manor Inc
65 W 30th, Eugene, OR 97405
(503) 342-5901, ext 521
Admin Ruth E Anderson RN NHA. Dir of
Nursing Donna Schoonhoven RN. Medical
Dir Keith McMilan MD.
Licensure Intermediate care; Retirement;
Alzheimer's care. Beds ICF 22; Retirement
120. Private Pay Patients 100%.
Owner Nonprofit organization/foundation.
Admissions Requirements Physician's request.
Staff Physicians 1 (pt); RNs 4 (pt); LPNs 1
(pt); Nurses' aides 10 (ft), 4 (pt); Physical
therapists (contracted); Occupational
therapists (contracted); Speech therapists
(contracted); Activities coordinators 1 (pt);
Dietitians 1 (ft); Social service designees 1
(pt).
Facilities Dining room; Activities room;
Chapel; Crafts room; Laundry room; Barber/
Beauty shop; Library; Enclosed deck/Roof
garden; Wanderguard system.
Activities Arts & crafts; Cards; Games;
Reading groups; Prayer groups; Movies;
Shopping trips; Dances/Social/Cultural
gatherings; Intergenerational programs; Pet
therapy; Private companions.

Emerald Nursing Center
2360 Chambers St, Eugene, OR 97405
(503) 687-1310
Admin Don Buel. Dir of Nursing Carolyn
Walter RN. Medical Dir Gordon Anderson
MD.
Licensure Skilled care; Intermediate care;
Alzheimer's care. Beds SNF 22; ICF 116.
Certified Medicaid; Medicare; VA.
Owner Nonprofit corp (Adventist Living
Centers).
Admissions Requirements Medical
examination; Physician's request.
Staff Physicians 1 (pt); RNs 6 (ft), 5 (pt);
LPNs 7 (ft), 6 (pt); Nurses' aides 36 (ft), 3
(pt); Physical therapists 1 (pt); Reality
therapists 1 (pt); Recreational therapists 2
(ft); Occupational therapists 1 (pt); Speech
therapists 1 (pt); Activities coordinators 1
(ft); Dietitians 1 (ft); Dentists 1 (pt).
Affiliation Seventh-Day Adventist.
Facilities Dining room; Physical therapy
room; Activities room; Crafts room; Laundry
room; Barber/Beauty shop; Library.
Activities Arts & crafts; Cards; Games;
Reading groups; Prayer groups; Movies;
Shopping trips; Dances/Social/Cultural
gatherings; Bowling; Van trips; Picnics;
Fishing; Ice cream socials; Summer
barbeques; Sewing clubs; Cooking clubs.

Eugene Good Samaritan Center
3500 Hilyard St, Eugene, OR 97405
(503) 687-9211
Admin David Horazdovsky. Dir of Nursing
Barbara Rock RN. Medical Dir Richard A
Anderson MD.

Licensure Skilled care; Intermediate care. Beds
SNF 34; ICF 120. Certified Medicaid;
Medicare.
Owner Nonprofit corp (Evangelical Lutheran/
Good Samaritan Society).
Staff RNs; LPNs; Nurses' aides; Physical
therapists; Occupational therapists; Activities
coordinators; Dietitians.
Facilities Dining room; Physical therapy
room; Activities room; Chapel; Crafts room;
Laundry room; Barber/Beauty shop.
Activities Arts & crafts; Cards; Games;
Reading groups; Prayer groups; Movies;
Shopping trips.

Green Valley Care Center
1735 Adkins St, Eugene, OR 97401
(503) 683-5032
Admin Wayne Dunbar. Dir of Nursing Helen
Schaefer RN. Medical Dir Jeffery Beckwith
MD.
Licensure Skilled care; Intermediate care. Beds
SNF 25; ICF 79. Private Pay Patients 30%.
Certified Medicaid; Medicare.
Owner Proprietary corp (Beverly Enterprises).
Admissions Requirements Medical
examination; Physician's request.
Staff RNs; LPNs; Nurses' aides; Physical
therapists; Recreational therapists;
Occupational therapists; Activities
coordinators; Dietitians.
Languages German.
Facilities Dining room; Physical therapy
room; Activities room; Crafts room; Laundry
room; Barber/Beauty shop.
Activities Arts & crafts; Games; Reading
groups; Prayer groups; Movies; Dances/
Social/Cultural gatherings; Intergenerational
programs.

Hillside Heights Convalescent Center
1201 McLean Blvd, Eugene, OR 97405
(503) 683-2155
Admin Martha J Jensen. Dir of Nursing Diane
Banos RN. Medical Dir Dr Dwight Johnson.
Licensure Skilled care; Intermediate care. Beds
SNF 22; ICF 61. Certified Medicaid;
Medicare.
Owner Proprietary corp (Beverly Enterprises).
Admissions Requirements Medical
examination.
Staff RNs 7 (ft); LPNs 5 (ft); Nurses' aides 25
(ft), 5 (pt); Physical therapists 1 (ft);
Occupational therapists 1 (pt); Speech
therapists 1 (pt); Activities coordinators 1
(ft); Dietitians 1 (ft).
Languages Spanish.
Facilities Dining room; Physical therapy
room; Activities room; Chapel; Crafts room;
Laundry room; Barber/Beauty shop.
Activities Arts & crafts; Games; Reading
groups; Prayer groups; Movies; Shopping
trips; Dances/Social/Cultural gatherings.

Ivorena Care Center
687 Cheshire, Eugene, OR 97402
(503) 484-2117, 344-4154 FAX
Admin R Leland Gilliand. Dir of Nursing
Beth Holmes, Interum. Medical Dir Terry
Copperman MD PC.
Licensure Skilled care; Intermediate care;
Alzheimer's care. Beds SNF 20; ICF 82.
Private Pay Patients 25%. Certified
Medicaid; Medicare.
Owner Proprietary corp (Beverly Enterprises).
Admissions Requirements Minimum age 65;
Medical examination; Physician's request.
Staff RNs 8 (ft), 2 (pt); LPNs 6 (ft), 3 (pt);
Nurses' aides 60 (ft), 12 (pt); Physical
therapists 1 (ft); Reality therapists 1 (ft);
Recreational therapists 1 (pt); Occupational
therapists 1 (pt); Speech therapists 1 (ft);
Activities coordinators 1 (ft), 1 (pt);
Dietitians 1 (pt); Ophthalmologists 1 (pt);
Podiatrists 1 (pt); Audiologists 1 (pt).
Languages Spanish, Italian.

Facilities Dining room; Physical therapy
room; Activities room; Chapel; Crafts room;
Laundry room; Barber/Beauty shop; Library.
Activities Arts & crafts; Cards; Games;
Reading groups; Prayer groups; Movies;
Shopping trips; Dances/Social/Cultural
gatherings; Pet therapy.

Riverpark Living Center
425 Alexander Loop, Eugene, OR 97401
(503) 345-6199
Admin Millicent Redford. Dir of Nursing
Mary Ann Fix RN. Medical Dir Dwayne
Rice MD.
Licensure Skilled care; Intermediate care;
Retirement. Beds SNF 9; ICF 57. Certified
Medicaid; Medicare.
Owner Privately owned.
Admissions Requirements Minimum age 18;
Physician's request.
Staff Physicians; RNs; LPNs; Nurses' aides;
Activities coordinators; Dietitians.
Languages German.
Facilities Dining room; Physical therapy
room; Activities room; Chapel; Crafts room;
Laundry room; Barber/Beauty shop; Library.
Activities Arts & crafts; Cards; Games;
Reading groups; Prayer groups; Shopping
trips; Dances/Social/Cultural gatherings.

South Hills Health Care Center
PO Box 5051, 1166 E 28th, Eugene, OR
97403
(503) 345-0534
Admin Lee Garber.
Medical Dir Donald England MD.
Licensure Skilled care; Intermediate care; Day
care. Beds SNF 24; ICF 76; Day care 10.
Certified Medicaid; Medicare.
Admissions Requirements Medical
examination; Physician's request.
Staff Physicians 1 (pt); RNs 6 (ft), 1 (pt);
LPNs 1 (ft), 1 (pt); Nurses' aides 31 (ft), 2
(pt); Physical therapists 1 (pt); Occupational
therapists 1 (pt); Speech therapists 1 (pt);
Activities coordinators 1 (ft); Dietitians 1
(pt); Podiatrists 1 (pt).
Facilities Dining room; Activities room;
Laundry room; Barber/Beauty shop.
Activities Arts & crafts; Cards; Games;
Reading groups; Prayer groups; Movies;
Shopping trips; Dances/Social/Cultural
gatherings.

Twilight Acres Nursing Home Inc
85434 Dilley Ln, Eugene, OR 97405
(503) 746-7611
Admin Anita Hays. Dir of Nursing Katherine
Bell RN. Medical Dir James McHan MD.
Licensure Intermediate care; Alzheimer's care.
Beds ICF 60. Certified Medicaid.
Owner Privately owned.
Admissions Requirements Medical
examination; Physician's request.
Staff Physicians 1 (pt); RNs 3 (ft), 2 (pt);
LPNs 2 (ft), 2 (pt); Nurses' aides 24 (ft), 6
(pt); Physical therapists 1 (pt); Recreational
therapists 1 (pt); Speech therapists 1 (pt);
Activities coordinators 1 (ft); Dietitians 1
(pt).
Facilities Dining room; Activities room;
Crafts room; Laundry room; Barber/Beauty
shop.
Activities Arts & crafts; Cards; Games;
Reading groups; Prayer groups; Movies;
Shopping trips; Dances/Social/Cultural
gatherings; Intergenerational programs; Pet
therapy.

Valley West Health Care Center
2300 Warren Ave, Eugene, OR 97405
(503) 686-2828
Admin John Bragg.
Medical Dir Dwayne Rice MD.
Licensure Skilled care; Intermediate care; Day
care; Alzheimer's care. Beds SNF 14; ICF
107; Day care 15. Certified Medicare.

Owner Proprietary corp (Life Care Centers of America).
Admissions Requirements Medical examination; Physician's request.
Staff Physicians 3 (pt); RNs 18 (ft); Nurses' aides 50 (ft); Physical therapists 1 (pt); Recreational therapists 2 (ft); Occupational therapists 1 (pt); Speech therapists 1 (pt); Activities coordinators 2 (ft); Dietitians 1 (pt); Ophthalmologists 1 (pt); Dentists 1 (pt).
Facilities Dining room; Physical therapy room; Activities room; Crafts room; Laundry room; Barber/Beauty shop; Library.
Activities Arts & crafts; Cards; Games; Reading groups; Prayer groups; Movies; Shopping trips; Dances/Social/Cultural gatherings; Alzheimer's activities.

Florence

Siuslaw Care Center
1951 21st St, Florence, OR 97439
(503) 997-8436
Admin Meldra Hanks.
Medical Dir Becky Landcaster.
Licensure Skilled care; Intermediate care; Retirement; Alzheimer's care. **Beds** SNF 8; ICF 57. **Certified** Medicaid; Medicare.
Owner Proprietary corp (Beverly Enterprises).
Staff Physicians 1 (pt); RNs 3 (ft), 2 (pt); LPNs 6 (ft), 3 (pt); Nurses' aides 28 (ft), 12 (pt); Physical therapists 2 (pt); Recreational therapists 1 (ft); Occupational therapists 1 (pt); Speech therapists 1 (pt); Activities coordinators 1 (ft); Dietitians 1 (pt); Ophthalmologists 1 (pt); Podiatrists 1 (pt); Dentists 1 (pt).
Activities Arts & crafts; Cards; Games; Reading groups; Prayer groups; Movies; Shopping trips; Dances/Social/Cultural gatherings.

Forest Grove

Camelot Care Center
3900 Pacific Ave, Forest Grove, OR 97116
(503) 359-0449
Admin Mary J Prentice. **Dir of Nursing** Winona Oswald. **Medical Dir** Dr Randolph Pitts.
Licensure Skilled care; Intermediate care; Retirement. **Beds** SNF 23; ICF 91; Retirement 14. **Private Pay Patients** 20%. **Certified** Medicaid; Medicare.
Owner Proprietary corp (Beverly Enterprises).
Admissions Requirements Physician's request.
Staff Physicians 12 (pt); RNs 7 (ft), 3 (pt); LPNs 10 (ft), 3 (pt); Nurses' aides 60 (ft), 20 (pt); Physical therapists 1 (pt); Occupational therapists 2 (pt); Speech therapists 1 (pt); Activities coordinators 1 (ft); Dietitians 1 (pt); Podiatrists 1 (pt).
Facilities Dining room; Physical therapy room; Activities room; Laundry room; Barber/Beauty shop.
Activities Arts & crafts; Cards; Games; Reading groups; Prayer groups; Movies; Shopping trips; Dances/Social/Cultural gatherings; Intergenerational programs; Pet therapy; Geri-psychiatric program.

Forest View Care Center
3300 19th Ave, Forest Grove, OR 97116
(503) 357-7119
Admin Bob Houghton. **Dir of Nursing** Dorothy Jurgensen.
Licensure Intermediate care; Day/Respite care. **Beds** ICF 114; Day/Respite care 5. **Certified** Medicaid.
Owner Proprietary corp (Beverly Enterprises).
Admissions Requirements Minimum age 18; Physician's request.
Staff RNs 4 (ft), 3 (pt); LPNs 3 (ft), 2 (pt); Nurses' aides 33 (ft), 13 (pt); Activities coordinators 1 (ft); Dietitians 1 (pt).

Facilities Dining room; Physical therapy room; Activities room; Laundry room; Barber/Beauty shop.
Activities Arts & crafts; Cards; Games; Reading groups; Prayer groups; Movies.

Lou Del Nursing Home Inc
2122 Oak St, Forest Grove, OR 97116
(503) 357-9780
Admin Joyce Gallovich.
Medical Dir Dr Robert Martens.
Licensure Intermediate care. **Beds** ICF 40. **Certified** Medicaid.
Admissions Requirements Minimum age 18; Medical examination; Physician's request.
Staff RNs 1 (ft); LPNs 5 (pt); Nurses' aides 14 (ft), 5 (pt); Activities coordinators 1 (ft); 1 (ft).
Facilities Dining room; Laundry room.
Activities Arts & crafts; Games; Reading groups; Prayer groups; Movies; Shopping trips; Dances/Social/Cultural gatherings.

Masonic & Eastern Star Home of Oregon
3505 Pacific Ave, Forest Grove, OR 97116
(503) 359-4465
Admin Josephine Wu.
Licensure Intermediate care; Day care; Respite care. **Beds** ICF 52; Day care 10; Respite care 6.
Affiliation Masons.

Gaston

Laurelwood Manor Nursing Home
Rte 2 Box 145, Gaston, OR 97119-9511
(503) 985-7484
Admin Ruth J Moreno.
Licensure Intermediate care. **Beds** 20. **Certified** Medicaid.

Gladstone

Franklin Care Center
220 E Hereford, Gladstone, OR 97027
(503) 656-0393, 656-3251 FAX
Admin Richard A Dillon. **Dir of Nursing** Cindy Mead.
Licensure Skilled care; Intermediate care. **Beds** SNF 16; ICF 75. **Certified** Medicaid; Medicare.
Owner Proprietary corp.
Admissions Requirements Medical examination.
Staff RNs 3 (ft), 1 (pt); LPNs 4 (ft), 1 (pt); Nurses' aides 30 (ft), 3 (pt); Activities coordinators 1 (ft).
Facilities Dining room; Activities room; Chapel; Crafts room; Laundry room; Barber/Beauty shop; Library.
Activities Arts & crafts; Cards; Games; Reading groups; Prayer groups; Movies; Shopping trips; Dances/Social/Cultural gatherings; Intergenerational programs; Pet therapy.

Gladstone Convalescent Care Facility
18000 SE Webster Rd, Gladstone, OR 97027
(503) 656-1644
Admin Joan Holbrook. **Dir of Nursing** Caroline Mills. **Medical Dir** Roy Payne MD.
Licensure Intermediate care; Day care; Respite care. **Beds** ICF 130; Day care 10; Respite care 20. **Certified** Medicaid.
Owner Proprietary corp (Beverly Enterprises).
Admissions Requirements Medical examination; Physician's request.
Staff Physicians 1 (pt); RNs 6 (ft), 1 (pt); LPNs 3 (ft), 2 (pt); Nurses' aides 50 (ft), 13 (pt); Physical therapists 1 (pt); Occupational therapists 1 (pt); Speech therapists 1 (pt); Activities coordinators 2 (ft); Dietitians 1 (pt).
Facilities Dining room; Physical therapy room; Activities room; Crafts room; Laundry room; Barber/Beauty shop.

Activities Arts & crafts; Cards; Games; Reading groups; Prayer groups; Movies; Shopping trips; Dances/Social/Cultural gatherings.

Grants Pass

Highland House Nursing Center
2201 NW Highland, Grants Pass, OR 97526
(503) 474-1901, 479-6046 FAX
Admin Philip Stephens. **Dir of Nursing** Betty Lavada RN. **Medical Dir** Dr George Bailey.
Licensure Skilled care; Intermediate care; Alzheimer's care. **Beds** SNF 23; ICF 111. **Private Pay Patients** 56%. **Certified** Medicaid; Medicare.
Owner Proprietary corp.
Admissions Requirements Medical examination; Physician's request.
Staff RNs 6 (ft), 5 (pt); LPNs 5 (ft), 6 (pt); Nurses' aides 46 (ft), 28 (pt); Physical therapists 1 (pt); Reality therapists 2 (ft); Recreational therapists 2 (ft); Occupational therapists 1 (pt); Speech therapists 1 (pt); Activities coordinators 1 (ft); Dietitians 1 (pt); Podiatrists 1 (pt).
Languages Spanish, German.
Facilities Dining room; Physical therapy room; Activities room; Chapel; Crafts room; Laundry room; Barber/Beauty shop; Library; TTY; Alzheimer's locked and secure wing with garden.
Activities Arts & crafts; Cards; Games; Reading groups; Prayer groups; Movies; Shopping trips; Dances/Social/Cultural gatherings; Intergenerational programs; Pet therapy.

Laurel Hill Nursing Center
859 NE 6th, Grants Pass, OR 97526
(503) 479-3700
Admin Dave Slaght. **Dir of Nursing** Ardythe Hoffman.
Licensure Intermediate care; Alzheimer's care. **Beds** ICF 41. **Certified** Medicaid.
Owner Proprietary corp.
Admissions Requirements Physician's request.
Staff Physicians 1 (ft), 4 (pt); RNs 2 (ft), 4 (pt); LPNs 1 (ft), 4 (pt); Nurses' aides 5 (ft), 4 (pt); Physical therapists 1 (ft), 4 (pt); Activities coordinators 1 (ft), 4 (pt); Dietitians 1 (ft), 4 (pt); Podiatrists 1 (ft), 4 (pt).
Languages Spanish.
Facilities Dining room; Activities room; Laundry room.
Activities Arts & crafts; Cards; Games; Reading groups; Prayer groups; Movies.

Mariola Nursing Center
1450 NE Fairview Ave, Grants Pass, OR 97526
(503) 479-2606
Admin Kenneth B Selvey.
Licensure Skilled care; Intermediate care. **Beds** SNF 12; ICF 90. **Certified** Medicaid; Medicare.

Royale Gardens Healthcare Facility
2075 NW Highland Ave, Grants Pass, OR 97526
(503) 476-8891
Admin Dennis L Will. **Dir of Nursing** Lois Greene RN. **Medical Dir** Thomas M Turek MD.
Licensure Skilled care; Intermediate care; Residential and respite care. **Beds** SNF 18; ICF 154; Residential and respite care 22. **Private Pay Patients** 46%. **Certified** Medicaid; Medicare.
Owner Privately owned.
Admissions Requirements Minimum age 18.
Staff Physicians; RNs 8 (ft), 5 (pt); LPNs 8 (ft), 7 (pt); Nurses' aides 62 (ft), 32 (pt); Physical therapists 1 (ft); Recreational therapists 2 (ft), 1 (pt); Occupational therapists 1 (pt); Speech therapists

(contracted); Activities coordinators 1 (ft); Dietitians (contracted); Podiatrists (contracted).
Languages German, Spanish.
Facilities Dining room; Physical therapy room; Activities room; Chapel; Crafts room; Laundry room; Barber/Beauty shop.
Activities Arts & crafts; Cards; Games; Reading groups; Prayer groups; Movies; Shopping trips; Dances/Social/Cultural gatherings; Intergenerational programs; Pet therapy.

Gresham

Fairlawn Care Center
3457 NE Division, Gresham, OR 97030
(503) 667-1965
Admin Robert Dennis.
Medical Dir Dr MacKay.
Licensure Skilled care; Intermediate care. *Beds* SNF 48; ICF 49. *Certified* Medicaid; Medicare.
Admissions Requirements Minimum age 60; Medical examination; Physician's request.
Staff RNs 4 (ft), 17 (pt); LPNs 3 (ft), 6 (pt); Nurses' aides 46 (ft), 25 (pt); Recreational therapists 2 (ft); Activities coordinators 1 (ft); Dietitians 1 (ft).
Affiliation Lutheran.
Facilities Dining room; Physical therapy room; Activities room; Chapel; Laundry room; Barber/Beauty shop; Library.
Activities Arts & crafts; Cards; Games; Prayer groups; Movies; Shopping trips; Current events; Bus trips; Music appreciation; Gardening; Church services; Grandparent program.

Neighbors of Woodcraft Home
1250 SE Roberts, Gresham, OR 97030
(503) 667-5430
Admin Jessie Johnson, Jr.
Licensure Intermediate care. *Beds* 4.

Pacific Crest Rehabilitation Center & Specialty Care
405 NE 5th St, Gresham, OR 97030
(503) 666-5600, 667-9633 FAX
Admin Jim Rockenbach. *Dir of Nursing* Linda Rader. *Medical Dir* Rick Tuscher DO.
Licensure Skilled care; Rehabilitation (head injury, spinal, CVA, ortho, congenital, neuro). *Beds* SNF 80. *Private Pay Patients* 10%. *Certified* Medicaid; Medicare.
Owner Privately owned (American Medical Services).
Staff RNs 9 (ft); LPNs 10 (ft); Nurses' aides 35 (ft); Physical therapists 3 (ft); Reality therapists 1 (ft); Recreational therapists 2 (ft); Occupational therapists 3 (ft); Speech therapists 1 (ft); Activities coordinators 1 (ft); Dietitians 1 (ft).
Facilities Dining room; Physical therapy room; Activities room; Crafts room; Laundry room; Barber/Beauty shop.
Activities Arts & crafts; Cards; Games; Reading groups; Prayer groups; Movies; Shopping trips; Dances/Social/Cultural gatherings; Intergenerational programs; Pet therapy; Sports; Aerobics.

Rest Harbor Extended Care Center
PO Box 525, 5905 E Powell Valley Blvd, Gresham, OR 97030
(503) 665-1151
Admin Greg Dempsey. *Dir of Nursing* Ruthann Eaton. *Medical Dir* Thomas Hickerson MD.
Licensure Skilled care; Intermediate care; Day care; Retirement. *Beds* SNF 42; ICF 86; Day care 25. *Certified* Medicaid; Medicare.
Owner Proprietary corp.
Admissions Requirements Medical examination; Physician's request.
Staff Physicians 3 (pt); RNs 9 (ft), 3 (pt); LPNs 5 (ft), 6 (pt); Nurses' aides 40 (ft), 17 (pt); Physical therapists 3 (pt); Reality

therapists 1 (pt); Recreational therapists 1 (ft), 1 (pt); Occupational therapists 2 (pt); Speech therapists 3 (pt); Activities coordinators 1 (ft); Dietitians 1 (pt).
Affiliation Seventh-Day Adventist.
Facilities Dining room; Physical therapy room; Activities room; Crafts room; Laundry room; Barber/Beauty shop; Library; Pharmacy.
Activities Arts & crafts; Cards; Games; Reading groups; Prayer groups; Movies; Shopping trips; Dances/Social/Cultural gatherings; Puppy therapy; Traveling zoo; Dining.

Village Convalescent Center
3955 SE 182nd, Gresham, OR 97030
(503) 665-0183, 666-6609 FAX
Admin Maureen Chaklai. *Dir of Nursing* Faith Scheill. *Medical Dir* Dr Thomas Hickerson.
Licensure Skilled care; Intermediate care. *Beds* SNF 34; ICF 72. *Private Pay Patients* 40%. *Certified* Medicaid; Medicare.
Owner Nonprofit corp (Pleasant Valley Health Services).
Admissions Requirements Medical examination; Physician's request.
Staff RNs 10 (ft), 2 (pt); LPNs 7 (ft), 2 (pt); Nurses' aides 45 (ft), 5 (pt); Physical therapists; Recreational therapists 1 (ft), 1 (pt); Dietitians.
Languages Spanish.
Facilities Dining room; Physical therapy room; Activities room; Laundry room; Barber/Beauty shop.
Activities Arts & crafts; Cards; Games; Reading groups; Prayer groups; Movies; Shopping trips; Dances/Social/Cultural gatherings; Intergenerational programs; Pet therapy; Music therapy.

Willow Tree Care Center Inc
PO Box 1379, 311 NE Division, Gresham, OR 97030
(503) 667-8050
Admin Van Wilson.
Licensure Intermediate care. *Beds* ICF 40. *Certified* Medicaid.

Heppner

Pioneer Memorial Hospital—Heppner
564 Pioneer Dr, Heppner, OR 97836
(503) 676-9133
Admin Ernest R Wick.
Medical Dir Jeanne Berretta MD.
Licensure Intermediate care; Day care. *Beds* ICF 32; Day care 3. *Certified* Medicaid.
Owner Publicly owned.
Admissions Requirements Medical examination.
Staff Physicians 2 (ft); RNs 2 (ft), 8 (pt); LPNs 3 (ft), 2 (pt); Nurses' aides 15 (ft), 5 (pt); Physical therapists 1 (pt); Activities coordinators 2 (pt); Dietitians 1 (ft).
Facilities Dining room; Activities room; Crafts room; Laundry room; Barber/Beauty shop; Solarium; Patio.
Activities Arts & crafts; Cards; Games; Reading groups; Prayer groups; Movies; Shopping trips.

Hermiston

Hermiston Good Samaritan
970 W Juniper Ave, Hermiston, OR 97838
(503) 567-8337
Admin Richard L Alexander. *Dir of Nursing* Pat Duff. *Medical Dir* Fisher MD.
Licensure Skilled care; Intermediate care; Alzheimer's care; Retirement. *Beds* SNF 10; ICF 73; Alzheimer's care 22; Retirement 15. *Certified* Medicaid; Medicare.
Owner Nonprofit corp (Evangelical Lutheran/ Good Samaritan Society).

Staff RNs 6 (ft); LPNs 6 (ft), 3 (pt); Nurses' aides 25 (ft), 15 (pt); Physical therapists 1 (pt); Recreational therapists 2 (ft), 1 (pt); Speech therapists 1 (pt); Activities coordinators 1 (pt); Dietitians 1 (pt).
Languages Spanish.
Affiliation Lutheran.
Facilities Dining room; Physical therapy room; Activities room; Chapel; Crafts room; Laundry room; Barber/Beauty shop.
Activities Arts & crafts; Cards; Games; Reading groups; Prayer groups; Movies; Shopping trips; Dances/Social/Cultural gatherings; Intergenerational programs.

Hillsboro

Extended Care Rehabilitation Center
335 SE 8th Ave, Hillsboro, OR 97123
(503) 681-1339
Admin Manuel Berman. *Dir of Nursing* Christine Chandler RN BSN. *Medical Dir* Peter Schluderman MD.
Licensure Skilled care. *Beds* SNF 20. *Private Pay Patients* 5%. *Certified* Medicaid; Medicare.
Owner Nonprofit corp.
Admissions Requirements Medical examination; Physician's request.
Staff RNs 3 (ft), 3 (pt); LPNs 2 (ft), 2 (pt); Nurses' aides 6 (ft), 6 (pt); Physical therapists 1 (ft), 1 (pt); Recreational therapists 1 (pt); Occupational therapists 1 (ft), 2 (pt); Speech therapists 2 (pt); Activities coordinators 1 (pt).
Languages Interpreters available.
Facilities Dining room; Physical therapy room; Activities room; Chapel; Library.
Activities Arts & crafts; Cards; Games; Reading groups.

Gardenview Care Center
33465 SW Tualatin Valley Hwy, Hillsboro, OR 97123
(503) 648-7181
Admin Donald V Terry.
Medical Dir Marjorie Thaanum.
Licensure Intermediate care; Day care; Respite care; Alzheimer's care. *Beds* ICF 36; Day care 6; Respite care 3. *Certified* Medicaid.
Owner Privately owned.
Admissions Requirements Physician's request.
Staff RNs 2 (ft), 2 (pt); Nurses' aides 10 (ft), 4 (pt); Activities coordinators 1 (ft); Dietitians 1 (pt); MRQs 1 (pt).
Facilities Dining room; Activities room; Crafts room; Laundry room; Patio.
Activities Arts & crafts; Games; Reading groups; Prayer groups; Dining out; Bingo; Music; Dancing; Exercises.

Hillaire Care Center
1778 NE Cornell Rd, Hillsboro, OR 97124
(503) 648-6621
Admin Theresa Heis.
Licensure Intermediate care. *Beds* ICF 56. *Certified* Medicaid.

Oak Villa Health Care Center
650 Oak St E, Hillsboro, OR 97123
(503) 648-8588
Admin Gary Wart.
Licensure Skilled care; Intermediate care; Day care; Respite care. *Beds* SNF 31; ICF 73; Day care 3; Respite care 3. *Certified* Medicaid; Medicare.

Hood River

Hood River Care Center
729 Henderson Rd, Hood River, OR 97031
(503) 386-2688
Admin Darryl Fisher. *Dir of Nursing* Linda Grunke RN. *Medical Dir* Paul Hamada MD.

Licensure Skilled care; Intermediate care; Day/Respite care. *Beds* SNF 25; ICF 103; Day/Respite care 13. *Certified* Medicaid; Medicare.
Owner Proprietary corp (Care Center Inc).
Admissions Requirements Physician's request.
Staff RNs 5 (ft); LPNs 6 (ft); Nurses' aides 23 (ft), 3 (pt); Physical therapists 1 (pt); Recreational therapists 1 (ft); Occupational therapists 1 (pt); Speech therapists 1 (pt); Activities coordinators 1 (ft); Dietitians 1 (pt); Ophthalmologists 1 (pt); Podiatrists 1 (pt); Dentists 1 (pt).
Facilities Dining room; Physical therapy room; Activities room; Crafts room; Laundry room; Barber/Beauty shop; Library.
Activities Arts & crafts; Cards; Games; Reading groups; Prayer groups; Movies; Shopping trips; Dances/Social/Cultural gatherings.

Independence

Cedarwood Care Center
1525 Monmouth Ave, Independence, OR 97351
(503) 838-0001
Admin Betty Martin.
Licensure Intermediate care; Day care. *Beds* ICF 80; Day care 5. *Certified* Medicaid.
Owner Proprietary corp (Beverly Enterprises).

Junction City

Grandview Manor Care Center
530 Birch St, Junction City, OR 97448
(503) 998-2395
Admin Loretta Grudt.
Licensure Intermediate care; Day care. *Beds* ICF 72; Day care 14. *Certified* Medicaid.

Keizer

Keizer Retirement & Health Care Village
5210 River Rd N, Keizer, OR 97303
(503) 393-3624
Admin Loretta Androes. *Dir of Nursing* Dana Murphy. *Medical Dir* Paul Young.
Licensure Intermediate care; Residential care; Retirement; Alzheimer's care. *Beds* ICF 36; Residential care 108; Retirement 150. *Private Pay Patients* 97%.
Owner Privately owned.
Admissions Requirements Minimum age 55; Medical examination; Physician's request.
Staff Physicians 1 (pt); RNs 4 (ft); LPNs 5 (ft), 2 (pt); Nurses' aides 18 (ft), 15 (pt); Physical therapists 1 (pt); Occupational therapists 1 (pt); Speech therapists 1 (pt); Activities coordinators 1 (ft); Dietitians 1 (pt).
Languages Spanish, German.
Facilities Dining room; Physical therapy room; Activities room; Chapel; Crafts room; Laundry room; Barber/Beauty shop; Library.
Activities Arts & crafts; Cards; Games; Reading groups; Prayer groups; Movies; Shopping trips; Dances/Social/Cultural gatherings; Intergenerational programs; Pet therapy.

Klamath Falls

Mountain View Oregon
711 Washburn Way, Klamath Falls, OR 97603
(503) 882-4471
Admin Helen Forner. *Dir of Nursing* H Mauer RN. *Medical Dir* Al Glidden.
Licensure Skilled care; Intermediate care; Day/Respite care. *Beds* SNF 32; ICF 82; Day/Respite care 114. *Certified* Medicaid; Medicare.
Owner Proprietary corp (Unicare).
Admissions Requirements Physician's request.

Staff Physicians; RNs; LPNs; Nurses' aides; Physical therapists; Occupational therapists; Speech therapists; Activities coordinators; Dietitians; Podiatrists.
Facilities Dining room; Physical therapy room; Activities room; Crafts room; Laundry room; Barber/Beauty shop.
Activities Arts & crafts; Cards; Games; Reading groups; Prayer groups; Movies; Shopping trips; Dances/Social/Cultural gatherings.

Oregon Health Care Center—Highland
2555 Main St, Klamath Falls, OR 97601
(503) 882-6341, 882-9804 FAX
Admin Daniel Lopez MEd MA. *Dir of Nursing* Linda Taylor RN. *Medical Dir* Raymond Tice MD.
Licensure Skilled care; Intermediate care; Residential care; Alzheimer's care. *Beds* Swing beds SNF/ICF 78; Residential care 14. *Private Pay Patients* 35%. *Certified* Medicaid; Medicare.
Owner Proprietary corp (Unicare).
Admissions Requirements Minimum age 18; Physician's request.
Staff RNs 4 (ft); LPNs 6 (ft); Nurses' aides 20 (ft), 5 (pt); Physical therapists; Recreational therapists 1 (ft); Activities coordinators 1 (ft); Dietitians.
Languages Spanish, German.
Facilities Dining room; Physical therapy room; Activities room; Laundry room; Barber/Beauty shop.
Activities Arts & crafts; Cards; Games; Reading groups; Prayer groups; Movies; Intergenerational programs; Pet therapy.

West Care Home
1401 Campus Dr, Klamath Falls, OR 97601
(503) 882-6691
Admin Julia K Roberson. *Dir of Nursing* Linda Barnett. *Medical Dir* Dr Charles Bury.
Licensure Skilled care; Intermediate care. *Beds* SNF 70; ICF 60. *Certified* Medicaid; Medicare.
Owner Nonprofit organization/foundation.
Admissions Requirements Physician's request.
Staff RNs 10 (ft), 17 (pt); LPNs 6 (ft), 2 (pt); Nurses' aides 58 (ft), 2 (pt); Physical therapists 1 (ft), 1 (pt); Occupational therapists 1 (ft); Activities coordinators 2 (ft), 1 (pt).
Facilities Dining room; Physical therapy room; Activities room; Chapel; Crafts room; Laundry room; Barber/Beauty shop; Library; Multi-purpose room; Sun room.
Activities Arts & crafts; Cards; Games; Reading groups; Prayer groups; Movies; Shopping trips; Dances/Social/Cultural gatherings; Pet therapy.

LaGrande

Mountain Vista Care Center
95 Aries Way, LaGrande, OR 97850
(503) 963-8678
Admin Karl "Rick" Miller.
Licensure Intermediate care. *Beds* ICF 80. *Certified* Medicaid.

Valley View Care Center
103 Adams Ave, LaGrande, OR 97850
(503) 963-4184
Admin Judith A Nitz. *Dir of Nursing* Arlette Patrow RN.
Licensure Skilled care; Intermediate care. *Beds* SNF 15; ICF 69. *Certified* Medicaid; Medicare.
Owner Proprietary corp.
Admissions Requirements Physician's request.
Staff RNs 3 (ft), 1 (pt); LPNs 4 (ft); Nurses' aides 26 (ft), 7 (pt); Activities coordinators 1 (ft), 1 (pt); Dietitians 1 (pt).
Facilities Dining room; Physical therapy room; Activities room; Laundry room; Barber/Beauty shop.

Activities Arts & crafts; Cards; Games; Reading groups; Prayer groups; Movies; Dances/Social/Cultural gatherings; Drives.

Lake Oswego

Mountain Park Convalescent Care Facility
PO Box 527, 4 Greenridge Ct, Lake Oswego, OR 97034
(503) 636-9614
Admin Dennis Rickert. *Dir of Nursing* Mary Doak RN. *Medical Dir* Gary Geddes MD.
Licensure Intermediate care; Day care; Respite care; Retirement. *Beds* ICF 182; Day care 5; Respite care 5. *Certified* Medicaid.
Owner Proprietary corp (Beverly Enterprises).
Admissions Requirements Medical examination; Physician's request.
Staff Physicians 1 (pt); RNs; LPNs; Nurses' aides; Physical therapists; Occupational therapists; Speech therapists; Activities coordinators; Dietitians; Ophthalmologists.
Facilities Dining room; Physical therapy room; Activities room; Crafts room; Laundry room; Barber/Beauty shop; Library.
Activities Arts & crafts; Cards; Games; Reading groups; Prayer groups; Movies; Shopping trips; Dances/Social/Cultural gatherings.

Lakeview

Lake District Hospital & Skilled Nursing Facility
700 S "J" St, Lakeview, OR 97630
(503) 947-2114, 947-2912 FAX
Admin Richard T Moore. *Dir of Nursing* Ann Murphy RN. *Medical Dir* William Striby MD.
Licensure Skilled care; Intermediate care. *Beds* SNF 47; ICF 47. *Private Pay Patients* 40%. *Certified* Medicaid; Medicare.
Owner Nonprofit organization/foundation.
Admissions Requirements Physician's request.
Staff Physicians 5 (pt); RNs 3 (ft), 6 (pt); LPNs 1 (ft), 1 (pt); Nurses' aides 10 (ft), 12 (pt); Physical therapists 1 (ft); Activities coordinators 1 (ft); Dietitians 1 (pt).
Facilities Dining room; Physical therapy room; Activities room; Chapel; Crafts room; Laundry room; Barber/Beauty shop.
Activities Arts & crafts; Cards; Games; Reading groups.

Lebanon

Villa Cascade Care Center
350 S 8th St, Lebanon, OR 97355
(503) 259-1221, 451-1349 FAX
Admin Greg Gortmaker. *Dir of Nursing* Ruth Speaker RN. *Medical Dir* Kenneth Orwick MD.
Licensure Skilled care; Intermediate care; Alzheimer's care. *Beds* SNF 25; ICF 85. *Private Pay Patients* 31%. *Certified* Medicaid; Medicare.
Owner Nonprofit corp (Pleasant Valley Health Services).
Admissions Requirements Medical examination.
Staff RNs 7 (ft); LPNs 9 (ft); Nurses' aides 29 (ft); Physical therapists 1 (pt); Occupational therapists 1 (pt); Speech therapists 1 (pt); Activities coordinators 1 (ft); Dietitians 1 (pt).
Facilities Dining room; Physical therapy room; Activities room; Chapel; Barber/Beauty shop; TV room; Alzheimer's secured area.
Activities Arts & crafts; Games; Reading groups; Prayer groups; Movies; Dances/Social/Cultural gatherings; Intergenerational programs; Pet therapy.

Lincoln City

Oregon Health Care Center—Evergreen
3011 NE 28th, Lincoln City, OR 97367
(503) 994-8111
Admin Shirley Weissenbuehler. *Dir of Nursing* Pam DeYoung RN. *Medical Dir* Erhling Oksenholt DO.
Licensure Skilled care; Intermediate care. *Beds* SNF 7; ICF 73. *Certified* Medicaid; Medicare.
Owner Proprietary corp (United Health Facilities).
Admissions Requirements Minimum age 16; Medical examination; Physician's request.
Facilities Dining room; Physical therapy room; Activities room; Crafts room; Barber/Beauty shop.
Activities Arts & crafts; Cards; Games; Reading groups; Prayer groups; Movies; Shopping trips; Dances/Social/Cultural gatherings; Intergenerational programs; Pet therapy.

Madras

Mountain View Hospital & Nursing Home
1270 A St, Madras, OR 97741
(503) 475-3882, 475-3882, ext 291 FAX
Admin Ronald W Barnes. *Dir of Nursing* Karen Potampa.
Licensure Skilled care; Intermediate care. *Beds* SNF 21; ICF 47. *Certified* Medicaid; Medicare.
Owner Publicly owned.

Mallala

Lutheran Pioneer Home
32746 Shooge Rd, Mallala, OR 97038
(503) 824-3311
Admin Beverly Rice.
Licensure Intermediate care. *Beds* 28. *Certified* Medicaid.
Affiliation Lutheran.

McMinnville

Careousel Care Center
1309 E 27th St, McMinnville, OR 97128
(503) 472-4678, 472-2896 FAX
Admin William Hoard. *Dir of Nursing* Del Lewis. *Medical Dir* Dr Lautenbach.
Licensure Skilled care; Intermediate care. *Beds* SNF 35; ICF 75. *Certified* Medicaid; Medicare.
Owner Proprietary corp (Unicare).
Admissions Requirements Minimum age 18; Medical examination; Physician's request.
Staff RNs; LPNs; Nurses' aides; Physical therapists; Occupational therapists; Speech therapists; Activities coordinators; Dietitians.
Languages French, Spanish, Japanese.
Facilities Dining room; Physical therapy room; Activities room; Crafts room; Laundry room; Barber/Beauty shop; Sculpture yard.
Activities Arts & crafts; Cards; Games; Reading groups; Prayer groups; Movies; Shopping trips; Dances/Social/Cultural gatherings; Intergenerational programs; Pet therapy.

Hillside Manor
900 N Hill Rd, McMinnville, OR 97128
(503) 472-9534
Admin Robert Donohue.
Medical Dir Donalda Webster.
Licensure Intermediate care; Retirement. *Beds* ICF 19.
Owner Nonprofit corp.
Staff RNs 3 (ft), 3 (pt); LPNs 3 (ft); Nurses' aides 14 (ft).
Facilities Dining room; Activities room; Chapel; Crafts room; Barber/Beauty shop; Library.

Activities Arts & crafts; Cards; Games; Reading groups; Prayer groups; Movies.

Oak Glen Care Center
421 S Evans St, McMinnville, OR 97128
(503) 472-3141
Admin Jan Buffa Temp.
Medical Dir Mark Olson MD.
Licensure Intermediate care; Alzheimer's care; Retirement. *Beds* ICF 109. *Certified* Medicaid.
Owner Privately owned.
Admissions Requirements Minimum age 18; Physician's request.
Staff RNs 3 (ft), 3 (pt); LPNs 5 (ft), 2 (pt); Nurses' aides 30 (ft), 5 (pt); Activities coordinators 3 (ft), 1 (pt).
Facilities Dining room; Physical therapy room; Activities room; Laundry room; Barber/Beauty shop.
Activities Arts & crafts; Cards; Games; Reading groups; Prayer groups; Movies; Shopping trips; Dances/Social/Cultural gatherings.

Medford

Hearthstone Manor
2901 E Barnett Rd, Medford, OR 97501
(503) 779-4221
Admin Dan Gregory. *Dir of Nursing* Mary Ellen Mower RN. *Medical Dir* Warren G Bishop MD.
Licensure Skilled care; Intermediate care; Alzheimer's care. *Beds* SNF 30; ICF 131. *Certified* Medicaid; Medicare.
Owner Nonprofit corp.
Admissions Requirements Medical examination; Physician's request.
Staff Physicians; RNs; LPNs; Nurses' aides; Physical therapists; Reality therapists; Recreational therapists; Occupational therapists; Speech therapists; Activities coordinators.
Facilities Dining room; Physical therapy room; Activities room; Crafts room; Barber/Beauty shop.
Activities Arts & crafts; Cards; Games; Reading groups; Prayer groups; Movies; Shopping trips; Dances/Social/Cultural gatherings; College classes.

Rogue Valley Care Center
3693 S Pacific Hwy, Medford, OR 97502
(503) 535-4636
Admin Jacqualine Connell. *Dir of Nursing* Dell Dewett. *Medical Dir* Dr John Shonerd.
Licensure Intermediate care. *Beds* ICF 36. *Certified* Medicaid.
Owner Privately owned.
Admissions Requirements Medical examination; Physician's request.
Staff Physicians 1 (pt); RNs 1 (ft), 1 (pt); LPNs 4 (ft), 3 (pt); Nurses' aides 10 (ft), 2 (pt); Physical therapists 1 (pt); Reality therapists 1 (pt); Occupational therapists 1 (ft); Activities coordinators 1 (ft); Dietitians 2 (pt).
Languages Spanish.
Facilities Dining room; Physical therapy room; Activities room; Laundry room; Barber/Beauty shop; Library.
Activities Arts & crafts; Cards; Games; Reading groups; Prayer groups; Movies; Shopping trips; Dances/Social/Cultural gatherings; Intergenerational programs; Pet therapy.

Rogue Valley Manor
1200 Mira Mar Ave, Medford, OR 97501
(503) 773-7411
Admin Roger Stevens.
Medical Dir Patricia Kauffman.
Licensure Intermediate care; Retirement. *Beds* ICF 60.
Owner Nonprofit corp.
Admissions Requirements Minimum age 62.

Staff Physicians; RNs; LPNs; Nurses' aides; Physical therapists; Recreational therapists; Occupational therapists; Speech therapists; Activities coordinators; Dietitians; Ophthalmologists; Podiatrists; Dentists.
Facilities Dining room; Physical therapy room; Activities room; Chapel; Crafts room; Laundry room; Barber/Beauty shop; Library; Pool; Fitness center.
Activities Arts & crafts; Cards; Games; Prayer groups; Movies; Shopping trips; Dances/ Social/Cultural gatherings; Swimming; Exercise.

Three Fountains Inc
835 Crater Lake Ave, Medford, OR 97504
(503) 773-7717
Admin Shirley A Inge CFACHCA. *Dir of Nursing* Susan Lewis RN BS. *Medical Dir* Warren Bishop MD.
Licensure Skilled care. *Beds* SNF 156. *Private Pay Patients* 60%. *Certified* Medicaid; Medicare.
Owner Proprietary corp.
Admissions Requirements Minimum age 12; Physician's request.
Staff RNs 16 (ft); LPNs 4 (ft); Nurses' aides 78 (ft), 4 (pt); Physical therapists 1 (ft); Occupational therapists 1 (ft); Speech therapists 1 (ft); Activities coordinators 3 (ft); Dietitians 1 (ft).
Facilities Dining room; Physical therapy room; Activities room; Crafts room; Barber/Beauty shop; Library.
Activities Arts & crafts; Cards; Games; Reading groups; Prayer groups; Movies; Shopping trips; Dances/Social/Cultural gatherings.

Villa Royal Health Care Center
625 Stevens St, Medford, OR 97504-6797
(503) 779-3551
Admin Jon Deason. *Dir of Nursing* Pam Cross. *Medical Dir* Steven Brummer.
Licensure Skilled care; Intermediate care. *Beds* SNF 34; ICF 96. *Certified* Medicaid; Medicare.
Owner Proprietary corp (Hillhaven Corp).
Staff Physicians; RNs; LPNs; Nurses' aides; Physical therapists; Reality therapists; Recreational therapists; Occupational therapists; Speech therapists; Activities coordinators; Dietitians.
Languages Spanish.
Facilities Dining room; Physical therapy room; Activities room; Crafts room; Laundry room; Barber/Beauty shop; Library.
Activities Arts & crafts; Cards; Games; Reading groups; Prayer groups; Movies; Shopping trips; Dances/Social/Cultural gatherings.

Merlin

Merlin Health Retreat
PO Box 340, 816 Sanitarium Rd, Merlin, OR 97532
(503) 476-5300
Admin Charles Werner.
Licensure Intermediate care. *Beds* ICF 40. *Certified* Medicaid.
Facilities Dining room; Activities room; Chapel.
Activities Games; Prayer groups; Movies; Dances/Social/Cultural gatherings.

Milton-Freewater

Elzora Manor
PO Box 498, 120 Elzora St, Milton-Freewater, OR 97862
(503) 938-3318
Admin Uva Berry. *Dir of Nursing* Pat Gomes. *Medical Dir* Dr Ronald Zleck.
Licensure Skilled care; Intermediate care; Retirement. *Beds* SNF 15; ICF 112. *Certified* Medicaid; Medicare.

Owner Proprietary corp.
Admissions Requirements Physician's request.
Staff Physicians 1 (pt); RNs 9 (ft); LPNs 5 (ft), 3 (pt); Nurses' aides 35 (ft); Physical therapists 1 (pt); Reality therapists 1 (pt); Recreational therapists 1 (pt); Occupational therapists 1 (pt); Speech therapists 1 (pt); Activities coordinators 2 (ft); Dietitians 1 (pt); Ophthalmologists 1 (pt); Podiatrists 1 (pt); Dentists 1 (pt).
Languages Spanish.
Facilities Dining room; Physical therapy room; Activities room; Crafts room; Laundry room; Barber/Beauty shop; Library.
Activities Arts & crafts; Cards; Games; Reading groups; Prayer groups; Movies; Shopping trips; Dances/Social/Cultural gatherings.

Milwaukie

Milwaukie Convalescent Center Inc
12045 SE Stanley, Milwaukie, OR 97222
(503) 659-2323
Admin Nash J Barinaga. Dir of Nursing Darlene Goode.
Licensure Intermediate care; Residential care. Beds ICF 75; Residential care 28. Private Pay Patients 75%. Certified Medicaid.
Owner Proprietary corp.
Admissions Requirements Medical examination.
Staff RNs 3 (ft), 2 (pt); LPNs 3 (ft), 2 (pt); Nurses' aides 10 (ft), 20 (pt); Activities coordinators; Dietitians; Maintenance 1 (ft), 1 (pt).
Languages Italian, Spanish.
Facilities Dining room; Physical therapy room; Activities room; Crafts room; Laundry room.
Activities Arts & crafts; Games; Movies; Dances/Social/Cultural gatherings; Pet therapy.

Rose Villa Health Care Inc
13505 SE River Rd, Milwaukie, OR 97222
(503) 654-3171
Admin James Sturgis.
Licensure Intermediate care. Beds ICF 55.

Willamette View Convalescent Center
13021 SE River Rd, Milwaukie, OR 97222
(503) 652-6200
Admin Virginia L Gaines. Dir of Nursing Judy de Maria. Medical Dir Dr Roy Payne.
Licensure Skilled care; Intermediate care; Retirement; Alzheimer's care. Beds SNF 6; ICF 113; Retirement 600. Private Pay Patients 98%.
Owner Nonprofit organization/foundation.
Admissions Requirements Medical examination; Physician's request.
Staff Physicians; RNs 10 (ft), 5 (pt); LPNs 3 (ft), 1 (pt); Nurses' aides 49 (ft), 12 (pt); Physical therapists (contracted); Occupational therapists 1 (ft); Activities coordinators 1 (ft); Dietitians 1 (pt); Podiatrists 1 (pt); Dentists 1 (pt).
Languages German, French, Dutch, Indonesian, Cambodian/Vietnamese.
Facilities Dining room; Physical therapy room; Activities room; Chapel; Crafts room; Barber/Beauty shop; Library.
Activities Arts & crafts; Games; Reading groups; Prayer groups; Movies; Dances/Social/Cultural gatherings; Intergenerational programs; Pet therapy.

Molalla

Molalla Manor Care Center
301 Ridins Ave, Molalla, OR 97038
(503) 829-5591
Admin Susan Maxwell. Dir of Nursing Kathleen A Williams. Medical Dir A B Willeford MD.

Licensure Skilled care; Intermediate care. Beds SNF 21; ICF 69. Certified Medicaid; Medicare.
Owner Proprietary corp (Care Center Inc).
Admissions Requirements Medical examination; Physician's request.
Staff RNs 3 (ft); LPNs 7 (ft); Nurses' aides 15 (ft), 13 (pt); Physical therapists 1 (pt); Occupational therapists 1 (pt); Speech therapists 1 (pt); Activities coordinators 1 (ft); Dietitians 1 (pt); Ophthalmologists 1 (pt).
Languages Spanish.
Facilities Dining room; Physical therapy room; Activities room; Laundry room; Barber/Beauty shop; Fireside; Multi-purpose Room.
Activities Arts & crafts; Games; Prayer groups; Movies; Dances/Social/Cultural gatherings.

Mount Angel

Benedictine Nursing Center
540 S Main St, Mount Angel, OR 97362
(503) 845-6841
Admin John H Hogan. Dir of Nursing Joy Smith. Medical Dir Dr Virgil Peters.
Licensure Skilled care; Intermediate care. Beds SNF 19; Swing beds SNF/ICF 111. Private Pay Patients 50%. Certified Medicaid; Medicare.
Owner Nonprofit corp.
Admissions Requirements Medical examination; Physician's request.
Staff RNs 13 (ft), 20 (pt); LPNs 2 (ft), 1 (pt); Nurses' aides 50 (ft), 45 (pt); Physical therapists 5 (ft), 4 (pt); Occupational therapists 2 (ft); Speech therapists 1 (ft); Activities coordinators 1 (ft), 1 (pt); Dietitians 1 (ft).
Languages Spanish, German.
Affiliation Roman Catholic.
Facilities Dining room; Physical therapy room; Activities room; Chapel; Crafts room; Barber/Beauty shop; Programs for care of the confused, care of the dying, adult care, child care.
Activities Cards; Games; Reading groups; Prayer groups; Movies; Dances/Social/Cultural gatherings; Intergenerational programs; Pet therapy; Reminiscence; Exercise; Music; SERVE; Pastoral care.

Myrtle Point

Myrtle Point Care Center
637 Ash St, Myrtle Point, OR 97458
(503) 572-2066, 572-5477 FAX
Admin Donald L Veverka. Dir of Nursing Jeanette Shorb RN. Medical Dir Reed Gurney MD.
Licensure Intermediate care; Residential care. Beds ICF 35; Residential care 20. Private Pay Patients 30-55%. Certified Medicaid.
Owner Proprietary corp (Care Centers West Inc).
Admissions Requirements Medical examination; Physician's request.
Staff RNs 2 (ft), 1 (pt); LPNs 1 (ft), 1 (pt); Nurses' aides 10 (ft), 9 (pt); Activities coordinators 1 (pt).
Facilities Dining room; Activities room; Crafts room; Laundry room; Barber/Beauty shop; Library; Sun room.
Activities Arts & crafts; Cards; Games; Prayer groups; Movies; Dances/Social/Cultural gatherings; Weekly van rides.

Newberg

Chehalem Convalescent Care Center
1900 Fulton St, Newberg, OR 97132
(503) 538-2108
Admin John Shafer.
Medical Dir Barbara Monroe.

Licensure Skilled care; Intermediate care; Day/Respite care. Beds SNF 22; ICF 77. Certified Medicaid.
Owner Proprietary corp (Beverly Enterprises).
Admissions Requirements Medical examination; Physician's request.
Staff RNs 8 (ft), 2 (pt); LPNs 2 (ft), 2 (pt); Nurses' aides 30 (ft); Recreational therapists 1 (ft); Activities coordinators 1 (ft); Dietitians 1 (ft).
Facilities Dining room; Physical therapy room; Activities room; Laundry room; Barber/Beauty shop.
Activities Arts & crafts; Cards; Games; Prayer groups; Movies; Dances/Social/Cultural gatherings.

Friendsview Manor Infirmary
1301 E Fulton St, Newberg, OR 97132
(503) 538-3144
Admin Stuart C Willcuts. Dir of Nursing LaVina Stram.
Licensure Intermediate care; Retirement; Alzheimer's care. Beds ICF 37; Retirement 240.
Owner Nonprofit corp.
Admissions Requirements Minimum age 65; Medical examination; Physician's request.
Staff RNs 2 (ft), 7 (pt); LPNs 1 (ft); Nurses' aides 10 (ft), 6 (pt); Reality therapists 1 (ft); Activities coordinators 1 (ft); Dietitians 1 (ft).
Languages Spanish, Portuguese.
Affiliation Society of Friends.
Facilities Dining room; Activities room; Chapel; Crafts room; Laundry room; Barber/Beauty shop; Library; Sun room.
Activities Arts & crafts; Cards; Games; Reading groups; Prayer groups; Movies; Shopping trips; Dances/Social/Cultural gatherings; Dining out; Church meetings.

Newberg Care Home
1500 E 1st St, Newberg, OR 97132
(503) 538-9436
Admin John Paul Jones.
Medical Dir John Cummings.
Licensure Skilled care; Intermediate care; Alzheimer's care. Beds SNF 13; ICF 54. Certified Medicaid; Medicare.
Owner Proprietary corp.
Admissions Requirements Minimum age Geriatrics; Medical examination; Physician's request.
Staff Physicians 1 (pt); RNs 4 (ft); LPNs 3 (ft); Nurses' aides 35 (ft), 5 (pt); Physical therapists 1 (pt); Activities coordinators 1 (ft), 1 (pt); Dietitians 1 (pt).
Facilities Dining room; Physical therapy room; Activities room; Chapel; Crafts room; Laundry room; Barber/Beauty shop.
Activities Arts & crafts; Cards; Games; Reading groups; Prayer groups; Movies; Shopping trips; Dances/Social/Cultural gatherings.

Newport

Yaquina Care Center Inc
835 SW 11th, Newport, OR 97365
(503) 265-5356
Admin John Palmer.
Licensure Skilled care; Intermediate care. Beds SNF 17; ICF 63. Certified Medicaid; Medicare.

North Bend

St Catherine's Residence & Nursing Center
3959 Sheridan Ave, North Bend, OR 97459
(503) 756-4151
Admin Tom Harter, Prov. Dir of Nursing Sr Mary Flavian. Medical Dir Charles Lindsay MD.
Licensure Skilled care; Intermediate care; Retirement; Alzheimer's care. Beds SNF 19; ICF 142. Certified Medicaid; Medicare.

Owner Nonprofit corp (Catholic Health Corp).
Admissions Requirements Medical examination; Physician's request.
Staff Physicians 1 (pt); RNs 10 (ft), 1 (pt); LPNs 6 (ft), 4 (pt); Nurses' aides 83 (ft), 7 (pt); Physical therapists 1 (pt); Activities coordinators 1 (ft); Dietitians 1 (ft).
Affiliation Roman Catholic.
Facilities Dining room; Physical therapy room; Activities room; Chapel; Crafts room; Barber/Beauty shop; Library.
Activities Arts & crafts; Cards; Games; Prayer groups; Movies; Shopping trips; Dances/Social/Cultural gatherings.

Nyssa

Malheur Memorial Hospital
1109 Park Ave, Nyssa, OR 97913
(503) 372-2211
Admin Ernest M Steelsmith. *Dir of Nursing* Charlene Bonner. *Medical Dir* David W Sarazin MD.
Licensure Skilled care. *Beds* SNF 51. *Private Pay Patients* 15%. *Certified* Medicaid; Medicare.
Owner Publicly owned.
Admissions Requirements Physician's request.
Staff Physicians 1 (pt); RNs 2 (ft); LPNs 6 (ft); Nurses' aides 18 (ft); Physical therapists (contracted); Recreational therapists 1 (pt); Activities coordinators 1 (pt); Dietitians 1 (ft).
Languages Spanish.
Facilities Dining room; Physical therapy room; Activities room; Crafts room; Laundry room; Barber/Beauty shop; Library.
Activities Arts & crafts; Cards; Games; Reading groups; Prayer groups; Movies; Shopping trips; Dances/Social/Cultural gatherings.

Ontario

Presbyterian Community Care Center
1085 N Oregon, Ontario, OR 97914
(503) 889-9133
Admin Cathleen Sullivan. *Dir of Nursing* Irene Haney. *Medical Dir* Dr Paul Snyder.
Licensure Skilled care; Intermediate care. *Beds* SNF 24; ICF 99. *Private Pay Patients* 30%. *Certified* Medicaid; Medicare.
Owner Nonprofit organization/foundation.
Admissions Requirements Physician's request.
Staff RNs 7 (ft); LPNs 12 (ft), 2 (pt); Nurses' aides 74 (ft), 12 (pt); Physical therapists; Speech therapists 1 (pt); Activities coordinators 3 (ft); Dietitians 16 (ft).
Affiliation Presbyterian.
Facilities Dining room; Physical therapy room; Activities room; Chapel; Crafts room; Laundry room; Barber/Beauty shop; Library.
Activities Arts & crafts; Games; Reading groups; Prayer groups; Movies; Shopping trips.

Oregon City

Golden Age Care Center
1506 Division St, Oregon City, OR 97045
(503) 656-1973
Admin Diane Matheny.
Medical Dir Joseph Intile.
Licensure Intermediate care; Respite care. *Beds* ICF 48; Respite care 3. *Certified* Medicaid.
Admissions Requirements Minimum age 18.
Staff RNs 2 (ft), 2 (pt); LPNs 1 (ft); Nurses' aides 25 (ft), 5 (pt); Activities coordinators 1 (ft).
Facilities Dining room; Activities room.
Activities Arts & crafts; Cards; Games; Prayer groups; Movies.

Mountain View Convalescent Care Center
1400 Division St, Oregon City, OR 97045
(503) 656-0367
Admin Rene' Dumas. *Dir of Nursing* Linda Campbell-Thurman RN. *Medical Dir* Dr Payne.
Licensure Skilled care; Intermediate care. *Beds* SNF 39; ICF 85. *Certified* Medicaid; Medicare.
Owner Proprietary corp (Beverly Enterprises).
Admissions Requirements Physician's request.
Staff Physicians 20 (pt); RNs 15 (ft), 5 (pt); LPNs 5 (ft), 2 (pt); Nurses' aides 40 (ft); Physical therapists 1 (ft); Occupational therapists; Speech therapists; Activities coordinators 1 (ft), 1 (pt); Dietitians 1 (pt); Ophthalmologists 1 (pt); Dentists 1 (pt).
Facilities Dining room; Physical therapy room; Activities room; Crafts room; Barber/Beauty shop.
Activities Arts & crafts; Cards; Games; Reading groups; Prayer groups; Movies; Shopping trips; Dances/Social/Cultural gatherings; Rhythm band.

Oregon City Care Center Inc
148 Hood St, Oregon City, OR 97045
(503) 656-4035
Admin Paul Johnson.
Medical Dir Dr Julian Markin.
Licensure Intermediate care; Day care. *Beds* ICF 53; Day care 5. *Certified* Medicaid.
Admissions Requirements Physician's request.
Staff RNs 1 (ft); LPNs 6 (ft); Nurses' aides 22 (ft); Activities coordinators 1 (ft); Dietitians 1 (pt); Podiatrists 1 (pt); Dentists 1 (pt).
Facilities Dining room; Activities room; Crafts room; Laundry room; Barber/Beauty shop.
Activities Arts & crafts; Games; Prayer groups; Movies; Shopping trips.

Sierra Vista Care Center
1680 Molalla Ave, Oregon City, OR 97045
(503) 655-2588
Admin Ans Van Gent.
Licensure Intermediate care. *Beds* ICF 102. *Certified* Medicaid.
Admissions Requirements Medical examination; Physician's request.
Staff Physicians 5 (pt); RNs 3 (ft); LPNs 6 (ft); Nurses' aides 35 (ft), 10 (pt); Physical therapists 1 (pt); Recreational therapists 1 (pt); Speech therapists 1 (pt); Activities coordinators 1 (ft); Dietitians 1 (pt).
Facilities Dining room; Activities room; Crafts room; Laundry room; Barber/Beauty shop.
Activities Arts & crafts; Movies; Shopping trips.

Pendleton

Amber Valley Care Center
707 SW 37th St, Pendleton, OR 97801
(503) 276-3374
Admin Harold Delamarter.
Licensure Intermediate care; Respite care; Day care. *Beds* ICF 84; Respite care 6; Day care 4. *Certified* Medicaid.

Delamarter Care Center
Rte 1 Box 35, Pendleton, OR 97801
(503) 276-7157, 276-3093 FAX
Admin Elizabeth Delamarter RN BSN. *Dir of Nursing* Delores McLaren RN. *Medical Dir* Dale Brandt MD.
Licensure Skilled care; Intermediate care; Alzheimer's care; Child day care. *Beds* SNF 14; ICF 54. *Private Pay Patients* 46%. *Certified* Medicaid; Medicare.
Owner Proprietary corp (Care Center Inc).
Admissions Requirements Medical examination; Physician's request.
Staff Physicians 4 (pt); RNs 4 (ft), 2 (pt); LPNs 4 (ft), 1 (pt); Physical therapists 2 (pt); Recreational therapists 1 (ft); Occupational therapists 1 (pt); Speech therapists 1 (pt);

Activities coordinators 1 (ft); Dietitians 1 (pt); Ophthalmologists 1 (pt); Podiatrists 1 (pt).
Languages Spanish.
Facilities Dining room; Physical therapy room; Activities room; Crafts room; Laundry room; Barber/Beauty shop; Library.
Activities Arts & crafts; Cards; Games; Reading groups; Prayer groups; Movies; Shopping trips; Dances/Social/Cultural gatherings; Intergenerational programs; Pet therapy.

Portland

Baptist Manor
900 NE 81st Ave, Portland, OR 97213
(503) 255-0860
Admin Lawrence G Bienert. *Dir of Nursing* Lois Williamson.
Licensure Intermediate care; Retirement. *Beds* ICF 94; Retirement 100. *Private Pay Patients* 80%.
Owner Nonprofit corp.
Admissions Requirements Medical examination; Physician's request.
Staff RNs 4 (ft), 3 (pt); LPNs 7 (ft), 4 (pt); Nurses' aides 32 (ft), 2 (pt); Activities coordinators 1 (ft), 1 (pt); Dietitians 1 (ft).
Languages German, Spanish.
Affiliation Baptist.
Facilities Dining room; Activities room; Chapel; Crafts room; Laundry room; Barber/Beauty shop; Library.
Activities Arts & crafts; Cards; Games; Reading groups; Prayer groups; Movies; Dances/Social/Cultural gatherings; Pet therapy.

Care Center East
11325 NE Weidler, Portland, OR 97220
(503) 253-1181
Admin Richard Herington.
Licensure Intermediate care. *Beds* ICF 93. *Certified* Medicaid.

Care West Nursing Center
2250 NW Kearney St, Portland, OR 97210
(503) 224-3910
Admin Dan Wellman.
Licensure Skilled care; Intermediate care. *Beds* SNF 49; ICF 83. *Certified* Medicaid; Medicare.

Cascade Terrace Nursing Center
5601 SE 122, Portland, OR 97236
(503) 761-3181
Admin Charles D Fogg. *Dir of Nursing* Juni Bailey. *Medical Dir* Dr Fennesseey.
Licensure Intermediate care; Retirement; Residential care. *Beds* ICF 95; Residential care 10. *Certified* Medicaid.
Owner Proprietary corp.
Staff RNs; LPNs; Nurses' aides; Physical therapists; Occupational therapists; Speech therapists; Activities coordinators; Dietitians.
Facilities Dining room; Physical therapy room; Activities room; Chapel; Crafts room; Laundry room; Barber/Beauty shop.
Activities Arts & crafts; Cards; Games; Reading groups; Prayer groups; Movies; Shopping trips; Dances/Social/Cultural gatherings.

Centennial Health Care Center
725 SE 202nd Ave, Portland, OR 97233
(503) 665-3118
Admin Ray Finch. *Dir of Nursing* Faith Schiell.
Licensure Skilled care; Intermediate care. *Beds* SNF 20; ICF 86. *Certified* Medicaid; Medicare.
Owner Proprietary corp (Beverly Enterprises).
Admissions Requirements Medical examination.
Staff RNs; LPNs; Nurses' aides; Activities coordinators; Dietitians.

Facilities Dining room; Physical therapy room; Activities room; Chapel; Laundry room; Barber/Beauty shop.
Activities Arts & crafts; Cards; Games; Reading groups; Prayer groups; Movies; Shopping trips; Dances/Social/Cultural gatherings.

Columbia Manor Convalescent Center
6010 SW Shattuck Rd, Portland, OR 97221
(503) 246-8811
Admin Eleanor M Johnson.
Medical Dir William Spisak MD.
Licensure Intermediate care; Respite care. *Beds* ICF 102; Respite care 3. *Certified* Medicaid.
Admissions Requirements Medical examination; Physician's request.
Staff RNs 2 (ft); LPNs 6 (ft); Reality therapists 1 (ft); Recreational therapists 1 (ft); Activities coordinators 1 (ft).
Facilities Dining room; Activities room; Crafts room; Laundry room; Barber/Beauty shop; Library.
Activities Arts & crafts; Cards; Games; Reading groups; Prayer groups; Movies; Shopping trips; Dances/Social/Cultural gatherings.

Crestview Convalescent
6530 SW 30th Ave, Portland, OR 97201
(503) 244-7533
Admin Jean Glanz.
Licensure Skilled care; Intermediate care. *Beds* SNF 28; ICF 79. *Certified* Medicare.

Del's Care Center Inc
319 NE Russett, Portland, OR 97211
(503) 289-5571
Admin Lin Neff. *Dir of Nursing* Barbara Olsen RN. *Medical Dir* David Klubert MD.
Licensure Skilled care; Intermediate care. *Beds* SNF 10; ICF 80. *Private Pay Patients* 25%. *Certified* Medicaid; Medicare.
Owner Proprietary corp (Prestige Care).
Staff RNs 3 (ft); LPNs 4 (ft); Nurses' aides 20 (ft); Activities coordinators 1 (ft), 1 (pt).
Facilities Dining room; Physical therapy room; Activities room; Laundry room; Barber/Beauty shop.
Activities Arts & crafts; Games; Reading groups; Prayer groups; Movies; Dances/Social/Cultural gatherings; Intergenerational programs; Pet therapy.

Fernhill Manor
5737 NE 37th, Portland, OR 97211
(503) 288-5967
Admin Caroline Schie. *Dir of Nursing* Ruth McKeown. *Medical Dir* Dr Wilcox.
Licensure Intermediate care. *Beds* ICF 63. *Certified* Medicaid.
Owner Proprietary corp.
Facilities Dining room; Activities room; Laundry room; Barber/Beauty shop; Library.
Activities Arts & crafts; Cards; Games; Reading groups; Prayer groups; Movies.

Friendship Health Center
3320 SE Holgate, Portland, OR 97202
(503) 231-1411
Admin Harvey Young.
Medical Dir H Lenox H Dick MD.
Licensure Skilled care; Intermediate care. *Beds* SNF 55; ICF 45. *Certified* Medicaid; Medicare.
Admissions Requirements Minimum age 18; Medical examination.
Staff Physicians 5 (pt); RNs 12 (ft), 5 (pt); LPNs 5 (ft), 4 (pt); Nurses' aides 47 (ft), 13 (pt); Physical therapists 1 (ft); Recreational therapists 2 (ft); Occupational therapists 1 (pt); Speech therapists 1 (pt); Dietitians 1 (ft); Podiatrists 1 (pt); Audiologists 1 (pt); Dentists 1 (pt).
Facilities Dining room; Physical therapy room; Activities room; Chapel; Crafts room; Laundry room; Barber/Beauty shop; Library.

Activities Arts & crafts; Cards; Games; Reading groups; Prayer groups; Movies; Shopping trips; Dances/Social/Cultural gatherings.

Gateway Care Center
39 NE 102nd Ave, Portland, OR 97220
(503) 252-2461, 254-6918 FAX
Admin Daniel Harding RRT. *Dir of Nursing* Cindi Thornton RN. *Medical Dir* Richard Orth DO.
Licensure Intermediate care; Residential care; Retirement. *Beds* ICF 46; Residential care 15; Retirement 23. *Private Pay Patients* 50%. *Certified* Medicaid.
Owner Proprietary corp.
Admissions Requirements Medical examination; Physician's request.
Staff Physicians 1 (pt); RNs 3 (ft); LPNs 2 (pt); Nurses' aides 20 (ft), 2 (pt); Activities coordinators 1 (ft); Dietitians 1 (pt); Podiatrists 1 (pt); Respiratory therapists (consultant).
Facilities Dining room; Physical therapy room; Activities room; Crafts room; Laundry room; Barber/Beauty shop; Chronic pulmonary and cardiac problems program.
Activities Arts & crafts; Games; Reading groups; Prayer groups; Movies; Dances/Social/Cultural gatherings; Pet therapy.

Glisan Care Center Inc
9750 NE Glisan St, Portland, OR 97220
(503) 256-3920
Admin Julie Carlson.
Medical Dir Bonnie Butler.
Licensure Skilled care; Intermediate care; Retirement; Alzheimer's care. *Beds* SNF 25; ICF 75. *Certified* Medicaid; Medicare.
Owner Proprietary corp (Care Center Inc).
Admissions Requirements Physician's request.
Staff RNs 4 (ft), 2 (pt); LPNs 5 (ft), 1 (pt); Nurses' aides 39 (ft), 3 (pt); Physical therapists 2 (ft); Reality therapists 1 (ft); Recreational therapists 1 (ft); Occupational therapists 1 (ft); Speech therapists 1 (ft); Activities coordinators 1 (ft); Dietitians 1 (pt).
Languages Japanese.
Facilities Dining room; Physical therapy room; Activities room; Crafts room; Barber/Beauty shop.
Activities Arts & crafts; Cards; Games; Reading groups; Prayer groups; Movies; Shopping trips; Dances/Social/Cultural gatherings.

Graystone Manor Convalescent Center
12640 SE Bush, Portland, OR 97236
(503) 761-6621
Admin Lily Diamalanta.
Licensure Intermediate care. *Beds* ICF 36. *Certified* Medicaid.

Gracelen Terrace Care Center
10948 SE Boise St, Portland, OR 97266
(503) 760-1727
Admin Linda M Glidden.
Medical Dir Dr Julia Markin.
Licensure Intermediate care; Alzheimer's care. *Beds* ICF 80. *Certified* Medicaid.
Owner Proprietary corp.
Staff Physicians 1 (ft); RNs 4 (ft); LPNs 3 (ft); Nurses' aides 63 (ft), 12 (pt); Physical therapists 1 (ft); Reality therapists 1 (ft); Recreational therapists 1 (ft); Activities coordinators 1 (ft); Dietitians 1 (ft); Ophthalmologists 1 (ft); Podiatrists 1 (ft); Dentists 1 (ft).
Facilities Dining room; Activities room; Crafts room; Laundry room; Barber/Beauty shop; Library; Patio; Yard.
Activities Arts & crafts; Cards; Games; Reading groups; Prayer groups; Movies; Shopping trips; Dances/Social/Cultural gatherings; Community events.

Hillside Convalescent Inc
800 NW 25th, Portland, OR 97210
(503) 224-0535
Admin JoAnn Bavier RN. *Dir of Nursing* Lisa Claunch RN. *Medical Dir* David Perry MD.
Licensure Intermediate care. *Beds* ICF 25. *Private Pay Patients* 100%.
Owner Proprietary corp.
Staff RNs; LPNs; Nurses' aides; Physical therapists; Occupational therapists (consultant); Activities coordinators; Dietitians (consultant); Podiatrists (consultant).
Facilities Dining room; Activities room; Barber/Beauty shop; Private rooms only.
Activities Arts & crafts; Cards; Games; Reading groups; Prayer groups; Pet therapy.

Holladay Park Medical Center Skilled Nursing Facility Unit
1224 NE 2nd Ave, Portland, OR 97232
(503) 233-4567
Admin Edwin Gante.
Licensure Long term care. *Beds* Long term care 24.

Holladay Park Plaza
1300 NE 16th Ave, Portland, OR 97232
(503) 288-6671
Admin Kathleen A Park. *Dir of Nursing* Marian Danley RN.
Licensure Intermediate care; Retirement. *Beds* ICF 33.
Owner Nonprofit corp.
Admissions Requirements Minimum age 62; Physician's request.
Staff RNs 3 (ft), 5 (pt); LPNs 1 (pt); Nurses' aides 8 (ft), 8 (pt); Activities coordinators 1 (ft); Dietitians 1 (ft).
Affiliation Presbyterian.
Facilities Dining room; Physical therapy room; Chapel; Barber/Beauty shop; Library.
Activities Arts & crafts; Cards; Games; Reading groups; Prayer groups; Movies; Shopping trips; Dances/Social/Cultural gatherings; Pleasure trips; Cooking sessions; Good grooming sessions.

House of Care
PO Box 66130, 6003 SE 136th, Portland, OR 97266
(503) 761-1155
Admin Janice Hill. *Dir of Nursing* Russ Shannon RN. *Medical Dir* Edward R Tallman MD.
Licensure Intermediate care; Residential care; Alzheimer's care. *Beds* ICF 76; Residential care 66. *Private Pay Patients* 80%. *Certified* Medicaid.
Owner Privately owned.
Staff Physicians 2 (pt); RNs 2 (ft); LPNs 6 (ft); Nurses' aides 36 (ft); Activities coordinators 4 (ft); Dietitians 1 (pt).
Facilities Dining room; Activities room; Crafts room; Barber/Beauty shop.
Activities Arts & crafts; Cards; Games; Reading groups; Prayer groups; Movies; Shopping trips; Dances/Social/Cultural gatherings; Pet therapy.

Karrington Care Center
PO Box 16159, Portland, OR 97233
(503) 255-7040
Admin Tom Pollock Temp.
Medical Dir Estill Deitz.
Licensure Intermediate care; Day/Respite care. *Beds* ICF 105; Day/Respite care 5. *Certified* Medicaid.
Admissions Requirements Medical examination; Physician's request.
Staff RNs 4 (ft), 1 (pt); LPNs 4 (ft), 1 (pt); Nurses' aides 34 (ft), 2 (pt); Activities coordinators 1 (ft).
Facilities Dining room; Activities room; Laundry room.
Activities Arts & crafts; Games; Prayer groups; Movies.

Laurelhurst Care Center
2827 SE Salmon St, Portland, OR 97214
(503) 232-8504
Admin James Dodd.
Medical Dir Stephen Jones MD.
Licensure Intermediate care. *Beds* ICF 85.
 Certified Medicaid.
Owner Proprietary corp (Beverly Enterprises).
Admissions Requirements Physician's request.
Staff RNs 4 (ft); LPNs 2 (ft); Nurses' aides 20
 (ft); Activities coordinators 1 (ft).
Facilities Dining room; Physical therapy
 room; Activities room; Laundry room;
 Barber/Beauty shop; Solarium.
Activities Arts & crafts; Cards; Games;
 Reading groups; Prayer groups; Movies.

Lawrence Convalescent Center
812 SE 48th, Portland, OR 97215
(503) 236-2624
Admin Jessie Curtis.
Medical Dir Martha Gail DO.
Licensure Intermediate care. *Beds* ICF 40.
 Certified Medicaid.
Admissions Requirements Medical
 examination; Physician's request.
Staff RNs 1 (ft); LPNs 2 (ft), 1 (pt); Nurses'
 aides 22 (ft); Reality therapists 1 (ft);
 Recreational therapists 1 (ft); Occupational
 therapists 1 (pt); Speech therapists 1 (pt);
 Activities coordinators 1 (ft); Dietitians 1
 (pt); Podiatrists 1 (pt); Dentists 1 (pt).
Facilities Dining room; Laundry room;
 Barber/Beauty shop.
Activities Arts & crafts; Games; Prayer groups;
 Movies.

Menlo Park Health Care Center
745 NE 122nd Ave, Portland, OR 97230
(503) 252-0241
Admin Judy Dove. *Dir of Nursing* Esther
 Murphy RN. *Medical Dir* T Hickerson MD.
Licensure Skilled care; Intermediate care. *Beds*
 SNF 12; ICF 71. *Certified* Medicaid;
 Medicare.
Owner Proprietary corp.
Admissions Requirements Medical
 examination; Physician's request.
Staff RNs 4 (ft), 7 (pt); LPNs 2 (ft), 1 (pt);
 Nurses' aides 25 (ft); Activities coordinators
 1 (ft).
Facilities Dining room; Physical therapy
 room; Activities room; Crafts room; Laundry
 room; Barber/Beauty shop; Library.
Activities Arts & crafts; Cards; Games;
 Reading groups; Prayer groups; Movies;
 Dances/Social/Cultural gatherings.

Midway Care Center Inc
5601 SE 122nd, Portland, OR 97236
(503) 761-3181
Admin Antonette Petrecca.
Licensure Intermediate care. *Beds* 43.
 Certified Medicaid.

Bishop Morris Care Center
2430 NW Marshall, Portland, OR 97210
(503) 227-3791
Admin John Allen. *Dir of Nursing* Kenda
 Carter RN. *Medical Dir* Stephen R Jones
 MD.
Licensure Intermediate care; Alzheimer's care.
 Beds ICF 110. *Certified* Medicaid.
Owner Proprietary corp (Hillhaven Corp).
Admissions Requirements Medical
 examination.
Staff Physicians; RNs; LPNs; Nurses' aides;
 Physical therapists; Reality therapists;
 Recreational therapists; Occupational
 therapists; Speech therapists; Activities
 coordinators; Dietitians.
Affiliation Episcopal.
Activities Arts & crafts; Cards; Games;
 Reading groups; Prayer groups; Movies;
 Shopping trips; Dances/Social/Cultural
 gatherings.

**Mt St Joseph Residence & Extended Care
Center**
3060 SE Stark St, Portland, OR 97214
(503) 232-6193, 235-2772 FAX
Admin James E Bagley. *Dir of Nursing*
 Carolyn Love RN. *Medical Dir* Charles
 Darby MD.
Licensure Skilled care; Intermediate care;
 Residential care; Respite care. *Beds* SNF 22;
 ICF 168; Residential care 99. *Private Pay
 Patients* 60%. *Certified* Medicaid; Medicare.
Owner Nonprofit corp (Sisters of Mercy).
Admissions Requirements Medical
 examination; Physician's request.
Languages Spanish, Cambodian, Filipino,
 Rumanian.
Affiliation Roman Catholic.
Facilities Dining room; Physical therapy
 room; Activities room; Chapel; Crafts room;
 Laundry room; Barber/Beauty shop; Gift
 shop.
Activities Arts & crafts; Cards; Games;
 Reading groups; Prayer groups; Movies;
 Shopping trips; Dances/Social/Cultural
 gatherings; Intergenerational programs; Pet
 therapy.

Mt Tabor Care Center
7100 SE Division, Portland, OR 97206
(503) 775-8601
Admin David Johnson.
Medical Dir Richard Orth DO.
Licensure Intermediate care; Alzheimer's care.
 Beds ICF 120. *Certified* Medicaid.
Owner Proprietary corp (American Health
 Care Inc).
Admissions Requirements Medical
 examination; Physician's request.
Staff RNs 4 (ft), 2 (pt); LPNs 5 (ft), 2 (pt);
 Nurses' aides 27 (ft), 15 (pt); Restorative
 aides.
Facilities Dining room; Physical therapy
 room; Activities room; Laundry room.
Activities Arts & crafts; Cards; Games;
 Reading groups; Prayer groups; Movies;
 Shopping trips; Dances/Social/Cultural
 gatherings.

Park Forest Care Center
8643 NE Beech St, Portland, OR 97220
(503) 256-2151
Admin David Park.
Licensure Intermediate care; Day care. *Beds*
 ICF 43; Day care 15. *Certified* Medicaid.

Park View Care Center Inc
2425 SW 6th Ave, Portland, OR 97201
(503) 228-6684
Admin Marion Wilson.
Licensure Skilled care; Intermediate care. *Beds*
 SNF 24; ICF 78. *Certified* Medicare.

Parkrose Nursing Home
10336 NE Wygant, Portland, OR 97220
(503) 255-7677
Admin Bernie Hartnell.
Medical Dir Sharon Faulk.
Licensure Skilled care; Intermediate care. *Beds*
 SNF 24; ICF 34. *Certified* Medicaid;
 Medicare.
Admissions Requirements Minimum age 14;
 Medical examination; Physician's request.
Staff RNs 3 (ft); LPNs 2 (ft); Nurses' aides 14
 (ft), 5 (pt); Activities coordinators 1 (ft).
Facilities Dining room.
Activities Arts & crafts; Cards; Games;
 Reading groups; Prayer groups; Movies;
 Dances/Social/Cultural gatherings;
 Individualized activities.

Porthaven Care Center
5330 NE Prescott, Portland, OR 97218
(503) 288-6585
Admin Jacquelyn H Janes. *Dir of Nursing*
 Jean Lynch. *Medical Dir* Dr Wiebe.
Licensure Skilled care; Retirement. *Beds* SNF
 99; Retirement 100. *Private Pay Patients*
 90%. *Certified* Medicaid; Medicare.

Owner Proprietary corp (Hesco Inc).
Admissions Requirements Medical
 examination; Physician's request.
Staff RNs 15 (ft); LPNs 3 (ft); Nurses' aides
 32 (ft); Physical therapists 1 (ft);
 Recreational therapists 1 (ft); Occupational
 therapists 1 (ft); Speech therapists 1 (ft);
 Activities coordinators 1 (ft); Dietitians 1
 (pt).
Facilities Dining room; Physical therapy
 room; Activities room; Laundry room;
 Barber/Beauty shop.
Activities Arts & crafts; Cards; Games;
 Reading groups; Prayer groups; Movies;
 Shopping trips; Intergenerational programs;
 Pet therapy.

Portland Adventist Convalescent Center
6040 SE Belmont, Portland, OR 97215
(503) 231-7166
Admin Harley Clendenon. *Dir of Nursing*
 Judy DePrada. *Medical Dir* John Griffin
 MD.
Licensure Skilled care; Intermediate care; Day
 care. *Beds* SNF 85; ICF 90; Day care 15.
 Certified Medicaid; Medicare.
Owner Nonprofit corp (Adventist Health Sys-
 USA).
Admissions Requirements Minimum age 2;
 Medical examination; Physician's request.
Staff Physicians 1 (pt); RNs 11 (ft), 16 (pt);
 LPNs 13 (ft), 20 (pt); Nurses' aides 63 (ft),
 16 (pt); Physical therapists 2 (ft), 3 (pt);
 Occupational therapists 1 (ft), 1 (pt); Speech
 therapists 1 (ft), 1 (pt); Activities
 coordinators 1 (ft); Dietitians 1 (pt).
Languages Spanish.
Affiliation Seventh-Day Adventist.
Activities Arts & crafts; Cards; Games;
 Reading groups; Prayer groups; Movies;
 Shopping trips; Dances/Social/Cultural
 gatherings.

Powellhurst Nursing Home
13033 SE Holgate Blvd, Portland, OR 97236
(503) 761-1533
Admin Peter Snoey.
Medical Dir Martha Gail DO.
Licensure Intermediate care. *Beds* ICF 77.
 Certified Medicaid.
Owner Proprietary corp (Beverly Enterprises).
Facilities Dining room; Physical therapy
 room; Activities room; Crafts room; Laundry
 room; Barber/Beauty shop.
Activities Arts & crafts; Cards; Games;
 Reading groups; Prayer groups; Movies;
 Shopping trips; Dances/Social/Cultural
 gatherings.

Providence Children's Nursing Center
830 NE 47th Ave, Portland, OR 97213
(503) 234-9991
Admin Charles Hawley, Temp.
Medical Dir Margaret M Wayson MD.
Licensure Intermediate care. *Beds* ICF 54.
 Certified Medicaid.
Owner Proprietary corp (Sisters of Providence
 Healthcare).
Admissions Requirements Medical
 examination; Physician's request.
Staff Physicians 1 (pt); RNs 6 (ft), 6 (pt);
 LPNs 3 (ft); Nurses' aides 40 (ft), 28 (pt);
 Physical therapists 1 (pt); Speech therapists
 1 (ft); Activities coordinators 1 (ft);
 Dietitians 1 (ft), 2 (pt).
Affiliation Roman Catholic.
Facilities Physical therapy room; Activities
 room; Chapel; Laundry room.
Activities Games; Reading groups; Shopping
 trips; Dances/Social/Cultural gatherings;
 Outings; Swimming.

**Providence Medical Center Skilled Nursing
Facility**
4805 NE Glisan, Portland, OR 97213
(503) 230-1111

Admin John P Lee. *Dir of Nursing* Dolores
Dolan RN. *Medical Dir* Patrick Fitzgerald
MD.
Licensure Skilled care. *Beds* SNF 20. *Private
Pay Patients* 0%. *Certified* Medicaid;
Medicare.
Owner Nonprofit organization/foundation.
Admissions Requirements Physician's request.
Staff RNs 3 (ft), 4 (pt); LPNs 2 (ft), 1 (pt);
Nurses' aides 5 (ft), 3 (pt); Physical
therapists 1 (pt); Recreational therapists 1
(pt); Occupational therapists 1 (pt); Speech
therapists 1 (pt); Dietitians 1 (pt).
Languages Language pool available.
Affiliation Roman Catholic.
Facilities Dining room; Physical therapy
room; Activities room; Chapel; Crafts room;
Laundry room; Library.
Activities Arts & crafts; Cards; Games;
Reading groups; Prayer groups; Dances/
Social/Cultural gatherings; Pet therapy;
Exercise groups; Cooking groups.

Raleigh Care Center
6630 SW Beaverton-Hillsdale Hwy, Portland,
OR 97225
(503) 292-4488
Admin Stan Smith.
Medical Dir Juliana Markin MD.
Licensure Intermediate care. *Beds* ICF 90.
Certified Medicaid.
Owner Proprietary corp (Beverly Enterprises).
Staff Physicians 1 (pt); RNs 4 (ft), 1 (pt);
LPNs 3 (ft), 3 (pt); Nurses' aides 20 (ft), 25
(pt); Physical therapists 1 (pt); Speech
therapists 1 (pt); Activities coordinators 1
(ft); Dietitians 1 (pt); Podiatrists 1 (pt);
Dentists 1 (pt).
Facilities Dining room; Physical therapy
room; Activities room; Laundry room;
Barber/Beauty shop.
Activities Arts & crafts; Cards; Games;
Reading groups; Prayer groups; Movies;
Shopping trips; Dances/Social/Cultural
gatherings.

Reedwood Extended Care Center
3540 SE Francis St, Portland, OR 97202
(503) 232-5767
Admin Alice R Nelson; Julie Harris, Asst. *Dir
of Nursing* Ofelia dela Rosa.
Licensure Skilled care. *Beds* SNF 65. *Certified*
Medicare.
Owner Proprietary corp.
Admissions Requirements Minimum age 18.
Staff Physicians 1 (pt); RNs 5 (ft), 3 (pt);
LPNs 1 (ft), 2 (pt); Nurses' aides 26 (ft), 2
(pt); Physical therapists 1 (pt); Occupational
therapists 1 (pt); Speech therapists 1 (pt);
Activities coordinators 1 (ft); Dietitians 1
(pt); Podiatrists 1 (pt).
Facilities Dining room; Physical therapy
room; Activities room; Chapel; Laundry
room; Solarium.
Activities Arts & crafts; Cards; Games;
Reading groups; Prayer groups; Movies; Pet
therapy.

Robison Jewish Home
6125 SW Boundary St, Portland, OR 97221
(503) 246-7706, 228-5816 FAX
Admin Al A Mendlovitz, Exec Dir; Linda
Duggan, Asst. *Dir of Nursing* Linda Duggan,
Acting. *Medical Dir* Sam Miller MD.
Licensure Skilled care; Intermediate care;
Residential care; Retirement; Alzheimer's
care; Hospice. *Beds* Swing beds SNF/ICF 88;
Residential 35; Retirement apartments 20.
Private Pay Patients 32%. *Certified*
Medicaid; Medicare.
Owner Nonprofit organization/foundation.
Admissions Requirements Minimum age 65;
Medical examination.
Staff Physicians 2 (pt); RNs 16 (ft); LPNs 15
(ft); Nurses' aides 52 (ft); Physical therapists
3 (ft), 1 (pt); Occupational therapists 1 (ft), 1

(pt); Speech therapists 1 (pt); Activities
coordinators 3 (ft), 2 (pt); Dietitians 1 (ft);
Podiatrists 1 (pt); Audiologists 1 (pt).
Languages Yiddish, Hebrew, Spanish.
Affiliation Jewish.
Facilities Physical therapy room; Activities
room; Chapel; Crafts room; Barber/Beauty
shop; Library; Auditorium; Kosher kitchen;
5 Dining rooms; Alzheimer's unit;
Rehabilitation unit; Hospice unit.
Activities Arts & crafts; Cards; Games;
Reading groups; Prayer groups; Movies;
Shopping trips; Dances/Social/Cultural
gatherings; Intergenerational programs; Pet
therapy; Reminiscing; Music groups; Drama;
Volunteer program.

Rose City Nursing Home
34 NE 20th Ave, Portland, OR 97232
(503) 231-0276
Admin Harry Geistlinger.
Medical Dir Dr Gerald Durris.
Licensure Intermediate care. *Beds* ICF 30.
Certified Medicaid.
Staff Physicians; RNs 1 (ft), 4 (pt); LPNs 2
(ft), 2 (pt); Nurses' aides 15 (ft); Activities
coordinators 1 (ft).
Facilities Dining room; Activities room;
Laundry room; Barber/Beauty shop.
Activities Arts & crafts; Cards; Games;
Reading groups; Prayer groups; Movies;
Shopping trips; Dances/Social/Cultural
gatherings.

Seaside Care Center
111 SW Columbia, No 725, Portland, OR
97201-5862
(503) 738-8383
Admin Eleanor M Johnson. *Dir of Nursing*
Linda Briggs RN.
Licensure Intermediate care. *Beds* ICF 100.
Certified Medicaid.
Owner Proprietary corp (Summit Health Ltd).
Admissions Requirements Minimum age 18;
Medical examination; Physician's request.
Staff Physicians; RNs; LPNs; Nurses' aides;
Physical therapists; Reality therapists;
Activities coordinators; Dietitians.
Facilities Dining room; Physical therapy
room; Activities room; Crafts room; Laundry
room; Barber/Beauty shop.
Activities Arts & crafts; Cards; Games;
Reading groups; Prayer groups; Movies;
Dances/Social/Cultural gatherings.

Sunny Vista Care Center
10435 SE Cora St, Portland, OR 97266
(503) 760-1737
Admin Theresa M Heis. *Dir of Nursing*
Phyllis Bell RN. *Medical Dir* Dr Lombos.
Licensure Intermediate care; Alzheimer's unit.
Beds ICF 53. *Private Pay Patients* 100%.
Owner Proprietary corp (National Heritage).
Admissions Requirements Medical
examination; Physician's request.
Staff RNs 3 (ft); LPNs 4 (ft); Nurses' aides 16
(ft); Activities coordinators 1 (ft).
Languages Spanish.
Facilities Dining room; Activities room;
Crafts room; Laundry room; Barber/Beauty
shop; Library; Enclosed-secure garden/
courtyard.
Activities Arts & crafts; Cards; Games;
Reading groups; Prayer groups; Movies;
Dances/Social/Cultural gatherings;
Intergenerational programs; Pet therapy.

Tabor Villa Inc
4914 SE Belmont St, Portland, OR 97215
(503) 235-3179
Admin Sandra Wood. *Dir of Nursing* Baya
Young. *Medical Dir* Carl Wilcox MD.
Licensure Intermediate care; Alzheimer's care.
Beds ICF 59. *Certified* Medicaid.
Owner Privately owned.

Staff RNs 2 (ft); LPNs 3 (ft), 2 (pt); Nurses'
aides 26 (ft); Recreational therapists 1 (ft), 1
(pt); Activities coordinators 1 (ft), 1 (pt);
Dietitians 1 (ft).
Facilities Dining room; Activities room;
Crafts room; Laundry room; Barber/Beauty
shop; Library.
Activities Arts & crafts; Cards; Games;
Reading groups; Prayer groups; Movies;
Shopping trips; Dances/Social/Cultural
gatherings.

Terwilliger Plaza Inc
2545 SW Terwilliger Blvd, Portland, OR
97201
(503) 226-4911
Admin Mark Hammer. *Dir of Nursing*
Carmen Lawson RN.
Licensure Intermediate care; Retirement. *Beds*
ICF 9.
Owner Nonprofit corp.
Admissions Requirements Must be a member
of Terwilliger Plaza.
Staff RNs 1 (pt); LPNs 6 (pt); Nurses' aides 1
(ft), 6 (pt); Activities coordinators;
Dietitians; Ophthalmologists.
Activities Arts & crafts; Cards; Games;
Reading groups; Prayer groups.

Tri-City Health Care Center
8323 SE Franklin, Portland, OR 97266
(503) 656-1646
Admin Maureen Kehoe.
Licensure Intermediate care. *Beds* ICF 126.
Certified Medicaid.
Owner Proprietary corp (Beverly Enterprises).

Victoria Nursing Home
3339 SE Division St, Portland, OR 97202
(503) 235-4135
Admin Esther Pearson.
Licensure Intermediate care. *Beds* 44.
Certified Medicaid.

West Hills Convalescent Center
5701 SW Multnomah Blvd, Portland, OR
97219
(503) 244-1107
Admin Bill Danner.
Medical Dir Hester Fieldhouse MD.
Licensure Skilled care; Intermediate care; Day
care. *Beds* SNF 20; ICF 140; Day care 10.
Certified Medicaid; Medicare.
Admissions Requirements Physician's request.
Staff RNs 10 (ft); LPNs 6 (ft); Nurses' aides
35 (ft); Physical therapists 2 (ft);
Recreational therapists 1 (pt); Speech
therapists 1 (pt); Activities coordinators 1
(ft); Dietitians 1 (pt).
Facilities Dining room; Physical therapy
room; Activities room; Crafts room; Laundry
room; Barber/Beauty shop; Library.
Activities Arts & crafts; Cards; Games;
Reading groups; Prayer groups; Movies;
Shopping trips; Dances/Social/Cultural
gatherings.

Willamette Nursing Home Inc
3125 N Willamette Blvd, Portland, OR 97217
(503) 285-8334
Admin Miriam M Drake.
Licensure Intermediate care. *Beds* 43.
Certified Medicaid.

Prairie City

Blue Mountain Nursing Home
112 E 5th St, Prairie City, OR 97869
(503) 820-3541
Admin Phyllis McCarthy.
Licensure Intermediate care. *Beds* ICF 52.
Certified Medicaid.
Admissions Requirements Minimum age 16;
Medical examination; Physician's request.
Staff RNs 2 (ft), 1 (pt); LPNs 1 (ft), 1 (pt);
Nurses' aides 18 (ft), 2 (pt); Occupational
therapists 1 (pt); Activities coordinators 1
(ft), 1 (pt).

Facilities Dining room; Physical therapy room; Activities room; Laundry room; Barber/Beauty shop.
Activities Cards; Games; Reading groups; Prayer groups; Movies; Shopping trips; Dances/Social/Cultural gatherings.

Prineville

Crook County Nursing Home
1201 N Elm, Prineville, OR 97754
(503) 447-1287
Admin Jose A Gorbea. *Dir of Nursing* Craig Wilson RN.
Licensure Intermediate care; Residential care. *Beds* 42.
Owner Publicly owned.
Admissions Requirements Medical examination; Physician's request.
Staff RNs 3 (ft); LPNs 3 (ft), 5 (pt); Nurses' aides 9 (ft), 5 (pt); Activities coordinators 1 (ft), 1 (pt); Dietitians 1 (ft).
Facilities Dining room; Activities room; Chapel; Crafts room; Laundry room; Barber/Beauty shop; Library; Sun room.
Activities Arts & crafts; Cards; Games; Reading groups; Prayer groups; Movies; Shopping trips; Dances/Social/Cultural gatherings; Outdoor activity.

Ochoco Nursing Home
950 N Elm, Prineville, OR 97754
(503) 447-7667
Admin Tim Brown. *Dir of Nursing* Dorothy Robertson. *Medical Dir* Dr Rinehart.
Licensure Intermediate care; Retirement. *Beds* ICF 63; Retirement 20. *Certified* Medicaid.
Owner Proprietary corp (ARJO Enterprises Inc).
Admissions Requirements Physician's request.
Staff RNs 1 (ft), 1 (pt); LPNs 5 (ft), 2 (pt); Nurses' aides 19 (ft), 2 (pt); Activities coordinators 1 (ft); Dietitians 1 (pt).
Languages Spanish.
Affiliation Kiwanis Club.
Facilities Dining room; Physical therapy room; Activities room; Laundry room; Barber/Beauty shop.
Activities Arts & crafts; Games; Reading groups; Prayer groups; Movies; Shopping trips; Dances/Social/Cultural gatherings; Pet therapy.

Redmond

Opportunity Foundation of Central Oregon
605 E Evergreen, Redmond, OR 97756
(503) 548-8444
Admin John Halstead.
Medical Dir Laura Brown.
Licensure Intermediate care for mentally retarded. *Beds* ICF/MR 16. *Certified* Medicaid.
Owner Nonprofit organization/foundation.
Admissions Requirements Minimum age 18; Medical examination.
Staff RNs 1 (ft); LPNs 7 (ft); Recreational therapists 1 (ft).
Facilities Dining room; Activities room; Laundry room.
Activities Arts & crafts; Cards; Games; Movies; Shopping trips; Dances/Social/Cultural gatherings.

Redmond Health Care Center
3025 SW Reservoir Dr, Redmond, OR 97756
(503) 548-5066
Admin Randall Arnett. *Dir of Nursing* Shelia Dwiggins. *Medical Dir* Dr James Detwiler.
Licensure Intermediate care. *Beds* ICF 67. *Private Pay Patients* 25%. *Certified* Medicaid.
Owner Proprietary corp (ARJO Enterprises Inc).

Staff Physicians 1 (ft); RNs 5 (ft); LPNs 3 (ft); Nurses' aides 22 (ft); Physical therapists 1 (pt); Activities coordinators 1 (ft); Dietitians 1 (pt); Podiatrists 1 (pt).
Languages Spanish.
Facilities Dining room; Physical therapy room; Activities room; Laundry room; Barber/Beauty shop.
Activities Arts & crafts; Cards; Games; Reading groups; Prayer groups; Movies; Shopping trips; Dances/Social/Cultural gatherings; Intergenerational programs; Pet therapy.

Reedsport

Lower Umpqua Hospital
PO Box 6, Reedsport, OR 97567
(503) 271-2171
Admin Michelle Pelt Prov.
Licensure Skilled care; Intermediate care. *Beds* SNF 4; ICF 18. *Certified* Medicaid; Medicare.

Roseburg

Grandview Care Center
1199 NW Grandview Dr, Roseburg, OR 97490
(503) 672-1638
Admin Jerry Yost. *Dir of Nursing* Betty Farris RN. *Medical Dir* Matthew Sacks MD.
Licensure Intermediate care; Day care; Respite care. *Beds* ICF 83; Day care 5; Respite care 6. *Certified* Medicaid.
Owner Proprietary corp.
Admissions Requirements Physician's request.
Staff RNs 6 (ft), 2 (pt); LPNs 2 (ft), 2 (pt); Nurses' aides 20 (ft), 9 (pt); Activities coordinators 1 (ft).
Facilities Dining room; Activities room; Laundry room; Barber/Beauty shop.
Activities Arts & crafts; Cards; Games; Reading groups; Prayer groups; Movies; Shopping trips; Dances/Social/Cultural gatherings.

Mercy Care Center
525 W Umpqua, Roseburg, OR 97470
(503) 440-2199
Admin Gerard Meier. *Dir of Nursing* Debbie Rinaker RN. *Medical Dir* Cliff Babbitt MD.
Licensure Skilled care; Intermediate care. *Beds* SNF 46; ICF 76. *Private Pay Patients* 30%. *Certified* Medicaid; Medicare.
Owner Nonprofit organization/foundation.
Staff RNs 12 (ft), 11 (pt); LPNs 6 (ft), 3 (pt); Nurses' aides 52 (ft), 19 (pt); Physical therapists 1 (pt); Occupational therapists 1 (pt); Speech therapists 1 (pt); Activities coordinators 1 (ft); Dietitians 1 (pt); Ophthalmologists 1 (pt); Podiatrists 1 (pt).

Rose Haven Nursing Center
740 NW Hill Pl, Roseburg, OR 97470
(503) 672-1631
Admin Debbie Ebner. *Dir of Nursing* Debbie Ebner. *Medical Dir* Dr Timothy Powell.
Licensure Skilled care; Intermediate care; Day care; Respite care; Alzheimer's care. *Beds* SNF 24; ICF 169; Day care 10; Respite care 10. *Certified* Medicaid; Medicare.
Owner Privately owned.
Admissions Requirements Medical examination.
Staff RNs 10 (ft); Nurses' aides 90 (ft); Physical therapists 2 (ft); Reality therapists; Recreational therapists; Occupational therapists; Speech therapists; Activities coordinators 3 (ft).
Facilities Dining room; Physical therapy room; Activities room; Crafts room; Laundry room; Barber/Beauty shop.
Activities Arts & crafts; Cards; Games; Reading groups; Prayer groups; Movies; Shopping trips; Dances/Social/Cultural gatherings.

Saint Helens

OHCC—Meadow Park
75 Shore Dr, Saint Helens, OR 97051
(503) 397-2713, 397-2669 FAX
Admin John Hempel. *Dir of Nursing* Melinda Palmquist RN. *Medical Dir* J W Partuadgo MD.
Licensure Intermediate care. *Beds* ICF 92. *Private Pay Patients* 26%. *Certified* Medicaid.
Owner Proprietary corp (Unicare).
Admissions Requirements Medical examination; Physician's request.
Staff Physicians 1 (pt); RNs 3 (ft), 3 (pt); LPNs 3 (ft), 3 (pt); Nurses' aides 29 (ft), 4 (pt); Physical therapists 1 (pt); Occupational therapists 1 (pt); Speech therapists 1 (pt); Activities coordinators 1 (ft); Dietitians 1 (pt); Ophthalmologists 1 (pt); Podiatrists 1 (pt); Audiologists 1 (pt).
Facilities Dining room; Physical therapy room; Activities room; Crafts room; Laundry room; Barber/Beauty shop; TV room.
Activities Arts & crafts; Cards; Games; Prayer groups; Movies; Dances/Social/Cultural gatherings; Birthday parties; Anniversary parties.

Salem

Capitol Manor Health Care Center
PO Box 5000, 955 Dallas Hwy NW, Salem, OR 97304
(503) 362-4101
Admin Scott Ferguson.
Licensure Intermediate care. *Beds* ICF 58.

Capitol View Health Care Center
875 Oak, Salem, OR 97301
(503) 581-1457
Admin Victor D Kintz. *Dir of Nursing* Edie Cowan RN. *Medical Dir* Paul Young MD.
Licensure Skilled care; Intermediate care. *Beds* SNF 52; ICF 17. *Certified* Medicaid; Medicare.
Owner Proprietary corp (Beverly Enterprises).
Admissions Requirements Physician's request.
Staff RNs 8 (ft); LPNs 8 (ft); Nurses' aides 37 (ft); Physical therapists 1 (ft); Occupational therapists 1 (ft); Speech therapists 1 (ft); Activities coordinators 1 (ft); Dietitians 1 (ft).
Facilities Dining room; Physical therapy room; Activities room; Crafts room; Laundry room; Barber/Beauty shop; Dayroom.
Activities Arts & crafts; Cards; Games; Reading groups; Prayer groups; Movies; Shopping trips; Dances/Social/Cultural gatherings; Van outings to the coast; Zoo trips.

Cedar Hall
555 20th St NE, Salem, OR 97301
(503) 399-7924
Admin Anson Bell.
Licensure Intermediate care for mentally retarded. *Beds* ICF/MR 10. *Certified* Medicaid.

Fairview Training Center—Crestview Group Home
2250 Strong Rd SE, Salem, OR 97310
(503) 378-5101
Admin Mike Lincicum, Prov.
Licensure Intermediate care for mentally retarded. *Beds* ICF/MR 1060. *Certified* Medicaid.

Magnolia Manor
2630 Church St NE, Salem, OR 97303
(503) 585-5612
Admin A Jeanine Knight. *Dir of Nursing* Erma Stevenson. *Medical Dir* Dr Paul Young.
Licensure Intermediate care. *Beds* ICF 65. *Private Pay Patients* 36%. *Certified* Medicaid.

Owner Privately owned.
Staff RNs 2 (ft), 1 (pt); LPNs 4 (ft), 2 (pt); Nurses' aides 25 (ft), 6 (pt); Activities coordinators 1 (ft); Dietitians 1 (pt).
Facilities Dining room; Activities room; Barber/Beauty shop.
Activities Arts & crafts; Cards; Games; Reading groups; Prayer groups; Movies; Shopping trips; Dances/Social/Cultural gatherings; Pet therapy.

Oak Crest Care Center
2933 Center St NE, Salem, OR 97301
(503) 585-5850
Admin Kathryn Gustaveson.
Medical Dir Dr Casterline.
Licensure Intermediate care. *Beds* ICF 110. *Certified* Medicaid.
Owner Proprietary corp (Hillhaven Corp).
Staff Physicians; RNs; LPNs; Nurses' aides; Physical therapists; Recreational therapists; Activities coordinators; Dietitians; Dentists.
Facilities Dining room; Activities room; Crafts room; Laundry room; Barber/Beauty shop.
Activities Arts & crafts; Cards; Games; Reading groups; Prayer groups; Movies; Shopping trips; Dances/Social/Cultural gatherings.

Plantation Care Center Inc
820 Cottage St NE, Salem, OR 97301
(503) 399-1135
Admin Joe Stynes.
Medical Dir Ruth Speaker.
Licensure Intermediate care; Respite care. *Beds* ICF 100; Respite care 5. *Certified* Medicaid.
Owner Proprietary corp (National Heritage).
Admissions Requirements Medical examination; Physician's request.
Staff RNs; LPNs; Nurses' aides; Physical therapists; Activities coordinators; Dietitians.
Facilities Dining room; Activities room; Laundry room; Barber/Beauty shop.
Activities Arts & crafts; Cards; Games; Reading groups; Prayer groups; Movies; Shopping trips; Dances/Social/Cultural gatherings.

Shangri-La Corporation
2887 74th SE, Salem, OR 97301
(503) 581-1732
Admin Zachary Caulkins.
Licensure Intermediate care for mentally retarded. *Beds* ICF/MR 60. *Certified* Medicaid.
Admissions Requirements Minimum age 6; Medical examination; Physician's request.
Staff Physicians 1 (pt); RNs 2 (ft), 1 (pt); Physical therapists 1 (pt); Recreational therapists 5 (ft); Occupational therapists 1 (pt); Speech therapists 1 (pt); Activities coordinators 1 (ft); Dietitians 1 (pt).
Facilities Dining room; Activities room; Laundry room.
Activities Arts & crafts; Cards; Games; Movies; Shopping trips; Dances/Social/Cultural gatherings.

Sherwood Park Nursing Home Inc
4062 Arleta Ave NE, Salem, OR 97303
(503) 390-2271
Admin Scott Fredrickson. *Dir of Nursing* Moira L Hughes RN. *Medical Dir* Bruce Duffy.
Licensure Intermediate care. *Beds* ICF 44. *Private Pay Patients* 62%. *Certified* Medicaid.
Owner Proprietary corp (Sherwood Park Nursing Home Inc).
Staff RNs 2 (ft); LPNs 4 (ft); Nurses' aides 19 (ft); Physical therapists (consultant); Activities coordinators 1 (ft); Dietitians (consultant).

Facilities Dining room; Activities room; Laundry room; Sun room.
Activities Arts & crafts; Games; Reading groups; Prayer groups; Movies; Shopping trips; Pet therapy.

South Salem Care Center
4120 Kurth St S, Salem, OR 97302
(503) 581-8667
Admin Julie Tullock.
Medical Dir Chris Edwardson.
Licensure Intermediate care. *Beds* ICF 72. *Certified* Medicaid.
Owner Proprietary corp (National Heritage).
Admissions Requirements Medical examination.
Staff Physicians 1 (pt); RNs 2 (ft); LPNs 5 (ft); Nurses' aides 30 (ft), 4 (pt); Physical therapists 1 (pt); Reality therapists 1 (pt); Recreational therapists 1 (ft); Occupational therapists 1 (pt); Speech therapists 1 (pt); Activities coordinators 1 (pt); Dietitians 1 (pt); Ophthalmologists 1 (pt); Podiatrists 1 (pt); Audiologists 1 (pt); Dentists 1 (pt).
Facilities Dining room; Activities room; Laundry room; Barber/Beauty shop.
Activities Arts & crafts; Cards; Games; Reading groups; Prayer groups; Movies; Shopping trips; Dances/Social/Cultural gatherings.

Spruce Villa
1960 Center St, Salem, OR 97301
(503) 399-7924
Admin Anson Bell.
Medical Dir Pat Seeber.
Licensure Intermediate care for mentally retarded. *Beds* ICF/MR 22. *Certified* Medicaid.
Owner Nonprofit corp.
Admissions Requirements Minimum age 18.
Staff Physicians 1 (pt); RNs 1 (ft); Nurses' aides 28 (ft); Recreational therapists 1 (ft); Activities coordinators 1 (ft); Skill trainers 7 (ft).
Languages Sign.
Facilities Apartments and homes.
Activities Shopping trips; Dances/Social/Cultural gatherings; Counseling; Behavior management; Skill acquisition; Support.

Sunnyside Care Center
4515 Sunnyside Rd SE, Salem, OR 97302
(503) 370-8284, 370-8024 FAX
Admin Ross J Monaco. *Dir of Nursing* David Duffield. *Medical Dir* Paul Young MD.
Licensure Skilled care; Intermediate care. *Beds* SNF 16; ICF 108. *Private Pay Patients* 40%. *Certified* Medicaid; Medicare.
Owner Proprietary corp (Senior Living Services of Oregon Inc).
Admissions Requirements Medical examination; Physician's request.
Staff RNs 6 (ft), 2 (pt); LPNs 5 (ft), 1 (pt); Nurses' aides 37 (ft), 2 (pt); Physical therapists; Recreational therapists; Occupational therapists; Speech therapists; Activities coordinators 1 (ft); Podiatrists 1 (ft).
Facilities Dining room; Physical therapy room; Activities room; Laundry room; Barber/Beauty shop.
Activities Arts & crafts; Cards; Games; Reading groups; Prayer groups; Movies; Shopping trips; Dances/Social/Cultural gatherings; Intergenerational programs; Pet therapy.

Tierra Rose Care Center
4254 Weathers NE, Salem, OR 97301
(503) 585-4602
Admin Mabel Baughman.
Licensure Intermediate care. *Beds* ICF 51. *Certified* Medicaid.

Willamette Lutheran Home
PO Box 169, 7693 Wheatland Rd NE, Salem, OR 97303
(503) 393-1491
Admin Monica M Roy. *Dir of Nursing* Bette Weaver. *Medical Dir* Dr John Ross.
Licensure Intermediate care; Retirement. *Beds* ICF 22; Retirement center 100. *Private Pay Patients* 100%.
Owner Nonprofit organization/foundation.
Admissions Requirements Minimum age 62; Medical examination.
Staff RNs 1 (ft); LPNs 4 (ft); Nurses' aides 10 (ft); Recreational therapists 1 (ft); Dietitians.
Affiliation Lutheran.
Facilities Dining room; Activities room; Chapel; Crafts room; Laundry room; Barber/Beauty shop; Library.
Activities Arts & crafts; Cards; Games; Prayer groups; Movies; Shopping trips; Dances/Social/Cultural gatherings; Intergenerational programs; Pet therapy; Shuffleboard.

Sandy

Bishop's Health Care
39641 Scenic St, Sandy, OR 97055
(503) 668-4108
Admin Tom DeJardin.
Licensure Intermediate care. *Beds* ICF 63. *Certified* Medicaid.

Orchard Crest Care Center
Box 1318, Sandy, OR 97055
(503) 668-5551
Admin Steve Shupe. *Dir of Nursing* Jean Lerch RN. *Medical Dir* Dr Levenburg.
Licensure Intermediate care; Alzheimer's care. *Beds* ICF 28. *Certified* Medicaid.
Owner Privately owned.
Admissions Requirements Physician's request.
Staff RNs 1 (ft), 1 (pt); LPNs 2 (ft), 4 (pt); Nurses' aides 9 (ft), 2 (pt); Activities coordinators 1 (ft).
Facilities Dining room; Activities room; Crafts room; Laundry room; Barber/Beauty shop.
Activities Arts & crafts; Cards; Games; Reading groups; Prayer groups; Movies; Shopping trips; Dances/Social/Cultural gatherings; Pet therapy; Horticultural therapy.

Scappoose

Columbia Care Center
PO Box 1068, 33910 E Columbia Blvd, Scappoose, OR 97056
(503) 543-7131
Admin Kathleen Schwerzler.
Licensure Intermediate care; Day care. *Beds* ICF 41; Day care 15. *Certified* Medicaid.
Admissions Requirements Minimum age 18; Medical examination; Physician's request.
Staff RNs 1 (ft); LPNs 3 (pt); Nurses' aides 5 (ft), 15 (pt); Activities coordinators 1 (ft), 1 (pt).
Facilities Dining room; Activities room; Barber/Beauty shop.
Activities Arts & crafts; Games; Reading groups; Prayer groups; Movies; Dances/Social/Cultural gatherings.

Seaside

Ocean Park Nursing Home
1420 E 10th, PO Box 836, Seaside, OR 97138
(503) 738-6142
Admin Kathy Park.
Licensure Intermediate care. *Beds* 22. *Certified* Medicaid.
Admissions Requirements Physician's request.
Staff RNs 1 (ft), 1 (pt); LPNs 1 (ft), 3 (pt); Nurses' aides 9 (ft), 9 (pt); Activities coordinators 1 (ft).

Facilities Dining room; Activities room; Laundry room.
Activities Arts & crafts; Cards; Games; Reading groups; Prayer groups; Movies; Shopping trips; Dances/Social/Cultural gatherings.

Sheridan

Sheridan Care Center
411 SE Sheridan Rd, Sheridan, OR 97378
(503) 843-2204, 843-4612 FAX
Admin Linda Hill. *Dir of Nursing* Letha Steinke-Isbell RN. *Medical Dir* Richard Nelson MD.
Licensure Intermediate care. *Beds* ICF 55. *Certified* Medicaid.
Owner Proprietary corp.
Admissions Requirements Medical examination; Physician's request; Nonsmokers.
Staff RNs 2 (ft); LPNs 2 (ft); Nurses' aides 16 (ft), 5 (pt); Physical therapists 1 (pt); Activities coordinators 2 (ft); Dietitians 1 (pt); Podiatrists 1 (pt).
Facilities Dining room; Physical therapy room; Activities room; Laundry room; Barber/Beauty shop; Limousine; 19 Private and 12 semi-private rooms.
Activities Arts & crafts; Cards; Games; Reading groups; Prayer groups; Movies; Shopping trips; Dances/Social/Cultural gatherings; Pet therapy; Beach trips; Barbecues.

Silverton

Riverview Convalescent Center
1164 S Water St, Silverton, OR 97381
(503) 873-5391
Admin Dorothy Yost.
Medical Dir Michael Grady MD.
Licensure Intermediate care. *Beds* ICF 57. *Certified* Medicaid.
Staff RNs 2 (ft); LPNs 3 (ft), 2 (pt); Nurses' aides 18 (ft), 4 (pt); Activities coordinators 1 (ft); Dietitians 1 (ft), 1 (pt).
Facilities Dining room; Physical therapy room; Activities room; Crafts room; Laundry room; Barber/Beauty shop; 2 Solariums.
Activities Arts & crafts; Cards; Games; Reading groups; Prayer groups; Movies; Shopping trips; Dances/Social/Cultural gatherings.

Silver Gardens Care Center
115 S James St, Silverton, OR 97381
(503) 873-5362
Admin Joseph D Mann. *Dir of Nursing* J MacLean. *Medical Dir* Michael Gabe.
Licensure Intermediate care; Alzheimer's care. *Beds* ICF 52. *Private Pay Patients* 58%. *Certified* Medicaid; Medicare.
Owner Proprietary corp.
Admissions Requirements Medical examination; Physician's request.
Staff Physicians 1 (pt); RNs 2 (ft); LPNs 6 (ft); Nurses' aides 21 (ft), 4 (pt); Physical therapists 1 (ft), 1 (pt); Reality therapists 1 (ft); Recreational therapists 1 (ft); Activities coordinators 1 (ft), 1 (pt); Dietitians 1 (pt); Podiatrists 1 (pt).
Facilities Dining room; Activities room; Crafts room; Laundry room; Barber/Beauty shop; Vehicle for outside travel.
Activities Arts & crafts; Cards; Games; Reading groups; Prayer groups; Movies; Dances/Social/Cultural gatherings; Intergenerational programs; Pet therapy.

Springfield

McKenzie Manor Living Center
1333 N 1st St, Springfield, OR 97477
(503) 746-6581

Admin James C Brown. *Dir of Nursing* Lynn Tromp. *Medical Dir* Wallace Baldwin MD.
Licensure Skilled care; Intermediate care. *Beds* SNF 34; ICF 119. *Certified* Medicaid; Medicare.
Owner Privately owned.
Admissions Requirements Medical examination; Physician's request.
Staff Physicians 1 (pt); RNs 8 (ft), 8 (pt); LPNs 7 (ft), 6 (pt); Nurses' aides 65 (ft), 21 (pt); Physical therapists 1 (pt); Reality therapists 1 (pt); Occupational therapists 1 (pt); Speech therapists 1 (pt); Activities coordinators 2 (ft); Dietitians 1 (pt); Ophthalmologists 1 (pt); Podiatrists 1 (pt); Dentists 1 (pt); Therapy aides 3 (ft).
Facilities Dining room; Physical therapy room; Activities room; Crafts room; Laundry room; Barber/Beauty shop; Library.
Activities Arts & crafts; Cards; Games; Reading groups; Movies; Shopping trips; Dances/Social/Cultural gatherings.

Sublimity

Marian Home
360 Church St, Sublimity, OR 97385
(503) 769-3499 Stayton, (503) 581-2006 Salem
Admin Maurice Reece.
Licensure Intermediate care. *Beds* ICF 174. *Certified* Medicaid.
Admissions Requirements Minimum age 43; Medical examination; Physician's request.
Staff Physicians 2 (pt); RNs 12 (ft); LPNs 14 (ft); Physical therapists 2 (pt); Occupational therapists 1 (pt); Speech therapists 1 (pt); Activities coordinators 2 (ft); Dietitians 1 (ft), 1 (pt); Ophthalmologists 1 (pt); Dentists 1 (pt).
Facilities Dining room; Activities room; Chapel; Crafts room; Laundry room; Barber/Beauty shop.
Activities Arts & crafts; Cards; Games; Reading groups; Prayer groups; Movies; Shopping trips; Dances/Social/Cultural gatherings; Short trips to mountains, coast park.

Sweet Home

Twin Oaks Care Center
950 Nandina St, Sweet Home, OR 97386
(503) 367-2191, 367-2630 FAX
Admin Alice Hyland. *Dir of Nursing* Noeleen Phillips. *Medical Dir* Dr H B Dowling.
Licensure Intermediate care. *Beds* ICF 48. *Private Pay Patients* 25%. *Certified* Medicaid.
Owner Proprietary corp.
Admissions Requirements Physician's request.
Staff RNs 1 (ft), 1 (pt); LPNs 2 (ft); Physical therapists 1 (pt); Recreational therapists 1 (ft); Occupational therapists 1 (pt); Speech therapists 1 (pt); Activities coordinators 1 (ft); Dietitians 1 (pt).
Facilities Dining room; Activities room; Laundry room.
Activities Arts & crafts; Cards; Games; Reading groups; Prayer groups; Movies; Intergenerational programs; Pet therapy.

Tigard

King City Convalescent Center
16485 SW Pacific Hwy, Tigard, OR 97223
(503) 620-5141
Admin Ron Preston. *Dir of Nursing* Dorothy Miles RN.
Licensure Skilled care; Intermediate care; Day care. *Beds* SNF 73; ICF 75; Day care 20. *Certified* Medicaid; Medicare.
Owner Proprietary corp (Beverly Enterprises).
Admissions Requirements Physician's request.

Staff RNs 14 (ft); LPNs 5 (ft); Nurses' aides 42 (ft); Physical therapists 3 (ft); Occupational therapists 2 (ft); Speech therapists 1 (ft); Activities coordinators 1 (ft); Dietitians 1 (ft).
Facilities Dining room; Physical therapy room; Activities room; Crafts room; Laundry room; Barber/Beauty shop.
Activities Arts & crafts; Reading groups; Prayer groups; Movies.

Tigard Care Center
14145 SW 105th St, Tigard, OR 97224
(503) 639-1144
Admin Pete Snoey. *Dir of Nursing* Deb Kistler. *Medical Dir* Lloyd Morita.
Licensure Skilled care; Intermediate care. *Beds* SNF 21; ICF 91. *Private Pay Patients* 37%. *Certified* Medicaid; Medicare.
Owner Proprietary corp (Beverly Enterprises).
Facilities Dining room; Physical therapy room; Activities room; Crafts room; Laundry room; Barber/Beauty shop.
Activities Arts & crafts; Cards; Games; Reading groups; Prayer groups; Movies; Shopping trips; Dances/Social/Cultural gatherings; Intergenerational programs; Pet therapy.

Tillamook

Tillamook Care Center
2500 Nielsen Rd, Tillamook, OR 97141
(503) 842-6664, 842-2116 FAX
Admin Warren R Yule. *Dir of Nursing* Mary Donaher. *Medical Dir* Dr William Brue.
Licensure Skilled care; Intermediate care. *Beds* SNF 15; ICF 67. *Private Pay Patients* 20%. *Certified* Medicaid; Medicare.
Owner Proprietary corp (Long Term Care Corp).
Admissions Requirements Medical examination; Physician's request.
Staff RNs 6 (ft), 1 (pt); LPNs 4 (ft), 1 (pt); Nurses' aides 24 (ft), 3 (pt); Activities coordinators 1 (ft); Dietitians 1 (pt).
Facilities Dining room; Physical therapy room; Activities room; Laundry room; Barber/Beauty shop.
Activities Arts & crafts; Cards; Games; Prayer groups; Movies; Shopping trips; Dances/Social/Cultural gatherings; Visits by religious groups.

Toledo

New Lincoln Hospital
PO Box 490, Toledo, OR 97391
(503) 336-2237
Admin David Bloomer, Jr.
Licensure Skilled care. *Beds* 18. *Certified* Medicare.

Troutdale

Wood Village Manor
2060 NE 238th Dr, Troutdale, OR 97060
(503) 666-3863
Admin Robbe Redford.
Medical Dir Laurel Demorest.
Licensure Intermediate care. *Beds* ICF 56. *Certified* Medicaid.
Owner Proprietary corp.
Admissions Requirements Minimum age 18.
Staff RNs 3 (ft); LPNs 2 (ft), 1 (pt); Nurses' aides 16 (ft); Activities coordinators 1 (ft); Audiologists CMAs 3 (ft); Social workers 1 (ft).
Facilities Dining room; Activities room; Laundry room; Barber/Beauty shop; Sun room.
Activities Arts & crafts; Cards; Games; Prayer groups; Movies; Shopping trips; Dances/Social/Cultural gatherings.

Vale

Pioneer Nursing Home Health District
1060 D St W, Vale, OR 97918
(503) 473-3131
Admin Gaynelle Edmondson.
Medical Dir D W Sarazin MD.
Licensure Intermediate care; Day care. *Beds* ICF 56; Day care 4. *Certified* Medicaid.
Admissions Requirements Medical examination; Physician's request.
Staff RNs 1 (ft), 1 (pt); LPNs 4 (ft), 3 (pt); Nurses' aides 17 (ft), 1 (pt); Activities coordinators 1 (ft).
Facilities Dining room; Physical therapy room; Activities room; Crafts room; Laundry room; Barber/Beauty shop.
Activities Arts & crafts; Cards; Games; Reading groups; Prayer groups; Movies; Shopping trips; Dances/Social/Cultural gatherings.

West Linn

West Linn Care Center Inc
2330 DeBok Rd, West Linn, OR 97068
(503) 655-6331
Admin Nancy Paulk. *Dir of Nursing* Rosemary Lee.
Licensure Intermediate care; Alzheimer's care. *Beds* ICF 62. *Certified* Medicaid.
Owner Proprietary corp (Care Center Inc).
Admissions Requirements Medical examination.
Staff RNs; LPNs; Nurses' aides.
Languages Spanish.

Facilities Dining room; Activities room; Laundry room.
Activities Arts & crafts; Games; Reading groups; Prayer groups; Movies; Shopping trips; Dances/Social/Cultural gatherings.

Wheeler

Nehalem Valley Care Center
PO Box 16, 278 Rowe St, Wheeler, OR 97147-0016
(503) 368-5119
Admin Ken Cafferty, Prov.
Medical Dir Dr Oscar Marin.
Licensure Intermediate care; Alzheimer's care. *Beds* ICF 50. *Certified* Medicaid.
Owner Publicly owned.
Admissions Requirements Medical examination; Physician's request.
Staff Physicians 4 (ft); RNs 2 (ft), 4 (pt); LPNs 1 (ft); Nurses' aides 21 (ft); Physical therapists 1 (ft); Recreational therapists 1 (ft); Occupational therapists 1 (pt); Speech therapists 1 (pt); Activities coordinators 1 (pt); Dietitians 1 (pt); Podiatrists 1 (pt); Dentists 1 (pt).
Facilities Dining room; Physical therapy room; Activities room; Chapel; Crafts room; Laundry room; Barber/Beauty shop; Library; Family room; Lounges.
Activities Arts & crafts; Games; Prayer groups; Dances/Social/Cultural gatherings; Exercise programs; Community education; Bus sight-seeing weekly; Pets.

Woodburn

French Prairie Care Center
601 Evergreen Rd, Woodburn, OR 97071
(503) 982-9946

Admin Duane Miner. *Dir of Nursing* Joyce Park RN. *Medical Dir* Gordon D Haynie MD.
Licensure Skilled care; Intermediate care; Day/Respite care. *Beds* SNF 14; ICF 66; Day/Respite care 5. *Certified* Medicaid; Medicare.
Owner Privately owned.
Admissions Requirements Physician's request; No pediatrics.
Staff RNs; LPNs; Nurses' aides; Activities coordinators; Dietitians.
Languages Spanish, German.
Facilities Dining room; Physical therapy room; Activities room; Crafts room; Laundry room; Barber/Beauty shop.
Activities Arts & crafts; Cards; Games; Reading groups; Prayer groups; Movies; Shopping trips; Dances/Social/Cultural gatherings.

TLC 1 Woodburn Care Center
540 Settlemier St, Woodburn, OR 97071
(503) 981-9566
Admin Cheryl Lacombe.
Licensure Intermediate care; Day/Respite care. *Beds* ICF 60; Day/Respite care 5. *Certified* Medicaid.
Admissions Requirements Minimum age 18; Physician's request.
Staff RNs 1 (ft), 1 (pt); LPNs 3 (ft), 2 (pt); Activities coordinators 1 (ft); Dietitians 1 (pt).
Facilities Dining room; Laundry room.
Activities Arts & crafts; Cards; Games; Reading groups; Prayer groups; Movies; Shopping trips; Dances/Social/Cultural gatherings.

PENNSYLVANIA

Akron

Maple Farm Nursing Center
Rte 272, Akron, PA 17501
(717) 859-1191
Admin Mary Ann Russell.
Medical Dir Ms McCloskey.
Licensure Skilled care; Alzheimer's care. *Beds*
SNF 123. *Certified* Medicaid; Medicare.
Owner Proprietary corp.
Admissions Requirements Medical
examination.
Facilities Dining room; Physical therapy
room; Activities room; Crafts room; Barber/
Beauty shop; Library.
Activities Arts & crafts; Games; Reading
groups; Movies; Shopping trips.

Aliquippa

Golfview Manor Nursing Home
616 Golfcourse Rd, Aliquippa, PA 15001
(412) 375-0345
Admin Judith L Young. *Dir of Nursing*
Roseann Langton. *Medical Dir* Dr Simmon
Wilcox.
Licensure Skilled care. *Beds* SNF 65. *Private
Pay Patients* 20%. *Certified* Medicaid;
Medicare.
Owner Proprietary corp.
Admissions Requirements Medical
examination.
Staff Physicians 1 (pt); RNs 1 (ft), 10 (pt);
LPNs 2 (pt); Nurses' aides 15 (ft), 12 (pt);
Physical therapists 1 (pt); Recreational
therapists 2 (ft); Speech therapists 1 (pt);
Activities coordinators 1 (pt); Dietitians 1
(pt); Podiatrists 2 (pt); Dentists 1 (pt).
Facilities Dining room; Activities room;
Crafts room; Laundry room; Barber/Beauty
shop.
Activities Arts & crafts; Cards; Games;
Reading groups; Prayer groups; Movies;
Shopping trips; Dances/Social/Cultural
gatherings; Intergenerational programs.

Allentown

Cedarbrook—Allentown
PO Box 508, 350 S Cedarbrook Rd,
Allentown, PA 18105-0508
(215) 395-3727
Admin Warren L Grasse. *Dir of Nursing* Janet
Kreller RN. *Medical Dir* Sam Bub MD.
Licensure Skilled care; Intermediate care. *Beds*
Swing beds SNF/ICF 624. *Certified*
Medicaid; Medicare.
Owner Publicly owned.
Admissions Requirements Minimum age 18;
Medical examination.
Staff RNs 35 (ft), 23 (pt); LPNs 45 (ft), 11
(pt); Nurses' aides 212 (ft), 78 (pt); Physical
therapists 1 (ft); Recreational therapists 2
(ft); Occupational therapists 1 (pt); Speech
therapists 1 (pt); Activities coordinators 1
(ft); Dietitians 1 (ft); Ophthalmologists 2
(pt); Podiatrists 1 (pt); Dentists 1 (pt).

Facilities Dining room; Physical therapy
room; Activities room; Chapel; Crafts room;
Barber/Beauty shop; Library.
Activities Arts & crafts; Cards; Games;
Reading groups; Prayer groups; Movies;
Shopping trips; Dances/Social/Cultural
gatherings.

**Good Shepherd Home Long-Term Care Facility
Inc**
6th & Saint John Sts, Allentown, PA 18103
(215) 776-3127, 776-3172 FAX
Admin Dr Dale Sandstrom. *Dir of Nursing*
Tina Helinsky. *Medical Dir* Dr E Joel
Carpenter IV.
Licensure Skilled care; Intermediate care. *Beds*
SNF 21; ICF 114. *Private Pay Patients* 4%.
Certified Medicaid; Medicare.
Owner Nonprofit corp.
Admissions Requirements Minimum age 12;
PASARR.
Staff Physicians 2 (pt); RNs 15 (ft), 9 (pt);
LPNs 11 (ft), 4 (pt); Nurses' aides 60 (ft), 30
(pt); Physical therapists 2 (ft); Recreational
therapists 2 (ft); Occupational therapists 3
(ft); Speech therapists 1 (ft), 1 (pt); Activities
coordinators 2 (ft); Dietitians 1 (pt).
Affiliation Lutheran.
Facilities Dining room; Physical therapy
room; Activities room; Chapel; Crafts room;
Laundry room; Barber/Beauty shop; Library;
Speech therapy area; Computer room;
Sewing room; Snack bar; Physical therapy/
Occupational therapy gym.
Activities Arts & crafts; Cards; Games;
Reading groups; Prayer groups; Movies;
Shopping trips; Dances/Social/Cultural
gatherings; Intergenerational programs; Pet
therapy; Resident education; Computer
access; Ceramics.

Leader Nursing & Rehabilitation—Allentown
1265 S Cedar Crest Blvd, Allentown, PA
18103

Liberty Nursing & Rehabilitation Center
17th & Allen Sts, Allentown, PA 18104
(215) 432-4351
Admin Dan Frost.
Medical Dir Linda Larrabee.
Licensure Skilled care; Hospice care; Respite
care. *Beds* SNF 150. *Certified* Medicaid;
Medicare.
Owner Proprietary corp (Health Care and
Retirement Corp).
Admissions Requirements Minimum age 17;
Medical examination; Physician's request.
Staff Physicians 4 (pt); RNs 15 (ft), 8 (pt);
LPNs 5 (ft), 5 (pt); Nurses' aides 42 (ft), 19
(pt); Physical therapists 1 (ft); Recreational
therapists 2 (ft), 1 (pt); Occupational
therapists 1 (ft), 1 (pt); Speech therapists 1
(pt); Activities coordinators 1 (ft); Dietitians
1 (pt); Ophthalmologists 2 (pt); Social
service 2 (ft), 2 (pt).
Languages Dutch, German, Italian, Greek,
Ukrainian, Spanish.

Facilities Dining room; Physical therapy
room; Activities room; Chapel; Crafts room;
Laundry room; Barber/Beauty shop; Library;
Occupational therapy room.
Activities Arts & crafts; Cards; Games;
Movies; Dances/Social/Cultural gatherings;
Lunch in restaurants; Pet shows.

Luther Crest
800 Hausman Rd, Allentown, PA 18104
(215) 398-8011, 398-4053 FAX
Admin Deborah L Reinhard NHA. *Dir of
Nursing* Jamie Fragnito RN. *Medical Dir*
Ward Becker MD.
Licensure Skilled care; Independent living.
Beds SNF 60; Independent living apts 302.
Private Pay Patients 80-90%. *Certified*
Medicaid; Medicare.
Owner Nonprofit corp.
Admissions Requirements Minimum age 60;
Medical examination.
Staff Physicians 1 (ft); RNs 5 (ft), 2 (pt);
LPNs 3 (ft), 4 (pt); Nurses' aides 24 (ft), 8
(pt); Physical therapists 1 (ft); Reality
therapists 1 (pt); Recreational therapists 1
(pt); Occupational therapists 1 (ft), 1 (pt);
Speech therapists 1 (pt); Activities
coordinators 1 (ft), 1 (pt); Dietitians 1 (pt);
Ophthalmologists 1 (pt); Podiatrists 1 (pt);
Audiologists 1 (pt).
Affiliation Lutheran.
Facilities Dining room; Physical therapy
room; Activities room; Chapel; Crafts room;
Laundry room; Barber/Beauty shop; Library.
Activities Arts & crafts; Cards; Games;
Reading groups; Prayer groups; Movies;
Shopping trips; Dances/Social/Cultural
gatherings; Intergenerational programs; Pet
therapy; Music therapy; Reality orientation.

Parkway Rest Home Inc
3600 Hamilton St, Allentown, PA 18104
(215) 395-3508, 395-4011
Admin Donald Lanquell.
Medical Dir Dr E Baum.
Licensure Intermediate care. *Beds* ICF 28.
Certified Medicaid.
Owner Proprietary corp.
Admissions Requirements Minimum age 35;
Medical examination.
Staff Physicians 4 (pt); RNs 4 (ft); LPNs 4
(ft); Nurses' aides 10 (ft); Physical therapists
1 (pt); Recreational therapists 1 (pt);
Occupational therapists 1 (pt); Activities
coordinators 1 (ft); Dietitians 1 (pt);
Podiatrists 1 (pt); Dentists 1 (pt).
Facilities Dining room; Activities room;
Laundry room.
Activities Arts & crafts; Cards; Games;
Reading groups; Prayer groups; Movies;
Dances/Social/Cultural gatherings.

Phoebe Home
1925 Turner St, Allentown, PA 18104
(215) 435-9037
Admin William C Soldrich NHA. *Dir of
Nursing* Lucinda Gurst RN. *Medical Dir*
Samuel W Criswell MD.

Licensure Skilled care; Intermediate care;
Personal care; Independent living. *Beds* SNF
102; ICF 288; Personal care 55; Independent
living 250. *Private Pay Patients* 60%.
Certified Medicaid; Medicare.
Owner Nonprofit organization/foundation.
Admissions Requirements Minimum age 62;
Medical examination.
Staff Physicians 1 (ft), 3 (pt); RNs 25 (ft), 31
(pt); LPNs 16 (ft), 3 (pt); Nurses' aides 104
(ft), 68 (pt); Physical therapists 1 (ft), 2 (pt);
Reality therapists 2 (ft); Recreational
therapists 2 (ft); Occupational therapists 2
(ft); Activities coordinators 1 (ft); Dietitians
2 (ft); Ophthalmologists 1 (pt); Dentists 1
(pt).
Languages Pennsylvania German.
Affiliation United Church of Christ.
Facilities Dining room; Physical therapy
room; Activities room; Chapel; Crafts room;
Laundry room; Barber/Beauty shop; Library;
Solariums; Nutrition kitchens; TV rooms;
Game rooms.
Activities Arts & crafts; Cards; Games;
Reading groups; Prayer groups; Movies;
Shopping trips; Dances/Social/Cultural
gatherings; Intergenerational programs; Pet
therapy.

Westminster Village
803 N Wahneta St, Allentown, PA 18103
(215) 434-6245
Admin James F Bernardo. *Dir of Nursing*
Jeraldine Kohut. *Medical Dir* George
Provost MD.
Licensure Skilled care; Intermediate care;
Independent living. *Beds* Swing beds SNF/
ICF 111; Independent living apartments 42.
Private Pay Patients 70%. *Certified*
Medicaid; Medicare.
Owner Nonprofit corp (Presbyterian Homes
Inc).
Admissions Requirements Minimum age 65;
Medical examination.
Staff Physicians; RNs; LPNs; Nurses' aides;
Physical therapists; Recreational therapists;
Occupational therapists; Speech therapists;
Activities coordinators; Dietitians;
Chaplains.
Languages Spanish.
Affiliation Presbyterian.
Facilities Dining room; Physical therapy
room; Activities room; Chapel; Crafts room;
Laundry room; Barber/Beauty shop; Activity
areas.
Activities Arts & crafts; Cards; Games;
Reading groups; Prayer groups; Movies;
Shopping trips; Dances/Social/Cultural
gatherings; Intergenerational programs; Pet
therapy; Cooking group; Lunch trips.

White Haven Center Annex—Allentown
1700 Hanover Ave, Allentown, PA 18103
(215) 821-6201
Licensure Intermediate care for mentally
retarded. *Beds* 43. *Certified* Medicaid.
Owner Nonprofit corp.

Allison Park

Regency Hall Nursing Home Inc
9399 Babcock Blvd, Allison Park, PA 15101
(412) 366-8540
Admin Sr M Carmelita Alvero; Daryl Hagen
RN, Asst. *Dir of Nursing* Louise
McDonough. *Medical Dir* David Sharp MD.
Licensure Skilled care; Personal care; Adult
day care. *Beds* SNF 136; Personal care 7.
Private Pay Patients 60%. *Certified*
Medicaid; Medicare.
Owner Nonprofit corp (Vincentian Sisters of
Charity).
Admissions Requirements Minimum age
Adult; Medical examination.
Staff Physicians 25 (pt); RNs 7 (ft), 12 (pt);
LPNs 4 (ft), 5 (pt); Nurses' aides 41 (ft), 23
(pt); Physical therapists 2 (pt); Occupational

therapists 1 (pt); Speech therapists 1 (pt);
Activities coordinators 3 (pt); Dietitians 1
(pt); Ophthalmologists 1 (pt); Podiatrists 1
(pt); Audiologists 1 (pt).
Languages Italian.
Affiliation Roman Catholic.
Facilities Dining room; Physical therapy
room; Activities room; Chapel; Crafts room;
Laundry room; Barber/Beauty shop.
Activities Arts & crafts; Cards; Games;
Reading groups; Prayer groups; Movies;
Dances/Social/Cultural gatherings;
Intergenerational programs; Pet therapy.

Altoona

Altoona Center
1515 4th St, Altoona, PA 16601
(814) 946-6900
Admin Barry C Benford.
Medical Dir Jules Netreba MD.
Licensure Intermediate care for mentally
retarded. *Beds* ICF/MR 138. *Certified*
Medicaid; Medicare.
Owner Publicly owned.
Staff Physicians 1 (ft); RNs 16 (ft); LPNs 3
(ft); Nurses' aides 93 (ft); Physical therapists
1 (ft); Recreational therapists 17 (ft);
Occupational therapists 1 (ft); Speech
therapists 2 (ft); Activities coordinators 1
(ft); Dietitians 1 (ft); Ophthalmologists 1
(pt); Dentists 1 (pt).
Facilities Dining room; Physical therapy
room; Activities room; Crafts room; Laundry
room; Barber/Beauty shop; Library.
Activities Arts & crafts; Games; Reading
groups; Prayer groups; Movies; Shopping
trips; Dances/Social/Cultural gatherings;
Individualized activities.

Hillview Care Center
700 S Cayuga Ave, Altoona, PA 16602
(814) 946-0471
Admin Virginia D Claar. *Dir of Nursing*
Charlene Monahan. *Medical Dir* Dr Sheedy.
Licensure Skilled care; Intermediate care;
Retirement. *Beds* SNF 30; ICF 98. *Certified*
Medicaid; Medicare.
Owner Proprietary corp (Beverly Enterprises).
Admissions Requirements Minimum age 65;
Medical examination; Physician's request.
Staff Physicians 1 (pt); RNs 6 (ft); LPNs 9
(ft); Nurses' aides 46 (ft); Physical therapists
1 (pt); Speech therapists 1 (pt); Activities
coordinators 1 (ft); Dietitians 1 (ft);
Ophthalmologists 1 (pt); Podiatrists 1 (pt);
Dentists 1 (pt).
Facilities Dining room; Physical therapy
room; Activities room; Chapel; Barber/
Beauty shop.
Activities Arts & crafts; Cards; Games;
Reading groups; Prayer groups; Dances/
Social/Cultural gatherings.

Mid State ICF/MR Broad
2605 Broad Ave, Altoona, PA 16601
(717) 946-4618
Licensure Residential MR care. *Beds* 8.
Certified Medicaid.
Owner Proprietary corp.

Mid State ICF/MR Inc
1908 8th Ave, Altoona, PA 16602
(814) 946-4623
Licensure Residential MR care. *Beds* 8.
Certified Medicaid.
Owner Proprietary corp.

Mid State ICF/MR Inc
2210 16th St, Altoona, PA 16601
(814) 946-4637
Licensure Residential MR care. *Beds* 8.
Certified Medicaid.
Owner Proprietary corp.

Valley View Home—Blair County
PO Box 1229, Altoona, PA 16603
(814) 944-0845

Licensure Skilled care; Intermediate care. *Beds*
SNF 78; ICF 166. *Certified* Medicaid;
Medicare.
Owner Publicly owned.

Ambler

Ambler Rest Center
32 S Bethlehem Pk, Ambler, PA 19002
(215) 646-7050, 646-6662 FAX
Admin Carol Olenek NHA. *Dir of Nursing*
Paula Moore RN. *Medical Dir* Barry Corson
MD.
Licensure Skilled care. *Beds* SNF 100. *Private
Pay Patients* 95%. *Certified* Medicare.
Owner Proprietary corp.
Staff Physicians; RNs 8 (ft), 4 (pt); LPNs 5
(ft), 2 (pt); Nurses' aides 30 (ft), 2 (pt);
Physical therapists 1 (pt); Recreational
therapists 1 (ft); Occupational therapists 1
(pt); Speech therapists 1 (pt); Activities
coordinators 1 (ft); Dietitians 1 (pt);
Ophthalmologists 1 (pt); Podiatrists 1 (pt);
Audiologists 1 (pt).
Facilities Dining room; Physical therapy
room; Activities room; Chapel; Crafts room;
Barber/Beauty shop; Lounges; Patios
overlooking wooded areas with a creek;
Farm.
Activities Arts & crafts; Cards; Games;
Reading groups; Movies; Shopping trips;
Intergenerational programs; Pet therapy;
Concerts; Cocktail parties; Picnics, barbecues
& parties for guests and families.

Artman Lutheran Home
250 Behtlehem Pike, Ambler, PA 19002
(215) 643-6333
Admin Florence D Thaler NHA. *Dir of
Nursing* Anne Gattuso RN. *Medical Dir*
Henry Borska MD.
Licensure Skilled care; Retirement. *Beds* SNF
30. *Certified* Medicaid.
Owner Nonprofit corp.
Admissions Requirements Minimum age 65.
Staff Physicians 1 (pt); RNs 3 (ft), 7 (pt);
LPNs 3 (pt); Nurses' aides 8 (ft), 5 (pt);
Recreational therapists 1 (ft), 1 (pt);
Activities coordinators 1 (ft); Dietitians 1
(pt); Ophthalmologists 1 (pt); Dentists 1 (pt).
Affiliation Lutheran.
Facilities Dining room; Activities room;
Chapel; Laundry room; Barber/Beauty shop;
Library.
Activities Arts & crafts; Cards; Games;
Reading groups; Prayer groups; Movies;
Shopping trips; Dances/Social/Cultural
gatherings.

Annville

Lebanon Valley Home
550 E Main St, Annville, PA 17003
(717) 867-4467
Licensure Skilled care. *Beds* SNF 53. *Certified*
Medicaid.
Owner Nonprofit corp.

United Christian Church Home
Rte 1 Box 629, Annville, PA 17003
(717) 867-4636
Admin Mary Ellen Rohrer. *Dir of Nursing*
Cecilia Myers. *Medical Dir* Dr Glenn
Hoffman.
Licensure Skilled care; Intermediate care;
Personal care; Retirement. *Beds* Swing beds
SNF/ICF 31; Personal care 24; Retirement
cottages 20. *Private Pay Patients* 91%.
Certified Medicaid; Medicare.
Owner Nonprofit corp.
Admissions Requirements Minimum age 65.
Staff RNs 3 (ft), 2 (pt); LPNs 4 (ft), 1 (pt);
Nurses' aides 9 (ft), 5 (pt); Physical
therapists (contracted); Reality therapists
(contracted); Recreational therapists
(contracted); Occupational therapists
(contracted); Speech therapists (contracted);

Activities coordinators (contracted); Dietitians (contracted); Ophthalmologists (contracted); Podiatrists (contracted); Audiologists (contracted).
Facilities Dining room; Physical therapy room; Activities room; Chapel; Crafts room; Laundry room; Barber/Beauty shop; Library.
Activities Arts & crafts; Games; Reading groups; Prayer groups; Movies; Shopping trips; Dances/Social/Cultural gatherings; Pet therapy.

Apollo

West Haven Nursing Home
PO Box 278, 151 Goodview Dr, Apollo, PA 15613
(412) 727-3451
Admin Sylvia J Smith. *Dir of Nursing* Pat Anthony RN. *Medical Dir* Dr Pal Muthappan.
Licensure Skilled care; Intermediate care; Retirement. *Beds* SNF 118; ICF 61; Retirement 100. *Private Pay Patients* 30%. *Certified* Medicaid; Medicare.
Owner Privately owned.
Admissions Requirements Medical examination.
Staff Physicians 8 (pt); RNs 5 (ft), 7 (pt); LPNs 9 (ft), 10 (pt); Nurses' aides 52 (ft), 20 (pt); Physical therapists 1 (pt); Recreational therapists 1 (ft), 2 (pt); Occupational therapists 1 (pt); Speech therapists 2 (pt); Activities coordinators 1 (pt); Dietitians 1 (pt); Ophthalmologists 1 (pt); Podiatrists 1 (pt); Audiologists 1 (pt).
Facilities Dining room; Physical therapy room; Activities room; Chapel; Crafts room; Laundry room; Barber/Beauty shop.
Activities Arts & crafts; Cards; Games; Reading groups; Prayer groups; Movies; Dances/Social/Cultural gatherings; Intergenerational programs; Pet therapy; Cooking.

Ashland

Ashland State General Hospital Geriatric Center
Rte 61, Ashland, PA 17921
(717) 875-2000, 875-6015 FAX
Admin Joan A Medlinsky NHA. *Dir of Nursing* Marilyn Connell RN MSR. *Medical Dir* Vincent Mirarchi MD.
Licensure Skilled care; Intermediate care. *Beds* Swing beds SNF/ICF 18. *Private Pay Patients* 2%. *Certified* Medicaid; Medicare.
Owner Publicly owned.
Admissions Requirements Minimum age 16; Medical examination; Physician's request.
Staff Physicians 1 (pt); RNs 5 (ft), 4 (pt); LPNs 4 (ft); Nurses' aides 3 (ft), 1 (pt); Physical therapists 2 (pt); Recreational therapists 1 (pt); Occupational therapists 1 (pt); Speech therapists (contracted); Dietitians (consultant); Ophthalmologists; Podiatrists; Audiologists (contracted); Dentists (contracted).
Facilities Dining room; Physical therapy room; Activities room; Chapel; Crafts room; Barber & beautician services available.
Activities Arts & crafts; Cards; Games; Reading groups; Prayer groups; Movies; Dances/Social/Cultural gatherings; Pet therapy.

Athens

Heritage Nursing Home Inc
200 S Main St, Athens, PA 18810
(717) 888-5805
Licensure Skilled care; Intermediate care. *Beds* 141. *Certified* Medicaid; Medicare.
Owner Proprietary corp.

Bala Cynwyd

Mary J Drexel Home
238 Belmont Ave, Bala Cynwyd, PA 19004
(215) 664-5967
Admin Katrina Kane Wise NHA, Exec Dir. *Dir of Nursing* Angela Standen RN. *Medical Dir* William Miller MD.
Licensure Skilled care; Intermediate care; Personal care. *Beds* Swing beds SNF/ICF 30; Personal care 43. *Private Pay Patients* 70%. *Certified* Medicaid.
Owner Nonprofit corp.
Admissions Requirements Minimum age 65; Medical examination.
Staff Physicians 1 (pt); RNs 3 (ft), 2 (pt); LPNs 2 (ft), 2 (pt); Nurses' aides 16 (ft), 4 (pt); Physical therapists 1 (pt); Recreational therapists 2 (ft), 1 (pt); Occupational therapists 1 (pt); Speech therapists 1 (pt); Activities coordinators 1 (ft); Dietitians 1 (pt); Ophthalmologists 1 (pt); Podiatrists 1 (pt); Audiologists 1 (pt).
Languages German, French.
Affiliation Evangelical Lutheran.
Facilities Dining room; Physical therapy room; Activities room; Chapel; Crafts room; Laundry room; Barber/Beauty shop; Library; Porch; Living room; Outside walking area.
Activities Arts & crafts; Cards; Games; Reading groups; Prayer groups; Movies; Shopping trips; Dances/Social/Cultural gatherings; Intergenerational programs; Pet therapy; Entertainment; Cultural events.

Bangor

Slate Belt Nursing & Rehabilitation Center
701 Slate Belt Blvd, Bangor, PA 18103
(215) 588-6161
Admin Joseph H Fortenbaugh III. *Dir of Nursing* Alicia Schutack RN. *Medical Dir* John G Oliver MD.
Licensure Skilled care; Drug & alcohol detox & rehabilitation. *Beds* SNF 94; Drug & alcohol detox & rehabilitation 26. *Certified* Medicaid; Medicare.
Owner Nonprofit corp (Healtheast).
Staff Physicians 1 (pt); RNs 15 (ft), 13 (pt); LPNs 7 (ft), 3 (pt); Physical therapists 1 (ft); Occupational therapists 1 (ft); Speech therapists 1 (pt); Activities coordinators 1 (ft); Dietitians 1 (pt); Podiatrists 1 (pt); Audiologists 1 (pt).
Facilities Dining room; Physical therapy room; Activities room; Chapel; Laundry room; Barber/Beauty shop; Library.
Activities Arts & crafts; Cards; Games; Reading groups; Prayer groups; Movies; Shopping trips; Dances/Social/Cultural gatherings; Intergenerational programs; Pet therapy.

Bear Creek

Bear Creek Health Care Center
PO Box 58 Rte 115, Bear Creek, PA 18602-0058
(717) 472-3785
Admin Leslie Gower NHA. *Dir of Nursing* Pamela Drury RN BSN. *Medical Dir* Dr Gregory Fino.
Licensure Intermediate care. *Beds* ICF 32. *Private Pay Patients* 33%. *Certified* Medicaid.
Owner Privately owned.
Admissions Requirements Medical examination; Physician's request.
Staff RNs 1 (ft), 2 (pt); LPNs 2 (ft), 2 (pt); Nurses' aides 7 (ft), 8 (pt); Physical therapists (consultant); Reality therapists (consultant); Recreational therapists (consultant); Occupational therapists (consultant); Speech therapists (consultant);

Activities coordinators 1 (ft); Dietitians 1 (pt); Ophthalmologists (consultant); Podiatrists 1 (pt); Audiologists (consultant).
Facilities Dining room; Activities room; Crafts room; Laundry room; Barber/Beauty shop.
Activities Arts & crafts; Cards; Games; Reading groups; Prayer groups; Movies; Dances/Social/Cultural gatherings; Intergenerational programs; Pet therapy.

Beaver

Beaver Valley Geriatric Center
Dutch Ridge Rd, Beaver, PA 15009
(412) 775-7100
Admin William R Jubeck NHA. *Dir of Nursing* Cynthia Phillips. *Medical Dir* Nicholas Vasilopoulos MD.
Licensure Skilled care; Intermediate care; HCI. *Beds* SNF 463; ICF 97; HCI 101. *Certified* Medicaid; Medicare.
Owner Publicly owned.
Admissions Requirements Medical examination.
Staff Physicians 1 (ft), 2 (pt); RNs 52 (ft), 29 (pt); LPNs 39 (ft), 19 (pt); Nurses' aides 192 (ft), 81 (pt); Physical therapists 1 (ft); Occupational therapists 1 (pt); Speech therapists 1 (pt); Activities coordinators 1 (ft); Dietitians 1 (ft); Ophthalmologists 1 (pt); Podiatrists 1 (pt); Audiologists 1 (pt).
Facilities Physical therapy room; Activities room; Chapel; Crafts room; Laundry room; Barber/Beauty shop; Library.
Activities Arts & crafts; Cards; Games; Movies; Dances/Social/Cultural gatherings; Pet therapy.

Medical Center Beaver Pennsylvania—Long-Term Care Unit
1000 Dutch Ridge Rd, Beaver, PA 15009

Beaver Falls

Beaver Valley Nursing Center
RD 1, Georgetown Rd, Beaver Falls, PA 15010
(412) 846-8200, 846-5609 FAX
Admin John D Hughes. *Dir of Nursing* Norma Shephard. *Medical Dir* Dr Damazo.
Licensure Skilled care; Intermediate care. *Beds* SNF 60; ICF 60. *Private Pay Patients* 18%. *Certified* Medicaid; Medicare.
Owner Proprietary corp (Unicare Health Facilities).
Admissions Requirements Medical examination.
Staff Physicians 6 (pt); RNs 4 (ft), 6 (pt); LPNs 3 (ft), 7 (pt); Nurses' aides 35 (ft), 20 (pt); Physical therapists 1 (pt); Occupational therapists 1 (ft); Speech therapists 1 (ft); Activities coordinators 1 (ft); Dietitians 1 (ft); Podiatrists 1 (pt).
Languages German, Italian.
Facilities Dining room; Physical therapy room; Activities room; Chapel; Crafts room; Laundry room; Barber/Beauty shop.
Activities Arts & crafts; Cards; Games; Reading groups; Prayer groups; Movies; Shopping trips; Dances/Social/Cultural gatherings; Intergenerational programs; Pet therapy; Other physical and mental activities; Religious services.

Blair Nursing Home Inc
RD 2, Mercer Rd, Beaver Falls, PA 15010
(412) 843-2209
Admin M W Blair. *Dir of Nursing* Margaret Elaine Blair RN. *Medical Dir* Dr E D Damazo.
Licensure Skilled care; Personal care; Retirement; Alzheimer's care. *Beds* SNF 28; Personal care 50; Retirement 50.
Owner Proprietary corp (Blair Nursing Home Inc).

Admissions Requirements Minimum age NH 50, PCH 21.
Staff Physicians 2 (pt); RNs 3 (ft), 2 (pt); LPNs 2 (ft), 1 (pt); Nurses' aides 3 (ft), 13 (pt); Physical therapists 1 (pt); Speech therapists 1 (pt); Activities coordinators 1 (ft); Dietitians 1 (pt); Ophthalmologists 1 (pt); Podiatrists 1 (pt).
Facilities Dining room; Activities room; Barber/Beauty shop; Library.
Activities Arts & crafts; Cards; Games; Prayer groups; Movies; Intergenerational programs; Pet therapy.

Providence Health Care Center
PO Box 140, 900 3rd Ave, Beaver Falls, PA 15010
(412) 846-8504
Admin Bruce T Pickens. *Dir of Nursing* Karen Haynes. *Medical Dir* Dr William Fiden.
Licensure Skilled care; Intermediate care. *Beds* Swing beds SNF/ICF 180. *Private Pay Patients* 18%. *Certified* Medicaid; Medicare.
Owner Proprietary corp.
Staff RNs; LPNs; Nurses' aides; Physical therapists; Activities coordinators; Dietitians.
Facilities Dining room; Physical therapy room; Activities room; Crafts room; Laundry room; Barber/Beauty shop.
Activities Arts & crafts; Cards; Games; Reading groups; Prayer groups; Movies; Intergenerational programs; Pet therapy.

Bedford

Donahoe Manor
Rte 5 Box 55, Bedford, PA 15522
(814) 623-9075
Licensure Skilled care; Intermediate care. *Beds* SNF 48; ICF 24. *Certified* Medicaid; Medicare.
Owner Proprietary corp (Health Care and Retirement Corp).

Bellefonte

Centre Crest
502 E Haward St, Bellefonte, PA 16823
(814) 355-6777
Admin Geraldine S Kline RN NHA.
Medical Dir Dr Mark A Knox.
Licensure Skilled care; Intermediate care. *Beds* SNF 24; ICF 201. *Certified* Medicaid; Medicare.
Owner Publicly owned.
Admissions Requirements Medical examination; Physician's request.
Staff Physicians 1 (ft); RNs 3 (ft), 11 (pt); LPNs 40 (ft), 10 (pt); Nurses' aides 40 (ft), 10 (pt); Physical therapists 1 (ft); Reality therapists 1 (ft); Recreational therapists 3 (ft); Occupational therapists 1 (pt); Speech therapists 1 (pt); Activities coordinators 1 (ft); Dietitians 1 (pt); Ophthalmologists 1 (pt); Dentists 1 (pt).
Facilities Dining room; Physical therapy room; Activities room; Chapel; Crafts room; Laundry room; Barber/Beauty shop; Library.
Activities Arts & crafts; Cards; Games; Reading groups; Prayer groups; Movies; Shopping trips; Dances/Social/Cultural gatherings; Boating; Fishing; Theatre.

Belleville

Valley View Retirement Community
PO Box 827, Belleville, PA 17004
(717) 935-2105
Admin Isabelle Felmlee; R David Metzler, Exec Dir. *Dir of Nursing* Connie Page RN.
Licensure Skilled care; Retirement. *Beds* SNF 120. *Certified* Medicaid.
Owner Nonprofit corp.
Admissions Requirements Minimum age 21; Medical examination.

Staff RNs 2 (ft), 6 (pt); LPNs 10 (ft), 13 (pt); Nurses' aides 29 (ft), 35 (pt); Activities coordinators 1 (ft), 1 (pt).
Facilities Dining room; Physical therapy room; Activities room; Chapel; Laundry room; Barber/Beauty shop.
Activities Arts & crafts; Games; Reading groups; Prayer groups; Movies; Shopping trips; Dances/Social/Cultural gatherings.

Bellwood

Morans Home Inc
402 Maple Ave, Bellwood, PA 16617
(814) 742-8947
Licensure Intermediate care. *Beds* ICF 17.
Owner Proprietary corp.

Berlin

Maple Mountain Manor
1401 Hay St, Berlin, PA 15530
(814) 267-4212
Admin John Lamont. *Dir of Nursing* Detra Webb. *Medical Dir* Deborah Baceski.
Licensure Intermediate care. *Beds* ICF 162. *Certified* Medicaid.
Owner Publicly owned.
Admissions Requirements Medical examination.
Facilities Dining room; Physical therapy room; Activities room; Chapel; Crafts room; Laundry room; Barber/Beauty shop; Library.
Activities Arts & crafts; Cards; Games; Reading groups; Prayer groups; Movies; Shopping trips; Dances/Social/Cultural gatherings; Intergenerational programs; Pet therapy; Reality orientation; Sensory stimulation.

Berwick

Berwick Retirement Village Nursing Home
801 E 16th St, Berwick, PA 18603
(717) 759-5400
Admin Ann Fletcher. *Dir of Nursing* Diane Krolikowski RN. *Medical Dir* Frank Gegwich MD.
Licensure Skilled care; Intermediate care. *Beds* SNF 60; ICF 60. *Private Pay Patients* 42%. *Certified* Medicaid; Medicare.
Owner Nonprofit organization/foundation.
Admissions Requirements Medical examination; Physician's request.
Staff Physicians; RNs 5 (ft), 7 (pt); LPNs 6 (ft), 11 (pt); Nurses' aides 27 (ft), 31 (pt); Physical therapists 1 (pt); Recreational therapists 2 (ft); Occupational therapists 1 (pt); Speech therapists 1 (pt); Activities coordinators 1 (ft); Dietitians 1 (pt); Ophthalmologists 1 (pt); Podiatrists 1 (pt); Dentists 1 (pt).
Facilities Dining room; Physical therapy room; Activities room; Crafts room; Laundry room; Barber/Beauty shop.
Activities Arts & crafts; Cards; Games; Reading groups; Prayer groups; Movies; Shopping trips; Dances/Social/Cultural gatherings; Intergenerational programs; Pet therapy.

Bethel Park

Leader Nursing & Rehabilitation Center—Bethel Park
60 Highland Rd, Bethel Park, PA 15102
(412) 831-6050
Licensure Skilled care. *Beds* SNF 120. *Certified* Medicaid; Medicare.
Owner Proprietary corp (Manor Care Inc).

Meadow Crest Inc
1200 Braun Rd, Bethel Park, PA 15102
(412) 854-5500

Admin Kathleen Hess. *Dir of Nursing* Kathleen Gastan. *Medical Dir* Walter Hoover MD.
Licensure Skilled care; Intermediate care. *Beds* Swing beds SNF/ICF 50. *Certified* Medicaid; Medicare.
Owner Proprietary corp.
Staff RNs 5 (ft), 1 (pt); LPNs 2 (pt); Nurses' aides 10 (ft), 6 (pt); Physical therapists 1 (pt); Recreational therapists 1 (ft); Occupational therapists 1 (pt); Speech therapists 1 (pt); Activities coordinators 1 (ft); Dietitians 1 (ft); Ophthalmologists 1 (pt); Podiatrists 1 (pt); Audiologists 1 (pt).
Facilities Dining room; Physical therapy room; Activities room; Barber/Beauty shop; Library; Center courtyard.
Activities Arts & crafts; Cards; Games; Reading groups; Movies; Intergenerational programs; Pet therapy.

Bethlehem

Blough Nursing Home Inc
316 E Market St, Bethlehem, PA 18018
(215) 868-4982
Admin Sandra A Massetti. *Dir of Nursing* Maryann Ginder RN. *Medical Dir* Dr Ronald Julia.
Licensure Skilled care; Intermediate care; Personal care. *Beds* SNF 18; ICF 29; Personal care 15. *Private Pay Patients* 75%. *Certified* Medicare.
Owner Proprietary corp.
Admissions Requirements Medical examination; Physician's request.
Staff Physicians 1 (pt); RNs 8 (ft), 4 (pt); LPNs 2 (pt); Nurses' aides 20 (ft), 10 (pt); Physical therapists 2 (pt); Occupational therapists 1 (pt); Speech therapists 1 (pt); Activities coordinators 1 (ft); Dietitians 1 (pt); Ophthalmologists 1 (pt); Podiatrists 1 (pt); Audiologists 1 (pt).
Facilities Dining room; Physical therapy room; Activities room; Crafts room; Laundry room; Barber/Beauty shop.
Activities Arts & crafts; Cards; Games; Prayer groups; Movies; Dances/Social/Cultural gatherings; Intergenerational programs; Pet therapy.

Cedarbrook Fountain Hill Annex
724 Delaware Ave, Bethlehem, PA 18015
(215) 691-6379
Admin Hilda Pope. *Dir of Nursing* Sara Wright RN. *Medical Dir* Gavin Barr MD.
Licensure Skilled care; Intermediate care. *Beds* SNF 118; ICF 79. *Private Pay Patients* 1%. *Certified* Medicaid; Medicare.
Owner Publicly owned.
Admissions Requirements Medical examination.
Staff Physicians 5 (pt); RNs 18 (ft), 8 (pt); LPNs 25 (ft), 6 (pt); Nurses' aides 67 (ft), 26 (pt); Physical therapists (contracted); Reality therapists 2 (ft); Recreational therapists 6 (ft); Occupational therapists (consultant); Speech therapists (consultant); Activities coordinators 1 (ft); Dietitians 1 (ft); Podiatrists (consultant); Audiologists (consultant); Social service 2 (ft); PT aides 2 (ft), 1 (pt); Ward clerks 6 (ft); Medical records 1 (ft); CSRs 3 (ft); URs 1 (ft).
Languages Spanish.
Facilities Dining room; Physical therapy room; Activities room; Chapel; Crafts room; Laundry room; Barber/Beauty shop.
Activities Arts & crafts; Cards; Games; Reading groups; Prayer groups; Movies; Shopping trips; Dances/Social/Cultural gatherings; Intergenerational programs; Pet therapy.

Holy Family Manor Inc
1200 Spring St, Bethlehem, PA 18018
(215) 865-5595

Admin Constance C Stair NHA. *Dir of Nursing* Marie Morano RN. *Medical Dir* Joseph Bartos MD.
Licensure Skilled care; Intermediate care. *Beds* SNF 99; ICF 99. *Private Pay Patients* 60%. *Certified* Medicaid; Medicare.
Owner Nonprofit corp.
Staff Physicians; RNs; LPNs; Nurses' aides; Physical therapists; Reality therapists; Recreational therapists; Occupational therapists; Speech therapists; Activities coordinators; Dietitians; Ophthalmologists (consultant); Podiatrists (consultant); Audiologists (consultants).
Affiliation Roman Catholic.

Leader Nursing & Rehabilitation Center II—Bethlehem
2029 Westgate Dr, Bethlehem, PA 18017
(215) 861-0100
Licensure Skilled care. *Beds* SNF 221. *Certified* Medicaid; Medicare.
Owner Proprietary corp (Manor Care Inc).

Leader Nursing & Rehabilitation Center I—Bethlehem
Westgate Dr & Catasauqua Rd, Bethlehem, PA 18017
(215) 865-6077
Admin Ann Molesevich. *Dir of Nursing* Deborah Csaszar. *Medical Dir* William Hemmerly MD.
Licensure Skilled care; Intermediate care. *Beds* SNF 152; ICF 61. *Private Pay Patients* 30%. *Certified* Medicaid; Medicare.
Owner Proprietary corp (Manor Care Inc).
Admissions Requirements Medical examination.
Staff RNs 11 (ft), 15 (pt); LPNs 24 (ft), 15 (pt); Nurses' aides 67 (ft), 43 (pt); Physical therapists 1 (ft); Recreational therapists (consultant); Occupational therapists 1 (ft); Speech therapists (consultant); Activities coordinators 1 (ft); Dietitians (consultant); Ophthalmologists (consultant); Podiatrists (consultant); Audiologists (consultant); Chaplains 1 (ft), 1 (pt).
Facilities Dining room; Physical therapy room; Activities room; Chapel; Laundry room; Barber/Beauty shop.
Activities Arts & crafts; Cards; Games; Reading groups; Prayer groups; Movies; Shopping trips; Dances/Social/Cultural gatherings; Intergenerational programs; Pet therapy; Chaplaincy program.

Bloomsburg

Bloomsburg Health Care Center
211 E 1st St, Bloomsburg, PA 17815
(717) 784-5930
Licensure Skilled care. *Beds* 154. *Certified* Medicaid; Medicare.
Owner Proprietary corp.

Blue Ball

Wetzler Convalescent Home Inc
Box 400, Blue Ball, PA 17506
(717) 354-7601
Licensure Skilled care. *Beds* SNF 17. *Certified* Medicaid.
Owner Proprietary corp.

Blue Bell

Normandy Farms Estates Nursing Care Facility
PO Box 1108, 1801 Morris Rd, Blue Bell, PA 19422
(215) 699-8727
Licensure Skilled care; Independent living. *Beds* SNF 55. *Certified* Medicare.
Owner Proprietary corp.

Boothwyn

Longwood Villa Geriatric Nursing Center
1194 Naamans Creek Rd, Boothwyn, PA 19061
(215) 459-9150
Admin Elizabeth A Thummel. *Dir of Nursing* Elizabeth Hisler. *Medical Dir* Dr John Giuliano.
Licensure Skilled care; Intermediate care. *Beds* SNF 28; ICF 25. *Certified* Medicaid.
Owner Proprietary corp.
Admissions Requirements Medical examination; Physician's request.
Staff Physicians; RNs; LPNs; Nurses' aides; Physical therapists; Reality therapists; Recreational therapists; Occupational therapists; Speech therapists; Activities coordinators; Dietitians; Ophthalmologists; Dentists.
Facilities Dining room; Activities room; Chapel; Crafts room; Laundry room; Barber/Beauty shop.
Activities Arts & crafts; Cards; Games; Reading groups; Prayer groups; Movies; Shopping trips; Dances/Social/Cultural gatherings.

Brackenridge

Highland Nursing & Rehabilitation Center
1050 Broadview Blvd, Brackenridge, PA 15014
(412) 224-9200
Admin Helen E Kunca RN NHA. *Dir of Nursing* Virginia Bialas. *Medical Dir* Dr Frank Kush.
Licensure Skilled care. *Beds* SNF 97. *Private Pay Patients* 30%. *Certified* Medicaid; Medicare.
Owner Proprietary corp (Genesis Health Ventures).
Staff RNs 5 (ft), 2 (pt); LPNs 10 (ft), 10 (pt); Nurses' aides 29 (ft), 9 (pt); Physical therapists; Dietitians.
Facilities Dining room; Physical therapy room; Activities room; Laundry room; Barber/Beauty shop.
Activities Arts & crafts; Cards; Games; Reading groups; Prayer groups; Movies; Shopping trips; Dances/Social/Cultural gatherings; Cardiac support group; Alzheimer's support group.

Bradford

Bradford Manor
50 Langmaid Ln, Bradford, PA 16701
(814) 362-6090
Admin Robert C Lytle.
Medical Dir Fayez Roumani MD.
Licensure Skilled care; Intermediate care. *Beds* Swing beds SNF/ICF 121. *Private Pay Patients* 10%. *Certified* Medicaid; Medicare.
Owner Proprietary corp (HCF Inc).
Admissions Requirements Medical examination.
Facilities Dining room; Physical therapy room; Activities room; Laundry room; Barber/Beauty shop; Library; Ice cream parlor.
Activities Arts & crafts; Cards; Games; Reading groups; Prayer groups; Movies; Shopping trips; Dances/Social/Cultural gatherings; Pet therapy.

Bradford Nursing Pavilion
200 Pleasant St, Bradford, PA 16701
(814) 368-4143
Admin Michael G Guley. *Dir of Nursing* Karen Cordner Quigg. *Medical Dir* Edward Roche MD.
Licensure Skilled care. *Beds* SNF 95. *Private Pay Patients* 40%. *Certified* Medicaid; Medicare.
Owner Nonprofit corp.
Admissions Requirements Minimum age 18.

Staff Physicians 1 (ft); RNs 6 (ft), 1 (pt); LPNs 8 (ft), 1 (pt); Nurses' aides 33 (ft); Physical therapists 1 (ft); Recreational therapists 2 (ft); Occupational therapists 1 (ft); Speech therapists 1 (ft); Dietitians 1 (ft); Ophthalmologists 1 (pt); Podiatrists 1 (pt).
Facilities Dining room; Activities room; Laundry room; Barber/Beauty shop.
Activities Arts & crafts; Games; Reading groups; Prayer groups; Movies; Shopping trips; Intergenerational programs; Pet therapy.

Hannum Memorial Rest Home Inc
PO Box 34, Bradford, PA 16701-0034
(814) 368-5648
Admin Deborah M Sprague.
Licensure Intermediate care. *Beds* ICF 34. *Certified* Medicaid.
Owner Nonprofit corp.
Staff Physicians 1 (pt); RNs 2 (ft), 2 (pt); LPNs 1 (ft), 2 (pt); Nurses' aides 8 (ft), 4 (pt); Physical therapists 1 (pt); Speech therapists 1 (pt); Activities coordinators 1 (ft); Dietitians 1 (pt); Podiatrists 1 (pt); Audiologists 1 (pt).
Affiliation Baptist.
Facilities Dining room; Activities room; Laundry room; Barber/Beauty shop.
Activities Arts & crafts; Cards; Games; Reading groups; Movies; Shopping trips; Dances/Social/Cultural gatherings.

Ramsbottom Center Inc
800 E Main St, Bradford, PA 16701
(814) 362-7401
Licensure Intermediate care for mentally retarded. *Beds* 24. *Certified* Medicaid.
Owner Nonprofit corp.

Bridgeville

Country Meadows of South Hills
3590 Washington Pike, Bridgeville, PA 15017
(412) 257-2474
Licensure Skilled care. *Beds* SNF 180. *Certified* Medicaid; Medicare.
Owner Proprietary corp.

Mayview State Hospital
Bridgeville, PA 15017
(412) 221-7500
Licensure Intermediate care for mentally retarded. *Beds* 120. *Certified* Medicaid.
Owner Publicly owned.

Mayview State Hospital—Long-Term Care Unit
Bridgeville, PA 15017
(412) 343-2700
Admin Joan Malarbey.
Medical Dir Charles L Squires MD.
Licensure Intermediate care. *Beds* 184. *Certified* Medicaid.
Owner Publicly owned.
Staff Physicians 2 (ft); RNs 17 (ft), 1 (pt); LPNs 9 (ft); Nurses' aides 70 (ft).
Facilities Dining room; Activities room; Chapel; Crafts room; Laundry room; Barber/Beauty shop; Conference room.
Activities Arts & crafts; Cards; Games; Reading groups; Prayer groups; Movies; Shopping trips; Dances/Social/Cultural gatherings; Bowling.

Haig S Temple Geriatric Center II
1601 Mayview Rd, Bridgeville, PA 15017
(412) 257-6354
Licensure Skilled care. *Beds* SNF 92. *Certified* Medicaid.
Owner Publicly owned.

Bristol

Silver Lake Nursing & Rehabilitation Center
King St at Fayette Dr, Bristol, PA 19007
(215) 785-3201, 785-5310 FAX

Admin Dennis H Gregory. *Dir of Nursing*
Gloria Boring.
Licensure Skilled care. *Beds* SNF 174. *Private
Pay Patients* 17%. *Certified* Medicaid;
Medicare.
Owner Proprietary corp.
Admissions Requirements Medical
examination; Physician's request.
Staff Physical therapists 1 (pt); Recreational
therapists 1 (ft); Occupational therapists 1
(pt); Speech therapists 1 (pt); Activities
coordinators 2 (ft); Dietitians 1 (ft);
Audiologists 1 (pt).
Facilities Dining room; Physical therapy
room; Activities room; Barber/Beauty shop.
Activities Arts & crafts; Cards; Games;
Reading groups; Prayer groups; Movies;
Dances/Social/Cultural gatherings;
Intergenerational programs.

Brookville

Jefferson Manor
RD 5, Brookville, PA 15825
(814) 849-8026
Licensure Skilled care; Intermediate care. *Beds*
SNF 112; ICF 112. *Certified* Medicaid;
Medicare.
Owner Proprietary corp (Unicare).

Pennsylvania Memorial Home
51 Euclid Ave, Brookville, PA 15825
(814) 849-3615
Licensure Skilled care; Intermediate care. *Beds*
SNF 51; ICF 49. *Certified* Medicaid;
Medicare.
Owner Nonprofit corp.

Broomall

Broomall Presbyterian Home
146 Marple Road, Broomall, PA 19008
(215) 356-0100
Licensure Skilled care; Alzheimer's care. *Beds*
SNF 147. *Certified* Medicaid; Medicare.
Owner Nonprofit corp (Philadelphia
Presbyterian Homes).
Admissions Requirements Minimum age 65;
Medical examination.
Staff Physicians 3 (pt); RNs 7 (ft), 15 (pt);
LPNs 7 (ft), 2 (pt); Nurses' aides 70 (ft), 20
(pt); Physical therapists 1 (pt); Recreational
therapists 1 (ft); Speech therapists 1 (pt);
Activities coordinators 1 (ft); Dietitians 1
(pt); Ophthalmologists 1 (pt); Podiatrists 1
(pt).
Affiliation Presbyterian.
Facilities Dining room; Physical therapy
room; Activities room; Crafts room; Laundry
room; Barber/Beauty shop; Library.
Activities Arts & crafts; Cards; Games;
Reading groups; Prayer groups; Movies;
Shopping trips; Dances/Social/Cultural
gatherings; Remotivation therapy; Touch
therapy.

Central Park Lodge—Broomall
50 N Malin Rd, Broomall, PA 19008
(215) 356-0800
Admin David Z Ross. *Dir of Nursing* Dolores
Jaquith RN. *Medical Dir* Madeline Long
MD.
Licensure Skilled care; Alzheimer's care. *Beds*
SNF 286. *Certified* Medicaid; Medicare.
Owner Proprietary corp.
Admissions Requirements Minimum age 60;
Medical examination.
Staff RNs 10 (ft), 15 (pt); LPNs 6 (ft), 10 (pt);
Nurses' aides 75 (ft), 40 (pt); Physical
therapists 1 (pt); Recreational therapists 3
(ft); Occupational therapists 1 (pt); Speech
therapists 1 (pt); Dietitians 1 (pt);
Ophthalmologists 2 (pt); Podiatrists 1 (pt).
Facilities Dining room; Physical therapy
room; Activities room; Crafts room; Laundry
room; Barber/Beauty shop.

Activities Arts & crafts; Cards; Games;
Reading groups; Prayer groups; Movies;
Shopping trips; Dances/Social/Cultural
gatherings; Sports events.

Church Lane Health Care Center
43 Church Ln, Broomall, PA 19008
(215) 356-3003
Admin Robert Kopansky. *Dir of Nursing* N
Kopitsig. *Medical Dir* Dr William Kozin.
Licensure Skilled care. *Beds* SNF 132.
Certified Medicaid; Medicare.
Owner Proprietary corp.
Admissions Requirements Minimum age 65.
Staff RNs; LPNs; Nurses' aides; Physical
therapists; Recreational therapists;
Occupational therapists; Speech therapists;
Activities coordinators; Dietitians;
Ophthalmologists; Podiatrists; Dentists.
Facilities Dining room; Physical therapy
room; Activities room; Crafts room; Laundry
room; Barber/Beauty shop.
Activities Arts & crafts; Cards; Games;
Reading groups; Prayer groups; Movies;
Shopping trips; Dances/Social/Cultural
gatherings.

Brownsville

Brownsville Golden Age
501 Church St, Brownsville, PA 15417
(412) 785-3900
Licensure Skilled care. *Beds* 68. *Certified*
Medicaid; Medicare.
Owner Proprietary corp.

Bryn Mawr

Beaumont at Bryn Mawr
601 N Ithan Ave, Bryn Mawr, PA 19010
(215) 526-7000
Admin Joseph H Fortenbaugh III MBA NHA.
Dir of Nursing Catherine Casey MSN RN.
Medical Dir Douglas Raymond MD.
Licensure Skilled care; Personal care;
Alzheimer's care; Retirement. *Beds* SNF 28;
Personal care 22; Retirement 300. *Private
Pay Patients* 95%. *Certified* Medicare.
Owner Nonprofit organization/foundation.
Admissions Requirements Minimum age adult;
Medical examination; Physician's request.
Staff RNs; LPNs; Nurses' aides; Physical
therapists (contracted); Recreational
therapists; Occupational therapists
(contracted); Speech therapists (contracted);
Activities coordinators; Dietitians;
Podiatrists (contracted); Audiologists
(contracted); Unit clerks.
Facilities Dining room; Physical therapy
room; Activities room; Crafts room; Laundry
room; Barber/Beauty shop; Library; Private
rooms with baths/showers.
Activities Arts & crafts; Cards; Games;
Reading groups; Prayer groups; Movies;
Dances/Social/Cultural gatherings;
Intergenerational programs; Pet therapy;
Picnics; Trips.

Bryn Mawr Terrace Convalescent Center
Haverford & Rugby Rds, Bryn Mawr, PA
19010
(215) 525-8300
Licensure Skilled care. *Beds* SNF 160.
Certified Medicare.
Owner Proprietary corp.

Chateau Nursing & Rehabilitation Center
956 Railroad Ave, Bryn Mawr, PA 19010
(215) 525-8412
Admin Anne A O'Rourke. *Dir of Nursing*
Jeanne Schell. *Medical Dir* Dr Koryeni.
Licensure Skilled care; Alzheimer's care. *Beds*
SNF 170. *Certified* Medicaid; Medicare.
Owner Proprietary corp.

Admissions Requirements Minimum age;
Medical examination.
Facilities Dining room; Physical therapy
room; Activities room; Crafts room; Laundry
room; Barber/Beauty shop.

Buckingham

Buckingham Valley Nursing Home
PO Box 447, Buckingham, PA 18912
(215) 598-7181
Licensure Skilled care. *Beds* SNF 100.
Certified Medicaid; Medicare.
Owner Proprietary corp.

Butler

Sunnyview Home
711 Morton Ave Ext, Butler, PA 16001
(412) 282-1800
Admin Thomas S Finucane. *Dir of Nursing*
Sheila A Scanlon RN. *Medical Dir* William
A Dicuccio MD.
Licensure Skilled care; Intermediate care. *Beds*
SNF 60; ICF 180. *Certified* Medicaid.
Owner Publicly owned.
Admissions Requirements Minimum age 18;
Medical examination; Physician's request.
Staff Physicians 3 (pt); RNs 7 (ft), 11 (pt);
LPNs 33 (ft), 5 (pt); Nurses' aides 98 (ft), 6
(pt); Physical therapists 4 (pt); Recreational
therapists 3 (ft); Speech therapists 1 (pt);
Activities coordinators 1 (ft); Dietitians 1
(pt); Ophthalmologists 1 (pt); Podiatrists 1
(pt).
Facilities Dining room; Physical therapy
room; Activities room; Chapel; Crafts room;
Laundry room; Barber/Beauty shop; Library.
Activities Arts & crafts; Cards; Games;
Reading groups; Prayer groups; Movies;
Shopping trips; Dances/Social/Cultural
gatherings.

Cabot

Lutheran Welfare Concordia Home
615 N Pike Rd, Cabot, PA 16023
(412) 352-1571
Admin Kieth E Frndak. *Dir of Nursing*
Michelene Neubert. *Medical Dir* Fred
Fioravanti MD.
Licensure Skilled care; Intermediate care;
Independent living. *Beds* SNF 60; ICF 66;
Independent living 20. *Certified* Medicaid;
Medicare.
Owner Nonprofit corp.
Admissions Requirements Minimum age 65;
Medical examination.
Staff Physicians 1 (pt); RNs 5 (ft), 3 (pt);
LPNs 6 (ft), 9 (pt); Nurses' aides 31 (ft), 15
(pt); Physical therapists 1 (pt); Speech
therapists 1 (pt); Dietitians 1 (pt).
Languages German.
Affiliation Lutheran.
Facilities Dining room; Physical therapy
room; Activities room; Chapel; Crafts room;
Laundry room; Barber/Beauty shop.
Activities Arts & crafts; Cards; Games;
Reading groups; Movies; Shopping trips.

Cambridge Springs

Presbyterian Home
229 N Main St, Cambridge Springs, PA 16403
(814) 398-2813
Admin Karen M Daughenbaugh NHA.
Medical Dir Edward J Owens DO; Dr Ronald
Martin.
Licensure Intermediate care; Personal care.
Beds ICF 10; Personal care 15. *Private Pay
Patients* 15%. *Certified* Medicaid.
Owner Nonprofit corp (Presbyterian Homes of
Lake Erie).
Admissions Requirements Medical
examination.

Staff Physicians; RNs 2 (ft), 3 (pt); LPNs 2 (ft), 4 (pt); Nurses' aides 3 (ft), 8 (pt); Activities coordinators; Dietitians (consultant).
Facilities Dining room; Laundry room; Barber/Beauty shop.
Activities Arts & crafts; Cards; Games; Reading groups; Prayer groups; Movies; Shopping trips; Dances/Social/Cultural gatherings; Intergenerational programs; Pet therapy.

Springs Manor Care Center
110 Canfield St, Cambridge Springs, PA 16403
(814) 398-4626
Admin Don McDowell. *Dir of Nursing* S Kathleen Varner RN. *Medical Dir* Dr Edward Owens.
Licensure Skilled care; Retirement. *Beds* SNF 91. *Certified* Medicaid; Medicare.
Owner Proprietary corp (Beverly Enterprises).
Admissions Requirements Medical examination; Physician's request.
Staff RNs 1 (ft); LPNs 1 (ft); Nurses' aides 1 (ft), 1 (pt); Physical therapists 1 (ft); Speech therapists 1 (pt); Activities coordinators 1 (ft); Dietitians 1 (ft).
Facilities Dining room; Physical therapy room; Activities room; Chapel; Laundry room; Barber/Beauty shop.
Activities Arts & crafts; Cards; Games; Reading groups; Prayer groups; Movies; Bowling league.

Camp Hill

Blue Ridge Haven—West
770 Poplar Church Rd, Camp Hill, PA 17011
(717) 763-7070
Licensure Skilled care; Intermediate care. *Beds* SNF 120; ICF 214. *Certified* Medicaid; Medicare.
Owner Proprietary corp (Beverly Enterprises).

Camp Hill Care Center
46 Erford Rd, Camp Hill, PA 17011
(717) 763-7361
Admin Sandra K Griffin. *Dir of Nursing* Jean Peterson. *Medical Dir* Dr Tzanis.
Licensure Skilled care; Intermediate care. *Beds* SNF 31; ICF 87. *Private Pay Patients* 10%. *Certified* Medicaid; Medicare.
Owner Proprietary corp (Meritcare).
Staff RNs 5 (ft), 2 (pt); LPNs 6 (ft), 4 (pt); Nurses' aides 40 (ft), 10 (pt); Physical therapists (contracted); Activities coordinators 2 (ft); Dietitians 1 (ft).
Facilities Dining room; Physical therapy room; Activities room; Laundry room; Barber/Beauty shop; Library.
Activities Arts & crafts; Cards; Games; Reading groups; Prayer groups; Movies; Shopping trips; Dances/Social/Cultural gatherings; Intergenerational programs; Pet therapy.

Leader Nursing & Rehabilitation Center—Camp Hill
1700 Market St, Camp Hill, PA 17011
(717) 737-8551
Admin Stacey E Radcliff MGS NHA. *Dir of Nursing* Sonna Schneider RN. *Medical Dir* Earl Moyer MD.
Licensure Skilled care; Retirement; Alzheimer's care. *Beds* 60. *Certified* Medicaid; Medicare.
Owner Proprietary corp (Manor Care Inc).
Staff Physicians 1 (ft); RNs; LPNs; Nurses' aides; Physical therapists; Speech therapists; Activities coordinators 1 (ft); Dietitians 2 (ft); Ophthalmologists.
Facilities Dining room; Physical therapy room; Activities room; Barber/Beauty shop.
Activities Arts & crafts; Cards; Games; Reading groups; Prayer groups; Movies; Shopping trips; Dances/Social/Cultural gatherings.

Campbelltown

Twin Oaks Nursing Home
90 W Main St, Campbelltown, PA 17010
(717) 838-2231
Admin Mary Snyder. *Dir of Nursing* Audry Scipioni. *Medical Dir* Harold Engle MD.
Licensure Intermediate care. *Beds* ICF 42. *Certified* Medicaid.
Owner Privately owned.
Admissions Requirements Medical examination; Physician's request.
Staff LPNs 4 (ft), 1 (pt); Nurses' aides 10 (ft), 5 (pt); Activities coordinators 1 (ft).
Facilities Dining room; Activities room; Barber/Beauty shop.
Activities Arts & crafts; Cards; Games; Reading groups.

Canonsburg

Canonsburg General Hospital Skilled Nursing Unit
RD 2 Rte 519 Box 147, Canonsburg, PA 15317
(412) 745-6100
Licensure Skilled care. *Beds* SNF 32. *Certified* Medicaid; Medicare.
Owner Proprietary corp.

Horizon Senior Care
300 Bair St, Canonsburg, PA 15317
Washington

Meadowlands Rehabilitation Center
RD 1 Box 146, Rte 519 S, Canonsburg, PA 15317
(412) 745-8000
Admin James O'Shea.
Medical Dir Patience Grummick.
Licensure Skilled care; Intermediate care. *Beds* SNF 120. *Certified* Medicaid; Medicare.
Owner Proprietary corp (New Medico Assoc).
Admissions Requirements Minimum age 16.
Staff Physicians 1 (ft), 4 (pt); RNs 12 (ft), 4 (pt); LPNs 12 (ft), 8 (pt); Nurses' aides 41 (ft), 16 (pt); Physical therapists 4 (ft); Recreational therapists 6 (ft); Occupational therapists 4 (ft); Speech therapists 4 (ft); Activities coordinators 1 (ft); Dietitians 1 (pt); Ophthalmologists 1 (pt); Podiatrists 1 (pt); Dentists 1 (pt); Adaptive equipment technicians 1 (ft); Family counselors 3 (ft); Case managers 3 (ft); Behavior specialists 1 (ft).
Facilities Dining room; Physical therapy room; Activities room; Crafts room; Laundry room; Barber/Beauty shop; Library.
Activities Arts & crafts; Cards; Games; Reading groups; Prayer groups; Movies; Shopping trips; Dances/Social/Cultural gatherings; Adaptive aquatics; Equestrian therapy.

South Hills Convalescent Center
201 Village Dr, Canonsburg, PA 15317
(412) 746-1300
Medical Dir Robert G Lesnock MD.
Licensure Skilled care. *Beds* SNF 104. *Certified* Medicaid; Medicare.
Owner Proprietary corp (Beverly Enterprises).
Admissions Requirements Minimum age 18; Medical examination.
Staff Physicians 1 (ft); RNs 7 (ft), 5 (pt); LPNs 6 (ft), 13 (pt); Nurses' aides 32 (ft), 21 (pt); Physical therapists 1 (pt); Speech therapists 1 (pt); Activities coordinators 1 (ft); Dietitians 1 (pt).
Facilities Dining room; Physical therapy room; Activities room; Chapel; Crafts room; Laundry room; Barber/Beauty shop; Library.
Activities Arts & crafts; Cards; Games; Reading groups; Prayer groups; Movies; Shopping trips; Dances/Social/Cultural gatherings.

Western Center
333 Curry Hill Rd, Canonsburg, PA 15317
(412) 745-0700
Licensure Intermediate care for mentally retarded. *Beds* 474. *Certified* Medicaid.
Owner Nonprofit corp.

Carbondale

Carbondale Nursing Home Inc
57 N Main St, Carbondale, PA 18407
(717) 282-1020
Medical Dir Dr John W Keyes.
Licensure Skilled care. *Beds* SNF 105. *Certified* Medicaid; Medicare.
Owner Proprietary corp.
Staff Physicians 1 (ft), 6 (pt); RNs 10 (ft); LPNs 15 (ft); Nurses' aides 15 (ft); Physical therapists 2 (pt); Recreational therapists 1 (ft); Occupational therapists 2 (pt); Speech therapists 2 (pt); Activities coordinators 1 (ft); Dietitians 1 (pt); Podiatrists 1 (pt); Dentists 1 (pt).

Carlisle

Alliance Home of Carlisle, PA
770 S Hanover St, Carlisle, PA 17013
(717) 249-1363
Admin Jack R Seward NHA ACSW. *Dir of Nursing* Beverly Osborn. *Medical Dir* Dr Robert Hollen.
Licensure Skilled care; Personal care; Apartments. *Beds* SNF 59; Personal care 73; Apts 48. *Private Pay Patients* 40%. *Certified* Medicaid.
Owner Nonprofit corp.
Admissions Requirements Minimum age 65.
Staff Physicians 1 (pt); RNs 6 (ft); LPNs 6 (ft); Nurses' aides 28 (ft); Activities coordinators 1 (ft).
Affiliation Christian & Missionary Alliance Foundation.
Facilities Dining room; Physical therapy room; Activities room; Chapel; Crafts room; Laundry room; Barber/Beauty shop; Library.
Activities Arts & crafts; Games; Reading groups; Prayer groups; Movies; Shopping trips; Dances/Social/Cultural gatherings; Pet therapy.

Church of God Home Inc
801 N Hanover St, Carlisle, PA 17013
(717) 249-5322, 258-5060 FAX
Admin Ronald F Madeira NHA; James E Domen Sr, Asst. *Dir of Nursing* Eleanor Hartman. *Medical Dir* Michael O Daniels MD.
Licensure Skilled care; Personal care; Retirement. *Beds* SNF 109; Personal care 30; Retirement 20. *Private Pay Patients* 60%. *Certified* Medicaid; Medicare.
Owner Nonprofit corp.
Admissions Requirements Medical examination.
Staff Physicians 1 (pt); RNs 6 (ft), 3 (pt); LPNs 11 (ft), 4 (pt); Nurses' aides 45 (ft), 14 (pt); Physical therapists 1 (pt); Recreational therapists 2 (ft); Occupational therapists 1 (pt); Speech therapists 1 (pt); Activities coordinators 1 (ft); Dietitians 1 (pt); Ophthalmologists 1 (pt); Podiatrists 1 (ft), 1 (pt); Audiologists 1 (pt).
Affiliation Church of God.
Facilities Dining room; Physical therapy room; Activities room; Chapel; Crafts room; Laundry room; Barber/Beauty shop.
Activities Arts & crafts; Games; Reading groups; Prayer groups; Movies; Shopping trips; Dances/Social/Cultural gatherings; Intergenerational programs; Pet therapy; Cooking; Dinner out; Men's club; Music appreciation; Choir.

Cumberland County Nursing Home
375 Claremont Dr, Carlisle, PA 17013
(717) 243-2031

Licensure Skilled care; Intermediate care. *Beds* 111. *Certified* Medicaid; Medicare.
Owner Publicly owned.

Forest Park Health Center
700 Walnut Bottom Rd, Carlisle, PA 17013
(717) 243-1032
Admin Denny Middleton NHA. *Dir of Nursing* Judith Hamlet RN. *Medical Dir* Dr Harold G Kretzing.
Licensure Skilled care. *Beds* SNF 104. *Private Pay Patients* 60%. *Certified* Medicaid; Medicare.
Owner Nonprofit corp.
Admissions Requirements Physician's request.
Staff Physicians 6 (pt); RNs 8 (ft); LPNs 8 (ft); Nurses' aides 35 (ft), 5 (pt); Physical therapists 1 (ft); Activities coordinators 1 (ft); Dietitians 1 (ft).
Affiliation Presbyterian.
Facilities Dining room; Physical therapy room; Activities room; Chapel; Crafts room; Laundry room; Barber/Beauty shop; Library.
Activities Arts & crafts; Cards; Games; Reading groups; Prayer groups; Movies; Shopping trips; Dances/Social/Cultural gatherings; Intergenerational programs; Pet therapy.

Leader Nursing & Rehabilitation Center—Carlisle
940 Walnut Bottom Rd, Carlisle, PA 17013
(717) 249-0085
Licensure Skilled care. *Beds* SNF 120. *Certified* Medicaid; Medicare.
Owner Proprietary corp (Manor Care Inc).

Thornwald Home
422 Walnut Bottom Rd, Carlisle, PA 17013
(717) 249-4118
Licensure Skilled care. *Beds* 79. *Certified* Medicaid.
Owner Nonprofit corp.

Sarah A Todd Memorial Home
1000 W South St, Carlisle, PA 17013
(717) 245-2187
Admin Susan B Hench. *Dir of Nursing* Jean Lane RN. *Medical Dir* Dr Kenneth Guistwite.
Licensure Skilled care; Intermediate care; Retirement. *Beds* SNF 11; ICF 49. *Certified* Medicaid; Medicare.
Owner Nonprofit corp.
Admissions Requirements Medical examination; Physician's request.
Staff RNs 3 (ft), 3 (pt); LPNs 4 (ft), 3 (pt); Nurses' aides 14 (ft), 18 (pt); Recreational therapists 1 (ft), 1 (pt); Dietitians 1 (pt).
Facilities Dining room; Physical therapy room; Activities room; Crafts room; Laundry room; Barber/Beauty shop; Library; Multi-purpose activity room.
Activities Arts & crafts; Cards; Games; Reading groups; Prayer groups; Movies; Shopping trips; Dances/Social/Cultural gatherings; Sensory groups; Adopt-a-grandparent.

Carnegie

Step by Step Inc
112 7th Ave, Carnegie, PA 15106
(412) 279-8943
Licensure Intermediate care for mentally retarded. *Beds* 8. *Certified* Medicaid.
Owner Nonprofit corp.

Woodville State Hospital Long-Term Care
Carnegie, PA 15106
(412) 645-6449
Licensure Skilled care. *Beds* SNF 183. *Certified* Medicaid; Medicare.
Owner Publicly owned.

Chambersburg

Franklin County Nursing Home
201 Franklin Farm Ln, Chambersburg, PA 17201
(717) 264-2715
Admin Joanne V Wible. *Dir of Nursing* Marcia Whitmore RN. *Medical Dir* Joseph Thornton MD; Martin Hudzinski MD.
Licensure Skilled care; Intermediate care. *Beds* SNF 40; ICF 184. *Private Pay Patients* 5%. *Certified* Medicaid; Medicare.
Owner Publicly owned.
Admissions Requirements Minimum age 18; Medical examination.
Staff Physicians (contracted); RNs 8 (ft), 3 (pt); LPNs 23 (ft), 15 (pt); Nurses' aides 50 (ft), 50 (pt); Activities coordinators 1 (ft); Dietitians 1 (pt); Ophthalmologists 2 (pt); Podiatrists 1 (pt).
Facilities Dining room; Physical therapy room; Activities room; Chapel; Crafts room; Laundry room; Barber/Beauty shop.
Activities Arts & crafts; Cards; Games; Reading groups; Prayer groups; Movies; Shopping trips; Pet therapy.

Leader Nursing & Rehabilitation Center—Chambersburg
1070 Stouffer Ave, Chambersburg, PA 17201
(717) 263-0463
Licensure Skilled care; Intermediate care. *Beds* 177. *Certified* Medicaid; Medicare.
Owner Proprietary corp (Manor Care Inc).

Menno-Haven
2075 Scotland Ave, Chambersburg, PA 17201
(717) 263-8545
Admin E Lewis Leaman. *Dir of Nursing* Joan Winter RN. *Medical Dir* James K Vankirk MD.
Licensure Skilled care; Intermediate care; Independent living; Alzheimer's care. *Beds* 132. *Certified* Medicaid; Medicare.
Owner Nonprofit corp.
Admissions Requirements Minimum age 55; Medical examination.
Staff Physicians 4 (pt); RNs 12 (ft); LPNs 12 (ft); Nurses' aides 40 (ft); Physical therapists 3 (pt); Reality therapists 1 (ft); Recreational therapists 1 (ft); Occupational therapists 1 (pt); Speech therapists 1 (pt); Activities coordinators 1 (ft); Dietitians 1 (ft); Ophthalmologists 2 (pt); Podiatrists 1 (pt).
Affiliation Mennonite.
Facilities Dining room; Physical therapy room; Activities room; Chapel; Crafts room; Laundry room; Barber/Beauty shop; Library; Therapy pool; Coffee shop; Corner store; Wood shop.
Activities Arts & crafts; Cards; Games; Reading groups; Prayer groups; Movies; Shopping trips; Dances/Social/Cultural gatherings.

John H Shook Home for the Aged
55 S 2nd St, Chambersburg, PA 17201
(717) 264-6815
Admin Edward T Parks. *Dir of Nursing* Lois C Bitner RN. *Medical Dir* Charles J Shapiro MD.
Licensure Intermediate care; Alzheimer's care. *Beds* ICF 64. *Certified* Medicaid.
Owner Nonprofit organization/foundation.
Admissions Requirements Minimum age 65; Medical examination.
Staff RNs 3 (ft), 2 (pt); LPNs 7 (ft), 7 (pt); Nurses' aides 28 (ft), 13 (pt); Activities coordinators 2 (ft), 2 (pt); Dietitians 1 (pt).
Facilities Dining room; Activities room; Laundry room; Barber/Beauty shop.
Activities Arts & crafts; Cards; Games; Reading groups; Prayer groups; Movies; Shopping trips; Dances/Social/Cultural gatherings; Pet therapy; Sunday school.

Chatham

Chatham Acres
PO Box 1, Chatham, PA 19318
(215) 869-2456, 869-9860 FAX
Admin Lisa Fiora Grech. *Dir of Nursing* Maureen Zagorskie RN. *Medical Dir* David Callahan DO.
Licensure Intermediate care. *Beds* ICF 121. *Private Pay Patients* 15%. *Certified* Medicaid.
Owner Proprietary corp.
Admissions Requirements Medical examination; Physician's request.
Staff Physicians; RNs; LPNs; Physical therapists (contracted); Dietitians; Podiatrists.
Facilities Dining room; Physical therapy room; Activities room; Crafts room; Laundry room; Barber/Beauty shop; Covered porch.
Activities Arts & crafts; Cards; Games; Reading groups; Prayer groups; Movies; Shopping trips; Dances/Social/Cultural gatherings; Intergenerational programs; Pet therapy.

Chester

Belvedere
2507 Chestnut St, Chester, PA 19013
(215) 872-5373
Admin Thomas P Connor. *Dir of Nursing* Mary Flacco RN. *Medical Dir* Barry Holms DO.
Licensure Skilled care; Residential care. *Beds* SNF 120; Residential care 28. *Private Pay Patients* 65%. *Certified* Medicaid; Medicare.
Owner Proprietary corp (Diversified Health Services).
Admissions Requirements Medical examination; Physician's request.
Staff RNs 8 (ft); LPNs 11 (ft); Nurses' aides 42 (ft); Physical therapists 2 (ft); Recreational therapists 2 (ft); Occupational therapists 1 (pt); Speech therapists 1 (pt); Activities coordinators 1 (ft); Dietitians 1 (ft); Ophthalmologists; Podiatrists; Audiologists 1 (pt); Dentists 1 (pt).
Facilities Dining room; Physical therapy room; Activities room; Laundry room; Barber/Beauty shop; Lounges.
Activities Arts & crafts; Cards; Games; Prayer groups; Movies; Shopping trips; Dances/Social/Cultural gatherings.

Chester Care Center
15th St & Shaw Terrace, Chester, PA 19013
(215) 499-8800, 499-8805 FAX
Admin Anna E Helfrich. *Dir of Nursing* Marian Ardinger RN. *Medical Dir* Edward Stankiewicz MD.
Licensure Skilled care; Intermediate care. *Beds* SNF 93; ICF 97. *Private Pay Patients* 5%. *Certified* Medicaid.
Owner Proprietary corp.
Admissions Requirements Minimum age 16; Medical examination; Physician's request.
Staff RNs 11 (ft), 3 (pt); LPNs 27 (ft), 8 (pt); Nurses' aides 88 (ft), 6 (pt); Physical therapists 1 (ft), 1 (pt); Reality therapists 1 (ft); Recreational therapists 1 (ft); Occupational therapists 1 (pt); Activities coordinators 1 (ft); Dietitians 1 (ft), 1 (pt).
Facilities Dining room; Physical therapy room; Activities room; Crafts room; Laundry room; Barber/Beauty shop.
Activities Arts & crafts; Cards; Games; Reading groups; Prayer groups; Movies; Shopping trips; Dances/Social/Cultural gatherings; Intergenerational programs.

Chester Care Center
210 W 14th St, Chester, PA 19013
Admin Aubrey C Smith.
Medical Dir Dr Leonard Haltrecht.
Licensure Intermediate care. *Beds* 97. *Certified* Medicaid.

Owner Proprietary corp.
Admissions Requirements Medical examination.
Staff Physicians 8 (pt); RNs 1 (pt); LPNs 9 (ft), 12 (pt); Nurses' aides 27 (ft), 20 (pt); Physical therapists 1 (pt); Reality therapists 1 (pt); Recreational therapists 1 (pt); Occupational therapists 1 (pt); Speech therapists 1 (pt); Activities coordinators 1 (ft); Dietitians 1 (pt); Podiatrists 1 (pt).
Facilities Dining room; Physical therapy room; Activities room; Crafts room; Laundry room; Barber/Beauty shop; Library.
Activities Arts & crafts; Cards; Games; Reading groups; Prayer groups; Movies; Shopping trips; Dances/Social/Cultural gatherings.

Cheswick

Valley View Nursing Home
RD 2, Box 234, Cheswick, PA 15024
(412) 767-4998
Admin Bonita L Readie. *Dir of Nursing* Mary Ann Montgomery RN. *Medical Dir* Dr Nick Bourdakos.
Licensure Skilled care; Intermediate care 79. *Beds* SNF 49; ICF 79. *Certified* Medicaid; Medicare; VA.
Owner Proprietary corp (Columbia Corp).
Staff Physicians 10 (pt); RNs 4 (ft), 7 (pt); LPNs 6 (ft), 5 (pt); Nurses' aides 36 (ft), 10 (pt); Physical therapists 1 (pt); Recreational therapists 1 (ft); Occupational therapists 1 (pt); Speech therapists 1 (pt); Activities coordinators 1 (ft); Dietitians 1 (pt); Ophthalmologists 1 (pt).
Facilities Dining room; Physical therapy room; Crafts room; Laundry room; Barber/Beauty shop.
Activities Arts & crafts; Cards; Games; Reading groups; Prayer groups; Movies; Dances/Social/Cultural gatherings; Adopt-a-grandparent program; Music therapy; Pet therapy; Horticulture.

Chicora

Chicora Medical Center
PO Box Q, Chicora, PA 16025
(412) 445-2000
Admin Yvonne De Bacco. *Dir of Nursing* Hazel Endlish. *Medical Dir* Scott S Piranian MD.
Licensure Skilled care; Intermediate care; Personal care. *Beds* SNF 54; ICF 48; Personal care 26. *Certified* Medicaid; Medicare.
Owner Proprietary corp.
Admissions Requirements Minimum age 16.
Staff RNs; LPNs; Nurses' aides; Activities coordinators.
Facilities Dining room; Physical therapy room; Activities room; Crafts room; Laundry room; Barber/Beauty shop; Library.
Activities Arts & crafts; Cards; Games; Reading groups; Prayer groups; Movies; Shopping trips; Dances/Social/Cultural gatherings.

Christiana

Harrison House
41 Newport Pike, Christiana, PA 17509
(219) 593-6901
Medical Dir Paul W Herr DO.
Licensure Skilled care; Independent living. *Beds* 139. *Certified* Medicare.
Owner Proprietary corp.
Admissions Requirements Minimum age 16.
Staff RNs 3 (ft), 10 (pt); LPNs 5 (ft), 10 (pt); Nurses' aides 24 (ft), 58 (pt); Activities coordinators 2 (ft); Dietitians 1 (ft); Physical therapists; Occupational therapists; Speech therapists.

Facilities Dining room; Physical therapy room; Activities room; Chapel; Crafts room; Laundry room; Barber/Beauty shop; Greenhouse.
Activities Arts & crafts; Cards; Games; Reading groups; Prayer groups; Movies; Shopping trips; Dances/Social/Cultural gatherings; Church; Sunday school.

Clairton

Lawson Nursing Home Inc
540 Coal Valley Rd, Clairton, PA 15025
(412) 466-1125
Admin Richard Lawson. *Dir of Nursing* Elaine Eckbreth. *Medical Dir* Robert Milligan.
Licensure Skilled care; Alzheimer's care. *Beds* SNF 55. *Private Pay Patients* 100%.
Owner Privately owned.
Admissions Requirements Minimum age 60.
Staff RNs 10 (ft); Nurses' aides 30 (ft), 20 (pt); Physical therapists; Recreational therapists 1 (ft); Activities coordinators 1 (ft); Dietitians.
Facilities Dining room; Activities room; Laundry room; Barber/Beauty shop.
Activities Arts & crafts; Cards; Games; Reading groups; Prayer groups; Movies; Dances/Social/Cultural gatherings; Intergenerational programs.

Clarion

Clarion Care Center
999 Heidrick St, Clarion, PA 16214
(814) 226-6380, 226-6391 FAX
Admin Karen Wilshire. *Dir of Nursing* Dennis Wickline RN. *Medical Dir* Michael Meyer DO.
Licensure Skilled care; Intermediate care. *Beds* SNF 45; ICF 107. *Private Pay Patients* 15%. *Certified* Medicaid; Medicare.
Owner Proprietary corp (Meritcare Inc).
Admissions Requirements Minimum age 18; Medical examination; Physician's request.
Staff RNs 4 (ft), 4 (pt); LPNs 20 (ft); Nurses' aides 59 (ft); Physical therapists (contracted); Occupational therapists (contracted); Speech therapists (contracted); Activities coordinators 3 (ft); Dietitians 1 (ft); Podiatrists (contracted); Audiologists (contracted).
Facilities Dining room; Physical therapy room; Activities room; Laundry room; Barber/Beauty shop.
Activities Arts & crafts; Cards; Games; Reading groups; Prayer groups; Movies; Shopping trips; Dances/Social/Cultural gatherings; Intergenerational programs; Pet therapy; Adopt-a-grandparent.

Clarks Summit

Abington Manor Nursing & Rehabilitation Center
100 Edella Rd, Clarks Summit, PA 18411
(717) 586-1002
Admin Michael Wylie.
Licensure Skilled care. *Beds* SNF 120. *Certified* Medicaid; Medicare.
Owner Proprietary corp (Genesis Health Ventures).

Clarks Summit State Hospital Long-Term Care Facility
1451 Hillside Dr, Clarks Summit, PA 18411
(717) 586-2011
Licensure Skilled care. *Beds* SNF 167. *Certified* Medicaid.
Owner Publicly owned.

White Haven Annex at Clark Summit
Clarks Summit State Hospital, Clarks Summit, PA 18411
(717) 586-2011

Licensure Intermediate care. *Beds* 52. *Certified* Medicaid.
Owner Nonprofit corp.

Clearfield

Clear Haven Nursing Center
700 Leonard St, Clearfield, PA 16830
(814) 765-7546
Licensure Skilled care; Intermediate care. *Beds* SNF 82; ICF 160. *Certified* Medicaid; Medicare.
Owner Proprietary corp (Unicare).

Mountain Laurel Nursing Center
700 Leonard St, Clearfield, PA 16830
(814) 765-7546
Licensure Skilled care. *Beds* SNF 242. *Certified* Medicaid; Medicare.
Owner Proprietary corp.

Coaldale

Coaldale State General Hospital Geriatric Center
7th St, Coaldale, PA 18218
(717) 645-2131
Licensure Skilled care. *Beds* SNF 48. *Certified* Medicaid; Medicare.
Owner Publicly owned.

Coatesville

Embreeville Center
Rte 162, Coatesville, PA 19320
(215) 486-8000
Admin Marguerite M Conley.
Medical Dir Resa Epel MD.
Licensure Intermediate care for mentally retarded. *Beds* ICF/MR 280. *Certified* Medicaid.
Owner Publicly owned.

Columbia

Heatherbank
745 Chiques Hill Rd, Columbia, PA 17512
(717) 684-7555
Admin Claire Nicholson. *Dir of Nursing* Judith G Garman RN. *Medical Dir* Ray Wilson MD.
Licensure Skilled care; Intermediate care; Rehabilitation. *Beds* SNF 98; ICF 82. *Certified* Medicaid; Medicare.
Owner Proprietary corp (Wilmac Corp).
Admissions Requirements Minimum age 12; Medical examination; Physician's request.
Staff RNs 7 (ft), 4 (pt); LPNs 18 (ft), 6 (pt); Nurses' aides 53 (ft), 15 (pt); Physical therapists 1 (pt); Recreational therapists 1 (ft); Occupational therapists 1 (pt); Speech therapists 1 (pt); Dietitians 1 (ft).
Languages Spanish.
Facilities Dining room; Physical therapy room; Activities room; Crafts room; Laundry room; Barber/Beauty shop; Library; Solarium; Conference room; Education room; 2 resident lounges; Patio; Staff dining room; Shrubbed grounds; Susquehanna River view.
Activities Arts & crafts; Cards; Games; Reading groups; Prayer groups; Movies; Shopping trips; Dances/Social/Cultural gatherings; Intergenerational programs; Pet therapy; Adopt-a-grandparent; Intrafacility events.

St Anne's Home
RD 2, Columbia, PA 17512
(717) 285-5443
Admin Sr Carmela Ginto. *Dir of Nursing* Sr M Daniele Brought. *Medical Dir* Dr William Landis.
Licensure Skilled care; Retirement. *Beds* SNF 121. *Certified* Medicaid.
Owner Nonprofit corp.

Admissions Requirements Medical examination; Physician's request.
Staff RNs; LPNs; Nurses' aides; Physical therapists; Recreational therapists; Occupational therapists; Activities coordinators; Dietitians.
Affiliation Roman Catholic.
Facilities Dining room; Physical therapy room; Activities room; Chapel; Crafts room; Laundry room; Barber/Beauty shop; Library; Occupational therapy room.
Activities Arts & crafts; Cards; Games; Reading groups; Prayer groups; Movies; Shopping trips; Dances/Social/Cultural gatherings.

Concordville

Concord Villa Convalescent Home
Rte 1, Concordville, PA 19331
(215) 459-2900
Admin Donald Tabb. *Dir of Nursing* Suzanne Gray. *Medical Dir* Ronald Carlucci MD.
Licensure Skilled care. *Beds* SNF 101. *Certified* Medicaid; Medicare.
Owner Privately owned.
Admissions Requirements Minimum age 16.
Staff Physicians; RNs 8 (ft); LPNs 4 (ft); Nurses' aides 40 (ft); Physical therapists 1 (pt); Recreational therapists 3 (ft); Occupational therapists 1 (pt); Speech therapists 1 (pt); Dietitians 1 (pt); Podiatrists 1 (pt).
Facilities Dining room; Physical therapy room; Activities room; Crafts room; Laundry room; Barber/Beauty shop.
Activities Arts & crafts; Cards; Games; Movies.

Conneautville

Rolling Fields Nursing Home Inc
PO Box D, Conneautville, PA 16406
(814) 587-2012
Admin Kimberly Braham-Moody.
Medical Dir Kimberly K Paterson MD.
Licensure Skilled care; Intermediate care. *Beds* SNF 30; ICF 91. *Certified* Medicaid; Medicare.
Owner Proprietary corp.
Admissions Requirements Medical examination.
Staff Physicians 1 (pt); RNs 8 (ft), 1 (pt); LPNs 7 (ft), 3 (pt); Nurses' aides; Physical therapists; Occupational therapists 1 (pt); Speech therapists 1 (pt); Activities coordinators; Dietitians 1 (pt); Ophthalmologists 1 (pt); Podiatrists 1 (pt); Dentists 1 (pt).
Facilities Dining room; Physical therapy room; Activities room; Chapel; Crafts room; Laundry room; Barber/Beauty shop; Library.
Activities Arts & crafts; Cards; Games; Reading groups; Prayer groups; Movies; Shopping trips; Dances/Social/Cultural gatherings; Pet therapy; Fishing.

Coopersburg

Valley Manor Nursing Center
Rte 309, Coopersburg, PA 18036
(215) 282-1919
Admin Thomas B Lyons NHA. *Dir of Nursing* Elizabeth Broadhead RN. *Medical Dir* Dr Garry Sussman DO.
Licensure Skilled care. *Beds* SNF 180. *Private Pay Patients* 20%. *Certified* Medicaid; Medicare.
Owner Proprietary corp (Unicare).
Admissions Requirements Medical examination; Physician's request.
Staff RNs 6 (ft), 6 (pt); LPNs 9 (ft), 10 (pt); Nurses' aides 45 (ft), 20 (pt); Physical therapists (contracted); Recreational therapists 2 (ft); Occupational therapists

(contracted); Speech therapists (contracted); Activities coordinators 1 (ft); Dietitians (contracted); Audiologists (contracted).
Languages Spanish, Pennsylvania Dutch.
Facilities Dining room; Physical therapy room; Activities room; Crafts room; Laundry room; Barber/Beauty shop; Courtyards.
Activities Arts & crafts; Cards; Games; Reading groups; Prayer groups; Movies; Shopping trips; Dances/Social/Cultural gatherings; Pet therapy; Famil council; Resident council.

Coraopolis

Allegheny Valley School for Exceptional Children
1992 Ewing Mill Rd, Coraopolis, PA 15108
(412) 262-3500
Licensure Intermediate care for mentally retarded. *Beds* 160. *Certified* Medicaid.
Owner Nonprofit corp.

Sycamore Creek Nursing Center
234 Coraopolis Rd, Coraopolis, PA 15108
(412) 331-6060
Admin Mark D Bondi. *Dir of Nursing* M Lorah. *Medical Dir* Dr Bader; Dr Dickinson.
Licensure Skilled care; Intermediate care. *Beds* SNF 60; ICF 60. *Certified* Medicaid; Medicare.
Owner Proprietary corp (Health Care Management).
Admissions Requirements Medical examination; Physician's request.
Staff Physicians 2 (pt); RNs 10 (ft); LPNs 19 (ft); Nurses' aides 30 (ft), 20 (pt); Physical therapists 1 (pt); Reality therapists 1 (pt); Recreational therapists 1 (ft), 1 (pt); Occupational therapists 1 (pt); Speech therapists 1 (pt); Activities coordinators 1 (ft); Dietitians 1 (ft), 1 (pt); Ophthalmologists 1 (pt); Podiatrists 1 (pt); Dentists 1 (pt).
Facilities Dining room; Physical therapy room; Activities room; Crafts room; Laundry room; Barber/Beauty shop.
Activities Arts & crafts; Cards; Games; Reading groups; Prayer groups; Movies; Shopping trips; Dances/Social/Cultural gatherings.

West Hills Health Care Center
951 Brodhead Rd, Coraopolis, PA 15108
(412) 269-1101
Licensure Skilled care. *Beds* SNF 120. *Certified* Medicaid; Medicare.
Owner Proprietary corp.

Cornwall

Cornwall Manor
Boyd St, Box 125, Cornwall, PA 17016
(717) 273-2647
Admin Steven Hassinger. *Dir of Nursing* Suzanne Hostetter. *Medical Dir* Robert Nielsen MD.
Licensure Skilled care; Intermediate care; Personal care; Independent living. *Beds* SNF 47; ICF 78; Personal care 50; Independent living 325. *Private Pay Patients* 60%. *Certified* Medicaid; Medicare.
Owner Nonprofit corp.
Admissions Requirements Medical examination; Physician's request.
Staff Physicians 6 (pt); RNs 5 (ft), 3 (pt); LPNs 19 (ft), 10 (pt); Nurses' aides 26 (ft), 26 (pt); Physical therapists 1 (pt); Activities coordinators 1 (ft), 1 (pt); Dietitians 1 (pt); Podiatrists 1 (pt).
Affiliation United Methodist.
Facilities Dining room; Physical therapy room; Activities room; Chapel; Crafts room; Laundry room; Barber/Beauty shop; Health center; Health clinic; Convenience stores; Banks; Public transportation available; Post office.

Activities Arts & crafts; Cards; Games; Reading groups; Prayer groups; Movies; Shopping trips; Dances/Social/Cultural gatherings; Intergenerational programs; Pet therapy.

Cornwell Heights

Muffett Nursing Home
958 Flushing Rd, Cornwell Heights, PA 19020
(215) 639-3568
Licensure Skilled care. *Beds* 23.
Owner Proprietary corp.

Corry

Corry Manor Nursing Home
640 Worth St, Corry, PA 16407
(814) 664-9606
Admin Hope Cousins. *Dir of Nursing* Marnie Hy RN. *Medical Dir* G R Lloyd MD.
Licensure Skilled care. *Beds* SNF 121. *Certified* Medicaid; Medicare.
Owner Proprietary corp (HCF Inc).
Admissions Requirements Medical examination; Physician's request.
Staff RNs; LPNs; Nurses' aides; Physical therapists 1 (pt); Speech therapists 1 (pt); Activities coordinators 1 (ft), 1 (pt).
Facilities Dining room; Physical therapy room; Activities room; Laundry room; Barber/Beauty shop; Library; Patios; Lounges; Soda shop.
Activities Arts & crafts; Cards; Games; Reading groups; Prayer groups; Movies; Shopping trips; Dances/Social/Cultural gatherings; Bowling; Bingo; Nail clinic.

Coudersport

Charles Cole Memorial Hospital
US Rte 6, Coudersport, PA 16915
(814) 274-9300, 274-7692 FAX
Admin Benjamin Stimaker. *Dir of Nursing* Judith Clark. *Medical Dir* Dr Michael E Callahan.
Licensure Skilled care; Intermediate care. *Beds* SNF 24; ICF 26. *Private Pay Patients* 5%. *Certified* Medicaid; Medicare.
Owner Nonprofit corp.
Admissions Requirements Medical examination; Physician's request.
Staff Physicians 8 (ft), 3 (pt); RNs 3 (ft), 4 (pt); LPNs 3 (ft), 4 (pt); Nurses' aides 7 (ft), 12 (pt); Physical therapists 2 (pt); Recreational therapists 1 (ft); Speech therapists 1 (pt); Dietitians 1 (ft); Ophthalmologists 1 (pt); Podiatrists 1 (pt); Audiologists 1 (pt).
Facilities Dining room; Physical therapy room; Activities room; Chapel; Crafts room; Laundry room; Barber/Beauty shop.
Activities Arts & crafts; Cards; Games; Reading groups; Prayer groups; Movies; Intergenerational programs.

Sweden Valley Manor
Rte 6 E, Coudersport, PA 16915
(814) 274-7610
Admin Edith Rothwell. *Dir of Nursing* Karen Saltsman. *Medical Dir* Howard J Miller MD.
Licensure Skilled care. *Beds* SNF 121. *Private Pay Patients* 15%. *Certified* Medicaid; Medicare.
Owner Proprietary corp (HCF Inc).
Admissions Requirements Medical examination.
Staff RNs 7 (ft), 2 (pt); LPNs 10 (ft), 3 (pt); Nurses' aides 80 (ft), 10 (pt); Activities coordinators 1 (ft), 1 (pt).
Facilities Dining room; Physical therapy room; Activities room; Laundry room; Barber/Beauty shop; Library.
Activities Arts & crafts; Games; Prayer groups; Movies; Shopping trips; Fishing trips.

Curwensville

Curwensville Nursing Home Inc
PO Box 372, Curwensville, PA 16833
(814) 236-0600
Licensure Skilled care. *Beds* SNF 121.
  Certified Medicaid; Medicare.
Owner Proprietary corp.

Dallas

Lakeside Nursing Center
PO Box 357, Rte 4, Old Lake Rd, Dallas, PA
  18612
(717) 639-1885
Admin Frank J Berleth. *Dir of Nursing*
  Patricia Shupp RN. *Medical Dir* Dr Gary
  Smith.
Licensure Skilled care; Retirement;
  Alzheimer's care. *Beds* SNF 30. *Certified*
  Medicaid; Medicare.
Owner Proprietary corp.
Admissions Requirements Medical
  examination; Physician's request.
Staff Physicians 6 (pt); RNs 1 (ft), 2 (pt);
  LPNs 4 (ft); Nurses' aides 7 (ft), 6 (pt);
  Physical therapists 1 (pt); Recreational
  therapists 1 (pt); Occupational therapists 1
  (pt); Speech therapists 1 (pt); Activities
  coordinators 1 (ft); Dietitians 3 (ft), 4 (pt);
  Ophthalmologists 2 (pt).
Facilities Dining room; Physical therapy
  room; Activities room; Laundry room.
Activities Arts & crafts; Cards; Games; Prayer
  groups; Movies; Shopping trips; Dances/
  Social/Cultural gatherings.

Maple Hill Nursing Home
PO Box 391, RD 2, Firehall Rd, Dallas, PA
  18612
(717) 675-1787
Admin Maureen Cerniglia NHA. *Dir of
  Nursing* Marlene Konopke RN. *Medical Dir*
  Ernest Gelb DO.
Licensure Intermediate care. *Beds* ICF 24.
  Certified Medicaid.
Owner Proprietary corp.
Admissions Requirements Medical
  examination; Physician's request.
Staff RNs 1 (ft); LPNs 5 (pt); Nurses' aides 5
  (ft), 4 (pt); Activities coordinators 1 (ft).
Facilities Dining room.
Activities Arts & crafts; Cards; Games;
  Reading groups; Prayer groups; Shopping
  trips.

Meadows Nursing Center
55 W Center Hill Rd, Dallas, PA 18612
(717) 675-8600
Admin Thomas J Sweeney. *Dir of Nursing*
  Bette Segrave-Daly. *Medical Dir* Dorothy
  Flynn MD.
Licensure Skilled care. *Beds* SNF 120.
  Certified Medicaid; Medicare.
Owner Nonprofit corp (Ecumenical
  Enterprises Inc).
Admissions Requirements Minimum age 18;
  Medical examination; Physician's request.
Staff RNs 6 (ft), 7 (pt); LPNs 11 (ft), 12 (pt);
  Nurses' aides 34 (ft), 34 (pt); Activities
  coordinators 1 (ft).
Facilities Dining room; Physical therapy
  room; Activities room; Chapel; Laundry
  room; Barber/Beauty shop.
Activities Arts & crafts; Games; Reading
  groups; Prayer groups; Movies; Shopping
  trips; Dances/Social/Cultural gatherings;
  Coffee klatch; Birthday parties; Exercises;
  Bingo; Music program.

Dallastown

**Leader Nursing & Rehabilitation
Center—Dallastown**
100 W Queen St, Dallastown, PA 19313
(717) 246-1671

Licensure Skilled care; Intermediate care. *Beds*
  SNF 120; ICF 60. *Certified* Medicaid;
  Medicare.
Owner Proprietary corp (Manor Care Inc).

Seitz Nursing Home
623 E Main St, Dallastown, PA 17313
(717) 244-2295
Admin Sylvia E Snyder. *Dir of Nursing* Maud
  Rupp. *Medical Dir* Edward F Holland MD.
Licensure Skilled care. *Beds* SNF 23.
Owner Privately owned.
Admissions Requirements Minimum age 16;
  Medical examination.
Staff RNs 1 (ft), 3 (pt); LPNs 1 (ft), 3 (pt);
  Nurses' aides 6 (ft), 6 (pt); Recreational
  therapists 1 (pt); Activities coordinators 1
  (pt).
Facilities Dining room; Activities room;
  Chapel; Crafts room; Laundry room.
Activities Arts & crafts; Cards; Games;
  Reading groups; Prayer groups; Movies;
  Shopping trips; Dances/Social/Cultural
  gatherings.

Danville

Gold Star Nursing Home
Schoolhouse Rd, Danville, PA 17821
(717) 275-4946
Licensure Intermediate care. *Beds* ICF 100.
  Certified Medicaid.
Owner Proprietary corp.
Admissions Requirements Medical
  examination.
Staff Physicians 11 (pt); RNs 4 (ft), 2 (pt);
  LPNs 6 (ft), 1 (pt); Nurses' aides 25 (ft), 1
  (pt); Physical therapists 1 (pt); Speech
  therapists 1 (pt); Activities coordinators 1
  (ft); Dietitians 1 (pt); Podiatrists 1 (pt);
  Dentists 1 (pt).
Facilities Dining room; Physical therapy
  room; Activities room; Crafts room; Laundry
  room; Barber/Beauty shop.
Activities Arts & crafts; Cards; Games;
  Reading groups; Prayer groups; Movies;
  Dances/Social/Cultural gatherings.

Grandview Health Homes Inc
Woodbine Ln, Danville, PA 17821
(717) 275-5240
Admin Jerry E Boone. *Dir of Nursing* Jane
  Campbell. *Medical Dir* Norman Ekberg MD.
Licensure Skilled care; Intermediate care. *Beds*
  SNF 20; ICF 130. *Certified* Medicaid;
  Medicare.
Owner Proprietary corp.
Admissions Requirements Medical
  examination.
Staff RNs 3 (ft), 3 (pt); LPNs 13 (ft), 3 (pt);
  Nurses' aides 43 (ft), 7 (pt); Physical
  therapists 1 (pt); Recreational therapists 3
  (pt); Speech therapists 1 (pt); Activities
  coordinators 1 (ft); Dietitians 1 (ft), 1 (pt);
  Ophthalmologists.
Facilities Dining room; Physical therapy
  room; Activities room; Crafts room; Laundry
  room; Barber/Beauty shop; Library.
Activities Arts & crafts; Cards; Games;
  Movies; Dances/Social/Cultural gatherings;
  Church; Group patient murals.

Maria Joseph Manor
RD 4 Box 3, Danville, PA 17821
(717) 275-4221
Admin Sr M Jeanette. *Dir of Nursing* Sr M
  Marguerite. *Medical Dir* John V McCormick
  MD.
Licensure Intermediate care; Personal care.
  Beds ICF 60; Personal care 36. *Private Pay
  Patients* 66%. *Certified* Medicaid; Medicare.
Owner Nonprofit corp.
Admissions Requirements Minimum age 65;
  Medical examination; Physician's request.
Staff Physicians 2 (pt); RNs 3 (ft), 7 (pt);
  LPNs 5 (pt), 3 (pt); Nurses' aides 22 (ft), 7
  (pt); Activities coordinators 1 (ft); Dietitians
  1 (ft).

Affiliation Roman Catholic.
Facilities Dining room; Physical therapy
  room; Activities room; Chapel; Crafts room;
  Laundry room; Barber/Beauty shop; Library;
  Outdoor pavilion/Patio.
Activities Arts & crafts; Cards; Games;
  Reading groups; Prayer groups; Movies;
  Shopping trips; Dances/Social/Cultural
  gatherings; Intergenerational programs; Pet
  therapy; Various parties.

Long Term Care Facility
PO Box 700, Danville State Hospital,
  Danville, PA 17821-0700
(717) 275-7133
Admin Barbara A Long. *Dir of Nursing* Jill
  Rhodes RN. *Medical Dir* Benjamin Corteza
  MD.
Licensure Skilled care; Intermediate care. *Beds*
  SNF 30; ICF 113. *Private Pay Patients* 0%.
  Certified Medicaid; Medicare.
Owner Publicly owned.
Admissions Requirements Minimum age 65;
  Medical examination; Physician's request.
Staff Physicians 1 (ft), 1 (pt); RNs 24 (ft), 2
  (pt); LPNs 18 (ft); Nurses' aides 43 (ft);
  Physical therapists 1 (pt); Occupational
  therapists 2 (pt); Speech therapists 1 (pt);
  Activities coordinators 3 (ft), 1 (pt);
  Dietitians 3 (pt); Podiatrists 1 (pt); Social
  workers 1 (ft); Dentists 1 (pt).
Facilities Dining room; Physical therapy
  room; Activities room; Chapel; Crafts room;
  Laundry room; Barber/Beauty shop; Library;
  Occupational therapy clinic.
Activities Arts & crafts; Cards; Games;
  Reading groups; Movies; Shopping trips;
  Dances/Social/Cultural gatherings;
  Intergenerational programs; Pet therapy.

Darby

Little Flower Manor
1201 Springfield Rd, Darby, PA 19023
(215) 534-6000
Admin Sr M Nicolette. *Dir of Nursing*
  Catherine Roche. *Medical Dir* Morris F
  Guirguis MD.
Licensure Skilled care; Alzheimer's care. *Beds*
  SNF 125. *Certified* Medicaid.
Owner Nonprofit corp.
Admissions Requirements Minimum age 65;
  Medical examination; Physician's request.
Staff Physicians 6 (pt); RNs 7 (ft), 18 (pt);
  LPNs 3 (ft), 4 (pt); Nurses' aides 23 (ft), 49
  (pt); Physical therapists 3 (pt); Recreational
  therapists 2 (ft), 1 (pt); Occupational
  therapists 1 (pt); Speech therapists 1 (pt);
  Activities coordinators 1 (ft); Dietitians 1
  (ft); Ophthalmologists 1 (pt); Podiatrists 1
  (pt); Dentists 1 (pt).
Affiliation Roman Catholic.
Facilities Dining room; Physical therapy
  room; Activities room; Chapel; Crafts room;
  Laundry room; Barber/Beauty shop; Library.
Activities Arts & crafts; Cards; Games;
  Reading groups; Prayer groups; Movies;
  Dances/Social/Cultural gatherings.

St Francis Country House
14th & Lansdowne Ave, Darby, PA 19023
(215) 461-6510
Admin Sr Anne Lutz CBS. *Dir of Nursing*
  Marion Nimey. *Medical Dir* Ronald E
  Rossman MD.
Licensure Skilled care; Alzheimer's care. *Beds*
  SNF 318. *Certified* Medicaid; Medicare.
Owner Nonprofit corp (Bon Secours Health
  Systems).
Admissions Requirements Medical
  examination.
Staff RNs 10 (ft), 10 (pt); LPNs 15 (ft), 15
  (pt); Nurses' aides 88 (ft), 88 (pt); Physical
  therapists 1 (pt); Occupational therapists 1
  (pt); Speech therapists 1 (pt); Activities
  coordinators 1 (ft); Dietitians 1 (ft).
Affiliation Roman Catholic.

Facilities Dining room; Physical therapy room; Activities room; Chapel; Crafts room; Barber/Beauty shop.
Activities Arts & crafts; Cards; Games; Reading groups; Prayer groups; Movies; Shopping trips.

Devon

Eliza Cathcart Home
445 N Valley Forge Rd, Devon, PA 19333
(215) 688-0833
Admin Jeffrey L Shireman NHA. *Dir of Nursing* Rita Harkins RN. *Medical Dir* Alexander O'Neal MD.
Licensure Skilled care; Retirement. *Beds* SNF 63. *Certified* Medicaid; Medicare.
Owner Nonprofit corp.
Admissions Requirements Medical examination; Physician's request.
Staff RNs; LPNs; Nurses' aides; Physical therapists; Speech therapists; Activities coordinators; Dietitians; Ophthalmologists.
Facilities Dining room; Physical therapy room; Activities room; Chapel; Laundry room; Barber/Beauty shop.
Activities Arts & crafts; Cards; Games; Prayer groups; Movies; Shopping trips.

Devon Manor
235 Lancaster Ave, Devon, PA 19333
(215) 688-8080
Admin Peter W Grim. *Dir of Nursing* Dorothy Riggs RN. *Medical Dir* Dr William Lander.
Licensure Skilled care; Retirement; Alzheimer's care. *Beds* SNF 90. *Certified* Medicare.
Owner Proprietary corp.
Admissions Requirements Medical examination.
Staff Physicians 4 (pt); RNs 14 (ft), 7 (pt); LPNs 3 (ft); Nurses' aides 26 (ft), 9 (pt); Physical therapists 1 (ft); Reality therapists 1 (pt); Recreational therapists 3 (ft), 1 (pt); Occupational therapists 2 (pt); Speech therapists 1 (pt); Activities coordinators 1 (ft); Dietitians 2 (ft), 1 (pt); Podiatrists 1 (pt); Dentists 1 (pt).
Languages French.
Facilities Dining room; Physical therapy room; Activities room; Chapel; Crafts room; Laundry room; Barber/Beauty shop; Library; Health club; Cocktail lounge; Billiards room.
Activities Arts & crafts; Cards; Games; Reading groups; Prayer groups; Movies; Shopping trips; Dances/Social/Cultural gatherings; Lectures; Shows; Classical music groups; Big band groups.

Doylestown

Briarleaf Nursing & Convalescent Center
252 Belmont Ave, Doylestown, PA 18901
(215) 348-2983
Admin Diane L McGerr. *Dir of Nursing* Pat Buess RN. *Medical Dir* Laudenslager MD.
Licensure Skilled care; Intermediate care. *Beds* 178. *Certified* Medicaid; Medicare.
Owner Privately owned.
Admissions Requirements Medical examination.
Staff RNs; LPNs; Nurses' aides; Physical therapists; Recreational therapists; Occupational therapists; Speech therapists; Activities coordinators; Dietitians.
Facilities Dining room; Physical therapy room; Activities room; Crafts room; Laundry room; Barber/Beauty shop; Library.
Activities Arts & crafts; Cards; Games; Reading groups; Prayer groups; Movies; Shopping trips; Dances/Social/Cultural gatherings.

Bucks County Association of Retarded Citizens
252 Belmont Dr, Doylestown, PA 18901
(215) 348-3524

Licensure Intermediate care for mentally retarded. *Beds* 8. *Certified* Medicaid.
Owner Nonprofit corp.

Doylestown Manor
Maple Ave at East St, Doylestown, PA 18901
(215) 345-1452
Admin Harry K Hobbs.
Licensure Skilled care; Intermediate care. *Beds* 120. *Certified* Medicaid; Medicare.
Owner Proprietary corp (Beverly Enterprises).
Staff RNs 8 (ft), 3 (pt); LPNs 5 (ft), 2 (pt); Nurses' aides 30 (ft), 10 (pt); Physical therapists 1 (ft), 1 (pt); Reality therapists 2 (ft); Activities coordinators 1 (ft).
Facilities Dining room; Physical therapy room; Activities room; Crafts room; Laundry room; Barber/Beauty shop.
Activities Arts & crafts; Cards; Games; Reading groups; Prayer groups; Movies; Shopping trips; Dances/Social/Cultural gatherings.

Greenleaf Nursing & Convalescent Center Inc
400 S Main St, Doylestown, PA 18901
(215) 348-2980
Admin David R Devereaux. *Dir of Nursing* Carol De Ricci. *Medical Dir* Dr E C Laudenslager.
Licensure Skilled care; Intermediate care. *Beds* SNF 16; ICF 114. *Certified* Medicaid; Medicare.
Owner Proprietary corp.
Facilities Dining room; Physical therapy room; Activities room; Laundry room; Barber/Beauty shop.
Activities Arts & crafts; Cards; Games; Prayer groups; Movies; Shopping trips.

Heritage Towers
200 Veterans Ln, Doylestown, PA 18901
(215) 345-4300
Admin Bruce L Lenich. *Dir of Nursing* Myra Berest RN. *Medical Dir* Charles W Burmeister MD.
Licensure Skilled care; Independent living. *Beds* SNF 60. *Certified* Medicaid; Medicare.
Owner Nonprofit corp.
Admissions Requirements Medical examination; Physician's request.
Staff Physicians; RNs 4 (ft), 4 (pt); LPNs 1 (ft), 2 (pt); Nurses' aides 9 (ft), 10 (pt); Physical therapists 1 (pt); Reality therapists 1 (pt); Recreational therapists 1 (pt); Occupational therapists 1 (pt); Speech therapists 1 (pt); Activities coordinators 1 (ft); Dietitians 1 (ft); Dentists 1 (pt).
Facilities Dining room; Physical therapy room; Activities room; Chapel; Crafts room; Laundry room; Barber/Beauty shop; Library; Auditorium.
Activities Arts & crafts; Cards; Games; Prayer groups; Dances/Social/Cultural gatherings.

Neshaminy Manor Home
Rte 611 & Almhouse Rd, Doylestown, PA 18901
(215) 345-3230
Admin James C Bailey LNHA.
Medical Dir Dr Vern Harrison.
Licensure Skilled care; Intermediate care. *Beds* SNF 60; ICF 300. *Certified* Medicaid; Medicare.
Owner Publicly owned.
Admissions Requirements Medical examination; Physician's request.
Staff Physicians 1 (ft), 3 (pt); RNs 50 (ft), 15 (pt); LPNs 20 (ft), 13 (pt); Nurses' aides 112 (ft), 43 (pt); Physical therapists 5 (ft); Recreational therapists 4 (ft); Occupational therapists 2 (pt); Speech therapists 1 (pt); Activities coordinators 1 (ft); Dietitians 3 (ft); Ophthalmologists 1 (pt); Dentists 1 (pt).
Facilities Dining room; Physical therapy room; Activities room; Chapel; Crafts room; Laundry room; Barber/Beauty shop; Library.

Activities Arts & crafts; Cards; Games; Reading groups; Prayer groups; Movies; Shopping trips; Dances/Social/Cultural gatherings.

Pine Run Medical Center
777 Ferry Rd, Doylestown, PA 18901
(215) 348-7770
Admin Patricia Demusz BSN NHA. *Dir of Nursing* Karen Guckavan RN BSN. *Medical Dir* James Blore MD.
Licensure Skilled care; Intermediate care; Personal care; Alzheimer's care. *Beds* SNF 118; ICF 68; Personal care 50. *Private Pay Patients* 70%. *Certified* Medicaid; Medicare.
Owner Proprietary corp.
Admissions Requirements Medical examination.
Staff Physicians 8 (pt); RNs 5 (ft), 9 (pt); LPNs 13 (ft), 8 (pt); Nurses' aides 52 (ft), 18 (pt); Physical therapists 1 (pt); Reality therapists 1 (ft); Recreational therapists 3 (ft), 2 (pt); Occupational therapists 1 (pt); Speech therapists 1 (pt); Activities coordinators 1 (ft); Dietitians 1 (ft); Ophthalmologists 3 (pt); Podiatrists 1 (pt); Audiologists 1 (pt).
Facilities Dining room; Physical therapy room; Activities room; Crafts room; Laundry room; Barber/Beauty shop; Library; Alzheimers unit; Garden apartments; Private and semi-private rooms with outside terraces and patios.
Activities Arts & crafts; Cards; Games; Reading groups; Prayer groups; Movies; Shopping trips; Dances/Social/Cultural gatherings; Intergenerational programs; Pet therapy; Residents' council; Garden club.

Dresher

Dresher Hill Nursing Center
1390 Camp Hill Rd, Dresher, PA 19034
(215) 641-1710
Licensure Skilled care. *Beds* SNF 120. *Certified* Medicaid; Medicare.
Owner Proprietary corp (Unicare).

Drums

Butler Valley Manor
RD 1 Box 206-A, Drums, PA 18222
(717) 788-4175, 788-4447 FAX
Admin Carolyn M Cummins. *Dir of Nursing* Jane Kujat. *Medical Dir* George Yurro.
Licensure Skilled care; Intermediate care; Personal care. *Beds* Swing beds SNF/ICF 37; Personal care 12. *Private Pay Patients* 40%. *Certified* Medicaid; Medicare.
Owner Privately owned.
Staff Physicians 5 (pt); RNs 2 (ft), 3 (pt); LPNs 3 (pt); Nurses' aides 15 (ft), 10 (pt); Physical therapists 1 (pt); Reality therapists 1 (pt); Recreational therapists 1 (pt); Occupational therapists 1 (pt); Speech therapists 1 (pt); Dietitians 1 (pt); Ophthalmologists 1 (pt); Podiatrists 2 (pt); Audiologists 1 (pt).
Facilities Dining room; Physical therapy room; Barber/Beauty shop.
Activities Cards; Games; Reading groups; Prayer groups; Movies; Pet therapy.

Dubois

Christ the King Manor
PO Box 448, Dubois, PA 15801
(814) 371-3180
Medical Dir Dr Stanley Lang.
Licensure Skilled care. *Beds* SNF 160. *Certified* Medicaid; Medicare.
Owner Nonprofit corp.
Admissions Requirements Medical examination.

Staff Physicians 3 (pt); RNs 11 (ft), 2 (pt); LPNs 20 (ft), 2 (pt); Nurses' aides 60 (ft), 16 (pt); Physical therapists 3 (pt); Recreational therapists 1 (ft); Occupational therapists 1 (pt); Speech therapists 1 (pt); Activities coordinators 1 (ft); Dietitians 1 (ft); Ophthalmologists 1 (pt); Podiatrists 1 (pt); Dentists 1 (pt).
Affiliation Roman Catholic.
Facilities Dining room; Physical therapy room; Activities room; Chapel; Crafts room; Laundry room; Barber/Beauty shop.
Activities Arts & crafts; Cards; Games; Reading groups; Prayer groups; Movies; Shopping trips; Dances/Social/Cultural gatherings.

DuBois Nursing Home
200 S 8th St, DuBois, PA 15801
(814) 375-9100, 375-0341 FAX
Admin David Gritzer. *Dir of Nursing* Bette Iley. *Medical Dir* Dr Jawahar Suvarnakar.
Licensure Skilled care; Alzheimer's care. *Beds* SNF 180. *Private Pay Patients* 14%. *Certified* Medicaid; Medicare.
Owner Nonprofit organization/foundation.
Admissions Requirements Medical examination; Physician's request.
Staff Physicians 7 (pt); RNs 8 (ft), 8 (pt); LPNs 12 (ft), 4 (pt); Nurses' aides 34 (ft), 15 (pt); Physical therapists 1 (pt); Recreational therapists 3 (ft); Speech therapists 1 (pt); Activities coordinators 3 (ft); Dietitians 1 (ft); Podiatrists 1 (pt); Dentists 1 (pt).
Facilities Dining room; Physical therapy room; Activities room; Chapel; Crafts room; Laundry room; Barber/Beauty shop; Library.
Activities Arts & crafts; Cards; Games; Reading groups; Prayer groups; Movies; Shopping trips; Dances/Social/Cultural gatherings; Intergenerational programs; Pet therapy.

Duncannon

Kinkora Pythian Home
25 Cove Rd, Duncannon, PA 17020
(717) 834-4887
Admin Marlin E Morgan Jr. *Dir of Nursing* Robert Ober RN. *Medical Dir* Joseph Kreiser MD.
Licensure Intermediate care; Residential care. *Beds* ICF 27; Residential care 8. *Certified* Medicaid.
Owner Nonprofit corp.
Admissions Requirements Minimum age 18; Medical examination.
Staff Physicians 1 (ft); RNs 4 (ft); LPNs 3 (ft); Nurses' aides 12 (ft); Activities coordinators 1 (ft); Dietitians 1 (ft); Podiatrists 1 (ft).
Affiliation Knights of Pythias.
Facilities Dining room; Activities room; Crafts room; Laundry room; Library; Living room.
Activities Arts & crafts; Cards; Games; Reading groups; Prayer groups; Movies; Shopping trips.

Victory Garden Nursing Home
RD 1, Duncannon, PA 17020

Dunmore

Laurel Hill Nursing Home
Smith & Mill Sts, Dunmore, PA 18512
(717) 342-7624
Admin Bruce N Harding. *Dir of Nursing* Mary Ann Alabovitz RN.
Licensure Skilled care; Intermediate care. *Beds* SNF 20; ICF 107. *Certified* Medicaid; Medicare.
Owner Proprietary corp.
Admissions Requirements Minimum age 21; Medical examination; Physician's request.
Staff RNs 5 (ft), 4 (pt); LPNs 6 (ft), 8 (pt); Nurses' aides 24 (ft), 20 (pt); Activities coordinators 3 (ft).

Facilities Dining room; Activities room; Laundry room.
Activities Arts & crafts; Games; Reading groups; Prayer groups; Movies; Shopping trips.

East Lansdowne

Lansdowne Rest Home
246 Melrose Ave, East Lansdowne, PA 19050
(215) 623-2233
Licensure Intermediate care. *Beds* 26.
Owner Proprietary corp.
Staff RNs 4 (pt); LPNs 2 (ft); Nurses' aides 4 (ft), 6 (pt); Activities coordinators 1 (pt); Dietitians 1 (pt).
Facilities Dining room; Activities room; Laundry room.
Activities Arts & crafts; Cards; Games; Reading groups; Dances/Social/Cultural gatherings.

East Stroudsburg

Stroud Manor Inc
221 E Brown St, East Stroudsburg, PA 18301
(717) 421-6200
Licensure Skilled care. *Beds* SNF 129.
Certified Medicaid; Medicare.
Owner Proprietary corp (Beverly Enterprises).

Easton

Easton Home for Aged Women
1022 Northampton St, Easton, PA 18042
(215) 258-7773
Admin Josephine Zeitner. *Dir of Nursing* Mary Linton. *Medical Dir* Thomas R Liberta MD.
Licensure Skilled care; Personal care. *Beds* SNF 26; Personal care 31. *Private Pay Patients* 100%.
Owner Nonprofit corp.
Admissions Requirements Females only; Medical examination.
Staff RNs; LPNs; Nurses' aides; Activities coordinators.
Facilities Dining room; Activities room; Chapel; Crafts room; Laundry room; Barber/Beauty shop; Library.
Activities Arts & crafts; Cards; Games; Reading groups; Movies; Shopping trips; Dances/Social/Cultural gatherings; Pet therapy.

Easton Nursing Center
498 Washington St, Easton, PA 18042
(215) 258-2985
Admin David T Boyer. *Dir of Nursing* Pauline Capparell. *Medical Dir* Dr Dominic Rasso.
Licensure Skilled care; Intermediate care. *Beds* SNF 77; ICF 104. *Private Pay Patients* 20%. *Certified* Medicaid; Medicare.
Owner Proprietary corp (Easton Nursing Center Association).
Admissions Requirements Minimum age 18; Medical examination.
Staff Physicians 1 (pt); RNs 10 (ft); LPNs 5 (ft); Physical therapists (contracted); Reality therapists (contracted); Recreational therapists 6 (ft); Occupational therapists (contracted); Speech therapists (contracted); Activities coordinators 1 (ft); Dietitians 1 (ft); Ophthalmologists (contracted); Podiatrists (contracted); Audiologists (contracted).
Facilities Dining room; Physical therapy room; Activities room; Chapel; Crafts room; Laundry room; Barber/Beauty shop.
Activities Arts & crafts; Cards; Games; Reading groups; Prayer groups; Movies; Shopping trips; Dances/Social/Cultural gatherings; Intergenerational programs; Pet therapy.

Eastwood Convalescent Home
2125 Fairview Ave, Easton, PA 18042
(215) 258-2801
Admin Mitchell L Richman. *Dir of Nursing* Marijane Ambrogi RN. *Medical Dir* Bruce Miles DO.
Licensure Skilled care. *Beds* SNF 107. *Certified* Medicare.
Owner Privately owned.
Admissions Requirements Medical examination.
Staff RNs 7 (ft), 5 (pt); LPNs 7 (ft), 3 (pt); Nurses' aides 38 (ft), 6 (pt); Recreational therapists 1 (ft), 2 (pt); Dietitians 1 (pt).
Facilities Dining room; Physical therapy room; Activities room; Laundry room; Barber/Beauty shop.
Activities Arts & crafts; Cards; Games; Prayer groups; Movies; Shopping trips; Pet therapy.

Leader Nursing & Rehabilitation Center
26 Northampton St, Easton, PA 18042
(215) 250-0150
Admin Donna Chamberlain. *Dir of Nursing* Barbara Fehr. *Medical Dir* Robert Silberman.
Licensure Skilled care; Intermediate care; Alzheimer's care. *Beds* SNF 180; ICF 40. *Private Pay Patients* 70%. *Certified* Medicaid; Medicare.
Owner Proprietary corp (Manor Care Inc).
Admissions Requirements Medical examination.
Staff Physicians; RNs; LPNs; Nurses' aides; Physical therapists; Reality therapists; Recreational therapists; Occupational therapists; Speech therapists; Activities coordinators; Dietitians; Ophthalmologists; Podiatrists; Audiologists.
Facilities Dining room; Physical therapy room; Activities room; Chapel; Crafts room; Laundry room; Barber/Beauty shop.
Activities Arts & crafts; Cards; Games; Reading groups; Prayer groups; Movies; Shopping trips; Dances/Social/Cultural gatherings; Intergenerational programs; Pet therapy.

Praxis Nursing Home
500 Washington St, Easton, PA 18042
(215) 253-3573, 253-0222 FAX
Admin Martha T Marino NHA. *Dir of Nursing* Marsha Schlegel RN. *Medical Dir* Dr Bijan Etemad.
Licensure Skilled care; Alzheimer's care. *Beds* SNF 115. *Private Pay Patients* 75%. *Certified* Medicaid; Medicare.
Owner Proprietary corp (Easton Nursing Center Association).
Admissions Requirements Medical examination; Must have Alzheimer's disease.
Staff Physicians 5 (pt); RNs 5 (ft), 4 (pt); LPNs 6 (ft), 4 (pt); Recreational therapists 1 (ft); Occupational therapists 1 (pt); Speech therapists 1 (pt); Activities coordinators 6 (ft), 3 (pt); Dietitians 1 (ft).
Languages Spanish, Italian.
Facilities Dining room; Physical therapy room; Activities room; Crafts room; Laundry room; Barber/Beauty shop.
Activities Arts & crafts; Cards; Games; Reading groups; Prayer groups; Movies; Shopping trips; Dances/Social/Cultural gatherings; Intergenerational programs; Pet therapy.

Ebensburg

Ebensburg Center
Rte 22, Ebensburg, PA 15931
(814) 472-6366
Admin Alan M Bellomo. *Dir of Nursing* Carole Sponsky. *Medical Dir* Edward Shertz MD.
Licensure Intermediate care for mentally retarded. *Beds* ICF/MR 528. *Private Pay Patients* 50%. *Certified* Medicare.

Owner Publicly owned.
Admissions Requirements Medical examination.
Staff Physicians 4 (ft); RNs 38 (ft); Nurses' aides 370 (ft); Physical therapists 5 (pt); Occupational therapists 1 (pt); Speech therapists 7 (ft); Activities coordinators 1 (ft); Dietitians 4 (ft); Ophthalmologists 1 (pt); Podiatrists 1 (ft); Audiologists 1 (pt).
Facilities Dining room; Physical therapy room; Activities room; Chapel; Crafts room; Laundry room; Barber/Beauty shop.
Activities Arts & crafts; Prayer groups; Movies; Shopping trips; Dances/Social/ Cultural gatherings; Pet therapy.

Laurel Crest Manor
Box 360, Loretto Rd, Ebensburg, PA 15931
(814) 472-8100, 472-8843 FAX
Admin Frank C Sciorilli. *Dir of Nursing* Janet Gerber RN. *Medical Dir* William P Hirsch MD.
Licensure Skilled care; Intermediate care. *Beds* SNF 187; ICF 428. *Private Pay Patients* 6%. *Certified* Medicaid; Medicare.
Owner Publicly owned.
Admissions Requirements Minimum age 21; Medical examination; Physician's request.
Staff Physicians 6 (pt); RNs 55 (ft), 7 (pt); LPNs 78 (ft), 4 (pt); Nurses' aides 242 (ft), 38 (pt); Physical therapists 1 (ft); Recreational therapists 1 (ft); Occupational therapists 4 (ft), 1 (pt); Speech therapists 2 (pt); Activities coordinators 14 (ft); Dietitians 3 (ft); Ophthalmologists 1 (pt); Podiatrists 3 (pt); Audiologists 1 (pt).
Facilities Dining room; Physical therapy room; Activities room; Crafts room; Laundry room; Barber/Beauty shop; Library.
Activities Arts & crafts; Cards; Games; Prayer groups; Movies; Shopping trips; Dances/ Social/Cultural gatherings; Intergenerational programs; Pet therapy.

Edinboro

Edinboro Manor
419 Waterford St, Edinboro, PA 16412
(814) 734-5021
Licensure Skilled care. *Beds* SNF 121. *Certified* Medicaid; Medicare.
Owner Proprietary corp (HCF Inc).

Effort

Brookmont Health Care Center Inc
PO Box 50, Brookmont Dr, Effort, PA 18330
(215) 681-4070
Admin Alan W Pedersen. *Dir of Nursing* Sherrill Rosetti. *Medical Dir* Thomas Harakal MD.
Licensure Skilled care; Intermediate care. *Beds* SNF 43; ICF 60. *Certified* Medicaid; Medicare.
Owner Privately owned.
Admissions Requirements Medical examination.
Staff Physicians 1 (pt); RNs 4 (ft), 2 (pt); LPNs 6 (ft), 2 (pt); Nurses' aides 30 (ft); Physical therapists 1 (ft); Recreational therapists 2 (ft).
Facilities Dining room; Physical therapy room; Activities room; Chapel; Crafts room; Laundry room; Barber/Beauty shop; Library.
Activities Arts & crafts; Cards; Games; Reading groups; Prayer groups; Movies; Shopping trips; Dances/Social/Cultural gatherings.

Elizabethtown

Leader Nursing & Rehabilitation Center—Elizabethtown
320 S Market St, Elizabethtown, PA 17022
(717) 367-1377

Admin Donald Allen. *Dir of Nursing* Minerva Ensminger RN. *Medical Dir* Henry Kreider MD.
Licensure Skilled care; Retirement. *Beds* SNF 61. *Certified* Medicaid; Medicare.
Owner Proprietary corp (Manor Care).
Admissions Requirements Medical examination.
Staff Physicians 1 (ft), 3 (pt); RNs 6 (ft), 1 (pt); LPNs 3 (ft), 1 (pt); Nurses' aides 34 (ft), 16 (pt); Physical therapists 1 (ft); Recreational therapists 1 (ft); Occupational therapists 1 (pt); Speech therapists 1 (pt); Activities coordinators 1 (ft); Dietitians 1 (ft); Ophthalmologists 1 (pt); Podiatrists 1 (pt); Dentists 1 (pt).
Facilities Dining room; Physical therapy room; Activities room; Chapel; Crafts room; Laundry room; Barber/Beauty shop; Library.
Activities Arts & crafts; Cards; Games; Reading groups; Prayer groups; Movies; Shopping trips; Dances/Social/Cultural gatherings.

Masonic Homes
Masonic Dr, Elizabethtown, PA 17022
(717) 367-1121, 367-6768 FAX
Admin Joseph E Murphy NHA, Exec Dir. *Dir of Nursing* Martha M Wess RN. *Medical Dir* William W Longenecker DO.
Licensure Skilled care; Intermediate care; Congregate living; Alzheimer's care. *Beds* SNF 348; ICF 134; Congregate living 256. *Private Pay Patients* 19%. *Certified* Medicaid; Medicare.
Owner Nonprofit organization/foundation.
Admissions Requirements Medical examination.
Staff Physicians 4 (ft); RNs 18 (ft), 11 (pt); LPNs 54 (ft), 12 (pt); Nurses' aides 155 (ft), 38 (pt); Physical therapists 1 (ft); Recreational therapists 1 (ft); Speech therapists 1 (pt); Activities coordinators 1 (ft); Dietitians 1 (ft); Ophthalmologists 2 (pt); Podiatrists 2 (pt); Dentists 2 (pt); Opticians 1 (pt).
Affiliation Masons.
Facilities Dining room; Physical therapy room; Activities room; Chapel; Crafts room; Laundry room; Barber/Beauty shop; Library; Museum; Post office; Snack shop; Ice cream parlor; Gift shop; Theater; Indoor swimming pool; Fishing lake.
Activities Arts & crafts; Cards; Games; Reading groups; Prayer groups; Movies; Shopping trips; Dances/Social/Cultural gatherings; Intergenerational programs; Pet therapy.

Elizabethville

Kepler Home Inc
44 S Market St, Elizabethville, PA 17023
(717) 362-8370
Admin Kathryn Hendershot. *Dir of Nursing* Sandra Mechling RN. *Medical Dir* Robert Ehlinger MD.
Licensure Intermediate care. *Beds* ICF 36. *Certified* Medicaid.
Owner Proprietary corp.
Admissions Requirements Medical examination.
Staff RNs 1 (ft), 6 (pt); LPNs 2 (ft), 2 (pt); Nurses' aides 9 (ft), 9 (pt); Activities coordinators 1 (ft); Dietitians 1 (pt).
Languages Pennsylvania Dutch.
Facilities Dining room; Activities room; Crafts room.
Activities Arts & crafts; Cards; Games; Reading groups; Prayer groups; Movies; Shopping trips; Dances/Social/Cultural gatherings; Intergenerational programs; Picnics; Sight-seeing trips.

Elkins Park

Rolling Hills Hospital Skilled Nursing Facility
60 E Township Line Rd, Elkins Park, PA 19117
(215) 663-6000
Licensure Skilled care. *Beds* SNF 24. *Certified* Medicare.
Owner Proprietary corp.

Township Manor Nursing Center
265 E Township Line Rd, Elkins Park, PA 19117
(215) 379-2700
Licensure Skilled care; Intermediate care. *Beds* SNF 102; ICF 48. *Certified* Medicaid; Medicare.
Owner Proprietary corp (Unicare).

Ellwood City

Mary Evans Extended Care Center
724 Pershing St, Ellwood City, PA 16117
(412) 752-0081
Licensure Skilled care. *Beds* SNF 19. *Certified* Medicaid; Medicare.
Owner Nonprofit corp.

Elmhurst

St Mary's Villa Nursing Home
Saint Mary's Villa Rd, Elmhurst, PA 18416-0193
(717) 842-7621
Admin Sr Mary Anne Kaporch NHA. *Dir of Nursing* Sandra Capooci RN. *Medical Dir* Joseph Demko MD.
Licensure Skilled care. *Beds* SNF 112. *Private Pay Patients* 31%. *Certified* Medicaid; Medicare.
Owner Nonprofit corp.
Admissions Requirements Minimum age 65; Medical examination; Physician's request.
Staff Physicians 11 (pt); RNs 5 (ft), 9 (pt); LPNs 7 (ft), 14 (pt); Nurses' aides 26 (ft), 42 (pt); Physical therapists (consultant); Speech therapists 1 (pt); Activities coordinators 1 (ft); Dietitians 1 (ft); Podiatrists 3 (pt); Audiologists 1 (pt); Dentists 1 (pt).
Languages Lithuanian.
Affiliation Roman Catholic.
Facilities Dining room; Physical therapy room; Activities room; Chapel; Laundry room; Barber/Beauty shop; Library; Lounges; Patio; Pavilion; Coffee/snack shop; Gift shop.
Activities Arts & crafts; Cards; Games; Reading groups; Prayer groups; Movies; Shopping trips; Dances/Social/Cultural gatherings; Intergenerational programs.

Elwyn

Elwyn Inc—Nevil Home
111 Elwyn Rd, Elwyn, PA 19063
(215) 891-2357
Admin Harry L Starr. *Dir of Nursing* Grace Johnson RN. *Medical Dir* Dr Robert A Schweizer.
Licensure Intermediate care. *Beds* ICF 41. *Private Pay Patients* 13%. *Certified* Medicaid.
Owner Proprietary corp.
Admissions Requirements Minimum age 55.
Staff Physicians 1 (pt); RNs 1 (ft), 1 (pt); LPNs 2 (ft), 2 (pt); Nurses' aides 20 (ft); Physical therapists 1 (pt); Recreational therapists 1 (ft); Occupational therapists 1 (pt); Dietitians 1 (pt); Ophthalmologists 1 (pt); Podiatrists 1 (pt); Audiologists 1 (pt); Dentists 1 (pt).
Languages Sign.
Facilities Dining room; Physical therapy room; Activities room; Crafts room; Laundry room; Barber/Beauty shop.

Emporium

Guy & Mary Felt Manor
110 E 4th St, Emporium, PA 15834
(814) 486-3736
Admin Nancy Umbenhauer. *Dir of Nursing*
David Wolfe. *Medical Dir* Dr J M
Blackburn.
Licensure Skilled care; Intermediate care. *Beds*
SNF 20; ICF 20. *Certified* Medicaid;
Medicare.
Owner Nonprofit corp.
Admissions Requirements Minimum age 18;
Medical examination; Physician's request.
Staff RNs 3 (ft), 1 (pt); LPNs 3 (ft), 2 (pt);
Nurses' aides 10 (ft), 10 (pt); Activities
coordinators 1 (ft); Dietitians 1 (pt).
Facilities Dining room; Physical therapy
room; Activities room; Crafts room; Laundry
room; Barber/Beauty shop.
Activities Arts & crafts; Cards; Games;
Reading groups; Prayer groups; Movies.

Ephrata

Ephrata Nursing Home
25 W Locust St, Ephrata, PA 17522
(717) 733-2189
Admin C M Wagner.
Medical Dir Dr William Noller.
Licensure Skilled care. *Beds* SNF 24. *Certified*
Medicaid; Medicare.
Owner Proprietary corp.
Admissions Requirements Minimum age 45;
Medical examination.
Staff Physicians 4 (pt); RNs 1 (ft), 2 (pt);
LPNs 2 (ft), 2 (pt); Nurses' aides 5 (ft), 6
(pt); Physical therapists 1 (pt); Reality
therapists 1 (pt); Recreational therapists 1
(ft); Occupational therapists 1 (pt); Speech
therapists 1 (pt); Activities coordinators 1
(ft); Dietitians 1 (pt); Ophthalmologists 1
(pt); Podiatrists 1 (pt); Dentists 1 (pt).
Facilities Dining room; Physical therapy
room; Activities room; Laundry room.
Activities Arts & crafts; Cards; Games;
Reading groups; Prayer groups.

Fairmont Rest Home
RD 4, Ephrata, PA 17522
(717) 354-4111
Licensure Skilled care. *Beds* 116. *Certified*
Medicaid.
Owner Nonprofit corp.

Erdenheim

Harston Hall Nursing & Convalescent Home Inc
350 Haws Ln, Erdenheim, PA 19118
(215) 233-0700
Licensure Skilled care. *Beds* SNF 120.
Certified Medicaid.
Owner Proprietary corp.

Erie

Alpine Manor Health Center
4114 Schaper Ave, Erie, PA 16509
(814) 868-0831
Admin Renee Brown.
Medical Dir Dr Merjia Wright.
Licensure Skilled care; Intermediate care;
Alzheimer's care. *Beds* SNF 60; ICF 69.
Certified Medicaid; Medicare.
Owner Proprietary corp (Integrated Health
Services Inc).
Admissions Requirements Medical
examination.

Staff Physicians 1 (ft), 1 (pt); RNs 12 (ft), 3
(pt); LPNs 2 (pt); Nurses' aides 30 (ft);
Physical therapists 2 (ft); Recreational
therapists 1 (ft); Occupational therapists 1
(ft); Speech therapists 1 (ft); Activities
coordinators 1 (ft); Dietitians 1 (ft);
Ophthalmologists 1 (pt).
Facilities Dining room; Physical therapy
room; Activities room; Laundry room;
Barber/Beauty shop.
Activities Arts & crafts; Cards; Games;
Reading groups; Prayer groups; Movies;
Dances/Social/Cultural gatherings.

Ball Pavilion
5416 E Lake Rd, Erie, PA 16511
(814) 899-8600
Licensure Skilled care; Intermediate care. *Beds*
SNF 31; ICF 53. *Certified* Medicaid;
Medicare.
Owner Nonprofit corp.

Dr Gertrude A Barber Center Inc
136 East Ave, Erie, PA 16507
(814) 453-7661
Admin Gertrude A Barber EdD. *Dir of
Nursing* Karen Hahn Berry RN MEd.
Medical Dir Joseph DeFranco MD.
Licensure Intermediate care for mentally
retarded. *Beds* ICF/MR 105. *Certified*
Medicaid.
Owner Nonprofit corp.
Admissions Requirements Minimum age 18;
Medical examination; Primary diagnosis of
mental retardation.
Staff Physicians; RNs; LPNs; Physical
therapists; Recreational therapists;
Occupational therapists; Speech therapists;
Activities coordinators; Dietitians;
Podiatrists; Audiologists.
Facilities Dining room; Physical therapy
room; Activities room; Chapel; Crafts room;
Laundry room; Library; Gymnasium;
Vocational workshops; Recreational area;
Pool.
Activities Arts & crafts; Games; Prayer groups;
Movies; Shopping trips; Dances/Social/
Cultural gatherings; Community activities;
Day program services; Therapeutic
recreation; Behavioral programming; Speech/
language development program.

Battersby Convalescent Center
2686 Peach St, Erie, PA 16508
(814) 453-6641
Licensure Skilled care. *Beds* SNF 115.
Certified Medicaid; Medicare.
Owner Proprietary corp (Beverly Enterprises).

Erie County Geriatric Center Annex
4728 Lake Pleasant Rd, Erie, PA 16504
(814) 825-0000
Licensure Skilled care. *Beds* SNF 80. *Certified*
Medicaid; Medicare.
Owner Publicly owned.

Lake Erie Institute of Rehabilitation
137 W 2nd St, Erie, PA 16507
(814) 453-5602
Admin Urban LaRiccia. *Dir of Nursing* Linda
Sproat RN CRRN. *Medical Dir* Thomas
Klaus MD.
Licensure Skilled care. *Beds* SNF 59. *Certified*
Medicaid; Medicare.
Owner Proprietary corp.
Staff Physicians 3 (ft), 2 (pt); RNs 25 (ft), 6
(pt); LPNs 7 (ft), 1 (pt); Nurses' aides 48
(ft), 19 (pt); Physical therapists 6 (ft);
Recreational therapists 5 (ft); Occupational
therapists 8 (ft); Speech therapists 8 (ft);
Dietitians 1 (pt); Respiratory therapists 1
(pt).
Facilities Dining room; Physical therapy
room; Activities room; Crafts room; Laundry
room; EEG & evoked potential lab; Research
department; Occupational therapy rooms;
Recreation therapy rooms; Speech therapy
rooms.

Activities Arts & crafts; Cards; Games;
Movies; Shopping trips; Dances/Social/
Cultural gatherings; Stimulation groups.

Lutheran Home for the Aged
149 W 22nd St, Erie, PA 16502
(814) 452-3271
Admin Joseph S Bieniek. *Dir of Nursing*
Virginia Shaffer RN NHA.
Licensure Skilled care; Intermediate care;
Retirement. *Beds* SNF 57; ICF 57. *Certified*
Medicaid; Medicare.
Owner Nonprofit corp.
Admissions Requirements Minimum age 65;
Medical examination.
Staff Physicians 1 (pt); RNs 1 (ft), 1 (pt);
LPNs 3 (pt); Nurses' aides 20 (ft), 8 (pt);
Physical therapists 1 (pt); Recreational
therapists 1 (pt); Occupational therapists 1
(pt); Speech therapists 1 (pt); Activities
coordinators 1 (ft); Dietitians 1 (ft);
Ophthalmologists 1 (pt); Podiatrists 1 (pt);
Dentists 1 (pt).
Languages Interpreters available.
Affiliation Lutheran.
Facilities Dining room; Physical therapy
room; Activities room; Chapel; Crafts room;
Laundry room; Barber/Beauty shop; Library.
Activities Arts & crafts; Cards; Games;
Reading groups; Prayer groups; Movies;
Shopping trips; Dances/Social/Cultural
gatherings.

Manor Home for the Aged Inc
3401 Poplar St, Erie, PA 16508
(814) 866-7449
Licensure Intermediate care. *Beds* ICF 33.
Certified Medicaid.
Owner Proprietary corp.

Mercy Health Care Center
1267 S Hill Rd, Erie, PA 16509
(814) 864-4081
Admin Mary Ann Balsign.
Medical Dir Dr Ronald W Pearson.
Licensure Skilled care; Intermediate care. *Beds*
SNF 50; ICF 30. *Certified* Medicaid;
Medicare.
Owner Proprietary corp (Unicare).
Admissions Requirements Minimum age 16;
Medical examination; Physician's request.
Staff RNs 4 (ft), 4 (pt); LPNs 4 (ft), 4 (pt);
Nurses' aides 21 (ft), 10 (pt); Physical
therapists 1 (pt); Recreational therapists 1
(ft); Activities coordinators 1 (ft).
Facilities Dining room; Physical therapy
room; Activities room; Chapel; Crafts room;
Barber/Beauty shop.
Activities Arts & crafts; Cards; Games;
Movies; Dances/Social/Cultural gatherings.

Pennsylvania Soldiers' & Sailors' Home
PO Box 6239, 570 E 3rd St, Erie, PA 16512-6239
(814) 871-4531
Admin Stanley E Snyder ACSW NHA. *Dir of
Nursing* R Jane Smith RN. *Medical Dir*
William A Rowane DO.
Licensure Skilled care; Intermediate care;
Personal care; Domiciliary care. *Beds* Swing
beds SNF/ICF 75; Personal care 60;
Domiciliary care 40. *Private Pay Patients*
3%.
Owner Publicly owned.
Admissions Requirements Medical
examination.
Staff Physicians 1 (ft); RNs 28 (ft); LPNs 9
(ft); Nurses' aides 33 (ft); Physical therapists
1 (ft); Speech therapists 1 (pt); Activities
coordinators 1 (ft); Dietitians 1 (ft);
Ophthalmologists 1 (pt).
Facilities Dining room; Physical therapy
room; Activities room; Chapel; Crafts room;
Laundry room; Barber/Beauty shop; Library.
Activities Arts & crafts; Cards; Games;
Movies; Shopping trips; Dances/Social/
Cultural gatherings; Pet therapy.

Activities Arts & crafts; Cards; Games;
Shopping trips; Dances/Social/Cultural
gatherings; Intergenerational programs; Pet
therapy.

Presbyterian Lodge
2628 Elmwood Ave, Erie, PA 16508
(814) 864-4802, 864-7929 FAX
Admin Doris E Johnson NHA. *Dir of Nursing*
Jean A Reichert RN. *Medical Dir* Ronald P
Leemhuis MD.
Licensure Skilled care; Intermediate care;
Personal care; Retirement. *Beds* SNF 18;
ICF 37; Personal care 22; Retirement apts 5.
Private Pay Patients 86%. *Certified*
Medicaid; Medicare.
Owner Nonprofit corp (Presbyterian Homes of
Lake Erie).
Admissions Requirements Minimum age 65;
Medical examination; Physician's request.
Staff Physicians; RNs; LPNs; Nurses' aides;
Physical therapists; Recreational therapists;
Occupational therapists; Speech therapists;
Activities coordinators; Dietitians;
Ophthalmologists.
Affiliation Presbyterian.
Facilities Dining room; Physical therapy
room; Activities room; Crafts room; Laundry
room; Barber/Beauty shop; Library.
Activities Arts & crafts; Cards; Games;
Reading groups; Prayer groups; Movies;
Shopping trips; Dances/Social/Cultural
gatherings; Intergenerational programs; Pet
therapy.

Sarah A Reed Retirement Center
227 W 22nd St, Erie, PA 16502-2689
(814) 453-6797, 454-3849 FAX
Admin Gale Magyar. *Dir of Nursing* Kathy
Gustafson. *Medical Dir* Robert R Stuart
MD.
Licensure Skilled care; Intermediate care;
Personal care; Alzheimer's care. *Beds* SNF
43; ICF 36; Personal care 54. *Private Pay
Patients* 90%. *Certified* Medicaid; Medicare.
Owner Nonprofit corp.
Admissions Requirements Medical
examination.
Staff Physicians; RNs; LPNs; Nurses' aides;
Physical therapists; Speech therapists;
Activities coordinators; Dietitians;
Podiatrists.
Facilities Dining room; Physical therapy
room; Activities room; Chapel; Crafts room;
Laundry room; Barber/Beauty shop; Library.
Activities Arts & crafts; Cards; Games;
Reading groups; Prayer groups; Movies;
Shopping trips; Dances/Social/Cultural
gatherings; Intergenerational programs; Pet
therapy.

St Marys Home of Erie
607 E 26th St, Erie, PA 16504
(814) 459-0621
Admin Sr Anastasia Valimont. *Dir of Nursing*
Sr Phyllis McCracken. *Medical Dir* Dr
Barabas Beresky.
Licensure Skilled care; Intermediate care;
Residential/Personal care; Adult/Alzheimer's
day care. *Beds* SNF 100; ICF 93;
Residential/Personal care 131. *Private Pay
Patients* 60%. *Certified* Medicaid; Medicare.
Owner Nonprofit corp.
Admissions Requirements Minimum age 65;
Medical examination.
Staff Physicians 1 (pt); RNs 14 (ft); LPNs 9
(ft); Nurses' aides 72 (ft); Physical therapists
(contracted); Recreational therapists 2 (ft);
Occupational therapists 1 (pt); Speech
therapists 1 (pt); Activities coordinators 2
(ft); Dietitians 2 (pt); Podiatrists 1 (pt).
Affiliation Roman Catholic.
Facilities Dining room; Physical therapy
room; Activities room; Chapel; Crafts room;
Laundry room; Barber/Beauty shop; Library.
Activities Arts & crafts; Cards; Games;
Reading groups; Prayer groups; Movies;
Dances/Social/Cultural gatherings;
Intergenerational programs; Pet therapy.

Twinbrook Medical Center
3805 Field St, Erie, PA 16511
(814) 899-0651

Admin Lloyd R Berkey. *Dir of Nursing* Julie
Breski RN.
Licensure Skilled care. *Beds* SNF 124.
Certified Medicaid; Medicare.
Owner Proprietary corp (Health Care and
Retirement Corp).
Facilities Dining room; Physical therapy
room; Activities room; Chapel; Crafts room;
Laundry room; Barber/Beauty shop; Library.
Activities Arts & crafts; Cards; Games;
Reading groups; Prayer groups; Movies;
Shopping trips; Dances/Social/Cultural
gatherings.

Western Reserve Convalescent Home
1521 W 54th St, Erie, PA 16509
(814) 864-0671
Licensure Skilled care. *Beds* SNF 133.
Certified Medicaid; Medicare.
Owner Proprietary corp (Beverly Enterprises).

Everett

Pennknoll Village Nursing Home
RD 1 Box 420, Everett, PA 15537
(814) 623-9018
Admin Brenda Barefoot. *Dir of Nursing* Kay
Will. *Medical Dir* Eyler MD.
Licensure Skilled care; Intermediate care;
Alzheimer's care. *Beds* SNF 29; ICF 104.
Certified Medicaid; Medicare.
Owner Nonprofit corp (Tressler-Lutheran
Services Assn).
Admissions Requirements Minimum age 65.
Staff RNs 6 (ft), 8 (pt); LPNs 8 (ft), 8 (pt);
Nurses' aides 37 (ft), 32 (pt); Activities
coordinators 1 (ft).
Facilities Dining room; Physical therapy
room; Activities room; Chapel; Crafts room;
Laundry room; Barber/Beauty shop; Library.
Activities Arts & crafts; Cards; Games;
Reading groups; Prayer groups; Movies;
Shopping trips; Dances/Social/Cultural
gatherings.

Exeter

Highland Manor Nursing Home
750 Schooley Ave, Exeter, PA 18643
(717) 655-3791
Licensure Skilled care. *Beds* SNF 120.
Certified Medicaid; Medicare.
Owner Proprietary corp (HBA Management
Inc).

Fairview

Fairview Manor
900 Manchester Rd, Fairview, PA 16415
(814) 838-4822
Admin Wallace E Warren. *Dir of Nursing*
Lynda Pazun RN. *Medical Dir* Thomas C
Klaus MD.
Licensure Skilled care. *Beds* SNF 120.
Certified Medicaid; Medicare.
Owner Proprietary corp (HCF Inc).
Admissions Requirements Medical
examination; Physician's request.
Staff RNs 6 (ft); LPNs 10 (ft), 1 (pt); Nurses'
aides 44 (ft), 12 (pt); Physical therapists;
Activities coordinators 1 (ft); Dietitians.
Facilities Dining room; Physical therapy
room; Activities room; Crafts room; Laundry
room; Barber/Beauty shop; Library.
Activities Arts & crafts; Cards; Games;
Reading groups; Prayer groups; Movies;
Shopping trips; Dances/Social/Cultural
gatherings.

Fayette City

Waddington Convalescent Home
Rte 1, Fayette City, PA 15438
(412) 326-4077
Licensure Skilled care. *Beds* 40.
Owner Proprietary corp.

Fayetteville

Caledonia Manor
3301 Lincoln Way E, Fayetteville, PA 17222
(717) 352-2101
Licensure Skilled care. *Beds* SNF 102.
Certified Medicaid; Medicare.
Owner Proprietary corp (Beverly Enterprises).

Guilford Convalesarium
3301 Lincoln Way East, Fayetteville, PA
17222
(717) 352-2101
Licensure Skilled care. *Beds* 64. *Certified*
Medicaid; Medicare.
Owner Proprietary corp.

Piney Mountain Home
6375 Chambersburg Rd, Fayetteville, PA
17222
(717) 352-2721
Licensure Skilled care; Intermediate care;
Independent living. *Beds* 92. *Certified*
Medicaid; Medicare.
Owner Nonprofit corp.

Feasterville

Ridge Crest Convalescent Center Inc
1730 Buck Rd N, Feasterville, PA 19047
(215) 355-3131
Admin Francis J Lee Jr NHA. *Dir of Nursing*
Edwina Lehman RN. *Medical Dir* Robert B
Davis MD.
Licensure Skilled care; Intermediate care. *Beds*
Swing beds SNF/ICF 128. *Private Pay
Patients* 20-25%. *Certified* Medicaid;
Medicare.
Owner Proprietary corp.
Admissions Requirements Minimum age 16.
Staff RNs 7 (ft), 2 (pt); LPNs 6 (ft), 2 (pt);
Nurses' aides 50 (ft), 15 (pt); Physical
therapists 2 (pt); Reality therapists 1 (pt);
Recreational therapists 1 (pt); Occupational
therapists 1 (pt); Speech therapists 1 (pt);
Activities coordinators 2 (ft); Dietitians 1
(pt); Ophthalmologists 1 (pt); Podiatrists 1
(pt); Audiologists 1 (pt).
Facilities Dining room; Physical therapy
room; Activities room; Crafts room; Laundry
room; Barber/Beauty shop; Library.
Activities Arts & crafts; Cards; Games;
Reading groups; Prayer groups; Movies;
Shopping trips; Intergenerational programs;
Pet therapy.

Flourtown

St Joseph Villa
Stenton & Wissahickon Aves, Flourtown, PA
19031
(215) 836-4179, 836-4222 FAX
Admin Sr Marie Rudegeair. *Dir of Nursing* Sr
Sean Marie. *Medical Dir* Jude Damian MD.
Licensure Skilled care; Intermediate care. *Beds*
SNF 54; ICF 54. *Certified* Medicare.
Owner Nonprofit corp.
Admissions Requirements Medical
examination; Physician's request.
Staff Physicians; RNs; LPNs; Nurses' aides;
Physical therapists; Recreational therapists;
Occupational therapists; Speech therapists;
Activities coordinators; Dietitians;
Ophthalmologists; Podiatrists; Audiologists.
Affiliation Roman Catholic.
Facilities Dining room; Physical therapy
room; Activities room; Chapel; Crafts room;
Laundry room; Barber/Beauty shop; Library.
Activities Arts & crafts; Cards; Games;
Reading groups; Prayer groups; Movies;
Shopping trips; Dances/Social/Cultural
gatherings; Intergenerational programs; Pet
therapy; Ceramics; Flower club.

Forest City

Forest City Nursing Center
915 Delaware St, Forest City, PA 18421
(717) 785-3005
Licensure Skilled care. *Beds* SNF 140.
  Certified Medicaid; Medicare.
Owner Proprietary corp.

Forksville

Dar-Way Nursing Home Inc
RD 1, Forksville, PA 18616
(717) 924-3411
Admin Dora A McCarty. *Dir of Nursing*
  Beverly Unruh RN.
Licensure Intermediate care. *Beds* ICF 70.
  Certified Medicaid; VA.
Owner Privately owned.
Admissions Requirements Medical
  examination; Physician's request.
Staff Physicians 3 (pt); RNs 3 (ft), 2 (pt);
  LPNs 3 (ft), 3 (pt); Nurses' aides 25 (ft), 7
  (pt); Occupational therapists 1 (ft); Dietitians
  1 (pt).
Facilities Dining room; Activities room;
  Chapel; Barber/Beauty shop.
Activities Arts & crafts; Cards; Games;
  Reading groups; Prayer groups; Movies.

Fort Washington

Fort Washington Estates
1264 Fort Washington Ave, Fort Washington,
PA 19034
(215) 542-8787
Admin Elaine R Reimet RN BSN NHA. *Dir
  of Nursing* Mary Hoffman RN. *Medical Dir*
  Arthur B Lintgen MD.
Licensure Skilled care; Retirement. *Beds* SNF
  62; Retirement 110. *Private Pay Patients* 8-
  10%. *Certified* Medicare.
Owner Nonprofit corp (ACTS Inc).
Admissions Requirements Medical
  examination; Physician's request.
Staff Physicians; RNs; LPNs; Nurses' aides;
  Physical therapists; Occupational therapists;
  Speech therapists; Activities coordinators;
  Dietitians; Ophthalmologists; Podiatrists;
  Audiologists.
Facilities Dining room; Physical therapy
  room; Activities room; Chapel; Crafts room;
  Laundry room; Barber/Beauty shop; Library.
Activities Arts & crafts; Cards; Games;
  Reading groups; Prayer groups; Movies;
  Shopping trips; Dances/Social/Cultural
  gatherings; Intergenerational programs; Pet
  therapy.

Frackville

Broad Mountain Nursing Home
500 W Laurel St, Frackville, PA 17931
(717) 874-0696
Admin Rose Ann Dyszel RN. *Dir of Nursing*
  Barbara Merwine. *Medical Dir* Gursharan
  Singh MD.
Licensure Skilled care. *Beds* SNF 129.
  Certified Medicaid; Medicare.
Owner Proprietary corp (Unicare).
Admissions Requirements Minimum age 18.
Staff RNs 4 (ft), 4 (pt); LPNs 6 (ft), 11 (pt);
  Nurses' aides 27 (ft), 24 (pt); Physical
  therapists 1 (ft); Activities coordinators 2
  (ft); Dietitians 2 (pt).
Facilities Dining room; Physical therapy
  room; Activities room; Crafts room; Laundry
  room; Barber/Beauty shop; Library; Outside
  patio.
Activities Arts & crafts; Cards; Games;
  Reading groups; Prayer groups; Movies;
  Shopping trips; Dances/Social/Cultural
  gatherings; Pet therapy; Birthday parties;
  Welcoming parties.

Franklin

Venango Manor
RD 3 Box 29, Franklin, PA 16323
(814) 437-6522
Admin Judith Billingsley RN NHA. *Dir of
  Nursing* Joyce Gibson RN BSN. *Medical Dir*
  Dr Kamal Aoun.
Licensure Skilled care; Intermediate care. *Beds*
  SNF 53; ICF 125. *Certified* Medicaid.
Owner Publicly owned.
Admissions Requirements Medical
  examination; Physician's request.
Staff Physicians; RNs; LPNs; Nurses' aides;
  Physical therapists; Recreational therapists;
  Speech therapists; Activities coordinators;
  Dietitians; Ophthalmologists; Podiatrists;
  Dentists.
Facilities Dining room; Physical therapy
  room; Activities room; Crafts room; Laundry
  room; Barber/Beauty shop.
Activities Arts & crafts; Cards; Games;
  Reading groups; Prayer groups; Movies;
  Shopping trips; Dances/Social/Cultural
  gatherings.

Frederick

Frederick Mennonite Home
Rte 73, Frederick, PA 19435
(215) 754-7878
Licensure Skilled care; Independent living.
  Beds SNF 60. *Certified* Medicaid; Medicare.
Owner Nonprofit corp.
Affiliation Mennonite.

Gettysburg

Gettysburg Lutheran Retirement Village
1075 Old Harrisburg Rd, Gettysburg, PA
17325-3199
(717) 334-6204
Admin Geary Milliken NHA. *Dir of Nursing*
  Sharon DeVivio. *Medical Dir* Dr Dwight
  Michael.
Licensure Skilled care; Intermediate care;
  Personal care. *Beds* SNF 19; ICF 81;
  Personal care 15. *Private Pay Patients* 70%.
  Certified Medicaid; Medicare.
Owner Nonprofit corp (Lutheran Social
  Services).
Admissions Requirements Minimum age 65;
  Medical examination; Physician's request.
Staff Physicians 1 (pt); RNs 6 (ft), 2 (pt);
  LPNs 13 (ft), 1 (pt); Nurses' aides 39 (ft), 14
  (pt); Physical therapists 1 (pt); Recreational
  therapists 1 (ft), 1 (pt); Occupational
  therapists 2 (pt); Speech therapists 1 (pt);
  Activities coordinators 1 (ft); Dietitians 1
  (ft); Podiatrists 1 (pt); Audiologists 1 (pt).
Affiliation Lutheran.
Facilities Dining room; Physical therapy
  room; Activities room; Chapel; Crafts room;
  Laundry room; Barber/Beauty shop; Library.
Activities Arts & crafts; Cards; Games;
  Reading groups; Prayer groups; Movies;
  Shopping trips; Dances/Social/Cultural
  gatherings; Intergenerational programs; Pet
  therapy.

Gettysburg Village Green Nursing Center
867 York Rd, Gettysburg, PA 17325
(717) 337-3238
Admin John D Giamber NHA. *Dir of Nursing*
  Claudia Brown RN. *Medical Dir* James
  Hammett DO.
Licensure Skilled care; Intermediate care. *Beds*
  SNF 40; ICF 80. *Private Pay Patients* 40%.
  Certified Medicaid; Medicare.
Owner Privately owned.
Admissions Requirements Medical
  examination; Physician's request.
Staff RNs 4 (ft); LPNs 8 (ft); Nurses' aides 50
  (ft); Physical therapists 1 (ft); Recreational
  therapists 1 (ft); Occupational therapists 1

(ft); Speech therapists 1 (ft); Activities
  coordinators 1 (ft); Dietitians 1 (ft);
  Audiologists 1 (ft).
Facilities Dining room; Physical therapy
  room; Activities room; Chapel; Crafts room;
  Laundry room; Barber/Beauty shop; Library.
Activities Arts & crafts; Cards; Games;
  Reading groups; Prayer groups; Movies;
  Dances/Social/Cultural gatherings;
  Intergenerational programs; Pet therapy.

Green Acres Adams County Home
595 Biglerville Rd, Gettysburg, PA 17325-
8002
(717) 334-3417
Admin Carol A Knisely. *Dir of Nursing*
  Barbara Reever. *Medical Dir* Robert S
  Lefever MD.
Licensure Skilled care; Intermediate care;
  Personal care; Adult day care; Respite care.
  Beds SNF 49; ICF 107; Personal care 6.
  Private Pay Patients 7%. *Certified* Medicaid;
  Medicare.
Owner Publicly owned.
Admissions Requirements Minimum age 18;
  Medical examination; Physician's request.
Staff Physicians 1 (pt); RNs 5 (ft), 4 (pt);
  LPNs 17 (ft), 9 (pt); Nurses' aides 45 (ft), 10
  (pt); Activities coordinators 1 (ft); Dietitians
  1 (pt).
Facilities Dining room; Physical therapy
  room; Activities room; Chapel; Laundry
  room; Barber/Beauty shop.
Activities Arts & crafts; Cards; Games;
  Reading groups; Prayer groups; Movies;
  Shopping trips; Dances/Social/Cultural
  gatherings; Intergenerational programs; Pet
  therapy; Floats for parades; Outside
  programs; Grandparent program.

Michael Manor
741 Chambersburg Rd, Gettysburg, PA 17325
(717) 334-6764
Admin Michelle Slotterback. *Dir of Nursing*
  Karen McDannell. *Medical Dir* Dr James
  Hammett.
Licensure Skilled care; Intermediate care. *Beds*
  SNF 50; ICF 56. *Private Pay Patients* 40%.
  Certified Medicaid; Medicare.
Owner Proprietary corp (Beverly Enterprises).
Admissions Requirements Medical
  examination; Physician's request.
Staff Physicians 1 (pt); RNs 6 (ft); LPNs 15
  (ft); Nurses' aides 60 (ft), 20 (pt); Physical
  therapists 1 (pt); Occupational therapists 2
  (pt); Speech therapists 1 (pt); Activities
  coordinators 2 (ft); Dietitians 1 (ft);
  Ophthalmologists 1 (pt); Podiatrists 1 (pt).
Facilities Dining room.
Activities Arts & crafts; Games; Reading
  groups; Prayer groups; Movies; Shopping
  trips; Dances/Social/Cultural gatherings;
  Intergenerational programs; Pet therapy.

Gibsonia

St Barnabas Nursing Home
5827 Meridian Rd, Gibsonia, PA 15044
(412) 443-1552
Admin William V Day. *Dir of Nursing* Karen
  Tabacchi. *Medical Dir* William F Schwerin
  MD.
Licensure Skilled care; Intermediate care;
  Independent living. *Beds* SNF 84; ICF 23;
  Independent living apts 252. *Certified*
  Medicaid; Medicare.
Owner Nonprofit organization/foundation.
Admissions Requirements Minimum age 10;
  Medical examination; Physician's request.
Staff Physicians 2 (pt); Physical therapists 2
  (pt); Recreational therapists 1 (ft); Activities
  coordinators 1 (ft); Dietitians 1 (ft);
  Podiatrists 1 (pt).
Facilities Dining room; Physical therapy
  room; Activities room; Chapel; Crafts room;
  Barber/Beauty shop.

Activities Arts & crafts; Cards; Games; Reading groups; Prayer groups; Movies; Shopping trips; Dances/Social/Cultural gatherings; Intergenerational programs; Pet therapy.

Girard

Erie County Geriatric Center
8300 W Ridge Rd, Girard, PA 16417
(814) 474-5521, 474-2307 FAX
Admin Robert Lethbridge, Exec Dir. *Dir of Nursing* Sandra L Nelson. *Medical Dir* E E Mercier MD.
Licensure Skilled care; Intermediate care; Alzheimer's care. *Beds* Swing beds SNF/ICF 519. *Certified* Medicaid; Medicare.
Owner Nonprofit organization/foundation.
Staff Physicians; RNs; LPNs; Nurses' aides; Physical therapists; Recreational therapists; Speech therapists; Activities coordinators; Dietitians; Ophthalmologists; Podiatrists.
Facilities Dining room; Physical therapy room; Activities room; Chapel; Crafts room; Laundry room; Barber/Beauty shop; Library.
Activities Arts & crafts; Cards; Games; Reading groups; Prayer groups; Movies; Shopping trips; Dances/Social/Cultural gatherings; Intergenerational programs; Pet therapy.

Gladwyne

Waverly Heights
1400 Waverly Rd, Gladwyne, PA 19035
(215) 645-8600
Licensure Skilled care; Independent living. *Beds* SNF 29. *Certified* Medicare.
Owner Proprietary corp.

Glenside

Edgehill Nursing & Rehabilitation Center
146 Edge Hill Rd, Glenside, PA 19038
(215) 886-1043
Admin Douglas Foulke. *Dir of Nursing* Betsy Sevitski. *Medical Dir* Dr Howard Fein.
Licensure Skilled care. *Beds* SNF 60. *Certified* Medicaid.
Owner Proprietary corp (GraceCare, Inc).
Admissions Requirements Medical examination.
Staff RNs 2 (ft), 5 (pt); LPNs 5 (ft); Nurses' aides 18 (ft), 4 (pt); Activities coordinators 1 (ft).
Facilities Dining room; Physical therapy room; Laundry room; Library; Multipurpose room used for chapel, activities room, and crafts room.
Activities Arts & crafts; Cards; Games; Reading groups; Prayer groups; Movies; Shopping trips; Dances/Social/Cultural gatherings.

Granville

Malta Home for the Aging
PO Box E, Malta Dr, Granville, PA 17029
(717) 248-3988
Admin Garry D Hennis. *Dir of Nursing* Greta J Hassinger RN. *Medical Dir* Dr Luis Velaquez.
Licensure Skilled care; Intermediate care; Personal care. *Beds* SNF 24; ICF 16; Personal care 20. *Private Pay Patients* 55%. *Certified* Medicaid; Medicare.
Owner Nonprofit organization/foundation.
Admissions Requirements Medical examination; Physician's request.
Staff RNs 3 (ft), 1 (pt); LPNs 10 (ft), 1 (pt); Nurses' aides 9 (ft), 6 (pt); Physical therapists 1 (pt); Recreational therapists 1 (ft); Speech therapists 1 (pt); Activities coordinators 1 (pt); Podiatrists 1 (pt).
Affiliation Knights of Malta.

Facilities Dining room; Physical therapy room; Activities room; Laundry room; Barber/Beauty shop; Library.
Activities Arts & crafts; Cards; Games; Reading groups; Prayer groups; Shopping trips; Intergenerational programs; Bingo; Bowling.

Greensburg

Greensburg Home—Redstone Presbytery
6 Garden Center Dr, Greensburg, PA 15601
(412) 832-8400
Admin John A Mobley.
Licensure Intermediate care; Independent living. *Beds* ICF 64. *Certified* Medicaid.
Owner Nonprofit corp.
Admissions Requirements Minimum age 62; Medical examination.
Staff Physicians 1 (pt); RNs 3 (ft), 3 (pt); LPNs 4 (ft), 3 (pt); Nurses' aides 16 (ft), 9 (pt); Activities coordinators 2 (ft), 1 (pt); Dietitians 1 (pt); Ophthalmologists 1 (pt).
Affiliation Presbyterian.
Facilities Dining room; Physical therapy room; Activities room; Chapel; Crafts room; Laundry room; Barber/Beauty shop; Library.
Activities Arts & crafts; Cards; Games; Reading groups; Prayer groups; Movies; Shopping trips; Dances/Social/Cultural gatherings.

Greensburg Nursing & Convalescent Center
Box 956, Donohoe & Luxor Rd, Greensburg, PA 15601-0956
(412) 836-2480
Admin Melba L Galonis. *Dir of Nursing* Eleanor Pennington. *Medical Dir* Thomas DeGregory MD.
Licensure Skilled care. *Beds* SNF 120. *Certified* Medicaid; Medicare.
Owner Privately owned.
Admissions Requirements Medical examination; Physician's request.
Staff RNs 3 (ft), 6 (pt); LPNs 8 (ft), 7 (pt); Nurses' aides 25 (ft), 21 (pt); Activities coordinators 1 (ft); Dietitians 1 (ft).
Languages German, Slavic, Italian.
Facilities Dining room; Physical therapy room; Activities room; Laundry room; Barber/Beauty shop.
Activities Arts & crafts; Cards; Games; Reading groups; Prayer groups; Movies; Dances/Social/Cultural gatherings.

Hopehill Nursing Home
RD 6, Woodward Dr, Greensburg, PA 15601
(412) 836-4424
Licensure Skilled care; Intermediate care. *Beds* SNF 120. *Certified* Medicaid; Medicare.
Owner Proprietary corp (HCF Inc).

Mt View Nursing & Rehabilitation Center
RD 7 Box 249, Greensburg, PA 15601
(412) 837-6499, 537-9645 FAX
Admin Janice C Reeping NHA. *Dir of Nursing* Joan A Silvis RN. *Medical Dir* Michael Zorch MD.
Licensure Skilled care; Intermediate care. *Beds* SNF 47; ICF 90. *Private Pay Patients* 65%. *Certified* Medicaid; Medicare.
Owner Proprietary corp (Integrated Health Services Inc).
Admissions Requirements Minimum age 16.
Staff Physicians 1 (pt); RNs 10 (ft), 6 (pt); LPNs 4 (ft), 7 (pt); Nurses' aides 28 (ft), 36 (pt); Physical therapists 2 (ft), 1 (pt); Recreational therapists 2 (ft); Occupational therapists 1 (ft), 1 (pt); Speech therapists 1 (pt); Activities coordinators 1 (ft); Dietitians 1 (pt); Ophthalmologists 1 (pt); Podiatrists 1 (pt); Audiologists 1 (pt).
Facilities Dining room; Physical therapy room; Activities room; Crafts room; Laundry room; Barber/Beauty shop.

Activities Arts & crafts; Cards; Games; Reading groups; Prayer groups; Movies; Shopping trips; Dances/Social/Cultural gatherings.

Oak Hill Home of Rest & Care Inc
Rte 7 Box 77A, Luxor Rd, Greensburg, PA 15601
(412) 837-7100
Licensure Skilled care. *Beds* SNF 48. *Certified* Medicaid; Medicare.
Owner Proprietary corp.

St Anne Home for the Elderly
685 Angela Dr, Greensburg, PA 15601
(412) 837-6070
Admin Sr Jean Francis Simok. *Dir of Nursing* Marie Cardella. *Medical Dir* Theodore A Schultz MD.
Licensure Skilled care; Intermediate care. *Beds* SNF 39; ICF 86. *Private Pay Patients* 60%. *Certified* Medicaid; Medicare.
Owner Nonprofit corp.
Admissions Requirements Minimum age 65; Medical examination.
Staff Physicians 2 (pt); RNs 2 (ft), 5 (pt); Physical therapists 1 (pt); Occupational therapists 1 (pt); Speech therapists 1 (pt); Activities coordinators 1 (pt); Dietitians 1 (pt); Ophthalmologists 1 (pt); Podiatrists 1 (pt); Audiologists 1 (pt); Inservice coordinators 1 (pt).
Affiliation Roman Catholic.
Facilities Dining room; Physical therapy room; Activities room; Chapel; Crafts room; Laundry room; Barber/Beauty shop; Library; Park.
Activities Arts & crafts; Cards; Games; Prayer groups; Movies; Dances/Social/Cultural gatherings; Intergenerational programs; Pet therapy.

Westmoreland Manor
2480 S Grande Blvd, Greensburg, PA 15601
(412) 834-0200
Licensure Skilled care. *Beds* SNF 540. *Certified* Medicaid; Medicare.
Owner Publicly owned.

Greenville

Gilmore's White-Cliff Nursing Home
110 Fredonia Rd, Greenville, PA 16125
(412) 588-8090
Licensure Skilled care. *Beds* SNF 134. *Certified* Medicaid; Medicare.
Owner Proprietary corp.

St Paul Homes
339 E Jamestown Rd, Greenville, PA 16125
(412) 588-7610
Admin G Bryan Oros NHA. *Dir of Nursing* Patricia Hilpert. *Medical Dir* Kathy Burcin DO.
Licensure Skilled care; Intermediate care; Retirement; Alzheimer's care. *Beds* SNF 53; ICF 173; Retirement 47. *Private Pay Patients* 40%. *Certified* Medicaid; Medicare.
Owner Nonprofit corp.
Admissions Requirements Minimum age 62; Medical examination; Physician's request.
Staff Physicians 15 (pt); RNs 8 (ft), 7 (pt); LPNs 22 (ft), 11 (pt); Nurses' aides 59 (ft), 42 (pt); Physical therapists 1 (pt); Reality therapists 4 (ft); Recreational therapists 3 (ft), 1 (pt); Speech therapists 1 (pt); Activities coordinators 1 (ft); Dietitians 1 (pt); Ophthalmologists 1 (pt); Podiatrists 1 (pt); Audiologists 1 (pt).
Affiliation United Church of Christ.
Facilities Dining room; Physical therapy room; Activities room; Chapel; Crafts room; Laundry room; Barber/Beauty shop; Library; Alzheimer's therapy unit.

Activities Arts & crafts; Cards; Games; Reading groups; Prayer groups; Movies; Shopping trips; Dances/Social/Cultural gatherings; Intergenerational programs; Pet therapy.

Grove City

Grove Manor
435 N Broad St, Grove City, PA 16127
(412) 458-7800
Admin Mary C Gray.
Licensure Skilled care. Beds SNF 59. Certified Medicaid; Medicare.
Owner Nonprofit corp.
Admissions Requirements Medical examination.
Staff RNs 2 (ft), 4 (pt); LPNs 2 (ft), 1 (pt); Nurses' aides 17 (ft), 8 (pt); Physical therapists 1 (ft); Speech therapists 1 (pt); Dietitians 1 (pt).
Affiliation Church of God.
Facilities Dining room; Physical therapy room; Chapel; Crafts room; Laundry room; Barber/Beauty shop.
Activities Arts & crafts; Games; Reading groups; Prayer groups; Movies.

Hillcrest Nursing Center
PO Box 1055, Grove City, PA 16127
(412) 458-9501
Licensure Skilled care. Beds SNF 121. Certified Medicaid; Medicare.
Owner Proprietary corp.

Orchard Manor
RD 3, Grove City, PA 16127
(412) 458-7760
Medical Dir William C Menzies MD.
Licensure Skilled care. Beds SNF 121. Certified Medicaid.
Owner Nonprofit corp.
Staff Physicians 2 (pt); RNs 8 (ft), 2 (pt); LPNs 5 (ft), 1 (pt); Nurses' aides 40 (ft), 3 (pt); Physical therapists 1 (pt); Activities coordinators 1 (ft); Dietitians 1 (pt); Ophthalmologists 1 (pt); Physical therapy aides 1 (ft).
Affiliation Independent Order of Odd Fellows & Rebekahs.
Facilities Dining room; Physical therapy room; Activities room; Chapel; Crafts room; Laundry room; Barber/Beauty shop; Library; Podiatry room.
Activities Arts & crafts; Cards; Games; Reading groups; Prayer groups; Movies; Shopping trips; Dances/Social/Cultural gatherings; Trips in van.

Gwynedd

Foulkeways at Gwynedd
1120 Meetinghouse Rd, Gwynedd, PA 19436
(215) 643-2200, 628-3682 FAX
Admin Douglas Tweddale NHA; Donald Moon Exec Dir. Dir of Nursing Linda Boston RN MSN MBA. Medical Dir Barbara Bell MD.
Licensure Skilled care; Personal care; Alzheimer's care. Beds SNF 68; Personal care 32. Certified Medicare.
Owner Nonprofit corp.
Admissions Requirements Minimum age 65; Medical examination.
Staff Physicians 3 (pt); RNs 7 (ft), 5 (pt); LPNs 7 (ft), 1 (pt); Nurses' aides 28 (ft), 4 (pt); Physical therapists 1 (pt); Recreational therapists 1 (ft); Occupational therapists 1 (pt); Speech therapists 1 (pt); Activities coordinators 2 (pt); Dietitians 3 (ft); Ophthalmologists 1 (pt); Podiatrists 1 (pt); Audiologists 1 (pt).
Affiliation Society of Friends.
Facilities Dining room; Physical therapy room; Activities room; Crafts room; Laundry room; Barber/Beauty shop; Library; Indoor swimming pool; Therapy pool.

Activities Arts & crafts; Cards; Games; Reading groups; Prayer groups; Movies; Shopping trips; Dances/Social/Cultural gatherings; Intergenerational programs; Pet therapy.

Hamburg

Hamburg Center
Old Rte 22, Hamburg, PA 19526
(215) 562-6000
Admin Carl E Elser.
Licensure Intermediate care for mentally retarded. Beds 448. Certified Medicaid.
Owner Publicly owned.
Staff Physicians 4 (ft); RNs 46 (ft), 5 (pt); LPNs 15 (ft); Physical therapists 1 (ft); Recreational therapists 5 (ft); Occupational therapists 1 (ft); Speech therapists 7 (ft); Activities coordinators 1 (ft); Dietitians 2 (ft); Podiatrists 1 (ft).
Facilities Dining room; Physical therapy room; Activities room; Chapel; Barber/Beauty shop; Library.
Activities Arts & crafts; Movies; Shopping trips; Dances/Social/Cultural gatherings; Therapeutic.

Laurel Living Center
Rte 3 Box 3835, Hamburg, PA 19526
(215) 562-2284, 562-0775 FAX
Admin Steve Bakken. Dir of Nursing Ludim Ortiz. Medical Dir Clifford Lyons MD.
Licensure Skilled care; Intermediate care; Personal care/Assisted living. Beds SNF 60; ICF 60; Personal care/Assisted living 40. Private Pay Patients 55%. Certified Medicaid; Medicare.
Owner Nonprofit corp (Adventist Living Centers).
Admissions Requirements Minimum age 18; Medical examination.
Staff Physicians 1 (pt); RNs 7 (ft), 9 (pt); LPNs 7 (ft), 14 (pt); Nurses' aides 17 (ft), 52 (pt); Physical therapists 1 (pt); Occupational therapists 1 (pt); Speech therapists 1 (pt); Activities coordinators 1 (ft); Dietitians 1 (pt); Podiatrists 1 (pt).
Languages Spanish.
Affiliation Seventh-Day Adventist.
Facilities Dining room; Physical therapy room; Activities room; Crafts room; Laundry room; Barber/Beauty shop; Respiratory therapy services.
Activities Arts & crafts; Cards; Games; Reading groups; Prayer groups; Movies; Shopping trips; Dances/Social/Cultural gatherings; Intergenerational programs; Pet therapy; Birding club.

Hanover

Hanover General Hospital—Hillview
300 Highland Ave, Hanover, PA 17331
(717) 637-3711
Licensure Skilled care. Beds SNF 41. Certified Medicaid; Medicare.
Owner Nonprofit corp.

Hanover Hall
267 Frederick St, Hanover, PA 17331
(717) 637-8937
Admin Christine F Lorah. Dir of Nursing Anita Buie. Medical Dir Dr James Miller.
Licensure Skilled care; Intermediate care; Retirement. Beds SNF 106; ICF 50. Certified Medicaid; Medicare.
Owner Proprietary corp (Wilmac Corp).
Admissions Requirements Medical examination & chest x-ray.
Staff RNs 5 (ft), 5 (pt); LPNs 12 (ft), 5 (pt); Nurses' aides 30 (ft), 28 (pt); Physical therapists 1 (ft); Recreational therapists 1 (ft), 2 (pt).
Facilities Dining room; Physical therapy room; Activities room; Chapel; Laundry room; Barber/Beauty shop; Lounges.

Activities Arts & crafts; Cards; Games; Reading groups; Prayer groups; Movies; Shopping trips; Dances/Social/Cultural gatherings; Pet therapy; Adopt-a-grandparent; Church services.

Homewood Retirement Center—Hanover
11 York St, Hanover, PA 17331
(717) 637-4166
Medical Dir Laurie Lojoi MD.
Licensure Intermediate care. Beds ICF 39. Certified Medicaid.
Owner Nonprofit corp (Homewood Retirement Centers).
Admissions Requirements Minimum age 60; Medical examination.
Staff Physicians 1 (pt); RNs 3 (ft), 2 (pt); LPNs 4 (ft), 3 (pt); Nurses' aides 11 (ft), 12 (pt); Physical therapists 1 (pt); Reality therapists 1 (pt); Activities coordinators 2 (ft); Dietitians 1 (pt); Ophthalmologists 1 (pt); Podiatrists 1 (pt); Audiologists 1 (pt); Dentists 1 (pt).
Affiliation Church of Christ.
Facilities Dining room; Physical therapy room; Activities room; Chapel; Crafts room; Laundry room; Barber/Beauty shop; Library.
Activities Arts & crafts; Cards; Games; Reading groups; Prayer groups; Movies; Shopping trips; Dances/Social/Cultural gatherings.

Harleysville

Peter Becker Community
800 Maple Ave, Harleysville, PA 19438
(215) 256-9501
Admin Ronald R M Moyer. Dir of Nursing Ruth Mumbauer. Medical Dir Ann Rudden MD.
Licensure Skilled care; Intermediate care; Personal care; Retirement. Beds Swing beds SNF/ICF 81; Personal care 35; Retirement apts 120. Private Pay Patients 75%. Certified Medicaid; Medicare.
Owner Nonprofit corp.
Admissions Requirements Minimum age 65; Medical examination.
Staff RNs; LPNs; Nurses' aides; Recreational therapists; Occupational therapists; Activities coordinators; Dietitians.
Affiliation Church of the Brethren.
Facilities Dining room; Physical therapy room; Activities room; Chapel; Crafts room; Laundry room; Barber/Beauty shop; Library.
Activities Arts & crafts; Cards; Games; Reading groups; Prayer groups; Movies; Shopping trips; Dances/Social/Cultural gatherings; Intergenerational programs; Pet therapy.

Harmony

Evergreen Nursing Center
RD 2 Box 56, Mill Rd, Harmony, PA 16037
(412) 452-6970, 452-1333 FAX
Admin Janice Marianna. Dir of Nursing Linda Long. Medical Dir De Channaputti.
Licensure Skilled care; Intermediate care; Personal care. Beds SNF 30; ICF 44; Personal care 44. Private Pay Patients 60%. Certified Medicaid; Medicare.
Owner Proprietary corp.
Admissions Requirements Physician's request.
Staff Physicians; RNs; LPNs; Nurses' aides; Physical therapists (contracted); Recreational therapists; Occupational therapists (contracted); Speech therapists (contracted); Dietitians (contracted); Ophthalmologists (contracted); Podiatrists (contracted); Audiologists (contracted).
Facilities Dining room; Physical therapy room; Activities room; Crafts room; Laundry room; Barber/Beauty shop; Library.
Activities Arts & crafts; Cards; Games; Prayer groups; Movies; Pet therapy.

Harrisburg

Aspin Center
1205 S 28th St, Harrisburg, PA 17111
(717) 558-1155
Admin Kathy Whitman. *Dir of Nursing*
Joanne MacCollum. *Medical Dir* Dr Anjana
Popat.
Licensure Intermediate care for mentally
retarded. *Beds* ICF/MR 22. *Private Pay
Patients* 0%. *Certified* Medicaid.
Owner Nonprofit organization/foundation.
Admissions Requirements Medical
examination; Nonambulatory.
Staff Physicians 1 (ft); RNs 3 (ft), 3 (pt);
LPNs 1 (ft), 2 (pt); Physical therapists 1 (pt);
Recreational therapists 1 (pt); Occupational
therapists 1 (pt); Speech therapists 2 (pt);
Activities coordinators 1 (ft); Dietitians 1
(pt); Ophthalmologists 1 (pt); Audiologists 1
(pt).
Facilities Dining room; Activities room;
Laundry room.
Activities Arts & crafts; Games; Reading
groups; Movies; Shopping trips;
Intergenerational programs; Pet therapy;
Active treatment; Developmental
programing.

Blue Ridge Haven East
3625 N Progress Ave, Harrisburg, PA 17110
(717) 652-2345
Admin Nancy Merisko. *Dir of Nursing* Terri L
Baker RN. *Medical Dir* Maurice Lewis MD.
Licensure Skilled care; Intermediate care. *Beds*
SNF 38; ICF 29. *Certified* Medicaid;
Medicare.
Owner Proprietary corp (Beverly Enterprises).
Admissions Requirements Minimum age 18;
Medical examination; Physician's request.
Staff RNs 3 (ft), 4 (pt); LPNs 2 (ft), 4 (pt);
Nurses' aides 13 (ft), 19 (pt); Physical
therapists 1 (pt); Speech therapists 1 (pt);
Activities coordinators 1 (pt); Dietitians 1
(pt); Ophthalmologists 1 (pt); Podiatrists 1
(pt); Dentists 1 (pt).
Facilities Dining room; Activities room;
Barber/Beauty shop.
Activities Arts & crafts; Cards; Games;
Reading groups; Prayer groups; Movies;
Shopping trips; Dances/Social/Cultural
gatherings.

Dauphin Manor
1205 S 28th St, Harrisburg, PA 17111
(717) 558-1000
Admin James H Hetrick. *Dir of Nursing* D L
Mengel RN. *Medical Dir* S Sava Macut MD.
Licensure Skilled care; Intermediate care. *Beds*
SNF 48; ICF 376. *Certified* Medicaid;
Medicare.
Owner Publicly owned.
Admissions Requirements Minimum age 18;
Females only.
Staff Physicians 9 (pt); RNs 29 (ft), 10 (pt);
LPNs 28 (ft), 3 (pt); Nurses' aides 133 (ft), 4
(pt); Physical therapists 2 (pt); Reality
therapists 1 (ft); Recreational therapists 5
(ft); Speech therapists 1 (pt); Activities
coordinators 1 (ft); Dietitians 2 (ft);
Ophthalmologists 1 (pt); Podiatrists 1 (pt);
Audiologists 1 (pt); Patient advocates 1 (ft).
Facilities Dining room; Physical therapy
room; Activities room; Chapel; Crafts room;
Laundry room; Barber/Beauty shop; Library.
Activities Arts & crafts; Cards; Games;
Reading groups; Prayer groups; Movies;
Shopping trips; Dances/Social/Cultural
gatherings; Gardening; Resident newspaper/
mailgrams.

Homeland Center
1901 N 5th St, Harrisburg, PA 17102
(717) 232-0883
Admin Mrs Isabelle C Smith. *Dir of Nursing*
Julie Giroux RN. *Medical Dir* Donald B
Freeman MD.

Licensure Skilled care; Intermediate care. *Beds*
60. *Certified* Medicaid; Medicare.
Owner Nonprofit corp.
Admissions Requirements Minimum age 65;
Medical examination.
Staff RNs 6 (ft), 5 (pt); LPNs 3 (ft), 1 (pt);
Nurses' aides 25 (ft), 15 (pt); Physical
therapists 1 (pt); Recreational therapists 2
(ft); Occupational therapists 1 (pt); Speech
therapists 1 (pt); Activities coordinators 1
(pt); Dietitians 1 (pt); Ophthalmologists 1
(pt); Podiatrists 1 (pt).
Facilities Dining room; Activities room;
Chapel; Crafts room; Laundry room; Barber/
Beauty shop; Library; Enclosed courtyard.
Activities Arts & crafts; Cards; Games;
Reading groups; Prayer groups; Movies;
Shopping trips; Dances/Social/Cultural
gatherings; Cooking groups.

Jewish Home of Greater Harrisburg
4000 Linglestown Rd, Harrisburg, PA 17112
(717) 657-0700
Medical Dir Dr Maurice Lewis.
Licensure Skilled care. *Beds* SNF 120.
Certified Medicaid; Medicare.
Owner Nonprofit corp.
Admissions Requirements Minimum age 18.
Staff RNs 6 (ft), 4 (pt); LPNs 3 (pt); Nurses'
aides 19 (ft), 17 (pt); Recreational therapists
2 (pt); Activities coordinators 1 (pt).
Affiliation Jewish.
Facilities Dining room; Physical therapy
room; Activities room; Chapel; Crafts room;
Laundry room; Barber/Beauty shop.
Activities Arts & crafts; Cards; Games;
Reading groups; Prayer groups; Movies;
Shopping trips; Dances/Social/Cultural
gatherings.

Leader Nursing & Rehabilitation Center
800 King Russ Rd, Harrisburg, PA 17109
(717) 657-1520, 657-3824 FAX
Admin Joanne Denise NHA. *Dir of Nursing*
Betty Bollinger. *Medical Dir* Peter Brier
MD.
Licensure Skilled care; Intermediate care. *Beds*
SNF 96; ICF 144. *Certified* Medicaid;
Medicare.
Owner Proprietary corp (Manor Care Inc).
Admissions Requirements Medical
examination; Physician's request.
Staff Physical therapists 2 (ft), 1 (pt);
Recreational therapists 1 (ft); Occupational
therapists 1 (ft); Speech therapists 2 (ft);
Activities coordinators 1 (ft); Dietitians 1
(ft).
Facilities Dining room; Physical therapy
room; Activities room; Chapel; Crafts room;
Laundry room; Barber/Beauty shop;
Lounges.
Activities Arts & crafts; Cards; Games;
Reading groups; Prayer groups; Movies;
Shopping trips; Dances/Social/Cultural
gatherings.

**Polyclinic Medical Center—Extended Care
Facility**
2601 N 3rd St, Harrisburg, PA 17110
(717) 782-2790
Admin Dennis V Reese NHA. *Dir of Nursing*
Vida Franklin RN. *Medical Dir* Duncan
MacLean MD.
Licensure Skilled care. *Beds* SNF 88. *Private
Pay Patients* 45%. *Certified* Medicaid;
Medicare.
Owner Nonprofit corp.
Admissions Requirements Minimum age 18.
Staff RNs 7 (ft), 8 (pt); LPNs 6 (ft), 4 (pt);
Nurses' aides 16 (ft), 24 (pt); Physical
therapists; Recreational therapists 1 (ft);
Occupational therapists 1 (pt); Speech
therapists 1 (pt); Dietitians 1 (pt).
Facilities Dining room; Physical therapy
room; Chapel; Crafts room; Laundry room;
Barber/Beauty shop.

Activities Arts & crafts; Cards; Games; Prayer
groups; Movies; Dances/Social/Cultural
gatherings; Intergenerational programs; Pet
therapy; One-on-one sensory stimulation;
Reality orientation.

**Susquehanna Center for Nursing &
Rehabilitation**
1909 N Front St, Harrisburg, PA 17102
(717) 234-4660
Admin Frank M Caswell Jr. *Dir of Nursing*
Betsy Garman RN. *Medical Dir* Dr
Lawrence Zimmerman.
Licensure Skilled care. *Beds* SNF 180.
Certified Medicaid; Medicare.
Owner Proprietary corp.
Admissions Requirements Minimum age 18;
Physician's request.
Staff Physicians 1 (pt); Physical therapists 1
(ft), 1 (pt); Recreational therapists 2 (ft);
Occupational therapists 1 (pt); Speech
therapists 1 (pt); Activities coordinators 1
(ft); Dietitians 1 (pt); Ophthalmologists 1
(pt); Podiatrists 1 (pt).
Facilities Dining room; Physical therapy
room; Activities room; Crafts room; Laundry
room; Barber/Beauty shop; TV room; Patio.
Activities Arts & crafts; Cards; Games;
Reading groups; Prayer groups; Movies;
Shopping trips; Dances/Social/Cultural
gatherings; Sing-alongs; Church groups;
River cruises.

Villa Teresa
1051 Avilla Rd, Harrisburg, PA 17109
(717) 652-5900
Licensure Skilled care; Intermediate care. *Beds*
184. *Certified* Medicaid; Medicare.
Owner Nonprofit corp.

Harrisville

Bonetti Health Care Center Inc
Main St, Harrisville, PA 16038
(412) 735-4224
Admin Larry G Bonetti. *Dir of Nursing* Helen
Rankin. *Medical Dir* A W Donan MD.
Licensure Skilled care. *Beds* SNF 103. *Private
Pay Patients* 50%. *Certified* Medicaid;
Medicare.
Owner Proprietary corp.
Admissions Requirements Medical
examination.
Staff RNs 4 (ft), 2 (pt); LPNs 3 (ft), 2 (pt);
Nurses' aides 43 (ft), 3 (pt); Physical
therapists 1 (ft); Recreational therapists 2
(ft); Speech therapists (contracted);
Dietitians (contracted); Ophthalmologists
(contracted); Podiatrists (contracted);
Audiologists (contracted).
Facilities Dining room; Physical therapy
room; Activities room; Laundry room;
Barber/Beauty shop.
Activities Arts & crafts; Cards; Games;
Reading groups; Prayer groups; Movies;
Shopping trips; Dances/Social/Cultural
gatherings; Pet therapy.

Hastings

Haida Manor
3rd Ave Ext, Hastings, PA 16646
(814) 247-6578, 247-8920 FAX
Admin Pauline Formeck RN NHA. *Dir of
Nursing* Joan Anna RN. *Medical Dir* Joseph
Sabo MD.
Licensure Skilled care; Intermediate care. *Beds*
SNF 52; ICF 50. *Private Pay Patients* 25%.
Certified Medicaid; Medicare.
Owner Proprietary corp (Beverly Enterprises).
Admissions Requirements Medical
examination; Physician's request.
Staff Physicians 7 (pt); RNs 8 (ft), 1 (pt);
LPNs 8 (ft), 8 (pt); Nurses' aides 35 (ft), 8
(pt); Physical therapists 1 (pt); Occupational
therapists 1 (ft); Speech therapists 1 (pt);

Activities coordinators 1 (ft), 1 (pt);
Dietitians 1 (ft); Ophthalmologists 1 (pt);
Podiatrists 1 (pt); Audiologists 1 (pt).
Languages Italian.
Facilities Dining room; Physical therapy
room; Activities room; Laundry room;
Barber/Beauty shop.
Activities Arts & crafts; Cards; Games;
Reading groups; Prayer groups; Dances/
Social/Cultural gatherings; Intergenerational
programs; Pet therapy.

Hatboro

Luther Woods Convalescent Center
313 County Line Rd, Hatboro, PA 19040
(215) 675-5005
Admin Ellen G Tetor. *Dir of Nursing* Patricia
Kiel RN. *Medical Dir* E Noble Wagner DO.
Licensure Skilled care. *Beds* SNF 140.
Certified Medicaid; Medicare.
Owner Privately owned.
Staff RNs 13 (ft), 4 (pt); LPNs 16 (ft), 7 (pt);
Nurses' aides 40 (ft), 23 (pt); Physical
therapists 3 (ft); Recreational therapists 4
(ft); Occupational therapists 2 (ft); Speech
therapists 2 (ft); Activities coordinators 1
(ft); Dietitians 1 (ft).
Facilities Dining room; Physical therapy
room; Activities room; Chapel; Laundry
room; Barber/Beauty shop.
Activities Arts & crafts; Cards; Games; Prayer
groups; Movies.

White Billet Nursing Home
412 S York Rd, Hatboro, PA 19040
(215) 675-2828
Admin Ellen Shraeger. *Dir of Nursing* Elaine
Streeper. *Medical Dir* R Bruce Lutz Jr MD.
Licensure Skilled care. *Beds* SNF 33.
Owner Proprietary corp (GraceCare, Inc).
Admissions Requirements Medical
examination.
Staff RNs 1 (ft), 5 (pt); LPNs 1 (ft), 3 (pt);
Nurses' aides 8 (ft), 9 (pt); Recreational
therapists 1 (pt).
Facilities Dining room; Activities room;
Chapel; Crafts room; Barber/Beauty shop.
Activities Arts & crafts; Cards; Games;
Reading groups; Movies; Dances/Social/
Cultural gatherings.

Haverford

Glenside Manor Haverford State Hospital LTC
3500 Darby Rd, Haverford, PA 19041
(215) 525-9620
Admin Beatrice M Cirillo RN BSN MSN.
Medical Dir Dr Elizabeth Bomeheur.
Licensure Skilled care; Intermediate care. *Beds*
SNF 39; ICF 37. *Certified* Medicaid;
Medicare.
Owner Publicly owned.
Admissions Requirements Minimum age 65;
Medical examination; Physician's request.
Staff Physicians 2 (pt); RNs 9 (ft), 7 (pt);
LPNs 5 (ft); Nurses' aides 38 (ft); Physical
therapists (contracted); Recreational
therapists 2 (ft); Occupational therapists
(consultant); Speech therapists (consultant);
Activities coordinators 1 (pt); Dietitians 1
(pt); Ophthalmologists (contracted);
Podiatrists (contracted); Audiologists
(contracted).
Languages Spanish.
Facilities Dining room; Physical therapy
room; Activities room; Laundry room;
Barber/Beauty shop.
Activities Arts & crafts; Cards; Games;
Reading groups; Prayer groups; Movies;
Shopping trips; Dances/Social/Cultural
gatherings; Intergenerational programs.

Havertown

Haverford Nursing & Rehabilitation Center
2050 Old West Chester Pike, Havertown, PA
19082
(215) 449-8600
Licensure Skilled care. *Beds* SNF 110.
Certified Medicare.
Owner Nonprofit corp.

Hazelton

Hazleton Nursing & Geriatric Center
PO Box 2307, 1000 W 27th St, Hazleton, PA
18201
(717) 454-8888
Licensure Skilled care. *Beds* SNF 183.
Certified Medicaid; Medicare.
Owner Proprietary corp.

**Mountain City Convalescent & Rehabilitation
Center**
PO Box 2307, 1000 W 27th St, Hazleton, PA
18201
(717) 459-9781
Licensure Skilled care. *Beds* SNF 120.
Certified Medicaid; Medicare.
Owner Proprietary corp.

St Luke Manor
1711 E Broad St, Hazleton, PA 18201
(717) 455-8571
Admin Susan M Dinofrio. *Dir of Nursing*
Augusta Ferdinand RN. *Medical Dir* Arthur
L Koch DO.
Licensure Skilled care; Intermediate care;
Alzheimer's care; Retirement. *Beds* SNF 34;
ICF 70; Alzheimer's care 26; Retirement 50.
Private Pay Patients 30%. *Certified*
Medicaid; Medicare.
Owner Nonprofit corp (Lutheran Welfare
Service).
Admissions Requirements Minimum age 16;
Medical examination.
Staff Physicians; RNs; LPNs; Nurses' aides;
Physical therapists (contracted);
Occupational therapists; Speech therapists;
Activities coordinators 1 (pt); Dietitians 1
(ft); Ophthalmologists; Podiatrists;
Audiologists; Chaplains 1 (ft).
Languages Slavic, Italian.
Affiliation Lutheran.
Facilities Dining room; Physical therapy
room; Activities room; Chapel; Laundry
room; Barber/Beauty shop; Enclosed outside
courtyard; Semi-private rooms.
Activities Arts & crafts; Cards; Games;
Reading groups; Prayer groups; Movies;
Shopping trips; Dances/Social/Cultural
gatherings; Intergenerational programs; Pet
therapy; Cooking class; Choir chime group.

St Luke Pavilion
1000 Stacie Dr, Hazleton, PA 18201
(717) 455-7578
Admin Edna P Reis. *Dir of Nursing* Jane
Guscott RN. *Medical Dir* Arthur L Koch
DO.
Licensure Skilled care; Intermediate care. *Beds*
SNF 60; ICF 60. *Private Pay Patients* 25%.
Certified Medicaid; Medicare.
Owner Nonprofit corp (Lutheran Welfare
Service).
Admissions Requirements Minimum age 16;
Medical examination.
Staff RNs 3 (ft), 5 (pt); LPNs 7 (ft), 6 (pt);
Nurses' aides 15 (ft), 30 (pt); Physical
therapists 1 (pt); Activities coordinators 1
(ft); Dietitians 1 (pt).
Affiliation Lutheran.
Facilities Dining room; Physical therapy
room; Activities room; Chapel; Laundry
room; Barber/Beauty shop.
Activities Arts & crafts; Games; Reading
groups; Prayer groups; Movies; Shopping
trips; Dances/Social/Cultural gatherings;
Intergenerational programs.

Hellertown

Mary Ellen Convalescent Home Inc
204 Leithsville Rd, Hellertown, PA 18055
(215) 838-7901
Licensure Intermediate care. *Beds* ICF 52.
Certified Medicaid.
Owner Proprietary corp.
Admissions Requirements Medical
examination.
Staff RNs 3 (ft), 3 (pt); LPNs 3 (ft), 3 (pt);
Nurses' aides 30 (ft); Physical therapists 1
(pt); Reality therapists 1 (pt); Recreational
therapists 1 (pt); Occupational therapists 1
(pt); Speech therapists 1 (pt); Activities
coordinators 1 (pt); Dietitians 1 (pt);
Ophthalmologists 1 (pt); Podiatrists 1 (pt);
Audiologists 1 (pt); Dentists 1 (pt).
Facilities Dining room; Activities room;
Library.
Activities Arts & crafts; Cards; Games;
Reading groups; Prayer groups; Shopping
trips; Dances/Social/Cultural gatherings.

Hermitage

Hospitality Care Center of Hermitage Inc
3726 E State St, Hermitage, PA 16148
(412) 342-5279
Admin Steven E Bible. *Dir of Nursing* Jean
Puhl. *Medical Dir* John Scmibli MD.
Licensure Skilled care. *Beds* SNF 28. *Certified*
Medicaid; Medicare.
Owner Privately owned.
Admissions Requirements Medical
examination; Physician's request.
Staff RNs 3 (ft), 1 (pt); LPNs 1 (ft), 4 (pt);
Nurses' aides 6 (ft), 4 (pt); Activities
coordinators 1 (ft); Dietitians 1 (ft).
Facilities Dining room; Activities room;
Laundry room.
Activities Arts & crafts; Cards; Games;
Reading groups; Prayer groups; Movies.

John XXIII Home
2250 Shenango Fwy, Hermitage, PA 16148
(412) 981-3200
Admin Sr Phyllis Schleicher OSB. *Dir of
Nursing* Irene Walsh RN. *Medical Dir* Dr
David D'Amore.
Licensure Skilled care; Intermediate care;
Personal care; Alzheimer's care. *Beds* SNF
37; ICF 53; Personal care 52. *Private Pay
Patients* 75%. *Certified* Medicaid; Medicare.
Owner Nonprofit corp.
Admissions Requirements Medical
examination.
Staff RNs 5 (ft), 5 (pt); LPNs 9 (ft), 7 (pt);
Nurses' aides 22 (ft), 31 (pt); Physical
therapists; Activities coordinators 2 (ft);
Dietitians.
Affiliation Roman Catholic.
Facilities Dining room; Physical therapy
room; Activities room; Chapel; Crafts room;
Laundry room; Barber/Beauty shop; Library;
Shuffleboard; Multi-purpose room.
Activities Arts & crafts; Cards; Games; Prayer
groups; Movies; Shopping trips; Dances/
Social/Cultural gatherings; Intergenerational
programs; Pet therapy.

Nugent Convalescent Home
500 Clarksville Rd, Hermitage, PA 16148
(412) 981-6610, 981-3224 FAX
Admin Lillian E Nugent. *Dir of Nursing*
Patricia Antus, Acting. *Medical Dir* T
Armour DO; W McDowell DO; J Bolotin
MD.
Licensure Skilled care; Intermediate care. *Beds*
SNF 48; ICF 53. *Private Pay Patients* 30%.
Certified Medicaid; Medicare.
Owner Proprietary corp.
Admissions Requirements Minimum age 18;
Medical examination.

Staff Physicians; RNs; LPNs; Nurses' aides; Physical therapists; Speech therapists; Activities coordinators; Dietitians; Podiatrists.
Facilities Dining room; Physical therapy room; Activities room; Crafts room; Laundry room.
Activities Arts & crafts; Cards; Games; Reading groups; Prayer groups; Movies; Dances/Social/Cultural gatherings; Pet therapy.

Hershey

Alpine Nursing & Rehabilitation
PO Box 377, Hershey, PA 17033
(717) 533-3351
Admin Carolyn Matson NHA. *Dir of Nursing* Julie Pearson RN. *Medical Dir* Dr William Heffley.
Licensure Skilled care; Intermediate care; Assisted living; Alzheimer's care. *Beds* SNF 88; ICF 75; Assisted living 38; Alzheimer's unit 40. *Certified* Medicaid; Medicare.
Owner Proprietary corp (Integrated Health Services Inc).
Admissions Requirements Medical examination.
Staff RNs 8 (ft); LPNs 17 (ft); Nurses' aides 62 (ft); Physical therapists 2 (ft); Recreational therapists (contracted); Occupational therapists 1 (ft); Speech therapists (contracted); Activities coordinators 2 (ft); Dietitians (contracted); Podiatrists (contracted); Audiologists (contracted).
Facilities Dining room; Physical therapy room; Activities room; Chapel; Crafts room; Laundry room; Barber/Beauty shop; Library; Ice cream parlor.
Activities Arts & crafts; Cards; Games; Reading groups; Prayer groups; Movies; Shopping trips; Dances/Social/Cultural gatherings; Intergenerational programs; Pet therapy.

Hillsdale

Mountain View Manor—Hillsdale
PO Box 138, Hillsdale, PA 15746
(814) 743-6614, (412) 254-2244
Admin Jeff Lee Rentner. *Dir of Nursing* Marlie Smith RN. *Medical Dir* Dr Chester Kauffman.
Licensure Skilled care; Intermediate care. *Beds* SNF 25; ICF 64. *Certified* Medicaid; Medicare.
Owner Proprietary corp (Beverly Enterprises).
Admissions Requirements Minimum age 21; Medical examination; Physician's request.
Staff Physicians 5 (pt); RNs 2 (ft), 3 (pt); LPNs 10 (ft), 8 (pt); Nurses' aides 25 (ft), 20 (pt); Physical therapists 3 (ft); Recreational therapists 1 (ft); Speech therapists 3 (pt); Activities coordinators 1 (ft); Dietitians 1 (ft).
Facilities Dining room; Physical therapy room; Activities room; Chapel; Crafts room; Laundry room; Barber/Beauty shop; Library; Enclosed garden/courtyard.
Activities Arts & crafts; Cards; Games; Reading groups; Prayer groups; Movies; Shopping trips; Dances/Social/Cultural gatherings; Special holiday events & outings.

Holland

St Joseph Home for the Aged
1182 Holland Rd, Holland, PA 18966
(215) 357-5511
Admin Sr Mary Lawrence SSC NHA. *Dir of Nursing* Wendy Harper RN. *Medical Dir* James Flanagan MD.
Licensure Intermediate care; Personal care. *Beds* ICF 38; Personal care 54. *Private Pay Patients* 60%. *Certified* Medicaid.

Owner Nonprofit corp.
Admissions Requirements Minimum age 65; Medical examination.
Staff Physicians 12 (pt); RNs 3 (ft), 3 (pt); LPNs 4 (ft), 3 (pt); Nurses' aides 9 (ft), 7 (pt); Physical therapists 1 (pt); Speech therapists; Activities coordinators 1 (ft); Dietitians 1 (pt); Audiologists.
Languages Lithuanian.
Affiliation Roman Catholic.
Facilities Dining room; Physical therapy room; Activities room; Chapel; Crafts room; Laundry room; Barber/Beauty shop.
Activities Arts & crafts; Cards; Games; Movies; Shopping trips; Dances/Social/Cultural gatherings; Pet therapy.

Twining Hall
280 Middle Holland Rd, Holland, PA 18966
(215) 322-6100
Licensure Skilled care; Independent living. *Beds* SNF 82. *Certified* Medicare.
Owner Proprietary corp.

Hollidaysburg

Allegheny Lutheran Home
916 Hickory St, Hollidaysburg, PA 16648
(814) 696-3501
Admin Lois J Gutshall. *Dir of Nursing* Connie Stoltz. *Medical Dir* Dr Johannes deKoning.
Licensure Skilled care; Intermediate care; Personal care; Retirement. *Beds* SNF 22; ICF 67; Personal care 23. *Private Pay Patients* 50%. *Certified* Medicaid; Medicare.
Owner Nonprofit corp.
Admissions Requirements Minimum age 65; Medical examination.
Staff RNs 3 (ft), 6 (pt); LPNs 8 (ft), 8 (pt); Nurses' aides 22 (ft), 10 (pt); Recreational therapists 2 (ft), 1 (pt); Speech therapists 1 (pt); Activities coordinators 1 (ft); Dietitians 1 (ft); Podiatrists 1 (pt).
Affiliation Lutheran.
Facilities Dining room; Physical therapy room; Activities room; Crafts room; Barber/Beauty shop; Library.
Activities Arts & crafts; Cards; Games; Reading groups; Prayer groups; Shopping trips; Pet therapy.

Garvey Manor Nursing Home
128 Logan Blvd, Hollidaysburg, PA 16648
(814) 695-5571
Medical Dir Dr John Sheedy.
Licensure Skilled care; Intermediate care. *Beds* 150. *Certified* Medicaid; Medicare.
Owner Nonprofit corp.
Admissions Requirements Minimum age 65; Medical examination; Physician's request.
Staff RNs 6 (ft), 3 (pt); LPNs 13 (ft), 9 (pt); Nurses' aides 56 (ft); Physical therapists 1 (pt); Reality therapists 1 (pt); Recreational therapists 1 (ft); Occupational therapists 1 (pt); Activities coordinators; Dietitians; Podiatrists.
Affiliation Roman Catholic.
Facilities Dining room; Physical therapy room; Activities room; Chapel; Crafts room; Laundry room; Barber/Beauty shop; Library.
Activities Arts & crafts; Cards; Games; Reading groups; Prayer groups; Movies; Shopping trips; Dances/Social/Cultural gatherings.

Hollidaysburg Veterans Home
PO Box 319, Hollidaysburg, PA 16648
(814) 696-5356
Admin David J Langguth MPA NHA. *Dir of Nursing* Mary Ellen Healy. *Medical Dir* Dr Edward Sarp.
Licensure Skilled care; Intermediate care; Retirement; Alzheimer's care. *Beds* Swing beds SNF/ICF 200; Retirement 179. *Certified* VA.
Owner Publicly owned.
Admissions Requirements Veterans of Pennsylvania.

Staff Physicians 2 (ft), 3 (pt); RNs 45 (ft); LPNs 6 (ft); Nurses' aides 20 (ft); Physical therapists 1 (ft); Recreational therapists 1 (ft); Occupational therapists 1 (pt); Activities coordinators 1 (ft); Dietitians 2 (ft).
Facilities Dining room; Physical therapy room; Activities room; Crafts room; Barber/Beauty shop; Library.
Activities Arts & crafts; Cards; Games; Movies; Shopping trips; Dances/Social/Cultural gatherings.

Presbyterian Homes of the Presbytery of Huntingdon
220 Newry St, Hollidaysburg, PA 16648
(814) 695-5095
Admin S Rae Eubank NHA. *Dir of Nursing* Donna Hess RN. *Medical Dir* K L Beers MD.
Licensure Skilled care; Personal care; Independent living. *Beds* SNF 67; Personal care 45; Independent living 20. *Private Pay Patients* 42%. *Certified* Medicaid; Medicare.
Owner Nonprofit corp.
Admissions Requirements Medical examination; Physician's request.
Staff Physicians 1 (pt); RNs 4 (ft), 5 (pt); LPNs 6 (ft), 6 (pt); Nurses' aides 30 (ft), 8 (pt); Physical therapists 1 (pt); Occupational therapists (consultant); Speech therapists (consultant); Activities coordinators 2 (ft); Dietitians (consultant); Podiatrists (fee service).
Affiliation Presbyterian.
Facilities Dining room; Physical therapy room; Activities room; Chapel; Barber/Beauty shop.
Activities Arts & crafts; Games; Reading groups; Prayer groups; Shopping trips.

Homestead

Willis Nursing Center
1800 West St, Homestead, PA 15120
(412) 464-6220
Admin Edith Smith NHA. *Dir of Nursing* John Bennett RN. *Medical Dir* Michael I Mallinger MD.
Licensure Skilled care. *Beds* SNF 74. *Private Pay Patients* 1%. *Certified* Medicaid; Medicare.
Owner Nonprofit corp.
Admissions Requirements Medical examination; Physician's request.
Staff RNs 8 (ft), 5 (pt); LPNs 9 (ft), 5 (pt); Nurses' aides 22 (ft), 15 (pt); Physical therapists 2 (ft); Recreational therapists 1 (ft); Occupational therapists 1 (ft); Speech therapists 1 (ft); Dietitians 1 (ft); Ophthalmologists 1 (pt); Podiatrists 1 (pt); Audiologists 1 (pt).
Facilities Dining room; Physical therapy room; Activities room; Chapel; Crafts room; Laundry room; Barber/Beauty shop; Library.
Activities Arts & crafts; Cards; Games; Reading groups; Movies; Dances/Social/Cultural gatherings; Intergenerational programs.

Honesdale

Ellen Memorial Health Care Center
RD 1 Box 1147, Honesdale, PA 18431
(717) 253-5690
Dir of Nursing Marilyn L Turner RN. *Medical Dir* Young Woo Lee MD.
Licensure Skilled care. *Beds* SNF 102. *Certified* Medicaid; Medicare.
Owner Proprietary corp.
Admissions Requirements Physician's request.
Staff Physicians 1 (pt); RNs 5 (ft), 4 (pt); Occupational therapists 3 (pt); Speech therapists 1 (pt); Activities coordinators 2 (ft); Dietitians 1 (pt).
Facilities Dining room; Physical therapy room; Activities room; Chapel; Crafts room; Laundry room; Barber/Beauty shop.

Activities Arts & crafts; Cards; Games; Reading groups; Prayer groups; Movies; Dances/Social/Cultural gatherings; Community plays; Concerts; Circus.

Wayne County Memorial Hospital Skilled Nursing Facility
Park & West Sts, Honesdale, PA 18431
(717) 253-1300
Admin John M Sherwood. *Dir of Nursing* Ellen Malloy RN. *Medical Dir* William F Davis MD.
Licensure Skilled care. *Beds* SNF 28. *Certified* Medicaid; Medicare.
Owner Nonprofit corp.
Admissions Requirements Medical examination; Physician's request.
Staff RNs; LPNs; Nurses' aides.
Facilities Dining room; Activities room; Chapel; Crafts room.
Activities Arts & crafts; Cards; Games; Reading groups; Prayer groups; Movies; Shopping trips; Dances/Social/Cultural gatherings.

Honey Brook

Hickory House Nursing Home
RD 3 Box 84, Honey Brook, PA 19344
(215) 273-2915, 273-3904 FAX
Admin David E Stott NHA. *Dir of Nursing* Mary E Magner RN. *Medical Dir* Dr Leonard Giunta.
Licensure Skilled care; Intermediate care; Independent and assisted living; Alzheimer's care. *Beds* SNF 70; ICF 30; Independent and assisted living 100. *Private Pay Patients* 70%. *Certified* Medicaid; Medicare.
Owner Proprietary corp (Life Care Centers of America).
Staff Physicians; RNs 3 (ft), 14 (pt); LPNs 2 (ft), 11 (pt); Nurses' aides 13 (ft), 35 (pt); Physical therapists (consultant); Recreational therapists (consultant); Occupational therapists (consultant); Speech therapists (consultant); Activities coordinators 1 (ft); Dietitians; Ophthalmologists (consultant); Podiatrists (consultant); Audiologists (consultant); Physical therapy assistants 1 (ft); Dietary; Housekeeping; Laundry; Maintenance.
Facilities Dining room; Physical therapy room; Activities room; Crafts room; Laundry room; Barber/Beauty shop; Library; 4 lounge areas; Wanderguard system.
Activities Arts & crafts; Cards; Games; Reading groups; Prayer groups; Movies; Shopping trips; Dances/Social/Cultural gatherings; Intergenerational programs; Pet therapy; Outings/Bus trips.

Tel Hai Nursing Center Inc
PO Box 190, Honey Brook, PA 19344
(215) 273-9333
Admin LeRoy Petersheim. *Dir of Nursing* Anna Skiles. *Medical Dir* Dr Richard Smith.
Licensure Skilled care; Retirement. *Beds* SNF 120. *Certified* Medicaid; Medicare.
Owner Nonprofit corp.
Admissions Requirements Medical examination.
Staff Physicians 15 (pt); RNs 8 (ft), 7 (pt); LPNs 6 (ft), 3 (pt); Nurses' aides 42 (ft), 21 (pt); Physical therapists 3 (pt); Recreational therapists 1 (pt); Occupational therapists 1 (pt); Speech therapists 1 (pt); Activities coordinators 3 (ft); Dietitians 1 (ft); Ophthalmologists 1 (pt); Podiatrists 1 (pt); Dentists 1 (pt); Chaplains.
Affiliation Mennonite.
Facilities Dining room; Physical therapy room; Activities room; Chapel; Crafts room; Laundry room; Barber/Beauty shop; Library.
Activities Arts & crafts; Cards; Games; Reading groups; Prayer groups; Movies; Shopping trips; Dances/Social/Cultural gatherings.

Huntingdon

Huntingdon County Nursing Home
Warm Springs Ave, Huntingdon, PA 16652
(814) 643-4210
Admin Sr M Constance Loeffler. *Dir of Nursing* Vera M Patton. *Medical Dir* Thomas Meloy MD.
Licensure Skilled care; Intermediate care. *Beds* SNF 15; ICF 78. *Certified* Medicaid; Medicare.
Owner Publicly owned.
Admissions Requirements Medical examination; Physician's request.
Staff RNs 4 (ft), 4 (pt); LPNs 6 (ft), 6 (pt); Nurses' aides 19 (ft), 19 (pt).
Facilities Dining room; Activities room; Crafts room; Laundry room; Barber/Beauty shop.
Activities Arts & crafts; Cards; Games; Prayer groups; Movies; Dances/Social/Cultural gatherings.

Huntingdon Valley

Combined Rehabilitation Services Inc
1633 Republic Rd, Huntingdon Valley, PA 19006
(215) 677-9500
Admin Joseph W Lista. *Dir of Nursing* Delores Redner RN. *Medical Dir* Richard Mirabelli MD.
Licensure Intermediate care for mentally retarded. *Beds* ICF/MR 161. *Certified* Medicaid.
Owner Nonprofit corp.
Admissions Requirements Medical examination.
Staff Physicians; RNs; LPNs; Nurses' aides; Physical therapists; Recreational therapists; Occupational therapists; Speech therapists; Activities coordinators; Dietitians; Ophthalmologists; Podiatrists; Dentists.
Facilities Dining room; Physical therapy room; Activities room; Crafts room; Laundry room.
Activities Arts & crafts; Cards; Games; Prayer groups; Movies; Shopping trips; Dances/Social/Cultural gatherings; Developmental training.

Immaculata

Camilla Hall
Immaculata, PA 19345
(215) 644-1152
Licensure Skilled care. *Beds* 150.
Owner Nonprofit corp.

Indiana

Beacon Manor
1515 Wayne Ave, Indiana, PA 15701
(412) 349-5300
Admin Denise McQuown-Hatter. *Dir of Nursing* Marcie Craig. *Medical Dir* Dr Ann Jesick.
Licensure Skilled care; Intermediate care. *Beds* SNF 57; ICF 65. *Private Pay Patients* 30%. *Certified* Medicaid; Medicare.
Owner Privately owned.
Admissions Requirements Medical examination; Physician's request.
Staff Physicians 1 (ft); RNs 3 (ft), 4 (pt); LPNs 14 (ft), 4 (pt); Nurses' aides 30 (ft), 4 (pt); Physical therapists 1 (ft); Occupational therapists 1 (ft); Speech therapists 1 (ft); Activities coordinators 2 (ft); Dietitians 1 (ft); Podiatrists 1 (ft); Audiologists 1 (ft).
Facilities Dining room; Physical therapy room; Activities room; Laundry room; Barber/Beauty shop; Living room.

Activities Arts & crafts; Cards; Games; Reading groups; Prayer groups; Movies; Shopping trips; Dances/Social/Cultural gatherings; Intergenerational programs; Pet therapy.

Indian Haven Nursing Home
PO Box 1377, 1671 Saltsburg Ave, Indiana, PA 15701
(412) 465-3900
Admin Ruth McCurdy RN NHA. *Dir of Nursing* Jean A Zbur RN. *Medical Dir* Dr William C Vernocy.
Licensure Skilled care; Intermediate care. *Beds* SNF 58; ICF 67. *Private Pay Patients* 3%. *Certified* Medicaid; Medicare.
Owner Publicly owned.
Admissions Requirements Minimum age Adult; Medical examination; Physician's request.
Staff Physicians 1 (pt); RNs 10 (ft), 1 (pt); LPNs 14 (ft), 1 (pt); Nurses' aides 56 (ft), 3 (pt); Physical therapists (contracted); Speech therapists 1 (pt); Activities coordinators 2 (ft); Dietitians 1 (ft), 1 (pt); Activities coordinators 2 (ft).
Facilities Dining room; Physical therapy room; Activities room; Chapel; Crafts room; Laundry room; Barber/Beauty shop; Library; Speech therapy room.
Activities Arts & crafts; Cards; Games; Reading groups; Prayer groups; Movies; Shopping trips; Dances/Social/Cultural gatherings; Intergenerational programs; Pet therapy.

Indiana Presbyterian Homes
1155 Indian Springs Rd, Indiana, PA 15701
(412) 349-4870
Licensure Skilled care; Intermediate care. *Beds* SNF 60; ICF 60. *Certified* Medicaid.
Owner Nonprofit corp.
Affiliation Presbyterian.

Julia Wilson Pound Health Care Center
1155 Indian Springs Rd, Indiana, PA 15701
(412) 349-4870
Licensure Skilled care. *Beds* SNF 120. *Certified* Medicaid; Medicare.
Owner Proprietary corp.

Scenery Hill Manor Inc
RD 5 Box 19, Lions Health Camp Rd, Indiana, PA 15701
(412) 463-7000
Licensure Skilled care. *Beds* SNF 58. *Certified* Medicaid; Medicare.
Owner Proprietary corp.

Jeannette

Trinity Haven
206 N 1st St, Jeannette, PA 15644
(412) 527-1509
Licensure Residential/Personal care; Alzheimer's care. *Beds* Residential/Personal care 27. *Certified* State licensed.
Owner Proprietary corp.
Admissions Requirements Minimum age 21.
Staff Nurses' aides 6 (ft), 6 (pt); Speech therapists 1 (ft); Activities coordinators 1 (ft).
Languages Italian, Polish, Spanish.
Facilities Dining room; Physical therapy room; Activities room; Crafts room; Laundry room; Sun room.
Activities Arts & crafts; Cards; Games; Reading groups; Prayer groups; Picnics.

Jersey Shore

Leader Nursing & Rehabilitation Center—Jersey Shore
Thompson Street & Kerr Ave, Jersey Shore, PA 17740
(717) 398-4747

Admin Charles J Miller. *Dir of Nursing* Lois Hensler. *Medical Dir* Lloyd R Forcey MD.
Licensure Skilled care; Intermediate care. *Beds* 180. *Certified* Medicaid; Medicare.
Owner Proprietary corp (Manor Care Inc).
Admissions Requirements Medical examination; Physician's request.
Staff Physicians 8 (pt); RNs 7 (ft), 3 (pt); LPNs 7 (ft), 3 (pt); Nurses' aides 60 (ft), 20 (pt); Speech therapists 1 (pt); Activities coordinators 1 (ft), 1 (pt); Dietitians 1 (ft); Ophthalmologists 1 (pt); Podiatrists 1 (pt).
Facilities Dining room; Activities room; Chapel; Laundry room; Barber/Beauty shop; Library.
Activities Arts & crafts; Cards; Games; Reading groups; Prayer groups; Movies; Shopping trips; Dances/Social/Cultural gatherings.

Johnstown

Allegheny Lutheran Home—Johnstown
807 Goucher St, Johnstown, PA 15905
(814) 255-6844
Admin Paula Schechter. *Dir of Nursing* Dorothy Charney RN. *Medical Dir* Victor Bantly MD.
Licensure Skilled care; Intermediate care; Retirement. *Beds* SNF 40; ICF 29. *Certified* Medicaid; Medicare.
Owner Nonprofit corp.
Admissions Requirements Minimum age 65; Medical examination.
Staff RNs 3 (ft), 4 (pt); LPNs 5 (ft), 4 (pt); Nurses' aides 16 (ft), 12 (pt); Activities coordinators 1 (ft); Audiologists 38 (ft), 19 (pt).
Affiliation Lutheran.
Facilities Dining room; Physical therapy room; Activities room; Chapel; Crafts room; Laundry room; Barber/Beauty shop; Library.
Activities Arts & crafts; Cards; Games; Reading groups; Prayer groups; Movies; Shopping trips; Dances/Social/Cultural gatherings; Remotivation; Reality orientation; Special interest groups; Cooking.

Hiram G Andrews Center
727 Goucher St, Johnstown, PA 15905
(814) 225-5881
Licensure Skilled care. *Beds* SNF 61. *Certified* Medicare.
Owner Publicly owned.

Arbutus Park Manor
207 Ottawa St, Johnstown, PA 15904
(814) 266-8621
Licensure Intermediate care; Independent living. *Beds* 122. *Certified* Medicaid.
Owner Nonprofit corp.

Mercy Hospital Nursing Care Center
1017 Franklin St, Johnstown, PA 15905
(814) 535-1934, 533-1819 FAX
Admin Sylvia Phillips. *Dir of Nursing* Dorothy Charney. *Medical Dir* Harry A Pote Jr.
Licensure Skilled care. *Beds* SNF 73. *Private Pay Patients* 33%. *Certified* Medicaid; Medicare.
Owner Nonprofit corp.
Admissions Requirements Medical examination; Physician's request.
Staff Physicians 2 (pt); RNs 6 (ft); LPNs 5 (ft), 7 (pt); Nurses' aides 20 (ft), 10 (pt); Physical therapists 1 (pt); Recreational therapists 1 (pt); Occupational therapists 1 (pt); Speech therapists 1 (pt); Activities coordinators 1 (ft); Dietitians 1 (pt).
Facilities Physical therapy room; Activities room; Laundry room.
Activities Arts & crafts; Cards; Games; Reading groups; Prayer groups; Movies; Dances/Social/Cultural gatherings; Intergenerational programs; Pet therapy.

Presbyterian Home of Redstone Presbytery
787 Goucher St, Johnstown, PA 15905
(814) 255-5539
Admin Leah H Williams. *Dir of Nursing* Kathleen Caldon RD. *Medical Dir* Dr Bruce Jeffries.
Licensure Intermediate care; Residential and personal care; Independent living. *Beds* ICF 23; Residential and personal care 31; Independent living units 14. *Private Pay Patients* 30%. *Certified* Medicaid.
Owner Nonprofit organization/foundation.
Admissions Requirements Minimum age 62; Medical examination.
Staff RNs 1 (ft), 3 (pt); LPNs 7 (ft); Nurses' aides 14 (ft); Activities coordinators 1 (pt); Dietitians 1 (pt).
Affiliation Presbyterian.
Facilities Dining room; Activities room; Chapel; Laundry room; Barber/Beauty shop; Library.
Activities Arts & crafts; Games; Reading groups; Prayer groups; Movies; Shopping trips; Intergenerational programs; Pet therapy.

Richland Manor
349 Vo-Tech Dr, Johnstown, PA 15904
(814) 266-9702
Licensure Skilled care. *Beds* SNF 73. *Certified* Medicaid; Medicare.
Owner Proprietary corp (Beverly Enterprises).

Kane

Lutheran Home at Kane
Clay St Ext, Kane, PA 16735
(814) 837-6706
Admin Linda D Carlson NHA. *Dir of Nursing* Mary Ellen Starner RN. *Medical Dir* Charles R Bentz MD.
Licensure Skilled care; Intermediate care; Residential care. *Beds* SNF 33; ICF 57; Residential care 42. *Private Pay Patients* 30%. *Certified* Medicaid; Medicare.
Owner Nonprofit corp.
Admissions Requirements Medical examination.
Staff Physicians 5 (pt); RNs 3 (ft), 3 (pt); LPNs 10 (ft), 8 (pt); Nurses' aides 28 (ft), 18 (pt); Physical therapists 1 (pt); Activities coordinators 1 (ft); Dietitians 1 (pt); Podiatrists 1 (pt).
Affiliation Lutheran.
Facilities Dining room; Physical therapy room; Activities room; Chapel; Crafts room; Laundry room; Barber/Beauty shop.
Activities Arts & crafts; Reading groups; Prayer groups; Movies.

Kennett Square

Crosslands
PO Box 100, Kennett Square, PA 19348
(215) 388-1441
Admin Paul M Lewis. *Dir of Nursing* Sandy Nething. *Medical Dir* Jeff Bell MD.
Licensure Skilled care; Intermediate care; Retirement; Alzheimer's care. *Beds* SNF 58; ICF 33; Retirement apts 250. *Certified* Medicare.
Owner Nonprofit organization/foundation.
Admissions Requirements Minimum age 65; Medical examination.
Facilities Dining room; Physical therapy room; Activities room; Crafts room; Laundry room; Barber/Beauty shop; Library.

Linden Hall
147 W State St, Kennett Square, PA 19348
(215) 444-0741
Admin Mary Lou Hovde. *Dir of Nursing* Rita MacEwen RN. *Medical Dir* Mary Ann Ost MD.
Licensure Skilled care; Retirement; Alzheimer's care. *Beds* SNF 16.
Owner Nonprofit corp.

Admissions Requirements Medical examination.
Staff RNs 1 (ft), 5 (pt); LPNs 1 (ft), 2 (pt); Nurses' aides 8 (ft); Activities coordinators 1 (pt).
Affiliation Society of Friends.
Facilities Dining room; Activities room; Crafts room; Barber/Beauty shop.
Activities Arts & crafts; Cards; Games; Reading groups; Movies; Dances/Social/Cultural gatherings.

King of Prussia

Fair Villa Nursing Home
PO Box 1030, King of Prussia, PA 19406-0477
(215) 275-6799
Medical Dir Dr Yu Jen Tsai.
Licensure Skilled care. *Beds* 57. *Certified* Medicaid.
Owner Proprietary corp.
Admissions Requirements Medical examination; Physician's request.
Staff Physicians 10 (pt); RNs 1 (ft), 1 (pt); LPNs 3 (ft), 1 (pt); Nurses' aides 31 (ft), 14 (pt); Physical therapists 1 (pt); Speech therapists 1 (pt); Activities coordinators 1 (ft); Dietitians 1 (pt); Podiatrists 1 (pt); Dentists 1 (pt).
Facilities Dining room; Activities room; Crafts room; Laundry room; Library.
Activities Arts & crafts; Cards; Games; Reading groups; Prayer groups; Movies; Shopping trips; Dances/Social/Cultural gatherings.

Kingston

Leader Nursing & Rehabilitation Center—East
200 2nd Ave, Kingston, PA 18704
(717) 299-9315
Licensure Skilled care; Intermediate care. *Beds* SNF 160; ICF 20. *Certified* Medicaid; Medicare.
Owner Proprietary corp (Manor Care Inc).

Leader Nursing & Rehabilitation Center—West
Wyoming Ave at Dorrance St, Kingston, PA 18704
(717) 288-5496
Admin Cathy Nally. *Dir of Nursing* Patricia Toole RN. *Medical Dir* Richard Crompton MD.
Licensure Skilled care. *Beds* SNF 153. *Certified* Medicaid; Medicare.
Owner Proprietary corp (Manor Care Inc).
Staff RNs 8 (ft), 2 (pt); LPNs 5 (ft), 7 (pt); Nurses' aides 44 (ft), 11 (pt); Physical therapists 1 (ft); Recreational therapists 3 (pt); Occupational therapists 1 (pt); Speech therapists 1 (pt); Activities coordinators 1 (ft).
Facilities Dining room; Physical therapy room; Activities room; Chapel; Laundry room; Barber/Beauty shop; Library.
Activities Arts & crafts; Cards; Games; Reading groups; Prayer groups; Movies; Shopping trips; Dances/Social/Cultural gatherings.

Kittanning

Armstrong County Health Center
265 S McKean St, Kittanning, PA 16201
(412) 548-2222
Admin James R Bender.
Medical Dir Dr Cyrus Slease.
Licensure Skilled care. *Beds* SNF 190. *Certified* Medicaid; Medicare.
Owner Publicly owned.
Admissions Requirements Medical examination; Physician's request.
Staff Physicians 1 (ft), 1 (pt); RNs 11 (ft), 3 (pt); LPNs 16 (ft), 4 (pt); Nurses' aides 57 (ft), 8 (pt); Physical therapists 1 (pt); Speech

therapists 1 (pt); Activities coordinators 1 (ft); Dietitians 1 (pt); Ophthalmologists 1 (pt); Podiatrists 1 (pt); Dentists 1 (pt).
Facilities Dining room; Physical therapy room; Activities room; Crafts room; Laundry room; Barber/Beauty shop.
Activities Arts & crafts; Cards; Games; Reading groups; Prayer groups; Movies; Shopping trips; Dances/Social/Cultural gatherings.

Wesley Manor Health Care Center
Rte 1, 422 E, Kittanning, PA 16201
(412) 545-2273
Admin Carol A Rohrabaugh.
Medical Dir Jeffrey Minteer MD.
Licensure Skilled care; Intermediate care. *Beds* SNF 60; ICF 60. *Certified* Medicaid; Medicare.
Owner Proprietary corp.
Admissions Requirements Medical examination.
Staff Physicians 2 (pt); RNs 5 (ft), 7 (pt); LPNs 5 (ft), 11 (pt); Nurses' aides 28 (ft), 20 (pt); Physical therapists; Speech therapists; Activities coordinators 1 (ft); Dietitians 1 (pt); Podiatrists; Dentists.
Facilities Dining room; Physical therapy room; Activities room; Crafts room; Laundry room; Barber/Beauty shop.
Activities Arts & crafts; Cards; Games; Prayer groups; Movies; Dances/Social/Cultural gatherings.

Kutztown

Kutztown Manor Inc
120 Trexler Ave, Kutztown, PA 19530
(215) 683-6220
Admin Jessica E Palazzi. *Dir of Nursing* Cheryl A Magee RN.
Licensure Skilled care; Intermediate care. *Beds* SNF 65; ICF 75. *Certified* Medicaid; Medicare.
Owner Proprietary corp.
Admissions Requirements Medical examination.
Staff RNs 9 (ft), 4 (pt); LPNs 10 (ft), 1 (pt); Nurses' aides 28 (ft), 29 (pt); Physical therapists 1 (ft); Occupational therapists 1 (ft); Speech therapists 1 (ft); Activities coordinators 1 (ft); Dietitians 1 (ft).
Languages Pennsylvania Dutch.
Facilities Dining room; Physical therapy room; Activities room; Crafts room; Laundry room; Barber/Beauty shop.
Activities Arts & crafts; Cards; Games; Reading groups; Prayer groups; Movies; Shopping trips; Dances/Social/Cultural gatherings; Garden group; Cooking.

Lafayette Hill

Masonic Home of Pennsylvania
801 Ridge Pike, Lafayette Hill, PA 19444
(215) 825-6100, 828-2803 FAX
Admin Kenneth R Mills NHA. *Dir of Nursing* Karen Fisher RN. *Medical Dir* Robert J Patterson MD.
Licensure Skilled care; Intermediate care; Residential/Personal care; Retirement; Alzheimer's care. *Beds* SNF 23; ICF 52; Residential/Personal care 155; Retirement apts 54. *Private Pay Patients* 17%. *Certified* Medicaid.
Owner Nonprofit corp.
Admissions Requirements Minimum age Personal care 75, Apartments 65.
Staff Physicians 2 (pt); RNs 12 (ft), 3 (pt); LPNs 6 (ft), 7 (pt); Nurses' aides 36 (ft), 9 (pt); Physical therapists 1 (pt); Reality therapists; Recreational therapists 2 (ft); Occupational therapists 1 (pt); Speech therapists 1 (pt); Activities coordinators 2 (ft); Dietitians 1 (pt); Podiatrists 2 (pt); Audiologists 1 (pt).
Affiliation Masons.

Facilities Dining room; Physical therapy room; Activities room; Chapel; Crafts room; Laundry room; Barber/Beauty shop; Library; Bowling alley; Putting green.
Activities Arts & crafts; Cards; Games; Prayer groups; Movies; Shopping trips; Dances/Social/Cultural gatherings; Intergenerational programs; Pet therapy; Bowling; Putting; Shuffleboard; Cocktail parties.

Lake Ariel

Julia Ribaudo Home
297-298 Center Dr, Lake Ariel, PA 18436
(717) 698-5647
Admin Ellen B Dennis. *Dir of Nursing* Anne Chinchar RN. *Medical Dir* Dr Gregory Salko.
Licensure Skilled care. *Beds* SNF 111. *Private Pay Patients* 50%. *Certified* Medicaid; Medicare.
Owner Proprietary corp (IFIDA Health Care Group).
Admissions Requirements Medical examination.
Staff RNs; LPNs; Nurses' aides; Physical therapists 1 (ft); Speech therapists 1 (ft); Activities coordinators; Dietitians.
Facilities Dining room; Physical therapy room; Activities room; Chapel; Laundry room; Barber/Beauty shop.
Activities Arts & crafts; Cards; Games; Prayer groups; Movies; Shopping trips.

Lancaster

Brethren Village
PO Box 5093, 3001 Lititz Pike, Lancaster, PA 17601
(717) 569-2657
Admin Gary N Clouser. *Dir of Nursing* Linda Sorrentino. *Medical Dir* Eugene Engle MD.
Licensure Skilled care; Intermediate care; Independent living. *Beds* SNF 67; ICF 81; Independent living 450. *Private Pay Patients* 90%. *Certified* Medicaid; Medicare.
Owner Nonprofit organization/foundation.
Admissions Requirements Minimum age 62; Medical examination.
Staff RNs; LPNs; Nurses' aides; Physical therapists; Recreational therapists; Activities coordinators; Dietitians.
Affiliation Church of the Brethren.
Facilities Dining room; Physical therapy room; Activities room; Chapel; Crafts room; Laundry room; Barber/Beauty shop; Library; Pool.
Activities Arts & crafts; Cards; Games; Reading groups; Prayer groups; Movies; Shopping trips; Dances/Social/Cultural gatherings; Intergenerational programs; Pet therapy; Swimming.

Calvary Fellowship Homes Inc
502 Elizabeth Dr, Lancaster, PA 17601
(717) 393-0711
Admin Clifford K Hurter. *Dir of Nursing* Elizabeth Greider. *Medical Dir* Richard Moncrief MD.
Licensure Skilled care; Retirement. *Beds* SNF 45; Retirement 220. *Private Pay Patients* 89%. *Certified* Medicaid; Medicare.
Owner Nonprofit corp.
Admissions Requirements Medical examination.
Staff RNs 4 (ft), 3 (pt); LPNs 1 (ft), 1 (pt); Nurses' aides 17 (ft), 6 (pt); Activities coordinators 1 (ft).
Facilities Dining room; Physical therapy room; Activities room; Chapel; Crafts room; Laundry room; Barber/Beauty shop; Library.
Activities Arts & crafts; Games; Prayer groups; Movies; Shopping trips; Intergenerational programs; Pet therapy.

Conestoga View
900 E King St, Lancaster, PA 17602
(717) 299-7853
Licensure Skilled care; Intermediate care. *Beds* SNF 132; ICF 320. *Certified* Medicaid.
Owner Publicly owned.

Duke Convalescent Residence
425 N Duke St, Lancaster, PA 17602
(717) 397-4281
Admin Joan Schwartz. *Dir of Nursing* Glenn Thomas RN. *Medical Dir* James Wolf.
Licensure Skilled care; Alzheimer's care. *Beds* 139. *Certified* Medicaid; Medicare.
Owner Proprietary corp (Beverly Enterprises).
Admissions Requirements Medical examination.
Staff RNs 5 (ft); LPNs 8 (ft), 4 (pt); Nurses' aides 27 (ft), 6 (pt); Physical therapists 1 (ft); Occupational therapists 1 (pt); Speech therapists 1 (pt); Activities coordinators 1 (ft); Dietitians 1 (ft).
Facilities Dining room; Physical therapy room; Activities room; Crafts room; Laundry room; Barber/Beauty shop.
Activities Arts & crafts; Cards; Games; Prayer groups; Movies; Shopping trips; Dances/Social/Cultural gatherings.

Hamilton Arms Nursing & Rehabilitation Center
336 S West End Ave, Lancaster, PA 17603
(717) 393-0419
Licensure Skilled care. *Beds* 120. *Certified* Medicaid; Medicare.
Owner Proprietary corp (Geriatric and Medical Centers).

Homestead Village Inc
1800 Village Cir, Lancaster, PA 17603
(717) 397-4831
Licensure Skilled care; Independent living. *Beds* SNF 60. *Certified* Medicaid; Medicare.
Owner Proprietary corp.

Lancashire Hall
2829 Lititz Pike, Lancaster, PA 17601
(717) 569-3211
Licensure Skilled care; Intermediate care. *Beds* 240. *Certified* Medicaid; Medicare.
Owner Proprietary corp.

Long Home
200 N West End Ave, Lancaster, PA 17603
(717) 397-3926
Medical Dir Peter J Altiman MD.
Licensure Skilled care. *Beds* 16.
Owner Nonprofit corp.
Admissions Requirements Minimum age 45; Medical examination.
Staff Physicians 4 (ft); RNs 3 (ft), 10 (pt); LPNs 1 (ft), 1 (pt); Nurses' aides 5 (ft), 2 (pt); Physical therapists 1 (pt); Reality therapists 1 (pt); Recreational therapists 1 (pt); Occupational therapists 1 (pt); Activities coordinators 1 (pt); Dietitians 1 (pt); Ophthalmologists 1 (pt); Podiatrists 1 (pt); Dentists 1 (pt).
Facilities Dining room; Physical therapy room; Activities room; Chapel; Crafts room; Laundry room; Barber/Beauty shop; Library.
Activities Cards; Games; Shopping trips.

Mennonite Home
1520 Harrisburg Pike, Lancaster, PA 17601
(717) 393-1301
Admin Paul G Leaman. *Dir of Nursing* Cynthia Stoner; Charlotte Yoder, Health Svcs Dir. *Medical Dir* Dr Harry H Hoffman.
Licensure Skilled care; Intermediate care; Personal care; Alzheimer's care. *Beds* SNF 170; ICF 92; Personal care 219. *Private Pay Patients* 85%. *Certified* Medicaid; Medicare.
Owner Nonprofit corp.
Admissions Requirements Minimum age 65; Medical examination.
Staff Physicians 3 (pt); RNs 8 (ft), 4 (pt); LPNs 23 (ft), 23 (pt); Nurses' aides 52 (ft), 42 (pt); Physical therapists (contracted);

Recreational therapists 7 (ft); Dietitians 1 (ft), 3 (pt); Podiatrists 1 (ft), 1 (pt); Physical therapy aides 1 (ft); Administrative, dietary, housekeeping, laundry, maintenance 55 (ft), 51 (pt).
Affiliation Mennonite.
Facilities Dining room; Physical therapy room; Activities room; Chapel; Crafts room; Laundry room; Barber/Beauty shop; Library; Therapy pool.
Activities Arts & crafts; Cards; Games; Reading groups; Prayer groups; Shopping trips; Dances/Social/Cultural gatherings; Intergenerational programs; Pet therapy; Pool therapy; Van trips.

Village Vista Skilled Nursing Facility
1941 Benmar Dr, Lancaster, PA 17603
(717) 397-5583
Medical Dir J D Kemrer MD.
Licensure Skilled care. *Beds* SNF 31. *Certified* Medicaid; Medicare.
Owner Proprietary corp.
Staff RNs 1 (ft), 3 (pt); LPNs 4 (ft), 1 (pt); Nurses' aides 6 (ft), 9 (pt); Physical therapists; Activities coordinators 1 (pt); Dietitians.
Facilities Dining room; Activities room; Laundry room.
Activities Arts & crafts; Games; Reading groups; Prayer groups.

Whitehall—Leader
100 Abbeyville Rd, Lancaster, PA 17603
(717) 397-4261
Admin Lori Mason. *Dir of Nursing* Teresa Long. *Medical Dir* Ervin Ellison.
Licensure Skilled care; Intermediate care; Alzheimer's care. *Beds* SNF 123; ICF 50. *Private Pay Patients* 70%. *Certified* Medicaid; Medicare.
Owner Proprietary corp (Manor Care Inc).
Staff Physicians; RNs; LPNs; Nurses' aides; Physical therapists; Recreational therapists; Occupational therapists; Speech therapists; Activities coordinators; Dietitians.
Facilities Dining room; Physical therapy room; Activities room; Crafts room; Laundry room; Barber/Beauty shop; Family and social areas; Alzheimer's unit.
Activities Arts & crafts; Cards; Games; Reading groups; Prayer groups; Movies; Shopping trips; Dances/Social/Cultural gatherings; Intergenerational programs; Pet therapy.

Willow Valley Manor
211 Willow Valley Square, Lancaster, PA 17602
(717) 464-5478
Admin Ada M Hallman. *Dir of Nursing* Barbara Lease. *Medical Dir* Jon Schrock MD.
Licensure Skilled care; Personal care; Retirement; Alzheimer's care. *Beds* SNF 50; Personal care 10; Retirement 500. *Certified* Medicare.
Owner Nonprofit corp.
Admissions Requirements Physician's request.
Staff RNs 4 (ft), 6 (pt); LPNs 8 (ft), 4 (pt); Nurses' aides 15 (ft), 10 (pt); Physical therapists (contracted); Recreational therapists 1 (ft), 3 (pt); Occupational therapists (contracted); Dietitians (consultant); Podiatrists (consultant); Audiologists (consultant).
Facilities Dining room; Physical therapy room; Activities room; Barber/Beauty shop.
Activities Arts & crafts; Cards; Games; Reading groups; Prayer groups; Movies; Shopping trips; Dances/Social/Cultural gatherings; Intergenerational programs; Pet therapy; Alzheimer's programing.

Landisville

Community Services Inc—Main
180 Main St, Landisville, PA 17538
(717) 898-6323
Licensure Intermediate care for mentally retarded. *Beds* 6. *Certified* Medicaid.
Owner Proprietary corp.

Langhorne

Attleboro Nursing & Rehabilitation Center
300 Winchester Ave, Langhorne, PA 19047
(215) 757-3739
Admin Henry R Gureck. *Dir of Nursing* Judy Wagner RN. *Medical Dir* Frank Madden MD.
Licensure Skilled care; Intermediate care; Retirement. *Beds* SNF 60; ICF 120. *Certified* Medicaid; Medicare.
Owner Proprietary corp (Wilmac Corp).
Admissions Requirements Minimum age 18.
Staff RNs; LPNs; Nurses' aides; Physical therapists 1 (ft); Recreational therapists 1 (ft); Activities coordinators 1 (ft); Dietitians 1 (ft).
Facilities Dining room; Physical therapy room; Activities room; Crafts room; Laundry room; Barber/Beauty shop; Library.
Activities Arts & crafts; Cards; Games; Reading groups; Movies; Shopping trips; Dances/Social/Cultural gatherings.

Crestview North Nursing & Rehabilitation Center
262 Tollgate Rd, Langhorne, PA 19047
(215) 968-4650, 860-5336 FAX
Admin Frank Marchese III NHA. *Dir of Nursing* Cynthia Berke RN. *Medical Dir* Harvey Goldberg MD.
Licensure Skilled care; Intermediate care. *Beds* SNF 60; ICF 120. *Private Pay Patients* 1%. *Certified* Medicaid; Medicare.
Owner Proprietary corp (Geriatric and Medical Centers Inc).
Admissions Requirements Medical examination.
Staff Physicians 22 (pt); RNs 4 (ft), 15 (pt); LPNs 9 (ft), 18 (pt); Nurses' aides 60 (ft); Physical therapists 1 (ft), 1 (pt); Recreational therapists 1 (ft), 3 (pt); Occupational therapists 1 (pt); Speech therapists 1 (pt); Activities coordinators 1 (ft); Dietitians 1 (pt); Ophthalmologists 1 (pt); Podiatrists 1 (pt); Audiologists 1 (pt); Dentists; Dermatologists; Psychologists 3 (pt).
Facilities Dining room; Physical therapy room; Activities room; Laundry room; Barber/Beauty shop; TV room; Resident lounges.
Activities Arts & crafts; Cards; Games; Prayer groups; Movies; Dances/Social/Cultural gatherings; Intergenerational programs; Pet therapy; Trips to social & cultural events; Investors club; Newsletter; Residents council; Exercise; Remotivation; Reality therapy.

Langhorne Gardens Nursing Center
350 Manor Ave, Langhorne, PA 19047
(215) 757-7667, 750-1426 FAX
Admin David Kinder. *Dir of Nursing* Geraldine Azmus RN. *Medical Dir* Arnold Goldstein MD.
Licensure Skilled care; Intermediate care; Alzheimer's care. *Beds* SNF 60; ICF 60. *Certified* Medicaid; Medicare.
Owner Proprietary corp (Unicare).
Admissions Requirements Minimum age 16; Medical examination.
Staff Physicians 16 (pt); RNs 8 (pt); LPNs 4 (ft), 6 (pt); Nurses' aides 23 (ft), 19 (pt); Physical therapists 1 (pt); Recreational therapists 1 (ft), 1 (pt); Speech therapists 1 (pt); Dietitians 1 (pt); Podiatrists 1 (pt).
Facilities Dining room; Physical therapy room; Activities room; Chapel; Crafts room; Laundry room; Barber/Beauty shop; Library.

Activities Arts & crafts; Games; Prayer groups; Movies; Shopping trips.

Lansdale

Dock Terrace
275 Dock Dr, Lansdale, PA 19446
(215) 362-5757
Admin Marcus A Clemens. *Dir of Nursing* Judy Truscott RN.
Licensure Skilled care; Retirement. *Beds* SNF 72. *Certified* Medicaid; Medicare.
Owner Nonprofit corp.
Staff RNs 4 (ft), 7 (pt); LPNs 1 (ft); Nurses' aides 26 (ft); Physical therapists 1 (pt); Occupational therapists 1 (pt); Speech therapists 1 (pt); Activities coordinators 1 (pt); Dietitians 1 (ft).
Affiliation Mennonite.
Facilities Dining room; Physical therapy room; Activities room; Chapel; Crafts room; Laundry room; Barber/Beauty shop.
Activities Arts & crafts; Cards; Games; Reading groups; Prayer groups; Movies.

Elm Terrace Gardens
660 N Broad St, Lansdale, PA 19446
(215) 362-6087
Admin Mike Metropole NHA. *Dir of Nursing* Barbara Leo RN.
Licensure Skilled care; Independent living. *Beds* SNF 45. *Certified* Medicaid; Medicare.
Owner Nonprofit corp.
Admissions Requirements Minimum age 60; Medical examination; Physician's request.
Staff RNs; LPNs; Nurses' aides; Activities coordinators.
Facilities Dining room; Physical therapy room; Activities room; Crafts room; Laundry room; Barber/Beauty shop; Library.
Activities Arts & crafts; Cards; Games; Reading groups; Prayer groups; Movies.

Gwynedd Square Center for Nursing & Convalescent Care
773 Sumneytown Pike, Lansdale, PA 19446
(215) 699-7571
Admin Sr Miriam Denis. *Dir of Nursing* Gladys Fuller RNC. *Medical Dir* Dr Michael Seldner.
Licensure Skilled care; Intermediate care; Alzheimer's care. *Beds* SNF 141; ICF 40. *Certified* Medicaid; Medicare.
Owner Proprietary corp.
Staff Physicians; RNs; LPNs; Nurses' aides; Physical therapists; Reality therapists; Recreational therapists; Occupational therapists; Speech therapists; Activities coordinators; Dietitians; Podiatrists.
Facilities Dining room; Physical therapy room; Chapel; Crafts room; Laundry room; Barber/Beauty shop; 3 lounges; 2 activities rooms; 2 interior courtyards with gardens.
Activities Arts & crafts; Cards; Games; Reading groups; Prayer groups; Movies; Dances/Social/Cultural gatherings; Intergenerational programs; Pet therapy.

Normandy Farms Estates West
1001 Valley Forge Rd, Lansdale, PA 19446
(215) 855-9700, 855-4360 FAX
Admin W Jean Abdollahian RN NHA. *Dir of Nursing* Janet Lorraine RN MSN. *Medical Dir* Charles Macey MD.
Licensure Skilled care; Retirement. *Beds* SNF 82; Retirement apts 243. *Private Pay Patients* 98%. *Certified* Medicare.
Owner Nonprofit corp (Adult Communities Total Services Inc).
Admissions Requirements Minimum age 18; Medical examination; Physician's request.
Staff RNs 4 (ft), 6 (pt); LPNs 1 (ft), 2 (pt); Nurses' aides 17 (ft), 10 (pt); Physical therapists (consultant); Occupational therapists (consultant); Speech therapists (consultant); Activities coordinators 1 (ft);

Dietitians 1 (ft); Ophthalmologists (consultant); Podiatrists (consultant); Audiologists (consultant).
Facilities Dining room; Physical therapy room; Activities room; Chapel; Crafts room; Laundry room; Barber/Beauty shop; Library.
Activities Arts & crafts; Cards; Games; Reading groups; Prayer groups; Movies; Dances/Social/Cultural gatherings; Intergenerational programs; Pet therapy.

North Pennsylvania Convalescent Center
25 W 5th St, Lansdale, PA 19446
(215) 855-9765, 368-1863 FAX
Admin Thomas E Howells. *Dir of Nursing* Clare Haubenstein. *Medical Dir* Dr Thomas Detweiler.
Licensure Skilled care; Intermediate care. *Beds* Swing beds SNF/ICF 126. *Private Pay Patients* 11%. *Certified* Medicaid; Medicare.
Owner Proprietary corp (Beverly Enterprises).
Admissions Requirements Minimum age 16.
Staff RNs 7 (ft), 2 (pt); LPNs 8 (ft), 3 (pt); Nurses' aides 38 (ft), 6 (pt); Physical therapists 1 (ft); Activities coordinators 2 (ft); Dietitians 1 (pt).
Facilities Dining room; Physical therapy room; Barber/Beauty shop.
Activities Arts & crafts; Cards; Games; Reading groups; Movies; Shopping trips; Intergenerational programs.

St Mary's Manor
701 Lansdale Ave, Lansdale, PA 19446
(215) 368-0900, 362-2891 FAX
Admin George C Stauffer NHA. *Dir of Nursing* Pamela Henderson RN. *Medical Dir* Leonardo V Arano MD.
Licensure Skilled care; Personal care. *Beds* SNF 70; Personal care 75. *Certified* Medicaid; Medicare.
Owner Nonprofit corp.
Admissions Requirements Minimum age 60; Medical examination.
Staff Physicians 1 (pt); RNs 4 (ft), 17 (pt); LPNs 1 (ft), 7 (pt); Nurses' aides 15 (ft), 18 (pt); Physical therapists 1 (pt); Recreational therapists 1 (ft), 1 (pt); Occupational therapists 1 (pt); Speech therapists 1 (pt); Activities coordinators 1 (ft); Dietitians 2 (ft); Ophthalmologists 1 (pt); Podiatrists 1 (pt); Audiologists 1 (pt).
Facilities Dining room; Physical therapy room; Activities room; Chapel; Crafts room; Laundry room; Barber/Beauty shop; Library.
Activities Arts & crafts; Cards; Games; Reading groups; Prayer groups; Movies; Shopping trips; Dances/Social/Cultural gatherings; Intergenerational programs; Pet therapy.

LaPorte

LaPorte United Methodist Home
Rte 42, LaPorte, PA 18626
(717) 946-7700
Licensure Skilled care. *Beds* SNF 120. *Certified* Medicaid; Medicare.
Owner Proprietary corp.

Laureldale

Leader Nursing & Rehabilitation Center—Laureldale
2125 Elizabeth Ave, Laureldale, PA 19605
(215) 921-9292
Admin Lisa Quinlan. *Dir of Nursing* Sue Hoch RN.
Licensure Skilled care; Intermediate care. *Beds* SNF 120; ICF 60. *Certified* Medicaid; Medicare.
Owner Proprietary corp (Manor Care Inc).
Admissions Requirements Medical examination.
Staff RNs 10 (ft), 5 (pt); LPNs 7 (ft), 14 (pt); Nurses' aides 44 (ft), 37 (pt); Physical therapists 5 (ft), 1 (pt); Recreational

therapists 3 (ft), 1 (pt); Occupational therapists 1 (ft); Activities coordinators 1 (ft).
Facilities Dining room; Physical therapy room; Activities room; Chapel; Crafts room; Laundry room; Barber/Beauty shop; Kosher kitchen.
Activities Arts & crafts; Cards; Games; Reading groups; Prayer groups; Shopping trips; Dances/Social/Cultural gatherings.

Laurelton

Laurelton Center
Rte 45, Laurelton, PA 17835-0300
(717) 922-3311
Admin S Reeves Power. *Dir of Nursing* Lynn Libby RN. *Medical Dir* James R Kodlick.
Licensure Intermediate care for mentally retarded. *Beds* ICF/MR 400. *Certified* Medicaid.
Owner Nonprofit organization/foundation.
Admissions Requirements Medical examination.
Staff Physicians 1 (pt); RNs 13 (ft); LPNs 43 (ft), 2 (pt); Recreational therapists 5 (ft); Occupational therapists 1 (ft); Speech therapists 3 (ft); Dietitians 2 (ft); Podiatrists 2 (ft); Residential services aides 172 (ft), 1 (pt).
Facilities Dining room; Physical therapy room; Activities room; Chapel; Crafts room; Barber/Beauty shop; Library.
Activities Arts & crafts; Cards; Games; Prayer groups; Movies; Shopping trips; Dances/Social/Cultural gatherings.

Lebanon

Cedar Haven—Lebanon County Home
590 S 5th Ave, Lebanon, PA 17042
(717) 274-0421
Admin Lee A Stickler. *Dir of Nursing* Ellen M Walker RN. *Medical Dir* Peter B Flowers MD.
Licensure Skilled care; Intermediate care. *Beds* SNF 40; ICF 320. *Certified* Medicaid; Medicare.
Owner Publicly owned.
Staff Physicians 2 (pt); RNs 10 (ft), 3 (pt); LPNs 26 (ft), 10 (pt); Nurses' aides 100 (ft), 50 (pt); Activities coordinators 3 (ft), 4 (pt).
Facilities Dining room; Physical therapy room; Activities room; Chapel; Crafts room; Laundry room; Barber/Beauty shop; Library.
Activities Arts & crafts; Cards; Games; Reading groups; Prayer groups; Movies; Shopping trips; Dances/Social/Cultural gatherings; Patio picnics; Exercise.

Leader Nursing & Rehabilitation Center—Lebanon
900 Tuck St, Lebanon, PA 17042
(717) 273-8595
Admin William G Boyer Jr.
Medical Dir Dale Brown-Bieber MD.
Licensure Skilled care; Intermediate care. *Beds* SNF 62; ICF 72. *Certified* Medicaid; Medicare.
Owner Proprietary corp (Manor Care).
Admissions Requirements Medical examination.
Staff RNs 3 (ft), 10 (pt); LPNs 11 (ft), 7 (pt); Nurses' aides 37 (ft), 42 (pt); Physical therapists 1 (ft); Recreational therapists 1 (ft); Occupational therapists 1 (ft), 1 (pt); Speech therapists 1 (pt); Activities coordinators 1 (ft).
Facilities Dining room; Physical therapy room; Activities room; Chapel; Crafts room; Laundry room; Barber/Beauty shop.
Activities Arts & crafts; Cards; Games; Reading groups; Prayer groups; Movies; Shopping trips; Dances/Social/Cultural gatherings; Field trips; Intergenerational groups.

Lebanon County Life Support
25 Metro Dr, Lebanon, PA 17042
(717) 274-0493
Medical Dir Bruce Yeamans MD & Drew Coutney MD.
Licensure Intermediate care for mentally retarded. *Beds* 25. *Certified* Medicaid.
Owner Nonprofit corp.
Admissions Requirements Medical examination; Physician's request.
Staff Nurses' aides 15 (ft), 5 (pt); Speech therapists 1 (pt); Activities coordinators 1 (pt); Dietitians 1 (pt); Program assistants 3 (ft).
Facilities Activities room.
Activities Arts & crafts; Games; Movies; Shopping trips.

Oakview
1407 Oak St, Lebanon, PA 17042
(717) 273-5541
Admin C Franklin Helt. *Dir of Nursing* Sandra Geib RN. *Medical Dir* Dr Glenn Hirsch.
Licensure Skilled care; Intermediate care; Retirement. *Beds* 28. *Certified* Medicaid; Medicare.
Owner Nonprofit corp.
Admissions Requirements Medical examination; Physician's request.
Staff RNs 1 (ft), 2 (pt); LPNs 1 (ft), 4 (pt); Nurses' aides 8 (ft), 4 (pt); Recreational therapists 1 (ft); Occupational therapists 1 (pt).
Facilities Dining room; Activities room; Chapel; Crafts room; Laundry room; Barber/Beauty shop; Library.
Activities Arts & crafts; Cards; Games; Reading groups; Prayer groups; Movies; Shopping trips; Dances/Social/Cultural gatherings; Pet therapy; Kitchen band; Morning exercises.

Spang Crest Nursing Home
945 Duke St, Lebanon, PA 17042
(717) 274-1495
Licensure Skilled care; Intermediate care. *Beds* SNF 35; ICF 70. *Certified* Medicaid; Medicare.
Owner Nonprofit corp.

Lehighton

Gnaden Huetten Nursing & Convalescent Center
11th & Hamilton Sts, Lehighton, PA 18229
(215) 377-1300
Admin Delores L Zaengle RN. *Dir of Nursing* Jean E Everett RN. *Medical Dir* Dr Robert Frantz.
Licensure Skilled care; Intermediate care. *Beds* SNF 46; ICF 45. *Certified* Medicaid; Medicare.
Owner Nonprofit corp.
Staff Physicians 20 (pt); RNs 5 (ft), 5 (pt); LPNs 7 (ft), 9 (pt); Nurses' aides 17 (ft), 18 (pt); Physical therapists 1 (ft); Recreational therapists 1 (ft); Occupational therapists 1 (ft); Speech therapists 1 (pt); Activities coordinators 1 (ft); Dietitians 1 (ft), 1 (pt); Ophthalmologists 4 (pt); Podiatrists 1 (pt); Audiologists 1 (pt).
Languages German, Pennsylvania Dutch, Slovak.
Facilities Dining room; Physical therapy room; Laundry room; Barber/Beauty shop; 2 lounge areas; Activities/Crafts room.
Activities Arts & crafts; Games; Reading groups; Prayer groups; Movies; Shopping trips; Dances/Social/Cultural gatherings; Yearly long-term Olympics.

Mahoning Valley Nursing & Rehabilitation Center
Rte 1 Box 46, Lehighton, PA 18235
(717) 386-5522
Medical Dir Dr Robert Frantz.

Licensure Skilled care; Intermediate care. *Beds* SNF 59; ICF 61. *Certified* Medicaid; Medicare.
Owner Proprietary corp.
Staff Physicians 3 (pt); RNs 4 (ft), 2 (pt); LPNs 9 (ft); Nurses' aides 28 (ft); Physical therapists 1 (pt); Occupational therapists 1 (pt); Speech therapists 1 (pt); Activities coordinators 1 (ft); Dietitians 1 (pt); Ophthalmologists 1 (pt); Podiatrists 1 (pt); Audiologists 1 (pt); Dentists 1 (pt).
Facilities Dining room; Physical therapy room; Activities room; Crafts room; Barber/Beauty shop.
Activities Arts & crafts; Cards; Games; Reading groups; Movies; Shopping trips.

Leola

Community Services Inc
312 Pleasant Valley Dr, Leola, PA 17540
(717) 656-8005
Licensure Intermediate care for mentally retarded. *Beds* 5. *Certified* Medicaid.
Owner Proprietary corp.

Levittown

Statesman Nursing Center
2629 Trenton Rd, Levittown, PA 19056
(215) 943-7777
Licensure Skilled care; Intermediate care. *Beds* SNF 70; ICF 31. *Certified* Medicaid; Medicare.
Owner Proprietary corp (Unicare).

Lewisberry

Fairview Village Nursing Center
780 Woodland Ave, Lewisberry, PA 17339
(717) 938-9370
Licensure Skilled care. *Beds* SNF 120. *Certified* Medicaid; Medicare.
Owner Proprietary corp.

Lewisburg

Buffalo Valley Lutheran Village
Fairground Rd, Lewisburg, PA 17837
(717) 524-2221
Admin Dennis E Horn. *Dir of Nursing* Carol L Moyer RN.
Licensure Skilled care; Intermediate care. *Beds* SNF 21; ICF 89. *Certified* Medicaid; Medicare.
Owner Nonprofit corp (Tressler-Lutheran Services Assn).
Admissions Requirements Minimum age 65; Medical examination.
Staff RNs 4 (ft), 3 (pt); LPNs 4 (ft), 3 (pt); Nurses' aides 24 (ft), 24 (pt); Activities coordinators 1 (ft).
Affiliation Lutheran.
Facilities Dining room; Physical therapy room; Activities room; Chapel; Crafts room; Laundry room; Barber/Beauty shop.
Activities Arts & crafts; Cards; Games; Reading groups; Prayer groups; Movies; Shopping trips; Dances/Social/Cultural gatherings.

Lewisburg United Methodist Homes
Lewisburg, PA 17837
(717) 524-2271, 524-5137 FAX
Admin Bonnie Haas. *Dir of Nursing* Sylvia Betzer RN. *Medical Dir* John H Persing MD.
Licensure Skilled care; Intermediate care; Retirement. *Beds* SNF 90; ICF 140. *Certified* Medicaid; Medicare.
Owner Nonprofit corp.
Admissions Requirements Minimum age 65; Medical examination.
Staff RNs; LPNs; Nurses' aides; Physical therapists; Activities coordinators.
Affiliation United Methodist.

Facilities Dining room; Physical therapy room; Activities room; Crafts room; Laundry room; Barber/Beauty shop; Library.
Activities Arts & crafts; Cards; Games; Reading groups; Prayer groups; Movies; Shopping trips; Dances/Social/Cultural gatherings; Intergenerational programs; Pet therapy.

Lewistown

Ohesson Manor
350 Green Ave Ext, Lewistown, PA 17044
(717) 242-1416
Licensure Skilled care; Intermediate care. *Beds* SNF 35; ICF 99. *Certified* Medicaid; Medicare.
Owner Nonprofit corp (Tressler-Lutheran Services Assn).

William Penn Nursing Center
163 Summit Dr, Lewistown, PA 17044
(717) 248-3941
Admin Stephen K Ott. *Dir of Nursing* Ramona Byler RN. *Medical Dir* Dr John Zornosa.
Licensure Skilled care; Intermediate care. *Beds* SNF 31; ICF 90. *Certified* Medicaid; Medicare.
Owner Proprietary corp (Beverly Enterprises).
Admissions Requirements Medical examination; Physician's request.
Staff RNs 5 (ft), 5 (pt); LPNs 9 (ft), 7 (pt); Nurses' aides 25 (ft), 31 (pt); Physical therapists 1 (pt); Recreational therapists 1 (ft), 1 (pt); Speech therapists 1 (pt).
Facilities Dining room; Physical therapy room; Activities room; Crafts room; Laundry room; Barber/Beauty shop; Lounges.
Activities Arts & crafts; Cards; Games; Reading groups; Prayer groups; Movies; Shopping trips; Dances/Social/Cultural gatherings; Individual programs.

Ligonier

Bethlen Home of the Hungarian Federation of America
PO Box 657, Ligonier, PA 15658
(412) 238-6711
Admin Rev Paul Kovacs.
Medical Dir G Jeanie Short.
Licensure Skilled care; Intermediate care; Retirement. *Beds* SNF 45; ICF 58; Retirement 20. *Private Pay Patients* 45%. *Certified* Medicaid; Medicare.
Owner Nonprofit corp.
Admissions Requirements Medical examination; Physician's request.
Staff RNs 3 (ft), 10 (pt); LPNs 1 (ft), 2 (pt); Nurses' aides; Activities coordinators; Dietitians 1 (ft).
Languages Hungarian.
Affiliation Presbyterian.
Facilities Dining room; Physical therapy room; Activities room; Chapel; Crafts room; Laundry room; Barber/Beauty shop.
Activities Arts & crafts; Cards; Games; Reading groups; Prayer groups; Movies; Shopping trips; Dances/Social/Cultural gatherings.

Pine Hurst Nursing & Convalescent Home
Rte 4, Ligonier, PA 15658
(412) 593-7720
Licensure Skilled care. *Beds* 23.
Owner Proprietary corp.

Lima

Fair Acres Geriatric Center
Middletown Rd, Lima, PA 19037
(215) 891-5600
Licensure Skilled care; Intermediate care. *Beds* SNF 700; ICF 211. *Certified* Medicaid; Medicare.
Owner Publicly owned.

Lima Estates Medical Care Facility
411 N Middletown Rd, Lima, PA 19037
(215) 565-8717
Licensure Skilled care; Independent living. *Beds* SNF 60. *Certified* Medicare.
Owner Nonprofit corp.

Lititz

Audubon Villa
125 S Broad St, Lititz, PA 17543
(717) 626-0211
Licensure Skilled care. *Beds* SNF 33. *Certified* Medicare.
Owner Proprietary corp.

Friendship Community
1149 E Oregon Rd, Lititz, PA 17543
(717) 656-2466
Admin Charles Bauman. *Dir of Nursing* Audrey Groff.
Licensure Intermediate care for mentally retarded; Retirement. *Beds* ICF/MR 33; Retirement 34. *Private Pay Patients* 0%. *Certified* Medicaid.
Owner Nonprofit organization/foundation.
Admissions Requirements Minimum age 17; Medical examination; Physician's request.
Staff RNs 3 (pt); LPNs 2 (ft), 2 (pt); Physical therapists (contracted); Activities coordinators 1 (pt); Dietitians; Resident advisors 15 (ft), 15 (pt).
Affiliation Mennonite.
Facilities Dining room.
Activities Arts & crafts; Games; Prayer groups; Shopping trips.

Landis Homes Retirement Community
Rte 3, Lititz, PA 17543
(717) 569-3271
Admin Edward M Longenecker. *Dir of Nursing* Ruth Johnson RN. *Medical Dir* John Wolgemuth MD.
Licensure Skilled care; Intermediate care; Independent living. *Beds* 111. *Certified* Medicaid.
Owner Nonprofit corp.
Admissions Requirements Minimum age 65.
Staff RNs 4 (ft), 6 (pt); LPNs 14 (ft), 9 (pt); Nurses' aides 12 (ft), 47 (pt); Recreational therapists 3 (ft), 1 (pt); Activities coordinators.
Languages Pennsylvania Dutch.
Affiliation Mennonite.
Facilities Dining room; Physical therapy room; Activities room; Chapel; Crafts room; Laundry room; Barber/Beauty shop; Library.
Activities Arts & crafts; Games; Reading groups; Prayer groups; Movies; Shopping trips; Dances/Social/Cultural gatherings; Cooking.

Luther Acres
600 E Main St, Lititz, PA 17543
(717) 626-1171
Licensure Skilled care; Intermediate care. *Beds* SNF 19; ICF 87. *Certified* Medicaid; Medicare.
Owner Nonprofit corp.
Affiliation Lutheran.

Moravian Manor
300 W Lemon St, Lititz, PA 17543
(717) 626-0214
Admin Nancy H O'Hara CFACHCA. *Dir of Nursing* Lillian Podlesny RN NHA, Res Svcs Dir. *Medical Dir* Gary Scibal MD.
Licensure Skilled care; Intermediate care; Personal care. *Beds* SNF 55; ICF 55; Personal care 88. *Certified* Medicaid; Medicare.
Owner Nonprofit corp.
Admissions Requirements Minimum age 62; Medical examination.
Staff RNs 8 (ft), 8 (pt); LPNs 6 (ft), 6 (pt); Nurses' aides 55 (ft), 22 (pt); Physical therapists 1 (pt); Recreational therapists 1 (ft); Occupational therapists (consultant);

Speech therapists (consultant); Activities coordinators 1 (ft); Dietitians (consultant); Podiatrists (consultant); Chaplains 1 (pt); Social workers 1 (ft); Beauticians-Barbers 1 (ft), 1 (pt).
Affiliation Moravian.
Facilities Dining room; Physical therapy room; Activities room; Chapel; Crafts room; Laundry room; Barber/Beauty shop; Library.
Activities Arts & crafts; Cards; Games; Reading groups; Prayer groups; Movies; Shopping trips; Dances/Social/Cultural gatherings; Intergenerational programs; Pet therapy; Ceramics; Community outings; Bowling; Current events groups; Exercises; Picnics; Afternoon teas; Cooking groups; Therapeutic activities.

United Zion Home Inc
722 Furnace Hills Pike, Lititz, PA 17543
(717) 626-2071
Licensure Skilled care. *Beds* SNF 46. *Certified* Medicaid; Medicare.
Owner Nonprofit corp.

Liverpool

Good Samaritan Home
PO Box C, Front St, Liverpool, PA 17045
(717) 444-3713
Admin Esther J Mohler.
Medical Dir Dr James Minahan.
Licensure Intermediate care. *Beds* ICF 24. *Certified* Medicaid.
Owner Proprietary corp.
Admissions Requirements Minimum age 16; Medical examination.
Staff RNs 1 (ft), 2 (pt); LPNs 4 (pt); Nurses' aides 8 (pt); Recreational therapists 1 (pt); Activities coordinators 1 (pt).
Facilities Dining room.
Activities Arts & crafts; Cards; Games; Reading groups; Prayer groups; Movies; Shopping trips; Dances/Social/Cultural gatherings.

Nipple Convalescent Home
100 S Front St, Liverpool, PA 17045
(717) 444-3413, 444-3421 FAX
Admin Rae A Adams NHA. *Dir of Nursing* Gale A Ulanoski. *Medical Dir* Joseph R Kreiser MD.
Licensure Intermediate care. *Beds* ICF 37. *Private Pay Patients* 34%. *Certified* Medicaid.
Owner Proprietary corp (Briarcliff Associates).
Admissions Requirements Minimum age 18; Medical examination; Physician's request.
Staff Physicians 1 (pt); RNs 1 (ft), 3 (pt); LPNs 2 (ft), 2 (pt); Nurses' aides 8 (ft), 4 (pt); Physical therapists 1 (pt); Recreational therapists 1 (ft); Speech therapists 1 (pt); Dietitians 1 (pt); Ophthalmologists 1 (pt); Podiatrists 1 (pt); Audiologists 1 (pt).
Facilities Dining room; Activities room; Crafts room; Laundry room; Barber/Beauty shop; Porch.
Activities Arts & crafts; Cards; Games; Reading groups; Prayer groups; Movies; Shopping trips; Intergenerational programs.

Lock Haven

Lock Haven Hospital
24 Cree Dr, Lock Haven, PA 17745
(717) 893-5000
Licensure Skilled care. *Beds* SNF 117. *Certified* Medicaid; Medicare.
Owner Proprietary corp.

Lock Haven Hospital—Extended Care Facility
Fourth & Nelson Sts, Lock Haven, PA 17745
(717) 748-7721
Licensure Skilled care; Intermediate care. *Beds* SNF 60; ICF 60. *Certified* Medicaid; Medicare.
Owner Nonprofit corp.

Susque View Home Inc
Cree Dr, Lock Haven, PA 17745
(717) 748-9377
Admin Jack Spayd. *Dir of Nursing* Barbara Jackson. *Medical Dir* James Dolan MD.
Licensure Skilled care; Intermediate care. *Beds* 164. *Certified* Medicaid; Medicare.
Owner Nonprofit corp.
Admissions Requirements Medical examination; Physician's request.
Staff Physicians 10 (pt); RNs 6 (ft), 4 (pt); LPNs 15 (ft), 8 (pt); Nurses' aides 44 (ft), 24 (pt); Physical therapists 2 (pt); Reality therapists 1 (pt); Recreational therapists 1 (ft); Occupational therapists 1 (pt); Speech therapists 1 (pt); Activities coordinators 1 (ft); Dietitians 1 (pt); Ophthalmologists 1 (pt); Podiatrists 1 (pt); Dentists 1 (pt).
Facilities Dining room; Physical therapy room; Activities room; Chapel; Crafts room; Laundry room; Barber/Beauty shop; Library.
Activities Arts & crafts; Cards; Games; Reading groups; Prayer groups; Movies; Shopping trips; Dances/Social/Cultural gatherings.

Lower Burrell

Belair Nursing Center
Chester Dr & Little Rd, Lower Burrell, PA 15068
(412) 339-1071, 339-2882 FAX
Admin John P Hughes. *Dir of Nursing* Mary Sharon Bielski. *Medical Dir* Dr Michael Mesoras; Valley Family Practice Center.
Licensure Skilled care; Intermediate care. *Beds* SNF 31; ICF 76. *Private Pay Patients* 50%. *Certified* Medicaid; Medicare.
Owner Proprietary corp (Unicare).
Admissions Requirements Medical examination.
Staff Physicians; RNs; LPNs; Nurses' aides; Physical therapists; Reality therapists; Recreational therapists; Occupational therapists; Speech therapists; Activities coordinators; Dietitians; Ophthalmologists; Podiatrists; Audiologists.
Facilities Dining room; Physical therapy room; Activities room; Crafts room; Laundry room; Barber/Beauty shop.
Activities Arts & crafts; Cards; Games; Reading groups; Prayer groups; Movies; Shopping trips; Dances/Social/Cultural gatherings; Pet therapy.

Lower Merion

Saunders House
City Line & Lancaster Aves, Lower Merion, PA 19151
(215) 896-7955
Admin Milton Jacobs. *Dir of Nursing* Nichy Ceasar RN. *Medical Dir* Bruce G Silver MD.
Licensure Skilled care; Intermediate care; Retirement; Alzheimer's care. *Beds* SNF 90; ICF 90; Retirement apts 30. *Certified* Medicaid; Medicare.
Owner Nonprofit corp.
Admissions Requirements Medical examination; Physician's request.
Staff RNs 12 (ft), 15 (pt); LPNs 4 (ft), 5 (pt); Nurses' aides 75 (ft); Physical therapists 1 (pt); Reality therapists 1 (ft); Recreational therapists 3 (ft); Occupational therapists 1 (pt); Speech therapists 1 (pt); Activities coordinators 1 (ft); Dietitians 2 (ft); Ophthalmologists 1 (pt); Podiatrists 1 (pt); Audiologists 1 (pt); Psychiatrists 1 (pt).
Facilities Dining room; Physical therapy room; Activities room; Chapel; Crafts room; Laundry room; Barber/Beauty shop; Library; Dental unit.

Activities Arts & crafts; Cards; Games; Reading groups; Prayer groups; Movies; Shopping trips; Dances/Social/Cultural gatherings.

Manheim

Mt Hope Dunkard Brethren Church Home
3026 Mount Hope Home Rd, Manheim, PA 17545
(717) 665-6365
Admin Glen K Ziegler. *Dir of Nursing* Anna S Keller RN. *Medical Dir* William J Stout MD.
Licensure Skilled care; Independent living. *Beds* SNF 59; Independent living 12. *Private Pay Patients* 60%. *Certified* Medicaid.
Owner Nonprofit corp.
Admissions Requirements Minimum age 65; Medical examination.
Staff RNs 1 (ft), 5 (pt); LPNs 4 (ft), 1 (pt); Nurses' aides 14 (ft), 30 (pt); Physical therapists; Dietitians.
Facilities Dining room; Activities room; Chapel; Crafts room; Laundry room.
Activities Arts & crafts; Cards; Games; Reading groups; Prayer groups; Shopping trips; Intergenerational programs; Pet therapy.

Pleasant View Home Inc
PO Box 487, 450 Penryn Rd, Manheim, PA 17545
(717) 665-2445
Medical Dir Dr Terrence Jones.
Licensure Skilled care. *Beds* SNF 130. *Certified* Medicaid.
Owner Nonprofit corp.
Admissions Requirements Medical examination.
Staff Physicians; RNs; LPNs; Nurses' aides; Physical therapists; Reality therapists; Recreational therapists; Activities coordinators; Dietitians; Ophthalmologists; Podiatrists; Dentists.
Facilities Dining room; Physical therapy room; Activities room; Chapel; Crafts room; Laundry room; Barber/Beauty shop.
Activities Arts & crafts; Games; Reading groups; Prayer groups; Movies; Shopping trips.

Marienville

Snyder Memorial Health Care Center
Rte 66 Box 680, Marienville, PA 16239
(814) 927-6670, 927-6966 FAX
Admin Richard P Faber. *Dir of Nursing* Wendy McKinnis. *Medical Dir* Dr R Saquin.
Licensure Skilled care; Intermediate care. *Beds* SNF 33; ICF 67. *Private Pay Patients* 31%. *Certified* Medicaid; Medicare.
Owner Proprietary corp (Windsor Corp).
Admissions Requirements Minimum age 5; Medical examination.
Staff RNs 5 (ft), 2 (pt); LPNs 10 (ft), 2 (pt); Nurses' aides 40 (ft), 8 (pt); Physical therapists 1 (pt); Speech therapists 1 (pt); Activities coordinators 1 (pt); Dietitians 1 (pt); Podiatrists 1 (pt); Audiologists 1 (pt).
Facilities Dining room; Physical therapy room; Activities room; Crafts room; Laundry room; Barber/Beauty shop.
Activities Arts & crafts; Cards; Games; Reading groups; Prayer groups; Movies; Shopping trips; Dances/Social/Cultural gatherings; Intergenerational programs; Pet therapy; Outdoor activities; Prom; Fishing; Cultural programs; Theater; Community parades.

Markleysburg

Henry Clay Villa
RD 1 Box 63-A, Markleysburg, PA 15459
(412) 329-5545
Licensure Skilled care. *Beds* SNF 74. *Certified* Medicaid.
Owner Proprietary corp.

Spear Convalescent Home
PO Box 37, Markleysburg, PA 15459
(412) 329-4830
Licensure Skilled care. *Beds* SNF 79. *Certified* Medicaid.
Owner Proprietary corp.

Mars

St John Lutheran Care Center
PO Box 928, 500 Wittenberg Way, Mars, PA 16046
(412) 625-1571, 625-1571, ext 210 FAX
Admin Judith Comer. *Dir of Nursing* Ann Rice RN. *Medical Dir* Dr Ira Baumgartel.
Licensure Skilled care; Intermediate care; Personal care; Residential care; Alzheimer's care. *Beds* SNF 103; ICF 215; Personal care 33; Residential care 9; Alzheimer's care 17. *Private Pay Patients* 54%. *Certified* Medicaid; Medicare.
Owner Nonprofit corp.
Admissions Requirements Minimum age 60; Medical examination.
Staff Physicians 3 (pt); RNs 10 (ft), 13 (pt); LPNs 28 (ft), 19 (pt); Nurses' aides 74 (ft), 36 (pt); Physical therapists 2 (pt); Reality therapists 2 (ft), 2 (pt); Recreational therapists 3 (ft); Occupational therapists 1 (pt); Speech therapists 1 (pt); Activities coordinators 1 (ft); Dietitians 2 (ft); Podiatrists 1 (pt); Audiologists 1 (pt); Optometrists 1 (pt); Dentists 1 (pt).
Affiliation Lutheran.
Facilities Dining room; Physical therapy room; Activities room; Chapel; Crafts room; Laundry room; Barber/Beauty shop; Library; Dental office.
Activities Arts & crafts; Cards; Games; Reading groups; Prayer groups; Movies; Shopping trips; Dances/Social/Cultural gatherings; Intergenerational programs; Pet therapy; Music therapy; Remotivation therapy; Choir.

Sherwood Oaks
100 Norman Dr, Mars, PA 16046
(412) 776-8100
Admin Jace Gerie.
Medical Dir Dr J Robert Love.
Licensure Skilled care; Independent living. *Beds* SNF 59; Independent living 37. *Certified* Medicaid; Medicare.
Owner Nonprofit corp.
Admissions Requirements Medical examination.
Staff Physicians 2 (pt); RNs 5 (ft), 4 (pt); LPNs 3 (ft), 3 (pt); Nurses' aides 14 (ft), 8 (pt); Recreational therapists 1 (ft); Occupational therapists 1 (pt); Speech therapists 1 (pt); Dietitians 1 (pt); Ophthalmologists; Podiatrists 1 (pt); Dentists 1 (pt); Occupational therapy aides 1 (pt); Physical therapy aides 1 (pt).
Facilities Dining room; Physical therapy room; Activities room; Chapel; Crafts room; Laundry room; Barber/Beauty shop; Library; Indoor heated pool & jacuzzi; Greenhouse; Bank; Convenience store; Woodworking shop; Lapidary shop.
Activities Arts & crafts; Cards; Games; Reading groups; Prayer groups; Movies; Shopping trips; Dances/Social/Cultural gatherings; Bible study.

Martinsburg

Homewood Retirement Center
430 S Market St, Martinsburg, PA 16662
(814) 793-3728
Admin Linda N Frederick RN NHA. *Dir of Nursing* Diane K Golomb RN. *Medical Dir* Richard H Bulger MD.
Licensure Intermediate care. *Beds* ICF 67. *Certified* Medicaid.
Owner Nonprofit corp (Homewood Retirement Centers).
Admissions Requirements Medical examination.
Staff Physicians 4 (pt); RNs 3 (ft), 4 (pt); LPNs 5 (ft), 5 (pt); Nurses' aides 16 (ft), 17 (pt); Physical therapists (consultant); Activities coordinators 1 (ft); Dietitians (consultant); Podiatrists 1 (pt).
Affiliation United Church of Christ.
Facilities Physical therapy room; Barber/Beauty shop; Activities/Crafts room; Dining room/Chapel; Private & semi-private rooms.
Activities Arts & crafts; Games; Reading groups; Prayer groups; Movies; Shopping trips; Dances/Social/Cultural gatherings; Intergenerational programs; Pet therapy.

Morrisons Cove Home
429 S Market St, Martinsburg, PA 16662
(814) 793-2104
Admin Lona B Norris. *Dir of Nursing* Ada Spaeth. *Medical Dir* Lunda Weaver MD.
Licensure Skilled care; Intermediate care; Retirement. *Beds* SNF 47; ICF 57. *Certified* Medicaid; Medicare.
Owner Nonprofit corp.
Admissions Requirements Minimum age 65; Medical examination.
Staff RNs 3 (ft), 8 (pt); LPNs 8 (ft), 10 (pt); Nurses' aides 29 (ft), 25 (pt); Activities coordinators 1 (ft).
Affiliation Church of the Brethren.
Facilities Dining room; Activities room; Chapel; Crafts room; Laundry room; Barber/Beauty shop; Library.
Activities Arts & crafts; Cards; Games; Reading groups; Prayer groups; Shopping trips; Dances/Social/Cultural gatherings.

McConnellsburg

Fulton County Medical Center
216 S 1st St, McConnellsburg, PA 17233
(717) 485-3155, 485-5605 FAX
Admin Cathleen A Otto RN. *Dir of Nursing* Sandra Kulakowski RN. *Medical Dir* James E Witt DO.
Licensure Skilled care; Intermediate care. *Beds* SNF 15; ICF 42. *Certified* Medicaid; Medicare.
Owner Nonprofit corp.
Admissions Requirements Medical examination.
Staff Physicians 1 (ft), 5 (pt); RNs 1 (ft), 2 (pt); LPNs 7 (ft), 8 (pt); Nurses' aides 9 (ft), 23 (pt); Physical therapists 3 (pt); Speech therapists 1 (pt); Activities coordinators 1 (ft), 1 (pt); Dietitians 1 (ft); Podiatrists 1 (pt).
Facilities Dining room; Physical therapy room; Activities room; Chapel; Laundry room; Barber/Beauty shop.
Activities Arts & crafts; Cards; Games; Reading groups; Prayer groups; Movies; Shopping trips; Dances/Social/Cultural gatherings; Intergenerational programs; Pet therapy.

McKees Rocks

Robinson Developmental Center
Clever Rd, McKees Rocks, PA 15136
(412) 787-2350
Admin Donald D DiMichele. *Dir of Nursing* Carol A Neuman RN. *Medical Dir* Louis D Pietragallo MD.
Licensure Intermediate care for mentally retarded. *Beds* 132. *Certified* Medicaid.
Owner Nonprofit corp.
Admissions Requirements Minimum age 21; Medical examination.
Staff Physicians 6 (pt); RNs 5 (ft); LPNs 6 (ft); Recreational therapists 1 (ft); Occupational therapists 1 (pt); Speech therapists 3 (ft); Activities coordinators 3 (ft); Dietitians 1 (ft); Dentists 1 (pt); Physical therapy aides 3 (ft), 1 (pt).
Languages Sign.
Facilities Dining room; Physical therapy room; Activities room; Laundry room; Library.
Activities Active developmental programming.

McKeesport

John J Kane Regional Center
100 9th St, McKeesport, PA 15132
(412) 675-8600, 675-8671 FAX
Admin D J Murphy. *Dir of Nursing* J Coates. *Medical Dir* F L Fontana MD.
Licensure Skilled care; Intermediate care; Alzheimer's care; Day care. *Beds* SNF 300; ICF 60. *Private Pay Patients* 1%. *Certified* Medicaid; Medicare.
Owner Publicly owned.
Admissions Requirements Minimum age 18; Medicaid eligible.
Staff Physicians (contracted); RNs 14 (ft), 3 (pt); LPNs 42 (ft), 4 (pt); Nurses' aides 128 (ft), 28 (pt); Physical therapists (contracted); Recreational therapists 4 (ft); Occupational therapists (contracted); Speech therapists (contracted); Activities coordinators 1 (ft); Dietitians 3 (ft); Ophthalmologists (contracted); Podiatrists (contracted); Audiologists (contracted).
Facilities Dining room; Physical therapy room; Activities room; Chapel; Crafts room; Laundry room; Barber/Beauty shop; Library; Snack shop; Day care room.
Activities Arts & crafts; Cards; Games; Reading groups; Prayer groups; Movies; Shopping trips; Dances/Social/Cultural gatherings; Intergenerational programs; Pet therapy; Fishing; Therapeutic recreation; Volunteer program; Pastoral care.

Riverside Nursing Center
100 8th Ave, McKeesport, PA 15132
(412) 664-8860
Admin Antoinette M Coury. *Dir of Nursing* Sandra Ramsey. *Medical Dir* James Camagna.
Licensure Skilled care; Intermediate care. *Beds* SNF 60; ICF 60. *Private Pay Patients* 40%. *Certified* Medicaid; Medicare.
Owner Proprietary corp.
Admissions Requirements Minimum age 16; Medical examination; Physician's request.
Staff Physicians 5 (pt); RNs 10 (pt); LPNs 14 (pt); Nurses' aides; Physical therapists 1 (pt); Recreational therapists 1 (ft); Occupational therapists 1 (pt); Speech therapists 1 (pt); Activities coordinators 1 (ft); Dietitians 1 (ft); Ophthalmologists 1 (pt); Podiatrists 1 (pt); Audiologists 1 (pt).
Facilities Dining room; Physical therapy room; Activities room; Crafts room; Laundry room; Barber/Beauty shop; Library.
Activities Arts & crafts; Cards; Games; Reading groups; Prayer groups; Movies; Shopping trips; Pet therapy.

McMurray

McMurray Hills Manor
249 W McMurray Rd, McMurray, PA 15317
(412) 941-1750
Admin Paul D Kwiecinski.
Medical Dir Jon Adler MD.
Licensure Skilled care; Intermediate care. *Beds* SNF 97; ICF 22. *Certified* Medicare.
Owner Proprietary corp.

Admissions Requirements Minimum age 40; Medical examination.
Staff Physicians 3 (pt); RNs 16 (ft), 6 (pt); LPNs 3 (pt); Nurses' aides 1 (pt); Physical therapists 1 (pt); Recreational therapists 1 (pt); Occupational therapists 1 (pt); Speech therapists 1 (pt); Activities coordinators 1 (ft); Dietitians 1 (pt); Ophthalmologists 1 (pt); Podiatrists 1 (pt); Dentists 1 (pt).
Facilities Dining room; Physical therapy room; Activities room; Crafts room; Laundry room; Barber/Beauty shop.
Activities Arts & crafts; Cards; Games; Reading groups; Prayer groups; Movies; Shopping trips; Dances/Social/Cultural gatherings.

Meadowbrook

St Joseph's Manor
1616 Huntingdon Pike, Meadowbrook, PA 19046
(215) 938-4000
Admin Benjamin J Pieczynski; Joseph F Mugford, Asst Admin.
Medical Dir Robert V Peruzzi Jr MD.
Licensure Skilled care; Retirement. *Beds* SNF 197. *Certified* Medicaid; Medicare.
Owner Nonprofit corp.
Admissions Requirements Minimum age 65; Medical examination.
Staff Physicians; RNs; LPNs; Nurses' aides; Activities coordinators; Dietitians.
Facilities Dining room; Physical therapy room; Activities room; Chapel; Crafts room; Laundry room; Barber/Beauty shop.
Activities Arts & crafts; Cards; Games; Reading groups; Prayer groups; Movies; Shopping trips; Dances/Social/Cultural gatherings.

Meadville

Mead Nursing Home
N Park Ave Extension, Meadville, PA 16335
(814) 337-4229
Licensure Skilled care. *Beds* 150. *Certified* Medicaid.
Owner Proprietary corp (Beverly Enterprises).

Meadville Care Center
RD 3 Box 350, Meadville, PA 16335
(814) 337-4228
Licensure Skilled care. *Beds* SNF 150. *Certified* Medicaid; Medicare.
Owner Proprietary corp.

Meadville Hillside Home
535 Williamson Rd, Meadville, PA 16335
(814) 724-3117
Licensure Intermediate care. *Beds* ICF 17. *Certified* Medicaid.
Owner Nonprofit corp.

Wesbury United Methodist Community
31 N Park Ave, Meadville, PA 16335
(814) 724-8000
Admin Rev William L Brown. *Dir of Nursing* Cathi Hanson. *Medical Dir* Dr Spiro E Moutsos.
Licensure Skilled care; Intermediate care; Residential care; Alzheimer's care. *Beds* Swing beds SNF/ICF 210; Residential care 130. *Private Pay Patients* 60%. *Certified* Medicaid; Medicare.
Owner Nonprofit corp.
Admissions Requirements Minimum age 65; Medical examination; Physician's request.
Staff RNs 10 (ft), 10 (pt); LPNs 19 (ft), 11 (pt); Nurses' aides 47 (ft), 69 (pt); Physical therapists; Occupational therapists 1 (ft); Activities coordinators 3 (pt); Dietitians 1 (ft).
Affiliation United Methodist.

Facilities Dining room; Physical therapy room; Activities room; Chapel; Crafts room; Laundry room; Barber/Beauty shop; Library; Nature trail.
Activities Arts & crafts; Cards; Games; Reading groups; Prayer groups; Movies; Shopping trips; Dances/Social/Cultural gatherings; Intergenerational programs; Pet therapy; Music therapy.

Mechanicsburg

Bethany Village Retirement Center
325 Wesley Dr, Mechanicsburg, PA 17055
(717) 766-0279, 763-7617 FAX
Admin James R Wilkins NHA. *Dir of Nursing* Bonnie Robbins RN. *Medical Dir* Donald J Lowry MD.
Licensure Skilled care; Intermediate care; Personal care; Residential care; Independent living. *Beds* Swing beds SNF/ICF 69; Personal care 56; Residential care 94; Independent living 95. *Private Pay Patients* 92%. *Certified* Medicaid; Medicare.
Owner Nonprofit corp (United Methodist Homes for the Aging Inc).
Admissions Requirements Minimum age 62; Medical examination; Physician's request.
Staff Physicians 2 (pt); RNs 3 (ft), 12 (pt); LPNs 7 (ft), 5 (pt); Nurses' aides 24 (ft), 10 (pt); Physical therapists 1 (ft), 1 (pt); Recreational therapists 3 (ft), 1 (pt); Occupational therapists 1 (pt); Speech therapists 1 (pt); Activities coordinators 1 (ft); Dietitians 1 (pt); Ophthalmologists 1 (pt); Podiatrists 2 (pt); Audiologists 1 (pt).
Affiliation Methodist.
Facilities Dining room; Physical therapy room; Activities room; Chapel; Crafts room; Laundry room; Barber/Beauty shop; Library.
Activities Arts & crafts; Cards; Games; Reading groups; Prayer groups; Movies; Shopping trips; Dances/Social/Cultural gatherings; Intergenerational programs; Pet therapy.

Messiah Village
PO Box 2015, 100 Mount Allen Dr, Mechanicsburg, PA 17055-2015
(717) 697-4666, 790-8200 FAX
Admin George K Kibler. *Dir of Nursing* Mary Lou Kuntzweiler. *Medical Dir* Lawrence Zimmerman MD.
Licensure Skilled care; Intermediate care; Alzheimer's care; Sheltered care; Personal care; Independent living. *Beds* Swing beds SNF/ICF 100; Alzheimer's care 53; Sheltered care 100; Personal care 42; Independent living 44. *Private Pay Patients* 19%. *Certified* Medicaid; Medicare.
Owner Nonprofit corp.
Admissions Requirements Minimum age 65; Medical examination; Physician's request.
Staff RNs 12 (ft), 24 (pt); LPNs 6 (ft), 3 (pt); Nurses' aides 48 (ft), 50 (pt); Activities coordinators 6 (ft), 7 (pt).
Affiliation Brethren In Christ Church.
Facilities Dining room; Physical therapy room; Activities room; Chapel; Crafts room; Laundry room; Barber/Beauty shop; Library; Swimming pool; Bowling lanes; Putting Green.
Activities Arts & crafts; Games; Reading groups; Prayer groups; Movies; Shopping trips; Intergenerational programs; Pet therapy.

Renova Center for Special Services
4950 Wilson Ln, Mechanicsburg, PA 17055
(717) 697-7706
Admin Christina Papacostas NHA. *Dir of Nursing* Louise Deal RN. *Medical Dir* Jay J Cho MD.
Licensure Skilled care; Sub-acute care. *Beds* SNF 98. *Private Pay Patients* 40%. *Certified* Medicaid; Medicare.
Owner Proprietary corp.

Admissions Requirements Minimum age 12; Medical examination.
Staff RNs 10 (ft), 12 (pt); LPNs 15 (ft), 20 (pt); Nurses' aides 20 (ft), 10 (pt); Physical therapists 3 (ft); Recreational therapists 1 (ft); Occupational therapists 2 (ft); Speech therapists 2 (ft); Activities coordinators 1 (ft); Dietitians 1 (pt).
Facilities Dining room; Physical therapy room; Activities room; Crafts room; Laundry room; Barber/Beauty shop; Ventilator unit; Oncology unit; Head injury care; Coma stimulation.
Activities Arts & crafts; Cards; Games; Reading groups; Movies; Shopping trips; Dances/Social/Cultural gatherings; Intergenerational programs; Pet therapy.

Seidle Memorial Hospital
120 S Filbert St, Mechanicsburg, PA 17055
(717) 766-7691
Licensure Skilled care. *Beds* 35. *Certified* Medicaid; Medicare.
Owner Nonprofit corp.

Media

Bishop Nursing Home
318 S Orange St, Media, PA 19063
(215) 565-3880
Medical Dir Peter Binnion MD.
Licensure Skilled care. *Beds* SNF 164. *Certified* Medicaid.
Owner Proprietary corp.
Staff Physicians 1 (pt); RNs 4 (ft), 8 (pt); LPNs 5 (ft), 8 (pt); Nurses' aides 56 (ft), 8 (pt); Physical therapists 1 (pt); Occupational therapists 1 (pt); Activities coordinators 1 (ft); Dietitians 1 (pt).
Facilities Dining room; Physical therapy room; Activities room; Chapel; Crafts room; Laundry room; Barber/Beauty shop; Library.
Activities Arts & crafts; Cards; Games; Reading groups; Prayer groups; Movies; Shopping trips; Dances/Social/Cultural gatherings; Van trips; Bus trips; Special parties; Weekly Barbeque; Community speakers.

Care Center at Martins Run
11 Martins Run, Media, PA 19063
(215) 353-7660
Admin Joan H Rarick RN NHA. *Dir of Nursing* Elena DiPlacido RNC. *Medical Dir* Sarle Cohen MD.
Licensure Skilled care; Retirement. *Beds* SNF 60; Retirement 250. *Private Pay Patients* 10%. *Certified* Medicaid; Medicare.
Owner Nonprofit corp.
Staff Physicians 3 (ft); RNs 2 (ft), 6 (pt); LPNs 3 (ft), 3 (pt); Nurses' aides 17 (ft), 6 (pt); Physical therapists (contracted); Occupational therapists 1 (ft); Recreational therapists (contracted); Speech therapists (contracted); Activities coordinators 1 (ft); Dietitians (contracted); Podiatrists (contracted); Audiologists (contracted).
Affiliation Jewish.
Facilities Dining room; Physical therapy room; Activities room; Laundry room; Barber/Beauty shop; Kosher kitchen.
Activities Cards; Games; Movies; Discussion groups ; Religious services.

Manchester House Nursing Convalescent Center
411 Manchester Ave, Media, PA 19063
(215) 565-1800
Licensure Skilled care. *Beds* SNF 297. *Certified* Medicaid.
Owner Proprietary corp.

Riddle Memorial Hospital-Based Skilled Nursing Facility
1068 W Baltimore Pike, Media, PA 19083-5177
(215) 891-3207, 891-3592 FAX

Admin Robert J Santilli. *Dir of Nursing*
Kathleen Lumley RN. *Medical Dir* Ronald
Andersen MD.
Licensure Skilled care. *Beds* SNF 22. *Private
Pay Patients* 3%. *Certified* Medicare.
Owner Nonprofit corp.
Admissions Requirements Medical
examination; Physician's request.
Staff Physicians 1 (pt); RNs 3 (ft), 18 (pt);
LPNs 2 (ft), 4 (pt); Nurses' aides 4 (ft), 2
(pt); Physical therapists 1 (ft); Reality
therapists 1 (pt); Recreational therapists 1
(pt); Occupational therapists 1 (pt); Speech
therapists 1 (pt); Activities coordinators 1
(pt); Dietitians 1 (pt); Ophthalmologists 1
(pt); Podiatrists 1 (pt); Audiologists 1 (pt).
Facilities Dining room; Activities room;
Laundry room.
Activities Arts & crafts; Cards; Games;
Movies.

Workmen's Circle Home
3rd & Jackson Sts, Media, PA 19063
(215) 566-8703, 566-5768 FAX
Admin L Wayne Tarlecki. *Dir of Nursing*
Helen Lit. *Medical Dir* Dr Diwan.
Licensure Intermediate care; Personal care.
Beds ICF 32. *Certified* Medicaid.
Owner Nonprofit corp.
Admissions Requirements Medical
examination; Physician's request.
Staff Physicians; RNs; LPNs; Nurses' aides;
Physical therapists; Reality therapists;
Recreational therapists; Occupational
therapists; Speech therapists; Activities
coordinators; Dietitians; Ophthalmologists;
Podiatrists; Audiologists (consultant).
Affiliation Workmen's Circle.
Facilities Dining room; Physical therapy
room; Activities room; Crafts room; Laundry
room; Barber/Beauty shop; Library.
Activities Arts & crafts; Cards; Games;
Reading groups; Movies; Shopping trips; Pet
therapy.

Mercer

Countryside Convalescent Home Inc
RD 7 Box 7146, Mercer, PA 16137
(412) 662-5860
Admin Gerald Furma.
Medical Dir V A Ciambotti DO.
Licensure Skilled care. *Beds* SNF 48.
Owner Proprietary corp.
Admissions Requirements Medical
examination; Physician's request.
Staff RNs 4 (ft); LPNs 5 (ft); Nurses' aides 22
(ft); Physical therapists 1 (ft); Recreational
therapists 2 (ft); Activities coordinators 1
(ft); Dietitians 1 (ft); Podiatrists 1 (pt);
Dentists 1 (pt).
Facilities Dining room; Physical therapy
room; Activities room; Chapel; Crafts room;
Laundry room; Barber/Beauty shop.
Activities Arts & crafts; Cards; Games;
Reading groups; Prayer groups; Movies;
Dances/Social/Cultural gatherings.

Mercer County Living Center
RD 2, Box 2060, Mercer, PA 16137
(412) 662-5400
Admin D C Hogue.
Medical Dir Connie Eves.
Licensure Skilled care; Intermediate care. *Beds*
SNF 21; ICF 104. *Certified* Medicaid.
Owner Publicly owned.
Staff Physicians 3 (pt); RNs 6 (ft), 3 (pt);
LPNs 14 (ft), 1 (pt); Nurses' aides 41 (ft), 12
(pt); Physical therapists 2 (ft); Recreational
therapists 1 (ft); Activities coordinators 1
(ft); Dietitians 1 (pt); Ophthalmologists 1
(pt); Dentists 1 (pt).
Facilities Dining room; Physical therapy
room; Activities room; Chapel; Crafts room;
Barber/Beauty shop; Library.

Activities Arts & crafts; Cards; Games;
Reading groups; Prayer groups; Movies;
Dances/Social/Cultural gatherings.

Meyersdale

Meyersdale Manor
201 Hospital Dr, Meyersdale, PA 15552
(814) 634-5966
Licensure Skilled care. *Beds* SNF 99. *Certified*
Medicaid; Medicare.
Owner Proprietary corp (Beverly Enterprises).

Middletown

Frey Village
1020 N Union St, Middletown, PA 17057
(717) 944-0451
Admin H Dixon Hemma. *Dir of Nursing*
Cheri Kroboth RN BSN; Fay Henry RN,
Asst. *Medical Dir* Joseph P Leaser MD.
Licensure Skilled care; Intermediate care;
Retirement. *Beds* SNF 25; ICF 110;
Retirement 93. *Private Pay Patients* 55%.
Certified Medicaid; Medicare.
Owner Nonprofit corp (Tressler-Lutheran
Services).
Admissions Requirements Minimum age 65;
Medical examination.
Staff Physicians 1 (pt); RNs 6 (ft), 10 (pt);
LPNs 7 (ft), 6 (pt); Nurses' aides 30 (ft), 30
(pt); Physical therapists 1 (pt); Speech
therapists 1 (pt); Activities coordinators 1
(ft), 2 (pt); Dietitians 1 (pt);
Ophthalmologists 1 (pt); Podiatrists 2 (pt);
Audiologists 1 (pt); Dentists 1 (pt).
Affiliation Lutheran.
Facilities Dining room; Physical therapy
room; Activities room; Chapel; Crafts room;
Laundry room; Barber/Beauty shop; Library;
Guest house.
Activities Arts & crafts; Cards; Games;
Reading groups; Prayer groups; Movies;
Shopping trips; Dances/Social/Cultural
gatherings; Intergenerational programs.

Odd Fellows Home of Pennsylvania
999 W Harrisburg Pike, Middletown, PA
17057
(717) 944-3351
Licensure Skilled care; Intermediate care. *Beds*
SNF 51; ICF 51. *Certified* Medicaid;
Medicare.
Owner Nonprofit corp.
Affiliation Independent Order of Odd Fellows
& Rebekahs.
Facilities Dining room; Physical therapy
room; Activities room; Chapel; Crafts room;
Laundry room; Barber/Beauty shop; Library.
Activities Arts & crafts; Cards; Games;
Reading groups; Prayer groups; Movies;
Shopping trips; Dances/Social/Cultural
gatherings.

Mifflin

Locust Grove Retirement Village
Box 7, HCR 67, Mifflin, PA 17058
(717) 436-8921
Admin Homer P Smith. *Dir of Nursing* Jane
Yohn RN. *Medical Dir* L G Guiser MD.
Licensure Skilled care; Intermediate care;
Retirement. *Beds* SNF 14; ICF 65. *Certified*
Medicaid; Medicare.
Owner Nonprofit corp (Tressler-Lutheran
Services Assn).
Admissions Requirements Minimum age 65.
Staff RNs; LPNs; Nurses' aides; Recreational
therapists; Activities coordinators; Dietitians;
Ophthalmologists.
Facilities Dining room; Physical therapy
room; Activities room; Chapel; Crafts room;
Laundry room; Barber/Beauty shop.
Activities Arts & crafts; Cards; Games;
Reading groups; Prayer groups; Movies.

Mifflintown

Brookline Manor Convalescent Rest Home
Rte 1 Box 63, Mifflintown, PA 17059
(717) 436-2178
Licensure Skilled care; Intermediate care. *Beds*
85. *Certified* Medicaid; Medicare.
Owner Proprietary corp.

Milford

Head Injury Recovery Center at Hillcrest
404 E Harford St, Milford, PA 18337
(717) 296-9261
Licensure Skilled care. *Beds* SNF 68. *Certified*
Medicaid; Medicare.
Owner Proprietary corp.

Milford Valley Convalescent Home Inc
Star Rte Box 379, Milford, PA 18337
(717) 491-4121
Admin Constance A Pizzoli. *Dir of Nursing*
Yvonne Krieger. *Medical Dir* Dr Harrison
Murray.
Licensure Skilled care. *Beds* SNF 80. *Private
Pay Patients* 60%. *Certified* Medicaid;
Medicare.
Owner Proprietary corp (North American
Medical Centers Inc).
Staff RNs 6 (ft), 5 (pt); LPNs 2 (ft), 2 (pt);
Nurses' aides 19 (ft), 12 (pt); Physical
therapists; Activities coordinators 1 (ft), 1
(pt); Dietitians.
Facilities Dining room; Physical therapy
room; Activities room; Crafts room; Laundry
room; Barber/Beauty shop.
Activities Arts & crafts; Cards; Games;
Reading groups; Prayer groups; Movies;
Dances/Social/Cultural gatherings;
Intergenerational programs; Pet therapy.

Millersburg

Susquehanna Lutheran Village
990 Medical Rd, Millersburg, PA 17061
(717) 692-4751
Admin Lori A Gerhard. *Dir of Nursing* Diann
Snyder. *Medical Dir* Robert A Ettlinger MD.
Licensure Skilled care; Intermediate care;
Retirement; Alzheimer's care. *Beds* SNF 47;
ICF 158; Retirement apts. *Private Pay
Patients* 40%. *Certified* Medicaid; Medicare.
Owner Nonprofit corp (Tressler-Lutheran
Services).
Staff RNs 9 (ft), 9 (pt); LPNs 13 (ft), 3 (pt);
Nurses' aides 40 (ft), 39 (pt); Activities
coordinators 1 (ft).
Affiliation Lutheran.
Facilities Dining room; Physical therapy
room; Activities room; Chapel; Crafts room;
Laundry room; Barber/Beauty shop.
Activities Reading groups; Prayer groups;
Movies; Shopping trips; Dances/Social/
Cultural gatherings; Intergenerational
programs; Pet therapy.

Millmont

Rolling Hills Manor
Rte 1, Millmont, PA 17845
(717) 922-3351
Medical Dir Dr Charles Fasano.
Licensure Skilled care. *Beds* SNF 60. *Certified*
Medicaid; Medicare.
Owner Proprietary corp.
Admissions Requirements Medical
examination.
Staff RNs 1 (ft), 1 (pt); LPNs 4 (ft), 3 (pt);
Nurses' aides 9 (ft), 13 (pt); Physical
therapists 1 (pt); Recreational therapists 1
(ft); Dietitians 1 (pt).
Facilities Dining room; Activities room;
Chapel; Crafts room; Laundry room.
Activities Arts & crafts; Games; Reading
groups; Prayer groups; Movies; Shopping
trips.

Millville

Boone Nursing Home
Rte 1 Box 340, Eyers Grove, Millville, PA
17846
(717) 458-6751
Medical Dir Dr Clark.
Licensure Intermediate care. *Beds* ICF 60.
Certified Medicaid.
Owner Proprietary corp.
Admissions Requirements Minimum age 18;
Medical examination; Physician's request.
Staff Physicians 1 (pt); RNs 3 (ft), 2 (pt);
LPNs 2 (ft), 2 (pt); Nurses' aides 18 (ft), 8
(pt); Physical therapists 1 (pt); Occupational
therapists 1 (pt); Speech therapists 1 (pt);
Activities coordinators 1 (ft); Dietitians 1
(pt); Podiatrists 1 (pt); Dentists 1 (pt).

Millville Health Center
Box 320, State St, Millville, PA 17846
(717) 458-5566
Licensure Skilled care. *Beds* SNF 112.
Certified Medicaid.
Owner Proprietary corp.

Milton

Kramm Healthcare—Broadway
560 Broadway, Milton, PA 17847
(717) 742-7651
Admin Shirley Stamm. *Dir of Nursing* Kathy
Felmey. *Medical Dir* Stephen Wood.
Licensure Intermediate care. *Beds* ICF 40.
Private Pay Patients 10%. *Certified*
Medicaid.
Owner Privately owned.
Admissions Requirements Medical
examination; Physician's request.
Staff Physicians 9 (pt); RNs 1 (ft); LPNs 3
(ft), 2 (pt); Nurses' aides 8 (ft), 10 (pt);
Physical therapists 1 (pt); Speech therapists
1 (pt); Activities coordinators 1 (ft);
Dietitians 1 (pt); Ophthalmologists 1 (pt);
Podiatrists 1 (pt).
Facilities Dining room; Physical therapy
room; Activities room; Laundry room;
Barber/Beauty shop.
Activities Arts & crafts; Cards; Games;
Reading groups; Prayer groups; Movies;
Dances/Social/Cultural gatherings; Pet
therapy.

Kramm Healthcare Center Inc
743 Mahoning St, Milton, PA 17847
(717) 742-2681
Admin Randall D Kramm.
Medical Dir Dr Robert Yannaccone.
Licensure Skilled care; Intermediate care. *Beds*
SNF 61; ICF 59. *Certified* Medicaid;
Medicare.
Owner Proprietary corp.
Admissions Requirements Medical
examination.
Staff Physicians 10 (pt); RNs 3 (ft), 4 (pt);
LPNs 3 (ft), 4 (pt); Nurses' aides 20 (ft), 20
(pt); Physical therapists 1 (pt); Recreational
therapists 1 (ft); Activities coordinators 1
(ft); Dietitians 1 (pt); Podiatrists 1 (pt);
Dentists 1 (pt).
Facilities Dining room; Physical therapy
room; Activities room; Crafts room; Laundry
room; Barber/Beauty shop.
Activities Arts & crafts; Cards; Games;
Reading groups; Prayer groups; Movies;
Shopping trips; Dances/Social/Cultural
gatherings.

Monongahela

Haven Crest Inc
1277 Country Club Rd, Monongahela, PA
15063
(412) 258-3000
Licensure Skilled care. *Beds* SNF 48. *Certified*
Medicare.
Owner Proprietary corp.

Monroeville

Beverly Manor of Monroeville
4142 Monroeville Blvd, Monroeville, PA
15146
(412) 856-7570
Licensure Skilled care. *Beds* SNF 120.
Certified Medicaid; Medicare.
Owner Proprietary corp (Beverly Enterprises).

Woodhaven Care Center
2400 McGinley Rd, Monroeville, PA 15146
(412) 856-4770
Licensure Skilled care. *Beds* SNF. *Certified*
Medicaid; Medicare.
Owner Proprietary corp (Meritcare).

Mont Clare

Janney House
Rte 29, River Crest Center, Mont Clare, PA
19453
(215) 935-1581
Licensure Intermediate care for mentally
retarded. *Beds* 6. *Certified* Medicaid.
Owner Nonprofit corp.

Ye Olde House
Rte 29, River Crest Center, Mont Clare, PA
19453
(215) 935-1581
Licensure Intermediate care for mentally
retarded. *Beds* 8. *Certified* Medicaid.
Owner Nonprofit corp.

Montoursville

Lysock View Nursing Home
RD 2 Box 26, Montoursville, PA 17754-9618
(717) 433-3161, 433-3882 FAX
Admin Richard Greene. *Dir of Nursing*
Roberta McClintock. *Medical Dir* Dr Edith
Murphy.
Licensure Skilled care; Intermediate care. *Beds*
SNF 44; ICF 164. *Private Pay Patients* 6%.
Certified Medicaid; Medicare.
Owner Publicly owned.
Admissions Requirements Minimum age 15;
Medical examination.
Staff Physicians 1 (ft); RNs 8 (ft), 1 (pt);
LPNs 26 (ft), 7 (pt); Nurses' aides 57 (ft), 30
(pt); Physical therapists 1 (pt); Reality
therapists 1 (ft); Recreational therapists 1
(ft); Occupational therapists 1 (pt); Speech
therapists 1 (pt); Activities coordinators 1
(ft); Dietitians 1 (pt); Podiatrists 3 (pt);
Audiologists 1 (pt).
Facilities Dining room; Physical therapy
room; Activities room; Chapel; Crafts room;
Laundry room; Barber/Beauty shop.
Activities Arts & crafts; Cards; Games;
Reading groups; Prayer groups; Movies;
Shopping trips; Dances/Social/Cultural
gatherings; Pet therapy.

Sycamore Manor Health Center
1445 Sycamore Rd, Montoursville, PA 17754
(717) 326-2037, 326-7378 FAX
Admin LeAnn J Rock. *Dir of Nursing* Carol A
Kopp RN. *Medical Dir* Dr Nancy Story.
Licensure Skilled care; Intermediate care. *Beds*
SNF 40; ICF 83. *Private Pay Patients* 50%.
Certified Medicaid; Medicare.
Owner Nonprofit corp.
Staff RNs 7 (ft), 5 (pt); LPNs 9 (ft), 4 (pt);
Nurses' aides 35 (ft), 13 (pt); Physical
therapists 1 (ft), 1 (pt); Occupational
therapists 2 (pt); Speech therapists 1 (pt);
Activities coordinators 1 (ft); Dietitians 1
(pt); Podiatrists 1 (pt); Beauticians 1 (ft).
Affiliation Presbyterian.
Facilities Dining room; Physical therapy
room; Activities room; Chapel; Laundry
room; Barber/Beauty shop; Library; Mini-
bus.

Activities Arts & crafts; Games; Prayer groups;
Movies; Shopping trips; Dances/Social/
Cultural gatherings; Intergenerational
programs; Pet therapy; Exercises.

Montrose

Medical Arts Nursing Center Inc
Park St, Montrose, PA 18801
(717) 278-3836
Admin Nancy Landes RN. *Dir of Nursing*
Janet Daniels RN. *Medical Dir* Paul B Kerr
MD.
Licensure Skilled care. *Beds* SNF 63. *Certified*
Medicaid; Medicare.
Owner Proprietary corp.
Admissions Requirements Medical
examination; Physician's request.
Staff Physicians 5 (ft); RNs 6 (ft), 7 (pt);
LPNs 2 (ft), 2 (pt); Nurses' aides 16 (ft), 16
(pt); Physical therapists 1 (pt); Recreational
therapists 1 (ft), 1 (pt); Speech therapists 1
(pt); Activities coordinators 1 (pt); Dietitians
1 (pt); Ophthalmologists 1 (pt); Dentists 1
(pt).
Facilities Dining room; Physical therapy
room; Activities room; Chapel; Crafts room;
Laundry room; Barber/Beauty shop.
Activities Arts & crafts; Cards; Games; Prayer
groups; Movies; Dances/Social/Cultural
gatherings.

Mount Carmel

Mt Carmel Nursing Center
PO Box 427, 700 W 3rd St, Mount Carmel,
PA 17851
(717) 339-2501, 339-0430 FAX
Admin Deanna H Gessner. *Dir of Nursing*
Susan Reed. *Medical Dir* Dennis Mychak.
Licensure Skilled care; Intermediate care. *Beds*
SNF 60; ICF 61. *Private Pay Patients* 30%.
Certified Medicaid; Medicare.
Owner Proprietary corp.
Admissions Requirements Medical
examination.
Staff RNs 8 (pt); LPNs 15 (pt); Physical
therapists 1 (pt); Occupational therapists 1
(pt); Speech therapists 1 (pt); Activities
coordinators 1 (ft); Dietitians.
Facilities Dining room; Physical therapy
room; Activities room; Laundry room;
Barber/Beauty shop.
Activities Arts & crafts; Cards; Games; Prayer
groups; Movies; Shopping trips; Dances/
Social/Cultural gatherings.

Mount Penn

Beverly Manor of Mt Penn
RD 3 Box 3559, Mount Penn, PA 19508
(215) 779-8522
Licensure Skilled care. *Beds* SNF 124.
Certified Medicaid; Medicare.
Owner Proprietary corp (Beverly Enterprises).

Mount Pleasant

Harmon House
601 S Church St, Mount Pleasant, PA 15666
(412) 547-1890, 547-1893 FAX
Admin Joseph E Huchko. *Dir of Nursing*
Doralee Geyer RN. *Medical Dir* Richard
Lynn MD.
Licensure Skilled care; Intermediate care;
Personal care. *Beds* SNF 45; ICF 29;
Personal care 104. *Private Pay Patients* 54%.
Certified Medicare.
Owner Proprietary corp (Grane Healthcare).
Admissions Requirements Medical
examination; Physician's request.
Staff RNs 4 (ft), 7 (pt); LPNs 6 (ft), 4 (pt);
Nurses' aides 14 (ft), 22 (pt); Physical
therapists 1 (ft); Occupational therapists 1
(ft); Speech therapists 2 (pt); Activities

coordinators 1 (ft); Dietitians 1 (ft); Occupational therapy assistants 2 (pt); Activities aides 3 (pt).
Facilities Dining room; Physical therapy room; Laundry room; Barber/Beauty shop; Lounges.
Activities Arts & crafts; Cards; Games; Reading groups; Prayer groups; Movies; Shopping trips; Dances/Social/Cultural gatherings; Pet therapy; Exercises; Parties.

Mountain Top

Davis Nursing Home Inc
185 S Mountain Blvd, Mountain Top, PA 18707
(717) 474-6377
Medical Dir Dr Basil Rudusky.
Licensure Skilled care. *Beds* SNF 79. *Certified* Medicaid; Medicare.
Owner Proprietary corp.
Staff Physicians; RNs 11 (ft); LPNs 8 (ft); Nurses' aides 40 (ft), 15 (pt); Physical therapists; Reality therapists 1 (ft), 1 (pt); Recreational therapists 1 (pt); Occupational therapists 1 (pt); Speech therapists 1 (pt); Activities coordinators 1 (ft), 1 (pt); Dietitians 1 (pt); Ophthalmologists 1 (pt); Podiatrists 1 (ft); Audiologists 1 (pt); Dentists 1 (pt).
Facilities Dining room; Physical therapy room; Activities room; Crafts room; Laundry room; Barber/Beauty shop.
Activities Arts & crafts; Cards; Games; Prayer groups; Shopping trips; Dances/Social/Cultural gatherings.

Smith Nursing & Convalescent Home Inc
453 Main Rd, Mountain Top, PA 18707
(717) 868-3664
Licensure Skilled care. *Beds* SNF 16. *Certified* Medicaid; Medicare.
Owner Proprietary corp.

Muncy

Muncy Valley Hospital—Skilled Nursing Facility
215 E Water St, Muncy, PA 17756
(717) 546-8282
Admin Sybil R Harriman.
Medical Dir Howard Weaner Jr MD.
Licensure Skilled care. *Beds* SNF 59. *Certified* Medicaid; Medicare.
Owner Nonprofit corp.
Admissions Requirements Medical examination; Physician's request.
Staff RNs 3 (ft); LPNs 4 (ft), 6 (pt); Nurses' aides 15 (ft), 6 (pt); Speech therapists; Activities coordinators; Dietitians; Ophthalmologists; Podiatrists; Dentists.
Facilities Dining room; Physical therapy room; Activities room; Crafts room; Laundry room; Barber/Beauty shop.
Activities Arts & crafts; Cards; Games; Reading groups; Prayer groups; Movies; Shopping trips; Dances/Social/Cultural gatherings.

Munhall

Elder Crest Inc
2600 W Run Rd, Munhall, PA 15120
(412) 462-8002
Admin Clara Radesausz.
Medical Dir John C Wain MD.
Licensure Skilled care. *Beds* SNF 48. *Certified* Medicare.
Owner Proprietary corp.
Admissions Requirements Minimum age 17.
Staff Physicians 1 (pt); RNs 2 (ft), 6 (pt); Nurses' aides 12 (ft), 13 (pt); Physical therapists 1 (pt); Activities coordinators 1 (ft); Dietitians 1 (pt); Ophthalmologists 1 (pt); Podiatrists 1 (pt); Dentists 1 (pt).

Facilities Dining room; Physical therapy room; Activities room; Crafts room; Laundry room; Barber/Beauty shop.
Activities Arts & crafts; Cards; Games; Reading groups; Dances/Social/Cultural gatherings.

Murraysville

Murray Manor Convalescent Center
3300 Logan Ferry Rd, Murraysville, PA 15668
(412) 325-1500
Admin Daniel Landis.
Medical Dir Walter Beam MD.
Licensure Skilled care; Intermediate care. *Beds* SNF 35; ICF 88. *Certified* Medicaid; Medicare.
Owner Proprietary corp (Beverly Enterprises).
Admissions Requirements Medical examination.
Staff RNs 8 (ft), 4 (pt) 13C 5 (ft), 3 (pt); Nurses' aides 25 (ft), 20 (pt); Physical therapists 1 (pt); Occupational therapists 1 (pt); Speech therapists 1 (pt); Activities coordinators 1 (ft), 1 (pt); Dietitians 1 (ft); Ophthalmologists 1 (pt); Dentists 1 (pt).
Facilities Dining room; Physical therapy room; Activities room; Laundry room; Barber/Beauty shop; Library.
Activities Arts & crafts; Cards; Games; Reading groups; Prayer groups; Movies; Shopping trips; Dances/Social/Cultural gatherings; Stroke group; Adopt-a-grandparent program.

Myerstown

Evangelical Congregational Church Retirement Village
S Railroad St & W Park Ave, Myerstown, PA 17067
(717) 866-6541
Admin Franklin H Schock. *Dir of Nursing* Carol Johnston. *Medical Dir* Dr Jose Sayson.
Licensure Skilled care; Alzheimer's care. *Beds* SNF 152. *Certified* Medicaid; Medicare.
Owner Nonprofit corp.
Admissions Requirements Minimum age 65 for residential; Medical examination.
Staff RNs 15 (ft); LPNs 13 (ft), 5 (pt); Nurses' aides 40 (ft), 40 (pt); Physical therapists 1 (ft); Recreational therapists 3 (ft), 1 (pt); Occupational therapists 1 (pt); Speech therapists 1 (pt); Activities coordinators 1 (ft); Dietitians 1 (pt); Ophthalmologists 1 (pt); Podiatrists 1 (pt); Dentists 1 (pt).
Affiliation Congregational.
Facilities Dining room; Physical therapy room; Activities room; Chapel; Crafts room; Laundry room; Barber/Beauty shop; Library.
Activities Arts & crafts; Cards; Games; Reading groups; Prayer groups; Movies; Shopping trips; Dances/Social/Cultural gatherings.

Nanticoke

Birchwood Nursing Center Limited
395 E Middle Rd, Nanticoke, PA 18634
(717) 735-2973
Admin Michael P Kelly.
Medical Dir Michael Kotch MD.
Licensure Skilled care; Intermediate care; Alzheimer's care. *Beds* SNF 60; ICF 61. *Certified* Medicaid; Medicare.
Owner Proprietary corp.
Staff Physicians 3 (pt); RNs 5 (ft), 3 (pt); LPNs 7 (ft), 4 (pt); Nurses' aides 25 (ft), 20 (pt); Physical therapists 1 (pt); Occupational therapists 2 (pt); Activities coordinators 1 (ft), 2 (pt); Dietitians 1 (pt).
Languages Polish.

Facilities Dining room; Physical therapy room; Activities room; Crafts room; Laundry room; Barber/Beauty shop; Smoking room; Occupational therapy room.
Activities Arts & crafts; Cards; Games; Reading groups; Prayer groups; Movies; Shopping trips; Dances/Social/Cultural gatherings; Baking; Photography; Music.

Mercy Health Care Center
Newport St, Nanticoke, PA 18634
(717) 735-7300
Admin Robert D Williams. *Dir of Nursing* Donald McHale. *Medical Dir* Dr John Kennedy.
Licensure Skilled care. *Beds* SNF 100. *Certified* Medicaid; Medicare.
Owner Nonprofit corp.
Staff Physicians 5 (pt); RNs 7 (ft), 3 (pt); LPNs 14 (ft), 1 (pt); Nurses' aides 23 (ft), 19 (pt); Physical therapists 1 (pt); Recreational therapists 1 (ft); Occupational therapists 1 (ft), 1 (pt); Speech therapists 1 (pt); Activities coordinators 1 (ft); Dietitians 1 (pt); Ophthalmologists 1 (pt); Podiatrists 1 (pt); Dentists 1 (pt).
Affiliation Roman Catholic.
Facilities Dining room; Physical therapy room; Activities room; Chapel; Laundry room; Library.
Activities Arts & crafts; Cards; Games; Prayer groups; Movies; Dances/Social/Cultural gatherings; Musical events.

Narvon

Zerbe Sisters Nursing Center Inc
RD 1 Box 209, Hammertown Rd, Narvon, PA 17557
(215) 445-4551
Admin Helen L Zerbe. *Dir of Nursing* Nancy Groff RN. *Medical Dir* Richard Bacon MD.
Licensure Skilled care; Intermediate care. *Beds* 81. *Certified* Medicaid; Medicare.
Owner Proprietary corp.
Admissions Requirements Medical examination; Financial statement.
Staff Physicians 4 (pt); RNs 5 (ft), 5 (pt); LPNs 3 (ft), 1 (pt); Nurses' aides 24 (ft), 20 (pt); Occupational therapists 1 (pt); Speech therapists 1 (pt); Activities coordinators 1 (ft); Dietitians 1 (pt); Ophthalmologists 1 (pt).
Languages Pennsylvania Dutch.
Facilities Dining room; Physical therapy room; Activities room; Crafts room; Laundry room; Barber/Beauty shop; Recreation room.
Activities Arts & crafts; Cards; Games; Reading groups; Prayer groups; Movies; Dances/Social/Cultural gatherings; Recreational day trips.

Nazareth

County of Northampton—Gracedale
Gracedale Ave, Nazareth, PA 18064
(215) 759-3200
Licensure Skilled care. *Beds* SNF 791. *Certified* Medicaid; Medicare.
Owner Publicly owned.

Moravian Hall Square
175 W North St, Nazareth, PA 18064
(215) 746-1000
Admin Susan E Cooper. *Dir of Nursing* Alice E Snyder RN BS. *Medical Dir* Dr Ralph Shields.
Licensure Skilled care; Intermediate care; Personal care; Apartment living; Alzheimer's care. *Beds* SNF 28; ICF 33; Personal care 68; Apartment living 219. *Private Pay Patients* 95%. *Certified* Medicaid; Medicare.
Owner Nonprofit organization/foundation.
Admissions Requirements Minimum age 62; Medical examination.

Staff Physicians 1 (pt); RNs 6 (ft), 2 (pt); LPNs 9 (ft), 1 (pt); Nurses' aides 23 (ft), 17 (pt); Physical therapists (consultant); Reality therapists (consultant); Recreational therapists (consultant); Occupational therapists (consultant); Speech therapists (consultant); Activities coordinators 2 (ft), 1 (pt); Dietitians 1 (ft); Ophthalmologists (consultant); Podiatrists (consultant); Audiologists (consultant).
Affiliation Moravian.
Facilities Dining room; Physical therapy room; Activities room; Laundry room; Barber/Beauty shop; Crafts room (apartments); Library (apartments).
Activities Arts & crafts; Cards; Games; Reading groups; Prayer groups; Movies; Shopping trips; Dances/Social/Cultural gatherings; Intergenerational programs; Pet therapy.

Northhampton County Home—Gracedale
Gracedale Avenue, Nazareth, PA 18064-9213
(215) 759-3200
Admin Harold W Russell Jr. *Dir of Nursing* Marjorie M Milanak. *Medical Dir* Wesley R Stancombe MD.
Licensure Skilled care; Intermediate care. *Beds* SNF 200; ICF 591. *Certified* Medicaid; Medicare.
Owner Nonprofit corp.
Staff Physicians 1 (ft), 3 (pt); RNs 53 (ft), 50 (pt); LPNs 69 (ft), 41 (pt); Nurses' aides 154 (ft), 189 (pt); Physical therapists 1 (ft); Recreational therapists 7 (ft); Occupational therapists 3 (ft); Speech therapists 1 (ft); Activities coordinators 1 (ft); Dietitians 1 (ft); Ophthalmologists 1 (ft); Podiatrists 1 (ft); Audiologists 1 (ft); Dentists 1 (ft).
Facilities Dining room; Physical therapy room; Activities room; Chapel; Crafts room; Laundry room; Barber/Beauty shop; Library.
Activities Arts & crafts; Cards; Games; Reading groups; Prayer groups; Movies; Shopping trips; Dances/Social/Cultural gatherings.

New Bloomfield

Perry Village Nursing Home
Rte 2 Box 68, New Bloomfield, PA 17068
(717) 582-4346
Admin Willis A Smith Jr.
Medical Dir Dr H Robert Gasull.
Licensure Skilled care; Intermediate care; Alzheimer's care. *Beds* SNF 13; ICF 110. *Certified* Medicaid; Medicare.
Owner Nonprofit corp (Tressler-Lutheran Services).
Admissions Requirements Minimum age 65.
Staff Physicians 3 (pt); RNs 3 (ft), 10 (pt); LPNs 4 (ft), 10 (pt); Nurses' aides 22 (ft), 35 (pt); Physical therapists 1 (pt); Speech therapists 1 (pt); Activities coordinators 1 (ft), 1 (pt); Dietitians 1 (pt); Ophthalmologists 1 (pt); Podiatrists 1 (pt); Dentists 1 (pt).
Affiliation Lutheran.
Facilities Dining room; Physical therapy room; Activities room; Chapel; Crafts room; Laundry room; Barber/Beauty shop.
Activities Arts & crafts; Cards; Games; Reading groups; Prayer groups; Movies; Shopping trips; Dances/Social/Cultural gatherings; Bus tours.

New Brighton

McGuire Memorial Home for Retired Children
2119 Mercer Rd, New Brighton, PA 15066
(412) 843-3400
Licensure Intermediate care for mentally retarded. *Beds* 99. *Certified* Medicaid.
Owner Nonprofit corp.

New Castle

Almira Home
1001 E Washington St, New Castle, PA 16101
(412) 652-4131
Licensure Intermediate care. *Beds* ICF 17.
Owner Nonprofit corp.

Golden Hill Nursing Home Inc
520 Friendship St, New Castle, PA 16101
(412) 654-7791
Licensure Skilled care. *Beds* SNF 204. *Certified* Medicaid; Medicare.
Owner Proprietary corp.

Haven Convalescent Home Inc
725 Paul St, New Castle, PA 16101
(412) 654-8833
Admin Charles Tanner. *Dir of Nursing* Jean Dzemyan RN. *Medical Dir* M Abul Ela MD.
Licensure Intermediate care; Alzheimer's care. *Beds* ICF 91. *Certified* Medicaid.
Owner Proprietary corp.
Admissions Requirements Minimum age 16; Medical examination; Physician's request.
Staff Physicians; RNs; LPNs; Nurses' aides; Physical therapists; Reality therapists; Speech therapists; Activities coordinators; Ophthalmologists; Dentists.
Languages Italian.
Facilities Dining room; Physical therapy room; Activities room; Chapel; Crafts room; Laundry room; Barber/Beauty shop.
Activities Arts & crafts; Cards; Games; Reading groups; Prayer groups; Movies; Shopping trips; Dances/Social/Cultural gatherings.

Highland Hall Care Center
239 W Pittsburgh Rd, New Castle, PA 16101
(412) 658-4781
Admin Linda M Plowey NHA. *Dir of Nursing* Rita June Hainer RN. *Medical Dir* Dr Raymond Seniow.
Licensure Intermediate care. *Beds* ICF 83. *Certified* Medicaid; Medicare.
Owner Proprietary corp.
Admissions Requirements Medical examination.
Staff RNs 3 (ft); LPNs 6 (ft), 1 (pt); Nurses' aides 24 (ft), 3 (pt); Recreational therapists 1 (ft); Activities coordinators 1 (ft); Dietitians 1 (ft).
Facilities Dining room; Activities room; Crafts room; Laundry room; TV lounge.
Activities Arts & crafts; Cards; Games; Reading groups; Movies; Shopping trips; Dances/Social/Cultural gatherings; Special theme days.

Hill View Manor
2801 Ellwood Rd, New Castle, PA 16101
(412) 658-1521
Admin Mary Lou Corsi. *Dir of Nursing* Mildred Pearsall. *Medical Dir* Mohammad Ali MD.
Licensure Intermediate care. *Beds* ICF 136. *Private Pay Patients* 2%. *Certified* Medicaid.
Owner Publicly owned.
Admissions Requirements Medical examination.
Staff Physicians 1 (pt); RNs 5 (ft), 2 (pt); LPNs 12 (ft); Nurses' aides 31 (ft), 7 (pt); Recreational therapists 2 (ft); Activities coordinators 1 (ft); Dietitians 1 (pt); Activities aides 2 (ft).
Facilities Dining room; Activities room; Chapel; Crafts room; Laundry room; Barber/Beauty shop; Library.
Activities Arts & crafts; Cards; Games; Reading groups; Prayer groups; Movies; Shopping trips; Dances/Social/Cultural gatherings; Adopt-a-grandparent.

Indian Creek Nursing Center
222 W Edison Ave, New Castle, PA 16101
(412) 652-6340

Licensure Skilled care; Intermediate care. *Beds* SNF 61; ICF 59. *Certified* Medicaid; Medicare.
Owner Proprietary corp (Health Care Management).

Jack Rees Nursing & Rehabilitation Center
715 Harbor St, New Castle, PA 16101
(412) 652-3863
Medical Dir Dr Ross Houston.
Licensure Skilled care; Intermediate care. *Beds* SNF 51; ICF 33. *Certified* Medicaid; Medicare.
Owner Proprietary corp.
Admissions Requirements Minimum age 18.
Staff Physicians 2 (pt); RNs 3 (ft), 3 (pt); LPNs 3 (ft), 4 (pt); Physical therapists 2 (pt); Recreational therapists 1 (pt); Speech therapists 1 (pt); Activities coordinators 1 (ft); Dietitians 1 (ft); Podiatrists 1 (pt).
Facilities Dining room; Physical therapy room; Activities room; Crafts room; Laundry room; Barber/Beauty shop; Library.
Activities Arts & crafts; Cards; Games; Reading groups; Prayer groups; Movies; Shopping trips; Dances/Social/Cultural gatherings.

Silver Oaks Nursing Center
715 Harbor St, New Castle, PA 16101
(412) 652-3863
Licensure Skilled care. *Beds* SNF 84. *Certified* Medicaid; Medicare.
Owner Proprietary corp.

New Galilee

St Francis Hospital of New Castle Skilled Nursing Center
RD 1, New Galilee, PA 16101
(412) 658-3511
Admin Mary Lou Mackievich. *Dir of Nursing* Elizabeth Richards. *Medical Dir* B Y Linganna MD.
Licensure Skilled care. *Beds* SNF 45. *Private Pay Patients* 20%. *Certified* Medicaid; Medicare.
Owner Nonprofit corp.
Admissions Requirements Medical examination; Physician's request.
Staff Physicians; RNs 5 (ft); LPNs 4 (ft); Nurses' aides 15 (ft); Physical therapists (contracted); Reality therapists; Occupational therapists; Speech therapists; Activities coordinators 1 (ft); Dietitians (contracted); Ophthalmologists; Podiatrists; Audiologists.
Facilities Dining room; Physical therapy room; Activities room; Chapel; Crafts room; Laundry room.
Activities Arts & crafts; Cards; Games; Reading groups; Prayer groups; Movies; Intergenerational programs; Pet therapy.

New Oxford

Brethren Home
PO Box 128, 2990 Carlisle Pike, New Oxford, PA 17350
(717) 624-2161
Admin Carl E Herr, Pres. *Dir of Nursing* Ruth R Carpenter RN. *Medical Dir* David E Zickafoose MD.
Licensure Skilled care; Intermediate care; Personal care; Retirement. *Beds* SNF 83; ICF 207; Personal care 111; Retirement 200-300. *Private Pay Patients* 65%. *Certified* Medicaid; Medicare.
Owner Nonprofit organization/foundation.
Admissions Requirements Minimum age 65; Medical examination.
Staff Physicians 1 (ft); RNs 13 (ft), 5 (pt); LPNs 28 (ft), 21 (pt); Nurses' aides 68 (ft), 56 (pt); Physical therapists 1 (ft); Activities coordinators.
Affiliation Church of the Brethren.

Facilities Dining room; Physical therapy room; Activities room; Chapel; Crafts room; Laundry room; Barber/Beauty shop; Library; Meeting house; Greenhouse.
Activities Arts & crafts; Cards; Games; Reading groups; Prayer groups; Movies; Shopping trips; Dances/Social/Cultural gatherings.

New Wilmington

Overlook Medical Clinic
New Castle Rd, New Wilmington, PA 16142
(412) 946-3511
Licensure Skilled care. Beds SNF 115. Certified Medicaid; Medicare.
Owner Proprietary corp.

Shenango Presbyterian Home
238 S Market St, New Wilmington, PA 16142
(412) 946-3516
Admin Celeste Golonski. Dir of Nursing Alice Sopher. Medical Dir Timothy Heilmann.
Licensure Intermediate care; Personal care. Beds ICF 25; Personal care 41.
Owner Nonprofit corp.
Admissions Requirements Minimum age 65; Medical examination.
Staff RNs 1 (ft), 3 (pt); LPNs 1 (ft), 4 (pt); Nurses' aides 7 (ft), 9 (pt); Recreational therapists 1 (ft); Dietitians 1 (pt).
Affiliation Presbyterian.
Facilities Dining room; Activities room; Chapel; Crafts room; Laundry room; Barber/Beauty shop; Library; Lounges.
Activities Arts & crafts; Cards; Games; Reading groups; Prayer groups; Movies; Shopping trips; Dances/Social/Cultural gatherings; Intergenerational programs; Pet therapy; Entertainment by college & churches; Volunteer program.

Newtown

Chandler Hall
Barclay St & Buck Rd, Newtown, PA 18940
(215) 860-4000
Licensure Skilled care. Beds SNF 57. Certified Medicaid; Medicare.
Owner Nonprofit corp.

Pennswood Village
Rte 413, Newtown, PA 18940
(215) 968-9110
Admin Michael Levengood. Dir of Nursing Patricia Smith. Medical Dir James C Alden MD.
Licensure Skilled care; Independent living. Beds SNF 45; Independent living 252. Certified Medicare.
Owner Nonprofit corp.
Admissions Requirements Minimum age 65.
Staff Physicians 1 (ft), 1 (pt); RNs 6 (ft), 7 (pt); LPNs 9 (ft), 4 (pt); Nurses' aides 17 (ft), 10 (pt); Physical therapists 1 (ft); Occupational therapists 1 (pt); Speech therapists 1 (pt); Activities coordinators 2 (ft); Dietitians 2 (ft).
Affiliation Society of Friends.
Facilities Dining room; Physical therapy room; Activities room; Crafts room; Laundry room; Barber/Beauty shop; Library; Game room; Auditorium; Greenhouse; Resident meeting rooms.
Activities Arts & crafts; Cards; Games; Reading groups; Movies; Shopping trips; Dances/Social/Cultural gatherings.

Pickering Manor Home
226 N Lincoln Ave, Newtown, PA 18940
(215) 968-3878
Medical Dir Blaine R Garner MD.
Licensure Skilled care. Beds SNF 47. Certified Medicaid; Medicare.
Owner Nonprofit corp.
Admissions Requirements Minimum age 18.

Facilities Dining room; Physical therapy room; Activities room; Laundry room; Barber/Beauty shop; Library.
Activities Arts & crafts; Cards; Games; Reading groups; Prayer groups; Movies; Shopping trips; Dances/Social/Cultural gatherings.

Newtown Square

Dunwoody Home
3500 West Chester Pike, Newtown Square, PA 19073
(215) 359-4400
Licensure Skilled care. Beds SNF 71. Certified Medicare.
Owner Nonprofit corp.

Newville

Swaim Health Center
210 Big Spring Rd, Newville, PA 17241
(717) 776-3192
Admin Linda H Bunning. Dir of Nursing Vicky Donson. Medical Dir J A Townsend MD.
Licensure Skilled care; Intermediate care; Continuing care; Independent living; Alzheimer's care. Beds Swing beds SNF/ICF 60; Continuing care 14; Independent living 84. Private Pay Patients 56%. Certified Medicaid; Medicare.
Owner Nonprofit corp (Presbyterian Homes Inc).
Admissions Requirements Minimum age 55; Medical examination; Physician's request.
Staff RNs 3 (ft), 3 (pt); LPNs 1 (ft), 6 (pt); Nurses' aides 14 (ft), 12 (pt); Physical therapists 1 (pt); Activities coordinators 1 (ft), 3 (pt); Dietitians 1 (ft).
Affiliation Presbyterian.
Facilities Dining room; Physical therapy room; Activities room; Chapel; Crafts room; Laundry room; Barber/Beauty shop; Library; Conference room; Community room.
Activities Arts & crafts; Cards; Games; Reading groups; Prayer groups; Shopping trips; Dances/Social/Cultural gatherings; Intergenerational programs; Pet therapy.

Norristown

Leader Health Care & Rehabilitation Center II
2004 Old Arch Rd, Norristown, PA 19401
(215) 277-0380
Medical Dir John McLoone MD.
Licensure Skilled care. Beds SNF 120. Certified Medicaid; Medicare.
Owner Proprietary corp (Manor Care Inc).
Admissions Requirements Medical examination.
Staff RNs 14 (ft); LPNs 11 (ft); Nurses' aides 45 (ft); Physical therapists 1 (ft); Reality therapists 1 (ft); Recreational therapists 1 (ft); Occupational therapists 1 (pt); Speech therapists 1 (pt); Activities coordinators 1 (ft); Dietitians 1 (ft); Audiologists 1 (pt).

Leader Nursing & Rehabilitation Center I
205 E Johnson Hwy, Norristown, PA 19401
(215) 275-6410
Admin Mary Beth Schwartz NHA. Dir of Nursing Mark Wlotko RN. Medical Dir John Maerz MD.
Licensure Skilled care; Intermediate care. Beds SNF 60; ICF 60. Private Pay Patients 49%. Certified Medicaid; Medicare.
Owner Proprietary corp (Manor Care Inc).
Admissions Requirements Medical examination.
Staff RNs; LPNs; Nurses' aides; Physical therapists; Recreational therapists; Occupational therapists; Speech therapists; Activities coordinators; Dietitians.

Facilities Dining room; Physical therapy room; Activities room; Chapel; Laundry room; Barber/Beauty shop.
Activities Arts & crafts; Cards; Games; Reading groups; Prayer groups; Shopping trips; Dances/Social/Cultural gatherings; Intergenerational programs; Pet therapy; Cooking groups.

Norristown State Hospital Long-Term Care Unit
Stanbridge & Sterigere Sts, Bldg 9, Norristown, PA 19401
(215) 270-1331
Licensure Skilled care. Beds SNF 75. Certified Medicaid; Medicare.
Owner Publicly owned.

Plymouth House Health Care Center
900 E Germantown Pike, Norristown, PA 19401
(215) 279-7300
Admin Sally Lucas. Dir of Nursing Barbara Koch RN. Medical Dir James Bard MD.
Licensure Skilled care; Intermediate care; Alzheimer's care. Beds SNF 30; ICF 127. Certified Medicaid; Medicare.
Owner Proprietary corp.
Admissions Requirements Minimum age 18; Medical examination.
Staff Physicians 54 (pt); RNs 12 (ft), 8 (pt); LPNs 7 (ft), 3 (pt); Nurses' aides 52 (ft), 21 (pt); Physical therapists 1 (pt); Recreational therapists 1 (ft), 1 (pt); Occupational therapists 1 (pt); Speech therapists 1 (pt); Activities coordinators 1 (ft); Dietitians 1 (ft); Ophthalmologists 1 (pt); Podiatrists 1 (pt); Dentists 1 (pt).
Facilities Dining room; Physical therapy room; Activities room; Chapel; Crafts room; Laundry room; Barber/Beauty shop; Library.
Activities Arts & crafts; Cards; Games; Reading groups; Prayer groups; Movies; Shopping trips; Dances/Social/Cultural gatherings.

Regina Community Nursing Center
550 E Fornance St, Norristown, PA 19401
(215) 272-5600
Admin Joseph Stimmler. Dir of Nursing Alice M Hagel RN. Medical Dir Charles Cutler MD.
Licensure Skilled care. Beds SNF 121. Certified Medicaid; Medicare.
Owner Nonprofit corp.
Facilities Dining room; Physical therapy room; Activities room; Crafts room; Laundry room; Barber/Beauty shop.
Activities Arts & crafts; Cards; Games; Prayer groups; Movies; Shopping trips; Dances/Social/Cultural gatherings.

North Huntingdon

Baldock Health Care Center
8850 Barns Lake Rd, North Huntingdon, PA 15642
(412) 864-7190, 864-6063 FAX
Admin John Belko NHA. Dir of Nursing Michelle Mick. Medical Dir Clark Kerr MD.
Licensure Skilled care. Beds SNF 120. Certified Medicaid; Medicare.
Owner Proprietary corp.
Admissions Requirements Medical examination; Physician's request.
Facilities Dining room; Physical therapy room; Activities room; Crafts room; Laundry room; Barber/Beauty shop.
Activities Arts & crafts; Cards; Games; Reading groups; Prayer groups; Movies; Shopping trips; Dances/Social/Cultural gatherings; Intergenerational programs; Pet therapy.

Briarcliff Pavilion
249 Maus Dr, North Huntingdon, PA 15642
(412) 863-4374

Admin Janet Maxwell. *Dir of Nursing* Mary Ann Nye RN. *Medical Dir* John M Aber MD.
Licensure Skilled care; Intermediate care. *Beds* SNF 55; ICF 65. *Certified* Medicaid; Medicare; VA.
Owner Proprietary corp.
Admissions Requirements Minimum age 18; Medical examination; Physician's request.
Staff Physicians 1 (pt); RNs 7 (ft), 3 (pt); LPNs 6 (ft), 3 (pt); Nurses' aides 33 (ft), 14 (pt); Physical therapists 1 (pt); Reality therapists 1 (pt); Occupational therapists 1 (pt); Speech therapists 1 (pt); Activities coordinators 2 (ft); Dietitians 1 (pt); Podiatrists 1 (pt); Dentists 1 (pt); Psychiatrists 1 (pt); Social workers 1 (ft).
Facilities Dining room; Physical therapy room; Activities room; Crafts room; Laundry room; Barber/Beauty shop.
Activities Arts & crafts; Cards; Games; Reading groups; Prayer groups; Movies; Shopping trips; Dances/Social/Cultural gatherings; Nationality day each month.

North Wales

Angeline Nursing Home Inc
Rte 309 & N Wales Rd, North Wales, PA 19454
(215) 855-8670
Licensure Skilled care. *Beds* 32. *Certified* Medicaid.
Owner Proprietary corp.

Northumberland

Nottingham Village
PO Box 32, Strawbridge Rd, Northumberland, PA 17857
(717) 473-8366
Licensure Skilled care; Independent living. *Beds* SNF 121. *Certified* Medicaid; Medicare.
Owner Proprietary corp.

Pleasant View Convalescent Home
Rte 1, Northumberland, PA 17857
(717) 473-9433
Licensure Skilled care. *Beds* 26. *Certified* Medicaid.
Owner Proprietary corp.

Oakmont

Oakmont Nursing Center
26 Ann St, Oakmont, PA 15139
(412) 828-7300, 828-2669 FAX
Admin Stephen K Ott MHSA NHA. *Dir of Nursing* Delores Bracco RN. *Medical Dir* T J Ferguson MD.
Licensure Skilled care; Intermediate care; Alzheimer's care. *Beds* Swing beds SNF/ICF 81; Medicare 24. *Private Pay Patients* 20%. *Certified* Medicaid; Medicare.
Owner Proprietary corp (Beverly Enterprises).
Staff Physicians 10 (pt); RNs 6 (ft), 5 (pt); LPNs 6 (ft), 6 (pt); Nurses' aides 35 (ft), 10 (pt); Physical therapists 1 (pt); Recreational therapists 1 (ft); Occupational therapists 1 (pt); Speech therapists 1 (pt); Activities coordinators 1 (ft); Dietitians 1 (pt); Ophthalmologists 1 (pt); Podiatrists 1 (pt); Audiologists 1 (pt).
Facilities Dining room; Physical therapy room; Activities room; Laundry room; Barber/Beauty shop; Secure patio/Grounds.
Activities Arts & crafts; Cards; Games; Reading groups; Prayer groups; Movies; Shopping trips; Dances/Social/Cultural gatherings; Intergenerational programs; Pet therapy.

Presbyterian Medical Center of Oakmont
1205 Hulton Rd, Oakmont, PA 15139
(412) 828-5600, 826-6121 FAX

Admin Paul M Winkler. *Dir of Nursing* Judith Ferguson RNC. *Medical Dir* Daniel R Steiner MD.
Licensure Skilled care; Intermediate care; Retirement. *Beds* SNF 46; ICF 156; Retirement 160. *Private Pay Patients* 35%. *Certified* Medicaid; Medicare.
Owner Nonprofit corp (Presbyterian Association on Aging).
Admissions Requirements Minimum age 18; Medical examination.
Staff Physicians 10 (pt); RNs 7 (ft), 8 (pt); LPNs 11 (ft), 7 (pt); Nurses' aides 54 (ft), 20 (pt); Physical therapists 1 (ft), 1 (pt); Recreational therapists 1 (ft); Occupational therapists 1 (ft); Speech therapists 1 (pt); Activities coordinators 1 (ft); Dietitians 1 (ft), 2 (pt); Ophthalmologists 1 (pt); Podiatrists 1 (pt).
Affiliation Presbyterian.
Facilities Dining room; Physical therapy room; Activities room; Chapel; Laundry room; Barber/Beauty shop; Library; Soda fountain; Private rooms.
Activities Arts & crafts; Cards; Games; Reading groups; Prayer groups; Movies; Shopping trips; Dances/Social/Cultural gatherings; Intergenerational programs; Pet therapy.

Oil City

Grandview Health Care
1293 Grandview Rd, Oil City, PA 16301
(814) 676-8208
Medical Dir Dr Gold.
Licensure Skilled care; Intermediate care. *Beds* SNF 25; ICF 124. *Certified* Medicaid; Medicare.
Owner Proprietary corp (Beverly Enterprises).
Admissions Requirements Minimum age 16; Medical examination.
Staff Physicians 1 (pt); RNs 3 (ft), 1 (pt); LPNs 1 (ft), 3 (pt); Nurses' aides 13 (ft), 5 (pt); Speech therapists 1 (pt); Activities coordinators 1 (ft), 1 (pt); Dietitians 1 (ft).
Facilities Dining room; Physical therapy room; Activities room; Crafts room; Laundry room; Barber/Beauty shop.
Activities Arts & crafts; Cards; Games; Reading groups; Movies; Shopping trips; Dances/Social/Cultural gatherings.

Presbyterian Home—Oil City
10 Vo Tech Dr, Oil City, PA 16301
(814) 676-8686
Admin Yvonne D Atkinson. *Dir of Nursing* Sandra Leta. *Medical Dir* Edward Kepp MD.
Licensure Skilled care; Intermediate care. *Beds* SNF 31; ICF 90. *Certified* Medicaid; Medicare.
Owner Nonprofit corp.
Admissions Requirements Minimum age 18; Medical examination.
Staff Physicians 1 (pt); RNs 6 (ft), 2 (pt); LPNs 8 (ft), 11 (pt); Nurses' aides 35 (ft), 19 (pt); Activities coordinators 1 (ft), 2 (pt).
Affiliation Presbyterian.
Facilities Dining room; Physical therapy room; Activities room; Crafts room; Laundry room; Barber/Beauty shop; Library.
Activities Arts & crafts; Cards; Games; Reading groups; Prayer groups; Movies; Shopping trips; Dances/Social/Cultural gatherings.

Olyphant

Lackawanna County Health Care Center
Sturges Rd, Olyphant, PA 18447-2501
(717) 489-8611
Admin Helen Cordelli NHA. *Dir of Nursing* Marie Ross. *Medical Dir* Dr Thomas Clauss.
Licensure Skilled care; Intermediate care. *Beds* Swing beds SNF/ICF 204. *Private Pay Patients* 12%. *Certified* Medicaid; Medicare.

Owner Publicly owned.
Admissions Requirements Minimum age 18.
Staff Physicians 3 (pt); RNs 9 (ft), 7 (pt); LPNs 14 (ft), 2 (pt); Nurses' aides 63 (ft), 52 (pt); Physical therapists 1 (ft); Reality therapists 1 (ft); Recreational therapists 1 (ft); Occupational therapists 1 (pt); Speech therapists 1 (pt); Activities coordinators 2 (ft); Dietitians; Ophthalmologists; Podiatrists; Audiologists; Social services 1 (ft), 2 (pt).
Facilities Dining room; Physical therapy room; Activities room; Chapel; Crafts room; Laundry room; Barber/Beauty shop; Library.
Activities Arts & crafts; Cards; Games; Reading groups; Prayer groups; Movies; Shopping trips; Dances/Social/Cultural gatherings; Intergenerational programs; Pet therapy.

Orangeville

Char Mund Nursing Home
Rte 2 Box 72, Orangeville, PA 17859
(717) 683-5333
Licensure Skilled care. *Beds* SNF 36. *Certified* Medicaid; Medicare.
Owner Proprietary corp.

Klingerman Nursing Center
Rte 2, Orangeville, PA 17859
(717) 683-5036
Admin Mahlon L Fritz, Sr.
Medical Dir Richard Delp; Gayl Klingerman.
Licensure Intermediate care. *Beds* ICF 118. *Certified* Medicaid.
Owner Proprietary corp.
Admissions Requirements Physician's request.
Staff Physicians 2 (ft), 5 (pt); RNs 4 (ft), 6 (pt); LPNs 4 (ft), 1 (pt); Nurses' aides 28 (ft), 13 (pt); Physical therapists 1 (pt); Reality therapists 1 (ft), 1 (pt); Recreational therapists 1 (ft), 1 (pt); Activities coordinators 1 (ft), 1 (pt); Dietitians 1 (pt); Podiatrists 2 (pt); Dentists 1 (pt).
Facilities Dining room; Activities room; Chapel; Crafts room; Laundry room; Barber/Beauty shop.
Activities Arts & crafts; Cards; Games; Reading groups; Prayer groups; Movies; Shopping trips; Dances/Social/Cultural gatherings.

Orbisonia

Woodland Retirement Center
PO Box 280, Orbisonia, PA 17243
(814) 447-5563
Admin Phyllis J Bard NHA. *Dir of Nursing* Sandra Whitsel. *Medical Dir* Dr Gary Wertman DO.
Licensure Skilled care; Intermediate care. *Beds* Swing beds SNF/ICF 124. *Private Pay Patients* 30%. *Certified* Medicaid; Medicare; VA.
Owner Privately owned.
Admissions Requirements Minimum age 18; Medical examination; Physician's request.
Staff Physicians 1 (ft); RNs 5 (ft), 3 (pt); LPNs 12 (ft), 14 (pt); Nurses' aides 33 (ft), 36 (pt); Physical therapists 1 (pt); Recreational therapists 1 (ft), 2 (pt); Occupational therapists 1 (pt); Speech therapists 1 (pt); Dietitians 1 (pt); Podiatrists 1 (pt); Audiologists 1 (pt).
Facilities Dining room; Physical therapy room; Activities room; Chapel; Crafts room; Laundry room; Barber/Beauty shop; Library (Medical).
Activities Arts & crafts; Cards; Games; Reading groups; Prayer groups; Movies; Shopping trips; Dances/Social/Cultural gatherings.

Oxford

Oxford Manor Nursing Home
7 E Locust St, Oxford, PA 19363
(215) 932-2900
Admin Geoffrey L Henry. *Dir of Nursing*
Roberta Zaffarano RN. *Medical Dir* Dr Faye
R Doyle.
Licensure Skilled care; Intermediate care;
Continuing care retirement community;
Alzheimer's care. *Beds* Swing beds SNF/ICF
100; PCB 40; ILU 34. *Certified* Medicaid;
Medicare.
Owner Nonprofit corp.
Admissions Requirements Medical
examination.
Staff Physicians 10 (pt); RNs 4 (ft), 5 (pt);
LPNs 2 (ft), 2 (pt); Nurses' aides 40 (ft);
Physical therapists 1 (pt); Occupational
therapists 1 (pt); Activities coordinators 1
(ft); Dietitians 1 (ft).
Affiliation Presbyterian.
Facilities Dining room; Physical therapy
room; Activities room; Crafts room; Laundry
room; Barber/Beauty shop; Library.
Activities Arts & crafts; Cards; Games;
Reading groups; Prayer groups; Movies;
Shopping trips; Dances/Social/Cultural
gatherings.

Palmyra

Lebanon Valley Brethren Home
1200 Grubb St, Palmyra, PA 17078
(717) 838-5406
Licensure Skilled care; Intermediate care;
Residential care; Retirement. *Beds* SNF 42;
ICF 58; Residential care 40; Retirement 185.
Certified Medicaid; Medicare.
Owner Nonprofit corp.
Admissions Requirements Minimum age 62;
Medical examination; Physician's request.
Facilities Dining room; Physical therapy
room; Activities room; Chapel; Crafts room;
Laundry room; Barber/Beauty shop; Library.
Activities Arts & crafts; Cards; Games;
Reading groups; Prayer groups; Movies;
Shopping trips; Dances/Social/Cultural
gatherings; Intergenerational programs; Pet
therapy.

Palmyra Nursing Home
341 N Railroad St, Palmyra, PA 17078
(717) 838-3011
Admin Jean B Blouch. *Dir of Nursing* Mary C
Hraborsky RN. *Medical Dir* Harold H Engle
MD.
Licensure Skilled care. *Beds* SNF 39. *Certified*
Medicaid; Medicare.
Owner Privately owned.
Admissions Requirements Minimum age 16;
Medical examination; Physician's request.
Staff Physicians 1 (pt); RNs 3 (ft), 2 (pt);
LPNs 2 (pt); Nurses' aides 9 (ft), 7 (pt);
Physical therapists 1 (pt); Reality therapists
1 (pt); Recreational therapists 1 (ft);
Occupational therapists 1 (pt); Speech
therapists 1 (pt); Activities coordinators 1
(ft); Dietitians 1 (pt); Ophthalmologists 1
(pt); Podiatrists 1 (pt); Audiologists 1 (pt).
Languages Italian, Pennsylvania Dutch.
Facilities Dining room; Physical therapy
room; Activities room; Crafts room; Laundry
room; Barber/Beauty shop.
Activities Arts & crafts; Cards; Games;
Reading groups; Prayer groups; Movies;
Shopping trips; Dances/Social/Cultural
gatherings; Intergenerational programs; Pet
therapy; Sight-seeing trip.

Paoli

Main Line Nursing & Rehabilitation Center
283 E Lancaster Ave, Paoli, PA 19301
(215) 296-4170

Admin Donna M Howard RN. *Dir of Nursing*
Sandra C Lutte RN. *Medical Dir* Ernest F
Gillan MD.
Licensure Skilled care; Intermediate care. *Beds*
SNF 120; ICF 60. *Certified* Medicaid;
Medicare.
Owner Nonprofit corp.
Staff Physicians 1 (ft); RNs 14 (ft); LPNs 19
(ft), 3 (pt); Nurses' aides 55 (ft); Physical
therapists 1 (ft); Recreational therapists 2
(ft); Occupational therapists 1 (ft); Speech
therapists 1 (pt); Activities coordinators 1
(ft); Dietitians 1 (pt); Ophthalmologists 1
(pt); Dentists 1 (pt).
Languages Spanish, Italian, German, Polish.
Facilities Dining room; Physical therapy
room; Activities room; Crafts room; Laundry
room; Barber/Beauty shop.
Activities Arts & crafts; Cards; Games;
Reading groups; Prayer groups; Movies;
Dances/Social/Cultural gatherings.

Pennsburg

Pennsburg Manor
5th & Macoby St, Pennsburg, PA 18073
(215) 679-8076
Admin Carole L Monahan RN. *Dir of Nursing*
Donna Cruz RN. *Medical Dir* Norbert Leska
MD.
Licensure Skilled care. *Beds* SNF 120. *Private
Pay Patients* 50%. *Certified* Medicaid;
Medicare.
Owner Proprietary corp (GraceCare Corp).
Admissions Requirements Medical
examination; OBRA form.
Staff Physicians 10 (pt); RNs 7 (ft), 5 (pt);
LPNs 3 (ft), 9 (pt); Physical therapists 1 (pt);
Occupational therapists 1 (pt); Speech
therapists 1 (pt); Activities coordinators 1
(ft), 3 (pt); Dietitians 1 (ft);
Ophthalmologists 1 (pt); Podiatrists 1 (pt).
Languages Spanish.
Facilities Dining room; Physical therapy
room; Activities room; Laundry room;
Barber/Beauty shop.
Activities Arts & crafts; Cards; Games;
Reading groups; Movies; Shopping trips;
Dances/Social/Cultural gatherings;
Intergenerational programs.

Philadelphia

Ashton Hall Nursing & Rehabilitation
2109 Red Lion Rd, Philadelphia, PA 19115
(215) 673-7000
Licensure Skilled care. *Beds* SNF 148.
Certified Medicaid; Medicare.
Owner Proprietary corp.

Bala Retirement & Rehabilitation
4001 Ford Rd, Philadelphia, PA 19131
(215) 877-5400
Admin Arnold Leof. *Dir of Nursing* Evelyn
Ebora RN. *Medical Dir* Dr Eric Shore.
Licensure Skilled care; Intermediate care. *Beds*
SNF 30; ICF 85. *Certified* Medicaid;
Medicare.
Owner Nonprofit corp.
Admissions Requirements Minimum age 65;
Medical examination; Physician's request.
Staff Physicians; RNs 5 (ft); LPNs 7 (ft);
Nurses' aides 40 (ft); Physical therapists;
Recreational therapists 1 (ft); Speech
therapists; Activities coordinators 1 (ft);
Dietitians; Ophthalmologists; Podiatrists;
Dentists.
Languages Hebrew, Yiddish.
Affiliation Jewish.
Facilities Dining room; Physical therapy
room; Activities room; Chapel; Crafts room;
Laundry room; Barber/Beauty shop; Library.
Activities Arts & crafts; Cards; Games;
Reading groups; Prayer groups; Movies;
Shopping trips; Dances/Social/Cultural
gatherings.

Baptist Home of Philadelphia
8301 Roosevelt Blvd, Philadelphia, PA 19152
(215) 624-7575
Admin David A Smiley NHA. *Dir of Nursing*
Emily Cervonka. *Medical Dir* Dr Vernando
Jaurique.
Licensure Skilled care; Intermediate care;
Independent living. *Beds* SNF 111; ICF 98;
Independent living 176. *Certified* Medicaid;
Medicare.
Owner Nonprofit corp.
Admissions Requirements Minimum age 65;
Medical examination.
Staff Physicians 5 (pt); RNs 4 (ft), 1 (pt);
LPNs 12 (ft), 11 (pt); Nurses' aides 59 (ft),
18 (pt); Physical therapists 1 (ft);
Recreational therapists 4 (ft), 1 (pt);
Activities coordinators 2 (ft); Dietitians 1
(ft).
Affiliation Baptist.
Facilities Dining room; Physical therapy
room; Activities room; Chapel; Crafts room;
Laundry room; Barber/Beauty shop; Library;
Gift shop.
Activities Arts & crafts; Cards; Games; Prayer
groups; Shopping trips; Dances/Social/
Cultural gatherings; Bingo; Basketball (with
Nurf ball); Gardening.

Boulevard Nursing Home
7950 Roosevelt Blvd, Philadelphia, PA 19152
(215) 332-3700
Admin Catherine Dowd. *Dir of Nursing* Mary
Antonio RN. *Medical Dir* Bernard Cramer
MD.
Licensure Skilled care; Intermediate care;
Alzheimer's care. *Beds* SNF 90; ICF 45.
Certified Medicaid; Medicare.
Owner Proprietary corp (Continental Health
Affiliates).
Admissions Requirements Minimum age 25;
Medical examination; Physician's request.
Staff Physicians; RNs; LPNs; Nurses' aides;
Physical therapists; Recreational therapists;
Occupational therapists; Speech therapists;
Activities coordinators; Dietitians;
Ophthalmologists; Podiatrists; Dentists.
Facilities Dining room; Physical therapy
room; Activities room; Crafts room; Laundry
room; Barber/Beauty shop.
Activities Arts & crafts; Cards; Games;
Reading groups; Prayer groups; Movies;
Shopping trips; Dances/Social/Cultural
gatherings.

Care Pavilion
6212 Walnut St, Philadelphia, PA 19139
(215) 476-6264
Medical Dir Dr R Weisberg.
Licensure Skilled care; Intermediate care. *Beds*
SNF 258; ICF 120. *Certified* Medicaid;
Medicare.
Owner Proprietary corp (Geriatric and
Medical Centers).
Staff Physicians 6 (pt); RNs 20 (ft), 6 (pt);
LPNs 30 (ft), 10 (pt); Nurses' aides 180 (ft),
20 (pt); Physical therapists 1 (ft), 1 (pt);
Recreational therapists 4 (ft), 1 (pt);
Occupational therapists 1 (ft); Speech
therapists 1 (ft); Activities coordinators 1
(ft); Dietitians 1 (ft).
Facilities Dining room; Physical therapy
room; Activities room; Laundry room;
Barber/Beauty shop.
Activities Arts & crafts; Cards; Games;
Reading groups; Prayer groups; Movies;
Shopping trips; Dances/Social/Cultural
gatherings.

Cathedral Village
600 E Cathedral Rd, Philadelphia, PA 19128
(215) 487-1300
Admin Judith A Hernan MSN NHA. *Dir of
Nursing* Carol Joyce RN. *Medical Dir*
Robert V Smith MD.

Licensure Skilled care; Intermediate care; Retirement; Alzheimer's care. *Beds* Swing beds SNF/ICF 148; Retirement apartments 245. *Certified* Medicaid; Medicare.
Owner Nonprofit organization/foundation.
Admissions Requirements Minimum age 65.
Staff Physicians 2 (pt); RNs 5 (ft), 20 (pt); LPNs 2 (ft), 4 (pt); Nurses' aides 32 (ft), 47 (pt); Physical therapists 1 (ft); Recreational therapists 1 (ft), 1 (pt); Occupational therapists 1 (ft); Speech therapists 1 (pt); Activities coordinators 1 (ft), 1 (pt); Dietitians 1 (ft); Ophthalmologists 1 (pt); Podiatrists 1 (pt); Audiologists 1 (pt); Dentists 1 (pt).
Affiliation Episcopal.
Facilities Dining room; Physical therapy room; Activities room; Crafts room; Laundry room; Barber/Beauty shop; Library; Lounges; Security system for wanderers.
Activities Arts & crafts; Cards; Games; Reading groups; Prayer groups; Movies; Shopping trips; Dances/Social/Cultural gatherings; Intergenerational programs; Pet therapy; Exercise group; Current events group; Music; Alzheimer's programs and activity.

Central Park Lodge—Chestnut Hill
8833 Stenton Ave, Philadelphia, PA 19118
(215) 836-2100
Dir of Nursing Carolyn Baxter RN. *Medical Dir* Lawrence Kessel MD.
Licensure Skilled care; Intermediate care. *Beds* Swing beds SNF/ICF 195. *Certified* Medicaid; Medicare.
Owner Proprietary corp (Central Park Lodges).
Staff Physicians 45 (pt); RNs 8 (ft), 10 (pt); LPNs 10 (ft), 4 (pt); Nurses' aides 57 (ft), 11 (pt); Physical therapists 1 (pt); Occupational therapists 1 (pt); Speech therapists 1 (pt); Activities coordinators 3 (ft); Dietitians 1 (pt); Ophthalmologists 1 (pt); Podiatrists 1 (pt); Audiologists 1 (pt).
Facilities Dining room; Physical therapy room; Activities room; Crafts room; Laundry room; Barber/Beauty shop.
Activities Arts & crafts; Cards; Games; Reading groups; Prayer groups; Movies; Shopping trips; Dances/Social/Cultural gatherings; Intergenerational programs; Pet therapy; Family support group.

Central Park Lodge—Whitemarsh
9209 Ridge Pike, Philadelphia, PA 19128
(215) 825-6560, 825-0531 FAX
Admin Jeanne V Bund. *Dir of Nursing* Josefa Clinton RN. *Medical Dir* Lawrence Kessel MD.
Licensure Skilled care. *Beds* SNF 247. *Private Pay Patients* 45%. *Certified* Medicaid; Medicare.
Owner Proprietary corp (Central Park Lodge).
Staff RNs 45 (ft), 10 (pt); LPNs 19 (ft), 5 (pt); Nurses' aides 90 (ft), 10 (pt); Physical therapists (contracted); Reality therapists (contracted); Recreational therapists (contracted); Occupational therapists (contracted); Speech therapists (contracted); Activities coordinators 3 (ft); Dietitians 1 (ft); Ophthalmologists 1 (pt); Podiatrists 1 (pt).
Facilities Dining room; Physical therapy room; Activities room; Crafts room; Laundry room; Barber/Beauty shop; Patios; Gazebo.
Activities Arts & crafts; Cards; Games; Reading groups; Prayer groups; Movies; Shopping trips; Dances/Social/Cultural gatherings; Intergenerational programs; Pet therapy.

Chapel Manor Nursing & Rehabilitation Center
1104 Welsh Rd, Philadelphia, PA 19115
(215) 676-9191

Licensure Skilled care. *Beds* SNF 240. *Certified* Medicaid; Medicare.
Owner Proprietary corp.

Cheltenham Nursing & Rehabilitation Center
600 W Cheltenham Ave, Philadelphia, PA 19126
(215) 927-7300
Admin Virginia Buchenhorst RN NHA. *Dir of Nursing* Cheryl Fida RN. *Medical Dir* O Frank Waxman DO.
Licensure Skilled care; Intermediate care; Alzheimer's care. *Beds* Swing beds SNF/ICF 255. *Certified* Medicaid; Medicare; VA.
Owner Proprietary corp (Geriatric and Medical Centers).
Admissions Requirements Medical examination; Physician's request.
Staff Physicians; RNs; LPNs; Nurses' aides; Physical therapists; Occupational therapists; Speech therapists; Activities coordinators; Dietitians; Ophthalmologists; Podiatrists; Audiologists; Recreational therapists; Reality therapists; Pastors (consultant).
Facilities Dining room; Physical therapy room; Activities room; Chapel; Crafts room; Laundry room; Barber/Beauty shop; Library; Rehabilitation therapy department.
Activities Arts & crafts; Cards; Games; Reading groups; Prayer groups; Movies; Shopping trips; Dances/Social/Cultural gatherings; Intergenerational programs; Religious services; Pastoral counseling.

Cheltenham-York Road Nursing & Rehabilitation Center
7107 Old York Rd, Philadelphia, PA 19126
(215) 424-4090
Licensure Skilled care. *Beds* SNF 240. *Certified* Medicaid; Medicare.
Owner Proprietary corp (Geriatric and Medical Centers).

Cliveden Convalescent Center
6400 Greene St, Philadelphia, PA 19119
(215) 844-6400
Licensure Skilled care. *Beds* SNF 180. *Certified* Medicaid; Medicare.
Owner Proprietary corp.

Cobbs Creek Nursing Center
6900 Cobbs Creek Pkwy, Philadelphia, PA 19142
(215) 729-1414
Licensure Skilled care. *Beds* SNF 205. *Certified* Medicaid.
Owner Proprietary corp (Geriatric and Medical Centers).

Courtland Center for Continuing Care
39th & Market Sts, Philadelphia, PA 19104

Mercy Douglass Human Services Center
4508-38 Chestnut St, Philadelphia, PA 19139
(215) 382-9495
Admin Jessie D James.
Medical Dir Nathaniel H Copeland MD.
Licensure Skilled care. *Beds* SNF 180. *Certified* Medicaid; Medicare.
Owner Nonprofit corp.
Admissions Requirements Minimum age 60; Medical examination; Physician's request.
Staff Physicians 5 (pt); RNs 6 (ft), 3 (pt); LPNs 10 (ft), 3 (pt); Nurses' aides 50 (ft), 15 (pt); Physical therapists 1 (pt); Recreational therapists 3 (ft); Speech therapists 1 (pt); Activities coordinators 1 (pt); Dietitians 1 (ft), 1 (pt); Ophthalmologists 1 (pt); Podiatrists 1 (pt); Audiologists 1 (pt); Dentists 2 (pt).
Facilities Dining room; Physical therapy room; Activities room; Chapel; Crafts room; Laundry room; Barber/Beauty shop; Library.
Activities Arts & crafts; Cards; Games; Reading groups; Prayer groups; Movies.

Albert Einstein Medical Center—Willowcrest-Bamberger Division
York & Tabor Rds, Philadelphia, PA 19141
(215) 456-8615, 456-8299 FAX
Admin Robert V Stutz. *Dir of Nursing* Michael Rose RN. *Medical Dir* Raymond Cogen MD.
Licensure Skilled care. *Beds* SNF 102. *Private Pay Patients* 2%. *Certified* Medicaid; Medicare.
Owner Nonprofit corp.
Admissions Requirements Minimum age 18; Medical examination; Physician's request.
Staff Physicians 1 (pt); RNs 11 (ft), 5 (pt); LPNs 9 (ft), 1 (pt); Nurses' aides 24 (ft), 7 (pt); Physical therapists 1 (ft); Recreational therapists 1 (ft); Occupational therapists 1 (ft), 1 (pt); Dietitians 1 (pt).
Facilities Dining room; Physical therapy room; Activities room.
Activities Arts & crafts; Cards; Games; Reading groups; Prayer groups; Movies; Dances/Social/Cultural gatherings.

Evangelical Manor
8401 Roosevelt Blvd, Philadelphia, PA 19152
(215) 624-5800, 335-1477 FAX
Admin James E Tallman. *Dir of Nursing* Irene Contino RN. *Medical Dir* Dr Venerando Jaurique.
Licensure Skilled care; Intermediate care; Personal care; Retirement. *Beds* SNF 60; ICF 60; Retirement 200. *Private Pay Patients* 60%. *Certified* Medicaid; Medicare.
Owner Nonprofit organization/foundation.
Admissions Requirements Minimum age 65; Medical examination.
Staff Physicians 4 (pt); RNs 12 (ft), 5 (pt); LPNs 2 (pt); Nurses' aides 45 (ft), 20 (pt); Physical therapists (consultant); Recreational therapists 1 (pt); Occupational therapists 1 (pt); Speech therapists 1 (pt); Activities coordinators 1 (ft); Dietitians (consultant); Ophthalmologists 1 (pt); Podiatrists 1 (pt); Audiologists 1 (pt).
Affiliation Methodist.
Facilities Dining room; Physical therapy room; Activities room; Chapel; Crafts room; Laundry room; Barber/Beauty shop; Library; Fitness trail.
Activities Arts & crafts; Cards; Games; Reading groups; Movies; Shopping trips; Dances/Social/Cultural gatherings; Intergenerational programs; Theme dinners; Rhythm band.

Fairview Care Center of Bethlehem Pike
184 Bethlehem Pike, Philadelphia, PA 19118
(215) 247-5311
Admin Frank J Marchese III. *Dir of Nursing* Laura Stauffer RN. *Medical Dir* Harry Borgersen DO.
Licensure Intermediate care; Alzheimer's care. *Beds* ICF 153. *Certified* Medicaid.
Owner Proprietary corp (Geriatric & Medical Centers).
Admissions Requirements Medical examination; Physician's request.
Staff Physicians 1 (pt); RNs 3 (ft), 2 (pt); LPNs 5 (ft), 2 (pt); Nurses' aides 65 (ft), 25 (pt); Physical therapists 2 (ft); Recreational therapists 2 (ft), 1 (pt); Activities coordinators 1 (ft); Dietitians 1 (ft); Ophthalmologists 1 (pt); Podiatrists 1 (pt); Dentists 1 (pt).
Facilities Dining room; Physical therapy room; Activities room; Crafts room; Laundry room; Barber/Beauty shop.
Activities Arts & crafts; Cards; Games; Reading groups; Prayer groups.

Fairview Care Center of Papermill Road
850 Papermill Rd, Philadelphia, PA 19118
(215) 233-0920, 836-1247 FAX
Admin R June Hudak. *Dir of Nursing* Pat Fritz RN. *Medical Dir* Louis A Pegel MD.

Licensure Skilled care; Intermediate care. *Beds* SNF 77; ICF 67. *Private Pay Patients* 10%. *Certified* Medicaid; Medicare.
Owner Proprietary corp (Geriatric and Medical Services Inc).
Admissions Requirements Medical examination.
Staff Physicians 20 (pt); RNs 9 (ft), 10 (pt); LPNs 8 (ft), 6 (pt); Nurses' aides 50 (ft), 25 (pt); Physical therapists (contracted); Recreational therapists 2 (ft), 1 (pt); Occupational therapists 1 (pt); Speech therapists 1 (pt); Activities coordinators 1 (ft); Dietitians 1 (ft); Ophthalmologists 1 (pt); Podiatrists 3 (pt); Audiologists 1 (pt).
Facilities Dining room; Physical therapy room; Activities room; Laundry room; Barber/Beauty shop.
Activities Arts & crafts; Cards; Games; Reading groups; Prayer groups; Movies; Shopping trips; Dances/Social/Cultural gatherings; Intergenerational programs; Pet therapy.

Germantown Home
6950 Germantown Ave, Philadelphia, PA 19119
(215) 848-3306
Admin Rev John G Huber. *Dir of Nursing* Mary Bayer RN. *Medical Dir* Bruce Silver MD.
Licensure Skilled care; Intermediate care; Personal care; Apartment living; Alzheimer's care. *Beds* SNF 20; ICF 149; Personal care 14; Apartment living 118. *Certified* Medicaid; Medicare.
Owner Nonprofit corp.
Admissions Requirements Minimum age 62; Medical examination; Physician's request.
Staff Physicians 3 (pt); Physical therapists 1 (ft); Reality therapists 1 (ft); Recreational therapists 3 (ft); Activities coordinators 1 (ft); Dietitians 1 (pt); Ophthalmologists 2 (pt); Dentists 1 (pt); Optometrists 1 (pt).
Affiliation Lutheran.
Facilities Dining room; Physical therapy room; Activities room; Chapel; Laundry room; Barber/Beauty shop; Library; Greenhouse.
Activities Arts & crafts; Games; Reading groups; Prayer groups; Movies; Shopping trips; Dances/Social/Cultural gatherings; Food fun; Ceramics; Manicure magic; Bedside sensory stimulation; Senior Olympics; Food fun; Gardening; Sewing groups; Music appreciation & therapy; Flower arranging.

Germantown Hospital Skilled Nursing Facility
1 Penn Bldg, Philadelphia, PA 19144

Golden Slipper Club Uptown Home
7800 Bustleton Ave, Philadelphia, PA 19152
(215) 722-2300
Licensure Skilled care. *Beds* SNF 240. *Certified* Medicaid; Medicare.
Owner Proprietary corp.

Greystone on the Greene Inc
6400 Greene St, Philadelphia, PA 19119
(215) 844-6401
Licensure Skilled care. *Beds* 180. *Certified* Medicaid; Medicare.
Owner Proprietary corp.

George L Harrison House Episcopal Hospital
Front St & Lehigh Ave, Philadelphia, PA 19125
(215) 427-7483
Admin Thomas P Schultz. *Dir of Nursing* Jane L Altland. *Medical Dir* Richard Adler.
Licensure Skilled care. *Beds* SNF 35. *Private Pay Patients* 2%. *Certified* Medicaid; Medicare.
Owner Nonprofit corp.
Admissions Requirements Medical examination; Physician's request.

Staff Physicians 4 (pt); RNs 3 (ft), 1 (pt); LPNs 1 (ft), 4 (pt); Nurses' aides 13 (ft), 5 (pt); Physical therapists (contracted); Recreational therapists 1 (ft); Occupational therapists 1 (pt); Speech therapists 1 (pt); Dietitians (contracted); Ophthalmologists 1 (pt); Podiatrists 1 (pt); Audiologists 1 (pt).
Languages Spanish.
Facilities Dining room.
Activities Arts & crafts; Cards; Games; Prayer groups; Movies; Intergenerational programs.

Holy Family Home
5300 Chester Ave, Philadelphia, PA 19143
(215) 729-5153
Admin Sr Joseph Grenon. *Dir of Nursing* Sr Gabrielle Garrett. *Medical Dir* Ronald Fronduti MD.
Licensure Skilled care; Intermediate care; Personal care; Independent living. *Beds* SNF 15; ICF 57; Personal care 31; Independent living apts 12. *Private Pay Patients* 2%. *Certified* Medicaid; Medicare.
Owner Nonprofit corp.
Admissions Requirements Minimum age 60; Medical examination; Physician's request.
Staff Physicians 3 (pt); RNs 3 (ft), 1 (pt); LPNs 6 (ft), 3 (pt); Nurses' aides 39 (ft), 13 (pt); Physical therapists 1 (pt); Occupational therapists 1 (pt); Speech therapists 1 (pt); Activities coordinators 1 (ft); Dietitians; Ophthalmologists 1 (pt); Podiatrists 1 (pt); Audiologists 1 (pt).
Languages French, Spanish, Italian.
Affiliation Roman Catholic.
Facilities Dining room; Physical therapy room; Activities room; Chapel; Crafts room; Laundry room; Barber/Beauty shop; Library; Tea room; Ceramics room; Gardens; Lawn; Porch.
Activities Arts & crafts; Cards; Games; Reading groups; Prayer groups; Movies; Shopping trips; Dances/Social/Cultural gatherings; Intergenerational programs; Pet therapy.

Home for the Jewish Aged
5301 Old York Rd, Philadelphia, PA 19141
(215) 456-2900
Licensure Skilled care; Intermediate care. *Beds* SNF 443; ICF 75. *Certified* Medicaid; Medicare.
Owner Nonprofit corp.
Affiliation Jewish.

Immaculate Mary Home
Holme Cir & Welsh Rd, Philadelphia, PA 19136
(215) 335-2100
Admin Sr Corda Marie OSF. *Dir of Nursing* Helen A Turchi RN. *Medical Dir* Herbert M Bergman MD.
Licensure Skilled care; Intermediate care; Adult day care. *Beds* SNF 196; ICF 100. *Private Pay Patients* 40-45%. *Certified* Medicaid; Medicare.
Owner Nonprofit corp.
Admissions Requirements Minimum age 60; Medical examination.
Staff Physicians; RNs; LPNs; Nurses' aides; Physical therapists; Recreational therapists; Occupational therapists; Speech therapists; Activities coordinators; Dietitians; Ophthalmologists; Podiatrists; Audiologists.
Languages Spanish, Polish, Italian.
Affiliation Roman Catholic.
Facilities Dining room; Physical therapy room; Activities room; Chapel; Crafts room; Laundry room; Barber/Beauty shop; Library.
Activities Arts & crafts; Cards; Games; Reading groups; Prayer groups; Movies; Shopping trips; Dances/Social/Cultural gatherings; Intergenerational programs; Pet therapy.

Inglis House, Philadelphia Home for Physically Disabled Persons
2600 Belmont Ave, Philadelphia, PA 19131
(215) 878-5600
Admin Kevin Jones.
Medical Dir Dr David Romanoff.
Licensure Skilled care. *Beds* SNF 297. *Certified* Medicaid; Medicare.
Owner Proprietary corp.
Admissions Requirements Minimum age 17; Medical examination; Physically disabled; Mentally alert.
Staff Physicians 1 (ft), 5 (pt); RNs 28 (ft), 11 (pt); LPNs 40 (ft), 2 (pt); Nurses' aides 169 (ft), 27 (pt); Physical therapists 2 (ft), 2 (pt); Recreational therapists 4 (ft); Occupational therapists 5 (ft); Speech therapists 1 (pt); Dietitians 1 (ft); Ophthalmologists 2 (pt); Dentists 1 (pt); Social workers 5 (ft); Teachers 4 (ft).
Facilities Physical therapy room; Activities room; Chapel; Laundry room; Barber/Beauty shop; Library; Occupational therapy room; Recreational therapy room; Pet room; Work activities room; Computer lab.
Activities Arts & crafts; Cards; Games; Reading groups; Prayer groups; Movies; Shopping trips; Dances/Social/Cultural gatherings; Pet therapy; Ham radio club; Photography; Gardening; GED & college classes.

Interim Care—Metropolitan Hospital
1331 E Wyoming Ave, Philadelphia, PA 19124
(215) 537-7400
Admin Henry R Gureck NHA. *Dir of Nursing* Loren Heiser RN. *Medical Dir* Gene Geld DO.
Licensure Skilled care. *Beds* SNF 19. *Private Pay Patients* 0%. *Certified* Medicare.
Owner Nonprofit organization/foundation.
Admissions Requirements Minimum age 65.
Staff RNs; LPNs; Nurses' aides; Physical therapists; Recreational therapists; Occupational therapists; Speech therapists; Activities coordinators; Dietitians; Ophthalmologists; Podiatrists; Audiologists.
Languages Interpreters available.
Facilities Dining room; Physical therapy room; Activities room; Laundry room; Library.
Activities Arts & crafts; Cards; Games; Movies.

Ivy Ridge Care Center
5627 Ridge Ave, Philadelphia, PA 19128
(215) 483-7522
Admin Annette Fabriean.
Medical Dir Mark Warren Cohen DO.
Licensure Intermediate care. *Beds* 47. *Certified* Medicaid.
Owner Proprietary corp.
Staff RNs 1 (ft); LPNs 3 (ft); Nurses' aides 8 (ft); Activities coordinators 1 (ft), 1 (pt).
Facilities Dining room; Activities room; Laundry room.
Activities Arts & crafts; Cards; Games; Reading groups; Prayer groups; Movies; Dances/Social/Cultural gatherings; Bazaars.

Elmira Jeffries Memorial Home Inc
1500-1514 N 15th St, Philadelphia, PA 19121
(215) 232-4290
Admin Mark T Lane. *Dir of Nursing* Dora Gray. *Medical Dir* Richard Brantz.
Licensure Skilled care. *Beds* SNF 180. *Private Pay Patients* 1%. *Certified* Medicaid; Medicare.
Owner Nonprofit corp (HBA Management Inc).
Admissions Requirements Medical examination.
Staff Physicians 2 (ft); RNs 4 (ft), 4 (pt); LPNs 16 (ft); Nurses' aides 49 (ft), 22 (pt); Physical therapists 1 (pt); Recreational therapists 1 (ft); Occupational therapists 1 (pt); Speech therapists 1 (pt); Activities

coordinators 1 (ft); Dietitians 1 (pt); Ophthalmologists 1 (pt); Podiatrists 1 (pt); Audiologists 1 (pt).
Facilities Dining room; Physical therapy room; Activities room; Laundry room; Barber/Beauty shop.
Activities Arts & crafts; Cards; Games; Prayer groups; Movies; Dances/Social/Cultural gatherings.

Kearsley—Christ Church Hospital
2100 N 49th St, Philadelphia, PA 19131-2698
(215) 877-1565
Admin Pamela A DeLissio-Johnson NHA. *Dir of Nursing* Santina J Beckius RN. *Medical Dir* Mary C DeJoseph DO.
Licensure Skilled care; Intermediate care; Independent living. *Beds* Swing beds SNF/ICF 20; Independent living 87. *Private Pay Patients* 20%. *Certified* Medicaid.
Owner Nonprofit corp.
Admissions Requirements Minimum age 62; Medical examination.
Staff Physicians 1 (pt); RNs 2 (ft), 1 (pt); LPNs 1 (ft); Nurses' aides 7 (ft), 1 (pt); Activities coordinators 1 (ft); Dietitians 1 (pt); Chaplains 1 (pt).
Affiliation Episcopal.
Facilities Dining room; Chapel; Laundry room; Barber/Beauty shop.
Activities Cards; Games; Prayer groups; Movies; Shopping trips; Dances/Social/Cultural gatherings; Intergenerational programs.

Lafayette Health Care Center
8580 Verree Rd, Philadelphia, PA 19111
(215) 728-8168
Admin Kate Jameson. *Dir of Nursing* Rebecca Wilkes. *Medical Dir* Dr Albert Paul.
Licensure Skilled care; Intermediate care; Alzheimer's care; Retirement. *Beds* SNF 60; ICF 60. *Certified* Medicaid; Medicare.
Owner Proprietary corp (Forum Group).
Staff RNs 5 (ft), 3 (pt); LPNs 10 (ft), 10 (pt); Nurses' aides 23 (ft), 15 (pt); Physical therapists 1 (pt); Recreational therapists 1 (ft); Occupational therapists 1 (pt); Speech therapists 1 (pt); Activities coordinators 1 (ft); Dietitians 1 (ft); Ophthalmologists 1 (pt); Podiatrists 1 (pt).
Languages Spanish.
Facilities Dining room; Physical therapy room; Activities room; Laundry room; Barber/Beauty shop; Library; Dayrooms; Screened porches; Country store.
Activities Arts & crafts; Cards; Games; Reading groups; Prayer groups; Movies; Shopping trips; Dances/Social/Cultural gatherings; Resident council.

Logan Square East Care Center
2 Franklintown Blvd, Philadelphia, PA 19124
(215) 563-1800
Admin John J Hurley. *Dir of Nursing* Diane Rojewski. *Medical Dir* Dr Sarle Cohen.
Licensure Skilled care; Independent living; Alzheimer's care. *Beds* SNF 148. *Certified* Medicaid; Medicare.
Owner Nonprofit corp.
Admissions Requirements Medical examination.
Staff Physicians; RNs; LPNs; Nurses' aides; Physical therapists; Occupational therapists; Speech therapists; Activities coordinators; Dietitians; Ophthalmologists; Dentists.
Facilities Dining room; Physical therapy room; Laundry room; Barber/Beauty shop.
Activities Arts & crafts; Cards; Games; Reading groups; Movies; Dances/Social/Cultural gatherings.

Maplewood Manor Convalescent Center Inc
125 W Schoolhouse Ln, Philadelphia, PA 19144
(215) 844-8806

Admin Jonathan A Schultz. *Dir of Nursing* Verna Womack RN. *Medical Dir* Paul Moyer MD.
Licensure Intermediate care. *Beds* ICF 180. *Certified* Medicaid.
Owner Proprietary corp.
Admissions Requirements Minimum age 18; Medical examination.
Staff Physicians 4 (pt); RNs 5 (ft), 3 (pt); LPNs 15 (ft), 8 (pt); Nurses' aides 65 (ft), 40 (pt); Physical therapists 1 (pt); Recreational therapists 2 (ft), 2 (pt); Speech therapists 1 (pt); Activities coordinators 1 (ft); Dietitians 2 (ft); Ophthalmologists 1 (pt); Podiatrists 1 (pt); Dentists 1 (pt).
Facilities Dining room; Physical therapy room; Activities room; Laundry room; Barber/Beauty shop.
Activities Arts & crafts; Cards; Games; Reading groups; Prayer groups; Movies; Shopping trips; Dances/Social/Cultural gatherings.

Marwood Rest Home Inc
1020 Oak Lane Ave, Philadelphia, PA 19126
(215) 224-9898
Admin R Lyle Carpenter.
Medical Dir Mortimer Strong DO; Ira Sharp MD.
Licensure Skilled care; Intermediate care. *Beds* Swing beds SNF/ICF 87. *Certified* Medicaid; Medicare.
Owner Proprietary corp.
Admissions Requirements Minimum age 65; Medical examination.
Staff Physicians 3 (pt); RNs 5 (ft), 5 (pt); LPNs 6 (ft), 5 (pt); Nurses' aides 24 (ft), 10 (pt); Physical therapists 1 (pt); Reality therapists 1 (pt); Occupational therapists 1 (pt); Speech therapists 1 (pt); Activities coordinators 1 (ft); Dietitians 1 (ft); Ophthalmologists 1 (pt); Podiatrists 1 (pt); Audiologists 1 (pt); Dentists 1 (pt).
Languages Indian.
Facilities Dining room; Physical therapy room; Activities room; Crafts room; Laundry room; Barber/Beauty shop; Outdoor areas.
Activities Arts & crafts; Cards; Games; Reading groups; Prayer groups; Movies; Shopping trips; Dances/Social/Cultural gatherings; Intergenerational programs; Pet therapy; Music; Exercise groups.

Mayo Nursing & Convalescent Center
650 Edison Ave, Philadelphia, PA 19116
(213) 673-5700
Admin Liz Kopman. *Dir of Nursing* Eileen McGlynn. *Medical Dir* R J Kane DO.
Licensure Skilled care. *Beds* SNF 241. *Certified* Medicaid; Medicare.
Owner Proprietary corp (Geriatric and Medical Centers).
Admissions Requirements Medical examination.
Staff Physicians 4 (ft); RNs 6 (ft), 3 (pt); LPNs 10 (ft), 4 (pt); Nurses' aides 70 (ft), 15 (pt); Physical therapists 1 (pt); Recreational therapists 1 (ft); Occupational therapists 1 (pt); Speech therapists 1 (pt); Activities coordinators 1 (ft); Dietitians 1 (pt); Ophthalmologists 1 (pt); Podiatrists 1 (pt); Dentists 1 (pt).
Facilities Dining room; Physical therapy room; Activities room; Barber/Beauty shop.
Activities Arts & crafts; Cards; Games; Movies; Dances/Social/Cultural gatherings.

New Ralston House
3609 Chestnut St, Philadelphia, PA 19104
(215) 386-2942
Admin Peter A Laudenslager RN NHA.
Licensure Skilled care; Intermediate care. *Beds* SNF 62; ICF 62. *Private Pay Patients* 30%. *Certified* Medicaid; Medicare.
Owner Nonprofit corp.

Staff RNs 7 (ft); LPNs 13 (ft); Nurses' aides 37 (ft); Physical therapists 1 (ft); Recreational therapists 1 (ft); Activities coordinators 1 (ft).
Facilities Dining room; Physical therapy room; Activities room; Laundry room; Barber/Beauty shop.
Activities Arts & crafts; Cards; Games; Reading groups; Prayer groups; Movies; Intergenerational programs; Pet therapy.

Northwood Nursing Center
4621 Castor Ave, Philadelphia, PA 19124
(215) 744-6464, 289-5991 FAX
Admin Sidney Malamut. *Dir of Nursing* Emily Cervonka. *Medical Dir* Terry Waldman MD.
Licensure Skilled care; Intermediate care. *Beds* SNF 72; ICF 76. *Certified* Medicaid; Medicare.
Owner Proprietary corp.
Admissions Requirements Medical examination; Physician's request.
Staff Physicians 10 (pt); Physical therapists 1 (pt); Occupational therapists 1 (pt); Speech therapists 1 (pt); Activities coordinators 1 (ft), 2 (pt); Dietitians 1 (pt); Ophthalmologists 1 (pt); Podiatrists 3 (pt); Audiologists 1 (pt).
Facilities Dining room; Physical therapy room; Activities room; Laundry room; Barber/Beauty shop.
Activities Arts & crafts; Cards; Games; Reading groups; Prayer groups; Movies; Intergenerational programs; Pet therapy.

Park Pleasant Inc
PO Box 19990, 4712 Chester Ave, Philadelphia, PA 19143
(215) 727-4450
Licensure Skilled care. *Beds* SNF 123. *Certified* Medicaid; Medicare.
Owner Proprietary corp.

Paul's Run
9896 Bustleton Ave, Philadelphia, PA 19115
(215) 934-3000
Admin Suzanne K Stevens. *Dir of Nursing* Gayle Sanders. *Medical Dir* Todd Sagin.
Licensure Skilled care; Independent living; Personal care. *Beds* SNF 60; Independent living 321; Personal care 44. *Private Pay Patients* 50%. *Certified* Medicare.
Owner Nonprofit corp.
Admissions Requirements Minimum age 65; Medical examination; Physician's request.
Staff Physicians 4 (pt); RNs 4 (ft), 5 (pt); LPNs 4 (ft), 6 (pt); Nurses' aides 20 (ft), 15 (pt); Physical therapists 1 (pt); Reality therapists 1 (ft); Recreational therapists 1 (ft); Occupational therapists 1 (pt); Speech therapists 1 (pt); Activities coordinators 1 (ft); Dietitians 1 (pt); Ophthalmologists (consultant); Podiatrists; Audiologists; Recreational therapy aides 2 (pt); Dentists 1 (pt); Physical therapy aides 2 (pt); Chaplains 1 (ft); Social workers 1 (ft); Psychiatric social workers 1 (pt).
Affiliation Lutheran.
Facilities Dining room; Physical therapy room; Activities room; Chapel; Crafts room; Laundry room; Barber/Beauty shop; Library.
Activities Arts & crafts; Cards; Games; Prayer groups; Movies; Shopping trips; Dances/Social/Cultural gatherings; Intergenerational programs; Pet therapy; Patient council.

Penny Pack Manor Nursing Home Inc
8015 Lawndale St, Philadelphia, PA 19111
(215) 725-2525
Admin Kathleen W Manning. *Dir of Nursing* Michelle Dominick. *Medical Dir* Edwin Merow.
Licensure Skilled care; Alzheimer's care. *Beds* SNF 56. *Private Pay Patients* 90%. *Certified* Medicare.
Owner Proprietary corp.

Facilities Dining room; Physical therapy room; Activities room; Crafts room.
Activities Arts & crafts; Cards; Games; Movies; Dances/Social/Cultural gatherings; Intergenerational programs; Pet therapy.

Perkins Convalescent Home
2107 W Tioga St, Philadelphia, PA 19140
(215) 226-0407
Licensure Skilled care. *Beds* 27. *Certified* Medicaid.
Owner Proprietary corp.

Philadelphia Nursing Home
Girard & Corinthian Aves, Philadelphia, PA 19130
(215) 978-2100
Admin Charles H Jordan, Exec Dir. *Dir of Nursing* Yvonne Campbell. *Medical Dir* Dr Richard Gibbons.
Licensure Skilled care; Intermediate care. *Beds* SNF 185; ICF 315. *Certified* Medicaid; Medicare.
Owner Publicly owned.
Admissions Requirements Physician's request.
Staff Physicians 3 (ft); RNs 21 (ft); LPNs 62 (ft); Nurses' aides 159 (ft); Physical therapists 1 (ft); Recreational therapists 3 (ft); Occupational therapists 1 (ft); Speech therapists 1 (ft); Activities coordinators 1 (ft); Dietitians 2 (ft); Ophthalmologists 1 (pt); Podiatrists 1 (pt); Audiologists 1 (pt).
Facilities Dining room; Physical therapy room; Activities room; Chapel; Crafts room; Laundry room; Barber/Beauty shop; Library.
Activities Arts & crafts; Cards; Games; Reading groups; Prayer groups; Movies; Shopping trips; Dances/Social/Cultural gatherings; Intergenerational programs; Pet therapy.

Philadelphia Nursing Home
7979 State Rd, Philadelphia, PA 19136
(215) 335-8715
Medical Dir Richard Gibbons MD.
Licensure Intermediate care. *Beds* 129. *Certified* Medicaid.
Owner Publicly owned.
Admissions Requirements Medical examination; Physician's request.
Staff Physicians 1 (ft), 1 (pt); RNs 8 (ft), 4 (pt); Recreational therapists 1 (ft); Dietitians 1 (pt); Ophthalmologists 1 (pt); Podiatrists 1 (pt); Audiologists 1 (pt); Dentists 1 (pt).
Facilities Dining room; Physical therapy room; Chapel; Crafts room; Laundry room; Barber/Beauty shop.
Activities Arts & crafts; Cards; Games; Reading groups; Prayer groups; Movies; Shopping trips; Dances/Social/Cultural gatherings.

Philadelphia Protestant Home
6500 Tabor Rd, Philadelphia, PA 19111
(215) 697-8000
Admin Rev Nevin L Kershner. *Dir of Nursing* Peter Ojeda. *Medical Dir* Dr Anthony Palazzola.
Licensure Intermediate care; Residential/personal care; Independent living. *Beds* ICF 106; Residential/personal care 126; Independent living 277. *Certified* Medicaid.
Owner Nonprofit corp.
Admissions Requirements Minimum age 62; Medical examination.
Staff Physicians 3 (pt); RNs 9 (ft); LPNs 15 (ft); Nurses' aides 2 (ft); Physical therapists 2 (ft); Recreational therapists 3 (pt); Occupational therapists 1 (pt); Speech therapists 1 (pt); Activities coordinators 1 (ft); Dietitians 3 (ft); Ophthalmologists 1 (pt); Podiatrists 2 (pt); Audiologists 1 (pt).
Languages German, Spanish.
Facilities Dining room; Physical therapy room; Activities room; Chapel; Crafts room; Laundry room; Barber/Beauty shop; Library; Pool; Fitness center.

Activities Arts & crafts; Cards; Games; Reading groups; Prayer groups; Movies; Shopping trips; Dances/Social/Cultural gatherings; Intergenerational programs; Pet therapy; Swimming; Fitness classes.

Presbyterian Home at 58th Street
58th St & Greenway Ave, Philadelphia, PA 19143
(215) 724-2218
Admin Thomas F Rockenbach Jr. *Dir of Nursing* Julia Bright. *Medical Dir* Donald J Corey MD.
Licensure Skilled care; Intermediate care; Independent living. *Beds* Swing beds SNF/ICF 50; Independent living 148. *Private Pay Patients* 47%. *Certified* Medicaid; Medicare.
Owner Nonprofit corp.
Admissions Requirements Medical examination.
Staff Physicians 2 (pt); RNs 4 (ft), 7 (pt); LPNs 3 (ft), 5 (pt); Nurses' aides 15 (ft); Occupational therapists 1 (pt); Speech therapists 1 (pt); Activities coordinators 1 (pt); Dietitians 1 (pt); Ophthalmologists 1 (pt); Podiatrists 1 (pt).
Affiliation Presbyterian.
Facilities Dining room; Physical therapy room; Chapel; Crafts room; Laundry room; Barber/Beauty shop; Library.
Activities Arts & crafts; Cards; Games; Reading groups; Prayer groups; Movies; Shopping trips; Dances/Social/Cultural gatherings.

Presbyterian Home for Aged
4700 City Line Ave, Philadelphia, PA 19131
(215) 877-8929
Licensure Independent living. *Beds* Independent living 30.
Owner Proprietary corp.

Ralston House
3615 Chestnut St, Philadelphia, PA 19104
(215) 386-2984
Medical Dir Dr Herb Cohen.
Licensure Skilled care; Intermediate care. *Beds* SNF 120; ICF 12. *Certified* Medicaid.
Owner Nonprofit corp.
Staff Physicians 1 (pt); RNs 7 (ft); LPNs 5 (ft), 6 (pt); Nurses' aides 50 (ft), 9 (pt); Physical therapists 1 (ft); Recreational therapists 2 (ft); Occupational therapists 1 (ft); Activities coordinators 1 (ft); Dietitians 1 (ft).
Facilities Dining room; Physical therapy room; Activities room; Chapel; Crafts room; Laundry room; Barber/Beauty shop; Library.
Activities Arts & crafts; Games; Reading groups; Prayer groups; Movies; Shopping trips; Dances/Social/Cultural gatherings.

Regina Community Nursing Center at 65th Street
230 N 65th St, Philadelphia, PA 19139
(215) 472-0541
Admin Philomena Cummins RN NHA. *Dir of Nursing* Mary Coyne RN. *Medical Dir* Martin J Kearney MD.
Licensure Skilled care. *Beds* SNF 44. *Certified* Medicaid.
Owner Nonprofit corp.
Admissions Requirements Minimum age 40; Medical examination.
Staff Physicians 4 (pt); RNs 3 (ft), 2 (pt); LPNs 1 (ft), 2 (pt); Nurses' aides 11 (ft), 8 (pt); Physical therapists 1 (pt); Recreational therapists 1 (pt); Dietitians 1 (pt).
Languages Italian.
Facilities Dining room; Physical therapy room; Activities room.
Activities Cards; Games; Prayer groups; Movies.

Rittenhouse Care Center
1526 Lombard St, Philadelphia, PA 19146
(215) 546-5960

Licensure Skilled care. *Beds* SNF 198. *Certified* Medicaid; Medicare.
Owner Proprietary corp (Geriatric and Medical Centers).

River's Edge Nursing & Rehabilitation Center
9501 State Rd, Philadelphia, PA 19114
(215) 632-5700, 632-3380 FAX
Admin Diane M Berlanda NHA. *Dir of Nursing* Carol Vogt RN. *Medical Dir* Mark Benjamin MD.
Licensure Skilled care. *Beds* SNF 120. *Private Pay Patients* 55%. *Certified* Medicaid; Medicare.
Owner Proprietary corp.
Admissions Requirements Medical examination.
Staff RNs 3 (ft), 9 (pt); LPNs 8 (ft), 14 (pt); Nurses' aides 32 (ft), 15 (pt); Physical therapists 1 (ft); Recreational therapists 1 (ft); Activities coordinators 1 (ft); Dietitians 1 (ft).
Facilities Dining room; Physical therapy room; Activities room; Laundry room; Barber/Beauty shop.
Activities Arts & crafts; Cards; Games; Reading groups; Prayer groups; Movies; Dances/Social/Cultural gatherings; Pet therapy; Intergenerational programs.

Sacred Heart Free Home for Incurable Cancer
1315 W Hunting Park Ave, Philadelphia, PA 19140
(215) 329-3222
Licensure Skilled care. *Beds* SNF 45.
Owner Nonprofit corp.
Admissions Requirements Must have terminal cancer.

Sacred Heart Manor—Philadelphia
6445 Germantown Ave, Philadelphia, PA 19119
(215) 438-5268, 951-0798
Admin Sr M Patricia Michael Sweeney. *Dir of Nursing* Sr Jeanne Francis. *Medical Dir* Wilfreta Baugh MD.
Licensure Skilled care; Intermediate care. *Beds* SNF 57; ICF 114. *Private Pay Patients* 40%. *Certified* Medicaid; Medicare.
Owner Nonprofit corp (Carmelite Sisters for the Aged and Infirm).
Admissions Requirements Minimum age 65; Medical examination.
Staff Physicians; RNs 8 (ft); LPNs 15 (ft); Nurses' aides 64 (ft); Physical therapists 1 (ft); Recreational therapists 1 (ft), 1 (pt); Occupational therapists 1 (pt); Speech therapists 1 (pt); Activities coordinators 1 (ft); Dietitians 1 (ft), 1 (pt); Ophthalmologists 3 (pt); Podiatrists 3 (pt); Audiologists 1 (pt).
Affiliation Roman Catholic.
Facilities Dining room; Physical therapy room; Activities room; Chapel; Crafts room; Laundry room; Barber/Beauty shop; Library.
Activities Arts & crafts; Cards; Games; Reading groups; Prayer groups; Movies; Shopping trips; Dances/Social/Cultural gatherings; Intergenerational programs; Pet therapy.

St Ignatius Nursing Home
4401 Haverford Ave, Philadelphia, PA 19104
(215) 349-8800
Admin Sr Mary Agatha Cebula. *Dir of Nursing* P Sturgis RN. *Medical Dir* L Walker MD.
Licensure Skilled care; Intermediate care. *Beds* SNF 62; ICF 114. *Certified* Medicaid; Medicare.
Owner Nonprofit corp.
Staff RNs 3 (ft), 7 (pt); LPNs 12 (ft), 6 (pt); Nurses' aides 63 (ft), 8 (pt); Physical therapists 1 (pt); Activities coordinators 1 (ft); Dietitians 1 (ft), 1 (pt); Dentists 1 (pt).

St John Neumann Nursing Home
10400 Roosevelt Blvd, Philadelphia, PA
19116-3999
(215) 698-5600
Admin Sr M Beata NHA. *Dir of Nursing*
Angela Clark BSN RN. *Medical Dir* Robert
E Chmielewski MD.
Licensure Skilled care. *Beds* SNF 224. *Private
Pay Patients* 30%. *Certified* Medicaid;
Medicare.
Owner Nonprofit corp.
Admissions Requirements Minimum age 16;
Medical examination; Physician's request.
Staff Physicians 10 (pt); RNs 6 (ft), 8 (pt);
LPNs 11 (ft), 13 (pt); Nurses' aides 89 (ft),
32 (pt); Physical therapists 1 (pt);
Occupational therapists 1 (pt); Speech
therapists 1 (pt); Activities coordinators 1
(ft); Dietitians 1 (ft); Ophthalmologists 2
(pt); Podiatrists 3 (pt); Audiologists 2 (pt).
Languages Polish, Spanish, Italian.
Affiliation Roman Catholic.
Facilities Dining room; Physical therapy
room; Activities room; Chapel; Crafts room;
Laundry room; Barber/Beauty shop; Library.
Activities Arts & crafts; Cards; Games; Prayer
groups; Movies; Shopping trips; Dances/
Social/Cultural gatherings; Pet therapy.

Simpson House Inc
Belmont Ave & Monument Rd, Philadelphia,
PA 19131
(215) 878-3600
Admin Rev David W Powell, Pres. *Dir of
Nursing* James J Kelly RN MSN. *Medical
Dir* Mary DeJoseph DO.
Licensure Skilled care; Intermediate care;
Independent living. *Beds* SNF 31; ICF 95;
Independent living 160. *Certified* Medicaid;
Medicare.
Owner Nonprofit corp.
Admissions Requirements Minimum age 65;
Medical examination; Physician's request.
Staff Physicians 3 (pt); RNs; LPNs; Nurses'
aides; Physical therapists (contracted);
Recreational therapists; Occupational
therapists; Speech therapists; Activities
coordinators; Dietitians (contracted);
Ophthalmologists; Podiatrists.
Affiliation Methodist.
Facilities Dining room; Physical therapy
room; Activities room; Chapel; Crafts room;
Laundry room; Barber/Beauty shop; Library.
Activities Arts & crafts; Cards; Games;
Reading groups; Prayer groups; Movies;
Shopping trips; Dances/Social/Cultural
gatherings; Intergenerational programs; Pet
therapy.

Stephen Smith Home for the Aged
4400 Girard Ave, Philadelphia, PA 19104
(215) 477-1170
Licensure Skilled care. *Beds* SNF 180.
Certified Medicaid.
Owner Nonprofit corp.

Stapeley In Germantown
6300 Greene St, Philadelphia, PA 19144
(215) 844-0700
Licensure Skilled care. *Beds* SNF 120.
Certified Medicaid; Medicare.

Stenton Hall
7310 Stenton Ave, Philadelphia, PA 19150
(215) 242-2727
Admin Ronnie R Scicchitano NHA. *Dir of
Nursing* Rick Keller RN. *Medical Dir*
Richard Rosenfeld MD.
Licensure Skilled care. *Beds* SNF 95. *Certified*
Medicaid; Medicare.
Owner Proprietary corp (Beverly Enterprises).
Staff Physicians 1 (pt); RNs 5 (ft), 1 (pt);
LPNs 4 (ft), 2 (pt); Nurses' aides 30 (ft);
Physical therapists 1 (pt); Recreational
therapists 1 (ft); Occupational therapists 1
(pt); Speech therapists 1 (pt); Activities
coordinators 1 (pt); Dietitians 1 (pt);
Podiatrists 1 (pt); Dentists 1 (pt).

Affiliation Jewish.
Facilities Dining room; Physical therapy
room; Activities room; Laundry room;
Barber/Beauty shop.
Activities Arts & crafts; Cards; Games;
Reading groups; Prayer groups; Movies;
Shopping trips; Dances/Social/Cultural
gatherings.

Tucker House II
1001 Wallace St, Philadelphia, PA 19123
(215) 235-1600, 763-4144 FAX
Admin Paula M Burroughs ACSW NHA. *Dir
of Nursing* Joanie Alston RN BSN.
Medical Dir Nathaniel Copeland MD.
Licensure Skilled care; Intermediate care;
Alzheimer's care. *Beds* SNF 60; ICF 120.
Private Pay Patients 2%. *Certified* Medicaid;
Medicare.
Owner Nonprofit corp.
Admissions Requirements Chest X-ray; CBC;
Urinalysis; Pre-admission screening.
Staff Physicians 1 (ft), 5 (pt); RNs 3 (ft), 7
(pt); LPNs 20 (ft); Nurses' aides 75 (ft);
Physical therapists 1 (ft); Recreational
therapists 2 (ft), 1 (pt); Occupational
therapists 1 (pt); Speech therapists 1 (pt);
Activities coordinators 2 (ft), 1 (pt);
Dietitians 1 (pt); Ophthalmologists 1 (pt);
Podiatrists 2 (pt); Audiologists 1 (pt).
Languages Spanish.
Facilities Dining room; Physical therapy
room; Activities room; Chapel; Crafts room;
Laundry room; Barber/Beauty shop;
Occupational therapy room.
Activities Arts & crafts; Cards; Games;
Reading groups; Prayer groups; Movies;
Shopping trips; Dances/Social/Cultural
gatherings; Intergenerational programs.

Unitarian Universalist House
224 W Tulpehocken St, Philadelphia, PA
19144
(215) 843-0809
Admin Beth Proukou MSN NHA. *Dir of
Nursing* Delores Salamone RNC. *Medical
Dir* Norman Stahlheber MD.
Licensure Skilled care; Intermediate care;
Residential care. *Beds* Swing beds SNF/ICF
39; Residential care 26. *Certified* Medicaid.
Owner Nonprofit corp.
Admissions Requirements Minimum age 65;
Medical examination.
Staff RNs 3 (ft), 3 (pt); LPNs 2 (ft), 3 (pt);
Nurses' aides 8 (ft), 10 (pt); Activities
coordinators 1 (ft); Dietitians 1 (pt).
Affiliation Unitarian Universalist.
Facilities Dining room; Activities room;
Barber/Beauty shop; Library; Enclosed
garden.
Activities Arts & crafts; Cards; Games;
Reading groups; Prayer groups; Movies;
Shopping trips; Dances/Social/Cultural
gatherings; Intergenerational programs; Pet
therapy; Concerts.

University Nursing & Rehabilitation Center
747 S Broad St, Philadelphia, PA 19147
(215) 985-0555
Licensure Skilled care. *Beds* SNF 248.
Certified Medicaid; Medicare.
Owner Proprietary corp.

Uptown Home for the Aged
7800 Bustleton Ave, Philadelphia, PA 19152
(215) 722-2300
Admin Samuel T Lewis.
Medical Dir Sidney Brenner MD.
Licensure Skilled care; Intermediate care. *Beds*
SNF 84; ICF 156. *Certified* Medicaid;
Medicare.
Owner Nonprofit corp.
Admissions Requirements Minimum age 65;
Medical examination.
Staff Physicians 2 (pt); RNs 7 (ft), 6 (pt);
LPNs 11 (ft), 17 (pt); Nurses' aides 51 (ft),
26 (pt); Physical therapists 1 (pt);
Recreational therapists 1 (ft); Occupational

therapists 1 (pt); Speech therapists 1 (pt);
Activities coordinators 1 (ft); Dietitians 1
(pt); Ophthalmologists 1 (pt); Podiatrists 1
(pt); Audiologists 1 (pt); Dentists 1 (pt);
Ward clerks 3 (ft).
Facilities Dining room; Physical therapy
room; Activities room; Chapel; Crafts room;
Laundry room; Barber/Beauty shop; Library.
Activities Arts & crafts; Cards; Games;
Reading groups; Prayer groups; Movies;
Shopping trips; Dances/Social/Cultural
gatherings.

Walt Whitman Convalescent Center
4th & Porter Sts, Philadelphia, PA 19148
(215) 271-1080
Admin Roxanne Bambach. *Dir of Nursing*
Frances Cunningham RN. *Medical Dir* Dr
Wolgin.
Licensure Skilled care; Intermediate care. *Beds*
SNF 60; ICF 60. *Certified* Medicaid;
Medicare.
Owner Nonprofit organization/foundation.
Staff Physicians 6 (pt); RNs 5 (ft); LPNs 5
(ft), 1 (pt); Nurses' aides 29 (ft); Physical
therapists (contracted); Recreational
therapists 1 (ft); Occupational therapists 1
(pt); Speech therapists 1 (pt); Activities
coordinators 2 (ft), 1 (pt); Dietitians 1 (ft);
Ophthalmologists (contracted); Podiatrists 2
(pt); Audiologists 1 (pt); Per diem RNs &
LPNs 9 (ft).
Facilities Dining room; Physical therapy
room; Activities room; Crafts room; Laundry
room; Barber/Beauty shop; Library.
Activities Arts & crafts; Cards; Games;
Reading groups; Prayer groups; Movies;
Dances/Social/Cultural gatherings;
Intergenerational programs; Pet therapy.

Philipsburg

Moshannon Heights
PO Box 551, Presqueisle & 2nd Sts,
Philipsburg, PA 16866
(814) 342-0340
Licensure Skilled care. *Beds* 38. *Certified*
Medicaid; Medicare.
Owner Nonprofit corp.
Affiliation Presbyterian.

Presbyterian Home of Moshannon Valley
PO Box 551, Philipsburg, PA 16866
(814) 342-6090
Licensure Skilled care. *Beds* SNF 120.
Certified Medicaid; Medicare.
Owner Proprietary corp.

Phoenixville

Phoenixville Convalescent Manor
833 S Main St, Phoenixville, PA 19460
(215) 933-5867
Licensure Skilled care. *Beds* SNF 144.
Certified Medicaid; Medicare.
Owner Proprietary corp (Beverly Enterprises).

Pitman

Friendly Nursing Home
RD 1, Box 118, Pitman, PA 17964
(717) 644-0489
Admin Dolly A Straight. *Dir of Nursing* Carol
Sidleck RN. *Medical Dir* Dr Peter McNeil.
Licensure Skilled care. *Beds* SNF 48. *Private
Pay Patients* 14%. *Certified* Medicaid.
Owner Proprietary corp (AmCare Inc).
Staff RNs 1 (ft), 5 (pt); LPNs 3 (pt); Nurses'
aides 3 (ft), 18 (pt); Activities coordinators 1
(ft); Dietitians.
Facilities Dining room; Activities room.
Activities Arts & crafts; Cards; Games;
Reading groups; Prayer groups; Movies;
Shopping trips; Dances/Social/Cultural
gatherings.

Pittsburgh

Angelus Convalescent Center Inc
200 Amber St, Pittsburgh, PA 15206
(412) 362-6300
Licensure Skilled care. *Beds* SNF 84. *Certified*
Medicaid; Medicare.
Owner Proprietary corp.

Asbury Heights
700 Bower Hill Rd, Mount Lebanon,
Pittsburgh, PA 15243
(412) 341-1030
Admin Howard F Peters.
Medical Dir Lawrence Wilson MD.
Licensure Skilled care; Intermediate care;
Personal care; Independent care. *Beds* SNF
55; ICF 90; Personal care 22. *Certified*
Medicaid; Medicare.
Owner Nonprofit corp.
Admissions Requirements Minimum age 65;
Medical examination.
Staff Physicians 1 (ft); RNs 12 (ft), 15 (pt);
LPNs 10 (ft), 17 (pt); Nurses' aides 35 (ft),
34 (pt); Physical therapists 1 (ft);
Recreational therapists 2 (ft); Occupational
therapists 1 (ft); Speech therapists 1 (ft);
Activities coordinators 4 (ft); Dietitians 1
(ft); Ophthalmologists 1 (ft); Dentists 1 (ft).
Affiliation Methodist.
Facilities Dining room; Physical therapy
room; Activities room; Chapel; Crafts room;
Laundry room; Barber/Beauty shop; Library;
Ice cream shop; Country store; Medical
complex; Skylight mall.
Activities Arts & crafts; Cards; Games;
Reading groups; Prayer groups; Movies;
Shopping trips; Dances/Social/Cultural
gatherings; Trips to local points of interest.

Baldwin Health Center
1717 Skyline Dr, Pittsburgh, PA 15227
(412) 885-8400, 885-0772 FAX
Admin Hollis Garfield Esq. *Dir of Nursing*
Nina Gigliotti RN. *Medical Dir* Thomas
Schaefer MD.
Licensure Skilled care; Intermediate care. *Beds*
SNF 100; ICF 100. *Private Pay Patients*
40%. *Certified* Medicaid; Medicare.
Owner Proprietary corp.
Admissions Requirements Medical
examination.
Staff Physicians 2 (ft), 10 (pt); RNs 6 (ft), 5
(pt); LPNs 11 (ft), 7 (pt); Nurses' aides 48
(ft), 15 (pt); Physical therapists 1 (ft);
Recreational therapists 2 (ft); Occupational
therapists 1 (ft); Speech therapists 1 (ft);
Activities coordinators 2 (ft); Dietitians 1
(ft); Ophthalmologists 1 (pt); Podiatrists 1
(pt); Audiologists 1 (pt); Dentists; Music
therapists; General surgeons.
Facilities Dining room; Physical therapy
room; Activities room; Chapel; Crafts room;
Laundry room; Barber/Beauty shop; Library;
Family room; Vending room; 4 lounges;
Hydrotherapy pool.
Activities Arts & crafts; Cards; Games;
Reading groups; Prayer groups; Movies;
Shopping trips; Dances/Social/Cultural
gatherings; Intergenerational programs; Pet
therapy; Music therapy; Ethnic/Therapeutic
meals.

Baptist Homes Nursing Center
489 Castle Shannon Blvd, Pittsburgh, PA
15234
(412) 563-6550
Admin Kathleen S Anderson. *Dir of Nursing*
Jean Wengryn RN. *Medical Dir* Dr Joyce
Sandberg.
Licensure Skilled care; Intermediate care;
Retirement; Alzheimer's care. *Beds* SNF 42;
ICF 84. *Certified* Medicaid; Medicare.
Owner Nonprofit corp.
Admissions Requirements Medical
examination; Physician's request.

Staff RNs 7 (ft), 14 (pt); LPNs 8 (ft), 3 (pt);
Nurses' aides 24 (ft), 38 (pt); Physical
therapists 1 (ft); Recreational therapists 1
(ft); Occupational therapists 1 (pt); Activities
coordinators 1 (ft); Dietitians 1 (ft).
Affiliation Baptist.
Facilities Dining room; Physical therapy
room; Activities room; Chapel; Crafts room;
Laundry room; Barber/Beauty shop;
Lounges; Solarium; Family rooms; Gift shop.
Activities Arts & crafts; Cards; Games;
Reading groups; Prayer groups; Movies;
Shopping trips; Dances/Social/Cultural
gatherings; Sewing; Cooking; Exercise
classes.

Canterbury Place
4001 Penn Ave, Pittsburgh, PA 15224
(412) 682-0153
Admin Kathleen S Martindale NHA. *Dir of
Nursing* June Tyniec RN. *Medical Dir* Dr
David Martin.
Licensure Skilled care; Retirement. *Beds* SNF
28. *Certified* Medicaid; Medicare.
Owner Nonprofit corp.
Admissions Requirements Minimum age 65;
Medical examination.
Staff Physicians 2 (pt); RNs 2 (ft), 2 (pt);
LPNs 3 (ft), 4 (pt); Nurses' aides 13 (ft), 7
(pt); Physical therapists 1 (pt); Activities
coordinators 1 (ft); Ophthalmologists 1 (pt);
Physical therapy aides 1 (pt); Social workers
1 (pt); Nurse practitioners 1 (pt).
Languages Polish, Slavic.
Affiliation Episcopal.
Facilities Dining room; Physical therapy
room; Activities room; Chapel; Laundry
room; Barber/Beauty shop; Library.
Activities Arts & crafts; Cards; Games;
Reading groups; Prayer groups; Movies;
Shopping trips; Dances/Social/Cultural
gatherings; Pet therapy; Resident council;
Music therapy.

Collins Nursing Home
5511 Baum Blvd, Pittsburgh, PA 15232
(412) 661-1740
Medical Dir Dr Maranatti.
Licensure Skilled care; Intermediate care. *Beds*
SNF 31; ICF 40. *Certified* Medicaid.
Owner Proprietary corp (Brian Center
Management Corp).
Admissions Requirements Minimum age 65;
Medical examination; Physician's request.
Staff Physicians 1 (pt); RNs 4 (ft), 3 (pt);
LPNs 6 (ft), 3 (pt); Physical therapists 1 (ft);
Recreational therapists 1 (ft); Speech
therapists 1 (pt); Activities coordinators 1
(ft); Dietitians 1 (ft); Ophthalmologists 1
(pt); Podiatrists 1 (pt); Dentists 1 (pt).
Facilities Dining room; Physical therapy
room; Activities room; Laundry room;
Barber/Beauty shop.
Activities Arts & crafts; Cards; Games;
Reading groups.

Forbes Center for Gerontology
Frankstown Ave at Washington Blvd,
Pittsburgh, PA 15206
(412) 665-3232
Medical Dir Dr J F O'Keefe & Dr J R Friday.
Licensure Skilled care. *Beds* SNF 134.
Certified Medicaid; Medicare.
Owner Nonprofit corp.
Admissions Requirements Minimum age 16;
Medical examination; Physician's request.
Staff Physicians 2 (ft); RNs 8 (ft), 4 (pt);
LPNs 12 (ft); Nurses' aides 30 (ft); Physical
therapists 1 (ft); Reality therapists 1 (ft);
Recreational therapists 2 (ft); Occupational
therapists 1 (pt); Speech therapists 1 (pt);
Activities coordinators 1 (ft); Dietitians 1
(ft).
Facilities Dining room; Physical therapy
room; Activities room; Chapel; Laundry
room; Barber/Beauty shop; Library; Music
therapy room.

Activities Arts & crafts; Games; Prayer groups;
Movies; Shopping trips; Dances/Social/
Cultural gatherings.

Friendship Village of South Hills
1290 Boyce Rd, Pittsburgh, PA 15241-2931
(412) 941-3100, 941-8069 FAX
Admin Mary E Meindl NHA. *Dir of Nursing*
Judith G DiGorio RN. *Medical Dir* Walter
Robison MD.
Licensure Skilled care; Retirement. *Beds* SNF
60; Retirement 260. *Private Pay Patients*
94%. *Certified* Medicaid; Medicare.
Owner Nonprofit corp (Life Care Services
Corp).
Admissions Requirements Minimum age 18;
Physician's request.
Staff Physicians 3 (pt); RNs 4 (ft), 4 (pt);
LPNs 4 (ft), 3 (pt); Nurses' aides 17 (ft), 7
(pt); Physical therapists 1 (pt); Recreational
therapists 1 (pt); Occupational therapists 1
(pt); Speech therapists 1 (pt); Activities
coordinators 1 (ft); Dietitians 1 (pt);
Ophthalmologists 1 (pt); Podiatrists 1 (pt);
Audiologists 1 (pt).
Facilities Dining room; Physical therapy
room; Activities room; Laundry room;
Barber/Beauty shop.
Activities Arts & crafts; Cards; Games;
Reading groups; Prayer groups; Movies;
Dances/Social/Cultural gatherings.

Glen Hazel Regional Center
955 Rivermont Dr, Pittsburgh, PA 15207
(412) 422-6800
Admin Dr Jacqueline H Mikell. *Dir of Nursing*
Dayna Colaizzi. *Medical Dir* Dr Alan
Steckel.
Licensure Skilled care; Intermediate care. *Beds*
SNF 300; ICF 60. *Private Pay Patients* 0%.
Certified Medicaid; Medicare.
Owner Publicly owned.
Staff Physicians (attending); RNs 20 (ft), 20
(pt); LPNs 38 (ft); Nurses' aides 144 (ft);
Physical therapists 1 (ft); Recreational
therapists 1 (ft); Occupational therapists 1
(ft); Speech therapists 1 (pt); Activities
coordinators 3 (ft); Dietitians 2 (ft);
Ophthalmologists 1 (pt); Podiatrists 1 (pt);
Audiologists 1 (pt); Medical consultants 25
(pt).

Heritage Shadyside
5702 Phillips Ave, Pittsburgh, PA 15217
(412) 422-5100
Licensure Skilled care. *Beds* SNF 159.
Certified Medicare.
Owner Proprietary corp.

Home for Aged Protestant Women
900 Rebecca Ave, Pittsburgh, PA 15221
(412) 731-2338
Medical Dir Noel Gillette MD.
Licensure Intermediate care. *Beds* 37.
Owner Nonprofit corp.
Admissions Requirements Minimum age 65;
Females only; Medical examination;
Physician's request.
Staff Physicians 1 (pt); RNs 1 (ft), 4 (pt);
LPNs 3 (ft), 2 (pt); Nurses' aides 8 (ft), 5
(pt); Physical therapists 1 (pt); Speech
therapists 1 (pt); Activities coordinators 1
(ft).
Facilities Dining room; Physical therapy
room; Activities room; Chapel; Crafts room;
Laundry room; Barber/Beauty shop; Library.
Activities Arts & crafts; Cards; Games;
Reading groups; Prayer groups; Movies;
Dances/Social/Cultural gatherings.

Jefferson Hills Manor Inc
PO Box 10805, 1448 Old Clairton Rd,
Pittsburgh, PA 15236
(412) 653-1128
Admin Doris Koehler. *Dir of Nursing* Sharron
Sonny. *Medical Dir* Dick Maley.

Licensure Skilled care; Personal care. *Beds* SNF 68; Personal care 19. *Private Pay Patients* 75%. *Certified* Medicare.
Owner Proprietary corp.
Facilities Dining room; Physical therapy room; Activities room; Chapel; Crafts room; Laundry room; Barber/Beauty shop; Library.
Activities Arts & crafts; Cards; Games; Prayer groups; Movies; Shopping trips; Dances/Social/Cultural gatherings; Pet therapy.

John J Kane Allegheny County Home
Vanadium Rd, Pittsburgh, PA 15243
(412) 928-1400
Licensure Skilled care; Intermediate care. *Beds* SNF 1087; ICF 378. *Certified* Medicaid; Medicare.
Owner Nonprofit corp.

John J Kane Regional Center—Ross Township
110 McIntyre Rd, Pittsburgh, PA 15237
(412) 369-2020
Licensure Skilled care. *Beds* SNF 360. *Certified* Medicaid; Medicare.
Owner Publicly owned.

John J Kane Regional Center—Scott Township
300 Kane Blvd, Pittsburgh, PA 15243
(412) 429-3020
Licensure Skilled care. *Beds* SNF 60. *Certified* Medicaid; Medicare.
Owner Publicly owned.

Ladies Grand Army of the Republic Home
2622 Woodstock Ave, Pittsburgh, PA 15218
(412) 271-1316
Medical Dir Dr Mangan.
Licensure Intermediate care. *Beds* ICF 66. *Certified* Medicaid.
Owner Nonprofit corp.
Admissions Requirements Females only; Medical examination.
Staff Physicians 2 (ft); RNs 1 (ft), 4 (pt); LPNs 2 (ft), 2 (pt); Nurses' aides 15 (ft); Physical therapists 1 (pt); Reality therapists 1 (ft); Occupational therapists 1 (ft); Activities coordinators 1 (ft); Dietitians 1 (ft); Dentists 1 (ft).
Facilities Dining room; Activities room; Chapel; Crafts room; Laundry room; Barber/Beauty shop; Library.
Activities Arts & crafts; Cards; Games; Reading groups; Prayer groups; Movies; Shopping trips; Dances/Social/Cultural gatherings.

Leader Nursing & Rehabilitation Center—Green Tree
1848 Greentree Rd, Pittsburgh, PA 15220
(412) 344-7744
Licensure Skilled care. *Beds* SNF 120. *Certified* Medicaid; Medicare.
Owner Proprietary corp (Manor Care Inc).

Lemington Home for the Aged
1625 Lincoln Ave, Pittsburgh, PA 15206
(412) 441-3700
Admin Delores M Cureton.
Medical Dir Labib Rizk; Yvonne Bankston.
Licensure Intermediate care. *Beds* ICF 180. *Certified* Medicaid.
Owner Nonprofit corp.
Admissions Requirements Minimum age 60; Medical examination; Physician's request.
Staff Physicians 3 (pt); RNs 4 (ft), 4 (pt); LPNs 15 (ft), 1 (pt); Nurses' aides 50 (ft), 2 (pt); Physical therapists 2 (pt); Recreational therapists 1 (ft); Activities coordinators 1 (ft); Dietitians 1 (pt); Ophthalmologists 1 (pt); Podiatrists 1 (pt); Dentists 1 (pt); Social workers 1 (ft).
Facilities Dining room; Physical therapy room; Activities room; Chapel; Crafts room; Laundry room; Barber/Beauty shop.
Activities Arts & crafts; Cards; Games; Reading groups; Prayer groups; Movies; Shopping trips; Dances/Social/Cultural gatherings.

Little Sisters of the Poor Home for the Aged
1028 Benton Ave, Pittsburgh, PA 15212
(412) 761-5373
Admin Sr Regina.
Medical Dir Sr Anne Joseph Doyle.
Licensure Skilled care; Retirement. *Beds* SNF 62. *Certified* Medicaid.
Owner Nonprofit corp.
Admissions Requirements Minimum age 60; Medical examination.
Staff RNs 3 (ft), 6 (pt); LPNs 6 (ft), 7 (pt); Nurses' aides 24 (ft), 20 (pt); Physical therapists 1 (pt); Activities coordinators 2 (ft); Dietitians 1 (pt).
Languages Italian, Spanish, French.
Affiliation Roman Catholic.
Facilities Dining room; Physical therapy room; Activities room; Chapel; Crafts room; Laundry room; Barber/Beauty shop; Library.
Activities Arts & crafts; Cards; Games; Reading groups; Prayer groups; Movies; Shopping trips; Dances/Social/Cultural gatherings.

Marian Manor Corporation
2695 Winchester Dr, Pittsburgh, PA 15220
(412) 563-6866
Licensure Skilled care; Intermediate care. *Beds* SNF 72; ICF 50. *Certified* Medicaid.
Owner Nonprofit corp.

McDonough Home
1540 Evergreen Ave, Pittsburgh, PA 15209
(412) 821-3088
Licensure Intermediate care. *Beds* 25.
Owner Proprietary corp.

Mt Lebanon Manor
350 Old Gilkeson Rd, Pittsburgh, PA 15228
(412) 257-4444
Admin David W Thomas. *Dir of Nursing* Shirley Jenkins RN. *Medical Dir* Michael Kavic MD.
Licensure Skilled care; Intermediate care; Independent living; Alzheimer's care. *Beds* SNF 60; ICF 61; Independent living 5. *Certified* Medicaid; Medicare.
Owner Proprietary corp (Beverly Enterprises).
Admissions Requirements Medical examination; Physician's request.
Staff Physicians 11 (pt); RNs 6 (ft), 6 (pt); LPNs 6 (ft), 6 (pt); Nurses' aides 20 (ft), 20 (pt); Activities coordinators; Dietitians 1 (ft).
Facilities Dining room; Physical therapy room; Activities room; Crafts room; Laundry room; Barber/Beauty shop; Library.
Activities Arts & crafts; Cards; Games; Reading groups; Prayer groups; Movies; Shopping trips; Dances/Social/Cultural gatherings.

Negley Nursing & Rehabilitation Center
550 S Negley Ave, Pittsburgh, PA 15232
(412) 665-2400
Admin Linda Keith. *Dir of Nursing* Peggy S Means RN. *Medical Dir* Grant J Shevchik MD.
Licensure Skilled care; Intermediate care. *Beds* SNF 76; ICF 148. *Certified* Medicaid; Medicare.
Owner Proprietary corp (Health Care and Retirement Corp).
Admissions Requirements Medical examination.
Staff RNs; LPNs; Nurses' aides; Physical therapists; Recreational therapists; Occupational therapists; Speech therapists; Activities coordinators; Dietitians; Ophthalmologists (consultant); Podiatrists (consultant).
Facilities Dining room; Physical therapy room; Activities room; Crafts room; Laundry room; Barber/Beauty shop.
Activities Arts & crafts; Cards; Games; Reading groups; Prayer groups; Movies; Shopping trips; Intergenerational programs; Pet therapy.

Northcoast Care Center
PO Box 27290, Pittsburgh, PA 15235
(216) 431-6200
Licensure Skilled care; Intermediate care. *Beds* Swing beds SNF/ICF 209. *Certified* Medicaid; Medicare.
Owner Proprietary corp.

Rebecca Residence for Protestant Ladies
900 Rebecca Ave, Pittsburgh, PA 15221
(412) 731-2338
Admin Mary E Wilson. *Dir of Nursing* H Terry RN. *Medical Dir* A J Zido MD.
Licensure Intermediate care; Independent living. *Beds* ICF 37.
Owner Nonprofit corp.
Admissions Requirements Minimum age 65; Females only; Medical examination.
Staff Physicians 1 (pt); RNs 3 (ft), 1 (pt); LPNs 3 (ft), 1 (pt); Nurses' aides 5 (ft), 3 (pt); Recreational therapists; Activities coordinators 1 (ft); Dietitians 1 (pt); Podiatrists 1 (pt).
Facilities Dining room; Physical therapy room; Activities room; Chapel; Crafts room; Laundry room; Barber/Beauty shop; Library.
Activities Arts & crafts; Cards; Games; Prayer groups; Movies; Shopping trips; Dances/Social/Cultural gatherings.

Reformed Presbyterian Home
2344 Perrysville Ave, Pittsburgh, PA 15214
(412) 321-4139
Admin William J Weir NHA. *Dir of Nursing* Marjorie Russell RN.
Licensure Skilled care. *Beds* SNF 58. *Certified* Medicaid; Medicare.
Owner Nonprofit corp.
Staff RNs; LPNs; Nurses' aides; Physical therapists; Recreational therapists; Activities coordinators; Dietitians.
Affiliation Presbyterian.

Riverview Center for Jewish Seniors
4724 Brown's Hill Rd, Pittsburgh, PA 15217
(412) 521-5900, 521-7210 FAX
Admin Stanley M Schiffman. *Dir of Nursing* Patricia Fallon RN. *Medical Dir* David P Segel MD.
Licensure Skilled care; Intermediate care; Retirement; Alzheimer's care. *Beds* SNF 188; ICF 202; Retirement 250. *Private Pay Patients* 35%. *Certified* Medicaid; Medicare.
Owner Nonprofit corp.
Admissions Requirements Minimum age 62; Medical examination.
Staff RNs; LPNs; Nurses' aides 152 (ft), 59 (pt); Physical therapists 5 (ft), 2 (pt); Reality therapists 1 (ft); Recreational therapists 5 (ft), 7 (pt); Occupational therapists 2 (pt); Speech therapists 1 (pt); Activities coordinators 1 (ft); Dietitians 1 (ft).
Languages Yiddish, Hebrew, Russian.
Affiliation Jewish.
Facilities Dining room; Physical therapy room; Activities room; Chapel; Crafts room; Laundry room; Barber/Beauty shop; Library.
Activities Arts & crafts; Cards; Games; Reading groups; Prayer groups; Movies; Shopping trips; Dances/Social/Cultural gatherings; Intergenerational programs; Pet therapy; Alzheimer's activity program; Day care for Alzheimer's and memory impaired adults.

St Francis Nursing Center—East
745 N Highland Ave, Pittsburgh, PA 15206

St Joseph Nursing & Health Care Center
5324 Penn Ave, Pittsburgh, PA 15224
(412) 665-5100
Admin Sr Maria Goretti Zamberlan RSM. *Dir of Nursing* Nadine Plummer RN. *Medical Dir* Frank Kush MD.
Licensure Skilled care; Adult day care. *Beds* SNF 158. *Private Pay Patients* 40%. *Certified* Medicaid; Medicare.
Owner Nonprofit corp.

Admissions Requirements Minimum age Primarily 60; Medical examination.
Staff Physicians (consultants); RNs 6 (ft), 3 (pt); LPNs 11 (ft), 6 (pt); Nurses' aides 50 (ft), 13 (pt); Physical therapists (consultant); Occupational therapists (consultant); Speech therapists (consultant); Activities coordinators 1 (ft); Dietitians (consultant); Ophthalmologists (consultant); Podiatrists (consultants); Audiologists (consultant).
Affiliation Roman Catholic.
Facilities Dining room; Physical therapy room; Activities room; Chapel; Crafts room; Laundry room; Barber/Beauty shop; Library; Activities of daily living room.
Activities Arts & crafts; Cards; Games; Reading groups; Prayer groups; Movies; Shopping trips; Dances/Social/Cultural gatherings; Intergenerational programs; Pet therapy; Birthday & holiday parties; Exercise classes.

Shadyside Nursing & Rehabilitation Center
5609 5th Ave, Pittsburgh, PA 15232
(412) 362-3500
Admin M Murray NHA. *Dir of Nursing* P Bernd RN. *Medical Dir* Margaret Kush MD.
Licensure Skilled care; Intermediate care. *Beds* SNF 100; ICF 50. *Certified* Medicaid; Medicare.
Owner Proprietary corp (Health Care & Retirement Corp).
Admissions Requirements Minimum age 18; Medical examination.
Staff Physicians; RNs; LPNs; Nurses' aides; Physical therapists; Recreational therapists; Occupational therapists; Speech therapists; Activities coordinators; Dietitians; Audiologists.
Facilities Dining room; Physical therapy room; Activities room; Barber/Beauty shop.
Activities Arts & crafts; Cards; Games; Reading groups; Prayer groups; Movies; Shopping trips; Dances/Social/Cultural gatherings; Intergenerational programs; Pet therapy.

Sidney Square Convalescent Center
2112 Sidney St, Pittsburgh, PA 15203
(412) 481-5566
Admin David W Thomas. *Dir of Nursing* Charlotte Sarles RN. *Medical Dir* D Michael I Mallinger MD.
Licensure Skilled care; Intermediate care; Personal care. *Beds* Swing beds SNF/ICF 85; Personal care 72. *Private Pay Patients* 72%. *Certified* Medicare.
Owner Proprietary corp.
Staff Physical therapists 1 (pt); Recreational therapists 1 (pt); Occupational therapists 1 (pt); Speech therapists 1 (pt); Activities coordinators 1 (ft); Dietitians 1 (pt); Ophthalmologists 1 (pt); Podiatrists 1 (pt); Audiologists 1 (pt).
Facilities Dining room; Physical therapy room; Activities room; Crafts room; Laundry room; Barber/Beauty shop.
Activities Arts & crafts; Cards; Games; Reading groups; Prayer groups; Movies; Shopping trips; Dances/Social/Cultural gatherings; Intergenerational programs; Pet therapy.

Sky Vue Terrace Nursing Center
2170 Rhine St, Pittsburgh, PA 15212
(412) 323-0420
Admin Conne Civiterla. *Dir of Nursing* Callie Todhunter. *Medical Dir* Dr Harry L Heck.
Licensure Skilled care; Intermediate care. *Beds* SNF 60; ICF 40. *Certified* Medicaid; Medicare; VA.
Owner Proprietary corp (Health Care and Retirement Corp).
Admissions Requirements Medical examination.
Staff Physicians 1 (ft), 5 (pt); RNs 5 (ft), 7 (pt); LPNs 6 (ft), 5 (pt); Nurses' aides 32 (ft), 4 (pt); Physical therapists 1 (ft);

Occupational therapists 1 (ft); Speech therapists 1 (ft); Activities coordinators 1 (ft); Dietitians 1 (ft); Ophthalmologists 1 (pt); Podiatrists 1 (pt); Dentists 1 (pt).
Facilities Dining room; Physical therapy room; Chapel; Laundry room; Barber/Beauty shop; Patient lounges.
Activities Arts & crafts; Cards; Games; Prayer groups; Movies; Shopping trips; Dances/Social/Cultural gatherings.

Southwestern Nursing Home & Rehabilitation Center
PO Box 18056, 500 Lewis Run Rd, Pittsburgh, PA 15236
(412) 466-0600
Admin Mark D Bondi. *Dir of Nursing* R Hofmann. *Medical Dir* A C Repepi MD.
Licensure Skilled care; Intermediate care; Alzheimer's care. *Beds* SNF 59; ICF 59. *Private Pay Patients* 34%. *Certified* Medicaid; Medicare.
Owner Proprietary corp.
Admissions Requirements Medical examination; Physician's request.
Staff Physicians (consultants); RNs 10 (ft), 5 (pt); LPNs 15 (ft), 10 (pt); Nurses' aides 45 (ft), 10 (pt); Physical therapists (consultant); Recreational therapists 2 (ft), 1 (pt); Dietitians.
Facilities Dining room; Physical therapy room; Activities room; Crafts room; Laundry room; Barber/Beauty shop; Library; Outpatient surgery center; Clinical laboratory; Physical therapy practice; Pharmacy; 40 physician offices; Cardiac assessment unit; X-ray facilities; Restaurant.
Activities Arts & crafts; Cards; Games; Reading groups; Prayer groups; Movies; Shopping trips; Dances/Social/Cultural gatherings; Intergenerational programs; Pet therapy.

United Methodist Health Center
700 Bower Hill Rd, Pittsburgh, PA 15243
(412) 341-1030
Licensure Skilled care; Independent living. *Beds* SNF 145. *Certified* Medicaid; Medicare.
Owner Proprietary corp.

United Presbyterian Home for Aged People
306 Pennsylvania Ave, Pittsburgh, PA 15221
(412) 242-3606
Admin Georgette Renze Miller. *Dir of Nursing* C Gehringer. *Medical Dir* J Gleason MD.
Licensure Skilled care; Independent living. *Beds* SNF 29.
Owner Nonprofit corp.
Admissions Requirements Minimum age 65; Medical examination.
Affiliation Presbyterian.
Facilities Dining room; Activities room; Chapel; Crafts room; Laundry room; Barber/Beauty shop; Library.
Activities Arts & crafts; Cards; Games; Reading groups; Prayer groups; Movies; Shopping trips.

Villa De Marillac Nursing Home
5300 Stanton Ave, Pittsburgh, PA 15206
(412) 361-2833
Admin Sr Theresa Novak NHA. *Dir of Nursing* Rita Farrell RN. *Medical Dir* Dr Linda Roberts.
Licensure Skilled care; Intermediate care. *Beds* Swing beds SNF/ICF 50. *Private Pay Patients* 76%. *Certified* Medicaid.
Owner Nonprofit corp.
Admissions Requirements Medical examination.
Staff RNs 2 (ft), 2 (pt); LPNs 2 (ft), 2 (pt); Nurses' aides 10 (ft), 10 (pt); Physical therapists; Activities coordinators 1 (ft); Dietitians 1 (ft).
Affiliation Roman Catholic.

Facilities Dining room; Physical therapy room; Activities room; Chapel; Laundry room; Barber/Beauty shop.
Activities Arts & crafts; Cards; Games; Prayer groups; Movies; Shopping trips; Dances/Social/Cultural gatherings; Intergenerational programs; Pet therapy.

Vincentian Home for Chronically Ill
Perrymont Rd, Pittsburgh, PA 15237
(412) 366-5600
Admin Sr Anne Kull VSC.
Licensure Skilled care. *Beds* SNF 219. *Certified* Medicaid; Medicare.
Owner Nonprofit corp (Vincentian Sisters of Charity).
Admissions Requirements Medical examination.
Affiliation Roman Catholic.
Facilities Dining room; Physical therapy room; Activities room; Chapel; Barber/Beauty shop.
Activities Cards; Games; Reading groups; Prayer groups; Movies; Shopping trips; Dances/Social/Cultural gatherings.

Western Pennsylvania Eastern Star Home
226 Bellevue Rd, Pittsburgh, PA 15229
(412) 931-8300
Licensure Skilled care. *Beds* SNF 39.
Owner Nonprofit corp.
Affiliation Order of Eastern Star.

Western Restoration Center
2851 Bedford Ave, Pittsburgh, PA 15219
(412) 683-5000
Licensure Skilled care; Intermediate care. *Beds* SNF 66; ICF 35. *Certified* Medicaid.
Owner Nonprofit corp.

Wightman Center for Nursing & Rehabilitation
2025 Wightman St, Pittsburgh, PA 15217
(412) 421-8443
Medical Dir Martin H Nalrath III MD.
Licensure Skilled care; Intermediate care. *Beds* SNF 134; ICF 47. *Certified* Medicaid; Medicare.
Owner Proprietary corp (Hannover Healthcare).
Admissions Requirements Minimum age 16; Medical examination.
Staff Physicians 6 (pt); RNs 7 (ft), 8 (pt); LPNs 15 (ft), 2 (pt); Nurses' aides 58 (ft), 2 (pt); Physical therapists 1 (ft); Recreational therapists 1 (ft); Occupational therapists 1 (ft), 1 (pt); Speech therapists 1 (pt); Activities coordinators 3 (ft); Dietitians 1 (pt).
Facilities Dining room; Physical therapy room; Activities room; Crafts room; Laundry room; Barber/Beauty shop; Library; Dental office; Occupational therapy room.
Activities Arts & crafts; Cards; Games; Prayer groups; Movies; Shopping trips; Dances/Social/Cultural gatherings.

Pittston

Wesley Village
Laflin Rd, Pittston, PA 18640
(717) 655-2891
Admin Mrs R Campenni NHA. *Dir of Nursing* Margaret Loefflad RN. *Medical Dir* Joseph Lombardo MD.
Licensure Skilled care; Retirement. *Beds* SNF 183. *Certified* Medicaid; Medicare.
Owner Nonprofit corp.
Admissions Requirements Minimum age 65.
Staff RNs; LPNs; Nurses' aides; Physical therapists 2 (ft); Dietitians 1 (ft), 1 (pt).
Affiliation Methodist.
Facilities Dining room; Physical therapy room; Activities room; Chapel; Crafts room; Laundry room; Barber/Beauty shop; Library; Gift shop; Wheelchair van.
Activities Arts & crafts; Cards; Games; Reading groups; Prayer groups; Movies; Nature trips.

Plymouth Meeting

Clara Burke Nursing Home
251 Stenton Ave, Plymouth Meeting, PA 19462
(215) 828-2272
Admin Dawn Delore. *Dir of Nursing* Judith Shearer. *Medical Dir* Dr Stewart McCracken.
Licensure Skilled care. *Beds* SNF 69.
Owner Proprietary corp (Integrated Health Services Inc).
Staff RNs; LPNs; Nurses' aides; Physical therapists; Reality therapists; Recreational therapists; Occupational therapists; Speech therapists; Activities coordinators; Dietitians; Private duty nurses.
Facilities Dining room; Activities room; Library.
Activities Arts & crafts; Cards; Games; Reading groups; Prayer groups; Movies; Shopping trips; Dances/Social/Cultural gatherings; Shows; Concerts.

Pottstown

Coventry Manor Nursing Home Inc
Star Rte, Pottstown, PA 19464
(215) 469-6228, 323-3798
Admin David T Boyer. *Dir of Nursing* Vinga Brown RN. *Medical Dir* Jack Wennersten MD.
Licensure Skilled care; Alzheimer's care. *Beds* SNF 41. *Certified* Medicaid.
Owner Proprietary corp.
Admissions Requirements Minimum age 18; Medical examination.
Staff Physicians 1 (pt); RNs 2 (ft), 3 (pt); LPNs 4 (pt); Nurses' aides 11 (ft), 12 (pt); Physical therapists 1 (pt); Occupational therapists 1 (pt); Speech therapists 1 (pt); Activities coordinators 1 (ft); Dietitians 1 (pt); Ophthalmologists 1 (pt); Podiatrists 1 (pt); Dentists 1 (pt).
Facilities Dining room; Physical therapy room; Activities room; Chapel; Crafts room; Laundry room; Barber/Beauty shop; Library.
Activities Arts & crafts; Cards; Games; Reading groups; Prayer groups; Movies; Shopping trips; Dances/Social/Cultural gatherings.

Leader Nursing & Rehabilitation Center—Pottstown
724 N Charlotte St, Pottstown, PA 19464
(215) 323-1837
Admin Lisa D Quinby. *Dir of Nursing* Sally Speicher RN. *Medical Dir* Joseph Zukoski MD.
Licensure Skilled care; Retirement. *Beds* SNF 165; Retirement 64. *Certified* Medicaid; Medicare.
Owner Proprietary corp (Manor Care Inc).
Staff Physical therapists 1 (ft), 1 (pt); Occupational therapists 1 (ft), 1 (pt); Speech therapists 1 (pt); Activities coordinators 1 (ft); Dietitians 2 (ft); Podiatrists 1 (pt).
Facilities Dining room; Physical therapy room; Activities room; Chapel; Laundry room; Barber/Beauty shop.
Activities Arts & crafts; Cards; Games; Reading groups; Prayer groups; Movies; Shopping trips; Dances/Social/Cultural gatherings.

Manatawny Manor Inc
Box 799, Old Schuylkill Rd & Rte 724, Pottstown, PA 19464
(215) 327-0840
Admin Deborah Dollar-Reid RN NHA. *Dir of Nursing* Debra Phillips RN. *Medical Dir* John A Lupas MD.
Licensure Skilled care; Alzheimer's care. *Beds* SNF 99. *Certified* Medicaid; Medicare.
Owner Proprietary corp.
Admissions Requirements Minimum age 18; Medical examination; Physician's request.

Staff RNs 7 (ft), 16 (pt); LPNs 6 (ft), 10 (pt); Nurses' aides 39 (ft), 23 (pt); Nurses' aides 2 (pt); Recreational therapists 1 (ft); Occupational therapists 2 (pt); Speech therapists 2 (pt); Activities coordinators 2 (ft); Dietitians 1 (pt); Ophthalmologists 1 (pt).
Facilities Dining room; Physical therapy room; Activities room; Chapel; Crafts room; Laundry room; Barber/Beauty shop; Library; Greenhouse; Gift shop.
Activities Arts & crafts; Cards; Games; Reading groups; Prayer groups; Movies; Shopping trips; Dances/Social/Cultural gatherings; Exercise class; Remotivation; Sensory stimulation.

Pottsville

Leader Nursing & Rehabilitation Center—Pottsville
Pulaski & Leader Dr, Pottsville, PA 17901
(717) 622-9582
Admin Jim Williams. *Dir of Nursing* Virginia Troutman. *Medical Dir* Dr Rashid.
Licensure Skilled care; Intermediate care. *Beds* SNF 121; ICF 61. *Private Pay Patients* 60%. *Certified* Medicaid; Medicare.
Owner Proprietary corp (Manor Care Inc).
Staff RNs 12 (ft), 6 (pt); LPNs 18 (ft), 12 (pt); Nurses' aides 50 (ft), 28 (pt); Physical therapists 1 (ft); Recreational therapists 3 (ft); Occupational therapists 1 (ft); Speech therapists 1 (pt); Activities coordinators 1 (ft); Dietitians 1 (pt); Ophthalmologists 1 (pt); Podiatrists 1 (pt); Audiologists 1 (pt).
Facilities Dining room; Physical therapy room; Activities room; Crafts room; Laundry room; Barber/Beauty shop.
Activities Arts & crafts; Cards; Games; Reading groups; Prayer groups; Movies; Shopping trips; Dances/Social/Cultural gatherings; Intergenerational programs.

York Terrace
24th & W Market St, Pottsville, PA 17901
(717) 622-3982
Admin Arlene S Postupak. *Dir of Nursing* Mary Goodman RN. *Medical Dir* Benjamin B Platt MD, Certified Geriatrician.
Licensure Skilled care; Intermediate care. *Beds* SNF 32; ICF 48. *Private Pay Patients* 25%. *Certified* Medicaid; Medicare; VA.
Owner Proprietary corp (Beverly Enterprises).
Admissions Requirements Medical examination.
Staff Physicians (contracted); RNs 3 (ft), 4 (pt); LPNs 4 (ft), 3 (pt); Nurses' aides 24 (ft), 20 (pt); Physical therapists 1 (pt); Occupational therapists (contracted); Speech therapists (contracted); Activities coordinators 1 (ft); Dietitians 1 (ft); Ophthalmologists (contracted); Podiatrists (contracted); Audiologists (contracted); Dentists (contracted); Business office 2 (ft); Barbers-Beauticians (contracted).
Languages Slavic.
Facilities Dining room; Physical therapy room; Activities room; Laundry room; Barber/Beauty shop; Courtyard; Patio.
Activities Arts & crafts; Cards; Games; Reading groups; Prayer groups; Movies; Shopping trips; Dances/Social/Cultural gatherings; Intergenerational programs; Pet therapy; Adopt-a-grandparent; Resident council; Family council.

Prospect Park

Prospect Park Care Center
815 Chester Pike, Prospect Park, PA 19076
(215) 586-6262, 586-4133 FAX
Admin Rosemary Kuhlman. *Dir of Nursing* Valerie Engelman. *Medical Dir* Dr Barry Chase.

Licensure Skilled care; Intermediate care; Alzheimer's care. *Beds* SNF 120; ICF 60. *Private Pay Patients* 20%. *Certified* Medicaid; Medicare.
Owner Nonprofit corp (RHA).
Admissions Requirements Minimum age 75; Medical examination.
Staff Physicians; RNs; LPNs; Nurses' aides; Physical therapists; Recreational therapists; Occupational therapists; Speech therapists; Activities coordinators; Dietitians; Ophthalmologists; Podiatrists.
Facilities Dining room; Physical therapy room; Activities room; Crafts room; Laundry room; Barber/Beauty shop.
Activities Arts & crafts; Cards; Games; Reading groups; Prayer groups; Movies; Shopping trips; Dances/Social/Cultural gatherings; Intergenerational programs; Pet therapy; Ceramics; Music therapy.

Punxsutawney

Blose-McGregor Health Care Center Inc
407 1/2 W Mahoning St, Punxsutawney, PA 15767
(814) 938-6020
Admin Barbara P Blose NHA. *Dir of Nursing* Andrew Farkas. *Medical Dir* Dr Joseph Kernich; Dr Jay Elder.
Licensure Skilled care. *Beds* SNF 94. *Certified* Medicaid; Medicare.
Owner Proprietary corp.
Admissions Requirements Medical examination; Physician's request.
Staff RNs 2 (ft), 3 (pt); LPNs 11 (ft), 7 (pt); Nurses' aides 27 (ft), 15 (pt); Physical therapists (contracted); Activities coordinators 1 (ft), 1 (pt); Dietitians.
Facilities Dining room; Physical therapy room; Activities room; Crafts room; Laundry room; Barber/Beauty shop.
Activities Arts & crafts; Cards; Games; Prayer groups; Movies; Dances/Social/Cultural gatherings; Intergenerational programs.

Quakertown

Belle Haven
1320 Mill Rd, Quakertown, PA 18951
(215) 536-7666
Admin Heather M Stamm. *Dir of Nursing* Rose Oxenford. *Medical Dir* Jon Schwartz MD.
Licensure Skilled care. *Beds* SNF 59. *Private Pay Patients* 70%. *Certified* Medicaid; Medicare.
Owner Proprietary corp.
Admissions Requirements Minimum age 18; Medical examination.
Staff Physicians 12 (pt); RNs 2 (ft), 5 (pt); LPNs 4 (ft), 2 (pt); Nurses' aides 14 (ft), 8 (pt); Physical therapists 1 (pt); Reality therapists 1 (ft); Recreational therapists 1 (ft); Occupational therapists 1 (pt); Speech therapists 1 (pt); Activities coordinators 1 (ft); Dietitians 1 (ft); Ophthalmologists 2 (pt); Podiatrists 3 (pt); Audiologists 1 (pt).
Facilities Dining room; Physical therapy room; Activities room; Crafts room; Laundry room; Barber/Beauty shop; Fenced yard.
Activities Arts & crafts; Cards; Games; Reading groups; Prayer groups; Movies; Shopping trips; Dances/Social/Cultural gatherings; Intergenerational programs; Pet therapy.

Quakertown Manor Convalescent & Rehabilitation Center
1020 S Main St, Quakertown, PA 18951
(215) 536-9300
Licensure Skilled care. *Beds* SNF 138. *Certified* Medicaid; Medicare.
Owner Proprietary corp.

Lifequest Nursing Center
Rte 663, Quakertown, PA 18951
(215) 536-0770
Licensure Skilled care. *Beds* SNF 120.
  Certified Medicaid; Medicare.
Owner Nonprofit corp.

Yingst Nursing Home Inc
Rte 663, Quakertown, PA 18951
(215) 536-4240
Licensure Skilled care. *Beds* 41. *Certified*
  Medicaid.
Owner Proprietary corp.

Quarryville

Quarryville Presbyterian Home
625 Robert Fulton Hwy, Quarryville, PA
  17566
(717) 786-7321
Admin G Keith Mitchell Jr. *Dir of Nursing*
  Bertelle Rintz. *Medical Dir* William D L
  Hunt.
Licensure Skilled care; Continuing care. *Beds*
  SNF 160; Continuing care 215. *Certified*
  Medicaid; Medicare.
Owner Nonprofit corp.
Admissions Requirements Minimum age 65;
  Medical examination.
Staff RNs 8 (ft), 8 (pt); LPNs 10 (ft), 18 (pt);
  Nurses' aides 32 (ft), 27 (pt); Activities
  coordinators 3 (ft); Dietitians 1 (ft), 1 (pt).
Affiliation Presbyterian.
Facilities Dining room; Physical therapy
  room; Activities room; Chapel; Crafts room;
  Laundry room; Barber/Beauty shop; Library.
Activities Arts & crafts; Games; Reading
  groups; Prayer groups; Movies; Shopping
  trips; Dances/Social/Cultural gatherings.

Quincy

Donely House ICF/MR
PO Box 217, Quincy, PA 17247
(717) 749-3151
Licensure Intermediate care for mentally
  retarded. *Beds* 8. *Certified* Medicaid.
Owner Nonprofit corp.

Quincy United Methodist Home
PO Box 217, Quincy, PA 17247
(717) 749-3151
Admin Kathleen R Pell. *Dir of Nursing*
  Elizabeth Kaiser RN. *Medical Dir* Dr
  Douglas Hess.
Licensure Skilled care; Intermediate care;
  Retirement; Alzheimer's care. *Beds* SNF 94;
  ICF 101. *Certified* Medicaid; Medicare.
Owner Nonprofit corp.
Admissions Requirements Medical
  examination.
Staff Physicians 1 (pt); RNs 12 (ft), 5 (pt);
  LPNs 18 (ft), 15 (pt); Nurses' aides 46 (ft),
  45 (pt); Physical therapists 1 (pt); Activities
  coordinators 1 (ft); Dietitians 1 (pt); Ophthalmologists 2
  (pt); Dentists 1 (pt).
Affiliation Methodist.
Facilities Dining room; Physical therapy
  room; Activities room; Chapel; Crafts room;
  Laundry room; Barber/Beauty shop; Library.
Activities Arts & crafts; Cards; Games;
  Reading groups; Prayer groups; Movies;
  Shopping trips; Dances/Social/Cultural
  gatherings; Weekly worship services.

Reading

Berks County Home Berks Heim
PO Box 1495, Reading, PA 19603
(215) 376-4841
Medical Dir Lynwood V Keller MD.
Licensure Skilled care; Intermediate care. *Beds*
  SNF 125; ICF 674. *Certified* Medicaid;
  Medicare.
Owner Publicly owned.

Admissions Requirements Minimum age 55;
  Medical examination.
Staff Physicians 14 (pt); RNs 32 (ft), 6 (pt);
  LPNs 73 (ft), 6 (pt); Nurses' aides 309 (ft),
  90 (pt); Physical therapists 1 (ft), 1 (pt);
  Recreational therapists 2 (ft); Occupational
  therapists 1 (pt); Speech therapists 1 (ft);
  Activities coordinators 1 (ft); Dietitians 2
  (ft), 1 (pt); Ophthalmologists 1 (pt);
  Podiatrists 1 (pt); Audiologists 1 (pt);
  Dentists 1 (pt).
Facilities Dining room; Physical therapy
  room; Activities room; Chapel; Crafts room;
  Laundry room; Barber/Beauty shop; Library.
Activities Arts & crafts; Cards; Games;
  Reading groups; Prayer groups; Movies;
  Shopping trips; Dances/Social/Cultural
  gatherings.

Hawthorne
1501 Mineral Spring Rd, Reading, PA 19602
(215) 375-2221
Admin Margaret Layland. *Dir of Nursing*
  Elizabeth Jozwiak. *Medical Dir* Irving H
  Jones MD.
Licensure Personal care boarding home. *Beds*
  Personal care boarding home 44.
Owner Privately owned.
Admissions Requirements Medical
  examination; Physician's request.
Staff RNs 1 (ft); LPNs 1 (ft), 1 (pt); Nurses'
  aides 4 (ft); Student nurses 2 (pt).
Facilities Dining room; Activities room;
  Laundry room; Barber/Beauty shop; Library.
Activities Cards; Games; Prayer groups;
  Shopping trips.

**Transitional Level of Care Center at
Community General Hospital**
PO Box 1728, 145 N 6th St, Reading, PA
  19603-1728
(215) 378-8393
Admin Robert Fetterolf RN MSN NHA. *Dir
  of Nursing* Beverly Flatt RN. *Medical Dir*
  Dr Jeffrey Hassel.
Licensure Skilled care. *Beds* SNF 34. *Private
  Pay Patients* 1%. *Certified* Medicare.
Owner Nonprofit organization/foundation.
Staff Physicians 1 (ft); RNs 5 (ft), 5 (pt);
  LPNs 3 (ft), 3 (pt); Nurses' aides 7 (ft), 11
  (pt); Physical therapists; Recreational
  therapists 1 (ft); Speech therapists 1 (ft);
  Activities coordinators 1 (ft); Dietitians.
Facilities Dining room; Physical therapy
  room; Activities room; Crafts room; Laundry
  room; Barber/Beauty shop.
Activities Arts & crafts; Prayer groups;
  Movies; Intergenerational programs; Pet
  therapy.

Wyomissing Lodge
1000 E Wyomissing Blvd, Reading, PA 19611
(215) 376-3991
Medical Dir Robert Demby MD.
Licensure Skilled care. *Beds* SNF 107.
  Certified Medicare.
Owner Proprietary corp.
Staff Physicians 20 (pt); RNs 5 (ft), 12 (pt);
  LPNs 4 (ft), 3 (pt); Nurses' aides 27 (ft), 10
  (pt); Physical therapists 1 (pt); Recreational
  therapists 1 (pt); Occupational therapists 1
  (pt); Speech therapists 1 (pt); Activities
  coordinators 1 (pt); Dietitians 1 (pt);
  Podiatrists 1 (pt).
Facilities Dining room; Physical therapy
  room; Activities room; Crafts room; Barber/
  Beauty shop; Library.
Activities Arts & crafts; Cards; Games; Prayer
  groups; Movies; Shopping trips; Wine &
  cheese gatherings.

Renovo

Bucktail Medical Center
1001 Pine St, Renovo, PA 17764
(717) 923-1000

Admin Donna C Paloskey. *Dir of Nursing*
  Barbara Allen RN. *Medical Dir* F L Conly
  MD.
Licensure Skilled care; Intermediate care. *Beds*
  Swing beds SNF/ICF 37. *Private Pay
  Patients* 5%. *Certified* Medicaid; Medicare.
Owner Nonprofit corp.
Admissions Requirements Medical
  examination; Physician's request.
Staff Physicians 2 (pt); RNs 1 (ft), 1 (pt);
  LPNs 3 (ft), 2 (pt); Nurses' aides 9 (ft), 12
  (pt); Physical therapists 1 (pt); Speech
  therapists 1 (pt); Activities coordinators 1
  (ft); Dietitians 1 (pt); Ophthalmologists 1
  (pt); Podiatrists 1 (pt).
Facilities Dining room; Physical therapy
  room; Activities room; Chapel; Laundry
  room; Barber/Beauty shop.
Activities Arts & crafts; Cards; Games;
  Reading groups; Prayer groups; Movies;
  Shopping trips; Dances/Social/Cultural
  gatherings; Intergenerational programs; Pet
  therapy.

Rheems

Rheems Guest & Nursing Home
PO Box 8, Rheems, PA 17570
(717) 367-1831
Admin Patricia G Baker.
Licensure Skilled care; Intermediate care;
  Retirement. *Beds* SNF 18; ICF 20.
Owner Proprietary corp.
Staff Physicians 1 (pt); RNs 2 (ft), 3 (pt);
  LPNs 2 (ft), 2 (pt); Nurses' aides 4 (ft), 6
  (pt); Recreational therapists 1 (pt); Activities
  coordinators 1 (ft); Dietitians 1 (pt).
Facilities Dining room; Activities room;
  Laundry room; Barber/Beauty shop.
Activities Arts & crafts; Cards; Games;
  Reading groups; Prayer groups; Shopping
  trips.

Richboro

Richboro Care Center
253 Twining Ford Rd, Richboro, PA 18954
(215) 357-2032
Admin Charles A Kane NHA. *Dir of Nursing*
  Estella Ortego RN. *Medical Dir* Wm
  Saponaro DO.
Licensure Skilled care. *Beds* SNF 64. *Certified*
  Medicaid; Medicare.
Owner Proprietary corp (Continental Medical
  Systems).
Admissions Requirements Medical
  examination; Physician's request.
Staff RNs 4 (ft), 5 (pt); LPNs 6 (ft), 7 (pt);
  Nurses' aides 20 (ft), 12 (pt); Physical
  therapists 1 (pt); Reality therapists 1 (pt);
  Recreational therapists 1 (ft); Occupational
  therapists 1 (pt); Speech therapists 1 (pt);
  Activities coordinators 1 (pt); Dietitians 1
  (ft); Podiatrists 1 (pt).
Facilities Dining room; Physical therapy
  room; Activities room; Laundry room.
Activities Arts & crafts; Cards; Games;
  Reading groups; Prayer groups; Movies;
  Dances/Social/Cultural gatherings.

Richfield

Zendt Home
Main St, Box 248, Richfield, PA 17086
(717) 694-3434, 694-3148 FAX
Admin Diana Sheaffer. *Dir of Nursing* Sandra
  Sherniniski. *Medical Dir* Dr David Aldinger.
Licensure Intermediate care; Personal care.
  Beds ICF 46; Personal care 8. *Certified*
  Medicaid.
Owner Proprietary corp (AnCare Inc).
Admissions Requirements Medical
  examination.
Staff RNs 1 (ft), 2 (pt); LPNs 1 (ft), 5 (pt);
  Nurses' aides 5 (ft), 19 (pt); Activities
  coordinators 2 (pt).

Facilities Dining room; Activities room; Laundry room; Barber/Beauty shop; Library.
Activities Arts & crafts; Cards; Games; Reading groups; Movies; Shopping trips; Dances/Social/Cultural gatherings; Pet therapy.

Richlandtown

Zohlman Nursing Home
108 S Main St, Richlandtown, PA 18955
(215) 536-2252
Admin Debora Bartsch RN LNHA.
Medical Dir Dr Alfred Vasta.
Licensure Skilled care; Alzheimer's care. *Beds* SNF 169. *Certified* Medicaid; Medicare.
Owner Proprietary corp.
Admissions Requirements Minimum age 16; Medical examination.
Staff RNs 7 (ft), 15 (pt); LPNs 7 (ft), 4 (pt); Nurses' aides 40 (ft), 11 (pt); Recreational therapists 2 (pt); Activities coordinators 1 (ft).
Languages Spanish.
Facilities Dining room; Physical therapy room; Activities room; Crafts room; Laundry room; Barber/Beauty shop.
Activities Arts & crafts; Cards; Games; Reading groups; Prayer groups; Movies; Shopping trips; Dances/Social/Cultural gatherings.

Ridley Park

Conner Williams Nursing Home
103 Morton Ave, Ridley Park, PA 19078
(215) 521-1331
Admin H Skiddell.
Licensure Intermediate care. *Beds* ICF 52. *Certified* Medicaid.
Owner Privately owned.
Admissions Requirements Medical examination.
Facilities Dining room; Activities room; Laundry room; Barber/Beauty shop.
Activities Arts & crafts; Cards; Games; Movies.

Ross Manor Nursing Home
316 E Hinckley Ave, Ridley Park, PA 19078
(215) 521-0193
Licensure Skilled care. *Beds* SNF 25.
Owner Proprietary corp.

Rochester

Rochester Manor
174 Virginia Ave, Rochester, PA 15074

Rosemont

Rosemont Manor
35 Rosemont Ave, Rosemont, PA 19010
(215) 525-1500
Admin Susan L Ulmer.
Medical Dir Dr Ian C Deener.
Licensure Skilled care. *Beds* SNF 76. *Certified* Medicaid; Medicare.
Owner Proprietary corp (Beverly Enterprises).
Admissions Requirements Minimum age 16.
Staff RNs; LPNs; Nurses' aides; Physical therapists; Recreational therapists; Occupational therapists; Speech therapists; Activities coordinators; Dietitians; Podiatrists; Audiologists; Dentists; Social workers.
Facilities Dining room; Physical therapy room; Activities room; Crafts room; Laundry room; Barber/Beauty shop.
Activities Arts & crafts; Cards; Games; Reading groups; Prayer groups; Movies; Dances/Social/Cultural gatherings; Adopt-a-grandparent.

Roslyn

Roslyn Nursing & Rehabilitation Center
2630 Woodland Rd, Roslyn, PA 19001
(215) 884-6776
Admin Albert Konrad. *Dir of Nursing* Joan Tribolet RN. *Medical Dir* Leonard A Winegrad DO.
Licensure Skilled care. *Beds* SNF 85. *Private Pay Patients* 60%. *Certified* Medicaid; Medicare.
Owner Proprietary corp (GraceCare Inc).
Admissions Requirements Medical examination.
Staff RNs 6 (ft), 10 (pt); LPNs 1 (ft), 3 (pt); Nurses' aides 22 (ft), 24 (pt); Activities coordinators 1 (ft), 2 (pt); Dietitians 1 (pt).
Languages German, Italian.
Facilities Dining room; Activities room; Laundry room; Barber/Beauty shop.
Activities Arts & crafts; Cards; Games; Reading groups; Prayer groups; Movies; Shopping trips; Dances/Social/Cultural gatherings; Intergenerational programs; Pet therapy.

Royersford

Montgomery County Geriatric & Rehabilitation Center
1600 Black Rock Rd, Royersford, PA 19468
(215) 948-8800, 948-7431 FAX
Admin Jean L John NHA. *Dir of Nursing* L A Ciarletta RN. *Medical Dir* John J Maron MD.
Licensure Skilled care; Intermediate care; Alzheimer's care. *Beds* SNF 250; ICF 341. *Certified* Medicaid; Medicare.
Owner Publicly owned.
Admissions Requirements Medical examination; Physician's request.
Staff Physicians; RNs; LPNs; Nurses' aides; Physical therapists; Recreational therapists; Occupational therapists; Speech therapists; Activities coordinators; Dietitians; Ophthalmologists; Podiatrists; Audiologists; Dentists.
Facilities Dining room; Physical therapy room; Activities room; Chapel; Crafts room; Laundry room; Barber/Beauty shop; Library.
Activities Arts & crafts; Cards; Games; Reading groups; Prayer groups; Movies; Shopping trips; Dances/Social/Cultural gatherings; Pet therapy.

Rydal

Rydal Park of Philadelphia Presbyterian Homes on the Fairway
1515 The Fairway, Rydal, PA 19046
(215) 885-6800
Admin Nancy W Weikert. *Dir of Nursing* Carol Gerhart. *Medical Dir* Charles Ewing MD.
Licensure Skilled care; Independent living. *Beds* SNF 120. *Certified* Medicaid; Medicare.
Owner Nonprofit corp (Philadelphia Presbyterian Homes).
Admissions Requirements Minimum age 65.
Staff Physicians 1 (ft); RNs 10 (ft), 9 (pt); LPNs 4 (ft), 3 (pt); Nurses' aides 34 (ft), 45 (pt); Recreational therapists 1 (ft); Occupational therapists 1 (ft); Activities coordinators 1 (ft); Dietitians 1 (ft); Ophthalmologists 1 (pt).
Affiliation Presbyterian.
Facilities Dining room; Physical therapy room; Activities room; Chapel; Crafts room; Laundry room; Barber/Beauty shop; Library.
Activities Arts & crafts; Cards; Games; Reading groups; Prayer groups; Movies; Shopping trips; Dances/Social/Cultural gatherings.

Saegertown

Crawford County Home
RD 1 Box 9, Saegertown, PA 16433
(814) 763-4061
Admin Gordon C Foltz NHA. *Dir of Nursing* Sandra K Travis RN. *Medical Dir* Dr Gerald M Brooks.
Licensure Intermediate care; Retirement. *Beds* ICF 179. *Certified* Medicaid.
Owner Publicly owned.
Admissions Requirements Medical examination; Physician's request.
Staff Physicians 1 (ft); RNs 3 (ft), 3 (pt); LPNs 9 (ft), 2 (pt); Nurses' aides 60 (ft), 4 (pt); Recreational therapists 2 (ft); Activities coordinators 1 (ft); Dietitians 1 (ft), 1 (pt).
Languages Polish.
Facilities Dining room; Physical therapy room; Activities room; Crafts room; Laundry room; Barber/Beauty shop; Library.
Activities Arts & crafts; Cards; Games; Reading groups; Prayer groups; Movies; Shopping trips; Dances/Social/Cultural gatherings.

Saint Marys

Elk Haven Nursing Home Association Inc
Rte 255 PO Box 271, Saint Marys, PA 15857
(814) 834-2618
Licensure Skilled care; Intermediate care. *Beds* SNF 60; ICF 60. *Certified* Medicaid; Medicare.
Owner Proprietary corp (Unicare).

Andrew Kaul Memorial Hospital—Extended Care Facility
763 Johnsonburg Rd, Saint Marys, PA 15857-3417
(814) 781-7500, 834-8592 FAX
Admin Michael V Fragale NHA. *Dir of Nursing* Mary Beth Ireland RN. *Medical Dir* Bernard L Coppolo MD.
Licensure Skilled care. *Beds* SNF 138. *Private Pay Patients* 22%. *Certified* Medicaid; Medicare.
Owner Nonprofit corp.
Admissions Requirements Medical examination; Physician's request.
Staff Physicians 1 (pt); RNs 11 (ft), 2 (pt); LPNs 15 (ft), 7 (pt); Nurses' aides 36 (ft), 36 (pt); Physical therapists 1 (ft), 1 (pt); Recreational therapists 1 (ft); Occupational therapists 2 (ft), 1 (pt); Speech therapists 1 (pt); Activities coordinators 1 (ft); Dietitians 1 (pt).
Languages Italian, German, Spanish.
Facilities Dining room; Physical therapy room; Activities room; Chapel; Crafts room; Laundry room; Barber/Beauty shop; Library; Occupational therapy; Industrial medicine.
Activities Arts & crafts; Cards; Games; Reading groups; Prayer groups; Movies; Shopping trips; Dances/Social/Cultural gatherings.

Salisbury

Greenleaf House Nursing Home
335 Elm St, Salisbury, PA 01952
(717) 462-3111
Admin Marcella A Costin.
Licensure Intermediate care. *Beds* ICF 60. *Certified* Medicaid.
Owner Proprietary corp.
Admissions Requirements Minimum age 21; Medical examination.
Staff Physicians 1 (pt); RNs 2 (ft), 3 (pt); LPNs 2 (ft); Nurses' aides 12 (ft), 14 (pt); Physical therapists 1 (pt); Occupational therapists 1 (pt); Activities coordinators 1 (ft), 1 (pt); Dietitians 1 (pt).

Facilities Dining room; Activities room;
Crafts room; Laundry room.
Activities Arts & crafts; Cards; Games;
Reading groups; Prayer groups; Movies;
Shopping trips; Dances/Social/Cultural
gatherings.

Sarver

Fair Winds
126 Iron Bridge Rd, Sarver, PA 16055
(412) 353-1531
Licensure Skilled care. *Beds* SNF 66. *Certified*
Medicaid; Medicare.
Owner Proprietary corp.

Saxonburg

Saxony Health Center
PO Box 458, Pittsburgh St, Saxonburg, PA
16056
(412) 352-9445
Admin Marjorie Hankey. *Dir of Nursing*
Marlene Huss. *Medical Dir* H William Knab
DO.
Licensure Skilled care; Personal care. *Beds*
SNF 51; Personal care 17. *Private Pay
Patients* 62%. *Certified* Medicaid; Medicare.
Owner Proprietary corp (Senior Living
Centers).
Admissions Requirements Minimum age 18.
Staff Physicians 2 (pt); RNs 3 (ft), 5 (pt);
LPNs 3 (ft), 3 (pt); Nurses' aides 17 (ft), 14
(pt); Physical therapists 3 (pt); Speech
therapists 1 (pt); Activities coordinators 1
(ft); Dietitians 1 (pt); Ophthalmologists 1
(pt); Podiatrists 1 (pt); Audiologists 1 (pt).
Facilities Dining room; Physical therapy
room; Activities room; Crafts room; Laundry
room; Barber/Beauty shop; Library.
Activities Arts & crafts; Cards; Games;
Reading groups; Movies; Dances/Social/
Cultural gatherings; Pet therapy; Ceramics;
Volunteer program.

Sayre

Sayre House Inc
N Elmer Ave, Sayre, PA 18840
(717) 888-2192
Licensure Skilled care. *Beds* SNF 50. *Certified*
Medicaid; Medicare.
Owner Proprietary corp.

Schuylkill Haven

Green View Nursing & Convalescent Center
RD 1, Schuylkill Haven, PA 17972
(717) 366-0554
Licensure Skilled care. *Beds* SNF 31. *Certified*
Medicaid; Medicare.
Owner Proprietary corp.

Rest Haven Nursing Home
Rte 61 Box 401, Schuylkill Haven, PA 17972
(717) 385-0331
Admin James R Bender. *Dir of Nursing* Elaine
M Schaeffer RN. *Medical Dir* Dr Joseph
Weber.
Licensure Skilled care; Intermediate care. *Beds*
SNF 68; ICF 194. *Private Pay Patients* 3%.
Certified Medicaid; Medicare.
Owner Publicly owned.
Admissions Requirements Minimum age 16;
Medical examination; Physician's request.
Staff Physicians 1 (ft); RNs 14 (ft), 2 (pt);
LPNs 28 (ft), 8 (pt); Nurses' aides 84 (ft), 29
(pt); Physical therapists 1 (ft); Recreational
therapists 2 (ft); Occupational therapists 1
(pt); Speech therapists 1 (pt); Activities
coordinators 1 (ft); Dietitians 2 (pt);
Podiatrists 1 (pt); Audiologists 1 (pt).
Facilities Dining room; Physical therapy
room; Activities room; Chapel; Crafts room;
Laundry room; Barber/Beauty shop; Library.

Activities Arts & crafts; Cards; Games;
Reading groups; Prayer groups; Movies;
Shopping trips; Dances/Social/Cultural
gatherings; Pet therapy.

Scottdale

Westview Nursing Home
900 Porter Ave, Scottdale, PA 15683
(412) 887-5010
Admin Arthur L Cullen. *Dir of Nursing*
Evelyn J Snyder. *Medical Dir* Efren
Leonida.
Licensure Skilled care; Intermediate care;
Retirement; Alzheimer's care. *Beds* SNF 21;
ICF 8; Retirement 50. *Certified* Medicaid;
Medicare.
Owner Proprietary corp.
Admissions Requirements Medical
examination.
Staff Physicians 5 (pt); RNs 3 (ft), 2 (pt);
LPNs 2 (ft); Nurses' aides 20 (ft); Physical
therapists 1 (ft); Reality therapists 1 (ft);
Recreational therapists 1 (ft); Occupational
therapists 1 (ft); Speech therapists 1 (ft);
Activities coordinators 1 (ft); Dietitians 1
(pt); Ophthalmologists 2 (pt); Podiatrists 1
(pt); Audiologists 1 (pt).
Facilities Dining room; Activities room;
Laundry room; Barber/Beauty shop.
Activities Arts & crafts; Cards; Games;
Reading groups; Prayer groups; Movies;
Shopping trips; Dances/Social/Cultural
gatherings; Intergenerational programs; Pet
therapy.

Wolfe Nursing Home Inc
521 Overholt St, Scottdale, PA 15683
(412) 887-7680
Licensure Skilled care. *Beds* 20.
Owner Proprietary corp.

Scranton

Adams Manor
824 Adams Ave, Scranton, PA 18510
(717) 346-5704
Admin Susan A York. *Dir of Nursing* Peg
Shaughnessy RN. *Medical Dir* Dr Kondash.
Licensure Skilled care; Intermediate care. *Beds*
SNF 35; ICF 104. *Certified* Medicaid;
Medicare.
Owner Proprietary corp (Beverly Enterprises).
Facilities Dining room; Physical therapy
room; Crafts room; Laundry room; Barber/
Beauty shop.
Activities Arts & crafts; Cards; Games;
Reading groups; Prayer groups; Movies;
Shopping trips; Dances/Social/Cultural
gatherings.

Allied Services—Long-Term Care Facility
PO Box 1103, 303 Smallcombe Dr, Scranton,
PA 18501
(717) 348-1424
Admin Ann P Rebar. *Dir of Nursing* Diane
Breslin RN. *Medical Dir* Richard Gratz MD.
Licensure Skilled care; Intermediate care;
Alzheimer's care. *Beds* SNF 240; ICF 120.
Certified Medicaid; Medicare.
Owner Nonprofit corp.
Admissions Requirements Minimum age 18;
Medical examination; Physician's request.
Staff RNs 18 (ft); LPNs 27 (ft); Nurses' aide
131 (ft); Physical therapists 1 (ft);
Recreational therapists 5 (ft); Activities
coordinators 1 (ft); Dietitians 1 (ft).
Facilities Dining room; Physical therapy
room; Activities room; Chapel; Crafts room;
Laundry room; Barber/Beauty shop.
Activities Arts & crafts; Cards; Games; Prayer
groups; Movies; Shopping trips; Dances/
Social/Cultural gatherings.

Allied Services—Lynett Village
475 Morgan Hwy, Scranton, PA 18508
(717) 347-1373

Medical Dir Daniel Parsick MD.
Licensure Intermediate care for mentally
retarded. *Beds* 89. *Certified* Medicaid.
Owner Nonprofit corp.
Admissions Requirements Minimum age 18;
Medical examination.
Staff Physicians 1 (pt); RNs 7 (ft), 12 (pt);
Recreational therapists 3 (ft); Dietitians 1
(ft).
Facilities Dining room; Physical therapy
room; Laundry room; Barber/Beauty shop.
Activities Arts & crafts; Games; Prayer groups;
Movies; Shopping trips; Dances/Social/
Cultural gatherings.

Ellen Memorial Convalescent Home
1554 Sanderson Ave, Scranton, PA 18509
(717) 343-8688
Admin Marilyn L Turner. *Dir of Nursing*
Margaret Hilderbrandt. *Medical Dir* Dr
Eugene Stec.
Licensure Skilled care. *Beds* SNF 34. *Certified*
Medicaid; Medicare.
Owner Proprietary corp.
Admissions Requirements Medical
examination; Physician's request.
Staff RNs 2 (ft), 1 (pt); LPNs 2 (ft), 2 (pt);
Nurses' aides 10 (ft), 6 (pt); Activities
coordinators 1 (ft).
Facilities Dining room; Activities room;
Laundry room.
Activities Arts & crafts; Cards; Games;
Reading groups; Prayer groups; Movies;
Shopping trips; Dances/Social/Cultural
gatherings.

Green Ridge Nursing Home
1530 Sanderson Ave, Scranton, PA 18509
(717) 344-6121
Admin Carmen D Scrimalli. *Dir of Nursing*
Dolores Trycinski RN. *Medical Dir* Michael
J Turock MD.
Licensure Skilled care; Intermediate care;
Alzheimer's care. *Beds* SNF 16; ICF 49.
Certified Medicaid; Medicare.
Owner Privately owned.
Admissions Requirements Medical
examination; Physician's request.
Staff Physicians; RNs; LPNs; Nurses' aides;
Physical therapists; Reality therapists;
Recreational therapists; Occupational
therapists; Speech therapists; Activities
coordinators; Dietitians; Ophthalmologists.
Facilities Dining room; Physical therapy
room; Activities room; Crafts room; Laundry
room; Barber/Beauty shop.
Activities Arts & crafts; Cards; Games;
Reading groups; Prayer groups; Movies;
Shopping trips; Dances/Social/Cultural
gatherings.

Holiday Manor Nuring Home
Franklin & Mulberry Sts, Scranton, PA 18503
(717) 347-3303
Licensure Intermediate care. *Beds* ICF 154.
Certified Medicaid.
Owner Proprietary corp.

Holy Family Residence
2500 Adams Ave, Scranton, PA 18509
(717) 343-4065
Medical Dir Dr Thomas Clause.
Licensure Skilled care; Intermediate care. *Beds*
78. *Certified* Medicaid; Medicare.
Owner Nonprofit corp (Little Sisters of the
Poor).
Admissions Requirements Minimum age 60;
Medical examination.
Affiliation Roman Catholic.
Facilities Dining room; Physical therapy
room; Activities room; Chapel; Crafts room;
Laundry room; Barber/Beauty shop; Library.
Activities Arts & crafts; Games; Reading
groups; Prayer groups; Movies; Shopping
trips; Dances/Social/Cultural gatherings.

Jewish Home of Eastern Pennsylvania
1101 Vine St, Scranton, PA 18510
(717) 344-6177
Licensure Skilled care. *Beds* SNF 175.
  Certified Medicaid; Medicare.
Owner Nonprofit corp.
Affiliation Jewish.

**Moses Taylor Hospital—Skilled Nursing
Facility**
700 Quincy Ave, Scranton, PA 18510
(717) 963-2100
Licensure Skilled care. *Beds* SNF 32. *Certified*
  Medicaid; Medicare.
Owner Nonprofit corp.

Mountain Rest Nursing Home
Linwood Ave, Scranton, PA 18505
(717) 346-7381
Admin Colleen M Lando NHA. *Dir of Nursing*
  Keverne Zavislak. *Medical Dir* Alfonso
  Gomar MD.
Licensure Skilled care; Intermediate care. *Beds*
  SNF 58; ICF 50. *Certified* Medicaid;
  Medicare.
Owner Proprietary corp (AmCare Inc).
Admissions Requirements Medical
  examination; Physician's request.
Staff RNs 9 (ft); LPNs 13 (ft); Nurses' aides
  35 (ft); Activities coordinators 1 (ft), 1 (pt);
  Food service supervisors 1 (ft).
Facilities Dining room; Activities room;
  Crafts room; Laundry room; Barber/Beauty
  shop; Library.
Activities Arts & crafts; Cards; Games;
  Reading groups; Prayer groups; Movies;
  Shopping trips; Dances/Social/Cultural
  gatherings; Intergenerational programs; Pet
  therapy.

St Josephs Center
2010 Adams Ave, Scranton, PA 18509
(717) 342-8379
Licensure Intermediate care for mentally
  retarded. *Beds* 85. *Certified* Medicaid.
Owner Nonprofit corp.

Secane

Haskins Nursing Home
1009 Rhoads Ave, Secane, PA 19018
(215) 623-3624
Admin Elizabeth M Vernot NHA. *Dir of
  Nursing* P Dolan RN. *Medical Dir* Joseph J
  Armao MD.
Licensure Skilled care. *Beds* SNF 22. *Certified*
  Medicaid.
Owner Privately owned.
Admissions Requirements Physician's request.
Staff Physicians; RNs; Nurses' aides;
  Activities coordinators; Dietitians.
Facilities Dining room; Laundry room.
Activities Arts & crafts; Cards; Reading
  groups; Prayer groups; Movies; Shopping
  trips.

Selinsgrove

Penn Lutheran Village
800 Broad St, Selinsgrove, PA 17870
(717) 374-8181
Admin Rae A Adams.
Medical Dir Robert A Grubb MD.
Licensure Skilled care; Intermediate care. *Beds*
  SNF 79; ICF 118. *Certified* Medicaid;
  Medicare.
Owner Nonprofit corp.
Staff Physicians 1 (ft), 1 (pt); RNs 4 (ft), 12
  (pt); LPNs 10 (ft), 13 (pt); Nurses' aides 48
  (ft), 34 (pt); Physical therapists 3 (pt);
  Recreational therapists 1 (ft), 1 (pt); Speech
  therapists 1 (pt); Dietitians 1 (ft); Podiatrists
  1 (pt).
Facilities Dining room; Physical therapy
  room; Activities room; Chapel; Crafts room;
  Laundry room; Barber/Beauty shop; Library.

Activities Arts & crafts; Cards; Games;
  Reading groups; Prayer groups; Movies;
  Shopping trips; Dances/Social/Cultural
  gatherings.

Rathfon Convalescent Home Inc
308 S Market St, Selinsgrove, PA 17870
(717) 374-8507
Admin Jean A Rathfon.
Medical Dir Dr Robert Heinback.
Licensure Intermediate care. *Beds* ICF 44.
  Certified Medicaid.
Owner Proprietary corp.
Admissions Requirements Medical
  examination.
Staff Physicians 1 (pt); RNs 2 (ft), 1 (pt);
  LPNs 1 (ft), 3 (pt); Nurses' aides 14 (ft);
  Physical therapists 1 (pt); Activities
  coordinators 1 (pt); Dietitians 1 (pt).
Facilities Dining room; Activities room.
Activities Arts & crafts; Cards; Games;
  Reading groups; Prayer groups; Shopping
  trips.

Selinsgrove Center
Box 500, Selinsgrove, PA 17870
(717) 374-2911
Admin Joseph J Scartelli. *Dir of Nursing* Jane
  Gallagher RN. *Medical Dir* William J
  Yingling MD.
Licensure Intermediate care for mentally
  retarded. *Beds* ICF/MR 900. *Certified*
  Medicaid.
Owner Publicly owned.
Admissions Requirements Mental retardation.
Staff Physicians 7 (ft), 2 (pt); RNs 45 (ft);
  LPNs 30 (ft); Physical therapists 2 (ft);
  Recreational therapists 1 (ft); Occupational
  therapists 2 (ft); Speech therapists 10 (ft);
  Activities coordinators 10 (ft); Dietitians 4
  (ft); Podiatrists 1 (ft); Aides 700 (ft).
Languages Spanish.
Facilities Dining room; Physical therapy
  room; Activities room; Chapel; Laundry
  room; Barber/Beauty shop; Library.
Activities Arts & crafts; Games; Prayer groups;
  Movies; Shopping trips; Dances/Social/
  Cultural gatherings.

Sellersville

**Community Foundation for Human
Development**
22 Almont Rd, Sellersville, PA 18960
(215) 257-1155
Admin David W S Austin PhD. *Dir of
  Nursing* Kathryn Becker. *Medical Dir* Dr
  Joseph Gerone.
Licensure Intermediate care for mentally
  retarded. *Beds* ICF/MR 37. *Certified*
  Medicaid.
Owner Nonprofit corp.
Admissions Requirements Minimum age Birth.
Staff Physicians 9 (pt); RNs 3 (ft), 1 (pt);
  LPNs 3 (ft), 4 (pt); Nurses' aides 21 (ft), 20
  (pt); Physical therapists 1 (pt); Recreational
  therapists 1 (pt); Occupational therapists 1
  (pt); Speech therapists 1 (pt); Dietitians 1
  (pt); Ophthalmologists 1 (pt); Podiatrists 1
  (pt); Dentists 1 (pt).
Facilities Dining room; Activities room;
  Laundry room.
Activities Arts & crafts; Games; Movies;
  Shopping trips; Dances/Social/Cultural
  gatherings.

Grand View Hospital Skilled Nursing Facility
700 Lawn Ave, Sellersville, PA 18960
(215) 257-3611
Admin Elyse Fox. *Dir of Nursing* Beverly J
  Ewer.
Licensure Skilled care; Alzheimer's care. *Beds*
  SNF 20. *Certified* Medicaid; Medicare.
Owner Nonprofit corp.
Admissions Requirements Medical
  examination; Physician's request.

Staff RNs 10 (ft), 15 (pt); Nurses' aides 3 (ft),
  3 (pt); Physical therapists 1 (ft); Recreational
  therapists 1 (ft); Occupational therapists 1
  (ft); Speech therapists 1 (pt); Activities
  coordinators 1 (ft); Dietitians 1 (ft);
  Podiatrists 1 (pt).
Languages German, Pennsylvania Dutch,
  Spanish.
Facilities Dining room; Physical therapy
  room; Activities room; Chapel; Crafts room;
  Barber/Beauty shop; Library.
Activities Arts & crafts; Cards; Games;
  Reading groups; Prayer groups; Movies;
  Dances/Social/Cultural gatherings.

Rockhill Mennonite Community
PO Box 21, Rte 152, Sellersville, PA 18960
(215) 257-2751
Admin Randy L Shelly. *Dir of Nursing* Susan
  Stubbs RN. *Medical Dir* Dr Winfield
  Hedrick.
Licensure Skilled care; Retirement. *Beds* SNF
  96. *Certified* Medicaid; Medicare.
Owner Nonprofit corp.
Admissions Requirements Minimum age 62;
  Medical examination.
Staff RNs 4 (ft), 4 (pt); LPNs 2 (ft), 2 (pt);
  Nurses' aides 10 (ft), 20 (pt); Recreational
  therapists 1 (ft); Activities coordinators 1
  (ft); Dietitians 1 (ft).
Languages Spanish.
Affiliation Mennonite.
Facilities Dining room; Physical therapy
  room; Activities room; Chapel; Crafts room;
  Laundry room; Barber/Beauty shop; Library.
Activities Arts & crafts; Cards; Games;
  Reading groups; Prayer groups; Movies;
  Shopping trips; Social gatherings.

Sewickley

Valley Care Nursing Home Inc
Merriman Rd, Sewickley, PA 15143
(412) 741-1400, 741-0555 FAX
Admin Diane K Martinez RN NHA. *Dir of
  Nursing* Linda Letrick RN MSN. *Medical
  Dir* Chris T O'Donnell MD.
Licensure Skilled care; Intermediate care;
  Alzheimer's care. *Beds* SNF 62; ICF 66;
  Alzheimer's care 20. *Private Pay Patients*
  50%. *Certified* Medicaid; Medicare.
Owner Nonprofit organization/foundation.
Admissions Requirements Medical
  examination.
Staff Physicians 2 (pt); RNs 9 (ft), 6 (pt);
  LPNs 12 (ft), 4 (pt); Nurses' aides 27 (ft), 10
  (pt); Physical therapists (contracted);
  Recreational therapists 2 (ft); Occupational
  therapists (contracted); Speech therapists
  (contracted); Activities coordinators 1 (ft);
  Dietitians 1 (ft); Podiatrists (contracted);
  Dentists (contracted).
Facilities Dining room; Physical therapy
  room; Activities room; Crafts room; Laundry
  room; Barber/Beauty shop; Library;
  Nourishment stations; TV lounges; Outdoor
  patios; Wheelchair path.
Activities Arts & crafts; Cards; Games; Prayer
  groups; Movies; Shopping trips; Dances/
  Social/Cultural gatherings; Intergenerational
  programs; Pet therapy; Socials; Outings;
  Musical programs; One-on-one programs.

Verland Foundation Inc
Iris Rd, RD 2, Sewickly, PA 15143
(412) 741-2375
Admin Carol B Mitchell.
Medical Dir Maureen Sleben.
Licensure Intermediate care for mentally
  retarded. *Beds* ICF/MR 99. *Certified*
  Medicaid.
Owner Nonprofit corp.

Staff RNs 15 (ft); Nurses' aides 120 (ft); Physical therapists 3 (ft); Recreational therapists 3 (ft); Occupational therapists 3 (ft); Speech therapists 3 (ft); Activities coordinators 1 (ft); Dietitians 1 (ft).
Facilities Dining room; Physical therapy room; Activities room; Laundry room; Library.
Activities Arts & crafts; Games; Shopping trips; Dances/Social/Cultural gatherings.

Shamokin

Mountain View Manor
RD 1, Box 228, Shamokin, PA 17872
(717) 644-4400
Admin Una M Kinchella. *Dir of Nursing* Kay Doty. *Medical Dir* Dr James C Gehris.
Licensure Skilled care; Intermediate care. *Beds* Swing beds SNF/ICF 317. *Private Pay Patients* 5%. *Certified* Medicaid; Medicare.
Owner Publicly owned.
Admissions Requirements Minimum age 40; Medical examination.
Staff Physicians 6 (pt); RNs 11 (ft), 8 (pt); LPNs 38 (ft), 2 (pt); Nurses' aides 128 (ft), 4 (pt); Physical therapists; Occupational therapists 1 (ft); Speech therapists 1 (pt); Activities coordinators 1 (ft); Dietitians 1 (pt); Podiatrists 1 (pt).
Facilities Dining room; Physical therapy room; Activities room; Chapel; Crafts room; Barber/Beauty shop; Library.
Activities Arts & crafts; Cards; Games; Reading groups; Prayer groups; Movies; Shopping trips; Dances/Social/Cultural gatherings; Pet therapy.

Sharon

Clepper Convalescent Home Inc
959 E State St, Sharon, PA 16146
(412) 981-2750
Licensure Skilled care. *Beds* SNF 61. *Certified* Medicaid; Medicare.
Owner Proprietary corp.

Sharon General Hospital Long-Term Care Unit
740 E State St, Sharon, PA 16146
(412) 983-3895, 983-3958 FAX
Admin Diane H Sizgorich RN NHA. *Dir of Nursing* Cynthia Majtrian RN. *Medical Dir* Morre J Greenburg MD.
Licensure Skilled care. *Beds* SNF 40. *Private Pay Patients* 0%. *Certified* Medicare.
Owner Nonprofit corp.
Staff Physicians 40 (pt); RNs 8 (ft), 7 (pt); LPNs 9 (ft), 2 (pt); Nurses' aides 9 (ft), 2 (pt); Physical therapists 3 (ft); Occupational therapists 1 (pt); Speech therapists 1 (pt); Activities coordinators 1 (ft); Dietitians 1 (ft); Ophthalmologists 1 (pt); Podiatrists 1 (pt); Audiologists 1 (pt).
Facilities Dining room; Physical therapy room; Activities room; Chapel; Laundry room.
Activities Arts & crafts; Cards; Games; Reading groups; Prayer groups; Movies; Dances/Social/Cultural gatherings; Intergenerational programs.

Shenandoah

Locust Mountain Health Care Facility Inc
Pennsylvania Ave, Shenandoah, PA 17976
(717) 462-1921
Admin Barbara Whalen RN NHA. *Dir of Nursing* Helene Choplick RN. *Medical Dir* Dr Roy Green.
Licensure Intermediate care; Personal care. *Beds* ICF 38; Personal care 14. *Private Pay Patients* 5%. *Certified* Medicaid.
Owner Nonprofit organization/foundation.
Admissions Requirements Minimum age 16; Medical examination; Physician's request.

Staff RNs 1 (ft), 8 (pt); LPNs 5 (ft), 2 (pt); Nurses' aides 10 (ft), 7 (pt); Activities coordinators 1 (ft).
Facilities Dining room; Activities room; Laundry room; Barber/Beauty shop.
Activities Arts & crafts; Cards; Games; Reading groups; Prayer groups; Movies; Shopping trips; Dances/Social/Cultural gatherings; Pet therapy.

Shenandoah Manor Nursing Center
101 E Washington St, Shenandoah, PA 17976
(717) 462-1908, 462-1457 FAX
Admin Mary Lou Legg NHA. *Dir of Nursing* Marjorie Carithers RN BSN. *Medical Dir* Dr G Singh.
Licensure Skilled care; Intermediate care. *Beds* SNF 37; ICF 89. *Certified* Medicaid; Medicare.
Owner Proprietary corp.
Admissions Requirements Minimum age 18; Medical examination; Physician's request.
Staff Physicians (consultant); RNs 5 (ft), 3 (pt); LPNs 6 (ft), 11 (pt); Nurses' aides 20 (ft), 36 (pt); Physical therapists 1 (pt); Occupational therapists 1 (pt); Speech therapists (consultant); Activities coordinators 2 (ft); Dietitians (consultant); Ophthalmologists (consultant); Podiatrists (consultant); Audiologists (consultant).
Facilities Dining room; Physical therapy room; Activities room; Crafts room; Laundry room; Barber/Beauty shop.
Activities Arts & crafts; Cards; Games; Reading groups; Prayer groups; Movies; Shopping trips; Dances/Social/Cultural gatherings; Intergenerational programs; Pet therapy.

Shillington

Mifflin Healthcare Center
500 E Philadelphia Ave, Shillington, PA 19607
(215) 777-7841
Admin Carl N Kline.
Medical Dir Brooke Cutler.
Licensure Skilled care; Intermediate care. *Beds* SNF 96; ICF 40. *Certified* Medicaid; Medicare.
Owner Proprietary corp (Genesis Health Ventures).
Admissions Requirements Minimum age 16.
Staff RNs; LPNs; Nurses' aides; Physical therapists; Occupational therapists; Speech therapists; Activities coordinators; Dietitians; Ophthalmologists; Podiatrists.
Facilities Dining room; Physical therapy room; Activities room; Crafts room; Laundry room; Barber/Beauty shop.
Activities Arts & crafts; Cards; Games; Reading groups; Prayer groups; Movies; Shopping trips; Dances/Social/Cultural gatherings; Adopt-a-grandparent.

Shinglehouse

Hewitt Manor Inc
59 Honeoye St, Shinglehouse, PA 16748
(814) 697-6340
Admin Evelyn P Thomson. *Dir of Nursing* Arlene Risser RN. *Medical Dir* Dilbagh Singh MD.
Licensure Skilled care; Intermediate care. *Beds* SNF 24; ICF 4. *Certified* Medicaid; Medicare.
Owner Proprietary corp.
Admissions Requirements Minimum age 60; Medical examination; Physician's request.
Staff Physicians 2 (pt); RNs 3 (ft), 1 (pt); LPNs 2 (ft), 3 (pt); Nurses' aides 11 (ft), 10 (pt).

Facilities Dining room; Activities room; Crafts room; Laundry room.
Activities Arts & crafts; Cards; Games; Reading groups; Prayer groups; Movies; Shopping trips; Dances/Social/Cultural gatherings.

Shippenville

Allegheny Manor
RD 2, Box 426, Shippenville, PA 16254
(814) 226-5660
Admin Brad Nowlen. *Dir of Nursing* Karen Wilshire. *Medical Dir* Angelo Amadio.
Licensure Skilled care; Intermediate care. *Beds* SNF 61; ICF 61. *Private Pay Patients* 17%. *Certified* Medicaid; Medicare.
Owner Proprietary corp (Beverly Enterprises).
Admissions Requirements Minimum age 30; Medical examination; Physician's request.
Staff Physicians; RNs; LPNs; Nurses' aides; Physical therapists; Reality therapists; Recreational therapists; Occupational therapists; Speech therapists; Activities coordinators; Dietitians; Podiatrists; Audiologists.
Facilities Dining room; Physical therapy room; Activities room; Chapel; Crafts room; Laundry room; Barber/Beauty shop; Lounges.
Activities Arts & crafts; Cards; Games; Reading groups; Prayer groups; Movies; Shopping trips; Dances/Social/Cultural gatherings; Intergenerational programs; Pet therapy.

Shrewsbury

Shrewsbury Lutheran Retirement Village
200 Luther Rd, Shrewsbury, PA 17361
(717) 235-6895
Admin Barbara J Egan.
Licensure Skilled care; Intermediate care; Retirement. *Beds* SNF 6; ICF 94. *Certified* Medicaid; Medicare.
Owner Nonprofit corp.
Admissions Requirements Minimum age 65.
Staff RNs 7 (ft), 10 (pt); LPNs 4 (ft), 4 (pt); Nurses' aides 42 (ft), 13 (pt); Physical therapists 1 (pt); Activities coordinators 1 (ft); Dietitians 1 (ft), 1 (pt).
Affiliation Lutheran.
Facilities Dining room; Physical therapy room; Activities room; Chapel; Crafts room; Laundry room; Barber/Beauty shop; Library.
Activities Arts & crafts; Cards; Games; Reading groups; Prayer groups; Movies; Shopping trips; Dances/Social/Cultural gatherings.

Sinking Spring

Leader Nursing & Rehabilitation Center—Sinking Spring
3000 Windmill Rd, Sinking Spring, PA 19608
(215) 670-2100
Admin Richard C Raffensperger.
Medical Dir Brian Wummer.
Licensure Skilled care; Intermediate care. *Beds* SNF 122; ICF 62. *Certified* Medicaid; Medicare.
Owner Proprietary corp (Manor Care Inc).
Staff RNs 6 (ft), 9 (pt); LPNs 16 (ft), 11 (pt); Nurses' aides 44 (ft), 39 (pt); Physical therapists 2 (ft); Occupational therapists 1 (ft); Speech therapists 1 (ft); Activities coordinators 1 (ft); Dietitians 1 (ft); Ophthalmologists 1 (pt); Podiatrists 1 (pt).
Facilities Dining room; Physical therapy room; Activities room; Chapel; Crafts room; Laundry room; Barber/Beauty shop; Library.
Activities Arts & crafts; Cards; Games; Reading groups; Prayer groups; Movies; Shopping trips; Dances/Social/Cultural gatherings; Cooking; Picnics; Field trips.

Sligo

Clarview
RD 1, Sligo, PA 16255
(814) 745-2031, 745-3010 FAX
Admin Brett Rothwell. *Dir of Nursing* Korona Say. *Medical Dir* Dr Arthur J Dostost.
Licensure Skilled care; Intermediate care. *Beds* SNF 60; ICF 60. *Private Pay Patients* 17%. *Certified* Medicaid; Medicare.
Owner Proprietary corp (Unicare).
Staff Physicians 7 (pt); RNs 4 (ft), 5 (pt); LPNs 8 (ft), 8 (pt); Nurses' aides 29 (ft), 24 (pt); Physical therapists; Activities coordinators 2 (ft); Dietitians 1 (ft); Social service coordinators 1 (ft); Nursing unit coordinators 1 (ft).

Smethport

Sena Kean Manor
Marvin St, RD 1, Smethport, PA 16749
(814) 887-5601
Admin Linda Babola. *Dir of Nursing* Linda Babuln. *Medical Dir* Dr Fayez Roumani.
Licensure Skilled care; Intermediate care. *Beds* SNF 27; ICF 131. *Certified* Medicaid.
Owner Publicly owned.
Admissions Requirements Minimum age 18; Medical examination; Physician's request.
Staff Physicians 4 (pt); RNs 5 (ft), 5 (pt); LPNs 11 (ft), 10 (pt); Nurses' aides 41 (ft), 16 (pt); Physical therapists 1 (pt); Speech therapists 1 (pt); Activities coordinators 2 (ft); Dietitians 1 (pt); Ophthalmologists 1 (pt); Dentists 1 (pt).
Facilities Dining room; Physical therapy room; Activities room; Crafts room; Laundry room; Barber/Beauty shop; Library; TV lounges.
Activities Arts & crafts; Cards; Games; Reading groups; Prayer groups; Movies; Shopping trips; Dances/Social/Cultural gatherings; Gardening; Fishing.

C-K Stone's Manor Inc
15 W Willow St, Smethport, PA 16749
(814) 887-5716
Admin Kathryn N Neumann NHA.
Licensure Intermediate care. *Beds* ICF 34. *Certified* Medicaid.
Owner Proprietary corp.
Admissions Requirements Medical examination.
Staff RNs 1 (ft), 2 (pt); LPNs 2 (ft), 3 (pt); Nurses' aides 4 (ft), 14 (pt); Physical therapists (consultant); Speech therapists (consultant); Activities coordinators 1 (ft); Dietitians (consultant); Ophthalmologists (consultant); Podiatrists (consultant); Dental (consultant).
Facilities Dining room; Activities room; Chapel; Laundry room; Barber/Beauty shop; Library.
Activities Arts & crafts; Cards; Games; Reading groups; Prayer groups; Movies; Shopping trips; Dances/Social/Cultural gatherings; Intergenerational programs; Pet therapy.

Somerset

Siemon Nursing Home Inc
Rte 7 Box 195A, Somerset, PA 15501
(814) 443-2811
Medical Dir Dr Wayne McKee.
Licensure Skilled care; Intermediate care. *Beds* SNF 30; ICF 90. *Certified* Medicaid; Medicare.
Owner Proprietary corp.
Admissions Requirements Minimum age 18.
Facilities Dining room; Physical therapy room; Activities room; Crafts room; Laundry room; Barber/Beauty shop.
Activities Arts & crafts; Cards; Games; Reading groups; Prayer groups; Movies; Shopping trips; Dances/Social/Cultural gatherings; Fishing.

Somerset Community Hospital
225 S Center Ave, Somerset, PA 15501
(814) 443-2626
Admin Nancy A Rayman.
Licensure Skilled care. *Beds* SNF 18. *Certified* Medicaid; Medicare.
Owner Nonprofit corp.
Staff Physicians; RNs; LPNs; Nurses' aides; Physical therapists; Recreational therapists; Occupational therapists; Speech therapists; Dietitians.
Facilities Dining room; Physical therapy room; Activities room; Crafts room; Acute care facility adjacent to skilled nursing facility.
Activities Arts & crafts; Cards; Games; Reading groups; Prayer groups.

Somerset State Hospital—Mentally Retarded Unit
PO Box 631, Somerset, PA 15501
(814) 445-6501
Licensure Intermediate care for mentally retarded. *Beds* 127. *Certified* Medicaid.
Owner Nonprofit corp.

Souderton

Souderton Mennonite Homes
207 W Summit St, Souderton, PA 18964
(215) 723-9881
Admin Paul D Moyer. *Dir of Nursing* Shirley Beaver. *Medical Dir* Dr John D Nuschke.
Licensure Skilled care; Retirement. *Beds* SNF 59; Retirement 200. *Private Pay Patients* 65%. *Certified* Medicaid; Medicare.
Owner Nonprofit corp.
Admissions Requirements Medical examination.
Staff RNs 3 (ft), 4 (pt); LPNs 2 (ft), 1 (pt); Nurses' aides 11 (ft), 13 (pt); Activities coordinators 1 (ft), 2 (pt); Dietitians.
Affiliation Mennonite.
Facilities Dining room; Physical therapy room; Activities room; Chapel; Barber/Beauty shop; Library; Multi-purpose room.
Activities Arts & crafts; Games; Reading groups; Prayer groups; Movies; Shopping trips; Intergenerational programs.

South Mountain

South Mountain Restoration Center
10058 South Mountain Rd, South Mountain, PA 17261
(717) 749-3121
Admin Bruce Darney. *Dir of Nursing* Nancy L Evans RN. *Medical Dir* Emmett P Davis MD.
Licensure Skilled care; Intermediate care. *Beds* 940. *Certified* Medicaid; Medicare.
Owner Publicly owned.
Admissions Requirements Minimum age 40; Medical examination; Physician's request.
Staff Physicians 3 (ft), 3 (pt); RNs 27 (ft); LPNs 94 (ft); Nurses' aides 220 (ft); Physical therapists 1 (pt); Occupational therapists 1 (ft); Speech therapists 1 (ft); Activities coordinators 4 (ft); Dietitians 4 (ft); Ophthalmologists 1 (pt); Dentists 1 (ft).
Facilities Dining room; Physical therapy room; Activities room; Chapel; Crafts room; Laundry room; Barber/Beauty shop; Library.
Activities Arts & crafts; Cards; Games; Reading groups; Prayer groups; Movies; Shopping trips; Dances/Social/Cultural gatherings.

Southampton

Southampton Estates
238 Street Rd, Southampton, PA 19090
(215) 364-2550
Admin Mary Kohler NHA; Jeanne Oski, Asst. *Dir of Nursing* Jill McCabe. *Medical Dir* Arthur Lintgen MD.
Licensure Skilled care; Intermediate care; Retirement. *Beds* SNF 60; ICF 40; Retirement 550. *Private Pay Patients* 20%. *Certified* Medicare.
Owner Nonprofit corp (ACTS Inc).
Admissions Requirements Minimum age 65; Medical examination.
Staff RNs 4 (ft), 5 (pt); LPNs 3 (ft), 3 (pt); Nurses' aides 25 (ft), 10 (pt); Physical therapists 1 (pt); Occupational therapists 1 (pt); Speech therapists 1 (pt); Activities coordinators 1 (ft); Dietitians 1 (pt); Podiatrists 1 (pt); Audiologists 1 (pt).
Facilities Dining room; Physical therapy room; Activities room; Crafts room; Laundry room; Barber/Beauty shop.
Activities Arts & crafts; Games; Reading groups; Prayer groups; Movies; Pet therapy.

Spring City

Pennhurst Modular Home Community
Spring City, PA 19475
(215) 948-3500
Licensure Intermediate care for mentally retarded. *Beds* 150. *Certified* Medicaid.
Owner Nonprofit corp.

Spring House

Silver Stream Nursing & Rehabilitation Center
905 Pennllyn Pike, Spring House, PA 19477
(215) 646-1500
Admin Florence Werlinsky. *Dir of Nursing* Jean Mundy. *Medical Dir* Dr Robert Leopold.
Licensure Skilled care; Intermediate care; Retirement. *Beds* SNF 51; ICF 57. *Certified* Medicaid; Medicare.
Owner Proprietary corp (Geriatric & Medical Centers).
Admissions Requirements Medical examination.
Staff Physicians 20 (pt); RNs 7 (ft), 4 (pt); LPNs 4 (ft), 4 (pt); Nurses' aides 26 (ft), 10 (pt); Physical therapists 1 (ft); Recreational therapists 1 (ft), 3 (pt); Occupational therapists 1 (pt); Speech therapists 1 (pt); Dietitians 1 (pt); Ophthalmologists 2 (pt); Podiatrists 1 (pt); Dentists 1 (pt).
Facilities Dining room; Physical therapy room; Activities room; Crafts room; Laundry room; Barber/Beauty shop; Library.
Activities Arts & crafts; Cards; Games; Reading groups; Prayer groups; Movies; Shopping trips; Dances/Social/Cultural gatherings.

Spring House Estates Medical Facility
Norristown & McKean St, Spring House, PA 19477
(215) 628-3545, 628-3546
Admin Elaine R Reimet. *Dir of Nursing* Beverly Whitman RN. *Medical Dir* Arthur B Lintgen MD.
Licensure Skilled care; Independent living. *Beds* SNF 60. *Certified* Medicare.
Owner Nonprofit corp.
Admissions Requirements Physician's request.
Staff RNs 3 (ft), 6 (pt); LPNs 1 (ft), 3 (pt); Nurses' aides 17 (ft), 22 (pt); Recreational therapists 1 (ft); Activities coordinators 1 (ft); Dietitians 1 (ft).
Facilities Dining room; Physical therapy room; Activities room; Crafts room; Laundry room; Barber/Beauty shop.

Activities Arts & crafts; Cards; Games; Reading groups; Prayer groups; Movies; Shopping trips; Dances/Social/Cultural gatherings.

Springfield

C R Center
1799 S Sproul Rd, Springfield, PA 19064
(215) 543-3380
Medical Dir Dr Rocco Sciubba.
Licensure Intermediate care for mentally retarded. *Beds* 93. *Certified* Medicaid.
Owner Nonprofit corp.
Admissions Requirements Minimum age 21; Males only; Medical examination.
Staff Physicians 1 (ft); RNs 1 (ft), 1 (pt); LPNs 1 (ft); Occupational therapists 1 (ft); Speech therapists 2 (ft); Activities coordinators 1 (ft); Dietitians 1 (ft).
Affiliation Roman Catholic.
Facilities Dining room; Activities room; Chapel; Crafts room; Laundry room; Barber/Beauty shop; Library.
Activities Arts & crafts; Cards; Games; Reading groups; Prayer groups; Movies; Shopping trips; Dances/Social/Cultural gatherings.

Harlee Manor
463 W Sproul Rd, Springfield, PA 19064
(215) 544-2200
Admin Bennett Balmer. *Dir of Nursing* Susan Straff. *Medical Dir* Dr Edwin Arsht.
Licensure Skilled care; Intermediate care; Alzheimer's care; Vacation care. *Beds* Swing beds SNF/ICF 180. *Private Pay Patients* 98%. *Certified* Medicare.
Owner Proprietary corp.
Staff Physicians 1 (pt); RNs 9 (ft), 13 (pt); LPNs 4 (ft), 6 (pt); Nurses' aides 55 (ft), 7 (pt); Physical therapists 1 (pt); Recreational therapists 1 (ft); Occupational therapists 1 (pt); Speech therapists 1 (pt); Activities coordinators 2 (ft), 1 (pt); Dietitians 1 (pt); Podiatrists 3 (pt).
Facilities Dining room; Physical therapy room; Activities room; Crafts room; Laundry room; Barber/Beauty shop.
Activities Arts & crafts; Cards; Games; Reading groups; Prayer groups; Movies; Shopping trips; Dances/Social/Cultural gatherings; Intergenerational programs; Pet therapy; Religious services; Outings; Christmas bazaar.

State College

Fairways at Brookline
1950 Cliffside Dr, State College, PA 16801

State College Manor Ltd
450 Waupelani Dr, State College, PA 16801
(814) 238-5065
Admin Gerald J Boyle. *Dir of Nursing* Eleanor Kraft RN. *Medical Dir* Thomas Bem MD.
Licensure Skilled care; Intermediate care. *Beds* SNF 41; ICF 132. *Certified* Medicaid; Medicare.
Owner Proprietary corp (Brian Center Management Corp).
Admissions Requirements Physician's request.
Staff Physicians 12 (pt); RNs 5 (ft), 8 (pt); LPNs 12 (ft), 11 (pt); Nurses' aides 33 (ft), 31 (pt); Physical therapists 1 (ft); Recreational therapists 1 (ft); Speech therapists 1 (ft); Activities coordinators 1 (ft), 2 (pt); Dietitians 1 (ft); Ophthalmologists 1 (pt).
Facilities Dining room; Physical therapy room; Activities room; Laundry room; Barber/Beauty shop.
Activities Arts & crafts; Games; Reading groups; Prayer groups; Movies; Shopping trips.

Stevens

Denver Nursing Home
400 Lancaster Ave, Stevens, PA 17578
(215) 267-3878, 267-3637 FAX
Admin Walter L Wentzel Jr. *Dir of Nursing* Judi Bachman RN. *Medical Dir* Dr Ronald B Laukaitis.
Licensure Skilled care; Intermediate care; Personal care. *Beds* SNF 24; ICF 51; Personal care 28. *Certified* Medicaid; Medicare.
Owner Proprietary corp.
Admissions Requirements Medical examination.
Staff Physicians 6 (pt); RNs 3 (ft), 6 (pt); LPNs 4 (ft), 6 (pt); Nurses' aides 25 (ft), 15 (pt); Physical therapists 1 (pt); Reality therapists 1 (pt); Recreational therapists 1 (pt); Occupational therapists 1 (pt); Speech therapists 1 (pt); Activities coordinators 1 (ft); Dietitians 1 (pt); Podiatrists 1 (pt).
Facilities Dining room; Physical therapy room; Activities room; Crafts room; Laundry room; Barber/Beauty shop; Library.
Activities Arts & crafts; Cards; Games; Prayer groups; Movies; Shopping trips; Pet therapy.

Stillwater

Bonham Nursing Center
RD 1, Stillwater, PA 17878
(717) 864-3174
Medical Dir Robert Campbell MD.
Licensure Skilled care. *Beds* SNF 58. *Certified* Medicaid; Medicare; VA.
Owner Proprietary corp.
Staff Physicians 4 (ft); RNs 2 (ft), 4 (pt); LPNs 4 (pt); Nurses' aides 15 (ft), 16 (pt); Physical therapists 1 (pt); Activities coordinators 1 (ft), 1 (pt); Dietitians 1 (pt); Ophthalmologists 1 (pt); Dentists 1 (pt).
Facilities Dining room; Activities room; Laundry room; Barber/Beauty shop; Ambulance; Recreational park; Bus.
Activities Arts & crafts; Games; Prayer groups; Movies; Shopping trips; Dances/Social/Cultural gatherings; Fairs; Circus; Bible study.

Stroudsburg

Laurel Manor Nursing Home
1170 W Main St, Stroudsburg, PA 18360
(717) 421-1240
Medical Dir James G Kitchen II MD.
Licensure Intermediate care. *Beds* ICF 59.
Owner Nonprofit corp.
Admissions Requirements Medical examination.
Staff Physicians 1 (pt); RNs 10 (ft); LPNs 5 (ft); Nurses' aides 13 (ft); Reality therapists 1 (pt); Activities coordinators 1 (ft); Dietitians 1 (pt).
Facilities Dining room; Activities room; Crafts room.
Activities Arts & crafts; Cards; Games; Reading groups; Prayer groups; Movies; Dances/Social/Cultural gatherings.

Pleasant Valley Manor
RD 2 Box 2338, Stroudsburg, PA 18360
(717) 992-4172, 992-6150 FAX
Admin Pamela K Reimer. *Dir of Nursing* Sarah Jacoby. *Medical Dir* Dr Meyer Halperin.
Licensure Skilled care; Intermediate care. *Beds* SNF 60; ICF 144. *Private Pay Patients* 2%. *Certified* Medicaid; Medicare.
Owner Publicly owned.
Admissions Requirements Medical examination.
Staff Physicians 3 (pt); RNs 7 (ft), 3 (pt); LPNs 16 (ft), 3 (pt); Nurses' aides 59 (ft), 8 (pt); Physical therapists (contracted); Recreational therapists 1 (ft); Occupational

therapists 1 (ft), 1 (pt); Speech therapists 1 (pt); Dietitians (contracted); Podiatrists 1 (pt); Audiologists 1 (pt).
Facilities Dining room; Physical therapy room; Activities room; Chapel; Crafts room; Laundry room; Barber/Beauty shop; Library.
Activities Arts & crafts; Cards; Games; Reading groups; Prayer groups; Movies; Shopping trips; Dances/Social/Cultural gatherings; Intergenerational programs; Pet therapy; Reality orientation.

Sunbury

Leader Nursing & Rehabilitation Center
800 Court St, Sunbury, PA 17801
(717) 286-7121
Admin Sandra Deppen. *Dir of Nursing* Alice Marks. *Medical Dir* Mohammed Munir MD.
Licensure Skilled care; Intermediate care. *Beds* SNF 46; ICF 76. *Private Pay Patients* 30%. *Certified* Medicaid; Medicare.
Owner Proprietary corp (Manor Care Inc).
Admissions Requirements Medical examination.
Staff RNs 6 (ft), 3 (pt); LPNs 7 (ft), 10 (pt); Nurses' aides 32 (ft), 30 (pt); Physical therapists 1 (ft); Recreational therapists 1 (ft), 1 (pt); Occupational therapists 1 (ft).
Facilities Dining room; Physical therapy room; Activities room; Chapel; Crafts room; Laundry room; Barber/Beauty shop.
Activities Arts & crafts; Cards; Games; Reading groups; Prayer groups; Movies; Shopping trips; Dances/Social/Cultural gatherings; Intergenerational programs; Pet therapy.

Mansion Nursing & Convalescent Home
1040 Market St, Sunbury, PA 17801
(717) 286-6922
Licensure Skilled care. *Beds* SNF 71. *Certified* Medicaid; Medicare.
Owner Proprietary corp (Beverly Enterprises).

Sunbury Community Hospital—Skilled Nursing Unit
PO Box 737, 305 N 11th St, Sunbury, PA 17801
(717) 286-3333
Admin Sherwin O Albert Jr NHA.
Licensure Skilled care; Intermediate care. *Beds* 29. *Certified* Medicaid; Medicare.
Owner Nonprofit corp.
Admissions Requirements Medical examination; Physician's request.
Staff RNs 3 (ft); LPNs 17 (ft); Physical therapists 1 (ft), 1 (pt); Recreational therapists 1 (pt); Dietitians 1 (ft).
Activities Arts & crafts; Cards; Games; Reading groups; Prayer groups; Movies; Shopping trips; Dances/Social/Cultural gatherings.

Susquehanna

Barnes-Kasson County Hospital Skilled Nursing Facility
400 Turnpike St, Susquehanna, PA 18847
(717) 853-3135
Admin Sara C Iveson. *Dir of Nursing* Joan Hurley RN. *Medical Dir* Robert M Shelly MD.
Licensure Skilled care. *Beds* SNF 49. *Certified* Medicaid; Medicare.
Owner Nonprofit corp.
Admissions Requirements Physician's request.
Staff Physicians 1 (pt); RNs 3 (ft), 2 (pt); LPNs 5 (ft), 1 (pt); Nurses' aides 14 (ft), 8 (pt); Physical therapists 2 (ft), 1 (pt); Speech therapists 1 (pt); Activities coordinators 1 (ft), 2 (pt); Dietitians 1 (ft); Ophthalmologists 1 (pt); Dentists 2 (pt).
Facilities Dining room; Physical therapy room; Activities room; Crafts room; Barber/Beauty shop; Solarium.

Activities Arts & crafts; Cards; Games; Reading groups; Prayer groups; Movies; Shopping trips; Dances/Social/Cultural gatherings; Activities for bed-bound.

Taylor

Taylor Nursing & Rehabilitation Center
500 W Hospital St, Taylor, PA 18517
(717) 562-2102
Licensure Skilled care. *Beds* SNF 159. *Certified* Medicaid; Medicare.
Owner Proprietary corp.

Telford

Lutheran Home at Telford
235 N Washington Ave, Telford, PA 18969
(215) 723-9819
Licensure Skilled care; Independent living. *Beds* SNF 75. *Certified* Medicaid.
Owner Nonprofit corp.
Affiliation Lutheran.

Thompsontown

Meda Nipple Convalescent Home
RD 1, Box 109, Thompsontown, PA 17094
(717) 463-2632
Licensure Skilled care. *Beds* 23. *Certified* Medicaid; Medicare.
Owner Proprietary corp.
Staff RNs 2 (ft), 1 (pt); LPNs 1 (ft), 1 (pt); Nurses' aides 2 (ft), 5 (pt); Physical therapists 1 (pt); Recreational therapists 1 (pt); Occupational therapists 1 (pt); Speech therapists 1 (pt); Activities coordinators 1 (ft); Dietitians 1 (pt); Podiatrists 1 (pt); Audiologists 1 (pt); Dentists 1 (pt).

Titusville

Sunset Manor
81 Dillon Dr, Titusville, PA 16354
(814) 827-2727
Admin Arlene Greenawalt. *Dir of Nursing* Susan Hollo RN. *Medical Dir* William Sonnenberg MD.
Licensure Intermediate care. *Beds* ICF 65. *Certified* Medicaid.
Owner Proprietary corp (Beverly Enterprises).
Admissions Requirements Minimum age 18; Medical examination.
Staff RNs 2 (ft), 1 (pt); LPNs 4 (ft), 2 (pt); Nurses' aides 15 (ft), 5 (pt); Activities coordinators 1 (ft); Dietitians 1 (ft).
Facilities Dining room; Physical therapy room; Activities room; Laundry room.
Activities Arts & crafts; Cards; Games; Reading groups; Prayer groups; Movies; Shopping trips; Dances/Social/Cultural gatherings; Bingo; Exercises; Family socials; Resident council.

Topton

Lutheran Home at Topton
Home Ave, Topton, PA 19562
(215) 682-2145, 682-1055 FAX
Admin Jean Fox. *Dir of Nursing* Marlene Fink. *Medical Dir* Raymond Hauser MD.
Licensure Skilled care; Independent living; Alzheimer's care. *Beds* SNF 229; Independent living 750. *Certified* Medicaid; Medicare.
Owner Nonprofit corp.
Admissions Requirements Minimum age 62; Medical examination; Physician's request.
Staff Physicians 3 (ft); RNs 16 (ft), 11 (pt); LPNs 16 (ft); Nurses' aides 42 (ft), 92 (pt); Physical therapists 2 (ft); Reality therapists 1 (pt); Recreational therapists 1 (ft); Occupational therapists 4 (ft); Speech

therapists 1 (pt); Activities coordinators 2 (ft); Dietitians 1 (pt); Ophthalmologists 1 (pt); Podiatrists 1 (pt); Audiologists 1 (pt).
Languages German, Spanish.
Affiliation Lutheran.
Facilities Dining room; Physical therapy room; Activities room; Chapel; Crafts room; Laundry room; Barber/Beauty shop; Library; Gift shop.
Activities Arts & crafts; Cards; Games; Reading groups; Prayer groups; Movies; Shopping trips; Dances/Social/Cultural gatherings; Intergenerational programs.

Torrance

Torrance State Hospital—Long-Term Care Facility
PO Box 103, Torrance, PA 15779
(412) 459-8000
Licensure Skilled care; Intermediate care; Intermediate care for mentally retarded. *Beds* SNF 134; ICF/MR 94. *Certified* Medicaid; Medicare.
Owner Publicly owned.

Towanda

Memorial Hospital Skilled Nursing Unit
1 Hospital Dr, Towanda, PA 18848
(717) 265-2191
Admin William B Donatelli. *Dir of Nursing* Carol Sager RN, Nurse Mgr. *Medical Dir* Raymond A Perry MD.
Licensure Skilled care. *Beds* SNF 44. *Certified* Medicaid; Medicare.
Owner Nonprofit corp.
Admissions Requirements Physician's request.
Staff Physicians 15 (ft); RNs 1 (ft), 2 (pt); LPNs 4 (ft), 5 (pt); Nurses' aides 13 (ft), 6 (pt); Physical therapists 2 (ft), 1 (pt); Speech therapists 1 (pt); Activities coordinators 1 (ft); Dietitians 1 (ft), 1 (pt).
Facilities Dining room; Physical therapy room; Activities room; Laundry room; Barber/Beauty shop.
Activities Arts & crafts; Cards; Games; Prayer groups; Movies; Dances/Social/Cultural gatherings; Pet therapy.

Tremont

Tremont Nursing Center
44 Donaldson Rd, Tremont, PA 17981
(717) 695-3141, 695-2623 FAX
Admin Mary Ann Chaklos. *Dir of Nursing* Gail O'Dell. *Medical Dir* Sung H Park MD.
Licensure Skilled care; Intermediate care. *Beds* SNF 60; ICF 60. *Private Pay Patients* 23%. *Certified* Medicaid; Medicare.
Owner Proprietary corp (Unicare).
Admissions Requirements Medical examination.
Staff Physicians; RNs 4 (ft), 10 (pt); LPNs 5 (ft), 11 (pt); Nurses' aides 33 (ft), 27 (pt); Physical therapists; Activities coordinators; Dietitians.
Languages Pennsylvania Dutch.
Facilities Dining room; Physical therapy room; Activities room; Laundry room; Barber/Beauty shop.
Activities Arts & crafts; Cards; Games; Reading groups; Prayer groups; Movies; Shopping trips; Dances/Social/Cultural gatherings; Intergenerational programs; Pet therapy.

Trexlertown

Mosser Nursing Home
Mosser Rd, Box 133, Trexlertown, PA 18087
(215) 395-5661
Admin Richard J Shaak. *Dir of Nursing* Linda Pope RN. *Medical Dir* Dr John Robertson.

Licensure Skilled care; Intermediate care. *Beds* Swing beds SNF/ICF 54. *Private Pay Patients* 95%. *Certified* Medicare.
Owner Nonprofit corp (Life Quest).
Languages Pennsylvania German.
Facilities Dining room; Physical therapy room; Activities room; Laundry room; Barber/Beauty shop.
Activities Arts & crafts; Cards; Games; Reading groups; Prayer groups; Movies; Intergenerational programs; Pet therapy.

Troy

Bradford County Manor
Rte 3 Box 322, Troy, PA 16947
(717) 297-4111
Admin Dale L Nolen. *Dir of Nursing* Sonya Powell RN. *Medical Dir* Vance A Good MD.
Licensure Skilled care; Intermediate care. *Beds* SNF 40; ICF 186. *Certified* Medicaid; Medicare.
Owner Publicly owned.
Admissions Requirements Medical examination; Physician's request.
Staff Physicians 7 (pt); RNs 8 (ft), 4 (pt); LPNs 20 (ft), 10 (pt); Nurses' aides 64 (ft), 35 (pt); Physical therapists 1 (pt); Speech therapists 1 (pt); Activities coordinators 1 (ft), 4 (pt); Dietitians 1 (ft); Ophthalmologists 1 (pt); Podiatrists 1 (pt); Optometrists 1 (pt); Pharmacists 1 (pt).
Facilities Dining room; Physical therapy room; Activities room; Chapel; Crafts room; Laundry room; Barber/Beauty shop.
Activities Arts & crafts; Cards; Games; Reading groups; Prayer groups; Movies; Shopping trips; Dances/Social/Cultural gatherings.

Martha Lloyd School—Camelot ICF/MR
W Main St, Troy, PA 16947
(717) 297-2185
Admin LuAnn Simcoe.
Licensure Intermediate care for mentally retarded. *Beds* 18.
Owner Nonprofit corp.
Admissions Requirements Females only; Medical examination.
Staff RNs 1 (pt); LPNs 3 (ft), 1 (pt); Nurses' aides 9 (ft), 3 (pt); Activities coordinators 1 (ft).
Facilities Dining room; Activities room; Crafts room; Laundry room; Barber/Beauty shop; Library; Gym; Workshop; School store; Home economics room.
Activities Arts & crafts; Cards; Games; Prayer groups; Movies; Shopping trips; Dances/Social/Cultural gatherings; Ceramics; Music.

Tunkhannock

Carpenter Care Center
RD 7 Box 12, Tunkhannock, PA 18657
(717) 836-5166
Admin Virginia Carpenter.
Medical Dir Dr Arthur Sherwood.
Licensure Skilled care. *Beds* SNF 124. *Certified* Medicaid; Medicare.
Owner Proprietary corp (Beverly Enterprises).
Admissions Requirements Minimum age 18; Medical examination.
Staff Physicians 7 (pt); Physical therapists 1 (ft); Reality therapists 1 (ft); Recreational therapists 3 (ft), 1 (pt); Occupational therapists 2 (ft), 1 (pt); Speech therapists 1 (pt); Activities coordinators 1 (pt); Dietitians 1 (ft); Ophthalmologists 1 (pt); Podiatrists 1 (pt); Audiologists 1 (pt); Dentists 1 (pt).
Facilities Dining room; Physical therapy room; Activities room; Chapel; Crafts room; Laundry room; Barber/Beauty shop; Library.
Activities Arts & crafts; Cards; Games; Reading groups; Prayer groups; Movies; Shopping trips; Dances/Social/Cultural gatherings.

Tyrone

Epworth Manor
951 Washington Ave, Tyrone, PA 16686
(814) 684-0320
Admin Paul D Schroeder.
Medical Dir Carlos A Wiegering MD.
Licensure Skilled care; Intermediate care. *Beds*
SNF 68; ICF 34. *Certified* Medicaid;
Medicare.
Owner Nonprofit corp.
Admissions Requirements Minimum age 62;
Medical examination.
Staff Physicians 1 (pt); RNs 1 (ft); LPNs 3
(ft); Nurses' aides 13 (ft); Physical therapists
1 (pt); Speech therapists 1 (pt); Activities
coordinators 1 (ft); Dietitians 1 (pt);
Ophthalmologists 1 (pt); Podiatrists 1 (pt);
Dentists 1 (pt).
Affiliation Methodist.
Facilities Dining room; Physical therapy
room; Activities room; Chapel; Crafts room;
Laundry room; Barber/Beauty shop.
Activities Arts & crafts; Cards; Games;
Reading groups; Prayer groups; Movies;
Shopping trips; Dances/Social/Cultural
gatherings.

Uniontown

Fayette Health Care Center
RD 4, Box 30, Franklin Ave Ext, Uniontown,
PA 15401-8906
(412) 439-5700, 439-8039 FAX
Admin James A Filippone NHA. *Dir of
Nursing* Maryellen Gumro RN. *Medical Dir*
Honorio Pineda MD.
Licensure Skilled care; Intermediate care. *Beds*
SNF 25; ICF 95. *Certified* Medicaid;
Medicare.
Owner Proprietary corp (Beverly Enterprises).
Admissions Requirements Medical
examination; Physician's request.
Staff Physicians 1 (ft); RNs 6 (ft), 1 (pt);
LPNs 11 (ft), 1 (pt); Nurses' aides 38 (ft), 20
(pt); Activities coordinators 2 (ft); Dietitians
1 (ft).
Facilities Dining room; Physical therapy
room; Activities room; Crafts room; Laundry
room.
Activities Arts & crafts; Cards; Games;
Reading groups; Prayer groups; Movies;
Shopping trips; Dances/Social/Cultural
gatherings.

Lafayette Manor Inc
Box 682 LM RD 4, Uniontown, PA 15401
(412) 437-9804
Licensure Skilled care. *Beds* SNF 98. *Certified*
Medicaid.
Owner Nonprofit corp.

Laurel Health Center
75 Hickle St, Uniontown, PA 15401
(412) 437-9871
Admin Kathleen Scarmazzi.
Licensure Skilled care; Retirement. *Beds* SNF
55; Retirement 8. *Certified* Medicare.
Owner Proprietary corp.
Admissions Requirements Minimum age 18;
Medical examination; Physician's request.
Staff RNs 3 (ft), 2 (pt); LPNs 5 (ft), 1 (pt);
Nurses' aides 20 (ft), 3 (pt); Physical
therapists 2 (pt); Reality therapists 1 (ft);
Recreational therapists 1 (ft); Occupational
therapists 1 (pt); Speech therapists 1 (pt);
Activities coordinators 1 (ft); Dietitians 1
(pt); Ophthalmologists 1 (pt).
Facilities Dining room; Physical therapy
room; Activities room; Laundry room;
Barber/Beauty shop.
Activities Arts & crafts; Cards; Games;
Reading groups; Prayer groups.

Mt Macrina Manor Nursing Home
PO Box 548, 520 W Main St, Uniontown, PA
15401
(412) 437-1303
Admin Sr Dorothy Balock.
Licensure Skilled care. *Beds* SNF 54. *Certified*
Medicaid; Medicare.
Owner Nonprofit corp.
Admissions Requirements Medical
examination; Physician's request.
Staff Physicians 5 (pt); RNs 3 (ft), 1 (pt);
LPNs 10 (ft), 1 (pt); Nurses' aides 26 (ft), 3
(pt); Physical therapists 1 (pt); Occupational
therapists 1 (pt); Speech therapists 1 (pt);
Activities coordinators 2 (ft); Dietitians 1
(ft); Ophthalmologists 1 (pt).
Languages Slavic.
Affiliation Roman Catholic.
Facilities Dining room; Physical therapy
room; Activities room; Chapel; Laundry
room; Barber/Beauty shop; Lounge;
Solarium; Porches.
Activities Arts & crafts; Cards; Games;
Reading groups; Prayer groups; Movies;
Exercises; Bowling.

Valencia

Graham's Nursing Home Inc
RD 1 Box 504, Sandyhill Rd, Valencia, PA
16059
(412) 898-1594
Admin Herbert S White.
Medical Dir Donald L Kelley MD.
Licensure Intermediate care. *Beds* ICF 24.
Certified Medicaid.
Owner Proprietary corp.
Staff Physicians 1 (pt); RNs 4 (ft), 1 (pt);
LPNs 2 (ft), 2 (pt); Nurses' aides 22 (ft);
Physical therapists 1 (pt); Reality therapists
1 (pt); Recreational therapists 1 (pt);
Activities coordinators 1 (ft); Dietitians 1
(pt).
Facilities Dining room; Physical therapy
room; Activities room; Crafts room; Laundry
room.
Activities Arts & crafts; Cards; Games;
Reading groups; Prayer groups; Movies;
Shopping trips; Dances/Social/Cultural
gatherings.

Valencia Woods Nursing Center
RD 4, Box 357, Valencia, PA 16059
(412) 625-1561
Admin Mary Pat Braudis. *Dir of Nursing*
Garnetta Simmons. *Medical Dir* Dr Jack
Heck III.
Licensure Skilled care. *Beds* SNF 75. *Private
Pay Patients* 25%. *Certified* Medicaid;
Medicare.
Owner Nonprofit organization/foundation.
Admissions Requirements Medical
examination.
Staff Physicians 1 (pt); RNs 6 (ft), 3 (pt);
LPNs 5 (pt); Nurses' aides 17 (ft), 15 (pt);
Physical therapists 2 (pt); Occupational
therapists 1 (pt); Speech therapists 1 (pt);
Activities coordinators 1 (ft), 1 (pt);
Dietitians 1 (ft); Ophthalmologists 1 (pt);
Podiatrists 1 (pt); Audiologists 1 (pt).
Facilities Dining room; Physical therapy
room; Barber/Beauty shop.
Activities Arts & crafts; Cards; Games;
Reading groups; Prayer groups; Movies;
Shopping trips; Dances/Social/Cultural
gatherings; Pet therapy.

Wallingford

Wallingford Nursing & Rehabilitation Center
115 S Providence Rd, Wallingford, PA 19086
(215) 565-3232
Licensure Skilled care. *Beds* SNF 207.
Certified Medicaid; Medicare.
Owner Proprietary corp (Health Care and
Retirement Corp).

Warminster

Centennial Spring Health Care Center
333 Newtown Rd, Warminster, PA 18974
(215) 672-9082, 675-6999 FAX
Admin Richard Shank RN NHA. *Dir of
Nursing* M Bereanda. *Medical Dir* Dr H
Stein.
Licensure Skilled care; Intermediate care. *Beds*
SNF 60; ICF 120. *Private Pay Patients* 30%.
Certified Medicaid; Medicare.
Owner Proprietary corp.
Admissions Requirements Medical
examination; Physician's request.
Staff RNs 12 (ft), 1 (pt); LPNs 12 (ft), 1 (pt);
Nurses' aides 59 (ft); Recreational
therapistsActivities coordinators 4 (ft).
Languages Spanish, French.
Facilities Dining room; Physical therapy
room; Activities room; Chapel; Crafts room;
Laundry room; Barber/Beauty shop; Library;
Van; Patio; Wheelchair garden; Closed-
circuit TV in rooms.
Activities Arts & crafts; Cards; Games;
Reading groups; Prayer groups; Movies;
Shopping trips; Dances/Social/Cultural
gatherings; Intergenerational programs; Pet
therapy.

Christ's Home Retirement Center
1220 W Street Rd, Warminster, PA 18974
(215) 956-2270
Admin Richard B Barnes. *Dir of Nursing*
Carol Baltera. *Medical Dir* Alan J Miller
MD.
Licensure Skilled care; Retirement. *Beds* SNF
18. *Certified* Medicaid; Medicare.
Owner Nonprofit corp.
Admissions Requirements Minimum age 65;
Medical examination; Physician's request.
Staff Physicians 2 (pt); RNs 4 (ft), 5 (pt);
LPNs 2 (ft), 3 (pt); Nurses' aides 9 (ft), 10
(pt); Physical therapists 1 (pt); Occupational
therapists 1 (pt); Speech therapists 1 (pt);
Activities coordinators 1 (ft); Dietitians 1
(pt); Ophthalmologists 1 (pt); Podiatrists 1
(pt); Dentists 1 (pt).
Languages German.
Facilities Dining room; Activities room;
Chapel; Crafts room; Laundry room; Barber/
Beauty shop.
Activities Arts & crafts; Games; Reading
groups; Prayer groups; Movies; Shopping
trips.

Eastern Pennsylvania Eastern Star Home
850 Norristown Rd, Warminster, PA 18974
(215) 672-2500
Admin Lorraine M Lardani. *Dir of Nursing*
Jane Delaney. *Medical Dir* David Davis DO.
Licensure Skilled care; Intermediate care;
Personal care. *Beds* SNF 26; ICF 8; Personal
care 26.
Owner Nonprofit organization/foundation.
Admissions Requirements Minimum age 65;
Medical examination; Must be member of
the Eastern Star.
Staff Physicians 2 (pt); RNs 2 (ft), 4 (pt);
LPNs 1 (ft), 9 (pt); Nurses' aides 10 (ft), 12
(pt); Physical therapists (consultant);
Recreational therapists 1 (ft), 2 (pt);
Occupational therapists (consultant); Speech
therapists (consultant); Dietitians
(consultant); Ophthalmologists (consultant);
Podiatrists 1 (pt); Audiologists (consultant).
Affiliation Eastern Star.
Facilities Dining room; Activities room;
Chapel; Crafts room; Laundry room; Barber/
Beauty shop; Library.
Activities Arts & crafts; Cards; Games;
Reading groups; Prayer groups; Movies;
Shopping trips; Dances/Social/Cultural
gatherings; Intergenerational programs; Pet
therapy.

Warminster Hospital-Based Skilled Nursing Facility
225 Newtown Rd, Warminster, PA 18974
(215) 441-6800
Licensure Skilled care. *Beds* SNF 19. *Certified* Medicaid; Medicare.
Owner Proprietary corp.

Warren

Central Care Center
121 Central Ave, Warren, PA 16365
(814) 726-1420
Admin Arlene Greenawalt. *Dir of Nursing* Margaret Burkett RN. *Medical Dir* Dr Ronald Simonsen.
Licensure Intermediate care. *Beds* ICF 48. *Private Pay Patients* 23%. *Certified* Medicaid.
Owner Proprietary corp (Meritcare Inc).
Admissions Requirements Minimum age 18; Medical examination; Physician's request.
Staff RNs 1 (ft), 2 (pt); LPNs 4 (ft), 1 (pt); Nurses' aides 18 (ft), 4 (pt); Activities coordinators 1 (ft); Dietitians.
Facilities Dining room; Activities room.
Activities Arts & crafts; Games; Reading groups; Prayer groups; Shopping trips; Pet therapy.

Kinzua Valley Health Care
205 Water St, Warren, PA 16365
(814) 726-0820
Licensure Skilled care. *Beds* SNF 111. *Certified* Medicaid; Medicare.
Owner Proprietary corp.

Warren Manor
682 Pleasant Dr, Warren, PA 16365
(814) 723-7060
Admin Royce E Freebourn. *Dir of Nursing* Donna Fellows. *Medical Dir* Dr Stephen Mory.
Licensure Skilled care. *Beds* SNF 100. *Certified* Medicaid; Medicare.
Owner Proprietary corp (HCF Inc).
Admissions Requirements Medical examination.
Staff Physicians 11 (pt); RNs 8 (ft), 4 (pt); LPNs 5 (ft), 8 (pt); Nurses' aides 32 (ft), 18 (pt); Physical therapists 5 (pt); Recreational therapists 2 (ft), 2 (pt); Speech therapists 2 (pt); Activities coordinators 1 (ft); Dietitians 3 (pt); Ophthalmologists 1 (pt); Podiatrists 1 (pt); Dentists 1 (pt); Respiratory therapists 2 (pt); EKG technicians 1 (pt); X-ray technicians 1 (pt).
Facilities Dining room; Physical therapy room; Activities room; Crafts room; Laundry room; Barber/Beauty shop; Library; 2 Lounges; 7 Patios; 7 acres of land; Therapy rooms; Soda shop.
Activities Arts & crafts; Cards; Games; Reading groups; Prayer groups; Movies; Shopping trips; Dances/Social/Cultural gatherings.

Warren Medical Services
205 Water St, Warren, PA 16365
(814) 726-0820)
Admin Joseph P Darrington.
Medical Dir Dr Robert Donaldson.
Licensure Skilled care. *Beds* 111. *Certified* Medicaid; Medicare.
Owner Proprietary corp (Beverly Enterprises).
Admissions Requirements Medical examination; Physician's request.
Staff Physicians 1 (pt); RNs 3 (ft), 6 (pt); LPNs 6 (ft), 5 (pt); Nurses' aides 26 (ft), 18 (pt); Physical therapists 1 (pt); Reality therapists 1 (ft); Recreational therapists 1 (ft); Occupational therapists 1 (pt); Speech therapists 1 (pt); Dietitians 1 (pt); Ophthalmologists 1 (pt); Podiatrists 1 (pt); Audiologists 1 (pt); Dentists 1 (pt).
Facilities Dining room; Physical therapy room; Activities room; Laundry room; Barber/Beauty shop.

Activities Arts & crafts; Cards; Games; Reading groups; Movies; Shopping trips; Dances/Social/Cultural gatherings; Music therapy.

Warren State Hospital Long-Term Care Facility
PO Box 249, Warren, PA 16365
(814) 723-5500
Admin Gizella Bunce. *Dir of Nursing* Victoria Schmader. *Medical Dir* Dr William S Wolters.
Licensure Intermediate care. *Beds* ICF 24. *Certified* Medicaid.
Owner Publicly owned.
Admissions Requirements Minimum age 21; Medical examination.
Staff Physicians 2 (pt); RNs 4 (ft); LPNs 7 (ft); Nurses' aides 6 (ft); Recreational therapists 1 (ft); Occupational therapists 2 (ft); Speech therapists 1 (ft); Activities coordinators 1 (ft); Dietitians 3 (ft).
Facilities Dining room; Activities room; Chapel; Crafts room; Laundry room; Barber/Beauty shop; Library.
Activities Arts & crafts; Cards; Games; Reading groups; Prayer groups; Movies; Shopping trips; Dances/Social/Cultural gatherings.

Warrington

Fox Nursing & Rehabilitation Center
PO Box 678, 2644 Bristol Rd, Warrington, PA 18976
(215) 343-2700
Admin Margaret W Crighton NHA RN. *Dir of Nursing* Sandi Meadow. *Medical Dir* Dr Paul Moyer.
Licensure Skilled care. *Beds* SNF 43. *Certified* Medicare.
Owner Proprietary corp (GraceCare, Inc).
Admissions Requirements Minimum age 25; Medical examination.
Staff RNs 6 (ft), 6 (pt); LPNs 7 (ft), 3 (pt); Nurses' aides 8 (ft), 9 (pt); Recreational therapists 1 (pt); Dietitians 1 (pt).
Facilities Dining room; Physical therapy room; Activities room; Crafts room; Laundry room.
Activities Arts & crafts; Cards; Games; Reading groups; Movies; Shopping trips; Dances/Social/Cultural gatherings.

Washington

Humbert Lane Health Care Center
90 Humbert Ln, Washington, PA 15301
(412) 228-4740
Licensure Skilled care. *Beds* SNF 120. *Certified* Medicaid; Medicare.
Owner Proprietary corp.

Kade Nursing Home
PO Box 1100, Washington, PA 15301
(412) 222-2148
Admin Janice Marianna.
Medical Dir Dr John McCarrell.
Licensure Skilled care. *Beds* SNF 62. *Certified* Medicaid; Medicare.
Owner Proprietary corp.
Staff RNs; LPNs; Nurses' aides; Physical therapists; Speech therapists; Activities coordinators; Dietitians.
Facilities Dining room; Physical therapy room; Activities room; Laundry room; Barber/Beauty shop.
Activities Arts & crafts; Cards; Games; Prayer groups; Shopping trips.

Presbyterian Medical Center of Washington Pennsylvania
835 S Main St, Washington, PA 15301
(412) 222-4300
Admin Evelyn M Vandever. *Dir of Nursing* Jeanne H Steele RN. *Medical Dir* Jesus S Evangelista MD.

Licensure Skilled care; Intermediate care; Retirement; Alzheimer's care. *Beds* SNF 48; ICF 102. *Certified* Medicaid; Medicare.
Owner Nonprofit corp.
Admissions Requirements Minimum age 62; Medical examination; Physician's request.
Staff Physicians 1 (pt); RNs 11 (ft); LPNs 15 (ft); Nurses' aides 59 (ft); Physical therapists 1 (ft); Recreational therapists 1 (ft); Occupational therapists 1 (pt); Speech therapists 1 (pt); Activities coordinators 2 (pt); Dietitians 1 (pt); Ophthalmologists 1 (pt); Podiatrists 1 (pt); Dentists 1 (pt).
Affiliation Presbyterian.
Facilities Dining room; Physical therapy room; Activities room; Crafts room; Laundry room; Barber/Beauty shop; Library; Soda fountain; Conference rooms; Patios; Atrium; Community rooms; Walkways.
Activities Arts & crafts; Cards; Games; Reading groups; Prayer groups; Movies; Shopping trips; Dances/Social/Cultural gatherings; Vesper services; Sewing.

Washington County Health Center
RD 1 Box 94, Washington, PA 15301
(412) 228-5010, 228-1619 FAX
Admin Barry W Parks DEd NHA. *Dir of Nursing* Margaret Buxton RN. *Medical Dir* Dennis Davis MD.
Licensure Skilled care; Intermediate care; Adult day care; Alzheimer's care. *Beds* SNF 100; ICF 150; Adult day care 20. *Private Pay Patients* 6%. *Certified* Medicaid; Medicare.
Owner Publicly owned.
Admissions Requirements Minimum age 21; Medical examination.
Staff Physicians 3 (pt); RNs 12 (ft), 6 (pt); LPNs 14 (ft), 8 (pt); Nurses' aides 100 (ft); Physical therapists 1 (pt); Recreational therapists 5 (ft); Occupational therapists 1 (pt); Speech therapists 1 (pt); Activities coordinators 1 (ft); Dietitians 1 (pt); Podiatrists 1 (pt).
Facilities Dining room; Physical therapy room; Activities room; Chapel; Crafts room; Laundry room; Barber/Beauty shop; Library.
Activities Arts & crafts; Games; Prayer groups; Movies; Shopping trips; Dances/Social/Cultural gatherings; Pet therapy; Rhythm band.

Watsontown

Kramm Nursing Home Inc
245 E 8th St, Watsontown, PA 17777
(717) 538-2561
Admin Randall D Kramm.
Medical Dir Dr Robert Yannaccone.
Licensure Intermediate care. *Beds* ICF 74. *Certified* Medicaid.
Owner Proprietary corp.
Admissions Requirements Medical examination.
Staff Physicians 9 (pt); RNs 2 (ft), 2 (pt); LPNs 2 (ft), 3 (pt); Nurses' aides 20 (ft), 14 (pt); Physical therapists 1 (pt); Activities coordinators 1 (ft); Dietitians 1 (pt); Ophthalmologists 1 (pt); Podiatrists 1 (pt); Dentists 1 (pt).
Facilities Dining room; Physical therapy room; Activities room; Crafts room; Laundry room; Barber/Beauty shop; Library.
Activities Arts & crafts; Cards; Games; Reading groups; Prayer groups; Movies; Shopping trips; Dances/Social/Cultural gatherings.

Wawa

Granite Farms Estates Medical Facility
1343 W Baltimore Pike, Wawa, PA 19063
(215) 358-0510
Licensure Skilled care; Independent living. *Beds* SNF 44. *Certified* Medicare.
Owner Proprietary corp.

Wayne

Wayne Nursing & Rehabilitation Center
30 West Ave, Wayne, PA 19087
(215) 688-3635
Admin Marjorie Walker.
Medical Dir Ian Ballard MD.
Licensure Skilled care. *Beds* SNF 108.
  Certified Medicaid; Medicare.
Owner Proprietary corp (Genesis Health
  Ventures).
Staff Physicians 3 (pt); RNs 9 (ft), 8 (pt);
  LPNs 4 (ft), 2 (pt); Nurses' aides 25 (ft), 20
  (pt); Physical therapists 1 (ft); Recreational
  therapists 1 (ft); Occupational therapists 1
  (pt); Speech therapists 1 (pt); Activities
  coordinators 1 (ft); Dietitians 1 (pt);
  Ophthalmologists 1 (pt); Podiatrists 1 (pt);
  Audiologists 1 (pt); Dentists 1 (pt).
Facilities Dining room; Physical therapy
  room; Activities room; Laundry room;
  Barber/Beauty shop; Library.
Activities Arts & crafts; Cards; Games;
  Reading groups; Prayer groups; Movies;
  Shopping trips; Wine & cheese parties;
  Theme lunches; Weekend & evening
  activities.

Waynesburg

Curry Memorial Home
RD 2, Box 60, Waynesburg, PA 15370
(412) 627-3153
Admin Diane W McCauley NHA. *Dir of
  Nursing* Cathy Brezovsky. *Medical Dir* Dr
  Jeffrey Smith.
Licensure Skilled care; Intermediate care. *Beds*
  SNF 37; ICF 74. *Certified* Medicaid;
  Medicare.
Owner Publicly owned.
Staff Physicians 1 (pt); RNs 7 (ft), 5 (pt);
  LPNs 22 (ft), 8 (pt); Nurses' aides 37 (ft), 10
  (pt); Physical therapists 1 (pt); Speech
  therapists 1 (pt); Activities coordinators 1
  (ft); Dietitians 1 (pt); Ophthalmologists 1
  (pt); Podiatrists 1 (pt); Dentists 1 (pt).
Facilities Dining room; Physical therapy
  room; Activities room; Chapel; Crafts room;
  Laundry room; Barber/Beauty shop; Library.
Activities Arts & crafts; Cards; Games;
  Reading groups; Prayer groups; Movies;
  Shopping trips; Dances/Social/Cultural
  gatherings.

Franklin Care Center
300 Center Ave, Waynesburg, PA 15370
(412) 852-2020
Licensure Skilled care. *Beds* SNF 120.
  Certified Medicaid; Medicare.
Owner Proprietary corp (Beverly Enterprises).

Weatherly

Carbon County Home for the Aged
Evergreen Ave, Weatherly, PA 18255
(717) 427-8683
Admin Frank E Wehr. *Dir of Nursing*
  Margaret Lewis. *Medical Dir* Dr Larry
  Antolick.
Licensure Skilled care; Intermediate care. *Beds*
  SNF 50; ICF 150. *Certified* Medicaid;
  Medicare.
Owner Publicly owned.
Admissions Requirements Minimum age 17;
  Medical examination; Physician's request.
Staff Physicians 1 (ft), 1 (pt); RNs 8 (ft), 6
  (pt); LPNs 15 (ft), 2 (pt); Nurses' aides 62
  (ft), 24 (pt); Physical therapists 1 (ft);
  Ophthalmologists 1 (ft); Podiatrists 1 (ft);
  Dentists 1 (ft).
Facilities Dining room; Physical therapy
  room; Activities room; Chapel; Crafts room;
  Laundry room; Barber/Beauty shop; Game
  room.

Activities Arts & crafts; Cards; Games;
  Reading groups; Prayer groups; Movies;
  Shopping trips; Dances/Social/Cultural
  gatherings; Olympics; Fishing trips; Picnics.

Wellsboro

Broad Acres Nursing Home Association
RD 3, Wellsboro, PA 16901
(717) 724-3559
Admin Maureen Phelps NHA. *Dir of Nursing*
  Jeanine Coolidge RN. *Medical Dir* Preston
  Erway MD.
Licensure Skilled care; Intermediate care. *Beds*
  SNF 60; ICF 60. *Certified* Medicaid;
  Medicare.
Owner Publicly owned.
Admissions Requirements Medical
  examination.
Staff RNs 4 (ft), 3 (pt); LPNs 11 (ft), 2 (pt);
  Nurses' aides 33 (ft), 13 (pt); Activities
  coordinators 2 (ft); Dietitians 1 (ft).
Facilities Dining room; Physical therapy
  room; Activities room; Crafts room; Laundry
  room; Barber/Beauty shop.
Activities Arts & crafts; Cards; Games; Prayer
  groups; Movies; Shopping trips; Dances/
  Social/Cultural gatherings; Resident
  committees; Music therapy.

Carleton Nursing Home
10 West Ave, Wellsboro, PA 16901
(717) 724-2631
Licensure Skilled care. *Beds* SNF 26. *Certified*
  Medicaid; Medicare.
Owner Proprietary corp.

Green Home Inc
PO Box 836, 37 Central Ave, Wellsboro, PA
16901
(717) 724-3131
Admin Graydon E Fanning.
Medical Dir Anne K Butler MD.
Licensure Skilled care. *Beds* SNF 122.
  Certified Medicaid; Medicare; VA.
Owner Nonprofit corp.
Admissions Requirements Medical
  examination; Physician's request.
Staff Physicians 1 (pt); RNs 6 (ft), 5 (pt);
  LPNs 10 (ft), 2 (pt); Nurses' aides 40 (ft), 27
  (pt); Physical therapists 1 (pt); Speech
  therapists 1 (pt); Activities coordinators 2
  (ft); Dietitians 1 (pt); Ophthalmologists 1
  (pt).
Facilities Dining room; Physical therapy
  room; Activities room; Laundry room;
  Barber/Beauty shop.
Activities Arts & crafts; Cards; Games;
  Reading groups; Prayer groups; Movies;
  Dances/Social/Cultural gatherings.

Wernersville

Hamburg Center Annex
Wernersville, PA 19565
(215) 678-3411
Admin Todd M Carsen.
Medical Dir Dr Richard Bick.
Licensure Skilled care; Intermediate care;
  Alzheimer's care. *Beds* SNF 214; ICF 86.
  Certified Medicaid; Medicare.
Owner Proprietary corp (Beverly Enterprises).
Admissions Requirements Minimum age 16;
  Physician's request.
Staff Physicians; RNs; LPNs; Nurses' aides;
  Physical therapists; Recreational therapists;
  Occupational therapists; Speech therapists;
  Activities coordinators; Dietitians;
  Ophthalmologists; Podiatrists; Dentists.
Facilities Dining room; Physical therapy
  room; Activities room; Chapel; Crafts room;
  Laundry room; Barber/Beauty shop.
Activities Arts & crafts; Games; Prayer groups;
  Movies; Shopping trips; Dances/Social/
  Cultural gatherings; Adopt-a-grandparent.

Long Term Care Unit
Wernersville State Hospital, Wernersville, PA
  19565-0300
(215) 678-3411
Admin John D Sholly Jr NHA. *Dir of Nursing*
  Fern R Wawrzyniak RN. *Medical Dir*
  Franklin E Gable DO.
Licensure Skilled care; Intermediate care. *Beds*
  SNF 33; ICF 113. *Certified* Medicaid;
  Medicare.
Owner Publicly owned.
Admissions Requirements Minimum age 65;
  Medical examination; Physician's request.
Staff Physicians 1 (ft), 1 (pt); RNs 25 (ft), 4
  (pt); LPNs 27 (ft), 2 (pt); Nurses' aides 24
  (ft), 2 (pt); Physical therapists 3 (ft);
  Recreational therapists 3 (ft); Dietitians.
Languages Spanish translator on contract.
Facilities Dining room; Physical therapy
  room; Activities room; Chapel; Laundry
  room; Barber/Beauty shop; Library.
Activities Arts & crafts; Cards; Games;
  Reading groups; Movies; Shopping trips;
  Dances/Social/Cultural gatherings; Pet
  therapy.

West Chester

Brandywine Hall Care Center
800 W Miner St, West Chester, PA 19382
(215) 696-3120
Admin Lois Eltonhead. *Dir of Nursing* Julia
  Thomson. *Medical Dir* Philip Kistler MD.
Licensure Skilled care. *Beds* SNF 120.
  Certified Medicaid; Medicare.
Owner Proprietary corp (Geriatric and
  Medical Centers).
Admissions Requirements Medical
  examination; Physician's request.
Staff Physicians; RNs; LPNs; Nurses' aides;
  Physical therapists; Reality therapists;
  Recreational therapists; Occupational
  therapists; Speech therapists; Activities
  coordinators; Dietitians; Podiatrists.
Facilities Dining room; Physical therapy
  room; Activities room; Crafts room; Laundry
  room; Barber/Beauty shop; Library;
  Occupational therapy room; Dietary exam
  room; Physician's room.
Activities Arts & crafts; Cards; Games;
  Reading groups; Prayer groups; Movies;
  Shopping trips; Dances/Social/Cultural
  gatherings; Rhythm band; Bell choir.

Friends Hall at West Chester
424 N Matlack St, West Chester, PA 19380
(215) 696-5211
Licensure Intermediate care. *Beds* ICF 80.
Owner Proprietary corp.

Pocopson Home
1695 Lenape Rd, West Chester, PA 19382
(215) 793-1212
Admin Peter S Perry NHA. *Dir of Nursing*
  Helen P McFarland RN MS. *Medical Dir*
  Dan S Butoi MD.
Licensure Skilled care; Intermediate care. *Beds*
  SNF 46; ICF 315. *Private Pay Patients* 5%.
  Certified Medicaid; Medicare.
Owner Nonprofit organization/foundation.
Admissions Requirements Minimum age 18;
  Medical examination.
Staff Physicians 3 (ft); RNs 13 (ft), 11 (pt);
  LPNs 25 (ft), 11 (pt); Nurses' aides 130 (ft),
  3 (pt); Physical therapists 1 (ft); Recreational
  therapists 7 (pt); Speech therapists 2 (pt);
  Activities coordinators 1 (ft); Dietitians 1
  (ft); Ophthalmologists 1 (pt); Podiatrists 1
  (pt); Audiologists 1 (pt); Chaplains.
Languages Spanish.
Facilities Dining room; Physical therapy
  room; Activities room; Chapel; Crafts room;
  Laundry room; Barber/Beauty shop; Library.
Activities Arts & crafts; Cards; Games;
  Reading groups; Prayer groups; Movies;
  Shopping trips; Dances/Social/Cultural
  gatherings; Pet therapy.

West Chester Arms Nursing & Rehabilitation Center
1130 West Chester Pike, West Chester, PA 19382
(215) 692-3636
Medical Dir Dr Ben Reniello.
Licensure Skilled care; Intermediate care. *Beds* SNF 90; ICF 150. *Certified* Medicaid; Medicare.
Owner Proprietary corp (Geriatric and Medical Centers).
Staff Physical therapists 1 (ft); Recreational therapists 3 (ft); Occupational therapists; Speech therapists; Activities coordinators; Dietitians; Podiatrists; Dentists.
Facilities Physical therapy room; Activities room; Crafts room; Laundry room; Barber/Beauty shop.
Activities Arts & crafts; Cards; Games; Reading groups; Prayer groups; Movies; Shopping trips; Dances/Social/Cultural gatherings.

West Reading

Leader Nursing & Rehabilitation Center—West Reading
425 Buttonwood St, West Reading, PA 19611
(215) 373-5166
Licensure Skilled care; Intermediate care. *Beds* SNF 120; ICF 60. *Certified* Medicaid; Medicare.
Owner Proprietary corp (Manor Care Inc).
Admissions Requirements Medical examination; Physician's request.
Staff RNs 8 (ft), 8 (pt); LPNs 14 (ft), 6 (pt); Nurses' aides 54 (ft), 36 (pt); Physical therapists 1 (ft); Reality therapists 1 (ft); Recreational therapists 1 (ft), 2 (pt); Activities coordinators 1 (ft); Dietitians 1 (ft).
Facilities Dining room; Physical therapy room; Activities room; Chapel; Laundry room; Barber/Beauty shop; Library.
Activities Arts & crafts; Cards; Reading groups; Prayer groups; Shopping trips; Dances/Social/Cultural gatherings.

Reading Nursing Center
4th & Spruce Sts, West Reading, PA 19611
(215) 374-5175
Admin Diane G Fonzone.
Medical Dir Dr Henry Bialas.
Licensure Skilled care; Intermediate care. *Beds* SNF 50; ICF 150. *Certified* Medicaid; Medicare.
Owner Proprietary corp (Unicare).
Staff RNs 6 (ft), 4 (pt); LPNs 11 (ft), 12 (pt); Nurses' aides 41 (ft), 43 (pt); Physical therapists 1 (ft); Occupational therapists 1 (pt); Speech therapists 1 (pt); Activities coordinators 4 (ft); Dietitians 1 (ft); Podiatrists 1 (pt); Audiologists 1 (pt).
Facilities Dining room; Physical therapy room; Activities room; Crafts room; Laundry room; Barber/Beauty shop.
Activities Arts & crafts; Cards; Games; Reading groups; Prayer groups; Movies; Shopping trips; Dances/Social/Cultural gatherings.

West Sunbury

Allegheny Valley School—Butler Campus
RR 2 Box 2017, West Sunbury, PA 16061
(412) 637-2981
Licensure Intermediate care for mentally retarded. *Beds* 15. *Certified* Medicaid.
Owner Nonprofit corp.

Wexford

Pine View Manor Inc
Box K, Swinderman Rd, Wexford, PA 15090
(412) 935-3781
Admin Louis R Meola. *Dir of Nursing* Marjorie Davis. *Medical Dir* Dr Rad Agrawal.
Licensure Skilled care; Intermediate care; Residential care; Alzheimer's care. *Beds* Swing beds SNF/ICF 55; Residential care 10.
Owner Proprietary corp.
Admissions Requirements Medical examination.
Facilities Dining room; Physical therapy room; Activities room; Chapel; Crafts room; Laundry room; Barber/Beauty shop.
Activities Arts & crafts; Cards; Games; Reading groups; Prayer groups; Movies; Shopping trips; Dances/Social/Cultural gatherings; Pet therapy; Music therapy.

Wexford House Nursing Center
9850 Old Perry Hwy, Wexford, PA 15090
(412) 366-7900
Admin Joel F Camp.
Medical Dir Arlene Moran.
Licensure Skilled care; Retirement; Alzheimer's care. *Beds* SNF 224. *Certified* Medicaid; Medicare.
Owner Proprietary corp.
Admissions Requirements Medical examination; Physician's request.
Staff Physicians; RNs; LPNs; Nurses' aides; Physical therapists; Recreational therapists; Occupational therapists; Speech therapists; Activities coordinators; Dietitians; Podiatrists.
Facilities Dining room; Physical therapy room; Activities room; Chapel; Crafts room; Laundry room; Barber/Beauty shop; Library.
Activities Arts & crafts; Cards; Games; Reading groups; Prayer groups; Movies; Shopping trips; Dances/Social/Cultural gatherings.

White Haven

White Haven Center
Oley Valley Rd, White Haven, PA 18661
(717) 443-9564
Licensure Intermediate care for mentally retarded. *Beds* 567. *Certified* Medicaid.
Owner Nonprofit corp.

Whitehall

Fellowship Manor
3000 Fellowship Dr, Whitehall, PA 18052
(215) 799-3000
Admin Dr David J Smock. *Dir of Nursing* Mary Carmargo. *Medical Dir* Dr Robert Vaughn.
Licensure Skilled care. *Beds* SNF 120. *Private Pay Patients* 80%. *Certified* Medicaid; Medicare.
Owner Nonprofit organization/foundation.
Admissions Requirements Medical examination; Physician's request.
Staff RNs 10 (ft), 4 (pt); LPNs 4 (ft), 3 (pt); Nurses' aides 40 (ft), 35 (pt); Dietitians 1 (pt).
Affiliation Bible Fellowship Church.
Facilities Dining room; Physical therapy room; Activities room; Laundry room; Barber/Beauty shop.
Activities Arts & crafts; Cards; Games; Prayer groups; Movies; Dances/Social/Cultural gatherings; Intergenerational programs; Pet therapy.

Wilkes-Barre

Hampton House
1548 Sans Souci Pkwy, Wilkes-Barre, PA 18702
(717) 825-8725

Licensure Skilled care. *Beds* SNF 104. *Certified* Medicaid; Medicare.
Owner Proprietary corp (Health Care and Retirement Corp).

Heritage House
80 E Northampton St, Wilkes-Barre, PA 18701
(717) 826-1031
Admin Margaret R Spencer. *Dir of Nursing* Barbara Aleo RN. *Medical Dir* Dr Joseph M Lombardo.
Licensure Skilled care; Retirement. *Beds* SNF 50. *Certified* Medicaid; Medicare.
Owner Nonprofit corp.
Admissions Requirements Minimum age 62; Medical examination; Physician's request.
Staff Physicians 1 (pt); RNs 3 (ft), 3 (pt); LPNs 3 (ft), 2 (pt); Nurses' aides 11 (ft), 14 (pt); Physical therapists 1 (pt); Occupational therapists 1 (pt); Speech therapists 1 (pt); Activities coordinators 1 (pt); Dietitians 1 (pt); Ophthalmologists 1 (pt); Dentists 1 (pt).
Facilities Dining room; Physical therapy room; Activities room; Crafts room; Laundry room; Barber/Beauty shop; Library; Outdoor patio.
Activities Arts & crafts; Cards; Games; Reading groups; Prayer groups; Movies; Shopping trips; Dances/Social/Cultural gatherings.

Little Flower Manor—Diocese of Scranton
200 S Meade St, Wilkes-Barre, PA 18702
(717) 823-6131
Medical Dir John Valenti MD.
Licensure Skilled care. *Beds* SNF 133. *Certified* Medicaid; Medicare.
Owner Nonprofit corp.
Staff Physicians 3 (ft); RNs 6 (ft), 4 (pt); LPNs 13 (ft), 6 (pt); Nurses' aides 36 (ft), 30 (pt); Recreational therapists 1 (ft); Dietitians 1 (ft); Ophthalmologists 1 (pt); Podiatrists 1 (pt); Dentists 1 (pt).
Affiliation Roman Catholic.
Facilities Dining room; Physical therapy room; Activities room; Chapel; Crafts room; Laundry room; Barber/Beauty shop.
Activities Arts & crafts; Cards; Games; Prayer groups; Movies; Shopping trips; Dances/Social/Cultural gatherings.

Riverstreet Manor Nursing & Rehabilitation Center
440 N River St, Wilkes-Barre, PA 18702
(717) 825-5611
Admin Paul Davies.
Licensure Skilled care. *Beds* SNF 122. *Certified* Medicaid; Medicare.
Owner Proprietary corp (Genesis Health Ventures).

Step by Step Inc
293 S Franklin St, Wilkes-Barre, PA 18702
(717) 823-6891
Admin Ann Chester.
Licensure Intermediate care for mentally retarded. *Beds* ICF/MR 16. *Certified* Medicaid.
Owner Nonprofit corp.
Admissions Requirements Medical examination; Physician's request.
Staff Physicians 2 (pt); RNs 1 (ft); LPNs 3 (pt); Physical therapists 1 (pt); Occupational therapists 1 (pt); Speech therapists 1 (pt); Activities coordinators 1 (pt); Dietitians 1 (pt); Ophthalmologists 1 (pt); Podiatrists 1 (pt); Dentists 1 (pt).
Facilities Dining room; Activities room; Laundry room.
Activities Arts & crafts; Games; Movies; Shopping trips; Dances/Social/Cultural gatherings.

Summit Health Care Center
50 N Pennsylvania Ave, Wilkes-Barre, PA 18701
(714) 825-3488

Admin Lori Gerhard. *Dir of Nursing* Diane Hazur. *Medical Dir* Isadore Robbins MD.
Licensure Skilled care; Intermediate care. *Beds* SNF 60; ICF 60. *Certified* Medicaid; Medicare.
Owner Proprietary corp (Beverly Enterprises).
Admissions Requirements Medical examination.
Facilities Dining room; Physical therapy room; Activities room; Laundry room; Barber/Beauty shop.
Activities Arts & crafts; Games; Prayer groups; Movies; Shopping trips; Dances/Social/Cultural gatherings.

Valley Crest Nursing Home
1551 East End Blvd, Wilkes-Barre, PA 18711
(717) 826-1011
Admin Robert A Reed.
Medical Dir David W Greenwald MD.
Licensure Skilled care. *Beds* SNF 384. *Certified* Medicaid; Medicare.
Owner Publicly owned.
Admissions Requirements Minimum age 18.
Staff Physicians 7 (ft); RNs 30 (ft), 2 (pt); LPNs 45 (ft); Nurses' aides 177 (ft); Physical therapists 1 (pt); Occupational therapists 1 (pt); Speech therapists 1 (pt); Activities coordinators 1 (ft); Dietitians 2 (ft); Ophthalmologists 1 (pt); Podiatrists 1 (pt); Audiologists 1 (pt); Dentists 1 (pt).
Facilities Dining room; Physical therapy room; Activities room; Chapel; Crafts room; Laundry room; Barber/Beauty shop; Library.
Activities Arts & crafts; Cards; Games; Reading groups; Prayer groups; Movies; Shopping trips; Dances/Social/Cultural gatherings.

Wyoming Valley Health Care
101 E Mountain Dr, Plains Township, Wilkes-Barre, PA 18702
(717) 825-5892
Licensure Skilled care. *Beds* SNF 120. *Certified* Medicaid; Medicare.
Owner Proprietary corp (Beverly Enterprises).

Williamsport

Divine Providence—Extended Care Facility
1100 Gramrion Blvd, Williamsport, PA 17701
(717) 326-8181
Licensure Skilled care. *Beds* 34. *Certified* Medicaid; Medicare.
Owner Nonprofit corp.

Hope Intermediate Residences Inc
PO Box 1837, Williamsport, PA 17703-1837
(717) 326-3745, 326-1258 FAX
Admin A Louise Forsha, VP. *Dir of Nursing* Christine Whiteman RN.
Licensure Intermediate care for mentally retarded. *Beds* ICF/MR 23. *Private Pay Patients* 3%. *Certified* Medicaid.
Owner Nonprofit corp.
Admissions Requirements Medical examination.
Staff RNs 1 (ft); LPNs 8 (ft); Nurses' aides 12 (ft); Physical therapists (contracted); Dietitians (contracted).
Languages Sign.
Facilities Dining room; Physical therapy room; Activities room; Crafts room; Laundry room.
Activities Arts & crafts; Cards; Games; Reading groups; Movies; Shopping trips; Dances/Social/Cultural gatherings; Pet therapy; Prayer groups through community churches.

Leader Nursing & Rehabilitation Center—North
300 Leader Dr, Williamsport, PA 17701
(717) 323-8627, 322-5820 FAX
Admin Sandra Trout. *Dir of Nursing* Sally Sherman RN. *Medical Dir* James Montague MD.

Licensure Skilled care; Intermediate care. *Beds* SNF 76; ICF 74. *Private Pay Patients* 38%. *Certified* Medicaid; Medicare.
Owner Proprietary corp (Manor Care Inc).
Admissions Requirements Physician's request.
Staff RNs 6 (ft), 4 (pt); LPNs 15 (ft), 4 (pt); Nurses' aides 37 (ft), 23 (pt); Physical therapists 1 (ft); Recreational therapists 1 (ft).
Facilities Dining room; Physical therapy room; Activities room; Chapel; Laundry room; Barber/Beauty shop.
Activities Arts & crafts; Cards; Games; Prayer groups; Movies; Dances/Social/Cultural gatherings; Intergenerational programs; Pet therapy.

Leader Nursing & Rehabilitation Center—South
101 Leader Dr, Williamsport, PA 17701
(717) 323-3758
Admin Roberta McClintock. *Dir of Nursing* Judy Sullivan. *Medical Dir* Dr Tobias.
Licensure Skilled care; Intermediate care; Retirement. *Beds* 184. *Certified* Medicaid; Medicare.
Owner Proprietary corp (Manor Care Inc).
Staff RNs 6 (ft), 4 (pt); LPNs 5 (ft), 6 (pt); Nurses' aides 28 (ft), 26 (pt); Physical therapists 1 (ft); Recreational therapists 1 (ft), 2 (pt).
Facilities Dining room; Physical therapy room; Activities room; Chapel; Crafts room; Laundry room; Barber/Beauty shop; Library.
Activities Arts & crafts; Cards; Games; Reading groups; Prayer groups; Movies; Shopping trips; Dances/Social/Cultural gatherings.

Rose View Manor
1201 Rural Ave, Williamsport, PA 17701
(717) 323-4340
Admin Dorothy J Dangle NHA. *Dir of Nursing* Virginia Campbell. *Medical Dir* David A Lindsay MD.
Licensure Skilled care; Alzheimer's care. *Beds* SNF 120. *Private Pay Patients* 80%. *Certified* Medicaid; Medicare.
Owner Privately owned.
Admissions Requirements Physician's request.
Staff RNs 6 (ft), 2 (pt); LPNs 15 (ft), 3 (pt); Nurses' aides 40 (ft), 15 (pt); Physical therapists 2 (ft); Recreational therapists 3 (ft), 1 (pt); Occupational therapists 2 (ft); Speech therapists 2 (pt); Activities coordinators 1 (ft); Dietitians 1 (pt); Ophthalmologists 1 (pt); Podiatrists 1 (pt); Audiologists 1 (pt).
Facilities Dining room; Physical therapy room; Activities room; Chapel; Crafts room; Laundry room; Barber/Beauty shop; Library.
Activities Arts & crafts; Cards; Games; Reading groups; Prayer groups; Movies; Shopping trips; Dances/Social/Cultural gatherings; Intergenerational programs; Pet therapy; Cocktail hour; Daily activity program for Alzheimer's patients.

Williamsport Home
1900 Ravine Rd, Williamsport, PA 17701
(717) 323-8781
Licensure Skilled care; Intermediate care. *Beds* SNF 8; ICF 141. *Certified* Medicaid; Medicare.
Owner Nonprofit corp.

Willow Grove

Homestead Nursing & Rehabilitation Center
1113 N Easton Rd, Willow Grove, PA 19090
(215) 659-3060
Admin Dennis H Gregory. *Dir of Nursing* Carol Lichtenwalner. *Medical Dir* Walter Krantz MD.
Licensure Skilled care. *Beds* SNF 185. *Certified* Medicaid; Medicare.
Owner Proprietary corp (Genesis Health Ventures).

Admissions Requirements Medical examination; Physician's request.
Staff RNs 6 (ft), 2 (pt); LPNs 9 (ft), 6 (pt); Nurses' aides 40 (ft), 50 (pt); Physical therapists 1 (ft); Recreational therapists 4 (ft); Occupational therapists 1 (ft); Speech therapists 1 (ft); Activities coordinators; Dietitians 1 (pt).
Facilities Dining room; Physical therapy room; Activities room; Barber/Beauty shop.
Activities Arts & crafts; Games; Reading groups; Prayer groups; Movies; Shopping trips.

Willow Street

Willow Valley Lakes Manor Healthcare
300 Willow Valley Lakes Dr, Willow Street, PA 17584

Windber

Church of the Brethren Home
1005 Hoffman Ave, Windber, PA 15963
(814) 467-5505, 467-6437 FAX
Admin Thomas J Reckner. *Dir of Nursing* Donna Tvardzik. *Medical Dir* Dr Svastava.
Licensure Skilled care; Intermediate care; Personal care; Retirement. *Beds* SNF 38; ICF 109; Personal care 75; Retirement cottages 9. *Private Pay Patients* 50%. *Certified* Medicaid; Medicare.
Owner Nonprofit corp.
Staff RNs 10 (ft), 7 (pt); LPNs 16 (ft), 29 (pt); Nurses' aides 38 (ft), 26 (pt); Physical therapists; Activities coordinators 1 (ft); Dietitians (consultant).
Affiliation Church of the Brethren.
Facilities Dining room; Physical therapy room; Activities room; Chapel; Crafts room; Laundry room; Barber/Beauty shop.
Activities Arts & crafts; Cards; Games; Reading groups; Prayer groups; Movies; Shopping trips; Dances/Social/Cultural gatherings; Intergenerational programs; Pet therapy.

Worcester

Meadowood
PO Box 670, 3205 Skippack Pike, Worcester, PA 19490
(617) 584-1000
Admin Christine A Clarke. *Dir of Nursing* Fran Moretti. *Medical Dir* Ed Buonocore MD.
Licensure Skilled care; Personal care; Independent living. *Beds* SNF 32; Personal care 49; Independent living units 256. *Certified* Medicare.
Owner Nonprofit corp.
Admissions Requirements Medical examination.
Staff Physicians; RNs; LPNs; Nurses' aides; Physical therapists; Occupational therapists; Speech therapists; Activities coordinators; Dietitians; Ophthalmologists; Podiatrists; Audiologists.
Facilities Dining room; Physical therapy room; Activities room; Crafts room; Laundry room; Barber/Beauty shop; Library.
Activities Arts & crafts; Cards; Games; Reading groups; Prayer groups; Movies; Shopping trips; Dances/Social/Cultural gatherings; Intergenerational programs; Pet therapy; Church services.

Worthington

Sugar Creek Rest Inc
RD 2 Box 80, Worthington, PA 16262
(412) 445-3146
Admin Kenneth Tack. *Dir of Nursing* Kathy James. *Medical Dir* Dr D W Minteer.

Licensure Skilled care; Intermediate care; Retirement; Alzheimer's care. *Beds* SNF 30; ICF 73. *Certified* Medicaid; Medicare.
Owner Proprietary corp.
Staff Physicians 4 (pt); RNs 5 (ft), 4 (pt); LPNs 3 (ft), 8 (pt); Nurses' aides 23 (ft), 17 (pt); Physical therapists 2 (ft); Reality therapists 1 (pt); Recreational therapists 2 (ft); Occupational therapists 1 (pt); Speech therapists 1 (pt); Activities coordinators 1 (ft); Dietitians 1 (ft); Ophthalmologists 1 (pt); Podiatrists 1 (pt); Dentists 1 (pt).
Facilities Dining room; Physical therapy room; Activities room; Crafts room; Laundry room; Barber/Beauty shop; Library.
Activities Arts & crafts; Cards; Games; Reading groups; Prayer groups; Movies; Dances/Social/Cultural gatherings.

Wyncote

Crestview Convalescent Home
Church Rd, Wyncote, PA 19095
(215) 884-9990, 884-5579 FAX
Admin Florence Werlinsky. *Dir of Nursing* Efrat Miodovnik. *Medical Dir* Dr Barry Chase.
Licensure Skilled care; Intermediate care; Alzheimer's care. *Beds* SNF 120; ICF 60. *Private Pay Patients* 20%. *Certified* Medicaid; Medicare.
Owner Proprietary corp (Geriatric and Medical Centers).
Admissions Requirements Minimum age adult; Medical examination.
Staff Physicians 30 (pt); RNs 7 (ft), 6 (pt); LPNs 12 (ft), 7 (pt); Nurses' aides 56 (ft), 2 (pt); Physical therapists 1 (ft); Recreational therapists 1 (ft); Occupational therapists 1 (pt); Speech therapists 1 (pt); Activities coordinators 2 (ft); Dietitians 1 (ft); Ophthalmologists 1 (pt); Podiatrists 1 (pt); Audiologists 1 (pt).
Languages Polish, Russian.
Facilities Dining room; Physical therapy room; Activities room; Crafts room; Laundry room; Barber/Beauty shop; Library; Solarium; Community room; Lounges; Nourishment rooms with microwaves; Lobby.
Activities Arts & crafts; Cards; Games; Reading groups; Prayer groups; Movies; Shopping trips; Dances/Social/Cultural gatherings; Intergenerational programs; Pet therapy; Religious services; Ethnic dinners.

Hopkins House Nursing & Rehabilitation Center
8100 Washington Ln, Wyncote, PA 19095
(215) 576-8000
Admin Arlene S Monroe. *Dir of Nursing* Nancy Randolph RN. *Medical Dir* Dr Leonard Winegrad.
Licensure Skilled care; Alzheimer's care; Respite care. *Beds* SNF 99. *Certified* Medicaid; Medicare.
Owner Proprietary corp (Columbia Corp).
Admissions Requirements Medical examination; Physician's request.
Staff RNs 4 (ft), 6 (pt); LPNs 10 (ft), 7 (pt); Nurses' aides 27 (ft), 24 (pt); Physical therapists 1 (ft); Reality therapists 1 (ft); Occupational therapists 1 (pt); Speech therapists 1 (pt); Activities coordinators 1 (ft); Dietitians 1 (ft); Ophthalmologists 1 (pt); Podiatrists 1 (pt); Dentists 1 (pt); Social services 1 (ft), 1 (pt).
Facilities Dining room; Physical therapy room; Activities room; Laundry room; Barber/Beauty shop; Library; Occupational therapy room; Speech therapy room.
Activities Arts & crafts; Cards; Games; Prayer groups; Movies; Shopping trips; Dances/Social/Cultural gatherings; Religious services.

Oaks Nursing & Rehabilitation Center
240 Barker Rd, Wyncote, PA 19095
(215) 884-3639
Admin Susan Montague RN NHA. *Dir of Nursing* Daun Barrett RN. *Medical Dir* Dr Giammanco.
Licensure Skilled care. *Beds* SNF 55. *Certified* Medicaid; Medicare.
Owner Proprietary corp (Genesis Health Ventures).
Staff RNs 1 (ft), 2 (pt); LPNs 4 (ft), 2 (pt); Nurses' aides 20 (ft), 10 (pt); Physical therapists 1 (pt); Recreational therapists 1 (ft); Occupational therapists 1 (pt); Speech therapists; Dietitians 1 (pt).

Wyncote Church Home
Fernbrook & Maple Aves, Wyncote, PA 19095
(215) 885-2620
Admin Donald R Fulmer. *Dir of Nursing* Elizabeth A Geiger RN. *Medical Dir* Earl S Krick MD.
Licensure Skilled care; Intermediate care; Independent living. *Beds* SNF 29; ICF 31; Independent living 70. *Certified* Medicaid; Medicare.
Owner Nonprofit corp.
Admissions Requirements Minimum age 65; Medical examination.
Staff Physicians 1 (pt); RNs 2 (ft), 9 (pt); LPNs 2 (pt); Nurses' aides 21 (ft), 11 (pt); Physical therapists 1 (pt); Recreational therapists 2 (pt); Occupational therapists 1 (pt); Speech therapists 1 (pt); Activities coordinators 1 (pt); Dietitians 1 (ft); Ophthalmologists 1 (pt); Podiatrists 1 (pt); Dentists 1 (pt).
Affiliation Church of Christ.
Facilities Dining room; Activities room; Chapel; Crafts room; Laundry room; Barber/Beauty shop; Library.
Activities Arts & crafts; Cards; Games; Reading groups; Prayer groups; Movies; Shopping trips; Dances/Social/Cultural gatherings; Remotivation; Choir groups.

Wyndmoor

All Sts Rehabilitation Hospital/Springfield Retirement Residence
8601 Stenton Ave, Wyndmoor, PA 19118
(215) 233-6200
Medical Dir Richard A Sullivan MD.
Licensure Skilled care; Rehabilitation hospital. *Beds* SNF 31; Rehab hospital 52. *Certified* Medicaid; Medicare.
Owner Nonprofit corp.
Admissions Requirements Physician's request.
Staff Physicians 5 (ft), 1 (pt); RNs 24 (ft); LPNs 3 (ft); Nurses' aides 20 (ft), 10 (pt); Physical therapists 6 (ft), 2 (pt); Recreational therapists 3 (ft); Occupational therapists 6 (ft); Speech therapists 1 (ft); Dietitians 1 (ft); Podiatrists 1 (pt); Dentists 1 (pt).
Affiliation Episcopal.
Facilities Dining room; Physical therapy room; Activities room; Chapel; Crafts room; Laundry room; Barber/Beauty shop; Library; Various sitting areas.
Activities Arts & crafts; Cards; Games; Reading groups; Prayer groups; Movies; Shopping trips; Dances/Social/Cultural gatherings.

Chestnut Hill Rehabilitation Hospital Skilled Nursing Facility
8601 Stenton Ave, Wyndmoor, PA 19118
(215) 233-6200
Licensure Skilled care; Independent living. *Beds* SNF 31. *Certified* Medicaid; Medicare.
Owner Proprietary corp.

Green Acres Rehabilitation Nursing Center
1401 Ivy Hill Rd, Wyndmoor, PA 19150
(215) 233-5605
Licensure Skilled care. *Beds* SNF 130. *Certified* Medicaid; Medicare.
Owner Proprietary corp.

Yeadon

Leader Nursing & Rehabilitation Center—Yeadon
Lansdowne & Lincoln Aves, Yeadon, PA 19050
(215) 626-7700
Admin Regina MacArthur. *Dir of Nursing* Jane Wenzinger. *Medical Dir* Elliott Schaffer MD.
Licensure Skilled care; Intermediate care; Personal care; Retirement. *Beds* SNF 142; ICF 36; Personal care 20; Retirement 30. *Private Pay Patients* 70%. *Certified* Medicaid; Medicare.
Owner Proprietary corp (Manor Care Inc).
Admissions Requirements Minimum age 16; Medical examination.
Staff RNs 4 (ft), 8 (pt); LPNs 15 (ft), 12 (pt); Nurses' aides 50 (ft), 28 (pt); Physical therapists 1 (ft); Reality therapists 1 (ft); Recreational therapists 1 (ft); Occupational therapists 1 (ft); Speech therapists 1 (pt); Activities coordinators 1 (ft), 3 (pt); Dietitians (consultant); Ophthalmologists (consultant); Podiatrists (consultant); Audiologists (consultant).
Facilities Dining room; Physical therapy room; Activities room; Chapel; Crafts room; Laundry room; Barber/Beauty shop; Library.
Activities Arts & crafts; Cards; Games; Reading groups; Prayer groups; Movies; Shopping trips; Dances/Social/Cultural gatherings; Intergenerational programs; Pet therapy.

York

Barley Convalescent Home—North
1775 Barley Rd, York, PA 17404
(717) 767-6530
Licensure Skilled care. *Beds* 121. *Certified* Medicaid; Medicare.
Owner Proprietary corp.

Colonial Manor Nursing Home
970 Colonial Ave, York, PA 17403
(717) 845-2661
Admin George R Lorah. *Dir of Nursing* Toni Schreiber. *Medical Dir* Dr Ray Wilson.
Licensure Skilled care; Intermediate care. *Beds* SNF 123; ICF 96. *Certified* Medicaid; Medicare.
Owner Proprietary corp.
Admissions Requirements Medical examination.
Staff Physicians 2 (ft); RNs 8 (ft), 4 (pt); LPNs 26 (ft), 11 (pt); Nurses' aides 54 (ft), 22 (pt); Physical therapists 1 (ft); Recreational therapists 1 (ft); Occupational therapists 1 (ft); Speech therapists 1 (ft); Activities coordinators 1 (ft); Dietitians 1 (pt); Office, dietary, laundry, housekeeping, maintenance, therapists 42 (ft), 13 (pt).
Facilities Dining room; Physical therapy room; Activities room; Chapel; Crafts room; Laundry room; Barber/Beauty shop.
Activities Arts & crafts; Cards; Games; Reading groups; Prayer groups; Movies; Shopping trips; Dances/Social/Cultural gatherings; Intergenerational programs; Pet therapy.

Manor Care of Barley Kingston
2400 Kingston Ct, York, PA 17402
(717) 755-8811
Medical Dir Merle Bacastow.
Licensure Skilled care. *Beds* SNF 121. *Certified* Medicaid; Medicare.
Owner Proprietary corp (Manor Care Inc).
Admissions Requirements Minimum age 16; Medical examination.
Staff RNs; LPNs; Nurses' aides; Physical therapists; Recreational therapists 1 (ft); Occupational therapists; Speech therapists; Activities coordinators 1 (ft).

Facilities Dining room; Physical therapy room; Activities room; Crafts room; Laundry room; Barber/Beauty shop; 4 Lounges/TV rooms.
Activities Arts & crafts; Cards; Games; Reading groups; Prayer groups; Movies; Shopping trips; Dances/Social/Cultural gatherings; Resident council; Current events; Discussion group; Spelling bees; Pokeno; Chaplaincy program.

Manor Care of Barley North
1770 Barley Rd, York, PA 17404
(717) 767-6530
Licensure Skilled care. *Beds* SNF 151.
Certified Medicaid; Medicare.
Owner Proprietary corp (Manor Care Inc).

Manor Care South Nursing & Rehabilitation Center
200 Pauline Dr, York, PA 17402
(717) 741-0824, 741-1274 FAX
Admin Marion Chiadis. *Dir of Nursing* Yvonne Gemmill. *Medical Dir* Dr Charles Schlager.
Licensure Skilled care. *Beds* SNF 102. *Private Pay Patients* 68%. *Certified* Medicaid; Medicare.
Owner Proprietary corp (Manor Care Inc).
Admissions Requirements Medical examination.
Staff Physicians 1 (pt); RNs 5 (ft), 3 (pt); LPNs 7 (ft); Nurses' aides 34 (ft), 5 (pt); Physical therapists 1 (ft); Recreational therapists 1 (ft); Occupational therapists 1 (pt); Speech therapists 1 (pt); Activities coordinators 1 (ft); Dietitians (consultant); Ophthalmologists (consultant); Podiatrists (consultant); Audiologists (consultant).
Languages Pennsylvania Dutch, German.
Facilities Dining room; Physical therapy room; Activities room; Chapel; Laundry room; Barber/Beauty shop; Telephone room; Occupational therapy room; Conference room.
Activities Arts & crafts; Cards; Games; Reading groups; Prayer groups; Movies; Shopping trips; Dances/Social/Cultural gatherings; Intergenerational programs; Pet therapy.

Misericordia Convalescent Home
998 S Russell St, York, PA 17402
(717) 755-1964
Admin Sr Rosella Marie DM. *Dir of Nursing* Sr M Concepta DM. *Medical Dir* Edward T Lis MD.
Licensure Skilled care. *Beds* SNF 55.
Owner Proprietary corp.
Admissions Requirements Medical examination; Physician's request.
Staff Physicians 2 (pt); RNs 3 (ft), 2 (pt); LPNs 2 (ft), 3 (pt); Nurses' aides 18 (ft), 15 (pt); Physical therapists 2 (pt); Recreational therapists 1 (ft), 1 (pt); Activities coordinators 1 (ft), 1 (pt); Dietitians 4 (ft), 1 (pt); Ophthalmologists 1 (pt).
Affiliation Roman Catholic.
Facilities Dining room; Activities room; Chapel; Crafts room; Laundry room; Barber/Beauty shop.
Activities Games; Prayer groups; Movies; Dances/Social/Cultural gatherings; Sing-alongs.

Margaret E Moul Home
2050 Barley Rd, York, PA 17404
(717) 767-6463
Admin Dennis V Reese.
Medical Dir James Harberger MD.
Licensure Intermediate care. *Beds* ICF 52.
Certified Medicaid.
Owner Nonprofit corp.
Admissions Requirements Minimum age 18; Medical examination; Physician's request.

Staff RNs 3 (ft), 3 (pt); LPNs 3 (ft), 4 (pt); Nurses' aides 16 (ft), 13 (pt); Physical therapists 1 (ft), 1 (pt); Recreational therapists 1 (ft), 1 (pt); Speech therapists 1 (pt); Dietitians 1 (pt).
Facilities Dining room; Physical therapy room; Activities room; Chapel; Crafts room; Laundry room.
Activities Arts & crafts; Cards; Games; Reading groups; Prayer groups; Movies; Shopping trips; Dances/Social/Cultural gatherings.

Rest Haven—York
1050 S George St, York, PA 17403
(717) 843-9866
Admin Margaret B Miller. *Dir of Nursing* Geraldine Stoltzfus. *Medical Dir* Dr Andrew Hickey.
Licensure Skilled care. *Beds* SNF 167.
Certified Medicaid; Medicare.
Owner Proprietary corp.
Staff Physicians 1 (ft); RNs 10 (ft), 4 (pt); LPNs 22 (ft), 4 (pt) 13E 29 (ft), 27 (pt); Recreational therapists 1 (ft); Occupational therapists 2 (pt); Speech therapists 1 (pt); Activities coordinators 1 (ft), 4 (pt); Dietitians 1 (pt); Ophthalmologists 1 (pt); Podiatrists 1 (pt); Dentists 1 (pt); Psychologists 1 (pt).
Facilities Dining room; Physical therapy room; Activities room; Chapel; Crafts room; Laundry room; Barber/Beauty shop.
Activities Arts & crafts; Games; Reading groups; Prayer groups; Movies; Shopping trips; Dances/Social/Cultural gatherings.

York County Hospital & Home
118 Pleasant Acres Rd, York, PA 17402
(717) 771-9100
Admin Patricia Konhaus.
Medical Dir Dr Andrew Hickey.
Licensure Skilled care; Intermediate care. *Beds* Swing beds SNF/ICF 495. *Private Pay Patients* 2%. *Certified* Medicaid; Medicare.
Owner Publicly owned.
Admissions Requirements Medical examination.
Staff Physicians 3 (pt); RNs 22 (ft), 11 (pt); LPNs 41 (ft), 18 (pt); Nurses' aides 197 (ft), 99 (pt); Physical therapists 1 (ft); Reality therapists 2 (ft); Recreational therapists 7 (ft); Occupational therapists 1 (pt); Speech therapists 1 (pt); Dietitians 1 (pt); Ophthalmologists 1 (pt); Podiatrists 3 (pt); Audiologists 1 (pt).
Facilities Dining room; Physical therapy room; Activities room; Chapel; Crafts room; Laundry room; Barber/Beauty shop; Library.
Activities Arts & crafts; Cards; Games; Reading groups; Prayer groups; Movies; Shopping trips; Dances/Social/Cultural gatherings; Intergenerational programs; Pet therapy; Bowling.

York Lutheran Home
750 Kelly Dr, York, PA 17404
(717) 848-2585
Admin Jeanne M Wildasin RN NHA. *Dir of Nursing* Janet Huber RN. *Medical Dir* James Harberger MD.
Licensure Skilled care; Intermediate care; Residential care; Independent living. *Beds* SNF 33; ICF 100; Residential care 26; Independent living 58. *Private Pay Patients* 64%.
Owner Nonprofit corp (Lutheran Social Services SR).
Admissions Requirements Minimum age 65; Medical examination.
Staff RNs; LPNs; Nurses' aides; Physical therapists 1 (pt); Recreational therapists 1 (ft); Occupational therapists 1 (pt); Speech therapists 1 (pt); Activities coordinators 1 (ft); Dietitians 1 (pt); Podiatrists 1 (pt); Audiologists 1 (pt); Chaplains 1 (ft); Volunteer coordinators 1 (ft).
Affiliation Lutheran.

Facilities Dining room; Physical therapy room; Activities room; Chapel; Crafts room; Laundry room; Barber/Beauty shop; Library; Plant room; Pharmacy; Volunteer suite; Sewing room; Gift shop; Clothing bank; Game room.
Activities Arts & crafts; Cards; Games; Reading groups; Prayer groups; Movies; Shopping trips; Dances/Social/Cultural gatherings; Intergenerational programs; Pet therapy.

Youngstown

Edgewood Nursing Center
PO Box 277, E Main St, Youngstown, PA 15696
(412) 537-4441
Admin Grace Mitchell. *Dir of Nursing* Brenda Sherer. *Medical Dir* Francis Meyers DO.
Licensure Intermediate care. *Beds* ICF 107.
Certified Medicaid.
Owner Proprietary corp.
Admissions Requirements Minimum age 16; Medical examination; Physician's request.
Staff Physicians 3 (pt); RNs 8 (ft), 2 (pt); LPNs 8 (ft), 4 (pt); Nurses' aides 30 (ft), 7 (pt); Physical therapists 1 (pt); Occupational therapists 1 (pt); Speech therapists 1 (pt); Activities coordinators 2 (ft); Dietitians 1 (pt); Podiatrists 1 (pt); Audiologists 1 (pt).
Facilities Dining room; Activities room; Crafts room; Laundry room; Barber/Beauty shop; Library.
Activities Arts & crafts; Cards; Games; Reading groups; Prayer groups; Movies; Dances/Social/Cultural gatherings; Intergenerational programs; Pet therapy.

Youngsville

Rouse-Warren County Home
PO Box 207, Youngsville, PA 16371
(814) 563-7561, 563-7431 FAX
Admin David A Metcalf NHA. *Dir of Nursing* Barbara Greenlund RN NHA. *Medical Dir* Stanley J Sivak MD.
Licensure Skilled care; Intermediate care; Alzheimer's care. *Beds* SNF 82; ICF 97. *Private Pay Patients* 12%. *Certified* Medicaid; Medicare.
Owner Publicly owned.
Admissions Requirements Medical examination; Physician's request.
Staff Physicians 1 (ft); RNs 8 (ft), 3 (pt); LPNs 19 (ft), 7 (pt); Nurses' aides 56 (ft), 32 (pt); Physical therapists (contracted); Occupational therapists; Speech therapists (contracted); Activities coordinators 1 (ft); Dietitians 2 (ft); Ophthalmologists (referral); Podiatrists (contracted); Audiologists (referral); Music therapists 1 (ft); Social workers 3 (ft); Chaplains 1 (pt).
Languages Sign interpreter contracted.
Facilities Dining room; Physical therapy room; Activities room; Chapel; Crafts room; Laundry room; Barber/Beauty shop; Residents' gardens.
Activities Arts & crafts; Cards; Games; Reading groups; Prayer groups; Movies; Shopping trips; Dances/Social/Cultural gatherings; Intergenerational programs; Pet therapy.

Zelienople

Passavant Retirement & Health Center
401 S Main St, Zelienople, PA 16063
(412) 452-5400, 452-5400, ext 4289 FAX
Admin William T Pratt. *Dir of Nursing* Bernadette Mehno. *Medical Dir* Linda Raymundo MD.
Licensure Skilled care; Intermediate care; Retirement. *Beds* Swing beds SNF/ICF 184; Retirement 350. *Private Pay Patients* 37%. *Certified* Medicaid; Medicare.

Owner Nonprofit corp.
Admissions Requirements Minimum age 65; Medical examination; Physician's request.
Staff Physicians 3 (pt); RNs 13 (ft), 2 (pt); LPNs 19 (ft), 5 (pt); Nurses' aides 58 (ft), 12 (pt); Physical therapists 1 (ft); Occupational therapists 1 (pt); Speech therapists 1 (pt); Activities coordinators 4 (ft), 4 (pt); Dietitians 1 (ft); Podiatrists 1 (pt); Audiologists 1 (pt).
Affiliation Lutheran.
Facilities Dining room; Physical therapy room; Activities room; Chapel; Crafts room; Laundry room; Barber/Beauty shop; Library.
Activities Arts & crafts; Cards; Games; Reading groups; Prayer groups; Movies; Shopping trips; Dances/Social/Cultural gatherings; Intergenerational programs; Pet therapy.

RHODE ISLAND

Bristol

Metacom Manor Health Center
1 Dawn Hill, Bristol, RI 02809
(401) 252-2300
Admin Ursula M Beauregard. *Dir of Nursing* Stephanie Barrette RN. *Medical Dir* Dr Chase.
Licensure Skilled care; Intermediate care; Alzheimer's care. *Beds* SNF 52; ICF 77. *Certified* Medicaid; Medicare.
Owner Proprietary corp.
Admissions Requirements Physician's request.
Languages Portuguese, French.
Facilities Dining room; Physical therapy room; Activities room; Chapel; Crafts room; Laundry room; Barber/Beauty shop; Library; Child care; Petting zoo; Greenhouse.
Activities Arts & crafts; Cards; Games; Reading groups; Prayer groups; Movies; Shopping trips; Dances/Social/Cultural gatherings; Intergenerational programs; Pet therapy; Resident council.

Silver Creek Manor
7 Creek Ln, Bristol, RI 02809
(401) 253-3000
Admin Gerald P Romano.
Medical Dir Paul Agatiello MD.
Licensure Skilled care; Intermediate care. *Beds* SNF 80; ICF 48. *Certified* Medicaid; Medicare.
Owner Privately owned.
Staff Physicians 20 (pt); RNs 6 (ft), 3 (pt); LPNs 3 (ft), 3 (pt); Nurses' aides 27 (ft), 20 (pt); Physical therapists 1 (pt); Recreational therapists 1 (ft); Speech therapists 1 (pt); Activities coordinators 1 (ft), 1 (pt); Dietitians 1 (pt); Ophthalmologists 2 (pt); Podiatrists 1 (pt); Dentists 1 (pt).
Languages French, Portuguese, Polish.
Facilities Dining room; Physical therapy room; Activities room; Crafts room; Laundry room; Barber/Beauty shop.
Activities Arts & crafts; Cards; Games; Reading groups; Prayer groups; Movies; Shopping trips; Dances/Social/Cultural gatherings.

Burrillville

Nicole Manor
130 Sayles Ave, Burrillville, RI 02859
(401) 568-6978
Admin Joan Sabella.
Licensure Intermediate care. *Beds* 14. *Certified* Medicaid.
Staff Physicians 3 (pt); RNs 1 (pt); LPNs 1 (ft), 1 (pt); Nurses' aides 2 (ft), 3 (pt); Recreational therapists 1 (ft); Activities coordinators 1 (ft); Ophthalmologists 2 (pt); Podiatrists 1 (pt); Dentists 2 (pt).
Facilities Dining room; Activities room; Crafts room; Laundry room; Barber/Beauty shop; Library.

Activities Arts & crafts; Cards; Games; Reading groups; Prayer groups; Movies; Shopping trips; Dances/Social/Cultural gatherings.

Overlook Nursing Home
14 Rock Ave, Burrillville, RI 02859
(401) 568-2549
Admin Harold Kenoian.
Licensure Skilled care; Intermediate care. *Beds* SNF 14; ICF 86. *Certified* Medicaid; Medicare.

Central Falls

Cartie's Health Center
21 Lincoln Ave, Central Falls, RI 02863
(401) 727-0900
Admin John Prew.
Medical Dir Eugene Gaudet MD.
Licensure Skilled care; Intermediate care. *Beds* SNF 33; ICF 180. *Certified* Medicaid; Medicare.
Admissions Requirements Minimum age 14; Medical examination; Physician's request.
Staff Physicians 35 (pt); RNs 5 (ft), 8 (pt); LPNs 14 (ft), 11 (pt); Nurses' aides 77 (ft), 23 (pt); Physical therapists 1 (ft), 1 (pt); Occupational therapists 1 (pt); Speech therapists 1 (pt); Activities coordinators 3 (ft); Dietitians 1 (pt); Ophthalmologists 1 (pt); Podiatrists 1 (pt); Audiologists 1 (ft); Dentists 1 (pt); Bed makers 2 (ft), 3 (pt).
Facilities Dining room; Physical therapy room; Activities room; Crafts room; Laundry room; Barber/Beauty shop.
Activities Arts & crafts; Cards; Games; Reading groups; Prayer groups; Movies; Dances/Social/Cultural gatherings.

Frigon Nursing Home Inc
60 Eben Brown Ln, Central Falls, RI 02863
(401) 726-0371
Admin James H Frigon.
Licensure Intermediate care. *Beds* ICF 27. *Certified* Medicaid.

Mansion Nursing Home
104 Clay St, Central Falls, RI 02863
(401) 722-0830, 726-5020
Admin Teresa Chopoorian EdD RN. *Dir of Nursing* Darlene Elkas RN. *Medical Dir* Eugene Gaudette MD.
Licensure Intermediate care. *Beds* ICF 62. *Private Pay Patients* 15%. *Certified* Medicaid.
Owner Proprietary corp.
Staff RNs 4 (ft); LPNs 3 (ft); Nurses' aides 11 (ft); Activities coordinators 1 (ft).
Languages French, Portuguese, Armenian, Spanish.
Facilities Dining room; Activities room; Laundry room; Porches; Yard with picnic table; Benches; Vegetable patch.
Activities Arts & crafts; Cards; Games; Prayer groups; Movies; Shopping trips; Dances/Social/Cultural gatherings; Intergenerational

programs; Picnics; Trips to park; Christmas lights; Penny socials; Auctions; Birthday parties; Family days.

Paquette Home Inc
649 Broad St, Central Falls, RI 02863
(401) 725-7045
Admin Ronald Paquette.
Licensure Intermediate care. *Beds* ICF 30. *Certified* Medicaid.

Rose Cottage Health Care Center
151 Hunt St, Central Falls, RI 02863
(401) 722-4610
Admin Leonard Lamphear.
Licensure Skilled care; Intermediate care. *Beds* SNF 17; ICF 87. *Certified* Medicaid; Medicare.

Coventry

Alpine Rest Home Inc
PO Box 457, Weaver Hill Rd, Coventry, RI 02816
(401) 397-5001
Admin Rodney J Gauvin. *Dir of Nursing* Mary Joan Smith RN. *Medical Dir* Alfred Arland MD.
Licensure Intermediate care. *Beds* ICF 29. *Certified* Medicaid.
Owner Proprietary corp.
Admissions Requirements Minimum age 50; Medical examination.
Staff Physicians; RNs 1 (ft), 1 (pt); Nurses' aides 4 (ft), 5 (pt); Activities coordinators 1 (ft); Dietitians 1 (pt); Podiatrists 1 (pt).
Languages French.
Facilities Dining room; Activities room; Laundry room; Barber/Beauty shop.
Activities Arts & crafts; Cards; Games; Prayer groups; Movies; Shopping trips.

Coventry Health Center
10 Woodland Dr, Coventry, RI 02816
(401) 826-2000
Admin Carol Belanger. *Dir of Nursing* Kathleen LaPorte RN. *Medical Dir* Anthony Kazlauskas MD.
Licensure Skilled care; Intermediate care. *Beds* SNF 102; ICF 204. *Certified* Medicaid; Medicare.
Owner Proprietary corp.
Admissions Requirements Medical examination.
Staff RNs; LPNs; Nurses' aides; Physical therapists; Recreational therapists; Occupational therapists; Speech therapists; Activities coordinators; Dietitians.
Facilities Dining room; Physical therapy room; Activities room; Chapel; Crafts room; Laundry room; Barber/Beauty shop; Library.
Activities Arts & crafts; Cards; Games; Prayer groups; Movies; Shopping trips; Dances/Social/Cultural gatherings; Pet therapy.

Laurel Foster Home Inc
51 Laurel Ave, Coventry, RI 02816
(401) 821-0136

Admin Eileen Hathaway.
Medical Dir Dr Anthony Kazlauskas.
Licensure Intermediate care. *Beds* ICF 60.
 Certified Medicaid.
Admissions Requirements Females only;
 Medical examination; Physician's request.
Staff RNs 1 (pt); LPNs 1 (ft), 1 (pt); Nurses'
 aides 8 (ft), 10 (pt); Activities coordinators 1
 (ft); Dietitians 1 (pt).
Facilities Dining room; Activities room;
 Chapel; Crafts room; Barber/Beauty shop;
 Library.
Activities Arts & crafts; Cards; Games;
 Reading groups; Prayer groups; Movies;
 Shopping trips; Dances/Social/Cultural
 gatherings; Resident council; Gardening
 club; Weekly bowling trips.

Riverview Nursing Home Inc
546 Main St, Coventry, RI 02816
(401) 821-6837
Admin Lois Richards.
Medical Dir Dr J Winters.
Licensure Skilled care; Intermediate care. *Beds*
 SNF 6; ICF 59. *Certified* Medicaid;
 Medicare.
Staff Physicians 5 (pt); RNs 5 (ft); LPNs 7
 (ft); Nurses' aides 20 (ft); Activities
 coordinators 1 (ft); Dietitians 1 (pt);
 Ophthalmologists 1 (pt); Podiatrists 1 (pt);
 Dentists 1 (pt).
Facilities Dining room; Activities room;
 Crafts room; Barber/Beauty shop.
Activities Arts & crafts; Games; Prayer groups;
 Movies; Outings; Gardening; Sing-alongs;
 Parties.

Cranston

Cedar Crest Nursing Centre Inc
125 Scituate Ave, Cranston, RI 02920
(401) 944-8500
Admin Pasquale Pezzelli.
Licensure Skilled care; Intermediate care. *Beds*
 SNF 40; ICF 95. *Certified* Medicaid;
 Medicare.

Cra-Mar Nursing Home Inc
575 7-Mile Rd, Cranston, RI 02831
(401) 828-5010
Admin Thomas J Grzych.
Licensure Skilled care; Intermediate care. *Beds*
 SNF 6; ICF 34. *Certified* Medicaid;
 Medicare.

Scandinavian Home for the Aged
1811 Broad St, Cranston, RI 02905
(401) 461-1433
Admin John C Woulfe. *Dir of Nursing* Lois
 Goff RN. *Medical Dir* Perry Garber MD.
Licensure Skilled care; Intermediate care. *Beds*
 SNF 16; ICF 54. *Private Pay Patients* 55%.
 Certified Medicaid; Medicare.
Owner Nonprofit organization/foundation.
Admissions Requirements Medical
 examination.
Staff RNs 4 (ft), 9 (pt); LPNs 1 (ft), 2 (pt);
 Nurses' aides 14 (ft), 17 (pt); Physical
 therapists 1 (pt); Activities coordinators 1
 (ft); Dietitians 1 (pt).
Facilities Dining room; Activities room;
 Chapel; Crafts room; Laundry room; Barber/
 Beauty shop; Lawns; Gardens; Walkways.
Activities Arts & crafts; Cards; Games;
 Reading groups; Prayer groups; Movies;
 Shopping trips.

Cumberland

Diamond Hill Nursing Center Inc
3579 Diamond Hill Rd, Cumberland, RI
 02864
(401) 333-5050
Admin Jeanne Abbruzzese. *Dir of Nursing*
 Gerri Lammertink RN.
Licensure Intermediate care. *Beds* ICF 48.
 Certified Medicaid.

Owner Privately owned.
Admissions Requirements Medical
 examination; Physician's request.
Staff RNs; LPNs; Nurses' aides; Activities
 coordinators.
Facilities Dining room; Activities room;
 Chapel; Laundry room.
Activities Arts & crafts; Cards; Games; Prayer
 groups; Movies; Shopping trips;
 Intergenerational programs; Pet therapy.

Grandview Nursing Home Inc
Chambers & John Sts, Cumberland, RI 02864
(401) 724-7500
Admin Frances McDermott RN.
Licensure Skilled care; Intermediate care. *Beds*
 SNF 59; ICF 13. *Certified* Medicaid;
 Medicare.

Mt St Rita Health Center
15 Sumner Brown Rd, Cumberland, RI 02864
(401) 333-6352
Admin Sr Joan Bailey. *Dir of Nursing* Edith
 Forrest. *Medical Dir* Patrick Levesque MD.
Licensure Intermediate care. *Beds* ICF 70.
 Private Pay Patients 90%. *Certified*
 Medicaid.
Owner Nonprofit organization/foundation.
Staff Physicians (consultants); RNs 4 (ft), 6
 (pt); LPNs 2 (ft), 4 (pt); Nurses' aides 17
 (ft), 37 (pt); Physical therapists 2 (ft);
 Recreational therapists 1 (ft); Activities
 coordinators 1 (ft); Dietitians 1 (ft);
 Podiatrists 1 (ft).
Affiliation Roman Catholic.
Facilities Dining room; Physical therapy
 room; Activities room; Chapel; Crafts room;
 Laundry room; Barber/Beauty shop.
Activities Arts & crafts; Cards; Games;
 Reading groups; Prayer groups; Movies;
 Shopping trips; Dances/Social/Cultural
 gatherings; Pet therapy.

East Greenwich

Greenwich Bay Manor
945 Main St, East Greenwich, RI 02818
(401) 885-3334
Admin Raymond Maxwell.
Licensure Intermediate care. *Beds* ICF 45.

Royal Manor Inc
159 Division St, East Greenwich, RI 02818
(401) 884-5590
Admin Annette M DeBaene.
Licensure Intermediate care. *Beds* ICF 55.

East Providence

Hattie Ide Chaffee Home
200 Wampanoag Trail, East Providence, RI
 02914
(401) 434-1520
Admin Adeline Frederick-Schwartz. *Dir of
 Nursing* Paula Wright. *Medical Dir* Fred
 Vohr MD.
Licensure Skilled care. *Beds* SNF 59. *Certified*
 Medicaid; Medicare.
Owner Nonprofit organization/foundation.
Admissions Requirements Minimum age 16;
 Preference given to cancer patients.
Staff Physicians 7 (pt); RNs 12 (ft), 6 (pt);
 Nurses' aides 27 (ft), 16 (pt); Physical
 therapists 1 (pt); Recreational therapists 2
 (ft); Speech therapists 1 (pt); Dietitians 1
 (pt); Ophthalmologists 1 (pt); Podiatrists 1
 (pt); Audiologists 1 (pt).
Languages French, Portuguese, Italian,
 German, Chinese.
Facilities Dining room; Physical therapy
 room; Activities room; Chapel; Crafts room;
 Barber/Beauty shop.
Activities Arts & crafts; Cards; Games;
 Reading groups; Movies; Dances/Social/
 Cultural gatherings; Intergenerational
 programs; Pet therapy; Church services;
 Trips; Parties.

Eastgate Nursing & Recovery Center Inc
198 Waterman Ave, East Providence, RI
 02914
(401) 431-2087
Admin Donna St Ours.
Licensure Skilled care; Intermediate care. *Beds*
 SNF 7; ICF 69. *Certified* Medicaid;
 Medicare.
Staff Physicians 4 (pt); RNs 3 (ft); LPNs 1 (ft)
 13E 18 (ft); Activities coordinators 1 (ft);
 Dietitians 1 (pt); Podiatrists 1 (pt).
Facilities Dining room; Activities room;
 Laundry room; Library.
Activities Arts & crafts; Cards; Games;
 Reading groups; Movies; Shopping trips;
 Dances/Social/Cultural gatherings.

Evergreen House Health Center
1 Evergreen Dr, East Providence, RI 02914
(401) 438-3250
Admin Diane Ashley.
Licensure Skilled care; Intermediate care. *Beds*
 SNF 52; ICF 104. *Certified* Medicaid;
 Medicare.
Owner Proprietary corp (National Heritage).

Fellowship House
2424 Pawtucket Ave, East Providence, RI
 02914
(401) 438-6925
Admin George Von Housen.
Licensure Intermediate care. *Beds* 12.
 Certified Medicaid.

Harris Health Center
833 Broadway, East Providence, RI 02914
(401) 434-7404
Admin Charles L Harris.
Medical Dir Peter J Sansone MD.
Licensure Intermediate care; Alzheimer's care.
 Beds ICF 36. *Certified* Medicaid.
Owner Proprietary corp.
Admissions Requirements Medical
 examination; Physician's request.
Staff Physicians 1 (pt); RNs 1 (ft), 2 (pt);
 LPNs 4 (ft), 2 (pt); Nurses' aides 10 (ft), 6
 (pt); Physical therapists 1 (pt); Reality
 therapists 1 (pt); Recreational therapists 1
 (pt); Occupational therapists 1 (pt); Speech
 therapists 1 (pt); Activities coordinators 1
 (ft), 1 (pt); Dietitians 1 (pt);
 Ophthalmologists 1 (pt); Podiatrists 1 (pt);
 Dentists 1 (pt).
Languages French, Portuguese.
Facilities Dining room; Activities room;
 Crafts room.
Activities Arts & crafts; Cards; Games;
 Reading groups; Prayer groups; Movies;
 Shopping trips; Dances/Social/Cultural
 gatherings.

Health Havens Nursing Center
100 Wampanoag Trail, East Providence, RI
 02915
(401) 438-4275
Admin Christopher P Mulrooney MPS. *Dir of
 Nursing* Carol A Calise RN. *Medical Dir*
 David N Newhall MD.
Licensure Skilled care; Intermediate care. *Beds*
 SNF 41; ICF 19. *Private Pay Patients* 54%.
 Certified Medicaid; Medicare.
Owner Proprietary corp (Personacare).
Admissions Requirements Medical
 examination.
Staff RNs 5 (ft), 7 (pt); LPNs 2 (ft), 3 (pt);
 Nurses' aides 20 (ft), 14 (pt); Physical
 therapists (consultant); Occupational
 therapists (consultant); Speech therapists
 (consultant); Activities coordinators 2 (pt);
 Dietitians (consultant); Podiatrists
 (consultant).
Languages Portuguese, French.
Facilities Dining room; Activities room;
 Landscaped green.
Activities Arts & crafts; Games; Reading
 groups; Prayer groups; Movies; Shopping
 trips; Dances/Social/Cultural gatherings;

Intergenerational programs; Pet therapy; Senior Center outings; One-on-one visits; Volunteer program.

Orchard View Manor
135 Tripps Ln, East Providence, RI 02915
(401) 438-2250, 438-0635 FAX
Admin Orlando J Bisbano Jr. *Dir of Nursing* Joann S Cardullo RN. *Medical Dir* Jacob Stone MC.
Licensure Skilled care; Intermediate care. *Beds* SNF 46; ICF 134. *Certified* Medicaid; Medicare.
Owner Privately owned.
Facilities Dining room; Physical therapy room; Activities room; Chapel; Crafts room; Laundry room; Barber/Beauty shop; Orchard; Gardens.
Activities Arts & crafts; Cards; Games; Reading groups; Movies; Shopping trips; Dances/Social/Cultural gatherings; Intergenerational programs; Pet therapy.

Riverside Nursing Home
336 Willett Ave, East Providence, RI 02915
(401) 433-0844
Admin Barbara Monteleone.
Medical Dir Dr Howard Perrone.
Licensure Intermediate care. *Beds* ICF 27. *Certified* Medicaid.
Staff Physicians 7 (pt); RNs 1 (ft), 4 (pt); LPNs 1 (ft), 3 (pt); Nurses' aides 3 (ft), 12 (pt); Activities coordinators 1 (ft); Dietitians 1 (pt); Ophthalmologists 1 (pt); Podiatrists 1 (pt); Audiologists 1 (pt); Dentists 1 (pt).
Facilities Dining room; Activities room; Laundry room.
Activities Arts & crafts; Cards; Games; Reading groups; Prayer groups; Movies; Shopping trips.

United Methodist Health Care Center
30 Alexander Ave, East Providence, RI 02914
(401) 438-7210
Admin Thomas J Peters.
Medical Dir Dr John Demicco.
Licensure Intermediate care; Retirement. *Beds* ICF 83; Retirement 125. *Private Pay Patients* 30%. *Certified* Medicaid.
Admissions Requirements Medical examination; Physician's request.
Staff Physicians 1 (pt); RNs 4 (ft), 2 (pt); LPNs 2 (ft), 1 (pt); Nurses' aides 24 (ft), 4 (pt); Reality therapists 1 (pt); Recreational therapists 1 (ft), 1 (pt); Activities coordinators 1 (ft); Dietitians 1 (pt).
Affiliation Methodist.
Facilities Dining room; Activities room; Chapel; Crafts room; Laundry room; Barber/Beauty shop; Library.
Activities Arts & crafts; Cards; Games; Reading groups; Prayer groups; Movies; Shopping trips; Dances/Social/Cultural gatherings.

Waterview Villa
1275 S Broadway, East Providence, RI 02914
(401) 438-7020
Admin Michael Monteleone. *Dir of Nursing* Ena Ward. *Medical Dir* Dr Rocco Marzilli.
Licensure Skilled care; Intermediate care. *Beds* SNF 44; ICF 88. *Certified* Medicaid; Medicare.
Owner Proprietary corp.
Admissions Requirements Medical examination.
Staff Physicians 44 (pt); RNs 9 (ft), 5 (pt); LPNs 7 (ft), 3 (pt); Nurses' aides 40 (ft), 20 (pt); Physical therapists 1 (pt); Occupational therapists 1 (pt); Speech therapists 1 (pt); Activities coordinators 1 (ft), 2 (pt); Dietitians 1 (pt); Ophthalmologists 1 (pt); Podiatrists 4 (pt).
Languages Portuguese.
Facilities Dining room; Physical therapy room; Activities room; Chapel; Crafts room; Laundry room; Barber/Beauty shop; Library; Dining facilities on 3 floors.

Activities Arts & crafts; Cards; Games; Reading groups; Prayer groups; Movies; Shopping trips; Dances/Social/Cultural gatherings; Intergenerational programs; Pet therapy; Spelling groups; Monthly restaurant night; Weekly cocktail hours with music.

Foster

Nancy Ann Convalescent Home
E Killingly Rd, Foster, RI 02825
(401) 647-2170
Admin Esther O'Dette.
Licensure Intermediate care. *Beds* ICF 18. *Certified* Medicaid.
Admissions Requirements Minimum age 50; Medical examination; Physician's request.
Staff RNs 1 (pt); LPNs 3 (ft); Nurses' aides 2 (ft), 4 (pt); Recreational therapists 1 (pt); Activities coordinators 1 (pt); Podiatrists 1 (pt).
Facilities Dining room; Laundry room; Barber/Beauty shop; Multi-purpose room.
Activities Arts & crafts; Cards; Games; Prayer groups; Movies; Dances/Social/Cultural gatherings.

Greene

Woodpecker Hill Nursing Home
2052 Plainfield Pike, Greene, RI 02827
(401) 397-7504
Admin Thomas Haynes. *Dir of Nursing* Claire Sonner. *Medical Dir* Dr Robert F Spencer.
Licensure Intermediate care. *Beds* ICF 31. *Certified* Medicaid.
Owner Privately owned.
Admissions Requirements Medical examination.
Staff Physicians 1 (pt); RNs 1 (ft); LPNs 4 (ft), 3 (pt); Nurses' aides 6 (ft), 6 (pt); Activities coordinators 1 (pt); Dietitians 1 (pt); Ophthalmologists 1 (pt); Podiatrists 1 (pt).
Facilities Dining room; Activities room; Laundry room.
Activities Arts & crafts; Cards; Games; Movies; Shopping trips; Dances/Social/Cultural gatherings.

Harrisville

Lakeview Health Center
Steere Farm Rd, Harrisville, RI 02859
(401) 568-6242
Admin Michael Monteleone.
Medical Dir Clayton Lanphear DO.
Licensure Skilled care; Intermediate care. *Beds* SNF 37; ICF 168. *Certified* Medicaid; Medicare.
Owner Privately owned.
Staff RNs 8 (ft), 4 (pt); LPNs 6 (ft), 10 (pt); Nurses' aides 40 (ft), 60 (pt); Activities coordinators 1 (ft), 1 (pt).
Facilities Dining room; Physical therapy room; Activities room; Chapel; Crafts room; Barber/Beauty shop.
Activities Arts & crafts; Cards; Games; Prayer groups; Movies; Cooking classes.

Johnston

Briarcliffe Healthcare Facility
PO Box 19550, Johnston, RI 02919
(401) 944-2450
Admin Mark Tordoff.
Licensure Skilled care; Intermediate care. *Beds* SNF 19; ICF 101. *Certified* Medicaid; Medicare.
Admissions Requirements Medical examination; Physician's request.
Staff RNs 3 (ft), 5 (pt); LPNs 6 (ft), 4 (pt); Nurses' aides 28 (ft), 26 (pt); Activities coordinators 1 (ft), 3 (pt).

Facilities Dining room; Physical therapy room; Activities room; Chapel; Crafts room; Laundry room; Barber/Beauty shop; Library.
Activities Arts & crafts; Cards; Games; Reading groups; Prayer groups; Movies; Dances/Social/Cultural gatherings.

Cherry Hill Manor
2 Cherry Hill Rd, Johnston, RI 02919
(401) 231-3102, 232-5520 FAX
Admin Elena Pisaturo RN. *Dir of Nursing* Bernice Coutu RN. *Medical Dir* Michael Baccari MD.
Licensure Skilled care; Intermediate care; Retirement. *Beds* SNF 68; ICF 100. *Certified* Medicaid; Medicare; VA.
Owner Proprietary corp.
Staff Physicians; RNs; LPNs; Nurses' aides; Physical therapists; Recreational therapists; Occupational therapists; Speech therapists; Activities coordinators; Dietitians; Ophthalmologists; Podiatrists; Audiologists; Dentists.
Facilities Dining room; Physical therapy room; Activities room; Chapel; Crafts room; Laundry room; Barber/Beauty shop; Library.
Activities Arts & crafts; Cards; Games; Reading groups; Prayer groups; Movies; Shopping trips; Dances/Social/Cultural gatherings; Intergenerational programs; Pet therapy.

Morgan Health Center
80 Morgan Ave, Johnston, RI 02919
(401) 944-7800
Admin Eugene Abbruzzese. *Dir of Nursing* Joyce Morton RN. *Medical Dir* Dr Kazlauskas.
Licensure Skilled care; Intermediate care. *Beds* SNF 40; ICF 80. *Certified* Medicaid; Medicare.
Owner Proprietary corp (Health Concepts).
Staff RNs; LPNs; Activities coordinators; Ophthalmologists.
Languages Italian.
Facilities Dining room; Activities room; Crafts room; Laundry room; Barber/Beauty shop; Library; Dining rooms; Gift shop.
Activities Arts & crafts; Cards; Games; Reading groups; Prayer groups; Movies; Shopping trips; Dances/Social/Cultural gatherings; An array of social groups & clubs.

Lincoln

Neighborhood Convalescent Home Inc
222 Old River Rd, Lincoln, RI 02865-1117
(401) 724-2111
Admin Raymond Dumas.
Medical Dir R Boucher MD.
Licensure Intermediate care. *Beds* ICF 17. *Certified* Medicaid.
Admissions Requirements Medical examination.
Staff RNs 1 (ft), 1 (pt); LPNs 2 (ft), 4 (pt); Nurses' aides 3 (ft), 4 (pt); Activities coordinators 1 (ft).
Facilities Dining room; Activities room; Laundry room.
Activities Arts & crafts; Cards; Games; Prayer groups; Movies; Shopping trips; Dances/Social/Cultural gatherings.

Manville

Holiday Retirement Home Inc
30 Sayles Hill Rd, Manville, RI 02838
(401) 765-1440, 521-4590
Admin Julie H Richard. *Dir of Nursing* Claire Dunton RN. *Medical Dir* Hao Huang MD.
Licensure Skilled care; Intermediate care. *Beds* SNF 4; ICF 125. *Private Pay Patients* 25%. *Certified* Medicaid; Medicare.
Owner Proprietary corp.
Admissions Requirements Medical examination.

Staff Physicians (contracted); RNs 8 (ft), 4 (pt); Nurses' LPNs 4 (ft), 4 (pt); Nurses' aides 19 (ft), 33 (pt); Physical therapists (contracted); Recreational therapists 1 (ft); Occupational therapists (contracted); Speech therapists (contracted); Activities coordinators 1 (pt); Dietitians (contracted); Ophthalmologists (contracted); Podiatrists (contracted); Audiologists (contracted); Social workers 1 (ft), 1 (pt).
Languages French, Polish, Portuguese.
Facilities Dining room; Activities room; Chapel; Barber/Beauty shop; Library.
Activities Arts & crafts; Cards; Games; Reading groups; Prayer groups; Movies; Shopping trips; Dances/Social/Cultural gatherings; Intergenerational programs; Pet therapy; Outings; Religious services.

Middletown

Carriage House Nursing Home Inc
93 Miantonomi Ave, Middletown, RI 02840
(401) 847-6300
Admin Brenda Nagle.
Medical Dir Suzanne E Grant.
Licensure Intermediate care. *Beds* ICF 51. *Certified* Medicaid.
Owner Privately owned.
Staff Physicians 1 (pt); RNs 2 (ft), 3 (pt); LPNs 2 (pt); Nurses' aides 11 (ft), 13 (pt); Activities coordinators 1 (ft); Dietitians 1 (pt).
Facilities Dining room; Activities room; Laundry room.
Activities Arts & crafts; Cards; Games; Reading groups; Prayer groups; Movies; Shopping trips; Dances/Social/Cultural gatherings.

John Clarke Retirement Center
600 Valley Rd, Middletown, RI 02840
(401) 846-0743
Admin Rev M Harry Randall. *Dir of Nursing* Charlotte Monk RN.
Licensure Skilled care; Intermediate care; Retirement. *Beds* SNF 10; ICF 50; Retirement 50. *Certified* Medicaid; Medicare.
Owner Nonprofit corp.
Admissions Requirements Minimum age 62; Medical examination.
Staff RNs; LPNs; Nurses' aides; Activities coordinators; Dietitians.
Languages Portuguese.
Affiliation Baptist.
Facilities Dining room; Physical therapy room; Activities room; Chapel; Crafts room; Laundry room; Barber/Beauty shop.
Activities Arts & crafts; Cards; Games; Reading groups; Movies; Shopping trips; Dances/Social/Cultural gatherings.

Forest Farm Health Care Centre Inc
201 Forest Ave, Middletown, RI 02840
(401) 847-2786
Admin Karl Lyon.
Licensure Skilled care; Intermediate care. *Beds* SNF 32; ICF 35. *Certified* Medicaid; Medicare.

Grand Islander Health Care Center
333 Green End Ave, Middletown, RI 02840
(401) 849-7100
Admin Jeffrey S Waddell. *Dir of Nursing* Janice Letiecq RN. *Medical Dir* Dr Anthony Caputi.
Licensure Skilled care; Intermediate care. *Beds* SNF 80; ICF 68. *Certified* Medicaid; Medicare.
Owner Proprietary corp.
Staff RNs; LPNs; Nurses' aides; Recreational therapists; Activities coordinators.
Facilities Dining room; Physical therapy room; Activities room; Crafts room; Laundry room; Barber/Beauty shop; Library; 5 Dayrooms.

Activities Arts & crafts; Cards; Games; Reading groups; Prayer groups; Movies; Shopping trips; Dances/Social/Cultural gatherings.

Newport

Catherine Manor
44 Catherine St, Newport, RI 02840
(401) 847-7455
Admin Edwina Sebest PhD. *Dir of Nursing* Susan Stafford RN.
Licensure Intermediate care. *Beds* ICF 19. *Private Pay Patients* 100%.
Owner Proprietary corp.
Admissions Requirements Medical examination.
Staff RNs 1 (ft); LPNs 2 (pt); Nurses' aides 3 (ft), 5 (pt); Activities coordinators 1 (pt); Dietitians 1 (pt); Podiatrists (consultant).
Facilities Dining room; Activities room; Laundry room; Library; Porch; Yard.
Activities Arts & crafts; Cards; Games; Prayer groups; Intergenerational programs; Pet therapy; Sing-alongs; Dance; Exercise class; Weekly rap group; Religious services; Visitations by Rabbi.

Oakwood Health Care Center Inc
Bellevue Ave, Newport, RI 02840
(401) 849-6600
Admin Michele V Thurman.
Licensure Skilled care; Intermediate care. *Beds* SNF 30; ICF 84. *Certified* Medicaid; Medicare.
Owner Proprietary corp (Oakwood Living Center).

St Clare's Home for Aged
309 Spring St, Newport, RI 02840
(401) 849-3204
Admin Mary Ann Altrui. *Dir of Nursing* Sr Marjorie Furze RN.
Licensure Intermediate care. *Beds* ICF 44. *Certified* Medicaid.
Owner Nonprofit corp.
Admissions Requirements Medical examination.
Staff RNs 1 (ft), 3 (pt); LPNs 1 (ft), 1 (pt); Nurses' aides 10 (ft), 4 (pt); Activities coordinators 1 (ft); Dietitians 1 (pt).
Facilities Dining room; Activities room; Chapel; Crafts room; Laundry room; Barber/Beauty shop; Library.
Activities Arts & crafts; Cards; Games; Reading groups; Prayer groups; Movies; Shopping trips; Dances/Social/Cultural gatherings.

Village House
70 Harrison Ave, Newport, RI 02840
(401) 849-5222
Admin Sally J Ryan.
Medical Dir Elizabeth A Lord.
Licensure Skilled care; Intermediate care; Alzheimer's care. *Beds* SNF 4; ICF 46. *Certified* Medicaid; Medicare.
Owner Proprietary corp.
Staff RNs 3 (ft), 6 (pt); LPNs 2 (pt); Nurses' aides 20 (ft), 10 (pt); Physical therapists 1 (pt); Reality therapists 1 (pt); Recreational therapists 1 (pt); Occupational therapists 1 (pt); Speech therapists 1 (pt); Activities coordinators 1 (ft); Dietitians 1 (pt).
Facilities Dining room; Activities room; Laundry room; Barber/Beauty shop.
Activities Arts & crafts; Games; Prayer groups; Movies; Shopping trips; Dances/Social/Cultural gatherings.

North Kingstown

Lafayette Nursing Home Inc
691 10-Rod Rd, North Kingstown, RI 02852
(401) 295-8816
Admin Hugh Hall.

Licensure Skilled care; Intermediate care. *Beds* SNF 25; ICF 27. *Certified* Medicaid; Medicare.

Roberts Health Centre Inc
990 10-Rod Rd, North Kingstown, RI 02852
(401) 884-6661
Admin Richard A Catallozzi.
Medical Dir Dr Capalbo.
Licensure Intermediate care. *Beds* ICF 61. *Certified* Medicaid.
Staff Physicians 1 (pt); RNs 2 (ft), 6 (pt); LPNs 3 (ft), 2 (pt); Nurses' aides 15 (ft), 8 (pt); Physical therapists 1 (pt); Reality therapists 1 (pt); Recreational therapists 1 (ft); Occupational therapists 1 (pt); Speech therapists 1 (pt); Activities coordinators 1 (ft); Dietitians 1 (pt); Ophthalmologists 1 (pt); Podiatrists 1 (pt); Audiologists 1 (pt); Dentists 1 (pt).
Facilities Dining room; Physical therapy room; Activities room; Chapel; Crafts room; Laundry room; Barber/Beauty shop; Library.
Activities Arts & crafts; Cards; Games; Reading groups; Prayer groups; Movies; Shopping trips.

Scalabrini Villa
860 N Quidnesset Rd, North Kingstown, RI 02852
(401) 884-1802
Admin Fr Edward J Marino. *Dir of Nursing* Barbara Mercurio. *Medical Dir* Dr Samuel Hassid.
Licensure Skilled care; Intermediate care. *Beds* SNF 9; ICF 61. *Private Pay Patients* 25%. *Certified* Medicaid; Medicare.
Owner Nonprofit organization/foundation.
Admissions Requirements Medical examination.
Staff RNs 6 (ft), 4 (pt); LPNs 1 (ft), 4 (pt); Nurses' aides 17 (ft), 13 (pt); Physical therapists; Activities coordinators 1 (ft); Dietitians 1 (pt).
Languages Italian, Spanish.
Affiliation Roman Catholic.
Facilities Dining room; Activities room; Chapel; Crafts room; Laundry room; Barber/Beauty shop; Library.
Activities Arts & crafts; Cards; Games; Prayer groups; Movies; Shopping trips; Dances/Social/Cultural gatherings; Intergenerational programs; Pet therapy.

South County Nursing Centre
Rte 4 & Oak Hill Rd, North Kingstown, RI 02852
(401) 294-4545
Admin Simone LeCroix.
Medical Dir Charles Sawson MD.
Licensure Skilled care; Intermediate care. *Beds* SNF 11; ICF 109. *Certified* Medicaid; Medicare.
Staff RNs 7 (ft), 12 (pt); LPNs 3 (ft), 3 (pt); Nurses' aides 80 (ft), 80 (pt); Activities coordinators 2 (ft); Dietitians 1 (ft).
Facilities Dining room; Physical therapy room; Activities room; Chapel; Crafts room; Laundry room; Barber/Beauty shop.
Activities Arts & crafts; Cards; Games; Reading groups; Prayer groups; Movies; Shopping trips; Dances/Social/Cultural gatherings.

North Providence

Golden Crest Nursing Center Inc
100 Smithfield Rd, North Providence, RI 02904
(401) 353-1710, 353-1711
Admin Paul Pezzelli.
Licensure Skilled care; Intermediate care. *Beds* SNF 33; ICF 114. *Certified* Medicaid; Medicare.

Hopkins Health Center
610 Smithfield Rd, North Providence, RI
02904
(401) 353-6300
Admin Carole Silva.
Medical Dir Dr Robert Brochu.
Licensure Skilled care; Intermediate care. *Beds*
SNF 104; ICF 106. *Certified* Medicaid;
Medicare.
Admissions Requirements Medical
examination.
Staff Physicians 1 (ft); RNs 8 (ft), 5 (pt);
LPNs 6 (ft), 8 (pt); Nurses' aides 55 (ft), 33
(pt); Physical therapists 1 (ft); Reality
therapists 1 (ft); Recreational therapists 2
(ft), 1 (pt); Occupational therapists 1 (pt);
Speech therapists 1 (pt); Dietitians 1 (ft);
Social workers 2 (ft).
Facilities Dining room; Physical therapy
room; Activities room; Chapel; Crafts room;
Barber/Beauty shop; Library.
Activities Arts & crafts; Cards; Games;
Reading groups; Prayer groups; Movies;
Dances/Social/Cultural gatherings.

North Side Manor
1373 Smith St, North Providence, RI 02911
(401) 353-1404
Admin Angela Squillante.
Licensure Intermediate care. *Beds* ICF 25.

North Scituate

Oak Crest Manor Inc
1057 Chopmist Hill Rd, North Scituate, RI
02857
(401) 647-7424
Admin Robert J DuClau. *Dir of Nursing*
Judith I DuClau. *Medical Dir* Dr Robert
Brochu.
Licensure Intermediate care. *Beds* ICF 46.
Private Pay Patients 12%. *Certified*
Medicaid.
Owner Privately owned.
Admissions Requirements Medical
examination; Physician's request.
Staff Physicians 1 (ft); RNs 1 (ft); LPNs 3 (ft),
3 (pt); Nurses' aides 9 (ft), 9 (pt); Activities
coordinators 1 (pt); Dietitians 1 (pt).
Facilities Dining room; Activities room;
Crafts room; Laundry room; Barber/Beauty
shop.
Activities Arts & crafts; Cards; Games;
Movies; Shopping trips; Dances/Social/
Cultural gatherings; Pet therapy.

North Smithfield

St Antoine Residence
400 Mendon Rd, North Smithfield, RI 02895
(401) 767-3500
Admin Mary Ann Altrui. *Dir of Nursing*
Jacqueline A Nerbonne RN.
Licensure Intermediate care. *Beds* ICF 243.
Certified Medicaid.
Owner Nonprofit corp.
Admissions Requirements Medical
examination; Physician's request.
Staff Physicians 14 (pt); RNs 4 (ft), 10 (pt);
LPNs 8 (ft), 8 (pt); Nurses' aides 60 (ft), 58
(pt); Physical therapists 1 (pt); Activities
coordinators 1 (ft), 2 (pt); Dietitians 1 (pt);
Podiatrists 3 (pt).
Languages French, Italian.
Affiliation Roman Catholic.
Facilities Dining room; Activities room;
Chapel; Crafts room; Laundry room; Barber/
Beauty shop; Library.
Activities Arts & crafts; Cards; Games;
Reading groups; Prayer groups; Movies;
Shopping trips; Dances/Social/Cultural
gatherings; Pet therapy.

Woodland Convalescent Center Inc
70 Woodland St, North Smithfield, RI 02895
(401) 765-0499

Admin Mary Ann Abbruzzi.
Licensure Intermediate care. *Beds* ICF 40.
Certified Medicaid.

Pascoag

Bayberry Commons Inc
1 Davis Dr, Pascoag, RI 02859
(401) 568-0600
Admin T Lloyd Ryan.
Licensure Skilled care; Intermediate care. *Beds*
SNF 24; ICF 96. *Certified* Medicaid;
Medicare.

Jolly Rest Home Inc
RFD 1, Box A33, S Main St, Pascoag, RI
02859
(401) 568-3091
Admin Rosemarie Johnson.
Medical Dir Dr Louis Moran.
Licensure Intermediate care. *Beds* ICF 36.
Certified Medicaid.
Staff Physicians 1 (ft), 5 (pt); RNs 1 (ft);
LPNs 2 (pt); Nurses' aides 1 (ft), 11 (pt);
Physical therapists 1 (pt); Reality therapists
1 (pt); Recreational therapists 1 (pt);
Occupational therapists 1 (pt); Speech
therapists 1 (pt); Activities coordinators 1
(ft); Dietitians 1 (ft), 3 (pt);
Ophthalmologists 3 (pt); Podiatrists 1 (pt);
Audiologists 1 (pt); Dentists 1 (pt).
Facilities Dining room; Activities room;
Crafts room; Laundry room; Library.
Activities Arts & crafts; Cards; Games; Prayer
groups; Movies; Shopping trips; Dances/
Social/Cultural gatherings.

Lakeview Health Center
RFD 1, Box 50A, Pascoag, RI 02859
(401) 568-6242
Admin James Donatelli.
Licensure Skilled care; Intermediate care. *Beds*
SNF 27; ICF 168. *Certified* Medicaid;
Medicare.

Pawtucket

Darlington Care Center
123 Armistice Blvd, Pawtucket, RI 02860
(401) 725-2400
Admin Susan Gesualdi.
Medical Dir William Reeves MD.
Licensure Sheltered care. *Beds* Sheltered care
20.
Owner Privately owned.
Admissions Requirements Medical
examination.
Staff Physicians (consultant); RNs
(consultant); Nurses' aides; Activities
coordinators; Dietitians; Ophthalmologists;
Podiatrists.
Affiliation Roman Catholic.
Facilities Dining room; Laundry room;
Barber/Beauty shop; Transportation for
doctor appointments.
Activities Arts & crafts; Cards; Games; Prayer
groups; Movies; Shopping trips; Dining out;
Home cooked meals daily.

Elsie May's Rest Home Inc
105 Beechwood Ave, Pawtucket, RI 02860
(401) 722-2630
Admin Stella Mandolfi.
Licensure Intermediate care. *Beds* 14.
Certified Medicaid.

Jeanne Jugan Residence
964 Main St, Pawtucket, RI 02860
(401) 723-4314
Admin Sr Patricia Metzgar.
Licensure Skilled care; Intermediate care. *Beds*
SNF 7; ICF 92. *Certified* Medicaid;
Medicare.
Owner Nonprofit corp (Little Sisters of the
Poor).

Maynard Rest Home
56 Maynard St, Pawtucket, RI 02860
(401) 725-0517
Admin George Peters.
Licensure Intermediate care. *Beds* ICF 18.
Certified Medicaid.
Staff Physicians 1 (ft); RNs 1 (pt); LPNs 2
(ft); Nurses' aides 3 (ft), 4 (pt); Activities
coordinators 1 (ft); Podiatrists 1 (pt);
Dentists 1 (pt).
Facilities Dining room; Activities room;
Crafts room; Laundry room.
Activities Arts & crafts; Cards; Games;
Reading groups; Prayer groups; Movies;
Shopping trips; Dances/Social/Cultural
gatherings.

Oak Hill Nursing Center
544 Pleasant St, Pawtucket, RI 02860
(401) 725-8888
Admin Stephen Rykiel. *Dir of Nursing* Lynn
Tammany RN. *Medical Dir* Dr Phillip
Lappin.
Licensure Skilled care; Intermediate care. *Beds*
SNF 78; ICF 26. *Certified* Medicaid;
Medicare.
Owner Proprietary corp (PersonaCare Inc).
Staff RNs; LPNs; Nurses' aides; Physical
therapists (consultant); Recreational
therapists; Dietitians (consultant).
Facilities Laundry room; Barber/Beauty shop;
Multi-purpose room.
Activities Arts & crafts; Cards; Games;
Reading groups; Prayer groups; Movies;
Dances/Social/Cultural gatherings;
Intergenerational programs; Pet therapy.

Pawtucket Institute for Health Services
70 Gill Ave, Pawtucket, RI 02861
(401) 722-7900
Admin George Dassenko. *Dir of Nursing*
Mildred Golembiesky RN. *Medical Dir*
Biswa N Paul MD.
Licensure Skilled care; Intermediate care. *Beds*
SNF 42; ICF 118. *Certified* Medicaid;
Medicare.
Owner Nonprofit corp.
Admissions Requirements Minimum age 14;
Medical examination; Physician's request.
Staff Physicians 1 (pt); RNs 8 (ft), 4 (pt);
LPNs 6 (ft), 5 (pt); Nurses' aides 60 (ft), 12
(pt); Physical therapists 1 (pt); Speech
therapists 1 (pt); Activities coordinators 1
(ft); Dietitians 1 (pt); Ophthalmologists 1
(pt); Podiatrists 1 (pt); Dentists 1 (pt).
Languages Portuguese, French.
Affiliation Seventh-Day Adventist.
Facilities Dining room; Physical therapy
room; Activities room; Chapel; Barber/
Beauty shop.
Activities Arts & crafts; Cards; Games; Prayer
groups; Movies; Shopping trips; Dances/
Social/Cultural gatherings.

Providence

Ann's Rest Home
599 Broad St, Providence, RI 02907
(401) 421-7576
Admin Diane Arzoumanian.
Licensure Intermediate care. *Beds* ICF 14.
Certified Medicaid.

Bannister Nursing Care Center
135 Dodge St, Providence, RI 02907
(401) 521-9600
Admin Richard E Miller.
Licensure Skilled care; Intermediate care. *Beds*
SNF 20; ICF 150. *Certified* Medicaid;
Medicare.

Bay Tower Nursing Center
101 Plain St, Providence, RI 02903
(401) 351-4444
Admin Genevieve A Francis.
Medical Dir John Demicco MD.

Licensure Skilled care; Intermediate care. Beds SNF 40; ICF 120. *Certified* Medicaid; Medicare.
Owner Proprietary corp.
Admissions Requirements Physician's request.
Staff Physicians 6 (pt); RNs 8 (ft), 3 (pt); LPNs 8 (ft), 3 (pt); Nurses' aides 1 (pt); Physical therapists 1 (pt); Occupational therapists 1 (pt); Speech therapists 1 (pt); Activities coordinators 2 (ft), 1 (pt); Dietitians 1 (pt); Ophthalmologists 1 (pt); Podiatrists 1 (pt); Dentists 1 (pt).
Facilities Dining room; Physical therapy room; Activities room; Chapel; Laundry room; Barber/Beauty shop.

Bethany Home of Rhode Island
111 S Angell St, Providence, RI 02906
(401) 831-2870
Admin Margaret Shippee.
Licensure Intermediate care. Beds ICF 30. *Certified* Medicaid.

Charlesgate Nursing Center
100 Randall St, Providence, RI 02904
(401) 861-5858
Admin Lucille Massemino.
Licensure Skilled care; Intermediate care. Beds SNF 40; ICF 160. *Certified* Medicaid; Medicare.

Elmhurst Extended Care Facility
50 Maude St, Providence, RI 02908
(401) 456-2600
Admin Richard Fishpaw.
Licensure Skilled care; Intermediate care. Beds SNF 34; ICF 151. *Certified* Medicaid; Medicare.

Elmwood Health Center Inc
225 Elmwood Ave, Providence, RI 02907
(401) 272-0600
Admin Norma J Ryan.
Medical Dir Hao Huang MD.
Licensure Skilled care; Intermediate care. Beds SNF 6; ICF 70. *Certified* Medicaid; Medicare.
Owner Privately owned.
Facilities Dining room; Physical therapy room; Activities room; Chapel; Crafts room; Laundry room; Barber/Beauty shop; Library.
Activities Arts & crafts; Cards; Games; Reading groups; Prayer groups; Movies; Shopping trips; Dances/Social/Cultural gatherings.

Hallworth House
66 Benefit St, Providence, RI 02904
(401) 274-4505
Admin Donald C Baker.
Medical Dir Paul J Conley MD.
Licensure Skilled care. Beds SNF 51. *Certified* Medicaid; Medicare.
Admissions Requirements Medical examination; Physician's request.
Staff RNs 16 (ft); LPNs 1 (ft); Nurses' aides 22 (ft); Physical therapists 1 (pt); Recreational therapists 1 (pt); Dietitians 1 (pt).
Facilities Dining room; Physical therapy room; Activities room; Chapel; Crafts room; Barber/Beauty shop; Library.
Activities Arts & crafts; Cards; Games; Reading groups; Prayer groups; Movies.

Jewish Home for the Aged
99 Hillside Ave, Providence, RI 02906
(401) 351-4750
Admin Saul Zeichner. *Dir of Nursing* Alicebelle Maxson Rubotzsky RN MS. *Medical Dir* Henry Izeman MD.
Licensure Skilled care; Intermediate care; Retirement; Day care; Alzheimer's care. Beds Swing beds SNF/ICF 254; Retirement 100. *Private Pay Patients* 22%. *Certified* Medicaid; Medicare.
Owner Nonprofit organization/foundation.
Admissions Requirements Minimum age 62, can be waived.

Staff Physicians 1 (pt); RNs 23 (ft); LPNs 23 (ft); Nurses' aides 103 (ft); Physical therapists 1 (ft); Recreational therapists 2 (ft), 3 (pt); Occupational therapists 1 (pt); Speech therapists (contracted); Dietitians 1 (ft), 1 (pt); Ophthalmologists 1 (pt); Podiatrists 2 (pt); Audiologists (contracted); Physical therapy aides 2 (ft), 1 (pt).
Languages Hebrew, Yiddish, Portuguese, Spanish.
Affiliation Jewish.
Facilities Dining room; Physical therapy room; Activities room; Crafts room; Barber/Beauty shop; Library; Synagogue.
Activities Arts & crafts; Cards; Games; Reading groups; Prayer groups; Movies; Shopping trips; Dances/Social/Cultural gatherings; Intergenerational programs; Pet therapy.

Park View Nursing Home
PO Box 3287, 31 Parade St, Providence, RI 02909
(401) 351-2600
Admin Lloyd H Turoff. *Dir of Nursing* Rosanna Fontaine RN. *Medical Dir* Dr Hao Huang.
Licensure Skilled care; Intermediate care. Beds SNF 20; ICF 55. *Certified* Medicaid; Medicare.
Owner Proprietary corp.
Staff Physicians 2 (ft); RNs 2 (ft); LPNs 2 (ft); Nurses' aides 28 (ft); Physical therapists 1 (pt); Recreational therapists 1 (ft); Occupational therapists 1 (pt); Speech therapists 1 (pt); Activities coordinators 2 (ft); Dietitians 1 (pt).
Facilities Dining room; Physical therapy room; Activities room; Crafts room; Barber/Beauty shop; Library.
Activities Arts & crafts; Cards; Games; Prayer groups; Movies; Shopping trips; Dances/Social/Cultural gatherings.

St Elizabeth Home
109 Melrose St, Providence, RI 02907
(401) 941-0200
Admin Steven J Horowitz. *Dir of Nursing* Ann Schwarber. *Medical Dir* Daniel Moore MD.
Licensure Skilled care; Intermediate care. Beds SNF 24; ICF 85. *Certified* Medicaid; Medicare.
Admissions Requirements Medical examination.
Staff RNs 11 (ft); LPNs 5 (ft); Physical therapists 2 (ft); Nurses' aides 52 (ft); Occupational therapists 1 (ft); Dietitians 1 (ft); Nurse practitioners 1 (pt).
Facilities Dining room; Physical therapy room; Activities room; Chapel; Crafts room; Barber/Beauty shop; Library; Solarium; Dental and podiatry clinics.
Activities Arts & crafts; Cards; Games; Reading groups; Movies; Dances/Social/Cultural gatherings.

Steere House
807 Broad St, Providence, RI 02907
(401) 461-3340
Admin Harmon P B Jordan Jr.
Licensure Intermediate care. Beds ICF 90. *Certified* Medicaid.

Summit Medical Center Inc
1085 N Main St, Providence, RI 02904
(401) 272-9600
Admin Thelma Kerzner.
Licensure Skilled care; Intermediate care. Beds SNF 23; ICF 119. *Certified* Medicaid; Medicare.

Tockwotton Home
180 George M Cohan Memorial Blvd, Providence, RI 02903
(401) 272-5280, 751-1550
Admin Joseph T Runner.
Medical Dir Richard Perry MD.

Licensure Intermediate care. Beds ICF 48. *Certified* Medicaid.
Owner Nonprofit corp.
Admissions Requirements Minimum age 65; Females only; Medical examination.
Staff Physicians 2 (pt); RNs 5 (ft), 3 (pt); Nurses' aides 8 (ft), 6 (pt); Physical therapists 1 (pt); Occupational therapists 1 (pt); Activities coordinators 1 (pt); Dietitians 1 (pt); Ophthalmologists 2 (pt); Dentists 1 (pt).
Facilities Dining room; Activities room; Crafts room; Laundry room; Barber/Beauty shop; Library.
Activities Arts & crafts; Cards; Movies; Shopping trips; Dances/Social/Cultural gatherings.

Wayland Health Center
140 Pitman St, Providence, RI 02906
(401) 274-4200
Admin Nicholas Passarelli. *Dir of Nursing* Rosemary DerHagopian RN. *Medical Dir* Dr Jacob Stone.
Licensure Skilled care; Intermediate care. Beds SNF 56; ICF 94. *Private Pay Patients* 10%. *Certified* Medicaid; Medicare.
Owner Proprietary corp.
Staff RNs 11 (ft); LPNs 10 (ft); Nurses' aides 47 (ft), 5 (pt); Physical therapists; Recreational therapists 1 (ft); Activities coordinators 1 (ft), 2 (pt); Dietitians 1 (ft), 1 (pt).
Facilities Dining room; Physical therapy room; Activities room; Crafts room; Laundry room; Barber/Beauty shop; Library.
Activities Arts & crafts; Cards; Games; Prayer groups; Movies; Shopping trips; Dances/Social/Cultural gatherings.

Smithfield

Elm Brook Home Inc
40 Farnum Pike, Smithfield, RI 02917
(401) 231-4646
Admin Liza Pezzelli. *Dir of Nursing* Lorraine Laprey. *Medical Dir* Dr C K Lee.
Licensure Intermediate care. Beds ICF 65. *Certified* Medicaid.
Owner Proprietary corp.
Admissions Requirements Medical examination; Physician's request.
Staff RNs 4 (ft); LPNs 3 (ft); Nurses' aides 26 (ft); Activities coordinators 1 (ft); Dietitians 1 (pt); Dentists 1 (pt).
Facilities Dining room; Activities room; Crafts room.
Activities Arts & crafts; Cards; Games; Prayer groups; Shopping trips; Dances/Social/Cultural gatherings.

Hebert's Nursing Home Inc
Log Rd, Smithfield, RI 02917
(401) 231-7016
Admin Paul J Hebert.
Licensure Skilled care; Intermediate care. Beds SNF 6; ICF 80. *Certified* Medicaid; Medicare.

Heritage Hills Nursing Centre
RFD 3, Douglas Pike, Smithfield, RI 02917
(401) 231-2700
Admin John W Sormanti.
Medical Dir Dr Ovid Vezza.
Licensure Skilled care; Intermediate care. Beds SNF 24; ICF 86. *Certified* Medicaid; Medicare.
Staff RNs 5 (ft), 6 (pt); LPNs 4 (ft), 3 (pt); Nurses' aides 20 (ft), 24 (pt); Physical therapists 1 (ft); Activities coordinators 2 (pt); Dietitians 1 (pt); Podiatrists 1 (pt).
Facilities Dining room; Physical therapy room; Activities room; Chapel; Crafts room; Laundry room; Barber/Beauty shop; Library.
Activities Arts & crafts; Games; Prayer groups; Movies; Dances/Social/Cultural gatherings; Cooking.

Waterman Heights Nursing Home Ltd
Putnam Pike, Smithfield, RI 02828
(401) 949-1200
Admin Claire Thibeault. *Dir of Nursing* Judith
  Robidoux RN. *Medical Dir* Robert F
  Spencer MD.
Licensure Skilled care; Intermediate care. *Beds*
  SNF 34; ICF 71. *Certified* Medicaid;
  Medicare.
Owner Proprietary corp.
Admissions Requirements Minimum age 14;
  Medical examination.
Staff RNs 5 (ft), 20 (pt); LPNs 5 (ft), 5 (pt);
  Nurses' aides 30 (ft), 27 (pt); Physical
  therapists 1 (pt); Activities coordinators 1
  (ft); Ophthalmologists 1 (pt).
Facilities Dining room; Physical therapy
  room; Activities room; Chapel; Barber/
  Beauty shop; Lounge.
Activities Arts & crafts; Cards; Games; Prayer
  groups; Movies; Dances/Social/Cultural
  gatherings; Annual western day.

South Kingstown

Allen's Health Centre Inc
S County Trail, South Kingstown, RI 02892
(401) 884-0425
Admin Mary Green.
Licensure Skilled care; Intermediate care. *Beds*
  SNF 29; ICF 73. *Certified* Medicaid;
  Medicare.

Scallop Shell Nursing Home Inc
Kingstown Rd, South Kingstown, RI 02883
(401) 789-3006
Admin Neil Mahoney.
Licensure Skilled care; Intermediate care. *Beds*
  SNF 17; ICF 51. *Certified* Medicaid;
  Medicare.

Warren

Grace Barker Nursing Home Inc
54 Barker Ave, Warren, RI 02885
(401) 245-9100
Admin Joseph E Sousa. *Dir of Nursing*
  Marilyn Serbst RN. *Medical Dir* Dr Victor
  Medeiros.
Licensure Skilled care; Intermediate care;
  Alzheimer's care. *Beds* SNF 28; ICF 58.
  Private Pay Patients 20%. *Certified*
  Medicaid; Medicare.
Owner Privately owned.
Staff Physicians; RNs; LPNs; Nurses' aides;
  Physical therapists; Activities coordinators;
  Dietitians.
Languages Portuguese.
Facilities Dining room; Physical therapy
  room; Activities room; Chapel; Crafts room;
  Laundry room; Barber/Beauty shop.
Activities Arts & crafts; Cards; Games; Prayer
  groups; Movies; Shopping trips; Dances/
  Social/Cultural gatherings; Pet therapy.

Crestwood Nursing & Convalescent Home Inc
568 Child St, Warren, RI 02885
(401) 245-1574
Admin Betty A Walsh. *Dir of Nursing* Agnes
  M Medeiros RN. *Medical Dir* Dr Howard
  Perrone.
Licensure Skilled care; Intermediate care. *Beds*
  SNF 15; ICF 61. *Certified* Medicaid;
  Medicare.
Owner Privately owned.
Admissions Requirements Minimum age 18.
Staff RNs 12 (ft), 5 (pt); LPNs 6 (ft), 5 (pt);
  Nurses' aides 38 (ft), 24 (pt); Activities
  coordinators 2 (ft).
Languages Italian, Portuguese, Polish.
Facilities Dining room; Activities room;
  Crafts room; Barber/Beauty shop; Library.
Activities Arts & crafts; Cards; Games;
  Reading groups; Prayer groups; Movies;
  Shopping trips; Dances/Social/Cultural
  gatherings; Cruises; Senior Olympics;
  Exercise program.

Desilets Nursing Home Inc
642 Metacom Ave, Warren, RI 02885
(401) 245-2860
Admin Richard Desilets.
Licensure Skilled care; Intermediate care. *Beds*
  SNF 8; ICF 72. *Certified* Medicaid;
  Medicare.

Warwick

Avalon Nursing Home Inc
57 Stokes St, Warwick, RI 02886
(401) 738-1200
Admin Francis Kowalik. *Dir of Nursing* A
  Susanne Kowalik.
Licensure Skilled care; Intermediate care. *Beds*
  SNF 6; ICF 24. *Private Pay Patients* 6%.
  Certified Medicaid; Medicare.
Owner Privately owned.
Admissions Requirements Medical
  examination; Physician's request.
Staff RNs 1 (ft), 4 (pt); LPNs 2 (ft), 3 (pt);
  Nurses' aides 5 (ft), 5 (pt); Activities
  coordinators 1 (pt); Dietitians 1 (ft), 2 (pt).
Facilities Dining room; Activities room;
  Laundry room; TV room.
Activities Arts & crafts; Cards; Games; Prayer
  groups; Live entertainment.

Brentwood Nursing Home Inc
3986 Post Rd, Warwick, RI 02886
(401) 884-8020
Admin Richard Miga.
Licensure Skilled care; Intermediate care. *Beds*
  SNF 24; ICF 72. *Certified* Medicaid;
  Medicare.

Burdick Convalescent Home
57 Fair St, Warwick, RI 02888
(401) 781-6628
Admin Elizabeth Moone. *Dir of Nursing*
  Carolyn Bell. *Medical Dir* Rapheal Perez
  MD.
Licensure Intermediate care. *Beds* ICF 13.
  Private Pay Patients 10%. *Certified*
  Medicaid.
Owner Proprietary corp.
Admissions Requirements Medical
  examination.
Staff Physicians 1 (pt); RNs 1 (pt); LPNs 2
  (ft); Nurses' aides 8 (ft); Ophthalmologists 1
  (pt); Podiatrists 1 (pt); Audiologists 1 (pt).
Facilities Dining room; Activities room;
  Chapel; Crafts room; Laundry room;
  Library.
Activities Arts & crafts; Cards; Games;
  Reading groups; Prayer groups; Shopping
  trips; Dances/Social/Cultural gatherings; Pet
  therapy.

Buttonwoods Crest Home
139 Hemlock Ave, Warwick, RI 02886
(401) 737-7325
Admin Roger A Handy.
Medical Dir Stanley Cate MD.
Licensure Intermediate care. *Beds* ICF 31.
  Certified Medicaid.
Owner Privately owned.
Staff RNs 1 (ft), 7 (pt); LPNs 4 (pt); Nurses'
  aides 2 (ft), 11 (pt); Physical therapists 1
  (pt); Recreational therapists 1 (pt); Activities
  coordinators 1 (pt); Dietitians 1 (pt);
  Ophthalmologists 1 (pt).
Facilities Dining room; Activities room;
  Crafts room; Laundry room.
Activities Arts & crafts; Cards; Games; Prayer
  groups; Shopping trips; Dances/Social/
  Cultural gatherings.

Evergreens Nursing Home Inc
163 Capron Farm Dr, Warwick, RI 02886-
  7701
(401) 769-8042
Admin Jeannette Kelly.
Licensure Intermediate care. *Beds* ICF 35.
  Certified Medicaid.

Greenwood House Nursing Home Inc
1139 Main Ave, Warwick, RI 02886
(401) 739-6600, 737-9609
Admin George A Cooper Jr.
Licensure Skilled care; Intermediate care. *Beds*
  SNF 60; ICF 62. *Certified* Medicaid;
  Medicare.

Greenwood Oaks Rest Home
14 Lake St, Warwick, RI 02886
(401) 739-3297
Admin Hope Lonetti, acting.
Licensure Intermediate care. *Beds* ICF 16.
  Certified Medicaid.

Kent Nursing Home Inc
660 Commonwealth Ave, Warwick, RI 02886
(401) 739-4241
Admin Carol A Sloan.
Medical Dir Dr Hossein Shushtari.
Licensure Skilled care; Intermediate care. *Beds*
  SNF 143; ICF 10. *Certified* Medicaid;
  Medicare.
Facilities Dining room; Physical therapy
  room; Activities room; Crafts room; Laundry
  room; Barber/Beauty shop.
Activities Arts & crafts; Cards; Games;
  Reading groups; Prayer groups; Movies;
  Shopping trips.

Pawtuxet Village Nursing Home Inc
270 Post Rd, Warwick, RI 02888
(401) 467-3555
Admin Steven H McLeod. *Dir of Nursing* Pat
  Bonn RN.
Licensure Skilled care; Intermediate care;
  Alzheimer's care. *Beds* SNF 51; ICF 80.
  Certified Medicaid; Medicare.
Owner Proprietary corp.
Facilities Dining room; Activities room;
  Chapel; Crafts room; Laundry room; Barber/
  Beauty shop.
Activities Arts & crafts; Cards; Games;
  Movies; Shopping trips; Dances/Social/
  Cultural gatherings.

Royal Manor Inc
159 Division St, Warwick, RI 02818
(401) 884-5590
Admin Jeannette E Del Padre.
Licensure Intermediate care. *Beds* 55.
Admissions Requirements Medical
  examination; Physician's request.
Staff RNs 5 (ft); Nurses' aides 24 (ft);
  Activities coordinators 1 (ft); Dietitians 1
  (pt).
Facilities Dining room; Barber/Beauty shop.
Activities Arts & crafts; Cards; Prayer groups;
  Movies; Shopping trips; Dances/Social/
  Cultural gatherings.

Sunny View Nursing Home
83 Corona St, Warwick, RI 02886
(401) 737-9193
Admin Patricia Miga, RN.
Licensure Skilled care; Intermediate care. *Beds*
  SNF 24; ICF 33. *Certified* Medicaid;
  Medicare.

Warwick Health Centre
109 W Shore Rd, Warwick, RI 02889
(401) 739-9440
Admin Harry Nahigian. *Dir of Nursing*
  Dorothy Wilmot. *Medical Dir* Nicholas
  Turilli.
Licensure Skilled care; Intermediate care. *Beds*
  SNF 27; ICF 122. *Certified* Medicaid;
  Medicare.
Owner Proprietary corp.
Admissions Requirements Medical
  examination.
Staff Physicians 2 (pt); RNs 18 (ft), 12 (pt);
  LPNs 10 (ft), 8 (pt); Nurses' aides 60 (ft), 20
  (pt); Physical therapists 1 (pt); Speech
  therapists 1 (pt); Activities coordinators 2
  (ft); Dietitians 1 (pt); Ophthalmologists 1
  (pt); Podiatrists 1 (pt).

Facilities Dining room; Physical therapy room; Activities room; Chapel; Crafts room; Laundry room; Barber/Beauty shop.
Activities Arts & crafts; Cards; Games; Prayer groups; Movies; Intergenerational programs.

Warwick Rest Home Inc
348 Warwick Neck Ave, Warwick, RI 02889
(401) 737-4909
Admin Pasquale P Squillante Jr.
Licensure Intermediate care. *Beds* ICF 16. *Certified* Medicaid.

West Bay Manor
2783 W Shore Rd, Warwick, RI 02886
(401) 739-7300
Admin Raymond L Tetrault.
Licensure Intermediate care. *Beds* ICF 45.

West Warwick

West View Nursing Home Inc
239 Legris Ave, West Warwick, RI 02983
(401) 828-9000
Admin Howard Mackey.
Medical Dir Frank Fallon DO.
Licensure Skilled care; Intermediate care. *Beds* SNF 22; ICF 98. *Certified* Medicaid; Medicare.
Staff Physicians 23 (pt); RNs 6 (ft), 4 (pt); LPNs 6 (ft), 3 (pt); Nurses' aides 40 (ft), 25 (pt); Physical therapists 1 (pt); Recreational therapists 2 (ft); Speech therapists 1 (pt); Activities coordinators 1 (ft); Dietitians 1 (pt); Ophthalmologists 1 (pt); Podiatrists 2 (pt); Audiologists 1 (pt); Dentists 1 (pt).
Facilities Dining room; Physical therapy room; Activities room; Chapel; Laundry room; Barber/Beauty shop.
Activities Arts & crafts; Cards; Games; Reading groups; Prayer groups; Movies; Shopping trips; Dances/Social/Cultural gatherings.

Westerly

Watch Hill Manor Ltd
83 Watch Hill Rd, Westerly, RI 02891
(401) 596-2664
Admin Robert E Horton Jr.
Medical Dir Bruce M Gillie MD.
Licensure Skilled care; Intermediate care. *Beds* SNF 10; ICF 49. *Certified* Medicaid; Medicare.
Admissions Requirements Medical examination; Physician's request.
Staff Recreational therapists.
Facilities Dining room; Activities room; Barber/Beauty shop.
Activities Arts & crafts; Games; Prayer groups; Shopping trips.

Westerly Health Center
RR4, Box 81A, Potter Hill Rd, Westerly, RI 02891
(401) 348-0020

Admin Thomas Whipple. *Dir of Nursing* Andrea Sellins RN. *Medical Dir* Dr Walter J Lentz.
Licensure Skilled care; Intermediate care. *Beds* SNF 60; ICF 60. *Certified* Medicaid; Medicare.
Owner Proprietary corp (Health Concepts Corp).
Staff RNs 8 (ft), 4 (pt); LPNs 6 (ft), 3 (pt); Nurses' aides 32 (ft), 17 (pt); Physical therapists 1 (pt); Activities coordinators 1 (ft), 2 (pt).
Facilities Dining room; Physical therapy room; Activities room; Crafts room; Laundry room; Barber/Beauty shop; Library.
Activities Arts & crafts; Cards; Games; Reading groups; Prayer groups; Movies; Dances/Social/Cultural gatherings.

Westerly Nursing Home Inc
81 Beach St, Westerly, RI 02891
(401) 596-4925
Admin Paul V Martin. *Dir of Nursing* Starlyne Davis RN. *Medical Dir* R Bruce Gillie MD.
Licensure Skilled care; Intermediate care; Alzheimer's care. *Beds* SNF 55; ICF 5. *Certified* Medicaid; Medicare.
Owner Proprietary corp.
Admissions Requirements Physician's request.
Staff Physicians; RNs; Nurses' aides; Physical therapists; Recreational therapists; Speech therapists; Activities coordinators; Dietitians; Ophthalmologists; Podiatrists.
Facilities Dining room; Activities room; Crafts room; Laundry room; Barber/Beauty shop.
Activities Arts & crafts; Cards; Games; Reading groups; Prayer groups; Movies; Shopping trips; Dances/Social/Cultural gatherings; Intergenerational programs; Pet therapy; Candlelight holiday dinners.

Woonsocket

Ballou Home for the Aged
60 Mendon Rd, Woonsocket, RI 02895
(401) 767-3315
Admin Jeannette T Gaudreau RN. *Dir of Nursing* Lorraine Laprey RN. *Medical Dir* Juan P Mallari MD.
Licensure Intermediate care. *Beds* ICF 27. *Private Pay Patients* 50%. *Certified* Medicaid.
Owner Nonprofit organization/foundation.
Admissions Requirements Minimum age 65; Medical examination.
Staff Physicians (contracted); RNs; LPNs; Nurses' aides; Physical therapists (contracted); Reality therapists (contracted); Recreational therapists; Occupational therapists (contracted); Speech therapists (contracted); Dietitians (contracted); Ophthalmologists (contracted); Podiatrists (contracted); Audiologists (contracted).
Languages French, Italian.

Facilities Dining room; Activities room; Laundry room; Barber/Beauty shop; Library; Porches; Outdoor area; Private rooms.
Activities Arts & crafts; Cards; Games; Reading groups; Movies; Shopping trips; Dances/Social/Cultural gatherings; Intergenerational programs; Pet therapy; Current events; Volunteer program; Exercise.

Friendly Home Inc
303 Rhodes Ave, Woonsocket, RI 02895
(401) 769-7220
Admin Angelo S Rotella.
Medical Dir Catello Scarano; Catherine Schenk.
Licensure Skilled care; Intermediate care. *Beds* SNF 24; ICF 102. *Certified* Medicaid; Medicare.
Owner Proprietary corp.
Staff RNs; LPNs; Nurses' aides; Activities coordinators.
Languages French.
Facilities Dining room; Physical therapy room; Activities room; Laundry room; Barber/Beauty shop; Library.
Activities Arts & crafts; Cards; Games; Prayer groups; Movies; Shopping trips; Dances/Social/Cultural gatherings.

Mt St Francis Health Center
4 Saint Joseph St, Woonsocket, RI 02895
(401) 765-5844
Admin Carol F Sabella RN. *Dir of Nursing* Lucille Falco RN. *Medical Dir* Dr Stanley Balm.
Licensure Skilled care; Intermediate care. *Beds* SNF 36; ICF 162. *Certified* Medicaid; Medicare.
Owner Privately owned.
Admissions Requirements Minimum age 18.
Staff Physicians; RNs; LPNs; Nurses' aides; Physical therapists (consultant); Reality therapists; Recreational therapists; Occupational therapists; Speech therapists; Activities coordinators; Dietitians; Ophthalmologists; Podiatrists; Audiologists.
Languages French.
Affiliation Roman Catholic.
Facilities Dining room; Physical therapy room; Activities room; Chapel; Crafts room; Laundry room; Barber/Beauty shop; Multi-purpose room.
Activities Arts & crafts; Cards; Games; Reading groups; Prayer groups; Movies; Shopping trips; Dances/Social/Cultural gatherings; Pet therapy; Outings; Exercise groups; Cooking groups; Adopt-a-grandparent program.

Woonsocket Health Centre
262 Poplar St, Woonsocket, RI 02895
(401) 765-2100
Admin Norma Pezzelli.
Licensure Skilled care; Intermediate care. *Beds* SNF 75; ICF 209. *Certified* Medicaid; Medicare.

SOUTH CAROLINA

Abbeville

Abbeville Nursing Home
Thomson Cir, Abbeville, SC 29620
(803) 459-5122
Admin Ethel L Hughes. *Dir of Nursing*
Jeannie Agan RN. *Medical Dir* Robert S
Clarke Jr MD.
Licensure Skilled care; Intermediate care. *Beds*
Swing beds SNF/ICF 94. *Certified* Medicaid;
Medicare.
Owner Proprietary corp.
Admissions Requirements Medical
examination; Physician's request.
Staff Physicians 8 (pt); RNs 7 (ft), 1 (pt);
LPNs 26 (ft), 2 (pt); Nurses' aides 40 (ft), 3
(pt); Physical therapists 1 (pt); Occupational
therapists (consultant); Speech therapists
(contracted); Activities coordinators 1 (ft);
Dietitians (consultant); Podiatrists 1 (pt).
Facilities Dining room; Physical therapy
room; Activities room; Crafts room; Barber/
Beauty shop.
Activities Arts & crafts; Cards; Games;
Reading groups; Prayer groups; Movies;
Shopping trips; Dances/Social/Cultural
gatherings; Intergenerational programs.

Aiken

Aiken Nursing Home
123 DuPont Dr, Aiken, SC 29801
(803) 648-0434
Admin David D Phillips. *Dir of Nursing* Hope
Rebecca Hastings.
Licensure Skilled care; Intermediate care. *Beds*
SNF 43; ICF 43. *Private Pay Patients* 10%.
Certified Medicaid; Medicare.
Owner Proprietary corp (Beverly Enterprises).
Admissions Requirements Minimum age 12;
Medical examination.
Staff RNs 4 (ft), 1 (pt); LPNs 9 (ft), 3 (pt);
Nurses' aides 34 (ft), 2 (pt); Physical
therapists 1 (ft); Recreational therapists 1
(ft); Occupational therapists 1 (ft); Speech
therapists 1 (ft); Activities coordinators 1
(ft); Dietitians 1 (ft); Podiatrists 1 (pt);
Audiologists 1 (pt).
Facilities Dining room; Physical therapy
room; Activities room; Chapel; Laundry
room; Barber/Beauty shop; Grounds;
Porches; Gazebo.
Activities Arts & crafts; Cards; Games;
Reading groups; Prayer groups; Movies;
Shopping trips; Dances/Social/Cultural
gatherings; Intergenerational programs; Pet
therapy.

Mattie C Hall Health Care Center
830 Laurens St, Aiken, SC 29801
(803) 649-6264
Admin Vicki Lollis Major NHA. *Dir of
Nursing* Shirley S Cooper RN. *Medical Dir*
T Mark Meyer MD.
Licensure Skilled care; Intermediate care;
Alzheimer's care. *Beds* SNF 88; ICF 88.
Private Pay Patients 37%. *Certified*
Medicaid; Medicare.

Owner Publicly owned.
Admissions Requirements Minimum age 18;
Medical examination; Physician's request.
Staff RNs 6 (ft), 4 (pt); LPNs 17 (ft), 6 (pt);
Nurses' aides 87 (ft), 13 (pt); Physical
therapists 1 (pt); Recreational therapists 3
(ft), 1 (pt); Occupational therapists 1 (pt);
Speech therapists 1 (pt); Dietitians 1 (ft);
Podiatrists 1 (pt).
Facilities Dining room; Physical therapy
room; Activities room; Laundry room;
Barber/Beauty shop; Semi-private and
private rooms.
Activities Arts & crafts; Games; Prayer groups;
Movies; Shopping trips; Dances/Social/
Cultural gatherings; Intergenerational
programs; Pet therapy.

Laurens State Community Residence
625 Cushman Dr, Aiken, SC 29801
(803) 649-7712, 758-4432
Admin Sally James.
Medical Dir Randy Watson MD.
Licensure Intermediate care for mentally
retarded. *Beds* ICF/MR 8. *Certified*
Medicaid.
Owner Nonprofit organization/foundation.
Admissions Requirements Minimum age 21;
Males only; Medical examination.
Staff Physicians 1 (pt); RNs 1 (pt); LPNs 1
(ft); Physical therapists 1 (pt); Recreational
therapists 1 (pt); Occupational therapists 1
(pt); Speech therapists 1 (pt); Dietitians 1
(pt); Mental retardation specialists 5 (ft).
Facilities Dining room; Activities room;
Laundry room; Basketball court.
Activities Arts & crafts; Games; Movies;
Shopping trips; Dances/Social/Cultural
gatherings.

Richland State Community Residence
1111 Richland St, Aiken, SC 29801
(803) 649-7590, 758-4432
Admin Sally James.
Licensure Intermediate care for mentally
retarded. *Beds* ICF/MR 8. *Certified*
Medicare.
Owner Publicly owned.
Admissions Requirements Minimum age 16;
Females only.
Staff Physicians 8 (pt); RNs 1 (ft), 16 (pt);
LPNs 3 (ft), 8 (pt); MRSs 3 (ft), 8 (pt).
Facilities Activities room; Laundry room;
Family type home.
Activities Arts & crafts; Games; Movies;
Shopping trips; Dances/Social/Cultural
gatherings.

Rudnick Community Residence
629 Chesterfield N, Aiken, SC 29801
(803) 649-7174, 758-4432
Admin Richard Weldon.
Licensure Intermediate care for mentally
retarded. *Beds* ICF/MR 8. *Certified*
Medicare.
Owner Publicly owned.
Admissions Requirements Minimum age 16;
Males only.

Staff Physicians 1 (ft), 16 (pt); RNs 1 (ft), 16
(pt); LPNs 3 (ft), 8 (pt); MRS's 3 (ft), 8 (pt).
Facilities Family style home.

Sanders Community Residence
625 Chesterfield N, Aiken, SC 29801
(803) 649-7315, 758-4432
Admin Richard M Weldon.
Medical Dir Randy Watson MD.
Licensure Intermediate care for mentally
retarded. *Beds* ICF/MR 8. *Certified*
Medicaid.
Owner Publicly owned.
Admissions Requirements Minimum age 21;
Females only; Medical examination.
Staff Physicians 1 (pt); RNs 1 (pt); LPNs 2
(ft); Physical therapists 1 (pt); Recreational
therapists 1 (pt); Occupational therapists 1
(pt); Speech therapists 1 (pt); Dietitians 1
(pt); Mental retardation specialists 5 (ft).
Facilities Dining room; Activities room;
Laundry room.
Activities Arts & crafts; Games; Movies;
Shopping trips; Dances/Social/Cultural
gatherings.

Anderson

Anderson Community Residence
1705 Holly St, Anderson, SC 29621
(803) 225-9943
Admin Mary Anderson.
Licensure Intermediate care for mentally
retarded. *Beds* ICF/MR 8.
Owner Publicly owned.

Anderson Health Care Center
PO Box 1327, 1501 E Greenville St,
Anderson, SC 29622
(803) 226-8356
Admin J B Kinney Jr.
Licensure Skilled care; Intermediate care. *Beds*
SNF 44; ICF 100; Swing beds SNF/ICF 146.
Certified Medicaid; Medicare.
Owner Proprietary corp (National Health
Corp).

Anderson Place
311 Simpson Rd, Anderson, SC 29621
(803) 261-3875
Admin Arlis Hinson.
Licensure Skilled care; Intermediate care. *Beds*
Swing beds SNF/ICF 44.
Owner Proprietary corp.

Ellenburg Nursing Center Inc
611 E Hampton St, Anderson, SC 29624
(803) 226-5054
Admin M L Ellenburg. *Dir of Nursing* Jo Ann
Cameron RN. *Medical Dir* Dr Warren
White.
Licensure Skilled care; Intermediate care. *Beds*
Swing beds SNF/ICF 88. *Certified* Medicaid;
Medicare.
Owner Proprietary corp.
Admissions Requirements Medical
examination; Physician's request.

Facilities Dining room; Physical therapy room; Activities room; Laundry room; Barber/Beauty shop.
Activities Arts & crafts; Games; Prayer groups; Movies; Pet therapy.

Latham Nursing Home
208 James St, Anderson, SC 29625
(803) 226-3427
Admin Debbie P Hembree. *Dir of Nursing* Virginia Reid RN. *Medical Dir* Warren W White MD.
Licensure Skilled care; Intermediate care. *Beds* Swing beds SNF/ICF 44. *Certified* Medicaid; Medicare.
Owner Proprietary corp (Lillian L Latham).
Admissions Requirements Medical examination; Physician's request.
Staff Physicians 20 (pt); RNs 3 (ft), 2 (pt); LPNs 2 (ft), 3 (pt); Nurses' aides 15 (ft); Physical therapists 1 (pt); Speech therapists 1 (pt); Activities coordinators 1 (pt); Dietitians 1 (pt); Podiatrists 1 (pt).
Facilities Dining room; Physical therapy room; Activities room; Laundry room; Barber/Beauty shop; Library.
Activities Arts & crafts; Cards; Games; Reading groups; Prayer groups; Dances/Social/Cultural gatherings; Pet therapy.

Bamberg

Bamberg County Memorial Nursing Center
PO Drawer 507, North & McGee Sts, Bamberg, SC 29003
(803) 245-4321
Admin Charles V Morgan. *Dir of Nursing* Mary Crawford. *Medical Dir* Dr Michael C Watson.
Licensure Skilled care; Intermediate care. *Beds* Swing beds SNF/ICF 22. *Certified* Medicaid; Medicare.
Owner Nonprofit organization/foundation.
Admissions Requirements Medical examination; Physician's request.
Activities Games; Reading groups.

Barnwell

Barnwell County Nursing Home
PO Box 807, Wren St, Barnwell, SC 29812
(803) 259-5547
Admin Paula E Birt. *Dir of Nursing* Nedra C Mobley.
Licensure Skilled care; Intermediate care. *Beds* Swing beds SNF/ICF 40. *Certified* Medicaid; Medicare.
Owner Publicly owned.
Admissions Requirements Medical examination; Physician's request.
Staff Physicians 4 (pt); RNs 4 (ft); LPNs 4 (ft); Nurses' aides 20 (ft); Physical therapists 1 (pt); Recreational therapists 1 (ft); Ophthalmologists 1 (pt).
Facilities Dining room; Physical therapy room; Activities room; Barber/Beauty shop.
Activities Arts & crafts; Cards; Games; Reading groups; Prayer groups; Movies; Shopping trips.

Lemon Park Community Residence
1904 Lemon Park, Barnwell, SC 29812
(803) 259-1682
Admin Brent Parker. *Dir of Nursing* Maxine Corley.
Licensure Intermediate care for mentally retarded. *Beds* ICF/MR 8. *Private Pay Patients* 0%. *Certified* Medicaid.
Owner Publicly owned.
Admissions Requirements Minimum age 18; Males only; Medical examination; Physician's request.
Staff RNs 1 (ft); LPNs 2 (ft), 1 (pt); Activities coordinators 2 (ft).

Facilities Dining room; Laundry room.
Activities Arts & crafts; Games; Reading groups; Movies; Shopping trips; Dances/Social/Cultural gatherings; Pet therapy.

Batesburg

Brookwood Residence
PO Box 190, Lex, 181 Brookwood Dr, Batesburg, SC 29072
(803) 359-9717
Admin Jon Bradford.
Licensure Intermediate care for mentally retarded. *Beds* ICF/MR 8.
Owner Proprietary corp.

Lexington West Inc—Batesburg Group Home
PO Box 3817, Cola, 99 David St, Batesburg, SC 29072
(803) 359-9717
Admin Jon Bradford.
Licensure Intermediate care for mentally retarded. *Beds* ICF/MR 8.
Owner Proprietary corp.

Beaufort

Bay View Nursing Center Inc
PO Box 1103, S Todd Dr, Beaufort, SC 29902
(803) 524-8911
Admin Sheila G Wright.
Licensure Skilled care; Intermediate care. *Beds* Swing beds SNF/ICF 132. *Certified* Medicaid; Medicare.

Bennettsville

Dundee Nursing Home
PO Box 858, Hwy 15, 401 Bypass, Bennettsville, SC 29512
(803) 479-6251
Admin Harold D Branton. *Dir of Nursing* Marie Hester. *Medical Dir* John May MD.
Licensure Skilled care; Intermediate care. *Beds* ICF 24; Swing beds SNF/ICF 87. *Certified* Medicaid; Medicare.
Owner Proprietary corp.
Staff Physicians 5 (ft); RNs 4 (ft), 3 (pt); LPNs 8 (ft), 7 (pt); Nurses' aides 28 (ft), 16 (pt); Dietitians; Dietitians 1 (ft).
Facilities Dining room; Physical therapy room; Activities room; Chapel; Laundry room; Barber/Beauty shop; Library.
Activities Arts & crafts; Cards; Games; Reading groups; Prayer groups; Movies; Shopping trips; Dances/Social/Cultural gatherings.

Bishopville

McLeod I
808 McLeod Rd, Bishopville, SC 29010
(803) 484-6987
Admin Mary Mack. *Dir of Nursing* Terry McCown. *Medical Dir* John Pate.
Licensure Intermediate care. *Beds* ICF 8. *Private Pay Patients* 0%. *Certified* Medicaid.
Owner Nonprofit organization/foundation (Lee County Special Housing).
Admissions Requirements Males only.
Staff Physicians 1 (pt); RNs 1 (pt); LPNs 2 (ft), 1 (pt); Physical therapists; Recreational therapists 1 (pt); Dietitians.
Facilities Dining room; Laundry room.
Activities Arts & crafts; Cards; Games; Movies; Shopping trips; Dances/Social/Cultural gatherings.

McLeod II Group Home
814 McLeod Rd, Bishopville, SC 29010
(803) 484-6995
Admin Mary Ann Mack QMRP. *Dir of Nursing* Terry McCown. *Medical Dir* John Date.

Licensure Intermediate care for mentally retarded. *Beds* ICF/MR 8. *Private Pay Patients* 0%. *Certified* Medicaid.
Owner Privately owned (Lee County Mental Retardation Board).
Admissions Requirements Females only.
Staff Physicians 1 (pt); RNs 1 (pt); LPNs 2 (ft), 1 (pt); Physical therapists 2 (pt); Recreational therapists 1 (pt); Occupational therapists 2 (pt); Dietitians 1 (pt).
Activities Arts & crafts; Cards; Games; Movies; Shopping trips; Dances/Social/Cultural gatherings; Work activity.

Blackville

Healing Springs Intermediate Care Facility Inc
PO Box 518, Rte 1, Blackville, SC 29817
(803) 284-3553
Admin Odom Grady.
Licensure Intermediate care. *Beds* ICF 26.
Owner Proprietary corp.

Meadow Brook
PO Box 215, Jonesbridge Rd, Blackville, SC 29817
(803) 284-2213
Admin Emily B Phail. *Dir of Nursing* Cheryl Steen, Acting. *Medical Dir* William B Clark.
Licensure Intermediate care. *Beds* ICF 85. *Private Pay Patients* 0%. *Certified* Medicaid; Medicare.
Owner Proprietary corp (Gencare Inc).
Staff Physicians 1 (ft); RNs 1 (ft); LPNs 5 (ft), 3 (pt); Nurses' aides 15 (ft), 10 (pt); Physical therapists 1 (pt); Occupational therapists 1 (pt); Speech therapists 1 (pt); Activities coordinators 1 (ft); Dietitians 1 (ft); Podiatrists 1 (pt).
Facilities Dining room; Activities room; Crafts room; Laundry room; Barber/Beauty shop.
Activities Arts & crafts; Cards; Games; Reading groups; Prayer groups; Movies; Shopping trips; Dances/Social/Cultural gatherings.

Blair

Ruby C Blair Residence
PO Box 3817, Columbia, Rte 1, Blair, SC 29230
(803) 359-9717
Admin Jon Bradford.
Licensure Intermediate care for mentally retarded. *Beds* ICF/MR 8.
Owner Proprietary corp.

Stuart L Blair Residence
PO Box 3817, Columbia, Rte 1, Blair, SC 29230
(803) 359-9717
Admin Jon Bradford.
Licensure Intermediate care for mentally retarded. *Beds* ICF/MR 8.
Owner Publicly owned.

Camden

Camden I Group Home
PO Box 190, 975 Wateree Blvd, Camden, SC 29072
(803) 359-9717
Admin Jon Bradford.
Licensure Intermediate care for mentally retarded. *Beds* ICF/MR 8.
Owner Proprietary corp.

Camden II Group Home
PO Box 190, 975 Wateree Blvd, Camden, SC 29072
(803) 359-9717
Admin Jon Bradford.
Licensure Intermediate care for mentally retarded. *Beds* ICF/MR 8.
Owner Proprietary corp.

A Sam Karesh Long-Term Care Center
1315 Roberts St, Camden, SC 29020
(803) 432-4311
Admin L H Young. *Dir of Nursing* Susan
Outen RN. *Medical Dir* John Dubose MD.
Licensure Skilled care; Intermediate care. *Beds*
Swing beds SNF/ICF 88. *Certified* Medicaid;
Medicare.
Owner Publicly owned.
Admissions Requirements Physician's request.
Staff Physicians 1 (pt); RNs 4 (ft), 1 (pt);
LPNs 13 (ft), 1 (pt); Nurses' aides 26 (ft), 4
(pt); Physical therapists 1 (pt); Speech
therapists 1 (pt); Activities coordinators 1
(ft); Dietitians 1 (pt).
Facilities Dining room; Physical therapy
room; Activities room; Laundry room;
Barber/Beauty shop.
Activities Arts & crafts; Cards; Games;
Reading groups; Prayer groups; Shopping
trips.

Springdale Village
PO Box 1619, 146 Battleship Rd, Camden, SC
29020
(803) 432-3741
Admin Frances Hendrix.
Licensure Skilled care; Intermediate care. *Beds*
Swing beds SNF/ICF 22.
Owner Proprietary corp.

Charleston

**Driftwood Health Care Center—Long-Term
Care Facility**
2375 Baker Hospital Blvd, Charleston, SC
29405
(803) 744-2750
Admin Calvin D Lipscomb.
Medical Dir Dr Alexander Marshall.
Licensure Nursing care. *Beds* 102. *Certified*
Medicaid; Medicare.
Staff Physicians; RNs; LPNs; Nurses' aides;
Physical therapists; Reality therapists;
Recreational therapists; Speech therapists;
Activities coordinators; Dietitians; Dentists.
Facilities Dining room; Activities room;
Laundry room; Barber/Beauty shop.
Activities Arts & crafts; Cards; Games;
Reading groups; Prayer groups; Movies;
Shopping trips; Dances/Social/Cultural
gatherings.

Firestone Road Community Residence
3641 Firestone Rd, Charleston, SC 29418
(803) 552-7201, 767-1007
Admin Thomas P Keating. *Dir of Nursing*
Claudia Freeman RN.
Licensure Intermediate care for mentally
retarded. *Beds* ICF/MR 14. *Certified*
Medicaid.
Owner Publicly owned.
Admissions Requirements Males only.
Staff Physicians 1 (pt); RNs 1 (pt); LPNs 1
(ft); Physical therapists 1 (pt); Recreational
therapists 1 (pt); Occupational therapists 1
(pt); Speech therapists 1 (pt); Dietitians 1
(pt); Podiatrists 1 (pt).
Facilities Dining room; Activities room;
Laundry room.
Activities Arts & crafts; Cards; Games;
Movies; Shopping trips; Dances/Social/
Cultural gatherings; Work activity.

Lenevar Community Residence
1435 W Lenevar Dr, Charleston, SC 29403
(803) 571-2916
Admin Susan Williams. *Dir of Nursing*
Eugenia Felsinger RN PhD.
Licensure Intermediate care for mentally
retarded. *Beds* ICF/MR 9. *Certified*
Medicaid.
Owner Publicly owned.
Admissions Requirements Males only.

Staff Physicians 1 (pt); RNs 1 (pt); LPNs 1
(ft); Physical therapists 1 (pt); Recreational
therapists 1 (pt); Occupational therapists 1
(pt); Speech therapists 1 (pt); Dietitians 1
(pt); Podiatrists 1 (pt).
Facilities Dining room; Activities room;
Laundry room.
Activities Arts & crafts; Cards; Games;
Movies; Shopping trips; Dances/Social/
Cultural gatherings; Work Activity.

Manor Care of Charleston
1137 Sam Rittenberg Blvd, Charleston, SC
29407
(803) 763-0233, 763-5774 FAX
Admin "Dee Dee" Claudia S Wright. *Dir of
Nursing* Dorothy Hodges. *Medical Dir* Dr
Donald Schweiger.
Licensure Skilled care; Assisted living. *Beds*
SNF 132; Assisted living 13. *Private Pay
Patients* 67%. *Certified* Medicaid; Medicare.
Owner Proprietary corp (Manor Care Inc).
Admissions Requirements Minimum age 16;
Medical examination; Physician's request.
Staff RNs 8 (ft), 5 (pt); LPNs 11 (ft), 4 (pt);
Nurses' aides 43 (ft), 21 (pt); Physical
therapists 2 (ft), 1 (pt); Recreational
therapists 1 (ft); Occupational therapists 1
(pt); Speech therapists 1 (ft); Activities
coordinators 2 (ft); Dietitians 1 (ft);
Ophthalmologists 1 (pt); Podiatrists 1 (pt).
Languages Spanish.
Facilities Dining room; Physical therapy
room; Activities room; Crafts room; Laundry
room; Barber/Beauty shop; Library.
Activities Arts & crafts; Cards; Games;
Reading groups; Prayer groups; Movies;
Shopping trips; Dances/Social/Cultural
gatherings; Intergenerational programs; Pet
therapy; "In Touch" program.

North Charleston Convalescent Center
9319 Medical Plaza Dr, Charleston, SC 29418
(803) 797-8282
Admin Beth Cliett. *Dir of Nursing* Lynn Giles.
Medical Dir Dr Paul Deaton.
Licensure Skilled care; Intermediate care;
Alzheimer's care. *Beds* Swing beds SNF/ICF
132. *Certified* Medicaid; Medicare.
Owner Proprietary corp (White Oak Manor).
Staff Physicians 2 (ft), 1 (pt); RNs 6 (ft), 1
(pt); LPNs 13 (ft), 8 (pt); Nurses' aides 48
(ft), 9 (pt); Physical therapists 3 (pt); Reality
therapists 1 (pt); Recreational therapists 2
(pt); Occupational therapists 1 (pt); Speech
therapists 1 (pt); Activities coordinators 1
(pt); Dietitians 1 (pt); Ophthalmologists 1
(pt).
Facilities Dining room; Physical therapy
room; Activities room; Crafts room; Laundry
room; Barber/Beauty shop.
Activities Arts & crafts; Cards; Games;
Reading groups; Prayer groups; Movies;
Shopping trips; Dances/Social/Cultural
gatherings.

Rutledge Avenue Community Residence
887 Rutledge Ave, Charleston, SC 29401
(803) 722-7547, 723-6078
Admin Thomas P Keating. *Dir of Nursing*
Claudia Freeman RN.
Licensure Intermediate care for mentally
retarded. *Beds* ICF/MR 8. *Certified*
Medicaid.
Owner Publicly owned.
Admissions Requirements Females only.
Staff Physicians 1 (pt); RNs 1 (pt); LPNs 1
(ft); Physical therapists 1 (pt); Recreational
therapists 1 (pt); Occupational therapists 1
(pt); Speech therapists 1 (pt); Dietitians 1
(pt); Podiatrists 1 (pt).
Facilities Dining room; Activities room;
Laundry room.
Activities Arts & crafts; Cards; Games;
Movies; Shopping trips; Dances/Social/
Cultural gatherings; Work activity.

Secessionville Community Residence
1217 Secessionville Rd, Charleston, SC 29403
(803) 762-2832
Admin Thomas P Keating.
Licensure Intermediate care for mentally
retarded. *Beds* ICF/MR 8.
Owner Publicly owned.

Cheraw

Cheraw Nursing Home Inc
PO Box 967, 114 Chesterfield Hwy, Cheraw,
SC 29520
(803) 537-5253, 537-4014 FAX
Admin Grady H Bethea. *Dir of Nursing* Mary
S Dever RN. *Medical Dir* Dr Frank Hyatt.
Licensure Skilled care; Intermediate care. *Beds*
Swing beds SNF/ICF 100. *Private Pay
Patients* 15%. *Certified* Medicaid; Medicare.
Owner Privately owned.
Admissions Requirements Medical
examination; Physician's request.
Staff Physicians 1 (ft), 5 (pt); RNs 3 (ft);
LPNs 11 (ft), 2 (pt); Nurses' aides 43 (ft), 2
(pt); Physical therapists (contracted); Reality
therapists 1 (ft); Activities coordinators 1
(ft), 1 (pt); Dietitians 1 (ft); Podiatrists 1
(pt).
Facilities Dining room; Physical therapy
room; Activities room; Laundry room;
Barber/Beauty shop.
Activities Arts & crafts; Games; Reading
groups; Prayer groups; Movies; Dances/
Social/Cultural gatherings; Intergenerational
programs; Pet therapy; Resident volunteer
meetings; Music therapy.

Charles M Ingram Sr Community Residence
Rte 3 Box 123M, State Rd, Cheraw, SC 29520
(803) 537-5122
Admin Margarete Davis.
Licensure Intermediate care for mentally
retarded. *Beds* ICF/MR 8.
Owner Proprietary corp.

Chester

Chester County Nursing Center
Great Falls Rd, Chester, SC 29706
(803) 377-3151
Admin Ron V Hunter. *Dir of Nursing* Gwen
Brown RN. *Medical Dir* J N Gaston Jr MD.
Licensure Skilled care; Intermediate care. *Beds*
Swing beds SNF/ICF 62.
Owner Nonprofit corp.
Staff Physicians 22 (ft); RNs 2 (ft); LPNs 10
(ft); Nurses' aides 33 (ft); Physical therapists
1 (ft); Activities coordinators 1 (ft);
Dietitians 1 (ft).
Facilities Dining room; Physical therapy
room; Activities room; Chapel; Barber/
Beauty shop.
Activities Arts & crafts; Games; Reading
groups; Prayer groups; Shopping trips;
Dances/Social/Cultural gatherings.

Clemson

Clemson Area Retirement Center
500 Downs Loop, Clemson, SC 29631
(803) 654-1155
Admin Diana B Jones. *Dir of Nursing* Anita
Davis RN. *Medical Dir* H P Cooper Jr MD.
Licensure Skilled care; Intermediate care;
Residential care. *Beds* Swing beds SNF/ICF
44; Residential care 200. *Certified* Medicare.
Owner Proprietary corp.
Admissions Requirements Minimum age 55;
Medical examination; Physician's request.
Staff Physicians 10 (pt); RNs 2 (ft), 4 (pt);
LPNs 4 (ft), 2 (pt); Nurses' aides 21 (ft), 5
(pt); Physical therapists 1 (pt); Occupational
therapists 1 (pt); Speech therapists 1 (pt);
Activities coordinators 1 (pt); Dietitians 1
(pt); Ophthalmologists 1 (pt); Podiatrists 1
(pt).

Facilities Dining room; Physical therapy room; Activities room; Crafts room; Laundry room; Barber/Beauty shop; Library; Patio; Sun room.
Activities Arts & crafts; Cards; Games; Reading groups; Prayer groups; Movies; Shopping trips; Dances/Social/Cultural gatherings; Intergenerational programs; Pet therapy; Theater trips.

Clinton

Bailey Nursing Home
PO Drawer 976, Jacobs Hwy, Clinton, SC 29325
(803) 833-2550
Admin Donnie Estes. *Dir of Nursing* Beth Redd RN. *Medical Dir* Holbrook Raynal MD.
Licensure Skilled care; Intermediate care. *Beds* Swing beds SNF/ICF 43. *Certified* Medicaid; Medicare.
Owner Publicly owned.
Admissions Requirements Physician's request.
Staff Physicians 1 (pt); RNs 3 (ft), 1 (pt); LPNs 5 (ft), 1 (pt); Nurses' aides 19 (ft); Physical therapists 1 (pt); Activities coordinators 1 (ft).
Facilities Dining room; Activities room; Laundry room; Barber/Beauty shop.
Activities Arts & crafts; Games; Reading groups; Prayer groups.

Presbyterian Home of South Carolina—Clinton
SC Hwy 56 N, Clinton, SC 29325
(803) 833-5190
Admin Joan V Young.
Licensure Skilled care. *Beds* SNF 66.
Owner Nonprofit corp.

Whitten Center—Campus Units 1, 2, 4-7, 9, 10
PO Box 239, Hwy 76 E, Clinton, SC 29325
(803) 833-2733
Admin Earl Anderson.
Licensure Intermediate care. *Beds* ICF 162.
Owner Publicly owned.

Whitten Center—Circle II, Units 19-22
PO Box 239, Hwy 76 E, Clinton, SC 29325
(803) 833-2733
Admin Wanda Hampton.
Licensure Intermediate care. *Beds* ICF 218.
Owner Publicly owned.

Whitten Center Med A, B, C, & D
PO Box 239, Hwy 76 E, Clinton, SC 29325
(803) 833-2733
Admin Bobby Haxel.
Licensure Intermediate care. *Beds* ICF 155.
Owner Publicly owned.

Whitten Center—Suber Center Units A1, 2, B1, 2
PO Box 239, Hwy 76 E, Clinton, SC 29325
(803) 833-2733
Admin Dianna Bowers.
Licensure Intermediate care. *Beds* ICF 144.
Owner Publicly owned.

Whitten Center—Webb, Units 26-29
PO Box 239, Hwy 76 E, Clinton, SC 29325
(803) 833-2733
Admin Tom Kirby.
Licensure Intermediate care. *Beds* ICF 224.
Owner Publicly owned.

Columbia

Archie Drive Group Home
PO Box 3817, 33 Archie Dr, Columbia, SC 29230
(803) 359-9717
Admin Kathy Bradley.
Licensure Intermediate care for mentally retarded. *Beds* ICF/MR 8. *Certified* Medicaid.
Owner Nonprofit corp.

Admissions Requirements Minimum age 18; Females only.
Staff RNs 1 (pt); LPNs 1 (ft); Nurses' aides 3 (ft), 1 (pt); Occupational therapists 1 (pt); Speech therapists 1 (pt); Dietitians 1 (pt).
Facilities Dining room; Activities room; Laundry room.
Activities Arts & crafts; Cards; Games; Prayer groups; Movies; Shopping trips; Dances/Social/Cultural gatherings.

Brian Center of Nursing Care Columbia
2451 Forest Dr, Columbia, SC 29204
(803) 254-5960
Admin Louise M Linder.
Licensure Skilled care; Intermediate care. *Beds* ICF 111; Swing beds SNF/ICF 146. *Certified* Medicaid; Medicare.
Owner Proprietary corp (Brian Center Management Corp).

Brian Center of Nursing Care—St Andrews
3514 Sidney Rd, Columbia, SC 29210
(803) 798-9715
Admin Dorothea C Moody.
Medical Dir Dr Shawn Chillag.
Licensure Skilled care; Intermediate care. *Beds* ICF 60; Swing beds SNF/ICF 60. *Certified* Medicaid; Medicare.
Owner Privately owned.
Staff Physicians 1 (pt); RNs 4 (ft), 4 (pt); LPNs 7 (ft), 3 (pt); Nurses' aides 34 (ft), 5 (pt); Physical therapists 1 (pt); Speech therapists; Activities coordinators 1 (ft), 1 (pt); Ophthalmologists; Podiatrists; Audiologists; Dentists.
Facilities Dining room; Physical therapy room; Activities room; Chapel; Crafts room; Laundry room; Barber/Beauty shop.
Activities Arts & crafts; Cards; Games; Reading groups; Prayer groups; Dances/Social/Cultural gatherings.

Capitol Convalescent Center
PO Box 4276, 3001 Beechaven Rd, Columbia, SC 29204
(803) 782-4363
Admin Patricia F Schneider. *Dir of Nursing* Nancy Skorupski. *Medical Dir* William Crigler.
Licensure Skilled care; Intermediate care. *Beds* Swing beds SNF/ICF 120. *Private Pay Patients* 25%. *Certified* Medicaid; Medicare.
Owner Proprietary corp (White Oak Manor).
Admissions Requirements Minimum age 12; Medical examination.
Staff Physicians 2 (pt); RNs 2 (ft), 3 (pt); LPNs 13 (ft), 8 (pt); Nurses' aides 40 (ft), 12 (pt); Physical therapists (contracted); Occupational therapists 1 (pt); Speech therapists 1 (pt); Activities coordinators 1 (ft), 1 (pt); Dietitians 1 (pt); Podiatrists 1 (pt).
Facilities Dining room; Physical therapy room; Activities room; Crafts room; Laundry room; Barber/Beauty shop; Recreation room.
Activities Arts & crafts; Cards; Games; Reading groups; Prayer groups; Movies; Shopping trips; Dances/Social/Cultural gatherings; Intergenerational programs; Pet therapy; Cookouts; Ceramics.

Carter Street Group Home
PO Box 3817, Cola, 1203 Carter St, Columbia, SC 29230
(803) 359-9717
Admin Kathy Bradley.
Licensure Intermediate care for mentally retarded. *Beds* ICF/MR 8.
Owner Proprietary corp.

Crafts-Farrow ICF/MR
7901 Farrow Rd, Columbia, SC 29203
(803) 737-7293
Admin Willie B Cantey.
Licensure Intermediate care for mentally retarded. *Beds* ICF/MR 80. *Certified* Medicaid.

Owner Publicly owned.
Admissions Requirements Minimum age; Medical examination.
Staff Physicians 1 (ft); RNs 2 (ft); LPNs 6 (ft); Physical therapists 1 (ft); Recreational therapists 5 (ft); Occupational therapists 1 (pt); Speech therapists 2 (ft); Dietitians 2 (pt); Ophthalmologists 1 (pt); Podiatrists 1 (pt); Audiologists 1 (pt); Mental retardation specialists 42 (ft); COTAs 1 (ft).
Activities Arts & crafts; Cards; Games; Reading groups; Prayer groups; Movies; Shopping trips; Dances/Social/Cultural gatherings.

Dowdy Gardner Nursing Care Center—Farmer
7901 Farrow Rd, State Park, Columbia, SC 29203
(803) 737-7121
Admin Thomas Cordan.
Licensure Skilled care; Intermediate care. *Beds* Swing beds SNF/ICF 166.
Owner Publicly owned.

Dowdy Gardner Nursing Care Center—McLendon
7901 Farrow Rd, Columbia, SC 29203
(803) 737-7802
Admin Monroe Risinger.
Licensure Skilled care; Intermediate care. *Beds* Swing beds SNF/ICF 132.
Owner Publicly owned.

First Midlands ICMRF
8301 Farrow Rd, Columbia, SC 29203
(803) 737-7504
Admin Dorothea Friday.
Licensure Intermediate care for mentally retarded. *Beds* ICF/MR 368.
Owner Publicly owned.

Kensington I Group Home
PO Box 3817, 100 Kensington Rd, Columbia, SC 29230
(803) 256-3360
Admin Kathy Bradley.
Licensure Intermediate care for mentally retarded. *Beds* ICF/MR 8.
Owner Proprietary corp.

Kensington II Group Home
PO Box 3817, 120 Kensington Rd, Columbia, SC 29230
(803) 359-9717
Admin Kathy Bradley.
Licensure Intermediate care for mentally retarded. *Beds* ICF/MR 8.
Owner Proprietary corp.

Manor Care of Columbia
2601 Forest Dr, Columbia, SC 29204
(803) 256-4983
Admin Joyce M Pyle. *Dir of Nursing* Beatrice R Mackey RN MSN. *Medical Dir* Dr James Vardell.
Licensure Skilled care; Intermediate care. *Beds* SNF 64; ICF 54. *Private Pay Patients* 90%. *Certified* Medicaid; Medicare.
Owner Proprietary corp (Manor Care Inc).
Admissions Requirements Minimum age 16; Medical examination.
Staff RNs 12 (ft), 8 (pt); LPNs 7 (ft), 5 (pt); Nurses' aides 2 (ft); Nurses' aides 40 (ft), 12 (pt); Physical therapists 1 (ft); Recreational therapists 2 (ft); Occupational therapists 1 (pt); Speech therapists 1 (pt); Activities coordinators 2 (ft); Dietitians 1 (ft); Chaplain.
Facilities Dining room; Physical therapy room; Activities room; Crafts room; Laundry room; Barber/Beauty shop.
Activities Arts & crafts; Cards; Games; Reading groups; Prayer groups; Movies; Shopping trips; Dances/Social/Cultural gatherings; Reality orientation; Happy hour; Family dinners.

Meridian Care Center
1007 N King St, Columbia, SC 29223
(803) 788-9596
Admin Melvin H Stepp.
Licensure Skilled care; Intermediate care. *Beds*
SNF 39; Swing beds SNF/ICF 44.
Owner Privately owned.

Midlands Center Infant Care Unit
8301 Farrow Rd, Columbia, SC 29203
(803) 758-4668
Admin Olieda B Ress.
Licensure Skilled care; Intermediate care. *Beds*
22. *Certified* Medicaid; Medicare.
Owner Publicly owned.

Pine Lake ICMRF—Babcock Center
PO Box 3817, 140 Flora Rd, Columbia, SC
29230
(803) 788-7872
Admin Dorothy Goodwin.
Medical Dir J William Pitts; JoAnn Bahelka.
Licensure Intermediate care for mentally
retarded. *Beds* ICF/MR 44. *Certified*
Medicaid.
Owner Nonprofit corp.
Admissions Requirements Medical
examination; Physician's request;
Psychological evaluation; Social evaluation.
Staff Physicians 1 (pt); RNs 2 (ft), 1 (pt);
LPNs 4 (ft); Physical therapists 2 (pt);
Recreational therapists 3 (ft); Occupational
therapists 1 (pt); Speech therapists 1 (pt);
Dietitians 1 (pt); Ophthalmologists 1 (pt);
Podiatrists 1 (pt); Dentists 1 (pt); Lifeguard
Secretary QMRPs 10 (ft), 10 (pt).
Languages Sign.
Facilities Dining room; Physical therapy
room; Activities room; Crafts room; Laundry
room; Lounges; Instruction areas; Work
activities center.
Activities Arts & crafts; Cards; Games;
Reading groups; Movies; Shopping trips;
Dances/Social/Cultural gatherings;
Habilitative training.

Richland Convalescent Center Inc
PO Drawer 4600, 4112 Hartford St,
Columbia, SC 29240
(803) 754-4203
Admin Claudia Waits.
Licensure Intermediate care. *Beds* ICF 152.
Certified Medicaid; Medicare.

Second Midlands ICMRF
8301 Farrow Rd, Columbia, SC 29203
(803) 737-7504
Admin Curtis Murph.
Licensure Intermediate care. *Beds* ICF 208.
Certified Medicaid; Medicare.
Owner Publicly owned.

**South Carolina Episcopal Retirement
Community**
100 7th St Ext, Columbia, SC 29169
(803) 796-6490
Admin Peggy Thibault. *Dir of Nursing* Jo Ann
Mitchell. *Medical Dir* Dr William Burnham.
Licensure Skilled care; Intermediate care;
Residential care; Retirement; Alzheimer's
care. *Beds* Swing beds SNF/ICF 44;
Residential care 45; Retirement cottages 30;
Retirement apts 50. *Private Pay Patients*
100%.
Owner Nonprofit corp.
Admissions Requirements Minimum age 55;
Medical examination; Physician's request.
Staff Physicians (contracted); RNs 2 (ft), 2
(pt); LPNs 3 (ft), 4 (pt); Nurses' aides 14
(ft), 1 (pt); Physical therapists (contracted);
Recreational therapists 1 (ft); Speech
therapists (consultant); Dietitians
(consultant); Podiatrists (consultant).
Affiliation Episcopal.
Facilities Dining room; Physical therapy
room; Activities room; Chapel; Crafts room;
Laundry room; Barber/Beauty shop; Library.

Activities Arts & crafts; Cards; Games;
Reading groups; Prayer groups; Movies;
Shopping trips; Dances/Social/Cultural
gatherings; Pet therapy; Spanish culture
classes.

Timberlane Drive Community Residence
PO Box 3817, 4246 Timberlane Dr,
Columbia, SC 29230
(803) 359-9717
Admin Kathy Bradley.
Licensure Intermediate care for mentally
retarded. *Beds* ICF/MR 8.
Owner Proprietary corp.

Transitional Living Center
1625 College St, Columbia, SC 29208
(803) 777-5178
Admin Marilyn B Chassie. *Dir of Nursing* Dr
Elizabeth Gross. *Medical Dir* Dr Terry King.
Licensure Skilled care; Intermediate care. *Beds*
Swing beds SNF/ICF 8. *Certified* Medicaid;
Medicare.
Owner Publicly owned.
Admissions Requirements Minimum age
college age; Medical examination;
Comprehensive evaluation & interview.
Staff Physicians 1 (pt); RNs 3 (ft), 2 (pt);
Nurses' aides 11 (ft), 2 (pt); Activities
coordinators 1 (ft); Dietitians 1 (pt).
Facilities Dining room; Library; All USC
facilities.
Activities All student-oriented activities
associated with the University of South
Carolina.

C M Tucker Jr Human Resources Center
2200 Harden St, Columbia, SC 29203
(803) 737-5301
Admin Robert Miller.
Medical Dir Charles N Still MD.
Licensure Skilled care; Intermediate care. *Beds*
SNF 100; ICF 458; Swing beds SNF/ICF 50.
Certified Medicaid; Medicare.
Owner Publicly owned.
Admissions Requirements Minimum age 18;
Medical examination; Physician's request.
Staff Physicians 6 (ft), 6 (pt); RNs 24 (ft), 4
(pt); LPNs 37 (ft), 2 (pt); Nurses' aides 213
(ft); Physical therapists 1 (ft); Recreational
therapists 8 (ft); Occupational therapists 1
(pt); Speech therapists 1 (ft); Activities
coordinators 1 (ft); Dietitians 2 (ft);
Audiologists 1 (ft); Dentists 1 (pt);
Pharmacists 4 (ft).
Facilities Dining room; Physical therapy
room; Activities room; Crafts room; Laundry
room; Barber/Beauty shop; Library.
Activities Arts & crafts; Cards; Games;
Reading groups; Movies; Shopping trips;
Dances/Social/Cultural gatherings.

Mary E White Developmental Center
8301 S Farrow Rd, Columbia, SC 29203
(803) 737-7504
Admin Donna K Vinson. *Dir of Nursing*
Carolyn Dukes RN. *Medical Dir* Louis Gold
MD.
Licensure Intermediate care for mentally
retarded. *Beds* ICF/MR 112. *Certified*
Medicaid; Medicare.
Owner Publicly owned.
Admissions Requirements Minimum age 18;
Must be classified as mentally retarded.
Staff Physicians 1 (ft); RNs 14 (ft); LPNs 19
(ft); Nurses' aides 64 (ft); Physical therapists
2 (pt); Recreational therapists 4 (pt);
Occupational therapists 2 (pt); Speech
therapists 2 (pt); Activities coordinators 1
(pt); Dietitians 1 (pt); Ophthalmologists 1
(pt); Podiatrists 1 (pt); Record clerk 2 (ft);
Chaplain 1 (pt).
Facilities Dining room; Physical therapy
room; Activities room; Chapel; Crafts room;
Laundry room; Medical clinic.
Activities Arts & crafts; Games; Reading
groups; Prayer groups; Movies; Shopping
trips; Dances/Social/Cultural gatherings.

Woodlawn Group Home
PO Box 3817, 1400 Woodlawn Ave,
Columbia, SC 29230
(803) 359-9717
Admin Kathy Bradley.
Licensure Intermediate care for mentally
retarded. *Beds* ICF/MR 8.
Owner Proprietary corp.

Conway

Conway Nursing Center Inc
3300 4th Ave, Conway, SC 29526
(803) 248-5728
Admin Melanie H Connelly. *Dir of Nursing*
Judith Russ. *Medical Dir* Dr R L Ramseur.
Licensure Skilled care; Intermediate care. *Beds*
Swing beds SNF/ICF 174. *Certified*
Medicaid; Medicare.
Owner Proprietary corp.
Admissions Requirements Minimum age 12;
Medical examination.
Staff RNs 5 (ft), 1 (pt); LPNs 11 (ft), 3 (pt);
Nurses' aides 47 (ft), 3 (pt); Physical
therapists 1 (pt); Occupational therapists 1
(pt); Activities coordinators 2 (ft); Dietitians
1 (pt).
Facilities Dining room; Physical therapy
room; Activities room; Crafts room; Laundry
room; Barber/Beauty shop; Library.
Activities Arts & crafts; Cards; Games;
Reading groups; Prayer groups; Movies;
Shopping trips; Dances/Social/Cultural
gatherings; Trips to restaurants & gardens.

Lois Eargle Community Residence
406 Webb St, Conway, SC 29526
(803) 248-5251
Admin Evelyn Califf.
Licensure Intermediate care for mentally
retarded. *Beds* ICF/MR 8.
Owner Publicly owned.

Horry County Community Residence
408 Webb St, Conway, SC 29526
(803) 248-3476
Admin Gene B Kemmers.
Licensure Intermediate care for mentally
retarded. *Beds* ICF/MR 8.
Owner Publicly owned.

Cowpens

Benchmark Home: Cowpens
204 Goforth St, Cowpens, SC 29330
(803) 585-0322, 591-0780 FAX
Admin Loren Libby. *Dir of Nursing* Joyce
Briggs RN. *Medical Dir* Marvin Hevener
MD.
Licensure Intermediate care for mentally
retarded; Supervised apartment living;
Retirement. *Beds* ICF/MR 12. *Certified*
Medicaid.
Owner Nonprofit corp (Charles Lea Center).
Admissions Requirements Minimum age 25;
Medical examination; Physician's request;
Admissions are through Case Management
recommendations.
Staff Physicians 1 (pt); RNs 1 (ft); LPNs 2
(ft); Physical therapists 1 (pt); Recreational
therapists 1 (ft); Occupational therapists 1
(pt); Speech therapists 1 (pt); Dietitians 1
(pt); Audiologists 1 (pt); Direct care 9 (ft);
Dentists 1 (pt); Pharmacists 1 (pt);
Psychologists 1 (ft); Medical records
administrators 1 (pt); QMRPs 1 (ft).
Facilities Dining room; Activities room;
Laundry room.
Activities Arts & crafts; Cards; Games;
Movies; Shopping trips; Dances/Social/
Cultural gatherings; Sheltered workshop
employment; Access to all community
resources.

Darlington

Bethea Baptist Home
PO Box 4000, Darlington, SC 29532
(803) 393-2867
Admin Horace L Hawes Jr. *Dir of Nursing*
Linda McIntyre. *Medical Dir* Dr James
McInnis; Dr Josiah Matthews.
Licensure Skilled care; Independent living.
Beds SNF 88; Independent living 150.
Private Pay Patients 100%.
Owner Nonprofit organization/foundation.
Admissions Requirements Minimum age 65;
Medical examination.
Staff RNs 4 (ft); LPNs 6 (ft), 6 (pt); Nurses'
aides 33 (ft), 4 (pt); Occupational therapists
1 (ft); Dietitians 3 (ft).
Affiliation Baptist.
Facilities Dining room; Activities room;
Chapel; Crafts room; Laundry room; Barber/
Beauty shop; Library.
Activities Arts & crafts; Games; Prayer groups.

Darlington Convalescent Center
PO Box 185, 352 Pearl St, Darlington, SC
29532
(803) 393-0401
Admin Patricia B McLeod.
Licensure Intermediate care. *Beds* ICF 44.
Certified Medicaid; Medicare.

Oakhaven Inc
PO Box 516, 131 Oak St, Darlington, SC
29532
(803) 393-5892
Admin Mary Lou Blackmon. *Dir of Nursing*
Phyllis Morris RN. *Medical Dir* George L
Timmons MD.
Licensure Skilled care; Intermediate care. *Beds*
Swing beds SNF/ICF 88. *Certified* Medicaid;
Medicare; VA.
Owner Proprietary corp.
Admissions Requirements Medical
examination; Physician's request.
Staff Physicians 1 (pt); RNs 4 (ft); LPNs 8
(ft), 4 (pt); Nurses' aides 30 (ft); Physical
therapists 1 (pt); Occupational therapists 1
(pt); Speech therapists 1 (pt); Activities
coordinators 1 (ft), 2 (pt); Dietitians 1 (pt);
Ophthalmologists 1 (pt); Social worker 1 (ft).
Facilities Dining room; Activities room;
Crafts room; Laundry room; Barber/Beauty
shop; Van.
Activities Arts & crafts; Cards; Games;
Reading groups; Prayer groups; Movies;
Shopping trips; Dances/Social/Cultural
gatherings; Holiday events.

Dillon

Pines Nursing & Convalescent Home
203 Lakeside Dr, Dillon, SC 29536
(803) 774-2741
Admin Richard C Cooke. *Dir of Nursing*
Margaret Arnette RN. *Medical Dir* S C
Black MD.
Licensure Skilled care; Intermediate care. *Beds*
Swing beds SNF/ICF 84. *Certified* Medicaid;
Medicare.
Owner Proprietary corp (Beverly Enterprises).
Admissions Requirements Medical
examination; Physician's request.
Staff Physicians; RNs; LPNs; Nurses' aides;
Physical therapists; Activities coordinators 1
(ft); Dietitians 1 (ft).
Facilities Dining room; Physical therapy
room; Laundry room; Barber/Beauty shop.
Activities Arts & crafts; Games; Prayer groups;
Movies; Dances/Social/Cultural gatherings.

Easley

Blue Ridge Health Care Inc
1800 Crestview Rd, Easley, SC 29640
(803) 859-3236
Admin Virginia Byrd.

Licensure Intermediate care. *Beds* ICF 67.
Owner Proprietary corp.

Easley Community Residence No 1
300 Nally St, Easley, SC 29671
(803) 859-5416
Admin Mary C Anderson.
Licensure Intermediate care for mentally
retarded. *Beds* ICF/MR 8.
Owner Publicly owned.

Easley Community Residence No 2
406 Olive St, Easley, SC 29640
(803) 859-4411
Admin Mary C Anderson.
Licensure Intermediate care for mentally
retarded. *Beds* ICF/MR 8.
Owner Publicly owned.

Easley Health Care
200 Anne Dr, Easley, SC 29640
(803) 859-9754
Admin Suzanne Amos Glymph. *Dir of Nursing*
Valerie Peterson RN. *Medical Dir* Dr Dexter
Rogers.
Licensure Skilled care; Intermediate care. *Beds*
Swing beds SNF/ICF 103. *Private Pay
Patients* 30%. *Certified* Medicaid; Medicare.
Owner Privately owned.
Admissions Requirements Minimum age 18;
Medical examination; Physician's request;
History and physical.
Staff RNs 4 (ft), 1 (pt); LPNs 8 (ft), 9 (pt);
Nurses' aides 48 (ft); Physical therapists 2
(pt); Speech therapists 1 (pt); Activities
coordinators 1 (ft); Dietitians 1 (ft).
Facilities Dining room; Physical therapy
room; Activities room; Laundry room;
Barber/Beauty shop.
Activities Arts & crafts; Cards; Games;
Reading groups; Prayer groups; Movies;
Intergenerational programs; Pet therapy.

Edgefield

Edgefield Health Care Center
PO Box 668, 1 Medical Park Dr, Edgefield,
SC 29824
(803) 637-5312
Admin Cynthia R Vann.
Medical Dir Dr H R Kylstra.
Licensure Intermediate care. *Beds* ICF 88.
Certified Medicaid; Medicare.
Owner Proprietary corp.
Admissions Requirements Medical
examination.
Staff RNs 3 (ft), 2 (pt); LPNs 2 (ft), 6 (pt);
Nurses' aides 23 (ft), 10 (pt); Physical
therapists 1 (pt); Activities coordinators 1
(ft); Dietitians 6 (ft), 1 (pt).
Facilities Dining room; Physical therapy
room; Laundry room; Barber/Beauty shop;
TV & recreation room.
Activities Arts & crafts; Games; Prayer groups;
Movies; Dances/Social/Cultural gatherings;
Cookouts; Pet therapy.

Estill

Stiles M Harper Convalescent Center
301 S Liberty St, Estill, SC 29918
(803) 625-3852
Admin Athalene B Mole. *Dir of Nursing*
Marie Benton LPN. *Medical Dir* Harrison L
Peeples MD.
Licensure Intermediate care. *Beds* ICF 44.
Certified Medicaid.
Owner Nonprofit organization/foundation.
Admissions Requirements Medical
examination.
Staff RNs 2 (pt); LPNs 4 (ft), 2 (pt); Nurses'
aides 12 (ft), 2 (pt); Activities coordinators 1
(ft); Dietitians 1 (pt).
Facilities Dining room; Activities room;
Crafts room; Laundry room; Barber/Beauty
shop.

Activities Arts & crafts; Cards; Games;
Reading groups; Prayer groups; Movies;
Dances/Social/Cultural gatherings.

Fairfax

John Edward Harter Nursing Center
PO Box 218, Hwy 278 W, Fairfax, SC 29827
(803) 632-3311
Admin M K Hiatt.
Medical Dir H L Laffitte MD.
Licensure Skilled care; Intermediate care. *Beds*
Swing beds SNF/ICF 44. *Certified* Medicaid;
Medicare.
Owner Publicly owned.
Admissions Requirements Medical
examination; Physician's request.
Staff RNs 2 (ft), 2 (pt); LPNs 5 (ft); Physical
therapists 1 (pt); Recreational therapists 1
(pt); Speech therapists 1 (pt); Activities
coordinators 1 (ft); Dietitians 1 (ft).
Facilities Dining room; Activities room.
Activities Arts & crafts; Games; Prayer groups;
Movies.

Florence

Acline Place
PO Box 12810, Florence, SC 29504
(803) 664-2821
Admin Belinda Calcutt NHA. *Dir of Nursing*
Teresa Deaver RN. *Medical Dir* David
Moon.
Licensure Intermediate care for mentally
retarded. *Beds* ICF/MR 8. *Private Pay
Patients* 0%. *Certified* Medicaid.
Owner Publicly owned.
Admissions Requirements Males only; SC
Dept MR eligibility requirements.
Staff Physicians; RNs; LPNs; Physical
therapists (contracted); Recreational
therapists; Occupational therapists; Speech
therapists; Activities coordinators; Dietitians
(contracted); Audiologists.
Facilities Dining room; Laundry room.
Activities Arts & crafts; Games; Movies;
Shopping trips; Dances/Social/Cultural
gatherings; Active treatment.

Carolina Place
PO Box 12810, Florence, SC 29504
(803) 664-2821
Admin Belinda Calcutt NHA. *Dir of Nursing*
Teresa Deaver RN. *Medical Dir* Dr David
Moon.
Licensure Intermediate care for mentally
retarded. *Beds* ICF/MR 8. *Private Pay
Patients* 0%. *Certified* Medicaid.
Owner Publicly owned.
Admissions Requirements Females only;
Medical examination; Must meet SC Dept of
MR eligibility requirements.
Staff Physicians; RNs; LPNs; Physical
therapists (contracted); Recreational
therapists; Occupational therapists; Speech
therapists; Activities coordinators; Dietitians
(contracted); Audiologists; QMRPs; MRs
staff; Psychologist.
Facilities Dining room; Laundry room.
Activities Arts & crafts; Games; Movies;
Shopping trips; Dances/Social/Cultural
gatherings; Active treatment therapy.

Clyde Street Home
PO Box 3209, 509 Clyde St, Florence, SC
29502
(803) 669-3661
Admin Kenneth Ward.
Licensure Intermediate care for mentally
retarded. *Beds* ICF/MR 20. *Certified*
Medicare.
Owner Publicly owned.

Coit Street Community Residence
654 S Coit St, Florence, SC 29502
(803) 669-3661

Admin Belinda Kaye Calcutt NHA. *Dir of Nursing* Bobbie Odum RN.
Licensure Intermediate care for mentally retarded. *Beds* ICF/MR 8. *Certified* Medicaid.
Owner Publicly owned.
Admissions Requirements Males only; Medical examination; MR.
Staff RNs 1 (pt) LPNs 1 (pt); Recreational therapists 1 (pt); Dietitians 1 (pt); QMRP 1 (pt) Nursing Home Aide 1 (pt) Social worker 1 (pt) Unit manager 1 (pt) Direct care 5 (ft).
Facilities Dining room; Laundry room.
Activities Arts & crafts; Games; Reading groups; Movies; Shopping trips; Dances/Social/Cultural gatherings; Habilitation - Active treatment.

Commander Nursing Center
Rte 3 Box 37, Pamplico Hwy, Florence, SC 29501
(803) 669-3502
Admin Joe Commander III.
Licensure Skilled care; Intermediate care. *Beds* Swing beds SNF/ICF 133. *Certified* Medicaid; Medicare.

Faith Nursing Home
PO Box 690, 617 W Marion St, Florence, SC 29503
(803) 669-9958
Admin Bonnie W Cockfield.
Licensure Skilled care; Intermediate care. *Beds* ICF 104; Swing beds SNF/ICF 44. *Certified* Medicaid; Medicare.

Florence Community Residence
PO Box 12810, Florence, SC 29504
(803) 664-2821
Admin Belinda Kaye Calcutt NHA. *Dir of Nursing* Teresa Deaver RN. *Medical Dir* Dr John Booth.
Licensure Intermediate care for mentally retarded. *Beds* ICF/MR 8. *Private Pay Patients* 0%. *Certified* Medicaid.
Owner Publicly owned.
Admissions Requirements Females only; Medical examination; SC Dept MR eligibility requirements.
Staff Physicians; RNs; LPNs; Physical therapists (contracted); Recreational therapists; Occupational therapists; Speech therapists; Activities coordinators; Dietitians (contracted); Audiologists.
Facilities Dining room; Laundry room.
Activities Arts & crafts; Active treatment programs.

Florence Convalescent Center
Rte 6 Box 165, Clark Rd, Florence, SC 29501
(803) 669-4374
Admin Genevieve M Lawrence.
Medical Dir Dr H H Jeter.
Licensure Skilled care; Intermediate care. *Beds* ICF 44; Swing beds SNF/ICF 44. *Certified* Medicaid.
Staff Physicians 5 (pt); RNs 2 (ft); LPNs 6 (ft), 1 (pt); Nurses' aides 20 (ft); Activities coordinators 1 (ft); Dietitians 7 (pt); Social workers 1 (ft).
Facilities Dining room; Activities room; Crafts room; Laundry room; Barber/Beauty shop.
Activities Arts & crafts; Cards; Games; Reading groups; Prayer groups; Movies; Shopping trips; Dances/Social/Cultural gatherings; Cookouts.

Folk Nursing Center
2385 Pamplico Hwy, Florence, SC 29501
(803) 669-4403
Admin Charles S Commander.
Licensure Skilled care; Intermediate care. *Beds* Swing beds SNF/ICF 88. *Certified* Medicaid; Medicare.

Graham Street Community Residence
PO Box 12810, 306 Graham St, Florence, SC 29504
(803) 669-3661
Admin Belinda Kaye Calcutt NHA.
Licensure Intermediate care for mentally retarded. *Beds* ICF/MR 8.
Owner Publicly owned.

HealthSouth Rehabilitation Center
722 S Dargan St, Florence, SC 29501
(803) 669-8891, 678-3750 FAX
Admin Allan Smith. *Dir of Nursing* Sue Dorsel. *Medical Dir* Dr Robert Kukla.
Licensure SNF rehabilitation. *Beds* SNF rehabilitation 88. *Private Pay Patients* 65%. *Certified* Medicaid; Medicare.
Owner Proprietary corp (HealthSouth Rehabilitation Corp).
Admissions Requirements Medical examination; Physician's request.
Staff Physicians 1 (ft); RNs 21 (ft), 4 (pt); LPNs 10 (ft), 4 (pt); Nurses' aides 25 (ft), 16 (pt); Physical therapists 7 (ft); Recreational therapists 3 (ft); Occupational therapists 9 (ft); Speech therapists 7 (ft); Dietitians 1 (ft), 1 (pt); Psychiatrists; Respiratory therapists; Neuropsychologists; Social workers.
Facilities Dining room; Physical therapy room; Activities room; Barber/Beauty shop; Occupational therapy room; Speech therapy rooms.
Activities Arts & crafts; Games; Prayer groups; Movies; Shopping trips; Dances/Social/Cultural gatherings; Pet therapy.

Heritage Home of Florence Inc
515 S Warley St, Florence, SC 29501
(803) 662-4573
Admin Sherwin D Welch.
Licensure Skilled care; Intermediate care. *Beds* Swing beds SNF/ICF 88. *Certified* Medicaid; Medicare.

Honorage Nursing Care
1207 N Cashua Rd, Florence, SC 29501
(803) 665-6172
Admin Howard W Clarke.
Medical Dir Harold H Jeter Jr MD.
Licensure Skilled care; Intermediate care. *Beds* Swing beds SNF/ICF 88. *Certified* Medicaid; Medicare.
Owner Proprietary corp.
Admissions Requirements Medical examination.
Staff RNs 7 (ft); LPNs 7 (ft); Nurses' aides 30 (ft); Activities coordinators 1 (ft).
Facilities Dining room; Activities room; Chapel; Crafts room; Laundry room; Barber/Beauty shop.
Activities Arts & crafts; Games; Reading groups; Prayer groups; Movies; Dances/Social/Cultural gatherings.

Mulberry Park
PO Box 3209, 714 National Cemetary Rd, Florence, SC 29502
(803) 669-3661
Admin Kenneth Ward.
Licensure Intermediate care for mentally retarded. *Beds* ICF/MR 112.
Owner Publicly owned.

Pamplico Highway Community Residence
PO Box 12810, Florence, SC 29504
(803) 664-2821
Admin Belinda K Calcutt NHA. *Dir of Nursing* Teresa Deaver RN. *Medical Dir* Dr John Booth.
Licensure Intermediate care for mentally retarded. *Beds* ICF/MR 8. *Private Pay Patients* 0%. *Certified* Medicaid.
Owner Publicly owned.
Admissions Requirements Females only; Medical examination; SC Dept MR eligibility requirements.

Staff Physicians; RNs; LPNs; Physical therapists (contracted); Recreational therapists; Occupational therapists; Speech therapists; Activities coordinators; Dietitians (contracted); Audiologists.
Facilities Homelike residence.
Activities Arts & crafts; Active treatment.

Pecan Lane
PO Box 3209, 714 National Cemetary Rd, Florence, SC 29502
(803) 669-3661
Admin Kenneth Ward.
Licensure Intermediate care for mentally retarded. *Beds* ICF/MR 160.
Owner Publicly owned.

Presbyterian Home of South Carolina—Florence
2350 Lucas St, Florence, SC 29501
(803) 665-2222
Admin Peggy Andrews.
Licensure Skilled care. *Beds* SNF 25.
Owner Nonprofit corp.

Thomas Drive Community Residence
PO Box 3209, 4 Thomas Dr, Florence, SC 29502
(803) 669-3661
Admin John Wiley.
Licensure Intermediate care for mentally retarded. *Beds* ICF/MR 8.
Owner Publicly owned.

Fork

Sunny Acres Nursing Home Inc
Rte 1 Box 115, Fork, SC 29543
(803) 464-6212
Admin Tony R Cooke.
Medical Dir Ira Barth MD.
Licensure Skilled care; Intermediate care. *Beds* ICF 54; Swing beds SNF/ICF 57. *Certified* Medicaid; Medicare.
Owner Proprietary corp.
Staff Physicians 3 (ft); RNs 4 (ft), 3 (pt); LPNs 11 (ft), 3 (pt); Nurses' aides 28 (ft), 4 (pt); Recreational therapists 2 (ft), 2 (pt); Dietitians 9 (ft).
Facilities Dining room; Physical therapy room; Activities room; Chapel; Crafts room; Laundry room; Barber/Beauty shop.
Activities Arts & crafts; Games; Reading groups; Prayer groups; Movies; Shopping trips; Dances/Social/Cultural gatherings.

Fountain Inn

Fountain Inn Convalescent Home
PO Box 67, 501 Gulliver St, Fountain Inn, SC 29644
(803) 862-2554
Admin Cecile McFarland RN.
Medical Dir Walter R McLawhorn MD.
Licensure Skilled care; Intermediate care. *Beds* Swing beds SNF/ICF 44. *Certified* Medicaid.
Owner Proprietary corp.
Admissions Requirements Medical examination.
Staff RNs 2 (ft); LPNs 2 (ft), 1 (pt); Nurses' aides 11 (ft), 2 (pt); Activities coordinators 1 (ft); Dietitians 1 (ft); Social worker 1 (ft).
Facilities Dining room; Activities room; Laundry room; Barber/Beauty shop.
Activities Arts & crafts; Cards; Games; Reading groups; Prayer groups; Movies; Dances/Social/Cultural gatherings.

Gaffney

Brookview House Inc
PO Box 1240, 510 Thompson St, Gaffney, SC 29342
(803) 489-3101
Admin Charles L Blanton Jr.
Medical Dir L L DuBose MD.

Licensure Skilled care; Intermediate care. *Beds* 44; Swing beds SNF/ICF 88. *Certified* Medicaid; Medicare.
Staff RNs 3 (ft), 4 (pt); LPNs 10 (ft), 5 (pt); Nurses' aides 35 (ft), 10 (pt); Activities coordinators 3 (pt); Dietitians 1 (ft).
Facilities Dining room; Activities room; Crafts room; Laundry room; Barber/Beauty shop; Library.
Activities Arts & crafts; Games; Movies; Dances/Social/Cultural gatherings.

Cherokee County Long-Term Care Facility
1420 N Limestone St, Gaffney, SC 29340
(803) 487-2716
Admin Jimmy L Snyder. *Dir of Nursing* Jamie L Patty RN. *Medical Dir* Charles P Stroup MD.
Licensure Skilled care; Intermediate care. *Beds* SNF 20; ICF 24. *Private Pay Patients* 44%. *Certified* Medicaid; Medicare.
Owner Publicly owned.
Admissions Requirements Medical examination.
Staff RNs 2 (ft); LPNs 4 (ft), 2 (pt); Nurses' aides 15 (ft), 1 (pt); Activities coordinators 1 (ft), 1 (pt).
Facilities Dining room; Activities room; Crafts room; Barber/Beauty shop.
Activities Arts & crafts; Games; Reading groups; Prayer groups; Movies; Shopping trips; Dances/Social/Cultural gatherings.

J Claude Fort Community Residence
816-818 W Montgomery St, Gaffney, SC 29340
(803) 487-4787, 487-4190
Admin J Arthur Bridges Jr. *Dir of Nursing* Kathryn Humphries RN.
Licensure Intermediate care for mentally retarded. *Beds* ICF/MR 16. *Certified* Medicaid.
Owner Publicly owned.
Admissions Requirements Minimum age 10; Males only; Medical examination.
Staff RNs 1 (ft), 2 (pt); LPNs 2 (ft); Nurses' aides 12 (ft), 2 (pt); Activities coordinators 1 (ft).
Facilities Dining room; Activities room; Laundry room.
Activities Arts & crafts; Cards; Games; Movies; Shopping trips; Dances/Social/Cultural gatherings; Sports.

Georgetown

Winyah Extended Care Center Inc
PO Box 8158, 2715 S Island Rd, Georgetown, SC 29440
(803) 546-4123
Admin W William Mitchell.
Licensure Skilled care; Intermediate care. *Beds* ICF 42; Swing beds SNF/ICF 42. *Certified* Medicaid; Medicare.

Greenville

Hillhaven Health Care
411 Ansel St, Greenville, SC 29601
(803) 232-5368
Admin Jane B Owings.
Licensure Skilled care; Intermediate care. *Beds* ICF 51; Swing beds SNF/ICF 78. *Certified* Medicaid; Medicare.
Owner Proprietary corp.

Grady H Hipp Nursing Center
661 Rutherford Rd, Greenville, SC 29609
(803) 233-7007, 232-2442
Admin Paula M Cargill, Exec Dir.
Licensure Skilled care; Intermediate care. *Beds* Swing beds SNF/ICF 112. *Certified* Medicaid; Medicare.

Oakmont East Nursing Center
601 Sulphur Springs Rd, Greenville, SC 29611
(803) 246-2721

Admin Michael H McBride.
Licensure Skilled care; Intermediate care. *Beds* Swing beds SNF/ICF 132. *Certified* Medicaid; Medicare.
Owner Proprietary corp (Health Care & Retirement Corp).

Oakmont West
600 Sulphur Springs Rd, Greenville, SC 29611
(803) 246-2721
Admin David S Harper.
Medical Dir W W Goodlett MD.
Licensure Intermediate care. *Beds* ICF 125. *Certified* Medicaid; Medicare.
Owner Proprietary corp (Health Care & Retirement Corp).
Staff Physicians 5 (ft); LPNs 8 (ft); Nurses' aides 40 (ft); Dietitians 1 (ft).
Facilities Dining room; Activities room; Chapel; Barber/Beauty shop.
Activities Arts & crafts; Cards; Games; Prayer groups; Movies; Shopping trips; Dances/Social/Cultural gatherings.

Piedmont Nursing Center
809 Laurens Rd, Greenville, SC 29607
(803) 232-8196
Admin Patsy P Jewell.
Licensure Skilled care; Intermediate care. *Beds* ICF 35; Swing beds SNF/ICF 44. *Certified* Medicaid; Medicare.

Resthaven Geriatric Center
2123 Grove Rd, Greenville, SC 29605
(803) 242-4730
Admin Joan T King.
Medical Dir Norris Boone MD.
Licensure Skilled care. *Beds* 30.
Admissions Requirements Minimum age 16; Medical examination; Physician's request.
Staff RNs 1 (ft), 1 (pt); LPNs 3 (ft), 2 (pt); Nurses' aides 10 (ft), 2 (pt).
Facilities Activities room; Laundry room.
Activities Prayer groups.

Ridge Road Residence
PO Box 17007-B, Rte 14 Ridge Rd, Greenville, SC 29606
(803) 297-0712
Admin Donald Shockley.
Licensure Intermediate care for mentally retarded. *Beds* ICF/MR 16.
Owner Publicly owned.

Rolling Green Village
1 Hoke Smith Blvd, Greenville, SC 29615
(803) 297-0558
Admin William S DuPree.
Licensure Skilled care; Intermediate care. *Beds* Swing beds SNF/ICF 44.
Owner Nonprofit corp.

Westside Health Care Inc
8 N Texas Ave, Greenville, SC 29611
(803) 295-1331
Admin Thelma James. *Dir of Nursing* Mary Bryan. *Medical Dir* James Gowan.
Licensure Skilled care; Intermediate care. *Beds* Swing beds SNF/ICF 88. *Private Pay Patients* 28%. *Certified* Medicaid; Medicare.
Owner Proprietary corp (Sentry Care Inc).
Admissions Requirements Minimum age 16; Medical examination; Physician's request.
Staff Physicians (contracted); RNs 4 (ft); LPNs 10 (ft); Nurses' aides 29 (ft), 4 (pt); Physical therapists (contracted); Reality therapists (contracted); Recreational therapists (contracted); Occupational therapists (contracted); Speech therapists (contracted); Activities coordinators 1 (ft); Dietitians 1 (ft); Podiatrists 1 (pt); Audiologists (contracted).
Facilities Dining room; Physical therapy room; Activities room; Crafts room; Laundry room; Barber/Beauty shop.
Activities Arts & crafts; Cards; Games; Prayer groups; Dances/Social/Cultural gatherings.

Greenwood

J Felton Burton Community Residence
PO Drawer 239, 308 Jenkins Spring Rd, Greenwood, SC 29646
(803) 223-8515
Admin Thomas F Kirby.
Licensure Intermediate care for mentally retarded. *Beds* ICF/MR 8.
Owner Publicly owned.

Greenbrook Manor
1415 Parkway, Greenwood, SC 29646
(803) 227-9500
Admin Edith Goforth.
Licensure Skilled care; Intermediate care. *Beds* Swing beds SNF/ICF 22.
Owner Proprietary corp.

Greenwood Health Care Center
PO Box 3109, 437 E Cambridge Ave, Greenwood, SC 29648
(803) 223-1950
Admin Brad W Moorhouse.
Licensure Skilled care; Intermediate care. *Beds* SNF 133; ICF 19. *Certified* Medicaid; Medicare.
Owner Proprietary corp (National Health Corp).

Nursing Center of Greenwood Methodist Home
1110 Marshall Rd, Greenwood, SC 29646
(803) 227-6655
Admin Ingrid L Speer. *Dir of Nursing* Lillian Thomas RN. *Medical Dir* O L Thomas MD.
Licensure Skilled care; Intermediate care; Retirement. *Beds* Swing beds SNF/ICF 102. *Certified* Medicaid; Medicare.
Owner Nonprofit organization/foundation.
Admissions Requirements Physician's request.
Staff Physicians 1 (pt); RNs 6 (ft), 3 (pt); LPNs 3 (ft); Nurses' aides 30 (ft), 9 (pt); Physical therapists 1 (pt); Activities coordinators 3 (ft); Dietitians 1 (ft).
Affiliation Methodist.
Facilities Dining room; Physical therapy room; Activities room; Chapel; Crafts room; Laundry room; Barber/Beauty shop.
Activities Arts & crafts; Cards; Games; Reading groups; Prayer groups; Movies; Shopping trips; Dances/Social/Cultural gatherings.

Dr Paul Baker Pritchard Jr Community Residence
PO Box 3004, 53 S Greenwood, Ware Shoals, Greenwood, SC 29646
(803) 223-4579
Admin Thomas F Kirby PhD.
Licensure Intermediate care for mentally retarded. *Beds* ICF/MR 12.
Owner Publicly owned.

South Main Community Residence
Rte 1 Box 146, S Main St, Greenwood, SC 29646
(803) 227-2441
Admin Linda L Gault.
Licensure Intermediate care for mentally retarded. *Beds* ICF/MR 8. *Certified* Medicaid.
Owner Publicly owned.

Greer

Roger Huntington Nursing Center
PO Box 1149, Forrest St, Greer, SC 29652
(803) 879-0130
Admin Michael W Massey. *Dir of Nursing* Martha Armstrong RN.
Licensure Skilled care; Intermediate care. *Beds* Swing beds SNF/ICF 88. *Private Pay Patients* 50%. *Certified* Medicaid; Medicare.
Owner Nonprofit organization/foundation.
Admissions Requirements Minimum age 21; Medical examination; Physician's request.

Staff RNs 10 (ft), 3 (pt); LPNs 3 (ft), 2 (pt); Nurses' aides 30 (ft), 15 (pt); Physical therapists 1 (ft); Activities coordinators 1 (ft); Dietitians 1 (ft).
Facilities Dining room; Physical therapy room; Activities room; Chapel; Crafts room; Barber/Beauty shop.
Activities Arts & crafts; Games; Reading groups; Movies; Shopping trips; Dances/ Social/Cultural gatherings; Pet therapy.

Pine Ridge Health Care Inc
Chandler Rd at Memorial Dr Ext, Greer, SC 29651
(803) 879-7474
Admin Larry D Lollis. *Dir of Nursing* Katherine Schuker RN. *Medical Dir* Lewis M Davis MD.
Licensure Skilled care; Intermediate care; Retirement. *Beds* Swing beds SNF/ICF 132. *Certified* Medicaid; Medicare.
Owner Proprietary corp.
Admissions Requirements Minimum age 13; Medical examination; Physician's request.
Staff Physicians 18 (pt); RNs 8 (ft); LPNs 16 (ft); Nurses' aides 56 (ft); Physical therapists 2 (pt); Recreational therapists 1 (pt); Occupational therapists 1 (pt); Speech therapists 1 (pt); Activities coordinators 1 (ft); Dietitians 2 (pt); Ophthalmologists 1 (pt); Podiatrists 1 (pt); Dentists 1 (pt); Psychiatrist 1 (pt); Social workers 2 (ft).
Facilities Dining room; Physical therapy room; Activities room; Crafts room; Laundry room; Barber/Beauty shop; Library.
Activities Arts & crafts; Cards; Games; Reading groups; Prayer groups; Movies; Shopping trips; Dances/Social/Cultural gatherings; Music therapy.

Hartsville

William W Bowen Residence
1045 Morrell Ave, Hartsville, SC 29550
(803) 332-1177
Admin Sylvia Johnson.
Licensure Intermediate care for mentally retarded. *Beds* ICF/MR 8.
Owner Proprietary corp.

Morrell Memorial Convalescent Center Inc
PO Box 1318, Hwy 15 N Bypass, Hartsville, SC 29550
(803) 383-5164
Admin Thomas S Stewart. *Dir of Nursing* Marcia B Stegner. *Medical Dir* Dr Darrel Gant.
Licensure Skilled care; Intermediate care. *Beds* SNF 44; ICF 44; Swing beds SNF/ICF 44. *Certified* Medicaid; Medicare.
Admissions Requirements Medical examination; Physician's request.
Staff Physicians 1 (ft); RNs 3 (ft), 1 (pt); LPNs 14 (ft), 3 (pt); Nurses' aides 48 (ft), 1 (pt); Activities coordinators 1 (ft).
Facilities Dining room; Physical therapy room; Activities room; Chapel; Crafts room; Laundry room; Barber/Beauty shop.
Activities Arts & crafts; Cards; Games; Reading groups; Prayer groups.

John A Reagan Residence
1100 Carolina Ave, Hartsville, SC 29550
(803) 332-4642
Admin Sylvia Johnson.
Licensure Intermediate care for mentally retarded. *Beds* ICF/MR 8.
Owner Publicly owned.

Thad E Saleeby Developmental Center
714 Lewellen Ave, Hartsville, SC 29550
(803) 332-4104
Admin Gail M Grainger. *Dir of Nursing* Celia Hinds RN. *Medical Dir* James O Morphis; Jesse T Cox MD.
Licensure Intermediate care for mentally retarded. *Beds* ICF/MR 132. *Certified* Medicare.

Owner Publicly owned.
Admissions Requirements Medical examination.
Staff Physicians 2 (ft); Physical therapists 1 (pt); Recreational therapists 1 (pt); Occupational therapists 1 (pt); Speech therapists 1 (ft); Activities coordinators 1 (ft); Dietitians 1 (ft); Podiatrists 1 (pt); Dentists 1 (pt).
Facilities Dining room; Physical therapy room; Activities room; Crafts room; Laundry room; Barber/Beauty shop; Library.
Activities Arts & crafts; Games; Reading groups; Movies; Shopping trips; Dances/ Social/Cultural gatherings.

Hilton Head Island

Healthcare of Hilton Head Inc
37 Bill Fries Dr, Hilton Head Island, SC 29926
(803) 681-6006
Medical Dir Dr England.
Licensure Skilled care; Intermediate care. *Beds* Swing beds SNF/ICF 44. *Private Pay Patients* 35%. *Certified* Medicaid; Medicare.
Owner Proprietary corp (Pruitt Corp).
Admissions Requirements Minimum age 50; Medical examination.
Staff RNs 3 (ft); LPNs 6 (ft); Nurses' aides 24 (ft); Physical therapists 1 (pt); Occupational therapists 1 (pt); Speech therapists 1 (pt); Activities coordinators 1 (pt); Dietitians 1 (pt).
Facilities Dining room; Physical therapy room; Activities room; Crafts room; Laundry room; Barber/Beauty shop.
Activities Arts & crafts; Cards; Games; Reading groups; Prayer groups; Movies; Shopping trips; Dances/Social/Cultural gatherings; Pet therapy.

Seabrook of Hilton Inc
300 Wood Haven Dr, Hilton Head Island, SC 29928
(803) 842-3747
Admin Annette R Martin. *Dir of Nursing* Carol Abbott. *Medical Dir* J Catlett MD.
Licensure Skilled care; Intermediate care; Residential care; Alzheimer's care. *Beds* Swing beds SNF/ICF 44; Residential care 200. *Certified* Medicare.
Owner Proprietary corp.
Admissions Requirements Minimum age 65; Medical examination.
Staff Physicians 1 (pt); RNs 2 (ft), 2 (pt); LPNs 4 (ft), 4 (pt); Nurses' aides 20 (ft), 10 (pt); Physical therapists 1 (pt); Recreational therapists 1 (pt); Speech therapists 1 (pt); Activities coordinators 1 (ft); Ophthalmologists 1 (pt).
Facilities Dining room; Physical therapy room; Activities room; Crafts room; Laundry room; Barber/Beauty shop; Library; Auditorium.
Activities Arts & crafts; Cards; Games; Reading groups; Prayer groups; Movies; Shopping trips; Dances/Social/Cultural gatherings; Concerts; Classes.

Hopkins

Stanton Pines Convalescent Home Inc
124 Ridge Rd, Hopkins, SC 29061
(803) 776-3536
Admin Daisey N Stanton RN.
Licensure Intermediate care. *Beds* ICF 26.
Owner Proprietary corp.
Admissions Requirements Medical examination; Physician's request.
Staff Physicians 3 (ft); RNs 1 (ft); LPNs 1 (ft); Nurses' aides 12 (ft); Dietitians 1 (ft).
Facilities Dining room; Activities room; Laundry room; Barber/Beauty shop.
Activities Cards; Games; Prayer groups; Movies.

Inman

Camp Care Inc
PO Box 847, Inman, SC 29349
(803) 472-2028
Admin Carole N Camp.
Medical Dir Dr Thomas Malone.
Licensure Intermediate care. *Beds* ICF 88. *Certified* Medicaid; Medicare.
Staff Physicians 1 (pt); RNs 1 (ft); LPNs 8 (ft), 2 (pt); Nurses' aides 24 (ft), 3 (pt); Recreational therapists 1 (ft); Activities coordinators 1 (ft); Dietitians 1 (pt); Dentists 1 (pt).
Facilities Dining room; Activities room; Crafts room; Laundry room; Barber/Beauty shop.
Activities Arts & crafts; Games; Prayer groups; Movies; Shopping trips; Dances/Social/ Cultural gatherings.

Camphaven Manor
63 Blackstock Rd, Inman, SC 29349
(803) 472-9055, 472-2619 FAX
Admin J David Niday. *Dir of Nursing* Lisa Laughter. *Medical Dir* David K Stokes Jr MD.
Licensure Skilled care. *Beds* SNF 176. *Private Pay Patients* 20%. *Certified* Medicaid; Medicare.
Owner Proprietary corp (Service Management Inc).
Admissions Requirements Minimum age 18; Medical examination.
Staff Physicians 1 (ft), 3 (pt); RNs 6 (ft); LPNs 20 (ft), 2 (pt); Nurses' aides 64 (ft), 10 (pt); Physical therapists 3 (pt); Recreational therapists 3 (ft); Occupational therapists 3 (pt); Speech therapists 1 (pt); Activities coordinators 1 (ft); Dietitians 1 (pt); Podiatrists 1 (pt).
Facilities Dining room; Physical therapy room; Activities room; Crafts room; Laundry room; Barber/Beauty shop.
Activities Arts & crafts; Cards; Games; Reading groups; Prayer groups; Movies; Dances/Social/Cultural gatherings; Pet therapy.

Inman Nursing Home
PO Box 266, 51 N Main St, Inman, SC 29349
(803) 472-9370
Admin H Wayne Johnson. *Dir of Nursing* Lisa Laughter RN. *Medical Dir* Dr Barry Henderson.
Licensure Skilled care; Intermediate care; Retirement. *Beds* Swing beds SNF/ICF 40. *Certified* Medicaid; Medicare.
Owner Proprietary corp.
Admissions Requirements Medical examination; Physician's request.
Staff Physicians 1 (ft); RNs 1 (ft), 2 (pt); LPNs 3 (ft), 2 (pt); Nurses' aides 15 (ft), 7 (pt); Activities coordinators 1 (ft), 1 (pt); Dietitians 1 (ft), 1 (pt).
Facilities Dining room; Activities room; Laundry room; Barber/Beauty shop.
Activities Arts & crafts; Cards; Games; Reading groups.

C W Johnson Intermediate Care Facility
82 N Main St, Inman, SC 29349
(803) 472-6636
Admin Timothy A Johnson. *Dir of Nursing* Dorothy High. *Medical Dir* Barry H Henderson.
Licensure Intermediate care. *Beds* ICF 44. *Private Pay Patients* 30%. *Certified* Medicaid.
Owner Proprietary corp.
Admissions Requirements Minimum age 21; Medical examination; Physician's request.
Staff Physicians 1 (pt); RNs 1 (pt); LPNs 4 (ft), 2 (pt); Nurses' aides 8 (ft), 6 (pt); Activities coordinators 1 (ft).

Facilities Dining room; Activities room; Laundry room; Barber/Beauty shop.
Activities Arts & crafts; Games; Reading groups; Movies; Shopping trips; Pet therapy; Religious services.

Iva

Golden Acres Intermediate Care Facility
PO Box 505, Hampton St, Iva, SC 29655
(803) 348-7433
Admin Loneta Dunn. *Dir of Nursing* Nell T Strickland, Nurse consultant. *Medical Dir* Gregory Baird MD.
Licensure Intermediate care. *Beds* ICF 26. *Private Pay Patients* 10%. *Certified* Medicaid.
Owner Privately owned.
Staff RNs; LPNs; Nurses' aides; Activities coordinators.
Facilities Dining room; Activities room; Chapel; Crafts room; Laundry room; Barber/Beauty shop.
Activities Arts & crafts; Games; Reading groups; Prayer groups; Movies; Shopping trips.

Johns Island

Hermina Traeye Memorial Nursing Home
PO Box 689, 3627 Maybank Hwy, Johns Island, SC 29457
(803) 559-5505
Admin Mary F Brown. *Dir of Nursing* Sharon Moore. *Medical Dir* Allan Rashford MD.
Licensure Skilled care; Intermediate care. *Beds* SNF 44; ICF 44. *Private Pay Patients* 10%. *Certified* Medicaid; Medicare.
Owner Nonprofit corp.
Admissions Requirements Physician's request.
Staff Physicians 2 (pt); RNs 2 (ft), 1 (pt); LPNs 3 (ft), 7 (pt); Nurses' aides 26 (ft), 4 (pt); Physical therapists 1 (pt); Speech therapists 1 (pt); Activities coordinators 1 (ft); Dietitians 1 (pt).
Facilities Dining room; Physical therapy room; Activities room; Crafts room; Laundry room; Barber/Beauty shop.
Activities Arts & crafts; Games; Reading groups; Prayer groups; Movies; Shopping trips; Dances/Social/Cultural gatherings; Pet therapy.

Kingstree

Kingstree Community Residence
PO Box 820, 1037-B Lexington St, Kingstree, SC 29556
(803) 354-9670
Admin Brent Koyle.
Licensure Intermediate care for mentally retarded. *Beds* ICF/MR 14. *Certified* Medicaid; Medicare.
Owner Publicly owned.
Admissions Requirements Minimum age 45.
Staff Physicians 1 (pt); RNs 1 (pt); LPNs 2 (ft), 3 (pt); Physical therapists 1 (pt); Occupational therapists 1 (pt); Speech therapists 1 (pt); Dietitians 1 (pt); Dentists 1 (pt).
Activities Work skills; Training in ADL, mobility, community awareness.

Kingstree Nursing Facility Inc
PO Box 359, 110 Mill St, Kingstree, SC 29556
(803) 354-6116
Admin Carlyle Cooke.
Licensure Skilled care; Intermediate care. *Beds* ICF 26; Swing beds SNF/ICF 44. *Certified* Medicaid; Medicare.
Owner Proprietary corp.

Ladson

Coastal Center—Department of Mental Retardation
12 Jamison Rd, Ladson, SC 29456
(803) 873-5750
Admin Jackson S Howell Jr; Erbert F Cicenia. *Dir of Nursing* Mary Christensen RN. *Medical Dir* John D Fletcher MD.
Licensure Skilled care; Intermediate care; Intermediate care for mentally retarded. *Beds* ICF/MR 336; Swing beds SNF/ICF 53. *Certified* Medicaid.
Owner Publicly owned.
Admissions Requirements Medical examination.
Staff Physicians 2 (ft); RNs 18 (ft); LPNs 45 (ft); Nurses' aides 351 (ft); Physical therapists 1 (ft); Recreational therapists 12 (ft); Occupational therapists 2 (ft); Speech therapists 4 (ft); Dietitians 2 (ft); Mental retardation specialists.
Facilities Dining room; Physical therapy room; Activities room; Library; Gymnasium.
Activities Arts & crafts; Games; Movies; Shopping trips; Dances/Social/Cultural gatherings; Pony carts; Annual summer camp; Rhythm band; Chorus.

Lancaster

Lancaster County Care Center
Rte 10 Box 379, Hwy 9 E, Lancaster, SC 29720
(803) 285-7907
Admin Iris Ann Shehan. *Dir of Nursing* Frances Jones RN. *Medical Dir* Lee Thomas MD.
Licensure Skilled care; Intermediate care. *Beds* ICF 66; Swing beds SNF/ICF 44. *Certified* Medicaid; Medicare.
Owner Publicly owned.
Admissions Requirements Medical examination; Physician's request.
Staff Physicians 3 (pt); RNs 4 (ft); LPNs 12 (ft), 4 (pt); Nurses' aides 38 (ft), 12 (pt); Physical therapists 1 (pt); Activities coordinators 2 (ft); Dietitians 2 (pt).
Facilities Dining room; Physical therapy room; Activities room; Laundry room; Barber/Beauty shop.
Activities Arts & crafts; Games; Reading groups; Prayer groups; Movies; Shopping trips; Dances/Social/Cultural gatherings.

Tom Mangum Home
223 S Plantation Rd, Lancaster, SC 29720
(803) 286-5771
Admin Danny L Hinson.
Licensure Intermediate care for mentally retarded. *Beds* ICF/MR 8.
Owner Publicly owned.

Nancy J McConnell Home
219 S Plantation Rd, Lancaster, SC 29720
(803) 286-5727
Admin Danny L Hinson.
Licensure Intermediate care for mentally retarded. *Beds* ICF/MR 8.
Owner Publicly owned.

Marion Sims Nursing Center
800 W Meeting St, Lancaster, SC 29720
(803) 286-1481
Admin Dace W Jones Jr.
Licensure Skilled care; Intermediate care. *Beds* Swing beds SNF/ICF 111. *Certified* Medicaid; Medicare.

Laurens

Martha Franks Baptist Retirement Center
1 Martha Franks Dr, Laurens, SC 29360
(803) 984-4541
Admin Joe R Babb.
Medical Dir Linda B Nelson.

Licensure Skilled care; Retirement. *Beds* SNF 30.
Owner Nonprofit corp.
Admissions Requirements Minimum age 65; Medical examination; Must be ambulatory.
Staff Physicians; RNs; LPNs; Nurses' aides; Physical therapists.
Affiliation Baptist.
Facilities Dining room; Physical therapy room; Activities room; Chapel; Crafts room; Laundry room; Barber/Beauty shop; Library.
Activities Arts & crafts; Cards; Games; Prayer groups; Movies; Shopping trips.

Laurens Health Care Center
PO Box 1197, 301 Pinehaven St Ext, Laurens, SC 29360
(803) 984-6584
Admin Rickie L Shearer. *Dir of Nursing* Kathy W Cheely RN. *Medical Dir* Julian Atkinson MD.
Licensure Skilled care; Intermediate care; Alzheimer's care. *Beds* ICF 44; Swing beds SNF/ICF 88. *Certified* Medicaid; Medicare; VA.
Owner Proprietary corp (National Health Corp).
Admissions Requirements Minimum age 18; Medical examination; Physician's request.
Staff Physicians 12 (pt); RNs 4 (ft), 4 (pt); LPNs 9 (ft), 2 (pt); Nurses' aides 26 (ft), 3 (pt); Physical therapists 1 (pt); Speech therapists 1 (pt); Activities coordinators 1 (ft); Dietitians 1 (pt); Podiatrists 1 (pt).
Facilities Dining room; Physical therapy room; Activities room; Chapel; Crafts room; Laundry room; Barber/Beauty shop; Library.
Activities Arts & crafts; Games; Reading groups; Prayer groups; Movies; Shopping trips; Dances/Social/Cultural gatherings.

Oak Grove Community Residence
Rte 2 Box 1070, Old Laurens Rd, Laurens, SC 29360
(803) 682-9734
Admin Von Sinclair.
Licensure Intermediate care for mentally retarded. *Beds* ICF/MR 8.
Owner Publicly owned.

South Harper Street Community Residence
817 S Harper St, Laurens, SC 29360
(803) 682-5469
Admin Von Sinclair.
Licensure Intermediate care for mentally retarded. *Beds* ICF/MR 8.
Owner Publicly owned.

Lexington

Bruton Smith Road Group Home
PO Box 190, 139 Bruton Smith Rd, Lexington, SC 29072
(803) 359-9717
Admin Jon Bradford.
Licensure Intermediate care for mentally retarded. *Beds* ICF/MR 8.
Owner Proprietary corp.

Clusters of Lexington
201 Duffie Dr, Lexington, SC 29072
(803) 359-5018
Admin Ralph E Courtney.
Medical Dir Joann Bahelka.
Licensure Intermediate care for mentally retarded. *Beds* ICF/MR 48. *Certified* Medicare.
Owner Nonprofit corp.
Admissions Requirements Minimum age 18; Males only.
Staff Physicians 1 (pt); RNs 2 (pt); LPNs 5 (ft), 2 (pt); Physical therapists 1 (pt); Recreational therapists 2 (ft); Occupational therapists 1 (pt); Speech therapists 1 (ft); Dietitians 1 (pt); Podiatrists 1 (pt); Dentists 1 (pt); Mental retardation specialists.
Languages Sign.

Facilities Dining room; Activities room;
Laundry room.
Activities Arts & crafts; Cards; Games; Prayer
groups; Movies; Shopping trips; Dances/
Social/Cultural gatherings.

Hendrix Street Group Home
PO Box 190, 425 Hendrix St, Lexington, SC
29072
(803) 359-9717
Admin Jon Bradford.
Licensure Intermediate care for mentally
retarded. *Beds* ICF/MR.
Owner Proprietary corp.

**Rikard Nursing Homes—Keisler & Holstedt
Bldgs**
815 Old Cherokee Rd, Lexington, SC 29072
(803) 359-5181
Admin Joseph D Wright.
Licensure Skilled care; Intermediate care. *Beds*
Swing beds SNF/ICF 256. *Certified*
Medicaid; Medicare.

**Rikard Nursing Homes—Rikard Convalescent
Bldg**
815 Old Cherokee Rd, Lexington, SC 29072
(803) 359-5181
Admin J Melvin Ellis.
Licensure Skilled care; Intermediate care. *Beds*
ICF 44; Swing beds SNF/ICF 19. *Certified*
Medicaid; Medicare.

Loris

Loris Hospital Extended Care Facility
3655 Mitchell St, Loris, SC 29569
(803) 756-4011, 756-4126 FAX
Admin Frank M Watts. *Dir of Nursing*
Ovaline Barberousse RN. *Medical Dir*
William A Stout MD.
Licensure Skilled care; Intermediate care. *Beds*
Swing beds SNF/ICF 40. *Private Pay
Patients* 1%. *Certified* Medicaid; Medicare.
Owner Publicly owned.
Admissions Requirements Physician's request.
Staff Physicians 6 (ft); RNs 3 (ft); LPNs 6 (ft),
2 (pt); Nurses' aides 15 (ft), 2 (pt); Physical
therapists 1 (ft); Recreational therapists 1
(ft); Activities coordinators 1 (ft); Podiatrists
1 (ft).
Facilities Dining room; Activities room;
Laundry room; Barber/Beauty shop.
Activities Arts & crafts; Games; Shopping
trips.

Manning

Briggs Nursing Home
Rte 5 Box 665, Manning, SC 29102
(803) 478-2323
Admin Mary W McLeod.
Licensure Skilled care; Intermediate care. *Beds*
ICF 26; Swing beds SNF/ICF 38. *Certified*
Medicare.

Vanguard Residential Services Inc I
PO Box 159, 200 E Hospital St, Manning, SC
29102
(803) 435-4208
Admin R J Aycock III.
Licensure Intermediate care for mentally
retarded. *Beds* ICF/MR 8.
Owner Proprietary corp.

Vanguard Residential Services Inc II
PO Box 159, 512 S Church St, Manning, SC
29102
(803) 435-4208
Admin R J Aycock III.
Licensure Intermediate care for mentally
retarded. *Beds* ICF/MR 7.
Owner Proprietary corp.

Marietta

Stroud Memorial Nursing Home
PO Box 216, 2906 Greer Hwy, Marietta, SC
29661
(803) 836-6381
Admin Earlene G Jones. *Dir of Nursing* Sallie
Barren RN. *Medical Dir* Dr James E
Barnett.
Licensure Intermediate care; Retirement. *Beds*
ICF 44; Retirement 24. *Private Pay Patients*
2%. *Certified* Medicaid.
Owner Nonprofit organization/foundation.
Admissions Requirements Medical
examination.
Staff RNs 2 (ft); LPNs 4 (ft); Nurses' aides 10
(ft), 2 (pt); Activities coordinators 1 (ft), 1
(pt); Dietitians 1 (ft).
Facilities Dining room; Activities room;
Chapel; Crafts room; Laundry room; Barber/
Beauty shop; Library.
Activities Arts & crafts; Cards; Games;
Reading groups; Prayer groups; Movies; Pet
therapy.

Marion

Jenkins Nursing Home Inc
PO Box 917, 401 Murray St, Marion, SC
29571
(803) 423-6947
Admin Simon M Jenkins.
Licensure Skilled care; Intermediate care. *Beds*
ICF 16; Swing beds SNF/ICF 42. *Certified*
Medicaid; Medicare.

Marion County Convalescent Center
PO Drawer 1106, Hwy 501, Marion, SC
29571
(803) 423-2601
Admin Crystal H Isom.
Licensure Skilled care; Intermediate care. *Beds*
ICF 26; Swing beds SNF/ICF 62. *Certified*
Medicaid; Medicare.
Owner Proprietary corp (National Healthcare).

Moncks Corner

Berkeley Convalescent Center
PO Box 1467, 505 S Live Oak Dr, Moncks
Corner, SC 29461
(803) 899-5292
Admin Richard L Ellickson. *Dir of Nursing*
Jan Polkow RN. *Medical Dir* John Fletcher
MD.
Licensure Skilled care; Intermediate care. *Beds*
ICF 44; Swing beds SNF/ICF 88. *Certified*
Medicaid; Medicare.
Owner Proprietary corp.
Admissions Requirements Physician's request.
Facilities Dining room; Physical therapy
room; Activities room; Crafts room; Laundry
room; Barber/Beauty shop.
Activities Arts & crafts; Cards; Games;
Reading groups; Prayer groups; Movies;
Shopping trips; Dances/Social/Cultural
gatherings.

Mount Pleasant

Cooper Hall Nursing Center
921 Bowman Rd, Mount Pleasant, SC 29464
(803) 884-8903
Admin James B Connelly.
Medical Dir George G Durst Sr MD.
Licensure Skilled care; Intermediate care. *Beds*
Swing beds SNF/ICF 132. *Certified*
Medicaid; Medicare.
Owner Proprietary corp.
Admissions Requirements Medical
examination; Physician's request.
Staff Physicians 1 (pt); RNs 6 (ft), 3 (pt);
LPNs 8 (ft), 4 (pt); Nurses' aides 46 (ft);
Physical therapists 1 (pt); Recreational

therapists 1 (pt); Occupational therapists 1
(pt); Speech therapists 1 (pt); Activities
coordinators 2 (ft); Dietitians 1 (ft).
Facilities Dining room; Physical therapy
room; Activities room; Laundry room;
Barber/Beauty shop.
Activities Arts & crafts; Cards; Games;
Reading groups; Prayer groups; Movies;
Shopping trips; Dances/Social/Cultural
gatherings.

Sandpiper Convalescent Center
1049 Anna Knapp Blvd, Mount Pleasant, SC
29464
(803) 881-3210
Admin Phillip Waters.
Licensure Skilled care; Intermediate care. *Beds*
Swing beds SNF/ICF 132. *Certified*
Medicaid.

Myrtle Beach

Covenant Towers Health Care
5001 Little River Rd, Myrtle Beach, SC 29577
(803) 449-2484
Admin Mack Brown.
Licensure Skilled care; Intermediate care. *Beds*
Swing beds SNF/ICF 30.
Owner Proprietary corp.

Myrtle Beach Manor
9201 N Kings Hwy, Myrtle Beach, SC 29577
(803) 449-5283
Admin Juana C Newber.
Licensure Skilled care; Intermediate care. *Beds*
Swing beds SNF/ICF 50. *Certified* Medicaid;
Medicare.
Owner Proprietary corp (Forum Group).

New Ellenton

New Ellenton Geriatric Center Inc
412 Main St, New Ellenton, SC 29809
(803) 652-2230
Admin Pace B Hungerford.
Licensure Intermediate care. *Beds* ICF 26.
Certified Medicaid; Medicare.

Newberry

Jesse Frank Hawkins Nursing Home
1330 Kinard St, Newberry, SC 29108
(803) 276-2601
Admin Fred K Taylor MEd. *Dir of Nursing*
Debbie Lipscomb RN. *Medical Dir* James A
Underwood Jr MD.
Licensure Skilled care; Intermediate care. *Beds*
Swing beds SNF/ICF 78. *Private Pay
Patients* 33%. *Certified* Medicaid; Medicare.
Owner Nonprofit organization/foundation.
Admissions Requirements Medical
examination.
Staff RNs 4 (ft), 1 (pt); LPNs 7 (ft), 3 (pt);
Nurses' aides 40 (ft), 1 (pt); Activities
coordinators 1 (ft); Dietitians 1 (pt).
Facilities Dining room; Activities room;
Chapel; Crafts room; Laundry room; Barber/
Beauty shop.
Activities Arts & crafts; Cards; Games;
Reading groups; Prayer groups; Movies;
Intergenerational programs.

Newberry Convalescent Center
PO Box 754, 2555 Kinard St, Newberry, SC
29108
(803) 276-6060, 276-6061 FAX
Admin Jo Ann Willard. *Dir of Nursing* Vicki
S Ruff RN. *Medical Dir* Dr E E Epting Jr.
Licensure Skilled care; Intermediate care. *Beds*
SNF 44; ICF 18. *Private Pay Patients* 10%.
Certified Medicaid; Medicare.
Owner Proprietary corp (White Oak Manor).
Admissions Requirements Minimum age 18;
Medical examination; Physician's request.
Staff Physicians 6 (pt); RNs 2 (ft), 2 (pt);
LPNs 6 (ft), 1 (pt); Nurses' aides 28 (ft);
Physical therapists 1 (pt); Recreational

therapists 1 (ft); Speech therapists 1 (pt);
Activities coordinators 1 (ft); Dietitians 1
(ft); Ophthalmologists 1 (pt).
Facilities Dining room; Activities room;
Crafts room; Laundry room; Barber/Beauty
shop.
Activities Arts & crafts; Cards; Games;
Reading groups; Prayer groups; Movies;
Shopping trips; Dances/Social/Cultural
gatherings; Intergenerational programs.

North Augusta

Anne Maria Medical Care Nursing Home Inc
1200 Talisman Dr, North Augusta, SC 29841
(803) 278-2170, 442-9344 FAX
Admin Marianne Luckey. *Dir of Nursing*
Annette Hobbs RN. *Medical Dir* Dr
Browning McRee; Dr Hy Sussman.
Licensure Skilled care; Intermediate care. *Beds*
Swing beds SNF/ICF 120. *Private Pay
Patients* 25%. *Certified* Medicaid; Medicare.
Owner Proprietary corp.
Admissions Requirements Medical
examination.
Staff Physicians 2 (ft); RNs 6 (ft); LPNs 14
(ft); Nurses' aides 53 (ft); Physical therapists
1 (ft); Reality therapists 1 (ft); Recreational
therapists 1 (ft); Speech therapists 1 (pt);
Activities coordinators 1 (ft); Dietitians 2
(ft); Podiatrists 1 (pt); Audiologists 1 (pt).
Facilities Dining room; Physical therapy
room; Activities room; Chapel; Crafts room;
Laundry room; Barber/Beauty shop; Library;
Ventilator unit; 2 courtyards.
Activities Arts & crafts; Cards; Games;
Reading groups; Prayer groups; Movies;
Shopping trips; Dances/Social/Cultural
gatherings; Pet therapy.

Orangeburg

Boulevard Community Residence
612 Boulevard St, Orangeburg, SC 29115
(803) 536-1361
Admin Sandra Gingrich RN.
Licensure Intermediate care for mentally
retarded. *Beds* ICF/MR 8. *Certified*
Medicaid.
Owner Publicly owned.
Admissions Requirements Minimum age 15;
Females only.
Staff Physicians 1 (pt); RNs 1 (ft); LPNs 2
(ft); Nurses' aides 3 (ft), 3 (pt); Physical
therapists 1 (pt); Recreational therapists 1
(ft); Occupational therapists 1 (pt); Speech
therapists 1 (pt); Activities coordinators 1
(ft); Dietitians 1 (pt); Ophthalmologists 1
(pt); Podiatrists 1 (pt); Dentists 1 (pt).
Facilities Dining room; Laundry room.
Activities Arts & crafts; Games; Movies;
Shopping trips; Dances/Social/Cultural
gatherings.

Edisto Convalescent Center
575 Stonewall Jackson Blvd SW, Orangeburg,
SC 29115
(803) 534-7771
Admin Ervin A Green. *Dir of Nursing* Betty O
Green. *Medical Dir* Dr Hyman Marcus.
Licensure Skilled care; Intermediate care;
Residential care. *Beds* SNF 70; ICF 43;
Residential care 17. *Private Pay Patients*
32%. *Certified* Medicaid; Medicare.
Owner Privately owned.
Admissions Requirements Medical
examination; Physician's request.
Staff RNs 5 (ft), 1 (pt); LPNs 6 (ft), 2 (pt);
Nurses' aides 30 (ft), 15 (pt); Activities
coordinators 2 (ft); Dietitians 1 (pt);
Pharmacists 1 (pt); Social services
(consultant).
Facilities Dining room; Physical therapy
room; Activities room; Crafts room; Laundry
room; Barber/Beauty shop; Library.

Activities Arts & crafts; Cards; Games;
Reading groups; Prayer groups; Movies;
Shopping trips; Dances/Social/Cultural
gatherings; Pet therapy.

Jolley Acres Nursing Home
PO Drawer 1909, 1180 Wolfe Trail,
Orangeburg, SC 29116
(803) 534-1001
Admin Deana Houser.
Licensure Skilled care; Intermediate care. *Beds*
Swing beds SNF/ICF 43. *Certified* Medicaid;
Medicare.
Owner Proprietary corp.

Methodist Home
PO Drawer 327, Hwy 215, Orangeburg, SC
29116
(803) 534-1212
Admin David D Phillips.
Medical Dir Vann Beth Shuler MD; James
Brunson MD.
Licensure Skilled care; Intermediate care;
Retirement. *Beds* ICF 80; Swing beds SNF/
ICF 52. *Certified* Medicaid; Medicare.
Owner Nonprofit organization/foundation.
Admissions Requirements Minimum age 62;
Medical examination.
Staff Physicians; RNs; LPNs; Nurses' aides;
Physical therapists; Reality therapists;
Recreational therapists; Occupational
therapists; Speech therapists; Activities
coordinators; Dietitians; Ophthalmologists;
Podiatrists; Dentists.
Affiliation Methodist.
Facilities Dining room; Physical therapy
room; Activities room; Chapel; Crafts room;
Laundry room; Barber/Beauty shop; Library.
Activities Arts & crafts; Cards; Games;
Reading groups; Prayer groups; Movies;
Shopping trips; Dances/Social/Cultural
gatherings.

Orangeburg Nursing Home Inc
755 Whitman SE, Orangeburg, SC 29115
(803) 534-7036
Admin Catherine D Young.
Medical Dir W O Whetsell MD.
Licensure Skilled care; Intermediate care. *Beds*
Swing beds SNF/ICF 88. *Certified* Medicaid;
Medicare.
Admissions Requirements Medical
examination; Physician's request.
Staff Physicians 5 (pt); RNs 4 (ft), 5 (pt);
LPNs 3 (ft), 4 (pt); Nurses' aides 23 (ft), 7
(pt); Physical therapists 1 (pt); Speech
therapists 1 (pt); Activities coordinators 1
(ft); Dietitians 1 (pt); Dentists 1 (pt).
Facilities Dining room; Laundry room;
Barber/Beauty shop.
Activities Arts & crafts; Cards; Games;
Reading groups; Prayer groups; Movies;
Shopping trips; Dances/Social/Cultural
gatherings.

Sifly Street Community Residence
PO Box 1812, 930 Sifly St, Orangeburg, SC
29116
(803) 536-1170
Admin Hester Wannamaker.
Licensure Intermediate care for mentally
retarded. *Beds* ICF/MR 8.
Owner Publicly owned.

Wannamaker Street Community Residence
PO Box 1812, 250 Wannamaker St,
Orangeburg, SC 29116
(803) 536-1170
Admin Hester Wannamaker.
Licensure Intermediate care for mentally
retarded. *Beds* ICF/MR 8.
Owner Proprietary corp.

Pageland

Pageland Community Residence
PO Box 6, 509 Sycamore St, Pageland, SC
29728
(803) 672-7905
Admin Margaret W Davis.
Licensure Intermediate care for mentally
retarded. *Beds* ICF/MR 8.
Owner Publicly owned.

Pickens

Laurel Hill Health Care
601 E Cedar Rock St, Pickens, SC 29671
(803) 878-4739
Admin Mary Reid. *Dir of Nursing* Christine
Wood. *Medical Dir* David W Mauldin.
Licensure Skilled care; Intermediate care. *Beds*
Swing beds SNF/ICF 80. *Private Pay
Patients* 30%. *Certified* Medicaid; Medicare.
Owner Proprietary corp.
Admissions Requirements Medical
examination; Physician's request.
Staff RNs 3 (ft), 1 (pt); LPNs 9 (ft), 3 (pt);
Nurses' aides 30 (ft), 12 (pt); Physical
therapists 1 (pt); Occupational therapists 1
(pt); Speech therapists 1 (pt); Activities
coordinators 1 (ft); Dietitians 1 (ft);
Podiatrists 1 (pt).
Facilities Dining room; Physical therapy
room; Activities room; Chapel; Crafts room;
Laundry room; Barber/Beauty shop.
Activities Arts & crafts; Cards; Games;
Reading groups; Prayer groups; Movies;
Dances/Social/Cultural gatherings.

McKinney Intermediate Care Facility
PO Box 895, 113 Rosemond St, Pickens, SC
29671
(803) 878-9620
Admin Iris L Robinson.
Licensure Intermediate care. *Beds* ICF 44.
Certified Medicaid; Medicare.
Owner Publicly owned.

Port Royal

Port Royal Community Residence
1508 Old Shell Rd, Port Royal, SC 29935
(803) 524-3001
Admin Susan C Long.
Licensure Intermediate care for mentally
retarded. *Beds* ICF/MR 16. *Certified*
Medicaid.
Owner Publicly owned.
Admissions Requirements Minimum age 17;
Medical examination; Physician's request;
Certification as MR.
Staff Physicians 1 (pt); RNs 1 (pt); LPNs 2
(ft); Speech therapists 1 (pt); Dietitians 1
(pt); Podiatrists 1 (pt); MRS Psychologist 1
(pt).
Facilities Dining room; Activities room;
Laundry room.
Activities Arts & crafts; Games; Shopping
trips; Dances/Social/Cultural gatherings; Skill
training.

Ridgeland

Ridgecrest Convalescent Center
PO Box 1570, Hwy 278, Ridgeland, SC 29936
(803) 726-5581
Admin Faye Cleland.
Licensure Skilled care; Intermediate care. *Beds*
Swing beds SNF/ICF 88. *Certified* Medicaid;
Medicare.

Ridgeway

Fairfield Homes
PO Drawer 157, Longtown Rd, Ridgeway, SC
29130
(803) 337-2257
Admin Annette B Cooper.

Licensure Skilled care; Intermediate care. *Beds* ICF 44; Swing beds SNF/ICF 68. *Certified* Medicaid; Medicare.

Tanglewood Health Care Center
PO Box 68, Third Rd, Ridgeway, SC 29130
(803) 337-3211
Admin Doris M Singley. *Dir of Nursing* Pattie Jones. *Medical Dir* Julius Campbell MD.
Licensure Skilled care; Intermediate care; Alzheimer's care. *Beds* ICF 107; Swing beds SNF/ICF 43. *Certified* Medicaid; Medicare; VA.
Owner Proprietary corp (Pruitt Corp).
Admissions Requirements Medical examination; Physician's request.
Staff Physicians; RNs; LPNs; Nurses' aides; Physical therapists (contracted); Recreational therapists (contracted); Occupational therapists (contracted); Speech therapists (contracted); Activities coordinators; Dietitians (contracted); Podiatrists (contracted).
Facilities Dining room; Physical therapy room; Activities room; Chapel; Laundry room; Barber/Beauty shop; Family room.
Activities Arts & crafts; Games; Reading groups; Prayer groups; Movies; Shopping trips; Dances/Social/Cultural gatherings; Pet therapy.

Rock Hill

Dowdy Gardner Nursing Care Center
101 Sedgewood Dr, Rock Hill, SC 29730
(803) 329-6500
Admin Douglas L Shuman.
Licensure Skilled care; Intermediate care. *Beds* ICF 88; Swing beds SNF/ICF 132.
Owner Publicly owned.

Ebenezer Nursing Home
111 Sedgewood Dr, Rock Hill, SC 29730
(803) 329-6565
Admin Jack Fallaw.
Licensure Skilled care; Intermediate care. *Beds* Swing beds SNF/ICF 37.
Owner Proprietary corp.

Magnolia Manor
127 Murrah Dr, Rock Hill, SC 29732
(803) 328-6518, 327-4638 FAX
Admin Brenda H Parris. *Dir of Nursing* Denise P Black. *Medical Dir* Eric Johnson MD.
Licensure Skilled care; Intermediate care. *Beds* SNF 44; ICF 62. *Private Pay Patients* 50%. *Certified* Medicaid; Medicare.
Owner Privately owned.
Admissions Requirements Minimum age 13; Medical examination; Physician's request.
Staff Physicians; RNs 5 (ft); LPNs 9 (ft), 6 (pt); Nurses' aides 34 (ft), 6 (pt); Physical therapists (contracted); Recreational therapists 2 (ft); Speech therapists (contracted); Activities coordinators 2 (ft); Dietitians (contracted); Ophthalmologists (contracted); Podiatrists (contracted); Audiologists (contracted).
Facilities Dining room; Activities room; Crafts room; Laundry room; Barber/Beauty shop; Library; Family room.
Activities Arts & crafts; Cards; Games; Reading groups; Prayer groups; Movies; Shopping trips; Dances/Social/Cultural gatherings; Intergenerational programs; Pet therapy; Sensory stimulation; Music therapy.

Magnolia Manor North
PO Box 3172-CRS, 127 Murrah Dr, Rock Hill, SC 29730
(803) 328-6518
Admin Brendon H Parris. *Dir of Nursing* Patricia Blanton.
Licensure Skilled care; Intermediate care. *Beds* ICF 62; Swing beds SNF/ICF 44. *Certified* Medicaid.
Owner Proprietary corp.

Admissions Requirements Minimum age 18; Medical examination; Physician's request.
Staff RNs 1 (pt); LPNs 6 (ft), 6 (pt); Nurses' aides 20 (ft), 12 (pt); Physical therapists 1 (pt); Recreational therapists 1 (pt); Occupational therapists 1 (pt); Speech therapists 1 (pt); Activities coordinators 1 (ft); Dietitians 1 (pt); Ophthalmologists 1 (pt).
Facilities Dining room; Physical therapy room; Activities room; Crafts room; Laundry room; Barber/Beauty shop.
Activities Arts & crafts; Cards; Games; Prayer groups; Movies; Shopping trips; Dances/Social/Cultural gatherings.

Marett Boulevard Community Residence
1723 Marett Blvd, Rock Hill, SC 29230
(803) 359-9717
Admin Risley E Linder.
Licensure Intermediate care for mentally retarded. *Beds* ICF/MR 8.
Owner Publicly owned.

Meadow Haven Nursing Center
PO Box 4478, 205 S Herlong Ave, Rock Hill, SC 29731
(803) 366-7133
Admin James J Burke. *Dir of Nursing* Lois Cox. *Medical Dir* J Luke Lentz.
Licensure Skilled care; Intermediate care. *Beds* ICF 88; Swing beds SNF/ICF 44. *Certified* Medicaid; Medicare.
Owner Proprietary corp (Beverly Enterprises).
Admissions Requirements Medical examination.
Facilities Dining room; Physical therapy room; Activities room; Crafts room; Laundry room; Barber/Beauty shop.
Activities Arts & crafts; Cards; Games; Reading groups; Prayer groups; Movies; Shopping trips; Dances/Social/Cultural gatherings.

Meadowlark Community Residence
PO Box 3817, Cola, 1183 Meadowlark Dr, Rock Hill, SC 29230
(803) 359-9717
Admin Risley E Linder.
Licensure Intermediate care for mentally retarded. *Beds* ICF/MR 8.
Owner Publicly owned.

Rock Hill Convalescent Center Inc
1915 Ebenezer Rd, Rock Hill, SC 29730
(803) 366-8155
Admin Amanda K Ashley. *Dir of Nursing* Sharlene Plyler RN. *Medical Dir* Dr Robert Patton.
Licensure Skilled care; Intermediate care. *Beds* Swing beds SNF/ICF 141. *Certified* Medicaid; Medicare.
Owner Proprietary corp (White Oak Manor).
Staff RNs 4 (ft), 2 (pt); LPNs 15 (ft), 1 (pt); Nurses' aides 51 (ft), 10 (pt); Physical therapists 2 (ft); Activities coordinators 1 (ft); Dietitians 1 (ft).
Facilities Dining room; Physical therapy room; Activities room; Laundry room; Barber/Beauty shop.
Activities Arts & crafts; Cards; Games; Reading groups; Prayer groups; Movies; Shopping trips; Dances/Social/Cultural gatherings.

Saint George

St George Health Care Center Inc
PO Box 187, 905 Dukes St, Saint George, SC 29477
(803) 563-4602
Admin William M Rogers Sr.
Licensure Skilled care; Intermediate care. *Beds* Swing beds SNF/ICF 88. *Certified* Medicaid.

Saint Matthews

Florence Gressette Residence
Rte 1 Box 31, 401 Milligan St, Saint Matthews, SC 29030
(803) 655-7585
Admin Anita G Linder.
Licensure Intermediate care for mentally retarded. *Beds* ICF/MR 8.
Owner Publicly owned.

Wylie-Brunson Residence
401 Milligan St, Saint Matthews, SC 29030
(803) 655-7559
Admin Risley E Linder.
Licensure Intermediate care for mentally retarded. *Beds* ICF/MR 8.
Owner Proprietary corp.

Saluda

Saluda Nursing Center
PO Box 398, Hwy 121, Saluda, SC 29138
(803) 445-2146
Admin Robert F Bowles.
Medical Dir Robert L Sawyer MD.
Licensure Skilled care; Intermediate care. *Beds* SNF 44; Swing beds SNF/ICF 88. *Certified* Medicaid; Medicare.
Owner Nonprofit organization/foundation.
Admissions Requirements Minimum age 14; Medical examination.
Staff Physicians 3 (ft); RNs 5 (ft), 4 (pt); LPNs 14 (ft); Nurses' aides 52 (ft), 2 (pt); Activities coordinators 2 (ft), 1 (pt).
Facilities Dining room; Physical therapy room; Activities room; Chapel; Crafts room; Laundry room; Barber/Beauty shop.
Activities Arts & crafts; Cards; Games; Reading groups; Prayer groups; Movies; Shopping trips; Dances/Social/Cultural gatherings.

Scranton

Lake City-Scranton Convalescent Center
PO Box 9, 9 Highhill Rd, Scranton, SC 29591
(803) 389-9201
Admin Laura Craft.
Licensure Skilled care; Intermediate care. *Beds* Swing beds SNF/ICF 88.
Owner Proprietary corp.

Seneca

Lila Doyle Nursing Care Facility
PO Box 858, Hwy 123, Seneca, SC 29678
(803) 882-3351
Admin W H Hudson.
Medical Dir D A Richardson MD.
Licensure Skilled care; Intermediate care. *Beds* ICF 39; Swing beds SNF/ICF 40. *Certified* Medicaid; Medicare.
Staff Physicians 20 (pt); RNs 3 (ft), 6 (pt); LPNs 9 (ft), 3 (pt); Nurses' aides 26 (ft), 9 (pt); Physical therapists 2 (pt); Activities coordinators 1 (ft); Dietitians 1 (ft).
Facilities Dining room; Physical therapy room; Activities room; Chapel; Crafts room; Barber/Beauty shop; Library.
Activities Arts & crafts; Cards; Games; Reading groups; Prayer groups; Movies; Shopping trips.

Oconee Community Residence No 1
Hwy 188, 330 Keowee School Rd, Seneca, SC 29678
(803) 882-2126
Admin Vickie A Thompson.
Licensure Intermediate care for mentally retarded. *Beds* ICF/MR 16. *Certified* Medicare.
Owner Publicly owned.

Oconee Community Residence No 2
Hwy 188, 350 Keowee School Rd, Seneca, SC 29678
(803) 882-7637
Admin Vickie A Thompson.
Licensure Intermediate care for mentally retarded. *Beds* ICF/MR 8.
Owner Publicly owned.

Pinnacle Care of Seneca
PO Box 189, Hwy 59 Rte 6, Seneca, SC 29679
(803) 882-1642
Admin Mark Bolding. *Dir of Nursing* Pam Smith RN. *Medical Dir* J R Hanahan Jr MD.
Licensure Skilled care; Intermediate care. *Beds* SNF 88; ICF 44. *Private Pay Patients* 20%. *Certified* Medicaid; Medicare.
Owner Proprietary corp (Pinnacle Care Corp).
Admissions Requirements Minimum age 18; Medical examination; Physician's request.
Staff RNs 4 (ft), 2 (pt); LPNs 12 (ft), 3 (pt); Nurses' aides 40 (ft), 5 (pt); Physical therapists 1 (ft); Occupational therapists 1 (ft); Speech therapists 1 (pt); Activities coordinators 1 (ft); Dietitians 1 (ft).
Languages Interpreters available for Spanish, French and Slavic languages.
Facilities Dining room; Physical therapy room; Activities room; Barber/Beauty shop.
Activities Arts & crafts; Cards; Games; Reading groups; Prayer groups; Movies; Dances/Social/Cultural gatherings.

Simpsonville

Palmetto Convalescent Center
721 W Curtis, Simpsonville, SC 29681
(803) 967-7191
Admin Otis Ridgeway Jr. *Dir of Nursing* Hilga Longino. *Medical Dir* Jim Richardson MD.
Licensure Intermediate care. *Beds* ICF 42. *Private Pay Patients* 8%. *Certified* Medicaid.
Owner Privately owned.
Staff Physicians; RNs; LPNs; Nurses' aides; Physical therapists (contracted); Reality therapists (contracted); Recreational therapists; Occupational therapists; Speech therapists (contracted); Activities coordinators; Dietitians; Ophthalmologists; Podiatrists.
Languages German, Spanish.
Activities Arts & crafts; Cards; Games; Reading groups; Prayer groups; Movies; Shopping trips; Dances/Social/Cultural gatherings; Intergenerational programs; Pet therapy.

Sentry Care Simpsonville Inc
807 SE Main St, Simpsonville, SC 29681
(803) 963-6069
Admin Debbie Lollis.
Licensure Skilled care; Intermediate care. *Beds* Swing beds SNF/ICF 88.
Owner Proprietary corp.

Six Mile

Harvey's Love & Care Inc
PO Box 160, Six Mile, SC 29682
(803) 868-2307
Admin Helen D Towe. *Dir of Nursing* Ann Shock RN. *Medical Dir* Dr David Mauldin.
Licensure Intermediate care. *Beds* ICF 40. *Certified* Medicaid.
Owner Privately owned.
Admissions Requirements Medical examination.
Staff RNs 1 (ft), 1 (pt); LPNs 2 (ft), 3 (pt); Nurses' aides 4 (ft), 6 (pt); Podiatrists (contracted).
Facilities Dining room; Activities room; Chapel; Crafts room; Laundry room; Barber/Beauty shop; Library.
Activities Arts & crafts; Games; Reading groups; Prayer groups; Movies; Dances/Social/Cultural gatherings; Pet therapy.

Spartanburg

Benchmark Home: Spartanburg
450 W Henry St, Spartanburg, SC 29301
(803) 585-0322, 571-0780 FAX
Admin Loren Libby. *Dir of Nursing* Joyce Briggs RN. *Medical Dir* Omri Kenneth Webb MD.
Licensure Intermediate care for mentally retarded; Supervised apartment living. *Beds* ICF/MR 12. *Certified* Medicaid.
Owner Nonprofit corp (Charles Lea Center).
Admissions Requirements Minimum age 13; Medical examination; Physician's request; Admissions are through Case Management recommendations.
Staff Physicians 1 (pt); RNs 1 (ft); LPNs 2 (ft); Physical therapists 1 (pt); Recreational therapists 1 (ft); Occupational therapists 1 (pt); Speech therapists 1 (pt); Dietitians 1 (pt); Audiologists 1 (pt); Direct care 9 (ft); Dentists 1 (pt); Pharmacists 1 (pt); Psychologists 1 (ft); Medical records administrators 1 (pt); QMRPs 1 (ft).
Facilities Dining room; Activities room; Laundry room.
Activities Arts & crafts; Cards; Games; Movies; Shopping trips; Dances/Social/Cultural gatherings; Sheltered workshop employment; Access to community resources; Independent living skills training.

Benchmark Homes—Cowpens
195 Burdette St, Spartanburg, SC 29302
(803) 585-0322
Admin Roy B Williams.
Licensure Intermediate care for mentally retarded. *Beds* ICF/MR 12.
Owner Proprietary corp.

Ferguson Community Residence No 1
123 Park Ave, Spartanburg, SC 29302
(803) 585-0322, 591-0780 FAX
Admin Loren Libby. *Dir of Nursing* Joyce Briggs RN. *Medical Dir* H Griffin Cupstid MD.
Licensure Intermediate care for mentally retarded; Supervised apartment living. *Beds* ICF/MR 8. *Certified* Medicaid.
Owner Publicly owned.
Admissions Requirements Minimum age 13; Males only; Medical examination; Physician's request; Recommendation of Case Management & the Interdisciplinary Admission Committee at Charles Lea Center.
Staff Physicians 1 (pt); RNs 1 (ft); LPNs 2 (ft); Physical therapists 1 (pt); Recreational therapists 1 (ft); Occupational therapists 1 (pt); Speech therapists 1 (pt); Dietitians 1 (pt); Audiologists 1 (pt); Direct care 9 (ft); Dentists 1 (pt); Pharmacists 1 (pt); Psychologists 1 (ft); Medical records administrators 1 (ft); QMRPs 1 (ft).
Facilities Dining room; Activities room; Laundry room.
Activities Arts & crafts; Cards; Games; Movies; Shopping trips; Dances/Social/Cultural gatherings; Sheltered workshop employment; Access to all community resources.

Ferguson Community Residence No 2
125 Park Ave, Spartanburg, SC 29302
(803) 585-0322, 591-0780 FAX
Admin Loren Libby. *Dir of Nursing* Joyce Briggs RN. *Medical Dir* H Griffin Cupstid MD.
Licensure Intermediate care for mentally retarded; Supervised apartment living. *Beds* ICF/MR 8. *Certified* Medicaid.
Owner Publicly owned.
Admissions Requirements Minimum age 13; Females only; Medical examination; Physician's request; Recommedation of Case Management & the Interdisciplinary Admission Committee at Charles Lea Center.

Staff Physicians 1 (pt); RNs 1 (ft); LPNs 2 (ft); Physical therapists 1 (pt); Recreational therapists 1 (ft); Occupational therapists 1 (pt); Speech therapists 1 (pt); Dietitians 1 (pt); Audiologists 1 (pt); Direct care 8 (ft); Dentists 1 (pt); Pharmacists 1 (pt); Psychologists 1 (ft); Medical records administrators 1 (ft); QMRPs 1 (ft).
Facilities Dining room; Activities room; Laundry room.
Activities Arts & crafts; Cards; Games; Movies; Shopping trips; Dances/Social/Cultural gatherings; Sheltered workshop employment; Access to all community resources.

Mountainview Nursing Home
340 Cedar Springs Rd, Spartanburg, SC 29302
(803) 582-4175
Admin Wilson K Dillard.
Licensure Skilled care; Intermediate care. *Beds* ICF 44; Swing beds SNF/ICF 88. *Certified* Medicaid; Medicare.

Pinewood Convalescent Center
PO Box 4127, Pinewood Station, 375 Serpentine Dr, Spartanburg, SC 29303
(803) 585-0218
Admin Geraldine G Finch. *Dir of Nursing* Shirley Kinsland RN. *Medical Dir* Warren C Lovett MD.
Licensure Skilled care; Intermediate care. *Beds* Swing beds SNF/ICF 95. *Certified* Medicaid; Medicare.
Owner Proprietary corp (Service Management Inc).
Admissions Requirements Minimum age 12; Physician's request.
Staff Physicians 1 (ft), 18 (pt); RNs 5 (ft), 4 (pt); LPNs 8 (ft), 3 (pt); Nurses' aides 34 (ft); Physical therapists 1 (pt); Reality therapists 1 (ft), 1 (pt); Recreational therapists 1 (pt); Occupational therapists 1 (pt); Speech therapists 1 (pt); Activities coordinators 1 (ft), 1 (pt); Dietitians 1 (ft); Ophthalmologists 1 (pt); Podiatrists 1 (pt).
Facilities Dining room; Physical therapy room; Activities room; Crafts room; Laundry room; Barber/Beauty shop; Bookmobile.
Activities Arts & crafts; Games; Reading groups; Prayer groups; Movies; Shopping trips.

Skyln Health Center
1705 Skyln Dr, Spartanburg, SC 29302
(803) 582-6838
Admin Gary D Catlett.
Licensure Skilled care. *Beds* SNF 22.
Owner Proprietary corp.

Spartanburg Community Residence Unit 1
29 Long St, Spartanburg, SC 29302
(803) 585-0322, 591-0780 FAX
Admin Loren L Libby. *Dir of Nursing* Joyce Briggs RN. *Medical Dir* Joseph R Hames MD.
Licensure Intermediate care for mentally retarded; Supervised apartment living. *Beds* ICF/MR 15. *Certified* Medicaid.
Owner Publicly owned.
Admissions Requirements Minimum age 13; Medical examination; Physician's request; Recommendation from Case Management & the Interdisciplinary Admissions Committee at Charles Lee Center.
Staff Physicians (contracted); RNs 1 (ft); LPNs 2 (ft); Physical therapists (contracted); Recreational therapists 1 (ft); Occupational therapists (contracted); Speech therapists (contracted); Dietitians (contracted); Audiologists (contracted); Direct care 16 (ft); Dentists (contracted); Pharmacists (contracted); Psychologists 1 (ft); Medical records administrators (contracted); QMRPs (contracted).

Facilities Dining room; Activities room; Laundry room.
Activities Arts & crafts; Cards; Games; Movies; Shopping trips; Dances/Social/Cultural gatherings; Sheltered workshop employment; Access to community resources.

Spartanburg Community Residence Unit 2
29 Long St, Spartanburg, SC 29302
(803) 585-0322, 591-0780 FAX
Admin Loren L Libby. *Dir of Nursing* Joyce Briggs RN. *Medical Dir* Joseph R Hames MD.
Licensure Intermediate care for mentally retarded; Supervised apartment living. *Beds* ICF/MR 15. *Certified* Medicaid.
Owner Publicly owned (South Carolina Department Mental Retardation).
Admissions Requirements Minimum age 13; Medical examination; Physician's request; Recommendation from Case Management & the Interdisciplinary Admissions Committee at Charles Lee Center.
Staff Physicians (contracted); RNs 1 (ft); LPNs 2 (ft); Physical therapists (contracted); Recreational therapists 1 (ft); Occupational therapists (contracted); Speech therapists (contracted); Dietitians (contracted); Audiologists (contracted); Direct care 13 (ft); Dentists (contracted); Pharmacists (contracted); Psychologists 1 (ft); Medical records administrators (contracted); QMRPs 1 (ft).
Facilities Dining room; Activities room; Laundry room.
Activities Arts & crafts; Cards; Games; Movies; Shopping trips; Dances/Social/Cultural gatherings; Sheltered workshop employment; Access to all community resources.

Spartanburg Convalescent Center Inc
295 E Pearl St, Spartanburg, SC 29303
(803) 585-0241
Admin Barbara H Adams. *Dir of Nursing* Millie Stein. *Medical Dir* Mark Knipfer.
Licensure Skilled care; Intermediate care; Adult medical day care; Alzheimer's care. *Beds* SNF 148; ICF 44; Adult Medical day care 20. *Private Pay Patients* 47%. *Certified* Medicaid; Medicare.
Owner Proprietary corp (White Oak Manor Inc).
Admissions Requirements Minimum age 18; Medical examination; Physician's request.
Staff Physicians 3 (pt); RNs 3 (ft), 5 (pt); LPNs 13 (ft), 8 (pt); Nurses' aides 65 (ft), 10 (pt); Physical therapists 2 (pt); Occupational therapists 1 (pt); Speech therapists 1 (pt); Activities coordinators 4 (ft), 1 (pt); Dietitians 1 (ft), 2 (pt); Podiatrists 1 (pt).
Facilities Dining room; Physical therapy room; Activities room; Crafts room; Laundry room; Barber/Beauty shop.
Activities Arts & crafts; Cards; Games; Reading groups; Prayer groups; Movies; Shopping trips; Dances/Social/Cultural gatherings; Intergenerational programs; Pet therapy; Augmentative communication therapy.

Valley Falls Terrace
223 Smith Rd, Spartanburg, SC 29303
(803) 585-2523
Admin Charles C Cecil.
Medical Dir Dr Barry Henderson.
Licensure Skilled care; Intermediate care. *Beds* Swing beds SNF/ICF 52. *Certified* Medicaid; Medicare; VA.
Owner Proprietary corp.
Admissions Requirements Minimum age 18; Medical examination; Physician's request.
Staff Physicians 1 (ft); RNs 2 (ft), 1 (pt); Nurses' aides 16 (ft), 7 (pt); Physical therapists 1 (pt); Speech therapists 1 (pt);

Activities coordinators 1 (ft); Dietitians 1 (ft), 1 (pt); Ophthalmologists 1 (pt); Dentists 1 (pt).
Facilities Dining room; Activities room; Crafts room.
Activities Arts & crafts; Cards; Games; Reading groups; Prayer groups; Movies; Dances/Social/Cultural gatherings.

White Oak Estates
400 Webber Rd, Spartanburg, SC 29304
(803) 582-7503
Admin B Terrell Ball.
Licensure Skilled care; Intermediate care. *Beds* Swing beds SNF/ICF 44.
Owner Proprietary corp (White Oak Manor Inc).

Summerville

Oakbrook Convalescent Center
920 Travelers Blvd, Summerville, SC 29483
(803) 875-9053
Admin Patricia H Gerwig.
Licensure Skilled care; Intermediate care. *Beds* Swing beds SNF/ICF 88.
Owner Proprietary corp.

Parsons I Group Home
707 Parsons St, Summerville, SC 29483
(803) 821-2876
Admin Risley E Linder.
Licensure Intermediate care for mentally retarded. *Beds* ICF/MR 8.
Owner Proprietary corp.

Parsons II Group Home
711 Parsons St, Summerville, SC 29483
(803) 821-2876
Admin Risley E Linder.
Licensure Intermediate care for mentally retarded. *Beds* ICF/MR 8.
Owner Proprietary corp.

Presbyterian Home of South Carolina—Summerville
CMR Box 140, 9 North St, Summerville, SC 29483
(803) 873-2550
Admin Keith D Stewart.
Licensure Skilled care. *Beds* SNF 90.
Owner Nonprofit corp.
Affiliation Presbyterian.

Sumter

Community Intermediate Care Facility
PO Box 6051, 703 Broad St, Sumter, SC 29150
(803) 773-6525
Admin Harold Hallums. *Dir of Nursing* Catherine D Davis. *Medical Dir* Brenda William MD.
Licensure Intermediate care. *Beds* ICF 20. *Private Pay Patients* 0%. *Certified* Medicaid.
Owner Nonprofit corp.
Admissions Requirements Medical examination; Physician's request.
Staff Physicians; LPNs 3 (ft), 2 (pt); Nurses' aides 5 (ft), 2 (pt); Activities coordinators 1 (ft).
Facilities Dining room; Activities room; Chapel; Crafts room; Laundry room.
Activities Arts & crafts; Games; Reading groups; Prayer groups; Movies; Shopping trips; Dances/Social/Cultural gatherings; Religious activities; Volunteer program; Community involvement.

Cypress Nursing Facility Inc
PO Box 1526, Carolina Ave, Sumter, SC 29151
(803) 775-5394
Admin Donna B Davis. *Dir of Nursing* Pat Boykin RN. *Medical Dir* R Lee Denny MD.
Licensure Skilled care. *Beds* SNF 88. *Certified* Medicaid; Medicare.
Owner Proprietary corp.

Admissions Requirements Minimum age 18; Medical examination.
Staff RNs 3 (ft); LPNs 10 (ft); Nurses' aides 26 (ft), 6 (pt); Physical therapists 2 (pt); Speech therapists 1 (pt); Activities coordinators 2 (ft); Dietitians 2 (pt).
Facilities Dining room; Physical therapy room; Activities room; Crafts room; Laundry room; Barber/Beauty shop.
Activities Arts & crafts; Cards; Games; Reading groups; Prayer groups; Movies; Dances/Social/Cultural gatherings.

Hampton Nursing Center Inc
PO Box 1568, 975 Miller Rd, Sumter, SC 29151
(803) 775-8376
Admin Emily C Mimms.
Medical Dir Lee Denny MD.
Licensure Skilled care; Intermediate care. *Beds* Swing beds SNF/ICF 88. *Certified* Medicaid; Medicare.
Admissions Requirements Medical examination.
Staff RNs; LPNs; Nurses' aides; Physical therapists; Occupational therapists.
Facilities Dining room; Physical therapy room; Activities room; Laundry room; Barber/Beauty shop.
Activities Arts & crafts; Cards; Games; Reading groups; Prayer groups.

Hopewell Health Care Center
PO Box 818, 1761 Pinewood Rd, Sumter, SC 29151
(803) 481-8591
Admin Mayes P Warr. *Dir of Nursing* Sandra J Minoughan RN. *Medical Dir* Samuel Perry Davis MD.
Licensure Intermediate care. *Beds* ICF 96. *Private Pay Patients* 6%. *Certified* Medicaid.
Owner Proprietary corp (National Health Corp).
Admissions Requirements Medical examination; Physician's request.
Staff Physicians; RNs; LPNs; Nurses' aides; Activities coordinators; Dietitians.
Facilities Dining room; Activities room; Chapel; Laundry room; Barber/Beauty shop.
Activities Arts & crafts; Cards; Games; Reading groups; Prayer groups; Movies; Shopping trips; Museum trips; Fairs.

National Health Care Center of Sumter
PO Box 1524, 1018 N Guignard Dr, Sumter, SC 29151
(803) 773-5567
Admin Eleanor Moses.
Licensure Skilled care; Intermediate care. *Beds* Swing beds SNF/ICF 100. *Certified* Medicaid; Medicare.

Travelers Rest

Oakmont North Nursing Center
601 Sulphur Springs Rd, Travelers Rest, SC 29611-1698
Admin Christine M Wechsler. *Dir of Nursing* Deborah Aiken RN. *Medical Dir* John Holliday MD.
Licensure Skilled care; Intermediate care; Alzheimer's care. *Beds* Swing beds SNF/ICF 22. *Certified* Medicaid; Medicare.
Owner Proprietary corp (Health Care & Retirement Corp).
Admissions Requirements Minimum age 18; Medical examination; Physician's request.
Staff RNs 1 (ft), 3 (pt); LPNs 2 (ft); Nurses' aides 6 (ft), 5 (pt); Activities coordinators 1 (pt); Dietitians 1 (pt).
Facilities Dining room; Activities room; Barber/Beauty shop.
Activities Arts & crafts; Games; Prayer groups; Remotivation therapy.

Union

Oakmont of Union
201 Rice St Ext, Union, SC 29379
(803) 427-0306, 427-0819 FAX
Admin William S Biggs NHA. *Dir of Nursing*
Irene Turner RN BSN. *Medical Dir* David
Keith MD.
Licensure Skilled care; Intermediate care;
Retirement. *Beds* SNF 44; ICF 44;
Retirement 36. *Private Pay Patients* 30%.
Certified Medicaid; Medicare.
Owner Proprietary corp (Health Care &
Retirement Corp).
Admissions Requirements Medical
examination; Physician's request.
Staff RNs 2 (ft), 4 (pt); LPNs 7 (ft), 1 (pt);
Nurses' aides 23 (ft), 18 (pt).
Facilities Dining room; Physical therapy
room; Activities room; Crafts room; Laundry
room; Barber/Beauty shop; Library.
Activities Arts & crafts; Cards; Games;
Reading groups; Prayer groups; Dances/
Social/Cultural gatherings.

Ellen Sagar Nursing Home
Rte 7 Box 138, Union, SC 29379
(803) 427-9533
Admin Anne O Winn. *Dir of Nursing* Rubye
Cheek. *Medical Dir* Dr Boyd Hames.
Licensure Skilled care; Intermediate care. *Beds*
Swing beds SNF/ICF 64. *Certified* Medicaid;
Medicare.
Owner Nonprofit organization/foundation.
Admissions Requirements Minimum age 15.
Staff RNs 4 (ft), 1 (pt); LPNs 6 (ft); Nurses'
aides 23 (ft), 2 (pt); Physical therapists 1
(pt); Speech therapists 1 (pt); Activities
coordinators 1 (ft); Dietitians 1 (pt).
Facilities Dining room; Physical therapy
room; Activities room; Chapel; Laundry
room; Barber/Beauty shop.
Activities Arts & crafts; Cards; Games;
Reading groups; Prayer groups; Movies;
Dances/Social/Cultural gatherings.

Walterboro

Oakwood Health Care Center
PO Drawer 1427, Walterboro, SC 29488
(803) 549-5546
Admin Christine Kirkman. *Dir of Nursing*
Terri Linder. *Medical Dir* William E Fender
Jr MD.
Licensure Skilled care; Intermediate care. *Beds*
SNF 74; ICF 58. *Private Pay Patients* 9%.
Certified Medicaid; Medicare.
Owner Proprietary corp (Pruitt Corp).
Admissions Requirements Minimum age 16;
Medical examination; Physician's request.
Staff RNs; LPNs; Nurses' aides; Activities
coordinators; Dietitians.
Facilities Dining room; Activities room;
Chapel; Laundry room; Barber/Beauty shop.
Activities Arts & crafts; Games; Reading
groups; Prayer groups; Movies; Pet therapy.

Ware Shoals

Marion P Carnell Residence
36 Saluda Ave, Ware Shoals, SC 29692
(803) 456-2294
Admin Linda Gault.
Licensure Intermediate care for mentally
retarded. *Beds* ICF/MR 8.
Owner Publicly owned.

Waterboro

Colleton Skilled Care Facility
501 Robertson Blvd, Waterboro, SC 29488
(803) 549-6371
Admin Charles Mitchener.
Licensure Skilled care; Intermediate care. *Beds*
Swing beds SNF/ICF 15.
Owner Nonprofit corp.

West Columbia

Manor Care Rehabilitation & Nursing Center
2416 Sunset Blvd, West Columbia, SC 29169
(803) 796-8024
Admin Jeff Bardo. *Dir of Nursing* Terri Smith
RN. *Medical Dir* Fred Clemenz MD.
Licensure Skilled care; Intermediate care. *Beds*
ICF 38; Swing beds SNF/ICF 82. *Certified*
Medicaid; Medicare.
Owner Proprietary corp (Manor Care Inc).
Admissions Requirements Medical
examination.
Staff Physicians 1 (pt); Physical therapists 1
(ft), 1 (pt); Recreational therapists 1 (ft);
Occupational therapists 1 (ft); Speech
therapists 2 (ft), 1 (pt); Activities
coordinators 1 (ft); Dietitians 1 (ft).
Languages French.
Facilities Dining room; Physical therapy
room; Activities room; Chapel; Crafts room;
Laundry room; Barber/Beauty shop; Library.
Activities Arts & crafts; Cards; Games;
Reading groups; Prayer groups; Movies;
Shopping trips; Dances/Social/Cultural
gatherings.

South Carolina Vocational Rehabilitation Comprehensive Center
1400 Boston Ave, West Columbia, SC 29169
(803) 758-8731
Admin Jack B Herndon.
Medical Dir J Robert Dunn III MD.
Licensure Intermediate care. *Beds* 18.
Certified Medicare.
Staff Physicians 1 (pt); RNs 1 (ft), 2 (pt);
LPNs 4 (ft), 1 (pt); Nurses' aides 1 (ft), 3
(pt); Physical therapists 1 (ft); Recreational
therapists 2 (ft); Occupational therapists 1
(ft); Speech therapists 1 (ft); Dietitians 1 (ft).
Facilities Dining room; Physical therapy
room; Activities room; Crafts room; Laundry
room; Library.
Activities Arts & crafts; Cards; Games;
Reading groups; Movies; Shopping trips;
Dances/Social/Cultural gatherings.

White Rock

Lowman Home
PO Box 444, White Rock, SC 29177
(803) 732-3000
Admin Louetta A Slice. *Dir of Nursing* Edna
McClain. *Medical Dir* Cooper Black MD.
Licensure Skilled care; Intermediate care;
Residential care; Retirement. *Beds* SNF 85;
ICF 44; Residential care 135; Retirement 36.
Private Pay Patients 60%. *Certified*
Medicaid; Medicare.
Owner Nonprofit organization/foundation.
Admissions Requirements Minimum age 18;
Medical examination; Physician's request.
Staff Physicians 3 (pt); RNs 8 (ft), 2 (pt);
LPNs 10 (ft), 2 (pt); Nurses' aides 100 (ft), 6
(pt); Physical therapists 1 (pt); Recreational
therapists 1 (ft); Speech therapists 1 (pt);
Activities coordinators 2 (ft); Dietitians 1
(pt).
Affiliation Lutheran.
Facilities Dining room; Activities room;
Chapel; Crafts room; Laundry room; Barber/
Beauty shop; Library.
Activities Arts & crafts; Cards; Games;
Reading groups; Prayer groups; Movies;
Shopping trips; Dances/Social/Cultural
gatherings; Intergenerational programs; Pet
therapy.

Williston

Academy Street Community Residence
311 Academy St, Williston, SC 29853
(803) 266-7833
Admin Brent Parker. *Dir of Nursing* Maxine
Corley.
Licensure Intermediate care for mentally
retarded. *Beds* ICF/MR 8. *Private Pay
Patients* 0%. *Certified* Medicaid.
Owner Publicly owned.
Admissions Requirements Minimum age 18;
Females only; Medical examination;
Physician's request.
Staff RNs 1 (ft); LPNs 2 (ft), 1 (pt); Activities
coordinators 2 (ft).
Facilities Dining room; Laundry room.
Activities Arts & crafts; Cards; Games;
Reading groups; Movies; Shopping trips;
Dances/Social/Cultural gatherings; Pet
therapy.

Black's Drive Community Residence
Rte 2 Box 163 B, Williston, SC 29853
(803) 266-3211
Admin Brent Parker. *Dir of Nursing* Maxine
Corley.
Licensure Intermediate care for mentally
retarded. *Beds* ICF/MR 8. *Private Pay
Patients* 0%. *Certified* Medicaid.
Owner Publicly owned.
Admissions Requirements Minimum age 18;
Males only; Medical examination;
Physician's request.
Staff RNs 1 (ft); LPNs 2 (ft), 1 (pt); Activities
coordinators 2 (ft).
Facilities Dining room; Laundry room.
Activities Arts & crafts; Cards; Games;
Reading groups; Movies; Shopping trips;
Dances/Social/Cultural gatherings; Pet
therapy.

Harley Road Community Residence
201 Harley Rd, Williston, SC 29853
(803) 266-3450
Admin Brent Parker. *Dir of Nursing* Maxine
Corley.
Licensure Intermediate care for mentally
retarded. *Beds* ICF/MR 8. *Private Pay
Patients* 0%. *Certified* Medicaid.
Owner Publicly owned.
Admissions Requirements Minimum age 18;
Males only; Medical examination;
Physician's request.
Staff RNs 1 (ft); LPNs 2 (ft), 1 (pt); Activities
coordinators 2 (ft).
Facilities Dining room; Laundry room.
Activities Arts & crafts; Cards; Games;
Reading groups; Movies; Shopping trips;
Dances/Social/Cultural gatherings; Pet
therapy.

Kirkland Convalescent Home Inc
PO Box 250, Rte 1 Hwy 78, Williston, SC
29853
(803) 266-3229
Admin Barbara T Kirkland.
Licensure Intermediate care. *Beds* ICF 20.
Certified Medicaid; Medicare.

Woodruff

Woodruff Health Care
PO Box 879, Rd 50, Woodruff, SC 29388
(803) 476-7092, 476-7094 FAX
Admin Terry Cash. *Dir of Nursing* Sheila
Walker RN. *Medical Dir* Warren Lovett
MD.
Licensure Skilled care; Intermediate care;
Alzheimer's care. *Beds* Swing beds SNF/ICF
88. *Certified* Medicaid; Medicare.
Owner Proprietary corp.
Admissions Requirements Minimum age 12;
Medical examination; Physician's request.
Staff Physicians; RNs; LPNs; Nurses' aides;
Physical therapists (contracted);
Occupational therapists; Speech therapists;
Activities coordinators; Dietitians
(contracted); Ophthalmologists; Podiatrists;
Audiologists.
Facilities Dining room; Physical therapy
room; Activities room; Crafts room; Laundry
room; Barber/Beauty shop; Exit door
security system for Alzheimer's patients.

Activities Arts & crafts; Cards; Games; Reading groups; Prayer groups; Movies; Shopping trips; Dances/Social/Cultural gatherings; Intergenerational programs; Pet therapy; Alzheimer's social & activities program; Alzheimer's support group; Psychosocial counseling for Alzheimer's patients.

York

Bon Secours—Divine Saviour Nursing Home
111 S Congress St, York, SC 29745
(803) 684-4231, 684-6288 FAX
Admin John B Davis, CEO. *Dir of Nursing* Connie Cothren RN. *Medical Dir* David O Holman MD.
Licensure Skilled care; Intermediate care. *Beds* Swing beds SNF/ICF 51. *Private Pay Patients* 30%. *Certified* Medicaid; Medicare.
Owner Nonprofit corp (Bon Secours Health System Inc).
Admissions Requirements Physician's request.

Staff RNs 5 (ft); LPNs 4 (ft); Nurses' aides 27 (ft), 2 (pt); Physical therapists 1 (ft); Recreational therapists 1 (ft); Speech therapists 1 (pt); Dietitians 1 (ft); Podiatrists (consultant).
Affiliation Roman Catholic.
Facilities Dining room; Activities room; Chapel; Crafts room.
Activities Arts & crafts; Cards; Games; Reading groups; Prayer groups; Movies; Shopping trips; Dances/Social/Cultural gatherings; Bingo; Parties; Reality orientation.

SOUTH DAKOTA

Aberdeen

Aberdeen Nursing Center
1700 N Hwy 281, Aberdeen, SD 57401
(605) 225-7315
Admin Craig Prokupek.
Medical Dir William Bormes MD.
Licensure Skilled care; Intermediate care. *Beds*
SNF 86; ICF 86. *Certified* Medicaid.

Americana Healthcare Center
400 8th Ave NW, Aberdeen, SD 57401
(605) 225-2550
Admin Dolores Inman.
Medical Dir William Bormes MD.
Licensure Skilled care. *Beds* SNF 69. *Certified*
Medicaid; Medicare.
Owner Proprietary corp (Manor Care Inc).

Bethesda Home of Aberdeen
1224 S High St, Aberdeen, SD 57401
(605) 225-7580
Admin Robert J Vevle.
Medical Dir Joe R Chang MD.
Licensure Skilled care; Retirement. *Beds* SNF
86. *Certified* Medicaid.
Owner Nonprofit corp.
Admissions Requirements Minimum age 60.
Staff RNs; LPNs; Nurses' aides; Activities
coordinators.
Affiliation Lutheran.
Facilities Dining room; Physical therapy
room; Activities room; Chapel; Crafts room;
Laundry room; Barber/Beauty shop; Library;
Children's day care.
Activities Arts & crafts; Cards; Games;
Reading groups; Prayer groups; Movies;
Shopping trips; Dances/Social/Cultural
gatherings.

Mother Joseph Manor
1002 N Jay St, Aberdeen, SD 57401
(605) 229-0550
Admin Gertrude Mangan.
Medical Dir Joe P Chang MD.
Licensure Skilled care; Intermediate care. *Beds*
SNF 50; ICF 31. *Certified* Medicaid.
Owner Nonprofit corp (Presentation Health
Systems).
Admissions Requirements Medical
examination; Physician's request.
Staff RNs 2 (ft), 3 (pt); LPNs 1 (ft), 4 (pt);
Nurses' aides 5 (ft), 15 (pt); Activities
coordinators 1 (ft); Dietitians 1 (ft).
Affiliation Roman Catholic.
Facilities Dining room; Physical therapy
room; Activities room; Chapel; Crafts room;
Laundry room; Barber/Beauty shop; Library.
Activities Arts & crafts; Cards; Games;
Reading groups; Prayer groups; Movies;
Shopping trips; Dances/Social/Cultural
gatherings.

Alcester

Morningside Manor
Box 188, Alcester, SD 57001
(605) 934-2011

Admin Joseph Ward.
Medical Dir James Daggett MD.
Licensure Skilled care; Intermediate care. *Beds*
SNF 50; ICF 38. *Certified* Medicaid;
Medicare.
Staff Physicians; RNs; LPNs; Nurses' aides;
Physical therapists; Recreational therapists;
Occupational therapists; Speech therapists;
Activities coordinators; Dietitians; Dentists.
Facilities Dining room; Physical therapy
room; Activities room; Crafts room; Laundry
room; Barber/Beauty shop; Library.
Activities Arts & crafts; Cards; Games;
Reading groups; Prayer groups; Movies;
Shopping trips; Dances/Social/Cultural
gatherings.

Arlington

Arlington Care Center
403 N 4th St, Arlington, SD 57212
(605) 983-5796
Admin Kathy Holland.
Medical Dir David J Halliday MD.
Licensure Skilled care. *Beds* SNF 52. *Certified*
Medicaid.
Owner Proprietary corp (Beverly Enterprises).
Staff RNs 3 (ft), 2 (pt); LPNs 1 (ft), 1 (pt);
Nurses' aides 8 (ft), 3 (pt); Activities
coordinators 2 (ft); Dietitians 1 (pt).
Facilities Dining room; Activities room;
Chapel; Crafts room; Laundry room; Barber/
Beauty shop.
Activities Arts & crafts; Cards; Games;
Reading groups; Prayer groups; Movies;
Shopping trips; Dances/Social/Cultural
gatherings.

Armour

Colonial Manor of Armour
PO Box 489, Hwy 281 S, Armour, SD 57313
(605) 724-2546
Admin Charlene R Nash. *Dir of Nursing* Mary
Mimmack. *Medical Dir* David Cruz MD.
Licensure Skilled care. *Beds* SNF 45. *Certified*
Medicaid.
Owner Proprietary corp (Beverly Enterprises).
Admissions Requirements Medical
examination; Physician's request.
Staff RNs 2 (ft), 2 (pt); LPNs 1 (ft), 3 (pt);
Nurses' aides 9 (ft), 6 (pt); Physical
therapists 1 (pt); Recreational therapists 1
(pt); Occupational therapists 1 (pt); Speech
therapists 1 (pt); Activities coordinators 1
(ft), 1 (pt); Dietitians 1 (pt).
Facilities Dining room; Physical therapy
room; Activities room; Chapel; Laundry
room; Barber/Beauty shop; Library.
Activities Arts & crafts; Cards; Games;
Reading groups; Prayer groups; Movies;
Shopping trips; Dances/Social/Cultural
gatherings; Competitive bowling.

Belle Fourche

**Belle Fourche Health Care Center—Long-Term
Care Unit**
2200 13th Ave, Belle Fourche, SD 57717
(605) 892-3331
Admin Ray Klein.
Medical Dir Michael Glanzer MD.
Licensure Skilled care; Intermediate care. *Beds*
SNF 50; ICF 50. *Certified* Medicaid.

Julia Olson Rest Home
1112 6th St, Belle Fourche, SD 57717
(605) 892-4187
Admin Julia Olson.
Licensure Supervised care. *Beds* 4.

Prairie Hills Home for Elderly
RR Box 567, Belle Fourche, SD 57717
(605) 892-3585
Admin Leone A Moncur.
Licensure Supervised living. *Beds* Supervised
living 12.

Beresford

Bethesda Home for Aged
606 W Cedar, Beresford, SD 57004
(605) 763-2050
Admin Jack Dahlseid. *Dir of Nursing* Diane
Landon. *Medical Dir* Mike Hogue MD.
Licensure Skilled care. *Beds* SNF 83. *Certified*
Medicaid.
Owner Nonprofit corp.
Admissions Requirements Medical
examination.
Staff RNs 5 (ft); LPNs 3 (ft); Nurses' aides 15
(ft), 20 (pt); Recreational therapists 2 (ft), 1
(pt); Activities coordinators 1 (ft).
Affiliation Lutheran.
Facilities Dining room; Physical therapy
room; Activities room; Chapel; Crafts room;
Laundry room; Barber/Beauty shop.
Activities Arts & crafts; Cards; Games;
Reading groups; Prayer groups; Movies;
Shopping trips; Dances/Social/Cultural
gatherings.

Bowdle

Bowdle Nursing Home
8061 5th St, Box 308, Bowdle, SD 57428
(605) 285-6391
Admin John L Jacobs. *Dir of Nursing* Colleen
Harner RN. *Medical Dir* John McFee Jr
MD.
Licensure Skilled care. *Beds* SNF 38. *Private
Pay Patients* 30%. *Certified* Medicaid.
Owner Nonprofit organization/foundation.
Admissions Requirements Physician's request.
Staff Physicians 1 (pt); RNs 5 (ft), 1 (pt);
LPNs 2 (ft), 1 (pt); Nurses' aides 12 (ft), 4
(pt); Physical therapists 1 (pt); Speech
therapists 1 (pt); Activities coordinators 1
(ft), 1 (pt); Dietitians 1 (ft), 1 (pt);
Audiologists 1 (pt).
Languages German.

Facilities Dining room; Physical therapy
room; Activities room; Chapel; Crafts room;
Laundry room; Barber/Beauty shop.
Activities Arts & crafts; Cards; Games;
Reading groups; Prayer groups; Movies;
Shopping trips; Dances/Social/Cultural
gatherings; Intergenerational programs; Pet
therapy.

Bridgewater

Diamond Care Center
PO Box 300, Bridgewater, SD 57319
(605) 729-2525
Admin Dave J Decker. *Dir of Nursing*
Dorothy Brendan.
Licensure Intermediate care. *Beds* ICF 56.
Certified Medicaid.
Owner Proprietary corp.
Staff Physicians; RNs; LPNs; Nurses' aides;
Recreational therapists; Activities
coordinators; Dietitians.

Bristol

Sun Dial Manor
PO Box 337, Bristol, SD 57219
(605) 492-3615
Admin Sally Damm. *Dir of Nursing* Diane
Warrington RN; Brenda Sletten RN. *Medical
Dir* Alfred Shousha MD.
Licensure Intermediate care. *Beds* ICF 37.
Certified Medicaid; Medicare.
Owner Nonprofit corp.
Admissions Requirements Medical
examination; Physician's request.
Staff RNs 2 (pt); LPNs 2 (pt); Nurses' aides 8
(ft), 20 (pt); Activities coordinators 1 (ft);
Dietitians 1 (ft).
Facilities Dining room; Activities room;
Chapel; Crafts room; Laundry room; Barber/
Beauty shop.
Activities Arts & crafts; Cards; Games;
Reading groups; Prayer groups; Movies;
Shopping trips; Dances/Social/Cultural
gatherings.

Britton

Marshall Manor
PO Box 939, W Hwy 10, Britton, SD 57430
(605) 448-2251
Admin Robert B Marx. *Dir of Nursing* J Bull.
Medical Dir Bruce Lushbough MD.
Licensure Intermediate care. *Beds* ICF 63.
Certified Medicaid.
Owner Proprietary corp.
Staff RNs 1 (ft), 1 (pt); LPNs 2 (ft); Nurses'
aides 18 (ft), 6 (pt); Activities coordinators 2
(ft); Dietitians 2 (ft), 3 (pt).
Facilities Dining room; Activities room;
Chapel; Laundry room; Barber/Beauty shop.
Activities Arts & crafts; Cards; Games;
Reading groups; Prayer groups; Movies;
Shopping trips; Dances/Social/Cultural
gatherings.

Brookings

Brookview Manor
300 22nd Ave, Brookings, SD 57006
(605) 692-6351
Admin David B Johnson. *Dir of Nursing*
Gloria Gerberding RN. *Medical Dir* Bruce
Lushbough MD.
Licensure Skilled care. *Beds* SNF 79. *Certified*
Medicaid.
Owner Publicly owned.
Admissions Requirements Physician's request.
Staff RNs 2 (ft), 11 (pt); LPNs 3 (ft), 4 (pt);
Nurses' aides 8 (ft), 24 (pt); Reality
therapists 1 (pt); Activities coordinators 1
(ft), 1 (pt); Dietitians 1 (pt).

Facilities Dining room; Physical therapy
room; Activities room; Chapel; Crafts room;
Laundry room; Barber/Beauty shop; Dental
room.
Activities Arts & crafts; Cards; Games;
Reading groups; Prayer groups; Movies;
Shopping trips; Dances/Social/Cultural
gatherings; Fishing; Camping.

United Retirement Center
405 1st Ave, Brookings, SD 57006
(605) 692-5351, 692-5982 FAX
Admin Arnold M Brown. *Dir of Nursing*
Brenda Johnson RN.
Licensure Intermediate care; Congregate
housing; Respite care; Adult day care; Home
health. *Beds* ICF 60; Congregate housing 22;
Respite care 1. *Private Pay Patients* 52%.
Certified Medicaid.
Owner Nonprofit corp.
Admissions Requirements Medical
examination; Physician's request;
Preadmissions assessment by state social
services.
Staff RNs; LPNs; Nurses' aides; Physical
therapists (contracted); Reality therapists 1
(pt); Recreational therapists 1 (pt);
Occupational therapists 1 (pt); Activities
coordinators 1 (ft); Dietitians 1 (pt); Social
services 1 (ft).
Languages Norwegian.
Facilities Dining room; Physical therapy
room; Activities room; Chapel; Laundry
room; Barber/Beauty shop; Library; Family
room.
Activities Arts & crafts; Cards; Games;
Reading groups; Prayer groups; Movies;
Shopping trips; Dances/Social/Cultural
gatherings; Intergenerational programs; Pet
therapy.

Bryant

Parkview Care Center
PO Box 247, Bryant, SD 57221
(605) 628-2771
Admin Robert E Gergen.
Medical Dir Dr G R Bell.
Licensure Intermediate care. *Beds* ICF 52.
Certified Medicaid.
Admissions Requirements Medical
examination.
Staff RNs 1 (ft), 3 (pt); LPNs 2 (ft), 2 (pt);
Nurses' aides 9 (ft), 12 (pt); Physical
therapists 1 (pt); Activities coordinators 1
(ft); Dietitians 1 (pt).
Facilities Dining room; Activities room;
Chapel; Crafts room; Laundry room; Barber/
Beauty shop.
Activities Arts & crafts; Cards; Games;
Reading groups; Prayer groups; Movies;
Shopping trips; Dances/Social/Cultural
gatherings.

Canistota

Canistota Good Samaritan Center
PO Box 6, 700 W Main, Canistota, SD 57012
(605) 296-3442
Admin Don Olson. *Dir of Nursing* Phyllis
Arends RN.
Licensure Intermediate care. *Beds* ICF 64.
Certified Medicaid.
Owner Nonprofit corp (Evangelical Lutheran/
Good Samaritan Society).
Admissions Requirements Medical
examination.
Staff RNs 2 (ft); LPNs 5 (ft); Nurses' aides 18
(ft); Physical therapists 1 (pt); Activities
coordinators 1 (ft), 1 (pt); Dietitians 1 (pt).
Facilities Dining room; Activities room;
Chapel; Crafts room; Laundry room; Barber/
Beauty shop.
Activities Arts & crafts; Cards; Games;
Reading groups; Prayer groups; Movies;
Shopping trips; Dances/Social/Cultural
gatherings.

Canton

Canton Good Samaritan Center
1022 N Oak Ave, Canton, SD 57013
(605) 987-2696
Admin Don W Toft. *Dir of Nursing* Joyce
Paulson. *Medical Dir* Gene Regier MD.
Licensure Skilled care; Intermediate care. *Beds*
SNF 68; ICF 10. *Private Pay Patients* 49%.
Certified Medicaid.
Owner Nonprofit corp (Evangelical Lutheran/
Good Samaritan Society).
Admissions Requirements Medical
examination; Physician's request.
Staff RNs 5 (ft), 5 (pt); LPNs 1 (ft), 1 (pt);
Nurses' aides 16 (ft), 19 (pt); Activities
coordinators 2 (ft), 2 (pt); Dietitians 7 (ft), 7
(pt); Physical therapists and aides 1 (ft), 2
(pt).
Languages Norwegian, German.
Affiliation Lutheran.
Facilities Dining room; Physical therapy
room; Activities room; Chapel; Crafts room;
Laundry room; Barber/Beauty shop.
Activities Arts & crafts; Cards; Games;
Reading groups; Prayer groups; Movies;
Shopping trips; Dances/Social/Cultural
gatherings; Intergenerational programs; Pet
therapy; Special days and events.

Centerville

Centerville Good Samaritan Center
PO Box 190, 500 Vermillion, Centerville, SD
57014
(605) 563-2251
Admin Eugene Mathison.
Licensure Intermediate care. *Beds* ICF 60.
Certified Medicaid.
Owner Nonprofit corp (Evangelical Lutheran/
Good Samaritan Society).
Admissions Requirements Medical
examination; Physician's request.
Staff RNs 1 (ft).
Facilities Dining room; Physical therapy
room; Activities room; Chapel; Crafts room;
Laundry room; Barber/Beauty shop; Library.
Activities Arts & crafts; Cards; Games;
Reading groups; Prayer groups; Movies;
Shopping trips; Dances/Social/Cultural
gatherings.

Chamberlain

Sunset Valley
PO Box 179, 111 W 16th Ave, Chamberlain,
SD 57325
(605) 734-6518
Admin Janet J Evangelisto. *Dir of Nursing*
Vickie L Mills RN. *Medical Dir* C F Binder
MD.
Licensure Skilled care. *Beds* SNF 58. *Private
Pay Patients* 50%. *Certified* Medicaid.
Owner Nonprofit corp.
Admissions Requirements Medical
examination; Physician's request.
Staff RNs 1 (ft), 3 (pt); LPNs 4 (pt); Nurses'
aides 6 (ft), 22 (pt); Activities coordinators 1
(ft), 1 (pt); Dietitians 1 (pt); Social service
designees 1 (ft); Maintenance supervisors 1
(ft); Housekeeping 2 (ft), 2 (pt); Cooks &
helpers 3 (ft), 5 (pt).
Facilities Dining room; Activities room;
Crafts room; Laundry room; Barber/Beauty
shop.
Activities Arts & crafts; Cards; Games;
Reading groups; Prayer groups; Movies;
Shopping trips; Dances/Social/Cultural
gatherings; Intergenerational programs; Pet
therapy; Transportation in community;
Alzheimer's support group.

Clark

Clark Care Center
201 NW 8th Ave, Clark, SD 57225
(605) 532-3431
Admin Joyce M Helkenn. *Dir of Nursing*
Betty Poppen RN. *Medical Dir* G R Bartron
MD.
Licensure Skilled care; Alzheimer's care. *Beds*
SNF 45. *Private Pay Patients* 40%. *Certified*
Medicaid.
Owner Proprietary corp (Beverly Enterprises).
Admissions Requirements Medical
examination; Physician's request.
Staff RNs 3 (ft), 4 (pt); LPNs 2 (ft), 1 (pt);
Nurses' aides 15 (ft), 14 (pt); Activities
coordinators 1 (ft).
Facilities Dining room; Physical therapy
room; Activities room; Crafts room; Laundry
room; Barber/Beauty shop.
Activities Arts & crafts; Cards; Games;
Reading groups; Prayer groups; Movies;
Shopping trips; Dances/Social/Cultural
gatherings; Intergenerational programs; Pet
therapy.

Clear Lake

Deuel County Good Samaritan Center
913 4th Ave S, Clear Lake, SD 57226
(605) 874-2159
Admin Daisy Bergjord. *Dir of Nursing* Julia V
Schumacher RN. *Medical Dir* H Dean
Hughes MD.
Licensure Skilled care; Intermediate care. *Beds*
SNF 42; ICF 38. *Certified* Medicaid.
Owner Nonprofit corp (Evangelical Lutheran/
Good Samaritan Society).
Admissions Requirements Medical
examination.
Staff RNs; LPNs; Nurses' aides; Activities
coordinators.
Affiliation Lutheran.
Facilities Dining room; Physical therapy
room; Activities room; Chapel; Crafts room;
Laundry room; Barber/Beauty shop.
Activities Arts & crafts; Cards; Games;
Reading groups; Prayer groups; Movies;
Shopping trips; Dances/Social/Cultural
gatherings.

Corsica

Pleasant View Good Samaritan
Rte 1 Box 300, Corsica, SD 57328
(605) 946-5467
Admin G M Nelson. *Dir of Nursing* Ruth Von
Heukelom.
Licensure Intermediate care. *Beds* ICF 62.
Certified Medicaid.
Owner Nonprofit corp (Evangelical Lutheran/
Good Samaritan Society).
Admissions Requirements Medical
examination; Physician's request.
Staff RNs 1 (ft), 3 (pt); LPNs 1 (ft), 2 (pt);
Nurses' aides 1 (ft), 20 (pt); Activities
coordinators 1 (ft).
Affiliation Lutheran.
Facilities Dining room; Physical therapy
room; Activities room; Laundry room;
Barber/Beauty shop.
Activities Arts & crafts; Cards; Games;
Reading groups; Prayer groups; Movies;
Shopping trips; Pet therapy.

Custer

Colonial Manor of Custer
1065 Montgomery St, Custer, SD 57730
(605) 673-2237
Admin Gerald W Woodford. *Dir of Nursing*
Brb Nordstrom RN. *Medical Dir* Dennis
Wicks MD.
Licensure Skilled care; Alzheimer's care. *Beds*
SNF 80. *Certified* Medicaid; Medicare.
Owner Proprietary corp (Beverly Enterprises).

examination; Physician's request.
Staff Physicians; RNs; LPNs; Nurses' aides;
Physical therapists; Recreational therapists;
Activities coordinators.
Facilities Dining room; Physical therapy
room; Activities room; Chapel; Crafts room;
Laundry room; Barber/Beauty shop.
Activities Arts & crafts; Cards; Games;
Reading groups; Prayer groups; Movies;
Shopping trips; Dances/Social/Cultural
gatherings.

Deadwood

Friendship Home
48 Highland, Deadwood, SD 57732
(605) 578-2482
Admin Douglas Baldwin; Teri Baldwin.
Medical Dir David Erickson MD.
Licensure Supervised care. *Beds* Supervised
care 8.

Dell Rapids

Odd Fellows Home
100 W 10th St, Dell Rapids, SD 57022
(605) 428-3043
Admin Robert Reiff. *Dir of Nursing* Gail
Syverson. *Medical Dir* Dr David Erickson.
Licensure Intermediate care. *Beds* ICF 50.
Private Pay Patients 40-50%. *Certified*
Medicaid.
Owner Nonprofit organization/foundation.
Admissions Requirements Medical
examination.
Staff RNs 2 (ft), 1 (pt); LPNs 4 (ft), 1 (pt);
Nurses' aides 20 (ft); Physical therapists;
Recreational therapists 1 (ft); Dietitians 3
(ft).
Affiliation Independent Order of Odd Fellows
& Rebekahs.
Facilities Dining room; Physical therapy
room; Activities room; Chapel; Crafts room;
Laundry room; Barber/Beauty shop; Private
rooms available.
Activities Arts & crafts; Cards; Games;
Reading groups; Movies; Dances/Social/
Cultural gatherings; Pet therapy; Exercise.

Terrace Manor
1400 Thresher Dr, Dell Rapids, SD 57022
(605) 428-5478
Admin Linda Ljunggren. *Dir of Nursing*
Loretta Coad RN. *Medical Dir* Dr Mitchell
Rydberg.
Licensure Skilled care; Intermediate care. *Beds*
Swing beds SNF/ICF 76. *Private Pay*
Patients 80%. *Certified* Medicaid.
Owner Proprietary corp.
Staff Physicians 4 (pt); RNs 2 (ft), 5 (pt);
LPNs 3 (pt); Nurses' aides 10 (ft), 26 (pt);
Physical therapists (contracted); Speech
therapists (contracted); Activities
coordinators 1 (ft), 1 (pt); Dietitians
(consultant).

DeSmet

DeSmet Good Samaritan Center
RR 1 Box 15A, DeSmet, SD 57231
(605) 854-3327
Admin Jerald D Keller.
Licensure Intermediate care; Supervised care.
Beds ICF 62; Supervised care 10. *Certified*
Medicaid.
Owner Nonprofit corp (Evangelical Lutheran/
Good Samaritan Society).
Staff RNs 1 (ft), 2 (pt); LPNs 1 (ft), 4 (pt);
Nurses' aides 10 (ft), 18 (pt); Activities
coordinators 1 (ft), 1 (pt).
Facilities Dining room; Activities room;
Chapel; Crafts room; Laundry room; Barber/
Beauty shop; Library.

Activities Arts & crafts; Cards; Games;
Reading groups; Prayer groups; Movies;
Shopping trips; Dances/Social/Cultural
gatherings.

Elk Point

Prairie Estates
Box 486, Elk Point, SD 57025
(605) 356-2622
Admin Alexander G Willford. *Dir of Nursing*
Janet Limoug. *Medical Dir* Janice Gallia
MD.
Licensure Intermediate care. *Beds* ICF 50.
Certified Medicaid.
Owner Proprietary corp.
Admissions Requirements Medical
examination; Physician's request.
Staff Physicians 2 (ft); RNs 4 (ft); LPNs 2 (ft);
Nurses' aides 20 (ft); Physical therapists 1
(ft); Speech therapists 1 (ft); Activities
coordinators 1 (ft); Dietitians 1 (ft).
Facilities Dining room; Activities room;
Chapel; Crafts room; Laundry room; Barber/
Beauty shop; Library.
Activities Arts & crafts; Games; Reading
groups; Prayer groups; Movies; Shopping
trips; Dances/Social/Cultural gatherings;
Field trips.

Elkton

Elkton Rest Home
205 W 3rd St, Elkton, SD 57026
(605) 542-7251
Admin Jim Cameron; Roween Cameron.
Licensure Supervised care. *Beds* Supervised
care 10.

Estelline

Estelline Nursing & Care Center
PO Box 130, N Main, Estelline, SD 57234
(605) 873-2278
Admin Evelyn Saathoff. *Dir of Nursing* Ginger
Casjens RN. *Medical Dir* Steven Feeney
MD.
Licensure Skilled care. *Beds* SNF 60. *Private*
Pay Patients 25%. *Certified* Medicaid.
Owner Publicly owned.
Admissions Requirements Medical
examination; Physician's request.
Staff RNs 2 (pt); LPNs 1 (ft), 6 (pt); Nurses'
aides 12 (ft), 13 (pt); Activities coordinators
1 (ft).
Facilities Dining room; Activities room;
Laundry room; Barber/Beauty shop.
Activities Arts & crafts; Cards; Games;
Reading groups; Prayer groups; Movies;
Shopping trips; Dances/Social/Cultural
gatherings; Intergenerational programs; Pet
therapy; Van outings in summer; Visits to
other nursing homes; Adopt-a-resident;
School programs.

Eureka

Lutheran Home (LHHS)
PO Box 40, Eureka, SD 57437
(605) 284-2534
Admin V R Just.
Medical Dir Susan Ostrowski MD.
Licensure Intermediate care. *Beds* ICF 62.
Certified Medicaid.
Owner Nonprofit corp (Lutheran Hospitals &
Homes Soctiey).
Admissions Requirements Medical
examination; Physician's request.
Staff Physicians 2 (ft); RNs 2 (ft), 1 (pt);
LPNs 2 (ft); Nurses' aides 16 (ft), 14 (pt);
Recreational therapists 1 (ft), 1 (pt);
Occupational therapists 1 (ft); Activities
coordinators 1 (ft), 1 (pt); Dietitians 1 (ft);
Ophthalmologists 1 (ft); Dentists 1 (ft).
Affiliation Lutheran.

Facilities Dining room; Activities room; Chapel; Crafts room; Laundry room; Barber/Beauty shop.
Activities Arts & crafts; Cards; Games; Reading groups; Prayer groups; Movies; Shopping trips; Dances/Social/Cultural gatherings; Fishing trips; Farm outings.

Faulkton

John P Shirk Memorial Home
PO Box 249, Pearl & 13th Sts, Faulkton, SD 57438
(605) 598-6214
Admin Karen R Collins RN BSN. *Dir of Nursing* Janet Melius RN BSN. *Medical Dir* Kenneth Bartholomew MD.
Licensure Skilled care; Intermediate care. *Beds* SNF 27; ICF 27. *Private Pay Patients* 31%. *Certified* Medicaid.
Owner Proprietary corp (North Central Health Services Inc).
Staff RNs 4 (ft); LPNs 2 (ft); Nurses' aides 14 (ft); Activities coordinators 1 (ft).
Facilities Dining room; Activities room; Laundry room; Barber/Beauty shop.
Activities Arts & crafts; Cards; Games; Reading groups; Prayer groups; Movies; Shopping trips; Dances/Social/Cultural gatherings; Intergenerational programs; Pet therapy.

Flandreau

Riverview Manor
611 E 2nd Ave, Flandreau, SD 57028
(605) 997-2481
Admin JoAnn Lind.
Medical Dir Tad Jacobs MD.
Licensure Skilled care. *Beds* SNF 80. *Certified* Medicaid.

Freeman

Freeman Nursing Home
510 E 8th St, Box 370, Freeman, SD 57029
(605) 925-4231, 925-4380 FAX
Admin James Krehbrel.
Medical Dir I Kaufman MD.
Licensure Skilled care; Intermediate care. *Beds* SNF 54; ICF 5. *Certified* Medicaid.
Owner Nonprofit organization/foundation.

Salem Mennonite Home for Aged
PO Box 140A, Freeman, SD 57029
(605) 925-4994
Admin Evelyn Hagemann. *Dir of Nursing* Evelyn Hagemann RN.
Licensure Supervised care; Retirement. *Beds* Supervised care 52. *Certified* Medicaid; Medicare.
Owner Proprietary corp.
Admissions Requirements Females only; Medical examination.
Staff RNs 2 (pt); Nurses' aides 10 (ft); Activities coordinators 2 (pt); Dietitians 1 (ft); Administrator 1 (ft); Maintenance 1 (ft); Diet aides & cooks 3 (ft), 3 (pt); Cleaning 3 (ft); Laundry 1 (ft), 1 (pt); Med aides 1 (ft), 3 (pt).
Languages German.
Affiliation Mennonite.
Facilities Dining room; Physical therapy room; Activities room; Chapel; Crafts room; Laundry room; Barber/Beauty shop; Library.
Activities Arts & crafts; Cards; Games; Reading groups; Prayer groups; Movies; Shopping trips; Dances/Social/Cultural gatherings.

Garretson

Palisade Manor
920 4th St, Garretson, SD 57030
(605) 594-3466
Admin Gloria M Schultz.

Medical Dir Marvin Wingert MD.
Licensure Skilled care; Intermediate care. *Beds* SNF 16; ICF 62. *Certified* Medicaid.

Gettysburg

Oahe Manor
700 E Garfield, Gettysburg, SD 57442
(605) 765-2461
Admin Timothy J Tracy.
Licensure Intermediate care. *Beds* ICF 70. *Certified* Medicaid.
Admissions Requirements Medical examination; Physician's request.
Staff RNs 1 (ft); LPNs 4 (ft); Nurses' aides 34 (ft); Activities coordinators 1 (ft); Dietitians 1 (ft).
Facilities Dining room; Activities room; Chapel; Crafts room; Laundry room; Barber/Beauty shop.
Activities Arts & crafts; Cards; Games; Reading groups; Prayer groups; Movies.

Gregory

Rosebud Nursing Home
PO Box 408, 300 Park, Gregory, SD 57533
(605) 835-8296, 835-9422 FAX
Admin Terry E Davis. *Dir of Nursing* Marlene Gellerman RN. *Medical Dir* Lloyd C Vogelgesang MD.
Licensure Skilled care. *Beds* SNF 58. *Private Pay Patients* 26%. *Certified* Medicaid; Medicare.
Owner Nonprofit corp (Lutheran Hospitals & Homes Society of America).
Staff RNs 6 (ft), 1 (pt); LPNs 2 (ft), 1 (pt); Nurses' aides 15 (ft), 8 (pt); Physical therapists 1 (pt); Activities coordinators 1 (ft); Dietitians 1 (pt).
Languages Bohemian.
Facilities Dining room; Activities room; Chapel; Crafts room; Barber/Beauty shop.
Activities Arts & crafts; Cards; Games; Reading groups; Prayer groups; Movies; Dances/Social/Cultural gatherings; Intergenerational programs.

Groton

Colonial Manor of Groton
PO Box 418, Groton, SD 57445
(605) 397-2365
Admin Bruce Glanzer.
Medical Dir David Ellerbusch MD.
Licensure Skilled care. *Beds* SNF 60. *Certified* Medicaid.
Owner Proprietary corp (Beverly Enterprises).

Herreid

Herreid Good Samaritan Center
PO Box 8, Herreid, SD 57632
(605) 437-2425
Admin Sandra Schanzenbach. *Dir of Nursing* Claraine Holmes.
Licensure Intermediate care; Basic care. *Beds* ICF 5; Basic care 22. *Private Pay Patients* 40%. *Certified* Medicaid.
Owner Nonprofit corp (Evangelical Lutheran/Good Samaritan Society).
Admissions Requirements Medical examination.
Staff RNs; LPNs; Nurses' aides; Activities coordinators.
Languages German.
Affiliation Lutheran.
Facilities Dining room; Laundry room.
Activities Arts & crafts; Cards; Games; Reading groups; Prayer groups.

Highmore

Highmore Healthcare Center
8th & Maple Sts, Highmore, SD 57345
(605) 852-2255
Admin Charlie Pesicka. *Dir of Nursing* Carol Schulz RN. *Medical Dir* Steve Schroeder MD.
Licensure Intermediate care. *Beds* ICF 48. *Private Pay Patients* 32%. *Certified* Medicaid.
Owner Proprietary corp (Tealwood Care Centers Inc).
Admissions Requirements Medical examination; Physician's request.
Staff Physicians 3 (pt); RNs 1 (ft), 2 (pt); LPNs 3 (pt); Nurses' aides 7 (ft), 16 (pt); Physical therapists 1 (pt); Reality therapists 1 (pt); Recreational therapists 1 (pt); Activities coordinators 1 (ft); Dietitians 1 (pt); Podiatrists 1 (pt).
Facilities Dining room; Activities room; Crafts room; Laundry room; Barber/Beauty shop.
Activities Arts & crafts; Cards; Games; Reading groups; Prayer groups; Movies; Shopping trips; Dances/Social/Cultural gatherings; Intergenerational programs; Pet therapy; Resident council; Family council.

Hosmer

Senior Citizens Home
PO Box 67, Hosmer, SD 57448
(605) 283-2203
Admin Paulette Gollnick Maursetter. *Dir of Nursing* Geralyn Malsom RN.
Licensure Intermediate care. *Beds* ICF 40. *Private Pay Patients* 30%. *Certified* Medicaid.
Owner Nonprofit organization/foundation.
Admissions Requirements Medical examination; Physician's request.
Staff Physicians 1 (ft); RNs 3 (ft); LPNs 2 (pt); Nurses' aides 10 (ft), 5 (pt); Activities coordinators 1 (ft); Dietitians 1 (ft).
Languages German.
Facilities Dining room; Activities room; Crafts room; Laundry room; Barber/Beauty shop.
Activities Arts & crafts; Cards; Games; Reading groups; Prayer groups; Movies; Shopping trips.

Hot Springs

Castle Manor
209 N 16th St, Hot Springs, SD 57747
(605) 745-5071
Admin Ronald J Cork. *Dir of Nursing* Irene Beard. *Medical Dir* Theodore Jacabson.
Licensure Intermediate care. *Beds* ICF 48. *Private Pay Patients* 47%. *Certified* Medicaid.
Owner Nonprofit corp (Lutheran Hospitals & Homes Society of America).
Admissions Requirements Physician's request.
Staff Physicians 6 (ft); RNs 1 (ft); LPNs 3 (ft); Nurses' aides 15 (ft), 3 (pt); Physical therapists (contracted); Activities coordinators 1 (ft); Dietitians 1 (ft).
Languages Native American.
Affiliation Lutheran.
Facilities Dining room; Physical therapy room; Activities room; Chapel; Crafts room; Laundry room; Barber/Beauty shop; Library.
Activities Arts & crafts; Cards; Games; Reading groups; Prayer groups; Movies; Shopping trips; Dances/Social/Cultural gatherings; Intergenerational programs; Pet therapy.

Howard

Howard Good Samaritan Center
PO Box 92, RR 1, Howard, SD 57349
(605) 772-4481
Admin Dennis Beeman. *Dir of Nursing* Lorna
Koch RN. *Medical Dir* Richard Sample MD.
Licensure Skilled care; Supervised care;
Retirement. *Beds* SNF 74; Supervised care
2. *Certified* Medicaid.
Owner Nonprofit corp (Evangelical Lutheran/
Good Samaritan Society).
Admissions Requirements Physician's request.
Staff Physicians 4 (pt); RNs 3 (ft), 7 (pt);
LPNs 1 (ft), 2 (pt); Nurses' aides 12 (ft), 23
(pt); Physical therapists 1 (pt); Activities
coordinators 1 (ft), 2 (pt); Dietitians 1 (pt).
Affiliation Lutheran.
Facilities Dining room; Physical therapy
room; Activities room; Crafts room; Laundry
room; Barber/Beauty shop.
Activities Arts & crafts; Cards; Games;
Reading groups; Prayer groups; Movies;
Shopping trips; Dances/Social/Cultural
gatherings.

Hudson

Colonial Manor of Hudson
PO Box 486, Hwy 46 W, Hudson, SD 57034
(605) 984-2244
Admin James Lewandowski.
Medical Dir K A Miller MD.
Licensure Intermediate care. *Beds* ICF 42.
Certified Medicaid.
Admissions Requirements Medical
examination; Physician's request.
Staff Physicians 1 (pt); RNs 1 (ft), 1 (pt);
LPNs 3 (pt); Nurses' aides 24 (pt); Activities
coordinators 1 (ft); Dietitians 1 (pt).
Facilities Dining room; Activities room;
Chapel; Crafts room; Laundry room; Barber/
Beauty shop; Library.
Activities Arts & crafts; Cards; Games;
Reading groups; Prayer groups; Movies;
Shopping trips.

Huron

Huron Nursing Home
15th & Michigan SW, Huron, SD 57350
(605) 352-8471
Admin Sharon Grayson.
Medical Dir Harold Adams MD.
Licensure Skilled care; Intermediate care. *Beds*
SNF 125; ICF 38. *Certified* Medicaid;
Medicare.
Owner Proprietary corp (Samcor).

Violet Tschetter Memorial Home
PO Box 946, 50 7th St SE, Huron, SD 57350
(605) 352-8533
Admin Peggy Roy. *Dir of Nursing* Joyce Kogel
RN. *Medical Dir* Paul Hohm MD.
Licensure Skilled care. *Beds* SNF 58. *Certified*
Medicaid.
Owner Nonprofit corp.
Admissions Requirements Medical
examination; Physician's request.
Staff RNs 1 (ft), 6 (pt); LPNs 1 (ft), 4 (pt);
Nurses' aides 16 (pt), 13 (pt); Activities
coordinators 1 (ft); Dietitians 1 (pt).
Facilities Dining room; Activities room;
Chapel; Crafts room; Laundry room; Barber/
Beauty shop.
Activities Arts & crafts; Cards; Games;
Reading groups; Prayer groups; Movies;
Shopping trips; Dances/Social/Cultural
gatherings.

Ipswich

Colonial Manor of Ipswich
617 Bloemendaal Dr, Ipswich, SD 57451
(605) 426-6622

Admin Carol Ulmer. *Dir of Nursing* Lydia
Leafgreen RN. *Medical Dir* John L McFee
MD.
Licensure Skilled care. *Beds* SNF 59. *Certified*
Medicaid.
Owner Proprietary corp (Beverly Enterprises).
Admissions Requirements Minimum age 16;
Medical examination.
Staff Physicians 1 (pt); RNs 3 (ft), 1 (pt);
LPNs 3 (ft), 2 (pt); Nurses' aides 20 (ft), 8
(pt); Physical therapists 1 (pt); Activities
coordinators 2 (ft), 2 (pt); Dietitians 1 (pt).
Languages German, French, Spanish.
Facilities Dining room; Physical therapy
room; Activities room; Crafts room; Laundry
room; Barber/Beauty shop.
Activities Arts & crafts; Cards; Games;
Reading groups; Prayer groups; Movies;
Shopping trips; Dances/Social/Cultural
gatherings; Current events; Ethnic
celebrations; Exercises.

Irene

Sunset Manor
PO Box 25, Irene, SD 57037
(605) 263-3318
Admin Kathleen Stanage.
Medical Dir C L Mark MD.
Licensure Intermediate care. *Beds* ICF 68.
Certified Medicaid.

Kadoka

Kadoka Nursing Home
PO Box 310, 104 Maple, Kadoka, SD 57543
(605) 837-2270
Admin Nona Prang. *Dir of Nursing* Nancy
Pettyjohn. *Medical Dir* L P Swisher MD.
Licensure Intermediate care. *Beds* ICF 34.
Private Pay Patients 50%. *Certified*
Medicaid.
Owner Nonprofit corp.
Admissions Requirements Medical
examination; Physician's request.
Staff Physicians 1 (pt); RNs 1 (pt); LPNs 2
(ft), 1 (pt); Nurses' aides 8 (ft), 4 (pt);
Activities coordinators 1 (ft); Dietitians 1
(pt).
Languages Sioux.
Facilities Dining room; Laundry room;
Barber/Beauty shop.
Activities Arts & crafts; Cards; Games;
Reading groups; Prayer groups; Movies;
Shopping trips; Dances/Social/Cultural
gatherings; Intergenerational programs; Pet
therapy.

Lake Andes

Lake Andes Health Care Center
PO Box 130, Lake Andes, SD 57356
(605) 487-7674
Admin Janice Schuman. *Dir of Nursing*
Marilyn Strehlow. *Medical Dir* Richard
Honke II.
Licensure Skilled care; Intermediate care. *Beds*
SNF 10; ICF 42. *Private Pay Patients* 35%.
Certified Medicaid.
Owner Proprietary corp.
Admissions Requirements Medical
examination.
Staff RNs 3 (ft), 2 (pt); LPNs 2 (ft), 1 (pt);
Nurses' aides 8 (ft), 15 (pt); Physical
therapists (consultant); Activities
coordinators 1 (ft); Dietitians (consultant).
Facilities Dining room; Activities room;
Crafts room; Laundry room; Barber/Beauty
shop.
Activities Arts & crafts; Cards; Games;
Movies; Shopping trips; Dances/Social/
Cultural gatherings; Pet therapy.

Lake Norden

Lake Norden Care Center
PO Box 38, West Side St, Lake Norden, SD
57248
(605) 783-3654
Admin Mike Gamet. *Dir of Nursing* Margaret
Boldt. *Medical Dir* G R Barton MD.
Licensure Skilled care. *Beds* SNF 63. *Certified*
Medicaid.
Owner Proprietary corp (Beverly Enterprises).
Admissions Requirements Medical
examination; Physician's request.
Staff Physicians 1 (pt); RNs 3 (ft); LPNs 3
(ft), 1 (pt); Nurses' aides 11 (ft), 10 (pt);
Physical therapists 1 (pt); Activities
coordinators 1 (ft), 1 (pt); Dietitians 1 (pt).
Facilities Dining room; Activities room;
Chapel; Crafts room; Laundry room; Barber/
Beauty shop.
Activities Arts & crafts; Cards; Games;
Reading groups; Prayer groups; Movies;
Shopping trips; Dances/Social/Cultural
gatherings; Outdoor outings.

Lake Preston

Kingsbury Memorial Manor (NCHS)
4th SE & Manor Ave, Lake Preston, SD
57249
(605) 847-4405
Admin Dixie Wilde. *Dir of Nursing* Sherry
Nielsen. *Medical Dir* David Halliday MD.
Licensure Skilled care; Intermediate care;
Retirement. *Beds* SNF 30; ICF 35. *Certified*
Medicaid.
Owner Proprietary corp (North Central Health
Services).
Admissions Requirements Medical
examination; Physician's request.
Staff Physicians 2 (ft); RNs 4 (ft), 1 (pt);
LPNs 2 (ft), 1 (pt); Nurses' aides 20 (ft), 15
(pt); Physical therapists 1 (pt); Recreational
therapists 2 (ft); Speech therapists 1 (pt);
Activities coordinators 1 (ft); Dietitians 1
(pt).
Facilities Dining room; Physical therapy
room; Activities room; Chapel; Crafts room;
Laundry room; Barber/Beauty shop; Library;
TV room.
Activities Arts & crafts; Cards; Games;
Reading groups; Prayer groups; Movies;
Shopping trips; Dances/Social/Cultural
gatherings.

Lemmon

Five Counties Nursing Home
401 6th Ave W, Lemmon, SD 57638
(605) 374-3871
Admin Helen S Lindquist. *Dir of Nursing*
Elizabeth Holm RN. *Medical Dir* Terrance
Mack MD.
Licensure Skilled care. *Beds* SNF 32. *Certified*
Medicaid.
Owner Nonprofit corp.
Admissions Requirements Physician's request.
Staff RNs; LPNs; Nurses' aides; Physical
therapists; Activities coordinators.
Facilities Dining room; Physical therapy
room; Laundry room.
Activities Arts & crafts; Cards; Games;
Reading groups; Prayer groups; Movies;
Picnics.

Lennox

Lennox Good Samaritan Center
PO Box 78, Lennox, SD 57039
(605) 647-2251
Admin J Lynn Thomas.
Medical Dir Larry Sittner MD.
Licensure Skilled care; Intermediate care. *Beds*
SNF 60; ICF 9. *Certified* Medicaid.
Owner Nonprofit corp (Evangelical Lutheran/
Good Samaritan Society).

Letcher

Storla Sunset Center
PO Box 46, RR 1, Letcher, SD 57359
(605) 248-2244
Admin L Burdell Nelson.
Medical Dir Roscoe Dean MD.
Licensure Intermediate care. *Beds* ICF 53.
Certified Medicaid.

Madison

Bethel Lutheran Home
1001 S Egan Ave, Madison, SD 57042
(605) 256-4539
Admin James T Iverson. *Dir of Nursing* Joan
Johnson RN. *Medical Dir* Richard Sample
MD.
Licensure Skilled care; Retirement;
Alzheimer's care. *Beds* SNF 59. *Certified*
Medicaid.
Owner Nonprofit corp.
Admissions Requirements Minimum age 18;
Medical examination; Physician's request.
Staff RNs 3 (ft), 4 (pt); LPNs 3 (ft); Nurses'
aides 20 (ft), 15 (pt); Activities coordinators
1 (ft), 1 (pt); Dietitians 1 (ft).
Affiliation Lutheran.
Facilities Dining room; Activities room;
Crafts room; Laundry room; Barber/Beauty
shop.
Activities Arts & crafts; Cards; Games;
Reading groups; Prayer groups; Movies;
Shopping trips; Dances/Social/Cultural
gatherings.

Evergreen Terrace Healthcare Center
718 NE 8th St, Madison, SD 57042
(605) 256-6621
Admin Jeanine Reed.
Medical Dir Richard Sample MD.
Licensure Skilled care; Intermediate care. *Beds*
SNF 42; ICF 20. *Certified* Medicaid.
Owner Proprietary corp (Waverly Group).
Affiliation Baptist.

Marion

Tieszen Memorial Home
RR 1 Box 209, Marion, SD 57043
(605) 648-3384
Admin Paul I Engbrecht. *Dir of Nursing* Kay
Weeldreyer.
Licensure Intermediate care; Retirement. *Beds*
ICF 64. *Certified* Medicaid.
Owner Nonprofit organization/foundation.
Admissions Requirements Medical
examination.
Languages German.
Facilities Dining room; Physical therapy
room; Activities room; Chapel; Crafts room;
Laundry room; Barber/Beauty shop; Library.
Activities Arts & crafts; Cards; Games;
Reading groups; Movies; Shopping trips;
Dances/Social/Cultural gatherings.

Martin

Bennett County Nursing Home
PO Box 70-D, Martin, SD 57551
(605) 685-6586
Admin Joseph A McFadden.
Medical Dir Carolos Torrent MD.
Licensure Skilled care; Intermediate care. *Beds*
SNF 40; ICF 8. *Certified* Medicaid.
Owner Publicly owned.
Staff Physicians 2 (ft); RNs 1 (ft), 2 (pt);
LPNs 2 (ft), 6 (pt); Nurses' aides 7 (ft), 9
(pt); Occupational therapists 1 (pt);
Activities coordinators 1 (ft); Dietitians 1
(pt).

Menno

Menno-Olivet Care Center
402 S Pine, Menno, SD 57045
(605) 387-5139
Admin Maxine Christensen. *Dir of Nursing*
Kathy Guthmiller. *Medical Dir* Kathy
Guthmiller.
Licensure Intermediate care. *Beds* ICF 49.
Private Pay Patients 50%. *Certified*
Medicaid.
Owner Nonprofit organization/foundation.
Admissions Requirements Medical
examination; Physician's request.
Staff Physicians 3 (pt); RNs 1 (ft), 1 (pt);
LPNs 4 (pt); Nurses' aides 4 (ft), 8 (pt);
Activities coordinators 1 (ft), 1 (pt);
Dietitians 1 (ft), 1 (pt).
Languages German.
Facilities Dining room; Physical therapy
room; Activities room; Chapel; Crafts room;
Laundry room; Barber/Beauty shop; Library.
Activities Arts & crafts; Cards; Games;
Reading groups; Prayer groups; Movies;
Shopping trips; Dances/Social/Cultural
gatherings; Intergenerational programs; Pet
therapy; Religious services.

Milbank

St William's Home for the Aged
901 E Virgil Ave, Milbank, SD 57252
(605) 432-4538
Admin Sr Margaret Mary Vogel. *Dir of
Nursing* Sr Martha Scheessele. *Medical Dir*
Kanya Vanadurongvan MD.
Licensure Intermediate care; Supervised care;
Retirement. *Beds* ICF 60; Supervised care
20. *Certified* Medicaid.
Owner Nonprofit corp (Daughters of St Mary
of Providence).
Admissions Requirements Medical
examination; Physician's request.
Staff Physicians (Med dir); RNs 1 (ft), 2 (pt);
LPNs 5 (ft), 5 (pt); Nurses' aides 24 (ft), 22
(pt); Physical therapists (contracted);
Recreational therapists 1 (ft); Activities
coordinators 1 (ft); Dietitians 1 (pt);
Ophthalmologists (contracted); Podiatrists
(contracted); Audiologists (contracted).
Languages German, Italian, Rumanian
interpreters available.
Affiliation Roman Catholic.
Facilities Dining room; Physical therapy
room; Activities room; Chapel; Crafts room;
Laundry room; Barber/Beauty shop; Library.
Activities Arts & crafts; Cards; Games;
Reading groups; Prayer groups; Movies;
Shopping trips; Dances/Social/Cultural
gatherings; Pet therapy.

Whetstone Valley Nursing Home
1103 S 2nd St, Milbank, SD 57252
(605) 432-4556
Admin Robert E Hanson. *Dir of Nursing*
Joyce Kasuske. *Medical Dir* Dr Michael
Coyle.
Licensure Skilled care. *Beds* SNF 83. *Certified*
Medicaid; Medicare.
Owner Proprietary corp (Beverly Enterprises).
Admissions Requirements Medical
examination.
Staff RNs 5 (ft); LPNs 9 (ft); Nurses' aides 40
(ft), 8 (pt); Physical therapists 1 (ft);
Recreational therapists 1 (ft); Dietitians.
Facilities Dining room; Physical therapy
room; Activities room; Crafts room; Laundry
room; Barber/Beauty shop.
Activities Arts & crafts; Cards; Games;
Reading groups; Prayer groups; Movies;
Shopping trips; Dances/Social/Cultural
gatherings.

Miller

Prairie Good Samaritan Center
421 E 4th St, Miller, SD 57362
(605) 853-2701
Admin Douglas B Cruff. *Dir of Nursing*
Mardelle Hoch RN. *Medical Dir* Stephan
Schroeder MD.
Licensure Skilled care. *Beds* SNF 78. *Private
Pay Patients* 30%. *Certified* Medicaid.
Owner Nonprofit corp (Evangelical Lutheran/
Good Samaritan Society).
Admissions Requirements Medical
examination; Physician's request.
Staff RNs 2 (ft), 5 (pt); LPNs 1 (ft), 4 (pt);
Nurses' aides 14 (ft), 25 (pt); Activities
coordinators 1 (ft).
Affiliation Lutheran.
Facilities Dining room; Physical therapy
room; Activities room; Chapel; Crafts room;
Laundry room; Barber/Beauty shop; Library;
Dayroom; Family room.
Activities Arts & crafts; Cards; Games;
Reading groups; Prayer groups; Movies;
Shopping trips; Dances/Social/Cultural
gatherings; Intergenerational programs; Bus
trips; Community programs.

Mitchell

Brady Memorial Home
500 S Ohlman, Box 430, Mitchell, SD 57301
(605) 996-7701
Admin Roberta Clark.
Medical Dir Lucio N Magullo MD.
Licensure Skilled care; Retirement. *Beds* SNF
61. *Certified* Medicaid.
Owner Nonprofit corp (Presentation Health
Systems).
Admissions Requirements Medical
examination.
Staff RNs 3 (ft), 4 (pt); LPNs 2 (pt); Nurses'
aides 6 (ft), 27 (pt); Activities coordinators 1
(ft), 1 (pt).
Affiliation Roman Catholic.
Facilities Dining room; Activities room;
Chapel; Crafts room; Laundry room; Barber/
Beauty shop.
Activities Arts & crafts; Cards; Games;
Reading groups; Movies; Dances/Social/
Cultural gatherings.

Firesteel Health Care Center
1120 E 7th St, Mitchell, SD 57301
(605) 996-6526
Admin Ronald D Gates Jr.
Medical Dir W Baas MD.
Licensure Skilled care. *Beds* SNF 117.
Certified Medicaid.
Admissions Requirements Medical
examination; Physician's request.
Facilities Dining room; Physical therapy
room; Activities room; Crafts room; Laundry
room; Barber/Beauty shop.
Activities Arts & crafts; Cards; Games;
Reading groups; Prayer groups; Movies;
Shopping trips; Dances/Social/Cultural
gatherings.

Mitchell Retirement Nursing Center
PO Box 190, 101 S Main St, Mitchell, SD
57301
(605) 996-6251
Admin Ronald D Gates Sr.
Licensure Intermediate care. *Beds* ICF 51.
Certified Medicaid.
Admissions Requirements Medical
examination; Physician's request.
Staff RNs 2 (ft), 1 (pt); LPNs 3 (ft), 5 (pt);
Nurses' aides 14 (ft), 8 (pt); Recreational
therapists 1 (ft); Activities coordinators 1
(ft); Dietitians 1 (pt).

Facilities Dining room; Activities room; Chapel; Crafts room.
Activities Arts & crafts; Cards; Games; Reading groups; Prayer groups; Movies; Shopping trips; Dances/Social/Cultural gatherings.

Mogck Home for Aged
1520 E 1st Ave, Mitchell, SD 57301
(605) 996-2221
Admin Dolores Juhnke Sheffield. Dir of Nursing Elsie Juhnke.
Licensure Supervised care. Beds Supervised care 11.
Owner Privately owned.
Admissions Requirements Females only.
Staff LPNs 1 (ft); Nurses' aides 3 (ft).
Facilities Dining room; Laundry room.
Activities Games; Movies; Shopping trips; Bingo.

Mogck's Rest Home
1510 E 1st Ave, Mitchell, SD 57301
(605) 996-2221
Admin Dolores Juhnke Sheffield. Dir of Nursing Elsie Juhnke.
Licensure Supervised care. Beds Supervised care 11.
Owner Privately owned.
Admissions Requirements Females only; Medical examination.
Staff LPNs; Nurses' aides.
Facilities Dining room; Laundry room.
Activities Cards; Movies; Bingo.

Wilge Memorial Home
619 N Kittridge, Mitchell, SD 57301
(605) 996-4280
Admin Roberta Clark. Dir of Nursing Marty Andrzejewski.
Licensure Intermediate care. Beds ICF 19. Certified Medicaid.
Owner Privately owned.
Admissions Requirements Medical examination.
Staff RNs 1 (ft); LPNs 1 (ft), 4 (pt); Nurses' aides 7 (pt); Activities coordinators 1 (pt); Dietitians 1 (pt).
Facilities Dining room; Activities room; Crafts room; Laundry room; Barber/Beauty shop.
Activities Arts & crafts; Cards; Games; Reading groups; Prayer groups; Movies; Shopping trips; Dances/Social/Cultural gatherings.

Mobridge

Mobridge Care Center
1100 4th Ave E, Mobridge, SD 57601
(605) 845-7201
Admin Gary Robertson.
Medical Dir Leonard Linde MD.
Licensure Skilled care. Beds SNF 117. Certified Medicaid.
Owner Proprietary corp (Beverly Enterprises).
Staff Physicians.
Facilities Dining room; Physical therapy room; Activities room; Chapel; Crafts room; Laundry room; Barber/Beauty shop.
Activities Arts & crafts; Cards; Games; Reading groups; Prayer groups; Movies; Shopping trips; Dances/Social/Cultural gatherings.

New Underwood

New Underwood Good Samaritan Center
PO Box 327, 412 S Madison, New Underwood, SD 57761
(605) 754-6489
Admin Bradley N Felix. Dir of Nursing Ann Simon. Medical Dir Ann Simon.
Licensure Intermediate care; Supervised care. Beds ICF 44; Supervised care 5. Private Pay Patients 50%. Certified Medicaid.

Owner Nonprofit corp (Evangelical Lutheran/ Good Samaritan Society).
Admissions Requirements Medical examination; Prescreening.
Staff Physicians 1 (ft); RNs 1 (ft), 2 (pt); LPNs 1 (ft), 2 (pt); Nurses' aides 11 (ft), 4 (pt); Activities coordinators 1 (ft); Dietitians 1 (ft).
Languages German.
Facilities Dining room; Activities room; Chapel; Crafts room; Laundry room; Barber/ Beauty shop; Library; Resident lounge.
Activities Arts & crafts; Cards; Games; Reading groups; Movies; Shopping trips; Intergenerational programs; Pet therapy.

Newell

Lee's Rest Home
218 S Girard, Newell, SD 57760
(605) 456-2108
Admin Norman & Joan Lee.
Licensure Intermediate care. Beds ICF 5.
Owner Privately owned.
Admissions Requirements Males only.
Staff RNs; Dietitians.
Facilities Dining room; Activities room; Laundry room.
Activities Arts & crafts; Shopping trips; Dances/Social/Cultural gatherings.

Parker

Hilltop Nursing Home
PO Box 218, Parker, SD 57053
(605) 297-3488
Admin Michael L Turner. Dir of Nursing Charlene Turner RN.
Licensure Intermediate care. Beds ICF 40. Certified Medicaid.
Owner Proprietary corp.
Admissions Requirements Medical examination; Physician's request.
Staff RNs 3 (ft), 1 (pt); LPNs 1 (ft), 3 (pt); Nurses' aides 28 (pt); Physical therapists 1 (pt); Reality therapists 2 (pt); Recreational therapists 1 (pt); Activities coordinators 1 (ft); Dietitians 1 (pt); Dentists 1 (pt).
Facilities Dining room; Activities room; Chapel; Crafts room; Laundry room; Barber/ Beauty shop; Library.
Activities Arts & crafts; Cards; Games; Reading groups; Prayer groups; Movies; Shopping trips; Dances/Social/Cultural gatherings.

Parkston

Parkston Nursing Center
501 W Main, Parkston, SD 57366
(605) 928-3384
Admin Gale N Walker.
Licensure Intermediate care. Beds ICF 47. Certified Medicaid.
Owner Nonprofit corp.
Admissions Requirements Medical examination; Physician's request.
Staff RNs 1 (ft); LPNs 4 (ft); Nurses' aides 4 (ft), 19 (pt); Activities coordinators 1 (ft), 1 (pt); Dietitians 1 (ft).
Affiliation Lutheran.
Facilities Dining room; Activities room; Chapel; Crafts room; Laundry room.
Activities Arts & crafts; Cards; Games; Reading groups; Movies; Dances/Social/ Cultural gatherings.

Parkston Supervised Living Center
PO Box 718, 205 E Ash, Parkston, SD 57366
(605) 928-3561
Admin Gale N Walker.
Licensure Supervised care. Beds Supervised care 26. Certified Medicaid.
Owner Nonprofit corp.
Admissions Requirements Medical examination; Physician's request.

Staff LPNs 1 (pt); Nurses' aides 7 (pt); Activities coordinators 1 (pt); Dietitians 1 (pt).
Affiliation Lutheran.
Facilities Dining room; Activities room; Chapel; Crafts room.
Activities Arts & crafts; Games; Movies; Dances/Social/Cultural gatherings.

Philip

Philip Nursing Home
PO Box 790, Philip, SD 57567
(605) 859-2511
Admin Joseph A McFadden. Dir of Nursing Jessica Dale RN. Medical Dir George Mangulis MD.
Licensure Skilled care. Beds SNF 30. Certified Medicaid.
Owner Nonprofit corp.
Admissions Requirements Medical examination; Physician's request.
Staff Physicians 1 (ft), 6 (pt); RNs 1 (ft), 5 (pt); LPNs 2 (ft), 4 (pt); Nurses' aides 4 (ft), 6 (pt); Physical therapists 1 (pt); Activities coordinators 1 (ft); Dietitians 1 (pt).
Facilities Dining room; Physical therapy room; Activities room; Laundry room; Barber/Beauty shop.
Activities Arts & crafts; Cards; Games; Reading groups; Prayer groups; Movies; Shopping trips; Dances/Social/Cultural gatherings.

Pierre

Kelly's Retirement Home
1014 E Park, Pierre, SD 57501
(605) 224-5261
Admin Dean Kelly; Peggy Kelly.
Licensure Supervised living. Beds Supervised living 6.

Maryhouse Inc
717 E Dakota, Pierre, SD 57501
(605) 224-8482
Admin Jane Vogt. Dir of Nursing Judy Schwartz RN. Medical Dir R C Jahraus MD.
Licensure Skilled care. Beds SNF 105. Private Pay Patients 50%. Certified Medicaid; Medicare.
Owner Nonprofit corp.
Admissions Requirements Medical examination; Physician's request.
Staff RNs 6 (ft), 3 (pt); LPNs 9 (ft), 2 (pt); Nurses' aides 37 (ft), 13 (pt); Physical therapists 1 (pt); Activities coordinators 2 (ft), 3 (pt); Dietitians 1 (pt).
Languages German, Lakota Sioux.
Affiliation Roman Catholic.
Facilities Dining room; Activities room; Chapel; Crafts room; Barber/Beauty shop; Library.
Activities Arts & crafts; Cards; Games; Reading groups; Prayer groups; Movies; Shopping trips; Dances/Social/Cultural gatherings; Intergenerational programs; Pet therapy; Creative seasonal events.

Missouri Valley Nursing Center
950 E Park, Pierre, SD 57501
(605) 224-8628
Admin Terry Rieck. Dir of Nursing Norma Newberger. Medical Dir P E Hoffsten MD.
Licensure Skilled care; Intermediate care; Alzheimer's care. Beds SNF 8; ICF 64. Private Pay Patients 32%. Certified Medicaid.
Owner Proprietary corp (Beverly Enterprises).
Admissions Requirements Medical examination; Physician's request.
Staff RNs 3 (ft); LPNs 3 (ft), 3 (pt); Nurses' aides 20 (ft), 12 (pt); Physical therapists (consultant); Activities coordinators 1 (ft), 2 (pt); Dietitians (consultant).

Facilities Dining room; Physical therapy room; Activities room; Laundry room; Barber/Beauty shop; Whirlpool & shower rooms.
Activities Arts & crafts; Cards; Games; Reading groups; Prayer groups; Movies; Dances/Social/Cultural gatherings; Intergenerational programs; Pet therapy; Alzheimer's support group.

Platte

Platte Nursing Home
609 E 7th, Platte, SD 57369
(605) 337-3131
Admin Patricia Biddle.
Medical Dir Jerome Bentz MD.
Licensure Skilled care; Intermediate care. *Beds* SNF 15; ICF 33. *Certified* Medicaid.
Admissions Requirements Physician's request.
Staff Physical therapists 1 (pt); Activities coordinators 1 (ft), 1 (pt); Dietitians 1 (pt).
Facilities Dining room; Activities room; Crafts room; Barber/Beauty shop.
Activities Arts & crafts; Cards; Games; Reading groups; Prayer groups; Shopping trips.

Quinn

Hilltop Retirement Home
PO Box 8, Quinn, SD 57775
(605) 386-2421
Admin Augusta Murphy.
Licensure Supervised care. *Beds* 8.

Rapid City

Bella Vista Nursing Center
302 Saint Cloud St, Rapid City, SD 57701
(605) 343-4738
Admin Doug Knutson.
Medical Dir Richard Finely MD.
Licensure Skilled care. *Beds* SNF 70. *Certified* Medicaid.
Owner Proprietary corp (Beverly Enterprises).
Admissions Requirements Medical examination.
Staff RNs 2 (ft), 2 (pt); LPNs 2 (ft), 2 (pt); Nurses' aides 21 (ft), 6 (pt); Physical therapists 1 (pt); Activities coordinators 2 (ft); Dietitians 1 (ft); Dentists 1 (pt).
Facilities Dining room; Physical therapy room; Activities room; Chapel; Crafts room; Laundry room; Barber/Beauty shop; Library.
Activities Arts & crafts; Games; Reading groups; Prayer groups; Movies; Shopping trips; Dances/Social/Cultural gatherings.

Black Hills Retirement Center
1620 N 7th St, Rapid City, SD 57701
(605) 343-4958
Admin Karen Jensen. *Dir of Nursing* Brenda Anton RN. *Medical Dir* Alvin Wessel MD.
Licensure Intermediate care. *Beds* ICF 74. *Certified* Medicaid.
Owner Proprietary corp (Beverly Enterprises).
Admissions Requirements Medical examination; Physician's request.
Staff RNs 1 (ft), 2 (pt); LPNs 2 (ft), 4 (pt); Nurses' aides 12 (ft), 14 (pt); Activities coordinators 1 (ft), 1 (pt).
Facilities Dining room; Activities room; Crafts room; Laundry room; Barber/Beauty shop; Dayroom; Solarium.
Activities Arts & crafts; Games; Reading groups; Prayer groups; Movies; Dances/Social/Cultural gatherings.

Boardman Community Care Home
6604 Green Willow Dr, Rapid City, SD 57701
(605) 342-0885
Admin Dottie Boardman.
Licensure Supervised care. *Beds* 7.

Clarkson Mountain View Guest Home (NCHS)
1015 Mountain View, Rapid City, SD 57702
(605) 343-5882
Admin Doris J McAndrews.
Medical Dir James Yackley MD.
Licensure Skilled care. *Beds* SNF 52. *Certified* Medicaid.
Owner Proprietary corp (North Central Health Services).

Meadowbrook Manor
2500 Arrowhead Dr, Rapid City, SD 57702
(605) 348-0285
Admin Lynn Burgad. *Dir of Nursing* Jean Wainwright. *Medical Dir* Reuben Bareis MD.
Licensure Skilled care. *Beds* SNF 76. *Private Pay Patients* 25%. *Certified* Medicaid.
Owner Proprietary corp (Beverly Enterprises).
Admissions Requirements Medical examination; Physician's request.
Staff RNs 6 (ft); LPNs 4 (ft); Nurses' aides 33 (ft); Physical therapists 1 (pt); Activities coordinators 1 (ft); Dietitians 1 (pt).
Facilities Dining room; Physical therapy room; Activities room; Crafts room; Laundry room; Barber/Beauty shop.
Activities Arts & crafts; Cards; Games; Reading groups; Prayer groups; Movies; Shopping trips; Dances/Social/Cultural gatherings; Intergenerational programs; Pet therapy.

O'Brien's Rest Home
1131 Wood Ave, Rapid City, SD 57701
(605) 342-4570
Admin Elizabeth O'Brien.
Licensure Supervised care. *Beds* 6.

Rapid City Care Center
916 Mountain View, Rapid City, SD 57702
(605) 343-8577
Admin John R Miller.
Medical Dir David Rieth MD.
Licensure Skilled care. *Beds* SNF 99. *Certified* Medicaid.
Owner Proprietary corp (Beverly Enterprises).

Rapid City Nursing Center
2908 5th St, Rapid City, SD 57701
(605) 343-8500
Admin Roland Marinkovic.
Licensure Skilled care. *Beds* 51. *Certified* Medicaid.

Wesleyan Health Care Center
2000 Wesleyan Blvd, Rapid City, SD 57701
(605) 343-3555
Admin Robert Bonato.
Licensure Skilled care; Intermediate care. *Beds* SNF 30; ICF 60.

Westhills Village Health Care Facility
255 Texas St, Rapid City, SD 57701
(605) 342-0255
Admin Daryl Reinicke.
Medical Dir Reuben Baries MD.
Licensure Skilled care; Intermediate care; Supervised living. *Beds* SNF 28; ICF 10; Supervised living 6.
Owner Proprietary corp (Health One Health Care).

Redfield

Eastern Star Home of South Dakota
126 W 12th Ave, Redfield, SD 57469
(605) 472-2255
Admin Mary Fountain. *Dir of Nursing* Judy Scnabel RN. *Medical Dir* Sterling Berg MD.
Licensure Intermediate care; Retirement. *Beds* ICF 30.
Owner Nonprofit corp.
Admissions Requirements Medical examination.
Staff RNs 1 (ft), 2 (pt); LPNs 2 (pt); Nurses' aides 3 (ft), 7 (pt); Activities coordinators 1 (ft).

Affiliation Eastern Star.
Facilities Dining room; Activities room; Chapel; Crafts room; Laundry room; Barber/Beauty shop; Library.
Activities Arts & crafts; Cards; Games; Reading groups; Prayer groups; Movies; Shopping trips; Dances/Social/Cultural gatherings.

James Valley Nursing Home
1015 3rd St E, Redfield, SD 57469
(605) 472-2289
Admin Joan Williams.
Medical Dir Joel Huber MD.
Licensure Skilled care. *Beds* SNF 87. *Certified* Medicaid.
Owner Proprietary corp (Beverly Enterprises).

Rosholt

Rosholt Nursing Home
PO Box 108, Rosholt, SD 57260
(605) 537-4272
Admin Shirleen Fossum. *Dir of Nursing* Carol Luebke LPN. *Medical Dir* Joseph Kass MD.
Licensure Intermediate care. *Beds* ICF 49. *Private Pay Patients* 66%. *Certified* Medicaid.
Owner Proprietary corp.
Admissions Requirements Medical examination.
Staff RNs 1 (pt); LPNs 1 (ft), 4 (pt); Nurses' aides 2 (ft), 24 (pt); Activities coordinators 1 (ft), 1 (pt).
Facilities Dining room; Activities room; Laundry room; Barber/Beauty shop.
Activities Arts & crafts; Cards; Games; Reading groups; Prayer groups; Movies; Dances/Social/Cultural gatherings.

Roslyn

Strand-Kjorsvig Community Rest Home
PO Box 195, Roslyn, SD 57261
(605) 486-4523
Admin Bernie H P Hanson. *Dir of Nursing* Barbara Stueland.
Licensure Intermediate care. *Beds* ICF 36. *Certified* Medicaid.
Owner Nonprofit corp.
Admissions Requirements Medical examination; Physician's request.
Staff RNs 1 (ft), 1 (pt); Nurses' aides 6 (ft), 11 (pt); Occupational therapists 1 (ft); Activities coordinators 1 (ft); Dietitians 1 (pt).
Facilities Dining room; Activities room; Chapel; Laundry room; Barber/Beauty shop.
Activities Arts & crafts; Cards; Games; Reading groups; Prayer groups; Dances/Social/Cultural gatherings.

Salem

Colonial Manor of Salem
500 Colonial Dr, Box 460, Salem, SD 57058
(605) 425-2203
Admin Dennis C Gourley.
Medical Dir Anthony Petres MD.
Licensure Skilled care. *Beds* SNF 63. *Certified* Medicaid.
Owner Proprietary corp (Beverly Enterprises).
Admissions Requirements Physician's request.
Staff RNs; LPNs; Nurses' aides; Activities coordinators; Dietitians.
Facilities Dining room; Physical therapy room; Activities room; Chapel; Laundry room; Barber/Beauty shop.
Activities Arts & crafts; Cards; Games; Reading groups; Prayer groups; Movies; Shopping trips; Dances/Social/Cultural gatherings.

Scotland

Scotland Good Samaritan Center
Box 428, Scotland, SD 57059
(605) 583-2216
Admin Thomas C Hoy. *Dir of Nursing* Gladys Hasz. *Medical Dir* Manuel Ramos MD.
Licensure Intermediate care; Alzheimer's care; Adult day care. *Beds* ICF 62. *Certified* Medicaid.
Owner Nonprofit corp (Evangelical Lutheran/ Good Samaritan Society).
Admissions Requirements Minimum age 18; Medical examination; Physician's request.
Staff RNs 2 (ft); LPNs 4 (pt); Nurses' aides 15 (ft), 15 (pt); Recreational therapists 2 (ft); Activities coordinators 1 (ft).
Languages German, Bohemian, Czech.
Affiliation Lutheran.
Facilities Dining room; Physical therapy room; Activities room; Chapel; Crafts room; Laundry room; Barber/Beauty shop; Library.
Activities Arts & crafts; Cards; Games; Reading groups; Prayer groups; Movies; Shopping trips; Dances/Social/Cultural gatherings; Worship services & devotions; Volunteer & auxiliary programs.

Selby

Selby Good Samaritan Center
4861 Lincoln Ave, Box 299, Selby, SD 57472
(605) 649-7663
Admin Sandra Schanzenbach. *Dir of Nursing* Chloe Stulken. *Medical Dir* L M Lindi MD.
Licensure Intermediate care. *Beds* ICF 64. *Certified* Medicaid.
Owner Nonprofit corp (Evangelical Lutheran/ Good Samaritan Society).
Admissions Requirements Medical examination.
Staff RNs; LPNs; Nurses' aides; Activities coordinators; Dietitians.
Languages German, Norwegian.
Affiliation Lutheran.
Facilities Dining room; Physical therapy room; Laundry room; Barber/Beauty shop.
Activities Arts & crafts; Cards; Games; Reading groups; Prayer groups; Movies; Dances/Social/Cultural gatherings; Pet therapy.

Sioux Falls

Bethany Lutheran Home
1901 S Holly, Sioux Falls, SD 57105
(605) 338-2351
Admin John B Roth.
Medical Dir Tim Hurley MD.
Licensure Skilled care. *Beds* SNF 112. *Certified* Medicaid.
Admissions Requirements Medical examination; Physician's request.
Staff RNs 9 (ft), 7 (pt); LPNs 5 (ft), 4 (pt); Nurses' aides 31 (ft), 49 (pt); Reality therapists 2 (ft), 1 (pt); Recreational therapists 2 (ft), 2 (pt); Activities coordinators 1 (ft); Dietitians 1 (pt).
Affiliation Lutheran.
Facilities Dining room; Physical therapy room; Activities room; Crafts room; Laundry room; Barber/Beauty shop; Hospitality room.
Activities Arts & crafts; Cards; Games; Reading groups; Prayer groups; Movies; Shopping trips; Exercises.

C & M Rest Haven
5405 Romar Dr, Sioux Falls, SD 57107
(605) 335-8237
Admin Carl Serr; Marion Serr.
Licensure Supervised care. *Beds* Supervised care 5.
Admissions Requirements Females only.
Facilities Dining room; Laundry room.

Covington Heights Health Care Center
3900 S Cathy Ave, Sioux Falls, SD 57106
(605) 361-8822
Admin Gary L Brink. *Dir of Nursing* Shelly Clauson RN. *Medical Dir* S Devick MD.
Licensure Skilled care; Retirement. *Beds* SNF 109. *Certified* Medicaid; Medicare.
Owner Proprietary corp (Beverly Enterprises).
Admissions Requirements Medical examination.
Staff RNs; LPNs; Nurses' aides; Activities coordinators; Dietitians.
Facilities Dining room; Physical therapy room; Activities room; Crafts room; Laundry room; Barber/Beauty shop.
Activities Arts & crafts; Cards; Games; Reading groups; Prayer groups; Movies; Shopping trips; Dances/Social/Cultural gatherings.

Dow-Rummel Village
1000 N Lake Ave, Sioux Falls, SD 57104
(605) 336-1490
Admin Ralph Jensen. *Dir of Nursing* Helen Carlson RN.
Licensure Intermediate care; Independent living. *Beds* ICF 40; Independent living units 97. *Private Pay Patients* 100%.
Owner Nonprofit organization/foundation.
Admissions Requirements Minimum age 65.
Staff RNs 3 (ft), 3 (pt); LPNs 2 (ft), 2 (pt); Nurses' aides 8 (ft), 4 (pt); Activities coordinators 1 (ft); Dietitians 1 (pt).
Facilities Dining room; Activities room; Chapel; Crafts room; Laundry room; Barber/ Beauty shop; Library.
Activities Arts & crafts; Cards; Games; Reading groups; Prayer groups; Movies; Shopping trips; Dances/Social/Cultural gatherings; Intergenerational programs; Pet therapy.

Good Samaritan Center
401 W 2nd St, Sioux Falls, SD 57104
(605) 336-6252
Admin Raymond Roti.
Medical Dir David Brechtelsbauer MD.
Licensure Skilled care. *Beds* SNF 141. *Certified* Medicaid.
Owner Nonprofit corp (Evangelical Lutheran/ Good Samaritan Society).
Admissions Requirements Minimum age 14; Medical examination.
Staff Physicians 1 (pt); RNs 7 (ft), 4 (pt); LPNs 7 (ft), 2 (pt); Nurses' aides 39 (ft), 28 (pt); Physical therapists 2 (pt); Recreational therapists 2 (ft); Occupational therapists 1 (pt); Speech therapists 1 (pt); Activities coordinators 1 (ft), 1 (pt); Dietitians 1 (pt); Podiatrists 1 (pt); Audiologists 1 (pt); Dentists 1 (pt).
Facilities Dining room; Physical therapy room; Activities room; Chapel; Crafts room; Laundry room; Barber/Beauty shop.
Activities Arts & crafts; Cards; Games; Reading groups; Prayer groups; Movies; Shopping trips; Dances/Social/Cultural gatherings; Bible study.

Good Samaritan Luther Manor
2900 S Lake Ave, Sioux Falls, SD 57105
(605) 336-1997
Admin Kayln H Johnson. *Dir of Nursing* Mina Hall. *Medical Dir* Dr Jerel Tieszen.
Licensure Skilled care; Alzheimer's care. *Beds* SNF 118. *Private Pay Patients* 50%. *Certified* Medicaid.
Owner Nonprofit corp (Evangelical Lutheran/ Good Samaritan Society).
Admissions Requirements Medical examination.
Staff Physicians 1 (pt); RNs 3 (ft), 11 (pt); LPNs 2 (ft), 6 (pt); Nurses' aides 28 (ft), 37 (pt); Physical therapists 4 (ft), 1 (pt); Reality therapists; Recreational therapists; Occupational therapists; Speech therapists;

Activities coordinators 1 (ft), 3 (pt); Dietitians 2 (pt); Ophthalmologists; Podiatrists; Audiologists.
Languages Spanish.
Affiliation Lutheran.
Facilities Dining room; Physical therapy room; Chapel; Laundry room; Barber/Beauty shop; Privacy room; Book mobile; Activities/ Crafts Room.
Activities Arts & crafts; Cards; Games; Reading groups; Prayer groups; Movies; Shopping trips; Dances/Social/Cultural gatherings; Pet therapy; Alzheimer's activities.

Good Samaritan Village
3901 S Marion Rd, Sioux Falls, SD 57106
(605) 361-3311
Admin John B Larson. *Dir of Nursing* Lael Smith RN. *Medical Dir* Larry L Sittner MD.
Licensure Skilled care; Intermediate care; Assisted living. *Beds* SNF 55; ICF 90; Assisted living 77. *Private Pay Patients* 62%. *Certified* Medicaid.
Owner Nonprofit corp (Evangelical Lutheran/ Good Samaritan Society).
Admissions Requirements Medical examination; Physician's request.
Staff RNs 4 (ft), 7 (pt); LPNs 8 (ft), 11 (pt); Nurses' aides 20 (ft), 35 (pt); Activities coordinators 1 (ft); Dietitians 1 (ft), 1 (pt).
Affiliation Lutheran.
Facilities Dining room; Activities room; Chapel; Crafts room; Laundry room; Barber/ Beauty shop; Library.
Activities Arts & crafts; Cards; Games; Reading groups; Prayer groups; Movies; Shopping trips; Dances/Social/Cultural gatherings.

Mom & Dad's Home & Health Care Center
3600 S Norton, Sioux Falls, SD 57105
(605) 338-9891
Admin Barbara Severson. *Dir of Nursing* Nita Birk RN. *Medical Dir* A P Reding MD.
Licensure Skilled care; Intermediate care. *Beds* SNF 109; ICF 50. *Certified* Medicaid.
Owner Proprietary corp (Samcor).
Admissions Requirements Medical examination.
Staff RNs 9 (ft); LPNs 11 (ft), 4 (pt); Nurses' aides 47 (ft), 34 (pt); Activities coordinators 2 (ft), 2 (pt); Dietitians 1 (ft).
Facilities Dining room; Physical therapy room; Activities room; Chapel; Crafts room; Laundry room; Barber/Beauty shop; Library.
Activities Arts & crafts; Cards; Games; Reading groups; Prayer groups; Movies; Shopping trips; Dances/Social/Cultural gatherings.

Prince of Peace Retirement Community
4500 Prince of Peace Pl, Sioux Falls, SD 57103
(605) 371-0700
Admin Gary O Tuschen. *Dir of Nursing* Lynda Wollman. *Medical Dir* Michael Tobin MD.
Licensure Skilled care; Retirement; Alzheimer's care. *Beds* SNF 90; Retirement apartments 25. *Certified* Medicaid.
Owner Nonprofit corp (Presentation Health System).
Admissions Requirements Medical examination; Physician's request.
Staff RNs 8 (ft), 7 (pt); LPNs 3 (ft), 3 (pt); Nurses' aides 23 (ft), 17 (pt); Physical therapists (consultant); Occupational therapists (consultant); Speech therapists (consultant); Activities coordinators 1 (ft), 1 (pt); Dietitians (consultant); Pharmacists (consultant).
Affiliation Roman Catholic.
Facilities Dining room; Physical therapy room; Activities room; Chapel; Crafts room; Laundry room; Barber/Beauty shop; Smoking & non-smoking resident lounges.

Activities Arts & crafts; Cards; Games;
Reading groups; Prayer groups; Movies;
Shopping trips; Dances/Social/Cultural
gatherings; Intergenerational programs; Pet
therapy; Resident council.

Sisseton

Tekakwitha Nursing Home
6 E Chestnut St, Sisseton, SD 57262
(605) 698-7693
Admin Dean Kidder. *Dir of Nursing* Carolyn
Hanson. *Medical Dir* David Oey MD.
Licensure Skilled care; Intermediate care. *Beds*
SNF 46; ICF 55. *Certified* Medicaid.
Owner Nonprofit corp (Missionary Oblates of
Mary Immaculate).
Admissions Requirements Medical
examination; Physician's request.
Staff RNs 2 (ft), 1 (pt); LPNs 5 (ft), 3 (pt);
Recreational therapists 1 (pt); Activities
coordinators 1 (ft), 1 (pt); Dietitians 1 (ft).
Facilities Dining room; Physical therapy
room; Activities room; Chapel; Crafts room;
Laundry room; Barber/Beauty shop.
Activities Arts & crafts; Cards; Games;
Reading groups; Prayer groups; Movies;
Shopping trips; Dances/Social/Cultural
gatherings.

Spearfish

David M Dorsett Health Care Facility
1020 10th St, Spearfish, SD 57783
(605) 642-2716
Admin James L Haeder. *Dir of Nursing*
Barbara Jordan RN. *Medical Dir* Warren
Golliher MD.
Licensure Skilled care; Intermediate care;
Alzheimer's care. *Beds* SNF 62; ICF 58.
Private Pay Patients 39%. *Certified*
Medicaid; Medicare.
Owner Nonprofit corp (North Central Health
Services Inc).
Admissions Requirements Medical
examination.
Staff RNs 6 (ft), 4 (pt); LPNs 2 (ft), 7 (pt);
Nurses' aides 36 (ft), 15 (pt); Physical
therapists 3 (ft); Recreational therapists 2
(ft), 1 (pt); Activities coordinators 1 (ft).
Facilities Dining room; Physical therapy
room; Activities room; Crafts room; Laundry
room; Barber/Beauty shop; Library;
Courtyard.
Activities Arts & crafts; Cards; Games;
Reading groups; Prayer groups; Movies;
Shopping trips; Dances/Social/Cultural
gatherings.

Serenity Corner
RR 1, Box 171, Spearfish, SD 57783
(605) 642-4029
Admin Marilyn Kessel; Steven Kindsfater. *Dir
of Nursing* Marilyn Kessel. *Medical Dir*
Shelley Paris.
Licensure Supervised living; Retirement. *Beds*
Supervised living 1; Retirement 4. *Private
Pay Patients* 90%. *Certified* Medicare.
Owner Privately owned.
Admissions Requirements Medical
examination; Physician's request.
Facilities Dining room; Activities room;
Laundry room.
Activities Cards; Games; Movies; Shopping
trips; Pet therapy.

Upper Valley Rest Home
PO Box 153, 262 Upper Valley Rd, Spearfish,
SD 57783
(605) 642-5021
Admin Joyce Carlson.
Licensure Supervised care. *Beds* Supervised
care 9. *Private Pay Patients* 2%. *Certified*
Medicaid.
Owner Privately owned.
Admissions Requirements Medical
examination.

Facilities Dining room; Activities room;
Laundry room; Barber/Beauty shop.
Activities Arts & crafts; Cards; Games; Prayer
groups; Shopping trips; Dances/Social/
Cultural gatherings; Pet therapy.

Walker's Veterans Home
1004 5th St, Spearfish, SD 57783
(605) 642-3911
Admin Ronald Walker; Jan Walker.
Licensure Supervised care. *Beds* Supervised
care 8.
Admissions Requirements Minimum age 18;
Medical examination.
Staff Nurses' aides; Recreational therapists;
Activities coordinators.
Facilities Dining room; Activities room;
Crafts room; Laundry room.
Activities Arts & crafts; Cards; Shopping trips.

Sturgis

B & C Rest Home
341 9th St, Sturgis, SD 57785
(605) 347-3659
Admin Charles E Jones.
Licensure Supervised care. *Beds* Supervised
care 24.
Owner Privately owned.
Admissions Requirements Medical
examination; Physician's request.
Staff Nurses' aides 2 (ft).
Facilities Dining room; Activities room;
Laundry room; Barber/Beauty shop.
Activities Arts & crafts; Cards; Games;
Movies; Shopping trips; Dances/Social/
Cultural gatherings.

Key City Retirement Home
1542 Davenport St, Sturgis, SD 57785
(605) 347-2770
Admin Thomas E Anderson; Cathie A
Anderson.
Licensure Supervised care. *Beds* Supervised
care 13.
Owner Privately owned.
Admissions Requirements Medical
examination.
Facilities Dining room.
Activities Cards; Games; Reading groups.

Nelson's Rest Home
1124 2nd St, Sturgis, SD 57785
(605) 347-2405
Admin Wayne Nelson; Betty Nelson.
Licensure Supervised care. *Beds* Supervised
care 10.

**Sturgis Community Health Care Center
(Nursing Home) NCHS**
Box 279, 949 Harmon St, Sturgis, SD 57785
(605) 347-2536
Admin Michael Penticoff.
Medical Dir L L Massa DO.
Licensure Skilled care; Intermediate care. *Beds*
SNF 39; ICF 45. *Certified* Medicaid.
Admissions Requirements Physician's request.
Staff RNs 2 (ft), 3 (pt); LPNs 2 (ft), 7 (pt);
Nurses' aides 21 (ft), 24 (pt); Physical
therapists 1 (pt); Activities coordinators 2
(ft); Dietitians 1 (pt).
Facilities Dining room; Physical therapy
room; Activities room; Chapel; Crafts room;
Laundry room; Barber/Beauty shop.
Activities Arts & crafts; Cards; Games;
Reading groups; Prayer groups; Movies;
Shopping trips; Dances/Social/Cultural
gatherings.

We Care Home for the Aged
1721 Davenport St, Sturgis, SD 57785-2342
(605) 347-2251
Admin Allen Moeller; Sandra Moeller.
Licensure Supervised care. *Beds* Supervised
care 8.

Tripp

Tripp Good Samaritan Center
PO Box 370, Tripp, SD 57376
(605) 935-6101
Admin Daniel J Fosness.
Licensure Intermediate care. *Beds* ICF 67.
Certified Medicaid.
Owner Nonprofit corp (Evangelical Lutheran/
Good Samaritan Society).

Tyndall

St Michael's Nursing Home
3rd & Broadway, Box 27, Tyndall, SD 57066
(605) 589-3341
Admin Gale N Walker.
Medical Dir Herb Saloum MD.
Licensure Intermediate care. *Beds* ICF 9.
Certified Medicaid.
Owner Proprietary corp (Health One Health
Care).

Tyndall Good Samaritan Center
PO Box 460, 800 N State St, Tyndall, SD
57066
(605) 589-3350
Admin Lynden R Heiman. *Dir of Nursing*
Teri VaVruska. *Medical Dir* Herb Saloum
MD.
Licensure Intermediate care. *Beds* ICF 71.
Certified Medicaid.
Owner Nonprofit corp (Evangelical Lutheran/
Good Samaritan Society).
Admissions Requirements Medical
examination; Physician's request.
Staff RNs 1 (ft), 1 (pt); LPNs 5 (ft); Nurses'
aides 20 (ft); Activities coordinators 1 (ft);
Restorative aides 1 (ft), 2 (pt).
Languages Czech, German, Dutch.
Affiliation Lutheran.
Facilities Dining room; Physical therapy
room; Activities room; Chapel; Crafts room;
Laundry room; Barber/Beauty shop; Library;
Family room; Solarium.
Activities Arts & crafts; Cards; Games;
Reading groups; Prayer groups; Movies;
Shopping trips; Dances/Social/Cultural
gatherings; Cooking; Baking.

Vermillion

Southeastern Dakota Nursing Home
102 S Plum St, Vermillion, SD 57069
(605) 624-2611
Admin William Wilson.
Licensure Intermediate care. *Beds* ICF 66.
Certified Medicaid.
Owner Nonprofit corp (Health One Health
Care).
Admissions Requirements Medical
examination.
Staff RNs 4 (ft), 4 (pt); LPNs 3 (ft), 1 (pt);
Nurses' aides 12 (ft), 20 (pt); Activities
coordinators 3 (ft).
Facilities Dining room; Physical therapy
room; Activities room; Chapel; Crafts room;
Barber/Beauty shop; Library on wheels.
Activities Arts & crafts; Cards; Games;
Reading groups; Prayer groups; Movies;
Shopping trips; Dances/Social/Cultural
gatherings.

Viborg

Pioneer Memorial Nursing Home
PO Box 368, Viborg, SD 57070
(605) 326-5161
Admin Joanne Powell.
Medical Dir E G Nelson MD.
Licensure Intermediate care; Alzheimer's care;
Retirement. *Beds* ICF 52. *Certified*
Medicaid.
Owner Proprietary corp (Health One Health
Care).

Staff RNs 2 (ft); LPNs 1 (ft), 2 (pt); Nurses'
aides 6 (ft), 17 (pt); Physical therapists 1
(pt); Activities coordinators 1 (ft); Dietitians
1 (pt).
Facilities Dining room; Physical therapy
room; Activities room; Chapel; Crafts room;
Laundry room; Barber/Beauty shop; Library.
Activities Arts & crafts; Cards; Games;
Reading groups; Prayer groups; Movies;
Shopping trips; Dances/Social/Cultural
gatherings; Current events; Bowling.

Volga

Parkview Health Center
125 W 2nd, Volga, SD 57071
(605) 627-9141
Admin Marilyn E Rice.
Licensure Supervised care. *Beds* Supervised
care 25. *Private Pay Patients* 60%. *Certified*
Medicaid.
Owner Proprietary corp (Omnilife Systems
Inc).
Admissions Requirements Medical
examination; Physician's request.
Staff Nurses' aides.
Facilities Dining room; Laundry room;
Barber/Beauty shop.
Activities Arts & crafts; Cards; Games;
Reading groups; Dances/Social/Cultural
gatherings; Pet therapy; Music; Spiritual.

Wagner

Wagner Good Samaritan Center
PO Box 550, Wagner, SD 57380
(605) 384-3661
Admin Sarah Jane Goldhammer. *Dir of
Nursing* Gloria Buhler RN.
Licensure Intermediate care. *Beds* ICF 77.
Certified Medicaid.
Owner Nonprofit corp (Evangelical Lutheran/
Good Samaritan Society).
Admissions Requirements Physician's request.
Staff RNs 1 (ft), 3 (pt); LPNs 1 (pt); Nurses'
aides 8 (ft), 9 (pt); Activities coordinators 1
(ft), 2 (pt); Dietitians 1 (pt).
Affiliation Lutheran.
Facilities Dining room; Physical therapy
room; Activities room; Chapel; Crafts room;
Laundry room; Barber/Beauty shop.
Activities Arts & crafts; Cards; Games;
Reading groups; Prayer groups; Movies;
Shopping trips.

Wakonda

Wakonda Heritage Manor
PO Box 327, Wakonda, SD 57073
(605) 267-2081
Admin Douglas R Ekeren. *Dir of Nursing*
Marilyn Rhymer.
Licensure Intermediate care; Supervised care.
Beds ICF 44; Supervised care 1. *Certified*
Medicare.
Owner Nonprofit corp.
Admissions Requirements Physician's request.
Staff RNs 4 (pt); LPNs 2 (ft); Nurses' aides 3
(ft), 10 (pt); Activities coordinators 2 (ft);
Dietitians 1 (pt).
Facilities Dining room; Activities room;
Crafts room; Laundry room; Barber/Beauty
shop; Library.
Activities Arts & crafts; Cards; Games;
Reading groups; Prayer groups; Movies;
Shopping trips; Dances/Social/Cultural
gatherings.

Watertown

Hazel's Rest Home
520 2nd Ave SE, Watertown, SD 57201
(605) 882-1768
Admin Hazel Pekelder.
Licensure Supervised care. *Beds* Supervised
care 6.

Owner Privately owned.
Admissions Requirements Medical
examination.
Facilities Dining room; Activities room.

Jenkins Methodist Home
12 2nd Ave SE, Watertown, SD 57201
(605) 886-5777
Admin Allen D Swan. *Dir of Nursing* Sharon
Klose. *Medical Dir* G Robert Bartron MD.
Licensure Skilled care; Intermediate care;
Retirement. *Beds* SNF 166; ICF 16;
Retirement apts 100. *Private Pay Patients*
34%. *Certified* Medicaid; Medicare.
Owner Nonprofit organization/foundation.
Admissions Requirements Medical
examination.
Staff RNs 1 (ft), 5 (pt); LPNs 8 (ft), 17 (pt);
Nurses' aides 46 (ft), 46 (pt); Recreational
therapists 4 (ft); Activities coordinators 1
(ft); Dietitians 1 (ft).
Affiliation Methodist.
Facilities Dining room; Physical therapy
room; Activities room; Chapel; Crafts room;
Barber/Beauty shop; Library.
Activities Arts & crafts; Cards; Games;
Reading groups; Prayer groups; Movies;
Shopping trips; Intergenerational programs;
Pet therapy.

**Prairie Lakes Health Care Center—Nursing
Home**
420 4th St NE, Watertown, SD 57201
(605) 886-8431
Admin Edmond L Weiland. *Dir of Nursing* Sr
Augusta Johnson. *Medical Dir* G R Bartron
MD.
Licensure Skilled care. *Beds* SNF 51. *Certified*
Medicaid.
Owner Nonprofit corp (Health One Health
Care).
Admissions Requirements Medical
examination; Physician's request.
Staff RNs 2 (ft), 1 (pt); LPNs 4 (ft), 6 (pt);
Nurses' aides 13 (ft), 8 (pt); Physical
therapists 1 (ft); Activities coordinators 1
(ft), 1 (pt); Dietitians 1 (ft).
Facilities Dining room; Physical therapy
room; Activities room; Chapel; Crafts room;
Laundry room; Barber/Beauty shop.
Activities Arts & crafts; Cards; Games;
Reading groups; Prayer groups; Movies;
Shopping trips; Dances/Social/Cultural
gatherings.

Waubay

Waubay Rest Home
PO Box 175, 1st Ave W, Waubay, SD 57273
(605) 947-4361
Admin Mildred Gregerson; Mary Warns.
Medical Dir Kevin Bjordahl MD.
Licensure Supervised care. *Beds* Supervised
care 9.
Admissions Requirements Medical
examination.
Staff Nurses' aides 2 (ft).
Facilities Dining room; Laundry room.
Activities Cards; Prayer groups; Shopping
trips; Dances/Social/Cultural gatherings.

Webster

Bethesda Home
W Hwy 12, Webster, SD 57274
(605) 345-3331
Admin Robert E Faehn. *Dir of Nursing* Carol
Richardt RN. *Medical Dir* Kevin Bjordahl
MD.
Licensure Skilled care. *Beds* SNF 58. *Private
Pay Patients* 50%. *Certified* Medicaid.
Owner Nonprofit organization/foundation.
Admissions Requirements Medical
examination; Physician's request.

Staff Physicians 1 (pt); RNs 2 (ft), 5 (pt);
LPNs 1 (ft), 1 (pt); Nurses' aides 32 (pt);
Physical therapists 1 (pt); Activities
coordinators 1 (ft), 2 (pt); Dietitians 1 (pt).
Facilities Dining room; Physical therapy
room; Activities room; Crafts room; Laundry
room; Barber/Beauty shop.
Activities Arts & crafts; Cards; Games;
Reading groups; Prayer groups; Movies;
Shopping trips.

Wessington Springs

Weskota Manor
PO Box S, 611 1st St NE, Wessington Springs,
SD 57382
(605) 539-1621
Admin Thomas V Richter. *Dir of Nursing*
Dorothy Willman RN. *Medical Dir* Roscoe
E Dean MD.
Licensure Intermediate care. *Beds* ICF 40.
Certified Medicaid.
Owner Nonprofit corp.
Admissions Requirements Medical
examination.
Staff RNs 2 (ft); LPNs 1 (pt); Nurses' aides 4
(ft), 17 (pt); Activities coordinators 1 (ft);
Dietitians 1 (ft).
Facilities Dining room; Activities room;
Chapel; Crafts room; Laundry room; Barber/
Beauty shop; Library; TV lounge.
Activities Cards; Games; Reading groups;
Prayer groups; Movies; Shopping trips;
School programs.

White

White Care Center Inc
PO Box 68, White, SD 57276
(605) 629-2881
Admin Allen P Svennes. *Dir of Nursing* Lori
Miller RN. *Medical Dir* LeRoy Mueller MD.
Licensure Intermediate care. *Beds* ICF 61.
Private Pay Patients 40%. *Certified*
Medicaid.
Owner Nonprofit corp.
Admissions Requirements Medical
examination; Physician's request.
Staff RNs 2 (ft), 2 (pt); LPNs 3 (ft), 1 (pt);
Nurses' aides 10 (ft), 15 (pt); Physical
therapists; Activities coordinators 1 (ft);
Dietitians.
Facilities Dining room; Physical therapy
room; Activities room; Chapel; Laundry
room; Barber/Beauty shop; Library.
Activities Cards; Games; Reading groups;
Prayer groups; Shopping trips; Dances/
Social/Cultural gatherings; Zoo trips; Picnics;
Fishing.

White Lake

Aurora-Brule Nursing Home
PO Box 217, White Lake, SD 57383
(605) 249-2216
Admin Larry L Fredericksen.
Medical Dir Tom Dean MD.
Licensure Intermediate care. *Beds* ICF 77.
Certified Medicaid.

White River

White River Health Care Center
Box 310, Investment Ave, White River, SD
57579
(605) 259-3161
Admin Tina Muller. *Dir of Nursing* Joan
Chamberlain RN. *Medical Dir* Tony Berg.
Licensure Intermediate care. *Beds* ICF 52.
Private Pay Patients 20%. *Certified*
Medicaid.
Owner Proprietary corp (Tealwood Care
Centers).
Admissions Requirements Medical
examination.

Staff Physicians 1 (pt); RNs 2 (ft), 1 (pt); LPNs 5 (ft); Nurses' aides 11 (ft), 6 (pt); Physical therapists 1 (pt); Activities coordinators 1 (ft); Dietitians 1 (pt).
Facilities Dining room; Physical therapy room; Activities room; Chapel; Crafts room; Laundry room; Barber/Beauty shop.
Activities Arts & crafts; Games; Reading groups; Prayer groups; Movies; Shopping trips; Dances/Social/Cultural gatherings.

Whitewood

Klima Kastle—Rock Home
Box 528, 1020 Ash, Whitewood, SD 57793
(605) 269-2422
Admin Debra Klima.
Licensure Supervised living. *Beds* Supervised living 8.
Owner Privately owned.
Admissions Requirements Males only; Medical examination.
Facilities Dining room; Activities room; Laundry room.
Activities Cards.

Wilmot

Wilmot Community Home
RR 2 Box 3, Wilmot, SD 57279
(605) 938-4418
Admin Audrey E Utley. *Dir of Nursing* Colette Weyh RN.
Licensure Intermediate care. *Beds* ICF 46. *Certified* Medicaid.
Owner Proprietary corp.
Admissions Requirements Medical examination; Physician's request.
Staff RNs 1 (ft); LPNs 2 (pt); Nurses' aides 23 (pt); Activities coordinators 1 (ft).
Facilities Dining room; Activities room; Crafts room; Laundry room; Barber/Beauty shop; Patio.
Activities Arts & crafts; Cards; Games; Reading groups; Prayer groups; Movies; Shopping trips; Dances/Social/Cultural gatherings; Residents council.

Winner

Winner Nursing Home
956 E 7th, Winner, SD 57580
(605) 842-3483
Admin Mark Kealy. *Dir of Nursing* Michelle Sachtjen. *Medical Dir* Tony Berg MD.
Licensure Intermediate care. *Beds* ICF 81. *Private Pay Patients* 35%. *Certified* Medicaid.
Owner Proprietary corp (Beverly Enterprises).
Admissions Requirements Medical examination; Physician's request.
Staff RNs 5 (ft), 1 (pt); LPNs 3 (ft); Nurses' aides 30 (ft), 4 (pt); Physical therapists 1 (pt); Activities coordinators 1 (ft); Dietitians 1 (pt).
Facilities Dining room; Physical therapy room; Activities room; Laundry room; Barber/Beauty shop.
Activities Arts & crafts; Cards; Games; Reading groups; Prayer groups; Movies; Shopping trips; Dances/Social/Cultural gatherings; Intergenerational programs; Pet therapy.

Woonsocket

Prairie View Care Center
PO Box 68, Woonsocket, SD 57385
(605) 796-4467
Admin Gerald Thorson.
Licensure Intermediate care. *Beds* ICF 52. *Certified* Medicaid.
Admissions Requirements Medical examination; Physician's request.
Staff RNs 1 (ft), 2 (pt); LPNs 3 (ft); Nurses' aides 7 (ft), 6 (pt); Activities coordinators 1 (ft), 1 (pt).
Facilities Dining room; Activities room; Chapel; Laundry room; Barber/Beauty shop.
Activities Arts & crafts; Cards; Games; Reading groups; Prayer groups; Movies; Shopping trips; Dances/Social/Cultural gatherings.

Yankton

Sister James' Nursing Home
1000 W 4th St, Yankton, SD 57078
(605) 665-9371
Admin Pamela Rezac RN. *Dir of Nursing* Lou Moore RN. *Medical Dir* T H Sattler MD.
Licensure Skilled care; Intermediate care; Intermediate care for mentally retarded. *Beds* SNF 48; ICF 65. *Certified* Medicaid.
Owner Nonprofit corp.
Admissions Requirements Medical examination; Physician's request.
Staff RNs 5 (ft), 4 (pt); LPNs 3 (ft), 2 (pt); Nurses' aides 18 (ft), 25 (pt).
Affiliation Roman Catholic.
Facilities Dining room; Activities room; Chapel; Crafts room; Laundry room; Barber/Beauty shop.
Activities Arts & crafts; Cards; Games; Prayer groups; Movies; Shopping trips; Dances/Social/Cultural gatherings.

Yankton Care Center
1212 W 8th, Box 714, Yankton, SD 57078
(605) 665-9429
Admin Patrick J Tomscha. *Dir of Nursing* Mary Hladky.
Licensure Intermediate care. *Beds* ICF 74. *Certified* Medicaid.
Owner Privately owned.
Admissions Requirements Medical examination.
Staff RNs 3 (ft), 2 (pt); LPNs 2 (ft), 2 (pt); Nurses' aides 12 (ft), 13 (pt); Physical therapists 1 (pt); Activities coordinators 1 (ft); Dietitians 1 (pt).
Facilities Dining room; Physical therapy room; Activities room; Chapel; Crafts room; Laundry room; Barber/Beauty shop; Library; Solarium; Lounge.
Activities Arts & crafts; Cards; Games; Reading groups; Prayer groups; Movies; Shopping trips; Dances/Social/Cultural gatherings; Fishing; Zoo; Picnics.

TENNESSEE

Adamsville

Tri-County Convalescent Home
PO Box 325, Park Ave, Adamsville, TN 38310
(901) 632-3301
Medical Dir Harry L Peeler MD.
Licensure Skilled care. *Beds* SNF 144.
  Certified Medicaid; Medicare.
Owner Publicly owned.
Admissions Requirements Minimum age 16;
  Medical examination; Physician's request.
Staff Physicians 7 (pt); RNs 1 (ft), 2 (pt);
  LPNs 9 (ft), 4 (pt); Nurses' aides 34 (ft), 2
  (pt); Physical therapists 1 (pt); Speech
  therapists 1 (pt); Activities coordinators 1
  (ft); Dietitians 1 (pt); Dentists 1 (pt).
Facilities Dining room; Physical therapy
  room; Activities room; Crafts room; Laundry
  room; Barber/Beauty shop.
Activities Arts & crafts; Cards; Games;
  Movies; Shopping trips; Dances/Social/
  Cultural gatherings; Daily devotions.

Alamo

Crockett County Nursing Home
372 W Main St, Alamo, TN 38001
(901) 696-4541
Admin G F Harber.
Licensure Intermediate care. *Beds* ICF 121.
  Certified Medicaid.
Owner Proprietary corp.
Admissions Requirements Minimum age 16;
  Medical examination.
Staff Physicians 2 (pt); RNs 1 (ft); LPNs 11
  (ft); Nurses' aides 42 (ft); Physical therapists
  1 (pt); Reality therapists 1 (pt); Recreational
  therapists 1 (ft); Activities coordinators 1
  (ft); Dietitians 1 (pt).
Facilities Dining room; Physical therapy
  room; Activities room; Chapel; Crafts room;
  Laundry room; Barber/Beauty shop.
Activities Arts & crafts; Cards; Games;
  Reading groups; Prayer groups; Movies;
  Shopping trips.

Algood

Masters Health Care Center
278 Dry Valley Rd, Algood, TN 38501
(615) 537-6524, 537-3013 FAX
Admin Laura Mansfield. *Dir of Nursing*
  Phyllis Cherry. *Medical Dir* J T Moore MD.
Licensure Skilled care; Intermediate care. *Beds*
  SNF 32; ICF 138. *Private Pay Patients* 14%.
  Certified Medicaid; Medicare.
Owner Proprietary corp (Hillhaven Corp).
Admissions Requirements Medical
  examination.
Staff Physicians 1 (pt); Physical therapists 1
  (ft); Occupational therapists 1 (pt); Speech
  therapists 1 (pt); Activities coordinators 1
  (ft); Dietitians 1 (pt); Ophthalmologists 1
  (pt); Podiatrists 1 (pt).

Facilities Dining room; Physical therapy
  room; Activities room; Crafts room; Laundry
  room; Barber/Beauty shop.
Activities Arts & crafts; Cards; Games;
  Reading groups; Prayer groups; Movies;
  Dances/Social/Cultural gatherings;
  Intergenerational programs; Music therapy.

Andersonville

Health Regency Care Center
Rte 2, Hwy 61, Andersonville, TN 37705
(615) 494-0986
Beds 90.
Owner Proprietary corp.

Antioch

Good Samaritan Convalescent Center
500 Hickory Hollow Terr, Antioch, TN 37013
(615) 731-7130
Admin C D Valdomar. *Dir of Nursing* Joy
  Fidel. *Medical Dir* Dr Maynard.
Licensure Skilled care. *Beds* SNF 120.
Owner Proprietary corp.
Staff RNs; LPNs; Nurses' aides; Physical
  therapists; Activities coordinators; Dietitians.

Ardmore

Ardmore Nursing Home Inc
Rte 1 Box 257, Ardmore, TN 38449
(615) 427-2143
Admin Ted Barnett.
Medical Dir A C Foronda.
Licensure Intermediate care. *Beds* ICF 70.
  Certified Medicaid.
Owner Proprietary corp.
Admissions Requirements Medical
  examination.
Staff Physicians 3 (pt); RNs 1 (pt); LPNs 2
  (ft), 4 (pt); Nurses' aides 16 (ft), 2 (pt);
  Physical therapists; Recreational therapists;
  Occupational therapists; Speech therapists;
  Activities coordinators 1 (ft); Dietitians 1
  (ft).
Facilities Dining room; Activities room;
  Laundry room; Lobby; 2 Sun rooms.
Activities Arts & crafts; Cards; Games;
  Reading groups; Prayer groups; Dances/
  Social/Cultural gatherings.

Ashland City

Cheatham County Rest Home
Rte 6, Ashland City, TN 37015
(615) 792-4948
Medical Dir James Baldwin MD.
Licensure Intermediate care. *Beds* ICF 100.
  Certified Medicaid.
Owner Proprietary corp.
Admissions Requirements Minimum age 14.
Facilities Dining room; Activities room;
  Chapel; Crafts room; Laundry room; Barber/
  Beauty shop.

Activities Arts & crafts; Cards; Games; Prayer
  groups; Shopping trips; Dances/Social/
  Cultural gatherings.

Montgomery County Nursing Home
Rte 5 Box 292, Ashland City, TN 37015
(615) 362-3203
Licensure Intermediate care. *Beds* ICF 81.
  Certified Medicaid.
Owner Publicly owned.

Athens

Athens Health Care Center
1204 Frye St, Athens, TN 37303
(615) 745-0434
Admin Walter H Heath.
Medical Dir Nancy Long.
Licensure Intermediate care. *Beds* ICF 96.
  Certified Medicaid; Medicare.
Owner Proprietary corp (National Health
  Corp).
Admissions Requirements Physician's request.
Facilities Dining room; Physical therapy
  room; Activities room; Crafts room; Laundry
  room; Barber/Beauty shop; Library.
Activities Arts & crafts; Cards; Games;
  Reading groups.

Life Care Center of Athens
1234 Frye St, Athens, TN 37303
(615) 745-8181, 745-9257 FAX
Admin William W Wright. *Dir of Nursing*
  Dorothy Greene RN. *Medical Dir* Jamie
  Cleveland MD.
Licensure Skilled care; Intermediate care. *Beds*
  SNF 24; ICF 104. *Private Pay Patients* 10%.
  Certified Medicaid; Medicare.
Owner Proprietary corp (Life Care Centers of
  America).
Admissions Requirements Medical
  examination; Physician's request.
Staff RNs 2 (ft); LPNs 12 (ft); Nurses' aides
  40 (ft); Physical therapists 1 (pt); Speech
  therapists 1 (pt); Activities coordinators 1
  (ft); Dietitians 1 (ft).
Facilities Dining room; Physical therapy
  room; Activities room; Crafts room; Laundry
  room; Barber/Beauty shop; Library.
Activities Arts & crafts; Cards; Games;
  Reading groups; Prayer groups; Shopping
  trips; Dances/Social/Cultural gatherings; Pet
  therapy.

Blountville

Greystone Healthcare Center
PO Box 1133 TCAS, Rte 3, Dunlap Rd,
  Blountville, TN 37617
(615) 323-7112
Medical Dir Dr T H Raberson.
Licensure Intermediate care. *Beds* ICF 170.
  Certified Medicaid.
Owner Proprietary corp.
Admissions Requirements Minimum age 14;
  Medical examination; Physician's request.

Staff Physicians 13 (ft); RNs 1 (ft), 1 (pt); LPNs 12 (ft), 3 (pt); Nurses' aides 44 (ft), 6 (pt); Physical therapists 1 (pt); Reality therapists 2 (pt); Speech therapists 1 (pt); Activities coordinators 1 (ft); Dietitians 1 (ft).
Facilities Dining room; Physical therapy room; Activities room; Laundry room; Barber/Beauty shop.
Activities Arts & crafts; Games; Reading groups; Prayer groups; Movies; Holiday parties; Western day; Mexican day.

Bolivar

Bolivar Health Care Center
214 N Water St, Bolivar, TN 38008
(901) 658-5287
Licensure Intermediate care. *Beds* ICF 51.
Certified Medicaid.
Owner Proprietary corp.

Hillhaven Convalescent Center—Bolivar
700 Nuckolls Rd, Bolivar, TN 38008
(901) 658-4707
Licensure Intermediate care. *Beds* ICF 132.
Certified Medicaid.
Owner Proprietary corp.

Bristol

Bristol Nursing Home Inc
261 North St, Bristol, TN 37620
(615) 764-6151
Licensure Intermediate care. *Beds* ICF 240.
Certified Medicaid.
Owner Proprietary corp.

Cedar Knoll Health Care Center
PO Box 3429, Raytheon Rd, Rte 1, Bristol, TN 37620
(615) 968-4123
Beds 110.

Brownsville

Crestview Nursing Home
704 Dupree St, Brownsville, TN 38012
(901) 772-3356
Admin Joyce Phillpott.
Medical Dir Jack G Pettigrew MD.
Licensure Intermediate care. *Beds* ICF 140.
Certified Medicaid.
Owner Proprietary corp (American Health Center Inc).
Admissions Requirements Medical examination.
Staff LPNs 8 (ft), 7 (pt); Nurses' aides 41 (ft), 8 (pt); Activities coordinators 1 (ft); Dietitians 7 (ft), 1 (pt).
Facilities Dining room; Activities room; Laundry room; Barber/Beauty shop.
Activities Arts & crafts; Cards; Games; Reading groups; Prayer groups; Movies; Dances/Social/Cultural gatherings.

Bruceton

Life Care Center of Bruceton—Hollow Rock
105 Rowland Ave, Bruceton, TN 38317
(901) 586-2061
Admin Peggy J Elkins. *Dir of Nursing* Brenda Woodruff. *Medical Dir* Dr Jerry Atkins.
Licensure Intermediate care. *Beds* ICF 90.
Certified Medicaid.
Owner Proprietary corp (Life Care Centers of America).
Admissions Requirements Medical examination; Physician's request.
Staff RNs 1 (ft); LPNs 8 (ft), 4 (pt); Nurses' aides 27 (ft), 9 (pt); Activities coordinators 1 (ft); Dietitians 1 (ft).
Facilities Dining room; Activities room; Crafts room; Laundry room; Barber/Beauty shop.

Activities Arts & crafts; Cards; Games; Reading groups; Prayer groups; Movies; Shopping trips; Dances/Social/Cultural gatherings.

Byrdstown

Pickett County Nursing Home
PO Box 388, Hillcrest Dr, Byrdstown, TN 38549
(615) 864-3162, 864-6260 FAX
Admin Erline S Myrick. *Dir of Nursing* Shelia Koger RN. *Medical Dir* Larry Mason MD.
Licensure Intermediate care. *Beds* ICF 48.
Certified Medicaid.
Owner Proprietary corp (Heritage Health Group Inc).
Admissions Requirements Minimum age 14; Medical examination; Physician's request.
Staff Physicians 1 (ft); RNs 1 (ft); LPNs 4 (ft); Nurses' aides 14 (ft), 3 (pt); Physical therapists 2 (pt); Occupational therapists 1 (pt); Activities coordinators 1 (ft); Dietitians 1 (ft); Podiatrists 1 (pt).
Facilities Dining room; Physical therapy room; Activities room; Laundry room; Barber/Beauty shop; Library.
Activities Arts & crafts; Cards; Games; Prayer groups; Shopping trips; Intergenerational programs; Pet therapy; Fourth of July celebration with family and friends.

Camden

Hillhaven Convalescent Center of Camden
197 Hospital Dr, Camden, TN 38320
(901) 584-3500
Admin Kathy Farmer.
Licensure Intermediate care. *Beds* ICF 186.
Certified Medicaid.
Owner Proprietary corp (Hillhaven Corp).
Admissions Requirements Medical examination.
Staff RNs 2 (ft); LPNs 15 (ft); Nurses' aides 60 (ft); Physical therapists 1 (pt); Activities coordinators 2 (ft); Dietitians 1 (pt).
Facilities Dining room; Activities room; Chapel; Crafts room; Laundry room; Barber/Beauty shop.
Activities Arts & crafts; Cards; Games; Reading groups; Prayer groups; Movies; Shopping trips; Dances/Social/Cultural gatherings.

Carthage

Smith County Health Care Center
100 Health Care Dr, Carthage, TN 37030
(615) 735-0569
Licensure Intermediate care. *Beds* ICF 128.
Certified Medicaid.
Owner Proprietary corp (Hillhaven Corp).

Celina

Clay County Manor Inc
Hwy 53, Pitcock Ln, Celina, TN 38551
(615) 243-3130
Admin Henry L Van Essen. *Dir of Nursing* Linda J Kendall. *Medical Dir* Dr R Mauricio.
Licensure Intermediate care. *Beds* ICF 66.
Certified Medicaid.
Owner Proprietary corp (American Health Center Inc).
Admissions Requirements Medical examination; Physician's request.
Staff Physicians 3 (pt); RNs 1 (pt); Physical therapists 1 (pt); Reality therapists 1 (ft); Recreational therapists 1 (ft); Speech therapists 1 (pt); Activities coordinators 1 (ft); Dietitians 1 (pt); Podiatrists 1 (pt).
Facilities Dining room; Physical therapy room; Activities room; Crafts room; Laundry room; Barber/Beauty shop; Library.

Activities Arts & crafts; Cards; Games; Reading groups; Prayer groups; Movies; Shopping trips; Dances/Social/Cultural gatherings; Picnics; Campouts; Parties.

Centerville

Centerville Health Care Center
112 Old Dickson Rd, Centerville, TN 37033
(615) 729-4236
Admin Charles P Harris Jr. *Dir of Nursing* Joyce Pace RN. *Medical Dir* Jeff Fosnes MD.
Licensure Intermediate care. *Beds* ICF 122.
Certified Medicaid.
Owner Proprietary corp.
Admissions Requirements Minimum age 14.
Staff Physicians 5 (pt); RNs 1 (ft); LPNs 9 (ft), 1 (pt); Nurses' aides 45 (ft); Activities coordinators 1 (ft); Dietitians 1 (pt).
Facilities Dining room; Physical therapy room; Activities room; Chapel; Crafts room; Laundry room; Barber/Beauty shop; Library.
Activities Arts & crafts; Games; Reading groups; Prayer groups; Movies; Shopping trips; Dances/Social/Cultural gatherings.

Hickman County Nursing Home
135 E Swan St, Centerville, TN 37033
(615) 729-4271
Medical Dir B L Holladay MD.
Licensure Intermediate care. *Beds* ICF 40.
Certified Medicaid.
Owner Proprietary corp.
Admissions Requirements Medical examination; Physician's request.
Staff Physicians 2 (pt); RNs 2 (ft); LPNs 2 (ft), 4 (pt); Nurses' aides 12 (ft), 3 (pt); Physical therapists; Occupational therapists; Speech therapists; Activities coordinators 1 (pt); Dietitians 1 (pt).
Facilities Dining room; Activities room; Barber/Beauty shop.
Activities Arts & crafts; Cards; Games; Prayer groups; Movies.

Chattanooga

Asbury Center at Oak Manor
716 Dodds Ave, Chattanooga, TN 37404
(615) 622-6424
Licensure Home for aged. *Beds* Home for aged 54.

Martin Boyd Christian Home
PO Box 22892, 6845 Standifer Gap Rd, Chattanooga, TN 37421
(615) 892-1020
Licensure Home for aged. *Beds* Home for aged 99.

Caldsted Foundation Inc
3701 Cherryton Dr, Chattanooga, TN 37411
(615) 624-9906
Admin Bernard Freedman. *Dir of Nursing* Wanda Vaughn.
Licensure Home for aged. *Beds* Home for aged 53. *Private Pay Patients* 100%.
Owner Nonprofit organization/foundation.
Admissions Requirements Minimum age 65; Medical examination.
Staff LPNs.
Facilities Dining room; Activities room; Laundry room; Barber/Beauty shop; Library.
Activities Cards; Games; Movies.

Cambridge Hall Ltd
825 Runyan Dr, Chattanooga, TN 37405
(615) 875-6723
Licensure Home for aged. *Beds* Home for aged 35.

Chattanooga Health Care Associates Ltd
8249 Standifer Gap Rd, Chattanooga, TN 37421
(615) 892-1716
Licensure Intermediate care. *Beds* ICF 120.

Friendship Haven
950 Dodson Ave, Chattanooga, TN 37406
(615) 629-2847
Admin Mabel Abernathy.
Licensure Home for aged. *Beds* Home for aged 25.
Admissions Requirements Minimum age 47; Females only; Medical examination.
Facilities Dining room; Laundry room.
Activities Prayer groups; Shopping trips; Exercise groups.

Hamilton County Nursing Home & Residential Care Unit
2626 Walker Rd, Chattanooga, TN 37421
(615) 892-9442, 899-1254
Admin H Doke Cage. *Dir of Nursing* Billie Watkins RN. *Medical Dir* Irene J Labrador MD.
Licensure Skilled care; Intermediate care; Home for aged. *Beds* 676; Home for aged 99. *Certified* Medicaid; Medicare.
Owner Nonprofit organization/foundation.
Admissions Requirements Minimum age 14; Medical examination.
Staff Physicians; RNs; LPNs; Nurses' aides; Physical therapists; Recreational therapists; Speech therapists; Activities coordinators; Dietitians.
Facilities Dining room; Physical therapy room; Activities room; Chapel; Crafts room; Laundry room; Barber/Beauty shop; Library.

HCA—Parkridge Medical Center Skilled Nursing Facility
2333 McCallie Ave, Chattanooga, TN 37404
(615) 698-6061
Beds 25.

Heritage Manor Nursing Home
708 Dwight St, Chattanooga, TN 37406
(615) 622-4301
Licensure Intermediate care. *Beds* ICF 78. *Certified* Medicaid.
Owner Proprietary corp (Life Care Centers of America).

Life Care Center of East Ridge
1500 Fincher Ave, Chattanooga, TN 37412
(615) 894-1254
Admin Joy Hambleton. *Dir of Nursing* Jeanine Gentry. *Medical Dir* Dr Winters.
Licensure Intermediate care. *Beds* ICF 120. *Certified* Medicaid.
Owner Proprietary corp (Life Care Centers of America).
Admissions Requirements Medical examination.
Staff Physicians 1 (pt); RNs 2 (ft); LPNs 6 (ft), 4 (pt); Nurses' aides 25 (ft), 15 (pt); Physical therapists 1 (pt); Recreational therapists 1 (ft); Activities coordinators 1 (ft); Dietitians 1 (ft), 1 (pt); Ophthalmologists 1 (pt).
Facilities Dining room; Physical therapy room; Activities room; Crafts room; Laundry room; Barber/Beauty shop.
Activities Arts & crafts; Cards; Games; Reading groups; Prayer groups; Movies; Shopping trips; Dances/Social/Cultural gatherings.

Memorial Hospital Skilled Nursing Unit
2500 Citico Ave, Chattanooga, TN 37404
(615) 629-8459
Beds 15.

Mountain Creek Manor
1005 Mountain Creek Rd, Chattanooga, TN 37405
(615) 875-4448
Beds 73.

Mountain View Rest Home
PO Box 2318, 5412 Lee Ave, Chattanooga, TN 37410
(615) 821-4836
Licensure Intermediate care. *Beds* 19. *Certified* Medicaid.

Parkwood Health Care Center
2700 Parkwood Ave, Chattanooga, TN 37404
(615) 624-1533
Medical Dir Dr Paul Hawkins.
Licensure Skilled care. *Beds* SNF 212. *Certified* Medicaid; Medicare.
Owner Proprietary corp (National Health Corp).
Admissions Requirements Minimum age 14; Medical examination.
Staff Physicians 2 (ft); RNs 7 (ft), 5 (pt); LPNs 14 (ft), 14 (pt); Nurses' aides 54 (ft), 12 (pt); Physical therapists 1 (ft); Recreational therapists 2 (ft); Speech therapists 1 (pt); Activities coordinators 1 (ft); Dietitians 1 (ft); Podiatrists 1 (pt); Dentists 1 (pt); Assistant physical therapists 3 (ft).
Facilities Dining room; Physical therapy room; Activities room; Chapel; Crafts room; Laundry room; Barber/Beauty shop; Library.
Activities Arts & crafts; Games; Movies; Shopping trips; Dances/Social/Cultural gatherings.

St Barnabas Nursing Home
600 Pine St, Chattanooga, TN 37402
(615) 267-3764
Admin John Smartt. *Dir of Nursing* Charlotte Burkhart RN. *Medical Dir* A Steven Ulin MD.
Licensure Skilled care; Intermediate care; Retirement. *Beds* SNF 29; ICF 58. *Private Pay Patients* 89%. *Certified* Medicaid; Medicare.
Owner Nonprofit corp.
Admissions Requirements Minimum age 14; Medical examination; Physician's request.
Staff Physicians 4 (ft), 3 (pt); RNs 4 (pt), 3 (pt); LPNs 5 (ft), 3 (pt); Nurses' aides 27 (ft), 16 (pt); Physical therapists 1 (pt); Activities coordinators 1 (ft); Dietitians 1 (ft).
Affiliation Episcopal.
Facilities Dining room; Physical therapy room; Activities room; Chapel; Barber/Beauty shop; Library.
Activities Arts & crafts; Cards; Games; Movies; Pet therapy.

Chuckey

Durham-Hensley Nursing Home Inc
Rte 3 Box 25, Chuckey, TN 37641
(615) 257-2291
Medical Dir Dr Ronald Cole.
Licensure Intermediate care. *Beds* ICF 110. *Certified* Medicaid.
Staff Physicians 7 (pt); RNs 2 (ft); LPNs 9 (ft); Nurses' aides 21 (ft), 6 (pt); Physical therapists 1 (pt); Speech therapists 1 (pt); Activities coordinators 1 (ft); Dietitians 1 (pt).
Facilities Dining room; Physical therapy room; Activities room; Laundry room; Barber/Beauty shop.
Activities Arts & crafts; Cards; Games; Reading groups; Prayer groups; Movies; Shopping trips; Dances/Social/Cultural gatherings.

Church Hill

Life Care Center of Church Hill
Rte 8, W Main St, Church Hill, TN 37642
(615) 357-7178
Admin James H Griffitt. *Dir of Nursing* Patty Schad RN. *Medical Dir* T H Roberson MD.
Licensure Intermediate care. *Beds* ICF 124. *Certified* Medicaid.
Owner Proprietary corp (Life Care Centers of America).
Admissions Requirements Minimum age 14; Medical examination; Physician's request.
Staff Physicians 6 (pt); RNs 2 (ft); LPNs 9 (ft), 3 (pt); Nurses' aides 30 (ft), 6 (pt); Physical therapists 1 (pt); Speech therapists

1 (pt); Activities coordinators 1 (ft); Dietitians 1 (pt); Ophthalmologists 1 (pt); Podiatrists 1 (pt).
Languages Spanish, German.
Facilities Dining room; Physical therapy room; Activities room; Crafts room; Laundry room; Barber/Beauty shop.
Activities Arts & crafts; Cards; Games; Reading groups; Prayer groups; Movies; Shopping trips; Dances/Social/Cultural gatherings.

Clarksville

Clarksville Manor Inc
2134 Old Ashland City Rd, Clarksville, TN 37043
(615) 552-3002
Admin Joyce P Boudreaux MEd. *Dir of Nursing* Patsy Coke RN. *Medical Dir* David Gullett MD.
Licensure Intermediate care. *Beds* ICF 83. *Private Pay Patients* 30%. *Certified* Medicaid.
Owner Proprietary corp (American Health Centers Inc).
Staff Physicians 1 (pt); RNs 1 (ft); LPNs 7 (ft); Nurses' aides 35 (ft); Activities coordinators 1 (ft).
Facilities Dining room; Activities room; Laundry room; Barber/Beauty shop.
Activities Arts & crafts; Cards; Games; Movies; Shopping trips; Dances/Social/Cultural gatherings.

General Care Convalescent Center
111 Ussery Rd, Clarksville, TN 37040
(615) 647-0269
Licensure Skilled care; Intermediate care. *Beds* 130. *Certified* Medicaid; Medicare.
Owner Proprietary corp (American Health Center Inc).

Spring Meadows Health Care Center
220 State Rte 76 I-24 Connector, Clarksville, TN 37043
(615) 552-0181, 552-0219 FAX
Admin Keith Smith. *Dir of Nursing* Pat Collins. *Medical Dir* David Gullett MD.
Licensure Intermediate care. *Beds* ICF 84. *Private Pay Patients* 56%. *Certified* Medicaid.
Owner Proprietary corp (Meadows Group).
Staff Physicians 1 (pt); RNs 1 (ft); LPNs 7 (ft); Physical therapists 1 (pt); Occupational therapists 1 (pt); Speech therapists 1 (pt); Activities coordinators 1 (pt); Dietitians 1 (ft).
Facilities Dining room; Physical therapy room; Activities room; Laundry room; Barber/Beauty shop.
Activities Arts & crafts; Cards; Games; Movies; Dances/Social/Cultural gatherings; Pet therapy.

Cleveland

Bradley County Nursing Home
2910 Peerless Rd NW, Cleveland, TN 37312
(615) 472-7116
Admin Ernest M Vincett. *Dir of Nursing* Cindy Johnson. *Medical Dir* Stanley Pettit MD.
Licensure Skilled care; Intermediate care. *Beds* SNF 50; ICF 185. *Private Pay Patients* 5%. *Certified* Medicaid; Medicare.
Owner Nonprofit organization/foundation.
Admissions Requirements Minimum age 14; Medical examination; Physician's request.
Staff RNs 5 (ft), 4 (pt); LPNs 14 (ft), 10 (pt); Nurses' aides 71 (ft), 26 (pt); Physical therapists 1 (ft); Activities coordinators 1 (ft); Dietitians 1 (ft).
Facilities Dining room; Physical therapy room; Activities room; Chapel; Crafts room; Laundry room; Barber/Beauty shop; Library.

Activities Arts & crafts; Cards; Games; Reading groups; Prayer groups; Movies; Shopping trips; Dances/Social/Cultural gatherings; Intergenerational programs; Pet therapy.

Life Care Center of Cleveland
3530 Keith St NW, Cleveland, TN 37311
(615) 476-3254
Admin Barbara C Kiser. *Dir of Nursing* Cindy Johnson. *Medical Dir* Dr Vance.
Licensure Intermediate care; Alzheimer's care. *Beds* ICF 163. *Certified* Medicaid.
Owner Proprietary corp (Life Care Centers of America).
Admissions Requirements Minimum age 14; Medical examination; Physician's request.
Staff RNs 2 (ft); LPNs 11 (ft), 2 (pt); Nurses' aides 41 (ft), 9 (pt); Activities coordinators 1 (pt); Recreational therapist aide 1 (ft).
Facilities Dining room; Physical therapy room; Activities room; Crafts room; Laundry room; Barber/Beauty shop; Library; Conference room.
Activities Arts & crafts; Cards; Games; Reading groups; Prayer groups; Movies; Shopping trips; Dances/Social/Cultural gatherings.

Royal Care of Cleveland Home for Aged
2750 Executive Park Pl, Cleveland, TN 37312
(615) 476-4444
Licensure Home for aged. *Beds* 60; Home for aged 40.

Clinton

Anderson County Health Care Center
220 Longmire Rd, Clinton, TN 37716
(615) 457-6925
Admin Sandra L Reynolds LNHA. *Dir of Nursing* Mary R Silcox RN. *Medical Dir* Dr R W Robinson.
Licensure Skilled care; Intermediate care. *Beds* SNF 30; ICF 90. *Certified* Medicaid; Medicare.
Owner Proprietary corp (Beverly Enterprises).
Admissions Requirements Medical examination.
Staff Physicians 3 (pt); RNs 2 (ft), 1 (pt); LPNs 10 (ft), 7 (pt); Nurses' aides 24 (ft), 16 (pt); Activities coordinators 1 (ft).
Facilities Dining room; Physical therapy room; Activities room; Laundry room; Barber/Beauty shop; (2) TV/sitting rooms.
Activities Arts & crafts; Cards; Games; Reading groups; Prayer groups; Movies; Shopping trips; Dances/Social/Cultural gatherings; Exercise class.

Collegedale

Heritage Manor of Collegedale
PO Box 658, 9210 Apison Pike, Collegedale, TN 37315
(615) 396-2182
Licensure Intermediate care. *Beds* ICF 124. *Certified* Medicaid.
Owner Proprietary corp (National Heritage).
Staff RNs 2 (ft), 1 (pt); LPNs 13 (ft), 3 (pt); Nurses' aides 33 (ft); Physical therapists 1 (ft); Reality therapists 1 (pt); Recreational therapists 1 (pt); Occupational therapists 1 (pt); Speech therapists 1 (pt); Activities coordinators 1 (ft); Dietitians 1 (ft).
Facilities Dining room; Physical therapy room; Activities room; Chapel; Laundry room; Barber/Beauty shop.
Activities Arts & crafts; Games; Movies; Shopping trips; Dances/Social/Cultural gatherings.

Collierville

Heritage Manor of Collierville
490 Hwy 57 W, Collierville, TN 38017
(901) 853-8561

Admin Brenda Stewart.
Medical Dir Rachel Kelsey.
Licensure Skilled care; Alzheimer's care. *Beds* SNF 114. *Certified* Medicaid; Medicare.
Owner Proprietary corp (National Heritage).
Admissions Requirements Physician's request.
Facilities Dining room; Activities room; Crafts room; Laundry room; Barber/Beauty shop; Library.
Activities Arts & crafts; Cards; Games; Reading groups; Prayer groups; Movies; Shopping trips; Dances/Social/Cultural gatherings.

Columbia

Bel-Air Health Care Center
105 N Campbell Blvd, Columbia, TN 38401
(615) 388-5035
Medical Dir Dr William A Robinson.
Licensure Intermediate care. *Beds* ICF 105. *Certified* Medicaid.
Owner Proprietary corp (Regency Health Care Centers).
Admissions Requirements Medical examination; Physician's request.
Staff RNs 1 (ft); LPNs 5 (ft), 3 (pt); Nurses' aides 23 (ft), 8 (pt); Physical therapists 1 (pt); Speech therapists 1 (pt); Activities coordinators 1 (pt); Dietitians 1 (pt); Podiatrists 1 (pt); Dentists 1 (pt).
Facilities Dining room; Activities room; Laundry room; Barber/Beauty shop.
Activities Arts & crafts; Cards; Games; Reading groups; Prayer groups; Movies; Shopping trips; Dances/Social/Cultural gatherings.

Columbia Health Care Center
101 Walnut Ln, Columbia, TN 38401
(615) 381-3112
Admin Mary K Sellars. *Dir of Nursing* Lynda Ponder. *Medical Dir* Dr C A Ball.
Licensure Skilled care; Intermediate care; Alzheimer's care. *Beds* SNF 48; ICF 72. *Certified* Medicaid; Medicare.
Owner Proprietary corp (National Health Corp).
Admissions Requirements Medical examination.
Staff RNs 3 (ft); LPNs 10 (ft); Nurses' aides 45 (ft); Physical therapists 1 (ft); Speech therapists 1 (ft); Activities coordinators 1 (ft), 5 (pt).
Facilities Dining room; Physical therapy room; Activities room; Laundry room; Barber/Beauty shop.

Heritage Manor of Columbia
1410 Trotwood Ave, Columbia, TN 38401
(615) 388-6443
Licensure Intermediate care. *Beds* ICF 181. *Certified* Medicaid.
Owner Proprietary corp (National Heritage).

Hillview Health Care Center
2710 Trotwood Ave, Columbia, TN 38401
(615) 388-7182
Medical Dir Dr Carl C Gardner.
Licensure Skilled care; Intermediate care. *Beds* 98. *Certified* Medicaid; Medicare.
Owner Proprietary corp (National Health Corp).
Admissions Requirements Minimum age 18; Physician's request.
Staff Physicians 1 (pt); RNs 6 (ft), 4 (pt); LPNs 5 (ft), 2 (pt); Nurses' aides 22 (ft), 5 (pt); Physical therapists 1 (ft); Speech therapists 1 (ft); Activities coordinators 1 (ft); Dietitians 1 (ft); Podiatrists 1 (pt); Audiologists 1 (pt); Dentists 1 (pt).
Facilities Dining room; Physical therapy room; Activities room; Chapel; Crafts room; Laundry room; Barber/Beauty shop; Library.
Activities Arts & crafts; Cards; Games; Reading groups; Prayer groups; Movies; Shopping trips; Dances/Social/Cultural gatherings.

Cookeville

Cookeville Health Care Center Inc
PO Box 2829, 815 Bunker Hill Rd, Cookeville, TN 38502
(615) 528-5516
Admin John R Strawn. *Dir of Nursing* Susan Adermann RN. *Medical Dir* Clarence Jones MD.
Licensure Skilled care; Intermediate care. *Beds* Swing beds SNF/ICF 96. *Certified* Medicaid; Medicare.
Owner Proprietary corp (National Health Corp).
Admissions Requirements Minimum age 18; Medical examination.
Staff Physicians 1 (pt); RNs 3 (pt); LPNs 9 (ft), 8 (pt); Nurses' aides 27 (ft), 15 (pt); Physical therapists 1 (ft), 1 (pt); Speech therapists 1 (pt); Activities coordinators 1 (ft); Dietitians 1 (ft).
Facilities Dining room; Physical therapy room; Activities room; Laundry room.
Activities Arts & crafts; Cards; Games; Reading groups; Prayer groups; Movies; Shopping trips; Dances/Social/Cultural gatherings.

Cookeville Manor Nursing Center
215 W 6th St, Cookeville, TN 38501
(615) 528-7466
Licensure Intermediate care. *Beds* ICF 49. *Certified* Medicaid.
Owner Proprietary corp (American Health Center Inc).

Cordova

Hillhaven Convalescent Center—Germantown
955 Germantown Rd, Cordova, TN 38018-9601
(901) 754-1393
Admin Cathy M Johnson MBA. *Dir of Nursing* Joyce Kiser RN. *Medical Dir* Patrick J Murphy MD.
Licensure Skilled care; Intermediate care. *Beds* SNF 34; ICF 240. *Certified* Medicaid; Medicare.
Owner Proprietary corp (Hillhaven Corp).
Admissions Requirements Medical examination; Physician's request.
Staff RNs 10 (ft); LPNs 30 (ft); Nurses' aides 150 (ft); Physical therapists 1 (pt); Recreational therapists 2 (ft); Activities coordinators 1 (ft); Dietitians 1 (ft); Physical therapy assistants 2 (ft).
Facilities Dining room; Physical therapy room; Activities room; Chapel; Crafts room; Barber/Beauty shop; Library.
Activities Arts & crafts; Cards; Games; Reading groups; Prayer groups; Movies; Shopping trips; Dances/Social/Cultural gatherings; Intergenerational programs; Pet therapy.

Covington

Covington Manor Nursing Center
PO Box 827, 1992 Hwy 51 S, Covington, TN 38019
(901) 476-1820
Admin Donald Lee Jones. *Dir of Nursing* Bettye Morgan. *Medical Dir* Dr N L Hyatt.
Licensure Intermediate care. *Beds* ICF 196. *Certified* Medicaid.
Owner Proprietary corp (American Health Center Inc).
Admissions Requirements Medical examination; Physician's request.
Staff RNs 1 (ft); LPNs; Nurses' aides; Physical therapists; Reality therapists; Recreational therapists; Occupational therapists; Speech therapists; Activities coordinators; Dietitians.
Facilities Dining room; Activities room; Crafts room; Laundry room; Barber/Beauty shop.

Activities Arts & crafts; Cards; Games; Reading groups; Prayer groups; Movies; Shopping trips; Dances/Social/Cultural gatherings; Beauty groups; Men's fellowship; Outings.

Crossville

Country Place Health Care Center
408 Justice St, Crossville, TN 38555
(615) 484-4782
Beds 120.

Life Care Center of Crossville
407 Wayne Ave, Crossville, TN 38555
(615) 484-6129
Licensure Intermediate care. *Beds* ICF 109.
Certified Medicaid.
Owner Proprietary corp (Life Care Centers of America).
Staff Physicians 8 (pt); RNs 1 (ft), 1 (pt); LPNs 8 (ft), 2 (pt); Nurses' aides 32 (ft), 6 (pt); Physical therapists 1 (pt); Activities coordinators 1 (ft); Dietitians 1 (pt); Dentists 1 (pt).
Facilities Dining room; Physical therapy room; Activities room; Crafts room; Laundry room; Barber/Beauty shop; Library.
Activities Arts & crafts; Cards; Games; Reading groups; Prayer groups; Movies; Shopping trips; Dances/Social/Cultural gatherings.

Dandridge

Jefferson County Nursing Home
Rte 5 Box 414, Dandridge, TN 37725
(615) 397-3163
Licensure Intermediate care. *Beds* ICF 103.
Certified Medicaid.

Dayton

Laurelbrook Sanitarium
Rte 3 Box 352, Ogden Rd, Dayton, TN 37321
(615) 775-0771, 775-3338 FAX
Admin Charles Hess. *Dir of Nursing* Donna Hansen. *Medical Dir* Lester Littell MD.
Licensure Intermediate care. *Beds* ICF 50.
Certified Medicaid.
Owner Nonprofit corp.
Admissions Requirements Medical examination; Physician's request.
Staff RNs 1 (ft), 1 (pt); LPNs 3 (ft), 3 (pt); Nurses' aides 5 (ft), 3 (pt); Activities coordinators 1 (ft); Dietitians 1 (ft).
Languages Spanish.
Affiliation Seventh-Day Adventist.
Facilities Dining room; Activities room; Chapel; Care for those w/tube feeders & tracheostomics feedings.
Activities Arts & crafts; Games; Prayer groups.

Rhea County Nursing Home
PO Box 629, Hwy 27 N, Dayton, TN 37321
(615) 775-1121
Admin Betty A Holland, Asst. *Dir of Nursing* Marilyn Thorla RN. *Medical Dir* Lester F Littell MD.
Licensure Intermediate care. *Beds* ICF 89.
Private Pay Patients 25%. *Certified* Medicaid.
Owner Publicly owned.
Staff Physicians 5 (ft); RNs 2 (ft); LPNs 11 (ft); Nurses' aides 26 (ft), 5 (pt); Physical therapists 1 (pt); Activities coordinators 1 (ft); Dietitians 1 (pt).
Facilities Dining room; Physical therapy room; Activities room; Chapel; Crafts room; Barber/Beauty shop; Library; Courtyard with barbecue pit; Large sunporch.
Activities Arts & crafts; Cards; Games; Reading groups; Prayer groups; Movies; Shopping trips; Dances/Social/Cultural gatherings; Intergenerational programs; Fishing trips; Character visits.

Decatur

Meadowbrook Manor of Decatur
PO Box 441, River Rd, Decatur, TN 37322
(615) 334-3002
Admin Sheila Eiche. *Dir of Nursing* Mildred Dale. *Medical Dir* Dr Steve Templeton.
Licensure Intermediate care. *Beds* ICF 86.
Private Pay Patients 10%. *Certified* Medicaid.
Owner Proprietary corp (Angell Group).
Admissions Requirements Medical examination; Physician's request.
Staff Physicians 1 (ft), 2 (pt); RNs 1 (pt); LPNs 7 (ft), 3 (pt); Nurses' aides 17 (ft), 9 (pt); Physical therapists 1 (pt); Reality therapists 1 (pt); Recreational therapists 1 (pt); Speech therapists 1 (pt); Activities coordinators 1 (ft); Dietitians 1 (ft).
Facilities Dining room; Physical therapy room; Activities room; Laundry room; Barber/Beauty shop; Library.
Activities Arts & crafts; Cards; Games; Reading groups; Prayer groups; Movies; Shopping trips; Dances/Social/Cultural gatherings; Intergenerational programs; Pet therapy.

Dickson

Dickson County Nursing Home
901 N Charlotte St, Dickson, TN 37055
(615) 446-5171
Admin JoAnn Brown. *Dir of Nursing* Betty Carpenter. *Medical Dir* Dr W A Bell.
Licensure Intermediate care. *Beds* ICF 70.
Certified Medicaid.
Owner Nonprofit organization/foundation.
Admissions Requirements Minimum age 18; Medical examination.
Staff Physicians 1 (pt); RNs 1 (pt); LPNs 8 (ft), 2 (pt); Nurses' aides 26 (ft), 4 (pt); Physical therapists 2 (ft); Recreational therapists (contracted); Speech therapists (contracted); Activities coordinators 1 (ft); Dietitians 1 (pt); Ophthalmologists (contracted); Podiatrists (contracted).
Facilities Dining room; Physical therapy room; Activities room; Laundry room; Barber/Beauty shop; Library.
Activities Arts & crafts; Cards; Games; Reading groups; Prayer groups; Movies; Dances/Social/Cultural gatherings.

Green Valley Health Care Center
PO Box 585, 812 Charlotte St, Dickson, TN 37055
(615) 446-8046
Admin Wesley Felts. *Dir of Nursing* Norma Wall RN; Faye Buchanan RN, Asst. *Medical Dir* W A Bell MD; John Salyer, Assoc.
Licensure Skilled care; Intermediate care. *Beds* SNF 80; ICF 77. *Private Pay Patients* 35%. *Certified* Medicaid; Medicare.
Owner Proprietary corp (National Health Corp).
Admissions Requirements Medical examination; Physician's request.
Staff RNs 7 (ft), 2 (pt); LPNs 18 (ft), 8 (pt); Nurses' aides 40 (ft), 20 (pt); Physical therapists 1 (ft), 1 (pt); Occupational therapists 1 (ft), 1 (pt); Speech therapists 1 (ft), 1 (pt); Activities coordinators 3 (ft); Dietitians 1 (ft), 1 (pt).
Facilities Dining room; Physical therapy room; Activities room; Crafts room; Laundry room; Barber/Beauty shop; Library.
Activities Arts & crafts; Cards; Games; Reading groups; Prayer groups; Movies; Shopping trips; Dances/Social/Cultural gatherings; Intergenerational programs.

Dover

Manor House of Dover
PO Box 399, Hwy 49 E, Dover, TN 37058
(615) 232-6902

Admin Patricia Lee. *Dir of Nursing* Marian Watson RN. *Medical Dir* Dr Robert Lee.
Licensure Skilled care; Intermediate care. *Beds* SNF 30; ICF 58. *Private Pay Patients* 20%. *Certified* Medicaid; Medicare; VA.
Owner Proprietary corp (Diversicare Corp).
Admissions Requirements Minimum age 14; Medical examination; Physician's request.
Staff Physicians 1 (ft), 1 (pt); RNs 2 (ft), 2 (pt); LPNs 6 (ft), 5 (pt); Nurses' aides 35 (ft), 20 (pt); Physical therapists 1 (pt); Occupational therapists 1 (pt); Speech therapists 1 (pt); Activities coordinators 1 (ft); Dietitians 1 (pt); Ophthalmologists 1 (pt); Podiatrists 1 (pt); Audiologists 1 (pt).
Facilities Dining room; Physical therapy room; Activities room; Crafts room; Laundry room; Barber/Beauty shop; Library.
Activities Arts & crafts; Cards; Games; Prayer groups; Movies; Shopping trips; Dances/Social/Cultural gatherings.

Dresden

Hillview Nursing Home
Rte 1 Box 377, Dresden, TN 38225
(901) 364-3886
Admin Mary Ellis.
Medical Dir Fran Allen.
Licensure Intermediate care. *Beds* ICF 70.
Certified Medicaid.
Owner Proprietary corp.
Admissions Requirements Medical examination.
Staff LPNs 7 (ft), 4 (pt); Nurses' aides 17 (ft), 6 (pt); Activities coordinators 1 (ft); Dietitians 1 (ft); Social service 1 (ft).
Facilities Dining room; Activities room; Chapel; Laundry room; Barber/Beauty shop; Patio.
Activities Arts & crafts; Cards; Games; Reading groups; Shopping trips.

Weakley County Nursing Home
Rte 1 Box 787, County Farm Rd, Dresden, TN 38225
(901) 364-3158
Admin Kenneth Wainscott. *Dir of Nursing* Pat Mitchell. *Medical Dir* Dr R E Owens.
Licensure Intermediate care. *Beds* ICF 139.
Certified Medicaid.
Owner Nonprofit organization/foundation.
Admissions Requirements Minimum age 14; Medical examination; Physician's request.
Staff RNs 1 (ft); LPNs 14 (ft), 4 (pt); Nurses' aides 46 (ft), 12 (pt); Activities coordinators 1 (ft), 1 (pt); Dietitians 1 (pt).
Facilities Dining room; Activities room; Laundry room; Barber/Beauty shop.
Activities Arts & crafts; Cards; Games; Movies; Shopping trips; Dances/Social/Cultural gatherings; Local parades; Fishing trips.

Ducktown

Life Care Center of Copper Basin
PO Box 518, Industrial Park Dr, Ducktown, TN 37326
(615) 496-3245
Beds 80.
Owner Proprietary corp (Life Care Centers of America).

Dunlap

Sequatchie Health Care Center
PO Box 685, Dunlap, TN 37327
(615) 949-4651
Admin Cheri Cropper. *Dir of Nursing* Susan Merriman. *Medical Dir* Dr Charles Graves.
Licensure Skilled care; Intermediate care. *Beds* SNF 22; ICF 38. *Private Pay Patients* 11%.
Certified Medicaid; Medicare.
Owner Proprietary corp (National Health Corp).

Staff RNs; LPNs; Nurses' aides; Physical therapists; Activities coordinators; Dietitians.
Facilities Dining room; Physical therapy room; Activities room; Barber/Beauty shop.
Activities Arts & crafts; Games; Reading groups; Prayer groups; Movies.

Dyersburg

Dyersburg Manor Nursing Center
1900 Parr Ave, Dyersburg, TN 38025-1048
(901) 286-1221
Beds 79.
Owner Proprietary corp (American Health Center Inc).

NuCare Convalescent
1636 Woodlawn, Dyersburg, TN 38024
(901) 285-6400
Admin Bettie Motley. *Dir of Nursing* Brenda Hollis.
Licensure Intermediate care. *Beds* ICF 50. *Certified* Medicaid.
Owner Proprietary corp (Southeastern Health Care).
Admissions Requirements Medical examination; Physician's request.
Staff RNs 1 (ft); LPNs 4 (ft), 3 (pt); Nurses' aides 15 (ft), 4 (pt); Activities coordinators 1 (ft); Social services 1 (ft).
Facilities Dining room; Activities room; Barber/Beauty shop.
Activities Arts & crafts; Cards; Games; Prayer groups; Shopping trips; Dances/Social/Cultural gatherings.

Parkview Convalescent Unit
350 Tickle St, Dyersburg, TN 38024
(901) 285-9710, 285-9545 FAX at hospital
Admin Sammy Copeland. *Dir of Nursing* Katie Coleman. *Medical Dir* Gregg Nicks.
Licensure Intermediate care. *Beds* ICF 113. *Private Pay Patients* 16%. *Certified* Medicaid.
Owner Nonprofit organization/foundation (Methodist Health Systems).
Admissions Requirements Medical examination; Physician's request.
Staff Physicians 13 (ft); RNs 2 (ft); LPNs 13 (ft), 1 (pt); Nurses' aides 31 (ft), 6 (pt); Activities coordinators 1 (ft); Dietitians 1 (ft).
Affiliation Methodist.
Facilities Dining room; Activities room; Laundry room; Barber/Beauty shop; Library.
Activities Arts & crafts; Games; Prayer groups; Movies.

Elizabethton

Heritage Manor of Elizabethton
PO Box 1510, 1641 Hwy 19 E, Elizabethton, TN 37643
(615) 542-4133, 542-3874 FAX
Admin Ed Killian. *Dir of Nursing* Annetta Nave RN. *Medical Dir* R Eugene Galloway MD; Jerry Gastineau MD.
Licensure Intermediate care. *Beds* ICF 158. *Private Pay Patients* 8%. *Certified* Medicaid.
Owner Proprietary corp (National Heritage).
Admissions Requirements Minimum age 18; Medical examination; Physician's request.
Staff RNs 2 (ft); LPNs 12 (ft), 1 (pt); Nurses' aides 48 (ft), 7 (pt); Physical therapists 1 (pt); Speech therapists 1 (pt); Activities coordinators 2 (ft); Dietitians 1 (ft), 1 (pt).
Facilities Dining room; Physical therapy room; Activities room; Laundry room; Barber/Beauty shop.
Activities Arts & crafts; Cards; Games; Reading groups; Prayer groups; Movies; Shopping trips; Dances/Social/Cultural gatherings.

Hermitage Nursing Home
1633 Hillview Dr, Elizabethton, TN 37643
(615) 543-2571

Admin Jeannette F Bradshaw.
Medical Dir Royce L Holsey Jr.
Licensure Intermediate care. *Beds* ICF 58. *Certified* Medicaid.
Admissions Requirements Minimum age 14; Medical examination; Physician's request.
Staff Physicians 1 (pt); RNs 1 (ft), 1 (pt); LPNs 3 (ft), 3 (pt); Nurses' aides 12 (ft), 7 (pt); Physical therapists 1 (pt); Activities coordinators 1 (ft); Dietitians 1 (pt).
Facilities Dining room; Physical therapy room; Activities room; Laundry room; Barber/Beauty shop; Library.
Activities Arts & crafts; Games; Reading groups; Prayer groups; Movies; Shopping trips; Dances/Social/Cultural gatherings.

Hillview Nursing Home
1666 Hillview Dr, Elizabethton, TN 37643
(615) 542-5061
Admin Carol Hutchins. *Dir of Nursing* Ruth S Holder RN. *Medical Dir* Dr Robert Walter.
Licensure Intermediate care. *Beds* ICF 42. *Private Pay Patients* 29%. *Certified* Medicaid.
Admissions Requirements Minimum age 14; Medical examination; Physician's request.
Staff Physicians; RNs 1 (ft), 1 (pt); LPNs 4 (ft), 2 (pt); Nurses' aides 10 (ft), 6 (pt); Physical therapists (contracted); Reality therapists (contracted); Recreational therapists (contracted); Speech therapists (contracted); Activities coordinators (contracted); Dietitians (contracted); Podiatrists (contracted).
Facilities Dining room; Laundry room; Outdoor activities shed; Dayroom.
Activities Arts & crafts; Cards; Games; Prayer groups; Shopping trips; Intergenerational programs; Pet therapy.

Ivy Hall Nursing Home Inc
301 Watauga Ave, Elizabethton, TN 37643
(615) 542-6512
Admin Judy C Taylor.
Medical Dir Dr E E Perry.
Licensure Intermediate care. *Beds* ICF 76. *Certified* Medicaid.
Admissions Requirements Medical examination; Physician's request.
Staff Physicians 1 (ft), 5 (pt); RNs 1 (ft); LPNs 6 (ft), 2 (pt); Nurses' aides 28 (ft), 5 (pt); Physical therapists 1 (pt); Speech therapists 1 (pt); Activities coordinators 1 (ft); Dietitians 1 (ft), 1 (pt); Ophthalmologists 1 (pt); Podiatrists 1 (pt); Audiologists 1 (pt); Recreational therapists Dentists 1 (pt).
Facilities Dining room; Physical therapy room; Activities room; Crafts room; Laundry room; Barber/Beauty shop; Library.
Activities Arts & crafts; Cards; Games; Reading groups; Prayer groups; Movies; Shopping trips; Dances/Social/Cultural gatherings.

Southwood Nursing Home
1200 Spruce Lane & Pine Ridge Cir, Elizabethton, TN 37643
(615) 543-3202
Admin Gerry Woods. *Dir of Nursing* Patsy McKinney. *Medical Dir* Dr Steve May.
Licensure Intermediate care. *Beds* ICF 92. *Certified* Medicaid.
Owner Proprietary corp (Southwood Health Care).
Admissions Requirements Medical examination.
Staff Physicians 1 (pt); RNs 1 (ft); LPNs 9 (ft); Nurses' aides 15 (ft), 15 (pt); Physical therapists 1 (pt); Activities coordinators 1 (ft); Dietitians 1 (ft).
Facilities Dining room; Physical therapy room; Activities room; Crafts room; Laundry room; Barber/Beauty shop.
Activities Arts & crafts; Cards; Games; Prayer groups; Movies; Shopping trips.

Erin

Royal Care of Erin Inc
Rte 3 Box 137-B, Knight Rd, Erin, TN 37061
(615) 289-4141
Admin Helen L Stout.
Medical Dir Daniel Martin MD.
Licensure Intermediate care. *Beds* ICF 160. *Certified* Medicaid.
Admissions Requirements Minimum age 18; Medical examination.
Staff Physicians 3 (ft), 1 (pt); RNs 3 (ft); LPNs 4 (ft), 4 (pt); Nurses' aides 20 (ft), 12 (pt); Physical therapists 1 (pt); Activities coordinators 1 (ft), 1 (pt); Dietitians 1 (pt).
Facilities Dining room; Physical therapy room; Activities room; Chapel; Crafts room; Laundry room; Barber/Beauty shop; Library.
Activities Arts & crafts; Games; Reading groups; Prayer groups; Movies; Dances/Social/Cultural gatherings.

Erwin

Life Care Center of Erwin
Stalling Ln, Erwin, TN 37650
(615) 743-4131
Admin Larry Hodge. *Dir of Nursing* Brenda Hutchings. *Medical Dir* Dr J W Colinger.
Licensure Skilled care; Intermediate care; Alzheimer's care. *Beds* SNF 46; ICF 80. *Certified* Medicaid; Medicare.
Owner Privately owned.
Admissions Requirements Physician's request.
Staff RNs 3 (ft), 1 (pt); LPNs 13 (ft), 4 (pt); Nurses' aides 50 (ft), 12 (pt); Physical therapists 1 (ft); Activities coordinators 1 (ft), 1 (pt); Dietitians 1 (ft); Podiatrists 1 (pt); Audiologists 1 (pt).
Facilities Dining room; Physical therapy room; Activities room; Laundry room; Barber/Beauty shop; Alzheimer's unit.
Activities Arts & crafts; Games; Prayer groups; Movies; Shopping trips; Dances/Social/Cultural gatherings.

Unicoi County Nursing Home
Greenway Cir, Erwin, TN 37650
(615) 743-3141
Licensure Skilled care; Intermediate care. *Beds* 46. *Certified* Medicaid; Medicare.

Etowah

Etowah Health Care Center
Old Grady Rd, Etowah, TN 37331
(615) 263-1138
Medical Dir Dr Thomas W Williams.
Licensure Intermediate care. *Beds* ICF 120. *Certified* Medicaid.
Admissions Requirements Minimum age 18; Medical examination; Physician's request.
Staff Physicians 1 (pt); RNs 1 (ft); LPNs 7 (ft), 3 (pt); Nurses' aides 30 (ft), 8 (pt); Physical therapists 1 (pt); Speech therapists 1 (pt); Activities coordinators 1 (ft), 1 (pt); Dietitians 1 (pt).
Facilities Dining room; Physical therapy room; Activities room; Laundry room; Barber/Beauty shop.
Activities Arts & crafts; Games; Prayer groups; Movies; Dances/Social/Cultural gatherings.

McMinn Memorial Nursing Home
PO Box 410, Old Grady Rd, Etowah, TN 37331
(615) 263-3647
Admin Wanda Watson. *Dir of Nursing* Judy Pickett RN. *Medical Dir* T W Williams MD.
Licensure Intermediate care. *Beds* ICF 44. *Private Pay Patients* 40%. *Certified* Medicaid.
Owner Publicly owned.
Admissions Requirements Physician's request.

Staff Physicians 7 (pt); RNs 1 (ft); LPNs 5 (ft); Nurses' aides 11 (ft), 4 (pt); Physical therapists 1 (pt); Reality therapists 1 (pt); Speech therapists 1 (pt); Activities coordinators 1 (pt); Dietitians 1 (pt).
Facilities Dining room; Activities room; Barber/Beauty shop.
Activities Arts & crafts; Cards; Games; Reading groups; Prayer groups; Movies; Shopping trips; Dances/Social/Cultural gatherings.

Fayetteville

Donalson Care Center
1681 Winchester Hwy 64 E, Fayetteville, TN 37334
(615) 433-7156, 433-6942 FAX
Admin Kathleen M Closson. *Dir of Nursing* Vicky Groce RN. *Medical Dir* Larry Barnes.
Licensure Skilled care; Intermediate care. *Beds* Swing beds SNF/ICF 78. *Private Pay Patients* 43%. *Certified* Medicaid; Medicare; VA.
Owner Nonprofit organization/foundation.
Admissions Requirements Minimum age 14; Medical examination; Physician's request.
Staff Physicians 1 (pt); RNs 1 (ft); LPNs 5 (ft), 5 (pt); Nurses' aides 20 (ft), 1 (pt); Activities coordinators 1 (ft).
Languages Spanish.
Facilities Dining room; Activities room; Crafts room.
Activities Arts & crafts; Cards; Games; Reading groups; Prayer groups; Movies; Shopping trips; Dances/Social/Cultural gatherings; Intergenerational programs; Pet therapy; Bus rides; One-on-one visits.

Health Inn
Rte 9 Box 173, Fayetteville, TN 37334
(615) 433-9973
Admin Jewell Barnett. *Dir of Nursing* Douie Meeks LPN. *Medical Dir* Dr Patel.
Licensure Intermediate care. *Beds* ICF 65. *Private Pay Patients* 25%. *Certified* Medicaid.
Owner Privately owned.
Staff RNs 1 (pt); LPNs 5 (ft), 3 (pt); Nurses' aides 14 (ft), 1 (pt); Activities coordinators 1 (ft); Dietitians 3 (ft), 3 (pt).
Facilities Dining room; Laundry room; Barber/Beauty shop.

Lincoln Care Center
501 Morgan Ave, Fayetteville, TN 37334
(615) 433-6146, 433-0816 FAX
Admin Kathleen M Closson. *Dir of Nursing* Gayle Sullivan RN, ICF; Lisa Riddle RN, SNF. *Medical Dir* Dr Larry Barnes.
Licensure Skilled care; Intermediate care. *Beds* SNF 37; ICF 139. *Certified* Medicaid; Medicare; VA.
Owner Nonprofit organization/foundation.
Admissions Requirements Medical examination; Physician's request.
Staff Physicians 1 (pt); RNs 6 (ft), 2 (pt); LPNs 15 (ft), 1 (pt); Nurses' aides 54 (ft), 8 (pt); Physical therapists 1 (ft); Occupational therapists 1 (ft); Speech therapists 1 (ft); Activities coordinators 1 (ft); Dietitians 1 (ft); Podiatrists 1 (pt).
Languages Spanish.
Facilities Dining room; Physical therapy room; Activities room; Crafts room; Barber/Beauty shop.
Activities Arts & crafts; Cards; Games; Prayer groups; Movies; Shopping trips; Dances/Social/Cultural gatherings; Intergenerational programs; Pet therapy; Bus rides; One-on-one visits; Special events; Quarterly family dinners.

Franklin

Claiborne & Hughes Convalescent Center Inc
200 Strahl St, Franklin, TN 37064
(615) 791-1103
Admin John W Jones. *Dir of Nursing* Pauline Pewitz RN. *Medical Dir* Robert Hollister MD.
Licensure Skilled care; Intermediate care; Alzheimer's care. *Beds* SNF 43; ICF 114. *Certified* Medicaid; Medicare.
Owner Proprietary corp.
Admissions Requirements Medical examination.
Staff RNs 2 (ft), 1 (pt); LPNs 13 (ft), 2 (pt); Nurses' aides 40 (ft), 15 (pt); Activities coordinators 2 (ft), 2 (pt).
Facilities Dining room; Physical therapy room; Activities room; Crafts room; Laundry room; Barber/Beauty shop.
Activities Arts & crafts; Cards; Games; Reading groups; Prayer groups; Movies; Shopping trips; Dances/Social/Cultural gatherings; Resident council.

Franklin Health Care Center
216 Fairground St, Franklin, TN 37064
(615) 790-0154
Licensure Skilled care; Intermediate care. *Beds* 84. *Certified* Medicaid; Medicare.
Owner Proprietary corp (National Health Corp).

Franklin Manor Nursing Home
1501 Columbia Ave, Franklin, TN 37064
(615) 794-2624
Beds 37.

Graystone Home Inc
157 4th Ave S, Franklin, TN 37064
(615) 794-4877
Admin Dorothy S Stone. *Dir of Nursing* Margurietta P Church RN.
Licensure Intermediate care; Alzheimer's care. *Beds* ICF 37.
Owner Proprietary corp.
Admissions Requirements Minimum age 14; Medical examination.
Staff Physicians 1 (pt); RNs 1 (ft); LPNs 3 (ft), 2 (pt); Nurses' aides 11 (ft), 4 (pt); Activities coordinators 1 (ft); Dietitians 1 (pt).
Facilities Activities room; Barber/Beauty shop.
Activities Arts & crafts; Cards; Games; Prayer groups; Group singing.

Harpeth Terrace Convalescent Center
1287 W Main St, Franklin, TN 37064
(615) 794-8417
Admin Boris Georgeff. *Dir of Nursing* Judy Michael. *Medical Dir* Dr H Bryant Savage.
Licensure Intermediate care. *Beds* ICF 89. *Certified* Medicaid; Medicare.
Owner Proprietary corp.
Admissions Requirements Medical examination.
Staff Physicians 3 (ft); RNs 3 (ft); LPNs 5 (ft); Nurses' aides 26 (ft); Activities coordinators 1 (ft); Dietitians 1 (pt); Social worker 1 (ft).
Facilities Dining room; Physical therapy room; Activities room; Laundry room; Barber/Beauty shop.
Activities Arts & crafts; Cards; Games; Reading groups; Prayer groups; Movies; Shopping trips; Dances/Social/Cultural gatherings.

Gainesboro

Theo Spivey Nursing Home
PO Box 553, Hwy 53 N, Gainesboro, TN 38562
(615) 268-0291
Licensure Intermediate care. *Beds* ICF 106. *Certified* Medicaid.

Gallatin

Brandywood Nursing Home
555 E Bledsoe St, Gallatin, TN 37066
(615) 452-7132
Licensure Skilled care; Intermediate care. *Beds* 100. *Certified* Medicaid; Medicare.
Owner Proprietary corp (Beverly Enterprises).

Gallatin Health Care Associates
438 N Water Ave, Gallatin, TN 37066
(615) 452-2322
Admin Marie Lane.
Medical Dir Family Practice Associates MD.
Licensure Skilled care; Intermediate care. *Beds* 215. *Certified* Medicaid; Medicare.
Owner Privately owned.
Admissions Requirements Physician's request.
Staff RNs 3 (ft); LPNs 25 (ft); Nurses' aides 100 (ft); Physical therapists 1 (ft); Occupational therapists 1 (ft); Speech therapists 1 (ft); Activities coordinators 1 (ft); Dietitians 1 (ft).
Facilities Dining room; Physical therapy room; Activities room; Crafts room; Laundry room; Barber/Beauty shop; Sun rooms.
Activities Arts & crafts; Prayer groups; Movies; Shopping trips; Dances/Social/Cultural gatherings.

L M Swanson Nursing Home
647 Pace St, Gallatin, TN 37066
(615) 452-0611
Licensure Intermediate care. *Beds* ICF 25. *Certified* Medicaid.

Gallaway

Layton W Watson Nursing Home
435 Old Brownsville Rd, Gallaway, TN 38036
(901) 867-2010
Admin Doris L Morris. *Dir of Nursing* Donna Beasley. *Medical Dir* Dr Patrick Murphy.
Licensure Intermediate care. *Beds* ICF 130. *Certified* Medicaid.
Owner Publicly owned.
Admissions Requirements Minimum age 14; Medical examination; Physician's request.
Staff LPNs 10 (ft), 5 (pt); Nurses' aides 33 (ft), 10 (pt); Activities coordinators 1 (ft).
Facilities Dining room; Physical therapy room; Activities room; Chapel; Crafts room; Laundry room; Barber/Beauty shop; Library.
Activities Arts & crafts; Cards; Games; Reading groups; Prayer groups; Movies; Shopping trips; Dances/Social/Cultural gatherings.

Goodlettsville

Vanco Manor Nursing Center
813 S Dickerson Rd, Goodlettsville, TN 37072
(615) 859-6600
Admin Billy R Talbert. *Dir of Nursing* Ema Hoove. *Medical Dir* Dr John Chauvin.
Licensure Intermediate care. *Beds* ICF 66. *Certified* Medicaid.
Owner Proprietary corp (American Health Centers Inc).
Admissions Requirements Medical examination.
Staff RNs 1 (ft); LPNs 6 (ft); Nurses' aides 18 (ft); Physical therapists 1 (pt); Speech therapists 1 (pt); Activities coordinators 1 (ft); Dietitians 1 (pt); Podiatrists 1 (pt); Audiologists 1 (pt).
Facilities Dining room; Activities room; Laundry room; Barber/Beauty shop.
Activities Arts & crafts; Cards; Games; Reading groups; Prayer groups; Shopping trips; Dances/Social/Cultural gatherings; Intergenerational programs; Pet therapy.

Gray

Anderson Healthcare Inc
PO Box 8275, Rte 15, Gray Station Rd, Gray,
TN 37615
(615) 477-7146
Admin Mrs Billie S Anderson. *Dir of Nursing*
Terri Nave RN. *Medical Dir* Jacqueline
Lloyd MD.
Licensure Skilled care; Intermediate care. *Beds*
SNF 20; ICF 85. *Certified* Medicaid;
Medicare.
Owner Proprietary corp.
Staff Physicians 14 (pt); RNs 2 (ft), 1 (pt);
LPNs 10 (ft), 2 (pt); Nurses 35 (ft), 10
(pt); Physical therapists 2 (pt); Speech
therapists 1 (pt); Activities coordinators 1
(ft); Dietitians 1 (ft); Ophthalmologists 1
(pt); Podiatrists 1 (pt); Dentists 1 (pt).
Facilities Dining room; Physical therapy
room; Activities room; Laundry room;
Barber/Beauty shop.
Activities Arts & crafts; Cards; Games;
Reading groups; Prayer groups; Dances/
Social/Cultural gatherings.

Graysville

Graysville Nursing Home
Star Rte, Graysville, TN 37338
(615) 775-1262
Licensure Nursing home. *Beds* 19.
Admissions Requirements Medical
examination.
Staff RNs 1 (pt); LPNs 1 (ft), 1 (pt); Nurses'
aides 6 (ft), 3 (pt).
Facilities Dining room; Laundry room.

Greeneville

Life Care Center of Greeneville
725 Crum St, Greeneville, TN 37743
(615) 639-8131
Licensure Intermediate care. *Beds* ICF 161.
Certified Medicaid.
Owner Proprietary corp (Life Care Centers of
America).
Facilities Dining room; Physical therapy
room; Activities room; Chapel; Crafts room;
Laundry room; Barber/Beauty shop; EKG;
X-ray; IPPB.
Activities Arts & crafts; Games; Reading
groups; Movies; Shopping trips; Dances/
Social/Cultural gatherings.

Life Care—West
210 Holt Court, Greeneville, TN 37743
(615) 639-0213
Admin Charles R Sherer. *Dir of Nursing* Betty
Laster. *Medical Dir* Dr Richard Aasheim.
Licensure Intermediate care. *Beds* ICF 124.
Certified Medicaid.
Owner Proprietary corp (Life Care Centers of
America).
Admissions Requirements Medical
examination; Physician's request.
Staff Physicians 1 (pt); RNs 2 (ft); LPNs 11
(ft); Nurses' aides 32 (ft), 10 (pt); Physical
therapists 1 (pt); Speech therapists 1 (pt);
Activities coordinators 1 (ft); Dietitians 1
(pt).
Facilities Dining room; Physical therapy
room; Activities room; Chapel; Crafts room;
Laundry room; Barber/Beauty shop.
Activities Arts & crafts; Cards; Games;
Reading groups; Prayer groups; Movies;
Shopping trips; Dances/Social/Cultural
gatherings; Fishing trips; Hayride; Bingo;
Christmas parade; County fair.

Harriman

Johnson's Health Care Center Inc
Rte 7 Box 290, Hannah Rd, Harriman, TN
37748
(615) 882-9159

Licensure Intermediate care. *Beds* ICF 170.
Certified Medicaid.

Marshall C Voss Health Care Facility
Rte 8 Box 68, Patton Ln, Harriman, TN
37748
(615) 354-3941
Beds 130.

Hartsville

Hartsville Convalescent Center
649 McMurry Blvd, Hartsville, TN 37074
(615) 374-2167
Admin Dorothy D Evins. *Dir of Nursing*
Lucille Seelow. *Medical Dir* E K Bratton
MD.
Licensure Intermediate care. *Beds* ICF 86.
Private Pay Patients 12%. *Certified*
Medicaid.
Owner Proprietary corp (Nursing Centers
Unlimited Inc).
Admissions Requirements Medical
examination; Physician's request.
Staff Physicians 1 (ft); LPNs 8 (ft), 1 (pt);
Nurses' aides 24 (ft); Activities coordinators
1 (ft); Dietitians 1 (ft).
Facilities Dining room; Laundry room;
Barber/Beauty shop.
Activities Arts & crafts; Cards; Games;
Reading groups; Prayer groups;
Intergenerational programs; Pet therapy;
Religious and social programs.

Henderson

Chester County Nursing Home
831 E Main St, Henderson, TN 38340
(901) 989-7598
Admin Tommie Archer. *Dir of Nursing*
Bonnie Hudson. *Medical Dir* R L Wilson
MD.
Licensure Intermediate care. *Beds* ICF 88.
Certified Medicaid.
Owner Privately owned.
Admissions Requirements Minimum age 18;
Medical examination; Physician's request.
Staff RNs 1 (ft); LPNs 7 (ft), 2 (pt); Nurses'
aides 20 (ft), 8 (pt); Activities coordinators 1
(ft); Dietitians 1 (pt).
Facilities Dining room; Activities room;
Laundry room; Barber/Beauty shop.
Activities Arts & crafts; Cards; Games;
Reading groups; Prayer groups; Movies;
Shopping trips; Dances/Social/Cultural
gatherings.

Hendersonville

Hendersonville Nursing Home Ltd
672 W Main St, Hendersonville, TN 37075
(615) 824-8301
Admin Randall Dodd. *Dir of Nursing* Linda
Fuqua. *Medical Dir* Millard Smith.
Licensure Intermediate care. *Beds* ICF 32.
Private Pay Patients 50%.
Owner Privately owned.
Staff LPNs 3 (ft), 1 (pt); Nurses' aides 8 (ft), 1
(pt); Activities coordinators 1 (pt).

National Health Care Center of Hendersonville
370 Old Shackle Island Rd, Hendersonville,
TN 37075
(615) 824-0720
Beds 97.
Owner Proprietary corp (National Health
Corp).

Hermitage

McKendree Village Inc
4343-47 Lebanon Rd, Hermitage, TN 37076
(615) 889-6990, 871-8699 FAX
Admin Dr Robert F Willner FACHE. *Dir of
Nursing* Barbara Bourne Davis RN. *Medical
Dir* Deborah Montgomery MD.

Licensure Skilled care; Intermediate care;
Retirement; Alzheimer's care. *Beds* SNF 50;
ICF 200; Retirement 430. *Certified*
Medicaid; Medicare.
Owner Nonprofit corp.
Admissions Requirements Minimum age 60;
Medical examination.
Staff Physicians (contracted); RNs 9 (ft), 5
(pt); LPNs 14 (ft), 12 (pt); Nurses' aides 77
(ft), 24 (pt); Physical therapists (contracted);
Occupational therapists 1 (pt); Activities
coordinators 6 (ft); Dietitians (contracted);
Podiatrists 1 (pt); Audiologists 1 (pt).
Affiliation United Methodist.
Facilities Dining room; Physical therapy
room; Activities room; Chapel; Crafts room;
Laundry room; Barber/Beauty shop; Library;
Fitness center with indoor pool, whirlpool,
exercise room; 100-bed Alzheimer's unit.
Activities Arts & crafts; Cards; Games;
Reading groups; Prayer groups; Movies;
Shopping trips; Dances/Social/Cultural
gatherings; Intergenerational programs; Pet
therapy; Educational opportunities.

Hohenwald

Lewis County Manor
PO Box 92, Linden Hwy, Hohenwald, TN
38462
(615) 796-3233
Admin Thelma Blocker.
Medical Dir Jean Allsop.
Licensure Intermediate care. *Beds* ICF 121.
Certified Medicaid.
Owner Proprietary corp (American Health
Center Inc).
Staff RNs 2 (pt); LPNs 4 (ft); Nurses' aides 13
(ft), 3 (pt); Activities coordinators 1 (ft);
Dietitians 1 (ft).
Facilities Dining room; Activities room;
Laundry room; Barber/Beauty shop.
Activities Arts & crafts; Cards; Games;
Reading groups; Movies; Shopping trips;
Dances/Social/Cultural gatherings.

Humboldt

NuCare Convalescent Center
2400 Mitchell St, Humboldt, TN 38343
(901) 784-5183
Admin Nichols L Nevius. *Dir of Nursing* M E
Duncan RN. *Medical Dir* Dr Robert
Routon.
Licensure Intermediate care. *Beds* ICF 142.
Certified Medicaid.
Owner Proprietary corp (Southeastern Health
Care).
Admissions Requirements Medical
examination; Physician's request.
Staff Physicians 14 (pt); RNs 1 (ft); LPNs 13
(ft); Nurses' aides 52 (ft); Physical therapists
1 (pt); Speech therapists 1 (pt); Activities
coordinators 1 (ft); Dietitians 1 (ft); Dentists
1 (pt).
Facilities Dining room; Physical therapy
room; Activities room; Laundry room;
Barber/Beauty shop; Library.
Activities Games; Dances/Social/Cultural
gatherings; Bingo; Ball games; Fishing trips.

Huntingdon

Hillhaven Convalescent Center of Huntingdon
635 High St, Huntingdon, TN 38344
(901) 986-8943
Admin William W Wright.
Licensure Intermediate care. *Beds* ICF 182.
Certified Medicaid.
Staff RNs 1 (ft); LPNs 13 (ft); Nurses' aides
26 (ft); Physical therapists 1 (pt); Activities
coordinators 1 (ft); Dietitians 1 (ft).
Facilities Dining room; Activities room;
Crafts room; Laundry room; Barber/Beauty
shop.

Activities Arts & crafts; Cards; Games; Reading groups; Prayer groups; Movies; Shopping trips; Dances/Social/Cultural gatherings.

Huntsville

Huntsville Manor
217A Baker St, Huntsville, TN 37756
(615) 663-3600
Admin Nancy Burton-Chitwood. *Dir of Nursing* Nita Miller. *Medical Dir* Dr George Kline.
Licensure Intermediate care. *Beds* ICF 96. *Private Pay Patients* 3-4%. *Certified* Medicaid.
Owner Proprietary corp (Angell Group).
Admissions Requirements Minimum age 14; Medical examination; Physician's request.
Staff Physicians 1 (pt); RNs 1 (ft); LPNs 6 (ft), 4 (pt); Nurses' aides 22 (ft), 10 (pt); Physical therapists 2 (pt); Activities coordinators 1 (ft); Dietitians 1 (pt); Social services 1 (ft).
Facilities Dining room; Physical therapy room; Activities room; Laundry room; Barber/Beauty shop; Dayroom with TV.
Activities Arts & crafts; Cards; Games; Reading groups; Prayer groups; Movies; Shopping trips; Dances/Social/Cultural gatherings; Intergenerational programs.

Jackson

Forest Cove Manor Inc
45 Forest Cove, Jackson, TN 38301
(901) 424-4200
Licensure Intermediate care. *Beds* ICF 157. *Certified* Medicaid.
Owner Proprietary corp (American Health Center Inc).
Admissions Requirements Minimum age 18.
Staff RNs 2 (ft); LPNs 12 (ft), 3 (pt); Nurses' aides 36 (ft), 13 (pt); Recreational therapists 1 (pt); Activities coordinators 1 (ft).
Facilities Dining room; Activities room; Crafts room; Barber/Beauty shop.
Activities Arts & crafts; Cards; Games; Prayer groups; Movies.

Jackson-Madison County General Hospital—Specialty Unit
670 Skyline Dr, Jackson, TN 38301
(901) 425-6708
Admin George Austin. *Dir of Nursing* Catherine Sue Martin. *Medical Dir* Dr William Satterfield.
Licensure Skilled care. *Beds* SNF 50. *Certified* Medicaid; Medicare.
Owner Publicly owned.
Admissions Requirements Minimum age 16; Medical examination; Physician's request.
Staff RNs 6 (ft); LPNs 8 (ft), 4 (pt); Nurses' aides 8 (ft), 1 (pt); Physical therapists 1 (pt); Occupational therapists 1 (pt); Speech therapists 1 (pt); Activities coordinators 1 (ft); Dietitians 1 (ft).
Facilities Dining room; Physical therapy room; Activities room; Crafts room; Laundry room.
Activities Arts & crafts; Cards; Games; Reading groups; Prayer groups; Movies; Dances/Social/Cultural gatherings.

Jackson Manor Inc
131 Cloverdale St, Jackson, TN 38301
(901) 423-8750
Admin Jane C Pendergrass. *Dir of Nursing* M Kirby Buchanan RN. *Medical Dir* Curtis Clark MD.
Licensure Intermediate care. *Beds* ICF 108. *Certified* Medicaid.
Owner Proprietary corp (Tullock Management).
Admissions Requirements Minimum age 14; Medical examination; Physician's request.

Staff Physicians 1 (pt); RNs 1 (ft); LPNs 8 (ft), 2 (pt); Nurses' aides 31 (ft), 6 (pt); Physical therapists 1 (pt); Activities coordinators 1 (ft), 1 (pt); Dietitians 1 (pt).
Facilities Dining room; Activities room; Crafts room; Laundry room; Barber/Beauty shop.
Activities Arts & crafts; Cards; Games; Prayer groups; Movies; Dances/Social/Cultural gatherings.

Laurelwood Health Care Center
PO Box 1467, 200 Birch St, Jackson, TN 38302
(901) 422-5641
Admin Di-Ann Jones. *Dir of Nursing* Marilyn Hayslett. *Medical Dir* Dr Robert Tucker.
Licensure Intermediate care. *Beds* ICF 73. *Private Pay Patients* 8%. *Certified* Medicaid.
Owner Proprietary corp.
Admissions Requirements Minimum age 14; Medical examination; Physician's request.
Staff Physicians; RNs 1 (ft); LPNs 8 (ft); Nurses' aides 27 (ft); Physical therapists 1 (ft); Activities coordinators 1 (ft); Dietitians 1 (ft).
Facilities Dining room; Activities room; Crafts room; Laundry room; Barber/Beauty shop.
Activities Arts & crafts; Cards; Games; Reading groups; Prayer groups; Movies; Shopping trips; Dances/Social/Cultural gatherings.

Maplewood Health Care Center
100 Cherrywood Pl, Jackson, TN 38301
(901) 668-1900
Licensure Intermediate care. *Beds* ICF 140. *Certified* Medicaid.

Mission Convalescent Home
118 Glass St, Jackson, TN 38301
(901) 424-2956
Admin F L Cherry. *Dir of Nursing* Brenda Bray LPN. *Medical Dir* Dr Ronald Weaver.
Licensure Intermediate care. *Beds* ICF 30. *Certified* Medicaid; Medicare.
Owner Nonprofit organization/foundation.
Admissions Requirements Minimum age 16; Medical examination; Physician's request.
Facilities Dining room; Activities room; Chapel; Laundry room.
Activities Arts & crafts; Cards; Games; Prayer groups; Movies; Dances/Social/Cultural gatherings.

Jamestown

Fentress County General Hospital Skilled Bed Facility
Hwy 52 W, Jamestown, TN 38556
(615) 879-8171
Beds 12.

Fentress County Nursing Home
Hwy 52 W, Jamestown, TN 38556
(615) 879-5859
Admin Gale C Potter. *Dir of Nursing* Glenna Hall RN. *Medical Dir* D N Joshi MD.
Licensure Intermediate care. *Beds* ICF 100. *Certified* Medicaid.
Owner Nonprofit organization/foundation.
Admissions Requirements Medical examination; Physician's request.
Staff Physicians 5 (pt); RNs 2 (ft); LPNs; Nurses' aides 27 (ft); Physical therapists 1 (pt); Speech therapists 1 (pt); Activities coordinators 1 (ft); Dietitians 1 (ft).
Facilities Dining room; Physical therapy room; Activities room; Laundry room; Barber/Beauty shop.
Activities Arts & crafts; Cards; Games; Reading groups; Prayer groups; Movies; Shopping trips; In-room visits.

Jefferson City

Hillhaven Health Care
Hwy 11 E, Jefferson City, TN 37760
(615) 475-9037, 475-5386 FAX
Admin Gina C Harris. *Dir of Nursing* Johnnie Michaels RN. *Medical Dir* Henry J Presutti MD.
Licensure Intermediate care. *Beds* ICF 186. *Private Pay Patients* 20%. *Certified* Medicaid.
Owner Proprietary corp (Hillhaven Corp).
Admissions Requirements Minimum age per state requirements; Medical examination; Physician's request.
Staff RNs 5 (ft), 1 (pt); LPNs 10 (ft), 8 (pt); Nurses' aides 40 (ft), 26 (pt); Activities coordinators 2 (ft); Dietitians 1 (ft).
Facilities Dining room; Activities room; Crafts room; Laundry room; Barber/Beauty shop.
Activities Arts & crafts; Cards; Games; Reading groups; Prayer groups; Movies; Shopping trips; Dances/Social/Cultural gatherings; Intergenerational programs; Pet therapy.

Johnson City

Appalachian Christian Village
2012 Sherwood Dr, Johnson City, TN 37601
(615) 928-3168
Admin Garry L Phillips.
Medical Dir Gwen Hendrix.
Licensure Intermediate care; Continuing care retirement community. *Beds* ICF 101. *Certified* Medicaid.
Owner Nonprofit organization/foundation.
Admissions Requirements Minimum age 62; Medical examination.
Staff RNs 2 (ft), 2 (pt); LPNs 10 (ft), 4 (pt); Nurses' aides 40 (ft), 6 (pt); Physical therapists 1 (pt); Activities coordinators 1 (ft), 1 (pt); Dietitians 1 (ft); Ophthalmologists 1 (pt); Podiatrists 1 (pt); Dentists 1 (pt); Ward clerks 2 (ft); Social worker 1.
Affiliation Church of Christ.
Facilities Dining room; Physical therapy room; Activities room; Chapel; Crafts room; Laundry room; Barber/Beauty shop; Library.
Activities Games; Movies; Dances/Social/Cultural gatherings.

Asbury Center
400 N Boone St, Johnson City, TN 37604
(615) 928-2475
Admin Sam W Ware, James R Deck. *Dir of Nursing* Nancy Hidalgo RN. *Medical Dir* Robert C Allen MD.
Licensure Skilled care; Intermediate care; Retirement facility. *Beds* SNF 22; ICF 152; Apartment units 90. *Certified* Medicaid; Medicare.
Owner Nonprofit corp.
Admissions Requirements Medical examination; Physician's request.
Staff RNs; LPNs; Nurses' aides; Physical therapists; Speech therapists; Activities coordinators; Dietitians.
Facilities Dining room; Physical therapy room; Activities room; Chapel; Crafts room; Laundry room; Barber/Beauty shop; Library; Garden with fountain; Gazebo; Shuffleboard; Putting green.
Activities Arts & crafts; Cards; Games; Reading groups; Prayer groups; Shopping trips; Dances/Social/Cultural gatherings.

Colonial Hill Health Care Center
PO Box 3218, 3209 Bristol Hwy, Johnson City, TN 37602
(615) 282-3311
Admin Ronald Dean. *Dir of Nursing* Joyce Walwick RN. *Medical Dir* Dr Richard Morrison.

Licensure Skilled care; Intermediate care; Retirement; Alzheimer's care. *Beds* SNF 74; ICF 103. *Certified* Medicaid; Medicare.
Owner Proprietary corp (National Health Corp).
Admissions Requirements Medical examination; Physician's request.
Staff Physicians 2 (pt); RNs 8 (ft), 3 (pt); LPNs 12 (ft), 12 (pt); Nurses' aides 43 (ft), 18 (pt); Physical therapists 2 (pt); Occupational therapists 2 (ft), 2 (pt); Speech therapists 2 (ft); Activities coordinators 2 (ft); Dietitians 1 (ft).
Facilities Dining room; Physical therapy room; Activities room; Crafts room; Laundry room; Barber/Beauty shop; Library.
Activities Arts & crafts; Cards; Games; Reading groups; Prayer groups; Movies; Shopping trips; Dances/Social/Cultural gatherings.

Jonesborough

Four Oaks Health Care Center
1101 Persimmon Ridge Rd, Jonesborough, TN 37659
(615) 753-8711
Admin Suzanne Ervin. *Dir of Nursing* Alice Ford RN. *Medical Dir* David Doane MD; Forrest Lang MD.
Licensure Skilled care; Intermediate care. *Beds* 80. *Certified* Medicaid; Medicare.
Owner Proprietary corp.
Admissions Requirements Medical examination.
Staff Physicians 2 (pt); RNs 1 (ft), 2 (pt); LPNs 4 (ft), 3 (pt); Nurses' aides 25 (ft), 5 (pt); Physical therapists 1 (pt); Recreational therapists 1 (ft); Occupational therapists 1 (pt); Speech therapists 1 (pt); Activities coordinators 1 (ft); Dietitians 1 (pt); Ophthalmologists 1 (pt); Podiatrists 1 (pt); Dentists 1 (pt).
Facilities Dining room; Physical therapy room; Activities room; Crafts room; Laundry room; Barber/Beauty shop; Library.
Activities Arts & crafts; Cards; Games; Reading groups; Prayer groups; Movies; Dances/Social/Cultural gatherings.

Jonesborough Nursing Home
300 W Jackson Blvd, Jonesborough, TN 37659
(615) 753-4281
Admin Linda Jennings. *Dir of Nursing* Sandy Timbs. *Medical Dir* Dr David Doane.
Licensure Intermediate care. *Beds* ICF 65. *Private Pay Patients* 2%. *Certified* Medicaid.
Owner Proprietary corp (Quality Care Management).
Admissions Requirements Medical examination; Physician's request.
Staff Physicians 2 (pt); RNs 1 (ft); LPNs 5 (ft), 1 (pt); Nurses' aides 18 (ft), 3 (pt); Activities coordinators 1 (ft); Dietitians 1 (pt).
Facilities Dining room; Activities room; Crafts room; Laundry room; Barber/Beauty shop.
Activities Arts & crafts; Cards; Games; Reading groups; Prayer groups; Dances/Social/Cultural gatherings; Pet therapy.

Kingsport

Asbury Center at Baysmont
100 Netherland Ln, Kingsport, TN 37660
(615) 245-0360
Admin Linda Jennings. *Dir of Nursing* Barbara Campbell. *Medical Dir* David Franzus.
Licensure Intermediate care; Alzheimer's care; Retirement. *Beds* ICF 40; Retirement 130.
Owner Nonprofit organization/foundation (Asbury Centers Inc).
Admissions Requirements Minimum age 14; Medical examination; Physician's request.

Staff LPNs 4 (ft), 3 (pt); Nurses' aides 25 (ft); Physical therapists (contracted); Reality therapists (contracted); Recreational therapists (contracted); Occupational therapists (contracted); Speech therapists (contracted); Dietitians (contracted); Podiatrists (contracted); Audiologists (contracted); Optometrists (contracted).
Affiliation United Methodist.
Facilities Dining room; Physical therapy room; Activities room; Laundry room; Barber/Beauty shop.
Activities Arts & crafts; Cards; Games; Reading groups; Prayer groups; Movies; Intergenerational programs; Nursing Home Enrichment program.

Hillside Manor
PO Box 3768, 3641 Memorial Blvd, Kingsport, TN 37664
(615) 246-2411
Beds 198.

Meadowbrook Manor of Kingsport
1 Brook Pl, Kingsport, TN 37660
(615) 246-8934
Beds 180.

Wessex House of Kingsport
2421 John B Dennis Pkwy, Kingsport, TN 37660
(615) 288-3988
Beds 120.

Knoxville

Brakebill Nursing Home Inc
5837 Lyons View Pike, Knoxville, TN 37919
(615) 584-3902
Admin W Lynn Brakebill.
Medical Dir Susan Titlow.
Licensure Skilled care; Intermediate care. *Beds* SNF 54; ICF 168. *Certified* Medicaid; Medicare.
Owner Privately owned.
Admissions Requirements Medical examination; Physician's request.
Staff Physicians 20 (pt); RNs 6 (ft), 2 (pt); LPNs 12 (ft), 2 (pt); Nurses' aides 50 (ft), 5 (pt); Physical therapists 1 (ft), 2 (pt); Speech therapists 1 (pt); Activities coordinators 3 (ft); Dietitians 1 (pt).
Facilities Dining room; Physical therapy room; Activities room; Crafts room; Laundry room; Barber/Beauty shop; Library.
Activities Arts & crafts; Cards; Games; Reading groups; Prayer groups; Movies; Shopping trips; Dances/Social/Cultural gatherings.

Farragut Health Care Center
12823 Kingston Pike, Knoxville, TN 37922
(615) 966-0600
Beds 88.

Hillcrest Central
5321 Tazewell Pike, Knoxville, TN 37918
(615) 687-1321
Admin Jeff Scott. *Dir of Nursing* Karen Kirk RN. *Medical Dir* Thomas B Drinnen MD.
Licensure Skilled care; Intermediate care. *Beds* SNF 83; ICF 90. *Private Pay Patients* 10%. *Certified* Medicaid; Medicare.
Owner Publicly owned.
Admissions Requirements Minimum age 18; Medical examination.
Facilities Dining room; Physical therapy room; Activities room; Crafts room; Laundry room; Barber/Beauty shop.
Activities Arts & crafts; Cards; Games; Reading groups; Prayer groups; Movies; Pet therapy.

Hillcrest North
5021 Maloneyville Rd, Knoxville, TN 37918
(615) 687-6881

Admin Thomas E Hicks. *Dir of Nursing* Jo Merrell RN. *Medical Dir* Dr Thomas B Drinnen.
Licensure Intermediate care. *Beds* ICF 386. *Private Pay Patients* 10%. *Certified* Medicaid.
Owner Publicly owned.
Admissions Requirements Minimum age 18; Medical examination.
Facilities Dining room; Activities room; Chapel; Crafts room; Laundry room; Barber/Beauty shop.
Activities Arts & crafts; Cards; Games; Reading groups; Prayer groups; Movies.

Hillcrest—South
1758 Hillwood Dr, Knoxville, TN 37920
(615) 573-9621
Licensure Intermediate care. *Beds* ICF 106. *Certified* Medicaid.

Hillcrest—West
6801 Middlebrook Pike, Knoxville, TN 37919
(615) 588-7661
Licensure Skilled care; Intermediate care. *Beds* 212. *Certified* Medicaid; Medicare.

Knoxville Convalescent Center
809 E Emerald Ave, Knoxville, TN 37917
(615) 524-7366
Licensure Skilled care; Intermediate care. *Beds* 152. *Certified* Medicaid; Medicare.
Owner Proprietary corp (National Health Corp).

Knoxville Health Care Center Inc
2120 Highland Ave, Knoxville, TN 37916
(615) 525-4131
Licensure Skilled care; Intermediate care. *Beds* 180. *Certified* Medicaid; Medicare.
Owner Proprietary corp (National Health Corp).

Little Creek Sanitarium
1810 Little Creek Ln, Knoxville, TN 37922
(615) 690-6727
Admin Ann Goodge. *Dir of Nursing* Ellen Dimick RN. *Medical Dir* Dr Paul Watson.
Licensure Skilled care. *Beds* SNF 38. *Private Pay Patients* 100%.
Owner Nonprofit organization/foundation.
Admissions Requirements Minimum age 14; Medical examination.
Staff RNs 2 (ft), 2 (pt); LPNs 3 (ft), 2 (pt); Nurses' aides 6 (ft), 25 (pt); Dietitians.
Affiliation Seventh-Day Adventist.
Facilities Dining room; Chapel; Barber/Beauty shop.
Activities Games; Reading groups; Prayer groups; Movies; Holiday and seasonal parties.

Northhaven Health Care Center
3300 Broadway NE, Knoxville, TN 37917
(615) 689-2052
Medical Dir Dr Mosley.
Licensure Intermediate care. *Beds* 96. *Certified* Medicaid.
Owner Proprietary corp (Hillhaven Corp).
Admissions Requirements Minimum age 14; Medical examination; Physician's request.
Staff RNs 2 (ft), 3 (pt); LPNs 2 (ft), 4 (pt); Nurses' aides 24 (ft), 8 (pt); Physical therapists 2 (pt); Activities coordinators 1 (ft); Dietitians 1 (ft); Ophthalmologists 1 (pt); Podiatrists 1 (pt); Audiologists 1 (pt); Dentists 1 (pt).
Facilities Dining room; Physical therapy room; Activities room; Crafts room; Laundry room; Barber/Beauty shop.
Activities Arts & crafts; Cards; Games; Reading groups; Prayer groups; Movies; Pet therapy.

Serene Manor Medical Center
970 Wray St, Knoxville, TN 37917
(615) 523-9171

Admin Rita Kidd. *Dir of Nursing* Nancy Bowman RNC. *Medical Dir* Dr Steve Masters.
Licensure Intermediate care. *Beds* ICF 75. *Private Pay Patients* 1%. *Certified* Medicaid.
Owner Nonprofit corp.
Admissions Requirements Minimum age 14; Medical examination; Physician's request.
Staff Physicians 1 (pt); RNs 2 (ft); LPNs 10 (ft); Nurses' aides 15 (ft), 12 (pt); Physical therapists 1 (pt); Recreational therapists 1 (pt); Activities coordinators 1 (ft); Dietitians 1 (ft); Ophthalmologists 1 (pt); Podiatrists 1 (pt).
Facilities Dining room; Physical therapy room; Activities room; Crafts room; Barber/Beauty shop.
Activities Arts & crafts; Cards; Games; Reading groups; Prayer groups; Movies; Shopping trips; Dances/Social/Cultural gatherings; Pet therapy; Birthday parties; Cook outs.

Shannondale Health Care & Retirement Center
801 Vanosdale Rd, Knoxville, TN 37919
(615) 690-3411
Medical Dir Dr Harry K Ogden.
Licensure Skilled care; Intermediate care; Home for aged. *Beds* 349. *Certified* Medicaid; Medicare.
Admissions Requirements Minimum age 62.
Staff Physicians 1 (pt); RNs 1 (ft), 2 (pt); LPNs 2 (ft), 1 (pt); Activities coordinators 1 (ft); Dietitians 1 (ft); Podiatrists 1 (pt).
Affiliation Presbyterian.
Facilities Dining room; Activities room; Chapel; Crafts room; Laundry room; Barber/Beauty shop; Library.
Activities Arts & crafts; Cards; Games; Prayer groups; Movies; Shopping trips; Dances/Social/Cultural gatherings; Theatre; Zoo; Dogwood Arts Festival; Art shows.

Lafayette

Janwynella Nursing Home Inc
405 Times Ave, Lafayette, TN 37083
(615) 666-3170
Medical Dir C C Chitwood Jr MD.
Beds 39.
Admissions Requirements Minimum age 14; Medical examination.
Staff RNs 1 (ft); LPNs 1 (ft); Nurses' aides 15 (ft); Activities coordinators 1 (ft); Dietitians 1 (pt).

LaFollette

LaFollette Community Nursing Home
106 E Ave, LaFollette, TN 37766
(615) 562-2211
Admin J B Wright. *Dir of Nursing* Carol Leach RN. *Medical Dir* Dr L J Seargeant.
Licensure Skilled care; Intermediate care. *Beds* SNF 50; ICF 48. *Certified* Medicaid; Medicare.
Owner Nonprofit organization/foundation.
Admissions Requirements Minimum age 14; Medical examination; Physician's request.
Staff Physicians 10 (ft); RNs 1 (ft), 1 (pt); LPNs 12 (ft), 7 (pt); Nurses' aides 27 (ft), 40 (pt); Physical therapists 1 (ft), 1 (pt); Speech therapists 1 (ft); Activities coordinators 2 (ft); Dietitians 1 (ft); Ophthalmologists 1 (ft); Dentists 1 (ft).
Facilities Dining room; Physical therapy room; Activities room; Chapel; Crafts room; Barber/Beauty shop; Library.
Activities Arts & crafts; Cards; Games; Reading groups; Prayer groups; Movies; Dances/Social/Cultural gatherings.

Meadowbrook Manor of LaFollette
155 Davis Rd, LaFollette, TN 37766
(615) 562-0760
Licensure Home for aged. *Beds* 168; Home for aged 14.

Lake City

Lake City Health Care Center
Industrial Park Rd, Lake City, TN 37769
(615) 426-2147
Admin Anita L Wilmoth. *Dir of Nursing* Elizabeth Templin RN. *Medical Dir* James Giles MD.
Licensure Intermediate care; Alzheimer's care. *Beds* ICF 115. *Certified* Medicaid.
Owner Privately owned.
Admissions Requirements Minimum age 18; Medical examination.
Staff RNs 1 (ft), 1 (pt); LPNs 8 (ft), 4 (pt); Nurses' aides 18 (ft), 15 (pt); Activities coordinators 1 (ft); Dietitians 1 (ft); Social service 1 (ft).
Facilities Dining room; Physical therapy room; Activities room; Crafts room; Laundry room; Barber/Beauty shop; Library.
Activities Arts & crafts; Cards; Games; Reading groups; Prayer groups; Movies; Shopping trips; Dances/Social/Cultural gatherings; Field trips.

Lawrenceburg

Lawrenceburg Health Care Center
PO Box 767, Lawrenceburg, TN 38464
(615) 762-9418
Admin James P Earle III. *Dir of Nursing* Donna Spears RN. *Medical Dir* Leon Everett MD.
Licensure Skilled care; Intermediate care. *Beds* SNF 18; ICF 19. *Private Pay Patients* 43%. *Certified* Medicaid; Medicare.
Owner Proprietary corp (National Health Corp).
Admissions Requirements Medical examination.
Staff Physicians; RNs; LPNs; Nurses' aides; Physical therapists; Speech therapists; Activities coordinators; Dietitians.
Facilities Dining room; Activities room.
Activities Arts & crafts; Cards; Games; Reading groups; Prayer groups; Movies.

Lawrenceburg Manor
Rte 1, 3051 Buffalo Rd, Lawrenceburg, TN 38464
(615) 762-7518
Admin Kaun Porter.
Medical Dir J Carmack Hudgins MD.
Licensure Skilled care; Intermediate care. *Beds* SNF 64; ICF 88. *Certified* Medicaid; Medicare.
Admissions Requirements Minimum age 14; Medical examination; Physician's request.
Staff RNs 4 (ft), 1 (pt); LPNs 11 (ft), 5 (pt); Nurses' aides 6 (ft), 35 (pt); Physical therapists; Speech therapists; Activities coordinators 1 (ft); Dietitians 1 (ft); Dentists; Social workers 1 (ft); Physical therapy aides 2 (ft).
Facilities Dining room; Physical therapy room; Activities room; Crafts room; Laundry room; Barber/Beauty shop; Library.
Activities Arts & crafts; Cards; Games; Reading groups; Prayer groups; Movies; Shopping trips; Dances/Social/Cultural gatherings; Painting classes; Quilting bees; Special singing; Church services.

National Healthcare Center of Lawrenceburg
374 Brink St, Lawrenceburg, TN 38464
(615) 762-6548
Licensure Intermediate care. *Beds* ICF 97. *Certified* Medicaid.

Lebanon

Cedars Health Care Center
932 Baddour Pkwy, Lebanon, TN 37087
(615) 449-5170
Dir of Nursing Betty Perkins. *Medical Dir* Morris Ferguson MD.
Licensure Skilled care; Intermediate care. *Beds* SNF 60; ICF 60. *Certified* Medicaid; Medicare.
Owner Proprietary corp.
Staff RNs 4 (ft), 1 (pt); LPNs 5 (ft); Nurses' aides 28 (ft); Physical therapists 1 (ft); Activities coordinators 1 (ft).
Facilities Dining room; Physical therapy room; Laundry room; Barber/Beauty shop.
Activities Arts & crafts; Cards; Games; Reading groups; Movies; Shopping trips; Dances/Social/Cultural gatherings.

Margie Anna Nursing Home Inc
152 S College St, Lebanon, TN 37087
(615) 444-2882
Admin Terry L Stafford. *Dir of Nursing* Louise Patterson. *Medical Dir* R C Kash MD.
Licensure Intermediate care. *Beds* ICF 46. *Certified* Medicaid.
Owner Proprietary corp.
Admissions Requirements Minimum age 16; Physician's request.
Staff RNs 1 (pt); LPNs 4 (ft), 3 (pt); Nurses' aides 15 (ft), 8 (pt); Activities coordinators 1 (ft); Dietitians 1 (pt).
Facilities Dining room; Laundry room.
Activities Arts & crafts; Games; Movies.

Quality Care Health Center
932 Baddour Pkwy, Lebanon, TN 37087
(615) 444-1836
Admin Dixie Taylor. *Dir of Nursing* Wilma Moore LPN. *Medical Dir* Morris Ferguson MD.
Licensure Intermediate care. *Beds* ICF 170. *Certified* Medicaid.
Owner Privately owned.
Staff Physicians 1 (ft); RNs 1 (ft); LPNs 11 (ft); Nurses' aides 53 (ft); Reality therapists 1 (pt); Activities coordinators 11 (ft); Dietitians 1 (pt).
Facilities Dining room; Physical therapy room; Barber/Beauty shop; Library.
Activities Arts & crafts; Cards; Games; Prayer groups; Dances/Social/Cultural gatherings.

Lenoir City

Baptist Health Care Center
Rte 1, Williams Ferry Rd, Lenoir City, TN 37771
(615) 986-3583, 986-1707 FAX
Admin Anita L Wilmoth. *Dir of Nursing* Susie Mynatt RN. *Medical Dir* Walter Shea MD.
Licensure Intermediate care; Private pay; Retirement; Alzheimer's care. *Beds* ICF 46; Private pay 58; Retirement 15. *Private Pay Patients* 44%. *Certified* Medicaid.
Owner Nonprofit organization/foundation.
Admissions Requirements Minimum age 18; Medical examination.
Staff RNs 2 (ft); LPNs 12 (ft); Nurses' aides 48 (ft), 2 (pt); Physical therapists 1 (pt); Occupational therapists 1 (pt); Speech therapists 1 (pt); Activities coordinators 1 (ft); Dietitians 1 (pt); Ophthalmologists 1 (pt); Podiatrists 1 (pt).
Affiliation Baptist.
Facilities Dining room; Physical therapy room; Activities room; Chapel; Crafts room; Laundry room; Barber/Beauty shop; Library.
Activities Arts & crafts; Cards; Games; Reading groups; Prayer groups; Movies; Shopping trips; Dances/Social/Cultural gatherings; Intergenerational programs.

Lewisburg

Merihil Health Care Center
PO Box 251, 1653 Mooresville Hwy, Lewisburg, TN 37091
(615) 359-4506
Admin Alecia E Pollock. *Dir of Nursing* Paulette Thacker. *Medical Dir* Jack Phelps MD.

Licensure Skilled care; Intermediate care. *Beds* SNF 41; ICF 54. *Certified* Medicaid; Medicare; VA.
Owner Proprietary corp (National Health Corp).
Admissions Requirements Medical examination; Physician's request.
Facilities Dining room; Physical therapy room; Activities room; Chapel; Crafts room; Laundry room; Barber/Beauty shop; Library.
Activities Arts & crafts; Cards; Games; Reading groups; Prayer groups; Movies; Dances/Social/Cultural gatherings.

Oakwood Health Care Center
PO Box 1667, 244 Oakwood Dr, Lewisburg, TN 37091
(615) 359-3563
Admin Howard J Nason Jr. *Dir of Nursing* Sudie Milam RN. *Medical Dir* Dr Joseph F Von Almen.
Licensure Skilled care; Intermediate care; Alzheimer's care. *Beds* SNF 32; ICF 30. *Private Pay Patients* 28%. *Certified* Medicaid; Medicare.
Owner Proprietary corp (National Health Corp).
Admissions Requirements Minimum age 14; Physician's request.
Staff Physicians 1 (ft); RNs 3 (ft); LPNs 7 (ft), 2 (pt); Nurses' aides 20 (ft), 3 (pt); Physical therapists 1 (pt); Recreational therapists 2 (pt); Occupational therapists 1 (pt); Speech therapists 1 (pt); Dietitians 1 (ft); Podiatrists 1 (pt).
Facilities Dining room; Physical therapy room; Activities room; Crafts room; Laundry room; Barber/Beauty shop.
Activities Arts & crafts; Cards; Games; Reading groups; Prayer groups; Movies; Shopping trips; Pet therapy.

Lexington

Lexington Manor Nursing Center
PO Box 1056, 727 E Church St, Lexington, TN 38351
(901) 968-2004, 968-2004 FAX
Admin Gail Crawford. *Dir of Nursing* Edna Robertson RN. *Medical Dir* Charles White MD.
Licensure Intermediate care. *Beds* ICF 121. *Private Pay Patients* 14%. *Certified* Medicaid.
Owner Proprietary corp (American Health Centers Inc).
Admissions Requirements Medical examination.
Staff RNs; LPNs; Nurses' aides; Physical therapists (consultant); Activities coordinators; Dietitians (consultant).
Facilities Dining room; Activities room; Crafts room; Laundry room; Barber/Beauty shop.
Activities Arts & crafts; Cards; Games; Reading groups; Prayer groups; Movies; Shopping trips; Dances/Social/Cultural gatherings.

NuCare Convalescent Center
PO Box 1077, 41 Hospital Dr, Lexington, TN 38351
(901) 968-6629
Admin Biddie J Smith. *Dir of Nursing* Joyce Thompson. *Medical Dir* Dr Tim Linder.
Licensure Intermediate care. *Beds* ICF 55. *Private Pay Patients* 15%. *Certified* Medicaid.
Owner Proprietary corp (Southeastern Health Care).
Admissions Requirements Medical examination; Physician's request.
Staff Physicians 1 (pt); RNs 1 (ft); LPNs 7 (ft); Nurses' aides 23 (ft); Activities coordinators 1 (ft); Dietitians 1 (ft).

Facilities Dining room; Activities room; Laundry room.
Activities Arts & crafts; Cards; Games; Reading groups; Prayer groups; Movies; Shopping trips; Dances/Social/Cultural gatherings; Intergenerational programs.

Limestone

John M Reed Nursing Home
Rte 2 Box 301, Limestone, TN 37681
(615) 257-6122, 257-2609 FAX
Admin Leon Dutka. *Dir of Nursing* Constance Fine. *Medical Dir* Newton F Garland MD.
Licensure Intermediate care. *Beds* ICF 56. *Private Pay Patients* 11%. *Certified* Medicaid.
Owner Nonprofit corp.
Admissions Requirements Medical examination; Physician's request.
Staff Physicians 2 (pt); RNs 1 (ft); LPNs 4 (ft), 2 (pt); Nurses' aides 17 (ft), 2 (pt); Physical therapists 1 (pt); Activities coordinators 1 (ft); Dietitians 1 (pt); Ophthalmologists 1 (pt); Podiatrists 1 (pt); Dentists 1 (pt).
Affiliation Church of the Brethren.
Facilities Dining room; Physical therapy room; Activities room; Crafts room; Laundry room; Barber/Beauty shop.
Activities Arts & crafts; Cards; Games; Reading groups; Prayer groups; Movies; Dances/Social/Cultural gatherings; Intergenerational programs; Pet therapy.

Linden

Perry County Nursing Home
Rte 4 Box 71, Linden, TN 37096
(615) 589-2134
Admin David Ramey. *Dir of Nursing* Peggie Ramey. *Medical Dir* Dr Stephen Averett.
Licensure Intermediate care. *Beds* ICF 72. *Certified* Medicaid.
Owner Proprietary corp.
Admissions Requirements Physician's request.
Staff Physicians 1 (pt); RNs 2 (ft); LPNs 7 (ft), 1 (pt); Nurses' aides 22 (ft), 3 (pt); Activities coordinators 1 (ft); Dietitians 1 (pt).
Facilities Dining room; Activities room; Laundry room; Barber/Beauty shop.
Activities Arts & crafts; Cards; Games; Prayer groups; Movies.

Livingston

Overton County Nursing Home
418 Bilbrey St, Livingston, TN 38570
(615) 823-6403
Admin R Gay Lane.
Medical Dir Dr J Roe.
Licensure Intermediate care. *Beds* ICF 164. *Certified* Medicaid.
Admissions Requirements Medical examination; Physician's request.
Staff Physicians 1 (pt); RNs 1 (ft), 1 (pt); LPNs 16 (ft), 5 (pt); Nurses' aides 36 (ft), 20 (pt); Recreational therapists 2 (ft); Activities coordinators 1 (ft); Dietitians 1 (pt).
Facilities Dining room; Physical therapy room; Activities room; Crafts room; Barber/ Beauty shop; Laundry services; Solarium; Whirpool bathing facilities.
Activities Arts & crafts; Games; Prayer groups; Movies; Ceramics; Prayer study.

Loudon

Loudon Healthcare Center
1320 Grove St, Loudon, TN 37774
(615) 458-5436
Licensure Intermediate care. *Beds* ICF 192. *Certified* Medicaid.
Admissions Requirements Medical examination.

Staff RNs 3 (ft); LPNs 9 (ft); Nurses' aides 23 (ft), 5 (pt); Activities coordinators 2 (ft); Dietitians 1 (ft).
Facilities Dining room; Physical therapy room; Activities room; Crafts room; Laundry room; Barber/Beauty shop.
Activities Arts & crafts; Cards; Games; Reading groups; Prayer groups; Movies; Shopping trips; Dances/Social/Cultural gatherings.

Madison

Hillhaven Convalescent Center
431 Larkin Springs Rd, Madison, TN 37115
(615) 865-8520
Licensure Skilled care; Intermediate care. *Beds* 96. *Certified* Medicaid; Medicare.
Owner Proprietary corp (Hillhaven Corp).

Imperial Manor Convalescent Center
300 W Due West Ave, Madison, TN 37115
(615) 865-5001
Licensure Skilled care; Intermediate care. *Beds* 201. *Certified* Medicaid; Medicare.
Owner Proprietary corp (Sunbelt Healthcare Centers Inc).

Madisonville

East Tennessee Health Care Center
Rte 2, 729 Isbill Rd, Madisonville, TN 37354
(615) 442-3990
Admin Steven H Martin. *Dir of Nursing* Ronda Hodge. *Medical Dir* Houston Lowry MD.
Licensure Intermediate care. *Beds* ICF 92. *Certified* Medicaid.
Owner Proprietary corp (American Health Center Inc).
Admissions Requirements Physician's request.
Staff RNs; LPNs; Nurses' aides; Activities coordinators.
Facilities Dining room; Activities room; Crafts room; Laundry room; Barber/Beauty shop.
Activities Arts & crafts; Cards; Games; Movies; Dances/Social/Cultural gatherings.

Manchester

Coffee Medical Center Nursing Home
1001 McArthur Dr, Manchester, TN 37355
(615) 728-3586, 728-6877 FAX
Admin James L Muse. *Dir of Nursing* Shirley M Price RN. *Medical Dir* Glenn A Davis MD.
Licensure Intermediate care. *Beds* ICF 72. *Private Pay Patients* 25%. *Certified* Medicaid.
Owner Publicly owned.
Admissions Requirements Minimum age 18; Medical examination.
Staff Physicians 8 (ft); RNs 1 (ft); LPNs 6 (ft), 5 (pt); Nurses' aides 23 (ft), 7 (pt); Physical therapists (contracted); Activities coordinators 1 (ft); Dietitians (consultant).
Facilities Dining room; Physical therapy room; Activities room; Barber/Beauty shop; Library.
Activities Arts & crafts; Cards; Games; Reading groups; Prayer groups; Movies; Dances/Social/Cultural gatherings.

Crestwood Nursing Home
Rte 1 Box 1001, Taylor St, Manchester, TN 37355
(615) 728-7549
Admin Rachel Carlene White. *Dir of Nursing* Mary Arwood. *Medical Dir* Harrison Yang MD.
Licensure Intermediate care. *Beds* ICF 59. *Certified* Medicaid.
Owner Privately owned.
Admissions Requirements Minimum age 18; Medical examination.

Staff Physicians; RNs 2 (pt); LPNs 7 (ft), 3 (pt); Nurses' aides 16 (ft), 6 (pt); Physical therapists (contracted); Reality therapists (contracted); Recreational therapists (contracted); Occupational therapists (contracted); Speech therapists (contracted); Activities coordinators 1 (ft); Dietitians 1 (pt); Laundry 1 (ft); Housekeeping 2 (ft); Maintenance 1 (ft).
Facilities Dining room; Activities room; Crafts room; Laundry room; Barber/Beauty shop.
Activities Arts & crafts; Cards; Games; Reading groups; Prayer groups; Movies; Shopping trips; Dances/Social/Cultural gatherings.

Martin

Cane Creek Center
18m Mount Pelia Rd, Martin, TN 38237
(901) 587-4231
Beds 36.

Van Ayer Manor Nursing Center
PO Box 1128, 640 Hannings Ln, Martin, TN 38237
(901) 587-3193, 587-9862 FAX
Admin Regina Danner. *Dir of Nursing* Debbie McDonald. *Medical Dir* Dr Kenneth Carr.
Licensure Intermediate care. *Beds* ICF 120. *Private Pay Patients* 20%. *Certified* Medicaid.
Owner Proprietary corp (American Health Center Inc).
Admissions Requirements Medical examination; Physician's request.
Staff Physicians 1 (pt); RNs 1 (ft); LPNs 10 (ft); Nurses' aides 28 (ft); Physical therapists 1 (ft); Recreational therapists 1 (ft); Speech therapists 1 (pt); Activities coordinators 1 (ft); Dietitians 6 (ft); Podiatrists 1 (pt).
Facilities Dining room; Activities room; Crafts room; Laundry room; Barber/Beauty shop.
Activities Arts & crafts; Cards; Games; Reading groups; Movies; Shopping trips; Dances/Social/Cultural gatherings; Pet therapy.

Maryville

Asbury Centers Inc
2648 Sevierville Rd, Maryville, TN 37801-3699
(615) 984-1660
Admin Melba B Bruce. *Dir of Nursing* Barbara Ann Blaylock. *Medical Dir* O L Simpson MD.
Licensure Skilled care; Intermediate care. *Beds* SNF 35; ICF 160. *Private Pay Patients* 52%. *Certified* Medicaid; Medicare.
Owner Nonprofit organization/foundation.
Admissions Requirements Minimum age 14; Medical examination; Physician's request.
Staff RNs 9 (ft), 3 (pt); LPNs 14 (ft), 5 (pt); Nurses' aides 68 (ft), 23 (pt); Physical therapists 1 (ft), 2 (pt); Recreational therapists 2 (ft); Activities coordinators 1 (ft); Dietitians 21 (ft), 5 (pt).
Affiliation Methodist.
Facilities Dining room; Physical therapy room; Activities room; Laundry room; Barber/Beauty shop.
Activities Arts & crafts; Cards; Games; Reading groups; Prayer groups; Movies; Shopping trips; Dances/Social/Cultural gatherings; Pet therapy; Current events.

Colonial Hills Nursing Center
2034 Cochran Rd, Maryville, TN 37801
(615) 982-6161
Admin Peggy G Savage. *Dir of Nursing* Annette Everett RN. *Medical Dir* J Thomas Mandrell MD.

Licensure Skilled care; Intermediate care; Retirement; Alzheimer's care. *Beds* SNF 6; ICF 197. *Certified* Medicaid; Medicare.
Owner Proprietary corp.
Admissions Requirements Minimum age 14; Medical examination.
Staff RNs 7 (ft); LPNs 20 (ft), 4 (pt); Nurses' aides 60 (ft), 6 (pt); Physical therapists 1 (pt); Speech therapists 1 (pt); Activities coordinators 2 (ft); Dietitians 1 (ft).
Languages Italian.
Facilities Dining room; Physical therapy room; Activities room; Crafts room; Laundry room; Barber/Beauty shop; Library; Solarium; Music room; Whirlpool baths.
Activities Arts & crafts; Cards; Games; Reading groups; Prayer groups; Movies; Shopping trips; Dances/Social/Cultural gatherings.

Fairpark Healthcare Center
PO Box 1355, Maryville, TN 37801
(615) 983-0261
Beds 66.
Owner Proprietary corp (Hillhaven Corp).

Hillhaven/Maryville Convalescent Center
1012 Jamestown Way, Maryville, TN 37801
(615) 984-7400
Licensure Intermediate care. *Beds* ICF 186. *Certified* Medicaid.
Owner Proprietary corp.

Montvale Health Center
Montvale Rd, Rte 6, Maryville, TN 37801
(615) 982-6161
Licensure Intermediate care. *Beds* 107. *Certified* Medicaid.

Maynardville

Meadowbrook Manor
Rte 1 Box 16C, Maynardville, TN 37807
(615) 992-5816
Dir of Nursing Juanita Honeycutt. *Medical Dir* Dr Larry Huskey.
Licensure Intermediate care. *Beds* ICF 68. *Certified* Medicaid.
Owner Proprietary corp (Angell Care Inc).
Admissions Requirements Medical examination; Physician's request.
Staff RNs 1 (pt); LPNs 7 (ft), 2 (pt); Nurses' aides 19 (ft), 4 (pt); Physical therapists 1 (pt); Speech therapists 1 (pt); Activities coordinators 1 (ft); Dietitians 1 (pt); Podiatrists 1 (pt).
Facilities Dining room; Activities room; Laundry room; Barber/Beauty shop.
Activities Arts & crafts; Games; Reading groups; Prayer groups; Movies; Shopping trips; Dances/Social/Cultural gatherings.

McMinnville

McMinnville Health Care Center
PO Box 528, Rte 1 Box 1, McMinnville, TN 37110
(615) 473-8431
Admin Clay F Crosson. *Dir of Nursing* Alma Stone RN. *Medical Dir* Dr J F Fisher.
Licensure Skilled care; Intermediate care. *Beds* SNF 52; ICF 30. *Certified* Medicaid; Medicare.
Owner Proprietary corp (National Health Corp).
Admissions Requirements Minimum age 18.
Staff Physicians 10 (pt); RNs 2 (ft), 2 (pt); LPNs 11 (ft), 4 (pt); Nurses' aides 30 (ft), 10 (pt); Physical therapists 1 (pt); Recreational therapists 1 (ft); Occupational therapists 1 (pt); Speech therapists 1 (pt); Activities coordinators 1 (pt); Dietitians 1 (ft); Ophthalmologists 1 (pt); Podiatrists 1 (pt); Dentists 1 (pt).
Facilities Dining room; Physical therapy room; Activities room; Crafts room; Laundry room; Barber/Beauty shop.

Activities Arts & crafts; Cards; Games; Reading groups; Prayer groups; Movies; Dances/Social/Cultural gatherings.

South Oaks Health Care Inc
Pace St, McMinnville, TN 37110
(615) 668-2011
Admin Gilbert E Salter.
Medical Dir Dr T L Pedigo.
Licensure Skilled care; Intermediate care. *Beds* 154. *Certified* Medicaid; Medicare.
Owner Proprietary corp.
Admissions Requirements Medical examination; Physician's request.
Staff Physicians 1 (pt); RNs 1 (ft); LPNs 7 (ft), 2 (pt); Nurses' aides 29 (ft), 15 (pt); Physical therapists 1 (pt); Speech therapists 1 (pt); Activities coordinators 1 (ft); Dietitians 1 (ft); Dentists 1 (pt).
Facilities Dining room; Physical therapy room; Activities room; Crafts room; Laundry room; Barber/Beauty shop; Library.
Activities Arts & crafts; Cards; Games; Reading groups; Prayer groups; Shopping trips; Dances/Social/Cultural gatherings.

Memphis

Allenbrooke Health Care Center
3933 Allenbrooke Cove, Memphis, TN 38118
(901) 795-2444
Admin Michael J. Carney.
Medical Dir Mark Hammond; Paula Bain.
Licensure Skilled care; Intermediate care; Alzheimer's care. *Beds* SNF 60; ICF 120. *Certified* Medicaid; Medicare.
Owner Proprietary corp (Beverly Enterprises).
Admissions Requirements Medical examination.
Staff Physicians; RNs; LPNs; Nurses' aides; Physical therapists; Reality therapists; Recreational therapists; Occupational therapists; Speech therapists; Activities coordinators; Dietitians; Ophthalmologists; Podiatrists.
Facilities Dining room; Physical therapy room; Activities room; Crafts room; Laundry room; Barber/Beauty shop; Library; Courtyard.
Activities Arts & crafts; Cards; Games; Reading groups; Prayer groups; Movies; Shopping trips.

Autumnfield East
1755 Eldridge Ave, Memphis, TN 38108
(901) 278-3840
Admin Bea Boyd.
Medical Dir Leslie Shumaker MD.
Licensure Intermediate care. *Beds* ICF 49. *Certified* Medicaid.
Admissions Requirements Minimum age 21; Medical examination; Physician's request.
Staff RNs 1 (pt); LPNs 6 (ft); Nurses' aides 20 (ft), 2 (pt); Physical therapists 1 (ft); Activities coordinators 1 (ft); Dietitians 1 (ft).
Facilities Dining room; Activities room; Laundry room.
Activities Arts & crafts; Cards; Games; Reading groups; Shopping trips.

Ave Maria Home
2805 Charles Bryan Rd, Memphis, TN 38134
(901) 386-3211
Admin Patricia Curtis. *Dir of Nursing* Charlotte Blair RN. *Medical Dir* Ed Hines III MD.
Licensure Intermediate care. *Beds* ICF 73. *Certified* Medicaid.
Owner Nonprofit corp.
Admissions Requirements Minimum age 60; Medical examination.
Staff Physicians 1 (pt); RNs 2 (ft), 1 (pt); LPNs 6 (ft), 1 (pt); Nurses' aides 22 (ft), 5 (pt); Activities coordinators 1 (ft); Dietitians 1 (pt); Ophthalmologists 1 (pt); Dentists 1 (pt).

Facilities Dining room; Activities room; Chapel; Barber/Beauty shop; Dental clinic; Landscaped grounds.
Activities Arts & crafts; Cards; Games; Prayer groups; Movies; Dances/Social/Cultural gatherings; Parties.

Baptist Memorial Hospital Skilled Nursing Unit
899 Madison Ave, Memphis, TN 38146
(901) 522-3900
Beds 44.

B'nai B'rith Home
131 N Tucker St, Memphis, TN 38104
(901) 726-5600
Admin Marvin Silver. *Dir of Nursing* Suzanne Meeks. *Medical Dir* Donald Schaffer.
Licensure Skilled care; Intermediate care; Alzheimer's care. *Beds* Swing beds SNF/ICF 159. *Private Pay Patients* 38%. *Certified* Medicaid; Medicare.
Owner Nonprofit organization/foundation.
Admissions Requirements Minimum age 45; Medical examination.
Staff RNs 6 (ft); LPNs 17 (ft); Nurses' aides 52 (ft), 2 (pt); Physical therapists 1 (pt); Recreational therapists 1 (ft); Activities coordinators 1 (ft); Dietitians 1 (pt); Podiatrists 1 (pt).
Languages German, Hebrew.
Affiliation Jewish.
Facilities Dining room; Physical therapy room; Activities room; Chapel; Crafts room; Laundry room; Barber/Beauty shop; Sun porches.
Activities Arts & crafts; Cards; Games; Reading groups; Movies; Shopping trips; Dances/Social/Cultural gatherings; Intergenerational programs; Pet therapy; Current events program; Happy hour.

Bright Glade Convalescent Center
5070 Sanderlin Ave, Memphis, TN 38117
(615) 682-5677
Medical Dir Saul Seigel MD.
Beds 85.
Owner Proprietary corp (American Health Center Inc).
Admissions Requirements Minimum age 16; Physician's request.
Staff Physicians 1 (ft), 1 (pt); RNs 2 (ft); LPNs 5 (ft), 1 (pt); Nurses' aides 11 (ft), 5 (pt); Physical therapists 1 (pt); Recreational therapists 1 (pt); Podiatrists 1 (pt).
Facilities Dining room; Activities room; Crafts room; Barber/Beauty shop.
Activities Cards; Games; Prayer groups.

Collins Chapel Health Care Center
409 N Ayers, Memphis, TN 38105
(615) 522-9243
Medical Dir Cary Anderson MD.
Licensure Intermediate care. *Beds* 88. *Certified* Medicaid.
Admissions Requirements Medical examination; Physician's request.
Staff Physicians 1 (ft), 1 (pt); RNs 1 (pt); LPNs 7 (ft); Nurses' aides 18 (ft); Physical therapists 1 (pt); Activities coordinators 1 (ft); Dietitians 6 (ft); Dentists 1 (pt).
Affiliation Christian Methodist Episcopal.
Facilities Dining room; Physical therapy room; Activities room; Crafts room; Laundry room; Barber/Beauty shop.
Activities Arts & crafts; Cards; Games; Reading groups; Prayer groups; Movies; Dances/Social/Cultural gatherings.

Court Manor Nursing Center
1414 Court St, Memphis, TN 38104
(901) 272-2492
Licensure Intermediate care. *Beds* ICF 98. *Certified* Medicaid.
Owner Proprietary corp (American Health Center Inc).

Durham Retirement Center
5050 Poplar Ave No 1522, Memphis, TN 38157
(901) 386-4531
Admin Thomas H Durham Jr.
Medical Dir Margaret Moffitt.
Licensure Independent living. *Beds* Retirement Community 80.
Owner Nonprofit organization/foundation.
Admissions Requirements Minimum age 55; Medical examination.
Staff Activities coordinators 1 (pt); Dietitians 1 (ft), 1 (pt).
Facilities Dining room; Activities room; Chapel; Barber/Beauty shop; Library; Patio; 3 sun porches; 4 open air porches; Walkpath.
Activities Cards; Games; Reading groups; Prayer groups; Movies; Shopping trips; Dances/Social/Cultural gatherings; Community & church interaction.

Heritage Manor of Memphis
2491 Joy Ln, Memphis, TN 38114
(901) 743-7700
Licensure Intermediate care. *Beds* ICF 110. *Certified* Medicaid.
Owner Proprietary corp (National Heritage).

Hillhaven Convalescent Center
6025 Primacy Pkwy, Memphis, TN 38119
(901) 767-1040
Admin Martha A Johnson. *Dir of Nursing* Sherian Black RN. *Medical Dir* Timothy Klein MD.
Licensure Skilled care; Intermediate care. *Beds* SNF 16; ICF 104. *Certified* Medicare.
Owner Proprietary corp (Hillhaven Corp).
Admissions Requirements Minimum age 12; Medical examination; Physician's request.
Staff RNs; LPNs; Nurses' aides; Physical therapists; Reality therapists; Recreational therapists; Occupational therapists; Speech therapists; Activities coordinators; Dietitians; Ophthalmologists (contracted); Podiatrists (contracted); Audiologists (contracted).
Facilities Dining room; Physical therapy room; Activities room; Laundry room; Barber/Beauty shop.
Activities Arts & crafts; Cards; Games; Reading groups; Prayer groups; Movies; Dances/Social/Cultural gatherings; Intergenerational programs; Pet therapy.

Hillhaven Health Care Center of Raleigh
3909 Covington Pike, Memphis, TN 38134
(901) 377-1011
Admin Susan P Morganelli. *Dir of Nursing* Christine Russell. *Medical Dir* Dr E E Hines.
Licensure Skilled care; Intermediate care; Alzheimer's care. *Beds* SNF 16; ICF 230. *Certified* Medicaid.
Owner Proprietary corp (Hillhaven Corp).
Admissions Requirements Medical examination; Physician's request.
Staff RNs; LPNs; Nurses' aides; Physical therapists; Reality therapists; Recreational therapists; Occupational therapists; Speech therapists; Activities coordinators; Dietitians; Ophthalmologists; Dentists.
Languages Spanish.
Facilities Dining room; Physical therapy room; Activities room; Chapel; Crafts room; Laundry room; Barber/Beauty shop.
Activities Arts & crafts; Cards; Games; Reading groups; Prayer groups; Movies; Shopping trips; Dances/Social/Cultural gatherings.

Johnson Care Home
1279 Peabody, Memphis, TN 38104
(901) 725-7821
Admin Neva H Johnson. *Dir of Nursing* Krister J Hobson. *Medical Dir* Dr Paul Drenning.

Licensure Intermediate care. *Beds* ICF 24. *Private Pay Patients* 50%. *Certified* Medicaid.
Owner Privately owned.
Admissions Requirements Minimum age 80; Females only; Medical examination; Physician's request.
Staff Physicians 24 (pt); RNs 2 (pt); LPNs 4 (pt); Nurses' aides 7 (pt); Physical therapists; Reality therapists; Recreational therapists; Occupational therapists; Speech therapists; Activities coordinators 1 (pt); Dietitians 1 (pt); Podiatrists 1 (pt).
Facilities Dining room; Activities room; Chapel; Laundry room; Barber/Beauty shop.
Activities Arts & crafts; Cards; Games; Reading groups; Prayer groups; Movies; Shopping trips; Dances/Social/Cultural gatherings; Intergenerational programs; Pet therapy.

King's Daughters & Sons Home
1467 E McLemore Ave, Memphis, TN 38016
(901) 272-7405, 272-7422 FAX
Admin Ronald B Arrison. *Dir of Nursing* Sharon Clay RN. *Medical Dir* J C Lougheed MD.
Licensure Skilled care; Intermediate care. *Beds* SNF 28; ICF 80. *Private Pay Patients* 6%. *Certified* Medicaid; Medicare.
Owner Nonprofit corp.
Admissions Requirements Minimum age 14; Medical examination; Physician's request.
Staff Physicians 1 (pt); RNs 3 (ft); LPNs 19 (ft), 5 (pt); Nurses' aides 40 (ft), 17 (pt); Dietitians 1 (pt).
Affiliation King's Daughters & Sons.
Facilities Dining room; Physical therapy room; Activities room; Chapel; Crafts room; Laundry room; Barber/Beauty shop; Library; Spinal cord injury/Head trauma unit.
Activities Arts & crafts; Cards; Games; Reading groups; Prayer groups; Movies; Shopping trips; Dances/Social/Cultural gatherings; Intergenerational programs; Pet therapy.

Kirby Pines Manor
3535 Kirby Rd, Memphis, TN 38115
(901) 365-0772 *Certified* Medicare.

Memphis Health Care Center
6733 Quince Rd, Memphis, TN 38119
(901) 755-3860
Admin Jeanette McKinion. *Dir of Nursing* Darla Grant. *Medical Dir* Mark Hammond MD.
Licensure Skilled care; Intermediate care. *Beds* SNF 28; ICF 152. *Certified* Medicaid; Medicare.
Owner Proprietary corp (Beverly Enterprises).
Admissions Requirements Minimum age 18; Medical examination; Physician's request.
Staff Physicians 1 (pt); RNs 2 (ft), 2 (pt); LPNs 13 (ft); Nurses' aides 67 (ft), 12 (pt); Activities coordinators 2 (ft); Social director 2 (ft); Dietary service manager 1 (ft).
Facilities Dining room; Physical therapy room; Activities room; Crafts room; Laundry room; Barber/Beauty shop.
Activities Arts & crafts; Cards; Games; Reading groups; Prayer groups; Movies; Shopping trips; Dances/Social/Cultural gatherings.

Methodist Hospitals of Memphis Skilled Care Facility
1265 Union Ave, Memphis, TN 38104
(901) 726-7955
Admin Thomas H Gee. *Dir of Nursing* Arlene Dugard RN. *Medical Dir* Rodney Holladay MD.
Licensure Skilled care. *Beds* SNF 22. *Private Pay Patients* 1%. *Certified* Medicaid; Medicare.
Owner Nonprofit organization/foundation (Methodist Hospitals of Memphis).

Admissions Requirements Minimum age 14; Medical examination; Physician's request; Generally accepts referrals from Methodist Health System hospitals.
Staff RNs 1 (ft), 1 (pt); LPNs 4 (ft), 2 (pt); Nurses' aides 6 (ft), 2 (pt); Physical therapists 1 (pt); Occupational therapists 1 (pt); Speech therapists 1 (pt); Activities coordinators 1 (pt); Dietitians 1 (pt).
Languages Outside translators available.
Activities Arts & crafts; Cards; Games; Reading groups; Dances/Social/Cultural gatherings.

Mid-City Care Center
1755 Eldridge Ave, Memphis, TN 38108-1115
(901) 726-5171
Medical Dir George Bassett.
Licensure Intermediate care. *Beds* ICF 79. *Certified* Medicaid.
Admissions Requirements Medical examination.
Staff Physicians 1 (ft); RNs 1 (ft); LPNs 12 (ft); Nurses' aides 25 (ft); Physical therapists 2 (ft); Reality therapists 2 (ft); Recreational therapists 2 (ft); Occupational therapists 1 (pt); Speech therapists 1 (pt); Activities coordinators 2 (ft); Dietitians 1 (ft); Ophthalmologists 1 (pt); Podiatrists 1 (pt); Audiologists 1 (pt); Dentists 1 (pt).
Facilities Dining room; Physical therapy room; Activities room; Chapel; Crafts room; Laundry room; Barber/Beauty shop; Library.
Activities Arts & crafts; Cards; Games; Reading groups; Prayer groups; Movies; Shopping trips; Dances/Social/Cultural gatherings.

Mid-South Christian Nursing Home
2380 James Rd, Memphis, TN 38127
(901) 358-1707
Admin John Faught.
Medical Dir Dr J H Ijams.
Licensure Intermediate care. *Beds* ICF 162. *Certified* Medicaid.
Owner Nonprofit corp.
Admissions Requirements Minimum age 25; Medical examination; Physician's request.
Staff Physicians 1 (pt); RNs 1 (ft); LPNs 13 (ft), 8 (pt); Nurses' aides 36 (ft), 27 (pt); Recreational therapists 1 (ft); Activities coordinators 2 (ft); Dietitians 1 (ft); Ophthalmologists 1 (pt).
Affiliation Church of Christ.
Facilities Dining room; Activities room; Chapel; Crafts room; Laundry room; Barber/Beauty shop.
Activities Arts & crafts; Cards; Games; Reading groups; Prayer groups; Movies; Shopping trips.

Allen Morgan Nursing Center
177 N Highland, Memphis, TN 38111
(901) 325-4003
Admin Rebecca D DeRousse. *Dir of Nursing* Suzanne Sydow RN. *Medical Dir* Charles L Clarke MD.
Licensure Skilled care; Retirement. *Beds* SNF 66; Retirement 200. *Private Pay Patients* 90%. *Certified* Medicare.
Owner Nonprofit organization/foundation.
Admissions Requirements Minimum age 15; Medical examination; Physician's request.
Staff Physicians 1 (pt); RNs 2 (ft), 6 (pt); LPNs 3 (ft), 3 (pt); Nurses' aides 19 (ft), 5 (pt); Physical therapists 1 (pt); Occupational therapists 1 (pt); Speech therapists 1 (pt); Activities coordinators 1 (ft); Dietitians 2 (pt); Podiatrists 1 (pt).
Facilities Dining room; Physical therapy room; Activities room; Chapel; Crafts room; Laundry room; Barber/Beauty shop; Library.
Activities Arts & crafts; Games; Reading groups; Prayer groups; Movies; Shopping trips; Dances/Social/Cultural gatherings.

Oakville Health Care Center
3391 Old Getwell Rd, Memphis, TN 38118
(901) 369-9100
Admin Paul C Chapman. *Dir of Nursing* Wanda Jane Alexander. *Medical Dir* George P Jones Jr MD.
Licensure Skilled care; Intermediate care. *Beds* 314. *Certified* Medicaid; Medicare.
Owner Publicly owned.
Admissions Requirements Physician's request.
Staff Physicians 2 (ft); RNs 13 (ft), 1 (pt); LPNs 56 (ft); Nurses' aides 126 (ft); Physical therapists 1 (pt); Recreational therapists 2 (ft); Occupational therapists 1 (pt); Activities coordinators 2 (ft); Dietitians 1 (ft).
Facilities Dining room; Physical therapy room; Activities room; Chapel; Crafts room; Barber/Beauty shop; Library.
Activities Arts & crafts; Cards; Games; Reading groups; Prayer groups; Movies; Shopping trips; Dances/Social/Cultural gatherings.

Resthaven Manor Nursing Center
300 N Bellevue, Memphis, TN 38105
(901) 726-9786
Medical Dir Billie Jeanne Johnson.
Beds 65.
Owner Proprietary corp (American Health Center Inc).
Admissions Requirements Minimum age 20; Medical examination; Physician's request.
Staff Physicians; RNs 2 (ft), 2 (pt); LPNs 2 (ft), 2 (pt); Nurses' aides 15 (ft), 2 (pt); Physical therapists 1 (pt); Recreational therapists 1 (ft); Occupational therapists 1 (pt); Speech therapists 1 (pt); Activities coordinators 1 (ft); Dietitians 1 (pt).
Facilities Dining room; Activities room; Laundry room; Barber/Beauty shop.
Activities Cards; Games; Reading groups; Prayer groups; Dances/Social/Cultural gatherings.

Rosewood Manor
3030 Walnut Grove Rd, Memphis, TN 38111
(901) 458-1146
Licensure Skilled care; Intermediate care. *Beds* 211. *Certified* Medicaid; Medicare.
Owner Proprietary corp (Health Care & Retirement Corp).

St Francis Hospital Nursing Home
5959 Park Ave, Memphis, TN 38119
(901) 765-1800
Admin Tom Hanlen. *Dir of Nursing* Lucille Place RN. *Medical Dir* Dr Mickey Busby.
Licensure Skilled care; Intermediate care. *Beds* Swing beds SNF/ICF 197. *Certified* Medicaid; Medicare.
Owner Nonprofit corp.
Admissions Requirements Physician's request.
Staff RNs 2 (ft); LPNs 21 (ft), 16 (pt); Nurses' aides 39 (ft), 41 (pt); Activities coordinators 1 (ft).
Facilities Dining room; Physical therapy room; Activities room; Chapel; Crafts room; Laundry room; Barber/Beauty shop.
Activities Arts & crafts; Cards; Games; Reading groups; Prayer groups; Movies; Dances/Social/Cultural gatherings.

St Peter Villa Nursing Home
141 N McLean, Memphis, TN 38104
(901) 276-2021, 274-8058 FAX
Admin Michael J Touchet. *Dir of Nursing* JoAnne Rains RN. *Medical Dir* Patrick J Murphy MD.
Licensure Skilled care; Intermediate care. *Beds* SNF 60; ICF 120. *Private Pay Patients* 25%. *Certified* Medicaid; Medicare.
Owner Nonprofit corp.
Admissions Requirements Minimum age 18.
Staff Physicians 1 (ft); RNs 3 (ft); LPNs 30 (ft), 1 (pt); Nurses' aides 60 (ft); Physical therapists 1 (ft); Recreational therapists 2 (ft); Occupational therapists 1 (pt); Speech therapists 1 (pt); Dietitians 1 (pt).

Affiliation Roman Catholic.
Facilities Dining room; Physical therapy room; Activities room; Chapel; Barber/Beauty shop.
Activities Arts & crafts; Cards; Games; Reading groups; Prayer groups; Movies; Shopping trips; Dances/Social/Cultural gatherings; Intergenerational programs; Pet therapy.

Shelby County Health Care Center
1075 Mullins Station Rd, Memphis, TN 38134
(901) 386-4361
Admin James D Brown. *Dir of Nursing* Nelda McCarter RN. *Medical Dir* George Jones MD.
Licensure Intermediate care. *Beds* ICF 575. *Certified* Medicaid.
Owner Publicly owned.
Admissions Requirements Medical examination; Physician's request.
Staff Physicians 2 (ft), 1 (pt); RNs 16 (ft); LPNs 56 (ft); Nurses' aides 255 (ft); Physical therapists 1 (pt); Recreational therapists 4 (ft); Activities coordinators 1 (ft); Dietitians 2 (ft), 1 (pt); Ophthalmologists 1 (pt); Dentists 1 (pt).
Facilities Dining room; Physical therapy room; Activities room; Chapel; Crafts room; Laundry room; Barber/Beauty shop; Library.
Activities Arts & crafts; Cards; Games; Reading groups; Prayer groups; Movies; Shopping trips; Dances/Social/Cultural gatherings; Fashion shows.

Sycamore View Nursing Home
1150 Dovecrest Rd, Memphis, TN 38134
(901) 382-1700
Licensure Intermediate care. *Beds* ICF 110. *Certified* Medicaid.
Owner Proprietary corp (Beverly Enterprises).

Wesley Highland Manor
3549 Norriswood, Memphis, TN 38111
(901) 458-7186, 327-8149 FAX
Admin Joyce Farnsworth. *Dir of Nursing* Jennell Monroe. *Medical Dir* Rodney Holladay MD; Connie Holladay MD.
Licensure Skilled care; Intermediate care; Personal care; Independent living. *Beds* ICF 10; Swing beds SNF/ICF 150. *Private Pay Patients* 50%. *Certified* Medicaid; Medicare.
Owner Nonprofit organization/foundation.
Admissions Requirements Minimum age 18; Medical examination.
Staff Physicians 2 (pt); RNs 2 (ft), 3 (pt); LPNs 11 (ft), 3 (pt); Nurses' aides 46 (ft), 9 (pt); Activities coordinators 1 (ft); Dietitians 1 (pt); Ophthalmologists.
Affiliation Methodist.
Facilities Dining room; Physical therapy room; Activities room; Laundry room; Barber/Beauty shop; Library.
Activities Games; Movies; Pet therapy.

Wesley Highland Place
3550 Watauga, Memphis, TN 38111
(901) 458-0086
Licensure Home for aged. *Beds* Home for aged 24.

Whitehaven Care Center
1076 Chambliss Rd, Memphis, TN 38116
(901) 396-8470
Admin Carole B Stengel. *Dir of Nursing* Vanessa Grant RN. *Medical Dir* Dr Kathi Clement.
Licensure Skilled care; Intermediate care. *Beds* SNF 16; ICF 76. *Certified* Medicaid; Medicare.
Owner Proprietary corp (Southeastern Health Care).
Admissions Requirements Minimum age 21; Medical examination; Physician's request.

Staff RNs 2 (ft); LPNs 13 (ft), 3 (pt); Nurses'
aides 46 (ft), 8 (pt); Physical therapists
(contracted); Activities coordinators 1 (ft);
Dietitians 1 (ft).
Facilities Dining room; Activities room;
Barber/Beauty shop.
Activities Arts & crafts; Cards; Games;
Reading groups; Prayer groups; Movies;
Shopping trips; Dances/Social/Cultural
gatherings; Intergenerational programs; Pet
therapy; Visits by religious groups; Family
council.

Milan

Douglas Nursing Home Inc
235 W Main St, Milan, TN 38358
(901) 686-8321
Licensure Intermediate care. *Beds* ICF 72.
Certified Medicaid.

Milan Health Care Inc
8060 Stinson St, Milan, TN 38358
(901) 686-8364
Admin Glenda McCartney. *Dir of Nursing*
Glenda Kilburn. *Medical Dir* J H Williams
MD.
Licensure Intermediate care. *Beds* ICF 66.
Private Pay Patients 6%. *Certified* Medicaid.
Owner Proprietary corp.
Admissions Requirements Physician's request.
Staff Physicians 1 (ft); RNs 1 (ft); LPNs 6 (ft);
Nurses' aides 23 (ft); Physical therapists
(contracted); Activities coordinators 1 (ft);
Dietitians 1 (ft).
Languages Sign.
Facilities Dining room; Activities room;
Laundry room; Barber/Beauty shop.
Activities Cards; Games; Reading groups;
Prayer groups; Movies; Shopping trips;
Dances/Social/Cultural gatherings;
Intergenerational programs.

Ridgewood Health Care Center
PO Box A, Dogwood Ln, Milan, TN 38358
(901) 686-8311
Admin Timothy Sullivan.
Medical Dir Fred Friedman MD.
Licensure Skilled care; Intermediate care. *Beds*
128. *Certified* Medicaid; Medicare.
Owner Proprietary corp (National Health
Corp).
Admissions Requirements Minimum age 21;
Medical examination; Physician's request.
Staff RNs 5 (ft), 1 (pt); LPNs 10 (ft), 1 (pt);
Nurses' aides 39 (ft), 4 (pt); Physical
therapists 1 (ft); Speech therapists 1 (ft);
Activities coordinators 1 (ft); Dietitians 1
(ft).
Facilities Dining room; Physical therapy
room; Activities room; Laundry room;
Barber/Beauty shop; Library.
Activities Arts & crafts; Cards; Games;
Reading groups; Prayer groups; Movies;
Dances/Social/Cultural gatherings.

Monteagle

Heritage Manor of Monteagle
218 2nd St NE, Monteagle, TN 37356
(615) 924-2041
Licensure Intermediate care. *Beds* ICF 150.
Certified Medicaid.
Owner Proprietary corp (National Heritage).
Admissions Requirements Minimum age 14.
Staff Physicians 5 (ft); RNs 4 (ft); LPNs 7 (ft);
Nurses' aides 45 (ft); Physical therapists 1
(pt); Occupational therapists 1 (pt); Speech
therapists 1 (pt); Activities coordinators 1
(ft); Dietitians 1 (pt).
Facilities Dining room; Physical therapy
room; Activities room; Crafts room; Laundry
room; Barber/Beauty shop; Library.
Activities Arts & crafts; Cards; Games;
Reading groups; Prayer groups; Movies;
Shopping trips; Dances/Social/Cultural
gatherings.

Monterey

Standing Stone Health Care Center
410 W Crawford Ave, Monterey, TN 38574
(615) 839-2244
Admin Joyce Hicks.
Medical Dir Danny Hall MD.
Licensure Intermediate care. *Beds* ICF 114.
Certified Medicaid.
Owner Proprietary corp.
Admissions Requirements Minimum age 14;
Medical examination; Physician's request.
Staff Physicians 5 (pt); RNs 2 (ft); LPNs 5
(ft), 6 (pt); Nurses' aides 24 (ft), 11 (pt);
Physical therapists 1 (pt); Speech therapists
1 (pt); Activities coordinators 1 (ft);
Dietitians 1 (pt).
Facilities Dining room; Physical therapy
room; Activities room; Chapel; Crafts room;
Laundry room; Barber/Beauty shop.
Activities Arts & crafts; Games; Reading
groups; Prayer groups; Shopping trips;
Dances/Social/Cultural gatherings.

Morristown

Life Care Center of Morristown
501 W Economy Rd, Morristown, TN 37814
(615) 581-5435
Admin Marvin Frey. *Dir of Nursing* Faye
Proffitt.
Licensure Intermediate care. *Beds* ICF 161.
Certified Medicaid.
Owner Proprietary corp (Life Care Centers of
America).
Admissions Requirements Medical
examination.
Staff RNs 2 (ft); LPNs 10 (ft), 4 (pt); Nurses'
aides 41 (ft), 11 (pt); Activities coordinators
1 (ft); Dietitians 1 (ft).
Facilities Dining room; Physical therapy
room; Activities room; Crafts room; Laundry
room; Barber/Beauty shop; Library.
Activities Arts & crafts; Cards; Games;
Reading groups; Prayer groups; Movies;
Shopping trips; Dances/Social/Cultural
gatherings.

Parkhurst Manor Ltd
739 E 2nd N St, Morristown, TN 37814
(615) 581-7075
Licensure Home for aged. *Beds* Home for
aged 60.

Mount Pleasant

Hidden Acres Manor Inc
904 Hidden Acres Dr, Mount Pleasant, TN
38474
(615) 379-5502
Licensure Intermediate care. *Beds* ICF 60.
Certified Medicaid.

Mountain City

Mountain City Health Care
919 Medical Park Dr, Mountain City, TN
37683
(615) 727-7800, 727-5508 FAX
Admin Anderson Greene. *Dir of Nursing*
Brenda Matheson. *Medical Dir* John
Whitlock MD.
Licensure Skilled care; Intermediate care. *Beds*
SNF 38; ICF 82. *Private Pay Patients* 5%.
Certified Medicaid; Medicare.
Owner Proprietary corp (Taylor and Bird).
Admissions Requirements Minimum age 14;
Medical examination; Physician's request.
Staff Physicians 6 (ft); RNs 2 (ft), 3 (pt);
LPNs 11 (ft); Nurses' aides 33 (ft), 3 (pt);
Physical therapists 1 (ft); Occupational
therapists 1 (ft); Speech therapists 1 (ft);
Activities coordinators 1 (ft); Dietitians 1
(ft); Ophthalmologists 1 (ft); Podiatrists 1
(ft).

Facilities Dining room; Physical therapy
room; Activities room; Crafts room; Laundry
room; Barber/Beauty shop; Library.
Activities Arts & crafts; Cards; Games;
Reading groups; Prayer groups; Movies;
Shopping trips; Dances/Social/Cultural
gatherings; Intergenerational programs.

Murfreesboro

Boulevard Terrace Nursing Home
915 S Tennessee Blvd, Murfreesboro, TN
37130
(615) 896-4504
Licensure Intermediate care. *Beds* ICF 100.
Certified Medicaid.
Admissions Requirements Medical
examination; Physician's request.
Facilities Dining room; Activities room;
Crafts room; Laundry room; Barber/Beauty
shop.
Activities Arts & crafts; Cards; Games;
Reading groups; Prayer groups; Movies;
Shopping trips; Dances/Social/Cultural
gatherings.

Community Care of Rutherford County Inc
901 County Farm Rd, Murfreesboro, TN
37130
(615) 893-2624, 898-0604 FAX
Admin H Leon Mansfield. *Dir of Nursing*
Mary J Mills. *Medical Dir* E C Tolbert MD.
Licensure Intermediate care. *Beds* ICF 131.
Private Pay Patients 17%. *Certified*
Medicaid.
Owner Nonprofit organization/foundation.
Admissions Requirements Medical
examination.
Staff RNs 1 (ft); LPNs 13 (ft), 2 (pt); Nurses'
aides 49 (ft), 1 (pt); Physical therapists;
Activities coordinators 1 (ft); Dietitians.
Facilities Dining room; Physical therapy
room; Activities room; Crafts room; Laundry
room; Barber/Beauty shop; Library.
Activities Arts & crafts; Cards; Games;
Reading groups; Prayer groups; Movies;
Dances/Social/Cultural gatherings;
Intergenerational programs.

Murfreesboro Health Care Center
420 N University St, Murfreesboro, TN 37130
(615) 893-2602
Medical Dir Dr Susan Andrews.
Licensure Skilled care. *Beds* SNF 190.
Certified Medicaid; Medicare.
Owner Proprietary corp (National Health
Corp).
Admissions Requirements Physician's request.
Staff RNs 10 (ft); LPNs 20 (ft); Nurses' aides
40 (ft); Physical therapists 2 (ft);
Recreational therapists 2 (ft); Occupational
therapists 1 (ft); Speech therapists 2 (ft);
Activities coordinators 1 (ft); Dietitians 1
(ft).
Facilities Dining room; Physical therapy
room; Activities room; Crafts room; Laundry
room; Barber/Beauty shop; Library.
Activities Arts & crafts; Games; Reading
groups; Prayer groups; Movies; Shopping
trips; Dances/Social/Cultural gatherings.

Nashville

Belcourt Terrace Nursing Home
1710 Belcourt Ave, Nashville, TN 37312
(615) 383-3570, 383-5209 FAX
Admin Nancy Meidinger. *Dir of Nursing*
Doris Billhorn RNC. *Medical Dir* Robert
Quinn MD.
Licensure Intermediate care; Alzheimer's care.
Beds ICF 49. *Private Pay Patients* 100%.
Owner Proprietary corp (Pinnacle Care Corp).
Staff Physicians; RNs 2 (ft), 2 (pt); LPNs 3
(ft), 2 (pt); Nurses' aides 20 (ft), 5 (pt);
Activities coordinators 1 (ft); Dietitians 1
(pt); Podiatrists 1 (pt).

Facilities Dining room; Laundry room.
Activities Arts & crafts; Cards; Games;
Reading groups; Prayer groups; Movies;
Dances/Social/Cultural gatherings;
Intergenerational programs; Pet therapy.

Bethany Health Care Center
421 Ocala Dr, Nashville, TN 37211
(615) 834-4214
Beds 180.
Owner Proprietary corp (Crowne
Management).

Brook Meade Health Care Inc
1000 St Luke Dr, Nashville, TN 37205
(615) 352-3430
Beds 120.

Carriage Health Care
1400 18th Ave S, Nashville, TN 37212
(615) 383-4715
Admin Brenda Dunn. *Dir of Nursing* Judy
Ferguson. *Medical Dir* Dr Dee Baker.
Licensure Intermediate care; Retirement. *Beds*
ICF 210. *Certified* Medicaid; Medicare.
Owner Proprietary corp (Sunbelt Healthcare
Centers Inc).
Admissions Requirements Medical
examination.
Staff Physicians 4 (ft); RNs 5 (ft); LPNs 20
(ft); Nurses' aides 60 (ft), 20 (pt); Physical
therapists 1 (ft); Reality therapists;
Recreational therapists 2 (ft); Speech
therapists 1 (ft); Activities coordinators 1
(ft); Dietitians 2 (ft); Ophthalmologists 1
(pt); Podiatrists 1 (pt); Dentists 1 (pt).
Facilities Dining room; Activities room;
Chapel; Crafts room; Laundry room; Barber/
Beauty shop.
Activities Arts & crafts; Cards; Games; Prayer
groups; Movies; Dances/Social/Cultural
gatherings; Exercise classes daily.

Church of Christ Home for Aged
1900 Eastland Ave, Nashville, TN 37206
(615) 227-9566
Licensure Home for aged. *Beds* Home for
aged 44.
Affiliation Church of Christ.

Crestview Nursing Home Inc
2030 25th Ave N, Nashville, TN 37208
(615) 256-4697
Licensure Intermediate care. *Beds* ICF 111.
Certified Medicaid.

Cumberland Manor Nursing Center
4343 Hydes Ferry Pike, Nashville, TN 37218
(615) 726-0492
Beds 120.

Eastland Health Care Center
701 Porter Rd, Nashville, TN 37206
(615) 226-3264, 226-3366 FAX
Admin Steven Neilson. *Dir of Nursing* Joan
Stover RN. *Medical Dir* Dr Charles Wiggins.
Licensure Intermediate care. *Beds* ICF 161.
Private Pay Patients 5%. *Certified* Medicaid.
Owner Privately owned.
Admissions Requirements Minimum age 14;
Medical examination; Physician's request.
Staff Physicians 8 (ft); RNs 2 (ft), 1 (pt);
LPNs 13 (ft), 3 (pt); Nurses' aides 50 (ft), 10
(pt); Physical therapists 1 (ft); Reality
therapists 2 (ft); Recreational therapists 2
(ft); Occupational therapists 2 (ft); Speech
therapists 1 (ft); Activities coordinators 1
(ft); Dietitians 1 (ft); Ophthalmologists 1 (ft);
Podiatrists 1 (ft); Activities coordinator
assistants 1 (ft); Mental health staff 1 (ft).
Facilities Dining room; Physical therapy
room; Activities room; Laundry room;
Barber/Beauty shop; Dayrooms; Private &
semi-private rooms.
Activities Arts & crafts; Cards; Games;
Reading groups; Prayer groups; Movies;
Shopping trips; Dances/Social/Cultural
gatherings; Intergenerational programs;
Weekly outings.

Jackson Park Christian Home
4107 Gallatin Rd, Nashville, TN 37216
(615) 228-0356
Licensure Skilled care; Intermediate care;
Home for aged. *Beds* 24; Home for aged 41.

Joseph B Knowles Home for the Aged
625 Benton Ave, Nashville, TN 37204
(615) 259-6429
Admin Caroline M Skelton.
Licensure Home for aged. *Beds* Home for
aged 70.
Owner Publicly owned.
Admissions Requirements Minimum age 55.
Staff RNs 1 (ft); Activities coordinators 1 (ft);
Group care workers 16 (ft); Custodians 3
(ft); Social workers 2 (ft).
Facilities Dining room; Activities room;
Chapel; Crafts room; Laundry room; Barber/
Beauty shop; Library.
Activities Arts & crafts; Cards; Games;
Reading groups; Prayer groups; Movies;
Shopping trips; Dances/Social/Cultural
gatherings; Exercise.

Lakeshore Heartland
3025 Fernbrook Ln, Nashville, TN 37214
(615) 885-2320
Admin George Chatfield Dir; David Grady,
Craig Underwood Adms.
Medical Dir Eva Rich.
Licensure Skilled care; Intermediate care;
Home for the aged; Assisted living;
Independent living. *Beds* SNF 28; ICF 164;
Home for the aged 88; Assisted living 48;
Independent living 173.
Owner Nonprofit corp.
Staff Physicians 1 (pt); RNs 10 (ft); LPNs 30
(ft); Nurses' aides 50 (ft); Activities
coordinators 3 (ft); Dietitians 3 (ft).

Lakeshore Nursing Home & Retirement Center
832 Wedgewood Ave, Nashville, TN 37203
(615) 383-4006
Admin David Grady. *Dir of Nursing* Eva
Rich. *Medical Dir* Dr Richard Garman.
Licensure Intermediate care; Independent
retirement rooms; Alzheimer's care. *Beds*
ICF 44; Independent retirement rooms 149.
Owner Nonprofit corp.
Admissions Requirements Medical
examination; Physician's request.
Staff Physicians; RNs; LPNs; Nurses' aides;
Physical therapists; Activities coordinators;
Dietitians; Ophthalmologists; Podiatrists.
Affiliation Church of Christ.
Facilities Dining room; Activities room;
Crafts room; Laundry room; Barber/Beauty
shop; Library.
Activities Arts & crafts; Cards; Games;
Reading groups; Prayer groups; Movies;
Shopping trips; Dances/Social/Cultural
gatherings.

Life Care Center of Donelson
2733 McCampbell Rd, Nashville, TN 37214
(615) 885-0483
Admin David L Tripp. *Dir of Nursing* Phyllis
Poe RN.
Licensure Skilled care; Intermediate care;
Alzheimer's care. *Beds* SNF 17; ICF 107.
Certified Medicaid; Medicare.
Owner Proprietary corp (National Heritage).
Admissions Requirements Minimum age 18;
Medical examination; Physician's request.
Staff Physicians 2 (pt); RNs 5 (ft); LPNs 10
(ft); Nurses' aides 25 (ft), 10 (pt); Physical
therapists 1 (ft), 1 (pt); Recreational
therapists 1 (ft); Occupational therapists 1
(pt); Speech therapists 1 (pt); Activities
coordinators 1 (ft); Dietitians 1 (ft); Social
workers 1 (ft).
Facilities Dining room; Physical therapy
room; Activities room; Crafts room; Laundry
room; Barber/Beauty shop; Library.

Activities Arts & crafts; Cards; Games;
Reading groups; Prayer groups; Movies;
Shopping trips; Dances/Social/Cultural
gatherings.

Meharry-Hubbard Hospital
PO Box 61-A, 1005 D B Todd Blvd,
Nashville, TN 37208
(615) 327-5550
Admin Duane Farnham Interim NHA. *Dir of
Nursing* Juanita J Polite RN. *Medical Dir*
Charles A Wiggins MD.
Licensure Skilled care; Retirement. *Beds* SNF
22. *Certified* Medicaid; Medicare.
Owner Nonprofit organization/foundation.
Admissions Requirements Physician's request.
Staff Physicians; RNs; LPNs; Physical
therapists; Recreational therapists;
Occupational therapists; Speech therapists;
Activities coordinators; Dietitians.
Facilities Dining room; Physical therapy
room; Activities room; Chapel.
Activities Arts & crafts; Cards; Games;
Reading groups; Prayer groups; Movies;
Dances/Social/Cultural gatherings; Quiet
hour.

Nashville Health Care Center
2215 Patterson St, Nashville, TN 37203
(615) 327-3011, 329-4727 FAX
Admin Martha A Ulm. *Dir of Nursing* Mary
Wentworth RN. *Medical Dir* Richard
Garman MD.
Licensure Skilled care; Intermediate care. *Beds*
SNF 52; ICF 50. *Certified* Medicaid;
Medicare.
Owner Proprietary corp (National Health
Corp).
Admissions Requirements Medical
examination.
Staff Physicians 1 (ft); RNs 5 (ft); LPNs 10
(ft); Nurses' aides 77 (ft); Physical therapists
2 (ft); Occupational therapists 2 (ft); Speech
therapists 1 (pt); Activities coordinators 2
(ft); Dietitians 1 (ft); Podiatrists 1 (pt);
Pharmacists 1 (pt); Chaplains 1 (ft); Geriatric
nurse practitioners 1 (ft).
Facilities Dining room; Physical therapy
room; Activities room; Crafts room; Laundry
room; Barber/Beauty shop; Pharmacy.
Activities Arts & crafts; Games; Movies;
Dances/Social/Cultural gatherings;
Intergenerational programs; Pet therapy.

Nashville Manor
1306 Katie Ave, Nashville, TN 37207
(615) 228-3494
Admin Mildred Ray. *Dir of Nursing* Delores
Burton. *Medical Dir* Charles Wiggins MD.
Licensure Intermediate care. *Beds* ICF 79.
Certified Medicaid.
Owner Privately owned.
Admissions Requirements Medical
examination; Physician's request.
Staff Physicians 1 (pt); RNs 1 (ft); Nurses'
aides 5 (ft); Activities coordinators 1 (pt);
Dietitians 1 (pt); Podiatrists 1 (pt).
Facilities Dining room; Activities room;
Crafts room; Laundry room; Barber/Beauty
shop.
Activities Arts & crafts; Cards; Games;
Reading groups; Prayer groups; Movies; Pet
therapy.

**Nashville Metropolitan Bordeaux
Hospital—Nursing Home**
1414 County Hospital Rd, Nashville, TN
37218
(615) 259-7000
Beds 636.

Trevecca Health Care Center
329 Murfreesboro Rd, Nashville, TN 37210
(615) 244-6900
Admin J W Tucker. *Dir of Nursing* M Bojuski
RN. *Medical Dir* Dr C Wiggins.

Licensure Skilled care; Intermediate care; Retirement. *Beds* SNF 120; ICF 120. *Private Pay Patients* 25%. *Certified* Medicaid; Medicare.
Owner Privately owned (Trevecca Ltd Partnership).
Admissions Requirements Minimum age 18; Medical examination; Physician's request.
Staff Physicians 8 (pt); RNs 7 (ft); LPNs 40 (ft); Nurses' aides 95 (ft); Physical therapists 1 (ft); Recreational therapists 1 (ft); Occupational therapists 1 (ft); Speech therapists 1 (pt); Activities coordinators 1 (ft); Dietitians 1 (ft); Podiatrists 1 (pt).
Affiliation Nazarene.
Facilities Dining room; Physical therapy room; Activities room; Chapel; Crafts room; Barber/Beauty shop.
Activities Arts & crafts; Cards; Games; Reading groups; Prayer groups; Movies; Shopping trips; Intergenerational programs.

University Health Care Center
2015 Terrace Pl, Nashville, TN 37203
(615) 327-2144
Medical Dir B H Webster MD.
Licensure Intermediate care. *Beds* ICF 49. *Certified* Medicaid.
Owner Proprietary corp (National Health Corp).
Staff Physicians 1 (pt); RNs 3 (ft); LPNs 4 (ft); Nurses' aides 14 (ft), 5 (pt); Physical therapists 1 (pt); Speech therapists 1 (pt); Activities coordinators 1 (pt); Dietitians 1 (ft).
Facilities Dining room; Physical therapy room; Activities room; Laundry room; Barber/Beauty shop.
Activities Games; Movies; Shopping trips.

West End Health Care Center
2818 Vanderbilt Pl, Nashville, TN 37212
(615) 327-4208
Beds 13.

New Tazewell

Laurel Manor Health Care
902 Buchanan Rd, New Tazewell, TN 37825
(615) 626-8215
Admin Mona G Ornduff. *Dir of Nursing* Brenda Bolinger. *Medical Dir* Dr William N Smith.
Licensure Skilled care; Intermediate care; Alzheimer's care. *Beds* SNF 67; ICF 67. *Private Pay Patients* 12%. *Certified* Medicaid; Medicare.
Owner Proprietary corp (Diversicare Corp).
Admissions Requirements Minimum age 14; Medical examination; Physician's request.
Staff Physicians 8 (pt); RNs 4 (ft); LPNs 12 (ft), 4 (pt); Nurses' aides 47 (ft), 2 (pt); Physical therapists 1 (pt); Reality therapists 1 (pt); Recreational therapists 1 (pt); Occupational therapists 1 (pt); Speech therapists 1 (ft); Activities coordinators 1 (ft); Dietitians 1 (pt); Ophthalmologists 1 (pt); Podiatrists 1 (pt); Audiologists 1 (pt).
Facilities Dining room; Physical therapy room; Activities room; Crafts room; Laundry room; Barber/Beauty shop.
Activities Arts & crafts; Cards; Games; Reading groups; Prayer groups; Movies; Shopping trips; Dances/Social/Cultural gatherings; Intergenerational programs; Pet therapy; Hay rides.

Newport

Cocke County Baptist Convalescent Center
603 College, Newport, TN 37821
(615) 625-2195, 625-2209 FAX
Admin Mary E Seay. *Dir of Nursing* Debra Holt RN. *Medical Dir* Dr Thomas Conway.
Licensure Intermediate care. *Beds* ICF 56. *Private Pay Patients* 25%. *Certified* Medicaid.

Owner Nonprofit organization/foundation.
Admissions Requirements Minimum age 18; Medical examination.
Staff Physicians 1 (pt); RNs 2 (ft); LPNs 6 (ft); Nurses' aides 19 (ft), 6 (pt); Physical therapists 1 (pt); Speech therapists 1 (pt); Activities coordinators 1 (ft); Dietitians 1 (pt).
Affiliation Baptist.
Facilities Dining room; Physical therapy room; Activities room; Crafts room; Laundry room; Barber/Beauty shop.
Activities Arts & crafts; Games; Prayer groups; Movies; Dances/Social/Cultural gatherings.

Regency Health Care Center—Newport
Hwy 25 at 70 & 411, Newport, TN 37821
(615) 623-0929
Admin Craig N Ethridge. *Dir of Nursing* Arnolene Seahorn RN. *Medical Dir* Kenneth Hill MD.
Licensure Skilled care; Intermediate care. *Beds* SNF 18; ICF 120. *Certified* Medicaid; Medicare.
Owner Proprietary corp (Regency Health Care Centers).
Admissions Requirements Minimum age 15; Medical examination; Physician's request.
Staff RNs 4 (ft); LPNs 12 (ft); Nurses' aides 30 (ft), 8 (pt); Physical therapists 1 (pt); Speech therapists 1 (ft); Activities coordinators 1 (ft); Dietitians 1 (ft).
Facilities Dining room; Physical therapy room; Activities room; Chapel; Crafts room; Laundry room; Barber/Beauty shop; Library.
Activities Arts & crafts; Cards; Games; Reading groups; Prayer groups; Movies; Shopping trips; Dances/Social/Cultural gatherings; Gardening.

Oak Ridge

Oak Ridge Health Care
300 Laboratory Rd, Oak Ridge, TN 37830
(615) 482-7698
Admin Kerry Trammell. *Dir of Nursing* Kim Hill. *Medical Dir* Dr Anthony Garton.
Licensure Skilled care; Intermediate care; Alzheimer's care. *Beds* SNF 46; ICF 84. *Private Pay Patients* 50%. *Certified* Medicaid; Medicare.
Owner Proprietary corp (National Health Corp).
Admissions Requirements Medical examination; Physician's request.
Staff RNs; LPNs; Nurses' aides; Physical therapists; Occupational therapists; Speech therapists; Activities coordinators; Dietitians.
Facilities Dining room; Physical therapy room; Activities room; Chapel; Crafts room; Laundry room; Barber/Beauty shop.
Activities Arts & crafts; Cards; Games; Reading groups; Prayer groups; Movies; Shopping trips; Dances/Social/Cultural gatherings; Pet therapy.

Oneida

Scott County Nursing Home
Alberta Dr, Oneida, TN 37841
(615) 569-8521
Admin Skip Flynn. *Dir of Nursing* Wilda Hazlett. *Medical Dir* Dr Maxwell Huff.
Licensure Intermediate care. *Beds* ICF 56. *Private Pay Patients* 5%. *Certified* Medicaid.
Owner Nonprofit organization/foundation.
Admissions Requirements Minimum age 16; Medical examination; Physician's request.
Staff RNs 1 (ft); LPNs 8 (ft); Nurses' aides 20 (ft); Physical therapists 1 (ft); Activities coordinators 1 (ft); Dietitians 1 (ft).
Facilities Dining room; Activities room; Crafts room; Laundry room; Barber/Beauty shop; Library.
Activities Arts & crafts; Games; Reading groups; Prayer groups; Movies; Shopping trips; Pet therapy.

Palmyra

Palmyra Intermediate Care Center
PO Box 8, Hwy 149, Palmyra, TN 37142
(615) 326-5252
Admin Frances H Warren.
Medical Dir Linda Newberry.
Licensure Skilled care; Intermediate care; Intermediate care for mentally retarded. *Beds* SNF 22; ICF 33; ICF/MR 20. *Certified* Medicaid; Medicare.
Owner Privately owned.
Admissions Requirements Minimum age 21; Medical examination; Physician's request.
Staff RNs 2 (ft), 2 (pt); LPNs 5 (ft), 4 (pt); Nurses' aides 8 (ft), 9 (pt); Recreational therapists 1 (ft), 1 (pt); Activities coordinators 1 (ft); Physical therapy aides 1 (ft); Developmental technicians 10 (ft), 13 (pt); Social workers 2 (ft); Medical records 1 (ft).
Languages Sign.
Facilities Dining room; Activities room; Crafts room; Laundry room; Barber/Beauty shop; Dental office; Training center for ADLS & vocational skills training.
Activities Arts & crafts; Cards; Games; Reading groups; Prayer groups; Movies; Shopping trips; Dances/Social/Cultural gatherings; Community service projects; Ceramics; Outings; Senior Olympics; Cook-outs.

Paris

Henry County Nursing Home
Hospital Cir, Paris, TN 38242
(901) 642-5700
Licensure Intermediate care. *Beds* ICF 114. *Certified* Medicaid.

Paris Manor Nursing Center
Rte 3 Box 1408, Old Murray Rd, Paris, TN 38242
(901) 642-2535
Admin Ramon C Snyder.
Licensure Intermediate care. *Beds* ICF 132. *Certified* Medicaid.
Owner Proprietary corp (American Health Center Inc).

Parsons

Decatur County Manor Nursing Center
1501 Kentucky Ave S, Parsons, TN 38363
(901) 847-6371
Admin Thomas E Feeback. *Dir of Nursing* Nancy Palmer.
Licensure Intermediate care. *Beds* ICF 98. *Certified* Medicaid.
Owner Proprietary corp (American Health Center Inc).
Admissions Requirements Medical examination.
Staff RNs 1 (ft); LPNs 11 (ft); Nurses' aides 27 (ft); Physical therapists 1 (pt); Recreational therapists 1 (ft); Activities coordinators 1 (ft).
Facilities Dining room; Activities room; Chapel; Crafts room; Laundry room; Barber/Beauty shop.
Activities Arts & crafts; Cards; Games; Reading groups; Prayer groups; Movies; Shopping trips; Dances/Social/Cultural gatherings.

Pigeon Forge

Royal Care of Pigeon Forge
447 Two View Rd, Pigeon Forge, TN 37863
(615) 428-5454
Beds 110.

Pikeville

Bledsoe County Nursing Home
Hwy 30 W, Pikeville, TN 37367
(615) 447-6811
Admin Gary Burton. *Dir of Nursing* Teda
Baron. *Medical Dir* A Quito MD.
Licensure Intermediate care. *Beds* ICF 50.
Private Pay Patients 12%. *Certified*
Medicaid.
Owner Publicly owned.
Admissions Requirements Medical
examination; Physician's request.
Staff RNs; LPNs; Nurses' aides; Activities
coordinators; Dietitians.
Facilities Dining room; Physical therapy
room; Activities room; Chapel; Barber/
Beauty shop.
Activities Cards; Games; Prayer groups;
Movies.

Pleasant Hill

May Cravath Wharton Nursing Home
PO Box 168, 20 Lake Dr, Pleasant Hill, TN
38578
(615) 277-3511
Admin Robin Gray. *Dir of Nursing* Verlee
Fischer RN. *Medical Dir* Fred Lake MD.
Licensure Intermediate care; Retirement. *Beds*
ICF 80; Retirement 30. *Private Pay Patients*
37%. *Certified* Medicaid.
Owner Nonprofit corp.
Admissions Requirements Medical
examination.
Staff Physicians 2 (pt); RNs 1 (ft), 2 (pt);
LPNs 4 (ft), 2 (pt); Nurses' aides 17 (ft), 13
(pt); Activities coordinators 1 (ft); Dietitians
1 (ft).
Affiliation Church of Christ.
Facilities Dining room; Activities room;
Crafts room; Laundry room; Barber/Beauty
shop; Library; Lounges; Patios.
Activities Arts & crafts; Cards; Games;
Reading groups; Prayer groups; Movies;
Shopping trips; Dances/Social/Cultural
gatherings; Pet therapy.

Portland

Highland Manor
215 Highland Circle Dr, Portland, TN 37148
(615) 325-9263
Admin Richard L Mountz. *Dir of Nursing*
Jean Crittenden RN. *Medical Dir* James
Ladd MD.
Licensure Intermediate care. *Beds* ICF 110.
Private Pay Patients 15%. *Certified*
Medicaid.
Owner Nonprofit corp (Sunbelt Health Care
Centers Inc).
Admissions Requirements Medical
examination; Physician's request.
Staff RNs 1 (ft), 1 (pt); LPNs 14 (ft), 2 (pt);
Nurses' aides 40 (ft), 2 (pt); Activities
coordinators 1 (ft).
Facilities Dining room; Activities room;
Barber/Beauty shop; Library; Family dining
room.
Activities Arts & crafts; Games; Movies; Pet
therapy.

Pulaski

Meadowbrook Nursing Center
PO Box 677, Pulaski, TN 38478
(615) 363-7548
Admin Christine Edwards.
Licensure Intermediate care. *Beds* ICF 83.
Certified Medicaid.
Owner Proprietary corp (American Health
Center Inc).
Admissions Requirements Minimum age 18;
Medical examination.
Staff RNs 1 (ft); LPNs 5 (ft); Nurses' aides 17
(ft); Activities coordinators 1 (ft).

Facilities Dining room; Activities room;
Laundry room; Barber/Beauty shop.
Activities Arts & crafts; Cards; Games;
Reading groups; Prayer groups; Movies;
Shopping trips; Dances/Social/Cultural
gatherings.

Pulaski Health Care Center
PO Box 638, 993 E College, Pulaski, TN
38478
(615) 363-3572
Admin Betty T Pope.
Medical Dir W K Owen MD.
Licensure Skilled care; Intermediate care. *Beds*
85. *Certified* Medicaid; Medicare.
Owner Proprietary corp (National Health
Corp).
Staff RNs 3 (ft), 1 (pt); LPNs 11 (ft); Nurses'
aides 13 (ft), 13 (pt); Physical therapists 1
(ft); Speech therapists 1 (pt); Activities
coordinators 1 (ft); Dietitians 1 (ft); Dentists
1 (pt).
Facilities Dining room; Activities room;
Barber/Beauty shop.
Activities Arts & crafts; Cards; Games;
Reading groups; Prayer groups; Movies.

Puryear

Puryear Nursing Home
223 W Chestnut St, Puryear, TN 38251
(901) 247-3205
Admin Peggy J Nichols. *Dir of Nursing*
Virginia A Sawyers. *Medical Dir* Dr D M
Norman.
Licensure Skilled care; Alzheimer's care. *Beds*
SNF 25. *Private Pay Patients* 100%.
Owner Privately owned.
Admissions Requirements Minimum age 14;
Medical examination.
Staff RNs 1 (ft); LPNs 4 (ft); Nurses' aides 10
(ft); Activities coordinators 1 (ft); Dietitians
4 (ft).
Facilities Dining room; Activities room;
Laundry room; Barber/Beauty shop; Library.
Activities Arts & crafts; Reading groups;
Movies.

Red Bank

Red Bank Health Care Center Inc
1020 Runyan Dr, Red Bank, TN 37405
(615) 877-1155
Beds 133.

Red Boiling Springs

Heritage Manor of Red Boiling Springs
Hwy 52, Red Boiling Springs, TN 37150
(615) 699-2238
Licensure Intermediate care. *Beds* ICF 119.
Certified Medicaid.
Owner Proprietary corp (National Heritage).

Ridgetop

Ridgetop Haven Inc
Woodruff, Ridgetop, TN 37152
(615) 643-4548, 859-5895
Beds 32.

Ripley

Hillhaven Convalescent Center of Ripley
118 Halliburton Dr, Ripley, TN 38063
(901) 635-5180
Admin Gregory H Mitchell. *Dir of Nursing*
Carolyn Drumwright RN. *Medical Dir*
William Tucker MD.
Licensure Skilled care; Intermediate care. *Beds*
SNF 10; ICF 168. *Certified* Medicaid;
Medicare.
Owner Proprietary corp (Hillhaven Corp).
Admissions Requirements Medical
examination; Physician's request.

Staff RNs 5 (ft); LPNs 16 (ft); Nurses' aides
65 (ft); Recreational therapists 1 (ft), 1 (pt);
Activities coordinators 1 (ft); Dietitians 1
(ft).
Facilities Dining room; Physical therapy
room; Activities room; Barber/Beauty shop.
Activities Arts & crafts; Games; Reading
groups; Prayer groups; Movies; Shopping
trips; Dances/Social/Cultural gatherings.

Lauderdale County Nursing Home
PO Box 186, 210 Tucker St, Ripley, TN
38063
(901) 635-5100
Licensure Intermediate care. *Beds* ICF 71.
Certified Medicaid.

Rockwood

Rockwood Health Care Center
Hwy 70 E, Rockwood, TN 37854
(615) 354-3366
Licensure Intermediate care. *Beds* ICF 150.
Certified Medicaid.

Rogersville

Heritage Manor of Rogersville
Rte 4 Box 30, Rogersville, TN 37857
(615) 272-3099, 272-6591 FAX
Admin A E Luttrell. *Dir of Nursing* Anna
Ethridge RN. *Medical Dir* Henry J Presutti
MD.
Licensure Intermediate care. *Beds* ICF 150.
Private Pay Patients 10%. *Certified*
Medicaid.
Owner Proprietary corp (National Heritage).
Admissions Requirements Medical
examination.
Staff RNs 3 (ft), 1 (pt); LPNs 11 (ft), 2 (pt);
Nurses' aides 43 (ft), 2 (pt); Activities
coordinators 1 (ft).
Facilities Dining room; Activities room;
Laundry room; Barber/Beauty shop.
Activities Arts & crafts; Games; Movies;
Shopping trips; Dances/Social/Cultural
gatherings.

Rutledge

**Ridgeview Terrace Convalescent & Nursing
Center**
PO Box 26, Coffey Ln, Rutledge, TN 37861
(615) 828-5295
Medical Dir Dr John Kinser.
Licensure Intermediate care. *Beds* ICF 132.
Certified Medicaid.
Owner Proprietary corp (National Heritage).
Staff Physicians 8 (pt); RNs 1 (ft); LPNs 9
(ft); Nurses' aides 8 (ft); Physical therapists 1
(pt); Reality therapists 1 (pt); Speech
therapists 1 (pt); Activities coordinators 1
(ft); Dietitians 1 (pt).
Facilities Dining room; Physical therapy
room; Activities room; Crafts room; Laundry
room; Barber/Beauty shop; Library.
Activities Arts & crafts; Games; Prayer groups;
Movies; Shopping trips.

Savannah

Harbert Hills Academy Nursing Home
Rte 2 Box 212, Lonesome Pine Rd, Savannah,
TN 38372
(901) 925-5495
Admin Lester L Dickman. *Dir of Nursing*
Geraldine Dickman RN. *Medical Dir* John
Lay MD.
Licensure Intermediate care. *Beds* ICF 49.
Certified Medicaid.
Owner Proprietary corp.
Staff Physicians 5 (pt); RNs 1 (ft); LPNs 5
(ft); Nurses' aides 60 (ft), 20 (pt); Activities
coordinators 1 (ft); Dietitians 1 (pt).

Facilities Dining room; Activities room; Chapel; Laundry room; Barber/Beauty shop.
Activities Arts & crafts; Movies; Shopping trips.

Hardin County Nursing Home
2006 Wayne Rd, Savannah, TN 38372
(901) 925-4954
Admin Johnny May. *Dir of Nursing* Margie Tall LPN. *Medical Dir* Janet K Lard MD.
Licensure Intermediate care. *Beds* ICF 48. *Certified* Medicaid.
Owner Publicly owned.
Admissions Requirements Medical examination; Physician's request.
Staff RNs 1 (pt); LPNs 6 (ft), 1 (pt); Nurses' aides 16 (ft), 6 (pt); Activities coordinators 1 (ft); Dietitians 1 (pt).
Facilities Dining room; Activities room; Laundry room; Barber/Beauty shop.
Activities Arts & crafts; Games; Movies; Dances/Social/Cultural gatherings.

Hardin Home Nursing Home
Hwy 64 E, Savannah, TN 38372
(901) 925-4004
Licensure Intermediate care. *Beds* ICF 57. *Certified* Medicaid.

Park Rest Hardin County Health Center
410 Shelby Dr, Savannah, TN 38372
(901) 925-1181
Beds 56.

Selmer

Maple Hill Nursing Home
6th St S, Selmer, TN 38375
(901) 645-7908
Licensure Intermediate care. *Beds* 31. *Certified* Medicaid.

McNairy County Health Care Center
PO Box 0349, Hwy 64 By-pass, Selmer, TN 38375
(901) 645-3201
Beds 73.

Sevierville

Fort Sanders—Sevier Medical Center Nursing Home
709 Middle Creek Rd, Sevierville, TN 37862
(615) 453-7111
Admin Samuel McGahn.
Medical Dir Charles H Bozeman MD.
Licensure Skilled care; Intermediate care. *Beds* 54. *Certified* Medicaid; Medicare.
Admissions Requirements Medical examination; Physician's request.
Staff Physicians 1 (pt); RNs 3 (ft), 3 (pt); LPNs 3 (ft), 4 (pt); Nurses' aides 19 (ft), 5 (pt); Physical therapists 3 (pt); Occupational therapists 1 (pt); Speech therapists 1 (pt); Activities coordinators 1 (ft); Dietitians 1 (pt); Dentists 1 (pt); Social workers 1 (pt).
Facilities Dining room; Physical therapy room; Activities room; Chapel; Crafts room; Barber/Beauty shop; Library.
Activities Arts & crafts; Cards; Games; Reading groups; Prayer groups; Movies; Shopping trips; Dances/Social/Cultural gatherings.

Markhill Manor Ltd
700 Markhill Dr, Sevierville, TN 37862
(615) 428-2445
Licensure Home for aged. *Beds* Home for aged 30.

Shelbyville

Bedford County Nursing Home
845 Union St, Shelbyville, TN 37160
(615) 685-5151

Admin Richard Graham. *Dir of Nursing* Jo Ann Warren RN. *Medical Dir* Sara Womack MD.
Licensure Skilled care; Intermediate care. *Beds* ICF 77; Swing beds SNF/ICF 30. *Certified* Medicaid; Medicare.
Owner Publicly owned.
Admissions Requirements Medical examination; Physician's request.
Staff Physicians; RNs; LPNs; Nurses' aides; Physical therapists; Occupational therapists; Speech therapists; Activities coordinators; Dietitians.
Facilities Dining room; Physical therapy room; Activities room; Chapel; Crafts room; Laundry room; Barber/Beauty shop; Library.
Activities Arts & crafts; Cards; Games; Reading groups; Shopping trips; Dances/Social/Cultural gatherings; Intergenerational programs; Pet therapy; Cooking.

Glen Oaks Convalescent Center
1101 Glen Oaks Rd, Shelbyville, TN 37160
(615) 684-8340
Admin Palyce W Jones. *Dir of Nursing* Rebecca Patterson RN. *Medical Dir* Dr A T Richards.
Licensure Intermediate care; Retirement. *Beds* ICF 130. *Certified* Medicaid.
Owner Privately owned.
Admissions Requirements Medical examination.
Staff Physicians 1 (pt); RNs 2 (ft); LPNs 14 (ft), 2 (pt); Nurses' aides 42 (ft), 6 (pt); Physical therapists 1 (pt); Occupational therapists 1 (pt); Speech therapists 1 (pt); Activities coordinators 1 (ft), 1 (pt); Dietitians 1 (pt).
Facilities Dining room; Physical therapy room; Activities room; Crafts room; Laundry room; Barber/Beauty shop.
Activities Arts & crafts; Cards; Games; Reading groups; Prayer groups; Movies; Shopping trips; Dances/Social/Cultural gatherings.

Signal Mountain

Alexian Village of Tennessee
100 James Blvd, Signal Mountain, TN 37377
(615) 886-0100, 886-0470 FAX
Admin Dan Gray. *Dir of Nursing* Chris Tarziers RN. *Medical Dir* Arch Y Smith MD.
Licensure Skilled care; Intermediate care; Apartments. *Beds* SNF 16; ICF 108; Apts 235. *Private Pay Patients* 77%. *Certified* Medicaid; Medicare.
Owner Nonprofit corp (Alexian Brothers Health Systems).
Admissions Requirements Medical examination; Physician's request.
Staff RNs 2 (ft), 1 (pt); LPNs 12 (ft), 2 (pt); Nurses' aides 37 (ft), 2 (pt); Physical therapists 1 (pt); Activities coordinators 1 (ft); Dietitians 1 (pt).
Affiliation Roman Catholic.
Facilities Dining room; Physical therapy room; Activities room; Chapel; Crafts room; Barber/Beauty shop; Library.
Activities Arts & crafts; Cards; Games; Reading groups; Prayer groups; Movies; Shopping trips; Dances/Social/Cultural gatherings; Intergenerational programs; Pet therapy; Fishing.

Smithville

Sunny Point Health Care Center
Rte 1, Spring St, Smithville, TN 37166
(615) 597-4284
Licensure Skilled care; Intermediate care. *Beds* 76. *Certified* Medicaid; Medicare.
Owner Proprietary corp (National Health Corp).

Smyrna

Cambridge Medical Center
PO Box 787, Smyrna, TN 37167-0787
(615) 355-0350, 242-3944
Beds 110.

Smyrna Nursing Center Inc
202 Enon Springs Rd, Smyrna, TN 37167
(615) 459-5621
Licensure Intermediate care. *Beds* ICF 89. *Certified* Medicaid.
Owner Proprietary corp (Wessex Corp).

Sneedville

Hancock Manor Nursing Home
E Main St, Sneedville, TN 37869
(615) 733-4783
Beds 50.

Somerville

Somerville Health Care Center
PO Box 229, 308 Lake Dr, Somerville, TN 38068
(901) 465-9861
Admin Brenda K Howell. *Dir of Nursing* Susan D Bohanon RN. *Medical Dir* Frank S McKnight MD.
Licensure Skilled care; Intermediate care. *Beds* SNF 42; ICF 42. *Private Pay Patients* 29%. *Certified* Medicaid; Medicare.
Owner Proprietary corp (National Health Corp).
Admissions Requirements Medical examination; Physician's request.
Staff Physicians; RNs; LPNs; Nurses' aides; Physical therapists; Speech therapists; Activities coordinators; Dietitians.
Facilities Dining room; Physical therapy room; Activities room; Crafts room; Laundry room; Barber/Beauty shop; Library; Private & semi-private rooms.
Activities Arts & crafts; Cards; Games; Reading groups; Prayer groups; Movies; Shopping trips; Intergenerational programs; Exercise.

South Pittsburg

Rivermont Convalescent & Nursing Center
201 E 10th St, South Pittsburg, TN 37380
(615) 837-7981
Admin Douglas L Malin. *Dir of Nursing* Rebecca Chambers. *Medical Dir* Dr Russ Adcock.
Licensure Intermediate care. *Beds* ICF 165. *Certified* Medicaid.
Owner Proprietary corp (National Heritage).
Admissions Requirements Medical examination.
Staff RNs 2 (ft); LPNs 14 (ft), 4 (pt); Nurses' aides 53 (ft), 14 (pt); Activities coordinators 1 (ft); Dietitians 1 (pt).
Facilities Dining room; Physical therapy room; Activities room; Crafts room; Laundry room; Barber/Beauty shop; Library.
Activities Arts & crafts; Cards; Games; Reading groups; Prayer groups; Movies; Shopping trips; Dances/Social/Cultural gatherings.

Sparta

Sparta Health Care Center
PO Box 98, 108 E Gracey St, Sparta, TN 38583
(615) 836-2211
Licensure Skilled care; Intermediate care. *Beds* 120. *Certified* Medicaid; Medicare.
Owner Proprietary corp (National Health Corp).

Spring City

Spring City Health Care Center
PO Box 730, Hinch St, Spring City, TN 37381
(615) 365-4355, 365-4809 FAX
Admin R Gay Lane. *Dir of Nursing* Betty
Whiteley RN. *Medical Dir* Dr John
Snodgrass.
Licensure Skilled care; Intermediate care. *Beds*
SNF 24; ICF 116. *Private Pay Patients* 25%.
Certified Medicaid; Medicare.
Owner Proprietary corp (Dixie Taylor et al).
Admissions Requirements Minimum age 14;
Medical examination; Physician's request.
Facilities Dining room; Physical therapy
room; Activities room; Chapel; Crafts room;
Laundry room; Barber/Beauty shop; Library.
Activities Arts & crafts; Cards; Games;
Reading groups; Prayer groups; Movies;
Shopping trips; Dances/Social/Cultural
gatherings; Intergenerational programs; Pet
therapy.

Springfield

Elm Hurst Nursing Home
704 5th Ave E, Springfield, TN 37172
(615) 384-7977
Admin Jane A Smithson. *Dir of Nursing*
Donna Henry. *Medical Dir* J R Quarles MD.
Licensure Intermediate care. *Beds* ICF 70.
Private Pay Patients 10%. *Certified*
Medicaid.
Owner Publicly owned.
Admissions Requirements Physician's request.
Staff Physicians 1 (pt); RNs 2 (pt); LPNs 10
(pt); Physical therapists (contracted);
Activities coordinators 1 (ft); Dietitians
(contracted); Podiatrists 1 (pt).
Facilities Dining room; Activities room;
Chapel; Crafts room; Laundry room; Barber/
Beauty shop; Library.
Activities Arts & crafts; Games; Reading
groups; Prayer groups; Movies; Dances/
Social/Cultural gatherings; Intergenerational
programs; Pet therapy.

Robertson County Health Care
2504 S Main, Springfield, TN 37172
(615) 384-9565
Admin Eleta Grimmett. *Dir of Nursing* Vicky
Thornton. *Medical Dir* John Bassel.
Licensure Skilled care; Intermediate care. *Beds*
SNF 34; ICF 86. *Certified* Medicaid;
Medicare.
Owner Proprietary corp (Beverly Enterprises).
Admissions Requirements Physician's request.
Staff RNs 3 (ft), 2 (pt); LPNs 10 (ft), 2 (pt);
Nurses' aides 55 (ft), 1 (pt); Physical
therapists 1 (pt); Recreational therapists 1
(ft); Occupational therapists 1 (pt); Speech
therapists 1 (pt); Activities coordinators 1
(ft); Dietitians 1 (ft); Podiatrists 1 (pt).
Facilities Dining room; Physical therapy
room; Activities room; Crafts room; Laundry
room; Barber/Beauty shop.
Activities Arts & crafts; Cards; Games;
Reading groups; Prayer groups; Movies;
Shopping trips; Dances/Social/Cultural
gatherings; Intergenerational programs; Pet
therapy.

Springfield Health Care Center
608 8th Ave E, Springfield, TN 37172
(615) 384-8453
Admin Edna McClurkan. *Dir of Nursing*
JoAnne Nicholson RN. *Medical Dir* John B
Turner MD.
Licensure Skilled care; Intermediate care;
Noncertified care. *Beds* SNF 33; ICF 52;
Noncertified 27. *Private Pay Patients* 35%.
Certified Medicaid; Medicare.
Owner Proprietary corp (National Health
Corp).
Admissions Requirements Minimum age 18;
Medical examination; Physician's request.

Staff RNs 3 (ft), 2 (pt); LPNs 6 (ft), 4 (pt);
Nurses' aides 34 (ft), 6 (pt); Physical
therapists 1 (ft); Recreational therapists 1
(ft); Occupational therapists 1 (ft); Activities
coordinators 1 (ft); Dietitians 1 (ft).
Facilities Dining room; Physical therapy
room; Activities room; Crafts room; Laundry
room; Barber/Beauty shop; Library.
Activities Arts & crafts; Cards; Games;
Reading groups; Prayer groups; Movies;
Shopping trips; Dances/Social/Cultural
gatherings; Intergenerational programs.

Sweetwater

**Sweetwater Valley Convalescent & Nursing
Home Inc**
Rte 2 Box 18, Sweetwater, TN 37874
(615) 337-6631
Licensure Intermediate care. *Beds* ICF 115.
Certified Medicaid.

Wood Presbyterian Home Inc
Rte 5 Box 700, Sweetwater, TN 37874
(615) 337-5326
Admin Richard Fields MPH. *Dir of Nursing*
Diane Honaker RN. *Medical Dir* Houston
Lowry MD.
Licensure Skilled care; Intermediate care;
Retirement; Residential care; Alzheimer's
care. *Beds* SNF 30; ICF 30; Residential care
15. *Certified* Medicaid; Medicare.
Owner Nonprofit organization/foundation.
Admissions Requirements Minimum age 14;
Medical examination; Physician's request.
Staff Physicians 6 (pt); RNs 1 (ft), 1 (pt);
LPNs 5 (ft), 2 (pt); Nurses' aides 20 (ft), 10
(pt); Physical therapists 1 (pt); Reality
therapists 1 (pt); Recreational therapists 1
(pt); Occupational therapists 1 (pt); Speech
therapists 1 (pt); Activities coordinators 1
(ft); Dietitians 1 (pt); Ophthalmologists 1
(pt); Podiatrists 1 (pt); Audiologists 1 (pt).
Languages Sign.
Affiliation Presbyterian.
Facilities Dining room; Physical therapy
room; Activities room; Crafts room; Laundry
room; Barber/Beauty shop; Library; Family
room.
Activities Arts & crafts; Cards; Games;
Reading groups; Prayer groups; Movies;
Shopping trips; Intergenerational programs;
Gardening.

Tazewell

Claiborne County Nursing Home
1000 Old Knoxville Rd, Tazewell, TN 37879
(615) 626-4211, 626-9926 FAX
Admin Patricia Gray. *Dir of Nursing* Edith
Noe. *Medical Dir* William Smith MD.
Licensure Skilled care; Intermediate care. *Beds*
Swing beds SNF/ICF 50. *Private Pay
Patients* 10%. *Certified* Medicaid; Medicare.
Owner Publicly owned.
Admissions Requirements Medical
examination; Physician's request.
Staff Physicians 9 (ft); RNs 4 (ft); LPNs 8 (ft);
Nurses' aides 25 (ft); Physical therapists 1
(ft); Activities coordinators 1 (ft); Dietitians
1 (ft); Podiatrists 1 (ft).
Facilities Dining room; Physical therapy
room; Activities room; Crafts room; Laundry
room; Barber/Beauty shop.
Activities Arts & crafts; Cards; Games;
Reading groups; Prayer groups; Movies;
Shopping trips; Dances/Social/Cultural
gatherings; Intergenerational programs.

Tiptonville

Reelfoot Manor Nursing Home
1034 Reelfoot Dr, Tiptonville, TN 38079-
9998
(901) 253-6681, 253-8014 FAX

Admin Johnny H Rea. *Dir of Nursing* Terry
Byrd RN. *Medical Dir* Sam Bradberry MD.
Licensure Intermediate care; Alzheimer's care.
Beds ICF 120. *Private Pay Patients* 7%.
Certified Medicaid.
Owner Proprietary corp (Beverly Enterprises).
Admissions Requirements Minimum age 18;
Medical examination; Physician's request.
Staff Physicians 3 (pt); RNs 1 (ft); LPNs 9
(ft), 3 (pt); Nurses' aides 28 (ft), 7 (pt);
Physical therapists 1 (pt); Reality therapists
1 (pt); Recreational therapists 1 (pt);
Occupational therapists 1 (pt); Speech
therapists 1 (pt); Activities coordinators 1
(ft); Dietitians 1 (pt); Ophthalmologists 1
(pt); Podiatrists 1 (pt).
Facilities Dining room; Physical therapy
room; Crafts room; Laundry room; Barber/
Beauty shop.
Activities Arts & crafts; Cards; Games; Prayer
groups; Movies; Shopping trips; Dances/
Social/Cultural gatherings; Fishing & boating
trips ; Winter trips; Eagle watching; Winter
programs; Picnics.

Trenton

Forum Convalescent Center
PO Box 168, Trenton, TN 38382
(901) 855-4500
Admin Karen Utley. *Dir of Nursing* Lorraine
Kail RN. *Medical Dir* William C Desouza
MD.
Licensure Intermediate care. *Beds* ICF 44.
Private Pay Patients 35%. *Certified*
Medicaid.
Owner Proprietary corp.
Admissions Requirements Medical
examination.
Staff Physicians 5 (pt); RNs 1 (ft); LPNs 4
(ft), 4 (pt); Nurses' aides 12 (ft), 10 (pt);
Physical therapists 1 (pt); Activities
coordinators 1 (ft); Dietitians 1 (pt);
Podiatrists 1 (pt).
Facilities Dining room; Activities room;
Crafts room; Barber/Beauty shop; Library.
Activities Arts & crafts; Cards; Games; Prayer
groups; Movies; Shopping trips; Dances/
Social/Cultural gatherings.

Tullahoma

Life Care Center of Tullahoma
1715 N Jackson St, Tullahoma, TN 37388
(615) 455-8557
Licensure Intermediate care. *Beds* ICF 169.
Certified Medicaid.
Owner Proprietary corp (Life Care Centers of
America).

Union City

Obion County Rest Home
Rte 1 Box 207, Union City, TN 38261
(901) 885-9065
Admin Bill Jordan.
Medical Dir Dr Grover Schleifer.
Licensure Intermediate care. *Beds* ICF 52.
Certified Medicaid.
Admissions Requirements Medical
examination; Physician's request.
Staff Physicians 1 (pt); RNs 1 (ft); LPNs 5
(ft); Nurses' aides 9 (ft); Activities
coordinators 1 (ft); Dietitians 1 (ft).
Facilities Dining room; Activities room;
Laundry room; Barber/Beauty shop.
Activities Arts & crafts; Games; Reading
groups; Prayer groups; Movies; Dances/
Social/Cultural gatherings.

Union City Health Care Center
1105 Sunswept Dr, Union City, TN 38261
(901) 885-6400
Licensure Skilled care; Intermediate care. *Beds*
120. *Certified* Medicaid; Medicare.
Owner Proprietary corp (Beverly Enterprises).

Union City Manor Nursing Center
PO Box 509, 1630 Reelfoot Ave, Union City,
TN 38261
(901) 885-8095
Admin Gary K Snyder. *Dir of Nursing* Beth
Huff. *Medical Dir* Dr Grover Schleifer.
Licensure Intermediate care. *Beds* ICF 83.
Private Pay Patients 26%. *Certified*
Medicaid.
Owner Proprietary corp (American Health
Centers Inc).
Admissions Requirements Minimum age 14.
Staff Physicians 1 (pt); RNs 1 (ft); LPNs 5
(ft), 2 (pt); Nurses' aides 22 (ft), 5 (pt);
Physical therapists 1 (pt); Occupational
therapists 1 (pt); Speech therapists 1 (pt);
Activities coordinators 1 (ft); Dietitians 1
(ft); Ophthalmologists 1 (pt); Podiatrists 1
(pt).
Facilities Dining room; Activities room;
Crafts room; Laundry room; Barber/Beauty
shop; Library.
Activities Arts & crafts; Cards; Games;
Reading groups; Prayer groups; Movies;
Shopping trips; Dances/Social/Cultural
gatherings; Intergenerational programs; Pet
therapy.

Wartburg

Life Care Center of Morgan County
419 Potters Falls Rd, Wartburg, TN 37887
(615) 346-6691, 346-7031 FAX
Admin Bryan Newmyer. *Dir of Nursing* Peggy
Vespie RN. *Medical Dir* Dwight Willett
MD.
Licensure Intermediate care. *Beds* ICF 124.
Private Pay Patients 18%. *Certified*
Medicaid.
Owner Proprietary corp (Life Care Centers of
America).
Admissions Requirements Minimum age 14;
Medical examination; Physician's request.
Staff Physicians 1 (pt); RNs 3 (ft); LPNs 10
(ft), 4 (pt); Nurses' aides 27 (ft), 14 (pt);
Physical therapists 1 (pt); Occupational
therapists 1 (pt); Speech therapists 1 (pt);
Activities coordinators 1 (pt); Dietitians 1
(pt); Podiatrists 2 (pt).
Facilities Dining room; Physical therapy
room; Activities room; Crafts room; Laundry
room; Barber/Beauty shop.
Activities Arts & crafts; Games; Prayer groups;
Movies; Dances/Social/Cultural gatherings.

Waverly

Humphreys County Nursing Home Inc
S Church St, Waverly, TN 37185
(615) 296-2532

Admin Steve Lee. *Dir of Nursing* Shelly
Jackson.
Licensure Intermediate care. *Beds* ICF 70.
Certified Medicaid.
Owner Nonprofit corp.
Admissions Requirements Minimum age 18;
Physician's request; Humphreys County
residents only.
Staff RNs; LPNs; Nurses' aides; Physical
therapists; Recreational therapists; Activities
coordinators; Dietitians.
Facilities Dining room; Activities room;
Crafts room; Laundry room; Barber/Beauty
shop.
Activities Arts & crafts; Cards; Games;
Reading groups; Prayer groups; Movies;
Shopping trips; Dances/Social/Cultural
gatherings.

Waynesboro

Wayne Care Nursing Home
505 S High St, Waynesboro, TN 38485
(615) 722-5832
Licensure Intermediate care. *Beds* ICF 46.
Certified Medicaid.
Owner Proprietary corp (National Healthcare
Inc).

Wayne County Nursing Home
PO Box 510, Hwy 64 E, Waynesboro, TN
38485
(615) 722-3641
Licensure Intermediate care. *Beds* ICF 79.
Certified Medicaid.

Whites Creek

**Brookside Manor Nursing Home & Home for
the Aged**
3425 Knight Rd, Whites Creek, TN 37189-
9189
(615) 876-2754
Admin Gerald D Williams.
Licensure Intermediate care; Home for aged.
Beds ICF 54; Home for aged 54. *Certified*
Medicaid.
Owner Privately owned.
Admissions Requirements Minimum age 14.
Facilities Dining room.
Activities Arts & crafts; Cards; Games;
Reading groups; Prayer groups; Movies;
Dances/Social/Cultural gatherings.

Winchester

Franklin County Health Care Center
Rte 3, 41-A Bypass, Winchester, TN 37398
(615) 967-7082

Admin Joseph R Hagan. *Dir of Nursing*
Vallerie Rose RN. *Medical Dir* Dudley Fort
MD.
Licensure Skilled care; Intermediate care. *Beds*
120. *Certified* Medicaid; Medicare.
Owner Proprietary corp (Beverly Enterprises).
Admissions Requirements Medical
examination.
Staff Physicians; RNs; LPNs; Nurses' aides;
Physical therapists; Activities coordinators;
Dietitians.
Facilities Dining room; Physical therapy
room; Activities room; Barber/Beauty shop;
Dayrooms on each wing.
Activities Arts & crafts; Cards; Games; Prayer
groups; Movies; Shopping trips; Dances/
Social/Cultural gatherings; Bingo; Bunko;
Daily coffee break; Birthday parties; Wine &
cheese parties.

Health Inn Nursing Home
PO Box 493, Shirley Dr, Winchester, TN
37398
(615) 967-0200
Beds 66.

Methodist Nursing Home of Middle Tennessee
Cowan Rd, Winchester, TN 37398
(615) 967-7249
Admin Robert Rose. *Dir of Nursing* Louvena
Glass.
Licensure Intermediate care. *Beds* ICF 40.
Certified Medicaid; Medicare.
Owner Nonprofit corp.
Admissions Requirements Medical
examination; Physician's request.
Staff RNs 3 (ft); LPNs 3 (ft), 1 (pt); Nurses'
aides 9 (ft), 3 (pt); Physical therapists;
Activities coordinators 1 (ft); Activities
coordinators.
Affiliation Methodist.
Facilities Dining room; Physical therapy
room; Activities room; Laundry room;
Barber/Beauty shop.
Activities Arts & crafts; Cards; Games;
Reading groups; Prayer groups; Movies;
Shopping trips; Dances/Social/Cultural
gatherings; Rhythm band.

Woodbury

Woodbury Nursing Center Inc
119 W High St, Woodbury, TN 37190
(615) 563-5939
Licensure Intermediate care. *Beds* ICF 84.
Certified Medicaid.

TEXAS

Abilene

Abilene Convalescent Center
2630 Old Anson Rd, Abilene, TX 79603
(915) 673-5101
Admin Lexie L Hutchison.
Licensure Intermediate care. *Beds* 114.
　Certified Medicaid.
Owner Proprietary corp.

Care Inn of Abilene
4934 S 7th St, Abilene, TX 79605
(915) 692-2172
Admin Joyce Pylant.
Licensure Intermediate care. *Beds* 106.
　Certified Medicaid.
Owner Proprietary corp (ARA Living
　Centers).

Coronado Nursing Center
1751 N 15th St, Abilene, TX 79603
(915) 673-8892
Admin Ernest C Valle.
Medical Dir S Daggubati MD.
Licensure Intermediate care. *Beds* 235.
　Certified Medicaid.
Staff RNs 3 (ft); LPNs 18 (ft); Nurses' aides
　70 (ft); Activities coordinators 1 (ft);
　Dietitians 1 (ft).
Facilities Dining room; Activities room;
　Crafts room; Laundry room; Barber/Beauty
　shop.
Activities Arts & crafts; Cards; Games;
　Reading groups; Prayer groups; Movies;
　Shopping trips; Dances/Social/Cultural
　gatherings.

Mesa Springs Health Care Center
7171 Buffalo Gap Rd, Abilene, TX 79606
(915) 692-8080
Licensure Nursing. *Beds* Nursing 90.

Radford Hills Convalescent Center
725 Medical Dr, Abilene, TX 79601
(915) 672-3236
Admin Carolyn Martin.
Licensure Intermediate care. *Beds* 118.
　Certified Medicaid.
Owner Proprietary corp.

Sears Memorial Methodist Center
3202 S Willis St, Abilene, TX 79605
(915) 692-6145
Admin Chris Spence. *Dir of Nursing* Pearl
　Merritt. *Medical Dir* W Kenneth Day MD.
Licensure Intermediate care; Custodial care;
　Retirement; Alzheimer's care. *Beds* ICF 159;
　Custodial 51. *Certified* Medicaid.
Owner Nonprofit corp.
Admissions Requirements Minimum age 62;
　Medical examination; Physician's request.
Staff Physicians 1 (pt); RNs 1 (ft); LPNs 20
　(ft), 4 (pt); Nurses' aides 48 (ft), 25 (pt);
　Activities coordinators 2 (ft); Dietitians 1
　(ft), 1 (pt).
Languages Spanish.
Affiliation Methodist.

Facilities Dining room; Physical therapy
　room; Activities room; Crafts room; Laundry
　room; Barber/Beauty shop; Library; Enclosed
　courtyard; Family parlor.
Activities Arts & crafts; Cards; Games; Prayer
　groups; Movies; Shopping trips; Dances/
　Social/Cultural gatherings; Birthday parties;
　Religious; Educational; Family activities.

Shady Oaks Manor 1
2722 Old Anson Rd, Abilene, TX 79603
(915) 676-1644
Admin Melba Fisher.
Licensure Intermediate care. *Beds* 114.
　Certified Medicaid.
Owner Proprietary corp.

Shady Oaks Manor 2
2722 Old Anson Rd, Abilene, TX 79603
(915) 676-1677
Admin Velda Howard.
Medical Dir Jack S Haynes MD.
Licensure Skilled care. *Beds* 100. *Certified*
　Medicaid.
Admissions Requirements Medical
　examination; Physician's request.
Staff Physicians 1 (pt); RNs 1 (ft), 3 (pt);
　LPNs 12 (ft), 2 (pt); Nurses' aides 26 (ft);
　Activities coordinators 1 (ft); Dietitians 1
　(pt); Dentists 1 (pt).
Facilities Dining room; Physical therapy
　room; Activities room; Crafts room; Laundry
　room; Barber/Beauty shop; Library.
Activities Arts & crafts; Cards; Games;
　Reading groups; Prayer groups; Movies;
　Shopping trips.

Starr Nursing Home
RR 2 Box 746, Abilene, TX 79602
(915) 928-5673
Admin Brenda J Quinn.
Licensure Intermediate care. *Beds* 45.
　Certified Medicaid.
Owner Proprietary corp.

Albany

Bluebonnet Nursing Home
PO Box 608, Baird Hwy, Albany, TX 76430
(915) 762-3329
Admin William D Wakefield.
Licensure Intermediate care; Alzheimer's care.
　Beds ICF 80. *Certified* Medicaid.
Owner Proprietary corp (Beverly Enterprises).
Admissions Requirements Minimum age 18;
　Medical examination; Physician's request.
Staff Physicians; RNs; LPNs; Nurses' aides;
　Physical therapists; Reality therapists;
　Recreational therapists; Occupational
　therapists; Speech therapists; Activities
　coordinators; Dietitians.
Languages Spanish.
Facilities Dining room; Physical therapy
　room; Activities room; Crafts room; Laundry
　room; Barber/Beauty shop.
Activities Arts & crafts; Cards; Games;
　Reading groups; Prayer groups; Movies;
　Dances/Social/Cultural gatherings.

Alice

Hospitality House Inc
PO Box 1458, 218-219 N King St, Alice, TX
78333
(512) 664-4366
Admin Terry E Drake. *Dir of Nursing*
　Yolanda Cruz RN BSM. *Medical Dir* Dr R
　O Albert.
Licensure Skilled care; Intermediate care;
　Personal care; Adult day care. *Beds* SNF 81;
　ICF 50; Personal care 15. *Private Pay
　Patients* 5%. *Certified* Medicaid; Medicare.
Owner Proprietary corp.
Admissions Requirements Medical
　examination; Physician's request.
Staff Physicians 9 (ft); RNs 2 (ft), 4 (pt);
　LPNs 15 (ft), 3 (pt); Nurses' aides 65 (ft), 15
　(pt); Physical therapists 4 (pt); Occupational
　therapists 1 (pt); Speech therapists 1 (pt);
　Activities coordinators 2 (ft); Dietitians 2
　(ft); Ophthalmologists 2 (pt); Podiatrists 1
　(pt).
Languages Spanish.
Facilities Dining room; Physical therapy
　room; Activities room; Barber/Beauty shop.
Activities Arts & crafts; Cards; Games;
　Reading groups; Prayer groups; Movies;
　Shopping trips; Dances/Social/Cultural
　gatherings; Intergenerational programs;
　Happy hour.

Retama Manor Nursing Center
606 Coyote Trail, Alice, TX 78332
(512) 664-5479
Admin Mary Lou Van Alstyne.
Licensure Intermediate care. *Beds* 140.
　Certified Medicaid.
Owner Proprietary corp (ARA Living
　Centers).

Alpine

Valle Star Nursing Home
1003 Loop Rd, Alpine, TX 79830
(915) 837-3343
Admin Tom Wright.
Medical Dir Ruth Apolinar.
Licensure Intermediate care. *Beds* 56.
　Certified Medicaid.
Admissions Requirements Physician's request.
Staff Physicians; RNs; Nurses' aides;
　Activities coordinators; Dietitians.
Facilities Dining room; Activities room;
　Crafts room; Laundry room; Barber/Beauty
　shop.
Activities Arts & crafts; Cards; Games;
　Reading groups; Prayer groups; Movies;
　Shopping trips; Dances/Social/Cultural
　gatherings; Field trips.

Alto

Carriage Park Nursing Center
PO Box 140, 305 Maggie Sessions, Alto, TX
75925
(409) 858-2255

Admin Patricia A Jeffcoat. *Dir of Nursing*
Elizabeth Amazeen RN. *Medical Dir* Dr
Robert Carroll.
Licensure Skilled care; Intermediate care. *Beds*
SNF 24; ICF 66. *Private Pay Patients* 2%.
Certified Medicaid; Medicare.
Owner Proprietary corp.
Admissions Requirements Medical
examination; Physician's request.
Staff RNs 1 (ft), 2 (pt); LPNs 8 (ft), 8 (pt);
Nurses' aides; Activities coordinators 1 (ft);
Dietitians.
Languages Spanish.
Facilities Dining room; Crafts room; Barber/
Beauty shop.
Activities Arts & crafts; Cards; Games;
Reading groups; Prayer groups; Movies;
Shopping trips; Intergenerational programs;
Pet therapy.

Alvarado

Alvarado Nursing Home
100 N Parkway, Alvarado, TX 76009
(817) 783-3304
Admin Genevieve H Tucker.
Licensure Skilled care. *Beds* 121. *Certified*
Medicaid.
Owner Proprietary corp.

Alvin

Alvin Convalescent Center
416 N Shirley, Alvin, TX 77511
(713) 585-8484
Admin Roberta Miller. *Dir of Nursing* Onella
Sue Moore LVN. *Medical Dir* Dale Messer
MD.
Licensure Intermediate care. *Beds* ICF 98.
Private Pay Patients 35%. *Certified*
Medicaid.
Owner Proprietary corp (Cantex Healthcare
Centers).
Admissions Requirements Medical
examination; Physician's request.
Staff Physicians 1 (pt); RNs 1 (pt); LPNs 5
(ft); Nurses' aides 17 (ft); Physical therapists
1 (pt); Occupational therapists 1 (pt); Speech
therapists 1 (pt); Activities coordinators 1
(ft); Dietitians 1 (pt).
Facilities Dining room; Crafts room; Laundry
room; Barber/Beauty shop.
Activities Arts & crafts; Cards; Games; Prayer
groups; Movies; Shopping trips; Dances/
Social/Cultural gatherings.

Winchester Lodge
1112 Smith Dr, Alvin, TX 77511
(713) 331-6125
Admin Sylvia Donelly. *Dir of Nursing* Lolly
Dickson RN.
Licensure Intermediate care; Personal care;
Supervised living. *Beds* ICF 96; Personal
care 25; Supervised living 21. *Certified*
Medicaid.
Owner Proprietary corp (ARA Living
Centers).
Admissions Requirements Medical
examination.
Staff RNs 1 (ft); LPNs 6 (ft); Nurses' aides 12
(ft); Activities coordinators 1 (ft); Dietitians
1 (ft).
Languages Spanish.
Facilities Dining room; Activities room;
Crafts room; Laundry room; Barber/Beauty
shop; Library.
Activities Arts & crafts; Cards; Games;
Reading groups; Prayer groups; Movies;
Shopping trips; Dances/Social/Cultural
gatherings.

Amarillo

Amarillo Good Samaritan Retirement Center
2200 7th St, Amarillo, TX 79106
(806) 374-6896

Admin Virginia Langston.
Medical Dir Mickey Suit.
Licensure Intermediate care; Alzheimer's care;
Retirement. *Beds* ICF 59. *Certified*
Medicaid.
Owner Proprietary corp.
Admissions Requirements Physician's request.
Staff RNs 1 (ft), 1 (pt); LPNs 6 (ft), 4 (pt);
Nurses' aides 22 (ft), 2 (pt); Activities
coordinators 1 (ft); Dietitians 1 (ft).
Facilities Dining room; Physical therapy
room; Activities room; Chapel; Crafts room;
Laundry room; Barber/Beauty shop; Library.
Activities Arts & crafts; Cards; Games;
Reading groups; Prayer groups; Movies;
Shopping trips; Dances/Social/Cultural
gatherings.

Amarillo Nursing Center
4033 W 51st St, Amarillo, TX 79109
(806) 355-4488
Admin Peggy Richburg.
Medical Dir Suzane Porter.
Licensure Intermediate care; Personal care.
Beds ICF 120; Personal 40. *Certified*
Medicaid.
Owner Proprietary corp (Beverly Enterprises).
Staff RNs 1 (ft); LPNs 5 (ft); Nurses' aides 10
(ft); Activities coordinators 1 (ft); Dietitians
1 (ft).
Facilities Dining room; Activities room;
Crafts room; Laundry room; Barber/Beauty
shop.
Activities Arts & crafts; Cards; Games;
Reading groups; Prayer groups; Movies;
Shopping trips; Dances/Social/Cultural
gatherings.

Elizabeth Jane Bivins Home for the Aged
PO Box 31450, 3115 Tee Anchor Blvd,
Amarillo, TX 79120
(806) 373-7671
Admin Maggie Cleo Cox. *Dir of Nursing*
Marquitta Elliott. *Medical Dir* Charles
Wright.
Licensure Intermediate care; Retirement. *Beds*
ICF 36; Retirement 7. *Private Pay Patients*
30%. *Certified* Medicaid.
Owner Nonprofit organization/foundation.
Admissions Requirements Medical
examination; Physician's request.
Staff LPNs; Nurses' aides; Physical therapists;
Activities coordinators; Dietitians.
Facilities Dining room; Physical therapy
room; Activities room; Chapel; Crafts room;
Laundry room; Barber/Beauty shop; Library.
Activities Arts & crafts; Cards; Games;
Reading groups; Prayer groups; Movies;
Shopping trips.

Bivins Memorial Nursing Home
1001 Wallace Blvd, Amarillo, TX 79106
(806) 355-7453
Admin Judy A Mosley. *Dir of Nursing* Bonnie
McMillan RN. *Medical Dir* Karen Holman
MD.
Licensure Skilled care; Intermediate care;
Alzheimer's care. *Beds* SNF 72; ICF 68.
Private Pay Patients 30%. *Certified*
Medicaid; Medicare.
Owner Nonprofit organization/foundation.
Admissions Requirements Medical
examination; Physician's request.
Staff Physicians 1 (pt); RNs 8 (ft), 1 (pt);
LPNs 34 (ft), 4 (pt); Nurses' aides 65 (ft), 10
(pt); Physical therapists 1 (ft), 1 (pt); Reality
therapists 1 (ft); Activities coordinators 1
(ft); Dietitians 1 (ft).
Facilities Dining room; Physical therapy
room; Activities room; Chapel; Crafts room;
Laundry room; Barber/Beauty shop; Library.
Activities Arts & crafts; Cards; Games;
Reading groups; Prayer groups; Movies;
Shopping trips; Dances/Social/Cultural
gatherings; Intergenerational programs.

Bryanwood Care Center
2423 Line Ave, Amarillo, TX 79106
(806) 376-7241
Admin Margurite Van Zandt.
Licensure Intermediate care. *Beds* 74.
Certified Medicaid.
Owner Proprietary corp.

Country Club Manor
9 Medical Dr, Amarillo, TX 79106
(806) 352-2731
Admin Wayne Campbell.
Medical Dir Rita Arthur.
Licensure Intermediate care. *Beds* ICF 102.
Certified Medicaid.
Owner Proprietary corp.
Staff LPNs; Nurses' aides; Physical therapists;
Speech therapists; Activities coordinators;
Dietitians.

Georgia Manor Nursing Home
2611 SW 46th St, Amarillo, TX 79110
(806) 355-6517
Admin Laverne Munoz. *Dir of Nursing* Mary
Amerson RN.
Licensure Intermediate care. *Beds* ICF 56.
Certified Medicaid; VA Contracts.
Owner Privately owned.
Admissions Requirements Medical
examination; Physician's request.
Staff LPNs 5 (ft), 1 (pt); Nurses' aides 8 (ft);
Activities coordinators; Dietitians.
Facilities Dining room; Activities room;
Laundry room; Barber/Beauty shop.
Activities Arts & crafts; Cards; Games;
Reading groups; Prayer groups; Movies;
Dances/Social/Cultural gatherings; Parties;
Resident Council; Family dinner night.

Golden Age Care Center
1601 Kirkland Dr, Amarillo, TX 79106
(806) 355-8281
Admin Sarah Rice. *Dir of Nursing* Terri Pace
RN.
Licensure Intermediate care. *Beds* ICF 98.
Certified Medicaid.
Owner Nonprofit organization/foundation.
Admissions Requirements Medical
examination; Physician's request.
Staff RNs 1 (pt); LPNs 8 (ft), 1 (pt); Nurses'
aides 22 (ft), 5 (pt); Activities coordinators 2
(ft); Dietitians 1 (pt).
Facilities Dining room; Activities room;
Laundry room; Barber/Beauty shop.
Activities Arts & crafts; Cards; Games;
Reading groups; Prayer groups; Shopping
trips; Dances/Social/Cultural gatherings.

Heritage Convalescent Center
1009 Clyde, Amarillo, TX 79106
(806) 352-5295
Admin Myrtis Mosley. *Dir of Nursing* Randall
Drumm RN. *Medical Dir* Donald Frank
MD.
Licensure Skilled care; Intermediate care. *Beds*
SNF 58; ICF 58. *Private Pay Patients* 33%.
Certified Medicaid; Medicare.
Owner Proprietary corp (Stebbins Five
Companies).
Admissions Requirements Medical
examination; Physician's request.
Staff RNs 3 (ft); LPNs 13 (ft), 2 (pt); Nurses'
aides 50 (ft); Physical therapists 1 (pt);
Occupational therapists 1 (pt); Speech
therapists 1 (pt); Activities coordinators 2
(ft); Dietitians 1 (pt).
Languages Sign.
Facilities Dining room; Activities room;
Crafts room; Laundry room; Barber/Beauty
shop.
Activities Arts & crafts; Cards; Games;
Reading groups; Prayer groups; Movies;
Dances/Social/Cultural gatherings;
Intergenerational programs; Pet therapy.

Olsen Manor Nursing Home
3350 Olsen Blvd, Amarillo, TX 79109
(806) 355-9726

Admin Phillip E Kielpinski.
Licensure Intermediate care; Custodial care.
  Beds ICF 120. *Certified* Medicaid.
Owner Proprietary corp.

Vida Nueva Care Center
1931 Medi Park Dr, Amarillo, TX 79106
(806) 353-7433
Admin Wayne Gray.
Medical Dir Harlan Wilson.
Licensure Intermediate care. *Beds* 124.
  Certified Medicaid.
Staff RNs 1 (ft); LPNs 9 (ft); Nurses' aides 25
  (ft); Physical therapists 1 (pt); Occupational
  therapists 1 (pt); Speech therapists 1 (pt);
  Activities coordinators 1 (ft); Dietitians 1
  (ft).
Facilities Dining room; Activities room;
  Crafts room; Laundry room; Barber/Beauty
  shop.
Activities Arts & crafts; Cards; Games;
  Reading groups; Prayer groups; Movies;
  Shopping trips; Dances/Social/Cultural
  gatherings.

Vivian's Nursing Home
508 N Taylor St, Amarillo, TX 79107
(806) 372-6822
Admin Jack D Rude.
Licensure Intermediate care. *Beds* 53.
  Certified Medicaid.
Owner Proprietary corp.

Ware Memorial Care Center
1300 S Harrison St, Amarillo, TX 79101
(806) 376-1177
Licensure Nursing. *Beds* Nursing 56.

Westcliff
5601 Plum Creek Dr, Amarillo, TX 79124
(806) 359-9666
Admin Gennell York. *Dir of Nursing* Shirley
  Plunk RN. *Medical Dir* Dr Harold Hartman.
Licensure Skilled care. *Beds* SNF 160.
Owner Proprietary corp (Retirement Living
  Affiliates).
Staff RNs; LPNs; Nurses' aides; Physical
  therapists; Occupational therapists; Speech
  therapists; Activities coordinators; Dietitians;
  Ophthalmologists; Podiatrists; Audiologists.

Amherst

Amherst Manor Nursing Home
PO Box 489, 700 Main St, Amherst, TX
  79312
(806) 246-3583
Admin Mamie Dangerfield.
Medical Dir Carol Warren.
Licensure Intermediate care; Alzheimer's care.
  Beds ICF 30. *Certified* Medicaid.
Owner Proprietary corp.
Admissions Requirements Medical
  examination; Physician's request.
Staff Nurses' aides 8 (ft); Activities
  coordinators 1 (ft); Dietitians; LVNs 4 (ft).
Facilities Dining room; Activities room;
  Crafts room; Laundry room; Lobby.
Activities Arts & crafts; Cards; Games;
  Reading groups; Prayer groups; Movies;
  Shopping trips; Dances/Social/Cultural
  gatherings.

Anahuac

Leisure Lodge
PO Drawer W, Front St, Anahuac, TX 77514
(409) 267-3164
Admin Minnie L Smith. *Dir of Nursing* Carol
  Waters RN. *Medical Dir* Raul Nadal MD.
Licensure Skilled care. *Beds* SNF 100. *Private
  Pay Patients* 2%. *Certified* Medicaid;
  Medicare.
Owner Proprietary corp (Beverly Enterprises).
Admissions Requirements Medical
  examination; Physician's request.

Staff RNs 1 (ft), 1 (pt); LPNs 4 (ft), 3 (pt);
  Nurses' aides 15 (ft), 6 (pt); Physical
  therapists 1 (pt); Activities coordinators 1
  (ft); Dietitians 1 (ft); Podiatrists 1 (pt).
Facilities Dining room; Chapel; Laundry
  room; Barber/Beauty shop.
Activities Arts & crafts; Cards; Games;
  Reading groups; Movies; Shopping trips;
  Dances/Social/Cultural gatherings;
  Intergenerational programs; Pet therapy.

Andrews

Andrews Nursing Center
620 Hospital Dr, Andrews, TX 79714
(915) 523-4986
Admin Virginia S Clegg.
Licensure Intermediate care. *Beds* 98.
  Certified Medicaid.
Owner Proprietary corp (Beverly Enterprises).

Angleton

Country Village Care Inc
721 W Mulberry St, Angleton, TX 77515
(409) 849-8281
Admin Joy Teague.
Licensure Intermediate care. *Beds* 103.
  Certified Medicaid.
Owner Proprietary corp.

Cypress Woods Care Center
135 1/2 Hospital Dr, Angleton, TX 77515
(409) 849-8221
Admin Velda Phelps-Wasson. *Dir of Nursing*
  Donna Britt. *Medical Dir* Ben Weiner MD.
Licensure Intermediate care. *Beds* ICF 104.
  Private Pay Patients 75%. *Certified*
  Medicaid.
Owner Privately owned.
Admissions Requirements Minimum age 70;
  Physician's request.
Staff RNs 2 (ft); LPNs 12 (ft); Nurses' aides
  45 (ft); Physical therapists; Activities
  coordinators 1 (ft), 2 (pt); Dietitians 1 (ft);
  chaplains.
Facilities Dining room; Activities room;
  Laundry room; Barber/Beauty shop.
Activities Arts & crafts; Games; Prayer groups;
  Movies; Pet therapy.

Anson

Briarstone Manor
125 Ave J, Anson, TX 79501
(915) 823-3471, 823-3131
Admin Lorene Beason.
Medical Dir Diana Moore.
Licensure Intermediate care. *Beds* ICF 70.
  Certified Medicaid.
Owner Proprietary corp (Beverly Enterprises).
Staff RNs 1 (pt); LPNs 5 (ft), 3 (pt); Nurses'
  aides 15 (ft), 3 (pt); Activities coordinators 1
  (ft).
Facilities Dining room; Activities room;
  Chapel; Laundry room; Barber/Beauty shop.
Activities Arts & crafts; Games; Prayer groups;
  Dances/Social/Cultural gatherings.

Valley View Care Center
101 Liberty Ln, Anson, TX 79501
(915) 823-2141
Admin Frances A Ward.
Licensure Intermediate care. *Beds* 36.
  Certified Medicaid.
Admissions Requirements Medical
  examination; Physician's request.
Staff RNs 1 (pt); LPNs 3 (ft), 2 (pt); Nurses'
  aides 9 (ft), 2 (pt); Activities coordinators 1
  (ft); Dietitians 1 (pt).
Facilities Dining room; Activities room;
  Chapel; Crafts room; Laundry room; Barber/
  Beauty shop.
Activities Arts & crafts; Cards; Games;
  Reading groups; Prayer groups; Shopping
  trips; Dances/Social/Cultural gatherings.

Aransas Pass

Aransas Pass Nursing & Convalescent Center
1661 W Yoakum St, Aransas Pass, TX 78336
(512) 758-7686
Admin Joyce Corry. *Dir of Nursing* Louise
  Wheeler RN.
Licensure Intermediate care. *Beds* 170.
  Certified Medicaid.
Owner Proprietary corp (Diversicare Corp).
Admissions Requirements Medical
  examination; Physician's request.
Staff RNs 1 (ft); LPNs 12 (ft), 2 (pt); Nurses'
  aides 20 (ft), 12 (ft); Activities coordinators
  1 (ft); Dietitians 1 (ft).
Languages Spanish.
Facilities Dining room; Activities room;
  Crafts room; Laundry room; Barber/Beauty
  shop.
Activities Arts & crafts; Cards; Games;
  Reading groups; Prayer groups; Movies;
  Shopping trips; Dances/Social/Cultural
  gatherings.

Archer City

Archer Nursing Home
PO Box 786, Archer City, TX 76351
(817) 574-4551
Admin Edith V Lawrence.
Licensure Intermediate care. *Beds* 46.
  Certified Medicaid.
Admissions Requirements Medical
  examination.
Staff RNs 1 (pt); LPNs 2 (ft), 1 (pt); Nurses'
  aides 13 (ft), 2 (pt); Activities coordinators 1
  (ft); Dietitians 1 (ft).
Facilities Dining room; Activities room;
  Laundry room.
Activities Arts & crafts; Cards; Games;
  Reading groups; Prayer groups; Movies;
  Dances/Social/Cultural gatherings; Church;
  Singing; Square dancing.

Arlington

All Seasons Nursing Center
301 W Randol Mill Rd, Arlington, TX 76011
(817) 460-2002
Licensure Nursing. *Beds* Nursing 120.

Arlington Nursing Center
301 W Randol Mill Rd, Arlington, TX 76010
(817) 460-2002
Admin Victoria Ray.
Licensure Intermediate care. *Beds* 120.
  Certified Medicaid.
Owner Proprietary corp.

Arlington Villa for Senior Citizens
2601 W Randol Mill Rd, Arlington, TX 76012
(817) 274-5571
Admin Genevieve Sims.
Licensure Intermediate care. *Beds* 148.
  Certified Medicaid.
Admissions Requirements Minimum age 62;
  Medical examination; Physician's request.
Staff RNs 1 (ft), 1 (pt); LPNs 7 (ft), 1 (pt);
  Nurses' aides 14 (ft); Activities coordinators
  1 (ft); Dietitians 1 (ft).
Facilities Dining room; Activities room;
  Chapel; Laundry room; Barber/Beauty shop;
  Library.
Activities Arts & crafts; Games; Prayer groups;
  Movies; Shopping trips; Dances/Social/
  Cultural gatherings.

Dal Worth Care Center
405 Duncan Perry, Arlington, TX 76011
(817) 649-3366
Admin Pat Koon. *Dir of Nursing* Ann Mann.
  Medical Dir James A McLaughlin.
Licensure Intermediate care; Alzheimer's care.
  Beds ICF 120. *Certified* Medicaid.
Owner Proprietary corp (Unicare).
Admissions Requirements Medical
  examination; Physician's request.

Staff Physicians 1 (pt); RNs 1 (ft); LPNs 13 (ft); Nurses' aides 42 (ft); Physical therapists 1 (pt); Reality therapists 1 (pt); Recreational therapists 1 (pt); Speech therapists 1 (pt); Activities coordinators 1 (ft); Dietitians 1 (ft); Podiatrists 1 (pt).
Facilities Dining room; Physical therapy room; Activities room; Chapel; Crafts room; Laundry room; Barber/Beauty shop; Library.
Activities Arts & crafts; Cards; Games; Reading groups; Prayer groups; Movies; Shopping trips; Dances/Social/Cultural gatherings; Intergenerational programs; Pet therapy; Volunteer program; Family program.

Eastern Star Home
1201 E Division, Arlington, TX 76011
(817) 265-1513
Admin Evelyn J Lutz. *Dir of Nursing* Vivian Barnett. *Medical Dir* Dr Edward Reichelt.
Licensure Noncertified infirmary; Retirement. *Beds* Noncertified infirmary 40; Retirement 100.
Owner Nonprofit organization/foundation.
Admissions Requirements Females only; Medical examination; Eastern Star member.
Staff Physicians (consultant); RNs; LPNs; Nurses' aides; Physical therapists (contracted); Reality therapists (contracted); Recreational therapists (contracted); Occupational therapists (contracted); Speech therapists (contracted); Activities coordinators; Dietitians; Ophthalmologists (contracted); Podiatrists (contracted); Audiologists (contracted).
Affiliation Order of Eastern Star.
Facilities Dining room; Activities room; Chapel; Laundry room; Barber/Beauty shop; Library.
Activities Arts & crafts; Cards; Games; Reading groups; Movies; Shopping trips; Dances/Social/Cultural gatherings; Intergenerational programs; Pet therapy.

Knights Templar Clinic
1501 W Division, Arlington, TX 76012
(817) 275-2893
Admin Dorothy B Health.
Licensure Intermediate care. *Beds* 60.
Owner Nonprofit corp.
Affiliation Masons.

Randol Mill Manor
2645 W Randol Mill Rd, Arlington, TX 76012
(817) 277-6789
Admin Barbara J Perkins.
Licensure Intermediate care. *Beds* 130. *Certified* Medicaid.
Owner Proprietary corp (Convalescent Services).
Admissions Requirements Medical examination.
Staff RNs 2 (ft); LPNs 8 (ft); Nurses' aides 30 (ft); Activities coordinators 1 (ft); Dietitians 1 (ft).
Facilities Dining room; Physical therapy room; Activities room; Laundry room; Barber/Beauty shop.
Activities Arts & crafts; Cards; Games; Prayer groups; Movies; Dances/Social/Cultural gatherings.

Aspermont

Gibson Nursing Center
PO Box 567, Aspermont, TX 79502
(817) 989-3526
Admin Beth Thomas. *Dir of Nursing* Mary Daniel.
Licensure Intermediate care. *Beds* ICF 80. *Certified* Medicaid.
Owner Proprietary corp (Beverly Enterprises).
Staff LPNs 4 (ft); Nurses' aides 6 (ft), 5 (pt); Activities coordinators 1 (ft); Dietitians 1 (pt).

Activities Arts & crafts; Cards; Games; Reading groups; Prayer groups; Movies; Dances/Social/Cultural gatherings.

Athens

Athens Nursing Home
305 S Palestine, Athens, TX 75751
(214) 675-2046, 675-8428 FAX
Admin Sam Hyden. *Dir of Nursing* Carolyn McPherson LVN. *Medical Dir* Robert M Eckert MD.
Licensure Intermediate care. *Beds* ICF 82. *Certified* Medicaid.
Owner Proprietary corp (Texas Health Enterprises).
Admissions Requirements Medical examination; Physician's request.
Staff LPNs 1 (ft), 16 (pt); Nurses' aides 1 (ft), 10 (pt).
Facilities Dining room; Activities room; Laundry room; Barber/Beauty shop.
Activities Arts & crafts; Cards; Games; Reading groups; Prayer groups; Movies.

Lakeside Convalescent Center
500 Valle Vista Rd, Athens, TX 75751
(214) 677-3434
Licensure Nursing. *Beds* Nursing 118.

Park Highlands
711 Lucas, Athens, TX 75751
(214) 675-7156, 8538
Admin Melba L Edwards.
Licensure Intermediate care. *Beds* 140. *Certified* Medicaid.
Owner Proprietary corp (ARA Living Centers).

South Place Nursing Center
Rte 2 Box 2827, 150 Gipson Rd, Athens, TX 75751
(214) 677-5864
Licensure Nursing. *Beds* Nursing 120.

Valvista Pavilion
500 Valle Vista Dr, Athens, TX 75751
(214) 675-8591
Admin Marie J Wood.
Medical Dir Dr A Dyphrone.
Licensure Intermediate care. *Beds* 118. *Certified* Medicaid.
Staff Physicians 1 (pt); RNs 1 (ft), 1 (pt); LPNs 8 (ft); Nurses' aides 33 (ft), 2 (pt); Activities coordinators 2 (ft); Dietitians 1 (ft), 1 (pt).
Facilities Dining room; Laundry room; Barber/Beauty shop.
Activities Arts & crafts; Games; Prayer groups; Movies; Shopping trips; Dances/Social/Cultural gatherings; Exercise class.

Woodlands Nursing Center
PO Box 1969, Hwy 31 W, Athens, TX 75751
(214) 677-5929
Licensure Nursing. *Beds* Nursing 120.

Atlanta

Pine Lodge Nursing Home
201 E 3rd, Atlanta, TX 75551
(214) 796-4461
Admin Betty Gardner. *Dir of Nursing* Glenda Page. *Medical Dir* Dr James Morris.
Licensure Intermediate care. *Beds* ICF 109. *Private Pay Patients* 25%. *Certified* Medicaid.
Owner Privately owned.
Admissions Requirements Minimum age 25; Medical examination; Physician's request.
Staff RNs 1 (ft); LPNs 8 (ft); Nurses' aides 38 (ft), 3 (pt); Physical therapists 1 (pt); Recreational therapists 1 (pt); Speech therapists 1 (pt); Activities coordinators 1 (ft); Dietitians 1 (pt); Podiatrists 1 (pt).

Facilities Dining room; Barber/Beauty shop.
Activities Arts & crafts; Games; Reading groups; Prayer groups; Movies; Dances/Social/Cultural gatherings; Pet therapy.

Rose Haven Retreat
Live Oak & S Williams, Atlanta, TX 75551
(214) 796-4127
Admin Leonard M Jester Jr.
Medical Dir James Morris MD.
Licensure Skilled care; Intermediate care. *Beds* SNF 45; ICF 63. *Certified* Medicaid.
Admissions Requirements Medical examination; Physician's request.
Staff Physicians 8 (pt); RNs 2 (ft), 1 (pt); LPNs 6 (ft), 2 (pt); Nurses' aides 22 (ft), 6 (pt); Activities coordinators 1 (ft); Dietitians 1 (pt); Ophthalmologists 1 (pt); Dentists 1 (pt).
Facilities Dining room; Physical therapy room; Activities room; Chapel; Crafts room; Laundry room; Barber/Beauty shop.
Activities Arts & crafts; Cards; Games; Reading groups; Prayer groups; Movies; Shopping trips; Dances/Social/Cultural gatherings.

Aubrey

Sundial Manors Nursing Home Inc
103 Surveyor Rd, Aubrey, TX 76227
(817) 686-2272
Admin Ray Dane.
Medical Dir Marion A Groff DO.
Licensure Skilled care. *Beds* 70. *Certified* Medicaid; Medicare.
Admissions Requirements Minimum age 18; Medical examination; Physician's request.
Staff RNs 2 (ft), 1 (pt); LPNs 11 (ft); Nurses' aides 13 (ft), 5 (pt); Physical therapists 1 (pt); Speech therapists 1 (pt); Activities coordinators 1 (ft); Dietitians 1 (ft), 1 (pt).
Facilities Dining room; Barber/Beauty shop; Library.
Activities Arts & crafts; Cards; Games; Reading groups; Prayer groups; Movies; Shopping trips; Dances/Social/Cultural gatherings.

Austin

Anderson Lane Care Center
7901 Lazy Ln, Austin, TX 78758
(512) 454-5621
Admin Janie Park. *Dir of Nursing* Patricia Hall LVN. *Medical Dir* Dr Peggy Russell.
Licensure Intermediate care. *Private Pay Patients* 20%. *Certified* Medicaid.
Owner Nonprofit corp.
Admissions Requirements Minimum age 17; Medical examination.
Staff LPNs 2 (ft), 4 (pt); Nurses' aides 12 (ft); Physical therapists (contracted); Activities coordinators 1 (ft); Dietitians.
Languages Spanish.
Facilities Dining room; Activities room; Crafts room; Laundry room; Barber/Beauty shop; Large fenced backyard.
Activities Arts & crafts; Cards; Games; Prayer groups; Movies; Shopping trips; Dances/Social/Cultural gatherings; Intergenerational programs; Pet therapy; Field trips.

Arnold's Care Center
3101 Govalle Ave, Austin, TX 78702
(512) 926-8117
Admin Marjorie D Austin.
Licensure Intermediate care. *Beds* 83. *Certified* Medicaid.
Owner Proprietary corp.

Austin Manor Nursing Home
5413 Guadalupe St, Austin, TX 78751
(512) 452-7316
Admin Lillian B Laughlin.

Licensure Intermediate care. Beds 60.
Certified Medicaid.
Owner Proprietary corp.

Austin Nursing Center
110 E Live Oak, Austin, TX 78704
(512) 444-3511
Admin Charles N Taylor. Dir of Nursing
Odilia San Miguel.
Licensure Intermediate care; Alzheimer's care.
Beds ICF 170. Certified Medicaid.
Owner Proprietary corp.
Admissions Requirements Medical
examination.
Staff RNs; Nurses' aides; Physical therapists;
Occupational therapists; Speech therapists;
Activities coordinators; Dietitians;
Ophthalmologists.
Languages Spanish.
Facilities Dining room; Activities room;
Crafts room; Laundry room; Barber/Beauty
shop; Library.
Activities Arts & crafts; Cards; Games;
Reading groups; Prayer groups; Movies;
Shopping trips; Dances/Social/Cultural
gatherings.

Barton Heights Nursing Home Inc
1606 Nash St, Austin, TX 78704
(512) 444-6708
Admin Mary E Zumwalt.
Licensure Intermediate care. Beds 60.
Certified Medicaid.
Owner Proprietary corp.

Buckner Monte Siesta Nursing Center
4501 Dudmar, Austin, TX 78735
(512) 892-1131
Admin David M Willson.
Licensure Intermediate care. Beds ICF 128.
Private Pay Patients 60%. Certified
Medicaid.
Owner Nonprofit corp (Buckner Baptist
Benevolences).
Admissions Requirements Minimum age 60;
Medical examination.
Staff RNs 1 (ft); LPNs 8 (ft), 3 (pt); Nurses'
aides 34 (ft); Activities coordinators 2 (ft);
Dietitians 1 (ft).
Affiliation Baptist.
Facilities Dining room; Activities room;
Laundry room; Barber/Beauty shop;
Solarium.
Activities Arts & crafts; Cards; Games;
Reading groups; Prayer groups; Movies;
Shopping trips; Dances/Social/Cultural
gatherings; Intergenerational programs; Pet
therapy.

Buckner Villa Siesta Home
1001 E Braker Ln, Austin, TX 78753
(512) 836-1515
Admin James H Cantrell.
Licensure Intermediate care. Beds 98.
Certified Medicaid.
Owner Nonprofit corp.
Affiliation Baptist.

Cameron Villa Rest Home
1109 E 52nd St, Austin, TX 78723
(512) 451-1673
Admin Charles Collins.
Licensure Intermediate care. Beds 41.
Certified Medicaid.
Owner Proprietary corp.

Capitol City Nursing Home
9052 Galewood Dr, Austin, TX 78758
(512) 836-9172
Admin Rita Balmforth.
Medical Dir Dr George Robison.
Licensure Skilled care. Beds 120. Certified
Medicaid.
Owner Proprietary corp (Beverly Enterprises).
Admissions Requirements Medical
examination.
Staff RNs 1 (ft), 1 (pt); LPNs 10 (ft), 5 (pt);
Nurses' aides 27 (ft), 2 (pt); Activities
coordinators 2 (ft); Dietitians 1 (ft).

Facilities Dining room; Activities room;
Laundry room; Barber/Beauty shop; Library.
Activities Arts & crafts; Cards; Games;
Reading groups; Prayer groups; Movies;
Shopping trips; Dances/Social/Cultural
gatherings.

Central Texas Care Center
8007 Burnet Rd, Austin, TX 78758
(512) 453-7389
Admin Mildred O Scheumack. Dir of Nursing
Elsie Dixon LVN.
Licensure Intermediate care. Beds ICF 96.
Certified Medicaid.
Owner Privately owned.
Admissions Requirements Medical
examination.
Staff Nurses' aides; Activities coordinators;
Dietitians; LVNs.
Languages Spanish.
Facilities Dining room; Activities room;
Laundry room; Barber/Beauty shop.
Activities Arts & crafts; Cards; Games;
Reading groups; Prayer groups; Movies;
Shopping trips; Dances/Social/Cultural
gatherings.

Cresthaven Childrens Center
4800 S 1st St, Austin, TX 78745
(512) 444-8551
Admin Robert Wolszon. Dir of Nursing
Debbie Robinson RN. Medical Dir Larry
Lewellyn DO.
Licensure Intermediate care for mentally
retarded. Beds 72. Certified Medicaid.
Owner Proprietary corp (Beverly Enterprises).
Admissions Requirements Minimum age 2 to
12.
Staff Physicians 1 (pt); RNs 1 (ft); LPNs 9
(ft); Nurses' aides 39 (ft), 8 (pt); Reality
therapists 1 (pt); Activities coordinators 2
(ft); Dietitians 1 (ft); Social worker 1 (ft).
Facilities Dining room; Physical therapy
room; Activities room; Laundry room.
Activities Games; Shopping trips; Dances/
Social/Cultural gatherings.

Cresthaven Nursing Center
6400 E Martin Luther King Blvd, Austin, TX
78724
(512) 926-5976
Admin Jerry Nelson. Dir of Nursing Linda
Trout RN.
Licensure Intermediate care for mentally
retarded. Beds ICF/MR 96. Certified
Medicaid.
Owner Nonprofit corp.
Admissions Requirements Minimum age 21.
Staff Physicians 3 (pt); RNs 3 (ft), 5 (pt);
LPNs 6 (ft), 4 (pt); Nurses' aides 80 (ft);
Physical therapists 1 (pt); Occupational
therapists 1 (pt); Speech therapists 1 (pt);
Activities coordinators 1 (ft); Dietitians 1
(ft); Ophthalmologists 1 (pt); Podiatrists 1
(pt); Dentists 1 (pt).
Languages Spanish.
Facilities Dining room; Activities room;
Crafts room; Laundry room.
Activities Arts & crafts; Cards; Games;
Reading groups; Prayer groups; Movies;
Shopping trips; Dances/Social/Cultural
gatherings; As required & meet needs &
abilities of clients.

Cullen Avenue Nursing Home
3509 Rogge Ln, Austin, TX 78723
(512) 454-6988
Admin Bobby Dockal.
Medical Dir Louise Eeds MD.
Licensure Intermediate care. Beds 60.
Certified Medicaid.
Staff Physicians 1 (ft), 2 (pt); RNs 1 (pt);
LPNs 2 (ft), 4 (pt); Nurses' aides 14 (ft), 3
(pt); Physical therapists 1 (pt); Speech
therapists 1 (pt); Activities coordinators 1
(ft); Dietitians 1 (pt); Podiatrists 1 (pt);
Dentists 1 (pt).

Facilities Dining room; Activities room;
Crafts room; Laundry room; Barber/Beauty
shop.
Activities Arts & crafts; Cards; Games;
Reading groups; Prayer groups; Movies;
Shopping trips; Dances/Social/Cultural
gatherings.

Delwood Nursing Center Inc
4407 Red River St, Austin, TX 78751
(512) 452-2533
Admin Billie G McGee.
Licensure Intermediate care. Beds 40.
Certified Medicaid.
Staff RNs 1 (ft); LPNs 2 (ft), 3 (pt); Nurses'
aides 11 (ft), 3 (pt); Activities coordinators 1
(pt).
Facilities Dining room; Activities room.
Activities Arts & crafts; Games; Prayer groups;
Dances/Social/Cultural gatherings.

Eastern Hills Convalescent Center
2806 Real St, Austin, TX 78722
(512) 474-1411
Licensure Nursing. Beds Nursing 204.

Four Seasons Nursing Center
500 E Saint Johns, Austin, TX 78752
(512) 454-9581
Admin Kenny Owings.
Medical Dir Alan Sonstien MD.
Licensure Skilled care; Intermediate care. Beds
233. Certified Medicaid; Medicare.
Owner Proprietary corp (Manor Care).
Admissions Requirements Medical
examination; Physician's request.
Staff RNs 9 (ft), 10 (pt); LPNs 4 (ft), 12 (pt);
Nurses' aides 18 (ft), 32 (pt); Physical
therapists 1 (pt); Reality therapists 2 (ft), 1
(pt); Occupational therapists 1 (pt); Speech
therapists 1 (pt); Ophthalmologists 1 (pt);
Activities coordinators 1 (pt); Dietitians 1
(pt); Dentists 1 (pt).
Facilities Dining room; Physical therapy
room; Activities room; Crafts room; Laundry
room; Barber/Beauty shop.
Activities Arts & crafts; Cards; Games;
Reading groups; Prayer groups; Movies;
Shopping trips; Dances/Social/Cultural
gatherings.

Lalla Convalescent Center
2915 Webberville Rd, Austin, TX 78702
(512) 477-0768
Licensure Nursing. Beds Nursing 120.

Maggie Johnson's Nursing Center
3406 E 17th St, Austin, TX 78721
(512) 926-4760
Admin Johnny E Slaughter.
Licensure Intermediate care. Beds 54.
Certified Medicaid.
Owner Proprietary corp.

Northwest Mediplex
5301 Duval Rd, Austin, TX 78759
(512) 345-1805
Admin Irene G Richter.
Medical Dir Ernest Schmatolla.
Licensure Intermediate care. Beds 388.
Certified Medicaid.
Owner Proprietary corp (Beverly Enterprises).
Facilities Dining room; Physical therapy
room; Activities room; Laundry room;
Barber/Beauty shop; Library.

Oakcrest Manor
9507 Hwy 290 E, Austin, TX 78724
(512) 272-5511
Admin Mary A Neal.
Licensure Intermediate care. Beds 66.
Certified Medicaid.
Owner Proprietary corp.

Pecan Grove Nursing Center
3101 Govalle, Austin, TX 78702
(512) 926-7871

Admin Beatrice V Burrell. *Dir of Nursing*
Shirley Nyberg RN, Acting. *Medical Dir* Dr
A Laurent.
Licensure Skilled care; Intermediate care. *Beds*
Swing beds SNF/ICF 83. *Private Pay
Patients* 2%. *Certified* Medicaid; Medicare.
Owner Proprietary corp (Masterhealth Care).
Staff Physicians; RNs; Nurses' aides; Physical
therapists; Activities coordinators; Dietitians.
Languages Spanish.
Facilities Dining room; Activities room;
Crafts room; Laundry room; Barber/Beauty
shop; Fenced backyard; Covered patio;
Pecan & fruit trees.
Activities Arts & crafts; Cards; Games;
Reading groups; Prayer groups; Movies;
Shopping trips; Dances/Social/Cultural
gatherings; Intergenerational programs; Pet
therapy; Religious services.

Retirement & Nursing Center
6909 Burnet Ln, Austin, TX 78757
(512) 452-5719, 452-3675 FAX
Admin Carolyn Perdue. *Dir of Nursing* Lisa
Balme RN.
Licensure Intermediate care. *Beds* ICF 104.
Private Pay Patients 100%.
Owner Proprietary corp (Stebbins Five
Companies).
Admissions Requirements Medical
examination; Physician's request.
Staff RNs 2 (ft), 1 (pt); LPNs 8 (ft), 2 (pt);
Nurses' aides 35 (ft), 5 (pt); Activities
coordinators 2 (ft), 2 (pt); Dietitians 1 (pt).
Facilities Dining room; Activities room;
Crafts room; Laundry room; Barber/Beauty
shop; 2 TV/Living rooms.
Activities Arts & crafts; Cards; Games;
Reading groups; Prayer groups; Movies;
Shopping trips; Dances/Social/Cultural
gatherings; Intergenerational programs; Pet
therapy.

Southwest Mediplex
1015 William Cannon Dr, Austin, TX 78745
(512) 443-1640
Admin Lisa Wilson.
Medical Dir Dr Allen Sonstein.
Licensure Intermediate care. *Beds* 182.
Certified Medicaid.
Owner Proprietary corp (Beverly Enterprises).
Admissions Requirements Medical
examination; Physician's request.
Staff RNs 2 (ft), 3 (pt); LPNs 6 (ft), 1 (pt);
Nurses' aides 21 (ft), 6 (pt); Activities
coordinators 1 (ft); Dietitians 1 (ft).
Facilities Dining room; Laundry room;
Barber/Beauty shop.
Activities Arts & crafts; Cards; Games;
Reading groups; Prayer groups; Movies;
Shopping trips; Dances/Social/Cultural
gatherings.

Southwood Nursing Home
3759 Valley View Rd, Austin, TX 78704
(512) 443-3436
Admin Irene G Richter.
Licensure Intermediate care. *Beds* 120.
Certified Medicaid.
Owner Proprietary corp.

Stonebrook Nursing Home
2806 Real St, Austin, TX 78722
(512) 474-1411
Admin Linda Matlock.
Licensure Skilled care; Intermediate care. *Beds*
204. *Certified* Medicaid; Medicare.
Owner Proprietary corp.

Walnut Hills Convalescent Center Inc
3509 Rogge Ln, Austin, TX 78723
(512) 926-2070
Admin Bobby Dockal.
Medical Dir Joyce Adams.
Licensure Intermediate care. *Beds* ICF 120.
Certified Medicaid.
Owner Proprietary corp.

Facilities Dining room; Physical therapy
room; Activities room; Chapel; Crafts room;
Laundry room; Barber/Beauty shop.
Activities Arts & crafts; Cards; Games;
Reading groups; Prayer groups; Movies;
Movies; Shopping trips; Dances/Social/
Cultural gatherings.

Westminster Health Care Center
4100 Jackson Ave, Austin, TX 78731
(512) 454-4645
Licensure Nursing. *Beds* Nursing 90.

Azle

Azle Manor Inc
225 Church St, Azle, TX 76020
(817) 444-2536
Admin McKinley Wayne Pack. *Dir of Nursing*
Janice Geisler. *Medical Dir* Jim Savage MD.
Licensure Skilled care. *Beds* SNF 127. *Private
Pay Patients* 30%. *Certified* Medicaid.
Owner Proprietary corp (Oak Management
Inc).
Staff RNs 2 (ft), 2 (pt); LPNs 11 (ft), 3 (pt);
Nurses' aides 35 (ft), 7 (pt); Activities
coordinators 1 (ft); Dietitians 1 (pt);
Ophthalmologists; Podiatrists.
Facilities Dining room; Activities room;
Crafts room; Laundry room; Barber/Beauty
shop.
Activities Arts & crafts; Cards; Games;
Reading groups; Prayer groups; Movies;
Shopping trips.

Baird

Canterbury Villa of Baird
240 E 6th St, Baird, TX 79504
(915) 854-1429
Admin Monica A Hawes.
Medical Dir Thelma Spann.
Licensure Intermediate care; Alzheimer's care.
Beds ICF 78. *Certified* Medicaid.
Owner Proprietary corp (Texas Health
Enterprises).
Admissions Requirements Minimum age 18;
Medical examination; Physician's request.
Staff LPNs 7 (ft); Nurses' aides; Activities
coordinators; Dietitians 1 (ft).
Languages Spanish.
Facilities Dining room; Activities room;
Crafts room; Laundry room; Barber/Beauty
shop.
Activities Arts & crafts; Cards; Games; Prayer
groups; Shopping trips; Dances/Social/
Cultural gatherings.

Balch Springs

Balch Springs Nursing Home
4200 Shepherd Ln, Balch Springs, TX 75180
(214) 286-0335
Admin Merril M Grey.
Medical Dir Paul Schorr.
Licensure Intermediate care. *Beds* 120.
Certified Medicaid.
Owner Proprietary corp (Beverly Enterprises).
Admissions Requirements Medical
examination; Physician's request.
Staff RNs 1 (ft); LPNs 10 (ft), 3 (pt); Nurses'
aides 22 (ft), 4 (pt); Activities coordinators 1
(ft); Dietitians 1 (ft).
Facilities Dining room; Activities room;
Chapel; Crafts room; Laundry room; Barber/
Beauty shop; Library.
Activities Arts & crafts; Cards; Games;
Reading groups; Prayer groups; Movies;
Shopping trips; Dances/Social/Cultural
gatherings.

Ballinger

Ballinger Nursing Center
1400 Country Club Ave, Ballinger, TX 76821
(915) 365-5666

Admin Darlene McDaniel.
Licensure Intermediate care. *Beds* 48.
Certified Medicaid.
Owner Proprietary corp.

Canterbury Villa of Ballinger
PO Box 309, Bronte Hwy, Ballinger, TX
76821
(915) 365-2538
Admin D W Sims.
Medical Dir Dr Antoine Albert.
Licensure Intermediate care. *Beds* 154.
Certified Medicaid.
Staff Physicians 4 (pt); LPNs 4 (ft), 2 (pt);
Nurses' aides 9 (ft), 7 (pt); Physical
therapists 1 (pt); Activities coordinators 1
(ft); Dietitians 2 (ft).
Facilities Dining room; Physical therapy
room; Activities room; Chapel; Crafts room;
Laundry room; Barber/Beauty shop; Library.
Activities Arts & crafts; Cards; Games;
Reading groups; Prayer groups; Movies;
Shopping trips; Dances/Social/Cultural
gatherings.

Bandera

Purple Hills Manor Inc
800 Montague Dr, Bandera, TX 78003
(512) 796-3767
Admin Preston Gray.
Medical Dir Alice Warnecke LVN.
Licensure Intermediate care; Alzheimer's care.
Beds ICF 62. *Certified* Medicaid.
Owner Privately owned.
Staff LPNs 3 (ft); Nurses' aides 18 (ft);
Physical therapists 1 (ft); Recreational
therapists 1 (ft); Activities coordinators 1
(ft); Dietitians 1 (ft).
Languages Spanish.
Facilities Dining room; Activities room;
Laundry room; Barber/Beauty shop.
Activities Cards; Games; Reading groups;
Prayer groups; Dances/Social/Cultural
gatherings; Music; Barbeques; Exercise.

Bangs

Bangs Nursing Home
PO Box 37, 1400 Fitzgerald St, Bangs, TX
76823
(915) 752-6321
Admin Glorris A Wolford.
Medical Dir Delores Daub.
Licensure Intermediate care. *Beds* ICF 48.
Certified Medicaid.
Owner Proprietary corp (ARA Living
Centers).
Admissions Requirements Physician's request.
Staff LPNs 4 (ft); Nurses' aides 7 (ft), 4 (pt);
Activities coordinators 1 (ft); Dietitians 3
(ft), 2 (pt).
Activities Arts & crafts; Cards; Games;
Reading groups; Prayer groups; Shopping
trips; Dances/Social/Cultural gatherings.

Twilight Nursing Home Inc
PO Box 130, Bangs, TX 76823
(915) 752-6322
Admin Wendell H Byler.
Licensure Intermediate care. *Beds* 41.
Certified Medicaid.
Owner Proprietary corp.

Bartlett

Will-O-Bell Inc
412 N Dalton, Bartlett, TX 76511
(817) 527-3371
Admin June D Fugate. *Dir of Nursing*
Hermania Vitek LVN. *Medical Dir* D W
Hopkins.
Licensure Intermediate care. *Beds* ICF 90.
Private Pay Patients 40%. *Certified*
Medicaid.
Owner Proprietary corp.

Admissions Requirements Medical examination; Physician's request.
Staff Physicians 1 (ft); RNs 1 (pt); LPNs 7 (ft); Nurses' aides 25 (ft); Physical therapists (contracted); Reality therapists (contracted); Recreational therapists (contracted); Occupational therapists (contracted); Speech therapists (contracted); Activities coordinators 1 (ft); Dietitians 1 (pt).
Languages Spanish, German, Czech.
Facilities Dining room; Activities room; Crafts room; Laundry room; Barber/Beauty shop.
Activities Arts & crafts; Cards; Games; Reading groups; Prayer groups; Movies; Shopping trips; Dances/Social/Cultural gatherings; Pet therapy.

Bastrop

Bastrop Nursing Center
PO Box 649, 400 Old Austin Hwy, Bastrop, TX 78602
(512) 321-2529
Admin Christopher C Bland. *Dir of Nursing* Anne Saegert. *Medical Dir* Dr Talley.
Licensure Intermediate care. *Beds* ICF 96. *Certified* Medicaid.
Owner Proprietary corp (ARA Living Centers).
Admissions Requirements Minimum age 18; Medical examination.
Staff RNs; LPNs; Nurses' aides; Recreational therapists; Activities coordinators; Dietitians.
Facilities Dining room; Activities room; Chapel; Laundry room; Barber/Beauty shop.
Activities Arts & crafts; Cards; Games; Reading groups; Prayer groups; Movies; Shopping trips; Dances/Social/Cultural gatherings; Fishing trips.

Bay City

Bay Villa Nursing Home
1800 13th St, Bay City, TX 77414
(409) 245-6327
Admin Polly Hedrick. *Dir of Nursing* Geraldine Sprys RN. *Medical Dir* Dr H C Matthes.
Licensure Skilled care; Intermediate care. *Beds* SNF 47; ICF 58. *Certified* Medicaid; Medicare.
Owner Proprietary corp (ARA Living Centers).
Admissions Requirements Medical examination; Physician's request.
Staff RNs 4 (ft); LPNs 11 (ft), 2 (pt); Nurses' aides 32 (ft), 3 (pt); Activities coordinators 1 (ft); Dietitians 1 (ft).
Languages Spanish.
Facilities Dining room; Activities room; Laundry room; Barber/Beauty shop.
Activities Arts & crafts; Cards; Games; Reading groups; Prayer groups; Movies; Shopping trips; Dances/Social/Cultural gatherings.

Matagorda House Nursing Home
1115 Ave G, Bay City, TX 77414
(409) 245-6383
Admin Pat Matthes. *Dir of Nursing* Louise Matthews RN. *Medical Dir* H C Matthes MD.
Licensure Skilled care. *Beds* SNF 28. *Certified* Medicaid; Medicare.
Owner Nonprofit corp.
Admissions Requirements Medical examination; Physician's request; TB screening.
Staff RNs 2 (ft); LPNs 4 (ft), 2 (pt); Nurses' aides 14 (ft); Physical therapists 1 (pt); Speech therapists 1 (pt); Activities coordinators 1 (ft); Dietitians 1 (pt); Ophthalmologists 1 (pt); Podiatrists 1 (pt); Audiologists 1 (pt); Dentists 1 (pt).
Languages Spanish.

Facilities Dining room; Chapel; Barber/Beauty shop.
Activities Cards; Games; Reading groups; Prayer groups; Parties.

Baytown

Allenbrook Healthcare Center
4109 Allenbrook Dr, Baytown, TX 77520
(713) 422-3546
Admin Jack E Hogston.
Medical Dir Susan Beth Shaffer.
Licensure Intermediate care. *Beds* ICF 120. *Certified* Medicaid.
Owner Proprietary corp (ARA Living Centers).
Admissions Requirements Medical examination.
Staff RNs 1 (ft); Nurses' aides 23 (ft), 1 (pt); Activities coordinators 1 (ft); Dietitians 1 (ft).
Facilities Dining room; Activities room; Crafts room; Laundry room; Barber/Beauty shop; Whirlpool room (2).
Activities Arts & crafts; Cards; Games; Movies; Shopping trips.

Baytown Nursing Home
1106 Park St, Baytown, TX 77520
(713) 427-1644, 1421
Admin Edward R Garrett.
Licensure Intermediate care. *Beds* 90. *Certified* Medicaid.
Owner Proprietary corp.

Green Acres Convalescent Center
2000 Beaumont, Baytown, TX 77520
(713) 427-4774
Admin Beverly Miller.
Licensure Intermediate care. *Beds* 100. *Certified* Medicaid.
Owner Proprietary corp (ARA Living Centers).

St James House of Baytown
5800 Baker Rd, Baytown, TX 77520
(713) 424-4541
Admin Elizabeth R Alexander. *Dir of Nursing* Leta Watkins. *Medical Dir* Keith Rapp MD.
Licensure Intermediate care; Semi-independent living ; Alzheimer's care. *Beds* ICF 68; Semi-independent living 37. *Private Pay Patients* 80%. *Certified* Medicaid.
Owner Nonprofit corp.
Admissions Requirements Minimum age 65; Medical examination.
Staff LPNs 13 (ft); Nurses' aides 45 (ft); Activities coordinators 1 (ft); Dietitians 1 (ft).
Languages Spanish.
Affiliation Episcopal.
Facilities Dining room; Activities room; Chapel; Crafts room; Laundry room; Barber/Beauty shop; 3 kitchens for residents' use; Restorative nursing room.
Activities Arts & crafts; Cards; Games; Reading groups; Prayer groups; Movies; Shopping trips; Dances/Social/Cultural gatherings; Pet therapy.

Beaumont

Adaptive Living Center—Southeast Texas
3755 Corley St, Beaumont, TX 77701
(713) 842-5900
Admin Martha Kirkpatrick.
Licensure Intermediate care for mentally retarded. *Beds* 130. *Certified* Medicaid.

Centerbury Villa of Beaumont
1175 Denton Dr, Beaumont, TX 77707
(409) 842-3120
Admin Margie Anders.
Medical Dir Dr J S Douglas.
Licensure Intermediate care. *Beds* 122. *Certified* Medicaid.
Owner Proprietary corp.

Staff Physicians 1 (pt); RNs 1 (ft); LPNs 8 (ft), 1 (pt); Nurses' aides 16 (ft), 2 (pt); Activities coordinators 1 (ft); Dietitians 1 (ft), 1 (pt); Podiatrists 1 (pt).
Facilities Dining room; Activities room; Crafts room; Laundry room; Barber/Beauty shop.
Activities Arts & crafts; Cards; Games; Reading groups; Prayer groups; Movies; Shopping trips; Dances/Social/Cultural gatherings.

College Street Nursing Center
4150 College St, Beaumont, TX 77707
(409) 842-0333
Admin Daniel G Wylie. *Dir of Nursing* Joann Reese LVN.
Licensure Intermediate care. *Beds* ICF 80. *Private Pay Patients* 30%. *Certified* Medicaid.
Owner Proprietary corp (Waverly Group).
Admissions Requirements Minimum age 16; Physician's request.
Staff LPNs 6 (ft); Nurses' aides 24 (ft); Physical therapists 3 (pt); Activities coordinators 1 (ft); Dietitians 1 (pt).
Facilities Dining room; Activities room; Crafts room; Laundry room; Barber/Beauty shop.
Activities Arts & crafts; Cards; Games; Prayer groups; Movies; Dances/Social/Cultural gatherings; Outreach program.

Glad Day Nursing Center
795 Lindberg Dr, Beaumont, TX 77707
(713) 842-0311
Admin Maggie E Davis.
Licensure Skilled care; Intermediate care. *Beds* 84. *Certified* Medicaid.
Facilities Dining room; Physical therapy room; Chapel; Crafts room.
Activities Arts & crafts; Cards; Games; Reading groups; Prayer groups; Movies; Shopping trips; Dances/Social/Cultural gatherings.

Green Acres Convalescent Center
11025 Old Voth Rd, Beaumont, TX 77708
(409) 892-9722
Admin Ruby L Marrero.
Licensure Intermediate care. *Beds* 146. *Certified* Medicaid.
Owner Proprietary corp (ARA Living Centers).

Hamilton Nursing Home
2660 Brickyard Rd, Beaumont, TX 77703
(409) 892-1533
Admin Martha Kirkpatrick. *Dir of Nursing* June Shell.
Licensure Intermediate care. *Beds* ICF 125. *Private Pay Patients* 90%. *Certified* Medicaid.
Owner Proprietary corp.
Admissions Requirements Minimum age 18; Physician's request.
Staff RNs 1 (ft); LPNs 10 (ft), 1 (pt); Nurses' aides 47 (ft), 5 (pt); Activities coordinators 2 (ft); Dietitians 1 (ft); Podiatrists 1 (ft), 1 (pt).
Facilities Dining room; Activities room; Laundry room; Barber/Beauty shop.
Activities Arts & crafts; Cards; Games; Prayer groups; Movies; Pet therapy.

Lindbergh Health Care Center
795 Lindbergh Dr, Beaumont, TX 77707
(409) 842-0311
Licensure Nursing. *Beds* Nursing 84.

Sabine Oaks Home
1945 Pennsylvania Ave, Beaumont, TX 77701
(409) 833-1989
Admin Rose M Stinnett. *Dir of Nursing* Cynthia Worthy.
Licensure Custodial care. *Beds* Custodial care 40. *Certified* Medicaid.
Owner Nonprofit corp.
Admissions Requirements Minimum age 60; Medical examination; Physician's request.

Staff RNs (consultant); LPNs; Nurses' aides; Activities coordinators; Dietitians (consultant).
Languages French.
Facilities Dining room; Activities room; Chapel; Crafts room; Laundry room; Barber/Beauty shop.
Activities Arts & crafts; Cards; Games; Reading groups; Prayer groups; Movies; Dances/Social/Cultural gatherings; Intergenerational programs; Pet therapy.

A W Schlesinger Geriatric Center Inc
PO Box 1990, 4195 Milan, Beaumont, TX 77707
(409) 842-4550
Admin Emma Jo Smith. *Dir of Nursing* Sybil Whitehead RN. *Medical Dir* Nicolas Rodriguez MD.
Licensure Skilled care; Intermediate care. *Beds* SNF 218; ICF 178. *Certified* Medicaid; Medicare.
Owner Nonprofit organization/foundation.
Admissions Requirements Minimum age 18; Medical examination; Physician's request.
Staff RNs 2 (ft), 1 (pt); LPNs 45 (ft), 5 (pt); Nurses' aides 100 (ft), 20 (pt); Physical therapists 1 (pt); Occupational therapists 1 (pt); Speech therapists 1 (pt); Activities coordinators 1 (ft); Dietitians 1 (ft).
Facilities Dining room; Physical therapy room; Activities room; Chapel; Crafts room; Laundry room; Barber/Beauty shop; Library; Greenhouse; Patios; Gift shop; Wheelchair-accessible van; Beauty/Barber shop.
Activities Arts & crafts; Cards; Games; Reading groups; Prayer groups; Movies; Shopping trips; Dances/Social/Cultural gatherings; Pet therapy; Bingo; Gardening; Outings; Monthly birthday party; Exercise programs; Religious services; Cooking program.

Bedford

H E B Nursing Center
2716 Tibbets Dr, Bedford, TX 76021
(817) 283-5511
Admin Sandra Hale.
Licensure Skilled care; Intermediate care. *Beds* 160. *Certified* Medicaid.
Owner Proprietary corp.

La Dora Lodge Nursing Home
1960 Bedford Rd, Bedford, TX 76021
(817) 283-4771
Admin Mary T Uebelhart.
Medical Dir Berradine Lupa.
Licensure Intermediate care. *Beds* ICF 66.
Owner Proprietary corp.
Admissions Requirements Medical examination.
Staff RNs 1 (ft); LPNs 5 (ft); Nurses' aides 15 (ft); Activities coordinators 1 (ft); Dietitians 1 (ft).
Facilities Dining room; Activities room; Crafts room; Laundry room; Barber/Beauty shop.
Activities Arts & crafts; Cards; Games; Reading groups; Prayer groups; Movies; Shopping trips; Dances/Social/Cultural gatherings.

Beeville

Arbor Care Center
4901 N Saint Mary's St, Beeville, TX 78102
(512) 358-5612
Admin Freddie Marie White. *Dir of Nursing* John C Coleman RN. *Medical Dir* Peter B Morgan.
Licensure Skilled care; Intermediate care. *Beds* Swing beds SNF/ICF 36. *Certified* Medicaid; Medicare.
Owner Proprietary corp (Arbor Living Centers).

Admissions Requirements Medical examination; Physician's request.
Staff Physicians 4 (pt); RNs 2 (ft), 3 (pt); LPNs 17 (ft), 5 (pt); Nurses' aides 27 (ft), 5 (pt); Physical therapists 2 (pt); Activities coordinators 1 (ft), 1 (pt); Dietitians.
Languages Spanish.
Facilities Dining room; Activities room; Crafts room; Laundry room; Barber/Beauty shop; Large patio.
Activities Arts & crafts; Cards; Games; Reading groups; Prayer groups; Pet therapy.

Hillside Lodge Nursing Home & Convalescent Center
600 Hillside Dr, Beeville, TX 78102
(512) 358-8880
Admin Judith Martin. *Dir of Nursing* Shirley R Jefferson RN. *Medical Dir* J L Reagan MD.
Licensure Intermediate care; Alzheimer's care. *Beds* 120. *Certified* Medicaid.
Owner Proprietary corp (Diversicare Corp).
Admissions Requirements Physician's request.
Staff Physicians; RNs; LPNs; Nurses' aides; Physical therapists; Activities coordinators; Dietitians; Ophthalmologists; Dentists.
Languages Spanish.
Facilities Dining room; Physical therapy room; Activities room; Laundry room; Barber/Beauty shop.
Activities Arts & crafts; Games; Prayer groups; Movies; Shopping trips; Dances/Social/Cultural gatherings.

Meridian Nursing Center—Beeville
4901 N St Marys, Beeville, TX 78102
(512) 358-5612
Admin William L Phelps Jr.
Medical Dir Tom Reagan MD.
Licensure Skilled care; Intermediate care. *Beds* SNF 50; ICF 50. *Certified* Medicaid.
Owner Proprietary corp (Meridian Healthcare).
Staff Physicians 1 (pt); RNs 3 (ft), 1 (pt); LPNs 3 (ft), 6 (pt); Nurses' aides 26 (ft), 10 (pt); Physical therapists 1 (pt); Reality therapists 1 (pt); Speech therapists 1 (pt); Activities coordinators 1 (ft); Dietitians 1 (pt); Podiatrists 1 (pt); Dentists 1 (pt).

Bellville

Colonial Belle Nursing Home
PO Box 59, Bellville, TX 77418
(409) 865-3689
Medical Dir J B Harle MD.
Licensure Skilled care. *Beds* 73. *Certified* Medicaid.
Admissions Requirements Medical examination; Physician's request.
Staff Physicians 4 (ft); RNs 2 (ft), 1 (pt); LPNs 9 (ft); Physical therapists 1 (pt); Recreational therapists 1 (pt); Activities coordinators 1 (pt); Dietitians 1 (pt); Ophthalmologists 1 (pt); Podiatrists 1 (pt); Dentists 1 (pt).
Facilities Dining room; Physical therapy room; Activities room; Chapel; Laundry room; Barber/Beauty shop; Library.
Activities Arts & crafts; Cards; Games; Reading groups; Prayer groups; Movies; Shopping trips; Dances/Social/Cultural gatherings.

Sweetbriar Nursing Home
PO Box 638, Hwy 36 N, Bellville, TX 77418
(409) 865-3145
Admin Lucile Kiemsteadt.
Medical Dir Katie Woods.
Licensure Intermediate care. *Beds* ICF 170. *Certified* Medicaid.
Owner Privately owned.
Admissions Requirements Physician's request.
Staff LPNs; Nurses' aides; Activities coordinators.
Languages German, Czech.

Facilities Dining room; Activities room; Laundry room; Barber/Beauty shop.
Activities Arts & crafts; Games; Reading groups; Prayer groups; Movies; Dances/Social/Cultural gatherings; Square dancing.

Belton

Crestview Manor Nursing Center
1103 Mary Jane St, Belton, TX 76513
(817) 939-9327
Admin Randell R Johnson. *Dir of Nursing* Barbara Sink RN. *Medical Dir* William B Long MD.
Licensure Skilled care; Intermediate care. *Beds* SNF 43; ICF 48. *Private Pay Patients* 22%. *Certified* Medicaid; Medicare.
Owner Proprietary corp (Beverly Enterprises).
Admissions Requirements Medical examination; Physician's request.
Staff RNs; LPNs; Nurses' aides; Activities coordinators.
Languages Spanish, German.
Facilities Dining room; Physical therapy room; Activities room; Crafts room; Laundry room; Barber/Beauty shop.
Activities Arts & crafts; Cards; Games; Reading groups; Prayer groups; Movies; Dances/Social/Cultural gatherings; Intergenerational programs.

Park Place Manor
810 E 13th Ave, Belton, TX 76513
(817) 939-1876
Licensure Nursing. *Beds* Nursing 120.

Bertram

Bertram Nursing Home
Hwy 29, Box 209, Bertram, TX 78605
(512) 355-2116
Admin Dixie Ann Westen.
Medical Dir H James Wall MD.
Licensure Intermediate care. *Beds* 32. *Certified* Medicaid.
Owner Nonprofit corp.
Admissions Requirements Medical examination; Physician's request.
Staff Physicians 1 (pt); RNs 1 (pt); LPNs 6 (pt); Nurses' aides 11 (ft), 6 (pt); Reality therapists 1 (pt); Recreational therapists 1 (pt); Occupational therapists 1 (pt); Speech therapists 1 (pt); Activities coordinators 1 (ft); Dietitians 1 (pt).
Facilities Dining room; Activities room; Laundry room; Barber/Beauty shop.
Activities Arts & crafts; Cards; Games; Reading groups; Movies; Shopping trips; Parties; Church; Sing-alongs; Recreational outings.

Big Lake

Reagan County Care Center
805 N Main, Big Lake, TX 76932
(915) 884-2561
Licensure Nursing. *Beds* Nursing 48.

Big Spring

Golden Plains Care Center
901 Goliad St, Big Spring, TX 79720
(915) 263-7633
Licensure Nursing. *Beds* Nursing 150.

Mountain View Lodge Inc
2009 Virginia, Big Spring, TX 79720
(915) 263-1271
Admin Billy M Hendrix.
Licensure Intermediate care. *Beds* 92. *Certified* Medicaid.
Owner Proprietary corp.

United Health Care Center
901 Goliad St, Big Spring, TX 79720
(915) 263-7633

Admin Raymond Junker.
Licensure Intermediate care. *Beds* 200.
  Certified Medicaid.
Owner Proprietary corp.

Blanco

Blanco Health Care Center
PO Box 327, 3rd & Elm St, Blanco, TX 78606
(512) 833-4710
Admin Sophie A Johnson.
Medical Dir Dorothy Wright.
Licensure Intermediate care; Retirement. *Beds*
  ICF 42; Personal care 20. *Certified*
  Medicaid.
Owner Proprietary corp.
Admissions Requirements Medical
  examination; Physician's request.
Staff RNs 1 (pt); Nurses' aides 12 (ft);
  Activities coordinators 1 (ft); LVNs 2 (ft), 2
  (pt).
Activities Arts & crafts; Cards; Games;
  Reading groups; Prayer groups; Movies;
  Shopping trips; Dances/Social/Cultural
  gatherings.

Live Oak Medical Nursing Center
PO Box 356, 618 E Live Oak St, Blanco, TX
  78606
(512) 833-4567
Admin Mary F Toms.
Medical Dir Mary Evans.
Licensure Intermediate care. *Beds* ICF 64.
  Certified Medicaid.
Owner Proprietary corp.
Admissions Requirements Medical
  examination; Physician's request.
Staff RNs 1 (ft); LPNs 4 (ft); Nurses' aides 15
  (ft); Physical therapists 1 (ft); Recreational
  therapists 1 (ft); Activities coordinators 2
  (ft); Dietitians 1 (ft).
Facilities Dining room; Activities room;
  Crafts room; Laundry room.
Activities Arts & crafts; Cards; Games;
  Reading groups; Prayer groups; Movies;
  Shopping trips.

Boerne

Hill Top Nursing Home
200 E Ryan St, Boerne, TX 78006
(512) 249-2594
Admin Betty Buel Price.
Licensure Intermediate care. *Beds* 74.
  Certified Medicaid.

Town & Country Manor Inc
625 N Main, Boerne, TX 78006
(512) 249-3085
Admin Lois F Wertheim.
Licensure Intermediate care. *Beds* 131.
  Certified Medicaid.
Owner Proprietary corp (Summit Health Ltd).

Bogata

Red River Haven Nursing Home Inc
319 Paris Rd, Bogata, TX 75417
(214) 632-5756
Admin Bobbie Lee Cawley.
Licensure Intermediate care. *Beds* 154.
  Certified Medicaid.
Owner Proprietary corp (Beverly Enterprises).

Bonham

Bonham Nursing Center
709 W 5th St, Bonham, TX 75418
(214) 583-8551
Admin Juanita Awbrey.
Licensure Intermediate care. *Beds* 65.
  Certified Medicaid.
Owner Proprietary corp (ARA Living
  Centers).
Admissions Requirements Physician's request.

Staff LPNs 8 (ft); Nurses' aides 10 (ft);
  Activities coordinators 1 (ft); Dietitians 3
  (ft), 2 (pt).
Facilities Dining room; Activities room;
  Crafts room; Laundry room; Barber/Beauty
  shop.
Activities Arts & crafts; Cards; Games;
  Reading groups; Prayer groups; Movies;
  Shopping trips; Dances/Social/Cultural
  gatherings; Exercise; Field trips.

Fairview Nursing Home
1500 Kennedy, Bonham, TX 75418
(214) 583-2148
Admin Betty West-Farley. *Dir of Nursing*
  Sharion Traylor. *Medical Dir* Walter Sisk
  MD.
Licensure Intermediate care. *Beds* ICF 103.
  Certified Medicaid.
Owner Proprietary corp (Texas Health
  Enterprises).
Admissions Requirements Medical
  examination; Physician's request.
Staff Physicians; RNs; LPNs; Nurses' aides;
  Physical therapists; Occupational therapists;
  Speech therapists; Activities coordinators;
  Dietitians; Ophthalmologists.
Facilities Dining room; Activities room;
  Chapel; Crafts room; Laundry room; Barber/
  Beauty shop.
Activities Arts & crafts; Cards; Games;
  Reading groups; Prayer groups; Movies;
  Shopping trips.

Seven Oaks Convalescent Care Center
901 Seven Oaks Rd, Bonham, TX 75418
(214) 583-2191
Admin K Ann Duckworth.
Medical Dir Hope Grantland.
Licensure Intermediate care. *Beds* 108.
  Certified Medicaid.
Owner Proprietary corp (Health Enter of
  America).
Admissions Requirements Physician's request.
Staff RNs 1 (ft); LPNs 9 (ft); Nurses' aides 36
  (ft), 3 (pt); Activities coordinators 1 (ft);
  Dietitians 1 (pt); Ophthalmologists 1 (pt);
  Podiatrists 1 (pt).
Languages Spanish.
Facilities Dining room; Laundry room;
  Barber/Beauty shop; Library.
Activities Arts & crafts; Cards; Games;
  Reading groups; Prayer groups; Movies;
  Shopping trips; Dances/Social/Cultural
  gatherings.

Borger

Borger Nursing Center
1316 S Florida, Borger, TX 79007
(806) 273-3785
Admin Dorothy Blumer. *Dir of Nursing* Elaine
  Cleek. *Medical Dir* A L Sherer MD.
Licensure Intermediate care. *Beds* 120.
Owner Proprietary corp (Beverly Enterprises).
Staff LPNs 8 (ft); Nurses' aides 24 (ft), 2 (pt);
  Activities coordinators 1 (ft); Dietitians 1
  (ft).
Languages Sign.
Facilities Dining room; Laundry room;
  Barber/Beauty shop.
Activities Arts & crafts; Games; Reading
  groups; Prayer groups; Movies; Dances/
  Social/Cultural gatherings.

Magic Star Nursing Home
PO Box 409, 200 Tyler St, Borger, TX 79009
(806) 273-3725
Admin Don F York.
Medical Dir Georgia Siebert.
Licensure Intermediate care. *Beds* ICF 49.
  Certified Medicaid.
Owner Proprietary corp.
Admissions Requirements Minimum age 18;
  Medical examination; Physician's request.
Staff RNs 1 (pt); LPNs 2 (ft), 3 (pt); Nurses'
  aides 10 (ft), 5 (pt); Activities coordinators 1
  (ft); Dietitians 1 (pt).

Languages Spanish, German.
Facilities Dining room; Activities room;
  Crafts room; Laundry room.
Activities Arts & crafts; Cards; Games;
  Reading groups; Prayer groups; Movies;
  Shopping trips; Dances/Social/Cultural
  gatherings.

Bowie

Bellmire Home
PO Box 1227, 1101 Rock St, Bowie, TX
  76230
(817) 872-2283
Admin Mary H Duvall.
Licensure Intermediate care. *Beds* 201.
  Certified Medicaid.
Owner Proprietary corp.

Bowie Nursing Center
601 Central Ave, Bowie, TX 76230
(817) 872-1231
Admin Carol S Brewer.
Licensure Intermediate care. *Beds* 95.
  Certified Medicaid.
Owner Proprietary corp.

Brady

Leisure Lodge of Brady
2201 Menard Hwy, Brady, TX 76825
(915) 597-2906
Admin Stephen M Goode. *Dir of Nursing*
  Carol Brawner. *Medical Dir* Dr McCullough.
Licensure Intermediate care. *Beds* ICF 110.
  Certified Medicaid.
Owner Proprietary corp (Beverly Enterprises).
Admissions Requirements Physician's request.
Staff Physicians 4 (ft), 1 (pt); LPNs 7 (ft);
  Nurses' aides 16 (ft); Activities coordinators
  1 (ft); Dietitians 1 (pt).
Languages Spanish.
Facilities Dining room; Barber/Beauty shop.
Activities Arts & crafts; Cards; Games; Prayer
  groups; Movies; Shopping trips; Picnics;
  Outings.

Shuffield Nursing Home Inc 1
1605 S Bradley, Brady, TX 76825
(915) 597-2916
Admin Eugene E Frost. *Dir of Nursing* Pam
  Wilkinson RN.
Licensure Intermediate care; Retirement. *Beds*
  ICF 67. *Certified* Medicaid.
Owner Proprietary corp.
Admissions Requirements Minimum age 18;
  Medical examination; Physician's request.
Staff RNs 1 (ft); LPNs 5 (ft), 2 (pt); Nurses'
  aides 25 (ft), 5 (pt); Activities coordinators 1
  (ft); Dietitians 1 (pt).
Languages Spanish.
Facilities Dining room; Physical therapy
  room; Activities room; Crafts room; Laundry
  room; Barber/Beauty shop.
Activities Arts & crafts; Cards; Games;
  Reading groups; Prayer groups; Movies;
  Shopping trips; Dances/Social/Cultural
  gatherings.

Shuffield Rest Home Inc No 2
PO Box 990, Brady, TX 76825
(915) 597-2947
Admin Patsy E Lohn. *Dir of Nursing* Ellen
  Johnson RN.
Licensure Intermediate care; Retirement. *Beds*
  ICF 60. *Certified* Medicaid.
Owner Proprietary corp.
Admissions Requirements Medical
  examination; Physician's request.
Staff RNs; LPNs; Nurses' aides; Activities
  coordinators.
Facilities Dining room; Activities room;
  Chapel; Crafts room; Laundry room; Barber/
  Beauty shop.

Activities Arts & crafts; Cards; Games;
Reading groups; Prayer groups; Movies;
Shopping trips; Dances/Social/Cultural
gatherings.

Breckenridge

Lake Country Manor
1901 W Elliott, Breckenridge, TX 76024
(817) 559-3302
Licensure Nursing. *Beds* Nursing 72.

Town Hall Estates
1900 W Elliott, Breckenridge, TX 76024
(817) 559-3303
Admin Kenneth V Campbell.
Licensure Intermediate care. *Beds* 72.
Certified Medicaid.
Owner Nonprofit corp.

Villa Haven Nursing Center
300 S Jackson, Breckenridge, TX 76024
(817) 559-3386
Admin Marjorie A Duncan.
Licensure Intermediate care. *Beds* 92.
Certified Medicaid.
Owner Proprietary corp (Unicare).
Staff RNs 2 (pt); LPNs 6 (ft), 3 (pt); Activities
coordinators 1 (ft); Dietitians 1 (pt).
Facilities Dining room; Activities room;
Crafts room; Laundry room; Barber/Beauty
shop.
Activities Arts & crafts; Cards; Games;
Reading groups; Prayer groups; Movies;
Shopping trips; Dances/Social/Cultural
gatherings.

Bremond

Bremond Nursing Center
PO Box 520, 200 N Main St, Bremond, TX
76629
(817) 746-7666
Admin Holis U McGee.
Medical Dir Dr Dan Saylak.
Licensure Intermediate care. *Beds* ICF 82.
Certified Medicaid.
Owner Proprietary corp (Unicare).
Staff Physicians 2 (pt); RNs 1 (pt); LPNs 4
(ft), 3 (pt); Nurses' aides 28 (ft), 5 (pt);
Activities coordinators 1 (ft); Dietitians 1
(pt); Dentists 1 (pt).
Facilities Dining room; Physical therapy
room; Activities room; Chapel; Crafts room;
Laundry room; Barber/Beauty shop; Library.
Activities Arts & crafts; Games; Reading
groups; Prayer groups; Movies; Shopping
trips; Dances/Social/Cultural gatherings.

Brenham

Brenham Rest Home Inc
406 Cottonwood St, Brenham, TX 77833
(409) 836-3434
Admin H S Hughes.
Licensure Intermediate care. *Beds* 108.
Certified Medicaid.
Admissions Requirements Medical
examination; Physician's request.
Staff RNs 1 (ft), 1 (pt); LPNs 7 (ft); Nurses'
aides 28 (ft), 12 (pt); Activities coordinators
1 (ft), 1 (pt).
Facilities Dining room; Activities room;
Crafts room; Laundry room.
Activities Arts & crafts; Cards; Games;
Reading groups; Prayer groups; Movies;
Dances/Social/Cultural gatherings.

Sweetbriar Nursing Home
401 E Horton, Brenham, TX 77833
(409) 836-6611
Admin Betty C Fife. *Dir of Nursing* Lu Ann
Hibbs. *Medical Dir* W F Hasskarl Jr MD.
Licensure Skilled care; Intermediate care. *Beds*
SNF 69; ICF 196. *Private Pay Patients* 30%.
Certified Medicaid; Medicare.
Owner Privately owned.

Admissions Requirements Minimum age 21.
Facilities Dining room; Physical therapy
room; Chapel; Crafts room; Laundry room;
Barber/Beauty shop.
Activities Arts & crafts; Games; Reading
groups; Prayer groups; Shopping trips.

Bridge City

Green Acres Convalescent Center
PO Box 606, 625 Meadowlawn, Bridge City,
TX 77611
(409) 735-3528
Admin James E Trussell Jr. *Dir of Nursing*
Joan Adams LVN. *Medical Dir* Dr Joseph
Vadas.
Licensure Intermediate care; Intermediate care
for mentally retarded. *Beds* ICF 106.
Certified Medicaid.
Owner Proprietary corp (ARA Devcon, Inc).
Admissions Requirements Minimum age 22;
Medical examination.
Staff Physicians 11 (pt); LPNs 11 (ft) 13E 38
(ft); Physical therapists 1 (pt); Recreational
therapists 1 (ft); Occupational therapists 1
(pt); Speech therapists 1 (pt); Activities
coordinators 1 (ft); Dietitians 1 (pt);
Ophthalmologists 1 (pt); Podiatrists 1 (pt);
Dentists 1 (pt); Psychologist 1 (pt).
Facilities Dining room; Activities room;
Chapel; Crafts room; Laundry room; Barber/
Beauty shop.
Activities Arts & crafts; Cards; Games;
Movies; Shopping trips; Dances/Social/
Cultural gatherings.

Bridgeport

Golden Years Retreat
1st at Cates, Bridgeport, TX 76026
(817) 683-5181
Admin Maxine Smith.
Licensure Intermediate care. *Beds* 98.
Certified Medicaid.
Owner Proprietary corp.

Bronte

Bronte Nursing Home
PO Drawer M, 900 S State St, Bronte, TX
76933
(915) 473-3621
Admin Pam Stokes. *Dir of Nursing* Pauline
Blair. *Medical Dir* Bill Bass MD.
Licensure Intermediate care. *Beds* ICF 40.
Private Pay Patients 25%. *Certified*
Medicaid.
Owner Publicly owned.
Admissions Requirements Minimum age 18;
Medical examination; Physician's request.
Staff LPNs; Nurses' aides; Activities
coordinators.
Languages Spanish.
Facilities Dining room; Activities room;
Crafts room; Laundry room; Barber/Beauty
shop; Library; 2 large outdoor patios with
picnic tables and barbecue pit.
Activities Arts & crafts; Cards; Games;
Reading groups; Prayer groups; Pet therapy;
Volunteer program.

Brookshire

Brookshire Arms Inc
PO Box 638, Hwy 359 S, Brookshire, TX
77423
(713) 934-2224
Admin Marvin E Cole.
Medical Dir Gail Bernhausen MD.
Licensure Intermediate care. *Beds* 134.
Certified Medicaid.
Admissions Requirements Medical
examination; Physician's request.
Staff RNs 2 (ft); LPNs 9 (ft); Nurses' aides 28
(ft), 7 (pt); Activities coordinators 2 (ft);
Dietitians 1 (ft); 27 (ft).

Facilities Dining room; Activities room;
Chapel; Laundry room.
Activities Arts & crafts; Cards; Games;
Shopping trips.

Brownfield

South Plains Nursing Center
1101 E Lake St, Brownfield, TX 79316
(806) 637-7561
Admin Julia Merrill.
Licensure Intermediate care. *Beds* 116.
Certified Medicaid.
Owner Proprietary corp (Beverly Enterprises).

Brownsville

Brownsville Good Samaritan Center
510 Parades Line Rd, Brownsville, TX 78521
(512) 546-5358
Admin Cletus M Solar.
Medical Dir Marcos Reis.
Licensure Skilled care; Intermediate care. *Beds*
112. *Certified* Medicaid.
Owner Nonprofit corp (Evangelical Lutheran/
Good Samaritan Society).
Admissions Requirements Physician's request.
Staff RNs; LPNs; Nurses' aides; Physical
therapists; Reality therapists; Recreational
therapists; Activities coordinators; Dietitians.
Facilities Dining room; Physical therapy
room; Activities room; Crafts room; Laundry
room; Barber/Beauty shop; Library.
Activities Arts & crafts; Cards; Games; Prayer
groups; Movies; Shopping trips; Dances/
Social/Cultural gatherings.

Mother of Perpetual Help Home
519 E Madison at 6th, Brownsville, TX 78520
(512) 546-6745
Admin Mary P Collins.
Licensure Intermediate care. *Beds* 38.
Certified Medicaid.

Retama Manor Nursing Center—Brownsville
1415 W Washington, Brownsville, TX 78520
(512) 546-3711
Admin Dalona Riggs Murphy.
Licensure Intermediate care; Intermediate care
for mentally retarded. *Beds* ICF 91; ICF/MR
74. *Certified* Medicaid.
Owner Proprietary corp (ARA Living
Centers).

Valley Grande Manor Inc
901 Wild Rose Ln, Brownsville, TX 78520
(512) 546-4568
Admin Ruben Mohan Raj Moses.
Medical Dir Gustavo F Stern.
Licensure Skilled care; Intermediate care;
Alzheimer's care. *Beds* SNF 121; ICF 59.
Certified Medicaid; Medicare.
Admissions Requirements Medical
examination; Physician's request.
Staff RNs 3 (ft), 2 (pt); LPNs 20 (ft), 4 (pt);
Nurses' aides 52 (ft), 3 (pt); Physical
therapists 1 (pt); Activities coordinators 2
(ft).
Languages Spanish.
Affiliation Seventh-Day Adventist.
Facilities Dining room; Physical therapy
room; Activities room; Chapel; Crafts room;
Laundry room; Barber/Beauty shop; Library.
Activities Arts & crafts; Cards; Games;
Reading groups; Prayer groups; Movies;
Shopping trips; Dances/Social/Cultural
gatherings; Zoo trips; Beach trips.

Brownwood

Brownwood Care Center
PO Box 1328, 101 Miller Dr, Brownwood, TX
76801
(915) 643-1596
Admin Betty F Turner.
Licensure Intermediate care. *Beds* 130.
Certified Medicaid.

Owner Proprietary corp.
Admissions Requirements Minimum age 18; Medical examination; Physician's request.
Staff RNs 1 (ft); LPNs 15 (ft); Nurses' aides 40 (ft), 5 (pt); Physical therapists 5 (pt); Activities coordinators 1 (ft); Dietitians 1 (ft).
Facilities Dining room; Activities room; Chapel; Crafts room; Laundry room; Barber/Beauty shop; TV room.
Activities Arts & crafts; Cards; Games; Prayer groups; Movies; Shopping trips; Dances/Social/Cultural gatherings; Bingo; Dominoes; Happy hour.

C.A.R.E. Inc Nursing Center
PO Box 6-A, Star Rte 3, Brownwood, TX 76801
(915) 646-5521
Admin Jerry D McGuffey. *Dir of Nursing* Margaret Copeland RN. *Medical Dir* Dr Fred Spencer.
Licensure Skilled care; Intermediate care; Retirement; Alzheimer's care. *Beds* SNF 21; ICF 76. *Certified* Medicaid.
Owner Proprietary corp.
Admissions Requirements Minimum age 16; Medical examination; Physician's request.
Staff Physicians 1 (ft); RNs 1 (ft), 1 (pt); LPNs 9 (ft), 5 (pt); Nurses' aides 25 (ft), 5 (pt); Activities coordinators 1 (ft); Dietitians 1 (ft).
Languages Spanish.
Facilities Dining room; Physical therapy room; Activities room; Chapel; Crafts room; Barber/Beauty shop; Library; Hydro therapy.
Activities Arts & crafts; Cards; Games; Reading groups; Prayer groups; Movies; Shopping trips; Dances/Social/Cultural gatherings.

Cross Country Care Center
1514 Indian Creek Rd, Brownwood, TX 76801
(915) 646-6529
Admin Mack Baldridge. *Dir of Nursing* Ann Padrone. *Medical Dir* Gary Butka MD.
Licensure Intermediate care; Alzheimer's care. *Beds* ICF 146. *Private Pay Patients* 15%. *Certified* Medicaid.
Owner Proprietary corp (Beverly Enterprises).
Admissions Requirements Medical examination; Physician's request.
Staff LPNs 8 (ft); Nurses' aides 24 (ft); Physical therapists 1 (pt); Activities coordinators 1 (ft), 1 (pt).
Facilities Dining room; Activities room; Chapel; Crafts room; Laundry room; Barber/Beauty shop.
Activities Arts & crafts; Cards; Games; Reading groups; Prayer groups; Movies; Shopping trips; Dances/Social/Cultural gatherings.

Plantation Nursing Home
PO Box 1768, Brownwood, TX 76804-1768
(915) 643-3606
Admin Patrick H McLaughlin III.
Licensure Intermediate care. *Beds* 46. *Certified* Medicaid.
Staff LPNs 3 (ft); Nurses' aides 12 (ft), 3 (pt); Activities coordinators 1 (ft).
Facilities Dining room; Laundry room.
Activities Arts & crafts; Cards; Games; Movies; Dances/Social/Cultural gatherings.

South Park Development Center
Morris-Sheppard Dr, Brownwood, TX 76801
(915) 646-9531
Admin Ann Daniel.
Licensure Intermediate care for mentally retarded. *Beds* 108. *Certified* Medicaid.
Admissions Requirements Minimum age 18.
Staff RNs 1 (ft); LPNs 5 (ft); Physical therapists 1 (ft); Reality therapists 1 (ft); Recreational therapists 1 (ft); Occupational therapists 1 (pt); Speech therapists 1 (pt);

Activities coordinators 1 (ft); Dietitians 1 (pt); Ophthalmologists 1 (pt); Podiatrists 1 (pt); Audiologists 1 (pt); Dentists 1 (pt).
Facilities Dining room; Physical therapy room; Activities room; Crafts room; Laundry room.
Activities Arts & crafts; Cards; Games; Reading groups; Movies; Shopping trips; Dances/Social/Cultural gatherings.

Bryan

Crestview Retirement Community
2501 Villa Maria Rd, Bryan, TX 77801
(409) 776-4778
Admin Rhonda M Morales. *Dir of Nursing* Madeline Klintworth RN.
Licensure Intermediate care; Independent living. *Beds* ICF 57; Independent living units 182. *Certified* Medicaid.
Owner Nonprofit corp.
Admissions Requirements Minimum age 62; Medical examination; Physician's request.
Staff RNs 1 (ft), 1 (pt); LPNs 6 (ft), 8 (pt); Nurses' aides 8 (ft), 6 (pt); Activities coordinators 2 (ft); Dietitians 1 (ft).
Affiliation Methodist.
Facilities Dining room; Physical therapy room; Activities room; Chapel; Crafts room; Laundry room; Barber/Beauty shop; Library.
Activities Arts & crafts; Cards; Games; Reading groups; Prayer groups; Movies; Shopping trips; Dances/Social/Cultural gatherings.

Sherwood Health Care
PO Box 3866, 1401 Memorial Dr, Bryan, TX 77805
(409) 776-7521, 774-7118 FAX
Admin Edwin P Sulik. *Dir of Nursing* Trisha Gary. *Medical Dir* Council Mills MD.
Licensure Skilled care; Intermediate care. *Beds* SNF 128; ICF 118. *Private Pay Patients* 44%. *Certified* Medicaid; Medicare.
Owner Privately owned.
Staff Physicians 4 (pt); RNs 5 (ft); LPNs 28 (ft); Nurses' aides 75 (ft), 10 (pt); Physical therapists 2 (ft); Recreational therapists 1 (pt); Occupational therapists 1 (pt); Speech therapists 1 (pt); Activities coordinators 3 (ft); Dietitians 2 (ft); Podiatrists 1 (pt).
Facilities Dining room; Physical therapy room; Activities room; Chapel; Crafts room; Laundry room; Barber/Beauty shop.
Activities Arts & crafts; Cards; Games; Reading groups; Prayer groups; Movies; Shopping trips; Dances/Social/Cultural gatherings; Intergenerational programs; Pet therapy.

University Hills Nursing Center
2001 E 29th St, Bryan, TX 77802
(713) 822-7361
Admin Loretta Henk.
Licensure Intermediate care. *Beds* 148. *Certified* Medicaid.
Owner Proprietary corp (Beverly Enterprises).
Facilities Dining room; Physical therapy room; Laundry room; Barber/Beauty shop.
Activities Arts & crafts; Cards; Games; Reading groups; Prayer groups; Shopping trips; Dances/Social/Cultural gatherings.

Buffalo

All Seasons Care Center—Buffalo
PO Drawer M, Pearlstone St at Hospital Dr, Buffalo, TX 75831
(214) 322-4208
Admin Pauline Bulen.
Licensure Intermediate care. *Beds* 60. *Certified* Medicaid.
Owner Proprietary corp (Beverly Enterprises).

Buna

Buna Nursing Home
PO Box 1088, Buna, TX 77612
(409) 994-3576
Admin Wayne Daniel Butchee. *Dir of Nursing* Pat Wiggins LVN. *Medical Dir* J L Sessions MD.
Licensure Intermediate care. *Beds* ICF 60. *Certified* Medicaid.
Owner Proprietary corp.

Burkburnett

Care Manor Nursing Center of Burkburnett
800 Red River Expwy, Burkburnett, TX 76354
(817) 569-1466
Admin Janice Sanders.
Medical Dir Ruby Lange.
Licensure Intermediate care. *Beds* ICF 74. *Certified* Medicaid.
Owner Proprietary corp.
Admissions Requirements Physician's request.
Staff RNs 1 (pt); LPNs 6 (ft); Nurses' aides 20 (ft); Activities coordinators 1 (ft); Dietitians 1 (pt); Ophthalmologists 1 (pt).
Facilities Dining room; Activities room; Laundry room; Barber/Beauty shop.
Activities Arts & crafts; Cards; Games; Reading groups; Prayer groups; Shopping trips; Dances/Social/Cultural gatherings.

Evergreen Care Center
406 E 7th, Burkburnett, TX 76354
(817) 569-2236
Admin Susie M Brown.
Licensure Intermediate care. *Beds* 60. *Certified* Medicaid.
Owner Proprietary corp (Beverly Enterprises).

Burleson

Burleson Nursing Center
144 SW Thomas, Burleson, TX 76028
(817) 295-2216
Admin Frank S Philbin. *Dir of Nursing* Joan L Philbin QMRP RN. *Medical Dir* Nelda Cunniff.
Licensure Skilled care; Intermediate care; Sub acute/Post op. *Beds* SNF 60; ICF 66. *Private Pay Patients* 10%. *Certified* Medicaid; Medicare; VA.
Owner Proprietary corp (Texas Health Enterprises).
Admissions Requirements Minimum age 6; Medical examination.
Staff Physicians 12 (pt); RNs 2 (ft); LPNs 14 (ft); Nurses' aides 28 (ft); Physical therapists 3 (pt); Reality therapists 1 (ft); Occupational therapists 3 (pt); Speech therapists 3 (pt); Activities coordinators 1 (ft); Dietitians 1 (pt); Ophthalmologists 2 (pt); Podiatrists 1 (pt); Audiologists 1 (pt).
Facilities Dining room; Physical therapy room; Activities room; Chapel; Crafts room; Laundry room; Barber/Beauty shop; Library; Head trauma.
Activities Arts & crafts; Cards; Games; Reading groups; Prayer groups; Movies; Shopping trips; Dances/Social/Cultural gatherings; Intergenerational programs; Pet therapy.

Silver Haven Care Center
600 Maple, Burleson, TX 76028
(817) 295-8118
Admin Andre F Villarreal. *Dir of Nursing* Judith Miles. *Medical Dir* Elvin Adams MD.
Licensure Intermediate care. *Beds* ICF 120. *Certified* Medicaid.
Owner Proprietary corp (Arbor Living Centers Inc).
Admissions Requirements Minimum age 18; Medical examination; Physician's request.
Staff RNs 1 (ft); LPNs 13 (ft); Nurses' aides 45 (ft); Ophthalmologists.

Languages Spanish.
Facilities Dining room; Activities room; Chapel; Crafts room; Laundry room; Barber/Beauty shop.
Activities Arts & crafts; Cards; Games; Reading groups; Prayer groups; Movies; Shopping trips; Dances/Social/Cultural gatherings; Pet therapy.

Burnet

Oaks Nursing Home
507 W Jackson, Burnet, TX 78611
(512) 756-6044
Admin Judy Edgar Allen.
Medical Dir Billy B Ozier MD.
Licensure Intermediate care. *Beds* 92.
   Certified Medicaid.
Owner Nonprofit corp.
Staff RNs 1 (ft); LPNs 5 (ft); Nurses' aides 32 (ft), 3 (pt); Activities coordinators 1 (ft); Dietitians 1 (pt).
Facilities Dining room; Activities room; Laundry room; Barber/Beauty shop.
Activities Cards; Games; Prayer groups; Movies; Shopping trips.

Caldwell

Leisure Lodge—Caldwell
701 N Broadway, Caldwell, TX 77836
(409) 567-3237
Admin LaVern E Balcar. *Dir of Nursing* Nancy Keller. *Medical Dir* D Barker Stigler MD.
Licensure Intermediate care. *Beds* ICF 156. *Private Pay Patients* 23%. *Certified* Medicaid; Medicare.
Owner Proprietary corp (Beverly Enterprises).
Admissions Requirements Minimum age 16; Medical examination; Physician's request.
Staff RNs 2 (ft); LPNs 9 (ft); Physical therapists 1 (pt); Activities coordinators 1 (ft); Dietitians 1 (pt); Social directors 1 (ft).
Languages Spanish, Czech.
Facilities Dining room; Physical therapy room; Activities room; Chapel; Crafts room; Laundry room; Barber/Beauty shop; Library.
Activities Arts & crafts; Games; Reading groups; Prayer groups; Movies; Shopping trips; Dances/Social/Cultural gatherings; Family council; Resident council; Ministerial alliance.

Calvert

Calvert Nursing Center
PO Box 159, 701 Browning, Calvert, TX 77837
(409) 364-2391, 364-2023
Admin Audrey G Williamson. *Dir of Nursing* Hazel L Brown.
Licensure Intermediate care; Alzheimer's care. *Beds* 32. *Certified* Medicaid.
Owner Privately owned.
Admissions Requirements Minimum age 21; Medical examination; Physician's request.
Staff LPNs; Nurses' aides; Physical therapists; Speech therapists; Activities coordinators.
Facilities Dining room; Laundry room; Barber/Beauty shop.
Activities Arts & crafts; Cards; Games; Reading groups; Prayer groups; Movies; Dances/Social/Cultural gatherings.

Cameron

Cameron Nursing Home
PO Box 831, 700 E 11th St, Cameron, TX 76520
(817) 697-6564
Admin Donna Sue Stephenson.
Licensure Intermediate care. *Beds* 43.
   Certified Medicaid.
Owner Proprietary corp.

Colonial Nursing Home
PO Box 831, 1002 E 10th St, Cameron, TX 76520
(817) 697-6578
Admin Connie Biffle.
Medical Dir Pat Kettett.
Licensure Intermediate care. *Beds* ICF 84.
   Certified Medicaid.
Owner Proprietary corp.
Admissions Requirements Minimum age 21; Medical examination; Physician's request.
Staff RNs 1 (ft); LPNs 8 (ft); Nurses' aides 18 (ft), 6 (pt); Recreational therapists 1 (ft); Activities coordinators 1 (ft); Dietitians 1 (pt).
Languages German.
Facilities Dining room; Activities room; Barber/Beauty shop; "Gathering" room; Living room.
Activities Arts & crafts; Cards; Games; Reading groups; Prayer groups; Movies; Shopping trips; Dances/Social/Cultural gatherings.

Canadian

Edward Abraham Memorial Home Inc
803 Birch, Canadian, TX 79014
(806) 323-6453
Admin Sue Flanagan Collier.
Licensure Intermediate care. *Beds* 59.
   Certified Medicaid.
Facilities Dining room; Activities room; Chapel; Laundry room; Barber/Beauty shop.
Activities Arts & crafts; Cards; Games; Reading groups; Prayer groups; Movies; Shopping trips; Dances/Social/Cultural gatherings.

Canton

Canton Nursing Center
1661 S Buffalo, Canton, TX 75103
(214) 567-4135
Admin John Grant. *Dir of Nursing* Johnnie Deshazo. *Medical Dir* Dr John Turner.
Licensure Intermediate care; Alzheimer's care. *Beds* ICF 66. *Private Pay Patients* 15%. *Certified* Medicaid.
Owner Proprietary corp (Beverly Enterprises).
Admissions Requirements Minimum age 62.
Staff LPNs; Nurses' aides; Activities coordinators.
Facilities Dining room; Activities room; Barber/Beauty shop.
Activities Arts & crafts; Cards; Games; Reading groups; Prayer groups; Movies; Shopping trips; Dances/Social/Cultural gatherings; Intergenerational programs; Pet therapy.

Canton Residential Center
1755 Elliott St, Canton, TX 75103
(214) 567-2901
Admin Debbie Davenport.
Licensure Intermediate care. *Beds* 42.
   Certified Medicaid.

Heritage Manor
PO Box 977, 901 W College St, Canton, TX 75103
(214) 567-4169
Admin Curtis D Bjornlie.
Licensure Intermediate care. *Beds* 110.
   Certified Medicaid.
Owner Proprietary corp.

Canyon

Golden Plains Care Center
15 Hospital Dr, Canyon, TX 79015
(806) 655-2161
Admin Fern B Yell. *Dir of Nursing* Betty Crawford RN.
Licensure Intermediate care. *Beds* ICF 90. *Private Pay Patients* 48%. *Certified* Medicaid.

Owner Privately owned.
Admissions Requirements Minimum age 21; Medical examination; Physician's request.
Staff RNs; LPNs; Nurses' aides; Activities coordinators; Dietitians.
Languages Spanish.
Facilities Dining room; Laundry room; Barber/Beauty shop.
Activities Arts & crafts; Cards; Games; Reading groups; Prayer groups; Movies; Shopping trips; Dances/Social/Cultural gatherings; Intergenerational programs; Pet therapy.

Carrizo Springs

Canterbury Villa of Carrizo Springs
8th & Clark Sts, Carrizo Springs, TX 78834
(512) 876-5011
Admin Anna M Howenstine. *Dir of Nursing* Felicitas Martinez LVN. *Medical Dir* Richard A Lankes MD.
Licensure Intermediate care; Personal care. *Beds* ICF 100; Personal care 24. *Private Pay Patients* 5%. *Certified* Medicaid.
Owner Proprietary corp (Texas Health Enterprises Inc).
Admissions Requirements Minimum age 18; Medical examination; Physician's request.
Staff LPNs; Nurses' aides; Activities coordinators; Dietitians.
Facilities Dining room; Activities room; Crafts room; Laundry room; Barber/Beauty shop.
Activities Arts & crafts; Games; Movies; Dances/Social/Cultural gatherings; Intergenerational programs.

Carrollton

Brookhaven Nursing Center
1855 Cheyenne, Carrollton, TX 75010
(214) 394-7141
Licensure Nursing. *Beds* Nursing 180.

Carrollton Manor
1618 Kirby, Carrollton, TX 75006
(214) 245-1573
Admin Sybil Perrin.
Licensure Intermediate care. *Beds* 120.
   Certified Medicaid.
Owner Proprietary corp (ARA Living Centers).

Northwood Manor Nursing Home
2135 Denton Dr, Carrollton, TX 75006
(214) 242-0666
Admin Charles William Hames.
Licensure Intermediate care. *Beds* 150.
   Certified Medicaid.
Owner Proprietary corp (Beverly Enterprises).

Carthage

Leisure Lodge
701 S Market, Carthage, TX 75633
(214) 693-6671
Admin Tommie Hight. *Dir of Nursing* Shirley Harris RN. *Medical Dir* Dr W C Smith.
Licensure Intermediate care. *Beds* ICF 104.
   Certified Medicaid.
Owner Proprietary corp (Beverly Enterprises).
Admissions Requirements Medical examination; Physician's request.
Staff RNs 1 (ft); LPNs 5 (ft), 4 (pt); Nurses' aides 20 (ft), 4 (pt); Physical therapists; Activities coordinators 1 (ft); Dietitians.
Facilities Dining room; Activities room; Chapel; Crafts room; Laundry room; Barber/Beauty shop.
Activities Arts & crafts; Cards; Games; Reading groups; Prayer groups; Movies; Shopping trips; Dances/Social/Cultural gatherings.

Panola Nursing Home
501 Cottage Rd, Carthage, TX 75633
(214) 693-7141
Admin Janet S Chamness. *Dir of Nursing*
June Alexander RN.
Licensure Skilled care; Intermediate care. *Beds*
108. *Certified* Medicaid; Medicare.
Owner Nonprofit corp.
Admissions Requirements Physician's request.
Staff RNs 1 (ft), 1 (pt); LPNs 10 (ft), 5 (pt);
Nurses' aides 32 (ft), 10 (pt); Activities
coordinators 1 (ft); Dietitians 1 (ft).
Facilities Dining room; Activities room;
Crafts room; Barber/Beauty shop.
Activities Arts & crafts; Cards; Games;
Reading groups; Prayer groups; Movies;
Shopping trips; Dances/Social/Cultural
gatherings.

Cedar Hill

Cedar Hill Nursing Center
303 S Clark Rd, Cedar Hill, TX 75104
(214) 291-7877
Admin Kerri G Etminan. *Dir of Nursing*
Deanna Green.
Licensure Intermediate care. *Beds* ICF 120.
Certified Medicaid.
Owner Proprietary corp (Beverly Enterprises).
Staff Physicians; RNs; LPNs; Nurses' aides;
Physical therapists; Reality therapists;
Recreational therapists; Occupational
therapists; Speech therapists; Activities
coordinators; Dietitians.

Celina

Belinda Care Center
PO Box 158, 601 Ohio Center, Celina, TX
75009
(214) 382-2356
Admin Peggy Jones. *Dir of Nursing* Jane
Sullivan RN. *Medical Dir* Glen Mitchell
MD.
Licensure Intermediate care. *Beds* ICF 88.
Certified Medicaid.
Owner Privately owned.
Admissions Requirements Medical
examination; Physician's request.
Staff RNs 1 (ft); LPNs 4 (ft); Nurses' aides 19
(ft); Activities coordinators 1 (ft); Dietitians
1 (ft).
Facilities Dining room; Activities room;
Crafts room; Laundry room; Barber/Beauty
shop.
Activities Arts & crafts; Cards; Games;
Reading groups; Prayer groups; Movies;
Shopping trips; Dances/Social/Cultural
gatherings.

Center

Green Acres Convalescent Center
501 Timpson, Center, TX 75935
(409) 598-2483
Admin Evelyn R Russell.
Licensure Intermediate care. *Beds* 102.
Certified Medicaid.
Owner Proprietary corp (ARA Living
Centers).
Admissions Requirements Medical
examination; Physician's request.
Staff RNs 1 (ft); LPNs 8 (ft); Nurses' aides 27
(ft); Physical therapists 1 (ft); Activities
coordinators 1 (ft); Podiatrists 1 (pt).
Facilities Dining room; Activities room;
Chapel; Crafts room; Laundry room; Barber/
Beauty shop.
Activities Arts & crafts; Cards; Games;
Reading groups; Prayer groups; Movies.

Holiday Nursing Center
PO Box 631, 100 Holiday Circle, Center, TX
75935
(713) 598-3371
Admin Gayla Adams.

Licensure Skilled care; Intermediate care. *Beds*
137. *Certified* Medicaid.
Owner Proprietary corp.

Pine Grove Nursing Center
Haley Ave at Loop 500, Center, TX 75935
(409) 598-6286
Licensure Nursing. *Beds* Nursing 120.

Centerville

Leisure Lodge Centerville
PO Drawer 158, 103 Teakwood Center,
Centerville, TX 75833
(214) 536-2596
Admin Beth J Rodell.
Licensure Intermediate care. *Beds* 100.
Certified Medicaid.
Owner Proprietary corp (Beverly Enterprises).

Chandler

Chandler Nursing Center
300 Cherry St, Chandler, TX 75758
(214) 849-2485
Licensure Nursing. *Beds* Nursing 60.

Childress

Childress Nursing Center
Box 1025, Childress, TX 79201
(817) 937-8668
Admin Shirley Southard.
Medical Dir Sharon Bowen.
Licensure Intermediate care; Personal care.
Beds ICF 110; Personal 10. *Certified*
Medicaid.
Owner Proprietary corp (Beverly Enterprises).
Admissions Requirements Physician's request.
Staff RNs 1 (ft); LPNs 8 (ft); Nurses' aides 18
(ft); Activities coordinators 1 (ft); Dietitians
1 (ft).
Facilities Dining room; Activities room;
Crafts room; Laundry room; Barber/Beauty
shop.
Activities Arts & crafts; Cards; Games; Prayer
groups; Movies.

Turner Nursing Home
PO Box 129, Childress, TX 79201
(817) 937-3675
Admin Linda Bohannon.
Licensure Intermediate care. *Beds* 60.
Certified Medicaid.
Admissions Requirements Medical
examination; Physician's request.
Staff RNs 2 (pt); LPNs 5 (ft); Nurses' aides 18
(ft), 2 (pt); Physical therapists 2 (pt); Speech
therapists 1 (pt); Activities coordinators 1
(ft); Dietitians 1 (pt); Ophthalmologists 1
(pt); Dentists 1 (pt).
Facilities Dining room; Activities room;
Laundry room; Barber/Beauty shop; Library.
Activities Arts & crafts; Cards; Games; Prayer
groups; Movies; Shopping trips; Dances/
Social/Cultural gatherings.

Chillicothe

Iris Haven Nursing & Convalescent Center
PO Box 667, 209 Ave I, Chillicothe, TX
79225
(817) 852-5151
Admin Helen W Holt. *Dir of Nursing* Betty
Clark LVN. *Medical Dir* Roy F Fisher DO.
Licensure Intermediate care. *Beds* ICF 36.
Private Pay Patients 20%. *Certified*
Medicaid.
Owner Proprietary corp (Wood Nursing
Home).
Admissions Requirements Minimum age 21;
Medical examination; Physician's request.
Staff LPNs; Nurses' aides; Physical therapists
(contracted); Activities coordinators 1 (ft);
Dietitians.

Facilities Dining room; Activities room;
Laundry room; Barber/Beauty shop.
Activities Arts & crafts; Cards; Games; Prayer
groups; Intergenerational programs.

Christoval

Christoval Golden Years Nursing Home Inc
PO Box 45, 116 McKee St, Christoval, TX
76935
(915) 896-2391
Admin Gilbert Aguirre. *Dir of Nursing* Linda
Leal RN. *Medical Dir* Betty Henry.
Licensure Intermediate care; Retirement. *Beds*
ICF 44; Retirement 12. *Certified* Medicaid.
Owner Proprietary corp.
Staff Physicians 1 (pt); RNs 3 (pt); LPNs 5
(pt); Nurses' aides 16 (pt); Activities
coordinators 1 (pt); Dietitians 1 (pt).
Languages Spanish.
Facilities Dining room; Activities room;
Laundry room.
Activities Arts & crafts; Cards; Games;
Reading groups; Prayer groups; Movies.

Cisco

Canterburry Villa of Cisco
PO Box 190, 1404 Front St, Cisco, TX 76437
(817) 442-4202
Admin Patricia R Monroe. *Dir of Nursing*
Nova George.
Licensure Intermediate care; Alzheimer's care.
Beds 106. *Certified* Medicaid.
Owner Proprietary corp (Texas Health
Enterprises).
Admissions Requirements Physician's request.
Staff Physicians 1 (pt); RNs 1 (pt); LPNs 8
(ft); Nurses' aides 25 (ft); Activities
coordinators 1 (ft); Dietitians 1 (ft), 1 (pt).
Facilities Dining room; Physical therapy
room; Activities room; Chapel; Crafts room;
Laundry room; Barber/Beauty shop; Library.
Activities Arts & crafts; Cards; Games;
Reading groups; Prayer groups; Shopping
trips; Dances/Social/Cultural gatherings.

Clarendon

Medical Center Nursing Home
Box 1007, Hwy 70 N, Clarendon, TX 79226
(806) 874-3760
Admin Larry White. *Dir of Nursing* Sue
Leeper RN.
Licensure Intermediate care. *Beds* 43.
Certified Medicaid.
Owner Nonprofit corp.
Admissions Requirements Medical
examination.
Staff Physicians 1 (pt); RNs 1 (ft), 1 (pt);
LPNs 9 (ft); Nurses' aides 27 (ft); Reality
therapists 1 (pt); Recreational therapists 1
(pt); Activities coordinators 2 (ft); Dietitians
1 (ft), 1 (pt).
Facilities Dining room; Physical therapy
room; Activities room; Crafts room; Laundry
room; Barber/Beauty shop.
Activities Arts & crafts; Cards; Games;
Reading groups; Prayer groups; Movies;
Dances/Social/Cultural gatherings.

Clarksville

Clarksville Nursing Center
PO Box 113, 300 E Baker St, Clarksville, TX
75426
(214) 427-2236
Admin Edna Nelson.
Medical Dir Dr B C Muthappa.
Licensure Intermediate care. *Beds* 132.
Certified Medicaid.
Owner Proprietary corp (Beverly Enterprises).
Staff RNs 1 (ft); LPNs 10 (ft), 2 (pt); Nurses'
aides 35 (ft); Physical therapists 1 (pt);
Activities coordinators 1 (ft); Dietitians 1
(pt).

Facilities Dining room; Chapel; Laundry room; Barber/Beauty shop.
Activities Arts & crafts; Games; Reading groups; Prayer groups; Movies; Shopping trips; Dances/Social/Cultural gatherings.

Claude

Palo Duro Convalescent Home Inc
PO Box 420, 405 S Collins St, Claude, TX 79019
(806) 226-5121
Admin Sharon K Kelley. *Dir of Nursing* Dianne Hill RN. *Medical Dir* Peter Knight MD.
Licensure Skilled care; Alzheimer's care. *Beds* SNF 56. *Certified* Medicaid; Medicare.
Owner Proprietary corp.
Admissions Requirements Minimum age 18; Medical examination; Physician's request.
Staff RNs 3 (ft), 2 (pt); LPNs 4 (ft), 2 (pt); Nurses' aides 18 (ft), 5 (pt); Activities coordinators 1 (ft); Dietitians 1 (pt).
Languages Spanish.
Facilities Dining room; Activities room; Crafts room; Laundry room; Barber/Beauty shop.
Activities Arts & crafts; Cards; Games; Reading groups; Prayer groups; Movies; Dances/Social/Cultural gatherings.

Cleburne

Cleburne Health Care Center
PO Box 138, 1108 W Kilpatrick St, Cleburne, TX 76031
(817) 645-3931
Licensure Nursing. *Beds* Nursing 120.

Colonial Manor Nursing Home
2035 N Granbury St, Cleburne, TX 76031
(817) 645-9134, 477-3009
Admin Harold D Werning.
Licensure Skilled care; Intermediate care. *Beds* 150. *Certified* Medicaid.
Owner Proprietary corp (Beverly Enterprises).

Fireside Lodge
301 Lincoln Park Dr, Cleburne, TX 76031
(817) 641-3433, 641-3434
Admin Wanda Dean.
Medical Dir Betty Huddleston.
Owner Proprietary corp (Golden Age Nursing Homes Inc).
Staff RNs 2 (ft), 1 (pt); Nurses' aides 32 (ft); Activities coordinators 2 (ft); LVNs 11 (ft), 1 (pt).

Golden Age Nursing Home Inc
1102 Williams Ave, Cleburne, TX 76031
(817) 645-8049
Admin Wanda Dean.
Licensure Intermediate care. *Beds* 102. *Certified* Medicaid.
Owner Proprietary corp.

Leisure Lodge—Cleburne
PO Box 138, 1108 W Kilpatrick St, Cleburne, TX 76031
(817) 645-3931
Admin Donna Poteet.
Licensure Intermediate care. *Beds* 120. *Certified* Medicaid.
Owner Proprietary corp.

Cleveland

Galaxy Manor Nursing Center
903 E Houston, Cleveland, TX 77327
(713) 592-8775
Admin Ann Yeager.
Licensure Intermediate care. *Beds* 157. *Certified* Medicaid.
Owner Proprietary corp (Beverly Enterprises).

Clifton

Clifton Lutheran Sunset Home
Box 71, Clifton, TX 76634
(817) 675-8637
Admin Rev Lauren C Endahl. *Dir of Nursing* Sarah Turner. *Medical Dir* Dr Donald A Gloff.
Licensure Skilled care; Intermediate care; Personal care; Residential care; Retirement living. *Beds* SNF 60; ICF 120; Personal care 48; Residential care 40; Retirement apts 41. *Private Pay Patients* 50%. *Certified* Medicaid; Medicare.
Owner Nonprofit corp.
Admissions Requirements Minimum age 62; Medical examination; Physician's request.
Staff RNs 3 (ft); LPNs 14 (ft); Nurses' aides 70 (ft), 10 (ft); Physical therapists 1 (pt); Activities coordinators 3 (ft); Dietitians 1 (pt).
Languages Spanish.
Affiliation Evangelical Lutheran.
Facilities Dining room; Physical therapy room; Activities room; Chapel; Crafts room; Laundry room; Barber/Beauty shop; Library.
Activities Arts & crafts; Cards; Games; Reading groups; Prayer groups; Movies; Shopping trips; Dances/Social/Cultural gatherings; Intergenerational programs; Pet therapy.

Clute

Cross Health Care Center
914 N Hwy 288, Clute, TX 77531
(409) 265-4794
Admin Glenna L Morlan.
Licensure Intermediate care. *Beds* 120. *Certified* Medicaid.
Owner Proprietary corp.

Wood Lake Nursing Home
603 E Plantation Rd, Clute, TX 77531
(409) 265-4221
Admin Polly Hedrick.
Licensure Intermediate care. *Beds* 98. *Certified* Medicaid.
Owner Proprietary corp (ARA Living Centers).

Clyde

Clyde Nursing Center
Rte 3 Box 148, Old Hwy 80, Clyde, TX 79510
(915) 893-4288
Admin Glenn R Gray.
Licensure Intermediate care. *Beds* 48. *Certified* Medicaid.
Owner Proprietary corp.

Coleman

Coleman Care Center
Box 392, Winter's Hwy 53, Coleman, TX 76834
(915) 625-4157
Admin Jimmy D Simpson.
Medical Dir Toni Burrage.
Licensure Intermediate care; Retirement. *Beds* ICF 74; Retirement apts 8. *Certified* Medicaid.
Owner Nonprofit corp.
Admissions Requirements Physician's request.
Staff LPNs 8 (ft), 2 (pt); Nurses' aides 26 (ft), 11 (pt); Activities coordinators 1 (ft); Dietitians 1 (pt).
Languages Spanish.
Facilities Dining room; Activities room; Chapel; Crafts room; Laundry room; Barber/Beauty shop.
Activities Arts & crafts; Games; Prayer groups.

Leisure Lodge—Coleman
2713 Commercial, Coleman, TX 76834
(915) 625-4105

Admin Joyce Williams. *Dir of Nursing* Tanna Gilbreath. *Medical Dir* Dr Mann.
Licensure Intermediate care. *Beds* ICF 64. *Private Pay Patients* 20%. *Certified* Medicaid.
Owner Proprietary corp (Beverly Enterprises).
Admissions Requirements Medical examination; Physician's request.
Staff LPNs; Nurses' aides; Physical therapists (contracted); Activities coordinators; Dietitians (contracted).
Languages Spanish.
Facilities Dining room; Physical therapy room; Activities room; Crafts room; Laundry room; Barber/Beauty shop; Library.
Activities Arts & crafts; Cards; Games; Reading groups; Prayer groups; Movies; Shopping trips; Dances/Social/Cultural gatherings; Intergenerational programs; Pet therapy.

College Station

Brazos Valley Geriatric Center
1115 Anderson, College Station, TX 77840
(409) 693-1515
Admin Freddie M White.
Medical Dir Sally Perez LVN.
Licensure Intermediate care. *Beds* 150. *Certified* Medicaid.
Owner Proprietary corp (ARA Living Centers).
Admissions Requirements Medical examination; Physician's request.
Staff LPNs 7 (ft), 3 (pt); Nurses' aides 16 (ft), 2 (pt); Activities coordinators 1 (ft); Dietitians 1 (ft).
Facilities Dining room; Physical therapy room; Activities room; Crafts room; Laundry room; Barber/Beauty shop.
Activities Arts & crafts; Cards; Games; Shopping trips; Dances/Social/Cultural gatherings; Birthday parties; Church; Singing.

Collinsville

Collinsville Care Center
PO Box 9, 400 Main St, Collinsville, TX 76233
(214) 429-6426
Admin Anita Murphree.
Medical Dir John Galewaler DO.
Licensure Intermediate care. *Beds* 88. *Certified* Medicaid.
Owner Proprietary corp.
Admissions Requirements Medical examination; Physician's request.
Staff RNs 1 (ft); LPNs 5 (ft); Nurses' aides 20 (ft), 6 (pt); Activities coordinators 1 (ft); Dietitians 1 (ft).
Facilities Dining room; Activities room; Chapel; Crafts room; Laundry room; Barber/Beauty shop.
Activities Arts & crafts; Games; Prayer groups; Movies; Shopping trips; Dances/Social/Cultural gatherings; Picnics; Olympics.

Colorado City

Kristi Lee Manor Inc
1941 Chestnut St, Colorado City, TX 79512
(915) 728-5247
Admin Chester C Moody.
Licensure Intermediate care. *Beds* 116. *Certified* Medicaid.
Owner Proprietary corp.

Valley Fair Lodge
1541 Chestnut St, Colorado City, TX 79512
(915) 728-2634
Admin Marsha Rickard. *Dir of Nursing* Elia Gonzalez. *Medical Dir* Thomas Aquillion MD.
Licensure Intermediate care. *Beds* ICF 50. *Certified* Medicaid.

Owner Publicly owned.
Admissions Requirements Medical examination; Physician's request.
Staff Physicians 1 (pt); RNs 1 (pt); LPNs 12 (ft); Nurses' aides 18 (ft); Physical therapists 1 (ft); Recreational therapists 1 (pt); Activities coordinators 1 (ft); Dietitians 1 (ft), 1 (pt).
Facilities Dining room; Physical therapy room; Activities room; Chapel; Laundry room; Barber/Beauty shop.
Activities Arts & crafts; Games; Reading groups; Prayer groups; Shopping trips; Dances/Social/Cultural gatherings.

Columbus

River Oaks Convalescent Center
300 N St, Columbus, TX 78934
(409) 732-2347
Admin Robert E Gay III.
Medical Dir R Cecil Marburger MD.
Licensure Intermediate care. *Beds* 90. *Certified* Medicaid.
Admissions Requirements Medical examination.
Staff Activities coordinators 1 (ft).
Facilities Dining room; Activities room; Laundry room; Barber/Beauty shop; Library.
Activities Cards; Games; Reading groups; Prayer groups; Movies; Shopping trips; Dances/Social/Cultural gatherings.

Sweetbriar Nursing Home
103 Sweetbriar Ln, Columbus, TX 78934
(409) 732-5716
Admin Marian J Werland.
Medical Dir R Cecil Marburger MD.
Licensure Intermediate care; Personal care; Alzheimer's unit. *Beds* ICF 116; Personal 24. *Certified* Medicaid.
Owner Proprietary corp (ARA Living Centers).
Admissions Requirements Minimum age 18; Medical examination; Physician's request.
Staff RNs; LPNs 6 (ft); Nurses' aides 18 (ft); Physical therapists; Speech therapists; Activities coordinators; Dietitians.
Languages Spanish, German.
Facilities Dining room; Activities room; Crafts room; Laundry room; Barber/Beauty shop.
Activities Arts & crafts; Cards; Games; Reading groups; Prayer groups; Movies; Shopping trips; Dances/Social/Cultural gatherings; Cook outs; Field trips; Costume days.

Comanche

Western Hills Nursing Home
Rte 5 Box 26, Comanche, TX 76442
(915) 356-2571
Admin Bobbie Nichols.
Licensure Skilled care; Intermediate care. *Beds* 166. *Certified* Medicaid.
Staff RNs 1 (ft); Physical therapists 1 (pt).
Facilities Dining room; Physical therapy room; Activities room; Crafts room; Laundry room; Barber/Beauty shop.
Activities Arts & crafts; Cards; Games; Reading groups; Prayer groups; Shopping trips.

Comfort

Comfort Garden Home
PO Box 509, 700 Faltin Ave, Comfort, TX 78013
(512) 995-3747
Admin Jerald W Myers Sr. *Dir of Nursing* Rita Wellington RN.
Licensure Intermediate care. *Beds* ICF 60. *Private Pay Patients* 50%. *Certified* Medicaid.
Owner Proprietary corp.

Languages German, Spanish.
Facilities Dining room; Activities room; Crafts room; Laundry room; Barber/Beauty shop.
Activities Arts & crafts; Cards; Games; Reading groups; Prayer groups; Movies; Shopping trips; Dances/Social/Cultural gatherings; Intergenerational programs; Pet therapy.

Commerce

Oak Manor Nursing Home
2901 Sterling Hart Dr, Commerce, TX 75428
(214) 886-2510
Admin Sybil Perrin. *Dir of Nursing* Terri Landers. *Medical Dir* Rick Selvaggi MD.
Licensure Intermediate care. *Beds* ICF 116. *Certified* Medicaid.
Owner Proprietary corp (Texas Health Enterprises).
Staff RNs 1 (pt); LPNs 10 (ft); Nurses' aides 26 (ft); Activities coordinators 1 (ft); Dietitians 1 (ft).

Conroe

Autumn Hills Convalescent Center—Conroe
2019 N Frazier, Conroe, TX 77301
(409) 756-5535
Admin Faye D Thompson. *Dir of Nursing* Joyce Coulter RN. *Medical Dir* Donald Stillwagon MD.
Licensure Intermediate care. *Beds* ICF 108. *Certified* Medicaid.
Owner Proprietary corp.
Admissions Requirements Minimum age 50; Medical examination; Physician's request.
Staff Physicians 1 (pt); RNs 1 (pt); LPNs 10 (ft); Nurses' aides 25 (ft).
Facilities Dining room; Activities room; Chapel; Crafts room; Laundry room; Barber/Beauty shop; Library.
Activities Arts & crafts; Cards; Games; Reading groups; Prayer groups; Movies; Shopping trips; Dances/Social/Cultural gatherings.

Woodland Manor Nursing Home
99 Rigby Owen Rd, Conroe, TX 77301
(409) 756-1240
Admin Charles T Smith.
Licensure Intermediate care. *Beds* 150. *Certified* Medicaid.
Admissions Requirements Medical examination.
Staff RNs; LPNs; Nurses' aides; Physical therapists; Speech therapists; Activities coordinators; Dietitians; Podiatrists.
Facilities Dining room; Activities room; Crafts room; Laundry room; Barber/Beauty shop; Library.
Activities Arts & crafts; Cards; Games; Prayer groups; Movies; Shopping trips; Dances/Social/Cultural gatherings.

Cooper

Birchwood Manor Nursing Home
Hwy 64 W, Cooper, TX 75432
(214) 395-2125
Admin Delma Wintermute.
Licensure Intermediate care. *Beds* 100. *Certified* Medicaid.

Delta Nursing Home
101 SE 8th St, Cooper, TX 75432
(214) 395-2184, 395-4844 FAX
Admin Delores Toon Cregg.
Licensure Intermediate care; Intermediate care for mentally retarded. *Beds* ICF 38; ICF/MR 24. *Certified* Medicaid.
Owner Privately owned.
Admissions Requirements Physician's request.
Staff LPNs 2 (ft), 2 (pt); Nurses' aides 9 (ft); Activities coordinators 1 (ft), 1 (pt).

Facilities Dining room; Activities room; Crafts room; Laundry room; Barber/Beauty shop.
Activities Arts & crafts; Cards; Games; Reading groups; Prayer groups; Movies; Shopping trips; Dances/Social/Cultural gatherings.

Copperas Cove

Wind Crest Nursing Center
607 W Ave B, Copperas Cove, TX 76522
(817) 547-1033
Admin Darrell Cross. *Dir of Nursing* Ann LaBounty RN. *Medical Dir* Dr Wesley Smith.
Licensure Skilled care. *Beds* SNF 128. *Private Pay Patients* 15%. *Certified* Medicaid; Medicare.
Owner Proprietary corp (Wind Crest Inc).
Admissions Requirements Physician's request.
Staff RNs 3 (ft), 2 (pt); LPNs 18 (ft), 4 (pt); Nurses' aides 45 (ft), 7 (pt); Physical therapists 1 (pt); Activities coordinators 1 (ft), 1 (pt); Dietitians 1 (pt).
Facilities Dining room; Physical therapy room; Laundry room; Barber/Beauty shop.
Activities Reading groups; Prayer groups; Movies; Shopping trips; Dances/Social/Cultural gatherings.

Corpus Christi

Alameda Oaks Nursing Center
1101 S Alameda, Corpus Christi, TX 78404
(512) 882-2711
Licensure Nursing. *Beds* Nursing 148.

Avante Villa
5607 Everhart, Corpus Christi, TX 78415
(512) 854-4601
Admin Elma G Gomez. *Dir of Nursing* Ann Nicholas. *Medical Dir* J M McCullough.
Licensure Skilled care; Intermediate care. *Beds* SNF 50; ICF 154. *Private Pay Patients* 30%. *Certified* Medicaid; Medicare.
Owner Proprietary corp (Avante Group).
Admissions Requirements Physician's request.
Staff RNs 1 (ft), 1 (pt); LPNs 18 (ft), 5 (pt); Nurses' aides 50 (ft), 4 (pt); Physical therapists 1 (pt); Reality therapists 1 (ft); Occupational therapists 1 (pt); Speech therapists 1 (pt); Activities coordinators 1 (ft); Dietitians 1 (ft); Ophthalmologists 1 (pt); Podiatrists 1 (pt); Audiologists 1 (pt).
Languages Spanish.
Facilities Dining room; Physical therapy room; Activities room; Chapel; Crafts room; Laundry room; Barber/Beauty shop; Library.
Activities Arts & crafts; Games; Movies; Dances/Social/Cultural gatherings; Intergenerational programs.

Del Mar Health Care Center
4130 Santa Elena, Corpus Christi, TX 78405
(512) 882-3655
Admin Chet Clark. *Dir of Nursing* Tony Nerios.
Licensure Intermediate care. *Beds* ICF 108. *Certified* Medicaid.
Owner Proprietary corp.
Admissions Requirements Medical examination.
Staff RNs 1 (ft); LPNs 6 (ft); Nurses' aides 11 (ft); Activities coordinators 1 (ft); Dietitians 1 (pt).
Languages Spanish.
Facilities Dining room; Physical therapy room; Activities room; Crafts room; Laundry room; Barber/Beauty shop.
Activities Arts & crafts; Cards; Games; Prayer groups; Movies; Shopping trips; Dances/Social/Cultural gatherings.

Heartland of Corpus Christi
202 Fortune Dr, Corpus Christi, TX 78405
(512) 289-0889

Licensure Nursing; Personal care. *Beds* Nursing 121; Personal care 66.

Hillhaven—Corpus Christi
1314 3rd St, Corpus Christi, TX 78404
(512) 888-5511
Admin Jerry E Bell.
Medical Dir Dr B B Grossman.
Licensure Skilled care; Intermediate care. *Beds* 174. *Certified* Medicaid; Medicare.
Owner Proprietary corp (Hillhaven Corp).
Admissions Requirements Physician's request.
Staff Physicians 1 (ft); RNs 4 (ft); LPNs 25 (ft); Nurses' aides 60 (ft); Physical therapists 1 (ft); Recreational therapists 1 (ft); Occupational therapists 1 (pt); Speech therapists 1 (pt); Activities coordinators 1 (ft); Dietitians 1 (ft).
Facilities Dining room; Physical therapy room; Activities room; Laundry room; Barber/Beauty shop; Library; Country store.
Activities Arts & crafts; Cards; Games; Prayer groups; Movies; Shopping trips; Dances/Social/Cultural gatherings; Happy hours; Religious services; Bowling.

Holmgreen Health Care Center
101 N Upper Broadway, Trinity Towers, Corpus Christi, TX 78401
(512) 887-2000
Admin Chris Rodrique. *Dir of Nursing* Cindy Keese RN MSN. *Medical Dir* Dr G Reeves.
Licensure Nursing; Personal care; Apartment living. *Beds* Nursing 30; Personal care 30; Apartment living 170. *Private Pay Patients* 100%.
Owner Nonprofit corp.
Admissions Requirements Medical examination.
Staff RNs 1 (ft), 1 (pt); LPNs 4 (ft), 5 (pt); Nurses' aides 24 (ft), 3 (pt); Activities coordinators 1 (ft); Dietitians 1 (pt).
Facilities Dining room; Physical therapy room; Activities room; Crafts room; Laundry room; Barber/Beauty shop; Library.
Activities Arts & crafts; Cards; Games; Prayer groups; Movies; Dances/Social/Cultural gatherings.

Human Development Center
3031 McArdle Rd, Corpus Christi, TX 78415
(512) 854-1458
Admin Lillie O Bryant. *Dir of Nursing* M Spencer RN. *Medical Dir* Dr Antonio Hernandez; Dr Girish Patel.
Licensure Intermediate care for mentally retarded. *Beds* ICF/MR 100. *Certified* Medicaid.
Owner Proprietary corp (ARA Living Centers).
Admissions Requirements Minimum age 1 yr.
Staff RNs 2 (ft); Nurses' aides 42 (ft), 11 (pt); Activities coordinators 1 (ft); LVNs 11 (ft), 6 (pt).
Facilities Dining room; Physical therapy room; Activities room; Recreation room.

Lynnhaven Nursing Center Inc
3030 Fig St, Corpus Christi, TX 78404
(512) 882-1948
Admin Robert W Harman. *Dir of Nursing* Yolanda Taylor RN.
Licensure Intermediate care. *Beds* ICF 180. *Certified* Medicaid.
Owner Proprietary corp.
Admissions Requirements Minimum age 20; Medical examination; Physician's request.
Staff RNs 1 (ft); LPNs 15 (ft); Nurses' aides 58 (ft); Dietitians 1 (pt).
Facilities Dining room; Activities room; Crafts room; Laundry room; Barber/Beauty shop.

Retama Manor Nursing Center—Corpus Christi
2322 Morgan Ave, Corpus Christi, TX 78405
(512) 882-4242
Admin Lillie O Bryant.

Licensure Skilled care; Intermediate care. *Beds* 180. *Certified* Medicaid.
Owner Proprietary corp (ARA Living Centers).

Retirement & Nursing Center—Corpus Christi
3050 Sunnybrook, Corpus Christi, TX 78415
(512) 853-9981
Admin Richard Stebbins.
Licensure Skilled care; Intermediate care. *Beds* 178. *Certified* Medicaid.
Owner Proprietary corp.

South Park Manor
3115 McArdle, Corpus Christi, TX 78415
(512) 853-2577
Admin F E Deere.
Licensure Intermediate care. *Beds* 194. *Certified* Medicaid.
Owner Proprietary corp.

Westwood Manor
801 Cantwell, Corpus Christi, TX 78408
(512) 882-4284
Admin Dorothy Westbrook. *Dir of Nursing* Marie Fischer RN.
Licensure Intermediate care; Alzheimer's care. *Beds* ICF 62. *Certified* Medicaid.
Owner Privately owned.
Admissions Requirements Minimum age 18; Medical examination; Physician's request.
Staff Physicians 1 (ft); RNs 1 (ft); LPNs 6 (ft); Nurses' aides 23 (ft); Activities coordinators 1 (ft); Dietitians 1 (ft).
Facilities Dining room; Activities room; Crafts room; Laundry room; Barber/Beauty shop.
Activities Arts & crafts; Games; Prayer groups; Shopping trips; Dances/Social/Cultural gatherings.

Wooldridge Place
7352 Wooldridge Rd, Corpus Christi, TX 78415
(512) 991-9633
Licensure Nursing. *Beds* Nursing 120.

Corrigan

Pineywood Acres
300 E Hospital St, Corrigan, TX 75939
(409) 398-2584, 398-2585
Admin Steve Devries. *Dir of Nursing* Brenda Harris.
Licensure Intermediate care. *Beds* ICF 90. *Certified* Medicaid.
Owner Proprietary corp.
Admissions Requirements Medical examination; Physician's request.
Staff Nurses' aides; Activities coordinators; Dietitians; LVNs.
Facilities Dining room; Activities room; Laundry room; Barber/Beauty shop; Library; Covered patio.
Activities Arts & crafts; Cards; Games; Reading groups; Prayer groups; Movies; Dances/Social/Cultural gatherings.

Corsicana

Corsicana Nursing Home
1500 N 45th, Corsicana, TX 75110
(214) 872-4606
Admin Todd E Mayfield. *Dir of Nursing* Pat Coppode. *Medical Dir* J H Barnebee MD.
Licensure Intermediate care. *Beds* ICF 120. *Certified* Medicaid.
Owner Proprietary corp (Beverly Enterprises).
Admissions Requirements Minimum age 18; Medical examination; Physician's request.
Staff Physicians 1 (ft); RNs 1 (pt); LPNs 8 (ft); Nurses' aides 21 (ft), 8 (pt); Physical therapists 2 (pt); Activities coordinators 1 (ft); Dietitians 1 (ft); Ophthalmologists 1 (pt); Podiatrists 1 (pt); Dentists 1 (pt); Medical aids 5 (ft), 2 (pt).

Facilities Dining room; Physical therapy room; Activities room; Crafts room; Laundry room; Barber/Beauty shop.
Activities Arts & crafts; Cards; Games; Reading groups; Prayer groups; Movies; Shopping trips; Dances/Social/Cultural gatherings.

Mel-Haven Convalescent Home
PO Box 510, 901 E 16th Ave, Corsicana, TX 75110
(214) 874-7454, 872-0260 FAX
Admin Mildred J Jennings. *Dir of Nursing* Wavis Hale RN. *Medical Dir* Dr Charles Biltz.
Licensure Intermediate care. *Beds* ICF 106. *Private Pay Patients* 7%. *Certified* Medicaid; VA.
Owner Proprietary corp.
Admissions Requirements Minimum age 18; Medical examination; Physician's request.
Staff RNs 1 (ft); Dietitians.
Facilities Dining room; Activities room; Laundry room; Barber/Beauty shop; Van with hydraulic lift.
Activities Arts & crafts; Cards; Games; Prayer groups; Shopping trips; Pet therapy.

Park Row Health Care Center
3301 Park Row, Corsicana, TX 75110
(214) 872-2455
Admin Donna Gordon. *Dir of Nursing* Wavis Hale RN.
Licensure Intermediate care. *Beds* ICF 102. *Private Pay Patients* 30%. *Certified* Medicaid.
Owner Proprietary corp (Waverly Group).
Admissions Requirements Medical examination; Physician's request.
Staff RNs 1 (ft); LPNs 7 (ft), 1 (pt); Nurses' aides 18 (ft); Activities coordinators 1 (ft); Dietitians 1 (ft).
Facilities Dining room; Activities room; Chapel; Crafts room; Laundry room; Barber/Beauty shop; Library.
Activities Arts & crafts; Cards; Games; Reading groups; Movies; Shopping trips; Pet therapy.

Twilight Home Inc
3001 W 4th Ave, Corsicana, TX 75110
(214) 872-2523
Admin Mary B Beamon LNHA. *Dir of Nursing* Marilyn Krantz RN. *Medical Dir* Charles I Biltz MD.
Licensure Intermediate care. *Beds* ICF 106. *Private Pay Patients* 48%. *Certified* Medicaid.
Owner Nonprofit corp.
Admissions Requirements Medical examination; Physician's request.
Staff RNs 3 (ft); LPNs 9 (ft), 3 (pt); Nurses' aides 31 (ft), 6 (pt); Activities coordinators 1 (ft); Dietitians.
Languages Spanish.
Facilities Dining room; Activities room; Crafts room; Laundry room; Barber/Beauty shop.
Activities Arts & crafts; Cards; Games; Reading groups; Prayer groups; Movies; Shopping trips; Dances/Social/Cultural gatherings; Intergenerational programs; Pet therapy.

Westside Development Center
421 N 40th St, Corsicana, TX 75110
(214) 874-6543
Admin Billy Bruce Apperson.
Licensure Intermediate care for mentally retarded. *Beds* 71. *Certified* Medicaid.

Crane

Golden Manor Nursing Home
1205 S Sue St, Crane, TX 79731
(915) 558-3888
Admin Carolyn Belshe.

Licensure Intermediate care. *Beds* 30.
  Certified Medicaid.
Owner Proprietary corp.

Crockett

Crockett Care Center
Loop 304 E, Crockett, TX 75835
(409) 544-2051
Admin Andrea K Hill.
Licensure Intermediate care. *Beds* 120.
  Certified Medicaid.
Owner Proprietary corp (Beverly Enterprises).
Staff RNs 1 (ft); LPNs 5 (ft); Nurses' aides 14
  (ft); Activities coordinators 2 (ft).
Facilities Dining room; Activities room;
  Laundry room; Barber/Beauty shop.
Activities Arts & crafts; Games; Prayer groups;
  Movies; Shopping trips; Dances/Social/
  Cultural gatherings.

Houston County Nursing Home
210 E Pease, Crockett, TX 75835
(409) 544-7884
Admin Dennis I Baker. *Dir of Nursing* Meg
  Foster RN. *Medical Dir* E P Ramsey.
Licensure Intermediate care. *Beds* ICF 60.
  Private Pay Patients 20%. *Certified*
  Medicaid.
Owner Proprietary corp.
Admissions Requirements Medical
  examination; Physician's request.
Staff RNs 1 (ft); LPNs 3 (ft), 3 (pt); Nurses'
  aides 15 (ft), 8 (pt); Physical therapists
  (contracted); Recreational therapists
  (contracted); Occupational therapists
  (contracted); Speech therapists (contracted);
  Activities coordinators 2 (ft); Dietitians.
Facilities Dining room; Activities room;
  Chapel; Crafts room; Laundry room; Barber/
  Beauty shop.
Activities Arts & crafts; Cards; Games;
  Reading groups; Prayer groups; Movies;
  Shopping trips; Dances/Social/Cultural
  gatherings; Intergenerational programs.

Whitehall Nursing Center Inc
PO Box 998, 1116 E Loop 304, Crockett, TX
  75835
(409) 544-2163
Admin Terri Smith Hutcherson.
Licensure Skilled care. *Beds* 71. *Certified*
  Medicaid.
Owner Proprietary corp.

Crosbyton

Crosbyton Care Center
222 N Farmer St, Crosbyton, TX 79322
(806) 675-2115
Admin Vickie Dian Griffin.
Licensure Intermediate care. *Beds* 62.
  Certified Medicaid.
Owner Proprietary corp.

Cross Plains

Colonial Oaks Nursing Home
PO Box 398, 1431 E 14th & Ave A, Cross
  Plains, TX 76443
(817) 725-6175
Admin Frances M Wolf. *Dir of Nursing* Peggy
  Hilburn LVN.
Licensure Intermediate care. *Beds* ICF 41.
  Certified Medicaid.
Owner Privately owned.
Admissions Requirements Medical
  examination; Physician's request.
Staff LPNs; Nurses' aides; Activities
  coordinators.
Languages German.
Facilities Dining room; Barber/Beauty shop.
Activities Games; Reading groups; Prayer
  groups; Dances/Social/Cultural gatherings.

Crowell

Crowell Nursing Center
PO Box 670, 200 S "B" Ave, Crowell, TX
  79227
(817) 684-1511
Admin Pat Keen.
Licensure Intermediate care. *Beds* 80.
  Certified Medicaid.
Owner Proprietary corp (Beverly Enterprises).
Staff Physicians; RNs; LPNs; Nurses' aides;
  Physical therapists; Reality therapists;
  Recreational therapists; Occupational
  therapists; Speech therapists; Activities
  coordinators; Dietitians.
Facilities Dining room; Physical therapy
  room; Activities room; Crafts room; Laundry
  room; Barber/Beauty shop; Library.
Activities Arts & crafts; Cards; Games;
  Reading groups; Prayer groups; Shopping
  trips; Shopping trips; Dances/Social/Cultural
  gatherings.

Cuero

Retama Manor Nursing Center—Cuero
PO Box 630, Hwy 77-A, Cuero, TX 77954
(512) 275-3421
Admin Orlo W Lang.
Licensure Intermediate care. *Beds* 98.
  Certified Medicaid.
Owner Proprietary corp (ARA Living
  Centers).

Retama Manor Nursing Center—East
1010 McArthur, Cuero, TX 77954
(512) 275-6133
Admin Kathrin Moore.
Medical Dir Barbara Nuckels.
Licensure Intermediate care; Personal care;
  Retirement. *Beds* ICF 86; Retirement 26.
  Certified Medicaid.
Owner Proprietary corp (ARA Living
  Centers).
Staff LPNs 5 (ft), 1 (pt); Nurses' aides 13 (ft);
  Activities coordinators 1 (ft).
Languages Spanish.
Facilities Dining room; Chapel; Crafts room;
  Laundry room; Barber/Beauty shop; Library.
Activities Arts & crafts; Cards; Games;
  Reading groups; Prayer groups; Movies;
  Shopping trips; Dances/Social/Cultural
  gatherings.

Retama Manor Nursing Center—West
PO Box 630, 108 Hospital Dr Hwy 77A,
  Cuero, TX 77954
(512) 275-3421
Licensure Nursing. *Beds* Nursing 98.
Owner Proprietary corp (ARA Living
  Centers).

Cushing

Cushing Care Center Inc
PO Box 338, Hwy 225 N, Cushing, TX 75760
(409) 326-4529
Admin Yvonne Williamson. *Dir of Nursing*
  Florence Barrett.
Licensure Intermediate care; Retirement. *Beds*
  ICF 90. *Certified* Medicaid.
Owner Proprietary corp.
Admissions Requirements Minimum age 18;
  Medical examination; Physician's request.
Staff RNs 1 (ft); Nurses' aides 20 (ft), 5 (pt);
  Activities coordinators 1 (ft); LVN 7 (ft), 1
  (pt).
Facilities Dining room; Activities room;
  Crafts room; Laundry room; Barber/Beauty
  shop.
Activities Arts & crafts; Games; Prayer groups;
  Movies; Shopping trips; Dances/Social/
  Cultural gatherings.

Daingerfield

Pinecrest Convalescent Home
PO Box 519, 507 E Watson Blvd,
  Daingerfield, TX 75638
(214) 645-3791, 645-3915
Admin Judy L Dodd. *Dir of Nursing* Linda
  Pilgrim. *Medical Dir* Dr Buddy Smith.
Licensure Intermediate care; Alzheimer's care.
  Beds ICF 117. *Certified* Medicaid.
Owner Proprietary corp (Hillhaven Corp).
Admissions Requirements Medical
  examination.
Staff Physicians Medical director; LPNs 6 (ft);
  Nurses' aides 13 (ft); Activities coordinators
  1 (ft); Dietitians 1 (pt); Ophthalmologists 1
  (pt).
Facilities Dining room; Activities room;
  Crafts room; Laundry room; Barber/Beauty
  shop; Library.
Activities Arts & crafts; Cards; Games; Prayer
  groups; Movies; Shopping trips; Dances/
  Social/Cultural gatherings.

Dalhart

Coon Memorial Home
210 Texas Blvd, Dalhart, TX 79022
(806) 249-4571
Admin Jimmie Sue Chisum. *Dir of Nursing*
  Elsie Sullivan RN.
Licensure Intermediate care. *Beds* ICF 111.
  Private Pay Patients 65%. *Certified*
  Medicaid.
Owner Publicly owned.
Admissions Requirements Medical
  examination; Physician's request.
Staff RNs 3 (ft); LPNs 7 (ft); Nurses' aides 40
  (ft); Activities coordinators 2 (ft); Dietitians
  1 (ft).
Languages Spanish.
Facilities Dining room; Activities room;
  Crafts room; Laundry room; Barber/Beauty
  shop; Library.
Activities Arts & crafts; Cards; Games;
  Reading groups; Prayer groups; Movies;
  Dances/Social/Cultural gatherings; Pet
  therapy.

Dallas

Autumn Care Cliff Gardens
801 W 10th St, Dallas, TX 75208
(214) 946-8709, 943-6827 FAX
Admin Sarah L Kennard. *Dir of Nursing*
  Wanella Warker LVN. *Medical Dir* Carl
  Williford.
Licensure Intermediate care. *Beds* ICF 34.
  Private Pay Patients 10%. *Certified*
  Medicaid.
Owner Proprietary corp (Americare).
Admissions Requirements Medical
  examination; Physician's request.
Staff LPNs 4 (ft), 1 (pt); Nurses' aides 10 (ft),
  2 (pt); Activities coordinators 1 (ft);
  Dietitians 1 (pt); 4 (ft), 1 (pt).
Facilities Dining room.
Activities Arts & crafts; Reading groups;
  Prayer groups; Movies; Shopping trips; Pet
  therapy.

Autumn Leaves
1010 Emerald Isle Dr, Dallas, TX 75218
(214) 328-4161
Admin Marvin Kayse. *Dir of Nursing* Diane
  Williams RN.
Licensure Skilled care; Intermediate care;
  Retirement. *Beds* Swing beds SNF/ICF 88;
  Retirement 150.
Owner Privately owned.
Staff RNs; LPNs; Nurses' aides; Physical
  therapists (contracted); Activities
  coordinators; Dietitians.
Facilities Dining room; Activities room;
  Chapel; Crafts room; Laundry room; Barber/
  Beauty shop; Library; Van.

Activities Arts & crafts; Cards; Games;
Reading groups; Movies; Shopping trips;
Dances/Social/Cultural gatherings.

Brentwood Place One
8069 Scyene Cir, Dallas, TX 75227
(214) 388-0609
Admin Lily P Gaban. *Dir of Nursing* Barbara
Dubose LVN. *Medical Dir* Dr James
McClean.
Licensure Intermediate care. *Beds* ICF 116.
Certified Medicaid.
Owner Proprietary corp (National Heritage).
Admissions Requirements Minimum age 16;
Physician's request.
Staff Physicians; LPNs; Activities
coordinators; Dietitians.
Languages Spanish.
Facilities Dining room; Activities room;
Chapel; Crafts room; Laundry room; Barber/
Beauty shop.
Activities Arts & crafts; Cards; Games;
Reading groups; Prayer groups; Movies;
Shopping trips; Dances/Social/Cultural
gatherings.

Brentwood Place Three
8039 Scyene Cir, Dallas, TX 75227
(214) 388-0424
Licensure Nursing. *Beds* Nursing 120.

Brentwood Place Two
8059 Scyene Cir, Dallas, TX 75227
(214) 388-0519
Licensure Nursing. *Beds* Nursing 120.

Bryan Manor Nursing Home
3401 Bryan St, Dallas, TX 75204
(214) 823-9071
Admin Bonnie B Gayton.
Licensure Intermediate care. *Beds* 80.
Certified Medicaid.
Owner Proprietary corp.

Buckner Baptist Trew Retirement Center
4800 Samuell Blvd, Dallas, TX 75228
(214) 388-2171
Admin Robert L Herring Jr.
Licensure Skilled care; Custodial care. *Beds*
SNF 104; Custodial care 75. *Certified*
Medicaid.
Owner Nonprofit corp (Buckner Bapt Retire
Vlg).
Affiliation Baptist.

Buckner Ryburn Nursing Center
4810 Samuell Blvd, Dallas, TX 75228
(214) 388-0426
Admin Larry W Stephens. *Dir of Nursing*
Lynn Craft RN. *Medical Dir* John Morgan
MD.
Licensure Intermediate care. *Beds* ICF 120.
Private Pay Patients 50%. *Certified*
Medicaid.
Owner Nonprofit organization/foundation
(Buckner Baptist Benevolences.
Admissions Requirements Minimum age 65;
Medical examination; Physician's request.
Staff RNs 3 (ft); LPNs 11 (ft); Nurses' aides
33 (ft); Activities coordinators 1 (ft);
Dietitians 1 (ft).
Affiliation Baptist.
Facilities Dining room; Physical therapy
room; Activities room; Laundry room;
Barber/Beauty shop; Library.
Activities Arts & crafts; Games; Prayer groups;
Movies; Dances/Social/Cultural gatherings;
Pet therapy.

Central Park Manor Inc
2355 Stemons No 505, Dallas, TX 75207
(214) 823-5641
Admin Sarah Kirkpatrick. *Dir of Nursing*
Robin Recer. *Medical Dir* Dr L S Thompson
Jr.
Licensure Skilled care. *Beds* 64.
Admissions Requirements Minimum age 16;
Medical examination; Physician's request.

Staff Physicians 1 (pt); RNs 1 (ft); LPNs 10
(ft), 2 (pt); Nurses' aides 18 (ft), 2 (pt);
Physical therapists 1 (pt); Occupational
therapists 1 (pt); Speech therapists 1 (pt);
Dietitians 1 (pt); Podiatrists 1 (pt); Dentists
1 (pt).
Facilities Dining room.

Christian Care Center North
9009 Forest Ln, Dallas, TX 75243
(214) 783-1771
Admin E Eugene Standifer.
Medical Dir Karen Cash.
Licensure Intermediate care. *Beds* ICF 120.
Certified Medicaid.
Owner Nonprofit corp.
Admissions Requirements Minimum age 21;
Medical examination; Physician's request.
Staff LPNs 12 (ft), 1 (pt); Nurses' aides 20
(ft); Physical therapists; Reality therapists;
Recreational therapists; Occupational
therapists; Speech therapists; Activities
coordinators 1 (ft); Dietitians 1 (ft).
Affiliation Church of Christ.
Facilities Dining room; Activities room;
Crafts room; Laundry room; Barber/Beauty
shop.
Activities Arts & crafts; Games; Reading
groups; Prayer groups; Movies; Shopping
trips; Dances/Social/Cultural gatherings;
Adopt-A-Friend.

Cliff Towers Nursing Home
329 E Colorado Blvd, Dallas, TX 75203
(214) 942-8425
Admin Jack L Anders.
Medical Dir B Northam DO & T V Nguyen
MD.
Licensure Skilled care; Intermediate care;
Custodial care. *Beds* SNF 214; Custodial
care 37. *Certified* Medicaid.
Admissions Requirements Medical
examination; Physician's request.
Staff LPNs 23 (ft), 4 (pt); Nurses' aides 55
(ft), 16 (pt); Physical therapists 1 (ft); Reality
therapists 1 (pt); Recreational therapists 1
(pt); Occupational therapists 1 (pt); Speech
therapists 1 (pt); Activities coordinators 2
(ft); Dietitians 1 (ft).
Facilities Dining room; Physical therapy
room; Activities room; Chapel; Crafts room;
Laundry room; Barber/Beauty shop.
Activities Arts & crafts; Cards; Games;
Reading groups; Prayer groups; Movies;
Shopping trips; Dances/Social/Cultural
gatherings.

Convalescent Center
4005 Gaston Ave, Dallas, TX 75246
(214) 826-3891
Admin W Edward McLendon. *Dir of Nursing*
Linda Bishop RN. *Medical Dir* Dr Ben
Northam.
Licensure Intermediate care; Intermediate care
for mentally retarded. *Beds* ICF 140; ICF/
MR 104. *Certified* Medicaid.
Owner Proprietary corp (Unicare).
Admissions Requirements Medical
examination; Physician's request.
Staff Physicians 1 (pt); RNs 2 (ft); LPNs 20
(ft); Physical therapists 1 (pt); Recreational
therapists 1 (pt); Occupational therapists 1
(pt); Speech therapists 1 (pt); Activities
coordinators 1 (ft); Dietitians 1 (ft);
Ophthalmologists 1 (pt); Podiatrists 1 (pt);
Dentists 1 (pt).
Facilities Dining room; Physical therapy
room; Activities room; Crafts room; Laundry
room; Barber/Beauty shop; Library.
Activities Arts & crafts; Cards; Games;
Reading groups; Prayer groups; Movies;
Shopping trips; Dances/Social/Cultural
gatherings.

Crystal Hill Nursing Home Inc
630 Elsbeth Ave, Dallas, TX 75208
(214) 948-3996

Admin Regina Rideaux. *Dir of Nursing* Helen
Evans LVN. *Medical Dir* William Preston
MD.
Licensure Intermediate care; Alzheimer's care.
Beds ICF 60. *Certified* Medicaid.
Owner Proprietary corp.
Admissions Requirements Medical
examination.
Staff Physicians 5 (pt); RNs 1 (ft); LPNs 5
(ft); Nurses' aides 19 (pt); Physical therapists
1 (pt); Occupational therapists 1 (pt); Speech
therapists 1 (pt); Activities coordinators 1
(ft); Dietitians 1 (pt); Ophthalmologists 1
(pt); Podiatrists 1 (pt); Dentists 1 (pt).
Languages Spanish.
Facilities Dining room; Activities room;
Laundry room; Barber/Beauty shop.
Activities Arts & crafts; Cards; Games;
Reading groups; Prayer groups; Movies;
Shopping trips; Dances/Social/Cultural
gatherings.

Dallas Home for Jewish Aged
2525 Centerville Rd, Dallas, TX 75228
(214) 327-4503
Admin Mary Jo Pompeo. *Dir of Nursing*
Justine Thompson RN. *Medical Dir* David
Bornstein MD.
Licensure Intermediate care; Retirement;
Alzheimer's care. *Beds* ICF 265. *Certified*
Medicaid.
Owner Nonprofit corp.
Staff Physicians 4 (pt); RNs 14 (ft); LPNs 40
(ft); Nurses' aides 95 (ft); Physical therapists
2 (ft); Recreational therapists 3 (ft);
Occupational therapists 4 (ft); Activities
coordinators 1 (ft); Dietitians 2 (ft);
Ophthalmologists 1 (pt); Social workers 4
(ft), 1 (pt).
Languages Yiddish, Hebrew, Russian.
Affiliation Jewish.
Activities Arts & crafts; Cards; Games;
Reading groups; Prayer groups; Movies;
Shopping trips; Dances/Social/Cultural
gatherings.

Doctor's Nursing Center Foundation Inc
9009 White Rock Trail, Dallas, TX 75238
(214) 348-8100
Admin Frank Jimenez. *Dir of Nursing* Janet
Boyden. *Medical Dir* Dr Jose Pilatovsky.
Licensure Intermediate care; Custodial care.
Beds ICF 283; Custodial care 45.
Admissions Requirements Minimum age 16;
Medical examination; Physician's request.
Staff Physicians 8 (ft), 1 (pt); RNs 8 (ft), 6
(pt); LPNs 16 (ft), 8 (pt); Nurses' aides 58
(ft), 24 (pt); Physical therapists 1 (ft);
Recreational therapists 1 (ft); Occupational
therapists 1 (pt); Speech therapists 1 (pt);
Activities coordinators 2 (ft); Dietitians 1
(ft); Podiatrists 1 (pt); Dentists 1 (pt);
Pharmacist 1 (ft).
Facilities Dining room; Activities room;
Chapel; Crafts room; Laundry room; Barber/
Beauty shop; Library; Pharmacy.
Activities Arts & crafts; Cards; Games;
Reading groups; Prayer groups; Movies;
Shopping trips; Dances/Social/Cultural
gatherings; Cocktail hours; Resident's
council.

Fair Park Health Care Center
2815 Martin Luther King Jr Blvd, Dallas, TX
75215
(214) 421-2159
Admin Peggy Higgins. *Dir of Nursing* Jewel
Holick RN.
Licensure Intermediate care. *Beds* ICF 120.
Certified Medicaid.
Owner Proprietary corp.
Admissions Requirements Medical
examination; Physician's request.
Staff Physicians; RNs 1 (ft), 1 (pt); LPNs 10
(ft); Nurses' aides 35 (ft); Physical therapists;
Reality therapists; Recreational therapists;

Occupational therapists; Speech therapists; Activities coordinators 2 (ft); Dietitians 1 (pt); Ophthalmologists 1 (pt).
Facilities Dining room; Activities room; Laundry room.
Activities Arts & crafts; Cards; Games; Reading groups; Prayer groups; Movies; Shopping trips; Dances/Social/Cultural gatherings.

Four Seasons Nursing Center—Dallas
3326 Burgoyne St, Dallas, TX 75233
(214) 330-9291
Admin Margaret V Wheeler. *Dir of Nursing* Pat Getman RN. *Medical Dir* J D Johnson MD.
Licensure Skilled care; Personal care. *Beds* 208. *Certified* Medicare.
Owner Proprietary corp (Manor Care).
Admissions Requirements Medical examination; Physician's request.
Staff RNs 5 (ft), 2 (pt); LPNs 15 (ft), 4 (pt); Nurses' aides 44 (ft), 1 (pt); Physical therapists 1 (ft); Activities coordinators 2 (ft); Physical therapist aides 2 (pt).
Languages Spanish.
Facilities Dining room; Physical therapy room; Activities room; Crafts room; Laundry room; Barber/Beauty shop; Library; TV rooms.
Activities Arts & crafts; Cards; Games; Reading groups; Prayer groups; Movies; Shopping trips; Dances/Social/Cultural gatherings.

Juliette Fowler Homes
PO Box 140129, 100 S Fulton St, Dallas, TX 75214
(214) 827-0813
Admin Marcela L Wentzel Ph D.
Licensure Intermediate care. *Beds* ICF 131. *Certified* Medicaid.
Owner Nonprofit corp (Natl Bnvlnt Assn of Chrstn Homes).
Admissions Requirements Medical examination.
Staff Physicians; RNs; LPNs; Nurses' aides; Physical therapists; Recreational therapists; Occupational therapists; Speech therapists; Activities coordinators; Dietitians; Ophthalmologists.
Affiliation Disciples of Christ.
Facilities Dining room; Activities room; Chapel; Crafts room; Laundry room; Barber/Beauty shop; Library.
Activities Arts & crafts; Cards; Games; Reading groups; Prayer groups; Movies; Shopping trips; Dances/Social/Cultural gatherings; Resident council; Resident food consultants committee; Extensive recreational/therapeutic activities.

Garrett Park Manor
1407 N Garrett, Dallas, TX 75206
(214) 824-8030, 824-8039 FAX
Admin Mark R Cummings. *Dir of Nursing* Rebecca Miller RN. *Medical Dir* Dr James McClain.
Licensure Intermediate care; AIDS patient care. *Beds* ICF 77. *Private Pay Patients* 20%. *Certified* Medicaid.
Owner Proprietary corp (Brun-Hisey Inc).
Admissions Requirements Minimum age 18; Medical examination; Physician's request.
Staff Physicians 4 (pt); RNs 1 (ft); LPNs 5 (ft); Nurses' aides 20 (ft), 5 (pt); Physical therapists 1 (pt); Occupational therapists 1 (pt); Speech therapists 1 (pt); Activities coordinators 1 (ft); Dietitians 1 (pt).
Languages Spanish.
Facilities Dining room; Physical therapy room; Activities room; Crafts room; Laundry room; Barber/Beauty shop.
Activities Arts & crafts; Cards; Games; Reading groups; Prayer groups; Movies; Shopping trips; Dances/Social/Cultural gatherings; Intergenerational programs; Pet therapy.

Grace Presbyterian Village
550 E Ann Arbor, Dallas, TX 75216
(214) 376-1701
Admin Galen K Ewer. *Dir of Nursing* Nancy Torrealba RN. *Medical Dir* Allen M Fain MD.
Licensure Intermediate care; Personal care; Independent living; Alzheimer's care. *Beds* ICF 160; Independent living 110. *Private Pay Patients* 80%. *Certified* Medicaid.
Owner Nonprofit corp.
Admissions Requirements Medical examination.
Staff Physicians 4 (pt); RNs 4 (ft), 1 (pt); LPNs 17 (ft), 2 (pt); Nurses' aides 35 (ft), 4 (pt); Physical therapists 1 (pt); Recreational therapists 3 (ft); Occupational therapists 1 (pt); Speech therapists 1 (pt); Activities coordinators 2 (ft); Dietitians 1 (ft); Podiatrists 1 (pt).
Languages Spanish.
Affiliation Presbyterian.
Facilities Dining room; Physical therapy room; Activities room; Chapel; Crafts room; Laundry room; Barber/Beauty shop; Library; Alzheimer's unit.
Activities Arts & crafts; Games; Prayer groups; Movies; Shopping trips; Pet therapy.

Greenery Rehabilitation Center
7850 Brookhollow Rd, Dallas, TX 75235
(214) 637-0000
Admin William J McGinley.
Licensure Skilled care. *Beds* SNF 66.
Owner Proprietary corp (Greenery Rehabilitation Group Inc).
Admissions Requirements Medical examination.
Staff Physicians; RNs; LPNs; Nurses' aides; Physical therapists; Recreational therapists; Occupational therapists; Speech therapists; Activities coordinators; Dietitians; Ophthalmologists; Podiatrists; Dentists; Psychiatrists; Neuropsychologists.
Languages Spanish.
Facilities Dining room; Physical therapy room; Activities room; Crafts room; Laundry room; Barber/Beauty shop; Library; Hydrotherapy department.
Activities Arts & crafts; Cards; Games; Reading groups; Prayer groups; Movies; Shopping trips; Dances/Social/Cultural gatherings.

Heritage Forest Lane
9009 Forest Ln, Dallas, TX 75243
(214) 783-1771
Admin Terry VanGundy. *Dir of Nursing* Sandra Pendergraph RN. *Medical Dir* S C Ong MD.
Licensure Intermediate care. *Beds* ICF 120. *Certified* Medicaid.
Owner Proprietary corp (People Care Inc).
Admissions Requirements Medical examination; Physician's request.
Staff RNs; LPNs; Nurses' aides; Physical therapists; Activities coordinators; Dietitians.
Facilities Dining room; Activities room; Chapel; Laundry room; Barber/Beauty shop; Library; Big screen TV room; Ice cream parlor; Private dining room; Lounge area with TV & stereo; Fenced patio; 2 additional patios.
Activities Arts & crafts; Games; Prayer groups; Movies; Shopping trips; Dances/Social/Cultural gatherings; Intergenerational programs; Pet therapy; Manicures; Library visits; Dietary council; Resident council; Family participation.

Holiday Hills Retirement Center
2428 Bahama, Dallas, TX 75211
(214) 948-3811
Admin Mae E Maddox.
Licensure Skilled care; Intermediate care. *Beds* 135. *Certified* Medicaid.
Owner Proprietary corp (Beverly Enterprises).

Kensington Manor
8039 Scyene Circle, Dallas, TX 75227
(214) 388-0424
Admin Billie C Hardin.
Licensure Intermediate care. *Beds* 120. *Certified* Medicaid.
Owner Proprietary corp (ARA Living Centers).

La Boure Care Center
1950 Record Crossing, Dallas, TX 75235
(214) 879-6400
Admin Douglas Daugherty.
Licensure Skilled care. *Beds* 155. *Certified* Medicaid; Medicare.
Owner Proprietary corp.

Lake Park Nursing & Retirement Center
329 E Colorado Blvd, Dallas, TX 75203
(214) 942-8425
Licensure Nursing. *Beds* Nursing 185.

Meadowgreen
8383 Meadow Rd, Dallas, TX 75231
(214) 369-7811
Admin Herman D Sabrsula. *Dir of Nursing* Earnestine Melton RN. *Medical Dir* Paul Cary MD.
Licensure Skilled care; Custodial care. *Beds* SNF 128; Custodial care 26. *Certified* Medicare.
Owner Proprietary corp.
Admissions Requirements Minimum age 18; Medical examination; Physician's request.
Staff Physicians 1 (ft); RNs 5 (ft); LPNs 18 (ft); Nurses' aides 33 (ft); Physical therapists 1 (ft); Activities coordinators 2 (ft); Dietitians 1 (ft).
Facilities Dining room; Physical therapy room; Laundry room; Barber/Beauty shop; Library; Covered patio.
Activities Arts & crafts; Cards; Games; Reading groups; Prayer groups; Movies; Shopping trips.

Northaven Nursing Center
11301 Dennis Rd, Dallas, TX 75229
(214) 247-4866
Admin Evelyn R Artall.
Medical Dir Stan Pull MD & S A Redfern MD.
Licensure Intermediate care. *Beds* 208. *Certified* Medicaid.
Owner Proprietary corp.
Admissions Requirements Minimum age 21; Medical examination; Physician's request.
Staff Physicians 1 (ft); RNs 3 (ft), 2 (pt); LPNs 14 (ft), 6 (pt); Nurses' aides 37 (ft), 10 (pt); Activities coordinators 1 (ft); Dietitians 1 (pt); Podiatrists 1 (pt); Dentists 1 (ft).
Facilities Dining room; Crafts room; Barber/Beauty shop; Library.
Activities Arts & crafts; Cards; Games; Reading groups; Prayer groups; Movies; Shopping trips; Dances/Social/Cultural gatherings.

Nottingham Manor
8059 Scyene Circle, Dallas, TX 75227
(214) 388-0519
Admin Jeanine Rutherford.
Medical Dir Dr Bill Morgan.
Licensure Intermediate care. *Beds* 120. *Certified* Medicaid.
Owner Proprietary corp (Beverly Enterprises).
Admissions Requirements Physician's request.
Staff Physicians 1 (ft); LPNs 6 (ft), 1 (pt); Nurses' aides 28 (ft), 4 (pt); Physical therapists 1 (pt); Recreational therapists 1 (ft); Occupational therapists 1 (pt); Activities coordinators 1 (ft); Podiatrists 1 (pt); Rehab LVNs 1 (ft).
Facilities Dining room; Activities room; Crafts room; Laundry room; Barber/Beauty shop; Rehab room.

Activities Arts & crafts; Cards; Games;
Reading groups; Prayer groups; Movies;
Shopping trips; Dances/Social/Cultural
gatherings.

Presbyterian Village North Health Services
8600 Skyline Dr, Dallas, TX 75243
(214) 349-3960
Admin C Lynn McGowan. *Dir of Nursing*
Ruth Matthews RN. *Medical Dir* Lisa Clark
MD.
Licensure Skilled care; Intermediate care;
Independent living; Personal care. *Beds* SNF
122; ICF 57.
Owner Nonprofit corp.
Admissions Requirements Minimum age 62;
Medical examination; Private Pay (financial
statement approval).
Staff Physicians 1 (pt); RNs 7 (ft), 1 (pt);
Nurses' aides 62 (ft), 1 (pt); Occupational
therapists 1 (ft); Activities coordinators 1
(ft); Dietitians 1 (pt); Chaplain 1 (ft);
Ambulation aide 1 (ft); Assistant
Administrator 1 (ft); LVNs 23 (ft), 2 (pt).
Facilities Dining room; Activities room;
Chapel; Crafts room; Laundry room; Barber/
Beauty shop; Library; Whirlpool; Pharmacy;
Gift shop.
Activities Arts & crafts; Cards; Games;
Reading groups; Prayer groups; Movies;
Shopping trips; Dances/Social/Cultural
gatherings; Cooking project; Current events;
Reality orientation; Exercise; In-room
activities for bed-fast.

St Joseph's Residence
330 W Pembroke, Dallas, TX 75208
(214) 948-3597
Admin Sr Adelaide R Bocanegra. *Dir of
Nursing* Billie Mokry. *Medical Dir* Dr Ross
M Carmichael.
Licensure Custodial care. *Beds* Custodial care
49. *Private Pay Patients* 100%.
Owner Nonprofit organization/foundation.
Admissions Requirements Minimum age 70;
Medical examination; Physician's request.
Staff Physicians; RNs; LPNs; Nurses' aides;
Activities coordinators; Dietitians;
Pharmacist.
Languages Spanish.
Affiliation Roman Catholic.
Facilities Dining room; Activities room;
Chapel; Crafts room; Laundry room; Barber/
Beauty shop; Library.
Activities Arts & crafts; Cards; Games;
Reading groups; Prayer groups; Movies;
Dances/Social/Cultural gatherings; Bus trips;
Sight-seeing.

South Dallas Nursing Home
3808 S Central Expwy, Dallas, TX 75215
(214) 428-2851
Admin Leona Hawkins.
Licensure Intermediate care. *Beds* 76.
Certified Medicaid.
Admissions Requirements Physician's request.
Staff RNs; LPNs; Nurses' aides; Occupational
therapists; Speech therapists; Activities
coordinators; Dietitians.
Facilities Dining room; Activities room;
Chapel; Crafts room; Laundry room.
Activities Arts & crafts; Cards; Games;
Reading groups; Prayer groups; Movies;
Dances/Social/Cultural gatherings.

Sunnyvale Manor
5300 Houston School Rd, Dallas, TX 75241
(214) 372-1496
Admin Don L Brewer.
Licensure Intermediate care. *Beds* ICF 200.
Certified Medicaid.
Owner Proprietary corp.

Sunset Manor
7626 Ferguson Rd, Dallas, TX 75228
(214) 327-9321
Licensure Nursing. *Beds* Nursing 92.

Tejas
3212 E Ledbetter, Dallas, TX 75216
(214) 374-0751
Licensure Nursing. *Beds* Nursing 62.

Traymore
7602 Culcourt, Dallas, TX 75209
(214) 358-3131
Admin Jessie E Wolkowicz.
Medical Dir James Walter Galbraith MD.
Licensure Skilled care; Intermediate care. *Beds*
150. *Certified* Private pay.
Owner Proprietary corp.
Admissions Requirements Medical
examination; Physician's request.
Languages Spanish.
Facilities Dining room; Activities room;
Crafts room; Laundry room; Barber/Beauty
shop; Library.
Activities Arts & crafts; Cards; Games;
Reading groups; Prayer groups; Movies;
Shopping trips; Dances/Social/Cultural
gatherings.

Tremont of Dallas
5550 Harvest Hill Rd, Dallas, TX 75230
(214) 661-1862
Admin Stephen Jones. *Dir of Nursing* Beth
Shapiro RN.
Licensure Skilled care; Intermediate care;
Custodial care. *Beds* 114.
Owner Proprietary corp.
Admissions Requirements Medical
examination; Physician's request.
Staff Physicians 2 (pt); RNs 5 (ft), 2 (pt);
LPNs 4 (ft), 1 (pt); Nurses' aides 18 (ft), 3
(pt); Physical therapists 1 (ft); Activities
coordinators 1 (ft), 1 (pt); Dietitians 1 (ft), 1
(pt); Podiatrists 1 (pt).
Facilities Dining room; Physical therapy
room; Activities room; Crafts room; Laundry
room; Barber/Beauty shop; Library.
Activities Arts & crafts; Cards; Games;
Reading groups; Prayer groups; Movies;
Shopping trips; Dances/Social/Cultural
gatherings.

Walnut Place
5515 Glen Lakes Dr, Dallas, TX 75231
(214) 361-8923
Admin Richard M Pratt. *Dir of Nursing* Gene
Ragsdale RN. *Medical Dir* Irwin Korngut
MD.
Licensure Skilled care; Personal care. *Beds*
SNF 285; Personal care 100.
Owner Privately owned.
Admissions Requirements Medical
examination; Physician's request.
Staff RNs; LPNs; Nurses' aides; Physical
therapists; Recreational therapists;
Occupational therapists; Activities
coordinators; Dietitians.
Facilities Dining room; Physical therapy
room; Activities room; Chapel; Crafts room;
Laundry room; Barber/Beauty shop; Library.
Activities Arts & crafts; Cards; Games;
Reading groups; Prayer groups; Movies;
Shopping trips; Dances/Social/Cultural
gatherings.

Westminster Manor
7979 Scyene Circle, Dallas, TX 75227
(214) 388-0549
Admin L Clay Stephenson.
Licensure Custodial care. *Beds* 96.
Owner Proprietary corp (National Heritage).

**C C Young Memorial Home—Young Health
Center**
4829 W Lawther Dr, Dallas, TX 75214
(214) 827-8080
Admin Julian D Thomas.
Licensure Intermediate care; Personal care.
Beds ICF 244; Personal 60. *Certified*
Medicaid.
Owner Nonprofit corp.
Affiliation Methodist.

Dayton

Heritage Manor Care Center
310 E Lawrence, Dayton, TX 77535
(409) 258-5562
Admin Jack Mallard.
Licensure Skilled care. *Beds* 60. *Certified*
Medicaid.
Owner Proprietary corp.

De Leon

Canterbury Villa—De Leon
PO Box 287, Hwy 6 E, De Leon, TX 76444
(817) 893-2075
Licensure Nursing. *Beds* Nursing 100.

De Leon Nursing Home
205 E Ayers, De Leon, TX 76444
(817) 893-6676
Admin Billie R Butler.
Licensure Intermediate care. *Beds* 53.
Certified Medicaid.
Admissions Requirements Medical
examination; Physician's request.
Staff RNs 1 (ft); LPNs 2 (ft); Nurses' aides 8
(ft); Activities coordinators 1 (ft); Dietitians
1 (pt).
Facilities Dining room; Activities room;
Laundry room; Barber/Beauty shop.
Activities Arts & crafts; Games; Reading
groups; Prayer groups; Shopping trips;
Dances/Social/Cultural gatherings.

Natatana Care Center
PO Box 287, Hwy 6 E, De Leon, TX 76444
(817) 893-2075
Admin Charles L Pollock.
Licensure Intermediate care. *Beds* 102.
Certified Medicaid.
Owner Proprietary corp.

De Soto

Park Manor
PO Box 945, 207 E Parkerville Rd, De Soto,
TX 75115
(214) 230-1000
Licensure Skilled care; Intermediate care;
Nursing care. *Beds* SNF 60; ICF 60; Nursing
care 30. *Certified* Medicaid; Medicare.
Owner Proprietary corp.

Decatur

Decatur Convalescent Center
PO Box 68, 605 W Mulberry St, Decatur, TX
76234
(817) 627-5444
Admin Geneva Galloway.
Licensure Intermediate care. *Beds* 60.
Certified Medicaid.
Owner Proprietary corp.

Golden Years Haven
PO Box 926, 1210 S Business Hwy 287,
Decatur, TX 76234
(817) 627-2234
Admin Lezlie McWhorter.
Medical Dir Verda Slimp.
Licensure Intermediate care. *Beds* 42.
Certified Medicaid.
Admissions Requirements Medical
examination.
Staff Physicians 5 (ft); RNs 1 (ft); LPNs 3 (ft),
1 (pt); Nurses' aides 16 (ft); Activities
coordinators 1 (ft); Dietitians 1 (ft); Dentists
1 (ft).
Facilities Dining room; Activities room;
Crafts room; Laundry room; Barber/Beauty
shop.
Activities Arts & crafts; Cards; Games; Prayer
groups; Movies.

Sunny Hills Nursing Center
200 E Thompson, Decatur, TX 76234
(817) 627-2165

Admin Gary M Hendrix.
Licensure Intermediate care. *Beds* 102.
  Certified Medicaid.
Owner Proprietary corp.

Deer Park

San Jacinto Heritage Manor
206 W Ave P, Deer Park, TX 77536
(713) 479-8471
Admin Pat Monroe.
Licensure Intermediate care. *Beds* 96.
  Certified Medicaid.
Owner Proprietary corp (National Heritage).

Dekalb

Sunny Acres
540 SE Front St, Dekalb, TX 75559
(214) 667-2572
Admin Dora S Perry. *Dir of Nursing* Donna
  Hawkins.
Licensure Intermediate care. *Beds* ICF 116.
  Private Pay Patients 15%. *Certified*
  Medicaid.
Owner Privately owned.
Admissions Requirements Minimum age 21;
  Physician's request.
Staff RNs; LPNs; Nurses' aides; Activities
  coordinators; Dietitians.
Facilities Dining room; Activities room;
  Chapel; Laundry room; Barber/Beauty shop.
Activities Arts & crafts; Cards; Games; Prayer
  groups; Movies; Dances/Social/Cultural
  gatherings.

Del Rio

Del Rio Nursing Home Inc
301 W Martin St, Del Rio, TX 78840
(512) 775-2459
Admin Nell T Gardner. *Dir of Nursing*
  Carleen White LVN. *Medical Dir* Ramon
  Garcia MD.
Licensure Intermediate care. *Beds* ICF 60.
  Private Pay Patients 33%. *Certified*
  Medicaid.
Owner Proprietary corp.
Admissions Requirements Minimum age 16;
  Medical examination; Physician's request.
Staff RNs 1 (pt); LPNs 5 (ft), 5 (pt); Nurses'
  aides 16 (ft), 1 (pt); Activities coordinators 1
  (ft); Dietitians 1 (pt).
Languages Spanish.
Facilities Dining room; Activities room;
  Crafts room; Laundry room; Barber/Beauty
  shop.
Activities Arts & crafts; Cards; Games;
  Reading groups; Prayer groups; Movies;
  Shopping trips; Dances/Social/Cultural
  gatherings; Intergenerational programs.

Retama Manor Nursing Center—Del Rio
100 Herrmann Dr, Del Rio, TX 78840
(512) 775-7477
Admin Janet Tennis.
Licensure Intermediate care. *Beds* 88.
  Certified Medicaid.
Owner Proprietary corp (ARA Living
  Centers).

Denison

Cantex Healthcare Center—Denison
801 W Washington St, Denison, TX 75020
(214) 465-9670
Admin Nancy Raulston.
Licensure Intermediate care. *Beds* 50.
  Certified Medicaid.
Owner Proprietary corp (Cantex Healthcare
  Centers).

Care Inn of Denison
1300 Memorial Dr, Denison, TX 75020
(214) 465-7442
Admin Adelia Shepherd.

Licensure Intermediate care. *Beds* 150.
  Certified Medicaid.
Owner Proprietary corp.

Denison Manor Inc
601 E Hwy 69, Denison, TX 75020
(214) 465-2438
Admin Ruth E Brinson.
Medical Dir M Y Stokes MD.
Licensure Skilled care; Intermediate care. *Beds*
  71. *Certified* Medicaid.
Owner Proprietary corp (ARA Living
  Centers).
Admissions Requirements Medical
  examination; Physician's request.
Staff RNs 2 (ft), 2 (pt); LPNs 5 (ft), 2 (pt);
  Nurses' aides 14 (ft), 4 (pt); Activities
  coordinators 1 (ft).
Facilities Dining room; Activities room;
  Crafts room; Barber/Beauty shop.
Activities Arts & crafts; Games.

Denton

Beaumont Nursing Home
2224 N Carroll Blvd, Denton, TX 76201
(817) 387-6656, 382-5713
Admin Pat B Kayser.
Licensure Intermediate care. *Beds* 55.
  Certified Medicaid.
Owner Proprietary corp.

Denton Good Samaritan Village
2500 Hinkle Dr, Denton, TX 76201
(817) 383-2651
Admin Douglas F Wuenschel.
Licensure Skilled care. *Beds* 92. *Certified*
  Medicaid.
Owner Nonprofit corp (Evangelical Lutheran/
  Good Samaritan Society).
Affiliation Lutheran.

Denton Nursing Center
2229 Carroll Blvd, Denton, TX 76201
(817) 387-8508
Admin Arveta M Shields.
Licensure Intermediate care. *Beds* 148.
  Certified Medicaid.
Owner Proprietary corp (Truco Inc).

**Lake Forest Good Samaritan Village Health
Care Center**
3901 Monecito Dr, Denton, TX 76205
(817) 383-1541
Licensure Nursing. *Beds* Nursing 60.

Vintage Health Center
205 N Bonnie Brae St, Denton, TX 76201
(817) 383-2361
Licensure Nursing; Personal care. *Beds*
  Nursing 110; Personal care 54.

Denver City

Canterbury Villa of Denver City
315 Mustang, Denver City, TX 79323
(806) 592-2127
Admin Virginia Clegg. *Dir of Nursing* Carol
  Jones RN.
Licensure Intermediate care. *Beds* 98.
  Certified Medicaid.

Deport

Deport Nursing Home
PO Box 396, Deport, TX 75435
(214) 652-7410
Admin Martha Castlebury; Charlene Borders.
  Dir of Nursing Marilyn Crawford.
Licensure Intermediate care. *Beds* ICF 102.
  Private Pay Patients 40%. *Certified*
  Medicaid.
Owner Proprietary corp.
Admissions Requirements Medical
  examination; Physician's request.

Staff RNs 2 (ft); LPNs 8 (ft); Nurses' aides 30
  (ft), 8 (pt); Physical therapists 1 (pt);
  Dietitians 1 (pt).
Languages Sign.
Facilities Dining room; Laundry room;
  Barber/Beauty shop.
Activities Arts & crafts; Cards; Games;
  Reading groups; Prayer groups; Movies;
  Shopping trips; Dances/Social/Cultural
  gatherings; Intergenerational programs; Pet
  therapy.

DeSoto

DeSoto Nursing Home
1101 N Hampton, DeSoto, TX 75115
(214) 223-3944
Admin Sylvia Bush. *Dir of Nursing* Rebecca
  Adams. *Medical Dir* Dr McLean.
Licensure Intermediate care. *Beds* ICF 120.
  Certified Medicaid; Private pay.
Owner Proprietary corp (Beverly Enterprises).
Admissions Requirements Medical
  examination; Physician's request.
Staff Physicians; RNs; LPNs; Nurses' aides;
  Physical therapists; Reality therapists;
  Recreational therapists; Occupational
  therapists; Speech therapists; Activities
  coordinators; Dietitians; Ophthalmologists;
  Podiatrists; Dentists.
Facilities Dining room; Activities room;
  Crafts room; Laundry room; Barber/Beauty
  shop.
Activities Arts & crafts; Cards; Games;
  Reading groups; Prayer groups; Movies;
  Shopping trips; Dances/Social/Cultural
  gatherings.

Skyline Nursing Home
1401 Meadow St, DeSoto, TX 75115
(214) 223-6311
Admin Henry C Hames. *Dir of Nursing* Mike
  Johnson RN. *Medical Dir* John Wright DO.
Licensure Skilled care; Intermediate care. *Beds*
  SNF 44; ICF 52. *Private Pay Patients* 30%.
  Certified Medicaid; Medicare.
Owner Proprietary corp (Cantex Healthcare
  Centers).
Admissions Requirements Minimum age 21;
  Medical examination; Physician's request.
Staff Physicians 5 (pt); RNs 1 (ft), 2 (pt);
  LPNs 12 (ft), 4 (pt); Nurses' aides 27 (ft), 2
  (pt); Physical therapists 1 (ft); Recreational
  therapists 1 (ft); Occupational therapists 1
  (pt); Speech therapists 1 (pt); Activities
  coordinators 1 (pt); Dietitians 1 (ft);
  Ophthalmologists 1 (pt); Podiatrists 1 (pt);
  Audiologists 1 (pt).
Languages Spanish.
Facilities Dining room; Physical therapy
  room; Crafts room; Laundry room; Barber/
  Beauty shop.
Activities Arts & crafts; Cards; Games;
  Reading groups; Movies; Dances/Social/
  Cultural gatherings; Intergenerational
  programs; Pet therapy; Bingo; Exercise.

Devine

Heritage Manor Inc
104 Enterprize, Devine, TX 78016
(512) 663-4451, 663-4452
Admin Eileen Lyall.
Licensure Intermediate care. *Beds* 100.
  Certified Medicaid.
Staff RNs 1 (ft); LPNs 4 (ft), 4 (pt); Activities
  coordinators 1 (ft); Dietitians 1 (pt).
Facilities Dining room; Physical therapy
  room; Activities room; Chapel; Crafts room;
  Laundry room; Barber/Beauty shop; Library.
Activities Arts & crafts; Cards; Games;
  Reading groups; Prayer groups; Movies;
  Shopping trips; Dances/Social/Cultural
  gatherings.

Heritage Residential Care Center
307 Briscoe Ave, Devine, TX 78016
(512) 663-2832
Admin Brenda Burford.
Medical Dir Angel Chapa.
Licensure Custodial care. *Beds* 45.
Owner Proprietary corp.
Staff LPNs; Nurses' aides; Activities
coordinators; Dietitians.
Facilities Dining room; Activities room;
Laundry room.
Activities Arts & crafts; Cards; Games;
Reading groups; Prayer groups; Movies;
Shopping trips; Dances/Social/Cultural
gatherings.

Diboll

South Meadows Nursing Home
PO Drawer BB, 900 S Temple Dr, Diboll, TX
75941
(409) 829-5581
Admin Jo Nell Placker.
Licensure Intermediate care. *Beds* 54.
Certified Medicaid.
Owner Proprietary corp.

Dimmitt

Canterbury Villa of Dimmitt
1621 Butler Blvd, Dimmitt, TX 79027
(806) 647-3117
Licensure Nursing. *Beds* Nursing 118.

South Hills Manor
1621 Butler Blvd, Dimmitt, TX 79027
(806) 647-3117
Admin Jean B Holt.
Licensure Intermediate care. *Beds* 118.
Certified Medicaid.
Owner Proprietary corp.

Dripping Springs

Hill Country Care Inc
Rte 4 Box 47BF, Hwy 290 W, Dripping
Springs, TX 78620
(512) 858-5624
Licensure Nursing. *Beds* Nursing 60.

Dublin

Dublin Nursing Center
715 Sheehan St, Dublin, TX 76446
(817) 445-2257
Admin C W Swanner.
Medical Dir Frances Rinehart.
Licensure Intermediate care. *Beds* 102.
Certified Medicaid.
Owner Privately owned.
Admissions Requirements Medical
examination.
Staff RNs; LPNs; Nurses' aides; Activities
coordinators; Dietitians; Ophthalmologists.
Languages Spanish.
Facilities Dining room; Activities room;
Laundry room; Barber/Beauty shop.
Activities Arts & crafts; Cards; Games;
Reading groups; Prayer groups; Movies;
Shopping trips; Dances/Social/Cultural
gatherings; Meals on Wheels.

Golden Age Manor
704 Dobkins, Dublin, TX 76446
(817) 445-3370
Admin Bobbie M Nichols. *Dir of Nursing*
Jimmie D Walker RN.
Licensure Skilled care; Intermediate care;
Retirement. *Beds* Swing beds SNF/ICF 90;
Retirement 6. *Certified* Medicaid; Medicare.
Owner Proprietary corp.
Admissions Requirements Medical
examination.
Staff RNs; LPNs; Nurses' aides; Activities
coordinators.

Facilities Dining room; Physical therapy
room; Activities room; Crafts room; Laundry
room; Barber/Beauty shop.
Activities Arts & crafts; Cards; Games;
Reading groups; Prayer groups; Movies;
Shopping trips; Dances/Social/Cultural
gatherings; Intergenerational programs.

Dumas

Dumas Nursing Center
1009 S Maddox, Dumas, TX 79029
(806) 935-4143, 935-4144
Admin Curt Osborn. *Dir of Nursing* Debbie
Ringo.
Licensure Intermediate care. *Beds* ICF 44.
Private Pay Patients 10%. *Certified*
Medicaid.
Owner Proprietary corp (Beverly Enterprises).
Admissions Requirements Medical
examination; Physician's request.
Staff Nurses' aides 15 (ft), 3 (pt); Activities
coordinators 1 (ft); Dietitians 1 (pt);
Podiatrists 1 (pt); LVNs 4 (ft), 2 (pt).
Languages Spanish.
Facilities Dining room; Activities room;
Barber/Beauty shop.
Activities Arts & crafts; Cards; Games; Prayer
groups; Intergenerational programs; Pet
therapy.

Duncanville

Shadyside Nursing Home
330 W Camp Wisdom Rd, Duncanville, TX
75116
(214) 298-3398
Admin Beverly V Johnson. *Dir of Nursing*
Krista R Denning RN. *Medical Dir* Don E
Christiansen DO.
Licensure Intermediate care. *Beds* ICF 60.
Private Pay Patients 100%.
Owner Proprietary corp.
Admissions Requirements Minimum age 50;
Medical examination.
Staff Physicians 5 (ft); RNs 2 (ft); Nurses'
aides 18 (ft); Physical therapists (contracted);
Reality therapists (contracted); Occupational
therapists (contracted); Speech therapists
(contracted); Activities coordinators 1 (ft);
Dietitians 1 (ft); Podiatrists (contracted).
Facilities Dining room; Activities room;
Crafts room; Barber/Beauty shop.
Activities Arts & crafts; Cards; Games; Prayer
groups; Pet therapy; Local entertainment.

Eagle Lake

Heritage House
200 Heritage Ln, Eagle Lake, TX 77434
(409) 234-3591
Admin Richard A Luebke.
Medical Dir Raymond R Thomas MD.
Licensure Intermediate care. *Beds* ICF 98.
Certified Medicaid.
Owner Proprietary corp (ARA Living
Centers).
Admissions Requirements Medical
examination; Physician's request.
Staff Physicians; LPNs; Nurses' aides;
Physical therapists; Occupational therapists;
Speech therapists; Activities coordinators;
Dietitians.
Languages Spanish, Czech, German.
Facilities Dining room; Activities room;
Crafts room; Laundry room; Barber/Beauty
shop.
Activities Arts & crafts; Cards; Games;
Reading groups; Prayer groups; Movies;
Shopping trips; Dances/Social/Cultural
gatherings; Senior Olympics.

Eagle Pass

Canterbury Villa of Eagle Pass
PO Box 1530, 2550 Zacatecas, Eagle Pass, TX
78852
(512) 773-4488
Admin Faye J Martin.
Medical Dir Doris Linder LVN.
Licensure Intermediate care. *Beds* ICF 120.
Certified Medicaid.
Owner Privately owned.
Admissions Requirements Medical
examination; Physician's request.
Staff RNs 1 (pt); LPNs 7 (ft); Nurses' aides 25
(ft); Reality therapists 1 (ft); Recreational
therapists 1 (ft); Activities coordinators 1
(ft); Dietitians 5 (ft).
Languages Spanish.
Facilities Dining room; Activities room;
Chapel; Laundry room; Barber/Beauty shop;
Library.
Activities Arts & crafts; Cards; Games;
Reading groups; Prayer groups; Movies;
Shopping trips; Dances/Social/Cultural
gatherings.

Eastland

Eastland Manor
PO Box 817, Eastland, TX 76448
(817) 629-2686
Admin Phillip Dalgleish.
Licensure Intermediate care. *Beds* 102.
Certified Medicaid.
Owner Proprietary corp (Beverly Enterprises).

Northview Development Center
411 W Moss St, Eastland, TX 76448
(817) 629-2624
Admin Lauretta Davis Lawler.
Licensure Intermediate care for mentally
retarded. *Beds* 54. *Certified* Medicaid.
Admissions Requirements Minimum age 18;
Medical examination; Physician's request.
Staff Physicians 1 (pt); RNs 1 (ft); LPNs 3
(ft), 3 (pt); Nurses' aides 14 (ft), 6 (pt);
Physical therapists 1 (ft); Recreational
therapists 1 (ft); Occupational therapists 1
(pt); Speech therapists 1 (pt); Dietitians 1
(pt); Ophthalmologists 1 (pt); Audiologists 1
(pt); Dentists 1 (pt).
Facilities Dining room; Activities room;
Crafts room; Laundry room; Barber/Beauty
shop.
Activities Arts & crafts; Cards; Games;
Reading groups; Movies; Shopping trips;
Dances/Social/Cultural gatherings; Camping;
Swimming; Hiking; Exercise classes; Make-
up classes.

Valley View Nursing Home
PO Box 552, 700 S Ostrom St, Eastland, TX
76448
(817) 629-1779
Admin Judith M Chaney.
Licensure Intermediate care. *Beds* 102.
Certified Medicaid.
Owner Proprietary corp (Beverly Enterprises).

Eden

Concho Nursing Center
PO Box 838, Eaker & Burleson Sts, Eden, TX
76837
(915) 869-5531
Admin Pearl Murrah.
Licensure Intermediate care. *Beds* 82.
Certified Medicaid.
Owner Proprietary corp (Unicare).

Edinburg

Colonial Manor
PO Box 308, 1401 S 2nd, Edinburg, TX
78540
(512) 383-4978

Admin Harlin L Sadler. *Dir of Nursing* Phyllis
   Karr. *Medical Dir* Dr Earnest Trevino.
Licensure Intermediate care. *Beds* ICF 44.
   Certified Medicaid.
Owner Privately owned.
Admissions Requirements Medical
   examination.
Staff Physicians; RNs; LPNs; Nurses' aides;
   Physical therapists; Reality therapists;
   Occupational therapists; Speech therapists;
   Activities coordinators; Dietitians;
   Podiatrists.
Languages Spanish.
Facilities Dining room; Activities room;
   Crafts room; Laundry room.
Activities Arts & crafts; Games; Prayer groups;
   Movies; Pet therapy.

Retama Manor Nursing Center
1505 S Closner, Edinburg, TX 78539
(512) 383-5656
Admin Leonides E Molina.
Licensure Intermediate care. *Beds* 104.
   Certified Medicaid.
Owner Proprietary corp (ARA Living
   Centers).
Staff LPNs 9 (ft); Nurses' aides 26 (ft);
   Activities coordinators 1 (ft); Dietitians 7
   (pt); Social workers 1 (ft).
Facilities Dining room; Activities room;
   Crafts room; Laundry room; Barber/Beauty
   shop.
Activities Arts & crafts; Cards; Games;
   Reading groups; Prayer groups; Movies;
   Shopping trips; Dances/Social/Cultural
   gatherings.

Edna

Care Inn of Edna
1204 N Wells, Edna, TX 77957
(512) 782-3581
Admin Henry L Langford. *Dir of Nursing*
   Pamela Pruitt. *Medical Dir* R Shenouda
   MD.
Licensure Intermediate care. *Beds* ICF 60.
   Private Pay Patients 11%. *Certified*
   Medicaid.
Owner Proprietary corp (ARA Living
   Centers).
Admissions Requirements Medical
   examination; Physician's request.
Staff LPNs 10 (ft), 2 (pt); Nurses' aides 20
   (pt); Physical therapists (contracted);
   Activities coordinators 1 (ft); Dietitians 1
   (ft); Podiatrists 1 (ft).
Languages Spanish, Czech.
Facilities Dining room; Activities room;
   Crafts room; Laundry room; Barber/Beauty
   shop.
Activities Arts & crafts; Cards; Games;
   Reading groups; Prayer groups; Movies;
   Shopping trips; Dances/Social/Cultural
   gatherings; Pet therapy; Holiday activities;
   Activities of daily living program.

El Campo

Czech Catholic Home for the Aged
Rte 3 Box 40, El Campo, TX 77437
(409) 648-2628
Admin Edith Sohrt Molberg.
Medical Dir Kathy Moore.
Licensure Intermediate care. *Beds* ICF 59.
   Certified Medicaid.
Owner Nonprofit corp.
Staff RNs 1 (pt); LPNs 7 (ft); Nurses' aides 20
   (ft), 4 (pt); Activities coordinators 1 (ft);
   Dietitians 1 (pt).
Affiliation Roman Catholic.

Garden Villa Nursing Home
106 Del Norte Dr, El Campo, TX 77437
(409) 543-6762
Admin Robert B Reeves.

Licensure Intermediate care. *Beds* 150.
   Certified Medicaid.
Owner Proprietary corp.

El Paso

Coronado Nursing Center Inc
223 S Resler, El Paso, TX 79912
(915) 584-9417
Admin William Jabalie.
Licensure Intermediate care. *Beds* 120.
   Certified Medicaid.
Facilities Dining room; Activities room;
   Laundry room; Barber/Beauty shop; Library.
Activities Arts & crafts; Games; Prayer groups;
   Movies; Dances/Social/Cultural gatherings.

El Paso Convalescent Center
11525 Vista Del Sol Dr, El Paso, TX 79936
(915) 855-3636
Admin Joyce Williams. *Dir of Nursing* Celia
   Duron.
Licensure Intermediate care. *Beds* ICF 150.
   Certified Medicaid.
Owner Proprietary corp (Beverly Enterprises).
Admissions Requirements Minimum age 21;
   Medical examination; Physician's request.
Staff LPNs; Nurses' aides; Physical therapists;
   Occupational therapists; Speech therapists;
   Activities coordinators; Dietitians.
Languages Spanish.
Facilities Dining room; Physical therapy
   room; Activities room; Crafts room; Laundry
   room; Barber/Beauty shop; Library.
Activities Arts & crafts; Cards; Games;
   Reading groups; Prayer groups; Movies;
   Shopping trips; Dances/Social/Cultural
   gatherings.

Four Seasons Nursing Center of El Paso
1600 Murchison Rd, El Paso, TX 79902
(915) 544-2002
Admin Betty Turner.
Licensure Skilled care; Intermediate care. *Beds*
   208. *Certified* Medicaid.
Owner Proprietary corp (Manor Care).

Hillhaven Convalescent Center
2301 N Oregon St, El Paso, TX 79902
(915) 532-8941
Admin Ann E Albert. *Dir of Nursing* Karen
   Fico RN. *Medical Dir* Robert Zurek MD.
Licensure Skilled care; Intermediate care;
   Alzheimer's care. *Beds* 247. *Certified*
   Medicaid; Medicare.
Owner Proprietary corp (Hillhaven Corp).
Admissions Requirements Minimum age 18;
   Medical examination; Physician's request.
Staff RNs; LPNs; Nurses' aides; Physical
   therapists; Speech therapists; Activities
   coordinators; Dietitians; Ophthalmologists;
   Podiatrists.
Languages Spanish.
Facilities Dining room; Physical therapy
   room; Activities room; Crafts room; Laundry
   room; Barber/Beauty shop.
Activities Arts & crafts; Cards; Games;
   Reading groups; Prayer groups; Movies;
   Shopping trips; Dances/Social/Cultural
   gatherings.

Montvista at Coronado
1575 Belvidere St, El Paso, TX 79912
(915) 833-2229
Licensure Nursing; Personal care. *Beds*
   Nursing 120; Personal care 15.

Mountain View Place
1600 Murchison Rd, El Paso, TX 79902
(915) 544-2002
Licensure Nursing. *Beds* Nursing 193.

Nazareth Hall
4614 Trowbridge Dr, El Paso, TX 79903
(915) 565-4677
Admin Sr Bernice B Juen. *Dir of Nursing*
   Colleen M Gillmouthe RN.

Licensure Intermediate care. *Beds* ICF 50.
   Certified Medicaid.
Owner Nonprofit corp.
Admissions Requirements Minimum age 18;
   Medical examination; Physician's request.
Staff Physicians 50 (pt); RNs; LPNs; Nurses'
   aides; Physical therapists; Activities
   coordinators; Ophthalmologists.
Languages Spanish.
Affiliation Roman Catholic.
Facilities Dining room; Activities room;
   Chapel; Crafts room; Laundry room; Barber/
   Beauty shop; Library.
Activities Arts & crafts; Games; Prayer groups;
   Movies.

Pebble Creek Nursing Center
11608 Scott Simpson, El Paso, TX 79936
(915) 857-0071
Admin Dioni Rivera. *Dir of Nursing* Suzanne
   Litterski. *Medical Dir* Frank Vilorio.
Licensure Skilled care; Intermediate care;
   Pediatrics. *Beds* SNF 60; ICF 60. *Private
   Pay Patients* 10%. *Certified* Medicaid;
   Medicare.
Owner Privately owned.
Admissions Requirements Medical
   examination.
Staff RNs 1 (ft), 2 (pt); LPNs 12 (ft), 1 (pt);
   Physical therapists 1 (pt); Recreational
   therapists 1 (pt); Speech therapists 1 (pt);
   Activities coordinators 1 (ft); Dietitians 1
   (pt); Podiatrists 1 (pt).
Languages Spanish, German.
Facilities Dining room; Physical therapy
   room; Activities room; Chapel; Laundry
   room; Barber/Beauty shop; 3 private dining
   rooms.
Activities Games; Prayer groups; Dances/
   Social/Cultural gatherings; Intergenerational
   programs; Pet therapy; Volleyball;
   Basketball; Bowling.

Rest Haven Nursing Home
2729 Porter Ave, El Paso, TX 79930
(915) 566-2111
Admin Joseph B Johns.
Licensure Intermediate care. *Beds* 51.
Owner Proprietary corp.

RN Nursing & Convalescent Home Inc
180 Croom Rd, El Paso, TX 79915
(915) 772-5480
Admin Joseph Johns. *Dir of Nursing* Tita S
   Vasquez. *Medical Dir* Dr W C Autrey.
Licensure Intermediate care. *Beds* ICF 48.
   Private Pay Patients 100%.
Owner Proprietary corp.
Admissions Requirements Medical
   examination.
Staff Physicians 1 (pt); RNs 1 (pt); LPNs 3
   (ft), 1 (pt); Nurses' aides 18 (ft); Physical
   therapists; Recreational therapists 1 (pt);
   Occupational therapists 1 (pt); Activities
   coordinators 1 (ft); Dietitians 1 (pt);
   Podiatrists 1 (pt).
Languages Spanish.
Facilities Dining room; Activities room;
   Crafts room; Laundry room; Barber/Beauty
   shop.
Activities Arts & crafts; Cards; Games;
   Reading groups; Prayer groups; Movies;
   Dances/Social/Cultural gatherings;
   Intergenerational programs; Pet therapy;
   Picnics; Barbecues; Gardening.

Sunset Haven
9001 N Loop Dr, El Paso, TX 79907
(915) 859-1650, 859-1653 FAX
Admin Jeanene Baucum LNHA. *Dir of
   Nursing* Joan Latimer LVN. *Medical Dir*
   David Carnes.
Licensure Intermediate care; Alzheimer's care.
   Beds ICF 120. *Private Pay Patients* 10-12%.
   Certified Medicaid.
Owner Proprietary corp.
Staff RNs 2 (ft); LPNs 1 (ft); Dietitians.

Languages Spanish.
Activities Arts & crafts; Cards; Games; Prayer groups; Movies; Dances/Social/Cultural gatherings; Pet therapy.

Vista Hills Health Care Center
1599 Lomaland Dr, El Paso, TX 79935
(915) 593-1131
Admin Miguel M Martinez.
Licensure Skilled care; Intermediate care. *Beds* 120. *Certified* Medicaid.
Owner Proprietary corp (Beverly Enterprises).

White Acres—Good Samaritan Retirement Village & Nursing Center
7304 Good Samaritan Ct, El Paso, TX 79912
(915) 581-4683
Admin Ronald Fechner. *Dir of Nursing* Rosa Ninojos.
Licensure Intermediate care; Retirement. *Beds* ICF 60. *Certified* Medicaid.
Owner Nonprofit corp (Evangelical Lutheran/Good Samaritan Society).
Admissions Requirements Medical examination; Physician's request.
Staff RNs 1 (ft); LPNs 7 (ft); Nurses' aides 15 (ft); Recreational therapists 1 (ft); Dietitians 1 (ft); Chaplains 1 (ft); Social workers 1 (ft).
Languages Spanish.
Affiliation Evangelical Lutheran.
Facilities Dining room; Activities room; Chapel; Laundry room; Barber/Beauty shop; Library.
Activities Arts & crafts; Games; Reading groups; Movies; Dances/Social/Cultural gatherings.

Eldorado

Schleicher County Medical Center
PO Box V, 400 Murchison St, Eldorado, TX 76936
(915) 853-2507
Admin Lilliam M Kroeger.
Medical Dir Dr H Shih.
Licensure Intermediate care. *Beds* 38. *Certified* Medicaid.
Admissions Requirements Medical examination.
Staff Physicians; RNs; LPNs 7 (ft); Nurses' aides 8 (ft); Activities coordinators 1 (ft); Dietitians 4 (ft).
Facilities Dining room; Activities room; Laundry room; Barber/Beauty shop.
Activities Arts & crafts; Cards; Games; Prayer groups; Shopping trips; Annual barbeque for residents' families; Monthly birthday parties.

Electra

Electra Nursing Center
511 S Bailey, Electra, TX 76367
(817) 495-2184
Admin Betty D Guyette. *Dir of Nursing* Gwen Latimer. *Medical Dir* Raymond Owen MD.
Licensure Intermediate care; Alzheimer's care. *Beds* ICF 69. *Private Pay Patients* 25%. *Certified* Medicaid.
Owner Proprietary corp (Beverly Enterprises).
Admissions Requirements Physician's request.
Staff RNs 1 (ft); LPNs 6 (ft), 2 (pt); Nurses' aides 16 (ft), 7 (pt); Activities coordinators 1 (ft); Dietitians 1 (pt); Food service supervisors 1 (ft).
Languages Spanish.
Facilities Dining room; Activities room; Crafts room; Laundry room; Barber/Beauty shop; Library.
Activities Arts & crafts; Cards; Games; Reading groups; Prayer groups; Movies; Dances/Social/Cultural gatherings; Intergenerational programs; Pet therapy; Bingo; Exercises.

Elgin

Elgin Golden Years Retirement & Nursing Home Inc
605 N US Hwy 290, Elgin, TX 78621
(512) 285-3444
Admin Patricia Ann McCullough.
Licensure Intermediate care. *Beds* 56. *Certified* Medicaid.
Staff RNs 1 (pt); LPNs 4 (ft); Nurses' aides 24 (ft), 2 (pt); Activities coordinators 1 (ft), 2 (pt); Dietitians 1 (pt).
Facilities Dining room; Activities room; Laundry room; Barber/Beauty shop.
Activities Arts & crafts; Cards; Games; Prayer groups.

Emory

Green Acres Nursing Home
Hwy 19 N, Emory, TX 75440
(214) 473-3752
Licensure Nursing. *Beds* Nursing 68.

Ennis

Claystone Manor Nursing Home
1107 S Clay St, Ennis, TX 75119
(214) 875-8411
Admin Dorothy Mahoney. *Dir of Nursing* Nancy Coffey RN. *Medical Dir* Dr Larry Jinks.
Licensure Skilled care; Intermediate care. *Beds* SNF 44; ICF 74. *Private Pay Patients* 10%. *Certified* Medicaid; Medicare.
Owner Proprietary corp (Beverly Enterprises).
Admissions Requirements Medical examination; Physician's request.
Staff Physicians 1 (ft); RNs 3 (ft); LPNs 8 (ft); Nurses' aides 26 (ft), 1 (pt); Physical therapists 1 (ft); Occupational therapists 1 (ft); Speech therapists 1 (ft); Activities coordinators 1 (ft); Dietitians 1 (ft); Ophthalmologists 1 (ft); Podiatrists 1 (ft).
Facilities Dining room; Physical therapy room; Activities room; Crafts room; Laundry room; Barber/Beauty shop; Library.
Activities Arts & crafts; Cards; Games; Reading groups; Prayer groups; Movies; Shopping trips; Dances/Social/Cultural gatherings; Intergenerational programs; Pet therapy.

Ennis Care Center
1200 S Hall St, Ennis, TX 75119
(214) 875-9051
Licensure Nursing. *Beds* Nursing 155.

Four Seasons Nursing Center
1200 S Hall St, Ennis, TX 75119
(214) 875-2673
Admin Mark R Cummings.
Medical Dir W D Kinzie MD.
Licensure Skilled care; Intermediate care. *Beds* 154. *Certified* Medicaid.
Admissions Requirements Minimum age 18.
Staff Physicians 9 (pt); RNs 6 (ft); LPNs 13 (ft), 6 (pt); Nurses' aides 39 (ft), 11 (pt); Physical therapists 2 (pt); Recreational therapists 1 (ft); Occupational therapists 1 (pt); Speech therapists 1 (pt); Activities coordinators 2 (ft); Dietitians 1 (pt); Ophthalmologists 1 (pt); Podiatrists 1 (pt); Audiologists 1 (pt); Dentists 1 (pt).
Facilities Dining room; Activities room; Chapel; Crafts room; Barber/Beauty shop; Library; Living & lounge rooms.
Activities Arts & crafts; Cards; Games; Reading groups; Prayer groups; Movies; Shopping trips; Dances/Social/Cultural gatherings; Outside trips; Garden club; College classes.

Odd Fellow & Rebekah Nursing Home
Rte 1, Oak Grove Rd, Ennis, TX 75119
(214) 875-8641
Admin David A Dunnahoo.

Licensure Intermediate care. *Beds* 58. *Certified* Medicaid.
Owner Nonprofit corp.
Affiliation Independent Order of Odd Fellows & Rebekahs.

Euless

Euless Nursing Center
901 Clinic Dr, Euless, TX 76039
(817) 283-5326
Admin Tina L Johnson.
Medical Dir Charles Maxville; Pam Homsher.
Licensure Intermediate care; Alzheimer's care. *Beds* ICF 120. *Certified* Medicaid.
Owner Proprietary corp (Beverly Enterprises).
Admissions Requirements Physician's request.
Staff RNs 1 (pt); LPNs 12 (ft); Nurses' aides 26 (ft); Activities coordinators 1 (ft).
Facilities Dining room; Crafts room; Laundry room; Barber/Beauty shop; Library.
Activities Arts & crafts; Cards; Games; Reading groups; Prayer groups; Movies; Dances/Social/Cultural gatherings; Monthly outings.

Evant

January Care Home Inc
506 Circle Dr, Evant, TX 76525
(817) 471-5526
Admin Sammie Lemons. *Dir of Nursing* Anita Lofland. *Medical Dir* C B Wright MD.
Licensure Intermediate care. *Beds* ICF 53. *Private Pay Patients* 30-40%. *Certified* Medicaid.
Owner Privately owned.
Admissions Requirements Medical examination; Physician's request.
Staff Physicians 1 (ft); RNs 1 (ft); Nurses' aides 15 (ft); Activities coordinators 2 (ft); Dietitians 1 (ft).
Facilities Dining room; Laundry room; Barber/Beauty shop.
Activities Arts & crafts; Cards; Games; Reading groups; Movies; Shopping trips; Dances/Social/Cultural gatherings.

Fairfield

Fairview Manor
PO Box 166, 601 Reunion St, Fairfield, TX 75840
(214) 389-4121
Admin Nellie H Halbert.
Licensure Intermediate care. *Beds* 90. *Certified* Medicaid.
Owner Proprietary corp.

Falfurrias

Canterbury Villa of Falfurrias
1301 S Terrell St, Falfurrias, TX 78355
(512) 325-3691
Admin Ann P Rotge.
Licensure Intermediate care. *Beds* 98. *Certified* Medicaid.
Owner Proprietary corp.

Farmers Branch

Brookhaven Nursing Center
5 Medical Pkwy, Farmers Branch, TX 75234
(214) 247-1000
Admin William A Rohloff.
Medical Dir Roger Beaudoing MD.
Licensure Skilled care. *Beds* 102. *Certified* Medicaid; Medicare.
Admissions Requirements Medical examination; Physician's request.
Staff RNs 7 (ft), 5 (pt); LPNs 8 (ft); Nurses' aides 30 (ft), 6 (pt); Physical therapists 2 (ft); Occupational therapists 1 (ft), 1 (pt); Speech

therapists 1 (ft); Activities coordinators 2
(ft); Dietitians 1 (ft); Ophthalmologists 2 (ft);
Dentists 1 (ft).
Affiliation Lutheran.
Facilities Dining room; Physical therapy
room; Activities room; Chapel; Crafts room;
Barber/Beauty shop.
Activities Arts & crafts; Cards; Games; Prayer
groups; Movies; Shopping trips; Dances/
Social/Cultural gatherings.

Farmersville

Hinton Home Inc
205 Beach St, Farmersville, TX 75031
(214) 782-6191
Admin Opal Hinton.
Licensure Intermediate care. *Beds* 74.
Certified Medicaid.
Staff RNs 1 (pt); Nurses' aides 28 (ft), 2 (pt);
Activities coordinators 1 (ft); Dietitians 1
(pt).
Facilities Dining room; Activities room;
Chapel; Laundry room; Barber/Beauty shop.
Activities Cards; Games; Prayer groups;
Movies; Shopping trips.

Ferris

Ferris Nursing Care Center
PO Box 427, 201 E 5th St, Ferris, TX 75125
(214) 544-2418
Admin Gabriel G Bach PhD. *Dir of Nursing*
Terri Palos RN. *Medical Dir* Dr B
Nordham.
Licensure Intermediate care; Retirement. *Beds*
ICF 88. *Certified* Medicaid.
Owner Proprietary corp.
Admissions Requirements Medical
examination; Physician's request.
Staff Physicians 1 (pt); RNs 2 (ft); LPNs 6
(ft); Nurses' aides 20 (ft); Activities
coordinators 1 (ft); Dietitians 1 (ft).
Languages Spanish, German.
Facilities Dining room; Activities room;
Laundry room; Barber/Beauty shop.
Activities Arts & crafts; Cards; Games;
Reading groups; Prayer groups; Movies;
Dances/Social/Cultural gatherings.

Flatonia

Oak Manor Nursing Center
PO Box 509, 624 Converse St, Flatonia, TX
78941
(512) 865-3571, 865-2591 FAX
Admin Ron Deshotels. *Dir of Nursing* Kathy
Koch. *Medical Dir* Dr M Wilkerson.
Licensure Intermediate care. *Beds* ICF 90.
Private Pay Patients 30%. *Certified*
Medicaid.
Owner Privately owned.
Staff Physicians 1 (pt); RNs 1 (ft), 1 (pt);
LPNs 5 (ft), 4 (pt); Nurses' aides 18 (ft), 6
(pt); Physical therapists 1 (pt); Speech
therapists 1 (pt); Activities coordinators 1
(ft); Dietitians 1 (ft), 1 (pt);
Ophthalmologists 1 (pt); Podiatrists 1 (pt).
Facilities Dining room; Activities room;
Crafts room; Laundry room; Barber/Beauty
shop; Library.
Activities Arts & crafts; Cards; Games;
Reading groups; Prayer groups; Movies;
Shopping trips; Dances/Social/Cultural
gatherings.

Floresville

Floresville Nursing Center
1811 6th St, Floresville, TX 78114
(512) 393-2561
Admin Norman J Custer. *Dir of Nursing*
Ofelia Morin. *Medical Dir* Dr Glen C
Coates.
Licensure Intermediate care. *Beds* ICF 144.
Certified Medicaid.

Owner Proprietary corp (Southwestern
Medical Centers).
Admissions Requirements Medical
examination; Physician's request.
Staff Physicians; RNs; LPNs; Nurses' aides;
Physical therapists (contracted); Activities
coordinators; Dietitians.
Languages Polish, Spanish, German.
Facilities Dining room; Physical therapy
room; Activities room; Crafts room; Laundry
room; Barber/Beauty shop; Library.
Activities Arts & crafts; Cards; Games;
Reading groups; Prayer groups; Movies;
Shopping trips; Dances/Social/Cultural
gatherings; Intergenerational programs.

Floydada

Floydada Nursing Home
PO Box 129, Floydada, TX 79235
(806) 983-3704
Admin Steve Westbrook.
Licensure Intermediate care. *Beds* 52.
Certified Medicaid.
Owner Proprietary corp.

Forest Hill

Forest Hill Nursing Center
4607 California Pkwy E, Forest Hill, TX
76119
(817) 535-0851
Licensure Nursing. *Beds* Nursing 120.

Fort Stockton

Comanche View Nursing Home
PO Box 1664, Fort Stockton, TX 79735
(915) 336-5261
Admin David B Herrell.
Licensure Intermediate care. *Beds* 68.
Certified Medicaid.
Owner Proprietary corp.

Fort Worth

All Seasons Central Care Center
921 W Cannon, Fort Worth, TX 76104
(817) 332-9261
Licensure Nursing. *Beds* Nursing 53.

All Seasons Nursing Center
PO Box 15522, 3825 Village Creek Rd, Fort
Worth, TX 76119
(817) 531-3696
Licensure Nursing. *Beds* Nursing 100.

Alta Mesa Nursing Center
5300 Alta Mesa Blvd, Fort Worth, TX 76133
(817) 346-1800, 346-0149 FAX
Admin Gabriel Bach PhD. *Dir of Nursing*
Teresa Manning RN. *Medical Dir* David
Engelking MD.
Licensure Intermediate care. *Beds* ICF 156.
Private Pay Patients 48%. *Certified*
Medicaid.
Owner Proprietary corp (Century Care Inc).
Admissions Requirements Physician's request.
Staff Physicians; RNs; Nurses' aides; Physical
therapists; Reality therapists; Recreational
therapists; Occupational therapists; Speech
therapists; Activities coordinators; Dietitians;
Ophthalmologists; Podiatrists; Audiologists.
Languages Spanish, German, French.
Facilities Dining room; Physical therapy
room; Activities room; Crafts room; Laundry
room; Barber/Beauty shop; Library; Enclosed
patios.
Activities Arts & crafts; Cards; Games;
Reading groups; Prayer groups; Movies;
Shopping trips; Dances/Social/Cultural
gatherings; Intergenerational programs; Pet
therapy.

Arlington Heights Nursing Center
4825 Wellesley St, Fort Worth, TX 76107
(817) 732-6608
Admin Lisbeth Miller.
Medical Dir Randall E Hayes DO.
Licensure Skilled care; Intermediate care. *Beds*
180. *Certified* Medicaid.
Owner Proprietary corp.
Admissions Requirements Medical
examination; Physician's request.
Staff RNs 3 (ft), 2 (pt); LPNs 22 (ft); Nurses'
aides 46 (ft); Activities coordinators 1 (ft);
Dietitians 1 (ft); Psychotherapist 1 (ft).
Facilities Dining room; Physical therapy
room; Activities room; Laundry room;
Barber/Beauty shop.
Activities Arts & crafts; Cards; Games;
Reading groups; Prayer groups; Movies;
Shopping trips; Dances/Social/Cultural
gatherings.

Autumn Care Cannon Manor
1617 W Cannon, Fort Worth, TX 76014
(817) 336-7283
Admin Betty J Ezell.
Licensure Skilled care; Intermediate care. *Beds*
104. *Certified* Medicaid.
Owner Proprietary corp.

Autumn Years Lodge Inc
424 S Adams, Fort Worth, TX 76104
(817) 335-5781
Admin Betty L Giaimo. *Dir of Nursing* Doris
Croyle. *Medical Dir* George McIlheran Jr
MD.
Licensure Skilled care; Intermediate care. *Beds*
SNF 111; ICF 84. *Certified* Medicaid;
Medicare.
Owner Proprietary corp.
Admissions Requirements Medical
examination; Physician's request.
Staff Physicians 3 (pt); RNs 3 (ft); LPNs 14
(ft), 3 (pt); Nurses' aides 54 (ft), 2 (pt);
Physical therapists 1 (pt); Recreational
therapists 1 (pt); Occupational therapists 1
(pt); Speech therapists 1 (pt); Activities
coordinators 1 (ft); Dietitians 1 (pt); Dentists
1 (pt).
Facilities Dining room; Physical therapy
room; Activities room; Chapel; Barber/
Beauty shop; Library; Sun lobby.
Activities Arts & crafts; Cards; Games;
Reading groups; Prayer groups; Movies;
Dances/Social/Cultural gatherings.

Brookhaven Nursing Center
4208 E Lancaster, Fort Worth, TX 76103
(817) 535-0816
Admin Jeannette Medlenka. *Dir of Nursing*
Therressa Houston LVN. *Medical Dir*
Harold Gaaitzer DO.
Licensure Intermediate care. *Beds* ICF 61.
Certified Medicaid.
Owner Proprietary corp (Summit Health Ltd).
Admissions Requirements Medical
examination; Physician's request.
Staff RNs 1 (ft); LPNs 6 (ft); Nurses' aides 16
(ft), 4 (pt); Activities coordinators 1 (ft);
Dietitians 1 (ft).
Facilities Dining room; Activities room;
Barber/Beauty shop; Sun room.
Activities Arts & crafts; Cards; Games;
Reading groups; Prayer groups; Movies;
Shopping trips; Dances/Social/Cultural
gatherings.

Cantebury Villa of Fort Worth
8401 Jacksboro Hwy, Fort Worth, TX 76135
(817) 237-3335
Admin Mary E Wolff. *Dir of Nursing*
Cameron Farris RN. *Medical Dir* Dr
Howard Graitzer.
Licensure Intermediate care. *Beds* ICF 104.
Certified Medicaid.
Owner Proprietary corp (Texas Health
Enterprises).

Staff Physicians 1 (ft), 4 (pt); RNs 1 (ft); LPNs 8 (ft), 2 (pt); Nurses' aides 24 (ft), 2 (pt); Physical therapists 1 (pt); Speech therapists 1 (pt); Activities coordinators 1 (ft); Dietitians 1 (pt); Ophthalmologists 1 (pt); Podiatrists 1 (pt); Dentists 1 (pt).
Languages Spanish.
Activities Arts & crafts; Cards; Games; Reading groups; Prayer groups; Movies; Dances/Social/Cultural gatherings.

Colonial Manor Nursing Center
400 S Beach St, Fort Worth, TX 76105
(817) 535-2135
Admin Ann E Williams.
Medical Dir Raj VenKatappan; Connie Fincher.
Licensure Skilled care; Intermediate care. *Beds* SNF 62; ICF 119. *Certified* Medicaid; Medicare.
Owner Proprietary corp.
Admissions Requirements Medical examination; Physician's request.
Staff RNs 2 (ft); LPNs 15 (ft); Nurses' aides 54 (ft); Activities coordinators 2 (ft); Dietitians 1 (ft); Dietary Manager 1 (ft).
Facilities Dining room; Activities room; Chapel; Crafts room; Laundry room; Barber/Beauty shop.
Activities Arts & crafts; Games; Movies; Shopping trips; Dances/Social/Cultural gatherings.

East Park Manor Nursing Center
1000 Park Manor Dr, Fort Worth, TX 76104
(817) 332-4042, 332-4044 FAX
Admin Gay Walters. *Dir of Nursing* Paula Farney. *Medical Dir* Raj Venkentappen.
Licensure Intermediate care; Alzheimer's care. *Beds* ICF 130. *Certified* Medicaid.
Owner Proprietary corp (Sensitive Care Inc).
Admissions Requirements Physician's request.
Staff RNs 1 (pt); LPNs 4 (ft), 4 (pt); Nurses' aides 20 (ft); Physical therapists 1 (pt); Recreational therapists 1 (pt); Occupational therapists 1 (pt); Speech therapists 1 (pt); Activities coordinators 1 (ft); Dietitians 1 (pt).
Languages Spanish.
Facilities Dining room; Activities room; Crafts room; Laundry room; Barber/Beauty shop.
Activities Arts & crafts; Cards; Games; Prayer groups; Movies; Shopping trips; Dances/Social/Cultural gatherings; Pet therapy.

Eastwood Village Nursing & Retirement Center
3825 Village Creek Rd, Fort Worth, TX 76119
(817) 531-3696
Admin Dovie J Webber.
Licensure Intermediate care. *Beds* 100. *Certified* Medicaid.
Owner Proprietary corp.

Fireside Lodge
4800 White Settlement Rd, Fort Worth, TX 76114
(817) 738-6556
Admin Terry McGrath FACHCA. *Dir of Nursing* Rita Prestage RN. *Medical Dir* Larry Sharp DO.
Licensure Skilled care; Intermediate care; Retirement; Alzheimer's care. *Beds* SNF 30; ICF 62; Retirement 50. *Private Pay Patients* 100%.
Owner Privately owned.
Admissions Requirements Minimum age 50; Medical examination; Physician's request.
Staff RNs 3 (ft); LPNs 4 (ft), 2 (pt); Nurses' aides 26 (ft), 6 (pt); Physical therapists 1 (pt); Recreational therapists 1 (ft); Occupational therapists 1 (ft); Speech therapists 1 (pt); Dietitians 1 (pt); Audiologists 1 (pt).
Facilities Dining room; Physical therapy room; Activities room; Chapel; Crafts room; Laundry room; Barber/Beauty shop; Library.

Activities Arts & crafts; Cards; Games; Reading groups; Movies; Shopping trips; Dances/Social/Cultural gatherings; Pet therapy.

Fireside Lodge Retirement Center
4800 White Settlement Rd, Fort Worth, TX 76114
(817) 738-6556
Admin Terry McGrath. *Dir of Nursing* Rita Prestage.
Licensure Skilled care; Retirement; Alzheimer's care. *Beds* SNF 92; Retirement apts 45.
Owner Proprietary corp.
Admissions Requirements Medical examination.
Staff Physicians; RNs; LPNs; Nurses' aides; Physical therapists; Reality therapists; Recreational therapists; Occupational therapists; Speech therapists; Activities coordinators; Dietitians; Ophthalmologists; Podiatrists; Audiologists.
Languages Spanish.
Facilities Dining room; Activities room; Chapel; Crafts room; Laundry room; Barber/Beauty shop; Library.
Activities Arts & crafts; Cards; Games; Reading groups; Prayer groups; Movies; Shopping trips; Dances/Social/Cultural gatherings; Pet therapy.

Forest Hill Nursing Center Inc
4607 California Pkwy E, Fort Worth, TX 76119
(817) 535-0851
Admin Lois M Jenkins.
Medical Dir William A Griffith DO.
Licensure Skilled care. *Beds* 120. *Certified* Medicaid.
Owner Proprietary corp (Summit Health Ltd).
Admissions Requirements Medical examination; Physician's request.
Staff RNs 1 (ft), 2 (pt); LPNs 12 (ft), 3 (pt); Nurses' aides 32 (ft), 2 (pt); Reality therapists 1 (pt); Dietitians 1 (pt).
Facilities Dining room; Activities room; Laundry room; Barber/Beauty shop.
Activities Arts & crafts; Cards; Games; Prayer groups; Shopping trips; Dances/Social/Cultural gatherings.

Four Seasons Nursing Center
7625 Glenview Dr, Fort Worth, TX 76180
(817) 284-1427
Admin Lisbeth Miller. *Dir of Nursing* Sue Bina RN. *Medical Dir* David Pillow MD.
Licensure Skilled care; Alzheimer's care; Private pay swing beds SNF/ICF. *Beds* SNF 24; Alzheimer's care 30; Private pay swing beds SNF/ICF 80. *Certified* Medicare.
Owner Proprietary corp (Manor Care).
Admissions Requirements Minimum age 18; Medical examination; Physician's request.
Staff RNs 8 (ft), 3 (pt); LPNs 7 (ft), 2 (pt); Nurses' aides 40 (ft); Physical therapists 1 (ft), 1 (pt); Activities coordinators 1 (ft), 2 (pt); Dietitians 1 (ft).
Facilities Dining room; Physical therapy room; Activities room; Barber/Beauty shop.
Activities Arts & crafts; Cards; Games; Reading groups; Prayer groups; Movies; Pet therapy.

Four Seasons Nursing Center of Fort Worth—Northwest
2129 Skyline Dr, Fort Worth, TX 76114
(817) 626-1956
Admin Kay Severson.
Medical Dir Barry Ungerleider DO.
Licensure Skilled care; Intermediate care. *Beds* 106. *Certified* Medicaid; Medicare.
Owner Proprietary corp (Manor Care).
Admissions Requirements Medical examination; Physician's request.
Staff Physicians 1 (ft); RNs 2 (ft), 3 (pt); LPNs 7 (ft), 3 (pt); Nurses' aides 27 (ft), 3 (pt); Activities coordinators 1 (ft).

Facilities Dining room; Physical therapy room; Activities room; Laundry room; Barber/Beauty shop.
Activities Games; Prayer groups; Shopping trips; Dances/Social/Cultural gatherings.

Francis Convalescent Center
1000 6th Ave, Fort Worth, TX 76104
(817) 336-2586
Admin Joan Bingman.
Licensure Skilled care; Intermediate care. *Beds* 130. *Certified* Medicaid.
Staff Physicians 2 (ft); RNs 2 (ft), 3 (pt); LPNs 9 (ft), 3 (pt); Nurses' aides 25 (ft), 4 (pt); Physical therapists 1 (ft); Occupational therapists 1 (pt); Speech therapists 1 (pt); Activities coordinators 2 (ft), 1 (pt); Dietitians 1 (ft), 1 (pt); Ophthalmologists 1 (pt); Podiatrists 1 (pt); Dentists 1 (pt); Medical aides 1 (ft), 1 (pt).
Facilities Dining room; Activities room; Crafts room; Laundry room; Barber/Beauty shop; Sun room.
Activities Arts & crafts; Cards; Games; Reading groups; Prayer groups; Movies; Shopping trips; Dances/Social/Cultural gatherings.

Haltom Convalescent Center
2936 Markum Dr, Fort Worth, TX 76117
(817) 831-0545
Admin Darrell R Smith. *Dir of Nursing* Carol Jenkinson RN. *Medical Dir* Donald E Pentecost MD.
Licensure Skilled care; Intermediate care. *Beds* SNF 22; ICF 124. *Private Pay Patients* 40%. *Certified* Medicaid; Medicare.
Owner Proprietary corp (Convalescent Services Inc).
Admissions Requirements Medical examination; Physician's request.
Staff RNs 2 (ft), 1 (pt); LPNs 11 (ft); Nurses' aides 64 (ft); Activities coordinators 1 (ft), 1 (pt).
Languages Spanish.
Facilities Dining room; Activities room; Laundry room; Barber/Beauty shop; Library.
Activities Arts & crafts; Cards; Games; Reading groups; Prayer groups; Movies; Intergenerational programs; Pet therapy.

Hearthstone Nursing Home
701 Saint Louis, Fort Worth, TX 76104
(817) 332-9962
Admin Elizabeth A Strange.
Licensure Intermediate care. *Beds* 103. *Certified* Medicaid.
Owner Proprietary corp.

Jackson Square Nursing Center of East Fort Worth
814 Weiler Blvd, Fort Worth, TX 76112
(817) 451-8111
Admin Mamie Jo Gentry.
Medical Dir Sherrie A Thomas.
Licensure Skilled care. *Beds* 60. *Certified* Medicaid; Medicare.
Owner Proprietary corp.
Admissions Requirements Females only.
Staff RNs; Nurses' aides; Activities coordinators; Dietitians; LVN.
Facilities Dining room; Activities room; Laundry room; Barber/Beauty shop.
Activities Games; Reading groups; Prayer groups; Movies; Dances/Social/Cultural gatherings.

Jackson Square Nursing Center of Texas Inc
921 W Cannon, Fort Worth, TX 76104
(817) 332-9261
Admin Linda M Hazel.
Licensure Intermediate care. *Beds* 53. *Certified* Medicaid.
Owner Proprietary corp.

Jarvis Heights Nursing Center
3601 Hardy St, Fort Worth, TX 76106
(817) 625-2739
Admin Carol M Egbert.

Medical Dir Harold C Shilling MD PA.
Licensure Skilled care. *Beds* 124. *Certified* Medicaid.
Owner Proprietary corp (Summit Health Ltd).
Admissions Requirements Medical examination; Physician's request.
Staff Physicians 1 (ft); RNs 3 (ft), 2 (pt); LPNs 10 (ft), 7 (pt); Nurses' aides 36 (ft), 5 (pt); Activities coordinators 1 (ft), 1 (pt).
Facilities Dining room; Activities room; Laundry room; Library.
Activities Arts & crafts; Cards; Games; Reading groups; Movies; Dances/Social/Cultural gatherings.

Kent Nursing Center
900 W Leuda St, Fort Worth, TX 76104
(817) 332-7003
Admin Cheryl L Killian.
Licensure Intermediate care. *Beds* ICF 107. *Certified* Medicaid.
Owner Proprietary corp.
Admissions Requirements Medical examination; Physician's request.
Staff RNs 1 (ft); LPNs 10 (ft); Nurses' aides 30 (ft); Activities coordinators 1 (ft), 1 (pt).
Languages Spanish.
Facilities Dining room; Activities room; Crafts room; Barber/Beauty shop; Library.
Activities Arts & crafts; Cards; Games; Reading groups; Prayer groups; Movies.

Lake Worth Nursing Home
4220 Wells Dr, Fort Worth, TX 76135
(817) 237-6101
Admin Eleanor Hewes.
Medical Dir H B Stilwell DO.
Licensure Skilled care. *Beds* 104. *Certified* Medicaid; Medicare; VA.
Admissions Requirements Minimum age 16; Medical examination; Physician's request.
Staff RNs 3 (ft); Nurses' aides 60 (ft); Activities coordinators 2 (ft); LVNs 15 (ft).
Languages Spanish.
Facilities Dining room; Laundry room.
Activities Arts & crafts; Cards; Games; Prayer groups; Movies; Shopping trips; Dances/Social/Cultural gatherings.

Lakewood Village
5100 Randol Mill Rd, Fort Worth, TX 76112
(817) 451-8001
Admin Dr M L Wentzel. *Dir of Nursing* Judy DesJardins RN.
Licensure Skilled care; Independent living. *Beds* SNF 30; Independent living 165. *Certified* Medicare.
Owner Nonprofit corp (Christian Care Centers).
Admissions Requirements Minimum age 62; Medical examination; Physician's request.
Staff Physicians 2 (pt); RNs 2 (ft); LPNs 5 (ft); Nurses' aides 13 (ft); Physical therapists 1 (pt); Reality therapists 1 (pt); Recreational therapists 1 (ft); Occupational therapists 1 (pt); Speech therapists 1 (pt); Activities coordinators 1 (ft); Dietitians 1 (ft); Ophthalmologists 1 (pt); Podiatrists 1 (pt); Audiologists 1 (pt); Dentists 1 (pt).
Languages Spanish.
Affiliation Church of Christ.
Facilities Dining room; Activities room; Chapel; Crafts room; Laundry room; Barber/Beauty shop; Library.
Activities Arts & crafts; Cards; Games; Reading groups; Prayer groups; Movies; Shopping trips; Dances/Social/Cultural gatherings; Intergenerational programs; Pet therapy; Music; Entertainment; Outings.

Parkview Care Center
3301 View St, Fort Worth, TX 76103
(817) 531-3616
Admin W O Newton. *Dir of Nursing* Geraldine Plasce. *Medical Dir* Dr Frank Jircik.

Licensure Skilled care; Intermediate care. *Beds* SNF 64; ICF 123. *Private Pay Patients* 15%. *Certified* Medicaid; Medicare.
Owner Proprietary corp (Beverly Enterprises).
Admissions Requirements Medical examination; Physician's request.
Staff Physicians (contracted); RNs 5 (ft); LPNs 12 (ft); Nurses' aides 50 (ft); Physical therapists (contracted); Recreational therapists 1 (ft); Occupational therapists (contracted); Speech therapists (contracted); Activities coordinators 1 (ft); Dietitians 1 (ft); Podiatrists (contracted).
Facilities Dining room; Physical therapy room; Activities room; Chapel; Crafts room; Laundry room; Barber/Beauty shop.
Activities Arts & crafts; Cards; Games; Reading groups; Prayer groups; Movies; Pet therapy.

Quality Convalescent Center
1000 6th Ave, Fort Worth, TX 76104
(817) 336-2586
Licensure Nursing. *Beds* Nursing 130.

Richland Hills Nursing Home
3109 Kings Ct, Fort Worth, TX 76118
(817) 589-2431
Admin Yvonne Jabri.
Medical Dir John Byarley MD.
Licensure Skilled care; Intermediate care. *Beds* 92. *Certified* Medicaid.
Owner Proprietary corp (Unicare).
Admissions Requirements Minimum age 16; Medical examination; Physician's request.
Staff RNs 1 (ft), 3 (pt); LPNs 6 (ft), 2 (pt); Nurses' aides 34 (ft); Activities coordinators 1 (ft); Dietitians 1 (pt).
Facilities Dining room; Activities room; Laundry room; Barber/Beauty shop.
Activities Arts & crafts; Cards; Games; Prayer groups; Movies; Shopping trips; Dances/Social/Cultural gatherings.

Ridgewood Manor Nursing Home
201 Sycamore School Rd, Fort Worth, TX 76134
(817) 293-7610
Admin Ruth Cahall.
Medical Dir David Engleking MD.
Licensure Intermediate care. *Beds* 150. *Certified* Medicaid.
Owner Proprietary corp (Beverly Enterprises).
Admissions Requirements Medical examination; Physician's request.
Staff Physicians 1 (pt); RNs 1 (ft), 2 (pt); LPNs 9 (ft), 3 (pt); Nurses' aides 31 (ft), 5 (pt); Physical therapists 1 (pt); Recreational therapists 1 (pt); Occupational therapists 1 (pt); Speech therapists 1 (pt); Activities coordinators 1 (ft); Dietitians 1 (pt); Ophthalmologists 1 (pt); Podiatrists 1 (pt); Dentists 1 (pt).
Facilities Dining room; Activities room; Chapel; Crafts room; Laundry room; Barber/Beauty shop; Library; Living room; Covered patio; Smoking areas.
Activities Arts & crafts; Cards; Games; Reading groups; Prayer groups; Movies; Shopping trips; Dances/Social/Cultural gatherings; Swimming; Baking group; Residents council; Meet the new residents.

River Oaks Care Center
2416 NW 18th St, Fort Worth, TX 76106
(817) 626-5454
Admin Betty L Giaimo. *Dir of Nursing* Doris Croyle RN. *Medical Dir* Charles Maxvill DO.
Licensure Intermediate care. *Beds* ICF 120. *Private Pay Patients* 25%. *Certified* Medicaid.
Owner Proprietary corp (National Heritage).
Admissions Requirements Minimum age 18; Medical examination; Physician's request.
Staff Physicians 1 (ft); RNs 1 (ft); LPNs 16 (ft); Nurses' aides 36 (ft); Physical therapists 1 (ft); Occupational therapists 1 (pt); Speech

therapists 1 (pt); Activities coordinators 1 (ft); Dietitians 1 (ft); Ophthalmologists; Podiatrists; Audiologists; Social services 1 (ft).
Facilities Dining room; Physical therapy room; Activities room; Barber/Beauty shop; Library.
Activities Arts & crafts; Cards; Games; Reading groups; Prayer groups; Movies; Dances/Social/Cultural gatherings; Intergenerational programs; Pet therapy.

Stanford Convalescent Center—Eighth Ave
1535 Pennsylvania, Fort Worth, TX 76104
(817) 336-2786
Admin Ollie C Wilson.
Licensure Intermediate care. *Beds* 89. *Certified* Medicaid.

Stanford Convalescent Center—Jennings
929 Hemphill St, Fort Worth, TX 76104
(817) 336-9191
Admin Linda Batchelor. *Dir of Nursing* Peggy Watts RN. *Medical Dir* Dr David Stone.
Licensure Intermediate care. *Beds* ICF 120. *Certified* Medicaid.
Owner Proprietary corp (Beverly Enterprises).
Admissions Requirements Minimum age 18; Medical examination; Physician's request.
Staff RNs 1 (ft); LPNs 4 (ft), 1 (pt); Nurses' aides 10 (ft); Activities coordinators 1 (ft).
Languages Spanish.
Facilities Dining room; Activities room; Crafts room; Laundry room; Barber/Beauty shop; Library.
Activities Arts & crafts; Cards; Games; Reading groups; Prayer groups; Movies; Dances/Social/Cultural gatherings.

Stanford Convalescent Center—Pennsylvania
901 Pennsyvlania, Fort Worth, TX 76104
(817) 335-3030
Admin Kathleen A Gerrity.
Licensure Intermediate care. *Beds* 125. *Certified* Medicaid.
Owner Proprietary corp (Beverly Enterprises).

Stanford—Hemphill
1617 Hemphill, Fort Worth, TX 76104
(817) 926-9201
Admin Patricia Sanders. *Dir of Nursing* Gloria Basey. *Medical Dir* Kenneth Jorns MD.
Licensure Skilled care; Intermediate care; Medicare certified. *Beds* SNF 59; ICF 73; Medicare certified 39. *Private Pay Patients* 10%. *Certified* Medicaid; Medicare; VA.
Owner Proprietary corp (Beverly Enterprises).
Admissions Requirements Medical examination; Physician's request.
Staff RNs 8 (ft); LPNs 8 (ft); Nurses' aides 30 (ft), 4 (pt); Physical therapists (contracted); Reality therapists (contracted); Recreational therapists (contracted); Occupational therapists (contracted); Speech therapists (contracted); Activities coordinators 1 (ft); Dietitians 1 (ft); Ophthalmologists (contracted); Podiatrists (contracted); Audiologists (contracted).
Languages Spanish.
Facilities Dining room; Physical therapy room; Activities room; Crafts room; Laundry room; Barber/Beauty shop; Dialysis unit; In-house lab and X-ray service.
Activities Arts & crafts; Cards; Games; Reading groups; Prayer groups; Movies; Shopping trips; Dances/Social/Cultural gatherings; Intergenerational programs; Pet therapy; One-on-one visits.

Trinity Terrace
1600 Texas St, Fort Worth, TX 76102
(817) 338-2400
Admin Wendell D Wilson. *Dir of Nursing* Candace Burks RN. *Medical Dir* Kendra Belfi MD.
Licensure Skilled care; Retirement. *Beds* SNF 60; Retirement 350. *Private Pay Patients* 5%.

Owner Nonprofit corp (The Cumberland Rest Inc).
Admissions Requirements Minimum age 62; Medical examination; Physician's request.
Staff RNs 3 (ft); LPNs 6 (ft), 3 (pt); Nurses' aides 20 (ft); Activities coordinators 1 (ft); Dietitians 1 (pt).
Affiliation Presbyterian.
Facilities Dining room; Activities room; Barber/Beauty shop; Library.
Activities Arts & crafts; Cards; Games; Reading groups; Prayer groups; Movies; Shopping trips; Dances/Social/Cultural gatherings; Pet therapy.

Watson Nursing Home
5000 E Lancaster, Fort Worth, TX 76102
(817) 535-3447
Admin Fred M Reed.
Medical Dir Tishey G Hughes LVN.
Licensure Intermediate care. *Beds* 69. *Certified* Medicaid.
Owner Proprietary corp.
Admissions Requirements Medical examination; Physician's request.
Facilities Activities room; Barber/Beauty shop.
Activities Arts & crafts; Cards; Games; Reading groups; Prayer groups; Movies.

Webber Nursing Center
4900 E Berry St, Fort Worth, TX 76105
(817) 531-3707
Admin Christene Moss. *Dir of Nursing* Patsy Dockery. *Medical Dir* Marion J Brooks MD.
Licensure Intermediate care; Alzheimer's care. *Beds* ICF 145. *Certified* Medicaid.
Owner Proprietary corp.
Admissions Requirements Medical examination; Physician's request.
Staff Physicians 1 (ft); RNs 1 (pt); LPNs 10 (ft); Nurses' aides 27 (ft), 1 (pt); Physical therapists 1 (pt); Recreational therapists 1 (pt); Occupational therapists 1 (pt); Recreational therapists 1 (pt); Activities coordinators 2 (ft); Dietitians 1 (pt); Ophthalmologists 1 (pt).
Languages Spanish.
Facilities Dining room; Activities room; Laundry room; Barber/Beauty shop.
Activities Arts & crafts; Cards; Games; Reading groups; Prayer groups; Movies; Shopping trips; Dances/Social/Cultural gatherings; Glee club; Newsletter.

Wedgewood Nursing Home
6621 Dan Danciger Rd, Fort Worth, TX 76133
(817) 292-6330
Admin Henry C Hames.
Licensure Skilled care. *Beds* 125. *Certified* Medicaid.
Owner Proprietary corp (Beverly Enterprises).

West Side Care Center
1950 Las Vegas Trail S, Fort Worth, TX 76108
(817) 246-4995, 246-1025 FAX
Admin Sharon Sullivan. *Dir of Nursing* Rosemary Endres RN. *Medical Dir* Dr Carl E Everett.
Licensure Skilled care; Intermediate care. *Beds* Swing beds SNF/ICF 240. *Certified* Medicaid; Medicare.
Owner Privately owned.
Admissions Requirements Medical examination; Physician's request.
Facilities Dining room; Physical therapy room; Activities room; Chapel; Crafts room; Laundry room; Barber/Beauty shop; Library.
Activities Arts & crafts; Cards; Games; Reading groups; Prayer groups; Dances/Social/Cultural gatherings; Intergenerational programs; Pet therapy.

Western Hills Nursing Home
8001 Western Hills Blvd, Fort Worth, TX 76108
(817) 246-4953

Admin Joan Bellah. *Dir of Nursing* Nelda Dixon RN. *Medical Dir* Charles Maxvill DO.
Licensure Skilled care; Intermediate care. *Beds* SNF 120; ICF 150. *Certified* Medicaid; Medicare; VA.
Owner Proprietary corp (National Heritage).
Admissions Requirements Minimum age 18; Medical examination; Physician's request.
Staff RNs 3 (ft), 2 (pt); LPNs 22 (ft), 1 (pt); Nurses' aides 93 (ft); Activities coordinators 2 (ft); Dietitians 1 (ft); Housekeeping, administration, dietary, maintenance personnel 37 (ft).
Languages Spanish.
Facilities Dining room; Physical therapy room; Activities room; Chapel; Crafts room; Laundry room; Barber/Beauty shop; TV lounges; Secured patio.
Activities Arts & crafts; Cards; Games; Reading groups; Prayer groups; Movies; Shopping trips; Dances/Social/Cultural gatherings; Pet therapy.

White Settlement Nursing Center
7820 Skyline Park Dr, Fort Worth, TX 76108
(817) 246-4671
Admin Betty S Martin. *Dir of Nursing* Marcia Spacher. *Medical Dir* Robert Irwin DO.
Licensure Skilled care. *Beds* 108. *Certified* Medicaid; Medicare.
Owner Proprietary corp (Beverly Enterprises).
Admissions Requirements Minimum age 21; Females only; Medical examination.
Staff Physicians 3 (ft); RNs 4 (ft); LPNs 100 (ft); Nurses' aides 29 (ft); Physical therapists 1 (ft); Reality therapists 1 (ft); Recreational therapists 1 (ft); Occupational therapists 1 (ft); Speech therapists 1 (ft); Activities coordinators 1 (ft); Dietitians 1 (ft); Ophthalmologists 1 (ft); Podiatrists 1 (ft).
Facilities Dining room; Activities room; Crafts room; Laundry room; Barber/Beauty shop.
Activities Arts & crafts; Cards; Games; Prayer groups; Movies; Shopping trips; Dances/Social/Cultural gatherings.

Franklin

Franklin Nursing Home
700 Hearne St, Franklin, TX 77856
(409) 828-5152
Licensure Nursing. *Beds* Nursing 90.

Frankston

Frankston Nursing Center
PO Box 66, Hwy 155, Frankston, TX 75763
(214) 876-3208, 876-3209
Admin Russ Weaver. *Dir of Nursing* Joann Baxter. *Medical Dir* Van Pham.
Licensure Intermediate care. *Beds* ICF 76. *Private Pay Patients* 10%. *Certified* Medicaid.
Owner Proprietary corp (Beverly Enterprises).
Admissions Requirements Medical examination; Physician's request.
Staff LPNs 3 (ft); Nurses' aides 12 (ft); Activities coordinators 1 (ft).
Facilities Dining room; Laundry room; Barber/Beauty shop.
Activities Games; Prayer groups; Movies; Dances/Social/Cultural gatherings.

Fredericksburg

Brown's Nursing Home Inc
619 W Live Oak Rd, Fredericksburg, TX 78624
(512) 997-4391
Admin Bernice Dryden.
Medical Dir Leona Black LVN.
Licensure Intermediate care. *Beds* 92. *Certified* Medicaid.

Staff RNs 1 (pt); Nurses' aides 24 (pt); Physical therapists 1 (pt); Occupational therapists 1 (pt); Speech therapists 1 (pt); Dietitians 1 (pt).
Facilities Dining room; Activities room; Chapel; Crafts room; Laundry room; Barber/Beauty shop.

Fredericksburg Nursing Home
1117 S Adams, Fredericksburg, TX 78624
(512) 997-4364
Admin Lynn J Hecht.
Licensure Intermediate care. *Beds* 90. *Certified* Medicaid.
Owner Nonprofit corp.
Affiliation Seventh-Day Adventist.

Knopp Nursing Home Inc 1
1208 N Llano, Fredericksburg, TX 78624
(512) 997-3704
Admin Irene Luckenbach.
Medical Dir Joan Lindley.
Licensure Skilled care; Intermediate care; VA contract; Retirement. *Beds* SNF 44; ICF 89. *Certified* Medicaid; Medicare.
Owner Proprietary corp.
Admissions Requirements Minimum age State req.
Staff RNs; LPNs; Nurses' aides; Activities coordinators; Dietitians.
Languages German, Spanish.
Facilities Dining room; Physical therapy room; Activities room; Crafts room; Laundry room; Barber/Beauty shop.
Activities Arts & crafts; Games; Reading groups; Prayer groups; Dances/Social/Cultural gatherings.

Knopp Nursing & Retirement Home 2 Inc
Rte 1 Box 311, 202 Hollmig Ln, Fredericksburg, TX 78624
(512) 997-7924
Admin Jerry M Luckenbach. *Dir of Nursing* Magdalena Wendel RN. *Medical Dir* Dr Lorence Fellen.
Licensure Intermediate care; Retirement. *Beds* ICF 60. *Certified* Medicaid.
Owner Proprietary corp.
Admissions Requirements Minimum age State req; Physician's request.
Staff LPNs 5 (ft), 3 (pt); Nurses' aides 12 (ft), 4 (pt); Activities coordinators 1 (ft); Dietitians 1 (ft).
Languages German, Spanish.
Facilities Dining room; Activities room; Crafts room; Laundry room; Barber/Beauty shop.
Activities Arts & crafts; Games; Reading groups; Prayer groups; Dances/Social/Cultural gatherings.

Friendswood

Friendswood Arms Convalescent Center
213 Heritage Dr, Friendswood, TX 77546
(713) 482-1281
Admin Patricia A Beem.
Licensure Skilled care; Intermediate care. *Beds* 119. *Certified* Medicaid.
Owner Proprietary corp.

Friona

Prairie Acres
201 E 15th St, Friona, TX 79035
(806) 247-3922
Admin Jo Gene Blackwell. *Dir of Nursing* Joan Ahrhart RN. *Medical Dir* R S Alexander MD.
Licensure Intermediate care. *Beds* ICF 83. *Private Pay Patients* 60%. *Certified* Medicaid.
Owner Publicly owned.
Admissions Requirements Medical examination; Physician's request.

Staff Physicians 1 (pt); RNs 1 (ft), 2 (pt); LPNs 6 (ft), 1 (pt); Nurses' aides 35 (ft), 3 (pt); Physical therapists 1 (pt); Activities coordinators 2 (ft); Dietitians 1 (ft), 1 (pt).
Facilities Dining room; Activities room; Chapel; Crafts room; Laundry room; Barber/Beauty shop; Library.
Activities Arts & crafts; Cards; Games; Reading groups; Prayer groups; Movies; Shopping trips; Dances/Social/Cultural gatherings; Pet therapy.

Gainesville

Frontier Manor
1907 Refinery Rd, Gainesville, TX 76240
(817) 665-0386
Admin Leo A Ladouceur.
Licensure Intermediate care. *Beds* 118. *Certified* Medicaid.
Owner Proprietary corp (ARA Living Centers).

Gainesville Convalescent Center
1900 O'Neal St, Gainesville, TX 76240
(817) 665-2826
Admin Milie P Belcher.
Licensure Intermediate care. *Beds* 120. *Certified* Medicaid.
Owner Proprietary corp (ARA Living Centers).

Oak Tree Lodge
PO Box 1199, Hwy 51, Black Hill Dr, Gainesville, TX 76240
(817) 665-5221
Admin Linda Edgett.
Medical Dir Dr William Powell.
Licensure Intermediate care. *Beds* 48. *Certified* Medicaid.
Owner Proprietary corp (Cantex Healthcare Centers).
Admissions Requirements Medical examination; Physician's request.
Staff Physicians 1 (ft); RNs 1 (ft); Nurses' aides 7 (ft), 2 (pt); Physical therapists 2 (ft); Activities coordinators 1 (ft); Dietitians 1 (ft); Dentists 1 (ft).

Galveston

Turner Geriatric Center
2228 Seawall Blvd, Galveston, TX 77550
(409) 765-4000
Admin Herman Sabrsula. *Dir of Nursing* Pat Pendleton. *Medical Dir* Dr Edgar Jones.
Licensure Intermediate care; Retirement; Alzheimer's care. *Beds* ICF 164. *Private Pay Patients* 70%. *Certified* Medicaid.
Owner Nonprofit organization/foundation.
Admissions Requirements Minimum age 62.
Staff Physicians 1 (ft); RNs 5 (ft); LPNs 5 (ft); Nurses' aides 12 (ft); Physical therapists 1 (ft), 1 (pt); Recreational therapists 1 (ft); Speech therapists 1 (ft); Dietitians 1 (ft); Podiatrists 1 (ft); Music therapists 1 (ft); Social workers 1 (ft); Volunteer coordinators 1 (pt); Pharmacists 1 (ft).
Affiliation United Methodist.
Facilities Dining room; Physical therapy room; Activities room; Chapel; Laundry room; Barber/Beauty shop; Library; Pharmacy clinic; Dental office.
Activities Arts & crafts; Cards; Games; Reading groups; Prayer groups; Movies; Shopping trips; Dances/Social/Cultural gatherings; Intergenerational programs; Pet therapy; Horseback riding; Sports; Lectures; Music therapy; Choir.

Ganado

Care Inn of Ganado
PO Drawer V, Ganado, TX 77962
(512) 771-3315

Licensure Intermediate care. *Beds* 57. *Certified* Medicaid.
Owner Proprietary corp (ARA Living Centers).

Garland

Castle Manor Nursing Home
1922 Castle Dr, Garland, TX 75040
(214) 494-1471
Admin Martin Tomerlin.
Licensure Intermediate care. *Beds* 100. *Certified* Medicaid.
Owner Proprietary corp (ARA Living Centers).
Admissions Requirements Medical examination.
Staff Physicians 3 (pt); RNs 1 (ft); LPNs 7 (ft), 3 (pt); Nurses' aides 20 (ft); Physical therapists 1 (pt); Occupational therapists 1 (pt); Speech therapists 1 (pt); Ophthalmologists 1 (pt).
Facilities Dining room; Activities room; Crafts room; Laundry room; Barber/Beauty shop.
Activities Arts & crafts; Cards; Prayer groups; Movies; Dances/Social/Cultural gatherings.

Garland Convalescent Center
321 N Shiloh Rd, Garland, TX 75042
(214) 276-9571
Admin Henry C Hames.
Medical Dir James R McLean DO.
Licensure Intermediate care. *Beds* 120. *Certified* Medicaid.
Owner Proprietary corp (Summit Health Ltd).
Admissions Requirements Minimum age 18; Physician's request.
Staff Physicians 1 (pt); RNs 1 (ft); LPNs 8 (ft), 1 (pt); Nurses' aides 22 (ft); Physical therapists 1 (pt); Reality therapists 1 (pt); Recreational therapists 1 (pt); Occupational therapists 1 (ft); Speech therapists 1 (ft); Activities coordinators 1 (ft); Dietitians 1 (pt).
Facilities Dining room; Activities room; Crafts room; Laundry room; Barber/Beauty shop.
Activities Arts & crafts; Cards; Games; Reading groups; Prayer groups; Movies; Shopping trips; Dances/Social/Cultural gatherings.

Serenity Haven Nursing Home
106 N Beltline Rd, Garland, TX 75040
(214) 495-7700
Admin Lois Y Jabri.
Licensure Skilled care; Intermediate care. *Beds* 120. *Certified* Medicaid.
Owner Proprietary corp (Beverly Enterprises).

Silver Leaves
505 W Centerville Rd, Garland, TX 75041
(214) 278-3566
Admin Jim Myrick. *Dir of Nursing* Penny Bennett RN BSN. *Medical Dir* Dr J R McLean DO.
Licensure Skilled care; Intermediate care. *Beds* SNF 59; ICF 52. *Private Pay Patients* 50%.
Owner Proprietary corp (Beverly Enterprises).
Admissions Requirements Minimum age 18; Medical examination; Physician's request.
Staff Physicians; RNs; LPNs; Nurses' aides; Physical therapists; Occupational therapists; Speech therapists; Activities coordinators; Dietitians.
Facilities Dining room; Physical therapy room; Laundry room; Barber/Beauty shop; IV therapy.
Activities Arts & crafts; Cards; Games; Reading groups; Prayer groups; Movies; Shopping trips; Dances/Social/Cultural gatherings; Intergenerational programs; Pet therapy; Entertainment.

Garrison

Garrison Nursing Home Inc
PO Box 600, Elm St, Garrison, TX 75946
(409) 347-2234
Admin Darrell G Yarbrough. *Dir of Nursing* Linda Williams.
Licensure Intermediate care. *Beds* ICF 43. *Certified* Medicaid.
Owner Proprietary corp.
Staff RNs; LPNs; Nurses' aides; Dietitians; Ophthalmologists.

Gatesville

Canterbury Villa of Gatesville
2525 Osage Rd, Gatesville, TX 76528
(817) 865-2231
Admin Truett Johnson. *Dir of Nursing* Rose Mary Colbet.
Licensure Skilled care; Intermediate care. *Beds* SNF 58; ICF 152. *Certified* Medicaid; Medicare.
Owner Proprietary corp (Truco Inc).
Admissions Requirements Physician's request.
Staff RNs; LPNs; Nurses' aides; Activities coordinators.
Facilities Dining room; Activities room; Laundry room; Barber/Beauty shop.
Activities Games; Prayer groups; Shopping trips.

Hillside Manor Nursing Center
101 S 34th St, Gatesville, TX 76528
(817) 865-8275
Admin Vicki Pressley.
Medical Dir William F Floyd MD.
Licensure Intermediate care. *Beds* 120. *Certified* Medicaid.
Owner Proprietary corp.
Admissions Requirements Physician's request.
Staff RNs 1 (pt); LPNs 5 (ft), 2 (pt); Nurses' aides 16 (ft); Activities coordinators 1 (ft); Dietitians 1 (ft).
Facilities Dining room; Activities room; Laundry room; Barber/Beauty shop.
Activities Arts & crafts; Games; Prayer groups.

Georgetown

Georgetown Sweetbriar Nursing Home Inc
N San Gabriel Park Dr, Georgetown, TX 78626
(512) 255-2746
Admin Linda L Duncan. *Dir of Nursing* Linda Johnson RN. *Medical Dir* James Shepherd MD.
Licensure Intermediate care. *Beds* ICF 120. *Private Pay Patients* 20%. *Certified* Medicaid.
Owner Privately owned.
Admissions Requirements Medical examination; Physician's request.
Staff RNs 1 (ft); LPNs 11 (ft), 1 (pt); Nurses' aides 40 (ft), 7 (pt).
Facilities Dining room; Laundry room; Barber/Beauty shop.
Activities Arts & crafts; Games; Reading groups; Prayer groups; Movies; Shopping trips; Dances/Social/Cultural gatherings; Pet therapy.

Wesleyan Nursing Home
2001 Scenic Dr, Georgetown, TX 78626
(512) 863-9511
Admin Chris G Spence. *Dir of Nursing* Elaine McAfee. *Medical Dir* Dr Douglas Benold.
Licensure Intermediate care; Retirement. *Beds* ICF 180; Retirmenet 100. *Certified* Medicaid.
Owner Nonprofit organization/foundation.
Admissions Requirements Medical examination; Physician's request.
Staff RNs 2 (ft); LPNs 12 (ft), 4 (pt); Nurses' aides 25 (ft), 12 (pt); Physical therapists 1 (pt); Activities coordinators 1 (ft); Dietitians 1 (ft).

Affiliation Methodist.
Facilities Dining room; Activities room;
Chapel; Laundry room; Barber/Beauty shop;
Library.
Activities Arts & crafts; Cards; Games;
Reading groups; Prayer groups; Movies;
Shopping trips.

Giddings

Giddings Convalescent Center
1747 E Hempstead, Giddings, TX 78942
(409) 542-2150
Admin Mary Halliburton.
Licensure Intermediate care. *Beds* 50.
Certified Medicaid.
Owner Proprietary corp.

Hennesey Nursing Center
PO Box 540, 1181 N Williamson St,
Giddings, TX 78942
(409) 542-3611
Admin Tommy G Jackson. *Dir of Nursing*
Linda Davis. *Medical Dir* Dr C M Burns.
Licensure Intermediate care. *Beds* ICF 92.
Private Pay Patients 33%. *Certified*
Medicaid.
Owner Nonprofit organization/foundation
(Advanced Living Technologies).
Admissions Requirements Physician's request.
Staff RNs; LPNs; Nurses' aides; Physical
therapists; Speech therapists; Activities
coordinators; Dietitians.
Languages German.
Facilities Dining room; Activities room;
Chapel; Crafts room; Laundry room; Barber/
Beauty shop.
Activities Arts & crafts; Cards; Games;
Reading groups; Prayer groups; Movies;
Shopping trips; Dances/Social/Cultural
gatherings; Intergenerational programs; Pet
therapy.

Gilmer

Gilmer Convalescent & Nursing Center
703 N Titus St, Gilmer, TX 75644
(214) 843-5529
Admin JoAnn Hinson. *Dir of Nursing* Anita
Steelman RN.
Licensure Skilled care; Intermediate care;
Alzheimer's care. *Beds* SNF 50; ICF 59.
Certified Medicaid; Medicare.
Owner Nonprofit organization/foundation.
Admissions Requirements Medical
examination; Physician's request.
Staff RNs 2 (ft), 2 (pt); LPNs 15 (ft); Nurses'
aides 33 (ft), 3 (pt); Activities coordinators 1
(ft); Dietitians 1 (pt).
Affiliation Baptist.
Facilities Dining room; Activities room;
Crafts room; Laundry room; Barber/Beauty
shop; Lounges.
Activities Arts & crafts; Cards; Games;
Reading groups; Prayer groups; Dances/
Social/Cultural gatherings.

Leisure Lodge
1704 Bradford, Gilmer, TX 75644
(214) 843-5696
Admin Alice Wyatt. *Dir of Nursing* Joyce
Goodson. *Medical Dir* Dr Rusty Warden; Dr
Joseph Bell.
Licensure Intermediate care. *Beds* ICF 100.
Certified Medicaid.
Owner Proprietary corp (Beverly Enterprises).
Staff RNs 1 (ft); LPNs 5 (ft), 3 (pt); Nurses'
aides 30 (ft); Physical therapists (contracted);
Recreational therapists 1 (ft); Activities
coordinators 1 (ft); Dietitians 1 (pt).
Facilities Dining room; Activities room;
Crafts room; Laundry room; Barber/Beauty
shop.
Activities Arts & crafts; Games; Prayer groups;
Intergenerational programs.

Gladewater

Care Inn of Gladewater
300 N Money St, Gladewater, TX 75647
(214) 845-2101
Licensure Nursing. *Beds* Nursing 80.

Oak Manor Nursing Home
PO Box 1467, Hwy 80 E, Gladewater, TX
75647
(214) 845-6933
Admin Alan Loyd.
Medical Dir Pat Steelman.
Licensure Intermediate care. *Beds* 120.
Certified Medicaid.
Owner Proprietary corp (Truco Inc).
Admissions Requirements Minimum age 21;
Medical examination; Physician's request.
Staff LPNs 10 (ft); Nurses' aides 65 (ft);
Activities coordinators 2 (ft).
Facilities Dining room; Activities room;
Crafts room; Laundry room; Barber/Beauty
shop.
Activities Arts & crafts; Cards; Games;
Reading groups; Prayer groups; Movies;
Shopping trips; Dances/Social/Cultural
gatherings.

Glen Rose

Glen Rose Nursing Home
PO Box 997, 1309 Holden St, Glen Rose, TX
76043
(817) 897-2215
Admin Gary A Marks. *Dir of Nursing* Jane
Wise RN.
Licensure Intermediate care. *Beds* ICF 42.
Certified Medicaid.
Owner Nonprofit corp.
Admissions Requirements Physician's request.
Staff RNs 1 (ft); LPNs 6 (ft), 2 (pt); Nurses'
aides 16 (ft); Activities coordinators 1 (ft);
Dietitians 1 (ft).
Affiliation Methodist.
Facilities Dining room; Activities room;
Crafts room; Laundry room; Barber/Beauty
shop; Library.
Activities Arts & crafts; Games; Reading
groups; Prayer groups; Movies; Dances/
Social/Cultural gatherings; Church services
twice weekly.

Goldthwaite

Gold Star Nursing Home
1207 Reynolds, Goldthwaite, TX 76844
(915) 648-2258
Admin Lovell Jewell. *Dir of Nursing* Kyla
Berry RN. *Medical Dir* Dr Richard Penly.
Licensure Skilled care; Intermediate care. *Beds*
SNF 50; ICF 84. *Certified* Medicaid; VA.
Owner Proprietary corp.
Admissions Requirements Medical
examination.
Staff RNs 1 (ft), 1 (pt); LPNs 11 (ft), 1 (pt);
Nurses' aides 25 (ft), 10 (pt); Activities
coordinators 1 (ft); Dietitians 1 (ft).
Facilities Dining room; Activities room;
Barber/Beauty shop; Library.
Activities Arts & crafts; Games; Reading
groups; Prayer groups; Movies; Dances/
Social/Cultural gatherings; Shopping trips.

Heritage Nursing Home Inc
1207 Reynolds, Goldthwaite, TX 76844
(915) 648-2258
Admin Beverly K Freeman.
Medical Dir Dr M A Childress.
Licensure Skilled care; Intermediate care. *Beds*
134. *Certified* Medicaid.
Staff RNs 1 (ft), 1 (pt); LPNs 6 (ft), 5 (pt);
Nurses' aides 22 (ft), 10 (pt); Activities
coordinators 1 (ft); Dietitians 1 (pt).
Facilities Dining room; Activities room;
Crafts room; Laundry room; Barber/Beauty
shop; Library.

Activities Games; Reading groups; Prayer
groups; Shopping trips; Dances/Social/
Cultural gatherings.

Hillview Manor
PO Box 588, 1110 Rice St, Goldthwaite, TX
76844
(915) 648-2247
Admin Beverly Yarborough.
Medical Dir Polly Womack.
Licensure Intermediate care. *Beds* ICF 60.
Certified Medicaid.
Owner Proprietary corp (ARA Living
Centers).
Admissions Requirements Medical
examination.
Staff RNs 1 (ft); LPNs 5 (ft), 1 (pt); Nurses'
aides 11 (ft), 3 (pt); Activities coordinators 1
(ft); Dietitians 1 (ft).
Facilities Dining room; Activities room;
Crafts room; Laundry room; Barber/Beauty
shop.
Activities Arts & crafts; Cards; Games;
Reading groups; Prayer groups; Movies;
Dances/Social/Cultural gatherings.

Goliad

Goliad Manor Inc
Rte 3 Box 106, Goliad, TX 77963
(512) 645-3352
Admin Dina Wood. *Dir of Nursing* Ina
Billups. *Medical Dir* Dr Diaz.
Licensure Intermediate care. *Beds* ICF 60.
Private Pay Patients 2%. *Certified* Medicaid.
Owner Proprietary corp (Diversicare Corp of
America).
Admissions Requirements Medical
examination; Physician's request.
Staff LPNs 6 (ft); Nurses' aides 22 (ft), 5 (pt);
Activities coordinators 1 (ft); Dietitians 1
(ft).
Languages Spanish.
Facilities Dining room; Activities room;
Laundry room; Barber/Beauty shop.
Activities Arts & crafts; Cards; Games; Prayer
groups; Movies; Shopping trips; Dances/
Social/Cultural gatherings; Pet therapy.

Gonzales

Care Inn of Gonzales
Box 145, Rte 4, Gonzales, TX 78629
(512) 672-2867
Admin Judith A Pleshek.
Medical Dir Lunetta Low.
Licensure Intermediate care. *Beds* ICF 90.
Certified Medicaid.
Owner Proprietary corp (ARA Living
Centers).
Admissions Requirements Minimum age 18;
Physician's request.
Staff RNs 1 (ft); LPNs 4 (ft), 1 (pt); Nurses'
aides 22 (ft), 3 (pt); Activities coordinators 1
(ft).
Languages Spanish.
Facilities Dining room; Laundry room.
Activities Arts & crafts; Cards; Games;
Reading groups; Prayer groups; Movies;
Shopping trips; Dances/Social/Cultural
gatherings; Exercise class; Reality
orientation.

Cartwheel Lodge of Gonzales
PO Box 659, 1800 Cartwheel Dr, Gonzales,
TX 78629
(512) 672-2887
Admin Kathy E Powell.
Licensure Intermediate care. *Beds* 98.
Certified Medicaid.
Owner Proprietary corp.

Gorman

Canterbury Villa of Gorman
PO Box 669, 600 W Roosevelt St, Gorman, TX 76454
(817) 734-2202
Admin Deane Christian.
Medical Dir Rena F Rhyne.
Licensure Intermediate care; Alzheimer's care. *Beds* ICF 97. *Certified* Medicaid.
Owner Proprietary corp (Texas Health Enterprises).
Admissions Requirements Physician's request.
Staff RNs 1 (ft); LPNs 8 (ft); Activities coordinators 1 (ft); Dietitians 1 (ft).
Languages Spanish.
Facilities Dining room; Activities room; Chapel; Laundry room; Barber/Beauty shop.
Activities Arts & crafts; Cards; Games; Reading groups; Prayer groups; Movies; Shopping trips; Dances/Social/Cultural gatherings.

Graham

Burgess Manor
1309 Brazos, Graham, TX 76046
(817) 549-3760
Admin Eileen Davis. *Dir of Nursing* Dena Walker.
Licensure Intermediate care. *Beds* ICF 64. *Private Pay Patients* 10%. *Certified* Medicaid.
Owner Proprietary corp (Beverly Enterprises).
Admissions Requirements Medical examination; Physician's request.
Staff RNs 1 (pt); Nurses' aides 15 (ft); Activities coordinators 1 (ft); Dietitians 1 (pt); LVNs 6 (ft).
Languages Spanish.
Facilities Dining room; Activities room; Crafts room; Laundry room; Barber/Beauty shop; Whirlpool.
Activities Arts & crafts; Cards; Games; Reading groups; Prayer groups; Movies; Shopping trips; Dances/Social/Cultural gatherings; Intergenerational programs; Pet therapy.

Cherry Oaks Nursing Center
1201 Cherry St, Graham, TX 76046
(817) 549-3677
Admin Brenda Freeman.
Medical Dir Dr R G McDaniels.
Licensure Intermediate care. *Beds* 66. *Certified* Medicaid.
Staff LPNs 5 (ft); Nurses' aides 11 (ft); Activities coordinators 1 (ft); Dietitians 1 (ft).
Facilities Dining room; Activities room; Chapel; Laundry room; Barber/Beauty shop.
Activities Arts & crafts; Games; Reading groups; Prayer groups; Movies; Shopping trips.

Garden Terrace Nursing Center
1224 Corvadura St, Graham, TX 76046
(817) 549-4646
Admin Mary L Shabay.
Licensure Intermediate care. *Beds* 120. *Certified* Medicaid.
Owner Proprietary corp (Beverly Enterprises).

Granbury

Granbury Care Center
PO Box 40, 301 Park Dr, Granbury, TX 76048
(817) 573-3726
Admin Millie L Westbrook. *Dir of Nursing* Janice Bianchi RN. *Medical Dir* Larry G Padget DO.
Licensure Intermediate care; Adult day care; Respite care. *Beds* ICF 181. *Private Pay Patients* 33%. *Certified* Medicaid.
Owner Proprietary corp.

Admissions Requirements Medical examination; Physician's request.
Staff Physicians 8 (ft); RNs 1 (ft); LPNs 15 (ft), 4 (pt); Nurses' aides 56 (ft), 3 (pt); Physical therapists 1 (pt); Recreational therapists 1 (pt); Speech therapists 1 (pt); Activities coordinators 2 (ft); Dietitians 1 (ft), 1 (pt); Ophthalmologists 1 (pt).
Languages German.
Facilities Dining room; Physical therapy room; Activities room; Chapel; Crafts room; Laundry room; Barber/Beauty shop; Visiting areas; Sitting areas.
Activities Arts & crafts; Cards; Games; Reading groups; Prayer groups; Movies; Shopping trips; Dances/Social/Cultural gatherings; Intergenerational programs; Pet therapy; Activities with community service groups.

Valley View Nursing Home
PO Box 998, 600 Reunion St, Granbury, TX 76048
(817) 573-3773
Admin Carolyn Sue Wilson.
Licensure Intermediate care. *Beds* 108. *Certified* Medicaid.
Owner Proprietary corp.

Grand Prairie

Great Southwest Convalescent Center
2337 Doreen St, Grand Prairie, TX 75050
(214) 647-1938
Admin Scott W Donaldson.
Medical Dir Ben Capote MD.
Licensure Skilled care. *Beds* 130. *Certified* Medicaid.
Owner Proprietary corp (Hillhaven Corp).
Staff RNs 1 (ft), 1 (pt); LPNs 8 (ft), 3 (pt); Nurses' aides 55 (ft); Activities coordinators 1 (ft); Dietitians 1 (pt).
Facilities Dining room; Activities room; Crafts room; Laundry room; Barber/Beauty shop.
Activities Arts & crafts; Cards; Games; Reading groups; Prayer groups; Movies.

Kern Place
820 Small St, Grand Prairie, TX 75050
(214) 262-1351
Admin Millie Westbrook. *Dir of Nursing* Nell Dees RN. *Medical Dir* Philip Pearson DO.
Licensure Skilled care; Intermediate care; Alzheimer's care. *Beds* SNF 150; ICF. *Certified* Medicaid; Medicare.
Owner Proprietary corp (Texas Health Enterprises).
Admissions Requirements Medical examination; Physician's request.
Staff Physicians; RNs 2 (ft); LPNs 7 (ft); Nurses' aides 13 (ft); Activities coordinators 1 (ft); Dietitians 1 (ft); Social services 1 (ft).
Facilities Dining room; Physical therapy room; Activities room; Chapel; Crafts room; Laundry room; Barber/Beauty shop; Library; 3 courtyards.
Activities Arts & crafts; Cards; Games; Reading groups; Prayer groups; Movies; Shopping trips; Dances/Social/Cultural gatherings.

Metroplex Care Center
658 SW 3rd St, Grand Prairie, TX 75051
(214) 264-2464
Admin Elma Gloria Gomez.
Licensure Intermediate care. *Beds* 150. *Certified* Medicaid.
Owner Proprietary corp (ARA Living Centers).

Grand Saline

Anderson Memorial Care Homes Inc
PO Drawer K, Bradburn Rd at High St, Grand Saline, TX 75140
(214) 962-4234

Admin Carolyn E La Prade.
Licensure Intermediate care. *Beds* 76. *Certified* Medicaid.
Owner Proprietary corp.

Grand Saline Manor
411 Spring Creek Rd, Grand Saline, TX 75140
(214) 962-4226
Admin James Fleet.
Licensure Intermediate care. *Beds* 76.
Owner Proprietary corp (Health Enter of America).

Grandview

Grandview Nursing Home
501 W Criner, Grandview, TX 76050
(817) 866-3367
Admin Linda Rae Smith.
Licensure Intermediate care. *Beds* 79. *Certified* Medicaid.
Owner Nonprofit corp.

Granger

Bluebonnet Nursing Center of Granger Inc
PO Box 666, Hwy 95 N, Granger, TX 76530
(512) 859-2800
Admin Lydia Kurtin.
Medical Dir Barbara Starling.
Licensure Intermediate care. *Beds* 68. *Certified* Medicaid.
Owner Proprietary corp.
Admissions Requirements Minimum age 18; Medical examination.
Staff RNs 1 (pt); LPNs 4 (ft), 2 (pt); Nurses' aides 13 (ft), 6 (pt); Activities coordinators 1 (ft).
Languages Spanish, Czech.
Facilities Dining room; Chapel; Laundry room; Barber/Beauty shop.
Activities Arts & crafts; Games; Reading groups; Prayer groups; Dances/Social/Cultural gatherings.

Grapeland

Grapeland Nursing Home
PO Box 368, US 287 at Church St, Grapeland, TX 75844
(409) 687-4655
Admin Patricia A Jeffcoat. *Dir of Nursing* Doris Brown RN.
Licensure Intermediate care. *Beds* ICF 68. *Certified* Medicaid.
Owner Proprietary corp.
Admissions Requirements Physician's request.
Staff RNs 1 (ft); LPNs 6 (ft), 3 (pt); Activities coordinators 1 (ft).
Facilities Dining room; Activities room; Laundry room; Barber/Beauty shop.
Activities Arts & crafts; Games; Reading groups; Movies; Shopping trips; Dances/Social/Cultural gatherings.

Grapevine

Brookhollow Manor
925 Minters Chapel Rd, Grapevine, TX 76051
(817) 488-5594
Admin Ralph Chinchurreta. *Dir of Nursing* Audie Owen RN. *Medical Dir* E L Lancaster MD.
Licensure Skilled care; Intermediate care. *Beds* SNF 45; ICF 33. *Private Pay Patients* 33%. *Certified* Medicaid; Medicare.
Owner Nonprofit organization/foundation.
Staff Physicians; RNs; LPNs; Nurses' aides; Physical therapists (contracted); Occupational therapists; Speech therapists; Activities coordinators; Dietitians.
Languages Spanish, German.

Facilities Dining room; Activities room; Laundry room; Barber/Beauty shop.
Activities Arts & crafts; Reading groups; Prayer groups; Movies; Shopping trips; Intergenerational programs; Pet therapy.

Woodridge Convalescent Center
1500 Autumn Dr, Grapevine, TX 76051
(817) 488-8585, 481-3622
Admin Terry J Barcelo.
Licensure Intermediate care. *Beds* 142. *Certified* Medicaid.
Owner Proprietary corp.

Greenville

Greencrest Manor Inc
6113 FM 1570, Greenville, TX 75401-6937
(214) 455-7942
Admin Martha L Ford. *Dir of Nursing* June Casey RN. *Medical Dir* John C Vallancey MD.
Licensure Intermediate care. *Beds* ICF 112. *Certified* Medicaid.
Owner Proprietary corp (Hillhaven Corp).
Admissions Requirements Medical examination; Physician's request.
Staff RNs 2 (ft); LPNs 9 (ft); Nurses' aides 17 (ft); Physical therapists 1 (pt); Speech therapists 1 (pt); Activities coordinators 1 (ft); Dietitians 1 (pt); Ophthalmologists 1 (pt); Podiatrists 1 (pt); Dentists 1 (pt).
Facilities Dining room; Activities room; Laundry room; Barber/Beauty shop.
Activities Arts & crafts; Cards; Games; Reading groups; Prayer groups; Movies; Shopping trips; Dances/Social/Cultural gatherings.

Greenville Nursing Home
4910 Wellington, Greenville, TX 75401
(214) 454-3772
Admin Delma Bowers. *Dir of Nursing* Frances Pitts.
Licensure Intermediate care. *Beds* ICF 120. *Certified* Medicaid.
Owner Proprietary corp (Beverly Enterprises).
Staff LPNs; Nurses' aides; Activities coordinators.
Activities Arts & crafts; Games; Reading groups; Movies; Shopping trips; Dances/Social/Cultural gatherings; Pet therapy.

Home for Aged Pythians
6017 Interstate 30, Greenville, TX 75401
(214) 455-0180
Admin Barbara Thomas. *Dir of Nursing* Stephanie Lamm LVN. *Medical Dir* John C Vallancey MD.
Licensure Intermediate care; Retirement. *Beds* ICF 48; Retirement 48.
Owner Nonprofit organization/foundation.
Admissions Requirements Minimum age 62; Physician's request.
Staff RNs; Nurses' aides 7 (ft), 1 (pt); Activities coordinators; Dietitians; LVNs 7 (ft), 1 (pt).
Languages Spanish.
Affiliation Knights of Pythias.
Facilities Dining room; Activities room; Crafts room; Laundry room; Barber/Beauty shop; Library; Courtyard with fountain and roses.
Activities Arts & crafts; Cards; Games; Reading groups; Prayer groups; Shopping trips; Dances/Social/Cultural gatherings; Intergenerational programs; Pet therapy.

Park Haven Nursing Center Inc
3500 Park St, Greenville, TX 75401
(214) 455-2220
Admin Carolyn Vinson. *Dir of Nursing* Lee Frazier RN. *Medical Dir* John C Vallancey MD.
Licensure Skilled care. *Beds* SNF 100. *Certified* Medicaid; Medicare.
Owner Proprietary corp (Hillhaven Corp).
Admissions Requirements Physician's request.

Staff Physicians 1 (pt); RNs 3 (ft), 1 (pt); LPNs 10 (ft), 2 (pt); Nurses' aides 30 (ft); Activities coordinators 1 (ft).
Facilities Dining room; Activities room; Chapel; Crafts room; Laundry room; Barber/Beauty shop; Library.
Activities Arts & crafts; Games; Reading groups; Prayer groups; Movies; Dances/Social/Cultural gatherings.

Groesbeck

Park Plaza Nursing Center
607 Parkside Dr, Groesbeck, TX 76642
(817) 729-3245
Admin Martha Saling.
Medical Dir Dorothy Outlaw.
Licensure Intermediate care. *Beds* ICF 90. *Certified* Medicaid.
Owner Proprietary corp.
Admissions Requirements Minimum age 18; Medical examination.
Staff Physicians 4 (ft); RNs 1 (ft); LPNs 6 (ft); Nurses' aides 18 (ft); Physical therapists 1 (ft); Speech therapists 1 (ft); Activities coordinators 1 (ft); Dietitians 1 (ft); Ophthalmologists 1 (ft); Podiatrists 1 (ft).
Facilities Dining room; Physical therapy room; Activities room; Crafts room; Laundry room; Barber/Beauty shop.
Activities Arts & crafts; Cards; Games; Reading groups; Prayer groups; Movies; Shopping trips; Dances/Social/Cultural gatherings; Picnics.

Groves

Cresthaven Nursing Residence
PO Box 878, 4400 Gulf Ave, Groves, TX 77619
(409) 962-5785
Admin Joyce N Lewis.
Medical Dir Dr H H Randolph Jr.
Licensure Skilled care; Intermediate care. *Beds* 138. *Certified* Medicaid.
Owner Proprietary corp (Cantex Healthcare Centers).
Staff Physicians 1 (pt); RNs 1 (ft), 2 (pt); LPNs 13 (ft); Nurses' aides 29 (pt); Activities coordinators 1 (ft), 1 (pt); Dietitians 1 (ft), 1 (pt); Dentists 1 (pt).
Facilities Dining room; Activities room; Chapel; Crafts room; Laundry room; Barber/Beauty shop.
Activities Arts & crafts; Cards; Games; Reading groups; Prayer groups; Movies; Dances/Social/Cultural gatherings.

Oak Grove Nursing Home Inc
6230 Warren St, Groves, TX 77619
(409) 963-1266
Admin Lois Rushing.
Licensure Intermediate care. *Beds* 100. *Certified* Medicaid.
Owner Proprietary corp.

Groveton

Groveton Nursing Home
PO Box 890, Hwy 287, Groveton, TX 75845
(409) 642-1221
Admin Beth Thornton.
Medical Dir Reatha Duke LVN.
Licensure Intermediate care. *Beds* ICF 35. *Certified* Medicaid.
Owner Nonprofit organization/foundation.
Admissions Requirements Minimum age 18.
Staff RNs; LPNs; Nurses' aides; Activities coordinators.
Facilities Dining room; Activities room; Barber/Beauty shop.
Activities Arts & crafts; Games; Prayer groups.

Gunter

Hilltop Haven
PO Box 323, 308 E College St, Gunter, TX 75058
(214) 433-2415
Admin Linda Morrison.
Licensure Intermediate care; Custodial care. *Beds* ICF 215. *Certified* Medicaid.
Admissions Requirements Minimum age 16; Medical examination; Physician's request.
Staff RNs 1 (ft); LPNs 13 (ft), 6 (pt); Nurses' aides 53 (ft), 7 (pt); Activities coordinators 2 (ft); Dietitians 18 (ft), 5 (pt).
Affiliation Church of Christ.
Facilities Dining room; Activities room; Chapel; Crafts room; Laundry room; Barber/Beauty shop; Library.
Activities Arts & crafts; Cards; Games; Prayer groups; Movies; Shopping trips.

Hale Center

Hi-Plains Nursing Home
202 W 3rd, Hale Center, TX 79041
(806) 839-2471
Admin Gordon Russell.
Licensure Intermediate care. *Beds* 44. *Certified* Medicaid.
Owner Nonprofit corp.

Hallettsville

Stevens Convalescent Center
106 Kahn, Hallettsville, TX 77964
(512) 798-3606
Admin Joseph C Bonck JR. *Dir of Nursing* Phyllis Valchar RN.
Licensure Intermediate care. *Beds* ICF 190. *Private Pay Patients* 63%. *Certified* Medicaid; VA.
Owner Proprietary corp (National Heritage).
Staff Physicians 4 (ft); RNs 1 (ft); LPNs 25 (ft); Nurses' aides 84 (ft); Physical therapists 1 (ft); Activities coordinators 3 (ft); Dietitians 1 (ft).
Languages Spanish, German.
Facilities Dining room; Physical therapy room; Activities room; Chapel; Crafts room; Laundry room; Barber/Beauty shop; Courtyard.
Activities Arts & crafts; Cards; Games; Reading groups; Prayer groups; Movies; Shopping trips; Dances/Social/Cultural gatherings; Pet therapy.

Haltom City

Crossroads
5700 Midway Rd, Haltom City, TX 76117
(817) 831-6471
Admin Lee A Brown. *Dir of Nursing* Cecelia Bost RN. *Medical Dir* Richard G LaMere MD.
Licensure Intermediate care for mentally retarded. *Beds* ICF/MR 80. *Private Pay Patients* 0%. *Certified* Medicaid.
Owner Nonprofit organization/foundation.
Admissions Requirements Minimum age 6-16.
Staff RNs 2 (ft); LPNs 5 (ft), 3 (pt); Nurses' aides 85 (ft), 5 (pt); Physical therapists; Recreational therapists 1 (ft); Speech therapists 1 (ft); Dietitians.
Facilities Dining room; Activities room; Laundry room.
Activities Arts & crafts; Cards; Games; Movies; Shopping trips.

Hamilton

Forest Oaks Nursing Home
726 E Coke St, Hamilton, TX 76531
(817) 386-5319
Admin Forrest S Tatum.
Licensure Intermediate care. *Beds* 28. *Certified* Medicaid.

Staff RNs 1 (pt); LPNs 3 (ft); Nurses' aides 5 (ft), 1 (pt); Activities coordinators 1 (ft); Dietitians 1 (pt).
Facilities Dining room; Activities room.
Activities Arts & crafts; Cards; Games; Movies; Dances/Social/Cultural gatherings.

Hamilton Nursing Home
205 W Gentry St, Hamilton, TX 76531
(817) 386-3106
Admin Georgia M Robinson.
Medical Dir Foster Lee Wilcox.
Licensure Intermediate care. *Beds* ICF 41.
Certified Medicare.
Owner Privately owned.
Admissions Requirements Minimum age 21.
Staff RNs 2 (ft); LPNs 4 (ft); Nurses' aides 10 (ft); Activities coordinators 1 (ft); Dietitians 1 (ft).
Facilities Dining room; Barber/Beauty shop.
Activities Arts & crafts; Games; Movies; Shopping trips; Dances/Social/Cultural gatherings.

Hillcrest Nursing Home
400 W Grogan, Hamilton, TX 76531
(817) 386-3171
Admin Martin R Hubbartt. *Dir of Nursing* Martha Willis RN. *Medical Dir* C B Wright.
Licensure Intermediate care; Alzheimer's care. *Beds* ICF 78. *Certified* Medicaid.
Owner Privately owned.
Admissions Requirements Medical examination; Physician's request.
Staff Physicians 2 (pt); RNs 1 (ft), 1 (pt); LPNs 5 (ft), 2 (pt); Nurses' aides 16 (ft), 4 (pt); Activities coordinators 1 (ft); Dietitians 1 (ft), 1 (pt); Chaplain 1 (ft).
Languages Spanish, Portuguese.
Facilities Dining room; Activities room; Chapel; Laundry room; Barber/Beauty shop; Billard room.
Activities Cards; Games; Prayer groups; Movies; Dances/Social/Cultural gatherings.

Leisure Lodge—Hamilton
910 E Pierson, Hamilton, TX 76531
(817) 386-8113
Admin Dennis P Dorton.
Licensure Intermediate care. *Beds* 96.
Certified Medicaid.
Owner Proprietary corp (Beverly Enterprises).

Hamlin

Holiday Lodge
425 SW Ave F, Hamlin, TX 79520
(915) 576-3643
Admin James B Crowley.
Licensure Intermediate care. *Beds* 60.
Certified Medicaid.
Owner Proprietary corp.

Hampstead

Hampstead Nursing Home
1111 San Antonio, Hampstead, TX 77445
(713) 816-3382, 816-6220
Admin Joyce Brokmeyer.
Licensure Skilled care; Intermediate care. *Beds* 110. *Certified* Medicaid; Medicare.
Owner Proprietary corp.

Harlingen

Golden Palms Retirement & Health Center
2101 Treasure Hills Blvd, Harlingen, TX 78552
(512) 421-4653
Licensure Nursing. *Beds* Nursing 60.

Harlingen Good Samaritan Center
4301 S "F" St, Harlingen, TX 78550
(512) 423-4959
Admin Darrold Nies. *Dir of Nursing* Betty Randgaard RN.

Licensure Intermediate care. *Beds* ICF 112.
Certified Medicaid.
Owner Nonprofit corp (Evangelical Lutheran/Good Samaritan Society).
Admissions Requirements Physician's request.
Staff RNs 1 (ft); LPNs 10 (ft), 4 (pt); Nurses' aides; Activities coordinators 1 (ft).
Languages Spanish, German.
Affiliation Lutheran.
Facilities Dining room; Physical therapy room; Laundry room; Barber/Beauty shop.
Activities Arts & crafts; Cards; Games; Prayer groups; Movies; Shopping trips.

Retama Manor Nursing Center—Harlingen
2201 Pease St, Harlingen, TX 78550
(512) 423-2663
Admin Edelmira Resendez.
Licensure Intermediate care. *Beds* 197.
Certified Medicaid.
Owner Proprietary corp (ARA Living Centers).

Sun Valley Health Care Center
2204 Pease St, Harlingen, TX 78550
(512) 425-2812
Admin Martha Ann Hamby.
Medical Dir Sam Carter MD.
Licensure Skilled care; Intermediate care. *Beds* 120. *Certified* Medicaid.
Owner Proprietary corp (Hillhaven Corp).
Admissions Requirements Medical examination.
Staff RNs 3 (ft), 4 (pt); LPNs 12 (ft), 3 (pt); Nurses' aides 24 (ft), 4 (pt); Activities coordinators 1 (ft), 1 (pt); Dietitians 1 (ft).
Facilities Dining room; Activities room; Crafts room; Laundry room; Barber/Beauty shop.

Haskell

Haskell Nursing Center
PO Box 1086, 1504 N 1st St, Haskell, TX 79521-1086
(817) 864-3556
Admin Lorene A Beason.
Licensure Intermediate care. *Beds* 68.
Certified Medicaid.
Owner Proprietary corp (Beverly Enterprises).

Rice Springs Care Home Inc
Rte 1 Box 640, 1302 N 1st St, Haskell, TX 79521
(817) 864-2652
Admin Ruth Ann Klose. *Dir of Nursing* Donna Tidrow.
Licensure Intermediate care. *Beds* ICF 82. *Private Pay Patients* 47%. *Certified* Medicaid.
Owner Proprietary corp.
Admissions Requirements Medical examination.
Staff LPNs; Nurses' aides; Activities coordinators; Dietitians.
Languages Spanish.
Facilities Dining room; Activities room; Laundry room; Barber/Beauty shop.
Activities Arts & crafts; Cards; Games; Reading groups; Prayer groups; Movies; Shopping trips; Dances/Social/Cultural gatherings; Intergenerational programs; Pet therapy.

Hawkins

Hawkins Care Center
PO Box 430, 230 S Beulah, Hawkins, TX 75765
(214) 769-2941
Admin Lavonia J Stone. *Dir of Nursing* Imarene Anders. *Medical Dir* Dr R A Lester III.
Licensure Intermediate care. *Beds* ICF 46.
Certified Medicaid.
Owner Proprietary corp (Health Enterprises of America).

Admissions Requirements Physician's request.
Staff Physicians 1 (ft); RNs 1 (pt); LPNs 4 (ft), 1 (pt); Nurses' aides 10 (ft), 3 (pt); Physical therapists 1 (pt); Reality therapists 1 (pt); Recreational therapists 1 (pt); Occupational therapists 1 (pt); Speech therapists 1 (pt); Activities coordinators 1 (ft); Dietitians 1 (ft); Ophthalmologists 1 (pt).
Facilities Dining room; Laundry room; Barber/Beauty shop.
Activities Arts & crafts; Cards; Games; Reading groups; Prayer groups; Movies; Shopping trips; Dances/Social/Cultural gatherings.

Hearne

Leisure Lodge—Hearne
1100 Brown St, Hearne, TX 77859
(409) 279-5361
Admin Velma Windham.
Licensure Intermediate care. *Beds* 148.
Certified Medicaid.
Owner Proprietary corp (Beverly Enterprises).

Hemphill

Hemphill Care Center
PO Box 1527, FM 83 W, Hemphill, TX 75948
(409) 787-3342
Licensure Nursing. *Beds* Nursing 90.

Hempstead

Retirement Care Center of Hempstead
1111 San Antonio, Hempstead, TX 77445
(409) 826-3382
Licensure Nursing. *Beds* Nursing 110.

Henderson

Leisure Lodge—Henderson
1010 W Main, Henderson, TX 75652
(214) 657-6513
Admin Marilyn A Johnson.
Licensure Intermediate care. *Beds* 179.
Certified Medicaid.
Owner Proprietary corp (Beverly Enterprises).
Staff LPNs 9 (ft), 2 (pt); Nurses' aides 44 (ft), 7 (pt).
Facilities Dining room; Laundry room; Barber/Beauty shop.
Activities Arts & crafts; Games; Reading groups; Prayer groups; Movies; Dances/Social/Cultural gatherings.

Southwood Convalescent Center Inc
PO Box 1066, Hwy 79 at 259, Henderson, TX 75653-1066
(214) 657-6506
Admin Loretta A Roberts. *Dir of Nursing* Barbara Tate.
Licensure Intermediate care. *Beds* ICF 160.
Certified Medicaid.
Owner Proprietary corp.
Admissions Requirements Medical examination.
Staff RNs; LPNs; Nurses' aides; Activities coordinators; Dietitians.
Facilities Dining room; Physical therapy room; Activities room; Barber/Beauty shop.
Activities Arts & crafts; Cards; Games; Prayer groups; Movies.

Henrietta

Care Manor Nursing Center of Henrietta
Hwy 287 E, Henrietta, TX 76365
(817) 538-5665
Admin Rebecca Rae Spikes.
Licensure Intermediate care. *Beds* 90.
Certified Medicaid.
Owner Nonprofit corp.

Henrietta Care Center
PO Box 7635, 807 W Bois D'Arc, Henrietta, TX 76365
(817) 538-4303
Admin Robert G Holmes.
Licensure Intermediate care. *Beds* 60. *Certified* Medicaid.
Owner Proprietary corp (Comprehensive Health Care Assn).

Hereford

Golden Plains Care Center
420 Ranger Dr, Hereford, TX 79045
(806) 364-3815
Licensure Nursing. *Beds* Nursing 90.

King's Manor Methodist Home Inc
PO Box 1999, 400 Ranger Dr, Hereford, TX 79045
(806) 364-0661
Admin Joyce L Lyons.
Licensure Intermediate care. *Beds* 79. *Certified* Medicaid.
Admissions Requirements Medical examination; Physician's request.
Staff Physicians 5 (ft); RNs 1 (ft), 1 (pt); LPNs 12 (ft); Nurses' aides 35 (ft); Activities coordinators 2 (ft); Dietitians 1 (pt).
Affiliation Methodist.
Facilities Dining room; Chapel; Laundry room; Barber/Beauty shop; Library.
Activities Arts & crafts; Cards; Games; Shopping trips.

Hico

Village Nursing Home
712 Railroad St, Hico, TX 76457
(817) 796-2111
Admin Velaine Swedelius.
Licensure Intermediate care. *Beds* 114. *Certified* Medicaid.
Admissions Requirements Physician's request.
Staff LPNs 8 (ft); Nurses' aides 32 (ft); Activities coordinators 1 (ft); Dietitians 1 (ft).
Facilities Dining room; Activities room; Laundry room.
Activities Arts & crafts; Cards; Games; Reading groups; Prayer groups; Movies; Shopping trips; Dances/Social/Cultural gatherings.

Hillsboro

Canterbury Villa of Hillsboro
Rte 3 Box 304, Old Brandon Rd, Hillsboro, TX 76645
(817) 582-8416
Admin Verna Gibson.
Medical Dir Nancy Coffey.
Licensure Intermediate care. *Beds* ICF 166. *Certified* Medicaid.
Owner Proprietary corp (Health Enter of America).
Admissions Requirements Medical examination; Physician's request.
Staff RNs 1 (ft); LPNs 11 (ft); Nurses' aides 50 (ft); Activities coordinators 1 (ft); Dietitians 1 (ft).
Facilities Dining room; Activities room; Chapel; Crafts room; Laundry room; Barber/Beauty shop.
Activities Arts & crafts; Cards; Games; Reading groups; Prayer groups; Movies; Dances/Social/Cultural gatherings.

Town Hall Estates
300 Happy Ln, Hillsboro, TX 76645
(817) 582-8482
Admin R Edward Lowe.
Medical Dir Sharon Maass.
Licensure Intermediate care. *Beds* 118. *Certified* Medicaid.
Owner Nonprofit corp.

Staff RNs 1 (pt); LPNs 11 (ft), 1 (pt); Nurses' aides 40 (ft), 10 (pt); Activities coordinators 1 (ft).
Facilities Dining room; Chapel; Barber/Beauty shop.
Activities Games; Dances/Social/Cultural gatherings.

Hiram

Locust Grove Nursing Home
Rte 5 Box 393, Hiram, TX 75169
(214) 563-9445
Licensure Nursing. *Beds* Nursing 60.

Hitchcock

Coastal Pines Care Center
6701 FM 2004, Hitchcock, TX 77563
(409) 986-6516
Admin Ann Wallace.
Licensure Intermediate care. *Beds* 61. *Certified* Medicaid.
Admissions Requirements Physician's request.
Staff Physicians 1 (pt); RNs 1 (pt); LPNs 4 (ft); Nurses' aides 15 (ft), 5 (pt); Physical therapists 1 (pt); Recreational therapists 1 (pt); Activities coordinators 1 (pt); Dietitians 1 (pt).
Facilities Dining room; Activities room; Crafts room; Laundry room; Barber/Beauty shop.
Activities Arts & crafts; Cards; Games; Prayer groups; Shopping trips; Dances/Social/Cultural gatherings.

Holland

K'Way Kare Nursing Home
PO Box 209, 610 Josephine, Holland, TX 76534
(817) 657-2494
Admin Gilbert W Goodnight. *Dir of Nursing* Cynthia Pacha LVN.
Licensure Intermediate care. *Beds* ICF 31. *Private Pay Patients* 40%. *Certified* Medicaid.
Owner Privately owned.
Admissions Requirements Medical examination.
Staff Physicians; LPNs; Nurses' aides; Recreational therapists; Activities coordinators; Dietitians.
Languages Spanish, Czech.
Facilities Dining room; Activities room; Crafts room; Laundry room.
Activities Arts & crafts; Cards; Games; Reading groups; Prayer groups; Movies; Dances/Social/Cultural gatherings; Pet therapy.

Hondo

Community Care Center of Hondo
2001 Ave E, Hondo, TX 78861
(512) 426-3087
Admin Virginia Lamza.
Medical Dir Betty Frieda.
Licensure Skilled care. *Beds* SNF 75. *Certified* Medicaid; Medicare.
Owner Proprietary corp (Columbia Corp).
Admissions Requirements Minimum age 14; Medical examination.
Staff Physicians 4 (pt); RNs 1 (ft), 1 (pt); LPNs 7 (ft), 1 (pt); Nurses' aides 30 (ft); Physical therapists 1 (pt); Reality therapists 1 (pt); Activities coordinators 1 (pt); Dietitians 1 (pt); Dentists 1 (pt).
Languages Spanish, German.
Facilities Dining room; Activities room; Crafts room; Laundry room; Barber/Beauty shop.
Activities Arts & crafts; Cards; Games; Reading groups; Prayer groups; Movies; Shopping trips; Dances/Social/Cultural gatherings.

Heritage Manor Care Center of Hondo
3002 Ave Q, Hondo, TX 78861
(512) 426-3057
Admin Myrtle Andrews. *Dir of Nursing* Gia Sabiat RN. *Medical Dir* Dr John Meyer.
Licensure Skilled care; Intermediate care; Alzheimer's care. *Beds* SNF 118; ICF. *Certified* Medicaid; Medicare.
Owner Proprietary corp.
Admissions Requirements Medical examination; Physician's request.
Staff RNs; LPNs 4 (ft); Nurses' aides 13 (ft); Activities coordinators 1 (ft).
Languages Spanish, Italian, German.
Facilities Dining room; Physical therapy room; Activities room; Laundry room; Barber/Beauty shop.
Activities Arts & crafts; Cards; Games; Reading groups; Prayer groups; Movies; Shopping trips; Dances/Social/Cultural gatherings; Picnics.

Honey Grove

Grove Manor Nursing Home
Rte 2, Honey Grove, TX 75446
(214) 378-2293
Admin John O'Connor. *Dir of Nursing* Wilma Thompson. *Medical Dir* Michael D Leddy.
Licensure Intermediate care. *Beds* ICF 90. *Private Pay Patients* 15%. *Certified* Medicaid.
Owner Proprietary corp (Monarch).
Admissions Requirements Minimum age 18; Medical examination; Physician's request.
Staff Physicians 4 (pt); RNs 1 (pt); LPNs 6 (ft), 3 (pt); Nurses' aides 17 (ft), 2 (pt); Physical therapists (consultant); Activities coordinators 1 (ft); Dietitians (consultant); Ophthalmologists 1 (pt); Podiatrists 1 (pt); Audiologists 1 (pt).
Facilities Dining room; Activities room; Chapel; Laundry room; Barber/Beauty shop; Library.
Activities Cards; Games; Reading groups; Prayer groups; Movies; Dances/Social/Cultural gatherings.

Houston

Afton Oaks Nursing Center
7514 Kingsley, Houston, TX 77087
(713) 644-8393
Admin Leonard C Goodin. *Dir of Nursing* Sherlyn Gidney RN. *Medical Dir* A O'Dwyer MD.
Licensure Skilled care; Intermediate care; Retirement. *Beds* 169. *Certified* Medicaid; Medicare.
Owner Proprietary corp.
Admissions Requirements Minimum age 21; Medical examination; Physician's request.
Staff Physicians 1 (pt); RNs 9 (ft); LPNs 28 (ft); Nurses' aides 42 (ft); Physical therapists 3 (pt); Recreational therapists 1 (pt); Occupational therapists 2 (pt); Speech therapists 1 (pt); Activities coordinators 1 (ft); Dietitians 1 (pt); Ophthalmologists 1 (pt); Podiatrists 1 (pt).
Facilities Dining room; Activities room; Chapel; Crafts room; Laundry room; Barber/Beauty shop; Library.
Activities Arts & crafts; Cards; Games; Reading groups; Prayer groups; Movies; Shopping trips; Dances/Social/Cultural gatherings.

Aldine Health Care Center Inc
10110 Airline Dr, Houston, TX 77037
(713) 447-0376
Licensure Nursing. *Beds* Nursing 197.

All Seasons Care Center
6150 S Loop E, Houston, TX 77087
(713) 643-2628
Licensure Nursing. *Beds* Nursing 120.

Autumn Hills Convalescent Center—Janisch
617 W Janisch, Houston, TX 77018
(713) 697-2891
Admin Mr Del Waggoner. *Dir of Nursing* Mrs Martha Sellers RN.
Licensure Intermediate care. *Beds* ICF 119. *Certified* Medicaid.
Owner Proprietary corp.
Admissions Requirements Medical examination; Physician's request.
Staff RNs; LPNs; Nurses' aides; Activities coordinators; Dietitians.
Facilities Dining room; Activities room; Crafts room; Laundry room; Barber/Beauty shop; Library.
Activities Arts & crafts; Cards; Games; Reading groups; Prayer groups; Movies; Shopping trips; Dances/Social/Cultural gatherings.

Bayou Glen-Jones Road
10851 Crescent Moon Rd, Houston, TX 77064
(713) 890-0171
Admin Sherry A Reid. *Dir of Nursing* Velma Gleason RN. *Medical Dir* B Vu MD.
Licensure Intermediate care. *Beds* ICF 120; Private 60. *Certified* Medicaid.
Owner Proprietary corp (Convalescent Services).
Admissions Requirements Medical examination.
Staff RNs 5 (ft), 4 (pt); LPNs 8 (ft), 3 (pt); Nurses' aides 50 (ft); Activities coordinators 2 (ft); Dietitians 1 (ft).
Facilities Dining room; Physical therapy room; Activities room; Crafts room; Laundry room; Barber/Beauty shop; Library; TV room.
Activities Arts & crafts; Cards; Games; Reading groups; Prayer groups; Movies; Shopping trips; Dances/Social/Cultural gatherings.

Bayou Glen—Northwest
7215 Windfern, Houston, TX 77040
(713) 466-8933
Admin Sherry Duke.
Licensure Skilled care; Intermediate care. *Beds* 180. *Certified* Medicaid.
Owner Proprietary corp (Convalescent Services).

Bayou Glen-Town Park
8820 Town Park Dr, Houston, TX 77036
(713) 777-7241
Admin Barbara L Martin.
Licensure Skilled care; Intermediate care. *Beds* 180. *Certified* Medicaid.
Owner Proprietary corp (Convalescent Services).

Bayou Manor
4141 S Braeswood, Houston, TX 77025
(713) 666-2651
Admin Vivian H Davis.
Medical Dir Dr John Borland.
Licensure Skilled care; Retirement. *Beds* SNF 26.
Owner Nonprofit organization/foundation (Brazos Presbyterian Homes Inc).
Admissions Requirements Minimum age 65; Must be a resident of Bayou Manor (a CCRC). Does not take patients from the community.
Staff RNs 3 (ft), 2 (pt); LPNs 2 (ft); Nurses' aides 10 (ft), 4 (pt); Activities coordinators 1 (ft); Dietitians 1 (pt).
Facilities Dining room; Activities room; Chapel; Crafts room; Laundry room; Barber/Beauty shop; Library.
Activities Arts & crafts; Cards; Games; Movies; Dances/Social/Cultural gatherings; Exercise.

Beechnut Manor Living Center
12777 Beechnut, Houston, TX 77072
(713) 879-8040
Licensure Nursing. *Beds* Nursing 146.

Benner Convalescent Center
3510 Sherman St, Houston, TX 77003
(713) 224-5344
Admin Elsie L Hawkins. *Dir of Nursing* Clydell Rhodes LVN.
Licensure Intermediate care. *Beds* ICF 117. *Certified* Medicaid.
Owner Proprietary corp.
Admissions Requirements Minimum age 18; Medical examination; Physician's request.
Staff LPNs 8 (ft), 3 (pt); Nurses' aides 22 (ft), 4 (pt); Activities coordinators 1 (ft).
Languages Spanish, Italian.
Facilities Dining room; Activities room; Crafts room; Laundry room; Barber/Beauty shop.
Activities Arts & crafts; Cards; Games; Reading groups; Prayer groups; Dances/Social/Cultural gatherings.

Blalock Nursing Home—East
1405 Holland Ave, Houston, TX 77029
(713) 455-1744
Admin Golden Wiltz.
Licensure Intermediate care. *Beds* 160. *Certified* Medicaid.
Owner Proprietary corp.

Blalock Nursing Home—North
5329 N Freeway, Houston, TX 77022
(713) 695-5821
Admin Claude Anderson.
Licensure Skilled care; Intermediate care. *Beds* 169. *Certified* Medicaid.
Owner Proprietary corp.

Canterbury Villa of Houston
4225 Denmark, Houston, TX 77016
(713) 631-0200
Licensure Nursing. *Beds* Nursing 83.

Center for the Retarded—Cullen
810 Marston, Houston, TX 77019
(713) 523-6741
Admin Dalona L Riggs.
Licensure Intermediate care for mentally retarded. *Beds* 86. *Certified* Medicaid.

Clarewood House
7400 Clarewood Dr, Houston, TX 77036
(713) 774-5821
Admin Janice Jones MS MEd. *Dir of Nursing* R Marie Dickey MSN RNC. *Medical Dir* Dr Jean Samaan.
Licensure Intermediate care; Personal care; Independent living. *Beds* ICF 24; Personal care 60; Independent living apts 200. *Private Pay Patients* 100%.
Owner Nonprofit corp.
Admissions Requirements Minimum age 65; Medical examination; Physician's request.
Staff RNs 3 (ft), 5 (pt); LPNs 1 (ft), 1 (pt); Nurses' aides 5 (ft), 6 (pt); Activities coordinators 1 (ft); Dietitians 1 (ft); CSWs 1 (pt).
Affiliation Methodist.
Facilities Dining room; Activities room; Chapel; Crafts room; Laundry room; Barber/Beauty shop; Library.
Activities Arts & crafts; Cards; Games; Prayer groups; Movies; Shopping trips; Dances/Social/Cultural gatherings; Pet therapy.

Courtyard Convalescent Center
7499 Stanwick Dr, Houston, TX 77087
(713) 644-8048
Admin Delight L Finnell.
Medical Dir J Winston Morrison MD.
Licensure Intermediate care. *Beds* 120. *Certified* Medicaid.
Owner Proprietary corp (Beverly Enterprises).
Admissions Requirements Minimum age 21; Medical examination; Physician's request.
Staff Physicians 1 (pt); RNs 1 (ft); LPNs 8 (ft), 4 (pt); Nurses' aides 30 (ft), 2 (pt); Physical therapists 1 (pt); Occupational therapists 1 (pt); Speech therapists 1 (pt);

Activities coordinators 1 (ft); Dietitians 1 (pt); Ophthalmologists 1 (pt); Podiatrists 1 (pt); Audiologists 1 (pt); Dentists 1 (pt).
Facilities Dining room; Activities room; Barber/Beauty shop.
Activities Arts & crafts; Cards; Games; Reading groups; Prayer groups; Movies; Shopping trips; Dances/Social/Cultural gatherings.

Dever Nursing Home
3310 W Main St, Houston, TX 77098
(713) 529-1218
Admin Grace French.
Licensure Intermediate care. *Beds* 37.
Owner Proprietary corp.

Golden Age Manor—Holmes
6150 S Loop E, Houston, TX 77087
(713) 643-2628
Admin Mildred M Stanley.
Licensure Intermediate care. *Beds* 120. *Certified* Medicaid.
Owner Proprietary corp (Hillhaven Corp).

Golden Age Manor—Long Point
8810 Long Point Rd, Houston, TX 77055
(713) 468-7833
Admin Marion L Martin.
Licensure Intermediate care. *Beds* 174. *Certified* Medicaid.
Owner Proprietary corp.

Golden Age Manor—North Loop
1737 North Loop W, Houston, TX 77008
(713) 869-5551
Admin Robert A Kalin.
Medical Dir Dr William Cruce.
Licensure Skilled care; Intermediate care. *Beds* 200. *Certified* Medicaid; Medicare.
Owner Proprietary corp.
Admissions Requirements Medical examination; Physician's request.
Staff Physicians 1 (pt); RNs 4 (ft), 1 (pt); LPNs 15 (ft), 5 (pt); Nurses' aides 62 (ft), 5 (pt); Physical therapists 2 (pt); Occupational therapists 1 (pt); Speech therapists 1 (pt); Activities coordinators 2 (ft); Dietitians 1 (ft); Ophthalmologists 1 (pt); Podiatrists 1 (pt); Dentists 1 (pt).
Facilities Dining room; Physical therapy room; Activities room; Crafts room; Laundry room; Barber/Beauty shop; Library.
Activities Arts & crafts; Cards; Games; Reading groups; Prayer groups; Movies; Shopping trips; Dances/Social/Cultural gatherings; Exercise classes.

Golden Age Manor—Rookin
6500 Rookin St, Houston, TX 77074
(713) 774-9736
Admin H Sparks Dorris.
Medical Dir Margaret Saw MD.
Licensure Skilled care; Intermediate care; Alzheimer's care. *Beds* SNF 57; ICF 189. *Certified* Medicaid; Medicare.
Owner Proprietary corp (Hillhaven Corp).
Staff RNs 13 (ft), 2 (pt); LPNs 19 (ft), 3 (pt); Nurses' aides 90 (ft); Physical therapists 1 (ft); Activities coordinators 3 (ft); Dietitians 1 (ft).
Languages Spanish, Hindi, Nigerian, Chinese, Tagalog, Vietnamese.
Facilities Dining room; Physical therapy room; Activities room; Crafts room; Laundry room; Barber/Beauty shop; Library.
Activities Arts & crafts; Cards; Games; Prayer groups; Movies; Dances/Social/Cultural gatherings; Intergenerational programs; Pet therapy; Cooking classes; Spanish movies; Music therapy; Reminiscence; Sensory stimulation; One-on-one interaction.

Graystone Manor Nursing Home 2
1911 Aldine Mail Rte, Houston, TX 77039
(713) 442-8436
Admin Mary Lou McMillan.

Licensure Intermediate care. *Beds* 49.
Certified Medicaid.
Owner Proprietary corp.

Greentree Health Center Inc
7210 Northline Dr, Houston, TX 77076
(713) 697-4771
Licensure Nursing. *Beds* Nursing 204.

Hallmark Anderson Health Care Center
4718 Hallmark Ln, Houston, TX 77056
(713) 622-6633
Admin Helen S Hampton. *Dir of Nursing*
Lucy C Shields.
Licensure Private nursing; Retirement. *Beds*
Private nursing 42.
Owner Nonprofit corp.
Admissions Requirements Minimum age 65;
Medical examination.
Staff Physicians 4 (ft); RNs 2 (ft); LPNs 5 (ft);
Nurses' aides 20 (ft); Activities coordinators
1 (ft); Dietitians 2 (ft); Ophthalmologists 1
(pt).
Facilities Dining room; Activities room;
Crafts room; Laundry room; Barber/Beauty
shop; Library; Swimming pool.
Activities Arts & crafts; Games; Reading
groups; Prayer groups; Movies; Shopping
trips; Dances/Social/Cultural gatherings.

Hermann Park Manor
5600 Chenevert St, Houston, TX 77004
(713) 523-6831, 524-8271 FAX
Admin Leonard C Goodin. *Dir of Nursing*
Sharon L Goodin RN QMRP. *Medical Dir*
Dr M Saw.
Licensure Skilled care; Intermediate care;
Hospice; Retirement; Alzheimer's care. *Beds*
SNF 129; ICF 56. *Private Pay Patients* 28%.
Certified Medicaid; Medicare; VA.
Owner Proprietary corp (American Health
Centers Inc).
Admissions Requirements Minimum age 25;
Medical examination; Physician's request.
Staff Physicians 2 (ft), 10 (pt); RNs 4 (ft);
LPNs 28 (ft), 7 (pt); Nurses' aides 60 (ft), 10
(pt); Physical therapists 7 (pt); Occupational
therapists 5 (pt); Speech therapists 2 (pt);
Activities coordinators 2 (ft); Dietitians 1
(ft), 2 (pt); Ophthalmologists 1 (pt);
Podiatrists 1 (pt); Audiologists 1 (pt).
Languages Spanish.
Facilities Dining room; Physical therapy
room; Activities room; Crafts room; Laundry
room; Barber/Beauty shop; Library.
Activities Arts & crafts; Cards; Games;
Reading groups; Prayer groups; Movies;
Shopping trips; Dances/Social/Cultural
gatherings; Intergenerational programs; Pet
therapy.

Highland Park Care Center
2714 Morrison, Houston, TX 77009
(713) 862-1616
Admin Charlene Hinton.
Licensure Intermediate care. *Beds* 67.
Certified Medicaid.
Admissions Requirements Medical
examination; Physician's request.
Staff RNs 1 (pt); LPNs 4 (ft); Nurses' aides 16
(ft); Activities coordinators 1 (ft); Podiatrists
1 (pt).
Facilities Dining room; Activities room;
Laundry room; Barber/Beauty shop.
Activities Arts & crafts; Cards; Games; Prayer
groups; Movies.

Holly Hall
8304 Knight Rd, Houston, TX 77054
(713) 799-9031
Admin Wesley F Stevens. *Dir of Nursing*
Juliette Buchanan.
Licensure Skilled care; Intermediate care;
Independent living. *Beds* SNF 46; ICF 24;
Independent living 85; Cottages 12;
Duplexes 4.
Owner Nonprofit corp.

Admissions Requirements Minimum age 65;
Medical examination.
Staff RNs 2 (ft), 1 (pt); LPNs 8 (ft), 2 (pt);
Nurses' aides 15 (ft), 3 (pt); Dietitians 2 (ft).
Facilities Dining room; Activities room;
Chapel; Barber/Beauty shop; Library.
Activities Arts & crafts; Games; Prayer groups;
Shopping trips.

Jewish Home for the Aged
6200 N Braeswood, Houston, TX 77074
(713) 771-4111
Admin Anita Cabelli.
Licensure Skilled care; Intermediate care. *Beds*
218. *Certified* Medicaid.
Owner Nonprofit corp.
Affiliation Jewish.

Leisure Arms Nursing Home
4225 Denmark, Houston, TX 77016
(713) 631-0200
Admin Geraldine L McElroy.
Licensure Intermediate care. *Beds* 83.
Certified Medicaid.
Owner Proprietary corp (ARA Living
Centers).
Admissions Requirements Minimum age 20;
Medical examination; Physician's request.
Staff Physicians 1 (ft); LPNs 4 (ft), 3 (pt);
Nurses' aides 12 (ft), 6 (pt).
Facilities Dining room; Activities room;
Crafts room; Laundry room.
Activities Arts & crafts; Cards; Games; Prayer
groups; Movies; Shopping trips; Dances/
Social/Cultural gatherings.

Manda Ann Convalescent Home Inc
7441 Coffee St, Houston, TX 77033
(713) 733-9471
Admin Grace Thomas.
Medical Dir Jo Ann Hampton.
Licensure Intermediate care. *Beds* ICF 216.
Certified Medicaid.
Owner Proprietary corp.
Admissions Requirements Physician's request.
Staff Physicians; RNs; Nurses' aides; Physical
therapists; Occupational therapists; Activities
coordinators; Dietitians; Ophthalmologists.
Facilities Dining room; Activities room;
Crafts room; Laundry room; Barber/Beauty
shop; Courtyard.
Activities Arts & crafts; Cards; Games;
Reading groups; Prayer groups; Movies;
Shopping trips; Dances/Social/Cultural
gatherings.

Manor Care Sharpview
7505 Bellerive, Houston, TX 77036
(713) 774-9611, 774-5421 FAX
Admin Peggy Wheeler. *Dir of Nursing* Lynette
Lawson RN. *Medical Dir* Arvind Bhandari
MD.
Licensure Skilled care; Intermediate care;
Alzheimer's care. *Beds* SNF 48; ICF 50;
Alzheimer's care 30. *Certified* Medicare.
Owner Proprietary corp (Manor Care Inc).
Admissions Requirements Physician's request.
Staff Physicians 6 (pt); RNs 4 (ft), 2 (pt);
LPNs 9 (ft), 7 (pt); Nurses' aides 40 (ft), 3
(pt); Physical therapists 1 (pt); Occupational
therapists 1 (pt); Speech therapists 1 (pt);
Activities coordinators 1 (ft), 1 (pt);
Dietitians 1 (pt).
Facilities Dining room; Physical therapy
room; Activities room; Crafts room; Laundry
room; Barber/Beauty shop; Private & semi-
private rooms available.
Activities Arts & crafts; Cards; Games;
Reading groups; Prayer groups; Movies;
Shopping trips; Dances/Social/Cultural
gatherings; Intergenerational programs; Pet
therapy; Family nights; Special events.

Mercy Nursing Home Inc
3901 Los Angeles St, Houston, TX 77026
(713) 672-7654
Admin Brenda Joyce H Edwards.

Licensure Intermediate care. *Beds* 63.
Certified Medicaid.
Owner Proprietary corp.

Montrose Care Center
3508 Milam St, Houston, TX 77002
(713) 529-3071
Admin Ronald Betterton.
Licensure Intermediate care. *Beds* 148.
Certified Medicaid.
Owner Proprietary corp (ARA Living
Centers).

North Shores Healthcare Center
12350 Wood Bayou Dr, Houston, TX 77013
(713) 453-0446
Admin Catherine A Golden. *Dir of Nursing*
Cynthia Douglas RN.
Licensure Intermediate care. *Beds* ICF 150.
Certified Medicaid; Medicare.
Owner Proprietary corp (ARA Living
Centers).
Admissions Requirements Minimum age 18;
Medical examination.
Staff RNs 1 (ft); LPNs 12 (ft), 2 (pt); Nurses'
aides 30 (ft), 8 (pt); Activities coordinators 1
(ft), 1 (pt).
Facilities Dining room; Activities room;
Crafts room; Laundry room; Barber/Beauty
shop; Library.
Activities Arts & crafts; Cards; Games;
Movies; Dances/Social/Cultural gatherings;
Stroke group.

Northline Manor
7210 Northline Dr, Houston, TX 77076
(713) 697-4771
Admin W William Jahn.
Licensure Intermediate care; Personal care.
Beds ICF 180; Personal 24. *Certified*
Medicaid.
Owner Proprietary corp (Cantex Healthcare
Centers).
Admissions Requirements Minimum age 18;
Medical examination.
Staff RNs 1 (ft); LPNs 10 (ft); Nurses' aides
65 (ft); Physical therapists 1 (ft);
Occupational therapists 1 (pt); Speech
therapists 1 (pt); Activities coordinators 1
(ft), 1 (pt); Dietitians 1 (pt).
Facilities Dining room; Physical therapy
room; Activities room; Chapel; Laundry
room; Barber/Beauty shop; Library.
Activities Arts & crafts; Cards; Games;
Reading groups; Prayer groups; Movies;
Shopping trips; Dances/Social/Cultural
gatherings.

Northway Healthcare Center
5329 N Freeway, Houston, TX 77022
(713) 695-5821
Admin Debbie Sehlke-Runnebs. *Dir of Nursing*
B Vachani. *Medical Dir* Dr M Vakil.
Licensure Skilled care; Intermediate care. *Beds*
SNF 111; ICF 56. *Certified* Medicaid;
Medicare.
Owner Proprietary corp (ARA Living
Centers).
Admissions Requirements Medical
examination; Physician's request.
Facilities Dining room; Physical therapy
room; Activities room; Chapel; Barber/
Beauty shop.
Activities Cards; Games; Reading groups;
Prayer groups; Movies; Shopping trips;
Dances/Social/Cultural gatherings; Pet
therapy; Bingo.

St Anthony Center
PO Box 14708, 6301 Almeda Rd, Houston,
TX 77021
(713) 748-5021
Admin Sr Mary Alma Murphy.
Medical Dir Bernard Flanz MD.
Licensure Skilled care; Intermediate care. *Beds*
325. *Certified* Medicaid; Medicare.
Admissions Requirements Physician's request.

Staff Physicians 2 (ft); RNs 24 (ft); LPNs 48 (ft); Nurses' aides 128 (ft); Physical therapists 7 (ft); Recreational therapists 2 (ft); Occupational therapists 9 (ft), 2 (pt); Speech therapists 2 (ft); Activities coordinators 1 (ft); Dietitians 1 (ft); Podiatrists 1 (pt); Audiologists 2 (ft); Dentists 2 (ft).
Affiliation Roman Catholic.
Facilities Dining room; Physical therapy room; Activities room; Chapel; Crafts room; Laundry room; Barber/Beauty shop; Library.
Activities Arts & crafts; Games; Prayer groups; Movies; Shopping trips.

St Dominic Nursing Home
6502 Grand Blvd, Houston, TX 77021
(713) 741-8701
Admin Ruth Whigham. *Dir of Nursing* Lucy Lloyd RN. *Medical Dir* Jean Samaan MD.
Licensure Intermediate care; Retirement. *Beds* ICF 120; Retirement 80. *Private Pay Patients* 75%. *Certified* Medicaid.
Owner Nonprofit corp.
Admissions Requirements Medical examination; Physician's request.
Staff RNs 2 (ft), 1 (pt); LPNs 19 (ft); Nurses' aides 41 (ft); Activities coordinators 2 (ft); Dietitians 1 (pt).
Languages Spanish.
Affiliation Roman Catholic.
Facilities Dining room; Activities room; Chapel; Laundry room; Barber/Beauty shop.
Activities Arts & crafts; Cards; Games; Prayer groups; Movies; Shopping trips; Dances/ Social/Cultural gatherings; Pet therapy.

St Thomas Convalescent Center
5925 Almeda Rd, Houston, TX 77004
(713) 522-5107
Admin Majorie Turner.
Licensure Intermediate care. *Beds* 125. *Certified* Medicaid.
Owner Proprietary corp.

Seven Acres Jewish Geriatric Center
6200 N Braeswood, Houston, TX 77074
(713) 778-5700, 778-0823 FAX
Admin Malcolm P Slatko. *Dir of Nursing* Dorothy Fields RN. *Medical Dir* Carlos Vallbona MD.
Licensure Intermediate care; Alzheimer's care; Adult day care. *Beds* ICF 294. *Private Pay Patients* 40%. *Certified* Medicaid.
Owner Nonprofit organization/foundation.
Admissions Requirements Minimum age 65; Medical examination; Physician's request.
Staff Physicians; RNs; LPNs; Nurses' aides; Physical therapists; Reality therapists; Recreational therapists; Occupational therapists; Speech therapists; Activities coordinators; Dietitians; Ophthalmologists; Podiatrists; Audiologists.
Languages Yiddish.
Affiliation Jewish.
Facilities Dining room; Physical therapy room; Activities room; Chapel; Crafts room; Laundry room; Barber/Beauty shop; Library; Outside patio.
Activities Arts & crafts; Cards; Games; Reading groups; Prayer groups; Movies; Shopping trips; Dances/Social/Cultural gatherings; Intergenerational programs; Pet therapy; Classes.

Silver Threads Nursing Center
3402 Vintage St, Houston, TX 77026
(713) 675-8105
Admin Helen M Spencer.
Licensure Intermediate care. *Beds* 82. *Certified* Medicaid.
Owner Proprietary corp (Beverly Enterprises).

Spring Branch Healthcare Center
8955 Long Point Rd, Houston, TX 77055
(713) 464-7625
Admin Carolyn Barten. *Dir of Nursing* Donna DiIorio RN.

Licensure Intermediate care. *Beds* ICF/MR 106. *Certified* Medicaid.
Owner Proprietary corp (ARA Living Centers).
Admissions Requirements Medical examination.
Staff Physicians; RNs; LPNs; Nurses' aides; Physical therapists; Occupational therapists; Speech therapists; Activities coordinators; Dietitians; Ophthalmologists; Podiatrists; Dentists.
Facilities Dining room; Activities room; Laundry room; Barber/Beauty shop; Van with wheelchair lift; individual a/c units.
Activities Arts & crafts; Cards; Games; Reading groups; Prayer groups; Movies; Shopping trips; Dances/Social/Cultural gatherings; Fieldtrips; Stroke support group.

Spring Shadows Pines
3033 Gessner, Houston, TX 77080
(713) 460-8222
Licensure Nursing. *Beds* Nursing 228.

Stoneybrook Healthcare Center
2808 Stoney Brook, Houston, TX 77063
(713) 782-4355
Admin Olive Moffit RN. *Dir of Nursing* Oneta Poole RN. *Medical Dir* P R Pingitore MD.
Licensure Intermediate care. *Beds* ICF 112. *Certified* Medicaid.
Owner Proprietary corp (ARA Living Centers).
Admissions Requirements Minimum age 18; Medical examination; Physician's request.
Staff RNs 1 (ft); LPNs 6 (ft); Nurses' aides 25 (ft); Activities coordinators 1 (ft); Dietitians 1 (ft).
Languages Spanish.
Facilities Dining room; Activities room; Barber/Beauty shop; Library.
Activities Arts & crafts; Cards; Games; Reading groups; Prayer groups; Movies; Shopping trips; Dances/Social/Cultural gatherings.

Thomas Care Centers Inc
3827 W Fuqua St, Houston, TX 77045
(713) 433-7206
Admin James R Hale.
Medical Dir Dr William L Mize.
Licensure Intermediate care; Intermediate care for mentally retarded. *Beds* 100. *Certified* Medicaid.
Owner Proprietary corp (ARA Living Centers).
Staff Physicians 2 (ft), 4 (pt); RNs 8 (ft), 12 (pt); LPNs 10 (ft), 10 (pt); Nurses' aides 25 (ft), 35 (pt); Physical therapists 3 (ft); Recreational therapists 4 (ft); Occupational therapists 4 (ft); Speech therapists 2 (ft); Activities coordinators 2 (ft); Dietitians 2 (ft); Ophthalmologists 1 (pt); Podiatrists 1 (pt); Audiologists 1 (ft); Dentists 1 (ft).
Facilities Dining room; Physical therapy room; Activities room; Crafts room; Laundry room; Barber/Beauty shop.
Activities Arts & crafts; Cards; Games; Reading groups; Prayer groups; Movies; Shopping trips; Dances/Social/Cultural gatherings.

Total Life Care Center
105 Drew, Houston, TX 77006
(713) 529-8922
Admin Joyce I Flaugher (Roe). *Dir of Nursing* Shirley Wyatt RN. *Medical Dir* Dr V Adam.
Licensure Skilled care. *Beds* SNF 40. *Private Pay Patients* 100%.
Owner Proprietary corp.
Staff Physicians 1 (ft); RNs 3 (ft); LPNs 13 (ft); Nurses' aides 28 (ft); Physical therapists 1 (pt); Recreational therapists 1 (ft); Speech therapists 1 (pt); Dietitians 1 (pt); Podiatrists 1 (pt); Respiratory therapists 4 (ft).
Languages Spanish, Polish.

Facilities Dining room; Activities room.
Activities Cards; Games; Prayer groups; Movies; Shopping trips.

Town Park Convalescent Center
5925 Almeda Rd, Houston, TX 77004
(713) 522-5107
Licensure Nursing. *Beds* Nursing 125.

Treemont Health Care Center
2501 Westerland Dr, Houston, TX 77063
(713) 783-4100
Admin Jean C Rogers.
Medical Dir William J Wylie.
Licensure Intermediate care; Custodial care. *Beds* ICF 125.
Admissions Requirements Minimum age 60; Medical examination; Physician's request.
Staff RNs 2 (ft); LPNs 10 (ft), 1 (pt); Nurses' aides 40 (ft), 3 (pt); Recreational therapists 1 (ft); Dietitians 1 (ft).
Facilities Dining room; Activities room; Crafts room; Laundry room; Barber/Beauty shop; Library.
Activities Arts & crafts; Cards; Games; Prayer groups; Movies; Shopping trips; Dances/Social/Cultural gatherings.

Isla Carroll Turner Health Care Center
4141 S Braeswood, Houston, TX 77025
(713) 666-2651
Admin Vivian H Davis. *Dir of Nursing* Kelly Langford RN.
Licensure Skilled care; Retirement. *Beds* 25.
Owner Nonprofit organization/foundation.
Admissions Requirements Minimum age 65; Medical examination.
Staff RNs 1 (ft), 2 (pt); LPNs 3 (ft), 1 (pt); Nurses' aides 12 (ft); Activities coordinators 1 (ft).
Facilities Dining room; Activities room; Chapel; Crafts room; Laundry room; Barber/ Beauty shop; Library.
Activities Arts & crafts; Cards; Games; Prayer groups; Movies; Shopping trips.

Villa Northwest Convalescent Center
17600 Cali Dr, Houston, TX 77090
(713) 440-9000
Admin Arthur C Johnson III. *Dir of Nursing* Patsy Tschudy. *Medical Dir* M Javed Aslam MD.
Licensure Skilled care; Intermediate care; Alzheimer's care. *Beds* 165. *Certified* Medicaid.
Owner Proprietary corp (Convalescent Services).
Admissions Requirements Minimum age 21.
Staff Physicians 1 (pt); RNs 7 (ft), 1 (pt); LPNs 10 (ft), 2 (pt); Nurses' aides 43 (ft), 6 (pt); Activities coordinators 1 (ft), 2 (pt); Dietitians 11 (ft), 1 (pt).
Facilities Dining room; Physical therapy room; Activities room; Laundry room; Barber/Beauty shop.
Activities Arts & crafts; Cards; Games; Reading groups; Prayer groups; Movies; Exercise; Church services; Special entertainment; Music therapy; Resident's council.

Village Healthcare Center
1341 Blalock Rd, Houston, TX 77055
(713) 468-7821
Admin Sue Morgan. *Dir of Nursing* Colleen Caswell RN.
Licensure Intermediate care; Alzheimer's care. *Beds* ICF 240. *Certified* Medicaid.
Owner Proprietary corp (ARA Living Centers).
Admissions Requirements Medical examination.
Staff RNs 1 (ft); LPNs 12 (ft); Nurses' aides 40 (ft); Physical therapists 1 (pt); Reality therapists 1 (ft); Occupational therapists 1 (pt); Speech therapists 1 (pt); Activities

coordinators 2 (ft); Dietitians 1 (pt);
Ophthalmologists 1 (pt); Podiatrists 1 (pt);
Dentists 1 (pt).
Languages French, Spanish.
Facilities Dining room; Activities room;
Crafts room; Laundry room; Barber/Beauty
shop; Library.
Activities Arts & crafts; Cards; Games;
Reading groups; Prayer groups; Movies;
Shopping trips; Dances/Social/Cultural
gatherings.

Manda Ann/Watkins Convalescent Home
730 W 23rd Rd, Houston, TX 77008
(713) 862-9584
Admin Betty Philips. *Dir of Nursing* Irene
Adams. *Medical Dir* B Echols MD.
Licensure Intermediate care. *Beds* ICF 116.
Certified Medicaid.
Owner Privately owned.
Admissions Requirements Medical
examination.
Staff Physicians 1 (ft); LPNs 6 (ft); Nurses'
aides 50 (ft); Physical therapists 2 (ft);
Reality therapists 1 (ft); Recreational
therapists 1 (ft); Occupational therapists 1
(ft); Speech therapists 1 (ft); Activities
coordinators 1 (ft); Dietitians 1 (ft);
Ophthalmologists 1 (ft); Dentists 1 (ft).
Languages Spanish.
Facilities Dining room; Physical therapy
room; Activities room; Laundry room;
Barber/Beauty shop.
Activities Arts & crafts; Cards; Games;
Reading groups; Prayer groups; Shopping
trips; Dances/Social/Cultural gatherings.

Westbury Place
5201 S Willow Dr, Houston, TX 77035
(713) 721-0297
Admin Hazel Reaves. *Dir of Nursing*
Margueritte Sluder RN.
Licensure Private Pay; Retirement;
Alzheimer's care. *Beds* 112. *Certified* Private
Pay.
Owner Proprietary corp (Convalescent
Services).
Admissions Requirements Medical
examination; Physician's request.
Staff Physicians; RNs; LPNs; Nurses' aides;
Physical therapists; Activities coordinators;
Dietitians; Ophthalmologists.
Languages Spanish, Italian, German.
Facilities Dining room; Physical therapy
room; Activities room; Chapel; Crafts room;
Laundry room; Barber/Beauty shop; Library.
Activities Arts & crafts; Cards; Games;
Reading groups; Prayer groups; Movies;
Shopping trips; Dances/Social/Cultural
gatherings.

Wileyvale Community Nursing Home
7915 Wileyvale Rd, Houston, TX 77016
(713) 633-2890
Admin Claude Anderson.
Licensure Intermediate care. *Beds* 130.
Certified Medicaid.
Staff Physicians 3 (pt); RNs 1 (pt); LPNs 15
(pt); Nurses' aides 35 (pt); Activities
coordinators 1 (ft), 1 (pt); Dietitians 1 (ft);
Ophthalmologists 1 (pt); Podiatrists 1 (pt);
Dentists 3 (pt).
Facilities Dining room; Activities room;
Laundry room.
Activities Cards; Games; Prayer groups.

Winter Haven Nursing Home
6534 Stuebner Airline Dr, Houston, TX 77091
(713) 692-5137
Admin Glenda C Donahue.
Licensure Intermediate care. *Beds* 151.
Certified Medicaid.
Staff RNs 1 (ft); LPNs 10 (ft), 4 (pt); Nurses'
aides 42 (ft); Physical therapists 3 (pt);
Activities coordinators 2 (ft); Dietitians 1
(ft); Medical aides 4 (pt).

Facilities Dining room; Physical therapy
room; Activities room; Crafts room; Laundry
room; Barber/Beauty shop; Library; Gift
shop.
Activities Arts & crafts; Cards; Games; Prayer
groups; Movies; Shopping trips; Dances/
Social/Cultural gatherings.

Hubbard

Oakview Manor Nursing Center
PO Box 561, 6th & Hickory, Hubbard, TX
76648
(817) 576-2518
Admin Janet C Marek. *Dir of Nursing* Patsy R
Reeves.
Licensure Intermediate care; Retirement. *Beds*
ICF 60. *Certified* Medicaid.
Owner Proprietary corp (Marwitz Brothers
Inc).
Staff LPNs; Nurses' aides; Recreational
therapists; Activities coordinators; Dietitians.
Facilities Dining room; Activities room;
Crafts room; Laundry room; Barber/Beauty
shop; Library.
Activities Arts & crafts; Cards; Games;
Reading groups; Prayer groups; Movies;
Shopping trips; Dances/Social/Cultural
gatherings; Intergenerational programs; Pet
therapy.

Hughes Springs

Theron Grainger Nursing Home
PO Box 1390, Hwy 161 South, Hughes
Springs,, TX 75656
(214) 639-2561
Admin Betty Traylor.
Medical Dir Kathryn Brimhall.
Licensure Intermediate care. *Beds* ICF 69.
Certified Medicaid.
Owner Proprietary corp.
Admissions Requirements Physician's request.
Staff LPNs 9 (ft); Nurses' aides 25 (ft);
Activities coordinators 1 (ft).
Facilities Dining room; Activities room;
Laundry room; Barber/Beauty shop.
Activities Arts & crafts; Cards; Games;
Reading groups; Prayer groups; Movies;
Shopping trips; Dances/Social/Cultural
gatherings.

Hughes Springs Nursing Home
N Taylor St, Hughes Springs, TX 75656
(214) 639-2531
Admin Betty M McCarley.
Licensure Intermediate care. *Beds* 60.
Certified Medicaid.
Owner Proprietary corp (Hillhaven Corp).
Staff RNs 1 (pt); LPNs 4 (ft); Nurses' aides 25
(ft); Physical therapists 1 (pt); Occupational
therapists 1 (pt); Speech therapists 1 (pt);
Activities coordinators 1 (ft).
Facilities Dining room; Activities room;
Crafts room; Laundry room; Barber/Beauty
shop.
Activities Arts & crafts; Games; Prayer groups;
Movies; Shopping trips; Dances/Social/
Cultural gatherings.

Humble

Green Acres Convalescent Center
93 Isaacks Rd, Humble, TX 77338
(713) 446-7159
Admin Jo Doerre. *Dir of Nursing* Georgia
Olson. *Medical Dir* Dr Joseph Guerrini.
Licensure Intermediate care; Alzheimer's care.
Beds ICF 134. *Certified* Medicaid.
Owner Proprietary corp (ARA Living
Centers).
Admissions Requirements Medical
examination; Physician's request.

Staff Physicians; RNs; LPNs; Nurses' aides;
Physical therapists (contracted);
Occupational therapists; Speech therapists;
Activities coordinators; Dietitians;
Podiatrists.
Facilities Dining room; Physical therapy
room; Activities room; Crafts room; Laundry
room; Barber/Beauty shop.
Activities Arts & crafts; Cards; Games;
Reading groups; Movies; Shopping trips;
Dances/Social/Cultural gatherings;
Intergenerational programs.

Humble Skilled Care Facility
18903 Memorial S, Humble, TX 77338
Medical Dir Dr N N Izzat.
Admissions Requirements Minimum age 6
months; Medical examination; Physician's
request.
Staff Physicians 22 (ft), 8 (pt); RNs 11 (ft), 5
(pt); LPNs 26 (ft), 7 (pt); Nurses' aides 43
(ft), 15 (pt); Physical therapists 14 (ft), 7
(pt); Recreational therapists 1 (ft);
Occupational therapists 9 (ft); Speech
therapists 3 (ft); Activities coordinators 1
(ft); Dietitians 1 (ft); Ophthalmologists 2 (ft);
Podiatrists 2 (ft); Audiologists 1 (ft); Dentists
4 (ft).
Facilities Dining room; Physical therapy
room; Activities room; Chapel; Crafts room;
Laundry room; Barber/Beauty shop; Library.
Activities Cards; Games; Reading groups;
Prayer groups; Dances/Social/Cultural
gatherings.

Renaissance Place—Humble
8450 Will Clayton Pkwy, Humble, TX 77338
(713) 446-8484
Admin Michael Bermes. *Dir of Nursing* Mrs
Johnson; Mrs Ramsey,. *Medical Dir* Dr
Greenie.
Licensure Skilled care; Intermediate care. *Beds*
SNF 60; ICF 60. *Certified* Medicaid;
Medicare.
Owner Proprietary corp (Atrium Living
Centers).
Facilities Dining room; Physical therapy
room; Activities room; Crafts room; Laundry
room; Barber/Beauty shop; Library.
Activities Arts & crafts; Cards; Games; Prayer
groups; Movies; Shopping trips; Pet therapy.

Huntsville

Fair Park Nursing Center
2628 Milam St, Huntsville, TX 77340
(409) 295-6464
Medical Dir Pam Jeffcoat.
Licensure Skilled care; Intermediate care. *Beds*
109. *Certified* Medicaid; Medicare.
Owner Proprietary corp (Beverly Enterprises).
Admissions Requirements Minimum age 18;
Medical examination; Physician's request.
Staff Physicians 1 (pt); RNs 2 (ft), 4 (pt);
LPNs 12 (ft), 3 (pt); Nurses' aides 51 (ft), 4
(pt); Physical therapists 1 (pt); Recreational
therapists 1 (pt); Occupational therapists 1
(pt); Speech therapists 1 (pt); Activities
coordinators 1 (ft); Dietitians 1 (pt);
Ophthalmologists 1 (pt); Podiatrists 1 (pt);
Dentists 1 (pt).
Languages Spanish.
Facilities Dining room; Physical therapy
room; Activities room; Chapel; Laundry
room; Barber/Beauty shop; Library; Den;
Sitting rooms.
Activities Arts & crafts; Cards; Games;
Reading groups; Prayer groups; Movies;
Shopping trips; Dances/Social/Cultural
gatherings; Reality orientation;
Individualized activities.

Green Acres Convalescent Center
1302 Inverness, Huntsville, TX 77340
(713) 295-6313
Admin Anna E Carpenter.
Medical Dir Hugh Poindexter MD.

Licensure Intermediate care. *Beds* 102.
Certified Medicaid.
Owner Proprietary corp (ARA Living
Centers).
Staff Physicians 1 (pt); RNs 1 (ft); Nurses'
aides 15 (ft); Reality therapists 1 (pt);
Recreational therapists 1 (pt); Activities
coordinators 1 (ft); Dietitians 1 (ft); LVNs 8
(ft).
Facilities Dining room; Activities room;
Chapel; Crafts room; Laundry room; Barber/
Beauty shop.
Activities Arts & crafts; Cards; Games;
Reading groups; Prayer groups; Movies;
Shopping trips; Dances/Social/Cultural
gatherings.

Ella Smither Geriatric Center
1115 Ave O, Huntsville, TX 77340
(409) 295-0216
Admin Geri Farris.
Medical Dir Dalia Harrelson.
Licensure Skilled care; Intermediate care;
Residential. *Beds* SNF 46; ICF 50;
Residential 13. *Certified* Medicaid;
Medicare.
Owner Nonprofit corp.
Admissions Requirements Physician's request.
Staff RNs 5 (ft), 2 (pt); LPNs 11 (ft), 7 (pt);
Nurses' aides 25 (ft), 14 (pt); Activities
coordinators 1 (ft); Dietitians 1 (ft).
Facilities Dining room; Activities room;
Chapel; Barber/Beauty shop.
Activities Arts & crafts; Cards; Games;
Reading groups; Prayer groups; Movies;
Dances/Social/Cultural gatherings.

Hurst

Bishop Davies Center Inc
2712 N Hurstview, Hurst, TX 76054
(817) 281-6708
Admin Robert C Murphy Jr. *Dir of Nursing*
Sara C Vaughan RN.
Licensure Skilled care. *Beds* SNF 100.
Certified Medicaid; Medicare.
Owner Nonprofit corp.
Admissions Requirements Minimum age 55;
Physician's request.
Staff Physicians 1 (pt); RNs 3 (ft), 3 (pt);
LPNs 12 (ft), 2 (pt); Nurses' aides 27 (ft);
Physical therapists 1 (pt); Recreational
therapists 1 (ft); Occupational therapists 1
(pt); Speech therapists 1 (pt); Activities
coordinators 1 (ft); Dietitians 1 (ft).
Affiliation Episcopal.
Facilities Dining room; Physical therapy
room; Activities room; Chapel; Crafts room;
Laundry room; Barber/Beauty shop; Library;
Parlour.
Activities Arts & crafts; Cards; Games;
Reading groups; Prayer groups; Movies;
Shopping trips; Dances/Social/Cultural
gatherings; Family nights; Family sharing
sessions; Van; Registered music therapist.

Hurst Care Center
215 E Plaza Blvd, Hurst, TX 76053
(817) 282-6777
Admin Mary Tharp.
Licensure Skilled care; Intermediate care. *Beds*
116. *Certified* Medicaid.
Owner Proprietary corp (ARA Living
Centers).

Iowa Park

Heritage Manor of Iowa Park
1109 N 3rd St, Iowa Park, TX 76367
(817) 592-4139
Admin Novella Gilbreath.
Licensure Intermediate care. *Beds* 77.
Certified Medicaid.
Owner Proprietary corp.
Staff Physicians 3 (pt); RNs 1 (pt); LPNs 9
(ft); Nurses' aides 34 (ft), 6 (pt); Activities
coordinators 1 (ft); Dietitians 1 (ft).

Facilities Dining room; Laundry room;
Barber/Beauty shop.
Activities Arts & crafts; Games; Prayer groups;
Movies; Shopping trips; Dances/Social/
Cultural gatherings.

Irving

Irving Care Center
619 N Britain Rd, Irving, TX 75060
(214) 438-4161
Admin Lisa J Dillard.
Licensure Intermediate care. *Beds* 86.
Certified Medicaid.
Owner Proprietary corp (Manor Care).

Irving Living Center
2021 Shoaf, Irving, TX 75061
(817) 579-1919
Admin Caryl Abshire. *Dir of Nursing* Betty
Tillman RN. *Medical Dir* James Galbraith
MD.
Licensure Skilled care; Alzheimer's care. *Beds*
SNF 330. *Certified* Medicaid; Medicare.
Owner Proprietary corp (Texas Health Care
Corp).
Admissions Requirements Minimum age 21.
Staff Physicians 2 (ft); RNs 7 (ft); LPNs 15
(ft); Nurses' aides 112 (ft); Activities
coordinators 3 (ft); Dietitians 1 (ft);
Ophthalmologists 1 (ft); Podiatrists 1 (ft);
Audiologists 1 (ft).
Facilities Dining room; Physical therapy
room; Activities room; Chapel; Crafts room;
Laundry room; Barber/Beauty shop; Library;
Alzhimer's unit.
Activities Arts & crafts; Cards; Games;
Reading groups; Prayer groups; Movies;
Shopping trips; Dances/Social/Cultural
gatherings; Intergenerational programs.

Pioneer Place Nursing Home
225 Sowers Rd, Irving, TX 75061
(214) 253-4173
Admin Robbi Stewart.
Medical Dir James Galbraith MD.
Licensure Intermediate care. *Beds* ICF 120.
Certified Medicaid.
Owner Proprietary corp (Beverly Enterprises).
Admissions Requirements Medical
examination; Physician's request.
Staff Physicians 1 (ft); LPNs 10 (ft); Nurses'
aides 28 (ft); Activities coordinators 1 (ft);
Dietitians 1 (ft); Ophthalmologists 1 (ft).
Facilities Dining room; Activities room;
Laundry room; Barber/Beauty shop; Library;
Large living room; Front & back patios.
Activities Arts & crafts; Cards; Games;
Reading groups; Prayer groups; Shopping
trips; Dances/Social/Cultural gatherings;
Sing-alongs; Manicures; Adopt-a-grandparent
program; Residents council; Reminiscence
therapy; Exercise.

Italy

Italy Convalescent Center
601 Mosley, Italy, TX 76651
(214) 483-6369
Admin Billie Farrington.
Medical Dir Zenaida Robles.
Licensure Intermediate care. *Beds* 61.
Certified Medicaid.
Owner Proprietary corp (National Heritage).
Admissions Requirements Medical
examination; Physician's request.
Staff Physicians 1 (pt); RNs 1 (pt); LPNs 8
(ft), 3 (pt); Nurses' aides 18 (ft), 6 (pt);
Physical therapists 1 (pt); Activities
coordinators 1 (ft); Dietitians 1 (pt);
Podiatrists 1 (pt); Dentists 1 (pt).
Facilities Dining room; Laundry room;
Barber/Beauty shop; Library.
Activities Arts & crafts; Cards; Games;
Reading groups; Prayer groups; Movies;
Shopping trips; Dances/Social/Cultural
gatherings.

Itasca

Itasca Nursing Home
409 S Files St, Itasca, TX 76055
(817) 687-2383
Admin Elizabeth Dianne Taylor. *Dir of
Nursing* Martha McWhorter RN. *Medical
Dir* Charles Allen MD.
Licensure Intermediate care; Alzheimer's care.
Beds ICF 82. *Certified* Medicaid.
Owner Proprietary corp (Health Enter of
America).
Staff RNs; LPNs; Nurses' aides; Activities
coordinators; Dietitians.
Facilities Dining room; Activities room;
Chapel; Crafts room; Laundry room; Barber/
Beauty shop; Library.
Activities Arts & crafts; Cards; Games;
Reading groups; Prayer groups; Movies;
Shopping trips; Dances/Social/Cultural
gatherings; Fishing trips; Picnics; Safari
trips; Adopt-a-grandparent; Resident council;
Family council.

Jacinto City

Jacinto City Healthcare Center
1405 Holland Ave, Jacinto City, TX 77029
(713) 455-1744
Licensure Nursing. *Beds* Nursing 160.

Jacksboro

Convalescent Care Center
527 W Belknap, Jacksboro, TX 76056
(817) 567-2371
Admin Pat Snow. *Dir of Nursing* Joyce
Guthrie.
Licensure Intermediate care. *Beds* ICF 46.
Private Pay Patients 5%. *Certified* Medicaid.
Owner Privately owned.
Admissions Requirements Medical
examination.
Facilities Dining room; Activities room;
Crafts room; Laundry room; Barber/Beauty
shop.
Activities Arts & crafts; Cards; Games; Prayer
groups; Movies; Shopping trips; Dances/
Social/Cultural gatherings.

Jacksboro Nursing Center
211 E Jasper, Jacksboro, TX 76056
(817) 567-2686
Admin Patsy Snow.
Licensure Intermediate care. *Beds* 108.
Certified Medicaid.
Owner Proprietary corp (Beverly Enterprises).

Jacksonville

Gardendale Nursing Home
PO Box 911, Hwy 79 E, Jacksonville, TX
75766
(214) 586-3626
Admin Pattie Gray.
Medical Dir D B Turner MD.
Licensure Skilled care; Intermediate care. *Beds*
120. *Certified* Medicaid.
Owner Proprietary corp (Beverly Enterprises).
Admissions Requirements Physician's request.

Sunset Care Center
PO Box 1512, 407 Bonita St, Jacksonville, TX
75766
(214) 586-3616
Admin Jean C Allen.
Licensure Intermediate care. *Beds* 53.
Certified Medicaid.
Owner Proprietary corp (Beverly Enterprises).

Twin Oaks Convalescent Center
PO Box 1271, 1123 N Bolton, Jacksonville,
TX 75766
(214) 586-9031
Admin Martha Bevel. *Dir of Nursing* Barbara
Trotter. *Medical Dir* Gregory Kotheimer
MD.

Licensure Intermediate care. *Beds* ICF 120. *Private Pay Patients* 10%. *Certified* Medicaid.
Owner Proprietary corp.
Admissions Requirements Medical examination; Physician's request.
Staff RNs 1 (ft); LPNs 14 (ft); Nurses' aides 40 (ft); Physical therapists 1 (pt); Speech therapists 1 (pt); Activities coordinators 1 (ft); Dietitians 1 (ft).
Facilities Dining room; Activities room; Crafts room; Laundry room; Barber/Beauty shop; Library.
Activities Arts & crafts; Cards; Games; Reading groups; Prayer groups; Movies; Shopping trips.

Jasper

Hines Health Care Center
315 W Gibson, Jasper, TX 75951
(409) 384-5768
Licensure Nursing. *Beds* Nursing 120.

Jasper Convalescent Center
350 Springhill Rd, Jasper, TX 75951
(409) 384-5411
Admin Lillie Carrell.
Licensure Intermediate care. *Beds* 88. *Certified* Medicaid.
Admissions Requirements Medical examination.
Staff RNs 2 (ft); LPNs 6 (ft), 3 (pt); Nurses' aides 25 (ft), 3 (pt); Physical therapists 1 (pt); Occupational therapists 1 (pt); Speech therapists 1 (pt); Activities coordinators 1 (ft); Dietitians 1 (ft); Podiatrists 1 (pt).
Facilities Dining room; Activities room; Laundry room; Barber/Beauty shop.
Activities Arts & crafts; Cards; Games; Movies; Shopping trips; Dances/Social/Cultural gatherings.

Pinewood Manor Nursing Home
315 W Gibson, Jasper, TX 75951
(713) 384-5768
Admin Doris Evelyn Chapman.
Licensure Intermediate care. *Beds* 120. *Certified* Medicaid.
Owner Proprietary corp.

Jayton

Kent County Nursing Home
Box 86, Hwy 70, Jayton, TX 79528
(806) 237-3036
Admin Sandy Hudson. *Dir of Nursing* Jackie Carr LVN. *Medical Dir* R Healing MD.
Licensure Intermediate care. *Beds* ICF 33. *Private Pay Patients* 50%. *Certified* Medicaid.
Owner Privately owned.
Admissions Requirements Medical examination; Physician's request.
Staff RNs 1 (ft); LPNs 3 (ft); Nurses' aides 8 (ft), 1 (pt); Activities coordinators 1 (ft); Dietitians 1 (pt).
Languages Spanish.
Facilities Dining room; Activities room; Laundry room; Barber/Beauty shop.
Activities Arts & crafts; Cards; Games; Prayer groups; Movies; Dances/Social/Cultural gatherings.

Jefferson

Magnolia Manor
510 E Bonham St, Jefferson, TX 75657
(214) 665-3903
Admin Brenda J Cox. *Dir of Nursing* Mary Green LVN. *Medical Dir* Dr Bernice Hoehn.
Licensure Intermediate care. *Beds* ICF 60. *Private Pay Patients* 19%. *Certified* Medicaid.
Owner Proprietary corp (American Manor).
Admissions Requirements Medical examination; Physician's request.

Staff RNs 1 (pt); LPNs 6 (ft), 2 (pt); Nurses' aides 18 (ft), 2 (pt); Physical therapists (contracted); Activities coordinators 1 (ft); Dietitians.
Facilities Dining room; Laundry room; Barber/Beauty shop.
Activities Arts & crafts; Cards; Games; Prayer groups; Movies; Shopping trips; Pet therapy; Field trips.

Johnson City

Lyndon B Johnson Medical Nursing Center
PO Box 415, Johnson City, TX 78636
(512) 868-4093
Admin Patricia J McDonnell. *Dir of Nursing* Carol Smith LVN.
Licensure Intermediate care; Personal care. *Beds* ICF 30; Personal care 30. *Private Pay Patients* 40%. *Certified* Medicaid.
Owner Privately owned (R L Toms Inc).
Admissions Requirements Medical examination.
Staff LPNs; Nurses' aides; Activities coordinators; Dietitians.
Languages Spanish, German.
Facilities Dining room; Activities room; Laundry room; Barber/Beauty shop.
Activities Arts & crafts; Cards; Games; Reading groups; Prayer groups; Movies; Shopping trips; Dances/Social/Cultural gatherings; Intergenerational programs.

Jourdanton

Retama Manor Nursing Center Inc—Jourdanton
1504 Oak, Jourdanton, TX 78026
(512) 569-2138
Admin Zettie B McLerran.
Licensure Skilled care. *Beds* 48. *Certified* Medicaid.
Owner Proprietary corp (ARA Living Centers).
Admissions Requirements Minimum age 21.
Staff Physicians 1 (pt); RNs 2 (ft); LPNs 4 (ft); Nurses' aides 12 (ft), 4 (pt); Physical therapists 1 (pt); Reality therapists 1 (pt); Recreational therapists 1 (pt); Occupational therapists 1 (pt); Speech therapists 1 (pt); Activities coordinators 1 (ft); Dietitians 1 (pt).
Facilities Dining room; Crafts room; Laundry room; Barber/Beauty shop.
Activities Arts & crafts; Cards; Games; Reading groups; Prayer groups; Movies; Dances/Social/Cultural gatherings.

Junction

Leisure Lodge—Junction
111 Hospital Dr, Junction, TX 76849
(915) 446-3351
Admin Rosemary Grissom. *Dir of Nursing* Louise Whitson LVN. *Medical Dir* Ronald A Graham MD.
Licensure Intermediate care. *Beds* ICF 70. *Private Pay Patients* 32%. *Certified* Medicaid.
Admissions Requirements Medical examination; Physician's request.
Staff LPNs 4 (ft), 2 (pt); Nurses' aides 14 (ft), 3 (pt); Activities coordinators 1 (pt); Dietitians 1 (ft).
Languages Spanish.
Facilities Dining room; Activities room; Crafts room; Laundry room; Barber/Beauty shop.
Activities Arts & crafts; Cards; Games; Reading groups; Prayer groups; Movies; Shopping trips; Dances/Social/Cultural gatherings; Intergenerational programs; Pet therapy.

Karnes City

Karnes City Care Center
209 Country Club Dr, Karnes City, TX 78118
(512) 780-2426, 780-4248 FAX
Admin Helen Brister. *Dir of Nursing* Patricia A Bednorz RN. *Medical Dir* Roberto Ramirez MD.
Licensure Skilled care. *Beds* SNF 60. *Certified* Medicaid; Medicare.
Owner Proprietary corp.
Admissions Requirements Medical examination; Physician's request.
Staff RNs; LPNs; Nurses' aides; Activities coordinators.
Facilities Dining room; Activities room; Laundry room; Barber/Beauty shop.
Activities Arts & crafts; Cards; Games; Reading groups; Prayer groups; Movies; Shopping trips; Dances/Social/Cultural gatherings; Intergenerational programs; Pet therapy.

Katy

Katyville Healthcare Center
5129 E 5th St, Katy, TX 77450
(713) 391-7087
Admin Lera E Phillips. *Dir of Nursing* Cheryl Crozier RN.
Licensure Intermediate care. *Beds* ICF 96. *Certified* Medicaid.
Owner Proprietary corp.
Admissions Requirements Minimum age 18.
Staff RNs; LPNs; Nurses' aides; Activities coordinators; Dietitians.
Facilities Dining room; Activities room; Crafts room; Laundry room; Barber/Beauty shop; Library.
Activities Arts & crafts; Cards; Games; Reading groups; Prayer groups; Movies; Shopping trips; Dances/Social/Cultural gatherings.

Renaissance Place—Katy
1525 Tull Dr, Katy, TX 77449
(713) 578-1600
Admin Nancy L Wood. *Dir of Nursing* Gail Becker-Steenberg. *Medical Dir* Mark Bing MD.
Licensure Skilled care; Intermediate care. *Beds* SNF 64; ICF 66. *Certified* Medicaid; Medicare.
Owner Proprietary corp.
Admissions Requirements Medical examination.
Staff RNs 8 (ft), 2 (pt); LPNs 18 (ft), 3 (pt); Nurses' aides 53 (ft), 7 (pt); Activities coordinators 1 (ft), 1 (pt); Dietitians 1 (ft).
Facilities Dining room; Physical therapy room; Activities room; Crafts room; Barber/Beauty shop; Library.
Activities Arts & crafts; Cards; Games; Reading groups; Prayer groups; Movies; Shopping trips; Dances/Social/Cultural gatherings; Intergenerational programs; Pet therapy.

Kaufman

Leisure Lodge
PO Box 191, 3001 S Houston, Kaufman, TX 75142
(214) 932-2118
Admin Ada East. *Dir of Nursing* Linda Braddy. *Medical Dir* David Ellis MD.
Licensure Intermediate care; Day care; Respite care. *Beds* ICF 115. *Certified* Medicaid.
Owner Proprietary corp (Beverly Enterprises).
Admissions Requirements Minimum age 18; Medical examination; Physician's request.
Staff Physicians; LPNs; Nurses' aides; Reality therapists; Recreational therapists; Activities coordinators; Podiatrists.

Facilities Dining room; Crafts room; Barber/
Beauty shop; Library.
Activities Arts & crafts; Cards; Games; Prayer
groups; Movies; Shopping trips; Dances/
Social/Cultural gatherings; Intergenerational
programs; Pet therapy.

Rose Haven of Kaufman Inc
102 E 9th St, Kaufman, TX 75142
(214) 932-2326
Admin Richard Mullin.
Licensure Intermediate care. *Beds* 37.
Certified Medicaid.
Owner Proprietary corp.

Keene

Town Hall Estates
PO Box 588, 213 Old Betsy Rd, Keene, TX
76059
(817) 641-8888
Admin Alberta Ann Bunnell.
Licensure Intermediate care. *Beds* 75.
Certified Medicaid.
Staff RNs 2 (ft); LPNs 5 (ft); Nurses' aides 23
(ft); Activities coordinators 1 (ft); Dietitians
1 (pt).
Facilities Dining room; Laundry room;
Barber/Beauty shop.
Activities Arts & crafts; Games; Reading
groups; Prayer groups; Movies.

Keller

Mimosa Manor
PO Box 485, 459 E Price, Keller, TX 76248
(817) 431-2518
Admin Yvonne Jabri. *Dir of Nursing* Patty
Azima. *Medical Dir* Dr Benjamin Domigos.
Licensure Intermediate care. *Beds* ICF 150.
Private Pay Patients 33%. *Certified*
Medicaid.
Owner Proprietary corp (Arbor Living
Centers).
Admissions Requirements Minimum age 16.
Staff RNs; Nurses' aides; Physical therapists;
Recreational therapists; Occupational
therapists; Activities coordinators; Dietitians;
Podiatrists; Audiologists.
Facilities Dining room; Crafts room; Laundry
room; Barber/Beauty shop.
Activities Arts & crafts; Cards; Games;
Reading groups; Prayer groups; Movies;
Shopping trips; Dances/Social/Cultural
gatherings; Intergenerational programs; Pet
therapy.

Kemp

Kemp Care Center
PO Box 409, 600 N Adams St, Kemp, TX
75143
(214) 498-5701
Admin A W Baldwin.
Licensure Intermediate care. *Beds* 60.
Certified Medicaid.
Admissions Requirements Medical
examination; Physician's request.
Staff Physicians; RNs; LPNs; Nurses' aides;
Physical therapists; Reality therapists;
Recreational therapists; Occupational
therapists; Speech therapists; Activities
coordinators; Dietitians; Podiatrists.
Facilities Dining room; Physical therapy
room; Activities room; Chapel; Crafts room;
Laundry room; Barber/Beauty shop; Library.
Activities Cards; Games; Prayer groups;
Movies; Shopping trips.

Kenedy

Green's Nursing Center
505 W Main St, Kenedy, TX 78119
(512) 583-3406
Admin Patsy L Marchant.
Medical Dir Stephanie Martignoni.

Licensure Intermediate care. *Beds* ICF 61.
Certified Medicaid; Medicare.
Owner Proprietary corp.
Admissions Requirements Minimum age 16;
Physician's request.
Staff LPNs; Nurses' aides.
Languages Spanish.
Facilities Dining room; Activities room;
Crafts room; Laundry room; Barber/Beauty
shop.
Activities Arts & crafts; Games; Reading
groups; Prayer groups; Movies; Shopping
trips; Dances/Social/Cultural gatherings.

John Paul II Nursing Center
PO Box 359, 215 Tilden, Kenedy, TX 78119
(512) 583-9841
Admin Pauline Wernli.
Licensure Intermediate care; Personal care.
Beds ICF 73; Personal 21. *Certified*
Medicaid.
Owner Nonprofit corp.
Affiliation Roman Catholic.

Restful Acres Care Center
Box E, Hwy 181 S, Kenedy, TX 78119
(512) 583-3421
Admin Lana K Green.
Licensure Intermediate care. *Beds* 60.
Certified Medicaid.
Owner Proprietary corp.

Kennedale

Kennedale Nursing Home
PO Box 447, 413 E Mansfield, Kennedale, TX
76060
(817) 478-5454
Admin Mildred K Garrett.
Licensure Skilled care. *Beds* 60. *Certified*
Medicaid.
Owner Proprietary corp (Summit Health Ltd).

Kerens

Maywood Manor Inc
Rte 1 Box 30, Kerens, TX 75144
(214) 396-2905
Admin Joan K Kilcrease. *Dir of Nursing* Sue
Farmer RN.
Licensure Intermediate care. *Beds* ICF 73.
Private Pay Patients 30%. *Certified*
Medicaid.
Owner Proprietary corp.
Admissions Requirements Medical
examination; Physician's request.
Staff RNs 1 (ft); LPNs 4 (ft), 2 (pt); Nurses'
aides 20 (ft), 5 (pt); Activities coordinators 1
(ft), 1 (pt); Dietitians 1 (pt).
Facilities Dining room; Laundry room;
Barber/Beauty shop.
Activities Arts & crafts; Games; Prayer groups;
Dances/Social/Cultural gatherings; Pet
therapy.

Kermit

Kermit Nursing Center
PO Box 1035, School St, Kermit, TX 79745
(915) 586-6665
Admin Jemmie Nell Cooke.
Licensure Nursing; Personal Care. *Beds*
Nursing 78; Personal care 22. *Certified*
Medicaid.
Owner Proprietary corp.

Kerrville

Alpine Terrace
746 Alpine Dr, Kerrville, TX 78028
(512) 896-2323
Admin Andrew B Seibert. *Dir of Nursing*
Mary Ann Parker RN. *Medical Dir* Gregory
G McKenzie MD.
Licensure Intermediate care; Custodial care;
Retirement. *Beds* ICF 60; Custodial care 60.

Owner Proprietary corp (Vari-Care Inc).
Admissions Requirements Medical
examination.
Staff Physicians 1 (pt); RNs 1 (ft); LPNs 5
(ft), 2 (pt); Nurses' aides 15 (ft), 3 (pt);
Activities coordinators 2 (ft); Dietitians 1
(pt).
Facilities Dining room; Physical therapy
room; Activities room; Crafts room; Laundry
room; Barber/Beauty shop; Library;
Courtyard.
Activities Arts & crafts; Cards; Games;
Reading groups; Prayer groups; Movies;
Shopping trips; Dances/Social/Cultural
gatherings.

Edgewater Care Center
1213 Water St, Kerrville, TX 78028
(512) 896-2411
Admin Chester G Freeman. *Dir of Nursing*
Ann K Hardee RN. *Medical Dir* Dan W
Bacon MD.
Licensure Skilled care; Intermediate care;
Alzheimer's care. *Beds* SNF 79; ICF 104.
Certified Medicaid; Medicare.
Owner Proprietary corp (Vari-Care Inc).
Admissions Requirements Minimum age 55;
Medical examination; Physician's request.
Staff Physicians 1 (pt); RNs 1 (ft), 1 (pt);
LPNs 10 (ft), 8 (pt); Nurses' aides 38 (ft), 8
(pt); Physical therapists 1 (pt); Activities
coordinators 1 (ft), 2 (pt); Dietitians 1 (ft), 1
(pt); Ophthalmologists 1 (pt).
Languages Spanish, German.
Facilities Dining room; Physical therapy
room; Activities room; Crafts room; Laundry
room; Barber/Beauty shop; Library.
Activities Arts & crafts; Cards; Games;
Reading groups; Prayer groups; Movies;
Shopping trips; Dances/Social/Cultural
gatherings.

Hilltop Village
1400 Hilltop Circle, Kerrville, TX 78028
(512) 895-3200
Admin Jack Reynolds.
Licensure Intermediate care; Custodial care.
Beds ICF 90; Custodial care 60. *Certified*
Medicaid.
Owner Proprietary corp (Vari-Care Inc).
Admissions Requirements Medical
examination; Physician's request.
Staff RNs 3 (ft), 1 (pt); LPNs 14 (ft), 2 (pt);
Nurses' aides 39 (ft), 5 (pt); Activities
coordinators 2 (ft); Dietitians 1 (ft).
Facilities Dining room; Activities room;
Chapel; Crafts room; Laundry room; Barber/
Beauty shop; Library.
Activities Arts & crafts; Cards; Games; Prayer
groups; Movies; Shopping trips; Dances/
Social/Cultural gatherings.

Meadowview Care Center
600 Leslie Dr, Kerrville, TX 78028
(512) 896-3711
Admin Paul Toops.
Licensure Intermediate care; Personal care.
Beds ICF 96; Personal care 22. *Certified*
Medicaid.
Admissions Requirements Medical
examination; Physician's request.
Staff RNs 1 (ft); Activities coordinators 1 (ft).
Facilities Dining room; Activities room;
Crafts room; Laundry room; Barber/Beauty
shop.
Activities Arts & crafts; Cards; Games;
Reading groups; Prayer groups; Movies;
Shopping trips; Exercise groups.

Kilgore

Gregg Home for the Aged Inc
Rte 5 Box 135, Hwy 42 N, Kilgore, TX 75662
(214) 984-5688, 984-4391
Admin Barbara A Garner. *Dir of Nursing*
Sharon L McCabe LVN.
Licensure Intermediate care; Alzheimer's care.
Beds ICF 62. *Certified* Medicaid.

Owner Nonprofit corp.
Admissions Requirements Minimum age 21;
Medical examination; Physician's request.
Staff RNs 1 (pt); LPNs 6 (ft); Nurses' aides 12
(ft); Physical therapists; Reality therapists;
Occupational therapists; Speech therapists;
Activities coordinators 1 (ft); Dietitians 1
(ft); Ophthalmologists; Podiatrists; Dentists.
Facilities Dining room; Activities room;
Chapel; Crafts room; Laundry room; Barber/
Beauty shop; Library; Sun rooms.
Activities Arts & crafts; Cards; Games;
Reading groups; Prayer groups; Movies;
Shopping trips; Dances/Social/Cultural
gatherings; Field trips; Mini-golf; Volleyball.

Kilgore Nursing Center
2700 S Henderson Blvd, Kilgore, TX 75662
(214) 984-3511
Admin Mike Chaney.
Medical Dir Linda Hutchison.
Licensure Skilled care. *Beds* SNF 115.
Certified Medicaid; Medicare.
Owner Proprietary corp.
Admissions Requirements Physician's request.
Staff RNs; LPNs; Nurses' aides; Activities
coordinators.
Facilities Dining room; Activities room;
Laundry room; Barber/Beauty shop.
Activities Arts & crafts; Cards; Games; Prayer
groups; Movies; Shopping trips; Dances/
Social/Cultural gatherings.

Stone Road Nursing Center Inc
PO Box 1317, 3607 Stone Rd, Kilgore, TX
75662
(214) 984-5036
Admin Glenda R Jones.
Medical Dir Sue Braswell LVN.
Licensure Intermediate care; Alzheimer's care.
Beds ICF 60. *Certified* Medicaid.
Owner Proprietary corp.
Staff LPNs; Nurses' aides; Activities
coordinators.
Activities Arts & crafts; Cards; Games;
Reading groups; Prayer groups; Movies;
Shopping trips; Dances/Social/Cultural
gatherings; Picnics; Outings.

Killeen

**Bell Haven Convalescent & Nursing Care
Center**
1002 Medical Dr, Killeen, TX 76543
(817) 634-0374
Admin Rollin House.
Medical Dir Dr Precha Suvunrungsi.
Licensure Skilled care. *Beds* SNF 150. *Private
Pay Patients* 33%. *Certified* Medicaid;
Medicare.
Owner Proprietary corp (House/Cross
Associates).
Admissions Requirements Physician's request.
Staff Physicians 5 (pt); RNs 1 (ft), 2 (pt);
LPNs 15 (ft), 6 (pt); Nurses' aides 45 (ft), 10
(pt); Physical therapists 2 (pt); Reality
therapists 1 (pt); Occupational therapists 1
(pt); Speech therapists 1 (pt); Activities
coordinators 1 (ft), 1 (pt); Dietitians 1 (pt);
Ophthalmologists 1 (pt); Podiatrists 1 (pt);
Audiologists 1 (pt).
Facilities Dining room; Activities room;
Crafts room; Laundry room; Barber/Beauty
shop; Library; Enclosed patios.
Activities Arts & crafts; Cards; Games;
Reading groups; Prayer groups; Movies;
Shopping trips; Dances/Social/Cultural
gatherings; Intergenerational programs; Pet
therapy; Happy hour; Bingo.

Killeen Nursing Center
710 W Rancier Ave, Killeen, TX 76541
(817) 526-3130
Admin Henry A Randolph. *Dir of Nursing*
Jackie Young RN. *Medical Dir* Victor K
Seghers MD.
Licensure Skilled care. *Beds* SNF 50. *Certified*
Medicaid; Medicare.

Owner Proprietary corp (Beverly Enterprises).
Admissions Requirements Medical
examination; Physician's request.
Staff Physicians 1 (pt); RNs 2 (ft), 1 (pt);
LPNs 5 (ft); Nurses' aides 20 (ft), 1 (pt);
Activities coordinators 1 (ft).
Facilities Dining room; Activities room;
Barber/Beauty shop.
Activities Cards; Games; Reading groups;
Prayer groups; Movies; Dances/Social/
Cultural gatherings; Pet therapy.

Kingsland

Kingsland Hills Care Center
PO Drawer 1079, Hwy 1431, Kingsland, TX
78639
(915) 388-4538
Admin Wanda M Laxson. *Dir of Nursing*
Wilma Dehnel RN. *Medical Dir* David
Hoerster MD.
Licensure Intermediate care. *Beds* ICF 108.
Private Pay Patients 50%. *Certified*
Medicaid.
Owner Proprietary corp (Care Givers Inc).
Admissions Requirements Medical
examination; Physician's request.
Staff RNs 1 (ft), 1 (pt); LPNs 10 (ft), 3 (pt);
Nurses' aides 34 (ft), 3 (pt); Activities
coordinators 1 (ft); Dietitians 1 (ft).
Languages Spanish.
Facilities Dining room; Activities room;
Laundry room; Barber/Beauty shop; Library.
Activities Games; Reading groups; Movies;
Shopping trips; Dances/Social/Cultural
gatherings.

Kingsville

Canterbury Villa of Kingsville
316 Military Hwy, Kingsville, TX 78363
(512) 592-9366
Admin Emma Aguilar.
Licensure Intermediate care; Custodial care.
Beds ICF 162; Custodial care 32. *Certified*
Medicaid.
Owner Proprietary corp (ARA Living
Centers).
Admissions Requirements Medical
examination; Physician's request.
Staff RNs 1 (ft); LPNs 8 (ft), 2 (pt); Activities
coordinators 1 (ft).
Facilities Dining room; Activities room;
Chapel; Crafts room; Laundry room; Barber/
Beauty shop.
Activities Arts & crafts; Cards; Games; Prayer
groups; Movies.

Kirbyville

Avalon Place
700 Blk of N Herndon, Kirbyville, TX 75956
(409) 423-6111
Licensure Nursing; Personal care. *Beds*
Nursing 90; Personal care 28.

Knox City

Brazos Valley Care Home
Rte 1 Box 87C, Knox City, TX 79529
(817) 658-3543
Admin Lorene Beason. *Dir of Nursing* Jean
Lagslow LVN. *Medical Dir* Terry Springer
MD.
Licensure Intermediate care. *Beds* ICF 70.
Certified Medicaid.
Owner Privately owned (D & D Health Care).
Admissions Requirements Minimum age 18;
Medical examination.
Staff Physicians 1 (pt); RNs 1 (pt); LPNs 5
(ft); Nurses' aides 25 (ft); Activities
coordinators 1 (ft); Dietitians 1 (pt).
Facilities Dining room; Activities room;
Crafts room; Laundry room; Barber/Beauty
shop.

Activities Arts & crafts; Games; Prayer groups;
Shopping trips; Pet therapy; Volunteer
program.

Kountze

Kountze Nursing Center
PO Box 940, FM 1293, Kountze, TX 77625
(409) 246-3418, 755-2121
Admin Sue McCain. *Dir of Nursing* Dawn
Murray RN. *Medical Dir* H A Hooks MD.
Licensure Skilled care. *Beds* SNF 60. *Private
Pay Patients* 12%. *Certified* Medicaid;
Medicare.
Owner Proprietary corp (ARA Living
Centers).
Admissions Requirements Medical
examination; Physician's request.
Staff RNs 1 (ft), 2 (pt); LPNs 3 (ft), 3 (pt);
Nurses' aides 20 (ft); Physical therapists 1
(pt); Occupational therapists 1 (pt); Speech
therapists 1 (pt); Activities coordinators 1
(ft); Dietitians 1 (pt).
Facilities Dining room; Activities room;
Crafts room; Laundry room; Barber/Beauty
shop.
Activities Arts & crafts; Cards; Games;
Reading groups; Prayer groups; Movies;
Shopping trips; Dances/Social/Cultural
gatherings; Intergenerational programs; Pet
therapy.

La Grange

Care Inn of La Grange
PO Box 398, 457 N Main, La Grange, TX
78945
(409) 968-5865
Licensure Intermediate care. *Beds* ICF 98.
Certified Medicaid.
Owner Proprietary corp (ARA Living
Centers).

Monument Hill Nursing Center
Spur 92 & Hwy 77, La Grange, TX 78945
(409) 968-3144, 968-6610 FAX
Admin Donald Cain. *Dir of Nursing* Vivian
DesHotels RN. *Medical Dir* Bill Nolen DO.
Licensure Skilled care; Intermediate care;
Alzheimer's care. *Beds* SNF 31; ICF 85.
Certified Medicaid; Medicare.
Owner Privately owned.
Admissions Requirements Medical
examination; Physician's request.
Staff RNs; LPNs; Nurses' aides; Physical
therapists; Occupational therapists; Speech
therapists; Activities coordinators; Dietitians.
Facilities Dining room; Physical therapy
room; Activities room; Crafts room; Laundry
room; Barber/Beauty shop.
Activities Arts & crafts; Cards; Games; Prayer
groups; Shopping trips; Dominoes.

La Porte

Happy Harbor Methodist Home
PO Box 1337, 1106 Bayshore Dr, La Porte,
TX 77571
(713) 471-1210
Admin H Frank Carter.
Licensure Intermediate care. *Beds* 140.
Certified Medicaid.
Owner Nonprofit corp.
Affiliation Methodist.

La Porte Care Center
PO Box 1376, 208 S Utah, La Porte, TX
77571
(713) 471-1810
Admin Elva Ramariz.
Licensure Intermediate care. *Beds* 58.
Certified Medicaid.
Owner Proprietary corp (Beverly Enterprises).
Staff RNs 1 (pt); LPNs 4 (ft); Nurses' aides 13
(ft); Activities coordinators 1 (ft); Dietitians
1 (ft); 8 (ft).

Facilities Dining room; Chapel; Laundry
room; Barber/Beauty shop.
Activities Arts & crafts; Cards; Games;
Reading groups; Prayer groups; Movies;
Shopping trips; Dances/Social/Cultural
gatherings.

Lake Jackson

Lake Jackson Nursing Home
413 Garland Dr, Lake Jackson, TX 77566
(409) 297-3266
Admin Rebecca Grether.
Medical Dir A O McCary MD.
Licensure Skilled care; Intermediate care. *Beds*
120. *Certified* Medicaid; Medicare.
Owner Proprietary corp (Beverly Enterprises).
Admissions Requirements Medical
examination; Physician's request.
Staff Physicians 1 (ft), 2 (pt); RNs 4 (ft);
LPNs 11 (ft); Nurses' aides 45 (ft); Physical
therapists 1 (pt); Occupational therapists 1
(pt); Speech therapists 1 (pt); Activities
coordinators 1 (ft); Dietitians 1 (pt);
Podiatrists 1 (pt); Dentists 1 (pt).
Facilities Dining room; Activities room;
Crafts room; Laundry room; Barber/Beauty
shop.
Activities Arts & crafts; Cards; Games;
Reading groups; Prayer groups; Movies;
Shopping trips; Dances/Social/Cultural
gatherings.

Lake Worth

Canterbury Villa of Fort Worth
Rte 2 Box 935-A 8401 Jacksboro Hwy, Lake
Worth, TX 76135
(817) 237-3335
Licensure Nursing. *Beds* Nursing 104.

Lake Lodge
3800 Marina Dr, Lake Worth, TX 76135
(817) 237-7231
Admin Donna J Snyder.
Medical Dir Charles Maxville; Myrna Jurica.
Licensure Intermediate care; Quadriplegic
wing. *Beds* 150. *Certified* Medicaid.
Owner Proprietary corp (Texas Health
Enterprises).
Admissions Requirements Medical
examination.
Staff Physicians 1 (pt); RNs 2 (ft); LPNs 10
(ft); Physical therapists 1 (pt); Occupational
therapists 1 (pt); Speech therapists 1 (pt);
Activities coordinators 1 (ft); Dietitians 1
(ft); Ophthalmologists 1 (pt); Podiatrists 1
(pt); Dentists 1 (pt).
Facilities Dining room; Activities room;
Crafts room; Laundry room; Barber/Beauty
shop; Library; 2 sunrooms; Sun deck; Large
patio.
Activities Arts & crafts; Cards; Games;
Reading groups; Prayer groups; Movies;
Shopping trips; Dances/Social/Cultural
gatherings.

Lake Worth Nursing Home
4220 Wells Dr, Lake Worth, TX 76135
(817) 237-7184
Licensure Nursing. *Beds* Nursing 104.

Lamesa

Heritage Nursing Manor
PO Box 1285, 1201 N 15th St, Lamesa, TX
79331
(806) 872-2141
Admin David O Crowson.
Licensure Intermediate care. *Beds* 80.
Certified Medicaid.
Owner Proprietary corp (Beverly Enterprises).

Lamesa Nursing Center
1818 N 7th St, Lamesa, TX 79331
(806) 872-8351
Admin Eugenia F Herrin.

Licensure Intermediate care. *Beds* 48.
Certified Medicaid.
Owner Proprietary corp (Beverly Enterprises).

Lampasas

Lampasas Manor
PO Box 970, 611 N Broad St, Lampasas, TX
76550
(512) 556-3588
Admin William A Reich. *Dir of Nursing*
Debra Wallace RN. *Medical Dir* Morris K
Patteson MD.
Licensure Skilled care. *Beds* SNF 68. *Private
Pay Patients* 20%. *Certified* Medicaid;
Medicare.
Owner Proprietary corp (DiversiCare—Texas).
Admissions Requirements Medical
examination; Physician's request.
Staff RNs 2 (ft); LPNs 7 (ft), 1 (pt); Nurses'
aides 20 (ft), 4 (pt); Activities coordinators 1
(ft); Dietitians.
Facilities Dining room; Physical therapy
room; Activities room; Laundry room;
Barber/Beauty shop.
Activities Arts & crafts; Cards; Games;
Reading groups; Prayer groups; Shopping
trips; Dances/Social/Cultural gatherings;
Intergenerational programs.

Leisure Lodge—Lampasas
FM Rd 580 E, Lampasas, TX 76550
(512) 556-6267
Admin Cheryl Fulton. *Dir of Nursing* Linda
Hattenbach. *Medical Dir* Alton Bishop.
Licensure Intermediate care. *Beds* ICF 96.
Certified Medicaid.
Owner Proprietary corp (Beverly Enterprises).
Facilities Dining room; Barber/Beauty shop.
Activities Arts & crafts; Cards; Games;
Reading groups; Prayer groups; Movies;
Shopping trips; Dances/Social/Cultural
gatherings; Intergenerational programs; Pet
therapy.

Lancaster

Lancaster Nursing Home Inc
1515 N Elm, Lancaster, TX 75134
(214) 227-6066
Admin Mina L Ellison.
Medical Dir Charles Waldrop MD.
Licensure Skilled care; Intermediate care. *Beds*
120. *Certified* Medicaid.
Owner Proprietary corp (Beverly Enterprises).
Admissions Requirements Medical
examination; Physician's request.
Facilities Dining room; Activities room;
Laundry room; Barber/Beauty shop.
Activities Arts & crafts; Games; Prayer groups;
Shopping trips; Dances/Social/Cultural
gatherings.

Lancaster Residential Center
3901 N Dallas Ave, Lancaster, TX 75134
(214) 224-3554
Admin James L Roberts Jr.
Licensure Intermediate care for mentally
retarded. *Beds* 68. *Certified* Medicaid.

Silent Night Nursing Home
346 W Redbud St, Lancaster, TX 75146
(214) 227-1205, 227-1255
Admin Gabriel G Bach PhD. *Dir of Nursing* J
J Devron RN. *Medical Dir* Dr J Waldrop.
Licensure Skilled care; Intermediate care;
Medicare. *Beds* SNF 26; ICF 124; Medicare
28. *Private Pay Patients* 25%. *Certified*
Medicaid; Medicare.
Owner Privately owned.
Admissions Requirements Minimum age 65
exceptions; Medical examination; Physician's
request.
Staff Physicians 3 (ft); RNs 2 (ft); LPNs 14
(ft); Nurses' aides 63 (ft); Physical therapists
2 (ft); Reality therapists 1 (ft); Recreational
therapists 1 (ft); Occupational therapists 1

(ft); Speech therapists 1 (ft); Activities
coordinators 1 (ft); Dietitians 2 (ft);
Ophthalmologists 1 (ft); Podiatrists 1 (ft);
Audiologists 1 (ft).
Languages French, German, Spanish.
Facilities Dining room; Physical therapy
room; Activities room; Chapel; Crafts room;
Laundry room; Barber/Beauty shop.
Activities Arts & crafts; Cards; Games;
Reading groups; Prayer groups; Movies;
Shopping trips; Dances/Social/Cultural
gatherings; Pet therapy.

Westridge Nursing Center
1241 Westridge, Lancaster, TX 75146
(214) 227-5110
Admin Joyce Steuer.
Licensure Intermediate care. *Beds* 120.
Certified Medicaid.
Owner Proprietary corp.

Laredo

Retama Manor Nursing Center—East
2520 Arkansas, Laredo, TX 78040
(512) 722-0584
Admin Virginia Rodriguez.
Licensure Skilled care. *Beds* 100. *Certified*
Medicaid.
Owner Proprietary corp (ARA Living
Centers).

Retama Manor Nursing Center—South
1102 Galveston, Laredo, TX 78040
(512) 723-2068
Admin Virginia Rodriguez.
Licensure Intermediate care. *Beds* 120.
Certified Medicaid.
Owner Proprietary corp (ARA Living
Centers).

Retama Manor Nursing Center—West
1200 Lane, Laredo, TX 78040
(512) 722-0031
Admin Betty Funkhouser.
Licensure Intermediate care; Custodial care.
Beds ICF 168; Custodial care 40. *Certified*
Medicaid.
Owner Proprietary corp (ARA Living
Centers).

League City

Baywind Village Convalescent Center
411 Alabama, League City, TX 77573
(713) 332-9588
Licensure Nursing. *Beds* Nursing 96.

Leon Valley

Leon Valley Lodge
6518 Samaritan Dr, Leon Valley, TX 78238
(512) 684-0308
Admin Faye Lobert.
Licensure Intermediate care. *Beds* 66.
Certified Medicaid.
Owner Proprietary corp.

Leonard

Leonard Nursing Home
PO Box 546, Leonard, TX 75452
(214) 587-2282, 587-2594 FAX
Admin M Nancee Manning. *Dir of Nursing*
Nora Ross. *Medical Dir* R Franklin.
Licensure Intermediate care. *Beds* ICF 80.
Private Pay Patients 25%. *Certified*
Medicaid.
Owner Nonprofit corp (Amer Manor).
Staff LPNs 6 (ft); Nurses' aides 22 (ft);
Activities coordinators 1 (ft).
Activities Arts & crafts; Cards; Games;
Reading groups; Prayer groups; Movies;
Shopping trips; Dances/Social/Cultural
gatherings; Intergenerational programs; Pet
therapy.

Levelland

Levelland Development Center
1515 5th St, Levelland, TX 79336
(806) 894-4902
Admin Don Whiteside.
Licensure Intermediate care for mentally retarded. *Beds* 42. *Certified* Medicaid.

Levelland Nursing Home
210 W Ave, Levelland, TX 79336
(806) 894-5053
Admin Charlene T Turner. *Dir of Nursing* Judy Choate RN. *Medical Dir* Dr W Wiri.
Licensure Intermediate care; Alzheimer's care. *Beds* ICF 89. *Certified* Medicaid.
Owner Proprietary corp (ARA Living Centers).
Admissions Requirements Medical examination; Physician's request.
Staff RNs 1 (ft); LPNs 9 (ft), 1 (pt); Nurses' aides 26 (ft), 3 (pt); Activities coordinators 1 (ft).
Facilities Dining room; Physical therapy room; Activities room; Crafts room; Laundry room; Barber/Beauty shop.
Activities Arts & crafts; Cards; Games; Reading groups; Prayer groups; Movies; Shopping trips; Dances/Social/Cultural gatherings; Intergenerational programs; Pet therapy.

Lewisville

Autumn Oaks Care Center
740 Edmonds, Lewisville, TX 75067
(214) 436-3314, 436-6919 FAX
Admin Priscilla Nelson. *Dir of Nursing* Wanda Parsons. *Medical Dir* Dr Jerry Damon.
Licensure Intermediate care. *Beds* ICF 60. *Private Pay Patients* 50%. *Certified* Medicaid.
Owner Proprietary corp (Americare Corp).
Admissions Requirements Minimum age 18; Medical examination.
Staff RNs; LPNs; Nurses' aides; Activities coordinators.
Facilities Dining room; Activities room; Crafts room; Laundry room; Barber/Beauty shop.
Activities Arts & crafts; Cards; Games; Reading groups; Prayer groups; Movies; Shopping trips; Dances/Social/Cultural gatherings; Intergenerational programs; Pet therapy.

Edmond Oaks Center
1680 Edmonds Ln, Lewisville, TX 75067
(214) 436-4538
Admin Douglas L Adams. *Dir of Nursing* Claire Ruffin RN.
Licensure Intermediate care for mentally retarded. *Beds* ICF/MR 116. *Certified* Medicaid.
Owner Proprietary corp.
Admissions Requirements Minimum age 16.
Staff Physicians 1 (pt); RNs 1 (pt); LPNs 6 (ft); Nurses' aides 120 (ft); Physical therapists 1 (ft); Recreational therapists 1 (ft); Occupational therapists 1 (pt); Speech therapists 1 (pt); Dietitians 1 (pt); Ophthalmologists 1 (pt); Podiatrists 1 (pt); Dentists 1 (pt).
Facilities Dining room; Physical therapy room; Activities room; Off-campus training center.
Activities Arts & crafts; Cards; Games; Dances/Social/Cultural gatherings; Habilitative training.

Twin Pines Nursing Center
169 Lake Park Rd, Lewisville, TX 75067
(214) 436-7571
Admin Michelle Roberts. *Dir of Nursing* Marie Konecny RN.

Licensure Intermediate care. *Beds* ICF 120. *Certified* Medicaid.
Owner Privately owned.
Admissions Requirements Medical examination.
Staff RNs; Nurses' aides; Physical therapists; Recreational therapists; Occupational therapists; Speech therapists; Activities coordinators; Dietitians; Ophthalmologists.
Languages Spanish.
Facilities Dining room; Activities room; Crafts room; Laundry room; Barber/Beauty shop; Library.
Activities Arts & crafts; Cards; Games; Reading groups; Prayer groups; Movies; Shopping trips; Dances/Social/Cultural gatherings.

Liberty

Golden Charm Nursing Center
1206 N Travis, Liberty, TX 77575
(713) 336-7247
Admin Rita Aalund.
Medical Dir Dr Sergio Rodriquez.
Licensure Skilled care; Intermediate care. *Beds* 120. *Certified* Medicaid.
Owner Proprietary corp (Beverly Enterprises).
Admissions Requirements Minimum age 21; Medical examination; Physician's request.
Staff Physicians 6 (pt); RNs 1 (ft), 1 (pt); LPNs 9 (ft); Nurses' aides 19 (ft); Physical therapists 1 (pt); Speech therapists 1 (pt); Activities coordinators 1 (pt); Dietitians 1 (pt); Podiatrists 1 (pt); Dentists 1 (pt).
Facilities Dining room; Activities room; Laundry room; Barber/Beauty shop.
Activities Arts & crafts; Games; Movies; Shopping trips; Dances/Social/Cultural gatherings.

Lindale

Colonial Nursing Center
PO Box 1630, 508 Pierce St, Lindale, TX 75771
(214) 882-6169
Admin Ralph J King. *Dir of Nursing* Carol Synder LVN. *Medical Dir* Wendell Hand DO.
Licensure Intermediate care; Alzheimer's care. *Beds* ICF 60. *Private Pay Patients* 50%. *Certified* Medicaid.
Owner Proprietary corp.
Admissions Requirements Medical examination; Physician's request.
Staff Physicians 1 (pt); RNs 1 (pt); LPNs 5 (ft); Nurses' aides 18 (ft); Physical therapists 1 (pt); Activities coordinators 1 (ft); Dietitians 1 (pt); Podiatrists 1 (pt).
Facilities Dining room; Activities room; Barber/Beauty shop; Library; TV room.
Activities Arts & crafts; Cards; Games; Reading groups; Prayer groups; Movies; Shopping trips; Dances/Social/Cultural gatherings; Pet therapy.

Lindale Nursing Center
PO Box 188, 215 Margaret, Lindale, TX 75771
(214) 882-3118, 882-6037
Admin Billie Pittman.
Licensure Intermediate care. *Beds* 89. *Certified* Medicaid.
Owner Proprietary corp (Beverly Enterprises).

Linden

Oak Manor Nursing Home
PO Box 551, Hwy 11 W, Linden, TX 75563
(214) 756-5575
Admin Wallace D Roberts Jr.
Licensure Intermediate care. *Beds* 107. *Certified* Medicaid.
Owner Proprietary corp (Truco Inc).

Facilities Dining room; Activities room; Barber/Beauty shop.
Activities Arts & crafts; Cards; Games; Prayer groups; Movies; Dances/Social/Cultural gatherings.

Littlefield

Knight's Nursing Home
Box 328, 520 Ash, Littlefield, TX 79339
(806) 385-3921
Admin Nelda Jean Cheshier. *Dir of Nursing* Nita Henley. *Medical Dir* Barney E Klein MD.
Licensure Intermediate care. *Beds* ICF 65. *Private Pay Patients* 50%. *Certified* Medicaid.
Owner Privately owned.
Staff Physicians 7 (ft); RNs 2 (ft); LPNs 6 (ft), 1 (pt); Nurses' aides 30 (ft); Dietitians 1 (ft); Ophthalmologists 1 (ft).
Languages Spanish, German.
Facilities Dining room; Activities room; Chapel; Crafts room; Laundry room.
Activities Arts & crafts; Cards; Games; Reading groups; Prayer groups; Dances/Social/Cultural gatherings.

Littlefield Hospitality House
PO Box 589, 1609 W 10th St, Littlefield, TX 79339
(806) 385-4544
Admin Vera L Reynolds.
Licensure Intermediate care. *Beds* 63. *Certified* Medicaid.
Owner Proprietary corp.

Livingston

Bur-Mont Nursing Center
154 Banks Dr, Livingston, TX 77351
(409) 327-5415
Admin Velma Walker.
Licensure Intermediate care. *Beds* 120. *Certified* Medicaid.
Staff LPNs 10 (ft); Nurses' aides 30 (ft); Activities coordinators 1 (ft); Dietitians 2 (ft).
Facilities Dining room; Activities room; Chapel; Crafts room; Laundry room; Barber/Beauty shop.
Activities Arts & crafts; Prayer groups; Movies; Dances/Social/Cultural gatherings.

Livingston Convalescent Center
PO Box 929, 1810 N Washington, Livingston, TX 77351
(409) 327-4341
Admin Virginia L Williams.
Licensure Intermediate care. *Beds* 52. *Certified* Medicaid.
Owner Proprietary corp (Cantex Healthcare Centers).

Llano

Care Inn of Llano
800 W Haynie, Llano, TX 78643
(915) 247-4194
Admin Audrey Sue Rice.
Licensure Intermediate care. *Beds* 122. *Certified* Medicaid.
Owner Proprietary corp (ARA Living Centers).

Hill Country Manor
507 E Green St, Llano, TX 78643
(915) 247-4115
Admin Mildred Overstreet. *Dir of Nursing* Patsy Dick.
Licensure Intermediate care. *Beds* ICF 86. *Private Pay Patients* 18%. *Certified* Medicaid.
Owner Proprietary corp (Beverly Enterprises).
Admissions Requirements Medical examination; Physician's request.

Staff RNs 1 (ft); LPNs 6 (ft); Nurses' aides 13
(ft); Physical therapists (consultant); Speech
therapists (consultant); Dietitians 1 (ft).
Languages Spanish, German.
Facilities Dining room; Activities room;
Crafts room; Laundry room; Barber/Beauty
shop.
Activities Arts & crafts; Cards; Games;
Reading groups; Prayer groups; Movies;
Shopping trips; Dances/Social/Cultural
gatherings; Intergenerational programs; Pet
therapy; Musicals; Bingo; Volunteer
program.

Lockhart

Cartwheel Lodge—Lockhart
107 N Medina, Lockhart, TX 78644
(512) 398-5213
Admin Mr Jack Keys. *Dir of Nursing* Mary
Soliz LVN.
Licensure Intermediate care. *Beds* ICF 100.
Certified Medicaid.
Owner Proprietary corp (Diversicare Corp).
Admissions Requirements Physician's request.
Staff LPNs 4 (ft), 1 (pt); Nurses' aides 22 (ft),
1 (pt); Activities coordinators 1 (ft);
Dietitians 1 (ft).
Languages Spanish.
Facilities Dining room; Activities room;
Laundry room; Barber/Beauty shop.
Activities Arts & crafts; Cards; Games;
Reading groups; Prayer groups; Movies;
Shopping trips; Dances/Social/Cultural
gatherings.

Golden Age Home
PO Box 870, 1505 S Main, Lockhart, TX
78644
(512) 398-2362
Admin Deborah Blackwell. *Dir of Nursing*
Elva Maurer. *Medical Dir* Dr Randall
Kirtley.
Licensure Intermediate care; Personal care;
Alzheimer's care. *Beds* ICF 120; Personal
care 65. *Private Pay Patients* 50%. *Certified*
Medicaid.
Owner Nonprofit organization/foundation.
Admissions Requirements Minimum age 62.
Staff Physicians 1 (ft); RNs 2 (ft), 3 (pt);
LPNs 5 (ft), 2 (pt); Nurses' aides 30 (ft), 5
(pt); Physical therapists (contracted);
Activities coordinators 1 (ft); Dietitians 1
(ft).
Languages Spanish.
Affiliation Methodist.
Facilities Dining room; Physical therapy
room; Activities room; Chapel; Crafts room;
Laundry room; Barber/Beauty shop; Library.
Activities Arts & crafts; Cards; Games;
Reading groups; Prayer groups; Movies;
Shopping trips; Dances/Social/Cultural
gatherings; Intergenerational programs; Pet
therapy.

Lockney

Lockney Care Center
401 N Main, Lockney, TX 79241
(806) 652-2502, 652-2513
Admin Lavona Pitchford.
Medical Dir Marilyn Ellis.
Licensure Intermediate care. *Beds* ICF 52.
Certified Medicaid.
Owner Proprietary corp (Unicare).
Admissions Requirements Medical
examination; Physician's request.
Staff LPNs 4 (ft); Nurses' aides 13 (ft), 2 (pt);
Activities coordinators 1 (ft).
Facilities Dining room; Laundry room;
Barber/Beauty shop.
Activities Arts & crafts; Cards; Games;
Reading groups; Prayer groups; Movies;
Shopping trips.

Longview

Clairmont
3201 N 4th St, Longview, TX 75601
(214) 236-4291
Admin Sharon Robb. *Dir of Nursing* Kay
Fudge. *Medical Dir* Jimmie Bagley.
Licensure Skilled care. *Beds* SNF 128.
Certified Medicaid; Medicare.
Owner Proprietary corp (American Health
Services Inc).
Facilities Dining room; Activities room;
Crafts room; Laundry room; Barber/Beauty
shop; Library.

Cleaver Memorial Convalescent Center
1000 Sapphire St, Longview, TX 75601
(214) 753-8608
Admin Edwin C Cuington.
Medical Dir Edna M McNeil.
Licensure Intermediate care. *Beds* ICF 100.
Certified Medicaid.
Owner Proprietary corp.
Admissions Requirements Physician's request.
Staff RNs 2 (ft); LPNs 8 (ft), 2 (pt); Nurses'
aides 10 (ft), 5 (pt); Activities coordinators 1
(ft); Dietitians 2 (ft).
Facilities Dining room; Activities room;
Chapel; Crafts room; Laundry room; Barber/
Beauty shop.
Activities Arts & crafts; Cards; Games; Prayer
groups; Dances/Social/Cultural gatherings.

Highland Pines Nursing Home
1100 N 4th St, Longview, TX 75601
(214) 753-7661
Admin John T DeLorme. *Dir of Nursing* Beth
Sangrey RN. *Medical Dir* Donald Pierson
MD.
Licensure Intermediate care. *Beds* ICF 171.
Private Pay Patients 60%. *Certified*
Medicaid.
Owner Proprietary corp (Stebbins Five Co).
Admissions Requirements Medical
examination; Physician's request.
Staff RNs 2 (ft); LPNs 14 (ft); Nurses' aides
55 (ft); Physical therapists 1 (pt); Reality
therapists 1 (pt); Speech therapists 1 (pt);
Activities coordinators 2 (ft); Dietitians 1
(pt); Ophthalmologists 1 (pt); Podiatrists 1
(pt); Audiologists 1 (pt).
Languages Spanish.
Facilities Dining room; Activities room;
Chapel; Crafts room; Laundry room; Barber/
Beauty shop; Library; TV room; Sun rooms.
Activities Arts & crafts; Cards; Games;
Reading groups; Prayer groups; Movies;
Shopping trips; Dances/Social/Cultural
gatherings; Intergenerational programs; Pet
therapy.

Holiday Lodge
1301 Eden Dr, Longview, TX 75601
(214) 753-7651
Admin Billie Sue Cooper. *Dir of Nursing*
Marilyn Sexton RN. *Medical Dir* Dr Scott
Hunter.
Licensure Skilled care; Intermediate care;
Retirement. *Beds* SNF 56; ICF 102;
Retirement 150. *Private Pay Patients* 25%.
Certified Medicaid; Medicare.
Owner Proprietary corp (ARA Living
Centers).
Admissions Requirements Minimum age 16;
Medical examination; Physician's request.
Staff RNs; LPNs; Nurses' aides; Physical
therapists; Occupational therapists; Speech
therapists; Activities coordinators; Dietitians;
Podiatrists.
Languages Spanish.
Facilities Dining room; Activities room;
Crafts room; Laundry room; Barber/Beauty
shop; Secure unit.
Activities Arts & crafts; Cards; Games;
Reading groups; Prayer groups; Movies;
Shopping trips; Dances/Social/Cultural
gatherings; Intergenerational programs; Pet
therapy.

Lynn Lodge Nursing Home
111 Ruthlynn Dr, Longview, TX 75601
(214) 757-2557
Admin Benjamin C Delmonico Jr. *Dir of
Nursing* Hilda Wallin RN. *Medical Dir*
Kenneth Marshall MD.
Licensure Intermediate care; Alzheimer's care.
Beds ICF 118. *Certified* Medicaid.
Owner Proprietary corp (ARA Living
Centers).
Admissions Requirements Medical
examination.
Staff RNs 1 (ft); LPNs 10 (ft); Nurses' aides
25 (ft); Activities coordinators 1 (ft).
Facilities Dining room; Activities room;
Laundry room; Barber/Beauty shop.
Activities Arts & crafts; Cards; Games; Prayer
groups; Movies; Dances/Social/Cultural
gatherings.

Pine Tree Lodge Nursing Center
2711 Pine Tree Rd, Longview, TX 75604
(214) 759-3994, 759-1439 FAX
Admin Marian Carlisle. *Dir of Nursing*
Johnnie Pace. *Medical Dir* Larry Huffman.
Licensure Intermediate care. *Beds* ICF 92.
Certified Medicaid.
Owner Privately owned.
Admissions Requirements Medical
examination; Physician's request.
Staff Physicians; RNs; LPNs; Nurses' aides;
Physical therapists; Activities coordinators;
Dietitians.
Facilities Dining room; Activities room;
Chapel; Crafts room; Laundry room; Barber/
Beauty shop.
Activities Arts & crafts; Cards; Games;
Reading groups; Prayer groups; Movies;
Shopping trips; Dances/Social/Cultural
gatherings; Pet therapy.

Summer Meadows
301 Hollybrook, Longview, TX 75601
(214) 758-7764
Admin Lois M Jenkins. *Dir of Nursing*
Elizabeth Cobb RN. *Medical Dir* George
Saikin MD.
Licensure Skilled care. *Beds* SNF 90. *Private
Pay Patients* 78%. *Certified* Medicaid;
Medicare.
Owner Proprietary corp.
Admissions Requirements Medical
examination; Physician's request.
Staff RNs; LPNs; Nurses' aides; Physical
therapists; Recreational therapists; Activities
coordinators; Dietitians.
Facilities Dining room; Physical therapy
room; Activities room; Chapel; Crafts room;
Laundry room; Barber/Beauty shop; Library.
Activities Arts & crafts; Cards; Games;
Reading groups; Prayer groups; Shopping
trips; Dances/Social/Cultural gatherings;
Intergenerational programs; Pet therapy.

Willowbrook Manor Nursing Home
112 Ruthlynn Dr, Longview, TX 75601
(214) 753-8611
Admin Bob E Standard. *Dir of Nursing*
Bonnie Castle. *Medical Dir* Dr Roger Kiser.
Licensure Skilled care; Intermediate care. *Beds*
SNF 70; ICF 80. *Certified* Medicaid;
Medicare.
Owner Proprietary corp (Beverly Enterprises).
Admissions Requirements Minimum age 18;
Medical examination.
Staff Physicians 2 (ft); RNs 2 (ft); LPNs 15
(ft); Nurses' aides 35 (ft); Physical therapists
1 (ft); Reality therapists 1 (ft); Recreational
therapists 1 (ft); Activities coordinators 1
(ft); Dietitians 1 (ft).
Languages Spanish.
Facilities Dining room; Physical therapy
room; Activities room; Crafts room; Laundry
room; Barber/Beauty shop.

Activities Arts & crafts; Cards; Games; Reading groups; Prayer groups; Movies; Shopping trips; Dances/Social/Cultural gatherings; Outdoor activities; Current events; Quilting.

Loraine

Loraine Nursing Home
PO Box 219, 219 Campbell Ave, Loraine, TX 79532
(915) 737-2209
Admin Linda Barrick.
Medical Dir Marie Graham DNS.
Licensure Intermediate care. *Beds* ICF 60. *Certified* Medicaid.
Owner Proprietary corp (Beverly Enterprises).
Admissions Requirements Medical examination; Physician's request.
Staff RNs 1 (pt); LPNs 4 (ft), 2 (pt); Nurses' aides 8 (ft), 1 (pt); Activities coordinators 1 (ft); Dietitians 1 (pt).
Languages Spanish.
Facilities Dining room; Activities room; Laundry room; Barber/Beauty shop.
Activities Arts & crafts; Cards; Games; Reading groups; Prayer groups; Movies; Shopping trips; Dances/Social/Cultural gatherings; Exercise.

Lubbock

Bender Terrace Nursing Home
4510 27th St, Lubbock, TX 79410
(806) 795-4368
Admin Deborah R Moore.
Licensure Intermediate care. *Beds* 60. *Certified* Medicaid.
Owner Proprietary corp (Summit Health Ltd).
Staff RNs 1 (pt); LPNs 4 (ft); Nurses' aides 15 (ft); Activities coordinators 1 (ft); Dietitians 1 (pt).
Facilities Dining room; Activities room; Laundry room; Barber/Beauty shop.
Activities Arts & crafts; Cards; Games; Reading groups; Prayer groups; Movies; Shopping trips; Dances/Social/Cultural gatherings.

Golden Age Nursing Home
2613 34th St, Lubbock, TX 79410
(806) 792-2196
Admin Sidney Z Pospisil.
Licensure Intermediate care. *Beds* 42. *Certified* Medicaid.
Owner Proprietary corp.

John Knox Village of Lubbock Inc
1717 Norfolk Ave, Lubbock, TX 79416
(806) 797-4305
Admin Rita E Mullins. *Dir of Nursing* Linda Villalobos.
Licensure Private pay; Retirement. *Beds* 62. *Certified* Medicaid; Medicare.
Owner Nonprofit organization/foundation.
Admissions Requirements Medical examination; Physician's request.
Staff Physicians 1 (ft); RNs 1 (ft); LPNs 8 (ft); Nurses' aides 20 (ft); Activities coordinators 1 (ft); Dietitians 1 (ft).
Facilities Dining room; Activities room; Chapel; Barber/Beauty shop.
Activities Arts & crafts; Cards; Games; Reading groups; Prayer groups; Movies; Shopping trips; Dances/Social/Cultural gatherings.

Lakeside Care Center
4306 24th St, Lubbock, TX 79410
(806) 793-2555
Admin Norma E Visage.
Licensure Intermediate care. *Beds* 93. *Certified* Medicaid.
Owner Proprietary corp.

Lubbock Health Care Center
4120 22nd Pl, Lubbock, TX 79407
(806) 793-3252
Admin Judy D Bobbitt.
Licensure Skilled care. *Beds* 120. *Certified* Medicaid.
Owner Proprietary corp.

Lubbock Hospitality House
4710 Slide Rd, Lubbock, TX 79414
(806) 797-3481
Admin Lois E Hays.
Licensure Intermediate care. *Beds* 117. *Certified* Medicaid.
Staff Physicians 1 (pt); RNs 2 (ft), 1 (pt); LPNs 9 (ft); Nurses' aides 28 (ft), 2 (pt); Activities coordinators 1 (ft); Dietitians 1 (ft).
Facilities Dining room; Activities room; Crafts room; Laundry room; Barber/Beauty shop; Library.
Activities Arts & crafts; Cards; Games; Reading groups; Prayer groups; Movies; Shopping trips; Dances/Social/Cultural gatherings.

Lutheran Home of West Texas
2418 6th St, Lubbock, TX 79401
(806) 744-5775
Admin Mary Nell Griffin. *Dir of Nursing* Nita Terry RN.
Licensure Intermediate care; Alzheimer's care. *Beds* 67. *Certified* Medicaid.
Owner Nonprofit organization/foundation.
Admissions Requirements Medical examination.
Languages German, Spanish.
Facilities Dining room; Activities room; Crafts room; Laundry room; Barber/Beauty shop; Library.
Activities Arts & crafts; Cards; Games; Reading groups; Prayer groups; Movies; Shopping trips; Dances/Social/Cultural gatherings.

Parkway Manor Care Center
114 Cherry Ave, Lubbock, TX 79403
(806) 763-4186
Admin Lisa L Owens. *Dir of Nursing* Shelley Arick RN. *Medical Dir* Patrick H Pappas MD.
Licensure Skilled care. *Beds* SNF 61. *Certified* Medicaid; Medicare.
Owner Proprietary corp (Southeastern Health Care).
Admissions Requirements Medical examination; Physician's request.
Languages Spanish.
Facilities Dining room; Physical therapy room; Laundry room; Barber/Beauty shop.
Activities Arts & crafts; Cards; Games; Reading groups; Prayer groups; Movies; Shopping trips; Dances/Social/Cultural gatherings.

Quaker Villa
4403 74th St, Lubbock, TX 79424
(806) 795-0668, 795-4250 FAX
Admin James T Swanner. *Dir of Nursing* Louise Kennedy RN. *Medical Dir* Carl Page MD.
Licensure Intermediate care. *Beds* ICF 96. *Private Pay Patients* 19%. *Certified* Medicaid.
Owner Proprietary corp (Texas Health Enterprises).
Admissions Requirements Physician's request.
Staff Physicians 1 (pt); RNs 2 (ft); Physical therapists 1 (pt); Speech therapists 1 (pt); Activities coordinators 1 (ft); Dietitians 1 (ft); Podiatrists 1 (pt).
Facilities Dining room; Activities room; Laundry room; Barber/Beauty shop.
Activities Arts & crafts; Games; Shopping trips.

Sherwood Health Care of Lubbock Inc
5502 W 4th St, Lubbock, TX 79416
(806) 739-1111
Admin Nell Casey.
Medical Dir Richard Mayer DO.
Licensure Intermediate care. *Beds* 150. *Certified* Medicaid.
Admissions Requirements Medical examination; Physician's request.
Staff LPNs 6 (ft); Nurses' aides 26 (ft); Activities coordinators 1 (ft).
Facilities Dining room; Chapel; Laundry room; Barber/Beauty shop.
Activities Arts & crafts; Cards; Games; Prayer groups; Movies; Shopping trips; Dances/ Social/Cultural gatherings.

University Manor
2400 Quaker, Lubbock, TX 79410
(806) 792-2831
Admin Nell Casey. *Dir of Nursing* Yvonne Langston RN. *Medical Dir* Carl F Page MD.
Licensure Skilled care; Intermediate care. *Beds* SNF 45; ICF 50. *Certified* Medicaid; Medicare.
Owner Privately owned.
Admissions Requirements Medical examination.
Staff Physicians; RNs; LPNs; Nurses' aides; Activities coordinators; Dietitians.
Languages Spanish.
Facilities Dining room; Laundry room; Barber/Beauty shop.
Activities Arts & crafts; Cards; Games; Reading groups; Prayer groups; Movies; Shopping trips.

Lufkin

Angelina Nursing Home Inc
504 N John Redditt Dr, Lufkin, TX 75901
(713) 632-3331
Admin Patricia R Culbertson.
Licensure Intermediate care. *Beds* 132. *Certified* Medicaid.
Owner Proprietary corp.

Cantex Convalescent Center of Lufkin
1514 Ellis Ave, Lufkin, TX 75901
(409) 632-5571
Admin Dr John H Barnes. *Dir of Nursing* La Dell Dominey.
Licensure Intermediate care. *Beds* ICF 68. *Certified* Medicaid; Medicare.
Owner Proprietary corp (Cantex Healthcare Centers).
Staff RNs 1 (pt); LPNs 8 (ft); Nurses' aides 15 (ft); Physical therapists 1 (pt); Activities coordinators 1 (ft); Dietitians 1 (pt); Ophthalmologists 1 (pt); Podiatrists 1 (pt); Dentists 1 (pt).
Facilities Dining room; Activities room; Laundry room; Barber/Beauty shop; Library.
Activities Arts & crafts; Games; Reading groups; Prayer groups; Movies; Shopping trips; Dances/Social/Cultural gatherings.

Lufkin Nursing Center
2313 N Raguet St, Lufkin, TX 75901
(713) 634-2264
Admin Jesse B Pugh.
Licensure Intermediate care. *Beds* 150. *Certified* Medicaid.
Owner Proprietary corp (Beverly Enterprises).
Admissions Requirements Medical examination; Physician's request.
Staff Physicians 1 (ft); RNs 1 (ft); LPNs 5 (ft); Nurses' aides 15 (ft); Occupational therapists 1 (ft); Speech therapists 1 (ft); Activities coordinators 1 (ft); Dietitians 1 (ft).
Facilities Dining room; Physical therapy room; Activities room; Laundry room; Barber/Beauty shop.
Activities Cards; Games; Reading groups; Prayer groups; Movies; Shopping trips; Dances/Social/Cultural gatherings.

Parkwood Place
300 N Bynum, Lufkin, TX 75901
(409) 637-7215
Licensure Nursing; Personal care. *Beds*
Nursing 115; Personal care 42.

Pine Haven Nursing Home
1712 N Timberland Dr, Lufkin, TX 75901
(409) 632-3346
Admin Linda B Jones. *Dir of Nursing* Peggy
Mettlen. *Medical Dir* Jansen Todd DO; C A
Allen MD.
Licensure Intermediate care; Alzheimer's care.
Beds ICF 92. *Private Pay Patients* 5%.
Certified Medicaid.
Owner Proprietary corp (Cantex Healthcare
Centers).
Admissions Requirements Minimum age 18
months; Physician's request.
Staff LPNs; Nurses' aides; Activities
coordinators.
Languages Spanish.
Facilities Dining room; Activities room;
Laundry room; Barber/Beauty shop; Secured
Alzheimer's-related dementias unit.
Activities Arts & crafts; Cards; Games;
Reading groups; Prayer groups; Movies;
Shopping trips; Dances/Social/Cultural
gatherings; Intergenerational programs; Pet
therapy; Outings such as picnics, and trips to
zoo.

Progressive Living Center
PO Box 2427, 2404 Medford Dr, Lufkin, TX
75901
(713) 639-1206
Admin David Milem.
Medical Dir Philis Costner.
Licensure Intermediate care for mentally
retarded. *Beds* ICF/MR 60. *Certified*
Medicaid; Medicare.
Owner Privately owned.
Staff Physicians 1 (ft); RNs 1 (pt); LPNs 5
(ft); Nurses' aides 27 (ft); Physical therapists
1 (pt); Recreational therapists 1 (ft);
Occupational therapists 1 (pt); Speech
therapists 1 (pt); Activities coordinators 1
(ft); Dietitians 1 (pt); Ophthalmologists 1
(pt); Podiatrists 1 (pt); Dentists 1 (ft).
Facilities Dining room; Physical therapy
room; Activities room; Crafts room; Laundry
room; Barber/Beauty shop; Recreation room;
Training room.
Activities Arts & crafts; Cards; Games;
Reading groups; Movies; Shopping trips;
Dances/Social/Cultural gatherings;
Community events.

Luling

Cartwheel Lodge of Luling
PO Drawer 912, Hwy 183 N, Luling, TX
78648
(512) 875-5606
Admin Jon L Miller.
Licensure Intermediate care. *Beds* 96.
Certified Medicaid; Medicare.

Hillcrest Manor
PO Box 230, Hwy 90 E, Luling, TX 78648
(512) 875-5219
Admin Beth Thomas. *Dir of Nursing* Opal
Valenta LVN.
Licensure Intermediate care. *Beds* ICF 60.
Private Pay Patients 35%. *Certified*
Medicaid.
Owner Proprietary corp (Diversicare Corp of
America).
Admissions Requirements Medical
examination; Physician's request.
Staff RNs; LPNs; Nurses' aides; Activities
coordinators; Dietitians.
Languages Spanish.
Facilities Dining room; Activities room;
Laundry room; Barber/Beauty shop;
Spacious grounds; Van.

Activities Arts & crafts; Games; Reading
groups; Prayer groups; Shopping trips;
Dances/Social/Cultural gatherings;
Intergenerational programs; Pet therapy;
Picnics.

Luling Care Center
PO Box 312, 501 W Austin St, Luling, TX
78648
(512) 875-5628
Admin Genevieve McCleary. *Dir of Nursing*
Sue Clay.
Licensure Intermediate care. *Beds* ICF 56.
Certified Medicaid.
Owner Privately owned.
Admissions Requirements Medical
examination.
Staff RNs 1 (pt); LPNs 5 (ft); Nurses' aides 14
(ft); Activities coordinators 1 (ft); Dietitians
1 (ft).
Facilities Dining room; Activities room;
Crafts room; Laundry room; Barber/Beauty
shop.
Activities Arts & crafts; Games; Prayer groups;
Movies; Shopping trips; Dances/Social/
Cultural gatherings.

Lytle

Lytle Nursing Home Inc
614 Oak St, Lytle, TX 78052
(512) 772-3557
Admin Nancy L Pawelek.
Medical Dir Dr Emanuel DeNoia.
Licensure Intermediate care. *Beds* 70.
Certified Medicaid.
Staff RNs 1 (pt); LPNs 5 (ft); Nurses' aides 18
(ft); Activities coordinators 1 (ft); Dietitians
1 (pt).
Facilities Dining room; Activities room;
Chapel; Crafts room; Laundry room; Barber/
Beauty shop.
Activities Arts & crafts; Games; Movies;
Shopping trips; Dances/Social/Cultural
gatherings.

Mabank

Mabank Nursing Home
Rte 1 Box 9, 110 W Trouple, Mabank, TX
75147
(214) 887-2436
Admin Johnny M Adams.
Licensure Intermediate care. *Beds* 60.
Certified Medicaid.
Owner Proprietary corp.

Madisonville

Madisonville Nursing Home No 1
PO Box 40, 411 E Collard St, Madisonville,
TX 77864
(409) 348-2735
Admin Norman G Morris.
Licensure Intermediate care; Nursing home.
Beds ICF 52. *Certified* Medicaid; Private
Pay.
Owner Privately owned.
Admissions Requirements Medical
examination; Physician's request.
Staff RNs; LPNs; Nurses' aides; Activities
coordinators; Dietitians.
Facilities Dining room; Activities room;
Laundry room; Barber/Beauty shop.
Activities Arts & crafts; Cards; Games;
Reading groups; Movies; Parties; Special
gatherings, etc.

Madisonville Nursing Home No 2
PO Box 40, 410 E Collard St, Madisonville,
TX 77864
(409) 348-6166
Admin Susanne Morris.
Licensure Intermediate care. *Beds* ICF 54.
Certified Medicaid; Private Pay.
Owner Privately owned.

Admissions Requirements Medical
examination; Physician's request.
Staff RNs; LPNs; Nurses' aides; Activities
coordinators; Dietitians.
Facilities Dining room; Activities room;
Laundry room; Barber/Beauty shop.
Activities Arts & crafts; Cards; Games;
Reading groups; Movies; Parties; Special
gatherings, etc.

Madisonville Nursing Home No 3
PO Box 40, 413 E Collard St, Madisonville,
TX 77864
(409) 348-3860
Admin Larry Goodrum.
Licensure Intermediate care. *Beds* ICF 30.
Certified Medicaid; Private Pay.
Owner Privately owned.
Admissions Requirements Medical
examination; Physician's request.
Staff RNs; LPNs; Nurses' aides; Activities
coordinators; Dietitians.
Facilities Dining room; Activities room;
Laundry room; Barber/Beauty shop.
Activities Arts & crafts; Cards; Games;
Reading groups; Movies; Parties; Special
gatherings, etc.

Malakoff

Cedar Lake Nursing Home
Rte 3 Box 3045, Hwy 31 W, Malakoff, TX
75148
(214) 489-1702, 489-1706
Admin Douglas B Humble III.
Medical Dir Jo Sparks.
Licensure Intermediate care; Retirement;
Alzheimer's care. *Beds* ICF 60. *Certified*
Medicaid.
Owner Proprietary corp.
Admissions Requirements Medical
examination; Physician's request.
Staff Physicians 1 (pt); RNs 2 (ft); Nurses'
aides 15 (ft), 5 (pt); Physical therapists 1
(pt); Activities coordinators 1 (pt); Dietitians
1 (pt); Ophthalmologists 1 (pt); Dentists 1
(pt); 25 (ft); LVNs 6 (ft).
Languages Spanish.
Facilities Dining room; Physical therapy
room; Activities room; Crafts room; Laundry
room; Barber/Beauty shop; Library.
Activities Arts & crafts; Cards; Games;
Reading groups; Prayer groups; Movies;
Shopping trips; Dances/Social/Cultural
gatherings; Newspaper.

Manchaca

Marbridge Villa
Box 250, FM 1626 & Bliss Spiller, Manchaca,
TX 78652
(512) 282-3233
Licensure Nursing. *Beds* Nursing 52.

Mansfield

Mansfield Nursing Home
1402 E Broad St, Mansfield, TX 76063
(817) 477-2176
Admin Peggy M Snow.
Medical Dir Larry Myer MD.
Licensure Skilled care. *Beds* 127. *Certified*
Medicaid.
Owner Proprietary corp (Summit Health Ltd).
Admissions Requirements Minimum age 21;
Medical examination; Physician's request.
Staff RNs 1 (ft), 3 (pt); Activities coordinators
1 (ft); Dietitians 1 (pt).
Facilities Dining room; Physical therapy
room; Activities room; Chapel; Crafts room;
Laundry room; Barber/Beauty shop.
Activities Arts & crafts; Cards; Games;
Reading groups; Prayer groups; Movies;
Shopping trips; Dances/Social/Cultural
gatherings.

Marble Falls

Northwood Health Care Center
1109 Northwood Dr, Marble Falls, TX 78654
(512) 693-3551
Admin Darlene Cayce. *Dir of Nursing* Carol
Klotz. *Medical Dir* Richard Repert MD.
Licensure Intermediate care. *Beds* ICF 110.
Certified Medicaid.
Owner Proprietary corp (ARA Living
Centers).
Admissions Requirements Minimum age 16;
Medical examination; Physician's request.
Staff RNs 1 (ft); LPNs 8 (ft), 2 (pt); Nurses'
aides 26 (ft); Activities coordinators 1 (ft);
Dietitians 1 (ft).
Languages Spanish, German.
Facilities Dining room; Physical therapy
room; Activities room; Laundry room;
Barber/Beauty shop.
Activities Arts & crafts; Cards; Games;
Reading groups; Prayer groups; Movies;
Shopping trips; Dances/Social/Cultural
gatherings.

Marlin

Elmwood Nursing Center
221 Virginia St, Marlin, TX 76661
(817) 883-5548
Admin William E Hazel. *Dir of Nursing*
Regina Koslosky RN. *Medical Dir* Dr D R
Sweatland.
Licensure Intermediate care. *Beds* ICF 141.
Private Pay Patients 50%. *Certified*
Medicaid.
Owner Proprietary corp.
Admissions Requirements Medical
examination; Physician's request.
Staff Physicians 1 (ft); RNs 1 (ft); LPNs 14
(ft); Nurses' aides 25 (ft); Dietitians 1 (ft).
Facilities Dining room; Activities room;
Crafts room; Laundry room; Barber/Beauty
shop.
Activities Arts & crafts; Cards; Games;
Reading groups; Prayer groups; Movies;
Shopping trips.

Golden Years Rest Home
PO Box 272, 351 Coleman St, Marlin, TX
76661
(817) 883-5508
Admin Carolyn Liberty.
Medical Dir William F McKinley.
Licensure Intermediate care. *Beds* 96.
Certified Medicaid.
Owner Proprietary corp (ARA Living
Centers).
Staff RNs 1 (ft); Nurses' aides 15 (ft), 4 (pt);
Activities coordinators 1 (ft); Dietitians 1
(pt).
Facilities Dining room; Activities room;
Crafts room; Laundry room; Barber/Beauty
shop.
Activities Arts & crafts; Cards; Games;
Reading groups; Prayer groups; Movies;
Shopping trips; Dances/Social/Cultural
gatherings.

Marshall

Colonial Park Nursing Home
PO Box 1869, 509 S Grove, Marshall, TX
75670
(214) 935-7886
Admin Douglas R Mehling. *Dir of Nursing*
Nancy Pringle RN.
Licensure Skilled care; Intermediate care. *Beds*
SNF 160. *Certified* Medicaid; Medicare.
Owner Proprietary corp (Beverly Enterprises).
Staff RNs 3 (ft), 2 (pt); LPNs 22 (ft), 4 (pt);
Nurses' aides 42 (ft), 4 (pt); Activities
coordinators 2 (ft).
Facilities Dining room; Physical therapy
room; Activities room; Chapel; Crafts room;
Laundry room; Barber/Beauty shop; Library.

Activities Arts & crafts; Cards; Games;
Movies; Shopping trips; Dances/Social/
Cultural gatherings.

Marshall Manor Nursing Home Inc
1007 S Washington St, Marshall, TX 75670
(214) 935-7971
Admin Julius E Cox Jr. *Dir of Nursing*
Patricia Salituro RN. *Medical Dir* George E
Bennett MD.
Licensure Skilled care; Intermediate care. *Beds*
SNF 50; ICF 129. *Certified* Medicaid;
Medicare.
Owner Proprietary corp.
Admissions Requirements Physician's request.
Staff RNs 3 (ft), 1 (pt); LPNs 22 (ft), 1 (pt);
Nurses' aides 45 (ft), 6 (pt); Activities
coordinators 4 (ft), 1 (pt).
Facilities Dining room; Activities room;
Crafts room; Laundry room; Barber/Beauty
shop; Library.
Activities Arts & crafts; Cards; Games;
Reading groups; Prayer groups; Movies;
Shopping trips; Dances/Social/Cultural
gatherings.

Merritt Plaza Nursing Home
207 W Merritt, Marshall, TX 75670
(214) 938-3793
Admin Tom Bowen.
Medical Dir Dr George E Bennett.
Licensure Intermediate care. *Beds* 170.
Certified Medicaid.
Owner Proprietary corp (Beverly Enterprises).
Admissions Requirements Medical
examination; Physician's request.
Staff RNs 1 (ft); LPNs 15 (ft); Nurses' aides
34 (ft); Physical therapists 1 (ft); Speech
therapists 1 (ft); Activities coordinators 2
(ft); Dietitians 1 (ft).
Facilities Dining room; Activities room;
Laundry room; Barber/Beauty shop.
Activities Arts & crafts; Games; Reading
groups; Prayer groups; Movies; Shopping
trips; Dances/Social/Cultural gatherings.

Suburban Acres Nursing Center
PO Box 366, Elysian Fields Rd, Marshall, TX
75670
(214) 938-6679
Admin Gloria J Johnson.
Licensure Intermediate care. *Beds* 74.
Certified Medicaid.
Owner Proprietary corp.

Mart

Park Plaza Nursing Home
1201 McLennan Ave, Mart, TX 76664
(817) 876-2531
Admin John W O'Connor.
Licensure Intermediate care. *Beds* 121.
Certified Medicaid.
Owner Proprietary corp.

Mason

Mason Care Center
PO Drawer D, 101 College, Mason, TX 76856
(915) 347-5181
Admin Harvey W Zombro Sr.
Medical Dir Michael Richey MD.
Licensure Intermediate care. *Beds* 60.
Certified Medicaid.
Admissions Requirements Minimum age 18;
Medical examination; Physician's request.
Staff Physicians 2 (ft); LPNs 6 (ft); Nurses'
aides 12 (ft); Physical therapists 1 (ft);
Speech therapists 1 (ft); Activities
coordinators 1 (ft); Dietitians 1 (pt); Dentists
1 (pt).
Facilities Dining room; Physical therapy
room; Activities room; Crafts room; Laundry
room; Barber/Beauty shop.

Activities Arts & crafts; Cards; Games;
Reading groups; Prayer groups; Movies;
Shopping trips; Dances/Social/Cultural
gatherings.

McAllen

Colonial Manor of McAllen
209 Hackberry, McAllen, TX 78501
(512) 686-2243
Admin Elma N Martinez. *Dir of Nursing*
Rosemary Knowles RN.
Licensure Intermediate care; Retirement. *Beds*
ICF 59. *Certified* Medicaid.
Owner Proprietary corp (Beverly Enterprises).
Admissions Requirements Physician's request.
Staff Physicians 1 (pt); RNs 1 (ft); LPNs 5
(ft), 3 (pt); Nurses' aides 14 (ft), 5 (pt);
Activities coordinators 1 (ft); Dietitians 1
(pt).
Languages Spanish.
Facilities Dining room; Activities room;
Crafts room; Laundry room.
Activities Cards; Games; Prayer groups;
Movies; Shopping trips; Dances/Social/
Cultural gatherings.

McAllen Good Samaritan Center
812 Houston Ave, McAllen, TX 78501
(512) 682-6331
Admin Josefina R Zarate. *Dir of Nursing*
Marie Hemmer.
Licensure Skilled care. *Beds* SNF 100. *Private
Pay Patients* 15%. *Certified* Medicaid;
Medicare.
Owner Nonprofit corp (Evangelical Lutheran/
Good Samaritan Society).
Admissions Requirements Resident assessment
only.
Staff RNs; LPNs; Nurses' aides; Physical
therapists; Activities coordinators; Dietitians.
Languages Spanish.
Affiliation Lutheran.
Facilities Dining room; Physical therapy
room; Activities room; Crafts room; Laundry
room; Barber/Beauty shop.
Activities Arts & crafts; Games; Reading
groups; Prayer groups; Dances/Social/
Cultural gatherings; Family involvement;
Community involvement.

McAllen Nursing Center
600 N Cynthia, McAllen, TX 78501
(512) 631-2265
Admin Betty Lofton. *Dir of Nursing* Ronnie
Barrera RN. *Medical Dir* Dr Popek.
Licensure Skilled care. *Beds* SNF 100.
Certified Medicaid; Medicare.
Owner Proprietary corp (Beverly Enterprises).
Admissions Requirements Physician's request.
Staff Physicians 2 (ft), 20 (pt); RNs 3 (ft), 1
(pt); LPNs 15 (ft), 4 (pt); Nurses' aides 20
(ft), 6 (pt); Speech therapists 1 (pt);
Activities coordinators 1 (ft); Dietitians 1
(ft); Ophthalmologists 1 (pt); Dentists 1 (pt).
Languages Spanish.
Facilities Dining room; Physical therapy
room; Activities room; Crafts room; Laundry
room; Barber/Beauty shop.
Activities Arts & crafts; Cards; Games; Prayer
groups; Movies; Outings.

Retama Manor Nursing Center
900 S 12th St, McAllen, TX 78501
(512) 682-4171
Admin Maria Dalia Welch. *Dir of Nursing*
Alta Quiroz RN. *Medical Dir* Richard
Barrera MD.
Licensure Skilled care; Intermediate care;
Supervised living; Personal care; Alzheimer's
care. *Beds* SNF 40; ICF 60; Personal 27.
Certified Medicaid; Medicare.
Owner Proprietary corp (ARA Living
Centers).
Admissions Requirements Minimum age 18;
Medical examination; Physician's request.
Staff RNs 1 (ft); LPNs 12 (ft); Nurses' aides
30 (ft), 4 (pt); Activities coordinators 1 (ft).

Facilities Dining room; Physical therapy room; Activities room; Chapel; Crafts room; Laundry room; Barber/Beauty shop; Library.
Activities Arts & crafts; Cards; Games; Reading groups; Prayer groups; Movies; Shopping trips; Dances/Social/Cultural gatherings; Entertainment.

Twinbrooke South—McAllen
1000 N McColl Rd, McAllen, TX 78501
(512) 682-6101
Admin Carl F Lueg Jr. *Dir of Nursing* Betty S Lueg.
Licensure Intermediate care; Alzheimer's care. *Beds* ICF 63. *Certified* Medicaid.
Owner Proprietary corp.
Admissions Requirements Physician's request.
Staff Physicians 1 (pt); RNs 1 (pt); LPNs 5 (ft); Nurses' aides 42 (ft), 3 (pt); Physical therapists 1 (pt); Activities coordinators 1 (ft); Dietitians 1 (pt); Ophthalmologists 1 (pt); Podiatrists 1 (pt).
Facilities Dining room; Activities room; Chapel; Laundry room; Barber/Beauty shop; Library.
Activities Arts & crafts; Cards; Games; Reading groups; Prayer groups; Movies; Shopping trips; Dances/Social/Cultural gatherings; Intergenerational programs; Pet therapy.

Village Convalescent Center
615 N Ware Rd, McAllen, TX 78501
(512) 682-4161, 682-8047 FAX
Admin Coral Ann Rung. *Dir of Nursing* Joy Hagne RN. *Medical Dir* Monique Popek MD.
Licensure Skilled care; Intermediate care. *Beds* SNF 60; ICF 54. *Private Pay Patients* 30%. *Certified* Medicaid; Medicare.
Owner Proprietary corp (American Manor Inc).
Admissions Requirements Physician's request.
Staff RNs 3 (ft), 1 (pt); LPNs 10 (ft), 3 (pt); Nurses' aides 35 (ft), 6 (pt); Physical therapists (contracted); Recreational therapists 1 (pt); Occupational therapists 1 (pt); Speech therapists 1 (pt); Activities coordinators 1 (ft); Dietitians 1 (pt).
Languages Spanish.
Facilities Dining room; Physical therapy room; Activities room; Crafts room; Laundry room; Barber/Beauty shop; Library; IV therapy; Respirator care; Critical care.
Activities Arts & crafts; Cards; Games; Reading groups; Prayer groups; Movies; Shopping trips; Dances/Social/Cultural gatherings; Intergenerational programs; Pet therapy.

McCamey

Upton County Convalescent Center
PO Box 1200, 305 S Burleson, McCamey, TX 79752
(915) 652-8626
Admin James R Queen Jr. *Dir of Nursing* Beverly J Nichols LVN.
Licensure Intermediate care. *Beds* ICF 30. *Certified* Medicaid.
Owner Publicly owned.
Admissions Requirements Medical examination.
Staff Physicians 5 (pt); RNs 1 (pt); LPNs 3 (ft), 3 (pt); Nurses' aides 10 (ft); Activities coordinators 1 (ft); Dietitians 2 (pt).
Languages Spanish.
Facilities Dining room; Activities room; Chapel; Laundry room; Barber/Beauty shop.
Activities Arts & crafts; Cards; Games; Prayer groups; Dances/Social/Cultural gatherings.

McGregor

Westview Manor
414 Johnson Dr, McGregor, TX 76657
(817) 840-3281

Admin Ray Dean Elliott.
Licensure Skilled care; Intermediate care. *Beds* 154. *Certified* Medicaid.
Owner Proprietary corp.

McKinney

Pavilion Nursing Home
PO Box 556, 1720 N McDonald, McKinney, TX 75069
(214) 542-3565, 542-4418
Admin Peggy Jones.
Licensure Intermediate care. *Beds* 140. *Certified* Medicaid.
Owner Proprietary corp (ARA Living Centers).

University Nursing Center
2030 W University Dr, McKinney, TX 75069
(214) 542-2695
Admin Billy Hill.
Licensure Skilled care. *Beds* 112. *Certified* Medicaid.
Owner Proprietary corp.

McLean

McLean Care Center
PO Box 280, 605 W 7th, McLean, TX 79057
(806) 779-2469
Admin Billy W Thomas. *Dir of Nursing* Tina L Thomas LVN. *Medical Dir* H F Fabian MD.
Licensure Intermediate care. *Beds* ICF 59. *Private Pay Patients* 40%. *Certified* Medicaid.
Owner Proprietary corp (Centex).
Admissions Requirements Minimum age 18.
Staff RNs; LPNs; Nurses' aides; Activities coordinators; Dietitians.
Facilities Dining room; Activities room; Crafts room; Laundry room; Barber/Beauty shop.
Activities Arts & crafts; Cards; Games; Reading groups; Prayer groups; Movies.

Memphis

Memphis Convalescent Center
PO Box 670, 1415 N 18th St, Memphis, TX 79245
(806) 259-3566
Admin Henry W Hall.
Licensure Intermediate care. *Beds* 80. *Certified* Medicaid.
Admissions Requirements Physician's request.
Staff RNs 1 (pt); LPNs 7 (ft); Activities coordinators 1 (ft).
Facilities Dining room; Activities room; Laundry room; Barber/Beauty shop.
Activities Arts & crafts; Games; Reading groups; Prayer groups; Shopping trips; Dances/Social/Cultural gatherings.

Menard

Menard Manor
PO Box 608, 100 Gay St, Menard, TX 76859
(915) 396-4515
Admin Edward Zachary.
Licensure Intermediate care. *Beds* 40. *Certified* Medicaid.
Staff LPNs 3 (ft), 1 (pt); Nurses' aides 11 (ft), 6 (pt); Activities coordinators 1 (ft).
Facilities Dining room; Physical therapy room; Activities room; Chapel; Laundry room; Barber/Beauty shop.
Activities Arts & crafts; Cards; Games; Reading groups; Prayer groups; Movies; Shopping trips; Dances/Social/Cultural gatherings.

Meridian

Meridian Geriatric Center
PO Box 437, 1110 N Main, Meridian, TX 76665
(817) 435-2357
Admin Truett Johnson. *Dir of Nursing* Kathryn Hallmark. *Medical Dir* Dr Dewayne Helms.
Licensure Intermediate care. *Beds* ICF 92. *Private Pay Patients* 10%. *Certified* Medicaid.
Owner Publicly owned.
Admissions Requirements Medical examination.
Staff RNs 1 (pt); LPNs 8 (ft), 1 (pt); Nurses' aides 35 (ft); Activities coordinators 1 (ft); Dietitians 1 (pt).
Facilities Dining room; Laundry room; Barber/Beauty shop.
Activities Arts & crafts; Games; Prayer groups; Movies; Shopping trips; Dances/Social/Cultural gatherings; Intergenerational programs.

Mesquite

Christian Care Center
1000 Wiggins Pkwy, Mesquite, TX 75150
(214) 686-3000
Admin Lucy Withrow. *Dir of Nursing* David Forgy RN. *Medical Dir* Roy Wagoner MD.
Licensure Skilled care; Intermediate care; Private pay; Independent living; Personal care. *Beds* SNF 60; ICF 60; Private pay 60; Independent living apartments 149; Personal care units 61. *Private Pay Patients* 61%. *Certified* Medicaid; Medicare.
Owner Nonprofit corp (Christian Care Centers Inc).
Admissions Requirements Medical examination; Physician's request.
Staff Physicians 3 (pt); RNs 3 (ft); LPNs 18 (ft); Nurses' aides 54 (ft); Physical therapists (contracted); Reality therapists (contracted); Recreational therapists (contracted); Occupational therapists (contracted); Speech therapists (contracted); Activities coordinators 2 (ft); Dietitians 1 (pt).
Languages Spanish.
Affiliation Church of Christ.
Facilities Dining room; Physical therapy room; Activities room; Chapel; Crafts room; Laundry room; Barber/Beauty shop; Library.
Activities Arts & crafts; Cards; Games; Reading groups; Prayer groups; Shopping trips; Dances/Social/Cultural gatherings; Intergenerational programs.

Heritage Place
825 W Kearney, Mesquite, TX 75149
(214) 288-7668
Admin Harvey Junker. *Dir of Nursing* Lynn Craft RN. *Medical Dir* John Pataki MD.
Licensure Intermediate care. *Beds* ICF 152. *Certified* Medicare.
Owner Proprietary corp.
Admissions Requirements Minimum age 60; Medical examination; Physician's request.
Staff RNs 3 (ft), 1 (pt); LPNs 8 (ft), 5 (pt); Nurses' aides 27 (ft), 6 (pt); Physical therapists; Recreational therapists; Speech therapists; Activities coordinators 1 (ft); Dietitians 1 (pt).
Facilities Dining room; Activities room; Chapel; Laundry room; Barber/Beauty shop; Library.
Activities Arts & crafts; Cards; Games; Reading groups; Prayer groups; Movies; Shopping trips; Dances/Social/Cultural gatherings.

Mesquite Tree Nursing Center
434 Paza Dr, Mesquite, TX 75149
(214) 288-6489

Admin Barbara A Roblin. *Dir of Nursing*
Tony Jackson. *Medical Dir* Linus Miller
MD.
Licensure Intermediate care. *Beds* ICF 148.
Certified Medicaid.
Owner Proprietary corp (Beverly Enterprises).
Admissions Requirements Medical
examination; Physician's request.
Staff LPNs; Nurses' aides; Physical therapists
(contracted); Occupational therapists
(contracted); Speech therapists (contracted);
Activities coordinators; Dietitians;
Ophthalmologists (contracted); Podiatrists
(contracted); Audiologists (contracted).
Languages Sign.
Facilities Dining room; Laundry room;
Barber/Beauty shop.
Activities Arts & crafts; Cards; Games; Prayer
groups; Movies; Shopping trips; Dances/
Social/Cultural gatherings; Intergenerational
programs; Programs and services for deaf
residents.

Willow Bend Care Center
2231 Hwy 80 E, Mesquite, TX 75150
(214) 279-3601
Licensure Nursing. *Beds* Nursing 251.

Mexia

Haven Nursing Home
601 Terrace Ln, Mexia, TX 76667
(817) 562-5400
Admin Lola M Compton. *Dir of Nursing*
Margaret Bumpas RN.
Licensure Intermediate care. *Beds* ICF 74.
Certified Medicaid.
Owner Privately owned.
Admissions Requirements Medical
examination; Physician's request.
Staff Physicians; RNs; LPNs; Nurses' aides;
Physical therapists; Reality therapists;
Recreational therapists; Occupational
therapists; Speech therapists; Activities
coordinators; Dietitians; Ophthalmologists.
Facilities Dining room; Activities room;
Crafts room; Laundry room; Barber/Beauty
shop.
Activities Arts & crafts; Cards; Games;
Reading groups; Prayer groups; Movies;
Shopping trips; Dances/Social/Cultural
gatherings.

Manor Retirement & Convalescent Center
PO Box 710, 831 Tehuacana Hwy, Mexia, TX
76667
(817) 562-3867
Admin Ronald R Huggins.
Licensure Intermediate care. *Beds* 80.
Certified Medicaid.
Owner Proprietary corp.

Mexia Nursing Home
501 E Sumpter St, Mexia, TX 76667
(817) 562-5542
Admin John Thomas Wright.
Licensure Intermediate care. *Beds* 40.
Certified Medicaid.
Admissions Requirements Medical
examination; Physician's request.
Staff Physicians 1 (ft); LPNs 3 (ft), 4 (pt);
Nurses' aides 5 (ft), 8 (pt); Activities
coordinators 1 (ft).
Facilities Dining room; Activities room;
Laundry room.
Activities Arts & crafts; Cards; Games; Prayer
groups; Shopping trips; Dances/Social/
Cultural gatherings; Community events.

Mico

Wood Nursing Home
Star Rte Box 64, Mico, TX 78056
(512) 924-8183
Admin Yvonne B Wood. *Dir of Nursing* Anita
Esparza.
Licensure Intermediate care. *Beds* ICF 49.

Owner Privately owned.
Admissions Requirements Physician's request.
Staff Physicians; RNs 1 (pt); LPNs 4 (ft);
Nurses' aides 13 (ft), 4 (pt); Activities
coordinators 1 (ft); Dietitians 1 (pt).
Languages Spanish.
Facilities Dining room; Physical therapy
room; Activities room; Laundry room.
Activities Arts & crafts; Cards; Games; Prayer
groups; Shopping trips; Dances/Social/
Cultural gatherings.

Midland

Lutheran Home—Permian Basin
3203 Sage, Midland, TX 79701
(915) 683-5403
Admin Marion Seba.
Medical Dir Debbie Shultz LVN.
Licensure Intermediate care; Retirement. *Beds*
ICF 114. *Certified* Medicaid.
Owner Nonprofit organization/foundation.
Admissions Requirements Minimum age 18;
Medical examination; Physician's request.
Affiliation Lutheran.
Facilities Dining room; Activities room;
Chapel; Laundry room; Barber/Beauty shop.
Activities Arts & crafts; Cards; Games;
Reading groups; Prayer groups; Movies;
Shopping trips; Dances/Social/Cultural
gatherings.

Mabee Health Care Center
2208 N Loop 250 W, Midland, TX 79707
(915) 689-9898
Licensure Nursing. *Beds* Nursing 120.

Midland Care Center Inc
2000 N Main, Midland, TX 79701
(915) 684-6613
Admin Betty R Gardner.
Licensure Intermediate care. *Beds* 118.
Certified Medicaid.
Owner Proprietary corp.

Sage Healthcare Center
3203 Sage, Midland, TX 79701
(915) 683-5403
Admin Edna Goodin.
Licensure Intermediate care. *Beds* 114.
Certified Medicaid.
Owner Proprietary corp.

Terrace Gardens Nursing Home
2901 W Ohio, Midland, TX 79701
(915) 694-8831
Admin Delores T Cregg.
Licensure Skilled care. *Beds* 60. *Certified*
Medicaid.
Owner Proprietary corp (Hillhaven Corp).

Terrace West Nursing Center
2800 N Midland Dr, Midland, TX 79707
(915) 697-3108
Admin J H Black.
Medical Dir Dr H F Page.
Licensure Intermediate care. *Beds* 150.
Certified Medicaid.
Owner Proprietary corp (Hillhaven Corp).
Admissions Requirements Medical
examination.
Staff Physicians 1 (pt); RNs 4 (ft); LPNs 12
(ft); Nurses' aides 31 (ft); Physical therapists
1 (pt); Occupational therapists 1 (pt); Speech
therapists 1 (pt); Activities coordinators 1
(ft); Dietitians 1 (pt); Dentists 1 (pt).
Facilities Dining room; Physical therapy
room; Activities room; Chapel; Crafts room;
Laundry room; Barber/Beauty shop.
Activities Arts & crafts; Cards; Games;
Reading groups; Prayer groups; Movies;
Shopping trips; Dances/Social/Cultural
gatherings.

Trinity Towers
2800 W Illinois, Midland, TX 79701
(915) 694-1691
Admin William G Saxton.

Licensure Intermediate care; Custodial care.
Beds ICF 60.
Owner Nonprofit corp.
Affiliation Presbyterian.

West Texas Care Center
2000 N Main, Midland, TX 79705
(915) 684-6613
Licensure Nursing. *Beds* Nursing 112.

Mineola

Hillview Nursing Home Inc
716 Mimosa Dr, Mineola, TX 75773
(214) 569-5366
Licensure Nursing. *Beds* Nursing 82.

Wood Memorial Nursing Center
PO Box 480, 320 Greenville Ave, Mineola,
TX 75773
(214) 569-3852
Admin Dana L Gentry. *Dir of Nursing* Mary
Cloud RN. *Medical Dir* R O Moore MD.
Licensure Intermediate care. *Beds* ICF 113.
Certified Medicaid.
Owner Proprietary corp.
Staff RNs 2 (ft); LPNs 4 (ft); Nurses' aides 20
(ft); Physical therapists 1 (pt); Recreational
therapists 1 (pt); Occupational therapists 1
(pt); Speech therapists 1 (pt); Activities
coordinators 1 (ft); Dietitians 1 (pt);
Ophthalmologists 1 (pt); Podiatrists 1 (pt).
Facilities Dining room; Barber/Beauty shop.
Activities Arts & crafts; Cards; Games; Prayer
groups; Movies; Shopping trips; Dances/
Social/Cultural gatherings.

Mineral Wells

Mineral Wells Care Center
316 SW 25th Ave, Mineral Wells, TX 76067
(817) 325-1358, 325-5802 FAX
Admin Linda Ratzlaff. *Dir of Nursing* Beth
Hott. *Medical Dir* William O'Quin.
Licensure Skilled care; Intermediate care. *Beds*
SNF 61; ICF 61. *Certified* Medicaid;
Medicare.
Owner Proprietary corp (Texas Health
Enterprises Inc).
Admissions Requirements Medical
examination; Physician's request.
Staff RNs; LPNs; Nurses' aides; Physical
therapists; Occupational therapists; Speech
therapists; Activities coordinators; Dietitians;
Podiatrists; Audiologists.
Languages Spanish.
Facilities Dining room; Laundry room;
Barber/Beauty shop.
Activities Arts & crafts; Cards; Games;
Reading groups; Prayer groups; Movies;
Shopping trips; Dances/Social/Cultural
gatherings; Intergenerational programs; Pet
therapy.

Palo Pinto Nursing Center
Star Rte Box 23, Mineral Wells, TX 76067
(817) 325-7813
Admin Terry W Matthews.
Licensure Intermediate care. *Beds* 106.
Certified Medicaid.
Owner Proprietary corp (Beverly Enterprises).

Resort Lodge Inc
401 NW 4th St, Mineral Wells, TX 76067
(817) 325-3744
Admin Florence W Kearby.
Licensure Skilled care. *Beds* 52. *Certified*
Medicaid.
Owner Proprietary corp.

Missouri City

Buckner Baptist Haven
2223 Glenn Lakes Ln, Missouri City, TX
77459-4436
(713) 465-3406

Admin Elaine W Brewer. *Dir of Nursing* Mary Ellen Gay.
Licensure Intermediate care; Custodial care; Retirement. *Beds* ICF 60; Custodial care 93. *Certified* Medicaid.
Owner Nonprofit corp (Buckner Bapt Retire Vlg).
Admissions Requirements Minimum age 65; Medical examination.
Affiliation Baptist.
Facilities Dining room; Activities room; Chapel; Crafts room; Laundry room; Barber/Beauty shop; Library.
Activities Cards; Games; Movies; Dances/Social/Cultural gatherings; Church services in chapel.

Colony House
4710 Lexington Blvd, Missouri City, TX 77459
(713) 499-4710
Licensure Nursing. *Beds* Nursing 105.

Monahans

West Wind Care Center
PO Box 1025, 1200 W 15th St, Monahans, TX 79756
(915) 943-2741
Admin Julia Martinez.
Licensure Intermediate care. *Beds* 98. *Certified* Medicaid.
Admissions Requirements Medical examination; Physician's request.
Staff RNs 1 (pt); LPNs 5 (pt); Nurses' aides 10 (ft); Activities coordinators 1 (ft); Dietitians 1 (pt).
Facilities Dining room; Activities room; Crafts room; Laundry room; Barber/Beauty shop.
Activities Arts & crafts; Cards; Games; Reading groups; Prayer groups; Movies; Shopping trips; Dances/Social/Cultural gatherings.

Moody

Moody Care Center
PO Box 218, 7th & Church Sts, Moody, TX 76557
(817) 853-2631
Admin Juanita Lightfoot. *Dir of Nursing* Jane Smith.
Licensure Intermediate care. *Beds* ICF 57. *Certified* Medicaid.
Owner Proprietary corp (Campbell, White & Associates).
Admissions Requirements Minimum age 18; Medical examination; Physician's request.
Staff LPNs; Nurses' aides; Physical therapists; Occupational therapists; Speech therapists; Activities coordinators; Dietitians.
Facilities Dining room; Activities room; Crafts room; Laundry room.
Activities Arts & crafts; Cards; Games; Reading groups; Prayer groups; Movies; Shopping trips; Dances/Social/Cultural gatherings.

Morton

Roberts Memorial Nursing Home
PO Box 952, 211 W Garfield, Morton, TX 79346
(806) 266-8866
Admin Clota M Templeton.
Licensure Intermediate care. *Beds* 30. *Certified* Medicaid.
Owner Proprietary corp.

Moulton

Shady Oak Nursing Home Inc
PO Drawer D, 101 S Lancaster, Moulton, TX 77975
(512) 596-7777

Admin Edward A Darilek.
Licensure Intermediate care. *Beds* 61. *Certified* Medicaid.
Admissions Requirements Minimum age 21; Medical examination; Physician's request.
Staff RNs 1 (pt); LPNs 7 (ft); Nurses' aides 13 (ft), 8 (pt); Activities coordinators 1 (ft); Dietitians 1 (pt).
Facilities Dining room; Activities room; Laundry room.
Activities Arts & crafts; Cards; Games.

Mount Pleasant

Currey Nursing Home Inc
901 N Jefferson, Mount Pleasant, TX 75455
(214) 572-4361
Admin Thelma Lee Landers. *Dir of Nursing* Reba Jefferson. *Medical Dir* G B Taylor DO.
Licensure Intermediate care; Alzheimer's care. *Beds* ICF 56. *Certified* Medicaid.
Owner Proprietary corp.
Admissions Requirements Physician's request.
Staff LPNs; Nurses' aides; Dietitians.
Facilities Dining room; Activities room; Laundry room; Barber/Beauty shop; Library.
Activities Arts & crafts; Cards; Games; Reading groups; Prayer groups; Shopping trips; Dances/Social/Cultural gatherings.

Geras Nursing Home
316 W 7th St, Mount Pleasant, TX 75455
(214) 572-3693
Admin Janice K Graham.
Licensure Intermediate care. *Beds* 101. *Certified* Medicaid.
Owner Proprietary corp (Summit Health Ltd).
Staff RNs 1 (ft); LPNs 7 (ft), 1 (pt); Nurses' aides 23 (ft), 2 (pt); Activities coordinators 1 (ft); Dietitians 1 (ft).
Facilities Dining room; Activities room; Crafts room.
Activities Arts & crafts; Cards; Games; Prayer groups; Dances/Social/Cultural gatherings.

Golden Years Lodge
1606 Memorial St, Mount Pleasant, TX 75455
(214) 572-3618
Admin Margaret R Strain. *Dir of Nursing* Georgia Lide RN.
Licensure Skilled care. *Beds* SNF 128. *Certified* Medicaid; Medicare.
Owner Proprietary corp (Truco Inc).
Admissions Requirements Physician's request.
Staff Physicians 1 (pt); RNs 2 (ft), 10 (pt); LPNs 11 (ft); Nurses' aides 30 (ft), 5 (pt); Reality therapists 1 (ft); Activities coordinators 1 (ft); Dietitians 2 (pt).
Languages Spanish.
Facilities Dining room; Physical therapy room; Activities room; Chapel; Laundry room; Barber/Beauty shop.
Activities Arts & crafts; Cards; Games; Prayer groups; Movies; Shopping trips; Dances/Social/Cultural gatherings.

Mt Pleasant Hospitality House
804 W 16th, Mount Pleasant, TX 75455
(214) 572-9893
Licensure Nursing. *Beds* Nursing 128.

Physicians Nursing & Convalescent Center
2101 N Mulberry, Mount Pleasant, TX 75455
(214) 572-6621
Admin Mary Sue Quarles.
Licensure Skilled care; Intermediate care. *Beds* 80. *Certified* Medicaid; Medicare.
Owner Proprietary corp (Beverly Enterprises).
Admissions Requirements Physician's request.
Staff RNs 2 (ft); LPNs 7 (ft); Nurses' aides 20 (ft), 4 (pt); Physical therapists; Speech therapists; Activities coordinators 1 (ft); Dietitians.
Facilities Dining room; Activities room; Laundry room; Barber/Beauty shop.
Activities Arts & crafts; Games; Prayer groups; Movies; Dances/Social/Cultural gatherings.

Villa Nursing Center
PO Box 1597, FM 1734 & I30, Mount Pleasant, TX 75455
(214) 572-5511, 572-4328
Admin Milton R Kelley. *Dir of Nursing* Phyllis Aurty RN. *Medical Dir* Gary Taylor MD.
Licensure Skilled care; Retirement. *Beds* SNF 90. *Certified* Medicaid; Medicare.
Owner Proprietary corp.
Admissions Requirements Physician's request.
Staff Physicians; RNs; LPNs; Nurses' aides; Physical therapists; Reality therapists; Occupational therapists; Speech therapists; Activities coordinators; Dietitians; Ophthalmologists; Podiatrists; Dentists.
Facilities Dining room; Physical therapy room; Activities room; Chapel; Crafts room; Laundry room; Barber/Beauty shop; Library.
Activities Arts & crafts; Cards; Games; Reading groups; Prayer groups; Movies; Shopping trips; Dances/Social/Cultural gatherings.

Mount Vernon

Mission Manor Nursing Home
PO Box 600, Mount Vernon, TX 75457
(214) 537-4424
Admin Diane Newsom. *Dir of Nursing* Ivey Moore. *Medical Dir* Larry Balzer MD.
Licensure Intermediate care. *Beds* ICF 101. *Private Pay Patients* 39%. *Certified* Medicare.
Owner Privately owned.
Admissions Requirements Physician's request.
Staff Physicians 6 (pt); RNs 1 (pt); LPNs 8 (ft), 2 (pt); Nurses' aides 30 (ft), 5 (pt); Physical therapists 1 (pt); Speech therapists 1 (pt); Activities coordinators 1 (ft); Dietitians 1 (ft); Podiatrists 1 (pt).
Languages Spanish by request.
Facilities Dining room; Physical therapy room; Activities room; Crafts room; Laundry room; Barber/Beauty shop; Parlor.
Activities Arts & crafts; Cards; Games; Reading groups; Prayer groups; Movies; Dances/Social/Cultural gatherings; Intergenerational programs.

Terry Haven Nursing Home
PO Box 519, Mount Vernon, TX 75457
(214) 537-4332, 537-2571, 537-4865 FAX
Admin Irma Morris. *Dir of Nursing* Patsy Smith. *Medical Dir* Otto C Walling Jr MD.
Licensure Intermediate care. *Beds* ICF 65. *Certified* Medicaid.
Owner Proprietary corp (Texas Health Enterprises Inc).
Admissions Requirements Medical examination; Physician's request.
Staff Physicians 4 (pt); LPNs 6 (ft), 2 (pt); Nurses' aides 14 (ft), 3 (pt); Activities coordinators 1 (ft); Dietitians 1 (pt); Ophthalmologists 1 (pt).
Facilities Dining room; Activities room; Crafts room; Laundry room; Barber/Beauty shop; Library.
Activities Arts & crafts; Cards; Games; Reading groups; Prayer groups; Movies; Shopping trips; Dances/Social/Cultural gatherings.

Muenster

St Richard's Villa Inc
US Hwy 82 W, Muenster, TX 76252
(817) 759-2219
Admin Wesley D Fuson.
Licensure Intermediate care. *Beds* 30. *Certified* Medicaid.
Owner Proprietary corp.

Muleshoe

Muleshoe Nursing Home
106 W Ave H, Muleshoe, TX 79347
(806) 272-3861
Admin Jim Swanner.
Medical Dir Helen Bayless.
Licensure Intermediate care. *Beds* ICF 57.
  Certified Medicare.
Owner Nonprofit corp.
Admissions Requirements Minimum age 16;
  Medical examination; Physician's request.
Staff LPNs 4 (ft); Activities coordinators 1
  (ft); Dietitians 1 (ft).
Languages Spanish.
Facilities Dining room; Activities room;
  Crafts room; Laundry room; Barber/Beauty
  shop.
Activities Arts & crafts; Cards; Games;
  Reading groups; Movies; Dances/Social/
  Cultural gatherings.

Munday

Munday Nursing Center
PO Box 199, 421 W "F" St, Munday, TX
76371
(817) 422-4541
Admin Joyce Hardin.
Licensure Intermediate care. *Beds* 61.
  Certified Medicaid.
Owner Proprietary corp (Beverly Enterprises).

Nacogdoches

Nacogdoches Convalescent Center
PO Box 603, 3305 N St, Nacogdoches, TX
75961
(409) 564-0256
Admin Cynthia Motley.
Medical Dir Gwen McClendon.
Licensure Intermediate care. *Beds* ICF 68.
  Certified Medicaid.
Owner Proprietary corp (Cantex Healthcare
  Centers).
Facilities Dining room; Laundry room;
  Barber/Beauty shop.
Activities Arts & crafts; Games; Prayer groups;
  Movies.

North Place Nursing Center
227 Russell Blvd, Nacogdoches, TX 75961
(409) 564-4596, 564-6824 FAX
Admin Joyce Lewis. *Dir of Nursing* Karen
  Stange RNC BSN. *Medical Dir* L W Snider
  MD.
Licensure Skilled care; Intermediate care. *Beds*
  SNF 34; ICF 116. *Private Pay Patients* 50%.
  Certified Medicaid; Medicare.
Owner Privately owned.
Admissions Requirements Medical
  examination.
Staff RNs; LPNs; Nurses' aides; Physical
  therapists; Occupational therapists; Speech
  therapists; Activities coordinators; Dietitians.
Facilities Dining room; Physical therapy
  room; Activities room; Laundry room;
  Barber/Beauty shop; Library.
Activities Arts & crafts; Games; Prayer groups;
  Movies; Shopping trips; Pet therapy.

Oak Manor Nursing Home
1200 Ferguson, Nacogdoches, TX 75961
(409) 564-7359
Admin Debbie Y Williams. *Dir of Nursing*
  Curtisa Christian.
Licensure Intermediate care; Alzheimer's care.
  Beds ICF 64. *Certified* Medicaid.
Owner Proprietary corp (ARA Living
  Centers).
Facilities Dining room; Activities room;
  Laundry room; Barber/Beauty shop.
Activities Arts & crafts; Cards; Games;
  Reading groups; Prayer groups; Movies;
  Shopping trips; Dances/Social/Cultural
  gatherings.

Pine Crest Nursing Home
2612 Williams St, Nacogdoches, TX 75961
(713) 564-7603
Admin Charles F Williams.
Licensure Intermediate care. *Beds* 56.
  Certified Medicaid.
Admissions Requirements Medical
  examination; Physician's request.
Staff Physicians 1 (pt); RNs 2 (pt); LPNs
  (LVN) 2 (ft), 2 (pt); Nurses' aides 10 (ft);
  Activities coordinators 1 (ft); Dietitians 3
  (ft), 2 (pt); Dentists 1 (pt).
Facilities Dining room; Activities room;
  Laundry room; Library.
Activities Arts & crafts; Games; Prayer groups;
  Movies; Shopping trips.

Rock Haven Nursing Center
401 SE Stallings Dr, Nacogdoches, TX 75961
(713) 569-9411
Admin C Wayne Hopson.
Licensure Skilled care. *Beds* 60. *Certified*
  Medicaid.
Owner Proprietary corp.

Westridge Manor Inc
PO Box 1951, 611 W Stallings Dr,
  Nacogdoches, TX 75961
(409) 564-1138
Admin Edward Williamson.
Medical Dir Jean Nichols.
Licensure Intermediate care; Personal care;
  Alzheimer's care. *Beds* ICF 86; Personal 10.
  Certified Medicaid.
Owner Proprietary corp.
Staff RNs 1 (pt); LPNs 8 (ft), 2 (pt); Nurses'
  aides 21 (ft), 4 (pt); Activities coordinators 1
  (ft); Dietitians 1 (pt).
Facilities Dining room; Barber/Beauty shop.
Activities Arts & crafts; Games; Prayer groups;
  Movies; Shopping trips; Dances/Social/
  Cultural gatherings.

Naples

Redbud Retreat Nursing Home
Rte 2 Box 2, Floyd St, Naples, TX 75568
(214) 897-5694
Admin Faye Sullivan.
Licensure Intermediate care. *Beds* ICF 86.
  Certified Medicaid.
Owner Privately owned.
Admissions Requirements Minimum age 21;
  Medical examination; Physician's request.
Staff Physicians 1 (pt); RNs 2 (pt); LPNs 10
  (pt); Nurses' aides 40 (pt); Physical
  therapists; Recreational therapists 1 (pt);
  Activities coordinators 1 (pt); Dietitians 1
  (pt).
Facilities Dining room; Physical therapy
  room; Activities room; Crafts room; Laundry
  room; Barber/Beauty shop.
Activities Arts & crafts; Cards; Games;
  Reading groups; Prayer groups; Movies;
  Shopping trips.

Navasota

Canterbury Villa of Navasota
1405 E Washington, Navasota, TX 77868
(713) 825-6463
Admin Irene E Higdon.
Licensure Intermediate care. *Beds* 172.
  Certified Medicaid.
Owner Proprietary corp (Health Enter of
  America).
Admissions Requirements Minimum age 18;
  Medical examination.
Staff RNs 1 (ft); LPNs 6 (ft), 2 (pt); Nurses'
  aides 48 (ft), 6 (pt); Activities coordinators 2
  (ft).
Facilities Dining room; Physical therapy
  room; Activities room; Crafts room; Laundry
  room; Barber/Beauty shop.
Activities Arts & crafts; Cards; Games; Prayer
  groups; Shopping trips; Dances/Social/
  Cultural gatherings.

Nederland

Nederland Nursing Home
3600 N Twin City Hwy, Nederland, TX
77627
(409) 727-3143
Admin Emma Aguilar. *Dir of Nursing* Levinia
  Benjamin. *Medical Dir* Dr G G Dunkerley;
  Dr Ray Benski.
Licensure Intermediate care. *Beds* ICF 110.
  Private Pay Patients 30%. *Certified*
  Medicaid.
Owner Proprietary corp (Beverly Enterprises).
Staff Physicians; RNs; LPNs; Nurses' aides;
  Activities coordinators; Dietitians;
  Podiatrists.

Needville

SPJST Rest Home 2
PO Box 347, 8611 Main St, Needville, TX
77461
(409) 793-4256
Admin Harvey L Marx.
Licensure Intermediate care. *Beds* 58.
  Certified Medicaid.
Owner Nonprofit corp.

New Boston

New Boston Nursing Center
210 Rice St, New Boston, TX 75570
(214) 628-5551
Admin James R Goodwin. *Dir of Nursing*
  JoAnn Clark. *Medical Dir* Balbir Singh.
Licensure Skilled care. *Beds* SNF 120. *Private
  Pay Patients* 30%. *Certified* Medicaid;
  Medicare.
Owner Proprietary corp (Truco Properties).
Admissions Requirements Minimum age 19;
  Medical examination.
Staff RNs 1 (ft), 2 (pt); Nurses' aides 42 (ft), 3
  (pt); Activities coordinators 1 (ft), 1 (pt);
  Dietitians 1 (ft); LVNs 14 (ft), 3 (pt).
Facilities Dining room; Activities room;
  Chapel; Crafts room; Laundry room; Barber/
  Beauty shop; Handicapped-lift van; Living
  room.
Activities Arts & crafts; Cards; Games;
  Reading groups; Prayer groups; Movies;
  Shopping trips; Pet therapy; Auxiliary.

New Braunfels

Colonial Manor Care Center
821 US Hwy 81 W, New Braunfels, TX 78130
(512) 625-7526
Admin Joyce Corry. *Dir of Nursing* Bonnie
  Wilson. *Medical Dir* Dr Stanley Woodward.
Licensure Skilled care; Intermediate care;
  Respite care. *Beds* SNF 96; ICF 64. *Certified*
  Medicaid; Medicare.
Owner Proprietary corp (Summit Health Ltd).
Admissions Requirements Medical
  examination; Physician's request.
Staff RNs 4 (ft), 2 (pt); LPNs 9 (ft), 3 (pt);
  Nurses' aides 18 (ft), 6 (pt); Physical
  therapists; Activities coordinators 1 (ft);
  Dietitians 1 (ft).
Languages Spanish.
Facilities Dining room; Physical therapy
  room; Activities room; Crafts room; Laundry
  room; Barber/Beauty shop.
Activities Arts & crafts; Cards; Games;
  Reading groups; Prayer groups; Shopping
  trips; Dances/Social/Cultural gatherings; Pet
  therapy.

Eden Home Inc
631 Lakeview Blvd, New Braunfels, TX 78130
(512) 625-6291
Admin Rev Rodney W Wells. *Dir of Nursing*
  Lorraine Kennemer RN. *Medical Dir*
  Charles Berger MD.

Licensure Skilled care; Intermediate care; Retirement; Alzheimer's care. *Beds* SNF 166; ICF 134. *Private Pay Patients* 60%. *Certified* Medicaid; Medicare.
Owner Nonprofit corp (South Central Conference of United Church of Christ).
Admissions Requirements Minimum age 62; Medical examination; Physician's request.
Staff RNs 4 (ft); LPNs 25 (ft); Nurses' aides 113 (ft), 2 (pt); Physical therapists 1 (ft); Recreational therapists 2 (ft); Dietitians 2 (pt).
Languages Spanish, German.
Affiliation United Church of Christ.
Facilities Dining room; Physical therapy room; Activities room; Chapel; Crafts room; Laundry room; Barber/Beauty shop; Library.
Activities Arts & crafts; Cards; Games; Reading groups; Prayer groups; Dances/Social/Cultural gatherings; Intergenerational programs; Pet therapy.

Kirkwood Manor
2590 Loop 337 N, New Braunfels, TX 78130
(512) 620-0509
Admin Sharon L Sutton. *Dir of Nursing* Patsy A Castillo. *Medical Dir* Dr Carlos Campos.
Licensure Skilled care. *Beds* SNF 120. *Private Pay Patients* 55%. *Certified* Medicaid; Medicare.
Owner Proprietary corp.
Staff RNs; LPNs; Nurses' aides; Activities coordinators; Dietitians.
Activities Arts & crafts; Cards; Games; Reading groups; Prayer groups; Movies; Shopping trips; Dances/Social/Cultural gatherings; Intergenerational programs; Pet therapy.

Oak Crest Inn
1310 Hwy 35 W, New Braunfels, TX 78130
(512) 625-6941
Admin Winona Oberkampf.
Licensure Intermediate care. *Beds* ICF 139. *Certified* Medicaid.
Owner Proprietary corp (ARA Living Centers).
Admissions Requirements Medical examination.
Staff RNs 12 (ft); LPNs 2 (ft); Nurses' aides 30 (ft); Reality therapists 1 (ft); Activities coordinators 1 (ft); Dietitians 1 (ft).
Languages German, Spanish.
Facilities Dining room; Activities room; Crafts room; Barber/Beauty shop.
Activities Arts & crafts; Cards; Games; Reading groups; Prayer groups; Movies; Shopping trips; Dances/Social/Cultural gatherings; Cooking clubs; Resident council; In-room activities.

New London

Sunshine Nursing Home
PO Box 378, New London, TX 75682
(214) 895-4884
Admin Gladys Riggs. *Dir of Nursing* Janis Jordan. *Medical Dir* J M Hamilton MD.
Licensure Intermediate care. *Beds* ICF 69. *Private Pay Patients* 15%. *Certified* Medicaid.
Owner Proprietary corp.
Admissions Requirements Medical examination; Physician's request.
Staff RNs 1 (pt); LPNs 9 (ft); Nurses' aides 22 (ft), 6 (pt); Physical therapists (contracted); Reality therapists (contracted); Recreational therapists (contracted); Occupational therapists (contracted); Speech therapists (contracted); Activities coordinators 1 (ft); Dietitians 1 (ft); Ophthalmologists 1 (pt).
Facilities Dining room; Activities room; Chapel; Crafts room; Laundry room; Barber/Beauty shop; Library.

Activities Arts & crafts; Cards; Games; Reading groups; Prayer groups; Movies; Shopping trips; Dances/Social/Cultural gatherings; Intergenerational programs.

Newton

Shady Acres Health Care Center
PO Drawer E, Shady Acres Ln, Newton, TX 75966
(409) 379-8911
Admin Betty L Hines. *Dir of Nursing* Carolyn Reed RN.
Licensure Skilled care; Alzheimer's care. *Beds* SNF 82. *Certified* Medicaid; Medicare.
Owner Proprietary corp.
Admissions Requirements Medical examination.
Staff RNs 1 (ft), 1 (pt); LPNs 4 (ft), 2 (pt); Nurses' aides 19 (ft), 4 (pt); Activities coordinators 1 (ft); Dietitians 1 (pt).
Facilities Dining room; Physical therapy room; Activities room; Chapel; Crafts room; Laundry room; Barber/Beauty shop; Library.
Activities Arts & crafts; Cards; Games; Reading groups; Prayer groups; Movies; Shopping trips.

Nixon

Colonial Convalescent & Nursing Home
406 S Parker, Nixon, TX 78140
(512) 582-1811, 582-1081
Admin Mike Millington. *Dir of Nursing* Rose Anne Medina RN. *Medical Dir* Dr W G Millington.
Licensure Intermediate care; Alzheimer's care. *Beds* ICF 89. *Certified* Medicaid.
Owner Proprietary corp.
Admissions Requirements Minimum age 21.
Staff Physicians 1 (pt); RNs 1 (pt); LPNs 6 (ft); Nurses' aides 29 (ft), 7 (pt); Activities coordinators 1 (ft); Dietitians 1 (pt); Ophthalmologists 1 (pt).
Languages Spanish.
Facilities Dining room; Activities room; Laundry room; Barber/Beauty shop.
Activities Arts & crafts; Games; Reading groups; Prayer groups; Movies; Shopping trips; Dances/Social/Cultural gatherings.

Nocona

Horizon Manor Nursing Center
Rte 2 Box 1000, Nocona, TX 76255
(817) 825-3258
Admin Mary Adams.
Licensure Intermediate care. *Beds* 64. *Certified* Medicaid.
Owner Proprietary corp (Comprehensive Health Care Assn).

Nocona Nursing Home
306 Carolyn Rd, Nocona, TX 76255
(817) 825-3288
Admin Becky Spikes. *Dir of Nursing* Mary Rose Underwood.
Licensure Intermediate care. *Beds* ICF 91. *Certified* Medicaid.
Owner Privately owned.
Admissions Requirements Medical examination; Physician's request.
Staff LPNs 6 (ft), 2 (pt); Nurses' aides 12 (ft), 4 (pt); Activities coordinators 1 (ft); Dietitians 1 (pt).
Facilities Dining room; Activities room; Chapel; Crafts room; Laundry room; Barber/Beauty shop.
Activities Arts & crafts; Games; Reading groups; Prayer groups.

Odessa

Avalon Place—Odessa Nursing Center
3800 Englewood Ln, Odessa, TX 79762
(915) 362-2583

Admin Charlene Allmon. *Dir of Nursing* Peggy Abel RN. *Medical Dir* Kirby Tatum MD.
Licensure Intermediate care; Alzheimer's care. *Beds* ICF 113. *Certified* Medicaid.
Owner Proprietary corp.
Admissions Requirements Medical examination; Physician's request.
Staff RNs 1 (ft), 1 (pt); LPNs 6 (ft), 1 (pt); Nurses' aides 19 (ft), 2 (pt); Reality therapists 1 (pt); Activities coordinators 1 (ft); Dietitians 1 (pt).
Facilities Dining room; Activities room; Laundry room; Barber/Beauty shop.
Activities Arts & crafts; Cards; Games; Reading groups; Prayer groups; Movies; Dances/Social/Cultural gatherings.

Deerings West Nursing Center
2510 W 8th St, Odessa, TX 79763
(915) 333-4511
Admin Daniel Lopez.
Medical Dir Kim Thompson.
Licensure Skilled care; Intermediate care. *Beds* 150. *Certified* Medicaid; Medicare.
Owner Proprietary corp (Hillhaven Corp).
Admissions Requirements Medical examination; Physician's request.
Staff RNs; LPNs; Nurses' aides; Activities coordinators; Dietitians.
Languages Spanish, Sign.
Facilities Dining room; Physical therapy room; Activities room; Laundry room; Barber/Beauty shop.
Activities Arts & crafts; Cards; Games; Reading groups; Prayer groups; Movies; Shopping trips; Dances/Social/Cultural gatherings.

Parks Good Samaritan Village
7801 San Machell Dr, Odessa, TX 79765
(915) 563-5707
Admin Melissa Smith. *Dir of Nursing* Lori Wingate RN. *Medical Dir* Dr Albert Finch.
Licensure Skilled care; Retirement. *Beds* SNF 60; Retirement units 35. *Private Pay Patients* 50%. *Certified* Medicaid; Medicare.
Owner Nonprofit corp (Evangelical Lutheran/ Good Samaritan Society).
Admissions Requirements Medical examination.
Staff RNs 2 (ft), 1 (pt); Nurses' aides 25 (ft); Physical therapists (contracted); Activities coordinators 1 (ft); Dietitians 1 (ft).
Languages Spanish.
Affiliation Evangelical Lutheran.
Facilities Dining room; Physical therapy room; Activities room; Chapel; Crafts room; Laundry room; Barber/Beauty shop; Library.
Activities Arts & crafts; Cards; Games; Dances/Social/Cultural gatherings; Intergenerational programs; Pet therapy; Singing.

Seabury Center
2443 W 16th St, Odessa, TX 79763
(915) 333-2904
Licensure Nursing. *Beds* Nursing 97.

Westview Manor
2443 W 16th St, Odessa, TX 79763
(915) 333-2904
Admin William L Ketcham.
Licensure Intermediate care. *Beds* 97. *Certified* Medicaid; Medicare.

Olney

Olney Nursing Center
1302 W Payne, Olney, TX 76374
(817) 564-5626
Admin John L Golden.
Medical Dir Dr Mark Mankins.
Licensure Intermediate care. *Beds* ICF 72. *Certified* Medicaid.

Owner Proprietary corp (Beverly Enterprises).
Staff RNs 1 (pt); LPNs 4 (ft), 2 (pt); Nurses' aides 12 (ft); Activities coordinators 1 (ft); Dietitians 1 (pt).

Seven Oaks Nursing Home Inc
PO Box 188, 1402 W Elm St, Olney, TX 76374
(817) 564-5631
Admin Katherine B Bennett.
Licensure Skilled care. *Beds* 99. *Certified* Medicaid.
Owner Proprietary corp (Comprehensive Health Care Assn).

Omaha

Elmwood Nursing Home
PO Box 1087, Giles St, Omaha, TX 75571
(214) 884-2341
Admin Clayton D Elliott.
Licensure Intermediate care. *Beds* 65.
Certified Medicaid.
Owner Proprietary corp (Truco Inc).

Orange

Jones Health Center
3000 Cardinal Dr, Orange, TX 77630
(409) 883-5727
Admin Mary F Dupuy.
Licensure Skilled care; Intermediate care. *Beds* 111. *Certified* Medicaid.
Owner Proprietary corp.

Oaks Living Center
501 N 3rd St, Orange, TX 77630
(409) 886-8677
Admin Rose Marie Gordon.
Licensure Intermediate care. *Beds* 112.
Certified Medicaid.
Owner Proprietary corp.

Overton

Leisure Lodge—Overton
PO Drawer K, Hwy 135 S, Overton, TX 75684
(214) 834-6166
Admin Linda B Jones. *Dir of Nursing* Carolyn Smith RN. *Medical Dir* James Hamilton MD.
Licensure Skilled care; Intermediate care. *Beds* 100. *Certified* Medicaid; Medicare.
Owner Proprietary corp (Beverly Enterprises).
Admissions Requirements Minimum age 18 months; Medical examination; Physician's request.
Staff RNs 2 (ft), 3 (pt); LPNs 10 (ft); Nurses' aides 44 (ft), 4 (pt); Activities coordinators 1 (ft); Dietitians 1 (ft).
Facilities Dining room; Activities room; Crafts room; Laundry room; Barber/Beauty shop.
Activities Arts & crafts; Cards; Games; Reading groups; Prayer groups; Movies; Shopping trips; Dances/Social/Cultural gatherings.

Ozona

Crockett County Care Center
103 N Ave H, Ozona, TX 76943
(915) 392-3096
Admin Doris Hull. *Dir of Nursing* Deena Ramos. *Medical Dir* Marcus Sims DO.
Licensure Intermediate care. *Beds* ICF 42.
Private Pay Patients 50%. *Certified* Medicaid.
Owner Publicly owned.
Admissions Requirements Minimum age 16; Medical examination; Physician's request.
Staff Physicians 2 (pt); RNs 1 (pt); Nurses' aides 23 (ft); Activities coordinators 1 (ft); Dietitians 1 (pt); LVNs 5 (ft).
Languages Spanish.

Facilities Dining room; Activities room; Chapel; Crafts room; Laundry room; Barber/Beauty shop.
Activities Arts & crafts; Cards; Games; Reading groups; Prayer groups; Movies; Shopping trips; Dances/Social/Cultural gatherings; Intergenerational programs; Pet therapy.

Paducah

Wood Convalescent Center
PO Box 627, 800 7th St, Paducah, TX 79248
(806) 492-3516
Admin Gwynna Marie Stofel. *Dir of Nursing* Doris Glidewell.
Licensure Intermediate care; Personal care. *Beds* ICF 46; Personal care 100. *Private Pay Patients* 10%. *Certified* Medicaid.
Owner Proprietary corp.
Staff RNs (consultant); LPNs 6 (ft); Nurses' aides 16 (ft); Activities coordinators 1 (ft); Dietitians (consultant).
Languages Spanish.
Activities Cards; Games; Reading groups; Prayer groups; Movies; Shopping trips; Dances/Social/Cultural gatherings.

Palacios

Leisure Lodge—Palacios
PO Box 819, Palacios, TX 77465
(512) 972-2542
Admin Minnie Smith.
Licensure Intermediate care. *Beds* 102.
Certified Medicaid.
Owner Proprietary corp (Beverly Enterprises).
Staff LPNs 4 (ft); Nurses' aides 12 (ft); Physical therapists 1 (pt); Occupational therapists 1 (pt); Speech therapists 1 (pt); Activities coordinators 1 (ft); Dietitians 1 (pt).
Facilities Dining room; Activities room; Chapel; Laundry room; Barber/Beauty shop.
Activities Arts & crafts; Games; Prayer groups; Movies; Shopping trips; Dances/Social/Cultural gatherings.

Palestine

Cartmell Home for Aged
2212 W Reagan, Palestine, TX 75801
(214) 729-2268
Admin Peggy Howland.
Licensure Intermediate care; Custodial care. *Beds* ICF 44; Custodial care 16.
Admissions Requirements Minimum age 65; Medical examination.
Staff Physicians 1 (pt); LPNs 4 (ft), 4 (pt); Nurses' aides 13 (ft), 3 (pt); Activities coordinators 1 (ft); Dietitians 1 (pt).
Facilities Dining room; Physical therapy room; Activities room; Crafts room; Laundry room; Barber/Beauty shop; Garden.
Activities Arts & crafts; Cards; Games; Prayer groups; Movies; Shopping trips; Local trips; Picnics.

Oak Haven Nursing Home
606 E Kolstad, Palestine, TX 75801
(214) 729-6901
Admin Patricia A Jeffcoat.
Licensure Intermediate care. *Beds* 54.
Certified Medicaid.
Owner Proprietary corp.

Palestine Nursing Center
PO Box 1428, 2404 Hwy 155, Palestine, TX 75801
(214) 729-6024
Admin Sue Lombright. *Dir of Nursing* Pattie Gray. *Medical Dir* Dr Stan Skrepnek.
Licensure Intermediate care; Alzheimer's care. *Beds* ICF 120. *Private Pay Patients* 28%. *Certified* Medicaid.
Owner Proprietary corp (Arbor Living Centers).

Admissions Requirements Medical examination.
Staff LPNs 8 (ft); Nurses' aides 30 (ft); Physical therapists 1 (pt); Recreational therapists 1 (ft); Occupational therapists 1 (pt); Speech therapists 1 (pt); Activities coordinators 2 (ft); Dietitians 1 (ft); Ophthalmologists 1 (pt); Podiatrists 1 (pt).
Facilities Dining room; Physical therapy room; Laundry room; Barber/Beauty shop.
Activities Arts & crafts; Cards; Games; Reading groups; Prayer groups; Movies; Shopping trips; Dances/Social/Cultural gatherings.

Park Place Nursing Home
505 Sylvan Ave, Palestine, TX 75801
(214) 729-3246
Admin Steven Hicks. *Dir of Nursing* Sue Carter. *Medical Dir* Lee Roy Mathis MD.
Licensure Intermediate care. *Beds* ICF 108.
Certified Medicaid.
Owner Proprietary corp.
Admissions Requirements Medical examination; Physician's request.
Facilities Dining room; Activities room; Crafts room; Laundry room; Barber/Beauty shop.
Activities Arts & crafts; Games; Prayer groups; Movies.

Villa Inn Nursing Center
1816 Tile Factory Rd, Palestine, TX 75801
(214) 729-2261
Admin Gary Parker. *Dir of Nursing* Pat Ramirez RN. *Medical Dir* David L Thompson MD.
Licensure Skilled care; Intermediate care; Alzheimer's care. *Beds* SNF 54; ICF 50.
Private Pay Patients 10%. *Certified* Medicaid; Medicare.
Owner Proprietary corp (Beverly Enterprises).
Admissions Requirements Physician's request.
Staff RNs 2 (ft), 1 (pt); LPNs 15 (ft); Nurses' aides 30 (ft), 15 (pt); Physical therapists 1 (pt); Activities coordinators 1 (ft), 1 (pt); Dietitians 1 (ft).
Facilities Dining room; Activities room; Crafts room; Laundry room; Barber/Beauty shop.
Activities Arts & crafts; Cards; Games; Reading groups; Prayer groups; Movies; Shopping trips; Dances/Social/Cultural gatherings; Intergenerational programs; Pet therapy; Community interaction.

Pampa

Coronado Nursing Center
1504 W Kentucky St, Pampa, TX 79065
(806) 665-5746
Admin Jimmie Lee Moore.
Licensure Intermediate care. *Beds* 120.
Certified Medicaid.
Owner Proprietary corp (Beverly Enterprises).

Pampa Nursing Center
PO Box 582, 1321 W Kentucky St, Pampa, TX 79065-0582
(806) 669-2551
Admin Dorris Houck.
Medical Dir Jesse Hardy.
Licensure Intermediate care. *Beds* 100.
Certified Medicaid.
Owner Proprietary corp (ARA Living Centers).
Admissions Requirements Medical examination; Physician's request.
Staff LPNs 4 (ft); Nurses' aides 14 (ft); Activities coordinators 1 (ft); Dietitians 1 (ft).

Panhandle

St Ann's Nursing Home
PO Box 1179, Spur 293, Panhandle, TX 79068
(806) 537-3194
Admin Sr M Consilia Feuchtenhofer.
Licensure Skilled care. *Beds* 52. *Certified* Medicaid.
Owner Nonprofit corp.
Affiliation Roman Catholic.

Paris

Cherry Street Annex
2185 E Cherry St, Paris, TX 75460
(214) 784-7108
Admin Raymond G Nixon. *Dir of Nursing* Pat Calk RN. *Medical Dir* Bert G Strom MD.
Licensure Intermediate care. *Beds* ICF 182. *Private Pay Patients* 35%. *Certified* Medicaid.
Owner Proprietary corp (Convalescent Management Inc).
Admissions Requirements Physician's request.
Staff Physicians 1 (pt); RNs 1 (ft); LPNs 9 (ft); Nurses' aides 35 (ft); Physical therapists 1 (pt); Activities coordinators 1 (ft); Dietitians 1 (pt).
Facilities Dining room; Activities room; Crafts room; Laundry room; Barber/Beauty shop; TV lobbies; Conversation area.
Activities Arts & crafts; Cards; Games; Reading groups; Prayer groups; Movies; Shopping trips; Dances/Social/Cultural gatherings.

Cherry Street Manor
2193 E Cherry St, Paris, TX 75460
(214) 784-2244
Admin Gerald E Hinkle. *Dir of Nursing* Pamela A Nicholson RN. *Medical Dir* G Bert Strom MD.
Licensure Intermediate care; Alzheimer's care. *Beds* ICF 182. *Private Pay Patients* 35%. *Certified* Medicaid.
Owner Proprietary corp (Convalescent Management Inc).
Admissions Requirements Medical examination; Physician's request.
Staff Physicians; RNs; LPNs; Nurses' aides; Physical therapists; Reality therapists; Recreational therapists; Occupational therapists; Speech therapists; Activities coordinators; Dietitians; Ophthalmologists; Podiatrists; Audiologists.
Facilities Dining room; Activities room; Crafts room; Laundry room; Barber/Beauty shop.
Activities Arts & crafts; Cards; Games; Reading groups; Prayer groups; Movies; Dances/Social/Cultural gatherings; Intergenerational programs; Pet therapy.

Medical Plaza Nursing Center
610 De Shong Dr, Paris, TX 75460
(214) 784-6638, 784-0606 FAX
Admin Doris Waters. *Dir of Nursing* Barbara Rose RN. *Medical Dir* Dr P R Bercher.
Licensure Skilled care. *Beds* SNF 98. *Private Pay Patients* 10%. *Certified* Medicaid; Medicare.
Owner Proprietary corp (Beverly Enterprises).
Admissions Requirements Medical examination.
Staff Physicians 1 (pt); RNs 2 (ft); LPNs 8 (ft); Nurses' aides 24 (ft); Physical therapists 1 (pt); Activities coordinators 1 (ft); Dietitians 1 (pt); Podiatrists 1 (pt).
Facilities Dining room; Physical therapy room; Laundry room; Barber/Beauty shop; Library.
Activities Arts & crafts; Cards; Games; Reading groups; Prayer groups; Movies; Shopping trips; Dances/Social/Cultural gatherings; Intergenerational programs; Pet therapy.

Paris Nursing Home
3055 Clarksville St, Paris, TX 75460
(214) 785-1601
Admin Robbi Ann Stewart.
Licensure Intermediate care; Personal care. *Beds* ICF 144. *Certified* Medicaid.
Owner Proprietary corp.

Parkview Convalescent Center
2895 Lewis Ln, Paris, TX 75460
(214) 784-4111
Admin Vi Burchfield. *Dir of Nursing* Georgia Hoskins. *Medical Dir* E S White.
Licensure Intermediate care. *Beds* ICF 102. *Private Pay Patients* 20%. *Certified* Medicaid.
Owner Proprietary corp (Convalescent Management Inc).
Admissions Requirements Medical examination; Physician's request.
Staff Physicians 1 (pt); RNs 1 (pt); LPNs 7 (ft), 1 (pt); Nurses' aides 17 (ft), 3 (pt); Physical therapists 1 (pt); Recreational therapists 1 (ft); Occupational therapists 1 (pt); Speech therapists 1 (pt); Activities coordinators 1 (ft); Dietitians 1 (pt); Ophthalmologists 1 (pt); Podiatrists 1 (pt); Audiologists 1 (pt).
Languages Spanish.
Facilities Dining room; Activities room; Crafts room; Laundry room; Barber/Beauty shop.
Activities Arts & crafts; Cards; Games; Reading groups; Prayer groups; Movies; Shopping trips; Dances/Social/Cultural gatherings; Intergenerational programs; Picnics; Harvest festival.

Pasadena

Blalock Nursing Home—Southeast
802 Fresa St, Pasadena, TX 77501
(713) 946-3360
Admin Karen Young.
Licensure Skilled care; Intermediate care. *Beds* 210. *Certified* Medicaid.
Owner Proprietary corp.

Faith Memorial Nursing Home
811 Garner Rd, Pasadena, TX 77502
(713) 473-8573
Admin Phyllis C Ayres.
Licensure Intermediate care. *Beds* 120. *Certified* Medicaid.
Owner Proprietary corp (ARA Living Centers).
Facilities Dining room; Activities room; Crafts room.
Activities Arts & crafts; Cards; Games; Reading groups; Prayer groups; Movies; Shopping trips; Dances/Social/Cultural gatherings.

Pasadena Care Center
4006 Vista Rd, Pasadena, TX 77504
(713) 943-1592
Admin Jerald W Myers Sr.
Licensure Intermediate care. *Beds* 120. *Certified* Medicaid.
Owner Proprietary corp (ARA Living Centers).

Southfield Healthcare Center
802 Fresa, Pasadena, TX 77502
(713) 946-3360
Admin Christopher C Bland. *Dir of Nursing* Shirley Walker. *Medical Dir* Dr Byron Herlong.
Licensure Skilled care; Intermediate care; Personal care. *Beds* SNF 32; ICF 130; Personal care 44. *Private Pay Patients* 30%. *Certified* Medicaid; Medicare.
Owner Proprietary corp (ARA Living Centers).
Staff RNs; LPNs; Nurses' aides; Physical therapists (contracted); Reality therapists (contracted); Recreational therapists (contracted); Occupational therapists (contracted); Speech therapists (contracted); Activities coordinators; Dietitians.
Facilities Dining room; Physical therapy room; Activities room; Crafts room; Laundry room; Barber/Beauty room.
Activities Arts & crafts; Cards; Games; Reading groups; Prayer groups; Movies; Shopping trips; Dances/Social/Cultural gatherings; Intergenerational programs; Pet therapy; Religious groups.

Vista Continuing Care Center
4300 Vista Rd, Pasadena, TX 77504
(713) 946-6787
Admin Coral Ann Rung. *Dir of Nursing* Elaine Burnham RN. *Medical Dir* W B Herlong MD.
Licensure Intermediate care. *Beds* ICF 131. *Certified* Medicaid; VA.
Owner Proprietary corp.
Staff Physicians 1 (pt); RNs 1 (ft); LPNs 9 (ft), 1 (pt); Nurses' aides 37 (ft), 2 (pt); Physical therapists 1 (pt); Occupational therapists 1 (pt); Speech therapists 1 (pt); Activities coordinators 1 (ft), 1 (pt); Dietitians 1 (pt); Ophthalmologists 1 (pt); Podiatrists 1 (pt).

Pearland

Windsong Village Convalescent Center
3400 E Walnut St, Pearland, TX 77581
(713) 485-2776
Admin Cecil W Barcelo.
Licensure Intermediate care. *Beds* 96. *Certified* Medicaid.
Owner Proprietary corp.

Pearsall

Amistad Care Center of Frio County
311 Hackberry, Pearsall, TX 78061
(512) 334-3371
Admin Beverly Roberts.
Licensure Intermediate care. *Beds* 104. *Certified* Medicaid.
Owner Proprietary corp.

Pearsall Manor
PO Drawer U, 320 S Ash, Pearsall, TX 78061
(512) 334-4197
Admin William D Mutzig.
Licensure Intermediate care. *Beds* 52. *Certified* Medicaid.
Owner Proprietary corp.

Pecos

Pecos Nursing Home
1819 Memorial Dr, Pecos, TX 79772
(915) 447-2183
Admin Elizabeth Z Peters. *Dir of Nursing* Gloria Gonzales LVN. *Medical Dir* Bruce Hay MD.
Licensure Intermediate care; Retirement. *Beds* ICF 60. *Certified* Medicaid.
Owner Privately owned.
Admissions Requirements Minimum age 53; Medical examination; Physician's request.
Staff RNs 1 (pt); LPNs 4 (ft); Nurses' aides 15 (ft); Activities coordinators 1 (ft); Dietitians 1 (pt).
Facilities Dining room; Activities room; Laundry room; Barber/Beauty shop.
Activities Arts & crafts; Cards; Games; Reading groups; Prayer groups; Movies; Shopping trips; Dances/Social/Cultural gatherings.

Perryton

Senior Village Nursing Home
Hwy 83 S, Perryton, TX 79070
(806) 435-5403
Admin Rita A Hargrove.

Medical Dir Pat Atkinson.
Licensure Intermediate care. *Beds* 60.
  Certified Medicaid.
Owner Proprietary corp (Beverly Enterprises).
Admissions Requirements Physician's request.
Staff LPNs 4 (ft), 2 (pt); Nurses' aides 15 (ft),
  1 (pt); Activities coordinators 1 (ft);
  Dietitians 1 (pt).
Facilities Dining room; Activities room;
  Laundry room; Barber/Beauty shop.
Activities Arts & crafts; Games; Reading
  groups; Prayer groups; Movies; Shopping
  trips; Dances/Social/Cultural gatherings.

Pharr

Pharr Nursing Home
PO Drawer D, 204 S Casa Rd, Pharr, TX
78577
(512) 787-2735
Admin Dorothy Sadler.
Medical Dir Socorro Rodriguez.
Licensure Intermediate care. *Beds* ICF 45.
  Certified Medicaid.
Owner Privately owned.
Admissions Requirements Medical
  examination.
Staff RNs 1 (ft); LPNs 3 (ft); Nurses' aides 14
  (ft); Activities coordinators 1 (ft); Dietitians
  1 (ft).
Languages Spanish.
Facilities Dining room; Activities room;
  Crafts room; Laundry room.
Activities Arts & crafts; Cards; Games;
  Reading groups; Prayer groups; Movies;
  Shopping trips; Dances/Social/Cultural
  gatherings.

Pineland

Hines Nursing Home
PO Box 806, Hwy 83, Pineland, TX 75968
(409) 584-2174
Admin Patricia Bradberry.
Licensure Intermediate care. *Beds* 90.
  Certified Medicaid.
Owner Proprietary corp.

Pittsburg

Moore's Nursing Home
PO Drawer 742, 618 Quitman St, Pittsburg,
TX 75686
(214) 856-3510
Admin Elizabeth Massie.
Medical Dir Betty L London.
Licensure Intermediate care. *Beds* 24.
  Certified Medicaid.
Owner Privately owned.
Admissions Requirements Minimum age 16;
  Medical examination; Physician's request.
Staff LPNs; Nurses' aides 4 (ft), 1 (pt);
  Activities coordinators 1 (ft); Podiatrists 1
  (pt).
Activities Arts & crafts; Cards; Games;
  Reading groups; Prayer groups; Movies;
  Shopping trips; Dances/Social/Cultural
  gatherings.

Pittsburg Nursing Center
123 Pecan Grove, Pittsburg, TX 75686
(214) 856-3633
Admin Billie Pittman.
Licensure Intermediate care. *Beds* 106.
  Certified Medicaid.
Owner Proprietary corp (Beverly Enterprises).

Plainview

Care Inn of Plainview
224 Saint Louis, Plainview, TX 79072
(806) 293-5201
Admin Janie W Rogers. *Dir of Nursing*
  Marilyn Ellis. *Medical Dir* Dr Tony Loggins.
Licensure Intermediate care. *Beds* ICF 68.
  Private Pay Patients 5%. *Certified* Medicaid.

Owner Proprietary corp (ARA Living
  Centers).
Admissions Requirements Medical
  examination; Physician's request.
Staff RNs; LPNs; Nurses' aides; Activities
  coordinators; Dietitians.
Languages Spanish.
Facilities Dining room; Activities room;
  Crafts room; Laundry room; Barber/Beauty
  shop; Library.
Activities Arts & crafts; Cards; Games;
  Reading groups; Movies; Shopping trips;
  Dances/Social/Cultural gatherings.

Heritage Home
2510 W 24th St, Plainview, TX 79072
(806) 296-5584
Admin Lila R Hawkins. *Dir of Nursing*
  Joquita Linquist RN.
Licensure Skilled care; Intermediate care;
  Alzheimer's care. *Beds* SNF 62; ICF 50.
  Certified Medicaid; Medicare.
Owner Proprietary corp (National Heritage).
Admissions Requirements Medical
  examination.
Staff RNs 1 (ft); LPNs 10 (ft); Nurses' aides
  20 (ft), 10 (pt); Activities coordinators 1 (ft).
Languages Spanish.
Facilities Dining room; Activities room;
  Crafts room; Laundry room; Barber/Beauty
  shop; Library.
Activities Arts & crafts; Cards; Games;
  Reading groups; Prayer groups; Movies;
  Shopping trips; Dances/Social/Cultural
  gatherings.

Plains Convalescent Center
2813 W 8th, Plainview, TX 79072
(806) 293-2581
Admin Victoria (Vickie) Hutton. *Dir of
  Nursing* Melba Dolois (Lois) Palmer.
  Medical Dir Mary Bublis MD.
Licensure Intermediate care. *Beds* ICF 52.
  Private Pay Patients 30%. *Certified*
  Medicaid.
Owner Nonprofit organization/foundation.
Admissions Requirements Medical
  examination; Physician's request.
Staff LPNs 5 (ft), 2 (pt); Nurses' aides 10 (ft);
  Activities coordinators 1 (ft), 1 (pt);
  Dietitians 1 (ft).
Languages Spanish.
Facilities Dining room; Activities room;
  Crafts room; Laundry room; Barber/Beauty
  shop.
Activities Arts & crafts; Cards; Games;
  Reading groups; Prayer groups; Movies;
  Shopping trips; Dances/Social/Cultural
  gatherings; Pet therapy.

Plano

Collin Care Center
3100 S Rigsbee Dr, Plano, TX 75074
(214) 423-6217
Admin Deborah R Renfro. *Dir of Nursing*
  Nickie McCurry. *Medical Dir* Dr Ben
  Northam.
Licensure Intermediate care. *Beds* ICF 120.
  Certified Medicaid.
Owner Proprietary corp.
Admissions Requirements Physician's request.
Staff RNs 1 (pt); LPNs 10 (ft); Nurses' aides
  50 (ft); Physical therapists 1 (pt);
  Occupational therapists 1 (pt); Speech
  therapists 1 (pt); Activities coordinators 1
  (ft); Dietitians 2 (ft).
Activities Arts & crafts; Games; Reading
  groups; Prayer groups; Movies; Shopping
  trips; Dances/Social/Cultural gatherings; Pet
  therapy.

Heritage Manor
1621 Coit Rd, Plano, TX 75074
(214) 596-7930
Admin Bobbie Sechovec RN. *Dir of Nursing*
  Lyn Goerot RN. *Medical Dir* A A Acosta
  MD.

Licensure Intermediate care; Alzheimer's care.
  Beds ICF 152. *Certified* Medicaid.
Owner Privately owned.
Admissions Requirements Medical
  examination; Physician's request.
Staff Physicians 25 (pt); RNs 3 (pt), 3 (pt);
  LPNs 8 (ft), 2 (pt); Nurses' aides 26 (ft), 7
  (pt); Physical therapists 1 (pt); Recreational
  therapists 1 (pt); Occupational therapists 1
  (pt); Speech therapists 1 (pt); Activities
  coordinators 1 (ft); Dietitians 1 (ft);
  Ophthalmologists 2 (pt); Podiatrists 1 (pt);
  Dentists 2 (pt).
Facilities Dining room; Physical therapy
  room; Activities room; Chapel; Laundry
  room; Barber/Beauty shop; Library; Sun
  rooms.
Activities Arts & crafts; Games; Reading
  groups; Prayer groups; Movies; Shopping
  trips; Dances/Social/Cultural gatherings;
  Music therapy; Pet therapy.

Heritage Park
3208 Thunderbird, Plano, TX 75075
(214) 422-2214
Admin Evelyn R Artall. *Dir of Nursing* Mary
  McDermott. *Medical Dir* Dr Lester Cannon.
Licensure Intermediate care. *Beds* ICF 120.
  Certified Medicaid; VA.
Owner Proprietary corp (People Care Corp).
Admissions Requirements Minimum age 21;
  Medical examination; Physician's request.
Staff Physicians 1 (ft); RNs 2 (ft); LPNs 11
  (ft); Nurses' aides 34 (ft); Activities
  coordinators 1 (ft); Dietitians 1 (ft).
Languages Spanish.
Facilities Dining room; Activities room;
  Laundry room; Barber/Beauty shop; Library.
Activities Arts & crafts; Cards; Games;
  Reading groups; Prayer groups; Movies; Pet
  therapy.

Plano Nursing Home
3100 S Rigsbee Dr, Plano, TX 75074
(214) 423-6217
Admin Ann Bridges.
Licensure Intermediate care. *Beds* 120.
  Certified Medicaid.
Owner Proprietary corp (Beverly Enterprises).

Pleasanton

Retama Manor North—Pleasanton
404 Goodwin St, Pleasanton, TX 78064
(512) 569-2138
Admin Marilyn Sweeten. *Dir of Nursing* Linda
  Mann LVN. *Medical Dir* Richard M Burgess
  MD.
Licensure Intermediate care. *Beds* ICF 48.
  Private Pay Patients 20%. *Certified*
  Medicaid.
Owner Proprietary corp (ARA Living
  Centers).
Admissions Requirements Physician's request.
Staff Physicians 1 (pt); RNs 1 (pt); LPNs 4
  (ft), 2 (pt); Nurses' aides 8 (ft), 3 (pt);
  Physical therapists 1 (pt); Speech therapists
  1 (pt); Activities coordinators 1 (ft);
  Dietitians 1 (ft), 1 (pt); Podiatrists 2 (ft);
  Beauticians 1 (pt); Barbers 1 (pt).
Facilities Dining room; Activities room;
  Laundry room; Barber/Beauty shop.
Activities Arts & crafts; Cards; Games; Prayer
  groups; Movies; Shopping trips; Dances/
  Social/Cultural gatherings; Intergenerational
  programs; Pet therapy; Gardening; Bird
  watching and feeding; Religious services.

Retama Manor Nursing Center—South
905 Oaklawn, Pleasanton, TX 78064
(512) 569-3861
Admin Sue Hines.
Licensure Intermediate care. *Beds* 96.
  Certified Medicaid.
Owner Proprietary corp (ARA Living
  Centers).

Port Arthur

Gaspard's Nursing Care Center Inc
PO Drawer 5639, 2689 65th St, Port Arthur,
TX 77640
(409) 736-1541
Admin Velma M Gaspard.
Licensure Skilled care. *Beds* 102. *Certified*
Medicaid.
Owner Proprietary corp.

Golden Triangle Convalescent Center
8825 Lamplighter, Port Arthur, TX 77640
(409) 727-1651
Admin Hulon A Walker.
Licensure Intermediate care. *Beds* 200.
Certified Medicaid.
Owner Proprietary corp.

Park Central Nursing Home
4225 Lake Arthur Dr, Port Arthur, TX 77642
(409) 724-7808, 724-2935 FAX
Admin Robert E French. *Dir of Nursing* Betty
Moran LVN. *Medical Dir* Dr Vadas.
Licensure Intermediate care. *Beds* ICF 120.
Certified Medicaid.
Owner Proprietary corp (Park Central Inc).
Staff LPNs 8 (ft); Nurses' aides 41 (ft);
Activities coordinators 1 (ft); Dietitians 1
(ft).
Facilities Dining room; Activities room;
Chapel; Laundry room; Barber/Beauty shop.
Activities Arts & crafts; Cards; Games;
Reading groups; Prayer groups; Movies;
Dances/Social/Cultural gatherings; Pet
therapy; Family participation.

Port Lavaca

Coastal Healthcare Center
524 Village Rd, Port Lavaca, TX 77979
(512) 552-3741
Admin Hannah M Kinsey. *Dir of Nursing*
Barbara Turk RN.
Licensure Intermediate care. *Beds* ICF 120.
Certified Medicaid.
Owner Proprietary corp (ARA Living
Centers).
Admissions Requirements Medical
examination.
Staff RNs 1 (ft), 1 (pt); LPNs 9 (ft); Nurses'
aides 35 (ft); Activities coordinators 1 (ft);
Dietitians 1 (ft).
Languages Spanish.
Facilities Dining room; Physical therapy
room; Activities room; Laundry room;
Barber/Beauty shop.
Activities Arts & crafts; Cards; Games; Prayer
groups; Movies; Dances/Social/Cultural
gatherings.

Porter

Pine Shadow Retreat
PO Box 889, 123 Pine Shadow Ln, Porter, TX
77365
(713) 354-2155
Admin Betty Swabado.
Licensure Intermediate care. *Beds* 106.
Certified Medicaid.
Owner Proprietary corp.

Post

Golden Plains Care Center
605 W 7th St, Post, TX 79356
(806) 495-2848
Licensure Nursing. *Beds* Nursing 75.

Twin Cedar Nursing Home
107 W 7th, Post, TX 79356
(806) 495-2022
Admin Bobbie Self. *Dir of Nursing* Bonnie
Medlin.
Licensure Intermediate care. *Beds* ICF 24.
Certified Medicaid.
Owner Privately owned.

Admissions Requirements Physician's request.
Staff LPNs 3 (ft); Nurses' aides 6 (ft);
Activities coordinators 1 (ft).
Languages Spanish.
Facilities Dining room; Activities room;
Crafts room; Laundry room; Barber/Beauty
shop.
Activities Arts & crafts; Games; Prayer groups;
Movies; Shopping trips.

United Convalescent of Post
605 W 7th St, Post, TX 79356
(806) 495-2848
Admin Bobbie Edler.
Licensure Intermediate care. *Beds* 75.
Certified Medicaid.
Owner Proprietary corp.

Poteet

Poteet Nursing Home
PO Box 995, 101 School Dr, Poteet, TX
78065
(512) 742-3525
Admin Rebecca M Parker. *Dir of Nursing*
Debra J Buck RN. *Medical Dir* Gerald
Phillips MD.
Licensure Skilled care. *Beds* SNF 60. *Certified*
Medicaid.
Owner Proprietary corp.
Admissions Requirements Physician's request.
Staff RNs 1 (ft); LPNs 6 (ft), 2 (pt); Nurses'
aides 15 (ft), 1 (pt); Activities coordinators 1
(ft); Rehabilitation Aide 1 (ft).
Languages Spanish.
Facilities Dining room; Activities room;
Laundry room.
Activities Arts & crafts; Cards; Games; Prayer
groups; Movies; Shopping trips; Dances/
Social/Cultural gatherings; Bingo.

Premont

Premont Nursing Home Inc
431 NW 3rd St, Premont, TX 78375
(512) 348-3812
Admin Janie S Dunn.
Licensure Intermediate care. *Beds* 48.
Certified Medicaid.
Owner Proprietary corp.

Quanah

Wood Convalescent Center of Quanah
1106 W 14th St, Quanah, TX 79252
(817) 663-5369
Admin Mary Catherine Morgan.
Medical Dir Dr W A Brooks.
Licensure Intermediate care. *Beds* 62.
Certified Medicaid.
Admissions Requirements Minimum age 21;
Medical examination; Physician's request.
Staff RNs 1 (pt); LPNs 3 (ft), 2 (pt); Nurses'
aides 12 (ft); Physical therapists 1 (ft), 2 (pt);
Speech therapists 1 (pt); Activities
coordinators 1 (ft); Dietitians 1 (pt); 17 (ft),
4 (pt).
Facilities Dining room; Laundry room;
Barber/Beauty shop.
Activities Arts & crafts; Cards; Games;
Reading groups; Prayer groups; Movies;
Shopping trips; Dances/Social/Cultural
gatherings.

Quitman

Heritage Nursing Home
1026 E Goode St, Quitman, TX 75783
(214) 763-2284
Admin Annette Simpkins.
Medical Dir Ben F Merritt MD.
Licensure Intermediate care. *Beds* 120.
Certified Medicaid.
Owner Proprietary corp.
Admissions Requirements Minimum age 18;
Medical examination; Physician's request.

Staff RNs 2 (ft); LPNs 8 (ft), 2 (pt); Nurses'
aides 35 (ft), 2 (pt); Physical therapists 1
(pt); Speech therapists 1 (pt); Activities
coordinators 1 (ft), 1 (pt); Dietitians 1 (ft);
Podiatrists 1 (pt).
Facilities Dining room; Physical therapy
room; Activities room; Crafts room; Laundry
room; Barber/Beauty shop; Library; Multi-
purpose room; Gift shop; Training center.
Activities Arts & crafts; Cards; Games;
Reading groups; Prayer groups; Movies;
Shopping trips; Dances/Social/Cultural
gatherings.

Village Manor Nursing Home
PO Box 894, 503 N College St, Quitman, TX
75783
(214) 763-2753
Admin Jo Ann Petrea. *Dir of Nursing* Brenda
Krodel LVN. *Medical Dir* Ronald L Daniels
DO, consultant.
Licensure Intermediate care. *Beds* ICF 62.
Private Pay Patients 30%. *Certified*
Medicaid.
Owner Nonprofit corp.
Admissions Requirements Medical
examination; Physician's request.
Staff RNs 1 (ft); LPNs 4 (ft), 3 (pt); Nurses'
aides 16 (ft); Activities coordinators 1 (ft);
Dietitians 1 (ft).
Facilities Dining room; Laundry room;
Barber/Beauty shop; Library.
Activities Arts & crafts; Cards; Games; Prayer
groups; Movies; Intergenerational programs;
Pet therapy; Sunday school; Church services.

Ralls

Ralls Nursing Home
PO Box 460, 1111 Ave P, Ralls, TX 79357
(806) 253-2314, 253-2415
Admin Lavona Pitchford. *Dir of Nursing*
Betty Kelsey. *Medical Dir* Dr Dale Rhoades.
Licensure Intermediate care. *Beds* ICF 46.
Certified Medicaid.
Owner Proprietary corp (ARA Living
Centers).
Admissions Requirements Medical
examination.
Staff RNs; LPNs; Nurses' aides; Activities
coordinators; Dietitians; Podiatrists.
Languages Spanish.
Facilities Dining room; Laundry room.
Activities Arts & crafts; Cards; Games;
Reading groups; Prayer groups; Shopping
trips; Intergenerational programs; Pet
therapy; Exercise group; Church services;
Bible study; Singing.

Ranger

Western Manor
460 W Main St, Ranger, TX 76470
(817) 647-3111, 647-5183 FAX
Admin Lauretta Lawler. *Dir of Nursing*
Lavelle Hallmark. *Medical Dir* L R Gohlke
MD.
Licensure Intermediate care. *Beds* ICF 54.
Private Pay Patients 20%. *Certified*
Medicaid.
Owner Proprietary corp (Clarence Stroh).
Admissions Requirements Minimum age 18;
Medical examination; Physician's request.
Staff RNs 1 (pt); LPNs 5 (ft), 2 (pt); Nurses'
aides 18 (ft), 3 (pt); Activities coordinators 1
(ft); Dietitians 1 (pt).
Languages Spanish.
Facilities Dining room; Activities room;
Laundry room.
Activities Arts & crafts; Cards; Games; Prayer
groups; Shopping trips; Dances/Social/
Cultural gatherings.

Raymondville

Retama Manor Nursing Center
PO Box 445, 1700 S Expy 77, Raymondville, TX 78580
(512) 689-2126
Admin Jimmy W Lowe. *Dir of Nursing* Pamela J Harrington.
Licensure Intermediate care. *Beds* ICF 91. *Certified* Medicaid.
Owner Proprietary corp (ARA Living Centers).
Admissions Requirements Medical examination; Physician's request.
Staff RNs 2 (pt); LPNs 5 (ft), 2 (pt); Nurses' aides 22 (ft), 8 (pt); Activities coordinators 1 (ft); Dietitians 1 (pt).
Languages Spanish.
Facilities Dining room; Activities room; Crafts room; Laundry room; Barber/Beauty shop.
Activities Arts & crafts; Cards; Games; Prayer groups; Movies; Shopping trips; Dances/Social/Cultural gatherings; Intergenerational programs.

Refugio

Refugio Manor
109 Swift St, Refugio, TX 78377
(512) 526-4641
Admin Joyce L Cox. *Dir of Nursing* Frances Poland LVN.
Licensure Intermediate care. *Beds* ICF 64. *Certified* Medicaid.
Owner Proprietary corp (Diversicare Corp of America).
Admissions Requirements Medical examination; Physician's request.
Staff LPNs 7 (ft), 3 (pt); Nurses' aides 17 (ft), 3 (pt); Activities coordinators 1 (ft); Dietitians 1 (pt).
Facilities Dining room; Activities room; Laundry room; Barber/Beauty shop.
Activities Arts & crafts; Cards; Games; Prayer groups; Shopping trips.

Richardson

Heritage Village Nursing Home
1111 Rockingham Dr, Richardson, TX 75080
(214) 231-8833
Admin Beverly J Holt.
Medical Dir Jean Atwood.
Licensure Intermediate care. *Beds* ICF 280. *Certified* Medicaid.
Owner Privately owned.
Admissions Requirements Medical examination; Physician's request.
Staff RNs 6 (ft), 1 (pt); LPNs 19 (ft), 3 (pt); Nurses' aides 49 (ft), 2 (pt); Physical therapists 1 (ft); Occupational therapists 1 (ft); Speech therapists 1 (ft); Activities coordinators 1 (ft), 1 (pt); Dietitians 1 (ft); Ophthalmologists 1 (ft); Podiatrists 1 (ft); Dentists 1 (ft); Social worker 1 (ft).
Languages Spanish.
Facilities Dining room; Physical therapy room; Activities room; Chapel; Crafts room; Laundry room; Barber/Beauty shop; Library; Ice cream parlor; Outdoor enclosed patio.
Activities Arts & crafts; Cards; Games; Reading groups; Prayer groups; Movies; Shopping trips; Dances/Social/Cultural gatherings.

Richardson Manor Care Center
1510 N Plano Rd, Richardson, TX 75080
(214) 234-4786
Admin Gabriel G Bach. *Dir of Nursing* Dee Kaulbach RN.
Licensure Intermediate care; Alzheimer's care. *Beds* ICF 142. *Certified* Medicaid.
Owner Proprietary corp.
Admissions Requirements Medical examination; Physician's request.

Staff Physicians 1 (ft); RNs 2 (ft); LPNs 12 (ft); Nurses' aides 38 (ft); Physical therapists 1 (pt); Reality therapists 1 (pt); Recreational therapists 1 (pt); Occupational therapists 1 (pt); Speech therapists 1 (pt); Activities coordinators 1 (pt); Dietitians 1 (pt); Ophthalmologists 1 (pt); Podiatrists 1 (pt); Dentists 1 (pt).
Languages Spanish, German, French.
Facilities Dining room; Activities room; Crafts room; Laundry room; Barber/Beauty shop.
Activities Arts & crafts; Cards; Games; Reading groups; Prayer groups.

Richland Hills

Boulevard Manor Care Center
7146 Baker Blvd, Richland Hills, TX 76118
(817) 284-1484
Admin Catherine M Costa.
Licensure Intermediate care. *Beds* 122. *Certified* Medicaid; Medicare.

Richland Hills Nursing Home
3109 Kings Ct, Richland Hills, TX 76118
(817) 589-2431
Licensure Nursing. *Beds* Nursing 92.

Richmond

Autumn Hills Convalescent Center
705 Jackson, Richmond, TX 77469
(713) 342-5493
Admin Mildred M Stanley. *Dir of Nursing* Catherine Stearns.
Licensure Intermediate care. *Beds* ICF 99. *Certified* Medicaid.
Owner Proprietary corp.
Admissions Requirements Medical examination; Physician's request.
Staff RNs 1 (ft); LPNs 10 (ft); Nurses' aides 24 (ft), 2 (pt); Physical therapists (outside resource); Recreational therapists 1 (pt); Occupational therapists 1 (pt); Activities coordinators 1 (ft); Dietitians 1 (pt); Ophthalmologists 1 (pt); Podiatrists 1 (pt); Audiologists 1 (pt).
Languages Spanish.
Facilities Dining room; Activities room; Crafts room; Laundry room; Barber/Beauty shop.
Activities Arts & crafts; Cards; Games; Reading groups; Prayer groups; Movies; Shopping trips; Dances/Social/Cultural gatherings; Intergenerational programs; Pet therapy.

Brazosview Healthcare Center
2127 Preston Rd, Richmond, TX 77469
(713) 342-2801
Admin Robin Baschnagel.
Licensure Intermediate care. *Beds* 56. *Certified* Medicaid.
Owner Proprietary corp (ARA Living Centers).

Rio Grande City

Retama Manor Nursing Center—Rio Grande City
400 S Pete Diaz, Jr, Rio Grande City, TX 78582
(512) 487-2513
Admin Rosemary Decker.
Licensure Intermediate care. *Beds* 100. *Certified* Medicaid; Medicare.
Owner Proprietary corp (ARA Living Centers).

Rising Star

Rising Star Nursing Center
411 S Miller, Rising Star, TX 76471
(817) 643-2691
Admin Glenn R Gray.

Medical Dir Terry Horton.
Licensure Intermediate care. *Beds* 61. *Certified* Medicaid.
Admissions Requirements Medical examination; Physician's request.
Staff LPNs 6 (ft), 1 (pt); Nurses' aides 15 (ft); Activities coordinators 1 (ft), 1 (pt).
Facilities Dining room; Activities room; Laundry room; Barber/Beauty shop.
Activities Arts & crafts; Cards; Games; Prayer groups; Shopping trips; Dances/Social/Cultural gatherings.

Robert Lee

West Coke County Hospital District Nursing Home
PO Box 66, 307 W 8th St, Robert Lee, TX 76945
(915) 453-2511
Admin Jeanene Andrews Baucum. *Dir of Nursing* Golda Brown LVN. *Medical Dir* Guno Kletter MD.
Licensure Intermediate care. *Beds* ICF 86. *Certified* Medicaid.
Owner Publicly owned.
Admissions Requirements Physician's request.
Staff Physicians 1 (pt); LPNs 8 (ft), 2 (pt); Nurses' aides 30 (ft), 2 (pt); Activities coordinators 1 (ft); Dietitians 1 (pt).
Languages Spanish.
Facilities Dining room; Physical therapy room; Activities room; Chapel; Crafts room; Laundry room; Barber/Beauty shop; Library; Physician exam room; X-Ray.
Activities Arts & crafts; Cards; Games; Prayer groups; Movies; Dances/Social/Cultural gatherings.

Robinson

Robinson Nursing Center
305 S Andrews, Robinson, TX 76706
(817) 662-4010
Admin Ann Duckworth.
Licensure Intermediate care. *Beds* 72. *Certified* Medicaid.
Owner Proprietary corp (ARA Living Centers).
Staff Physicians; RNs; Nurses' aides; Physical therapists; Occupational therapists; Speech therapists; Dietitians.
Facilities Dining room; Activities room; Crafts room; Laundry room; Barber/Beauty shop.
Activities Arts & crafts; Reading groups; Shopping trips.

Robstown

Retama Manor—Robstown
603 E Ave J, Robstown, TX 78380
(512) 387-1568
Admin Peggy McCullough. *Dir of Nursing* Patty Glass. *Medical Dir* Dr William Meiser.
Licensure Skilled care; Intermediate care; Medicare. *Beds* SNF 32; ICF 50; Medicare 12. *Private Pay Patients* 14%. *Certified* Medicaid; Medicare.
Owner Proprietary corp (ARA Living Centers).
Admissions Requirements Medical examination; Physician's request.
Staff RNs 2 (ft), 2 (pt); LPNs 7 (ft), 2 (pt); Nurses' aides 18 (ft), 5 (pt); Activities coordinators 1 (ft); Dietitians 6 (ft), 3 (pt).
Languages Spanish.
Facilities Dining room; Activities room; Laundry room; Barber/Beauty shop; Security fence.
Activities Arts & crafts; Cards; Games; Prayer groups; Movies; Dances/Social/Cultural gatherings.

Rockdale

Rockdale Nursing Home
700 Dyer St, Rockdale, TX 76567
(512) 446-2548
Admin Esta Faye Lay. *Dir of Nursing* Alice
Duncum RN. *Medical Dir* Dr Philip M
Young.
Licensure Intermediate care. *Beds* ICF 59.
Certified Medicaid.
Admissions Requirements Physician's request.
Staff RNs 1 (ft); LPNs 4 (ft); Nurses' aides 16
(ft), 3 (pt); Physical therapists 1 (pt);
Activities coordinators 1 (ft); Dietitians 1
(pt); Ophthalmologists 1 (pt); Dentists 1 (pt).
Facilities Dining room; Activities room;
Crafts room; Barber/Beauty shop; TV room;
Piano room.
Activities Arts & crafts; Cards; Games;
Reading groups; Prayer groups; Shopping
trips; Dances/Social/Cultural gatherings;
Daily exercise program.

Rockport

Rockport Nursing Center
1004 Young Ave, Rockport, TX 78382
(512) 729-1228
Licensure Nursing. *Beds* Nursing 90.

Rockwall

Rockwall Nursing Care Center
PO Box 930, 206 Storr's St, Rockwall, TX
75087
(214) 722-8101
Admin Don E Miller.
Licensure Intermediate care. *Beds* 192.
Certified Medicaid.
Admissions Requirements Medical
examination; Physician's request.
Staff Physicians 1 (pt); RNs 4 (ft); LPNs ; 6
(ft); Nurses' aides 35 (ft); Physical therapists
1 (pt); Reality therapists 1 (pt); Recreational
therapists 1 (pt); Occupational therapists 1
(pt); Speech therapists 1 (pt); Activities
coordinators 1 (ft); Dietitians 1 (pt).
Facilities Dining room; Laundry room;
Barber/Beauty shop.
Activities Arts & crafts; Cards; Games;
Reading groups; Prayer groups; Movies;
Dances/Social/Cultural gatherings.

Roscoe

Roscoe Nursing Center
201 Cypress, Roscoe, TX 79545
(915) 766-3374
Admin Shelly Peterson. *Dir of Nursing*
Patricia Featherston. *Medical Dir* Dr Larry
McEachern.
Licensure Intermediate care. *Beds* ICF 60.
Certified Medicaid.
Owner Proprietary corp (Beverly Enterprises).
Admissions Requirements Physician's request.
Staff Physicians; RNs; LPNs 6 (ft); Nurses'
aides 11 (ft); Activities coordinators 1 (ft);
Dietitians 1 (pt).
Facilities Dining room; Activities room;
Crafts room; Laundry room; Barber/Beauty
shop; Designated areas serve as library,
chapel, physical therapy and treatment
rooms.
Activities Arts & crafts; Cards; Games;
Reading groups; Prayer groups; Movies;
Shopping trips; Dances/Social/Cultural
gatherings; Adopt-a-grandparent.

Rosebud

Heritage House
PO Drawer 656, College & Ave F, Rosebud,
TX 76570
(817) 583-7904, 583-2830 FAX
Admin Judy S Robison. *Dir of Nursing* Jane
Sammon. *Medical Dir* Clarence D Snyder
MD.
Licensure Skilled care; Intermediate care;
Retirement. *Beds* SNF 60; ICF 64;
Retirement 8. *Private Pay Patients* 27%.
Certified Medicaid; Medicare.
Owner Nonprofit organization/foundation.
Staff Physicians 2 (pt); RNs 1 (ft), 2 (pt);
LPNs 12 (ft), 1 (pt); Nurses' aides 40 (ft);
Physical therapists 1 (pt); Reality therapists
(contracted); Recreational therapists
(contracted); Occupational therapists
(contracted); Speech therapists (contracted);
Activities coordinators 1 (ft), 1 (pt);
Dietitians 1 (pt).
Languages Spanish, Czech, German.
Facilities Dining room; Laundry room;
Barber/Beauty shop; Activities and crafts
room/Library.
Activities Arts & crafts; Cards; Games;
Reading groups; Prayer groups; Movies;
Shopping trips; Dances/Social/Cultural
gatherings; Pet therapy.

Rosenberg

Fort Bend Nursing Home
3010 Bamore Rd, Rosenberg, TX 77471
(713) 342-2142
Admin Tamara D Hall.
Licensure Intermediate care. *Beds* 56.
Certified Medicaid.
Owner Proprietary corp.

Leisure Lodge—Rosenberg
1419 Mahlman St, Rosenberg, TX 77471
(713) 232-6471
Admin Olivia Manning.
Medical Dir R L Yelderman MD.
Licensure Intermediate care. *Beds* 148.
Certified Medicaid.
Owner Proprietary corp (Beverly Enterprises).
Staff RNs 1 (ft); LPNs 8 (ft); Nurses' aides 30
(ft); Activities coordinators 1 (ft); Dietitians
1 (pt).
Facilities Dining room; Laundry room;
Barber/Beauty shop.
Activities Arts & crafts; Games; Reading
groups; Prayer groups; Movies; Shopping
trips.

Rotan

Fisher County Nursing Home
110 W Johnson, Rotan, TX 79546
(915) 735-3291
Admin Mary Sue Hitt.
Licensure Intermediate care. *Beds* 35.
Certified Medicaid.
Owner Proprietary corp.

Rotan Nursing Center
711 E 5th, Rotan, TX 79546
(915) 735-2233
Admin Sandra Givens. *Dir of Nursing* Juanita
Underhill. *Medical Dir* Maurice Callan MD.
Licensure Intermediate care. *Beds* ICF 48.
Private Pay Patients 33%. *Certified*
Medicaid.
Owner Proprietary corp (Beverly Enterprises).
Admissions Requirements Medical
examination; Physician's request.
Staff LPNs 5 (ft), 1 (pt); Nurses' aides 11 (ft),
2 (pt); Activities coordinators 1 (ft);
Dietitians 1 (pt).
Languages Spanish.
Facilities Dining room; Laundry room;
Barber/Beauty shop.
Activities Arts & crafts; Cards; Games;
Reading groups; Prayer groups; Movies;
Shopping trips; Dances/Social/Cultural
gatherings.

Round Rock

Trinity Lutheran Home
PO Box 849, 1000 E Main Ave, Round Rock,
TX 78680
(512) 255-2521
Admin Kenneth M Keller.
Medical Dir Dr Hal Gaddy.
Licensure Intermediate care; Retirement. *Beds*
ICF 119; Personal care 40. *Certified*
Medicaid.
Owner Nonprofit corp.
Admissions Requirements Medical
examination; Physician's request.
Staff Physicians 1 (pt); RNs 1 (ft); LPNs 10
(ft), 2 (pt); Nurses' aides 24 (ft), 6 (pt);
Physical therapists 1 (pt); Reality therapists
1 (pt); Activities coordinators 1 (ft);
Dietitians 1 (pt).
Languages Spanish.
Affiliation Lutheran.
Facilities Dining room; Physical therapy
room; Activities room; Chapel; Crafts room;
Laundry room; Barber/Beauty shop; Library;
Many extra dayrooms; 3 enclosed
courtyards.
Activities Arts & crafts; Cards; Games;
Reading groups; Prayer groups; Movies;
Shopping trips; Dances/Social/Cultural
gatherings; Picnic; Open house; Bazaar;
Fishing.

Rusk

Leisure Lodge—Rusk
2205 E Johnson, Rusk, TX 75785
(214) 683-5444
Admin Elizabeth Doss.
Medical Dir Dr Roger McLarry.
Licensure Intermediate care. *Beds* 96.
Certified Medicaid.
Owner Proprietary corp (Beverly Enterprises).
Staff LPNs 5 (ft), 2 (pt); Nurses' aides 18 (ft),
4 (pt); Activities coordinators 1 (ft);
Dietitians 1 (ft).
Facilities Dining room; Physical therapy
room; Activities room; Laundry room;
Barber/Beauty shop.
Activities Arts & crafts; Games; Prayer groups;
Movies.

Rusk Nursing Home Inc
PO Box 347, 1216 W 6th St, Rusk, TX 75785
(214) 683-5421
Admin Eleanor E Gabbert.
Licensure Intermediate care. *Beds* 42.
Certified Medicaid.
Owner Proprietary corp.

Town Hall Estates
PO Box 517, 1900 E Bagley Rd, Rusk, TX
75785
(214) 683-5438
Admin Steven M Tandy. *Dir of Nursing*
Nancy DeFoor. *Medical Dir* Roger A
Meharry MD.
Licensure Skilled care; Intermediate care;
Private. *Beds* SNF 56; ICF 60; Private 24.
Certified Medicaid; Medicare.
Owner Nonprofit corp.
Admissions Requirements Medical
examination; Physician's request.
Staff RNs 3 (ft); LPNs 22 (ft); Nurses' aides
56 (ft); Physical therapists 1 (ft); Activities
coordinators 1 (ft), 1 (pt).
Affiliation American Religious Town Hall
Meeting.
Facilities Dining room; Physical therapy
room; Activities room; Crafts room; Laundry
room; Barber/Beauty shop; Library; Books
on wheels; Lobby.
Activities Arts & crafts; Games; Reading
groups; Prayer groups; Movies; Shopping
trips; Dances/Social/Cultural gatherings.

Saint Jo

St Jo Nursing Center
PO Box 70, 405 W Boggess St, Saint Jo, TX 76265
(817) 995-2302
Licensure Nursing. *Beds* Nursing 61.

San Angelo

Baptist Memorials Geriatric Center
PO Box 5661, 902 N Main St, San Angelo, TX 76902
(915) 655-7391
Admin Walter D McDonald; Marguerite H Gailey, Asst. *Dir of Nursing* Carolyn Owings RN. *Medical Dir* Charles Michael Jones MD.
Licensure Skilled care; Intermediate care; Long-term care hospital; Retirement. *Beds* SNF 100; ICF 108; Long-term care hospital 110; Retirement 463. *Private Pay Patients* 55%. *Certified* Medicaid; Medicare.
Owner Nonprofit organization/foundation.
Admissions Requirements Physician's request.
Staff Physicians 61 (ft) (by invitation); RNs 4 (ft), 4 (pt); LPNs 48 (ft), 2 (pt); Nurses' aides 116 (ft), 2 (pt); Physical therapists (consultant); Reality therapists 2 (ft); Recreational therapists 2 (ft); Activities coordinators 1 (ft); Dietitians (consultant).
Languages Spanish.
Facilities Dining room; Physical therapy room; Activities room; Chapel; Crafts room; Laundry room; Barber/Beauty shop; Library.
Activities Arts & crafts; Cards; Games; Reading groups; Prayer groups; Movies; Visits by community religious groups.

Colonial Nursing Home
4215 Armstrong, San Angelo, TX 76903
(915) 655-8986
Admin Stephen Hicks.
Medical Dir Marlene Keith.
Licensure Intermediate care. *Beds* 60. *Certified* Medicaid.
Owner Proprietary corp.
Admissions Requirements Physician's request.
Staff RNs 1 (ft); LPNs 4 (ft), 2 (pt); Nurses' aides 12 (ft), 3 (pt); Activities coordinators 1 (ft); Dietitians 1 (ft).
Languages Spanish.
Facilities Dining room; Physical therapy room; Activities room; Crafts room; Laundry room; Barber/Beauty shop.
Activities Arts & crafts; Cards; Games; Reading groups; Prayer groups; Movies; Shopping trips; Dances/Social/Cultural gatherings.

Meadow Creek Nursing Center
4343 Oak Grove Blvd, San Angelo, TX 76904
(915) 949-2559
Licensure Nursing. *Beds* Nursing 80.

Park Plaza Nursing Center Inc
2210 Howard St, San Angelo, TX 76901
(915) 944-0561
Admin James D Loudermilk.
Licensure Intermediate care. *Beds* 90. *Certified* Medicaid.
Owner Proprietary corp.

River Oaks Nursing Care Center Inc
1915 Greenwood, San Angelo, TX 76901
(915) 942-0677
Admin Lois Jones. *Dir of Nursing* Sherrie Jones. *Medical Dir* Dr James Womack.
Licensure Intermediate care. *Beds* ICF 90.
Owner Privately owned.
Staff Activities coordinators 2 (ft); Dietitians.

Riverside Manor
609 Rio Concho Dr, San Angelo, TX 76903
(915) 653-1266
Admin J W Kendall.
Medical Dir Dr Lloyd Downing.

Licensure Intermediate care. *Beds* 148. *Certified* Medicaid.
Owner Proprietary corp (Beverly Enterprises).
Admissions Requirements Physician's request.
Staff Physicians 1 (pt); RNs 2 (ft); LPNs 6 (ft); Nurses' aides 40 (ft); Reality therapists 1 (ft); Activities coordinators 1 (ft); Dietitians 1 (pt).
Facilities Dining room; Physical therapy room; Activities room; Chapel; Laundry room; Barber/Beauty shop.
Activities Arts & crafts; Cards; Games; Prayer groups; Movies; Shopping trips; Dances/ Social/Cultural gatherings; Parties.

San Antonio

Air Force Village Foundation—Health Care Center
4917 Ravenswood Dr, San Antonio, TX 78227
(512) 673-0325
Admin Jean Nagle.
Medical Dir Patricia Hague.
Licensure Intermediate care; Retirement. *Beds* ICF 68.
Owner Nonprofit organization/foundation.
Admissions Requirements Minimum age 62; Physician's request.
Staff Physicians 2 (pt); RNs 3 (ft), 2 (pt); LPNs 3 (ft), 2 (pt); Nurses' aides 9 (ft), 12 (pt); Occupational therapists 1 (pt); Activities coordinators 1 (ft); Dietitians 1 (pt); Ophthalmologists 1 (pt).
Languages Spanish.
Facilities Dining room; Activities room; Chapel; Laundry room; Barber/Beauty shop.
Activities Arts & crafts; Cards; Reading groups; Movies; Birthday parties; Dining out; Exercise class; Social hour.

Air Force Village II
5100 John D Ryan Blvd, San Antonio, TX 78245
(512) 677-8666
Admin Phil Newsom. *Dir of Nursing* Janet Honig RN. *Medical Dir* Dr Patrick Peters.
Licensure Private pay; Retirement; Alzheimer's care. *Beds* Private pay 68; Retirement 632. *Private Pay Patients* 100%.
Owner Nonprofit organization/foundation.
Admissions Requirements Minimum age 62; Medical examination; Physician's request; Generally limited to retired military officers and their spouses.
Staff Physicians (consultant); RNs 2 (ft); LPNs 5 (ft), 2 (pt); Nurses' aides 14 (ft), 7 (pt); Activities coordinators 1 (ft); Dietitians 1 (ft); Podiatrists (consultant).
Facilities Dining room; Activities room; Chapel; Crafts room; Laundry room; Barber/ Beauty shop; Library; Secured care system for wanderers.
Activities Arts & crafts; Cards; Games; Movies; Shopping trips; Dances/Social/ Cultural gatherings; Pet therapy; Monthly birthday parties; Exercise class.

Alamo Heights Manor
8223 Broadway, San Antonio, TX 78209
(512) 828-0606, 826-7766 FAX
Admin Myrna J Eavenson. *Dir of Nursing* Richard Farmer RN. *Medical Dir* Delio Romeu.
Licensure Skilled care; Intermediate care. *Beds* SNF 171; ICF 66. *Private Pay Patients* 25%. *Certified* Medicaid; Medicare.
Owner Proprietary corp.
Admissions Requirements Minimum age 18; Medical examination; Physician's request.
Staff RNs 3 (ft), 2 (pt); LPNs 25 (ft); Nurses' aides 63 (ft), 2 (pt); Physical therapists (contracted); Occupational therapists 1 (pt); Speech therapists 1 (pt); Activities coordinators 2 (pt); Dietitians 1 (pt); Ophthalmologists 1 (pt); Podiatrists 1 (pt).
Languages Spanish.

Facilities Dining room; Physical therapy room; Activities room; Chapel; Crafts room; Laundry room; Barber/Beauty shop; Library; Enclosed landscaped courtyards; Lobby.
Activities Arts & crafts; Cards; Games; Reading groups; Prayer groups; Movies; Shopping trips; Dances/Social/Cultural gatherings; Intergenerational programs; Pet therapy; Cooking; Dominoes; Sea World and zoo trips.

Alta Vista Nursing Center
616 W Russell, San Antonio, TX 78212
(512) 735-9233
Licensure Nursing. *Beds* Nursing 108.

Arms of Mercy Care Center Inc
225 W Laurel, San Antonio, TX 78212
(512) 227-0267
Admin Mary Eleanor Foreman.
Licensure Intermediate care. *Beds* 75. *Certified* Medicaid.
Owner Proprietary corp.

Army Residence Community Health Care Center
7400 Crestway Dr, San Antonio, TX 78239
(512) 646-5200
Admin Dena Castle-Adams. *Dir of Nursing* Catherine Hilgendorf RN. *Medical Dir* Dr Harvey Richey.
Licensure Skilled care; Retirement. *Beds* SNF 59; Retirement 532. *Private Pay Patients* 100%.
Owner Nonprofit organization/foundation.
Admissions Requirements Minimum age 62; Medical examination; Physician's request; Retired military officers and their spouses.
Staff RNs 3 (ft); LPNs 6 (ft), 4 (pt); Nurses' aides 23 (ft), 3 (pt); Physical therapists (contracted); Occupational therapists (contracted); Speech therapists (contracted); Activities coordinators 1 (ft); Dietitians 1 (ft); Podiatrists (consultant); Audiologists (consultant).
Facilities Dining room; Physical therapy room; Activities room; Chapel; Crafts room; Laundry room; Barber/Beauty shop; Library.
Activities Arts & crafts; Cards; Games; Reading groups; Prayer groups; Movies; Shopping trips; Dances/Social/Cultural gatherings; Intergenerational programs; Pet therapy.

Bethesda Care Center
1939 Bandera Rd, San Antonio, TX 78228
(512) 434-0671
Admin Paul Richard Love.
Licensure Intermediate care. *Beds* 144. *Certified* Medicaid.
Owner Nonprofit corp.

Broadway Lodge
1841 Flamingo, San Antonio, TX 78209
(512) 824-5324, 824-5326
Admin Jeaneane Enke.
Licensure Intermediate care; Personal care. *Beds* ICF 66; Personal 26. *Certified* Medicaid.
Owner Proprietary corp (ARA Living Centers).

Camlu Care Center—Louis Pasteur
7602 Louis Pasteur Dr, San Antonio, TX 78229
(512) 690-9974
Admin Paul W Nettle.
Medical Dir Emanuel P DeNoia MD.
Licensure Skilled care. *Beds* 87. *Certified* Medicaid.
Admissions Requirements Physician's request.
Staff RNs 2 (ft), 1 (pt); LPNs 12 (ft), 1 (pt); Nurses' aides 18 (ft), 4 (pt); Physical therapists 1 (pt); Recreational therapists 1 (ft); Occupational therapists 1 (pt); Activities coordinators 1 (ft), 1 (pt); Dietitians 1 (ft).
Facilities Dining room; Physical therapy room; Activities room; Chapel; Crafts room; Laundry room; Barber/Beauty shop; Library.

Activities Arts & crafts; Cards; Games; Reading groups; Prayer groups; Movies; Shopping trips; Dances/Social/Cultural gatherings; Outside events—rides, ball games, park outings.

Camlu Care Center of Oak Hills
7302 Oak Manor Dr, San Antonio, TX 78229
(512) 344-8537
Admin Susan Distelhorst.
Medical Dir Dr Norman Jacobson.
Licensure Skilled care; Intermediate care; Alzheimer's unit. Beds SNF 192; Alzheimer's unit 48. Certified Medicaid.
Admissions Requirements Minimum age 18; Medical examination.
Staff Physical therapists; Occupational therapists; Speech therapists; Dietitians; Podiatrists.
Facilities Dining room; Physical therapy room; Activities room; Chapel; Crafts room; Laundry room; Barber/Beauty shop; Library.
Activities Arts & crafts; Cards; Games; Reading groups; Prayer groups; Movies; Shopping trips; Dances/Social/Cultural gatherings.

Camlu Care Center of Woodlawn Hills
3031 W Woodlawn Ave, San Antonio, TX 78228
(512) 432-2381
Admin Paul W Nettle.
Medical Dir Luis E Perez-Montes MD.
Licensure Skilled care; Intermediate care. Beds 204. Certified Medicaid.
Admissions Requirements Minimum age 18; Physician's request.
Staff RNs 3 (ft), 1 (pt); LPNs 22 (ft), 7 (pt); Nurses' aides 34 (ft), 12 (pt); Physical therapists 1 (ft); Reality therapists 1 (ft); Recreational therapists 2 (ft); Occupational therapists 1 (pt); Activities coordinators 1 (ft), 1 (pt); Dietitians 1 (pt).
Facilities Dining room; Physical therapy room; Activities room; Chapel; Crafts room; Laundry room; Barber/Beauty shop; Library.
Activities Arts & crafts; Cards; Games; Reading groups; Prayer groups; Movies; Shopping trips; Dances/Social/Cultural gatherings; Van rides; Outings.

Carriage Square Nursing Home
8020 Blanco Rd, San Antonio, TX 78216
(512) 344-4553
Admin Carolyn A Barten.
Licensure Skilled care. Beds 143. Certified Medicaid.
Owner Proprietary corp.

Casa de San Antonio
603 Corinne, San Antonio, TX 78218
(512) 824-4891
Admin Myrna J Eavenson.
Medical Dir Carol Ann Chamberlain.
Licensure Intermediate care. Beds ICF 80; Private pay 40. Certified Medicaid.
Owner Privately owned.
Admissions Requirements Medical examination.
Staff RNs; LPNs; Nurses' aides; Activities coordinators; Dietitians; Podiatrists.
Facilities Dining room; Activities room; Laundry room; Barber/Beauty shop; Library.
Activities Arts & crafts; Cards; Games; Reading groups; Prayer groups; Movies; Shopping trips; Dances/Social/Cultural gatherings; Van rides.

Castle Hills Manor
8020 Blanco Rd, San Antonio, TX 78216
(512) 344-4553
Licensure Nursing. Beds Nursing 143.

Chandler Memorial Home
137 W French Pl, San Antonio, TX 78213
(512) 737-5110
Admin John L Poteete. Dir of Nursing Mary McDowell. Medical Dir Rowan Fisher.

Licensure Intermediate care; Retirement. Beds ICF 120; Retirement units 39. Certified Medicaid.
Owner Nonprofit organization/foundation.
Admissions Requirements Medical examination; Physician's request.
Staff Physicians 1 (pt); RNs 2 (ft); LPNs 9 (ft); Nurses' aides 32 (ft); Activities coordinators 1 (ft); Dietitians 1 (pt).
Languages Spanish.
Facilities Dining room; Activities room; Crafts room; Laundry room; Barber/Beauty shop; Library.
Activities Arts & crafts; Games; Prayer groups; Movies; Shopping trips; Dances/Social/Cultural gatherings; Intergenerational programs; Pet therapy; Senior center.

Chavaneaux Care Center
1339 W Chavaneaux, San Antonio, TX 78224
(512) 924-6211
Licensure Nursing. Beds Nursing 90.

Cresthaven Childrens Center
3018 E Commerce St, San Antonio, TX 78220
(512) 224-4271
Admin Joe Ward.
Medical Dir Janet Phillips; Yolanda Threat.
Licensure Intermediate care for mentally retarded. Beds ICF/MR 208. Certified Medicaid.
Owner Proprietary corp (Beverly Enterprises).
Admissions Requirements Minimum age 5.
Staff Physicians 3 (pt); RNs 3 (ft); Physical therapists 1 (pt); Occupational therapists 1 (pt); Speech therapists 1 (pt); Activities coordinators 2 (ft); Dietitians 1 (ft); LVNs 15 (ft); Qualified Mental Retardation Professionals 8 (ft).
Languages Spanish.
Facilities Dining room; Physical therapy room; Activities room; Crafts room; Laundry room.
Activities Arts & crafts; Games; Reading groups; Movies; Shopping trips; Dances/Social/Cultural gatherings.

Desha's Rest Home
135 Ridge Dr, San Antonio, TX 78228-3755
(512) 532-5841
Admin Beatrice W Desha.
Licensure Intermediate care. Beds 22. Certified Medicaid.
Admissions Requirements Medical examination; Physician's request.
Staff RNs 1 (pt); LPNs 1 (ft), 6 (pt); Nurses' aides 5 (ft), 4 (pt); Activities coordinators 1 (ft); Dietitians 1 (pt).
Facilities Dining room; Laundry room.
Activities Arts & crafts; Cards; Games; Reading groups; Prayer groups; Shopping trips; Dances/Social/Cultural gatherings.

Four Seasons Nursing Center—North
7703 Briaridge, San Antonio, TX 78230
(512) 341-6121
Admin Peggy Brisgill. Dir of Nursing Thelma Fisher. Medical Dir Dr John Matlock.
Licensure Skilled care; Intermediate care. Beds Swing beds SNF/ICF 106. Private Pay Patients 88%. Certified Medicare.
Owner Proprietary corp (Manor Care Inc).
Admissions Requirements Medical examination.
Staff RNs 6 (ft); LPNs 10 (ft); Nurses' aides 30 (ft), 2 (pt); Physical therapists; Activities coordinators 1 (ft); Dietitians 1 (ft).
Languages Spanish.
Facilities Dining room; Physical therapy room; Activities room; Laundry room; Barber/Beauty shop; Library.
Activities Arts & crafts; Cards; Games; Prayer groups; Shopping trips; Dances/Social/Cultural gatherings; Intergenerational programs; Pet therapy.

Four Seasons Nursing Center of San Antonio—Babcock
1975 Babcock Rd, San Antonio, TX 78229
(512) 341-8681
Admin Catherine Ferguson. Dir of Nursing E Parker RN. Medical Dir E DeNoia MD.
Licensure Skilled care; Intermediate care. Beds SNF 224; ICF; Non Certified. Certified Medicaid; Medicare.
Owner Proprietary corp (Manor Care).
Admissions Requirements Minimum age 21; Medical examination; Physician's request.
Staff RNs 8 (ft), 3 (pt); LPNs 14 (ft), 1 (pt); Nurses' aides 59 (ft), 7 (pt); Physical therapists 1 (ft); Occupational therapists 1 (ft); Speech therapists 1 (ft); Activities coordinators 2 (ft).
Languages Spanish.
Facilities Dining room; Physical therapy room; Activities room; Laundry room; Barber/Beauty shop.
Activities Arts & crafts; Cards; Games; Reading groups; Prayer groups; Movies; Shopping trips; Dances/Social/Cultural gatherings.

Four Seasons Nursing Center of San Antonio—Northwest
8300 Wurzbach Rd, San Antonio, TX 78229
(512) 690-1040
Admin Ruth Anne VanBlaricum.
Medical Dir Dr Norman Jacobson.
Licensure Intermediate care. Beds 164. Certified Medicaid.
Owner Proprietary corp (Manor Care).
Admissions Requirements Medical examination; Physician's request.
Staff RNs; LPNs; Nurses' aides; Physical therapists; Reality therapists; Recreational therapists; Activities coordinators; Dictitians; Podiatrists; Dentists.
Facilities Dining room; Activities room; Crafts room; Barber/Beauty shop; Library.
Activities Arts & crafts; Cards; Games; Reading groups; Prayer groups; Movies; Shopping trips; Dances/Social/Cultural gatherings.

Four Seasons Nursing Center of San Antonio—Pecan Valley
5027 Pecan Grove, San Antonio, TX 78222
(512) 333-6815
Admin Linda K Young.
Licensure Skilled care; Intermediate care. Beds 206. Certified Medicaid.
Owner Proprietary corp (Manor Care).

Four Seasons Nursing Center of San Antonio—Windcrest
8800 Fourwinds Dr, San Antonio, TX 78239
(512) 656-7800
Admin Della M Torres.
Licensure Skilled care; Intermediate care. Beds 208. Certified Medicaid.
Owner Proprietary corp (Manor Care).

Four Seasons Nursing Center—South
1339 W Chavaneaux Rd, San Antonio, TX 78224
(512) 924-6211
Admin Jeannie M Warren.
Licensure Intermediate care. Beds 90. Certified Medicaid.
Owner Proprietary corp (Manor Care).

Sarah Roberts French Home
1315 Texas Ave, San Antonio, TX 78201
(512) 736-4238
Admin Myrtle E Andrews. Dir of Nursing Janna Morgan Loyd. Medical Dir Orlando Suris MD.
Licensure Intermediate care. Beds ICF 60. Private Pay Patients 33%. Certified Medicaid.
Owner Nonprofit organization/foundation.
Staff RNs 1 (ft); LPNs 6 (ft); Nurses' aides 20 (ft); Activities coordinators 1 (ft).
Languages Spanish, German.

Facilities Dining room; Activities room; Laundry room; Barber/Beauty shop; Library.
Activities Arts & crafts; Games; Reading groups; Prayer groups; Movies; Shopping trips; Dances/Social/Cultural gatherings; Pet therapy.

Golden Manor Jewish Home for the Aged
130 Spencer Ln, San Antonio, TX 78201
(512) 736-4544
Admin Sue S Bornstein.
Licensure Skilled care. *Beds* 59. *Certified* Medicaid.
Owner Nonprofit corp.
Affiliation Jewish.

Grayson Square Health Care Center Inc
818 E Grayson, San Antonio, TX 78208
(512) 226-8181
Admin Terrence R Hayes.
Medical Dir Allen Ritch MD.
Licensure Intermediate care. *Beds* 81. *Certified* Medicaid.
Admissions Requirements Physician's request.
Staff RNs 1 (ft); LPNs 8 (ft); Nurses' aides 19 (ft); Activities coordinators 2 (ft); Dietitians 1 (ft).

Heartland of North East San Antonio
15175 Judson Rd, San Antonio, TX 78247
(512) 653-1219
Licensure Nursing; Personal care. *Beds* Nursing 121; Personal care 66.
Owner Proprietary corp (Health Care and Retirement Corp).

Highland Nursing Home
5819 Pecan Valley Dr, San Antonio, TX 78223
(512) 532-1911
Admin Michael A Triana.
Licensure Skilled care; Custodial care. *Beds* SNF 59; Custodial 22. *Certified* Medicaid.
Owner Proprietary corp.

King William Health Care Center
323 E Johnson St, San Antonio, TX 78204
(512) 222-0171
Licensure Nursing. *Beds* Nursing 142.

Louis Pasteur Care Center
7602 Louis Pasteur Dr, San Antonio, TX 78229
(512) 690-9974
Licensure Nursing. *Beds* Nursing 87.

Manor Square Convalescent Home
414 N Hackberry, San Antonio, TX 78202
(512) 226-6397
Admin Jeannette Cade.
Licensure Intermediate care. *Beds* 41. *Certified* Medicaid.

Memorial Medical Nursing Center
315 Lewis St, San Antonio, TX 78212
(512) 223-5521
Admin Robert W Knoebel.
Medical Dir J Rolando Rojas.
Licensure Skilled care; Intermediate care; Personal care. *Beds* SNF 60; ICF 119; Personal 26. *Certified* Medicaid.
Owner Proprietary corp (ARA Living Centers).
Admissions Requirements Minimum age 18; Medical examination; Physician's request.
Staff Physicians 1 (pt); RNs 2 (ft), 4 (pt); Nurses' aides 44 (ft); Physical therapists; Occupational therapists; Speech therapists; Activities coordinators 1 (ft), 1 (pt); Dietitians 1 (ft); Ophthalmologists 1 (pt); Podiatrists 1 (pt); Dentists 1 (pt).
Facilities Dining room; Physical therapy room; Activities room; Barber/Beauty shop.
Activities Arts & crafts; Cards; Games; Prayer groups; Movies; Dances/Social/Cultural gatherings.

Morningside Manor
602 Babcock Rd, San Antonio, TX 78284
(512) 734-7271
Admin Glenn Brown. *Dir of Nursing* Caroline Sorensen. *Medical Dir* Rowan Fisher MD.
Licensure Skilled care; Intermediate care; Personal care; Alzheimer's care. *Beds* SNF 95; ICF 202; Personal 78. *Certified* Medicaid; Medicare.
Owner Nonprofit corp.
Admissions Requirements Minimum age 62; Medical examination; Physician's request.
Staff Physicians 1 (pt); RNs 5 (ft), 3 (pt); LPNs 28 (ft), 5 (pt); Nurses' aides 90 (ft), 12 (pt); Physical therapists 1 (pt); Occupational therapists 4 (ft); Activities coordinators 5 (ft); Dietitians 1 (pt).
Languages Spanish.
Facilities Dining room; Physical therapy room; Activities room; Chapel; Crafts room; Laundry room; Barber/Beauty shop; Library.
Activities Arts & crafts; Cards; Games; Reading groups; Prayer groups; Movies; Shopping trips; Dances/Social/Cultural gatherings.

Normandy Terrace Inc
841 Rice Rd, San Antonio, TX 78220
(512) 648-0101
Admin Betty Lou Roberts.
Medical Dir Dr Ruskin Norman.
Licensure Skilled care; Intermediate care. *Beds* 320. *Certified* Medicaid; Medicare.
Admissions Requirements Medical examination; Physician's request.
Staff RNs 6 (ft), 4 (pt); LPNs 21 (ft); Nurses' aides 109 (ft); Physical therapists 3 (ft); Recreational therapists 2 (ft); Occupational therapists 2 (ft); Activities coordinators 1 (ft); Dietitians 1 (ft).
Facilities Dining room; Physical therapy room; Activities room; Chapel; Crafts room; Laundry room; Barber/Beauty shop.
Activities Arts & crafts; Cards; Games; Reading groups; Prayer groups; Movies; Shopping trips; Dances/Social/Cultural gatherings.

Normandy Terrace Inc—Northeast
8607 Village Dr, San Antonio, TX 78217
(512) 656-6733
Admin Charles H Koll.
Licensure Skilled care. *Beds* 240. *Certified* Medicaid.
Owner Proprietary corp.

Northgate Manor
5757 N Knoll, San Antonio, TX 78240
(512) 699-8535
Licensure Nursing. *Beds* Nursing 120.

Oak Hills Care Center
7302 Oak Manor Dr, San Antonio, TX 78229
(512) 344-8537
Licensure Nursing. *Beds* Nursing 186.

Retama Manor Nursing Center—North
501 Ogden, San Antonio, TX 78212
(512) 225-4588
Admin Mary S Jakob.
Licensure Intermediate care. *Beds* 136. *Certified* Medicaid.
Owner Proprietary corp (ARA Living Centers).

Retama Manor Nursing Center—South
3030 S Roosevelt, San Antonio, TX 78214
(512) 924-8151
Admin Billy Bruce Apperson.
Licensure Intermediate care. *Beds* 150. *Certified* Medicaid.
Owner Proprietary corp (ARA Living Centers).

Retama Manor Nursing Center—West
636 Cupples Rd, San Antonio, TX 78237
(512) 434-0611
Admin Deborah L Lally.

Licensure Intermediate care. *Beds* 150. *Certified* Medicaid.
Owner Proprietary corp (ARA Living Centers).

St Benedict Nursing Home
323 E Johnson St, San Antonio, TX 78204
(512) 222-0171
Admin Sr Mary John Sapp.
Licensure Skilled care; Intermediate care. *Beds* 197. *Certified* Medicaid; Medicare.
Owner Nonprofit corp.
Affiliation Roman Catholic.

St Francis Nursing Home
2717 N Flores, San Antonio, TX 78212
(512) 736-3177
Admin Patsy Sue Block.
Licensure Intermediate care. *Beds* 143. *Certified* Medicaid.
Owner Nonprofit corp.
Affiliation Roman Catholic.

San Jose Nursing Center
406 Sharmain, San Antonio, TX 78221
(512) 924-8136
Admin Marilyn Kowalik.
Licensure Intermediate care. *Beds* ICF 70. *Certified* Medicaid.
Owner Privately owned.
Staff LPNs; Nurses' aides; Activities coordinators.

San Pedro Manor
515 W Ashby Pl, San Antonio, TX 78212
(512) 732-5181
Admin Bessie B Parkin. *Dir of Nursing* Patricia Perritano RN.
Licensure Skilled care; Intermediate care. *Beds* 152. *Certified* Medicaid; Medicare; Private pay.
Owner Proprietary corp.
Admissions Requirements Physician's request.
Staff RNs 5 (ft), 3 (pt); LPNs 13 (ft), 6 (pt); Nurses' aides 30 (ft), 15 (pt); Activities coordinators 1 (ft), 1 (pt); Dietitians 1 (ft).
Languages Spanish.
Facilities Dining room; Barber/Beauty shop.
Activities Arts & crafts; Cards; Games; Prayer groups; Movies; Exercise groups; Resident council.

Silver Creek Manor
9014 Timberpath, San Antonio, TX 78250
(512) 523-2455
Admin Deborah L Lally. *Dir of Nursing* Linda Ybarra. *Medical Dir* Rodney Carry MD.
Licensure Skilled care. *Beds* SNF 120. *Private Pay Patients* 30%. *Certified* Medicaid; Medicare.
Owner Proprietary corp (Vari-Care Inc).
Staff RNs 5 (ft); LPNs 12 (ft), 5 (pt); Nurses' aides 56 (ft), 13 (pt); Physical therapists (contracted); Reality therapists (contracted); Occupational therapists (contracted); Speech therapists (contracted); Activities coordinators 1 (ft); Dietitians (contracted); Podiatrists (contracted).
Languages Spanish.
Activities Arts & crafts; Cards; Games; Reading groups; Prayer groups; Movies; Shopping trips; Dances/Social/Cultural gatherings; Intergenerational programs.

Skyview Living Center—San Antonio
4703 Goldfield, San Antonio, TX 78218
(512) 661-6751
Admin Joyce M Latham.
Licensure Intermediate care for mentally retarded. *Beds* 150. *Certified* Medicaid.

Southeast Nursing Center
4302 E Southcross, San Antonio, TX 78222
(512) 333-1223
Admin Jean Harrison. *Dir of Nursing* Connie Speaks. *Medical Dir* Dr Rodney Carry.
Licensure Skilled care. *Beds* SNF 120. *Private Pay Patients* 8%. *Certified* Medicaid; Medicare.

Owner Proprietary corp (Beverly Enterprises).
Admissions Requirements Minimum age 18; Medical examination; Physician's request.
Staff RNs 1 (ft), 1 (pt); LPNs 15 (ft); Nurses' aides 50 (ft), 10 (pt); Activities coordinators 1 (ft), 1 (pt); Dietitians 1 (ft).
Languages Spanish.
Facilities Dining room; Activities room; Chapel; Crafts room; Laundry room; Barber/Beauty shop.
Activities Arts & crafts; Games; Prayer groups; Movies; Shopping trips; Dances/Social/Cultural gatherings; Pet therapy.

Southwest Care Centers Inc
PO Box 21156, 903 Leahy St, San Antonio, TX 78221
(512) 922-2761
Admin Samuel W Hardy.
Licensure Intermediate care. *Beds* 92. *Certified* Medicaid.
Owner Proprietary corp.

Sunrise Convalescent Center
50 Briggs, San Antonio, TX 78224
(512) 921-0184
Licensure Nursing. *Beds* Nursing 120.

Villa Care Center
1939 Bandera Rd, San Antonio, TX 78228
(512) 434-0671
Licensure Nursing. *Beds* Nursing 144.

Village at Vance Jackson
1975 Babcock, San Antonio, TX 78229
(512) 344-3047
Admin Donna M Weimer. *Dir of Nursing* Nancy Spilka. *Medical Dir* Dr Edward Sargent.
Licensure Custodial assisted living center. *Beds* Custodial 120.
Owner Proprietary corp (Manor Care).
Admissions Requirements Medical examination.
Staff RNs; LPNs; Nurses' aides; Activities coordinators.
Languages Spanish.
Facilities Dining room; Activities room; Crafts room; Laundry room; Barber/Beauty shop; Library; Garden.
Activities Arts & crafts; Cards; Games; Prayer groups; Movies; Shopping trips; Dances/Social/Cultural gatherings; Cocktail hour.

Village on the Heights
5000 Fawn Meadow, San Antonio, TX 78240
(512) 696-6005
Licensure Nursing; Personal care. *Beds* Nursing 60; Personal care 30.

Walden Oaks Health Care Center
5100 Newcome Dr, San Antonio, TX 78229
(512) 680-2280
Licensure Nursing. *Beds* Nursing 60.

Woodlawn Hills Care Center
3031 W Woodlawn Ave, San Antonio, TX 78228
(512) 432-2381
Licensure Nursing. *Beds* Nursing 186.

Wright Nursing Home Inc
328 W Mayfield Blvd, San Antonio, TX 78221
(512) 924-5533
Admin Georgia W Holmes. *Dir of Nursing* Susan Quezada. *Medical Dir* Dr David Madonsky.
Licensure Intermediate care; Personal. *Beds* ICF 60; Personal 20. *Certified* Medicaid.
Owner Proprietary corp.
Admissions Requirements Minimum age 21.
Staff LPNs 5 (ft), 3 (pt); Nurses' aides 15 (ft), 5 (pt); Activities coordinators 1 (ft); Dietitians 1 (pt).
Languages Spanish.

Facilities Dining room; Activities room; Library.
Activities Arts & crafts; Cards; Games; Reading groups; Prayer groups; Movies; Shopping trips; Dances/Social/Cultural gatherings; Picnics.

San Augustine

Hines Health Care Center
806 N Clark St, San Augustine, TX 75972
(409) 275-2522, 275-5609
Admin Jeanette B Davidson.
Licensure Intermediate care. *Beds* 70. *Certified* Medicaid.
Owner Proprietary corp.

San Augustine Nursing Center
Hwy 96 at FM 1277, San Augustine, TX 75972
(409) 275-3466
Admin Patsy R Thomas. *Dir of Nursing* Carol Moore.
Licensure Intermediate care; Intermediate care for mentally retarded. *Beds* ICF 58. *Certified* Medicaid; Medicare.
Owner Proprietary corp (ARA Living Centers).
Admissions Requirements Minimum age 21; Medical examination; Physician's request.
Staff RNs 3 (ft); Nurses' aides (ft); Recreational therapists 1 (ft); Activities coordinators 1 (ft); Dietitians 1 (pt); LVN 8 (ft).
Activities Arts & crafts; Cards; Games; Reading groups; Prayer groups; Movies; Shopping trips; Dances/Social/Cultural gatherings.

Twin Lakes Care Center
Rte 1 Box 725, Hwy 96, San Augustine, TX 75972
(409) 275-2900
Admin Jeanette Davidson.
Medical Dir Diana Whitehead.
Licensure Intermediate care. *Beds* ICF 90. *Certified* Medicaid.
Owner Privately owned (D & H Enterprises Inc).
Admissions Requirements Medical examination.
Staff RNs 1 (ft); LPNs 6 (ft); Nurses' aides 40 (ft); Activities coordinators 1 (ft).
Facilities Dining room; Activities room; Chapel; Crafts room; Laundry room; Barber/Beauty shop; Library.
Activities Arts & crafts; Prayer groups; Shopping trips; Dances/Social/Cultural gatherings.

San Benito

Twinbrooke South
502 E Expressway 83, San Benito, TX 78586-3097
(512) 399-3732
Admin Rebecca M Berry. *Dir of Nursing* Barbara Elliff.
Licensure Intermediate care. *Beds* ICF 52. *Private Pay Patients* 5%. *Certified* Medicaid.
Owner Proprietary corp (Rio Grande Resident Care Corp).
Admissions Requirements Medical examination; Physician's request.
Staff RNs 2 (pt); Nurses' aides 14 (ft), 2 (pt); Physical therapists; Occupational therapists; Activities coordinators; Dietitians (consultant).
Languages Spanish.
Facilities Dining room; Laundry room.
Activities Arts & crafts; Cards; Games; Reading groups; Prayer groups; Movies; Dances/Social/Cultural gatherings; Pet therapy.

San Diego

La Hacienda Nursing Home Inc
4408 Hwy 44 E, San Diego, TX 78384
(512) 279-3860
Admin James M Baker.
Licensure Skilled care; Intermediate care. *Beds* 114. *Certified* Medicaid.
Owner Proprietary corp.

San Juan

San Juan Nursing Home Inc
PO Box 1238, 300 N Nebraska Ave, San Juan, TX 78589
(512) 787-1771
Admin Sr Lucille M Belisle.
Licensure Skilled care. *Beds* 124. *Certified* Medicaid.
Owner Nonprofit corp.
Affiliation Roman Catholic.

San Marcos

Care Inn of San Marcos
1600 N IH 35, San Marcos, TX 78666
(512) 353-5026
Licensure Nursing. *Beds* Nursing 118; Personal care 28.

Hillside Manor of San Marcos Inc
Thorpe Ln, San Marcos, TX 78666
(512) 353-8988
Admin George E Dimmick; Karen Kersh, Assist Admin. *Dir of Nursing* Mary Spurlock. *Medical Dir* Ken Long MD.
Licensure Skilled care; Intermediate care. *Beds* SNF 45; ICF 99; Non-certified 5. *Private Pay Patients* 40%. *Certified* Medicaid; Medicare.
Owner Privately owned.
Admissions Requirements Medical examination; Physician's request.
Staff RNs; LPNs; Nurses' aides; Physical therapists; Recreational therapists; Activities coordinators; Dietitians.
Languages Spanish.
Facilities Dining room; Physical therapy room; Activities room; Crafts room; Laundry room; Barber/Beauty shop; Library.
Activities Arts & crafts; Cards; Games; Reading groups; Prayer groups; Movies; Shopping trips; Dances/Social/Cultural gatherings; Intergenerational programs; Pet therapy; S.T.A.I.R.S. to Health.

San Saba

Eventide Nursing Home
1405 W Storey, San Saba, TX 76877
(915) 372-3675
Admin Alice M Brown. *Dir of Nursing* Marietta Adams.
Licensure Intermediate care. *Beds* ICF 80. *Certified* Medicaid.
Owner Privately owned.
Admissions Requirements Medical examination; Physician's request.
Staff Physicians; RNs; LPNs; Nurses' aides; Physical therapists; Activities coordinators; Dietitians.
Facilities Dining room; Activities room; Laundry room; Barber/Beauty shop; Picnic grounds.
Activities Arts & crafts; Cards; Games; Reading groups; Prayer groups; Movies; Shopping trips.

San Saba Nursing Home Inc
608 S Edgewood St, San Saba, TX 76877
(915) 372-5179
Admin Joyce Lusty.
Licensure Intermediate care. *Beds* 63. *Certified* Medicaid.
Owner Proprietary corp.

Sanger

Care Inn of Sanger
PO Box 786, 600 N Stemmons Fwy, Sanger, TX 76266
(817) 458-3202
Admin Opal Faye Morrison.
Medical Dir J Clyde Chapman DO.
Licensure Intermediate care. *Beds* 67. *Certified* Medicaid.
Owner Proprietary corp (ARA Living Centers).
Admissions Requirements Minimum age 18.
Staff RNs 1 (ft); LPNs 7 (ft), 2 (pt); Nurses' aides 12 (ft), 1 (pt).
Facilities Dining room; Activities room; Crafts room; Laundry room; Barber/Beauty shop; Library.
Activities Arts & crafts; Games; Reading groups; Dances/Social/Cultural gatherings.

Santa Anna

Ranger Park Inn
PO Box 159, Brownwood Hwy, Santa Anna, TX 76878
(915) 348-3105
Admin Herbert C Houser. *Dir of Nursing* Lila Tucker RN.
Licensure Skilled care; Retirement. *Beds* SNF 70. *Certified* Medicaid; Medicare.
Owner Proprietary corp.
Admissions Requirements Medical examination; Physician's request.
Staff RNs 1 (ft); LPNs 6 (ft); Nurses' aides 11 (ft); Physical therapists 1 (pt); Activities coordinators 1 (ft); Dietitians 1 (pt).
Facilities Dining room; Activities room; Crafts room; Laundry room; Barber/Beauty shop.
Activities Arts & crafts; Games; Prayer groups; Dances/Cultural gatherings.

Savoy

Country View Nursing Center
Hwy 82 E, Savoy, TX 75479
(214) 965-4285
Admin Joan F Pierce.
Licensure Intermediate care. *Beds* 96. *Certified* Medicaid.
Owner Proprietary corp (Health Enter of America).
Admissions Requirements Medical examination.
Staff RNs 1 (ft); LPNs 2 (ft); Nurses' aides 20 (ft); Activities coordinators 1 (ft); Dietitians 1 (ft).
Facilities Dining room; Physical therapy room; Activities room; Chapel; Crafts room; Laundry room; Barber/Beauty shop.
Activities Arts & crafts; Cards; Games; Shopping trips; Dances/Social/Cultural gatherings.

Mullican Nursing Home
PO Box 426, Main St, Savoy, TX 75479
(214) 965-4964
Admin Mary A Little.
Licensure Intermediate care. *Beds* 93. *Certified* Medicaid.
Owner Proprietary corp.

Schertz

Autumn Winds Retirement Lodge
FM 3009, Schertz, TX 78154
(512) 658-6338
Admin Darlene T Pruitt.
Licensure Custodial care. *Beds* 96. *Certified* Medicaid.
Staff RNs 2 (ft); LPNs 7 (ft); Nurses' aides 19 (ft); Activities coordinators 2 (ft); Dietitians 1 (ft).

Facilities Dining room; Activities room; Crafts room; Laundry room; Barber/Beauty shop; Library.
Activities Arts & crafts; Cards; Prayer groups; Movies; Shopping trips; Dances/Social/Cultural gatherings.

Schulenburg

Colonial Nursing Home Inc
507 West Ave, Schulenburg, TX 78956
(409) 743-4150
Admin Rita Brossmann. *Dir of Nursing* Evelyn Meyer.
Licensure Intermediate care; Alzheimer's care. *Beds* ICF 90. *Certified* Medicaid.
Owner Proprietary corp.
Admissions Requirements Medical examination; Physician's request.
Staff Nurses' aides; Physical therapists; Recreational therapists; Occupational therapists; Speech therapists; Activities coordinators; Dietitians.
Languages Spanish, Czech, German.
Facilities Dining room; Activities room; Chapel; Crafts room; Laundry room; Barber/Beauty shop.
Activities Arts & crafts; Cards; Games; Reading groups; Prayer groups; Movies; Shopping trips; Dances/Social/Cultural gatherings.

Seagoville

Carter Nursing Home Corporation
111 Fisk Rd, Seagoville, TX 75159
(214) 287-2322
Admin Doyle J Graham.
Licensure Intermediate care. *Beds* ICF 126. *Certified* Medicaid.
Owner Proprietary corp.
Admissions Requirements Minimum age 21; Medical examination; Physician's request.
Staff Physicians 3 (ft); RNs 2 (ft); LPNs 6 (ft); Nurses' aides 28 (ft); Physical therapists 1 (ft); Reality therapists 1 (ft); Recreational therapists 1 (ft); Speech therapists 1 (ft); Activities coordinators 1 (ft); Dietitians 1 (ft); Ophthalmologists 1 (ft); Podiatrists 1 (ft).
Languages Spanish.
Facilities Dining room; Activities room; Crafts room; Laundry room; Barber/Beauty shop.
Activities Arts & crafts; Cards; Games; Reading groups; Prayer groups; Movies; Shopping trips; Dances/Social/Cultural gatherings.

Seago Manor
2416 Elizabeth Ln, Seagoville, TX 75159
(214) 287-1201
Admin Barbara Perryman.
Medical Dir Larry Stubblefield MD.
Licensure Intermediate care. *Beds* ICF 142. *Certified* Medicaid.
Owner Proprietary corp (Cantex Healthcare Centers).
Admissions Requirements Minimum age 18; Medical examination; Physician's request.
Staff RNs 1 (pt); LPNs 8 (ft), 1 (pt); Nurses' aides 31 (ft); Activities coordinators 1 (ft); Dietitians 1 (ft), 1 (pt).
Facilities Dining room; Physical therapy room; Activities room; Chapel; Crafts room; Laundry room; Barber/Beauty shop; Library.
Activities Arts & crafts; Cards; Games; Reading groups; Prayer groups; Movies; Shopping trips; Dances/Social/Cultural gatherings.

Sealy

Azalea Manor Nursing Home
207 N Meyer, Sealy, TX 77474
(409) 885-2937

Admin Phylis Avant.
Licensure Intermediate care. *Beds* 90. *Certified* Medicaid.
Admissions Requirements Medical examination; Physician's request.
Staff RNs 1 (ft); LPNs 5 (ft), 2 (pt); Nurses' aides 20 (ft), 4 (pt); Activities coordinators 1 (ft); Dietitians 1 (pt).
Facilities Dining room; Physical therapy room; Laundry room; Barber/Beauty shop.
Activities Arts & crafts; Cards; Games; Reading groups; Prayer groups; Shopping trips; Dances/Social/Cultural gatherings.

Seguin

Care Inn of Seguin
1219 Eastwood Dr, Seguin, TX 78155
(512) 379-7777
Admin Jeaneane Y Enke.
Medical Dir Dr Robert Fretz.
Licensure Intermediate care. *Beds* 136. *Certified* Medicaid.
Owner Proprietary corp (ARA Living Centers).
Admissions Requirements Medical examination; Physician's request.
Staff Physicians; RNs; LPNs; Nurses' aides; Activities coordinators; Dietitians.
Facilities Dining room; Activities room; Laundry room; Barber/Beauty shop; Restorative care room.
Activities Arts & crafts; Cards; Games; Reading groups; Prayer groups; Shopping trips; Ceramics; One-to-one activities; Country western band; Family night dinners.

Nesbit Nursing Home
PO Box 1509, 1215 E Ashby, Seguin, TX 78155
(512) 379-1606
Admin David W Nesbit.
Licensure Intermediate care. *Beds* 120. *Certified* Medicaid.
Admissions Requirements Medical examination; Physician's request.
Staff RNs 1 (ft); LPNs 10 (ft), 2 (pt); Nurses' aides 37 (ft), 4 (pt); Activities coordinators 2 (ft); Dietitians 1 (ft).
Facilities Dining room; Activities room; Crafts room; Laundry room; Barber/Beauty shop.
Activities Arts & crafts; Cards; Games; Reading groups; Prayer groups; Movies; Shopping trips; Dances/Social/Cultural gatherings.

Seguin Convalescent Home
1637 N King, Seguin, TX 78155
(512) 379-3784
Admin Julie Hetherington. *Dir of Nursing* Jeanette Muenich RN. *Medical Dir* John Mueller MD.
Licensure Skilled care; Intermediate care. *Beds* SNF 44; ICF 69. *Private Pay Patients* 50%. *Certified* Medicaid; VA.
Owner Proprietary corp (Care Givers Inc).
Admissions Requirements Minimum age 18.
Staff RNs 3 (ft); LPNs 10 (ft); Nurses' aides 25 (ft); Physical therapists 1 (ft); Reality therapists 1 (ft); Recreational therapists 1 (ft); Occupational therapists; Speech therapists 1 (ft); Activities coordinators 1 (ft); Dietitians 1 (ft); Ophthalmologists 1 (ft).
Languages German, Spanish.
Facilities Dining room; Activities room; Chapel; Laundry room; Barber/Beauty shop; Van with lift.
Activities Arts & crafts; Cards; Games; Reading groups; Prayer groups; Movies; Shopping trips; Dances/Social/Cultural gatherings; Intergenerational programs; Pet therapy.

Seminole

Seminole Nursing Center
PO Box 811, 308 NW 3rd St, Seminole, TX
79360
(915) 758-3022
Admin David O Crowson.
Licensure Intermediate care. *Beds* 33.
Certified Medicaid.
Admissions Requirements Minimum age 18;
Medical examination; Physician's request.
Staff LPNs 4 (ft); Nurses' aides 12 (ft);
Activities coordinators 1 (ft).
Facilities Dining room; Laundry room;
Barber/Beauty shop.
Activities Arts & crafts; Cards; Games;
Reading groups; Prayer groups; Movies;
Shopping trips; Dances/Social/Cultural
gatherings.

Seymour

Westview Care Center
PO Box 1291, 1100 Westview Dr, Seymour,
TX 76380
(817) 888-3176
Admin W Faye Hollar.
Licensure Intermediate care. *Beds* 100.
Certified Medicaid.
Owner Proprietary corp (Beverly Enterprises).
Admissions Requirements Minimum age 18.
Staff RNs 1 (pt); LPNs 8 (ft); Nurses' aides 25
(ft), 3 (pt); Activities coordinators 1 (ft).
Languages Spanish.
Facilities Dining room; Activities room;
Crafts room; Laundry room; Barber/Beauty
shop.
Activities Arts & crafts; Cards; Games;
Reading groups; Prayer groups; Movies;
Shopping trips; Dances/Social/Cultural
gatherings.

Shamrock

Care Inn of Shamrock
Hwy 83 S, Shamrock, TX 79079
(806) 256-2153
Admin Daniel G Wylie.
Licensure Intermediate care. *Beds* 64.
Certified Medicaid.
Owner Proprietary corp (ARA Living
Centers).

Sherman

Chapel of Care Nursing Center
1518 S Sam Rayburn Fwy, Sherman, TX
75090
(214) 893-5553
Admin Judith A Pleshek. *Dir of Nursing*
Charlotte Henry RN. *Medical Dir* Dr David
Garvin.
Licensure Skilled care; Intermediate care;
Alzheimer's care. *Beds* SNF 89; ICF 111.
Certified Medicaid; Medicare; VA.
Owner Proprietary corp.
Staff Physicians 27 (ft); RNs 3 (ft); LPNs 22
(ft); Nurses' aides 66 (ft); Physical therapists
2 (ft); Reality therapists 2 (ft); Recreational
therapists 2 (ft); Occupational therapists 2
(ft); Speech therapists 2 (ft); Activities
coordinators 2 (ft); Dietitians 1 (ft);
Ophthalmologists 1 (ft); Podiatrists 1 (ft);
Audiologists 1 (ft).
Languages Spanish.
Facilities Dining room; Activities room;
Chapel; Laundry room; Barber/Beauty shop.
Activities Arts & crafts; Cards; Games;
Reading groups; Prayer groups; Movies;
Shopping trips; Dances/Social/Cultural
gatherings; Intergenerational programs; Pet
therapy.

Heritage Manor Nursing Home
315 W McLain, Sherman, TX 75090
(214) 893-0149

Admin Annabelle Grissom.
Licensure Intermediate care; Intermediate care
for mentally retarded. *Beds* ICF 64; ICF/MR
66. *Certified* Medicaid.
Owner Proprietary corp (ARA Living
Centers).

Shady Oaks Nursing Center
Loy Lake Rd & Hwy 82, Sherman, TX 75090
(214) 893-9636
Admin Wanda J Howard.
Medical Dir Stanley Monroe MD.
Licensure Skilled care. *Beds* 195. *Certified*
Medicaid.
Owner Proprietary corp (Meridan Healthcare).
Admissions Requirements Minimum age 18.
Staff Physicians 1 (pt); RNs 1 (ft), 3 (pt);
LPNs 11 (ft); Nurses' aides 39 (ft); Activities
coordinators 1 (ft); Dietitians 1 (ft).
Facilities Dining room; Physical therapy
room; Activities room; Chapel; Crafts room;
Laundry room; Barber/Beauty shop; Library;
Greenhouse.
Activities Arts & crafts; Cards; Games; Prayer
groups; Movies; Dances/Social/Cultural
gatherings.

Sherman Nursing Center
817 W Center St, Sherman, TX 75090
(214) 893-6348
Admin Jerry L Jones.
Licensure Intermediate care. *Beds* 122.
Certified Medicaid.
Owner Proprietary corp (Truco Inc).

Shiner

Trinity Lutheran Home
Rte 3 Box 19, 1213 N Ave B, Shiner, TX
77984
(512) 594-4101
Admin Mary Lynn Campbell. *Dir of Nursing*
Georgie Herman. *Medical Dir* Dr Maurice G
Wilkinson.
Licensure Intermediate care; Retirement. *Beds*
ICF 91; Retirement 28. *Private Pay Patients*
38%. *Certified* Medicaid.
Owner Nonprofit corp (Lutheran Social
Services of Texas Inc).
Admissions Requirements Medical
examination; Physician's request.
Staff Nurses' aides 19 (ft), 7 (pt); Activities
coordinators 1 (ft), 1 (pt); LVNs 9 (ft), 1
(pt).
Languages Czech, German, Spanish.
Affiliation Lutheran.
Facilities Dining room; Activities room;
Chapel; Crafts room; Laundry room; Barber/
Beauty shop.
Activities Arts & crafts; Games; Reading
groups; Prayer groups; Movies; Dances/
Social/Cultural gatherings; Pet therapy.

Silsbee

Bur-Mont Nursing Center
1680 Hwy 327 W, Silsbee, TX 77656
(409) 385-5571
Admin Anna L Tanton.
Licensure Skilled care. *Beds* 120. *Certified*
Medicaid; VA.
Owner Proprietary corp.
Staff Physicians; RNs; LPNs; Nurses' aides;
Physical therapists; Occupational therapists;
Speech therapists; Activities coordinators.

Silsbee Convalescent Center
1105 W Hwy 418, Silsbee, TX 77656
(713) 385-3784
Admin Martha J Reeves.
Licensure Intermediate care. *Beds* 68.
Certified Medicaid.
Owner Proprietary corp (Cantex Healthcare
Centers).

Sinton

Sinton Manor
936 W 4th St, Sinton, TX 78387
(512) 364-3478
Admin Norma Apple. *Dir of Nursing* Vee
Marez. *Medical Dir* Dr Rene Acuna.
Licensure Intermediate care; Alzheimer's care.
Beds ICF 60. *Private Pay Patients* 40%.
Certified Medicaid.
Owner Proprietary corp (F E Deere Inc).
Staff Physicians 1 (pt); RNs 1 (pt); LPNs 4
(ft), 2 (pt); Nurses' aides 21 (ft), 1 (pt);
Activities coordinators 1 (ft); Dietitians 1
(pt).
Facilities Dining room; Activities room;
Crafts room; Laundry room.
Activities Arts & crafts; Games; Reading
groups; Prayer groups; Movies; Shopping
trips; Dances/Social/Cultural gatherings.

Taft Hospital & Convalescent Center
San Pat Courthouse, Sinton, TX 78387-2450
(512) 528-2545
Admin Douglas Langley. *Dir of Nursing*
Cynthia Keese. *Medical Dir* Y S Jenkins
MD.
Licensure Private. *Beds* Private 30.
Owner Publicly owned.
Admissions Requirements Minimum age 18;
Medical examination; Physician's request.
Staff RNs 1 (ft); LPNs 4 (ft); Nurses' aides 4
(ft); Physical therapists 1 (pt); Activities
coordinators 1 (pt); Dietitians 1 (pt).
Facilities Dining room; Physical therapy
room; Activities room; Chapel; Crafts room;
Laundry room; Library.
Activities Arts & crafts; Cards; Games;
Reading groups; Prayer groups.

Slaton

Slaton Care Center
630 S 19th St, Slaton, TX 79364
(806) 828-6268
Admin Wanda Barclay. *Dir of Nursing* June
Wilson RN.
Licensure Intermediate care. *Beds* ICF 120.
Certified Medicaid.
Owner Proprietary corp (Centex).
Admissions Requirements Medical
examination; Physician's request.
Staff RNs 1 (ft); LPNs 5 (ft), 4 (pt); Nurses'
aides 20 (ft), 10 (pt); Activities coordinators
1 (ft); Dietitians 1 (ft).
Languages Spanish.
Facilities Dining room; Activities room;
Crafts room; Laundry room; Barber/Beauty
shop.
Activities Arts & crafts; Cards; Games; Prayer
groups; Movies; Shopping trips; Dances/
Social/Cultural gatherings; Pet therapy.

Smithville

Towers Nursing Home
907 Garwood, Smithville, TX 78957
(512) 237-4606
Admin Jean Satterfield. *Dir of Nursing*
Rosemary Galpin.
Licensure Intermediate care. *Beds* ICF 90.
Private Pay Patients 35%. *Certified*
Medicaid.
Owner Nonprofit corp.
Activities Arts & crafts; Cards; Games;
Reading groups; Prayer groups; Movies;
Shopping trips; Dances/Social/Cultural
gatherings; Intergenerational programs; Pet
therapy.

Snyder

Snyder Nursing Center
5311 Big Spring Hwy, Snyder, TX 79549
(915) 573-6332
Admin Jerry Miller.

Licensure Intermediate care; Personal care.
Beds ICF 80; Personal 20. *Certified* Medicaid.
Owner Proprietary corp (Beverly Enterprises).
Staff LPNs 4 (ft); Nurses' aides 25 (ft); Reality therapists 1 (ft); Activities coordinators 1 (ft); Dietitians 4 (ft).
Facilities Dining room; Physical therapy room; Activities room; Laundry room; Barber/Beauty shop.
Activities Arts & crafts; Cards; Games; Reading groups; Prayer groups; Movies; Shopping trips; Dances/Social/Cultural gatherings.

Snyder Oaks Care Center
210 E 37th St, Snyder, TX 79549
(915) 573-9377
Admin Nelda Pearl Kruger.
Licensure Intermediate care. *Beds* 97. *Certified* Medicaid.
Owner Proprietary corp.

Sonora

Lillian M Hudspeth Nursing Home
PO Box 455, 310 Hudspeth, Sonora, TX 76950
(915) 387-2521
Admin M Scott Gilmore. *Dir of Nursing* Rebecca Becknell. *Medical Dir* Gregory Lind MD.
Licensure Intermediate care. *Beds* ICF 39. *Certified* Medicaid.
Owner Nonprofit corp.
Admissions Requirements Minimum age 18; Physician's request.
Staff Physicians 2 (ft); LPNs 6 (ft); Nurses' aides 14 (ft); Activities coordinators 1 (ft); Dietitians 1 (ft); Ophthalmologists 1 (pt).
Languages Spanish.
Facilities Dining room; Activities room; Chapel; Laundry room; Barber/Beauty shop.
Activities Arts & crafts; Cards; Games; Reading groups; Movies; Dances/Social/ Cultural gatherings.

Spearman

Hansford Manor
707 S Roland, Spearman, TX 79081
(806) 659-5535
Admin Raymond Wasil.
Licensure Intermediate care. *Beds* 84. *Certified* Medicaid.
Owner Publicly owned.
Admissions Requirements Medical examination.
Staff LPNs 6 (ft); Nurses' aides 16 (ft), 1 (pt); Physical therapists 1 (pt); Activities coordinators 1 (ft).
Facilities Dining room; Physical therapy room; Activities room; Crafts room; Barber/ Beauty shop.
Activities Arts & crafts; Cards; Games; Reading groups; Prayer groups; Movies; Shopping trips.

Spur

Spur Care Center
PO Box 239, E Hwy 70, Spur, TX 79370
(806) 271-3324
Admin Margurite Van Zandt.
Licensure Intermediate care. *Beds* 40. *Certified* Medicaid.
Admissions Requirements Medical examination; Physician's request.
Staff LPNs; Nurses' aides; Activities coordinators; Dietitians.
Facilities Dining room; Activities room; Laundry room; Barber/Beauty shop.
Activities Arts & crafts; Games; Prayer groups; Movies; Shopping trips; Dances/Social/ Cultural gatherings.

Stamford

Skyview Living Center of Stamford
1101 Columbia, Stamford, TX 79553
(915) 773-2791
Admin Patsy R Newland.
Licensure Intermediate care for mentally retarded. *Beds* 102. *Certified* Medicaid.

Teakwood Manor
PO Box 232, 1003 Columbia, Stamford, TX 79553
(915) 773-3671
Admin Judy Doster.
Medical Dir Vickie Wilhelm.
Licensure Intermediate care. *Beds* 150. *Certified* Medicaid.
Owner Proprietary corp (Truco Inc).
Admissions Requirements Minimum age 18.
Staff RNs 1 (pt); LPNs 4 (ft); Nurses' aides 30 (ft); Physical therapists; Reality therapists; Recreational therapists; Occupational therapists; Speech therapists; Activities coordinators 1 (ft); Dietitians 1 (pt).
Facilities Dining room; Activities room; Chapel; Crafts room; Laundry room; Barber/ Beauty shop.
Activities Arts & crafts; Cards; Games; Reading groups; Prayer groups; Movies; Shopping trips.

Stanton

Stanton Care Center
PO Box 400, 1100 W Broadway, Stanton, TX 79782
(915) 756-3387
Admin. Richard C Melville. *Dir of Nursing* Toni Rodriguez. *Medical Dir* Dr Dipakpatel.
Licensure Intermediate care. *Beds* ICF 65. *Private Pay Patients* 8%. *Certified* Medicaid.
Owner Proprietary corp (Honorcare Corp).
Admissions Requirements Medical examination; Physician's request.
Staff RNs; LPNs; Nurses' aides; Activities coordinators; Dietitians.
Languages Spanish.
Facilities Dining room; Activities room; Laundry room; Barber/Beauty shop.
Activities Arts & crafts; Cards; Games; Reading groups; Prayer groups; Movies; Shopping trips; Exercises.

Stephenville

Canterbury Villa of Stephenville
2309 W Washington St, Stephenville, TX 76401
(817) 968-4191
Admin Deltha McDonald.
Licensure Intermediate care. *Beds* ICF 88. *Certified* Medicaid; VA; Private pay.
Owner Proprietary corp.
Admissions Requirements Medical examination.
Staff RNs 1 (ft); LPNs 6 (ft); Nurses' aides 12 (ft); Physical therapists 1 (ft); Speech therapists 1 (ft); Activities coordinators 1 (ft); Dietitians 1 (ft); Ophthalmologists 1 (ft); Podiatrists 1 (ft); Dentists 1 (ft).
Facilities Dining room; Activities room; Laundry room; Barber/Beauty shop.
Activities Arts & crafts; Games; Reading groups; Prayer groups; Shopping trips; Dances/Social/Cultural gatherings.

Community Nursing Home
2025 NW Loop, Stephenville, TX 76401
(817) 968-4649
Admin Erma Cooper. *Dir of Nursing* Judy Cranford RN.
Licensure Intermediate care. *Beds* ICF 105. *Certified* Medicaid.
Owner Privately owned (CareTech Management).

Staff RNs 1 (ft); LPNs 10 (ft), 2 (pt); Nurses' aides 30 (ft); Activities coordinators; Dietitians.
Facilities Dining room; Physical therapy room; Activities room; Chapel; Laundry room; Barber/Beauty shop.
Activities Arts & crafts; Games; Prayer groups; Movies; Dances/Social/Cultural gatherings.

Mulberry Manor
1670 Lingleville Rd, Stephenville, TX 76401
(817) 968-2158
Admin Bill Wakefield.
Licensure Skilled care. *Beds* 118. *Certified* Medicaid.
Owner Proprietary corp (ARA Living Centers).

Stephenville Nursing Home Inc
2311 W Washington St, Stephenville, TX 76401
(817) 968-3313
Admin Helen Allen.
Licensure Intermediate care. *Beds* 46. *Certified* Medicaid.
Staff RNs 1 (ft); LPNs 1 (ft), 2 (pt); Activities coordinators 1 (ft).
Facilities Dining room; Laundry room; Barber/Beauty shop.
Activities Arts & crafts; Cards; Games; Reading groups; Prayer groups; Movies; Shopping trips; Dances/Social/Cultural gatherings.

Sterling City

Sterling County Nursing Home
Box 3, 5th Ave, Sterling City, TX 76951
(915) 378-3201
Admin Cindy Stokes.
Licensure Intermediate care. *Beds* 29. *Certified* Medicaid.
Owner Publicly owned.

Stockdale

Stockdale Nursing Home
PO Box 36, 300 Solomon St, Stockdale, TX 78160
(512) 996-3721
Admin Jonnie L Staggs.
Licensure Skilled care. *Beds* 68. *Certified* Medicaid.
Owner Proprietary corp.

Stratford

Coldwater Manor Nursing Home
PO Box 1189, 1111 Beaver, Stratford, TX 79084
(806) 396-5568
Admin Theresa Ward. *Dir of Nursing* Susie Jeffries RN. *Medical Dir* Claude Harlow MD.
Licensure Intermediate care. *Beds* ICF 38. *Private Pay Patients* 50%. *Certified* Medicaid.
Owner Nonprofit organization/foundation.
Admissions Requirements Medical examination.
Staff Physicians 1 (ft); RNs 1 (ft); LPNs 4 (ft); Nurses' aides 18 (ft); Activities coordinators 1 (ft); Dietitians 1 (ft).
Facilities Dining room; Activities room; Chapel; Crafts room; Laundry room; Barber/ Beauty shop; Library.
Activities Arts & crafts; Cards; Games; Reading groups; Movies; Shopping trips; Dances/Social/Cultural gatherings; Intergenerational programs.

Sugar Land

Autumn Hills Convalescent Center
333 Matlage Way, Sugar Land, TX 77478
(713) 491-3011

Admin Paul A Smith. *Dir of Nursing* Pat Wilson.
Licensure Intermediate care. *Beds* ICF 151. *Private Pay Patients* 50%. *Certified* Medicaid.
Owner Proprietary corp.
Admissions Requirements Minimum age 65; Medical examination; Physician's request.
Staff RNs 1 (ft); LPNs 12 (ft); Nurses' aides 40 (ft); Activities coordinators 2 (ft); Dietitians 1 (ft).
Facilities Dining room; Activities room; Crafts room; Barber/Beauty shop; Living room; 2 Lounges.
Activities Arts & crafts; Cards; Games; Reading groups; Prayer groups; Movies; Dances/Social/Cultural gatherings.

Sulphur Springs

Hopkins County Nursing Home
1333 Jefferson St, Sulphur Springs, TX 75482
(214) 885-7642
Admin Alvie L Morgan. *Dir of Nursing* Loretta McKay. *Medical Dir* Charles Jones.
Licensure Intermediate care. *Beds* ICF 119. *Private Pay Patients* 30%. *Certified* Medicaid.
Owner Proprietary corp (Woodhaven Inc).
Admissions Requirements Medical examination; Physician's request.
Staff Physicians 1 (pt); RNs 1 (ft); LPNs 7 (ft); Nurses' aides 24 (ft), 1 (pt); Physical therapists 1 (pt); Occupational therapists 1 (pt); Speech therapists 1 (pt); Activities coordinators 1 (ft); Dietitians 1 (pt); Podiatrists 1 (pt).
Facilities Dining room; Activities room; Chapel; Crafts room; Laundry room; Barber/Beauty shop.
Activities Arts & crafts; Cards; Games; Reading groups; Prayer groups; Movies; Shopping trips; Dances/Social/Cultural gatherings; Intergenerational programs; Pet therapy; Individual and group.

Leisure Lodge—Sulphur Springs
411 Airport Rd, Sulphur Springs, TX 75482
(214) 885-7668
Admin Brian Bailey. *Dir of Nursing* Miriam Carpenter. *Medical Dir* Dr Claude Reynolds.
Licensure Skilled care; Intermediate care. *Beds* SNF 130. *Certified* Medicaid.
Owner Proprietary corp (Beverly Enterprises).
Admissions Requirements Medical examination; Physician's request.
Staff RNs 3 (ft); LPNs 8 (ft); Nurses' aides 30 (ft); Activities coordinators 1 (ft); Dietitians 1 (pt).
Facilities Dining room; Activities room; Chapel; Crafts room; Laundry room; Barber/Beauty shop.
Activities Arts & crafts; Cards; Games; Reading groups; Prayer groups; Movies; Shopping trips; Dances/Social/Cultural gatherings; Exercise; Resident council; Family council; Birthday parties.

Sulphur Springs Nursing Home
301 Oak Ave, Sulphur Springs, TX 75482
(214) 885-3596
Admin Mary Pamela Folowell.
Medical Dir Pam Burnett.
Licensure Intermediate care. *Beds* ICF 60. *Certified* Medicaid.
Owner Privately owned.
Admissions Requirements Medical examination; Physician's request.
Staff RNs 1 (ft); LPNs 3 (ft), 1 (pt); Nurses' aides 24 (ft), 3 (pt); Activities coordinators 1 (ft).
Facilities Dining room; Activities room; Laundry room; Barber/Beauty shop.
Activities Arts & crafts; Cards; Games; Reading groups; Movies; Shopping trips; Dances/Social/Cultural gatherings.

Woodhaven Nursing Home
1200 N Jackson, Sulphur Springs, TX 75482
(214) 885-6571
Admin William Frank Rettmann. *Dir of Nursing* Auzie Pate.
Licensure Intermediate care. *Beds* ICF 95. *Private Pay Patients* 40%. *Certified* Medicaid.
Owner Proprietary corp (Nursing Centers Management Corp).
Admissions Requirements Medical examination; Physician's request.
Staff LPNs; Nurses' aides; Activities coordinators.
Facilities Dining room; Activities room; Crafts room; Laundry room; Barber/Beauty shop.
Activities Arts & crafts; Games; Prayer groups; Movies; Shopping trips; Dances/Social/Cultural gatherings.

Sweeny

Sweeny House
109 N McKinney, Sweeny, TX 77480
(409) 548-3383
Admin Connie Shaw. *Dir of Nursing* Donna Winebrenner. *Medical Dir* T J Milian.
Licensure Intermediate care; Personal care; Retirement. *Beds* ICF 75; Personal care 16; Retirement 20. *Certified* Medicaid.
Owner Proprietary corp (ARA Living Centers).
Admissions Requirements Medical examination; Physician's request.
Staff RNs 1 (ft); LPNs 8 (ft); Nurses' aides 35 (ft), 4 (pt); Activities coordinators 1 (ft).
Languages Spanish.
Facilities Dining room; Activities room; Laundry room; Barber/Beauty shop; In-house doctor's office.
Activities Arts & crafts; Cards; Games; Reading groups; Prayer groups; Movies; Shopping trips; Dances/Social/Cultural gatherings; In-room activities; Awareness; Dominoes; Holiday activities; Field trips; Residents council.

Sweetwater

Holiday Retirement Center
PO Box 1369, 1901 Lamar, Sweetwater, TX 79556
(915) 235-5417
Admin Katherine Owen.
Licensure Skilled care. *Beds* 78. *Certified* Medicaid.
Owner Proprietary corp (Hillhaven Corp).

Sweetwater Nursing Center
1600 Josephine, Sweetwater, TX 79556
(915) 236-6653
Admin Linda Barrick. *Dir of Nursing* Marie Graham. *Medical Dir* Judy Clayton DO.
Licensure Intermediate care. *Beds* ICF 100. *Certified* Medicaid.
Owner Proprietary corp (Beverly Enterprises).
Admissions Requirements Physician's request.
Staff LPNs 9 (ft), 3 (pt); Nurses' aides 21 (ft), 3 (pt); Physical therapists (contracted); Activities coordinators 1 (ft); Dietitians 1 (ft).
Languages Spanish.
Facilities Dining room; Activities room; Crafts room; Laundry room; Barber/Beauty shop; Exercise trail.
Activities Arts & crafts; Cards; Games; Reading groups; Prayer groups; Movies; Shopping trips; Dances/Social/Cultural gatherings; "Walk and Dine".

Taft

Shoreline Healthcare Center
1201 Gregory St, Taft, TX 78390
(512) 528-2523

Admin Norma Brandt.
Licensure Intermediate care. *Beds* 152. *Certified* Medicaid.
Owner Proprietary corp (ARA Living Centers).

Tahoka

Tahoka Care Center
PO Box 449, 1829 S 7th St, Tahoka, TX 79373
(806) 998-5018
Admin Diana Riojas. *Dir of Nursing* Lucy Perez.
Licensure Intermediate care. *Beds* ICF 46. *Certified* Medicaid.
Owner Nonprofit organization/foundation (MSC Associates).
Admissions Requirements Physician's request.
Staff LPNs; Nurses' aides; Activities coordinators; Dietitians.
Languages Spanish.
Facilities Dining room; Activities room; Laundry room; Barber/Beauty shop.
Activities Arts & crafts; Cards; Games; Prayer groups; Movies; Shopping trips; Dances/Social/Cultural gatherings; Intergenerational programs; Pet therapy.

Taylor

SPJST Rest Home 1
500 E Lake Dr, Taylor, TX 76574
(512) 352-6337
Admin Frances Schwenker. *Dir of Nursing* Ilyn Kaspar.
Licensure Intermediate care. *Beds* ICF 72. *Private Pay Patients* 59%. *Certified* Medicaid.
Owner Nonprofit corp.
Admissions Requirements Physician's request.
Staff LPNs 10 (ft); Nurses' aides 50 (ft); Activities coordinators 1 (ft); Dietitians 1 (ft).
Facilities Dining room; Activities room; Laundry room.
Activities Arts & crafts; Cards; Games; Reading groups; Prayer groups; Movies; Shopping trips.

Sunnyside Retirement Center 2
PO Box 1129, 212 E Lake Dr, Taylor, TX 76574
(512) 352-2700
Admin Bholanath B Nadkarni.
Medical Dir Melissa Kelley.
Licensure Intermediate care; Alzheimer's care. *Beds* ICF 89. *Certified* Medicaid.
Owner Proprietary corp.
Admissions Requirements Minimum age 18; Medical examination.
Staff Physicians 1 (pt); RNs 1 (pt); LPNs 5 (ft); Nurses' aides 16 (pt); Physical therapists 1 (pt); Occupational therapists 1 (pt); Speech therapists 1 (pt); Activities coordinators 1 (ft), 1 (pt); Dietitians 1 (ft), 1 (pt); Ophthalmologists 1 (pt); Podiatrists 1 (pt); Dentists 1 (pt).
Languages Spanish, German, French, Czech.
Facilities Dining room; Laundry room; Barber/Beauty shop; Library.
Activities Arts & crafts; Cards; Games; Reading groups; Prayer groups; Shopping trips; Dances/Social/Cultural gatherings; Wheelchair basketball; Sports.

Sweetbriar Nursing Home
PO Box 831, Granger Hwy, Taylor, TX 76574
(512) 352-3684
Admin Dorothy Phillips.
Medical Dir Pat Maxwell.
Licensure Intermediate care; Personal care. *Beds* ICF 150; Personal care 40; Licensed 66. *Certified* Medicaid.
Owner Proprietary corp (ARA Living Centers).

Admissions Requirements Medical examination.
Staff Physicians; RNs; LPNs; Nurses' aides; Physical therapists; Reality therapists; Recreational therapists; Occupational therapists; Speech therapists; Activities coordinators; Dietitians; Ophthalmologists; Podiatrists; Dentists.
Languages Czech, German, Spanish.
Facilities Dining room; Activities room; Crafts room; Laundry room; Barber/Beauty shop; Library.
Activities Arts & crafts; Cards; Games; Reading groups; Prayer groups; Shopping trips; Dances/Social/Cultural gatherings; Alzheimer's support group.

Teague

McGee Nursing Home
615 S 8th Ave, Teague, TX 75860
(817) 739-2566
Beds 82. *Certified* Medicaid.
Admissions Requirements Minimum age 21.
Staff Physicians 1 (ft); RNs 1 (ft); LPNs 4 (ft); Nurses' aides 30 (ft); Activities coordinators 1 (ft); Dietitians 1 (ft); Dentists 1 (ft).
Facilities Dining room; Activities room; Crafts room; Laundry room; Barber/Beauty shop; Library.
Activities Arts & crafts; Cards; Games; Reading groups; Prayer groups; Movies; Shopping trips.

Teague Nursing Home
PO Box 89, E Hwy 84, Teague, TX 75860
(817) 739-2541
Admin Eugenia Lummus.
Medical Dir Marion Williams.
Licensure Intermediate care. *Beds* ICF 102. *Certified* Medicaid.
Owner Proprietary corp.
Admissions Requirements Physician's request.
Staff Nurses' aides 20 (ft), 3 (pt); Activities coordinators 1 (ft); LVN 7 (ft), 1 (pt).
Facilities Dining room; Chapel; Laundry room; Barber/Beauty shop.
Activities Arts & crafts; Games; Prayer groups; Movies; Shopping trips; Dances/Social/Cultural gatherings.

Temple

Bur-Mont Nursing Center
612 Industrial Blvd, Temple, TX 76501
(817) 773-5640
Admin Rose M Mondrik. *Dir of Nursing* Debbie Quinton. *Medical Dir* Jack S Weinblatt.
Licensure Intermediate care. *Beds* ICF 120. *Certified* Medicaid.
Owner Proprietary corp.
Admissions Requirements Physician's request.
Staff Physicians (contracted); RNs; LPNs; Nurses' aides; Physical therapists (contracted); Occupational therapists (contracted); Speech therapists (contracted); Activities coordinators; Dietitians (consultant); Podiatrists (contracted); Social workers.
Facilities Dining room.
Activities Arts & crafts; Cards; Games; Reading groups; Prayer groups; Movies; Shopping trips; Dances/Social/Cultural gatherings; Pet therapy.

Camlu Care Centers—Temple
1802 S 31st St, Temple, TX 76501
(817) 778-4231
Licensure Nursing. *Beds* Nursing 145.

Four Seasons Nursing Center of Temple
1700 Marland Wood Rd, Temple, TX 76502
(817) 773-1591
Admin C D Elliott. *Dir of Nursing* Jackie Young. *Medical Dir* Jack Weinblatt MD.

Licensure Skilled care; Private-intermediate care. *Beds* SNF 24; Private 81. *Certified* Medicaid; Medicare.
Owner Proprietary corp (Manor Care).
Staff RNs 2 (ft), 2 (pt); LPNs 9 (ft); Nurses' aides 27 (ft), 3 (pt); Activities coordinators 1 (ft).
Languages Spanish, Tagalog.
Facilities Dining room; Physical therapy room; Activities room; Crafts room; Laundry room; Barber/Beauty shop; Heritage lounge.
Activities Arts & crafts; Games; Reading groups; Movies; Shopping trips; Dances/Social/Cultural gatherings.

Golden Heritage Care Center
1511 Marland Wood Rd, Temple, TX 76501
(817) 778-6616
Admin Ruth Haptonstall.
Licensure Intermediate care. *Beds* 91. *Certified* Medicaid.
Owner Proprietary corp.

Regency Manor Nursing Center
3011 W Adams, Temple, TX 76504
(817) 773-1626
Admin G Jo Beach.
Medical Dir Jack Weinblott MD.
Licensure Intermediate care. *Beds* 140. *Certified* Medicaid.
Owner Proprietary corp (Beverly Enterprises).
Admissions Requirements Medical examination.
Staff RNs; LPNs; Nurses' aides; Physical therapists; Recreational therapists; Occupational therapists; Speech therapists; Activities coordinators; Dietitians.
Facilities Dining room; Activities room; Crafts room; Laundry room; Barber/Beauty shop.
Activities Arts & crafts; Cards; Games; Reading groups; Prayer groups; Movies; Shopping trips; Dances/Social/Cultural gatherings.

Southern Manor Inc
1802 S 31st St, Temple, TX 76501
(817) 778-4231
Admin Barbara A Doyle.
Medical Dir Jack Weinblatt MD.
Licensure Skilled care; Intermediate care. *Beds* 145. *Certified* Medicaid.
Admissions Requirements Medical examination; Physician's request.
Staff RNs 1 (ft), 2 (pt); LPNs 9 (ft), 4 (pt); Nurses' aides 43 (ft), 3 (pt); Activities coordinators 1 (ft); Dietitians 1 (ft).
Facilities Dining room; Physical therapy room; Activities room; Crafts room; Laundry room; Barber/Beauty shop.
Activities Arts & crafts; Cards; Games; Prayer groups; Movies; Shopping trips; Dances/Social/Cultural gatherings.

Southland Villa Nursing Center
2222 S 5th, Temple, TX 76501
(817) 773-1641
Admin Margaret F Jackson.
Medical Dir James D Wilson Sr MD.
Licensure Skilled care. *Beds* 134. *Certified* Medicaid.
Owner Proprietary corp (Summit Health Ltd).
Admissions Requirements Medical examination.
Staff Physicians 6 (ft); RNs 3 (ft); LPNs 29 (ft); Nurses' aides 42 (ft); Physical therapists 1 (ft); Reality therapists 1 (ft); Recreational therapists 1 (ft); Activities coordinators 1 (ft); Dietitians 1 (ft); Dentists 1 (ft).
Facilities Dining room; Activities room; Crafts room; Laundry room; Barber/Beauty shop.
Activities Arts & crafts; Cards; Games; Reading groups; Prayer groups; Movies; Shopping trips; Dances/Social/Cultural gatherings; Picnics; Trips to park; Rides out to the lake & countryside; Dining out.

Temple Care Center
1511 Marland Wood Rd, Temple, TX 76501
(817) 778-6616
Licensure Nursing. *Beds* Nursing 150.

Tutor Nursing Home Inc
119 S 33rd St, Temple, TX 76501
(817) 778-3301
Admin Ray Van Tutor. *Dir of Nursing* Renie Conway.
Licensure Intermediate care. *Beds* ICF 45. *Private Pay Patients* 45%. *Certified* Medicaid.
Owner Proprietary corp.
Admissions Requirements Minimum age 18.
Staff RNs 1 (ft); LPNs 4 (ft); Nurses' aides 6 (ft), 3 (pt); Activities coordinators 1 (ft); Dietitians 1 (pt).
Languages Spanish, Czech.
Facilities Dining room; Activities room; Chapel; Crafts room; Laundry room; Library.
Activities Arts & crafts; Cards; Games; Prayer groups; Movies; Shopping trips; Dances/Social/Cultural gatherings.

Village on Canyon Creek
4312 S 31st St, Temple, TX 76501
(817) 771-1226
Licensure Nursing. *Beds* Nursing 60.

Terrell

Rose Hill Personal Care Center
1010 Rose Hill Rd, Terrell, TX 75160
(214) 563-5796
Admin Billie R Simmons.
Licensure Intermediate care. *Beds* 68. *Certified* Medicaid.
Owner Proprietary corp (National Heritage).

Terrell Care Center
204 W Nash, Terrell, TX 75160
(214) 563-7668
Admin Berneice Hill.
Medical Dir Becky Slagle.
Licensure Intermediate care. *Beds* ICF 94. *Certified* Medicaid.
Owner Proprietary corp (National Heritage).
Admissions Requirements Medical examination; Physician's request.
Staff LPNs 20 (ft); Nurses' aides 35 (ft); Activities coordinators 1 (ft); Dietitians 7 (ft).
Facilities Dining room; Activities room; Chapel; Crafts room; Barber/Beauty shop.
Activities Cards; Games; Reading groups; Prayer groups; Movies; Dances/Social/Cultural gatherings.

Terrell Convalescent Center 1
1800 N Frances, Terrell, TX 75160
(214) 563-2652
Admin Jean A Bishop SW. *Dir of Nursing* Catherine Bradford. *Medical Dir* Neil Saytu MD.
Licensure Intermediate care. *Beds* ICF 129. *Certified* Medicaid.
Owner Proprietary corp (National Heritage Inc).
Admissions Requirements Medical examination; Physician's request.
Staff Physicians; RNs; LPNs; Nurses' aides; Physical therapists; Reality therapists; Recreational therapists; Occupational therapists; Speech therapists; Activities coordinators; Dietitians; Ophthalmologists; Podiatrists; Audiologists.
Facilities Dining room; Activities room; Crafts room; Barber/Beauty shop.
Activities Arts & crafts; Cards; Games; Reading groups; Prayer groups; Movies; Shopping trips; Dances/Social/Cultural gatherings; Intergenerational programs; Pet therapy.

Terrell Convalescent Center 2
1900 N Frances, Terrell, TX 75160
(214) 563-6428
Admin Marjorie D Looker.
Licensure Intermediate care. *Beds* 122.
 Certified Medicaid.
Owner Proprietary corp (National Heritage).

Texarkana

Edgewood Manor Nursing Home
4925 Elizabeth St, Texarkana, TX 75503
(214) 793-4645
Admin Peggy Fomby. *Dir of Nursing* Jo Ann
 Griffin. *Medical Dir* Dr Charles Marrow.
Licensure Intermediate care. *Beds* ICF 120.
 Certified Medicaid.
Admissions Requirements Physician's request.
Staff LPNs 10 (ft); Nurses' aides 32 (ft);
 Activities coordinators 1 (ft); Dietary Staff
 10 (ft); Housekeeping, laundry and
 maintenance staff 9 (ft).
Facilities Dining room; Activities room;
 Crafts room; Laundry room; Barber/Beauty
 shop; Library.
Activities Arts & crafts; Games; Reading
 groups; Prayer groups; Movies; Shopping
 trips; Dances/Social/Cultural gatherings.

Four States Nursing Home
PO Box 5368, 8 E Midway Dr, Texarkana,
 TX 75504-5368
(214) 838-9526
Admin Norma Z Dozier. *Dir of Nursing*
 Donna Murphy. *Medical Dir* Dr Donald
 Middleton.
Licensure Intermediate care. *Beds* ICF 180.
 Certified Medicaid.
Owner Proprietary corp (Hillhaven Corp).
Admissions Requirements Medical
 examination; Physician's request.
Staff RNs; LPNs; Nurses' aides; Activities
 coordinators.
Facilities Dining room; Laundry room;
 Barber/Beauty shop.
Activities Arts & crafts; Games; Reading
 groups; Prayer groups; Movies; Dances/
 Social/Cultural gatherings.

Leisure Lodge Texarkana
4808 Elizabeth, Texarkana, TX 75503
(214) 794-3826
Admin Erma Cooper. *Dir of Nursing* Kathy
 Wilson LVN.
Licensure Intermediate care. *Beds* 120.
 Certified Medicaid.
Owner Proprietary corp (Beverly Enterprises).
Admissions Requirements Medical
 examination.
Staff RNs 1 (ft); LPNs 10 (ft); Nurses' aides;
 Activities coordinators.
Facilities Dining room; Activities room;
 Crafts room; Laundry room; Barber/Beauty
 shop; Library.
Activities Arts & crafts; Cards; Games;
 Reading groups; Prayer groups; Movies;
 Shopping trips; Dances/Social/Cultural
 gatherings.

Oak Manor Nursing Home
210 N Kenwood, Texarkana, TX 75501
(214) 838-7566
Admin Ronald E Duke.
Licensure Intermediate care. *Beds* 56.
 Certified Medicaid.
Owner Proprietary corp.

Texarkana Nursing Center
4920 Elizabeth, Texarkana, TX 75503
(214) 792-3812
Admin Alandra Needham. *Dir of Nursing*
 Barbara McDonell. *Medical Dir* Dr Thomas
 Alston.
Licensure Intermediate care. *Beds* ICF 120.
 Private Pay Patients 30%. *Certified*
 Medicaid.
Owner Proprietary corp (Beverly Enterprises).

examination; Physician's request.
Staff RNs 2 (ft); LPNs 10 (ft); Nurses' aides
 30 (ft); Activities coordinators 1 (ft);
 Dietitians 1 (ft).
Facilities Dining room; Physical therapy
 room; Activities room; Crafts room; Laundry
 room; Barber/Beauty shop; Library.
Activities Arts & crafts; Cards; Games;
 Reading groups; Prayer groups; Movies;
 Shopping trips; Dances/Social/Cultural
 gatherings.

Texas City

Avalon Place
210 Gulf Fwy, Texas City, TX 77591
(409) 938-4271
Admin Herbert Houser. *Dir of Nursing* Ann
 Wright. *Medical Dir* R E Sullivan MD.
Licensure Skilled care; Intermediate care. *Beds*
 SNF 52; ICF 58. *Certified* Medicaid;
 Medicare.
Owner Nonprofit organization/foundation.
Admissions Requirements Medical
 examination.
Staff RNs 3 (ft), 3 (pt); LPNs 9 (ft), 6 (pt);
 Nurses' aides 32 (ft), 9 (pt); Physical
 therapists 1 (pt); Occupational therapists 1
 (pt); Speech therapists 1 (pt); Activities
 coordinators 1 (ft); Dietitians 1 (ft);
 Ophthalmologists 1 (pt); Podiatrists 1 (pt).
Facilities Dining room.
Activities Arts & crafts; Cards; Games;
 Reading groups; Prayer groups; Movies;
 Shopping trips; Dances/Social/Cultural
 gatherings.

Bay Brook Villa
501 8th Ave N, Texas City, TX 77590
(409) 948-3502, 948-6873 FAX
Admin Betty Phillips. *Dir of Nursing* Anna
 Wilson RN.
Licensure Intermediate care. *Beds* ICF 117.
 Private Pay Patients 10%. *Certified*
 Medicaid.
Owner Proprietary corp (Texas Health
 Enterprises Inc).
Admissions Requirements Medical
 examination; Physician's request.
Staff Physicians 5 (pt); RNs 1 (ft); LPNs 8
 (ft), 1 (pt); Nurses' aides 25 (ft), 5 (pt);
 Activities coordinators 1 (ft); Dietitians 1
 (ft).
Languages Spanish.
Facilities Dining room; Activities room;
 Crafts room; Laundry room; Barber/Beauty
 shop.
Activities Arts & crafts; Cards; Games;
 Reading groups; Prayer groups; Movies;
 Shopping trips; Dances/Social/Cultural
 gatherings; Intergenerational programs.

College Park Care Center
424 N Tarpey Rd, Texas City, TX 77590
(409) 938-8431
Admin Peggy E Thomas.
Medical Dir Weldon Kolb MD.
Licensure Skilled care; Intermediate care. *Beds*
 120. *Certified* Medicaid.
Owner Proprietary corp (Beverly Enterprises).
Staff Physicians 1 (pt); RNs 2 (ft); LPNs 10
 (ft); Nurses' aides 30 (ft), 5 (pt); Physical
 therapists 1 (pt); Occupational therapists 1
 (pt); Speech therapists 1 (pt); Activities
 coordinators 1 (ft); Dietitians 1 (pt); Dentists
 1 (pt).
Facilities Dining room; Activities room;
 Crafts room; Laundry room; Barber/Beauty
 shop.
Activities Arts & crafts; Cards; Games;
 Reading groups; Movies; Shopping trips;
 Dances/Social/Cultural gatherings.

Fifth Avenue Care Center
815 5th Ave N, Texas City, TX 77590
(409) 945-7429

Admin Janice Kline. *Dir of Nursing* Gayle
 Freeman. *Medical Dir* Dr Reeves.
Licensure Intermediate care. *Beds* ICF 65.
 Certified Medicaid.
Owner Proprietary corp (Southeastern Health
 Care).
Admissions Requirements Medical
 examination; Physician's request.
Staff LPNs; Nurses' aides; Occupational
 therapists; Speech therapists; Activities
 coordinators; Dietitians.
Facilities Dining room; Activities room;
 Laundry room; Barber/Beauty shop.
Activities Arts & crafts; Cards; Games;
 Reading groups; Prayer groups; Movies;
 Dances/Social/Cultural gatherings.

Seabreeze Care Center
6602 Memorial Dr, Texas City, TX 77590
(409) 935-2451
Admin Nancy Gail van Cleave.
Licensure Intermediate care. *Beds* 103.
 Certified Medicaid.
Owner Proprietary corp (ARA Living
 Centers).

Three Rivers

Roma Memorial Nursing Home
PO Drawer 807, Smith Blvd, Three Rivers,
 TX 78071
(512) 786-2256
Admin Evelyn Huebotter. *Dir of Nursing*
 Gloria Gonzales. *Medical Dir* G F Carralho
 MD.
Licensure Intermediate care. *Beds* ICF 74.
 Certified Medicaid.
Owner Proprietary corp.
Admissions Requirements Physician's request.
Staff RNs 1 (ft), 1 (pt); LPNs 4 (ft), 1 (pt);
 Nurses' aides 15 (ft); Dietitians 1 (ft).
Facilities Dining room; Activities room;
 Laundry room; Barber/Beauty shop.
Activities Arts & crafts; Cards; Games.

Throckmorton

Throckmorton Nursing Center
1000 Minter Ave, Throckmorton, TX 76083
(817) 849-2861
Admin Betty Mahan.
Licensure Intermediate care. *Beds* 58.
 Certified Medicaid.
Owner Proprietary corp (Beverly Enterprises).

Tomball

Autumn Hills Convalescent Center—Tomball
615 Lawrence St, Tomball, TX 77375
(713) 351-7231
Admin Martha G Conn.
Medical Dir George Murillo MD.
Licensure Skilled care; Intermediate care. *Beds*
 150. *Certified* Medicaid.
Admissions Requirements Medical
 examination.
Staff Physicians 12 (ft); RNs 4 (ft), 1 (pt);
 LPNs 15 (ft), 2 (pt); Nurses' aides 33 (ft);
 Activities coordinators 2 (ft); Dietitians 1
 (ft); Podiatrists 1 (ft); Dentists 1 (ft).
Facilities Dining room; Activities room;
 Laundry room; Barber/Beauty shop.
Activities Arts & crafts; Cards; Games;
 Reading groups; Prayer groups; Shopping
 trips; Dances/Social/Cultural gatherings.

**Louise & John L Winslow Memorial Nursing
Home**
815 N Peach St, Tomball, TX 77375
(713) 351-5443
Admin Evelyn Bolds.
Medical Dir Arvind Pai MD.
Licensure Skilled care; Intermediate care. *Beds*
 SNF 60; ICF 62. *Certified* Medicaid.
Owner Proprietary corp (Cantex Healthcare
 Centers).

Admissions Requirements Minimum age 16; Medical examination; Physician's request.
Staff Physicians 1 (pt); RNs 1 (ft); LPNs 6 (ft); Nurses' aides 12 (ft); Activities coordinators 1 (ft), 1 (pt); Dietitians 1 (ft).
Facilities Dining room; Activities room; Chapel; Laundry room; Barber/Beauty shop.
Activities Arts & crafts; Cards; Games; Reading groups; Prayer groups; Movies; Shopping trips; Dances/Social/Cultural gatherings.

Trinity

Avalon Place—Trinity
PO Box 631, Hwy 19 S, Trinity, TX 75862
(409) 594-7521
Licensure Nursing. *Beds* Nursing 120.

Trinity Memorial Hospital
PO Box 471, 900 Prospect Dr, Trinity, TX 75862
(713) 594-3588
Admin Glea Ramey Jr.
Licensure Intermediate care. *Beds* 28.
Certified Medicaid.
Owner Publicly owned.

Troup

Westwood Convalescent Home Inc
PO Box 399, 1204 W Noble St, Troup, TX 75789
(214) 842-3118
Admin Arthur P Mowery.
Licensure Intermediate care. *Beds* 60.
Certified Medicaid.
Owner Proprietary corp.

Tulia

Tulia Care Center
714 S Austin, Tulia, TX 79088
(806) 995-4810
Admin Mary Ann Resch.
Licensure Intermediate care. *Beds* 52.
Certified Medicaid.
Admissions Requirements Medical examination.
Staff RNs 1 (ft), 1 (pt); LPNs 4 (ft); Nurses' aides 10 (ft), 2 (pt); Speech therapists 1 (pt); Activities coordinators 1 (ft), 1 (pt); Dietitians 1 (pt).
Facilities Dining room; Physical therapy room; Activities room; Laundry room; Barber/Beauty shop.
Activities Arts & crafts; Games; Prayer groups; Movies; Shopping trips; Dances/Social/Cultural gatherings.

Tyler

All Seasons Care Center
2901 E Front St, Tyler, TX 75702
(214) 592-6584
Admin Betty Hill.
Medical Dir Juanita White; Carole Monday.
Licensure Intermediate care. *Beds* ICF 148.
Certified Medicaid.
Owner Proprietary corp (Texas Health Enterprises).
Staff Physicians; RNs; LPNs; Nurses' aides; Activities coordinators.
Facilities Dining room; Activities room; Crafts room; Laundry room; Barber/Beauty shop; Library; TV Lounge.
Activities Arts & crafts; Cards; Games; Reading groups; Prayer groups; Movies; Shopping trips; Dances/Social/Cultural gatherings.

Briarcliff Village Health Center
3403 S Vine, Tyler, TX 75701
(214) 581-5714
Licensure Nursing. *Beds* Nursing 150.

Clairmont
900 S Baxter, Tyler, TX 75701
(214) 597-8192
Licensure Nursing. *Beds* Nursing 120.

Colonial Manor of Tyler
930 S Baxter St, Tyler, TX 75701
(214) 597-2068
Admin Sue Burford.
Medical Dir Dr Irving Brown.
Licensure Skilled care; Intermediate care. *Beds* 174. *Certified* Medicaid; Medicare.
Activities Arts & crafts; Cards; Games; Reading groups; Prayer groups; Shopping trips; Dances/Social/Cultural gatherings.

Eastview Nursing Center
2902 Hwy 31 E, Tyler, TX 75702
(214) 597-1323
Admin Ralph J King LNHA. *Dir of Nursing* Kay Ritch LVN.
Licensure Intermediate care. *Beds* ICF 120. *Certified* Medicaid.
Owner Proprietary corp.
Staff Physicians 1 (pt); LPNs 8 (ft); Nurses' aides 20 (ft); Activities coordinators 1 (ft).

Glenview of Tyler Nursing Home Inc
PO Box 4878, 3526 W Erwin, Tyler, TX 75712
(214) 593-6441
Admin Barbara Gill.
Licensure Intermediate care. *Beds* 120. *Certified* Medicaid.
Admissions Requirements Medical examination; Physician's request.
Facilities Dining room; Activities room; Crafts room; Laundry room; Barber/Beauty shop; Library.
Activities Arts & crafts; Cards; Games; Movies; Dances/Social/Cultural gatherings.

Melrose Nursing Center
1501 W 29th, Tyler, TX 75702
(214) 592-8148, 595-1253 FAX
Admin Eivis C Luter. *Dir of Nursing* Elaine Mosley. *Medical Dir* R A Lester III.
Licensure Intermediate care. *Beds* ICF 106. *Certified* Medicaid.
Owner Proprietary corp (American Manor Inc).
Admissions Requirements Medical examination; Physician's request.
Staff LPNs; Nurses' aides; Physical therapists; Occupational therapists; Speech therapists; Activities coordinators; Dietitians; Ophthalmologists; Podiatrists.
Activities Arts & crafts; Cards; Games; Reading groups; Prayer groups; Movies; Shopping trips; Dances/Social/Cultural gatherings.

Park Place Nursing Center
2450 E 5th St, Tyler, TX 75701
(214) 592-6745
Admin Mary Wintters. *Dir of Nursing* Sharon Shakleford RN. *Medical Dir* Charles Albright MD.
Licensure Skilled care; Private pay; Alzheimer's care. *Beds* SNF 20; Private pay 100. *Certified* Medicare.
Owner Proprietary corp.
Admissions Requirements Physician's request.
Languages Spanish.
Facilities Dining room; Physical therapy room; Activities room; Chapel; Crafts room; Laundry room; Barber/Beauty shop; Library.
Activities Arts & crafts; Cards; Games; Reading groups; Prayer groups; Movies; Shopping trips; Dances/Social/Cultural gatherings; Intergenerational programs; Pet therapy.

Southview Nursing Center
3505 Old Jacksonville Rd, Tyler, TX 75701
(214) 561-2011
Licensure Nursing. *Beds* Nursing 120.

Woodcreek Nursing Center
810 S Porter, Tyler, TX 75701
(214) 593-2463
Admin Joyce Handorf.
Licensure Intermediate care. *Beds* 196. *Certified* Medicaid.
Owner Proprietary corp (Beverly Enterprises).

Uvalde

Amistad II Care Center
535 N Park St, Uvalde, TX 78801
(512) 278-2505
Admin Lisa R Morse. *Dir of Nursing* Linda Brown RN. *Medical Dir* J M Barton MD.
Licensure Intermediate care. *Beds* ICF 118. *Private Pay Patients* 35%. *Certified* Medicaid.
Owner Proprietary corp.
Admissions Requirements Physician's request.
Staff RNs 1 (ft); LPNs 10 (ft); Nurses' aides 45 (ft), 2 (pt); Activities coordinators 1 (ft), 1 (pt).
Languages Spanish.
Facilities Dining room; Activities room; Laundry room; Barber/Beauty shop.
Activities Arts & crafts; Cards; Games; Prayer groups; Movies; Shopping trips; Intergenerational programs; Pet therapy.

Amistad Nursing Home Inc
PO Drawer 2450, 615 Garden St, Uvalde, TX 78801
(512) 278-5641
Admin Glenda Wade. *Dir of Nursing* Debrah Jainik RN. *Medical Dir* J M Barton MD.
Licensure Skilled care. *Beds* SNF 118. *Private Pay Patients* 4%. *Certified* Medicaid; Medicare.
Owner Proprietary corp.
Admissions Requirements Minimum age 16; Physician's request.
Staff RNs 2 (ft); LPNs 6 (ft).
Languages Spanish.
Facilities Dining room; Activities room; Barber/Beauty shop.
Activities Arts & crafts; Cards; Games; Reading groups; Prayer groups; Movies; Pet therapy.

Valley Mills

Valley Mills Care Center
PO Box 138, 1st St & Ave E, Valley Mills, TX 76689
(817) 932-6288
Admin Cleo D Jones.
Licensure Intermediate care. *Beds* 61. *Certified* Medicaid.
Owner Proprietary corp.

Van

Country Inn Care Center
PO Box 1020, 615 E Main, Van, TX 75790
(214) 963-8646
Admin Dana L Fleming.
Licensure Intermediate care. *Beds* 61. *Certified* Medicaid.
Owner Proprietary corp (Beverly Enterprises).

Villa Siesta Nursing Home
PO Box 1030, 201 S Oak, Van, TX 75790
(214) 963-8642
Admin Valta L Carcamo.
Licensure Intermediate care. *Beds* 60. *Certified* Medicaid.
Owner Proprietary corp (Beverly Enterprises).

Van Alstyne

Meadowbrook Care Center
PO Box 307, 100 Windsor Dr, Van Alstyne, TX 75095
(214) 482-5941, 532-6543
Admin Cheryl Ann Littrell.

Licensure Intermediate care. *Beds* 60.
  Certified Medicaid.
Owner Proprietary corp.

Vernon

Vernon Care Center
2301 Texas St, Vernon, TX 76384
(817) 552-9316
Admin Norma J Gatewood.
Licensure Intermediate care. *Beds* 90.
  Certified Medicaid.
Owner Proprietary corp (Beverly Enterprises).

Wood Nursing & Convalescent Center
4301 Hospital Dr, Vernon, TX 76384
(817) 552-2568
Admin James L Wood.
Licensure Intermediate care. *Beds* 206.
  Certified Medicaid.
Owner Proprietary corp.

Victoria

Linwood Place
3401 E Airline Dr, Victoria, TX 77901
(512) 573-2467
Admin Linda L Hoffman. *Dir of Nursing*
  Nancy Kolafa RN.
Licensure Private pay. *Beds* Private pay 80.
  Certified Medicaid.
Owner Proprietary corp (ARA Living
  Centers).
Admissions Requirements Physician's request;
  All private pay.
Staff Physicians 1 (pt); RNs 1 (ft); LPNs 6
  (ft); Nurses' aides 30 (ft); Physical therapists
  1 (pt); Reality therapists 1 (pt); Recreational
  therapists 1 (pt); Occupational therapists 1
  (pt); Speech therapists 1 (pt); Activities
  coordinators 1 (ft), 1 (pt); Dietitians 1 (ft), 1
  (pt); Ophthalmologists 1 (pt); Podiatrists 1
  (pt); Dentists 1 (pt).
Activities Arts & crafts; Cards; Games;
  Reading groups; Prayer groups; Movies;
  Shopping trips; Dances/Social/Cultural
  gatherings.

Retama Manor Nursing Center—West
3007 N Navarro, Victoria, TX 77901
(512) 575-2356
Admin William McMullen.
Licensure Intermediate care. *Beds* 184.
  Certified Medicaid.
Owner Proprietary corp (ARA Living
  Centers).

Retama Manor—South
3103 Airline Dr, Victoria, TX 77901
(512) 575-6457
Admin Kathy Moore. *Dir of Nursing* Pat
  Jacob RN.
Licensure Intermediate care. *Beds* ICF 170.
  Certified Medicaid.
Owner Proprietary corp (ARA Living
  Centers).
Admissions Requirements Minimum age 18;
  Medical examination; Physician's request.
Staff RNs 2 (ft); LPNs 10 (ft), 10 (pt); Nurses'
  aides 45 (ft), 5 (pt); Activities coordinators 1
  (ft); Dietitians 1 (ft).
Languages Spanish, Czech, Russian.
Facilities Dining room; Activities room;
  Crafts room; Laundry room; Barber/Beauty
  shop.
Activities Arts & crafts; Cards; Games;
  Reading groups; Prayer groups; Movies;
  Shopping trips; Dances/Social/Cultural
  gatherings.

Twin Pines Nursing Home
3301 Mockingbird Ln, Victoria, TX 77901
(512) 573-3201
Admin Betty J Hedgclough.
Licensure Intermediate care. *Beds* 160.
  Certified Medicaid.
Owner Nonprofit corp.

Victoria Nursing & Rehabilitation Center
114 Medical Dr, Victoria, TX 77904
(512) 576-6128
Licensure Nursing. *Beds* Nursing 122.

Vidor

Changing Seasons Community Care Center
545 Denver St, Vidor, TX 77662
(409) 769-4542, 769-4510
Admin Neda E Wilson.
Licensure Intermediate care. *Beds* 55.
  Certified Medicaid.
Owner Proprietary corp.

Green Acres Convalescent Center
470 Moore St, Vidor, TX 77662
(713) 769-2454
Admin Maybelle Chandler.
Licensure Intermediate care. *Beds* 146.
  Certified Medicaid.
Owner Proprietary corp (ARA Living
  Centers).

Oakwood Manor Nursing Home
225 S Main St, Vidor, TX 77662
(409) 769-3692, 769-5697
Admin Charlene Evans.
Licensure Intermediate care. *Beds* 61.
  Certified Medicaid.
Owner Proprietary corp (Cantex Healthcare
  Centers).

Waco

Adaptive Livng Center—Central Texas
1916 Seley St, Waco, TX 76705
(817) 799-6291
Admin Ruby Faye Sumerior.
Licensure Intermediate care for mentally
  retarded. *Beds* 100. *Certified* Medicaid.

Bellmead Family Care Inc
4601 Wisconsin, Waco, TX 76705
(817) 799-5581
Admin Helen E Moser LNHA. *Dir of Nursing*
  Lynn Aven RN BSN. *Medical Dir* Dr
  Michael Stones.
Licensure Intermediate care. *Beds* ICF 49.
  Private Pay Patients 48%. *Certified*
  Medicaid.
Owner Proprietary corp.
Admissions Requirements Minimum age 21;
  Medical examination; Physician's request.
Staff Physicians 1 (pt); RNs 1 (ft); LPNs 4
  (ft), 5 (pt); Nurses' aides 10 (ft), 3 (pt);
  Physical therapists 1 (pt); Reality therapists
  1 (pt); Recreational therapists 1 (pt);
  Occupational therapists 1 (pt); Speech
  therapists 1 (pt); Activities coordinators 1
  (ft), 1 (pt); Dietitians 1 (ft), 1 (pt);
  Podiatrists 1 (pt); Audiologists 1 (pt).
Languages Spanish.
Facilities Dining room; Activities room;
  Barber/Beauty shop.
Activities Arts & crafts; Cards; Games;
  Reading groups; Prayer groups; Movies;
  Dances/Social/Cultural gatherings;
  Intergenerational programs; Pet therapy.

Care Inn of Waco
5900 Clover Ln, Waco, TX 76710
(817) 772-0610, 772-9191 FAX
Admin Helen Atkinson. *Dir of Nursing* Edna
  Tucker LVN. *Medical Dir* E W Schwartze
  MD.
Licensure Intermediate care. *Beds* ICF 74.
  Private Pay Patients 31%. *Certified*
  Medicaid.
Owner Proprietary corp (ARA Living
  Centers).
Admissions Requirements Medical
  examination.

Staff RNs 1 (ft); Nurses' aides 24 (ft); Physical
  therapists (contracted); Occupational
  therapists (contracted); Speech therapists
  (contracted); Activities coordinators 1 (ft);
  Dietitians 1 (ft); LVNs 10 (ft).
Facilities Dining room; Activities room;
  Laundry room; Barber/Beauty shop; Patio.
Activities Arts & crafts; Cards; Games;
  Reading groups; Prayer groups; Movies;
  Shopping trips; Dances/Social/Cultural
  gatherings; Intergenerational programs; Pet
  therapy; Outings; Silver Key Club.

**Crestview Manor Retirement & Convalescent
Center**
PO Drawer 5301, 1400 Lake Shore Dr, Waco,
  TX 76708
(817) 753-0291
Admin Ruby Faye Sumerour.
Licensure Intermediate care. *Beds* 150.
  Certified Medicaid.
Owner Proprietary corp.

Greenview Manor
401 Owen Ln, Waco, TX 76710
(817) 772-8900
Admin Helen Goss.
Licensure Intermediate care. *Beds* 136.
  Certified Medicaid.
Owner Proprietary corp (ARA Living
  Centers).

Haven Manor
1701 W Waco Dr, Waco, TX 76707
(817) 754-2347
Admin Millie L Westbrook. *Dir of Nursing*
  Leah Bailey. *Medical Dir* Richard Kleiman
  MD.
Licensure Intermediate care. *Beds* ICF 102.
  Private Pay Patients 18%. *Certified*
  Medicaid.
Owner Proprietary corp (Texas Health
  Enterprises).
Admissions Requirements Medical
  examination; Physician's request.
Staff Physicians (contracted); RNs
  (contracted); LPNs; Nurses' aides; Physical
  therapists (contracted); Recreational
  therapists (contracted); Occupational
  therapists (contracted); Speech therapists
  (contracted); Activities coordinators;
  Dietitians; Podiatrists (contracted);
  Audiologists (contracted); Chaplains (3 days
  a week); Counselors (3 days a week).
Languages Spanish.
Facilities Dining room; Activities room;
  Laundry room; Barber/Beauty shop.
Activities Arts & crafts; Cards; Games;
  Reading groups; Prayer groups; Movies;
  Shopping trips; Dances/Social/Cultural
  gatherings; Intergenerational programs; Pet
  therapy; Grandparent's day out.

Hillcrest Manor Nursing Center
PO Drawer 5070, 3008 Lyle Ave, Waco, TX
  76708
(817) 752-2596
Admin Larry Overstreet. *Dir of Nursing*
  Johnetta Chapman. *Medical Dir* Monnie
  Williams.
Licensure Intermediate care. *Beds* ICF 60.
  Private Pay Patients 23%. *Certified*
  Medicaid.
Owner Proprietary corp (Marwitz Brothers
  Inc).
Admissions Requirements Physician's request.
Staff Physicians 1 (pt); RNs 1 (ft), 1 (pt);
  LPNs 3 (ft), 4 (pt); Nurses' aides 15 (ft), 3
  (pt); Activities coordinators 1 (ft); Dietitians
  1 (ft).
Facilities Dining room; Laundry room;
  Barber/Beauty shop.
Activities Arts & crafts; Games; Reading
  groups; Movies; Individual activities.

Jeffrey Place Nursing Center
820 Jeffrey Dr, Waco, TX 76710
(817) 772-9480

Admin Sandra Balcar.
Licensure Intermediate care. *Beds* 106.
  Certified Medicaid.
Owner Proprietary corp (Beverly Enterprises).

Parkview Nursing Home
2120 N 4th St, Waco, TX 76708
(817) 756-5446
Admin Marian A Garcia.
Licensure Intermediate care. *Beds* 57.
  Certified Medicaid.
Owner Proprietary corp (ARA Living
  Centers).

Quality Care of Waco
2501 Maple Ave, Waco, TX 76707
(817) 752-0311
Admin Geraldine Hatchett.
Medical Dir Robert Gassler MD.
Licensure Intermediate care. *Beds* 121.
  Certified Medicare.
Admissions Requirements Medical
  examination; Physician's request.
Staff RNs 5 (ft), 7 (pt); LPNs 6 (ft), 6 (pt);
  Nurses' aides 21 (ft), 18 (pt); Occupational
  therapists 1 (pt); Speech therapists 1 (pt);
  Activities coordinators 1 (ft); Dietitians 1
  (pt); Dentists 1 (pt).
Facilities Dining room; Activities room;
  Crafts room; Laundry room; Barber/Beauty
  shop.
Activities Arts & crafts; Cards; Games;
  Reading groups; Prayer groups; Movies;
  Shopping trips; Dances/Social/Cultural
  gatherings.

Ridgecrest
1900 Hwy 6 W, Waco, TX 76712
(817) 776-9681
Admin Beverly Huntsman. *Dir of Nursing*
  Anne Patterson RN. *Medical Dir* David
  Lockhart MD.
Licensure Skilled care; Personal care;
  Retirement. *Beds* SNF 80; Personal care
  120; Retirement 30. *Private Pay Patients*
  98%. *Certified* Medicare.
Owner Privately owned.
Admissions Requirements Minimum age 55;
  Medical examination; Physician's request.
Staff Physicians; RNs 3 (ft); LPNs 9 (ft);
  Nurses' aides 30 (ft); Physical therapists;
  Occupational therapists; Speech therapists;
  Activities coordinators 2 (ft); Dietitians.
Languages German, Spanish, others by
  contract.
Facilities Dining room; Physical therapy
  room; Activities room; Chapel; Crafts room;
  Laundry room; Barber/Beauty shop.
Activities Arts & crafts; Cards; Games; Prayer
  groups; Shopping trips; Dances/Social/
  Cultural gatherings; Pet therapy.

St Elizabeth Nursing Home
PO Box 1909, 406 Austin Ave, Waco, TX
  76701
(817) 756-5441
Admin Keith Perry. *Dir of Nursing* Jan Irons
  RN FNP.
Licensure Intermediate care; Retirement. *Beds*
  179. *Certified* Medicaid.
Owner Nonprofit corp.
Staff Physicians 1 (pt); RNs 4 (ft), 1 (pt);
  LPNs 17 (ft); Nurses' aides 42 (ft); Physical
  therapists 1 (pt); Speech therapists 1 (pt);
  Activities coordinators 3 (ft); Dietitians 1
  (pt); Pastoral counselor 1 (ft); Social worker
  2 (ft).
Affiliation Roman Catholic.
Facilities Dining room; Physical therapy
  room; Activities room; Chapel; Crafts room;
  Laundry room; Barber/Beauty shop; Library.
Activities Arts & crafts; Cards; Games;
  Reading groups; Prayer groups; Movies;
  Shopping trips; Dances/Social/Cultural
  gatherings.

Twin Oaks Retirement Center
2329 N 39th St, Waco, TX 76708
(817) 756-3701
Admin Stephen Adams.
Licensure Intermediate care; Alzheimer's care.
  Beds ICF 98. *Certified* Medicaid.
Owner Proprietary corp (ARA Living
  Centers).
Facilities Dining room; Activities room;
  Crafts room; Laundry room; Barber/Beauty
  shop.
Activities Arts & crafts; Cards; Games;
  Reading groups; Prayer groups; Movies;
  Shopping trips; Dances/Social/Cultural
  gatherings; Pool; Crochet; Chartered trips.

Woodland Springs Nursing Center
1010 Dallas St, Waco, TX 76704
(817) 752-9774
Admin Virginia Atkinson. *Dir of Nursing*
  Carolyn C B Harmon RN.
Licensure Intermediate care. *Beds* ICF 148.
  Private Pay Patients 96%. *Certified*
  Medicaid.
Owner Nonprofit corp.
Admissions Requirements Minimum age 55;
  Medical examination; Physician's request.
Staff RNs; LPNs; Nurses' aides; Activities
  coordinators; Dietitians; Podiatrists.
Languages Spanish.
Facilities Dining room; Activities room;
  Crafts room; Laundry room; Barber/Beauty
  shop.
Activities Arts & crafts; Cards; Games;
  Reading groups; Prayer groups; Movies;
  Shopping trips; Dances/Social/Cultural
  gatherings; Intergenerational programs; Pet
  therapy.

Waxahachie

Pleasant Manor Nursing Home
Access Rd, S Hwy 35, Waxahachie, TX 75165
(214) 937-7320
Admin Steven V Cook.
Licensure Intermediate care. *Beds* ICF 102.
  Certified Medicaid.
Owner Privately owned.
Admissions Requirements Minimum age 18;
  Medical examination; Physician's request.
Staff RNs 1 (ft); LPNs 8 (ft), 2 (pt); Nurses'
  aides 24 (ft), 6 (pt); Activities coordinators 1
  (ft); Dietitians 1 (ft).
Facilities Dining room; Activities room;
  Chapel; Laundry room; Barber/Beauty shop.
Activities Arts & crafts; Cards; Games;
  Reading groups; Prayer groups; Movies;
  Shopping trips; Dances/Social/Cultural
  gatherings.

Renfro Nursing Home
1413 W Main St, Waxahachie, TX 75165
(214) 937-2298
Admin Larry L Walker.
Medical Dir John G Compton MD.
Licensure Skilled care; Intermediate care. *Beds*
  SNF 58; ICF 98. *Certified* Medicaid;
  Medicare.
Owner Proprietary corp (Beverly Enterprises).
Admissions Requirements Physician's request.
Staff Physicians 7 (ft); RNs 2 (ft), 1 (pt);
  LPNs 5 (ft), 4 (pt); Nurses' aides 17 (ft), 3
  (pt); Physical therapists 1 (ft); Reality
  therapists 1 (ft); Recreational therapists 1
  (ft); Occupational therapists 1 (ft); Speech
  therapists 1 (ft); Activities coordinators 1
  (ft), 1 (pt); Dietitians 1 (pt);
  Ophthalmologists 1 (pt); Podiatrists 1 (pt);
  Dentists 1 (pt).
Facilities Dining room; Activities room;
  Laundry room; Barber/Beauty shop.
Activities Arts & crafts; Cards; Games;
  Reading groups; Prayer groups; Movies;
  Shopping trips.

Weatherford

Keeneland Nursing Home
700 S Bowie, Weatherford, TX 76086
(817) 594-2715
Admin Luther Shuffield.
Licensure Skilled care. *Beds* 72. *Certified*
  Medicaid.
Owner Proprietary corp (National Heritage).

Leisure Lodge—Weatherford
1205 Santa Fe Dr, Weatherford, TX 76086
(817) 594-2786
Admin Janelle Lynch.
Medical Dir Dr John L Roan.
Licensure Intermediate care. *Beds* 120.
  Certified Medicaid.
Owner Proprietary corp (Beverly Enterprises).
Admissions Requirements Medical
  examination; Physician's request.
Staff Physicians 19 (pt); RNs 1 (ft); LPNs 9
  (ft); Nurses' aides 28 (ft); Activities
  coordinators 1 (ft); Dietitians 1 (ft).
Facilities Dining room; Physical therapy
  room; Laundry room; Barber/Beauty shop.
Activities Arts & crafts; Cards; Games;
  Reading groups; Prayer groups; Movies;
  Shopping trips; Dances/Social/Cultural
  gatherings.

Peach Tree Place
315 Anderson St, Weatherford, TX 76086
(817) 599-4181
Licensure Nursing. *Beds* Nursing 59.

Weatherford Care Center 1
521 W 7th St, Peaster Hwy, Weatherford, TX
  76086
(817) 594-8713
Admin John DeGrand.
Medical Dir Dr John Roon.
Licensure Skilled care; Intermediate care. *Beds*
  122. *Certified* Medicaid.
Owner Proprietary corp (ARA Living
  Centers).
Staff RNs 2 (ft); LPNs 10 (ft); Activities
  coordinators 1 (ft); Dietitians 1 (ft).
Facilities Dining room; Physical therapy
  room; Activities room; Laundry room;
  Barber/Beauty shop.
Activities Arts & crafts; Cards; Games; Prayer
  groups; Movies.

Weatherford Care Center 2
315 Anderson St, Weatherford, TX 76086
(817) 594-6461
Admin Deborah L Whitaker.
Licensure Intermediate care. *Beds* 59.
  Certified Medicaid.
Owner Proprietary corp.

Webster

Manor Care of Webster
750 W Texas Ave, Webster, TX 77598
(713) 332-3496
Admin Sharan Nunn. *Dir of Nursing* Mollie
  Jamison RN. *Medical Dir* Michael J Austin
  MD.
Licensure Skilled care; Intermediate care;
  Non-certified; Alzheimer's care. *Beds* SNF
  28; ICF 65; Non-certified 26. *Certified*
  Medicaid; Medicare.
Owner Proprietary corp (Manor Care).
Admissions Requirements Minimum age 18;
  Medical examination; Physician's request.
Staff Physicians; RNs; LPNs; Nurses' aides;
  Physical therapists; Recreational therapists;
  Occupational therapists; Speech therapists;
  Activities coordinators; Dietitians;
  Ophthalmologists.
Facilities Dining room; Physical therapy
  room; Activities room; Laundry room;
  Barber/Beauty shop.
Activities Arts & crafts; Cards; Games;
  Reading groups; Prayer groups; Movies;
  Shopping trips; Dances/Social/Cultural
  gatherings; Happy hour; Pet therapy.

Weimar

Parkview Manor
206 N Smith St, Weimar, TX 78962
(409) 725-8564
Admin Carolyn D Poenitzsch. *Dir of Nursing*
Ottillia Klare RN.
Licensure Intermediate care; Alzheimer's care.
Beds ICF 68. *Private Pay Patients* 50%.
Certified Medicaid.
Owner Nonprofit organization/foundation.
Admissions Requirements Medical
examination; Physician's request.
Staff RNs; LPNs; Nurses' aides; Physical
therapists (contracted); Activities
coordinators; Dietitians (contracted).
Languages Czech, German, Spanish.
Affiliation Methodist.
Facilities Dining room; Physical therapy
room; Activities room; Chapel; Crafts room;
Laundry room; Barber/Beauty shop; Library.
Activities Arts & crafts; Cards; Games;
Reading groups; Prayer groups; Movies;
Shopping trips; Dances/Social/Cultural
gatherings; Intergenerational programs; Pet
therapy.

Wellington

Wellington Care Center
1506 Childress St, Wellington, TX 79095
(806) 447-2777
Admin Angelin Anderson.
Medical Dir Dr K N Kumar.
Licensure Intermediate care. *Beds* ICF 84.
Certified Medicaid.
Owner Proprietary corp.
Admissions Requirements Physician's request.
Staff RNs 1 (pt); LPNs 6 (ft), 2 (pt); Nurses'
aides 23 (ft), 2 (pt); Activities coordinators 1
(ft); Dietitians 1 (pt).
Facilities Dining room; Activities room;
Crafts room; Laundry room; Barber/Beauty
shop.
Activities Arts & crafts; Cards; Games;
Reading groups; Prayer groups; Shopping
trips; Dances/Social/Cultural gatherings.

Wells

Wells Nursing Home
PO Box 359, May St at 2nd St, Wells, TX
75976
(409) 867-4707
Admin Robert D Winfield.
Licensure Intermediate care. *Beds* 60.
Certified Medicaid.
Owner Proprietary corp.

Weslaco

John Knox Village Medical Center
1300 S Border Ave, Weslaco, TX 78596
(512) 968-4575
Admin Audrey L Earl. *Dir of Nursing* Barbara
Jackson RN.
Licensure Life care Retirement Community.
Beds SNF 60. *Certified* Medicare.
Owner Nonprofit corp.
Staff RNs; LPNs; Nurses' aides; Activities
coordinators; Dietitians.
Facilities Dining room; Activities room;
Chapel; Crafts room; Laundry room; Barber/
Beauty shop; Library; Billards; Ice cream
parlor; Exercise room; Swimming pool;
Jacuzzi.
Activities Arts & crafts; Cards; Games;
Reading groups; Prayer groups; Movies;
Shopping trips; Dances/Social/Cultural
gatherings.

Retama Manor Nursing Center—Weslaco
721 Airport Dr, Weslaco, TX 78596
(512) 968-8502
Admin William N Lowe.

Licensure Intermediate care. *Beds* 120.
Certified Medicaid.
Owner Proprietary corp (ARA Living
Centers).

Valley Grande Manor
1212 S Bridge Ave, Weslaco, TX 78596
(512) 968-2121
Admin Diane Butler. *Dir of Nursing* Janet
Louitt RN.
Licensure Skilled care; Intermediate care. *Beds*
SNF 143. *Certified* Medicaid; Medicare.
Owner Nonprofit corp.
Admissions Requirements Medical
examination; Physician's request.
Staff RNs; LPNs; Nurses' aides; Activities
coordinators; Dietitians.
Languages Spanish.
Affiliation Seventh-Day Adventist.
Facilities Dining room; Physical therapy
room; Activities room; Chapel; Crafts room;
Laundry room; Barber/Beauty shop; Library.
Activities Arts & crafts; Cards; Games;
Reading groups; Prayer groups; Movies;
Dances/Social/Cultural gatherings.

West

West Rest Haven Inc
300 Haven St, West, TX 76691
(817) 826-5354
Admin Zona M Donohue. *Dir of Nursing*
Helen Kubacak. *Medical Dir* Dr George
Smith.
Licensure Skilled care; Intermediate care. *Beds*
SNF 105. *Certified* Medicaid; Medicare.
Owner Proprietary corp.
Admissions Requirements Medical
examination; Physician's request.
Staff Physicians 1 (ft); RNs 2 (ft); Nurses'
aides 22 (ft); Physical therapists 1 (ft);
Occupational therapists 1 (ft); Speech
therapists 1 (ft); Activities coordinators 1
(ft); Dietitians 1 (ft).
Facilities Dining room; Activities room;
Chapel; Crafts room; Laundry room; Barber/
Beauty shop.
Activities Arts & crafts; Dances/Social/Cultural
gatherings; Pet therapy.

West Columbia

Sweetbriar Development Center
212 N 14th, West Columbia, TX 77486
(713) 345-3191
Admin Leanne M K Martinsen.
Licensure Intermediate care for mentally
retarded. *Beds* 120. *Certified* Medicaid.

Wharton

Wharton Manor
418 N Rusk St, Wharton, TX 77488
(409) 532-5020
Admin Willa Dean Roades.
Licensure Intermediate care. *Beds* 116.
Certified Medicaid.
Owner Proprietary corp (ARA Living
Centers).

Wheeler

Wheeler Care Center
PO Box 525, 1000 S Kiowa, Wheeler, TX
79096
(806) 826-3397
Admin B A Hyatt. *Dir of Nursing* La Vonda
Durham.
Licensure Intermediate care. *Beds* ICF 90.
Private Pay Patients 26%. *Certified*
Medicaid.
Owner Privately owned.
Admissions Requirements Physician's request.
Staff RNs 1 (pt); LPNs 8 (ft), 5 (pt); Nurses'
aides 23 (ft), 3 (pt); Activities coordinators 1
(ft); Dietitians 1 (pt).

Facilities Dining room; Activities room;
Laundry room; Barber/Beauty shop;
Smoking lounge.
Activities Arts & crafts; Games; Prayer groups;
Movies; Shopping trips; Field trips.

White Settlement

White Settlement Nursing Center
7820 Skyline Park Dr, White Settlement, TX
76108
(817) 246-4671
Admin Betty Martin. *Dir of Nursing* Marcia
Spacher RN. *Medical Dir* James T Hawa.
Licensure Skilled care. *Beds* SNF 108. *Private
Pay Patients* 20%.
Owner Proprietary corp (Beverly Enterprises).
Staff Physicians 10 (pt); RNs 3 (ft), 2 (pt);
LPNs 8 (ft), 3 (pt); Nurses' aides 20 (ft), 4
(pt); Activities coordinators 1 (ft); Food
service supervisors 1 (ft).

Whitesboro

Whitesboro Nursing Home Inc
PO Box 250, 1204 Sherman Dr, Whitesboro,
TX 76273
(214) 564-3508
Admin Darrell Reed. *Dir of Nursing* Macel
Hood.
Licensure Skilled care. *Beds* ICF 82. *Certified*
Medicaid.
Owner Proprietary corp.
Admissions Requirements Minimum age 21;
Medical examination.
Staff RNs 1 (pt); LPNs 10 (ft), 2 (pt); Nurses'
aides 21 (ft), 2 (pt); Activities coordinators 1
(ft), 1 (pt).
Facilities Dining room; Physical therapy
room; Activities room; Chapel; Crafts room;
Laundry room; Barber/Beauty shop; Library.
Activities Arts & crafts; Games; Reading
groups; Prayer groups; Movies; Dances/
Social/Cultural gatherings.

Whitewright

Campbell Care of Whitewright
PO Box 808, 400 S Bond St, Whitewright, TX
75491
(214) 364-2772, 364-2774
Admin Rosalie S Geers.
Licensure Skilled care; Custodial care. *Beds*
SNF 137; Custodial care 12. *Certified*
Medicaid.
Owner Proprietary corp.

Whitney

Park Plaza Nursing Home
1244 State Park Rd, Whitney, TX 76692
(817) 694-2239
Admin Millie L Westbrook. *Dir of Nursing*
Sherry Jumper. *Medical Dir* Morris R Hill
MD.
Licensure Intermediate care; Retirement. *Beds*
ICF 110. *Certified* Medicaid.
Owner Proprietary corp (Health Enter of
America).
Admissions Requirements Physician's request.
Staff RNs; LPNs; Nurses' aides; Physical
therapists; Recreational therapists; Speech
therapists; Activities coordinators; Dietitians;
Ophthalmologists; Podiatrists.
Facilities Dining room; Activities room;
Laundry room; Barber/Beauty shop.
Activities Arts & crafts; Cards; Games;
Reading groups; Prayer groups; Movies;
Shopping trips; Dances/Social/Cultural
gatherings.

Town Hall Estates Health Care Facility
PO Box 1830, 101 San Marcos, Whitney, TX
76692
(817) 694-2233

Admin Sue Murphy. *Dir of Nursing* Marsha Middlebrook.
Licensure Intermediate care; Private pay. *Beds* ICF 60; Private pay 30. *Private Pay Patients* 33%. *Certified* Medicaid.
Owner Nonprofit corp (American Religious Town Hall Meeting Inc).
Admissions Requirements Medical examination.
Staff RNs 1 (pt); LPNs 14 (ft); Nurses' aides 30 (ft); Physical therapists (contracted); Reality therapists (contracted); Recreational therapists (contracted); Occupational therapists (contracted); Speech therapists (contracted); Activities coordinators 1 (ft), 1 (pt); Dietitians 1 (pt).
Languages Spanish.
Affiliation Seventh-Day Adventist.
Facilities Dining room; Activities room; Chapel; Crafts room; Laundry room; Barber/Beauty shop.
Activities Arts & crafts; Cards; Games; Reading groups; Prayer groups; Movies; Dances/Social/Cultural gatherings; Intergenerational programs.

Wichita Falls

Canterbury Villa of Wichita Falls
1908 6th St, Wichita Falls, TX 76301
(817) 322-2193
Admin Carlton Jack Lane.
Licensure Intermediate care. *Beds* 62. *Certified* Medicaid.
Owner Proprietary corp.

Deerings Nursing Home
1604 Filmore St, Wichita Falls, TX 76309
(915) 332-0371
Admin Fred Cullens. *Dir of Nursing* Phyllis Young.
Licensure Intermediate care. *Beds* ICF 89; Private 22. *Certified* Medicaid.
Owner Proprietary corp (Hillhaven Corp).
Staff LPNs; Nurses' aides; Activities coordinators; Dietitians.

Denver Manor Nursing Home
608 Denver, Wichita Falls, TX 76301
(817) 322-7852
Admin Frederick D Lane.
Licensure Intermediate care. *Beds* 81. *Certified* Medicaid.
Owner Proprietary corp.

Highland Nursing Center
4411 Henry S Grace Fwy, Wichita Falls, TX 76302
(817) 692-2820
Admin Eileen M Addison.
Medical Dir Georgia Cargal.
Licensure Intermediate care; Personal care. *Beds* ICF 90; Personal 24. *Certified* Medicaid.
Owner Proprietary corp.
Staff LPNs 8 (ft); Nurses' aides 34 (ft); Activities coordinators 1 (ft); Dietitians 1 (pt).
Activities Arts & crafts; Games; Reading groups; Prayer groups; Movies; Shopping trips.

Midwestern Parkway Heritage Manor
601 Midwestern Pkwy, Wichita Falls, TX 76302
(817) 723-0885
Admin David Reaves.
Licensure Intermediate care. *Beds* ICF 120. *Certified* Medicaid.
Owner Proprietary corp (National Heritage).

Monterey Care Center
3101 10th St, Wichita Falls, TX 76309
(817) 766-0281
Admin Marjorie Sue Moncrief.
Licensure Skilled care. *Beds* 91. *Certified* Medicaid.
Owner Proprietary corp (Beverly Enterprises).

Pleasant Hill Nursing Home
1420 Tanbark Rd, Wichita Falls, TX 76305
(817) 692-3977
Admin Freeda Patterson.
Medical Dir A Chitale; Karen Liss.
Licensure Intermediate care. *Beds* ICF 35. *Certified* Medicaid.
Staff Physicians 1 (ft); RNs 1 (pt); LPNs 3 (ft), 1 (pt); Nurses' aides 5 (ft), 2 (pt); Physical therapists 1 (pt); Reality therapists 1 (pt); Activities coordinators 1 (ft); Dietitians 1 (ft); Ophthalmologists 1 (pt).
Languages Spanish.
Facilities Dining room; Activities room; Crafts room; Laundry room.
Activities Arts & crafts; Cards; Games; Reading groups; Prayer groups; Movies; Shopping trips; Dances/Social/Cultural gatherings.

Presbyterian Manor
4600 Taft Blvd, Wichita Falls, TX 76308
(817) 691-1710
Admin Jimmy Oakley. *Dir of Nursing* Helen Talley.
Licensure Intermediate care; Custodial care. *Beds* ICF 43; Custodial care 14.
Owner Nonprofit corp.
Staff RNs 2 (ft), 3 (pt); LPNs 5 (ft), 4 (pt); Nurses' aides 15 (ft), 6 (pt); Activities coordinators 2 (ft); Dietitians 1 (ft).
Affiliation Presbyterian.

Ridgeview Nursing & Convalescent Center
4411 Henry S Grace Fwy S, Wichita Falls, TX 76302
(817) 767-8322
Admin Dennis Ferguson.
Licensure Intermediate care. *Beds* 148. *Certified* Medicaid.
Owner Proprietary corp (Hillhaven Corp).

River Oaks Care Center
100 Bailey St, Wichita Falls, TX 76307
(817) 766-0279
Admin Stephen Taras Jr.
Licensure Intermediate care. *Beds* 58. *Certified* Medicaid.
Owner Proprietary corp (Beverly Enterprises).

Rolling Meadows Health Care Center
3006 McNeil, Wichita Falls, TX 76309
(817) 691-7511
Licensure Nursing. *Beds* Nursing 78; Personal care 8.

Texhoma Christian Care Center
300 Loop 11, Wichita Falls, TX 76305
(817) 723-8420
Admin Kale Martin. *Dir of Nursing* Myrle Taylor LVN.
Licensure Intermediate care; Alzheimer's care. *Beds* ICF 301. *Certified* Medicaid.
Owner Nonprofit corp.
Admissions Requirements Minimum age 18; Medical examination.
Staff Physicians 1 (pt); RNs 1 (ft); LPNs 21 (ft); Nurses' aides 130 (ft); Activities coordinators 3 (ft); Dietitians 1 (pt).
Affiliation Church of Christ.
Facilities Dining room; Activities room; Chapel; Crafts room; Laundry room; Barber/Beauty shop.
Activities Arts & crafts; Cards; Games; Prayer groups; Movies; Dances/Social/Cultural gatherings.

University Park Heritage Manor
4511 Coronado, Wichita Falls, TX 76301
(817) 692-8001
Admin Frank Conyea.
Licensure Intermediate care. *Beds* 100. *Certified* Medicaid.
Owner Proprietary corp (National Heritage).

Wichita Falls Convalescent Center
1501 7th St, Wichita Falls, TX 76301
(817) 322-0741
Admin Elisha Y Ashcraft.

Licensure Intermediate care. *Beds* 197. *Certified* Medicaid.
Owner Proprietary corp.

Wood Convalescent
2400 Southwest Pkwy, Wichita Falls, TX 76308
(817) 691-5301
Admin Mary F Wood. *Dir of Nursing* Dixie Price. *Medical Dir* Gary Ozier.
Licensure Intermediate care. *Beds* ICF 98. *Certified* Medicaid.
Owner Proprietary corp.
Admissions Requirements Medical examination; Physician's request.
Staff Physicians 1 (pt); RNs 1 (ft); LPNs 7 (ft), 3 (pt); Nurses' aides 36 (ft), 9 (pt); Physical therapists 1 (pt); Activities coordinators 1 (ft); Dietitians 1 (pt).
Facilities Dining room; Activities room; Laundry room; Barber/Beauty shop.
Activities Arts & crafts; Cards; Games; Reading groups; Prayer groups; Movies; Shopping trips; Dances/Social/Cultural gatherings; Intergenerational programs; Pet therapy.

Willis

Willis Convalescent Center
3000 N Danville, Willis, TX 77378
(409) 856-4312, 856-7013
Admin Jeanne Young.
Licensure Intermediate care. *Beds* 114. *Certified* Medicaid.
Owner Proprietary corp (ARA Living Centers).

Wills Point

Free State Crestwood Inc
PO Box 368, 1448 Houston St, Wills Point, TX 75169
(214) 873-2542
Admin Mike Henrie.
Medical Dir Sherry Martin.
Licensure Intermediate care. *Beds* ICF 120. *Certified* Medicaid.
Owner Proprietary corp.
Admissions Requirements Physician's request.
Staff RNs 1 (pt); LPNs 12 (ft); Nurses' aides 38 (ft), 3 (pt); Activities coordinators 1 (ft); Dietitians 1 (pt).
Languages Spanish.
Facilities Dining room; Activities room; Chapel; Crafts room; Laundry room; Barber/Beauty shop; Library.
Activities Arts & crafts; Cards; Games; Reading groups; Prayer groups; Movies; Shopping trips; Dances/Social/Cultural gatherings.

Locust Grove Nursing Home
Rte 5 Box 393, Wills Point, TX 75169
(214) 563-9445
Admin William A Reed.
Licensure Intermediate care. *Beds* 60. *Certified* Medicaid.
Owner Proprietary corp.

Wimberley

Deer Creek Nursing Center
Rte 2 Box 6, Kyle Hwy at Flite Acres, Wimberley, TX 78676
(512) 847-5540
Licensure Nursing. *Beds* Nursing 122.

Winnsboro

Whispering Pines Nursing Home Inc
PO Box 47, 910 Beech St, Winnsboro, TX 75494
(214) 342-5243
Admin Jo Ann Milner.
Medical Dir Lynda Combs.

Licensure Intermediate care. *Beds* ICF 120.
Certified Medicaid.
Owner Proprietary corp.
Admissions Requirements Physician's request.
Staff LPNs 8 (ft), 6 (pt); Nurses' aides 25 (ft),
10 (pt); Activities coordinators 1 (ft);
Dietitians 1 (ft).
Facilities Dining room; Activities room;
Crafts room; Laundry room; Barber/Beauty
shop.
Activities Arts & crafts; Cards; Games;
Reading groups; Prayer groups; Shopping
trips.

Winnsboro Nursing Home
PO Box 554, 402 S Chestnut, Winnsboro, TX
75494
(214) 342-6156
Admin Pam Hollingsworth. *Dir of Nursing*
Helen Martin LVN. *Medical Dir* David
Murley MD.
Licensure Intermediate care. *Beds* ICF 60.
Private Pay Patients 10%. *Certified*
Medicaid.
Owner Proprietary corp (Texas Life Care Inc).
Admissions Requirements Medical
examination; Physician's request.
Staff Physicians 2 (ft); RNs 1 (ft); LPNs 6 (ft);
Nurses' aides 30 (ft); Physical therapists 1
(ft); Activities coordinators 1 (ft); Dietitians
1 (ft).
Facilities Dining room; Activities room;
Crafts room; Laundry room; Barber/Beauty
shop.
Activities Arts & crafts; Cards; Games;
Reading groups; Prayer groups; Movies;
Dances/Social/Cultural gatherings; Pet
therapy; Kid therapy.

Winnwood Nursing Home Inc
PO Box 24, 502 E Coke Rd, Winnsboro, TX
75494
(214) 342-6951, 342-3387 FAX
Admin Edna Nelson. *Dir of Nursing* Cathy
McGill. *Medical Dir* Dr W Massey.
Licensure Intermediate care. *Beds* ICF 60.
Private Pay Patients 50%. *Certified*
Medicaid.
Owner Proprietary corp.
Admissions Requirements Physician's request.
Staff LPNs 4 (ft), 2 (pt); Nurses' aides 12 (ft),
2 (pt); Physical therapists 1 (pt); Podiatrists
1 (pt).
Facilities Dining room; Physical therapy
room; Activities room; Laundry room;
Barber/Beauty shop; Library.
Activities Arts & crafts; Cards; Games;
Reading groups; Prayer groups; Movies;
Shopping trips; Dances/Social/Cultural
gatherings; Intergenerational programs; Pet
therapy.

Winters

Senior Citizens Nursing Home
PO Box 66, 506 Van Ness St, Winters, TX
79567
(915) 754-4566
Admin Wanda M Laxson. *Dir of Nursing*
Tommye J O'Dell. *Medical Dir* Dr Y K Lee.
Licensure Intermediate care. *Beds* ICF 48.
Certified Medicaid.
Owner Proprietary corp.
Admissions Requirements Medical
examination; Physician's request.
Staff RNs 1 (pt); LPNs 6 (ft), 1 (pt); Nurses'
aides 14 (ft), 3 (pt); Physical therapists 1
(pt); Activities coordinators 1 (ft), 1 (pt);
Dietitians 1 (pt).
Facilities Dining room; Physical therapy
room; Activities room; Chapel; Laundry
room; Barber/Beauty shop; Whirlpool/spa.
Activities Arts & crafts; Cards; Games;
Reading groups; Prayer groups; Movies;
Shopping trips; Dances/Social/Cultural
gatherings.

Wolfe City

Smith's Nursing Home
PO Box 107, 300 Crockett, Wolfe City, TX
75496
(214) 496-2261
Admin S E Smith.
Licensure Intermediate care. *Beds* 46.
Certified Medicaid.
Owner Proprietary corp.

The Woodlands

Heritage Manor
4650 S Panther Creek Rd, The Woodlands,
TX 77381
(713) 363-3535, 292-7970 FAX
Admin Mattie Locke. *Dir of Nursing* Dianne
B McCage.
Licensure Skilled care; Intermediate care;
Alzheimer's care. *Beds* Swing beds SNF/ICF
206. *Private Pay Patients* 47%. *Certified*
Medicaid; Medicare.
Owner Privately owned.
Admissions Requirements Medical
examination.
Languages Spanish.
Facilities Dining room; Physical therapy
room; Activities room; Chapel; Crafts room;
Laundry room; Barber/Beauty shop; Library;
Gardens; Patios; Fountains; Game room.
Activities Arts & crafts; Cards; Games;
Reading groups; Prayer groups; Movies;
Shopping trips; Dances/Social/Cultural
gatherings; Intergenerational programs; Pet
therapy.

Woodville

Holiday Pines Manor
1201 Cardinal Dr, Woodville, TX 75979
(409) 283-3397
Admin Sondra Lankford.
Licensure Intermediate care. *Beds* 112.
Certified Medicaid.
Admissions Requirements Medical
examination.
Staff Physicians 1 (pt); RNs 1 (ft); LPNs 6
(ft); Nurses' aides 60 (ft); Physical therapists
1 (pt); Occupational therapists 1 (pt); Speech
therapists 1 (pt); Activities coordinators 1
(ft); Dietitians 1 (pt); Podiatrists 1 (pt);
Dentists 1 (pt).
Facilities Dining room; Physical therapy
room; Activities room; Chapel; Crafts room;
Laundry room; Barber/Beauty shop.
Activities Arts & crafts; Cards; Games;
Reading groups; Prayer groups; Movies;
Shopping trips; Dances/Social/Cultural
gatherings; Gardening.

Woodville Convalescent Center
102 N Beach St, Woodville, TX 75979
(409) 283-2555
Admin Judy G McKee.
Licensure Intermediate care. *Beds* 98.
Certified Medicaid.
Owner Proprietary corp (Cantex Healthcare
Centers).

Wortham

Leisure Lodge—Wortham
PO Box 368, Twin Circle Addition, Wortham,
TX 76693
(817) 765-3377
Admin Margaret W Brown. *Dir of Nursing*
Janet McDade. *Medical Dir* N D Buchmeyer
MD.
Licensure Intermediate care. *Beds* ICF 102.
Certified Medicaid.
Owner Proprietary corp (Beverly Enterprises).
Admissions Requirements Physician's request.
Staff RNs 1 (ft); LPNs 5 (ft), 1 (pt); Nurses'
aides 14 (ft), 3 (pt); Activities coordinators 1
(ft); Dietitians 1 (ft).

Facilities Dining room; Physical therapy
room; Chapel; Laundry room; Barber/Beauty
shop.
Activities Arts & crafts; Cards; Games; Prayer
groups; Shopping trips.

Wylie

Hillcrest Manor
300 E Brown, Wylie, TX 75098
(214) 442-3553
Admin Ania Rost. *Dir of Nursing* Debbie
Logan. *Medical Dir* Dr Ben Northam.
Licensure Intermediate care. *Beds* ICF 102.
Certified Medicaid.
Owner Proprietary corp (Campbell, White &
Associates).
Admissions Requirements Medical
examination; Physician's request.
Staff Physicians 4 (ft), 8 (pt); RNs 1 (pt);
LPNs 10 (ft), 3 (pt); Nurses' aides 45 (ft), 5
(pt); Physical therapists 1 (ft); Reality
therapists 1 (pt); Recreational therapists 1
(pt); Occupational therapists 1 (pt); Speech
therapists 1 (pt); Activities coordinators 1
(ft); Dietitians 1 (ft); Ophthalmologists 1
(pt); Podiatrists 1 (pt); Audiologists 1 (pt).
Languages Spanish, Polish.
Facilities Dining room; Physical therapy
room; Activities room; Laundry room;
Barber/Beauty shop; 2 sunrooms.
Activities Arts & crafts; Cards; Games;
Reading groups; Prayer groups; Movies;
Dances/Social/Cultural gatherings;
Intergenerational programs; Pet therapy;
Catered lunches from local restaurants;
Country fair.

Yoakum

Stevens Nursing Home
205 Walter St, Yoakum, TX 77995
(512) 293-3544
Admin Chesley Stevens. *Dir of Nursing*
Viringia Flatmann. *Medical Dir* F L Merian
MD.
Licensure Skilled care; Intermediate care. *Beds*
SNF 46; ICF 60. *Private Pay Patients* 30%.
Certified Medicaid; Medicare.
Owner Proprietary corp (Care Givers Inc).
Admissions Requirements Minimum age 16.
Staff RNs 2 (ft); LPNs 8 (ft), 6 (pt); Nurses'
aides 38 (ft); Activities coordinators 1 (ft), 1
(pt); Dietitians 1 (ft).
Facilities Dining room; Activities room;
Chapel; Crafts room; Laundry room; Barber/
Beauty shop.
Activities Arts & crafts; Cards; Games;
Reading groups; Prayer groups; Movies; Pet
therapy.

Yoakum Memorial Nursing Home Inc
PO Box 512, Hwy 77-A Business Rte,
Yoakum, TX 77995
(512) 293-2533
Admin C R Jamison.
Licensure Intermediate care. *Beds* 60.
Certified Medicaid.
Staff RNs 1 (pt); LPNs 2 (ft), 3 (pt); Nurses'
aides 10 (ft), 4 (pt); Activities coordinators 1
(ft); 12 (ft), 5 (pt).
Facilities Dining room; Activities room;
Laundry room; Barber/Beauty shop.
Activities Arts & crafts; Games; Prayer groups;
Shopping trips.

Yorktown

Yorktown Manor Home
670 W 4th St, Yorktown, TX 78164
(512) 564-2275
Admin Lyndal S Pattillo.
Medical Dir Gloria Suggs LVN.
Licensure Intermediate care. *Beds* ICF 92.
Certified Medicaid; Medicare.
Owner Proprietary corp (Diversicare Corp).

Admissions Requirements Minimum age 16; Physician's request.

Staff Physicians 2 (ft); RNs 1 (pt); LPNs 3 (ft); Nurses' aides 17 (ft); Physical therapists 1 (pt); Activities coordinators 2 (ft); Dietitians 1 (ft); Podiatrists 1 (pt); Dentists 1 (ft).
Languages Spanish, Polish.

Facilities Dining room; Activities room; Chapel; Laundry room; Barber/Beauty shop.
Activities Arts & crafts; Cards; Games; Reading groups; Prayer groups; Movies; Shopping trips; Dances/Social/Cultural gatherings; Parties.

UTAH

American Fork

Heritage Convalescent Center
350 E 300 N, American Fork, UT 84003
(801) 756-5293
Admin Shirley Garrett.
Licensure Skilled care. *Beds* SNF 60. *Certified*
Medicaid; Medicare.

Utah State Training School
795 N 900 E, American Fork, UT 84003
(801) 763-4000
Admin Jeremiah R Dandoy.
Medical Dir David Green MD.
Licensure Intermediate care for mentally
retarded. *Beds* ICF/MR 511. *Certified*
Medicaid; Medicare.
Owner Publicly owned.
Staff Physicians 2 (ft), 20 (pt); RNs 16 (ft);
LPNs 45 (ft); Physical therapists 4 (ft);
Recreational therapists 10 (ft); Occupational
therapists 4 (ft); Speech therapists 10 (ft);
Dietitians 2 (ft).

Blanding

Four Corners Regional Care Center
930 N 400 W, Blanding, UT 84511
(801) 678-2251
Admin Rayburn E Jack. *Dir of Nursing*
Kathleen G Lyman. *Medical Dir* Roland D
Benedict.
Licensure Skilled care. *Beds* SNF 80. *Private*
Pay Patients 21%. *Certified* Medicaid;
Medicare; VA.
Owner Proprietary corp (Westcare
Management Inc).
Admissions Requirements Medical
examination; Physician's request.
Staff RNs 5 (ft), 1 (pt); LPNs 6 (ft), 6 (pt);
Nurses' aides 26 (ft), 7 (pt); Physical
therapists 1 (pt); Recreational therapists 1
(ft); Activities coordinators 2 (ft).
Languages Ute, Navajo, Spanish.
Facilities Dining room; Physical therapy
room; Activities room; Crafts room; Laundry
room; Barber/Beauty shop; Library.
Activities Arts & crafts; Cards; Games;
Reading groups; Movies; Shopping trips;
Dances/Social/Cultural gatherings.

Bountiful

Bountiful Nursing Home
130 E 100 N, Bountiful, UT 84010
(801) 295-3003
Admin Sybel Simmonds.
Licensure Intermediate care. *Beds* ICF 23.

CareWest—Bountiful
350 S 400 E, Bountiful, UT 84010
(801) 298-2291
Admin Lollie Green RN, acting. *Dir of*
Nursing Lollie Green RN. *Medical Dir* Dr
Joseph Jensen.
Licensure Skilled care; Alzheimer's care; Adult
day care. *Beds* SNF 104. *Private Pay*
Patients 25%. *Certified* Medicaid; Medicare.
Owner Proprietary corp (Care Enterprises).
Admissions Requirements Medical
examination; Physician's request.
Staff RNs 6 (ft), 4 (pt); LPNs 6 (ft), 1 (pt);
Nurses' aides 80 (ft); Physical therapists 1
(ft); Recreational therapists 1 (ft);
Occupational therapists 1 (pt); Speech
therapists 1 (pt); Activities coordinators 3
(ft); Dietitians 1 (pt); Podiatrists 1 (pt);
Audiologists 1 (pt).
Languages Spanish.
Facilities Dining room; Physical therapy
room; Activities room; Crafts room; Laundry
room; Barber/Beauty shop; Library; Lobby;
Alzheimer's unit.
Activities Arts & crafts; Cards; Games;
Reading groups; Prayer groups; Movies;
Shopping trips; Dances/Social/Cultural
gatherings; Intergenerational programs;
Exercises.

Ivy Manor
340 N 100 W, Bountiful, UT 84010
(801) 295-8112
Admin Sharon C Barber.
Licensure Intermediate care. *Beds* ICF 24.

Life Care Center of Bountiful
460 W 2600 S, Bountiful, UT 84010
(801) 295-3135
Admin Dennis F Gehring. *Dir of Nursing*
Barbara Stratford. *Medical Dir* Dr Scott
Southworth.
Licensure Skilled care. *Beds* SNF 120. *Private*
Pay Patients 35%. *Certified* Medicaid;
Medicare.
Owner Proprietary corp.
Admissions Requirements Medical
examination; Physician's request.
Staff Physicians 1 (pt); RNs 3 (ft), 7 (pt);
LPNs 6 (ft), 3 (pt); Nurses' aides 25 (ft), 12
(pt); Physical therapists 1 (pt); Recreational
therapists 1 (ft); Occupational therapists 1
(pt); Speech therapists 1 (pt); Activities
coordinators 1 (ft); Dietitians 1 (pt);
Podiatrists 1 (pt); Audiologists 1 (pt).
Facilities Dining room; Physical therapy
room; Activities room; Chapel; Crafts room;
Laundry room; Barber/Beauty shop.
Activities Arts & crafts; Cards; Games;
Reading groups; Prayer groups; Movies;
Shopping trips; Dances/Social/Cultural
gatherings; Intergenerational programs; Pet
therapy.

Park View Nursing Home
PO Box 520, Bountiful, UT 84011
(801) 298-2234
Admin Dean Allen Bithell.
Medical Dir Annette Bithell.
Licensure Intermediate care; Alzheimer's care.
Beds ICF 38. *Certified* Medicaid.
Owner Privately owned.
Admissions Requirements Medical
examination; Physician's request.

Staff Physicians 1 (pt); RNs 1 (pt); LPNs 5
(ft); Nurses' aides 12 (ft); Recreational
therapists 1 (ft); Dietitians 1 (pt).
Languages Spanish, German.
Facilities Dining room; Activities room;
Crafts room; Laundry room; Barber/Beauty
shop.
Activities Arts & crafts; Cards; Games;
Reading groups; Prayer groups; Movies;
Shopping trips; Dances/Social/Cultural
gatherings; Touring rides; Picnic outings.

South Davis Community Hospital Inc
401 S 400 E, Bountiful, UT 84010
(801) 295-2361
Admin Gordon W Bennet; Rosemary Lindsay,
Asst. *Dir of Nursing* Ione Callahan; Michelle
Duerden. *Medical Dir* Scott Southworth
MD.
Licensure Skilled care; Intermediate care;
Chronic specialty care; Alzheimer's care.
Beds Swing beds SNF/ICF 44; Hospital 34.
Private Pay Patients 41%. *Certified*
Medicaid; Medicare.
Owner Nonprofit corp.
Admissions Requirements Medical
examination; Physician's request.
Staff RNs 8 (ft), 3 (pt); LPNs 14 (ft), 11 (pt);
Nurses' aides 26 (ft), 20 (pt); Physical
therapists (contracted); Recreational
therapists 3 (ft); Occupational therapists
(contracted); Speech therapists (contracted);
Dietitians 1 (ft).
Facilities Dining room; Physical therapy
room; Activities room; Crafts room; Laundry
room; Barber/Beauty shop.
Activities Arts & crafts; Cards; Games;
Reading groups; Prayer groups; Movies;
Shopping trips; Dances/Social/Cultural
gatherings; Van rides.

Brigham City

Godfrey's Foothill Retreat
775 N 200 E, Brigham City, UT 84302
(801) 723-6038
Admin Michael J Godfrey Sr.
Medical Dir John R Markeson.
Licensure Skilled care; Intermediate care. *Beds*
SNF 24; ICF 26. *Certified* Medicaid.
Facilities Dining room; Physical therapy
room; Activities room; Chapel; Crafts room;
Laundry room; Barber/Beauty shop.
Activities Arts & crafts; Cards; Games;
Reading groups; Prayer groups; Movies;
Shopping trips.

Pioneer Care Center
815 S 200 W, Brigham City, UT 84302
(801) 723-5289
Admin Margo S Eberhard. *Dir of Nursing*
Marie Olsen RN. *Medical Dir* Dr Lynn Q
Beard.
Licensure Skilled care; Intermediate care;
Alzheimer's care. *Beds* SNF 32; ICF 42.
Certified Medicaid; Medicare.
Owner Publicly owned.

Admissions Requirements Medical examination; Physician's request.
Staff RNs 2 (ft), 5 (pt); LPNs 2 (ft), 3 (pt); Nurses' aides 21 (ft), 6 (pt); Physical therapists 1 (pt); Recreational therapists 2 (ft); Occupational therapists 1 (pt); Speech therapists 1 (pt); Activities coordinators; Dietitians 1 (pt); Dentists.
Facilities Dining room; Physical therapy room; Activities room; Crafts room; Laundry room; Barber/Beauty shop.
Activities Arts & crafts; Cards; Games; Reading groups; Movies; Shopping trips; Dances/Social/Cultural gatherings; Bus rides; Exercises; Church service.

Cedar City

Cedar Care Center
PO Box 1028, 679 S Sunset Dr, Cedar City, UT 84720
(801) 586-6481
Admin Robert R Larsen HFA. *Dir of Nursing* Karyn Klein HSS. *Medical Dir* Robert D Corry MD.
Licensure Intermediate care; Alzheimer's care. *Beds* ICF 44. *Private Pay Patients* 52%. *Certified* Medicaid.
Owner Proprietary corp.
Admissions Requirements Medical examination; Physician's request.
Staff Physicians 2 (pt); RNs 1 (pt); LPNs 5 (ft); Nurses' aides 16 (ft); Physical therapists 1 (pt); Reality therapists 1 (ft); Recreational therapists 1 (ft); Occupational therapists 1 (pt); Speech therapists 1 (pt); Activities coordinators 1 (ft), 2 (pt); Dietitians 1 (pt); Ophthalmologists 1 (pt); Podiatrists 1 (pt); Audiologists 1 (pt).
Languages German.
Facilities Dining room; Physical therapy room; Activities room; Chapel; Crafts room; Laundry room; Barber/Beauty shop.
Activities Arts & crafts; Cards; Games; Reading groups; Prayer groups; Movies; Shopping trips; Dances/Social/Cultural gatherings; Intergenerational programs; Pet therapy; Horticulture.

Valley View Medical Center
595 S 75 E, Cedar City, UT 84720
(801) 586-6587
Admin Mark Dalley. *Dir of Nursing* Nancy Willets RN.
Licensure Skilled care. *Beds* 48. *Certified* Medicaid; Medicare.
Owner Nonprofit organization/foundation.
Admissions Requirements Physician's request.
Staff Physicians 21 (ft); RNs 32 (ft); LPNs 2 (ft); Nurses' aides 3 (ft); Physical therapists 1 (ft); Recreational therapists 1 (ft); Speech therapists 1 (ft); Activities coordinators 1 (ft); Dietitians 1 (ft); Ophthalmologists 1 (ft); Podiatrists 1 (ft); Dentists 1 (ft).
Languages Spanish.
Facilities Dining room; Physical therapy room; Activities room; Crafts room; Laundry room.
Activities Arts & crafts; Cards; Games; Reading groups; Movies; Dances/Social/ Cultural gatherings.

Clearfield

Care West—Clearfield Nursing & Rehabilitation Center
1450 S 1500 E, Clearfield, UT 84015
(801) 773-6553
Admin Ernest J Nielsen. *Dir of Nursing* Rose Bauman RN. *Medical Dir* Dr De J Cutler.
Licensure Skilled care; Retirement. *Beds* SNF 108. *Certified* Medicaid; Medicare.
Owner Proprietary corp (Care Enterprises).
Admissions Requirements Medical examination; Physician's request.

Staff Physicians 1 (pt); RNs 6 (ft); LPNs 7 (ft); Nurses' aides 50 (ft); Physical therapists 2 (ft); Recreational therapists 1 (ft); Occupational therapists 1 (pt); Speech therapists 1 (pt); Dietitians 1 (ft); Ophthalmologists 1 (ft).
Languages Spanish, Sign.
Facilities Dining room; Physical therapy room; Activities room; Chapel; Crafts room; Laundry room; Barber/Beauty shop; Library.
Activities Arts & crafts; Cards; Games; Reading groups; Prayer groups; Movies; Shopping trips; Dances/Social/Cultural gatherings; Barbeques.

Delta

West Millard Care Center
275 W 100 S, Delta, UT 84624
(801) 864-2944
Admin Gary E Stay. *Dir of Nursing* Margaret Baker RN. *Medical Dir* Brent Black MD.
Licensure Intermediate care; Retirement. *Beds* ICF 36. *Certified* Medicaid; Medicare.
Admissions Requirements Medical examination; Physician's request.
Staff Physicians 1 (ft); RNs 1 (ft); LPNs 4 (ft); Nurses' aides 10 (ft); Physical therapists; Recreational therapists; Dietitians.
Languages Spanish, German, French.
Facilities Dining room; Physical therapy room; Activities room; Crafts room; Laundry room; Library.
Activities Arts & crafts; Games; Reading groups; Movies; Shopping trips; Visits to parks.

Draper

Lanore's Nursing Home
12702 S 950 E, Draper, UT 84020
(801) 571-2704
Admin Tony B Wrigley.
Licensure Skilled care. *Beds* SNF 82. *Certified* Medicaid.

Ferron

Emery County Nursing Home
Box 936, 455 W Mill Rd, Ferron, UT 84523
(801) 384-2301, 384-2303
Admin John W Bramall. *Dir of Nursing* Marianna Pugmire RN. *Medical Dir* Konrad Kotrady MD.
Licensure Skilled care; Intermediate care; Alzheimer's care. *Beds* Swing beds SNF/ICF 50. *Private Pay Patients* 25-33%. *Certified* Medicaid; Medicare; VA.
Owner Publicly owned.
Admissions Requirements Medical examination.
Staff Physicians 1 (pt); RNs 1 (ft), 2 (pt); LPNs 4 (ft), 4 (pt); Nurses' aides 9 (ft), 8 (pt); Physical therapists 1 (pt); Reality therapists 1 (pt); Recreational therapists 1 (ft); Occupational therapists 1 (pt); Speech therapists 1 (pt); Activities coordinators 1 (ft); Dietitians 1 (ft); Podiatrists (contracted); Audiologists (contracted).
Languages Dutch, Spanish.
Facilities Dining room; Physical therapy room; Activities room; Crafts room; Laundry room; Barber/Beauty shop; Library; Dayroom.
Activities Arts & crafts; Cards; Games; Reading groups; Prayer groups; Movies; Shopping trips; Dances/Social/Cultural gatherings; Intergenerational programs; Pet therapy; Drives.

Gunnison

Gunnison Valley Hospital
60 E 1st N, Gunnison, UT 84634
(801) 528-7246
Admin Dale A Rosenlund.

Licensure Skilled care; Intermediate care. *Beds* SNF 12; ICF 9.

Heber City

London Springs Care Center
160 W 500 N, Heber City, UT 84032
(801) 654-5500
Admin Rebecca B Hepworth. *Dir of Nursing* Janet Matthews. *Medical Dir* Dr Wain Allen.
Licensure Intermediate care; Alzheimer's care. *Beds* ICF 49. *Private Pay Patients* 25%. *Certified* Medicaid.
Owner Privately owned (Provider Management Systems).
Admissions Requirements Medical examination; Physician's request.
Staff RNs; LPNs; Nurses' aides; Recreational therapists.
Languages Spanish.
Facilities Dining room; Activities room; Laundry room; Barber/Beauty shop; Resident park.
Activities Arts & crafts; Games; Reading groups; Prayer groups; Movies; Dances/ Social/Cultural gatherings; Intergenerational programs; Pet therapy.

Wasatch County Hospital—Skilled Nursing Facility
55 S 500 E, Heber City, UT 84032
(801) 654-2500
Admin Wayne Terry.
Medical Dir Dr G D Pitts.
Licensure Skilled care; Intermediate care. *Beds* 15. *Certified* Medicaid; Medicare.
Admissions Requirements Medical examination; Physician's request.
Staff RNs 1 (ft); LPNs 1 (ft), 1 (pt); Nurses' aides 5 (ft); Physical therapists 1 (ft); Recreational therapists 1 (ft); Speech therapists 1 (pt); Activities coordinators 1 (ft); Dietitians 1 (pt).
Facilities Dining room; Physical therapy room; Activities room.
Activities Arts & crafts; Cards; Games; Reading groups; Prayer groups; Movies.

Hurricane

Birk's Mountain Home
416 N State 38-13, Hurricane, UT 84737
(801) 635-2558
Admin Norene Birk.
Licensure Intermediate care. *Beds* 24. *Certified* Medicaid.
Staff Physicians 1 (pt); RNs 1 (ft); LPNs 2 (ft); Nurses' aides 7 (ft), 2 (pt); Recreational therapists 1 (pt); Dietitians 1 (pt); Ophthalmologists 1 (pt); Podiatrists 1 (pt); Dentists 1 (pt).
Facilities Dining room; Physical therapy room; Activities room; Laundry room; Barber/Beauty shop.
Activities Arts & crafts; Games; Reading groups; Movies; Shopping trips.

Zions Health Care Complex
416 N State No 38, Hurricane, UT 84737
(801) 635-9833
Admin Reinhard Lawrence.
Licensure Skilled care; Intermediate care. *Beds* SNF 14; ICF 48. *Certified* Medicaid; Medicare.

Lehi

Larsen's Nursing Home
651 E 200 S, Lehi, UT 84043
(801) 768-3631
Admin Maxine H Larsen.
Licensure Intermediate care. *Beds* ICF 30. *Certified* Medicaid.

Logan

Logan Valley Nursing Center
1480 N 400 E, Logan, UT 84321
(801) 750-5501
Admin Peter Birkholz MHA. *Dir of Nursing*
Lorraine Lyle RN. *Medical Dir* Douglas
Hyldahl MD.
Licensure Skilled care; Intermediate care. *Beds*
SNF 72; ICF 48. *Private Pay Patients* 44%.
Certified Medicaid; Medicare.
Owner Proprietary corp (Paradigm Corp).
Admissions Requirements Medical
examination; Physician's request.
Staff Physicians 1 (pt); RNs 6 (ft), 10 (pt);
LPNs 6 (ft), 5 (pt); Nurses' aides 20 (ft), 22
(pt); Physical therapists 1 (pt); Recreational
therapists 1 (ft); Occupational therapists 1
(pt); Speech therapists 1 (pt); Activities
coordinators 1 (ft); Dietitians 1 (ft), 1 (pt);
Podiatrists 1 (pt).
Languages German, Spanish.
Affiliation Latter Day Saints.
Facilities Dining room; Physical therapy
room; Activities room; Laundry room;
Barber/Beauty shop.
Activities Arts & crafts; Games; Prayer groups;
Movies; Shopping trips; Dances/Social/
Cultural gatherings; Intergenerational
programs.

Sunshine Terrace Foundation
225 N 200 W, Logan, UT 84321
(801) 752-0411
Admin Sara V Sinclair. *Dir of Nursing* Alyn
Bosch RN. *Medical Dir* Merrill C Daines
MD.
Licensure Skilled care; Intermediate care;
Adult day center; Alzheimer's wing. *Beds*
SNF 96; ICF 76. *Certified* Medicaid;
Medicare; VA.
Owner Nonprofit organization/foundation.
Admissions Requirements Medical
examination; Physician's request; Must have
need for 24-hour care.
Staff RNs 12 (ft), 24 (pt); LPNs 16 (ft), 8 (pt);
Nurses' aides 12 (ft), 53 (pt); Recreational
therapists 6 (ft); Activities coordinators 1
(ft); Rehabilitation aides 10 (ft), 1 (pt);
Social workers 2 (ft).
Languages Spanish, French.
Facilities Dining room; Physical therapy
room; Activities room; Crafts room; Laundry
room; Barber/Beauty shop; Library;
Pharmacy; Dental room; Patios; Outdoor
walking paths; Handicapped van & bus;
Adult day center.
Activities Arts & crafts; Cards; Games;
Reading groups; Prayer groups; Movies;
Shopping trips; Dances/Social/Cultural
gatherings; Residents council; Family
council; Lecture series; Reality orientation;
Current events; Cooking; Woodworking;
Reminiscence group.

Mayfield

Mayfield Manor
11 S Main, Mayfield, UT 84643
(801) 528-3550
Admin Eugene S Bartholomew.
Licensure Intermediate care. *Beds* ICF 37.
Certified Medicaid.

Milford

Milford Valley Memorial Nursing Home
PO Box 640, 451 N Main St, Milford, UT
84751
(801) 387-2411
Admin Mary Wiseman. *Dir of Nursing*
Jacqueline Williams RN. *Medical Dir* David
A Symond MD.
Licensure Skilled care; Intermediate care. *Beds*
Swing beds SNF/ICF 34. *Private Pay
Patients* 15%. *Certified* Medicaid; Medicare.
Owner Nonprofit organization/foundation.

Staff Physicians; RNs; LPNs; Nurses' aides;
Recreational therapists; Activities
coordinators; Dietitians.
Facilities Dining room; Activities room;
Crafts room; Laundry room; Barber/Beauty
shop; Library.
Activities Arts & crafts; Cards; Games; Prayer
groups; Movies; Shopping trips; Dances/
Social/Cultural gatherings; Church services.

Murray

Bennion Care Center
6276 S Redwood Rd, Murray, UT 84107
(801) 969-1420
Admin Michael Daskalas.
Licensure Skilled care; Intermediate care. *Beds*
SNF 52; ICF 52. *Certified* Medicaid;
Medicare.

Plantation Care Center
835 Vine St, Murray, UT 84107
(801) 266-3852
Admin Richard J Shumway. *Dir of Nursing*
Elisa McMillan. *Medical Dir* King Udall.
Licensure Intermediate care. *Beds* ICF 80.
Certified Medicaid.
Owner Proprietary corp.
Admissions Requirements Medical
examination; Physician's request.
Staff Physicians; RNs; LPNs; Nurses' aides;
Physical therapists; Recreational therapists;
Occupational therapists; Speech therapists;
Activities coordinators; Dietitians;
Ophthalmologists; Podiatrists; Audiologists.
Facilities Dining room; Physical therapy
room; Activities room; Chapel; Crafts room;
Laundry room; Barber/Beauty shop.
Activities Arts & crafts; Cards; Games;
Reading groups; Prayer groups; Movies;
Shopping trips; Dances/Social/Cultural
gatherings; Intergenerational programs; Pet
therapy.

Quality Care Murray
404 E 5600 S, Murray, UT 84107
(801) 266-3588
Admin Dorthea Peak. *Dir of Nursing* Thelma
Ennis. *Medical Dir* Dr John Hylen.
Licensure Skilled care. *Beds* SNF 119.
Certified Medicaid; Medicare.
Owner Proprietary corp (Care Enterprises).
Staff Physicians; RNs 6 (ft), 1 (pt); Nurses'
aides 25 (ft), 10 (pt); Physical therapists 2
(ft); Reality therapists 1 (ft); Recreational
therapists 1 (ft); Occupational therapists 20
(pt); Speech therapists 20 (pt); Activities
coordinators 1 (ft); Dietitians 1 (ft);
Ophthalmologists 10 (pt).
Facilities Dining room; Physical therapy
room; Activities room; Laundry room;
Barber/Beauty shop.
Activities Arts & crafts; Cards; Games;
Reading groups; Prayer groups; Movies;
Shopping trips; Dances/Social/Cultural
gatherings.

Nephi

Canyon Hills Health Care Center
1100 N 400 E, Nephi, UT 84648
(801) 623-1721
Admin Daniel W Kostenko. *Dir of Nursing*
Louise Larson. *Medical Dir* James M
Besendorfer MD.
Licensure Skilled care; Intermediate care;
Retirement. *Beds* SNF 16; ICF 64;
Retirement 15. *Certified* Medicaid;
Medicare.
Owner Proprietary corp.
Admissions Requirements Medical
examination.
Staff RNs 6 (ft), 1 (pt); LPNs 6 (ft), 1 (pt);
Nurses' aides 19 (ft), 8 (pt); Physical
therapists; Recreational therapists 2 (ft), 1
(pt); Activities coordinators 1 (ft); Dietitians.
Languages Spanish.

Facilities Dining room; Physical therapy
room; Activities room; Chapel; Crafts room;
Laundry room; Barber/Beauty shop; Central
courtyard.
Activities Arts & crafts; Cards; Games;
Reading groups; Prayer groups; Movies;
Shopping trips; Dances/Social/Cultural
gatherings; Intergenerational programs.

Colonial Manor Health Care Center
71 N Main, Nephi, UT 84648
(801) 623-0511
Admin Juanita Crawford.
Medical Dir Dr Catrett.
Licensure Intermediate care. *Beds* ICF 64.
Certified Medicaid.
Admissions Requirements Medical
examination; Physician's request.
Staff RNs 2 (ft), 2 (pt); LPNs 2 (pt); Nurses'
aides 26 (ft); Recreational therapists 1 (ft);
Activities coordinators 1 (ft); Dietitians 1
(pt).
Facilities Dining room; Activities room;
Chapel; Laundry room; Barber/Beauty shop.
Activities Arts & crafts; Cards; Games;
Reading groups; Prayer groups; Movies;
Shopping trips; Dances/Social/Cultural
gatherings.

Ogden

Aspen Care Center
2325 Madison Ave, Ogden, UT 84401
(801) 399-5846
Admin Robert H Breinholt.
Medical Dir John Newton MD.
Licensure Intermediate care. *Beds* ICF 72.
Certified Medicaid; Medicare.
Admissions Requirements Medical
examination; Physician's request.
Staff Physicians 1 (ft); RNs 3 (ft); LPNs 13
(ft); Nurses' aides 24 (ft); Physical therapists
1 (pt); Reality therapists 1 (pt); Recreational
therapists 1 (pt); Occupational therapists 1
(pt); Speech therapists 1 (pt); Activities
coordinators 1 (ft); Dietitians 1 (ft);
Ophthalmologists 1 (pt); Podiatrists 1 (pt);
Audiologists 1 (pt); Dentists 1 (pt).
Facilities Dining room; Physical therapy
room; Activities room; Laundry room;
Barber/Beauty shop; Library; Lounge/
smoking area.
Activities Arts & crafts; Cards; Games;
Reading groups; Prayer groups; Movies;
Shopping trips; Dances/Social/Cultural
gatherings; Fishing trips; Song fest weekly.

Country Meadow Convalescent Center
5865 Wasatch Dr, Ogden, UT 84403
(801) 479-8480
Admin Carl W Barney.
Medical Dir LaMar Rogers MD.
Licensure Skilled care; Intermediate care. *Beds*
SNF 35; ICF 145. *Certified* Medicaid.
Staff Physicians 1 (ft), 6 (pt); RNs 3 (ft), 2
(pt); LPNs 5 (ft), 4 (pt); Nurses' aides 20
(ft), 14 (pt); Physical therapists 1 (ft);
Recreational therapists 1 (ft); Occupational
therapists 1 (ft); Speech therapists 1 (ft);
Activities coordinators 1 (ft); Dietitians 1
(ft); Podiatrists 1 (ft).

Crestwood Care Center
3665 Brinker Ave, Ogden, UT 84403
(801) 627-2532
Admin Allen Day. *Dir of Nursing* Monique
Poulsen. *Medical Dir* Michael Woolmann
MD.
Licensure Skilled care; Intermediate care. *Beds*
SNF 63; ICF 25. *Private Pay Patients* 40%.
Certified Medicaid; Medicare.
Owner Privately owned.
Admissions Requirements Medical
examination; Physician's request.
Staff RNs; LPNs; Nurses' aides; Recreational
therapists.
Languages Spanish, French.

Facilities Dining room; Physical therapy room; Activities room; Laundry room; Barber/Beauty shop.
Activities Arts & crafts; Cards; Games; Reading groups; Shopping trips; Dances/Social/Cultural gatherings; Intergenerational programs; Pet therapy.

Manor Care of South Ogden
5540 S 1050 E, Ogden, UT 84405
(801) 479-8455
Admin Sue Bowker. *Dir of Nursing* Pam Russel. *Medical Dir* Brent Wallace.
Licensure Skilled care; Alzheimer's care. *Beds* SNF 120. *Certified* Medicaid; Medicare.
Owner Proprietary corp (Manor Care).
Admissions Requirements Medical examination; Physician's request.
Staff RNs 10 (ft); LPNs 5 (ft); Nurses' aides 50 (ft); Physical therapists 1 (ft), 1 (pt); Recreational therapists 1 (ft); Occupational therapists 1 (ft); Speech therapists 1 (ft); Activities coordinators 2 (ft); Dietitians 1 (ft).
Languages Spanish.
Facilities Dining room; Physical therapy room; Activities room; Crafts room; Laundry room; Barber/Beauty shop; Library.
Activities Arts & crafts; Cards; Games; Reading groups; Prayer groups; Movies; Shopping trips; Dances/Social/Cultural gatherings; Pet therapy.

McKay-Dee Transitional Care Center
3939 Harrison Blvd, Ogden, UT 84409
(801) 625-2380, 625-2740 FAX
Admin Michelle Tippets RN. *Dir of Nursing* Michelle Tippets RN. *Medical Dir* Paul Southwick MD.
Licensure Skilled care. *Beds* SNF 31. *Certified* Medicaid; Medicare.
Owner Nonprofit organization/foundation.
Admissions Requirements Physician's request.
Staff RNs 4 (ft), 5 (pt); LPNs 1 (ft), 2 (pt); Nurses' aides 11 (ft), 3 (pt); Recreational therapists 1 (pt); Occupational therapists (consultant); Speech therapists (consultant); Dietitians.
Languages Spanish.
Facilities Dining room; Physical therapy room; Activities room; Barber/Beauty shop.
Activities Arts & crafts; Cards; Games.

Ogden Care Center North
524 E 800 N, Ogden, UT 84404
(801) 782-3740
Admin Patricia M Rothey. *Dir of Nursing* Keely Bunderson. *Medical Dir* Jack D Wahlen MD.
Licensure Skilled care; Intermediate care. *Beds* SNF 33; ICF 71. *Certified* Medicaid; Medicare.
Owner Proprietary corp.
Admissions Requirements Medical examination; Physician's request.
Staff Physicians 1 (ft); RNs 8 (ft); LPNs 7 (ft); Nurses' aides 32 (ft); Physical therapists 1 (ft); Recreational therapists 1 (ft); Occupational therapists 1 (ft); Speech therapists 1 (ft); Activities coordinators 1 (ft); Dietitians 1 (ft); Ophthalmologists 1 (ft); Podiatrists 1 (ft).
Languages Spanish.
Facilities Dining room; Physical therapy room; Activities room; Crafts room; Laundry room; Barber/Beauty shop; Library.
Activities Arts & crafts; Cards; Games; Reading groups; Prayer groups; Movies; Shopping trips; Dances/Social/Cultural gatherings.

Wasatch Care Center
3430 Harrison Blvd, Ogden, UT 84403
(801) 399-5609, 392-7372 FAX
Admin Inge Glover. *Dir of Nursing* Janet Moore RN. *Medical Dir* Dr Lee Schussman.
Licensure Skilled care. *Beds* SNF 69. *Certified* Medicaid; Medicare.

Owner Proprietary corp (Hillhaven Corp).
Admissions Requirements Minimum age 21; Medical examination; Physician's request.
Staff Physicians 1 (pt); RNs 3 (ft), 3 (pt); LPNs 2 (ft), 2 (pt); Nurses' aides 14 (ft), 6 (pt); Physical therapists 1 (pt); Recreational therapists 1 (ft); Occupational therapists 1 (pt); Speech therapists 1 (pt); Dietitians 1 (pt); Ophthalmologists 1 (pt); Podiatrists 1 (pt); Audiologists 1 (pt).
Facilities Dining room; Physical therapy room; Activities room; Crafts room; Laundry room; Barber/Beauty shop; Library; Hospice care.
Activities Arts & crafts; Cards; Games; Reading groups; Prayer groups; Movies; Shopping trips; Dances/Social/Cultural gatherings; Intergenerational programs; Pet therapy.

Washington Terrace Nursing Center
400 E 5350 S, Ogden, UT 84405
(801) 479-9855
Admin Jana Hazelbaker.
Licensure Skilled care; Intermediate care. *Beds* SNF 54; ICF 66. *Certified* Medicaid; Medicare.

Wide Horizons Care Center
910 Monroe Blvd, Ogden, UT 84404
(801) 399-5876
Admin Marcia Parisi.
Medical Dir Laureen Jacobson.
Licensure Intermediate care for mentally retarded. *Beds* ICF/MR 83. *Certified* Medicaid.
Owner Proprietary corp (National Heritage).
Staff RNs 1 (ft); LPNs 3 (ft), 1 (pt); Nurses' aides 31 (ft); Physical therapists 1 (ft), 1 (pt); Recreational therapists 1 (ft); Occupational therapists 1 (pt); Speech therapists 1 (pt); Activities coordinators 1 (ft); Dietitians 1 (pt); Ophthalmologists 1 (pt); Podiatrists 1 (pt); QMRPs 8 (ft).
Languages Spanish.
Facilities Dining room; Physical therapy room; Activities room; Crafts room; Laundry room; Barber/Beauty shop.
Activities Arts & crafts; Cards; Games; Reading groups; Movies; Shopping trips; Dances/Social/Cultural gatherings.

Orem

Care West—Orem
575 E 1400 S, Orem, UT 84058
(801) 225-4741
Admin Stan Magelby.
Licensure Skilled care. *Beds* SNF 120. *Certified* Medicaid; Medicare.
Owner Proprietary corp (Care Enterprises).

Hidden Hollow Care Center
261 W 2000 S, Orem, UT 84058
(801) 225-2145
Admin Kenneth Ekong.
Medical Dir Dr Kraig Jenson.
Licensure Intermediate care for mentally retarded. *Beds* ICF/MR 34. *Certified* Medicaid; Medicare.
Staff Physicians; RNs 1 (pt); LPNs 1 (ft), 3 (pt); Nurses' aides 8 (ft); Recreational therapists 1 (ft); Activities coordinators 1 (ft), 4 (pt).
Facilities Dining room; Physical therapy room; Activities room; Chapel; Crafts room; Laundry room.
Activities Arts & crafts; Cards; Games; Reading groups; Prayer groups; Movies; Shopping trips; Dances/Social/Cultural gatherings.

Lakecrest Development Care Center
394 W 400 N, Orem, UT 84057
(801) 225-9292
Admin Christian David Yeates.
Medical Dir Dr Robert Clark.

Licensure Intermediate care for mentally retarded. *Beds* ICF/MR 54. *Certified* Medicaid; Medicare.
Staff Physicians; RNs; LPNs; Nurses' aides; Physical therapists; Reality therapists; Recreational therapists; Occupational therapists; Speech therapists; Activities coordinators; Dietitians; Ophthalmologists; Podiatrists; Audiologists; Dentists.
Facilities Dining room; Physical therapy room; Activities room; Crafts room; Laundry room; Barber/Beauty shop.
Activities Arts & crafts; Cards; Games; Reading groups; Prayer groups; Movies; Shopping trips; Dances/Social/Cultural gatherings; Programing for the mentally retarded.

Timpanogos Care Center
740 N 300 E, Orem, UT 84057
(801) 224-0921
Admin Dan W Thomas.
Licensure Skilled care; Intermediate care. *Beds* SNF 48; ICF 41. *Certified* Medicaid; Medicare.
Staff Physicians 2 (ft); RNs 4 (ft), 2 (pt); LPNs 12 (ft), 8 (pt); Nurses' aides 14 (ft), 6 (pt); Physical therapists 1 (ft); Reality therapists 2 (ft); Recreational therapists 2 (ft); Occupational therapists 1 (ft); Speech therapists 2 (ft); Activities coordinators 1 (ft); Dietitians 1 (ft); Podiatrists 1 (ft); Audiologists 2 (ft); Dentists 1 (ft).
Facilities Dining room; Physical therapy room; Activities room; Chapel; Crafts room; Laundry room; Barber/Beauty shop.
Activities Arts & crafts; Cards; Games; Reading groups; Prayer groups; Movies; Shopping trips; Dances/Social/Cultural gatherings.

Topham's Tiny Tots Care Center
247 N 100 E, Orem, UT 84057
(801) 225-0323
Admin Lorraine Topham. *Dir of Nursing* Linda Hallet LPN. *Medical Dir* Richard Farnsworth MD.
Licensure Intermediate care for mentally retarded. *Beds* ICF/MR 50. *Certified* Medicaid.
Owner Proprietary corp.
Admissions Requirements Minimum age 0-11; Medical examination; Physician's request.
Staff Physicians 1 (pt); RNs 1 (pt); LPNs 5 (pt); Nurses' aides 40 (ft); Physical therapists 2 (pt); Recreational therapists 1 (pt); Occupational therapists 3 (pt); Speech therapists 1 (pt); Activities coordinators 1 (ft); Dietitians 1 (pt).
Facilities Dining room; Physical therapy room; Activities room; Chapel; Crafts room; Laundry room; Barber/Beauty shop; Library.
Activities Arts & crafts; Games; Reading groups; Movies; Sunday school.

Panguitch

Garfield Memorial Hospital
PO Box 389, 224 N 400 E, Panguitch, UT 84759
(801) 676-8811
Admin Wayne R Ross. *Dir of Nursing* Linda Owen. *Medical Dir* E Terry Henrie MD.
Licensure Skilled care; Intermediate care. *Beds* Swing beds SNF/ICF 20. *Private Pay Patients* 20%. *Certified* Medicaid; Medicare.
Owner Nonprofit organization/foundation.
Admissions Requirements Physician's request.
Staff Physicians 1 (ft); RNs 4 (ft), 4 (pt); LPNs 3 (ft), 2 (pt); Nurses' aides 4 (ft), 6 (pt); Physical therapists 1 (ft); Recreational therapists 1 (pt); Dietitians 1 (ft).
Languages Spanish.
Activities Arts & crafts; Cards; Games; Reading groups; Movies; Pet therapy.

Parowan

Iron County Rest Home
PO Box 397, 69 E 100 S, Parowan, UT 84761
(801) 477-3615
Admin Clarence J Benson. *Dir of Nursing*
Elizabeth Burton LPN. *Medical Dir* C J
Thinnes MD.
Licensure Intermediate care. *Beds* ICF 31.
Private Pay Patients 50%. *Certified*
Medicaid.
Owner Privately owned.
Admissions Requirements Medical
examination; Physician's request.
Staff Physicians 3 (pt); RNs 1 (pt); LPNs 1
(ft), 2 (pt); Nurses' aides 9 (ft), 2 (pt);
Physical therapists 1 (pt); Reality therapists
1 (pt); Recreational therapists 1 (ft); Speech
therapists 1 (pt); Activities coordinators 1
(ft); Dietitians 1 (pt); Podiatrists 1 (pt);
Audiologists 1 (pt).
Facilities Dining room; Physical therapy
room; Activities room; Chapel; Crafts room;
Laundry room; Barber/Beauty shop; Library.
Activities Arts & crafts; Cards; Games;
Reading groups; Prayer groups; Movies;
Shopping trips; Dances/Social/Cultural
gatherings; Intergenerational programs; Pet
therapy.

Payson

El Rancho Nursing Home
E Hwy 91, Box 860, Payson, UT 84651
(801) 465-9211
Admin Steve A Lassen.
Licensure Intermediate care. *Beds* ICF 51.
Certified Medicaid.

Mountain View Hospital
1000 E Hwy 91, Payson, UT 84057
(801) 465-9201
Admin Val Christensen.
Licensure Skilled care; Intermediate care. *Beds*
SNF 5; ICF 89.

Pleasant Grove

Alpine Valley Care Center
25 E Alpine Dr, Pleasant Grove, UT 84062
(801) 785-3568
Admin Lauren Dinehart.
Licensure Skilled care. *Beds* SNF 52. *Certified*
Medicaid.
Owner Proprietary corp (National Heritage).

Lindon Care & Training Center
PO Box 457, Pleasant Grove, UT 84062
(801) 785-2179
Admin Joyce L Halling.
Medical Dir William Parker MD.
Licensure Intermediate care for mentally
retarded. *Beds* ICF/MR 66. *Certified*
Medicaid.
Admissions Requirements Minimum age 12;
Females only; Medical examination;
Physician's request.
Staff Physicians 1 (pt); RNs 1 (pt); LPNs 6
(ft); Nurses' aides 25 (ft), 25 (pt); Physical
therapists 1 (pt); Reality therapists 1 (ft);
Recreational therapists 1 (ft); Occupational
therapists 1 (pt); Speech therapists 1 (pt);
Activities coordinators 1 (ft); Dietitians 1
(pt); Ophthalmologists 1 (pt); Podiatrists 1
(pt); Dentists 1 (pt).
Facilities Dining room; Activities room;
Crafts room; Laundry room; Barber/Beauty
shop.
Activities Arts & crafts; Cards; Games;
Reading groups; Prayer groups; Movies;
Shopping trips; Dances/Social/Cultural
gatherings.

Price

Castle Country Care Center
PO Box 791, Price, UT 84501
(801) 637-9213
Admin Tracy Sadler. *Dir of Nursing* Kathy
Paddock. *Medical Dir* Fred Feurstein.
Licensure Skilled care; Intermediate care;
Alzheimer's care; Adult day care. *Beds* SNF
26; ICF 74. *Private Pay Patients* 25%.
Certified Medicaid; Medicare.
Owner Privately owned.
Staff RNs; LPNs; Nurses' aides; Physical
therapists; Recreational therapists; Speech
therapists; Dietitians.
Facilities Dining room.
Activities Arts & crafts; Cards; Games;
Reading groups; Prayer groups; Movies;
Shopping trips; Dances/Social/Cultural
gatherings; Intergenerational programs;
Recreational therapy.

Parkdale Care Center
250 E 600 N, Price, UT 84501
(801) 637-2621
Admin Patricia J Richardson. *Dir of Nursing*
May Marchello. *Medical Dir* Sterling Potter
MD.
Licensure Skilled care; Intermediate care;
Alzheimer's care. *Beds* SNF 17; ICF 41.
Private Pay Patients 30%. *Certified*
Medicaid; Medicare.
Owner Proprietary corp (Westcare
Management Inc).
Staff Physicians; RNs; LPNs; Nurses' aides;
Physical therapists; Recreational therapists;
Speech therapists; Activities coordinators;
Dietitians; Podiatrists.
Facilities Dining room; Physical therapy
room; Activities room; Crafts room; Laundry
room; Barber/Beauty shop; Library.
Activities Arts & crafts; Cards; Games;
Reading groups; Prayer groups; Movies;
Shopping trips; Dances/Social/Cultural
gatherings; Intergenerational programs; Pet
therapy; Family socials; Resident council.

Provo

Bunce Care Center II
552 W 1560 S, Provo, UT 84601
(801) 375-5832
Admin Kim Bunce.
Licensure Intermediate care. *Beds* ICF 34.
Certified Medicaid.

Bunce Convalescent Center
1530 S 500 W, Provo, UT 84601
(801) 374-1468
Admin Nilda Bunce.
Medical Dir Kim Bunce.
Licensure Intermediate care; Alzheimer's care.
Beds ICF 34. *Certified* Medicaid; Medicare.
Owner Privately owned.
Admissions Requirements Medical
examination; Physician's request.
Staff Physicians; RNs; LPNs; Nurses' aides;
Physical therapists; Reality therapists;
Recreational therapists; Occupational
therapists; Speech therapists; Occupational
therapists; Dietitians; Ophthalmologists;
Podiatrists.
Facilities Dining room; Physical therapy
room; Activities room; Chapel; Crafts room;
Laundry room; Barber/Beauty shop.
Activities Arts & crafts; Cards; Games;
Reading groups; Prayer groups; Movies;
Shopping trips; Dances/Social/Cultural
gatherings.

Crestview Convalescent Center
1053 W 1020 S, Provo, UT 84601
(801) 373-2630
Admin Barbara Adams. *Dir of Nursing* Gail
James RN. *Medical Dir* Dr Jeffrey Johnson.
Licensure Skilled care. *Beds* SNF 99. *Certified*
Medicaid.

Owner Proprietary corp (National Heritage).
Staff Physicians; RNs; LPNs; Nurses' aides;
Physical therapists; Recreational therapists;
Occupational therapists; Speech therapists;
Activities coordinators; Dietitians;
Ophthalmologists; Podiatrists.

East Lake Care Center
1001 N 500 W, Provo, UT 84601
(801) 377-9661
Admin Craig Johnson.
Licensure Skilled care. *Beds* SNF 120.
Certified Medicaid; Medicare.

Medallion Manor
1701 W 600 S, Provo, UT 84601
(801) 375-2710
Admin Dennis R Wright.
Licensure Intermediate care for mentally
retarded. *Beds* ICF/MR 40. *Certified*
Medicaid.

Phillips Nursing Home
2901 W Center St, Provo, UT 84601
(801) 373-5079
Admin J James Rutter. *Dir of Nursing* Dee
Gren. *Medical Dir* Dr Bruce Guernsey.
Licensure Intermediate care. *Beds* ICF 58.
Certified Medicaid.
Owner Privately owned.
Facilities Dining room; Activities room;
Crafts room; Laundry room; Barber/Beauty
shop.
Activities Arts & crafts; Cards; Games;
Reading groups; Prayer groups; Movies;
Shopping trips; Dances/Social/Cultural
gatherings; Intergenerational programs;
Bowling; Van rides; Special Olympics.

Provo Care Center
PO Box 1933, Provo, UT 84603
(801) 373-8771
Admin Maria Wiggins CSW QMRP. *Dir of
Nursing* Paula Mortensen LPN. *Medical Dir*
Dan Purser MD.
Licensure Intermediate care for mentally
retarded. *Beds* ICF/MR 35. *Private Pay
Patients* 10%. *Certified* Medicaid.
Owner Proprietary corp (David & Joyce
Halling).
Admissions Requirements Minimum age 30;
Medical examination; MR diagnosis.
Staff Physicians 1 (pt); RNs 1 (pt); LPNs 3
(ft); Physical therapists 1 (pt); Recreational
therapists 1 (ft); Occupational therapists 1
(pt); Speech therapists 1 (pt); Activities
coordinators 1 (ft); Dietitians 1 (pt);
Podiatrists 1 (pt); Habilitation technicians
12 (ft), 2 (pt).
Languages Sign.
Affiliation Latter Day Saints.
Facilities Dining room; Activities room;
Crafts room; Laundry room; Barber/Beauty
shop; Library.
Activities Arts & crafts; Cards; Games;
Reading groups; Movies; Shopping trips;
Dances/Social/Cultural gatherings;
Intergenerational programs; Pet therapy;
Banking.

Transitional Care Unit at UVRMC
1034 N 5th W, Provo, UT 84603
(801) 373-7850
Admin Ron Liston.
Licensure Skilled care. *Beds* SNF 14. *Certified*
Medicaid; Medicare.

Richfield

Richfield Care Center
83 E 1100 N, Richfield, UT 84701
(801) 896-8211
Admin Ronald L Nielsen. *Dir of Nursing*
Elaine Blackburn. *Medical Dir* Michael
Travers.
Licensure Skilled care; Intermediate care. *Beds*
SNF 76; ICF 22. *Private Pay Patients* 15%.
Certified Medicaid; Medicare.

Owner Proprietary corp (Heritage Health Management).
Admissions Requirements Minimum age 18; Medical examination; Physician's request.
Staff RNs 3 (ft), 2 (pt); LPNs 8 (ft), 3 (pt); Nurses' aides 25 (ft), 5 (pt); Physical therapists 2 (pt); Recreational therapists 1 (ft); Activities coordinators 1 (pt).
Facilities Dining room; Physical therapy room; Activities room; Crafts room; Laundry room; Barber/Beauty shop; Library.
Activities Arts & crafts; Cards; Games; Reading groups; Prayer groups; Movies; Shopping trips; Dances/Social/Cultural gatherings; Intergenerational programs; Pet therapy.

Roosevelt

Cedar Crest Convalescent Center
187 W Lagoon St, Roosevelt, UT 84066
(801) 722-2497
Admin Jams E Zeim.
Medical Dir Gary White MD.
Licensure Skilled care; Intermediate care. *Beds* SNF 18; ICF 29. *Certified* Medicaid.
Admissions Requirements Medical examination; Physician's request.
Staff Physicians; RNs; LPNs; Nurses' aides; Recreational therapists; Activities coordinators; Dietitians; Ophthalmologists; Podiatrists; Dentists.
Facilities Dining room; Activities room; Crafts room; Laundry room; Barber/Beauty shop.
Activities Arts & crafts; Cards; Games; Reading groups; Prayer groups; Movies; Shopping trips; Dances/Social/Cultural gatherings.

Roy

Heritage Park Care Center
2700 W 5600 S, Roy, UT 84067
(801) 825-9731
Admin Mark F Dunn.
Licensure Skilled care. *Beds* SNF 176.
Certified Medicaid; Medicare.
Owner Proprietary corp (National Heritage).

Saint George

Color Country Care Center
233 S 1000 E, Saint George, UT 84770
(801) 673-4310
Admin Alice S Barlow.
Licensure Intermediate care. *Beds* ICF 25.
Certified Medicaid; Medicare.

Porter's Nursing Home
126 W 200 N, Saint George, UT 84770
(801) 628-1601
Admin James L Porter. *Dir of Nursing* Carol Wood LPN. *Medical Dir* M K McGregor MD.
Licensure Intermediate care; Alzheimer's care. *Beds* ICF 53. *Private Pay Patients* 41%.
Certified Medicaid.
Owner Privately owned.
Admissions Requirements Minimum age 21; Medical examination.
Staff Physicians 1 (pt); RNs 1 (pt); LPNs 4 (ft), 2 (pt); Nurses' aides 13 (ft), 5 (pt); Physical therapists 1 (pt); Reality therapists 1 (pt); Recreational therapists 1 (ft); Occupational therapists 1 (pt); Speech therapists 1 (pt); Activities coordinators 1 (ft); Dietitians 1 (pt); Podiatrists 1 (pt); Audiologists 1 (pt); Social workers 1 (pt); Social service aides 1 (pt).
Languages Spanish.
Facilities Dining room; Activities room; Chapel; Crafts room; Laundry room; Barber/Beauty shop; Fenced yard.

Activities Arts & crafts; Cards; Games; Reading groups; Prayer groups; Movies; Shopping trips; Dances/Social/Cultural gatherings; Intergenerational programs; Pet therapy.

St George Care Center
1032 E 100 S, Saint George, UT 84770
(801) 628-0488
Admin Terry Granger.
Licensure Skilled care; Intermediate care. *Beds* SNF 50; ICF 102. *Certified* Medicaid; Medicare.
Owner Proprietary corp (Hillhaven Corp).

Southern Hospitality Living Center
35 S 100 E, Saint George, UT 84770
(801) 673-3682
Admin Laurel C Stinson. *Dir of Nursing* Rebecca Reardon.
Licensure Intermediate care; Alzheimer's care. *Beds* ICF 34. *Private Pay Patients* 28%.
Certified Medicaid; Medicare.
Owner Proprietary corp.
Admissions Requirements Minimum age 18; Medical examination; Physician's request.
Staff RNs 1 (ft); LPNs 2 (ft), 2 (pt); Nurses' aides 20 (ft), 3 (pt); Reality therapists 1 (ft); Recreational therapists 1 (ft); Activities coordinators 1 (ft); Dietitians 1 (ft).
Facilities Dining room; Activities room; Crafts room; Laundry room.
Activities Arts & crafts; Cards; Games; Reading groups; Movies; Shopping trips; Dances/Social/Cultural gatherings.

Salt Lake City

A & E Nursing Home
3094 S State St, Salt Lake City, UT 84115
(801) 487-6127
Admin John R Burton. *Dir of Nursing* Jo Anne Cheney. *Medical Dir* King S Udall.
Licensure Intermediate care; Alzheimer's care. *Beds* ICF 37. *Private Pay Patients* 20%.
Certified Medicaid.
Owner Proprietary corp.
Admissions Requirements Minimum age 21; Medical examination; Physician's request.
Staff Physicians 1 (pt); RNs 1 (pt); LPNs 5 (ft); Nurses' aides 13 (ft); Physical therapists 1 (pt); Recreational therapists 1 (ft); Speech therapists 1 (pt); Activities coordinators 1 (ft); Dietitians 1 (pt); Ophthalmologists 1 (pt); Podiatrists 1 (pt); Audiologists 1 (pt); 1 (pt).
Facilities Dining room; Activities room; Laundry room; Separate smoking area.
Activities Arts & crafts; Cards; Games; Reading groups; Prayer groups; Movies; Shopping trips; Dances/Social/Cultural gatherings; Intergenerational programs; Pet therapy.

Alta Care Center
4035 S 500 E, Salt Lake City, UT 84107
(801) 262-9181
Admin Dirk Anjewierden.
Medical Dir Randall Daynes MD.
Licensure Skilled care; Intermediate care. *Beds* SNF 40; ICF 59. *Certified* Medicaid; Medicare.
Owner Proprietary corp.
Admissions Requirements Minimum age 25; Medical examination; Physician's request.
Staff Physicians 2 (pt); RNs 2 (ft), 3 (pt); LPNs 4 (ft), 4 (pt); Nurses' aides 23 (ft), 8 (pt); Physical therapists 1 (pt); Recreational therapists 1 (ft), 1 (pt); Occupational therapists 1 (pt); Speech therapists 1 (pt); Activities coordinators 1 (ft); Dietitians 1 (pt); Ophthalmologists 1 (pt); Podiatrists 1 (pt).
Languages Spanish, German.
Facilities Dining room; Physical therapy room; Activities room; Crafts room; Laundry room; Library; TV room.

Activities Arts & crafts; Cards; Games; Reading groups; Prayer groups; Movies; Shopping trips; Dances/Social/Cultural gatherings.

Ann's Rest Home Inc
3944 S 400 E, Salt Lake City, UT 84107
(801) 266-4339
Admin Ann Roos.
Licensure Intermediate care. *Beds* ICF 60.
Certified Medicaid.
Admissions Requirements Males only.

Autumn Living Care Center
3750 S Highland Dr Wing B, Salt Lake City, UT 84106
(801) 277-1900
Admin Steven Frasier.
Licensure Intermediate care. *Beds* ICF 34.

Care West—Salt Lake
165 S 10th E, Salt Lake City, UT 84102
(801) 322-5521
Admin Gina Yates. *Dir of Nursing* Karen Stokes. *Medical Dir* Victor Kassel MD.
Licensure Skilled care; Alzheimer's care. *Beds* SNF 106. *Private Pay Patients* 20%. *Certified* Medicaid; Medicare.
Owner Proprietary corp (Care Enterprises).
Admissions Requirements Medical examination; Physician's request.
Staff RNs 6 (ft), 2 (pt); LPNs 8 (ft), 2 (pt); Nurses' aides 39 (ft), 2 (pt); Physical therapists 2 (ft); Recreational therapists 2 (ft).
Languages Spanish.
Facilities Dining room; Physical therapy room; Activities room; Crafts room; Laundry room; Barber/Beauty shop.
Activities Arts & crafts; Cards; Games; Reading groups; Prayer groups; Movies; Shopping trips; Dances/Social/Cultural gatherings; Intergenerational programs; Pet therapy.

Creekside Care Center
1205 E 4725 S, Salt Lake City, UT 84117
(801) 262-2908
Admin Kenneth Depew. *Dir of Nursing* Kay Staring. *Medical Dir* Randall P Daynes.
Licensure Skilled care; Intermediate care. *Beds* SNF 38; ICF 48. *Private Pay Patients* 20%. *Certified* Medicaid; Medicare.
Owner Proprietary corp (Beverly Enterprises).
Staff Physicians; RNs; LPNs; Nurses' aides; Physical therapists; Reality therapists; Recreational therapists; Occupational therapists; Speech therapists; Activities coordinators; Dietitians; Podiatrists.

Eva Dawn Care Center
1001 N Featherstone Dr, Salt Lake City, UT 84116
(801) 596-2810
Admin Donna Featherstone; Kent Featherstone. *Dir of Nursing* Shelby Frye RN. *Medical Dir* Clel Jensen MD.
Licensure Skilled care; Intermediate care; Alzheimer's care. *Beds* SNF 6; ICF 54.
Certified Medicaid; Medicare.
Owner Privately owned.
Admissions Requirements Medical examination; Physician's request; Family request.
Staff Physicians 1 (pt); RNs 1 (ft), 2 (pt); LPNs 5 (ft), 1 (pt); Nurses' aides 16 (ft), 6 (pt); Physical therapists 1 (pt); Reality therapists 1 (pt); Recreational therapists 1 (ft); Occupational therapists 1 (pt); Speech therapists 1 (pt); Activities coordinators 1 (ft); Dietitians 1 (pt); Ophthalmologists 1 (pt); Podiatrists 1 (pt); Audiologists 1 (pt).
Languages Spanish, French.
Facilities Dining room; Physical therapy room; Activities room; Crafts room; Laundry room; Barber/Beauty shop; Library.

Activities Arts & crafts; Cards; Games;
Reading groups; Prayer groups; Movies;
Shopping trips; Dances/Social/Cultural
gatherings; Intergenerational programs; Pet
therapy.

Doxey-Hatch Medical Center
1255 E 3900 S, Salt Lake City, UT 84124
(801) 262-3401
Admin Brad J Mikesell. *Dir of Nursing* Gayla
Littlefield. *Medical Dir* Dr Glen Wilson.
Licensure Skilled care; Intermediate care;
Chronic disease. *Beds* SNF 30; ICF 138;
Chronic disease 12. *Private Pay Patients*
20%. *Certified* Medicaid; Medicare.
Owner Proprietary corp.
Admissions Requirements Physician's request.
Staff RNs 10 (ft), 3 (pt); LPNs 10 (ft), 2 (pt);
Nurses' aides 50 (ft), 10 (pt); Physical
therapists; Recreational therapists 2 (ft), 1
(pt).
Facilities Dining room; Physical therapy
room; Activities room; Crafts room; Barber/
Beauty shop; Library.
Activities Arts & crafts; Cards; Games;
Reading groups; Prayer groups; Movies;
Shopping trips; Dances/Social/Cultural
gatherings; Pet therapy.

Fairview Care Center East
455 S 900 E, Salt Lake City, UT 84102
(801) 355-6891
Admin Joseph D Petersen.
Licensure Intermediate care. *Beds* ICF 36.
Certified Medicaid.

Fairview Care Center West
876 W 700 S, Salt Lake City, UT 84104
(801) 355-9649
Admin Dale E Petersen.
Licensure Intermediate care. *Beds* ICF 36.
Certified Medicaid.

Fay Case Nursing Home
294 E Robert Ave, Salt Lake City, UT 84115
(801) 466-2211
Admin Judy B Heaps. *Dir of Nursing* Rose T
Gillespie. *Medical Dir* David W Fiegal MD.
Licensure Intermediate care. *Beds* ICF 68.
Certified Medicaid.
Admissions Requirements Medical
examination.
Staff LPNs 10 (ft); Nurses' aides 20 (ft);
Recreational therapists 1 (ft).
Facilities Dining room; Activities room;
Laundry room; Barber/Beauty shop.
Activities Arts & crafts; Cards; Games;
Reading groups; Prayer groups; Movies;
Shopping trips; Dances/Social/Cultural
gatherings.

Glenwood Care
404 E 5600 S, Salt Lake City, UT 84107
(801) 266-3588
Admin Sue Bowker.
Medical Dir Dr Burtis Evans.
Licensure Skilled care; Intermediate care. *Beds*
119. *Certified* Medicaid; Medicare.
Admissions Requirements Medical
examination; Physician's request.
Staff Physicians 20 (pt); RNs 6 (ft), 2 (pt);
LPNs 8 (ft); Physical therapists 1 (ft);
Reality therapists 1 (ft); Recreational
therapists 1 (ft); Occupational therapists 1
(ft); Speech therapists 1 (ft); Activities
coordinators 1 (ft); Dietitians 1 (pt);
Ophthalmologists 1 (pt); Podiatrists 1 (pt);
Audiologists 1 (pt); Dentists 1 (pt).
Facilities Dining room; Physical therapy
room; Activities room; Crafts room; Laundry
room; Barber/Beauty shop.
Activities Arts & crafts; Cards; Games;
Reading groups; Prayer groups; Movies;
Shopping trips; Dances/Social/Cultural
gatherings.

Highland Care Center
4285 Highland Dr, Salt Lake City, UT 84124
(801) 278-2839

Admin Terry A Lemmon. *Dir of Nursing* Pam
Wolf RN. *Medical Dir* John Hylen MD.
Licensure Skilled care. *Beds* SNF 60. *Certified*
Medicaid; Medicare.
Owner Proprietary corp.
Admissions Requirements Minimum age 65;
Medical examination; Physician's request.
Staff Physicians; RNs 2 (ft), 2 (pt); LPNs 3
(ft), 2 (pt); Nurses' aides 15 (ft), 5 (pt);
Physical therapists 2 (pt); Recreational
therapists 1 (ft); Speech therapists 1 (pt);
Activities coordinators; Dietitians 1 (pt);
Ophthalmologists 1 (pt).
Languages Spanish.
Affiliation Church of Latter-Day Saints
(Mormon).
Facilities Dining room; Physical therapy
room; Activities room; Laundry room;
Barber/Beauty shop.
Activities Arts & crafts; Cards; Games;
Reading groups; Prayer groups; Movies;
Shopping trips; Dances/Social/Cultural
gatherings.

Hillhaven Convalescent Center
41 S 900 E, Salt Lake City, UT 84102
(801) 532-3539
Admin Saundra R BeBout.
Licensure Skilled care. *Beds* SNF 154.
Certified Medicaid; Medicare.
Owner Proprietary corp (Hillhaven Corp).

Hillside Villa Care Center
1216 E 1300 S, Salt Lake City, UT 84105
(801) 487-5865
Admin Erich S Linner.
Medical Dir James Pearl MD.
Licensure Intermediate care; Alzheimer's care.
Beds ICF 120. *Certified* Medicaid.
Owner Proprietary corp.
Admissions Requirements Medical
examination; Physician's request.
Staff RNs 3 (ft); LPNs 7 (ft); Nurses' aides 26
(ft); Activities coordinators 2 (ft);
Ophthalmologists 1 (ft); Podiatrists 1 (ft).
Facilities Dining room; Physical therapy
room; Activities room; Crafts room; Laundry
room; Barber/Beauty shop; Library.
Activities Arts & crafts; Cards; Games;
Reading groups; Movies; Shopping trips;
Dances/Social/Cultural gatherings; Outings;
Picnics.

Holladay Healthcare Center
4782 S Holladay Blvd, Salt Lake City, UT
84117
(801) 277-7002
Admin Owen Gustafsen.
Licensure Skilled care. *Beds* SNF 120.
Certified Medicaid; Medicare.

Johanna Nursing Home
433 E 2700 S, Salt Lake City, UT 84115
(801) 487-2248
Admin Johanna M Syms.
Medical Dir John Tudor MD.
Licensure Intermediate care. *Beds* ICF 41.
Certified Medicaid.
Staff Physicians; RNs; LPNs; Nurses' aides;
Recreational therapists; Activities
coordinators; Dietitians.
Facilities Dining room; Activities room;
Laundry room; Barber/Beauty shop; Library.
Activities Arts & crafts; Cards; Games;
Reading groups; Prayer groups; Movies;
Shopping trips.

L D S Hospital Transitional Care Center
8th Ave & C St, Salt Lake City, UT 84143
(801) 321-5400
Admin Connie Frisch.
Licensure Skilled care. *Beds* SNF 14. *Certified*
Medicaid; Medicare.

Latham Nursing Home
642 University St, Salt Lake City, UT 84102
(801) 582-2195
Admin Belinda Latham.
Licensure Intermediate care. *Beds* 16.

Midtown Manor
125 S 900 W, Salt Lake City, UT 84101
(801) 363-6340
Admin John N Papadakis.
Medical Dir Leo Sotiriou.
Licensure Intermediate care. *Beds* ICF 79.
Certified Medicaid.
Admissions Requirements Minimum age 18.
Staff Physicians; RNs; LPNs; Nurses' aides;
Physical therapists; Recreational therapists;
Occupational therapists; Speech therapists;
Activities coordinators; Dietitians;
Ophthalmologists; Podiatrists; Audiologists;
Dentists; Medical records; Social worker;
Food service supervisor.
Facilities Dining room; Physical therapy
room; Activities room; Crafts room; Laundry
room; Barber/Beauty shop; Dayroom.
Activities Arts & crafts; Cards; Games; Prayer
groups; Movies; Shopping trips; Dances/
Social/Cultural gatherings.

Olympus Care Center
950 E 3300 S, Salt Lake City, UT 84106
(801) 486-5121
Admin Teresa Ann Fagot. *Dir of Nursing*
Carol Davis. *Medical Dir* Margaret Hect
MD.
Licensure Intermediate care. *Beds* ICF 72.
Certified Medicaid.
Owner Proprietary corp.
Admissions Requirements Medical
examination; Physician's request.
Staff LPNs 8 (ft); Nurses' aides 12 (ft), 3 (pt);
Recreational therapists 1 (ft); Activities
coordinators 1 (ft).
Languages Spanish.
Facilities Dining room; Activities room;
Crafts room; Laundry room; Barber/Beauty
shop.
Activities Arts & crafts; Cards; Games;
Reading groups; Prayer groups; Movies;
Shopping trips; Dances/Social/Cultural
gatherings; Trips; Camping; Bowling;
Fishing; Cook-outs.

Rosewood Terrace
158 N 600 W, Salt Lake City, UT 84116
(801) 363-4222
Admin Debbie Holling.
Medical Dir King Udall; Jan Brotherton.
Licensure Skilled care. *Beds* SNF 79. *Certified*
Medicaid; Medicare.
Owner Proprietary corp.
Admissions Requirements Physician's request.
Staff RNs 4 (ft); LPNs 6 (ft); Nurses' aides;
Activities coordinators 1 (ft); Dietitians 1
(pt).
Facilities Dining room; Physical therapy
room; Laundry room; Barber/Beauty shop;
TV/smoking room.
Activities Arts & crafts; Cards; Games; Prayer
groups; Movies; Shopping trips; Dances/
Social/Cultural gatherings.

St Joseph Villa
475 Ramona Ave, Salt Lake City, UT 84115
(801) 487-7557
Admin G Richard Erick. *Dir of Nursing* Paula
Siciliano RN. *Medical Dir* Victor Kassel
MD.
Licensure Skilled care; Intermediate care;
Residential care. *Beds* Swing beds SNF/ICF
165. *Certified* Medicaid; Medicare.
Owner Nonprofit organization/foundation.
Admissions Requirements Minimum age 55;
Medical examination; Physician's request.
Staff RNs 5 (ft), 7 (pt); LPNs 17 (ft), 11 (pt);
Nurses' aides 55 (ft), 9 (pt); Physical
therapists (contracted); Recreational
therapists 1 (ft), 1 (pt); Occupational
therapists (contracted); Speech therapists
(contracted); Activities coordinators 1 (ft);
Dietitians 1 (ft); Ophthalmologists
(contracted); Podiatrists (contracted);
Audiologists (contracted).
Affiliation Roman Catholic.

Facilities Dining room; Physical therapy room; Activities room; Chapel; Crafts room; Laundry room; Barber/Beauty shop; Library; Arboretum.
Activities Arts & crafts; Cards; Games; Prayer groups; Movies; Dances/Social/Cultural gatherings; Intergenerational programs; Pet therapy; Pastoral care program.

Terrace Villa Care Center
4600 Highland Dr, Salt Lake City, UT 84117
(801) 272-4411
Admin Mark D Bybee. *Dir of Nursing* Clarine Moffit RN. *Medical Dir* Dr John M Tudor.
Licensure Skilled care; Intermediate care for mentally retarded; Alzheimer's care. *Beds* SNF 54; ICF/MR 42. *Certified* Medicaid; Medicare.
Owner Proprietary corp (Chartham Management).
Staff RNs 3 (ft), 2 (pt); Nurses' aides 50 (ft); Physical therapists 2 (ft); Reality therapists 1 (ft); Recreational therapists 1 (ft); Dietitians 1 (ft).
Facilities Dining room; Physical therapy room; Activities room; Chapel; Crafts room; Laundry room; Barber/Beauty shop; Library.
Activities Arts & crafts; Cards; Games; Reading groups; Prayer groups; Movies; Dances/Social/Cultural gatherings.

Twin Pines Care Center
3520 S Highland Dr, Salt Lake City, UT 84106
(801) 484-7638
Admin Janene Daskalas.
Licensure Intermediate care. *Beds* 57. *Certified* Medicaid.

Wasatch Villa Convalescent Nursing Home
2200 E 3300 S, Salt Lake City, UT 84109
(801) 486-2096, 486-0105 FAX
Admin Karen L Stoddard. *Dir of Nursing* Lois Laine. *Medical Dir* John C Hylen.
Licensure Skilled care. *Beds* SNF 118. *Private Pay Patients* 35%. *Certified* Medicaid; Medicare.
Owner Proprietary corp (Hillhaven Corp).
Admissions Requirements Minimum age 21; Medical examination; Physician's request.
Staff Physicians 1 (pt); RNs 8 (ft), 1 (pt); LPNs 12 (ft), 1 (pt); Nurses' aides 36 (ft), 6 (pt); Physical therapists 1 (ft), 1 (pt); Recreational therapists 1 (ft), 1 (pt); Occupational therapists 1 (ft); Speech therapists 1 (pt); Activities coordinators 1 (pt); Dietitians 2 (pt); Ophthalmologists 1 (pt); Podiatrists 1 (pt); Audiologists 1 (pt).
Affiliation Church of Latter-Day Saints (Mormon).
Facilities Dining room; Physical therapy room; Activities room; Chapel; Crafts room; Laundry room; Barber/Beauty shop; Library.
Activities Arts & crafts; Cards; Games; Reading groups; Prayer groups; Movies; Shopping trips; Dances/Social/Cultural gatherings.

Woodland Park Care Center
3855 S 700 E, Salt Lake City, UT 84106
(801) 268-4766
Admin Revel J McPhie. *Dir of Nursing* Carole Housekeeper. *Medical Dir* Clel L Jensen.
Licensure Skilled care. *Beds* SNF 100. *Certified* Medicaid; Medicare.
Owner Proprietary corp.
Admissions Requirements Minimum age 18; Medical examination; Physician's request.
Staff Physicians 1 (pt); RNs 3 (ft), 3 (pt); LPNs 4 (ft), 4 (pt); Nurses' aides 25 (ft); Physical therapists 1 (ft), 1 (pt); Recreational therapists 2 (ft); Activities coordinators 1 (ft); Dietitians.
Languages Spanish.
Facilities Dining room; Physical therapy room; Activities room; Chapel; Crafts room; Laundry room; Barber/Beauty shop; Library; Head trauma and neuro care.

Activities Arts & crafts; Cards; Games; Reading groups; Prayer groups; Movies; Shopping trips; Dances/Social/Cultural gatherings; Intergenerational programs; Pet therapy.

Zion's Care Center
2730 E 3300 S, Salt Lake City, UT 84109
(801) 487-0896
Admin Michael Sparks.
Licensure Skilled care; Intermediate care. *Beds* SNF 52; ICF 61. *Certified* Medicaid.
Staff Physicians 1 (ft); RNs 1 (ft); LPNs 6 (ft), 1 (pt); Nurses' aides 45 (ft); Recreational therapists 1 (ft); Dietitians 1 (pt); Podiatrists 1 (pt).
Facilities Dining room; Laundry room; Barber/Beauty shop.
Activities Arts & crafts; Games; Reading groups; Movies; Shopping trips; Dances/Social/Cultural gatherings.

Sandy

Crosslands Health Care Center
575 E 11000 S, Sandy, UT 84070
(801) 571-7600
Admin Terry Lemmon. *Dir of Nursing* Shauna Stevenson RN. *Medical Dir* Richard Brown MD.
Licensure Skilled care. *Beds* SNF 120. *Private Pay Patients* 38%. *Certified* Medicaid; Medicare.
Owner Proprietary corp (Hillhaven Corp).

Hillcrest Care Center
348 E 8000 S, Sandy, UT 84091
(801) 566-4191
Admin Dottie Gonthier. *Dir of Nursing* Sharon Jeffs RN.
Licensure Intermediate care for mentally retarded. *Beds* ICF/MR 60. *Certified* Medicaid; Medicare.
Owner Proprietary corp (National Heritage).
Admissions Requirements Minimum age 21.
Staff Physicians 1 (pt); RNs 1 (pt); LPNs 4 (ft), 2 (pt); Nurses' aides 25 (ft); Physical therapists 1 (pt); Recreational therapists 1 (ft), 2 (pt); Occupational therapists 1 (ft); Speech therapists 1 (ft); Dietitians 1 (ft), 1 (pt); Podiatrists 1 (pt).
Facilities Dining room; Activities room; Crafts room; Laundry room.
Activities Arts & crafts; Cards; Games; Movies; Shopping trips; Dances/Social/Cultural gatherings; Special Olympics.

Sandy Regional Convalescent & Rehabilitation
50 E 9000 S, Sandy, UT 84070
(801) 561-9839
Admin Teresa Ann Fagot RN.
Medical Dir Warren Stadler MD.
Licensure Skilled care; Intermediate care; Alzheimer's care. *Beds* Swing beds SNF/ICF 138. *Private Pay Patients* 20%. *Certified* Medicaid; Medicare.
Owner Proprietary corp (Westcare Management Inc).
Admissions Requirements Medical examination; Physician's request.
Staff RNs 3 (ft), 2 (pt); LPNs 12 (ft), 2 (pt); Physical therapists; Recreational therapists 2 (ft); Occupational therapists 1 (pt); Speech therapists 1 (pt); Activities coordinators 1 (ft); Dietitians (consultant); Ophthalmologists (consultant); Podiatrists (consultant); Audiologists (consultant).
Facilities Dining room; Physical therapy room; Activities room; Laundry room; Barber/Beauty shop; 2 dayrooms; 2 common areas.
Activities Arts & crafts; Games; Reading groups; Movies; Shopping trips; Pet therapy; Religious services.

Spanish Fork

Hales Rest Home
46 N 100 E, Spanish Fork, UT 84660
(801) 798-6220
Admin Steven A Bona.
Licensure Intermediate care. *Beds* ICF 28. *Certified* Medicaid.
Admissions Requirements Females only; Medical examination; Physician's request.
Staff Physicians 3 (pt); RNs 1 (pt); LPNs 4 (ft); Nurses' aides 9 (ft); Physical therapists 1 (pt); Recreational therapists 1 (ft); Occupational therapists 1 (pt); Speech therapists 1 (pt); Activities coordinators 1 (pt); Dietitians 1 (pt); Ophthalmologists 1 (pt); Podiatrists 1 (pt); Audiologists 1 (pt); Dentists 1 (pt).
Facilities Dining room; Activities room; Crafts room; Laundry room; Barber/Beauty shop.
Activities Arts & crafts; Cards; Games; Reading groups; Movies; Shopping trips.

Springville

Ann's Siesta Villa
469 N Main, Springville, UT 84663
(801) 489-9409
Admin Sharon Maestas. *Dir of Nursing* Dee Crook. *Medical Dir* Kevin Colver.
Licensure Intermediate care. *Beds* ICF 44. *Private Pay Patients* 20%. *Certified* Medicaid.
Admissions Requirements Males only; Medical examination; Physician's request.
Staff Physicians; RNs; LPNs; Nurses' aides; Physical therapists; Reality therapists; Recreational therapists; Occupational therapists; Speech therapists; Activities coordinators; Dietitians; Ophthalmologists; Podiatrists; Audiologists.
Facilities Dining room; Activities room; Crafts room; Laundry room; Barber/Beauty shop; Library.
Activities Arts & crafts; Cards; Games; Reading groups; Prayer groups; Movies; Shopping trips; Dances/Social/Cultural gatherings; Pet therapy.

Todholm Care Center
321 E 800 S, Springville, UT 84663
(801) 489-9461
Admin Margaret M Boyack.
Medical Dir L Colledge.
Licensure Intermediate care; Alzheimer's care. *Beds* ICF 67. *Certified* Medicaid.
Owner Proprietary corp.
Admissions Requirements Medical examination; Physician's request.
Staff LPNs 4 (ft), 3 (pt); Nurses' aides 12 (ft), 8 (pt); Activities coordinators 1 (ft).
Facilities Dining room; Activities room; Laundry room; Barber/Beauty shop; Library; Outdoor recreational facilities.
Activities Arts & crafts; Cards; Games; Reading groups; Movies; Shopping trips; Dances/Social/Cultural gatherings; Various church groups.

Tooele

Tooele Valley Nursing Home
140 E 2nd S, Tooele, UT 84074
(801) 882-6130
Admin Beth W Vowles. *Dir of Nursing* Betty Sumner RN. *Medical Dir* W Kim Sullivan MD.
Licensure Skilled care. *Beds* SNF 82. *Private Pay Patients* 22%. *Certified* Medicaid; Medicare.
Owner Publicly owned.
Admissions Requirements Medical examination; Physician's request.
Staff Physicians 5 (pt); RNs 3 (ft), 1 (pt); LPNs 3 (ft), 1 (pt); Nurses' aides 24 (ft), 6 (pt); Physical therapists 1 (pt); Reality

therapists 1 (pt); Recreational therapists 1 (ft), 1 (pt); Occupational therapists 1 (pt); Speech therapists 1 (pt); Activities coordinators 1 (ft); Dietitians 1 (ft); Ophthalmologists 1 (pt); Podiatrists 1 (pt); Audiologists 1 (pt).
Languages Spanish, Indian, Japanese.
Facilities Dining room; Physical therapy room; Activities room; Chapel; Crafts room; Laundry room; Barber/Beauty shop; Library; Patio.
Activities Arts & crafts; Cards; Games; Reading groups; Prayer groups; Movies; Shopping trips; Dances/Social/Cultural gatherings; Intergenerational programs; Pet therapy; Bus trips; Cookouts.

Tremonton

Box Elder County Nursing Home
460 W 600 N, Tremonton, UT 84337
(801) 257-5356
Admin Robert F Jex. *Dir of Nursing* Carma Bradshaw RN. *Medical Dir* Jack S Johnson MD.
Licensure Intermediate care. *Beds* ICF 38. *Certified* Medicaid.
Owner Publicly owned.
Admissions Requirements Medical examination; Physician's request.
Staff RNs; LPNs; Nurses' aides; Activities coordinators; Dietitians; Dentists.
Facilities Dining room; Physical therapy room; Activities room; Crafts room; Laundry room; Barber/Beauty shop.
Activities Arts & crafts; Cards; Games; Reading groups; Movies; Shopping trips; Dances/Social/Cultural gatherings.

Vernal

Uintah Care Center
510 S 500 W, Vernal, UT 84078
(801) 789-8851
Admin Rossa Simmons.
Medical Dir Dr Paul Stringham.
Licensure Skilled care; Intermediate care; Alzheimer's care. *Beds* SNF 25; ICF 25.
Owner Proprietary corp (Chartham Management).
Admissions Requirements Medical examination; Physician's request.

Staff RNs; LPNs; Nurses' aides; Physical therapists; Reality therapists; Recreational therapists; Occupational therapists; Speech therapists; Activities coordinators; Dietitians; Ophthalmologists; Podiatrists; Dentists.
Facilities Dining room; Physical therapy room; Activities room; Crafts room; Laundry room; Barber/Beauty shop; Library; Smoking room; Large covered patio & backyard.
Activities Arts & crafts; Cards; Games; Reading groups; Prayer groups; Movies; Shopping trips; Dances/Social/Cultural gatherings; Reality orientation; Cooking classes; Wood shop.

Washington Terrace

Care West—Mt Ogden
375 E 5350 S, Washington Terrace, UT 84403
(801) 479-5700
Admin William Wortley. *Dir of Nursing* Pam Russell; Janet Akins RN. *Medical Dir* Dr J Newton.
Licensure Skilled care. *Beds* SNF 120. *Certified* Medicaid; Medicare.
Owner Proprietary corp (Care Enterprises).
Admissions Requirements Medical examination; Physician's request.
Staff RNs 16 (ft), 2 (pt); LPNs 2 (ft), 1 (pt); Nurses' aides 45 (ft), 5 (pt); Physical therapists 5 (ft), 1 (pt); Reality therapists 1 (ft), 1 (pt); Recreational therapists 1 (ft), 1 (pt); Occupational therapists 1 (pt); Speech therapists 1 (pt); Activities coordinators 1 (pt); Dietitians 1 (pt).
Facilities Dining room; Physical therapy room; Activities room; Crafts room; Laundry room; Barber/Beauty shop; Library.
Activities Arts & crafts; Cards; Games; Reading groups; Prayer groups; Movies; Shopping trips; Dances/Social/Cultural gatherings.

West Jordan

South Valley Health Center
3706 W 9000 S, West Jordan, UT 84084
(801) 569-2273
Admin Paula Miles.
Licensure Skilled care; Intermediate care. *Beds* SNF 59; ICF 61. *Certified* Medicaid; Medicare.

West Jordan Care Center
3350 W 7800 S, West Jordan, UT 84084
(801) 566-0686

Admin Donald R Maxwell.
Medical Dir Dr J Mumford.
Licensure Intermediate care for mentally retarded. *Beds* ICF/MR 80. *Certified* Medicaid; Medicare.
Admissions Requirements Minimum age 5; Medical examination; Physician's request.
Staff Physicians 1 (ft); RNs 2 (ft); LPNs 5 (ft), 1 (pt); Nurses' aides 25 (ft), 4 (pt); Physical therapists 1 (ft); Reality therapists 1 (ft); Recreational therapists 1 (ft).
Facilities Dining room; Physical therapy room; Activities room; Crafts room; Laundry room; Barber/Beauty shop.
Activities Arts & crafts; Cards; Games; Reading groups; Prayer groups; Movies; Shopping trips; Dances/Social/Cultural gatherings.

West Valley City

Care West—Valley View
4150 W 3375 S, West Valley City, UT 84120
(801) 968-9028
Admin Ray Wilde.
Licensure Skilled care. *Beds* SNF 72. *Certified* Medicaid; Medicare.
Owner Proprietary corp (Care Enterprises).

Hazen Nursing Facility Inc
2520 S Redwood Rd, West Valley City, UT 84119
(801) 972-1050
Admin Romaine P Tuft.
Medical Dir Dr David Feigal.
Licensure Intermediate care; Alzheimer's care. *Beds* ICF 26. *Certified* Medicaid.
Owner Proprietary corp.
Admissions Requirements Females only; Medical examination.
Staff Physicians 1 (pt); RNs 1 (pt); LPNs 2 (ft), 2 (pt); Nurses' aides 12 (ft), 7 (pt); Recreational therapists 1 (ft); Activities coordinators 1 (ft); Dietitians 1 (pt).
Facilities Dining room; Activities room; Laundry room.
Activities Arts & crafts; Cards; Games; Reading groups; Prayer groups; Movies; Shopping trips; Dances/Social/Cultural gatherings; Van rides; Daily exercise class.

Pfeiffer's Community Home
4028 S 4800 W, West Valley City, UT 84120
(801) 968-8122
Admin Rosemarie T Rohde.
Licensure Intermediate care. *Beds* 28.

VERMONT

Barre

Berlin Convalescent Center
PO Box 6684, RR 3, Airport Rd, Barre, VT
05641
(802) 229-0308
Admin Carol C Carey. *Dir of Nursing* Nancy
Plunket. *Medical Dir* Harry L Columbo MD.
Licensure Skilled care; Intermediate care. *Beds*
SNF 48; ICF 104. *Certified* Medicare.
Admissions Requirements Minimum age 16;
Medical examination; Physician's request.
Staff RNs 19 (ft), 11 (pt); LPNs 2 (ft), 7 (pt);
Nurses' aides 18 (ft), 53 (pt); Physical
therapists 1 (ft); Recreational therapists 1
(ft), 1 (pt); Speech therapists 1 (pt);
Activities coordinators 1 (ft); Dietitians 1
(pt); Dentists 1 (pt).
Facilities Dining room; Physical therapy
room; Activities room; Chapel; Crafts room;
Laundry room; Barber/Beauty shop.
Activities Arts & crafts; Cards; Games;
Reading groups; Prayer groups; Movies;
Shopping trips; Dances/Social/Cultural
gatherings.

McFarland House
71 Washington Hwy, Barre, VT 05641
(802) 476-4164
Admin Daria V Mason. *Dir of Nursing* Arlene
MacPherson.
Licensure Intermediate care. *Beds* ICF 92.
Certified Medicaid.

Rowan Court Nursing Home
Prospect St, Barre, VT 05641
(802) 476-4166
Admin Carol Carey. *Dir of Nursing* Maureen
Bertrand. *Medical Dir* Dr George Lucchina.
Licensure Intermediate care. *Beds* ICF 104.
Admissions Requirements Minimum age 16;
Medical examination; Physician's request.
Staff RNs 8 (ft); LPNs 7 (ft); Nurses' aides 69
(ft); Activities coordinators 1 (ft); Dietitians
1 (pt); Ophthalmologists 2 (pt); Podiatrists 2
(pt); Audiologists 1 (pt); Dentists 2 (pt).
Facilities Dining room; Physical therapy
room; Activities room; Chapel; Crafts room;
Laundry room; Barber/Beauty shop; Library;
Greenhouse.
Activities Arts & crafts; Cards; Games;
Reading groups; Prayer groups; Movies;
Shopping trips; Dances/Social/Cultural
gatherings; Bus with wheelchair lift for
outings.

Barton

Maple Lane Nursing Home
PO Box 291, Barton Hill Rd, Barton, VT
05822
(802) 754-8575
Admin Gary Marcotte. *Dir of Nursing* Barbara
Fontaine.
Licensure Intermediate care. *Beds* ICF 64.
Certified Medicaid.

Bellows Falls

McGirr Nursing Home
33 Atkinson St, Bellows Falls, VT 05101
(802) 463-4387
Admin Margaret M Perry. *Dir of Nursing* Leta
Abbott.
Licensure Intermediate care. *Beds* ICF 30.

Bennington

Bennington Convalescent Center
360 Dewey St, Bennington, VT 05201
(802) 442-8526
Admin Neil H Gruber. *Dir of Nursing* Betty-
Jean DeVries. *Medical Dir* Peter Peff MD.
Licensure Skilled care; Intermediate care. *Beds*
SNF 51; ICF 49. *Certified* Medicaid;
Medicare.
Owner Proprietary corp.
Admissions Requirements Medical
examination.
Staff RNs 5 (ft), 5 (pt); LPNs 10 (ft), 10 (pt);
Nurses' aides 15 (ft), 25 (pt); Physical
therapists 1 (pt); Recreational therapists 2
(ft); Dietitians 1 (pt); Dentists 1 (pt).
Facilities Dining room; Physical therapy
room; Activities room; Crafts room; Barber/
Beauty shop.
Activities Arts & crafts; Cards; Games;
Reading groups; Prayer groups; Movies;
Shopping trips; Dances/Social/Cultural
gatherings.

Crescent Manor Nursing Home
312 Crescent Blvd, Bennington, VT 05201
(802) 447-1501
Admin Brendan Coogan. *Dir of Nursing*
Patricia Babcock.
Licensure Intermediate care. *Beds* ICF 72.
Owner Proprietary corp.
Facilities Dining room; Activities room;
Barber/Beauty shop.
Activities Arts & crafts; Cards; Games;
Reading groups; Prayer groups; Movies;
Shopping trips; Dances/Social/Cultural
gatherings.

Weston Hadden Convalescent Center
160 Hospital Dr, Bennington, VT 05201
(802) 447-1547
Admin Robert M Stair. *Dir of Nursing* Gail
Harbour.
Licensure Skilled care; Intermediate care. *Beds*
SNF 60; ICF 40. *Certified* Medicare.

Bradford

Brookside Nursing Home of Bradford
PO Box 729, Bradford, VT 05033
(802) 222-5203
Admin Thomas E Rice. *Dir of Nursing* Jenny
Lamoureux.
Licensure Skilled care; Intermediate care. *Beds*
SNF 20; ICF 52. *Certified* Medicare.

Brattleboro

Eden Park Nursing Home
Pine Heights, Brattleboro, VT 05301
(802) 257-0307
Admin David G Selover. *Dir of Nursing*
Lorraine Fahey. *Medical Dir* Dr Christopher
J Schmidt.
Licensure Skilled care; Intermediate care. *Beds*
SNF 40; ICF 84. *Certified* Medicaid;
Medicare.
Owner Proprietary corp (Eden Park
Management Inc).
Admissions Requirements Minimum age 16;
Medical examination; Physician's request.
Staff RNs 4 (ft), 8 (pt); LPNs 9 (ft), 10 (pt);
Nurses' aides 38 (ft), 9 (pt); Physical
therapists 1 (ft); Occupational therapists
(consultant); Speech therapists 1 (pt);
Activities coordinators 1 (ft); Dietitians
(consultant); Ophthalmologists (consultant);
Podiatrists (consultant); Audiologists
(consultant).
Facilities Dining room; Physical therapy
room; Activities room; Laundry room;
Barber/Beauty shop; Patio.
Activities Arts & crafts; Cards; Games;
Reading groups; Prayer groups; Movies;
Dances/Social/Cultural gatherings; Pet
therapy; Picnics.

Linden Lodge Nursing Home
75 Linden St, Brattleboro, VT 05301
(802) 254-9692
Admin Roberta Bremmer RN. *Dir of Nursing*
Betty McCormick. *Medical Dir* Dr R
Walker.
Licensure Intermediate care. *Beds* ICF 117.

Thompson House
30 Maple St, Brattleboro, VT 05301-1117
(802) 254-4977
Admin Janet J Henningsen, CFACHCA. *Dir
of Nursing* Annette Vigneau RN. *Medical
Dir* John R Bookwalter MD.
Licensure Intermediate care; Residential care;
Alzheimer's care. *Beds* ICF 35; Residential
care 24. *Private Pay Patients* 70%. *Certified*
Medicaid.
Owner Nonprofit corp (Brattleboro Mutual
Aid Association Inc).
Admissions Requirements Minimum age 18;
Medical examination.
Staff RNs 2 (ft); LPNs 4 (ft); Nurses' aides 18
(ft); Recreational therapists 2 (ft); Activities
coordinators 1 (ft).
Facilities Dining room; Activities room;
Crafts room; Laundry room; Barber/Beauty
shop; Library.
Activities Arts & crafts; Cards; Games;
Reading groups; Prayer groups; Movies;
Shopping trips; Dances/Social/Cultural
gatherings; Intergenerational programs; Pet
therapy; Cooking group; Current events;
Alzheimer's day program.

Burlington

Birchwood Terrace Healthcare
43 Starr Farm Rd, Burlington, VT 05401
(802) 863-6384
Admin Carole Howe-Glidden. *Dir of Nursing*
Joan K Bombard RN. *Medical Dir* Maurice
Walsh MD.
Licensure Skilled care; Intermediate care. *Beds*
SNF 60; ICF 100. *Certified* Medicare.
Owner Proprietary corp (Hillhaven Corp).

Burlington Convalescent Center
300 Pearl St, Burlington, VT 05401
(802) 658-4200
Admin Richard Morley.
Licensure Skilled care; Intermediate care. *Beds*
SNF 42; ICF 126. *Certified* Medicare.

Medical Center Nursing Home—DeGoesbriand Unit
Medical Center Hospital of Vermont,
Burlington, VT 05401
(802) 656-3909
Admin Carol Trombley.
Licensure Skilled care. *Beds* 42. *Certified*
Medicaid; Medicare.

Starr Farm Nursing Center
98 Starr Farm Rd, Burlington, VT 05401
(802) 658-6717
Admin Kevin Henry. *Dir of Nursing* Anne
Johnson.
Licensure Skilled care; Intermediate care. *Beds*
SNF 18; ICF 82. *Certified* Medicare.

Colchester

Green Mountain Nursing Home
1120 Ethan Allen Ave, Colchester, VT 05446
(802) 655-1025
Admin Robert Sterling. *Dir of Nursing* Kim
Ebel. *Medical Dir* John Lantman MD.
Licensure Skilled care; Intermediate care. *Beds*
SNF 13; ICF 60.
Admissions Requirements Minimum age 18;
Physician's request.
Staff Physicians 1 (pt); RNs 7 (ft), 6 (pt);
LPNs 3 (ft), 3 (pt); Nurses' aides 28 (ft), 15
(pt); Physical therapists 1 (pt); Recreational
therapists 3 (ft); Activities coordinators 1
(ft); Dietitians 1 (pt); Dentists 1 (pt).
Facilities Dining room; Physical therapy
room; Activities room; Chapel; Crafts room;
Laundry room; Barber/Beauty shop; Library;
TV lounges.
Activities Arts & crafts; Games; Reading
groups; Prayer groups; Movies; Shopping
trips; Dances/Social/Cultural gatherings;
Cooking group.

Derby

Derby Green Nursing Home
Main St, Derby, VT 05829
(802) 766-2201
Admin Kim Channell. *Dir of Nursing* Diane
Clowery. *Medical Dir* Dr F P Fiermonte.
Licensure Intermediate care. *Beds* ICF 21.
Staff Physicians 1 (pt); RNs 1 (ft), 1 (pt);
LPNs 4 (ft); Nurses' aides 4 (ft); Physical
therapists 1 (pt); Speech therapists 1 (pt);
Dietitians 1 (pt).
Facilities Dining room; Activities room.

Fair Haven

Sager Nursing Home
28 Prospect St, Fair Haven, VT 05743
(802) 265-3263
Admin Leon Dion. *Dir of Nursing* Ellen
Salvato. *Medical Dir* Edward C Stannard.
Licensure Intermediate care. *Beds* ICF 36.
Admissions Requirements Medical
examination; Physician's request.

Staff RNs 2 (ft), 6 (pt); LPNs 1 (pt); Nurses'
aides 6 (ft), 6 (pt); Reality therapists 1 (ft);
Recreational therapists 1 (ft); Occupational
therapists 1 (pt); Activities coordinators 1
(pt); Dietitians 1 (pt).
Facilities Dining room; Activities room;
Crafts room; Laundry room; Barber/Beauty
shop.
Activities Arts & crafts; Cards; Games;
Reading groups; Prayer groups; Dances/
Social/Cultural gatherings.

Glover

Union House Nursing Home Inc
RR 2 Box 1, Main St, Glover, VT 05839
(802) 525-6600, 525-3452 FAX
Admin Patricia E Russell. *Dir of Nursing*
Betty Austin. *Medical Dir* Dr George
Linton.
Licensure Intermediate care. *Beds* ICF/MR
31. *Private Pay Patients* 5%. *Certified*
Medicaid.
Owner Privately owned.
Admissions Requirements Minimum age 18.
Staff Physicians 1 (ft), 1 (pt); RNs 2 (ft);
LPNs 5 (ft), 1 (pt); Nurses' aides 14 (ft), 7
(pt); Physical therapists (contracted); Reality
therapists 1 (pt); Recreational therapists 1
(pt); Occupational therapists 1 (pt); Speech
therapists 1 (pt); Activities coordinators 1
(ft); Dietitians (contracted);
Ophthalmologists 1 (pt); Podiatrists 1 (pt);
Audiologists 1 (pt).
Languages French.
Facilities Dining room; Activities room;
Crafts room; Laundry room.
Activities Arts & crafts; Cards; Games;
Reading groups; Prayer groups; Movies;
Shopping trips; Dances/Social/Cultural
gatherings; Intergenerational programs; Pet
therapy; Picnics; Gardening.

Greensboro

Greensboro Nursing Home
RR 1 Box 460, Cemetary Rd, Greensboro, VT
05841
(802) 533-7051
Admin David Yacovone. *Dir of Nursing* Ila
Hunt. *Medical Dir* Mark Lichenstein.
Licensure Intermediate care. *Beds* ICF 30.
Private Pay Patients 25%. *Certified*
Medicaid.
Owner Nonprofit organization/foundation.
Staff RNs 3 (pt); LPNs 3 (ft), 5 (pt); Nurses'
aides 12 (ft), 8 (pt); Physical therapists 1
(pt); Recreational therapists 1 (ft), 1 (pt);
Dietitians 1 (pt).
Facilities Dining room; Physical therapy
room; Activities room; Chapel; Crafts room;
Laundry room; Barber/Beauty shop; Library.
Activities Arts & crafts; Cards; Games;
Reading groups; Prayer groups; Movies;
Shopping trips; Dances/Social/Cultural
gatherings; Intergenerational programs; Pet
therapy.

Ludlow

Gill Odd Fellows Home
PO Box K, 8 Gill Terr, Ludlow, VT 05149
(802) 228-4571
Admin Joseph J Girouard. *Dir of Nursing*
Betty A Demers. *Medical Dir* Christopher
Allen.
Licensure Intermediate care; Residential care;
Apartment living. *Beds* ICF 52; Residential
care 10; Apartment living 24. *Private Pay
Patients* 50%. *Certified* Medicaid.
Owner Nonprofit organization/foundation.
Admissions Requirements Medical
examination; Physician's request.
Affiliation Independent Order of Odd Fellows
& Rebekahs.

Facilities Dining room; Physical therapy
room; Activities room; Crafts room; Laundry
room; Barber/Beauty shop.
Activities Arts & crafts; Cards; Games;
Reading groups; Prayer groups; Movies;
Shopping trips; Dances/Social/Cultural
gatherings; Intergenerational programs; Pet
therapy.

Lyndonville

Pine Knoll Nursing Home
RR 1 Box 94, Kirby Rd, Lyndonville, VT
05851
(802) 626-3361
Admin Francis E Cheney. *Dir of Nursing*
Nancy Bean.
Licensure Intermediate care. *Beds* ICF 52.

Middlebury

Helen Porter Nursing Home
South St, Middlebury, VT 05753
(802) 388-7901
Admin Susan J Bormolini. *Dir of Nursing*
Susan J Bormolini; Joan Dupree. *Medical
Dir* Dr Clark W Bryant.
Licensure Skilled care. *Beds* SNF 50. *Certified*
Medicare.
Owner Proprietary corp (Health One Health
Care).
Admissions Requirements Minimum age 21;
Medical examination; Physician's request.
Staff RNs 2 (ft), 12 (pt); LPNs 1 (ft), 5 (pt);
Nurses' aides 13 (ft), 18 (pt); Activities
coordinators 1 (ft); Dietitians 1 (ft).
Facilities Dining room; Activities room;
Barber/Beauty shop.
Activities Arts & crafts; Games; Reading
groups; Prayer groups; Movies; Dances/
Social/Cultural gatherings; Resident council.

Montpelier

Heaton House
Heaton St, Montpelier, VT 05602
(802) 223-3424
Admin Daria Mason. *Dir of Nursing* Sherry
Easterbrooks.
Licensure Skilled care. *Beds* SNF 61.

Morrisville

Manor Nursing Home
RR 3 Box 630, Morrisville, VT 05661
(802) 888-5201
Admin Lorraine A Comi. *Dir of Nursing*
Judith Deming. *Medical Dir* Lincoln Jacobs
MD.
Licensure Intermediate care. *Beds* ICF 50.
Owner Proprietary corp.
Admissions Requirements Medical
examination.
Staff RNs 3 (ft), 1 (pt); LPNs 2 (ft), 4 (pt);
Nurses' aides 20 (ft); Physical therapists 1
(pt); Activities coordinators 2 (pt); Dietitians
1 (pt).
Facilities Dining room; Activities room;
Chapel; Crafts room; Laundry room; Barber/
Beauty shop.
Activities Arts & crafts; Cards; Games;
Reading groups; Prayer groups; Movies;
Shopping trips; Dances/Social/Cultural
gatherings.

McKerley Health Care Center—Morrisville Inc
PO Box 960, Harrel St, Morrisville, VT 05661
(802) 888-3131
Admin Carolyn Smith. *Dir of Nursing* Debra
Pryme.
Licensure Intermediate care. *Beds* ICF 90.
Owner Proprietary corp (Beverly Enterprises).

Newport

Bel-Aire Quality Care Nursing Home
Bel-Aire Dr, Newport, VT 05855
(802) 334-2878
Admin Rose Mary Mayhew. *Dir of Nursing*
Joanne Massey RN. *Medical Dir* Dr Ferial
Barber.
Licensure Intermediate care; Assisted living.
Beds ICF 44; Assisted living 14. *Private Pay
Patients* 50%. *Certified* Medicaid.
Owner Proprietary corp (Northwestern Service
Corp).
Admissions Requirements Medical
examination.
Staff RNs 2 (ft); LPNs 5 (ft), 3 (pt); Nurses'
aides 10 (ft), 8 (pt); Physical therapists;
Activities coordinators 1 (ft); Dietitians.
Languages French.
Facilities Dining room; Activities room;
Barber/Beauty shop; Library; Outside
courtyards.
Activities Arts & crafts; Cards; Games;
Reading groups; Prayer groups; Movies;
Shopping trips; Dances/Social/Cultural
gatherings; Intergenerational programs; Pet
therapy; Monthly birthday parties; Special
events for all holidays.

Newport Health Care Center
RR 2, Box 123, Newport, VT 05855
(802) 334-7321
Admin David L Silver. *Dir of Nursing* Edna
Silver.
Licensure Skilled care; Intermediate care. *Beds*
SNF 25; ICF 35. *Certified* Medicare.
Owner Proprietary corp.
Admissions Requirements Minimum age 16.
Staff RNs 3 (ft), 2 (pt); LPNs 5 (ft), 5 (pt);
Nurses' aides 12 (ft), 12 (pt); Reality
therapists 1 (pt); Activities coordinators 1
(ft).
Facilities Dining room; Physical therapy
room; Activities room; Crafts room; Laundry
room; Barber/Beauty shop; Library.
Activities Arts & crafts; Games; Prayer groups;
Movies.

North Bennington

Prospect Nursing Home
34 Prospect St, North Bennington, VT 05257
(802) 447-7144
Admin Peter J Morris. *Dir of Nursing* Lillian
McNichol. *Medical Dir* Oliver Durand MD.
Licensure Intermediate care. *Beds* ICF 20.
Admissions Requirements Medical
examination.
Staff Physicians 1 (pt); RNs 1 (ft); LPNs 3
(ft); Nurses' aides 5 (ft); Physical therapists 1
(pt); Recreational therapists 1 (ft); Activities
coordinators 1 (ft); Dietitians 1 (pt).
Facilities Dining room; Activities room;
Chapel; Crafts room; Laundry room; Barber/
Beauty shop; Library.
Activities Arts & crafts; Games; Prayer groups;
Movies; Shopping trips.

Northfield

Mayo Memorial Nursing Home
1 Richardson Ave, Northfield, VT 05663
(802) 485-3161
Admin Lorraine R Day. *Dir of Nursing*
Maureen Bertrand. *Medical Dir* Dr Roger
Kellogg.
Licensure Skilled care; Intermediate care;
Retirement. *Beds* SNF 20; ICF 30.
Owner Nonprofit corp.
Admissions Requirements Medical
examination; Physician's request.
Staff Physicians 3 (pt); RNs 8 (ft); LPNs 2
(ft); Nurses' aides 20 (ft), 12 (pt); Physical
therapists 2 (pt); Recreational therapists 1
(ft); Speech therapists 1 (pt); Activities
coordinators 1 (pt); Dietitians 1 (pt);
Ophthalmologists 2 (pt).

Facilities Dining room; Physical therapy
room; Activities room; Crafts room; Laundry
room; Barber/Beauty shop; Library.
Activities Arts & crafts; Cards; Games;
Reading groups; Prayer groups; Movies;
Shopping trips; Dances/Social/Cultural
gatherings; Newspaper.

Randolph

Tranquility Nursing Home
50 Randolph Ave, Randolph, VT 05060
(802) 728-5607
Admin E Ingrid Anderson. *Dir of Nursing*
Mary K Wawrzyniak. *Medical Dir* Sandra
Patterson.
Licensure Intermediate care. *Beds* ICF 53.
Owner Proprietary corp.
Staff RNs 4 (ft); LPNs 3 (ft); Nurses' aides 20
(ft); Activities coordinators 1 (ft), 1 (pt);
Dietitians 1 (pt).
Facilities Dining room; Activities room;
Chapel; Crafts room; Laundry room; Barber/
Beauty shop.
Activities Arts & crafts; Cards; Games;
Reading groups; Prayer groups; Movies;
Shopping trips; Dances/Social/Cultural
gatherings.

Rutland

Eden Park Nursing Home of Rutland
99 Allen St, Rutland, VT 05701
(802) 775-2331
Admin Joan B Fletcher. *Dir of Nursing* Sandra
Hare.
Licensure Skilled care; Intermediate care. *Beds*
SNF 40; ICF 84. *Certified* Medicare.
Owner Proprietary corp (Eden Park
Management).

McKerley Health Care Center
9 Haywood Ave, Rutland, VT 05701
(802) 775-0007
Admin Susan J Salmon. *Dir of Nursing* Jane
Charron. *Medical Dir* Dr Gordon Smith.
Licensure Skilled care; Intermediate care. *Beds*
SNF 49; ICF 117. *Private Pay Patients* 20%.
Certified Medicaid; Medicare.
Owner Proprietary corp (McKerley Health
Care Inc).
Admissions Requirements Minimum age 18;
Medical examination; Physician's request.
Staff Physicians 1 (pt); RNs; LPNs; Nurses'
aides; Physical therapists 1 (ft); Recreational
therapists 1 (ft); Activities coordinators 2
(ft), 1 (pt); Dietitians 1 (pt).
Languages French, Italian.
Facilities Dining room; Physical therapy
room; Activities room; Barber/Beauty shop;
Library.
Activities Arts & crafts; Cards; Games;
Reading groups; Prayer groups; Movies;
Shopping trips; Dances/Social/Cultural
gatherings; Intergenerational programs; Pet
therapy.

Pleasant Manor Nursing Home
46 Nichols St, Rutland, VT 05701
(802) 775-2941
Admin Joanne Turnbell. *Dir of Nursing* Ann
Pollock.
Licensure Intermediate care. *Beds* ICF 119.

Vermont Achievement Center
88 Park St, Rutland, VT 05701
(802) 775-2395
Admin Faith Brothers. *Dir of Nursing* Judy
Fuller RN. *Medical Dir* P M Costello MD.
Licensure Skilled care. *Beds* SNF 20.
Owner Nonprofit corp.
Admissions Requirements Minimum age 0-21.
Staff Physicians 2 (pt); RNs 5 (ft), 7 (pt);
LPNs 1 (pt); Nurses' aides 12 (ft), 5 (pt);
Physical therapists 1 (ft); Occupational

therapists 1 (ft); Speech therapists 1 (pt);
Activities coordinators 1 (ft); Dietitians 1
(pt).
Facilities Dining room; Physical therapy
room; Activities room; Crafts room; Laundry
room; Library; Gym; School; Grass
playgrounds.
Activities Arts & crafts; Cards; Games;
Reading groups; Movies; Shopping trips;
Dances/Social/Cultural gatherings.

Saint Albans

Holiday House
RR 1 Box 79, Sheldon Rd, Saint Albans, VT
05478
(802) 524-2996
Admin Phillip H Condon. *Dir of Nursing*
Helen Hibbard.
Licensure Intermediate care. *Beds* ICF 64.

Redstone Villa
7 Forest Hill Dr, Saint Albans, VT 05478
(802) 524-3498
Admin Irene Witoski. *Dir of Nursing* Anna
Tisdale. *Medical Dir* Albert Brosseau MD.
Licensure Intermediate care. *Beds* ICF 30.
Admissions Requirements Medical
examination; Physician's request.
Staff Physicians 7 (ft); RNs 2 (ft); LPNs 4
(ft), 2 (pt); Nurses' aides 15 (ft), 6 (pt);
Reality therapists 1 (ft); Recreational
therapists 1 (ft); Activities coordinators 1
(ft); Dietitians 1 (ft).
Facilities Dining room; Laundry room;
Barber/Beauty shop.
Activities Arts & crafts; Games; Reading
groups; Prayer groups; Dances/Social/
Cultural gatherings.

VerDelle Village Inc
Box 80, Sheldon Rd, Saint Albans, VT 05478
(802) 524-6534
Admin Paul F Richards. *Dir of Nursing*
Phyllis Lucas RN. *Medical Dir* Frank J
Zsoldos MD.
Licensure Skilled care; Intermediate care. *Beds*
SNF 24; ICF 96. *Certified* Medicare.
Owner Proprietary corp.
Staff Physicians 3 (pt); RNs 6 (ft), 3 (pt);
LPNs 15 (ft), 6 (pt); Nurses' aides 60 (ft), 20
(pt); Physical therapists 1 (ft); Recreational
therapists 2 (ft); Occupational therapists 1
(pt); Speech therapists 1 (pt); Activities
coordinators 1 (pt); Dietitians 1 (ft);
Ophthalmologists 1 (pt).
Languages French.
Activities Arts & crafts; Cards; Games;
Reading groups; Prayer groups; Movies;
Shopping trips; Dances/Social/Cultural
gatherings.

Saint Johnsbury

St Johnsbury Convalescent Center
Hospital Dr, Saint Johnsbury, VT 05819
(802) 748-8757
Admin Florence Gauthier. *Dir of Nursing*
Mary Allen RN. *Medical Dir* shared
directorship.
Licensure Skilled care; Intermediate care. *Beds*
SNF 27; ICF 83. *Private Pay Patients* 45%.
Certified Medicaid; Medicare.
Owner Privately owned.
Staff Physicians 6 (ft); RNs 9 (ft); LPNs 14
(ft); Nurses' aides 35 (ft); Physical therapists
1 (ft); Speech therapists (contracted);
Activities coordinators 1 (ft); Dietitians
(consultant); Podiatrists (contracted).
Facilities Dining room; Physical therapy
room; Activities room; Chapel; Crafts room;
Laundry room; Barber/Beauty shop; Large
grounds; Child day care.

Activities Arts & crafts; Cards; Games; Reading groups; Prayer groups; Movies; Shopping trips; Dances/Social/Cultural gatherings; Intergenerational programs; Pet therapy; Private parties.

South Barre

Girouard St Jude Nursing Home
PO Box 300, South Barre, VT 05641
(802) 476-7442
Admin Normand E Girouard. *Dir of Nursing* Judith Libby.
Licensure Intermediate care. *Beds* ICF 36.
Admissions Requirements Medical examination.
Staff RNs 2 (ft), 2 (pt); LPNs 2 (ft), 4 (pt); Nurses' aides 10 (ft), 6 (pt); Activities coordinators.
Facilities Dining room; Activities room; Crafts room; Laundry room; 2 TV rooms.
Activities Arts & crafts; Cards; Games; Prayer groups; Movies; Shopping trips; Dances/ Social/Cultural gatherings.

Springfield

Hanson Court Convalescent Center
365 Summer St, Springfield, VT 05156
(802) 885-3408
Admin Stephen Main. *Dir of Nursing* Phyllis Peterson RN. *Medical Dir* Mark Hamilton MD.
Licensure Intermediate care. *Beds* ICF 42. *Private Pay Patients* 34%. *Certified* Medicaid.
Owner Proprietary corp.
Admissions Requirements Medical examination; Physician's request.
Staff RNs 1 (ft), 1 (pt); LPNs 4 (ft), 2 (pt); Nurses' aides 14 (ft), 4 (pt); Activities coordinators 1 (ft); Dietitians 1 (pt).
Facilities Dining room; Activities room; Barber/Beauty shop.
Activities Arts & crafts; Cards; Games; Reading groups; Prayer groups; Movies; Shopping trips; Dances/Social/Cultural gatherings; Intergenerational programs; Pet therapy; Grooming classes; Barbecues; Music.

Springfield Convalescent Center
105 Chester Rd, Springfield, VT 05156
(802) 885-5741
Admin Martha Chesley. *Dir of Nursing* Sue Rogstad. *Medical Dir* Mark Hamilton; Judith Trout.
Licensure Skilled care; Intermediate care; Adult day care. *Beds* SNF 26; ICF 76. *Certified* Medicare.
Owner Proprietary corp.
Admissions Requirements Physician's request.
Staff RNs 5 (ft), 3 (pt); LPNs 7 (ft), 8 (pt); Nurses' aides 34 (ft), 27 (pt); Physical therapists 1 (pt); Recreational therapists 1 (ft); Occupational therapists 1 (pt); Speech therapists 1 (pt); Activities coordinators 1 (ft); Dietitians 1 (pt).
Facilities Dining room; Physical therapy room; Activities room; Crafts room; Laundry room; Barber/Beauty shop; Library.
Activities Arts & crafts; Cards; Games; Reading groups; Prayer groups; Movies; Shopping trips; Dances/Social/Cultural gatherings; Cooking; Activities; Day care.

Townshend

Stratton House
PO Box 216, Townshend, VT 05353
(802) 365-7304
Admin Effie B Chamberlin. *Dir of Nursing* Richard Davis RN. *Medical Dir* Timothy Shafer MD.

Licensure Intermediate care; Retirement. *Beds* ICF 18. *Private Pay Patients* 20%. *Certified* Medicaid.
Owner Nonprofit organization/foundation.
Staff Physicians 3 (ft); RNs 1 (ft), 3 (pt); LPNs 8 (pt); Nurses' aides 3 (ft), 8 (pt); Physical therapists 2 (pt); Occupational therapists 1 (pt); Speech therapists 1 (pt); Activities coordinators 2 (ft); Dietitians 1 (pt).
Facilities Dining room; Physical therapy room; Activities room.
Activities Arts & crafts; Cards; Games; Reading groups; Prayer groups; Movies; Shopping trips; Dances/Social/Cultural gatherings; Intergenerational programs; Pet therapy; Van rides; Various outings; Fashion shows; Apple picking.

Vergennes

Clark Nursing Home
34 North St, Vergennes, VT 05491
(802) 877-3562
Admin Donald B Clark. *Dir of Nursing* Theresa Clark.
Licensure Intermediate care. *Beds* ICF 17.

Vernon

Vernon Green Nursing Home
Rte 142, Vernon, VT 05354
(802) 254-6041
Admin Lawrence B Knowles. *Dir of Nursing* Carol Puffer-Shippee. *Medical Dir* R Keith Clarke MD.
Licensure Skilled care; Intermediate care. *Beds* SNF 39; ICF 20. *Certified* Medicare.
Admissions Requirements Physician's request.
Staff RNs 3 (ft), 2 (pt); LPNs 3 (ft), 5 (pt); Nurses' aides 18 (ft), 8 (pt); Physical therapists 1 (pt); Occupational therapists 1 (pt); Speech therapists 1 (pt); Activities coordinators 1 (ft).
Facilities Dining room; Physical therapy room; Activities room; Chapel; Crafts room; Laundry room; Barber/Beauty shop; Library.
Activities Arts & crafts; Cards; Games; Reading groups; Prayer groups; Movies; Shopping trips; Dances/Social/Cultural gatherings.

Waterbury

Vermont State Nursing Home
103 S Main St, Waterbury, VT 05676
(802) 241-1000
Admin Claudia P Stone. *Dir of Nursing* Denise Hydok.
Licensure Intermediate care. *Beds* ICF 36.

White River Junction

Brookside of White River
PO Box 135 RR2, White River Junction, VT 05001
(802) 295-7511
Admin Thomas Rice. *Dir of Nursing* Joyce Potter RN. *Medical Dir* Royal Whitney MD.
Licensure Skilled care; Intermediate care. *Beds* SNF 40; ICF 120. *Certified* Medicaid; Medicare; VA.
Owner Proprietary corp (Brookside Nursing Home Inc).
Languages Spanish, French.
Activities Arts & crafts; Cards; Games; Reading groups; Prayer groups; Movies; Shopping trips; Dances/Social/Cultural gatherings; Intergenerational programs; Pet therapy.

Windsor

Cedar Hill Health Care Center
HCR 72 Box 93, Ascutney Blvd, Windsor, VT 05089
(802) 674-6609
Admin Mary Louise Horn. *Dir of Nursing* Judith B Brogren RN. *Medical Dir* Dale Gephart MD.
Licensure Intermediate care. *Beds* ICF 31. *Certified* Medicaid.
Owner Privately owned.
Admissions Requirements Minimum age 18; Medical examination; Physician's request.
Staff RNs 2 (pt); LPNs 1 (ft), 2 (pt); Nurses' aides 8 (ft), 4 (pt); Physical therapists; Activities coordinators; Dietitians; Social workers; Housekeepers 2 (ft); Cooks 1 (ft), 1 (pt); Diet aides 1 (ft), 1 (pt).
Facilities Dining room; Activities room; Laundry room; Barber/Beauty shop.
Activities Arts & crafts; Cards; Games; Reading groups; Prayer groups; Movies; Shopping trips; Dances/Social/Cultural gatherings; Intergenerational programs; Pet therapy; Rhythm band; Ceramics; Family involvement.

Cedar Manor Nursing Home Inc
Star Rte 1, Windsor, VT 05089
(802) 674-2050
Admin E Ingrid Anderson.
Medical Dir Dale Gephart MD.
Licensure Intermediate care. *Beds* 31. *Certified* Medicaid.
Admissions Requirements Minimum age 16; Medical examination.
Staff RNs 2 (ft), 1 (pt); LPNs 2 (ft), 3 (pt); Nurses' aides 9 (ft), 4 (pt).
Facilities Dining room; Laundry room; Gardens; Swimming pool; Large yard; Picnic area.
Activities Arts & crafts; Cards; Games; Reading groups; Prayer groups; Movies; Shopping trips; Dances/Social/Cultural gatherings; Swimming pool; Outdoor programs (picnics, games, walks); Educational programs; Exercise class; Gardening; Bird-watching.

Mt Ascutney Hospital & Health Center
RR 1 Box 6, County Rd, Windsor, VT 05089
(802) 674-6711, 674-5360 FAX
Admin Jeannette Lynch RN. *Dir of Nursing* Jeannette Lynch. *Medical Dir* Robert Wilson MD.
Licensure Skilled care. *Beds* SNF 32. *Certified* Medicaid; Medicare.
Owner Nonprofit organization/foundation.
Admissions Requirements Minimum age 16; Medical examination; Physician's request.
Staff Physicians; RNs; LPNs; Nurses' aides; Physical therapists; Occupational therapists; Speech therapists; Activities coordinators; Dietitians; Ophthalmologists; Podiatrists.
Facilities Dining room; Physical therapy room; Activities room; Crafts room; Laundry room; Barber/Beauty shop; Library.
Activities Arts & crafts; Cards; Games; Reading groups; Prayer groups; Movies; Shopping trips; Dances/Social/Cultural gatherings; Exercise; Current events; Horticulture; Painting; Bowling; Sing-alongs; Cooking programs; Contact with VT State Library.

Woodstock

Mertens House
73 River St, Woodstock, VT 05091
(802) 457-4411
Admin Elizabeth D Canning BS RN. *Dir of Nursing* Judith Jones RN. *Medical Dir* Steven Smith MD.
Licensure Intermediate care. *Beds* ICF 14. *Private Pay Patients* 100%.
Owner Nonprofit organization/foundation.

Admissions Requirements Minimum age 65 preferred; Medical examination.

Staff Physicians 1 (pt); RNs 1 (ft), 3 (pt); LPNs 1 (ft), 4 (pt); Nurses' aides 7 (ft), 3 (pt); Physical therapists 1 (pt); Occupational therapists 1 (pt); Speech therapists 1 (pt); Activities coordinators 1 (ft); Dietitians 1 (pt); Podiatrists 1 (pt); Dentists (consultant).

Facilities Dining room; Physical therapy room; Activities room; Crafts room; Laundry room; Barber/Beauty shop; Whirlpool bath; Private telephones; Cable TV; Private rooms with 1/2 baths.

Activities Arts & crafts; Cards; Games; Reading groups; Prayer groups; Movies; Dances/Social/Cultural gatherings; Pet therapy; Wine and tea socials; Bingo.

VIRGINIA

Abingdon

Cedar Lawn Convalescent Center
600 Walden Rd, Abingdon, VA 24210
(703) 628-2111
Admin Herman A Hogston. *Dir of Nursing*
Maureen Guckert. *Medical Dir* Dr J S
Shaffer.
Licensure Intermediate care. *Beds* ICF 120.
Private Pay Patients 68%. *Certified*
Medicaid.
Owner Privately owned.
Admissions Requirements Minimum age 14;
Medical examination.
Staff Physicians 4 (ft); RNs 1 (ft); LPNs 17
(ft); Nurses' aides 47 (ft); Physical therapists
1 (pt); Activities coordinators 1 (ft);
Dietitians 1 (pt).
Facilities Dining room; Activities room;
Chapel; Crafts room; Laundry room; Barber/
Beauty shop; Library.
Activities Arts & crafts; Cards; Games;
Reading groups; Prayer groups; Movies;
Dances/Social/Cultural gatherings; Pet
therapy.

Alexandria

Alexandria Residential Care Home
718 N Columbus, Alexandria, VA 22314
(703) 838-4243
Medical Dir Barbara Williams Admis.
Licensure Home for adults. *Beds* Home for
adults 10.

Dogwood Drive Home for Adults
1521 Dogwood Dr, Alexandria, VA 22302
(703) 836-5751
Medical Dir Charles Howard Admis.
Licensure Home for adults. *Beds* Home for
adults 7.

Goodwin House
4800 Fillmore Ave, Alexandria, VA 22311
(703) 578-1000, 824-1353 FAX
Admin James K Meharg Jr. *Dir of Nursing*
Robin O'Connell. *Medical Dir* James R
Brayshaw MD.
Licensure Skilled care; Intermediate care;
Retirement; Life care. *Beds* SNF 60; ICF 34;
Retirement 329; Life care 362. *Private Pay
Patients* 25%. *Certified* Medicaid; Medicare.
Owner Nonprofit organization/foundation.
Admissions Requirements Minimum age 65;
Medical examination; Physician's request.
Staff RNs 8 (ft), 11 (pt); LPNs 10 (ft), 6 (pt);
Nurses' aides 52 (ft), 13 (pt); Physical
therapists (contracted); Recreational
therapists 1 (ft); Occupational therapists
(contracted); Speech therapists (contracted);
Activities coordinators 1 (ft); Dietitians 1
(pt); Podiatrists 1 (pt).
Affiliation Episcopal.
Facilities Dining room; Physical therapy
room; Activities room; Chapel; Crafts room;
Laundry room; Barber/Beauty shop; Library.

Activities Arts & crafts; Cards; Games;
Reading groups; Prayer groups; Movies;
Shopping trips; Dances/Social/Cultural
gatherings; Intergenerational programs; Pet
therapy.

Hermitage in Northern Virginia
5000 Fairbanks Ave, Alexandria, VA 22311
(703) 820-2434, 820-1816 FAX
Admin Edwin G Burch. *Dir of Nursing* Helene
McHugh RN MSN. *Medical Dir* Dr Richard
Kelly.
Licensure Intermediate care; Independent
living. *Beds* ICF 109; Independent living
apts 225. *Private Pay Patients* 100%.
Owner Nonprofit corp (Virginia United
Methodist Homes Inc).
Admissions Requirements Minimum age 65;
Medical examination.
Staff RNs 10 (ft), 10 (pt); LPNs 9 (ft), 8 (pt);
Nurses' aides 53 (ft), 11 (pt); Activities
coordinators 2 (ft); Dietitians 1 (ft).
Affiliation United Methodist.
Facilities Dining room; Physical therapy
room; Activities room; Chapel; Crafts room;
Laundry room; Barber/Beauty shop; Library;
Auditorium; Solariums on each floor;
Penthouse.
Activities Arts & crafts; Cards; Games;
Reading groups; Prayer groups; Movies;
Shopping trips; Dances/Social/Cultural
gatherings; Intergenerational programs; Pet
therapy; Music programs.

Mt Vernon Nursing Center
8111 Tiswell Dr, Alexandria, VA 22306
(703) 360-4000, 780-5118 FAX
Admin Betty G Solomonson CNP. *Dir of
Nursing* Dorothy Bainter RN. *Medical Dir*
Scott Robson MD.
Licensure Intermediate care; Respite care;
Alzheimer's care. *Beds* ICF 130. *Private Pay
Patients* 52%. *Certified* Medicaid.
Owner Privately owned.
Staff Physicians 1 (pt); RNs 5 (ft), 2 (pt);
LPNs 8 (ft), 6 (pt); Nurses' aides 36 (ft), 11
(pt); Physical therapists 1 (pt); Occupational
therapists 1 (pt); Speech therapists 1 (pt);
Activities coordinators 2 (ft); Dietitians 1
(ft), 1 (pt); Podiatrists 1 (pt).
Languages Spanish, German.
Facilities Dining room; Physical therapy
room; Activities room; Crafts room; Barber/
Beauty shop; Library; Solariums; Conference
room.
Activities Arts & crafts; Cards; Games;
Reading groups; Prayer groups; Movies;
Shopping trips; Dances/Social/Cultural
gatherings; Intergenerational programs; Pet
therapy; Current events; Exercise programs;
Alzheimer's support group; Dining for
residents and guests.

Oak Meadow Nursing Center
1510 Collingwood Rd, Alexandria, VA 22308
(703) 765-6107
Admin Sandra L Reynolds. *Dir of Nursing*
Patsy McLaurin RN. *Medical Dir* Scott
Robson MD.

Licensure Skilled care; Intermediate care. *Beds*
SNF 31; ICF 65. *Certified* Medicaid;
Medicare.
Owner Proprietary corp (Health Care and
Retirement Corp).
Admissions Requirements Medical
examination.
Staff RNs 5 (ft), 3 (pt); LPNs 4 (ft), 5 (pt);
Nurses' aides 19 (ft), 31 (pt); Activities
coordinators 1 (ft), 1 (pt).
Languages Spanish.
Facilities Dining room; Physical therapy
room; Activities room; Chapel; Crafts room;
Laundry room; Barber/Beauty shop;
Dayrooms with TVs.
Activities Arts & crafts; Cards; Games;
Reading groups; Prayer groups; Movies;
Shopping trips; Dances/Social/Cultural
gatherings; Monthly lunch out.

Paul Spring Retirement Community
7116 Fort Hunt Rd, Alexandria, VA 22307
(703) 768-0234
Medical Dir Tracey Kane Admis.
Licensure Home for adults.

Taylor Run Group Home
1105 E Taylor Run Pkwy, Alexandria, VA
22314
(703) 838-4593
Admin Chuck Perso Div Dir for MR.
Licensure Intermediate care for mentally
retarded. *Beds* ICF/MR 7.

Washington House
5100 Fillmore Ave, Alexandria, VA 22311
(703) 379-9000
Admin Doris Sunday.
Medical Dir Dr Ronald Apter.
Licensure Private pay; Domiciliary care. *Beds*
Private pay 68; Domiciliary care 215.
Owner Nonprofit corp.
Admissions Requirements Medical
examination.
Staff Physicians 2 (pt); Physical therapists 2
(pt); Recreational therapists 1 (ft); Activities
coordinators 1 (ft); Dietitians 1 (pt);
Podiatrists 1 (pt); Dentists 1 (pt).

Woodbine Nursing & Convalescent Center
2729 King St, Alexandria, VA 22302
(703) 836-8838
Admin Vivian V Hewett.
Medical Dir Natalie Segal Admis.
Licensure Skilled care; Intermediate care;
Private pay. *Beds* SNF 70; ICF 186; Private
pay 51.
Owner Proprietary corp.

Altavista

Autumn Care of Altavista
1317 Lola Ave, Altavista, VA 24517
(804) 369-5161
Admin Nanci B Woody.
Licensure Skilled care; Intermediate care. *Beds*
SNF 10; ICF 50.
Owner Proprietary corp.

Amherst

Ryan Nursing Center
PO Box 590, Rte 60, Amherst, VA 24521
(804) 946-7781
Admin Claudette Canter.
Medical Dir Fay Cox.
Licensure Intermediate care. *Beds* ICF 51.
 Certified Medicaid.
Owner Proprietary corp.
Admissions Requirements Medical
 examination; Physician's request.
Staff RNs; LPNs; Nurses' aides; Recreational
 therapists; Activities coordinators.
Facilities Dining room; Physical therapy
 room; Activities room; Crafts room; Laundry
 room; Library.
Activities Arts & crafts; Cards; Games;
 Reading groups; Prayer groups; Movies;
 Dances/Social/Cultural gatherings.

Annandale

Leewood Nursing Home
7120 Braddock Rd, Annandale, VA 22003
(703) 256-9770
Admin Denny G Dennis. *Dir of Nursing*
 Joann Dawson RN. *Medical Dir* M Roy
 Nicholson MD.
Licensure Intermediate care; Home for adults;
 Adult day care. *Beds* ICF 132; Home for
 adults 44. *Certified* Medicaid.
Owner Privately owned.
Admissions Requirements Minimum age 16;
 Medical examination; Physician's request.
Staff Physicians; RNs; LPNs; Nurses' aides;
 Physical therapists; Recreational therapists;
 Occupational therapists; Speech therapists;
 Activities coordinators; Dietitians; Social
 workers.
Facilities Dining room; Physical therapy
 room; Activities room; Chapel; Barber/
 Beauty shop.
Activities Arts & crafts; Cards; Games;
 Reading groups; Prayer groups; Movies;
 Dances/Social/Cultural gatherings;
 Intergenerational programs; Pet therapy.

Sleepy Hollow Manor Nursing Home
6700 Columbia Pike, Annandale, VA 22003
(703) 256-7000
Admin Julia Huffman.
Medical Dir Marcia Matthias Admis.
Licensure Skilled care; Intermediate care. *Beds*
 SNF 20; ICF 210. *Certified* Medicaid;
 Medicare.
Owner Proprietary corp (Beverly Enterprises).

Appomattox

Appomattox Health Care Center
Rte 4 Box 800, Appomattox, VA 24522
(804) 352-7420
Admin T Michael Shelor. *Dir of Nursing* Leta
 Hunter RN. *Medical Dir* Dr Kenneth
 Powell; Dr A A Fratrick.
Licensure Skilled care; Intermediate care. *Beds*
 SNF 6; ICF 54. *Private Pay Patients* 25%.
 Certified Medicaid; Medicare.
Owner Proprietary corp (Medical Facilities of
 America).
Admissions Requirements Medical
 examination; Physician's request.
Staff RNs 2 (ft), 3 (pt); LPNs 3 (ft), 4 (pt);
 Nurses' aides 15 (ft), 20 (pt); Physical
 therapists; Activities coordinators 1 (ft);
 Dietitians.
Facilities Dining room; Physical therapy
 room; Activities room; Laundry room;
 Barber/Beauty shop.
Activities Arts & crafts; Cards; Games;
 Reading groups; Prayer groups; Movies;
 Shopping trips; Dances/Social/Cultural
 gatherings; Intergenerational programs; Pet
 therapy.

Arlington

Camelot Hall—Cherrydale
3710 Lee Hwy, Arlington, VA 22207
(703) 243-7640
Admin Robert D Fabian. *Dir of Nursing*
 Robert Spencer RN. *Medical Dir* Robert G
 Bullock MD.
Licensure Skilled care; Intermediate care. *Beds*
 SNF 10; ICF 230. *Certified* Medicaid;
 Medicare.
Owner Proprietary corp (Medical Facilities of
 America).
Admissions Requirements Medical
 examination.
Staff RNs 8 (ft), 8 (pt); LPNs 18 (ft), 2 (pt);
 Nurses' aides 71 (ft), 7 (pt); Physical
 therapists 1 (ft); Occupational therapists 1
 (ft); Speech therapists 1 (ft); Activities
 coordinators 1 (ft); Dietitians 1 (pt).
Facilities Dining room; Physical therapy
 room; Activities room; Chapel; Crafts room;
 Laundry room; Barber/Beauty shop.
Activities Arts & crafts; Cards; Games;
 Reading groups; Prayer groups; Movies;
 Shopping trips; Stroke support club;
 Reminiscing workshop.

Crystal City Nursing Center
1785 S Hayes St, Arlington, VA 22202
(703) 920-5700
Admin W J Delaney.
Medical Dir Myron Lenkon MD.
Licensure Skilled care; Intermediate care. *Beds*
 SNF 30; ICF 210. *Certified* Medicaid;
 Medicare.
Owner Proprietary corp (Genesis Health
 Ventures).
Admissions Requirements Minimum age 14;
 Medical examination; Physician's request.
Staff Physicians; RNs; LPNs; Nurses' aides;
 Physical therapists; Recreational therapists;
 Occupational therapists 1 (pt); Speech
 therapists 1 (ft); Activities coordinators 1
 (ft); Dietitians 2 (ft).
Facilities Dining room; Physical therapy
 room; Activities room; Chapel; Crafts room;
 Laundry room; Barber/Beauty shop.
Activities Arts & crafts; Cards; Games;
 Reading groups; Prayer groups; Movies;
 Shopping trips; Dances/Social/Cultural
 gatherings; Special events; Cherry Blossom
 Trip; Dining out in local restaurants.

Manor Care Nursing & Rehabilitation Center
550 S Carlin Springs Rd, Arlington, VA 22204
(703) 379-7200, 820-1048 FAX
Admin Kathryn A Heflin. *Dir of Nursing*
 Kathleen Beeman RN. *Medical Dir* James
 Ambury MD.
Licensure Skilled care; Intermediate care. *Beds*
 SNF 58; ICF 138. *Private Pay Patients* 65%.
 Certified Medicaid; Medicare.
Owner Proprietary corp (Manor Care Inc).
Admissions Requirements Minimum age 16;
 Medical examination; Physician's request.
Staff Physicians 1 (pt); RNs 11 (ft), 7 (pt);
 LPNs 14 (ft), 21 (pt); Nurses' aides 60 (ft),
 12 (pt); Physical therapists 3 (ft);
 Occupational therapists 1 (ft); Speech
 therapists 2 (ft); Dietitians 1 (pt); Podiatrists
 1 (pt); Audiologists 1 (pt); Recreational
 therapistsActivities coordinators 5 (ft).
Facilities Dining room; Physical therapy
 room; Activities room; Crafts room; Barber/
 Beauty shop; Head trauma and spinal cord
 injury unit.
Activities Arts & crafts; Cards; Games;
 Reading groups; Prayer groups; Movies;
 Shopping trips; Dances/Social/Cultural
 gatherings; Intergenerational programs; Pet
 therapy; Ballroom dancing; Family/Resident
 dinners.

North 16th Street Group Home
5563 N 16th St, Arlington, VA 22205
(703) 536-3248, 536-3411
Admin Laura Young PhD Clin Dir.
Licensure Intermediate care for mentally
 retarded. *Beds* ICF/MR 8.

Oak Springs
2000 S 5th St, Arlington, VA 22204
(703) 685-0606
Medical Dir M Davidson Admis.
Licensure Home for adults. *Beds* Home for
 adults 63.

Sunrise Retirement Home of Arlington
2000 N Glebe Rd, Arlington, VA 22207
(703) 524-5300
Medical Dir Jacqueline Reid Admis.
Licensure Home for adults. *Beds* Home for
 adults 50.

Aroda

Mountain View Nursing Home Inc
Star Rte 5 Box 186, Aroda, VA 22709
(703) 948-6831
Admin Eldon Hochstetler. *Dir of Nursing*
 Hilda Zook RN. *Medical Dir* William B
 Cave MD.
Licensure Intermediate care. *Beds* ICF 40.
 Certified Medicaid.
Owner Nonprofit corp.
Admissions Requirements Medical
 examination.
Staff Physicians 3 (pt); RNs 2 (ft), 2 (pt);
 LPNs 2 (ft); Nurses' aides 11 (ft); Activities
 coordinators 1 (ft); Dietitians 1 (ft).
Affiliation Mennonite.
Facilities Dining room; Activities room;
 Crafts room; Laundry room; Barber/Beauty
 shop.
Activities Arts & crafts; Games; Reading
 groups; Prayer groups; Movies; Shopping
 trips.

Ashland

Ashland Convalescent Center Inc
PO Box 2050, Rte 54 W, Ashland, VA 23005
(804) 798-3291
Admin Edward L Grubb.
Licensure Skilled care; Intermediate care. *Beds*
 SNF 25; ICF 155. *Certified* Medicaid;
 Medicare.
Owner Proprietary corp.

Bastian

George B Kegley Manor
Rte 1 Box 105, Bastian, VA 24314
(703) 688-4141
Admin Phillip Castleberg.
Licensure Skilled care; Intermediate care. *Beds*
 SNF 10; ICF 47.
Owner Proprietary corp.

Bedford

Bedford County Memorial Hospital—Oakwood Manor Nursing Home
1613 Oakwood St, Bedford, VA 24523
(703) 586-2441, 586-4342 FAX
Admin John H Fretz. *Dir of Nursing* Ardeth
 Hall RN. *Medical Dir* Brian Buchanan MD.
Licensure Skilled care; Intermediate care. *Beds*
 SNF 24; ICF 87. *Private Pay Patients* 14%.
 Certified Medicaid; Medicare.
Owner Nonprofit corp (Carilion Health
 System).
Admissions Requirements Medical
 examination; Physician's request.
Staff Physicians; RNs; LPNs; Nurses' aides;
 Activities coordinators; Dietitians.
Facilities Dining room; Physical therapy
 room; Activities room; Chapel; Crafts room;
 Barber/Beauty shop.
Activities Arts & crafts; Cards; Games;
 Reading groups; Prayer groups.

Bedford County Nursing Home
Rte 7 Box 70, Bedford, VA 24523
(703) 586-7658
Admin Janet S Beahm. *Dir of Nursing* Lou P
Brown RN. *Medical Dir* Village Family
Physicians.
Licensure Intermediate care. *Beds* ICF 56.
Private Pay Patients 25%. *Certified*
Medicaid.
Owner Publicly owned.
Staff RNs 1 (ft), 2 (pt); LPNs 4 (ft), 4 (pt);
Nurses' aides 16 (ft), 8 (pt); Physical
therapists 1 (pt); Activities coordinators 1
(ft); Dietitians 1 (pt).
Facilities Dining room; Activities room;
Chapel; Crafts room; Laundry room; Barber/
Beauty shop.
Activities Arts & crafts; Cards; Games;
Movies; Dances/Social/Cultural gatherings;
Pet therapy.

Berryville

Rose Hill Nursing Home
110 Chalmers Ct, Berryville, VA 22611
(703) 955-9995
Admin Joseph Lemon. *Dir of Nursing* Sylvia
Heishman RN.
Licensure Skilled care; Intermediate care. *Beds*
SNF 18; ICF 102. *Certified* Medicaid;
Medicare; VA.
Owner Proprietary corp (Beverly Enterprises).
Staff RNs; LPNs; Nurses' aides; Physical
therapists; Occupational therapists; Speech
therapists; Activities coordinators; Dietitians;
Ophthalmologists; Podiatrists; Dentists.
Facilities Dining room; Physical therapy
room; Activities room; Crafts room; Barber/
Beauty shop.
Activities Arts & crafts; Cards; Games; Prayer
groups; Movies; Shopping trips; Dances/
Social/Cultural gatherings.

Big Stone Gap

Heritage Hall Big Stone Gap
2045 Valley View Dr, Big Stone Gap, VA
24219
(703) 523-3000
Admin Pat H Stallard. *Dir of Nursing* Linda
Ramesy RN. *Medical Dir* Dr Lawrence
Fleenor.
Licensure Skilled care; Intermediate care. *Beds*
SNF 22; ICF 158. *Certified* Medicaid;
Medicare.
Owner Proprietary corp.
Admissions Requirements Minimum age 14;
Medical examination; Physician's request.
Staff Physicians 11 (ft); RNs 3 (ft), 2 (pt);
LPNs 21 (ft), 6 (pt); Nurses' aides 34 (ft), 32
(pt); Activities coordinators 1 (ft); Dietitians
1 (ft).
Facilities Dining room; Physical therapy
room; Activities room; Crafts room; Laundry
room; Barber/Beauty shop; Library.
Activities Arts & crafts; Games; Prayer groups;
Dances/Social/Cultural gatherings.

Blackstone

Heritage Hall Health Care
800 S Main St, Blackstone, VA 23824
(804) 292-5301
Admin Richard Scott. *Dir of Nursing* Betty
Pomfrey. *Medical Dir* Dr Stuart B White.
Licensure Intermediate care. *Beds* ICF 180.
Private Pay Patients 8%. *Certified* Medicaid;
Medicare.
Owner Proprietary corp (HCMF Corp).
Admissions Requirements Medical
examination; Physician's request.
Staff Physicians 3 (ft), 6 (pt); RNs 5 (ft);
LPNs 14 (ft), 3 (pt); Nurses' aides 58 (ft), 12
(pt); Physical therapists 1 (ft), 2 (pt); Reality

therapists 1 (pt); Occupational therapists 1
(pt); Activities coordinators 2 (ft); Dietitians
1 (pt); Podiatrists 1 (pt).
Facilities Dining room; Physical therapy
room; Activities room; Laundry room;
Barber/Beauty shop; 8 private and 86 semi-
private rooms.
Activities Arts & crafts; Games; Prayer groups;
Movies; Dances/Social/Cultural gatherings;
Residents council; Volunteer groups.

Bloxom

Bi-County Clinic & Nursing Home Inc
Rte 13, PO Box 85, Bloxom, VA 23308
(804) 665-5005
Admin Isaac S White.
Medical Dir Edward S White.
Beds 24.
Owner Proprietary corp.
Staff Physicians 2 (ft); RNs 1 (ft); LPNs 2 (ft),
2 (pt); Nurses' aides 6 (ft); Activities
coordinators 1 (pt); Dietitians 1 (pt);
Podiatrists 1 (pt); Dentists 1 (pt).
Facilities Dining room; Activities room.
Activities Games; Movies.

Bluefield

Westwood Health Care Center
307 Cumberland Rd, Bluefield, VA 24605
(703) 322-5439
Admin Nile Cutlip.
Licensure Skilled care; Intermediate care. *Beds*
SNF 12; ICF 44.
Owner Proprietary corp.

Bowling Green

Bowling Green Health Care Center
PO Box 967, 120 Anderson Ave, Bowling
Green, VA 22427
(804) 633-4839
Admin Laura N Sims. *Dir of Nursing* Betsy
MacDonald. *Medical Dir* Dr Stephen
Mandell; Dr David Kelly.
Licensure Intermediate care. *Beds* ICF 55.
Certified Medicaid.
Owner Proprietary corp (Medical Facilities of
America).
Admissions Requirements Medical
examination; Physician's request.
Staff RNs 1 (ft), 1 (pt); LPNs 5 (ft), 4 (pt);
Nurses' aides 12 (ft), 10 (pt); Physical
therapists 1 (pt); Recreational therapists 1
(ft); Activities coordinators 1 (ft); Dietitians
1 (pt).
Facilities Dining room; Physical therapy
room; Activities room; Barber/Beauty shop;
Private and semi-private rooms.
Activities Arts & crafts; Games; Reading
groups; Prayer groups; Movies; Shopping
trips; Pet therapy.

Bridgewater

Bridgewater Home Inc Health Care Unit
302 N 2nd St, Bridgewater, VA 22812-1799
(703) 828-2531
Admin John R Garber.
Licensure Intermediate care. *Beds* ICF 200.
Certified Medicaid.
Owner Nonprofit corp.
Admissions Requirements Minimum age 14;
Medical examination; Physician's request.
Staff RNs 11 (ft), 16 (pt); LPNs 7 (ft), 5 (pt);
Physical therapists 1 (pt); Speech therapists
1 (pt); Activities coordinators 1 (ft);
Dietitians 1 (pt); Audiologists 1 (pt).
Affiliation Church of the Brethren.
Facilities Dining room; Physical therapy
room; Activities room; Chapel; Crafts room;
Laundry room; Barber/Beauty shop; Library.
Activities Arts & crafts; Cards; Games;
Reading groups; Prayer groups; Movies;
Shopping trips.

Bristol

Bristol Health Care Center
245 North St, Bristol, VA 24201
(703) 669-4711
Admin William D Bishop. *Dir of Nursing*
Betty Carrier RN. *Medical Dir* Fred Greear
MD.
Licensure Skilled care; Intermediate care. *Beds*
SNF 30; ICF 90. *Private Pay Patients* 30%.
Certified Medicaid; Medicare.
Owner Proprietary corp (National Health
Corp).
Admissions Requirements Minimum age 14;
Physician's request.
Staff RNs 7 (ft), 4 (pt); LPNs 18 (ft), 5 (pt);
Nurses' aides 44 (ft), 2 (pt); Physical
therapists 1 (ft); Occupational therapists 1
(pt); Speech therapists 1 (pt); Activities
coordinators 1 (ft); Dietitians 1 (ft).
Facilities Dining room; Physical therapy
room; Activities room; Crafts room; Laundry
room; Barber/Beauty shop; Family rooms;
Dayrooms.
Activities Arts & crafts; Games; Reading
groups; Prayer groups; Movies; Shopping
trips; Dances/Social/Cultural gatherings; Pet
therapy.

Memorial Hall—Bristol Memorial Hospital
North St, Bristol, VA 24201
(615) 968-1121
Admin W W Fanning.
Licensure Skilled care. *Beds* 40. *Certified*
Medicaid; Medicare.
Owner Nonprofit corp.

Buena Vista

Shenandoah Valley Health Care Center
PO Box 711, 3737 Catalpa Ave, Buena Vista,
VA 24416
(703) 261-7444
Admin Judy Knecht.
Licensure Skilled care; Intermediate care. *Beds*
SNF 13; ICF 80.
Owner Proprietary corp.

Burkeville

Piedmont Geriatric Hospital
Burkeville, VA 23922
(804) 767-4401
Admin Willard R Pierce Jr Dir.
Licensure Intermediate care for mentally
retarded. *Beds* LTC 290.

Catawba

Catawba Hospital
PO Box 200, Catawba, VA 24070
(703) 387-1157
Admin R Michael Marsh PhD Dir.
Licensure Intermediate care for mentally
retarded. *Beds* Long-term care 250; IPT 40.

Charlottesville

Cedars Nursing Home
1242 Cedars Ct, Charlottesville, VA 22901-
3684
(804) 296-5611
Admin Dave Paul. *Dir of Nursing* Barbara
Gruber RN. *Medical Dir* Dr David Chester.
Licensure Skilled care; Intermediate care. *Beds*
SNF 14; ICF 129. *Certified* Medicaid;
Medicare.
Owner Proprietary corp (Beverly Enterprises).
Admissions Requirements Minimum age 14.
Staff RNs 10 (ft), 4 (pt); LPNs 12 (ft), 4 (pt);
Nurses' aides 59 (ft), 1 (pt); Physical
therapists 1 (ft); Occupational therapists 1
(ft); Speech therapists 1 (ft); Activities
coordinators 2 (ft); Dietitians 1 (ft).

Activities Arts & crafts; Cards; Games;
Reading groups; Prayer groups; Movies;
Shopping trips; Dances/Social/Cultural
gatherings.

Eldercare Gardens
1150 Northwest Dr, Charlottesville, VA 22901
(804) 973-7933
Admin Larry M Lucas. *Dir of Nursing* Allene
Brighton RN. *Medical Dir* Dr William
Tompkins.
Licensure Skilled care; Intermediate care. *Beds*
SNF 60; ICF 120. *Certified* Medicaid;
Medicare; VA.
Owner Proprietary corp.
Admissions Requirements Medical
examination; Physician's request.
Facilities Dining room; Physical therapy
room; Activities room; Crafts room; Laundry
room; Barber/Beauty shop; Library.
Activities Arts & crafts; Cards; Games;
Reading groups; Prayer groups; Movies;
Shopping trips; Dances/Social/Cultural
gatherings.

Heritage Hall—Charlottesville
505 W Rio Rd, Charlottesville, VA 22901
(804) 978-7015
Admin Richard C Baker.
Licensure Skilled care; Intermediate care. *Beds*
SNF 12; ICF 108.
Owner Proprietary corp.

**Martha Jefferson House Infirmary Health Care
Unit**
1600 Gordon Ave, Charlottesville, VA 22903
(804) 293-6136
Admin Marie J Groh.
Licensure Private pay. *Beds* Private pay 34.
Owner Nonprofit corp.

Paul Victorious House
515 Park St, Charlottesville, VA 22901
(804) 295-0692
Admin John Pezzoli Dir.
Licensure Intermediate care for mentally
retarded. *Beds* ICF/MR 8.

**Piedmont Health Care Center—Health Care
Unit**
PO Box 3815, 1214 Jefferson Park Ave,
Charlottesville, VA 22903
(804) 295-1161
Admin Pamela E Doshier.
Medical Dir Dr Joseph May.
Licensure Intermediate care. *Beds* ICF 173.
Certified Medicaid.
Owner Proprietary corp (National Healthcare
Affiliates Inc).
Admissions Requirements Medical
examination; Physician's request.
Facilities Dining room; Physical therapy
room; Activities room; Chapel; Crafts room;
Laundry room; Barber/Beauty shop; Library.
Activities Arts & crafts; Cards; Games;
Reading groups; Prayer groups; Movies;
Dances/Social/Cultural gatherings.

Chesapeake

Autumn Care of Chesapeake
PO Box 13780, 2701 Border Rd, Chesapeake,
VA 23325
(804) 545-2487, 545-5267 FAX
Admin Juanita L Snell. *Dir of Nursing* Carol
Rampale RN. *Medical Dir* Dr Rudolph
Schuster.
Licensure Intermediate care. *Beds* ICF 54.
Certified Medicaid.
Owner Proprietary corp (Autumn Corp).
Admissions Requirements Minimum age 18;
Medical examination; Physician's request.
Staff RNs 1 (ft); LPNs 3 (ft), 2 (pt); Nurses'
aides 21 (ft), 5 (pt); Recreational therapists 1
(ft); Dietitians 1 (ft).
Facilities Dining room; Activities room;
Crafts room; Laundry room; Barber/Beauty
shop.

Activities Arts & crafts; Cards; Games;
Reading groups; Prayer groups; Movies;
Shopping trips; Pet therapy.

Autumn Care of Great Bridge
PO Box 15224, 821 Cedar Rd, Chesapeake,
VA 23320
(804) 547-4528
Admin Delores G Dickinson.
Licensure Intermediate care. *Beds* ICF 55.
Certified Medicaid.
Owner Proprietary corp (Autumn Corp).

Brent-Lox Hall Nursing Center
1017 George Washington Hwy, Chesapeake,
VA 23323
(804) 485-5500
Admin Kelly A Thornton. *Dir of Nursing*
Marite Pelverts RN. *Medical Dir* Jonathan
Marven MD.
Licensure Intermediate care. *Beds* ICF 120.
Certified Medicaid.
Owner Proprietary corp (Libbie Rehabilitation
Centers Inc).
Admissions Requirements Medical
examination; Physician's request.
Staff Physicians (consultant); RNs 2 (ft); LPNs
12 (ft), 2 (pt); Nurses' aides 40 (ft), 3 (pt);
Physical therapists 2 (pt); Recreational
therapists 1 (ft); Occupational therapists 1
(pt); Speech therapists 1 (pt); Dietitians 1
(pt); Podiatrists 1 (pt).
Facilities Dining room; Physical therapy
room; Activities room; Crafts room; Laundry
room; Barber/Beauty shop; Smoking room.
Activities Arts & crafts; Cards; Games;
Reading groups; Prayer groups; Movies;
Dances/Social/Cultural gatherings; Pet
therapy.

Camelot Hall Nursing Home
688 Kingsborough Sq, Chesapeake, VA 23320
(804) 547-9111
Admin Jay L Underwood.
Licensure Skilled care; Intermediate care. *Beds*
SNF 10; ICF 230. *Certified* Medicaid;
Medicare.
Owner Proprietary corp (Medical Facilities of
America).
Admissions Requirements Minimum age 16;
Medical examination; Physician's request.
Staff Physicians; RNs; LPNs; Nurses' aides;
Physical therapists; Recreational therapists;
Speech therapists; Activities coordinators;
Dietitians; Ophthalmologists.
Facilities Dining room; Physical therapy
room; Activities room; Chapel; Crafts room;
Laundry room; Barber/Beauty shop; Library.
Activities Arts & crafts; Cards; Games;
Reading groups; Prayer groups; Movies;
Shopping trips; Dances/Social/Cultural
gatherings.

Sentara Nursing Center—Chesapeake
PO Box 1277, 776 Oak Grove Rd,
Chesapeake, VA 23320
(804) 547-5156, 548-0119 FAX
Admin Jeffrey D Custer. *Dir of Nursing* Sonia
Dansenco. *Medical Dir* L Jonathan Marven
MD.
Licensure Intermediate care; Retirement. *Beds*
ICF 120; Retirement 61. *Private Pay
Patients* 21%. *Certified* Medicaid.
Owner Nonprofit organization/foundation.
Admissions Requirements Minimum age 18;
Medical examination; Physician's request.
Staff Physicians 6 (pt); RNs 2 (ft); LPNs 16
(ft), 4 (pt); Nurses' aides 46 (ft); Physical
therapists (contracted); Reality therapists
(contracted); Recreational therapists 2 (ft);
Occupational therapists (contracted); Speech
therapists (contracted); Activities
coordinators 1 (ft); Dietitians 1 (pt);
Ophthalmologists (contracted); Podiatrists
(contracted); Audiologists (contracted).

Facilities Dining room; Activities room;
Barber/Beauty shop.
Activities Arts & crafts; Cards; Games;
Reading groups; Prayer groups; Movies;
Shopping trips; Dances/Social/Cultural
gatherings; Intergenerational programs; Pet
therapy.

Southeastern Virginia Training Center
2100 Steppingstone Sq, Chesapeake, VA
23320
(804) 424-8240
Admin Robert D Shrewsberry PhD Dir.
Licensure Intermediate care for mentally
retarded. *Beds* ICF/MR 200.

Chesterfield

Chesterfield County Lucy Corr Nursing Home
PO Drawer 170, 6800 Lucy Corr Ct,
Chesterfield, VA 23832
(804) 748-1511
Admin Jacob W Mast Jr. *Dir of Nursing*
Susan Phalen RN. *Medical Dir* Scott
Woogen MD.
Licensure Skilled care; Intermediate care;
Alzheimer's unit; Adult day care. *Beds* SNF
30; ICF 164. *Private Pay Patients* 47%.
Certified Medicaid; Medicare.
Owner Publicly owned.
Admissions Requirements Medical
examination.
Staff Physicians 4 (pt); Physical therapists 1
(ft), 1 (pt); Occupational therapists 1 (ft);
Speech therapists (contracted); Activities
coordinators 1 (ft); Dietitians 1 (ft);
Podiatrists 1 (pt).
Facilities Dining room; Physical therapy
room; Activities room; Crafts room; Laundry
room; Barber/Beauty shop.
Activities Arts & crafts; Cards; Games;
Reading groups; Prayer groups; Movies;
Shopping trips; Dances/Social/Cultural
gatherings; Intergenerational programs; Pet
therapy; Camping; Kings Dominion; Fishing.

Chilhowie

Valley Health Care Center
PO Box 746, Hwy 11 & Pine St, Chilhowie,
VA 24319
(703) 646-8911
Admin Douglas R Wright.
Medical Dir William N Greever MD.
Licensure Skilled care; Intermediate care;
Residential home for adults. *Beds* SNF 20;
ICF 160; Home for adults 27. *Certified*
Medicaid; Medicare.
Owner Proprietary corp (Convalescent Care
Inc).
Admissions Requirements Medical
examination.
Staff RNs 6 (ft), 5 (pt); LPNs 20 (ft), 2 (pt);
Nurses' aides 48 (ft), 4 (pt); Activities
coordinators 2 (ft).
Facilities Dining room; Physical therapy
room; Activities room; Laundry room;
Barber/Beauty shop.
Activities Arts & crafts; Cards; Games;
Reading groups; Prayer groups; Movies;
Dances/Social/Cultural gatherings; Ceramics.

Clifton Forge

Liberty House Nursing Home
PO Box 167, Rte 60 E, Clifton Forge, VA
24422
(703) 862-5791
Admin Mae S Tucker.
Medical Dir Dr R S Goings.
Licensure Skilled care; Intermediate care. *Beds*
SNF 20; ICF 30. *Certified* Medicaid.
Owner Proprietary corp (Beverly Enterprises).
Admissions Requirements Medical
examination; Physician's request.

Staff Physicians 1 (pt); RNs 9 (ft); LPNs 7 (ft); Physical therapists 1 (pt); Activities coordinators 1 (ft); Dietitians 1 (pt); Podiatrists 1 (pt); Dentists 1 (pt).
Facilities Dining room; Physical therapy room; Activities room; Chapel; Crafts room; Laundry room; Barber/Beauty shop; Library.
Activities Arts & crafts; Games; Movies; Shopping trips; Dances/Social/Cultural gatherings.

Shenandoah Manor Nursing Home
PO Drawer 603, Fairview Heights, Clifton Forge, VA 24426
(703) 863-4096
Admin James Clowser. *Dir of Nursing* Carol B Andrews. *Medical Dir* Raymond Claterbaugh.
Licensure Intermediate care; Retirement. *Beds* ICF 60; Retirement 30. *Private Pay Patients* 50%. *Certified* Medicaid; Medicare.
Owner Proprietary corp.
Staff Physicians 1 (ft); RNs 2 (ft), 2 (pt); LPNs 4 (ft), 3 (pt); Nurses' aides 19 (ft), 8 (pt); Physical therapists (consultant); Activities coordinators 1 (ft); Dietitians 1 (ft).
Facilities Dining room; Physical therapy room; Activities room; Laundry room; Barber/Beauty shop; Large dining room; Visitors lounge.
Activities Arts & crafts; Cards; Games; Reading groups; Prayer groups; Movies; Shopping trips; Dances/Social/Cultural gatherings; Music.

Clintwood

Heritage Hall—Clintwood
Rte 607 Box 909, Clintwood, VA 24228
(703) 926-4693
Admin John R Vance. *Dir of Nursing* Glenna (Ginger) Kennedy. *Medical Dir* Ram Singh MD.
Licensure Intermediate care. *Beds* ICF 100. *Private Pay Patients* 2%. *Certified* Medicaid.
Owner Proprietary corp (HCMF Corp).
Admissions Requirements Minimum age 14; Medical examination; Physician's request.
Staff Physicians 1 (pt); RNs 1 (ft), 1 (pt); LPNs 7 (ft), 4 (pt); Nurses' aides 24 (ft), 5 (pt); Physical therapists 1 (pt); Reality therapists 1 (pt); Recreational therapists 1 (ft); Speech therapists 1 (pt); Activities coordinators 1 (ft); Dietitians 1 (pt); Ophthalmologists 2 (pt); Podiatrists 1 (pt); Audiologists 1 (pt).
Facilities Dining room; Physical therapy room; Activities room; Crafts room; Laundry room; Barber/Beauty shop; Courtyard with rose garden.
Activities Arts & crafts; Cards; Games; Reading groups; Prayer groups; Movies; Shopping trips; Dances/Social/Cultural gatherings; Intergenerational programs; Pet therapy.

Colonial Heights

Colonial Heights Convalescent Center
831 E Ellerslie Ave, Colonial Heights, VA 23834
(804) 526-6851
Admin Anne B McDaniel. *Dir of Nursing* Martha Mabe. *Medical Dir* Dr Scott Knowles.
Licensure Skilled care; Intermediate care. *Beds* SNF 24; ICF 172. *Certified* Medicaid; Medicare.
Owner Proprietary corp (Convalescent Care Inc).
Admissions Requirements Medical examination; Physician's request.
Staff Physicians 20 (pt); RNs 8 (ft), 1 (pt); LPNs 18 (ft), 8 (pt); Nurses' aides 86 (ft), 5 (pt); Physical therapists 1 (pt); Recreational therapists 1 (ft); Occupational therapists 1

(pt); Speech therapists 1 (pt); Activities coordinators 2 (ft); Dietitians 1 (pt); Ophthalmologists 1 (pt); Podiatrists 1 (pt); Audiologists 1 (pt).
Facilities Dining room; Physical therapy room; Activities room; Crafts room; Laundry room; Barber/Beauty shop; Library; Lounges; 2 outside courtyards; 4 dayrooms.
Activities Arts & crafts; Cards; Games; Reading groups; Prayer groups; Movies; Shopping trips; Dances/Social/Cultural gatherings; Intergenerational programs; Pet therapy; Resident council; Ceramics.

Culpeper

Culpeper Baptist Retirement Community—Dorothy Finney Health Care Unit
PO Box 191, Culpeper, VA 22701
(703) 825-2411
Admin R Stephen McElmurray.
Medical Dir Evelyn B Cunningham.
Licensure Intermediate care. *Beds* ICF 47.
Owner Nonprofit corp.
Admissions Requirements Minimum age 65; Medical examination.
Staff Physicians 1 (pt); RNs 2 (ft), 3 (pt); LPNs 8 (ft), 1 (pt); Nurses' aides 22 (ft), 16 (pt); Activities coordinators 1 (ft); Dietitians 1 (pt); Ophthalmologists 1 (pt).
Affiliation Baptist.
Facilities Dining room; Activities room; Chapel; Crafts room; Laundry room; Barber/ Beauty shop; Library.
Activities Arts & crafts; Cards; Games; Reading groups; Prayer groups; Shopping trips; Dances/Social/Cultural gatherings.

Culpeper Health Care Center
602 Madison Rd, Culpeper, VA 22701
(703) 825-2884
Admin Paul Clements.
Licensure Intermediate care. *Beds* ICF 180.
Owner Proprietary corp.

Danville

Camelot Hall Nursing Home
450 Piney Forest Rd, Danville, VA 24540
(804) 799-1565
Admin Robert A Giannini. *Dir of Nursing* Deborah Hawkins RN. *Medical Dir* Dr Vincent Falgui; Dr Thomas Alabanza.
Licensure Skilled care; Intermediate care. *Beds* SNF 14; ICF 106. *Certified* Medicaid; Medicare.
Owner Proprietary corp (Medical Facilities of America).
Admissions Requirements Minimum age 14; Medical examination; Physician's request.
Staff Physicians 21 (pt); RNs 5 (ft), 4 (pt); LPNs 11 (ft), 7 (pt); Nurses' aides 32 (ft), 19 (pt); Physical therapists 1 (pt); Occupational therapists 1 (pt); Speech therapists 1 (pt); Activities coordinators 1 (ft); Dietitians 1 (pt); Podiatrists 1 (pt).
Facilities Dining room; Physical therapy room; Activities room; Laundry room; Barber/Beauty shop; Dayrooms.
Activities Arts & crafts; Games; Reading groups; Prayer groups; Movies; Shopping trips; Dances/Social/Cultural gatherings; Intergenerational programs; Pet therapy.

Memorial Hospital of Danville Long-Term Care Unit
142 S Main St, Danville, VA 24541
(804) 799-3700
Admin Hunter A Grumbles Pres.
Licensure Skilled care. *Beds* SNF 46.
Owner Nonprofit corp.

Riverside Health Care Center
2344 Riverside Dr, Danville, VA 24540
(804) 791-3800
Admin Dan E Dailey.

Licensure Intermediate care. *Beds* ICF 180. *Certified* Medicare.
Owner Proprietary corp (Medical Facilities of America).

Roman Eagle Memorial Home Inc
2526 N Main St, Danville, VA 24540
(804) 793-0111
Admin Dan R Setliff.
Medical Dir G V Thompson Jr.
Licensure Skilled care; Intermediate care. *Beds* SNF 48; ICF 264. *Certified* Medicaid; Medicare.
Owner Nonprofit corp.
Admissions Requirements Medical examination; Physician's request.
Staff RNs 12 (ft), 4 (pt); LPNs 24 (ft), 12 (pt); Nurses' aides 112 (ft), 27 (pt); Physical therapists 1 (pt); Speech therapists 1 (pt); Activities coordinators 3 (ft); Dietitians 1 (ft).
Facilities Dining room; Physical therapy room; Activities room; Chapel; Crafts room; Laundry room; Barber/Beauty shop; Library; Pharmacy; Speech therapy room.
Activities Arts & crafts; Cards; Games; Reading groups; Prayer groups; Movies; Shopping trips.

Southern Virginia Mental Health Institute
382 Taylor Dr, Danville, VA 24541
(804) 799-6220
Admin Constance N Fletcher PhD Dir.
Licensure Intermediate care for mentally retarded. *Beds* IPT 96.

Dillwyn

Heritage Hall
9 Brickyard Dr, Dillwyn, VA 23936
(804) 983-2058
Admin Nancy H Downey. *Dir of Nursing* Marjorie R Dixon. *Medical Dir* Dr Irving Epperson.
Licensure Intermediate care. *Beds* ICF 60. *Private Pay Patients* 3%. *Certified* Medicaid.
Owner Proprietary corp (HCMF Corp).
Admissions Requirements Medical examination; Physician's request.
Staff RNs 2 (ft); LPNs 6 (ft), 3 (pt); Nurses' aides 9 (ft), 13 (pt); Activities coordinators 1 (ft); Dietitians 1 (pt); Podiatrists 1 (pt).
Facilities Dining room; Physical therapy room; Crafts room; Laundry room; Barber/ Beauty shop.
Activities Arts & crafts; Cards; Games; Reading groups; Prayer groups; Movies; Shopping trips; Dances/Social/Cultural gatherings; Intergenerational programs.

Dryden

Carter Hall Nursing Home
PO Box 59, Alt Rte 58, Dryden, VA 24243
(703) 546-4114
Admin Dennis E Bowen.
Licensure Intermediate care. *Beds* ICF 50. *Certified* Medicaid.
Owner Proprietary corp (Beverly Enterprises).

Dublin

Highland Manor Nursing Home
PO Box 1087, Hanks St, Dublin, VA 24084
(703) 674-4193
Admin Irene L Seeley.
Medical Dir James L Patterson Jr MD.
Licensure Intermediate care; Alzheimer's care. *Beds* ICF 132. *Certified* Medicaid.
Owner Proprietary corp.
Admissions Requirements Minimum age 18; Medical examination; Physician's request.
Staff Physicians 6 (ft); RNs 3 (ft); LPNs 16 (ft), 1 (pt); Nurses' aides 39 (ft), 3 (pt); Physical therapists 1 (ft), 1 (pt); Recreational

therapists 1 (ft); Speech therapists 2 (pt); Dietitians 1 (ft), 1 (pt); Ophthalmologists 1 (pt); Podiatrists 1 (pt).
Facilities Dining room; Physical therapy room; Activities room; Crafts room; Barber/Beauty shop; Library; Dayrooms; Enclosed outside courts; Laboratory; Whirlpool baths; Wheelchair lift bus; Walking trails.
Activities Arts & crafts; Cards; Games; Reading groups; Prayer groups; Movies; Shopping trips; Dances/Social/Cultural gatherings; Intergenerational programs; Pet therapy; Picnics; Planned outings; Birthday parties; Coffee groups; Fishing trips; Exercise classes; Monthly newspaper published; Resident council; Current events groups; Bingo; Mini productions.

Duffield

Ridgecrest Manor Nursing Home
PO Box 280, Thomas Village, Duffield, VA 24244
(703) 431-2841
Admin Jim R Daugherty.
Licensure Skilled care; Intermediate care. *Beds* SNF 30; ICF 90. *Certified* Medicare.
Owner Proprietary corp (Beverly Enterprises).

Dunn Loring

Iliff Nursing Home
8000 Iliff Dr, Dunn Loring, VA 22027
(703) 560-1000
Admin Ruth M Peterson. *Dir of Nursing* Barbara Arnold. *Medical Dir* Otto Kurz MD.
Licensure Intermediate care; Skilled care for pediatrics. *Beds* SNF 10; ICF 120. *Certified* Medicaid.
Owner Proprietary corp (Continental Medical Systems).
Admissions Requirements Medical examination.
Staff Physicians; RNs 9 (ft); LPNs 6 (ft); Nurses' aides 33 (ft); Physical therapists 1 (ft); Recreational therapists 1 (ft); Occupational therapists 1 (pt); Speech therapists 1 (pt); Dietitians 1 (pt); Podiatrists 1 (pt).
Facilities Dining room; Physical therapy room; Activities room; Chapel; Crafts room; Laundry room; Barber/Beauty shop; Library; Child day care.
Activities Arts & crafts; Cards; Games; Reading groups; Prayer groups; Movies; Shopping trips; Dances/Social/Cultural gatherings; Intergenerational programs; Pet therapy.

Emporia

Avis B Adams Christian Convalescent Center
200 Weaver Ave, Emporia, VA 23847
(804) 634-6581
Admin Janet C White. *Dir of Nursing* Sandra C Matthews RN. *Medical Dir* Dr James A Kirkland.
Licensure Intermediate care; ACF. *Beds* ICF 120; ACF 10. *Private Pay Patients* 20%. *Certified* Medicaid.
Owner Proprietary corp (PKR Convalescent Centers).
Admissions Requirements Minimum age 18; Medical examination; Physician's request.
Staff Physicians 1 (pt); RNs 1 (ft); LPNs 10 (ft), 2 (pt); Nurses' aides 28 (ft), 26 (pt); Physical therapists (consultant); Speech therapists (consultant); Activities coordinators 1 (ft); Dietitians (consultant); Podiatrists (consultant).
Facilities Dining room; Physical therapy room; Activities room; Chapel; Crafts room; Laundry room; Barber/Beauty shop.

Activities Arts & crafts; Cards; Games; Reading groups; Prayer groups; Movies; Shopping trips; Intergenerational programs; Pet therapy.

Fairfax

Commonwealth Care Center
4315 Chain Bridge Rd, Fairfax, VA 22030
(703) 934-5000
Admin Joan H Bishop.
Medical Dir Paula Macerollo Admis.
Licensure Skilled care; Intermediate care. *Beds* SNF 24; ICF 96. *Certified* Medicaid; Medicare.
Owner Nonprofit corp.

Fairfax Nursing Center
10701 Main St, Fairfax, VA 22030
(703) 273-7705, 273-8077 FAX
Admin Renee Houle. *Dir of Nursing* Beth Kleb RN. *Medical Dir* Dr Alan Machintosh.
Licensure Skilled care; Intermediate care; Retirement; Respite care; Alzheimer's care. *Beds* SNF 24; ICF 176; Retirement 48. *Private Pay Patients* 80%. *Certified* Medicaid; Medicare.
Owner Proprietary corp (Robert Bainum).
Admissions Requirements Medical examination; Physician's request.
Staff RNs 12 (ft), 20 (pt); LPNs 20 (ft), 12 (pt); Nurses' aides 20 (ft), 12 (pt); Physical therapists 3 (ft); Recreational therapists 6 (ft); Occupational therapists 1 (ft); Speech therapists 1 (pt); Activities coordinators 1 (ft); Dietitians 3 (ft); Podiatrists 1 (pt); Chaplains 1 (ft).
Facilities Dining room; Physical therapy room; Activities room; Chapel; Crafts room; Laundry room; Barber/Beauty shop; Patio.
Activities Arts & crafts; Cards; Games; Prayer groups; Movies; Shopping trips; Dances/Social/Cultural gatherings; Intergenerational programs; Pet therapy; Outings; Beach trips; Religious services; Family support groups.

Lee Manor Home for the Retired
2900 Maple Ln, Fairfax, VA 22031
(703) 560-1752
Medical Dir Ruby Broyhill Admis.
Licensure Home for adults. *Beds* Home for adults 9.

Northern Virginia Training Center
9901 Braddock Rd, Fairfax, VA 22032
(703) 323-4000
Admin David H Lawson PhD Dir.
Licensure Intermediate care for mentally retarded. *Beds* ICF/MR 299.

Virginian Health Care Unit
9229 Arlington Blvd, Fairfax, VA 22031
(703) 385-0555
Admin Sonia Y Weaver. *Dir of Nursing* Mary Fisher.
Licensure Private Pay; Life care; Alzheimer's care; Retirement. *Beds* Private pay 100; Life care 300.
Owner Nonprofit organization/foundation.
Admissions Requirements Medical examination.
Staff Physicians 5 (pt); RNs; LPNs; Nurses' aides; Physical therapists 1 (pt); Recreational therapists 1 (ft); Activities coordinators 2 (ft), 1 (pt); Dietitians 1 (pt); Ophthalmologists 1 (ft); Dentists 1 (ft).
Facilities Dining room; Physical therapy room; Activities room; Chapel; Crafts room; Laundry room; Barber/Beauty shop; Library.
Activities Arts & crafts; Cards; Games; Reading groups; Prayer groups; Movies; Shopping trips; Dances/Social/Cultural gatherings.

Falls Church

Barcroft Institute
2960 Sleepy Hollow Rd, Falls Church, VA 22044
(703) 536-2000
Admin Karen A Sartiano. *Dir of Nursing* Regina Freestone. *Medical Dir* William Hart MD.
Licensure Intermediate care. *Beds* ICF 46. *Certified* Medicaid.
Owner Proprietary corp.
Admissions Requirements Minimum age 16; Medical examination; Physician's request.
Staff Physicians 30 (pt); RNs 5 (ft), 2 (pt); LPNs 5 (ft), 2 (pt); Nurses' aides 17 (ft), 7 (pt); Physical therapists 1 (pt); Occupational therapists 1 (pt); Speech therapists 1 (pt); Activities coordinators 1 (ft); Dietitians 1 (ft), 1 (pt); Ophthalmologists 1 (pt); Podiatrists 1 (pt); Dentists 1 (pt).
Facilities Dining room; Activities room; Barber/Beauty shop; Library.
Activities Arts & crafts; Cards; Games; Reading groups; Prayer groups; Movies; Shopping trips; Dances/Social/Cultural gatherings; Van rides; Planned activities off grounds.

Powhatan Nursing Home
2100 Powhatan St, Falls Church, VA 22043
(703) 538-2400
Admin J T Butler. *Dir of Nursing* Sally Palatko Admis. *Medical Dir* Robert Communale MD.
Licensure Private pay. *Beds* Private pay 160.
Owner Proprietary corp.
Admissions Requirements Minimum age 18.
Staff Physicians 48 (pt); RNs 21 (ft), 9 (pt); LPNs 7 (ft), 2 (pt); Nurses' aides 71 (ft), 11 (pt); Physical therapists 1 (ft), 1 (pt); Reality therapists 1 (ft); Recreational therapists 3 (ft); Speech therapists 1 (pt); Activities coordinators 2 (ft); Dietitians 1 (pt); Ophthalmologists 1 (pt); Podiatrists 1 (pt); Audiologists 1 (pt); Dentists 1 (pt).
Facilities Dining room; Physical therapy room; Activities room; Chapel; Crafts room; Laundry room; Barber/Beauty shop; Library.
Activities Arts & crafts; Cards; Games; Reading groups; Prayer groups; Movies; Shopping trips; Dances/Social/Cultural gatherings.

Farmville

Eldercare of Farmville
PO Box 487, Rte 4 Scott Dr, Farmville, VA 23901
(804) 392-8806
Admin Floyd Beard.
Medical Dir Carrill Benhoff.
Licensure Intermediate care. *Beds* ICF 120. *Certified* Medicare.
Owner Proprietary corp.
Facilities Dining room; Physical therapy room; Activities room; Crafts room; Laundry room; Barber/Beauty shop.
Activities Arts & crafts; Cards; Games; Reading groups; Prayer groups; Movies; Shopping trips; Dances/Social/Cultural gatherings.

Holly Manor Nursing Home
2003 Cobb St, Farmville, VA 23901
(804) 392-6106
Admin Earl B Lee. *Dir of Nursing* Marsha Whitehurst. *Medical Dir* Dr R A Moore Jr.
Licensure Intermediate care; Retirement; Alzheimer's care. *Beds* ICF 115; Retirement 80.
Owner Proprietary corp.
Admissions Requirements Medical examination.
Staff RNs 3 (ft); LPNs 18 (ft), 2 (pt); Nurses' aides 45 (ft), 3 (pt); Recreational therapists 2 (ft); Activities coordinators 1 (pt).

Languages Spanish.
Facilities Dining room; Physical therapy room; Activities room; Crafts room; Laundry room; Barber/Beauty shop.
Activities Arts & crafts; Cards; Games; Reading groups; Prayer groups; Movies; Shopping trips; Dances/Social/Cultural gatherings.

Southside Community Hospital
800 Oak St, Farmville, VA 23901
(804) 392-8811, 392-6666 FAX
Admin Thomas J Rice III. *Dir of Nursing* Dr Linda C Aleksa. *Medical Dir* Dr Girish Purohit.
Licensure Intermediate care. *Beds* ICF 20. *Private Pay Patients* 15%. *Certified* Medicaid.
Owner Nonprofit corp.
Admissions Requirements Medical examination; Physician's request.
Staff Physicians 19 (ft); RNs 1 (ft); LPNs 3 (ft), 3 (pt); Nurses' aides 4 (ft), 3 (pt); Physical therapists 1 (ft); Speech therapists 1 (pt); Activities coordinators 1 (pt); Dietitians 1 (ft); Ophthalmologists 1 (ft).
Facilities Dining room; Physical therapy room; Activities room; Chapel; Barber/Beauty shop.
Activities Arts & crafts; Cards; Games; Movies.

Floyd

Skyline Manor Nursing Home
PO Box 508, St Rte 681, Floyd, VA 24091
(703) 745-2016
Admin Karen T Thompson. *Dir of Nursing* Brenda Smithson RN. *Medical Dir* Clarence W Taylor Jr MD.
Licensure Intermediate care. *Beds* ICF 60. *Private Pay Patients* 10%. *Certified* Medicaid.
Owner Proprietary corp.
Admissions Requirements Medical examination.
Staff Physicians 5 (pt); RNs 2 (ft); LPNs 6 (ft), 3 (pt); Nurses' aides 18 (ft), 11 (pt); Physical therapists 1 (pt); Speech therapists 1 (pt); Activities coordinators 1 (ft), 1 (pt); Dietitians 1 (ft).
Facilities Physical therapy room; Laundry room; Barber/Beauty shop; Dining/Activities room.
Activities Arts & crafts; Cards; Games; Reading groups; Prayer groups; Movies; Shopping trips; Dances/Social/Cultural gatherings; Intergenerational programs; Pet therapy; Music; Spelling bees; Resident council; Bookmobile.

Fort Belvoir

Belvoir Woods Healthcare Center
9160 Belvoir Woods Pkwy, Fort Belvoir, VA 22060
(703) 799-1333
Admin Robert DeMaria.
Licensure Skilled care; Intermediate care. *Beds* SNF 12; ICF 48.
Owner Proprietary corp.

Franklin

Southampton Memorial Hospital—East Pavilion
PO Drawer 817, 100 Fairview Dr, Franklin, VA 23852
(804) 562-5165
Admin Esther Barksdale RN.
Medical Dir Michael Ponder MD.
Licensure Skilled care. *Beds* SNF 131. *Certified* Medicaid; Medicare.
Owner Nonprofit corp.
Admissions Requirements Minimum age 14; Medical examination.

Staff RNs 2 (ft), 3 (pt); LPNs 12 (ft), 7 (pt); Nurses' aides 32 (ft), 14 (pt); Physical therapists 1 (ft); Activities coordinators 2 (pt); Dietitians 1 (ft).
Facilities Dining room; Physical therapy room; Activities room; Crafts room; Laundry room; Barber/Beauty shop; Library.
Activities Arts & crafts; Cards; Games; Prayer groups; Movies; Dances/Social/Cultural gatherings; Bingo; Resident council.

Fredericksburg

Carriage Hill Nursing Home & Residential Care Center
5040 Plank Rd, Fredericksburg, VA 22401
(703) 786-4549
Admin Mary L Peebles.
Licensure Intermediate care. *Beds* ICF 90.
Owner Nonprofit corp.

Fredericksburg Nursing Home
3900 Plank Rd, Fredericksburg, VA 22401
(703) 786-8351
Admin Sharon Bartlett. *Dir of Nursing* Louise Burch.
Licensure Intermediate care. *Beds* ICF 177. *Certified* Medicaid.
Owner Proprietary corp (Beverly Enterprises).
Admissions Requirements Minimum age 18; Medical examination; Physician's request.
Staff Physicians; RNs; LPNs; Nurses' aides; Physical therapists (contracted); Recreational therapists; Occupational therapists (contracted); Speech therapists (contracted); Activities coordinators; Dietitians; Ophthalmologists (contracted); Podiatrists (contracted); Audiologists (contracted).
Facilities Dining room; Physical therapy room; Activities room; Crafts room; Laundry room; Barber/Beauty shop.
Activities Arts & crafts; Cards; Games; Reading groups; Prayer groups; Movies; Shopping trips; Dances/Social/Cultural gatherings; Intergenerational programs; Pet therapy.

Woodmont Nursing Home
PO Box 366, 120 King Hwy, Fredericksburg, VA 22404
(703) 371-9414
Admin Lucille B Merritt.
Licensure Intermediate care. *Beds* ICF 122. *Certified* Medicaid.
Owner Proprietary corp (National Healthcare Affiliates Inc).

Front Royal

Heritage Hall—Front Royal
400 W Strasburg Rd, Front Royal, VA 22630
(703) 636-3700
Admin Sharon L Carte.
Licensure Intermediate care. *Beds* ICF 60.
Owner Proprietary corp.

Lynn Care Center
Shenandoah Ave, Front Royal, VA 22630
(703) 636-0264
Admin C Douglas Rosen. *Dir of Nursing* Patricia Richardson. *Medical Dir* Roger K Westfall MD.
Licensure Intermediate care. *Beds* ICF 40. *Private Pay Patients* 20%. *Certified* Medicaid; Medicare.
Owner Nonprofit organization/foundation.
Admissions Requirements Medical examination.
Staff Physicians; RNs; LPNs; Nurses' aides; Physical therapists; Reality therapists; Recreational therapists; Speech therapists; Activities coordinators; Dietitians; Ophthalmologists; Podiatrists; Audiologists.

Facilities Physical therapy room; Activities room; Barber/Beauty shop.
Activities Arts & crafts; Games; Reading groups; Prayer groups; Movies; Shopping trips; Dances/Social/Cultural gatherings; Volunteer program.

Galax

Blue Ridge Highlands Nursing Home
PO Box 229, 836 Glendale Rd, Galax, VA 24333
(703) 236-9991
Admin Laurence L Newell. *Dir of Nursing* Faye E Cole.
Licensure Intermediate care. *Beds* ICF 120. *Certified* Medicaid.
Owner Proprietary corp (Beverly Enterprises).
Admissions Requirements Minimum age 18; Medical examination; Physician's request.
Staff RNs 4 (ft); LPNs 8 (ft), 6 (pt); Nurses' aides 51 (ft), 18 (pt); Activities coordinators 1 (ft).
Facilities Dining room; Physical therapy room; Activities room; Crafts room; Laundry room; Barber/Beauty shop.
Activities Arts & crafts; Cards; Games; Reading groups; Prayer groups; Movies; Shopping trips; Dances/Social/Cultural gatherings.

Waddell Nursing Home
202 Painter St, Galax, VA 24333
(703) 236-5164
Admin Kimberly R Cox. *Dir of Nursing* Doris W Morris. *Medical Dir* Dr William Waddell.
Licensure Skilled care; Intermediate care; Retirement. *Beds* SNF 32; ICF 103. *Certified* Medicaid; Medicare.
Owner Proprietary corp.
Admissions Requirements Medical examination; Physician's request.
Staff RNs 2 (ft), 2 (pt); LPNs 18 (ft), 4 (pt); Nurses' aides 55 (ft), 15 (pt); Physical therapists 1 (pt); Speech therapists 1 (pt); Activities coordinators 1 (ft); Dietitians 1 (ft).
Languages German, Spanish.
Facilities Dining room; Physical therapy room; Activities room; Crafts room; Laundry room; Barber/Beauty shop; 3 Courtyards.
Activities Arts & crafts; Cards; Games; Reading groups; Prayer groups; Movies; Shopping trips; Dances/Social/Cultural gatherings.

Glen Allen

Elizabeth Adam Crump Manor
PO Box 1458, 3600 Mountain Rd, Glen Allen, VA 23060
(804) 672-8725, 755-6863 FAX
Admin Herbert R Woodall. *Dir of Nursing* Katherine Roberts RN. *Medical Dir* Dr Forrest Pitts.
Licensure Intermediate care; Private pay. *Beds* ICF 169; Private pay 11. *Private Pay Patients* 40%. *Certified* Medicaid.
Owner Nonprofit corp.
Staff Physicians; RNs 7 (ft); LPNs 15 (ft); Nurses' aides 60 (ft); Physical therapists 1 (ft); Occupational therapists 1 (ft); Speech therapists 1 (ft); Activities coordinators 2 (ft); Dietitians 1 (ft); Podiatrists 1 (ft).
Facilities Dining room; Physical therapy room; Activities room; Chapel; Crafts room; Laundry room; Barber/Beauty shop; Library.
Activities Arts & crafts; Games; Reading groups; Prayer groups; Shopping trips; Dances/Social/Cultural gatherings; Intergenerational programs; Pet therapy.

Gloucester

Horn Harbor Nursing Home Inc
Box 887, Gloucester, VA 23061
(804) 725-7830
Admin Hal D Bourque.
Licensure Intermediate care. *Beds* 77.
Certified Medicaid.
Owner Proprietary corp.

Walter Reed Convalescent Center
PO Box 887, Rte 17 & Meredith Dr,
Gloucester, VA 23061
(804) 693-6503
Admin Hal D Bourque. *Dir of Nursing* Sonya
Krista RN. *Medical Dir* Sam R Stanford Jr
MD.
Licensure Intermediate care. *Beds* ICF 161.
Certified Medicaid.
Owner Proprietary corp.
Admissions Requirements Physician's request.
Staff RNs 6 (ft), 7 (pt); LPNs 8 (ft), 10 (pt);
Nurses' aides 42 (ft), 35 (pt); Physical
therapists 1 (ft); Activities coordinators 2
(ft); Dietitians 1 (ft).
Facilities Dining room; Physical therapy
room; Activities room; Crafts room; Laundry
room; Barber/Beauty shop; Library.
Activities Arts & crafts; Cards; Games; Prayer
groups; Movies; Dances/Social/Cultural
gatherings.

Francis N Sanders Nursing Home Inc
PO Box 130, Walker Ave, Gloucester, VA
23061
(804) 693-2000
Admin Merlin R Steider. *Dir of Nursing*
Frances F Jackson RN. *Medical Dir* Dr
Raymond S Brown.
Licensure Intermediate care. *Beds* ICF 55.
Owner Nonprofit corp.
Admissions Requirements Minimum age 16;
Medical examination; Physician's request.
Staff RNs 2 (ft), 4 (pt); LPNs 1 (ft), 3 (pt);
Nurses' aides 16 (ft), 17 (pt); Activities
coordinators 1 (pt); Dietitians 1 (pt).
Facilities Dining room; Activities room;
Chapel; Crafts room; Laundry room; Barber/
Beauty shop.
Activities Arts & crafts; Games; Reading
groups; Prayer groups; Movies; Dances/
Social/Cultural gatherings.

Grafton

Regency Health Care Center
112 N Constitution Dr, Grafton, VA 23692
(804) 890-0675
Admin Lynn O Lohrmann.
Licensure Skilled care; Intermediate care. *Beds*
SNF 6; ICF 54.
Owner Proprietary corp (Regency Health Care
Centers).

Gwynn

Rosewood Convalescent Center
Henry's Rd, Gwynn, VA 23066
(804) 725-5200
Admin Guy K Shelton Jr.
Licensure Intermediate care. *Beds* 24.
Certified Medicaid.
Owner Proprietary corp.

Hampton

Coliseum Park Nursing Home
305 Marcella Dr, Hampton, VA 23666
(804) 827-8953
Admin Patricia N Miller. *Dir of Nursing*
Gloria Kenerley RN. *Medical Dir* Dr Frank
Robert.
Licensure Intermediate care; Alzheimer's care.
Beds ICF 180. Certified Medicaid.
Owner Privately owned.

Admissions Requirements Minimum age 16;
Medical examination; Physician's request.
Staff Physicians 38 (ft); RNs 7 (ft); LPNs 10
(ft), 8 (pt); Nurses' aides 25 (ft), 40 (pt);
Activities coordinators 2 (ft); Dietitians 1
(ft).
Facilities Dining room; Activities room;
Laundry room; Barber/Beauty shop.
Activities Arts & crafts; Cards; Games;
Reading groups; Prayer groups; Movies;
Shopping trips; Dances/Social/Cultural
gatherings.

Sarah Bonwell Hudgins
PO Box 7394, 51 Battle Rd, Hampton, VA
23666
(804) 826-6461
Admin Roger J Warner Exec Dir.
Licensure Intermediate care for mentally
retarded. *Beds* ICF/MR 20.

Riverside Convalescent Center—Hampton
414 Algonquin Rd, Hampton, VA 23661
(804) 722-9881
Admin Guy K Shelton Jr. *Dir of Nursing*
Maureen Cash RN. *Medical Dir* Louis
Parham MD.
Licensure Intermediate care. *Beds* ICF 160.
Certified Medicaid.
Owner Nonprofit corp.
Admissions Requirements Medical
examination; Physician's request.
Staff RNs 3 (ft), 3 (pt); LPNs 15 (ft), 14 (pt);
Nurses' aides 33 (ft), 26 (pt); Activities
coordinators 1 (ft).
Facilities Dining room; Physical therapy
room; Activities room; Crafts room; Laundry
room; Barber/Beauty shop.
Activities Arts & crafts; Cards; Games;
Reading groups; Prayer groups; Movies;
Shopping trips; Dances/Social/Cultural
gatherings.

Sentara—Hampton General Hospital
PO Box 640 NE, 3120 Victoria Blvd,
Hampton, VA 23669
(804) 727-7554
Admin Roger M Eitelman.
Licensure Skilled care. *Beds* SNF 26.
Owner Nonprofit corp.

Harrisonburg

Camelot Hall Nursing Home
1225 Reservoir St, Harrisonburg, VA 22801
(703) 433-2623
Admin J S Parker Jones IV.
Licensure Skilled care; Intermediate care. *Beds*
SNF 13; ICF 67. Certified Medicaid;
Medicare.
Owner Proprietary corp (Medical Facilities of
America).
Staff RNs 15 (ft); LPNs 9 (ft); Physical
therapists 1 (pt); Speech therapists 1 (pt);
Activities coordinators 1 (ft); Dietitians 1
(ft); Audiologists 1 (pt); Dentists 1 (pt).
Facilities Dining room; Physical therapy
room; Activities room; Chapel; Crafts room;
Laundry room; Barber/Beauty shop.
Activities Arts & crafts; Cards; Games;
Reading groups; Prayer groups; Movies;
Shopping trips; Dances/Social/Cultural
gatherings.

Harrison Intermediate Care Residence
1631 Virginia Ave, Harrisonburg, VA 22801
(703) 433-0965
Admin Terry L Whitmore Exec Dir.
Licensure Intermediate care for mentally
retarded. *Beds* ICF/MR 15.

Liberty House Nursing Home
94 South Ave, Harrisonburg, VA 22801
(703) 433-2791
Admin James H Anderson.
Medical Dir Mark Kniss MD.

Licensure Skilled care; Intermediate care. *Beds*
SNF 10; ICF 107. Certified Medicaid;
Medicare.
Owner Proprietary corp (Beverly Enterprises).
Admissions Requirements Medical
examination.
Staff Physicians 2 (pt); RNs 3 (ft); LPNs 7
(ft), 2 (pt); Nurses' aides 31 (ft), 12 (pt);
Physical therapists 1 (pt); Speech therapists
1 (ft); Activities coordinators 1 (ft);
Dietitians 1 (ft); Ophthalmologists 1 (pt);
Podiatrists 1 (pt).
Facilities Dining room; Physical therapy
room; Activities room; Chapel; Laundry
room; Barber/Beauty shop; Library.
Activities Arts & crafts; Cards; Games;
Reading groups; Prayer groups; Movies;
Shopping trips; Dances/Social/Cultural
gatherings.

Oak Lea Nursing Home
1475 Virginia Ave, Harrisonburg, VA 22801
(703) 434-0084
Admin Glendon L Heatwole. *Dir of Nursing*
Kathy Suter. *Medical Dir* Dr James R
Brunk.
Licensure Intermediate care; Retirement;
Alzheimer's care. *Beds* ICF 120; Retirement
300. Certified Medicaid.
Owner Nonprofit organization/foundation.
Admissions Requirements Medical
examination.
Staff RNs 7 (ft), 5 (pt); LPNs 8 (ft), 3 (pt);
Nurses' aides 35 (ft), 39 (pt); Recreational
therapists 3 (ft); Activities coordinators 1
(ft); Dietitians 1 (ft).
Affiliation Mennonite.
Facilities Dining room; Physical therapy
room; Activities room; Chapel; Crafts room;
Laundry room; Barber/Beauty shop; Library.
Activities Arts & crafts; Cards; Games;
Reading groups; Prayer groups; Movies;
Dances/Social/Cultural gatherings.

**Sunnyside Presbyterian Home Health Care
Unit**
Box 928, Harrisonburg, VA 22801
(703) 568-8200
Admin Dick Lyons.
Medical Dir Karen Shiflet.
Licensure Intermediate care; Retirement. *Beds*
ICF 120. Certified Medicaid.
Owner Nonprofit corp.
Admissions Requirements Minimum age 65.
Staff RNs 18 (ft); LPNs 20 (ft).
Affiliation Presbyterian.
Facilities Dining room; Physical therapy
room; Activities room; Chapel; Crafts room;
Laundry room; Barber/Beauty shop; Library;
Dental operatory.
Activities Arts & crafts; Cards; Games;
Reading groups; Prayer groups; Movies;
Shopping trips; Dances/Social/Cultural
gatherings.

Highland Springs

Henrico Health Care Center
561 N Airport Dr, Highland Springs, VA
23075
(804) 737-0172
Admin Sheena Mackenzie.
Licensure Skilled care; Intermediate care. *Beds*
SNF 10; ICF 110.
Owner Proprietary corp.

Hillsville

Carroll House
Rte 1 Box 340, Hillsville, VA 24343
(703) 728-4301
Admin Darlene Douglas Prog Coord.
Licensure Intermediate care for mentally
retarded. *Beds* ICF/MR 12.

Eldercare of Hillsville
222 Fulcher St, Hillsville, VA 24343
(703) 728-5002
Admin Rebecca Phillips.
Licensure Skilled care; Intermediate care. *Beds*
SNF 20; ICF 40.
Owner Proprietary corp.

Southwestern Virginia Training Center
Rte 1 Box 415, Hillsville, VA 24343
(703) 728-3121, 728-3127 FAX
Admin Benjamin H Allen PhD Dir. *Dir of
Nursing* Sandra Watkins RN. *Medical Dir*
Barry M Mayberry MD.
Licensure Intermediate care for mentally
retarded. *Beds* ICF/MR 223. *Private Pay
Patients* 5%. *Certified* Medicaid.
Owner Publicly owned.
Staff Physicians 1 (ft); RNs 15 (ft), 1 (pt);
LPNs 12 (ft), 2 (pt); Physical therapists
(contracted); Recreational therapists 4 (ft);
Occupational therapists (contracted); Speech
therapists 2 (ft); Activities coordinators 5
(ft); Dietitians (contracted); Audiologists
(contracted).
Facilities Dining room; Physical therapy
room; Activities room; Crafts room; Laundry
room; Barber/Beauty shop; Library; Gym.
Activities Arts & crafts; Games; Movies;
Shopping trips; Dances/Social/Cultural
gatherings; Intergenerational programs;
Exercise groups; Self-help skills; Social skills.

Hopewell

Hopewell Convalescent Center
905 Cousin Ave, Hopewell, VA 23860
(804) 458-6325
Admin Betsy L Merrell.
Licensure Skilled care; Intermediate care. *Beds*
SNF 19; ICF 111. *Certified* Medicaid;
Medicare.
Owner Proprietary corp.

John Randolph Nursing Home Inc
409 W Randolph Rd, Hopewell, VA 23860
(804) 541-3651
Admin Paula S Poole RN. *Dir of Nursing*
Gwendolyn Cosslett RN. *Medical Dir* Dr
Lee Weathington.
Licensure Skilled care; Intermediate care. *Beds*
SNF 22; ICF 102. *Certified* Medicaid;
Medicare.
Owner Nonprofit corp.
Admissions Requirements Physician's request.
Staff RNs 6 (ft), 8 (pt); LPNs 12 (ft), 12 (pt);
Nurses' aides 35 (ft), 22 (pt); Activities
coordinators 1 (ft); Dietitians 1 (pt).
Facilities Dining room; Activities room;
Crafts room; Laundry room; Barber/Beauty
shop.
Activities Arts & crafts; Games; Reading
groups; Prayer groups; Movies; Shopping
trips; Dances/Social/Cultural gatherings.

Irvington

Rappahannock Westminster-Canterbury Inc
Rte 646, 10 Lancaster Dr, Irvington, VA
22480
(804) 438-4000
Admin Rexford F Beckwith III. *Dir of Nursing*
Evelyn Johnston RN. *Medical Dir* Ralph
Robertson MD.
Licensure Skilled care; Intermediate care;
Home for adults; Retirement living;
Alzheimer's care. *Beds* SNF 10; ICF 32;
Home for adults 66; Retirement living 78.
Certified Medicaid; Medicare.
Owner Nonprofit corp (Rappahannock
Westminster-Canterbury Inc).
Admissions Requirements Minimum age 65
Retirement living; 14 Nursing home;
Medical examination; Physician's request
Nursing home.

Staff Physicians 5 (pt); RNs 5 (ft); LPNs 4
(ft); Nurses' aides 22 (ft); Physical therapists
1 (pt); Activities coordinators 2 (ft);
Dietitians 1 (ft); Ophthalmologists 1 (pt);
Podiatrists 1 (pt).
Affiliation Episcopal.
Facilities Dining room; Physical therapy
room; Activities room; Crafts room; Laundry
room; Barber/Beauty shop; Library; Store;
Bank; Clinic; Auditorium; Private meeting
rooms; Snack bar/cafe.
Activities Arts & crafts; Cards; Games;
Reading groups; Prayer groups; Movies;
Shopping trips; Dances/Social/Cultural
gatherings; Trips; Lectures.

Keen Mountain

Keen Mountain House
PO Box 621, Keen Mountain, VA 24624
(703) 498-4549
Admin Ronald A Allison Exec Dir.
Licensure Intermediate care for mentally
retarded. *Beds* ICF/MR 12.

Kilmarnock

Lancashire Nursing Home
PO Box 1509, 287 School St, Kilmarnock, VA
22482
(804) 435-1684
Admin George W Crenshaw Jr. *Dir of Nursing*
Patricia P Crenshaw RN. *Medical Dir* A B
Gravath MD; Steven Hamilton MD.
Licensure Intermediate care; Residential care;
Alzheimer's care. *Beds* ICF 120. *Private Pay
Patients* 50%. *Certified* Medicaid.
Owner Privately owned.
Admissions Requirements Minimum age 30;
Medical examination; Physician's request.
Staff Physicians 2 (ft); RNs 4 (ft), 1 (pt);
LPNs 8 (ft), 5 (pt); Nurses' aides 42 (ft), 12
(pt); Activities coordinators 1 (ft), 1 (pt);
Dietitians 10 (ft), 4 (pt); Podiatrists 1 (pt).
Facilities Dining room; Physical therapy
room; Activities room; Chapel; Crafts room;
Laundry room; Barber/Beauty shop.
Activities Arts & crafts; Games; Reading
groups; Prayer groups; Movies.

King George

Heritage Hall—King George
PO Box 495, State Rte 3, King George, VA
22485
(703) 775-4000
Admin Tracy E Horton.
Licensure Intermediate care. *Beds* ICF 130.
Owner Proprietary corp.

Lawrenceville

Brian Center Nursing Care/Lawrenceville Inc
PO Box 105, Lawrenceville, VA 23868
(804) 848-4766
Admin Nancy Fisher.
Licensure Skilled care; Intermediate care. *Beds*
SNF 10; ICF 67.
Owner Proprietary corp.

Leesburg

Edwards Ferry House
112 Edwards Ferry Rd NE, Leesburg, VA
22075
(703) 777-0453
Admin Cindy Christensen Res Dev Coord.
Licensure Intermediate care for mentally
retarded. *Beds* ICF/MR 6.

Heritage Hall Leesburg
122 Morven Park Rd NW, Leesburg, VA
22075
(703) 777-8700
Admin Peggy Davies.
Medical Dir Hope Carbaugh Admis.

Licensure Intermediate care. *Beds* ICF 120.
Owner Proprietary corp.
Admissions Requirements Minimum age 14;
Medical examination.
Staff RNs 5 (ft), 3 (pt); LPNs 4 (ft), 4 (pt);
Nurses' aides 35 (ft), 4 (pt); Activities
coordinators 1 (ft); Dietitians 1 (ft); Social
workers 1 (ft).
Facilities Dining room; Physical therapy
room; Activities room; Crafts room; Laundry
room; Barber/Beauty shop.
Activities Arts & crafts; Games; Prayer groups;
Movies; Shopping trips; Dances/Social/
Cultural gatherings.

Leesburg Sunrise Retirement Homes
246 W Market St, Leesburg, VA 22075
(703) 777-1971
Admin Mary Ann Koppmann.
Licensure Assisted living. *Beds* Assisted living
33.
Owner Proprietary corp.
Admissions Requirements Medical
examination.
Staff RNs; Nurses' aides; Activities
coordinators; Dietitians.
Facilities Dining room; Activities room;
Laundry room; Library; Porch; Gardens.
Activities Arts & crafts; Cards; Games;
Reading groups; Prayer groups; Movies;
Shopping trips; Dances/Social/Cultural
gatherings; Intergenerational programs; Pet
therapy.

Loudoun Long-Term Care Center
224 Cornwall St NW, Leesburg, VA 22075
(703) 771-2841
Admin Margaret W Mallon. *Dir of Nursing*
Cynthia H Mazurkiewicz RNC. *Medical Dir*
Warren Johnson.
Licensure Intermediate care. *Beds* ICF 100.
Private Pay Patients 30-40%. *Certified*
Medicaid.
Owner Nonprofit organization/foundation.
Admissions Requirements Minimum age 16;
Medical examination.
Staff RNs 4 (ft), 3 (pt); LPNs 5 (ft), 4 (pt);
Nurses' aides 25 (ft), 10 (pt); Activities
coordinators 1 (ft).
Facilities Dining room; Physical therapy
room; Activities room; Crafts room; Laundry
room; Barber/Beauty shop.
Activities Arts & crafts; Games; Reading
groups; Prayer groups; Movies; Shopping
trips; Dances/Social/Cultural gatherings;
Intergenerational programs.

Lexington

**Stonewall Jackson Hospital Long-Term Care
Unit**
Spotswood Rd, Lexington, VA 24450
(703) 463-9141
Admin L E Richardson. *Dir of Nursing*
Barbara N Cathey BSN RN.
Licensure Skilled care; Intermediate care. *Beds*
SNF 25; ICF 25. *Certified* Medicaid;
Medicare.
Owner Nonprofit corp.
Staff Physicians 23 (ft); RNs 2 (ft); LPNs 10
(ft); Nurses' aides 23 (ft); Physical therapists
2 (ft); Occupational therapists 1 (pt); Speech
therapists 1 (pt); Activities coordinators 1
(ft); Dietitians 1 (pt); Ophthalmologists 2
(pt); Podiatrists 1 (pt).
Facilities Dining room; Physical therapy
room; Activities room; Laundry room;
Barber/Beauty shop.
Activities Arts & crafts; Cards; Games;
Reading groups; Prayer groups; Movies;
Shopping trips; Dances/Social/Cultural
gatherings; Intergenerational programs.

Locust Hill

Mizpah Nursing Home Inc
PO Box 70, Locust Hill, VA 23092
(804) 758-5260
Admin Myrtle D Faulkner.
Licensure Intermediate care. *Beds* ICF 64.
  Certified Medicaid.
Owner Proprietary corp.

Louisa

Louisa Health Care Center
PO Box 1310, Hwy 208 S, Louisa, VA 23093
(703) 967-2250
Admin Charles E Rehnborg Interim.
Licensure Intermediate care. *Beds* ICF 90.
Owner Proprietary corp.

Lovettsville

Woodland Retirement Home of Loudoun County
Rte 2 Box 55A, Lovettsville, VA 22080
(703) 822-5462
Medical Dir Shauna Hyatt Admis.
Licensure Home for adults. *Beds* Home for
  adults 12.

Lovingston

Lovingston Health Care Center
PO Box 398, Business Hwy 29, Lovingston,
  VA 22949-0398
(804) 263-4823
Admin Brian R Carlton. *Dir of Nursing*
  Darlene M Sirois RN. *Medical Dir* Dr
  Henry B Larzelere.
Licensure Intermediate care; Alzheimer's care.
  Beds ICF 60. *Private Pay Patients* 13%.
  Certified Medicaid.
Owner Privately owned (Medical Facilities of
  America).
Admissions Requirements Medical
  examination; Physician's request.
Staff Physicians 3 (pt); RNs 1 (ft), 3 (pt);
  LPNs 3 (ft), 6 (pt); Nurses' aides 16 (ft), 7
  (pt); Physical therapists 1 (pt); Activities
  coordinators 1 (ft), 1 (pt); Dietitians 1 (ft);
  Podiatrists 1 (pt).
Facilities Dining room; Physical therapy
  room; Laundry room; Barber/Beauty shop;
  Library; Meditation room; Dayroom.
Activities Arts & crafts; Cards; Games;
  Reading groups; Prayer groups; Movies;
  Shopping trips; Dances/Social/Cultural
  gatherings; Intergenerational programs; Pet
  therapy; Exercise class; Sing-alongs; Hymn
  singing; Bible study; Holiday parties; County
  parade; Picnics; Outings.

Luray

MontVue Nursing Home
MontVue Dr, Luray, VA 22835
(703) 743-4571
Admin Beverly Arington. *Dir of Nursing*
  Elsymar Cross. *Medical Dir* James R
  Holsinger MD.
Licensure Intermediate care. *Beds* ICF 120.
  Private Pay Patients 13%. *Certified*
  Medicaid.
Owner Proprietary corp (Hillhaven Corp).
Admissions Requirements Minimum age 16;
  Medical examination.
Staff Physicians 3 (pt); RNs 4 (ft); LPNs 10
  (ft); Nurses' aides 34 (ft); Physical therapists
  1 (pt); Activities coordinators 1 (ft);
  Dietitians (contracted); Ophthalmologists
  (contracted); Podiatrists (contracted).
Facilities Dining room; Physical therapy
  room; Activities room; Crafts room; Laundry
  room; Barber/Beauty shop.
Activities Arts & crafts; Cards; Games;
  Reading groups; Prayer groups; Movies;
  Dances/Social/Cultural gatherings.

Lynchburg

Camelot Hall Nursing Home
5615 Seminole Ave, Lynchburg, VA 24502
(804) 239-2657
Admin Elizabeth E Kail.
Medical Dir Dr Alan Podosek.
Licensure Skilled care; Intermediate care. *Beds*
  SNF 9; ICF 171. *Certified* Medicaid;
  Medicare.
Owner Proprietary corp.
Admissions Requirements Minimum age Birth-
  14; Medical examination; Physician's
  request.
Staff RNs 9 (ft), 12 (pt); LPNs 7 (ft), 12 (pt);
  Nurses' aides 48 (ft), 8 (pt); Physical
  therapists 1 (pt); Activities coordinators 1
  (ft); Dietitians 1 (pt).
Facilities Dining room; Physical therapy
  room; Activities room; Crafts room; Laundry
  room; Barber/Beauty shop; Library.
Activities Arts & crafts; Games; Prayer groups;
  Movies; Shopping trips; Dances/Social/
  Cultural gatherings.

Central Virginia Training Center
PO Box 1098, Lynchburg, VA 24505
(703) 528-6327, 947-6326 Scats
Admin B R Walker PhD Dir.
Licensure Skilled care; Intermediate care;
  Intermediate care for mentally retarded.
  Beds SNF 129; ICF 219; ICF/MR 1362; M/
  S 46.

Grace Lodge Health Care Unit
PO Box 820, 1503 Grace St, Lynchburg, VA
  24505
(804) 528-0969
Admin Charles E Rehnborg.
Licensure Intermediate care. *Beds* ICF 44.
Owner Proprietary corp.

Guggenheimer Nursing Home
1902 Grace St, Lynchburg, VA 24504-3524
(804) 528-5100
Admin Judith N Gates. *Dir of Nursing* Joyce
  Wade. *Medical Dir* Dr Charles V Ashworth
  Jr; Dr Alan M Podosek.
Licensure Intermediate care. *Beds* ICF 110.
  Certified Medicaid.
Owner Nonprofit organization/foundation.
Staff Physicians 2 (pt); RNs 3 (ft), 3 (pt);
  LPNs 17 (ft), 6 (pt); Nurses' aides 34 (ft), 5
  (pt); Activities coordinators 2 (ft).
Facilities Dining room; Physical therapy
  room; Activities room; Chapel; Crafts room;
  Laundry room; Barber/Beauty shop.
Activities Arts & crafts; Games; Reading
  groups; Prayer groups; Movies; Shopping
  trips; Dances/Social/Cultural gatherings; Pet
  therapy; Ceramics; Trips to concerts, plays,
  lunch, minor league baseball games,
  community senior programs.

Lynchburg Nursing Home
701 Hollins St, Lynchburg, VA 24504
(804) 847-1341
Admin Robert H Gerndt. *Dir of Nursing*
  Clarice W Mitchell RN. *Medical Dir* Lewis
  F Somers MD.
Licensure Intermediate care. *Beds* ICF 89.
  Private Pay Patients 1%. *Certified* Medicaid.
Owner Publicly owned.
Admissions Requirements Medical
  examination; Physician's request.
Staff Physicians 1 (pt); RNs 5 (ft); LPNs 7
  (ft), 2 (pt); Nurses' aides 29 (ft), 3 (pt);
  Physical therapists 1 (pt); Activities
  coordinators 1 (ft); Dietitians 1 (pt).
Facilities Dining room; Activities room;
  Chapel; Crafts room; Laundry room; Barber/
  Beauty shop.
Activities Arts & crafts; Cards; Games;
  Reading groups; Prayer groups; Movies;
  Shopping trips; Dances/Social/Cultural
  gatherings; Pet therapy.

Medical Care Center
2200 Landover Pl, Lynchburg, VA 24501
(804) 846-4626
Admin Chuck Rehnborg. *Dir of Nursing*
  Becky Jones RN. *Medical Dir* Charles
  Ashworth MD.
Licensure Skilled care; Intermediate care. *Beds*
  SNF 15; ICF 101. *Private Pay Patients* 45-
  50%. *Certified* Medicaid; Medicare.
Owner Proprietary corp (Health Care and
  Retirement Corp).
Admissions Requirements Medical
  examination.
Staff Physicians 57 (pt); RNs 4 (ft), 5 (pt);
  LPNs 9 (ft), 6 (pt); Nurses' aides 38 (ft), 5
  (pt); Physical therapists (consultant);
  Occupational therapists (consultant); Speech
  therapists; Activities coordinators; Dietitians;
  Podiatrists (consultant); Dentists
  (consultant).
Facilities Dining room; Physical therapy
  room; Activities room; Crafts room; Laundry
  room; Barber/Beauty shop; 2 patios.
Activities Arts & crafts; Cards; Games;
  Reading groups; Prayer groups; Movies;
  Shopping trips; Dances/Social/Cultural
  gatherings; Pet therapy.

St John's Nursing Home Inc
3500 Powhatan St, Lynchburg, VA 24501
(804) 845-6045
Admin Karen S Green.
Licensure Private pay. *Beds* Private pay 45.
Owner Proprietary corp.

Seven Hills Health Care Center
2081 Langhorne Rd, Lynchburg, VA 24501
(804) 846-8437
Admin Justine C Stadtherr.
Medical Dir Doris Justice.
Licensure Skilled care; Intermediate care. *Beds*
  SNF 16; ICF 93. *Certified* Medicaid;
  Medicare.
Owner Proprietary corp (Beverly Enterprises).
Admissions Requirements Physician's request.
Staff RNs; LPNs; Nurses' aides; Activities
  coordinators; Social Services Coordinator.
Facilities Dining room; Physical therapy
  room; Activities room; Crafts room; Laundry
  room; Barber/Beauty shop.
Activities Arts & crafts; Cards; Games; Prayer
  groups; Movies; Shopping trips; Dances/
  Social/Cultural gatherings.

Virginia Baptist Hospital—Skilled Nursing Unit
3300 Rivermont Ave, Lynchburg, VA 24503
(804) 384-4511
Admin Thomas C Jividen Pres.
Medical Dir Sandra Lewis.
Licensure Skilled care. *Beds* SNF 36. *Certified*
  Medicaid; Medicare.
Owner Nonprofit corp.
Admissions Requirements Minimum age 18;
  Physician's request.
Staff RNs 7 (ft), 4 (pt); LPNs 4 (ft), 6 (pt);
  Nurses' aides 12 (ft), 3 (pt); Physical
  therapists 7 (ft), 1 (pt); Recreational
  therapists 2 (ft); Occupational therapists 6
  (ft); Speech therapists 3 (ft), 1 (pt);
  Dietitians 3 (ft); Podiatrists 2 (ft), 1 (pt).
Languages Spanish.
Facilities Activities room; Laundry room;
  Barber/Beauty shop.
Activities Arts & crafts; Games; Prayer groups;
  Dances/Social/Cultural gatherings.

Westminster-Canterbury of Lynchburg Inc—Health Care Unit
501 VES Rd, Lynchburg, VA 24503
(804) 386-3505
Admin Hunsdon Cary III.
Licensure Skilled care; Intermediate care. *Beds*
  SNF 19; ICF 61. *Certified* Medicaid;
  Medicare.
Owner Nonprofit corp.

Madison

Autumn Care of Madison
PO Drawer 420, 1 Autumn Ct, Madison, VA 22727
(703) 948-3054
Admin Gloria B Shifflett. *Dir of Nursing* Marilyn Brand. *Medical Dir* Dr Harold Jenkins.
Licensure Intermediate care; Home for adults. *Beds* ICF 44; Home for adults 16. *Private Pay Patients* 45%.
Owner Proprietary corp (Autumn Corp).

Manassas

Annaburg Manor
9201 Maple St, Manassas, VA 22110
(703) 335-8300, 335-8309 FAX
Admin Harley L Tabak; Mandy L Gannon, Asst. *Dir of Nursing* Alice V Love. *Medical Dir* Dr J L Mathews Jr.
Licensure Skilled care; Intermediate care; Retirement; Alzheimer's care. *Beds* SNF 29; ICF 216. *Private Pay Patients* 30%. *Certified* Medicaid; Medicare.
Owner Nonprofit corp.
Staff Physicians 4 (ft); RNs 11 (ft); LPNs 29 (ft); Nurses' aides 104 (ft); Physical therapists 1 (ft); Occupational therapists 2 (ft); Speech therapists 1 (ft); Activities coordinators 1 (ft); Dietitians 1 (pt); Ophthalmologists; Podiatrists; Audiologists; Dentists; Physical therapy aides 1 (ft); Activities aides 2 (ft).
Facilities Dining room; Physical therapy room; Activities room; Chapel; Crafts room; Laundry room; Barber/Beauty shop; Library.
Activities Arts & crafts; Cards; Games; Reading groups; Prayer groups; Movies; Shopping trips; Dances/Social/Cultural gatherings; Intergenerational programs; Pet therapy.

District Home
8605 Centreville Rd, Manassas, VA 22111
(703) 361-3196
Medical Dir Mrs Dillon Admis.
Licensure Home for adults. *Beds* Home for adults 73.

Marion

Francis Marion Manor
PO Box 880, Park Blvd, Marion, VA 24354
(703) 783-3141
Admin Sherrell H Sauls.
Licensure Intermediate care. *Beds* ICF 60. *Certified* Medicaid.
Owner Nonprofit corp.

Porterfield Geriatric Treatment Center
502 E Main St, Marion, VA 23453
(703) 783-6921
Admin R Michael Jones PhD Unit Dir.
Licensure Intermediate care for mentally retarded. *Beds* ICF/MR 96.

Smyth County Community Hospital Inc—Long-Term Care Unit
PO Box 880, Park Blvd, Marion, VA 24354
(703) 783-3141
Admin Garland G Scott Jr.
Licensure Skilled care. *Beds* SNF 16.
Owner Nonprofit corp.

Southwestern Virginia Mental Health Institute
502 E Main St, Marion, VA 23454
(703) 783-1200, 783-9712 FAX
Admin David A Rosenquist MHA. *Dir of Nursing* Agnes Hurt RN. *Medical Dir* Michael L Connell MD.
Licensure Intermediate care; Medical & Surgical. *Beds* ICF 48; Medical & Surgical 8. *Private Pay Patients* 5%.

Owner Publicly owned.
Staff Physicians 1 (ft), 1 (pt); RNs 12 (ft); LPNs 9 (ft); Nurses' aides 20 (ft); Recreational therapists 1 (ft), 1 (pt); Occupational therapists 1 (ft); Dietitians 1 (pt).

Martinsville

Blue Ridge Nursing Center of Martinsville & Henry County
15 Starling Ave, Martinsville, VA 24112
(703) 638-8701
Admin Mona K Clark.
Medical Dir John Kasterintious.
Licensure Intermediate care; Home for aged. *Beds* ICF 182; Home for aged 102. *Certified* Medicaid.
Owner Proprietary corp.
Admissions Requirements Minimum age 18; Medical examination; Physician's request.
Staff Physicians 2 (pt); RNs 6 (ft); LPNs 22 (pt); Nurses' aides 110 (pt); Speech therapists 1 (pt); Activities coordinators 1 (ft); Dietitians 1 (pt); Ophthalmologists 1 (pt); Podiatrists 1 (pt); Audiologists 1 (pt); Dentists 1 (pt).
Facilities Dining room; Activities room; Chapel; Crafts room; Laundry room; Barber/Beauty shop; Library.
Activities Arts & crafts; Cards; Games; Reading groups; Prayer groups; Movies; Shopping trips; Dances/Social/Cultural gatherings.

Martinsville Convalescent Center
PO Box 3191, Martinsville, VA 24115
(703) 632-7146, 632-1112
Admin Genevieve C Jones. *Dir of Nursing* Toby L Myers. *Medical Dir* John D French MD.
Licensure Skilled care; Intermediate care. *Beds* SNF 16; ICF 126. *Certified* Medicaid; Medicare.
Owner Proprietary corp (Beverly Enterprises).
Admissions Requirements Medical examination; Physician's request.
Staff Physicians 2 (pt); RNs 4 (ft), 1 (pt); LPNs 14 (ft); Nurses' aides 62 (ft), 8 (pt); Physical therapists 2 (pt); Recreational therapists 1 (ft); Occupational therapists 1 (pt); Speech therapists 1 (pt); Activities coordinators 1 (ft); Dietitians 1 (ft); Podiatrists 1 (pt).
Facilities Dining room; Physical therapy room; Activities room; Chapel; Crafts room; Laundry room; Barber/Beauty shop; Library.
Activities Arts & crafts; Cards; Games; Reading groups; Prayer groups; Movies; Shopping trips; Dances/Social/Cultural gatherings; Intergenerational programs; Pet therapy.

Mathews

Riverside Convalescent Center—Mathews
PO Box 370, Mathews, VA 23109
(80k) 725-9443
Admin Judith A Wright.
Licensure Intermediate care. *Beds* ICF 59.
Owner Proprietary corp.

Midlothian

Health Care Center at Brandermill Woods
2100 Brandermill Pkwy, Midlothian, VA 23112
(804) 744-1700
Admin Janet R Salmon.
Licensure Skilled care; Intermediate care. *Beds* SNF 30; ICF 30.
Owner Proprietary corp.

Montvale

Woodhaven Village Inc
PO Box 168, Rte 460 E, Montvale, VA 24122
(703) 947-2207
Admin Malcolm A Pace.
Licensure Private pay. *Beds* Private pay 48.
Owner Proprietary corp.

Nassawadox

Heritage Hall Nassawadox
PO Box 176, Hospital Rd, Nassawadox, VA 23413
(804) 442-5600
Admin Michael D Payne. *Dir of Nursing* Lorraine Williams. *Medical Dir* Dr John Snyder.
Licensure Intermediate care. *Beds* ICF 125. *Certified* Medicaid.
Owner Proprietary corp.
Admissions Requirements Minimum age 18; Medical examination; Physician's request.
Staff RNs 2 (ft), 1 (pt); LPNs 8 (ft), 5 (pt); Nurses' aides 28 (ft), 33 (pt); Activities coordinators 1 (ft).
Facilities Dining room; Activities room; Crafts room; Laundry room; Barber/Beauty shop.
Activities Arts & crafts; Cards; Games; Prayer groups; Movies; Shopping trips; Dances/Social/Cultural gatherings.

Northampton—Accomack Memorial Hospital
Nassawadox, VA 23413
(804) 442-8765
Admin Roy G Layne.
Licensure Skilled care. *Beds* SNF 13.
Owner Nonprofit corp.

Nelsonia

Arcadia Nursing Center
PO Box 97, Nelsonia, VA 23414
(804) 665-5555
Admin Thomas P Malik.
Medical Dir Dr Edward White.
Licensure Intermediate care. *Beds* ICF 60. *Private Pay Patients* 20%. *Certified* Medicaid.
Owner Privately owned.
Admissions Requirements Medical examination; Physician's request.
Staff RNs 2 (ft), 1 (pt); LPNs 6 (ft), 6 (pt); Nurses' aides 15 (ft), 10 (pt); Physical therapists; Activities coordinators 2 (pt); Dietitians 1 (pt).
Facilities Dining room; Physical therapy room; Activities room; Laundry room; Barber/Beauty shop.
Activities Arts & crafts; Cards; Games; Prayer groups; Dances/Social/Cultural gatherings; Pet therapy.

New Market

Life Care Center of New Market
PO Box 1100, Hwy 211 E, New Market, VA 22844
(703) 740-8041
Admin David Beaver.
Licensure Skilled care; Intermediate care. *Beds* SNF 28; ICF 90.
Owner Proprietary corp.

Newport News

Huntington Convalescent Center
5015 Huntington Ave, Newport News, VA 23607
(804) 244-1734
Admin John E Ferguson.
Licensure Skilled care; Intermediate care. *Beds* SNF 32; ICF 232. *Certified* Medicaid.
Owner Proprietary corp (Vantage Healthcare).

James River Convalescent Center
540 Aberthaw Ave, Newport News, VA 23601
(804) 595-2273
Admin Jeffrey L Mendelsohn Pres.
Licensure Intermediate care. *Beds* ICF 195.
  Certified Medicaid; Medicare.
Owner Proprietary corp.

Newport Convalescent Center Inc
11141 Warwick Blvd, Newport News, VA
  23601
(804) 595-3733
Admin John R Tew.
Licensure Private pay. *Beds* Private pay 50.
Owner Proprietary corp.

**Newport News Baptist Retirement Community
Health Care Unit**
955 Harpersville Rd, Newport News, VA
  23601
(804) 599-4376
Admin David H Hassenpflug. *Dir of Nursing*
  Judy Dozier RN.
Licensure Intermediate care; Retirement. *Beds*
  ICF 52. *Certified* Medicaid.
Owner Nonprofit corp.
Admissions Requirements Minimum age 65;
  Medical examination.
Staff Physicians; RNs; LPNs; Nurses' aides;
  Physical therapists; Recreational therapists;
  Activities coordinators; Dietitians.
Affiliation Baptist.
Facilities Dining room; Physical therapy
  room; Activities room; Chapel; Crafts room;
  Laundry room; Barber/Beauty shop; Library;
  Large carpeted patio.
Activities Arts & crafts; Games; Reading
  groups; Prayer groups; Movies; Shopping
  trips; Bowling; Sing-alongs.

Riverside Regional Convalescent Center
1000 Old Denbigh Blvd, Newport News, VA
  23602
(804) 875-2000
Admin Patricia A Iannetta. *Dir of Nursing*
  Lynda Burton. *Medical Dir* Dr G S Mitchell.
Licensure Skilled care; Intermediate care. *Beds*
  SNF 60; ICF 325. *Certified* Medicaid;
  Medicare.
Owner Nonprofit corp.
Admissions Requirements Medical
  examination.
Staff Physicians 12 (pt); RNs 19 (ft), 5 (pt);
  LPNs 25 (ft), 25 (pt); Nurses' aides 123 (ft),
  6 (pt); Physical therapists 1 (ft), 1 (pt);
  Recreational therapists 1 (ft); Occupational
  therapists 1 (ft); Speech therapists 1 (pt);
  Dietitians 1 (ft), 1 (pt); Ophthalmologists 1
  (pt); Podiatrists 1 (pt); Dentists 1 (ft).
Facilities Physical therapy room; Activities
  room; Chapel; Crafts room; Barber/Beauty
  shop.
Activities Arts & crafts; Cards; Games;
  Reading groups; Prayer groups; Movies;
  Dances/Social/Cultural gatherings.

Norfolk

DePaul Hospital
150 Kingsley Ln, Norfolk, VA 23505
(804) 489-5000
Admin Sr Mary Carroll.
Licensure Skilled care. *Beds* SNF 12.
Owner Nonprofit corp.

**Hillhaven Rehabilitation & Convalescent
Center**
1005 Hampton Blvd, Norfolk, VA 23507
(804) 623-5602, 623-4646 FAX
Admin Vickie A Archer. *Dir of Nursing* Robin
  Phillips RNC. *Medical Dir* Robert F Mann
  MD.
Licensure Skilled care; Intermediate care. *Beds*
  SNF 46; ICF 126. *Certified* Medicaid;
  Medicare.
Owner Proprietary corp (Hillhaven Corp).
Admissions Requirements Physician's request.

Staff RNs 7 (ft), 8 (pt); LPNs 13 (ft), 17 (pt);
  Nurses' aides 46 (ft), 40 (pt); Physical
  therapists 2 (ft); Recreational therapists 2
  (ft); Occupational therapists 1 (ft); Speech
  therapists 1 (ft); Activities coordinators 1
  (ft); Dietitians 1 (ft).
Facilities Dining room; Physical therapy
  room; Activities room; Laundry room;
  Barber/Beauty shop.
Activities Arts & crafts; Games; Prayer groups;
  Movies; Pet therapy.

Lafayette Villa Health Care
3900 Llewellyn Ave, Norfolk, VA 23504
(804) 625-5363
Admin Gary W Seay. *Dir of Nursing* Betty
  Chamberlin. *Medical Dir* Mary Ann Lucas.
Licensure Intermediate care. *Beds* ICF 242.
  Certified Medicaid.
Owner Proprietary corp.
Admissions Requirements Minimum age 18.
Staff RNs 3 (ft), 2 (pt); LPNs 32 (ft); Nurses'
  aides 95 (ft), 5 (pt); Physical therapists 1
  (pt); Activities coordinators 1 (pt); Dietitians
  1 (pt).
Facilities Dining room; Physical therapy
  room; Activities room; Chapel; Crafts room;
  Laundry room; Barber/Beauty shop.
Activities Arts & crafts; Cards; Games;
  Reading groups; Prayer groups; Movies;
  Dances/Social/Cultural gatherings; Outside
  entertainment.

Lake Taylor Hospital—Long-Term Care Unit
1309 Kempsville Rd, Norfolk, VA 23502
(804) 461-5001, 461-4282 FAX
Admin Dean F Martin. *Dir of Nursing* Sandy
  Whitaker. *Medical Dir* Robert Morton.
Licensure Skilled care; Intermediate care; Sub-
  acute care. *Beds* SNF 108; ICF 120; Sub-
  acute care 104. *Private Pay Patients* 10%.
  Certified Medicaid; Medicare.
Owner Publicly owned.
Admissions Requirements Physician's request.
Staff Physicians 5 (ft); RNs 24 (ft), 13 (pt);
  LPNs 31 (ft), 20 (pt); Nurses' aides 32 (ft),
  55 (pt); Physical therapists 1 (ft), 1 (pt);
  Recreational therapists 1 (ft); Occupational
  therapists 1 (ft); Speech therapists 1 (ft);
  Dietitians 3 (ft); Podiatrists 1 (ft).
Facilities Dining room; Physical therapy
  room; Activities room; Chapel; Crafts room;
  Laundry room; Barber/Beauty shop.
Activities Arts & crafts; Cards; Games;
  Reading groups; Prayer groups; Movies;
  Shopping trips; Dances/Social/Cultural
  gatherings; Intergenerational programs; Pet
  therapy.

Norfolk Community Hospital
3539 Corprew Ave, Norfolk, VA 23504
(804) 628-1400
Admin Phillip D Brooks.
Licensure Skilled care. *Beds* SNF 13.
Owner Nonprofit corp.

Richardson Nursing Home
419 W 28th St, Norfolk, VA 23508
(804) 622-1094
Admin Lillian T Moseley.
Medical Dir Sandra Thorogood.
Licensure Intermediate care. *Beds* 43.
  Certified Medicaid.
Owner Proprietary corp.
Admissions Requirements Medical
  examination; Physician's request.
Staff RNs 1 (ft); LPNs 3 (ft), 1 (pt); Nurses'
  aides 14 (ft), 2 (pt); Activities coordinators 1
  (ft).
Facilities Dining room; Activities room;
  Laundry room.

St Mary's Infant Home Inc
317 Chapel St, Norfolk, VA 23504
(804) 622-2208
Admin William M Jolly.

Licensure Intermediate care for mentally
  retarded. *Beds* ICF/MR 88; Specialty infants
  birth thru 11 years. *Certified* Medicaid.
Owner Nonprofit corp.

Sentara Nursing Center—Norfolk
249 S Newtown Rd, Norfolk, VA 23502
(804) 461-8500
Admin Jeffrey D Custer.
Licensure Skilled care; Intermediate care. *Beds*
  SNF 23; ICF 200. *Certified* Medicaid.
Owner Nonprofit corp.
Admissions Requirements Minimum age 50.
Staff Physicians 2 (ft); RNs 1 (ft), 2 (pt);
  LPNs 4 (ft), 4 (pt); Nurses' aides 13 (ft), 7
  (pt); Physical therapists 1 (pt); Activities
  coordinators 1 (ft); Dietitians 1 (ft);
  Podiatrists 1 (ft).
Facilities Dining room; Activities room;
  Laundry room; Barber/Beauty shop; Library.
Activities Arts & crafts; Cards; Games;
  Reading groups; Prayer groups; Movies;
  Dances/Social/Cultural gatherings.

Thorton Hall Health Care Unit
827 Norview Ave, Norfolk, VA 23509
(804) 853-6281
Admin G F Rowe.
Licensure Intermediate care. *Beds* ICF 60.
Owner Proprietary corp.

Norton

St Mary's Hospital
3rd St NE, Norton, VA 24273
(703) 679-9100
Admin Gary DelForge. *Dir of Nursing* Betty
  Elswick. *Medical Dir* Tom Renfro MD.
Licensure Intermediate care. *Beds* ICF 44.
  Certified Medicaid; Medicare.
Owner Nonprofit organization/foundation.
Admissions Requirements Medical
  examination; Physician's request.
Staff Physicians 12 (ft); RNs 1 (ft); LPNs 7
  (ft), 2 (pt); Nurses' aides 23 (ft); Physical
  therapists 1 (ft); Speech therapists 1 (pt);
  Activities coordinators 1 (ft); Dietitians 1
  (pt); Pastors 1 (ft).
Affiliation Roman Catholic.
Facilities Dining room; Physical therapy
  room; Activities room; Crafts room; Laundry
  room; Barber/Beauty shop.
Activities Arts & crafts; Cards; Games;
  Reading groups; Prayer groups; Movies;
  Shopping trips; Dances/Social/Cultural
  gatherings; Intergenerational programs; Pet
  therapy.

Oakton

Sunrise Terrace Retirement Home
10322 Blake Ln, Oakton, VA 22124
(703) 255-2050
Medical Dir Lillian Boes Admis.
Licensure Home for adults. *Beds* Home for
  adults 50.

Onancock

Hermitage on the Eastern Shore
North St Ext, Onancock, VA 23417
(804) 787-4343
Admin Charles M Johnson. *Dir of Nursing*
  Elizabeth S Perry RNC. *Medical Dir* E W
  Bosworth MD.
Licensure Intermediate care; Retirement. *Beds*
  ICF 35; Retirement 138. *Private Pay
  Patients* 100%.
Owner Nonprofit corp (Virginia United
  Methodist Homes Inc).
Admissions Requirements Minimum age 65;
  Medical examination.
Staff RNs 1 (ft); LPNs 5 (ft), 5 (pt); Nurses'
  aides 17 (ft), 17 (pt); Activities coordinators
  1 (ft), 1 (pt); Dietitians 1 (pt).
Affiliation Methodist.

Facilities Dining room; Physical therapy room; Activities room; Chapel; Crafts room; Laundry room; Barber/Beauty shop; Library; Social hall; Lounges.
Activities Arts & crafts; Cards; Games; Reading groups; Prayer groups; Movies; Shopping trips; Dances/Social/Cultural gatherings; Pet therapy; Bible study; Vespers; Special outings.

Orange

Orange County Nursing Home & Home for Adults
120 Dogwood Ln, Orange, VA 22960
(703) 672-2611
Admin Delores C Darnell RNC. Dir of Nursing Shirley A Stone RN. Medical Dir Dr R S LeGarde.
Licensure Intermediate care; Home for aged. Beds ICF 134; Home for aged 34. Certified Medicaid.
Owner Publicly owned.
Admissions Requirements Medical examination.
Staff RNs 5 (ft); LPNs 20 (ft), 4 (pt); Nurses' aides 68 (ft), 18 (pt); Physical therapists 1 (pt); Recreational therapists 2 (ft), 1 (pt); Occupational therapists 1 (pt); Speech therapists 1 (pt); Activities coordinators 1 (ft); Dietitians 1 (pt); Ophthalmologists 1 (pt).
Facilities Dining room; Physical therapy room; Activities room; Chapel; Crafts room; Laundry room; Barber/Beauty shop; Library.
Activities Arts & crafts; Cards; Games; Reading groups; Prayer groups; Movies; Shopping trips; Dances/Social/Cultural gatherings.

Parksley

Accomack County Nursing Home
PO Box 185, Rte 1, Parksley, VA 23421
(804) 665-5133
Admin W J Bundick Jr.
Medical Dir Edward S White MD.
Licensure Intermediate care. Beds ICF 136. Certified Medicaid.
Owner Publicly owned.
Admissions Requirements Minimum age 14; Medical examination; Physician's request.
Staff Physicians 1 (pt); RNs 2 (ft), 2 (pt); LPNs 11 (ft), 4 (pt); Nurses' aides 32 (ft), 17 (pt); Occupational therapists 1 (pt); Activities coordinators 1 (ft); Dietitians 1 (pt); Ophthalmologists 1 (pt).
Facilities Dining room; Physical therapy room; Activities room; Chapel; Crafts room; Laundry room; Barber/Beauty shop; Library.
Activities Arts & crafts; Cards; Games; Reading groups; Prayer groups; Movies; Dances/Social/Cultural gatherings.

Petersburg

Battlefield Park Convalescent Center
250 Flank Rd, Petersburg, VA 23805
(804) 861-2223
Admin Phyllis J Watson. Dir of Nursing Martha Spain RN. Medical Dir William S Sloan MD.
Licensure Intermediate care. Beds ICF 120. Private Pay Patients 25-30%. Certified Medicaid.
Owner Proprietary corp (Beverly Enterprises).
Admissions Requirements Medical examination; Physician's request.
Staff Physicians; RNs; LPNs; Nurses' aides; Activities coordinators; Dietitians.
Facilities Dining room; Physical therapy room; Activities room; Crafts room; Laundry room; Barber/Beauty shop; Courtyard.

Activities Arts & crafts; Cards; Games; Reading groups; Prayer groups; Movies; Shopping trips; Dances/Social/Cultural gatherings; Intergenerational programs; Pet therapy.

Hiram W Davis Medical Center
PO Box 4030, Petersburg, VA 23803
(804) 524-7000
Admin Silas Burnette Jr Dir.
Licensure Skilled care; Intermediate care for mentally retarded. Beds SNF 60; ICF 10; M/S 17.

Southside Regional Medical Center
801 S Adams St, Petersburg, VA 23803
(804) 862-5903
Admin Kirby H Smith Exec Dir.
Licensure Skilled care. Beds SNF 20.
Owner Nonprofit corp.

Southside Virginia Training Center
PO Box 4110, Petersburg, VA 23803
(804) 524-7333
Admin Richard E Buckley PhD. Dir of Nursing Conroy Johnson RN. Medical Dir Patricia Hunt MD MPH.
Licensure Skilled care; Intermediate care for mentally retarded. Beds SNF 48; ICF/MR 808. Private Pay Patients 0%. Certified Medicaid.
Owner Publicly owned.
Staff Physicians 6 (ft), 1 (pt); RNs 38 (ft); LPNs 70 (ft), 2 (pt); Nurses' aides 702 (ft); Physical therapists 3 (ft); Recreational therapists 9 (ft); Occupational therapists 7 (ft); Speech therapists 6 (ft); Dietitians 6 (ft); Audiologists 2 (ft); Chaplains.
Facilities Dining room; Physical therapy room; Activities room; Chapel; Crafts room; Laundry room; Barber/Beauty shop; Library.
Activities Arts & crafts; Games; Prayer groups; Movies; Shopping trips; Dances/Social/Cultural gatherings; Vocational and educational services; Religious services; Foster grandparent program.

Walnut Hill Convalescent Center
287 South Blvd, Petersburg, VA 23805
(804) 733-1190
Admin Elizabeth C Croxton. Dir of Nursing Fred Long. Medical Dir Peter Ault MD.
Licensure Skilled care; Intermediate care; Alzheimer's care. Beds SNF 28; ICF 92. Certified Medicaid; Medicare.
Owner Proprietary corp (Beverly Enterprises).
Admissions Requirements Medical examination.
Staff RNs 4 (ft); LPNs 20 (ft); Nurses' aides 50 (ft); Physical therapists 1 (pt); Recreational therapists 1 (ft), 1 (pt); Activities coordinators 1 (ft), 1 (pt); Dietitians 1 (pt); Ophthalmologists 1 (pt).
Facilities Dining room; Physical therapy room; Activities room; Crafts room; Laundry room; Barber/Beauty shop.
Activities Arts & crafts; Cards; Games; Prayer groups; Movies; Shopping trips; Dances/Social/Cultural gatherings.

Poquoson

Bayside of Poquoson Convalescent Center
1 Vantage Dr, Poquoson, VA 23662
(804) 868-9960
Admin Mary T Ward.
Licensure Intermediate care. Beds ICF 60.
Owner Proprietary corp.

Portsmouth

Autumn Care of Portsmouth
3610 Winchester Dr, Portsmouth, VA 23707
(804) 397-0725
Admin Thelma J Wilson. Dir of Nursing Janice Turner RN. Medical Dir Boniface Costa MD.

Licensure Skilled care; Intermediate care; Alzheimer's care. Beds SNF 10; ICF 98. Certified Medicaid.
Owner Proprietary corp (Autumn Corp).
Admissions Requirements Medical examination; Physician's request.
Staff RNs 1 (ft); LPNs 5 (ft), 5 (pt); Nurses' aides 26 (ft); Activities coordinators 1 (ft); Dietitians 1 (ft); Restorative nursing aides 3 (ft) Social worker 1 (ft).
Facilities Dining room; Activities room; Crafts room; Laundry room; Barber/Beauty shop; Social services; Staff development.
Activities Arts & crafts; Cards; Games; Reading groups; Prayer groups; Movies; Shopping trips; Dances/Social/Cultural gatherings; Picnics; Ferry trips; Dinning out.

Beverly Manor of Portsmouth
900 London Blvd, Portsmouth, VA 23704
(804) 393-6864
Admin Roderick Williams.
Medical Dir Faith Dajao MD.
Licensure Skilled care; Intermediate care. Beds SNF 10; ICF 110.
Owner Proprietary corp (Beverly Enterprises).
Admissions Requirements Minimum age 14; Medical examination; Physician's request.
Staff RNs 5 (ft), 5 (pt); LPNs 9 (ft), 8 (pt); Nurses' aides 26 (ft), 30 (pt); Physical therapists; Occupational therapists; Speech therapists; Activities coordinators 1 (ft).
Facilities Dining room; Physical therapy room; Activities room; Chapel; Laundry room; Barber/Beauty shop.
Activities Arts & crafts; Cards; Games; Reading groups; Prayer groups; Movies; Shopping trips; Dances/Social/Cultural gatherings; Picnics & other outings.

William T Hall Memorial Convalescent Home
4201 Greenwood Dr/Sentara, Portsmouth, VA 23701
(804) 399-0691
Admin Anthony L Fludd. Dir of Nursing Aleurta Hughes. Medical Dir Dr J Marven.
Licensure Intermediate care. Beds 32. Certified Medicaid.
Owner Nonprofit organization/foundation.
Staff RNs 1 (ft); LPNs 3 (ft), 6 (pt); Nurses' aides 4 (ft), 9 (pt); Activities coordinators 1 (ft); Dietitians 1 (ft).
Facilities Dining room; Activities room; Laundry room.

Holiday House of Portsmouth
4211 County St, Portsmouth, VA 23707
(804) 397-6352
Admin Lois Ziegler Exec Dir. Dir of Nursing Amanda Powell.
Licensure Intermediate care for mentally retarded. Beds ICF/MR 28. Certified Medicaid.
Owner Nonprofit organization/foundation.
Admissions Requirements Minimum age 4-21; Medical examination; Physician's request.
Staff Physicians (family practice); RNs 1 (ft); LPNs 3 (ft); Nurses' aides 18 (ft); Physical therapists 2 (ft); Recreational therapists 2 (ft); Occupational therapists 2 (ft); Speech therapists 2 (ft); Activities coordinators 1 (ft); Dietitians 1 (ft).
Facilities Dining room; Physical therapy room; Activities room; Crafts room; Laundry room.
Activities Arts & crafts; Games; Movies; Shopping trips; Dances/Social/Cultural gatherings.

Manning Convalescent Home Inc
PO Box 430, 175 Hatton St, Portsmouth, VA 23705
(804) 399-1321
Admin Thurman W Manning.
Medical Dir Dr E A Barham Jr.
Licensure Skilled care; Intermediate care. Beds SNF 96; ICF 162. Certified Medicaid; Medicare.

Owner Privately owned.
Admissions Requirements Minimum age 14; Medical examination; Physician's request.
Staff Physicians 64 (ft); RNs 14 (ft), 9 (pt); LPNs 20 (ft), 7 (pt); Nurses' aides 97 (ft), 16 (pt); Physical therapists 1 (ft); Occupational therapists 1 (ft); Speech therapists 1 (ft); Activities coordinators 1 (ft); Dietitians 1 (ft), 1 (pt); Ophthalmologists 2 (pt); Dentists 2 (pt).
Facilities Dining room; Physical therapy room; Activities room; Chapel; Crafts room; Laundry room; Barber/Beauty shop; Library; Dental Office.
Activities Arts & crafts; Cards; Games; Reading groups; Prayer groups; Movies; Shopping trips.

Sentara Nursing Center—Portsmouth
4201 Greenwood Dr, Portsmouth, VA 23701
(804) 488-4400
Admin Anthony L Fludd.
Licensure Intermediate care; Private pay. *Beds* ICF 122; Private pay 10.
Owner Privately owned.

Pulaski

Pulaski Health Care Center Health Care Unit
2401 Lee Hwy, Pulaski, VA 24301
(703) 980-3111
Admin Deidra S White.
Licensure Intermediate care; Retirement. *Beds* ICF 60. *Certified* Medicaid; Medicare.
Owner Proprietary corp (Medical Facilities of America).
Admissions Requirements Minimum age 14; Medical examination.
Facilities Dining room; Physical therapy room; Activities room; Crafts room; Laundry room; Barber/Beauty shop.
Activities Arts & crafts; Cards; Games; Reading groups; Prayer groups; Movies; Shopping trips; Dances/Social/Cultural gatherings; Success therapy; Flower cart; Visitation program.

Purcellville

Loudon Valley Country Manor I & II
763 E Main St, Purcellville, VA 22132
(703) 338-5615
Medical Dir Mr Robin Admis; Deborah Johns Admis.
Licensure Home for adults. *Beds* Home for adults 24.

Radford

Fairlawn Group Home
1206 Norwood, Radford, VA 24073
(703) 831-5916
Admin Lynn H Chenault.
Licensure Intermediate care for mentally retarded. *Beds* ICF/MR 12. *Private Pay Patients* 0%. *Certified* Medicaid.
Owner Publicly owned.
Admissions Requirements Minimum age 18; Medical examination; Physician's request.
Staff Physicians 1 (pt); RNs 1 (pt); LPNs 1 (pt); Physical therapists 1 (pt); Speech therapists 1 (pt); Activities coordinators 1 (pt); Dietitians 1 (pt); Ophthalmologists 1 (pt); Podiatrists 1 (pt); Audiologists 1 (pt).
Facilities Dining room; Activities room; Laundry room.
Activities Arts & crafts; Cards; Games; Movies; Shopping trips; Dances/Social/ Cultural gatherings; Intergenerational programs; Pet therapy.

Radford Community Hospital
8th & Randolph Sts, Radford, VA 24141
(703) 731-2502
Admin Lester L Lamb Pres.

Licensure Skilled care; Intermediate care. *Beds* SNF 3; ICF 9.
Owner Nonprofit corp.

Wheatland Hills Retirement Center Inc
Rte 11 W, Fairlawn, Radford, VA 24141
(703) 639-2411
Admin Benjamin F Holstein Jr.
Licensure Intermediate care. *Beds* ICF 24.
Owner Proprietary corp.

Reston

Cameron Glen Care Center
1800 Cameron Glen Dr, Reston, VA 22090
(703) 834-5800, 834-5851 FAX
Admin John A Olmstead. *Dir of Nursing* Jane C Decker. *Medical Dir* Nicholas B Cirillo MD.
Licensure Skilled care; Intermediate care; Home for adults with dementia; Alzheimer's care. *Beds* SNF 14; ICF 106; Home for adults with dementia 120. *Private Pay Patients* 50%. *Certified* Medicaid; Medicare.
Owner Nonprofit corp.
Admissions Requirements Medical examination.
Staff RNs 10 (ft), 3 (pt); LPNs 12 (ft), 6 (pt); Nurses' aides; Physical therapists 1 (pt); Recreational therapists 1 (ft); Occupational therapists 1 (pt); Speech therapists 1 (pt); Activities coordinators 2 (ft); Dietitians 1 (pt); Podiatrists (contracted).
Facilities Dining room; Physical therapy room; Activities room; Chapel; Crafts room; Laundry room; Barber/Beauty shop; Library.
Activities Arts & crafts; Cards; Games; Reading groups; Prayer groups; Movies; Shopping trips; Dances/Social/Cultural gatherings; Intergenerational programs; Pet therapy.

Tall Oaks Fellowship House
12052 N Shore Dr, Reston, VA 22090
(703) 834-5420
Medical Dir Helen Hessler Admis.
Licensure Home for adults. *Beds* Home for adults 169.

Rich Creek

Riverview Nursing Home Inc
PO Box 327, 120 Virginia Ave, Rich Creek, VA 24147
(703) 726-2328
Admin W F Lambert. *Dir of Nursing* Laurie Dobbs RN. *Medical Dir* L E Delap MD.
Licensure Intermediate care; Retirement. *Beds* ICF 60; Retirement 35. *Certified* Medicaid.
Owner Proprietary corp.
Admissions Requirements Medical examination.
Staff Physicians 5 (pt); RNs 2 (ft), 2 (pt); LPNs 3 (ft), 4 (pt); Nurses' aides 18 (ft), 9 (pt); Physical therapists 1 (pt); Activities coordinators 1 (ft); Dietitians 1 (pt); Podiatrists 1 (pt); Dentists 1 (pt); Social workers 1 (ft).
Facilities Dining room; Activities room; Chapel; Crafts room; Laundry room; Barber/ Beauty shop.
Activities Arts & crafts; Cards; Games; Reading groups; Prayer groups; Movies; Shopping trips; Dances/Social/Cultural gatherings.

Richlands

Humana Hospital—Clinch Valley Long-Term Care Unit
2949 W Front St, Richlands, VA 24641
(703) 963-0811
Admin William A Gillespie Exec Dir.
Licensure Skilled care. *Beds* SNF 10.
Owner Proprietary corp.

Richmond

Beth Shalom Home of Central Virginia
12000 Gayton Rd, Richmond, VA 23233
(804) 750-2183, 750-1078 FAX
Admin Barbara K Gottlieb. *Dir of Nursing* Marian L Baxter RN MS. *Medical Dir* Sheldon Retchin MD.
Licensure Intermediate care; Alzheimer's care. *Beds* ICF 116. *Private Pay Patients* 33%. *Certified* Medicaid.
Owner Nonprofit corp (Beth Shalom Geriatric Services of Virginia).
Admissions Requirements Minimum age 65; Medical examination.
Staff Physicians 2 (pt); RNs 11 (ft); LPNs 18 (ft); Nurses' aides 62 (ft); Physical therapists 1 (pt); Recreational therapists 2 (ft); Occupational therapists 1 (pt); Speech therapists 1 (pt); Activities coordinators 1 (ft); Dietitians 1 (pt); Ophthalmologists 1 (pt); Podiatrists 2 (pt).
Languages Yiddish, Hebrew.
Affiliation Jewish.
Facilities Dining room; Physical therapy room; Activities room; Chapel; Crafts room; Laundry room; Barber/Beauty shop; Library; Gift shop.
Activities Arts & crafts; Cards; Games; Reading groups; Prayer groups; Movies; Shopping trips; Dances/Social/Cultural gatherings; Intergenerational programs; Pet therapy.

Cambridge Manor
1776 Cambridge Dr, Richmond, VA 23233
(804) 740-6174
Admin E Robert Thomas.
Licensure Intermediate care. *Beds* ICF 196. *Certified* Medicaid; Medicare.
Owner Proprietary corp.

Camelot Hall Nursing Home
2400 E Parham Rd, Richmond, VA 23228
(804) 264-9185
Admin Charles B Puckett.
Licensure Skilled care; Intermediate care. *Beds* SNF 22; ICF 58. *Certified* Medicaid; Medicare.
Owner Proprietary corp (Medical Facilities of America).

Chippenham Manor Nursing Center
7246 Forest Hill Ave, Richmond, VA 23225
(804) 320-7901
Admin Irvin D Winebrenner MA NHA. *Dir of Nursing* Pat Miller. *Medical Dir* Justo T Perez MD.
Licensure Intermediate care. *Beds* ICF 196. *Private Pay Patients* 26%. *Certified* Medicaid.
Owner Nonprofit organization/foundation (Keystone Healthcare/Delco Systems Services Inc).
Admissions Requirements Medical examination; Physician's request.
Staff Physicians 1 (pt); RNs 8 (ft), 7 (pt); LPNs 10 (ft), 4 (pt); Nurses' aides 71 (ft), 3 (pt); Physical therapists 1 (pt); Reality therapists 1 (pt); Recreational therapists 1 (ft); Occupational therapists 1 (pt); Speech therapists 1 (pt); Activities coordinators 1 (ft); Dietitians 1 (pt); Podiatrists 1 (pt); Audiologists 1 (pt).
Facilities Dining room; Physical therapy room; Activities room; Crafts room; Laundry room; Barber/Beauty shop.
Activities Arts & crafts; Cards; Games; Reading groups; Prayer groups; Movies; Shopping trips; Dances/Social/Cultural gatherings; Intergenerational programs; Pet therapy.

Convalescent Care Inc
7204 Glen Forest Dr, Ste 101, Richmond, VA 23226
(804) 285-7600
Admin W W Willis Pres.

Licensure Skilled care; Intermediate care;
Home for adults. *Beds* SNF 60; ICF 785;
Home for adults 55. *Certified* Medicaid;
Medicare.
Owner Proprietary corp.
Admissions Requirements Minimum age 14;
Medical examination; Physician's request.
Facilities Dining room; Physical therapy
room; Activities room; Chapel; Crafts room;
Laundry room; Barber/Beauty shop; Library.
Activities Arts & crafts; Cards; Games;
Reading groups; Prayer groups; Movies;
Shopping trips; Dances/Social/Cultural
gatherings.

Forest Hill Convalescent Center
4403 Forest Hill Ave, Richmond, VA 23225
(804) 231-0231
Admin Matthew C Farmer.
Licensure Intermediate care. *Beds* ICF 174.
Certified Medicaid.
Owner Proprietary corp.

Imperial Health Center
1717 Bellevue Ave, Richmond, VA 23227
(804) 262-7364
Admin James D Gillentine.
Licensure Intermediate care; Private pay. *Beds*
ICF 34; Private pay 34. *Certified* Medicaid.
Owner Proprietary corp.

**Lakewood Manor Baptist Retirement
Community Inc**
1900 Lauderdale Dr, Richmond, VA 23233
(804) 740-2900
Admin Robert E Dowd.
Licensure Private pay. *Beds* Private pay 110.
Owner Nonprofit corp.

Libbie Convalescent Center
PO Box 17190, 1901 Libbie Ave, Richmond,
VA 23226
(804) 282-9767
Admin Morris W Rooke.
Licensure Skilled care; Intermediate care;
Private pay. *Beds* SNF 45; ICF 109; Private
pay 41.
Owner Proprietary corp.

**Little Sisters of the Poor—St Joseph's Home
for the Aged Health Care Unit**
1503 Michael Rd, Richmond, VA 23229-4899
(804) 288-6245
Admin Sr Marie Candide McCabe.
Licensure Intermediate care. *Beds* ICF 50.
Certified Medicaid.
Owner Nonprofit corp.
Affiliation Roman Catholic.

Masonic Home of Virginia—Health Care Unit
4101 Nine Mile Rd, Richmond, VA 23223
(804) 222-1694
Admin Charles O Franck Jr.
Medical Dir J Earle Smith.
Beds Private pay 42.
Owner Nonprofit corp.
Admissions Requirements Minimum age 65;
Medical examination.
Affiliation Masons.
Facilities Dining room; Physical therapy
room; Activities room; Chapel; Crafts room;
Laundry room; Barber/Beauty shop; Library.
Activities Arts & crafts; Games; Prayer groups;
Movies; Shopping trips; Dances/Social/
Cultural gatherings.

Richmond Home for Ladies Health Care Unit
2620 Stuart Ave, Richmond, VA 23220
(804) 254-8021
Admin Nancy L Richardson.
Licensure Private pay. *Beds* Private pay 22.
Owner Nonprofit corp.

Richmond Nursing Home
1900 Cool Ln, Richmond, VA 23223
(804) 780-4914
Admin Joyce A Kauffmann, acting. *Dir of
Nursing* Alvina S Bey RN. *Medical Dir*
Hayes E Willis MD.

Licensure Skilled care; Intermediate care. *Beds*
SNF 56; ICF 113. *Certified* Medicaid;
Medicare.
Owner Publicly owned.
Staff Physicians 4 (pt); RNs 6 (ft), 4 (pt);
LPNs 22 (ft), 3 (pt); Nurses' aides 56 (ft), 6
(pt); Physical therapists 1 (pt); Recreational
therapists 1 (ft); Occupational therapists 2
(ft); Speech therapists 1 (pt); Activities
coordinators 1 (ft); Dietitians 1 (ft);
Ophthalmologists 1 (pt); Podiatrists 2 (pt);
Audiologists 1 (pt).

Stratford Hall Nursing Center
2125 Hilliard Rd, Richmond, VA 23228
(804) 266-9666
Admin Vivian D Thomas.
Medical Dir Thomas W Murrell Jr MD.
Licensure Skilled care; Intermediate care;
Private pay. *Beds* SNF 54; ICF 22; Private
pay 118. *Certified* Medicaid; Medicare.
Owner Proprietary corp (Manor Care Inc).
Staff RNs 7 (ft), 7 (pt); LPNs 10 (ft), 4 (pt);
Nurses' aides 60 (ft), 5 (pt); Physical
therapists 1 (ft), 1 (pt); Recreational
therapists 2 (ft); Occupational therapists 1
(pt); Speech therapists 1 (ft); Activities
coordinators 1 (ft); Dietitians 1 (ft).
Facilities Dining room; Physical therapy
room; Activities room; Crafts room; Laundry
room; Barber/Beauty shop; Library.
Activities Arts & crafts; Cards; Games;
Reading groups; Prayer groups; Movies;
Shopping trips; Dances/Social/Cultural
gatherings.

University Park
2420 Pemberton Rd, Richmond, VA 23233-
2099
(804) 747-9200
Admin Walter W Regirer.
Medical Dir H Chesley Decker MD.
Licensure Skilled care; Intermediate care;
Home of adults; Club homes; Home health
care; Retirement. *Beds* SNF 8; ICF 182;
Home of adults 18; Club homes 6. *Certified*
Medicaid; Medicare; VA.
Owner Proprietary corp.
Admissions Requirements Medical
examination; Physician's request.
Staff Physicians 83 (pt); RNs 18 (ft); LPNs 20
(ft); Nurses' aides 69 (ft); Physical therapists
2 (ft); Reality therapists 1 (ft); Recreational
therapists 4 (ft); Occupational therapists 2
(ft); Speech therapists 1 (pt); Activities
coordinators 1 (ft); Dietitians 1 (ft);
Ophthalmologists 1 (pt); Podiatrists 1 (pt);
Dentists 1 (pt).
Facilities Dining room; Physical therapy
room; Activities room; Chapel; Crafts room;
Laundry room; Barber/Beauty shop; Library;
Tavern; Dental; Gift shop.
Activities Arts & crafts; Cards; Games;
Reading groups; Prayer groups; Movies;
Shopping trips; Dances/Social/Cultural
gatherings.

**Via Health Care Center/The Hermitage
Richmond Virginia United Methodist Homes
Inc**
1600 Westwood Ave, Richmond, VA 23227
(804) 355-5721
Admin C Bruce Pfeiffer. *Dir of Nursing*
Lethea Hague RN. *Medical Dir* Dr Ronald
Artz.
Licensure Private pay. *Beds* Private pay 115.
Owner Nonprofit corp.
Admissions Requirements Minimum age 65;
Medical examination.
Staff Physicians 1 (pt); RNs 5 (ft); LPNs 9
(ft), 3 (pt); Nurses' aides 56 (ft), 13 (pt);
Physical therapists 1 (ft), 1 (pt); Activities
coordinators 1 (ft); Dietitians 1 (ft).
Affiliation Methodist.
Facilities Dining room; Physical therapy
room; Activities room; Chapel; Crafts room;
Laundry room; Barber/Beauty shop; Library.

Activities Arts & crafts; Cards; Games;
Reading groups; Prayer groups; Movies;
Shopping trips; Dances/Social/Cultural
gatherings.

Virginia Home
1101 Hampton St, Richmond, VA 23220
(804) 359-4093
Admin Robert A Crouse. *Dir of Nursing*
Cornelia Fields. *Medical Dir* Dr Gile
Robertson.
Licensure Intermediate care. *Beds* ICF 113.
Certified Medicaid.
Owner Nonprofit corp.
Admissions Requirements Minimum age 18;
Medical examination; Physician's request.
Staff Physicians 4 (pt); RNs 5 (ft), 3 (pt);
LPNs 9 (ft), 7 (pt); Physical therapists 1 (pt);
Recreational therapists 3 (ft); Occupational
therapists 1 (ft); Speech therapists 1 (pt);
Activities coordinators 1 (ft); Dietitians 1
(ft); Ophthalmologists 1 (pt); Podiatrists 1
(pt); Dentists 1 (pt).
Facilities Dining room; Physical therapy
room; Activities room; Chapel; Crafts room;
Laundry room; Barber/Beauty shop; Library;
Recreation room; Sun parlors; Solarium;
Medical room; Dental room.
Activities Arts & crafts; Cards; Games;
Reading groups; Prayer groups; Movies;
Shopping trips; Dances/Social/Cultural
gatherings; Outings with vehicles.

Westminster Canterbury House
1600 Westbrook Ave, Richmond, VA 23227
(804) 264-6000, 264-3529 FAX
Admin W Thomas Cunningham Jr, Pres;
Marion B Hunter, Health Svcs Adm. *Dir of
Nursing* Phyllis Moore RN. *Medical Dir*
Fleming W Gill MD.
Licensure Skilled care; Intermediate care;
Independent living; Personal care. *Beds* SNF
30; ICF 103; Independent living apts 367;
Personal care apts 130. *Private Pay Patients*
13%. *Certified* Medicaid; Medicare.
Owner Nonprofit corp.
Admissions Requirements Minimum age 65.
Staff RNs 12 (ft), 10 (pt); LPNs 11 (ft), 5 (pt);
Nurses' aides 66 (ft), 5 (pt); Physical
therapists; Recreational therapists 1 (ft);
Activities coordinators 1 (ft); Dietitians 1
(ft); Podiatrists 1 (pt); 3-11 evening
managers 1 (ft); RN clinical institute 1 (ft);
Unit secretaries 5 (ft).
Facilities Dining room; Physical therapy
room; Activities room; Chapel; Crafts room;
Laundry room; Barber/Beauty shop; Library;
Exercise room; Jacuzzi; Pharmacy; Pic n'
Pay Shop; Bank; Voting precinct; Private
rooms; Van.
Activities Arts & crafts; Cards; Games;
Reading groups; Prayer groups; Movies;
Shopping trips; Dances/Social/Cultural
gatherings; Intergenerational programs; Pet
therapy; Bazaars.

Westport Convalescent Center
7300 Forest Ave, Richmond, VA 23226
(804) 288-3152
Admin Margaret L Stowe.
Medical Dir Melvin Fratkin MD.
Licensure Intermediate care. *Beds* ICF 225.
Certified Medicaid.
Owner Proprietary corp.
Admissions Requirements Minimum age 14;
Medical examination; Physician's request.
Staff RNs 13 (ft); LPNs 14 (ft); Nurses' aides
61 (ft); Physical therapists 1 (ft); Reality
therapists 2 (ft); Activities coordinators 1
(ft).
Facilities Dining room; Physical therapy
room; Activities room; Chapel; Crafts room;
Laundry room; Barber/Beauty shop.
Activities Arts & crafts; Cards; Games;
Reading groups; Prayer groups; Movies;
Shopping trips.

Westwood Transitional Care Unit—Richmond Memorial Hospital
1300 Westwood Ave, Richmond, VA 23227
(804) 254-6129
Admin Samuel F Lillard Pres.
Licensure Skilled care; Intermediate care. *Beds* SNF 15; ICF 5.
Owner Nonprofit corp.

Windsor
3600 Grove Ave, Richmond, VA 23221
(804) 353-3881
Admin Ms Walter W Regirer.
Licensure Skilled care; Intermediate care. *Beds* SNF 4; ICF 71. *Certified* Medicaid; Medicare.
Owner Proprietary corp.

Roanoke

Friendship Manor Nursing Home
327 Hershberger Rd NW, Roanoke, VA 24012
(703) 366-7641
Admin H Lawrence Rice.
Medical Dir Dr Anthony R Stavola.
Licensure Skilled care; Intermediate care; Retirement; Alzheimer's care. *Beds* SNF 47; ICF 326. *Certified* Medicaid; Medicare.
Owner Nonprofit corp.
Admissions Requirements Minimum age 50.
Staff Physicians; RNs 13 (ft), 8 (pt); LPNs 22 (ft), 11 (pt); Nurses' aides 101 (ft), 40 (pt); Physical therapists 1 (ft), 2 (pt); Reality therapists 1 (ft); Recreational therapists 1 (ft); Occupational therapists 1 (ft); Speech therapists 1 (pt); Activities coordinators 2 (ft); Dietitians 1 (ft), 1 (pt).
Facilities Dining room; Physical therapy room; Activities room; Chapel; Crafts room; Laundry room; Barber/Beauty shop; Library.
Activities Arts & crafts; Cards; Games; Reading groups; Prayer groups; Movies; Shopping trips; Dances/Social/Cultural gatherings.

Hazelridge Road Residence
5220 Hazelridge Rd, Roanoke, VA 24012
(703) 366-9156
Admin Fred Rossel Jr Exec Dir.
Licensure Intermediate care for mentally retarded. *Beds* ICF/MR 12.

Liberty House Nursing Home
324 King George Ave SW, Roanoke, VA 24016
(703) 345-8139
Admin Kenneth E Vest.
Medical Dir A M Jacobson MD.
Licensure Intermediate care. *Beds* ICF 141. *Certified* Medicaid.
Owner Proprietary corp (Beverly Enterprises).
Admissions Requirements Medical examination.
Staff Nurses' aides; Physical therapists; Speech therapists; Social services.
Facilities Dining room; Physical therapy room; Activities room; Laundry room; Barber/Beauty shop.
Activities Arts & crafts; Cards; Games; Reading groups; Prayer groups; Movies; Shopping trips; Dances/Social/Cultural gatherings.

Roanoke City Nursing Home
4365 Coyner Springs Rd, Roanoke, VA 24012
(703) 977-1018
Admin R F Hyatt. *Dir of Nursing* Martha Hartley. *Medical Dir* Ronald Overstreet.
Licensure Intermediate care. *Beds* ICF 58. *Private Pay Patients* 5%. *Certified* Medicaid.
Owner Publicly owned.
Admissions Requirements Medical examination.
Staff Physicians 1 (ft); RNs 3 (ft); LPNs 4 (ft), 1 (pt); Nurses' aides 20 (ft), 2 (pt); Activities coordinators 1 (ft); Dietitians 1 (ft).

Facilities Dining room; Activities room.
Activities Arts & crafts; Cards; Games; Movies; Shopping trips; Dances/Social/Cultural gatherings.

Roanoke United Methodist Home
PO Box 6339, 1009 Old Country Club Rd NW, Roanoke, VA 24017
(703) 344-6248
Admin Thomas H Au.
Medical Dir Dr William Ward.
Licensure Private pay; Retirement. *Beds* Private pay 40.
Owner Nonprofit corp.
Admissions Requirements Minimum age 65; Medical examination.
Staff Physicians 4 (pt); RNs 4 (ft), 4 (pt); LPNs 4 (ft), 7 (pt); Nurses' aides 21 (ft), 5 (pt); Physical therapists 1 (pt); Activities coordinators 1 (ft); Dietitians 1 (ft); Ophthalmologists 2 (pt); Dentists 1 (pt).
Affiliation Methodist.
Facilities Dining room; Activities room; Chapel; Crafts room; Laundry room; Barber/Beauty shop; Library.
Activities Arts & crafts; Cards; Games; Reading groups; Prayer groups; Movies; Shopping trips; Dances/Social/Cultural gatherings; Shuffleboard; Greenhouse.

South Roanoke Nursing Home Inc
3823 Franklin Rd SW, Roanoke, VA 24014
(703) 344-4325
Admin Charles E Carter Jr.
Licensure Skilled care. *Beds* SNF 104. *Certified* Medicaid; Medicare.
Owner Proprietary corp.

Virginia Synod Lutheran Home at Roanoke
3804 Brandon Ave SW, Roanoke, VA 24018
(703) 774-1661
Admin Rev Janet L Ramsey. *Dir of Nursing* Doloris B Dutton RN. *Medical Dir* Keith Edmunds MD, Advisor.
Licensure Intermediate care; Alzheimer's care. *Beds* ICF 62. *Certified* Medicaid.
Owner Nonprofit corp.
Admissions Requirements Physician's request.
Staff RNs; LPNs; Nurses' aides; Activities coordinators; Dietitians; Chaplains; Social workers.
Affiliation Evangelical Lutheran.
Facilities Dining room; Physical therapy room; Activities room; Chapel; Crafts room; Barber/Beauty shop.
Activities Arts & crafts; Cards; Games; Reading groups; Prayer groups; Movies; Shopping trips; Dances/Social/Cultural gatherings; Intergenerational programs; Pet therapy; Support for family members; Volunteer program; Transportation to church.

Rocky Mount

Eldercare of Franklin County
PO Drawer 739, 500 Hatcher St, Rocky Mount, VA 24151
(703) 483-9261
Admin Vicki D Clark.
Medical Dir Robert S Strong.
Licensure Skilled care; Intermediate care. *Beds* SNF 12; ICF 168. *Certified* Medicaid; Medicare.
Owner Proprietary corp.
Admissions Requirements Medical examination.
Staff Physicians; RNs; LPNs; Nurses' aides; Physical therapists; Speech therapists; Activities coordinators; Dietitians; Ophthalmologists; Podiatrists; Dentists.
Facilities Dining room; Physical therapy room; Activities room; Crafts room; Laundry room; Barber/Beauty shop.
Activities Arts & crafts; Cards; Games; Reading groups; Prayer groups; Movies; Shopping trips; Dances/Social/Cultural gatherings.

Salem

Camelot Hall Nursing Home
1945 Roanoke Blvd, Salem, VA 24153
(703) 345-3894
Admin Ron Covington.
Medical Dir H J Minarik & Esther Brown.
Licensure Skilled care; Intermediate care. *Beds* SNF 20; ICF 220. *Certified* Medicaid; Medicare.
Owner Proprietary corp (Medical Facilities of America).
Admissions Requirements Medical examination; Physician's request.
Staff Physicians 2 (pt); RNs 16 (ft), 3 (pt); LPNs 20 (ft), 8 (pt); Nurses' aides 70 (ft), 4 (pt); Physical therapists 1 (pt); Reality therapists 1 (ft); Recreational therapists 1 (ft); Speech therapists; Activities coordinators; Ophthalmologists; Podiatrists; Dentists.
Facilities Dining room; Physical therapy room; Activities room; Chapel; Crafts room; Laundry room; Barber/Beauty shop; Library.
Activities Arts & crafts; Cards; Games; Reading groups; Movies; Shopping trips; Dances/Social/Cultural gatherings.

McVitty House Inc
US Rte 460 W, PO Box 1240, Salem, VA 24153
(703) 389-0271
Admin William K Anglim.
Medical Dir Howard Lebow MD.
Licensure Skilled care; Intermediate care. *Beds* 327. *Certified* Medicaid; Medicare.
Owner Nonprofit corp.
Admissions Requirements Medical examination; Physician's request.
Staff Physicians 12 (pt); LPNs 20 (ft); LPNs 25 (ft); Nurses' aides 120 (ft); Physical therapists 1 (ft); Speech therapists 2 (pt); Activities coordinators 2 (ft); Dietitians 1 (ft); Podiatrists 1 (pt); Dentists 1 (pt).
Facilities Dining room; Physical therapy room; Activities room; Chapel; Crafts room; Laundry room; Barber/Beauty shop.
Activities Arts & crafts; Games; Reading groups; Prayer groups; Movies.

Richfield Nursing Center
PO Box 3240, 3615 W Main St, Salem, VA 24153
(703) 380-4500
Admin Charles M LeMaster.
Licensure Skilled care; Intermediate care. *Beds* SNF 50; ICF 277.
Owner Nonprofit corp.

Snyder Nursing Home Inc
11 N Broad St, Salem, VA 24153
(703) 389-0160
Admin Wanda L Warner.
Licensure Intermediate care. *Beds* ICF 45. *Certified* Medicaid.
Owner Nonprofit corp.

Saluda

Riverside Convalescent Center—Saluda
PO Box 303, US Rte 17, Saluda, VA 23149
(804) 758-2363
Admin Robert F Yeomans.
Licensure Intermediate care. *Beds* ICF 60. *Certified* Medicaid.
Owner Nonprofit corp.

Shawsville

Meadowbrook Nursing Home
PO Box 497, Rte 460 E, Shawsville, VA 24162
(703) 268-2203
Admin George R Smith III.
Medical Dir Dr G R Smith Jr.
Licensure Intermediate care. *Beds* ICF 120. *Certified* Medicaid.

Owner Proprietary corp.
Admissions Requirements Medical examination; Physician's request.
Staff Physicians 3 (ft); RNs 4 (ft); LPNs 6 (ft); Nurses' aides 30 (ft); Physical therapists 1 (pt); Speech therapists 1 (pt); Activities coordinators 1 (ft); Dietitians 1 (pt); Dentists 1 (pt).
Facilities Dining room; Physical therapy room; Activities room; Chapel; Crafts room; Laundry room; Barber/Beauty shop; Library; Enclosed courtyard.
Activities Arts & crafts; Cards; Games; Reading groups; Prayer groups; Dances/Social/Cultural gatherings.

Smithfield

Riverside Convalescent-Smithfield—Health Care Unit
200 Lumar Rd, Smithfield, VA 23430
(804) 357-3282, 357-0870 FAX
Admin Milton M Katz. *Dir of Nursing* Ellen La Bonte RN. *Medical Dir* Dr Bernard F Jamison.
Licensure Intermediate care; Home for aged; Retirement; Alzheimer's care. *Beds* ICF 95; Home for aged 34. *Certified* Medicaid; Medicare.
Owner Nonprofit organization/foundation.
Staff Physicians; RNs; LPNs; Nurses' aides; Physical therapists; Recreational therapists; Occupational therapists; Speech therapists; Activities coordinators; Dietitians; Podiatrists.
Activities Arts & crafts; Cards; Games; Reading groups; Prayer groups; Movies; Shopping trips; Pet therapy.

South Boston

Berry Hill Nursing Home Inc
PO Box 779, 621 Berry Hill Rd, South Boston, VA 24592
(804) 572-8901
Admin G Carlton Stevens.
Licensure Intermediate care. *Beds* ICF 120. *Certified* Medicaid.
Owner Proprietary corp.

Twin Oaks Convalescent Home
406 Oak Ln, South Boston, VA 24592
(804) 572-2925
Admin Connie S Zamora. *Dir of Nursing* Gladys Beaver. *Medical Dir* Dr Warren C Hagood.
Licensure Intermediate care. *Beds* ICF 54. *Private Pay Patients* 10%. *Certified* Medicaid.
Owner Proprietary corp.
Admissions Requirements Medical examination.
Staff Physicians (consultant); RNs 1 (ft), 2 (pt); LPNs 6 (ft), 7 (pt); Nurses' aides 14 (ft), 13 (pt); Physical therapists (contracted); Occupational therapists (contracted); Speech therapists (contracted); Activities coordinators 1 (ft); Dietitians (consultant).
Facilities Dining room; Activities room; Laundry room; Barber/Beauty shop.
Activities Arts & crafts; Cards; Games; Reading groups; Prayer groups; Movies; Dances/Social/Cultural gatherings; Intergenerational programs; Pet therapy; Variety of outings; Cooking group; Church services; Sunday school.

Woodview
103 Rosehill Dr, South Boston, VA 24592
(804) 572-4906
Admin Harvey B Newbill. *Dir of Nursing* Winnifred A Boger RN. *Medical Dir* Cecil B Dixon MD.
Licensure Skilled care; Intermediate care. *Beds* SNF 19; ICF 161. *Private Pay Patients* 24%. *Certified* Medicaid; Medicare.
Owner Nonprofit organization/foundation.

Admissions Requirements Medical examination; Physician's request.
Staff Physicians 8 (pt); RNs 4 (ft), 1 (pt); LPNs 22 (ft), 6 (pt); Nurses' aides 56 (ft), 8 (pt); Physical therapists 2 (ft), 1 (pt); Reality therapists 1 (pt); Recreational therapists 1 (pt); Activities coordinators 1 (ft), 3 (pt); Dietitians 1 (pt).
Facilities Dining room; Physical therapy room; Activities room; Chapel; Crafts room; Laundry room; Barber/Beauty shop; Library.
Activities Arts & crafts; Cards; Games; Reading groups; Prayer groups; Movies; Shopping trips; Dances/Social/Cultural gatherings.

South Hill

Community Memorial Healthcenter & W S Hundley Annex
PO Box 90, 125 Buena Vista Cir, South Hill, VA 23970
(804) 447-3151
Admin Allene Reese. *Dir of Nursing* Mary Ann Hager RN. *Medical Dir* F C Sturmer MD.
Licensure Skilled care; Intermediate care. *Beds* SNF 15; ICF 140. *Certified* Medicaid; Medicare.
Owner Nonprofit corp.
Admissions Requirements Medical examination; Special needs not provided by this facility.
Staff Physicians; RNs; LPNs; Nurses' aides; Physical therapists; Speech therapists; Activities coordinators; Dietitians.
Facilities Dining room; Physical therapy room; Activities room; Chapel; Laundry room; Barber/Beauty shop; Library; Lounges; Patios.
Activities Arts & crafts; Cards; Games; Reading groups; Prayer groups; Movies; Shopping trips; Dances/Social/Cultural gatherings; Cookouts; Music.

Stafford

Brookwood Nursing Home
PO Box 85, 140 Andrew Chapel Rd, Stafford, VA 22554
(703) 659-4670
Admin Patricia D Bagley. *Dir of Nursing* Lynn Deans. *Medical Dir* Dr Joel Koslow.
Licensure Intermediate care. *Beds* ICF 34. *Certified* Medicaid; Medicare.
Owner Privately owned.
Admissions Requirements Medical examination.
Staff RNs; LPNs; Nurses' aides; Activities coordinators; Dietitians.
Facilities Dining room; Activities room; Crafts room; Laundry room.
Activities Arts & crafts; Cards; Games; Reading groups; Prayer groups; Movies; Shopping trips; Dances/Social/Cultural gatherings; Pet therapy.

Staunton

Oak Hill Nursing Home Health Care Unit
PO Box 2565, 512 Houston St, Staunton, VA 24401
(703) 886-2335
Admin Mary Lou DiGrassie.
Medical Dir Dr Leon Lenker.
Licensure Intermediate care. *Beds* ICF 130. *Certified* Medicaid.
Owner Proprietary corp (National Healthcare Affiliates Inc).
Admissions Requirements Medical examination.
Facilities Dining room; Activities room; Crafts room; Laundry room; Barber/Beauty shop.

Activities Arts & crafts; Cards; Games; Reading groups; Prayer groups; Movies; Shopping trips; Dances/Social/Cultural gatherings.

Shenandoah Geriatric Treatment Center
Box 2500, Staunton, VA 24401
(703) 332-8000
Admin Alberta J McGrogan Dir.
Licensure Intermediate care for mentally retarded. *Beds* ICF/MR 160.

Staunton Manor Nursing Home Inc
1734 Churchville Ave, Staunton, VA 24401
(703) 885-3611
Admin Daniel Sheets.
Medical Dir Myrtle Summers.
Licensure Intermediate care. *Beds* ICF 89. *Certified* Medicaid.
Owner Proprietary corp.
Staff RNs; LPNs; Nurses' aides; Activities coordinators; Dietitians.
Facilities Dining room; Activities room; Chapel; Crafts room; Laundry room.
Activities Arts & crafts; Cards; Games; Reading groups; Prayer groups; Movies; Dances/Social/Cultural gatherings.

Western State Hospital
Box 2500, Staunton, VA 24401
(703) 332-8000
Admin Lynwood F Harding Dir.
Licensure Intermediate care for mentally retarded. *Beds* M/S 30; IPT 25.

Stuart

Blue Ridge Nursing Home Inc
Commerce St, Stuart, VA 24171
(703) 694-7161
Admin D Victor Williams LNHA. *Dir of Nursing* Sandra Harris RN. *Medical Dir* Sam P Massie; Dr Robert Bowman.
Licensure Intermediate care. *Beds* ICF 120. *Certified* Medicaid.
Owner Proprietary corp.
Staff Physicians 3 (pt); RNs 8 (ft), 2 (pt); LPNs 3 (ft); Nurses' aides 28 (ft), 23 (pt); Physical therapists 2 (pt); Speech therapists 1 (pt); Activities coordinators 1 (ft), 1 (pt); Dietitians 1 (pt).
Facilities Dining room; Physical therapy room; Activities room; Chapel; Crafts room; Laundry room; Barber/Beauty shop; Library.
Activities Arts & crafts; Games; Reading groups; Prayer groups; Movies; Dances/Social/Cultural gatherings.

R J Reynolds—Patrick County Memorial Hospital Inc
Rte 2 Box 11, Stuart, VA 24171
(703) 694-3153
Admin Felix Fraraccio.
Licensure Skilled care. *Beds* SNF 25.
Owner Nonprofit corp.

Suffolk

Autumn Care of Suffolk
PO Box 1548, 2580 Pruden Blvd, Suffolk, VA 23434
(804) 934-2363
Admin Mary G Taychert.
Medical Dir Beverly Holladay MD.
Licensure Intermediate care. *Beds* ICF 120. *Certified* Medicaid.
Owner Proprietary corp (Autumn Corp).
Admissions Requirements Minimum age 18; Medical examination; Physician's request.
Staff RNs 1 (ft); LPNs 11 (ft); Nurses' aides 47 (ft); Recreational therapists; Activities coordinators 1 (ft); Dietitians 1 (pt); Podiatrists 1 (pt).
Facilities Dining room; Physical therapy room; Activities room; Crafts room; Laundry room; Barber/Beauty shop.

Activities Arts & crafts; Cards; Games; Reading groups; Prayer groups; Movies; Shopping trips; Dances/Social/Cultural gatherings.

Finney Avenue Residence
404 Finney Ave, Suffolk, VA 23434
(804) 925-2408
Admin Vince Doheny Exec Dir.
Licensure Intermediate care for mentally retarded. *Beds* ICF/MR 12.

Nansemond Convalescent Center Inc Health Care Unit
200 W Constance Rd, Suffolk, VA 23434
(804) 539-8744
Admin Audrey B Butler.
Licensure Intermediate care. *Beds* ICF 100. *Certified* Medicaid.
Owner Proprietary corp (Hillhaven Corp).

Tappahannock

Riverside Tappahannock Hospital
Rte 2 Box 612, Tappahannock, VA 22560
(804) 443-3311
Admin Glenn D Waters V Pres/Admin.
Licensure Skilled care. *Beds* SNF 17.
Owner Nonprofit corp.

Tappahannock Manor Convalescent Center & Home for Adults Health Care Unit
PO Box 1488, Tappahannock, VA 22560
(804) 443-4308
Admin Mary G Davis.
Licensure Intermediate care. *Beds* ICF 60. *Certified* Medicaid.
Owner Proprietary corp.
Admissions Requirements Minimum age 18.
Staff Physicians 7 (pt); RNs 1 (ft), 2 (pt); LPNs 4 (ft), 5 (pt); Nurses' aides 13 (ft), 10 (pt); Physical therapists 1 (pt); Activities coordinators 1 (ft), 1 (pt); Dietitians 1 (pt).
Facilities Dining room; Physical therapy room; Activities room; Crafts room; Barber/Beauty shop.
Activities Arts & crafts; Cards; Games; Prayer groups; Movies; Shopping trips.

Tazewell

Heritage Hall Tazewell
121 Ben Bolt Ave, Tazewell, VA 24651
(703) 988-2515
Admin Joy C Myers. *Dir of Nursing* Delores Troupe. *Medical Dir* Dr James Thompson.
Licensure Skilled care; Intermediate care. *Beds* SNF 14; ICF 166. *Certified* Medicaid.
Owner Proprietary corp.
Staff Physicians 14 (pt); RNs 3 (ft), 2 (pt); LPNs 12 (ft), 7 (pt); Nurses' aides 48 (ft), 23 (pt); Activities coordinators 2 (ft); Dentists 2 (pt).
Facilities Dining room; Physical therapy room; Activities room; Chapel; Crafts room; Laundry room; Barber/Beauty shop.
Activities Arts & crafts; Cards; Games; Prayer groups; Movies; Shopping trips; Dances/Social/Cultural gatherings.

Vienna

Ayr Hill Adult Home
112 Ayr Hill Ave NW, Vienna, VA 22180
(703) 938-8200
Medical Dir Brenda Scott Admis; Etta Stalker Admis.
Licensure Home for adults. *Beds* Home for adults 16.

Courthouse Road Intermediate Care Facility
137 Courthouse Rd, Vienna, VA 22180
(703) 255-4785
Admin Susan Perlik Dir.
Licensure Intermediate care for mentally retarded. *Beds* ICF/MR 4.

Minerva Fisher Hall Group Home
8207 Wolftrap Rd, Vienna, VA 22180
(703) 573-8631
Admin Allan Phillips Dir.
Licensure Intermediate care for mentally retarded. *Beds* ICF/MR 12.

Weakleys Home for Adults No 1
736 Ninovan Rd, Vienna, VA 22180
(703) 938-8519
Medical Dir Pat Hickerson Admis.
Licensure Home for adults. *Beds* Home for adults 18.

Weakleys Home for Adults No 2
732 Ninovan Rd, Vienna, VA 22180
(703) 938-8519
Medical Dir Pat Hickerson Admis.
Licensure Home for adults. *Beds* Home for adults 18.

Vinton

Berkshire
705 Clearview Dr, Vinton, VA 24179
(703) 982-6691
Admin Jacqueline H Wood. *Dir of Nursing* Toni Pierce RN. *Medical Dir* Robert Bondurant MD.
Licensure Intermediate care. *Beds* ICF 180. *Certified* Medicaid.
Owner Proprietary corp (Medical Facilities of America).
Admissions Requirements Minimum age 14; Medical examination; Physician's request.
Staff RNs; LPNs; Nurses' aides; Activities coordinators.
Facilities Dining room; Physical therapy room; Activities room; Laundry room; Barber/Beauty shop; Meditation room; Treatment room.
Activities Arts & crafts; Cards; Games; Reading groups; Prayer groups; Movies; Dances/Social/Cultural gatherings.

Virginia Beach

Beth Shalom Home of Eastern Virginia
6401 Auburn Dr, Virginia Beach, VA 23464
(804) 420-2512
Admin Lee H Olitsky.
Licensure Skilled care; Adult day care. *Beds* SNF 120. *Certified* Medicaid.
Owner Nonprofit corp (Beth Shalom Homes of Virginia).
Affiliation Jewish.

Camelot Hall Nursing Home
1801 Camelot Dr, Virginia Beach, VA 23454
(804) 481-3500
Admin Charles Weiden. *Dir of Nursing* Mrs Jean Mann. *Medical Dir* Dr Gregory Edinger.
Licensure Intermediate care. *Beds* ICF 240. *Certified* Medicaid; Medicare.
Owner Proprietary corp (Medical Facilities of America).
Admissions Requirements Minimum age 18; Medical examination.
Facilities Dining room; Physical therapy room; Activities room; Barber/Beauty shop.
Activities Arts & crafts; Cards; Games; Reading groups; Prayer groups; Movies; Shopping trips; Dances/Social/Cultural gatherings; Special programs.

Holmes Convalescent Center
4142 Bonney Rd, Virginia Beach, VA 23452
(804) 340-0620
Admin Joseph G Cicatko Jr.
Licensure Intermediate care. *Beds* ICF 160. *Certified* Medicaid.
Owner Proprietary corp (Hillhaven Corp).

Lynn Shores Manor
340 Lynn Shores Dr, Virginia Beach, VA 23452
(804) 340-6611

Admin Tom Orsini.
Medical Dir Gregory Edinger MD.
Licensure Skilled care; Intermediate care. *Beds* SNF 28; ICF 214. *Certified* Medicaid; Medicare.
Owner Proprietary corp (Beverly Enterprises).
Admissions Requirements Minimum age 14; Medical examination; Physician's request.
Staff RNs 8 (ft), 6 (pt); LPNs 20 (ft), 10 (pt); Nurses' aides 62 (ft), 92 (pt); Activities coordinators 1 (ft), 3 (pt); Dietitians 1 (ft), 2 (pt).
Facilities Dining room; Physical therapy room; Activities room; Crafts room; Laundry room; Barber/Beauty shop; Library.
Activities Arts & crafts; Cards; Games; Reading groups; Prayer groups; Movies; Shopping trips; Dances/Social/Cultural gatherings; Outings.

Medicenter—Virginia Beach
1148 1st Colonial Rd, Virginia Beach, VA 23454
(804) 481-3321
Admin Berit Kuntz.
Medical Dir Marc Gaines.
Licensure Skilled care; Intermediate care. *Beds* SNF 40; ICF 78. *Certified* Medicaid; Medicare.
Owner Proprietary corp (Hillhaven Corp).
Admissions Requirements Medical examination; Physician's request.
Staff RNs 7 (ft); LPNs 8 (ft), 9 (pt); Nurses' aides 33 (ft), 16 (pt); Physical therapists 2 (ft); Recreational therapists 1 (ft); Occupational therapists 1 (ft); Speech therapists 1 (ft); Activities coordinators 1 (ft); Dietitians 1 (ft); Ophthalmologists 1 (pt); Podiatrists 1 (pt); Audiologists 1 (pt); Dentists 1 (pt).
Facilities Dining room; Physical therapy room; Activities room; Laundry room; Barber/Beauty shop.
Activities Arts & crafts; Cards; Games; Reading groups; Prayer groups; Movies; Shopping trips; Dances/Social/Cultural gatherings.

Westminster-Canterbury of Hampton Roads Inc
3100 Shore Dr, Virginia Beach, VA 23451
(804) 496-1100
Admin Thomas E Clements.
Medical Dir Thomas Manser MD.
Licensure Skilled care; Intermediate care; Lifecare retirement. *Beds* SNF 15; ICF 60. *Certified* Medicaid; Medicare.
Owner Nonprofit corp.
Admissions Requirements Medical examination; Physician's request.
Staff Physicians 2 (pt); RNs 10 (ft), 8 (pt); LPNs 8 (ft), 6 (pt); Nurses' aides 25 (ft), 20 (pt); Physical therapists 1 (ft); Recreational therapists 1 (ft); Occupational therapists 1 (pt); Speech therapists 1 (pt); Activities coordinators 2 (ft); Dietitians 1 (ft); Ophthalmologists 1 (pt).
Affiliation Episcopal.
Facilities Dining room; Physical therapy room; Activities room; Chapel; Crafts room; Laundry room; Barber/Beauty shop; Library; Woodworking shop; Convenience store; Clinic.
Activities Arts & crafts; Cards; Games; Reading groups; Prayer groups; Movies; Shopping trips; Dances/Social/Cultural gatherings; Weekly chapel services; Travelogues; Display of collections & hobbies.

Warrenton

District Nursing Home
32 Waterloo St, Warrenton, VA 22186
(703) 347-1881
Admin Bryan P Graham. *Dir of Nursing* Ms Tavenner. *Medical Dir* Dr Iden.

Licensure Intermediate care. *Beds* ICF 51.
Private Pay Patients 1%. *Certified* Medicaid.
Owner Publicly owned.
Admissions Requirements Medical
examination; Physician's request.
Staff RNs 1 (ft), 1 (pt); LPNs 6 (ft), 1 (pt);
Nurses' aides 22 (pt); Activities coordinators
1 (pt).
Facilities Dining room; Physical therapy
room; Barber/Beauty shop.
Activities Arts & crafts; Games; Prayer groups;
Pet therapy.

Oak Springs of Warrenton
1066 Hastings Ln, Warrenton, VA 22186
(703) 347-4770
Admin Timothy J McCagh. *Dir of Nursing*
Louann Toomey RN. *Medical Dir* Dr
Douglas Morris.
Licensure Intermediate care; Alzheimer's care.
Beds ICF 130. *Certified* Medicaid.
Owner Proprietary corp.
Admissions Requirements Minimum age 17;
Medical examination.
Staff RNs 5 (ft); LPNs 16 (ft), 3 (pt); Nurses'
aides 56 (ft), 7 (pt); Physical therapists 1
(pt); Recreational therapists 1 (ft);
Occupational therapists 1 (pt); Speech
therapists 1 (pt); Activities coordinators 1
(ft); Dietitians 1 (pt).
Facilities Dining room; Physical therapy
room; Activities room; Crafts room; Laundry
room; Barber/Beauty shop.
Activities Arts & crafts; Games; Reading
groups; Prayer groups; Movies; Shopping
trips; Dances/Social/Cultural gatherings.

Warsaw

Warsaw Health Care Center
Rte 1 Box 39, 302 W Richmond Rd, Warsaw,
VA 22572
(804) 333-3616
Admin Dennis C Hill. *Dir of Nursing* Carolyn
Neale. *Medical Dir* Niels Oster MD.
Licensure Skilled care; Intermediate care. *Beds*
SNF 10; ICF 170. *Private Pay Patients* 18%.
Certified Medicaid; Medicare.
Owner Privately owned (Medical Facilities of
America).
Admissions Requirements Minimum age 18;
Medical examination; Physician's request.
Staff RNs 4 (ft), 8 (pt); LPNs 16 (ft), 10 (pt);
Nurses' aides 49 (ft), 30 (pt); Physical
therapists; Activities coordinators 1 (ft);
Dietitians (consultant).
Languages Spanish, German, French, Sign.
Facilities Dining room; Physical therapy
room; Activities room; Crafts room; Laundry
room; Barber/Beauty shop.
Activities Arts & crafts; Cards; Games;
Reading groups; Prayer groups; Movies;
Shopping trips; Dances/Social/Cultural
gatherings; Intergenerational programs.

Waverly

Waverly Health Care Center
PO Box 641, 456 E Main St, Waverly, VA
23890
(804) 834-3975
Admin Rae E Leslie. *Dir of Nursing* Hope
Butler. *Medical Dir* Dr David Weinstein.
Licensure Skilled care; Intermediate care;
Alzheimer's care. *Beds* SNF 24; ICF 96.
Private Pay Patients 16%. *Certified*
Medicaid; Medicare.
Owner Proprietary corp (Medical Facilities of
America).
Admissions Requirements Medical
examination; Physician's request.
Staff Physicians 4 (ft); RNs 1 (ft), 2 (pt);
LPNs 5 (ft), 2 (pt); Nurses' aides 29 (ft), 11
(pt); Physical therapists 1 (ft); Recreational
therapists 1 (pt); Occupational therapists 1

(ft); Speech therapists 1 (ft); Activities
coordinators 1 (ft); Dietitians 1 (ft);
Podiatrists 1 (ft).
Languages German.
Facilities Dining room; Physical therapy
room; Activities room; Crafts room; Laundry
room; Barber/Beauty shop; Library; 2
dayrooms.
Activities Arts & crafts; Games; Prayer groups;
Movies; Dances/Social/Cultural gatherings.

Waynesboro

District Home
1400 District Home Dr, Waynesboro, VA
22980-9305
(703) 942-5237
Admin Jerry B Layman. *Dir of Nursing*
Brenda Q Novene BS RN. *Medical Dir* G C
Ayers MD.
Licensure Intermediate care; Home for adults;
Retirement. *Beds* ICF 91; Home for adults
60. *Certified* Medicaid.
Owner Publicly owned.
Admissions Requirements Minimum age 18;
Medical examination.
Staff Physicians 1 (pt); RNs 3 (ft); LPNs 14
(ft), 2 (pt); Nurses' aides 41 (ft), 4 (pt);
Physical therapists 1 (pt); Recreational
therapists 1 (pt); Speech therapists 1 (pt);
Activities coordinators 1 (ft); Dietitians 1
(pt); Ophthalmologists 1 (pt); Dentists 1 (pt).
Facilities Dining room; Activities room;
Chapel; Crafts room; Barber/Beauty shop;
Library.
Activities Arts & crafts; Cards; Games;
Reading groups; Prayer groups; Movies;
Shopping trips; Dances/Social/Cultural
gatherings.

Liberty House Nursing Home
1221 Rosser Ave, Waynesboro, VA 22980
(703) 949-7191
Admin John G Lambert.
Licensure Skilled care; Intermediate care. *Beds*
SNF 14; ICF 95. *Certified* Medicaid.
Owner Proprietary corp (Beverly Enterprises).

West Point

Riverside Convalescent Center—West Point
2960 Cheslea Rd, West Point, VA 23181
(804) 843-4323
Admin Barbara Fowler.
Licensure Intermediate care. *Beds* ICF 60.
Owner Nonprofit corp.

Williamsburg

Eastern State Hospital
Drawer A, Williamsburg, VA 23187
(804) 253-5161
Admin David C Pribble Dir.
Licensure Intermediate care for mentally
retarded. *Beds* M/S 50.

Hancock Geriatric Treatment Center
Drawer A, Williamsburg, VA 23187
(804) 253-5326
Admin Chris L Bowman Dir.
Licensure Skilled care; Intermediate care. *Beds*
SNF 25; ICF 433.

Pines Convalescent Center
1235 Mount Vernon Ave, Williamsburg, VA
23185
(804) 229-4121, 229-6625 FAX
Admin William Cifaratta. *Dir of Nursing*
Joyce Tewksbury. *Medical Dir* Joseph D
Brown MD.
Licensure Intermediate care. *Beds* ICF 157.
Private Pay Patients 20%. *Certified*
Medicaid.

Owner Proprietary corp (National Healthcare
Affiliates Inc).
Staff Physical therapists 1 (pt); Occupational
therapists 1 (pt); Speech therapists 1 (pt);
Activities coordinators 1 (ft); Dietitians 1
(pt).

Williamsburg Landing
5700 Williamsburg Landing Dr, Williamsburg,
VA 23185
(804) 253-0303
Admin Ben Puckett; William A Doig, Exec
Dir. *Dir of Nursing* Charlene Crostley RN.
Medical Dir James E Barton MD.
Licensure Skilled care; Intermediate care;
Residential care. *Beds* SNF 5; ICF 32;
Residential care 350. *Certified* Medicare.
Owner Nonprofit corp.
Admissions Requirements Physician's request.
Staff RNs; LPNs; Nurses' aides; Activities
coordinators; Dietitians.
Facilities Dining room; Physical therapy
room; Activities room; Chapel; Barber/
Beauty shop; Library.
Activities Arts & crafts; Cards; Games;
Reading groups; Prayer groups; Movies;
Shopping trips; Dances/Social/Cultural
gatherings; Intergenerational programs; Pet
therapy.

Winchester

Hillcrest Manor Nursing Home Inc
1000 Lauck Dr, Sunnyside Station,
Winchester, VA 22601
(703) 667-7830
Admin Doris Traylor.
Licensure Intermediate care. *Beds* ICF 62.
Owner Proprietary corp.

Shawnee Springs Nursing Home
PO Box 2338, 380 Millwood Ave, Winchester,
VA 22601
(703) 667-7010
Admin B Wendell Raby. *Dir of Nursing*
Sherlyn B Armistead. *Medical Dir* James B
York.
Licensure Skilled care; Intermediate care. *Beds*
SNF 20; ICF 156. *Private Pay Patients* 10%.
Certified Medicaid; Medicare.
Owner Proprietary corp (Beverly Enterpriss).
Admissions Requirements Minimum age 18;
Medical examination.
Staff Physicians 15 (pt); Physical therapists 1
(pt); Occupational therapists 1 (pt); Speech
therapists 1 (pt); Activities coordinators 2
(pt); Dietitians 1 (pt); Podiatrists 1 (pt).
Facilities Dining room; Physical therapy
room; Activities room; Crafts room; Barber/
Beauty shop.
Activities Arts & crafts; Cards; Games;
Reading groups; Prayer groups; Movies;
Shopping trips; Dances/Social/Cultural
gatherings; Pet therapy.

Westminster-Canterbury of Winchester Inc
956 Westminster-Canterbury Dr, Winchester,
VA 22601
(804) 665-0156
Admin Estelle V Bauer.
Licensure Skilled care; Intermediate care. *Beds*
SNF 5; ICF 35.
Owner Nonprofit corp.

Wise

Heritage Hall—Wise
PO Box 1009, College Rd, Wise, VA 24293
(703) 328-2721
Admin M Robin Miles. *Dir of Nursing* Leta
Holden RN. *Medical Dir* Dr E Capalad.
Licensure Intermediate care. *Beds* ICF 62.
Private Pay Patients 10%. *Certified*
Medicaid.
Owner Proprietary corp (Heritage Hall).
Admissions Requirements Medical
examination; Physician's request.

Staff RNs 1 (ft); LPNs 5 (ft), 6 (pt); Nurses' aides 14 (ft), 5 (pt); Physical therapists 1 (ft); Activities coordinators 1 (ft); Dietitians.
Facilities Dining room; Activities room; Crafts room; Laundry room; Barber/Beauty shop.
Activities Arts & crafts; Cards; Games; Prayer groups; Shopping trips.

Woodbridge

Woodbridge Nursing Center
14906 Jefferson Davis Hwy, Woodbridge, VA 22191
(703) 491-6167
Admin W Russell Rodgers Jr. *Dir of Nursing* Jane Klein, Admin. *Medical Dir* William McCarthy MD.
Licensure Intermediate care. *Beds* ICF 120.
Owner Proprietary corp.
Admissions Requirements Medical examination; Physician's request.
Staff Physicians 14 (pt); RNs 4 (ft), 6 (pt); LPNs 9 (ft), 4 (pt); Nurses' aides 38 (ft), 26 (pt); Physical therapists 2 (ft), 1 (pt); Reality therapists 1 (ft); Recreational therapists 1 (pt); Speech therapists 2 (pt); Dietitians 1 (ft); Ophthalmologists 2 (pt); Podiatrists 1 (pt); Dentists 2 (pt); Social workers 1 (ft).
Facilities Dining room; Physical therapy room; Activities room; Crafts room; Laundry room; Barber/Beauty shop.
Activities Arts & crafts; Cards; Games; Reading groups; Prayer groups; Movies; Shopping trips; Dances/Social/Cultural gatherings.

Woodstock

Susan B Miller Nursing Homes Inc
118 N Muhlenberg St, Woodstock, VA 22664
(703) 459-2118

Admin Marian E Foltz.
Licensure Intermediate care. *Beds* ICF 54.
Certified Medicaid.
Owner Proprietary corp.

Shenandoah County Memorial Hospital—Long-Term Care Unit
Rte 11, Woodstock, VA 22664
(703) 459-4021
Admin Edwin E Hurysz.
Licensure Intermediate care. *Beds* ICF 34.
Certified Medicaid.
Owner Nonprofit corp.

Skyline Terrace Convalescent Home
PO Box 191, US 11 S & Lakeview Rd, Woodstock, VA 22664
(703) 459-3738
Admin Jessee D Funkhouser.
Licensure Intermediate care. *Beds* ICF 70.
Certified Medicaid.
Owner Proprietary corp.

Wytheville

Asbury Center at Birdmont
990 Holston Rd, Wytheville, VA 24382
(703) 228-5595
Admin Judy P Viars. *Dir of Nursing* Julana K Whitlow.
Licensure Intermediate care; Retirement. *Beds* ICF 152; Retirement community 88. *Private Pay Patients* 20%. *Certified* Medicaid; Medicare.
Owner Nonprofit corp.
Admissions Requirements Minimum age 65; Medical examination; Physician's request.
Staff RNs 11 (ft), 4 (pt); LPNs 12 (ft), 2 (pt); Nurses' aides 79 (ft), 10 (pt); Physical therapists 4 (ft), 4 (pt); Occupational therapists 2 (pt); Speech therapists 1 (pt); Activities coordinators 2 (ft), 2 (pt); Dietitians 1 (pt); Podiatrists 1 (pt).

Affiliation Methodist.
Facilities Dining room; Physical therapy room; Chapel; Crafts room; Laundry room; Barber/Beauty shop; Ambulance service.
Activities Arts & crafts; Cards; Games; Reading groups; Prayer groups; Movies; Shopping trips; Dances/Social/Cultural gatherings; Pet therapy.

Malin Health Care Center
1550 Chapman Rd, Wytheville, VA 24382
(703) 228-7380
Admin Charles Gallimore.
Licensure Skilled care; Intermediate care. *Beds* SNF 10; ICF 50.
Owner Nonprofit corp.

Wythe County Community Hospital
600 Ridge Rd, Wytheville, VA 24382
(703) 228-2181
Admin Scott K Adams.
Licensure Skilled care; Intermediate care. *Beds* SNF 6; ICF 2.
Owner Nonprofit corp.

Wythe House
Rte 1 Box 62, Wytheville, VA 24382
(703) 228-7069
Admin Jack Wall Dir Comm Svcs Bd.
Licensure Intermediate care for mentally retarded. *Beds* ICF/MR 12.

Yorktown

York Convalescent Center
113 Battle Rd, Yorktown, VA 23692
(804) 898-1491
Admin Jerry M Carpenter.
Licensure Skilled care; Intermediate care. *Beds* SNF 10; ICF 50.
Owner Proprietary corp.

WASHINGTON

Aberdeen

Grays Harbor Convalescent Center
920 Anderson Dr, Aberdeen, WA 98520
(206) 532-5122
Admin Patty McMillan.
Medical Dir Dr James Baker.
Licensure Skilled care; Intermediate care. *Beds* 155. *Certified* Medicaid; Medicare.
Owner Proprietary corp (Beverly Enterprises).
Admissions Requirements Medical examination; Physician's request.
Staff RNs 7 (ft), 1 (pt); LPNs 12 (ft), 3 (pt); Nurses' aides 55 (ft), 10 (pt); Activities coordinators 3 (ft).
Facilities Dining room; Physical therapy room; Activities room; Chapel; Crafts room; Barber/Beauty shop; Library.
Activities Arts & crafts; Cards; Games; Reading groups; Prayer groups; Movies; Shopping trips; Dances/Social/Cultural gatherings.

Harbor Health Care
308 W King, Aberdeen, WA 98520
(206) 533-3000
Admin Tonja Myers. *Dir of Nursing* Lorena Westerback. *Medical Dir* Welland Orchard MD.
Licensure Skilled care; Intermediate care; Alzheimer's care. *Beds* Swing beds SNF/ICF 91. *Private Pay Patients* 12%. *Certified* Medicaid; Medicare.
Owner Proprietary corp (Beverly Enterprises).
Admissions Requirements Medical examination; Physician's request.
Staff Physical therapists 1 (pt); Reality therapists 1 (pt); Recreational therapists 1 (ft); Occupational therapists 1 (pt); Speech therapists 1 (ft), 1 (pt); Activities coordinators 1 (ft); Dietitians 1 (ft); Ophthalmologists 1 (pt); Podiatrists 1 (pt); Audiologists 1 (pt).
Languages Finnish, Spanish.
Facilities Dining room; Physical therapy room; Activities room; Crafts room; Laundry room; Barber/Beauty shop; Mini park.
Activities Arts & crafts; Games; Reading groups; Prayer groups; Movies; Shopping trips; Dances/Social/Cultural gatherings; Intergenerational programs; Pet therapy; Geriatric olympics; Beauty pageant; Parade.

St Joseph Hospital
1006 N "H" St, Aberdeen, WA 98520
(206) 533-0450
Admin Sr Charlotte Van Dyke.
Licensure Skilled care; Intermediate care. *Beds* 34. *Certified* Medicaid.
Owner Nonprofit corp.

Anacortes

Anacortes Convalescent Center
1105 26th St, Anacortes, WA 98221
(206) 293-3174
Admin John E Mock.
Licensure Skilled care; Intermediate care. *Beds* 119. *Certified* Medicaid; Medicare.
Owner Proprietary corp (HMH Associates Inc).

Barth Nursing Home
1407 5th St, Anacortes, WA 98221
(206) 293-6622
Admin Virginia Wiggins. *Dir of Nursing* Barbara Dunn. *Medical Dir* Joan Farmer.
Licensure Intermediate care. *Beds* ICF 26. *Private Pay Patients* 35%. *Certified* Medicaid.
Owner Privately owned.
Admissions Requirements Medical examination; Physician's request.
Staff RNs 1 (ft); LPNs 3 (ft), 2 (pt); Nurses' aides 6 (ft), 3 (pt); Activities coordinators 1 (ft); Dietitians 1 (pt).
Facilities Dining room; Activities room; Crafts room; Laundry room; Barber/Beauty shop.
Activities Arts & crafts; Cards; Games; Reading groups; Prayer groups; Movies; Shopping trips; Intergenerational programs.

San Juan Nursing Home
911 21st St, Anacortes, WA 98221
(206) 293-7222
Admin Stephen R Johnson. *Dir of Nursing* Gail Brown. *Medical Dir* Dr Clure.
Licensure Skilled care; Intermediate care. *Beds* Swing beds SNF/ICF 52. *Private Pay Patients* 60%. *Certified* Medicaid.
Owner Privately owned.
Admissions Requirements Medical examination; Physician's request.
Staff RNs; LPNs; Nurses' aides; Activities coordinators; Dietitians.
Facilities Dining room; Activities room; Laundry room; Barber/Beauty shop.
Activities Arts & crafts; Games; Reading groups; Prayer groups; Movies; Shopping trips; Pet therapy.

Arlington

Arlington Convalescent Center
Box 248, Florence & Hazel St, Arlington, WA 98223
(206) 435-5521
Admin David L Rogge. *Dir of Nursing* Ann Tennyson. *Medical Dir* Dr Mark Lucianna.
Licensure Skilled care; Intermediate care. *Beds* 96. *Certified* Medicaid.
Owner Privately owned.
Admissions Requirements Medical examination; Physician's request.
Staff Physicians; RNs; LPNs; Nurses' aides; Recreational therapists; Activities coordinators.
Facilities Dining room; Physical therapy room; Activities room; Chapel; Crafts room; Laundry room; Barber/Beauty shop.
Activities Arts & crafts; Cards; Games; Reading groups; Prayer groups; Movies; Dances/Social/Cultural gatherings; Reality orientation classes; Remotivation classes.

Auburn

Applegate Care Center
414 SE 17th St, Auburn, WA 98002
(206) 833-1740
Admin Norman F Allen. *Dir of Nursing* Ginny Whyte. *Medical Dir* Dr Zerr.
Licensure Skilled care; Intermediate care. *Beds* SNF 48; ICF 48. *Certified* Medicaid; Medicare.
Owner Proprietary corp.
Admissions Requirements Physician's request.
Staff RNs 2 (ft), 1 (pt); LPNs 11 (ft), 1 (pt); Nurses' aides 45 (ft), 7 (pt); Physical therapists 1 (pt); Recreational therapists 1 (ft); Occupational therapists 1 (pt); Speech therapists 1 (pt); Activities coordinators 1 (ft); Dietitians 1 (pt); Ophthalmologists 1 (pt); Podiatrists 1 (pt); Audiologists 1 (pt).
Facilities Dining room; Physical therapy room; Activities room; Crafts room; Laundry room; Barber/Beauty shop.
Activities Arts & crafts; Cards; Games; Reading groups; Prayer groups; Movies; Shopping trips; Pet therapy.

Canterbury House
502 29th St SE, Auburn, WA 98002
(206) 939-0090
Admin Barbara Altier.
Licensure Skilled care; Intermediate care. *Beds* 100. *Certified* Medicaid.
Owner Proprietary corp.

Green River Terrace Nursing Home
2830 I St NE, Auburn, WA 98002
(206) 854-4142
Admin David Masterjohn.
Licensure Skilled care; Intermediate care. *Beds* 139. *Certified* Medicaid; Medicare.
Owner Proprietary corp (Beverly Enterprises).

Bainbridge Island

Messenger House Care Center
10861 Manitou Park Blvd NE, Bainbridge Island, WA 98110
(206) 842-2654
Admin Ray Ramsdell. *Dir of Nursing* Elinor Ringland. *Medical Dir* Thomas Haggar MD.
Licensure Skilled care; Intermediate care; Alzheimer's care. *Beds* Swing beds SNF/ICF 96. *Private Pay Patients* 30%. *Certified* Medicaid.
Owner Proprietary corp (Soundcare Inc).
Admissions Requirements Medical examination; Physician's request.
Staff RNs 4 (ft), 7 (pt); LPNs 4 (ft), 4 (pt); Nurses' aides 25 (ft), 25 (pt); Physical therapists 1 (pt); Recreational therapists 1 (pt); Occupational therapists 1 (pt); Speech therapists 1 (pt); Activities coordinators 1 (ft); Dietitians 1 (pt); Ophthalmologists 1 (pt); Podiatrists 1 (pt).
Facilities Dining room; Physical therapy room; Activities room; Crafts room; Barber/Beauty shop.

Activities Arts & crafts; Cards; Games;
Reading groups; Prayer groups; Movies;
Shopping trips; Dances/Social/Cultural
gatherings.

Parkside Health Care Inc
9964 NE LaFayette, Bainbridge Island, WA
98110
(206) 322-2293
Admin Robert E Johnson.
Medical Dir William Stewart MD.
Licensure Skilled care; Intermediate care. *Beds*
79. *Certified* Medicaid.
Owner Proprietary corp.
Staff RNs 4 (ft); LPNs 4 (ft); Nurses' aides 28
(ft), 8 (pt); Recreational therapists 1 (ft);
Occupational therapists 1 (ft); Activities
coordinators 1 (ft); Dietitians 1 (pt).
Facilities Dining room; Physical therapy
room; Activities room; Laundry room.
Activities Arts & crafts; Cards; Games;
Reading groups; Prayer groups; Movies;
Shopping trips.

Winslow Convalescent Center
835 Madison Ave N, Bainbridge Island, WA
98110
(206) 842-4765
Admin Sandi Bush.
Medical Dir Dr Keyes.
Licensure Skilled care; Intermediate care. *Beds*
92. *Certified* Medicaid.
Owner Proprietary corp.
Admissions Requirements Medical
examination.
Staff RNs 8 (ft), 5 (pt); LPNs 1 (pt); Nurses'
aides 24 (ft), 14 (pt); Physical therapists 2
(pt); Reality therapists 1 (pt); Recreational
therapists 2 (pt); Occupational therapists 2
(pt); Speech therapists 1 (pt); Activities
coordinators 1 (ft), 1 (pt); Dietitians 1 (pt);
Ophthalmologists 1 (pt); Podiatrists 1 (pt);
Audiologists 1 (pt); Dentists 1 (pt).
Facilities Dining room; Physical therapy
room; Activities room; Laundry room;
Barber/Beauty shop.
Activities Arts & crafts; Cards; Games;
Movies; Shopping trips; Dances/Social/
Cultural gatherings; Church services; Current
events discussion group; Visiting musical
entertainment groups; Sensory stimulation
groups.

Battle Ground

Clark Institute of Restorative Tech
PO Box 218, 103 N Pkwy, Battle Ground,
WA 98604
(206) 687-3781
Admin James Morgan.
Licensure Intermediate care for mentally
retarded. *Beds* 57. *Certified* Medicaid.
Owner Proprietary corp.

Meadow Glade Manor
11117 NE 189th St, Battle Ground, WA
98604
(206) 687-3151
Admin Peter Merchant.
Medical Dir Dean Barth MD.
Licensure Skilled care. *Beds* SNF 65. *Certified*
Medicare.
Owner Proprietary corp (Beverly Enterprises).
Admissions Requirements Minimum age 21;
Medical examination; Physician's request.
Staff Physicians 1 (ft); RNs 5 (ft); LPNs 4 (ft);
Nurses' aides 33 (ft); Physical therapists 1
(pt); Reality therapists 1 (ft); Recreational
therapists 1 (ft); Occupational therapists 1
(pt); Speech therapists 1 (pt); Activities
coordinators 1 (pt); Dietitians 1 (pt);
Podiatrists 1 (pt); Dentists 1 (pt).
Facilities Dining room; Physical therapy
room; Activities room; Crafts room; Barber/
Beauty shop; Dayroom.
Activities Arts & crafts; Cards; Games;
Reading groups; Prayer groups; Movies;
Shopping trips; Dances/Social/Cultural

gatherings; Resident council; Church
services; Special entertainment; Dining out;
Beach trips; County fair; Relaxation;
Exercises; Pet therapy.

Parkway North Care Center
404 N Parkway, Battle Ground, WA 98604
(206) 687-5141
Admin Gail Davis RN. *Dir of Nursing* Mary
Ann Hart. *Medical Dir* Dr Dean Barth; Dr
Ross.
Licensure Skilled care; Intermediate care. *Beds*
Swing beds SNF/ICF 83. *Certified* Medicaid;
Medicare.
Owner Proprietary corp (National Heritage).
Admissions Requirements Medical
examination; Physician's request.
Staff Physicians 1 (pt); RNs 4 (ft), 2 (pt);
LPNs 4 (ft), 2 (pt); Nurses' aides 31 (ft), 3
(pt); Physical therapists 1 (pt); Reality
therapists 1 (pt); Recreational therapists 1
(ft); Occupational therapists 1 (pt); Speech
therapists 1 (pt); Activities coordinators 2
(ft); Dietitians 1 (pt); Podiatrists 1 (pt);
Audiologists 1 (pt).
Facilities Dining room; Physical therapy
room; Activities room; Laundry room;
Barber/Beauty shop.
Activities Arts & crafts; Cards; Games;
Reading groups; Prayer groups; Movies;
Shopping trips; Dances/Social/Cultural
gatherings; Intergenerational programs; Pet
therapy.

Bellevue

Bellevue Center DD Training Center
1640 148th Ave SE, Bellevue, WA 98007
(206) 746-8640
Admin Barbara Hancock.
Medical Dir H Angle MD.
Licensure Intermediate care for mentally
retarded. *Beds* ICF/MR 109. *Certified*
Medicaid.
Owner Proprietary corp.
Staff Physicians 5 (pt); RNs 8 (ft), 4 (pt);
LPNs 3 (ft), 1 (pt); Nurses' aides 48 (ft), 6
(pt); Physical therapists 1 (pt); Recreational
therapists 1 (ft); Occupational therapists 1
(ft); Speech therapists 1 (ft); Activities
coordinators 1 (ft); Dietitians 1 (pt); Dentists
1 (pt).
Facilities Dining room; Physical therapy
room; Activities room; Laundry room;
Sensory stimulation therapy room.
Activities Arts & crafts; Cards; Games;
Movies; Shopping trips; Dances/Social/
Cultural gatherings; Art therapy with artists;
Music therapy; Special Olympics;
Wheelchair games; Bowling; Swimming.

Bellevue Terrace Nursing Center
150 102nd SE, Bellevue, WA 98004
(206) 454-6166
Admin Frank Occhiuto.
Licensure Skilled care; Intermediate care;
Respite; Alzheimer's care. *Certified*
Medicaid; Medicare.
Owner Proprietary corp (Horizon Healthcare
Corp).
Admissions Requirements Minimum age;
Medical examination; Physician's request.
Staff Physicians 3 (pt); RNs 10 (ft), 5 (pt);
LPNs 11 (ft), 8 (pt); Nurses' aides 51 (ft), 9
(pt); Physical therapists 1 (pt); Reality
therapists 1 (pt); Recreational therapists 2
(ft); Occupational therapists 1 (pt); Speech
therapists 1 (pt); Activities coordinators 1
(ft); Dietitians 1 (pt); Ophthalmologists 1
(pt); Podiatrists 1 (pt); Dentists 1 (pt).
Languages Spanish, French, Chinese, Tagalog.
Facilities Dining room; Physical therapy
room; Activities room; Crafts room; Laundry
room; Barber/Beauty shop; Library.

Activities Arts & crafts; Cards; Games;
Reading groups; Prayer groups; Movies;
Shopping trips; Dances/Social/Cultural
gatherings.

Bellingham

Alderwood Park Convalescent Center
2726 Alderwood Ave, Bellingham, WA 98225
(206) 733-2322, 733-0713 FAX
Admin Donna Nylund RN. *Dir of Nursing*
Eunice Cole RN. *Medical Dir* Eugene
Rideout MD.
Licensure Skilled care; Intermediate care. *Beds*
Swing beds SNF/ICF 102. *Certified*
Medicaid; Medicare.
Owner Proprietary corp (Regency Care
Centers Inc).
Staff RNs 3 (ft), 1 (pt); LPNs 8 (ft), 2 (pt);
Nurses' aides 30 (ft); Recreational therapists
1 (ft); Activities coordinators 1 (ft).
Facilities Dining room; Physical therapy
room; Activities room; Laundry room;
Barber/Beauty shop.
Activities Arts & crafts; Cards; Games;
Reading groups; Prayer groups; Movies;
Shopping trips; Dances/Social/Cultural
gatherings; Intergenerational programs; Pet
therapy; Sensory stimulation; Reality
orientation.

Bellingham Care Center
1200 Birchwood, Bellingham, WA 98225
(206) 734-9295
Admin Wayne Gerner. *Dir of Nursing* Leta
Benfield. *Medical Dir* Dr Douglas Wynne.
Licensure Skilled care; Intermediate care;
Alzheimer's unit. *Beds* Swing beds SNF/ICF
120. *Private Pay Patients* 30%. *Certified*
Medicaid; Medicare.
Owner Proprietary corp (Hillhaven Corp).
Admissions Requirements Physician's request.
Staff RNs 5 (ft), 3 (pt); LPNs 8 (ft), 4 (pt);
Nurses' aides 23 (ft), 9 (pt); Physical
therapists 1 (ft); Recreational therapists 1
(ft), 2 (pt); Activities coordinators 1 (ft).
Facilities Dining room; Physical therapy
room; Activities room; Laundry room;
Barber/Beauty shop; Library.
Activities Arts & crafts; Cards; Games;
Reading groups; Prayer groups; Movies;
Shopping trips; Pet therapy.

Highland Convalescent Center
2400 Samish Way, Bellingham, WA 98226
(206) 734-4800
Admin Richard Chasteen. *Dir of Nursing*
Mary Kruze.
Licensure Skilled care; Intermediate care. *Beds*
44. *Certified* Medicaid; Medicare.
Owner Privately owned.
Admissions Requirements Minimum age;
Males only; Medical examination;
Physician's request.
Staff RNs 3 (ft); LPNs 2 (ft); Nurses' aides 9
(ft); Physical therapists 5 (pt); Recreational
therapists 1 (ft); Dietitians 1 (ft).
Facilities Dining room; Activities room;
Laundry room.
Activities Arts & crafts; Cards; Games;
Reading groups; Prayer groups; Movies;
Shopping trips.

Mt Baker Care Inc
5280 Northwest Rd, Bellingham, WA 98226
(206) 734-4181, 384-4180 FAX
Admin Terry A Unger. *Dir of Nursing* Ann
Tennyson. *Medical Dir* Dr Stuart Andrews.
Licensure Skilled care. *Beds* SNF 70. *Private
Pay Patients* 15%. *Certified* Medicaid.
Owner Proprietary corp (Regency Care
Centers Inc).
Admissions Requirements Medical
examination.
Staff RNs 2 (ft); LPNs 5 (ft); Nurses' aides 19
(ft); Activities coordinators 1 (ft).

Facilities Dining room; Activities room; Chapel; Barber/Beauty shop; TV room.
Activities Arts & crafts; Cards; Games; Movies; Shopping trips; Dances/Social/ Cultural gatherings.

Needham's Nursing Home Inc
1509 E Victor St, Bellingham, WA 98225
(206) 733-3141
Admin J F Wiley.
Medical Dir E Fairbanks MD.
Licensure Skilled care; Intermediate care. *Beds* 122. *Certified* Medicaid.
Owner Proprietary corp.
Facilities Dining room; Activities room; Crafts room; Laundry room; Barber/Beauty shop; Library.
Activities Arts & crafts; Cards; Games; Prayer groups; Movies; Shopping trips; Field trips.

St Francis Extended Health Care
PO Box 3150, 3121 Squalicum Pkwy, Bellingham, WA 98227
(206) 734-6760
Admin James O Hall.
Licensure Skilled care; Intermediate care. *Beds* 120. *Certified* Medicaid; Medicare.
Owner Privately owned.

Sehome Park Care Center
700 32nd St, Bellingham, WA 98225
(206) 734-9330
Admin William Klock.
Medical Dir Joan L Humen.
Licensure Skilled care; Intermediate care. *Beds* 137. *Certified* Medicaid; Medicare.
Owner Proprietary corp.
Admissions Requirements Medical examination; Physician's request.
Facilities Dining room; Physical therapy room; Activities room; Crafts room; Laundry room; Barber/Beauty shop; Library.
Activities Arts & crafts; Cards; Games; Reading groups; Prayer groups; Movies; Shopping trips; Dances/Social/Cultural gatherings.

Shuksan Convalescent Center
1530 James St, Bellingham, WA 98225
(206) 733-9161
Admin Everett Gimmaka. *Dir of Nursing* Sharon Landcastle RN. *Medical Dir* Marta Kazymyra MD.
Licensure Skilled care. *Beds* SNF 61. *Private Pay Patients* 30%. *Certified* Medicaid; Medicare.
Owner Proprietary corp.
Staff RNs 4 (ft); LPNs 4 (ft), 4 (pt); Nurses' aides 13 (ft), 2 (pt); Activities coordinators 1 (ft); Restorative aides 1 (ft).
Facilities Dining room; Physical therapy room; Activities room; Barber/Beauty shop; Library.
Activities Arts & crafts; Cards; Games; Reading groups; Prayer groups; Movies; Shopping trips; Intergenerational programs; Pet therapy.

Blaine

Stafholt Good Samaritan Center
PO Box Z, 360 D St, Blaine, WA 98230
(206) 332-8733
Admin Ann L Walter. *Dir of Nursing* Marilyn Matheson RN. *Medical Dir* Stuart Andrews MD.
Licensure Skilled care; Intermediate care; Alzheimer's care. *Beds* Swing beds SNF/ICF 65. *Certified* Medicaid.
Owner Nonprofit corp (Evangelical Lutheran/ Good Samaritan Society).
Admissions Requirements Medical examination.
Staff RNs 4 (ft), 1 (pt); LPNs 6 (ft), 1 (pt); Nurses' aides 18 (ft), 12 (pt); Recreational therapists 1 (ft); Activities coordinators 1 (ft); Dietitians 1 (pt).

Facilities Dining room; Physical therapy room; Activities room; Crafts room; Laundry room; Barber/Beauty shop; Library.
Activities Arts & crafts; Cards; Games; Reading groups; Prayer groups; Movies; Shopping trips; Dances/Social/Cultural gatherings.

Bothell

Eastern Star Nursing Home—Bothell
707 228th SW, Bothell, WA 98011
(206) 481-8500
Admin Vivian B Spore.
Licensure Skilled care; Intermediate care. *Beds* 99. *Certified* Medicaid.
Owner Nonprofit corp.

Northshore Manor
10909 NE 185th St, Bothell, WA 98011
(206) 486-7174
Admin David R Crawford.
Medical Dir Dr James Monahan.
Licensure Skilled care; Intermediate care. *Beds* 135. *Certified* Medicaid.
Owner Nonprofit corp.
Admissions Requirements Medical examination.
Staff RNs 11 (ft), 6 (pt); LPNs 5 (ft), 1 (pt); Nurses' aides 35 (ft), 27 (pt); Activities coordinators 2 (ft); Dietitians 1 (ft).
Facilities Dining room; Physical therapy room; Activities room; Chapel; Crafts room; Laundry room; Barber/Beauty shop.
Activities Arts & crafts; Cards; Games; Reading groups; Prayer groups; Movies; Dances/Social/Cultural gatherings.

Bremerton

Belmont Terrace Inc
560 Lebo Blvd, Bremerton, WA 98310
(206) 479-1515, 479-1517 FAX
Admin Sam Sutherland. *Dir of Nursing* Frankie Smith RN BS. *Medical Dir* T M Lang MD.
Licensure Skilled care; Intermediate care. *Beds* Swing beds SNF/ICF 102. *Private Pay Patients* 40%. *Certified* Medicaid; Medicare.
Owner Proprietary corp.
Admissions Requirements Medical examination; Physician's request.
Staff RNs 11 (ft), 6 (pt); LPNs 7 (ft), 4 (pt); Nurses' aides 40 (ft), 5 (pt); Physical therapists; Activities coordinators 1 (ft); Dietitians.
Facilities Dining room; Physical therapy room; Activities room; Laundry room; Barber/Beauty shop.
Activities Games; Prayer groups; Movies; Pet therapy; Volunteer musical groups.

Bremerton Convalescent Center
PO Box 2014, Bremerton, WA 98310
(206) 377-3951
Admin Roger P Bright.
Medical Dir Dr Robert Bright.
Licensure Skilled care; Intermediate care. *Beds* 140. *Certified* Medicaid; Medicare.
Owner Proprietary corp.
Admissions Requirements Medical examination; Physician's request.
Staff RNs 10 (ft); LPNs 5 (ft); Nurses' aides 60 (ft); Physical therapists 1 (pt); Recreational therapists 1 (ft); Occupational therapists 1 (pt); Speech therapists 1 (pt); Activities coordinators 1 (pt); Dietitians 1 (pt).
Facilities Dining room; Physical therapy room; Activities room; Chapel; Crafts room; Laundry room; Barber/Beauty shop; Library; TV.
Activities Arts & crafts; Cards; Games; Reading groups; Prayer groups; Movies; Dances/Social/Cultural gatherings.

Forest Ridge Convalescent Center
140 S Marion Ave, Bremerton, WA 98312
(206) 479-4747, 377-3736 FAX
Admin Kathleen J Reed BS RN. *Dir of Nursing* Elizabeth Ledbetter RN. *Medical Dir* Dr William Seal.
Licensure Skilled care; Intermediate care; Alzheimer's care. *Beds* Swing beds SNF/ICF 98. *Certified* Medicaid; Medicare.
Owner Proprietary corp (KLR Associates Inc).
Admissions Requirements Medical examination; Physician's request.
Staff RNs 10 (ft), 5 (pt); LPNs 3 (ft), 8 (pt); Nurses' aides 34 (ft), 8 (pt); Physical therapists 1 (ft); Recreational therapists 1 (ft); Occupational therapists 1 (pt); Speech therapists 1 (pt); Dietitians 1 (pt); Podiatrists 1 (pt); Audiologists 1 (pt).
Facilities Dining room; Physical therapy room; Activities room; Chapel; Crafts room; Laundry room; Barber/Beauty shop; Library.
Activities Arts & crafts; Cards; Games; Reading groups; Prayer groups; Movies; Shopping trips; Dances/Social/Cultural gatherings; Intergenerational programs; Pet therapy.

Resthaven Health Care Center
3517 11th St, Bremerton, WA 98310
(206) 377-5537
Admin Judith Ann Leaf.
Medical Dir Hugh Harkins MD.
Licensure Skilled care; Intermediate care. *Beds* 91. *Certified* Medicaid; Medicare.
Owner Proprietary corp.
Admissions Requirements Medical examination; Physician's request.
Staff RNs 5 (ft), 3 (pt); LPNs 3 (ft), 3 (pt); Nurses' aides 32 (ft), 3 (pt); Physical therapists 1 (pt); Recreational therapists 2 (pt); Occupational therapists 1 (pt); Speech therapists 1 (pt); Activities coordinators 1 (ft), 1 (pt); Dietitians 1 (pt).
Affiliation Lutheran.
Facilities Dining room; Physical therapy room; Activities room; Crafts room; Laundry room; Barber/Beauty shop.
Activities Arts & crafts; Games; Reading groups; Prayer groups; Movies; Shopping trips; Dances/Social/Cultural gatherings; Crafty cookers; Gardening; Resident council events; Special speakers & presentations.

301 Sylvan Way
5112 NW Taylor Rd, Bremerton, WA 98312
(206) 377-6153
Admin Molly Harris.
Licensure Intermediate care for mentally retarded. *Beds* 6.
Owner Nonprofit corp.

Brewster

Harmony House
PO Box 829, 100 River Plaza, Brewster, WA 98812
(509) 689-2546
Admin Jerry R Tretwold. *Dir of Nursing* Shirley McCoy. *Medical Dir* Jim Edwards MD.
Licensure Skilled care. *Beds* SNF 73. *Certified* Medicaid.
Owner Privately owned.
Staff Physicians; RNs; LPNs; Nurses' aides; Physical therapists; Recreational therapists; Occupational therapists; Speech therapists; Activities coordinators; Dietitians.
Activities Arts & crafts; Cards; Games; Reading groups; Prayer groups; Movies; Shopping trips; Dances/Social/Cultural gatherings.

Burlington

Burton Nursing Home
1036 Victoria Ave, Burlington, WA 98233
(206) 755-0711

Admin Stephen R Johnson. *Dir of Nursing* Cathy Waters. *Medical Dir* Dr Steven M Aldrich.
Licensure Intermediate care. *Beds* ICF 49. *Private Pay Patients* 50%. *Certified* Medicaid.
Owner Privately owned.
Admissions Requirements Medical examination; Physician's request.
Staff RNs 2 (ft), 1 (pt); LPNs 2 (ft), 3 (pt); Nurses' aides 16 (ft), 7 (pt); Physical therapists 1 (pt); Activities coordinators 1 (ft), 1 (pt); Dietitians 1 (ft); Restorative aides 1 (ft).
Facilities Dining room; Activities room; Living room; Solarium; Secure courtyard.
Activities Arts & crafts; Cards; Games; Reading groups; Prayer groups; Movies; Shopping trips; Dances/Social/Cultural gatherings; Pet therapy.

Camano Island

Camano Shores Nursing Home
1054 SW Camano Dr, Camano Island, WA 98292
(206) 387-4711
Admin Loren Fassett. *Dir of Nursing* Pat Danforth RN. *Medical Dir* Dr Fred Remington.
Licensure Intermediate care. *Beds* ICF 24. *Certified* Medicaid.
Owner Privately owned.
Admissions Requirements Minimum age 18; Medical examination; Physician's request.
Staff Physicians 3 (ft); RNs 2 (ft), 3 (pt); LPNs 1 (ft), 2 (pt); Nurses' aides 3 (ft), 2 (pt); Physical therapists 1 (pt); Activities coordinators 1 (ft); Dietitians 1 (pt); Ophthalmologists 1 (pt); Podiatrists 1 (pt); Audiologists 1 (pt).
Languages French, German.
Facilities Dining room; Laundry room; Barber/Beauty shop.
Activities Arts & crafts; Cards; Games; Reading groups; Prayer groups; Shopping trips; Dances/Social/Cultural gatherings; Intergenerational programs; Pet therapy; Services by local churches; Geriatric day treatment program.

Camas

Highland Terrace Nursing Center
PO Box 1148, 640 NE Everett St, Camas, WA 98607
(206) 834-5055
Admin Kathleen Dhanes.
Licensure Skilled care; Intermediate care. *Beds* 131. *Certified* Medicaid; Medicare.
Owner Proprietary corp (Beverly Enterprises).

Cashmere

Cashmere Convalescent Center
PO Box 626, 817 Pioneer Ave, Cashmere, WA 98815
(509) 782-1251
Admin William A Dronen.
Licensure Skilled care; Intermediate care. *Beds* 90. *Certified* Medicaid; Medicare.
Owner Proprietary corp.

Cathlamet

Columbia View Nursing Home
PO Box 338, 155 Alder, Cathlamet, WA 98612
(206) 795-3234
Admin Crystal Stanley.
Licensure Skilled care; Intermediate care. *Beds* 53. *Certified* Medicaid.
Owner Proprietary corp.
Admissions Requirements Medical examination; Physician's request.

Staff RNs 5 (ft); LPNs 3 (ft); Nurses' aides 20 (ft); Physical therapists 1 (pt); Speech therapists 1 (pt); Activities coordinators 1 (ft); Dietitians 1 (pt); Ophthalmologists 1 (pt); Podiatrists 1 (pt); Audiologists 1 (pt); Dentists 1 (pt).
Facilities Dining room; Activities room; Laundry room.
Activities Arts & crafts; Cards; Games; Reading groups; Prayer groups; Movies; Shopping trips; Dances/Social/Cultural gatherings.

Centralia

Centralia Convalescent Center
1015 Long Rd, Centralia, WA 98531
(206) 736-3381
Admin Debi L Thompson. *Dir of Nursing* Sharon Gadd RN. *Medical Dir* Dr Kenneth Burden.
Licensure Skilled care; Intermediate care. *Beds* 96. *Certified* Medicaid; Medicare.
Owner Nonprofit corp (Pleasant Valley Services Corp).
Admissions Requirements Medical examination; Physician's request.
Staff RNs; LPNs; Nurses' aides; Activities coordinators.
Facilities Dining room; Physical therapy room; Activities room; Crafts room; Laundry room; Barber/Beauty shop.
Activities Arts & crafts; Cards; Games; Prayer groups; Movies; Shopping trips; Dances/Social/Cultural gatherings; Exercises; Manicures; Grooming; Banquets.

Liberty Care & Rehabilitation Center
917 S Scheuber Rd, Centralia, WA 98531
(206) 736-2020
Admin Blossom Knudson. *Dir of Nursing* Marti Summer. *Medical Dir* Loren Cooper.
Licensure Skilled care; Intermediate care; Alzheimer's care. *Beds* Swing beds SNF/ICF 128. *Private Pay Patients* 20%. *Certified* Medicaid.
Owner Privately owned.
Admissions Requirements Minimum age 18; Medical examination; Physician's request.
Staff Physicians 1 (pt); RNs 5 (ft); LPNs 13 (ft); Nurses' aides 50 (ft); Physical therapists 1 (pt); Recreational therapists 1 (ft); Occupational therapists 1 (pt); Activities coordinators 1 (ft); Dietitians 1 (pt).
Facilities Dining room; Physical therapy room; Activities room; Crafts room; Laundry room; Barber/Beauty shop; Dayrooms; Private and semi-private rooms.
Activities Arts & crafts; Cards; Games; Reading groups; Prayer groups; Movies; Shopping trips; Dances/Social/Cultural gatherings; Intergenerational programs; Pet therapy.

Sharon Care Center Inc
1509 Harrison Ave, Centralia, WA 98531
(206) 736-0112
Admin William Hammond. *Dir of Nursing* Candy Hayertz RN. *Medical Dir* Dr Cooper.
Licensure Intermediate care; Alzheimer's care. *Beds* ICF 42. *Private Pay Patients* 50%. *Certified* Medicaid.
Owner Proprietary corp.
Admissions Requirements Minimum age 50.
Staff RNs 1 (ft); LPNs 3 (ft), 1 (pt); Nurses' aides 10 (ft); Physical therapists (contracted); Recreational therapists 1 (ft); Speech therapists (contracted); Activities coordinators 1 (ft); Dietitians (contracted); Podiatrists (contracted); Audiologists (contracted).
Facilities Dining room; Physical therapy room; Activities room; Crafts room; Laundry room; Barber/Beauty shop.

Activities Arts & crafts; Cards; Games; Reading groups; Prayer groups; Movies; Shopping trips; Dances/Social/Cultural gatherings; Intergenerational programs; Pet therapy.

Walker Care Center
408 S King, Centralia, WA 98531
(206) 736-1197
Admin Duane McCormies. *Dir of Nursing* Mary Farmer.
Licensure Skilled care; Intermediate care; Alzheimer's care. *Beds* Swing beds SNF/ICF 48. *Certified* Medicaid.
Owner Proprietary corp (Soundcare Inc).
Admissions Requirements Physician's request.
Staff RNs 2 (ft), 1 (pt); LPNs 3 (ft), 2 (pt); Nurses' aides 15 (ft), 9 (pt); Physical therapists 1 (pt); Occupational therapists 1 (pt); Activities coordinators 1 (ft); Dietitians 1 (pt).
Facilities Dining room; Activities room; Laundry room.
Activities Arts & crafts; Games; Reading groups; Prayer groups; Movies; Shopping trips; Dances/Social/Cultural gatherings.

Washington Health Care Center—Riverside
1305 Alexander, Centralia, WA 98531
(206) 736-2823, 736-1821 FAX
Admin Karin Rutt. *Dir of Nursing* Colleen Murray RN. *Medical Dir* Kenneth Burden MD.
Licensure Skilled care. *Beds* SNF 131. *Certified* Medicaid.
Owner Proprietary corp (Unicare).
Facilities Dining room; Physical therapy room; Activities room; Laundry room; Barber/Beauty shop; Library.
Activities Arts & crafts; Games; Reading groups; Prayer groups; Movies; Shopping trips; Dances/Social/Cultural gatherings; Intergenerational programs; Pet therapy.

Chehalis

Providence—Chehalis
500 SE Washington, Chehalis, WA 98532
(206) 748-4444
Admin Harold Brockman. *Dir of Nursing* Mitzi Vandewege. *Medical Dir* Dr David Fick.
Licensure Skilled care; Intermediate care. *Beds* SNF 16; ICF 25. *Private Pay Patients* 20%. *Certified* Medicaid; Medicare.
Owner Nonprofit organization/foundation (Sisters of Providence).

Chelan

Regency Manor
PO Box 609, 726 N Markeson, Chelan, WA 98816
(509) 682-2551, 682-4455 FAX
Admin David W Dickes. *Dir of Nursing* Larita Bigelow ARNP GNP. *Medical Dir* Charles F James MD.
Licensure Skilled care; Intermediate care. *Beds* Swing beds SNF/ICF 80. *Private Pay Patients* 10%. *Certified* Medicaid.
Owner Proprietary corp (Regency Care Centers Inc).
Staff RNs 8 (ft), 3 (pt); LPNs 5 (ft); Nurses' aides 21 (ft), 7 (pt); Recreational therapists 2 (ft); Dietitians 1 (ft).
Languages Spanish.
Facilities Dining room; Physical therapy room; Laundry room; Barber/Beauty shop.
Activities Arts & crafts; Cards; Games; Reading groups; Prayer groups; Movies; Shopping trips; Dances/Social/Cultural gatherings; Intergenerational programs; Pet therapy.

Cheney

Cheney Care Center
2219 N 6th, Cheney, WA 99004
(509) 235-6196, 235-2044 FAX
Admin Timothy C Lewis. *Dir of Nursing*
Carol Morgenstern. *Medical Dir* Roger
Garvin MD.
Licensure Skilled care; Alzheimer's care;
Retirement. *Beds* SNF 62. *Certified*
Medicaid; Medicare.
Owner Nonprofit organization/foundation.
Admissions Requirements Medical
examination; Physician's request.
Staff RNs 4 (ft), 2 (pt); LPNs 5 (ft), 6 (pt);
Nurses' aides 17 (ft), 25 (pt); Physical
therapists 1 (pt); Recreational therapists 1
(ft); Occupational therapists 1 (pt); Speech
therapists 1 (pt); Activities coordinators 1
(ft); Dietitians 1 (pt).
Facilities Dining room; Physical therapy
room; Activities room; Laundry room;
Barber/Beauty shop; Security system for
wanderers; Fenced backyard.
Activities Arts & crafts; Cards; Games;
Reading groups; Prayer groups; Movies;
Shopping trips; Dances/Social/Cultural
gatherings; Intergenerational programs; Pet
therapy.

Clarkston

Clarkston Care Center
PO Box 159, 1242 11th St, Clarkston, WA
99403
(509) 758-2523
Admin Larry Robeson.
Medical Dir Dr Walter Seibly.
Licensure Skilled care; Intermediate care. *Beds*
Swing beds SNF/ICF 85. *Certified* Medicaid;
Medicare.
Owner Privately owned.

Tri-State Convalescent Center
PO Box 429, 1255 Belmont Way, Clarkston,
WA 99403
(509) 758-5573
Admin Judith P Seubert. *Dir of Nursing*
Diana Berndt RN. *Medical Dir* Walter
Seibly MD.
Licensure Skilled care; Intermediate care. *Beds*
124. *Certified* Medicaid; Medicare.
Owner Privately owned.
Admissions Requirements Medical
examination; Physician's request.
Staff RNs 8 (ft); LPNs 9 (ft), 3 (pt); Nurses'
aides 33 (ft), 12 (pt); Activities coordinators
2 (ft), 1 (pt).
Facilities Dining room; Activities room;
Laundry room; Barber/Beauty shop.
Activities Arts & crafts; Cards; Games;
Reading groups; Prayer groups; Movies;
Dances/Social/Cultural gatherings.

Cle Elum

Pinecrest Manor Convalescent Home
601 Power St, Cle Elum, WA 98922
(509) 674-4401
Admin Carol Detwiler. *Dir of Nursing* Mary
Eggen RN. *Medical Dir* Dr Elizabeth Wise.
Licensure Skilled care; Intermediate care. *Beds*
61. *Certified* Medicaid.
Owner Proprietary corp.
Admissions Requirements Minimum age 18;
Medical examination; Physician's request.
Staff RNs 6 (ft); LPNs 7 (ft); Nurses' aides 32
(ft); Activities coordinators 1 (ft), 1 (pt).
Facilities Dining room; Physical therapy
room; Activities room; Laundry room;
Barber/Beauty shop.
Activities Arts & crafts; Cards; Games;
Reading groups; Prayer groups; Movies;
Shopping trips; Dances/Social/Cultural
gatherings; Cooking; Mental health sensory
stimulation; Music.

Colfax

Whitman Convalescent Center
PO Box 680, Almota Rd, Colfax, WA 99111
(509) 397-3433
Admin Dennis McDonald.
Licensure Skilled care; Intermediate care. *Beds*
74. *Certified* Medicaid; Medicare.
Owner Proprietary corp.

College Place

Blue Mountain Convalescent Center
1200 SE 12th, College Place, WA 99324
(509) 529-4080
Admin Edward Sorrels. *Dir of Nursing* Mary
Fowler RN. *Medical Dir* Michael Kilfoyle
MD.
Licensure Skilled care; Intermediate care. *Beds*
123. *Certified* Medicaid; Medicare.
Owner Proprietary corp (Horizon Health
Systems).
Admissions Requirements Medical
examination.
Staff RNs; LPNs; Nurses' aides; Physical
therapists; Activities coordinators; Dietitians.
Languages Spanish.
Facilities Dining room; Physical therapy
room; Activities room; Crafts room; Laundry
room; Barber/Beauty shop.
Activities Arts & crafts; Cards; Games;
Reading groups; Prayer groups; Movies;
Shopping trips; Dances/Social/Cultural
gatherings.

Colville

Buena Vista Inc
Rte 2 Box 17, Colville, WA 99114
(509) 684-4539
Admin Velda McCammon.
Medical Dir Dr J Herman.
Licensure Skilled care; Intermediate care. *Beds*
Swing beds SNF/ICF 40. *Certified* Medicaid;
Medicare.
Owner Proprietary corp.
Staff Physicians 6 (pt); RNs 6 (ft), 2 (pt);
LPNs 2 (ft); Nurses' aides 30 (ft); Physical
therapists 1 (pt); Recreational therapists 1
(pt); Occupational therapists 1 (pt);
Activities coordinators 1 (ft); Dietitians 1
(pt); Ophthalmologists 1 (pt).
Facilities Dining room; Activities room;
Crafts room; Barber/Beauty shop.
Activities Arts & crafts; Cards; Games;
Reading groups; Prayer groups; Movies;
Shopping trips; Dances/Social/Cultural
gatherings.

Pinewood Terrace Nursing Center
PO Box 559, 1000 E Elep St, Colville, WA
99114
(509) 684-2573
Admin Steven H Wilson. *Dir of Nursing*
Linda Winslow RN. *Medical Dir* William
Doyle MD.
Licensure Skilled care; Intermediate care;
Retirement. *Beds* 93. *Certified* Medicaid;
Medicare.
Owner Proprietary corp (Beverly Enterprises).
Admissions Requirements Minimum age 21;
Physician's request.
Staff RNs 3 (ft); LPNs 4 (ft), 1 (pt); Nurses'
aides 21 (ft), 1 (pt); Activities coordinators 1
(ft); Dietitians 1 (ft).
Facilities Dining room; Physical therapy
room; Activities room; Laundry room;
Barber/Beauty shop.
Activities Arts & crafts; Cards; Games;
Reading groups; Prayer groups; Movies;
Shopping trips; Dances/Social/Cultural
gatherings; Ceramics.

Coupeville

Careage of Whidbey
PO Box 1140, 311 NE Third, Coupeville, WA
98239
(206) 678-2273
Admin Carmen McFadyen.
Licensure Skilled care; Intermediate care. *Beds*
59. *Certified* Medicaid; Medicare.
Owner Proprietary corp.

Davenport

Lincoln Hospital
10 Nichols St, Davenport, WA 99122
(509) 725-7101
Admin Thomas J Martin. *Dir of Nursing*
Judith Van Pevenage RN. *Medical Dir* Dr
Dan Husky.
Licensure Intermediate care; Alzheimer's care.
Beds ICF 71. *Private Pay Patients* 55%.
Certified Medicaid.
Owner Publicly owned.
Admissions Requirements Medical
examination; Physician's request.
Staff Physicians 5 (ft); RNs 20 (ft); LPNs 4
(ft); Nurses' aides 20 (ft); Physical therapists
1 (ft); Recreational therapists 3 (ft);
Occupational therapists 1 (pt); Speech
therapists 1 (pt); Activities coordinators 1
(ft); Dietitians 1 (pt); Podiatrists 1 (pt).
Facilities Dining room; Physical therapy
room; Activities room; Crafts room; Laundry
room; Barber/Beauty shop.
Activities Arts & crafts; Cards; Games;
Reading groups; Prayer groups; Movies;
Shopping trips; Dances/Social/Cultural
gatherings; Intergenerational programs; Pet
therapy.

Dayton

Booker Convalescent Annex
1012 S 3rd, Dayton, WA 99328
(509) 382-2531
Admin Garvin G Olson.
Medical Dir S R Hevel MD.
Licensure Nursing home. *Beds* Nursing home
20.
Owner Publicly owned.
Admissions Requirements Medical
examination; Physician's request.
Staff RNs 2 (ft); LPNs 1 (ft), 1 (pt); Nurses'
aides 4 (ft), 2 (pt); Activities coordinators 1
(ft); Dietitians 1 (pt).
Facilities Dining room; Physical therapy
room; Activities room.
Activities Arts & crafts; Games; Prayer groups;
Movies; Dances/Social/Cultural gatherings.

Robison Nursing Home Inc
221 E Washington, Dayton, WA 99328
(509) 382-4621
Admin Garvin G Olson.
Medical Dir S R Hevel MD.
Licensure Skilled care; Intermediate care. *Beds*
46. *Certified* Medicaid.
Owner Publicly owned.
Admissions Requirements Medical
examination; Physician's request.
Staff RNs 4 (ft); LPNs 4 (ft), 1 (pt); Nurses'
aides 17 (ft), 3 (pt); Physical therapists 1
(pt); Activities coordinators 1 (ft); Dietitians
1 (pt).
Facilities Dining room; Physical therapy
room; Activities room.
Activities Arts & crafts; Games; Prayer groups;
Movies; Dances/Social/Cultural gatherings.

Des Moines

Judson Park Health Center
23620 Marine View Dr S, Des Moines, WA
98198
(206) 824-4000

Admin Ted Day. *Dir of Nursing* Louise Ellis
RN. *Medical Dir* Eleanor Sutherland MD.
Licensure Skilled care; Intermediate care;
Retirement. *Beds* 120. *Certified* Medicaid;
Medicare.
Owner Nonprofit corp.
Admissions Requirements Minimum age 62;
Medical examination; Physician's request.
Staff Physicians 1 (pt); RNs 4 (ft), 144 (pt);
LPNs 3 (ft), 4 (pt); Nurses' aides 39 (ft), 24
(pt); Physical therapists 1 (pt); Recreational
therapists 1 (pt); Speech therapists 1 (pt);
Dietitians 1 (pt); Ophthalmologists 1 (pt);
Dentists 1 (pt).
Affiliation Baptist.
Facilities Dining room; Physical therapy
room; Activities room; Chapel; Crafts room;
Laundry room; Barber/Beauty shop.
Activities Arts & crafts; Games; Reading
groups; Prayer groups; Movies; Drives;
Restaurants; Bowling.

Masonic Home of Washington
23660 Marine View Dr S, Des Moines, WA
98198
(206) 878-8434
Admin Donna Mae Ketten. *Dir of Nursing*
Kim Deitch RN. *Medical Dir* Dr Fred T
Yates.
Licensure Skilled care; Retirement. *Beds* SNF
72; Retirement 120.
Owner Nonprofit organization/foundation.
Admissions Requirements Medical
examination.
Staff Physicians 1 (pt); RNs 5 (ft), 4 (pt);
LPNs 1 (ft), 1 (pt); Nurses' aides 12 (ft), 5
(pt); Physical therapists 1 (pt); Recreational
therapists 1 (pt); Activities coordinators 1
(pt); Dietitians 1 (pt); Ophthalmologists 1
(pt); Podiatrists 1 (pt); Audiologists 1 (pt);
Dentists 1 (pt).
Languages French, Lao, East Indian, Korean,
Swedish, Norwegian.
Affiliation Masons.
Facilities Dining room; Physical therapy
room; Activities room; Chapel; Crafts room;
Laundry room; Barber/Beauty shop; Library.
Activities Arts & crafts; Cards; Games;
Reading groups; Prayer groups; Movies;
Shopping trips; Dances/Social/Cultural
gatherings; Intergenerational programs; Pet
therapy.

Seatoma Convalescent Center
2800 S 224th St, Des Moines, WA 98198
(206) 824-0600
Admin Kris F Bolt.
Medical Dir Dr Janet Hodge.
Licensure Skilled care; Intermediate care. *Beds*
265. *Certified* Medicaid; Medicare.
Owner Proprietary corp.
Admissions Requirements Medical
examination.
Staff Physicians 4 (ft), 8 (pt); RNs 15 (ft);
LPNs 12 (ft); Physical therapists 2 (ft);
Recreational therapists 2 (ft); Occupational
therapists 1 (ft); Speech therapists 1 (pt);
Activities coordinators 2 (ft); Dietitians 1
(pt); Podiatrists 1 (pt); Dentists 1 (pt).
Facilities Dining room; Physical therapy
room; Activities room; Chapel; Crafts room;
Laundry room; Barber/Beauty shop; TV
room; Solarium.
Activities Arts & crafts; Games; Reading
groups; Prayer groups; Movies; Shopping
trips; Dances/Social/Cultural gatherings.

Wesley Care Center
1122 S 216th St, Des Moines, WA 98198
(206) 824-3663
Admin Calvin A Groenenberg.
Licensure Skilled care. *Beds* SNF 98. *Certified*
Medicaid.
Owner Nonprofit corp (Wesley Homes).
Affiliation Methodist.

Wesley Homes—The Gardens
815 S 216th St, Des Moines, WA 98188
(206) 824-5000
Admin Leon F Bowers.
Medical Dir Stanley Harris MD.
Licensure Skilled care; Intermediate care. *Beds*
58. *Certified* Medicaid.
Owner Nonprofit corp (Wesley Homes).
Staff RNs; LPNs; Nurses' aides; Physical
therapists; Recreational therapists;
Occupational therapists; Speech therapists;
Dietitians; Ophthalmologists; Podiatrists;
Audiologists; Dentists.
Affiliation Methodist.
Facilities Dining room; Physical therapy
room; Activities room; Chapel; Crafts room;
Laundry room; Barber/Beauty shop; Library.

Wesley Homes—Wesley Terrace
816 S 216th St, Des Moines, WA 98188
(206) 824-5000
Admin Leon F Bowers.
Medical Dir Stanley Harris MD.
Licensure Skilled care; Intermediate care. *Beds*
35. *Certified* Medicaid.
Owner Nonprofit corp (Wesley Homes).
Staff RNs; LPNs; Nurses' aides; Physical
therapists; Recreational therapists;
Occupational therapists; Activities
coordinators; Dietitians; Podiatrists;
Audiologists; Dentists.
Facilities Dining room; Physical therapy
room; Activities room; Chapel; Crafts room;
Laundry room; Barber/Beauty shop; Library.

Duvall

Carlton Group Home
PO Box 61, Duvall, WA 98019
(206) 788-4489
Admin Steve Skeen.
Licensure Intermediate care for mentally
retarded. *Beds* ICF/MR 6. *Certified*
Medicaid.
Owner Nonprofit corp.

Chelsea Group Home
PO Box 1394, 317 1st Ave NE, Duvall, WA
98019
(206) 788-4585
Admin Steve Skeen.
Licensure Intermediate care for mentally
retarded. *Beds* ICF/MR 6. *Certified*
Medicaid.
Owner Nonprofit corp.

East Wenatchee

Highline Convalescent Center
609 Highline Dr, East Wenatchee, WA 98801
(509) 884-6602
Admin Terry Lee Mace. *Dir of Nursing*
Delores Peterson RN. *Medical Dir* Dr
Robert Hoxsey.
Licensure Skilled care; Intermediate care;
Alzheimer's care; Retirement. *Beds* 101.
Certified Medicaid; Medicare.
Owner Privately owned.
Admissions Requirements Medical
examination; Physician's request.
Staff Physicians; RNs; LPNs; Nurses' aides;
Physical therapists; Reality therapists;
Recreational therapists; Occupational
therapists; Speech therapists; Activities
coordinators; Dietitians; Ophthalmologists.
Activities Arts & crafts; Cards; Games;
Reading groups; Prayer groups; Movies;
Shopping trips; Dances/Social/Cultural
gatherings.

Edmonds

Aurora-Edmonds Nursing Home
8104 220th SW, Edmonds, WA 98020
(206) 778-5703

Admin James W Frymier Jr. *Dir of Nursing*
Margaret Smith RN. *Medical Dir* Dr David
Spiro.
Licensure Intermediate care; Assisted living.
Beds ICF 31; Assisted living 26. *Private Pay
Patients* 15%. *Certified* Medicaid.
Owner Proprietary corp (Habitats Association
LTD).
Admissions Requirements Physician's request.
Staff RNs 4 (ft), 3 (pt); LPNs 3 (ft), 2 (pt);
Nurses' aides 6 (ft), 6 (pt); Physical
therapists 1 (pt); Occupational therapists 1
(pt); Speech therapists 1 (pt); Activities
coordinators 1 (ft); Dietitians 1 (pt).
Languages Spanish.
Facilities Dining room; Activities room;
Laundry room.
Activities Arts & crafts; Cards; Games;
Reading groups; Prayer groups; Movies;
Dances/Social/Cultural gatherings; Pet
therapy.

Edmonds Care Center
21008 76th Ave W, Edmonds, WA 98020
(206) 778-0107
Admin Jane Whitaker. *Dir of Nursing* Ardelle
Marchand.
Licensure Skilled care; Intermediate care;
Alzheimer's care. *Beds* 98. *Certified*
Medicaid; Medicare.
Owner Proprietary corp (Hillhaven Corp).
Admissions Requirements Medical
examination; Physician's request History &
Physical.
Staff RNs 11 (ft); LPNs 4 (ft), 1 (pt); Nurses'
aides 30 (ft), 4 (pt); Activities coordinators 1
(ft), 1 (pt); Dietitians 1 (ft).
Facilities Dining room; Physical therapy
room; Activities room; Laundry room;
Barber/Beauty shop.
Activities Arts & crafts; Cards; Games;
Reading groups; Prayer groups; Movies;
Dances/Social/Cultural gatherings.

Washington Healthcare Center—Aldercrest
21400 72nd Ave W, Edmonds, WA 98020
(206) 775-1961
Admin Joanne L Wheaton.
Medical Dir Pamela Cooper MD.
Licensure Skilled care; Intermediate care;
Alzheimer's care. *Beds* 160. *Certified*
Medicaid; Medicare.
Owner Proprietary corp (Unicare).
Staff RNs; LPNs; Nurses' aides; Physical
therapists; Reality therapists; Recreational
therapists; Occupational therapists; Speech
therapists; Activities coordinators; Dietitians;
Ophthalmologists; Podiatrists; Dentists.
Facilities Dining room; Physical therapy
room; Activities room; Crafts room; Laundry
room; Barber/Beauty shop.
Activities Arts & crafts; Cards; Games;
Reading groups; Prayer groups; Movies;
Shopping trips; Dances/Social/Cultural
gatherings.

Ellensburg

Royal Vista Care Center
1506 Radio Rd, Ellensburg, WA 98926
(509) 925-1404
Admin Janice K Eidson.
Medical Dir Dr Messner.
Licensure Skilled care; Intermediate care. *Beds*
86. *Certified* Medicaid; Medicare.
Owner Proprietary corp.
Staff RNs 5 (ft); LPNs 6 (ft); Nurses' aides 60
(ft); Physical therapists 2 (ft); Reality
therapists 1 (ft); Recreational therapists 1
(ft), 1 (pt); Activities coordinators 1 (ft);
Dietitians 1 (ft).
Facilities Dining room; Physical therapy
room; Activities room; Crafts room; Laundry
room; Library.

Activities Arts & crafts; Cards; Games;
Reading groups; Prayer groups; Movies;
Shopping trips; Dances/Social/Cultural
gatherings.

Washington Healthcare Center Gold Leaf
1050 E Mountain View, Ellensburg, WA
98926
(509) 925-4171
Admin Sandra Bush. *Dir of Nursing* Claudia
Eattock RN. *Medical Dir* Dr Alfred Grose.
Licensure Skilled care; Intermediate care. *Beds*
80. *Certified* Medicaid; Medicare.
Owner Proprietary corp (Unicare).
Admissions Requirements Physician's request.
Staff RNs 4 (ft), 4 (pt); LPNs 6 (ft); Physical
therapists 1 (pt); Reality therapists 1 (pt);
Recreational therapists 1 (pt); Occupational
therapists 1 (pt); Speech therapists 1 (pt);
Activities coordinators 1 (ft); Dietitians 1
(ft); Ophthalmologists 1 (pt); Podiatrists 1
(pt); Dentists 1 (pt).
Facilities Dining room; Physical therapy
room; Activities room; Chapel; Laundry
room; Barber/Beauty shop; Library; TV
room; Lounge.
Activities Arts & crafts; Cards; Games;
Reading groups; Prayer groups; Movies;
Dances/Social/Cultural gatherings.

Elma

Beechwood Nursing Home
PO Box 759, 308 E Young St, Elma, WA
98541
(206) 482-3234
Admin Cable J Wolverton.
Licensure Intermediate care. *Beds* ICF 35.
Certified Medicaid.
Owner Privately owned.
Admissions Requirements Physician's request.
Staff RNs 1 (ft), 1 (pt); LPNs 5 (pt); Nurses'
aides 6 (ft), 6 (pt); Physical therapists;
Activities coordinators 1 (ft); Dietitians;
Ophthalmologists; Podiatrists; Dentists.
Facilities Dining room; Crafts room; Laundry
room.
Activities Arts & crafts; Cards; Games;
Reading groups; Movies; Shopping trips;
Dances/Social/Cultural gatherings.

Oakhurst Convalescent Center
PO Box 717, 506 E Young St, Elma, WA
98541
(206) 482-2941
Admin Sharon Genson. *Dir of Nursing* Kathy
McElroy. *Medical Dir* Tereasa Trygstad.
Licensure Skilled care; Intermediate care;
Alzheimer's care. *Beds* SNF 150; ICF 43.
Private Pay Patients 20%. *Certified*
Medicaid.
Owner Privately owned.
Admissions Requirements Medical
examination.
Staff Physicians 4 (ft); RNs 6 (ft); LPNs 20
(ft), 2 (pt); Nurses' aides 50 (ft), 35 (pt);
Physical therapists 3 (ft), 1 (pt); Reality
therapists 5 (ft); Recreational therapists 4
(ft); Occupational therapists 5 (ft); Speech
therapists 1 (ft); Activities coordinators 1
(ft); Dietitians 1 (ft); Podiatrists 2 (ft);
Audiologists 1 (ft).
Facilities Dining room; Physical therapy
room; Activities room; Crafts room; Laundry
room; Barber/Beauty shop; 5 acres of
parklike setting with 3 ponds.
Activities Arts & crafts; Cards; Games;
Reading groups; Prayer groups; Movies;
Shopping trips; Dances/Social/Cultural
gatherings; Intergenerational programs; Pet
therapy.

Enumclaw

Bethesda Manor
2323 Jensen St, Enumclaw, WA 98022
(206) 825-2541

Admin Donald H Sires.
Licensure Skilled care; Intermediate care. *Beds*
148. *Certified* Medicaid.
Owner Nonprofit corp.

Ephrata

Columbia Basin Hospital
200 Southeast Blvd, Ephrata, WA 98823
(509) 754-4631
Admin Gerard Fischer. *Dir of Nursing* Nadine
Mahler ARNP. *Medical Dir* Paul G Kinney
MD.
Licensure Skilled care; Intermediate care. *Beds*
Swing beds SNF/ICF 29. *Private Pay
Patients* 5%. *Certified* Medicaid.
Owner Publicly owned.
Admissions Requirements Physician's request.
Facilities Dining room; Physical therapy
room; Activities room; Crafts room; Laundry
room.
Activities Arts & crafts; Cards; Games;
Reading groups; Prayer groups.

Everett

Bethany of the Northwest
3322 Broadway, Everett, WA 98201
(206) 259-5508
Admin Mark C Peterson. *Dir of Nursing*
Barbara Tuck.
Licensure Skilled care; Intermediate care;
Retirement; Alzheimer's care. *Beds* 242.
Certified Medicaid.
Owner Nonprofit corp.
Admissions Requirements Medical
examination.
Staff RNs; LPNs; Nurses' aides; Physical
therapists; Activities coordinators; Dietitians.
Affiliation Lutheran.
Facilities Dining room; Physical therapy
room; Activities room; Chapel; Crafts room;
Laundry room; Barber/Beauty shop; Library.
Activities Arts & crafts; Cards; Games;
Reading groups; Prayer groups; Movies.

Colby Manor
4230 Colby Ave, Everett, WA 98203
(206) 259-5569
Admin Doris M Dewees.
Licensure Skilled care; Intermediate care. *Beds*
69. *Certified* Medicaid.
Owner Privately owned.

Pleasant Acres Nursing Home
5129 Hilltop Rd, Everett, WA 98203
(206) 258-4474
Admin Teresa Judge.
Licensure Skilled care; Intermediate care. *Beds*
60. *Certified* Medicaid.
Owner Proprietary corp (Beverly Enterprises).

Sunrise View Convalescent Center
2520 Madison, Everett, WA 98203
(206) 353-4040
Admin Charmaine Slattery.
Licensure Skilled care; Intermediate care. *Beds*
73. *Certified* Medicaid.
Owner Privately owned.

Virginia Manor Convalescent Home Inc
3515 Hoyt Ave, Everett, WA 98201
(206) 259-0242
Admin Ulysses Rowell Jr.
Medical Dir F J Reichmann MD.
Licensure Skilled care; Intermediate care. *Beds*
238. *Certified* Medicaid; Medicare.
Owner Proprietary corp.
Facilities Dining room; Activities room;
Laundry room; Barber/Beauty shop.
Activities Arts & crafts; Cards; Games;
Reading groups; Movies; Dances/Social/
Cultural gatherings.

Fairfield

Fairfield Good Samaritan Center
Rte 1 Box 131A, Fairfield, WA 99012
(509) 283-2118
Admin Donald Heeringa. *Dir of Nursing* Mary
Surdez RN. *Medical Dir* Francis Thiel MD.
Licensure Skilled care; Intermediate care;
Retirement; Alzheimer's care. *Beds* 80.
Certified Medicaid; Medicare.
Owner Nonprofit corp (Evangelical Lutheran/
Good Samaritan Society).
Admissions Requirements Medical
examination; Physician's request.
Staff RNs 3 (ft), 3 (pt); LPNs 3 (ft), 6 (pt);
Nurses' aides 14 (ft), 26 (pt); Activities
coordinators 1 (ft), 1 (pt); Dietitians 1 (ft).
Languages German.
Affiliation Lutheran.
Facilities Dining room; Physical therapy
room; Activities room; Chapel; Crafts room;
Laundry room; Barber/Beauty shop; Library.
Activities Arts & crafts; Cards; Games;
Reading groups; Prayer groups; Movies;
Shopping trips; Dances/Social/Cultural
gatherings.

Federal Way

Federal Way Convalescent Center
1045 S 308th, Federal Way, WA 98003
(206) 946-2273
Admin Richard Dickson. *Dir of Nursing*
Beverly Myers RN. *Medical Dir* Bertold
Bruell MD.
Licensure Skilled care; Intermediate care;
Alzheimer's care. *Beds* 157. *Certified*
Medicaid; Medicare.
Owner Privately owned.
Admissions Requirements Minimum age 16;
Medical examination; Physician's request.
Staff Physicians 30 (pt); RNs 12 (ft), 6 (pt);
LPNs 8 (ft), 8 (pt); Nurses' aides 32 (ft), 11
(pt); Physical therapists 1 (pt); Reality
therapists 1 (ft); Recreational therapists 2
(ft); Occupational therapists 1 (pt); Speech
therapists 1 (pt); Activities coordinators 1
(ft); Dietitians 1 (pt); Ophthalmologists 1
(pt); Dentists 1 (pt).
Languages Spanish, Vietnamese.
Facilities Dining room; Physical therapy
room; Activities room; Crafts room; Laundry
room; Barber/Beauty shop.
Activities Arts & crafts; Cards; Games;
Reading groups; Prayer groups; Movies;
Shopping trips; Dances/Social/Cultural
gatherings.

Hallmark Manor
32300 First Ave S, Federal Way, WA 98003
(206) 874-3580
Admin Steven H Schrieber.
Licensure Skilled care; Intermediate care. *Beds*
147. *Certified* Medicaid; Medicare.
Owner Privately owned.

Ferndale

Pioneer Ridge Healthcare
PO Box 608, 2185 Seamount St, Ferndale,
WA 98248
(206) 384-1277
Admin Nancy B Giordano.
Licensure Skilled care; Intermediate care. *Beds*
79. *Certified* Medicaid.
Owner Privately owned.
Staff RNs 3 (ft); LPNs 2 (ft); Nurses' aides 11
(ft); Activities coordinators 2 (ft); Dietitians
1 (pt).
Facilities Dining room; Activities room;
Barber/Beauty shop.
Activities Arts & crafts; Cards; Games;
Reading groups; Prayer groups; Movies;
Shopping trips; Dances/Social/Cultural
gatherings.

Forks

Forks Community Hospital
RR 3 Box 3575, Forks, WA 98331
(206) 374-6271
Admin Dave McIvor.
Medical Dir R Keith Dobyns DO.
Licensure Skilled care; Intermediate care. *Beds*
20. *Certified* Medicaid.
Owner Publicly owned.
Admissions Requirements Physician's request.
Staff RNs 1 (ft), 3 (pt); LPNs 3 (ft), 2 (pt);
Nurses' aides 5 (ft), 9 (pt); Activities
coordinators 1 (ft), 1 (pt); Dietitians 1 (pt).
Facilities Dining room; Activities room;
Crafts room; Laundry room; Barber/Beauty
shop.
Activities Arts & crafts; Games; Movies.

Freeland

Karin's Kottage
PO Box 1030, Freeland, WA 98249
(206) 321-6232
Admin Karin Rutt. *Dir of Nursing* Ann Rudd
RN. *Medical Dir* Dr Patrice Oneill.
Licensure Skilled care; Intermediate care. *Beds*
61. *Certified* Medicaid.
Owner Proprietary corp (Christopher Homes
Inc).
Admissions Requirements Medical
examination.
Facilities Dining room; Laundry room;
Barber/Beauty shop.
Activities Arts & crafts; Cards; Games;
Reading groups; Prayer groups; Movies;
Shopping trips; Dances/Social/Cultural
gatherings; Special luncheons; Dinners.

Friday Harbor

Islands Convalescent Center Inc
PO Box 489, 660 Spring St, Friday Harbor,
WA 98250
(206) 378-2117
Admin Gale B Carter; Doreen Carter. *Dir of
Nursing* Lynne Barnes ARNP. *Medical Dir*
Burk Gossom MD.
Licensure Skilled care; Intermediate care. *Beds*
53. *Certified* Medicaid.
Owner Privately owned.
Admissions Requirements Physician's request.
Staff RNs; LPNs; Nurses' aides; Recreational
therapists; Activities coordinators.
Facilities Dining room; Activities room;
Barber/Beauty shop.
Activities Arts & crafts; Cards; Games;
Reading groups; Prayer groups; Movies;
Dances/Social/Cultural gatherings.

Gig Harbor

Cottesmore Nursing Home Inc
2909 14th Ave NW, Gig Harbor, WA 98335
(206) 383-1268
Admin Inez L Glass RN. *Dir of Nursing* Luan
Lusk RN. *Medical Dir* Richard Gilbert MD.
Licensure Skilled care; Respite care; Day care;
Alzheimer's care. *Beds* SNF 108; Respite
care 4.
Owner Proprietary corp.
Admissions Requirements Minimum age 16;
Medical examination; Physician's request.
Staff Physicians (consultant); RNs 5 (ft), 8
(pt); LPNs 6 (ft), 9 (pt); Nurses' aides 44
(ft), 8 (pt); Occupational therapists
(consultant); Speech therapists (consultant);
Activities coordinators 1 (ft), 2 (pt);
Dietitians 1 (pt); Ophthalmologists 1 (pt);
Podiatrists 1 (pt); Audiologists 1 (pt).
Facilities Dining room; Physical therapy
room; Activities room; Chapel; Crafts room;
Laundry room; Barber/Beauty shop; Library.
Activities Arts & crafts; Games; Reading
groups; Prayer groups; Movies; Shopping
trips; Dances/Social/Cultural gatherings;
Intergenerational programs; Pet therapy;
Scandia Christmas; Scandia day; Community
participation.

Gig Harbor Group Home
6823 Soundview Dr, Gig Harbor, WA 98335
(206) 851-3716
Admin Cassandra S Kimble.
Licensure Intermediate care for mentally
retarded. *Beds* ICF/MR 5. *Certified*
Medicaid.
Owner Nonprofit corp.

Rocky Bay Health Care Facility
17526 Elgin Clifton Rd KPN, Gig Harbor,
WA 98335
(206) 884-2277
Admin Edith M Moore.
Licensure Intermediate care; Intermediate care
for mentally retarded. *Beds* ICF/MR 30.
Certified Medicaid; Medicare.
Owner Privately owned.
Admissions Requirements Medical
examination; Physician's request.
Staff Physicians 1 (pt); RNs 2 (ft); LPNs 1
(ft), 2 (pt); Nurses' aides 8 (ft), 7 (pt);
Physical therapists 1 (pt); Recreational
therapists 2 (pt); Occupational therapists 1
(pt); Speech therapists 1 (pt); Activities
coordinators 2 (ft); Dietitians 1 (pt).
Facilities Dining room; Activities room;
Laundry room.
Activities Arts & crafts; Cards; Games; Prayer
groups; Movies; Shopping trips; Dances/
Social/Cultural gatherings.

Goldendale

Mt Adams Care Center
216 E Simcoe Dr, Goldendale, WA 98620
(509) 773-5714, 773-6819 FAX
Admin Ray Hoffman. *Dir of Nursing* Miriam
Nielsen RN.
Licensure Skilled care; Intermediate care;
Retirement. *Beds* Swing beds SNF/ICF 80;
Retirement apts 8. *Private Pay Patients* 20%.
Certified Medicaid.
Owner Proprietary corp (Regency Care
Centers Inc).
Admissions Requirements Physician's request.
Staff RNs; LPNs; Nurses' aides; Activities
coordinators.
Facilities Dining room; Physical therapy
room; Activities room; Laundry room;
Barber/Beauty shop; Garden.
Activities Arts & crafts; Cards; Games;
Reading groups; Prayer groups; Movies;
Shopping trips; Pet therapy.

Grand Coulee

Coulee Community Hospital Nursing Home
PO Box H, 411 Fortuyn Rd, Grand Coulee,
WA 99133
(509) 633-1753
Admin Sigvard Barr RN. *Dir of Nursing* Betty
Jean Hauber RN. *Medical Dir* Vicki Black
MD.
Licensure Skilled care; Intermediate care. *Beds*
Swing beds SNF/ICF 25. *Certified* Medicaid.
Owner Nonprofit organization/foundation.
Admissions Requirements Minimum age 20;
Medical examination; Physician's request.
Staff Physicians 3 (ft); RNs 1 (ft), 3 (pt);
LPNs 1 (ft), 2 (pt); Nurses' aides 8 (ft), 3
(pt); Physical therapists 1 (pt); Occupational
therapists 1 (pt); Activities coordinators 1
(ft); Dietitians 1 (ft); Podiatrists 1 (ft).
Facilities Dining room; Activities room;
Crafts room; Barber/Beauty shop.
Activities Arts & crafts; Games; Reading
groups; Prayer groups; Movies; Dances/
Social/Cultural gatherings; Intergenerational
programs; Pet therapy.

Grandview

Hillcrest Nursing Home
912 Hillcrest Ave, Grandview, WA 98930
(509) 882-1200
Admin Ruth E Hall. *Dir of Nursing* Sarah
Baumgartel. *Medical Dir* Robert D Bush.
Licensure Skilled care. *Beds* SNF 80. *Private
Pay Patients* 7%. *Certified* Medicaid;
Medicare.
Owner Proprietary corp (Beverly Enterprises).
Admissions Requirements Medical
examination; Physician's request.
Staff RNs 5 (ft), 2 (pt); LPNs 4 (ft), 4 (pt);
Nurses' aides 35 (ft); Physical therapists;
Activities coordinators 1 (ft), 1 (pt);
Dietitians.
Facilities Dining room; Activities room;
Laundry room.
Activities Arts & crafts; Cards; Games;
Reading groups; Prayer groups; Movies;
Shopping trips; Pet therapy.

Walnut Grove
Rte 2 Box 2438, Hicks Rd, Grandview, WA
98930
(509) 882-2400, 786-3711, 882-4166 FAX
Admin Patricia Friedland. *Dir of Nursing*
Marie McClure. *Medical Dir* Robert Bush
MD.
Licensure Skilled care; Retirement;
Alzheimer's care. *Beds* SNF 71. *Certified*
Medicaid.
Owner Nonprofit corp (Pleasant Valley Health
Services).
Admissions Requirements Medical
examination; Physician's request.
Staff Physicians 5 (pt); RNs 5 (ft), 3 (pt);
LPNs 3 (ft), 2 (pt); Nurses' aides 30 (ft);
Physical therapists 1 (pt); Recreational
therapists 1 (ft); Occupational therapists 1
(pt); Speech therapists 1 (pt); Activities
coordinators 1 (ft); Dietitians 1 (pt);
Ophthalmologists 1 (pt); Podiatrists 1 (pt);
Audiologists 1 (pt).
Languages Spanish, German.
Facilities Dining room; Activities room;
Crafts room; Laundry room; Barber/Beauty
shop; Library.
Activities Arts & crafts; Cards; Games;
Reading groups; Prayer groups; Movies;
Shopping trips; Dances/Social/Cultural
gatherings; Intergenerational programs; Pet
therapy.

Greenacres

Spokane Valley Good Samaritan
17121 E 8th Ave, Greenacres, WA 99016
(509) 924-6161
Admin Rev Steven P Gutzman. *Dir of Nursing*
Penny Davis RN. *Medical Dir* Dr Robert
Matthies.
Licensure Skilled care; Retirement. *Beds* SNF
201; Retirement apts 86. *Private Pay
Patients* 25%. *Certified* Medicaid; Medicare.
Owner Nonprofit corp (Evangelical Lutheran/
Good Samaritan Society).
Admissions Requirements Medical
examination; Physician's request.
Staff RNs 14 (ft), 6 (pt); LPNs 14 (ft), 12 (pt);
Nurses' aides 75 (ft), 30 (pt); Physical
therapists 1 (pt); Activities coordinators 1
(ft); Dietitians 1 (pt).
Languages German, Swedish.
Affiliation Evangelical Lutheran.
Facilities Dining room; Physical therapy
room; Activities room; Chapel; Crafts room;
Laundry room; Barber/Beauty shop; Library.
Activities Arts & crafts; Cards; Games;
Reading groups; Prayer groups; Movies;
Shopping trips; Dances/Social/Cultural
gatherings; Intergenerational programs; Pet
therapy.

Hoquiam

Pacific Care Center
3035 Cherry St, Hoquiam, WA 98550
(206) 532-7882
Admin John L Mack.
Licensure Skilled care; Intermediate care. *Beds* 118. *Certified* Medicaid; Medicare.
Owner Proprietary corp.

Issaquah

Issaquah Care Center
805 Front St S, Issaquah, WA 98027
(206) 392-1271
Admin John W Nugent.
Licensure Skilled care; Intermediate care. *Beds* 182. *Certified* Medicaid; Medicare.
Owner Proprietary corp (Hillhaven Corp).

Marianwood Extended Healthcare Services
3725 Providence Point Rd SE, Issaquah, WA 98027
(206) 391-2800
Admin Eva Sullivan. *Dir of Nursing* Madeline Miller RN. *Medical Dir* Maurice Doerfler MD.
Licensure Skilled care; Intermediate care; Retirement; Alzheimer's care. *Beds* 120. *Certified* Medicaid; Medicare.
Owner Nonprofit corp.
Staff RNs; LPNs; Nurses' aides; Physical therapists; Recreational therapists 1 (ft), 1 (pt); Dietitians 1 (pt); Geriatric nurse practitioner 1 (ft).
Affiliation Roman Catholic.
Facilities Dining room; Physical therapy room; Activities room; Chapel; Laundry room; Barber/Beauty shop; Library.

Kelso

Monticello Hall
405 N 19th, Kelso, WA 98626
(206) 423-4140
Admin Gregory Middlestetter.
Licensure Intermediate care. *Beds* ICF 48. *Certified* Medicaid.
Owner Nonprofit corp (Pleasant Valley Health Services Corp).
Admissions Requirements Minimum age 20; Medical examination; Physician's request.

Kennewick

Life Care Center of Kennewick
1508 W 7th Ave, Kennewick, WA 99336
(509) 586-9185
Admin Ann E Albert. *Dir of Nursing* Judi Merkel. *Medical Dir* Thomas Cooper MD.
Licensure Skilled care; Intermediate care. *Beds* 136. *Certified* Medicaid; Medicare.
Owner Proprietary corp (Life Care Centers of America).
Admissions Requirements Medical examination; Physician's request.
Staff RNs 6 (ft), 4 (pt); LPNs 4 (ft), 6 (pt); Nurses' aides 36 (ft), 15 (pt); Activities coordinators 1 (ft).
Languages Spanish.
Facilities Dining room; Physical therapy room; Activities room; Laundry room; Barber/Beauty shop.
Activities Arts & crafts; Games; Reading groups; Prayer groups; Movies; Dances/Social/Cultural gatherings.

Vistavue Care Center
1213 Morain Loop, Kennewick, WA 99336
(509) 783-3213
Admin Hazel Batchelor. *Dir of Nursing* Agnes Barnett Rn. *Medical Dir* Dr Charles Krause.
Licensure Skilled care; Intermediate care; Alzheimer's care. *Beds* 53. *Certified* Medicaid.
Owner Privately owned.

Admissions Requirements Minimum age 21; Medical examination; Physician's request.
Staff Physicians 6 (ft), 53 (pt); LPNs 6 (ft); Nurses' aides 18 (ft); Physical therapists 1 (ft); Recreational therapists 1 (ft); Occupational therapists 1 (ft); Speech therapists 1 (ft); Activities coordinators 1 (ft); Dietitians 1 (ft); Ophthalmologists 1 (ft).
Languages Spanish, German.
Facilities Dining room; Physical therapy room; Activities room; TV lounge.
Activities Arts & crafts; Cards; Games; Reading groups; Prayer groups; Movies; Shopping trips; Dances/Social/Cultural gatherings.

Kent

Benson Heights Rehabilitation Center
22410 Benson Rd SE, Kent, WA 98037
(206) 852-7755
Admin Gary L Miller. *Dir of Nursing* Nancy McCulley. *Medical Dir* N Zemcuznikov.
Licensure Intermediate care. *Beds* ICF 91. *Certified* Medicaid.
Owner Proprietary corp (Beverly Enterprises).
Admissions Requirements Minimum age 18; Medical examination.
Staff RNs 7 (ft), 1 (pt); LPNs 9 (ft), 2 (pt); Nurses' aides 20 (ft), 3 (pt); Recreational therapists 3 (ft); Dietitians 1 (pt).
Facilities Dining room; Activities room; Chapel; Crafts room; Laundry room; Barber/Beauty shop; Library.
Activities Arts & crafts; Cards; Games; Reading groups; Prayer groups; Movies; Shopping trips; Dances/Social/Cultural gatherings; Reality orientation; Pet therapy.

Midway Manor Convalescent Center
24215 Pacific Hwy S, Kent, WA 98032
(206) 824-1490
Admin Clenet Merrifield. *Dir of Nursing* Charlotte Liddell. *Medical Dir* Dr Thomas Deal.
Licensure Intermediate care. *Beds* ICF 51. *Certified* Medicaid.
Owner Proprietary corp (PHM Health Care Group).
Admissions Requirements Minimum age 30; Medical examination; Physician's request.
Staff RNs 1 (ft); LPNs 4 (ft), 2 (pt); Nurses' aides 6 (ft), 1 (pt); Activities coordinators 1 (ft).
Facilities Dining room; Activities room; Crafts room; Laundry room; Pool room; Smoking room.
Activities Arts & crafts; Cards; Games; Prayer groups; Movies; Shopping trips; Dances/Social/Cultural gatherings; Day bus outings.

Kirkland

Evergreen Vista Convalescent Center
11800 NE 128th, Kirkland, WA 98034
(206) 821-0404
Admin Pearl Barnes.
Licensure Skilled care; Intermediate care. *Beds* 132. *Certified* Medicaid; Medicare.
Owner Proprietary corp.

Kirkland Convalescent Center
6505 Lakeview Dr, Kirkland, WA 98033
(206) 822-6096, 828-4923 FAX
Admin Elaine Salisbury. *Dir of Nursing* Nielna Griffith. *Medical Dir* Dr Marmostein.
Licensure Skilled care; Intermediate care; Alzheimer's care. *Beds* SNF 48; ICF 37. *Certified* Medicaid.
Owner Nonprofit corp (Pleasant Valley Health Services).
Admissions Requirements Physician's request; OBRA screening.
Staff Physicians 1 (pt); RNs 9 (ft); LPNs 4 (ft); Nurses' aides 39 (ft); Physical therapists 1 (pt); Recreational therapists 1 (ft); Occupational therapists 1 (pt); Activities coordinators 1 (ft); Dietitians 1 (pt); Ophthalmologists 1 (pt); Podiatrists 1 (pt).
Facilities Dining room; Physical therapy room; Activities room; Laundry room; Barber/Beauty shop.
Activities Arts & crafts; Cards; Games; Reading groups; Prayer groups; Movies; Shopping trips; Dances/Social/Cultural gatherings; Pet therapy; Social dining groups; Mobile library.

Lake Vue Gardens
10101 NE 120th, Kirkland, WA 98033
(206) 823-2323, 821-2892
Admin Leona Dalrymple. *Dir of Nursing* Nancy Zytcowitz.
Licensure Skilled care; Alzheimer's care. *Beds* SNF 190. *Private Pay Patients* 32%. *Certified* Medicaid; Medicare.
Owner Proprietary corp (Cascade Care Centers Inc).
Admissions Requirements Minimum age Adult; Medical examination; Physician's request.
Staff RNs 14 (ft), 6 (pt); LPNs 7 (ft), 6 (pt); Nurses' aides 85 (ft), 25 (pt); Physical therapists 1 (pt); Recreational therapists 1 (ft); Occupational therapists 1 (pt); Speech therapists 1 (pt); Activities coordinators 2 (ft), 4 (pt); Dietitians 1 (ft), 2 (pt); Geriatric nurse practitioners.
Languages German, Filipino.
Facilities Dining room; Physical therapy room; Activities room; Chapel; Crafts room; Laundry room; Barber/Beauty shop; Library.
Activities Arts & crafts; Cards; Games; Reading groups; Prayer groups; Movies; Shopping trips; Dances/Social/Cultural gatherings; Intergenerational programs; Pet therapy.

La Center

Moorehaven Care Center
PO Box 102, Rte 2 Box 440, La Center, WA 98629
(206) 263-2147
Admin Don Bottemiller. *Dir of Nursing* Carolyn Mott. *Medical Dir* Dean Barth.
Licensure Skilled care; Intermediate care; Retirement; Alzheimer's care. *Beds* SNF 46; ICF 7; Retirement 28. *Private Pay Patients* 0%. *Certified* Medicaid.
Owner Proprietary corp (Soundcare Inc).
Admissions Requirements Medical examination; Physician's request.
Staff Physicians 1 (pt); RNs 3 (ft), 2 (pt); LPNs 4 (ft), 3 (pt); Physical therapists 1 (pt); Occupational therapists 1 (pt); Speech therapists 1 (pt); Activities coordinators 1 (ft), 1 (pt); Dietitians 1 (pt); Ophthalmologists 1 (pt); Podiatrists 1 (pt); Audiologists 1 (pt).
Facilities Dining room; Physical therapy room; Activities room; Crafts room; Laundry room; Barber/Beauty shop; Fenced yard.
Activities Arts & crafts; Cards; Games; Reading groups; Prayer groups; Movies; Shopping trips; Dances/Social/Cultural gatherings; Intergenerational programs; Pet therapy.

Lacey

Panorama City Convalescent & Rehabilitation Center
150 Circle Dr SE, Lacey, WA 98503
(206) 456-0111, ext 4200
Admin Helen June Nelson. *Dir of Nursing* Pat Albright. *Medical Dir* Endre Mihalyi MD.
Licensure Skilled care; Intermediate care; Alzheimer's care; Retirement. *Beds* 155. *Certified* Medicaid; Medicare.
Owner Proprietary corp.
Admissions Requirements Medical examination; Physician's request.

Staff Physicians 1 (pt); RNs 6 (ft), 2 (pt);
LPNs 18 (ft), 2 (pt); Nurses' aides 69 (ft), 2
(pt); Physical therapists 1 (pt); Occupational
therapists 1 (pt); Speech therapists 1 (pt);
Activities coordinators 3 (ft), 1 (pt);
Dietitians 1 (pt); Ophthalmologists 1 (pt);
Podiatrists 1 (pt); Dentists 1 (pt); Mental
health workers 2 (pt).
Facilities Dining room; Physical therapy
room; Activities room; Chapel; Crafts room;
Laundry room; Barber/Beauty shop; Library.
Activities Arts & crafts; Cards; Games;
Reading groups; Prayer groups; Movies;
Shopping trips; Dances/Social/Cultural
gatherings.

Roo-Lan Healthcare Center
1505 SE Carpenter Rd, Lacey, WA 98503
(206) 491-1765
Admin Burton C Levee.
Licensure Skilled care; Intermediate care. *Beds*
102. *Certified* Medicaid; Medicare.
Owner Proprietary corp.

Long Beach

New Seaera Convalescent Home
PO Box 619, 800 W Washington St, Long
Beach, WA 98631
(206) 642-3173
Admin Steven Lane. *Dir of Nursing* Donna
Meed RN. *Medical Dir* M Stone MD.
Licensure Skilled care; Intermediate care. *Beds*
Swing beds SNF/ICF 53. *Certified* Medicaid;
Medicare.
Owner Proprietary corp (International Care
Centers of Washington Inc).
Admissions Requirements Medical
examination; Physician's request.
Staff Physicians 1 (pt); RNs 4 (ft), 1 (pt);
LPNs 3 (ft), 1 (pt); Nurses' aides 19 (ft), 2
(pt); Physical therapists 1 (pt); Recreational
therapists 1 (pt); Occupational therapists 1
(pt); Speech therapists 1 (pt); Activities
coordinators 1 (ft); Dietitians 1 (pt);
Ophthalmologists 1 (pt); Podiatrists 1 (pt);
Dentists 1 (pt).
Facilities Dining room; Physical therapy
room; Activities room; Crafts room; Laundry
room; Barber/Beauty shop.
Activities Arts & crafts; Cards; Games;
Reading groups; Prayer groups; Movies;
Shopping trips; Dances/Social/Cultural
gatherings.

Ocean View Convalescent Center
Rte 1 Box 580, 211 Pioneer Rd, Long Beach,
WA 98631
(206) 642-3123
Admin Mary Jo Strope. *Dir of Nursing*
Dorothy Owens. *Medical Dir* Dr L C Neace.
Licensure Skilled care; Intermediate care;
Congregate care facility; Alzheimer's care.
Beds 62; Congregate care 19. *Certified*
Medicaid.
Owner Privately owned.
Admissions Requirements Medical
examination; Physician's request.
Staff RNs 4 (ft); LPNs 6 (ft); Nurses' aides 18
(ft); Activities coordinators 1 (ft).
Facilities Dining room; Physical therapy
room; Activities room; Laundry room;
Barber/Beauty shop; Dayroom for visits.
Activities Arts & crafts; Cards; Games;
Reading groups; Prayer groups; Movies;
Shopping trips; Dances/Social/Cultural
gatherings; Individual activity plans.

Longview

Americana Convalescent Home
917 7th Ave, Longview, WA 98632
(206) 425-5910
Admin Mary Barnes.
Medical Dir Dr James Davis.
Licensure Skilled care; Intermediate care. *Beds*
82. *Certified* Medicaid.

Owner Nonprofit corp.
Admissions Requirements Medical
examination; Physician's request.
Staff Physicians 1 (pt); RNs 5 (ft), 3 (pt);
LPNs 3 (ft), 2 (pt); Nurses' aides 45 (ft), 12
(pt); Physical therapists 1 (pt); Occupational
therapists 1 (pt); Speech therapists 1 (pt);
Activities coordinators 2 (ft); Dietitians 1
(ft); Ophthalmologists 1 (pt); Podiatrists 1
(pt); Dentists 1 (pt).
Facilities Dining room; Physical therapy
room; Activities room; Chapel; Crafts room;
Laundry room; Barber/Beauty shop; Patios.
Activities Arts & crafts; Cards; Games;
Reading groups; Prayer groups; Movies;
Shopping trips; Dances/Social/Cultural
gatherings.

Cowlitz Convalescent Center
1541 11th Ave, Longview, WA 98632
(206) 425-5840
Admin Jim Rutt. *Dir of Nursing* Carolyn Mott
RN. *Medical Dir* L Hamilton MD.
Licensure Skilled care; Intermediate care. *Beds*
52. *Certified* Medicaid; Medicare.
Owner Proprietary corp (Christopher Homes
Inc).
Staff RNs 4 (ft), 1 (pt); LPNs 2 (ft), 1 (pt);
Nurses' aides 25 (ft), 6 (pt); Activities
coordinators 1 (ft); Rehabilitation aides 2
(ft).
Facilities Dining room; Activities room.
Activities Arts & crafts; Cards; Games;
Reading groups; Prayer groups; Movies;
Shopping trips; Dances/Social/Cultural
gatherings.

Frontier Extended Care Facility
1500 3rd Ave, Longview, WA 98632
(206) 423-8800
Admin Patricia E Walker.
Medical Dir Dr James Davis.
Licensure Skilled care; Intermediate care. *Beds*
146. *Certified* Medicaid; Medicare.
Owner Nonprofit corp (Pleasant Valley Health
Services Corp).
Admissions Requirements Medical
examination; Physician's request.
Staff Physicians 1 (pt); RNs 12 (ft), 5 (pt);
LPNs 8 (ft), 3 (pt); Nurses' aides 44 (ft), 40
(pt); Physical therapists 1 (pt); Reality
therapists 2 (pt); Recreational therapists 1
(ft), 1 (pt); Occupational therapists 1 (pt);
Speech therapists 1 (pt); Activities
coordinators 2 (ft); Dietitians 1 (ft);
Ophthalmologists 1 (pt); Podiatrists 1 (pt);
Dentists 1 (pt).
Languages Spanish, Vietnamese, Sign.
Facilities Dining room; Physical therapy
room; Activities room; Crafts room; Laundry
room; Barber/Beauty shop; Library.
Activities Arts & crafts; Cards; Games;
Reading groups; Prayer groups; Movies;
Shopping trips; Dances/Social/Cultural
gatherings.

Manor Nursing Home
1330 11th Ave, Longview, WA 98632
(206) 425-6706
Admin Gregory Middlestetter. *Dir of Nursing*
Karlene Peterson. *Medical Dir* Dr Frank
Marre.
Licensure Skilled care; Intermediate care. *Beds*
55. *Certified* Medicaid; Medicare.
Owner Nonprofit corp (Pleasant Valley Health
Services Corp).
Admissions Requirements Physician's request.
Staff RNs; LPNs; Nurses' aides; Activities
coordinators.
Facilities Dining room; Physical therapy
room; Activities room; Barber/Beauty shop.
Activities Arts & crafts; Cards; Games;
Reading groups; Prayer groups; Movies;
Shopping trips; Dances/Social/Cultural
gatherings.

Northwest Continuum Care Center
128 Beacon Hill Dr, Longview, WA 98632
(206) 423-4060
Admin Thomas B Deutsch. *Dir of Nursing*
Nancy Arnett RN. *Medical Dir* Jake
Bergstrom MD.
Licensure Skilled care; Intermediate care;
Retirement. *Beds* 74. *Certified* Medicaid;
Medicare.
Owner Proprietary corp.
Admissions Requirements Physician's request.
Staff RNs 4 (ft); LPNs 7 (ft); Nurses' aides 40
(ft); Activities coordinators 2 (ft).
Facilities Dining room; Physical therapy
room; Activities room; Crafts room; Laundry
room; Barber/Beauty shop; Library.
Activities Arts & crafts; Cards; Games;
Reading groups; Prayer groups; Movies;
Shopping trips; Dances/Social/Cultural
gatherings.

Park Royal Medical
910 16th Ave, Longview, WA 98632
(206) 423-2890
Admin Jim Rutt. *Dir of Nursing* Debbie Nida
RN.
Licensure Skilled care; Intermediate care. *Beds*
62. *Certified* Medicaid; Medicare.
Owner Privately owned (Christopher Homes
Inc).
Admissions Requirements Medical
examination; Physician's request.
Staff Physicians; RNs; LPNs; Nurses' aides;
Physical therapists; Reality therapists;
Recreational therapists; Occupational
therapists; Speech therapists; Activities
coordinators; Dietitians; Ophthalmologists;
Podiatrists; Dentists.
Facilities Dining room; Activities room;
Laundry room; Barber/Beauty shop; Library.
Activities Arts & crafts; Cards; Games;
Reading groups; Prayer groups; Movies;
Shopping trips; Dances/Social/Cultural
gatherings.

Lynden

Christian Rest Home
205 S British Columbia Ave, Lynden, WA
98264
(206) 354-4434
Admin Angeline J Brouwer.
Medical Dir Dr Steven Alexandar.
Licensure Skilled care; Intermediate care. *Beds*
150. *Certified* Medicaid.
Owner Nonprofit corp.
Admissions Requirements Minimum age 60;
Medical examination; Physician's request.
Staff Physicians 1 (ft); RNs 6 (ft), 9 (pt);
LPNs 3 (ft), 12 (pt); Nurses' aides 39 (ft), 66
(pt); Physical therapists 1 (ft), 1 (pt); Reality
therapists 1 (ft), 1 (pt); Recreational
therapists 1 (ft), 1 (pt); Activities
coordinators 1 (ft); Dietitians 1 (ft).
Facilities Dining room; Activities room;
Chapel; Crafts room; Barber/Beauty shop;
Library.
Activities Arts & crafts; Cards; Games;
Reading groups; Prayer groups; Movies;
Shopping trips; Dances/Social/Cultural
gatherings.

Lynnwood

Lynnwood Manor Health Care Center
5821 188th SW, Lynnwood, WA 98037
(206) 776-5512
Admin Yvonne Halvorson. *Dir of Nursing*
Denise Myers. *Medical Dir* Dr Petrin.
Licensure Skilled care; Intermediate care. *Beds*
109. *Certified* Medicaid.
Owner Proprietary corp (HMH Associates
Inc).
Admissions Requirements Medical
examination.

Staff RNs 5 (ft), 5 (pt); LPNs 5 (ft), 5 (pt); Nurses' aides 44 (ft); Activities coordinators 1 (ft).
Languages French, Spanish, Japanese.
Facilities Dining room; Physical therapy room; Activities room; Laundry room; Barber/Beauty shop; Library.
Activities Arts & crafts; Cards; Games; Prayer groups; Movies; Shopping trips; Dances/Social/Cultural gatherings.

Manor Care Convalescent Rehabilitation Center of Lynn
3701 188th St SW, Lynnwood, WA 98036
(206) 775-9222
Admin Helen Moloney.
Beds 113.
Owner Proprietary corp (Manor Care Inc).

Marysville

Havenwood Care Center Inc
1821 Grove, Marysville, WA 98270
(206) 659-3926
Admin Viola M Melnyk. *Dir of Nursing* Melinda Michalke.
Licensure Skilled care. *Beds* SNF 46. *Certified* Medicaid.
Owner Proprietary corp.
Admissions Requirements Medical examination; Physician's request.
Staff RNs 8 (ft); LPNs 3 (ft), 1 (pt); Nurses' aides 25 (ft), 2 (pt); Activities coordinators 1 (ft); Dietitians 5 (ft); Rehabilitation therapists 2 (ft).
Facilities Dining room; Activities room; Crafts room; Laundry room; Barber/Beauty shop; Music room.
Activities Arts & crafts; Cards; Games; Reading groups; Prayer groups; Movies.

Madeleine Villa Convalescent Center
2nd & Liberty, Marysville, WA 98270
(206) 659-1259
Admin Michael E Downey.
Licensure Skilled care; Intermediate care. *Beds* 108. *Certified* Medicaid.
Owner Proprietary corp.

McKenna

Nisqually Valley Care Center
PO Box B, 1 Main St, McKenna, WA 98558
(206) 458-3801
Admin John C Striker.
Medical Dir Cathrine Abbey.
Licensure Skilled care; Intermediate care; Alzheimer's care. *Beds* 133. *Certified* Medicaid.
Owner Proprietary corp (Soundcare Inc).
Admissions Requirements Medical examination; Physician's request.
Staff RNs 5 (ft); LPNs 10 (ft); Nurses' aides 35 (ft); Physical therapists 1 (pt); Reality therapists 1 (pt); Recreational therapists 1 (pt); Occupational therapists 1 (pt); Speech therapists 1 (pt); Activities coordinators 1 (ft); Dietitians 1 (pt).
Facilities Dining room; Activities room; Crafts room; Laundry room.
Activities Arts & crafts; Cards; Games; Reading groups; Prayer groups; Movies; Dances/Social/Cultural gatherings; Many trips & scheduled outings.

Mercer Island

Mercer Island Care Center
7445 SE 24th, Mercer Island, WA 98040
(206) 232-6600
Admin Linda M Larson.
Licensure Skilled care. *Beds* SNF 108. *Certified* Medicare.
Owner Proprietary corp (Hillhaven Corp).

Facilities Dining room; Physical therapy room; Activities room; Barber/Beauty shop.
Activities Arts & crafts; Cards; Games; Reading groups; Prayer groups; Movies; Shopping trips; Dances/Social/Cultural gatherings.

Monroe

Regency Care Center of Monroe
PO Box 819, 1355 W Main St, Monroe, WA 98272
(206) 794-4011
Admin Bryon Clay. *Dir of Nursing* Viola DeJonge. *Medical Dir* Dr Trotter.
Licensure Nursing home. *Beds* Nursing home 92. *Certified* Medicaid.
Owner Proprietary corp (Regency Health Care Centers Inc).
Admissions Requirements Minimum age 14.
Staff RNs 6 (ft), 4 (pt); LPNs 4 (ft), 4 (pt); Nurses' aides 21 (ft), 21 (pt); Physical therapists 1 (ft); Activities coordinators 1 (ft), 1 (pt).
Facilities Dining room; Physical therapy room; Activities room; Barber/Beauty shop.
Activities Arts & crafts; Cards; Games; Reading groups; Prayer groups; Movies; Shopping trips; Dances/Social/Cultural gatherings.

Montesano

Cedar Apartments
PO Box 325, 1301 E Cedar St, Montesano, WA 98563
(206) 249-3900
Admin William S Pine.
Licensure Intermediate care for mentally retarded. *Beds* ICF/MR 10. *Certified* Medicaid.
Owner Proprietary corp.

Edgewood Manor of Grays Harbor Inc
514 E Broadway, Montesano, WA 98563
(206) 249-4521
Admin Gerald A Cutler. *Dir of Nursing* Bernice Porter RN. *Medical Dir* Dr Lindel.
Licensure Intermediate care. *Beds* ICF 37. *Certified* Medicaid.
Owner Proprietary corp.
Admissions Requirements Medical examination; Physician's request.
Staff RNs 1 (ft); LPNs 1 (ft), 6 (pt); Nurses' aides 9 (ft), 6 (pt); Physical therapists 1 (pt); Activities coordinators 1 (ft); Dietitians 2 (ft), 3 (pt); Ophthalmologists 1 (pt); Podiatrists 1 (pt).
Facilities Dining room; Activities room; Crafts room; Laundry room.
Activities Arts & crafts; Cards; Games; Reading groups; Prayer groups; Movies; Shopping trips.

Woodland Terrace Residential Training Center
PO Box 129, 414 E Ferndale, Montesano, WA 98563
(206) 249-3822
Admin Carol Cutler.
Medical Dir Sandi Sikos.
Licensure Intermediate care for mentally retarded. *Beds* ICF/MR 34. *Certified* Medicaid.
Owner Proprietary corp.
Admissions Requirements Minimum age 18; Medical examination; Physician's request.
Staff Physicians 1 (pt); RNs 1 (pt); LPNs 2 (ft), 3 (pt); Nurses' aides 15 (ft), 5 (pt); Recreational therapists 1 (pt); Occupational therapists 1 (pt); Speech therapists; Activities coordinators 1 (ft), 1 (pt); Dietitians 1 (pt).
Languages Sign.
Facilities Dining room; Activities room; Laundry room; Dayroom.
Activities Arts & crafts; Games; Prayer groups; Movies; Shopping trips; Dances/Social/Cultural gatherings.

Morton

Morton Nursing Home
PO Box 249, 180 Adams St, Morton, WA 98356
(206) 496-5328
Admin Wilma M Milward. *Dir of Nursing* Wanda Murphy.
Licensure Intermediate care. *Beds* ICF 23. *Certified* Medicaid.
Owner Privately owned.
Admissions Requirements Medical examination.
Staff RNs; LPNs; Nurses' aides; Activities coordinators; Dietitians.
Facilities Dining room; Physical therapy room; Activities room; Crafts room; Laundry room; Library.
Activities Arts & crafts; Cards; Games; Reading groups; Prayer groups; Movies; Shopping trips; Pet therapy.

Moses Lake

Crestview Convalescent Center
817 E Plum, Moses Lake, WA 98837
(509) 765-7835, 765-7041 FAX
Admin James E McConnell. *Dir of Nursing* Kaye Harp. *Medical Dir* Dr Pease.
Licensure Skilled care; Intermediate care; Alzheimer's care. *Beds* Swing beds SNF/ICF 96. *Private Pay Patients* 13%. *Certified* Medicaid; Medicare.
Owner Proprietary corp (Regency Health Services).
Admissions Requirements Physician's request.
Staff Physicians 10 (pt); RNs 4 (ft); LPNs 8 (ft); Nurses' aides 30 (ft); Physical therapists 1 (pt); Reality therapists 1 (pt); Recreational therapists 1 (pt); Occupational therapists 1 (pt); Speech therapists 1 (pt); Activities coordinators 1 (ft); Dietitians 1 (pt); Ophthalmologists 1 (pt); Podiatrists 1 (pt); Audiologists 1 (pt).
Facilities Dining room; Physical therapy room; Activities room; Laundry room; Barber/Beauty shop.
Activities Arts & crafts; Cards; Games; Reading groups; Prayer groups; Movies; Shopping trips; Dances/Social/Cultural gatherings; Intergenerational programs; Pet therapy.

Mount Vernon

Evergreen Terrace Nursing Center
2120 E Division St, Mount Vernon, WA 98273
(206) 424-4258, 424-7722 FAX
Admin Vicki Weddle. *Dir of Nursing* Sharon Schmidt. *Medical Dir* Dr Wayne Martin.
Licensure Skilled care; Intermediate care. *Beds* Swing beds SNF/ICF 142. *Private Pay Patients* 20%. *Certified* Medicaid; Medicare.
Owner Proprietary corp.
Staff RNs 8 (ft); LPNs 15 (ft); Nurses' aides 45 (ft); Physical therapists 1 (ft); Activities coordinators 2 (ft); Dietitians 1 (ft).
Facilities Dining room; Physical therapy room; Activities room; Crafts room; Barber/Beauty shop; Family room.
Activities Arts & crafts; Cards; Games; Reading groups; Prayer groups; Movies; Dances/Social/Cultural gatherings; Intergenerational programs; Pet therapy.

Mira Vista Care Center
PO Box 1305, 300 S 18th, Mount Vernon, WA 98273
(206) 424-1320
Admin David W Miller.
Licensure Skilled care; Intermediate care. *Beds* 94. *Certified* Medicaid; Medicare.
Owner Proprietary corp.

Valley Homes
PO Box 576, 1005 S 3rd Ave, Mount Vernon,
WA 98273
(206) 336-5717
Admin George Q Wheeler Jr. *Dir of Nursing*
Sally Herman Rn. *Medical Dir* John W
Erbstoeszer MD.
Licensure Intermediate care for mentally
retarded; Retirement. *Beds* ICF/MR 8.
Certified Medicaid.
Owner Nonprofit corp.
Admissions Requirements Minimum age 18;
Medical examination.
Facilities Dining room; Laundry room.
Activities Arts & crafts; Games; Movies;
Shopping trips; Dances/Social/Cultural
gatherings.

Naches

Strawn Nursing Home Inc
30 Link Rd, Naches, WA 98937
(509) 966-5880
Admin Berdina M Faith. *Dir of Nursing* Doris
Worby RN. *Medical Dir* William Cox DO.
Licensure Intermediate care. *Beds* ICF 39.
Certified Medicaid.
Owner Proprietary corp.
Admissions Requirements Medical
examination; Physician's request.
Staff Physicians (consultant); RNs 3 (ft); LPNs
1 (ft), 3 (pt); Nurses' aides 7 (ft), 3 (pt);
Recreational therapists 1 (ft); Activities
coordinators 1 (ft), 1 (pt).
Facilities Dining room; Activities room;
Laundry room; Barber/Beauty shop.
Activities Arts & crafts; Cards; Games;
Reading groups; Prayer groups; Movies;
Shopping trips; Dances/Social/Cultural
gatherings; Field trips.

Nespelem

Colville Tribal Convalescent Center
PO Box 150, Colville Indian Agency Campus,
Nespelem, WA 99155
(509) 634-4788
Admin Eugene R Sajcich. *Dir of Nursing*
Helen Purdy RN. *Medical Dir* G D
Patterson DO.
Licensure Skilled care; Intermediate care. *Beds*
52. *Certified* Medicaid.
Owner Proprietary corp.
Admissions Requirements Medical
examination; Physician's request.
Staff Physicians 2 (ft); RNs 2 (ft); LPNs 4 (ft);
Nurses' aides 16 (ft), 2 (pt); Recreational
therapists 1 (pt); Activities coordinators 1
(ft); Dietitians 1 (pt); Physical thearpy aides
1 (ft).
Languages Indian.
Facilities Dining room; Physical therapy
room; Activities room; Chapel; Crafts room;
Laundry room; Barber/Beauty shop; Library.
Activities Arts & crafts; Cards; Games;
Reading groups; Prayer groups; Movies;
Shopping trips; Lunch outings.

Newport

Pend Oreille Pines
Box 669, 714 W Pine St, Newport, WA 99156
(509) 447-2464
Admin Judith A Emerson. *Dir of Nursing*
Sylvia Platts. *Medical Dir* A Peter Weir MD.
Licensure Skilled care. *Beds* SNF 50. *Private
Pay Patients* 8%. *Certified* Medicaid.
Owner Publicly owned.
Admissions Requirements Medical
examination; Physician's request.
Staff Physicians 2 (ft); RNs 4 (ft); LPNs 3 (ft);
Nurses' aides 13 (ft); Recreational therapists
1 (ft), 1 (pt); Dietitians (contracted); Physical
therapy aides.

Facilities Dining room; Physical therapy
room; Activities room; Crafts room; Laundry
room; Barber/Beauty shop.
Activities Arts & crafts; Cards; Games;
Reading groups; Movies; Dances/Social/
Cultural gatherings; Intergenerational
programs; Pet therapy.

North Bend

North Bend Nursing Center
PO Box 1405, 219 Cedar Ave S, North Bend,
WA 98045
(206) 888-2129
Admin Gary D Morical. *Dir of Nursing* Pat
Mittness Rn. *Medical Dir* Dr Maurice
Doerfler.
Licensure Skilled care; Intermediate care. *Beds*
94. *Certified* Medicaid; VA.
Owner Proprietary corp (Regency Health Care
Centers).
Admissions Requirements Minimum age 16;
Medical examination; Physician's request.
Staff Physicians 8 (pt); RNs 7 (ft); LPNs 6
(ft); Nurses' aides 25 (ft); Physical therapists
1 (pt); Reality therapists 2 (pt); Occupational
therapists 1 (pt); Speech therapists 1 (pt);
Activities coordinators 1 (ft); Dietitians 1
(pt); Podiatrists 1 (pt); Dentists 1 (pt).
Facilities Dining room; Physical therapy
room; Activities room; Crafts room; Laundry
room; Barber/Beauty shop; Dayroom.
Activities Arts & crafts; Cards; Games;
Reading groups; Prayer groups; Movies;
Dances/Social/Cultural gatherings; Van rides.

Oak Harbor

Whidbey Island Manor Inc
PO Box 1900, 5425 500th Ave W, Oak
Harbor, WA 98277
(206) 675-5913
Admin Mark S Wiggins. *Dir of Nursing* Pat
Koontz RN.
Licensure Skilled care; Intermediate care;
Retirement. *Beds* 62. *Certified* Medicaid.
Owner Proprietary corp.
Admissions Requirements Physician's request.
Staff RNs 4 (ft), 2 (pt); LPNs 3 (ft), 2 (pt);
Nurses' aides 30 (ft), 7 (pt); Physical
therapists 1 (pt); Reality therapists 1 (pt);
Recreational therapists 1 (ft); Occupational
therapists 1 (pt); Speech therapists 1 (pt);
Activities coordinators 1 (ft), 1 (pt);
Dietitians 1 (pt).
Facilities Dining room; Laundry room.
Activities Arts & crafts; Games; Reading
groups; Prayer groups; Movies; Dances/
Social/Cultural gatherings.

Odessa

Memorial Hospital
502 E Amende, Odessa, WA 99159
(509) 982-2611, 982-2614 FAX
Admin R O'Halloran. *Dir of Nursing* Marlene
Brendell. *Medical Dir* Dr James P Cornell.
Licensure Skilled care; Intermediate care. *Beds*
Swing beds SNF/ICF 23. *Private Pay
Patients* 20%. *Certified* Medicaid.
Owner Publicly owned.
Admissions Requirements Medical
examination.
Staff Physicians 1 (pt); RNs 1 (ft), 10 (pt);
LPNs 2 (pt); Nurses' aides 6 (ft), 12 (pt);
Physical therapists 1 (ft), 1 (pt); Recreational
therapists 1 (pt); Occupational therapists 1
(pt); Speech therapists 1 (pt); Activities
coordinators 1 (ft), 1 (pt); Dietitians 1 (pt);
Ophthalmologists 1 (pt); Podiatrists 1 (pt);
Audiologists 1 (pt).
Facilities Dining room; Physical therapy
room; Activities room; Crafts room; Laundry
room; Barber/Beauty shop.

Activities Arts & crafts; Cards; Games;
Reading groups; Prayer groups; Movies;
Shopping trips.

Okanogan

Valley Care Center
PO Box 977, 520 2nd Ave, Okanogan, WA
98840
(509) 422-3180
Admin Ann Kier. *Dir of Nursing* Sandra
Martellini RN. *Medical Dir* Dr Dengel.
Licensure Skilled care; Intermediate care;
Alzheimer's care. *Beds* 89. *Certified*
Medicaid; Medicare.
Owner Proprietary corp.
Admissions Requirements Physician's request.
Staff RNs 8 (ft); LPNs 13 (ft); Nurses' aides
45 (ft); Physical therapists 1 (pt);
Occupational therapists 1 (pt); Speech
therapists 1 (pt); Activities coordinators 1
(ft); Dietitians 1 (pt).
Facilities Dining room; Physical therapy
room; Activities room; Laundry room;
Barber/Beauty shop; Library.
Activities Arts & crafts; Cards; Games;
Reading groups; Prayer groups; Movies;
Shopping trips; Dances/Social/Cultural
gatherings; Reality orientation; Sensory
stimulation; Resident council; Music events;
Social hour; Exercise group.

Olympia

Evergreen Convalescent Center
430 Lilly Rd, Olympia, WA 98506
(206) 491-9700
Admin Carol Z Hall.
Licensure Skilled care; Intermediate care. *Beds*
151. *Certified* Medicaid; Medicare.
Owner Proprietary corp.

Olympia Manor
1811 E 22nd Ave, Olympia, WA 98501
(206) 943-0910
Admin Gordon Burns. *Dir of Nursing* Kara
Moore. *Medical Dir* Darrell W Craig.
Licensure Skilled care. *Beds* SNF 28; CON
158. *Private Pay Patients* 50%. *Certified*
Medicaid.
Owner Proprietary corp.
Admissions Requirements Medical
examination.
Staff RNs 2 (pt); LPNs 3 (ft), 3 (pt); Nurses'
aides 7 (ft); Physical therapists (consultant);
Reality therapists (consultant); Recreational
therapists (consultant); Occupational
therapists (consultant); Speech therapists
(consultant); Activities coordinators 1 (ft);
Dietitians (consultant).
Facilities Dining room; Activities room;
Laundry room; Barber/Beauty shop; Library.
Activities Arts & crafts; Cards; Games;
Reading groups; Prayer groups; Movies;
Shopping trips; Dances/Social/Cultural
gatherings; Pet therapy.

Puget Sound Healthcare Center
4001 Capitol Mall Dr, Olympia, WA 98502
Admin Richard Thomas Guthrie.
Licensure Skilled care; Intermediate care. *Beds*
100. *Certified* Medicaid; Medicare.
Owner Proprietary corp (Beverly Enterprises).

Othello

Othello Convalescent Center
495 N 13th St, Othello, WA 99344
(509) 488-9609
Admin Betty Drymonaz.
Medical Dir Diane Bolin.
Licensure Skilled care; Intermediate care. *Beds*
62. *Certified* Medicaid; Medicare.
Owner Proprietary corp (Beverly Enterprises).

Staff RNs 7 (ft), 2 (pt); LPNs 2 (ft); Nurses' aides 20 (ft); Physical therapists 1 (pt); Activities coordinators 1 (ft); Dietitians 1 (ft).
Languages Spanish.
Facilities Dining room; Activities room; Laundry room; Barber/Beauty shop.
Activities Arts & crafts; Cards; Games; Reading groups; Prayer groups; Movies; Shopping trips; Dances/Social/Cultural gatherings.

Pasco

Hillcrest Convalescent Center
2004 N 22nd St, Pasco, WA 99301
(509) 547-8811
Admin Betty Deymonaz.
Medical Dir Mark Campbell.
Licensure Skilled care; Intermediate care. *Beds* 125. *Certified* Medicaid; Medicare.
Owner Proprietary corp (Beverly Enterprises).
Facilities Dining room; Physical therapy room; Activities room; Laundry room; Barber/Beauty shop.
Activities Arts & crafts; Cards; Games; Reading groups; Prayer groups; Movies; Shopping trips.

Pomeroy

Garfield County Hospital District
66 N 6th St, Pomeroy, WA 99347
(509) 843-1591
Admin Moe Chaudry. *Dir of Nursing* Susan Morrow. *Medical Dir* D Shirley Richardson MD.
Licensure Skilled care; Acute care. *Beds* SNF 40; Acute care 14. *Private Pay Patients* 55%. *Certified* Medicaid; Medicare.
Owner Publicly owned.
Admissions Requirements Medical examination; Physician's request.
Staff Physicians 2 (ft), 1 (pt); RNs 8 (ft), 3 (pt); LPNs 4 (ft), 1 (pt); Nurses' aides 15 (ft), 5 (pt); Physical therapists 1 (ft), 1 (pt); Recreational therapists 1 (pt); Occupational therapists 1 (ft); Speech therapists 1 (pt); Activities coordinators 2 (ft); Dietitians 1 (pt); Ophthalmologists 1 (pt); Podiatrists 1 (pt); Audiologists 1 (pt).
Facilities Dining room; Physical therapy room; Activities room; Chapel; Crafts room; Laundry room; Barber/Beauty shop; Library.
Activities Arts & crafts; Cards; Games; Reading groups; Prayer groups; Movies; Shopping trips; Dances/Social/Cultural gatherings; Intergenerational programs; Pet therapy.

Port Angeles

Crestwood Convalescent Center
1116 E Lauridsen Blvd, Port Angeles, WA 98362
(206) 452-9206
Admin H B Folden. *Dir of Nursing* Sondyn Rose.
Licensure Skilled care; Intermediate care; Alzheimer's care. *Beds* 103. *Certified* Medicaid; Medicare.
Owner Privately owned.
Staff RNs 11 (ft); LPNs 14 (ft); Nurses' aides 25 (ft); Physical therapists 1 (ft); Reality therapists 1 (pt); Occupational therapists 1 (pt); Speech therapists 1 (pt); Activities coordinators 1 (ft); Dietitians 1 (pt).
Facilities Dining room; Physical therapy room; Activities room; Crafts room; Laundry room; Barber/Beauty shop; Library.
Activities Arts & crafts; Cards; Games; Reading groups; Prayer groups; Movies; Dances/Social/Cultural gatherings.

Port Angeles Care Center
825 E 5th, Port Angeles, WA 98362
(206) 452-6213
Admin Neil Peisley.
Medical Dir Tricia Hall.
Licensure Skilled care; Intermediate care; Alzheimer's care. *Beds* 115. *Certified* Medicaid; Medicare; VA.
Owner Privately owned.
Admissions Requirements Medical examination; Physician's request.
Staff RNs; LPNs; Nurses' aides; Activities coordinators.
Languages Spanish.
Facilities Dining room; Physical therapy room; Activities room; Crafts room; Laundry room; Barber/Beauty shop.
Activities Arts & crafts; Games; Reading groups; Prayer groups; Movies; Dances/Social/Cultural gatherings.

Port Orchard

Long Lake Manor Inc
7242 Long Lake Rd SE, Port Orchard, WA 98366
(206) 871-1210
Admin Ernest L Beals. *Dir of Nursing* Jeanne A Beals RN. *Medical Dir* Michael Butler MD.
Licensure Skilled care; Intermediate care; Alzheimer's care. *Beds* 46. *Certified* Medicaid.
Owner Proprietary corp.
Admissions Requirements Medical examination.
Staff RNs 3 (ft), 2 (pt); LPNs 3 (ft), 2 (pt); Nurses' aides 18 (ft), 2 (pt); Reality therapists 1 (ft); Recreational therapists 1 (ft); Activities coordinators 1 (ft).
Facilities Dining room; Activities room.
Activities Arts & crafts; Cards; Games; Reading groups; Prayer groups; Movies; Shopping trips; Dances/Social/Cultural gatherings.

Port Orchard Care Center
2031 Pottery Ave, Port Orchard, WA 98366
(206) 876-8035
Admin Keith Briggs.
Medical Dir Kitty Phillips.
Licensure Skilled care; Intermediate care; Alzheimer's care. *Beds* 125. *Certified* Medicaid; Medicare.
Owner Privately owned.
Admissions Requirements Medical examination; Physician's request.
Staff Physicians 1 (pt); RNs 7 (ft); LPNs 10 (ft), 3 (pt); Nurses' aides 35 (ft); Physical therapists 1 (pt); Reality therapists 1 (pt); Recreational therapists 1 (pt); Occupational therapists 1 (pt); Speech therapists 1 (pt); Activities coordinators 1 (ft); Dietitians 1 (pt); Ophthalmologists 1 (pt); Podiatrists 1 (pt); Dentists 1 (pt).
Languages Spanish.
Facilities Dining room; Physical therapy room; Activities room; Crafts room; Laundry room; Barber/Beauty shop; Special dining area.
Activities Arts & crafts; Cards; Games; Reading groups; Prayer groups; Movies; Shopping trips; Dances/Social/Cultural gatherings; Social dinners; Alzheimer's support group.

Ridgemont Terrace Inc
2051 Pottery Ave, Port Orchard, WA 98366
(206) 876-4461
Admin Eugene F Asa. *Dir of Nursing* Cheri Svensson. *Medical Dir* Dr Merley.
Licensure Skilled care; Intermediate care; Retirement; Alzheimer's care. *Beds* 119. *Certified* Medicaid; Medicare.
Owner Proprietary corp.
Admissions Requirements Medical examination.

Staff Physicians 1 (pt); RNs 11 (ft); LPNs 5 (ft); Nurses' aides 29 (ft); Physical therapists 1 (pt); Recreational therapists 1 (ft); Occupational therapists 1 (pt); Speech therapists 1 (pt); Activities coordinators 2 (pt); Dietitians 1 (pt); Podiatrists 1 (pt); Dentists 1 (pt).
Facilities Dining room; Physical therapy room; Activities room; Crafts room; Laundry room; Barber/Beauty shop.
Activities Arts & crafts; Cards; Games; Prayer groups; Movies; Shopping trips; Dances/Social/Cultural gatherings.

Port Townsend

Kah Tai Care Center
751 Kearney St, Port Townsend, WA 98368
(206) 385-3555
Admin George Avis.
Medical Dir Tiffany Benton.
Licensure Skilled care; Intermediate care; Alzheimer's care. *Beds* 94. *Certified* Medicaid; Medicare.
Owner Proprietary corp.
Admissions Requirements Medical examination; Physician's request.
Staff RNs 16 (ft); LPNs 3 (ft); Nurses' aides 35 (ft), 6 (pt); Occupational therapists 1 (pt); Activities coordinators 1 (ft); Dietitians 1 (pt); Ophthalmologists 1 (pt).
Facilities Dining room; Physical therapy room; Activities room; Barber/Beauty shop.
Activities Arts & crafts; Reading groups; Prayer groups; Movies; Resident council; Sing-alongs; Monthly birthday parties.

Poulsbo

Martha & Mary Nursing Home
Box 127, 19160 Front St NE, Poulsbo, WA 98370
(206) 779-4517
Admin Jaak Juhkentaal. *Dir of Nursing* Marcia Weedman. *Medical Dir* Dr Patrick Tracy.
Licensure Skilled care; Intermediate care; Retirement; Alzheimer's care. *Beds* 190. *Certified* Medicaid.
Owner Nonprofit corp.
Admissions Requirements Minimum age 18; Medical examination; Physician's request.
Staff RNs 10 (ft), 20 (pt); LPNs 4 (ft), 5 (pt); Nurses' aides 55 (ft), 30 (pt); Physical therapists 1 (pt); Recreational therapists 4 (ft); Occupational therapists 1 (pt); Speech therapists 1 (pt); Activities coordinators 1 (ft); Dietitians 1 (ft).
Affiliation Lutheran.
Facilities Dining room; Physical therapy room; Activities room; Chapel; Crafts room; Laundry room; Barber/Beauty shop; Library; Dayrooms.
Activities Arts & crafts; Cards; Games; Reading groups; Prayer groups; Movies; Shopping trips; Dances/Social/Cultural gatherings; Bus rides.

Prosser

Prosser Memorial Hospital
723 Memorial St, Prosser, WA 99350
(509) 786-2222
Admin Gerard Fischer.
Licensure Skilled care; Intermediate care. *Beds* 31. *Certified* Medicaid; Medicare.
Owner Publicly owned.

Pullman

Pullman Convalescent Center
NW 1310 Deane, Pullman, WA 99163
(509) 332-1566
Admin William Barrett.
Medical Dir David Magaret MD.

Licensure Skilled care; Intermediate care. *Beds* 74. *Certified* Medicaid; Medicare.
Owner Proprietary corp (PHM Health Care Group Inc).
Admissions Requirements Medical examination; Physician's request.
Staff Physicians 1 (pt); RNs 3 (ft), 2 (pt); LPNs 3 (ft), 2 (pt); Nurses' aides 26 (ft); Physical therapists 1 (pt); Recreational therapists 2 (ft); Occupational therapists 1 (pt); Activities coordinators 1 (ft); Dietitians 1 (ft).
Facilities Dining room; Physical therapy room; Activities room; Laundry room; Barber/Beauty shop.
Activities Arts & crafts; Cards; Games; Reading groups; Prayer groups; Movies; Shopping trips; Dances/Social/Cultural gatherings.

Puyallup

Pam Group Home
619 7th Ave SE, Puyallup, WA 98371
(206) 845-8871
Admin Peggy Wright.
Licensure Intermediate care for mentally retarded. *Beds* ICF/MR 8. *Certified* Medicaid.
Owner Nonprofit corp.
Admissions Requirements Minimum age 21; DDD referral.
Facilities Dining room; Laundry room.
Activities Arts & crafts; Games; Movies; Shopping trips; Dances/Social/Cultural gatherings.

Rainier Vista Care Center
920 12th Ave SE, Puyallup, WA 98372
(206) 841-3422
Admin Terry Almasi.
Licensure Skilled care; Intermediate care. *Beds* 100. *Certified* Medicaid; Medicare.
Owner Privately owned.

Riverwood Inn
114 4th Ave NW, Puyallup, WA 98371
(206) 848-4551
Admin Charlene Kissler. *Dir of Nursing* Diane Tooke RN. *Medical Dir* Scott Kronlund MD.
Licensure Skilled care; Intermediate care. *Beds* 80. *Certified* Medicaid.
Owner Nonprofit corp (Pleasant Valley Health Services Corp).
Admissions Requirements Minimum age 14.
Staff RNs 7 (ft); LPNs 4 (ft); Nurses' aides 22 (ft); Physical therapists 1 (pt); Occupational therapists 1 (pt); Speech therapists 1 (pt); Activities coordinators 2 (ft); Dietitians 1 (pt); Ophthalmologists 1 (pt); Podiatrists 1 (pt).
Languages German.
Facilities Dining room; Physical therapy room; Activities room; Crafts room; Laundry room; Barber/Beauty shop.
Activities Arts & crafts; Cards; Games; Reading groups; Prayer groups; Movies; Shopping trips; Dances/Social/Cultural gatherings.

Sunrise Haven
PO Box 459, 1701 13th St SE, Puyallup, WA 98371
(206) 845-1718
Admin Kenneth C Lane. *Dir of Nursing* Linda Tresaugue.
Licensure Nursing home. *Beds* Nursing home 50.
Owner Nonprofit corp.
Admissions Requirements Must rely totally on Christian Science for healing.
Staff Nurses' aides; Activities coordinators.
Affiliation Christian Science.

Facilities Dining room; Laundry room; Barber/Beauty shop; Library; Reading room.
Activities Arts & crafts; Games; Reading groups; Prayer groups; Movies; Shopping trips; Musical groups.

Valley Terrace Nursing Center
511 10th Ave SE, Puyallup, WA 98372
(206) 845-7566, 848-7703 FAX
Admin Patricia L Wood. *Dir of Nursing* Karen Carlton. *Medical Dir* Dr Charles Vaught.
Licensure Skilled care; Intermediate care; Retirement; Alzheimer's care. *Beds* SNF 21; ICF 181; Retirement 82. *Private Pay Patients* 25%. *Certified* Medicaid; Medicare.
Owner Privately owned.
Admissions Requirements Medical examination; Physician's request.
Staff Physicians 1 (pt); RNs 7 (ft), 3 (pt); LPNs 20 (ft); Nurses' aides 75 (ft), 11 (pt); Physical therapists (consultants); Activities coordinators 2 (ft); Dietitians (consultant); General nurse practitioners 1 (ft).
Facilities Dining room; Physical therapy room; Activities room; Laundry room; Barber/Beauty shop.
Activities Arts & crafts; Cards; Games; Reading groups; Prayer groups; Movies; Dances/Social/Cultural gatherings; Intergenerational programs; Pet therapy.

Wildwood Health Care Center
909 S Meridian, Puyallup, WA 98371
(206) 845-6631
Admin Terrell Leno.
Medical Dir D Thomas Clark MD.
Licensure Skilled care; Intermediate care. *Beds* 138. *Certified* Medicaid; Medicare.
Owner Proprietary corp (Beverly Enterprises).
Admissions Requirements Medical examination; Physician's request.
Staff Physicians 1 (pt); RNs 6 (ft); LPNs 13 (ft), 2 (pt); Nurses' aides 40 (ft), 5 (pt); Physical therapists 1 (ft); Occupational therapists 1 (ft); Speech therapists 1 (ft); Speech therapists 1 (ft); Activities coordinators 2 (ft); Dietitians 1 (ft); Ophthalmologists 1 (pt); Podiatrists 1 (pt); Social workers 1 (ft), 1 (pt).
Facilities Dining room; Physical therapy room; Activities room; Chapel; Crafts room; Crafts room; Laundry room; Barber/Beauty shop; Library.
Activities Arts & crafts; Cards; Games; Reading groups; Prayer groups; Movies; Shopping trips; Dances/Social/Cultural gatherings; Reality orientation; Special programs for low-functioning patients.

Raymond

Willapa Harbor Care Center
PO Box 432, 1100 Jackson St, Raymond, WA 98577
(206) 942-2424
Admin Paul Jeffers.
Medical Dir Frank Hing; Patsy Cook.
Licensure Skilled care; Intermediate care. *Beds* 80. *Certified* Medicaid.
Owner Proprietary corp (Beverly Enterprises).
Staff RNs 4 (ft); LPNs 7 (ft); Physical therapists 1 (pt); Activities coordinators 1 (ft); Dietitians 1 (ft); Ophthalmologists 1 (pt).

Redmond

Cascade Vista Convalescent Center
7900 Redmond Kirkland Hwy, Redmond, WA 98052
(206) 885-0808
Admin Pearl K Barnes.
Licensure Skilled care; Intermediate care. *Beds* 139. *Certified* Medicaid; Medicare.
Owner Proprietary corp.

Renton

Highlands Convalescent Center Inc
1110 Edmonds Ave NE, Renton, WA 98056
(206) 226-6120
Admin Phyllis Wallace RN. *Dir of Nursing* Carol Rigney. *Medical Dir* Frans Koning.
Licensure Skilled care; Intermediate care. *Beds* Swing beds SNF/ICF 100. *Certified* Medicaid.
Owner Privately owned.
Admissions Requirements Minimum age 60; Medical examination; Physician's request.
Staff RNs; LPNs; Nurses' aides; Physical therapists; Activities coordinators.
Facilities Dining room; Activities room; Chapel; Crafts room; Laundry room; Barber/ Beauty shop.
Activities Arts & crafts; Cards; Games; Reading groups; Prayer groups; Movies.

Renton Terrace Nursing Center
80 SW 2nd St, Renton, WA 98055
(206) 226-4610
Admin Joyce Kovell.
Medical Dir Dr Richard Niemann.
Licensure Skilled care; Intermediate care. *Beds* 160. *Certified* Medicaid; Medicare.
Owner Proprietary corp (Beverly Enterprises).
Staff Physicians 12 (pt); RNs 7 (ft); LPNs 12 (ft); Nurses' aides 31 (ft); Physical therapists 1 (ft); Recreational therapists 2 (ft); Occupational therapists 1 (ft); Speech therapists 1 (pt); Activities coordinators 2 (ft); Dietitians 1 (pt); Ophthalmologists 1 (pt); Podiatrists 1 (pt); Dentists 1 (pt).
Facilities Dining room; Physical therapy room; Activities room; Laundry room; Barber/Beauty shop.
Activities Arts & crafts; Cards; Games; Reading groups; Prayer groups; Movies; Shopping trips; Dances/Social/Cultural gatherings.

Valley Health Care Center
4430 Talbot Rd S, Renton, WA 98055
(206) 226-7500
Admin Linda Fernyhough.
Licensure Skilled care; Intermediate care. *Beds* 166. *Certified* Medicaid; Medicare.
Owner Proprietary corp (Hillhaven Corp).

Richland

Life Care Center of Richland
44 Goethals Dr, Richland, WA 99352
(509) 943-1117
Admin Paul Jensen. *Dir of Nursing* Shirlene Brown RNC. *Medical Dir* Justin Delos Santos MD.
Licensure Skilled care. *Beds* SNF 104. *Private Pay Patients* 30%. *Certified* Medicaid; Medicare.
Owner Proprietary corp (Life Care Centers of America).
Admissions Requirements Medical examination; Physician's request.
Staff Physicians; RNs; LPNs; Nurses' aides; Physical therapists; Occupational therapists; Speech therapists; Activities coordinators; Dietitians; Podiatrists; Restorative aides.
Languages Spanish.
Facilities Dining room; Physical therapy room; Activities room; Chapel; Crafts room; Laundry room; Barber/Beauty shop; Library; Dayrooms with TV.
Activities Arts & crafts; Games; Reading groups; Prayer groups; Movies; Shopping trips; Dances/Social/Cultural gatherings; Intergenerational programs; Pet therapy; Monthly lunches; Family gatherings; Daily living skills.

Ridgefield

Ridgefield Care Center
PO Box 399, 104 Pioneer Ave, Ridgefield,
WA 98642
(206) 887-3121
Admin Barbara Kachmarek. *Dir of Nursing*
Marlene Hickman. *Medical Dir* Dean Barth.
Licensure Intermediate care; Alzheimer's care.
Beds ICF 42. *Private Pay Patients* 10%.
Certified Medicaid; Medicare.
Owner Proprietary corp (Cascade Properties).
Admissions Requirements Minimum age 18;
Medical examination; Physician's request.
Staff RNs 2 (ft), 1 (pt); LPNs 3 (ft), 1 (pt);
Nurses' aides 10 (ft), 4 (pt); Activities
coordinators 1 (ft); Social service 1 (pt).
Facilities Dining room; Activities room;
Laundry room; Barber/Beauty shop.
Activities Arts & crafts; Cards; Games;
Reading groups; Prayer groups; Movies;
Shopping trips; Dances/Social/Cultural
gatherings; Intergenerational programs; Pet
therapy.

Ritzville

Life Care Center of Ritzville
506 S Jackson, Ritzville, WA 99169
(509) 659-1600
Admin Julie Schultz. *Dir of Nursing* Merrily
Fagg RN. *Medical Dir* James J Jardee MD.
Licensure Skilled care; Intermediate care. *Beds*
50. *Certified* Medicaid; Medicare.
Owner Proprietary corp (Life Care Centers of
America).
Staff Physicians 3 (ft); RNs 4 (ft); LPNs 3 (ft);
Nurses' aides 13 (ft), 5 (pt); Physical
therapists 1 (pt); Speech therapists 1 (pt);
Activities coordinators 1 (ft); Dietitians 1
(ft); Ophthalmologists 1 (pt); Dentists 2 (pt).
Facilities Dining room; Activities room;
Crafts room; Laundry room; Barber/Beauty
shop.
Activities Arts & crafts; Cards; Games;
Reading groups; Prayer groups; Movies;
Shopping trips; Dances/Social/Cultural
gatherings; One to one visits.

Seattle

Anderson House Inc
17127 15th Ave NE, Seattle, WA 98155
(206) 364-7131
Admin Larry Anderson.
Licensure Skilled care; Intermediate care;
Retirement. *Beds* SNF 112.
Owner Proprietary corp.
Admissions Requirements Physician's request.
Staff Physicians; RNs; LPNs; Nurses' aides;
Physical therapists; Reality therapists;
Recreational therapists; Occupational
therapists; Speech therapists; Activities
coordinators; Dietitians; Ophthalmologists;
Podiatrists; Dentists.
Facilities Dining room; Physical therapy
room; Activities room; Crafts room; Laundry
room; Barber/Beauty shop; Library.
Activities Arts & crafts; Cards; Games;
Reading groups; Prayer groups; Movies;
Shopping trips; Dances/Social/Cultural
gatherings.

Arden Nursing Home
16357 Aurora Ave N, Seattle, WA 98133
(206) 542-3103
Admin Felecia Bly RN. *Dir of Nursing* Anne
Walker RN.
Licensure Skilled care. *Beds* SNF 100.
Certified Medicare.
Owner Proprietary corp (Hillhaven Corp).
Staff RNs 6 (ft), 2 (pt); LPNs 3 (ft), 2 (pt);
Nurses' aides 26 (ft), 8 (pt); Physical
therapists 1 (ft); Recreational therapists 1
(ft); Occupational therapists 1 (ft); Dietitians
1 (ft).

Facilities Dining room; Physical therapy
room; Activities room; Barber/Beauty shop.
Activities Arts & crafts; Cards; Games;
Reading groups; Prayer groups; Movies;
Shopping trips; Dances/Social/Cultural
gatherings.

Austin Nursing Home
9005 Roosevelt Way NE, Seattle, WA 98115
(206) 523-4296
Admin Betty L Diedrich.
Licensure Private pay. *Beds* Private pay 44.
Owner Proprietary corp.

Ballard Convalescent Center
820 NW 95th, Seattle, WA 98117
(206) 782-0100
Admin Leny Sandbeck. *Dir of Nursing* Bonnie
Blachley. *Medical Dir* Dr Martin Burkland;
Dr Roger Higgs; Dr Laminack; Dr Leitzell.
Licensure Skilled care; Retirement. *Beds* SNF
210. *Certified* Medicare.
Owner Proprietary corp.
Admissions Requirements Physician's request.
Staff Physicians 4 (pt); RNs 16 (ft), 2 (pt);
LPNs 4 (ft), 2 (pt); Nurses' aides 65 (ft), 6
(pt); Physical therapists 2 (ft), 1 (pt); Reality
therapists 1 (ft); Recreational therapists 2
(ft), 2 (pt); Occupational therapists 1 (ft), 1
(pt); Speech therapists 1 (pt); Activities
coordinators 1 (ft); Dietitians 1 (ft);
Ophthalmologists 1 (pt).
Languages German, Spanish, Japanese.
Facilities Dining room; Physical therapy
room; Activities room; Crafts room; Laundry
room; Barber/Beauty shop.
Activities Arts & crafts; Cards; Games;
Reading groups; Prayer groups; Movies;
Shopping trips; Dances/Social/Cultural
gatherings.

Barclay Boarding Home
PO Box 33032, 1510 NE Perkins Way,
Seattle, WA 98133
(206) 365-9767
Admin Steve Skeen.
Licensure Intermediate care for mentally
retarded. *Beds* ICF/MR 6. *Certified*
Medicaid.
Owner Nonprofit corp.

Bayview Manor
11 W Aloha, Seattle, WA 98119
(206) 284-7330
Admin Elizabeth Zohn RNC BSN; Marshall C
Hjelte, Exec Dir. *Dir of Nursing* Janice
Edwards RN BSN. *Medical Dir* John
Addison MD.
Licensure Skilled care; Retirement. *Beds* SNF
50; Retirement 180. *Private Pay Patients*
85%. *Certified* Medicaid.
Owner Nonprofit corp.
Admissions Requirements Minimum age 62;
Medical examination; Physician's request.
Staff Physicians 1 (ft); RNs 4 (ft), 3 (pt);
LPNs 4 (ft), 2 (pt); Nurses' aides 15 (ft), 5
(pt); Physical therapists (consultant); Reality
therapists (consultant); Recreational
therapists 1 (ft); Occupational therapists 1
(ft); Speech therapists (consultant); Activities
coordinators 2 (pt); Dietitians 1 (ft);
Podiatrists (consultant); Audiologists
(consultant); Dentists (consultant).
Affiliation Methodist.
Facilities Dining room; Physical therapy
room; Activities room; Chapel; Crafts room;
Laundry room; Barber/Beauty shop; Library.
Activities Arts & crafts; Cards; Games;
Reading groups; Prayer groups; Movies;
Shopping trips; Dances/Social/Cultural
gatherings; Intergenerational programs; Pet
therapy.

Branch Villa Health Care Center
2611 S Dearborn, Seattle, WA 98144
(206) 325-6700
Admin Helen Sikor. *Dir of Nursing* S Slette.
Medical Dir K Hong MD.

Licensure Skilled care; Intermediate care;
Hospice care; Alzheimer's care. *Beds* Swing
beds SNF/ICF 175. *Private Pay Patients*
20%. *Certified* Medicaid.
Owner Proprietary corp.
Admissions Requirements Minimum age 18;
Medical examination; Physician's request.
Staff Physicians 22 (pt); RNs 13 (ft); LPNs 13
(ft); Nurses' aides 70 (ft), 16 (pt); Physical
therapists 1 (ft); Reality therapists 1 (pt);
Recreational therapists 1 (ft); Occupational
therapists 1 (pt); Speech therapists 1 (pt);
Activities coordinators 2 (ft); Dietitians 1
(ft); Ophthalmologists 1 (pt); Podiatrists 1
(pt); Audiologists 1 (pt).
Languages Tagalog, Chinese, Korean, East
Indian.
Facilities Dining room; Physical therapy
room; Activities room; Chapel; Crafts room;
Laundry room; Barber/Beauty shop; Library.
Activities Arts & crafts; Cards; Games;
Reading groups; Prayer groups; Movies;
Shopping trips; Dances/Social/Cultural
gatherings; Intergenerational programs; Pet
therapy; Community outings; Resident
council; Volunteer programs.

Burien Terrace Nursing Center
1031 SW 130th St, Seattle, WA 98146
(206) 242-3213
Admin Doris Barret. *Dir of Nursing* Carol
Juhnke. *Medical Dir* Dr Zerr.
Licensure Skilled care; Intermediate care;
Alzheimer's care. *Beds* 140. *Certified*
Medicaid; Medicare.
Owner Proprietary corp.
Admissions Requirements Medical
examination; Physician's request.
Staff Physicians 1 (pt); RNs 5 (ft); LPNs 11
(ft); Nurses' aides 50 (ft); Physical therapists
1 (pt); Recreational therapists 1 (ft);
Occupational therapists 1 (pt); Speech
therapists 1 (pt); Activities coordinators 1
(ft); Dietitians 1 (pt); Ophthalmologists 1
(pt); Podiatrists 1 (pt); Dentists 1 (pt).
Facilities Dining room; Physical therapy
room; Activities room; Laundry room;
Barber/Beauty shop; Library.
Activities Arts & crafts; Cards; Games;
Reading groups; Prayer groups; Movies;
Shopping trips; Dances/Social/Cultural
gatherings.

Camelot Group Home
9201 2nd NW, Seattle, WA 98117
(206) 783-2373
Admin Steve Skeen.
Licensure Intermediate care for mentally
retarded. *Beds* ICF/MR 8. *Certified*
Medicaid.
Owner Nonprofit corp.

Columbia Lutheran Home
4700 Phinney Ave N, Seattle, WA 98103
(206) 632-7400
Admin Jon Rorem.
Licensure Skilled care; Intermediate care. *Beds*
122. *Certified* Medicaid.
Owner Nonprofit corp.
Affiliation Lutheran.

Crista Senior Community
19303 Fremont Ave N, Seattle, WA 98133
(206) 546-7400
Admin Jeffrey L Crandall. *Dir of Nursing*
Vivian Johnson. *Medical Dir* Pamela Cooper
MD.
Licensure Skilled care; Intermediate care;
Alzheimer's care; Retirement. *Beds* 236.
Certified Medicaid; Medicare.
Owner Nonprofit corp.
Admissions Requirements Minimum age 62;
Medical examination.
Staff RNs 26 (ft), 17 (pt); LPNs 5 (ft), 2 (pt);
Nurses' aides 69 (ft), 17 (pt); Physical
therapists 1 (ft); Reality therapists 4 (ft);

Recreational therapists 4 (ft); Occupational therapists; Activities coordinators 1 (ft); Dietitians 1 (pt).
Facilities Dining room; Physical therapy room; Activities room; Chapel; Crafts room; Laundry room; Barber/Beauty shop; Library; Van service.
Activities Arts & crafts; Cards; Games; Reading groups; Prayer groups; Movies; Shopping trips; Dances/Social/Cultural gatherings; Ceramics; Discussion groups; Bible study; Chapel services; Art classes; Exercise classes; Missionary fellowship; Cooking classes.

Exeter House
720 Seneca St, Seattle, WA 98101
(206) 622-1300
Admin Arlene Temple. *Dir of Nursing* Helen Reed RN. *Medical Dir* Dr Robert Erickson.
Licensure Nursing home; Retirement. *Beds* Nursing home 130.
Owner Nonprofit corp (Presbyterian Ministries Inc).
Admissions Requirements Minimum age 62; Medical examination; Physician's request.
Staff RNs 4 (ft), 2 (pt); LPNs 1 (ft), 1 (pt); Nurses' aides 6 (ft), 4 (pt); Activities coordinators 1 (ft); Dietitians 1 (ft).
Affiliation Presbyterian.
Facilities Dining room; Activities room; Chapel; Crafts room; Laundry room; Barber/Beauty shop; Library.
Activities Arts & crafts; Cards; Games; Reading groups; Prayer groups; Movies; Shopping trips; Dances/Social/Cultural gatherings.

Fircrest School
15230 15th NE, Seattle, WA 98155
(206) 364-0300
Admin Norm Davis. *Dir of Nursing* Pat Buker.
Licensure Intermediate care for mentally retarded. *Beds* ICF/MR 496. *Certified* Medicaid; Medicare.
Owner Publicly owned.
Staff Physicians; RNs; LPNs; Physical therapists; Recreational therapists; Occupational therapists; Speech therapists; Activities coordinators; Dietitians; Ophthalmologists (contracted); Podiatrists (contracted); Audiologists (contracted).
Languages Sign.
Facilities Dining room; Physical therapy room; Activities room; Chapel; Crafts room; Laundry room.
Activities Arts & crafts; Games; Prayer groups; Movies; Shopping trips; Dances/Social/Cultural gatherings; Pet therapy.

First Hill Care Center
1334 Terry Ave, Seattle, WA 98101
(206) 624-1484
Admin Susan Peton. *Dir of Nursing* Ellen Gerson. *Medical Dir* John Addison MD.
Licensure Skilled care; Intermediate care. *Beds* 181. *Certified* Medicaid; Medicare.
Owner Proprietary corp (Hillhaven Corp).
Admissions Requirements Minimum age 18; Medical examination; Physician's request.
Staff Physicians 1 (ft); RNs 14 (ft); LPNs 18 (ft); Nurses' aides 48 (ft), 27 (pt); Physical therapists 2 (ft); Occupational therapists 1 (ft); Speech therapists 1 (pt); Activities coordinators 1 (ft), 3 (pt); Dietitians 1 (ft); Ophthalmologists 1 (pt); Podiatrists 1 (pt); Dentists 1 (pt).
Facilities Dining room; Physical therapy room; Activities room; Crafts room; Laundry room; Barber/Beauty shop; Library.
Activities Arts & crafts; Cards; Games; Reading groups; Prayer groups; Movies; Shopping trips; Dances/Social/Cultural gatherings.

Forest Glen Nursing Center
10344 14th Ave S, Seattle, WA 98168
(206) 762-8481, 763-8548 FAX
Admin Kenneth S Rehusch. *Dir of Nursing* Linda Harres. *Medical Dir* Dr Wallace Hodges.
Licensure Skilled care; Intermediate care. *Beds* Swing beds SNF/ICF 204. *Private Pay Patients* 25%. *Certified* Medicaid; Medicare.
Owner Nonprofit corp (Pleasant Valley Health Services Corp).

Foss Home
13023 Greenwood Ave N, Seattle, WA 98133
(206) 364-1300
Admin Joseph J Breznau.
Licensure Skilled care; Intermediate care. *Beds* 211. *Certified* Medicaid.
Owner Nonprofit corp.

Caroline K Galland Home
7500 Seward Park Ave S, Seattle, WA 98118
(206) 725-8800
Admin Joshua Gortler.
Licensure Skilled care; Intermediate care. *Beds* 145. *Certified* Medicaid.
Owner Nonprofit corp.

Greenery Rehabilitation Center—Seattle
555 16th Ave, Seattle, WA 98122
(206) 324-8200
Admin Marlyn M Hathaway. *Dir of Nursing* Lani Spencer. *Medical Dir* Richard Arnold MD.
Licensure Skilled care; Intermediate care; Alzheimer's care. *Beds* 150. *Certified* Medicaid; Medicare.
Owner Proprietary corp (Greenery Rehabilitation Group Inc).
Admissions Requirements Minimum age 12; Physician's request.
Staff Physicians; RNs; LPNs; Nurses' aides; Physical therapists; Recreational therapists; Occupational therapists; Speech therapists; Activities coordinators; Dietitians.
Languages Chinese, Vietnamese.
Facilities Dining room; Physical therapy room; Activities room; Crafts room; Laundry room; Barber/Beauty shop; Library.
Activities Arts & crafts; Cards; Games; Reading groups; Prayer groups; Movies; Shopping trips; Dances/Social/Cultural gatherings.

Greenwood Park Care Center Inc
13333 Greenwood Ave N, Seattle, WA 98133
(206) 362-0303, 367-4241 FAX
Admin Darlene DeMello-McEntire. *Dir of Nursing* Shirley Gilday. *Medical Dir* Joseph Pellicier.
Licensure Skilled care; Intermediate care; Alzheimer's care. *Beds* Swing beds SNF/ICF 136; Alzheimer's unit 14. *Private Pay Patients* 21%. *Certified* Medicaid; Medicare; VA.
Owner Proprietary corp (All Seasons Living Care).
Admissions Requirements Minimum age 18; Medical examination; Physician's request.
Staff RNs 5 (ft), 2 (pt); LPNs 9 (ft), 6 (pt); Nurses' aides 35 (ft), 12 (pt); Physical therapists (consultant); Reality therapists (consultant); Recreational therapists (consultant); Occupational therapists (consultant); Speech therapists (consultant); Activities coordinators 1 (ft), 1 (pt); Dietitians (consultant); Ophthalmologists (consultant); Podiatrists (consultant); Audiologists (consultant).
Languages Korean.
Facilities Dining room; Physical therapy room; Activities room; Crafts room; Barber/Beauty shop; Alzheimer's unit.
Activities Arts & crafts; Cards; Games; Reading groups; Prayer groups; Movies; Dances/Social/Cultural gatherings; Pet

therapy; Pastoral care; Candlelight dinners; Men's breakfast club; Occupational therapy kitchen teaching.

Harmony Gardens Care Center
10010 Des Moines Way S, Seattle, WA 98168
(206) 762-0166
Admin Michael Dorsey. *Dir of Nursing* Mary Mun. *Medical Dir* Thomas E Hulse MD.
Licensure Skilled care; Residential care; Alzheimer's care. *Beds* SNF 45; Residential care 4. *Private Pay Patients* 60%. *Certified* Medicaid; Medicare.
Owner Proprietary corp (Sunrise Health Care Corp).
Admissions Requirements Medical examination.
Staff RNs 4 (ft), 2 (pt); LPNs 1 (ft), 1 (pt); Nurses' aides 12 (ft); Physical therapists 1 (pt); Recreational therapists 1 (ft); Occupational therapists 1 (pt); Speech therapists 1 (pt); Activities coordinators 1 (ft); Dietitians 1 (pt); Ophthalmologists 1 (pt); Podiatrists 1 (pt); Audiologists 1 (pt).
Facilities Dining room; Physical therapy room; Activities room; Barber/Beauty shop; Library; Outdoor areas for walking.
Activities Cards; Games; Prayer groups; Movies; Dances/Social/Cultural gatherings; Intergenerational programs; Pet therapy; Facility has pet dog.

Hearthstone
6720 E Green Lake Way N, Seattle, WA 98103
(206) 525-9666
Admin Richard J Milsow.
Medical Dir Dr Robert Erickson.
Licensure Skilled care; Intermediate care. *Beds* Swing beds SNF/ICF 51. *Certified* Medicaid; Medicare.
Owner Nonprofit corp.
Admissions Requirements Minimum age 62; Medical examination; Physician's request.
Staff RNs 5 (ft), 5 (pt); LPNs 2 (ft), 2 (pt); Nurses' aides 17 (ft), 8 (pt); Physical therapists 1 (pt); Occupational therapists 1 (pt); Speech therapists 1 (pt); Activities coordinators 1 (ft), 1 (pt); Dietitians 1 (pt); Podiatrists 1 (pt).
Affiliation Lutheran.
Facilities Dining room; Activities room; Chapel; Crafts room; Laundry room; Barber/Beauty shop; Library.
Activities Arts & crafts; Cards; Games; Reading groups; Prayer groups; Movies; Shopping trips; Dances/Social/Cultural gatherings.

Highline Care Center Inc
220 SW 160th, Seattle, WA 98166
(206) 243-3056
Admin Elaine Salisbury. *Dir of Nursing* Judy McTaggart. *Medical Dir* Dr J M Claunch.
Licensure Intermediate care for mentally retarded. *Beds* ICF/MR 86. *Certified* Medicaid.
Owner Proprietary corp.
Admissions Requirements Developmental Disability.
Staff Physicians 20 (pt); RNs 3 (ft), 2 (pt); LPNs 6 (ft); Physical therapists 1 (pt); Recreational therapists 2 (ft), 3 (pt); Occupational therapists 1 (pt); Speech therapists 1 (pt); Dietitians 1 (pt); Ophthalmologists 1 (pt); Podiatrists 1 (pt); Dentists 1 (pt); QMRPs 3 (ft); Attendant counselors 29 (ft), 4 (pt); Van drivers 3 (ft), 2 (pt).
Facilities Dining room; Physical therapy room; Activities room; Barber/Beauty shop.
Activities Arts & crafts; Games; Movies; Shopping trips; Dances/Social/Cultural gatherings; Camping trips; Special Olympics; Field trips.

Horizon House
900 University St, Seattle, WA 98101
(206) 624-3700
Admin Audrey G Bowers. *Dir of Nursing* Lois A Kinney. *Medical Dir* Robert Y Erickson MD.
Licensure Skilled care; Continuing care residential; Alzheimer's care; Retirement. *Beds* SNF 56; Continuing care residential 450. *Certified* Medicare.
Owner Nonprofit corp.
Admissions Requirements Medical examination.
Staff Physicians 2 (pt); RNs 10 (ft); LPNs 4 (ft); Nurses' aides 30 (ft); Physical therapists 1 (ft); Recreational therapists 2 (ft); Occupational therapists 1 (pt); Speech therapists 1 (pt); Activities coordinators 1 (ft).
Affiliation United Church of Christ.
Facilities Dining room; Physical therapy room; Activities room; Chapel; Crafts room; Laundry room; Barber/Beauty shop; Library; Dental clinic; Doctors clinic; Physical fitness center; Overnight guest rooms for family members.
Activities Arts & crafts; Cards; Games; Reading groups; Prayer groups; Movies; Shopping trips; Dances/Social/Cultural gatherings; Pet therapy.

Jacobsen Nursing Home
1810 11th Ave, Seattle, WA 98122
(206) 323-5321
Admin Joan C Wong.
Licensure Nursing home. *Beds* Nursing home 45.
Owner Proprietary corp.

Kenney Presbyterian Home
7125 Fauntleroy Way SW, Seattle, WA 98136
(206) 937-2800
Admin Kenneth D Curry.
Medical Dir Samuel Peizer MD.
Licensure Skilled care; Intermediate care. *Beds* 53. *Certified* Medicaid.
Owner Nonprofit corp.
Admissions Requirements Minimum age 60; Medical examination; Physician's request.
Staff Physicians 1 (pt); RNs 3 (ft), 3 (pt); LPNs 1 (ft), 4 (pt); Nurses' aides 19 (ft), 3 (pt); Activities coordinators 1 (ft), 2 (pt).
Affiliation Presbyterian.
Facilities Dining room; Physical therapy room; Activities room; Chapel; Crafts room; Laundry room; Barber/Beauty shop; Library; Recreation room; Lounges; Sewing room; Wood shop.
Activities Arts & crafts; Cards; Games; Reading groups; Prayer groups; Movies; Shopping trips; Dances/Social/Cultural gatherings; Literary guild; Little theatre group; Service projects.

Kin ON Nursing Home
1700 24th Ave S, Seattle, WA 98144
(206) 322-0080
Admin Frederick Yee MBA MS. *Dir of Nursing* Eliane Dao RN ARNP. *Medical Dir* Dr Harry Lo.
Licensure Skilled care. *Beds* SNF 63. *Private Pay Patients* 5%. *Certified* Medicaid.
Owner Nonprofit corp.
Admissions Requirements Medical examination; Physician's request.
Staff RNs 4 (ft), 3 (pt); LPNs 2 (ft), 4 (pt); Nurses' aides 14 (ft), 13 (pt); Physical therapists (consultant); Activities coordinators 1 (ft), 1 (pt); Dietitians (consultant); Social workers 1 (ft), 1 (pt).
Languages Chinese (Mandarin, Cantonese, Toishanese), Filipino, Vietnamese.
Facilities Dining room; Physical therapy room; Activities room; Laundry room.
Activities Arts & crafts; Games; Prayer groups; Movies; Shopping trips; Dances/Social/Cultural gatherings; Chinese cultural program.

Magnolia Health Care
4646 36th Ave W, Seattle, WA 98199
(206) 283-9322
Admin Jan R Reinking. *Dir of Nursing* Karn Hardin.
Licensure Intermediate care; Alzheimer's care. *Beds* ICF 34. *Certified* Medicaid.
Owner Privately owned.
Admissions Requirements Medical examination; Physician's request.
Staff RNs 2 (ft), 1 (ft); LPNs 1 (ft); Nurses' aides 4 (ft), 2 (pt); Activities coordinators 1 (ft).
Facilities Dining room; Activities room; Crafts room; Laundry room; Barber/Beauty shop; Patio areas.
Activities Arts & crafts; Cards; Games; Reading groups; Prayer groups; Movies; Shopping trips; Dances/Social/Cultural gatherings; Outdoor recreation.

Malden Nursing Home
PO Box 12011, 526 Malden Ave E, Seattle, WA 98102
(206) 324-8133
Admin Donald D Dunnagan.
Medical Dir Danita Shelton.
Licensure Intermediate care. *Beds* ICF 23. *Certified* Medicaid.
Owner Privately owned.
Admissions Requirements Minimum age 35.
Staff RNs 1 (ft); LPNs 3 (ft); Nurses' aides 3 (ft); Activities coordinators 1 (ft); Dietitians 1 (ft).
Facilities Dining room; Activities room; Crafts room; Laundry room.
Activities Arts & crafts; Cards; Games; Reading groups; Prayer groups; Movies; Shopping trips; Dances/Social/Cultural gatherings; Van outing.

Meadowbrook Nursing & Convalescent Center
3540 NE 110th, Seattle, WA 98125
(206) 363-7733
Admin Louis E Sternberg. *Dir of Nursing* Janine Humphrey. *Medical Dir* Dr Robert Haining.
Licensure Nursing home; Retirement. *Beds* Nursing home 47.
Owner Proprietary corp.
Admissions Requirements Minimum age 18; Medical examination; Physician's request.
Staff RNs 6 (ft), 4 (pt); LPNs 2 (pt); Nurses' aides 12 (ft), 13 (pt); Activities coordinators 1 (ft).
Facilities Dining room; Physical therapy room; Activities room; Laundry room; Barber/Beauty shop; Library.
Activities Arts & crafts; Cards; Games; Reading groups; Prayer groups; Movies; Shopping trips.

Moderncare West Seattle Inc
4700 SW Admiral Way, Seattle, WA 98116
(206) 935-2480, 932-1467 FAX
Admin John W Kirk. *Dir of Nursing* Carol Juhnke RNC. *Medical Dir* Robert DeMonte MD.
Licensure Skilled care. *Beds* SNF 106. *Private Pay Patients* 35%. *Certified* Medicaid.
Owner Proprietary corp.
Admissions Requirements Minimum age 21; Medical examination; Physician's request.
Staff Physicians 6 (ft), 1 (pt); LPNs 4 (ft); Nurses' aides 25 (ft); Physical therapists 1 (pt); Reality therapists 1 (pt); Occupational therapists; Speech therapists; Activities coordinators 2 (ft); Dietitians; Ophthalmologists; Podiatrists; Dentists.
Facilities Dining room; Physical therapy room; Activities room; Laundry room; Barber/Beauty shop.
Activities Arts & crafts; Cards; Games; Reading groups; Prayer groups; Movies; Shopping trips; Dances/Social/Cultural gatherings; Intergenerational programs; Pet therapy.

Monarch Care Center
21428 Pacific Hwy S, Seattle, WA 98198
(206) 878-2042
Licensure Skilled care; Intermediate care. *Beds* 110. *Certified* Medicaid.
Owner Proprietary corp (Beverly Enterprises).
Facilities Dining room; Physical therapy room; Activities room; Crafts room; Laundry room; Barber/Beauty shop.
Activities Arts & crafts; Games; Reading groups; Prayer groups; Movies; Dances/Social/Cultural gatherings.

Mt St Vincent Nursing Center
4831 35th Ave SW, Seattle, WA 98126
(206) 937-3700
Admin Robert Wildenhaus. *Dir of Nursing* Margarita Prentice. *Medical Dir* Dr Joseph C M Downs.
Licensure Skilled care; Intermediate care; Retirement; Alzheimer's care. *Beds* 252. *Certified* Medicaid; Medicare.
Owner Nonprofit corp.
Admissions Requirements Minimum age 18; Females only; Medical examination.
Staff RNs 17 (ft); LPNs 17 (ft); Nurses' aides 83 (ft); Physical therapists 1 (ft); Reality therapists 5 (ft); Recreational therapists 5 (ft); Occupational therapists 1 (ft); Speech therapists 1 (ft); Dietitians 2 (ft); Podiatrists 1 (ft); Social workers 3 (ft).
Affiliation Roman Catholic.
Facilities Dining room; Physical therapy room; Activities room; Chapel; Crafts room; Laundry room; Barber/Beauty shop; Library; Adult Day Center.
Activities Arts & crafts; Cards; Games; Reading groups; Prayer groups; Movies; Shopping trips; Dances/Social/Cultural gatherings; Special events; Bingo; Music therapy; Volunteer programs; Thrift shop.

Norse Home Inc
5311 Phinney Ave N, Seattle, WA 98103
(206) 783-9600
Admin Dr Robert Solem. *Dir of Nursing* Donna Hawkings RN. *Medical Dir* Dr John Addison.
Licensure Skilled care; Intermediate care; Retirement. *Beds* 51. *Certified* Medicaid.
Owner Nonprofit corp.
Admissions Requirements Minimum age 65; Physician's request.
Staff RNs 3 (ft), 2 (pt); LPNs 3 (ft), 3 (pt); Nurses' aides 20 (ft), 7 (pt); Recreational therapists 1 (pt); Activities coordinators 1 (ft).
Facilities Dining room; Physical therapy room; Activities room; Barber/Beauty shop.
Activities Arts & crafts; Games; Reading groups; Movies; Dances/Social/Cultural gatherings; Music therapy; Pet therapy; Bible study.

Northgate Rehabilitation Center
10509 Stone Ave N, Seattle, WA 98133
(206) 524-8300
Admin Phyllis A Moss.
Licensure Skilled care; Intermediate care. *Beds* 142. *Certified* Medicaid.
Owner Proprietary corp (Beverly Enterprises).

Northwest Hospital Skilled Nursing Facility
1500 N 115th, Seattle, WA 98133
(206) 368-1996, 368-1949 FAX
Admin James Hornell. *Dir of Nursing* Bonnie Brian-Caldwell. *Medical Dir* Sarah Goodlin MD.
Licensure Skilled care; Hospice. *Beds* SNF 42; Hospice 10. *Private Pay Patients* 3%. *Certified* Medicare.
Owner Nonprofit corp.
Admissions Requirements Minimum age 18; Medical examination; Physician's request.
Staff Physicians; RNs 12 (ft); LPNs 12 (ft); Nurses' aides 20 (ft); Physical therapists 2 (ft); Recreational therapists 1 (ft);

Occupational therapists 2 (ft); Speech therapists 2 (pt); Dietitians 1 (ft); Social workers 1 (ft).
Facilities Dining room; Physical therapy room; Activities room; Crafts room; Laundry room; Barber/Beauty shop.
Activities Arts & crafts; Cards; Games; Reading groups; Movies; Pet therapy.

Park Ridge Care Center Inc
1250 NE 145th, Seattle, WA 98155
(206) 363-5856
Admin Joseph A Buck. *Dir of Nursing* Donna Chandler RN. *Medical Dir* Dr George Langmyhr.
Licensure Skilled care; Retirement; Alzheimer's care. *Beds* SNF 128. *Certified* Medicare.
Owner Proprietary corp.
Admissions Requirements Medical examination; Physician's request.
Staff Physicians 1 (ft); RNs 9 (ft); LPNs 6 (ft); Nurses' aides 37 (ft); Activities coordinators 1 (ft).
Facilities Dining room; Physical therapy room; Activities room; Crafts room; Laundry room; Barber/Beauty shop; Library.
Activities Arts & crafts; Cards; Games; Reading groups; Prayer groups; Movies; Shopping trips; Bingo; Pet therapy; Entertainment.

Park Shore
1630 43rd E, Seattle, WA 98112
(206) 329-0770
Admin Donald R Mickey. *Dir of Nursing* Kate Tesh RN. *Medical Dir* Dr Robert Bain.
Licensure Skilled care; Assisted living; Independent living. *Beds* SNF 34; Assisted living 10; Independent living 200.
Owner Nonprofit corp (Presbyterian Ministries Inc).
Admissions Requirements Minimum age 62; Medical examination.
Staff Physicians 1 (pt); RNs 4 (ft), 4 (pt); Nurses' aides 12 (ft), 6 (pt); Activities coordinators 2 (pt); Dietitians 1 (ft).
Affiliation Presbyterian.
Facilities Dining room; Activities room; Chapel; Crafts room; Laundry room; Barber/ Beauty shop; Library.
Activities Arts & crafts; Cards; Games; Prayer groups; Movies.

Park West Care Center
1703 California Ave SW, Seattle, WA 98116
(206) 937-9750
Admin C R Parmelee. *Dir of Nursing* Leslie Aronson. *Medical Dir* Dr Hugh Clark.
Licensure Skilled care; Alzheimer's care. *Beds* SNF 152. *Private Pay Patients* 42%. *Certified* Medicaid; Medicare.
Owner Proprietary corp (All Seasons Living Care).
Staff Physicians 3 (ft), 4 (pt); RNs 8 (ft); LPNs 12 (ft); Nurses' aides 60 (ft); Physical therapists 1 (pt); Occupational therapists 1 (pt); Speech therapists 1 (pt); Activities coordinators 1 (ft); Dietitians 1 (ft); Ophthalmologists 1 (pt); Podiatrists 1 (pt); Audiologists 1 (pt); Restorative aides 4 (ft).
Facilities Dining room; Physical therapy room; Activities room; Crafts room; Laundry room; Barber/Beauty shop.
Activities Arts & crafts; Cards; Games; Reading groups; Prayer groups; Movies; Pet therapy.

Pedersen Nursing Home Inc
414 10th Ave, Seattle, WA 98122
(206) 623-3635
Admin Ida E Israel. *Dir of Nursing* Leriza DeCastro. *Medical Dir* Thomas Deal MD.
Licensure Intermediate care. *Beds* ICF 37. *Certified* Medicaid.
Owner Proprietary corp.
Admissions Requirements Minimum age 18.

Staff RNs 1 (ft), 1 (pt); LPNs 1 (ft), 1 (pt); Nurses' aides 3 (ft), 3 (pt); Activities coordinators 1 (ft); Dietitians 1 (pt).
Languages Spanish.
Facilities Dining room; Activities room; Crafts room; Laundry room; Barber/Beauty shop.
Activities Arts & crafts; Cards; Games; Reading groups; Prayer groups; Movies; Shopping trips; Dances/Social/Cultural gatherings.

Pinehurst Convalescent Center
11039 17th NE, Seattle, WA 98125
(206) 363-5490, 361-2648 FAX
Admin Dan Platt. *Dir of Nursing* Viola Maziarski.
Licensure Intermediate care. *Beds* ICF 38. *Private Pay Patients* 10%. *Certified* Medicaid.
Owner Proprietary corp.
Admissions Requirements Physician's request.
Staff RNs 2 (ft); LPNs 4 (ft); Nurses' aides 9 (ft), 3 (pt); Physical therapists 1 (pt); Occupational therapists 1 (pt); Speech therapists 1 (pt); Activities coordinators 1 (ft); Dietitians 1 (pt); Podiatrists 1 (pt).
Facilities Dining room; Laundry room.
Activities Arts & crafts; Cards; Games; Reading groups; Prayer groups; Movies; Shopping trips; Dances/Social/Cultural gatherings; Pet therapy.

Pinehurst Park Terrace
2818 NE 145th St, Seattle, WA 98155
(206) 364-8810
Admin Denney J Austin.
Medical Dir George Zerr MD.
Licensure Skilled care; Intermediate care. *Beds* 200. *Certified* Medicaid.
Owner Proprietary corp (Beverly Enterprises).
Facilities Dining room; Physical therapy room; Activities room; Crafts room; Laundry room; Barber/Beauty shop.
Activities Arts & crafts; Cards; Games; Reading groups; Prayer groups; Movies; Shopping trips.

Queen Anne Care Center
2717 Dexter Ave N, Seattle, WA 98109
(206) 284-7012
Admin Charles R Parmelee.
Licensure Skilled care; Intermediate care. *Beds* 174. *Certified* Medicaid; Medicare.
Owner Proprietary corp (Hillhaven Corp).

Restorative Care Center
2821 S Walden St, Seattle, WA 98144
(206) 725-2800
Admin David Langdon. *Dir of Nursing* Shirley Gilday.
Licensure Skilled care; Intermediate care; Rehabilitation/Restorative/Specialty; Alzheimer's care. *Beds* 189. *Certified* Medicaid; Medicare.
Owner Proprietary corp.
Admissions Requirements Medical examination; Physician's request.
Staff Physicians 1 (pt); RNs 6 (ft), 7 (pt); LPNs 11 (ft), 6 (pt); Nurses' aides 70 (ft), 9 (pt); Physical therapists 1 (pt); Occupational therapists 1 (pt); Speech therapists 1 (pt); Activities coordinators 1 (ft); Dietitians 1 (pt); Ophthalmologists 1 (pt); Podiatrists 1 (pt); Dentists 1 (pt).
Facilities Dining room; Physical therapy room; Activities room; Chapel; Crafts room; Laundry room; Barber/Beauty shop.
Activities Arts & crafts; Cards; Games; Reading groups; Prayer groups; Movies; Shopping trips; Dances/Social/Cultural gatherings.

Riverton Heights Convalescent Home
2849 S 127th, Seattle, WA 98168
(206) 243-0200
Admin Henri G Trueba.

Licensure Skilled care; Intermediate care. *Beds* 70. *Certified* Medicaid.
Owner Proprietary corp.

St Cabrini Hospital Skilled Nursing Facility
Terry & Madison, Seattle, WA 98104
(206) 682-0500, 583-4331 FAX
Admin Ronald C M Bergstrom. *Dir of Nursing* Beth Buckley. *Medical Dir* John Carlson MD.
Licensure Skilled care. *Beds* SNF 33. *Private Pay Patients* 1%. *Certified* Medicaid; Medicare.
Owner Nonprofit corp.
Admissions Requirements Minimum age 19; Medical examination; Physician's request.
Staff Physicians 2 (ft); RNs; LPNs; Nurses' aides; Physical therapists; Recreational therapists; Occupational therapists; Speech therapists; Activities coordinators; Dietitians; Ophthalmologists; Podiatrists; Audiologists.
Languages Cantonese, Spanish, French, Danish.
Facilities Dining room; Physical therapy room; Activities room; Chapel; Crafts room; Laundry room; Barber/Beauty shop; Library.
Activities Arts & crafts; Cards; Games; Reading groups; Prayer groups; Movies; Dances/Social/Cultural gatherings; Intergenerational programs; Pet therapy.

Seattle Keiro
1601 E Yesler Way, Seattle, WA 98122-5640
(206) 323-7100
Admin Russell Akiyama. *Dir of Nursing* Mitsi Hara. *Medical Dir* Ben Uyeno MD.
Licensure Skilled care; Intermediate care. *Beds* Swing beds SNF/ICF 150. *Private Pay Patients* 20%. *Certified* Medicaid.
Owner Nonprofit organization/foundation.
Admissions Requirements Physician's request.
Staff Physicians 1 (ft); RNs 13 (ft); LPNs 7 (ft); Nurses' aides 62 (ft), 4 (pt); Physical therapists 1 (pt); Occupational therapists 1 (pt); Speech therapists 1 (pt); Activities coordinators 6 (ft); Dietitians 1 (pt).
Languages Japanese.
Facilities Dining room; Physical therapy room; Activities room; Chapel; Crafts room; Barber/Beauty shop.
Activities Arts & crafts; Cards; Games; Reading groups; Prayer groups; Movies; Dances/Social/Cultural gatherings; Intergenerational programs; Pet therapy; Flower arranging.

Seattle Specialized Group Home
7347 Dibble Ave NW, Seattle, WA 98117
(206) 782-0149
Admin C L Prochazka.
Licensure Intermediate care for mentally retarded. *Beds* ICF/MR 6.
Owner Nonprofit corp.

Sunshine Vista
1732 16th Ave, Seattle, WA 98122
(206) 329-5775
Admin George Wiemerslage. *Dir of Nursing* Mimi Castle RN. *Medical Dir* Jean Bourdeau MD.
Licensure Skilled care; Intermediate care. *Beds* Swing beds SNF/ICF 37. *Private Pay Patients* 55%. *Certified* Medicaid; Medicare.
Owner Proprietary corp.
Admissions Requirements Medical examination; Physician's request.
Staff RNs 2 (ft), 1 (pt); LPNs 4 (ft); Nurses' aides 14 (ft), 3 (pt); Physical therapists; Activities coordinators 1 (ft); Dietitians; Restorative aides 1 (ft); MSWs 1 (pt).
Facilities Dining room; Activities room; Laundry room; Barber/Beauty shop.
Activities Arts & crafts; Cards; Games; Reading groups; Prayer groups; Movies; Shopping trips; Dances/Social/Cultural gatherings; Intergenerational programs; Pet therapy; Van rides & outings.

Terrace View Convalescent Center
1701 18th Ave S, Seattle, WA 98144
(206) 329-9586
Admin Philip Gayton.
Medical Dir James B Bushyhead MD.
Licensure Skilled care; Intermediate care. *Beds* 115. *Certified* Medicaid; Medicare.
Owner Proprietary corp.
Admissions Requirements Minimum age 18; Medical examination; Physician's request.
Staff RNs 10 (ft), 2 (pt); LPNs 6 (ft), 2 (pt); Nurses' aides 30 (ft), 15 (pt); Physical therapists 1 (ft), 1 (pt); Activities coordinators 1 (ft); Dietitians 1 (ft), 1 (pt).
Facilities Dining room; Physical therapy room; Activities room; Chapel; Crafts room; Laundry room; Barber/Beauty shop; Library.
Activities Arts & crafts; Cards; Games; Reading groups; Prayer groups; Movies; Shopping trips; Dances/Social/Cultural gatherings.

United Cerebral Palsy Residential Center
PO Box 77048, 14910 1st Ave NE, Seattle, WA 98177
(206) 363-7303
Admin Richard R Roth. *Dir of Nursing* Barbara Benson. *Medical Dir* Kathryn Zufall-Larson MD.
Licensure Intermediate care for mentally retarded. *Beds* ICF/MR 110. *Certified* Medicaid.
Owner Nonprofit organization/foundation.
Admissions Requirements Minimum age 18.
Staff RNs; LPNs; Physical therapists; Recreational therapists; Occupational therapists; Speech therapists; Dietitians.
Facilities Dining room; Physical therapy room; Activities room; Chapel.
Activities Arts & crafts; Cards; Games; Reading groups; Movies; Shopping trips; Dances/Social/Cultural gatherings; Art programs.

Wedgwood Rehabilitation Center
9132 Ravenna Ave NE, Seattle, WA 98115
(206) 525-5845
Admin Beverly B Felton.
Licensure Skilled care; Intermediate care. *Beds* 81. *Certified* Medicaid.
Owner Proprietary corp.

Sedro Woolley

Skagit Valley Convalescent Center Inc
2019 Hwy 20, Sedro Woolley, WA 98233
(206) 856-6867
Admin Rich Kackmeister. *Dir of Nursing* Karen Axelson RN. *Medical Dir* Vanoy Smith MD.
Licensure Skilled care; Retirement. *Beds* SNF 104; Retirement 70. *Private Pay Patients* 25%. *Certified* Medicaid; Medicare.
Owner Proprietary corp (Village Concepts Inc).
Admissions Requirements Physician's request.
Staff RNs 6 (ft), 2 (pt); LPNs 10 (ft), 4 (pt); Nurses' aides 30 (ft), 8 (pt); Physical therapists (consultant); Speech therapists (consultant); Activities coordinators 2 (ft); Dietitians (consultant); Podiatrists (consultant); Audiologists (consultant).
Facilities Dining room; Physical therapy room; Activities room; Crafts room; Laundry room; Barber/Beauty shop.
Activities Arts & crafts; Cards; Games; Reading groups; Prayer groups; Movies; Shopping trips; Dances/Social/Cultural gatherings.

Selah

Selah Convalescent Home Inc
PO Box 157, 203 W Naches Ave, Selah, WA 98942
(509) 697-8503

Admin Carol J Hyatt. *Dir of Nursing* Sheila Gawlik. *Medical Dir* Paul Emmans DO.
Licensure Skilled care; Intermediate care. *Beds* Swing beds SNF/ICF 39. *Private Pay Patients* 30%. *Certified* Medicaid.
Owner Proprietary corp.
Admissions Requirements Medical examination; Physician's request.
Staff RNs 1 (ft), 2 (pt); LPNs 2 (ft), 3 (pt); Nurses' aides 12 (ft), 2 (pt); Activities coordinators 1 (ft), 1 (pt); Dietitians 1 (pt); Podiatrists 1 (pt).
Facilities Dining room; Activities room; Laundry room; Barber/Beauty shop.
Activities Arts & crafts; Cards; Games; Reading groups; Prayer groups; Movies; Pet therapy.

Sequim

Olympic Health Care
1000 5th Ave S, Sequim, WA 98382
(206) 683-1112
Admin Neal Peisley. *Dir of Nursing* Patricia Carr. *Medical Dir* Joe Corn MD.
Licensure Skilled care; Intermediate care; Alzheimer's care. *Beds* Swing beds SNF/ICF 60. *Private Pay Patients* 33%. *Certified* Medicaid; Medicare.
Owner Proprietary corp.
Admissions Requirements Physician's request.
Staff RNs; LPNs; Nurses' aides; Recreational therapists; Activities coordinators.
Facilities Dining room; Physical therapy room; Activities room; Crafts room; Laundry room; Barber/Beauty shop.
Activities Arts & crafts; Cards; Games; Reading groups; Prayer groups; Movies; Shopping trips; Dances/Social/Cultural gatherings; Pet therapy.

Sequim Nursing Center
PO Box 726, 408 W Washington, Sequim, WA 98382
(206) 683-4184
Admin Carl Helms. *Dir of Nursing* Iveigh B Erban RN. *Medical Dir* Allen Berry MD.
Licensure Skilled care; Intermediate care; Retirement; Alzheimer's care. *Beds* 102. *Certified* Medicaid; Medicare; VA; Private.
Owner Proprietary corp (International Care Centers of Washington).
Admissions Requirements Medical examination.
Staff Physicians 1 (ft); RNs 5 (ft); LPNs 7 (ft); Nurses' aides 40 (ft); Physical therapists 1 (ft); Reality therapists 1 (ft); Occupational therapists 1 (pt); Speech therapists 1 (pt); Activities coordinators 1 (ft); Dietitians 1 (pt); Ophthalmologists 1 (pt); Podiatrists 1 (pt); Dentists 1 (pt).
Facilities Dining room; Physical therapy room; Activities room; Crafts room; Laundry room; Barber/Beauty shop; Library.
Activities Arts & crafts; Cards; Games; Reading groups; Prayer groups; Movies; Shopping trips; Dances/Social/Cultural gatherings; Bingo; Teas; Barbeques.

Sherwood Manor Inc
PO Box 1630, 550 Hendrickson Rd, Sequim, WA 98382
(206) 683-3348
Admin Donald L Daniel. *Dir of Nursing* Sue Lynne. *Medical Dir* Stanton Berman MD.
Licensure Skilled care; Residential care; Alzheimer's care. *Beds* SNF 65; Residential care 60. *Private Pay Patients* 55%. *Certified* Medicaid.
Owner Proprietary corp.
Admissions Requirements Medical examination; Physician's request.
Staff RNs 8 (ft), 2 (pt); LPNs 1 (ft), 1 (pt); Nurses' aides 18 (ft), 6 (pt); Activities coordinators.

Facilities Dining room; Activities room; Laundry room; Barber/Beauty shop; Library.
Activities Arts & crafts; Games; Reading groups; Prayer groups; Movies; Shopping trips; Dances/Social/Cultural gatherings; Pet therapy.

Shelton

Fir Lane Terrace Convalescent Center
2430 N 13th St, Shelton, WA 98584
(206) 426-1651
Admin Roberta L Goodwin. *Dir of Nursing* Linda Elvin. *Medical Dir* Dr Tim Weber.
Licensure Skilled care; Intermediate care. *Beds* 159. *Certified* Medicaid; Medicare; VA.
Owner Proprietary corp.
Admissions Requirements Physician's request.
Facilities Dining room; Physical therapy room; Activities room; Crafts room; Laundry room; Barber/Beauty shop.
Activities Arts & crafts; Cards; Games; Reading groups; Prayer groups; Movies; Dances/Social/Cultural gatherings.

Silverdale

Martin Street Group Home
8814 Martin St, Silverdale, WA 98370
(206) 692-3062
Admin Stephen Hult.
Licensure Intermediate care for mentally retarded. *Beds* ICF/MR 6.
Owner Nonprofit corp.

Snohomish

Delta Rehabilitation Center
1705 Terrace, Snohomish, WA 98290
(206) 568-2168
Admin Wallace J Walsh.
Licensure Skilled care; Intermediate care. *Beds* 138. *Certified* Medicaid.
Owner Proprietary corp.

Hollycrest Home Inc
124 Ave B, Snohomish, WA 98290
(206) 568-1535
Admin Linda Moe.
Licensure Intermediate care for mentally retarded. *Beds* ICF/MR 32. *Certified* Medicaid.
Owner Nonprofit corp.

Merry Haven Health Care Center
PO Box 69, 800 10th St, Snohomish, WA 98290
(206) 568-3161
Admin Kathleen Taylor.
Medical Dir Karen Crawford.
Licensure Skilled care; Intermediate care. *Beds* 91. *Certified* Medicaid.
Owner Proprietary corp.
Admissions Requirements Minimum age 18; Medical examination.
Staff RNs 10 (ft); LPNs 10 (ft); Nurses' aides; Recreational therapists 2 (ft); Dietitians 1 (ft).
Facilities Dining room; Physical therapy room; Activities room; Chapel; Crafts room; Laundry room; Barber/Beauty shop.
Activities Arts & crafts; Cards; Games; Reading groups; Prayer groups; Movies; Shopping trips; Dances/Social/Cultural gatherings.

Parkway Nursing Center
525 13th St, Snohomish, WA 98290
(206) 568-8566
Admin Chris Nickerson.
Medical Dir Melvin Nelson MD.
Licensure Skilled care; Intermediate care. *Beds* 119. *Certified* Medicaid.
Owner Proprietary corp (HMH Associates Inc).
Admissions Requirements Medical examination; Physician's request.

Staff RNs 6 (ft), 3 (pt); LPNs 3 (ft), 3 (pt); Nurses' aides 37 (ft), 4 (pt); Physical therapists 1 (pt); Reality therapists 1 (ft); Recreational therapists 1 (ft); Occupational therapists 1 (pt); Speech therapists 1 (pt); Activities coordinators 1 (ft), 1 (pt); Dietitians 1 (pt); Dentists 1 (pt).
Facilities Dining room; Physical therapy room; Activities room; Chapel; Crafts room; Laundry room; Barber/Beauty shop; Library.
Activities Arts & crafts; Cards; Games; Reading groups; Prayer groups; Movies; Shopping trips; Dances/Social/Cultural gatherings.

Soap Lake

McKay Memorial
PO Box 818, 127 2nd Ave, Soap Lake, WA 98851
(509) 246-1111
Admin Dr Kenneth V Buell. *Dir of Nursing* Terriann Gates. *Medical Dir* Dr Azab.
Licensure Skilled care; Alzheimer's care; Retirement. *Beds* SNF 42; Retirement 9. *Certified* Medicaid; Medicare.
Owner Nonprofit organization/foundation.
Admissions Requirements Medical examination; Physician's request.
Staff Physicians 4 (pt); RNs 6 (ft); LPNs 5 (ft), 2 (pt); Nurses' aides 18 (ft), 6 (pt); Physical therapists 1 (pt); Activities coordinators 1 (ft); Dietitians 1 (ft).
Languages Russian, Spanish, German, Dutch, French, Lithuanian.
Facilities Dining room; Physical therapy room; Activities room; Chapel; Crafts room; Laundry room; Barber/Beauty shop; Library; Fenced yard with sidewalks; Gazebos; Pets.
Activities Arts & crafts; Cards; Games; Reading groups; Prayer groups; Movies; Shopping trips; Dances/Social/Cultural gatherings; Intergenerational programs; Pet therapy; Music groups; Adopt-a-grandparent program.

Spokane

Alderwood Manor
E 3600 Hartson, Spokane, WA 99203
(509) 535-2071
Admin Karen Burgerson. *Dir of Nursing* Sylvia Alexander. *Medical Dir* Eric Paulson MD.
Licensure Skilled care; Intermediate care; Retirement. *Beds* SNF 73; ICF 12; Retirement apts 9. *Certified* Medicaid; Medicare.
Owner Privately owned.
Admissions Requirements Medical examination; Physician's request.
Staff RNs; LPNs; Nurses' aides; Physical therapists; Recreational therapists; Occupational therapists; Activities coordinators; Dietitians; Podiatrists.
Facilities Dining room; Physical therapy room; Laundry room; Barber/Beauty shop.
Activities Arts & crafts; Cards; Games; Reading groups; Prayer groups; Movies; Dances/Social/Cultural gatherings; Intergenerational programs; Pet therapy.

Cliff Manor
W 427 7th Ave, Spokane, WA 99204
(509) 624-2324
Admin John Lanouette.
Licensure Skilled care; Intermediate care. *Beds* 85. *Certified* Medicaid.
Owner Proprietary corp.

Garden Terrace Manor
W 424 7th, Spokane, WA 99204
(509) 838-8233
Admin John Lanouette.
Licensure Skilled care; Intermediate care. *Beds* 120. *Certified* Medicaid; Medicare.
Owner Proprietary corp.

Hawthorne Manor
E 101 Hawthorne Rd, Spokane, WA 99218
(509) 466-0411
Admin Robert R Barwell; Marilyn Teets, in-training. *Dir of Nursing* Patricia L Tolbert RN.
Licensure Skilled care; Assisted living; Retirement. *Beds* SNF 20; Assisted living 15; Retirement 110. *Private Pay Patients* 100%.
Owner Nonprofit corp (Presbyterian Ministries Inc).
Admissions Requirements Minimum age 62.
Staff RNs 4 (ft), 5 (pt); Nurses' aides 8 (ft), 6 (pt); Activities coordinators 1 (ft), 1 (pt).
Affiliation Presbyterian.
Facilities Dining room; Activities room; Crafts room; Laundry room; Barber/Beauty shop; Library.
Activities Arts & crafts; Cards; Games; Reading groups; Prayer groups; Movies.

Keller Nursing Home
W 1117 10th Ave, Spokane, WA 99204
(509) 624-7632
Admin Patsy Keller.
Licensure Nursing home. *Beds* Nursing home 22.
Owner Proprietary corp.

Latah Center Inc
S 5913 Inland Empire Way, Spokane, WA 99204
(509) 448-2262
Admin Julie J Landwehr. *Dir of Nursing* Patti Hundeby RN. *Medical Dir* Hershel Zellman MD.
Licensure Intermediate care for mentally retarded. *Beds* ICF/MR 40. *Certified* Medicaid.
Owner Proprietary corp.
Admissions Requirements Minimum age 18.
Staff Physicians 1 (pt); RNs 2 (ft); LPNs 3 (ft); Nurses' aides 14 (ft), 4 (pt); Physical therapists 1 (pt); Recreational therapists 2 (ft); Occupational therapists 1 (pt); Speech therapists 1 (pt); Dietitians 1 (pt); Ophthalmologists 1 (pt); Podiatrists 1 (pt); Dentists 1 (pt).
Facilities Dining room; Activities room; Laundry room.
Activities Arts & crafts; Cards; Games; Movies; Shopping trips; Dances/Social/Cultural gatherings.

Lilac City Convalescent Center
E 1707 Rowan Ave, Spokane, WA 99207
(509) 489-1427
Admin Kerry Arbuckle. *Dir of Nursing* Jay Waddell RN. *Medical Dir* Leonard Vanderbosch MD.
Licensure Skilled care; Intermediate care. *Beds* 52. *Certified* Medicaid.
Owner Proprietary corp (Beverly Enterprises).
Admissions Requirements Minimum age 18; Physician's request.
Staff RNs 4 (ft), 1 (pt); LPNs 2 (ft); Nurses' aides 24 (ft); Activities coordinators 1 (ft); Office managers.
Facilities Dining room; Physical therapy room; Activities room; Laundry room; Barber/Beauty shop.
Activities Arts & crafts; Cards; Games; Reading groups; Prayer groups; Movies; Shopping trips; Dances/Social/Cultural gatherings.

Manor Care Convalescent Rehabilitation Center of Spokane
N 6025 Assembly, Spokane, WA 99205
(509) 326-8282
Admin Raymond Billings.
Licensure Skilled care; Intermediate care. *Beds* 125. *Certified* Medicaid; Medicare.
Owner Proprietary corp (Manor Care Inc).

Mansion House Nursing Home
E 3011 Wellesley, Spokane, WA 99207
(509) 489-8825
Admin Bonita Powers.
Medical Dir Dr Van Veen.
Licensure Skilled care; Intermediate care. *Beds* 67. *Certified* Medicaid.
Owner Proprietary corp (PHM Health Care Group Inc).
Staff RNs 3 (ft); LPNs 6 (ft); Nurses' aides 20 (ft); Physical therapists 1 (ft); Activities coordinators 1 (ft); Dietitians 1 (pt).
Facilities Dining room; Physical therapy room; Activities room; Crafts room; Laundry room; Barber/Beauty shop.
Activities Arts & crafts; Cards; Games; Reading groups; Prayer groups; Movies.

North-Central Care
W 618 Nora, Spokane, WA 99205
(509) 328-6030
Admin Claude Hill.
Licensure Skilled care; Intermediate care. *Beds* 101. *Certified* Medicaid.
Owner Proprietary corp.

Regency Care Center of Spokane
E 44 Cozza Dr, Spokane, WA 99208
(509) 489-5652
Admin Sharron Ahonen. *Dir of Nursing* Alice J Brown RN. *Medical Dir* Arthur Craig MD.
Licensure Skilled care; Intermediate care. *Beds* 137. *Certified* Medicaid; VA.
Owner Proprietary corp (Regency Health Care Centers Inc).
Admissions Requirements Medical examination; Physician's request.
Staff RNs 7 (ft), 5 (pt); LPNs 7 (ft), 7 (pt); Nurses' aides 49 (ft), 10 (pt); Occupational therapists 1 (pt); Speech therapists 1 (pt); Activities coordinators 2 (ft); Dietitians 1 (ft), 1 (pt); Ophthalmologists 1 (pt).
Facilities Dining room; Physical therapy room; Activities room; Laundry room; Barber/Beauty shop.
Activities Arts & crafts; Cards; Games; Reading groups; Prayer groups; Movies; Shopping trips; Dances/Social/Cultural gatherings.

Regency South Care Center
S 518 Browne, Spokane, WA 99204
(509) 455-9710, 455-9733 FAX
Admin Vicki McKenna. *Dir of Nursing* Cassandra Vent. *Medical Dir* Dr VanVeen.
Licensure Skilled care; Intermediate care. *Beds* Swing beds SNF/ICF 58. *Private Pay Patients* 10%. *Certified* Medicaid.
Owner Proprietary corp (Regency Health Care Centers Inc).
Admissions Requirements Minimum age 18.
Staff RNs 4 (ft); LPNs 5 (ft), 1 (pt); Nurses' aides 22 (ft); Physical therapists 1 (pt); Occupational therapists 1 (pt); Speech therapists 1 (pt); Activities coordinators 1 (ft); Dietitians 1 (pt); Ophthalmologists (consultant); Podiatrists (consultant); Audiologists (consultant).
Facilities Dining room; Activities room; Laundry room.
Activities Arts & crafts; Cards; Games; Prayer groups; Movies; Shopping trips; Dances/Social/Cultural gatherings; Intergenerational programs.

Riverpark Convalescent Center
W 4444 Downriver Dr, Spokane, WA 99205
(509) 326-6711
Admin Robert Avey Jr. *Dir of Nursing* Georgeen Golembiewski. *Medical Dir* Dr Frank Vanveen.
Licensure Skilled care; Intermediate care; Alzheimer's care. *Beds* Swing beds SNF/ICF 136. *Certified* Medicaid.
Owner Proprietary corp.

Staff RNs 5 (ft), 1 (pt); LPNs 7 (ft), 2 (pt); Nurses' aides 31 (ft); Physical therapists 1 (ft); Occupational therapists 1 (ft); Activities coordinators 1 (ft); Dietitians 1 (ft).
Facilities Dining room; Activities room; Laundry room; Library.
Activities Arts & crafts; Cards; Games; Reading groups; Prayer groups; Movies; Shopping trips; Dances/Social/Cultural gatherings.

Riverview Center for Retirement Living
E 1801 Upriver Dr, Spokane, WA 99207
(509) 482-8138, 483-5008 FAX
Admin Gene Larson. *Dir of Nursing* Sherri Adams. *Medical Dir* Alex Van Derwild MD.
Licensure Skilled care; Assisted living; Retirement. *Beds* SNF 75; Assisted living 20; Retirement apts 149; Retirement homes 60. *Private Pay Patients* 90%. *Certified* Medicaid; Medicare.
Owner Nonprofit organization/foundation.
Admissions Requirements Minimum age 60.
Staff Physicians 1 (pt); RNs 5 (ft); LPNs 12 (ft); Nurses' aides 35 (ft); Physical therapists 1 (ft); Reality therapists 2 (ft); Recreational therapists 1 (pt); Occupational therapists 1 (pt); Speech therapists 1 (pt); Activities coordinators 4 (ft); Dietitians 1 (ft); Podiatrists 1 (ft), 1 (pt); Audiologists 1 (pt); Chaplains 1 (ft), 1 (pt).
Affiliation Lutheran.
Facilities Dining room; Physical therapy room; Activities room; Chapel; Crafts room; Laundry room; Barber/Beauty shop; Library; Recreation building with swimming pool, jacuzzi, pool tables.
Activities Arts & crafts; Cards; Games; Reading groups; Prayer groups; Movies; Shopping trips; Dances/Social/Cultural gatherings; Intergenerational programs; Pet therapy.

Rockwood Manor Infirmary
E 2903 25th Ave, Spokane, WA 99223
(509) 536-6650
Admin Daniel M Chapman. *Dir of Nursing* Eric Mahnke RN.
Licensure Skilled care; Alzheimer's care; Retirement. *Beds* SNF 48. *Certified* Medicare.
Owner Nonprofit corp.
Admissions Requirements Minimum age 65; Medical examination.
Staff RNs 9 (ft); LPNs 8 (ft); Nurses' aides 15 (ft); Physical therapists 1 (pt); Recreational therapists 1 (ft); Occupational therapists 1 (pt); Speech therapists 1 (pt); Activities coordinators 1 (ft); Dietitians 1 (pt); Ophthalmologists 1 (pt); Podiatrists 1 (pt); Dentists 1 (pt).
Affiliation Methodist.
Facilities Dining room; Physical therapy room; Activities room; Chapel; Crafts room; Laundry room; Barber/Beauty shop; Library.
Activities Arts & crafts; Cards; Games; Reading groups; Prayer groups; Movies; Shopping trips; Dances/Social/Cultural gatherings.

St Brendan Care Center
E 17 8th Ave, Spokane, WA 99202
(509) 624-1161
Admin Thomas Gray. *Dir of Nursing* Linda Harrison. *Medical Dir* Dr Jeff Clode.
Licensure Skilled care; Intermediate care; Respite care. *Beds* Swing beds SNF/ICF 177. *Certified* Medicaid; Medicare; VA.
Owner Nonprofit corp.
Admissions Requirements Physician's request.
Staff Physicians 1 (pt); RNs 10 (ft); LPNs 15 (ft); Nurses' aides 90 (ft); Physical therapists 2 (ft); Occupational therapists 1 (pt); Speech therapists 2 (ft); Activities coordinators 3 (ft); Dietitians 1 (ft); Dentists 1 (pt).

Facilities Dining room; Physical therapy room; Activities room; Crafts room; Laundry room; Barber/Beauty shop; Library; Appolo bathing.
Activities Arts & crafts; Cards; Games; Reading groups; Prayer groups; Movies; Shopping trips; Dances/Social/Cultural gatherings.

St Joseph Care Center
W 20 9th Ave, Spokane, WA 99204
(509) 838-6437
Admin Sr Vincenza Dufresne.
Medical Dir Dr Richard Bale.
Licensure Skilled care; Intermediate care. *Beds* 103. *Certified* Medicaid.
Owner Nonprofit corp.
Admissions Requirements Medical examination; Physician's request.
Staff Physicians 1 (pt); RNs 12 (pt); LPNs 1 (pt); Nurses' aides 36 (ft), 10 (pt); Physical therapists 3 (ft), 1 (pt); Recreational therapists 1 (pt); Occupational therapists 1 (pt); Speech therapists 1 (pt); Dietitians 1 (pt); Ophthalmologists 1 (pt); Dentists 1 (pt).
Languages French.
Affiliation Roman Catholic.
Facilities Dining room; Physical therapy room; Activities room; Chapel; Crafts room; Laundry room; Barber/Beauty shop; Library.
Activities Arts & crafts; Cards; Games; Reading groups; Prayer groups; Movies; Shopping trips.

St Jude's Health Care Centre
1521 E Illinois, Spokane, WA 99207
(509) 484-3132
Admin Florence Davis Reynolds. *Dir of Nursing* Ronda Truppe RN. *Medical Dir* Dr Rodkey.
Licensure Intermediate care. *Beds* ICF 45. *Certified* Medicaid.
Owner Proprietary corp.
Admissions Requirements Medical examination; Physician's request.
Staff RNs 6 (ft); LPNs 2 (ft); Nurses' aides 15 (ft), 1 (pt); Activities coordinators 2 (ft).
Affiliation Roman Catholic.
Facilities Dining room; Physical therapy room; Activities room; Laundry room.
Activities Arts & crafts; Cards; Games; Reading groups; Prayer groups; Movies; Shopping trips; Dances/Social/Cultural gatherings; Intergenerational programs; Pet therapy; Civic theater; Picnics; Circus; Ice Capades; Catholic and Protestant services.

St Luke's Extended Care Center
E 222 5th Ave, Spokane, WA 99202
(509) 838-7940, 838-4743 FAX
Admin Ralph K Allen Jr PhD. *Dir of Nursing* Nancy J Stewart RNC, V Pres. *Medical Dir* C F Manning MD.
Licensure Skilled care; Intermediate care; Sub-acute care. *Beds* Swing beds SNF/ICF 102. *Private Pay Patients* 30%. *Certified* Medicaid; Medicare.
Owner Nonprofit organization/foundation.
Admissions Requirements Physician's request.
Staff RNs; LPNs; Nurses' aides; Physical therapists (contracted); Recreational therapists 1 (ft); Occupational therapists (contracted); Speech therapists (contracted); Activities coordinators 1 (pt); Dietitians (contracted); Ophthalmologists (contracted); Podiatrists (contracted); Audiologists (contracted); Chaplains 1 (ft).
Languages contracted as needed.
Facilities Dining room; Physical therapy room; Activities room; Chapel; Crafts room; Laundry room; Barber/Beauty shop.
Activities Arts & crafts; Cards; Games; Reading groups; Prayer groups; Movies; Shopping trips; Dances/Social/Cultural gatherings; Intergenerational programs; Pet therapy.

Senior Citizens Nursing Home
N 2659 Ash, Spokane, WA 99205
(509) 327-7728
Admin Carol Jean Jones.
Medical Dir Patricia A Friedland.
Licensure Nursing home; Alzheimer's care. *Beds* Nursing home 24.
Owner Proprietary corp (Regency Health Care Centers Inc).
Staff Physicians; RNs; LPNs; Nurses' aides; Physical therapists; Reality therapists; Recreational therapists; Occupational therapists; Speech therapists; Activities coordinators; Dietitians; Ophthalmologists; Podiatrists; Dentists.
Activities Arts & crafts; Cards; Games; Reading groups; Prayer groups; Movies.

Sunshine Gardens
10410 E 9th Ave, Spokane, WA 99206
(509) 926-3547
Admin Margaret C Dikes. *Dir of Nursing* Charles Morel. *Medical Dir* Dr Robert Eastwood.
Licensure Skilled care; Intermediate care; Alzheimer's care. *Beds* SNF 27; ICF 57. *Private Pay Patients* 25%. *Certified* Medicaid.
Owner Proprietary corp.
Facilities Dining room; Physical therapy room; Activities room; Laundry room; Barber/Beauty shop; Quiet lounge; Solarium; Occupational therapy room; Vans.
Activities Arts & crafts; Cards; Games; Reading groups; Prayer groups; Movies; Shopping trips; Dances/Social/Cultural gatherings; Pet therapy; Visitation therapy program for cognitively impaired residents.

Washington Healthcare Center—Northcrest
N 6021 Lidgerwood, Spokane, WA 99207
(509) 489-3323
Admin Vicki McKenna.
Medical Dir Lana Boteler.
Licensure Skilled care; Intermediate care; Retirement. *Beds* 163. *Certified* Medicaid; Medicare.
Owner Proprietary corp (Unicare).
Staff RNs 5 (ft), 5 (pt).
Facilities Dining room; Physical therapy room; Activities room; Laundry room; Barber/Beauty shop.
Activities Arts & crafts; Cards; Games; Reading groups; Prayer groups; Movies; Shopping trips; Dances/Social/Cultural gatherings.

Washington Healthcare Center—Unicrest
S 414 University Rd, Spokane, WA 99206
(509) 924-4650
Admin Monica Roy. *Dir of Nursing* Mary Olmsted. *Medical Dir* Robert Matthias.
Licensure Skilled care; Intermediate care; Retirement. *Beds* 115. *Certified* Medicaid; Medicare.
Owner Proprietary corp (Unicare).
Admissions Requirements Medical examination; Physician's request.
Staff Physicians; RNs 5 (ft), 2 (pt); LPNs 11 (ft), 1 (pt); Nurses' aides 66 (ft), 3 (pt); Activities coordinators 2 (ft); Dietitians 1 (ft); Ophthalmologists.
Facilities Dining room; Physical therapy room; Activities room; Laundry room; Barber/Beauty shop; Library.
Activities Arts & crafts; Cards; Games; Prayer groups; Movies; Shopping trips; Dances/Social/Cultural gatherings.

Washington Healthcare Center—Valley Crest
E 12715 Mission Ave, Spokane, WA 99216
(509) 924-3040
Admin Lawrence J Cirka. *Dir of Nursing* Kathi Wenzel. *Medical Dir* Laurina Worth MD.
Licensure Skilled care; Intermediate care. *Beds* 130. *Certified* Medicaid; Medicare.
Owner Proprietary corp (Unicare).

Staff RNs 7 (ft); LPNs 12 (ft); Nurses' aides 40 (ft); Recreational therapists 1 (ft); Activities coordinators 1 (ft); Dietitians 1 (ft); Dentists 1 (pt).
Facilities Dining room; Physical therapy room; Activities room; Barber/Beauty shop.
Activities Arts & crafts; Cards; Games; Prayer groups; Movies; Shopping trips; Dances/Social/Cultural gatherings.

Washington Rehabilitation Center Southcrest
W 110 Cliff, Spokane, WA 99204
(509) 456-8300
Admin David Murphy.
Medical Dir Dr F Claude Manning.
Licensure Skilled care; Intermediate care. *Beds* 212. *Certified* Medicaid; Medicare.
Owner Proprietary corp (Unicare).
Admissions Requirements Medical examination; Physician's request.
Staff RNs 15 (ft); LPNs 11 (ft); Nurses' aides 57 (ft); Physical therapists 2 (ft); Recreational therapists 2 (ft); Speech therapists; Dietitians 1 (ft); Podiatrists; Dentists.
Facilities Dining room; Physical therapy room; Activities room; Chapel; Crafts room; Laundry room; Barber/Beauty shop; Library.
Activities Arts & crafts; Cards; Games; Reading groups; Prayer groups; Movies; Shopping trips; Dances/Social/Cultural gatherings.

Stanwood

Josephine Sunset Home
9901 272nd Pl NW, Stanwood, WA 98292
(206) 629-2126
Admin Monica Mattson.
Licensure Skilled care; Intermediate care. *Beds* 160. *Certified* Medicaid.
Owner Nonprofit corp.
Admissions Requirements Minimum age 19.
Staff Physicians 1 (pt); RNs 9 (ft), 8 (pt); LPNs 6 (ft), 9 (pt); Nurses' aides 54 (ft), 10 (pt); Activities coordinators 1 (ft).
Affiliation Lutheran.
Facilities Dining room; Physical therapy room; Activities room; Chapel; Crafts room; Laundry room; Barber/Beauty shop; Library.
Activities Arts & crafts; Cards; Games; Reading groups; Prayer groups; Movies; Shopping trips; Dances/Social/Cultural gatherings.

Warm Beach Health Care Center
20420 Marine Dr NW, Stanwood, WA 98292
(206) 652-7585
Admin George J Avis. *Dir of Nursing* Sally McDougall. *Medical Dir* Dr Randall Miller.
Licensure Skilled care; Intermediate care; Residential care; Alzheimer's care. *Beds* Swing beds SNF/ICF 81; Residential care 300. *Private Pay Patients* 37%. *Certified* Medicaid.
Owner Nonprofit corp.
Admissions Requirements Medical examination; Physician's request.
Staff RNs 5 (ft), 4 (pt); LPNs 3 (ft), 2 (pt); Nurses' aides 30 (ft), 8 (pt); Physical therapists 1 (pt); Reality therapists 1 (pt); Occupational therapists 1 (pt); Activities coordinators 1 (ft); Dietitians 1 (pt).
Affiliation Free Methodist.
Facilities Dining room; Physical therapy room; Activities room; Crafts room; Laundry room; Barber/Beauty shop; Library; Swimming pool; Atrium; Gazebo.
Activities Arts & crafts; Games; Reading groups; Prayer groups; Movies; Shopping trips.

Sumner

Sumner Lodge
PO Box 1110, Sumner, WA 98390-1110
(206) 863-0433

Admin Kathleen A Kinkade.
Licensure Intermediate care for mentally retarded. *Beds* ICF/MR 43. *Certified* Medicaid.
Owner Proprietary corp.

Sunnyside

Hillcrest Manor—Sunnyside
PO Box 876, 721 Otis, Sunnyside, WA 98944
(509) 837-2122
Admin Mary Arthur.
Medical Dir Dr Arnold Tait.
Licensure Skilled care; Intermediate care. *Beds* 84. *Certified* Medicaid; Medicare.
Owner Proprietary corp (Beverly Enterprises).
Admissions Requirements Medical examination; Physician's request.
Staff RNs 6 (ft), 3 (pt); LPNs 4 (ft), 2 (pt); Nurses' aides 18 (ft), 12 (pt); Physical therapists 1 (pt); Recreational therapists 1 (ft); Activities coordinators 1 (ft), 1 (pt); Dietitians 1 (ft).
Facilities Dining room; Physical therapy room; Activities room; Chapel; Crafts room; Laundry room; Barber/Beauty shop; Dayroom.
Activities Arts & crafts; Cards; Games; Reading groups; Prayer groups; Movies; Shopping trips; Dances/Social/Cultural gatherings.

Sunny Haven Convalescent Center
1313 S 6th, Sunnyside, WA 98944
(509) 837-4200
Admin Chuck Gilman. *Dir of Nursing* Theresa Scofield RN. *Medical Dir* Arnold Tait MD.
Licensure Intermediate care for mentally retarded. *Beds* ICF/MR 60. *Certified* Medicaid.
Owner Proprietary corp (Beverly Enterprises).
Admissions Requirements Minimum age 18.
Staff Physicians 1 (pt); RNs 6 (ft); LPNs 3 (ft); Nurses' aides 31 (ft); Physical therapists 1 (ft); Occupational therapists 1 (pt); Speech therapists 1 (pt); Activities coordinators 1 (ft); Dietitians 1 (pt); Podiatrists 1 (pt).
Languages Spanish, Sign.
Facilities Dining room; Physical therapy room; Activities room; Laundry room; Barber/Beauty shop.
Activities Arts & crafts; Cards; Games; Reading groups; Prayer groups; Movies; Shopping trips; Dances/Social/Cultural gatherings; Special Olympics; 4-H Club; Shelter workshop developmental training classes.

Tacoma

Abilene House Inc
2901 Bridgeport Way W, Tacoma, WA 98466
(206) 564-1643
Admin James C Edwards. *Dir of Nursing* Marion Ray RN. *Medical Dir* William Wright MD.
Licensure Private pay; Retirement; Alzheimer's care. *Beds* Private pay 70.
Owner Proprietary corp.
Staff RNs 3 (ft), 4 (pt); LPNs 4 (ft), 4 (pt); Nurses' aides 30 (ft), 1 (pt); Physical therapists 1 (pt); Reality therapists 1 (pt); Recreational therapists 1 (pt); Occupational therapists 1 (pt); Speech therapists 1 (pt); Activities coordinators 2 (ft); Dietitians 1 (pt); Ophthalmologists 1 (pt).
Languages Lithuanian.
Facilities Dining room; Physical therapy room; Activities room; Crafts room; Laundry room; Barber/Beauty shop.
Activities Arts & crafts; Cards; Games; Reading groups; Prayer groups; Movies; Shopping trips; Dances/Social/Cultural gatherings.

Bel Air
630 S Pearl, Tacoma, WA 98465
(206) 564-7111
Admin Kenneth S Rehusch. *Dir of Nursing* Kimmi Munson-Walsh RN. *Medical Dir* James M Wilson Jr MD.
Licensure Skilled care; Intermediate care; Alzheimer's care. *Beds* 103. *Certified* Medicaid; Medicare.
Owner Privately owned (Quad Cities Healthcare Centers).
Admissions Requirements Minimum age 18; Medical examination.
Staff RNs 4 (ft), 2 (pt); LPNs 4 (ft), 2 (pt); Nurses' aides 21 (ft), 2 (pt); Activities coordinators 2 (ft); Dietitians 1 (ft).
Facilities Dining room; Physical therapy room; Activities room; Barber/Beauty shop.
Activities Arts & crafts; Cards; Games; Movies; Shopping trips; Dances/Social/Cultural gatherings; Baking; Exercise classes; Breakfast club.

Bellevue Care Center
515 S 64th St, Tacoma, WA 98408
(206) 472-4481
Admin Sandra A Reynoldson. *Dir of Nursing* Joene M Timmans RN. *Medical Dir* Dr John Comfort.
Licensure Skilled care; Intermediate care. *Beds* 51. *Certified* Medicaid.
Owner Proprietary corp.
Admissions Requirements Medical examination; Physician's request.
Staff RNs 5 (ft), 3 (pt); LPNs 4 (ft), 2 (pt); Nurses' aides 11 (ft), 4 (pt); Physical therapists 1 (ft); Occupational therapists 1 (ft); Activities coordinators 1 (ft).
Languages German, Korean.
Facilities Dining room; Activities room; Barber/Beauty shop; Library.
Activities Arts & crafts; Cards; Games; Reading groups; Prayer groups; Movies; Shopping trips; Dances/Social/Cultural gatherings.

Brentwood
1401 N 5th St, Tacoma, WA 98403
(206) 572-8141
Admin Nola Davis.
Medical Dir David Brown MD.
Licensure Skilled care; Intermediate care. *Beds* 50. *Certified* Medicaid.
Owner Privately owned (Quad Cities Healthcare Centers).
Admissions Requirements Medical examination.
Staff Physicians 1 (pt); RNs 3 (ft), 2 (pt); LPNs 5 (ft), 3 (pt); Nurses' aides 10 (ft), 5 (pt); Physical therapists 1 (pt); Activities coordinators 1 (ft), 1 (pt); Dietitians 1 (ft); Dentists 1 (pt).
Facilities Dining room; Physical therapy room; Activities room; Laundry room; Barber/Beauty shop.
Activities Arts & crafts; Cards; Games; Reading groups; Prayer groups; Movies; Shopping trips; Dances/Social/Cultural gatherings.

Clearview Manor Convalescent & Rehabilitation Center
6844 Portland Ave, Tacoma, WA 98404
(206) 474-9496
Admin Thomas E Imel.
Medical Dir Bryan M Archer MD.
Licensure Skilled care; Intermediate care. *Beds* 136. *Certified* Medicaid.
Owner Proprietary corp (Beverly Enterprises).
Admissions Requirements Medical examination; Physician's request.
Staff RNs; LPNs; Nurses' aides; Physical therapists; Reality therapists; Recreational therapists; Occupational therapists; Activities coordinators; Restorative technicians.
Facilities Dining room; Physical therapy room; Activities room; Crafts room; Barber/Beauty shop.

Activities Arts & crafts; Games; Reading groups; Prayer groups; Movies; Shopping trips; Dances/Social/Cultural gatherings.

Georgian House
8407 Steilacoom Blvd SW, Tacoma, WA 98498
(206) 588-2146
Admin Edward C Mawe.
Medical Dir Herman Judd MD.
Licensure Skilled care; Intermediate care; Retirement; Alzheimer's care. *Beds* 73. *Certified* Medicaid; Medicare.
Owner Privately owned (Quad Cities Healthcare Centers).
Admissions Requirements Minimum age 18.
Staff RNs 3 (ft), 6 (pt); LPNs 4 (ft), 3 (pt); Nurses' aides 30 (ft), 5 (pt); Physical therapists 1 (pt); Recreational therapists 1 (ft); Occupational therapists 1 (pt); Activities coordinators 1 (ft); Dietitians 1 (pt); Ophthalmologists 1 (pt); Dentists 1 (pt).
Facilities Dining room; Physical therapy room; Activities room; Crafts room; Barber/Beauty shop.
Activities Arts & crafts; Cards; Games; Reading groups; Prayer groups; Movies; Shopping trips; Dances/Social/Cultural gatherings.

Heritage
7411 Pacific Ave, Tacoma, WA 98408
(206) 474-8456
Admin Sandra E Crossland. *Dir of Nursing* Katherine Mikita ARNP GNP. *Medical Dir* James Wilson MD.
Licensure Skilled care; Intermediate care. *Beds* Swing beds SNF/ICF 89. *Private Pay Patients* 30%. *Certified* Medicaid; Medicare.
Owner Privately owned (Quad Cities Healthcare Centers).
Admissions Requirements Physician's request.
Staff Physicians 1 (pt); RNs 4 (ft), 2 (pt); LPNs 12 (ft), 3 (pt); Nurses' aides 30 (ft); Physical therapists 1 (pt); Reality therapists 1 (pt); Recreational therapists 1 (pt); Occupational therapists 1 (pt); Speech therapists 1 (pt); Activities coordinators 2 (ft), 1 (pt); Dietitians 1 (pt); Ophthalmologists 1 (pt); Podiatrists 1 (pt); Audiologists 1 (pt).
Facilities Dining room; Physical therapy room; Activities room; Crafts room; Barber/Beauty shop.
Activities Arts & crafts; Cards; Games; Reading groups; Prayer groups; Movies; Dances/Social/Cultural gatherings; Pet therapy.

Highlands
5954 N 26th, Tacoma, WA 98407
(206) 752-7713
Admin Sandra E Crossland.
Medical Dir David Munoz MD.
Licensure Skilled care; Intermediate care; Alzheimer's care. *Beds* 86. *Certified* Medicaid.
Owner Privately owned (Quad Cities Healthcare Centers).
Admissions Requirements Medical examination; Physician's request.
Staff Physical therapists 1 (pt); Activities coordinators 1 (ft).
Languages Italian.
Facilities Dining room; Activities room; Crafts room; Laundry room; Barber/Beauty shop.
Activities Arts & crafts; Cards; Games; Movies; Shopping trips; Dances/Social/Cultural gatherings; Small groups for severely impaired.

Jefferson House Care Center
1748 Jefferson Ave, Tacoma, WA 98402
(206) 383-5495
Admin Tim Moore. *Dir of Nursing* Kathryn Jensen. *Medical Dir* Bryan Archer.

Licensure Skilled care; Intermediate care. *Beds* Swing beds SNF/ICF 130. *Private Pay Patients* 5%. *Certified* Medicaid.
Owner Proprietary corp (Soundcare Inc).
Admissions Requirements Minimum age; Physician's request.
Staff RNs 4 (ft), 5 (pt); LPNs 5 (ft), 2 (pt); Nurses' aides 20 (ft), 1 (pt); Activities coordinators 1 (ft), 2 (pt); Dietitians 1 (pt).
Facilities Dining room; Activities room; Laundry room.
Activities Arts & crafts; Cards; Games; Reading groups; Movies; Shopping trips; Dances/Social/Cultural gatherings; Pet therapy.

Franke Tobey Jones Home
5340 N Bristol, Tacoma, WA 98407
(206) 752-6621
Admin Sarita Rebman. *Dir of Nursing* Jo An Head RN. *Medical Dir* Joseph Regimbal MD.
Licensure Nursing home; Retirement. *Beds* Nursing home 23.
Owner Nonprofit corp.
Admissions Requirements Minimum age 18 Nursing home, 65 Boarding home; Medical examination; Physician's request.
Staff Physicians 1 (pt); LPNs 3 (ft); Recreational therapists 1 (ft); Activities coordinators 1 (ft); Dietitians 1 (ft).
Languages German, Scandinavian.
Facilities Dining room; Activities room; Laundry room; Barber/Beauty shop; Library; Parlors; Spa with jacuzzi; Greenhouse.
Activities Arts & crafts; Cards; Games; Reading groups; Prayer groups; Movies; Shopping trips; Dances/Social/Cultural gatherings; Greenhouse.

Kitsap Peninsula House
3010 N McCarver St, Tacoma, WA 98403-3338
(206) 531-9684, 377-7231
Admin Stephen Hult.
Medical Dir Cynthia Wilson.
Licensure Intermediate care for mentally retarded. *Beds* ICF/MR 8. *Certified* Medicaid.
Owner Nonprofit corp.
Admissions Requirements Minimum age 18; Medical examination; Physician's request.
Staff Physicians 1 (pt); RNs 1 (pt); LPNs 1 (pt); Nurses' aides 5 (ft), 3 (pt); Physical therapists 1 (pt); Recreational therapists 1 (pt); Occupational therapists 1 (pt); Speech therapists 1 (pt); Dietitians 1 (pt); Ophthalmologists 2 (pt); Audiologists 2 (pt); Dentists 2 (pt).
Facilities Dining room; Physical therapy room; Activities room; Laundry room.
Activities Arts & crafts; Games; Movies; Shopping trips; Dances/Social/Cultural gatherings.

KPHA/Narrows Drive
3010 N McCarver St, Tacoma, WA 98403-3338
(206) 752-3696, 377-7231
Admin Stephen Hult.
Medical Dir Doug Jeffrey.
Licensure Intermediate care for mentally retarded. *Beds* ICF/MR 8. *Certified* Medicaid.
Owner Nonprofit corp.
Admissions Requirements Minimum age 18; Medical examination; Physician's request.
Staff Physicians 1 (pt); RNs 1 (pt); LPNs 1 (pt); Nurses' aides 5 (ft), 3 (pt); Physical therapists 1 (pt); Recreational therapists 1 (pt); Occupational therapists 1 (pt); Speech therapists 1 (pt); Dietitians 1 (pt); Ophthalmologists 2 (pt); Audiologists 2 (pt); Dentists 2 (pt).
Facilities Dining room; Physical therapy room; Activities room; Crafts room; Laundry room.

Activities Arts & crafts; Cards; Games; Reading groups; Movies; Shopping trips; Dances/Social/Cultural gatherings.

Manor Care of Meadow Park
5601 S Orchard St, Tacoma, WA 98409
(206) 474-8421
Admin Terrell Leno.
Licensure Skilled care; Intermediate care. *Beds* 125. *Certified* Medicaid; Medicare.
Owner Proprietary corp (Manor Care Inc).

Midland Manor
10816 18th Ave E, Tacoma, WA 98445
(206) 537-5395
Admin Judy Prunty. *Dir of Nursing* Judy Morford. *Medical Dir* Dr Thomas Bowden.
Licensure Intermediate care. *Beds* ICF 45. *Certified* Medicaid.
Owner Proprietary corp.
Admissions Requirements Medical examination.
Staff LPNs; Nurses' aides; Activities coordinators; Dietitians.
Facilities Dining room; Laundry room; Barber/Beauty shop.
Activities Arts & crafts; Cards; Games; Reading groups; Prayer groups; Movies; Shopping trips; Dances/Social/Cultural gatherings; Pet therapy.

Northwood
1415 N 5th St, Tacoma, WA 98403
(206) 272-1206
Admin Nola Davis.
Licensure Intermediate care. *Beds* ICF 35. *Certified* Medicaid.
Owner Privately owned (Quad Cities Healthcare Centers).

Orchard Park
4755 S 48th St, Tacoma, WA 98409
(206) 475-4611
Admin Edward C Mawe. *Dir of Nursing* Beverley Myers. *Medical Dir* James M Wilson.
Licensure Skilled care; Intermediate care; Retirement; Alzheimer's care. *Beds* SNF 39; ICF 104. *Private Pay Patients* 39%. *Certified* Medicaid; Medicare; VA.
Owner Privately owned (William Conley & William Chunyk).
Admissions Requirements Physician's request.
Staff RNs 1 (ft), 2 (pt); LPNs 15 (ft), 4 (pt); Nurses' aides 100 (ft); Physical therapists 1 (ft); Occupational therapists 1 (ft); Speech therapists 1 (ft); Activities coordinators 1 (ft); Dietitians 1 (ft); Podiatrists 1 (pt); Dentists 1 (pt).
Facilities Dining room; Physical therapy room; Activities room; Barber/Beauty shop.
Activities Arts & crafts; Cards; Games; Reading groups; Prayer groups; Movies; Dances/Social/Cultural gatherings; Intergenerational programs; Pet therapy; State & county resident council; DARE; Tours; Library books.

Park Rose Care Center
3919 S 19th, Tacoma, WA 98405
(206) 752-5677
Admin Leta Faust.
Licensure Skilled care; Intermediate care. *Beds* 85. *Certified* Medicaid; Medicare.
Owner Proprietary corp.

Parkland Care Center
321 S 116th St, Tacoma, WA 98444
(206) 537-3022
Admin William T Rowe Jr.
Medical Dir Dr Thomas Bowden.
Licensure Nursing home. *Beds* Nursing home 30.
Owner Proprietary corp.
Admissions Requirements Medical examination; Physician's request.
Staff RNs 1 (ft); LPNs 5 (pt); Nurses' aides 9 (ft), 1 (pt); Activities coordinators 1 (ft).

Facilities Dining room; Activities room; Laundry room.
Activities Arts & crafts; Cards; Games; Reading groups; Movies; Shopping trips; Dances/Social/Cultural gatherings; Church services; Special music.

Sherwood Terrace Nursing Center
2102 S 96th, Tacoma, WA 98444
(206) 582-4141
Admin Clarence Folsom.
Medical Dir George Zerr.
Licensure Skilled care; Intermediate care. *Beds* 236. *Certified* Medicaid; Medicare.
Owner Proprietary corp (PHM Health Care Group Inc).
Staff RNs; LPNs; Nurses' aides; Physical therapists; Reality therapists; Recreational therapists; Occupational therapists; Speech therapists; Activities coordinators; Dietitians; Ophthalmologists; Podiatrists; Audiologists; Dentists.
Facilities Dining room; Physical therapy room; Activities room; Chapel; Crafts room; Laundry room; Barber/Beauty shop.
Activities Arts & crafts; Cards; Games; Reading groups; Prayer groups; Movies; Shopping trips; Dances/Social/Cultural gatherings.

Tacoma Lutheran Home & Retirement Community
1301 Highlands Pkwy N, Tacoma, WA 98406
(206) 752-7112
Admin Paul M Opgrande, Pres. *Dir of Nursing* Patty White. *Medical Dir* Dr Ray Miller.
Licensure Skilled care; Intermediate care; Residential care; Alzheimer's care. *Beds* Swing beds SNF/ICF 220; Residential care 160. *Certified* Medicaid.
Owner Nonprofit organization/foundation.
Staff RNs 16 (ft), 8 (pt); LPNs 24 (ft), 9 (pt); Nurses' aides 134 (ft), 36 (pt); Physical therapists 1 (ft), 1 (pt); Occupational therapists 1 (pt); Speech therapists 1 (pt); Activities coordinators 1 (ft); Dietitians 1 (pt).
Affiliation Lutheran.
Facilities Dining room; Physical therapy room; Activities room; Chapel; Crafts room; Laundry room; Barber/Beauty shop; Library.
Activities Arts & crafts; Cards; Games; Movies; Shopping trips; Dances/Social/Cultural gatherings; Pet therapy.

Tacoma Terrace Convalescent Center
3625 E "B" St, Tacoma, WA 98404
(206) 475-2507
Admin Arnie Schoenmoser.
Medical Dir Sharon Harrison.
Licensure Skilled care; Intermediate care. *Beds* 139. *Certified* Medicaid; Medicare.
Owner Proprietary corp (Beverly Enterprises).
Admissions Requirements Medical examination; Physician's request.
Staff RNs 7 (ft); LPNs 2 (ft), 10 (pt); Dietitians 1 (pt); Ophthalmologists 1 (pt); Podiatrists 1 (pt); Dentists 1 (pt).
Facilities Dining room; Physical therapy room; Activities room; Laundry room; Barber/Beauty shop; Lounges.
Activities Arts & crafts; Cards; Games; Movies; Dances/Social/Cultural gatherings.

Tule Lake Manor
901 Tule Lake Rd, Tacoma, WA 98444
(206) 537-7887
Admin Linda Rouse.
Licensure Nursing home. *Beds* 15.
Owner Proprietary corp.
Staff LPNs 1 (ft); Nurses' aides 8 (ft).
Activities Arts & crafts; Cards; Games; Shopping trips.

Viewcrest Convalescent Center
4810 S Wilkeson St, Tacoma, WA 98408
(206) 474-0733, 473-6484 FAX

Admin Jacqueline Folsom. *Dir of Nursing* Christianne Addison. *Medical Dir* Dr Thomas Bowden.
Licensure Skilled care; Intermediate care. *Beds* Swing beds SNF/ICF 106. *Private Pay Patients* 6%. *Certified* Medicaid.
Owner Proprietary corp.
Admissions Requirements Minimum age 18; Medical examination; Physician's request.
Staff RNs 7 (ft); LPNs 8 (ft); Nurses' aides 41 (ft); Physical therapists 1 (pt); Recreational therapists 1 (ft); Occupational therapists 1 (pt); Speech therapists 1 (pt); Activities coordinators 1 (ft); Dietitians 1 (pt); Ophthalmologists 1 (pt); Audiologists 1 (pt); Dental Hygienists 1 (pt).
Facilities Dining room; Activities room; Crafts room; Laundry room; Barber/Beauty shop.
Activities Arts & crafts; Cards; Games; Reading groups; Prayer groups; Movies; Shopping trips; Dances/Social/Cultural gatherings; Pet therapy; Adopt-a-grandparent program.

Tekoa

Tekoa Care Center
Rte 1 Box 350, Tekoa, WA 99033-9712
(509) 284-4501
Admin Dorothy I Fletcher RN. *Dir of Nursing* Arlene Morgan RN. *Medical Dir* Francis Thiel MD.
Licensure Skilled care; Intermediate care; Apartments. *Beds* Swing beds SNF/ICF 71; Apts 18. *Private Pay Patients* 55%. *Certified* Medicaid.
Owner Proprietary corp.
Admissions Requirements Medical examination.
Staff Physicians 3 (pt); RNs 3 (ft), 1 (pt); LPNs 2 (ft), 2 (pt); Nurses' aides 16 (ft), 11 (pt); Physical therapists 1 (pt); Reality therapists 1 (pt); Recreational therapists 1 (pt); Occupational therapists 1 (pt); Speech therapists 1 (pt); Activities coordinators 1 (ft); Dietitians 1 (pt); Ophthalmologists 1 (pt); Podiatrists 1 (pt); Audiologists 1 (pt).
Facilities Dining room; Physical therapy room; Activities room; Chapel; Crafts room; Laundry room; Barber/Beauty shop; Family visiting rooms.
Activities Arts & crafts; Games; Reading groups; Prayer groups; Movies; Shopping trips; Dances/Social/Cultural gatherings; Ceramics.

Tonasket

North Valley Hospital
PO Box 488, 2nd & Western, Tonasket, WA 98855
(509) 486-2151
Admin Gordon McLean.
Licensure Skilled care; Intermediate care. *Beds* 70. *Certified* Medicaid.
Owner Publicly owned.

Toppenish

Valley Rehabilitation Center
PO Box 352, 802 W 3rd, Toppenish, WA 98948
(509) 865-3955, 865-3799 FAX
Admin Arnie Schoenmoser. *Dir of Nursing* Kris Schoenmoser. *Medical Dir* R O Shearer.
Licensure Skilled care. *Beds* SNF 100. *Private Pay Patients* 15%. *Certified* Medicaid; Medicare.
Owner Proprietary corp (Long Term Care Group).
Admissions Requirements Medical examination; Physician's request.

Staff RNs; LPNs; Nurses' aides; Physical therapists; Activities coordinators; Dietitians; Rehabilitation RNs.
Languages Spanish, German.
Facilities Dining room; Physical therapy room; Activities room; Crafts room; Laundry room; Barber/Beauty shop; Library; Family room.
Activities Arts & crafts; Cards; Games; Reading groups; Prayer groups; Movies; Shopping trips; Dances/Social/Cultural gatherings; Intergenerational programs; Pet therapy; Local merchants set up booths in facility for patients' holiday shopping; Family visits.

Union Gap

Parkside Nursing Care Center
308 W Emma, Union Gap, WA 98903
(509) 248-1985
Admin Clinton Neal Smith. *Dir of Nursing* Joan Funk.
Licensure Skilled care; Intermediate care. *Beds* Swing beds SNF/ICF 88. *Certified* Medicaid.
Owner Proprietary corp.
Staff RNs; LPNs; Nurses' aides; Recreational therapists; Activities coordinators; Dietitians; Ophthalmologists.
Facilities Dining room; Activities room; Crafts room; Laundry room; Barber/Beauty shop.
Activities Arts & crafts; Cards; Games; Reading groups; Prayer groups; Movies; Shopping trips; Dances/Social/Cultural gatherings.

Vancouver

Care Vista
PO Box 2462, Vancouver, WA 98668
(503) 777-5642
Admin Beverly Wilmoth.
Medical Dir Rebecca Stephens.
Licensure Intermediate care. *Beds* ICF 120. *Certified* Medicaid.
Owner Proprietary corp.
Staff Physicians 4 (pt); RNs 10 (ft), 2 (pt); LPNs 2 (ft); Nurses' aides 28 (ft); Physical therapists 1 (pt); Activities coordinators 2 (ft); Dietitians 1 (pt).
Facilities Dining room; Physical therapy room; Activities room; Crafts room; Laundry room; Barber/Beauty shop; Library.
Activities Arts & crafts; Cards; Games; Reading groups; Prayer groups; Movies; Shopping trips; Dances/Social/Cultural gatherings.

Emerald Terrace Nursing Center
1015 N Garrison Rd, Vancouver, WA 98664
(206) 694-7501
Admin James K Bennett.
Licensure Skilled care; Intermediate care. *Beds* 152. *Certified* Medicaid; Medicare.
Owner Proprietary corp (Beverly Enterprises).

Fort Vancouver Convalescent Center
804 NE 87th Ave, Vancouver, WA 98664
(206) 254-5335
Admin Steve C Jackson.
Medical Dir Dorothy Barnaby.
Licensure Skilled care; Intermediate care. *Beds* 92. *Certified* Medicaid; Medicare.
Owner Privately owned.
Admissions Requirements Physician's request.
Staff RNs; LPNs; Nurses' aides; Activities coordinators.
Facilities Dining room; Physical therapy room; Activities room; Chapel; Crafts room; Laundry room; Barber/Beauty shop.
Activities Arts & crafts; Games; Reading groups; Prayer groups; Movies; Exercises.

Hillhaven Convalescent Center
400 E 33rd St, Vancouver, WA 98663
(206) 696-2561

Admin Lennette Watson. *Dir of Nursing* Barbara Pederson. *Medical Dir* Dr Barth. *Licensure* Skilled care; Intermediate care. *Beds* 98. *Certified* Medicaid; Medicare.
Owner Proprietary corp (Hillhaven Corp).
Admissions Requirements Physician's request.
Staff RNs 10 (ft), 4 (pt); LPNs 4 (ft), 2 (pt); Nurses' aides 37 (ft), 6 (pt); Activities coordinators 1 (ft).
Facilities Dining room; Physical therapy room; Activities room; Barber/Beauty shop.

Hillhaven Nursing Home
3605 Y St, Vancouver, WA 98663
(206) 693-5839
Admin Brenda K Stewart.
Medical Dir Dr G Dean Barth.
Licensure Skilled care; Alzheimer's care. *Beds* SNF 53. *Private Pay Patients* 17%. *Certified* Medicaid; Medicare.
Owner Proprietary corp (Hillhaven Corp).
Admissions Requirements Medical examination; Physician's request.
Staff Physicians 1 (ft); RNs 6 (ft); LPNs 2 (ft); Nurses' aides 11 (ft); Physical therapists; Activities coordinators 1 (ft); Dietitians 1 (ft).
Facilities Dining room; Physical therapy room; Activities room; Crafts room; Fenced courtyard; Wanderguard alarm system.
Activities Arts & crafts; Cards; Games; Reading groups; Prayer groups; Movies; Dances/Social/Cultural gatherings; Intergenerational programs; Pet therapy.

Oregon-Washington Pythian Home
3409 Main St, Vancouver, WA 98663
(206) 696-4375
Admin David A Anderson. *Dir of Nursing* Daisy Sulit RN. *Medical Dir* Dr Dean Barth.
Licensure Skilled care; Intermediate care; Retirement. *Beds* Swing beds SNF/ICF 34; Retirement apts 166. *Private Pay Patients* 16%. *Certified* Medicaid.
Owner Nonprofit organization/foundation.
Admissions Requirements Medical examination; Physician's request.
Staff Physicians 2 (pt); RNs 2 (ft), 3 (pt); LPNs 3 (ft), 2 (pt); Nurses' aides 8 (ft), 6 (pt); Physical therapists 1 (pt); Reality therapists 1 (pt); Recreational therapists 1 (ft); Occupational therapists 1 (pt); Speech therapists 1 (pt); Activities coordinators 1 (ft); Dietitians 1 (pt).
Affiliation Knights of Pythias.
Facilities Dining room; Physical therapy room; Activities room; Chapel; Crafts room; Laundry room; Barber/Beauty shop; Library; Courtyard.
Activities Arts & crafts; Cards; Games; Reading groups; Prayer groups; Movies; Dances/Social/Cultural gatherings; Intergenerational programs; Pet therapy; Cookouts; Fashion show; Family night.

Rose Vista Nursing Center
5001 Columbia View Dr, Vancouver, WA 98661
(206) 696-0161
Admin Janice D Lehner.
Medical Dir G Dean Barth MD.
Licensure Skilled care; Intermediate care. *Beds* 210. *Certified* Medicaid; Medicare.
Owner Proprietary corp (Beverly Enterprises).
Admissions Requirements Physician's request.
Staff RNs 8 (ft), 2 (pt); LPNs 11 (ft), 3 (pt); Nurses' aides 65 (ft), 4 (pt); Activities coordinators 1 (ft).
Facilities Dining room; Physical therapy room; Activities room; Crafts room; Laundry room; Barber/Beauty shop; Library.
Activities Arts & crafts; Cards; Games; Reading groups; Prayer groups; Movies; Shopping trips; Dances/Social/Cultural gatherings.

Whispering Pines Care Center
5220 NE Hazel Dell Ave, Vancouver, WA 98663
(206) 693-1474
Admin Tom Ward.
Licensure Skilled care; Intermediate care. *Beds* 89. *Certified* Medicaid.
Owner Proprietary corp (PHM Health Care Group Inc).

Vashon Island

Island Manor Nursing Center
Rte 1 Box 20, 15401 99th Ave SW, Vashon Island, WA 98070
(206) 567-4421
Admin James Alexander. *Dir of Nursing* Mary Ruth Hughes RN. *Medical Dir* Janet Hodge MD.
Licensure Skilled care; Intermediate care; Alzheimer's care. *Beds* 52. *Certified* Medicaid.
Owner Privately owned.
Admissions Requirements Minimum age 50; Medical examination; Physician's request.
Staff RNs 4 (ft), 4 (pt); LPNs 2 (ft), 2 (pt); Nurses' aides 15 (ft), 10 (pt); Physical therapists 1 (pt); Activities coordinators 1 (ft), 2 (pt); Dietitians 1 (pt).
Facilities Dining room; Activities room; Laundry room; Barber/Beauty shop; Library; TV room.
Activities Arts & crafts; Cards; Games; Reading groups; Movies; Shopping trips; Dances/Social/Cultural gatherings.

Veradale

Rosewood Manor
4317 Ball Dr, Veradale, WA 99037-9105
(509) 326-5252
Admin Kay Corder.
Licensure Skilled care; Intermediate care. *Beds* 44. *Certified* Medicaid.
Owner Proprietary corp.

Walla Walla

Alderbrook Inn
1865 E Alder, Walla Walla, WA 99362
(509) 525-8762
Admin Rodger Wayne Schmerer. *Dir of Nursing* Deborah Townsend. *Medical Dir* John Conder.
Licensure Skilled care; Intermediate care. *Beds* Swing beds SNF/ICF 74. *Private Pay Patients* 60%. *Certified* Medicaid.
Owner Proprietary corp (North Pacific Health Services Inc).
Admissions Requirements Medical examination; Physician's request.
Staff RNs 8 (ft), 1 (pt); LPNs 2 (ft), 1 (pt); Nurses' aides 23 (ft), 7 (pt); Activities coordinators 2 (ft); Dietitians.
Languages Spanish.
Facilities Dining room; Physical therapy room; Activities room; Crafts room; Laundry room; Barber/Beauty shop.
Activities Arts & crafts; Cards; Games; Reading groups; Prayer groups; Movies; Shopping trips; Dances/Social/Cultural gatherings; Intergenerational programs; Pet therapy.

Park Manor Convalescent Center
1710 Plaza Way, Walla Walla, WA 99362
(509) 529-4218
Admin Dale Schell. *Dir of Nursing* Aileen Oye RN. *Medical Dir* Robert Candill MD.
Licensure Skilled care; Intermediate care. *Beds* 84. *Certified* Medicaid; Medicare.
Owner Proprietary corp (Hillhaven Corp).
Admissions Requirements Physician's request.

Staff RNs 5 (ft), 4 (pt); LPNs 2 (ft), 2 (pt); Nurses' aides 28 (ft), 7 (pt); Physical therapists 1 (ft); Occupational therapists 1 (pt); Speech therapists 1 (pt); Activities coordinators 2 (ft), 2 (pt); Dietitians 1 (pt).
Activities Arts & crafts; Cards; Games; Reading groups; Prayer groups; Movies.

Pleasant View Nursing Home
RR 8 Box 31, Walla Walla, WA 99362
(509) 529-1882
Admin Jerry Doctor. *Dir of Nursing* Aster Debeb.
Licensure Intermediate care. *Beds* ICF 17. *Certified* Medicaid.
Owner Privately owned.
Staff Physicians; RNs; LPNs; Nurses' aides; Dietitians.
Facilities Dining room; Activities room; Chapel; Crafts room; Laundry room; Barber/ Beauty shop.
Activities Arts & crafts; Cards; Games; Reading groups; Prayer groups; Movies; Dances/Social/Cultural gatherings.

Regency Care Walla Walla
225 Woodland Ave, Walla Walla, WA 99362
(509) 525-4480
Admin Roger A Joice.
Medical Dir Michael J Kilfoyle; Jan Schmidt.
Licensure Skilled care; Intermediate care; Alzheimer's care. *Beds* 102. *Certified* Medicaid; Medicare; VA.
Owner Proprietary corp.
Admissions Requirements Medical examination; Physician's request.
Staff Physicians 1 (pt); RNs 6 (ft), 4 (pt); LPNs 50 (ft), 5 (pt); Nurses' aides 23 (ft), 10 (pt); Physical therapists 1 (pt); Recreational therapists 1 (ft), 1 (pt); Dietitians 1 (pt).
Facilities Dining room; Physical therapy room; Activities room; Crafts room; Laundry room; Barber/Beauty shop.
Activities Arts & crafts; Cards; Games; Prayer groups; Movies; Shopping trips; Dances/ Social/Cultural gatherings; Barbeques; Picnics.

Washington Odd Fellows Home
534 Boyer Ave, Walla Walla, WA 99362
(509) 525-6463
Admin John R Brigham. *Dir of Nursing* Cecelia Liskey RN. *Medical Dir* Dr James Johnson.
Licensure Skilled care; Intermediate care; Boarding care; Independent living; Alzheimer's care. *Beds* Swing beds SNF/ICF 100; Boarding care 165; Independent living apts 33. *Private Pay Patients* 65%. *Certified* Medicaid.
Owner Nonprofit organization/foundation.
Admissions Requirements Minimum age 65; Medical examination; Physician's request.
Staff Physicians; RNs 16 (ft), 9 (pt); LPNs 1 (ft), 1 (pt); Nurses' aides 49 (ft), 7 (pt); Activities coordinators 3 (ft); Social workers 1 (ft).
Affiliation Independent Order of Odd Fellows & Rebekahs.
Facilities Dining room; Physical therapy room; Activities room; Crafts room; Laundry room; Barber/Beauty shop; Library.
Activities Arts & crafts; Cards; Games; Reading groups; Prayer groups; Movies; Shopping trips; Dances/Social/Cultural gatherings; Pet therapy.

Wapato

Emerald Circle Convalescent Center
209 N Ahtanum Ave, Wapato, WA 98951
(509) 877-3175
Admin Louis A Robert. *Dir of Nursing* Gladys Flournoy. *Medical Dir* Wallace A Donaldson.
Licensure Skilled care. *Beds* SNF 88. *Private Pay Patients* 7%. *Certified* Medicaid; Medicare.

Owner Proprietary corp.
Admissions Requirements Physician's request.
Staff RNs 4 (ft), 4 (pt); LPNs 5 (ft); Nurses' aides 32 (ft), 4 (pt); Physical therapists 1 (pt); Occupational therapists 1 (pt); Activities coordinators 1 (ft), 1 (pt); Dietitians 1 (pt); Podiatrists 1 (pt).
Languages Spanish.
Facilities Dining room; Physical therapy room; Activities room; Chapel; Crafts room; Laundry room; Barber/Beauty shop; Outdoor patios.
Activities Arts & crafts; Cards; Games; Reading groups; Prayer groups; Movies; Dances/Social/Cultural gatherings; Pet therapy.

Wenatchee

Colonial Vista Convalescent Center
625 Okanogan Ave, Wenatchee, WA 98801
(509) 663-1171
Admin Mel Everett. *Dir of Nursing* Lee Ann Matson. *Medical Dir* Dr Robert Hoxey.
Licensure Skilled care; Intermediate care; Personal care; Retirement. *Beds* Swing beds SNF/ICF 100; Personal care 48; Retirement apts 164. *Private Pay Patients* 50%. *Certified* Medicaid.
Owner Privately owned.
Admissions Requirements Medical examination; Physician's request.
Staff RNs 8 (ft), 4 (pt); LPNs 6 (ft), 2 (pt); Nurses' aides 28 (ft), 11 (pt); Physical therapists 1 (pt); Occupational therapists 1 (pt); Speech therapists 1 (pt); Activities coordinators 3 (ft); Dietitians 1 (pt); Podiatrists 2 (pt).
Languages Spanish.
Facilities Dining room; Physical therapy room; Activities room; Crafts room; Laundry room; Barber/Beauty shop; Classroom; Physicians exam room.
Activities Arts & crafts; Games; Reading groups; Movies; Shopping trips; Dances/Social/Cultural gatherings; Intergenerational programs; Pet therapy; Walking club.

Parkside Manor Convalescent Center
PO Box 2986, 1230 Monitor, Wenatchee, WA 98801
(509) 663-1628
Admin Benjamin E Colson. *Dir of Nursing* Dixie Wilkinson RN. *Medical Dir* Robert Hoxsey MD.
Licensure Skilled care; Intermediate care; Alzheimer's care. *Beds* SNF 156. *Certified* Medicaid.
Owner Privately owned.
Admissions Requirements Medical examination; Physician's request.
Staff Physicians 15 (pt); RNs 18 (ft); LPNs 10 (ft); Nurses' aides 45 (ft); Physical therapists 1 (pt); Occupational therapists 1 (pt); Speech therapists 1 (pt); Activities coordinators 3 (ft); Dietitians 1 (pt); Ophthalmologists 2 (pt); Podiatrists 1 (pt); Dentists 1 (pt).
Languages Spanish.
Facilities Dining room; Activities room; Crafts room; Laundry room; Barber/Beauty shop; Secure & protected courtyards.
Activities Arts & crafts; Cards; Games; Reading groups; Prayer groups; Movies; Shopping trips; Dances/Social/Cultural gatherings.

Woodinville

Bedford Group Home
12461 NE 173rd Pl, Woodinville, WA 98072
(206) 488-7764
Admin Steve Skeen.
Licensure Intermediate care for mentally retarded. *Beds* ICF/MR 6. *Certified* Medicaid.
Owner Nonprofit corp.

Admissions Requirements Minimum age 18; Medical examination.
Staff Physicians 1 (pt); RNs 1 (pt); Physical therapists 1 (pt); Recreational therapists 1 (pt); Occupational therapists 1 (pt); Speech therapists 1 (pt); Dietitians 1 (pt).
Facilities Dining room; Activities room; Laundry room.
Activities Arts & crafts; Cards; Games; Movies; Shopping trips; Dances/Social/Cultural gatherings.

Brookhaven Group Home
17235 126th Pl NE, Woodinville, WA 98072
(206) 488-8877
Admin Steve Skeen.
Licensure Intermediate care for mentally retarded. *Beds* ICF/MR 6. *Certified* Medicaid.
Owner Nonprofit corp.
Admissions Requirements Minimum age 18; Medical examination.
Staff Physicians 1 (pt); RNs 1 (pt); Physical therapists 1 (pt); Recreational therapists 1 (pt); Occupational therapists 1 (pt); Speech therapists 1 (pt); Dietitians 1 (pt).
Facilities Dining room; Activities room; Laundry room.
Activities Arts & crafts; Cards; Games; Movies; Shopping trips; Dances/Social/Cultural gatherings.

Woodland

Woodland Convalescent Center
PO Box 69, 310 4th St, Woodland, WA 98674
(206) 225-9443
Admin Patricia Madsen. *Dir of Nursing* Grace Horsch.
Licensure Skilled care; Intermediate care. *Beds* Swing beds SNF/ICF 62. *Certified* Medicaid; Medicare.
Owner Proprietary corp.
Admissions Requirements Medical examination; Physician's request.
Staff Physicians; RNs 8 (ft), 2 (pt); LPNs 2 (ft); Nurses' aides 27 (ft); Physical therapists (consultant); Occupational therapists (consultant); Speech therapists (consultant); Activities coordinators 1 (ft), 2 (pt); Dietitians (consultant); Podiatrists (consultant); Audiologists (consultant).
Languages Spanish by arrangement.
Facilities Dining room; Physical therapy room; Laundry room; Barber/Beauty shop; Activities and crafts room/Library.
Activities Arts & crafts; Games; Reading groups; Prayer groups; Shopping trips; Intergenerational programs; Pet therapy; Programs for disoriented patients.

Yakima

Central Convalescent
206 S 10th Ave, Yakima, WA 98902
(509) 453-4854
Admin David W Forsman.
Licensure Skilled care; Intermediate care. *Beds* 104. *Certified* Medicaid; Medicare.
Owner Nonprofit corp.

Chalet Healthcare
115 N 10th St, Yakima, WA 98901
(509) 248-4173
Admin Johnny Gross.
Licensure Skilled care; Intermediate care. *Beds* 109. *Certified* Medicaid.
Owner Proprietary corp.

Crescent Convalescent Center
505 N 40th Ave, Yakima, WA 98908
(509) 248-4446
Admin Dona George. *Dir of Nursing* Julie Barr RN. *Medical Dir* Stanley L Wilkinson MD.
Licensure Skilled care; Intermediate care. *Beds* 122. *Certified* Medicaid; Medicare; VA.

Owner Proprietary corp.
Admissions Requirements Medical examination; Physician's request.
Staff Physicians 1 (pt); RNs 10 (ft); LPNs 4 (ft); Nurses' aides 52 (ft); Physical therapists 1 (pt); Speech therapists 1 (pt); Activities coordinators 2 (ft); Dietitians 1 (pt); Rehabilitation Nurse 1 (ft).
Facilities Dining room; Physical therapy room; Activities room; Laundry room; Barber/Beauty shop; Library; Outside patios.
Activities Arts & crafts; Cards; Games; Reading groups; Movies; Shopping trips; Dances/Social/Cultural gatherings; Church services; Social outings.

Eastern Star Nursing Home Yakima
515 N 34th, Yakima, WA 98902
(509) 248-6220
Admin Richard E Exendine.
Medical Dir Molly Harrington.
Licensure Skilled care; Intermediate care. *Beds* 82. *Certified* Medicaid; Medicare.
Owner Proprietary corp.
Facilities Dining room; Physical therapy room; Activities room; Crafts room; Laundry room; Barber/Beauty shop; Library.
Activities Arts & crafts; Cards; Games; Reading groups; Prayer groups; Movies; Shopping trips; Dances/Social/Cultural gatherings.

Good Samaritan Health Care Center
702 N 16th Ave, Yakima, WA 98902
(509) 248-5320, 248-8103 FAX
Admin Richard Chasteen. *Dir of Nursing* Kathryn Armstrong. *Medical Dir* William W Robinson MD.
Licensure Skilled care; Intermediate care. *Beds* Swing beds SNF/ICF 120. *Private Pay Patients* 44%. *Certified* Medicaid; Medicare.
Owner Proprietary corp (Regency Health Care Centers Inc).
Admissions Requirements Minimum age 18; Medical examination; Physician's request.
Staff RNs 12 (ft); LPNs 6 (ft); Nurses' aides 44 (ft); Physical therapists 2 (pt); Recreational therapists 1 (pt); Occupational therapists 1 (pt); Speech therapists 1 (pt); Activities coordinators 2 (ft), 1 (pt); Dietitians 1 (pt).
Languages Spanish.
Facilities Dining room; Physical therapy room; Activities room; Laundry room; Barber/Beauty shop; Private dining room.
Activities Arts & crafts; Cards; Games; Prayer groups; Movies; Shopping trips; Intergenerational programs; Pet therapy.

Living Care Community
3905 Knobel Ave, Yakima, WA 98902
(509) 966-6240
Admin Doug Bault. *Dir of Nursing* Sherry Alexander. *Medical Dir* Dr Wilkinson.
Licensure Skilled care; Intermediate care; Retirement. *Beds* SNF 93; ICF 87; Retirement apartment 90. *Certified* Medicaid.
Owner Nonprofit organization/foundation (Living Care Centers).
Admissions Requirements Medical examination; Physician's request.
Staff RNs 13 (ft); LPNs 17 (ft); Nurses' aides 95 (ft); Physical therapists; Occupational therapists 2 (ft); Activities coordinators 4 (ft); Dietitians 1 (ft).
Languages Spanish.
Facilities Dining room; Physical therapy room; Activities room; Chapel; Crafts room; Laundry room; Barber/Beauty shop; Library; Classroom.
Activities Arts & crafts; Cards; Games; Reading groups; Prayer groups; Movies; Shopping trips; Dances/Social/Cultural gatherings; Pet therapy.

Renaissance Care Center
4007 Tieton Dr, Yakima, WA 98908
(509) 966-4500
Admin Randy Wirick. *Dir of Nursing* Carma
Dixon. *Medical Dir* William Von Stubbe
MD.
Licensure Skilled care; Intermediate care;
Residential care. *Beds* Swing beds SNF/ICF
84; Residential care 14. *Private Pay Patients*
25%. *Certified* Medicaid.
Owner Proprietary corp.
Admissions Requirements Medical
examination.
Staff Physicians 1 (pt); RNs 6 (ft); LPNs 4
(ft); Physical therapists 1 (pt); Speech
therapists 1 (pt); Activities coordinators 1
(ft); Dietitians 1 (pt); Rehabilitation nurse 1
(ft); Nursing assistants 20 (ft).
Languages Spanish, German.

Facilities Dining room; Physical therapy
room; Activities room; Laundry room;
Barber/Beauty shop; 39 private rooms.
Activities Arts & crafts; Cards; Games;
Reading groups; Prayer groups; Movies;
Shopping trips; Dances/Social/Cultural
gatherings; Intergenerational programs; Pet
therapy.

Yakima Convalescent
818 W Yakima Ave, Yakima, WA 98902
(509) 248-4104
Admin Doug Bault. *Dir of Nursing* Pauline
Groth. *Medical Dir* Stanley Wilkinson MD.
Licensure Skilled care; Intermediate care;
Retirement. *Beds* Swing beds SNF/ICF 93;
Retirement 36. *Private Pay Patients* 27%.
Certified Medicaid; Medicare.
Owner Nonprofit organization/foundation.

Admissions Requirements Medical
examination; Physician's request.
Staff RNs 8 (ft); LPNs 5 (ft); Nurses' aides 51
(ft); Physical therapists 1 (pt); Activities
coordinators 1 (ft); Dietitians 1 (ft).
Languages Spanish, German.
Facilities Dining room; Physical therapy
room; Activities room; Crafts room; Laundry
room; Barber/Beauty shop.
Activities Arts & crafts; Cards; Games;
Reading groups; Prayer groups; Movies;
Shopping trips; Dances/Social/Cultural
gatherings; Intergenerational programs; Pet
therapy.

WEST VIRGINIA

Ansted

Ansted Health Care Center
PO Drawer 400, Ansted, WV 25812
(304) 658-5271
Admin Marjorie J Tullins acting.
Licensure Intermediate care. *Beds* ICF 60.
Owner Proprietary corp (US Care Corp).

Baker

E A Hawse Continuous Care Center
PO Box 70, Baker, WV 26801-0070
(304) 897-5903, 897-5906 FAX
Admin Thomas C Wood. *Dir of Nursing*
Rebecca Grahovac RN. *Medical Dir* James
Fridley MD.
Licensure Intermediate care. *Beds* ICF 60.
Certified Medicaid.
Owner Proprietary corp (American Medical
Facilities Management Inc).
Admissions Requirements Medical
examination; Physician's request.
Staff Physicians 2 (pt); RNs 5 (ft), 1 (pt);
LPNs 4 (pt); Nurses' aides 15 (ft), 14 (pt);
Physical therapists 1 (pt); Activities
coordinators 1 (ft); Dietitians 1 (ft);
Ophthalmologists 1 (pt); Podiatrists 1 (pt);
Audiologists 1 (pt).
Facilities Dining room; Physical therapy
room; Activities room; Laundry room;
Barber/Beauty shop.
Activities Arts & crafts; Cards; Games;
Reading groups; Prayer groups; Movies;
Intergenerational programs; Pet therapy.

Beckley

**Americare Pine Lodge Nursing &
Rehabilitation Center**
405 Stanaford Rd, Beckley, WV 25801
(304) 252-6317
Admin Tammy Jo Bowen.
Medical Dir John M Daniel.
Licensure Skilled care; Intermediate care. *Beds*
Swing beds SNF/ICF 120. *Certified*
Medicaid; Medicare.
Owner Proprietary corp (Care Enterprises).
Staff Physicians 2 (ft); RNs 3 (ft); LPNs 13
(ft); Nurses' aides 40 (ft); Recreational
therapists 1 (ft); Activities coordinators 1
(ft); Dietitians 1 (ft); Ophthalmologists 1 (ft);
Dentists 1 (ft).
Facilities Dining room; Activities room;
Laundry room; Barber/Beauty shop.
Activities Arts & crafts; Games; Prayer groups;
Movies; Shopping trips.

Heartland of Beckley
300 Dry Hill Rd, Beckley, WV 25801
(304) 256-1650
Admin Rodney Dunn. *Dir of Nursing* Mary
Berry RN. *Medical Dir* Dr T Rojas.
Licensure Intermediate care. *Beds* ICF 220.
Certified Medicaid.
Owner Proprietary corp (Health Care &
Retirement Corp).

Admissions Requirements Minimum age 18;
Medical examination; Physician's request.
Staff Physicians 2 (pt); RNs 2 (ft), 1 (pt);
LPNs 14 (ft), 9 (pt); Nurses' aides 39 (ft), 15
(pt); Physical therapists 1 (pt); Activities
coordinators 2 (ft); Dietitians 1 (ft), 1 (pt);
Ophthalmologists 1 (pt); Podiatrists 1 (pt).
Facilities Dining room; Physical therapy
room; Activities room; Chapel; Crafts room;
Laundry room; Barber/Beauty shop; Library;
Patio; Landscaped grounds.
Activities Arts & crafts; Cards; Games;
Reading groups; Prayer groups; Movies;
Shopping trips; Dances/Social/Cultural
gatherings.

Belington

Barbour County Good Samaritan Center
Rte 3 Box 15C, Belington, WV 26250
(304) 823-2555
Admin Royce L Rall. *Dir of Nursing* Cheryl
Yoakum. *Medical Dir* Paul Nefflen.
Licensure Intermediate care. *Beds* ICF 60.
Private Pay Patients 29%. *Certified*
Medicaid.
Owner Nonprofit corp (Evangelical Lutheran/
Good Samaritan Society).
Admissions Requirements Medical
examination; Physician's request.
Staff RNs 4 (ft), 4 (pt); LPNs 1 (ft), 4 (pt);
Nurses' aides 14 (ft), 9 (pt); Physical
therapists; Activities coordinators 1 (ft), 1
(pt); Dietitians.
Affiliation Lutheran.
Facilities Dining room; Activities room;
Chapel; Laundry room; Barber/Beauty shop.
Activities Arts & crafts; Cards; Games; Prayer
groups; Movies; Shopping trips; Dances/
Social/Cultural gatherings.

Belmont

Care Haven of Pleasants
PO Box 625, Belmont, WV 26134
(304) 665-2065
Admin Tom Stalek.
Licensure Intermediate care. *Beds* ICF 62.

Berkeley Springs

Valley View Nursing Home
Rte 3 Box 277A, Berkeley Springs, WV 25411
(304) 258-3673
Admin John E Richards Jr.
Medical Dir Romulo J Estigoy.
Licensure Intermediate care. *Beds* ICF 122.
Staff Physicians 3 (ft); RNs 4 (ft); LPNs 9 (ft);
Nurses' aides 42 (ft), 16 (pt); Activities
coordinators 2 (ft); Ophthalmologists 1 (pt);
Podiatrists 1 (pt); Audiologists 1 (pt);
Dentists 1 (pt).
Facilities Dining room; Activities room;
Chapel; Crafts room; Laundry room; Barber/
Beauty shop; Library; Exercise room.

Activities Arts & crafts; Cards; Games;
Reading groups; Prayer groups; Movies;
Shopping trips; Dances/Social/Cultural
gatherings.

Bluefield

Cumberland Care Center Inc
Rogers & Pearis Sts, Bluefield, WV 24701
(304) 325-5448
Admin James R Wooddell.
Medical Dir David Bell.
Licensure Skilled care; Intermediate care. *Beds*
Swing beds SNF/ICF 105. *Certified*
Medicaid; Medicare.
Admissions Requirements Medical
examination.
Staff Physicians 1 (ft), 1 (pt); RNs 6 (ft), 4
(pt); LPNs 8 (ft), 1 (pt); Nurses' aides 43
(ft); Physical therapists 1 (pt); Reality
therapists 1 (pt); Recreational therapists 3
(ft); Speech therapists 1 (pt); Activities
coordinators 1 (ft); Dietitians 1 (pt);
Ophthalmologists 1 (pt); Podiatrists 1 (pt);
Dentists 1 (pt).
Facilities Dining room; Physical therapy
room; Activities room; Laundry room;
Barber/Beauty shop; Library.
Activities Arts & crafts; Cards; Games;
Reading groups; Prayer groups; Shopping
trips; Dances/Social/Cultural gatherings.

Maples Nursing Home
1600 Bland St, Bluefield, WV 24701
(304) 327-2485
Admin Sharon K Johnson. *Dir of Nursing*
Vera Tomlinson RN. *Medical Dir* John
Bryan MD.
Licensure Intermediate care. *Beds* ICF 60.
Certified Medicaid.
Owner Proprietary corp (US Care Corp).
Admissions Requirements Medical
examination; Physician's request.
Staff Physicians 1 (ft); RNs 1 (ft); LPNs 3 (ft),
1 (pt); Nurses' aides 6 (ft), 8 (pt);
Recreational therapists 1 (pt); Activities
coordinators 1 (ft); Dietitians 1 (pt);
Ophthalmologists 1 (pt); Dentists 1 (pt).
Facilities Dining room; Activities room;
Crafts room; Laundry room; Barber/Beauty
shop.
Activities Arts & crafts; Cards; Games;
Reading groups; Prayer groups; Movies;
Shopping trips; Dances/Social/Cultural
gatherings.

Bridgeport

Heritage Inc
Rte 3 Box 17, Bridgeport, WV 26330
(304) 842-4135
Admin Audrey Freeman.
Licensure Skilled care; Intermediate care. *Beds*
Swing beds SNF/ICF 51. *Certified* Medicaid.

Meadowview Manor Health Care
41 Crestview Terr, Bridgeport, WV 26330
(304) 842-7101, 842-7104 FAX

Admin Roxanne McDaniel. *Dir of Nursing* Lisa Griffith. *Medical Dir* Dr Louis F Ortenzio.
Licensure Intermediate care. *Beds* ICF 60. *Certified* Medicaid.
Owner Privately owned.
Admissions Requirements Medical examination; Physician's request.
Staff RNs 1 (ft), 3 (pt); LPNs 4 (ft), 7 (pt); Nurses' aides 15 (ft), 9 (pt); Activities coordinators 1 (ft), 1 (pt).
Languages German, Italian.
Facilities Physical therapy room; Activities room; Chapel; Crafts room; Laundry room; Barber/Beauty shop; Dining room/Chapel; Library/TV & recreation room.
Activities Arts & crafts; Cards; Games; Reading groups; Prayer groups; Movies; Shopping trips; Dances/Social/Cultural gatherings; Pet therapy.

Buckhannon

Holbrook Nursing Home Inc
346 S Florida St, Buckhannon, WV 26201
(304) 472-3280, 472-8774 FAX
Admin Bonnie L Hitt. *Dir of Nursing* Joanne Freeman. *Medical Dir* R L Chamberlain MD.
Licensure Skilled care; Intermediate care. *Beds* Swing beds SNF/ICF 120. *Private Pay Patients* 20%. *Certified* Medicaid; Medicare.
Owner Proprietary corp.
Admissions Requirements Medical examination; Physician's request.
Staff Physicians 11 (ft); RNs 6 (ft); LPNs 18 (pt); Nurses' aides 40 (ft), 10 (pt); Physical therapists 1 (pt); Speech therapists 1 (pt); Activities coordinators 1 (ft); Dietitians 1 (pt); Ophthalmologists 1 (pt); Podiatrists 1 (pt); Audiologists 1 (pt).
Facilities Dining room; Physical therapy room; Activities room; Chapel; Crafts room; Laundry room; Barber/Beauty shop; Library.
Activities Arts & crafts; Cards; Games; Reading groups; Prayer groups; Movies; Shopping trips; Dances/Social/Cultural gatherings; Intergenerational programs; Pet therapy.

Cameron

Cameron Health Care Center
PO Box 216, Cameron, WV 26033
(304) 686-3318
Admin James W Loew.
Licensure Intermediate care. *Beds* ICF 20.

McConaughey Guest Home
PO Box 56, Cameron, WV 26033
(304) 686-3644
Admin John C McConaughey.
Medical Dir Dr Meyer Sonneborn.
Licensure Intermediate care. *Beds* 19. *Certified* Medicaid.
Staff Physicians 1 (pt); RNs 1 (pt); LPNs 4 (ft); Nurses' aides 12 (ft); Activities coordinators 1 (ft); Dietitians 1 (pt); Dentists 1 (pt).
Facilities Dining room; Activities room; Laundry room.
Activities Prayer groups; Movies.

Ceredo

Aivert Nursing Home
PO Box 636, 953 Airport Rd, Ceredo, WV 25507-0636
(304) 453-1851
Admin Constance Hager.
Medical Dir W F Daniels Jr MD.
Licensure Intermediate care. *Beds* 20.
Admissions Requirements Medical examination; Physician's request.

Staff Physicians 1 (pt); RNs 1 (ft); LPNs 4 (ft); Nurses' aides 4 (ft); Recreational therapists 1 (pt); Activities coordinators 1 (pt); Dietitians 1 (pt).
Facilities Dining room; Activities room; Laundry room.
Activities Arts & crafts; Cards; Games; Reading groups; Prayer groups; Movies; Dances/Social/Cultural gatherings.

Charles Town

Jeffersonian Manor
Rte 9 Box 220, Charles Town, WV 25414
(304) 725-6575
Admin James S Hecker. *Dir of Nursing* Ellen D O'Bannon RN. *Medical Dir* Konrad Nau MD.
Licensure Intermediate care. *Beds* ICF 118. *Private Pay Patients* 40%. *Certified* Medicaid.
Owner Proprietary corp (Life Care Centers of America).
Admissions Requirements Medical examination.
Staff Physicians 1 (ft); RNs 3 (ft); LPNs 12 (ft); Nurses' aides 45 (ft); Physical therapists 1 (ft); Activities coordinators 1 (ft); Dietitians 1 (ft); Pharmacists (consultant).
Facilities Dining room; Physical therapy room; Activities room; Laundry room; Barber/Beauty shop; Library.
Activities Arts & crafts; Cards; Games; Reading groups; Prayer groups; Movies; Shopping trips; Dances/Social/Cultural gatherings; Church services.

Knott Nursing Home
115 W Congress St, Charles Town, WV 25414
(304) 725-5124
Admin Susan F Duel.
Licensure Nursing care. *Beds* Nursing care 30.

Charleston

Capital City Nursing Home
1301 Virginia St E, Charleston, WV 25301
(304) 346-5725
Admin Paul Browning.
Licensure Intermediate care. *Beds* ICF 87. *Certified* Medicaid.

Heartland of Charleston
3819 Chesterfield Ave, Charleston, WV 25304
(304) 925-4772
Admin Lynda G Kramer. *Dir of Nursing* Laurn Atkinson RN BSN. *Medical Dir* Joseph Farris MD.
Licensure Skilled care; Intermediate care. *Beds* Swing beds SNF/ICF 195. *Certified* Medicaid.
Owner Proprietary corp (Health Care & Retirement Corp).
Admissions Requirements Medical examination; Physician's request.
Staff Physicians 2 (pt); RNs 2 (ft), 1 (pt); LPNs 13 (ft), 3 (pt); Nurses' aides 46 (ft), 6 (pt); Physical therapists 1 (pt); Recreational therapists 1 (ft); Dietitians 1 (pt); Ophthalmologists 1 (pt).
Facilities Dining room; Activities room; Crafts room; Laundry room; Barber/Beauty shop.
Activities Arts & crafts; Cards; Games; Reading groups; Prayer groups; Movies; Shopping trips; Dances/Social/Cultural gatherings; Exercises.

Arthur B Hodges Center Inc
500 Morris St, Charleston, WV 25301
(304) 345-6560
Admin Diane T Gouhin. *Dir of Nursing* Joyce Durham. *Medical Dir* John W Byrd MD.
Licensure Skilled care; Intermediate care. *Beds* Swing beds SNF/ICF 120. *Private Pay Patients* 30%. *Certified* Medicaid; Medicare.
Owner Nonprofit corp.

Admissions Requirements Medical examination; Physician's request.
Staff Physicians 4 (pt); RNs 9 (ft); LPNs 16 (ft); Nurses' aides 52 (ft); Physical therapists 1 (ft); Recreational therapists 1 (ft); Occupational therapists 1 (pt); Speech therapists 1 (pt); Speech therapists 1 (pt); Activities coordinators 1 (ft); Dietitians 1 (ft); Podiatrists 1 (pt); Audiologists 1 (pt).
Languages Translators available.
Facilities Dining room; Physical therapy room; Activities room; Crafts room; Laundry room; Barber/Beauty shop; Library; Kitchen for cooking group.
Activities Arts & crafts; Cards; Games; Prayer groups; Movies; Shopping trips; Dances/Social/Cultural gatherings; Intergenerational programs; Pet therapy; Cooking group; Volunteer program.

Meadowbrook Acres
Rte 6 Box 544G, 3/4 Mile N Capitol Hwy, Charleston, WV 25311
(304) 344-4268
Admin Gwen F Ashley FACHCA. *Dir of Nursing* Judith J Wilson RN. *Medical Dir* Lester Labus MD.
Licensure Intermediate care. *Beds* ICF 60. *Private Pay Patients* 40%. *Certified* Medicaid.
Owner Proprietary corp (Nursing Care Management of America).
Admissions Requirements Medical examination; Physician's request.
Staff Physicians 1 (pt); RNs 3 (ft); LPNs 6 (ft), 3 (pt); Nurses' aides 22 (ft), 6 (pt); Physical therapists 1 (pt); Recreational therapists 1 (ft); Activities coordinators 1 (ft); Ophthalmologists 1 (pt); Podiatrists 1 (pt); Audiologists 1 (pt).
Facilities Dining room; Physical therapy room; Activities room; Crafts room; Laundry room; Barber/Beauty shop; Library; TV.
Activities Arts & crafts; Cards; Games; Reading groups; Prayer groups; Movies; Shopping trips; Dances/Social/Cultural gatherings; Pet therapy.

Chester

Fox Nursing Home Inc
RD 1 Box 2, Chester, WV 26034
(304) 387-0101
Admin James E Fox. *Dir of Nursing* Margaret Simmons RN.
Licensure Intermediate care. *Beds* ICF 60. *Certified* Medicaid.
Owner Proprietary corp.
Admissions Requirements Medical examination.
Staff RNs 4 (ft), 2 (pt); LPNs 3 (ft), 3 (pt); Nurses' aides 20 (ft), 10 (pt); Activities coordinators 1 (ft).
Facilities Dining room; Physical therapy room; Activities room; Chapel; Barber/Beauty shop.
Activities Arts & crafts; Cards; Games; Reading groups; Prayer groups; Dances/Social/Cultural gatherings; Pet therapy.

Clarksburg

Lida Clark Nursing Home
960 W Pike St, Clarksburg, WV 26301
(304) 622-2621
Admin Roxanne McDaniel.
Licensure Nursing home. *Beds* 36.

Clarksburg Continuous Care Center
Rte 5 Box 360, Clarksburg, WV 26301
(304) 624-6500
Admin Wanda Lou Rau.
Licensure Intermediate care. *Beds* ICF 90.

Heartland of Clarksburg
100 Parkway Dr, Clarksburg, WV 26301
(304) 624-6401

Admin Robert Pate.
Medical Dir Robert Hess MD.
Licensure Intermediate care. *Beds* ICF 120.
  Certified Medicaid.
Owner Proprietary corp (Health Care &
  Retirement Corp).
Admissions Requirements Medical
  examination.
Staff Physicians 10 (ft); RNs 4 (ft); LPNs 6
  (ft); Nurses' aides 100 (ft); Activities
  coordinators 1 (ft); Dietitians 1 (ft).
Facilities Dining room; Physical therapy
  room; Activities room; Crafts room; Laundry
  room; Barber/Beauty shop; Library;
  Conference room; TV Lounges.
Activities Arts & crafts; Cards; Games;
  Reading groups; Prayer groups; Movies;
  Shopping trips; Dances/Social/Cultural
  gatherings.

Cowen

Webster Continuous Care Center
PO Box 0820, Cowen, WV 26206
(304) 226-5301
Admin Mary Batton.
Licensure Intermediate care. *Beds* ICF 60.

Daniels

Care Haven of Raleigh
PO Drawer HH, Daniels, WV 25832
(304) 763-3051
Admin James O Strom.
Licensure Skilled care; Intermediate care. *Beds*
  60.

Dunbar

**Americare Dunbar Nursing & Rehabilitation
Center**
501 Caldwell Ln, Dunbar, WV 25064
(304) 744-4761
Admin Jerri Hartsock NHA. *Dir of Nursing*
  Emma Coleman RN. *Medical Dir* Dr John
  Merrifield; Dr Joseph Smith.
Licensure Skilled care; Intermediate care. *Beds*
  120. *Certified* Medicaid; Medicare.
Owner Proprietary corp (Care Enterprises).
Staff Physicians 3 (pt); RNs 4 (ft); LPNs 7
  (ft), 3 (pt); Nurses' aides 40 (ft), 9 (pt);
  Physical therapists; Speech therapists 1 (ft);
  Activities coordinators 1 (ft); Dietitians 1
  (pt); Ophthalmologists 1 (pt); Dentists 1 (pt).
Facilities Dining room; Physical therapy
  room; Activities room; Crafts room; Laundry
  room; Barber/Beauty shop; TV lounges.
Activities Arts & crafts; Games; Reading
  groups; Prayer groups; Movies; Shopping
  trips; Dances/Social/Cultural gatherings.

Elkins

Nella's Inc
PO Box 1639, Elkins, WV 26241
(304) 636-1008
Admin Thomas R Eidell.
Licensure Skilled care; Intermediate care. *Beds*
  Swing beds SNF/ICF 102. *Certified*
  Medicaid; Medicare.

Nella's Nursing Home
301 Central St, Elkins, WV 26241
(304) 636-2033
Admin Carolyn Eidell.
Medical Dir Dr Samuel J Bucher.
Licensure Intermediate care; Alzheimer's care.
  Beds ICF 84. *Certified* Medicaid.
Owner Proprietary corp.
Admissions Requirements Females only;
  Medical examination.
Staff RNs 2 (ft); LPNs 11 (ft); Nurses' aides
  38 (ft); Activities coordinators 1 (ft);
  Dietitians 1 (pt).

Facilities Dining room; Activities room;
  Chapel; Crafts room; Barber/Beauty shop.
Activities Arts & crafts; Cards; Games;
  Reading groups; Prayer groups; Movies;
  Shopping trips; Dances/Social/Cultural
  gatherings.

Ellenboro

Sheppard Health Care Inc
Star Rte 83 Box 10, Ellenboro, WV 26346
(304) 869-3344
Admin P G Sheppard NHA. *Dir of Nursing*
  Judy M Terrell RN. *Medical Dir* Asel P
  Hatfield MD.
Licensure Intermediate care. *Beds* ICF 26.
  Private Pay Patients 8-12%. *Certified*
  Medicaid.
Owner Proprietary corp.
Admissions Requirements Medical
  examination; Physician's request.
Staff Physicians 1 (pt); RNs 1 (ft), 1 (pt);
  LPNs 4 (ft); Nurses' aides 14 (ft), 2 (pt);
  Activities coordinators 1 (pt); Dietitians 1
  (pt).
Facilities Dining room; Activities room;
  Crafts room; Laundry room.
Activities Arts & crafts; Cards; Games; Prayer
  groups; Shopping trips; Dances/Social/
  Cultural gatherings; Intergenerational
  programs; Pet therapy.

Fairmont

Arbors at Fairmont
130 Kaufman Dr, Fairmont, WV 26554
(304) 363-5633
Admin Dora Grisinger.
Licensure Intermediate care. *Beds* ICF 120.
Owner Proprietary corp (Arbor Health Care).

Wishing Well Health Center
1539 Country Club Rd, Fairmont, WV 26554
(304) 366-9100
Admin Herman Haupstein.
Licensure Skilled care; Intermediate care. *Beds*
  Swing beds SNF/ICF 120. *Certified*
  Medicaid; Medicare.

Wishing Well Manor Inc
1543 Country Club Rd, Fairmont, WV 26554
(304) 363-2273
Admin George Haupstein.
Licensure Intermediate care. *Beds* ICF 60.

Fayetteville

Fayette Continuous Care Center
100 Hresan Blvd, Fayetteville, WV 25840
(304) 574-0770
Admin Darlene L Newell.
Licensure Intermediate care. *Beds* ICF 60.
  Certified Medicaid.
Owner Proprietary corp.
Admissions Requirements Medical
  examination.
Staff Physicians; RNs; LPNs; Nurses' aides;
  Physical therapists; Speech therapists;
  Activities coordinators; Dietitians; Dentists.
Facilities Dining room; Physical therapy
  room; Activities room; Crafts room; Laundry
  room; Barber/Beauty shop; Library.
Activities Arts & crafts; Cards; Games;
  Reading groups; Prayer groups; Movies.

Follansbee

Brightwood Nursing Home
840 Lee Rd, Follansbee, WV 26037
(304) 527-1100, 527-0909 FAX
Admin Winifred McCoy. *Dir of Nursing* Lisa
  Furioli. *Medical Dir* Dr Michael
  Giannamore.
Licensure Intermediate care; Adult day care.
  Beds ICF 128. *Certified* Medicaid.
Owner Proprietary corp.

Admissions Requirements Medical
  examination; Physician's request.
Staff Physicians 6 (pt); RNs 6 (ft); LPNs 14
  (ft); Nurses' aides 30 (ft); Physical therapists
  1 (pt); Speech therapists 1 (pt); Activities
  coordinators 1 (ft), 1 (pt); Dietitians 1 (ft), 1
  (pt); Ophthalmologists 1 (pt); Podiatrists 1
  (pt); Audiologists 1 (pt).
Languages Italian.
Facilities Dining room; Physical therapy
  room; Activities room; Chapel; Laundry
  room; Barber/Beauty shop; Lounges; Game
  preserve; Enclosed courtyards.
Activities Arts & crafts; Cards; Games;
  Reading groups; Prayer groups; Movies;
  Shopping trips; Dances/Social/Cultural
  gatherings; Intergenerational programs; Pet
  therapy.

Fort Ashby

Dawn View Manor
PO Box 686, Fort Ashby, WV 26719-0686
(304) 298-3602
Admin Mary E Billmyre.
Medical Dir Dr Robert R Brown.
Licensure Intermediate care. *Beds* ICF 60.
  Certified Medicaid.
Admissions Requirements Medical
  examination.
Staff RNs 2 (ft), 1 (pt); LPNs 6 (ft); Nurses'
  aides 12 (ft), 11 (pt); Activities coordinators
  1 (ft), 1 (pt).
Facilities Dining room; Physical therapy
  room; Activities room; Crafts room; Laundry
  room; Barber/Beauty shop.
Activities Arts & crafts; Cards; Games;
  Reading groups; Prayer groups; Shopping
  trips; Dances/Social/Cultural gatherings.

Franklin

Pendleton Nursing Home
PO Box 700, US 33 East, Franklin, WV 26807
(304) 358-2320
Admin Robert P Nixon. *Dir of Nursing* Ann
  M Cloud RNC. *Medical Dir* Dr H Luke Eye.
Licensure Intermediate care; Personal care;
  Independent living. *Beds* ICF 91; Personal
  care 10; Independent living apts 10. *Private
  Pay Patients* 20%. *Certified* Medicaid.
Owner Nonprofit corp (Evangelical Lutheran/
  Good Samaritan Society).
Admissions Requirements Medical
  examination.
Staff Physicians 2 (pt); Physical therapists 1
  (ft); Activities coordinators 1 (ft); Dietitians
  1 (ft).
Affiliation Evangelical Lutheran.
Facilities Dining room; Physical therapy
  room; Activities room; Chapel; Crafts room;
  Laundry room; Barber/Beauty shop.
Activities Arts & crafts; Cards; Games;
  Reading groups; Prayer groups; Movies;
  Shopping trips; Dances/Social/Cultural
  gatherings; Intergenerational programs; Pet
  therapy.

Gary

McDowell Continuous Care Center
PO Box 220, Rte 103, Gary, WV 24836
(304) 448-2121
Admin Jane Wade.
Licensure Intermediate care. *Beds* ICF 120.

Glasgow

Beverly Health Care Center
PO Box 350, Melrose Dr & US 60, Glasgow,
  WV 25086
(304) 595-1155, 949-6232 FAX
Admin Judith Diehl. *Dir of Nursing* Deborah
  Hill. *Medical Dir* Dr Mahmood Partoui.

Licensure Intermediate care. *Beds* ICF 120.
Private Pay Patients 5%.
Owner Proprietary corp (Beverly Enterprises).

Glenville

Americare Glenville Nursing & Rehabilitation Center
46 Fairground Rd, Glenville, WV 26351
(304) 462-5718
Admin David E Wilbur acting.
Licensure Intermediate care. *Beds* ICF 65.
Certified Medicaid.
Owner Proprietary corp (Care Enterprises).
Admissions Requirements Medical
examination; Physician's request.
Staff RNs 3 (ft), 2 (pt); LPNs 4 (ft), 2 (pt);
Nurses' aides 21 (ft), 6 (pt); Activities
coordinators 1 (ft).
Facilities Dining room; Physical therapy
room; Laundry room; Barber/Beauty shop.
Activities Arts & crafts; Cards; Games; Prayer
groups; Movies; Shopping trips; Dances/
Social/Cultural gatherings.

Grafton

Rosewood Health Care Center
8 Rose St, Grafton, WV 26354
(304) 265-0095, 265-0097 FAX
Admin Grace G Lewis. *Dir of Nursing* Pat
Shaw RN. *Medical Dir* David Grossman
MD.
Licensure Skilled care; Intermediate care;
Respite care; Alzheimer's care. *Beds* SNF
16; ICF 50; Respite care 3. *Private Pay
Patients* 19%. *Certified* Medicaid; Medicare.
Owner Proprietary corp (Glenmark
Associates).
Admissions Requirements Medical
examination; Physician's request.
Staff Physicians (consultant); RNs 3 (ft); LPNs
5 (ft), 2 (pt); Nurses' aides 23 (ft), 4 (pt);
Physical therapists 1 (ft); Occupational
therapists (consultant); Speech therapists
(consultant); Activities coordinators 1 (ft);
Dietitians (consultant); Ophthalmologists
(consultant); Podiatrists (consultant).
Facilities Dining room; Physical therapy
room; Activities room; Laundry room;
Barber/Beauty shop.
Activities Arts & crafts; Games; Reading
groups; Prayer groups; Movies; Shopping
trips; Dances/Social/Cultural gatherings;
Intergenerational programs; Pet therapy.

Hamlin

Lincoln Continuous Care Center
200 Monday Dr, Hamlin, WV 25523
(304) 824-3133
Admin Eric Nichols.
Licensure Intermediate care. *Beds* ICF 60.

Harrisville

Pine View Continuous Care Center
400 McKinley St, Harrisville, WV 26362
(304) 643-2712
Admin Wilma M Conaway NHA. *Dir of
Nursing* Lynda Conaway Kiek RN.
Licensure Intermediate care. *Beds* ICF 60.
Certified Medicaid.
Owner Proprietary corp.
Admissions Requirements Minimum age 40.
Staff Physicians 2 (ft); RNs 4 (ft); LPNs 12
(ft); Nurses' aides 37 (ft); Physical therapists
1 (ft); Reality therapists 1 (ft); Recreational
therapists 1 (ft); Speech therapists 1 (ft);
Activities coordinators 2 (ft); Dietitians 1
(ft).
Facilities Dining room; Physical therapy
room; Activities room; Chapel; Crafts room;
Laundry room; Barber/Beauty shop.

Activities Arts & crafts; Cards; Games;
Reading groups; Prayer groups; Movies;
Shopping trips; Dances/Social/Cultural
gatherings.

Hilltop

Hilltop Health Care Center
PO Box 125, Hilltop, WV 25855
(304) 469-2966
Admin Robert Cempella. *Dir of Nursing*
Gloria A Vest RN. *Medical Dir* D C Newell
Jr DO.
Licensure Skilled care; Intermediate care. *Beds*
Swing beds SNF/ICF 120. *Certified*
Medicaid; Medicare.
Owner Proprietary corp.
Admissions Requirements Medical
examination; Physician's request.
Staff Physicians 5 (pt); RNs 4 (ft), 1 (pt);
LPNs 12 (ft), 6 (pt); Nurses' aides 32 (ft), 11
(pt); Physical therapists 1 (pt); Speech
therapists 1 (pt); Activities coordinators 1
(ft); Dietitians 1 (pt); Ophthalmologists 1
(pt); Podiatrists 1 (pt); Dentists 1 (pt).
Facilities Dining room; Physical therapy
room; Activities room; Laundry room;
Barber/Beauty shop.
Activities Arts & crafts; Cards; Games;
Reading groups; Prayer groups; Movies;
Shopping trips; Dances/Social/Cultural
gatherings.

Hilltop Nursing Home
PO Box 207, Hilltop, WV 25855
(304) 469-2988
Admin Richard H Clelland.
Licensure Intermediate care. *Beds* 30.
Certified Medicaid.

Hinton

Summers County Continuous Care Center
PO Box 1240, Hinton, WV 25951
(304) 466-0332
Admin Linda K Turner.
Medical Dir Dr J D Woodrum.
Licensure Intermediate care. *Beds* ICF 120.
Certified Medicaid.
Owner Proprietary corp.
Admissions Requirements Minimum age 21;
Medical examination; Physician's request.
Staff Physicians 2 (pt); RNs 4 (ft), 1 (pt);
LPNs 18 (ft), 2 (pt); Nurses' aides 40 (ft), 4
(pt); Physical therapists 2 (pt); Speech
therapists 1 (pt); Activities coordinators 1
(ft); Dietitians 1 (pt); Podiatrists 1 (pt);
Dentists 1 (pt); Social workers 1 (ft).
Facilities Dining room; Physical therapy
room; Activities room; Chapel; Crafts room;
Laundry room; Barber/Beauty shop; Library.
Activities Arts & crafts; Cards; Games;
Reading groups; Prayer groups; Movies;
Shopping trips; Dances/Social/Cultural
gatherings.

Huntington

Fairhaven Rest Home
302 Adams Ave, Huntington, WV 25701
(304) 522-0032
Admin Barbara McCall.
Licensure Skilled care; Intermediate care. *Beds*
Swing beds SNF/ICF 41. *Certified* Medicaid;
Medicare.

Pinnacle Care Center Nursing & Rehabilitation
1720 17th St, Huntington, WV 25701
(304) 529-6031
Admin Carol Wellman NHA.
Licensure Skilled care; Intermediate care. *Beds*
Swing beds SNF/ICF 186. *Certified*
Medicaid; Medicare.

Pleasant View Manor
3100 Staunton Rd, Huntington, WV 25702
(304) 523-8429

Admin Mark Dillon.
Licensure Nursing home. *Beds* 34.

Presbyterian Manor
101 13th St, Huntington, WV 25716
(304) 525-7622
Admin Frank William Armstrong. *Dir of
Nursing* Joyce Seamonds RN. *Medical Dir*
Willard F Daniels MD.
Licensure Skilled care; Intermediate care. *Beds*
Swing beds SNF/ICF 120. *Certified*
Medicaid; Medicare.
Owner Nonprofit corp.
Admissions Requirements Minimum age 18;
Medical examination; Physician's request.
Staff Physicians 1 (pt); RNs 6 (ft), 1 (pt);
LPNs 10 (ft), 1 (pt); Nurses' aides 52 (ft), 3
(pt); Physical therapists 1 (pt); Speech
therapists 1 (pt); Activities coordinators 1
(ft); Dietitians 1 (pt); Social worker 1 (ft).
Affiliation Presbyterian.
Facilities Dining room; Physical therapy
room; Activities room; Chapel; Crafts room;
Laundry room; Barber/Beauty shop; Library;
Enclosed patio.
Activities Arts & crafts; Cards; Games;
Reading groups; Prayer groups; Movies;
Shopping trips; Dances/Social/Cultural
gatherings; Exercise class; Professional
entertainers.

Hurricane

Americare Putnam Nursing & Rehabilitation Center
300 Seville Rd, Hurricane, WV 25526
(304) 757-6805
Admin William Snook. *Dir of Nursing* Mary
Walker. *Medical Dir* Dr Robert Hively.
Licensure Skilled care; Intermediate care. *Beds*
Swing beds SNF/ICF 120. *Certified*
Medicaid; Medicare.
Owner Proprietary corp (Care Enterprises).
Admissions Requirements Minimum age 17;
Medical examination; Physician's request.
Staff Physicians 1 (ft); RNs 3 (ft), 3 (pt);
LPNs 7 (ft), 6 (pt); Nurses' aides 27 (ft), 26
(pt); Activities coordinators 1 (ft).
Facilities Dining room; Physical therapy
room; Activities room; Laundry room;
Barber/Beauty shop; TV room/Lounge.
Activities Arts & crafts; Cards; Games;
Reading groups; Prayer groups; Movies;
Shopping trips; Dances/Social/Cultural
gatherings.

Care Haven of Teays Valley
590 Poplar Fork Rd, Hurricane, WV 25526
(304) 757-7826
Admin David Wilbur.
Licensure Intermediate care. *Beds* ICF 94.

Jane Lew

Crestview Manor
PO Box 40, Jane Lew, WV 26378
(304) 884-7811, 884-7057 FAX
Admin Jerry Gallien. *Dir of Nursing* Sue A
Broadwater RN. *Medical Dir* Bennett D
Orvik MD.
Licensure Intermediate care. *Beds* ICF 68.
Certified Medicaid.
Owner Nonprofit corp.
Admissions Requirements Physician's request.
Staff Physicians 1 (pt); RNs 3 (ft), 2 (pt);
LPNs 5 (ft), 7 (pt); Nurses' aides 19 (ft), 12
(pt); Physical therapists 2 (pt); Speech
therapists 1 (pt); Activities coordinators 1
(ft); Dietitians 1 (pt); Ophthalmologists 1
(pt); Podiatrists 1 (pt).
Facilities Dining room; Physical therapy
room; Activities room; Chapel; Crafts room;
Laundry room; Barber/Beauty shop; Library.
Activities Arts & crafts; Cards; Games;
Reading groups; Prayer groups; Movies;
Shopping trips; Dances/Social/Cultural
gatherings.

Keyser

Heartland of Keyser
PO Box 848, 135 Southern Dr, Keyser, WV 26726
(304) 788-3415
Admin Sharon A Nicol. *Dir of Nursing* M Susan Harber. *Medical Dir* Dr Phillip Staggers.
Licensure Intermediate care. *Beds* ICF 120. *Certified* Medicaid.
Owner Proprietary corp (Health Care & Retirement Corp).
Admissions Requirements Medical examination; Physician's request.
Staff Physicians 8 (pt); RNs 7 (ft), 2 (pt); LPNs 5 (ft); Nurses' aides 39 (ft), 16 (pt); Physical therapists 1 (pt); Speech therapists 1 (pt); Activities coordinators 1 (ft); Dietitians 1 (ft); Podiatrists 1 (pt); Licensed Social worker 1 (ft).
Facilities Dining room; Physical therapy room; Activities room; Barber/Beauty shop; Nature trail.
Activities Arts & crafts; Cards; Games; Prayer groups; Movies; Dances/Social/Cultural gatherings.

Kingwood

Heartland of Preston County
300 Miller Rd, Kingwood, WV 26537
(304) 329-3195
Admin Anna R Ruckman.
Medical Dir Dr Frederick Conley; Dr Claude Shannon.
Licensure Skilled care; Intermediate care. *Beds* Swing beds SNF/ICF 120. *Certified* Medicaid; Medicare.
Owner Proprietary corp (Health Care & Retirement Corp).
Admissions Requirements Medical examination; Physician's request.
Staff Physicians 2 (pt); RNs 2 (ft), 3 (pt); LPNs 11 (ft), 1 (pt); Nurses' aides 39 (ft), 15 (pt); Physical therapists 1 (pt); Occupational therapists 1 (pt); Speech therapists 1 (pt); Activities coordinators 1 (ft); Dietitians 1 (pt).
Facilities Dining room; Physical therapy room; Activities room; Crafts room; Laundry room; Barber/Beauty shop.
Activities Arts & crafts; Cards; Games; Reading groups; Prayer groups; Movies; Shopping trips; Dances/Social/Cultural gatherings.

Lewisburg

Greenbrier Manor
Rte 2 Box 15A, Lewisburg, WV 24901
(304) 645-3076
Admin Brownie Dunn. *Dir of Nursing* Ann Canterbury. *Medical Dir* Martin Smith DO.
Licensure Intermediate care. *Beds* ICF 100. *Certified* Medicaid.
Owner Nonprofit organization/foundation.
Admissions Requirements Medical examination.
Staff Physicians 1 (pt); RNs 3 (ft); LPNs 12 (ft); Nurses' aides 42 (ft), 2 (pt); Physical therapists 2 (pt); Recreational therapists 2 (ft), 1 (pt); Speech therapists 1 (pt); Activities coordinators 1 (ft); Dietitians 1 (pt).
Facilities Dining room; Physical therapy room; Activities room; Chapel; Laundry room; Barber/Beauty shop; Outdoor deck.
Activities Arts & crafts; Games; Reading groups; Prayer groups; Movies; Shopping trips.

Lindside

Springfield Comprehensive Care Center
Rte 1 Box 101-A, Lindside, WV 24951
(304) 753-4332
Admin Kyle E Baker. *Dir of Nursing* Marrianne Blaheslee. *Medical Dir* Malcolm Harris.
Licensure Intermediate care; Alzheimer's care. *Beds* ICF 66. *Private Pay Patients* 20%. *Certified* Medicaid.
Owner Proprietary corp.
Admissions Requirements Minimum age 55; Medical examination.
Staff Physicians 3 (pt); RNs 2 (ft), 2 (pt); LPNs 5 (ft), 2 (pt); Nurses' aides 28 (ft), 6 (pt); Physical therapists 1 (pt); Occupational therapists 1 (pt); Speech therapists 1 (pt); Activities coordinators 2 (ft); Dietitians 1 (ft), 1 (pt); Ophthalmologists 1 (pt); Podiatrists 1 (pt); Audiologists 1 (pt).
Facilities Dining room; Physical therapy room; Activities room; Crafts room; Laundry room; Barber/Beauty shop; Library.
Activities Arts & crafts; Cards; Games; Reading groups; Prayer groups; Movies; Shopping trips; Pet therapy.

Logan

Logan Health Village
PO Box 540, Logan, WV 25601
(304) 752-2273
Admin Carolyn Mandala.
Licensure Intermediate care. *Beds* ICF 62.

Logan Park Care Center
PO Box 990, Logan, WV 25601
(304) 752-8724
Admin James P Martin.
Medical Dir Dr Erwin R Chillag.
Licensure Intermediate care. *Beds* ICF 120. *Certified* Medicaid.
Admissions Requirements Medical examination.
Staff Physicians 2 (pt); RNs 4 (ft); LPNs 12 (ft); Physical therapists 1 (pt); Activities coordinators 2 (ft), 1 (pt); Dietitians 1 (pt); Podiatrists 1 (pt); Dentists 1 (pt).
Facilities Dining room; Physical therapy room; Activities room; Crafts room; Laundry room; Barber/Beauty shop; Library; Resident lounges; Large visitors lounge.
Activities Arts & crafts; Cards; Games; Reading groups; Prayer groups; Movies; Shopping trips; Dances/Social/Cultural gatherings.

Marlinton

Pocahontas Continuous Care Center
RR 1, PO Box 500, Marlinton, WV 24954
(304) 799-7375
Admin Dana L Moyers. *Dir of Nursing* Susie Dolan RN. *Medical Dir* John Sharp MD.
Licensure Intermediate care; Personal care. *Beds* ICF 66; Personal care 2. *Certified* Medicaid.
Owner Proprietary corp (Glenmark Associates).
Admissions Requirements Medical examination; Physician's request.
Staff Physicians 6 (pt); RNs 4 (ft); LPNs 6 (ft); Nurses' aides 12 (ft), 10 (pt); Physical therapists 1 (pt); Reality therapists 1 (ft); Recreational therapists 1 (ft); Occupational therapists 1 (pt); Speech therapists 1 (pt); Activities coordinators 2 (pt); Dietitians 1 (ft); Podiatrists 1 (pt).
Facilities Dining room; Physical therapy room; Activities room; Chapel; Crafts room; Laundry room; Barber/Beauty shop; Library.
Activities Arts & crafts; Reading groups; Prayer groups; Movies; Shopping trips; Sing-along; Frankle exercises.

Marmet

Marmet Health Care Center
1 Sutphin Dr, Marmet, WV 25315
(304) 949-1580
Admin Bill J Crouch.
Licensure Intermediate care. *Beds* ICF 62.

Martinsburg

Care Haven of Berkeley
Rte 5 Box A-167, Martinsburg, WV 25401
(304) 263-0933
Admin Anthony J Cooper.
Licensure Intermediate care. *Beds* ICF 62.

Heartland of Martinsburg
210 Clover St, Martinsburg, WV 25401
(304) 263-8921
Admin Robert E Baer.
Medical Dir R Estgoy & R Crisp.
Licensure Skilled care; Intermediate care. *Beds* Swing beds SNF/ICF 116. *Certified* Medicaid; Medicare.
Owner Proprietary corp (Health Care & Retirement Corp).
Staff Physicians 2 (ft); RNs 8 (ft); LPNs 8 (ft); Nurses' aides 40 (ft); Physical therapists 1 (pt); Activities coordinators 1 (ft); Dietitians 1 (pt); Podiatrists 1 (pt); Dentists 1 (pt).
Facilities Dining room; Physical therapy room; Activities room; Chapel; Crafts room; Laundry room; Barber/Beauty shop.
Activities Arts & crafts; Cards; Games; Reading groups; Prayer groups; Movies; Shopping trips.

Milton

Morris Memorial Nursing & Convalescent Home
PO Box 6, Milton, WV 25541
(304) 743-6861
Admin John E Greene.
Licensure Nursing care. *Beds* Nursing care 185.

Monongah

St Barbara's Memorial Nursing Home
Off Rte 19, Maple Terrace, Lady Lane, Monongah, WV 26554
(304) 534-5220
Admin Sr Mary Stephen Reynolds PhD. *Dir of Nursing* Joyce Pellillo RN.
Licensure Skilled care; Intermediate care. *Beds* Swing beds SNF/ICF 57. *Certified* Medicaid; Medicare.
Owner Nonprofit corp.
Admissions Requirements Physician's request; Patients request.
Staff Physicians 1 (pt); RNs 4 (ft); Nurses' aides 18 (ft); Physical therapists 1 (ft), 1 (pt); Activities coordinators 1 (ft), 1 (pt); Dietitians 1 (ft), 1 (pt); Maintenance Technicians 1 (ft), 1 (pt).
Facilities Dining room; Physical therapy room; Activities room; Chapel; Barber/Beauty shop; Library.
Activities Arts & crafts; Games; Prayer groups; Movies; Dances/Social/Cultural gatherings.

Montgomery

Montgomery General Elderly Care
PO Box 1010, Montgomery, WV 25136
(304) 442-2460
Admin Bonnie S Wood.
Licensure Intermediate care. *Beds* ICF 60.

Morgantown

Americare Morgantown Nursing & Rehabilitation Center
995 Maple Dr, Morgantown, WV 26505
(304) 599-9378
Admin Mike Anderson.
Medical Dir Austin Thompson MD; Richard Emanuelson MD.
Licensure Skilled care; Intermediate care. *Beds* Swing beds SNF/ICF 111. *Certified* Medicare.
Owner Proprietary corp (Care Enterprises).
Admissions Requirements Medical examination; Physician's request.
Staff Physicians 2 (ft); RNs 3 (ft), 3 (pt); LPNs 6 (ft), 7 (pt); Nurses' aides 28 (ft), 18 (pt); Physical therapists 1 (pt); Recreational therapists 1 (ft); Occupational therapists 1 (pt); Speech therapists 1 (pt); Activities coordinators 1 (ft); Dietitians 1 (pt); Ophthalmologists 1 (pt); Podiatrists 1 (pt); Audiologists 1 (pt); Dentists 1 (pt).
Facilities Dining room; Physical therapy room; Activities room; Laundry room; Barber/Beauty shop; Library.
Activities Arts & crafts; Cards; Games; Reading groups; Prayer groups; Movies; Shopping trips; Dances/Social/Cultural gatherings.

Madison House
445 Van Voorhis Rd, Morgantown, WV 26505
(304) 598-2900
Admin Linda F Bair.
Licensure Intermediate care. *Beds* ICF 28.

Morgan Manor Convalescent Center
1379 Van Voorhis Rd, Morgantown, WV 26505
(304) 599-9480
Admin Patraicia A Daler acting.
Licensure Skilled care; Intermediate care. *Beds* Swing beds SNF/ICF 100. *Certified* Medicaid; Medicare.
Owner Proprietary corp (Beverly Enterprises).

Sundale
800 J D Anderson Dr, Morgantown, WV 26505
(304) 599-0497
Admin Sherry Rice.
Medical Dir Edwin Boso; Margaret Rog.
Licensure Skilled care; Intermediate care. *Beds* Swing beds SNF/ICF 120. *Certified* Medicaid.
Owner Nonprofit corp.
Admissions Requirements Medical examination; Physician's request.
Staff Physicians 2 (ft); RNs 2 (ft); LPNs 11 (ft), 6 (pt); Nurses' aides 23 (ft), 26 (pt); Physical therapists 1 (ft), 2 (pt); Speech therapists 3 (ft); Activities coordinators 1 (ft); Dietitians 1 (ft); Ophthalmologists 1 (pt).
Facilities Dining room; Physical therapy room; Activities room; Chapel; Crafts room; Laundry room; Barber/Beauty shop.
Activities Arts & crafts; Cards; Games; Prayer groups; Movies; Shopping trips; Dances/ Social/Cultural gatherings.

Moundsville

Mound View Health Care Center
PO Box F, Moundsville, WV 26101
(304) 843-1035
Admin Herman Conaway. *Dir of Nursing* Alma Cunningham. *Medical Dir* Dr Dolgovskij.
Licensure Skilled care; Intermediate care; Retirement; Alzheimer's care. *Beds* Swing beds SNF/ICF 174. *Certified* Medicaid; Medicare.
Owner Proprietary corp.
Admissions Requirements Minimum age 16.

Staff Physicians 1 (pt); RNs 12 (ft); LPNs 4 (ft); Nurses' aides 39 (ft); Physical therapists 1 (ft); Recreational therapists 1 (pt); Occupational therapists 1 (pt); Speech therapists 1 (pt); Activities coordinators 2 (ft); Dietitians 1 (ft); Podiatrists 1 (pt); Dentists 1 (pt).
Facilities Dining room; Physical therapy room; Activities room; Chapel; Crafts room; Laundry room; Barber/Beauty shop; Library.
Activities Arts & crafts; Cards; Games; Reading groups; Prayer groups; Movies; Shopping trips; Dances/Social/Cultural gatherings.

New Martinsville

New Martinsville Health Care Center
225 Russell Ave, New Martinsville, WV 26155-1532
(304) 455-2600, 455-2580 FAX
Admin George G Couch LNHA. *Dir of Nursing* Lameta Funari RN. *Medical Dir* Dr Robert D Morris.
Licensure Skilled care. *Beds* SNF 120. *Private Pay Patients* 25%. *Certified* Medicaid; Medicare.
Owner Proprietary corp (Mountain Care Inc).
Staff Physicians 2 (pt); RNs 12 (ft), 2 (pt); LPNs 10 (ft), 3 (pt); Nurses' aides 45 (ft), 10 (pt); Physical therapists 1 (pt); Speech therapists 1 (pt); Activities coordinators 1 (ft); Dietitians 1 (pt); Ophthalmologists 1 (pt); Podiatrists 1 (pt).
Facilities Dining room; Physical therapy room; Activities room; Crafts room; Laundry room; Barber/Beauty shop; Library; Courtyard.
Activities Arts & crafts; Cards; Games; Reading groups; Prayer groups; Movies; Dances/Social/Cultural gatherings; Intergenerational programs; Pet therapy.

New Richmond

Wyoming Continuous Care Center
PO Box 149, New Richmond, WV 24867
(304) 294-7584
Admin Paul H McNalley.
Licensure Intermediate care. *Beds* ICF 60.

Oak Hill

Hidden Valley Health Care
422 23rd St, Oak Hill, WV 25901
(304) 465-1903
Admin Evelyn Phelps.
Licensure Intermediate care. *Beds* ICF 62.

Parkersburg

Americare Arlington Nursing & Rehabilitation Center
1716 Gihon Rd, Parkersburg, WV 26101
(304) 485-5511
Admin Darlene Willis NHA.
Licensure Intermediate care. *Beds* ICF 66. *Certified* Medicaid.

Ohio Valley Health Care
Rte 5 Box 146, Parkersburg, WV 26101
(304) 485-5137
Admin Michael A Miller.
Licensure Intermediate care. *Beds* ICF 60. *Certified* Medicaid.

Parkview Healthcare Inc
1600 27th St, Parkersburg, WV 26101
(304) 485-6476
Admin Mary J Love.
Medical Dir R Biddle MD.
Licensure Skilled care; Intermediate care. *Beds* Swing beds SNF/ICF 155. *Certified* Medicare.
Owner Proprietary corp (ARA Living Centers).

Staff Physicians 3 (pt); RNs 4 (ft), 7 (pt); LPNs 7 (ft); Nurses' aides 29 (ft); Physical therapists 2 (ft); Occupational therapists 1 (pt); Speech therapists 1 (pt); Activities coordinators 2 (ft); Dietitians 1 (pt); Ophthalmologists 1 (pt); Podiatrists 2 (pt); Dentists 1 (pt).
Facilities Dining room; Physical therapy room; Activities room; Chapel; Crafts room; Laundry room; Barber/Beauty shop; Library.
Activities Arts & crafts; Cards; Games; Reading groups; Prayer groups; Movies; Shopping trips; Dances/Social/Cultural gatherings.

Willows
PO Box 3374, 723 Summers St, Parkersburg, WV 26101
(304) 428-5573
Admin A Martinez. *Dir of Nursing* P Westfall RN. *Medical Dir* B Powderly MD.
Licensure Skilled care; Intermediate care. *Beds* SNF 12; ICF 77. *Private Pay Patients* 50%. *Certified* Medicaid; Medicare.
Owner Proprietary corp (Glenmark Associates).
Admissions Requirements Minimum age 18; Medical examination.
Staff Physicians 1 (pt); RNs 4 (ft), 5 (pt); LPNs 3 (ft), 3 (pt); Nurses' aides 18 (ft), 12 (pt); Physical therapists 1 (pt); Activities coordinators 1 (ft); Dietitians 1 (ft).
Facilities Dining room; Physical therapy room; Activities room; Laundry room; Barber/Beauty shop.
Activities Arts & crafts; Cards; Games; Prayer groups; Movies; Shopping trips; Dances/ Social/Cultural gatherings.

Worthington Manor
PO Box 4010, 36th St & Core Rd, Parkersburg, WV 26104
(304) 485-7447
Admin Norma Dunn. *Dir of Nursing* Patricia Richardson RN. *Medical Dir* George McCarty MD.
Licensure Skilled care; Intermediate care. *Beds* Swing beds SNF/ICF 105. *Certified* Medicaid; Medicare.
Owner Privately owned.
Admissions Requirements Medical examination; Physician's request.
Staff Physicians 2 (pt); RNs 4 (ft), 2 (pt); LPNs 13 (ft); Nurses' aides 39 (ft), 3 (pt); Physical therapists 1 (pt); Speech therapists 2 (pt); Activities coordinators 1 (ft); Dietitians 1 (pt); Ophthalmologists 1 (pt); Dentists 1 (pt).
Facilities Dining room; Physical therapy room; Activities room; Crafts room; Laundry room; Barber/Beauty shop; Library.
Activities Arts & crafts; Cards; Games; Reading groups; Prayer groups; Movies; Shopping trips; Dances/Social/Cultural gatherings.

Petersburg

Grant County Nursing Home
27 Early Ave, Petersburg, WV 26847
(304) 257-4233
Admin Terry Shobe. *Dir of Nursing* Cynthia Kouf. *Medical Dir* Dewey Bensenhaver MD.
Licensure Intermediate care; Personal care. *Beds* ICF 110; Personal care 10. *Private Pay Patients* 18%. *Certified* Medicaid.
Owner Publicly owned.
Admissions Requirements Minimum age 18; Medical examination.
Staff Physicians 2 (pt); RNs 5 (ft), 3 (pt); LPNs 7 (ft), 8 (pt); Nurses' aides 29 (ft), 30 (pt); Physical therapists 1 (pt); Recreational therapists 1 (pt); Speech therapists 1 (pt); Activities coordinators 1 (ft); Dietitians 1 (pt); Ophthalmologists 1 (pt); Podiatrists 1 (pt); Medical records 1 (pt); Activities coordinator aides 1 (ft).

Facilities Dining room; Activities room;
Chapel; Laundry room; Barber/Beauty shop;
3 TV rooms; Patio; Courtyard with garden.
Activities Arts & crafts; Cards; Games;
Reading groups; Movies; Shopping trips;
Intergenerational programs; Pet therapy;
Weekly worship service; Bible study.

Point Pleasant

Care Haven of Point Pleasant
Rte 1 Box 326, Point Pleasant, WV 25550
(304) 675-3005
Admin Kathy Gessler.
Licensure Intermediate care. *Beds* ICF 62.

Princeton

Glenwood Park United Methodist Home
Rte 1 Box 464, Princeton, WV 24740
(304) 325-8164
Admin Daniel W Farley.
Licensure Skilled care; Intermediate care. *Beds*
Swing beds SNF/ICF 61.
Affiliation Methodist.

Princeton Health Care Center
315 Courthouse Rd, Princeton, WV 24740
(304) 487-3458
Admin Patrick A Smith. *Dir of Nursing* Diana
J Mills. *Medical Dir* Dr Charles J Mirabile.
Licensure Intermediate care; Alzheimer's care.
Beds ICF 120. *Private Pay Patients* 30%.
Certified Medicaid.
Owner Proprietary corp (Health Care &
Retirement Corp).
Admissions Requirements Medical
examination.
Staff Physicians 1 (ft); RNs 2 (ft); LPNs 13
(ft); Nurses' aides 26 (ft), 19 (pt); Physical
therapists 1 (pt); Reality therapists 1 (ft);
Recreational therapists 2 (ft); Speech
therapists 1 (pt); Activities coordinators 1
(ft); Dietitians 1 (ft); Ophthalmologists 1
(pt); Podiatrists 1 (pt); Audiologists 1 (pt).
Facilities Dining room; Physical therapy
room; Activities room; Crafts room; Laundry
room; Barber/Beauty shop.
Activities Arts & crafts; Cards; Games;
Reading groups; Prayer groups; Movies;
Shopping trips; Dances/Social/Cultural
gatherings; Intergenerational programs; Pet
therapy.

Rainelle

Heartland of Rainelle
606 Pennsylvania Ave, Rainelle, WV 25962
(304) 438-6127
Admin William Stone.
Licensure Intermediate care. *Beds* ICF 59.
Certified Medicaid.
Owner Proprietary corp (Health Care &
Retirement Corp).

Ranson

Shenandoah Home Inc
131 E 3rd St, Ranson, WV 25438
(304) 725-3404
Admin James Bryan.
Licensure Intermediate care. *Beds* ICF 48.
Certified Medicaid.

Ravenswood

Ravenswood Village Nursing Home
200 Ritchie St, Ravenswood, WV 26164
(304) 273-9385
Admin Deborah A Kelley.
Licensure Skilled care; Intermediate care. *Beds*
62.

Richwood

Nicholas County Health Care Center
18 4th St, Richwood, WV 26261
(304) 846-2668
Admin Richard A Lemons. *Dir of Nursing* Sue
Cogar RN. *Medical Dir* Clemente Diaz MD.
Licensure Intermediate care. *Beds* ICF 120.
Certified Medicaid.
Owner Proprietary corp (Unicare).
Staff Physicians 5 (pt); RNs 4 (ft), 1 (pt);
LPNs 5 (ft), 4 (pt); Nurses' aides 30 (ft), 8
(pt); Physical therapists 3 (pt); Recreational
therapists 1 (pt); Speech therapists 1 (pt);
Activities coordinators 1 (ft); Dietitians 1
(pt); Podiatrists 1 (pt).
Facilities Dining room; Physical therapy
room; Activities room; Crafts room; Laundry
room; Barber/Beauty shop.
Activities Arts & crafts; Cards; Games; Prayer
groups; Movies; Shopping trips; Dances/
Social/Cultural gatherings.

Ripley

Eldercare of West Virginia
107 Miller Dr, Ripley, WV 25271
(304) 372-5115
Admin Ken Overton.
Medical Dir Samuel Johnson MD.
Licensure Skilled care; Intermediate care. *Beds*
Swing beds SNF/ICF 120. *Certified*
Medicaid; Medicare.
Owner Proprietary corp (Beverly Enterprises).
Admissions Requirements Medical
examination.
Staff Physicians 2 (pt); RNs 6 (ft); LPNs 12
(ft); Nurses' aides 49 (ft); Physical therapists
1 (pt); Recreational therapists 1 (pt);
Activities coordinators 1 (ft); Dietitians 1
(pt); Ophthalmologists 1 (pt); Podiatrists 1
(pt); Dentists 2 (pt); Psychologists 1 (pt).
Facilities Dining room; Physical therapy
room; Activities room; Chapel; Laundry
room; Barber/Beauty shop.
Activities Arts & crafts; Games; Reading
groups; Prayer groups; Movies; Shopping
trips; Dances/Social/Cultural gatherings.

Romney

Kidwell Rest Home
550 Sioux Ln, Romney, WV 26757
(304) 822-5330
Admin Nellie Kidwell.
Licensure Intermediate care. *Beds* 18.
Certified Medicaid.

Ronceverte

Shenandoah Manor
608 Greenbrier Ave, Ronceverte, WV 24970
(304) 645-7270
Admin Melinda Utterback. *Dir of Nursing*
Sarah Hatton. *Medical Dir* Dorris Ragsdale
MD; Lynn Smith MD.
Licensure Intermediate care. *Beds* ICF 96.
Private Pay Patients 25%. *Certified*
Medicaid.
Owner Privately owned.
Admissions Requirements Medical
examination.
Staff Physicians 2 (ft), 1 (pt); RNs 3 (ft), 1
(pt); LPNs 12 (ft), 1 (pt); Nurses' aides 40
(ft); Physical therapists 1 (pt); Recreational
therapists 1 (ft); Speech therapists 1 (pt);
Activities coordinators 1 (ft); Dietitians 1
(pt); Ophthalmologists (consultant);
Podiatrists (consultant); Audiologists
(consultant).
Facilities Dining room; Physical therapy
room; Activities room; Laundry room;
Barber/Beauty shop.

Activities Arts & crafts; Cards; Games;
Reading groups; Prayer groups; Movies;
Shopping trips; Dances/Social/Cultural
gatherings; Intergenerational programs; Pet
therapy.

Saint Albans

Riverside Nursing Home
6500 MacCorkle Ave, Saint Albans, WV
25177
(304) 768-0002, 766-7916 FAX
Admin Ruth Duppee RN. *Dir of Nursing*
Deanna Pitchford RN. *Medical Dir* Donald
Klinestiver MD.
Licensure Skilled care. *Beds* SNF 98. *Private
Pay Patients* 20%. *Certified* Medicaid;
Medicare.
Owner Proprietary corp (Beverly Enterprises).
Admissions Requirements Minimum age 21;
Physician's request.
Staff Physicians 3 (pt); RNs 5 (ft), 2 (pt);
LPNs 8 (ft), 1 (pt); Nurses' aides 38 (ft), 3
(pt); Physical therapists 1 (pt); Recreational
therapists 1 (ft); Speech therapists 1 (pt);
Activities coordinators 1 (ft); Dietitians 1
(ft); Ophthalmologists 1 (pt); Podiatrists 1
(pt); Audiologists 1 (pt).
Facilities Dining room; Physical therapy
room; Activities room; Chapel; Crafts room;
Laundry room; Barber/Beauty shop.
Activities Arts & crafts; Cards; Games;
Reading groups; Prayer groups; Movies;
Shopping trips; Dances/Social/Cultural
gatherings; Intergenerational programs; Pet
therapy.

Salem

**Americare Salem Nursing & Rehabilitation
Center**
146 Water St, Salem, WV 26426
(304) 782-3000
Admin R K Cotrill.
Medical Dir Dr Arthur Calhoun; Dr Mark
Godenick; Dr Connie Godenick.
Licensure Skilled care; Intermediate care. *Beds*
SNF 28; ICF 100. *Certified* Medicaid;
Medicare.
Owner Proprietary corp (Care Enterprises).
Admissions Requirements Medical
examination.
Staff Physicians 3 (pt); RNs 4 (ft), 2 (pt);
LPNs 8 (ft), 3 (pt); Nurses' aides 35 (ft), 15
(pt); Physical therapists 1 (ft); Speech
therapists 1 (pt); Activities coordinators 1
(ft); Dietitians 1 (ft).
Facilities Dining room; Physical therapy
room; Activities room; Crafts room; Laundry
room; Barber/Beauty shop.
Activities Arts & crafts; Cards; Games;
Reading groups; Prayer groups; Movies;
Shopping trips; Dances/Social/Cultural
gatherings.

Sissonville

Cedar Ridge Health Care Center
302 Cedar Ridge Rd, Sissonville, WV 25360
(304) 984-0046
Admin Roy Drake.
Licensure Skilled care; Intermediate care. *Beds*
120.
Owner Proprietary corp (Glenmark Associates
Inc).

Sistersville

Care Haven of Sistersville
201 Wood St, Sistersville, WV 26175
(304) 652-1032
Admin Mary Ann Bowry. *Dir of Nursing*
Judith Lavelle RN. *Medical Dir* Dr Teresita
DeJosef.

Licensure Intermediate care. *Beds* ICF 62.
Private Pay Patients 10%. *Certified*
Medicaid.
Owner Proprietary corp (Glenmark Associates Inc).
Admissions Requirements Minimum age 18;
Medical examination.
Staff Physicians 1 (ft); RNs 2 (ft), 1 (pt);
LPNs 8 (ft), 2 (pt); Nurses' aides 19 (ft), 6
(pt); Physical therapists 1 (pt); Activities
coordinators 1 (ft); Dietitians 1 (pt);
Podiatrists 1 (pt); Audiologists 1 (pt).
Facilities Dining room; Physical therapy
room; Activities room; Chapel; Crafts room;
Laundry room; Barber/Beauty shop; Library;
Dayroom; TV room.
Activities Arts & crafts; Cards; Games;
Reading groups; Prayer groups; Movies;
Shopping trips; Dances/Social/Cultural
gatherings; Intergenerational programs; Pet
therapy.

South Charleston

Valley Health Village
1000 Lincoln Dr, South Charleston, WV
25309
(304) 768-4400
Admin Paula F Geer.
Licensure Skilled care; Intermediate care. *Beds*
62.

Spencer

Gordon Memorial Health Care Facility
400 Church St, Spencer, WV 25276
(304) 927-5331
Admin Marybelle Hersman.
Medical Dir H L Gamposia MD.
Licensure Intermediate care. *Beds* 66.
Certified Medicaid.
Owner Proprietary corp (Glenmark Associates Inc).
Admissions Requirements Medical
examination; Physician's request.
Staff Physicians 1 (ft), 3 (pt); RNs 2 (ft);
LPNs 6 (ft); Nurses' aides 17 (ft), 2 (pt);
Physical therapists 1 (pt); Recreational
therapists 1 (ft), 2 (pt); Occupational therapists 1
(ft), 2 (pt); Dietitians 1 (pt);
Ophthalmologists 1 (pt); Podiatrists 1 (pt);
Dentists 1 (pt).
Facilities Dining room; Activities room;
Laundry room; Barber/Beauty shop.
Activities Arts & crafts; Cards; Games;
Reading groups; Prayer groups; Movies;
Shopping trips; Dances/Social/Cultural
gatherings.

Miletree Health Care Center
825 Summit St, Spencer, WV 25276
(304) 927-1007
Admin Lawrence Kuczma.
Licensure Intermediate care. *Beds* ICF 60.

Sutton

Braxton Health Care Center
Rte 19/23, Old Dyer Rd, Sutton, WV 26601
(304) 765-2861
Admin Thelma Brydie. *Dir of Nursing* Patricia
Ridpath RN.
Licensure Intermediate care. *Beds* ICF 65.
Private Pay Patients 10%. *Certified*
Medicaid.
Owner Privately owned.
Admissions Requirements Medical
examination.
Staff Physicians; RNs; LPNs; Nurses' aides;
Physical therapists; Activities coordinators;
Dietitians.
Facilities Dining room; Physical therapy
room; Activities room; Laundry room;
Barber/Beauty shop.

Activities Arts & crafts; Cards; Games;
Reading groups; Prayer groups; Movies;
Dances/Social/Cultural gatherings;
Intergenerational programs; Pet therapy.

Thomas

Cortland Acres Nursing Home
PO Box 98, Thomas, WV 26292
(304) 463-4181
Admin Daniel Bucher. *Dir of Nursing* Anita
Flanigan RN. *Medical Dir* Samuel J Bucher
MD.
Licensure Skilled care; Intermediate care;
Independent living. *Beds* Swing beds SNF/
ICF 94; Independent living apartments 24.
Certified Medicaid; Medicare.
Owner Nonprofit corp.
Staff Physicians 6 (pt); RNs 6 (ft), 2 (pt);
LPNs 6 (ft), 5 (pt); Nurses' aides 21 (ft), 24
(pt); Physical therapists 1 (ft), 1 (pt);
Activities coordinators 1 (ft), 1 (pt);
Dietitians 1 (pt); Podiatrists 1 (pt).
Languages Polish, French.
Facilities Dining room; Physical therapy
room; Activities room; Chapel; Crafts room;
Laundry room; Barber/Beauty shop; Library;
TV.
Activities Arts & crafts; Cards; Games; Prayer
groups; Movies; Shopping trips; Pet therapy.

Wayne

Wayne Continuous Care Center
Rte 1 Box 1372, Wayne, WV 25570
(304) 697-7007
Admin W Frank Topping.
Licensure Intermediate care. *Beds* ICF 60.

Weirton

Weirton Geriatric Center
2525 Pennsylvania Ave, Weirton, WV 26062
(304) 723-4300
Admin Louis Serra. *Dir of Nursing* Nancy
Riggle RN. *Medical Dir* Antonio Licata MD.
Licensure Skilled care; Intermediate care;
Retirement. *Beds* Swing beds SNF/ICF 119.
Certified Medicaid; Medicare.
Owner Proprietary corp.
Staff Physicians 10 (pt); RNs 10 (ft), 4 (pt);
LPNs 2 (pt); Nurses' aides 55 (ft), 15 (pt);
Physical therapists 1 (pt); Speech therapists
1 (pt); Activities coordinators 1 (ft);
Dietitians 1 (pt); Ophthalmologists 1 (pt);
Podiatrists 1 (pt).
Facilities Dining room; Physical therapy
room; Activities room; Chapel; Crafts room;
Laundry room; Barber/Beauty shop.
Activities Arts & crafts; Cards; Games;
Reading groups; Prayer groups; Movies;
Shopping trips; Dances/Social/Cultural
gatherings Exercise Program.

Wellsburg

Valley Haven Geriatric Center Inc
RD 2, Box 44, Wellsburg, WV 26070
(304) 394-5322
Admin Nellie Baker. *Dir of Nursing* Judy
Sebroski. *Medical Dir* Dr Phillip Murray.
Licensure Intermediate care. *Beds* ICF 60.
Certified Medicaid.
Owner Privately owned.
Admissions Requirements Minimum age 18.
Staff Physicians 1 (pt); RNs 8 (ft), 2 (pt);
LPNs 6 (ft), 3 (pt); Nurses' aides 29 (ft), 2
(pt); Physical therapists 1 (pt); Recreational
therapists 1 (pt); Speech therapists 1 (pt);
Activities coordinators 1 (ft), 1 (pt);
Dietitians 1 (pt); Ophthalmologists 1 (pt);
Podiatrists 1 (pt); Dentists 1 (pt); Social
service 1 (ft).

Facilities Dining room; Physical therapy
room; Laundry room; Barber/Beauty shop.
Activities Arts & crafts; Cards; Games;
Reading groups; Prayer groups; Movies; Pet
therapy.

Wheeling

Good Shepherd Nursing Home
159 Edgington Blvd, Wheeling, WV 26003
(304) 242-1093
Admin Donald R Kirsch.
Medical Dir Dr John Battaglino.
Licensure Skilled care; Intermediate care. *Beds*
Swing beds SNF/ICF 192. *Certified*
Medicaid; Medicare.
Admissions Requirements Minimum age 55.
Staff RNs 4 (ft), 8 (pt); LPNs 19 (ft), 13 (pt);
Nurses' aides 63 (ft), 18 (pt); Physical
therapists 2 (pt); Speech therapists 1 (pt);
Activities coordinators 1 (ft); Dietitians 1
(pt).
Facilities Dining room; Physical therapy
room; Activities room; Chapel; Laundry
room.
Activities Arts & crafts; Cards; Games;
Reading groups; Prayer groups; Movies;
Shopping trips; Dances/Social/Cultural
gatherings.

**Bishop Joseph H Hodges Continuous Care
Center**
Medical Park, Wheeling, WV 26003
(304) 243-3800
Admin Michael Caruso. *Dir of Nursing*
Deborah Cox RN. *Medical Dir* John J
Battaglino Jr MD.
Licensure Skilled care; Intermediate care. *Beds*
SNF 60; ICF 60. *Certified* Medicaid;
Medicare.
Owner Nonprofit corp.
Admissions Requirements Physician's request.
Staff Physicians 1 (pt); RNs 10 (ft), 14 (pt);
LPNs 11 (ft), 7 (pt); Nurses' aides 26 (ft), 42
(pt); Physical therapists 1 (pt); Occupational
therapists 1 (pt); Speech therapists 1 (pt);
Activities coordinators 1 (ft); Dietitians 1
(pt); Audiologists 1 (pt).
Facilities Dining room; Physical therapy
room; Activities room; Chapel; Crafts room;
Laundry room; Barber/Beauty shop; Library.
Activities Arts & crafts; Cards; Games;
Reading groups; Prayer groups; Movies;
Shopping trips; Dances/Social/Cultural
gatherings; Intergenerational programs; Pet
therapy.

Wheeling Continuous Care Center
Medical Park, Wheeling, WV 26003
(304) 243-3800
Admin Patrick J Ward.
Licensure Skilled care; Intermediate care. *Beds*
76. *Certified* Medicaid; Medicare.

White Sulphur Springs

White Sulphur Springs Family Care Center
Box H, White Sulphur Springs, WV 24986
(304) 536-4661
Admin Dorothy N Lee ACSW NHA. *Dir of
Nursing* Shelbia H Bayne RN. *Medical Dir*
Lynn N Smith MD; Dorris A Ragsdale MD.
Licensure Skilled care; Intermediate care;
Personal care. *Beds* SNF 20; ICF 48;
Personal care 8. *Certified* Medicaid;
Medicare.
Owner Proprietary corp.
Admissions Requirements Medical
examination.
Facilities Dining room; Physical therapy
room; Activities room; Crafts room; Barber/
Beauty shop; Courtyard.
Activities Arts & crafts; Cards; Games;
Reading groups; Prayer groups; Movies;
Shopping trips; Dances/Social/Cultural

gatherings; Intergenerational programs; Pet therapy; Community service projects; Seasonal activities.

Williamson

Mingo Health Care Center Inc
Hillcrest Dr, Williamson, WV 25661
(304) 235-7005
Admin Willis M Elkins. *Dir of Nursing* Pat Harrah RN. *Medical Dir* Dr E R Chillag.

Licensure Skilled care; Intermediate care. *Beds* Swing beds SNF/ICF 120. *Certified* Medicaid; Medicare.
Owner Privately owned.
Admissions Requirements Medical examination; Physician's request.
Staff Physicians; RNs; LPNs; Nurses' aides; Physical therapists; Recreational therapists; Activities coordinators; Dietitians; Ophthalmologists; Dentists.

Facilities Dining room; Physical therapy room; Activities room; Crafts room; Laundry room; Barber/Beauty shop; Library; 3 lounges.
Activities Arts & crafts; Cards; Games; Reading groups; Prayer groups; Movies; Shopping trips; Dances/Social/Cultural gatherings.

WISCONSIN

Abbotsford

Continental Manor
600 E Elm St, Abbotsford, WI 54405
(715) 223-2359
Admin Margie Dolezel. *Dir of Nursing* Renee
Hinrichsen. *Medical Dir* Dr Paul Writz.
Licensure Skilled care. *Beds* SNF 60. *Private
Pay Patients* 25%. *Certified* Medicaid;
Medicare.
Owner Proprietary corp (Beverly Enterprises).
Admissions Requirements Medical
examination; Physician's request.
Staff RNs 3 (ft), 1 (pt); LPNs 4 (ft), 2 (pt);
Nurses' aides 15 (ft), 11 (pt); Physical
therapists; Activities coordinators 1 (ft);
Dietitians.
Facilities Dining room; Physical therapy
room; Activities room; Chapel; Laundry
room; Barber/Beauty shop.
Activities Arts & crafts; Cards; Games;
Reading groups; Dances/Social/Cultural
gatherings; Intergenerational programs; Pet
therapy.

Algoma

**Algoma Medical Center & Long-Term Care
Unit**
1510 Fremont St, Algoma, WI 54201
(414) 487-5511
Admin Mary L Dettman. *Dir of Nursing* Carol
Haasch. *Medical Dir* Jack F March MD.
Licensure Skilled care; Intermediate care;
Retirement. *Beds* Swing beds SNF/ICF 51.
Private Pay Patients 35%. *Certified*
Medicaid.
Owner Publicly owned.
Admissions Requirements Medical
examination; Physician's request.
Staff Physicians; RNs 2 (ft), 4 (pt); LPNs 2
(ft), 4 (pt); Nurses' aides 14 (ft), 11 (pt);
Physical therapists; Recreational therapists 1
(ft).
Languages Italian, German.
Facilities Dining room; Physical therapy
room; Activities room; Barber/Beauty shop;
X-ray; Laboratory.
Activities Arts & crafts; Games; Prayer groups;
Movies; Shopping trips; Pet therapy.

Altoona

Oakwood Villa
2512 New Pine Dr, Altoona, WI 54720
(715) 833-0400
Admin John C Halbleib. *Dir of Nursing*
Ronda Ziehr. *Medical Dir* Steven Cook.
Licensure Skilled care. *Beds* SNF 88. *Private
Pay Patients* 28%. *Certified* Medicaid;
Medicare.
Owner Proprietary corp (Heyde Health System
Inc).
Admissions Requirements Minimum age 18;
Medical examination; Physician's request.

Staff Physicians 1 (pt); RNs 3 (ft), 2 (pt);
LPNs 2 (ft), 4 (pt); Nurses' aides 12 (ft), 18
(pt); Physical therapists 1 (pt); Recreational
therapists 1 (ft), 3 (pt); Dietitians 1 (ft), 1
(pt).
Facilities Dining room; Physical therapy
room; Activities room; Chapel; Crafts room;
Laundry room; Barber/Beauty shop; Library.
Activities Arts & crafts; Cards; Games;
Reading groups; Prayer groups; Movies;
Shopping trips; Dances/Social/Cultural
gatherings; Intergenerational programs; Pet
therapy.

Amery

Golden Age Manor
220 Scholl St, Amery, WI 54001
(715) 268-7107
Admin Gary E Taxdahl.
Licensure Skilled care; Intermediate care. *Beds*
SNF 114. *Certified* Medicaid.
Owner Publicly owned.

Willow Ridge Inc
400 Deronda St, Amery, WI 54001
(715) 268-8171
Admin Dean H Dixon.
Medical Dir Bill Byrnes; Shannon Purinton.
Licensure Skilled care; Intermediate care. *Beds*
SNF 94. *Certified* Medicaid; Medicare.
Owner Proprietary corp.
Admissions Requirements Medical
examination.
Staff RNs 1 (ft), 3 (pt); LPNs 2 (ft), 4 (pt);
Nurses' aides 30 (ft), 14 (pt); Recreational
therapists 1 (ft); Activities coordinators 1
(ft); Dietitians 1 (pt).
Facilities Dining room; Activities room;
Laundry room; Barber/Beauty shop.
Activities Arts & crafts; Cards; Games;
Reading groups; Prayer groups; Movies;
Shopping trips; Dances/Social/Cultural
gatherings.

Antigo

Eastview Manor
729 Park St, Antigo, WI 54409
(715) 623-2356
Admin Mary Ellen Draeger.
Medical Dir John McKenna MD.
Licensure Skilled care; Intermediate care. *Beds*
SNF 173. *Certified* Medicaid.
Owner Proprietary corp (Hillhaven Corp).
Admissions Requirements Minimum age 18;
Medical examination; Physician's request.
Staff RNs 1 (ft), 12 (pt); LPNs 1 (ft), 8 (pt);
Nurses' aides 20 (ft), 47 (pt); Physical
therapists 1 (pt); Occupational therapists 1
(pt); Activities coordinators 1 (ft); Dietitians
1 (ft).
Facilities Dining room; Physical therapy
room; Activities room; Chapel; Crafts room;
Laundry room; Barber/Beauty shop.

Activities Arts & crafts; Cards; Games;
Reading groups; Prayer groups; Movies;
Shopping trips; Dances/Social/Cultural
gatherings.

Appleton

Americana Health Care Center
1335 S Oneida St, Appleton, WI 54915
(414) 731-6646
Admin Mary Sue Taylor. *Dir of Nursing* Jeff
Vander Venter. *Medical Dir* William Hale
MD.
Licensure Skilled care. *Beds* SNF 104.
Certified Medicaid; Medicare.
Owner Proprietary corp (Manor Care).
Admissions Requirements Medical
examination; Physician's request.
Staff Physicians 1 (pt); RNs 3 (ft), 3 (pt);
LPNs 2 (ft), 10 (pt); Nurses' aides 15 (ft), 32
(pt); Physical therapists 1 (pt); Recreational
therapists 1 (ft); Occupational therapists 1
(pt); Speech therapists 1 (pt); Dietitians 1
(pt); Ophthalmologists 1 (pt).
Facilities Dining room; Physical therapy
room; Activities room; Crafts room; Laundry
room; Barber/Beauty shop; Library.
Activities Arts & crafts; Cards; Games;
Reading groups; Prayer groups; Movies;
Shopping trips; Dances/Social/Cultural
gatherings; Community involvement.

Colony Oaks Care Center
601 Briarcliff Dr, Appleton, WI 54915
(414) 739-4466
Admin Mark Strautman.
Licensure Skilled care. *Beds* SNF 102.
Certified Medicaid; Medicare.
Owner Proprietary corp (Hillhaven Corp).

Franciscan Care Center Inc
2915 N Meade St, Appleton, WI 54911
(414) 731-3184
Admin Kathryn H Arthur.
Licensure Skilled care; Intermediate care. *Beds*
SNF 235. *Certified* Medicaid.
Owner Proprietary corp.

Outagamie County Health Center
3400 W Brewster St, Appleton, WI 54914-
1699
(414) 832-5400, 832-5416 FAX
Admin David Rothmann. *Dir of Nursing* John
Weyers RN. *Medical Dir* Dr Alan Laird.
Licensure Skilled care; Intermediate care;
Intermediate care for mentally retarded;
Alzheimer's care; Adult day care. *Beds* ICF/
MR 45; Swing beds SNF/ICF 211. *Private
Pay Patients* 5%. *Certified* Medicaid.
Owner Publicly owned.
Admissions Requirements Minimum age 18;
Medical examination; Physician's request.
Staff Physicians 24 (pt); RNs 16 (ft), 6 (pt);
LPNs 11 (ft), 11 (pt); Nurses' aides 45 (ft),
81 (pt); Physical therapists 1 (pt);
Occupational therapists 1 (ft), 1 (pt);
Activities coordinators 1 (ft); Dietitians 1
(pt); Dentists 2 (pt).

Facilities Dining room; Physical therapy room; Activities room; Chapel; Crafts room; Barber/Beauty shop; Library.
Activities Arts & crafts; Cards; Games; Reading groups; Prayer groups; Movies; Shopping trips; Dances/Social/Cultural gatherings; Intergenerational programs; Pet therapy.

Peabody Manor Inc
720 W 5th St, Appleton, WI 54914
(414) 733-3724
Admin Robert J Bastian.
Licensure Skilled care. Beds SNF 80.
Owner Nonprofit corp.

Arcadia

St Joseph Nursing Home
464 S Saint Joseph Ave, Arcadia, WI 54612
(608) 323-3341
Admin Bruce E Roesler.
Licensure Skilled care; Intermediate care. Beds SNF 75. Certified Medicaid.
Owner Nonprofit corp.

Arpin

Bethel Living Center
8014 Bethel Rd, Arpin, WI 54410
(715) 652-2103
Admin Walter A Schroeder. Dir of Nursing Linda Skilton. Medical Dir Robert Phillips MD.
Licensure Skilled care; Alzheimer's care. Beds SNF 111. Certified Medicaid; Medicare.
Owner Proprietary corp.
Admissions Requirements Minimum age 18; Medical examination; Physician's request.
Staff RNs 4 (ft), 4 (pt); LPNs 4 (ft), 4 (pt); Nurses' aides 30 (ft), 30 (pt); Physical therapists 1 (pt); Activities coordinators 1 (ft); Dietitians 1 (pt).
Affiliation Seventh-Day Adventist.
Facilities Dining room; Physical therapy room; Activities room; Chapel; Crafts room; Laundry room; Barber/Beauty shop; Library; Gym.
Activities Arts & crafts; Cards; Games; Reading groups; Prayer groups; Movies; Shopping trips; Dances/Social/Cultural gatherings; Bus rides.

Ashland

Ashland Health Care Center Inc
1319 Beaser Ave, Ashland, WI 54806
(715) 682-3468
Admin Richard R Andersen. Dir of Nursing Janet Bresette RN. Medical Dir Joseph M Jauquet MD.
Licensure Skilled care. Beds SNF 144. Certified Medicaid; Medicare.
Owner Privately owned.
Admissions Requirements Medical examination; Physician's request.
Staff RNs 6 (ft), 9 (pt); LPNs 7 (ft), 11 (pt); Nurses' aides 20 (ft), 32 (pt); Physical therapists 1 (pt); Activities coordinators 2 (ft), 1 (pt); Dietitians 1 (pt).
Languages German, Finnish, Swedish.
Facilities Dining room; Physical therapy room; Activities room; Chapel; Crafts room; Laundry room; Barber/Beauty shop; Physicians exam room; 15-passenger van with hydraulic wheelchar lift.
Activities Arts & crafts; Cards; Games; Reading groups; Prayer groups; Movies; Shopping trips; Dances/Social/Cultural gatherings; Religious services.

Court Manor
911 W 3rd St, Ashland, WI 54608
(715) 682-8172
Admin Roy T Shoemaker. Dir of Nursing Nancy Bissell RN. Medical Dir Joseph M Jauquet MD.

Licensure Skilled care. Beds SNF 150. Certified Medicaid; Medicare; VA.
Owner Proprietary corp (Beverly Enterprises).
Admissions Requirements Minimum age 18; Medical examination.
Staff Physicians 25 (pt); RNs 4 (ft), 5 (pt); LPNs 12 (ft), 3 (pt); Nurses' aides 48 (ft), 18 (pt); Physical therapists 1 (pt); Recreational therapists 2 (ft), 1 (pt); Speech therapists 1 (pt); Activities coordinators 1 (ft); Dietitians 1 (pt); Ophthalmologists 4 (pt); Podiatrists 1 (pt).
Languages German, Finnish, Swedish, Norwegian.
Facilities Dining room; Physical therapy room; Activities room; Chapel; Crafts room; Barber/Beauty shop; Library; Van.
Activities Arts & crafts; Cards; Games; Reading groups; Prayer groups; Movies; Shopping trips; Dances/Social/Cultural gatherings; Pet therapy.

Augusta

Augusta Nursing Home
619 Hudson, Augusta, WI 54722
(715) 286-2266
Admin Joyce Richards. Dir of Nursing Linda Kaurick.
Licensure Intermediate care. Beds ICF 62. Private Pay Patients 30%. Certified Medicaid.
Owner Nonprofit corp.
Admissions Requirements Minimum age 18; Medical examination; Physician's request.
Staff RNs 1 (ft), 4 (pt); LPNs 4 (pt); Nurses' aides 4 (ft), 16 (pt); Activities coordinators 1 (ft), 1 (pt).
Facilities Dining room; Activities room; Chapel; Laundry room; Barber/Beauty shop.
Activities Arts & crafts; Cards; Games; Reading groups; Prayer groups; Movies; Shopping trips; Dances/Social/Cultural gatherings; Intergenerational programs; Pet therapy.

Baldwin

Baldwin Care Center
640 Elm St, Baldwin, WI 54002
(715) 684-3231
Admin Eileen M Nowak. Dir of Nursing Tina McLeod RN. Medical Dir Dr Leonard B Torkelson.
Licensure Skilled care; Intermediate care; Retirement. Beds Swing beds SNF/ICF 76; Retirement apts 13. Private Pay Patients 40%. Certified Medicaid.
Owner Publicly owned.
Admissions Requirements Minimum age 18; Medical examination.
Staff Physicians (consultant); RNs 1 (ft), 1 (pt); LPNs 3 (ft), 4 (pt); Nurses' aides 16 (ft), 14 (pt); Physical therapists (consultant); Recreational therapists (consultant); Occupational therapists (consultant); Speech therapists (consultant); Activities coordinators 1 (ft); Dietitians (consultant); Podiatrists (consultant); Audiologists (consultant).
Facilities Dining room; Physical therapy room; Activities room; Laundry room; Barber/Beauty shop.
Activities Arts & crafts; Cards; Games; Reading groups; Prayer groups; Movies; Shopping trips; Dances/Social/Cultural gatherings; Intergenerational programs.

Baraboo

Jefferson Meadows Care Center
1414 Jefferson St, Baraboo, WI 53913
(608) 356-4838
Admin Craig Ubbelohde. Dir of Nursing Rita Miller RN. Medical Dir John J Siebert MD.

Licensure Skilled care; Retirement. Beds SNF 102. Certified Medicaid; Medicare.
Owner Nonprofit corp.
Admissions Requirements Minimum age 18; Medical examination; Physician's request.
Staff Physicians 1 (pt); RNs 2 (ft), 10 (pt); LPNs 1 (ft), 7 (pt); Nurses' aides 7 (ft), 45 (pt); Physical therapists 1 (pt); Reality therapists 1 (pt); Recreational therapists 4 (pt); Occupational therapists 1 (pt); Speech therapists 1 (pt); Activities coordinators 1 (pt); Dietitians 1 (pt); Podiatrists 1 (pt).
Facilities Dining room; Physical therapy room; Activities room; Laundry room; Barber/Beauty shop; Ice cream parlor.
Activities Arts & crafts; Cards; Games; Movies; Shopping trips; Dances/Social/Cultural gatherings.

Barron

Barron Memorial Medical Center Skilled Nursing Facility
1222 E Woodland Ave, Barron, WI 54812
(715) 537-3186
Admin Gerald C Olson.
Medical Dir Dr Michael Damroth.
Licensure Skilled care; Retirement; Alzheimer's care. Beds SNF 50. Certified Medicaid.
Owner Nonprofit corp.
Admissions Requirements Medical examination; Physician's request.
Staff Physicians 10 (pt); RNs 4 (ft); LPNs 4 (ft); Nurses' aides 18 (ft), 6 (pt); Physical therapists 1 (pt); Occupational therapists 1 (pt); Speech therapists 1 (pt); Activities coordinators 1 (ft); Dietitians 1 (pt); Ophthalmologists 1 (pt).
Languages Spanish.
Facilities Dining room; Physical therapy room; Activities room; Chapel; Crafts room; Barber/Beauty shop; Library.
Activities Arts & crafts; Cards; Games; Reading groups; Prayer groups; Movies; Shopping trips; Dances/Social/Cultural gatherings; Fishing; Family picnics; Pets day.

Barron Riverside Manor
660 E Birch Ave, Barron, WI 54812
(715) 537-5643
Admin Cora M Ayers. Dir of Nursing Phoebe Vik. Medical Dir J R Hoefert MD.
Licensure Skilled care; Alzheimer's care. Beds SNF 50. Certified Medicaid.
Owner Nonprofit corp.
Admissions Requirements Minimum age 18; Medical examination; Physician's request.
Staff RNs 2 (ft), 2 (pt); LPNs 2 (ft), 2 (pt); Nurses' aides 6 (ft), 16 (pt); Physical therapists 1 (pt); Recreational therapists 1 (pt); Occupational therapists 1 (pt); Speech therapists 1 (pt); Activities coordinators 1 (ft); Dietitians 1 (pt).
Facilities Dining room; Physical therapy room; Activities room; Crafts room; Laundry room; Barber/Beauty shop.
Activities Arts & crafts; Cards; Games; Reading groups; Prayer groups; Movies; Shopping trips; Dances/Social/Cultural gatherings; Gardening.

Beaver Dam

Beaver Dam Care Center
PO Box 617, 410 Roedl Ct, Beaver Dam, WI 53916
(414) 887-7191
Admin Richard F Rexrode Jr. Dir of Nursing Jessica Benlke RN. Medical Dir Fred Karsten MD.
Licensure Skilled care. Beds SNF 130. Private Pay Patients 35%. Certified Medicaid; Medicare.
Owner Proprietary corp (Beverly Enterprises).
Admissions Requirements Minimum age 18; Medical examination; Physician's request.

Staff RNs 6 (ft), 4 (pt); LPNs 9 (ft), 5 (pt); Nurses' aides 39 (ft), 14 (pt); Physical therapists; Activities coordinators 1 (ft); Dietitians 1 (ft).
Facilities Dining room; Physical therapy room; Activities room; Chapel; Crafts room; Laundry room; Barber/Beauty shop.
Activities Arts & crafts; Cards; Games; Reading groups; Prayer groups; Movies; Shopping trips; Dances/Social/Cultural gatherings; Intergenerational programs; Pet therapy.

Beaver Dam Lakeview Unit
208 Lacrosse St, Beaver Dam, WI 53916
(414) 887-7181
Admin Judson R Schultz.
Licensure Skilled care. *Beds* SNF 123. *Certified* Medicaid.
Owner Nonprofit corp.

Beloit

Beloit Convalescent Center
1905 W Hart Rd, Beloit, WI 53511
(608) 365-2554
Admin Darlene Sanchez.
Medical Dir Dr James Long.
Licensure Skilled care. *Beds* SNF 156. *Certified* Medicaid; Medicare.
Owner Proprietary corp (Unicare).
Admissions Requirements Medical examination.
Facilities Dining room; Physical therapy room; Activities room; Chapel; Crafts room; Laundry room; Barber/Beauty shop.
Activities Arts & crafts; Cards; Games; Reading groups; Prayer groups; Movies; Shopping trips; Dances/Social/Cultural gatherings.

Caravilla
PO Box 75, Beloit, WI 53511
(608) 365-8877
Admin Catherine H (Betty) Smith. *Dir of Nursing* Carol Cuff RN. *Medical Dir* James Miller MD.
Licensure Skilled care; Retirement; Alzheimer's care. *Beds* SNF 328; Retirement 76 ; Alzheimer's care. *Private Pay Patients* 32%. *Certified* Medicaid; Medicare.
Owner Proprietary corp.
Admissions Requirements Minimum age 18.
Staff Physicians; RNs 16 (ft); LPNs 20 (ft); Nurses' aides 120 (ft); Physical therapists 1 (ft); Recreational therapists 1 (ft); Occupational therapists 1 (pt); Speech therapists 1 (pt); Dietitians 1 (ft); Podiatrists 1 (pt).
Facilities Dining room; Physical therapy room; Activities room; Chapel; Crafts room; Laundry room; Barber/Beauty shop; Library.
Activities Arts & crafts; Cards; Games; Reading groups; Prayer groups; Movies; Shopping trips; Dances/Social/Cultural gatherings; Intergenerational programs; Pet therapy.

Carlyle
2121 Pioneer Dr, Beloit, WI 53511
(608) 365-9526
Admin Patricia Murphy. *Dir of Nursing* Sherri Mills. *Medical Dir* Dr Ram Das.
Licensure Skilled care; Alzheimer's care. *Beds* SNF 262. *Private Pay Patients* 12%. *Certified* Medicaid; Medicare.
Owner Proprietary corp (Wis-Care Inc).
Admissions Requirements Minimum age 18; Medical examination; Physician's request.
Staff RNs 10 (ft), 11 (pt); LPNs 4 (ft), 8 (pt); Nurses' aides 26 (ft), 33 (pt); Activities coordinators 1 (ft); Dietitians.
Facilities Dining room; Physical therapy room; Activities room; Laundry room; Barber/Beauty shop; Library.

Activities Arts & crafts; Cards; Games; Reading groups; Prayer groups; Movies; Shopping trips; Dances/Social/Cultural gatherings; Intergenerational programs; Pet therapy; Bowling; Boat rides; Baseball games.

NCF Eastridge House
2009 E Ridge Rd, Beloit, WI 53511
(608) 365-4511
Admin Nancy Fennema.
Licensure Intermediate care. *Beds* 4. *Certified* Medicaid.
Owner Nonprofit corp.

Berlin

Juliette Manor
169 E Huron St, Berlin, WI 54923
(414) 361-3092
Admin Miriam G Ownby.
Medical Dir William Piotrowski MD.
Licensure Skilled care; Intermediate care. *Beds* SNF 102. *Certified* Medicaid; Medicare.
Owner Nonprofit corp.
Admissions Requirements Medical examination; Physician's request.
Facilities Dining room; Physical therapy room; Activities room; Chapel; Crafts room; Laundry room; Barber/Beauty shop; Cocktail lounge.
Activities Arts & crafts; Cards; Games; Prayer groups; Movies; Shopping trips; Dances/Social/Cultural gatherings; Current events group.

Black Earth

Black Earth Manor
634 Center St, Black Earth, WI 53515
(608) 767-2572
Admin Mary E Reines.
Medical Dir Dr Gerald Kempthorne.
Licensure Intermediate care. *Beds* ICF 32. *Certified* Medicaid.
Owner Nonprofit corp (Good Shepherd Health Fac).
Admissions Requirements Minimum age 18; Medical examination; Physician's request.
Staff RNs 1 (ft), 2 (pt); LPNs 3 (pt); Nurses' aides 13 (pt); Activities coordinators 1 (pt); Dietitians 1 (pt).
Facilities Dining room; Several multipurpose lounge areas.
Activities Arts & crafts; Cards; Games; Reading groups; Prayer groups; Movies; Shopping trips; Dances/Social/Cultural gatherings; Outings & trips.

Black River Falls

Family Heritage Nursing Home
1311 Tyler St, Black River Falls, WI 54615
(715) 284-4396, 284-9580 FAX
Admin Charlotte Moore. *Dir of Nursing* LuAnne Flick. *Medical Dir* Dr Eugene Krohn.
Licensure Skilled care. *Beds* SNF 156. *Private Pay Patients* 20%. *Certified* Medicaid; Medicare.
Owner Proprietary corp (Health Enterprises of America).
Admissions Requirements Minimum age 18; Medical examination; Physician's request.
Staff RNs 2 (ft), 1 (pt); LPNs 3 (ft), 4 (pt); Nurses' aides 23 (ft), 16 (pt); Physical therapists 4 (pt); Recreational therapists 1 (ft), 1 (pt); Occupational therapists 3 (pt); Speech therapists 1 (pt); Activities coordinators 1 (ft); Dietitians 1 (pt).
Facilities Dining room; Physical therapy room; Activities room; Chapel; Crafts room; Laundry room; Barber/Beauty shop; Library; Meeting rooms.

Activities Arts & crafts; Cards; Games; Reading groups; Prayer groups; Movies; Shopping trips; Dances/Social/Cultural gatherings; Intergenerational programs; Pet therapy.

Pine View Nursing Home
400 Pine View Rd, Black River Falls, WI 54601
(715) 284-5396
Admin Flora G Nay. *Dir of Nursing* Diane Vlach. *Medical Dir* Gary Peterson.
Licensure Skilled care; Retirement. *Beds* SNF 141; Retirement 36. *Private Pay Patients* 48%. *Certified* Medicaid; Medicare.
Owner Publicly owned.
Admissions Requirements Minimum age 18.
Staff Physicians (contracted); RNs 5 (ft), 6 (pt); LPNs 2 (ft), 5 (pt); Nurses' aides 35 (ft), 25 (pt); Physical therapists 1 (pt); Recreational therapists 1 (ft); Occupational therapists 1 (pt); Speech therapists 1 (pt); Activities coordinators 1 (ft); Dietitians 1 (pt); HK, Laundry, Maintenance, Clerical 35 (ft), 17 (pt); Pharmacists 1 (pt).
Languages German, Spanish, Norwegian, Winnebago (Native American), Sign.
Facilities Dining room; Physical therapy room; Activities room; Crafts room; Laundry room; Barber/Beauty shop; TV lounges; Pool room.
Activities Arts & crafts; Cards; Games; Reading groups; Prayer groups; Movies; Shopping trips; Dances/Social/Cultural gatherings; Intergenerational programs; Exercises; Picnics; Outdoor walks; Wildlife watching; Gardening.

Blackwell

Nu-Roc Nursing Home
PO Laona, Blackwell, WI 54541
(715) 674-4477
Admin Craig R Newton.
Licensure Skilled care. *Beds* SNF 61.

Blair

Grand View Care Center Inc
PO Box 27, 620 Grand View Ave, Blair, WI 54616
(608) 989-2511
Admin Michael O Kittleson. *Dir of Nursing* Sandra Erickson RN.
Licensure Skilled care; Intermediate care. *Beds* SNF 101. *Certified* Medicaid.
Owner Nonprofit corp.
Admissions Requirements Medical examination.
Staff Physicians 2 (pt); RNs 3 (ft), 6 (pt); LPNs 1 (ft), 4 (pt); Nurses' aides 7 (ft), 46 (pt); Physical therapists 1 (pt); Recreational therapists 1 (ft), 1 (pt); Dietitians 1 (pt).
Facilities Dining room; Physical therapy room; Activities room; Crafts room; Laundry room; Barber/Beauty shop; Library.
Activities Arts & crafts; Cards; Games; Reading groups; Prayer groups; Movies; Shopping trips; Dances/Social/Cultural gatherings; Music.

Bloomer

Eagleton Nursing Home FDD
Rte 3, Bloomer, WI 54724
(715) 288-6311, 723-9341 FAX
Admin Thomas G Spagnoletti. *Dir of Nursing* Helen Tenley RN. *Medical Dir* John Layer MD.
Licensure Intermediate care for mentally retarded. *Beds* ICF/MR 28. *Private Pay Patients* 0%. *Certified* Medicaid.
Owner Proprietary corp.
Admissions Requirements Physician's request.

Staff Physicians 6 (pt); RNs 1 (ft), 2 (pt); LPNs 1 (ft), 2 (pt); Nurses' aides 6 (ft), 12 (pt); Physical therapists (contracted); Recreational therapists 1 (ft); Occupational therapists 1 (ft); Speech therapists (contracted); Activities coordinators 2 (pt); Dietitians (consultant).
Facilities Dining room; Activities room; Crafts room; Laundry room.
Activities Arts & crafts; Cards; Games; Reading groups; Prayer groups; Movies; Shopping trips; Dances/Social/Cultural gatherings; Intergenerational programs; Pet therapy.

Hetzel Care Center Inc
PO Box 227, 1840 Priddy St, Bloomer, WI 54724-0227
(715) 568-2503
Admin Gordon P Hetzel. *Dir of Nursing* Carol J Hable RN. *Medical Dir* M W Asplund MD.
Licensure Skilled care; Residential care. *Beds* SNF 31; Residential care 15. *Private Pay Patients* 40%. *Certified* Medicaid.
Owner Proprietary corp.
Admissions Requirements Minimum age 18; Medical examination; Physician's request.
Staff RNs 1 (ft), 4 (pt); LPNs 1 (ft), 1 (pt); Nurses' aides 5 (ft), 6 (pt); Activities coordinators 2 (pt).
Facilities Dining room; Physical therapy room; Activities room; Chapel; Crafts room; Laundry room; Barber/Beauty shop.
Activities Arts & crafts; Cards; Games; Reading groups; Prayer groups; Movies; Dances/Social/Cultural gatherings; Intergenerational programs.

Maple Wood Nursing Home
1501 Thompson Ave, Bloomer, WI 54724
(715) 568-2000
Admin Rae Kennedy. *Dir of Nursing* M D Crisp. *Medical Dir* R E Gladitsch MD.
Licensure Skilled care; Intermediate care; Retirement. *Beds* Swing beds SNF/ICF 75; Retirement 24. *Certified* Medicaid.
Owner Nonprofit organization/foundation.
Admissions Requirements Medical examination; Physician's request.
Staff Physicians 1 (pt); RNs 4 (ft), 1 (pt); LPNs 3 (ft), 3 (pt); Nurses' aides 16 (ft), 16 (pt); Physical therapists 1 (ft); Recreational therapists 2 (ft); Dietitians 1 (ft).
Facilities Dining room; Physical therapy room; Activities room; Crafts room; Laundry room; Barber/Beauty shop.
Activities Arts & crafts; Cards; Games; Reading groups; Prayer groups; Movies; Shopping trips; Dances/Social/Cultural gatherings; Intergenerational programs; Pet therapy.

Boscobel

Memorial Nursing Home of Boscobel
205 Parker St, Boscobel, WI 53805
(608) 375-4104
Admin Cathleen Connelly. *Dir of Nursing* Bonnie Qualey. *Medical Dir* Dr William Fast.
Licensure Skilled care; Intermediate care; Respite care. *Beds* Swing beds SNF/ICF 88. *Private Pay Patients* 26%. *Certified* Medicaid; Medicare.
Owner Nonprofit organization/foundation.
Admissions Requirements Medical examination; Physician's request.
Staff RNs; LPNs; Nurses' aides; Physical therapists 1 (ft); Recreational therapists 1 (ft); Speech therapists 1 (pt); Dietitians 1 (pt); Podiatrists 1 (pt); Audiologists 1 (pt).
Facilities Dining room; Physical therapy room; Activities room; Chapel; Crafts room; Barber/Beauty shop; Van.

Activities Arts & crafts; Cards; Games; Reading groups; Prayer groups; Movies; Shopping trips; Dances/Social/Cultural gatherings.

Brookfield

Congregational Home Inc
13900 W Burleigh Rd, Brookfield, WI 53005
(414) 781-0550
Admin Robert G Hankins. *Dir of Nursing* Nancy M Tabor. *Medical Dir* Dr Nicholas Owen.
Licensure Skilled care; Retirement. *Beds* SNF 88.
Owner Nonprofit corp.
Admissions Requirements Minimum age 18; Medical examination.
Staff Physicians 1 (pt); RNs 5 (ft), 11 (pt); LPNs 2 (ft), 11 (pt); Nurses' aides 11 (ft), 14 (pt); Physical therapists 1 (pt); Occupational therapists 1 (ft); Activities coordinators 1 (pt); Dietitians 1 (pt).
Affiliation Congregational.
Facilities Dining room; Physical therapy room; Activities room; Chapel; Crafts room; Laundry room; Barber/Beauty shop; Library.
Activities Arts & crafts; Cards; Games; Reading groups; Prayer groups; Movies; Shopping trips; Dances/Social/Cultural gatherings.

St Elizabeth Nursing Home
745 N Brookfield Rd, Brookfield, WI 53005
(414) 782-8118
Admin Mother Mary Rita Amrhein. *Dir of Nursing* Sr Angela Myers. *Medical Dir* Dr Thomas Mallory.
Licensure Intermediate care. *Beds* ICF 16. *Private Pay Patients* 100%.
Owner Nonprofit organization/foundation.
Admissions Requirements Minimum age 18; Females only; Medical examination; Physician's request.
Staff Physicians 1 (pt); RNs 1 (ft), 1 (pt); LPNs 1 (ft); Nurses' aides 4 (ft), 2 (pt); Physical therapists; Activities coordinators 1 (pt); Dietitians 1 (pt); Ophthalmologists; Podiatrists; Audiologists (consultant).
Languages German.
Affiliation Roman Catholic.
Facilities Activities room; Chapel; Solarium; Parlor.
Activities Cards; Games; Reading groups; Prayer groups; Movies; Dances/Social/Cultural gatherings; Intergenerational programs; One-to-one interaction.

Woodland Health Center
18740 W Bluemound Rd, Brookfield, WI 53005
(414) 782-0230, 782-9318 FAX
Admin Mark W Lawrence. *Dir of Nursing* Susie Jackson. *Medical Dir* James D Gardner.
Licensure Skilled care; Alzheimer's care. *Beds* SNF 226. *Private Pay Patients* 50%. *Certified* Medicaid; Medicare.
Owner Proprietary corp (American Medical Services).
Admissions Requirements Medical examination; Physician's request.
Staff Physicians 35 (pt); RNs 10 (ft), 5 (pt); LPNs 26 (ft), 10 (pt); Nurses' aides 60 (ft), 30 (pt); Physical therapists 1 (ft); Recreational therapists 5 (ft); Occupational therapists 1 (ft); Speech therapists 1 (pt); Activities coordinators 1 (ft); Dietitians 1 (pt).
Languages Spanish, German, Polish, French.
Facilities Dining room; Physical therapy room; Activities room; Chapel; Crafts room; Laundry room; Barber/Beauty shop; Library; Occupational therapy room; Music room; Nature trail.

Activities Arts & crafts; Cards; Games; Reading groups; Prayer groups; Movies; Shopping trips; Dances/Social/Cultural gatherings; Intergenerational programs; Pet therapy; Exercise groups.

Burlington

Mt Carmel Care Center
677 E State St, Burlington, WI 53105
(414) 763-9531
Admin Thomas W Polakowski. *Dir of Nursing* Ken Koth RN. *Medical Dir* R C Wheaton MD.
Licensure Skilled care; Intermediate care. *Beds* SNF 105. *Private Pay Patients* 65%. *Certified* Medicaid.
Owner Proprietary corp (Hillhaven Corp).
Staff Physicians 1 (pt); RNs 2 (ft); LPNs 4 (ft); Nurses' aides 8 (ft); Recreational therapists 1 (ft); Occupational therapists 1 (pt); Speech therapists 1 (pt); Activities coordinators 1 (ft); Dietitians 1 (ft).
Facilities Dining room; Physical therapy room; Activities room; Chapel; Crafts room; Laundry room; Barber/Beauty shop.
Activities Arts & crafts; Cards; Games; Reading groups; Prayer groups; Movies; Shopping trips; Dances/Social/Cultural gatherings; Annual resident senior pro.

Cedarburg

Lasata
W 76 N 677 Wauwatosa Rd, Cedarburg, WI 53012
(414) 377-5060
Admin Ralph G Luedtke. *Dir of Nursing* Marjorie Leach. *Medical Dir* Dr Celestino Perez.
Licensure Skilled care; Retirement; Alzheimer's care. *Beds* SNF 204. *Certified* Medicaid; Medicare.
Owner Publicly owned.
Admissions Requirements Minimum age 18; Medical examination.
Staff Physicians 1 (pt); RNs 17 (ft), 16 (pt); LPNs 6 (ft), 5 (pt); Nurses' aides 42 (ft), 35 (pt); Physical therapists 2 (ft); Occupational therapists 2 (ft); Speech therapists 1 (ft); Activities coordinators 1 (ft); Dietitians 1 (pt).
Facilities Dining room; Physical therapy room; Activities room; Chapel; Crafts room; Laundry room; Barber/Beauty shop; Library.
Activities Arts & crafts; Cards; Games; Reading groups; Prayer groups; Movies; Shopping trips; Dances/Social/Cultural gatherings.

Centuria

Centuria Care Center
300 Michigan Ave, Centuria, WI 54824
(715) 646-2010
Admin Darlene R Romportl. *Dir of Nursing* Wanda E Nelson. *Medical Dir* Dr Michael Schmidt.
Licensure Intermediate care. *Beds* ICF 41. *Private Pay Patients* 27%. *Certified* Medicaid.
Owner Proprietary corp (Malban Inc).
Admissions Requirements Medical examination.
Staff Physicians 1 (pt); RNs 1 (ft), 2 (pt); LPNs 2 (ft), 1 (pt); Nurses' aides 3 (ft), 10 (pt); Physical therapists (consultant); Activities coordinators 1 (pt); Dietitians (consultant).
Facilities Dining room; Chapel; Crafts room; Laundry room.
Activities Arts & crafts; Cards; Games; Reading groups; Movies; Shopping trips; Dances/Social/Cultural gatherings; Pet therapy.

Chetek

Knapp Haven
725 Knapp St, Chetek, WI 54728
(715) 924-4891
Admin Fred Schlosser, Jr. *Dir of Nursing*
Mary Huset. *Medical Dir* Howard Thalacker
MD.
Licensure Skilled care; Intermediate care;
Alzheimer's care. *Beds* SNF 99. *Certified*
Medicaid.
Owner Publicly owned.
Admissions Requirements Minimum age 18;
Medical examination; Physician's request.
Staff RNs 3 (ft), 7 (pt); LPNs 1 (ft), 5 (pt);
Nurses' aides 15 (ft), 38 (pt); Physical
therapists 1 (pt); Reality therapists 1 (pt);
Recreational therapists 1 (ft); Occupational
therapists 1 (pt); Speech therapists 1 (pt);
Activities coordinators 1 (pt); Dietitians 1
(pt).
Facilities Dining room; Physical therapy
room; Activities room; Chapel; Crafts room;
Laundry room; Barber/Beauty shop; Library.
Activities Arts & crafts; Cards; Games;
Reading groups; Prayer groups; Movies;
Shopping trips; Dances/Social/Cultural
gatherings.

Chilton

Chilton Village
810 Memorial Dr, Chilton, WI 53014
(414) 849-2308
Admin Wayne Weinschenk. *Dir of Nursing*
Dawn Holsen.
Licensure Skilled care. *Beds* SNF 106.
Certified Medicaid; Medicare.
Owner Proprietary corp (Beverly Enterprises).
Admissions Requirements Minimum age 18;
Physician's request.
Staff RNs 5 (ft); LPNs 9 (ft), 3 (pt); Nurses'
aides 39 (ft), 31 (pt); Physical therapists 1
(pt); Recreational therapists 1 (ft), 3 (pt);
Occupational therapists 1 (pt); Speech
therapists 1 (pt); Activities coordinators 1
(ft); Dietitians 1 (ft); Ophthalmologists 1
(pt); Podiatrists 1 (pt); Dentists 1 (pt).
Languages German.
Facilities Dining room; Physical therapy
room; Activities room; Chapel; Crafts room;
Laundry room; Barber/Beauty shop; Library.
Activities Arts & crafts; Cards; Games;
Reading groups; Prayer groups; Movies;
Shopping trips; Dances/Social/Cultural
gatherings.

Chippewa Falls

Chippewa Manor Nursing Home
222 Chapman Rd, Chippewa Falls, WI 54729
(715) 723-4437
Admin Karen Davis. *Dir of Nursing* Nancy L
Hanson. *Medical Dir* Robert L Hendrickson
MD.
Licensure Skilled care. *Beds* SNF 90. *Certified*
Medicaid.
Owner Privately owned.
Admissions Requirements Minimum age 18;
Medical examination; Physician's request.
Staff RNs 4 (ft), 5 (pt); Physical therapists 1
(pt); Activities coordinators 1 (ft), 1 (pt);
Dietitians 1 (pt); Chaplain 1 (ft).
Facilities Dining room; Physical therapy
room; Activities room; Chapel; Crafts room;
Laundry room; Barber/Beauty shop; Library.
Activities Arts & crafts; Cards; Games;
Reading groups; Prayer groups; Movies;
Shopping trips; Dances/Social/Cultural
gatherings.

Heyde Health System Inc
2821 County Trunk I, Chippewa Falls, WI
54729
(715) 723-9341
Admin Martin C Metten. *Dir of Nursing* Lois
Peloquin. *Medical Dir* John H Layer MD.

Licensure Skilled care; Alzheimer's units;
Hospice. *Beds* SNF 353; Alzheimer's units 3;
Hospice 4. *Private Pay Patients* 21%.
Certified Medicaid; Medicare.
Owner Proprietary corp (Heyde Health System
Inc).
Admissions Requirements Minimum age 18;
Medical examination; Physician's request.
Staff RNs 7 (ft), 17 (pt); LPNs 14 (ft), 13 (pt);
Nurses' aides 51 (ft), 110 (pt); Physical
therapists; Activities coordinators 1 (ft);
Dietitians 1 (ft).
Facilities Dining room; Physical therapy
room; Activities room; Chapel; Crafts room;
Laundry room; Barber/Beauty shop; Library;
Ventilator unit.
Activities Arts & crafts; Cards; Games;
Reading groups; Prayer groups; Movies;
Shopping trips; Dances/Social/Cultural
gatherings; Intergenerational programs; Pet
therapy.

Hannah M Rutledge Home for the Aged
300 Bridgewater Ave, Chippewa Falls, WI
54729
(715) 723-5566
Admin Mary Beth McLaughlin. *Dir of Nursing*
Carol Schaefer. *Medical Dir* Dr Steven
Paulson.
Licensure Skilled care. *Beds* SNF 100. *Private
Pay Patients* 50%. *Certified* Medicaid.
Owner Nonprofit organization/foundation.
Admissions Requirements Minimum age 65.
Staff RNs 3 (ft), 3 (pt); LPNs 6 (ft), 2 (pt);
Nurses' aides 28 (ft), 2 (pt); Activities
coordinators 1 (ft); Dietitians 1 (pt).
Facilities Dining room; Activities room;
Laundry room; Barber/Beauty shop.
Activities Arts & crafts; Cards; Games;
Reading groups; Prayer groups; Movies;
Shopping trips; Pet therapy.

Clinton

Clinton Meadows Park Nursing Home
PO Box 309, Clinton, WI 53525
(608) 676-2202
Admin David D Mickelson. *Dir of Nursing*
JoAnn Shibley RN. *Medical Dir* Dr James P
Long.
Licensure Skilled care; Alzheimer's care. *Beds*
SNF 99. *Certified* Medicaid.
Owner Proprietary corp.
Admissions Requirements Minimum age 18;
Medical examination; Physician's request.
Staff RNs 5 (ft), 3 (pt); LPNs 2 (ft), 5 (pt);
Nurses' aides 15 (ft), 30 (pt); Physical
therapists 1 (ft); Activities coordinators 1
(ft), 2 (pt); Dietitians 1 (ft).
Facilities Dining room; Physical therapy
room; Activities room; Chapel; Crafts room;
Laundry room; Barber/Beauty shop; Library.
Activities Arts & crafts; Cards; Games;
Reading groups; Prayer groups; Movies;
Shopping trips; Dances/Social/Cultural
gatherings.

Clintonville

Behling Memorial Home Inc
38 N Main St, Clintonville, WI 54929
(715) 823-3121, ext 276
Admin Andrew V Lagatta. *Dir of Nursing*
Sonya Adams RN. *Medical Dir* Cynthia
Egan MD.
Licensure Skilled care. *Beds* SNF 26. *Private
Pay Patients* 100%.
Owner Proprietary corp.
Admissions Requirements Medical
examination; Physician's request.
Staff Physicians 5 (ft); RNs 2 (ft), 1 (pt);
LPNs 3 (ft); Nurses' aides 10 (ft), 5 (pt);
Physical therapists 1 (pt); Activities
coordinators 1 (ft); Dietitians 1 (pt).

Facilities Dining room; Activities room;
Chapel; Barber/Beauty shop.
Activities Arts & crafts; Cards; Games;
Reading groups; Prayer groups; Movies;
Shopping trips; Dances/Social/Cultural
gatherings; Intergenerational programs; Pet
therapy.

Greentree Health Care Center
70 Greentree Rd, Clintonville, WI 54929
(715) 823-2194, 823-1306 FAX
Admin John Simonson. *Dir of Nursing*
Frances Heise. *Medical Dir* Dr Cynthia
Egan.
Licensure Skilled care. *Beds* SNF 78. *Certified*
Medicaid; Medicare.
Owner Proprietary corp (American Medical
Services Inc).
Admissions Requirements Minimum age 18;
Medical examination; Physician's request.
Staff Physicians 7 (pt); RNs 3 (ft), 2 (pt);
LPNs 4 (ft), 1 (pt); Nurses' aides 20 (ft);
Physical therapists; Recreational therapists 2
(ft), 4 (pt); Activities coordinators 1 (ft);
Dietitians 1 (ft).
Facilities Dining room; Physical therapy
room; Activities room; Chapel; Crafts room;
Barber/Beauty shop.
Activities Arts & crafts; Cards; Games;
Reading groups; Prayer groups; Movies;
Shopping trips; Dances/Social/Cultural
gatherings; Intergenerational programs.

Pine Manor Health Care Center
PO Box 30, Clintonville, WI 54929
(715) 823-3135, 823-1313 FAX
Admin Mathew J Oreskovich. *Dir of Nursing*
Mary Schlender. *Medical Dir* Dr T Thomas.
Licensure Skilled care; Intermediate care;
Intermediate care for mentally retarded.
Beds ICF/MR 26; Swing beds SNF/ICF 95.
Private Pay Patients 8%. *Certified* Medicaid.
Owner Proprietary corp (American Medical
Services Inc).
Admissions Requirements Medical
examination; Physician's request.
Staff Physicians (attending); RNs 5 (ft), 2 (pt);
LPNs 4 (ft), 3 (pt); Nurses' aides 28 (ft), 13
(pt); Physical therapists 1 (pt); Recreational
therapists 4 (pt); Occupational therapists 2
(pt); Speech therapists 1 (pt); Activities
coordinators 2 (pt); Dietitians 1 (pt).
Facilities Dining room; Physical therapy
room; Activities room; Chapel; Crafts room;
Laundry room; Barber/Beauty shop.
Activities Arts & crafts; Cards; Games;
Reading groups; Prayer groups; Movies;
Shopping trips; Dances/Social/Cultural
gatherings; Intergenerational programs; Pet
therapy.

Colby

Colonial House Living Center
702 W Dolf St, Colby, WI 54421
(715) 223-2352
Admin Paul E Kenyon. *Dir of Nursing* Sharon
Groschwitz. *Medical Dir* D Pfefferkorn.
Licensure Skilled care. *Beds* SNF 95. *Certified*
Medicaid; Medicare.
Owner Nonprofit corp (Adventist Health Sys-
USA).
Admissions Requirements Minimum age 18;
Medical examination; Physician's request.
Staff RNs 5 (ft), 3 (pt); LPNs 2 (ft), 2 (pt);
Nurses' aides 25 (ft), 14 (pt); Activities
coordinators 1 (ft); Dietitians 1 (ft).
Languages German.
Affiliation Seventh-Day Adventist.
Facilities Dining room; Physical therapy
room; Activities room; Chapel; Crafts room;
Laundry room; Barber/Beauty shop; Library.
Activities Arts & crafts; Cards; Games;
Reading groups; Prayer groups; Movies;
Shopping trips; Dances/Social/Cultural
gatherings; Fishing; Bingo.

Colfax

Area Nursing Home Inc
PO Box 515, Colfax, WI 54730
(715) 962-3186
Admin Jon A Suckow. *Dir of Nursing* Jean Fox. *Medical Dir* P Schleifer.
Licensure Skilled care. *Beds* SNF 97. *Certified* Medicaid.
Owner Proprietary corp.
Admissions Requirements Minimum age 18; Medical examination; Physician's request.
Staff Physicians 1 (pt); RNs 6 (ft); LPNs 7 (ft); Nurses' aides 30 (ft), 22 (pt); Physical therapists 1 (pt); Recreational therapists 2 (ft); Occupational therapists 1 (pt); Activities coordinators 1 (ft); Dietitians 1 (pt); Podiatrists.
Facilities Dining room; Physical therapy room; Activities room; Chapel; Crafts room; Laundry room; Barber/Beauty shop.
Activities Arts & crafts; Cards; Games; Reading groups; Prayer groups; Movies; Shopping trips; Dances/Social/Cultural gatherings.

Columbus

Columbus Care Center
825 Western Ave, Columbus, WI 53925
(414) 623-2520
Admin Darlene Thompson.
Licensure Skilled care. *Beds* SNF 99. *Certified* Medicaid.
Owner Proprietary corp (Hillhaven Corp).
Admissions Requirements Minimum age 18; Medical examination; Physician's request.
Facilities Dining room; Physical therapy room; Activities room; Chapel; Crafts room; Laundry room; Barber/Beauty shop.
Activities Arts & crafts; Cards; Games; Reading groups; Prayer groups; Movies; Shopping trips; Dances/Social/Cultural gatherings.

Cornell

Cornell Area Care Center Inc
PO Box 125, Cornell, WI 54732
(715) 239-6288
Admin Kenneth L Tayler.
Medical Dir Robert L Henrickson MD.
Licensure Skilled care. *Beds* SNF 50. *Certified* Medicaid.
Owner Proprietary corp.
Admissions Requirements Medical examination; Physician's request.
Facilities Dining room; Physical therapy room; Activities room; Chapel; Crafts room; Laundry room; Barber/Beauty shop.
Activities Arts & crafts; Cards; Games; Reading groups; Prayer groups; Movies; Shopping trips; Dances/Social/Cultural gatherings.

Crandon

Crandon Health Care Center Inc
PO Box 366, Crandon, WI 54520
(715) 478-3325
Admin Phillip J Orlenko.
Medical Dir Daniel Johnson MD.
Licensure Skilled care; Intermediate care. *Beds* 111. *Certified* Medicaid.
Owner Proprietary corp.
Staff RNs 4 (ft); LPNs 8 (ft); Nurses' aides 20 (ft), 5 (pt); Physical therapists 1 (pt); Occupational therapists 1 (pt); Activities coordinators 1 (ft); Dietitians 1 (pt).
Facilities Dining room; Physical therapy room; Activities room; Chapel; Crafts room; Laundry room; Barber/Beauty shop.
Activities Arts & crafts; Cards; Games; Movies; Shopping trips; Dances/Social/ Cultural gatherings.

Crandon Nursing Home
105 W Pioneer Ave, Crandon, WI 54520
(715) 478-3324
Admin Kathy Krause Palmer.
Licensure Skilled care. *Beds* SNF 89.

Crivitz

McVane Memorial Nursing Home
PO Box 220, Crivitz, WI 54114
(715) 854-2715
Admin Betty L Larsen. *Dir of Nursing* Lois Hudson.
Licensure Intermediate care. *Beds* ICF 64.
Private Pay Patients 20%. *Certified* Medicaid.
Owner Proprietary corp.
Admissions Requirements Minimum age 18; Medical examination.
Staff RNs 2 (ft), 2 (pt); LPNs 3 (ft), 2 (pt).
Facilities Dining room; Physical therapy room; Activities room; Chapel; Crafts room; Laundry room; Barber/Beauty shop.
Activities Arts & crafts; Cards; Games; Reading groups; Prayer groups; Movies; Shopping trips; Dances/Social/Cultural gatherings.

Cuba City

Southwest Health Center Nursing Home
808 S Washington St, Cuba City, WI 53807
(608) 744-2161
Admin Kenneth W Creswick. *Dir of Nursing* Pat Moxness RN. *Medical Dir* M F Stuessy MD.
Licensure Skilled care; Intermediate care. *Beds* SNF 94. *Certified* Medicaid; Medicare.
Owner Nonprofit corp.
Staff Physicians 1 (pt); RNs 2 (ft), 6 (pt); LPNs 2 (ft), 8 (pt); Nurses' aides 9 (ft), 38 (pt); Physical therapists 1 (pt); Occupational therapists 1 (pt); Speech therapists 1 (pt); Activities coordinators 1 (ft); Dietitians 1 (pt); Ophthalmologists 1 (pt); Podiatrists 1 (pt); Dentists 1 (pt).
Facilities Dining room; Physical therapy room; Activities room; Chapel; Crafts room; Laundry room; Barber/Beauty shop; Library.
Activities Arts & crafts; Cards; Games; Reading groups; Prayer groups; Movies; Dances/Social/Cultural gatherings.

Cumberland

Cumberland Memorial Hospital—Extended Care Unit
1110 7th Ave, Box 37, Cumberland, WI 54829
(715) 822-4521, ext 241, 822-2741 FAX
Admin Craig Kantos. *Dir of Nursing* Donna Olson. *Medical Dir* Dr Thomas Lingen.
Licensure Skilled care; Intermediate care. *Beds* Swing beds SNF/ICF 49. *Certified* Medicaid.
Owner Nonprofit organization/foundation.
Admissions Requirements Minimum age 18; Medical examination; Physician's request.
Staff RNs 2 (ft), 3 (pt); LPNs 1 (ft), 4 (pt); Nurses' aides 16 (ft), 20 (pt); Physical therapists 1 (pt) (plus consultant); Occupational therapists 1 (pt) (plus consultant); Activities coordinators 1 (ft), 1 (pt); Dietitians 1 (pt).
Facilities Dining room; Activities room; Barber/Beauty shop.
Activities Arts & crafts; Cards; Games; Reading groups; Prayer groups; Movies; Intergenerational programs; Pet therapy.

Dallas

Dallas Health & Rehabilitation Center
PO Box 165, Dallas, WI 54733
(715) 837-1222

Admin Gerald L Johnson. *Dir of Nursing* Barbara A Strangeway RN. *Medical Dir* Mark Rholl MD.
Licensure Skilled care. *Beds* SNF 60. *Certified* Medicaid.
Owner Nonprofit corp.
Admissions Requirements Medical examination; Physician's request.
Staff Physicians 1 (pt); RNs 1 (ft), 4 (pt); LPNs 7 (ft), 2 (pt); Nurses' aides 12 (ft), 5 (pt); Activities coordinators 1 (ft); Dietitians 1 (pt).
Facilities Dining room; Physical therapy room; Activities room; Crafts room; Laundry room; Barber/Beauty shop.
Activities Arts & crafts; Games; Reading groups; Prayer groups; Movies; Shopping trips; Dances/Social/Cultural gatherings.

Darlington

Lafayette Manor
719 E Catherine St, Box 167, Darlington, WI 53530
(608) 776-4472
Admin Gene Schwarze. *Dir of Nursing* Juanita Burke RN. *Medical Dir* David F Ruf MD.
Licensure Skilled care; Intermediate care. *Beds* Swing beds SNF/ICF 123. *Private Pay Patients* 40%. *Certified* Medicaid; Medicare.
Owner Publicly owned.
Admissions Requirements Minimum age 65; Medical examination; Physician's request.
Staff RNs 3 (ft), 6 (pt); LPNs 2 (ft), 3 (pt); Nurses' aides 25 (ft), 22 (pt); Physical therapists; Activities coordinators 3 (ft); Dietitians.
Facilities Dining room; Physical therapy room; Activities room; Chapel; Crafts room; Laundry room; Barber/Beauty shop; Visitors area.
Activities Arts & crafts; Cards; Games; Reading groups; Prayer groups; Movies; Dances/Social/Cultural gatherings; Intergenerational programs; Pet therapy.

De Pere

Anna John Home
828 EE Rd, De Pere, WI 54115
(414) 869-2797
Admin Whitney J Mills. *Dir of Nursing* Chris Parins.
Licensure Skilled care; Intermediate care. *Beds* 50. *Certified* Medicaid; Medicare.
Owner Publicly owned.
Admissions Requirements Minimum age 18.
Staff Physicians 1 (pt); RNs 1 (ft), 3 (pt); LPNs 7 (pt); Nurses' aides 10 (ft), 10 (pt); Physical therapists 1 (pt); Recreational therapists 1 (ft), 1 (pt); Activities coordinators 1 (ft); Dietitians 1 (pt).
Facilities Dining room; Physical therapy room; Activities room; Chapel; Crafts room; Laundry room; Barber/Beauty shop; Library.
Activities Arts & crafts; Cards; Games; Reading groups; Prayer groups; Movies; Shopping trips; Dances/Social/Cultural gatherings.

Rennes Health Center
PO Box 3218, De Pere, WI 54115
(414) 336-5680
Admin Nancy L Never.
Licensure Skilled care. *Beds* SNF 102.

Roseville of De Pere
Rte 1, De Pere, WI 54115
(414) 336-7733
Admin Kenneth J Secor. *Dir of Nursing* Brenda Ceasar RN. *Medical Dir* Michael Meyer MD.
Licensure Intermediate care. *Beds* ICF 38. *Certified* Medicaid.
Owner Proprietary corp.
Admissions Requirements Medical examination; Physician's request.

Staff RNs 1 (ft), 3 (pt); LPNs 1 (ft), 4 (pt); Nurses' aides 5 (ft), 7 (pt); Activities coordinators.
Facilities Dining room; Activities room.
Activities Arts & crafts; Cards; Games; Prayer groups; Movies; Dances/Social/Cultural gatherings; Pet therapy.

Delafield

Clearview Sanatorium
PO Box 189, Delafield, WI 53018
(414) 646-3361
Admin Wayne C Long.
Licensure Skilled care. *Beds* SNF 32.

Delavan

Willowfield
905 E Geneva, Delavan, WI 53115
(414) 728-6319
Admin Jeffrey Minor. *Dir of Nursing* Susan Scrima. *Medical Dir* John Martin.
Licensure Skilled care; Alzheimer's care. *Beds* SNF 51. *Certified* Medicaid; Medicare.
Owner Proprietary corp (Unicare).
Admissions Requirements Medical examination; Physician's request.
Staff Physicians 1 (pt); RNs 3 (ft), 4 (pt); LPNs 5 (pt); Nurses' aides 8 (ft), 9 (pt); Physical therapists 1 (pt); Occupational therapists 1 (pt); Speech therapists 1 (pt); Activities coordinators 1 (ft); Dietitians 1 (pt); Podiatrists 1 (pt).
Facilities Dining room; Physical therapy room; Activities room; Laundry room; Barber/Beauty shop.
Activities Arts & crafts; Cards; Games; Reading groups; Prayer groups; Movies; Dances/Social/Cultural gatherings; Intergenerational programs; Pet therapy.

Dodgeville

Bloomfield Manor Nursing Home
PO Box 55, Rte 3, Dodgeville, WI 53533
(608) 935-3321
Admin Barbara B Linscheid. *Dir of Nursing* Mary Moll. *Medical Dir* Harold P Breier.
Licensure Skilled care. *Beds* SNF 100. *Certified* Medicaid.
Owner Publicly owned.
Admissions Requirements Minimum age 18; Medical examination; Physician's request.
Staff Physicians 1 (pt); RNs 3 (ft), 7 (pt); LPNs 1 (ft), 6 (pt); Nurses' aides 6 (ft), 29 (pt); Physical therapists 1 (pt); Occupational therapists 1 (pt); Speech therapists 1 (pt); Activities coordinators 1 (ft); Dietitians 1 (pt).
Facilities Dining room; Physical therapy room; Activities room; Chapel; Crafts room; Laundry room; Barber/Beauty shop; Picnic areas.
Activities Arts & crafts; Cards; Games; Reading groups; Prayer groups; Shopping trips; Dances/Social/Cultural gatherings; Picnics; Camping.

Memorial Hospital Medical Care Facility
125 E North St, Dodgeville, WI 53533
(608) 935-2329
Admin Cheryl Ortiz RN.
Medical Dir Dr Imlehman.
Licensure Skilled care; Intermediate care. *Beds* SNF 44. *Certified* Medicaid; Medicare.
Owner Nonprofit corp.
Admissions Requirements Medical examination.
Staff Physicians 12 (ft); RNs 2 (ft), 4 (pt); LPNs 2 (ft), 3 (pt); Nurses' aides 7 (ft), 10 (pt); Physical therapists 2 (ft); Occupational therapists 1 (pt); Activities coordinators; Activities coordinators 1 (ft); Dietitians 1 (ft).

Facilities Dining room; Physical therapy room; Activities room; Crafts room; Laundry room; Barber/Beauty shop.
Activities Arts & crafts; Cards; Games; Reading groups; Prayer groups; Movies; Shopping trips; Dances/Social/Cultural gatherings; Lunch bunch; Religious services; Reality orientation; Exercise classes.

Dousman

Masonic Health Care Center Inc
400 N Main St, Dousman, WI 53118
(414) 965-2111, 965-9285
Admin Mark A Strautman NHA. *Dir of Nursing* Shirley Brown RN. *Medical Dir* Dan T Cleary MD.
Licensure Skilled care; Intermediate care; Retirement. *Beds* Swing beds SNF/ICF 84; Retirement 60-80. *Private Pay Patients* 50%. *Certified* Medicaid.
Owner Nonprofit organization/foundation.
Admissions Requirements Minimum age 18; Medical examination; Physician's request.
Staff Physicians 1 (pt); RNs 4 (ft), 14 (pt); LPNs 2 (ft), 7 (pt); Nurses' aides 10 (ft), 15 (pt); Physical therapists 1 (pt); Occupational therapists 1 (pt); Activities coordinators 1 (ft); Dietitians 1 (ft).
Facilities Dining room; Physical therapy room; Activities room; Barber/Beauty shop.
Activities Arts & crafts; Cards; Games; Reading groups; Prayer groups; Movies; Shopping trips; Dances/Social/Cultural gatherings; Intergenerational programs; Pet therapy.

Durand

Oakview Care Center
PO Box 224, 1220 3rd Ave W, Durand, WI 54736
(715) 672-4211, 672-5112 FAX
Admin Malcolm P Cole. *Dir of Nursing* Margie Ware RN. *Medical Dir* Robert L Dohlman MD.
Licensure Skilled care; Intermediate care. *Beds* Swing beds SNF/ICF 60. *Private Pay Patients* 25%. *Certified* Medicaid; Medicare.
Owner Nonprofit corp (Adventist Health System).
Admissions Requirements Medical examination; Physician's request.
Staff Physicians 6 (ft); RNs 1 (ft), 3 (pt); LPNs 5 (pt); Nurses' aides 4 (ft), 26 (pt); Physical therapists 2 (ft); Activities coordinators 1 (ft), 1 (pt); Dietitians 1 (ft).
Languages German.
Affiliation Seventh-Day Adventist.
Facilities Dining room; Physical therapy room; Activities room; Chapel; Crafts room; Laundry room; Barber/Beauty shop.
Activities Arts & crafts; Cards; Games; Reading groups; Prayer groups; Movies; Shopping trips; Dances/Social/Cultural gatherings; Intergenerational programs.

Eagle River

Eagle River Health Care Center Inc
Box 1149, 357 River St, Eagle River, WI 54521
(715) 479-7464
Admin Mildred M Kiefer.
Licensure Skilled care; Intermediate care. *Beds* SNF 97. *Certified* Medicaid.
Owner Proprietary corp.

East Troy

Kiwanis Manor Inc
PO Box 292, 3271 North St, East Troy, WI 53120
(414) 642-3995

Admin David B Henschel. *Dir of Nursing* Gayle Gramza. *Medical Dir* Dr Thomas Williams.
Licensure Skilled care; Intermediate care. *Beds* SNF 60. *Certified* Medicaid.
Owner Nonprofit corp.
Admissions Requirements Medical examination; Physician's request.
Staff Physicians 4 (pt); RNs 3 (ft), 4 (pt); LPNs 5 (ft), 1 (pt); Nurses' aides 22 (ft), 9 (pt); Physical therapists 1 (ft); Occupational therapists 1 (pt); Speech therapists 1 (pt); Activities coordinators 1 (ft); Dietitians 1 (ft).
Facilities Dining room; Physical therapy room; Activities room; Crafts room; Laundry room; Barber/Beauty shop; Multi-purpose rooms.
Activities Arts & crafts; Cards; Games; Reading groups; Prayer groups; Movies; Shopping trips; Dances/Social/Cultural gatherings.

Eau Claire

Center of Care
1405 Truax Blvd, Eau Claire, WI 54703
(715) 839-4844, 839-4875 FAX
Admin Avon R Karpenske RN. *Dir of Nursing* Donna M Scott RN. *Medical Dir* Dr L J Wilson.
Licensure Skilled care; Intermediate care. *Beds* Swing beds SNF/ICF 190. *Certified* Medicaid; Medicare.
Owner Publicly owned.
Admissions Requirements Minimum age 18; Medical examination; Physician's request.
Staff Physicians (contracted); RNs 8 (ft), 8 (pt); LPNs 3 (ft), 3 (pt); Nurses' aides 49 (ft), 35 (pt); Physical therapists (contracted); Occupational therapists (contracted); Speech therapists (contracted); Activities coordinators 1 (pt); Dietitians (contracted); Podiatrists (contracted); Social workers 2 (ft).
Facilities Dining room; Physical therapy room; Activities room; Chapel; Crafts room; Laundry room; Barber/Beauty shop; Library; IV therapy; Surveillance system.
Activities Arts & crafts; Cards; Games; Reading groups; Prayer groups; Movies; Shopping trips; Dances/Social/Cultural gatherings; Intergenerational programs; Pet therapy; Special Olympics; Active treatment; Volunteer program; Work therapy.

Clairemont
2120 Heights Dr, Eau Claire, WI 54701
(715) 832-1681
Admin John M Hartz. *Dir of Nursing* Bonnie Ackley. *Medical Dir* Robert N Leasum MD.
Licensure Skilled care; Intermediate care. *Beds* Swing beds SNF/ICF 223. *Certified* Medicaid; Medicare; VA.
Owner Proprietary corp.
Admissions Requirements Minimum age 18; Medical examination; Physician's request.
Staff RNs 1 (ft), 6 (pt); LPNs 3 (ft), 21 (pt); Nurses' aides 33 (ft), 66 (pt); Physical therapists (contracted); Occupational therapists (contracted); Speech therapists (contracted); Activities coordinators 2 (ft), 2 (pt); Dietitians 1 (ft), 1 (pt).
Facilities Dining room; Physical therapy room; Activities room; Chapel; Crafts room; Laundry room; Barber/Beauty shop; Library; Occupational therapy room; Speech therapy room; Relaxation/Solariums.
Activities Arts & crafts; Cards; Games; Reading groups; Prayer groups; Movies; Shopping trips; Dances/Social/Cultural gatherings; Intergenerational programs; Pet therapy; Ceramics; Woodworking; Religious services.

Syverson Lutheran Home
816 Porter St, Eau Claire, WI 54701
(715) 832-1644
Admin Mari Beth Fiandt.
Licensure Skilled care; Intermediate care. *Beds*
SNF 95. *Certified* Medicaid.
Owner Nonprofit corp.
Affiliation Lutheran.

Edgerton

**Memorial Community Hospital—Long-Term
Care Facility**
313 Stoughton Rd, Edgerton, WI 53534
(608) 884-3441
Admin Barbara J Kerchoff. *Dir of Nursing*
Sue Larson. *Medical Dir* Dr Victor E Falk.
Licensure Skilled care; Intermediate care;
Retirement. *Beds* Swing beds SNF/ICF 61;
Retirement 24. *Certified* Medicaid;
Medicare.
Owner Nonprofit organization/foundation.
Admissions Requirements Minimum age 18.
Staff Physicians 1 (ft); RNs 1 (ft), 2 (pt);
LPNs 8 (ft), 3 (pt); Nurses' aides 16 (ft), 5
(pt); Physical therapists 1 (pt); Occupational
therapists 1 (pt); Speech therapists 1 (pt);
Activities coordinators 1 (ft); Dietitians 1
(pt); Ophthalmologists 1 (pt); Podiatrists 1
(pt); Audiologists 1 (pt); Activity aides 1 (ft),
1 (pt).
Facilities Dining room; Physical therapy
room; Activities room; Crafts room.
Activities Arts & crafts; Cards; Games;
Reading groups; Prayer groups; Movies;
Shopping trips; Pet therapy.

Elkhorn

Holton Manor
638 N Broad St, Elkhorn, WI 53121
(414) 723-4963
Admin Maureen A Welch. *Dir of Nursing* Jill
Broihahn RN. *Medical Dir* Dr Irwin Bruhn.
Licensure Skilled care; Intermediate care. *Beds*
SNF 60. *Certified* Medicaid.
Owner Proprietary corp (Wis-Care Corp Inc).
Admissions Requirements Medical
examination; Physician's request.
Staff Physicians; RNs; LPNs; Nurses' aides;
Activities coordinators; Dietitians.
Facilities Dining room; Physical therapy
room; Activities room; Laundry room;
Barber/Beauty shop.
Activities Arts & crafts; Cards; Games;
Reading groups; Prayer groups; Movies;
Shopping trips; Dances/Social/Cultural
gatherings; Intergenerational programs; Pet
therapy.

Lakeland Nursing Home of Walworth County
Box 1003, Hwy NN, Elkhorn, WI 53121
(414) 741-3600
Admin Marilyn J Rantz. *Dir of Nursing* Tari
V Miller. *Medical Dir* Dr Menandro Tavera.
Licensure Skilled care. *Beds* SNF 328.
Certified Medicaid.
Owner Publicly owned.
Admissions Requirements Medical
examination; Physician's request.
Staff Physicians 1 (pt); RNs 17 (ft), 18 (pt);
LPNs 10 (ft), 17 (pt); Nurses' aides 101 (ft),
119 (pt); Recreational therapists 7 (ft);
Activities coordinators 2 (ft); Dietitians 2
(ft).
Facilities Dining room; Physical therapy
room; Activities room; Chapel; Crafts room;
Laundry room; Barber/Beauty shop.
Activities Arts & crafts; Cards; Games;
Reading groups; Prayer groups; Movies;
Shopping trips; Dances/Social/Cultural
gatherings.

Ellsworth

Ellsworth Care Centers Inc
403 N Maple St, Ellsworth, WI 54011
(715) 273-5821
Admin Larry Clausen.
Medical Dir F B Klaas MD.
Licensure Skilled care; Intermediate care. *Beds*
SNF 89. *Certified* Medicaid.
Owner Proprietary corp.
Admissions Requirements Minimum age 18;
Medical examination.
Staff Physicians 2 (pt); RNs 3 (ft), 4 (pt);
LPNs 3 (ft), 3 (pt); Nurses' aides 20 (ft), 21
(pt); Physical therapists 1 (pt); Reality
therapists 1 (pt); Occupational therapists 1
(pt); Speech therapists 1 (pt); Activities
coordinators 2 (ft); Dietitians 1 (ft).
Facilities Dining room; Physical therapy
room; Activities room; Crafts room; Laundry
room; Barber/Beauty shop.
Activities Arts & crafts; Cards; Games;
Reading groups; Prayer groups; Movies.

Group Home I
256 W Warner St, Ellsworth, WI 54011
(715) 273-5060
Admin Lucille M Strom.
Licensure Intermediate care for mentally
retarded. *Beds* ICF/MR 15. *Certified*
Medicaid.
Owner Proprietary corp.

Group Home III
256 W Warner St, Ellsworth, WI 54011
(715) 273-5060
Admin Lucille M Strom.
Licensure Intermediate care for mentally
retarded. *Beds* ICF/MR 14.

Piety Place
120 S Piety St, Ellsworth, WI 54011
(715) 273-3515
Admin James E Peterson.
Licensure Intermediate care. *Beds* ICF 20.
Certified Medicaid.
Owner Proprietary corp.

Elmwood

Heritage of Elmwood Nursing Home
232 E Eau Galle Ave, Elmwood, WI 54740
(715) 639-2911
Admin Rodney J Gilles. *Dir of Nursing* Jo
Anne Meyer RN. *Medical Dir* Frank
Springer MD.
Licensure Skilled care. *Beds* SNF 78. *Private
Pay Patients* 30%. *Certified* Medicaid.
Owner Nonprofit corp.
Admissions Requirements Minimum age 18;
Medical examination; Physician's request.
Staff RNs 1 (ft), 3 (pt); LPNs 9 (pt); Nurses'
aides 11 (ft), 30 (pt); Physical therapists;
Activities coordinators 1 (pt); Dietitians.
Facilities Dining room; Physical therapy
room; Activities room; Chapel; Laundry
room; Barber/Beauty shop; Occupational
therapy room.
Activities Arts & crafts; Cards; Games;
Reading groups; Prayer groups; Dances/
Social/Cultural gatherings; Music therapy.

Elroy

Heritage Manor
PO Box 167, Elroy, WI 53929
(608) 462-8491
Admin Patricia A Schulz. *Dir of Nursing* Mary
Wegner RN. *Medical Dir* Roy Balder MD.
Licensure Skilled care. *Beds* SNF 80. *Certified*
Medicaid.
Owner Proprietary corp (First American Care
Facility).
Admissions Requirements Minimum age 16;
Medical examination.

Staff RNs 5 (ft), 2 (pt); LPNs 5 (ft); Nurses'
aides 20 (ft), 20 (pt); Recreational therapists
1 (pt); Occupational therapists 1 (pt); Speech
therapists 1 (pt); Activities coordinators 1
(ft); Dietitians 1 (pt).
Facilities Dining room; Physical therapy
room; Activities room; Chapel; Crafts room;
Laundry room; Barber/Beauty shop; Library;
TV room.
Activities Arts & crafts; Cards; Games;
Reading groups; Prayer groups; Movies;
Shopping trips; Dances/Social/Cultural
gatherings.

Evansville

Evansville Manor
540 Garfield Ave, Evansville, WI 53536
(608) 882-5700
Admin Clifford D Woolever. *Dir of Nursing*
Barbara Buttchen RN. *Medical Dir* R S
Gray MD.
Licensure Skilled care; Intermediate care. *Beds*
SNF 83. *Certified* Medicaid.
Owner Proprietary corp.
Admissions Requirements Minimum age 18;
Medical examination; Physician's request.
Staff Physicians 1 (pt); RNs 3 (ft), 8 (pt);
LPNs 1 (ft), 4 (pt); Nurses' aides 17 (ft), 45
(pt); Physical therapists 1 (ft); Occupational
therapists 1 (pt); Speech therapists 1 (pt);
Activities coordinators 1 (ft), 1 (pt);
Dietitians 1 (pt); Ophthalmologists 1 (pt).
Languages German, Norwegian.
Facilities Dining room; Physical therapy
room; Activities room; Chapel; Crafts room;
Laundry room; Barber/Beauty shop; Library.
Activities Arts & crafts; Cards; Games;
Reading groups; Prayer groups; Movies;
Shopping trips; Dances/Social/Cultural
gatherings.

Fairchild

Fairchild Nursing Home
PO Box 99, N Front St, Fairchild, WI 54741
(715) 334-4311
Admin Kenneth P King.
Licensure Skilled care. *Beds* SNF 50. *Certified*
Medicaid.
Owner Proprietary corp.

Fall Creek

Fall Creek Valley Nursing Home
PO Box 398, 344 W Lincoln Ave, Fall Creek,
WI 54742
(715) 877-2411
Admin Barbara Sook. *Dir of Nursing* Donna
Hopkins. *Medical Dir* Dr Happe.
Licensure Skilled care. *Beds* SNF 76. *Private
Pay Patients* 30%. *Certified* Medicaid;
Medicare.
Owner Nonprofit organization/foundation.
Admissions Requirements Medical
examination; Physician's request.
Staff RNs 3 (ft); LPNs 7 (ft); Nurses' aides 25
(ft); Activities coordinators 1 (ft).
Facilities Dining room; Physical therapy
room; Activities room; Chapel; Laundry
room; Barber/Beauty shop.
Activities Arts & crafts; Cards; Games; Prayer
groups; Movies; Shopping trips; Dances/
Social/Cultural gatherings; Intergenerational
programs.

Fennimore

Fennimore Good Samaritan Center
1850 11th St, Fennimore, WI 53809
(608) 822-6100
Admin Douglas T Daechsel. *Dir of Nursing*
Donna Brugger. *Medical Dir* Dr Robert
Stader.

Licensure Skilled care; Intermediate care; Retirement; Alzheimer's care. *Beds* Swing beds SNF/ICF 88; Retirement 4. *Private Pay Patients* 60%. *Certified* Medicaid; Medicare.
Owner Nonprofit corp (Evangelical Lutheran/ Good Samaritan Society).
Admissions Requirements Minimum age 18; Medical examination.
Staff Physicians 3 (pt); RNs 3 (ft), 5 (pt); LPNs 3 (ft), 3 (pt); Nurses' aides 20 (ft), 16 (pt); Physical therapists 1 (pt); Occupational therapists 1 (pt); Speech therapists 1 (pt); Activities coordinators 1 (ft), 1 (pt); Dietitians 1 (ft); Podiatrists 1 (pt); Audiologists 1 (pt).
Affiliation Evangelical Lutheran.
Facilities Dining room; Physical therapy room; Activities room; Chapel; Crafts room; Laundry room; Barber/Beauty shop.
Activities Arts & crafts; Cards; Games; Reading groups; Prayer groups; Movies; Shopping trips; Dances/Social/Cultural gatherings; Intergenerational programs; Pet therapy.

Florence

Florence Villa
1000 Chapin St, Florence, WI 54121
(715) 528-4833
Admin Bruce R Schlei. *Dir of Nursing* Sheri Giordana.
Licensure Skilled care; Intermediate care. *Beds* Swing beds SNF/ICF 74. *Certified* Medicaid; Medicare.
Owner Proprietary corp (Beverly Enterprises).
Admissions Requirements Minimum age 18; Medical examination; Physician's request.
Staff RNs 3 (ft), 1 (pt); LPNs 4 (ft), 3 (pt); Nurses' aides 25 (ft), 5 (pt); Activities coordinators 1 (pt).
Facilities Dining room; Physical therapy room; Activities room; Laundry room; Barber/Beauty shop.
Activities Arts & crafts; Cards; Games; Reading groups; Prayer groups; Movies; Shopping trips; Dances/Social/Cultural gatherings; Intergenerational programs; Pet therapy.

Fond Du Lac

Americana Healthcare Center
265 S National Ave, Fond Du Lac, WI 54935
(414) 922-7342
Admin Lorie L Neumann.
Medical Dir Dr R L Waffle.
Licensure Skilled care. *Beds* SNF 108. *Certified* Medicaid; Medicare.
Owner Proprietary corp (Manor Care).
Admissions Requirements Medical examination.
Facilities Dining room; Physical therapy room; Activities room; Laundry room; Barber/Beauty shop; Occupational therapy room.
Activities Arts & crafts; Games; Reading groups; Prayer groups; Movies; Shopping trips; Dances/Social/Cultural gatherings.

Care Center East
PO Box 428, Fond Du Lac, WI 54936
(414) 923-7040
Admin Barbara Deitte. *Dir of Nursing* Genevieve Lewellyn. *Medical Dir* Alfred Pennings MD.
Licensure Skilled care. *Beds* SNF 131. *Certified* Medicaid; Medicare.
Owner Proprietary corp (Unicare).
Admissions Requirements Minimum age 18; Medical examination; Physician's request.
Staff RNs 3 (ft), 4 (pt); LPNs 3 (ft), 12 (pt); Nurses' aides 6 (ft), 39 (pt); Activities coordinators 1 (ft); Dietitians 1 (ft).
Facilities Dining room; Physical therapy room; Activities room; Chapel; Laundry room; Barber/Beauty shop.

Activities Arts & crafts; Cards; Games; Reading groups; Prayer groups; Movies; Shopping trips; Dances/Social/Cultural gatherings.

Fond Du Lac County Health Care Center
459 E 1st St, Fond Du Lac, WI 54935
(414) 929-3502
Admin Donn C Stout. *Dir of Nursing* Lorna Friess RN BSN. *Medical Dir* Dr J R Musunuru.
Licensure Skilled care; Intermediate care for mentally retarded. *Beds* SNF 123. *Certified* Medicaid; Medicare (acute only).
Owner Publicly owned.
Admissions Requirements Minimum age 18; Medical examination; Physician's request.
Staff Physicians 2 (ft), 3 (pt); RNs 5 (ft), 4 (pt); LPNs 9 (ft), 4 (pt); Recreational therapists 1 (ft); Occupational therapists 1 (ft); Dietitians 1 (pt).
Facilities Dining room; Activities room; Chapel; Crafts room; Laundry room; Barber/ Beauty shop; Library.
Activities Arts & crafts; Cards; Games; Reading groups; Prayer groups; Movies; Shopping trips; Dances/Social/Cultural gatherings.

Fond Du Lac Lutheran Home
244 N Macy St, Fond Du Lac, WI 54935
(414) 921-9520
Admin Leon C Tomchek.
Licensure Skilled care; Intermediate care. *Beds* SNF 150. *Certified* Medicaid.
Owner Nonprofit corp.
Affiliation Lutheran.

Grancare Nursing Center
517 E Division St, Fond Du Lac, WI 54935
(414) 921-6800
Admin Lori S Roth.
Medical Dir Robert E Cullen MD.
Licensure Skilled care. *Beds* SNF 75.
Owner Proprietary corp.
Staff Physicians 1 (pt); RNs 4 (ft), 3 (pt); LPNs 4 (ft), 4 (pt); Nurses' aides 10 (ft), 14 (pt); Recreational therapists 1 (ft), 1 (pt); Activities coordinators 1 (pt).
Facilities Dining room; Physical therapy room; Activities room; Chapel; Crafts room; Laundry room; Barber/Beauty shop; Library; Personal dayroom.
Activities Arts & crafts; Cards; Games; Reading groups; Prayer groups; Movies; Shopping trips; Dances/Social/Cultural gatherings; Picnics; Luncheons.

Rolling Meadows
PO Box 470, 1155 S Military Rd, Fond Du Lac, WI 54935
(414) 929-3585
Admin Genevieve Huck. *Dir of Nursing* Constance Atkinson RN. *Medical Dir* Gay D Trepanier MD.
Licensure Skilled care; Intermediate care. *Beds* SNF 177. *Certified* Medicaid.
Owner Publicly owned.
Admissions Requirements Medical examination; Physician's request.
Staff Physicians 1 (pt); RNs 7 (ft), 9 (pt); LPNs 2 (ft), 13 (pt); Nurses' aides 27 (ft), 62 (pt); Physical therapists 1 (pt); Occupational therapists 1 (pt); Speech therapists 1 (pt); Activities coordinators 2 (ft), 1 (pt); Dietitians 1 (ft); Dentists 1 (pt).
Facilities Dining room; Physical therapy room; Activities room; Chapel; Crafts room; Laundry room; Barber/Beauty shop; Library.
Activities Arts & crafts; Cards; Games; Reading groups; Prayer groups; Movies; Shopping trips; Dances/Social/Cultural gatherings.

St Frances Home
365 Gillett St, Fond Du Lac, WI 54935
(414) 921-2280

Admin Sr Irene Kohne. *Dir of Nursing* Eileen Dineen. *Medical Dir* Robert E Cullen MD.
Licensure Skilled care; Intermediate care; Retirement. *Beds* Swing beds SNF/ICF 70; Retirement 7. *Certified* Medicaid.
Owner Nonprofit corp.
Admissions Requirements Minimum age 65; Medical examination.
Staff RNs 1 (ft), 4 (pt); LPNs 1 (ft), 6 (pt); Nurses' aides 8 (ft), 16 (pt); Activities coordinators 1 (ft), 2 (pt); Dietitians 1 (ft).
Affiliation Roman Catholic.
Facilities Dining room; Physical therapy room; Activities room; Chapel; Crafts room; Laundry room; Barber/Beauty shop; Library.
Activities Arts & crafts; Cards; Games; Reading groups; Prayer groups; Movies; Shopping trips; Dances/Social/Cultural gatherings.

Fort Atkinson

Fort Atkinson Health Care Center
430 Wilcox, Fort Atkinson, WI 53538
(414) 563-5533
Admin Marilynn J Perry. *Dir of Nursing* Polly Schull. *Medical Dir* H Leering MD.
Licensure Skilled care. *Beds* SNF 126. *Private Pay Patients* 38%. *Certified* Medicaid; Medicare.
Owner Proprietary corp (Beverly Enterprises).
Admissions Requirements Minimum age 18; Medical examination; Physician's request.
Staff RNs 3 (ft), 3 (pt); LPNs 7 (ft), 8 (pt); Nurses' aides 27 (ft), 20 (pt); Physical therapists 1 (pt); Occupational therapists 1 (pt); Speech therapists 1 (pt); Activities coordinators 1 (ft), 1 (pt); Dietitians 1 (pt).
Facilities Dining room; Physical therapy room; Activities room; Barber/Beauty shop.
Activities Arts & crafts; Cards; Games; Reading groups; Movies; Shopping trips; Dances/Social/Cultural gatherings; Intergenerational programs.

Fountain City

St Michael's Evangelical Lutheran Home for the Aged
RR 2, 270 North St, Fountain City, WI 54629
(608) 687-7721
Admin Shirley Steckel. *Dir of Nursing* Christine Kafer. *Medical Dir* Dr Andrew Edin.
Licensure Skilled care; Intermediate care. *Beds* Swing beds SNF/ICF 55. *Private Pay Patients* 75%. *Certified* Medicaid.
Owner Nonprofit organization/foundation.
Admissions Requirements Minimum age 60; Medical examination.
Staff RNs 2 (ft), 1 (pt); LPNs 4 (ft), 4 (pt); Nurses' aides 10 (ft), 13 (pt); Physical therapists 1 (pt); Activities coordinators 1 (ft), 1 (pt); Dietitians 1 (pt).
Affiliation Evangelical Lutheran.
Facilities Dining room; Physical therapy room; Activities room; Chapel; Crafts room; Barber/Beauty shop; Library.
Activities Arts & crafts; Cards; Games; Reading groups; Prayer groups; Movies; Shopping trips; Dances/Social/Cultural gatherings; Intergenerational programs; Pet therapy.

Franksville

Oak Ridge Care Center
18100 65th Ct, Franksville, WI 53126
(414) 835-4809
Admin Kim Gallina. *Dir of Nursing* Karen Klein.
Licensure Intermediate care. *Beds* ICF 36. *Private Pay Patients* 33%. *Certified* Medicaid.
Owner Proprietary corp.

Admissions Requirements Minimum age 21;
Medical examination; Physician's request.
Staff RNs 1 (ft), 6 (pt); LPNs 1 (ft), 2 (pt);
Nurses' aides 7 (ft), 5 (pt); Activities
coordinators 2 (pt); Dietitians 1 (pt); FSS 1
(pt); Social workers 1 (pt).
Facilities Dining room; Activities room;
Crafts room; Laundry room; Barber/Beauty
shop; Living/dayroom.
Activities Arts & crafts; Cards; Games;
Reading groups; Prayer groups; Movies;
Shopping trips; Dances/Social/Cultural
gatherings; Intergenerational programs; Pet
therapy.

Frederic

Frederic Care Center Inc
PO Box 644, 107 E Oak St, Frederic, WI
54837
(715) 327-4297, 327-4950 FAX
Admin Nancy J Jappe. *Dir of Nursing* Richard
Hambacher. *Medical Dir* Dr James Mulry.
Licensure Intermediate care. *Beds* ICF 30.
Certified Medicaid.
Owner Proprietary corp.
Admissions Requirements Medical
examination; Physician's request.
Facilities Dining room; Activities room;
Laundry room; Barber/Beauty shop.
Activities Arts & crafts; Cards; Games;
Reading groups; Prayer groups; Movies;
Shopping trips; Dances/Social/Cultural
gatherings; Intergenerational programs; Pet
therapy.

Friendship

**Adams County Memorial Hospital Nursing
Care Unit**
PO Box 40, 402 W Lake, Friendship, WI
53934
(608) 339-3331
Admin Linda Gonzalez. *Dir of Nursing* Myrna
Garnett. *Medical Dir* Martin J Janssen MD.
Licensure Skilled care; Intermediate care. *Beds*
Swing beds SNF/ICF 18. *Certified* Medicaid.
Owner Nonprofit organization/foundation.
Admissions Requirements Minimum age 18;
Medical examination; Physician's request.
Staff RNs 1 (ft), 2 (pt); LPNs 1 (ft), 8 (pt);
Nurses' aides 3 (ft), 8 (pt); Physical
therapists 1 (pt); Occupational therapists 1
(pt); Speech therapists 1 (pt); Activities
coordinators 1 (pt); Dietitians 1 (pt);
Podiatrists 1 (pt).
Facilities Dining room; Physical therapy
room; Activities room; Laundry room;
Barber/Beauty shop; Century tub bather
room.
Activities Arts & crafts; Cards; Games;
Reading groups; Prayer groups; Movies;
Shopping trips; Dances/Social/Cultural
gatherings.

Villa Pines Living Center
201 S Park St, Friendship, WI 53934
(608) 339-3361
Admin Jeffrey G Helsius.
Medical Dir Dr Martin Janssen.
Licensure Skilled care; Intermediate care. *Beds*
SNF 124. *Certified* Medicaid; Medicare.
Owner Nonprofit corp (Adventist Health Sys-
USA).
Staff Physicians 6 (ft); RNs 11 (ft), 2 (pt);
LPNs 3 (ft), 1 (pt); Nurses' aides 20 (ft), 18
(pt); Physical therapists 1 (ft), 1 (pt);
Occupational therapists 1 (ft); Speech
therapists 1 (ft); Activities coordinators 2
(pt); Dietitians 1 (ft); Ophthalmologists 1
(ft); Dentists 1 (ft).
Affiliation Seventh-Day Adventist.
Facilities Dining room; Physical therapy
room; Activities room; Chapel; Crafts room;
Laundry room; Barber/Beauty shop.

Activities Arts & crafts; Cards; Games;
Reading groups; Prayer groups; Movies;
Shopping trips; Dances/Social/Cultural
gatherings.

Galesville

Marinuka Manor
PO Box 339, 100 Silver Creek Rd, Galesville,
WI 54630
(608) 582-2211
Admin Russ Heilman. *Dir of Nursing* Deb
Lamoreaux. *Medical Dir* James Richardson.
Licensure Skilled care; Semi-independent
apartment living. *Beds* SNF 59; Semi-
independent apartment living 28. *Private
Pay Patients* 40%. *Certified* Medicaid.
Owner Publicly owned.
Admissions Requirements Medical
examination.
Staff RNs; LPNs; Nurses' aides; Physical
therapists; Activities coordinators; Dietitians.
Facilities Dining room; Physical therapy
room; Activities room; Chapel; Laundry
room; Barber/Beauty shop.
Activities Arts & crafts; Cards; Games;
Reading groups; Prayer groups; Movies;
Dances/Social/Cultural gatherings; Pet
therapy.

Genoa City

Highland Home for the Aged
Rte 1 Box 2, Hwy H, Genoa City, WI 53128
(414) 279-3345
Admin Myrna A Webster. *Dir of Nursing*
Karen M Klein. *Medical Dir* C Dekker MD.
Licensure Intermediate care. *Beds* ICF 28.
Certified Medicaid.
Owner Proprietary corp.
Admissions Requirements Minimum age 18;
Medical examination; Physician's request.
Staff RNs 1 (ft), 2 (pt); Nurses' aides 6 (ft), 5
(pt); Activities coordinators 1 (pt); Dietitians
1 (pt).
Languages German, Spanish.
Facilities Dining room; Activities room;
Crafts room; Laundry room; Barber/Beauty
shop.
Activities Arts & crafts; Cards; Games;
Reading groups; Prayer groups; Movies;
Shopping trips; Dances/Social/Cultural
gatherings.

Gillett

Gillett Nursing Home
330 Robinhood Ln, Gillett, WI 54124
(414) 855-2136
Admin Betty I Jones. *Dir of Nursing* Barbara
M Smith. *Medical Dir* Dr Clyde Siefert.
Licensure Skilled care. *Beds* SNF 44. *Private
Pay Patients* 33%. *Certified* Medicaid.
Owner Privately owned.
Admissions Requirements Minimum age 18;
Medical examination.
Staff RNs 2 (ft), 1 (pt); LPNs 5 (ft), 1 (pt);
Nurses' aides 10 (ft), 6 (pt); Physical
therapists 1 (pt); Occupational therapists 1
(pt); Speech therapists 1 (pt); Activities
coordinators 1 (ft), 1 (pt); Dietitians 1 (pt).
Facilities Dining room; Physical therapy
room; Activities room; Crafts room; Laundry
room.
Activities Arts & crafts; Cards; Games;
Reading groups; Prayer groups; Movies;
Shopping trips; Dances/Social/Cultural
gatherings; Intergenerational programs; Pet
therapy; Church services.

Gilman

Gilman Nursing Home
2nd & Gramb St, Gilman, WI 54433
(715) 447-8217
Admin Wayne C Zastrow.

Medical Dir Robert L Hendrickson MD.
Licensure Intermediate care. *Beds* ICF 19.
Certified Medicaid.
Owner Proprietary corp.
Admissions Requirements Medical
examination; Physician's request.
Staff RNs 1 (ft); LPNs 1 (pt); Nurses' aides 3
(ft), 4 (pt); Physical therapists 1 (pt);
Occupational therapists 1 (pt); Speech
therapists 1 (pt); Activities coordinators 1
(ft); Dietitians 1 (pt); Dentists 1 (pt).
Facilities Dining room; Activities room;
Crafts room; Laundry room.
Activities Arts & crafts; Cards; Games;
Movies; Shopping trips; Dances/Social/
Cultural gatherings.

Zastrow Care Center Inc
N3531 Elder Dr, Gilman, WI 54433
(715) 447-8217
Admin Wayne C Zastrow.
Medical Dir Robert L Hendrickson MD.
Licensure Intermediate care. *Beds* ICF 24.
Certified Medicaid.
Owner Proprietary corp.
Admissions Requirements Medical
examination; Physician's request.
Staff Physicians 1 (pt); RNs 1 (ft); LPNs 2
(pt); Nurses' aides 3 (ft), 7 (pt); Physical
therapists 1 (pt); Speech therapists 1 (pt);
Activities coordinators 1 (ft); Dietitians 1
(pt); Dentists 1 (pt).
Facilities Dining room; Activities room;
Crafts room; Laundry room.
Activities Arts & crafts; Cards; Games;
Reading groups; Movies; Shopping trips;
Dances/Social/Cultural gatherings.

Glendale

AMS Green Tree Health Care Center
6925 N Port Washington Rd, Glendale, WI
53217
(414) 352-3300, 352-4087 FAX
Admin Thomas C Zwicker NHA. *Dir of
Nursing* Janet Horton RN. *Medical Dir*
Marshall Mirviss MD.
Licensure Skilled care; Intermediate care for
mentally retarded; Alzheimer's care. *Beds*
SNF 354; ICF/MR 49. *Private Pay Patients*
7%. *Certified* Medicaid; Medicare.
Owner Proprietary corp (American Medical
Services).
Admissions Requirements Minimum age 18;
Medical examination.
Staff RNs 32 (ft), 6 (pt); LPNs 36 (ft), 27 (pt);
Nurses' aides 130 (ft); Physical therapists 2
(ft); Recreational therapists 6 (ft), 3 (pt);
Occupational therapists 2 (ft), 2 (pt); Speech
therapists 1 (ft); Activities coordinators 1
(ft); Dietitians 2 (ft), 1 (pt).
Facilities Dining room; Physical therapy
room; Activities room; Crafts room; Laundry
room; Barber/Beauty shop; Library; Malt
shop; Conference center; Rehabilitation unit.
Activities Arts & crafts; Cards; Games;
Reading groups; Prayer groups; Movies;
Shopping trips; Dances/Social/Cultural
gatherings; Intergenerational programs; Pet
therapy; Wheelchair gardening; Residents
volunteer in community.

Colonial Manor
1616 W Bender Rd, Glendale, WI 53209
(414) 228-8700
Admin David M Mills. *Dir of Nursing*
Darlette Klienmann. *Medical Dir* Dr Larry
Dean.
Licensure Skilled care; Intermediate care. *Beds*
Swing beds SNF/ICF 225. *Private Pay
Patients* 30%. *Certified* Medicaid; Medicare.
Owner Proprietary corp (Beverly Enterprises).
Admissions Requirements Minimum age 65;
Medical examination; Physician's request.
Staff Physicians; RNs; LPNs; Nurses' aides;
Physical therapists; Reality therapists;
Recreational therapists; Occupational

therapists; Speech therapists; Activities coordinators; Dietitians; Ophthalmologists; Podiatrists; Audiologists.

Facilities Dining room; Physical therapy room; Activities room; Chapel; Crafts room; Laundry room; Barber/Beauty shop; Library; Courtyard; Garden area; Tea room.

Activities Arts & crafts; Cards; Games; Reading groups; Prayer groups; Movies; Shopping trips; Dances/Social/Cultural gatherings; Intergenerational programs; Pet therapy.

Glenwood City

Glenhaven Care Center
Rte 2 Box 153, Glenwood City, WI 54013
(715) 265-4555
Admin Alvin B Knutson. *Dir of Nursing* Karen Stoner. *Medical Dir* Dr Allen Limburg.
Licensure Skilled care; Intermediate care; Alzheimer's care. *Beds* Swing beds SNF/ICF 44. *Private Pay Patients* 43%. *Certified* Medicaid.
Owner Nonprofit corp.
Admissions Requirements Minimum age 18; Medical examination; Physician's request.
Staff RNs 3 (ft), 2 (pt); LPNs 2 (ft), 1 (pt); Nurses' aides 10 (ft), 9 (pt); Activities coordinators 1 (ft), 2 (pt); Dietitians 1 (ft), 1 (pt); Physical therapy aides 1 (ft); Housekeeping; Laundry; Maintenance; Social services.
Languages Spanish, Norwegian.
Facilities Dining room; Physical therapy room; Activities room; Chapel; Crafts room; Laundry room; Barber/Beauty shop; Child day care; Security system for wanderers.
Activities Arts & crafts; Cards; Games; Reading groups; Prayer groups; Movies; Shopping trips; Intergenerational programs; Pet therapy; Musical programs.

Grantsburg

Burnett General Hospital—LTC
Box 99, Grantsburg, WI 54840
(715) 463-5353
Admin Stanley J Gaynor.
Licensure Skilled care. *Beds* SNF 53. *Certified* Medicaid.
Owner Nonprofit corp.

Green Bay

Americana Healthcare Center—East
600 S Webster Ave, Green Bay, WI 54301
(414) 432-3213, 432-0614 FAX
Admin Vivian M De Seve. *Dir of Nursing* Marcella Rierdon. *Medical Dir* Fred Walbrun MD.
Licensure Skilled care. *Beds* SNF 79. *Certified* Medicaid; Medicare.
Owner Proprietary corp (Manor Care).
Admissions Requirements Medical examination; Physician's request.
Staff RNs 2 (ft), 3 (pt); LPNs 5 (ft), 3 (pt); Nurses' aides 18 (ft), 13 (pt); Physical therapists; Activities coordinators 1 (ft); Dietitians (contracted).
Facilities Dining room; Physical therapy room; Activities room; Laundry room; Barber/Beauty shop.
Activities Arts & crafts; Cards; Games; Reading groups; Prayer groups; Movies; Shopping trips; Dances/Social/Cultural gatherings; Intergenerational programs; Pet therapy.

Americana Healthcare Center—West
1760 Shawano Ave, Green Bay, WI 54303
(414) 499-5191
Admin Laura Kuber. *Dir of Nursing* Sandy Fenendael RN. *Medical Dir* Fred Walbrun MD.

Licensure Skilled care. *Beds* SNF 105. *Certified* Medicaid; Medicare.
Owner Proprietary corp (Manor Care).
Admissions Requirements Minimum age 18; Medical examination; Physician's request.
Staff RNs; LPNs; Nurses' aides; Physical therapists 1 (pt); Occupational therapists 1 (pt); Speech therapists 1 (pt); Activities coordinators 1 (pt); Dietitians 1 (pt); Ophthalmologists 1 (pt); Dentists 1 (pt).
Facilities Dining room; Physical therapy room; Activities room; Crafts room; Laundry room; Barber/Beauty shop; Lounges.
Activities Arts & crafts; Cards; Games; Reading groups; Prayer groups; Movies; Shopping trips; Dances/Social/Cultural gatherings.

Bornemann Nursing Home Inc
226 Bornemann St, Green Bay, WI 54302
(414) 468-8675
Admin Bonnie J Davis.
Licensure Skilled care. *Beds* SNF 146. *Certified* Medicaid.
Owner Privately owned.
Admissions Requirements Minimum age 18.
Staff RNs; LPNs; Nurses' aides; Activities coordinators.
Facilities Dining room; Physical therapy room; Activities room; Chapel; Crafts room; Laundry room; Barber/Beauty shop.
Activities Arts & crafts; Cards; Games; Reading groups; Prayer groups; Movies; Shopping trips; Dances/Social/Cultural gatherings.

Brown County Health Care Center
2900 Saint Anthony Dr, Green Bay, WI 54311
(414) 468-1136, 468-4213 FAX
Admin Dorothy E Riley MSN RN NHA. *Dir of Nursing* Nancy L Tess BSN RN. *Medical Dir* Enrique Manabat MD.
Licensure Skilled care; Intermediate care for mentally retarded; Alzheimer's care. *Beds* SNF 106; ICF/MR 84. *Private Pay Patients* 3%. *Certified* Medicaid.
Owner Publicly owned.
Admissions Requirements Minimum age 18; Medical examination; Physician's request; Unified Board approval.
Staff Physicians 1 (ft); RNs 7 (ft), 10 (pt); LPNs 13 (ft), 16 (pt); Nurses' aides 53 (ft), 53 (pt); Physical therapists (contracted); Recreational therapists 1 (ft); Occupational therapists 1 (ft), 1 (pt); Speech therapists (contracted); Activities coordinators 1 (ft); Dietitians 2 (ft); Podiatrists (contracted); Vocational services coordinator; Volunteer services coordinator; Psychology services; Psychiatrists (contracted); Support staff; Pharmacist (contracted); Social services; Laboratory (contracted); In-service education.
Facilities Dining room; Physical therapy room; Activities room; Chapel; Crafts room; Laundry room; Barber/Beauty shop; Library; Workshop; Canteen area; Recreation hall; Walking path; Patio areas.
Activities Arts & crafts; Cards; Games; Reading groups; Prayer groups; Movies; Shopping trips; Dances/Social/Cultural gatherings.

Cottonwood Center
PO Box 8065, 1311 N Danz Ave, Green Bay, WI 54308
(414) 468-4801, 468-5469 FAX
Admin Charles D Hawkins. *Dir of Nursing* Ruth Obry. *Medical Dir* Dr M Villwock.
Licensure Intermediate care for mentally retarded. *Beds* ICF/MR 53. *Private Pay Patients* 0%. *Certified* Medicaid.
Owner Nonprofit organization/foundation.
Admissions Requirements Minimum age 18; Medical examination.

Staff RNs 1 (ft); LPNs 2 (ft), 3 (pt); Nurses' aides 15 (ft), 10 (pt); Occupational therapists 1 (pt); Speech therapists 1 (pt); Activities coordinators 1 (ft); Dietitians 1 (pt); Ophthalmologists 1 (pt); Podiatrists 1 (pt).
Facilities Dining room; Physical therapy room; Activities room; Crafts room; Laundry room; Barber/Beauty shop.
Activities Arts & crafts; Cards; Games; Reading groups; Movies; Shopping trips; Dances/Social/Cultural gatherings; Intergenerational programs; Pet therapy; Active treatment.

Grancare Nursing Center
1555 Dousman St, Green Bay, WI 54303
(414) 494-4525
Admin Donna M Zunker.
Medical Dir Barb Long.
Licensure Skilled care; Alzheimer's care. *Beds* SNF 76.
Owner Proprietary corp.
Admissions Requirements Minimum age 18; Medical examination; Physician's request.
Staff Physicians 1 (pt); RNs 4 (ft), 4 (pt); LPNs 6 (ft), 2 (pt); Nurses' aides 20 (ft), 30 (pt); Physical therapists 1 (pt); Reality therapists 1 (pt); Recreational therapists 1 (ft); Occupational therapists 1 (pt); Speech therapists 1 (pt); Activities coordinators 2 (ft), 1 (pt); Dietitians 1 (pt); Ophthalmologists 1 (pt); Food service director 1 (ft).
Facilities Dining room; Physical therapy room; Activities room; Chapel; Crafts room; Laundry room; Barber/Beauty shop; Library.
Activities Arts & crafts; Cards; Games; Reading groups; Prayer groups; Movies; Shopping trips; Dances/Social/Cultural gatherings.

Guardian Angel Health Care Center
2997 Saint Anthony Dr, Green Bay, WI 54311
(414) 468-0734
Admin John Lippert.
Licensure Skilled care; Intermediate care. *Beds* SNF 66. *Certified* Medicaid.
Owner Proprietary corp (Beverly Enterprises).

Parkview Manor
2961 Saint Anthony Dr, Green Bay, WI 54301
(414) 468-0861
Admin Thomas R Morrison.
Medical Dir Dr Rahr.
Licensure Skilled care; Intermediate care. *Beds* SNF 142. *Certified* Medicaid; Medicare.
Owner Proprietary corp (Beverly Enterprises).
Staff RNs 4 (ft), 4 (pt); LPNs 8 (ft), 6 (pt); Nurses' aides 40 (ft), 38 (pt); Physical therapists 1 (ft); Occupational therapists 1 (pt); Speech therapists 1 (pt); Activities coordinators 1 (ft); Dietitians 1 (ft); Dentists 1 (pt).
Facilities Dining room; Physical therapy room; Activities room; Chapel; Laundry room; Barber/Beauty shop.
Activities Arts & crafts; Cards; Games; Reading groups; Prayer groups; Movies; Shopping trips; Dances/Social/Cultural gatherings.

San Luis Manor
2305 San Luis Pl, Green Bay, WI 54304
(414) 494-5231
Admin Laverne L Larson.
Medical Dir Fred Walburn.
Licensure Skilled care; Intermediate care. *Beds* SNF 180. *Certified* Medicaid.
Owner Proprietary corp (Hillhaven Corp).
Admissions Requirements Medical examination; Physician's request.
Staff Physicians 1 (pt); RNs 4 (ft), 7 (pt); LPNs 9 (ft), 9 (pt); Nurses' aides 40 (ft), 50 (pt); Physical therapists 1 (ft); Occupational therapists 1 (ft); Speech therapists 1 (pt); Activities coordinators 1 (ft); Dietitians 1 (pt); Podiatrists 1 (pt); Dentists 1 (pt).

Facilities Dining room; Physical therapy room; Activities room; Chapel; Crafts room; Laundry room; Barber/Beauty shop; Library.
Activities Arts & crafts; Cards; Games; Reading groups; Prayer groups; Movies; Shopping trips; Dances/Social/Cultural gatherings.

Santa Marie Nursing Home
430 S Clay St, Green Bay, WI 54301
(414) 432-5231
Admin Helen M Desotell.
Licensure Skilled care; Intermediate care. *Beds* SNF 59. *Certified* Medicaid.
Owner Proprietary corp.

Western Village
1640 Shawano Ave, Green Bay, WI 54303
(414) 499-5177
Admin Dale P Johnson.
Licensure Skilled care; Intermediate care. *Beds* SNF 125. *Certified* Medicaid; Medicare.
Owner Proprietary corp (Beverly Enterprises).

Wisconsin Odd Fellow-Rebekah Nursing Home
1229 S Jackson St, Green Bay, WI 54301
(414) 437-6523
Admin Leonard D Ferris.
Licensure Skilled care; Intermediate care. *Beds* SNF 82. *Certified* Medicaid.
Owner Nonprofit corp.
Affiliation Independent Order of Odd Fellows & Rebekahs.

Woodside Lutheran Home
1040 Pilgrim Way, Green Bay, WI 54304
(414) 499-1481
Admin Dale L Pauls.
Licensure Skilled care; Intermediate care. *Beds* SNF 168. *Certified* Medicaid.
Owner Nonprofit corp.
Affiliation Lutheran.

Greenfield

Clement Manor Health Care Center
3939 S 92nd St, Greenfield, WI 53228
(414) 321-1800, 546-7305 FAX
Admin Lawrence J Heicher. *Dir of Nursing* Linda Struhar. *Medical Dir* John Wisniewski MD.
Licensure Skilled care; Intermediate care; Retirement; Alzheimer's care. *Beds* Swing beds SNF/ICF 168. *Private Pay Patients* 58%. *Certified* Medicaid; Medicare.
Owner Nonprofit corp.
Admissions Requirements Minimum age 18; Medical examination; Physician's request.
Staff Physicians 1 (pt); RNs 8 (ft), 14 (pt); LPNs 6 (ft), 12 (pt); Nurses' aides 36 (ft), 64 (pt); Physical therapists 3 (ft), 1 (pt); Reality therapists 1 (ft); Recreational therapists 2 (ft), 2 (pt); Occupational therapists 2 (pt); Speech therapists 1 (pt); Activities coordinators 1 (ft), 2 (pt); Dietitians 1 (ft); Podiatrists 1 (pt).
Languages German, Polish.
Affiliation Roman Catholic.
Facilities Dining room; Physical therapy room; Activities room; Chapel; Crafts room; Laundry room; Barber/Beauty shop; Library.
Activities Arts & crafts; Cards; Games; Reading groups; Prayer groups; Movies; Shopping trips; Dances/Social/Cultural gatherings; Intergenerational programs; Pet therapy; Reality orientation; Remotivation; Woodworking.

Hales Corners

Tudor Oaks Health Center
S 77 W 12929 McShane Dr, Hales Corners, WI 53130-0901
(414) 529-0100
Admin Earl J Hoagberg. *Dir of Nursing* Karen A Boese. *Medical Dir* Dr Scott Tilleson.

Licensure Skilled care; Retirement. *Beds* SNF 61; Retirement apts 197. *Private Pay Patients* 60%. *Certified* Medicaid; Medicare.
Owner Nonprofit corp (American Baptist Homes of the Midwest).
Admissions Requirements Minimum age 65; Medical examination; Physician's request.
Staff RNs 2 (ft), 8 (pt); LPNs 1 (ft), 9 (pt); Nurses' aides 2 (ft), 35 (pt); Physical therapists 1 (pt); Occupational therapists 1 (pt); Speech therapists 1 (pt); Activities coordinators 1 (ft); Dietitians 1 (ft); Podiatrists 1 (pt).
Affiliation Baptist.
Facilities Dining room; Physical therapy room; Chapel; Barber/Beauty shop; Outdoor garden; Patio area; Living room.
Activities Arts & crafts; Games; Reading groups; Prayer groups; Movies; Shopping trips; Intergenerational programs; Pet therapy; Family participation.

Hammond

American Heritage Care Center
425 Davis St, Hammond, WI 54015
(715) 796-2218
Admin Bruce A Beckman. *Dir of Nursing* Virginia Lindus. *Medical Dir* Dr David DeGear.
Licensure Skilled care; Retirement. *Beds* SNF 67; Retirement apts 20. *Private Pay Patients* 60%. *Certified* Medicaid.
Owner Publicly owned.
Admissions Requirements Medical examination; Physician's request.
Staff Physicians 1 (pt); RNs 3 (ft), 4 (pt); LPNs 5 (ft); Nurses' aides 25 (ft), 10 (pt); Physical therapists 1 (pt); Occupational therapists 1 (pt); Speech therapists 1 (pt); Activities coordinators 1 (ft); Dietitians 1 (pt).
Facilities Dining room; Activities room; Crafts room; Laundry room; Barber/Beauty shop.
Activities Arts & crafts; Cards; Games; Prayer groups; Movies; Shopping trips; Dances/Social/Cultural gatherings; Baking; Parties; Dining out.

Hartford

Hartford Care Center
1202 E Sumner St, Hartford, WI 53027
(414) 673-2220
Admin Richard Sternke.
Licensure Skilled care; Intermediate care. *Beds* SNF 115. *Certified* Medicaid.
Owner Proprietary corp (Hillhaven Corp).

Hawthorne

Middle River Health Facility
Hwy 53, Hawthorne, WI 54842
(715) 398-3523
Admin Marvin L Benedict. *Dir of Nursing* Claudia Porter. *Medical Dir* Dr James Roberts.
Licensure Skilled care; Retirement. *Beds* SNF 124; Retirement 12. *Private Pay Patients* 30%. *Certified* Medicaid; Medicare.
Owner Publicly owned.
Admissions Requirements Medical examination; Physician's request.
Staff Physicians 1 (pt); RNs 2 (ft), 4 (pt); LPNs 6 (ft), 10 (pt); Nurses' aides 25 (ft), 22 (pt); Physical therapists 1 (pt); Occupational therapists 1 (pt); Speech therapists 1 (pt); Activities coordinators 1 (ft); Dietitians 1 (pt).
Facilities Dining room; Physical therapy room; Activities room; Chapel; Crafts room; Laundry room; Barber/Beauty shop; Library.

Activities Arts & crafts; Cards; Games; Reading groups; Prayer groups; Movies; Shopping trips; Dances/Social/Cultural gatherings.

Hayward

Hayward Nursing Home
Rte 3 Box 3999, Hayward, WI 54843
(715) 634-8911
Admin Karen Churitch.
Licensure Skilled care; Intermediate care. *Beds* SNF 76. *Certified* Medicaid.
Owner Nonprofit corp.

Valley Health Care Center
PO Box 779, Hayward, WI 54843
(715) 634-2202
Admin Jeffrey A Schueller. *Dir of Nursing* Jane Fox. *Medical Dir* Kathy J Keimig MD.
Licensure Skilled care. *Beds* SNF 62. *Private Pay Patients* 20%. *Certified* Medicaid; Medicare.
Owner Proprietary corp (Beverly Enterprises).
Admissions Requirements Minimum age 18; Medical examination; Physician's request.
Staff Physicians; RNs 3 (ft), 1 (pt); LPNs 5 (ft), 2 (pt); Nurses' aides 16 (ft), 7 (pt); Physical therapists 1 (pt); Occupational therapists 1 (pt); Speech therapists 1 (pt); Activities coordinators 1 (ft); Dietitians 1 (ft), 1 (pt).
Facilities Dining room; Physical therapy room; Activities room; Chapel; Crafts room; Laundry room; Barber/Beauty shop; Library.
Activities Arts & crafts; Cards; Games; Reading groups; Prayer groups; Movies; Shopping trips; Dances/Social/Cultural gatherings; Intergenerational programs; Pet therapy.

Hillsboro

St Joseph's Nursing Home
400 Water Ave, Hillsboro, WI 54634
(608) 489-2211
Admin Rolin H Johnson.
Licensure Skilled care; Intermediate care. *Beds* SNF 65. *Certified* Medicaid.
Owner Nonprofit corp.

Hudson

Christian Community Home of Hudson
1415 Laurel Ave, Hudson, WI 54016
(715) 386-9303
Admin Daniel C Dixon.
Medical Dir Dr Jeanne Diefenbach.
Licensure Skilled care. *Beds* SNF 75. *Certified* Medicaid.
Owner Nonprofit corp.
Admissions Requirements Medical examination; Physician's request.
Staff RNs 3 (ft), 2 (pt); LPNs 3 (ft), 5 (pt); Nurses' aides 28 (ft), 8 (pt); Activities coordinators 1 (ft); Dietitians 1 (ft).
Affiliation Methodist.
Facilities Dining room; Physical therapy room; Activities room; Chapel; Crafts room; Barber/Beauty shop; Library; Smokers lounge; Atrium.
Activities Arts & crafts; Cards; Games; Prayer groups; Movies; Dances/Social/Cultural gatherings; Dining out.

L O Simenstad Nursing Care Unit
Box 218, 301 River St, Hudson, WI 54020
(715) 294-2120
Admin Mark H Tibbetts. *Dir of Nursing* Cheryl Zempel RN. *Medical Dir* A S Potek MD.
Licensure Skilled care; Intermediate care. *Beds* SNF 40; ICF. *Certified* Medicaid.
Owner Nonprofit organization/foundation.
Admissions Requirements Medical examination; Physician's request.

Facilities Dining room; Physical therapy room; Activities room; Chapel; Crafts room; Laundry room; Barber/Beauty shop.
Activities Arts & crafts; Cards; Games; Reading groups; Prayer groups; Movies; Shopping trips; Outings; Fishing trips; Picnics; Sight-seeing.

Willow Park Care Facility
Rte 2 Box 385, Hudson, WI 54016
(715) 386-2222
Admin Colette Ruemmele.
Medical Dir Dr Frank H Hollar.
Licensure Intermediate care. *Beds* 39. *Certified* Medicaid.
Owner Proprietary corp.
Admissions Requirements Medical examination; Physician's request.
Staff Physicians 1 (pt); RNs 2 (ft); LPNs 2 (ft); Nurses' aides 2 (ft), 4 (pt); Reality therapists 1 (pt); Recreational therapists 1 (pt); Activities coordinators 1 (pt); Dietitians 1 (pt); Dentists 1 (pt).
Facilities Dining room; Activities room; Crafts room; Group meeting room.
Activities Arts & crafts; Cards; Games; Prayer groups; Movies; Shopping trips; Dances/Social/Cultural gatherings Library visits & mail-a-book service; AA in-house meetings.

Hurley

Sky View Nursing Center
309 Iron St, Hurley, WI 54534
(715) 561-5646
Admin Dean A Jivery.
Licensure Intermediate care. *Beds* ICF 36. *Certified* Medicaid.
Owner Proprietary corp.

Villa Maria Healthcare Center
Villa Dr, Hurley, WI 54534
(715) 561-3200
Admin Lawrence J Kutz.
Licensure Skilled care; Intermediate care. *Beds* SNF 70. *Certified* Medicaid.
Owner Proprietary corp.

Iola

Iola Hospital & Nursing Home
185 S Washington, Iola, WI 54945
(715) 445-2272
Admin Gregory W Loeser. *Dir of Nursing* Mary Bublitz RN. *Medical Dir* N J Hollero.
Licensure Skilled care. *Beds* SNF 38. *Private Pay Patients* 40%. *Certified* Medicaid; Medicare.
Owner Nonprofit organization/foundation.
Staff Physicians 2 (ft); RNs 1 (ft), 3 (pt); LPNs 2 (ft), 5 (pt); Nurses' aides 5 (ft), 10 (pt); Physical therapists 1 (pt); Recreational therapists 1 (ft); Activities coordinators 1 (ft); Dietitians 1 (pt).
Facilities Dining room; Physical therapy room; Activities room; Chapel; Crafts room; Laundry room; Barber/Beauty shop; Library.
Activities Arts & crafts; Cards; Games; Reading groups; Prayer groups; Movies; Shopping trips; Dances/Social/Cultural gatherings; Intergenerational programs; Pet therapy.

Janesville

Cedar Crest Health Center
1700 S River Rd, Janesville, WI 53545
(608) 756-0344
Admin Jay E Smoke. *Dir of Nursing* Dorothy Osborne RN. *Medical Dir* David Smith MD.
Licensure Skilled care. *Beds* SNF 95.
Owner Nonprofit corp.
Staff RNs 4 (ft), 12 (pt); LPNs 2 (pt); Nurses' aides 22 (ft), 31 (pt); Activities coordinators 1 (ft).

Dupoint House
1947 Dupoint Dr, Janesville, WI 53545
(608) 831-2055
Admin Nancy Fennema.
Licensure Skilled care; Intermediate care for mentally retarded. *Beds* 6. *Certified* Medicaid.
Owner Nonprofit corp.

Janesville Health Care Center
119 S Parker Dr, Janesville, WI 53545
(608) 756-0374
Admin Mary Ann Wright. *Dir of Nursing* Charlene Wittlieff. *Medical Dir* S Frazer MD.
Licensure Skilled care; Intermediate care; Medicare. *Beds* Swing beds SNF/ICF 86; Medicare 18. *Private Pay Patients* 25%. *Certified* Medicaid; Medicare.
Owner Proprietary corp (Health Enterprises of America).
Admissions Requirements Minimum age 18; Medical examination; Physician's request.
Staff RNs 5 (ft), 1 (pt); LPNs 3 (ft), 4 (pt); Nurses' aides 35 (ft), 10 (pt); Physical therapists 1 (pt); Recreational therapists 1 (pt); Occupational therapists 1 (pt); Speech therapists 1 (pt); Activities coordinators 1 (ft); Dietitians 1 (pt); Podiatrists 1 (pt).
Facilities Dining room; Physical therapy room; Activities room; Crafts room; Laundry room; Barber/Beauty shop.
Activities Arts & crafts; Cards; Games; Prayer groups; Movies; Shopping trips; Pet therapy.

Rock County Health Care Center
PO Box 351, N Parker Dr, Janesville, WI 53547
(608)' 755-2500
Admin Terry A Scieszinski. *Dir of Nursing* Lucy Vickerman MSN. *Medical Dir* Paul F Frechette MD.
Licensure Skilled care; Alzheimer's care. *Beds* SNF 388. *Private Pay Patients* 14%. *Certified* Medicaid; Medicare.
Owner Publicly owned.
Admissions Requirements Minimum age 18; Medical examination; Physician's request.
Staff Physicians 2 (ft), 3 (pt); RNs 11 (ft), 19 (pt); LPNs 8 (ft), 14 (pt); Nurses' aides 107 (ft), 71 (pt); Physical therapists 1 (ft); Recreational therapists 1 (ft); Occupational therapists 3 (ft), 1 (pt); Speech therapists 1 (ft); Dietitians 2 (ft), 1 (pt); Ophthalmologists 1 (pt); Podiatrists 1 (pt); Audiologists 1 (pt).
Facilities Dining room; Physical therapy room; Activities room; Chapel; Crafts room; Laundry room; Barber/Beauty shop; Library.
Activities Arts & crafts; Cards; Games; Reading groups; Prayer groups; Movies; Shopping trips; Dances/Social/Cultural gatherings; Intergenerational programs; Pet therapy.

St Elizabeth's Nursing Home
502 Saint Lawrence, Janesville, WI 53545
(608) 752-6709
Admin Sr Mary Denise Slocum. *Dir of Nursing* Sr Mary Jacinta. *Medical Dir* Dr Charles Baker.
Licensure Skilled care; Intermediate care; Alzheimer's care. *Beds* Swing beds SNF/ICF 41.
Owner Nonprofit organization/foundation.
Admissions Requirements Medical examination; Physician's request.
Staff RNs 2 (ft); LPNs 1 (ft); Nurses' aides 20 (ft); Physical therapists 1 (ft); Recreational therapists 2 (ft); Occupational therapists 1 (ft); Dietitians 1 (ft).
Affiliation Roman Catholic.
Activities Arts & crafts; Cards; Games; Reading groups; Prayer groups; Movies; Pet therapy.

Jefferson

Countryside Home
1425 Wisconsin Dr, Jefferson, WI 53549
(414) 674-3170
Admin Phyllis T Williams RN NHA. *Dir of Nursing* Sharon Erickson RN. *Medical Dir* Dr H Leering.
Licensure Skilled care. *Beds* SNF 353. *Certified* Medicaid; Medicare.
Owner Publicly owned.
Admissions Requirements Minimum age 18; Medical examination; Physician's request.
Staff Physicians 1 (ft); RNs 12 (ft), 5 (pt); LPNs 24 (ft), 19 (pt); Nurses' aides 84 (ft), 60 (pt); Recreational therapists 1 (ft); Activities coordinators 1 (ft); Dietitians 1 (pt).
Facilities Dining room; Physical therapy room; Activities room; Chapel; Crafts room; Laundry room; Barber/Beauty shop; Library.
Activities Arts & crafts; Cards; Games; Reading groups; Prayer groups; Movies; Shopping trips; Dances/Social/Cultural gatherings.

St Coletta School Alverno Cottage
W 4955 Hwy 18, Jefferson, WI 53549
(414) 674-2045
Admin Ellen Haines. *Dir of Nursing* Judith Kylmanen RN.
Licensure Intermediate care for mentally retarded. *Beds* ICF/MR 76. *Certified* Medicaid.
Owner Nonprofit corp.
Admissions Requirements Minimum age 18; Medical examination; Physician's request.
Staff RNs 1 (ft); LPNs 3 (pt); Nurses' aides 19 (ft), 15 (pt); Occupational therapists 1 (ft); Speech therapists 1 (pt); Dietitians 1 (pt).
Facilities Dining room; Physical therapy room; Activities room; Chapel; Crafts room; Laundry room; Barber/Beauty shop; Library.
Activities Arts & crafts; Cards; Games; Reading groups; Prayer groups; Movies; Shopping trips; Dances/Social/Cultural gatherings.

Juneau

Clearview
198 Home Rd, Juneau, WI 53039
(414) 386-2631
Admin Michael W Berry.
Medical Dir Frederick Haessley.
Licensure Skilled care. *Beds* SNF 243. *Certified* Medicaid.
Owner Publicly owned.
Admissions Requirements Minimum age 18; Medical examination; Physician's request.
Staff Physicians 1 (ft); RNs 4 (ft), 6 (pt); LPNs 13 (ft), 13 (pt); Nurses' aides 62 (ft), 13 (pt); Recreational therapists 3 (ft); Activities coordinators 1 (ft); Dietitians 1 (ft).
Facilities Dining room; Physical therapy room; Activities room; Chapel; Crafts room; Laundry room; Barber/Beauty shop; Library.
Activities Arts & crafts; Cards; Games; Reading groups; Prayer groups; Movies; Shopping trips; Dances/Social/Cultural gatherings.

Dodge County Community Health Center
199 Home Rd, Juneau, WI 53039
(414) 386-2655
Admin Michael W Berry.
Medical Dir John Smith.
Licensure Skilled care; Intermediate care; Intermediate care for mentally retarded. *Beds* SNF 141; ICF/MR 84. *Certified* Medicaid.
Owner Publicly owned.
Admissions Requirements Minimum age 18; Medical examination; Physician's request.

Staff Physicians 1 (ft); RNs 5 (ft), 6 (pt);
LPNs 11 (ft), 11 (pt); Nurses' aides 71 (ft), 6
(pt); Occupational therapists 1 (ft), 1 (pt).
Facilities Dining room; Physical therapy
room; Activities room; Chapel; Crafts room;
Laundry room; Barber/Beauty shop; Library.
Activities Arts & crafts; Cards; Games;
Reading groups; Prayer groups; Movies;
Shopping trips; Dances/Social/Cultural
gatherings.

Kaukauna

Riverview Health Center
200 Sanatorium Rd, Kaukauna, WI 54130
(414) 766-4241
Admin Harold Morris. *Dir of Nursing* Sharon
Magmin. *Medical Dir* James Jeffrey MD.
Licensure Skilled care. *Beds* SNF 77. *Certified*
Medicaid.
Owner Nonprofit corp.
Admissions Requirements Minimum age 18;
Medical examination; Physician's request.
Staff RNs 2 (ft), 3 (pt); LPNs 7 (pt); Nurses'
aides 36 (ft); Occupational therapists 3 (pt).
Facilities Dining room; Physical therapy
room; Activities room; Chapel; Crafts room;
Barber/Beauty shop.
Activities Arts & crafts; Cards; Games;
Reading groups; Prayer groups; Movies;
Shopping trips; Dances/Social/Cultural
gatherings.

St Paul Home Inc
1211 Oakridge Ave, Kaukauna, WI 54130
(414) 766-6020, 766-9161 FAX
Admin Sr Mary Kaye Winkler. *Dir of Nursing*
Dianne Niquette. *Medical Dir* W W
Wolfmeyer MD.
Licensure Skilled care; Intermediate care. *Beds*
Swing beds SNF/ICF 129. *Certified*
Medicaid.
Owner Nonprofit organization/foundation.
Staff RNs; LPNs; Nurses' aides; Physical
therapists (consultant); Occupational
therapists 1 (ft); Speech therapists
(consultant); Activities coordinators 1 (ft);
Dietitians 1 (ft); Podiatrists (consultant).
Affiliation Roman Catholic.
Facilities Dining room; Physical therapy
room; Activities room; Chapel; Crafts room;
Laundry room; Barber/Beauty shop.
Activities Arts & crafts; Cards; Games;
Reading groups; Prayer groups; Shopping
trips; Dances/Social/Cultural gatherings;
Intergenerational programs; Pet therapy.

Kenosha

Brookside Care Center
3506 Washington Rd, Kenosha, WI 53142
(414) 656-6700, 656-6762 FAX
Admin Juanita Roni Wethington. *Dir of
Nursing* Bernice Wikstrom. *Medical Dir* D
Boyd Horsley MD.
Licensure Skilled care; Intermediate care;
Intermediate care for mentally retarded.
Beds ICF/MR 37; Swing beds SNF/ICF 223.
Private Pay Patients 4%. *Certified* Medicaid.
Owner Publicly owned.
Admissions Requirements Minimum age 18;
Medical examination; Physician's request.
Staff Physicians 1 (pt); RNs 10 (ft), 6 (pt);
LPNs 7 (ft), 18 (pt); Nurses' aides 42 (ft), 67
(pt); Physical therapists 1 (ft); Recreational
therapists 5 (ft); Occupational therapists 2
(ft); Speech therapists 1 (pt); Activities
coordinators 1 (ft); Dietitians 1 (pt);
Podiatrists 1 (pt); Audiologists 1 (pt).
Facilities Dining room; Physical therapy
room; Activities room; Crafts room; Laundry
room; Barber/Beauty shop; Library.
Activities Arts & crafts; Cards; Games;
Reading groups; Prayer groups; Movies;
Shopping trips; Dances/Social/Cultural
gatherings; Pet therapy.

Clairidge House
1519 60th St, Kenosha, WI 53140
(414) 656-7500
Admin Bernice Wikstrom.
Medical Dir L Newman.
Licensure Skilled care. *Beds* SNF 96.
Owner Proprietary corp.
Admissions Requirements Minimum age 18;
Medical examination; Physician's request.
Staff RNs 3 (ft), 2 (pt); LPNs 4 (ft);
Recreational therapists 1 (ft), 1 (pt);
Occupational therapists 1 (ft); Activities
coordinators 1 (ft), 1 (pt); Dietitians 1 (pt).
Facilities Dining room; Physical therapy
room; Activities room; Chapel; Crafts room;
Laundry room.
Activities Arts & crafts; Cards; Games;
Reading groups; Prayer groups; Movies;
Shopping trips; Dances/Social/Cultural
gatherings.

Dayton Residential Care Facility
521 59th St, Kenosha, WI 53140
(414) 657-6121
Admin Robert R Ruffalo.
Licensure Intermediate care. *Beds* ICF 102.
Certified Medicaid.
Owner Proprietary corp.
Admissions Requirements Minimum age 18.
Staff LPNs; Nurses' aides; Activities
coordinators; Dietitians.
Facilities Dining room; Activities room;
Crafts room; Laundry room; Barber/Beauty
shop.
Activities Cards; Games; Dances/Social/
Cultural gatherings; Bingo; Exercise.

Hospitality Manor
8633 32nd Ave, Kenosha, WI 53142
(414) 627-9411, 694-0190 FAX
Admin Darlene Sanchez. *Dir of Nursing*
Rebecca Brehm. *Medical Dir* Suresh R Naik.
Licensure Skilled care. *Beds* SNF 133.
Certified Medicaid; Medicare.
Owner Proprietary corp (Unicare).
Admissions Requirements Minimum age 18;
Medical examination; Physician's request.
Staff RNs 3 (ft), 5 (pt); LPNs 5 (ft), 4 (pt);
Nurses' aides 20 (ft), 45 (pt); Physical
therapists 2 (ft); Recreational therapists 1
(ft); Occupational therapists 1 (ft); Speech
therapists 1 (ft); Activities coordinators 1
(ft); Dietitians 1 (ft).
Facilities Dining room; Physical therapy
room; Activities room; Crafts room; Laundry
room; Barber/Beauty shop; Library.
Activities Arts & crafts; Cards; Games;
Reading groups; Prayer groups; Movies;
Dances/Social/Cultural gatherings;
Intergenerational programs; Pet therapy;
Shopping cart.

St Joseph's Home
9244-29th Ave, Kenosha, WI 53140
(414) 694-0080
Admin Sr Mary E Apanites. *Dir of Nursing*
Rita Cox.
Licensure Skilled care. *Beds* SNF 93; ICF.
Certified Medicaid.
Owner Nonprofit organization/foundation.
Staff RNs 2 (ft), 4 (pt); LPNs 4 (ft), 7 (pt);
Nurses' aides 17 (ft), 16 (pt); Activities
coordinators 1 (ft); Dietitians 1 (pt).

Shady Lawn East
920 61st St, Kenosha, WI 53140
(414) 658-4346
Admin Judith A Riley. *Dir of Nursing* Barbara
Beardsley RN. *Medical Dir* Bonnie Wirfs.
Licensure Intermediate care; Respite care;
Alzheimer's care. *Beds* ICF 80. *Certified*
Medicaid.
Owner Proprietary corp.
Admissions Requirements Medical
examination; Physician's request.
Staff RNs; LPNs; Nurses' aides; Activities
coordinators.

Facilities Dining room; Activities room;
Chapel; Crafts room; Laundry room; Barber/
Beauty shop; Security system for confused &
disoriented residents.
Activities Arts & crafts; Cards; Games;
Reading groups; Prayer groups; Movies;
Shopping trips; Dances/Social/Cultural
gatherings; Intergenerational programs.

Shady Lawn West
1703 60th St, Kenosha, WI 53140
(414) 658-4125
Admin Mary A Obermeier. *Dir of Nursing*
David J Mueller RN. *Medical Dir* Bonnie
Wrfs MD.
Licensure Skilled care; Intermediate care. *Beds*
SNF 120. *Certified* Medicaid; Medicare.
Owner Proprietary corp (Vantage Healthcare).
Admissions Requirements Medical
examination; Physician's request.
Staff Physicians 1 (pt); RNs 6 (ft); LPNs 6
(ft), 3 (pt); Nurses' aides 30 (ft), 25 (pt);
Physical therapists 1 (ft); Recreational
therapists 1 (ft); Occupational therapists 1
(pt); Speech therapists 1 (pt); Activities
coordinators 1 (ft); Dietitians 1 (pt);
Podiatrists 1 (pt).
Facilities Dining room; Physical therapy
room; Activities room; Chapel; Crafts room;
Laundry room; Barber/Beauty shop; Library.
Activities Arts & crafts; Cards; Games;
Reading groups; Prayer groups; Movies.

Sheridan Nursing Home
8400 Sheridan Rd, Kenosha, WI 53140
(414) 658-4141
Admin Karen L Vincent. *Dir of Nursing* Ann
Gainey RN. *Medical Dir* Dr Mitchell
Ziarko.
Licensure Skilled care; Intermediate care. *Beds*
SNF 106. *Certified* Medicaid; Medicare.
Owner Proprietary corp (Hillhaven Corp).
Admissions Requirements Minimum age 18;
Medical examination; Physician's request.
Staff RNs; LPNs; Nurses' aides; Physical
therapists; Reality therapists; Recreational
therapists; Occupational therapists; Speech
therapists; Activities coordinators; Dietitians;
Ophthalmologists.
Languages Italian.
Facilities Dining room; Activities room;
Chapel; Crafts room; Barber/Beauty shop;
Library.
Activities Arts & crafts; Cards; Games;
Reading groups; Prayer groups; Movies;
Shopping trips; Dances/Social/Cultural
gatherings; Creative writing; Poetry.

Washington Manor
3100 Washington Rd, Kenosha, WI 53142
(414) 658-4622
Admin Thomas F O'Neal. *Dir of Nursing*
Nadene Loeffler RN. *Medical Dir* Dr David
Goldstein.
Licensure Skilled care; Intermediate care. *Beds*
Swing beds SNF/ICF 103. *Private Pay
Patients* 60%. *Certified* Medicaid; Medicare.
Owner Proprietary corp (Health Care &
Retirement Corp).
Admissions Requirements Minimum age 18;
Medical examination; Physician's request.
Staff RNs; LPNs; Nurses' aides; Physical
therapists; Recreational therapists;
Occupational therapists; Speech therapists;
Activities coordinators; Dietitians;
Ophthalmologists.
Facilities Dining room; Physical therapy
room; Activities room; Crafts room; Laundry
room; Barber/Beauty shop.
Activities Arts & crafts; Cards; Games;
Reading groups; Prayer groups; Movies;
Shopping trips; Dances/Social/Cultural
gatherings; Intergenerational programs; Pet
therapy.

Woodstock-Kenosha Health Center
3415 N Sheridan Rd, Kenosha, WI 53140
(414) 657-6175

Admin Stephen R La Pierre. *Dir of Nursing*
Janice Kafer RN. *Medical Dir* R Rustia
MD.
Licensure Skilled care. *Beds* SNF 183.
Certified Medicaid; Medicare.
Owner Proprietary corp (Hillhaven Corp).
Admissions Requirements Minimum age 18;
Medical examination; Physician's request.
Staff Physicians 3 (pt); RNs 3 (ft), 12 (pt);
LPNs 6 (ft), 15 (pt) 13 (ft), 66 (pt); Physical
therapists 2 (ft); Occupational therapists 2
(ft); Speech therapists 1 (ft); Activities
coordinators 1 (ft), 7 (pt); Dietitians 1 (pt);
Ophthalmologists 1 (pt); Podiatrists 1 (pt);
Dentists 1 (pt); Volunteer Coordinator 1
(pt).
Facilities Dining room; Physical therapy
room; Activities room; Crafts room; Laundry
room; Barber/Beauty shop.
Activities Arts & crafts; Cards; Games;
Reading groups; Prayer groups; Movies;
Shopping trips; Dances/Social/Cultural
gatherings; Van equipped for the
handicapped.

Kewaskum

Beechwood Rest Home
Rte 1, 16-98 Hwy A, Kewaskum, WI 53040
(414) 626-4258
Admin Lee L Rammer.
Licensure Intermediate care. *Beds* ICF 26.
Certified Medicaid.
Owner Proprietary corp.

Kewaunee

Kewaunee Health Care Center
1308 Lincoln St, Kewaunee, WI 54216
(414) 388-4111
Admin Steven Bavers. *Dir of Nursing*
Kathleen Zuege. *Medical Dir* Dr R M
Nesemann.
Licensure Skilled care; Intermediate care. *Beds*
Swing beds SNF/ICF 106. *Private Pay
Patients* 25%. *Certified* Medicaid; Medicare;
VA.
Owner Proprietary corp (Beverly Enterprises).
Admissions Requirements Minimum age 18;
Medical examination; Physician's request.
Staff Physicians 5 (pt); RNs 2 (ft), 2 (pt);
LPNs 5 (ft), 4 (pt); Nurses' aides 22 (ft), 26
(pt); Physical therapists 3 (pt); Occupational
therapists 3 (pt); Speech therapists 1 (pt);
Activities coordinators 1 (ft), 1 (pt);
Dietitians 1 (ft); Ophthalmologists 1 (pt);
Podiatrists 1 (pt); Audiologists 1 (pt).
Facilities Dining room; Physical therapy
room; Activities room; Crafts room; Laundry
room; Barber/Beauty shop.
Activities Arts & crafts; Cards; Games;
Reading groups; Prayer groups; Movies;
Shopping trips; Dances/Social/Cultural
gatherings; Intergenerational programs; Pet
therapy.

King

Wisconsin Veterans Home
Cty Hwy QQ, King, WI 54946
(715) 258-5586
Admin LaVern L Hanke, Interim. *Dir of
Nursing* Mary Tenant RN MSN. *Medical
Dir* Paul A Drinka MD.
Licensure Skilled care; Intermediate care;
Domiciliary care; Alzheimer's care. *Beds*
Swing beds SNF/ICF 709; Domiciliary care
28. *Private Pay Patients* 17%. *Certified*
Medicaid.
Owner Publicly owned.
Admissions Requirements Minimum age 50;
Medical examination; Physician's request.
Staff Physicians (contracted); RNs 29 (ft), 14
(pt); LPNs 34 (ft), 33 (pt); Nurses' aides 145
(ft), 96 (pt); Physical therapists (contracted);
Recreational therapists 2 (ft); Occupational

therapists (contracted); Speech therapists
(contracted); Activities coordinators 1 (ft);
Dietitians 2 (ft), 1 (pt); Ophthalmologists
(contracted); Podiatrists (contracted);
Audiologists (contracted); Dentists 1 (ft);
Pharmacists 3 (ft), 1 (pt).
Languages German, Spanish, Swedish,
Norwegian, Polish.
Facilities Dining room; Physical therapy
room; Activities room; Chapel; Crafts room;
Laundry room; Barber/Beauty shop; Library;
Bowling alley.
Activities Arts & crafts; Cards; Games;
Reading groups; Prayer groups; Movies;
Shopping trips; Dances/Social/Cultural
gatherings; Intergenerational programs; Pet
therapy; Bowling; Volunteer Program.

La Crosse

Bethany Riverside
2575 S 7th St, La Crosse, WI 54601
(608) 784-3380
Admin William Chad McGrath.
Medical Dir Bruce Polender MD.
Licensure Skilled care. *Beds* SNF 123.
Certified Medicaid.
Owner Proprietary corp.
Admissions Requirements Minimum age 21;
Medical examination.
Affiliation Lutheran.
Facilities Dining room; Physical therapy
room; Activities room; Chapel; Crafts room;
Laundry room; Barber/Beauty shop; Library.
Activities Arts & crafts; Cards; Games;
Reading groups; Prayer groups; Movies;
Shopping trips; Dances/Social/Cultural
gatherings; Outings.

Bethany St Joseph Care Center
2501 Shelby Rd, La Crosse, WI 54601
(608) 788-5700
Admin Thomas Rand. *Dir of Nursing* Beth
Olson RN. *Medical Dir* Phil Utz MD.
Licensure Skilled care; Retirement. *Beds* SNF
226. *Certified* Medicaid; Medicare.
Owner Proprietary corp.
Admissions Requirements Minimum age 18;
Medical examination; Physician's request.
Staff RNs 12 (ft), 20 (pt); LPNs 3 (ft), 21 (pt);
Nurses' aides 41 (ft), 63 (pt); Physical
therapists 1 (ft), 2 (pt); Recreational
therapists 1 (ft); Occupational therapists 2
(pt); Speech therapists 1 (ft); Activities
coordinators 1 (ft); Dietitians 1 (ft), 2 (pt).
Facilities Dining room; Physical therapy
room; Activities room; Chapel; Crafts room;
Laundry room; Barber/Beauty shop; Library.
Activities Arts & crafts; Cards; Games;
Reading groups; Prayer groups; Movies;
Shopping trips; Dances/Social/Cultural
gatherings; Music; Cooking.

Hillview Health Care Center
3501 Park Lane Dr, La Crosse, WI 54601
(608) 788-6650
Admin James E Ertz.
Medical Dir Teddy Wais.
Licensure Skilled care; Retirement. *Beds* SNF
228. *Certified* Medicaid.
Owner Publicly owned.
Admissions Requirements Medical
examination; Physician's request.
Staff Physicians 1 (pt); RNs 8 (ft), 11 (pt);
LPNs 5 (ft), 10 (pt); Nurses' aides 45 (ft), 63
(pt); Physical therapists 1 (ft); Recreational
therapists 1 (ft); Occupational therapists 1
(ft); Speech therapists 1 (pt); Activities
coordinators 1 (ft); Dietitians 1 (ft).
Facilities Dining room; Physical therapy
room; Activities room; Chapel; Crafts room;
Laundry room; Barber/Beauty shop; Library.
Activities Arts & crafts; Cards; Games;
Reading groups; Prayer groups; Movies;
Dances/Social/Cultural gatherings.

St Francis Home
620 S 11th St, La Crosse, WI 54601
(608) 785-0966
Admin Larry Alens. *Dir of Nursing* Richard
Berendes RN. *Medical Dir* Dr Phillip Utz.
Licensure Skilled care. *Beds* SNF 95. *Private
Pay Patients* 50%. *Certified* Medicaid;
Medicare; VA.
Owner Nonprofit corp.
Admissions Requirements Minimum age 18;
Medical examination; Physician's request.
Staff RNs 5 (ft), 4 (pt); LPNs 2 (ft), 10 (pt);
Nurses' aides 20 (ft), 24 (pt); Physical
therapists (contracted); Activities
coordinators 1 (ft), 3 (pt); Dietitians
(contracted).
Affiliation Roman Catholic.
Facilities Dining room; Activities room;
Chapel; Crafts room; Laundry room; Barber/
Beauty shop.
Activities Arts & crafts; Cards; Games;
Reading groups; Prayer groups; Movies;
Shopping trips; Dances/Social/Cultural
gatherings; Pet therapy.

St Joseph's Nursing Home
2902 East Ave S, La Crosse, WI 54601
(608) 788-9870
Admin James S Bialecki.
Licensure Skilled care; Intermediate care. *Beds*
SNF 80. *Certified* Medicaid.
Owner Publicly owned.
Affiliation Roman Catholic.

Ladysmith

Ladysmith Nursing Home
120 E 4th St, Ladysmith, WI 54848
(715) 532-5546
Admin Michael W Kelley.
Licensure Intermediate care. *Beds* ICF 42.
Certified Medicaid.
Owner Proprietary corp.

Rusk County Nursing Home
900 College Ave W, Ladysmith, WI 54848
(715) 532-5561
Admin J Michael Shaw. *Dir of Nursing*
Juanita Patten RN. *Medical Dir* Dr Douglas
Delong.
Licensure Skilled care. *Beds* SNF 117. *Private
Pay Patients* 20%. *Certified* Medicaid;
Medicare.
Owner Nonprofit organization/foundation.
Admissions Requirements Minimum age 18;
Medical examination; Physician's request.
Staff Physicians 8 (pt); RNs 8 (ft), 3 (pt);
LPNs 5 (pt); Nurses' aides 17 (ft), 34 (pt);
Physical therapists 1 (pt); Occupational
therapists 1 (pt); Speech therapists 1 (pt);
Activities coordinators 1 (ft), 1 (pt);
Dietitians 1 (pt).
Facilities Dining room; Physical therapy
room; Activities room; Chapel; Crafts room;
Laundry room; Barber/Beauty shop; Library;
Cable TV.
Activities Arts & crafts; Cards; Games;
Reading groups; Prayer groups; Movies;
Shopping trips; Dances/Social/Cultural
gatherings; Intergenerational programs; Pet
therapy.

Lake Geneva

Geneva Lake Manor
211 S Curtis, Lake Geneva, WI 53147
(414) 248-3145
Admin Stephanie Quass. *Dir of Nursing* Betty
J Dearing. *Medical Dir* Dr E Paul Gander.
Licensure Skilled care; Intermediate care. *Beds*
Swing beds SNF/ICF 60. *Certified* Medicaid.
Owner Proprietary corp (Wis-Care Inc).
Admissions Requirements Medical
examination; Physician's request.
Staff Physicians 14 (pt); RNs 4 (ft), 2 (pt);
LPNs 4 (ft), 2 (pt); Nurses' aides 16 (ft), 8
(pt); Physical therapists 1 (pt); Occupational

therapists 1 (pt); Speech therapists 1 (pt); Activities coordinators 1 (ft); Dietitians 1 (pt); Ophthalmologists 1 (pt); Podiatrists 1 (pt); Pharmacists 3 (pt).
Facilities Dining room; Physical therapy room; Activities room; Chapel; Laundry room; Barber/Beauty shop.
Activities Arts & crafts; Games; Reading groups; Movies; Dances/Social/Cultural gatherings.

Lake Mills

Willowbrook Nursing Home
901 Mulberry St, Lake Mills, WI 53551
(414) 648-8344
Admin Ellen E Fritsch. *Dir of Nursing* Margaret Merry RN. *Medical Dir* James P Wishow.
Licensure Skilled care; Intermediate care. *Beds* Swing beds SNF/ICF 60. *Certified* Medicaid; Medicare.
Owner Proprietary corp (Unicare Health).
Admissions Requirements Minimum age 18; Medical examination; Physician's request.
Staff RNs 1 (ft), 6 (pt); LPNs 2 (ft), 5 (pt); Nurses' aides 12 (ft), 15 (pt); Physical therapists (contracted); Occupational therapists (contracted); Speech therapists (contracted); Activities coordinators 1 (ft), 1 (pt); Dietitians (consultant); Podiatrists (contracted).
Facilities Dining room; Physical therapy room; Activities room; Laundry room; Barber/Beauty shop; Day care.
Activities Arts & crafts; Cards; Games; Reading groups; Prayer groups; Dances/Social/Cultural gatherings; Intergenerational programs; Pet therapy.

Lancaster

Lancaster Living Center
1350 S Madison St, Lancaster, WI 53813
(608) 723-4143
Admin Kenneth A Becker. *Dir of Nursing* Candice Auel. *Medical Dir* Leo Becher MD.
Licensure Skilled care; Intermediate care. *Beds* SNF 68; ICF 66. *Private Pay Patients* 32%. *Certified* Medicaid; Medicare.
Owner Nonprofit corp (Adventist Living Centers).
Staff Physicians 2 (pt); RNs 3 (ft), 1 (pt); LPNs 5 (ft), 4 (pt); Nurses' aides 30 (ft), 18 (pt); Physical therapists 1 (pt); Speech therapists 1 (pt); Activities coordinators 1 (ft), 1 (pt); Dietitians 5 (ft), 4 (pt).
Affiliation Seventh-Day Adventist.
Facilities Dining room; Physical therapy room; Activities room; Chapel; Crafts room; Laundry room; Barber/Beauty shop; Library.
Activities Arts & crafts; Cards; Games; Reading groups; Prayer groups; Movies; Shopping trips; Dances/Social/Cultural gatherings.

Orchard Manor—North
PO Box 431, Lancaster, WI 53813
(608) 723-2113
Admin Matteo T Furno, Jr.
Licensure Skilled care; Intermediate care for mentally retarded. *Beds* SNF 81; ICF/MR 62. *Certified* Medicaid; Medicare.
Owner Publicly owned.

Orchard Manor—South
PO Box 431, Lancaster, WI 53813
(608) 723-2113
Admin Matteo T Furno Jr.
Medical Dir Donna Peterson.
Licensure Skilled care. *Beds* SNF 30. *Certified* Medicaid; Medicare.
Owner Publicly owned.
Admissions Requirements Minimum age 18; Medical examination.

Facilities Dining room; Physical therapy room; Activities room; Chapel; Crafts room; Laundry room; Barber/Beauty shop; Library.
Activities Arts & crafts; Cards; Games; Reading groups; Prayer groups; Movies; Dances/Social/Cultural gatherings.

Laona

Nu-Roc Nursing Home
Rte 1, Laona, WI 54541
(715) 674-4477
Admin Craig R Newton.
Medical Dir Dr R D Niehause.
Licensure Skilled care; Intermediate care. *Beds* 61. *Certified* Medicaid.
Owner Proprietary corp.
Admissions Requirements Medical examination.
Staff RNs 3 (ft); LPNs 3 (ft), 1 (pt); Nurses' aides 6 (ft), 20 (pt); Physical therapists 1 (pt); Activities coordinators 1 (ft); Dietitians 1 (pt).
Facilities Dining room; Physical therapy room; Activities room; Laundry room; Barber/Beauty shop.
Activities Arts & crafts; Cards; Games; Prayer groups; Dances/Social/Cultural gatherings; Dinner club.

Little Chute

Parkside Care Center
1201 Garfield Ave, Little Chute, WI 54140
(414) 788-5806
Admin Thomas Lesselyong. *Dir of Nursing* Jana Clement. *Medical Dir* F X Van Lieshout MD.
Licensure Skilled care. *Beds* SNF 103. *Certified* Medicaid.
Owner Proprietary corp.
Admissions Requirements Minimum age 18; Medical examination; Physician's request.
Staff RNs 3 (ft), 1 (pt); LPNs 4 (ft), 4 (pt); Nurses' aides 12 (ft), 30 (pt); Activities coordinators 1 (ft), 2 (pt).
Facilities Dining room; Physical therapy room; Activities room; Chapel; Crafts room; Laundry room; Barber/Beauty shop.
Activities Arts & crafts; Cards; Games; Reading groups; Prayer groups; Movies; Dances/Social/Cultural gatherings.

Lodi

Lodi Good Samaritan Center
700 Clark St, Lodi, WI 53555
(608) 592-3241
Admin Gilbert M Singer. *Dir of Nursing* Cristi L Maier RN. *Medical Dir* Dr Dale Fanney.
Licensure Skilled care; Retirement; Alzheimer's care. *Beds* SNF 100. *Certified* Medicaid.
Owner Nonprofit corp (Evangelical Lutheran/ Good Samaritan Society).
Admissions Requirements Minimum age 18; Medical examination.
Staff Physicians 5 (ft); RNs 2 (ft), 8 (pt); LPNs 1 (ft), 10 (pt); Nurses' aides 16 (ft), 31 (pt); Physical therapists 1 (pt); Speech therapists 1 (pt); Occupational therapists 1 (pt); Activities coordinators 1 (ft), 2 (pt); Dietitians 1 (pt); Podiatrists 1 (pt); Dentists 1 (pt).
Affiliation Lutheran.
Facilities Dining room; Physical therapy room; Activities room; Chapel; Crafts room; Laundry room; Barber/Beauty shop.
Activities Arts & crafts; Cards; Games; Reading groups; Prayer groups; Movies; Shopping trips; Dances/Social/Cultural gatherings; Outings in van.

Lomira

Hope Nursing Home
438 Ashford Ave, Lomira, WI 53048
(414) 269-4386
Admin Sr Ann Josepha Lencioni. *Dir of Nursing* Elaine Muchlius RN. *Medical Dir* Dr G P Langenfeld.
Licensure Skilled care. *Beds* SNF 42. *Certified* Medicaid.
Owner Nonprofit corp.
Admissions Requirements Minimum age 21; Medical examination.
Staff Physicians 3 (pt); RNs 1 (ft), 3 (pt); LPNs 1 (ft), 4 (pt); Nurses' aides 6 (ft), 16 (pt); Recreational therapists 1 (pt); Activities coordinators 1 (pt); Dietitians 1 (pt).
Affiliation Roman Catholic.
Facilities Dining room; Activities room; Chapel; Laundry room; Barber/Beauty shop; Library; Living room.
Activities Cards; Games; Reading groups; Prayer groups; Movies; Dances/Social/ Cultural gatherings.

Luck

United Pioneer Home
Park Ave, Luck, WI 54853
(715) 472-2164
Admin Daniel A Valentine.
Medical Dir Dr Arnold Lagus.
Licensure Skilled care; Intermediate care. *Beds* SNF 98. *Certified* Medicaid.
Owner Nonprofit corp.
Staff RNs 5 (ft), 1 (pt); LPNs 2 (ft), 4 (pt); Nurses' aides 5 (ft), 20 (pt); Physical therapists 1 (pt); Reality therapists 1 (pt); Recreational therapists 1 (ft), 1 (pt); Occupational therapists 1 (pt); Activities coordinators 1 (ft); Dietitians 1 (pt).
Facilities Dining room; Physical therapy room; Activities room; Chapel; Crafts room; Laundry room; Barber/Beauty shop.
Activities Arts & crafts; Cards; Games; Reading groups; Movies; Shopping trips; Dances/Social/Cultural gatherings.

Madison

Arbor View Healthcare Center Inc
1347 Fish Hatchery Rd, Madison, WI 53715
(608) 257-0781
Admin Jeanne Hegerich.
Licensure Skilled care. *Beds* SNF 184. *Certified* Medicaid; Medicare.
Owner Proprietary corp.

Attic Angel
602-606 N Segoe Rd, Madison, WI 53705
(608) 238-8282
Admin Mary Ann Drescher. *Dir of Nursing* Joanne Elfman. *Medical Dir* Dr Warrick.
Licensure Skilled care; Retirement; Alzheimer's care. *Beds* SNF 64; Retirement 70. *Private Pay Patients* 100%.
Owner Nonprofit organization/foundation.
Admissions Requirements Minimum age 18; Medical examination; Physician's request.
Staff RNs 5 (ft), 2 (pt); LPNs 2 (pt); Nurses' aides 38 (ft), 20 (pt); Recreational therapists 1 (ft); Activities coordinators 1 (ft); Dietitians 1 (pt).
Facilities Dining room; Physical therapy room; Activities room; Chapel; Barber/ Beauty shop.
Activities Arts & crafts; Games; Reading groups; Prayer groups; Dances/Social/ Cultural gatherings; Pet therapy.

Central Wisconsin Center for the Developmentally Disabled
317 Knutson Dr, Madison, WI 53704-1197
(608) 249-2151, 249-0878 FAX
Admin Gerald E Dymond. *Dir of Nursing* Kathlyn J Steele, Acting. *Medical Dir* John B Toussaint MD.

Licensure Intermediate care for mentally retarded. *Beds* ICF/MR 629. *Private Pay Patients* 0%. *Certified* Medicaid; Medicare. *Owner* Publicly owned.
Admissions Requirements Minimum age birth; Physician's request.
Staff Physicians 6 (ft), 1 (pt); RNs 34 (ft), 15 (pt); LPNs 55 (ft), 15 (pt); Nurses' aides 419 (ft), 38 (pt); Physical therapists 10 (ft); Recreational therapists 8 (ft), 3 (pt); Occupational therapists 5 (ft), 6 (pt); Speech therapists 5 (ft), 1 (pt); Activities coordinators 1 (ft); Dietitians 2 (ft), 4 (pt).
Facilities Dining room; Physical therapy room; Activities room; Chapel; Crafts room; Library; Acute hospital unit.
Activities Arts & crafts; Games; Movies; Shopping trips; Dances/Social/Cultural gatherings; Pet therapy.

City View Nursing Home
Rte 10, 3737 Burke Rd, Madison, WI 53704
(608) 244-1313
Admin Thomas R Schroud.
Licensure Skilled care. *Beds* SNF 60. *Certified* Medicaid.
Owner Proprietary corp.

Colonial Manor
110 Belmont Rd, Madison, WI 53714
(608) 249-7391, 249-7020 FAX
Admin Lawana S Parks. *Dir of Nursing* Sandy Zeitlin. *Medical Dir* Dr Gary Bridgwater.
Licensure Skilled care. *Beds* SNF 144. *Private Pay Patients* 20%. *Certified* Medicaid; Medicare.
Owner Proprietary corp (Hillhaven Corp).
Admissions Requirements Minimum age 18; Medical examination; Physician's request.
Staff RNs; LPNs; Nurses' aides; Physical therapists 1 (ft), 1 (pt); Recreational therapists 1 (ft), 1 (pt); Occupational therapists 2 (ft); Speech therapists 1 (pt); Activities coordinators 1 (ft); Dietitians 1 (ft).
Facilities Dining room; Physical therapy room; Activities room; Laundry room; Barber/Beauty shop; Lounges.
Activities Arts & crafts; Cards; Games; Prayer groups; Movies; Shopping trips; Intergenerational programs; Pet therapy.

Karmenta Health Care Center
4502 Milwaukee St, Madison, WI 53714
(608) 249-2137
Admin Arlene Peterson.
Licensure Skilled care; Intermediate care. *Beds* SNF 105. *Certified* Medicaid; Medicare.
Owner Proprietary corp.

Leader Nursing & Rehabilitation Center
801 Braxton Pl, Madison, WI 53715
(608) 251-1010
Admin Mary Calhoun.
Medical Dir Dr Linda Farley.
Licensure Skilled care; Intermediate care. *Beds* SNF 173. *Certified* Medicaid; Medicare.
Owner Proprietary corp (Manor Care).
Staff RNs 10 (ft), 5 (pt); LPNs 6 (ft), 9 (pt); Physical therapists 2 (ft), 2 (pt); Recreational therapists 2 (ft), 1 (pt); Occupational therapists 2 (ft); Speech therapists 1 (pt); Dietitians 1 (pt); Podiatrists 1 (pt); Audiologists 1 (pt); Dentists 1 (pt).
Facilities Dining room; Physical therapy room; Activities room; Chapel; Crafts room; Laundry room; Barber/Beauty shop; Library.
Activities Arts & crafts; Cards; Games; Reading groups; Prayer groups; Movies; Shopping trips; Dances/Social/Cultural gatherings.

Madison Convalescent Center
2308 University Ave, Madison, WI 53705
(608) 238-8401
Admin Philip Tremain. *Dir of Nursing* Bonnie Fredrick. *Medical Dir* Dr Steven Babcock.

Licensure Skilled care; Intermediate care. *Beds* SNF 150. *Certified* Medicaid; Medicare.
Owner Proprietary corp (Unicare).
Admissions Requirements Minimum age 18; Medical examination; Physician's request.
Staff RNs 4 (ft), 8 (pt); LPNs 5 (ft), 6 (pt); Nurses' aides 20 (ft), 39 (pt); Activities coordinators 1 (ft).
Facilities Dining room; Physical therapy room; Activities room; Chapel; Crafts room; Laundry room; Barber/Beauty shop.
Activities Arts & crafts; Cards; Games; Reading groups; Prayer groups; Movies; Shopping trips; Dances/Social/Cultural gatherings; Community outings.

Methodist Health Center
334 W Doty St, Madison, WI 53703
(608) 258-2700
Admin Nancy B Anderson. *Dir of Nursing* Mary L Brueggeman. *Medical Dir* Dr Edward Kramper.
Licensure Skilled care; Adult day care; Retirement. *Beds* SNF 120; Adult day care 25. *Private Pay Patients* 65%. *Certified* Medicaid; Medicare.
Owner Nonprofit organization/foundation.
Admissions Requirements Minimum age 55; Medical examination.
Staff RNs 8 (ft), 12 (pt); LPNs 3 (ft), 5 (pt); Nurses' aides 24 (ft), 24 (pt); Physical therapists 1 (ft), 1 (pt); Occupational therapists 2 (pt); Speech therapists 1 (pt); Activities coordinators 1 (ft), 3 (pt); Dietitians 1 (ft).
Affiliation Methodist.
Facilities Dining room; Physical therapy room; Activities room; Chapel; Laundry room; Barber/Beauty shop.
Activities Arts & crafts; Cards; Games; Reading groups; Prayer groups; Movies; Shopping trips; Dances/Social/Cultural gatherings; Intergenerational programs; Pet therapy.

Oakwood Lutheran—Hebron Hall
6201 Mineral Point Rd, Madison, WI 53705
(608) 231-3453
Admin Charles K Lamson. *Dir of Nursing* Tracy Cisneros. *Medical Dir* John E Ewalt MD.
Licensure Skilled care; Intermediate care; Retirement. *Beds* SNF 137. *Certified* Medicaid; Medicare.
Owner Nonprofit corp.
Admissions Requirements Medical examination; Physician's request.
Staff RNs 6 (ft), 17 (pt); LPNs 2 (ft), 4 (pt); Nurses' aides 16 (ft), 52 (pt); Activities coordinators 1 (ft).
Affiliation Lutheran.
Facilities Dining room; Physical therapy room; Activities room; Chapel; Crafts room; Laundry room; Barber/Beauty shop; Pharmacy; 30 wooded acres.
Activities Arts & crafts; Cards; Games; Reading groups; Prayer groups; Movies; Shopping trips; Bible study.

Orchard Hill
2875 Fish Hatchery Rd, Madison, WI 53713
(608) 274-4350
Admin Stephen Jones PhD. *Dir of Nursing* Greta Janus RN. *Medical Dir* Ron Shaw MD.
Licensure Intermediate care for mentally retarded; Retirement. *Beds* ICF/MR 96. *Certified* Medicaid; Medicare.
Owner Nonprofit organization/foundation.
Admissions Requirements Minimum age 18; Medical examination.
Staff Physicians 1 (pt); RNs 3 (ft); Nurses' aides 2 (ft); Physical therapists 1 (ft); Recreational therapists 3 (ft), 1 (pt); Occupational therapists 2 (pt); Speech therapists 1 (pt); Activities coordinators 1 (ft); Dietitians 1 (pt); Social workers 2 (ft); Psychologist 1 (ft), 1 (pt).

Facilities Dining room; Activities room; Crafts room; Laundry room; Barber/Beauty shop; Gym.
Activities Arts & crafts; Cards; Games; Reading groups; Movies; Shopping trips; Dances/Social/Cultural gatherings; Horseback riding; Swimming; Bike hike; Bowling; Choir.

Sunny Hill Health Care Center
4325 Nakoma Rd, Madison, WI 53711
(608) 271-7321, 271-3946 FAX
Admin James E Enlund. *Dir of Nursing* Darla J Armstrong. *Medical Dir* Marilyn Adlin.
Licensure Skilled care; Intermediate care; Alzheimer's care. *Beds* Swing beds SNF/ICF 73. *Private Pay Patients* 70%. *Certified* Medicaid; Medicare.
Owner Proprietary corp (American Medical Services Inc).
Admissions Requirements Minimum age 18; Medical examination; Physician's request.
Staff RNs 6 (ft), 3 (pt); LPNs 3 (ft), 6 (pt); Nurses' aides 15 (ft), 17 (pt); Physical therapists 1 (ft), 1 (pt); Recreational therapists 3 (pt); Occupational therapists 1 (pt); Speech therapists 1 (pt); Activities coordinators 1 (ft); Food service directors 1 (ft).
Facilities Dining room; Physical therapy room; Activities room; Crafts room; Laundry room; Barber/Beauty shop; Library.
Activities Arts & crafts; Cards; Games; Reading groups; Prayer groups; Movies; Shopping trips; Dances/Social/Cultural gatherings; Intergenerational programs; Pet therapy.

Manawa

Manawa Community Nursing Center
400 E 4th, Manawa, WI 54949
(414) 596-2566, 596-2588 FAX
Admin Ann F Bonikowske NHA. *Dir of Nursing* Gayle Loberg RN. *Medical Dir* Lloyd Maasch MD.
Licensure Skilled care; Intermediate care. *Beds* Swing beds SNF/ICF 68. *Private Pay Patients* 22%. *Certified* Medicaid; Medicare.
Owner Proprietary corp.
Admissions Requirements Minimum age 18; Medical examination; Physician's request.
Staff Physicians 9 (pt); RNs 2 (ft), 2 (pt); LPNs 5 (ft), 2 (pt); Nurses' aides 15 (ft), 10 (pt); Physical therapists 1 (pt); Occupational therapists 1 (pt); Speech therapists 1 (pt); Activities coordinators 1 (ft); Dietitians 1 (pt).
Facilities Dining room; Physical therapy room; Activities room; Crafts room; Laundry room; Barber/Beauty shop.
Activities Arts & crafts; Cards; Games; Reading groups; Prayer groups; Movies; Shopping trips; Dances/Social/Cultural gatherings; Intergenerational programs; Pet therapy.

Manitowoc

Manitowoc Health Care Center
4200 Calumet Ave, Manitowoc, WI 54220
(414) 683-4100
Admin Frances M Anderson. *Dir of Nursing* Dawn Holsen.
Licensure Skilled care; Intermediate care for mentally retarded. *Beds* SNF 245; ICF/MR 49. *Certified* Medicaid; Medicare.
Owner Publicly owned.

Michigan Shores
1028 S 9th St, Manitowoc, WI 54220
(414) 682-0262
Admin Margaret R Schmeling. *Dir of Nursing* Jean Hinds. *Medical Dir* Edgar Stuntz MD.
Licensure Intermediate care. *Beds* ICF 41. *Private Pay Patients* 0%. *Certified* Medicaid.
Owner Proprietary corp (Beverly Enterprises).

Admissions Requirements Minimum age 18; Medical examination; Physician's request.
Staff RNs 2 (ft); LPNs 3 (ft), 3 (pt); Nurses' aides 5 (ft), 4 (pt); Physical therapists (contracted); Reality therapists (contracted); Recreational therapists (contracted); Occupational therapists (contracted); Speech therapists (contracted); Activities coordinators 1 (ft); Dietitians (contracted); Ophthalmologists (contracted); Podiatrists (contracted); Audiologists (contracted).
Facilities Dining room; Activities room; Laundry room; Living room.
Activities Arts & crafts; Cards; Games; Reading groups; Prayer groups; Movies; Shopping trips; Dances/Social/Cultural gatherings; Intergenerational programs; Pet therapy.

North Ridge Care Center
1445 N 7th St, Manitowoc, WI 54220
(414) 682-0316
Admin Kenneth Zade. *Dir of Nursing* Judy Holder. *Medical Dir* Dr J L Stoune.
Licensure Skilled care; Intermediate care. *Beds* SNF 164. *Certified* Medicaid; Medicare.
Owner Proprietary corp (Hillhaven Corp).
Staff Physicians 1 (pt); RNs 5 (ft), 3 (pt); LPNs 5 (ft), 8 (pt); Nurses' aides 13 (ft), 44 (pt); Physical therapists 1 (pt); Occupational therapists 1 (pt); Activities coordinators 1 (ft).
Facilities Dining room; Activities room; Barber/Beauty shop.
Activities Cards; Games; Reading groups; Prayer groups; Movies; Dances/Social/Cultural gatherings; Lunch outings; Rides.

Park Lawn Home
1308 S 22nd St, Manitowoc, WI 54220
(414) 684-1144
Admin Douglas Trost.
Licensure Skilled care; Intermediate care. *Beds* SNF 99. *Certified* Medicaid.
Owner Publicly owned.

Rainbow House
610 S 29th St, Manitowoc, WI 54220
(414) 684-4851
Admin Marcia M Christiansen. *Dir of Nursing* Sharon Van Ells. *Medical Dir* Steven Driggers MD.
Licensure Intermediate care for mentally retarded. *Beds* ICF/MR 15. *Certified* Medicaid.
Owner Privately owned.
Admissions Requirements Minimum age 18; Developmentally disabled & ambulatory.
Staff RNs 2 (pt); LPNs 1 (ft), 1 (pt); Nurses' aides 2 (ft), 4 (pt); Activities coordinators 1 (ft); Skill development aides 1 (ft), 2 (pt).
Facilities Dining room; Activities room; Laundry room.
Activities Arts & crafts; Cards; Games; Reading groups; Prayer groups; Movies; Shopping trips; Dances/Social/Cultural gatherings.

St Mary's Home for the Aged Inc
2005 Division St, Manitowoc, WI 54220
(414) 684-7171
Admin Sr Mary Claude. *Dir of Nursing* Sr Noel Marie. *Medical Dir* Dr Gary Schmidt.
Licensure Skilled care; Intermediate care; Retirement; Alzheimer's care. *Beds* Swing beds SNF/ICF 256; Retirement apts 64. *Private Pay Patients* 48%. *Certified* Medicaid.
Owner Nonprofit organization/foundation.
Admissions Requirements Minimum age 18; Medical examination.
Staff RNs 10 (ft), 7 (pt); LPNs 12 (ft), 9 (pt); Nurses' aides 91 (ft), 32 (pt); Activities coordinators 1 (pt); Dietitians 1 (ft).
Affiliation Roman Catholic.

Facilities Dining room; Physical therapy room; Activities room; Chapel; Crafts room; Laundry room; Barber/Beauty shop; Library; Swimming pool; Bowling alley; Coffee shop; Apparel shop; Gift shop; Alzheimer's unit.
Activities Arts & crafts; Cards; Games; Reading groups; Prayer groups; Movies; Shopping trips; Dances/Social/Cultural gatherings; Pet therapy; Swimming; Bowling.

Shady Lane Home Inc
1235 S 24th St, Manitowoc, WI 54220
(414) 682-8254
Admin Karen S Pesce. *Dir of Nursing* Karen Komoroski RN. *Medical Dir* Mary Govier MD.
Licensure Skilled care. *Beds* SNF 168. *Private Pay Patients* 50%. *Certified* Medicaid.
Owner Nonprofit organization/foundation.
Admissions Requirements Minimum age 62; Medical examination; Physician's request; Manitowoc County resident.
Staff RNs 8 (ft); LPNs 8 (ft); Nurses' aides 44 (ft); Physical therapists (contracted); Activities coordinators 1 (ft); Dietitians (consultant).
Facilities Dining room; Physical therapy room; Activities room; Chapel; Crafts room; Laundry room; Barber/Beauty shop; Library; Assisted feeding dining areas.
Activities Arts & crafts; Cards; Games; Reading groups; Prayer groups; Movies; Shopping trips; Dances/Social/Cultural gatherings; Intergenerational programs; Pet therapy.

Marinette

Luther Home
831 Pine Beach Rd, Marinette, WI 54143
(715) 732-0155
Admin Rev Kenneth Michaelis. *Dir of Nursing* Lydia Taylor RN. *Medical Dir* Dr Elwyn Mantei.
Licensure Skilled care; Intermediate care; Retirement. *Beds* Swing beds SNF/ICF 161; Retirement 175. *Certified* Medicaid.
Owner Nonprofit corp.
Admissions Requirements Minimum age 18; Medical examination; Physician's request.
Staff Physicians; RNs; LPNs; Nurses' aides; Physical therapists; Speech therapists; Activities coordinators; Dietitians.
Affiliation Evangelical Lutheran.
Facilities Dining room; Physical therapy room; Activities room; Chapel; Crafts room; Laundry room; Barber/Beauty shop.
Activities Arts & crafts; Cards; Games; Reading groups; Prayer groups; Movies; Dances/Social/Cultural gatherings; Intergenerational programs; Pet therapy.

Markesan

Riverdale Manor
150 S Bridge St, Markesan, WI 53946
(414) 398-2751
Admin Miriam G Ownby. *Dir of Nursing* Kathy Jerome RN. *Medical Dir* Paul Plueddemann MD.
Licensure Skilled care; Intermediate care; Retirement. *Beds* SNF 59; ICF 13. *Private Pay Patients* 62%. *Certified* Medicaid.
Owner Nonprofit organization/foundation.
Staff RNs 3 (ft), 3 (pt); LPNs 4 (ft), 4 (pt); Nurses' aides 15 (ft), 22 (pt); Physical therapists; Activities coordinators 1 (ft), 1 (pt); Dietitians 1 (pt).
Languages German, Polish.
Facilities Dining room; Physical therapy room; Activities room; Chapel; Crafts room; Laundry room; Barber/Beauty shop.
Activities Arts & crafts; Cards; Games; Reading groups; Prayer groups; Movies; Shopping trips; Dances/Social/Cultural gatherings; Intergenerational programs.

Marshfield

Marshfield Living Center
814 W 14th St, Marshfield, WI 54449
(715) 387-1188
Admin Gary Hixon. *Dir of Nursing* Beverly Kermitz RN. *Medical Dir* Scott Erickson MD.
Licensure Skilled care; Intermediate care. *Beds* SNF 206. *Certified* Medicaid; Medicare.
Owner Nonprofit corp (Adventist Living Centers).
Admissions Requirements Medical examination; Physician's request.
Staff Physicians 2 (pt); RNs 17 (ft), 5 (pt); LPNs 8 (ft), 8 (pt); Nurses' aides 61 (ft), 54 (pt); Physical therapists 1 (ft); Occupational therapists 1 (pt); Speech therapists 1 (pt); Activities coordinators 1 (ft); Dietitians 1 (ft); Ophthalmologists 1 (pt).
Affiliation Seventh-Day Adventist.
Facilities Dining room; Physical therapy room; Activities room; Chapel; Crafts room; Laundry room; Barber/Beauty shop; Library.
Activities Arts & crafts; Cards; Games; Reading groups; Prayer groups; Movies; Shopping trips; Dances/Social/Cultural gatherings; Outside meetings; Softball tournaments.

Norwood Health Center
1600 N Chestnut Ave, Marshfield, WI 54449-1499
(715) 384-2188
Admin Randy Bestul. *Dir of Nursing* Anne Kreeger. *Medical Dir* George A Pagels MD.
Licensure Skilled care; Intermediate care for mentally retarded; Acute psychiatric hospital. *Beds* SNF 16; ICF/MR 30; Acute psychiatric hospital 19. *Private Pay Patients* 1%. *Certified* Medicaid.
Owner Publicly owned.
Admissions Requirements Minimum age 18; Medical examination; Physician's request.
Staff Physicians 10 (pt); RNs 12 (ft), 4 (pt); LPNs 2 (pt); Nurses' aides 50 (ft), 25 (pt); Recreational therapists 1 (ft); Occupational therapists 1 (ft); Speech therapists 1 (ft); Activities coordinators 1 (ft); Dietitians 1 (pt); Ophthalmologists 1 (ft); Podiatrists 1 (ft); Audiologists 1 (pt); Dentists 1 (ft).
Languages Vietnamese, Polish.
Facilities Dining room; Activities room; Crafts room; Laundry room; Barber/Beauty shop; Library; Educational training center; Recreational area.
Activities Arts & crafts; Cards; Games; Reading groups; Prayer groups; Movies; Shopping trips; Dances/Social/Cultural gatherings; Pet therapy.

Mauston

Fair View Home
1050 Division St, Mauston, WI 53948
(608) 847-6161
Admin Daniel L Manders.
Medical Dir Dr E Heaney.
Licensure Skilled care; Intermediate care. *Beds* SNF 60. *Certified* Medicaid.
Owner Nonprofit corp.
Admissions Requirements Medical examination; Physician's request.
Staff Physicians 9 (ft); RNs 9 (ft); LPNs 3 (pt); Nurses' aides 10 (ft), 31 (pt); Physical therapists 2 (ft); Recreational therapists 2 (pt); Occupational therapists 1 (pt); Dietitians 1 (ft).
Facilities Dining room; Physical therapy room; Activities room; Barber/Beauty shop.
Activities Arts & crafts; Cards; Games; Reading groups; Prayer groups; Movies; Shopping trips; Dances/Social/Cultural gatherings.

Medford

Memorial Nursing Home Long-Term Care Unit
135 S Gibson St, Medford, WI 54451
(715) 748-8100
Admin Eugene W Arnett.
Licensure Skilled care; Intermediate care. *Beds*
SNF 104. *Certified* Medicaid.
Owner Nonprofit corp.
Staff RNs 4 (ft), 5 (pt); LPNs 3 (ft), 5 (pt);
Nurses' aides 32 (ft), 4 (pt); Physical
therapists 2 (pt); Occupational therapists 1
(pt); Activities coordinators 3 (ft); Dietitians
1 (pt).
Facilities Dining room; Physical therapy
room; Activities room; Chapel; Crafts room;
Laundry room; Barber/Beauty shop.
Activities Arts & crafts; Cards; Games;
Reading groups; Prayer groups; Movies;
Shopping trips; Dances/Social/Cultural
gatherings.

Mellen

Mellen Manor
450 Lake Dr, Mellen, WI 54546
(715) 274-5706
Admin Lorraine Daubner.
Licensure Skilled care. *Beds* SNF 40.

Menasha

Oakridge Gardens Nursing Center Inc
1700 Midway Rd, Menasha, WI 54952
(414) 739-0111
Admin Michael T Schanke. *Dir of Nursing*
Vivian A Schutte RN. *Medical Dir* G R
Mich MD.
Licensure Skilled care; Intermediate care. *Beds*
SNF 111. *Certified* Medicaid.
Owner Privately owned.
Staff RNs 3 (ft), 4 (pt); LPNs 2 (ft), 10 (pt);
Nurses' aides 9 (ft), 35 (pt); Activities
coordinators 1 (ft), 2 (pt).
Facilities Dining room; Physical therapy
room; Activities room; Crafts room; Laundry
room; Barber/Beauty shop.
Activities Arts & crafts; Games; Prayer groups;
Movies; Shopping trips; Bingo; Exercises.

Menomonee Falls

Linden Grove—Menomonee Falls
W 180 N 8071 Town Hall Rd, Menomonee
Falls, WI 53051
(414) 253-2700, 253-2283 FAX
Admin Mary A Obermeier. *Dir of Nursing*
Nancy Bruggeman. *Medical Dir* Dr
Dougherty; Dr Brody.
Licensure Skilled care; Alzheimer's care. *Beds*
SNF 135. *Certified* Medicaid; Medicare.
Owner Nonprofit corp (Linden Grove Inc).
Admissions Requirements Minimum age 65;
Medical examination; Physician's request.
Staff RNs 5 (ft), 5 (pt); LPNs 9 (ft), 23 (pt);
Nurses' aides 28 (ft), 33 (pt); Physical
therapists 1 (ft); Recreational therapists 1
(ft); Occupational therapists 1 (pt); Activities
coordinators 1 (ft); Dietitians 1 (ft).
Facilities Dining room; Physical therapy
room; Activities room; Crafts room; Laundry
room; Barber/Beauty shop.
Activities Arts & crafts; Cards; Games;
Reading groups; Prayer groups; Movies;
Shopping trips; Dances/Social/Cultural
gatherings; Intergenerational programs; Pet
therapy.

Menomonee Falls Health Care Center
N 84 W 17049 Menomonee Ave, Menomonee
Falls, WI 53051
(414) 255-1180, 255-2282 FAX
Admin Bill Smith. *Dir of Nursing* Barb
DeVajd RN. *Medical Dir* Steven L Merry
MD.
Licensure Skilled care; Intermediate care;
Retirement. *Beds* SNF 106. *Private Pay
Patients* 75%. *Certified* Medicaid; Medicare.
Owner Proprietary corp (Unicare).
Staff RNs; LPNs; Nurses' aides; Physical
therapists; Recreational therapists;
Occupational therapists; Speech therapists;
Activities coordinators; Dietitians;
Podiatrists.
Facilities Dining room; Physical therapy
room; Activities room; Laundry room;
Barber/Beauty shop; Lounges.
Activities Arts & crafts; Cards; Games; Prayer
groups; Movies; Shopping trips; Dances/
Social/Cultural gatherings; Intergenerational
programs; Pet therapy.

Menomonie

American Lutheran Home—Menomonie Unit
915 Elm Ave, Menomonie, WI 54751
(715) 235-9041
Admin Lanette M Flunker. *Dir of Nursing*
Margaret Kinderman. *Medical Dir* Dr
William Wright.
Licensure Skilled care; Retirement. *Beds* SNF
60. *Certified* Medicaid.
Owner Nonprofit corp.
Staff RNs 3 (ft), 2 (pt); LPNs 4 (ft), 1 (pt);
Nurses' aides 10 (ft), 22 (pt); Activities
coordinators 1 (ft); Dietitians 1 (ft).
Affiliation Lutheran.
Facilities Dining room; Activities room;
Chapel; Laundry room; Barber/Beauty shop.
Activities Cards; Games; Reading groups;
Prayer groups; Movies; Shopping trips.

Dunn County Health Care Center
Rte 2 Box 150, Menomonie, WI 54751
(715) 232-2661
Admin Gregory M Roberts. *Dir of Nursing*
Sharon Miller RN. *Medical Dir* Dr Daniel
Johnson.
Licensure Skilled care; Intermediate care for
mentally retarded; Alzheimer's care. *Beds*
SNF 185; ICF/MR 66. *Private Pay Patients*
10%. *Certified* Medicaid; Medicare.
Owner Publicly owned.
Admissions Requirements Physician's request.
Staff Physicians 5 (pt); RNs 6 (ft), 25 (pt);
LPNs 9 (ft), 4 (pt); Nurses' aides 49 (ft), 65
(pt); Recreational therapists 1 (ft); Activities
coordinators 1 (ft); Dietitians 1 (ft).
Facilities Dining room; Physical therapy
room; Activities room; Chapel; Crafts room;
Laundry room; Barber/Beauty shop.
Activities Arts & crafts; Cards; Games;
Reading groups; Prayer groups; Movies;
Shopping trips; Dances/Social/Cultural
gatherings.

Mequon

Mequon Care Center
10911 N Port Washington Rd, Mequon, WI
53092
(414) 241-3950
Admin Suzanne M Navin. *Dir of Nursing*
Doris Kingman RN. *Medical Dir* Russell
Robertson MD.
Licensure Skilled care; Alzheimer's care. *Beds*
SNF 213. *Certified* Medicaid; Medicare.
Owner Proprietary corp.
Admissions Requirements Minimum age 18;
Medical examination; Physician's request.
Staff RNs 12 (ft), 18 (pt); LPNs 15 (ft), 16
(pt); Nurses' aides 70 (ft), 63 (pt); Physical
therapists 1 (ft), 1 (pt); Activities
coordinators 1 (ft); Dietitians 1 (ft).
Languages German.
Facilities Dining room; Physical therapy
room; Activities room; Crafts room; Laundry
room; Barber/Beauty shop; Library; Private
room for family visits.

Activities Arts & crafts; Cards; Games;
Reading groups; Prayer groups; Movies;
Shopping trips; Dances/Social/Cultural
gatherings; Intergenerational programs; Pet
therapy.

Merrill

Pine Crest Nursing Home
2100 E 6th St, Merrill, WI 54452
(715) 536-0355
Admin Tim W Meehean. *Dir of Nursing*
Evelyn Sommi RN. *Medical Dir* Dr Roxana
Saeger.
Licensure Skilled care; Intermediate care;
Alzheimer's care. *Beds* SNF 180. *Certified*
Medicaid; Medicare.
Owner Publicly owned.
Admissions Requirements Minimum age 18;
Medical examination; Physician's request.
Staff RNs 7 (ft), 12 (pt); LPNs 4 (ft), 6 (pt);
Nurses' aides 43 (ft), 50 (pt); Physical
therapists 1 (pt); Recreational therapists 3
(ft); Occupational therapists 1 (pt); Speech
therapists 1 (pt); Activities coordinators 1
(ft); Dietitians 1 (ft); Podiatrists 1 (pt);
Dentists 1 (pt).
Facilities Dining room; Physical therapy
room; Activities room; Chapel; Crafts room;
Laundry room; Barber/Beauty shop; Library.
Activities Arts & crafts; Cards; Games;
Reading groups; Prayer groups; Movies;
Shopping trips; Dances/Social/Cultural
gatherings.

Middleton

Middleton Village Nursing Home
6201 Elmwood Ave, Middleton, WI 53562
(608) 831-8300
Admin Robert A Gorder.
Medical Dir Joyce Crates.
Licensure Skilled care; Alzheimer's care. *Beds*
SNF 80. *Certified* Medicaid; Medicare.
Owner Proprietary corp.
Admissions Requirements Minimum age 55;
Medical examination.
Staff Physicians 1 (pt); RNs 3 (ft), 6 (pt);
LPNs 3 (ft), 3 (pt); Nurses' aides 15 (ft), 44
(pt); Activities coordinators 1 (ft); Dietitians
1 (ft).
Facilities Dining room; Physical therapy
room; Activities room; Chapel; Crafts room;
Laundry room; Barber/Beauty shop; Library;
Lounges.
Activities Arts & crafts; Cards; Games;
Reading groups; Prayer groups; Movies;
Shopping trips; Dances/Social/Cultural
gatherings.

Milwaukee

Alexian Village of Milwaukee
9301 N 76th St, Milwaukee, WI 53223
(414) 355-9300, 357-5106 FAX
Admin Daniel C Krejci. *Dir of Nursing* Janet
I Fine RN. *Medical Dir* Dr Bruce Van
Cleave.
Licensure Skilled care; Retirement. *Beds* SNF
61; Independent apartment living 328.
Private Pay Patients 8%. *Certified* Medicaid.
Owner Nonprofit corp (Alexian Brothers
Health Systems Inc).
Admissions Requirements Minimum age 18.
Staff RNs 3 (ft), 4 (pt); LPNs 3 (ft), 4 (pt);
Nurses' aides 19 (ft), 10 (pt); Recreational
therapists 1 (pt); Activities coordinators 1
(ft).
Affiliation Roman Catholic.
Facilities Dining room; Physical therapy
room; Activities room; Chapel; Crafts room;
Laundry room; Barber/Beauty shop; Library;
Country store; Bank; Pharmacy.

Activities Arts & crafts; Cards; Games; Reading groups; Prayer groups; Movies; Shopping trips; Dances/Social/Cultural gatherings; Intergenerational programs; Pet therapy.

Bel Air Health Care Center
9350 W Fond Du Lac Ave, Milwaukee, WI 53225
(414) 438-4360, 464-3622
Admin Walter Bilski. *Dir of Nursing* Jane Clemente-Elliot. *Medical Dir* Michael Fehrer MD.
Licensure Skilled care. *Beds* SNF 310. *Private Pay Patients* 15%. *Certified* Medicaid; Medicare.
Owner Proprietary corp.
Admissions Requirements Minimum age 18; Medical examination; Physician's request.
Staff Physicians 1 (ft); RNs 21 (ft), 6 (pt); LPNs 34 (ft), 14 (pt); Nurses' aides 101 (ft), 21 (pt); Physical therapists 1 (ft), 2 (pt); Recreational therapists 1 (ft); Occupational therapists 1 (ft); Speech therapists 1 (ft); Activities coordinators 4 (ft), 4 (pt); Dietitians 1 (ft); Ophthalmologists 1 (pt); Podiatrists 1 (pt); Psychologists 1 (pt); COTAs 1 (pt); QMRPs 1 (pt).
Facilities Dining room; Physical therapy room; Activities room; Chapel; Crafts room; Laundry room; Barber/Beauty shop; Library; Patio.
Activities Arts & crafts; Cards; Games; Reading groups; Prayer groups; Movies; Shopping trips; Dances/Social/Cultural gatherings; Intergenerational programs; Pet therapy.

Bradley Convalescent Center
6735 W Bradley Rd, Milwaukee, WI 53223
(414) 354-3300
Admin Ada B Mara.
Licensure Skilled care. *Beds* SNF 270. *Certified* Medicaid; Medicare.
Owner Proprietary corp (Beverly Enterprises).

Cameo Convalescent Center
5790 S 27th St, Milwaukee, WI 53221
(414) 282-1300
Admin Borislav Kresovic.
Licensure Skilled care. *Beds* SNF 112. *Certified* Medicaid.
Owner Proprietary corp.

Colonial Manor
1616 W Bender Rd, Milwaukee, WI 53209
(414) 228-8700
Admin Mary B Lesjak.
Licensure Skilled care. *Beds* SNF 225.

Comstock Nursing Home
3025 W Mitchell, Milwaukee, WI 53215
(414) 384-8550
Admin Raymond J Herrmann.
Medical Dir John Palese MD.
Licensure Skilled care. *Beds* SNF 70. *Certified* Medicaid.
Owner Proprietary corp.
Admissions Requirements Minimum age 21; Medical examination.
Staff Physicians 4 (pt); RNs 3 (ft); LPNs 3 (ft), 6 (pt); Nurses' aides 8 (ft), 19 (pt); Physical therapists 1 (pt); Occupational therapists 1 (pt); Speech therapists 1 (pt); Activities coordinators 3 (pt); Dietitians 1 (pt); Podiatrists 1 (pt); Dentists 1 (pt).
Facilities Dining room; Physical therapy room; Activities room; Crafts room; Laundry room; Barber/Beauty shop.
Activities Arts & crafts; Cards; Games; Prayer groups; Movies; Shopping trips; Dances/ Social/Cultural gatherings.

De Paul Belleview Extended Care
1904 E Belleview Pl, Milwaukee, WI 53211
(414) 964-8200
Admin John E Stager. *Dir of Nursing* Paulette Herwig RN. *Medical Dir* William McDaniel MD.

Licensure Skilled care; Intermediate care. *Beds* Swing beds SNF/ICF 95. *Certified* Medicaid.
Owner Nonprofit corp.
Admissions Requirements Minimum age 18; Medical examination.
Staff Physicians 3 (pt); RNs 7 (ft), 6 (pt); LPNs 6 (ft), 8 (pt); Nurses' aides 7 (ft), 18 (pt); Physical therapists 2 (pt); Recreational therapists 2 (ft), 1 (pt); Occupational therapists 5 (ft); Speech therapists 1 (pt); Activities coordinators 1 (ft); Dietitians 1 (ft); Ophthalmologists 1 (pt); Podiatrists 1 (pt); Dentists 1 (pt); Counselors & social workers 11 (ft).
Facilities Dining room; Physical therapy room; Activities room; Chapel; Crafts room; Laundry room; Barber/Beauty shop; Library; Meeting rooms.
Activities Arts & crafts; Cards; Games; Reading groups; Prayer groups; Movies; Shopping trips; Dances/Social/Cultural gatherings; Community outings; Trips; AA; NA; OA; Support groups.

Family Nursing Home & Rehabilitation Center Inc
2801 W Wisconsin Ave, Milwaukee, WI 53208
(414) 937-8700
Admin Wayne Brow.
Medical Dir David Fischer.
Licensure Skilled care. *Beds* SNF 174. *Certified* Medicaid; Medicare.
Owner Proprietary corp.
Admissions Requirements Minimum age 18; Medical examination; Physician's request.
Staff Physicians 25 (pt); RNs 6 (ft), 3 (pt); LPNs 15 (ft), 6 (pt); Nurses' aides 20 (ft), 30 (pt); Physical therapists 1 (ft); Recreational therapists 1 (ft); Occupational therapists 1 (ft); Speech therapists 1 (ft); Activities coordinators 1 (ft); Dietitians 1 (pt); Ophthalmologists 1 (pt); Dentists.
Facilities Dining room; Physical therapy room; Activities room; Crafts room; Laundry room; Barber/Beauty shop; Library.
Activities Arts & crafts; Cards; Games; Reading groups; Prayer groups; Movies; Shopping trips; Dances/Social/Cultural gatherings.

Friendship Village
7300 W Dean Rd, Milwaukee, WI 53223
(414) 354-3700, 357-0375 FAX
Admin Susan Timmons. *Dir of Nursing* Jeanne Brandt. *Medical Dir* Dr James Hare.
Licensure Skilled care; CBRF; Retirement. *Beds* SNF 93; CBRF 22; Retirement apts 325. *Private Pay Patients* 100%.
Owner Nonprofit organization/foundation.
Admissions Requirements Minimum age 62; Medical examination; Physician's request.
Staff Physicians 1 (pt); RNs 4 (ft), 8 (pt); LPNs 3 (ft), 9 (pt); Nurses' aides 15 (ft), 21 (pt); Physical therapists (contracted); Activities coordinators 1 (ft); Dietitians (contracted).
Facilities Dining room; Physical therapy room; Activities room; Chapel; Crafts room; Laundry room; Barber/Beauty shop; Library.
Activities Arts & crafts; Cards; Games; Reading groups; Prayer groups; Movies; Shopping trips; Dances/Social/Cultural gatherings; Pet therapy.

Glen Field Health Care Center
1633 W Bender Rd, Milwaukee, WI 53209
(414) 228-9440
Admin Thomas D Pollock.
Licensure Skilled care; Intermediate care. *Beds* SNF 260. *Certified* Medicaid; Medicare.
Owner Proprietary corp (Beverly Enterprises).

Heartland of Milwaukee
3216 W Highland Blvd, Milwaukee, WI 53208
(414) 344-6515
Admin Betsy J Larsen.
Medical Dir Jean Neitzke.

Licensure Skilled care; Intermediate care; Alzheimer's care. *Beds* SNF 150. *Certified* Medicaid; Medicare.
Owner Proprietary corp (Health Care & Retirement Corp).
Admissions Requirements Minimum age 18; Medical examination; Physician's request.
Staff Physicians 1 (pt); RNs 12 (ft), 4 (pt); LPNs 6 (ft), 15 (pt); Nurses' aides 36 (ft), 84 (pt); Physical therapists 1 (pt); Recreational therapists 1 (ft), 2 (pt); Occupational therapists 1 (ft); Speech therapists 1 (pt); Activities coordinators 1 (ft); Dietitians 1 (pt).
Facilities Dining room; Physical therapy room; Activities room; Chapel; Crafts room; Laundry room; Barber/Beauty shop.
Activities Arts & crafts; Cards; Games; Reading groups; Prayer groups; Movies; Shopping trips; Dances/Social/Cultural gatherings.

Hillcrest Convalescent Home Inc
3281 N 15th St, Milwaukee, WI 53206
(414) 264-2720
Admin Thelma Henderson.
Licensure Skilled care; Intermediate care. *Beds* SNF 50. *Certified* Medicaid.
Owner Proprietary corp.

Hillside Health Care Center Inc
8726 W Mill Rd, Milwaukee, WI 53225
(414) 353-4100
Admin Wendy A Stevert. *Dir of Nursing* Pat Fuller RN. *Medical Dir* Nicholas C De Leo MD.
Licensure Skilled care. *Beds* SNF 39. *Certified* Medicaid.
Owner Proprietary corp.
Admissions Requirements Minimum age 50; Medical examination; Physician's request.
Staff RNs 1 (ft), 1 (pt); LPNs 3 (ft), 3 (pt); Nurses' aides 10 (ft), 10 (pt); Physical therapists; Recreational therapists 1 (ft); Occupational therapists; Speech therapists; Activities coordinators 1 (ft); Dietitians 1 (pt); Dentists.
Facilities Dining room; Physical therapy room; Activities room; Chapel; Laundry room; Barber/Beauty shop.
Activities Arts & crafts; Cards; Games; Reading groups; Prayer groups; Movies; Shopping trips; Dances/Social/Cultural gatherings.

Hillview Care Center Inc
1615 S 22nd St, Milwaukee, WI 53204
(414) 671-6830
Admin Gail L Wolf. *Dir of Nursing* Ms Walker. *Medical Dir* Dr Vinluan.
Licensure Skilled care. *Beds* SNF 114. *Certified* Medicaid.
Owner Propriatry corp.
Admissions Requirements Minimum age 45.
Facilities Dining room; Physical therapy room; Activities room; Barber/Beauty shop.
Activities Arts & crafts; Cards; Games; Reading groups; Prayer groups; Movies; Shopping trips; Dances/Social/Cultural gatherings.

Jackson Center Nursing Home
1840 N 6th St, Milwaukee, WI 53212
(414) 263-1933
Admin Joann Harris-Adams. *Dir of Nursing* Bernadette Pier. *Medical Dir* Dr Simplico Go.
Licensure Intermediate care for mentally retarded. *Beds* ICF/MR 125. *Certified* Medicaid.
Owner Proprietary corp (Unicare).
Admissions Requirements Minimum age 18; Medical examination.
Staff RNs 4 (ft); LPNs 10 (ft); Nurses' aides 48 (ft); Recreational therapists 6 (ft); Dietitians 1 (ft).

Facilities Dining room; Physical therapy
room; Activities room; Laundry room.
Activities Arts & crafts; Cards; Games;
Reading groups; Prayer groups; Movies;
Shopping trips; Dances/Social/Cultural
gatherings.

Kilbourn Care Center
2125 W Kilbourn Ave, Milwaukee, WI 53233
(414) 342-1312
Admin Lois M Lister RD NHA. *Dir of
Nursing* Maria Ponce. *Medical Dir*
Mohammed Sethi MD.
Licensure Skilled care; Intermediate care. *Beds*
SNF 98. *Private Pay Patients* 2%. *Certified*
Medicaid.
Owner Proprietary corp (Beverly Enterprises).
Admissions Requirements Minimum age 40;
Medical examination; Physician's request.
Staff Physicians 8 (pt); RNs 3 (ft), 5 (pt);
LPNs 6 (ft), 10 (pt); Nurses' aides 12 (ft), 16
(pt); Physical therapists 2 (pt); Recreational
therapists 1 (ft), 1 (pt); Occupational
therapists 1 (pt); Speech therapists 1 (pt);
Ophthalmologists 1 (pt); Dentists 1 (pt);
Dining Service Manager 1 (ft).
Facilities Dining room; Physical therapy
room; Activities room; Laundry room;
Barber/Beauty shop.
Activities Arts & crafts; Games; Prayer groups;
Movies; Shopping trips; Dances/Social/
Cultural gatherings; Pet therapy.

Lakewood Care Center
2115 E Woodstock Pl, Milwaukee, WI 53202
(414) 271-1020
Admin Michael Baskett.
Medical Dir Dr Lillich.
Licensure Skilled care; Intermediate care. *Beds*
SNF 246. *Certified* Medicaid.
Owner Proprietary corp (Beverly Enterprises).
Admissions Requirements Medical
examination; Physician's request.
Staff RNs 15 (ft), 5 (pt); LPNs 36 (ft), 4 (pt);
Nurses' aides 87 (ft), 8 (pt); Recreational
therapists 3 (ft); Activities coordinators 1
(ft); Dietitians 1 (ft).
Facilities Dining room; Physical therapy
room; Activities room; Chapel; Barber/
Beauty shop; Occupational Therapy; Speech
Therapy.
Activities Arts & crafts; Cards; Games;
Reading groups; Prayer groups; Movies;
Shopping trips; Dances/Social/Cultural
gatherings; Resident council; Family council.

Luther Manor
4545 N 92nd St, Milwaukee, WI 53225
(414) 464-3880
Admin Peter E Chang.
Licensure Skilled care; Intermediate care. *Beds*
SNF 201. *Certified* Medicaid; Medicare.
Owner Nonprofit corp.
Affiliation Lutheran.

Marian Catholic Home
3333 W Highland Blvd, Milwaukee, WI 53208
(414) 344-8100
Admin Susan O'Shea.
Medical Dir Dr Mary Gavinski.
Licensure Skilled care; Intermediate care. *Beds*
SNF 360. *Private Pay Patients* 45%. *Certified*
Medicaid; Medicare.
Owner Nonprofit corp.
Affiliation Roman Catholic.

Marian Franciscan Home
9632 W Appleton Ave, Milwaukee, WI 53225
(414) 461-8850
Admin James D Gresham. *Dir of Nursing*
Ruth N Springob RN.
Licensure Skilled care. *Beds* SNF 465.
Certified Medicaid.
Owner Nonprofit corp.
Admissions Requirements Minimum age 18.

Affiliation Roman Catholic.
Facilities Dining room; Physical therapy
room; Activities room; Crafts room; Laundry
room; Barber/Beauty shop.

Marina View Manor Inc
1522 N Prospect Ave, Milwaukee, WI 53202
(414) 273-4890, 273-2105 FAX
Admin John F Flynn. *Dir of Nursing* Beth
Huettig RN. *Medical Dir* Dr Marvin
Lauwasser.
Licensure Skilled care. *Beds* SNF 357. *Private
Pay Patients* 5%. *Certified* Medicaid;
Medicare.
Owner Proprietary corp (Health Care & Retire
Corp).
Admissions Requirements Minimum age 18.
Languages Polish, German, Spanish.
Facilities Dining room; Physical therapy
room; Activities room; Chapel; Crafts room;
Laundry room; Barber/Beauty shop; Library.
Activities Arts & crafts; Cards; Games;
Reading groups; Prayer groups; Movies;
Shopping trips; Dances/Social/Cultural
gatherings; Intergenerational programs; Pet
therapy.

Mercy Residential & Rehabilitation Center
2727 W Mitchell St, Milwaukee, WI 53215
(414) 383-3699
Admin Elaine K Lukas. *Dir of Nursing* Sandra
Baumgartner RN. *Medical Dir* Dr Gregory
Kuhr.
Licensure Skilled care; Alzheimer's care. *Beds*
SNF 60. *Private Pay Patients* 50%.
Owner Proprietary corp (Unicare).
Admissions Requirements Minimum age 65;
Medical examination; Physician's request.
Staff Physicians 1 (pt); RNs 5 (ft), 2 (pt);
LPNs 4 (ft), 2 (pt); Nurses' aides 24 (ft), 10
(pt); Physical therapists 1 (ft); Recreational
therapists 1 (ft); Occupational therapists 1
(ft); Speech therapists 1 (ft); Activities
coordinators 1 (ft); Dietitians 1 (pt);
Ophthalmologists (consultant); Podiatrists
(consultant); Audiologists (consultant);
Dietary, Housekeeping, and Laundry 7 (ft), 3
(pt).
Facilities Dining room; Physical therapy
room; Activities room; Laundry room;
Barber/Beauty shop.
Activities Arts & crafts; Cards; Games;
Reading groups; Prayer groups; Movies;
Shopping trips; Dances/Social/Cultural
gatherings; Intergenerational programs; Pet
therapy; Dinner trips.

Millway Nursing Home
8534 W Mill Rd, Milwaukee, WI 53225
(414) 353-2300
Admin Peter S Zlotocha.
Licensure Skilled care; Intermediate care. *Beds*
SNF 105. *Certified* Medicaid.
Owner Proprietary corp.

Milwaukee Catholic Home
2462 N Prospect Ave, Milwaukee, WI 53211
(414) 224-9700
Admin Paul J Connolly.
Licensure Skilled care; Intermediate care. *Beds*
SNF 44. *Certified* Medicaid.
Owner Nonprofit corp.
Affiliation Roman Catholic.

Milwaukee Jewish Convalescent Center
5151 W Silver Spring Dr, Milwaukee, WI
53218
(414) 464-2300
Admin Benjamin E Lane.
Medical Dir Sanford Mallin; Madonna
Booher.
Licensure Skilled care; Intermediate care;
Alzheimer's care. *Beds* SNF 48. *Certified*
Medicaid; Medicare.
Owner Nonprofit corp.
Admissions Requirements Medical
examination.

Staff Physicians 3 (pt); RNs 3 (ft); LPNs 3
(ft), 3 (pt); Nurses' aides 12 (ft), 4 (pt);
Physical therapists 2 (pt); Reality therapists
1 (pt); Recreational therapists 2 (ft), 5 (pt);
Occupational therapists 1 (pt); Dietitians 1
(pt).
Languages Yiddish, Hebrew.
Affiliation Jewish.
Facilities Dining room; Physical therapy
room; Activities room; Chapel; Crafts room;
Barber/Beauty shop; Library.
Activities Arts & crafts; Cards; Games;
Reading groups; Prayer groups; Movies;
Shopping trips; Dances/Social/Cultural
gatherings.

Milwaukee Jewish Home
1414 N Prospect Ave, Milwaukee, WI 53202
(414) 276-2627, 276-4828 FAX
Admin Nita L Corre NHA. *Dir of Nursing*
Walter J Vine RN MHA. *Medical Dir*
Richard Kane MD.
Licensure Skilled care; Alzheimer's care. *Beds*
SNF 208. *Certified* Medicaid; Medicare.
Owner Nonprofit organization/foundation.
Admissions Requirements Medical
examination.
Staff Physicians 28 (pt); RNs 10 (ft), 20 (pt);
LPNs 13 (ft), 17 (pt); Nurses' aides 72 (ft),
38 (pt); Physical therapists 1 (ft);
Occupational therapists 1 (ft); Activities
coordinators 4 (ft); Dietitians 1 (pt);
Podiatrists 1 (pt); Medical records
coordinators 1 (ft); Unit clerks 4 (ft), 4 (pt).
Languages Yiddish, Hebrew, Russian, Polish.
Affiliation Jewish.
Facilities Dining room; Physical therapy
room; Activities room; Crafts room; Barber/
Beauty shop; Library; Synagogue.
Activities Arts & crafts; Cards; Games;
Reading groups; Prayer groups; Movies;
Shopping trips; Dances/Social/Cultural
gatherings; Intergenerational programs; Pet
therapy; Sheltered workshop; Therapy
program for Alzheimer's patients.

Milwaukee Protestant Bradford Terrace
2429 E Bradford Ave, Milwaukee, WI 53211
(414) 332-8610
Admin James G Lehmkuhl.
Licensure Skilled care. *Beds* SNF 50. *Certified*
Medicare.
Owner Nonprofit corp.

Milwaukee Protestant Home Infirmary
2449 N Downer Ave, Milwaukee, WI 53211
(414) 332-8610
Admin James G Lehmkuhl.
Licensure Skilled care. *Beds* SNF 47.
Owner Nonprofit corp.

Mt Carmel Health Care Center
5700 W Layton Ave, Milwaukee, WI 53220
(414) 281-7200, 281-4620
Admin Richard J Lesjak NHA. *Dir of Nursing*
Carolyn Glocka RNC. *Medical Dir* Robert S
Chudnow MD.
Licensure Skilled care; Intermediate care;
Alzheimer's care. *Beds* SNF 692. *Certified*
Medicaid; Medicare.
Owner Proprietary corp (Hillhaven Corp).
Admissions Requirements Minimum age 18;
Medical examination.
Staff Ophthalmologists (consultant);
Podiatrists (consultant); Audiologists
(consultant).
Facilities Dining room; Physical therapy
room; Activities room; Chapel; Crafts room;
Laundry room; Barber/Beauty shop.
Activities Arts & crafts; Cards; Games;
Reading groups; Prayer groups; Movies;
Shopping trips; Dances/Social/Cultural
gatherings; Intergenerational programs; Pet
therapy.

North Shore Health Care Center
601 W Glencoe Pl, Milwaukee, WI 53217
(414) 351-3830, 351-3701 FAX

Admin James A Guschl. *Dir of Nursing* Jay
Wallace. *Medical Dir* Dr Asher Cornfield.
Licensure Skilled care; Intermediate care. *Beds*
SNF 44; ICF 238. *Private Pay Patients* 10%.
Certified Medicaid.
Owner Proprietary corp (Beverly Enterprises).
Admissions Requirements Medical
examination; Physician's request.
Staff RNs 8 (ft), 3 (pt); LPNs 25 (ft), 11 (pt);
Nurses' aides 68 (ft), 17 (pt); Physical
therapists 1 (pt); Occupational therapists 2
(ft); Speech therapists 1 (pt); Activities
coordinators 1 (ft); Dietitians 1 (ft).
Facilities Dining room; Physical therapy
room; Activities room; Crafts room; Laundry
room; Barber/Beauty shop.
Activities Arts & crafts; Cards; Games;
Reading groups; Prayer groups; Movies;
Shopping trips; Dances/Social/Cultural
gatherings.

Northwest Health Care Center
7800 W Fond Du Lac Ave, Milwaukee, WI
53218
(414) 464-3950
Admin Jack D Nelson. *Dir of Nursing* John
Navine. *Medical Dir* Dr Michael Fehrer.
Licensure Skilled care; Intermediate care;
HEAP Trauma Unit. *Beds* SNF 118; HEAP
Trauma Unit 32. *Private Pay Patients* 35%.
Certified Medicaid; Medicare.
Owner Proprietary corp (American Medical
Services Inc).
Admissions Requirements Minimum age 18.
Staff Physicians 1 (pt); RNs 8 (ft), 7 (pt);
LPNs 4 (ft), 10 (pt); Nurses' aides 23 (ft), 47
(pt); Physical therapists 1 (pt); Recreational
therapists 1 (ft), 2 (pt); Occupational
therapists 1 (ft), 1 (pt); Speech therapists 1
(pt); Activities coordinators 1 (pt); Dietitians
1 (ft); Ophthalmologists 1 (pt); Podiatrists 1
(pt); Audiologists 1 (pt).
Facilities Dining room; Physical therapy
room; Activities room; Chapel; Crafts room;
Laundry room; Barber/Beauty shop.
Activities Arts & crafts; Cards; Games;
Reading groups; Prayer groups; Movies;
Shopping trips; Dances/Social/Cultural
gatherings; Intergenerational programs; Pet
therapy.

Park Manor Health Care Center
1824 E Park Pl, Milwaukee, WI 53211
(414) 961-1115
Admin Dana E Bilder.
Medical Dir John Becker MD.
Licensure Skilled care; Intermediate care. *Beds*
SNF 118. *Certified* Medicaid; Medicare.
Owner Proprietary corp (American Medical
Services Inc).
Admissions Requirements Minimum age 18;
Medical examination; Physician's request.
Staff Physicians 22 (pt); RNs 3 (ft), 7 (pt);
LPNs 4 (ft), 7 (pt); Nurses' aides 9 (ft), 33
(pt); Physical therapists 3 (pt); Recreational
therapists 1 (ft), 1 (pt); Occupational
therapists 2 (pt); Speech therapists 1 (pt);
Dietitians 1 (pt); Podiatrists 1 (pt); Dentists
1 (pt).
Facilities Dining room; Physical therapy
room; Activities room; Chapel; Crafts room;
Laundry room; Barber/Beauty shop; Library;
Outdoor patio.
Activities Arts & crafts; Cards; Games;
Reading groups; Prayer groups; Movies;
Shopping trips; Dances/Social/Cultural
gatherings; Music.

Parkview Care Center Inc
4615 W Hampton Ave, Milwaukee, WI 53218
(414) 462-9590
Admin Thomas G Schanke. *Dir of Nursing*
Marge Gozdowiak RN. *Medical Dir* Dr
DeLeo.
Licensure Skilled care; Intermediate care. *Beds*
SNF 74. *Certified* Medicaid.
Owner Proprietary corp.

Staff RNs; LPNs; Nurses' aides; Activities
coordinators; Dietitians.
Facilities Dining room; Physical therapy
room; Activities room; Laundry room;
Barber/Beauty shop.
Activities Arts & crafts; Cards; Games; Prayer
groups; Movies; Shopping trips; Dances/
Social/Cultural gatherings.

Plymouth Manor Nursing Home
619 W Walnut St, Milwaukee, WI 53212
(414) 263-1770
Admin Cordelia Taylor.
Medical Dir M R Sethi MD.
Licensure Skilled care; Intermediate care. *Beds*
SNF 166. *Certified* Medicaid.
Owner Proprietary corp (Unicare).
Facilities Dining room; Physical therapy
room; Activities room; Crafts room; Barber/
Beauty shop; Occupational Therapy Room.
Activities Arts & crafts; Cards; Games;
Reading groups; Prayer groups; Movies;
Shopping trips; Dances/Social/Cultural
gatherings; Afro-American Studies.

Regency Terrace South
2919 W Parnell Ave, Milwaukee, WI 53221
(414) 231-2810
Admin Herbert J Wilson.
Licensure Intermediate care. *Beds* ICF 156.
Certified Medicaid.
Owner Proprietary corp.

River Hills East Health Care Center
1301 N Franklin Pl, Milwaukee, WI 53202
(414) 273-3560
Admin Daniel G Barrett.
Medical Dir Richard Fritz MD.
Licensure Skilled care. *Beds* SNF 308.
Certified Medicaid; Medicare.
Owner Proprietary corp (American Medical
Services Inc).
Admissions Requirements Minimum age 18;
Medical examination; Physician's request.
Staff RNs 18 (ft), 7 (pt); LPNs 8 (ft); Nurses'
aides 73 (ft), 28 (pt); Physical therapists 1
(ft); Recreational therapists 5 (ft), 1 (pt);
Occupational therapists 2 (ft); Speech
therapists 1 (ft); Dietitians 1 (ft).
Facilities Dining room; Physical therapy
room; Activities room.
Activities Arts & crafts; Cards; Games;
Reading groups; Prayer groups; Movies;
Shopping trips; Dances/Social/Cultural
gatherings.

River Hills South Health Care Center
2730 W Ramsey, Milwaukee, WI 53221
(414) 282-2600
Admin Judith N Stuver. *Dir of Nursing* Betty
Storm. *Medical Dir* Dr Richard Kane.
Licensure Skilled care; Intermediate care. *Beds*
SNF 196. *Certified* Medicaid; Medicare.
Owner Proprietary corp (National Heritage).
Admissions Requirements Minimum age 18;
Medical examination; Physician's request.
Staff Physicians 25 (pt); RNs 7 (ft), 7 (pt);
LPNs 7 (ft), 17 (pt); Nurses' aides 34 (ft), 37
(pt); Physical therapists 1 (ft), 1 (pt); Reality
therapists 1 (pt); Recreational therapists 3
(ft), 1 (pt); Occupational therapists 1 (pt);
Speech therapists 1 (pt); Activities
coordinators 1 (ft); Dietitians 1 (pt);
Podiatrists 1 (pt); Audiologists 1 (pt);
Dentists 1 (pt).
Facilities Dining room; Physical therapy
room; Activities room; Crafts room; Laundry
room; Barber/Beauty shop.
Activities Arts & crafts; Cards; Games;
Reading groups; Prayer groups; Movies;
Shopping trips; Dances/Social/Cultural
gatherings.

Roseville East
1825 N Prospect Ave, Milwaukee, WI 53202
(414) 271-9160
Admin Julie A McKnight.

Licensure Skilled care; Intermediate care. *Beds*
SNF 122. *Certified* Medicaid; Medicare.
Owner Proprietary corp.

Roseville Manor
8526 W Mill Rd, Milwaukee, WI 53225
(414) 358-1403
Admin Elizabeth Brunner RN NHA. *Dir of
Nursing* Mary Moll RN. *Medical Dir* Dr
Nicholas De Leo.
Licensure Skilled care; Alzheimer's care. *Beds*
SNF 65. *Private Pay Patients* 35%. *Certified*
Medicaid; Medicare.
Owner Proprietary corp (Julie McKnight).
Admissions Requirements Minimum age 65.
Staff Physicians; RNs; LPNs; Nurses' aides;
Physical therapists; Recreational therapists;
Occupational therapists; Speech therapists;
Activities coordinators; Dietitians;
Ophthalmologists; Podiatrists.
Facilities Dining room; Physical therapy
room; Activities room; Crafts room; Barber/
Beauty shop; Family dining area; Outdoor
patio; Garden.
Activities Arts & crafts; Cards; Games;
Reading groups; Prayer groups; Movies;
Shopping trips; Dances/Social/Cultural
gatherings; Intergenerational programs; Pet
therapy; Diners club; Newspaper; Church
services; Adopt-a-grandparent.

Roseville Nursing Home
6477 N 91st St, Milwaukee, WI 53224
(414) 353-5780
Admin Sandra Schmeling.
Licensure Intermediate care for mentally
retarded. *Beds* ICF/MR 16. *Certified*
Medicaid.
Owner Proprietary corp.

St Anne's Home for the Elderly
3800 N 92nd St, Milwaukee, WI 53222
(414) 463-7570
Admin Sr Cecilia Honigfort.
Licensure Skilled care; Intermediate care. *Beds*
SNF 116. *Certified* Medicaid.
Owner Nonprofit corp (Little Sisters of the
Poor).
Affiliation Roman Catholic.

St Ann's Rest Home
2020 S Muskego, Milwaukee, WI 53204
(414) 383-2630
Admin Sr Lis M Columba.
Licensure Intermediate care. *Beds* ICF 54.
Certified Medicaid.
Owner Nonprofit corp.
Affiliation Roman Catholic.

St John's Home of Milwaukee
1840 N Prospect Ave, Milwaukee, WI 53202
(414) 272-2022
Admin Dennis M Gralinski. *Dir of Nursing*
Carol Schrank RN. *Medical Dir* Parks
LeTellier MD.
Licensure Skilled care; Intermediate care;
Home health; Retirement. *Beds* SNF 95.
Certified Medicaid; Medicare.
Owner Nonprofit corp.
Admissions Requirements Minimum age 60;
Medical examination; Physician's request.
Staff Physicians 1 (pt); RNs 6 (ft), 2 (pt);
LPNs 5 (ft), 6 (pt); Nurses' aides 17 (ft), 30
(pt); Physical therapists 1 (pt); Occupational
therapists 1 (ft), 2 (pt); Activities
coordinators 2 (ft); Dietitians 1 (pt);
Podiatrists 1 (pt).
Affiliation Episcopal.
Facilities Dining room; Physical therapy
room; Activities room; Chapel; Crafts room;
Laundry room; Barber/Beauty shop; Library;
Dental services.
Activities Arts & crafts; Cards; Games;
Reading groups; Prayer groups; Movies;
Shopping trips; Dances/Social/Cultural
gatherings; Service club; Special events.

St Jude Nursing Home
6526 W Bluemound Rd, Milwaukee, WI 53213
(414) 774-4290
Admin Lynn M Vogt. *Dir of Nursing* Geri Klebenow. *Medical Dir* Dr A Moonilal Singh.
Licensure Skilled care; Intermediate care; Retirement. *Beds* SNF 44. *Certified* Medicaid.
Owner Privately owned.
Admissions Requirements Minimum age 35; Medical examination; Physician's request.
Staff Physicians 1 (pt); RNs 2 (ft), 3 (pt); LPNs 3 (ft), 3 (pt); Nurses' aides 9 (ft), 9 (pt); Physical therapists 1 (pt); Reality therapists 1 (ft); Recreational therapists 1 (ft); Occupational therapists 1 (pt); Activities coordinators 1 (pt); Dietitians 1 (pt); Podiatrists 1 (pt); Other staff 1 (pt).
Languages German, Norwegian, Italian, French, Spanish.
Facilities Dining room; Activities room; Crafts room; Laundry room; Smoking room.
Activities Arts & crafts; Cards; Games; Reading groups; Prayer groups; Movies; Shopping trips; Dances/Social/Cultural gatherings; Pet therapy.

St Marys Nursing Home
3516 W Center St, Milwaukee, WI 53210
(414) 873-9250
Admin Michael R Zimmerman. *Dir of Nursing* Bernadetta Kolbeck MSN. *Medical Dir* Dr Eric Conradson.
Licensure Skilled care. *Beds* SNF 130. *Certified* Medicaid.
Owner Nonprofit corp.
Admissions Requirements Minimum age 18.
Staff RNs 4 (ft), 7 (pt); LPNs 8 (ft), 2 (pt); Nurses' aides 46 (ft), 24 (pt); Physical therapists 1 (ft), 2 (pt); Recreational therapists 2 (ft); Occupational therapists 1 (ft); Activities coordinators 1 (ft); Dietitians 1 (pt).
Affiliation Roman Catholic.
Facilities Dining room; Physical therapy room; Activities room; Chapel; Crafts room; Laundry room; Barber/Beauty shop.
Activities Arts & crafts; Games; Reading groups; Prayer groups; Movies; Dances/Social/Cultural gatherings.

Silver Spring Convalescent Center
1300 W Silver Spring Dr, Milwaukee, WI 53209
(414) 228-8120
Admin Rodney Smith.
Licensure Skilled care; Intermediate care. *Beds* SNF 138. *Certified* Medicaid.
Owner Proprietary corp (Beverly Enterprises).

Sunrise Nursing Home for the Blind Inc
827 N 34th St, Milwaukee, WI 53208
(414) 933-6977
Admin Michael J Kern. *Dir of Nursing* Barbara A DeVaud RN. *Medical Dir* Dr P C Ghosh.
Licensure Skilled care; Alzheimer's care. *Beds* SNF 99. *Private Pay Patients* 1%. *Certified* Medicaid.
Owner Nonprofit corp.
Admissions Requirements Minimum age 18; Medical examination; Physician's request.
Staff Physicians 4 (pt); RNs 2 (ft), 5 (pt); LPNs 9 (ft), 2 (pt); Nurses' aides 15 (ft), 16 (pt); Physical therapists 3 (pt); Occupational therapists 2 (pt); Speech therapists 1 (pt); Activities coordinators 1 (ft); Dietitians 1 (ft).
Languages Spanish, Polish, German.
Facilities Dining room; Physical therapy room; Activities room; Chapel; Crafts room; Laundry room; Barber/Beauty shop; Blind guidance rails.
Activities Arts & crafts; Cards; Games; Prayer groups; Movies; Shopping trips; Dances/Social/Cultural gatherings; Pet therapy.

Town & Country Manor
9222 W Appleton, Milwaukee, WI 53225
(414) 464-3050
Admin John R Werner.
Licensure Skilled care; Intermediate care. *Beds* SNF 30. *Certified* Medicaid; Medicare.
Owner Proprietary corp.

Westview Nursing Home—IMD
3014 W McKinley, Milwaukee, WI 53208
(414) 933-5217
Admin Joan M Langen.
Medical Dir Dr Wiliam Kah.
Licensure Intermediiate IMD. *Beds* Intermediate-IMD 21. *Certified* Medicaid.
Owner Proprietary corp.
Admissions Requirements Minimum age 18; Females only; Medical examination; Physician's request.
Staff Physicians 2 (pt); RNs 1 (ft); LPNs 2 (pt); Nurses' aides 4 (ft), 6 (pt); Recreational therapists 1 (pt); Dietitians 1 (pt).
Facilities Dining room; Activities room; Chapel; Crafts room; Laundry room.
Activities Arts & crafts; Cards; Games; Reading groups; Prayer groups; Movies; Shopping trips.

Wisconsin Lutheran Child & Family Service
PO Box 23980, 6800 N 76th St, Milwaukee, WI 53223
(414) 353-5000
Admin Rev Ernst F Lehninger.
Medical Dir Marc Olsen MD.
Licensure Skilled care; Retirement. *Beds* SNF 161. *Certified* Medicaid.
Owner Nonprofit corp.
Admissions Requirements Medical examination; Physician's request.
Staff Physicians 1 (pt); RNs 7 (ft), 11 (pt); LPNs 2 (ft), 9 (pt); Nurses' aides 35 (ft), 53 (pt); Physical therapists 1 (pt); Occupational therapists 1 (pt); Speech therapists 1 (pt); Activities coordinators 1 (ft); Dietitians 1 (pt).
Affiliation Lutheran.
Facilities Dining room; Physical therapy room; Activities room; Chapel; Crafts room; Laundry room; Barber/Beauty shop.
Activities Arts & crafts; Cards; Games; Reading groups; Prayer groups; Movies; Shopping trips; Dances/Social/Cultural gatherings.

Mineral Point

Mineral Point Living Center
109 N Iowa St, Mineral Point, WI 53565
(609) 987-2381
Admin Edward M Sajdak. *Dir of Nursing* Colleen Watters. *Medical Dir* T A Correll.
Licensure Skilled care. *Beds* SNF 89. *Private Pay Patients* 28%. *Certified* Medicaid; Medicare.
Owner Nonprofit corp (Adventist Health Systems-USA).
Admissions Requirements Minimum age; Medical examination; Physician's request.
Staff RNs 4 (ft), 1 (pt); LPNs 4 (ft), 2 (pt); Nurses' aides 18 (ft), 15 (pt); Physical therapists (contracted) Occupational therapists (contracted) Speech therapists (contracted); Activities coordinators 1 (ft), 1 (pt); Dietitians 1 (ft); Podiatrists (contracted).
Affiliation Seventh-Day Adventist.
Facilities Dining room; Physical therapy room; Activities room; Chapel; Crafts room; Laundry room; Barber/Beauty shop.
Activities Arts & crafts; Games; Reading groups; Prayer groups; Movies; Shopping trips; Dances/Social/Cultural gatherings; Pet therapy; Family participation; Religious support from community.

Mondovi

American Lutheran Home
158 E Main, Mondovi, WI 54755
(715) 926-4962
Admin Sheila J Gibbs. *Dir of Nursing* Mary Jacobson. *Medical Dir* Dr William Wright.
Licensure Skilled care; Residential care; Alzheimer's care. *Beds* SNF 55; Residential care 14. *Certified* Medicaid.
Owner Nonprofit corp (American Lutheran Homes Inc).
Admissions Requirements Minimum age 18; Medical examination; Physician's request.
Staff RNs 3 (ft), 1 (pt); LPNs 2 (ft), 1 (pt); Nurses' aides 20 (ft), 6 (pt); Physical therapists 1 (pt); Occupational therapists 1 (pt); Speech therapists 1 (pt); Activities coordinators 1 (ft), 1 (pt); Dietitians 1 (pt).
Affiliation Evangelical Lutheran.
Facilities Dining room; Physical therapy room; Activities room; Chapel; Laundry room; Barber/Beauty shop.
Activities Arts & crafts; Games; Reading groups; Prayer groups; Movies; Shopping trips; Dances/Social/Cultural gatherings; Intergenerational programs; Pet therapy.

Memorial Manor
200 Memorial Dr, Mondovi, WI 54755
(715) 926-4201
Admin Jacqueline Pavelski.
Licensure Skilled care; Intermediate care. *Beds* SNF 119. *Certified* Medicaid.
Owner Nonprofit corp.

Monroe

Monroe Manor Nursing Home
516 26th Ave, Monroe, WI 53566
(608) 325-9141
Admin John Imming. *Dir of Nursing* Kathy Ramsey. *Medical Dir* Dr John Irvin.
Licensure Skilled care; Intermediate care; Alzheimer's care. *Beds* SNF 100. *Certified* Medicaid; Medicare.
Owner Proprietary corp (Unicare).
Admissions Requirements Minimum age 18; Medical examination.
Staff RNs 6 (ft), 2 (pt); LPNs 2 (ft), 2 (pt); Nurses' aides 4 (ft), 36 (pt); Physical therapists 1 (pt); Occupational therapists 1 (pt); Speech therapists 1 (pt); Activities coordinators 1 (ft), 2 (pt); Dietitians 1 (ft); Dentists 1 (pt).
Facilities Dining room; Physical therapy room; Activities room; Chapel; Crafts room; Laundry room; Barber/Beauty shop.
Activities Arts & crafts; Cards; Games; Reading groups; Prayer groups; Movies; Shopping trips; Dances/Social/Cultural gatherings.

Pleasant View Nursing Home
PO Box 768, Monroe, WI 53566
(608) 325-2171
Admin Don Stoor.
Medical Dir John Frantz MD.
Licensure Skilled care; Intermediate care. *Beds* SNF 196. *Certified* Medicaid; Medicare.
Owner Publicly owned.
Admissions Requirements Medical examination.
Staff RNs 8 (ft), 8 (pt); LPNs 6 (ft), 3 (pt); Nurses' aides 40 (ft), 70 (pt); Activities coordinators 3 (ft), 1 (pt); Dietitians 1 (pt).
Facilities Dining room; Physical therapy room; Activities room; Chapel; Crafts room; Laundry room; Barber/Beauty shop; Library.
Activities Arts & crafts; Cards; Games; Reading groups; Prayer groups; Movies; Dances/Social/Cultural gatherings.

Montello

Montello Care Center
251 Forest Ln, Montello, WI 53949
(608) 297-2153
Admin Ruth F Bornick. *Dir of Nursing*
Barbara Holtz RN. *Medical Dir* Renato
Baylon MD.
Licensure Skilled care; Intermediate care. *Beds*
SNF 62. *Certified* Medicaid.
Owner Proprietary corp.
Admissions Requirements Medical
examination; Physician's request.
Staff RNs 2 (ft), 3 (pt); LPNs 2 (ft), 5 (pt);
Nurses' aides 8 (ft), 22 (pt); Physical
therapists 1 (pt); Occupational therapists 1
(pt); Speech therapists 1 (pt); Activities
coordinators 1 (ft); Dietitians 1 (pt);
Podiatrists 1 (pt).
Facilities Dining room; Physical therapy
room; Activities room; Chapel; Crafts room;
Laundry room; Barber/Beauty shop; Library.
Activities Arts & crafts; Cards; Games;
Reading groups; Prayer groups; Movies;
Shopping trips; Dances/Social/Cultural
gatherings.

Mount Calvary

Villa Loretto Nursing Home
N8138 Calvary St, Mount Calvary, WI 53057
(414) 753-3211, 753-3100 FAX
Admin Sr Mary Rose Schulte NHA. *Dir of
Nursing* Sr Mary Stephen. *Medical Dir*
Jeffrey A Strong MD.
Licensure Skilled care; Intermediate care. *Beds*
SNF 50. *Private Pay Patients* 30%. *Certified*
Medicaid.
Owner Nonprofit corp.
Admissions Requirements Minimum age 55.
Staff RNs 1 (ft), 3 (pt); LPNs 1 (ft), 4 (pt);
Nurses' aides 5 (ft), 18 (pt); Recreational
therapists; Occupational therapists; Activities
coordinators 1 (ft), 2 (pt); Dietitians 1 (pt).
Affiliation Roman Catholic.
Facilities Dining room; Activities room;
Chapel; Laundry room; Barber/Beauty shop;
Library.
Activities Arts & crafts; Cards; Games; Prayer
groups; Movies; Pet therapy.

Mount Horeb

Ingleside
407 N 8th St, Mount Horeb, WI 53572
(608) 437-5511
Admin Michael J Rock. *Dir of Nursing* Pat
Stauss. *Medical Dir* Dr James Damos.
Licensure Skilled care; Retirement. *Beds* SNF
119. *Certified* VA.
Admissions Requirements Medical
examination; Physician's request.
Staff RNs 5 (ft), 7 (pt); LPNs 3 (ft), 5 (pt);
Nurses' aides 20 (ft), 44 (pt).
Facilities Dining room; Physical therapy
room; Activities room; Chapel; Crafts room;
Barber/Beauty shop.
Activities Arts & crafts; Cards; Games;
Reading groups; Prayer groups; Movies;
Shopping trips; Dances/Social/Cultural
gatherings.

Muscoda

Riverdale Manor
1000 N Wisconsin Ave, Muscoda, WI 53573
(608) 739-3186
Admin Ronald L Bingham. *Dir of Nursing*
Rosaleen Gibbons RN. *Medical Dir* Dale
Sinnett MD.
Licensure Skilled care; Intermediate care. *Beds*
SNF 80. *Certified* Medicaid; Medicare.
Owner Proprietary corp (Beverly Enterprises).
Admissions Requirements Medical
examination; Physician's request.

Staff Physicians 3 (pt); RNs 3 (ft), 1 (pt);
LPNs 3 (ft), 2 (pt); Nurses' aides 20 (ft), 20
(pt); Physical therapists 1 (pt); Reality
therapists 1 (pt); Recreational therapists 1
(ft), 1 (pt); Occupational therapists 1 (pt);
Speech therapists 1 (pt); Activities
coordinators 1 (ft); Dietitians 1 (pt);
Ophthalmologists 1 (pt).
Facilities Dining room; Physical therapy
room; Activities room; Chapel; Crafts room;
Laundry room; Barber/Beauty shop; Library.
Activities Arts & crafts; Cards; Games;
Reading groups; Prayer groups; Movies;
Shopping trips; Dances/Social/Cultural
gatherings.

Muskego

Muskego Nursing Home
S 77-W 18690 Janesville Rd, Muskego, WI
53150
(414) 679-0246
Admin Harold M Swanto Jr.
Medical Dir Dr John Buhl.
Licensure Skilled care; Intermediate care. *Beds*
SNF 49. *Certified* Medicaid.
Owner Proprietary corp.
Admissions Requirements Minimum age 18;
Medical examination; Physician's request.

Tudor Oaks Health Center
12929 McShane Dr, Muskego, WI 53150
(414) 529-0100
Admin Earl J Hoagberg. *Dir of Nursing* Karen
Boese RN. *Medical Dir* Dr Scott Tilleson.
Licensure Skilled care; Retirement. *Beds* SNF
61. *Certified* Medicaid; Medicare.
Owner Nonprofit corp (American Baptists
Homes of the Midwest).
Admissions Requirements Minimum age 18;
Medical examination; Physician's request.
Staff RNs 5 (ft), 6 (pt); LPNs 3 (ft), 6 (pt);
Nurses' aides 15 (ft), 16 (pt); Physical
therapists 1 (pt); Recreational therapists 1
(ft); Occupational therapists 1 (pt); Dietitians
1 (ft).
Affiliation Baptist.
Facilities Dining room; Physical therapy
room; Activities room; Chapel; Crafts room;
Barber/Beauty shop.
Activities Arts & crafts; Cards; Games;
Reading groups; Prayer groups; Movies;
Shopping trips; Dances/Social/Cultural
gatherings; Pet therapy.

Neenah

Vallhaven Care Center
125 Byrd Ave, Neenah, WI 54956
(414) 725-2714
Admin David Bertrand. *Dir of Nursing* Rose
Wendt RN. *Medical Dir* E Loftus MD.
Licensure Skilled care. *Beds* SNF 164.
Certified Medicaid.
Owner Proprietary corp (Hillhaven Corp).
Admissions Requirements Minimum age 18.
Staff Physicians 1 (pt); RNs 8 (ft), 3 (pt);
LPNs 5 (ft), 9 (pt); Nurses' aides 24 (ft), 33
(pt); Physical therapists 1 (pt); Occupational
therapists 1 (pt); Speech therapists 1 (pt);
Activities coordinators 2 (ft); Dietitians 1
(pt).
Facilities Dining room; Activities room;
Chapel; Crafts room; Laundry room; Barber/
Beauty shop; Library.
Activities Arts & crafts; Cards; Games;
Reading groups; Prayer groups; Movies;
Shopping trips; Dances/Social/Cultural
gatherings; Exercise.

Neillsville

Neillsville Memorial Home
216 Sunset Pl, Neillsville, WI 54456
(715) 743-3101
Admin Glen E Grady.

Licensure Skilled care; Intermediate care. *Beds*
SNF 176. *Certified* Medicaid.
Owner Nonprofit corp.

New Berlin

Linden Grove Health Care Center
13755 W Fieldpointe Dr, New Berlin, WI
53151
(414) 796-3660
Admin Judith A Riley. *Dir of Nursing* Evonne
Luebke. *Medical Dir* Dr Peter Geiss.
Licensure Skilled care; Alzheimer's care. *Beds*
SNF 135. *Certified* Medicaid; Medicare.
Owner Nonprofit organization/foundation.
Admissions Requirements Minimum age 65;
Medical examination; Physician's request.
Staff RNs; LPNs; Nurses' aides; Physical
therapists; Occupational therapists; Speech
therapists; Activities coordinators; Dietitians.
Facilities Dining room; Physical therapy
room; Activities room; Chapel; Crafts room;
Laundry room; Barber/Beauty shop; Gift
shop; Dayrooms.
Activities Arts & crafts; Cards; Games; Prayer
groups; Movies; Shopping trips; Dances/
Social/Cultural gatherings; Intergenerational
programs; Pet therapy; Bingo; One-on-one
interaction; Entertainment; Church services.

New Glarus

New Glarus Home Inc
600 2nd Ave, New Glarus, WI 53574
(608) 527-2126
Admin Roger L Goepfert. *Dir of Nursing* Jane
Phillipson. *Medical Dir* Dr Edmund Aquino.
Licensure Skilled care; Retirement. *Beds* SNF
97; Retirement 22. *Private Pay Patients*
70%. *Certified* Medicaid.
Owner Nonprofit corp.
Staff RNs 2 (ft), 5 (pt); LPNs 1 (ft), 9 (pt);
Nurses' aides; Physical therapists 2 (pt);
Activities coordinators 1 (ft); Dietitians 1
(ft).
Affiliation United Church of Christ.
Facilities Dining room; Physical therapy
room; Activities room; Chapel; Crafts room;
Laundry room; Barber/Beauty shop; Library.
Activities Arts & crafts; Cards; Games;
Reading groups; Prayer groups; Movies;
Shopping trips; Dances/Social/Cultural
gatherings; Pet therapy.

New Holstein

Calumet Homestead
1712 Monroe St, New Holstein, WI 53061
(414) 898-4296
Admin Nancy S Steinke. *Dir of Nursing*
Donna J Delrow RN. *Medical Dir* Denis J
Pleviak MD.
Licensure Skilled care; Intermediate care;
Alzheimer's care. *Beds* SNF 104. *Private Pay
Patients* 48%. *Certified* Medicaid.
Owner Publicly owned.
Admissions Requirements Medical
examination.
Staff Physicians 1 (pt); RNs 4 (ft), 8 (pt);
LPNs 5 (pt); Nurses' aides 16 (ft), 39 (pt);
Physical therapists (consultant);
Occupational therapists 1 (pt); Speech
therapists (consultant); Activities
coordinators 1 (ft); Dietitians (consultant);
Dentists (consultant).
Languages German.
Facilities Dining room; Physical therapy
room.
Activities Arts & crafts; Cards; Games;
Reading groups; Prayer groups; Movies;
Shopping trips occasional; Dances/Social/
Cultural gatherings; Intergenerational
programs; Pet therapy.

Willowdale Nursing Home
1610 Hoover St, New Holstein, WI 53061
(414) 898-5706
Admin Nola Feldkamp.
Licensure Skilled care. *Beds* SNF 51. *Certified* Medicaid.
Owner Proprietary corp (Unicare).

New Lisbon

Pleasant Acres
W8741, County B, New Lisbon, WI 53950
(608) 562-3667
Admin Herbert C Finger. *Dir of Nursing* Marian Fox. *Medical Dir* Dr Tim Hinton.
Licensure Skilled care; Intermediate care. *Beds* Swing beds SNF/ICF 70. *Private Pay Patients* 20%. *Certified* Medicaid.
Owner Publicly owned.
Admissions Requirements Medical examination; Physician's request.
Staff RNs 2 (ft), 5 (pt); LPNs 1 (ft), 4 (pt); Nurses' aides 12 (ft), 16 (pt); Activities coordinators 1 (ft); Dietitians 1 (ft).
Facilities Dining room; Physical therapy room; Activities room; Laundry room; Barber/Beauty shop.
Activities Arts & crafts; Cards; Games; Reading groups; Prayer groups; Movies; Shopping trips; Dances/Social/Cultural gatherings; Pet therapy.

New London

St Joseph Residence
1925 Division, New London, WI 54961
(414) 982-5310
Admin Daniel W Orr. *Dir of Nursing* Terrie Pralat RN. *Medical Dir* Alan Strobusch MD.
Licensure Skilled care; Intermediate care; Retirement. *Beds* SNF 107. *Certified* Medicaid.
Owner Nonprofit corp.
Admissions Requirements Medical examination; Physician's request.
Affiliation Roman Catholic.
Facilities Dining room; Physical therapy room; Activities room; Chapel; Crafts room; Laundry room; Barber/Beauty shop; Library.
Activities Arts & crafts; Cards; Games; Reading groups; Prayer groups; Movies; Shopping trips; Dances/Social/Cultural gatherings.

New Richmond

Maple Manor Health Care Center
505 W 8th St, New Richmond, WI 54017
(715) 246-6851
Admin Lee Larson. *Dir of Nursing* Judy Knox RN. *Medical Dir* Dr Joseph Powell.
Licensure Skilled care; Intermediate care. *Beds* SNF 80. *Certified* Medicaid; Medicare.
Owner Proprietary corp (Beverly Enterprises).
Admissions Requirements Minimum age 18; Medical examination; Physician's request.
Staff RNs 4 (ft), 3 (pt); LPNs 2 (ft), 3 (pt); Nurses' aides 16 (ft), 15 (pt); Physical therapists 1 (pt); Occupational therapists 1 (pt); Speech therapists 1 (pt); Activities coordinators 1 (ft); Dietitians 1 (pt).
Facilities Dining room; Physical therapy room; Activities room; Crafts room; Laundry room; Barber/Beauty shop.
Activities Arts & crafts; Cards; Games; Reading groups; Prayer groups; Movies; Shopping trips; Dances/Social/Cultural gatherings.

St Croix Health Center
Rte 5 Box 33A, New Richmond, WI 54017
(715) 246-6991
Admin Doris E Kuefler. *Dir of Nursing* Joyce Jurisch RN. *Medical Dir* Bruce Hanson MD.

Licensure Skilled care; Intermediate care. *Beds* Swing beds SNF/ICF 123. *Private Pay Patients* 6%. *Certified* Medicaid.
Owner Publicly owned.
Staff Physicians (consultant); RNs 1 (ft), 8 (pt); LPNs 4 (ft), 5 (pt); Nurses' aides 31 (ft), 29 (pt); Physical therapists (consultant); Recreational therapists 1 (ft), 1 (pt); Occupational therapists (consultant); Speech therapists (consultant); Activities coordinators 1 (ft); Dietitians (consultant); Audiologists (consultant).
Facilities Dining room; Physical therapy room; Activities room; Chapel; Crafts room; Laundry room; Barber/Beauty shop; Library.
Activities Arts & crafts; Cards; Games; Reading groups; Prayer groups; Movies; Shopping trips; Dances/Social/Cultural gatherings; Intergenerational programs; Pet therapy.

Niagara

Maryhill Manor
501 Madison Ave, Niagara, WI 54151
(715) 251-3178
Admin Joanne D Wall NHA, Pres. *Dir of Nursing* Dawn Lanich-Seidel. *Medical Dir* Dr Carl Reinighaus DO.
Licensure Skilled care; Assisted living. *Beds* SNF 49; Assisted living units 6. *Private Pay Patients* 10%. *Certified* Medicaid.
Owner Nonprofit corp (School Sisters of St Francis).
Admissions Requirements Minimum age 60; Medical examination.
Staff RNs 3 (ft), 2 (pt); LPNs 1 (ft), 5 (pt); Nurses' aides 5 (ft), 18 (pt); Physical therapists (consultant); Activities coordinators 1 (pt); Dietitians (consultant).
Languages Polish, French.
Affiliation Roman Catholic.
Facilities Dining room; Physical therapy room; Laundry room; Barber/Beauty shop; Activities & crafts room/Library; Chapel/Multi-purpose room; Private living room; Dayrooms; Devotional room; Wheelchair accessible patio & gazebo.
Activities Arts & crafts; Cards; Games; Reading groups; Prayer groups; Movies; Dances/Social/Cultural gatherings; Intergenerational programs; Pet therapy.

Oconomowoc

Shorehaven
PO Box 208, 1306 West Wisconsin Ave, Oconomowoc, WI 53066
(414) 567-8341
Admin Tim E Thiele. *Dir of Nursing* Lorna Gartzke RN. *Medical Dir* Dr Robert Ballman.
Licensure Skilled care; Intermediate care; Retirement. *Beds* SNF 242. *Certified* Medicaid.
Owner Nonprofit corp.
Admissions Requirements Medical examination; Physician's request.
Staff RNs; LPNs; Nurses' aides; Activities coordinators; Dietitians.
Affiliation Lutheran.
Facilities Dining room; Physical therapy room; Activities room; Chapel; Crafts room; Barber/Beauty shop.
Activities Arts & crafts; Cards; Games; Reading groups; Prayer groups; Movies; Shopping trips; Dances/Social/Cultural gatherings.

Oconto

Riverside Nursing Center
100 Scherer Ave, Oconto, WI 54153
(414) 834-4575
Admin Ed Brady. *Dir of Nursing* Nancy Gralewski. *Medical Dir* John S Honish.

Licensure Skilled care; Intermediate care. *Beds* Swing beds SNF/ICF 103. *Certified* Medicaid; Medicare.
Owner Proprietary corp (Beverly Enterprises).
Admissions Requirements Medical examination.
Staff RNs; LPNs; Nurses' aides; Physical therapists; Occupational therapists; Speech therapists; Activities coordinators; Dietitians.
Facilities Dining room; Physical therapy room; Activities room; Chapel; Crafts room; Laundry room; Barber/Beauty shop.
Activities Arts & crafts; Cards; Games; Reading groups; Prayer groups; Movies; Shopping trips; Dances/Social/Cultural gatherings; Intergenerational programs; Pet therapy.

Oconto Falls

Falls Nursing Home
PO Box 985, Oconto Falls, WI 54154
(414) 846-3272
Admin James M Sharpe. *Dir of Nursing* Lou Ann Brown RN. *Medical Dir* James R Wong MD.
Licensure Skilled care; Intermediate care. *Beds* SNF 115. *Certified* Medicaid.
Owner Proprietary corp.
Admissions Requirements Minimum age 18; Medical examination; Physician's request.
Staff RNs 4 (ft), 2 (pt); LPNs 4 (ft), 6 (pt); Nurses' aides 20 (ft), 25 (pt); Activities coordinators 1 (ft), 2 (pt); Dietitians 1 (ft).
Facilities Dining room; Physical therapy room; Activities room; Laundry room; Barber/Beauty shop.
Activities Arts & crafts; Cards; Games; Reading groups; Prayer groups; Movies; Shopping trips; Dances/Social/Cultural gatherings; Picnics; Sight-seeing; Dinner outings.

Omro

Omro Care Center
500 S Grant St, Omro, WI 54963
(414) 685-2755
Admin Penny J Place. *Dir of Nursing* Joyce Elliott. *Medical Dir* Donald McDonald MD.
Licensure Skilled care; Alzheimer's care. *Beds* SNF 124. *Certified* Medicaid; Medicare.
Owner Proprietary corp (Hillhaven Corp).
Admissions Requirements Minimum age 18; Medical examination; Physician's request.
Staff Physical therapists 1 (pt); Recreational therapists 3 (pt); Occupational therapists 1 (pt); Speech therapists 1 (pt); Activities coordinators 1 (ft); Dietitians 1 (pt).
Facilities Dining room; Physical therapy room; Activities room; Chapel; Crafts room; Laundry room; Barber/Beauty shop; Library.
Activities Arts & crafts; Cards; Games; Reading groups; Prayer groups; Movies; Shopping trips; Dances/Social/Cultural gatherings; Intergenerational programs; Pet therapy.

Onalaska

Onalaska Care Center
1600 Main St, Onalaska, WI 54650
(608) 783-4681
Admin Rick Buechner. *Dir of Nursing* Karen L McBeth RN. *Medical Dir* Philip H Utz MD.
Licensure Skilled care; Intermediate care; Alzheimer's care. *Beds* SNF 112. *Certified* Medicaid.
Owner Proprietary corp.
Admissions Requirements Minimum age 18; Medical examination; Physician's request.
Staff Physicians 2 (pt); RNs 5 (ft), 6 (pt); LPNs 4 (ft), 7 (pt); Nurses' aides 41 (ft), 27 (pt); Physical therapists 2 (pt); Reality therapists 1 (ft); Recreational therapists 1

(ft); Occupational therapists 1 (pt); Speech
therapists 1 (pt); Activities coordinators 1
(ft); Dietitians 1 (ft).
Facilities Dining room; Physical therapy
room; Activities room; Chapel; Crafts room;
Laundry room; Barber/Beauty shop; Library.
Activities Arts & crafts; Cards; Games;
Reading groups; Prayer groups; Movies;
Shopping trips; Dances/Social/Cultural
gatherings.

Oneida

Anna John Nursing Home
PO Box 365, Oneida, WI 54155
(414) 869-2797
Admin Whitney Mills.
Medical Dir Dr Fred H Walbrun.
Licensure Skilled care. *Beds* SNF 50. *Certified*
Medicaid.
Owner Nonprofit corp.
Admissions Requirements Minimum age 18;
Medical examination; Physician's request.
Facilities Dining room; Physical therapy
room; Activities room; Chapel; Crafts room;
Laundry room; Barber/Beauty shop; Library.
Activities Arts & crafts; Cards; Games;
Reading groups; Prayer groups; Movies;
Shopping trips; Dances/Social/Cultural
gatherings.

Oregon

Oregon Manor Ltd
354 N Main St, Oregon, WI 53575
(608) 835-3535
Admin Harlan Murphy.
Licensure Skilled care. *Beds* SNF 45. *Certified*
Medicaid.
Owner Proprietary corp.

Osceola

L O Simenstad Nursing Unit
Box 218, 301 River St, Osceola, WI 54020
(715) 294-2111
Admin Stephen J Hardman. *Dir of Nursing*
Kathy H Moberg. *Medical Dir* Arnold Potek
MD.
Licensure Skilled care. *Beds* SNF 40. *Certified*
Medicaid; Medicare.
Owner Nonprofit organization/foundation.
Facilities Dining room; Physical therapy
room; Activities room; Chapel; Crafts room;
Laundry room; Barber/Beauty shop.
Activities Arts & crafts; Cards; Games;
Reading groups; Prayer groups; Movies;
Shopping trips; Dances/Social/Cultural
gatherings; Intergenerational programs; Pet
therapy.

Oshkosh

Bethel Home
225 N Eagle St, Oshkosh, WI 54901
(414) 235-4653
Admin Roberta K Messer. *Dir of Nursing*
Barbara Kapel RN. *Medical Dir* T C Mork
MD.
Licensure Skilled care; Retirement. *Beds* SNF
200; Retirement apartments 274. *Certified*
Medicaid.
Owner Nonprofit corp.
Admissions Requirements Medical
examination; Physician's request.
Staff RNs; LPNs; Nurses' aides; Activities
coordinators.
Affiliation Lutheran.
Facilities Dining room; Physical therapy
room; Activities room; Chapel; Crafts room;
Laundry room; Barber/Beauty shop; Library;
Family lounges.
Activities Arts & crafts; Cards; Games; Prayer
groups; Movies; Shopping trips; Dances/
Social/Cultural gatherings; Intergenerational
programs; Music groups; Cooking groups.

Evergreen Manor
PO Box 1720, 1130 N Westfield St, Oshkosh,
WI 54902
(414) 233-2340
Admin David A Green. *Dir of Nursing* Carol
Mueller. *Medical Dir* Paul Plueddeman MD.
Licensure Skilled care; Intermediate care;
Alzheimer's care; Retirement. *Beds* SNF
106. *Certified* Medicaid.
Owner Nonprofit corp.
Admissions Requirements Minimum age 60.
Staff RNs 4 (ft), 14 (pt); LPNs 1 (ft), 14 (pt);
Nurses' aides 19 (ft), 47 (pt); Activities
coordinators 1 (ft).
Affiliation Methodist.
Facilities Dining room; Physical therapy
room; Activities room; Chapel; Crafts room;
Laundry room; Barber/Beauty shop; Library;
Kitchen available for residents use.
Activities Arts & crafts; Cards; Games;
Reading groups; Prayer groups; Movies;
Shopping trips; Dances/Social/Cultural
gatherings; Music appreciation; Dinner
clubs; Supper clubs; Kaffee Klatsch.

Oshkosh Care Center
1850 Bowen St, Oshkosh, WI 54901
(414) 233-4011
Admin David S Miller. *Dir of Nursing* Lynn
K Harron RN.
Licensure Skilled care; Alzheimer's care. *Beds*
SNF 186. *Certified* Medicaid; Medicare.
Owner Proprietary corp (Hillhaven Corp).
Admissions Requirements Medical
examination; Physician's request.
Staff RNs 9 (ft), 6 (pt); LPNs 9 (ft), 19 (pt);
Nurses' aides 125 (ft); Physical therapists 1
(ft), 2 (pt); Occupational therapists 2 (ft);
Activities coordinators 1 (ft); Dietitians 1
(ft).
Facilities Dining room; Physical therapy
room; Activities room; Chapel; Laundry
room; Barber/Beauty shop; Occupational
therapy room; Speech therapy; Privacy
room.
Activities Arts & crafts; Cards; Games;
Reading groups; Prayer groups; Movies;
Shopping trips; Dances/Social/Cultural
gatherings.

Osseo

**Osseo Area Municipal Hospital & Nursing
Home**
674 8th St, Osseo, WI 54758
(715) 597-3121
Admin James G Sokup. *Dir of Nursing* Arvis
Crump RN. *Medical Dir* Bradley G Garber.
Licensure Skilled care; Intermediate care. *Beds*
SNF 90. *Certified* Medicaid; Medicare.
Owner Nonprofit corp.
Admissions Requirements Physician's request.
Staff Physicians 3 (ft); RNs 2 (ft), 2 (pt);
LPNs 5 (ft); Nurses' aides 10 (ft), 18 (pt);
Physical therapists 1 (ft); Recreational
therapists 2 (ft); Activities coordinators 1
(ft); Dietitians 1 (ft).
Languages Norwegian.
Facilities Dining room; Physical therapy
room; Activities room; Chapel; Crafts room;
Laundry room; Barber/Beauty shop; Van for
travel.
Activities Arts & crafts; Cards; Games;
Reading groups; Prayer groups; Movies;
Shopping trips; Dances/Social/Cultural
gatherings.

Owen

Clark County Health Care Center
Hwy 29 E, Owen, WI 54460
(715) 229-2172
Admin Arlyn A Mills. *Dir of Nursing* Karen
Haselow. *Medical Dir* William Hopkins.

Licensure Skilled care; Intermediate care for
mentally retarded; Alzheimer's care. *Beds*
SNF 192; ICF/MR 61. *Private Pay Patients*
5%. *Certified* Medicaid; Medicare; VA.
Owner Publicly owned.
Admissions Requirements Minimum age 18;
Medical examination; Physician's request.
Staff RNs 15 (ft), 9 (pt); LPNs 5 (ft), 6 (pt);
Nurses' aides 81 (ft), 80 (pt); Recreational
therapists 9 (ft), 1 (pt); Occupational
therapists 1 (pt); Activities coordinators 1
(ft); Dietitians 2 (ft).
Facilities Dining room; Physical therapy
room; Activities room; Chapel; Crafts room;
Laundry room; Barber/Beauty shop; Library;
Multi-purpose gymnasium.
Activities Arts & crafts; Cards; Games;
Reading groups; Prayer groups; Movies;
Shopping trips; Dances/Social/Cultural
gatherings; Pet therapy.

Oxford

Oxford Convalescent Home
PO Box 47, Oxford, WI 53952
(608) 586-4211
Admin Thomas Kuehn.
Licensure Skilled care; Intermediate care. *Beds*
58. *Certified* Medicaid.
Owner Proprietary corp.

Park Falls

Park Manor
250 Lawrence Ave, Park Falls, WI 54552
(715) 762-2449
Admin Wanda Preisler. *Dir of Nursing* Jane
Sellers. *Medical Dir* James L Murphy MD.
Licensure Skilled care; Retirement. *Beds* SNF
171. *Certified* Medicaid.
Owner Proprietary corp.
Admissions Requirements Medical
examination; Physician's request.
Staff RNs 4 (ft), 6 (pt); LPNs 5 (ft), 7 (pt);
Nurses' aides 11 (ft), 66 (pt); Physical
therapists 1 (pt); Activities coordinators 2
(ft).
Facilities Dining room; Physical therapy
room; Activities room; Crafts room; Laundry
room; Barber/Beauty shop; Library.
Activities Arts & crafts; Cards; Games;
Reading groups; Prayer groups; Movies;
Shopping trips; Dances/Social/Cultural
gatherings.

Pepin

Pepin Manor Care Center
PO Box 218, 2nd & Locust St, Pepin, WI
54759
(715) 442-4811
Admin Twylah S Wieland.
Licensure Skilled care; Intermediate care. *Beds*
SNF 100. *Certified* Medicaid.
Owner Proprietary corp.

Peshtigo

Greenview Health Center
PO Box 148, Peshtigo, WI 54157
(715) 582-4148
Admin Gerard A Buser. *Dir of Nursing* Janine
Kinney. *Medical Dir* Tom Foley MD.
Licensure Skilled care. *Beds* SNF 77. *Private
Pay Patients* 15%. *Certified* Medicaid.
Owner Proprietary corp (Peshtigo Associates).
Admissions Requirements Minimum age 18;
Medical examination; Physician's request.
Staff RNs 2 (ft), 2 (pt); LPNs 1 (ft), 8 (pt);
Nurses' aides 14 (ft), 11 (pt); Physical
therapists 1 (pt); Speech therapists 1 (pt);
Activities coordinators 1 (ft); Dietitians 1
(pt); Podiatrists 1 (pt); Social worker, Ward
clerk, Medical record designee 2 (ft), 1 (pt).

Facilities Dining room; Physical therapy room; Activities room; Laundry room; Barber/Beauty shop.
Activities Arts & crafts; Cards; Games; Reading groups; Prayer groups; Movies; Shopping trips; Dances/Social/Cultural gatherings; Intergenerational programs; Pet therapy.

Pine View Health Care Center
PO Box 127, Peshtigo, WI 54157
(715) 582-3962
Admin Karla K Brabender. *Dir of Nursing* Georgetta Preg. *Medical Dir* Dr Tom Mack.
Licensure Skilled care; Intermediate care for mentally retarded; Adult day care; Alzheimer's care. *Beds* SNF 135; ICF/MR 20. *Private Pay Patients* 10%. *Certified* Medicaid.
Owner Publicly owned.
Admissions Requirements Minimum age 18; Medical examination; Physician's request.
Staff Physicians 2 (pt); RNs 8 (ft), 7 (pt); LPNs 1 (ft), 13 (pt); Nurses' aides 20 (ft), 64 (pt); Physical therapists 1 (pt); Occupational therapists 1 (pt); Speech therapists 2 (pt); Activities coordinators 1 (pt); Dietitians 1 (pt).
Facilities Dining room; Physical therapy room; Activities room; Crafts room; Laundry room; Barber/Beauty shop; Library; Enclosed courtyard.
Activities Arts & crafts; Cards; Games; Reading groups; Prayer groups; Movies; Shopping trips; Dances/Social/Cultural gatherings; Intergenerational programs; Pet therapy; Wine & Dine.

Rennes Health Center—Peshtigo
PO Box 147, 501 N Lake St, Peshtigo, WI 54157
(715) 582-3906
Admin Karen M Brechlin. *Dir of Nursing* Ruth Carriveau. *Medical Dir* Dr T Mack.
Licensure Skilled care; Retirement. *Beds* SNF 144; Retirement 8. *Certified* Medicaid; Medicare.
Owner Proprietary corp.
Admissions Requirements Minimum age 18; Medical examination; Physician's request.
Staff Physicians 4 (pt); RNs 4 (ft), 9 (pt); LPNs 2 (ft), 13 (pt); Nurses' aides 9 (ft), 65 (pt); Physical therapists 1 (pt); Recreational therapists 1 (ft); Occupational therapists 1 (pt); Speech therapists 1 (pt); Activities coordinators 1 (ft); Dietitians 1 (ft); Ophthalmologists 1 (pt); Dentists 1 (pt).
Facilities Dining room; Physical therapy room; Activities room; Chapel; Crafts room; Laundry room; Barber/Beauty shop; Library; Greenhouse; Whirlpool baths; Courtyards.
Activities Arts & crafts; Cards; Games; Reading groups; Prayer groups; Movies; Shopping trips; Dances/Social/Cultural gatherings; Community trips.

Pewaukee

River Hills West Health Care Center
321 Riverside Dr, Pewaukee, WI 53072
(414) 691-2300
Admin Barry Metevia. *Dir of Nursing* Bev Grams. *Medical Dir* David Imse MD.
Licensure Skilled care; Retirement; Alzheimer's care. *Beds* SNF 248. *Private Pay Patients* 28%. *Certified* Medicaid; Medicare.
Owner Proprietary corp (American Medical Services Inc).
Admissions Requirements Minimum age 60; Medical examination; Physician's request.
Staff Physicians outside provider; RNs 12 (ft), 27 (pt); LPNs 4 (ft), 27 (pt); Nurses' aides 33 (ft), 74 (pt); Physical therapists 3 (ft); Recreational therapists 4 (ft); Occupational therapists 3 (ft); Speech therapists outside provider; Activities coordinators 1 (ft);

Dietitians 1 (ft), 1 (pt); Ophthalmologists outside provider; Podiatrists outside provider; Audiologists outside provider.
Facilities Dining room; Physical therapy room; Activities room; Chapel; Crafts room; Laundry room; Barber/Beauty shop; Library; Child day care.
Activities Arts & crafts; Cards; Games; Reading groups; Prayer groups; Movies; Shopping trips; Dances/Social/Cultural gatherings; Intergenerational programs; Pet therapy.

Phelps

Lillian Kerr Nursing Home
PO Box 26, 2383 Hwy 17, Phelps, WI 54554
(715) 545-2589, 545-3216 FAX
Admin Curtis A Johnson NHA CPA. *Dir of Nursing* Sally Wysocki. *Medical Dir* Thomas Richards DO.
Licensure Skilled care; Intermediate care; Retirement. *Beds* Swing beds SNF/ICF 81; Retirement 32. *Private Pay Patients* 15%. *Certified* Medicaid.
Owner Nonprofit organization/foundation.
Admissions Requirements Minimum age 16; Medical examination; Physician's request.
Staff Physicians 4 (ft); RNs 4 (ft), 2 (pt); LPNs 3 (ft), 5 (pt); Nurses' aides 18 (ft), 15 (pt); Physical therapists 1 (pt); Recreational therapists 3 (pt); Occupational therapists 1 (pt); Speech therapists 1 (pt); Activities coordinators 1 (ft); Dietitians 1 (pt); Podiatrists 1 (pt); Audiologists 1 (pt).
Languages Spanish, Finnish, German.
Facilities Dining room; Physical therapy room; Activities room; Chapel; Crafts room; Laundry room; Barber/Beauty shop.
Activities Arts & crafts; Cards; Games; Reading groups; Prayer groups; Movies; Shopping trips; Dances/Social/Cultural gatherings; Intergenerational programs.

Phillips

Pleasant View Nursing Home
Peterson Dr, Phillips, WI 54555
(715) 339-3113
Admin Wayne R Sawallish.
Medical Dir Walter E Niebauer MD.
Licensure Skilled care; Intermediate care. *Beds* SNF 86. *Certified* Medicaid.
Owner Nonprofit corp.
Admissions Requirements Medical examination; Physician's request.
Staff Physicians 3 (pt); RNs 2 (ft), 4 (pt); LPNs 6 (pt); Nurses' aides 14 (ft), 28 (pt); Physical therapists 1 (pt); Speech therapists 1 (pt); Activities coordinators 1 (ft), 2 (pt); Dietitians 1 (ft), 1 (pt); Dentists 1 (pt).
Facilities Dining room; Physical therapy room; Activities room; Crafts room; Laundry room; Barber/Beauty shop; Library.
Activities Arts & crafts; Cards; Games; Reading groups; Prayer groups; Movies; Shopping trips; Dances/Social/Cultural gatherings.

Pigeon Falls

Pigeon Falls Nursing Home
PO Box 195, Pigeon Falls, WI 54760
(715) 983-2293
Admin Laurie J Haines. *Dir of Nursing* Doris A Johnson RN. *Medical Dir* Reuben Adams MD.
Licensure Skilled care; Intermediate care. *Beds* SNF 41. *Certified* Medicaid.
Owner Proprietary corp.

Platteville

Grays Nursing Home Inc
555 N Chestnut St, Platteville, WI 53818
(608) 349-6741

Admin Bernice M Gray. *Dir of Nursing* Karen Beckman RN. *Medical Dir* J Huekner.
Licensure Skilled care; Intermediate care; Retirement. *Beds* SNF 20. *Certified* Medicaid.
Owner Proprietary corp.
Admissions Requirements Medical examination; Physician's request.
Staff RNs 2 (ft), 3 (pt); LPNs 3 (pt); Nurses' aides 11 (pt); Activities coordinators 1 (ft); Dietitians 1 (pt); Social worker 1 (pt).
Facilities Dining room; Activities room; Chapel; Crafts room; Laundry room; Multi-purpose rooms.
Activities Arts & crafts; Cards; Games; Reading groups; Prayer groups; Movies; Shopping trips.

Parkview Terrace
1300 N Water St, Platteville, WI 53818
(608) 348-2453
Admin Mary Ann Floerke. *Dir of Nursing* Carol Patterson RN. *Medical Dir* Dr P Groben.
Licensure Skilled care; Adult day care. *Beds* SNF 100. *Certified* Medicaid; Medicare; VA.
Owner Proprietary corp (Health Care & Retirement Corp).
Admissions Requirements Minimum age 18; Medical examination; Physician's request.
Facilities Dining room; Physical therapy room; Activities room; Chapel; Crafts room; Laundry room; Barber/Beauty shop; Library.
Activities Arts & crafts; Cards; Games; Reading groups; Prayer groups; Movies; Dances/Social/Cultural gatherings; Art therapy; Poetry group; Cooking; Residents council.

Southwest Health Center Nursing Home
1100 5th Ave, Platteville, WI 53818
(608) 348-2331
Admin Kenneth W Creswick.
Medical Dir Milton F Stuessy MD.
Licensure Skilled care; Intermediate care. *Beds* 34. *Certified* Medicaid.
Owner Nonprofit corp.
Staff RNs 4 (pt); LPNs 3 (ft), 4 (pt); Nurses' aides 8 (ft), 15 (pt); Physical therapists 1 (pt); Occupational therapists 1 (pt); Activities coordinators 1 (pt); Dietitians 1 (pt).
Facilities Dining room; Physical therapy room; Activities room; Crafts room.
Activities Arts & crafts; Cards; Games; Prayer groups; Movies; Shopping trips; Dances/Social/Cultural gatherings.

Plum City

Plum City Care Center
301 Cherry St, Plum City, WI 54761
(715) 647-2401
Admin Kelly Murphy. *Dir of Nursing* Sherri Hydo. *Medical Dir* Dr C W Docter.
Licensure Skilled care. *Beds* SNF 42. *Private Pay Patients* 40%. *Certified* Medicaid; Medicare.
Owner Proprietary corp (Real Property Health).
Admissions Requirements Minimum age 18; Medical examination; Physician's request.
Staff Physicians 1 (pt); RNs 1 (ft), 3 (pt); LPNs 2 (ft), 5 (pt); Nurses' aides 7 (ft), 13 (pt); Physical therapists (contracted); Occupational therapists (contracted); Speech therapists (contracted); Activities coordinators 1 (ft); Dietitians (contracted).
Facilities Dining room; Physical therapy room; Activities room; Crafts room; Laundry room; Barber/Beauty shop.
Activities Arts & crafts; Games; Reading groups; Prayer groups; Movies; Shopping trips; Dances/Social/Cultural gatherings; Intergenerational programs.

Plymouth

Rocky Knoll Health Care Facility
Plymouth, WI 53073
(414) 893-6441
Admin William Schoen. *Dir of Nursing* Nancy
Slupski RN. *Medical Dir* Curtis Hancock
MD.
Licensure Skilled care; Intermediate care. *Beds*
SNF 228. *Private Pay Patients* 27%. *Certified*
Medicaid; Medicare; VA.
Owner Publicly owned.
Admissions Requirements Physician's request.
Staff RNs 10 (ft), 12 (pt); LPNs 14 (ft), 6 (pt);
Nurses' aides 45 (ft), 70 (pt); Recreational
therapists 4 (ft), 2 (pt); Activities
coordinators 1 (ft); Dietitians 1 (pt).
Facilities Dining room; Physical therapy
room; Activities room; Chapel; Crafts room;
Laundry room; Barber/Beauty shop; Library.
Activities Arts & crafts; Cards; Games;
Reading groups; Prayer groups; Movies;
Shopping trips; Dances/Social/Cultural
gatherings; Intergenerational programs; Pet
therapy.

Valley Manor Nursing Home
916 E Clifford St, Plymouth, WI 53073
(414) 893-1771
Admin Patrick J Trotter. *Dir of Nursing* K
Newell. *Medical Dir* Dr George Schroeder.
Licensure Skilled care; Retirement. *Beds* SNF
60. *Certified* Medicaid; Medicare.
Owner Nonprofit corp.
Admissions Requirements Medical
examination; Physician's request.
Staff Physicians 1 (pt); RNs 3 (ft), 1 (pt);
LPNs 3 (ft), 3 (pt); Nurses' aides 4 (ft), 10
(pt); Physical therapists 1 (pt); Recreational
therapists 1 (pt); Occupational therapists 1
(pt); Speech therapists 1 (pt); Activities
coordinators 1 (ft), 1 (pt); Dietitians 1 (pt);
Podiatrists 1 (pt); Dentists 1 (pt); Social
workers 2 (ft).
Facilities Dining room; Physical therapy
room; Activities room; Chapel; Laundry
room; Barber/Beauty shop; Solarium.
Activities Arts & crafts; Cards; Games;
Reading groups; Movies; Shopping trips.

Port Edwards

Edgewater Haven Nursing Home
1351 Wisconsin River Dr, Port Edwards, WI
54469
(715) 887-3200
Admin Steven R Sterzinger. *Dir of Nursing*
Carol J Dean. *Medical Dir* John E
Thompson MD.
Licensure Skilled care; Intermediate care. *Beds*
SNF 164. *Certified* Medicaid; Medicare.
Owner Publicly owned.
Admissions Requirements Medical
examination.
Staff RNs 4 (ft), 13 (pt); LPNs 3 (ft), 12 (pt);
Nurses' aides 44 (ft), 15 (pt); Physical
therapists 2 (pt); Recreational therapists 1
(ft); Dietitians 1 (pt).
Facilities Dining room; Physical therapy
room; Activities room; Chapel; Laundry
room; Barber/Beauty shop.
Activities Arts & crafts; Cards; Games; Prayer
groups; Movies; Shopping trips; Dances/
Social/Cultural gatherings.

Port Washington

Heritage Nursing Home
1119 N Wisconsin St, Port Washington, WI
53074
(414) 284-5892
Admin Janeen G Staveness NHA. *Dir of
Nursing* Bernice Lubner RN. *Medical Dir*
Mark Bostwick MD.
Licensure Skilled care. *Beds* SNF 54. *Certified*
Medicaid.
Owner Proprietary corp.

Staff RNs 1 (ft), 6 (pt); LPNs 4 (pt); Nurses'
aides 5 (ft), 38 (pt); Physical therapists 1
(pt); Recreational therapists 1 (pt); Speech
therapists 1 (pt); Activities coordinators 1
(pt); Dietitians 1 (pt).
Facilities Dining room.
Activities Arts & crafts; Cards; Games;
Reading groups; Prayer groups; Movies;
Dances/Social/Cultural gatherings;
Intergenerational programs; Pet therapy.

Portage

Divine Savior Hospital & Nursing Home
715 W Pleasant St, Portage, WI 53901
(608) 742-4131
Admin William L Bender. *Dir of Nursing*
Penny Finnegan. *Medical Dir* Dr Stuart
Taylor Sr.
Licensure Skilled care; Intermediate care. *Beds*
SNF 111. *Certified* Medicaid.
Owner Nonprofit corp.
Staff RNs 14 (ft); LPNs 5 (ft); Nurses' aides
38 (ft); Physical therapists 1 (ft);
Occupational therapists 1 (ft); Speech
therapists 1 (ft); Activities coordinators 1
(ft); Dietitians 1 (ft); Podiatrists 1 (ft).
Affiliation Roman Catholic.

Prairie du Chien

Prairie Health Care
1150 S 15th St, Prairie du Chien, WI 53821
(608) 326-8471
Admin Mikki Posten, acting. *Dir of Nursing*
Wanda Hanson. *Medical Dir* Dr Kirk D
Berger.
Licensure Skilled care; Intermediate care;
Alzheimer's wing; Retirement. *Beds* Swing
beds SNF/ICF 173. *Certified* Medicaid.
Owner Nonprofit corp (International Elderly
Health Care).
Admissions Requirements Medical
examination.
Staff RNs; LPNs; Nurses' aides; Physical
therapists; Occupational therapists; Activities
coordinators; Dietitians.
Facilities Dining room; Physical therapy
room; Chapel; Crafts room; Laundry room;
Barber/Beauty shop.
Activities Arts & crafts; Cards; Games;
Reading groups; Prayer groups; Movies;
Shopping trips; Pet therapy.

Prairie Farm

Pioneer Home
PO Box 95, Prairie Farm, WI 54762
(715) 455-1178, 455-1878
Admin David K West. *Dir of Nursing* Joanne
Griffiths. *Medical Dir* Dr Michael Damroth.
Licensure Skilled care; Intermediate care. *Beds*
Swing beds SNF/ICF 42. *Private Pay
Patients* 15%. *Certified* Medicaid.
Owner Publicly owned.
Admissions Requirements Minimum age 18.
Staff RNs 1 (ft), 5 (pt); LPNs 4 (pt); Nurses'
aides 1 (ft), 21 (pt); Physical therapists
(consultant); Activities coordinators 1 (ft);
Dietitians (consultant).
Facilities Dining room; Physical therapy
room; Activities room; Laundry room;
Barber/Beauty shop; Library.
Activities Arts & crafts; Cards; Games;
Reading groups; Prayer groups; Movies;
Shopping trips; Dances/Social/Cultural
gatherings; Intergenerational programs; Pet
therapy.

Prescott

St Croix Care Center
1505 Orrin Rd, Prescott, WI 54021
(715) 262-5661

Admin Gary D Dalzell. *Dir of Nursing* Lisa
Jacobsen RN. *Medical Dir* Paul Kerestes
MD.
Licensure Skilled care; Intermediate care;
Hospice care. *Beds* Swing beds SNF/ICF 74.
Private Pay Patients 50%. *Certified*
Medicaid; Medicare.
Owner Nonprofit organization/foundation.
Admissions Requirements Minimum age 18;
Medical examination.
Staff Physicians 1 (pt); RNs 4 (ft), 1 (pt);
LPNs 4 (ft), 4 (pt); Nurses' aides 14 (ft), 21
(pt); Physical therapists 1 (pt); Recreational
therapists 1 (pt); Occupational therapists 1
(pt); Speech therapists 1 (pt); Activities
coordinators 1 (ft); Dietitians 1 (ft);
Podiatrists 1 (pt); Audiologists 1 (pt);
Beauticians 1 (pt).
Facilities Dining room; Physical therapy
room; Activities room; Chapel; Crafts room;
Laundry room; Barber/Beauty shop; Lounge.
Activities Arts & crafts; Cards; Games;
Reading groups; Prayer groups; Movies;
Shopping trips; Pet therapy; Music
programs.

Princeton

Sunnyview Village
900 Sunnyview Ln, Princeton, WI 54968
(414) 295-6463
Admin Amy Pfeifer. *Dir of Nursing* Helen
Beckstrom. *Medical Dir* Robert House MD.
Licensure Skilled care. *Beds* SNF 66. *Certified*
Medicaid.
Owner Proprietary corp (Wisconsin Health
Systems Inc).
Admissions Requirements Medical
examination.
Staff RNs 4 (ft); LPNs 2 (ft), 4 (pt); Nurses'
aides 9 (ft), 16 (pt); Physical therapists 1
(pt); Occupational therapists 1 (pt);
Activities coordinators 1 (ft); Dietitians 1
(pt).
Facilities Dining room; Physical therapy
room; Activities room; Chapel; Barber/
Beauty shop; Library.
Activities Arts & crafts; Cards; Games; Prayer
groups; Movies; Dances/Social/Cultural
gatherings; Pet therapy.

Racine

Lincoln Lutheran Home
2015 Prospect St, Racine, WI 53404
(414) 637-6531
Admin Lee D Morey. *Dir of Nursing* Anita
Getty. *Medical Dir* Dr John Jamieson.
Licensure Skilled care; Intermediate care. *Beds*
SNF 167. *Private Pay Patients* 33%. *Certified*
Medicaid.
Owner Nonprofit corp (Lincoln Lutheran of
Racine WI).
Admissions Requirements Medical
examination; Physician's request.
Staff Physicians 1 (pt); RNs 7 (ft), 18 (pt);
LPNs 1 (ft), 11 (pt); Nurses' aides 23 (ft), 65
(pt); Physical therapists 1 (ft); Recreational
therapists 4 (pt); Activities coordinators 1
(ft); Dietitians 1 (pt); Podiatrists 1 (pt).
Facilities Dining room; Physical therapy
room; Activities room; Chapel; Laundry
room; Barber/Beauty shop; Library.
Activities Arts & crafts; Cards; Games;
Reading groups; Prayer groups; Movies;
Shopping trips; Dances/Social/Cultural
gatherings; Intergenerational programs; Pet
therapy.

Lincoln Village Convalescent Center
1700 C A Becker Dr, Racine, WI 53406
(414) 637-9751
Admin Joseph D Alexander.
Medical Dir Santiago Yllas MD.
Licensure Skilled care; Retirement. *Beds* SNF
122. *Certified* Medicaid; Medicare.

Owner Nonprofit corp (Lincoln Luth of Racine WI).
Admissions Requirements Minimum age 18; Medical examination; Physician's request.
Staff Physicians 1 (pt); RNs 4 (ft), 13 (pt); LPNs 15 (pt); Nurses' aides 30 (ft), 52 (pt); Physical therapists 1 (pt); Recreational therapists 3 (pt); Occupational therapists 1 (pt); Speech therapists 1 (pt); Activities coordinators 1 (ft); Dietitians 1 (pt); Ophthalmologists 1 (pt); Dentists 1 (pt) Chaplain 1 (ft).
Affiliation Lutheran.
Facilities Dining room; Physical therapy room; Activities room; Crafts room; Barber/Beauty shop; Library; Living room.
Activities Arts & crafts; Cards; Games; Reading groups; Prayer groups; Movies; Shopping trips; Dances/Social/Cultural gatherings.

Racine Residential Care
1719 Washington Ave, Racine, WI 53403
(414) 633-6348
Admin Norman L Steffen.
Licensure Intermediate care for mentally retarded. *Beds* ICF/MR 51. *Certified* Medicaid.
Owner Proprietary corp.
Admissions Requirements Minimum age 18; Medical examination.
Staff RNs 1 (ft), 1 (pt); LPNs 2 (ft), 2 (pt); Nurses' aides 9 (ft), 3 (pt); Recreational therapists 1 (ft); Occupational therapists 1 (ft); Dietitians 1 (ft); Social workers 2 (ft).
Facilities Dining room; Activities room.
Activities Arts & crafts; Games; Reading groups; Prayer groups; Movies; Shopping trips; Dances/Social/Cultural gatherings.

Ridgewood Care Center
5455 Durand Ave, Racine, WI 53406
(414) 554-6440
Admin Brenda E Danculovich. *Dir of Nursing* Frances Petrick. *Medical Dir* Dr William Haedike.
Licensure Skilled care; Intermediate care; Alzheimer's care. *Beds* SNF 210. *Certified* Medicaid.
Owner Publicly owned.
Admissions Requirements Minimum age 18; Medical examination; Physician's request.
Staff Physicians 3 (pt); RNs 10 (ft), 10 (pt); LPNs 13 (ft), 13 (pt); Nurses' aides 38 (ft), 42 (pt); Physical therapists 1 (pt); Recreational therapists 2 (ft); Occupational therapists 1 (ft); Speech therapists 1 (pt); Activities coordinators 1 (ft); Dietitians 1 (ft); Ophthalmologists 1 (pt); Optometrist 1 (pt).
Facilities Dining room; Physical therapy room; Activities room; Chapel; Crafts room; Laundry room; Barber/Beauty shop; Library; Locked unit for court-ordered protectively placed; Secure care system for wanderers.
Activities Arts & crafts; Cards; Games; Reading groups; Prayer groups; Movies; Shopping trips; Dances/Social/Cultural gatherings.

St Catherine's Infirmary
5635 Erie St, Racine, WI 53402
(414) 639-4100
Admin Sr Mae M Schellinger NHA. *Dir of Nursing* Mary Anne Bunkers RN. *Medical Dir* Dr Marvin G Parker.
Licensure Skilled care; Retirement. *Beds* SNF 41. *Private Pay Patients* 25%. *Certified* Medicaid.
Owner Nonprofit organization/foundation.
Admissions Requirements Physician's request.
Staff RNs; LPNs; Nurses' aides; Activities coordinators; Dietitians; Ophthalmologists; Podiatrists.
Languages Spanish, German.
Affiliation Roman Catholic.

Facilities Dining room; Activities room; Chapel; Laundry room; Barber/Beauty shop; Library.
Activities Arts & crafts; Games; Reading groups; Prayer groups; Dances/Social/Cultural gatherings.

Becker/Shoop Center
6101 16th St, Racine, WI 53406
(414) 637-7486
Admin Daniel W Langenwalter. *Dir of Nursing* Elaine M Oser RN. *Medical Dir* Dr John Jamieson.
Licensure Skilled care; Alzheimer's care; Retirement. *Beds* SNF 110. *Certified* Medicaid.
Owner Nonprofit corp (Lincoln Luth of Racine WI).
Admissions Requirements Medical examination; Physician's request.
Staff Physicians 1 (pt); RNs 8 (ft), 15 (pt); LPNs 1 (ft), 3 (pt); Nurses' aides 16 (ft), 62 (pt); Physical therapists 1 (pt); Recreational therapists 1 (ft); Occupational therapists 1 (pt); Speech therapists 1 (pt); Activities coordinators 1 (pt); Dietitians 1 (pt); Ophthalmologists 1 (pt); Podiatrists 1 (pt); Dentists 1 (pt).
Languages German, Polish, Danish.
Affiliation Lutheran.
Facilities Dining room; Physical therapy room; Activities room; Chapel; Crafts room; Laundry room; Barber/Beauty shop; Solarium; Outdoor courtyard.
Activities Arts & crafts; Cards; Games; Reading groups; Prayer groups; Movies; Shopping trips; Dances/Social/Cultural gatherings; Music; One-to-one interaction.

Westview Health Care Center Inc
1600 Ohio St, Racine, WI 53405
(414) 637-7491
Admin Ronald A Chrsitner.
Licensure Skilled care; Intermediate care. *Beds* SNF 320. *Certified* Medicaid; Medicare.
Owner Proprietary corp.

Radisson

Marian Nursing Home
Rte 1, Radisson, WI 54867
(715) 945-2203
Admin Frances A Mleczko.
Medical Dir Dr Larry Carlson.
Licensure Intermediate care. *Beds* ICF 28. *Certified* Medicaid.
Owner Proprietary corp.
Admissions Requirements Medical examination.
Staff Physicians 1 (pt); RNs 2 (ft), 2 (pt); LPNs 2 (pt); Nurses' aides 5 (ft), 6 (pt); Physical therapists 1 (pt); Occupational therapists 1 (pt); Speech therapists 1 (pt); Activities coordinators 1 (pt); Dietitians 1 (pt); Dentists 1 (pt).
Facilities Dining room; Activities room; Chapel; Crafts room; Laundry room; Barber/Beauty shop; Library.
Activities Arts & crafts; Cards; Games; Reading groups; Prayer groups; Movies; Shopping trips.

Randolph

Continental Manor of Randolph
502 S High St, Randolph, WI 53956
(414) 326-3171
Admin William H Disch. *Dir of Nursing* Marita Tietz RN. *Medical Dir* Dr John Poser.
Licensure Skilled care. *Beds* SNF 84. *Private Pay Patients* 30%. *Certified* Medicaid; Medicare.
Owner Proprietary corp (Beverly Enterprises).
Admissions Requirements Medical examination; Physician's request.

Staff RNs 2 (ft), 3 (pt); LPNs 4 (ft), 7 (pt); Nurses' aides 21 (ft), 21 (pt); Physical therapists; Activities coordinators 1 (pt); Dietitians.
Facilities Dining room; Physical therapy room; Activities room; Crafts room; Laundry room; Barber/Beauty shop; 2 dayrooms; Living room; Multi-purpose room.
Activities Arts & crafts; Cards; Games; Reading groups; Prayer groups; Movies; Dances/Social/Cultural gatherings; Intergenerational programs; Pet therapy; Monthly luncheons to local restaurants.

Reedsburg

Sauk County Health Care Center
S 4555 Hwy CH, Reedsburg, WI 53959
(608) 524-4371
Admin Donald W Erickson. *Dir of Nursing* Joan Petron RN. *Medical Dir* Frederick W Blancke MD.
Licensure Skilled care. *Beds* SNF 275. *Certified* Medicaid; Medicare.
Owner Publicly owned.
Admissions Requirements Minimum age 21; Medical examination; Physician's request.
Staff Physicians 13 (pt); RNs 8 (ft), 12 (pt); LPNs 4 (ft), 8 (pt); Nurses' aides 45 (ft), 80 (pt); Physical therapists 1 (pt); Recreational therapists 4 (ft), 6 (pt); Occupational therapists 1 (ft); Speech therapists 1 (pt); Activities coordinators 1 (ft); Dietitians 1 (pt); Podiatrists 1 (pt).
Facilities Dining room; Physical therapy room; Activities room; Chapel; Crafts room; Laundry room; Barber/Beauty shop; Library; In-house bakery.
Activities Arts & crafts; Cards; Games; Reading groups; Prayer groups; Movies; Shopping trips; Dances/Social/Cultural gatherings; Resident council.

Edward Snyder Old People's Home
1104 21st St, Reedsburg, WI 53959
(608) 524-6487
Admin George L Johnson.
Medical Dir Dr D Burnett.
Licensure Skilled care; Intermediate care. *Beds* SNF 50. *Certified* Medicaid.
Owner Nonprofit corp.
Admissions Requirements Medical examination; Physician's request.
Staff RNs 2 (ft), 4 (pt); LPNs 2 (ft), 1 (pt); Nurses' aides 8 (ft), 15 (pt); Physical therapists 1 (ft); Occupational therapists 1 (ft); Activities coordinators 1 (ft); Dietitians 1 (pt).
Facilities Dining room; Physical therapy room; Activities room; Chapel; Crafts room; Laundry room; Barber/Beauty shop.
Activities Arts & crafts; Cards; Games; Reading groups; Prayer groups; Movies; Shopping trips; Dances/Social/Cultural gatherings.

Zimmerman Nursing Home
617 4th St, Reedsburg, WI 53959
(608) 524-3664
Admin Marion K Zimmerman. *Dir of Nursing* Linda Splett RN. *Medical Dir* V G Vergara MD.
Licensure Intermediate care. *Beds* ICF 12. *Private Pay Patients* 7%. *Certified* Medicaid.
Owner Privately owned.
Admissions Requirements Medical examination; Physician's request.
Staff RNs 1 (ft), 2 (pt); LPNs 2 (ft), 3 (pt); Activities coordinators 1 (pt); Dietitians 1 (pt).
Facilities Dining room; Activities room; Chapel; Laundry room; Barber/Beauty shop.
Activities Arts & crafts; Cards; Games; Reading groups; Prayer groups; Movies; Dances/Social/Cultural gatherings; Intergenerational programs; Pet therapy; Family participation.

Rhinelander

Friendly Village
PO Box 857, Rhinelander, WI 54501
(715) 369-6900
Admin Carol Paradies. *Dir of Nursing* Rhae Ellen Schnoor. *Medical Dir* Dr M J Henry.
Licensure Skilled care; Intermediate care. *Beds* SNF 152. *Certified* Medicaid.
Owner Proprietary corp (Petersen Health Care of Wisconsin Inc).
Admissions Requirements Medical examination.
Staff RNs; LPNs; Nurses' aides; Physical therapists; Occupational therapists; Speech therapists; Activities coordinators; Dietitians.
Facilities Dining room; Physical therapy room; Activities room; Chapel; Crafts room; Laundry room; Barber/Beauty shop.
Activities Arts & crafts; Cards; Games; Reading groups; Prayer groups; Movies; Dances/Social/Cultural gatherings.

Horizons Unlimited
PO Box 857, Rhinelander, WI 54501
(715) 369-6900
Admin Kathy Bowers. *Dir of Nursing* Maureen Krouze. *Medical Dir* Dr Lynn D Eggman.
Licensure Intermediate care for mentally retarded; Group home for developmentally disabled; Retirement. *Beds* ICF/MR 198; Group home for developmentally disabled 6. *Certified* Medicaid.
Owner Proprietary corp (Petersen Health Care of Wisconsin Inc).
Admissions Requirements Minimum age 18; Medical examination.
Staff Physicians 3 (pt); RNs 6 (ft), 1 (pt); LPNs 6 (ft), 10 (pt); Nurses' aides 69 (ft); Physical therapists 1 (ft); Occupational therapists 1 (ft), 1 (pt); Speech therapists 2 (ft); Activities coordinators 5 (ft); Dietitians 1 (ft).
Facilities Dining room; Physical therapy room; Activities room; Chapel; Crafts room; Laundry room; Barber/Beauty shop.
Activities Arts & crafts; Cards; Games; Reading groups; Movies; Shopping trips; Dances/Social/Cultural gatherings.

Passport
PO Box 857, Rhinelander, WI 54501
(715) 369-6900
Admin Patricia Lietz. *Dir of Nursing* Cathy Weingarten. *Medical Dir* Dr L D Eggman.
Licensure Intermediate care for mentally retarded. *Beds* ICF/MR 20. *Certified* Medicaid.
Owner Proprietary corp (Petersen Health Care of Wisconsin Inc).
Admissions Requirements Minimum age 18; Medical examination.
Staff RNs 1 (pt); LPNs 1 (ft), 1 (pt); Nurses' aides 3 (ft), 3 (pt); Recreational therapists 1 (ft).
Facilities Dining room; Activities room; Crafts room; Laundry room.
Activities Arts & crafts; Cards; Games; Reading groups; Prayer groups; Movies; Shopping trips; Dances/Social/Cultural gatherings.

Taylor Park Health Care & Rehabilitation Center
PO Box 857, Rhinelander, WI 54501
(715) 369-6900
Admin Phyllis J Dable. *Dir of Nursing* Noreen Lamon. *Medical Dir* Dr M J Henry.
Licensure Skilled care. *Beds* SNF 100. *Private Pay Patients* 42%. *Certified* Medicaid; Medicare.
Owner Proprietary corp (Petersen Health Care of Wisconsin Inc).
Admissions Requirements Medical examination; Physician's request.

Staff RNs 5 (ft), 5 (pt); LPNs 4 (ft), 3 (pt); Nurses' aides 30 (ft), 15 (pt); Physical therapists 3 (ft), 1 (pt); Occupational therapists 1 (ft), 1 (pt); Speech therapists 1 (ft); Activities coordinators 1 (ft); Dietitians 1 (ft).
Facilities Dining room; Physical therapy room; Activities room; Chapel; Barber/Beauty shop.
Activities Arts & crafts; Cards; Games; Reading groups; Prayer groups; Movies; Shopping trips; Dances/Social/Cultural gatherings; Intergenerational programs; Pet therapy.

Rib Lake

Rib Lake Health Care Center
PO Box 308, Rib Lake, WI 54470
(715) 427-5291
Admin Jerry L Frese.
Licensure Skilled care; Intermediate care. *Beds* SNF 100. *Certified* Medicaid; Medicare.
Owner Proprietary corp (Beverly Enterprises).

Rice Lake

Heritage Manor
19 W Newton St, Rice Lake, WI 54868
(715) 234-2161
Admin Daniel C Dixon. *Dir of Nursing* Brenda Nelson RN. *Medical Dir* William Smith MD.
Licensure Skilled care; Intermediate care. *Beds* SNF 101. *Certified* Medicaid; Medicare.
Owner Proprietary corp.
Admissions Requirements Medical examination; Physician's request.
Staff RNs 5 (ft); LPNs 3 (ft); Nurses' aides 23 (ft), 22 (pt); Physical therapists 2 (pt); Activities coordinators 1 (ft), 1 (pt); Dietitians 1 (ft); Social worker 1 (ft); Medical Records 1 (ft).
Facilities Dining room; Physical therapy room; Activities room; Chapel; Crafts room; Laundry room; Barber/Beauty shop; Library; Family dining room.
Activities Arts & crafts; Cards; Games; Reading groups; Prayer groups; Movies; Shopping trips; Dances/Social/Cultural gatherings; Pet therapy; Church services; Community outings; Family oriented activities.

Heritage Manor
19 W Newton St, Rice Lake, WI 54868
(715) 234-2161
Admin Len Meysembourg.
Licensure Skilled care. *Beds* SNF 101.

Rice Lake Convalescent Center
1016 Lakeshore Dr, Rice Lake, WI 54868
(715) 234-9101
Admin Don L Fritz.
Medical Dir Dr Mark Nymo.
Licensure Skilled care. *Beds* SNF 100. *Certified* Medicaid.
Owner Proprietary corp (1st Am Care Fac).
Staff Physicians 1 (ft), 12 (pt); RNs 2 (ft), 9 (pt); LPNs 1 (ft), 3 (pt); Nurses' aides 20 (ft), 27 (pt); Physical therapists 1 (pt); Occupational therapists 1 (pt); Speech therapists 1 (pt); Activities coordinators 1 (ft); Dietitians 1 (ft); Ophthalmologists 1 (pt); Podiatrists 1 (pt); Audiologists 1 (pt); Dentists 1 (pt).
Facilities Dining room; Physical therapy room; Activities room; Chapel; Crafts room; Laundry room; Barber/Beauty shop; Library.
Activities Arts & crafts; Cards; Games; Reading groups; Prayer groups; Movies; Shopping trips; Dances/Social/Cultural gatherings; Pet therapy; Choir; Rhythm band.

Richland Center

Pine Valley Manor
PO Box 154, Richland Center, WI 53581
(608) 647-2138
Admin Charles Aber.
Medical Dir John Jordon MD.
Licensure Skilled care; Intermediate care; Retirement. *Beds* Swing beds SNF/ICF 176; Retirement 17. *Certified* Medicaid; Medicare.
Owner Publicly owned.
Admissions Requirements Minimum age 18; Medical examination.
Staff Physicians 6 (pt); RNs 1 (ft), 8 (pt); LPNs 12 (ft), 3 (pt); Nurses' aides 46 (ft), 32 (pt); Physical therapists 1 (ft); Recreational therapists 1 (ft); Occupational therapists 2 (ft); Speech therapists 1 (pt); Activities coordinators 1 (ft); Dietitians 1 (pt); Dentists 1 (pt).
Facilities Dining room; Physical therapy room; Activities room; Chapel; Laundry room; Barber/Beauty shop.
Activities Arts & crafts; Cards; Games; Reading groups; Prayer groups; Movies; Shopping trips; Dances/Social/Cultural gatherings.

Schmitt Woodland Hills Inc
1400 W Seminary St, Richland Center, WI 53581
(608) 647-8931
Admin Ruth L McVay. *Dir of Nursing* Shannon Trebus. *Medical Dir* Dr Thomas Richardson.
Licensure Skilled care; Intermediate care; Retirement. *Beds* SNF 25. *Certified* Medicaid.
Owner Nonprofit corp.
Admissions Requirements Minimum age 65; Medical examination.
Staff RNs 2 (ft), 2 (pt); LPNs 2 (ft), 2 (pt); Nurses' aides 5 (ft), 9 (pt); Activities coordinators 1 (ft); Dietitians 1 (ft).
Affiliation Methodist.
Facilities Dining room; Physical therapy room; Activities room; Chapel; Crafts room; Laundry room; Barber/Beauty shop; Library.
Activities Arts & crafts; Cards; Games; Movies; Shopping trips; Dances/Social/Cultural gatherings.

Ripon

Parkview Care Center Inc
PO Box 509, 50 Wolverton Ave, Ripon, WI 54971
(414) 748-5638, ext 14
Admin Lisa M Knuppel. *Dir of Nursing* Marlene Hautamauki. *Medical Dir* Dr Robert House.
Licensure Skilled care; Intermediate care. *Beds* Swing beds SNF/ICF 177. *Private Pay Patients* 35%. *Certified* Medicaid.
Owner Proprietary corp.
Admissions Requirements Medical examination; Physician's request.
Staff RNs 4 (ft), 8 (pt); LPNs 8 (ft), 12 (pt); Nurses' aides 32 (ft), 42 (pt); Physical therapists (contracted); Recreational therapists 1 (ft); Dietitians 1 (ft).
Facilities Dining room; Activities room; Chapel; Crafts room; Laundry room; Barber/Beauty shop; Library.
Activities Arts & crafts; Cards; Games; Reading groups; Prayer groups; Movies; Shopping trips; Dances/Social/Cultural gatherings; Intergenerational programs; Exercise groups; Volunteer program.

Ripon Area Residential Center
PO Box 538, 1002 Eureka St, Ripon, WI 54971
(414) 748-6252
Admin Lisa Selthofner. *Dir of Nursing* Barb Prellwitz. *Medical Dir* Paul Nelsen MD.

Licensure Intermediate care for mentally retarded; Retirement. *Beds* ICF/MR 60. *Certified* Medicaid.
Owner Nonprofit corp.
Admissions Requirements Minimum age 18; Medical examination; Physician's request; County Unified Services approval.
Staff RNs 2 (ft), 1 (pt); LPNs 2 (ft), 4 (pt); Nurses' aides 14 (ft), 10 (pt); Physical therapists 1 (pt); Recreational therapists 2 (ft); Occupational therapists 1 (pt); Speech therapists 1 (pt); Activities coordinators 1 (ft); Dietitians 1 (pt); Psychologist 1 (pt); Social worker 1 (pt); Work activity trainer 1 (ft), 1 (pt).
Facilities Dining room; Physical therapy room; Activities room; Crafts room; Laundry room; Barber/Beauty shop; Work activity; Visiting lounge; TV lounges.
Activities Cards; Games; Prayer groups; Movies; Shopping trips; Dances/Social/Cultural gatherings; Church; Bible study; Swimming; Bowling.

River Falls

Ridgewood
Rte 1, Hwy 35, River Falls, WI 54022
(715) 273-5060
Admin Lucille M Strom.
Licensure Intermediate care for mentally retarded. *Beds* ICF/MR 12.

River Falls Area Hospital Kinnic Long-Term Care
550 N Main, River Falls, WI 54022
(715) 425-6155, 425-6119 FAX
Admin Mary L Hanson. *Dir of Nursing* Dorothy Symes. *Medical Dir* Dr R Hammer.
Licensure Skilled care; Intermediate care. *Beds* Swing beds SNF/ICF 63. *Private Pay Patients* 40%. *Certified* Medicaid.
Owner Nonprofit corp.
Admissions Requirements Minimum age 18; Medical examination; Physician's request.
Staff RNs 3 (ft), 2 (pt); LPNs 3 (ft), 10 (pt); Nurses' aides 13 (ft), 21 (pt); Physical therapists 2 (ft); Occupational therapists 2 (pt); Speech therapists 1 (pt); Activities coordinators 1 (ft), 2 (pt); Dietitians 1 (pt).
Facilities Dining room; Physical therapy room; Activities room; Chapel; Laundry room; Barber/Beauty shop; Library; Occupational therapy room; Speech therapy room; Lab; X-ray; Emergency room; Pharmacy; Outpatient clinic.
Activities Arts & crafts; Cards; Games; Reading groups; Prayer groups; Movies; Shopping trips; Dances/Social/Cultural gatherings; Intergenerational programs; Pet therapy.

River Falls Care Center
640 N Main St, River Falls, WI 54022
(715) 425-5353
Admin Glenda Zielski. *Dir of Nursing* Jean Clausen RN. *Medical Dir* Robert Johnson MD.
Licensure Skilled care; Intermediate care; Retirement; Alzheimer's care. *Beds* Swing beds SNF/ICF 140; Retirement 60. *Certified* Medicaid; Medicare.
Owner Proprietary corp.
Admissions Requirements Minimum age 18; Medical examination; Physician's request.
Staff Physicians; RNs; LPNs; Nurses' aides; Physical therapists; Occupational therapists; Speech therapists; Activities coordinators; Dietitians.
Facilities Dining room; Physical therapy room; Activities room; Chapel; Barber/Beauty shop.
Activities Arts & crafts; Cards; Games; Reading groups; Prayer groups; Movies; Shopping trips; Dances/Social/Cultural gatherings.

Saint Croix Falls

St Croix Valley Good Samaritan Center
750 Louisiana E, Saint Croix Falls, WI 54024
(715) 483-9815
Admin Rev Max Dietze. *Dir of Nursing* Sharon Loaney RN. *Medical Dir* Dr William Riegel.
Licensure Skilled care; Intermediate care; Retirement. *Beds* SNF 68. *Certified* Medicaid.
Owner Nonprofit corp (Evangelical Lutheran/ Good Samaritan Society).
Admissions Requirements Minimum age 18; Medical examination; Physician's request.
Staff Physicians 2 (pt); RNs 3 (ft), 4 (pt); LPNs 2 (ft), 4 (pt); Nurses' aides 10 (ft), 17 (pt); Physical therapists 1 (pt); Occupational therapists 1 (ft); Speech therapists 1 (pt); Activities coordinators 1 (ft).
Affiliation Lutheran.
Facilities Dining room; Physical therapy room; Activities room; Chapel; Crafts room; Laundry room; Barber/Beauty shop; Library.
Activities Arts & crafts; Cards; Games; Reading groups; Prayer groups; Movies; Shopping trips; Dances/Social/Cultural gatherings.

Saint Francis

South Shore Manor
1915 E Tripoli Ave, Saint Francis, WI 53207
(414) 483-3611
Admin Patricia Maurer. *Dir of Nursing* Barbara Schmitz. *Medical Dir* Gregory Nierengarten DO.
Licensure Skilled care; Intermediate care; Alzheimer's care. *Beds* SNF 34. *Certified* Medicaid.
Owner Proprietary corp (Beverly Enterprises).
Admissions Requirements Minimum age 18; Medical examination.
Staff RNs 2 (ft), 2 (pt); LPNs 2 (ft), 6 (pt); Nurses' aides 7 (ft), 9 (pt); Physical therapists; Activities coordinators 2 (pt); Dietitians 1 (ft), 3 (pt); Ophthalmologists 1 (pt); Podiatrists 1 (pt).
Languages Polish.
Facilities Dining room; Physical therapy room; Activities room; Laundry room; Barber/Beauty shop.
Activities Arts & crafts; Cards; Games; Reading groups; Prayer groups; Movies; Shopping trips; Dances/Social/Cultural gatherings; Intergenerational programs; Pet therapy; Programs with day care, nursery school and grade school.

Sauk City

Maplewood of Sauk Prairie
245 Sycamore St, Sauk City, WI 53583
(608) 643-3383
Admin Scott A Nelson.
Licensure Skilled care; Intermediate care. *Beds* SNF 125. *Certified* Medicaid.
Owner Proprietary corp.

Schofield

Heritage Haven Care Center
6001 Alderson St, Schofield, WI 54476
(715) 359-4257
Admin Suzanne T Whitty.
Medical Dir C Grauer MD.
Licensure Skilled care; Intermediate care; Alzheimer's care. *Beds* SNF 164. *Certified* Medicaid.
Owner Proprietary corp (Hillhaven Corp).
Admissions Requirements Minimum age 18; Medical examination; Physician's request.
Facilities Dining room; Physical therapy room; Activities room; Chapel; Laundry room; Barber/Beauty shop; Books available; Social services.

Activities Arts & crafts; Cards; Games; Reading groups; Prayer groups; Movies; Shopping trips; Dances/Social/Cultural gatherings.

Seymour

Good Shepherd Home Ltd
Rte 2, 607 Bronson Rd, Seymour, WI 54165
(414) 833-6856
Admin Shirley K Mielke. *Dir of Nursing* Lori Schultz. *Medical Dir* Dr Lindy Eatwell.
Licensure Skilled care; Intermediate care. *Beds* SNF 97. *Certified* Medicaid.
Owner Nonprofit corp.
Admissions Requirements Minimum age 18; Medical examination; Physician's request.
Staff Physicians 8 (pt); RNs 1 (ft), 8 (pt); LPNs 3 (ft), 6 (pt); Nurses' aides 16 (ft), 32 (pt); Physical therapists 1 (pt); Occupational therapists 1 (pt); Speech therapists 1 (pt); Activities coordinators 1 (ft), 2 (pt); Dietitians 1 (pt); Ophthalmologists 1 (pt).
Facilities Dining room; Physical therapy room; Activities room; Chapel; Laundry room; Barber/Beauty shop; Senior citizen center; Conference room.
Activities Arts & crafts; Cards; Games; Reading groups; Prayer groups; Movies; Shopping trips; Dances/Social/Cultural gatherings; Exercise program; Music therapy.

Shawano

Birch Hill Health Care Center
1475 Birch Hill Ln, Shawano, WI 54166
(715) 526-3161
Admin Allen M Kratky.
Medical Dir Ronald Lageman; Gail Mader.
Licensure Skilled care. *Beds* SNF 102. *Certified* Medicaid; Medicare.
Owner Proprietary corp.
Admissions Requirements Medical examination; Physician's request.
Staff RNs 5 (ft), 3 (pt); LPNs 2 (ft), 2 (pt); Nurses' aides 21 (ft), 13 (pt); Activities coordinators 1 (ft); Dietitians 1 (pt).
Facilities Dining room; Physical therapy room; Activities room; Chapel; Crafts room; Laundry room; Barber/Beauty shop.
Activities Arts & crafts; Cards; Games; Reading groups; Prayer groups; Movies; Shopping trips; Dances/Social/Cultural gatherings.

Evergreen Health Care Center Inc
1250 Evergreen St, Shawano, WI 54166
(715) 526-3107
Admin Jane T Wuench. *Dir of Nursing* Kathleen Dey RN. *Medical Dir* R L Logemann MD.
Licensure Skilled care; Intermediate care. *Beds* SNF 103. *Certified* Medicaid; Medicare.
Owner Proprietary corp.
Admissions Requirements Medical examination; Physician's request.
Facilities Dining room; Physical therapy room; Activities room; Chapel; Crafts room; Laundry room; Barber/Beauty shop.
Activities Arts & crafts; Cards; Games; Reading groups; Prayer groups; Movies; Shopping trips; Dances/Social/Cultural gatherings.

Heartland of Shawano
1436 S Lincoln St, Shawano, WI 54166
(715) 526-6111
Admin Lisa J Schulte.
Medical Dir Patricia Stuff MD.
Licensure Skilled care; Intermediate care. *Beds* SNF 118. *Certified* Medicaid; Medicare.
Owner Proprietary corp (Health Care & Retirement Corp).
Admissions Requirements Minimum age 18; Medical examination; Physician's request.

Staff RNs 2 (ft), 2 (pt); LPNs 4 (ft), 4 (pt);
Nurses' aides 25 (ft), 15 (pt); Physical
therapists 1 (ft); Occupational therapists 1
(pt); Speech therapists 1 (pt); Activities
coordinators 1 (ft), 1 (pt); Dietitians 1 (pt).
Facilities Dining room; Physical therapy
room; Activities room; Chapel; Laundry
room; Barber/Beauty shop.
Activities Cards; Games; Reading groups;
Prayer groups; Movies; Shopping trips;
Dances/Social/Cultural gatherings.

Maple Lane Health Care Facility
PO Box 534, Shawano, WI 54166
(715) 526-3158
Admin Thomas W Arvey.
Medical Dir Alois J Sebesta; Mary Martin.
Licensure Skilled care. *Beds* SNF 102.
Certified Medicaid.
Owner Publicly owned.
Admissions Requirements Minimum age;
Medical examination.
Staff Physicians 1 (pt); RNs 3 (ft), 2 (pt);
LPNs 6 (pt); Nurses' aides 22 (ft), 14 (pt);
Activities coordinators 1 (ft); Dietitians 1
(pt).
Facilities Dining room; Activities room;
Chapel; Crafts room; Laundry room; Barber/
Beauty shop; Library; Woodshop; Kitchen;
Dental exam room; Canteen.
Activities Arts & crafts; Cards; Games; Prayer
groups; Movies; Shopping trips; Dances/
Social/Cultural gatherings; Woodworking;
Exercises; Current events; Socialization.

Sheboygan

Greendale Health Care Center
3129 Michigan Ave, Sheboygan, WI 53082
(414) 458-1155
Admin Suzanne M Groth.
Medical Dir Dr Stephen Wescott.
Licensure Skilled care; Intermediate care. *Beds*
SNF 64. *Certified* Medicaid.
Owner Proprietary corp.
Admissions Requirements Minimum age 18;
Medical examination; Physician's request.
Staff Physicians 1 (pt); Physical therapists 1
(pt); Reality therapists 1 (ft), 1 (pt);
Recreational therapists 1 (ft), 1 (pt);
Occupational therapists 1 (pt); Speech
therapists 1 (pt); Activities coordinators 1
(ft); Dietitians 1 (ft); Audiologists 1 (pt);
Dentists 1 (pt).
Facilities Dining room; Physical therapy
room; Activities room; Chapel; Crafts room;
Laundry room; Barber/Beauty shop; Library;
Luxurious lounges; Outside areas; Private
personal storage; Safety deposit box;
Specially equipped vans for patient
transportation or family use.
Activities Arts & crafts; Cards; Games;
Reading groups; Prayer groups; Movies;
Shopping trips; Dances/Social/Cultural
gatherings; Resident council; Geriatric/adult
day care; Outpatient physical therapy;
Occupational therapy; Speech therapy;
Outpatient activities program.

Heritage Nursing Center
1902 Mead St, Sheboygan, WI 53081
(414) 458-8333
Admin Virgil W Kalchthaler.
Medical Dir Dr Robert A Helminiak.
Licensure Skilled care; Intermediate care. *Beds*
SNF 156. *Certified* Medicaid.
Owner Proprietary corp.
Admissions Requirements Minimum age 18;
Medical examination; Physician's request.
Staff Physicians; RNs; LPNs; Nurses' aides;
Physical therapists; Reality therapists;
Recreational therapists; Occupational
therapists; Speech therapists; Activities
coordinators; Dietitians; Ophthalmologists;
Podiatrists; Audiologists; Dentists.

Facilities Dining room; Activities room;
Crafts room; Laundry room; Barber/Beauty
shop.
Activities Arts & crafts; Cards; Games;
Reading groups; Prayer groups; Shopping
trips.

Meadow View Manor Nursing Home Inc
PO Box 1127, 3613 S 13th St, Sheboygan, WI
53082
(414) 458-4040
Admin Marilyn L Schmidtke. *Dir of Nursing*
Jacolyn Stone.
Licensure Intermediate care. *Beds* ICF 74.
Certified Medicaid.
Owner Privately owned.
Admissions Requirements Physician's request.
Facilities Dining room; Activities room;
Laundry room; Barber/Beauty shop.
Activities Arts & crafts; Cards; Games;
Reading groups; Prayer groups; Movies;
Shopping trips; Dances/Social/Cultural
gatherings.

Morningside Health Center
3431 N 13th St, Sheboygan, WI 53083
(414) 457-5046
Admin Edith M Schmidt.
Licensure Skilled care; Intermediate care. *Beds*
SNF 72. *Certified* Medicaid.
Owner Proprietary corp.

**Sheboygan Retirement Home & Beach Health
Care Center Inc**
930 N 6th St, Sheboygan, WI 53081
(414) 458-2137
Admin Michael J Basch. *Dir of Nursing* Pat
Kolb RN. *Medical Dir* Vytas Kerpe MD.
Licensure Skilled care; Intermediate care;
Retirement. *Beds* SNF 82. *Certified*
Medicaid.
Owner Nonprofit organization/foundation.
Admissions Requirements Medical
examination.
Staff RNs 1 (ft), 3 (pt); LPNs 6 (ft), 11 (pt);
Physical therapists 1 (ft); Activities
coordinators 2 (ft), 1 (pt).
Affiliation Methodist.
Facilities Dining room; Physical therapy
room; Activities room; Chapel; Crafts room;
Laundry room; Barber/Beauty shop; Library;
Patio; Sun deck; Wood working shop.
Activities Arts & crafts; Cards; Games;
Reading groups; Prayer groups; Movies;
Shopping trips; Dances/Social/Cultural
gatherings.

Sunny Ridge
3014 Erie Ave, Sheboygan, WI 53081
(414) 459-3028, 459-4341 FAX
Admin Randall G Krentz. *Dir of Nursing*
Cecila Leutgeweger. *Medical Dir* Dr Curtis
Hancock.
Licensure Skilled care; Alzheimer's care. *Beds*
SNF 398. *Private Pay Patients* 39%. *Certified*
Medicaid.
Owner Publicly owned.
Admissions Requirements Minimum age 18.
Staff RNs 13 (ft), 13 (pt); LPNs 14 (ft), 14
(pt); Nurses' aides 85 (ft), 66 (pt); Dietitians.
Facilities Dining room; Physical therapy
room; Activities room; Chapel; Crafts room;
Laundry room; Barber/Beauty shop; Library.
Activities Arts & crafts; Cards; Games;
Reading groups; Movies; Shopping trips;
Dances/Social/Cultural gatherings;
Intergenerational programs; Pet therapy.

Sheboygan Falls

Pine Haven Christian Home
531 Giddings Ave, Sheboygan Falls, WI 53085
(414) 467-2401, 467-2573 FAX
Admin Daniel H Pastoor. *Dir of Nursing*
Mary Veenendaal. *Medical Dir* James B
Kuplic MD.

Licensure Skilled care; Retirement. *Beds* SNF
71. *Private Pay Patients* 28%. *Certified*
Medicaid.
Owner Nonprofit corp.
Admissions Requirements Minimum age 65;
Medical examination.
Staff RNs 1 (ft), 4 (pt); LPNs 1 (ft), 8 (pt);
Nurses' aides 41 (pt); Activities coordinators
1 (pt); Dietitians 1 (pt); Other staff 50 (pt).
Facilities Dining room; Activities room;
Laundry room; Barber/Beauty shop; Library.
Activities Arts & crafts; Games; Reading
groups; Prayer groups; Movies; Shopping
trips; Intergenerational programs.

**Sheboygan County Comprehensive Health
Center**
Rte 2 Box 265, Sheboygan Falls, WI 53085
(414) 467-4648
Admin John Van Der Male NHA. *Dir of
Nursing* Mary Jane Van Loon Rn. *Medical
Dir* A A Shah Psychiatrist.
Licensure Skilled care; Intermediate care for
mentally retarded; Alzheimer's care. *Beds*
SNF 115; ICF/MR 115. *Private Pay Patients*
2%. *Certified* Medicaid; Medicare.
Owner Nonprofit organization/foundation.
Admissions Requirements Minimum age 18.
Staff Physicians 3 (pt); RNs 6 (ft), 8 (pt);
LPNs 14 (ft), 12 (pt); Nurses' aides 48 (ft),
53 (pt); Occupational therapists 1 (ft);
Activities coordinators 3 (ft); Dietitians 1
(pt).
Facilities Dining room; Activities room;
Chapel; Crafts room; Barber/Beauty shop;
Library.
Activities Arts & crafts; Cards; Games;
Reading groups; Prayer groups; Movies;
Shopping trips; Dances/Social/Cultural
gatherings; Intergenerational programs; Pet
therapy.

Shell Lake

Terraceview Living Center
PO Box 379, County Trunk B "E", Shell Lake,
WI 54871
(715) 468-7292, 468-2820 FAX
Admin Lindell W Weathers. *Dir of Nursing*
Dorothy Peterson. *Medical Dir* Fred
Goetsch MD.
Licensure Skilled care. *Beds* SNF 70. *Private
Pay Patients* 20%. *Certified* Medicaid.
Owner Nonprofit corp.
Admissions Requirements Minimum age 18;
Medical examination; Physician's request.
Staff Physicians 10 (pt); RNs 3 (ft), 1 (pt);
LPNs 4 (ft), 6 (pt); Nurses' aides 11 (ft), 14
(pt); Physical therapists 1 (ft); Speech
therapists 1 (pt); Activities coordinators 1
(ft); Dietitians 1 (pt).
Facilities Dining room; Physical therapy
room; Activities room; Chapel; Crafts room;
Laundry room; Barber/Beauty shop.
Activities Arts & crafts; Cards; Games;
Reading groups; Prayer groups; Movies;
Shopping trips; Dances/Social/Cultural
gatherings.

Shorewood

Shorewood Heights Health Care Center
3710 N Oakland Ave, Shorewood, WI 53211
(414) 964-6200, 332-1948 FAX
Admin Judith A Goldberg. *Dir of Nursing*
Karlene Sorenson. *Medical Dir* Dr Richard
Kane.
Licensure Skilled care; Alzheimer's care. *Beds*
SNF 288. *Private Pay Patients* 5%. *Certified*
Medicaid.
Owner Proprietary corp (Beverly Enterprises).
Admissions Requirements Medical
examination.
Staff Physicians 5 (ft); RNs 9 (ft), 2 (pt);
LPNs 20 (ft), 8 (pt); Nurses' aides 57 (ft), 25
(pt); Physical therapists 1 (ft); Recreational
therapists 1 (ft); Occupational therapists 1

(ft); Speech therapists 1 (ft); Activities coordinators 1 (ft); Dietitians 1 (pt); Ophthalmologists 1 (pt); Podiatrists 1 (pt).
Facilities Dining room; Physical therapy room; Activities room; Laundry room; Barber/Beauty shop; Occupational therapy room.
Activities Arts & crafts; Cards; Games; Reading groups; Prayer groups; Movies; Shopping trips; Dances/Social/Cultural gatherings; Intergenerational programs; Pet therapy; Cooking; Exercises.

Siren

Capeside Cove Good Samaritan Center
PO Box 49, 23926 4th Ave S, Siren, WI 54872-0049
(715) 349-2292, 349-7218 FAX
Admin David F Boock. *Dir of Nursing* Paulette Kuehn. *Medical Dir* Dr Mark Bixby.
Licensure Skilled care. *Beds* SNF 100. *Private Pay Patients* 30%. *Certified* Medicaid.
Owner Nonprofit corp (Evangelical Lutheran/ Good Samaritan Society).
Admissions Requirements Medical examination; Physician's request.
Staff RNs 5 (ft), 6 (pt); LPNs 4 (ft), 4 (pt); Activities coordinators 1 (ft).
Affiliation Lutheran.
Facilities Dining room; Physical therapy room; Activities room; Chapel; Laundry room; Barber/Beauty shop.
Activities Arts & crafts; Cards; Games; Reading groups; Movies; Shopping trips.

Sister Bay

Scandia Village Retirement Center
290 Smith Dr, Sister Bay, WI 54234
(414) 854-2317
Admin Donald E Heeringa. *Dir of Nursing* Mary Kaye Gray. *Medical Dir* Dr William Meyer.
Licensure Skilled care; Intermediate care; CBRF; Retirement; Alzheimer's care. *Beds* Swing beds SNF/ICF 60; CBRF 20; Retirement apts 62. *Private Pay Patients* 59%. *Certified* Medicaid.
Owner Nonprofit corp.
Admissions Requirements Medical examination; Physician's request.
Staff RNs 2 (ft), 4 (pt); LPNs 1 (ft), 4 (pt); Nurses' aides 12 (ft), 15 (pt); Physical therapists (contracted); Activities coordinators 1 (ft); Dietitians (contracted).
Facilities Dining room; Physical therapy room; Activities room; Chapel; Crafts room; Laundry room; Barber/Beauty shop.
Activities Arts & crafts; Cards; Games; Reading groups; Prayer groups; Movies; Shopping trips; Dances/Social/Cultural gatherings; Community support.

Soldiers Grove

Sannes Skogdalen
Hwy 61, Soldiers Grove, WI 54655
(608) 624-5244
Admin Donald A Sannes. *Dir of Nursing* Marlene Norman. *Medical Dir* Timothy Devitt MD.
Licensure Skilled care; Intermediate care. *Beds* SNF 66. *Certified* Medicaid.
Owner Proprietary corp.
Admissions Requirements Medical examination.
Staff RNs; LPNs; Nurses' aides; Activities coordinators; Dietitians.
Facilities Dining room; Physical therapy room; Activities room; Chapel; Crafts room; Laundry room; Barber/Beauty shop; Library.

Activities Arts & crafts; Cards; Games; Reading groups; Prayer groups; Movies; Shopping trips; Dances/Social/Cultural gatherings.

South Milwaukee

Franciscan Villa
3601 S Chicago Ave, South Milwaukee, WI 53172
(414) 764-4100
Admin Sr Rita Kraemer OSF. *Dir of Nursing* Donna Phillips RN BSN. *Medical Dir* Antonio A Malapira MD.
Licensure Skilled care. *Beds* SNF 150. *Private Pay Patients* 35%. *Certified* Medicaid.
Owner Nonprofit corp.
Admissions Requirements Medical examination; Physician's request.
Staff RNs 13 (ft), 10 (pt); LPNs 6 (ft), 9 (pt); Nurses' aides 36 (ft), 33 (pt); Physical therapists 1 (ft); Occupational therapists 1 (ft); Activities coordinators 1 (ft); Dietitians 1 (pt); Art Therapists 1 (pt).
Affiliation Roman Catholic.
Facilities Dining room; Physical therapy room; Activities room; Chapel; Crafts room; Laundry room; Barber/Beauty shop; Occupational therapy.
Activities Arts & crafts; Cards; Games; Reading groups; Prayer groups; Movies; Shopping trips; Dances/Social/Cultural gatherings; Intergenerational programs.

Willowcrest
3821 S Chicago Ave, South Milwaukee, WI 53172
(414) 762-7336, 762-7105 FAX
Admin Marlene A Fieldbinder NHA. *Dir of Nursing* Kathy May-Rosiak RN. *Medical Dir* Wadie Abdallah MD.
Licensure Skilled care; Alzheimer's care. *Beds* SNF 51. *Private Pay Patients* 20%. *Certified* Medicaid; Medicare.
Owner Proprietary corp (Unicare).
Admissions Requirements Minimum age 18; Medical examination; Physician's request.
Staff Physicians (contracted); RNs 1 (ft), 2 (pt); LPNs 2 (ft), 10 (pt); Nurses' aides 12 (ft), 7 (pt); Physical therapists (contracted); Occupational therapists (contracted); Speech therapists (contracted); Activities coordinators; Dietitians 1 (ft); Ophthalmologists (contracted); Podiatrists (contracted); Audiologists (contracted).
Facilities Dining room; Physical therapy room; Activities room; Crafts room; Laundry room; Barber/Beauty shop.
Activities Arts & crafts; Cards; Games; Reading groups; Prayer groups; Movies; Dances/Social/Cultural gatherings; Intergenerational programs; Pet therapy.

Sparta

Morrow Memorial Home for the Aged
331 S Water St, Sparta, WI 54656
(608) 269-3168
Admin Anita Van Beek NHA. *Dir of Nursing* Pamela Semb RN. *Medical Dir* Paul G Albrecht MD.
Licensure Skilled care; Alzheimer's care. *Beds* SNF 115. *Private Pay Patients* 40%. *Certified* Medicaid.
Owner Nonprofit organization/foundation.
Admissions Requirements Minimum age 18; Medical examination; Physician's request.
Staff RNs 4 (ft), 5 (pt); LPNs 3 (ft), 7 (pt); Nurses' aides 15 (ft), 40 (pt); Physical therapists; Activities coordinators 1 (ft); Dietitians.
Affiliation United Methodist.
Facilities Dining room; Physical therapy room; Activities room; Chapel; Crafts room; Laundry room; Barber/Beauty shop; Library; Dayrooms; Party rooms; Activity kitchen; Whirlpool baths.

Activities Arts & crafts; Cards; Games; Reading groups; Prayer groups; Movies; Shopping trips; Dances/Social/Cultural gatherings; Intergenerational programs; Pet therapy.

Rolling Hills
Rte 2, Sparta, WI 54656
(608) 269-8800
Admin Barbara D Heuer.
Medical Dir Dr Patricia Raftery.
Licensure Skilled care; Intermediate care. *Beds* SNF 248. *Certified* Medicaid.
Owner Publicly owned.
Staff Physicians 3 (pt); RNs 11 (ft), 9 (pt); LPNs 6 (ft), 11 (pt); Nurses' aides 78 (ft), 32 (pt); Physical therapists 1 (pt); Occupational therapists 1 (pt); Speech therapists 1 (pt); Activities coordinators 2 (ft); Dietitians 1 (pt); Podiatrists 1 (pt); Dentists 1 (pt).
Facilities Dining room; Physical therapy room; Activities room; Chapel; Crafts room; Laundry room; Barber/Beauty shop; Library.
Activities Arts & crafts; Cards; Games; Reading groups; Prayer groups; Movies; Shopping trips; Dances/Social/Cultural gatherings.

St Mary's Nursing Home
K & W Main Sts, Sparta, WI 54656
(608) 269-2132
Admin Sr Julie Tydrich.
Medical Dir Susan Davis.
Licensure Skilled care; Retirement. *Beds* SNF 30. *Certified* Medicaid.
Owner Nonprofit corp.
Admissions Requirements Medical examination.
Staff RNs 1 (ft), 6 (pt); LPNs 1 (ft), 2 (pt); Nurses' aides 3 (ft), 9 (pt); Physical therapists 1 (ft), 1 (pt); Recreational therapists 1 (pt); Occupational therapists 1 (pt); Speech therapists 1 (pt); Activities coordinators 1 (pt); Dietitians 1 (pt).
Affiliation Roman Catholic.
Facilities Dining room; Physical therapy room; Activities room; Chapel; Crafts room; Laundry room; Barber/Beauty shop.
Activities Arts & crafts; Cards; Games; Reading groups; Prayer groups; Movies; Shopping trips; Dances/Social/Cultural gatherings.

Spooner

Community Memorial Hospital & Nursing Home
819 Ash St, Spooner, WI 54801
(715) 635-2111
Admin Craig J Barness. *Dir of Nursing* Nancy Detlefsen RN. *Medical Dir* Fredrick Goetsch MD.
Licensure Skilled care. *Beds* SNF 90. *Certified* Medicaid.
Owner Nonprofit corp.
Admissions Requirements Medical examination; Physician's request.
Staff Physicians 10 (ft); RNs 8 (ft); LPNs 10 (ft), 5 (pt); Nurses' aides 30 (ft), 15 (pt); Physical therapists 2 (ft), 1 (pt); Recreational therapists 2 (ft); Speech therapists 1 (ft); Activities coordinators 1 (ft); Dietitians 1 (ft); Ophthalmologists 2 (ft); Dentists 2 (ft).
Facilities Dining room; Physical therapy room; Activities room; Chapel; Crafts room; Laundry room; Barber/Beauty shop; Library.
Activities Arts & crafts; Cards; Games; Reading groups; Prayer groups; Movies; Shopping trips; Dances/Social/Cultural gatherings.

Spring Green

Greenway Manor
501 S Winsted, Spring Green, WI 53588
(608) 588-2586

Admin Mark W Scoles. *Dir of Nursing*
Theresa Young. *Medical Dir* Dr Gerald
Kempthorne.
Licensure Skilled care; Intermediate care. *Beds*
SNF 60. *Certified* Medicaid; Medicare.
Owner Proprietary corp.
Admissions Requirements Physician's request.
Staff RNs 2 (ft), 7 (pt); LPNs 1 (ft), 2 (pt);
Nurses' aides 10 (ft), 25 (pt); Physical
therapists 1 (ft); Recreational therapists 1
(ft), 1 (pt).
Facilities Dining room; Physical therapy
room; Activities room; Chapel; Crafts room;
Laundry room; Barber/Beauty shop; Library.
Activities Arts & crafts; Cards; Games;
Reading groups; Movies; Dances/Social/
Cultural gatherings.

Spring Valley

Spring Valley Health Care Center
W 500 Spring St, Hwy 29, Spring Valley, WI
54767
(715) 778-5545
Admin Kevin H Larson NHA. *Dir of Nursing*
Gayle A Schliep RN. *Medical Dir* L B
Torkelson MD.
Licensure Skilled care; Respite care. *Beds*
SNF 86. *Private Pay Patients* 35%. *Certified*
Medicaid; Medicare.
Owner Publicly owned.
Admissions Requirements Minimum age 18;
Medical examination; Physician's request.
Staff Physicians 3 (pt); RNs 2 (ft), 2 (pt);
LPNs 4 (ft), 4 (pt); Nurses' aides 16 (ft), 15
(pt); Physical therapists 1 (pt); Reality
therapists 1 (pt); Recreational therapists 1
(ft); Occupational therapists 1 (pt); Speech
therapists 1 (pt); Activities coordinators 1
(ft); Dietitians 1 (pt); Ophthalmologists 1
(pt); Podiatrists 1 (pt); Audiologists 1 (pt).
Languages Interpreters available.
Facilities Dining room; Physical therapy
room; Activities room; Chapel; Crafts room;
Laundry room; Barber/Beauty shop; Library;
Outdoor gazebo/patio.
Activities Arts & crafts; Cards; Games;
Reading groups; Prayer groups; Movies;
Shopping trips; Dances/Social/Cultural
gatherings; Intergenerational programs; Pet
therapy.

Stanley

Victory Memorial Hospital & Nursing Home
230 E 4th Ave, Stanley, WI 54768
(715) 644-5571
Admin John J Blahnik. *Dir of Nursing*
Roxanne Green RN CCRN, Nursing Home;
Jennifer Polnaszek RN CCRN, Hospital.
Medical Dir William Hopkins MD.
Licensure Skilled care; Acute care. *Beds* SNF
86; Acute care 41. *Private Pay Patients* 23%.
Certified Medicaid.
Owner Nonprofit organization/foundation.
Admissions Requirements Medical
examination; Physician's request.
Staff Physicians 1 (pt); RNs 5 (ft), 3 (pt);
LPNs 3 (ft), 8 (pt); Nurses' aides 17 (ft), 22
(pt); Physical therapists 1 (pt); Occupational
therapists 1 (pt); Activities coordinators 2
(ft); Dietitians 1 (pt).
Languages Polish, Spanish.
Facilities Dining room; Physical therapy
room; Activities room; Chapel; Crafts room;
Laundry room; Barber/Beauty shop; Library;
TV rooms.
Activities Arts & crafts; Cards; Games;
Reading groups; Prayer groups; Movies;
Shopping trips; Dances/Social/Cultural
gatherings; Intergenerational programs; Pet
therapy.

Stevens Point

Portage County Home
825 Whiting Ave, Stevens Point, WI 54481
(715) 346-1374
Admin William J Van Offeren. *Dir of Nursing*
Elizabeth Rollo. *Medical Dir* Dr Daniel
Brick.
Licensure Skilled care; Intermediate care. *Beds*
SNF 139. *Certified* Medicaid.
Owner Publicly owned.
Admissions Requirements Minimum age 18;
Medical examination; Physician's request.
Staff Physicians 1 (pt); RNs 3 (ft), 8 (pt);
LPNs 2 (ft), 6 (pt); Nurses' aides 28 (ft), 37
(pt); Physical therapists 1 (pt); Recreational
therapists 1 (pt); Occupational therapists 1
(pt); Activities coordinators 1 (pt); Dietitians
1 (pt); Ophthalmologists 1 (pt); Dentists 1
(pt).
Facilities Dining room; Physical therapy
room; Activities room; Chapel; Crafts room;
Laundry room; Barber/Beauty shop; Library.
Activities Arts & crafts; Cards; Games;
Reading groups; Prayer groups; Movies;
Shopping trips; Dances/Social/Cultural
gatherings.

River Pines Living Center
1800 Sherman Ave, Stevens Point, WI 54481
(715) 344-1800
Admin George R Ginsel. *Dir of Nursing*
Wanda Lamz RN. *Medical Dir* Daniel L
Brick MD.
Licensure Skilled care; Intermediate care;
Intermediate care for mentally retarded.
Beds ICF/MR 22; Swing beds SNF/ICF 216.
Certified Medicaid; Medicare.
Owner Nonprofit corp (Adventist Living
Centers).
Admissions Requirements Minimum age 18;
Medical examination.
Staff Physicians 8 (pt); RNs 4 (ft), 9 (pt);
LPNs 1 (ft), 21 (pt); Nurses' aides 107 (ft), 1
(pt); Physical therapists 1 (ft); Occupational
therapists 1 (ft); Speech therapists 1 (ft);
Activities coordinators 1 (ft); Dietitians 1
(ft).
Affiliation Seventh-Day Adventist.
Facilities Dining room; Physical therapy
room; Activities room; Chapel; Crafts room;
Laundry room; Barber/Beauty shop; Library.
Activities Arts & crafts; Cards; Games;
Reading groups; Prayer groups; Movies;
Shopping trips; Dances/Social/Cultural
gatherings.

Stoughton

McCarthy Nursing Home
124 S Monroe St, Stoughton, WI 53589
(608) 873-7462
Admin Michael J McCarthy.
Medical Dir Jean E Pecotte.
Licensure Intermediate care for mentally
retarded. *Beds* ICF/MR 18. *Certified*
Medicaid.
Owner Proprietary corp.
Staff RNs 1 (ft); LPNs 1 (ft); Nurses' aides 7
(ft); Activities coordinators 1 (pt); Dietitians
1 (pt).
Facilities Dining room; Activities room;
Laundry room.
Activities Arts & crafts; Cards; Games;
Reading groups; Prayer groups; Movies;
Shopping trips; Dances/Social/Cultural
gatherings.

Morningside Care Center
PO Box 313, Stoughton, WI 53589
(608) 873-6441
Admin Ruth C Jensen.
Licensure Intermediate care for mentally
retarded. *Beds* ICF/MR 15. *Certified*
Medicaid.
Owner Proprietary corp.

Nazareth House
814 Jackson St, Stoughton, WI 53589
(608) 873-6448
Admin Sr Rose Hoye.
Medical Dir Dr V W Nordholm.
Licensure Skilled care; Intermediate care. *Beds*
SNF 99. *Certified* Medicaid.
Owner Nonprofit corp.
Admissions Requirements Minimum age 65;
Medical examination.
Staff Physicians 2 (pt); RNs 4 (ft), 4 (pt);
LPNs 2 (ft), 2 (pt); Nurses' aides 30 (ft), 12
(pt); Physical therapists 1 (ft), 2 (pt); Reality
therapists 1 (ft); Recreational therapists 1
(pt); Activities coordinators 1 (ft), 3 (pt);
Dietitians 1 (ft); Dentists 1 (pt).
Affiliation Roman Catholic.
Facilities Dining room; Physical therapy
room; Activities room; Chapel; Crafts room;
Laundry room; Barber/Beauty shop; Sun
rooms.
Activities Arts & crafts; Cards; Games; Prayer
groups; Movies; Dances/Social/Cultural
gatherings.

Nygaard Manor
400 N Morris, Stoughton, WI 53589
(608) 873-9072
Admin Kristine Gabert. *Dir of Nursing*
Clarice Lyke.
Licensure Intermediate care; Alzheimer's care.
Beds ICF 16.
Owner Nonprofit corp.
Admissions Requirements Minimum age 65;
Females only; Medical examination;
Physician's request.
Staff Physicians 1 (pt); RNs 1 (ft), 1 (pt);
LPNs 1 (ft), 3 (pt); Nurses' aides 2 (ft), 4
(pt); Physical therapists 1 (pt); Occupational
therapists 1 (pt); Activities coordinators 1
(pt); Dietitians 1 (pt).
Languages Norwegian.
Affiliation Lutheran.
Facilities Dining room; Activities room;
Laundry room.
Activities Arts & crafts; Cards; Games;
Reading groups; Prayer groups; Movies;
Shopping trips; Dances/Social/Cultural
gatherings.

Skaalen Sunset Home
400 N Morris St, Stoughton, WI 53589
(608) 873-5651
Admin Mark Benson.
Medical Dir Dr David Nelson.
Licensure Skilled care; Retirement. *Beds* SNF
270; Retirement 200. *Private Pay Patients*
50%. *Certified* Medicaid.
Owner Nonprofit corp.
Admissions Requirements Minimum age 65;
Medical examination; Physician's request.
Staff RNs 7 (ft), 12 (pt); LPNs 5 (ft), 21 (pt);
Nurses' aides 33 (ft), 122 (pt); Recreational
therapists 2 (ft), 1 (pt); Occupational
therapists 1 (ft), 1 (pt); Activities
coordinators 1 (ft); Dietitians 1 (pt).
Affiliation Lutheran.
Facilities Dining room; Physical therapy
room; Activities room; Chapel; Crafts room;
Barber/Beauty shop; Library; In-service
education.
Activities Arts & crafts; Cards; Games;
Reading groups; Prayer groups; Movies;
Shopping trips; Dances/Social/Cultural
gatherings.

Strum

Strum Nursing Home
PO Box 217, 208 Elm St, Strum, WI 54770
(715) 695-2611
Admin Mary Gullicksrud. *Dir of Nursing*
Roberta Ross RN. *Medical Dir* Dr William
E Wright.
Licensure Skilled care; Intermediate care. *Beds*
SNF 44; ICF 6. *Private Pay Patients* 15%.
Certified Medicaid.

Owner Proprietary corp.
Admissions Requirements Minimum age 18; Medical examination.
Staff Physicians 3 (pt); RNs 4 (ft), 1 (pt); LPNs 1 (ft), 3 (pt); Nurses' aides 10 (ft), 13 (pt); Physical therapists 1 (pt); Occupational therapists 1 (pt); Speech therapists 1 (pt); Activities coordinators 1 (ft); Dietitians 1 (pt).
Languages Norwegian.
Facilities Dining room; Physical therapy room; Activities room; Chapel; Laundry room; Barber/Beauty shop.
Activities Arts & crafts; Cards; Games; Reading groups; Prayer groups; Movies; Dances/Social/Cultural gatherings.

Sturgeon Bay

Door County Memorial Hospital—Skilled Nursing Facility
330 S 16th Pl, Sturgeon Bay, WI 54235
(414) 743-5566
Admin Joan D Hauer. *Dir of Nursing* Karin Bellin RN. *Medical Dir* Jeffery J Brook.
Licensure Skilled care; Intermediate care; Alzheimer's care. *Beds* Swing beds SNF/ICF 30. *Private Pay Patients* 33%. *Certified* Medicaid; Medicare.
Owner Nonprofit corp.
Staff RNs 1 (ft), 6 (pt); LPNs 2 (ft), 3 (pt); Nurses' aides 3 (ft), 12 (pt); Physical therapists (contracted); Recreational therapists 1 (pt); Occupational therapists (contracted); Speech therapists (contracted); Dietitians 1 (pt).
Facilities Dining room; Activities room; Barber/Beauty shop.
Activities Arts & crafts; Cards; Games; Reading groups; Prayer groups; Movies; Shopping trips; Dances/Social/Cultural gatherings; Intergenerational programs; Pet therapy.

Dorchester Nursing Center
200 N 7th Ave, Sturgeon Bay, WI 54235
(414) 743-6274
Admin Jean Marsh. *Dir of Nursing* Judy Fischer RN. *Medical Dir* George Roenning MD.
Licensure Skilled care; Alzheimer's care. *Beds* SNF 149. *Private Pay Patients* 35%. *Certified* Medicaid; Medicare.
Owner Proprietary corp.
Admissions Requirements Minimum age 18; Medical examination; Physician's request.
Staff RNs 4 (ft), 8 (pt); LPNs 9 (ft), 6 (pt); Nurses' aides 32 (ft), 16 (pt); Physical therapists (contracted); Activities coordinators 1 (ft); Dietitians 1 (pt).
Facilities Dining room; Physical therapy room; Activities room; Chapel; Crafts room; Laundry room; Barber/Beauty shop.
Activities Arts & crafts; Cards; Games; Reading groups; Prayer groups; Movies; Shopping trips; Dances/Social/Cultural gatherings; Intergenerational programs; Pet therapy; One-to-one interaction.

Sun Prairie

Sun Prairie Health Care Center
228 W Main St, Sun Prairie, WI 53590
(608) 837-5959
Admin Lars Rogeberg.
Medical Dir M Schmidt MD.
Licensure Skilled care. *Beds* SNF 32. *Certified* Medicaid; Medicare.
Owner Proprietary corp.
Admissions Requirements Medical examination; Physician's request.
Staff Physicians 1 (pt); RNs 1 (ft), 3 (pt); LPNs 1 (ft), 4 (pt); Physical therapists 1 (pt); Occupational therapists 1 (ft); Speech therapists 1 (pt); Activities coordinators 1

(pt); Dietitians 1 (pt); Ophthalmologists 1 (pt); Podiatrists 1 (pt); Audiologists 1 (pt); Dentists 1 (pt).
Facilities Dining room; Physical therapy room; Activities room; Crafts room; Laundry room; Barber/Beauty shop; Library.
Activities Arts & crafts; Cards; Games; Reading groups; Prayer groups; Movies; Shopping trips; Dances/Social/Cultural gatherings.

Willows Nursing Home
41 Rickel Rd, Sun Prairie, WI 53590
(608) 837-8520
Admin Craig R Smith.
Medical Dir Dr William Russell.
Licensure Skilled care. *Beds* SNF 60. *Certified* Medicaid; Medicare.
Owner Proprietary corp (Unicare).
Admissions Requirements Minimum age 18; Medical examination; Physician's request.
Staff RNs 1 (ft), 6 (pt); LPNs 7 (pt); Nurses' aides 15 (ft), 10 (pt); Recreational therapists 1 (ft), 1 (pt).
Facilities Dining room; Physical therapy room; Activities room; Crafts room; Laundry room; Barber/Beauty shop; Library.
Activities Arts & crafts; Cards; Games; Reading groups; Prayer groups; Movies; Shopping trips; Dances/Social/Cultural gatherings; Discussion groups; Self-help groups; Stroke groups.

Superior

Chaffey Nursing Home Inc
1419 Hill Ave, Superior, WI 54880
(715) 392-6121
Admin D Joy Jurgensen NHA. *Dir of Nursing* Janice LeMay RN. *Medical Dir* R P Fruehauf MD.
Licensure Skilled care. *Beds* SNF 50. *Certified* Medicaid.
Owner Proprietary corp.
Admissions Requirements Minimum age 18 unless waivered; Medical examination; Physician's request.
Staff RNs 3 (ft), 1 (pt); LPNs 1 (ft), 9 (pt); Nurses' aides 6 (ft), 26 (pt); Physical therapists; Occupational therapists; Speech therapists; Activities coordinators 1 (ft), 1 (pt).
Facilities Dining room; Activities room; Crafts room; Laundry room; Barber/Beauty shop; Library; Patio area for outdoor enjoyment.
Activities Arts & crafts; Cards; Games; Reading groups; Prayer groups; Movies; Shopping trips; Dances/Social/Cultural gatherings; Music therapy; Resident council; Baking/cooking; Intergenerational programs.

Colonial Health Care Services Inc
3120 N 21st St, Superior, WI 54880
(715) 392-2922
Admin Patricia Ziburski.
Medical Dir Claudia Porter.
Licensure Intermediate care. *Beds* ICF 42. *Certified* Medicaid.
Owner Proprietary corp.
Admissions Requirements Medical examination; Physician's request.
Staff RNs 1 (ft); LPNs 2 (ft), 4 (pt); Nurses' aides 8 (ft), 4 (pt); Activities coordinators 1 (ft); Dietitians 1 (pt).
Facilities Dining room; Activities room; Crafts room; Laundry room; Barber/Beauty shop.
Activities Arts & crafts; Cards; Games; Reading groups; Prayer groups; Movies; Shopping trips; Dances/Social/Cultural gatherings.

Fieldview Manor
1612 N 37th St, Superior, WI 54880
(715) 392-5144
Admin Benjamin Prince.

Licensure Skilled care; Intermediate care. *Beds* SNF 119. *Certified* Medicaid.
Owner Proprietary corp (Beverly Enterprises).

St Francis Home Inc
1800 New York Ave, Superior, WI 54880
(715) 394-5591
Admin Kurt M Graves.
Medical Dir Dr Selleas.
Licensure Skilled care; Alzheimer's care. *Beds* SNF 192. *Certified* Medicaid; Medicare.
Owner Nonprofit corp.
Affiliation Roman Catholic.

Southdale Health Care Services Inc
3712 Tower Ave, Superior, WI 54880
(715) 392-6272
Admin Patricia Ziburski.
Medical Dir L Beth Carlson.
Licensure Intermediate care. *Beds* ICF 50. *Certified* Medicaid.
Owner Proprietary corp.
Admissions Requirements Medical examination; Physician's request.
Staff RNs 1 (ft); LPNs 5 (ft), 2 (pt); Nurses' aides 8 (ft), 9 (pt); Activities coordinators 1 (ft); Dietitians 1 (pt).
Facilities Dining room; Activities room; Crafts room; Laundry room; Barber/Beauty shop; Library.
Activities Arts & crafts; Cards; Games; Reading groups; Prayer groups; Movies; Shopping trips; Dances/Social/Cultural gatherings.

Suring

Woodland Village Nursing Home Inc
430 Manor Dr, Suring, WI 54174
(414) 842-2191, 842-4223 FAX
Admin Helen J Newbury. *Dir of Nursing* Carol Weber RN. *Medical Dir* Dr Randall Lewis.
Licensure Skilled care. *Beds* SNF 60. *Certified* Medicaid; Medicare.
Owner Proprietary corp.
Admissions Requirements Minimum age 18; Medical examination.
Staff Physicians 5 (ft); RNs 4 (ft); LPNs 6 (ft); Nurses' aides 32 (ft); Physical therapists 1 (ft); Recreational therapists 2 (ft); Occupational therapists 1 (ft); Speech therapists 1 (ft); Activities coordinators 1 (ft); Dietitians 1 (ft).
Languages Sign, Polish, German.
Facilities Dining room; Physical therapy room; Activities room; Chapel; Crafts room; Laundry room; Barber/Beauty shop; Library.
Activities Arts & crafts; Cards; Games; Reading groups; Prayer groups; Movies; Shopping trips; Dances/Social/Cultural gatherings; Pet therapy.

Thorp

Oakbrook Manor of Thorp
206 W Prospect St, Thorp, WI 54771
(715) 669-5321
Admin Lucille G Hoffman. *Dir of Nursing* Chris Dietrich. *Medical Dir* Dr William Hopkins.
Licensure Skilled care; Intermediate care. *Beds* SNF 43; ICF 8. *Private Pay Patients* 27%. *Certified* Medicaid.
Owner Proprietary corp.
Admissions Requirements Minimum age 18; Medical examination; Physician's request.
Staff Physicians; RNs; LPNs; Nurses' aides; Activities coordinators.
Languages Polish, Ukranian, German, Finnish.
Facilities Dining room; Physical therapy room; Activities room; Laundry room; Barber/Beauty shop.
Activities Arts & crafts; Cards; Games; Reading groups; Prayer groups; Movies; Intergenerational programs; Pet therapy.

Tomah

Tomah Care Center
1505 Butts Ave, Tomah, WI 54660
(608) 372-3241
Admin Todd Ramley. *Dir of Nursing* Janice Henry RN. *Medical Dir* Michael Saunders MD.
Licensure Skilled care; Alzheimer's care. *Beds* SNF 110. *Certified* Medicaid.
Owner Proprietary corp (Beverly Enterprises).
Admissions Requirements Minimum age 18; Medical examination; Physician's request.
Staff RNs 5 (ft), 2 (pt); LPNs 3 (ft), 3 (pt); Nurses' aides 32 (ft), 18 (pt); Physical therapists 1 (ft); Recreational therapists 1 (ft); Occupational therapists 1 (ft).
Facilities Dining room; Physical therapy room; Activities room; Crafts room; Laundry room; Barber/Beauty shop; Dayroom; Conference or visiting/privacy room; TV rooms.
Activities Arts & crafts; Cards; Games; Reading groups; Prayer groups; Movies; Shopping trips; Dances/Social/Cultural gatherings; Exercises; Small groups for sensory stimulation; Socialization skill level; Reminiscing; Church.

Tomahawk

Golden Age
720 E Kings Rd, Tomahawk, WI 54487
(715) 453-2164
Admin Peter E Merchant. *Dir of Nursing* Jean Richert. *Medical Dir* James L Carroll MD.
Licensure Skilled care; Alzheimer's cawre. *Beds* SNF 105. *Private Pay Patients* 22%. *Certified* Medicaid; Medicare.
Owner Proprietary corp (Beverly Enterprises).
Admissions Requirements Medical examination; Physician's request.
Staff Physicians 1 (pt); RNs 4 (ft), 3 (pt); LPNs 5 (ft), 2 (pt); Nurses' aides 22 (ft), 12 (pt); Physical therapists 1 (pt); Occupational therapists 1 (pt); Speech therapists 1 (pt); Activities coordinators 1 (ft); Dietitians 1 (pt).
Facilities Dining room; Physical therapy room; Activities room; Crafts room; Laundry room; Barber/Beauty shop; Library; Grounds with gazebo and pond; Security system for wanders.
Activities Arts & crafts; Cards; Games; Reading groups; Prayer groups; Movies; Shopping trips; Dances/Social/Cultural gatherings; Intergenerational programs.

Riverview Terrace
428 N 6th St, Tomahawk, WI 54487
(715) 453-2511
Admin John P Ley.
Medical Dir N L Bugarin.
Licensure Skilled care; Intermediate care. *Beds* SNF 64. *Certified* Medicaid; Medicare.
Owner Proprietary corp (Beverly Enterprises).
Admissions Requirements Minimum age 18; Medical examination; Physician's request.
Staff RNs 2 (ft), 1 (pt); LPNs 3 (ft), 2 (pt); Nurses' aides 30 (ft), 14 (pt); Physical therapists 1 (pt); Occupational therapists 1 (pt); Speech therapists 1 (pt); Activities coordinators 1 (ft); Dietitians 1 (pt).
Facilities Dining room; Physical therapy room; Activities room; Laundry room; Barber/Beauty shop.
Activities Arts & crafts; Cards; Games; Prayer groups; Movies; Shopping trips; Dances/Social/Cultural gatherings.

Twin Lakes

Hillcrest Nursing Home
100 E School St, Twin Lakes, WI 53181
(414) 877-2118

Admin Jeffrey R Minor. *Dir of Nursing* Kathleen Walker. *Medical Dir* Dr Richard Rodarte.
Licensure Intermediate care. *Beds* ICF 53. *Certified* Medicaid.
Owner Proprietary corp.
Admissions Requirements Minimum age 18; Medical examination.
Staff Physicians 6 (pt); RNs 3 (ft), 3 (pt); LPNs 4 (ft), 3 (pt); Physical therapists 1 (pt); Occupational therapists 1 (pt); Speech therapists 1 (pt); Activities coordinators 1 (ft); Dietitians 1 (ft); Ophthalmologists 1 (pt); Podiatrists 1 (pt); Dentists 1 (pt).
Facilities Dining room; Laundry room; Barber/Beauty shop.
Activities Arts & crafts; Cards; Games; Reading groups; Prayer groups; Movies; Shopping trips; Dances/Social/Cultural gatherings.

Two Rivers

Hamilton Memorial Home
1 Hamilton Dr, Two Rivers, WI 54241
(414) 793-2261
Admin Mary Budnik. *Dir of Nursing* Margaret Shikowski RN. *Medical Dir* John E Nilles MD.
Licensure Skilled care; Intermediate care. *Beds* SNF 85. *Certified* Medicaid.
Owner Nonprofit corp.
Admissions Requirements Minimum age 18; Medical examination; Physician's request.
Staff Physicians 8 (pt); RNs 3 (ft), 4 (pt); LPNs 3 (ft), 6 (pt); Nurses' aides 10 (ft), 30 (pt); Physical therapists 1 (pt); Occupational therapists 1 (pt); Activities coordinators 1 (ft); Dietitians 1 (pt).
Facilities Dining room; Activities room; Chapel; Crafts room; Laundry room; Barber/Beauty shop.
Activities Arts & crafts; Cards; Games; Reading groups; Prayer groups; Movies; Shopping trips; Dances/Social/Cultural gatherings; Pet therapy.

Union Grove

Southern Wisconsin Center for the Developmentally Disabled
21425 Spring St, Union Grove, WI 53182-9708
(414) 878-2411, ext 200, 878-5701 FAX
Admin Marlys S Griffiths, Dir. *Dir of Nursing* Barbara H Geitz RN. *Medical Dir* Miroslaw K Rogalski MD.
Licensure Intermediate care for mentally retarded. *Beds* ICF/MR 625. *Private Pay Patients* 0%. *Certified* Medicaid.
Owner Publicly owned.
Admissions Requirements Minimum age 22.
Staff Physicians 5 (ft); RNs 37 (ft), 9 (pt); LPNs 19 (ft), 7 (pt); Nurses' aides 448 (ft), 46 (pt); Physical therapists 6 (ft); Recreational therapists 13 (ft); Occupational therapists 7 (ft); Speech therapists 5 (ft), 3 (pt); Dietitians 3 (ft); Ophthalmologists 1 (ft); Podiatrists 1 (ft); Audiologists 1 (ft).
Facilities Dining room; Physical therapy room; Activities room; Chapel; Crafts room; Laundry room; Library.
Activities Arts & crafts; Cards; Games; Reading groups; Prayer groups; Movies; Shopping trips; Dances/Social/Cultural gatherings; Intergenerational programs; Pet therapy.

Verona

Badger Prairie Health Care Center
6748 Hwy 18 & 151, Verona, WI 53593
(608) 845-6601
Admin Stephen H Seybold. *Dir of Nursing* Sharon Burns. *Medical Dir* Stephen Babcock.

Licensure Skilled care; Institute for mental disease; Alzheimer's care. *Beds* SNF 96; IMD 82. *Private Pay Patients* 11%. *Certified* Medicaid.
Owner Publicly owned.
Admissions Requirements Minimum age 18; Medical examination; Physician's request.
Staff Physicians 2 (pt); RNs 16 (ft); LPNs 9 (ft); Nurses' aides 75 (ft); Recreational therapists 1 (ft); Occupational therapists 1 (ft); Speech therapists 1 (pt); Activities coordinators 1 (ft); Dietitians 2 (ft); Podiatrists 1 (pt); Audiologists 1 (pt); Psychologists 1 (pt); Psychiatrists 2 (pt).
Facilities Dining room; Physical therapy room; Activities room; Chapel; Crafts room; Laundry room; Barber/Beauty shop; Library.
Activities Arts & crafts; Cards; Games; Reading groups; Prayer groups; Movies; Shopping trips; Dances/Social/Cultural gatherings; Intergenerational programs.

Birchwood Court
6830 Hwys 18 & 151, Verona, WI 53593
(608) 845-8306
Licensure Custodial care. *Beds* Custodial care 101. *Private Pay Patients* 100%.
Owner Privately owned.
Admissions Requirements Medical examination.
Facilities Dining room; Activities room; Crafts room; Laundry room; Barber/Beauty shop; Library.
Activities Arts & crafts; Games; Shopping trips; Dances/Social/Cultural gatherings; Exercise class.

Four Winds Manor
303 S Jefferson, Verona, WI 53593
(608) 845-6465
Admin Max Arthur.
Licensure Skilled care; Intermediate care. *Beds* SNF 71. *Certified* Medicaid.
Owner Proprietary corp.

Rest Haven Health Care Center
7672 Mineral Point Rd, Verona, WI 53593
(608) 833-1691
Admin Marilyn J Rogeberg. *Dir of Nursing* Eleanor Abrams. *Medical Dir* Don Janicek MD.
Licensure Skilled care; Retirement. *Beds* SNF 21.
Owner Proprietary corp.
Admissions Requirements Medical examination; Physician's request.
Staff Physicians 1 (pt); RNs 1 (ft), 2 (pt); LPNs 1 (ft), 4 (pt); Nurses' aides 2 (ft), 8 (pt); Recreational therapists 1 (ft); Dietitians 1 (pt); Dentists 1 (pt).
Facilities Dining room; Physical therapy room; Activities room; Crafts room; Laundry room.
Activities Arts & crafts; Cards; Games; Reading groups; Prayer groups; Movies; Dances/Social/Cultural gatherings.

Viroqua

Bethel Home
614 S Rock Ave, Viroqua, WI 54665
(608) 637-2171
Admin James B Olson.
Medical Dir Dr Koons.
Licensure Skilled care; Retirement. *Beds* SNF 121. *Private Pay Patients* 30%. *Certified* Medicaid.
Owner Nonprofit organization/foundation.
Admissions Requirements Medical examination; Physician's request.
Staff RNs 5 (ft), 8 (pt); LPNs 2 (ft), 5 (pt); Nurses' aides 9 (ft), 50 (pt); Activities coordinators 1 (ft); Dietitians 1 (ft).
Languages Norwegian.
Affiliation Lutheran.
Facilities Dining room; Physical therapy room; Activities room; Chapel; Crafts room; Laundry room; Barber/Beauty shop; Library.

Activities Arts & crafts; Cards; Games; Reading groups; Prayer groups; Movies; Shopping trips; Dances/Social/Cultural gatherings; Intergenerational programs; Pet therapy.

Vernon Manor
Rte 3 Box 300, Viroqua, WI 54665
(608) 637-8311
Admin Myrtle M Jacobson. *Dir of Nursing* Carole Friske RN. *Medical Dir* DeVerne W Vig MD.
Licensure Skilled care. *Beds* SNF 120. *Private Pay Patients* 20%. *Certified* Medicaid.
Owner Publicly owned.
Admissions Requirements Minimum age 18; Medical examination; Physician's request.
Staff RNs 6 (ft), 1 (pt); LPNs 4 (ft), 3 (pt); Nurses' aides 28 (ft), 22 (pt); Physical therapists (contracted); Occupational therapists 1 (pt); Speech therapists 1 (pt); Activities coordinators 1 (ft); Dietitians (contracted).
Facilities Dining room; Physical therapy room; Activities room; Chapel; Crafts room; Barber/Beauty shop; Handicapped accessible plan.
Activities Arts & crafts; Cards; Games; Reading groups; Prayer groups; Movies; Shopping trips; Dances/Social/Cultural gatherings; Intergenerational programs.

Walworth

Christian League for the Handicapped
PO Box 948, Walworth, WI 53184
Admin Clark Dempsey. *Dir of Nursing* Sandra Anderson RN.
Licensure Residential care. *Beds* 68. *Certified* Medicaid.
Owner Nonprofit corp.
Admissions Requirements Minimum age 18.
Staff RNs 1 (ft), 3 (pt); Nurses' aides 3 (ft), 2 (pt); Activities coordinators 1 (ft).
Facilities Dining room; Physical therapy room; Activities room; Crafts room; Laundry room; Barber/Beauty shop; Library; Sheltered workshop; Conference & retreat center.
Activities Arts & crafts; Games; Reading groups; Prayer groups; Movies; Shopping trips; Dances/Social/Cultural gatherings; Camping sessions; Outings.

Golden Years Home
Rte 1 Box 91, Walworth, WI 53184
(414) 275-6103
Admin Richard T Austin.
Licensure Intermediate care. *Beds* ICF 26.
Owner Proprietary corp.

Washburn

Northern Lights Manor Nursing Home
322 Superior Ave, Washburn, WI 54891
(715) 373-5621
Admin Larry D Welsh. *Dir of Nursing* Laurel Gilbert RN. *Medical Dir* Edward Vandenberg MD.
Licensure Skilled care. *Beds* SNF 86. *Certified* Medicaid.
Owner Nonprofit corp.
Staff Physicians 7 (pt); RNs 5 (ft), 3 (pt); LPNs 5 (ft), 5 (pt); Nurses' aides 22 (ft), 19 (pt); Physical therapists 1 (ft); Reality therapists 1 (pt); Recreational therapists 1 (ft); Occupational therapists 1 (pt); Speech therapists 1 (pt); Activities coordinators 1 (ft); Dietitians 1 (ft), 1 (pt); Ophthalmologists 2 (pt); Podiatrists 1 (pt); Audiologists 1 (pt).
Facilities Dining room; Physical therapy room; Activities room; Crafts room; Barber/Beauty shop; Library.

Activities Arts & crafts; Cards; Games; Reading groups; Prayer groups; Movies; Shopping trips; Dances/Social/Cultural gatherings.

Waterford

New Medico Rehabilitation & Skilled Nursing Care of Wisconsin
1701 Sharp Rd, Waterford, WI 53185
(414) 534-2301
Admin Mary Lueck.
Licensure CBRF. *Beds* CBRF 19.

Watertown

Bethesda Lutheran Home
700 Hoffmann Dr, Watertown, WI 53094
(414) 261-3050, 261-8441 FAX
Admin Kathleen McGwin. *Dir of Nursing* Shila A Kuenzli. *Medical Dir* Dr C Panagis.
Licensure Intermediate care for mentally retarded. *Beds* ICF/MR 345. *Certified* Medicaid.
Owner Nonprofit corp.
Admissions Requirements Minimum age 8; Medical examination; Physician's request.
Staff Physicians 2 (ft), 1 (pt); RNs 13 (ft), 7 (pt); LPNs 15 (ft), 7 (pt); Nurses' aides 5 (ft), 4 (pt); Physical therapists 3 (ft); Reality therapists 14 (ft); Recreational therapists 10 (ft); Occupational therapists 3 (ft); Speech therapists 1 (ft), 1 (pt); Activities coordinators 2 (ft); Dietitians 1 (ft).
Affiliation Lutheran.
Facilities Dining room; Physical therapy room; Activities room; Chapel; Crafts room; Laundry room; Barber/Beauty shop; Library.
Activities Arts & crafts; Cards; Games; Reading groups; Prayer groups; Movies; Shopping trips; Dances/Social/Cultural gatherings; Intergenerational programs.

Beverly Terrace
121 Hospital Dr, Watertown, WI 53094
(414) 261-9220
Admin Duane Floyd.
Licensure Skilled care. *Beds* SNF 130. *Certified* Medicaid; Medicare.
Owner Proprietary corp (Beverly Enterprises).
Staff Physicians 6 (ft); RNs 4 (ft); LPNs 8 (ft); Nurses' aides 55 (ft); Physical therapists 1 (ft); Reality therapists 1 (pt); Recreational therapists 1 (pt); Occupational therapists 2 (pt); Speech therapists 1 (pt); Activities coordinators 1 (ft); Dietitians 1 (pt); Ophthalmologists 1 (pt); Podiatrists 1 (ft); Dentists 1 (ft).
Facilities Dining room; Physical therapy room; Activities room; Chapel; Crafts room; Laundry room; Barber/Beauty shop.
Activities Arts & crafts; Cards; Games; Reading groups; Movies; Dances/Social/Cultural gatherings.

Marquardt Memorial Manor Inc
1020 Hill St, Watertown, WI 53094
(414) 261-0400
Admin Boyd A Flater. *Dir of Nursing* Bonnie Zabel. *Medical Dir* Dr L W Nowack.
Licensure Skilled care; Retirement; Alzheimer's care. *Beds* SNF 140; Retirement apts & duplexes 188. *Certified* Medicaid.
Owner Nonprofit corp.
Staff RNs 5 (ft), 7 (pt); LPNs 8 (ft), 12 (pt); Nurses' aides 50 (ft), 15 (pt); Physical therapists 1 (pt); Recreational therapists 2 (ft); Occupational therapists 1 (pt); Speech therapists 1 (pt); Activities coordinators 1 (ft); Dietitians 1 (pt).
Affiliation Moravian.
Facilities Dining room; Physical therapy room; Activities room; Chapel; Crafts room; Laundry room; Barber/Beauty shop; Library.

Activities Arts & crafts; Cards; Games; Reading groups; Prayer groups; Movies; Shopping trips; Dances/Social/Cultural gatherings; Intergenerational programs; Pet therapy.

Welbourne Hall
1301 E Main St, Watertown, WI 53094
(414) 261-1211
Admin Kenneth M Mueller Jr.
Licensure Community based residential facility. *Beds* Community based residential facility 80. *Certified* Medicaid.

Clara Werner Dormitory
700 Hoffmann Dr, Watertown, WI 53094
(414) 261-3050
Admin Gerald A Born. *Dir of Nursing* Joan Sofinowski. *Medical Dir* John Heffelfinger MD.
Licensure Intermediate care for mentally retarded. *Beds* ICF/MR 46. *Certified* Medicaid.
Owner Nonprofit corp.
Admissions Requirements Medical examination; Physician's request.
Staff Physicians; RNs; LPNs; Nurses' aides; Physical therapists; Recreational therapists; Occupational therapists; Speech therapists; Activities coordinators; Dietitians.
Affiliation Lutheran.
Facilities Dining room; Physical therapy room; Activities room; Chapel; Crafts room; Laundry room; Barber/Beauty shop; Library.
Activities Arts & crafts; Cards; Games; Movies; Shopping trips; Dances/Social/Cultural gatherings; Special dinners; Concerts.

Waukesha

Avalon Manor Infirmary
222 Park Pl, Waukesha, WI 53186
(414) 547-6741
Admin Mary Joan Evans. *Dir of Nursing* Lynne M Engstrom RN. *Medical Dir* Warren Smirl MD.
Licensure Skilled care; Retirement. *Beds* SNF 22; Retirement 76. *Private Pay Patients* 100%.
Owner Nonprofit corp.
Admissions Requirements Minimum age 62; Medical examination; Physician's request.
Staff RNs 3 (ft), 4 (pt); Nurses' aides 14 (pt); Activities coordinators 1 (pt); Dietitians.
Facilities Dining room; Activities room; Crafts room; Laundry room; Barber/Beauty shop; Library.
Activities Arts & crafts; Cards; Games; Reading groups; Prayer groups; Movies; Shopping trips; Dances/Social/Cultural gatherings.

Linden Grove of Waukesha
425 N University Dr, Waukesha, WI 53188
(414) 524-6400
Admin Charles T Nelson.
Licensure Skilled care. *Beds* SNF 135.

Virginia
1471 Waukesha Ave, Waukesha, WI 53186
(414) 547-2123, 547-6204 FAX
Admin Susan Bischmann. *Dir of Nursing* Denise Scherer RN BSN. *Medical Dir* Thomas Gallagher MD.
Licensure Skilled care; Intermediate care; Alzheimer's care. *Beds* Swing beds SNF/ICF 102. *Private Pay Patients* 50%. *Certified* Medicaid.
Owner Proprietary corp (American Medical Services Inc).
Admissions Requirements Minimum age 65; Medical examination; Physician's request.
Staff RNs 1 (ft), 13 (pt); LPNs 3 (ft), 10 (pt); Nurses' aides 18 (ft), 28 (pt); Physical therapists 1 (pt); Recreational therapists 1

(ft); Occupational therapists 1 (pt); Speech therapists 1 (pt); Activities coordinators 1 (ft); Dietitians 1 (pt); Podiatrists 1 (pt).
Languages Laotian, Spanish, German.
Facilities Dining room; Physical therapy room; Activities room; Chapel; Crafts room; Barber/Beauty shop.
Activities Arts & crafts; Cards; Games; Reading groups; Prayer groups; Movies; Shopping trips; Dances/Social/Cultural gatherings; Intergenerational programs; Pet therapy.

Westmoreland Health Center
1810 Kensington Dr, Waukesha, WI 53188
(414) 548-1400
Admin Robert J Best. *Dir of Nursing* Susan Jackson RN. *Medical Dir* Wilbur Rosenkranz MD.
Licensure Skilled care; Alzheimer's care; Retirement. *Beds* SNF 245. *Certified* Medicaid; Medicare.
Owner Proprietary corp.
Admissions Requirements Minimum age 18; Medical examination; Physician's request.
Staff Physicians 48 (pt); RNs 7 (ft), 13 (pt); LPNs 10 (ft), 21 (pt); Nurses' aides 44 (ft), 58 (pt); Physical therapists 3 (ft); Reality therapists 1 (ft); Recreational therapists 2 (ft); Occupational therapists 2 (pt); Speech therapists 2 (pt); Activities coordinators 2 (ft), 10 (pt); Dietitians 1 (pt); Ophthalmologists 1 (pt); Podiatrists 1 (pt); Dentists 1 (pt).
Languages German, Spanish, Sign.
Facilities Dining room; Physical therapy room; Activities room; Chapel; Crafts room; Laundry room; Barber/Beauty shop; Library; Visitor dining area.
Activities Arts & crafts; Cards; Games; Reading groups; Prayer groups; Movies; Shopping trips; Dances/Social/Cultural gatherings; Oral history groups; Intergenerational programs.

Waunakee

Waunakee Manor Health Care Center
801 Klein Dr, Waunakee, WI 53597
(608) 849-5016
Admin Edwin M Kruchten. *Dir of Nursing* Roxanne Wermuth. *Medical Dir* Mel Rasen MD.
Licensure Skilled care; Retirement; Residential. *Beds* SNF 104; Retirement 14; Residential apts 28. *Certified* Medicaid; Medicare.
Owner Proprietary corp.
Admissions Requirements Medical examination; Physician's request.
Staff RNs 5 (ft); LPNs 3 (ft), 5 (pt); Physical therapists 1 (ft); Recreational therapists 1 (pt); Occupational therapists 1 (ft); Speech therapists 1 (pt); Dietitians 1 (pt); Podiatrists 1 (pt); COTAs 2 (ft).
Languages German.
Facilities Dining room; Physical therapy room; Activities room; Chapel; Crafts room; Laundry room; Barber/Beauty shop; Library.
Activities Arts & crafts; Cards; Games; Reading groups; Prayer groups; Movies; Shopping trips; Dances/Social/Cultural gatherings; Intergenerational programs; Pet therapy.

Waupaca

Bethany Home
1226 Berlin St, Waupaca, WI 54981
(715) 258-5521
Admin William N Parker.
Licensure Skilled care. *Beds* SNF 119. *Certified* Medicaid.
Owner Proprietary corp.

Pine Ridge Manor
Box 439, 1401 Churchill St, Waupaca, WI 54981
(715) 258-8131
Admin Darryl Koch. *Dir of Nursing* Jean Israels RN. *Medical Dir* G Burgstede MD.
Licensure Skilled care; Intermediate care. *Beds* SNF 80. *Certified* Medicaid; Medicare.
Owner Proprietary corp (Unicare).
Admissions Requirements Minimum age 18; Medical examination; Physician's request.
Staff RNs; LPNs; Nurses' aides; Physical therapists; Reality therapists; Occupational therapists; Speech therapists; Activities coordinators; Dietitians.
Facilities Dining room; Physical therapy room; Activities room; Chapel; Barber/Beauty shop.
Activities Arts & crafts; Cards; Games; Reading groups; Prayer groups; Movies; Shopping trips; Dances/Social/Cultural gatherings.

Waupun

Christian Home Inc
220 Grandview Ave, Waupun, WI 53963
(414) 324-9051
Admin Joyce Buytendorp. *Dir of Nursing* Ruth Schrank. *Medical Dir* Mariano Rosales MD.
Licensure Skilled care. *Beds* SNF 84. *Private Pay Patients* 48%. *Certified* Medicaid.
Owner Nonprofit corp.
Admissions Requirements Physician's request.
Staff RNs 1 (ft), 8 (pt); LPNs 16 (pt); Nurses' aides 6 (ft), 35 (pt); Occupational therapists 1 (pt); Activities coordinators 2 (pt); Dietitians 1 (pt).
Facilities Dining room; Activities room; Chapel; Crafts room; Laundry room; Barber/Beauty shop.
Activities Arts & crafts; Cards; Games; Reading groups; Prayer groups; Movies; Pet therapy.

Wausau

Colonial Manor of Wausau
1010 E Wausau Ave, Wausau, WI 54401
(715) 842-2028
Admin Norma Jean Burgener. *Dir of Nursing* Mary Ellen Schreiber. *Medical Dir* J V Flannery Sr MD.
Licensure Skilled care; Retirement; Alzheimer's care. *Beds* SNF 152. *Certified* Medicaid; Medicare.
Owner Proprietary corp (Hillhaven Corp).
Admissions Requirements Minimum age 18; Physician's request.
Staff Physicians 1 (pt); RNs 1 (ft), 12 (pt); LPNs 7 (pt); Nurses' aides 30 (ft), 27 (pt); Physical therapists 1 (pt); Recreational therapists 1 (ft), 3 (pt); Occupational therapists 1 (pt); Speech therapists 1 (pt); Activities coordinators 1 (ft); Dietitians 1 (ft); Podiatrists 1 (pt); Dentists 1 (pt).
Languages Polish, German.
Facilities Dining room; Physical therapy room; Activities room; Chapel; Crafts room; Laundry room; Barber/Beauty shop.
Activities Arts & crafts; Cards; Games; Reading groups; Prayer groups; Movies; Shopping trips.

Marywood Convalescent Center
1821 N 4th Ave, Wausau, WI 54401
(715) 675-9451
Admin Elaine A Roskos.
Licensure Skilled care; Intermediate care. *Beds* SNF 90. *Certified* Medicaid; Medicare.
Owner Nonprofit corp.

Mt View Nursing Home
2400 Marshall St, Wausau, WI 54401
(715) 848-4300
Admin William Chad McGrath.

Licensure Intermediate care. *Beds* 135. *Certified* Medicaid.
Owner Publicly owned.

North Central Health Care Facility
1100 Lake View Dr, Wausau, WI 54401
(715) 848-4600
Admin Tim H Steller. *Dir of Nursing* Molly Maguire RN. *Medical Dir* Dr S N Basu.
Licensure Skilled care; Intermediate care; Alzheimer's care. *Beds* SNF 382. *Certified* Medicaid; Medicare.
Owner Publicly owned.
Admissions Requirements Medical examination.
Staff Physicians 1 (ft), 2 (pt); RNs 19 (ft), 23 (pt); LPNs 9 (ft), 8 (pt); Nurses' aides 108 (ft), 86 (pt); Recreational therapists 1 (pt); Occupational therapists 4 (pt); Activities coordinators 1 (pt); Dietitians 2 (pt).
Facilities Dining room; Physical therapy room; Activities room; Chapel; Crafts room; Laundry room; Barber/Beauty shop; Library.
Activities Arts & crafts; Cards; Games; Reading groups; Prayer groups; Movies; Shopping trips; Dances/Social/Cultural gatherings.

Sunny Vale Nursing Home
1200 Lakeview Dr, Wausau, WI 54401
(715) 845-6725
Admin William Chad McGrath.
Medical Dir S N Basu.
Licensure Skilled care; Intermediate care. *Beds* 151. *Certified* Medicaid; Medicare.
Owner Publicly owned.
Staff Physicians 1 (pt); RNs 6 (ft), 10 (pt); LPNs 2 (ft), 5 (pt); Nurses' aides 51 (ft), 23 (pt); Physical therapists 2 (pt); Occupational therapists 1 (pt); Speech therapists 2 (pt); Dietitians 1 (pt); Dentists 1 (pt).
Facilities Dining room; Activities room; Crafts room.
Activities Arts & crafts; Cards; Games; Reading groups; Movies; Shopping trips; Dances/Social/Cultural gatherings.

Wausau Manor
3107 Westhill Dr, Wausau, WI 54401
(715) 842-0575
Admin Stan C Jones. *Dir of Nursing* Peggy Larson RN. *Medical Dir* Frank Rubino MD.
Licensure Skilled care; Alzheimer's care. *Beds* SNF 60. *Certified* Medicare.
Owner Privately owned.
Admissions Requirements Medical examination; Physician's request.
Staff Physicians 1 (pt); RNs 5 (ft), 4 (pt); LPNs 1 (ft), 1 (pt); Nurses' aides 20 (ft), 10 (pt); Physical therapists 2 (pt); Recreational therapists 1 (ft), 1 (pt); Occupational therapists 1 (pt); Speech therapists 1 (pt); Dietitians 1 (pt).
Facilities Dining room; Physical therapy room; Activities room; Crafts room; Laundry room; Barber/Beauty shop; Library.
Activities Arts & crafts; Cards; Games; Reading groups; Prayer groups; Movies; Shopping trips; Dances/Social/Cultural gatherings.

Wautoma

Wautoma Care Center Inc
327 Waupaca St, Box 720, Wautoma, WI 54982
(414) 787-3359, 787-4826 FAX
Admin Roger W Krueger. *Dir of Nursing* Sharon Voss RN. *Medical Dir* Alan L Taber MD.
Licensure Skilled care; Intermediate care. *Beds* Swing beds SNF/ICF 84. *Private Pay Patients* 30%. *Certified* Medicaid; Medicare.
Owner Proprietary corp.
Admissions Requirements Minimum age 18; Medical examination; Physician's request.

Staff Physicians 13 (pt); RNs 1 (ft), 5 (pt); LPNs 4 (ft), 2 (pt); Nurses' aides 21 (ft), 13 (pt); Physical therapists 1 (pt); Occupational therapists 1 (pt); Speech therapists 1 (pt); Activities coordinators 1 (ft); Dietitians 1 (pt); Ophthalmologists 1 (pt); Podiatrists 1 (pt).
Facilities Dining room; Physical therapy room; Activities room; Laundry room; Barber/Beauty shop.
Activities Arts & crafts; Cards; Games; Reading groups; Prayer groups; Movies; Shopping trips; Dances/Social/Cultural gatherings; Intergenerational programs; Pet therapy.

Wauwatosa

Luther Manor
4545 N 92nd St, Wauwatosa, WI 53226
(414) 464-3880
Admin Peter E Chang.
Medical Dir Dr Paul Nordin.
Licensure Skilled care; Intermediate care. *Beds* 201. *Certified* Medicaid.
Owner Nonprofit corp.
Admissions Requirements Minimum age 68; Medical examination; Physician's request.
Staff RNs 5 (ft), 22 (pt); LPNs 17 (pt); Recreational therapists 4 (ft); Occupational therapists 1 (pt); Dietitians 1 (ft); Podiatrists 1 (pt); Dentists 1 (pt).
Affiliation Lutheran.
Facilities Dining room; Physical therapy room; Activities room; Chapel; Crafts room; Laundry room; Barber/Beauty shop; Library.
Activities Arts & crafts; Cards; Games; Reading groups; Prayer groups; Movies; Shopping trips; Dances/Social/Cultural gatherings.

Lutheran Home for the Aging Inc
7500 W North Ave, Wauwatosa, WI 53213
(414) 258-6170, 258-1125 FAX
Admin Roger A Sievers. *Dir of Nursing* Eileen Hayeland. *Medical Dir* Peter Sigmon.
Licensure Skilled care. *Beds* SNF 290. *Certified* Medicaid.
Owner Nonprofit corp.
Admissions Requirements Minimum age 65; Medical examination; Physician's request.
Staff Physicians 1 (pt); RNs 23 (ft), 16 (pt); LPNs 19 (ft), 5 (pt); Nurses' aides 79 (ft), 25 (pt); Physical therapists 3 (pt); Recreational therapists 2 (ft); Occupational therapists 1 (ft), 2 (pt); Speech therapists 1 (pt); Activities coordinators 1 (ft); Dietitians 1 (ft); Ophthalmologists 1 (pt); Podiatrists 1 (pt).
Facilities Dining room; Physical therapy room; Activities room; Chapel; Laundry room; Barber/Beauty shop; Library.
Activities Arts & crafts; Cards; Games; Reading groups; Prayer groups; Movies; Shopping trips; Dances/Social/Cultural gatherings; Pet therapy.

Milwaukee County Mental Health Complex Rehabilitation Center—Central
9455 Watertown Plank Rd, Wauwatosa, WI 53226
(414) 257-6995
Admin Joan F Brown. *Dir of Nursing* Molly Kluth RN. *Medical Dir* Roger L Ruehl MD.
Licensure Skilled care; Intermediate care. *Beds* Swing beds SNF IMD/ICF IMD 192. *Private Pay Patients* 1%. *Certified* Medicaid.
Owner Publicly owned.
Admissions Requirements Minimum age 18; Referral request required.
Staff Physicians 3 (ft), 2 (pt); RNs 42 (ft), 6 (pt); LPNs 24 (ft), 4 (pt); Nurses' aides 64 (ft), 20 (pt); Physical therapists (contracted); Recreational therapists 1 (ft); Occupational therapists 10 (ft), 1 (pt); Activities coordinators 1 (ft); Dietitians 1 (ft).

Languages Spanish, other languages by request.
Facilities Dining room; Physical therapy room; Activities room; Chapel; Crafts room; Laundry room; Barber/Beauty shop; Library.
Activities Arts & crafts; Cards; Games; Reading groups; Prayer groups; Movies; Shopping trips; Dances/Social/Cultural gatherings; Pet therapy.

Milwaukee County Mental Health Complex Rehabilitation Center—South
802 N 94th St, Wauwatosa, WI 53226
(414) 257-7258
Admin Joan F Brown. *Dir of Nursing* Molly Kluth RN. *Medical Dir* Roger L Ruehl MD.
Licensure Intermediate care for mentally retarded. *Beds* ICF/MR 140.
Owner Publicly owned.
Admissions Requirements Minimum age 18; Dually diagnosed developmentally disabled/ mentally ill.
Staff Physicians 1 (ft), 2 (pt); RNs 46 (ft), 1 (pt); LPNs 32 (ft), 1 (pt); Nurses' aides 68 (ft), 14 (pt); Physical therapists (contracted); Occupational therapists 5 (ft); Activities coordinators 1 (ft); Dietitians 1 (ft); COTAs 14 (ft); Music therapists 1 (ft).
Languages Interpreters available.
Facilities Dining room; Activities room; Crafts room; Laundry room.
Activities Arts & crafts; Cards; Games; Reading groups; Prayer groups; Movies; Shopping trips; Dances/Social/Cultural gatherings.

Milwaukee County Mental Health Complex Rehabilitation Center—West
10437 Watertown Plank Rd, Wauwatosa, WI 53226
(414) 257-6617
Admin Joan Brown. *Dir of Nursing* Grace Reddy RN. *Medical Dir* Richard P Jahn MD.
Licensure Intermediate Care IMD. *Beds* Intermediate care IMD 220. *Private Pay Patients* 2%. *Certified* Medicaid.
Owner Publicly owned.
Admissions Requirements Minimum age 18.
Staff Physicians 1 (ft), 2 (pt); RNs 11 (ft), 3 (pt); LPNs 13 (ft), 2 (pt); Nurses' aides 64 (ft), 24 (pt); Recreational therapists 1 (ft); Occupational therapists 5 (ft); Activities coordinators 4 (ft); Dietitians 1 (ft); Podiatrists 1 (pt).
Languages Spanish interpreters.
Facilities Dining room; Activities room; Chapel; Crafts room; Laundry room; Barber/ Beauty shop; Library.
Activities Arts & crafts; Cards; Games; Reading groups; Prayer groups; Movies; Shopping trips; Dances/Social/Cultural gatherings; Pet therapy.

St Camillus Health Center
10100 W Blue Mound Rd, Wauwatosa, WI 53226
(414) 258-1814
Admin Rick L Johnson. *Dir of Nursing* Betty Brunner RN. *Medical Dir* Illuminado Millar MD.
Licensure Skilled care; Retirement. *Beds* SNF 188. *Certified* Medicaid; Medicare.
Owner Nonprofit corp.
Admissions Requirements Minimum age 18.
Staff Physicians 1 (pt); RNs 10 (ft), 13 (pt); LPNs 12 (ft), 13 (pt); Nurses' aides 39 (ft), 45 (pt); Physical therapists 1 (ft); Reality therapists 1 (ft); Recreational therapists 1 (ft); Occupational therapists 1 (ft); Speech therapists 1 (pt); Dietitians 1 (pt).
Affiliation Roman Catholic.
Facilities Dining room; Physical therapy room; Activities room; Chapel; Crafts room; Barber/Beauty shop.

Activities Arts & crafts; Cards; Games; Reading groups; Prayer groups; Movies; Shopping trips; Dances/Social/Cultural gatherings; Intergenerational programs; Pet therapy.

Wentworth

Parkland Health
PO Box 58, Wentworth, WI 54874
(715) 398-6616
Admin Jennifer Bieno NHA. *Dir of Nursing* Terri Winterberg RN. *Medical Dir* Dr Brian Swanson.
Licensure Skilled care; Intermediate care; Intermediate care for mentally retarded. *Beds* ICF/MR 25; Swing beds SNF/ICF 94. *Private Pay Patients* 3%. *Certified* Medicaid.
Owner Proprietary corp (Catholic Charities Bureau).
Admissions Requirements Medical examination; Physician's request.
Staff Physicians (consultant); RNs 6 (ft); LPNs 15 (ft); Nurses' aides 35 (ft); Physical therapists (consultant); Recreational therapists (consultant); Occupational therapists 1 (ft); Speech therapists (consultant); Activities coordinators 1 (ft); Dietitians (consultant); Ophthalmologists (consultant); Podiatrists (consultant); Audiologists (consultant).
Languages Sign.
Facilities Dining room; Physical therapy room; Activities room; Crafts room; Laundry room; Barber/Beauty shop; Auditorium.
Activities Arts & crafts; Cards; Games; Reading groups; Prayer groups; Movies; Shopping trips; Dances/Social/Cultural gatherings; Intergenerational programs; Pet therapy; LEEP programs; Woodworking.

West Allis

Hillcrest Nursing Home
1467 S 75th St, West Allis, WI 53214
(414) 476-2928
Admin Lynn M Vogt.
Medical Dir Dr Roger Ruehl.
Licensure Intermediate care. *Beds* ICF 16. *Certified* Medicaid.
Owner Proprietary corp.
Admissions Requirements Minimum age 18.
Staff Physicians 1 (pt); RNs 1 (ft); LPNs 2 (pt); Nurses' aides 1 (ft), 10 (pt); Activities coordinators 1 (pt); Dietitians 1 (pt).

Kappes Nursing Home
8300 W Beloit Rd, West Allis, WI 53219
(414) 321-2420
Admin Ralph P Hibbard.
Medical Dir Donna Mathis.
Licensure Intermediate care. *Beds* ICF 28. *Certified* Medicaid.
Owner Proprietary corp.
Admissions Requirements Minimum age 55.
Staff RNs 1 (ft), 2 (pt); LPNs 1 (ft), 2 (pt); Nurses' aides; Activities coordinators 2 (pt); Dietitians 1 (pt).
Facilities Dining room; Activities room; Barber/Beauty shop.
Activities Arts & crafts; Cards; Games; Prayer groups; Movies; Dances/Social/Cultural gatherings.

Mary-Jude Nursing Home
9806 W Lincoln Ave, West Allis, WI 53227
(414) 543-5330
Admin Lisa C Kolpin. *Dir of Nursing* Mary Copson RN. *Medical Dir* Louis Jermain MD.
Licensure Skilled care. *Beds* SNF 51. *Private Pay Patients* 50%. *Certified* Medicaid.
Owner Proprietary corp.
Admissions Requirements Medical examination; Physician's request.

Staff RNs 1 (ft), 5 (pt); LPNs 1 (ft), 4 (pt);
Nurses' aides 12 (ft), 8 (pt); Activities
coordinators 1 (ft); Dietitians 1 (pt).
Languages Polish, German.
Facilities Dining room; Activities room;
Laundry room; Barber/Beauty shop.
Activities Arts & crafts; Cards; Games;
Reading groups; Prayer groups; Movies;
Shopping trips; Dances/Social/Cultural
gatherings; Intergenerational programs; Pet
therapy.

Methodist Manor Health Center
8615 W Beloit Rd, West Allis, WI 53227
(414) 541-2600
Admin R A Wagner.
Licensure Skilled care. *Beds* SNF 168.

Methodist Manor Inc
3023 S 84th St, West Allis, WI 53227
(414) 541-2600
Admin R A Wagner.
Licensure Intermediate care. *Beds* ICF 20.

Rosewood Nursing Home
3161 S 112th St, West Allis, WI 53227
(414) 543-1809
Admin Elizabeth A Neer. *Dir of Nursing* June
Stummeier.
Licensure Intermediate care. *Beds* ICF 23.
Private Pay Patients 1%. *Certified* Medicaid.
Owner Nonprofit organization/foundation.
Admissions Requirements Minimum age 18;
Medical examination.
Staff RNs 1 (ft), 1 (pt); LPNs 2 (pt); Nurses'
aides 2 (ft), 5 (pt); Recreational therapists 1
(ft), 1 (pt); Dietitians 1 (ft).
Affiliation Lutheran.
Facilities Dining room; Activities room;
Laundry room.
Activities Arts & crafts; Cards; Games;
Reading groups; Prayer groups; Movies;
Shopping trips; Intergenerational programs;
Pet therapy.

St Joan Antida Home
6700 W Beloit Rd, West Allis, WI 53219
(414) 541-9840
Admin Sr Ann Catherine Veierstahler NHA.
Dir of Nursing Louise Besaw RN. *Medical
Dir* E Kuglitsch MD.
Licensure Skilled care. *Beds* SNF 73. *Private
Pay Patients* 25%. *Certified* Medicaid.
Owner Nonprofit organization/foundation.
Admissions Requirements Medical
examination; Physician's request.
Staff Physicians 1 (pt); RNs 4 (ft); LPNs 3
(ft), 4 (pt); Nurses' aides 20 (ft); Physical
therapists 1 (pt); Reality therapists 1 (pt);
Recreational therapists 1 (ft); Occupational
therapists 1 (pt); Activities coordinators 1
(ft); Dietitians 1 (pt); Podiatrists 1 (pt).
Languages Italian.
Affiliation Roman Catholic.
Facilities Dining room; Physical therapy
room; Activities room; Chapel; Crafts room;
Laundry room.
Activities Arts & crafts; Cards; Games; Prayer
groups; Pet therapy.

St Joseph's Home for the Aged
5301 W Lincoln Ave, West Allis, WI 53219
(414) 541-8444
Admin Sr Bridget Marie NHA. *Dir of Nursing*
Sr Mary Frances. *Medical Dir* Dr John
Palase.
Licensure Skilled care; Residential care; Adult
day care. *Beds* SNF 74; Residential care 49.
Private Pay Patients 75%. *Certified*
Medicaid.
Owner Nonprofit corp.
Admissions Requirements Minimum age 65;
Medical examination.
Staff RNs; LPNs; Nurses' aides; Physical
therapists; Reality therapists; Recreational
therapists; Occupational therapists; Speech
therapists; Activities coordinators; Dietitians;
Podiatrists.

Languages Polish, German, Slovene, French.
Affiliation Roman Catholic.
Facilities Dining room; Physical therapy
room; Activities room; Chapel; Crafts room;
Laundry room; Barber/Beauty shop; Library;
Social hall; Private rooms.
Activities Arts & crafts; Cards; Games;
Reading groups; Prayer groups; Movies;
Shopping trips; Dances/Social/Cultural
gatherings; Intergenerational programs; Pet
therapy; Religious services.

Villa Clement
9047 W Greenfield, West Allis, WI 53214
(414) 453-9290
Admin Georgina Dennik-Champion, RN,
MSN. *Dir of Nursing* Priscilla Rice RNMS.
Medical Dir John Wisniewski MD.
Licensure Skilled care. *Beds* SNF 194.
Certified Medicaid; Medicare.
Owner Nonprofit corp (School Sisters of St
Francis).
Staff Physicians 1 (pt); RNs 13 (ft), 22 (pt);
LPNs 8 (ft), 11 (pt); Physical therapists 1
(ft), 2 (pt); Recreational therapists 8 (pt);
Occupational therapists 1 (ft); Speech
therapists 3 (pt); Activities coordinators 1
(pt); Dietitians 1 (ft); Ophthalmologists 1
(pt).
Affiliation Roman Catholic.
Facilities Dining room; Physical therapy
room; Activities room; Chapel; Laundry
room; Barber/Beauty shop.
Activities Arts & crafts; Cards; Games;
Reading groups; Prayer groups; Movies;
Dances/Social/Cultural gatherings; Planting.

West Bend

Cedar Lake Home Campus
5595 Hwy Z, West Bend, WI 53095
(414) 334-9487, 334-9383 FAX
Admin Steven J Jaberg. *Dir of Nursing* Amy
Bauer RN. *Medical Dir* Dr Charles
Holmburg.
Licensure Skilled care; Alzheimer's care;
Retirement. *Beds* SNF 415; Alzheimer's care
128; Retirement homes & apts 397. *Private
Pay Patients* 60%. *Certified* Medicaid.
Owner Nonprofit corp.
Admissions Requirements Minimum age 18.
Staff RNs 15 (ft), 27 (pt); LPNs 9 (ft), 17 (pt);
Nurses' aides 81 (ft), 110 (pt); Physical
therapists 3 (ft); Recreational therapists 1
(ft); Occupational therapists 2 (ft), 1 (pt);
Speech therapists 1 (pt); Dietitians 2 (ft).
Languages Sign.
Affiliation United Church of Christ.
Facilities Dining room; Physical therapy
room; Activities room; Chapel; Crafts room;
Laundry room; Barber/Beauty shop; Library.
Activities Arts & crafts; Cards; Games;
Reading groups; Prayer groups; Movies;
Shopping trips; Dances/Social/Cultural
gatherings; Intergenerational programs; Pet
therapy; Music therapy.

Samaritan Home
531 E Washington St, West Bend, WI 53095
(414) 338-4500
Admin Anne Tilt. *Dir of Nursing* Donna Ash.
Medical Dir Dr Gary Herdrich.
Licensure Skilled care. *Beds* SNF 251.
Certified Medicaid; Medicare.
Owner Publicly owned.
Admissions Requirements Minimum age 21;
Medical examination; Physician's request.
Staff Physicians 1 (ft), 2 (pt); RNs 12 (ft);
LPNs 18 (ft), 6 (pt); Nurses' aides 66 (ft), 47
(pt); Physical therapists 1 (ft); Occupational
therapists 2 (pt); Speech therapists 1 (pt);
Activities coordinators 1 (pt); Dietitians 1
(pt); Dentists 1 (pt).

Facilities Dining room; Physical therapy
room; Activities room; Chapel; Crafts room;
Laundry room; Barber/Beauty shop; Library;
Occupational therapy department: Child day
care.
Activities Arts & crafts; Cards; Games;
Reading groups; Prayer groups; Movies;
Shopping trips; Dances/Social/Cultural
gatherings; Bus trips; Picnics.

West Salem

Lakeview Health Center
902 E Garland St, West Salem, WI 54669-
1399
(608) 786-1400, 786-1419 FAX
Admin Robert G Machotka NHA. *Dir of
Nursing* Lynn Borchert RN. *Medical Dir*
William D Bateman MD.
Licensure Skilled care; Intermediate care for
mentally retarded. *Beds* SNF 177; ICF/MR
78. *Certified* Medicaid.
Owner Publicly owned.
Admissions Requirements Minimum age 18;
Medical examination; Physician's request.
Staff Physicians 4 (pt); RNs 16 (ft), 7 (pt);
LPNs 6 (ft), 4 (pt); Nurses' aides 48 (ft), 44
(pt); Physical therapists 1 (pt); Occupational
therapists 1 (pt); Speech therapists 1 (pt);
Dietitians 1 (pt); Ophthalmologists 1 (pt);
Dentists 1 (pt).
Facilities Dining room; Physical therapy
room; Activities room; Chapel; Crafts room;
Laundry room; Barber/Beauty shop; Library.
Activities Arts & crafts; Cards; Games;
Reading groups; Prayer groups; Movies;
Shopping trips; Dances/Social/Cultural
gatherings; Pet therapy.

Mulder Health Care Facility
PO Box 850, 713 N Leonard St, West Salem,
WI 54669
(608) 786-1600
Admin Ronald G Gilbertson.
Licensure Skilled care; Intermediate care. *Beds*
SNF 106. *Certified* Medicaid; Medicare.
Owner Proprietary corp.

Westby

Norseland Nursing Home
323 Black River Rd, Westby, WI 54667
(608) 634-3747
Admin Ned P Barstad.
Licensure Skilled care; Intermediate care. *Beds*
SNF 59. *Certified* Medicaid.
Owner Publicly owned.

Weyauwega

Lakeview Manor
Rte 1 Box X, Weyauwega, WI 54983
(414) 867-2183
Admin Jeanne M Zempel.
Medical Dir Lloyd P Maasch MD.
Licensure Skilled care; Skilled IMD. *Beds*
SNF 51; Skilled IMD 52. *Certified*
Medicaid.
Owner Publicly owned.
Staff Physicians 2 (pt); RNs 6 (ft), 2 (pt);
LPNs 8 (ft); Nurses' aides 31 (ft); Physical
therapists 1 (pt); Recreational therapists 2
(ft), 5 (pt); Occupational therapists 2 (pt);
Activities coordinators 1 (ft); Dietitians 1
(pt); Podiatrists 1 (pt); Social workers 1 (ft),
1 (pt).
Facilities Dining room; Physical therapy
room; Activities room; Chapel; Crafts room;
Laundry room; Barber/Beauty shop;
Workshop; Greenhouse.
Activities Arts & crafts; Cards; Games;
Reading groups; Prayer groups; Movies;
Shopping trips; Dances/Social/Cultural
gatherings.

Weyauwega Health Care Center
PO Box 440, 717 E Alfred St, Weyauwega, WI 54983
(414) 867-3121, 867-3997 FAX
Admin Kathie Prust. *Dir of Nursing* Barb Sullivan. *Medical Dir* Dr Lloyd Maasch.
Licensure Skilled care; Intermediate care; Alzheimer's care. *Beds* Swing beds SNF/ICF 103. *Private Pay Patients* 30%. *Certified* Medicaid; Medicare.
Owner Proprietary corp (Unicare).
Admissions Requirements Minimum age 18; Medical examination; Physician's request.
Staff RNs 3 (ft), 2 (pt); LPNs 3 (ft), 4 (pt); Nurses' aides 16 (ft), 24 (pt); Physical therapists 2 (pt); Occupational therapists 2 (pt); Speech therapists 1 (pt); Activities coordinators 1 (ft); Dietitians 1 (pt).
Facilities Dining room; Physical therapy room; Activities room; Chapel; Laundry room; Barber/Beauty shop; Alzheimer's unit.
Activities Arts & crafts; Cards; Games; Reading groups; Prayer groups; Movies; Shopping trips; Dances/Social/Cultural gatherings; Intergenerational programs.

Whitehall

Trempealeau County Health Care Center
Rte 2 Box 150, Whitehall, WI 54773
(715) 538-4312
Admin Phillip J Borreson, J. M Smieja, Asst. *Dir of Nursing* Mary Jo Halama. *Medical Dir* Dr D Steele.
Licensure Skilled care; Intermediate care for mentally retarded; Skilled care IMD. *Beds* SNF 34; ICF/MR 44; Skilled care IMD 89. *Private Pay Patients* 1%. *Certified* Medicaid.
Owner Publicly owned.
Admissions Requirements Minimum age 18; Medical examination.
Staff Physicians 3 (pt); RNs 17 (ft), 2 (pt); LPNs 2 (ft), 2 (pt); Nurses' aides 60 (ft), 10 (pt); Recreational therapists 1 (ft); Occupational therapists 1 (pt); Speech therapists 1 (pt); Activities coordinators 1 (ft); Dietitians 1 (pt); Social workers 3 (ft), 1 (pt); Psychologists 1 (ft); QMRPs 1 (ft); Vocational rehabilitation 1 (ft).
Facilities Dining room; Activities room; Chapel; Crafts room; Laundry room; Barber/Beauty shop; Library; Education center; Recreation room.
Activities Arts & crafts; Cards; Games; Reading groups; Prayer groups; Movies; Shopping trips; Dances/Social/Cultural gatherings; Intergenerational programs; Pet therapy; Activities of daily living; School; Work therapy.

Tri-County Memorial Hospital—Nursing Home
1801 Lincoln St, Whitehall, WI 54773
(715) 538-4361
Admin Ronald B Fields.
Licensure Skilled care; Intermediate care. *Beds* SNF 68. *Certified* Medicaid.
Owner Nonprofit corp.

Whitewater

Fairhaven Corporation
435 Starin Rd, Whitewater, WI 53190
(414) 473-2140, 473-2140 FAX
Admin Rev David G Yochum. *Dir of Nursing* Olive Crawley RN. *Medical Dir* L F Nelson MD.
Licensure Skilled care; Intermediate care; Residential apartments. *Beds* Swing beds SNF/ICF 84. *Private Pay Patients* 75%. *Certified* Medicaid.
Owner Nonprofit corp.
Admissions Requirements Minimum age 65; Medical examination.
Staff RNs; LPNs; Nurses' aides; Recreational therapists; Activities coordinators; Dietitians.
Affiliation United Church of Christ.

Facilities Dining room; Physical therapy room; Activities room; Chapel; Crafts room; Laundry room; Barber/Beauty shop; Library.
Activities Arts & crafts; Cards; Games; Reading groups; Prayer groups; Movies; Shopping trips; Dances/Social/Cultural gatherings; Intergenerational programs; Life Long Learning with University of Wisconsin-Whitewater.

Wild Rose

Wild Rose Manor
PO Box 295, 625 Summit St, Wild Rose, WI 54984
(414) 622-4342
Admin Donna M Barbian. *Dir of Nursing* Carol Jankovich. *Medical Dir* Dr Teodoro Romana.
Licensure Skilled care. *Beds* SNF 84. *Private Pay Patients* 30%. *Certified* Medicaid.
Owner Proprietary corp (Wis-Care Inc).
Admissions Requirements Minimum age 18; Medical examination; Physician's request.
Staff RNs 2 (ft), 4 (pt); LPNs 2 (ft), 7 (pt); Nurses' aides 10 (ft), 30 (pt); Physical therapists 1 (pt); Occupational therapists 1 (pt); Activities coordinators 1 (ft); Dietitians 1 (pt).
Facilities Dining room; Physical therapy room; Activities room; Chapel; Laundry room; Barber/Beauty shop; Library.
Activities Arts & crafts; Cards; Games; Reading groups; Prayer groups; Movies; Shopping trips; Dances/Social/Cultural gatherings; Intergenerational programs; Pet therapy.

Williams Bay

Sherwood Care Center
PO Box 1170, 146 Clover St, Williams Bay, WI 53191
(414) 245-6400, 245-9271 FAX
Admin Frank E Urban. *Dir of Nursing* Steve Hyduke. *Medical Dir* Britton Kolar MD.
Licensure Skilled care; Retirement. *Beds* SNF 84. *Certified* Medicaid; Medicare.
Owner Proprietary corp (Pinnacle Care Corp).
Admissions Requirements Medical examination; Physician's request.
Staff Physicians 1 (ft), 6 (pt); RNs 9 (ft), 5 (pt); LPNs 5 (ft), 5 (pt); Nurses' aides 30 (ft), 24 (pt); Physical therapists 1 (ft); Recreational therapists 1 (ft); Occupational therapists 1 (ft); Speech therapists 1 (pt); Activities coordinators 1 (ft); Dietitians 1 (pt); Podiatrists 1 (pt); Audiologists 1 (pt).
Facilities Dining room; Physical therapy room; Activities room; Chapel; Crafts room; Laundry room; Barber/Beauty shop; Rehabilitation.
Activities Arts & crafts; Cards; Games; Reading groups; Prayer groups; Movies; Shopping trips; Dances/Social/Cultural gatherings; Intergenerational programs; Pet therapy.

Winnebago

Park View Health Center
725 Butler Ave, Winnebago, WI 54985
(414) 235-5100
Admin Charlene A Lowe. *Dir of Nursing* Marge Schock. *Medical Dir* Dr Weber.
Licensure Skilled care; Intermediate care; Alzheimer's care. *Beds* Swing beds SNF/ICF 362. *Certified* Medicare.
Owner Publicly owned.
Admissions Requirements Minimum age 18.
Facilities Dining room; Physical therapy room; Activities room; Chapel; Crafts room; Laundry room; Barber/Beauty shop; Library.

Activities Arts & crafts; Cards; Games; Reading groups; Prayer groups; Movies; Shopping trips; Dances/Social/Cultural gatherings; Intergenerational programs.

Wisconsin Dells

Continental Manor—Wisconsin Dells
300 Race St, Wisconsin Dells, WI 53965
(608) 254-2574, 254-2576 FAX
Admin Scott Martens. *Dir of Nursing* Barbara Drolson. *Medical Dir* Richard K Westphall MD.
Licensure Skilled care. *Beds* SNF 101. *Private Pay Patients* 22%. *Certified* Medicaid; Medicare.
Owner Proprietary corp (Beverly Enterprises).
Admissions Requirements Minimum age 18; Medical examination; Physician's request.
Staff Physicians 3 (pt); RNs 7 (ft); LPNs 4 (ft), 3 (pt); Nurses' aides 25 (ft), 15 (pt); Physical therapists 1 (ft); Occupational therapists 1 (pt); Speech therapists 1 (pt); Activities coordinators 1 (ft); Dietitians 1 (pt); Ophthalmologists 1 (pt); Podiatrists 2 (pt); Audiologists 1 (pt).
Facilities Dining room; Physical therapy room; Activities room; Laundry room; Barber/Beauty shop.
Activities Arts & crafts; Cards; Games; Reading groups; Prayer groups; Movies; Shopping trips; Dances/Social/Cultural gatherings; Intergenerational programs; Pet therapy.

Wisconsin Rapids

Family Heritage Nursing Home
130 Strawberry Ln, Wisconsin Rapids, WI 54494
(715) 424-1600, 423-4936 FAX
Admin David Green. *Dir of Nursing* Patricia Sorenson. *Medical Dir* Richard W Clasen.
Licensure Skilled care. *Beds* SNF 165. *Certified* Medicaid; Medicare.
Owner Proprietary corp (Hillhaven Corp).
Admissions Requirements Medical examination; Physician's request.
Staff RNs 8 (ft); LPNs 7 (ft), 9 (pt); Nurses' aides 34 (ft), 22 (pt); Occupational therapists 1 (ft); Activities coordinators 2 (ft).
Facilities Dining room; Activities room; Chapel; Laundry room; Barber/Beauty shop.
Activities Arts & crafts; Cards; Games; Prayer groups; Movies; Shopping trips; Dances/Social/Cultural gatherings; Pet therapy.

Riverview Manor
PO Box 8080, 921 3rd St S, Wisconsin Rapids, WI 54495
(715) 421-7468
Admin William C Schloer. *Dir of Nursing* Patricia Raymond RN. *Medical Dir* Clifford Stair MD.
Licensure Skilled care. *Beds* SNF 118. *Certified* Medicaid; Medicare.
Owner Nonprofit corp.
Admissions Requirements Minimum age 18; Medical examination; Physician's request.
Staff RNs 3 (ft), 5 (pt); LPNs 5 (ft), 6 (pt); Nurses' aides 21 (ft), 27 (pt); Physical therapists 1 (ft); Recreational therapists 1 (ft), 1 (pt); Occupational therapists 1 (pt); Speech therapists 1 (pt); Dietitians 1 (pt).
Languages Polish, German.
Facilities Dining room; Physical therapy room; Activities room; Crafts room; Barber/Beauty shop.
Activities Arts & crafts; Cards; Games; Reading groups; Prayer groups; Movies; Shopping trips; Dances/Social/Cultural gatherings.

Wittenberg

Homme Home for the Aging
607 Webb St, Wittenberg, WI 54499
(715) 253-2125
Admin Charles P Clarey. *Dir of Nursing*
Ramona Morehouse. *Medical Dir* Ralph
Tauke MD.
Licensure Skilled care; Alzheimer's care; Self-
care; Independent living. *Beds* SNF 136;
Alzheimer's unit 9; Self-care 59; Independent
living apts 6. *Private Pay Patients* 17%.
Certified Medicaid.
Owner Nonprofit corp.
Admissions Requirements Minimum age 18;
Medical examination.
Staff Physicians (contracted); RNs 10 (ft), 10
(pt); LPNs 9 (ft), 7 (pt); Nurses' aides 56
(ft), 34 (pt); Physical therapists (contracted);
Activities coordinators 1 (ft); Dietitians 1
(ft); Ophthalmologists (contracted);
Chaplains 1 (ft).
Languages German, Polish, Norwegian.
Affiliation Evangelical Lutheran.
Facilities Dining room; Physical therapy
room; Activities room; Chapel; Crafts room;
Laundry room; Barber/Beauty shop; Library.
Activities Arts & crafts; Cards; Games;
Reading groups; Prayer groups; Movies;
Shopping trips; Dances/Social/Cultural
gatherings; Intergenerational programs.

Woodruff

Doctor Kate's Woodland Manor
PO Box 859, Woodruff, WI 54568
(715) 356-5355
Admin David Rademacher.
Medical Dir George Nemec.
Licensure Skilled care; Intermediate care. *Beds*
SNF 61. *Certified* Medicaid.
Owner Proprietary corp.
Staff Physicians 1 (pt); RNs 4 (ft), 1 (pt);
LPNs 3 (ft), 2 (pt); Nurses' aides 15 (ft), 8
(pt); Physical therapists 1 (pt); Reality
therapists 1 (pt); Reality therapists 1 (pt);
Occupational therapists 1 (pt); Speech
therapists 1 (pt); Activities coordinators 1
(ft); Dietitians 1 (ft); Ophthalmologists 1
(pt); Podiatrists 1 (pt); Audiologists 1 (pt);
Dentists 1 (pt).
Facilities Dining room; Physical therapy
room; Activities room; Crafts room; Laundry
room; Barber/Beauty shop.
Activities Arts & crafts; Games; Reading
groups; Prayer groups; Movies; Shopping
trips; Dances/Social/Cultural gatherings.

Doctor Kate Newcomb Convalescent Center
PO Box 829, 301 Elm, Woodruff, WI 54568
(715) 356-8804
Admin Cynthia Eichman. *Dir of Nursing* Jill
Paczkowski RN. *Medical Dir* Dr George
Nemec.
Licensure Skilled care; Retirement. *Beds* SNF
65; Retirement apts 21. *Certified* Medicaid.
Owner Nonprofit organization/foundation.
Admissions Requirements Medical
examination.
Staff RNs 4 (ft), 1 (pt); LPNs 2 (ft), 3 (pt);
Nurses' aides 18 (ft), 11 (pt); Activities
coordinators 1 (ft), 1 (pt); Dietitians 1 (pt);
Social workers 1 (ft), 1 (pt).
Languages Sign.
Facilities Dining room; Physical therapy
room; Activities room; Crafts room; Laundry
room; Barber/Beauty shop; Library.
Activities Arts & crafts; Cards; Games;
Reading groups; Prayer groups; Movies;
Shopping trips; Dances/Social/Cultural
gatherings; Intergenerational programs; Pet
therapy.

Woodville

Park View Home
220 Lockwood St, Woodville, WI 54028
(715) 698-2451
Admin Jeannette V Howard.
Medical Dir Dr Arthur Heiser.
Licensure Skilled care; Retirement;
Alzheimer's care. *Beds* SNF 61. *Certified*
Medicaid.
Owner Nonprofit corp.
Admissions Requirements Minimum age 18;
Medical examination.
Staff Physicians 5 (pt); RNs 2 (ft), 1 (pt);
LPNs 5 (pt); Nurses' aides 6 (ft), 14 (pt);
Physical therapists 1 (pt); Recreational
therapists 1 (ft), 1 (pt); Occupational
therapists 1 (pt); Speech therapists 1 (pt);
Dietitians 1 (pt).
Facilities Dining room; Physical therapy
room; Activities room; Crafts room; Laundry
room; Barber/Beauty shop; Library; Living
room/lounge area.
Activities Arts & crafts; Cards; Games;
Reading groups; Prayer groups; Movies;
Dances/Social/Cultural gatherings.

Wyocena

Columbia County Home
Box 895, Wyocena, WI 53954
(608) 429-2181, 429-2281 FAX
Admin Gerald E Baldowin. *Dir of Nursing*
Jean Wadsworth RN. *Medical Dir* Bruce
Kraus MD.
Licensure Skilled care; Alzheimer's care. *Beds*
SNF 150. *Private Pay Patients* 33%. *Certified*
Medicaid; Medicare.
Owner Publicly owned.
Admissions Requirements Minimum age 18.
Staff Physicians 1 (pt); RNs 5 (ft), 14 (pt);
LPNs 6 (ft), 11 (pt); Nurses' aides 36 (ft), 50
(pt); Activities coordinators 1 (ft); Dietitians
1 (pt).
Facilities Dining room; Physical therapy
room; Activities room; Chapel; Crafts room;
Laundry room; Barber/Beauty shop; Library.
Activities Arts & crafts; Cards; Games;
Reading groups; Prayer groups; Movies;
Shopping trips; Dances/Social/Cultural
gatherings; Pet therapy.

WYOMING

Basin

A Touch of Kindness
PO Box 878, 4396 Orchard Bench Rd, Basin,
WY 82410
(307) 568-2232
Admin Donna J Butler.
Licensure Boarding home. *Beds* Boarding
home 5.

Wyoming Retirement Center
890 Hwy 20 S, Basin, WY 82410
(307) 568-2431
Admin Gerald E Bronnenberg. *Dir of Nursing*
Patricia K Fritz RN. *Medical Dir* Dr
Richard Heiss.
Licensure Skilled care; Intermediate care;
Alzheimer's care. *Beds* Swing beds SNF/ICF
120. *Private Pay Patients* 46%. *Certified*
Medicaid; Medicare.
Owner Publicly owned.
Admissions Requirements Medical
examination.
Staff RNs 6 (ft); LPNs 8 (ft), 3 (pt); Nurses'
aides 22 (ft), 8 (pt); Physical therapists 1
(pt); Recreational therapists 1 (ft);
Occupational therapists 1 (ft); Activities
coordinators 1 (ft); Dietitians 1 (pt).
Facilities Dining room; Physical therapy
room; Activities room; Chapel; Crafts room;
Laundry room; Barber/Beauty shop; Library.
Activities Arts & crafts; Cards; Games;
Reading groups; Prayer groups; Movies;
Shopping trips; Dances/Social/Cultural
gatherings; Intergenerational programs; Pet
therapy.

Big Horn

Big Horn Rest Home
Box 340, Big Horn, WY 82833
(307) 672-2625
Admin M C Faass.
Licensure Boarding home. *Beds* Boarding
home 8.

Buffalo

Amie Holt Care Center
497 W Lott St, Buffalo, WY 82834
(307) 684-5521
Admin Kent Ward. *Dir of Nursing* Phyllis
Hepp RN. *Medical Dir* Dr Pat Nolan.
Licensure Skilled care; Intermediate care. *Beds*
Swing beds SNF/ICF 54. *Certified* Medicaid.
Owner Publicly owned.
Staff RNs 2 (ft), 1 (pt); LPNs 4 (ft); Nurses'
aides 22 (ft), 3 (pt); Physical therapists 1
(pt); Speech therapists 1 (pt); Activities
coordinators 1 (ft), 1 (pt); Dietitians 1 (pt);
Podiatrists 1 (pt).
Facilities Dining room; Activities room;
Chapel; Crafts room; Barber/Beauty shop.
Activities Arts & crafts; Cards; Games;
Reading groups; Prayer groups; Movies;
Shopping trips; Dances/Social/Cultural
gatherings.

Casper

Maurice Griffith Manor
77 Gardenia, Casper, WY 82604
(307) 234-0572
Admin Lora Hill.
Licensure Independent living center. *Beds*
Independent living center 26. *Private Pay
Patients* 26%.
Owner Nonprofit corp (Luthercare Inc).
Admissions Requirements Minimum age
Seniors; Medical examination.
Staff Nurses' aides; Activities coordinators;
Podiatrists.
Facilities Dining room; Activities room;
Laundry room; Barber/Beauty shop; Cable
TV.
Activities Cards; Games; Prayer groups;
Movies; Shopping trips; Dances/Social/
Cultural gatherings.

Poplar Living Center
4305 S Poplar St, Casper, WY 82601
(307) 237-2561
Admin Richard Crowley. *Dir of Nursing* Judy
Banks RN. *Medical Dir* Dr Fred Deiss.
Licensure Skilled care; Intermediate care;
Alzheimer's care. *Beds* Swing beds SNF/ICF
120. *Certified* Medicaid; Medicare.
Owner Proprietary corp (ARA Living
Centers).
Admissions Requirements Minimum age 21;
Physician's request.
Staff RNs 6 (ft); LPNs 10 (ft); Nurses' aides
42 (ft); Activities coordinators 1 (ft), 1 (pt);
Dietitians 2 (pt).
Languages Spanish.
Facilities Dining room; Physical therapy
room; Activities room; Crafts room; Laundry
room; Barber/Beauty shop; Library.
Activities Arts & crafts; Cards; Games;
Reading groups; Prayer groups; Movies;
Shopping trips; Dances/Social/Cultural
gatherings; Ice cream social; Reality
orientation classes; Pie social.

Shepherd of the Valley Care Center
60 Magnolia Rd, Casper, WY 82604
(307) 234-9381
Admin Keith W Skatrud. *Dir of Nursing*
Eloise C Hensley RN.
Licensure Skilled care; Intermediate care. *Beds*
204.
Owner Nonprofit corp.

Cheyenne

Cheyenne Health Care Center
2700 E 12th St, Cheyenne, WY 82001
(307) 634-7986
Admin Brent Jones. *Dir of Nursing* Carolyn
May RN.
Licensure Skilled care; Intermediate care. *Beds*
108.
Owner Nonprofit corp.

Fox Adult Foster Care
1622 Madison Ave, Cheyenne, WY 82001
(307) 638-0292
Admin Kelly Fox.
Licensure Boarding home. *Beds* Boarding
home 6.

Homestead
4012 Columbia, Cheyenne, WY 82009
(307) 632-7406
Admin Deborah Franklin.
Licensure Boarding home. *Beds* Boarding
home 8.

Life Care of Cheyenne
1330 Prairie Ave, Cheyenne, WY 82009
(307) 778-8997
Licensure Skilled care; Intermediate care. *Beds*
150.

Mountain Towers Healthcare
3129 Acacia Dr, Cheyenne, WY 82001
(307) 634-7901
Admin Frank J Shaw. *Dir of Nursing* Marie
Hummel RN.
Licensure Skilled care; Intermediate care. *Beds*
Swing beds SNF/ICF 170. *Certified*
Medicaid.
Owner Proprietary corp (Hillhaven Corp).

S & R Foster Home
1416 Orchid Ct, Cheyenne, WY 82001
(307) 632-2742
Admin Sarah F Sanchez.
Licensure Boarding home. *Beds* Boarding
home 4.

S & R Foster Home
1422 Orchid Ct, Cheyenne, WY 82001
(307) 635-8730
Admin Sarah F Sanchez.
Licensure Boarding home. *Beds* Boarding
home 2.

Cody

West Park Long-Term Care Center
707 Sheridan Ave, Cody, WY 82414
(307) 578-2434
Admin Jeanne Kaiser. *Dir of Nursing* Donna
Meadows RN. *Medical Dir* Peter Rutherford
MD.
Licensure Skilled care; Intermediate care. *Beds*
SNF 47; ICF 58. *Private Pay Patients* 33%.
Certified Medicaid; Medicare.
Owner Publicly owned.
Admissions Requirements Medical
examination; Physician's request.
Staff RNs 4 (ft), 4 (pt); LPNs 8 (ft), 5 (pt);
Nurses' aides 33 (ft), 9 (pt); Physical
therapists 1 (pt); Activities coordinators 1
(ft); Dietitians 1 (ft).
Languages German, Spanish.
Facilities Dining room; Physical therapy
room; Activities room; Chapel; Crafts room;
Laundry room; Barber/Beauty shop; Library.

Activities Arts & crafts; Cards; Games; Reading groups; Prayer groups; Movies; Shopping trips; Dances/Social/Cultural gatherings; Intergenerational programs; Pet therapy.

Douglas

McComb Retirement/Boarding Center
1247 Village Dr, Douglas, WY 82633
(307) 632-5167
Admin Theo McComb.
Licensure Boarding home. *Beds* Boarding home 8.

McComb Retirement/Boarding Center
830 Richards St, Douglas, WY 82633
(307) 358-6790
Admin Theo McComb.
Licensure Boarding home. *Beds* Boarding home 14.

Michael Manor
1108 Birch St, Douglas, WY 82633
(307) 358-3397
Admin Patricia A Miller. *Dir of Nursing* Sheila Osborne RN.
Licensure Skilled care; Intermediate care. *Beds* 60.
Owner Proprietary corp.

Evanston

Uinta Healthcare Center Inc
475 Yellowcreek Rd, Evanston, WY 82930
(307) 789-0726
Admin Sterling G Loveland. *Dir of Nursing* Sandra Little.
Licensure Skilled care; Intermediate care. *Beds* 60.
Owner Proprietary corp.

Fort Washakie

Morning Star Manor
PO Box 859, 4 N Fork Rd, Fort Washakie, WY 82514
(307) 332-6902
Admin Bruce Odenthal. *Dir of Nursing* Sandy Daffron.
Licensure Intermediate care. *Beds* ICF 50. *Certified* Medicaid.
Owner Proprietary corp (Shoshoni Enterprises).
Admissions Requirements Minimum age 18; Physician's request.
Staff RNs 2 (ft); LPNs 1 (ft); Nurses' aides 8 (ft), 6 (pt); Physical therapists 1 (ft); Speech therapists 1 (pt); Activities coordinators 1 (ft), 1 (pt); Dietitians 1 (ft).
Languages Shoshoni, Arapahoe.
Facilities Dining room; Activities room; Chapel; Crafts room; Laundry room; Barber/Beauty shop.
Activities Arts & crafts; Cards; Games; Reading groups; Prayer groups; Dances/Social/Cultural gatherings.

Gillette

Pioneer Manor Board & Care
900 W 8th, Gillette, WY 82716
(307) 682-4709
Admin Charles R Willey. *Dir of Nursing* Ann Herman RN.
Licensure Skilled care; Board & care; Supervised living; Independent living; Alzheimer's care. *Beds* SNF 148; Board & care 15; Supervised living apartments 13; Independent living apartments 68. *Private Pay Patients* 43%. *Certified* Medicaid; Medicare.
Owner Nonprofit corp (North Central Health Services).
Admissions Requirements Medical examination; Physician's request.

Staff RNs; LPNs; Nurses' aides; Physical therapists; Recreational therapists; Occupational therapists; Speech therapists; Activities coordinators; Dietitians; Podiatrists.
Facilities Dining room; Physical therapy room; Activities room; Chapel; Crafts room; Laundry room; Barber/Beauty shop; Library; Control access unit for Alzheimer's patients.
Activities Arts & crafts; Cards; Games; Reading groups; Prayer groups; Movies; Shopping trips; Dances/Social/Cultural gatherings; Intergenerational programs; Pet therapy.

Pioneer Manor Nursing & Convalescent Home
900 W 8th St, Gillette, WY 82716
(307) 682-4709
Admin Charles R Willey. *Dir of Nursing* Ann M Swartz RN. *Medical Dir* J E Taylor MD.
Licensure Skilled care; Intermediate care. *Beds* Swing beds SNF/ICF 148. *Certified* Medicaid; Medicare.
Owner Nonprofit corp (Health One Health Care).
Staff RNs 7 (ft), 3 (pt); LPNs 6 (ft), 2 (pt); Nurses' aides 41 (ft), 4 (pt); Activities coordinators 1 (ft); Dietitians 1 (ft).
Facilities Dining room; Physical therapy room; Activities room; Chapel; Crafts room; Laundry room; Barber/Beauty shop; Library.
Activities Arts & crafts; Cards; Games; Reading groups; Prayer groups; Movies; Shopping trips; Dances/Social/Cultural gatherings.

Green River

Castle Rock Convalescent Center
1445 Uinta Dr, Green River, WY 82935
(307) 875-4030
Admin Auggie A Pepple.
Licensure Skilled care. *Beds* SNF 59.

Villa
1445 Uinta Dr, Green River, WY 82935
(307) 875-4030
Admin Auggie A Pepple.
Licensure Boarding home. *Beds* Boarding home 27.

Greybull

Bonnie Bluejacket Memorial Nursing Home
River Rte, Greybull, WY 82426
(307) 765-3311
Admin Jerry Peak. *Dir of Nursing* Donna Becker RN. *Medical Dir* Ben Mills MD.
Licensure Skilled care; Intermediate care. *Beds* Swing beds SNF/ICF 32. *Private Pay Patients* 84%. *Certified* Medicaid; Medicare.
Owner Publicly owned.
Admissions Requirements Medical examination.
Staff Physicians 2 (pt); RNs 1 (ft), 3 (pt); LPNs 3 (ft), 2 (pt); Nurses' aides 6 (ft), 6 (pt); Physical therapists 1 (pt); Speech therapists 1 (pt); Activities coordinators 1 (ft); Dietitians 1 (pt).
Facilities Dining room; Physical therapy room; Activities room; Chapel; Crafts room; Laundry room; Barber/Beauty shop.
Activities Arts & crafts; Cards; Games; Reading groups; Prayer groups; Movies; Shopping trips; Dances/Social/Cultural gatherings; Intergenerational programs; Pet therapy.

Jackson

St John's Hospital Long-Term Care Unit
PO Box 428, 555 E Broadway, Jackson, WY 83001
(307) 733-3636
Admin Dale Morgan. *Dir of Nursing* Linda Rode RN. *Medical Dir* Bruce Hayse MD.

Licensure Intermediate care. *Beds* ICF 12. *Certified* Medicaid.
Owner Publicly owned.
Admissions Requirements Physician's request.
Staff Physicians 20 (ft); RNs 1 (ft); LPNs 2 (ft); Nurses' aides 6 (ft); Physical therapists 1 (ft); Occupational therapists 1 (pt); Speech therapists 1 (pt); Activities coordinators 1 (pt); Dietitians 1 (pt).
Languages German, French.
Facilities Dining room; Physical therapy room; Activities room; Crafts room; Laundry room; Barber/Beauty shop; Library.
Activities Arts & crafts; Cards; Games; Reading groups; Prayer groups; Movies; Dances/Social/Cultural gatherings; Picnics; Bus trips.

Lander

Westward Heights Nursing Home
150 Buena Vista Dr, Lander, WY 82520
(307) 332-5560
Admin Michael J Mathison. *Dir of Nursing* Florence M Cox RN. *Medical Dir* Dr Charles McMahon.
Licensure Skilled care; Intermediate care. *Beds* Swing beds SNF/ICF 60. *Certified* Medicaid.
Owner Proprietary corp (Beverly Enterprises).
Admissions Requirements Medical examination; Physician's request.
Staff RNs; LPNs; Nurses' aides; Activities coordinators; Social service coordinator.
Facilities Dining room; Activities room; Chapel; Laundry room; Barber/Beauty shop; Library.
Activities Arts & crafts; Cards; Games; Reading groups; Prayer groups; Movies; Dances/Social/Cultural gatherings.

Laramie

Bethesda Care Center
1051 Bonita Rd, Laramie, WY 82070
(303) 742-3728
Admin Maxine S Chisholm. *Dir of Nursing* Nancy Findholt. *Medical Dir* Dr J Coates.
Licensure Skilled care; Alzheimer's care. *Beds* SNF 144. *Private Pay Patients* 50%. *Certified* Medicaid; Medicare.
Owner Proprietary corp (Meritcare).
Staff Physicians 13 (ft); RNs 15 (ft); LPNs 20 (ft); Nurses' aides 70 (ft); Physical therapists 1 (ft); Speech therapists 1 (ft); Activities coordinators 1 (ft); Dietitians 1 (ft); Ophthalmologists 2 (ft); Podiatrists 1 (ft); Audiologists 1 (ft).
Facilities Dining room; Physical therapy room; Activities room; Chapel; Laundry room; Barber/Beauty shop.
Activities Arts & crafts; Cards; Games; Reading groups; Prayer groups; Movies; Shopping trips; Dances/Social/Cultural gatherings; Intergenerational programs; Pet therapy.

Ivinson Memorial Hospital
255 N 30th, Laramie, WY 82070
(307) 742-2141
Admin Thomas Nord. *Dir of Nursing* Terry Huston.
Licensure Skilled care; Intermediate care. *Beds* 11.
Owner Publicly owned.

Lovell

New Horizons Care Center
PO Box 518, 100 E 10th St, Lovell, WY 82431
(307) 548-2771
Admin Imogene Hanson. *Dir of Nursing* Janice Hansen RN. *Medical Dir* John M Welch MD.

Licensure Skilled care; Intermediate care. *Beds* Swing beds SNF/ICF 60. *Certified* Medicaid; Medicare.
Owner Publicly owned.
Admissions Requirements Physician's request.
Staff RNs; LPNs; Nurses' aides; Recreational therapists; Activities coordinators; Dietitians.
Facilities Dining room; Physical therapy room; Activities room; Chapel; Crafts room; Laundry room; Barber/Beauty shop; Library.
Activities Arts & crafts; Cards; Games; Reading groups; Prayer groups; Movies; Shopping trips; Dances/Social/Cultural gatherings.

Lusk

Niobrara County Memorial Nursing Home
PO Box 780, 921 Ballancee Ave, Lusk, WY 82225
(307) 334-2900
Admin Jim D LeBrun. *Dir of Nursing* Ruth Schmidt RN. *Medical Dir* Darcy Turner MD.
Licensure Skilled care; Intermediate care. *Beds* Swing beds SNF/ICF 36. *Private Pay Patients* 25%. *Certified* Medicaid; Medicare.
Owner Publicly owned.
Admissions Requirements Medical examination; Physician's request.
Staff Physicians 2 (ft); RNs 4 (ft); LPNs 3 (ft); Nurses' aides 15 (ft); Physical therapists 1 (pt); Activities coordinators 1 (ft); Dietitians 1 (pt).
Languages German.
Facilities Dining room; Physical therapy room; Activities room; Chapel; Crafts room; Laundry room; Barber/Beauty shop.
Activities Arts & crafts; Cards; Games; Reading groups; Prayer groups; Movies; Dances/Social/Cultural gatherings; Intergenerational programs; Pet therapy.

Newcastle

Weston County Manor
1124 Washington Blvd, Newcastle, WY 82701
(307) 746-4491
Admin Evonne G Ulmer. *Dir of Nursing* Nancy Bair RN. *Medical Dir* Dr Chuck Franklin.
Licensure Skilled care; Intermediate care; Alzheimer's care. *Beds* SNF 41; Swing beds SNF/ICF 28. *Private Pay Patients* 50%. *Certified* Medicaid; Medicare.
Owner Publicly owned.
Admissions Requirements Medical examination.
Staff RNs 3 (ft), 1 (pt); LPNs 2 (ft); Nurses' aides 16 (ft), 4 (pt); Physical therapists 1 (pt); Recreational therapists 1 (ft); Activities coordinators 1 (ft); Dietitians 1 (pt).
Languages Italian.
Facilities Dining room; Physical therapy room; Activities room; Crafts room; Laundry room; Barber/Beauty shop; Library.
Activities Arts & crafts; Cards; Games; Reading groups; Prayer groups; Movies; Shopping trips; Dances/Social/Cultural gatherings; Intergenerational programs; Pet therapy; Dining club; Field trips.

Pine Bluffs

Whispering Pines Care Home
PO Box 808, 805 Pine St, Pine Bluffs, WY 82082
(307) 245-3814
Admin L Evelyn Fleming.
Licensure Boarding home. *Beds* Boarding home 8.

Pinedale

Sublette County Retirement Center
PO Box 788, 333 Bridger Ave, Pinedale, WY 82941
(307) 367-4161
Admin Ellen I Toth. *Dir of Nursing* Gaye Fletcher RN. *Medical Dir* Dr J T Johnston.
Licensure Skilled care; Intermediate care; Boarding care; Apartments. *Beds* Swing beds SNF/ICF 60; Boarding care 32; Apts 15. *Certified* Medicaid; Medicare.
Owner Nonprofit corp.
Admissions Requirements Minimum age 55; Medical examination; Physician's request.
Staff Physicians 3 (pt); RNs 3 (ft), 2 (pt); LPNs 2 (ft), 1 (pt); Nurses' aides 7 (ft), 3 (pt); Physical therapists 1 (pt); Reality therapists 1 (ft); Activities coordinators 1 (ft); Dietitians 1 (ft).
Facilities Dining room; Physical therapy room; Activities room; Chapel; Crafts room; Laundry room; Barber/Beauty shop; Library.
Activities Arts & crafts; Cards; Games; Reading groups; Prayer groups; Movies; Shopping trips; Dances/Social/Cultural gatherings.

Powell

Powell Nursing Home
639 Ave H, Powell, WY 82435
(307) 754-5704
Admin Elaine R Knudson RN. *Dir of Nursing* Mary Lois Jacobson RN. *Medical Dir* Lyle F Haberland.
Licensure Skilled care; Intermediate care; Retirement. *Beds* Swing beds SNF/ICF 98. *Certified* Medicaid.
Owner Publicly owned.
Admissions Requirements Physician's request.
Staff Physicians 4 (pt); RNs 6 (ft); LPNs 5 (ft), 2 (pt); Nurses' aides 35 (ft), 6 (pt); Physical therapists 1 (pt); Activities coordinators 1 (ft); Dietitians 1 (pt); Podiatrists 1 (pt); Activities aide 1 (ft); Restorative aide 1 (ft); Social service 1 (ft).
Languages Spanish, German.
Facilities Dining room; Physical therapy room; Activities room; Chapel; Crafts room; Laundry room; Barber/Beauty shop; Library.
Activities Arts & crafts; Games; Reading groups; Prayer groups; Movies; Shopping trips; Picnics; Bus rides; County fair; Birthday parties.

Ranchester

Case Golden Age Care
PO Box 275, Ranchester, WY 82839
(307) 655-9650
Admin Alice L Case.
Licensure Boarding home. *Beds* Boarding home 5.

Rawlins

Park Manor Nursing & Convalescent Home
542 16th St, Rawlins, WY 82301
(307) 324-2759
Admin Henry M Rae. *Dir of Nursing* Annette Fagnant RN.
Licensure Skilled care; Intermediate care. *Beds* Swing beds SNF/ICF 90. *Certified* Medicaid; Medicare.
Owner Proprietary corp (Hillhaven).
Admissions Requirements Physician's request.
Staff Physicians 3 (pt); RNs 4 (ft), 5 (pt); LPNs 8 (ft), 4 (pt); Nurses' aides 30 (ft), 7 (pt); Physical therapists 1 (pt); Speech therapists 1 (pt); Activities coordinators 1 (ft), 1 (pt); Dietitians 2 (pt).
Languages Spanish.
Facilities Dining room; Physical therapy room; Activities room; Chapel; Crafts room; Laundry room; Barber/Beauty shop.
Activities Arts & crafts; Cards; Games; Reading groups; Prayer groups; Movies; Shopping trips; Dances/Social/Cultural gatherings; Intergenerational programs.

Riverton

Fremont Manor Nursing & Convalescent Home
1002 Forest Dr, Riverton, WY 82501
(307) 856-9471
Admin Saundra Rene Bebout. *Dir of Nursing* Loretta F Ray RN.
Licensure Skilled care; Intermediate care. *Beds* 90.
Owner Proprietary corp.

Wyotech Group Home
960 Galloway, Riverton, WY 82501
(307) 856-1637
Admin Brenda Iden.
Licensure Intermediate care for mentally retarded. *Beds* ICF/MR 6. *Private Pay Patients* 100%.
Owner Privately owned.
Admissions Requirements Minimum age 18; Females only; Ambulatory.
Facilities Dining room; Activities room; Crafts room; Laundry room; Sun room.
Activities Arts & crafts; Cards; Games; Movies; Shopping trips; Dances/Social/Cultural gatherings; Reading.

Rock Springs

Sage View Care Center
1325 Sage St, Rock Springs, WY 82901
(307) 362-3780
Admin Glen Dunlap. *Dir of Nursing* Jill Stephens. *Medical Dir* Howard Greaves MD.
Licensure Intermediate care. *Beds* ICF 101. *Certified* Medicaid; Medicare.
Owner Proprietary corp (Hillhaven Corp).
Admissions Requirements Medical examination; Physician's request.
Staff RNs 6 (ft); LPNs 5 (ft); Activities coordinators 1 (ft), 1 (pt); Dietitians 1 (pt); Ophthalmologists; Podiatrists; Dentists.
Facilities Dining room; Physical therapy room; Activities room; Chapel; Crafts room; Laundry room; Barber/Beauty shop.
Activities Arts & crafts; Cards; Games; Reading groups; Prayer groups; Movies; Shopping trips; Dances/Social/Cultural gatherings.

Saratoga

Valley View Health Care Center
PO Box 630, 207 E Holly, Saratoga, WY 82331
(307) 326-8212
Admin Mary DeWaard.
Medical Dir Dr John Lunt.
Licensure Skilled care; Intermediate care. *Beds* Swing beds SNF/ICF 52. *Certified* Medicaid.
Owner Proprietary corp.
Admissions Requirements Physician's request.
Staff Physicians 1 (pt); RNs 1 (ft), 3 (pt); LPNs 1 (ft), 3 (pt); Nurses' aides 12 (ft), 2 (pt); Physical therapists 1 (pt); Activities coordinators 1 (ft), 1 (pt); Dietitians 1 (ft), 1 (pt).
Facilities Dining room; Physical therapy room; Laundry room; Barber/Beauty shop; Library.
Activities Arts & crafts; Cards; Games; Reading groups; Movies; Shopping trips; Dances/Social/Cultural gatherings.

Sheridan

Eventide of Sheridan
1851 Big Horn Ave, Sheridan, WY 82801
(307) 674-4416
Admin Richard Dunkley. *Dir of Nursing* Kay Causer RN.

Licensure Skilled care; Intermediate care. *Beds* Swing beds SNF/ICF 120. *Certified* Medicaid; Medicare.
Owner Proprietary corp (ARA Living Centers).
Staff RNs; LPNs; Nurses' aides.
Languages Spanish, German, Polish.
Facilities Dining room; Activities room; Chapel; Laundry room; Barber/Beauty shop; Library.
Activities Arts & crafts; Cards; Games; Reading groups; Prayer groups; Movies; Shopping trips; Dances/Social/Cultural gatherings.

Guest Ranch Utopia
14 Upper Rd No 113, Sheridan, WY 82801
(307) 674-8801
Admin John Cristler; Jean Cristler.
Licensure Boarding home. *Beds* Boarding home 9.

KJ's TLC
PO Box 7016, Sheridan, WY 82801
(307) 655-2266
Admin Kimberly Kalland.
Licensure Boarding home. *Beds* Boarding home 9. *Private Pay Patients* 95%.
Owner Privately owned.
Admissions Requirements Medical examination; Physician's request.
Staff Nurses' aides.
Facilities Dining room.
Activities Arts & crafts; Cards; Games; Movies; Shopping trips; Pet therapy.

Overlin Boarding Home
320 Gladstone St, Sheridan, WY 82801
(307) 672-3224
Admin William Overlin; Muriel Overlin.
Licensure Boarding home. *Beds* Boarding home 9.

Steigelman's Rest Home
Red Grade Rd No 91, Box 7219, Sheridan, WY 82801
(307) 672-2507
Admin Goldie Steigelman.
Licensure Boarding home. *Beds* Boarding home 5.

Story

Kessler Home
PO Box 8, 17 A Wagon Box Rd, Story, WY 82842
(307) 683-2285
Admin Glen Kessler; Hazel Kessler.
Licensure Boarding home. *Beds* Boarding home 10.

Sundance

Crook County Nursing Home
713 Oak, Box 517, Sundance, WY 82729
(307) 283-2725
Admin David Dick. *Dir of Nursing* Patricia Voll RN. *Medical Dir* Jeremi Villano MD.
Licensure Skilled care; Intermediate care. *Beds* Swing beds SNF/ICF 32. *Private Pay Patients* 40%. *Certified* Medicaid; Medicare.
Owner Publicly owned.
Admissions Requirements Physician's request.
Staff Physicians 2 (ft); RNs 3 (ft); LPNs 5 (ft); Nurses' aides 15 (ft), 5 (pt); Physical therapists 1 (pt); Activities coordinators 1 (ft); Dietitians 1 (pt).
Facilities Dining room; Physical therapy room; Chapel; Laundry room; Barber/Beauty shop; Library; Multi-purpose room.
Activities Arts & crafts; Cards; Games; Prayer groups; Movies; Shopping trips; Dances/Social/Cultural gatherings; Intergenerational programs; Pet therapy.

Thermopolis

Canyon Hills Manor
PO Box 1325, 1210 Canyon Hills Rd, Thermopolis, WY 82443
(307) 864-5591
Admin Patricia J Jemming. *Dir of Nursing* Jean Pinter RN. *Medical Dir* Dr Howard Willson.
Licensure Intermediate care. *Beds* ICF 80. *Private Pay Patients* 10%. *Certified* Medicaid.
Owner Nonprofit organization/foundation.
Admissions Requirements Physician's request.
Staff Physicians 1 (pt); RNs 3 (ft); LPNs 3 (ft); Nurses' aides 20 (ft); Recreational therapists 1 (ft); Activities coordinators 1 (ft); Dietitians 1 (pt).
Facilities Dining room; Activities room; Crafts room; Laundry room; Barber/Beauty shop.
Activities Arts & crafts; Cards; Games; Reading groups; Prayer groups; Movies; Shopping trips; Dances/Social/Cultural gatherings; Pet therapy; Swimming; Bathing in mineral springs.

Wyoming Pioneer Home
5 Pioneer Dr, Thermopolis, WY 82443
(307) 864-3151
Admin Carol Ann Barham, Supt. *Dir of Nursing* Peter R Person RN.
Licensure Boarding home. *Beds* Observation area 7: Boarding home 114. *Private Pay Patients* 100%.
Owner Publicly owned.
Admissions Requirements Minimum age 55; Medical examination; Under age 55 must be legally blind.
Staff RNs 4 (ft); LPNs 2 (ft); Nurses' aides 6 (ft); Activities coordinators 1 (ft); Dietitians (contracted).
Facilities Dining room; Activities room; Chapel; Crafts room; Laundry room; Barber/ Beauty shop; Library; Lapidary; Recreation.
Activities Arts & crafts; Cards; Games; Reading groups; Prayer groups; Movies; Shopping trips; Dances/Social/Cultural gatherings; Intergenerational programs; Pet therapy; Holiday programs; Transportation.

Torrington

Adult Foster Care Home
1019 W 25th Ave, Torrington, WY 82240
(307) 532-2368
Admin Barbara R Houk.
Licensure Boarding home. *Beds* Boarding home 3.

Country Villa
Rte 3 Box 24, Torrington, WY 82240
(307) 532-7414
Admin Carol Webb.
Licensure Boarding home. *Beds* Boarding home 16. *Private Pay Patients* 100%.
Owner Privately owned.
Admissions Requirements Minimum age 19; Medical examination; Physician's request.
Staff LPNs 1 (pt); Nurses' aides 2 (ft), 1 (pt).
Facilities Dining room; Activities room; Chapel; Crafts room; Laundry room; Barber/ Beauty shop; Gardens.
Activities Arts & crafts; Cards; Games; Reading groups; Prayer groups; Movies; Shopping trips; Pet therapy; Church.

Goshen County Memorial Nursing Home
536 E 20th Ave, Torrington, WY 82240
(307) 532-4038
Admin Jean M Zerwas. *Dir of Nursing* Shirley E Love RN.
Licensure Intermediate care. *Beds* ICF 75. *Certified* Medicaid.
Owner Publicly owned.

Staff RNs 3 (ft); LPNs 9 (ft); Nurses' aides 18 (ft), 7 (pt); Activities coordinators 2 (ft), 1 (pt); Dietitians 1 (ft).
Facilities Dining room; Activities room; Chapel; Crafts room; Barber/Beauty shop; Library; Ceramics room.
Activities Arts & crafts; Cards; Games; Reading groups; Prayer groups; Movies; Dances/Social/Cultural gatherings; One-on-one interaction; Bus rides; Sing-alongs.

Wheatland

William Irvine Home Trust
PO Box 1138, 855 Water St, Wheatland, WY 82201
(307) 322-3767
Admin Yvonne Pinney.
Licensure Boarding home. *Beds* Boarding home 11.

Platte County Memorial Nursing Home
201 14th St, Wheatland, WY 82201
(307) 322-3636
Admin Duaine C Kanwischer. *Dir of Nursing* Samuel Smerud RN. *Medical Dir* Jane Nickel.
Licensure Intermediate care. *Beds* ICF 43. *Certified* Medicaid.
Owner Publicly owned.
Admissions Requirements Medical examination; Physician's request.
Staff RNs 1 (ft); LPNs 3 (ft), 4 (pt); Nurses' aides 7 (ft), 14 (pt); Physical therapists 1 (pt); Speech therapists 1 (pt); Activities coordinators 2 (ft); Dietitians 1 (pt); Dentists 1 (pt).
Facilities Dining room; Physical therapy room; Activities room; Chapel; Crafts room; Laundry room; Barber/Beauty shop.
Activities Arts & crafts; Cards; Games; Reading groups; Prayer groups; Movies; Shopping trips; Dances/Social/Cultural gatherings.

Worland

Bethesda Care Center
1901 Howell Ave, Worland, WY 82401
(307) 347-4285
Admin Eric B Jensen NHA. *Dir of Nursing* Virginia E Basse RN.
Licensure Intermediate care; Retirement. *Beds* ICF 76. *Certified* Medicaid.
Owner Nonprofit corp (Bethesda Care Centers).
Admissions Requirements Medical examination; Physician's request.
Staff RNs 2 (ft), 4 (pt); LPNs 2 (ft), 4 (pt); Nurses' aides 20 (ft), 7 (pt); Physical therapists 1 (pt); Activities coordinators 2 (ft), 1 (pt); Dietitians 1 (pt); Social worker 1 (pt).
Languages Spanish.
Facilities Dining room; Physical therapy room; Activities room; Chapel; Barber/ Beauty shop; Library.
Activities Arts & crafts; Cards; Games; Reading groups; Prayer groups; Movies; Shopping trips; Dances/Social/Cultural gatherings; Van outings.

Wyarno

McKey Boarding Home
PO Box 8, Wyarno, WY 82845
(307) 737-2417
Admin Earl R McKey; Patsye E McKey.
Licensure Boarding home. *Beds* Boarding home 2.

PUERTO RICO

Caguas

Caguas Regional Skilled Nursing Facility
Box 1238, Caguas, PR 00625
Licensure Skilled care. *Beds* 24. *Certified*
Medicaid; Medicare.

Guayamas

Santa Rosa Extended Care Facility
PO Box 988, Guayamas, PR 00654
Licensure Acute. *Beds* 47. *Certified* Medicaid;
Medicare.

Hato Rey

Auxilio Mutuo Hospital
Ponce de Leon Ave, Stop 37, Hato Rey, PR
00919
Licensure Skilled care. *Beds* 66. *Certified*
Medicaid; Medicare.

Humacao

Ryder Memorial Skilled Nursing Facility
Call Box 859, Humacao, PR 00661
(809) 852-0768
Admin Saturnino Pena Flores.
Medical Dir Dr Jose Rafael Alvarez.
Licensure Skilled care; Retirement. *Beds* SNF
40. *Certified* Medicare.
Owner Nonprofit organization/foundation.
Admissions Requirements Medical
examination; Physician's request.
Staff Physicians 1 (ft); RNs 8 (ft), 2 (pt);
LPNs 15 (ft); Physical therapists 1 (ft), 1
(pt); Occupational therapists 1 (ft); Speech
therapists 1 (pt); Activities coordinators 1
(ft); Dietitians 1 (ft); Podiatrists 1 (pt);
Dentists 1 (pt).
Languages Spanish.
Affiliation Church of Christ.
Facilities Dining room; Physical therapy
room; Activities room; Chapel; Crafts room;
Laundry room; Library.
Activities Arts & crafts; Cards; Games;
Reading groups; Prayer groups; Movies;
Dances/Social/Cultural gatherings; Educative
conferences.

VIRGIN ISLANDS

Christiansted

Charles Harwood Memorial Hospital—Skilled Nursing Unit
Estate Orange Grove, Christiansted, VI 00820
Licensure Skilled care. *Beds* 115. *Certified* Medicaid; Medicare.
Owner Publicly owned.

Saint Thomas

Knud Hansen Memorial Hospital
Hospital Ln, Saint Thomas, VI 00801
Licensure Skilled care. *Beds* 201. *Certified* Medicaid; Medicare.
Owner Publicly owned.

AFFILIATION INDEX

ALABAMA

Baptist
Baptist Home for Senior Citizens Inc, Cook Springs, AL
Eufaula Geriatric Center, Eufaula, AL

Episcopal
St Martin's-in-the-Pines, Birmingham, AL

Methodist
Methodist Home for the Aging, Birmingham, AL
Wesley Manor Methodist Home for the Aging, Dothan, AL

Presbyterian
John Knox Manor Inc II, Montgomery, AL

Roman Catholic
Father Purcell Memorial Exceptional Children's Center, Montgomery, AL
Father Walter Memorial Child Care Center, Montgomery, AL
Mercy Medical, Daphne, AL
Resurrection Catholic Nursing Home, Marbury, AL

ALASKA

Lutheran
Heritage Place, Soldotna, AK
Kodiak Island Hospital, Kodiak, AK

Roman Catholic
Our Lady of Compassion Care Center, Anchorage, AK

ARIZONA

Baptist
Orangewood Health Facility—American Baptist Estates, Phoenix, AZ

Jewish
Handmaker Jewish Geriatric Center, Tucson, AZ
Kivel Care Center, Phoenix, AZ
Phoenix Jewish Care Center, Phoenix, AZ

Lutheran
Good Shepherd Retirement Center, Peoria, AZ
Prescott Samaritan Village, Prescott, AZ
Wooddale Health Centre, Sun City, AZ

Order of Eastern Star
Arizona Eastern Star Home, Phoenix, AZ

Roman Catholic
Carondelet Holy Cross Hospital & Geriatric Center, Nogales, AZ
Crestview Convalescent Lodge, Phoenix, AZ
St Joseph's Care Center, Phoenix, AZ
Villa Maria, Tucson, AZ

Seventh-Day Adventist
Pueblo Norte Nursing Center, Show Low, AZ

Volunteers of America
Westchester Care Center, Tempe, AZ

ARKANSAS

Baptist
Longmeadow Nursing Home of Malvern, Malvern, AR

Lutheran
Good Samaritan Cedar Lodge, Hot Springs Village, AR

Mennonite
Hillcrest Home, Harrison, AR
Hudson Memorial Nursing Home, El Dorado, AR

Methodist
Methodist Nursing Home Inc, Fort Smith, AR

Presbyterian
Presbyterian Village Health Care Center, Little Rock, AR

Roman Catholic
Pinewood Nursing Home, Waldron, AR

CALIFORNIA

Baptist
Piedmont Gardens Health Facility, Oakland, CA
Pilgrim Haven Health Facility, Los Altos, CA
Plymouth Village, Redlands, CA
Rosewood Health Facility, Bakersfield, CA
Valle Verde Health Facility, Santa Barbara, CA

Christian Reformed
Artesia Christian Home Inc, Artesia, CA

Church of Christ
Mt San Antonio Gardens, Pomona, CA
Plymouth Tower, Riverside, CA
Sunset Haven Health Center, Cherry Valley, CA

Church of God
Grace Nursing Home Inc, Livingston, CA

Congregational
Carmel Valley Manor, Carmel, CA

Disciples of Christ
Bethany Convalescent Hospital, San Jose, CA
Bethesda Convalescent Center, Los Gatos, CA
California Christian Home, Rosemead, CA

Dutch Reformed
Inland Christian Home Inc, Ontario, CA

Episcopal
Canterbury, Rancho Palos Verdes, CA
Canterbury Woods, Pacific Grove, CA
Home for the Aged of the Protestant Episcopal Church, Alhambra, CA
Los Gatos Meadows Geriatric Hospital, Los Gatos, CA

St Paul's Health Care Center, San Diego, CA
St Paul's Towers, Oakland, CA

Evangelical Covenant Church
Brandel Manor, Turlock, CA
Mt Miguel Covenant Village, Spring Valley, CA
Samarkand Health Center, Santa Barbara, CA

Jewish
Beverly Palms Rehabilitation Hospital, Los Angeles, CA
Hebrew Home for Aged Disabled, San Francisco, CA
Home for Jewish Parents, Oakland, CA
San Diego Hebrew Home for the Aged, San Diego, CA

Lutheran
Lutheran Health Facility, Alhambra, CA
Lutheran Health Facility of Anaheim, Anaheim, CA
Lutheran Health Facility of Carlsbad, Carlsbad, CA
St Luke Manor, Fortuna, CA
Salem Lutheran Home Skilled Nursing Facility, Oakland, CA
Solheim Lutheran Home, Los Angeles, CA
Southland Geriatric Center, Norwalk, CA
Sunny View Manor, Cupertino, CA

Mennonite
Pleasant View Manor, Reedley, CA
Sierra View Homes Inc, Reedley, CA

Methodist
Lake Park Retirement Residence, Oakland, CA
Pacific Grove Convalescent Hospital, Pacific Grove, CA

Order of Eastern Star
Eastern Star Home, Los Angeles, CA

Presbyterian
Buena Vista Manor, Duarte, CA
Casa Verdugo Convalescent Lodge, Glendale, CA
Monte Vista Grove, Pasadena, CA
Westminster Gardens, Duarte, CA
White Sands of La Jolla, La Jolla, CA

Reorganized Church of Jesus Christ of Latter-Day Saints
Pacific Haven Convalescent Home, Garden Grove, CA

Roman Catholic
Ave Maria Convalescent Hospital, Monterey, CA
Franciscan Convalescent Hospital, Merced, CA
High Valley Lodge, Sunland, CA
Lassen Community Skilled Nursing Facility, Susanville, CA
Little Sisters of the Poor, San Pedro, CA
Marian Extended Care Center, Santa Maria, CA
Marycrest Manor, Culver City, CA

Mercy Rehabilitation & Care Center, San Diego, CA
Nazareth House, San Diego, CA
Nazareth House, Fresno, CA
Nazareth House, Los Angeles, CA
Our Lady of Fatima Villa, Saratoga, CA
St Annes Home, San Francisco, CA
St Elizabeth Toluca Lake Convalescent Hospital, North Hollywood, CA
St John of God Nursing Hospital, Los Angeles, CA
St Joseph Medical Center Pavilion, Burbank, CA
St Joseph's Convalescent Hospital, Ojai, CA
St Theresa Convalescent Hospital, Pico Rivera, CA
Valley Manor Convalescent Hospital, North Hollywood, CA

Russian Orthodox
St John Kronstadt Convalescent Center, Castro Valley, CA

Seventh-Day Adventist
Adventist Convalescent Hospital, Glendora, CA
Paradise Valley Health Care Center, National City, CA
Ventura Estates Health Manor, Newbury Park, CA

Society of Friends
Quaker Gardens, Stanton, CA

United Church of Christ
Bixby Knolls Towers, Long Beach, CA

United Methodist
Prather Methodist Memorial Home, Alameda, CA

Volunteers of America
Imperial Manor, Imperial, CA

COLORADO

Baptist
Mountain Vista Nursing Home, Wheat Ridge, CO
Park Avenue Baptist Home, Denver, CO
Stovall Care Center, Denver, CO

Independent Order of Odd Fellows & Rebekahs
Hildebrand Care Center, Canon City, CO

Jewish
Beth Israel Health Care Center, Denver, CO

Lutheran
Boulder Good Samaritan Health Care Center, Boulder, CO
Eben Ezer Lutheran Care Center, Brush, CO
Fort Collins Good Samaritan Retirement Village, Fort Collins, CO
Good Shepard Lutheran Home of the West, Littleton, CO
Hampton Drive, Colorado Springs, CO
Hilltop Nursing Home & Community Clinic, Cripple Creek, CO
Loveland Good Samaritan Village, Loveland, CO
Simla Good Samaritan Center, Simla, CO

Mennonite
Arkansas Valley Regional Medical Center Nursing Care Center, La Junta, CO

Reformed Church
Christian Living Campus—University Hills, Denver, CO

Roman Catholic
Ivy Nursing Center, Denver, CO
St Francis Nursing Center, Colorado Springs, CO
St Joseph Manor, Florence, CO
St Joseph's Hospital & Nursing Home of Del Norte Inc, Del Norte, CO

St Thomas More Hospital & Progressive Care Center, Canon City, CO

Seventh-Day Adventist
Asbury Circle Living Center, Denver, CO
Eden Valley Nursing Home, Loveland, CO

United Methodist
Frasier Meadows Manor Health Care Center, Boulder, CO

CONNECTICUT

Baptist
Elim Park Baptist Home Inc, Cheshire, CT
Evangelical Baptist Home, Ashford, CT
Pierce Memorial Baptist Home Inc, Brooklyn, CT

Congregational
Miller Memorial Community—Edward Pavilion/Caroline Hall, Meriden, CT
Noble Building, Hartford, CT

Evangelical Covenant Church
Pilgrim Manor, Cromwell, CT

Independent Order of Odd Fellows & Rebekahs
Fairview, Groton, CT

Jewish
Hebrew Home & Hospital, Hartford, CT
Jewish Home for the Aged, New Haven, CT
Jewish Home for the Elderly of Fairfield County, Fairfield, CT

Lutheran
Lutheran Home of Middletown Inc, Middletown, CT
Lutheran Home of Southbury, Southbury, CT

Masons
Ashlar of Newtown, A Masonic Home, Newtown, CT
Masonic Home & Hospital, Wallingford, CT

Roman Catholic
Matulaitis Nursing Home, Putnam, CT
Mercyknoll Inc, West Hartford, CT
Notre Dame Convalescent Home Inc, Norwalk, CT
Rose Manor, Waterbury, CT
St Elizabeth Health Center, East Hartford, CT
St Joseph's Manor, Trumbull, CT
St Joseph's Residence, Enfield, CT
St Mary Home, West Hartford, CT
St Regis Health Center, New Haven, CT
Waterbury Extended Care Facility Inc, Watertown, CT

Salvation Army
Hughes Convalescent Inc, West Hartford, CT

United Methodist
United Methodist Convalescent Homes of Connecticut Inc, Shelton, CT

DELAWARE

Episcopal
Episcopal Church Home, Hockessin, DE

Jewish
Milton & Hattie Kutz Home, Wilmington, DE

Masons
Masonic Home, Wilmington, DE

Mennonite
Country Rest Home, Greenwood, DE

Methodist
Cokesbury Village, Hockessin, DE
Methodist Country House, Wilmington, DE
Methodist Manor House, Seaford, DE

Presbyterian
Westminster Village Health Center, Dover, DE

DISTRICT OF COLUMBIA

Baptist
Thomas House, Washington, DC

Masons
Medlantic Manor at Lamond—Riggs, Washington, DC

Methodist
Methodist Home of DC, Washington, DC

Presbyterian
Presbyterian Home of DC, Washington, DC

FLORIDA

Baptist
Florida Baptist Retirement Center Nursing Facility, Vero Beach, FL
Palm Shores Retirement Center, Saint Petersburg, FL

Christian & Missionary Alliance Foundation
Alliance Nursing Center, Deland, FL
Pavilion at Shell Point Village, Fort Myers, FL

Christian Science
Daystar Inc, Fort Lauderdale, FL

Church of Christ
Plymouth Harbor Inc, Sarasota, FL

Church of the Brethren
Palms Health Care Center, Sebring, FL

Disciples of Christ
Florida Christian Health Center, Jacksonville, FL

Episcopal
William L Hargrave Health Center, Davenport, FL
Suncoast Manor, Saint Petersburg, FL

Evangelical Lutheran
Fair Havens Center, Miami Springs, FL

Jewish
Aviva Manor, Lauderdale Lakes, FL
Hebrew Home for the Aged—North Dade, North Miami Beach, FL
King David Center at Palm Beach, West Palm Beach, FL
Menorah Manor, Saint Petersburg, FL
Miami Beach Hebrew Home for the Aged, Miami Beach, FL
Miami Jewish Home for the Aged at Douglas Gardens, Miami, FL
River Garden Hebrew Home for the Aged, Jacksonville, FL

Lutheran
Daytona Beach Olds Hall Good Samaritan Nursing Center, Daytona Beach, FL
Fair Havens Center, Miami Springs, FL
Kissimmee Good Samaritan Nursing Center, Kissimmee, FL
Lutheran Haven, Oviedo, FL
Olds Hall Good Samaritan Center, Daytona Beach, FL
Orlando Lutheran Towers, Orlando, FL
St Mark Village Inc, Palm Harbor, FL
Southwest Florida Retirement Center, Venice, FL
Swanholm Nursing & Rehabilitation Center, Saint Petersburg, FL

Masons
Masonic Home of Florida, Saint Petersburg, FL

Mennonite
Sunnyside Nursing Home, Sarasota, FL

Methodist
Sunny Shores Health Center, Saint Petersburg, FL

Wesley Manor Retirement Village, Jacksonville, FL

Presbyterian
Bay Village of Sarasota, Sarasota, FL
Bradenton Manor, Bradenton, FL
Johnson Health Center, Lakeland, FL
Leisure Manor, Saint Petersburg, FL
Osceola Inn, Clearwater, FL
Presbyterian Nursing Center, Lakeland, FL
Westminster Oaks Health Center, Tallahassee, FL
Westminster Towers, Orlando, FL
Winter Park Towers, Winter Park, FL

Roman Catholic
All Saints Catholic Nursing Home, Jacksonville, FL
Bon Secours Hospital/Villa Maria Nursing Center, North Miami, FL
Florida Manor, Orlando, FL
Haven of Our Lady of Peace, Pensacola, FL
Lourdes-Noreen McKeen Residence for Geriatric Care Inc, West Palm Beach, FL
Maria Manor Health Care, Saint Petersburg, FL
St Catherine Laboure Manor, Jacksonville, FL
St John's Health Care Center, Lauderdale Lakes, FL
St Jude Manor Nursing Home, Jacksonville, FL
Villa Maria Nursing & Rehabilitation Center Inc, North Miami, FL

Royal Order of Moose
Moosehaven Health Center, Orange Park, FL

Seventh-Day Adventist
Florida Living Nursing Center, Apopka, FL
Lake Alfred Restorium, Lake Alfred, FL
Lake Wales Convalescent Center, Lake Wales, FL

United Methodist
Asbury Towers, Bradenton, FL

GEORGIA

Baptist
Banks-Jackson-Commerce Nursing Home, Commerce, GA
Baptist Village Inc, Waycross, GA
Bethany Home for Men, Millen, GA
Harvest Heights, Decatur, GA

Eastern Star
Ware Avenue Personal Care Home, East Point, GA

Jewish
Jewish Home, Atlanta, GA

Methodist
Budd Terrace Intermediate Care Home, Atlanta, GA
Magnolia Manor Methodist Nursing Care, Americus, GA
Wesley Woods Health Center, Atlanta, GA

Presbyterian
Presbyterian Home Inc, Quitman, GA

Roman Catholic
Our Lady of Perpetual Help, Atlanta, GA

Seventh-Day Adventist
Lakeland Villa Convalescent Center, Lakeland, GA

HAWAII

Church of Christ
Arcadia, Honolulu, HI

Lutheran
Pohai Nani Care Center, Kaneohe, HI

Roman Catholic
St Francis Hospital, Honolulu, HI

IDAHO

Lutheran
Boise Samaritan Village, Boise, ID
Good Samaritan Center, Idaho Falls, ID
Good Samaritan Village, Moscow, ID
Silver Wood Good Samaritan, Silverton, ID

Roman Catholic
St Benedict's Family Medical Center Inc, Jerome, ID

ILLINOIS

Apostolic Christian
Apostolic Christian Home, Roanoke, IL
Apostolic Christian Resthaven, Elgin, IL
Apostolic Christian Restmor Inc, Morton, IL
Apostolic Morton, Morton, IL
Apostolic Peoria, Peoria, IL
Eureka Apostolic Christian Home, Eureka, IL
Fairview Haven Inc, Fairbury, IL

Assembly of God
Parkway Terrace Nursing Home, Wheaton, IL

Baha'i Faith
Baha'i Home Inc, Wilmette, IL

Baptist
Baptist Retirement Home, Maywood, IL
Central Baptist Home for the Aged, Norridge, IL
Country Care of Litchfield, Litchfield, IL
Fairview Baptist Home, Downers Grove, IL
General Baptist Nursing Home, Mount Carmel, IL

Christian Reformed
Rest Haven South Skilled Nursing Center, South Holland, IL
Rest Haven West Skilled Nursing Facility, Downers Grove, IL

Christian Science
Hill Top, Lake Bluff, IL

Church of Christ
Beulah Land Christian Home, Flanagan, IL
Eden Village Care Center, Edwardsville, IL
Fair Havens Christian Home, Decatur, IL
Faith Countryside Homes, Highland, IL
Good Samaritan Home of Quincy, Quincy, IL
Hitz Memorial Home, Alhambra, IL
Lewis Memorial Christian Village, Springfield, IL
Peotone Bensenville Home, Peotone, IL
Pine View Care Center, Saint Charles, IL
Plymouth Place Inc, La Grange Park, IL
Washington Christian Village, Washington, IL

Church of the Brethren
Pinecrest Manor, Mount Morris, IL

Evangelical Covenant Church
Covenant Health Care Center Inc, Batavia, IL
Covenant Health Care Center Inc, Northbrook, IL
Covenant Home, Batavia, IL
Covenant Home of Chicago, Chicago, IL
Michealsen Health Center, Batavia, IL

Evangelical Free Church
Fairhaven Christian Home, Rockford, IL

Franciscan Sisters of Chicago
Mother Theresa Home, Lemont, IL

Free Methodist
Sunset Manor, Woodstock, IL

Independent Order of Odd Fellows & Rebekahs
Odd Fellow-Rebekah Home, Mattoon, IL

Jewish
Jewish Home for the Blind, Chicago, IL
Jewish Peoples Convalescent Home, Chicago, IL
Lieberman Geriatric Health Centre, Skokie, IL

Selfhelp Home for the Aged, Chicago, IL

King's Daughters & Sons
Friendship Manor, Rock Island, IL

Lutheran
Bethesda Home & Retirement Center, Chicago, IL
Bethesda Lutheran Home, Springfield, IL
Carroll County Good Samaritan Center, Mount Carroll, IL
Country Health Inc, Gifford, IL
Good Samaritan Home of Flanagan, Flanagan, IL
Hoopeston Regional Nursing Home, Hoopeston, IL
Lutheran Care Center, Altamont, IL
Lutheran Home, Peoria, IL
Lutheran Home & Services for the Aged, Arlington Heights, IL
Mendota Lutheran Home, Mendota, IL
Metropolis Good Samaritan Home, Metropolis, IL
Moorings Health Center, Arlington Heights, IL
P A Peterson Home for the Aging, Rockford, IL
Pleasant View Luther Home, Ottawa, IL
Prairieview Lutheran Home, Danforth, IL
St Matthew Lutheran Home, Park Ridge, IL
Salem Village, Joliet, IL

Masons
Warren N Barr Pavilion/Illinois Masonic Medical Center, Chicago, IL
Illinois Knights Templar Home for Aged, Paxton, IL
Illinois Masonic Home, Sullivan, IL

Mennonite
Maple Lawn Health Center, Eureka, IL
Meadows Mennonite Home, Chenoa, IL

Methodist
Bethany Terrace Retirement & Nursing Home, Morton Grove, IL
Evenglow Lodge, Pontiac, IL
Methodist Home, Chicago, IL
North Rockford Convalescent Home, Rockford, IL
Oak Crest, De Kalb, IL
United Methodist Village, Lawrenceville, IL
Wesley Village U M C Health Care Center, Macomb, IL
Willows Health Center, Rockford, IL

Order of Eastern Star
Eastern Star Home, Macon, IL

Presbyterian
Illinois Presbyterian Home, Springfield, IL
Presbyterian Home, Evanston, IL
Titus Memorial Presbyterian Home, Sullivan, IL

Roman Catholic
Addolorata Villa, Wheeling, IL
Alvernia Manor, Lemont, IL
Brother James Court, Springfield, IL
Dammert Geriatric Center, Belleville, IL
Franciscan Nursing Home, Joliet, IL
Holy Family Health Center, Des Plaines, IL
Holy Family Villa, Lemont, IL
Little Sisters of the Poor, Chicago, IL
Maria Linden, Rockford, IL
McAuley Manor, Aurora, IL
A Merkle C Knipprath Nursing Home, Clifton, IL
Misericordia Home, Chicago, IL
Mt St Joseph, Lake Zurich, IL
Nazarethville, Des Plaines, IL
Our Lady of Angels Retirement Home, Joliet, IL
Our Lady of Victory, Bourbonnais, IL
Pershing Convalescent Home Inc, Stickney, IL
Rosary Hill Home, Justice, IL
Rose Marian Hall, Chicago, IL
St Anthonys Continuing Care Center, Rock Island, IL
St Benedict Home for Aged, Niles, IL

St Francis Extended Care Center, Evanston, IL
St Joseph Home of Chicago Inc, Chicago, IL
St Joseph's Home for the Elderly, Palatine, IL
St Joseph's Home of Peoria, Peoria, IL
St Joseph's Home of Springfield, Springfield, IL
St Patrick's Residence, Joliet, IL
Villa St Cyril—Home For Aged, Highland Park, IL
Villa Scalabrini, Northlake, IL

Seventh-Day Adventist
Applewood Living Center, Matteson, IL
Carington Living Center, Bloomingdale, IL
Colonial Hall Nursing Home, Princeton, IL
Crown Manor Living Center, Zion, IL
Douglas Living Center, Mattoon, IL
Elmwood Nursing Home, Aurora, IL
Lakewood Nursing Home, Plainfield, IL
Notre Dame Hills Living Center, Belleville, IL
Rivershores Living Center, Marseilles, IL
Snow Valley Living Center, Lisle, IL
White Pines Living Center, Oregon, IL

Slovak American Charitable Association
Rolling Hills Manor, Zion, IL

United Church of Christ
Anchorage, Bensenville, IL
Anchorage of Beecher, Beecher, IL
Peace Memorial Home, Evergreen Park, IL
Pine Acres Care Center, De Kalb, IL
St Pauls House/Grace Convalescent Home, Chicago, IL

United Methodist
Sunset Home of the United Methodist Church, Quincy, IL

INDIANA

Apostolic Christian
Parkview Haven, Francesville, IN

Baptist
St Paul Baptist Church Home for the Aged, Indianapolis, IN

Church of Christ
Evansville Protestant Home Inc, Evansville, IN
Golden Years Homestead Inc, Fort Wayne, IN
Maple Manor Christian Home Inc—Adult Division, Sellersburg, IN

Church of the Brethren
Brethren's Home of Indiana Inc, Flora, IN
Grace Village Health Care Facility, Winona Lake, IN
Timbercrest—Church of the Brethren Home Inc, North Manchester, IN

Civitan
Columbia Nursing Plaza Inc, Evansville, IN

Disciples of Christ
Flinn Memorial Home, Marion, IN
Kennedy Living Center, Martinsville, IN

Independent Order of Odd Fellows & Rebekahs
Odd Fellows Home, Greensburg, IN

Jewish
Hooverwood, Indianapolis, IN

Knights of Pythias
Indiana Pythian Home, Lafayette, IN

Lutheran
Lutheran Community Home Inc, Seymour, IN
Lutheran Home of Northwest Indiana Inc, Crown Point, IN
Lutheran Homes Inc, Fort Wayne, IN
Mulberry Lutheran Home, Mulberry, IN
North Wood Good Samaritan Center, Jasper, IN
Shakamak Good Samaritan Center, Jasonville, IN

Shepherd of the Hill, Kendallville, IN

Mennonite
Greencroft Nursing Center, Goshen, IN
Swiss Village Inc, Berne, IN

Methodist
Asbury Towers, Greencastle, IN
Hamilton Grove, New Carlisle, IN
United Methodist Memorial Home, Warren, IN
Wesley Manor, Frankfort, IN

Missionary Church
Hubbard Hill Estates Inc, Elkhart, IN

Presbyterian
Peabody Retirement Community, North Manchester, IN

Roman Catholic
Little Company of Mary Health Facility Inc, San Pierre, IN
Providence Retirement Home, New Albany, IN
Regina Continuing Care Center, Evansville, IN
Sacred Heart Home, Avilla, IN
St Anne Home, Fort Wayne, IN
St Anthony Health Care, Lafayette, IN
St Anthony Home, Crown Point, IN
St Augustine Home for the Aged, Indianapolis, IN
St Elizabeth Healthcare Center, Delphi, IN
St Elizabeth Hospital Medical Center Skilled Nursing Unit, Lafayette, IN
St John's Home for the Aged, Evansville, IN
St Joseph's Care Center—Morningside, South Bend, IN
St Joseph's Care Center West, South Bend, IN
St Paul Hermitage, Beech Grove, IN

Seventh-Day Adventist
Bethel Manor, Evansville, IN
Prairie Village Living Center, Washington, IN
River Valley Living Center, Madison, IN
Scott Villa Living Center, Scottsburg, IN
Swiss Villa Living Center, Vevay, IN

Society of Friends
Friends Fellowship Community Inc, Richmond, IN

United Church of Christ
Good Samaritan Home Inc, Evansville, IN

United Methodist
Franklin United Methodist Home, Franklin, IN

IOWA

Baptist
Baptist Memorial Home, Harlan, IA
Crest Group Home, Ottumwa, IA
Northcrest Retirement Community, Ames, IA
Salsbury Baptist Home, Charles City, IA

Disciples of Christ
Ramsey Home, Des Moines, IA

Evangelical Free Church
Evangelical Free Church Home, Boone, IA

Evangelical Lutheran
Good Neighbor Home, Manchester, IA

Independent Order of Odd Fellows & Rebekahs
I O O F Home, Mason City, IA

Jewish
Iowa Jewish Senior Life Center, Des Moines, IA

Lutheran
Bartel's Lutheran Home, Waverly, IA
Bethany Lutheran Home, Council Bluffs, IA
Bethany Manor, Story City, IA
Cedar Falls Lutheran Home, Cedar Falls, IA

Davenport Lutheran Home, Davenport, IA
Eventide Lutheran Home, Denison, IA
George Good Samaritan Center, George, IA
Good Samaritan Center, Postville, IA
Good Samaritan Center, Algona, IA
Good Samaritan Center, Ottumwa, IA
Good Samaritan Center, Forest City, IA
Aase Haugen Homes Inc, Decorah, IA
Holstein Good Samaritan Center, Holstein, IA
Lakeside Lutheran Home, Emmetsburg, IA
Luther Manor, Dubuque, IA
Luther Park Health Center, Des Moines, IA
Lutheran Home, Strawberry Point, IA
Lutheran Home, Muscatine, IA
Lutheran Home for the Aged, Vinton, IA
Lutheran Retirement Home Inc, Northwood, IA
Manson Good Samaritan, Manson, IA
Perry Lutheran Home, Perry, IA
St Luke's Lutheran Home, Spencer, IA
Salem Lutheran Home, Elk Horn, IA
Van Buren Good Samaritan Center, Keosauqua, IA
West Union Good Samaritan Center, West Union, IA

Masons
Iowa Masonic Nursing Home, Bettendorf, IA
Memorial Masonic Home, Perry, IA
Scottish Rite Park, Des Moines, IA

Mennonite
Parkview Home, Wayland, IA
Pleasantview Home, Kalona, IA

Methodist
Halcyon House, Washington, IA
Heritage House, Atlantic, IA
Meth-Wick Manor, Cedar Rapids, IA
Methodist Manor, Storm Lake, IA
St Luke's Methodist Hospital, Cedar Rapids, IA
Wesley Acres, Des Moines, IA
Western Home, Cedar Falls, IA

Order of Eastern Star
M A Barthell Order of Eastern Star Home, Decorah, IA
Eastern Star Masonic Home, Boone, IA

Presbyterian
Bethany Home, Dubuque, IA
United Presbyterian Home, Ackley, IA
United Presbyterian Home, Washington, IA

Roman Catholic
Alverno Health Care Facility, Clinton, IA
Covenant Medical Center, Waterloo, IA
Bishop Drumm Care Center, Johnston, IA
Hallmar, Mercy Medical Center, Cedar Rapids, IA
Happy Siesta Nursing Home, Remsen, IA
Kahl Home for the Aged & Infirm, Davenport, IA
Marian Home, Fort Dodge, IA
Mercy Health Center Skilled Nursing Unit, Dubuque, IA
Oakcrest Manor & Skilled Nursing Unit—St Mary's Unit, Dyersville, IA
St Anthony Nursing Home, Carroll, IA
St Francis Continuing Care & Nursing Home Center, Burlington, IA
Stonehill Care Center, Dubuque, IA

United Church of Christ
Mayflower Home, Grinnell, IA

United Methodist
Friendship Haven Inc, Fort Dodge, IA

KANSAS

Apostolic Christian
Apostolic Christian Home, Sabetha, KS

Baptist
Homestead Health Center Inc, Wichita, KS
Sunset Nursing Center, Concordia, KS

Church of Christ
Christ Villa Nursing Center, Wichita, KS
Winfield Rest Haven Inc, Winfield, KS

Church of the Brethren
Cedars Inc, McPherson, KS

Congregational
Brewster Place, Topeka, KS

Independent Order of Odd Fellows & Rebekahs
Rebekah—Odd Fellow Care Home,
    Hutchinson, KS

Lutheran
Bethany Home Association, Lindsborg, KS
Cedar View Good Samaritan Center,
    Wellington, KS
Decatur County Good Samaritan Center,
    Oberlin, KS
Ellis Good Samaritan Center, Ellis, KS
Ellsworth Good Samaritan Center—Villa
    Hope, Ellsworth, KS
Ellsworth Good Samaritan Village—Villa
    Grace, Ellsworth, KS
Good Samaritan Center, Junction City, KS
Good Samaritan Village, Saint Francis, KS
Good Samaritan Village, Winfield, KS
Hays Good Samaritan Center, Hays, KS
Hutchinson Good Samaritan Center,
    Hutchinson, KS
Liberal Good Samaritan Center, Liberal, KS
Linn Community Nursing Home Inc, Linn,
    KS
Lutheran Home Inc, Herington, KS
Lyons Good Samaritan Center, Lyons, KS
Manor Nursing Home, Independence, KS
Minneapolis Good Samaritan Center,
    Minneapolis, KS
Olathe Good Samaritan Center, Olathe, KS
Parsons Good Samaritan Center, Parsons, KS
Rush County Nursing Home, LaCrosse, KS
Shiloh Manor of Canton Inc, Canton, KS
Trinity Lutheran Manor, Merriam, KS
Valley Vista Good Samaritan Center,
    Wamego, KS

Masons
Kansas Masonic Home, Wichita, KS

Mennonite
Bethel Home for Aged, Newton, KS
Bethel Home Inc, Montezuma, KS
Buhler Sunshine Home Inc, Buhler, KS
Garden Valley Retirement Village, Garden
    City, KS
Lone Tree Lodge, Meade, KS
Memorial Home for the Aged, Moundridge,
    KS
Mennonite Friendship Manor Inc, South
    Hutchinson, KS
Moundridge Manor, Moundridge, KS
Parkside Homes Inc, Hillsboro, KS
Schowalter Villa, Hesston, KS

Methodist
Aldersgate Village Health Unit, Topeka, KS
Trinity Manor Adult Care Home, Dodge City,
    KS
United Methodist Home, Topeka, KS
Wesley Towers Inc, Hutchinson, KS

Presbyterian
Arkansas City Presbyterian Manor, Arkansas
    City, KS
Clay Center Presbyterian Manor, Clay Center,
    KS
Emporia Presbyterian Manor Inc, Emporia,
    KS
Hutchinson Heights, Hutchinson, KS
Kansas City Presbyterian Manor, Kansas City,
    KS
Lawrence Presbyterian Manor, Lawrence, KS
Newton Presbyterian Manor, Newton, KS
Parsons Presbyterian Manor, Parsons, KS
Salina Presbyterian Manor, Salina, KS
Sterling Presbyterian Manor, Sterling, KS
Topeka Presbyterian Manor Inc, Topeka, KS
Wichita Presbyterian Manor, Wichita, KS

Roman Catholic
Catholic Care Center, Wichita, KS
Mt Joseph Inc, Concordia, KS
Providence Place Inc, Kansas City, KS
St John's of Hays, Hays, KS
St Johns Rest Home, Victoria, KS
St Joseph Care Center, Kansas City, KS
Villa Maria Inc, Mulvane, KS

Seventh-Day Adventist
Overland Park Manor, Overland Park, KS
Paradise Valley Living Center, Belle Plaine,
    KS

United Methodist
Friendly Acres Inc, Newton, KS

KENTUCKY

Baptist
Baptist Convalescent Center, Newport, KY
Baptist Home East, Louisville, KY
Mary Harding Home, Owensboro, KY
Ruby's Rest Home, Middlesboro, KY

Church of Christ
Sayre Christian Village Nursing Home,
    Lexington, KY

Disciples of Christ
Christian Health Center, Louisville, KY

Episcopal
Episcopal Church Home, Louisville, KY

King's Daughters & Sons
Kings Daughters & Sons Home, Louisville,
    KY
King's Daughters & Sons Home for Aged Men
    & Women, Ashland, KY

Lutheran
Cedar Lake Lodge, LaGrange, KY
Louisville Lutheran Home, Jeffersontown, KY

Masons
Masonic Widows & Orphans Home,
    Louisville, KY
Old Masons' Home of Kentucky, Shelbyville,
    KY

Methodist
Lewis Memorial Methodist Home, Franklin,
    KY
Wesley Manor Nursing Center & Retirement
    Community, Louisville, KY

Order of Eastern Star
Eastern Star Home in Kentucky, Louisville,
    KY

Presbyterian
Rose Anna Hughes Presbyterian Home,
    Louisville, KY
Westminster Terrace—Rose Anna Hughes
    Campus, Louisville, KY

Roman Catholic
Carmel Home, Owensboro, KY
Carmel Manor, Fort Thomas, KY
Loretto Motherhouse Infirmary, Nerinx, KY
Marian Home—Ursuline Sisters, Louisville,
    KY
Nazareth Home, Louisville, KY
Sacred Heart Home, Louisville, KY
Sansbury Memorial Infirmary, Saint
    Catherine, KY
Taylor Manor Nursing Home, Versailles, KY

Seventh-Day Adventist
Friendship Manor Nursing Home, Pewee
    Valley, KY
Memorial Hospital Inc—SNF, Manchester,
    KY
Mills Manor, Mayfield, KY
Pinecrest Manor, Hopkinsville, KY

LOUISIANA

Assembly of God
Oak Park Care Center, Lake Charles, LA

Baptist
Arcadia Baptist Home, Arcadia, LA
Madison Parish Home for the Aged, Tallulah,
    LA

Episcopal
St James Place Nursing Care Center, Baton
    Rouge, LA

Jewish
Willow Wood New Orleans Home for Jewish
    Aged, New Orleans, LA

Lutheran
Lutheran Home of New Orleans, New
    Orleans, LA

Methodist
Lafon United Methodist Nursing Home, New
    Orleans, LA

Presbyterian
Evergreen Manor, Minden, LA
Presbyterian Village of Homer Inc, Homer,
    LA

Roman Catholic
Bethany MHS Health Care Center, Lafayette,
    LA
Consolata Home, New Iberia, LA
Lafon Nursing Home of the Holy Family,
    New Orleans, LA
Martin dePorres Nursing Home Inc, Lake
    Charles, LA
Mary Joseph Residence—Little Sisters of the
    Poor, New Orleans, LA
Our Lady of Prompt Succor Nursing Home,
    Opelousas, LA
St Joseph's Home for Infirm & Aged, Monroe,
    LA
St Margaret's Daughters Nursing Home, New
    Orleans, LA
St Mary's Residential Training School,
    Alexandria, LA

MAINE

Jewish
Jewish Home for the Aged, Portland, ME

Latter Day Saints
Resthaven Nursing Home, Jonesport, ME

Roman Catholic
D'Youville Pavilion, Lewiston, ME
Mt St Joseph Nursing Home, Waterville, ME
St Andre Health Care Facility, Biddeford, ME
St Casimir Health Care Facility, Lewiston, ME
St Joseph Nursing Home, Upper Frenchville,
    ME
St Joseph's Manor, Portland, ME

Seventh-Day Adventist
Ledgeview Nursing Home, West Paris, ME

MARYLAND

Baptist
Maryland Baptist Aged Home, Baltimore, MD

Episcopal
Uplands Home for Church Women,
    Baltimore, MD

Jewish
Hebrew Home of Greater Washington,
    Rockville, MD
Hurwitz House, Baltimore, MD
Jewish Convalescent Center—Scotts Level,
    Baltimore, MD
Levindale Hebrew Geriatric Center & Hospital
    Inc, Baltimore, MD

Milford Manor Nursing Home, Baltimore, MD
Pikesville Nursing & Convalescent Center, Pikesville, MD

Lutheran
Augsburg Lutheran Home of Maryland, Pikesville, MD
Brighton Manor Nursing & Geriatric Center, Baltimore, MD
Deaton Hospital & Medical Center, Baltimore, MD
Frostburg Village of Allegany County, Frostburg, MD
National Lutheran Home for the Aged, Rockville, MD
Ravenwood Lutheran Village, Hagerstown, MD
Roland Park Place Inc, Baltimore, MD
St Luke Lutheran Home, Baltimore, MD

Masons
Maryland Masonic Homes, Cockeysville, MD

Mennonite
Goodwill Mennonite Home Inc, Grantsville, MD

Roman Catholic
Bon Secours Extended Care, Ellicott City, MD
Cardinal Shehan Center, Towson, MD
Carroll Manor Inc, Hyattsville, MD
Jenkins Memorial Inc, Baltimore, MD
Stella Maris, Baltimore, MD
St Joseph's Nursing Home, Catonsville, MD
Villa Rosa Nursing Home, Mitchellville, MD

Seventh-Day Adventist
Shady Grove Adventist Nursing Center, Rockville, MD

Society of Friends
Broadmead, Cockeysville, MD
Friends Nursing Home Inc, Sandy Spring, MD

MASSACHUSETTS

Afro-American
Hurstdale Rest Home, Springfield, MA

Baptist
Baptist Home of Massachusetts, Newton, MA

Episcopal
Taber Street Nursing Home, New Bedford, MA

German Ladies Aid Society
Deutsches Altenheim Inc, Boston, MA

Hellenic Women's Benevolent Society
Hellenic Nursing Home for the Aged, Canton, MA

Independent Order of Odd Fellows & Rebekahs
Odd Fellows Home of Massachusetts, Worcester, MA

Jewish
Chelsea Jewish Nursing Home, Chelsea, MA
Fall River Jewish Home, Fall River, MA
Jewish Home for the Aged, Worcester, MA
Jewish Nursing Home of Western Massachusetts, Longmeadow, MA
Jewish Rehabilitation Center for Aged of the North Shore Inc, Swampscott, MA
New Bedford Jewish Convalescent Home, New Bedford, MA

Lutheran
Fair Havens Rest Home Inc, Middleborough, MA
Gronna Good Samaritan Center, Worcester, MA
Lutheran Home of Brockton Inc, Brockton, MA
Lutheran Home of Worcester Inc, Worcester, MA

Masons
Masonic Home, Charlton, MA

Methodist
Rivercrest Long-Term Care Facility, Concord, MA

Roman Catholic
Campion Residence & Renewal Center, Weston, MA
Catholic Memorial Home, Fall River, MA
D'Youville Manor Nursing Home, Lowell, MA
Harborview Manor—A Long-Term Care Facility, Dartmouth, MA
Rose Hawthorne Lathrop Home, Fall River, MA
Madonna Manor Nursing Home, North Attleboro, MA
Marian Manor, Boston, MA
Maristhill Nursing Home, Waltham, MA
MI Nursing & Restorative Center, Lawrence, MA
Mt St Vincent Home, Holyoke, MA
Notre Dame Long-Term Care Center, Worcester, MA
Our Lady's Haven, Fairhaven, MA
Sacred Heart Nursing Home, New Bedford, MA
St Francis Home, Worcester, MA
St Joseph's Manor, Boston, MA
St Patricks Manor Inc, Framingham, MA
Tower Hill Rest Home, Fitchburg, MA

Society of Friends
New England Friends Home, Hingham, MA

Unitarian Universalist
Doolittle Home Inc, Foxborough, MA

MICHIGAN

Apostolic Christian Church
Woodhaven of Livonia, Livonia, MI

Baptist
Inter-City Christian Manor, Allen Park, MI
Michigan Christian Home, Grand Rapids, MI

Christian Reformed
Holland Home—Raybrook Manor, Grand Rapids, MI

Church of Christ
Church of Christ Care Center, Mount Clemens, MI
Evangelical Home—Detroit, Detroit, MI

Episcopal
St Luke's Episcopal Church Home, Highland Park, MI

Evangelical Lutheran
Luther Haven, Detroit, MI

Independent Order of Odd Fellows & Rebekahs
Odd Fellow & Rebekah Home, Jackson, MI

Jewish
Jewish Home for Aged—Prentis Manor, Southfield, MI
Jewish Home for the Aged 2, Detroit, MI

Lutheran
Luther Home, Grand Rapids, MI
Luther Manor Nursing Home, Saginaw, MI
Martin Luther—Holt Home, Holt, MI
Martin Luther Memorial Home—South Haven, South Haven, MI
Martin Luther Memorial Home, South Lyon, MI
Martin Luther—Saginaw Home, Saginaw, MI
Lutheran Home, Frankenmuth, MI
Lutheran Home, Monroe, MI

Masons
Michigan Masonic Home, Alma, MI

Mennonite
Ausable Valley Home, Fairview, MI

Thurston Woods Village, Sturgis, MI

Presbyterian
Porter Hills Presbyterian Village, Grand Rapids, MI
Presbyterian Village East, New Baltimore, MI

Roman Catholic
Dowagiac Nursing Home, Dowagiac, MI
Grand Blanc Convalescent Center, Grand Blanc, MI
Lourdes Inc, Pontiac, MI
Marycrest Manor, Livonia, MI
Bishop Noa Home, Escanaba, MI
Our Lady of Mercy Convalescent Home, Hubbell, MI
River Forest Nursing Care Center, Three Rivers, MI
St Anthony Nursing Center, Warren, MI
St Francis Home, Saginaw, MI
St Jude Convalescent Center, Livonia, MI
St Lawrence Dimondale Center, Dimondale, MI
St Martin Deporres Nursing Home, Detroit, MI
Villa Elizabeth, Grand Rapids, MI

Royal Order of Moose
Whitehall Convalescent Home, Novi, MI

Seventh-Day Adventist
Riveridge Manor Inc, Niles, MI

United Church of Christ
Evangelical Home—Port Huron, Port Huron, MI
Pilgrim Manor, Grand Rapids, MI

United Methodist
Boulevard Temple United Methodist Retirement Home, Detroit, MI
Chelsea United Methodist Retirement Home, Chelsea, MI

MINNESOTA

Baptist
Maranatha Baptist Care Center, Brooklyn Center, MN
Thorne Crest Retirement Center, Albert Lea, MN
Winnebago Baptist Home, Winnebago, MN

Christian Science
Clifton House, Minneapolis, MN

Church of Christ
Christian Manor Nursing Home, Tracy, MN
St Lucas Convalescent & Geriatric Center, Faribault, MN
St Paul's Church Home Inc, Saint Paul, MN

Episcopal
Episcopal Church Home of Minnesota, Saint Paul, MN

Evangelical Covenant Church
Colonial Acres Health Care Center, Golden Valley, MN
Ebenezer Covenant Home, Buffalo, MN

Evangelical Free Church
Elim Home, Milaca, MN
Elim Home, Princeton, MN
Elim Home, Watertown, MN

Evangelical Lutheran
Bethany Good Samaritan Village, Brainerd, MN
Good Samaritan Center, Clearbrook, MN
Kelliher Good Samaritan, Kelliher, MN
Pioneer Home Inc, Fergus Falls, MN

Independent Order of Odd Fellows & Rebekahs
Minnesota Odd Fellows Home, Northfield, MN

Jewish
Minnesota Jewish Group Home II—Tikvah,
Saint Paul, MN
Shalom Home, Saint Paul, MN

Lutheran
Adams Group Home, Adams, MN
Albert Lea Good Samaritan Center, Albert
Lea, MN
Arlington Good Samaritan Center, Arlington,
MN
Augustana Home of Minneapolis,
Minneapolis, MN
Bethany Home, Alexandria, MN
Bethany Home, Litchfield, MN
Bethany Samaritan Heights, Rochester, MN
Bethesda Lutheran Care Center, Saint Paul,
MN
Board of Social Ministry, Saint Paul, MN
Brainerd Good Samaritan Center, Brainerd,
MN
Broen Memorial Home, Fergus Falls, MN
Mary J Brown Good Samaritan Center,
Luverne, MN
Clinton Good Samaritan Center, Clinton, MN
Crest View Lutheran Home, Columbia
Heights, MN
Ebenezer Hall, Minneapolis, MN
Ebenezer Ridges Geriatric Care Center,
Lakeville, MN
Ebenezer Society Luther & Field, Minneapolis,
MN
Elders' Home Inc, New York Mills, MN
Emmanuel Home, Litchfield, MN
Emmanuel Nursing Home, Detroit Lakes, MN
Eventide Lutheran Home, Moorhead, MN
Gethsemane Group Home, Virginia, MN
Glenwood Retirement Home Inc, Glenwood,
MN
Good Samaritan Center, Jackson, MN
Good Samaritan Center, Pelican Rapids, MN
Good Samaritan Center, East Grand Forks,
MN
Good Samaritan Village, Pipestone, MN
Good Shepherd Lutheran Home, Rushford,
MN
Good Shepherd Lutheran Home, Sauk Rapids,
MN
Halstad Lutheran Memorial Home, Halstad,
MN
Kenyon Sunset Home, Kenyon, MN
Lafayette Good Samaritan Center, Lafayette,
MN
Lakeshore Lutheran Home, Duluth, MN
Luther Haven Nursing Home, Montevideo,
MN
Martin Luther Manor, Bloomington, MN
Luther Memorial Home, Madelia, MN
Lutheran Home, Belle Plaine, MN
Lutheran Memorial Nursing Home, Twin
Valley, MN
Lutheran Retirement Home of Southern
Minnesota, Truman, MN
Lyngblomsten Care Center, Saint Paul, MN
Madison Lutheran Home, Madison, MN
Mankato Lutheran Home, Mankato, MN
Minnewaska Lutheran Home, Starbuck, MN
Mountain Lake Good Samaritan Village,
Mountain Lake, MN
Northern Pines Good Samaritan Center,
Blackduck, MN
Northfield Retirement Center, Northfield, MN
Paynesville Good Samaritan Home,
Paynesville, MN
Pelican Valley Health Center, Pelican Rapids,
MN
Pleasant View Good Samaritan Center, Saint
James, MN
Red Wing Group Home, Red Wing, MN
St John Lutheran Home, Springfield, MN
St Johns Lutheran Home, Albert Lea, MN
St Marks Lutheran Home, Austin, MN
St Olaf Residence, Minneapolis, MN
St Stephen Group Homes A & B,
Bloomington, MN
Seminary Memorial Home, Red Wing, MN
Sogge Good Samaritan Center, Windom, MN
Tuff Memorial Home, Hills, MN

Tweeten Lutheran Health Care Center, Spring
Grove, MN
Whispering Pines Good Samaritan Center,
Pine River, MN

Masonic, Eastern Star
Minnesota Masonic Home Care Center,
Minneapolis, MN

Methodist
Chapel View Inc, Hopkins, MN
Lakeview Methodist Health Care Center,
Fairmont, MN
Walker Methodist Health Center, Minneapolis,
MN

Moravian
Auburn Manor, Chaska, MN

Presbyterian
Johanna Shores, Arden Hills, MN
Langton Place, Saint Paul, MN
Outreach Minneapolis—Stevens Group Home,
Minneapolis, MN
Presbyterian Homes Johanna Shores, Saint
Paul, MN

Roman Catholic
Assumption Home, Cold Spring, MN
Divine Providence Community Home, Sleepy
Eye, MN
Divine Providence Hospital & Home,
Ivanhoe, MN
Health One St Mary's, Winsted, MN
Little Sisters of the Poor, Saint Paul, MN
Madonna Towers Inc, Rochester, MN
Mille Lacs Hospital & Home, Onamia, MN
Mother of Mercy Nursing Home, Albany, MN
Mother Teresa Home, Cold Spring, MN
Our Lady of Good Counsel, Saint Paul, MN
Sacred Heart Hospice, Austin, MN
St Annes Hospice, Winona, MN
St Anthony Elder Center on Main,
Minneapolis, MN
St Benedict's Center, Saint Cloud, MN
St Elizabeth Hospital, Wabasha, MN
St Francis Home, Waite Park, MN
St Francis Home, Breckenridge, MN
St Mary's Home, Saint Paul, MN
St Marys Nursing Center, Detroit Lakes, MN
St Marys Villa Nursing Home, Pierz, MN
St Ottos Care Center, Little Falls, MN
St Therese Home, New Hope, MN
Villa of St Francis Nursing Home, Morris,
MN
Villa St Vincent, Crookston, MN

Seventh-Day Adventist
Karlstad Memorial Nursing Center, Karlstad,
MN

Volunteers of America
Crystal Care Center, Crystal, MN
Sleepy Eye Care Center, Sleepy Eye, MN

MISSISSIPPI

Baptist
Crawford's Nursing Home Inc, Jackson, MS

King's Daughters & Sons
King's Daughters & Sons Rest Home Inc,
Meridian, MS
Silver Cross Home, Brookhaven, MS

Roman Catholic
Mercy Extended Care Facility, Vicksburg, MS

Seventh-Day Adventist
Adventist Health Center, Lumberton, MS

MISSOURI

Assembly of God
Maranatha Village, Springfield, MO

Baptist
Baptist Home, Chillicothe, Chillicothe, MO

Baptist Home Inc, Ironton, MO
General Baptist Nursing Home, Independence,
MO
General Baptist Nursing Home, Campbell,
MO
Lacoba Homes Inc, Monett, MO
West Vue Home Inc, West Plains, MO

Christian Science
Great Oaks Inc, Kansas City, MO

Disciples of Christ
Foxwood Springs Living Center, Raymore,
MO
Lenoir Health Care Center, Columbia, MO

Evangelical Lutheran
Pine View Manor Inc, Stanberry, MO

Independent Order of Odd Fellows & Rebekahs
Odd Fellows Home Association Inc, Liberty,
MO

Jewish
Jewish Center for Aged, Chesterfield, MO
Shalom Geriatric Center Inc, Kansas City,
MO

King's Daughters & Sons
King's Daughters Home, Mexico, MO

Latter Day Saints
Resthaven, Independence, MO

Lutheran
Beautiful Savior Home, Belton, MO
Luther Manor Retirement & Nursing Center,
Hannibal, MO
Lutheran Altenheim Society of Missouri, Saint
Louis, MO
Lutheran Good Shepherd Home & Nursing
Home, Concordia, MO
Lutheran Health Care Association, Saint
Louis, MO
Lutheran Home, Cape Girardeau, MO

Methodist
Ozarks Methodist Manor, Marionville, MO

Presbyterian
Fulton Presbyterian Manor, Fulton, MO
Presbyterian Manor at Farmington,
Farmington, MO
Presbyterian Manor at Rolla, Rolla, MO

**Reorganized Church of Jesus Christ of Latter-
Day Saints**
Independence Regional Health
Center—Extended Care, Independence,
MO

Roman Catholic
DePaul Health Center St Anne's Division,
Bridgeton, MO
ExPerius Health Care Inc, Kansas City, MO
La Verna Heights Retirement Center,
Savannah, MO
La Verna Village Nursing Home Inc,
Savannah, MO
Little Sisters of the Poor, Saint Louis, MO
Mary Queen & Mother Center, Saint Louis,
MO
Mother of Good Counsel Home, Saint Louis,
MO
Our Lady of Mercy Home, Kansas City, MO
St Agnes Home, Kirkwood, MO
St John's Mercy Villa, Springfield, MO
St Joseph's Hill Infirmary Inc, Eureka, MO

United Church of Christ
Good Samaritan Home, Saint Louis, MO
Parkside Meadows Inc, Saint Charles, MO

MONTANA

Evangelical Lutheran
St John's Lutheran Home—Billings Heights,
Billings, MT

Lutheran
Carbon County Memorial Nursing Home, Red Lodge, MT
Faith Lutheran Home Inc, Wolf Point, MT
Immanuel Lutheran Home, Kalispell, MT
Lutheran Home of the Good Shepherd, Havre, MT
Mountain View Manor Good Samaritan, Eureka, MT
Mountainview Memorial Nursing Home, White Sulphur Springs, MT
St John's Lutheran Home, Billings, MT
Valley View Home, Glasgow, MT

NEBRASKA

Baptist
Maple-Crest, Omaha, NE

Evangelical Free Church
Christian Homes Inc, Holdrege, NE

Evangelical Lutheran
Scribner Good Samaritan Center, Scribner, NE

Jewish
Rose Blumkin Jewish Home, Omaha, NE
Doctor Philip Sher Jewish Home, Omaha, NE

Lutheran
Atkinson Good Samaritan Center, Atkinson, NE
Beatrice Good Samaritan Center, Beatrice, NE
Bethphage at Axtell, Axtell, NE
Bloomfield Good Samaritan Center, Bloomfield, NE
Blue Valley Lutheran Home, Hebron, NE
Callaway Good Samaritan Center, Callaway, NE
Colonial Villa Good Samaritan Center, Alma, NE
Good Samaritan Center, Nelson, NE
Good Samaritan Center, Syracuse, NE
Good Samaritan Village, Alliance, NE
Good Samaritan Village—Perkins Pavilion, Hastings, NE
Good Samaritan Village—Villa Grace, Hastings, NE
Good Shepherd Lutheran Home, Blair, NE
Gordon Good Samaritan Center, Gordon, NE
Lutheran Home, Omaha, NE
Mid Nebraska Lutheran Home, Newman Grove, NE
Millard Good Samaritan Center, Omaha, NE
C A Mues Memorial Good Samaritan Center, Arapahoe, NE
Nemaha County Good Samaritan Center, Auburn, NE
Pine View Good Samaritan Center, Valentine, NE
Ravenna Good Samaritan Center, Ravenna, NE
St John's Center, Kearney, NE
St Luke's Good Samaritan Village, Kearney, NE
Superior Good Samaritan Center, Superior, NE
Tabitha Nursing Home, Lincoln, NE
Wolf Memorial Good Samaritan Center, Albion, NE
Wymore Good Samaritan Center, Wymore, NE

Methodist
Crowell Memorial Home, Blair, NE
M & S Anderson Health Care Unit, Holdrege, NE

Reformed Church
Lakeview Rest Home, Firth, NE

Roman Catholic
Madonna Centers, Lincoln, NE
Mt Carmel Home—Keens Memorial, Kearney, NE
St Joseph Gerontology Center, Alliance, NE
St Joseph's Villa Inc, David City, NE

Women's Christian Temperance Union
Mother Hull Home Inc, Kearney, NE

NEW HAMPSHIRE

Independent Order of Odd Fellows & Rebekahs
New Hampshire Odd Fellows Home, Concord, NH

Masons
Masonic Home, Manchester, NH

Roman Catholic
Mt Carmel Nursing Home, Manchester, NH
St Francis Home, Laconia, NH

United Church of Christ
Havenwood-Heritage Heights, Concord, NH

NEW JERSEY

Jewish
Central New Jersey Jewish Home for the Aged, Somerset, NJ
Daughters of Israel Pleasant Valley Home, West Orange, NJ
Jewish Geriatric Center, Cherry Hill, NJ
Westwood Hall Hebrew Home, Long Branch, NJ

Lutheran
Lutheran Home at Ocean View, Ocean View, NJ

Masons
Masonic Home of New Jersey, Burlington, NJ

Presbyterian
Grove Health Care Center, Neptune, NJ
Haddonfield Presbyterian Home, Haddonfield, NJ
Robert Wood Johnson Jr Health Care, Plainfield, NJ
Lodge, Neptune, NJ

Roman Catholic
Mater Dei Nursing Home, Newfield, NJ
Bishop McCarthy Residence, Vineland, NJ
Our Lady's Residence, Pleasantville, NJ
St Vincent's Nursing Home, Montclair, NJ

Society of Friends
Cadbury Health Care Center, Cherry Hill, NJ
Friends Home at Woodstown, Woodstown, NJ
Greenleaf, Moorestown, NJ
Medford Leas, Medford, NJ

NEW MEXICO

Church of Christ
Lakeview Christian Home of the Southwest Inc, Carlsbad, NM
Northgate Unit of Lakeview Christian Home of the Southwest Inc, Carlsbad, NM

Evangelical Lutheran
Betty Dare Good Samaritan Center, Alamogordo, NM

Lutheran
Four Corners Good Samaritan Center, Aztec, NM
Grants Good Samaritan Center, Grants, NM
Lovington Good Samaritan Center, Lovington, NM
Manzano del Sol Good Samaritan Village, Albuquerque, NM
Socorro Good Samaritan Village, Socorro, NM
University Terrace Good Samaritan Village, Las Cruces, NM

Methodist
Landsun Homes Inc, Carlsbad, NM

Presbyterian
La Residencia NC, Santa Fe, NM
Retirement Ranch of Clovis, Clovis, NM

Roman Catholic
Casa Angelica, Albuquerque, NM
Casa Maria Health Care Centre, Roswell, NM
St Francis Gardens, Albuquerque, NM

NEW YORK

American Legion
New Medico Highgate Manor of Cortland, Cortland, NY

Baptist
Baptist Home of Brooklyn New York, Rhinebeck, NY
Baptist Retirement Center, Scotia, NY
Fairport Baptist Home, Fairport, NY

Congregational
New York Congregational Home for the Aged, Brooklyn, NY

Episcopal
Child's Nursing Home, Albany, NY
St John's Episcopal Homes for the Aged & the Blind, Brooklyn, NY
St Mary's Hospital for Children, Bayside, NY
24 Rhode Island Street Nursing Home, Buffalo, NY

Evangelical Lutheran
Niagara Lutheran Home Inc, Buffalo, NY

Free Methodist
Heritage Village Health Center, Gerry, NY

Independent Order of Odd Fellows & Rebekahs
Odd Fellow & Rebekah Nursing Home Inc, Lockport, NY
United Odd Fellow & Rebekah Home, Bronx, NY

Jewish
Aishel Avraham Residential Health Facility Inc, Brooklyn, NY
Beth Abraham Hospital, New York, NY
Bezalel Nursing Home Company, Far Rockaway, NY
Bialystoker Home & Infirmary for the Aged, New York, NY
Rosa Coplon Jewish Home, Buffalo, NY
Daughters of Jacob Nursing Home Company Inc, Bronx, NY
Daughters of Sarah Nursing Home, Albany, NY
Fort Tryon Nursing Home, New York, NY
Rosalind & Joseph Gurwin Jewish Geriatric Center of Long Island, Commack, NY
Haym Salomon Home for the Aged, Brooklyn, NY
Hebrew Home for the Aged at Riverdale, New York, NY
Hebrew Home for the Aged at Riverdale—Fairfield Division, Bronx, NY
Hebrew Hospital for the Chronic Sick, Bronx, NY
Jewish Home & Hospital for Aged—Bronx Division, Bronx, NY
Jewish Home & Hospital for Aged—Manhattan Division, New York, NY
Jewish Home of Central New York, Syracuse, NY
Jewish Home of Rochester, Rochester, NY
JHMCB Center for Nursing & Rehabilitation Inc, Brooklyn, NY
Menorah Home & Hospital for the Aged & Infirm, Brooklyn, NY
Menorah Nursing Home Inc, Brooklyn, NY
Metropolitan Jewish Geriatric Center, Brooklyn, NY
MJG Nursing Home, Brooklyn, NY
Parker Jewish Geriatric Institute, New Hyde Park, NY
Port Chester Nursing Home, Port Chester, NY
Prospect Park Nursing Home Inc, Brooklyn, NY
Rego Park Nursing Home, Flushing, NY
Rutland Nursing Home Co Inc, Brooklyn, NY

Sephardic Home for the Aged Inc, Brooklyn, NY
Charles T Sitrin Nursing Home Company Inc, New Hartford, NY
United Hebrew Geriatric Center, New Rochelle, NY
Workmen's Circle Home & Infirmary, Bronx, NY

Lutheran
Augustana Lutheran Home, Brooklyn, NY
Eger Lutheran Homes, Staten Island, NY
Good Samaritan Nursing Home Company Inc, Delmar, NY
Martin Luther Nursing Home, Clinton, NY
Lutheran Center for the Aging, Smithtown, NY
Lutheran Retirement Home, Jamestown, NY
Wartburg Home of the Evangelical Lutheran Church, Mount Vernon, NY
Wartburg Lutheran Home for the Aging, Brooklyn, NY

Masons
German Masonic Home Corp, New Rochelle, NY
Masonic Home & Health Facility, Utica, NY

Methodist
Beechwood Residence, Getzville, NY
Bethany Nursing Home & Health Related Facility Inc, Horseheads, NY
Bethel Methodist Home, Ossining, NY
Brooklyn Methodist Church Home, Brooklyn, NY
Elizabeth Church Manor, Binghamton, NY
Folts Home, Herkimer, NY
Methodist Church Home for the Aged, Bronx, NY
Wesley Health Care Center Inc, Saratoga Springs, NY

Order of Eastern Star
Eastern Star Home & Infirmary, Oriskany, NY

Presbyterian
Amherst Presbyterian Nursing Center, Williamsville, NY
Kirkhaven, Rochester, NY
Presbyterian Home for Central New York, New Hartford, NY
St Lukes Presbyterian Nursing Center, Buffalo, NY

Roman Catholic
A Barton Hepburn Hospital Skilled Nursing Facility, Ogdensburg, NY
Brothers of Mercy Nursing & Rehabilitation Center, Clarence, NY
Consolation Nursing Home Inc, West Islip, NY
Terence Cardinal Cooke Health Care Center, New York, NY
Ferncliff Nursing Home Co Inc, Rhinebeck, NY
Good Samaritan Nursing Home, Sayville, NY
Holy Family Home for the Aged, Brooklyn, NY
Jeanne Jugan Residence, Bronx, NY
Kateri Residence, New York, NY
Kenmore Mercy Hospital Skilled Nursing Facility, Kenmore, NY
Lyden Nursing Home, Astoria, NY
Madonna Home of Mercy Hospital of Watertown, Watertown, NY
Madonna Residence Inc, Brooklyn, NY
Mercy Health & Rehabilitation Center Nursing Home Company Inc, Auburn, NY
Mercy Healthcare Center, Tupper Lake, NY
Mercy Hospital—Skilled Nursing Facility, Buffalo, NY
Monsignor Fitzpatrick Pavilion for Skilled Nursing Care, Jamaica, NY
Mt Loretto Nursing Home, Amsterdam, NY
Mt St Mary's Long-Term Care Facility Inc, Niagara Falls, NY
Nazareth Nursing Home & Health Related Facility, Buffalo, NY

Our Lady of Hope Residence—Little Sisters of the Poor, Latham, NY
Ozanam Hall of Queens Nursing Home Inc, Bayside, NY
Sacred Heart Home, Bronx, NY
Sacred Heart Home Inc, Plattsburgh, NY
St Cabrini Nursing Home Inc, Dobbs Ferry, NY
St Camillus Residential Health Care Facility, Syracuse, NY
St Clare Manor, Lockport, NY
St Josephs Hospital Nursing Home of Yonkers New York Inc, Yonkers, NY
St Josephs Home, Ogdensburg, NY
St Josephs Manor, Olean, NY
St Luke Manor of Batavia, Batavia, NY
St Luke Nursing Home Company Inc, Oswego, NY
St Patricks Home for the Aged & Infirm, Bronx, NY
St Teresas Nursing Home Inc, Middletown, NY
Frances Schervier Home & Hospital, New York, NY
Sisters of Charity Hospital Skilled Nursing Facility, Buffalo, NY
Teresian House Nursing Home Company Inc, Albany, NY
Tibbits Health Related Facility, White Plains, NY
Uihlein Mercy Center, Lake Placid, NY
Villa Mary Immaculate, Albany, NY

Seventh-Day Adventist
Adventist Nursing Home Inc, Livingston, NY

United Church of Christ
United Church Colony Homes Inc, Gasport, NY

Volunteer Firefighting Service
Firemen's Home of the State of New York, Hudson, NY

NORTH CAROLINA

Baptist
Baptist Retirement Homes of North Carolina Inc, Winston-Salem, NC

Church of Christ
J W Abernethy Center—United Church Retirement Homes Inc, Newton, NC

Episcopal
Deerfield Episcopal Retirement Community Inc, Asheville, NC

First Wesleyan Church
Wesleyan Arms Inc, High Point, NC

Jewish
Bluementhal Jewish Home, Clemmons, NC

Lutheran
Lutheran Nursing Homes Inc—Albemarle Unit, Albemarle, NC
Lutheran Nursing Homes Inc—Hickory Unit, Hickory, NC
Lutheran Nursing Homes Inc—Salisbury Unit, Salisbury, NC
Twin Lakes Center, Burlington, NC

Masons
Masonic & Eastern Star Home of North Carolina Inc, Greensboro, NC

Methodist
Brooks-Howell Home, Asheville, NC
Methodist Retirement Homes Inc, Durham, NC
Wesley Pines, Lumberton, NC

Moravian
Moravian Home Inc, Winston-Salem, NC

Presbyterian
Covenant Village Inc, Gastonia, NC

Presbyterian Home of Hawfields Inc, Mebane, NC
Presbyterian Home of High Point, High Point, NC
Sharon Towers, Charlotte, NC

Roman Catholic
Maryfield Nursing Home, High Point, NC
St Joseph of the Pines Inc, Southern Pines, NC

Seventh-Day Adventist
Pisgah Manor Health Care Center, Candler, NC

Society of Friends
Friends Homes Inc, Greensboro, NC

United Church of Christ
Piedmont Retirement Center, Thomasville, NC

NORTH DAKOTA

Church of Christ
Wishek Home for the Aged, Wishek, ND

Evangelical Free Church
Elim Home, Fargo, ND

Evangelical Lutheran
Good Shepherd Home, Watford City, ND
Mountrail Bethel Home, Stanley, ND

Lutheran
Arthur Good Samaritan Center, Arthur, ND
Enderlin Hillcrest Manor Ltd, Enderlin, ND
Good Samaritan, Rugby, ND
Good Samaritan Center, Osnabrock, ND
Lake Region Lutheran Home, Devils Lake, ND
Larimore Good Samaritan Center, Larimore, ND
Luther Memorial Home, Mayville, ND
Lutheran Home of the Good Shepherd, New Rockford, ND
Lutheran Sunset Home, Grafton, ND
Missouri Slope Lutheran Care Center, Bismarck, ND
Mott Good Samaritan Nursing Center, Mott, ND
New Town Nursing Home, New Town, ND
Northwood Deaconess Hospital & Home Association, Northwood, ND
Oakes Manor Good Samaritan Center, Oakes, ND
Parkside Lutheran Home, Lisbon, ND
Pembina County Memorial Nursing Home, Cavalier, ND
St Luke's Home, Dickinson, ND
Souris Valley Care Center, Velva, ND
Sunset Care Corporation, Bowman, ND
Tri-County Retirement & Nursing Home, Hatton, ND
Valley Memorial Home—Almonte, Grand Forks, ND
Valley Memorial Home—Medical Park, Grand Forks, ND
Westhope Home, Westhope, ND

Roman Catholic
Carrington Health Center—SNF, Carrington, ND
Garrison Memorial Hospital—ICF, Garrison, ND
Garrison Nursing Center, Garrison, ND
La Moure Healthcare Manor, La Moure, ND
St Aloisius Medical Center, Harvey, ND
St Andrew's Nursing Home, Bottineau, ND
St Vincent's Nursing Home, Bismarck, ND

United Church of Christ
Elm Crest Manor, New Salem, ND

OHIO

Apostolic Christian
Apostolic Christian Home Inc, Rittman, OH

Baptist
Judson Village, Cincinnati, OH

Christian Reformed Hungarian Church
Lorantffy Care Center Inc, Akron, OH

Christian Science
Overlook House, Cleveland, OH

Church of Christ
Canton Christian Home, Canton, OH
Fairhaven Retirement & Health Care
  Community, Upper Sandusky, OH
Mt Healthy Christian Home, Cincinnati, OH
Trinity Home, Dayton, OH
Willow Brook Christian Home, Columbus,
  OH

Church of God
Hester Memorial Nursing Home, Dayton, OH
Winebrenner Extended Care Facility, Findlay,
  OH
Winebrenner Haven, Findlay, OH

Church of the Brethren
Brethren Care Inc, Ashland, OH
Brethren's Home, Greenville, OH
Good Shepherd Home, Fostoria, OH
West View Manor, Wooster, OH

Episcopal
Marjorie P Lee Home for the Aged,
  Cincinnati, OH
St Luke Center, Cincinnati, OH
Whetstone Convalescent Center, Columbus,
  OH

First Community Church
First Community Village Healthcare Center,
  Columbus, OH

Independent Order of Odd Fellows & Rebekahs
Odd Fellows Home of Ohio, Springfield, OH

Jewish
Darlington House, Toledo, OH
Glen Manor, Cincinnati, OH
Heritage House-Columbus Jewish Home for
  the Aged, Columbus, OH
Heritage Manor, Jewish Home for Aged,
  Youngstown, OH
Jewish Home for Aged, Dayton, OH
Montefiore Home, Cleveland Heights, OH
Orthodox Jewish Home for the Aged,
  Cincinnati, OH

Knights of Pythias
K W Hess Ohio Pythian Home of Springfield
  Ohio, Springfield, OH
Sophia Huntington Parker Home, Medina,
  OH

Lutheran
Bethany Lutheran Village, Dayton, OH
Filling Memorial Home of Mercy, Napoleon,
  OH
Luther Home of Mercy, Williston, OH
Lutheran Home, Napoleon, OH
Lutheran Home, Westlake, OH
Lutheran Memorial Home, Sandusky, OH
Lutheran Old Folks Home, Toledo, OH
Lutheran Senior City Inc, Columbus, OH
St Luke Lutheran Home, North Canton, OH
Shepherd of the Valley Nursing Home, Niles,
  OH

Masons
Ohio Masonic Home, Springfield, OH

Mennonite
Fairlawn Haven, Archbold, OH
Mennonite Memorial Home, Bluffton, OH

Methodist
Crandall Medical Center, Sebring, OH
Elyria United Methodist Home, Elyria, OH
Healthaven Nursing Home, Akron, OH
Lake Park Nursing Care Center, Sylvania, OH
Otterbein-Lebanon Home, Lebanon, OH
Portage Valley Inc, Pemberville, OH
Riverside United Methodist Hospital's
  Extended Care Unit, Columbus, OH
Wesley Glen Inc, Columbus, OH
Wesley Hall Inc, Cincinnati, OH

Missionary Church
Dayview Care Center, New Carlisle, OH

Order of Eastern Star
Eastern Star Home of Cuyahoga County, East
  Cleveland, OH
Hamilton County Eastern Star Home Inc,
  Cincinnati, OH
Ohio Eastern Star Home, Mount Vernon, OH

Presbyterian
Fairmount Health Center of Breckenridge
  Village, Willoughby, OH
Dorothy Love Retirement Community,
  Sidney, OH
Marietta Manor, Cleveland, OH
Mt Pleasant Nursing Home, Cleveland, OH
Mt Pleasant Village, Monroe, OH
Park Vista Unit, Ohio Presbyterian Home,
  Youngstown, OH
Rockynol Retirement Community, Akron, OH
Westminster-Thurber Retirement Community,
  Columbus, OH

Roman Catholic
Archbishop Leibold Home, Cincinnati, OH
Assumption Nursing Home, Youngstown, OH
Good Samaritan Hospital, Zanesville, OH
Health Center at Oakwood Village,
  Springfield, OH
Jennings Hall Inc, Garfield Heights, OH
Little Sisters of the Poor, Oregon, OH
Little Sisters of the Poor—Home for the Aged,
  Cleveland, OH
Madonna Hall, Cleveland, OH
Maria-Joseph Center, Dayton, OH
Mother Margaret Hall, Mount Saint Joseph,
  OH
Mt Alverna Home Inc, Parma, OH
St Alexis Hospital Skilled Nursing Facility,
  Cleveland, OH
St Ann Skilled Nursing Center, Sandusky, OH
St Clare Retirement Community, Cincinnati,
  OH
St Edward Home, Akron, OH
St Francis Home, Tiffin, OH
St Francis Rehabilitation Hospital & Nursing
  Home, Green Springs, OH
St John's Center, Springfield, OH
St Joseph Hospice, Louisville, OH
St Raphaels Home for the Aged, Columbus,
  OH
St Rita's Home for the Aged Inc, Columbus,
  OH
St Theresa Home, Cincinnati, OH
Villa Santa Anna Home for the Aged Inc,
  Beachwood, OH

Seventh-Day Adventist
Meadowbrook Living Center, Montgomery,
  OH
Northside Manor Living Center, Mount
  Vernon, OH

Society of Friends
Quaker Heights Nursing Home, Waynesville,
  OH

Swedenborgian
New Dawn Convalescent Center, Furnace, OH

United Methodist
Bethesda Scarlet Oaks, Cincinnati, OH
Hill View Health Care Facility, Portsmouth,
  OH
Twin Towers, Cincinnati, OH

Volunteers of America
Bethesda Care Center, Fremont, OH
Kettering Convalescent Center, Kettering, OH
Leisure Oaks Convalescent Center, Defiance,
  OH

OKLAHOMA

Baptist
Evergreen Care Center, Owasso, OK
Lackey Manor Nursing Home, Oklahoma
  City, OK

Church of Christ
Central Oklahoma Christian Home, Oklahoma
  City, OK
Cordell Christian Home, Cordell, OK
Tulsa Christian Home Inc, Tulsa, OK

Disciples of Christ
Oklahoma Christian Home, Edmond, OK

Episcopal
Canterbury Health Center, Oklahoma City,
  OK
St Simeon's Episcopal Home Inc, Tulsa, OK

Independent Order of Odd Fellows & Rebekahs
Odd Fellows Rest Home, Checotah, OK

Jewish
Tulsa Jewish Community Retirement &
  Health Care Center Inc, Tulsa, OK

King's Daughters & Sons
King's Daughters & Sons Nursing Home,
  Durant, OK

Lutheran
Hobart Good Samaritan Home, Hobart, OK

Mennonite
Corn Heritage Village, Corn, OK
Maple Lawn Manor, Hydro, OK

Methodist
Dr W F & Mada Dunaway Manor Nursing
  Home of Guymon Inc, Guymon, OK
Methodist Home of Enid Inc, Enid, OK
United Methodist Health Care Center,
  Clinton, OK

Oral Roberts Ministries
University Village Inc, Tulsa, OK

Pentecostal Holiness
Carmen Home, Carmen, OK

Roman Catholic
Franciscan Villa, Broken Arrow, OK
St Ann's Home, Oklahoma City, OK
St John Medical Center, Tulsa, OK
Westminster Village Inc, Ponca City, OK

United Methodist
Oklahoma Methodist Home for the Aged,
  Tulsa, OK

OREGON

Baptist
Baptist Manor, Portland, OR

Episcopal
Bishop Morris Care Center, Portland, OR

Jewish
Robison Jewish Home, Portland, OR

Kiwanis Club
Ochoco Nursing Home, Prineville, OR

Lutheran
Fairlawn Care Center, Gresham, OR
Good Shepherd Lutheran Home, Cornelius,
  OR
Hermiston Good Samaritan, Hermiston, OR
Lutheran Pioneer Home, Mallala, OR
Willamette Lutheran Home, Salem, OR

Masons
Masonic & Eastern Star Home of Oregon,
Forest Grove, OR

Mennonite
Dallas Nursing Home, Dallas, OR
Mennonite Home, Albany, OR

Presbyterian
Holladay Park Plaza, Portland, OR
Presbyterian Community Care Center,
Ontario, OR

Roman Catholic
Benedictine Nursing Center, Mount Angel, OR
Maryville Nursing Home, Beaverton, OR
Mt St Joseph Residence & Extended Care
Center, Portland, OR
Providence Children's Nursing Center,
Portland, OR
Providence Medical Center Skilled Nursing
Facility, Portland, OR
St Catherine's Residence & Nursing Center,
North Bend, OR
St Elizabeth Health Care Center, Baker, OR

Seventh-Day Adventist
Emerald Nursing Center, Eugene, OR
Portland Adventist Convalescent Center,
Portland, OR
Rest Harbor Extended Care Center, Gresham,
OR

Society of Friends
Friendsview Manor Infirmary, Newberg, OR

PENNSYLVANIA

Baptist
Baptist Home of Philadelphia, Philadelphia,
PA
Baptist Homes Nursing Center, Pittsburgh, PA
Hannum Memorial Rest Home Inc, Bradford,
PA

Bible Fellowship Church
Fellowship Manor, Whitehall, PA

Brethren In Christ Church
Messiah Village, Mechanicsburg, PA

Christian & Missionary Alliance Foundation
Alliance Home of Carlisle, PA, Carlisle, PA

Church of Christ
Homewood Retirement Center—Hanover,
Hanover, PA
Wyncote Church Home, Wyncote, PA

Church of God
Church of God Home Inc, Carlisle, PA
Grove Manor, Grove City, PA

Church of the Brethren
Peter Becker Community, Harleysville, PA
Brethren Home, New Oxford, PA
Brethren Village, Lancaster, PA
Church of the Brethren Home, Windber, PA
Morrisons Cove Home, Martinsburg, PA

Congregational
Evangelical Congregational Church Retirement
Village, Myerstown, PA

Eastern Star
Eastern Pennsylvania Eastern Star Home,
Warminster, PA

Episcopal
All Sts Rehabilitation Hospital/Springfield
Retirement Residence, Wyndmoor, PA
Canterbury Place, Pittsburgh, PA
Cathedral Village, Philadelphia, PA
Kearsley—Christ Church Hospital,
Philadelphia, PA

Evangelical Lutheran
Mary J Drexel Home, Bala Cynwyd, PA

Independent Order of Odd Fellows & Rebekahs
Odd Fellows Home of Pennsylvania,
Middletown, PA
Orchard Manor, Grove City, PA

Jewish
Bala Retirement & Rehabilitation,
Philadelphia, PA
Care Center at Martins Run, Media, PA
Home for the Jewish Aged, Philadelphia, PA
Jewish Home of Eastern Pennsylvania,
Scranton, PA
Jewish Home of Greater Harrisburg,
Harrisburg, PA
Riverview Center for Jewish Seniors,
Pittsburgh, PA
Stenton Hall, Philadelphia, PA

Knights of Malta
Malta Home for the Aging, Granville, PA

Knights of Pythias
Kinkora Pythian Home, Duncannon, PA

Lutheran
Allegheny Lutheran Home, Hollidaysburg, PA
Allegheny Lutheran Home—Johnstown,
Johnstown, PA
Artman Lutheran Home, Ambler, PA
Buffalo Valley Lutheran Village, Lewisburg,
PA
Frey Village, Middletown, PA
Germantown Home, Philadelphia, PA
Gettysburg Lutheran Retirement Village,
Gettysburg, PA
Good Shepherd Home Long-Term Care
Facility Inc, Allentown, PA
Luther Acres, Lititz, PA
Luther Crest, Allentown, PA
Lutheran Home at Kane, Kane, PA
Lutheran Home at Telford, Telford, PA
Lutheran Home at Topton, Topton, PA
Lutheran Home for the Aged, Erie, PA
Lutheran Welfare Concordia Home, Cabot,
PA
Passavant Retirement & Health Center,
Zelienople, PA
Paul's Run, Philadelphia, PA
Perry Village Nursing Home, New Bloomfield,
PA
St John Lutheran Care Center, Mars, PA
St Luke Manor, Hazelton, PA
St Luke Pavilion, Hazelton, PA
Shrewsbury Lutheran Retirement Village,
Shrewsbury, PA
Susquehanna Lutheran Village, Millersburg,
PA
York Lutheran Home, York, PA

Masons
Masonic Home of Pennsylvania, Lafayette
Hill, PA
Masonic Homes, Elizabethtown, PA

Mennonite
Dock Terrace, Lansdale, PA
Frederick Mennonite Home, Frederick, PA
Friendship Community, Lititz, PA
Landis Homes Retirement Community, Lititz,
PA
Menno-Haven, Chambersburg, PA
Mennonite Home, Lancaster, PA
Rockhill Mennonite Community, Sellersville,
PA
Souderton Mennonite Homes, Souderton, PA
Tel Hai Nursing Center Inc, Honey Brook, PA

Methodist
Asbury Heights, Pittsburgh, PA
Bethany Village Retirement Center,
Mechanicsburg, PA
Epworth Manor, Tyrone, PA
Evangelical Manor, Philadelphia, PA
Quincy United Methodist Home, Quincy, PA
Simpson House Inc, Philadelphia, PA
Wesley Village, Pittston, PA

Moravian
Moravian Hall Square, Nazareth, PA

Moravian Manor, Lititz, PA

Order of Eastern Star
Western Pennsylvania Eastern Star Home,
Pittsburgh, PA

Presbyterian
Bethlen Home of the Hungarian Federation of
America, Ligonier, PA
Broomall Presbyterian Home, Broomall, PA
Forest Park Health Center, Carlisle, PA
Greensburg Home—Redstone Presbytery,
Greensburg, PA
Indiana Presbyterian Homes, Indiana, PA
Moshannon Heights, Philipsburg, PA
Oxford Manor Nursing Home, Oxford, PA
Presbyterian Home at 58th Street,
Philadelphia, PA
Presbyterian Home of Redstone Presbytery,
Johnstown, PA
Presbyterian Home—Oil City, Oil City, PA
Presbyterian Homes of the Presbytery of
Huntingdon, Hollidaysburg, PA
Presbyterian Lodge, Erie, PA
Presbyterian Medical Center of Oakmont,
Oakmont, PA
Presbyterian Medical Center of Washington
Pennsylvania, Washington, PA
Quarryville Presbyterian Home, Quarryville,
PA
Reformed Presbyterian Home, Pittsburgh, PA
Rydal Park of Philadelphia Presbyterian
Homes on the Fairway, Rydal, PA
Shenango Presbyterian Home, New
Wilmington, PA
Swaim Health Center, Newville, PA
Sycamore Manor Health Center,
Montoursville, PA
United Presbyterian Home for Aged People,
Pittsburgh, PA
Westminster Village, Allentown, PA

Roman Catholic
C R Center, Springfield, PA
Christ the King Manor, Dubois, PA
Garvey Manor Nursing Home, Hollidaysburg,
PA
Holy Family Home, Philadelphia, PA
Holy Family Manor Inc, Bethlehem, PA
Holy Family Residence, Scranton, PA
Immaculate Mary Home, Philadelphia, PA
John XXIII Home, Hermitage, PA
Maria Joseph Manor, Danville, PA
Little Flower Manor, Darby, PA
Little Flower Manor—Diocese of Scranton,
Wilkes-Barre, PA
Little Sisters of the Poor Home for the Aged,
Pittsburgh, PA
Mercy Health Care Center, Nanticoke, PA
Misericordia Convalescent Home, York, PA
Mt Macrina Manor Nursing Home,
Uniontown, PA
Regency Hall Nursing Home Inc, Allison Park,
PA
Sacred Heart Manor—Philadelphia,
Philadelphia, PA
St Anne Home for the Elderly, Greensburg,
PA
St Anne's Home, Columbia, PA
St Francis Country House, Darby, PA
St John Neumann Nursing Home,
Philadelphia, PA
St Joseph Home for the Aged, Holland, PA
St Joseph Nursing & Health Care Center,
Pittsburgh, PA
St Joseph Villa, Flourtown, PA
St Marys Home of Erie, Erie, PA
St Mary's Villa Nursing Home, Elmhurst, PA
Villa De Marillac Nursing Home, Pittsburgh,
PA
Vincentian Home for Chronically Ill,
Pittsburgh, PA

Seventh-Day Adventist
Laurel Living Center, Hamburg, PA

Society of Friends
Foulkeways at Gwynedd, Gwynedd, PA

Linden Hall, Kennett Square, PA
Pennswood Village, Newtown, PA

Unitarian Universalist
Unitarian Universalist House, Philadelphia, PA

United Church of Christ
Homewood Retirement Center, Martinsburg, PA
Phoebe Home, Allentown, PA
St Paul Homes, Greenville, PA

United Methodist
Cornwall Manor, Cornwall, PA
Lewisburg United Methodist Homes, Lewisburg, PA
Wesbury United Methodist Community, Meadville, PA

Workmen's Circle
Workmen's Circle Home, Media, PA

RHODE ISLAND

Baptist
John Clarke Retirement Center, Middletown, RI

Jewish
Jewish Home for the Aged, Providence, RI

Methodist
United Methodist Health Care Center, East Providence, RI

Roman Catholic
Darlington Care Center, Pawtucket, RI
Mt St Francis Health Center, Woonsocket, RI
Mt St Rita Health Center, Cumberland, RI
St Antoine Residence, North Smithfield, RI
Scalabrini Villa, North Kingstown, RI

Seventh-Day Adventist
Pawtucket Institute for Health Services, Pawtucket, RI

SOUTH CAROLINA

Baptist
Bethea Baptist Home, Darlington, SC
Martha Franks Baptist Retirement Center, Laurens, SC

Episcopal
South Carolina Episcopal Retirement Community, Columbia, SC

Lutheran
Lowman Home, White Rock, SC

Methodist
Methodist Home, Orangeburg, SC
Nursing Center of Greenwood Methodist Home, Greenwood, SC

Presbyterian
Presbyterian Home of South Carolina—Summerville, Summerville, SC

Roman Catholic
Bon Secours—Divine Saviour Nursing Home, York, SC

SOUTH DAKOTA

Baptist
Evergreen Terrace Healthcare Center, Madison, SD

Eastern Star
Eastern Star Home of South Dakota, Redfield, SD

Independent Order of Odd Fellows & Rebekahs
Odd Fellows Home, Dell Rapids, SD

Lutheran
Bethany Lutheran Home, Sioux Falls, SD

Bethel Lutheran Home, Madison, SD
Bethesda Home for Aged, Beresford, SD
Bethesda Home of Aberdeen, Aberdeen, SD
Canton Good Samaritan Center, Canton, SD
Castle Manor, Hot Springs, SD
Deuel County Good Samaritan Center, Clear Lake, SD
Good Samaritan Luther Manor, Sioux Falls, SD
Good Samaritan Village, Sioux Falls, SD
Herreid Good Samaritan Center, Herreid, SD
Howard Good Samaritan Center, Howard, SD
Lutheran Home (LHHS), Eureka, SD
Parkston Nursing Center, Parkston, SD
Parkston Supervised Living Center, Parkston, SD
Pleasant View Good Samaritan, Corsica, SD
Prairie Good Samaritan Center, Miller, SD
Scotland Good Samaritan Center, Scotland, SD
Selby Good Samaritan Center, Selby, SD
Tyndall Good Samaritan Center, Tyndall, SD
Wagner Good Samaritan Center, Wagner, SD

Mennonite
Salem Mennonite Home for Aged, Freeman, SD

Methodist
Jenkins Methodist Home, Watertown, SD

Roman Catholic
Brady Memorial Home, Mitchell, SD
Maryhouse Inc, Pierre, SD
Mother Joseph Manor, Aberdeen, SD
Prince of Peace Retirement Community, Sioux Falls, SD
St William's Home for the Aged, Milbank, SD
Sister James' Nursing Home, Yankton, SD

TENNESSEE

Baptist
Baptist Health Care Center, Lenoir City, TN
Cocke County Baptist Convalescent Center, Newport, TN

Christian Methodist Episcopal
Collins Chapel Health Care Center, Memphis, TN

Church of Christ
Appalachian Christian Village, Johnson City, TN
Church of Christ Home for Aged, Nashville, TN
Lakeshore Nursing Home & Retirement Center, Nashville, TN
Mid-South Christian Nursing Home, Memphis, TN
May Cravath Wharton Nursing Home, Pleasant Hill, TN

Church of the Brethren
John M Reed Nursing Home, Limestone, TN

Episcopal
St Barnabas Nursing Home, Chattanooga, TN

Jewish
B'nai B'rith Home, Memphis, TN

King's Daughters & Sons
King's Daughters & Sons Home, Memphis, TN

Methodist
Asbury Centers Inc, Maryville, TN
Methodist Nursing Home of Middle Tennessee, Winchester, TN
Parkview Convalescent Unit, Dyersburg, TN
Wesley Highland Manor, Memphis, TN

Nazarene
Trevecca Health Care Center, Nashville, TN

Presbyterian
Shannondale Health Care & Retirement Center, Knoxville, TN

Wood Presbyterian Home Inc, Sweetwater, TN

Roman Catholic
Alexian Village of Tennessee, Signal Mountain, TN
St Peter Villa Nursing Home, Memphis, TN

Seventh-Day Adventist
Laurelbrook Sanitarium, Dayton, TN
Little Creek Sanitarium, Knoxville, TN

United Methodist
Asbury Center at Baysmont, Kingsport, TN
McKendree Village Inc, Hermitage, TN

TEXAS

American Religious Town Hall Meeting
Town Hall Estates, Rusk, TX

Baptist
Buckner Baptist Haven, Missouri City, TX
Buckner Baptist Trew Retirement Center, Dallas, TX
Buckner Monte Siesta Nursing Center, Austin, TX
Buckner Ryburn Nursing Center, Dallas, TX
Buckner Villa Siesta Home, Austin, TX
Gilmer Convalescent & Nursing Center, Gilmer, TX

Church of Christ
Christian Care Center, Mesquite, TX
Christian Care Center North, Dallas, TX
Hilltop Haven, Gunter, TX
Lakewood Village, Fort Worth, TX
Texhoma Christian Care Center, Wichita Falls, TX

Disciples of Christ
Juliette Fowler Homes, Dallas, TX

Episcopal
Bishop Davies Center Inc, Hurst, TX
St James House of Baytown, Baytown, TX

Evangelical Lutheran
Clifton Lutheran Sunset Home, Clifton, TX
Parks Good Samaritan Village, Odessa, TX
White Acres—Good Samaritan Retirement Village & Nursing Center, El Paso, TX

Independent Order of Odd Fellows & Rebekahs
Odd Fellow & Rebekah Nursing Home, Ennis, TX

Jewish
Dallas Home for Jewish Aged, Dallas, TX
Golden Manor Jewish Home for the Aged, San Antonio, TX
Jewish Home for the Aged, Houston, TX
Seven Acres Jewish Geriatric Center, Houston, TX

Knights of Pythias
Home for Aged Pythians, Greenville, TX

Lutheran
Brookhaven Nursing Center, Farmers Branch, TX
Denton Good Samaritan Village, Denton, TX
Harlingen Good Samaritan Center, Harlingen, TX
Lutheran Home—Permian Basin, Midland, TX
McAllen Good Samaritan Center, McAllen, TX
Trinity Lutheran Home, Round Rock, TX
Trinity Lutheran Home, Shiner, TX

Masons
Knights Templar Clinic, Arlington, TX

Methodist
Clarewood House, Houston, TX
Crestview Retirement Community, Bryan, TX
Glen Rose Nursing Home, Glen Rose, TX
Golden Age Home, Lockhart, TX

Happy Harbor Methodist Home, La Porte, TX
King's Manor Methodist Home Inc, Hereford, TX
Parkview Manor, Weimar, TX
Sears Memorial Methodist Center, Abilene, TX
Wesleyan Nursing Home, Georgetown, TX
C C Young Memorial Home—Young Health Center, Dallas, TX

Order of Eastern Star
Eastern Star Home, Arlington, TX

Presbyterian
Grace Presbyterian Village, Dallas, TX
Presbyterian Manor, Wichita Falls, TX
Trinity Terrace, Fort Worth, TX
Trinity Towers, Midland, TX

Roman Catholic
Czech Catholic Home for the Aged, El Campo, TX
John Paul II Nursing Center, Kenedy, TX
Nazareth Hall, El Paso, TX
St Ann's Nursing Home, Panhandle, TX
St Anthony Center, Houston, TX
St Benedict Nursing Home, San Antonio, TX
St Dominic Nursing Home, Houston, TX
St Elizabeth Nursing Home, Waco, TX
St Francis Nursing Home, San Antonio, TX
St Joseph's Residence, Dallas, TX
San Juan Nursing Home Inc, San Juan, TX

Seventh-Day Adventist
Fredericksburg Nursing Home, Fredericksburg, TX
Town Hall Estates Health Care Facility, Whitney, TX
Valley Grande Manor, Weslaco, TX
Valley Grande Manor Inc, Brownsville, TX

United Church of Christ
Eden Home Inc, New Braunfels, TX

United Methodist
Turner Geriatric Center, Galveston, TX

UTAH

Church of Latter-Day Saints (Mormon)
Highland Care Center, Salt Lake City, UT
Wasatch Villa Convalescent Nursing Home, Salt Lake City, UT

Latter Day Saints
Logan Valley Nursing Center, Logan, UT
Provo Care Center, Provo, UT

Roman Catholic
St Joseph Villa, Salt Lake City, UT

VERMONT

Independent Order of Odd Fellows & Rebekahs
Gill Odd Fellows Home, Ludlow, VT

VIRGINIA

Baptist
Culpeper Baptist Retirement Community—Dorothy Finney Health Care Unit, Culpeper, VA
Newport News Baptist Retirement Community Health Care Unit, Newport News, VA

Church of the Brethren
Bridgewater Home Inc Health Care Unit, Bridgewater, VA

Episcopal
Goodwin House, Alexandria, VA
Rappahannock Westminster-Canterbury Inc, Irvington, VA
Westminster-Canterbury of Hampton Roads Inc, Virginia Beach, VA

Evangelical Lutheran
Virginia Synod Lutheran Home at Roanoke, Roanoke, VA

Jewish
Beth Shalom Home of Central Virginia, Richmond, VA
Beth Shalom Home of Eastern Virginia, Virginia Beach, VA

Masons
Masonic Home of Virginia—Health Care Unit, Richmond, VA

Mennonite
Mountain View Nursing Home Inc, Aroda, VA
Oak Lea Nursing Home, Harrisonburg, VA

Methodist
Asbury Center at Birdmont, Wytheville, VA
Hermitage on the Eastern Shore, Onancock, VA
Roanoke United Methodist Home, Roanoke, VA
Via Health Care Center/The Hermitage Richmond Virginia United Methodist Homes Inc, Richmond, VA

Presbyterian
Sunnyside Presbyterian Home Health Care Unit, Harrisonburg, VA

Roman Catholic
Little Sisters of the Poor—St Joseph's Home for the Aged Health Care Unit, Richmond, VA
St Mary's Hospital, Norton, VA

United Methodist
Hermitage in Northern Virginia, Alexandria, VA

WASHINGTON

Baptist
Judson Park Health Center, Des Moines, WA

Christian Science
Sunrise Haven, Puyallup, WA

Evangelical Lutheran
Spokane Valley Good Samaritan, Greenacres, WA

Free Methodist
Warm Beach Health Care Center, Stanwood, WA

Independent Order of Odd Fellows & Rebekahs
Washington Odd Fellows Home, Walla Walla, WA

Knights of Pythias
Oregon-Washington Pythian Home, Vancouver, WA

Lutheran
Bethany of the Northwest, Everett, WA
Columbia Lutheran Home, Seattle, WA
Fairfield Good Samaritan Center, Fairfield, WA
Hearthstone, Seattle, WA
Josephine Sunset Home, Stanwood, WA
Martha & Mary Nursing Home, Poulsbo, WA
Resthaven Health Care Center, Bremerton, WA
Riverview Center for Retirement Living, Spokane, WA
Tacoma Lutheran Home & Retirement Community, Tacoma, WA

Masons
Masonic Home of Washington, Des Moines, WA

Methodist
Bayview Manor, Seattle, WA
Rockwood Manor Infirmary, Spokane, WA
Wesley Care Center, Des Moines, WA

Wesley Homes—The Gardens, Des Moines, WA

Presbyterian
Exeter House, Seattle, WA
Hawthorne Manor, Spokane, WA
Kenney Presbyterian Home, Seattle, WA
Park Shore, Seattle, WA

Roman Catholic
Marianwood Extended Healthcare Services, Issaquah, WA
Mt St Vincent Nursing Center, Seattle, WA
St Joseph Care Center, Spokane, WA
St Jude's Health Care Centre, Spokane, WA

United Church of Christ
Horizon House, Seattle, WA

WEST VIRGINIA

Evangelical Lutheran
Pendleton Nursing Home, Franklin, WV

Lutheran
Barbour County Good Samaritan Center, Belington, WV

Methodist
Glenwood Park United Methodist Home, Princeton, WV

Presbyterian
Presbyterian Manor, Huntington, WV

WISCONSIN

Baptist
Tudor Oaks Health Center, Hales Corners, WI
Tudor Oaks Health Center, Muskego, WI

Congregational
Congregational Home Inc, Brookfield, WI

Episcopal
St John's Home of Milwaukee, Milwaukee, WI

Evangelical Lutheran
American Lutheran Home, Mondovi, WI
Fennimore Good Samaritan Center, Fennimore, WI
Homme Home for the Aging, Wittenberg, WI
Luther Home, Marinette, WI
St Michael's Evangelical Lutheran Home for the Aged, Fountain City, WI

Independent Order of Odd Fellows & Rebekahs
Wisconsin Odd Fellow-Rebekah Nursing Home, Green Bay, WI

Jewish
Milwaukee Jewish Convalescent Center, Milwaukee, WI
Milwaukee Jewish Home, Milwaukee, WI

Lutheran
American Lutheran Home—Menomonie Unit, Menomonie, WI
Bethany Riverside, La Crosse, WI
Bethel Home, Oshkosh, WI
Bethel Home, Viroqua, WI
Bethesda Lutheran Home, Watertown, WI
Capeside Cove Good Samaritan Center, Siren, WI
Fond Du Lac Lutheran Home, Fond Du Lac, WI
Lincoln Village Convalescent Center, Racine, WI
Lodi Good Samaritan Center, Lodi, WI
Luther Manor, Wauwatosa, WI
Luther Manor, Milwaukee, WI
Nygaard Manor, Stoughton, WI
Oakwood Lutheran—Hebron Hall, Madison, WI
Rosewood Nursing Home, West Allis, WI
St Croix Valley Good Samaritan Center, Saint Croix Falls, WI
Shorehaven, Oconomowoc, WI

Skaalen Sunset Home, Stoughton, WI
Syverson Lutheran Home, Eau Claire, WI
Becker/Shoop Center, Racine, WI
Clara Werner Dormitory, Watertown, WI
Wisconsin Lutheran Child & Family Service,
    Milwaukee, WI
Woodside Lutheran Home, Green Bay, WI

Methodist
Christian Community Home of Hudson,
    Hudson, WI
Evergreen Manor, Oshkosh, WI
Methodist Health Center, Madison, WI
Schmitt Woodland Hills Inc, Richland Center,
    WI
Sheboygan Retirement Home & Beach Health
    Care Center Inc, Sheboygan, WI

Moravian
Marquardt Memorial Manor Inc, Watertown,
    WI

Roman Catholic
Alexian Village of Milwaukee, Milwaukee, WI
Clement Manor Health Care Center,
    Greenfield, WI
Divine Savior Hospital & Nursing Home,
    Portage, WI
Franciscan Villa, South Milwaukee, WI
Hope Nursing Home, Lomira, WI
Marian Catholic Home, Milwaukee, WI
Marian Franciscan Home, Milwaukee, WI
Maryhill Manor, Niagara, WI
Milwaukee Catholic Home, Milwaukee, WI
Nazareth House, Stoughton, WI
St Anne's Home for the Elderly, Milwaukee,
    WI
St Ann's Rest Home, Milwaukee, WI
St Camillus Health Center, Wauwatosa, WI
St Catherine's Infirmary, Racine, WI
St Elizabeth Nursing Home, Brookfield, WI
St Elizabeth's Nursing Home, Janesville, WI
St Frances Home, Fond Du Lac, WI
St Francis Home, La Crosse, WI
St Francis Home Inc, Superior, WI
St Joan Antida Home, West Allis, WI
St Joseph Residence, New London, WI
St Joseph's Home for the Aged, West Allis,
    WI
St Joseph's Nursing Home, La Crosse, WI
St Mary's Home for the Aged Inc, Manitowoc,
    WI
St Marys Nursing Home, Milwaukee, WI
St Mary's Nursing Home, Sparta, WI
St Paul Home Inc, Kaukauna, WI
Villa Clement, West Allis, WI
Villa Loretto Nursing Home, Mount Calvary,
    WI

Seventh-Day Adventist
Bethel Living Center, Arpin, WI
Colonial House Living Center, Colby, WI
Lancaster Living Center, Lancaster, WI
Marshfield Living Center, Marshfield, WI
Mineral Point Living Center, Mineral Point,
    WI
Oakview Care Center, Durand, WI
River Pines Living Center, Stevens Point, WI
Villa Pines Living Center, Friendship, WI

United Church of Christ
Cedar Lake Home Campus, West Bend, WI
Fairhaven Corporation, Whitewater, WI
New Glarus Home Inc, New Glarus, WI

United Methodist
Morrow Memorial Home for the Aged, Sparta,
    WI

PUERTO RICO

Church of Christ
Ryder Memorial Skilled Nursing Facility,
    Humacao, PR

ALPHABETICAL LISTING OF FACILITIES

A & E Nursing Home, Salt Lake City, UT
Aaron Convalescent Home, Cincinnati, OH
Aaron Convalescent Home, Reading, OH
Aaron Manor Health Care Facility, Chester, CT
Abbe Center for Community Care, Marion, IA
Abbeville Heritage Manor, Abbeville, LA
Abbeville Nursing Home, Abbeville, SC
Abbey Convalescent Center, Warren, MI
Abbey Forest Nursing Home, Waltham, MA
Abbey Hill Nursing Home, Saugus, MA
Abbey Manor Inc, Windham, CT
Abbey Nursing Home, Kenmore, NY
Abbey Nursing Home Inc, Saint Petersburg, FL
Abbey of LeMars, LeMars, IA
Abbington House, Roselle, IL
Abbot Group Home, Abbot, ME
Abbott House, Highland Park, IL
Abbott House Nursing Home, Lynn, MA
Abbott Manor Convalescent Center, Plainfield, NJ
Abbott Northwestern Hospital, Minneapolis, MN
Abbott Terrace Health Center, Waterbury, CT
ABC Community Services Inc, Duluth, MN
ABC Health Center, Harrisonville, MO
Aberdeen Nursing Center, Aberdeen, SD
Aberdeen Nursing Home, Rochester, NY
Aberjona Nursing Center Inc, Winchester, MA
J W Abernethy Center—United Church Retirement Homes Inc, Newton, NC
Abilene Convalescent Center, Abilene, TX
Abilene House Inc, Tacoma, WA
Abilene Nursing Center, Abilene, KS
Abington Manor Nursing & Rehabilitation Center, Clarks Summit, PA
Able Manor Nursing Home, Cincinnati, OH
Edward Abraham Memorial Home Inc, Canadian, TX
Absecon Manor Nursing & Rehabilitation Center, Absecon, NJ
Acacias Care Center Inc, Ojai, CA
Academy Manor of Andover, Andover, MA
Academy Street Community Residence, Williston, SC
Acadia Manor Nursing Home, Acadia, LA
Acadia—St Landry Guest Home Inc, Church Point, LA
Acadia—St Landry Hospital, Church Point, LA
Acadian House Care Center, Baton Rouge, LA
Acadian Nursing Home, Gonzales, LA
Acadian Oaks Living Center, Harvey, LA
Acadiana Nursing Home, Lafayette, LA
Accomack County Nursing Home, Parksley, VA
Achenbach Learning Center, Macksville, KS
Acline Place, Florence, SC
Acushnet Nursing Home, Acushnet, MA
Ada Municipal Hospital, Ada, MN
Ada Retirement & Care Center, Ada, OK
Ada 1, Ada, MN
Ada 2, Ada, MN
Adair Community Health Center, Adair, IA
Adams & Kinton Nursing Home, Lillington, NC

Avis B Adams Christian Convalescent Center, Emporia, VA
Adams County Manor, West Union, OH
Adams County Memorial Hospital Nursing Care Unit, Friendship, WI
Adams County Nursing Center, Natchez, MS
Adams Group Home, Adams, MN
Adams Health Care Center, Adams, MN
Adams House Group Home, Westminster, CO
Adams House Healthcare, Torrington, CT
John Adams Nursing Home, Quincy, MA
Adams Manor, Scranton, PA
Adams Nursing Home, Alexander City, AL
Adams Plaza, Jacksonville, FL
Adams Rest Home Inc, Adams, MA
Adaptive Living Center—Southeast Texas, Beaumont, TX
Adaptive Livng Center—Central Texas, Waco, TX
Adare Medical Center, Rockledge, FL
ADD—1167 Neil, Columbus, OH
ADD—Hampstead, Columbus, OH
ADD—Ida, Columbus, OH
ADD—Indianola, Columbus, OH
ADD—Kimberly, Columbus, OH
ADD—Lane Avenue, Columbus, OH
ADD—Maize Road, Columbus, OH
ADD—Teakwood, Columbus, OH
ADD—1299 Neil, Columbus, OH
ADD—Whittier, Columbus, OH
Addolorata Villa, Wheeling, IL
Adel Acres Care Center, Adel, IA
Adin Manor Convalescent Home, Hopedale, MA
Adirondack Tri-County Nursing Home Inc, North Creek, NY
Adkins Nursing Home, Weleetka, OK
Adkins-Weleetka Nursing Home, Weleetka, OK
Adrian Health Care Center, Adrian, MI
Adrian Manor Inc, Adrian, MO
Adult Foster Care Home, Torrington, WY
Adult Living Center East, Muskogee, OK
Advance Nursing & Residential Care Center, Advance, MO
Advance Nursing Center Inc, Inkster, MI
Adventist Convalescent Hospital, Glendora, CA
Adventist Health Center, Lumberton, MS
Adventist Nursing Home Inc, Livingston, NY
Aftenro Home, Duluth, MN
Afton Care Center, Afton, IA
Afton Oaks Nursing Center, Houston, TX
Ah-Gwah-Ching Nursing Home, Ah Gwah Ching, MN
Ahimsa Care Center, Laguna Beach, CA
Aicota Nursing Home, Aitkin, MN
Aiken Nursing Home, Aiken, SC
Air Force Village Foundation—Health Care Center, San Antonio, TX
Air Force Village II, San Antonio, TX
Air Force Village West Health Care Center, Riverside, CA
Aishel Avraham Residential Health Facility Inc, Brooklyn, NY
Aitkin Community Hospital, Aitkin, MN
Aivert Nursing Home, Ceredo, WV
Akin's Convalescent Hospital, Long Beach, CA

Akron City Convalescent Care Center, Akron, IA
Aksarben Manor, Omaha, NE
Al Mar Residence, Julesburg, CO
Ala Fern Nursing Home, Russell, KS
Alaimo Nursing Home, Rochester, NY
Alamance Memorial Hospital Skilled Nursing Division, Burlington, NC
Alameda Oaks Nursing Center, Corpus Christi, TX
Alamitos Belmont Rehabilitation Hospital, Long Beach, CA
Alamitos West Convalescent Hospital, Los Alamitos, CA
Alamo Heights Manor, San Antonio, TX
Alamo Nursing Home Inc, Kalamazoo, MI
Barry Alan Nursing Home, Saint Louis, MO
Alaska Nursing Home, Cincinnati, OH
Alba Nursing Home, Lynn, MA
Albany Avenue Nursing Home, Kingston, NY
Albany Care Center, Albany, OR
Albany County Nursing Home, Albany, NY
Albany House, Evanston, IL
Albany Nursing Care Inc, Albany, IN
Albemarle, Tarboro, NC
Albemarle Villa, Williamston, NC
Albermarle Health Care Center, Jackson, MS
Albert Lea Good Samaritan Center, Albert Lea, MN
Albert's Nursing & Residential Facility, Warren, OH
Albert's Nursing Home, Warren, OH
Albertville Nursing Home Inc, Albertville, AL
Albia Manor, Albia, IA
Albion Manor Care Center, Albion, MI
Albuquerque Manor Inc, Albuquerque, NM
Alby Residence, Godfrey, IL
Alcoholic Clinic of Youngstown, Youngstown, OH
Alcott Rehabilitation Hospital, Los Angeles, CA
Alden Nursing Center—Heather, Harvey, IL
Alden Nursing Center—Lakeland, Chicago, IL
Alden Nursing Center—Morrow, Chicago, IL
Alden Nursing Center—Naperville, Naperville, IL
Alden Nursing Center—Princeton, Chicago, IL
Alden Nursing Center—Wentworth, Chicago, IL
Alden—Poplar Creek, Hoffman Estates, IL
Alden Terrace Convalescent Hospital, Los Angeles, CA
Alderbrook Inn, Walla Walla, WA
Aldersgate Village Health Unit, Topeka, KS
Aldersly Inc—Danish Home Senior Citizens, San Rafael, CA
Alderson Convalescent Hospital, Woodland, CA
Alderwood Health Care Center, South Elgin, IL
Alderwood Manor, Spokane, WA
Alderwood Manor Convalescent Hospital, San Gabriel, CA
Alderwood Park Convalescent Center, Bellingham, WA
Aldine Health Care Center Inc, Houston, TX
Aldrich Board & Care, Minneapolis, MN
Aledo Health Care Center, Aledo, IL

Aletha Lodge Nursing Home Inc, Booneville, MS

Alexander Continuing Care Center, Royal Oak, MI

Alexander Home, Willmar, MN

Alexander Human Development Center, Alexander, AR

Alexandria Convalescent Center, Alexandria, IN

Alexandria Convalescent Hospital, Los Angeles, CA

Alexandria Residential Care Home, Alexandria, VA

Alexian Village of Milwaukee, Milwaukee, WI

Alexian Village of Tennessee, Signal Mountain, TN

Mildred Alford Nursing Home, Abington, MA

Algart Health Care Inc, Cleveland, OH

Algoma Medical Center & Long-Term Care Unit, Algoma, WI

Algona Manor Care Center, Algona, IA

Alhambra Convalescent Home, Alhambra, CA

Alhambra Convalescent Hospital, Martinez, CA

Alhambra Nursing Home Inc, Saint Petersburg, FL

Alice Manor, Baltimore, MD

Aliceville Manor Nursing Home, Aliceville, AL

All American Health Care, Oklahoma City, OK

All American Nursing Home, Chicago, IL

All Saints Catholic Nursing Home, Jacksonville, FL

All Saints Convalescent Center, North Hollywood, CA

All Sts Rehabilitation Hospital/Springfield Retirement Residence, Wyndmoor, PA

All Seasons Care Center, Houston, TX

All Seasons Care Center, Tyler, TX

All Seasons Care Center—Buffalo, Buffalo, TX

All Seasons Central Care Center, Fort Worth, TX

All Seasons Nursing Center, Arlington, TX

All Seasons Nursing Center, Fort Worth, TX

Allegan County Medical Care Facility, Allegan, MI

Allegany County Nursing Home, Cumberland, MD

Allegany Nursing Home, Allegany, NY

Allegheny Lutheran Home, Hollidaysburg, PA

Allegheny Lutheran Home—Johnstown, Johnstown, PA

Allegheny Manor, Shippenville, PA

Allegheny Valley School—Butler Campus, West Sunbury, PA

Allegheny Valley School for Exceptional Children, Coraopolis, PA

Allen-Calder Skilled Nursing Facility, Utica, NY

Allen County Inn, Lima, OH

Allen Court, Clinton, IL

Allen Hall, Milledgeville, GA

Allen Memorial Home, Mobile, AL

Allen Memorial Hospital, Waterloo, IA

Allen Oaks, Oakdale, LA

Allen Parish Hospital, Kinder, LA

Allen Park Convalescent Home, Allen Park, MI

S D Allen Intermediate Care Facility, Northport, AL

Allenbrook Healthcare Center, Baytown, TX

Allenbrooke Health Care Center, Memphis, TN

Allendale Nursing Home, Allendale, NJ

Allen's Health Centre Inc, South Kingstown, RI

Alliance Home of Carlisle, PA, Carlisle, PA

Alliance Nursing Center, Deland, FL

Alliance Nursing Home Inc, Alliance, OH

Allied Services—Long-Term Care Facility, Scranton, PA

Allied Services—Lynett Village, Scranton, PA

Allison Health Care Center, Lakewood, CO

Allison Health Care Center, Allison, IA

Allison Healthcare Corp, Poseyville, IN

Alma Manor, Alma, KS

Alma Nelson Manor Inc, Rockford, IL

Almeida Rest Home, Boston, MA

Almira Home, New Castle, PA

Aloha Health Care, Kaneohe, HI

Alois Alzheimer Center, Cincinnati, OH

Alpha & Omega Personal Care, Jackson, MS

Alpha Annex Nursing Center, Detroit, MI

Alpha Community House, Charleston, IL

Alpha Health Services Inc No 1, Post Falls, ID

Alpha Health Services Inc No 2, Post Falls, ID

Alpha Health Services Inc No 3, Post Falls, ID

Alpha Home, Indianapolis, IN

Alpha Home, Moorhead, MN

Alpha Manor Nursing Home, Detroit, MI

Alpha Village Long-Term Care Facility, Middleborough, MA

Alpine Convalescent Center, Alpine, CA

Alpine Fireside Health Center, Rockford, IL

Alpine Guest Care Center, Ruston, LA

Alpine Manor, Thornton, CO

Alpine Manor, Grand Rapids, MI

Alpine Manor Health Center, Erie, PA

Alpine North Nursing & Rehabilitation Center, Kansas City, MO

Alpine Nursing & Rehabilitation, Hershey, PA

Alpine Nursing Center, Saint Petersburg, FL

Alpine Rest Home Inc, Coventry, RI

Alpine Terrace, Kerrville, TX

Alpine Valley Care Center, Pleasant Grove, UT

Alpine Village, Verdigre, NE

Alps Manor Nursing Home, Wayne, NJ

Alshore House, Chicago, IL

Alta Care Center, Salt Lake City, UT

Alta Loma Convalescent Hospital, Alta Loma, CA

Alta Mesa Nursing Center, Fort Worth, TX

Alta Mira Nursing Home, Tiffin, OH

Alta Nursing Home Inc, Dayton, OH

Alta Vista Healthcare, Arlington, CA

Alta Vista Nursing Center, San Antonio, TX

Altamaha Convalescent Center, Jesup, GA

Altamont Nursing Center & Retirement Home, Birmingham, AL

Altenheim, Forest Park, IL

Altenheim, Strongsville, OH

Altenheim Community United Church Homes Inc, Indianapolis, IN

Altenheim Inc, Oakland, CA

Altercare of Big Rapids, Big Rapids, MI

Altercare of Mason, Mason, OH

Altercare of Millersburg, Millersburg, OH

Altercare of North Ridgeville, North Ridgeville, OH

Altercare of Ravenna, Ravenna, OH

Alternative Residences Two Inc— Cadiz Home, Cadiz, OH

Alternative Residence Two Inc—Middleton Estates, Gallipolis, OH

Alternative Residences Inc, Columbus, OH

Alternative Residences Inc—C & W Home, Columbus, OH

Alternative Residences Inc—1834 Home, Columbus, OH

Alternative Residences Inc—Indian Trail, West Carrollton, OH

Alternative Residences Inc—James Road Home, Columbus, OH

Alternative Residences Inc—McEwen Road Home, Centerville, OH

Alternative Residences Inc—Norcross Home, Columbus, OH

Alternative Residences Inc—Ottawa Home, Ottawa, OH

Alternative Residences Inc—Putnam Home, Ottawa, OH

Alternative Residences Inc—Regency Ridge Home, Dayton, OH

Alternative Residences Inc—Saville Row Home, Columbus, OH

Alternative Residences Inc—Sidney Home, Sidney, OH

Alternative Residences Three Inc—Hillsboro Home, Hillsboro, OH

Alternative Residences Three Inc—Taylor Home, Hillsboro, OH

Alternative Residences Three Inc—Willetsville Home, Hillsboro, OH

Alternative Residences Two Inc—19th Street Home, Massillon, OH

Alternative Residences Two Inc—346 Waterside Home, Canal Fulton, OH

Alternative Residences Two Inc—Tremont Avenue Home, Massillon, OH

Altoona Center, Altoona, PA

Altoona Health Care Center, Altoona, AL

Altoona Manor Care Center, Altoona, IA

Altus House Nursing Home, Altus, OK

Alum Crest Nursing Home, Columbus, OH

Alvarado Convalescent & Rehabilitation Hospital, San Diego, CA

Alvarado Nursing Home, Alvarado, TX

Alvernia Manor, Lemont, IL

Alverno Health Care Facility, Clinton, IA

Alvin Convalescent Center, Alvin, TX

Alvira Heights Manor, Oklahoma City, OK

Alvis House Mental Retardation Unit, Columbus, OH

Alvista Care Home Inc, Greenville, GA

Amador Hospital D/P, Jackson, CA

Amarillo Good Samaritan Retirement Center, Amarillo, TX

Amarillo Nursing Center, Amarillo, TX

Ambassador, Omaha, NE

Ambassador Convalescent Hospital, West Covina, CA

Ambassador Health Care Center, New Hope, MN

Ambassador Manor Nursing Center Inc, Tulsa, OK

Ambassador Manor South, Jenks, OK

Ambassador North, Cincinnati, OH

Ambassador Nursing Center, Chicago, IL

Ambassador Nursing Center, East Cleveland, OH

Ambassador South, Cincinnati, OH

Amber Health Care Center, Cincinnati, OH

Amber Valley Care Center, Pendleton, OR

Amberwood Convalescent Hospital, Los Angeles, CA

Ambler Rest Center, Ambler, PA

Amboy Care Center, Perth Amboy, NJ

Ambrosia Home Inc, Tampa, FL

AMC Cancer Research Center & Hospital, Lakewood, CO

Amelia Island Care Center, Fernandina Beach, FL

Amelia Manor Nursing Home Inc, Lafayette, LA

Amenity Manor, Topsham, ME

American Beauty Nursing Home, West Frankfort, IL

American Care Center, Perryville, MO

American Finnish Nursing Home Finnish-American Rest Home Inc, Lake Worth, FL

American Heritage Care Center, Hammond, WI

American Indian Nursing Home, Laveen, AZ

American Lutheran Home, Mondovi, WI

American Lutheran Home—Menomonie Unit, Menomonie, WI

American Nursing Home, New York, NY

American Village, Indianapolis, IN

Americana Convalescent Home, Longview, WA

Americana-Family Tree Healthcare Center, Anderson, IN

Americana Health Care Center, Decatur, GA

Americana Health Care Center, Appleton, WI

Americana Health Care Center of Naples, Naples, FL

Americana Health Care Center of Orlando, Orlando, FL

Americana Healthcare Center, Marietta, GA

Americana Healthcare Center, Danville, IL

Americana Healthcare Center, Kankakee, IL

Americana Healthcare Center, Anderson, IN

Americana Healthcare Center, Elkhart, IN

Americana Healthcare Center, Kokomo, IN

Americana Healthcare Center, Cedar Rapids, IA

Americana Healthcare Center, Davenport, IA

Americana Healthcare Center, Mason City, IA

Americana Healthcare Center, Waterloo, IA

Americana Healthcare Center, Kingsford, MI
Americana Healthcare Center, Florissant, MO
Americana Healthcare Center, Springfield, MO
Americana Healthcare Center, Fargo, ND
Americana Healthcare Center, Minot, ND
Americana Healthcare Center, Aberdeen, SD
Americana Healthcare Center, Fond Du Lac, WI
Americana Healthcare Center—East, Green Bay, WI
Americana Healthcare Center—Indianapolis, Indianapolis, IN
Americana Healthcare Center—Indianapolis Midtown, Indianapolis, IN
Americana Healthcare Center—Indianapolis North, Indianapolis, IN
Americana Healthcare Center of Arlington Heights, Arlington Heights, IL
Americana Healthcare Center of Champaign, Champaign, IL
Americana Healthcare Center of Decatur, Decatur, IL
Americana Healthcare Center of Elgin, Elgin, IL
Americana Healthcare Center of Elk Grove Village, Elk Grove Village, IL
Americana Healthcare Center of Jacksonville, Jacksonville, FL
Americana Healthcare Center of Libertyville, Libertyville, IL
Americana Healthcare Center of Naperville, Naperville, IL
Americana Healthcare Center of Normal, Normal, IL
Americana Healthcare Center of Oak Lawn, Oak Lawn, IL
Americana Healthcare Center of Palos Heights, Palos Heights, IL
Americana Healthcare Center of Peoria, Peoria, IL
Americana Healthcare Center of Rolling Meadows, Rolling Meadows, IL
Americana Healthcare Center of South Holland, South Holland, IL
Americana Healthcare Center of Urbana, Urbana, IL
Americana Healthcare Center of Westmont, Westmont, IL
Americana Healthcare Center of Winter Park, Winter Park, FL
Americana Healthcare Center South, Indianapolis, IN
Americana Healthcare Center—West, Green Bay, WI
Americana—Monticello Convalescent Center, Oak Lawn, IL
Americare Arlington Nursing & Rehabilitation Center, Parkersburg, WV
Americare—Circleville, Circleville, OH
Americare Columbus Nursing Center, Columbus, OH
Americare Convalescent Center, Detroit, MI
Americare Dunbar Nursing & Rehabilitation Center, Dunbar, WV
Americare Glenville Nursing & Rehabilitation Center, Glenville, WV
Americare Golden Age Nursing Center, Clovis, NM
Americare—Homestead Nursing & Rehabilitation Center, Lancaster, OH
Americare—Lancaster Nursing & Rehabilitation Center, Lancaster, OH
Americare—Marion, Marion, OH
Americare Morgantown Nursing & Rehabilitation Center, Morgantown, WV
Americare—New Lexington Nursing & Rehabilitation Center, New Lexington, OH
Americare Oregon Nursing & Rehabilitation Center, Oregon, OH
Americare Pine Lodge Nursing & Rehabilitation Center, Beckley, WV
Americare Pomeroy, Pomeroy, OH
Americare Putnam Nursing & Rehabilitation Center, Hurricane, WV
Americare Rio Rancho Nursing Center, Rio Rancho, NM

Americare Rittman Nursing & Rehabilitation Center, Rittman, OH
Americare Salem Nursing & Rehabilitation Center, Salem, WV
Americare—Toledo Nursing & Rehabilitation Center, Toledo, OH
Americare—Woodsfield, Woodsfield, OH
Americas Health Care, Greenville, NC
Americas Health Care of Fayetteville, Fayetteville, NC
Americas Health Care of Oxford, Oxford, NC
Americas Healthcare of Greensboro, Greensboro, NC
Ames Way House, Arvada, CO
Amherst Manor, Amherst, OH
Amherst Manor Nursing Home, Amherst, TX
Amherst Nursing & Convalescent Home, Amherst, NY
Amherst Nursing Home Inc, Amherst, MA
Amherst Presbyterian Nursing Center, Williamsville, NY
Amistad Care Center of Frio County, Pearsall, TX
Amistad II Care Center, Uvalde, TX
Amistad Nursing Home Inc, Uvalde, TX
Amite Nursing Home Inc, Amite, LA
Amory Manor Nursing Home, Amory, MS
AMS Green Tree Health Care Center, Glendale, WI
Amsterdam Memorial Hospital Related Health Care Facility, Amsterdam, NY
Amsterdam Nursing Home Corp, New York, NY
Anacortes Convalescent Center, Anacortes, WA
Anaheim Convalescent Center, Anaheim, CA
Anaheim Terrace Care Center, Anaheim, CA
Anamosa Care Center, Anamosa, IA
Anchor Lodge Nursing Home Inc, Lorain, OH
Anchorage, Bensenville, IL
Anchorage Convalescent Home Inc, Detroit, MI
Anchorage Nursing Home, Shelburne Falls, MA
Anchorage of Beecher, Beecher, IL
Anchorage Pioneers Home, Anchorage, AK
Andbe Home Inc, Norton, KS
Anderson Care Center, Anderson, CA
Anderson Community Residence, Anderson, SC
Anderson County Health Care Center, Clinton, TN
Anderson Health Care Center, Anderson, SC
Anderson Health Center, Miami, FL
Anderson Healthcare Center, Anderson, IN
Anderson Healthcare Inc, Gray, TN
Anderson House Inc, Seattle, WA
Anderson Lane Care Center, Austin, TX
Anderson Memorial Care Homes Inc, Grand Saline, TX
Anderson Place, Anderson, SC
Andover Health Care Center Inc, Andover, KS
Andover Intermediate Care Center, Andover, NJ
Andrew House Healthcare, New Britain, CT
Andrew Residence, Minneapolis, MN
Hiram G Andrews Center, Johnstown, PA
Andrews Nursing Center, Andrews, TX
Andrus Retirement Community, Hastings on Hudson, NY
Aneskarn IV, Brookston, MN
Aneta Good Samaritan Center, Aneta, ND
Angelina Nursing Home Inc, Lufkin, TX
Angeline Nursing Home Inc, North Wales, PA
Angels Nursing Center, Los Angeles, CA
Angels of Mercy Nursing Home, Kansas City, MO
Angelus Convalescent Center East, Inglewood, CA
Angelus Convalescent Center Inc, Pittsburgh, PA
Angelus Convalescent Center West, Inglewood, CA
Angelus Convalescent Home, Minneapolis, MN
Angola Nursing Home, Angola, IN
Anlaw Nursing Home, Lawrence, MA
AnMac IV Group Home, Millersburg, OH

AnMac Home I, Newark, OH
AnMac Home II, Newark, OH
AnMac Home III, Heath, OH
AnMac Home V, Massillon, OH
AnMac Home VI, Massillon, OH
Ann Pearl, Kaneohe, HI
Anna-Henry Nursing Home, Edwardsville, IL
Anna John Home, De Pere, WI
Anna Maria of Aurora Inc, Aurora, OH
Annaburg Manor, Manassas, VA
Annandale Care Center, Annandale, MN
Annapolis Convalescent Center, Annapolis, MD
Anne Maria Medical Care Nursing Home Inc, North Augusta, SC
Annemark Nursing Home, Revere, MA
Annie Mae Matthews Memorial Nursing Home, Alexandria, LA
Anniston Nursing Home, Anniston, AL
Ann's Personal Care Home, Jackson, MS
Ann's Rest Home, Dorchester, MA
Ann's Rest Home, Providence, RI
Ann's Rest Home Inc, Salt Lake City, UT
Ann's Siesta Villa, Springville, UT
Anoka Maple Manor Care Center, Anoka, MN
Ansley Pavilion, Atlanta, GA
Anson County Hospital—SNF, Wadesboro, NC
Ansted Health Care Center, Ansted, WV
Antelope Valley Convalescent Hospital & Nursing Home, Lancaster, CA
Antioch Convalescent Hospital, Antioch, CA
Antlers Nursing Home, Antlers, OK
Marie Antoinette Pavilion, Marietta, OH
Anza Convalescent Hospital, El Cajon, CA
Apache Junction Health Center, Apache Junction, AZ
Apalachicola Health Care Center Inc, Apalachicola, FL
Apalachicola Valley Nursing Center, Blountstown, FL
Apostolic Christian Home, Roanoke, IL
Apostolic Christian Home, Sabetha, KS
Apostolic Christian Home Inc, Rittman, OH
Apostolic Christian Resthaven, Elgin, IL
Apostolic Christian Restmor Inc, Morton, IL
Apostolic Lutheran Home, Calumet, MI
Apostolic Morton, Morton, IL
Apostolic Peoria, Peoria, IL
Appalachian Christian Village, Johnson City, TN
Appalachian Regional Hospital Skilled Nursing Facility, South Williamson, KY
Apple Creek Developmental Center, Apple Creek, OH
Apple Geriatric Care, Castro Valley, CA
Apple Tree Inn, Fayetteville, AR
Apple Tree Lane Ltd, Romulus, MI
Apple Valley Convalescent, Sebastopol, CA
Apple Valley Health Center, Apple Valley, MN
Applegarth Care Center, Hightstown, NJ
Applegate Care Center, Auburn, WA
Applegate East, Galesburg, IL
Appleton Municipal Hospital, Appleton, MN
Applewood Care Center Inc, Chanute, KS
Applewood Healthcare Center, Winchester, NH
Applewood Inn, Redding, CA
Applewood Living Center, Longmont, CO
Applewood Living Center, Matteson, IL
Applewood Manor, McMillan, MI
Applewood Manor, Freehold, NJ
Applewood Nursing Center, Woodhaven, MI
Applin Nursing Home, Springfield, OH
Appling County Nursing Home, Baxley, GA
Appomattox Health Care Center, Appomattox, VA
Approved Home Inc, Chicago, IL
Arah's Acres, Hallsville, MO
Aransas Pass Nursing & Convalescent Center, Aransas Pass, TX
Ararat Convalescent Hospital, Los Angeles, CA
Arbor Care Center, Beeville, TX
Arbor Convalescent Hospital, Lodi, CA
Arbor Glen Care Center, Glendora, CA
Arbor Home, Detroit, MI

Arbor Inn, Warren, MI
Arbor Manor, Fremont, NE
Arbor Manor Care Center, Spring Arbor, MI
Arbor of Itasca, Itasca, IL
Arbor View Healthcare Center Inc, Madison, WI
Arboridge Care Center, Galesburg, MI
Arboridge Care Center, Kalamazoo, MI
Arbors at Canton, Canton, OH
Arbors at Fairlawn, Fairlawn, OH
Arbors at Fairmont, Fairmont, WV
Arbors at Hilliard, Hilliard, OH
Arbors at Marietta, Marietta, OH
Arbors at Toledo, Toledo, OH
Arbors Health Care Center, Camp Verde, AZ
Arborway Manor Inc, Boston, MA
Arbour Health Care Center Ltd, Chicago, IL
Arbutus Park Manor, Johnstown, PA
ARCA Group Home—615 Louisiana, Albuquerque, NM
ARCA Group Home—1120 Louisiana, Albuquerque, NM
ARCA Group Home A Centro Familiar, Albuquerque, NM
ARCA Group Home A Copper, Albuquerque, NM
ARCA Group Home B Centro Familiar, Albuquerque, NM
ARCA Group Home B Copper, Albuquerque, NM
ARCA Group Home—Corrales, Albuquerque, NM
ARCA Group Home Gibson 3, Albuquerque, NM
ARCA Group Home Gibson 2, Albuquerque, NM
ARCA Group Home—Gun Club, Albuquerque, NM
ARCA Group Home—Trumbull, Albuquerque, NM
Arcadia, Honolulu, HI
Arcadia Acres, Logan, OH
Arcadia Baptist Home, Arcadia, LA
Arcadia Care Manor, Evansville, IN
Arcadia Children's Home, Arcadia, IN
Arcadia Convalescent Hospital, Arcadia, CA
Arcadia Manor, Cincinnati, OH
Arcadia Nursing Center, Coolville, OH
Arcadia Nursing Center, Nelsonia, VA
Arcadia Nursing Home, Lowell, MA
Arch Creek Nursing Home, North Miami, FL
Archbishop Leibold Home, Cincinnati, OH
Archer Nursing Home, Archer City, TX
Archie Drive Group Home, Columbia, SC
Archuse Convalescent Center Inc, Quitman, MS
Arden Hill Life Care Center, Goshen, NY
Arden House, Hamden, CT
Arden Nursing Home, Seattle, WA
Ardis Nursing Home, Farwell, MI
Ardmore Memorial Convalescent Home, Ardmore, OK
Ardmore Nursing Home Inc, Ardmore, TN
Area Nursing Home Inc, Colfax, WI
Argyle, Denver, CO
Argyle House, Springfield, IL
Aristocrat Berea, Berea, OH
Aristocrat Lakewood, Lakewood, OH
Aristocrat South, Parma Heights, OH
Arizona Eastern Star Home, Phoenix, AZ
Arizona Elks Long-Term Care, Tucson, AZ
Arizona Pioneers' Home, Prescott, AZ
Arizona Rehabilitation Center—SNF, Sun City, AZ
Arizona William-Wesley Nursing Home, Tucson, AZ
Arkadelphia Human Developmental Center, Arkadelphia, AR
Arkansas City Presbyterian Manor, Arkansas City, KS
Arkansas Convalescent Center, Texarkana, AR
Arkansas Convalescent Center—Pine Bluff, Pine Bluff, AR
Arkansas Easter Seal Residential Center, Little Rock, AR
Arkansas Health Care, Hot Springs, AR
Arkansas Healthcare Nursing Center, Hot Springs, AR

Arkansas Manor Nursing Home Inc, Denver, CO
Arkansas Valley Regional Medical Center Nursing Care Center, La Junta, CO
Arkhaven at Altamont, Altamont, KS
Arkhaven at Erie, Erie, KS
Arkhaven at Fort Scott, Fort Scott, KS
Arkhaven at Garnett, Garnett, KS
Arkhaven at Iola, Iola, KS
Arlington Care Center, Arlington, SD
Arlington Convalescent Center, Arlington, WA
Arlington Court Nursing Home, Columbus, OH
Arlington Gardens Convalescent Hospital, Riverside, CA
Arlington Good Samaritan Center, Arlington, MN
Arlington Good Samaritan Center, Arlington, OH
Arlington Green Eldercare, Quincy, MA
Arlington Heights Nursing Center, Fort Worth, TX
Arlington Home, Fergus Falls, MN
Arlington Manor, Lawton, OK
Arlington Manor Care Center, Jacksonville, FL
Arlington Nursing Center, Arlington, TX
Arlington Nursing Home Inc, Newark, OH
Arlington Villa for Senior Citizens, Arlington, TX
Armacost Nursing Home Inc, Baltimore, MD
Armenian Nursing Home, Jamaica Plain, MA
Armour Heights Nursing Home Inc, Fort Smith, AR
Armour Home, Kansas City, MO
Arms of Mercy Care Center Inc, San Antonio, TX
Armstrong County Health Center, Kittanning, PA
Armstrong Nursing Home, Worcester, MA
Armstrong's Personal Care Home I, Jackson, MS
Armstrong's Personal Care Home II, Jackson, MS
Army Residence Community Health Care Center, San Antonio, TX
Arnett Pritchett Foundation Home, Lexington, KY
Arnold Avenue Nursing Home, Greenville, MS
Arnold Home Inc, Detroit, MI
Arnold House Incorporated, Stoneham, MA
Arnold Memorial Nursing Home, Adrian, MN
Arnold's Care Center, Austin, TX
Arnot-Ogden Memorial Hospital Skilled Nursing Unit, Elmira, NY
Arolyn Heights Nursing Home, Chanute, KS
Aroostook Medical Center—Community General Hospital Division, Fort Fairfield, ME
Aroostook Residential Center, Presque Isle, ME
Arrise Group Home for Young Adults—Autism, Oak Park, IL
Arrowhead Health Care Center, Eveleth, MN
Arrowhead Health Care Center, Virginia, MN
Arrowhead Home, San Bernardino, CA
Arrowhead Nursing Center, Jonesboro, GA
Arrowood Nursing Center, Battle Creek, MI
Arroyo Vista Convalescent Center, San Diego, CA
Arterburn Home Inc, West Haven, CT
Artesia Christian Home Inc, Artesia, CA
Artesia General Hospital, Artesia, NM
Artesia Good Samaritan Center, Artesia, NM
Artesian Home, Sulphur, OK
Arthur Good Samaritan Center, Arthur, ND
Arthur Home, Arthur, IL
Artman Lutheran Home, Ambler, PA
Artrips Personal Care Home, Ashland, KY
Arundel Geriatric & Nursing Center, Glen Burnie, MD
Arvada Health Center, Arvada, CO
Asbury Center at Baysmont, Kingsport, TN
Asbury Center at Birdmont, Wytheville, VA
Asbury Center at Oak Manor, Chattanooga, TN
Asbury Center, Johnson City, TN

Asbury Centers Inc, Maryville, TN
Asbury Circle Living Center, Denver, CO
Asbury Heights, Pittsburgh, PA
Asbury Towers, Bradenton, FL
Asbury Towers, Greencastle, IN
Ash Flat Convalescent Center, Ash Flat, AR
Ash Grove Nursing Home Inc, Ash Grove, MO
Ashbrook Nursing Home, Scotch Plains, NJ
Ashburn Health Care Inc, Ashburn, GA
Ashburnham Rest Home Inc, Ashburnham, MA
Ashburton Nursing Home, Baltimore, MD
Ashby Geriatric Hospital Inc, Berkeley, CA
Ashland Avenue Nursing Home, Toledo, OH
Ashland Convalescent Center Inc, Ashland, VA
Ashland Health Care Center Inc, Ashland, WI
Ashland Manor, Ashland, OH
Ashland Manor Nursing Home, Ashland, MA
Ashland State General Hospital Geriatric Center, Ashland, PA
Ashland Terrace, Lexington, KY
Ashlar of Newtown, A Masonic Home, Newtown, CT
Ashley Manor Care Center, Boonville, MO
Ashley Manor Care Center Inc, Miami, FL
Ashley Medical Center, Ashley, ND
Ashley Place Health Care Inc, Youngstown, OH
Ashmere Manor Nursing Home, Hinsdale, MA
Ashmore Estates, Ashmore, IL
Ashtabula County Nursing Home, Kingsville, OH
Ashtabula Medicare Nursing Center, Ashtabula, OH
Ashton Hall Nursing & Rehabilitation, Philadelphia, PA
Ashton Memorial, Ashton, ID
Ashton Woods Convalescent Center, Atlanta, GA
Ashville Manor Nursing Home, Ashville, AL
Ashwood Health Care Center, Willmar, MN
Asian Community Nursing Home, Sacramento, CA
Asistencia Villa Convalescent Center, Redlands, CA
Aspen Care Center, Ogden, UT
Aspen Care Center—West, Glenwood Springs, CO
Aspen Living Center, Colorado Springs, CO
Aspen Siesta, Denver, CO
Aspenwood Health Care Center, Silvis, IL
Aspin Center, Harrisburg, PA
Assembly Nursing Home, Poplar Bluff, MO
Assumption General Hospital, Napoleonville, LA
Assumption Health Care Center, Napoleonville, LA
Assumption Home, Cold Spring, MN
Assumption Nursing Home, Youngstown, OH
Asthmatic Childrens Foundation of New York Inc, Ossining, NY
Aston Park Health Care Center Inc, Asheville, NC
Astor Gardens Nursing Home, Bronx, NY
Astoria Convalescent Hospital, Sylmar, CA
Astoria Healthcare Center, Astoria, IL
Atchison Senior Village, Atchison, KS
Athena Manor, Newark, OH
Athens Convalescent Center Inc, Athens, AL
Athens Group Home, Athens, ME
Athens Health Care Center, Athens, TN
Athens Health Care Center Inc, Athens, GA
Athens Heritage Home Inc, Athens, GA
Athens Nursing Home, Athens, TX
Atkinson Good Samaritan Center, Atkinson, NE
Georgia Atkison Convalescent Center, El Monte, CA
Atlanta Health Care Center, Austell, GA
Atlantacare Convalescent Center Intermediate Care Unit, Decatur, GA
Atlantic Care Center, Atlantic, IA
Atlantic Highlands Nursing Home, Atlantic Highlands, NJ
Atlantic Rest Home, Lynn, MA
AtlantiCare Nursing Home, Revere, MA

Atlantis Nursing Center, Lantana, FL
Atmore Nursing Care Center, Atmore, AL
Atoka Care Center, Atoka, OK
Atoka Colonial Manor Inc, Atoka, OK
Atrium Health Care Center Ltd, Chicago, IL
Atrium Village, Hills, IA
Attala County Nursing Center, Kosciusko, MS
Attalla Health Care Inc, Attalla, AL
Attic Angel, Madison, WI
Attleboro Nursing & Rehabilitation Center, Langhorne, PA
Atwater House, Atwater, MN
Atwood Manor Nursing Center, Galion, OH
Atwood Nursing Center, Carrollton, OH
Auburn Gardens Convalescent Hospital, Auburn, CA
Auburn House Nursing Home, Boston, MA
Auburn Manor, Chaska, MN
Auburn Manor, Washington Court House, OH
Auburn Nursing Center Inc, Auburn, KY
Auburn Nursing Home, Auburn, ME
Auburn Nursing Home, Auburn, NY
Auburn Park Club, Chicago, IL
Auburn Ravine Terrace, Auburn, CA
Audubon Guest House, Thibodaux, LA
Audubon Living Center, Hammond, LA
Audubon Villa, Lititz, PA
Auglaize Acres, Wapakoneta, OH
Augsburg Lutheran Home of Maryland, Pikesville, MD
Augusta Convalescent Center, Augusta, ME
Augusta Health Care, Augusta, GA
Augusta Mental Health Institute, Augusta, ME
Augusta Nursing Home, Augusta, WI
Augustana Home of Minneapolis, Minneapolis, MN
Augustana Lutheran Home, Brooklyn, NY
Aurora Australis Lodge, Columbus, MS
Aurora-Brule Nursing Home, White Lake, SD
Aurora Care Center, Aurora, CO
Aurora Community Living Facility, Aurora, IL
Aurora-Edmonds Nursing Home, Edmonds, WA
Aurora House, Saint Paul, MN
Aurora Manor, Aurora, IL
Aurora Nursing Center, Aurora, MO
Aurora Park Health Center Inc, East Aurora, NY
Aurora Road Home, Solon, OH
Ausable Valley Home, Fairview, MI
Austin Home Inc, Warner, NH
Austin Manor Nursing Home, Austin, TX
Moses Austin Group Care Home Inc, Potosi, MO
Austin Nursing Center, Austin, TX
Austin Nursing Home, Seattle, WA
Austin Woods Nursing Center, Austintown, OH
Austin's Rest Haven Nursing Home, Metairie, LA
Autauga Health Care Center, Prattville, AL
Autumn Aegis Nursing Home, Lorain, OH
Autumn Breeze Health Care Center, Eight Mile, AL
Autumn Breeze Nursing Home, Marietta, GA
Autumn Care Cannon Manor, Fort Worth, TX
Autumn Care Cliff Gardens, Dallas, TX
Autumn Care of Altavista, Altavista, VA
Autumn Care of Biscoe, Biscoe, NC
Autumn Care of Castleton, Indianapolis, IN
Autumn Care of Chesapeake, Chesapeake, VA
Autumn Care of Clark's Creek, Plainfield, IN
Autumn Care of Drexel, Drexel, NC
Autumn Care of Great Bridge, Chesapeake, VA
Autumn Care of Ladoga, Ladoga, IN
Autumn Care of Madison, Madison, VA
Autumn Care of Marion, Marion, NC
Autumn Care of Marshville, Marshville, NC
Autumn Care of Mocksville, Mocksville, NC
Autumn Care of Portsmouth, Portsmouth, VA
Autumn Care of Raeford, Raeford, NC
Autumn Care of Salisbury, Salisbury, NC
Autumn Care of Saluda, Saluda, NC
Autumn Care of Suffolk, Suffolk, VA
Autumn Care of Waynesville, Waynesville, NC

Autumn Court Nursing Center, Columbia, MO
Autumn Heights Health Care Center, Denver, CO
Autumn Hills Care Center Inc, Niles, OH
Autumn Hills Convalescent Center, Richmond, TX
Autumn Hills Convalescent Center, Sugar Land, TX
Autumn Hills Convalescent Center—Conroe, Conroe, TX
Autumn Hills Convalescent Center—Janisch, Houston, TX
Autumn Hills Convalescent Center—Tomball, Tomball, TX
Autumn Hills Convalescent Hospital, Glendale, CA
Autumn Leaves, Dallas, TX
Autumn Leaves Care Center of Shreveport, Shreveport, LA
Autumn Leaves Nursing Home, Winnfield, LA
Autumn Leaves Nursing Home Inc, Greenville, MS
Autumn Living Care Center, Salt Lake City, UT
Autumn Nursing Centers Inc 1, Vinita, OK
Autumn Nursing Centers Inc 2, Vinita, OK
Autumn Oaks Care Center, Lewisville, TX
Autumn Splendor Health Care, Mountain View, OK
Autumn View Manor, Hamburg, NY
Autumn Villa Care Center, Canton, OH
Autumn Winds Retirement Lodge, Schertz, TX
Autumn Woods Residential Health Care Facility, Warren, MI
Autumn Years Lodge Inc, Fort Worth, TX
Autumn Years Nursing Center, Sabina, OH
Autumnfield East, Memphis, TN
Autumnfield Inc of Lowell, Gastonia, NC
Autumnfield of Asheville, Asheville, NC
Autumnfield of Danville, Danville, KY
Autumnwood Care Center, Tiffin, OH
Autumnwood of Deckerville, Deckerville, MI
Autumnwood of McBain, McBain, MI
Autumnwood of Sylvania, Toledo, OH
Autumnwood Villa, McPherson, KS
Auventine Retirement & Nursing Center, Saint Louis, MO
Auxilio Mutuo Hospital, Hato Rey, PR
Avalon Garden, Saint Louis, MO
Avalon Manor Inc, Hagerstown, MD
Avalon Manor Infirmary, Waukesha, WI
Avalon Nursing Home Inc, Warwick, RI
Avalon Place, Kirbyville, TX
Avalon Place, Texas City, TX
Avalon Place—Odessa Nursing Center, Odessa, TX
Avalon Place—Trinity, Trinity, TX
Avante Villa, Corpus Christi, TX
Avante Villa at Jacksonville Beach, Jacksonville Beach, FL
Ave Maria Convalescent Hospital, Monterey, CA
Ave Maria Home, Memphis, TN
Avenue Care Center Inc, Chicago, IL
Avery Nursing Home, Hartford, CT
Aveyron Homes Inc, Hutchinson, MN
Aviston Countryside Manor, Aviston, IL
Aviston Terrace, Aviston, IL
Aviva Manor, Lauderdale Lakes, FL
Avon Convalescent Home, Avon, CT
Avon Nursing Home, Avon, NY
Avon Nursing Home Inc, Avon, IL
Avon Oaks Nursing Home, Avon, OH
Avondale Convalescent Home, Rochester, MI
Avonside Nursing Home, Detroit, MI
Avoyelles Manor Inc, Plaucheville, LA
Ayer-Lar Sanitarium, Gardena, CA
Ayers Nursing Home, Snyder, OK
Ayr Hill Adult Home, Vienna, VA
Azalea Gardens Nursing Center, Wiggins, MS
Azalea Manor Nursing Home, Sealy, TX
Azalea Park Manor, Muskogee, OK
Azalea Trace, Pensacola, FL
Azalea Villa Nursing Home, New Iberia, LA
Azalealand Nursing Home Inc, Savannah, GA
Azle Manor Inc, Azle, TX

B & B Nursing Home, Comanche, OK
B & C Rest Home, Sturgis, SD
B & K Nursing Center, Hobart, OK
Bachelor Butte Nursing Home, Bend, OR
Bacon Nursing Home Inc, Harrisburg, IL
Badger Prairie Health Care Center, Verona, WI
Badillo Convalescent Hospital, Covina, CA
Baggott House, Chicago, IL
Bagwell Nursing Home, Carrollton, GA
Baha'i Home Inc, Wilmette, IL
Bailey Nursing Home, Clinton, SC
Bailie's Rest Home, Fairhaven, MA
Bainbridge Health Care Inc, Bainbridge, GA
Bainbridge Nursing Home, Bronx, NY
Baird Nursing Home, Rochester, NY
Baker Katz Nursing Home, Haverhill, MA
Baker Manor Nursing Home, Baker, LA
Baker-Sumser Health Care Center, Canton, OH
Baker's Rest Haven, Boonville, IN
Bakersfield Convalescent Hospital, Bakersfield, CA
Bala Retirement & Rehabilitation, Philadelphia, PA
Balch Springs Nursing Home, Balch Springs, TX
Baldock Health Care Center, North Huntingdon, PA
Baldwin Care Center, Baldwin, WI
Baldwin Health Center, Pittsburgh, PA
Baldwin Manor Nursing Home Inc, Cleveland, OH
Baldwinville Nursing Home, Templeton, MA
Ball Pavilion, Erie, PA
Ballard Convalescent Center, Seattle, WA
Ballard Nursing Center, Ada, OK
Ballard Nursing Center Inc, Des Plaines, IL
Ballinger Nursing Center, Ballinger, TX
Ballou Home for the Aged, Woonsocket, RI
Balmoral Care Center, Tucson, AZ
Balmoral Nursing Centre Inc, Chicago, IL
Balmoral Skilled Nursing Home, Trenton, MI
Balowen Care Center, Van Nuys, CA
Baltic Country Manor, Baltic, OH
Bamberg County Memorial Nursing Center, Bamberg, SC
Bancroft Convalescent Hospital, San Leandro, CA
Bancroft Family Care Home, Toledo, OH
Bancroft House Healthcare Nursing Home, Worcester, MA
Bangor City Nursing Facility, Bangor, ME
Bangor Convalescent Center, Bangor, ME
Bangor Mental Health Institute, Bangor, ME
Bangs Nursing Home, Bangs, TX
Banks-Jackson-Commerce Nursing Home, Commerce, GA
Bannister Nursing Care Center, Providence, RI
Bannochie Nursing Home, Minneapolis, MN
Bannock County Nursing Home, Pocatello, ID
Baptist Convalescent Center, Newport, KY
Baptist Health Care Center, Lenoir City, TN
Baptist Home, Chillicothe, Chillicothe, MO
Baptist Home East, Louisville, KY
Baptist Home for Senior Citizens Inc, Cook Springs, AL
Baptist Home for the Aged, Bronx, NY
Baptist Home Inc, Ironton, MO
Baptist Home Inc, Bismarck, ND
Baptist Home of Brooklyn New York, Rhinebeck, NY
Baptist Home of Maryland Del Inc, Owings Mills, MD
Baptist Home of Massachusetts, Newton, MA
Baptist Home of Philadelphia, Philadelphia, PA
Baptist Homes Nursing Center, Pittsburgh, PA
Baptist Manor, Portland, OR
Baptist Manor Inc, Pensacola, FL
Baptist Medical Center & Skilled Nursing Unit—Montclair, Birmingham, AL
Baptist Memorial Home, Harlan, IA
Baptist Memorial Hospital Skilled Nursing Unit, Memphis, TN
Baptist Memorials Geriatric Center, San Angelo, TX

Baptist Regional Health Center SNF, Miami, OK
Baptist Residence, Minneapolis, MN
Baptist Retirement Center, Scotia, NY
Baptist Retirement Home, Maywood, IL
Baptist Retirement Homes of North Carolina Inc, Winston-Salem, NC
Baptist Village Inc, Waycross, GA
Baraga County Memorial Hospital, L'Anse, MI
Dr Gertrude A Barber Center Inc, Erie, PA
Barberton Citizens Hospital, Barberton, OH
Barbour County Good Samaritan Center, Belington, WV
BARC Housing Inc, Davie, FL
Barclay Boarding Home, Seattle, WA
Barcroft Institute, Falls Church, VA
Barfield Health Care Inc, Guntersville, AL
Grace Barker Nursing Home Inc, Warren, RI
Barker Rest Home, Galena, KS
Barley Convalescent Home—North, York, PA
Barn Hill Convalescent Center, Newton, NJ
Barnard Nursing Home, Calais, ME
Barnard Rest Home, Westfield, MA
Barnegat Nursing Center, Barnegat, NJ
Barnes-Kasson County Hospital Skilled Nursing Facility, Susquehanna, PA
Barnesville Care Center, Barnesville, MN
Barnesville Health Care Center, Barnesville, OH
Barnesville Home, Barnesville, OH
Barnett Multi-Health Care Facility, Bridgeport, CT
Barnett's Stilhaven Nursing Home, Dayton, OH
Barnsdall Nursing Home, Barnsdall, OK
Barnwell County Nursing Home, Barnwell, SC
Barnwell Nursing Home, Valatie, NY
Barr House, Canon, CO
Warren N Barr Pavilion/Illinois Masonic Medical Center, Chicago, IL
Barren County Health Care Center, Glasgow, KY
Barrett Care Center Inc, Barrett, MN
Barrett Convalescent Hospital, Hayward, CA
Barrington Terrace Nursing Home, Orlando, FL
Barron Center, Portland, ME
Barron Memorial Medical Center Skilled Nursing Facility, Barron, WI
Barron Riverside Manor, Barron, WI
Barry Community Care Center, Barry, IL
Barry County Care Center, Cassville, MO
Bartel's Lutheran Home, Waverly, IA
Barth Nursing Home, Anacortes, WA
M A Barthell Order of Eastern Star Home, Decorah, IA
Bartholomew County Home, Columbus, IN
Bartlett Manor Nursing Home, Malden, MA
Bartley Manor Convalescent Center, Jackson, NJ
Bartmann Health Care Center, Atlanta, IL
Clara Barton Terrace, Flint, MI
Barton Heights Nursing Home Inc, Austin, TX
A Barton Hepburn Hospital Skilled Nursing Facility, Ogdensburg, NY
Barton House, Indianapolis, IN
Kathryn Barton Nursing Home, Wayland, MA
Barton Nursing Home, Detroit, MI
Barton W Stone Christian Home, Jacksonville, IL
Bartow Convalescent Center, Bartow, FL
Bashford East Health Care Facility, Louisville, KY
Basile Care Center Inc, Basile, LA
Bass Memorial Baptist Hospital, Enid, OK
Bassard Convalescent Hospital Inc, Hayward, CA
Basswood Health Care Center, Princeton, IL
Bastrop Nursing Center, Bastrop, TX
Batavia Nursing & Convalescent Inn, Batavia, OH
Batavia Nursing Home Inc, Batavia, NY
Batavia Nursing Home Inc, Batavia, OH
Batesville Manor Nursing Home, Batesville, MS
Bath Nursing Home, Bath, ME

Baton Rouge Extensive Care, Baton Rouge, LA
Baton Rouge General Medical Center Skilled Nursing Facility, Baton Rouge, LA
Baton Rouge Health Care Center, Baton Rouge, LA
Baton Rouge Heritage House Nursing Home II, Baton Rouge, LA
Battersby Convalescent Center, Erie, PA
Batterson Convalescent Hospital, Santa Cruz, CA
Battle Lake Care Center, Battle Lake, MN
Battlefield Park Convalescent Center, Petersburg, VA
Battles Home, Lowell, MA
Bauer Residential Care Facility, Rocky Ford, CO
Baxley Manor Inc, Baxley, GA
Baxter Manor Nursing Home, Mountain Home, AR
Bay Breeze Nursing & Retirement Center, Gulf Breeze, FL
Bay Brook Villa, Texas City, TX
Bay Convalescent Center, Panama City, FL
Bay Convalescent Hospital, Long Beach, CA
Bay County Medical Care Facility, Essexville, MI
Bay Crest Care Center, Torrance, CA
Bay Harbor Rehabilitation Center, Torrance, CA
Bay Heritage Nursing & Convalescent Center, Niceville, FL
Bay Manor Health Care Center, Mobile, AL
Bay Manor Nursing Home Inc, Arnold, MD
Bay Path at Duxbury Nursing Rehabilitation, Duxbury, MA
Bay Pointe Nursing Pavilion, Saint Petersburg, FL
Bay St Joseph Care Center, Port Saint Joseph, FL
Bay Shore Sanitarium, Tujunga, CA
Bay Shores Nursing Care Center, Bay City, MI
Bay to Bay Nursing Center Inc, Tampa, FL
Bay Tower Nursing Center, Providence, RI
Bay View Nursing Center Inc, Beaufort, SC
Bay View Nursing Home, Winthrop, MA
Bay Villa Nursing Home, Bay City, TX
Bay Village of Sarasota, Sarasota, FL
Bay Vista, Santa Monica, CA
Bayard Care Center, Bayard, IA
Bayberry Commons Inc, Pascoag, RI
Bayberry Convalescent Hospital, Concord, CA
Bayberry Nursing Home, New Rochelle, NY
Bayboro Health Care Center & Britthaven of Pamlico, Grantsboro, NC
Bayless Boarding Home, Farmington, MO
Bayou Chateau Nursing Center, Simmesport, LA
Bayou Glen-Jones Road, Houston, TX
Bayou Glen—Northwest, Houston, TX
Bayou Glen-Town Park, Houston, TX
Bayou Manor, Houston, TX
Bayou Manor Health Care, Saint Petersburg, FL
Bayou Village Nursing Center, Crowley, LA
Bayou Vista Manor, Bunkie, LA
Bayshore Convalescent Center, North Miami Beach, FL
Bayshore Health Care Center, Holmdel, NJ
Bayside Nursing Center, Lexington Park, MD
Bayside Nursing Home, Boston, MA
Bayside of Poquoson Convalescent Center, Poquoson, VA
Bayside Terrace, Waukegan, IL
Baytown Nursing Home, Baytown, TX
Baytree Nursing Center, Palm Harbor, FL
Bayview Convalescent Center, Bayville, NJ
Bayview Manor, Seattle, WA
Bayview Nursing Home, Island Park, NY
Baywind Village Convalescent Center, League City, TX
Baywood Convalescent Hospital, Pleasant Hill, CA
Baywood Nursing Home, Ludington, MI
Beach Cliff Lodge Nursing Home, Michigan City, IN
Beach Convalescent Home, Saint Petersburg Beach, FL

Beach Convalescent Hotel, Saint Petersburg, FL
Beach Haven Health Care Center, Beachwood, OH
Beach Nursing Home, Monroe, MI
Beachview Intermediate Care Facility, Keansburg, NJ
Beachwood, Kennebunk, ME
Beacon-Donegan Manor, Fort Myers, FL
Beacon Hill, Lombard, IL
Beacon Hill Nursing Home, Kansas City, MO
Beacon Manor, Indiana, PA
Beadles Rest Home, Alva, OK
Bear Creek Health Care Center, Bear Creek, PA
Bear Creek House, Rochester, MN
Bear Creek Nursing Center, Morrison, CO
Bear Creek Nursing Center Inc, Hudson, FL
Bear Hill Nursing Center at Wakefield, Stoneham, MA
Bear Lake Memorial Nursing Home, Montpelier, ID
Beardstown Health Care Complex, Beardstown, IL
Beatitudes Campus of Care, Phoenix, AZ
Beatrice Catherine Rest Home, Boston, MA
Beatrice Good Samaritan Center, Beatrice, NE
Beatrice Manor Care Center, Beatrice, NE
Beauclerc Manor, Jacksonville, FL
Beaulieu Convalescent Center Inc, Newnan, GA
Beaumont at Bryn Mawr, Bryn Mawr, PA
Beaumont at the Willows A Skilled Nursing Facility, Westborough, MA
Beaumont Convalescent Hospital, Beaumont, CA
Beaumont Nursing Home, Northbridge, MA
Beaumont Nursing Home, Denton, TX
Beauregard Nursing Home Inc, DeRidder, LA
Beautiful Savior Home, Belton, MO
Beaver City Manor, Beaver City, NE
Beaver County Nursing Home, Beaver, OK
Beaver Dam Care Center, Beaver Dam, WI
Beaver Dam Health Care Manor, Beaver Dam, KY
Beaver Dam Lakeview Unit, Beaver Dam, WI
Beaver Valley Geriatric Center, Beaver, PA
Beaver Valley Nursing Center, Beaver Falls, PA
Peter Becker Community, Harleysville, PA
Beckwood Manor, Anniston, AL
Bedford County Memorial Hospital—Oakwood Manor Nursing Home, Bedford, VA
Bedford County Nursing Home, Shelbyville, TN
Bedford County Nursing Home, Bedford, VA
Bedford Group Home, Woodinville, WA
Bedford Manor, Bedford, IA
Bedford Nursing Center, Gardner, KS
Bedford Nursing Home, Bedford, IN
Bedford Village Nursing Home Inc, New Bedford, MA
Beech Grove Healthcare Center, Beech Grove, IN
Beech Manor Rest Home, Springfield, MA
Beech Street ICF/MR, Claremont, NH
Beecher Manor, Flint, MI
Beechknoll Convalescent Center, Cincinnati, OH
Beechknoll Terrace Retirement Center, Cincinnati, OH
Beechnut Manor Living Center, Houston, TX
Beechwood Health Care Center, Pekin, IL
Beechwood Home, Cincinnati, OH
Beechwood Manor Inc, New London, CT
Beechwood Nursing Home, Elma, WA
Beechwood Residence, Getzville, NY
Beechwood Rest Home, Kewaskum, WI
Beechwood Sanitarium, Rochester, NY
Beeman Place, Lake Elmo, MN
Beemans Sanitarium, Whittier, CA
Beggs Nursing Center, Beggs, OK
Behling Memorial Home Inc, Clintonville, WI
Bel Air, Tacoma, WA
Bel-Air Care Center, Alliance, OH
Bel Air Convalescent Center Inc, Bel Air, MD
Bel-Air Health Care Center, Columbia, TN

Bel Air Health Care Center, Milwaukee, WI
Bel-Air Lodge Convalescent Hospital, Turlock, CA
Bel-Air Manor, Newington, CT
Bel-Air Nursing Home, Goffstown, NH
Bel-Aire Quality Care Nursing Home, Newport, VT
Bel Arbor Medical Care, Macon, GA
Bel Forest Nursing & Rehabilitation Center, Forest Hill, MD
Bel Isle Nursing Home, Phoenix, AZ
Bel Tooren Villa Convalescent Hospital, Bellflower, CA
Bel Vista Convalescent Hospital, Long Beach, CA
Bel-Wood Nursing Home, Peoria, IL
Belair Convalesarium, Baltimore, MD
Belair Nursing Center, Lower Burrell, PA
Belair Nursing Home, North Bellmore, NY
Belchertown State School, Belchertown, MA
Belcourt Terrace Nursing Home, Nashville, TN
Belding Christian Nursing Home, Belding, MI
Belen Health Care Center, Belen, NM
Belgrade Nursing Home, Belgrade, MN
Belhaven Inc, Chicago, IL
Belhaven Nursing Home, Jackson, MS
Belinda Care Center, Celina, TX
Belknap County Nursing Home, Laconia, NH
Bell Convalescent Hospital, Bell, CA
Bell Crest Inc, Cool Valley, MO
Bell Gardens Convalescent Center, Bell Gardens, CA
Bell Haven Convalescent & Nursing Care Center, Killeen, TX
Bell Hill Recovery Center, Wadena, MN
Bell Manor Inc, Normandy, MO
Bell-Minor Home Inc, Gainesville, GA
Bell Nursing Home, Kimbolton, OH
Bell Nursing Home Inc, Belmont, OH
Bella Vista Convalescent Hospital, Ontario, CA
Bella Vista Nursing Center, Rapid City, SD
Bella Vita Towers Inc, Denver, CO
Belle Fourche Health Care Center—Long-Term Care Unit, Belle Fourche, SD
Belle Haven, Quakertown, PA
Belle Maison Nursing Home, Hammond, LA
Belle Manor Nursing Home, New Carlisle, OH
Belle Reeve Health Care Center, Lakewood, NJ
Belleair East Health Care Center, Clearwater, FL
Bellefontaine Place, Waterloo, IL
Bellerose Convalescent Hospital, San Jose, CA
Belleview Valley Nursing Home Inc, Belleview, MO
Belleville Health Care Center, Belleville, KS
Bellevue Care Center, Tacoma, WA
Bellevue Center DD Training Center, Bellevue, WA
Bellevue Nursing Center, Oklahoma City, OK
Bellevue Nursing Home, Bellevue, OH
Bellevue Terrace Nursing Center, Bellevue, WA
Bellflower Convalescent Hospital, Bellflower, CA
Bellingham Care Center, Bellingham, WA
Bellmead Family Care Inc, Waco, TX
Bellmire Home, Bowie, TX
Bells Lodge, Phoenix, AZ
Belmond Health Care Center, Belmond, IA
Belmont Convalescent Hospital, Belmont, CA
Belmont County Oakview Nursing Home, Saint Clairsville, OH
Belmont Habilitation Center, Saint Clairsville, OH
Belmont Home, Worcester, MA
Belmont Lodge, Pueblo, CO
Belmont Manor Nursing Home Inc, Belmont, MA
Belmont Nursing Center, Perrysburg, OH
Belmont Nursing Home Inc, Chicago, IL
Belmont Terrace Inc, Bremerton, WA
Beloit Convalescent Center, Beloit, WI
Beltrami Nursing Home, Bemidji, MN
Belvedere, Chester, PA

Belvoir Woods Healthcare Center, Fort Belvoir, VA
Bement Manor, Bement, IL
Ben Hur Home, Crawfordsville, IN
Benchmark Home: Cowpens, Cowpens, SC
Benchmark Home: Spartanburg, Spartanburg, SC
Benchmark Homes—Cowpens, Spartanburg, SC
Bender Terrace Nursing Home, Lubbock, TX
Benedictine Health Center, Duluth, MN
Benedictine Nursing Center, Mount Angel, OR
Beneva Nursing Pavilion, Sarasota, FL
Benner Convalescent Center, Houston, TX
Bennett County Nursing Home, Martin, SD
Bennington Convalescent Center, Bennington, VT
Bennion Care Center, Murray, UT
Benson Heights Rehabilitation Center, Kent, WA
Benson's Nursing Home Inc, Nashville, AR
Bent County Memorial Nursing Home, Las Animas, CO
Bentley Gardens Health Care Center, West Haven, CT
Bentley Village Health Care Facility, Naples, FL
Benton Care Center, Kansas City, MO
Benton Services Center Nursing Home, Benton, AR
Bentonville Manor, Bentonville, AR
Benzie County Medical Care Facility, Frankfort, MI
Berea Health Care Center, Berea, KY
Berea Hospital—Skilled Nursing Facility, Berea, KY
Berea North Quality Care Nursing Center, Berea, OH
Berea Quality Care Nursing Center, Berea, OH
Bergen County Intermediate Care Facility, Rockleigh, NJ
Berkeley Convalescent Center, Moncks Corner, SC
Berkeley Hall Nursing Home, Berkeley Heights, NJ
Berkeley Heights Convalescent Center, Berkeley Heights, NJ
Berkeley Pines Skilled Nursing Facility, Berkeley, CA
Berkeley Retirement Home, Lawrence, MA
Berkley East Convalescent Hospital, Santa Monica, CA
Berkley Manor, Denver, CO
Berkley West Convalescent Hospital, Santa Monica, CA
Berks County Home Berks Heim, Reading, PA
Berkshire Hills North, Lee, MA
Berkshire Nursing Center, West Babylon, NY
Berkshire Nursing Home Inc, Pittsfield, MA
Berkshire Place, Pittsfield, MA
Berkshire Residence, Osseo, MN
Berkshire Sanitarium, Santa Monica, CA
Berkshire, Vinton, VA
Berlin Convalescent Center, Barre, VT
Berlin Nursing Home, Berlin, MD
Bernard West Pine Nursing Home Inc, Saint Louis, MO
Berrien General Hospital, Berrien Center, MI
Berrien Nursing Center Inc, Nashville, GA
Berry Hill Nursing Home Inc, South Boston, VA
Martha T Berry Memorial Medical Care Facility, Mount Clemens, MI
Berryman Health—East Whittier, Whittier, CA
Berryman Health—West Whittier, Whittier, CA
Berryville Health Care Center, Berryville, AR
Bert Anne Annex, West Chesterfield, NH
Bert Anne Home for the Aged, West Chesterfield, NH
Bertram Nursing Home, Bertram, TX
Bertran Home for Aged Men, Salem, MA
Bertrand Nursing Home, Bertrand, NE
Bertrand Retirement Home Inc, Bertrand, MO
Berwick Retirement Village Nursing Home, Berwick, PA
Bescare Nursing Home, Columbus, OH

Best Care Convalescent Hospital, Torrance, CA
Best Care Nursing Facility, Wheelersburg, OH
Beth Abraham Hospital, New York, NY
Beth-Haven Nursing Home, Hannibal, MO
Beth Israel Health Care Center, Denver, CO
Beth Shalom Home of Central Virginia, Richmond, VA
Beth Shalom Home of Eastern Virginia, Virginia Beach, VA
Bethalto Care Center Inc, Bethalto, IL
Bethamy Gardens, Clearwater, FL
Bethany Care Center, Lakewood, CO
Bethany Care Center, Bethany, MO
Bethany Convalescent Hospital, San Jose, CA
Bethany Covenant Home, Minneapolis, MN
Bethany Good Samaritan Village, Brainerd, MN
Bethany Health Care Center, Nashville, TN
Bethany Home, Dubuque, IA
Bethany Home, New Orleans, LA
Bethany Home, Alexandria, MN
Bethany Home, Litchfield, MN
Bethany Home, Minden, NE
Bethany Home, Waupaca, WI
Bethany Home Association, Lindsborg, KS
Bethany Home for Ladies, Vidalia, GA
Bethany Home for Men, Millen, GA
Bethany Home of Rhode Island, Providence, RI
Bethany Home Society San Joaquin County, Ripon, CA
Bethany Homes, Fargo, ND
Bethany Inc, Albion, ME
Bethany Lutheran Home, Council Bluffs, IA
Bethany Lutheran Home, Sioux Falls, SD
Bethany Lutheran Village, Dayton, OH
Bethany Manor, Story City, IA
Bethany MHS Health Care Center, Lafayette, LA
Bethany Nursing Home, Bloomingdale, MI
Bethany Nursing Home, Canton, OH
Bethany Nursing Home & Health Related Facility Inc, Horseheads, NY
Bethany of the Northwest, Everett, WA
Bethany Riverside, La Crosse, WI
Bethany St Joseph Care Center, La Crosse, WI
Bethany Samaritan Heights, Rochester, MN
Bethany Terrace Retirement & Nursing Home, Morton Grove, IL
Bethany Village Health Care Center, Bethany, OK
Bethany Village Nursing Home, Indianapolis, IN
Bethany Village Retirement Center, Mechanicsburg, PA
Bethea Baptist Home, Darlington, SC
Bethel Care Center, Saint Paul, MN
Bethel Home, Oshkosh, WI
Bethel Home, Viroqua, WI
Bethel Home for Aged, Newton, KS
Bethel Home Inc, Montezuma, KS
Bethel Living Center, Arpin, WI
Bethel Lutheran Home, Williston, ND
Bethel Lutheran Home, Madison, SD
Bethel Lutheran Home Inc, Selma, CA
Bethel Lutheran Home Inc, Selma, CA
Bethel Manor, Evansville, IN
Bethel Methodist Home, Ossining, NY
Bethel Nursing Home Company Inc, Ossining, NY
Bethei Rest Home, Cuyahoga Falls, OH
Bethesda Care Center, Canon City, CO
Bethesda Care Center, Delta, CO
Bethesda Care Center, Grand Junction, CO
Bethesda Care Center, Paonia, CO
Bethesda Care Center, Saint Maries, ID
Bethesda Care Center, Clarinda, IA
Bethesda Care Center, Mediapolis, IA
Bethesda Care Center, Muscatine, IA
Bethesda Care Center, Toledo, IA
Bethesda Care Center, Winterset, IA
Bethesda Care Center, Smith Center, KS
Bethesda Care Center, Ainsworth, NE
Bethesda Care Center, Ashland, NE
Bethesda Care Center, Aurora, NE
Bethesda Care Center, Central City, NE
Bethesda Care Center, Edgar, NE

Bethesda Care Center, Exeter, NE
Bethesda Care Center, Sutherland, NE
Bethesda Care Center, Utica, NE
Bethesda Care Center, Fremont, OH
Bethesda Care Center, San Antonio, TX
Bethesda Care Center, Laramie, WY
Bethesda Care Center, Worland, WY
Bethesda Care Center of Bassett, Colorado
   Springs, CO
Bethesda Care Center of Blue Hill, Blue Hill,
   NE
Bethesda Care Center of Colorado Springs,
   Colorado Springs, CO
Bethesda Care Center of Grand Junction,
   Grand Junction, CO
Bethesda Care Center of Gretna, Gretna, NE
Bethesda Care Center of Seward, Seward, NE
Bethesda Care Centers, Colorado Springs, CO
Bethesda Convalescent Center, Los Gatos, CA
Bethesda-Dilworth Memorial Home, Saint
   Louis, MO
Bethesda Health Care Facility, Fayetteville,
   NC
Bethesda Heritage Center, Willmar, MN
Bethesda Home, Hayward, CA
Bethesda Home, Goessel, KS
Bethesda Home, Webster, SD
Bethesda Home & Retirement Center,
   Chicago, IL
Bethesda Home for Aged, Beresford, SD
Bethesda Home of Aberdeen, Aberdeen, SD
Bethesda Lutheran Care Center, Saint Paul,
   MN
Bethesda Lutheran Home, Springfield, IL
Bethesda Lutheran Home, Watertown, WI
Bethesda Lutheran Home—Montgomery,
   Aurora, IL
Bethesda Manor, Enumclaw, WA
Bethesda Nursing Center, Chanute, KS
Bethesda Nursing Home—Pleasantview,
   Willmar, MN
Bethesda Retirement Nursing Center, Chevy
   Chase, MD
Bethesda Scarlet Oaks, Cincinnati, OH
Bethesda Skilled Nursing Facility, Saint Louis,
   MO
Bethlen Home of the Hungarian Federation of
   America, Ligonier, PA
Bethphage at Axtell, Axtell, NE
Bethphage No 1, Des Moines, IA
Bethphage No 2, Des Moines, IA
Bethphage No 3, Des Moines, IA
Bethshan Association, Palos Heights, IL
Bethshan Association II, Palos Heights, IL
Bethshan Association—Tibstra House, South
   Holland, IL
Bethune Plaza Inc, Chicago, IL
Bettendorf Health Care Center, Bettendorf, IA
Betty Ann Nursing Home, Grove, OK
Betz Nursing Home Inc, Auburn, IN
Beulah Community Nursing Home, Beulah,
   ND
Beulah Land Christian Home, Flanagan, IL
Beverly Farm Foundation, Godfrey, IL
Beverly Health Care Center, Birmingham, AL
Beverly Health Care Center, Tarboro, NC
Beverly Health Care Center, Glasgow, WV
Beverly Health Care Center—West, Fairfield,
   AL
Beverly La Cumbre Convalescent Hospital,
   Santa Barbara, CA
Beverly Manor, Burbank, CA
Beverly Manor, Santa Clara, CA
Beverly Manor, Saint Joseph, MO
Beverly Manor Convalescent Center, Augusta,
   GA
Beverly Manor Convalescent Center,
   Honolulu, HI
Beverly Manor Convalescent Center, Belle
   Plaine, IA
Beverly Manor Convalescent Center, Iowa
   City, IA
Beverly Manor Convalescent Center,
   Southgate, MI
Beverly Manor Convalescent Hospital,
   Bakersfield, CA
Beverly Manor Convalescent Hospital,
   Burbank, CA

Beverly Manor Convalescent Hospital, Canoga
   Park, CA
Beverly Manor Convalescent Hospital,
   Capistrano Beach, CA
Beverly Manor Convalescent Hospital, Chico,
   CA
Beverly Manor Convalescent Hospital, Costa
   Mesa, CA
Beverly Manor Convalescent Hospital,
   Escondido, CA
Beverly Manor Convalescent Hospital, Fresno,
   CA
Beverly Manor Convalescent Hospital, La
   Mesa, CA
Beverly Manor Convalescent Hospital, Laguna
   Hills, CA
Beverly Manor Convalescent Hospital, Los
   Altos, CA
Beverly Manor Convalescent Hospital, Los
   Angeles, CA
Beverly Manor Convalescent Hospital,
   Monrovia, CA
Beverly Manor Convalescent Hospital,
   Monterey, CA
Beverly Manor Convalescent Hospital,
   Panorama City, CA
Beverly Manor Convalescent Hospital,
   Redding, CA
Beverly Manor Convalescent Hospital,
   Redlands, CA
Beverly Manor Convalescent Hospital,
   Riverside, CA
Beverly Manor Convalescent Hospital, San
   Francisco, CA
Beverly Manor Convalescent Hospital, Santa
   Barbara, CA
Beverly Manor Convalescent Hospital, Seal
   Beach, CA
Beverly Manor Convalescent Hospital, Van
   Nuys, CA
Beverly Manor Convalescent Hospital, West
   Covina, CA
Beverly Manor Convalescent Hospital, Yreka,
   CA
Beverly Manor Convalescent Hospital of
   Glendale, Glendale, CA
Beverly Manor Convalescent No 53, Decatur,
   GA
Beverly Manor Healthcare Center, Ridgecrest,
   CA
Beverly Manor of Charlotte, Charlotte, NC
Beverly Manor of Margate, Margate, FL
Beverly Manor of Monroeville, Monroeville,
   PA
Beverly Manor of Mt Penn, Mount Penn, PA
Beverly Manor of Petaluma, Petaluma, CA
Beverly Manor of Plymouth Nursing Home,
   Plymouth, MA
Beverly Manor of Portsmouth, Portsmouth,
   VA
Beverly Manor of Stockton, Stockton, CA
Beverly Manor Sanitarium, Riverside, CA
Beverly Nursing Center, Pittsburg, KS
Beverly Nursing Home, Beverly, MA
Beverly Palms Rehabilitation Hospital, Los
   Angeles, CA
Beverly Terrace, Watertown, WI
Beverly Towers Nursing Home, Chicago, IL
Beverwyck Nursing Home, Parsippany, NJ
Bey Lea Village, Toms River, NJ
Bezalel Nursing Home Company, Far
   Rockaway, NY
Bi-County Clinic & Nursing Home Inc,
   Bloxom, VA
Bialystoker Home & Infirmary for the Aged,
   New York, NY
Bibb Medical Center Hospital & Nursing
   Home, Centreville, AL
Bickford Convalescent Home, Windsor Locks,
   CT
Bicknell Health Care, Bicknell, IN
Bienville General Hospital, Bienville, LA
Big Bend Retreat Inc, Slater, MO
Big Horn County Memorial Nursing Home,
   Hardin, MT
Big Horn Rest Home, Big Horn, WY
Big Meadows Inc, Savanna, IL
Big Pine Convalescent Hospital, Big Pine, CA

Big Sandy Medical Center—Long Term Care,
   Big Sandy, MT
Big Sky Care Center, Helena, MT
Big Spring Manor, Huntsville, AL
Big Spring Nursing Home, Humansville, MO
Biggs-Gridley Memorial Hospital Hovlid
   Community Care Center, Gridley, CA
Billdora, Tylertown, MS
Billings Fairchild Center Inc, Billings, OK
Biltmore Manor Inc, Asheville, NC
Binger Nursing Home, Binger, OK
Bingham County Nursing Home, Blackfoot,
   ID
Birch Hill Health Care Center, Shawano, WI
Birch Manor Nursing Home, Chicopee, MA
Birch Street Manor, Dallas, OR
Birch View Nursing Center, Birch Tree, MO
Birchway Health Care, Saint Louis, MO
Birchwood Care Center, Marne, MI
Birchwood Care Center A Long-Term Care
   Facility, Fitchburg, MA
Birchwood Care Home, Minneapolis, MN
Birchwood Cluter Manor Inc, Waterbury, CT
Birchwood Court, Verona, WI
Birchwood Health Care Center, Belleville, IL
Birchwood Health Care Center, Forest Lake,
   MN
Birchwood Health Care Center Inc, Liverpool,
   NY
Birchwood Manor, North Bend, NE
Birchwood Manor—Holland, Holland, MI
Birchwood Manor Nursing Home, Cooper, TX
Birchwood Nursing & Convalescent Center,
   Edison, NJ
Birchwood Nursing Center, Traverse City, MI
Birchwood Nursing Center Limited,
   Nanticoke, PA
Birchwood Nursing Home, Casey, IL
Birchwood Nursing Home, Derry Village, NH
Birchwood Nursing Home, Huntington
   Station, NY
Birchwood Plaza Nursing & Rehabilitation
   Center, Chicago, IL
Birchwood Terrace Healthcare, Burlington, VT
Bird Island Manor Healthcare Center, Bird
   Island, MN
Birk's Mountain Home, Hurricane, UT
Bishop Nursing Home, Media, PA
Bishop Soenneker Home, Philpot, KY
Bishop's Glen, Holly Hill, FL
Bishop's Health Care, Sandy, OR
Emily P Bissell Hospital, Wilmington, DE
Bittersweet Home, Whitehouse, OH
Elizabeth Jane Bivins Home for the Aged,
   Amarillo, TX
Bivins Memorial Nursing Home, Amarillo,
   TX
Bixby Knolls Towers, Long Beach, CA
Bixby Manor Nursing Home, Bixby, OK
Black Earth Manor, Black Earth, WI
Black Hawk County Health Care, Waterloo,
   IA
Black Hills Retirement Center, Rapid City,
   SD
Black Mountain Center, Black Mountain, NC
Blackfeet Nursing Home, Browning, MT
Black's Drive Community Residence,
   Williston, SC
Black's Nursing Home, Tulsa, OK
Blackstone Nursing Home, Blackstone, MA
Blackwell Nursing Home Inc, Blackwell, OK
Blaine Manor, Hailey, ID
Blair House, Augusta, GA
Blair Nursing Home Inc, Beaver Falls, PA
Ruby C Blair Residence, Blair, SC
Stuart L Blair Residence, Blair, SC
Blaire House Long-Term Care Facility,
   Milford, MA
Blaire House Long-Term Care Facility
   Tewksbury, Tewksbury, MA
Blaire House of New Bedford, New Bedford,
   MA
Blaire House of Worcester, Worcester, MA
Blakely Care Center, North Baltimore, OH
Blalock Nursing Home—East, Houston, TX
Blalock Nursing Home—North, Houston, TX
Blalock Nursing Home—Southeast, Pasadena,
   TX

Blanchard Valley Residential Center, Findlay, OH
Blanchester Care Center, Blanchester, OH
Blanco Health Care Center, Blanco, TX
Bland Residential Care Home, Erie, CO
Bledsoe County Nursing Home, Pikeville, TN
Blenwood Nursing Home, Methuen, MA
Blevins Retirement & Care Center, McAlester, OK
Blind Girl's Home, Kirkwood, MO
Ely Bloomenson Community Hospital & Nursing Home, Ely, MN
Bloomfield Care Center, Bloomfield, IA
Bloomfield Convalescent Home, Bloomfield, CT
Bloomfield Good Samaritan Center, Bloomfield, NE
Bloomfield Health Care Center, Bloomfield, IN
Bloomfield Hills Care Center, Bloomfield Hills, MI
Bloomfield Manor Nursing Home, Dodgeville, WI
Bloomfield Nursing Center, Bloomfield, MO
Bloomfield Nursing Home Inc, Macon, GA
Bloomingdale Pavilion, Bloomingdale, IL
Bloomington Convalescent Center, Bloomington, IN
Bloomington Maple Manor, Bloomington, MN
Bloomington Nursing & Rehabilitation Center, Bloomington, IL
Bloomington Nursing Home, Bloomington, MN
Bloomington Outreach Home, Bloomington, MN
Bloomsburg Health Care Center, Bloomsburg, PA
Bloomville Nursing Care Center, Bloomville, OH
Blose-McGregor Health Care Center Inc, Punxsutawney, PA
Blossom Health Care Center, Rochester, NY
Blossom Hill Nursing Home, Huntsburg, OH
Blossom Nursing Center, Alliance, OH
Blossom View Nursing Home, Sodus, NY
Blough Nursing Home Inc, Bethlehem, PA
Blowing Rock Hospital—SNF/ICF, Blowing Rock, NC
Blu-Fountain Manor, Godfrey, IL
Blue Ash Nursing & Convalescent Home Inc, Blue Ash, OH
Blue Hills Centre, Kansas City, MO
Blue Hills Convalescent Home, Stoughton, MA
Blue Island Nursing Home, Blue Island, IL
Blue Mountain Convalescent Center, College Place, WA
Blue Mountain Nursing Home, Prairie City, OR
Blue Ridge Haven East, Harrisburg, PA
Blue Ridge Haven—West, Camp Hill, PA
Blue Ridge Health Care Inc, Easley, SC
Blue Ridge Highlands Nursing Home, Galax, VA
Blue Ridge Manor, Raleigh, NC
Blue Ridge Nursing Center of Martinsville & Henry County, Martinsville, VA
Blue Ridge Nursing Home, Kansas City, MO
Blue Ridge Nursing Home Inc, Stuart, VA
Blue Springs Care Center, Blue Springs, MO
Blue Spruce Rest Home, Springfield, MA
Blue Valley Lutheran Home, Hebron, NE
Blue Valley Nursing Home Inc, Blue Rapids, KS
Blueberry Hill Healthcare Nursing Home, Beverly, MA
Blueberry Hill Rest Home, Kingston, MA
Bluebonnet Nursing Center of Granger Inc, Granger, TX
Bluebonnet Nursing Home, Albany, TX
Bluegrass Personal Care Home, Lexington, KY
Bonnie Bluejacket Memorial Nursing Home, Greybull, WY
Bluementhal Jewish Home, Clemmons, NC
Bluff Nursing Center, Poplar Bluff, MO
Bluffs Nursing Home, Pensacola, FL
Rose Blumkin Jewish Home, Omaha, NE
Blythe Nursing Care Center, Blythe, CA

Blytheville Nursing Center Inc, Blytheville, AR
B'nai B'rith Home, Memphis, TN
Board of Social Ministry, Saint Paul, MN
Boardman Community Care Home, Rapid City, SD
Boca Raton Convalescent Center, Boca Raton, FL
Boddy Nursing Center, Woodstock, GA
Bohannon Nursing Home Inc, Lebanon, IL
Bohemian Home for the Aged, Chicago, IL
Boise Group Home 1, Boise, ID
Boise Group Home 2, Boise, ID
Boise Group Home 3, Boise, ID
Boise Group Home 4, Boise, ID
Boise Group Home 5, Boise, ID
Boise Group Home 6, Boise, ID
Boise Samaritan Village, Boise, ID
Boley Intermediate Care Facility, Boley, OK
Bolingreen Nursing Center, Macon, GA
Bolivar County Hospital—Long-Term Care Facility, Cleveland, MS
Bolivar Health Care Center, Bolivar, TN
Bolster Heights Health Care Facility, Auburn, ME
Bolton Convalescent Home, Bratenahl, OH
Bolton Manor Nursing Home, Marlborough, MA
Bon Air Nursing Home, Coca, FL
Bon-Ing Inc, Columbus, OH
Bon-Ing Inc, Gahanna, OH
Bon Secours—Divine Saviour Nursing Home, York, SC
Bon Secours Extended Care, Ellicott City, MD
Bon Secours Hospital/Villa Maria Nursing Center, North Miami, FL
Bond Nursing Care Center, Lutesville, MO
Willard F Bond Home, Madison, MS
Bonell Good Samaritan Center, Greeley, CO
Bonetti Health Care Center Inc, Harrisville, PA
Bonham Nursing Center, Stillwater, PA
Bonham Nursing Center, Bonham, TX
Bonifay Nursing Home, Bonifay, FL
Bonne Terre Rest Home Inc, Bonne Terre, MO
Bonner Health Center, Bonner Springs, KS
Bonnie Brae's, Tucson, AZ
Bonnie's Nursing Home, Westchester, OH
Bonnie's Nursing Home Inc, West Chester, OH
Bono Nursing Home, Henryetta, OK
Bonterra Nursing Center, East Point, GA
Booker Convalescent Annex, Dayton, WA
Boone Guest Home, Boone, CO
Boone Nursing Home, Millville, PA
Boone Retirement Center Inc, Columbia, MO
Boonville Convalescent Center Inc, Boonville, IN
Borderview Manor Inc, Van Buren, ME
Borger Nursing Center, Borger, TX
Borgess Nursing Home, Kalamazoo, MI
Bornemann Nursing Home Inc, Green Bay, WI
Bortz Health Care of Oakland, Pontiac, MI
Bortz Health Care of Petoskey, Petoskey, MI
Bortz Health Care of Rose City, Rose City, MI
Bortz Health Care of Traverse City, Traverse City, MI
Bortz Health Care of Warren, Warren, MI
Bortz Health Care of West Bloomfield, West Bloomfield, MI
Bortz Health Care of West Branch, West Branch, MI
Bortz Health Care of Ypsilanti, Ypsilanti, MI
Bossier Health Care Center, Bossier City, LA
Bossier Medical Center Skilled Nursing Facility, Bossier City, LA
Boston Home Inc, Boston, MA
Boswell Retardation Center—W L Jaquith ICF/MR, Sanatorium, MS
Bottineau Good Samaritan Center, Bottineau, ND
Boulder City Care Center, Boulder City, NV
Boulder City Hospital—Skilled Nursing Facility, Boulder City, NV

Boulder Good Samaritan Health Care Center, Boulder, CO
Boulder Manor, Boulder, CO
Boulevard Care Center Inc, Chicago, IL
Boulevard Community Residence, Orangeburg, SC
Boulevard Home for the Aged, Detroit, MI
Boulevard Manor Care Center, Richland Hills, TX
Boulevard Manor Nursing Center, Boynton Beach, FL
Boulevard Nursing Home, Philadelphia, PA
Boulevard Temple United Methodist Retirement Home, Detroit, MI
Boulevard Terrace Nursing Home, Murfreesboro, TN
Boundary County Nursing Home, Bonners Ferry, ID
Bountiful Nursing Home, Bountiful, UT
Bourbon Heights Nursing Home, Paris, KY
Bourbonnais Terrace, Bourbonnais, IL
Bowden Nursing Home, Wilmington, NC
Bowdle Nursing Home, Bowdle, SD
Bowen Health Center, Raytown, MO
William W Bowen Residence, Hartsville, SC
Bowerston Health Care Center, Bowerston, OH
Bowie Nursing Center, Bowie, TX
Bowling Green Health Care Center, Bowling Green, VA
Bowling Green Manor, Bowling Green, OH
Bowman-Harrison Convalescent Hospital, San Francisco, CA
Bowman Nursing Home, Midlothian, IL
Bowman's Nursing Center, Ormond Beach, FL
Box Elder County Nursing Home, Tremonton, UT
Boxwood Health Care Center, Newman, IL
Boyce Manor Inc, Holdenville, OK
Robert E Boyce Pavilion, East Liverpool, OH
Martin Boyd Christian Home, Chattanooga, TN
Boyd's Kinsman, Kinsman, OH
Bozeman Care Center, Bozeman, MT
Bracken Center Inc, Augusta, KY
Bradbury Manor, Belfast, ME
Bradenton Convalescent Center, Bradenton, FL
Bradenton Manor, Bradenton, FL
Bradford County Manor, Troy, PA
Bradford Living Care Center, Bradford, OH
Bradford Manor, Bradford, PA
Bradford Nursing Pavilion, Bradford, PA
Bradford Oaks Nursing & Retirement Centre, Clinton, MD
Bradford Square, Frankfort, KY
Bradlee Rest Home, Boston, MA
Bradley Convalescent Center, Milwaukee, WI
Bradley County Nursing Home, Cleveland, TN
Bradley Home Infirmary, Meriden, CT
Bradley Nursing Home, Jamaica Plain, MA
Bradley Road Nursing Home, Bay Village, OH
Bradley Royale Inc, Bradley, IL
Bradner Village Health Care Center Inc, Marion, IN
Brady Memorial Home, Mitchell, SD
Bonnie Brae Convalescent Hospital, Los Angeles, CA
Brae Burn Inc, Bloomfield Hills, MI
Brae Burn Nursing Home, Whitman, MA
Brae Loch Manor, Rochester, NY
Brae View Manor Health Care Facility, Euclid, OH
Braeburn Nursing Home, Newton, MA
Braeburn Nursing Home, Waban, MA
Braemoor Nursing Home Inc, Brockton, MA
Bragg Residential Care Home Inc, Denver, CO
Brainerd Good Samaritan Center, Brainerd, MN
Brainerd Regional Human Services Center, Brainerd, MN
Braintree Manor, Braintree, MA
Brakebill Nursing Home Inc, Knoxville, TN
Branch Villa Health Care Center, Seattle, WA
Brandel Manor, Turlock, CA

Joseph D Brandenburg Center, Cumberland, MD
Brandon Woods, Lawrence, KS
Brandon Woods Long-Term Care Facility, Dartmouth, MA
Brandewine Convalescent Home, Wilmington, DE
Brandywine Hall Care Center, West Chester, PA
Brandywine Manor, Greenfield, IN
Brandywine Nursing Home Inc, Briarcliff Manor, NY
Brandywood Nursing Home, Gallatin, TN
Brandywyne Convalescent Center, Winter Haven, FL
Branford Hills Health Care Center, Branford, CT
Braswell's Colonial Care, Redlands, CA
Braswell's Community Convalescent Center, Yucaipa, CA
Braswell's Ivy Retreat, Mentone, CA
Braswell's Yucaipa Valley Convalescent Hospital, Yucaipa, CA
Braun's Nursing Home Inc, Evansville, IN
Braxton Health Care Center, Sutton, WV
Brazos Valley Care Home, Knox City, TX
Brazos Valley Geriatric Center, College Station, TX
Brazosview Healthcare Center, Richmond, TX
Breckinridge Health Care Inc, Lexington, KY
Breckinridge Health Care Inc, Lexington, KY
Breese Nursing Home, Breese, IL
Bremen Health Care Center, Bremen, IN
Bremerton Convalescent Center, Bremerton, WA
Bremond Nursing Center, Bremond, TX
Brendan House Skilled Nursing Facility, Kalispell, MT
Brenham Rest Home Inc, Brenham, TX
Brenn-Field Nursing Center, Orrville, OH
Brent-Lox Hall Nursing Center, Chesapeake, VA
Brentwood, Tacoma, WA
Brentwood Care Center, Denver, CO
Brentwood Convalescent Center, Evansville, IN
Brentwood Convalescent Hospital, Red Bluff, CA
Brentwood Good Samaritan Center, Le Mars, IA
Brentwood Hills Nursing Center, Asheville, NC
Brentwood Manor, Yarmouth, ME
Brentwood North Nursing & Rehabilitation Center, Riverwoods, IL
Brentwood Nursing & Rehabilitation Center, Burbank, IL
Brentwood Nursing Home Inc, Brookline, MA
Brentwood Nursing Home Inc, Warwick, RI
Brentwood Park Nursing Home, Rome, GA
Brentwood Place One, Dallas, TX
Brentwood Place Three, Dallas, TX
Brentwood Place Two, Dallas, TX
Brentwood Terrace Health Center, Waynesboro, GA
Brethren Care Inc, Ashland, OH
Brethren Home, New Oxford, PA
Brethren Village, Lancaster, PA
Brethren's Home, Greenville, OH
Brethren's Home of Indiana Inc, Flora, IN
Brevin Nursing Home Inc, Havre de Grace, MD
Albert P Brewer Developmental Center, Mobile, AL
Brewer Convalescent Center—Head Injury Treatment Program, Brewer, ME
Brewster Manor Nursing & Retirement Home, Brewster, MA
Brewster Parke Convalescent Center, Brewster, OH
Brewster Place, Topeka, KS
Brian Center Health & Retirement, Mooresville, NC
Brian Center Health & Retirement—Asheville, Asheville, NC
Brian Center Health & Retirement—Brevard, Brevard, NC

Brian Center Health & Retirement—Charlotte, Charlotte, NC
Brian Center Health & Retirement—Eden, Eden, NC
Brian Center Health & Retirement—Hickory East, Hickory, NC
Brian Center Health & Retirement—Lincolnton, Lincolnton, NC
Brian Center Health & Retirement—Spruce Pine, Spruce Pines, NC
Brian Center Health & Retirement—Yanceyville, Yanceyville, NC
Brian Center Nursing Care—Raleigh, Raleigh, NC
Brian Center Nursing Care—Asheboro, Asheboro, NC
Brian Center Nursing Care—Gastonia Inc, Gastonia, NC
Brian Center Nursing Care—Hertford, Hertford, NC
Brian Center Nursing Care—Hickory, Hickory, NC
Brian Center Nursing Care/Lawrenceville Inc, Lawrenceville, VA
Brian Center Nursing Care—Lexington, Lexington, NC
Brian Center Nursing Care of LaGrange, LaGrange, GA
Brian Center Nursing Care of Lumber City, Lumber City, GA
Brian Center Nursing Care—Salisbury, Salisbury, NC
Brian Center Nursing Care—Shamrock, Charlotte, NC
Brian Center of Health & Retirement, Statesville, NC
Brian Center of Nursing Care—Austell, Austell, GA
Brian Center of Nursing Care Columbia, Columbia, SC
Brian Center of Nursing Care—St Andrews, Columbia, SC
Briar Crest Home, Ossining, NY
Briar Hill Nursing Home, Middlefield, OH
Briar Hill Rest Home Inc, Florence, MS
Briar Place Ltd, Indian Head Park, IL
Briarcliff Haven, Atlanta, GA
Briarcliff Manor, New London, CT
Briarcliff Manor Inc, Topeka, KS
Briarcliff Nursing Home, Alabaster, AL
Briarcliff Pavilion, North Huntingdon, PA
Briarcliff Village Health Center, Tyler, TX
Briarcliffe Healthcare Facility, Johnston, RI
Briarfield Inc, Sylvania, OH
Briarleaf Nursing & Convalescent Center, Doylestown, PA
Briarstone Manor, Anson, TX
Briarwood Convalescent Center, Needham, MA
Briarwood Health Care Center, Denver, CO
Briarwood Manor, Coldwater, OH
Briarwood Manor Nursing Home, Flint, MI
Briarwood Nursing & Convalescent Center, Louisville, KY
Briarwood Nursing Center Inc, Tucker, GA
Briarwood Way, Lakewood, CO
Bridge View Nursing Home, Whitestone, NY
Bridgeport Terrace, Bridgeport, IL
Bridgeton Nursing Center, Bridgeton, MO
Bridgeton Nursing Center, Bridgeton, NJ
Bridgeview Convalescent Center, Bridgeview, IL
Bridgeville Group Home, Bridgeville, DE
Bridgewater Home Inc Health Care Unit, Bridgewater, VA
Bridgewater Nursing Home, Bridgewater, MA
Bridgeway Convalescent Center, Bridgewater, NJ
Bridgewood Manor, Plainwell, MI
Bridgton Health Care Center, Bridgton, ME
Brier Oak Terrace Care Center, Los Angeles, CA
Briggs Nursing Home, Manning, SC
Brigham Manor Convalescent Home, Newburyport, MA
Bright Glade Convalescent Center, Memphis, TN
Brighter Day Residence, Mora, MN

Brightmoor Medical Care Home, Griffin, GA
Brighton Care Center, Brighton, CO
Brighton Hall Nursing Center, New Haven, IN
Brighton Manor Nursing & Geriatric Center, Baltimore, MD
Brighton Place North, Topeka, KS
Brighton Place West Inc, Topeka, KS
Brightonian, Rochester, NY
Brightview Care Center Inc, Chicago, IL
Brightview Nursing & Retirement Center, Avon, CT
Brightwood Nursing Home, Follansbee, WV
Briody Nursing Home, Lockport, NY
Bristol Health Care Center, Bristol, VA
Bristol Manor Health Care Center, Rochelle Park, NJ
Bristol Nursing Home, Attleboro, MA
Bristol Nursing Home Inc, Bristol, TN
British Home, Brookfield, IL
Brittany Convalescent Home, Natick, MA
Brittany Farms Health Center, New Britain, CT
Britthaven of Benton, Benton, KY
Britthaven of Bowling Green, Bowling Green, KY
Britthaven of Chapel Hill, Chapel Hill, NC
Britthaven of Charlotte, Charlotte, NC
Britthaven of Clyde, Clyde, NC
Britthaven of Davidson, Thomasville, NC
Britthaven of Edenton, Edenton, NC
Britthaven of Franklin, Franklin, NC
Britthaven of Goldsboro, Goldsboro, NC
Britthaven of Gulfport, Gulfport, MS
Britthaven of Hamlet, Hamlet, NC
Britthaven of Jacksonville, Jacksonville, NC
Britthaven of Kernersville, Kernersville, NC
Britthaven of Kinston, Kinston, NC
Britthaven of Madison, Madison, NC
Britthaven of Morganton, Morganton, NC
Britthaven of New Bern, New Bern, NC
Britthaven of Onslow, Jacksonville, NC
Britthaven of Outer Banks, Nags Head, NC
Britthaven of Piedmont, Albemarle, NC
Britthaven of Pineville, Pineville, KY
Britthaven of Prospect, Prospect, KY
Britthaven of Raleigh, Raleigh, NC
Britthaven of Smithfield, Smithfield, NC
Britthaven of Snow Hill, Snow Hill, NC
Britthaven of Somerset, Somerset, KY
Britthaven of South Louisville, Louisville, KY
Britthaven of Washington, Washington, NC
Britthaven of Wilkesboro Inc, Wilkesboro, NC
Britthaven of Wilmington, Wilmington, NC
Britthaven of Wilson, Wilson, NC
Broad Acres Nursing Home Association, Wellsboro, PA
Broad Mountain Nursing Home, Frackville, PA
Broad Ripple Nursing Home, Indianapolis, IN
Broadacres, Utica, NY
Broadfield Manor Nursing & Convalescent Home, Madison, OH
Broadlawn Manor, Purcell, OK
Broadlawn Manor Nursing Home, Amityville, NY
Broadmead, Cockeysville, MD
Broadmoor Health Care Center Inc, Meridian, MS
Broadstreet Nursing Center, Detroit, MI
Broadview Developmental Center, Broadview Heights, OH
Broadview Nursing Home, Parma, OH
Broadwater County Rest Home, Townsend, MT
Broadwater Health Center Nursing Home, Townsend, MT
Broadway, San Gabriel, CA
Broadway Arms Community Living Center, Lewistown, IL
Broadway Convalescent Home, Methuen, MA
Broadway Lodge, San Antonio, TX
Broadway Manor, Muskogee, OK
Broadway Manor Convalescent Hospital, Glendale, CA
Broadway Nursing Home, Joliet, IL
Broadway Residential Treatment Center, Winona, MN

Brockwood Health Care Nursing Home, Brockton, MA

Brockton Ridge Long-Term Care Center, Brockton, MA

Broderick Convalescent Hospital, San Francisco, CA

Broen Memorial Home, Fergus Falls, MN

Broken Arrow Nursing Home Inc, Broken Arrow, OK

Broken Bow Nursing Home, Broken Bow, OK

Brommer Manor, Santa Cruz, CA

Charles Bronstien Home, Minneapolis, MN

Bronte Nursing Home, Bronte, TX

Brook Haven Rest Home, West Brookfield, MA

Brook Hollow Health Care Center, Wallingford, CT

Brook Manor Nursing Center, Brookhaven, MS

Brook Meade Health Care Inc, Nashville, TN

Brook Wood Convalescent Home, Saddle Brook, NJ

Brookcrest Nursing Home, Grandville, MI

Brooke Grove Nursing Home, Olney, MD

Brookfield Manor, Hopkinsville, KY

Brookfield Nursing Center, Brookfield, MO

Brookhaven Beach Health Related Facility, Far Rockaway, NY

Brookhaven Care Center, Kalamazoo, MI

Brookhaven Group Home, Woodinville, WA

Brookhaven Health Care Center, East Orange, NJ

Brookhaven Medical Care Facility, Muskegon, MI

Brookhaven Nursing & Care Center, Brookville, OH

Brookhaven Nursing Center, Carrollton, TX

Brookhaven Nursing Center, Farmers Branch, TX

Brookhaven Nursing Center, Fort Worth, TX

Brookhaven Nursing Home, Brooklyn, IA

Brookhollow Manor, Grapevine, TX

Brookhouse Home for Aged Women, Salem, MA

Brooking Park Geriatric Center, Sedalia, MO

Brookline Manor Convalescent Rest Home, Mifflintown, PA

Brooklyn Center Outreach Home, Brooklyn Center, MN

Brooklyn Methodist Church Home, Brooklyn, NY

Brooklyn Rest Home, Brooklyn, CT

Brookmont Health Care Center Inc, Effort, PA

Brooks Center Health Care Facility, Marquette, MI

Brooks-Howell Home, Asheville, NC

Brookshire Arms Inc, Brookshire, TX

Brookside Care Center, Kenosha, WI

Brookside Convalescent Hospital, San Mateo, CA

Brookside Manor, Overbrook, KS

Brookside Manor Inc, Centralia, IL

Brookside Manor Nursing Home, Madill, OK

Brookside Manor Nursing Home & Home for the Aged, Whites Creek, TN

Brookside Nursing Home of Bradford, Bradford, VT

Brookside of White River, White River Junction, VT

Brooksville Nursing Manor, Brooksville, FL

Brookview, West Hartford, CT

Brookview House Inc, Gaffney, SC

Brookview Manor, Indianapolis, IN

Brookview Manor, Brookings, SD

Brookview Nursing Home Inc, Maryland Heights, MO

Brookwood Care Center, Downey, CA

Brookwood Gardens Convalescent Center, Homestead, FL

Brookwood Nursing Home, Stafford, VA

Brookwood Residence, Batesburg, SC

Brookwood Retirement Community, Cincinnati, OH

Broomall Presbyterian Home, Broomall, PA

Brother James Court, Springfield, IL

Brothers of Mercy Nursing & Rehabilitation Center, Clarence, NY

Broughton Hospital—Intermediate Care Facility, Morganton, NC

Broward Convalescent Home, Fort Lauderdale, FL

Brown County Community Care Center Inc, Nashville, IN

Brown County Detox & Evaluation Center, New Ulm, MN

Brown County Health Care Center, Green Bay, WI

Mary Ann Brown Residential Facility, Lima, OH

Mary J Brown Good Samaritan Center, Luverne, MN

Brown Memorial Convalescent Center, Royston, GA

Brown Memorial Home Inc, Circleville, OH

Brown Nursing Home, Alexander City, AL

Brown Nursing Home, Evart, MI

Brown Rest Home, Madisonville, KY

Browning Care Center, Waterville, OH

Hannah Browning Home, Mount Vernon, OH

Browning House, Durango, CO

Browning Manor Convalescent Hospital, Delano, CA

Browns Nursing Home, Statesboro, GA

Brown's Nursing Home, Lincoln Heights, OH

Brown's Nursing Home Inc, Fredericksburg, TX

Browns Valley Community Nursing Home, Browns Valley, MN

Brownsboro Hills Nursing Home, Louisville, KY

Brownsburg Health Care Center, Brownsburg, IN

Brownsville Golden Age, Brownsville, PA

Brownsville Good Samaritan Center, Brownsville, TX

Brownwood Care Center, Brownwood, TX

Brownwood Life Care Center Inc, Fort Smith, AR

Brownwood Manor Inc, Van Buren, AR

Brownwood Nursing Home, Moultrie, GA

Bruce Manor, Clearwater, FL

Bruceville Terrace (D/P of Methodist), Sacramento, CA

Bruckner Nursing Home, Bronx, NY

Brunswick Convalescent Center, Brunswick, ME

Brunswick Manor, Brunswick, ME

Brunswick Nursing Home, Amityville, NY

Brush Creek Manor, Kansas City, MO

Brushwood Care Center, Albuquerque, NM

Bruton Smith Road Group Home, Lexington, SC

Bry-Fern Care Center, Berrien Center, MI

Bryan County Manor, Durant, OK

Bryan Manor, Salem, IL

Bryan Manor Nursing Home, Dallas, TX

Bryan Nursing Care Center, Bryan, OH

Bryans Memorial Extended Care Center, Phoenix, AZ

Bryant Avenue Residence, South Saint Paul, MN

Bryant-Butler-Kitchen Nursing Home, Kansas City, KS

Eliza Bryant Center, Cleveland, OH

Bryant Health Center Inc, Ironton, OH

Lee Alan Bryant Health Care Facilities Inc, Rockville, IN

Mary Bryant Home for the Visually Impaired, Springfield, IL

Bryant Nursing Center, Cochran, GA

Bryant Nursing Center, Edmond, OK

Bryanwood Care Center, Amarillo, TX

Bryden Manor Nursing Home, Columbus, OH

Brykirk Extended Care Hospital, Alhambra, CA

Bryn Mawr Health Care Center, Minneapolis, MN

Bryn Mawr Terrace Convalescent Center, Bryn Mawr, PA

June Buchanan Primary Care Center, Hindman, KY

Buchanan Nursing Home, Chisholm, MN

Buchanan Nursing Home of Okeene Inc, Okeene, OK

Buchanon Nursing Home Inc, Malden, MA

Buckeye Community Services—Bidwell Home, Bidwell, OH

Buckeye Community Services—Childrens Transitional Facility, The Plains, OH

Buckeye Community Services—Culver Street Home, Logan, OH

Buckeye Community Services—Grandview Avenue Homes, Waverly, OH

Buckeye Community Services—Hunter Street Home, Logan, OH

Buckeye Community Services—South Street Home, Jackson, OH

Buckeye Community Services—Transitional Facility, Gallipolis, OH

Buckeye Community Services—Walnut Street Home, Logan, OH

Buckeye Nursing Home, Clyde, OH

Buckingham Pavilion Nursing & Rehabilitation Center Inc, Chicago, IL

Buckingham-Smith Memorial Home, Saint Augustine, FL

Buckingham Valley Nursing Home, Buckingham, PA

Buckley Convalescent Home, Hartford, CT

Buckley Nursing & Retirement Home, Holyoke, MA

Buckley Nursing Home, Greenfield, MA

Buckner Baptist Haven, Missouri City, TX

Buckner Baptist Trew Retirement Center, Dallas, TX

Buckner Monte Siesta Nursing Center, Austin, TX

Buckner Ryburn Nursing Center, Dallas, TX

Buckner Villa Siesta Home, Austin, TX

Bucks County Association of Retarded Citizens, Doylestown, PA

Bucktail Medical Center, Renovo, PA

Buckwell Rest Home, Warren, MA

Budd Terrace Intermediate Care Home, Atlanta, GA

Buena Park Nursing Center, Buena Park, CA

Buena Ventura Convalescent Hospital, Los Angeles, CA

Buena Vista Care Center, Anaheim, CA

Buena Vista Home for the Aged, Sedalia, MO

Buena Vista Inc, Colville, WA

Buena Vista Manor, Duarte, CA

Buena Vista Manor, Storm Lake, IA

Buena Vista Nursing, Lexington, NC

Bueno's Group Home, Las Animas, CO

Buerra Vista Hospital, Truth or Consequences, NM

Buffalo Lake Nursing Home, Buffalo Lake, MN

Buffalo Valley Lutheran Village, Lewisburg, PA

Buford Manor Nursing Home, Buford, GA

Buhler Sunshine Home Inc, Buhler, KS

Bullock County Nursing Home, Union Springs, AL

Buna Nursing Home, Buna, TX

Bunce Care Center II, Provo, UT

Bunce Convalescent Center, Provo, UT

Bunkie General Hospital, Bunkie, LA

Bur-Mont Nursing Center, Livingston, TX

Bur-Mont Nursing Center, Silsbee, TX

Bur-Mont Nursing Center, Temple, TX

Burbank Convalescent Hospital, Burbank, CA

Burcham Hills Retirement Center II, East Lansing, MI

Ollie Steele Burden Manor, Baton Rouge, LA

Burdick Convalescent Home, Warwick, RI

Bureau of Habilitation Services—Forest Haven, Laurel, MD

Burford Manor, Davis, OK

Burgess Manor, Graham, TX

Burgess Nursing Home, Birmingham, AL

Burgess Square Healthcare Centre, Westmont, IL

Joe Anne Burgin Nursing Home, Cuthbert, GA

Burgin Manor, Olney, IL

Burgoyne Rest Home, Boston, MA

Burien Terrace Nursing Center, Seattle, WA

Burleson Nursing Center, Burleson, TX

Burley Care Center, Burley, ID

Burling House, Charles City, IA

Burlington Care Center, Burlington, IA

Burlington Convalescent Center, Burlington, VT
Burlington Convalescent Hospital, Los Angeles, CA
Burlington Medical Center, Burlington, IA
Burlington Medical Center, Burlington, IA
Burlington Medical Center—Klein Unit, Burlington, IA
Burlington Woods Convalescent Center, Burlington, NJ
Burncoat Plains Rest Home, Worcester, MA
Burnett General Hospital—LTC, Grantsburg, WI
Burnham Terrace Care Center, Chicago, IL
Burnham Terrace Ltd, Burnham, IL
Burns Manor Nursing Home, Hutchinson, MN
Burns Nursing Home, Burns, OR
Burns Nursing Home Inc, Russellville, AL
Burnside Convalescent Home Inc, East Hartford, CT
Burnsides Nursing Home, Marshall, IL
Burnt Tavern Convalescent Center, Bricktown, NJ
Burr Oak Manor, Austin, MN
Burroughs Home Inc, Bridgeport, CT
Burt Manor, DeSoto, MO
Burt Sheltered Care Home, Alton, IL
Burton Family Care Home, Denver, CO
J Felton Burton Community Residence, Greenwood, SC
Burton Nursing Home, Burlington, WA
Burzenski Nursing Home, Sarasota, FL
Butler County Care Facility, Hamilton, OH
Butler Valley Manor, Drums, PA
Butte Convalescent Center, Butte, MT
Butte Nursing Home, Butte, NE
Butte Park Royal, Butte, MT
Buttonwood Hospital of Burlington County, New Lisbon, NJ
Buttonwoods Crest Home, Warwick, RI
Byrd Haven Nursing Home, Searcy, AR
Byrd Memorial Hospital, Leesville, LA
Byrnebrook Nursing Home, Toledo, OH
Byrnes Convalescent Center Inc, Cincinnati, OH
Byron Health Center, Fort Wayne, IN
Bywood East Health Care, Minneapolis, MN
C & M Rest Haven, Sioux Falls, SD
C R Center, Springfield, PA
Cabarrus Nursing Center, Concord, NC
Cabot Manor Nursing Center, Cabot, AR
Cabrillo Extended Care Hospital, San Luis Obispo, CA
Cabs Nursing Home Company Inc, Brooklyn, NY
Cadbury Health Care Center, Cherry Hill, NJ
Caddo Nursing Home, Caddo, OK
Cadillac Nursing Home, Detroit, MI
Caguas Regional Skilled Nursing Facility, Caguas, PR
Cahokia Health Care Center, Cahokia, IL
Cal Haven Convalescent Hospital, Glendale, CA
Caldsted Foundation Inc, Chattanooga, TN
Caldwell Care Center, Caldwell, ID
Caldwell Manor Nursing Home, Kansas City, MO
Caldwell Memorial Hospital, Columbia, LA
Stephen Caldwell Memorial Convalescent Home Inc, Ipswich, MA
Caledonia Health Care Center, Caledonia, MN
Caledonia Manor, Fayetteville, PA
Calera Manor Nursing Home, Calera, OK
Calhoun Care Center, Hardin, IL
Calhoun County Medical Care Facility, Battle Creek, MI
Calhoun County Nursing Home, Calhoun, MS
Calhoun Nursing Home, Edison, GA
California Care Center, California, MO
California Christian Home, Rosemead, CA
California Convalescent Center 1, Los Angeles, CA
California Convalescent Center 2, Los Angeles, CA
California Convalescent Hospital, San Francisco, CA
California Gardens Nursing Center, Chicago, IL

California Home for the Aged Inc, Fresno, CA
California Nursing & Rehabilitation Center, Palm Springs, CA
California P E O Home, Alhambra, CA
California PEO Home—San Jose Unit, San Jose, CA
California Special Care Center Inc, La Mesa, CA
Californian Care Center, Bakersfield, CA
Californian—Pasadena Convalescent Hospital, Pasadena, CA
Callaway Good Samaritan Center, Callaway, NE
Callaway Nursing Home, Sulphur, OK
Calumet Homestead, New Holstein, WI
Calusa Harbour, Fort Myers, FL
Calvary Fellowship Homes Inc, Lancaster, PA
Calvary Manor Nursing Home, Ottawa, OH
Calvert City Convalescent Center, Calvert City, KY
Calvert County Nursing Center, Prince Frederick, MD
Calvert House Corp, Prince Frederick, MD
Calvert Nursing Center, Calvert, TX
Virgil L Calvert Care Center, East Saint Louis, IL
Calvin Manor, Des Moines, IA
Camano Shores Nursing Home, Camano Island, WA
Camargo Manor Nursing Home, Cincinnati, OH
Camarillo Convalescent Hospital, Camarillo, CA
Cambridge Bedford, Southfield, MI
Cambridge Convalescent Center, Tampa, FL
Cambridge Court, Great Falls, MT
Cambridge Court Manor Inc, Charleston, IL
Cambridge East, Madison Heights, MI
Cambridge Hall Ltd, Chattanooga, TN
Cambridge Health Care Center, Lakewood, CO
Cambridge Health Care Center, Indianapolis, IN
Cambridge Health Care Center, Cambridge, MN
Cambridge Health Care Center, Cambridge, OH
Cambridge Health Care Facility of Montgomery Inc, Montgomery, AL
Cambridge Homes, Cambridge, MA
Cambridge Manor, Richmond, VA
Cambridge Medical Center, Smyrna, TN
Cambridge North, Clawson, MI
Cambridge Nursing Home, Cambridge, MA
Cambridge South, Birmingham, MI
Cambridge West, Redford, MI
Camden Care Center, Minneapolis, MN
Camden Community Health Care Center, Camden, ME
Camden Convalescent Hospital, Campbell, CA
Camden County Health Service Center, Blackwood, NJ
Camden Health Care Center, Monett, MO
Camden Health Center, Harrisonville, MO
Camden I Group Home, Camden, SC
Camden II Group Home, Camden, SC
Camden Nursing Facility, Camden, AL
Camden Nursing Home, Camden, ME
Camdenton Windsor Estates, Camdenton, MO
Camellia Care Center, Aurora, CO
Camellia Garden Nursing Home, Pineville, LA
Camellia Garden of Life Care, Thomasville, GA
Camelot Arms Care Center, Youngstown, OH
Camelot Care Center, Sun City, AZ
Camelot Care Center, Forest Grove, OR
Camelot Care Centers, Logansport, IN
Camelot Care Intermediate Care Facility, Gainesville, GA
Camelot Group Home, Seattle, WA
Camelot Hall—Cherrydale, Arlington, VA
Camelot Hall Convalescent Center, Livonia, MI
Camelot Hall Nursing Home, Chesapeake, VA
Camelot Hall Nursing Home, Danville, VA
Camelot Hall Nursing Home, Harrisonburg, VA
Camelot Hall Nursing Home, Lynchburg, VA

Camelot Hall Nursing Home, Richmond, VA
Camelot Hall Nursing Home, Salem, VA
Camelot Hall Nursing Home, Virginia Beach, VA
Camelot Lake, Fairfield, OH
Camelot Manor, Peoria, AZ
Camelot Manor, Streator, IL
Camelot Manor Nursing Care Facility Inc, Granite Falls, NC
Camelot Nursing Center, Farmington, MO
Camelot Nursing Home, New London, CT
Cameo Convalescent Center, Milwaukee, WI
Cameron Glen Care Center, Reston, VA
Cameron Health Care Center, Cameron, WV
Cameron Manor, Cameron, MO
Cameron Nursing Home, Cameron, TX
Cameron Villa Rest Home, Austin, TX
Camilia Rose Convalescent Center, Coon Rapids, MN
Camilia Rose Group Home, Coon Rapids, MN
Camilla Hall, Immaculata, PA
Camilla Street Intermediate Care Home, Atlanta, GA
Camlu Care Center—Louis Pasteur, San Antonio, TX
Camlu Care Center of Oak Hills, San Antonio, TX
Camlu Care Center of Woodlawn Hills, San Antonio, TX
Camlu Care Centers—Temple, Temple, TX
Camp Care Inc, Inman, SC
Camp Hill Care Center, Camp Hill, PA
Campbell Care of Whitewright, Whitewright, TX
Mary Campbell Center, Wilmington, DE
Campbell's Ingersoll Rest Home, Springfield, MA
Camphaven Manor, Inman, SC
Camphill Village Minnesota Inc, Sauk Centre, MN
Campion Residence & Renewal Center, Weston, MA
Canby Care Center, Canby, OR
Canby Community Health Services, Canby, MN
Candlelight Care Center, Columbia, MO
Candlewood Care Center, Long Beach, CA
Candlewood Valley Care Center, New Milford, CT
Cane Creek Center, Martin, TN
Caney Nursing Center, Caney, KS
Canistota Good Samaritan Center, Canistota, SD
Cannon Falls Manor Nursing Home, Cannon Falls, MN
Canoga Care Center, Canoga Park, CA
Canon Lodge, Canon City, CO
Canonsburg General Hospital Skilled Nursing Unit, Canonsburg, PA
Cantabridgia Health Care Nursing Facility, Cambridge, MA
Cantebury Villa of Fort Worth, Fort Worth, TX
Canterburry Villa of Cisco, Cisco, TX
Canterbury, Rancho Palos Verdes, CA
Canterbury Care Center, New Lebanon, OH
Canterbury Court Intermediate Care Unit, Atlanta, GA
Canterbury Health Center, Oklahoma City, OK
Canterbury House, Auburn, WA
Canterbury Manor, Rochester, IN
Canterbury Manor Nursing Center, Waterloo, IL
Canterbury Place, Valparaiso, IN
Canterbury Place, Pittsburgh, PA
Canterbury Towers, Tampa, FL
Canterbury Villa—De Leon, De Leon, TX
Canterbury Villa of Alliance, Alliance, OH
Canterbury Villa of Baird, Baird, TX
Canterbury Villa of Ballinger, Ballinger, TX
Canterbury Villa of Bloomfield, Bloomfield, CT
Canterbury Villa of Carrizo Springs, Carrizo Springs, TX
Canterbury Villa of Centerburg, Centerburg, OH

Canterbury Villa of Denver City, Denver City, TX
Canterbury Villa of Dimmitt, Dimmitt, TX
Canterbury Villa of Eagle Pass, Eagle Pass, TX
Canterbury Villa of Falfurrias, Falfurrias, TX
Canterbury Villa of Fort Worth, Lake Worth, TX
Canterbury Villa of Gatesville, Gatesville, TX
Canterbury Villa of Gorman, Gorman, TX
Canterbury Villa of Hillsboro, Hillsboro, TX
Canterbury Villa of Houston, Houston, TX
Canterbury Villa of Kingsville, Kingsville, TX
Canterbury Villa of Milan, Milan, OH
Canterbury Villa of Navasota, Navasota, TX
Canterbury Villa of Seville, Seville, OH
Canterbury Villa of Stephenville, Stephenville, TX
Canterbury Villa of Wichita Falls, Wichita Falls, TX
Canterbury Woods, Pacific Grove, CA
Cantex Convalescent Center of Lufkin, Lufkin, TX
Cantex Healthcare Center—Denison, Denison, TX
Canton Care Center, Troy, MI
Canton Christian Home, Canton, OH
Canton Good Samaritan Center, Canton, SD
Canton Harbor Nursing Centre, Baltimore, MD
Canton Health Care Center, Canton, NC
Canton Health Care Center, Canton, OH
Canton Manor, Canton, MS
Canton Nursing Center, Canton, GA
Canton Nursing Center, Canton, TX
Canton Regency Health Care Center, Canton, OH
Canton Residential Center, Canton, TX
Canyon Hills Health Care Center, Nephi, UT
Canyon Hills Manor, Thermopolis, WY
Canyon Manor, Novato, CA
Canyonwood Nursing Center, Redding, CA
Cape Cod Nursing & Retirement Home, Wareham, MA
Cape Coral Nursing Pavilion, Cape Coral, FL
Cape End Manor, Provincetown, MA
Cape Girardeau Care Center, Cape Girardeau, MO
Cape Girardeau Nursing Center, Cape Girardeau, MO
Cape Heritage Nursing Home, Sandwich, MA
Cape May Care Center, Cape May Court House, NJ
Cape Regency Nursing Home, Barnstable, MA
Capeside Cove Good Samaritan Center, Siren, WI
Capital Care Center, Boise, ID
Capital Care Healthcare Center, Indianapolis, IN
Capital City Nursing Home, Charleston, WV
Capital Health Care Center, Tallahassee, FL
Capital Region Ford Nursing Home, Cohoes, NY
Capitol City Nursing Home, Austin, TX
Capitol Convalescent Center, Columbia, SC
Capitol Health Care Center Inc, Washington, DC
Capitol Hill Healthcare Center, Montgomery, AL
Capitol Manor Health Care Center, Salem, OR
Capitol Nursing Home, Baton Rouge, LA
Capitol South Care Center, Columbus, OH
Capitol View Health Care Center, Salem, OR
Capri Nursing Home, Phoenix, AZ
Caravilla, Beloit, WI
Carbon County Health Care Center, Red Lodge, MT
Carbon County Home for the Aged, Weatherly, PA
Carbon County Memorial Nursing Home, Red Lodge, MT
Carbon Hill Health Care Inc, Carbon Hill, AL
Carbondale Manor, Carbondale, IL
Carbondale Nursing Home Inc, Carbondale, PA
CARC Fara—Lineberry, Carlsbad, NM
CARC Fara—Scarborough, Carlsbad, NM
CARC Fara—Spence Home, Carlsbad, NM

CARC Fara—Washington Ranch 1, Carlsbad, NM
CARC Fara—Washington Ranch 2, Carlsbad, NM
Carci Hall, Chicago, IL
Cardigan Nursing Home, Scituate, MA
Cardinal Drive Home, Bryan, OH
Cardinal Healthcare of Danville, Danville, IN
Cardinal Shehan Center, Towson, MD
Care Center at Martins Run, Media, PA
Care Center East, Portland, OR
Care Center East, Fond Du Lac, WI
Care Center of Abingdon, Abingdon, IL
Care Center of Iowa Inc, Creston, IA
Care Center of Lopatcong, Phillipsburg, NJ
Care Center of Phillipsburg, Phillipsburg, NJ
Care Center, Baton Rouge, LA
Care Haven of Berkeley, Martinsburg, WV
Care Haven of Pleasants, Belmont, WV
Care Haven of Point Pleasant, Point Pleasant, WV
Care Haven of Raleigh, Daniels, WV
Care Haven of Sistersville, Sistersville, WV
Care Haven of Teays Valley, Hurricane, WV
Care House, Medina, OH
C.A.R.E. Inc Nursing Center, Brownwood, TX
Care Inn—Alcorn County, Corinth, MS
Care Inn Convalescent Center, La Salle, IL
Care Inn Convalescent Center of Litchfield, Litchfield, IL
Care Inn of Abilene, Abilene, TX
Care Inn of Denison, Denison, TX
Care Inn of Edna, Edna, TX
Care Inn of Ganado, Ganado, TX
Care Inn of Gladewater, Gladewater, TX
Care Inn of Gonzales, Gonzales, TX
Care Inn of La Grange, La Grange, TX
Care Inn of Llano, Llano, TX
Care Inn of Plainview, Plainview, TX
Care Inn of San Marcos, San Marcos, TX
Care Inn of Sanger, Sanger, TX
Care Inn of Seguin, Seguin, TX
Care Inn of Shamrock, Shamrock, TX
Care Inn of Voorhees, Voorhees, NJ
Care Inn of Waco, Waco, TX
Care Manor Nursing Center of Burkburnett, Burkburnett, TX
Care Manor Nursing Center of Henrietta, Henrietta, TX
Care Manor of Farmington, Farmington, CT
Care Nursing Home, Miami, OK
Care Pavilion, Philadelphia, PA
Care Vista, Vancouver, WA
Care Well Manor Nursing Home, Malden, MA
Care West—Alondra Nursing Center, Gardena, CA
Care West—Arizona Nursing Center, Santa Monica, CA
Care West—Banning Nursing Center, Banning, CA
Care West—Bayside Nursing & Rehabilitation Center, Kentfield, CA
Care West—Burlingame Nursing & Rehabilitation Center, Burlingame, CA
Care West—Calistoga Nursing & Rehabilitation Center, Calistoga, CA
Care West—Cedars Nursing Center, Red Bluff, CA
Care West—Citrus Nursing Center, Fontana, CA
Care West—Claremont Nursing Center, Pomona, CA
Care West—Clearfield Nursing & Rehabilitation Center, Clearfield, UT
Care West—Garfield Nursing Center, Huntington Beach, CA
Care West—Haster Nursing Center, Garden Grove, CA
Care West Intercommunity Nursing Center, Norwalk, CA
Care West—Kingsburg Nursing Center, Kingsburg, CA
Care West—La Mariposa Nursing & Rehabilitation Center, Fairfield, CA
Care West—Madrone Nursing Center, Saint Helena, CA
Care West—Manteca, Manteca, CA

Care West—Mission Nursing Center, Riverside, CA
Care West—Montebello Convalescent Hospital, Montebello, CA
Care West—Mt Ogden, Washington Terrace, UT
Care West—North Valley Nursing Center, Chico, CA
Care West Northbrook, Willits, CA
Care West—Northridge, Reseda, CA
Care West Nursing Center, Portland, OR
Care West—Orem, Orem, UT
Care West—Palm Springs Nursing Center, Palm Springs, CA
Care West—Palomar Nursing Center, Inglewood, CA
Care West—Park Central Nursing Center, Fremont, CA
Care West—Playa Del Rey Nursing Center, Playa Del Rey, CA
Care West—Pomona Vista Nursing Center, Pomona, CA
Care West—Quincy Nursing Center, Quincy, CA
Care West Rio Hondo Nursing Center, Montebello, CA
Care West—Salt Lake, Salt Lake City, UT
Care West—Santa Monica Nursing Center, Santa Monica, CA
Care West—Sierra Nursing Center, Roseville, CA
Care West—Sonoma Nursing & Rehabilitation Center, Sonoma, CA
Care West—South Bay Nursing Center, Signal Hill, CA
Care West—Susanville Nursing Center, Susanville, CA
Care West—Valley View, West Valley City, UT
Care West—Warner Mountain Nursing Center, Alturas, CA
Care West—Washington Manor Nursing Center, San Leandro, CA
Care West—Weed Nursing Center, Weed, CA
Care West—Wyngate Nursing Center, Tujunga, CA
Care With Dignity Convalescent Hospital, San Diego, CA
Careage of Avondale, Avondale, AZ
Careage of Banning, Banning, CA
Careage of Chico, Chico, CA
Careage of Tracy, Tracy, CA
Careage of Whidbey, Coupeville, WA
Careco Apartments, Inver Grove Heights, MN
Carehouse Convalescent Hospital, Santa Ana, CA
Careousel Care Center, McMinnville, OR
Careview Home Inc, Minneapolis, MN
Carewell Rest Home, New Haven, CT
CareWest—Bountiful, Bountiful, UT
CareWest—Fullerton Nursing Center, Fullerton, CA
CareWest—Gateway Nursing Center, Hayward, CA
CareWest-Hollister Nursing Center, Hollister, CA
CareWest—Huntington Valley, Huntington Beach, CA
CareWest—Manzanita Nursing Center, Cloverdale, CA
CareWest—Petaluma, Petaluma, CA
CareWest—Redlands, Redlands, CA
Carey Nursing Home, Carey, OH
Caribou Memorial Nursing Home, Soda Springs, ID
Caribou Nursing Home, Caribou, ME
Carillon House Nursing Home, Huntington, NY
Carington Living Center, Bloomingdale, IL
Carle Arbours, Savoy, IL
Carleton Nursing Home, Wellsboro, PA
Carleton-Willard Village Nursing Center, Bedford, MA
Carlin Park Healthcare Center, Angola, IN
Carlinville Terrace Ltd, Carlinville, IL
Carlisle Care Center, Carlisle, IA
Carlisle Manor, Franklin, OH
Carlisle Manor Health Care Inc, Carlisle, OH

Carlmont Convalescent Hospital, Belmont, CA
Carlotta, Palm Desert, CA
Carlson Drake House, Bloomington, MN
Carlton Group Home, Duvall, WA
Carlton House Nursing Center, Chicago, IL
Carlton Nursing Home, Carlton, MN
Carlton Nursing Home, Brooklyn, NY
Carlyle, Beloit, WI
Carlyle Health Care Center, South Bend, IN
Carlyle Healthcare Center Inc, Carlyle, IL
Carlyle Nursing Home Inc, Framingham, MA
Carmel Care Center, Carmel, IN
Carmel Convalescent Hospital, Carmel, CA
Carmel Home, Owensboro, KY
Carmel Ltd, Boulder, CO
Carmel Manor, Fort Thomas, KY
Carmel Mountain Healthcare Center, San Diego, CA
Carmel Richmond Nursing Home Inc, Staten Island, NY
Carmel Valley Manor, Carmel, CA
Carmen Home, Carmen, OK
Carmen Manor, Chicago, IL
Carmen Nursing Home, Crawfordsville, IN
Carmichael Convalescent Hospital Inc, Carmichael, CA
Carnegie Care Center, Cleveland, OH
Carnegie Gardens Nursing Center, Melbourne, FL
Carnegie Nursing Home, Carnegie, OK
Marion P Carnell Residence, Ware Shoals, SC
Carol Woods, Chapel Hill, NC
Carolina Care Center, Cherryville, NC
Carolina Place, Florence, SC
Carolina Village Inc, Hendersonville, NC
Caroline Nursing Home Inc, Denton, MD
Carolton Chronic & Convalescent Hospital Inc, Fairfield, CT
Caromin House—Dodge, Duluth, MN
Caromin House—Tioga, Duluth, MN
Caromin House Two Harbors, Two Harbors, MN
Carondelet Holy Cross Hospital & Geriatric Center, Nogales, AZ
Carondelet Holy Family Center, Tucson, AZ
Carondelet Manor, Kansas City, MO
Carpenter Care Center, Tunkhannock, PA
Carriage Hill Nursing Home & Residential Care Center, Fredericksburg, VA
Carriage by the Lake Nursing Center, Bellbrook, OH
Carriage Health Care, Nashville, TN
Carriage Hill—Bethesda Inc, Bethesda, MD
Carriage Hill—Silver Spring, Silver Spring, MD
Carriage House Manor, Fullerton, CA
Carriage House Manor, Morgan, NJ
Carriage House Nursing Home Inc, Middletown, RI
Carriage House of Bay City, Bay City, MI
Carriage Inn Convalescent Center, Coldwater, MI
Carriage Inn of Cadiz Inc, Cadiz, OH
Carriage Inn of Steubenville Inc, Steubenville, OH
Carriage Manor Care Center, Farmington, MO
Carriage Park Nursing Center, Alto, TX
Carriage Square Health Care Center, Saint Joseph, MO
Carriage Square Nursing Home, San Antonio, TX
Carrier Mills Nursing Home Inc, Carrier Mills, IL
Carrington Convalescent Hospital, Stockton, CA
Carrington Health Center—SNF, Carrington, ND
Ann Carroll Nursing Home, Lynn, MA
Carroll Convalescent Center, Carrollton, GA
Carroll County Good Samaritan Center, Mount Carroll, IL
Carroll Health Care Center Inc, Carrollton, OH
Carroll Health Center, Carroll, IA
Carroll House, Hillsville, VA
Carroll Lutheran Nursing Home, Westminster, MD
Carroll Manor, Carroll, IA

Carroll Manor Inc, Hyattsville, MD
Carroll Nursing Home Inc, Oak Grove, LA
Carroll's Intermediate Care, El Cajon, CA
Carroll's Intermediate Care—Anza, El Cajon, CA
Carrollton House, Carrollton, OH
Carrollton Manor, Carrollton, GA
Carrollton Manor, Carrollton, KY
Carrollton Manor, Carrollton, TX
Carrollton Nursing Center, Carrollton, MO
Carrolton of Nash County Inc, Rocky Mount, NC
Carson Convalescent Center, Carson City, NV
Carson Retirement Home, Benton Harbor, MI
Carter Hall Nursing Home, Dryden, VA
Carter Health Care Center, Grayson, KY
Carter Nursing Home Corporation, Seagoville, TX
Carter Nursing Home Inc, Jonesboro, LA
Carter Street Group Home, Columbia, SC
Walter P Carter Center—Mental Retardation Unit, Baltimore, MD
Carter's Guest Home Inc, Jackson, MS
Carter's Nursing Home, Oberlin, OH
Carthage Area Hospital, Carthage, NY
Carthage Health Care Center Inc, Carthage, MS
Carthage Nursing Home, Carthage, AR
Cartie's Health Center, Central Falls, RI
Cartmell Home for Aged, Palestine, TX
Cartwheel Lodge—Lockhart, Lockhart, TX
Cartwheel Lodge of Gonzales, Gonzales, TX
Cartwheel Lodge of Luling, Luling, TX
Caruthersville Nursing Center, Caruthersville, MO
Carvel Building—Delaware State Hospital, Wilmington, DE
Casa Angelica, Albuquerque, NM
Casa Arena Blanca, Alamogordo, NM
Casa Arena Blanca Nursing Center, Alamogordo, NM
Casa Bonita Convalescent Hospital, San Dimas, CA
Casa Central Center, Chicago, IL
Casa Coloma Health Care Center, Rancho Cordova, CA
Casa de las Campanas, San Diego, CA
Casa De Modesto, Modesto, CA
Casa De Paz, Sioux City, IA
Casa de San Antonio, San Antonio, TX
Casa De Vida, San Luis Obispo, CA
Casa del Sol Senior Care Center, Las Cruces, NM
Casa Delmar, Scottsdale, AZ
Casa Dorinda, Montecito, CA
Casa Dorinda, Santa Barbara, CA
Casa Grande Intermediate Care Facility, Anaheim, CA
Casa Inc, Scarborough, ME
Casa Loma Convalescent Center, Payette, ID
Casa Maria Convalescent Hospital, Fontana, CA
Casa Maria Health Care Centre, Roswell, NM
Casa Metropolitan, Fresno, CA
Casa Olga Intermediate Health Care Facility, Palo Alto, CA
Casa Pacifica, Anaheim, CA
Casa Palmera Care Center, Del Mar, CA
Casa Real, Santa Fe, NM
Casa San Miguel, Concord, CA
Casa Serena Skilled Nursing & Rehabilitation Hospital, Salinas, CA
Casa Serena Skilled Nursing & Rehabilitation Hospital, San Jose, CA
Casa Verdugo Convalescent Lodge, Glendale, CA
Casa Willis, Sterling, IL
Cascade Care Center, Caldwell, ID
Cascade Care Center, Grand Rapids, MI
Cascade County Convalescent Nursing Home, Great Falls, MT
Cascade Manor Inc, Eugene, OR
Cascade Terrace Nursing Center, Portland, OR
Cascade Vista Convalescent Center, Redmond, WA
Case Convalescent Center, Washington Court House, OH

Case Golden Age Care, Ranchester, WY
Casey Care Center, Mount Vernon, IL
Casey Nursing Home, Piketon, OH
Caseyville Health Care Center, Caseyville, IL
Cashmere Convalescent Center, Cashmere, WA
Casitas Care Center, Granada Hills, CA
Cass County Medical Care Facility, Cassopolis, MI
Cass County Memorial Hospital, Atlantic, IA
Cassia Memorial Hospital Long-Term Care Unit, Burley, ID
Castle Acres Nursing Home Inc, Hillsboro, MO
Castle Country Care Center, Price, UT
Castle Garden Nursing Home, Northglenn, CO
Castle Hills Manor, San Antonio, TX
Castle Manor, Hot Springs, SD
Castle Manor Convalescent Center, National City, CA
Castle Manor Nursing Home, Garland, TX
Castle Park Nursing Home, Worcester, MA
Castle Rest Nursing Home, Syracuse, NY
Castle Ridge Care Center, Eden Prairie, MN
Castle Rock Care Center, Castle Rock, CO
Castle Rock Convalescent Center, Green River, WY
Castle Shannon Nursing Home, Rockville, IN
Castlehaven Nursing Center, Belleville, IL
Caswell Annex, Goldsboro, NC
Caswell Center, Kinston, NC
Catalpa Manor, Dayton, OH
Catawba Hospital, Catawba, VA
Catered Manor, Long Beach, CA
Eliza Cathcart Home, Devon, PA
Cathedral Convalescent Center, Jacksonville, FL
Cathedral Village, Philadelphia, PA
Catherine Manor, Newport, RI
Catholic Care Center, Wichita, KS
Catholic Memorial Home, Fall River, MA
Caton Park Nursing Home, Brooklyn, NY
Cattaraugus County Home & Infirmary, Machias, NY
Cattaraugus County Public Nursing Home, Olean, NY
Cavallo Convalescent Hospital, Antioch, CA
Cayuga County Nursing Home, Auburn, NY
Cedar I, Austin, MN
Cedar Apartments, Montesano, WA
Cedar Care Center, Cedar City, UT
Cedar Care Center Inc, Cedar Springs, MI
Cedar Creek Living Center, Norman, OK
Cedar Crest, Montgomery, AL
Cedar Crest Convalescent Center, Roosevelt, UT
Cedar Crest Health Center, Janesville, WI
Cedar Crest Health Center Inc, Indianapolis, IN
Cedar Crest Manor, Lawton, OK
Cedar Crest Nursing Centre Inc, Cranston, RI
Cedar Falls Health Care Center, Cedar Falls, IA
Cedar Falls Lutheran Home, Cedar Falls, IA
Cedar Glen Nursing Home, Danvers, MA
Cedar Grove Manor, Cedar Grove, NJ
Cedar Grove Nursing Home, Hillsboro, MO
Cedar Hall, Salem, OR
Cedar Haven—Lebanon County Home, Lebanon, PA
Cedar Hedge Nursing Home, Rouses Point, NY
Cedar Hill Care Center, Zanesville, OH
Cedar Hill Health Care Center, Windsor, VT
Cedar Hill Nursing Center, Cedar Hill, TX
Cedar Hills Nursing Center, Jacksonville, FL
Cedar Home, Fergus Falls, MN
Cedar II, Austin, MN
Cedar III, Austin, MN
Cedar IV, Austin, MN
Cedar Knoll Health Care Center, Bristol, TN
Cedar Knoll Rest Home, Grass Lake, MI
Cedar Lake Home Campus, West Bend, WI
Cedar Lake Lodge, LaGrange, KY
Cedar Lake Nursing Home, Malakoff, TX
Cedar Lane Rehabilitation & Health Care Center, Waterbury, CT

Cedar Lawn Convalescent Center, Abingdon, VA
Cedar Lodge Nursing Center, Marvell, AR
Cedar Lodge Nursing Home, Center Moriches, NY
Cedar Manor, Tipton, IA
Cedar Manor Nursing Home, Ossining, NY
Cedar Manor Nursing Home Inc, Windsor, VT
Cedar Oaks Care Center Inc, South Plainfield, NJ
Cedar Pines Nursing Home, Minneapolis, MN
Cedar Ridge Health Care Center, Sissonville, WV
Cedar Ridge Inc, Skowhegan, ME
Cedar Springs Nursing Center, Cedar Springs, MI
Cedar Street Home, Helena, MT
Cedar Vale Nursing Center, Cedar Vale, KS
Cedar View Good Samaritan Center, Wellington, KS
Cedar Wood Living Center, Lawrence, KS
Cedarbrook—Allentown, Allentown, PA
Cedarbrook Fountain Hill Annex, Bethlehem, PA
Cedarcrest Inc, Keene, NH
Cedarcrest Manor, Washington, MO
Cedarcroft Nursing Home, Valley Park, MO
Cedardale Health Care Facility, Wray, CO
Cedargate, Poplar Bluff, MO
Cedars—Glen Care Center, El Monte, CA
Cedars Health Care Center, Lakewood, CO
Cedars Health Care Center, Cedar Hill, MO
Cedars Health Care Center, Lebanon, TN
Cedars Health Center, Tupelo, MS
Cedars Inc, McPherson, KS
Cedars Intermediate Care Facility, Columbia, MS
Cedars Manor Inc, Checotah, OK
Cedars Nursing Home, Charlottesville, VA
Cedars of Lebanon, Lebanon, OH
Cedars of Lebanon Rest Home, Lebanon, KY
Cedartown Health Care, Cedartown, GA
Cedarview Nursing Home, Owatonna, MN
Cedarwood Care Center, Independence, OR
Cedarwood Health Care Center, Decatur, IL
Cedarwood Health Care Center Inc, Colorado Springs, CO
Celebrity Care Center, Des Moines, IA
Celina Manor, Celina, OH
Centenary Heritage Manor, Shreveport, LA
Centennial Health Care Center, Greeley, CO
Centennial Health Care Center, Portland, OR
Centennial Homestead Inc, Washington, KS
Centennial Park Retirement Village, North Platte, NE
Centennial Spring Health Care Center, Warminster, PA
Center at Manatee Springs, Bradenton, FL
Center for the Retarded—Cullen, Houston, TX
Center Green Rest Home, Fairhaven, MA
Center Haven Health Center, Hamilton, OH
Center of Care, Eau Claire, WI
Center of Family Love, Okarche, OK
Center Ridge Nursing Home, North Ridgeville, OH
Center Skilled Nursing Facility, Sacramento, CA
Centerburg Nursing Center, Centerburg, OH
Centerbury Villa of Beaumont, Beaumont, TX
Centerclair Inc, Lexington, NC
Centerville Care Center, Tallahassee, FL
Centerville Care Center, Centerville, IA
Centerville Good Samaritan Center, Centerville, SD
Centerville Health Care Center, Centerville, TN
Centerville Nursing Home, Centerville, MA
Centinela Park Convalescent Hospital, Inglewood, CA
Central Baptist Home for the Aged, Norridge, IL
Central Care Center, Minneapolis, MN
Central Care Center, Warren, PA
Central Convalescent, Yakima, WA
Central Dakota Nursing Home, Jamestown, ND

Central Dutchess Nursing Home Inc, Wappingers Falls, NY
Central Gardens, San Francisco, CA
Central Health Care Inc, Le Center, MN
Central Healthcare Center, Indianapolis, IN
Central Island Nursing Home, Plainview, NY
Central Montana Nursing Home, Lewistown, MT
Central New Jersey Jewish Home for the Aged, Somerset, NJ
Central Nursing, Chicago, IL
Central Ohio Rehabilitation Center, Columbus, OH
Central Oklahoma Christian Home, Oklahoma City, OK
Central Oregon Health Care Center, Bend, OR
Central Park Lodge—Broomall, Broomall, PA
Central Park Lodge—Chestnut Hill, Philadelphia, PA
Central Park Lodge Nursing Center, Auburndale, FL
Central Park Lodge Nursing Center, Pinellas Park, FL
Central Park Lodge—Tarpon Springs, Tarpon Springs, FL
Central Park Lodge—Whitemarsh, Philadelphia, PA
Central Park Manor Inc, Dallas, TX
Central Park Village Health Care Center, Orlando, FL
Central Piedmont Nursing Center, Burlington, NC
Central Plaza Residential Home, Chicago, IL
Central Point Care Center, Central Point, OR
Central State Hospital, Milledgeville, GA
Central State Hospital, Milledgeville, GA
Central Suffolk Hospital Skilled Nursing Facility, Riverhead, NY
Central Texas Care Center, Austin, TX
Central Todd County Care Center, Clarissa, MN
Central Virginia Training Center, Lynchburg, VA
Central Wisconsin Center for the Developmentally Disabled, Madison, WI
Centralia Care Center, Centralia, IL
Centralia Convalescent Center, Centralia, WA
Centralia Convalescent Hospital, Long Beach, CA
Centralia Fireside House, Centralia, IL
Centralia Friendship House, Centralia, IL
Centre Crest, Bellefonte, PA
Centreville Health Care Center, Centreville, MS
Centuria Care Center, Centuria, WI
Century Care Center Inc, Whiteville, NC
Century Care of Laurinburg Inc, Laurinburg, NC
Century Home Inc, Baltimore, MD
Century Villa Health Care, Greentown, IN
Cerri's Painesville Nursing Home, Painesville, OH
Cerro Gordo County Care Facility, Mason City, IA
Hattie Ide Chaffee Home, East Providence, RI
Jennie B Richmond Chaffee Nursing Home Company Inc, Springville, NY
Chaffee Nursing Center, Chaffee, MO
Chaffey Nursing Home Inc, Superior, WI
Chalet Healthcare, Yakima, WA
Chalet Village, Berne, IN
Chalkville Health Care Inc, Birmingham, AL
Chamberlain Nursing Home, Brookline, MA
Chambers Nursing Home Inc, Carlisle, AR
Sarah Jane Chambers Geriatric Center, Delphos, OH
Chamness Square, Bourbonnais, IL
Chamor Nursing Center, Tulsa, OK
Champaign Children's Home, Champaign, IL
Champaign County Nursing Home, Urbana, IL
Champaign County Residential Services Inc, Urbana, OH
Champaign Nursing Home, Urbana, OH
Champaign Opportunity House, Champaign, IL
Champaign Terrace, Saint Joseph, IL
Champion Childrens Home, Duluth, MN

Champlain Valley Physicians Hospital Medical Center—Skilled Nursing Facility, Plattsburgh, NY
Chandler Care Center—Ramona, El Monte, CA
Chandler Convalescent Hospital, Glendale, CA
Chandler Convalescent Hospital, North Hollywood, CA
Chandler Hall, Newtown, PA
Chandler Haven, Detroit, MI
Chandler Healthcare Center, Chandler, AZ
Chandler Hillcrest Manor Inc, Chandler, OK
Chandler Manor Rest Home, Somerville, MA
Chandler Memorial Home, San Antonio, TX
Chandler Nursing Center, Chandler, TX
Changing Seasons Community Care Center, Vidor, TX
Channing House, Palo Alto, CA
Chaparral House, Berkeley, CA
Chapel Hill Convalescent Home, Randallstown, MD
Chapel Hill Home, Canal Fulton, OH
Chapel Hill Nursing Home, Holyoke, MA
Chapel Manor Nursing & Rehabilitation Center, Philadelphia, PA
Chapel of Care Nursing Center, Sherman, TX
Chapel View Inc, Hopkins, MN
Chapin Center Skilled Nursing Facility, Springfield, MA
Chapin Home for the Aging, Jamaica, NY
Chaplinwood Nursing Home, Milledgeville, GA
Chapman Convalescent Hospital, Riverside, CA
Chapman Harbor Skilled Nursing Center, Garden Grove, CA
Chapman Nursing Home Inc, Alexander City, AL
Chapman Valley Manor, Chapman, KS
Char-Lotte Nursing Home Inc, Rock Creek, OH
Char Mund Nursing Home, Orangeville, PA
Chariot Nursing & Convalescent Home, Wilmington, DE
Charis House, Brainerd, MN
Charis House, Brainerd, MN
Chariton Manor, Chariton, IA
Chariton Park, Salisbury, MO
Charity Nursing Facility, Dennison, OH
Charlene Manor Extended Care Facility, Greenfield, MA
Charles County Nursing Home, La Plata, MD
Charles Court Health Care Center, Newton Falls, OH
Charles Harwood Memorial Hospital—Skilled Nursing Unit, Christiansted, VI
Charles the First Medical Center Inc, Saint Louis, MO
Charlesgate Manor Convalescent Home Inc, Watertown, MA
Charlesgate Nursing Center, Providence, RI
Charless Home, Saint Louis, MO
Charleston Group Home, Charleston, NH
Charleston Health Care Center, Las Vegas, NV
Charleston Manor, Charleston, IL
Charleston Manor, Charleston, MO
Charlestown Retirement Community, Catonsville, MD
Charlevoix Nursing Center, Saint Charles, MO
Charlotte Hall Veterans Home, Charlotte Hall, MD
Charlotte Stephenson Home, Adrian, MI
Charlton Manor Rest Home Inc, Charlton, MA
Charlwell House, Norwood, MA
Charter House Health Center, Rochester, MN
Chase Centeer, Logansport, IN
Chase County Nursing Center, Cottonwood Falls, KS
Chase Memorial Nursing Home Co Inc, New Berlin, NY
Chateau Convalescent Centre, Muncie, IN
Chateau Convalescent Hospital, Stockton, CA
Chateau D'Arbonne Nursing Care Center, Farmerville, LA
Chateau de Notre Dame, New Orleans, LA
Chateau Gardens, Flint, MI

Chateau Girardeau Health Center, Cape Girardeau, MO
Chateau Healthcare Center, Minneapolis, MN
Chateau Lake San Marcos Health Center, Lake San Marcos, CA
Chateau Living Center, Kenner, LA
Chateau Nursing & Rehabilitation Center, Bryn Mawr, PA
Chateau Village Living Center, Willowbrook, IL
Chatham Acres, Chatham, PA
Hugh Chatham Memorial Hospital—SNF, Elkin, NC
Chatham Nursing Home I, Savannah, GA
Chatham Nursing Home II, Savannah, GA
Chatsworth Health & Rehabilitation Center, Chatsworth, CA
Chatsworth Health Care Center, Chatsworth, GA
Chatsworth Park Convalescent Hospital, Chatsworth, CA
Chattahoochee Health Services, Atlanta, GA
Chattanooga Health Care Associates Ltd, Chattanooga, TN
Chautauqua County Home, Dunkirk, NY
Chautauqua Guest Home 1, Charles City, IA
Chautauqua Guest Home 2, Charles City, IA
Chautauqua Guest Home 3, Charles City, IA
Chavaneaux Care Center, San Antonio, TX
Cheatham County Rest Home, Ashland City, TN
Cheboygan Health Care Center, Cheboygan, MI
Checotah Manor Inc, Checotah, OK
Chehalem Convalescent Care Center, Newberg, OR
Chelsea Group Home, Duvall, WA
Chelsea Jewish Nursing Home, Chelsea, MA
Chelsea United Methodist Retirement Home, Chelsea, MI
Cheltenham Nursing & Rehabilitation Center, Philadelphia, PA
Cheltenham-York Road Nursing & Rehabilitation Center, Philadelphia, PA
Chemung County Health Center—Nursing Facility, Elmira, NY
Chenango Memorial Hospital—Skilled Nursing Facility, Norwich, NY
Cheney Care Center, Cheney, WA
Cheney Golden Age Home Inc, Cheney, KS
Chenita Nursing Home, Mansfield, OH
Chenita Nursing Home No 1, Mansfield, OH
Cheraw Nursing Home Inc, Cheraw, SC
Cherish Nursing Center, Richmond, IN
Cherokee County Long-Term Care Facility, Gaffney, SC
Cherokee County Nursing Home, Centre, AL
Cherokee Lodge Adult Care Home, Oskaloosa, KS
Cherokee Manor, Cherokee, OK
Cherokee Nursing Home, Calhoun, GA
Cherokee Villa, Cherokee, IA
Cherrelyn Manor Health Care Center, Littleton, CO
Cherry-Carecentre Inc, Springfield, MO
Cherry Creek Nursing Center, Aurora, CO
Cherry Creek Village Nursing Center, Wichita, KS
Cherry Hill Convalescent Center, Cherry Hill, NJ
Cherry Hill Home, Mansfield, OH
Cherry Hill Manor, Johnston, RI
Cherry Hills Nursing Home, Englewood, CO
Cherry Hospital—ICF, Goldsboro, NC
Cherry Nursing Home, Montclair, NJ
Cherry Oaks Nursing Center, Graham, TX
Cherry Park Health Care Facility, Englewood, CO
Cherry Ridge Guest Care Center, Bastrop, LA
Cherry Street Annex, Paris, TX
Cherry Street Manor, Paris, TX
Cherry Village, Great Bend, KS
Cherrylee Lodge Sanitarium, El Monte, CA
Cherryvale Medi-Lodge, Cherryvale, KS
Cherrywood Extended Care Centre, Reisterstown, MD
Cherrywood Health Care Center, Vandalia, IL

Chesaning Nursing Care Center, Chesaning, MI
Chesapeake Group Home, Saint Georges, DE
Chesapeake Manor Extended Care, Arnold, MD
Cheshire Convalescent Center, Cheshire, CT
Cheshire County Maplewood Nursing Home, Westmoreland, NH
Cheshire Home, Summit, NJ
Chestelm Convalescent Home, Moodus, CT
Chester Care Center, Chester, PA
Chester Care Center, Chester, PA
Chester County Nursing Center, Chester, SC
Chester County Nursing Home, Henderson, TN
Chesterfield County Lucy Corr Nursing Home, Chesterfield, VA
Chesterfield Manor Inc, Chesterfield, MO
Chesterfields Chronic & Convalescent Hospital, Chester, CT
Chesterton Health Care Center, Chesterton, IN
Chestnut Corner Sheltered Care, Louisville, IL
Chestnut Hill Convalescent Center, Passaic, NJ
Chestnut Hill Nursing Home, East Longmeadow, MA
Chestnut Hill Rehabilitation Hospital Skilled Nursing Facility, Wyndmoor, PA
Chestnut Knoll Inc, Springfield, MA
Chestor House, Boulder, CO
Chetwynde Convalescent Home, Newton, MA
Chetwynde Nursing Home, Newton, MA
Cheviot Garden Convalescent Hospital, Los Angeles, CA
Chevy Chase Nursing Center, Chicago, IL
Cheyenne Convalescent Home, Cheyenne, OK
Cheyenne Health Care Center, Cheyenne, WY
Cheyenne Lodge Nursing Home, Jamestown, KS
Cheyenne Manor, Cheyenne Wells, CO
Cheyenne Mountain Nursing Center, Colorado Springs, CO
Cheyenne Village Inc, Manitou Springs, CO
Chez Nous—St Anthony Park, Saint Paul, MN
Chicago Ridge Nursing Center, Chicago Ridge, IL
Chickasha Nursing Center Inc, Chickasha, OK
Chicopee Municipal Home, Chicopee, MA
Chicora Medical Center, Chicora, PA
Children's Convalescent Center, Bethany, OK
Children's Extended Care Center, Groton, MA
Children's Habilitation Center, Johnston, IA
Childress Nursing Center, Childress, TX
Child's Nursing Home, Albany, NY
Mary Chiles Hospital, Mount Sterling, KY
Chilton Village, Chilton, WI
Chimney Rock Villa, Bayard, NE
Chinle Nursing Home, Chinle, AZ
Chipeta Drive, Montrose, CO
Chippendale Nursing Home, Kansas City, MO
Chippenham Manor Nursing Center, Richmond, VA
Chippewa County War Memorial Hospital Inc, Sault Sainte Marie, MI
Chippewa Manor Nursing Home, Chippewa Falls, WI
Chisago Lakes Hospital, Chisago City, MN
Choctaw County Nursing Home, Ackerman, MS
Choctaw Residential Center, Philadelphia, MS
Chosen Valley Care Center, Chatfield, MN
Chouteau County District Hospital & Nursing Home, Fort Benton, MT
Chouteau Nursing Center, Chouteau, OK
Chowan Hospital Inc—Skilled Nursing Facility, Edenton, NC
Chowchilla Convalescent Hospital, Chowchilla, CA
Chris Ridge Village Health Center, Phoenix, AZ
Christ the King Manor, Dubois, PA
Christ Villa Nursing Center, Wichita, KS
Christel Manor Nursing Home, Fairborn, OH
Christian Buehler Memorial Home, Peoria, IL
Christian Care Center, Mesquite, TX
Christian Care Center North, Dallas, TX
Christian Care Nursing Center, Phoenix, AZ

Christian Care of Cincinnati Inc, Cincinnati, OH
Christian Care Retirement Village, Chickasha, OK
Christian City Convalescent Center, Atlanta, GA
Christian Community Home of Hudson, Hudson, WI
Christian Convalescent Home, Muskegon, MI
Christian Haven, Grand Haven, MI
Christian Health Care Center, Wyckoff, NJ
Christian Health Center, Corbin, KY
Christian Health Center, Hopkinsville, KY
Christian Health Center, Louisville, KY
Christian Hill Rest Home, Barre, MA
Christian Home for the Aged, Muskegon, MI
Christian Home for the Aged, Columbus, OH
Christian Home Inc, Waupun, WI
Christian Homes Inc, Holdrege, NE
Christian League for the Handicapped, Walworth, WI
Christian Living Campus—Johnson Center, Littleton, CO
Christian Living Campus—University Hills, Denver, CO
Christian Manor Nursing Home, Tracy, MN
Christian Nursing Center, Grand Rapids, MI
Christian Nursing Center Inc, Kentwood, MI
Christian Nursing Home Inc, Lincoln, IL
Christian Nursing & Living Center, Willmar, MN
Christian Old People's Home, Ferguson, MO
Christian Park Health Care Center, Escanaba, MI
Christian Park Village, Escanaba, MI
Christian Rest Home, Lynden, WA
Christian Rest Home Association, Grand Rapids, MI
Christian Shelticenter, Quincy, IL
Christian Villa Nursing Home, Crowley, LA
Christopher—East Health Care Facility, Louisville, KY
Christopher East Living Center, Evansville, IN
Christopher House Nursing Home, Wheat Ridge, CO
Christoval Golden Years Nursing Home Inc, Christoval, TX
Christ's Home Retirement Center, Warminster, PA
Christus Group Home, Little Falls, MN
Chrystal's Country Home Inc, Parker City, IN
Chula Vista Nursing Home, Mesa, AZ
Church Creek—A Marriott Retirement Community & Health Care Center, Arlington Heights, IL
Church Home for the Aged, Perry, GA
Church Lane Convalescent Hospital, San Pablo, CA
Church Lane Health Care Center, Broomall, PA
Church of Christ Care Center, Mount Clemens, MI
Church of Christ Home for Aged, Nashville, TN
Church of God Home Inc, Carlisle, PA
Church of the Brethren Home, Windber, PA
Church Street Manor, Saint Joseph, MO
Churchman Manor, Indianapolis, IN
Churchmans Village Inc, Newark, DE
Churchview Health Center Retirement Home, Haverhill, MA
Cicero Children's Center Inc, Cicero, IN
Cimarron Nursing Center, Kingfisher, OK
Cimarron Nursing Home, Boise City, OK
Cimarron Pointe Care Center, Mannford, OK
Cinnaminson Manor Nursing & Convalescent Center, Cinnaminson, NJ
Cinnamon Hill Manor Inc, Lanagan, MO
Circle Manor Nursing Home, Kensington, MD
Circle Manor Nursing Home, Boston, MA
Cisne Manor, Cisne, IL
Citadel Care Center, Mesa, AZ
Citadel Health Care, Pueblo, CO
Citadel Health Care Pavilion, Saint Joseph, MO
Citizens Medical Center, Columbia, LA
Citizens Memorial Healthcare Facility, Bolivar, MO

Citizens Nursing Home of Frederick County, Frederick, MD
Citizens Nursing Home of Harford County, Havre de Grace, MD
Citronelle Convalescent Center, Citronelle, AL
City Care Center, Anna, IL
City Hospital at Elmhurst Public Home Infirmary, Elmhurst, NY
City View Nursing Home, Madison, WI
City View Nursing Home Inc, Brookline, MA
Civic Center Nursing Home, Birmingham, AL
Cla-Clif Home for the Aged Inc, Brinkley, AR
Claiborne & Hughes Convalescent Center Inc, Franklin, TN
Claiborne County Nursing Home, Tazewell, TN
Claiborne Manor Nursing Home Inc, Homer, LA
Clairemont, Eau Claire, WI
Clairidge House, Kenosha, WI
Clairmont, Longview, TX
Clairmont, Tyler, TX
Clanton Health Care Center Inc, Clanton, AL
Clapp's Convalescent Nursing Home Inc, Asheboro, NC
Clapp's Nursing Center Inc, Pleasant Garden, NC
Clara Burke Nursing Home, Plymouth Meeting, PA
Clara City Community Nursing Home, Clara City, MN
Clara Doerr-Lindley Hall, Minneapolis, MN
Clara Manor Nursing Home, Kansas City, MO
Clare Home, Montevideo, MN
Clare Nursing Home, Clare, MI
Claremont Care Center, Point Pleasant, NJ
Claremont Convalescent Hospital, Berkeley, CA
Claremont Convalescent Hospital, Claremont, CA
Claremore Nursing Home Inc, Claremore, OK
Claremore Regional Medical Center SNF, Claremore, OK
Clarence Nursing Home, Clarence, IA
Clarence Nursing Home District, Clarence, MO
Clarendon Hill Nursing Home, Somerville, MA
Clarewood House, Houston, TX
Claridge House, North Miami, FL
Clarion Care Center, Clarion, IA
Clarion Care Center, Clarion, PA
Clark Care Center, Clark, SD
Clark County Health Care Center, Owen, WI
Clark County Nursing Home, Kahoka, MO
Clark Fork Valley Nursing Home, Plains, MT
Clark Institute of Restorative Tech, Battle Ground, WA
Lida Clark Nursing Home, Clarksburg, WV
Clark-Lindsey Village, Urbana, IL
M J Clark Memorial Home, Grand Rapids, MI
Clark Manor Convalescent Center, Chicago, IL
Clark Manor Nursing Home Inc, Worcester, MA
Clark Memorial Home, Springfield, OH
Clark Nursing Home, Vergennes, VT
John Clarke Retirement Center, Middletown, RI
Clarkfield Care Center, Clarkfield, MN
Clark's Mountain Nursing Center, Piedmont, MO
Clarks Summit State Hospital Long-Term Care Facility, Clarks Summit, PA
Clarksburg Continuous Care Center, Clarksburg, WV
Clarkson Mountain View Guest Home (NCHS), Rapid City, SD
Clarkston Care Center, Clarkston, WA
Clarkston Court, Springfield, IL
Clarksville Convalescent Home Inc, Clarksville, AR
Clarksville Healthcare Center, Clarksville, IN
Clarksville Manor Inc, Clarksville, TN
Clarksville Nursing Center, Clarksville, TX
Clarview, Sligo, PA
Clarytona Manor, Lewistown, IL

Classic Care South, Sandusky, OH
Classic Center, Sandusky, OH
Clatsop Care & Rehabilitation Center, Astoria, OR
Claxton Nursing Home, Claxton, GA
Clay Center Presbyterian Manor, Clay Center, KS
Clay County Health Center Inc, Brazil, IN
Clay County Hospital & Nursing Home, Ashland, AL
Clay County Manor Inc, Celina, TN
Clay County Residence, Hawley, MN
Clay County Residence II, Moorhead, MN
Henry Clay Villa, Markleysburg, PA
Clayberg, Cuba, IL
Claystone Manor Nursing Home, Ennis, TX
Clayton House Health Care & Terrace, Ballwin, MO
Clayton-on-the-Green Nursing Center, Ballwin, MO
Clayton Residential Home, Chicago, IL
Claywest House, Saint Charles, MO
Clear Creek Care Center, Westminster, CO
Clear Haven Nursing Center, Clearfield, PA
Clear View Convalescent Center, Gardena, CA
Clear View Sanitarium, Gardena, CA
Clearbrook Center, Rolling Meadows, IL
Clearbrook Center East, Rolling Meadows, IL
Clearbrook Center West, Rolling Meadows, IL
Clearbrook House, Arlington Heights, IL
Clearview, Juneau, WI
Clearview Convalescent Center, Columbus, OH
Clearview Home, Clearfield, IA
Clearview Home, Mount Ayr, IA
Clearview Manor, Prairie City, IA
Clearview Manor Convalescent & Rehabilitation Center, Tacoma, WA
Clearview Nursing Care, Thomaston, GA
Clearview Nursing Home, Whitestone, NY
Clearview Nursing Home Inc, Hagerstown, MD
Clearview Sanatorium, Delafield, WI
Clearwater Care Center, Twin Falls, ID
Clearwater Convalescent Center, Clearwater, FL
Cleaver Memorial Convalescent Center, Longview, TX
Cleburne Community Hospital & Nursing Home, Heflin, AL
Cleburne Health Care Center, Cleburne, TX
Clement Manor Health Care Center, Greenfield, WI
Clemson Area Retirement Center, Clemson, SC
Clepper Convalescent Home Inc, Sharon, PA
Clermont Nursing & Convalescent Center, Milford, OH
Cleveland County Nursing Home, Rison, AR
Cleveland Golden Age Nursing Home, Cleveland, OH
Cleveland Health Care Center, Cleveland, MS
Cleveland Health Care Center, Kansas City, MO
Cleveland Manor Nursing Home, Cleveland, OK
Cleveland Memorial Hospital—Skilled Nursing Facility, Shelby, NC
Clewiston Health Care Center, Clewiston, FL
Cliff Gables Nursing Home, Fall River, MA
Cliff Haven Nursing Home, Fall River, MA
Cliff Heights Nursing Home, Fall River, MA
Cliff House, Englewood Cliffs, NJ
Cliff House Nursing Home Inc, Winthrop, MA
Cliff Lawn Nursing Home, Fall River, MA
Cliff Manor, Spokane, WA
Cliff Manor Nursing Home, Fall River, MA
Cliff Towers Nursing Home, Dallas, TX
Cliffside Health Care Center, Cliffwood Beach, NJ
Cliffside Nursing Home, Flushing, NY
Clifton Care Center Inc, Cincinnati, OH
Clifton Geriatric Center Long-Term Care Facility, Somerset, MA
Clifton House, Park Ridge, IL
Clifton House, Minneapolis, MN
Clifton Lutheran Sunset Home, Clifton, TX

Clifton Springs Hospital & Clinic Extended Care, Clifton Springs, NY
Clifton Villa, Cincinnati, OH
Clifty Falls Convalescent Center, Madison, IN
Clinic Convalescent Center, Madisonville, KY
Clinton-Aire Nursing Center, Mount Clemens, MI
Clinton Convalescent Center, Clinton, MD
Clinton Country Manor, Clinton, MS
Clinton County Nursing Home, Plattsburgh, NY
Clinton Cove Convalescent Center, Macon, GA
Clinton Good Samaritan Center, Clinton, MN
Clinton Health Care Center, Clinton, CT
Clinton-Hickman County Hospital—IC/PC Facility, Clinton, KY
Clinton Home for Aged People, Clinton, MA
Clinton House Inc, Frankfort, IN
Clinton Manor Inc, Plattsburg, MO
Clinton Manor Living Center, New Baden, IL
Clinton Manor Nursing Home, Clinton, MA
Clinton Meadows Park Nursing Home, Clinton, WI
Clinton Nursing Home, Clinton, IN
Clinton Retirement Village, Clinton, IA
Clinton Village Convalescent Hospital, Oakland, CA
Clio Convalescent Center, Clio, MI
Clipper Home of North Conway, North Conway, NH
Clipper Home of Portsmouth, Portsmouth, NH
Clipper Home of Rochester Inc, Rochester, NH
Clipper Home of Wolfeboro, Wolfeboro, NH
Cliveden Convalescent Center, Philadelphia, PA
Clock Tower Village, Sergeant Bluff, IA
Cloisters of La Jolla, La Jolla, CA
Cloisters of Mission Hills Convalescent Hospital, San Diego, CA
Clove Lakes Nursing Home & Health Related Facility, Staten Island, NY
Clover Manor Inc, Auburn, ME
Clover Rest Home, Columbia, NJ
Clover Rest Nursing Home, Montclair, NJ
Cloverleaf Healthcare, Hemet, CA
Cloverlodge Care Center, Saint Edward, NE
Clovernook Inc, Cincinnati, OH
Clovis Convalescent Hospital, Clovis, CA
Clovis Nursing Home, Clovis, CA
Clusters of Lexington, Lexington, SC
Clyatt Memorial Center, Daytona Beach, FL
Clyde Nursing Center, Clyde, TX
Clyde Street Home, Florence, SC
Coaldale State General Hospital Geriatric Center, Coaldale, PA
Coalinga Convalescent Center, Coalinga, CA
Coast Care Convalescent Center, Baldwin Park, CA
Coast Fork Nursing Center, Cottage Grove, OR
Coastal Healthcare Center, Port Lavaca, TX
Coastal Manor, Yarmouth, ME
Coastal Pines Care Center, Hitchcock, TX
Cobalt Lodge Convalescent Home, Cobalt, CT
Cobb Health Care Center, Comer, GA
Cobble Hill Nursing Home, Brooklyn, NY
Cobbs Creek Nursing Center, Philadelphia, PA
Coberly Green Intermediate Care Facility, Oakland, CA
Coburn Charitable Society, Ipswich, MA
Thomas A Coccomo Memorial, Meriden, CT
Cochituate Nursing Home Inc, Wayland, MA
Cocke County Baptist Convalescent Center, Newport, TN
Coffee Medical Center Nursing Home, Manchester, TN
Coffman Home for the Aging Inc, Hagerstown, MD
Cogburn Health Center Inc, Mobile, AL
Cohasset Knoll Skilled Nursing & Rehabilitation, Cohasset, MA
Cohen's Retreat, Savannah, GA
Coit Street Community Residence, Florence, SC
Cojeunaze Nursing Center, Chicago, IL

Cokato Manor Inc, Cokato, MN
Coker Intermediate Care Home, Canton, GA
Martha Coker Convalescent Home, Yazoo City, MS
Cokesbury Village, Hockessin, DE
Colby Center, Glendale, CA
Colby Manor, Everett, WA
Colchester Health Care, Colchester, CT
Colchester Nursing Center, Colchester, IL
Coldwater Manor Nursing Home, Stratford, TX
Coldwell Nursing Home, Mexico, MO
Charles Cole Memorial Hospital, Coudersport, PA
Coleman Care Center, Coleman, TX
Coleman's Personal Care Home, Jackson, MS
Coler Memorial Hospital Skilled Nursing Facility, New York, NY
Cole's Rest Haven Nursing Home, Guthrie, OK
Colfax General Hospital—Intermediate Care Facility, Springer, NM
Coliseum Park Nursing Home, Hampton, VA
College Harbor Inc, Saint Petersburg, FL
College Hill Skilled Nursing Center, Manhattan, KS
College Nursing Home—Waterview Nursing Care Center, Flushing, NY
College Park Care Center, Texas City, TX
College Park Convalescent Home, College Park, GA
College Park Convalescent Hospital, Menlo Park, CA
College Park Village, Salina, KS
College Street Nursing Center, Beaumont, TX
College Vista Convalescent Hospital, Los Angeles, CA
Colleton Skilled Care Facility, Waterboro, SC
Collier Manor, Highland, KS
Collier's Health Care Center, Ellsworth, ME
Collin Care Center, Plano, TX
Collingswood Nursing Center, Rockville, MD
Collington Episcopal Life Care Center, Mitchellville, MD
Collingwood Manor, Chula Vista, CA
Collingwood Nursing Home, Toledo, OH
Collins Chapel Health Care Center, Memphis, TN
Collins Nursing Home, Pittsburgh, PA
Collins Rest Home Inc, Ashburnham, MA
Collins Square, Bradley, IL
Collinsville Care Center, Collinsville, TX
Collinsville Manor Nursing Home, Collinsville, OK
Collinsville Nursing Home Inc, Collinsville, AL
Colonial Acres Health Care Center, Golden Valley, MN
Colonial Acres Inc, Rock Falls, IL
Colonial Acres Nursing Home, Lincoln, ME
Colonial Acres Nursing Home, Humboldt, NE
Colonial Apartments, Centralia, IL
Colonial Belle Nursing Home, Bellville, TX
Colonial Care Center, Saint Petersburg, FL
Colonial Care Center A Long-Term Care Facility, Norwood, MA
Colonial Care Home, Somerset, KY
Colonial Columns Nursing Center, Colorado Springs, CO
Colonial Convalescent & Nursing Home, Nixon, TX
Colonial Convalescent Home Inc, Wynnewood, OK
Colonial Convalescent Hospital, Bakersfield, CA
Colonial Convalescent Hospital, San Jacinto, CA
Colonial Estates, Guthrie, OK
Colonial Gardens Health Care Center, Boonville, MO
Colonial Gardens Inc, Tallmadge, OH
Colonial Gardens Nursing Home, Pico Rivera, CA
Colonial Hall Manor, Shelbyville, KY
Colonial Hall Nursing Home, Princeton, IL
Colonial Haven, Beemer, NE
Colonial Haven Nursing Home Inc, Granite City, IL

Colonial Health Care Services Inc, Superior, WI
Colonial Heights Convalescent Center, Colonial Heights, VA
Colonial Hill Health Care Center, Johnson City, TN
Colonial Hills Nursing Center, Maryville, TN
Colonial House, Bardstown, KY
Colonial House Living Center, Colby, WI
Colonial House Manor, Waterville, ME
Colonial House Nursing Home, Framingham, MA
Colonial House of Shepherdsville, Shepherdsville, KY
Colonial Lodge Nursing Home, Independence, KS
Colonial Lodge Nursing Home, McAlester, OK
Colonial Manor, Amana, IA
Colonial Manor, Anita, IA
Colonial Manor, Avoca, IA
Colonial Manor, Baxter, IA
Colonial Manor, Corning, IA
Colonial Manor, Kingsley, IA
Colonial Manor, LaPorte City, IA
Colonial Manor, Zearing, IA
Colonial Manor, Lawrence, KS
Colonial Manor, Clarkson, NE
Colonial Manor, Middletown, OH
Colonial Manor, Youngstown, OH
Colonial Manor, Chelsea, OK
Colonial Manor, Edinburg, TX
Colonial Manor, Glendale, WI
Colonial Manor, Madison, WI
Colonial Manor, Milwaukee, WI
Colonial Manor 45, Elma, IA
Colonial Manor I, Hollis, OK
Colonial Manor II, Hollis, OK
Colonial Manor Care Center, New Braunfels, TX
Colonial Manor—Columbus Junction, Columbus Junction, IA
Colonial Manor Convalescent Hospital, Long Beach, CA
Colonial Manor Convalescent Hospital, West Covina, CA
Colonial Manor Guest House, Rayville, LA
Colonial Manor Health Care Center, Loudonville, OH
Colonial Manor Health Care Center Inc II, Loudonville, OH
Colonial Manor Inc, Danville, IL
Colonial Manor Living Center, La Grange, IL
Colonial Manor Nursing & Care Center, Lansing, KS
Colonial Manor Nursing & Care Center, Wathena, KS
Colonial Manor Health Care Center, Nephi, UT
Colonial Manor Nursing Center, Fort Worth, TX
Colonial Manor Nursing Home, Bowling Green, KY
Colonial Manor Nursing Home, Lakefield, MN
Colonial Manor Nursing Home, Appleton City, MO
Colonial Manor Nursing Home, Midwest City, OK
Colonial Manor Nursing Home, Tulsa, OK
Colonial Manor Nursing Home, York, PA
Colonial Manor Nursing Home, Cleburne, TX
Colonial Manor Nursing Home of Woodward Inc, Woodward, OK
Colonial Manor of Albany, Albany, MO
Colonial Manor of Armour, Armour, SD
Colonial Manor of Balaton, Balaton, MN
Colonial Manor of Correctionville, Correctionville, IA
Colonial Manor of Custer, Custer, SD
Colonial Manor of Deer Lodge, Deer Lodge, MT
Colonial Manor of Glasgow, Glasgow, MO
Colonial Manor of Groton, Groton, SD
Colonial Manor of Hudson, Hudson, SD
Colonial Manor of Ipswich, Ipswich, SD
Colonial Manor of McAllen, McAllen, TX
Colonial Manor of Odebolt, Odebolt, IA

Colonial Manor of Randolph Inc, Randolph, NE
Colonial Manor of Salem, Salem, SD
Colonial Manor of Tyler, Tyler, TX
Colonial Manor of Wausau, Wausau, WI
Colonial Manor of Whitefish, Whitefish, MT
Colonial Nursing & Rehabilitation Center, Weymouth, MA
Colonial Nursing & Retirement Center, Pauls Valley, OK
Colonial Nursing Center, Canton, OH
Colonial Nursing Center, Lindale, TX
Colonial Nursing Home, Crown Point, IN
Colonial Nursing Home, Kansas City, MO
Colonial Nursing Home, Rockford, OH
Colonial Nursing Home, Cameron, TX
Colonial Nursing Home, San Angelo, TX
Colonial Nursing Home Inc, Nashville, AR
Colonial Nursing Home Inc, Marksville, LA
Colonial Nursing Home Inc, Schulenburg, TX
Colonial Oaks Health Care Center, Marion, IN
Colonial Oaks Living Center, Metairie, LA
Colonial Oaks Nursing Home, Cross Plains, TX
Colonial Palms East Nursing Home, Pompano Beach, FL
Colonial Palms—West, Pompano Beach, FL
Colonial Park Nursing Home, McAlester, OK
Colonial Park Nursing Home, Marshall, TX
Colonial Park Nursing Home Inc, Okemah, OK
Colonial Pines Health Care Center, Oxford, AL
Colonial Plaza, Nashville, IL
Colonial Plaza Nursing Home Inc, Cushing, OK
Colonial Poplin Nursing Home, Fremont, NH
Colonial Rest Home, Owingsville, KY
Colonial Rest Home, Lowell, MA
Colonial Retirement Center Inc, Bismarck, MO
Colonial Terrace, Independence, KS
Colonial Terrace Care Center Inc, Pryor, OK
Colonial Terrace Intermediate Care, Sebree, KY
Colonial Villa Good Samaritan Center, Alma, NE
Colonial Villa Nursing Home, Silver Spring, MD
Colonial Village, Grandfield, OK
Colonial Vista Convalescent Center, Wenatchee, WA
Colonnades, Granite City, IL
Colony House, Missouri City, TX
Colony House Healthcare Nursing Home, Abington, MA
Colony Oaks Care Center, Appleton, WI
Colony Park Care Center, Modesto, CA
Color Country Care Center, Saint George, UT
Colorado Lutheran Health Care Center, Arvada, CO
Colorado State Veterans Nursing Home, Florence, CO
Colorado State Veterans Nursing Home, Rifle, CO
Colorow Care Center, Olathe, CO
Colter Village, Glendale, AZ
Colton Care Center, Colton, OR
Colton Villa Nursing Center, Hagerstown, MD
Columbia Basin Hospital, Ephrata, WA
Columbia Basin Nursing Home, The Dalles, OR
Columbia Care Center, Scappoose, OR
Columbia City Community Care Center, Columbia City, IN
Columbia City Nursing Home, Columbia City, IN
Columbia Convalescent Home, Los Angeles, CA
Columbia County Home, Wyocena, WI
Columbia-Greene Medical Center Long-Term Care Division, Catskill, NY
Columbia Health Care Center, Columbia, TN
Columbia Heights Nursing Home Inc, Columbia, LA
Columbia House, Springfield, OH
Columbia House Healthcare, Columbia, MO

Columbia Lutheran Home, Seattle, WA
Columbia Manor Care Center, Columbia, MO
Columbia Manor Convalescent Center, Portland, OR
Columbia Nursing Home, Lima, OH
Columbia Nursing Plaza Inc, Evansville, IN
Columbia Regional Medical Center & Nursing Home, Mobile, AL
Columbia State School, Columbia, LA
Columbia View Nursing Home, Cathlamet, WA
Columbine Care Center, Fort Collins, CO
Columbine Care Center West, Fort Collins, CO
Columbine Manor, Salida, CO
Columbine Manor Inc, Wheat Ridge, CO
Columbus Care Center, Columbus, WI
Columbus Center for Human Services Inc, Columbus, OH
Columbus Colony for the Elderly Care Inc, Westerville, OH
Columbus Convalescent Center, Columbus, IN
Columbus Health Care Center, Columbus, GA
Columbus Manor, Columbus, NE
Columbus Manor Residential Care Home, Chicago, IL
Columbus Quality Care Nursing Center, Columbus, OH
Colville Tribal Convalescent Center, Nespelem, WA
Colwich Health Center, Colwich, KS
Comanche View Nursing Home, Fort Stockton, TX
Combined Rehabilitation Services Inc, Huntingdon Valley, PA
J W Comer Nursing Home, Carlisle, AR
Comforcare Care Center, Austin, MN
Comfort Garden Home, Comfort, TX
Comfort Harbor Home, Milan, IL
Comfort Retirement & Nursing Home Inc, Lafayette, IN
Commander Nursing Center, Florence, SC
Commodore Inn Inc, Chicago, IL
Commonwealth Care Center, Des Moines, IA
Commonwealth Care Center, Fairfax, VA
Commonwealth Health Care Center, Saint Paul, MN
Communicare Inc No 2, Nampa, ID
Communicare Inc No 5, Kuna, ID
Communicare Inc No 6, Weiser, ID
Communicare Inc No 4, Boise, ID
Communicare Inc No 3, Boise, ID
Communicare Nursing Center, Cleveland, OH
Community Access—Edmund, Saint Paul, MN
Community Care Center, Duarte, CA
Community Care Center, Stuart, IA
Community Care Center, El Dorado Springs, MO
Community Care Center, Chickasha, OK
Community Care Center Inc, Chicago, IL
Community Care Center of Anderson, Anderson, IN
Community Care Center of Cuba Inc, Cuba, MO
Community Care Center of Dale, Dale, IN
Community Care Center of Festus, Festus, MO
Community Care Center of Hondo, Hondo, TX
Community Care Center of Lemay, Lemay, MO
Community Care Center of North Vernon, North Vernon, IN
Community Care Center of Seymour, Seymour, IN
Community Care Center of Winchester, Winchester, IN
Community Care Nursing & Geriatric Center, Baltimore, MD
Community Care of Rutherford County Inc, Murfreesboro, TN
Community Center, De Kalb, IL
Community Center, Decatur, IL
Community Comfort Cottage Nursing Home, Rayville, LA
Community Convalescent Center, Martinez, CA

Community Convalescent Center, Riverside, CA
Community Convalescent Center, Gainesville, FL
Community Convalescent Center, Plant City, FL
Community Convalescent Center—Naperville, Naperville, IL
Community Convalescent Hospital, Lynwood, CA
Community Convalescent Hospital of Glendora, Glendora, CA
Community Convalescent Hospital of La Mesa, La Mesa, CA
Community Convalescent Hospital of Montclair, Montclair, CA
Community Convalescent Hospital of San Gabriel, San Gabriel, CA
Community Foundation for Human Development, Sellersville, PA
Community General Hospital of Greater Syracuse Nursing Home Unit, Syracuse, NY
Community General Hospital of Sullivan County, Harris, NY
Community Health Center, Wakita, OK
Community Healthcare of Indianapolis, Indianapolis, IN
Community Intermediate Care Facility, Sumter, SC
Community Living, Des Moines, IA
Community Living—Alpha, Des Moines, IA
Community Living—Beta, Des Moines, IA
Community Living Concepts, Saint Paul, MN
Community Living Inc, Victoria, MN
Community Living Inc—Cottage 6, Coon Rapids, MN
Community Living Inc—Cottage 5, Coon Rapids, MN
Community Memorial Healthcenter & W S Hundley Annex, South Hill, VA
Community Memorial Home, Osakis, MN
Community Memorial Hospital, Hartley, IA
Community Memorial Hospital, Postville, IA
Community Memorial Hospital, Cloquet, MN
Community Memorial Hospital, Winona, MN
Community Memorial Hospital & Community Nursing Care, Spring Valley, MN
Community Memorial Hospital—Extended Care Facility, Cheboygan, MI
Community Memorial Hospital Inc—Nursing Home Unit, Hamilton, NY
Community Memorial Hospital & Nursing Home, Spooner, WI
Community Memorial Hospital San Buenaventura, Ventura, CA
Community Memorial Nursing Home, Lisbon, ND
Community Multicare Center, Fairfield, OH
Community Nursing & Rehabilitation Facility, Missoula, MT
Community Nursing Center, Marion, OH
Community Nursing Home, Clarksville, IA
Community Nursing Home, Jackson, MS
Community Nursing Home, Bowling Green, OH
Community Nursing Home, Stephenville, TX
Community Nursing Home of Anaconda, Anaconda, MT
Community Options, Fridley, MN
Community Pride Care Center, Battle Creek, NE
Community Services Inc, Leola, PA
Community Services Inc—Main, Landisville, PA
Community Skilled Nursing Centre of Warren, Warren, OH
Community Skilled Nursing Facility, Stamford, NY
Compere's Nursing Home Inc, Jackson, MS
Comprehensive Systems Inc, Charles City, IA
Compton Convalescent Hospital, Compton, CA
Compton's Oak Grove Lodge, Mountain View, AR
Comstock Nursing Home, Milwaukee, WI
Con Lea Nursing Home, Geneva, OH
Concerned Services Inc, Stanberry, MO
Concho Nursing Center, Eden, TX

Concord Care Center, Garner, IA
Concord Extended Care, Oak Lawn, IL
Concord Manor Nursing Home, Cleveland, OH
Concord Nursing Center, Concord, NC
Concord Nursing Home Inc, Brooklyn, NY
Concord Villa Convalescent Home, Concordville, PA
Concordia Care Center, Bella Vista, AR
Concordia Manor, Saint Petersburg, FL
Concordia Nursing Center, Concordia, KS
Concordia Parish Rest Home, Ferriday, LA
Concourse Nursing Home, Bronx, NY
Conejos County Hospital, La Jara, CO
Conestoga View, Lancaster, PA
Conesus Lake Nursing Home, Livonia, NY
Congregational Home Inc, Brookfield, WI
Congress Care Center, Chicago, IL
Congress Convalescent of Huntington Memorial Hospital, Pasadena, CA
Conner Nursing Home, Glenwood, GA
Conner Williams Nursing Home, Ridley Park, PA
Connersville Nursing Home, Connersville, IN
Conser House, Overland Park, KS
Consolata Home, New Iberia, LA
Consolation Nursing Home Inc, West Islip, NY
Continana Convalescent Hospital, National City, CA
Continental Care Center, Chicago, IL
Continental Convalescent Center, Indianapolis, IN
Continental Manor, Abbotsford, WI
Continental Manor Nursing & Rehabilitation Center, Blanchester, OH
Continental Manor of Randolph, Randolph, WI
Continental Manor—Wisconsin Dells, Wisconsin Dells, WI
Conv-A-Center, Neptune, NJ
Conva-Rest Northgate—Warren Hall, Hattiesburg, MS
Conva-Rest Northgate—Monroe Hall, Hattiesburg, MS
Conva-Rest of Hattiesburg, Hattiesburg, MS
Conva-Rest of Mendenhall, Mendenhall, MS
Conva-Rest of Newton Inc, Newton, MS
Conva-Rest of Petal, Petal, MS
Convalescent Care Center, Los Angeles, CA
Convalescent Care Center, Saint Petersburg, FL
Convalescent Care Center, Jacksboro, TX
Convalescent Care Center of Mattoon, Mattoon, IL
Convalescent Care Inc, Richmond, VA
Convalescent Care of Enfield Inc, Enfield, NC
Convalescent Center, Dallas, TX
Convalescent Center 2, East Liverpool, OH
Convalescent Center Inc, Tulsa, OK
Convalescent Center Mission Street, San Francisco, CA
Convalescent Center of Grady County, Chickasha, OK
Convalescent Center of Honolulu, Honolulu, HI
Convalescent Center of Lee County Inc, Sanford, NC
Convalescent Center of Norwich Inc, Norwich, CT
Convalescent Center of Oklahoma City, Oklahoma City, OK
Convalescent Center of Reseda, Reseda, CA
Convalescent Center of Sanford Inc, Sanford, NC
Convalescent Center of Shattuck, Shattuck, OK
Convalescent Center of the Palm Beaches, West Palm Beach, FL
Convalescent Hospital Casa Descanso, Los Angeles, CA
Convalescent Hospital University Branch, Menlo Park, CA
Convention Street Nursing Center, Baton Rouge, LA
Convoy Care Center, Convoy, OH
Conway Nursing Center Inc, Conway, SC
Cook Community Hospital, Cook, MN

Cook County Northshore Hospital, Grand Marais, MN
Cook Health Care, Youngtown, AZ
Cook-Willow Convalescent Hospital Inc, Plymouth, CT
Terence Cardinal Cooke Health Care Center, New York, NY
Cookeville Health Care Center Inc, Cookeville, TN
Cookeville Manor Nursing Center, Cookeville, TN
G B Cooley Services, West Monroe, LA
Coolidge Center, Palmer, NE
Coolidge Corner Convalescent Center, Brookline, MA
Coon Memorial Home, Dalhart, TX
Cooney Convalescent Home, Helena, MT
Cooper Community Care Center, Bluffton, IN
Cooper Hall Nursing Center, Mount Pleasant, SC
Cooper Nursing Home No 2, Tallmadge, OH
Cooper River Convalescent Center, Pennsauken, NJ
Coos County Nursing Home, Berlin, NH
Coos County Nursing Hospital, West Stewartstown, NH
Coosa Valley Healthcare Inc, Glencoe, AL
Coosa Valley Medical Center & Coosa Valley Nursing Home, Sylacauga, AL
Coplin Manor Convalescent Home, Ferndale, MI
Rosa Coplon Jewish Home, Buffalo, NY
Copper Queen Community Hospital, Bisbee, AZ
Coquille Care Center, Coquille, OR
Coral Gables Convalescent Center, Miami, FL
Coral Trace Manor, Cape Coral, FL
Cordele Royal Care Center, Cordele, GA
Cordell Care Center, Cordell, OK
Cordell Christian Home, Cordell, OK
Cordilleras Mental Health Center, Redwood City, CA
Cordova Community Hospital, Cordova, AK
Cordova Health Care Center, Cordova, AL
Cordova Residential Care, Pueblo, CO
Corey Hill Nursing Home, Boston, MA
Cori Manor Nursing Home, Fenton, MO
Corinthian, Kenton, OH
Cormon Health Care, Canton, OH
Corn Heritage Village, Corn, OK
Cornell Area Care Center Inc, Cornell, WI
Cornell Hall Convalescent Center, Union, NJ
Corner House Nursing Inc, Meriden, CT
Cornerstone Home, Monticello, IL
Cornerstone Services Inc, Joliet, IL
Cornerstone Village Infirmary, Lafayette, LA
Corning Nursing Home, Corning, AR
Cornwall Manor, Cornwall, PA
Corona Community Care Center, Corona, CA
Corona Gables Retirement Home & Convalescent Hospital, Corona, CA
Coronado Nursing Center, Abilene, TX
Coronado Nursing Center, Pampa, TX
Coronado Nursing Center Inc, El Paso, TX
Coronado Sanitarium, Mission Hills, CA
Corry Manor Nursing Home, Corry, PA
Corsicana Nursing Home, Corsicana, TX
Cortland Acres Nursing Home, Thomas, WV
Cortland Nursing Home, Cortland, NY
Cortland Quality Care Nursing Center, Cortland, OH
Cortlandt Nursing Care Center Inc, Peekskill, NY
Corvallis Care Center, Corvallis, OR
Corvallis Manor, Corvallis, OR
Corydon Care Center, Corydon, IA
Corydon Nursing Home, Clarksville, IN
Cosada Delmar Nursing Center of Green Valley, Henderson, NV
Cosada Villa Nursing Center, Mesa, AZ
Cosada Villa Nursing Center, Kansas City, MO
Coshocton County Home, Coshocton, OH
Coshocton County Memorial Hospital, Coshocton, OH
Coshocton Health Care Center, Coshocton, OH
Cosmos Healthcare Center, Cosmos, MN

Costigan Family Care Home, Denver, CO
Cotillion Ridge Nursing Center, Robinson, IL
Cottage-Belmont Nursing Center, Harper Woods, MI
Cottage Grove Hospital Skilled Nursing Facility, Cottage Grove, OR
Cottage Grove Nursing Home, Jackson, MS
Cottage Healthcare Inc, Monroe, LA
Cottage Hill Health Care Center, Pleasant Grove, AL
Cottage Hill Nursing Home, Pleasant Grove, AL
Cottage Manor Nursing Home, Chelsea, MA
Cotter Residence, Richfield, MN
Cottesmore Nursing Home Inc, Gig Harbor, WA
Cottingham Retirement Community, Cincinnati, OH
Cottonwood Care Center, Brighton, CO
Cottonwood Care Center, Gardnerville, NV
Cottonwood Center, Green Bay, WI
Cottonwood Health Care Center, Galesburg, IL
Cottonwood Manor, Columbus, IN
Cottonwood Manor Nursing Home, Yukon, OK
Coulee Community Hospital Nursing Home, Grand Coulee, WA
Council Bluffs Care Center, Council Bluffs, IA
Country Brook Living Center, Brookhaven, MS
Country Care, Williamsport, IN
Country Care Center, Gillespie, IL
Country Care Convalescent Hospital, Atascadero, CA
Country Care Manor Inc, Effingham, IL
Country Care of Carlinville, Carlinville, IL
Country Care of Litchfield, Litchfield, IL
Country Care of Pana, Pana, IL
Country Care of Staunton, Staunton, IL
Country Club Center, Dover, OH
Country Club Center II, Mount Vernon, OH
Country Club Center III, Ashtabula, OH
Country Club Convalescent Hospital Inc, Santa Ana, CA
Country Club Home, Council Grove, KS
Country Club Manor, Amarillo, TX
Country Club Retirement Center IV, Bellaire, OH
Country Court, Mount Vernon, OH
Country Estate, Cleveland, OH
Country Gardens Nursing Home, Swansea, MA
Country Haven Adult Care Center, Paola, KS
Country Haven Healthcare, Cynthiana, IN
Country Haven Nursing Home, Norton, MA
Country Health Inc, Gifford, IL
Country House, Pomona, CA
Country Inn Care Center, Van, TX
Country Lawn Nursing Home, Navarre, OH
Country Life Manor, Clayton, NM
Country Manor, Louisville, IL
Country Manor, Sartell, MN
Country Manor Convalescent Home, Newburyport, MA
Country Manor Convalescent Hospital, San Fernando, CA
Country Manor—Dover Inc, Toms River, NJ
Country Manor Health Care Center, Prospect, CT
Country Manor Nursing Home, Coopers Mills, ME
Country Manor of Todd County, Elkton, KY
Country Meadow Convalescent Center, Ogden, UT
Country Meadows of South Hills, Bridgeville, PA
Country Meadows Rest Haven, Providence, KY
Country Meadows Retirement Center, Flat River, MO
Country Park Health Care Center, Long Beach, CA
Country Place Health Care Center, Crossville, TN
Country Place of Clearwater, Clearwater, FL
Country Rest Home, Greenwood, DE
Country Rest Home, Dartmouth, MA

Country Trace Healthcare Center, Indianapolis, IN
Country View, Waterloo, IA
Country View Care Center, Longmont, CO
Country View Care Village, Genoa, NE
Country View Convalescent Hospital, Fresno, CA
Country View Estates, Seneca, KS
Country View Manor Inc, Sibley, IA
Country View Nursing Center, Savoy, TX
Country View Nursing Home, Billerica, MA
Country Villa, Rockingham, NC
Country Villa, Torrington, WY
Country Villa North Convalescent Hospital, Los Angeles, CA
Country Villa Plaza Convalescent Center, Santa Ana, CA
Country Villa South Convalescent Center, Los Angeles, CA
Country Villa Westwood Center, Los Angeles, CA
Country Villa Wilshire Convalescent Center, Los Angeles, CA
Country Village Care Inc, Angleton, TX
Country Village Health Care Center, Lancaster, NH
Countryside Care Center, Jackson, MI
Countryside Continuing Care Center, Fremont, OH
Countryside Convalescent Home Inc, Mercer, PA
Countryside Elderly Care, Billings, MT
Countryside Estates, Cherokee, IA
Countryside Estates, Iola, KS
Countryside Estates Inc, Warner, OK
Countryside Health Care Center, Palm Harbour, FL
Countryside Health Center, Buchanan, GA
Countryside Health Center, Topeka, KS
Countryside Healthcare, Muncie, IN
Countryside Healthcare Center, Aurora, IL
Countryside Home, Madison, NE
Countryside Home, Jefferson, WI
Countryside Intermediate Care Facility, Woodland, CA
Countryside Manor, Bristol, CT
Countryside Manor, Elgin, IL
Countryside Manor, Stokesdale, NC
Countryside Manor Healthcare Center, Anderson, IN
Countryside Nursing Center, Terre Haute, IN
Countryside Nursing Home, South Haven, MI
Countryside Nursing Home Inc, Framingham, MA
Countryside Place, Knox, IN
Countryside Place, LaPorte, IN
Countryside Place, Mishawaka, IN
Countryside Plaza, Dolton, IL
Countryside Retirement Home, Sioux City, IA
Countryview Living Center, Latham, IL
County Manor, Tenafly, NJ
County of Northampton—Gracedale, Nazareth, PA
Courage Homes, Sioux City, IA
Courage Residence, Golden Valley, MN
Court House Manor, Washington Court House, OH
Court Manor, Ashland, WI
Court Manor Nursing Center, Memphis, TN
Courtenay Springs Nursing Home, Merritt Island, FL
Courthouse Convalescent Center, Cape May Court House, NJ
Courthouse Road Intermediate Care Facility, Vienna, VA
Courtland Center for Continuing Care, Philadelphia, PA
Courtland Gardens Health Center, Stamford, CT
Courtland Manor Nursing & Convalescent Home, Dover, DE
Courtyard Convalescent Center, Houston, TX
Courville at Nashua Inc, Nashua, NH
Cove Manor Convalescent Center Inc, New Haven, CT
Covenant Health Care Center Inc, Batavia, IL
Covenant Health Care Center Inc, Northbrook, IL

Covenant Home, Batavia, IL
Covenant Home, New Orleans, LA
Covenant Home of Chicago, Chicago, IL
Covenant Medical Center, Waterloo, IA
Covenant Medical Center, Waterloo, IA
Covenant Towers Health Care, Myrtle Beach, SC
Covenant Village Inc, Gastonia, NC
Coventry Health Center, Coventry, RI
Coventry Manor, Indianapolis, IN
Coventry Manor Nursing Home Inc, Pottstown, PA
Covina Convalescent Center, Covina, CA
Covington Care Center, Covington, OH
Covington County Nursing Center, Collins, MS
Covington Heights Health Care Center, Sioux Falls, SD
Covington House Inc, Youngstown, OH
Covington Ladies Home, Covington, KY
Covington Manor, Covington, GA
Covington Manor Health Care Center, Covington, IN
Covington Manor Inc, Opp, AL
Covington Manor Nursing Center, Fort Wayne, IN
Covington Manor Nursing Center, Covington, TN
Covington Rest Home, Covington, MI
Covingtons Convalescent Center, Hopkinsville, KY
Coweta Manor, Coweta, OK
Cowlitz Convalescent Center, Longview, WA
Cozy Corner Nursing Home Inc, Sunderland, MA
Cozy Inn Nursing Home, Rumford, ME
CPC Coliseum Medical Center Skilled Nursing Facility, New Orleans, LA
CR Homes on Cummings, Arden Hills, MN
Cra-Mar Nursing Home Inc, Cranston, RI
Crabel Court Community Living Facility, Chillicothe, IL
Craft Care Center, Panora, IA
Crafts-Farrow ICF/MR, Columbia, SC
Craighead Nursing Center, Jonesboro, AR
Craigmont Care Center, Des Moines, IA
Cranbrook Geriatric Village, Detroit, MI
Crandall Medical Center, Sebring, OH
Crandon Health Care Center Inc, Crandon, WI
Crandon Nursing Home, Crandon, WI
Crane Health Care Center, Crane, MO
Cranford Hall, Cranford, NJ
Cranford Health & Extended Care Center, Cranford, NJ
Crawford County Convalescent Center, Robinson, IL
Crawford County Home, Saegertown, PA
Crawford House Convalescent Home, Fall River, MA
Crawford Retreat Inc, Baltimore, MD
Crawford's Convalescent Home, Haleiwa, HI
Crawford's Nursing Home Inc, Jackson, MS
Creal Springs Nursing Home, Creal Springs, IL
Creekside Care Center, Salt Lake City, UT
Creekside Care Convalescent Hospital, Vacaville, CA
Creekside Convalescent Hospital, Santa Rosa, CA
Creekside Terrace Intermediate Care Facility Inc, Hayward, CA
Creighton Care Centre, Creighton, NE
Crescent Bay Convalescent Hospital, Santa Monica, CA
Crescent Care Center, Crescent, OK
Crescent City Convalescent, Crescent City, CA
Crescent City Health Care Center, New Orleans, LA
Crescent Convalescent Center, Yakima, WA
Crescent Court Nursing Home, Lodi, CA
Crescent Farm Nursing & Convalescent Home, Dover, DE
Crescent Hill Nursing Home, Springfield, MA
Crescent Manor, Greenfield, IN
Crescent Manor Nursing Home, Bennington, VT
Crescent Manor Rest Home, Grafton, MA

Cresco Care Center, Cresco, IA
Crest Group Home, Ottumwa, IA
Crest Hall Health Related Facility, Middle Island, NY
Crest Haven, Cape May Court House, NJ
Crest Home of Albert Lea, Albert Lea, MN
Crest Manor Nursing Center, Lake Worth, FL
Crest Manor Nursing Home, Fairport, NY
Crest Nursing Home, Butte, MT
Crest View Lutheran Home, Columbia Heights, MN
Crest View Manor, Chadron, NE
Crest View Manor Inc, Houlton, ME
Cresta Loma Convalescent & Guest Home, Lemon Grove, CA
Crestfield Convalescent Home—Fenwood, Manchester, CT
Cresthaven Childrens Center, Austin, TX
Cresthaven Childrens Center, San Antonio, TX
Cresthaven Nursing Center, Austin, TX
Cresthaven Nursing Home, Santa Cruz, CA
Cresthaven Nursing Residence, Groves, TX
Crestline Nursing Home Inc, Crestline, OH
Crestmont Medical Care Facility, Fenton, MI
Crestmont Nursing Home Inc, Cleveland, OH
Crestmont Nursing Home North Inc, Lakewood, OH
Creston Manor, Creston, IA
Crestpark Inn of Forrest City, Forrest City, AR
Crestpark Inn of Helena Skilled Nursing Facility, Helena, AR
Crestpark Inn of Stuttgart Inc, Stuttgart, AR
Crestpark of Wynne Skilled Nursing Facility, Wynne, AR
Crestpark Retirement Inn, Helena, AR
Crestpark Retirement Inn, Marianna, AR
Crestridge, Maquoketa, IA
Crestview Acres, Marion, IA
Crestview Care Center, West Branch, IA
Crestview Care Center, Milford, NE
Crestview Care Center, Astoria, OR
Crestview Convalescent, Portland, OR
Crestview Convalescent Center, Provo, UT
Crestview Convalescent Center, Moses Lake, WA
Crestview Convalescent Home, Vincennes, IN
Crestview Convalescent Home, Wyncote, PA
Crestview Convalescent Hospital, Petaluma, CA
Crestview Convalescent Hospital, Rialto, CA
Crestview Convalescent Lodge, Phoenix, AZ
Crestview Health Care Facility, Indianapolis, IN
Crestview Healthcare, Ava, MO
Crestview Healthcare Center, Shelbyville, KY
Crestview Healthcare Facility, Quincy, MA
Crestview Home, Thief River Falls, MN
Crestview Home Inc, Bethany, MO
Crestview Manor, Webster City, IA
Crestview Manor, Seneca, KS
Crestview Manor, Wyoming, MI
Crestview Manor, Jane Lew, WV
Crestview Manor Inc, Evansville, MN
Crestview Manor Nursing Center, Belton, TX
Crestview Manor Nursing Home, Lynn, MA
Crestview Manor Nursing Home I, Lancaster, OH
Crestview Manor Nursing Home II, Lancaster, OH
Crestview Manor Retirement & Convalescent Center, Waco, TX
Crestview North Nursing & Rehabilitation Center, Langhorne, PA
Crestview Nursing & Convalescent Home, Crestview, FL
Crestview Nursing Center, Clinton, IL
Crestview Nursing Home, Atlanta, GA
Crestview Nursing Home, Ottawa, KS
Crestview Nursing Home, Cincinnati, OH
Crestview Nursing Home, Brownsville, TN
Crestview Nursing Home II, Dayton, OH
Crestview Nursing Home Inc, Nashville, TN
Crestview Personal Care Home, Richmond, KY
Crestview Personal Care Home, Somerset, KY
Crestview Retirement Community, Bryan, TX

Crestwood Care Center, Shelby, OH
Crestwood Care Center, Ogden, UT
Crestwood Care Center Inc, Fairfield, OH
Crestwood Care Center, Mansfield, Mansfield, OH
Crestwood Convalescent Center, Port Angeles, WA
Crestwood Convalescent Home, Fall River, MA
Crestwood Convalescent Hospital, Chico, CA
Crestwood Convalescent Hospital, Redding, CA
Crestwood Convalescent Hospital, Sylmar, CA
Crestwood Convalescent Hospital, Vallejo, CA
Crestwood Convalescent Pasadena, Pasadena, CA
Crestwood Geriatric Treatment Center, Angwin, CA
Crestwood Geriatric Treatment Center, Fremont, CA
Crestwood Geriatric Treatment Center, Redding, CA
Crestwood Healthcare Center, Milford, NH
Crestwood Heights Nursing Center, Midlothian, IL
Crestwood Manor, Eureka, CA
Crestwood Manor, Modesto, CA
Crestwood Manor, Stockton, CA
Crestwood Manor—Bakersfield, Stockton, CA
Crestwood Manor—San Jose, San Jose, CA
Crestwood Manor—Vallejo, Vallejo, CA
Crestwood Nursing & Convalescent Home Inc, Warren, RI
Crestwood Nursing Home, Valdosta, GA
Crestwood Nursing Home, Whippany, NJ
Crestwood Nursing Home, Manchester, TN
Crestwood Rehabilitation & Convalescent Hospital, Fremont, CA
Crestwood Rehabilitation & Convalescent Hospital, Stockton, CA
Crestwood Terrace, Crestwood, IL
Crestwood Terrace, Midlothian, IL
Creswell Care Center, Creswell, OR
Creswell Convalescent Center, Rome, GA
Crete Manor, Crete, NE
Cridersville Nursing Home, Cridersville, OH
Crisis Receiving Unit, Rochester, MN
Crisp County Medical Nursing Center, Cordele, GA
Crista Senior Community, Seattle, WA
Crites Nursing Home 2, Lancaster, OH
Crittenden County Convalescence Center, Marion, KY
Crocker Family Care Home, Commerce City, CO
Crockett Care Center, Crockett, TX
Crockett County Care Center, Ozona, TX
Crockett County Nursing Home, Alamo, TN
Crofton Convalescent Center, Crofton, MD
Croixdale Residence, Bayport, MN
Cromwell Crest Convalescent Home, Cromwell, CT
Crook County Nursing Home, Prineville, OR
Crook County Nursing Home, Sundance, WY
Crookston Group Home 1, Crookston, MN
Crookston Group Home 2, Crookston, MN
Crookston Group Home 3, Crookston, MN
Crosby Good Samaritan Center, Crosby, ND
Crosbyton Care Center, Crosbyton, TX
Cross Country Care Center, Brownwood, TX
Cross Creek Health Care Center, Pensacola, FL
Cross Health Care Center, Clute, TX
Cross Key Manor, Lehigh Acres, FL
Cross Roads Intermediate Care Facility, Cleveland, GA
Crossgate Manor Inc, Brandon, MS
Crosslands, Kennett Square, PA
Crosslands Health Care Center, Sandy, UT
Crossroads, Haltom City, TX
Crossville Nursing Home Inc, Crossville, AL
Crotinger Nursing Home, Union City, OH
Crowell Memorial Home, Blair, NE
Crowell Nursing Center, Crowell, TX
Crowley County Nursing Center, Ordway, CO
Crowley Guest House, Crowley, LA
Crowley Ridge Care Center, Dexter, MO
Crown Manor Living Center, Zion, IL

Crown Nursing Home, Saint Petersburg Beach, FL
Crown Nursing Home, Saint Petersburg Beach, FL
Crown Nursing Home, Brooklyn, NY
Elizabeth Adam Crump Manor, Glen Allen, VA
Crystal Care Center, Napa, CA
Crystal Care Center, Crystal, MN
Crystal City Nursing Center, Arlington, VA
Crystal Hill Nursing Home Inc, Dallas, TX
Crystal Lake Health Care Center, Robbinsdale, MN
Crystal Manor, Crystal Falls, MI
Crystal Manor Care Center, Des Moines, IA
Crystal Pines Nursing Home, Crystal Lake, IL
Crystal River Geriatric Center, Crystal River, FL
Crystal Springs Rehabilitation Center, San Mateo, CA
Crystal Valley Care Center, Goshen, IN
Crystle Springs Nursing Home Inc, Commerce, GA
Cuba Memorial Hospital Skilled Nursing Facility, Cuba, NY
Cullen Avenue Nursing Home, Austin, TX
Victor Cullen Center, Sabillasville, MD
Cullman Health Care Center, Cullman, AL
Culpeper Baptist Retirement Community—Dorothy Finney Health Care Unit, Culpeper, VA
Culpeper Health Care Center, Culpeper, VA
Culver West Convalescent Hospital, Los Angeles, CA
Cumberland Care Center Inc, Bluefield, WV
Cumberland Convalescent Center Inc, Vineland, NJ
Cumberland County Nursing Home, Carlisle, PA
Cumberland Manor, Lowell, MI
Cumberland Manor, Bridgeton, NJ
Cumberland Manor Nursing Center, Nashville, TN
Cumberland Manor Rest Home, Parker's Lake, KY
Cumberland Memorial Hospital—Extended Care Unit, Cumberland, WI
Cumberland Nursing Center, Greenup, IL
Cumberland Nursing Center, Cumberland, MD
Cumberland Valley Manor, Burkesville, KY
Cumbernauld Village, Winfield, KS
Cumming Convalescent Home, Cumming, GA
Cummings Health Care Facility Inc, Howland, ME
Cupola Nursing Home, Brockport, NY
Cuppett & Weeks Nursing Home, Oakland, MD
Currey Nursing Home Inc, Mount Pleasant, TX
Curry Good Samaritan Center, Brookings, OR
Curry Memorial Home, Waynesburg, PA
Carl T Curtis Health Education Center, Macy, NE
Curtis Home—St Elizabeth Center, Meriden, CT
Curtis Manor Retirement Home, Dalton, MA
Curwensville Nursing Home Inc, Curwensville, PA
Cushing Care Center Inc, Cushing, TX
Cushing Regional Hospital, Cushing, OK
Cushing Retirement Home, Boston, MA
Custer County Rest Home, Miles City, MT
Cuy-La Home, Euclid, OH
Cuyahoga County Hospital—Sunny Acres, Warrensville, OH
Cuyahoga County Nursing Home, Cleveland, OH
Cuyahoga Falls Country Place, Cuyahoga Falls, OH
Cuyuna Range District Nursing Home, Crosby, MN
Cypress Acres Convalescent Hospital, Paradise, CA
Cypress Acres Intermediate Care Facility, Paradise, CA
Cypress Care Center, Santa Cruz, CA
Cypress Cove Care Center, Crystal River, FL

Cypress Gardens Convalescent Hospital, Riverside, CA
Cypress Manor, Fort Myers, FL
Cypress Manor Nursing Home, Hancock, MI
Cypress Nursing Facility Inc, Sumter, SC
Cypress Woods Care Center, Angleton, TX
Cyril Nursing Home, Cyril, OK
Czech Catholic Home for the Aged, El Campo, TX
Dacotah Alpha, Mandan, ND
Dade City Geriatric Center, Dade City, FL
Dade County Nursing Home District, Greenfield, MO
Dadeville Convalescent Home, Dadeville, AL
Dadeville Health Care, Dadeville, AL
D'Adrian Convalescent Center, Godfrey, IL
Daggett-Crandall-Newcomb Home, Norton, MA
Dahl Memorial Nursing Home, Ekalaka, MT
Dakota County Receiving Center, Hastings, MN
Dakota's Children Home, West Saint Paul, MN
Dal Worth Care Center, Arlington, TX
Daleview Nursing Home & Manor, Farmingdale, NY
Dallas County Nursing Home, Fordyce, AR
Dallas Health & Rehabilitation Center, Dallas, WI
Dallas Home for Jewish Aged, Dallas, TX
Dallas Lamb Foundation Home, Payne, OH
Dallas Nursing Home, Dallas, OR
Dalton Nursing Home Inc, Dalton, MA
Dalton Rest Home, Worcester, MA
Daly Parks Geriatric Center, Cincinnati, OH
Dammert Geriatric Center, Belleville, IL
D'Amore Rest Haven Inc, East Windsor, CT
Dana Home of Lexington, Lexington, MA
Danbury Pavilion Healthcare, Danbury, CT
Danforth Habilitation Residential Center, Danforth, ME
Danforth House, Chicago, IL
Danforth Nursing Home Inc, Danforth, ME
Dania Nursing Home, Dania, FL
Kathleen Daniel Health Care SNF, Framingham, MA
Daniel Nursing Home, Fulton, MS
Daniel's House Nursing Home, Reading, MA
Daniels Memorial Nursing Home, Scobey, MT
Danish Convalescent Hospital, Atascadero, CA
Danridge Nursing Home, Youngstown, OH
Dans Boarding Care Home, Saint Cloud, MN
Danvers Twin Oaks Nursing Home, Danvers, MA
Danville Care Center, Danville, IA
Danville Care Center Ltd, Danville, IL
Danville Independent Living Center, Danville, IL
Danville Manor, Danville, IL
Dar-Way Nursing Home Inc, Forksville, PA
Darby Square, Lexington, KY
Darcy Hall, West Palm Beach, FL
Dardanelle Nursing Center Inc, Dardanelle, AR
Betty Dare Good Samaritan Center, Alamogordo, NM
Darien Convalescent Center, Darien, CT
Darlington Care Center, Pawtucket, RI
Darlington Convalescent Center, Darlington, SC
Darlington House, Toledo, OH
Dartmouth Manor Rest Home, Dartmouth, MA
Dassel Lakeside Community Home, Dassel, MN
Daughters of Israel Pleasant Valley Home, West Orange, NJ
Daughters of Jacob Nursing Home Company Inc, Bronx, NY
Daughters of Sarah Nursing Home, Albany, NY
Dauphin Health Care Facility, Mobile, AL
Dauphin Manor, Harrisburg, PA
Dautrive Hospital Skilled Nursing Facility, New Iberia, LA
Davenport Good Samaritan Center, Davenport, IA
Davenport Lutheran Home, Davenport, IA

Davenport Memorial Home, Malden, MA
David Nursing Home, Detroit, MI
David Place, David City, NE
Bishop Davies Center Inc, Hurst, TX
Davies Square, Pekin, IL
Daviess County Nursing Home Corp, Gallatin, MO
Cornelia Nixon Davis Health Care Center, Wilmington, NC
Davis County Hospital, Bloomfield, IA
Davis Gardens Health Center, Terre Haute, IN
George Davis Manor, West Lafayette, IN
Davis Home for the Aged, Oak Hill, OH
Davis House, Chicago, IL
Davis Nursing Home, Tahlequah, OK
Davis Nursing Home Inc, Mountain Top, PA
Davis Skilled Nursing Facility, Pine Bluff, AR
Davison Rest Home Inc, Laurel, MS
Eva Dawn Care Center, Salt Lake City, UT
Dawn View Manor, Fort Ashby, WV
Dawson Manor, Dawson, GA
Dawson Place Inc, Hill City, KS
Dawson Springs Health Care Center, Dawson Springs, KY
William L Dawson Nursing Home, Chicago, IL
Daystar Care Center, Cairo, IL
Daystar Home, Needham, MA
Daystar Inc, Fort Lauderdale, FL
Dayton Boarding Care Home, Saint Paul, MN
Dayton Health Care Center, Dayton, OH
Dayton House of People Inc, Saint Paul, MN
Dayton Mental Health Center—Building 64, Dayton, OH
Dayton Residential Care Facility, Kenosha, WI
Daytona Beach Geriatric Center, Daytona Beach, FL
Daytona Beach Olds Hall Good Samaritan Nursing Center, Daytona Beach, FL
Daytona Manor Nursing Home, South Daytona, FL
Dayview Care Center, New Carlisle, OH
DC Village Nursing Home, Washington, DC
DCI Dakota Adults, Mendota Heights, MN
De Baca General Hospital, Fort Sumner, NM
De Kalb County Nursing Home, De Kalb, IL
De Leon Nursing Home, De Leon, TX
De Paul Belleview Extended Care, Milwaukee, WI
DePaul Health Center St Anne's Division, Bridgeton, MO
Deacon Home Ltd, Rockford, IL
Deaconess Manor, Saint Louis, MO
Deaconess Skilled Nursing Center, Great Falls, MT
Deaconess Skilled Nursing Facility, Buffalo, NY
Deal Nursing Home Inc, Jackson, MO
Dearborn Heights Health Care Center, Dearborn Heights, MI
Deaton Hospital & Medical Center, Baltimore, MD
Deaton Hospital & Medical Center of Christ Lutheran Church—South, Baltimore, MD
Deauville Health Care Center, Chicago, IL
DeBary Manor, DeBary, FL
DeBoer Nursing Home, Muskegon, MI
Deborah House, Chicago, IL
Decatur Community Care Center, Decatur, IN
Decatur Convalescent Center, Decatur, TX
Decatur County Good Samaritan Center, Oberlin, KS
Decatur County Manor Nursing Center, Parsons, TN
Decatur Nursing & Rehabilitation Center, Indianapolis, IN
Dee-Maret Nursing Home, Akron, OH
Deep River Convalescent Home Inc, Deep River, CT
Deer Creek Nursing Center, Wimberley, TX
Deer Parke Nursing Home, Cincinnati, OH
Deerbrook Nursing Centre, Joliet, IL
Deerfield Episcopal Retirement Community Inc, Asheville, NC
Deering Nursing Home Inc, Hingham, MA
Deerings Nursing Home, Wichita Falls, TX

Deerings West Nursing Center, Odessa, TX
Deer's Head Center, Salisbury, MD
Defiance Health Care Center, Defiance, OH
Degraff Memorial Hospital—Skilled Nursing Facility, North Tonawanda, NY
Deiber Nursing Home Inc, Sabina, OH
DeKalb General Nursing Unit, Decatur, GA
DeKalb Health Care Center, Auburn, IN
Del Amo Gardens Convalescent Hospital, Torrance, CA
Del Capri Terrace Convalescent, San Diego, CA
Del City Cerebral Palsy Center, Del City, OK
Del Manor Nursing Home Inc, Rockland, MA
Del Mar Convalescent Hospital, Rosemead, CA
Del Mar Health Care Center, Corpus Christi, TX
Del Mar Nursing Home Inc, Indianapolis, IN
Del Rio Convalescent Center, Bell Gardens, CA
Del Rio Nursing Home Inc, Del Rio, TX
Del Rio Sanitarium, Bell Gardens, CA
Del Rosa Convalescent Hospital, San Bernardino, CA
Del Rosa Villa, San Bernardino, CA
Delaire Nursing & Convalescent Home, Linden, NJ
Delamarter Care Center, Pendleton, OR
Deland Convalescent Center, Deland, FL
Delano Healthcare Center, Delano, MN
Delano Regional Medical Center, Delano, CA
Delaware Care Center, Milford, DE
Delaware Care Center, Milford, DE
Delaware County Health Center, Muncie, IN
Delaware County Home & Infirmary, Delhi, NY
Delaware County Memorial Hospital & Memorial Care Center, Manchester, IA
Delaware Court Inc, Delaware, OH
Delaware Elwyn Hockessin, Wilmington, DE
Delaware Elwyn Lauren Farms, Bear, DE
Delaware Health Care Facility, Indianapolis, IN
Delaware Hospital for the Chronically Ill, Smyrna, DE
Delaware Park Care Center, Delaware, OH
Delhaven Manor, Saint Louis, MO
Delhi Guest Home, Delhi, LA
Thomas Dell Nursing Home & Manor Inc, Farmington, MO
Dellridge Nursing Home, Paramus, NJ
Dells Place Inc, Delano, MN
Delmar, Aurora, CO
Delmar Gardens East Inc, University City, MO
Delmar Gardens North, Florissant, MO
Delmar Gardens of Chesterfield, Chesterfield, MO
Delmar Gardens of Lenexa, Lenexa, KS
Delmar Gardens of Olathe Inc, Olathe, KS
Delmar Gardens of Overland Park, Overland Park, KS
Delmar Gardens of South County Inc, Saint Louis, MO
Delmar Gardens West, Chesterfield, MO
Delphi, Shakopee, MN
Delphi Nursing Home, Delphi, IN
Delphos Memorial Home, Delphos, OH
Delphos Rest Home Inc, Delphos, KS
Del's Care Center Inc, Portland, OR
Delta Care Center, Delta, CO
Delta Convalescent Hospital, Lodi, CA
Delta Convalescent Hospital, Visalia, CA
Delta Haven Nursing Home, Tallulah, LA
Delta Manor, Clarksdale, MS
Delta Nursing Home, Cooper, TX
Delta Rehabilitation Center, Snohomish, WA
Delta Valley Convalescent Hospital, Stockton, CA
Deltona Health Care Center, Deltona, FL
Deluxe Care Inn, South Pasadena, FL
Delwood Nursing Center Inc, Austin, TX
Demars Childrens Home, Coon Rapids, MN
Den-Mar Nursing Home, Rockport, MA
Denali Center, Fairbanks, AK
Denison Care Center, Denison, IA
Denison Manor Inc, Denison, TX

Dennett Road Manor Inc, Oakland, MD
Denny House Nursing Home Inc, Norwood, MA
Denton Good Samaritan Village, Denton, TX
Denton Nursing Center, Denton, TX
Denver Manor Nursing Home, Wichita Falls, TX
Denver Nursing Home, Stevens, PA
Denver Sunset Home, Denver, IA
DePaul Hospital, Norfolk, VA
Deport Nursing Home, Deport, TX
Mary Lee Depugh Nursing Home, Winter Park, FL
DeQueen Manor Nursing Center, DeQueen, AR
DeQuincy Memorial Hospital, DeQuincy, LA
Derby Green Nursing Home, Derby, VT
Derby Nursing Center, Derby, CT
Des Arc Convalescent Center, Des Arc, AR
Des Moines General Hospital Skilled Nursing Facility, Des Moines, IA
Des Peres Health Care, Des Peres, MO
Desert Cove Nursing Center, Chandler, AZ
Desert Developmental Center, Las Vegas, NV
Desert Haven Nursing Center, Phoenix, AZ
Desert Knolls Convalescent Hospital, Victorville, CA
Desert Lane Care Center, Las Vegas, NV
Desert Life Health Care Center, Tucson, AZ
Desert Palms Convalescent Hospital, Indio, CA
Desert SunQuest Care Center, Mesa, AZ
Desert Terrace Nursing Center, Phoenix, AZ
Desert Valley Care Center, Casa Grande, AZ
Desert Valley Rehabilitation Medical Center, Phoenix, AZ
Desha's Rest Home, San Antonio, TX
Desilets Nursing Home Inc, Warren, RI
Desloge Health Care Center, Flat River, MO
DeSmet Good Samaritan Center, DeSmet, SD
DeSoto General Hospital, Mansfield, LA
DeSoto Manor Nursing Home, Arcadia, FL
DeSoto Nursing Home, DeSoto, TX
Desserich House, Lakewood, CO
Detroiter Residence, Detroit, MI
Dettmer Hospital/Koester ECF, Troy, OH
Detwiler Manor, Wauseon, OH
Deuel County Good Samaritan Center, Clear Lake, SD
Deutsches Altenheim Inc, Boston, MA
Dever Nursing Home, Houston, TX
Paul A Dever State School, Taunton, MA
Devereux House Nursing Home, Marblehead, MA
Devils Lake Good Samaritan Center, Devils Lake, ND
Devine Haven Convalescent Center, Elkton, MD
Joseph B Devlin Public Medical Institute, Lynn, MA
Devon Gables Health Care Center, Tucson, AZ
Devon Manor, Devon, PA
Devonshire Acres Ltd, Sterling, CO
Devonshire Nursing Care Center, Portland, ME
Devonshire Oaks, Redwood City, CA
Dewhurst, West Lafayette, OH
DeWitt City Nursing Home, DeWitt, AR
Dewitt Community Hospital, Dewitt, IA
Dewitt County Nursing Home, Clinton, IL
Dewitt Nursing Home, New York, NY
Dexter House Nursing Facility, Malden, MA
Dexter Nursing Center, Dexter, MO
Dexter Nursing Home, Dexter, ME
Diablo Convalescent Hospital, Danville, CA
Diamond Care Center, Bridgewater, SD
Diamond Hill Nursing Center Inc, Cumberland, RI
Diamondhead Extended Care Center 2, North Lima, OH
Diana Lynn Lodge, Sunland, CA
Dickey Nursing Home Inc, Elwood, IN
Todd Dickey Medical Center, Leavenworth, IN
Dickinson Nursing Center, Dickinson, ND
Jane Dickman Center, Woodbury, MN
Dickson County Nursing Home, Dickson, TN

Dighton Nursing Center, Dighton, MA
Dillsboro Manor, Dillsboro, IN
Grover C Dils Medical Center, Caliente, NV
Dinan Memorial Center, Bridgeport, CT
Dinuba Convalescent Hospital, Dinuba, CA
Directors Hall, Kalamazoo, MI
Dirksen House Healthcare, Springfield, IL
Dishman Personal Care Home, Monticello, KY
District Home, Manassas, VA
District Home, Waynesboro, VA
District Nursing Home, Warrenton, VA
Divine Providence Community Home, Sleepy Eye, MN
Divine Providence—Extended Care Facility, Williamsport, PA
Divine Providence Hospital & Home, Ivanhoe, MN
Divine Savior Hospital & Nursing Home, Portage, WI
Dixfield Health Care Center, Dixfield, ME
Dixie Manor Sheltered Care, Harvey, IL
Dixon Health Care Center, Dixon, IL
Dixon Health Care Center, Wintersville, OH
Dixon Home Care Center, Martinsville, IN
Doanes Nursing Home, Campbell Hall, NY
Dobbins Nursing Home Inc, New Richmond, OH
Dobson Plaza Inc, Evanston, IL
Dock Terrace, Lansdale, PA
Docsa Home for the Aged, Springfield, MI
Doctor Kate's Woodland Manor, Woodruff, WI
Doctor's Convalescent Hospital, Whittier, CA
Doctors Hospital, Denver, CO
Doctors Hospital of Opelousas—Skilled Nursing Facility, Opelousas, LA
Doctors' Hospital SNF, Tulsa, OK
Doctor's Nursing Center Foundation Inc, Dallas, TX
Doctors Nursing Home, Salem, IL
Dodge County Community Health Center, Juneau, WI
Dodge Park Rest Home, Worcester, MA
Dogwood Acres Intermediate Care Facility, Durham, CT
Dogwood Drive Home for Adults, Alexandria, VA
Dogwood Health Care Center, Sandwich, IL
Dolly Mount Nursing Home, Clifton, NJ
Dolton Healthcare Center, Dolton, IL
Don Orione Nursing Home, Boston, MA
Donahoe Manor, Bedford, PA
Donalson Care Center, Fayetteville, TN
Donely House ICF/MR, Quincy, PA
Doniphan Retirement Home, Doniphan, MO
Donna Kay Rest Home, Worcester, MA
Donnellson Manor Care Center, Donnellson, IA
Doolittle Home Inc, Foxborough, MA
Door County Memorial Hospital—Skilled Nursing Facility, Sturgeon Bay, WI
Dorchester Nursing Center, Sturgeon Bay, WI
David M Dorsett Health Care Facility, Spearfish, SD
Dorvin Convalescent & Nursing Center, Livonia, MI
Doty House of Middletown Inc, Middletown, OH
Douglas Home, Fergus Falls, MN
Douglas Living Center, Mattoon, IL
Douglas Manor Care Center, Douglas, AZ
Douglas Manor Nursing Complex, Tuscola, IL
Douglas Nursing Home Inc, Milan, TN
Mercy Douglass Human Services Center, Philadelphia, PA
Dove Nursing Facility, Uhrichsville, OH
Dove Tree Nursing Home, Indianapolis, IN
Dover Christian Nursing Home, Dover, NJ
Dover House Healthcare, Dover, NH
Dover Manor Nursing Home, Georgetown, KY
Dover Nursing Home, Brooklyn, NY
Dover Nursing Home, Westlake, OH
Dow-Rummel Village, Sioux Falls, SD
Dowagiac Nursing Home, Dowagiac, MI
Dowdy Gardner Nursing Care Center, Rock Hill, SC

Dowdy Gardner Nursing Care Center—Farmer, Columbia, SC
Dowdy Gardner Nursing Care Center—McLendon, Columbia, SC
Dowling Convalescent Hospital, Oakland, CA
Downey Care Center, Downey, CA
Downey Community Health Center, Downey, CA
Downs Nursing Center, Downs, KS
Dows Care Center, Dows, IA
Doxey-Hatch Medical Center, Salt Lake City, UT
Lila Doyle Nursing Care Facility, Seneca, SC
Doylestown Health Care Center, Doylestown, OH
Doylestown Manor, Doylestown, PA
Daniel Drake Memorial Hospital, Cincinnati, OH
Drake Nursing Home, Zanesville, OH
Draper Plaza, Joliet, IL
Dreier's Sanitarium, Glendale, CA
Dresher Hill Nursing Center, Dresher, PA
Drew Village Nursing Center, Clearwater, FL
Mary J Drexel Home, Bala Cynwyd, PA
Elsie M Dreyer Nursing Home II, Brookville, IN
Dreyerhaus, Batesville, IN
Driftwood Care Center, Yuba City, CA
Driftwood Convalescent Center, Torrance, CA
Driftwood Convalescent Hospital, Davis, CA
Driftwood Convalescent Hospital, Fremont, CA
Driftwood Convalescent Hospital, Gilroy, CA
Driftwood Convalescent Hospital, Monterey, CA
Driftwood Convalescent Hospital, Salinas, CA
Driftwood Convalescent Hospital, San Jose, CA
Driftwood Convalescent Hospital, Santa Cruz, CA
Driftwood Health Care Center—Long-Term Care Facility, Charleston, SC
Driftwood Manor, Hayward, CA
Bishop Drumm Care Center, Johnston, IA
Drumright Nursing Home, Drumright, OK
Dry Harbor Nursing Home, Middle Village, NY
Dry Ridge Personal Care Home, Dry Ridge, KY
Elsie Dryer Nursing Home I, Brookville, IN
Du Page Convalescent Center, Wheaton, IL
Dublin Nursing Center, Dublin, TX
Dublinaire Nursing Home, Dublin, GA
DuBois Nursing Home, DuBois, PA
Dubuque Health Care Center, Dubuque, IA
Duff Memorial Nursing Home, Nebraska City, NE
Dugan Memorial Home, West Point, MS
Duke Convalescent Residence, Lancaster, PA
Duluth Regional Care Center 1, Duluth, MN
Duluth Regional Care Center II, Duluth, MN
Duluth Regional Care Center III, Duluth, MN
Duluth Regional Care Center IV, Duluth, MN
Dumas Nursing Center, Dumas, AR
Dumas Nursing Center, Dumas, TX
Dumont Masonic Home, New Rochelle, NY
Dumont Nursing Home, Dumont, IA
Dr W F & Mada Dunaway Manor Nursing Home of Guymon Inc, Guymon, OK
Duncan Care Center, Duncan, OK
Duncan Regional Hospital SNF, Duncan, OK
Dundee Nursing Home, Bennettsville, SC
Dunedin Care Center, Dunedin, FL
Dungarvin II Camara, Roseville, MN
Dungarvin III—Balbriggen, Saint Paul, MN
Dungarvin V Tyrothy, Crystal, MN
Dungarvin VII, New Hope, MN
Dungarvin IX, Maple Grove, MN
Dungarvin XI Urlingford, Lester Prairie, MN
Dungarvin VIII, Hugo, MN
Dunlap Care Center, Dunlap, IA
Dunlap Sanitarium, Los Angeles, CA
Dunn County Health Care Center, Menomonie, WI
Dunn Nursing Home, Selma, AL
Dunroven Nursing Home, Cresskill, NJ
Dunseith Community Nursing Home, Dunseith, ND

Dunwoody Home, Newtown Square, PA
Duplin General Hospital—Skilled Nursing Facility, Kenansville, NC
Dupoint House, Janesville, WI
Durand Convalescent Center, Durand, MI
Durham-Hensley Nursing Home Inc, Chuckey, TN
Durham Retirement Center, Memphis, TN
Hannah Duston Long-Term Health Care Center, Haverhill, MA
Dutchess County Health Care Facility, Millbrook, NY
Duvall Home, Glenwood, FL
Duxbury House Nursing Home, Duxbury, MA
D'Ville House Inc, Donaldsonville, LA
Dyball Sunshine Home, Fairfield, IL
Dyersburg Manor Nursing Center, Dyersburg, TN
D'Youville Manor Nursing Home, Lowell, MA
D'Youville Pavilion, Lewiston, ME
Eagle Creek Nursing Center, West Union, OH
Eagle Crest Nursing Center, Jacksonville, FL
Eagle Lake Home, Eagle Lake, ME
Eagle Nursing Home, Bloomington, MN
Eagle Pond Nursing Home, South Dennis, MA
Eagle River Health Care Center Inc, Eagle River, WI
Eagle Valley Children's Home, Carson City, NV
Eagle Valley Healthcare Center, Indianapolis, IN
Eagleton Nursing Home FDD, Bloomer, WI
Eaglewood Village—Care Center, Springfield, OH
Lois Eargle Community Residence, Conway, SC
Earle Street Personal Care Home, Jackson, MS
Earlham Manor Care Center, Earlham, IA
Earlwood Care Center, Torrance, CA
Early Memorial Nursing Home, Blakley, GA
Easley Community Residence No 1, Easley, SC
Easley Community Residence No 2, Easley, SC
Easley Health Care, Easley, SC
Eason Nursing Home, Lake Worth, FL
East Broad Manor, Columbus, OH
East Carroll Care Center Inc, Lake Providence, LA
East Carroll Nursing Home, Kensington, OH
East End Convalescent Home, Waterbury, CT
East Galbraith Health Care Center & Nursing Home, Cincinnati, OH
East Galbraith Nursing Home, Deer Park, OH
East Grand Forks Group Home I, East Grand Forks, MN
East Grand Forks Group Home II, East Grand Forks, MN
East Grand Nursing Home, Detroit, MI
East Haven Health Care, Birmingham, AL
East Haven Health Related Facility, Bronx, NY
East Haven Rest Home, East Haven, CT
East Jefferson Hospital Skilled Nursing Facility, Metairie, LA
East Lake Care Center, Provo, UT
East Lansing Health Care Center, East Lansing, MI
East Liverpool Convalescent Center, East Liverpool, OH
East Liverpool Extended Care Center, East Liverpool, OH
East Longmeadow Nursing Home, East Longmeadow, MA
East Los Angeles Convalescent Hospital, Los Angeles, CA
East Manor Medical Care Center, Sarasota, FL
East Manor Nursing Center, El Dorado, AR
East Mesa Care Center, Mesa, AZ
East Moline Care Center, East Moline, IL
East Moline Garden Plaza, East Moline, IL
East Moore Nursing Center, Moore, OK
East Neck Nursing Center, West Babylon, NY
East Ohio Regional Hospital Long-Term Care Unit, Martins Ferry, OH
East Orange Nursing Home, East Orange, NJ

East Park Manor Nursing Center, Fort Worth, TX
East Prairie Nursing Center, East Prairie, MO
East Ridge Retirement Village Inc, Miami, FL
East Rockaway Nursing Home, Lynbrook, NY
East Side Nursing Home, Warsaw, NY
East Tennessee Health Care Center, Madisonville, TN
East Towne Care Center, Independence, IA
East Valley Pavilion, San Jose, CA
East View Nursing Center, Enid, OK
East Village Nursing Home, Lexington, MA
Eastbrooke Health Care Center, Brooksville, FL
Eastchester Park Nursing Home, Bronx, NY
Eastern Hills Convalescent Center, Austin, TX
Eastern Maine Medical Center (Ross Division), Bangor, ME
Eastern Oklahoma Skilled Nursing Facility, Poteau, OK
Eastern Pennsylvania Eastern Star Home, Warminster, PA
Eastern Pines Convalescent Center, Atlantic City, NJ
Eastern Shore Health Care, Fairhope, AL
Eastern Shore Nursing/Convalescent Center, Cape May Court House, NJ
Eastern Star Home, Los Angeles, CA
Eastern Star Home, Macon, IL
Eastern Star Home, Arlington, TX
Eastern Star Home & Infirmary, Oriskany, NY
Eastern Star Home in Kentucky, Louisville, KY
Eastern Star Home of Cuyahoga County, East Cleveland, OH
Eastern Star Home of South Dakota, Redfield, SD
Eastern Star Masonic Home, Boone, IA
Eastern Star Nursing Home—Bothell, Bothell, WA
Eastern Star Nursing Home Yakima, Yakima, WA
Eastern State Hospital, Williamsburg, VA
Easter's Home of Ruth Inc, Farmington, MO
Eastgate Health Care Center, Cincinnati, OH
Eastgate Manor Nursing & Residential Center Inc, Washington, IN
Eastgate Nursing & Recovery Center Inc, East Providence, RI
Eastgate Village Retirement Center, Muskogee, OK
Easthaven Care Center, New Orleans, LA
Eastland Care Center, Columbus, OH
Eastland Health Care Center, Nashville, TN
Eastland Manor, Eastland, TX
Eastmont Human Services Center, Glendive, MT
Easton Home for Aged Women, Easton, PA
Easton—Lincoln Nursing Home, North Easton, MA
Easton Manor, Easton, KS
Easton Nursing Center, Easton, PA
Eastpoint Nursing Home, Baltimore, MD
Eastport Memorial Nursing Home, Eastport, ME
Eastside Healthcare Center, Indianapolis, IN
Eastview Manor, Antigo, WI
Eastview Manor Care Center, Trenton, MO
Eastview Manor Inc, Prospect, CT
Eastview Manor Nursing Home, Dayton, OH
Eastview Nursing Center, Tyler, TX
Eastview Nursing Home, Macon, GA
Eastwood Care Center A Long-Term Care Facility, Dedham, MA
Eastwood Convalescent Home, Easton, PA
Eastwood Convalescent Hospital, Long Beach, CA
Eastwood Manor, Commerce, OK
Eastwood Nursing Center, Detroit, MI
Eastwood Pines Nursing Home, Gardner, MA
Eastwood Village Nursing & Retirement Center, Fort Worth, TX
Eaton County Medical Care Facility, Charlotte, MI
Eaton Manor Inc, Charlotte, MI
Eatontown Convalescent Center, Eatontown, NJ
Eben Ezer Lutheran Care Center, Brush, CO

Ebenezer Caroline, Minneapolis, MN
Ebenezer Covenant Home, Buffalo, MN
Ebenezer Hall, Minneapolis, MN
Ebenezer Nursing Home, Rock Hill, SC
Ebenezer Ridges, Burnsville, MN
Ebenezer Ridges Geriatric Care Center,
  Lakeville, MN
Ebenezer Society Luther & Field, Minneapolis,
  MN
Ebensburg Center, Ebensburg, PA
EBI Inc, Duluth, MN
Echo Manor Extended Care Center,
  Pickerington, OH
Echo Park Skilled Nursing Facility Hospital
  Inc, Los Angeles, CA
Echoing Hills Residential Center, Warsaw, OH
Echoing Ridge Residential Center, Canal
  Fulton, OH
Echoing Valley Residential Home, Dayton,
  OH
Echoing Woods Residential Home, Dayton,
  OH
Eckfield Rest Home Inc, Medina, OH
Eddington Group Home, Brewer, ME
James A Eddy Memorial Geriatric Center,
  Troy, NY
Eden Gardens Nursing Center, Shreveport, LA
Eden Home Inc, New Braunfels, TX
Eden Manor Nursing Home, Sabina, OH
Eden Park Health Services Inc, Cobleskill, NY
Eden Park Health Services Inc, Troy, NY
Eden Park Nursing Home, Albany, NY
Eden Park Nursing Home, Catskill, NY
Eden Park Nursing Home, Hudson, NY
Eden Park Nursing Home, Poughkeepsie, NY
Eden Park Nursing Home, Brattleboro, VT
Eden Park Nursing Home & Health Related
  Facility, Glens Falls, NY
Eden Park Nursing Home & HRF, Utica, NY
Eden Park Nursing Home of Rutland,
  Rutland, VT
Eden Valley Nursing Home, Loveland, CO
Eden Village Care Center, Edwardsville, IL
Eden West Convalescent Hospital, Hayward,
  CA
Edenwald, Towson, MD
Edgebrook Rest Center Inc, Edgerton, MN
Edgecombe Nursing Home, Lenox, MA
Edgefield Health Care Center, Edgefield, SC
Edgehill Nursing & Rehabilitation Center,
  Glenside, PA
Edgell Rest Home, Framingham, MA
Edgemont Manor Nursing Home, Cynthiana,
  KY
Edgemoor Geriatric Hospital, Santee, CA
Edgerton Manor, West Lafayette, OH
Edgewater Care Center, Kerrville, TX
Edgewater Convalescent Hospital, Long Beach,
  CA
Edgewater Haven Nursing Home, Port
  Edwards, WI
Edgewater Home Inc, Saint Louis, MO
Edgewater Nursing & Geriatric Center,
  Chicago, IL
Edgewater Pointe Estates Medical Facility,
  Boca Raton, FL
Edgewater Quality Care Nursing Center, Lake
  Milton, OH
Edgewood Convalescent Home, Edgewood, IA
Edgewood Convalescent Home, Boston, MA
Edgewood Healthcare, Oxford, IN
Edgewood Manor, Farmington, ME
Edgewood Manor, Portsmouth, NH
Edgewood Manor Nursing Center, Port
  Clinton, OH
Edgewood Manor Nursing Home, Texarkana,
  TX
Edgewood Manor of Fostoria, Fostoria, OH
Edgewood Manor of Grays Harbor Inc,
  Montesano, WA
Edgewood Manor of Greenfield Inc,
  Greenfield, OH
Edgewood Manor of Lucasville Inc, Lucasville,
  OH
Edgewood Manor of Wellston Inc, Wellston,
  OH
Edgewood Manor of Westerville, Westerville,
  OH

Edgewood Nursing Center, Hopkins, MN
Edgewood Nursing Center, Youngstown, PA
Edgewood Nursing Home, Toledo, OH
Edgewood Nursing Home Inc, Grafton, MA
Edgewood Rest Home, Pittsfield, MA
Edina Care Center, Edina, MN
Edinboro Manor, Edinboro, PA
Edison Estates, Edison, NJ
Edisto Convalescent Center, Orangeburg, SC
Edmond Nursing Center, Edmond, OK
Edmond Oaks Convalescent, Lewisville, TX
Edmonds Care Center, Edmonds, WA
Jennie Edmundson Memorial Hospital,
  Council Bluffs, IA
Edson Convalescent Hospital, Modesto, CA
Edwards Ferry House, Leesburg, VA
Edwards Redeemer Nursing Center, Oklahoma
  City, OK
Edwardsville Care Center, Edwardsville, IL
Edwardsville Care Center East, Edwardsville,
  IL
Edwardsville Convalescent Center,
  Edwardsville, KS
Edwardsville Manor, Edwardsville, KS
Effingham County—ECF, Springfield, GA
Effingham Terrace, Effingham, IL
Effingham Terrace, Effingham, IL
Eger Lutheran Homes, Staten Island, NY
Egle Nursing Home, Lonaconing, MD
Egly Drive Family Home, West Unity, OH
Albert Einstein Medical Center—Willowcrest-
  Bamberger Division, Philadelphia, PA
Eisenhower Nursing & Convalescent Hospital,
  Pasadena, CA
El Cajon Valley Convalescent Hospital, El
  Cajon, CA
El Camino Convalescent Hospital,
  Carmichael, CA
El Centro Villa Nursing Center, Albuquerque,
  NM
El Dorado Convalescent Hospital, Placerville,
  CA
El Dorado Manor, Trenton, NE
El Dorado Nursing Center, El Dorado, KS
El Encanto Convalescent Hospital, City of
  Industry, CA
El Jen Convalescent Hospital, Las Vegas, NV
El Jen Convalescent Hospital—Rehabilitation,
  Las Vegas, NV
El Monte Care Center, El Monte, CA
El Monte Convalescent Hospital, El Monte,
  CA
El Paso Convalescent Center, El Paso, TX
El Paso Health Care, El Paso, IL
El Ponce De Leon Convalescent Center,
  Miami, FL
El Rancho Nursing Home, Payson, UT
El Rancho Vista Convalescent Center, Pico
  Rivera, CA
El Reno Nursing Center, El Reno, OK
El Reposo Sanitarium, Florence, AL
Elba General Hospital & Nursing Home, Elba,
  AL
Elberta Health Care, Warner Robins, GA
Elcor Health Home, Horseheads, NY
Elcor's Marriott Manor Health Related
  Facility, Horseheads, NY
Elder Crest Inc, Munhall, PA
Elder House, Fenton, MI
Eldercare Gardens, Charlottesville, VA
Eldercare of Alton, Alton, IL
Eldercare of Farmville, Farmville, VA
Eldercare of Franklin County, Rocky Mount,
  VA
Eldercare of Hillsville, Hillsville, VA
Eldercare of West Virginia, Ripley, WV
Elders' Home Inc, New York Mills, MN
Eldon Health Care Center, Eldon, MO
Eldora Manor, Eldora, IA
Eldorado Nursing Home Inc, Eldorado, IL
Electra Nursing Center, Electra, TX
Eleven Seven, New Ulm, MN
Elgin Community Living Facility, Elgin, IL
Elgin Golden Years Retirement & Nursing
  Home Inc, Elgin, TX
Elim Home, Milaca, MN
Elim Home, Princeton, MN
Elim Home, Watertown, MN

Elim Home, Fargo, ND
Elim Park Baptist Home Inc, Cheshire, CT
Eliot Falls Nursing Home, Newton Centre,
  MA
Elite Nursing Home, Cincinnati, OH
Elizabeth Carelton House, Boston, MA
Elizabeth Catherine Retirement Facility,
  Weymouth, MA
Elizabeth Church Manor, Binghamton, NY
Jane Elizabeth House Nursing Home,
  Cambridge, MA
Elizabeth Manor Skilled Nursing Facility, Los
  Angeles, CA
Elizabeth Nursing Home, Elizabeth, NJ
Elizabeth Nursing Home Inc, Elizabeth, IL
Elizabethtown Nursing Center Inc,
  Elizabethtown, NC
Elk City Nursing Centre, Elk City, OK
Elk Grove Convalescent Hospital, Elk Grove,
  CA
Elk Haven Nursing Home Association Inc,
  Saint Marys, PA
Elk Manor Home, Moline, KS
Elk River Nursing Home, Elk River, MN
Elkader Care Center, Elkader, IA
Elkhart Healthcare Center, Elkhart, IN
Elkhorn Manor, Elkhorn, NE
Elkton Rest Home, Elkton, SD
Ellen Memorial Convalescent Home, Scranton,
  PA
Ellen Memorial Health Care Center,
  Honesdale, PA
Ellenburg Nursing Center Inc, Anderson, SC
Ellendale Nursing Center, Ellendale, ND
Ellen's Convalescent Health Center, Fort
  Dodge, IA
Ellen's Memorial Convalescent Hospital,
  Richmond, CA
Ellet Manor, Akron, OH
Elliot Avenue Boarding Care Home,
  Minneapolis, MN
Elliot Manor Nursing Home, Newton, MA
Ellis Good Samaritan Center, Ellis, KS
Ellis Nursing Center, Norwood, MA
Ellisville State School—Clover Circle ICF/MR,
  Ellisville, MS
Ellisville State School—Hillside SNF/ICF,
  Ellisville, MS
Ellisville State School—Peacan Grove,
  Ellisville, MS
Ellner Terrace, Evansville, IL
Ellsworth Care Centers Inc, Ellsworth, WI
Ellsworth Convalescent Center, Ellsworth, ME
Ellsworth Good Samaritan Center—Villa
  Hope, Ellsworth, KS
Ellsworth Good Samaritan Village—Villa
  Grace, Ellsworth, KS
Elm Brook Home Inc, Smithfield, RI
Elm Creek Nursing Center, West Carrollton,
  OH
Elm Crest Manor, New Salem, ND
Elm Heights—Parkcrest, Shenandoah, IA
Elm Hill Nursing Center, Rocky Hill, CT
Elm Hill Nursing Home, Boston, MA
Elm Hurst Nursing Home, Springfield, TN
Elm Manor Convalescent Center, Walnut
  Creek, CA
Elm Manor Nursing Home, Canandaigua, NY
Elm North Inc, Waseca, MN
Elm Residence, Waseca, MN
Elm Terrace Gardens, Lansdale, PA
Elm View Care Center, Burlington, IA
Elmbrook Home, Ardmore, OK
Elmcrest Convalescent Hospital, El Monte, CA
Elmhaven, Parsons, KS
Elmhaven Convalescent Hospital, Stockton,
  CA
Elmhurst Extended Care Center Inc, Elmhurst,
  IL
Elmhurst Extended Care Facility, Providence,
  RI
Elmhurst Nursing Home, Melrose, MA
Elmhurst Nursing Home, Canby, OR
Elmore Memorial Nursing Home, Mountain
  Home, ID
Elms, Macomb, IL
Elms Convalescent Hospital, Glendale, CA
Elms Haven Care Center, Thornton, CO

Elms Health Care, Ponca, NE
Elms Manor Nursing Home, Chicopee, MA
Elms Nursing Home, Cranbury, NJ
Elms Nursing Home, Wellington, OH
Elms Residence Nursing Home, Old Orchard Beach, ME
Elmwood Care Center, Onawa, IA
Elmwood Convalescent Hospital, Berkeley, CA
Elmwood Geriatric Village, Detroit, MI
Elmwood Health Care Center, Marysville, IL
Elmwood Health Center Inc, Providence, RI
Elmwood Manor Inc, Wewoka, OK
Elmwood Manor Nursing Home, Worcester, MA
Elmwood Manor Nursing Home Inc, Nanuet, NY
Elmwood Nursing Center, Marlin, TX
Elmwood Nursing Home, Aurora, IL
Elmwood Nursing Home, Green Springs, OH
Elmwood Nursing Home, Omaha, TX
Elmwood Village of Ashland, Ashland, KY
Elness Convalescent Hospital, Turlock, CA
Elsberry Missouri Health Care Center, Elsberry, MO
Elsie May's Rest Home Inc, Pawtucket, RI
Elston Nursing Center, Chicago, IL
Elwyn Inc—Nevil Home, Elwyn, PA
Elwood Care Center, Elwood, NE
Elyria United Methodist Home, Elyria, OH
Elzora Manor, Milton-Freewater, OR
Emanuel County Nursing Home, Swainsboro, GA
Embassy House Health Care Nursing Home, Brockton, MA
Embassy Manor Care Center, Newton, IA
Embreeville Center, Coatesville, PA
Emerald Circle Convalescent Center, Wapato, WA
Emerald Estates, Canton, IL
Emerald Gardens Health Care, Lebanon, IL
Emerald Health & Progressive Alzheimers Enhancement Center, Taylorsville, NC
Emerald Health Care of Ashe, Jefferson, NC
Emerald Hills Skilled Nursing, Ukiah, CA
Emerald Nursing Center, Eugene, OR
Emerald Terrace Nursing Center, Vancouver, WA
Emerson Boarding Care Home, Minneapolis, MN
Emerson Convalescent Center, Emerson, NJ
Emerson Convalescent Home, Watertown, MA
Emerson Nursing Home, Indianapolis, IN
Emerson Place North, Minneapolis, MN
Emery County Nursing Home, Ferron, UT
Emery Manor Nursing Home, Matawan, NJ
Emery Retirement & Convalescent Home, Medford, MA
Emery Street Community Residence, Portland, ME
Emmanuel Home, Litchfield, MN
Emmanuel Nursing Home, Detroit Lakes, MN
Emmet County Medical Care Facility, Harbor Springs, MI
Emmetsburg Care Center, Emmetsburg, IA
Emmett Care Center, Emmett, ID
Emory Nursing Center, Atlanta, GA
Emporia Presbyterian Manor Inc, Emporia, KS
Empress Convalescent Center, Long Beach, CA
Empress Convalescent Home 1, Cincinnati, OH
Empress Convalescent Home 2, Cincinnati, OH
Empress Convalescent Hospital, San Jose, CA
Enderlin Hillcrest Manor Ltd, Enderlin, ND
Enfield Memorial Center, Enfield, CT
England Manor, England, AR
England Nursing Center, England, AR
Englewood Health Care Center, Monroeville, AL
Englewood Health Care Center, Englewood, FL
Englewood House, Englewood, CO
Englewood Manor Inc, Englewood, OH
Englewood Nursing Home, Boston, MA
English Nursing Home, Lebanon, IN

English Oaks Convalescent Hospital & Rehabilitation Center, Modesto, CA
English Valley Nursing Care Center, North English, IA
English Village Manor Inc, Altus, OK
Enid Memorial Hospital SNF, Enid, OK
Enid State School, Enid, OK
Ennis Care Center, Ennis, TX
Ennoble Center of Long Beach, Long Beach, CA
Ennoble Manor Care Center, Dubuque, IA
Enterprise Estates Nursing Center, Enterprise, KS
Enterprise Hospital & Nursing Home, Enterprise, AL
Ephrata Nursing Home, Ephrata, PA
Episcopal Church Home, Hockessin, DE
Episcopal Church Home, Louisville, KY
Episcopal Church Home, Rochester, NY
Episcopal Church Home of Minnesota, Saint Paul, MN
Epsom Manor, Epsom, NH
Epworth Manor, Tyrone, PA
Erick Nursing Home, Erick, OK
Erie County Care Facility, Huron, OH
Erie County Geriatric Center, Girard, PA
Erie County Geriatric Center Annex, Erie, PA
Erie County Home & Infirmary, Alden, NY
Erie County Medical Center—Skilled Nursing Facility, Buffalo, NY
Erinkay Dungarvin XIII, Robbinsdale, MN
Escambia County Nursing Home, Pensacola, FL
Escondido Convalescent Center, Escondido, CA
Eskaton Glenwood Manor, Sacramento, CA
Eskaton Manzanita Manor, Carmichael, CA
Essex Convalescent Home, Lynn, MA
Essex County Geriatric Center, Belleville, NJ
Essex Manor, Lebanon, IN
Estelle's Nursing Home, Clifton, KS
Estelline Nursing & Care Center, Estelline, SD
Estes Health Care Center—East, Birmingham, AL
Estes Health Care Center—Glen Haven, Northport, AL
Estes Health Care Center—North, Northport, AL
Estes Health Care Center—Park Manor, Northport, AL
Estes Health Care Center—Riverchase, Birmingham, AL
Estes Health Care—North, Northport, AL
Estes Nursing Facility—Civic Center, Birmingham, AL
Estes Nursing Facility—Northway, Birmingham, AL
Estes Nursing Facility—Oak Knoll, Birmingham, AL
Estes Nursing Facility—South, Birmingham, AL
Esther House, Grand Rapids, MN
Esther Marie Nursing Center, Geneva, OH
Etowah Health Care Center, Etowah, TN
Euclid Convalescent Center, San Diego, CA
Euclid General Hospital, Euclid, OH
Euclid Manor Nursing Home, Cleveland, OH
Eudora Nursing Center, Eudora, KS
Eufaula Geriatric Center, Eufaula, AL
Eufaula Manor, Eufaula, OK
Eugene Good Samaritan Center, Eugene, OR
Euless Nursing Center, Euless, TX
Eunice Care Center Inc, Eunice, LA
Eupora Health Care Center Inc, Eupora, MS
Eureka Apostolic Christian Home, Eureka, IL
Eureka Springs Convalescent Center, Eureka Springs, AR
Eustis Manor Inc, Eustis, FL
Evamor Manor, Worcester, MA
Evangelical Baptist Home, Ashford, CT
Evangelical Congregational Church Retirement Village, Myerstown, PA
Evangelical Free Church Home, Boone, IA
Evangelical Home—Detroit, Detroit, MI
Evangelical Home—Port Huron, Port Huron, MI
Evangelical Home—Saline, Saline, MI

Evangelical Home—Sterling Heights, Sterling Heights, MI
Evangelical Manor, Philadelphia, PA
Evangeline Oaks Guest House, Carencro, LA
Evangeline of Natchitoches, Natchitoches, LA
Evangeline of Ormond, Destrehan, LA
Evangeline Village Nursing Home, Houma, LA
Evans Health Care, Evans, GA
Helen Evans Home for Retarded Children, Hacienda Heights, CA
Evans Manor Nursing Home, Worcester, MA
Mary Evans Extended Care Center, Ellwood City, PA
Evans Memorial Home, Cresco, IA
Evansville Manor, Evansville, WI
Evansville Protestant Home Inc, Evansville, IN
Eveleth Hospital Community & Nursing Care Unit, Eveleth, MN
Evenglow Lodge, Pontiac, IL
Evening Star Nursing Home, Bethany, OK
Eventide Convalescent Center Inc, Topeka, KS
Eventide Home, Mountain Lake, MN
Eventide Home Inc, Exeter, NH
Eventide Lutheran Home, Denison, IA
Eventide Lutheran Home, Moorhead, MN
Eventide Nursing Home, Massillon, OH
Eventide Nursing Home, San Saba, TX
Eventide of Sheridan, Sheridan, WY
Everett Court Community, Lakewood, CO
Evergreen Care Center, Montrose, CO
Evergreen Care Center, Medina, OH
Evergreen Care Center, Owasso, OK
Evergreen Care Center, Burkburnett, TX
Evergreen Convalescent Center, Olympia, WA
Evergreen Convalescent Center Inc, Temple City, CA
Evergreen Convalescent Hospital Inc, Modesto, CA
Evergreen Health Care Center Inc, Shawano, WI
Evergreen Health Center, Phillipsburg, KS
Evergreen Hills Nursing Center, Ypsilanti, MI
Evergreen House Health Center, East Providence, RI
Evergreen Manor, Minden, LA
Evergreen Manor, Saco, ME
Evergreen Manor, Delaware, OH
Evergreen Manor, Oshkosh, WI
Evergreen Manor Nursing Home, Montpelier, OH
Evergreen North Nursing Home, Montpelier, OH
Evergreen Nursing Center, Harmony, PA
Evergreen Nursing Home, Evergreen, AL
Evergreen Nursing Home, Evergreen, AL
Evergreen Nursing Home, Alamosa, CO
Evergreen Nursing Home, Del City, OK
Evergreen Nursing Home & Rehabilitation Center Inc, Creve Coeur, MO
Evergreen Place, Texarkana, AR
Evergreen Place A Rest Home, Springfield, MA
Evergreen Residential Care Home, Pontiac, MI
Evergreen Terrace Healthcare Center, Madison, SD
Evergreen Terrace Nursing Center, Mount Vernon, WA
Evergreen Vista Convalescent Center, Kirkland, WA
Evergreen Woods, Spring Hill, FL
Evergreens—High Point, High Point, NC
Evergreens Inc—Greensboro, Greensboro, NC
Evergreens Nursing Home Inc, Warwick, RI
Evergren Terrace Care Center, Lakewood, CO
Ewing Nursing Home, Terre Haute, IN
Ewing Nursing Home, Trenton, NJ
Excelsior Nursing Home, Excelsior, MN
Excelsior Springs Care Center, Excelsior Springs, MO
Exceptional Care & Training Center, Sterling, IL
Excepticon—Lexington Campus, Lexington, KY
Exeter Healthcare Inc, Exeter, NH

Exeter House, Seattle, WA
Exira Care Center, Exira, IA
ExPerius Health Care Inc, Kansas City, MO
Extended Care Hospital of Anaheim, Anaheim, CA
Extended Care Hospital of Riverside, Riverside, CA
Extended Care Rehabilitation Center, Hillsboro, OR
Extendicare Health Center, Dothan, AL
Faber Nursing Home, Cortland, OH
Fair Acres Geriatric Center, Lima, PA
Fair Acres Nursing Home, Armada, MI
Fair Acres Nursing Home Inc, Du Quoin, IL
Fair Haven Shelby County Home, Sidney, OH
Fair Havens Center, Miami Springs, FL
Fair Havens Center,°Miami Springs, FL
Fair Havens Christian Home, Decatur, IL
Fair Havens Rest Home Inc, Middleborough, MA
Fair Lawn Manor Nursing Home, Fair Lawn, NJ
Fair Lodge Health Care Center, Louisville, KY
Fair Meadow Nursing Home, Fertile, MN
Fair Oaks, Greenville, IL
Fair Oaks Health Care Center, Crystal Lake, IL
Fair Oaks Nursing Home, South Beloit, IL
Fair Oaks Nursing Home, Jamestown, KY
Fair Oaks Nursing Home, Hineston, LA
Fair Park Health Care Center, Dallas, TX
Fair Park Nursing Center, Huntsville, TX
Fair View Home, Mauston, WI
Fair View Nursing Home, Sedalia, MO
Fair Villa Nursing Home, King of Prussia, PA
Fair Winds, Sarver, PA
Fairacres Manor Inc, Greeley, CO
Fairbanks Pioneers Home, Fairbanks, AK
Fairborn Family Care Home, Fairborn, OH
Fairburn Health Care Center, Fairburn, GA
Fairchild Manor Nursing Home, Lewiston, NY
Fairchild Nursing Home, Fairchild, WI
Fairfax Community Home, Fairfax, MN
Fairfax Health Care Center, Berwyn, IL
Fairfax Nursing Center, Fairfax, VA
Fairfax Nursing Home, Fairfax, OK
Fairfax Rest Home, Boston, MA
Fairfield Center, Fairfield, OH
Fairfield Convalescent Hospital, Fairfield, CA
Fairfield Good Samaritan Center, Fairfield, WA
Fairfield Health Care Center, Fairfield, AL
Fairfield Homes, Ridgeway, SC
Fairfield Manor Health Care Center, Norwalk, CT
Fairfield Nursing Center Inc, Crownsville, MD
Fairhaven Christian Home, Rockford, IL
Fairhaven Corporation, Whitewater, WI
Fairhaven Nursing Home, Sykesville, MD
Fairhaven Nursing Home, Lowell, MA
Fairhaven Rest Home, Huntington, WV
Fairhaven Retirement & Health Care Community, Upper Sandusky, OH
Fairland Nursing & Rehabilitation Center, Silver Spring, MD
Fairland Nursing Home, Fairland, OK
Fairlane Memorial Convalescent Home, Detroit, MI
Fairlawn Care Center, Gresham, OR
Fairlawn Convalescent Home Inc, Norwich, CT
Fairlawn Group Home, Radford, VA
Fairlawn Haven, Archbold, OH
Fairlawn Heights Nursing Center, Topeka, KS
Fairlawn Nursing Home, Leominster, MA
Fairlawn Nursing Home Inc, Lexington, MA
Fairmont Community Hospital, Fairmont, MN
Fairmont Rehabilitation Hospital, Lodi, CA
Fairmont Rest Home, Ephrata, PA
Fairmount Community Access, Saint Paul, MN
Fairmount Health Center of Breckenridge Village, Willoughby, OH
Fairmount Nursing Center, Baltimore, MD
Fairmount Rest Home, Leominster, MA

Fairmount Rest Home Inc, Boston, MA
Fairpark Healthcare Center, Maryville, TN
Fairport Baptist Home, Fairport, NY
Fairview, Groton, CT
Fairview Baptist Home, Downers Grove, IL
Fairview Care Center East, Salt Lake City, UT
Fairview Care Center of Bethlehem Pike, Philadelphia, PA
Fairview Care Center of Papermill Road, Philadelphia, PA
Fairview Care Center West, Salt Lake City, UT
Fairview Castle Nursing Home, Millersburg, OH
Fairview Fellowship Home for Senior Citizens Inc, Fairview, OK
Fairview Gardens, Creve Coeur, MO
Fairview Haven Inc, Fairbury, IL
Fairview Health Care Center, La Grange Park, IL
Fairview Home, Carlisle, OH
Fairview House, Rosiclare, IL
Fairview Manor, Belvidere, IL
Fairview Manor, Fairmont, NE
Fairview Manor, Fairview, PA
Fairview Manor, Fairfield, TX
Fairview Manor Nursing Center, Toledo, OH
Fairview Manor Nursing Center, Oklahoma City, OK
Fairview Manor Nursing Home Inc, Newark, OH
Fairview Medical Care Facility, Centreville, MI
Fairview Nursing & Convalescent Home, Birmingham, AL
Fairview Nursing Center, Du Quoin, IL
Fairview Nursing Home, Dodge Center, MN
Fairview Nursing Home, Forest Hills, NY
Fairview Nursing Home, Cincinnati, OH
Fairview Nursing Home, Bonham, TX
Fairview Nursing Home Inc, Hudson, NH
Fairview Plaza Limited Partnership, Rockford, IL
Fairview Receiving Center, Eden Prairie, MN
Fairview Training Center—Crestview Group Home, Salem, OR
Fairview Village Nursing Center, Lewisberry, PA
Fairway Convalescent Center, Fullerton, CA
Fairways at Brookline, State College, PA
Faith Countryside Homes, Highland, IL
Faith Handicap Village 1, 2, 3, Shawnee Mission, KS
Faith Haven Care Center, Jackson, MI
Faith Lutheran Home, Osage, IA
Faith Lutheran Home Inc, Wolf Point, MT
Faith Medical Care Center, Saint Clair, MI
Faith Memorial Nursing Home, Pasadena, TX
Faith Nursing Home, Edinburg, IN
Faith Nursing Home, Florence, SC
Falkville Health Care Center, Falkville, AL
Fall Creek Valley Nursing Home, Fall Creek, WI
Fall River Jewish Home, Fall River, MA
Fall River Nursing Home Inc, Fall River, MA
Fallbrook Convalescent Hospital, Fallbrook, CA
Fallon Convalescent Center, Fallon, NV
Fallon County Medical Complex—Nursing Home, Baker, MT
Falls Care Center, International Falls, MN
Falls City Healthcare Center, Falls City, NE
Falls Nursing Home, South Hadley, MA
Falls Nursing Home, Oconto Falls, WI
Falmouth by the Sea, Falmouth, ME
Falmouth Nursing Home, Falmouth, MA
Falmouth Rest Home, Falmouth, KY
Family Health West, Fruita, CO
Family Heritage Nursing Home, Black River Falls, WI
Family Heritage Nursing Home, Wisconsin Rapids, WI
Family House, North Mankato, MN
Family Life Enrichment Center, High Shoals, GA
Family Nursing Home & Rehabilitation Center Inc, Milwaukee, WI
Familystyle Homes, Saint Paul, MN

Fannin County Nursing Home, Blue Ridge, GA
Far Rockaway Nursing Home, Far Rockaway, NY
Fargo Nursing Home, Fargo, ND
Faribault Manor, Faribault, MN
Faribault Regional Center, Faribault, MN
Farmington Convalescent Home, Farmington, CT
Farmington Hills Inn, Farmington Hills, MI
Farmington Nursing Home, Farmington, IL
Farmington Nursing Home, Farmington Hills, MI
Farnsworth Nursing Home, Peabody, MA
Farragut Health Care Center, Knoxville, TN
Farwell Convalescent Center, Omaha, NE
Father Murray Nursing Center, Centerline, MI
Father Purcell Memorial Exceptional Children's Center, Montgomery, AL
Father Walter Memorial Child Care Center, Montgomery, AL
Fauskee Nursing Home Inc, Worthington, MN
Faxton Sunset St Luke's Home, Utica, NY
Fay Case Nursing Home, Salt Lake City, UT
Fayette Continuous Care Center, Fayetteville, WV
Fayette County Hospital & Nursing Home, Fayette, IA
Fayette Health Care Center, Uniontown, PA
Fayetteville City Hospital Geriatrics Center, Fayetteville, AR
Federal Hill Manor Nursing/Convalescent Center, Bardstown, KY
Federal Way Convalescent Center, Federal Way, WA
Fejervary Health Care Center, Davenport, IA
Fellowship Deaconry Inc, Bernardsville, NJ
Fellowship House, East Providence, RI
Fellowship Manor, Whitehall, PA
Fellowship Nursing Home Inc, Warrenton, MO
Guy & Mary Felt Manor, Emporium, PA
Felton Convalescent Home, Felton, DE
Fennimore Good Samaritan Center, Fennimore, WI
Fenton Extended Care Center, Fenton, MI
Fenton Park Health Related Facility, Greenhurst, NY
Fenton Park Nursing Home, Jamestown, NY
Fentress County General Hospital Skilled Bed Facility, Jamestown, TN
Fentress County Nursing Home, Jamestown, TN
Fenwood Manor Inc, Manchester, CT
Fergus Falls Regional Treatment Center, Fergus Falls, MN
Ferguson Community Residence No 1, Spartanburg, SC
Ferguson Community Residence No 2, Spartanburg, SC
Ferguson Convalescent Home, Lapeer, MI
Ferguson Rest Home, Clinton, MA
Fern Terrace Lodge of Bowling Green, Bowling Green, KY
Fern Terrace Lodge of Mayfield, Mayfield, KY
Fern Terrace Lodge of Murray, Murray, KY
Fern Terrace Lodge of Owensboro, Owensboro, KY
Fernandez Nursing Home Inc, Saint Bernard, LA
Ferncliff Nursing Home Co Inc, Rhinebeck, NY
Ferncrest Manor Nursing Home, New Orleans, LA
Fernhill Manor, Portland, OR
Fernview Convalescent Hospital, San Gabriel, CA
Fernwood Health Care Center, Dwight, IL
Fernwood House Retirement & Nursing Center, Bethesda, MD
Ferris Nursing Care Center, Ferris, TX
J Ferry Nursing Home, Elyria, OH
Ferry Point—SNCF, Old Saybrook, CT
Festus Manor, Festus, MO
FHP Westminster Skilled Nursing Facility, Westminster, CA

Fiddlers Green Manor Nursing Home, Springville, NY

Field Crest Nursing Home, Hayfield, MN

Field Home—Holy Comforter, Peekskill, NY

Field House, Canon City, CO

Fieldcrest Manor Nursing Home, Waldoboro, ME

Fieldston Lodge Nursing Home, Bronx, NY

Fieldview Manor, Superior, WI

Fieser Nursing Home, Fenton, MO

Fifth Avenue Care Center, Texas City, TX

Fifth Avenue Convalescent Hospital, San Rafael, CA

Fifth Avenue Health Care Center, Rome, GA

58th Avenue, Arvada, CO

Filling Memorial Home of Mercy, Napoleon, OH

Fillmore Convalescent Center, Fillmore, CA

Fillmore County Long-Term Care, Geneva, NE

Millard Fillmore Skilled Nursing Facility, Buffalo, NY

Fillmore Place, Preston, MN

Filosa Convalescent Home Inc, Danbury, CT

Filson Care Home, Louisville, KY

Hazel I Findlay Country Manor, Saint Johns, MI

Finley Hospital, Dubuque, IA

Finney Avenue Residence, Suffolk, VA

Finnie Good Shepherd Nursing Home Inc, Galatia, IL

Fir Lane Terrace Convalescent Center, Shelton, WA

Fircrest Convalescent Hospital, Sebastopol, CA

Fircrest School, Seattle, WA

Firelands Nursing Center, New London, OH

Firemen's Home of the State of New York, Hudson, NY

Fireside Convalescent Hospital, Santa Monica, CA

Fireside Foster Inn, Mora, MN

Fireside Lodge, Cleburne, TX

Fireside Lodge, Fort Worth, TX

Fireside Lodge Retirement Center, Fort Worth, TX

Firesteel Health Care Center, Mitchell, SD

Firestone Road Community Residence, Charleston, SC

First Christian Church Residence, Minneapolis, MN

First Community Village Healthcare Center, Columbus, OH

First Hill Care Center, Seattle, WA

First Midlands ICMRF, Columbia, SC

First Shamrock Care Center, Kingfisher, OK

Firwood Health Care Center, Batavia, IL

Fisher Convalescent Home, Mayville, MI

Fisher County Nursing Home, Rotan, TX

Fishkill Health Related Center Inc, Beacon, NY

Fitch Rest Home, Melrose, MA

Fitzgerald Nursing Home, Fitzgerald, GA

Thomas Fitzgerald Veterans Home, Omaha, NE

Five Counties Nursing Home, Lemmon, SD

Five Oaks Nursing Center Inc, Concord, NC

Five Star Industries Inc, Du Quoin, IL

Flagship Healthcare Center, Newport Beach, CA

Flambeau—Dungarvin XII, Minneapolis, MN

Flannery Oaks Guest House, Baton Rouge, LA

Flannery's Health Care Center, Portsmouth, OH

Flatbush Manor Care Center, Brooklyn, NY

Flathead County Care Center, Kalispell, MT

Fleetcrest Manor Inc, Waterbury, CT

Fletcher Living Center, Fletcher, NC

Mary Fletcher Health Care Center, Salem, OH

Fleur de Lis, Farmington, MO

Flinn Memorial Home, Marion, IN

Flint City Nursing Home Inc, Decatur, AL

Flint Hills Manor, Emporia, KS

Flor Haven Home, Missoula, MT

Flora Care Center, Flora, IL

Flora Manor, Flora, IL

Flora Nursing Center, Flora, IL

Flora Terrace Convalescent Hospital Inc, Los Angeles, CA

Flora Terrace West Convalescent Hospital Inc, Los Angeles, CA

Florence Community Residence, Florence, SC

Florence Convalescent Center, Florence, SC

Florence Gressette Residence, Saint Matthews, SC

Florence Hand Home, LaGrange, GA

Florence Heights Village Nursing Center, Omaha, NE

Florence Home, Omaha, NE

Florence Nursing Home, Marengo, IL

Florence Nursing Home, Riverside, NJ

Florence Park Care Center, Florence, KY

Florence Villa, Florence, WI

Floresville Nursing Center, Floresville, TX

Florida Baptist Retirement Center Nursing Facility, Vero Beach, FL

Florida Christian Health Center, Jacksonville, FL

Florida Club Care Center, Miami, FL

Florida Living Nursing Center, Apopka, FL

Florida Manor, Orlando, FL

Floridean Nursing Home Inc, Miami, FL

Florin Convalescent Hospital, Sacramento, CA

Florissant Nursing Center, Florissant, MO

Flower Square Health Care Center, Tucson, AZ

Flowery Branch Nursing Center, Flowery Branch, GA

Floy Dyer Manor, Houston, MS

J H Floyd Sunshine Manor, Sarasota, FL

Floydada Nursing Home, Floydada, TX

Flushing Manor Care Center, Flushing, NY

Flushing Manor Nursing Home Inc, Flushing, NY

Foley Nursing Center, Foley, MN

Foley Nursing Home, Foley, AL

Folk Nursing Center, Florence, SC

Folsom Convalescent Hospital, Folsom, CA

Folts Home, Herkimer, NY

Fond Du Lac County Health Care Center, Fond Du Lac, WI

Fond Du Lac Lutheran Home, Fond Du Lac, WI

Fonda Care Center, Fonda, IA

Fondulac Woods Health Care Center, East Peoria, IL

Fontaine Woods Nursing Home, Saint Louis, MO

Fontanbleu Nursing Center, Bloomington, IN

Fontanelle Good Samaritan Center, Fontanelle, IA

Foothill Acres Inc, Neshanic, NJ

Foothill Health & Rehabilitation Center, Sylmar, CA

Foothill Oaks Care Center, Auburn, CA

Foothills Care Center Inc, Longmont, CO

Foothills ICF/MR Group Home, Morganton, NC

For-Rest Convalescent Home, Hattiesburg, MS

Forbes Center for Gerontology, Pittsburgh, PA

Ford County Nursing Home, Paxton, IL

Henry Ford Continuing Care—Roseville, Roseville, MI

Ford-Hull-Mar, Yorkville, OH

Forest City Nursing Center, Forest City, PA

Forest Cove Manor Inc, Jackson, TN

Forest Del Convalescent Center, Princeton, IN

Forest Farm Health Care Centre Inc, Middletown, RI

Forest Glen Nursing Center, Seattle, WA

Forest Haven Care Center, Maryland Heights, MO

Forest Haven Nursing Home, Catonsville, MD

Forest Hill, A Zandex Retirement Community, Saint Clairsville, OH

Forest Hill Convalescent Center, Richmond, VA

Forest Hill Manor Inc, Fort Kent, ME

Forest Hill Nursing Center, Forest Hill, TX

Forest Hill Nursing Center Inc, Fort Worth, TX

Forest Hills Nursing Home, Forest Hills, NY

Forest Hills Nursing Home, Cleveland, OH

Forest Lane Group Home, Newark, DE

Forest Manor Health Care Center, Hope, NJ

Forest Manor Health Related Facility Inc, Glen Cove, NY

Forest Manor Inc, Northport, AL

Forest Manor Nursing Home, Covington, LA

Forest Manor Rest Home, Gardner, MA

Forest Oaks Nursing Home, Hamilton, TX

Forest Park Health Center, Carlisle, PA

Forest Park Healthcare Center, Kokomo, IN

Forest Park Nursing Center, Plant City, FL

Forest Ridge Convalescent Center, Bremerton, WA

Forest View Care Center, Forest Grove, OR

Forest View Nursing Home, Forest Hills, NY

Forest Villa Nursing Center, Niles, IL

Forestdale Health Care, Birmingham, AL

Forestdale Nursing Home, Boston, MA

Forester Haven, San Fernando, CA

Forester Nursing Home Inc, Wintersville, OH

Forestview Nursing Home, Cincinnati, OH

Forestview Sunlen, Bloomington, MN

Forge Pond Nursing Home, East Bridgewater, MA

Forks Community Hospital, Forks, WA

Forrest Lake Health Care, Martinez, GA

Forrest Manor Nursing Home, Dewey, OK

Forsyth Nursing Home, Forsyth, GA

Fort Atkinson Health Care Center, Fort Atkinson, WI

Fort Bayard Medical Center, Fort Bayard, NM

Fort Bend Nursing Home, Rosenberg, TX

Fort Collins Good Samaritan Retirement Village, Fort Collins, CO

Fort Collins Health Care Center, Fort Collins, CO

Fort Dodge Villa Care Center, Fort Dodge, IA

Fort Gaines Nursing Home, Fort Gaines, GA

Fort Gibson Nursing Home, Fort Gibson, OK

Fort Hudson Nursing Home Inc, Fort Edward, NY

Fort Logan Hospital, Stanford, KY

Fort Madison Nursing Care Center, Fort Madison, IA

Fort Myers Care Center, Fort Myers, FL

Fort Oglethorpe Nursing Center, Fort Oglethorpe, GA

Fort Pierce Care Center, Fort Pierce, FL

Fort Sanders—Sevier Medical Center Nursing Home, Sevierville, TN

Fort Scott Manor, Fort Scott, KS

Fort Stanton Hospital & Training School, Fort Stanton, NM

Fort Tryon Nursing Home, New York, NY

Fort Valley Health Care Center, Fort Valley, GA

Fort Vancouver Convalescent Center, Vancouver, WA

Fort Walton Developmental Center, Fort Walton Beach, FL

Fort Washington Estates, Fort Washington, PA

Fort Washington Rehabilitation Center, Fort Washington, MD

Fort Wayne Nursing Home, Fort Wayne, IN

Forum at the Crossing, Indianapolis, IN

Forum Convalescent Center, Trenton, TN

Forwood Manor, Wilmington, DE

Foss Home, Seattle, WA

Fosston Group Home, Fosston, MN

Fosston Municipal Hospital & Home, Fosston, MN

Wendell Foster Center, Owensboro, KY

Foster's Nursing Home, Springfield, MO

Fostrian Manor, Flushing, MI

Foulk Manor North, Wilmington, DE

Foulk Manor South, Wilmington, DE

Foulkeways at Gwynedd, Gwynedd, PA

Founders Pavilion, Corning, NY

Fountain Care Center, Orange, CA

Fountain Gardens Convalescent Hospital, Los Angeles, CA

Fountain Inn Convalescent Home, Fountain Inn, SC

Fountain Lake Treatment Center, Albert Lea, MN

Fountain Manor Nursing Home, Hicksville, OH

Fountain Nursing Home, Reform, AL

Fountain Park Nursing Home Inc, Woodstock, OH

Fountain Terrace, Loves Park, IL

Fountain Terrace, Rockford, IL

Fountain Valley Regional Care Center of FVRH, Fountain Valley, CA

Fountain View Convalescent Hospital, Los Angeles, CA

Fountain View Manor, Henryetta, OK

Fountain View Nursing Home, Springhill, LA

Fountain View Villa, Ashland, KS

Fountain Villa Care Center, Sabetha, KS

Fountain West Health Center, West Des Moines, IA

Fountainbleau Nursing Centre, Anaheim, CA

Fountainbleau Nursing Home, Little Rock, AR

Fountainhead Manor, Florissant, MO

Fountainhead Nursing & Convalescent Home, North Miami, FL

Fountainhead Nursing Center, North Miami, FL

Fountainhead Nursing Home, Franklin Furnace, OH

Fountains, Daytona Beach, FL

Fountains Nursing Home, Boca Raton, FL

Fountains Nursing Home, Marion, IL

Fountainview Convalescent Center, Atlanta, GA

Fountainview Inc, Eldorado, IL

Fountainview Place, Elkhart, IN

Fountainview Place, Indianapolis, IN

Fountainview Place, Muncie, IN

Fountainview Place, Portage, IN

Fountainview Place—Goshen, Goshen, IN

Fountainview Place of Mishawaka, Mishawaka, IN

Fountainview Terrace, LaPorte, IN

Four Chaplains Convalescent Center, Westland, MI

Four Corners Good Samaritan Center, Aztec, NM

Four Corners Health Care Center, Durango, CO

Four Corners Regional Care Center, Blanding, UT

Four Courts, Louisville, KY

Four Fountains Convalescent Center, Belleville, IL

Four Freedoms Manor, Miami, FL

Four Oaks Health Care Center, Jonesborough, TN

Four Pines Retirement Home Inc, Independence, MO

Four Seasons Care Center—Capitol, Saint Paul, MN

Four Seasons Care Center—Central, Saint Paul, MN

Four Seasons Care Center—Metro, Minneapolis, MN

Four Seasons Care Center—Richfield, Richfield, MN

Four Seasons Health Care, Bad Axe, MI

Four Seasons Health Care Center, Fort Collins, CO

Four Seasons Nursing Center, Pueblo, CO

Four Seasons Nursing Center, Tulsa, OK

Four Seasons Nursing Center, Austin, TX

Four Seasons Nursing Center, Ennis, TX

Four Seasons Nursing Center, Fort Worth, TX

Four Seasons Nursing Center—Dallas, Dallas, TX

Four Seasons Nursing Center—North, San Antonio, TX

Four Seasons Nursing Center of Durant, Durant, OK

Four Seasons Nursing Center of El Paso, El Paso, TX

Four Seasons Nursing Center of Fort Worth—Northwest, Fort Worth, TX

Four Seasons Nursing Center of Midwest City, Midwest City, OK

Four Seasons Nursing Center of Norman, Norman, OK

Four Seasons Nursing Center of Northwest Oklahoma City, Oklahoma City, OK

Four Seasons Nursing Center of San Antonio—Babcock, San Antonio, TX

Four Seasons Nursing Center of San Antonio—Northwest, San Antonio, TX

Four Seasons Nursing Center of San Antonio—Pecan Valley, San Antonio, TX

Four Seasons Nursing Center of San Antonio—Windcrest, San Antonio, TX

Four Seasons Nursing Center of Southwest Oklahoma City, Oklahoma City, OK

Four Seasons Nursing Center of Temple, Temple, TX

Four Seasons Nursing Center of Warr Acres, Oklahoma City, OK

Four Seasons Nursing Center of Windsor Hills, Oklahoma City, OK

Four Seasons Nursing Center—South, San Antonio, TX

Four Seasons Residential Care, Moscow Mills, MO

Four Seasons Retirement & Health Care Center, Columbus, IN

Four States Nursing Home, Texarkana, TX

Four Winds Manor, Verona, WI

Four Winds Nursing Facility, Jackson, OH

Fourth Street Care Center, Monett, MO

Fowler Convalescent Hospital, Fowler, CA

Fowler Health Care Center, Fowler, CO

Fowler House, Cuyahoga Falls, OH

Juliette Fowler Homes, Dallas, TX

Fowler Nursing Center Inc, Guilford, CT

Fowler Nursing Home, Fowler, KS

Fox Adult Foster Care, Cheyenne, WY

Aurelia Osborn Fox Memorial Hospital, Oneonta, NY

Fox Chase Rehabilitation & Nursing Center, Silver Spring, MD

Fox Crest Manor, West Chicago, IL

Fox Nursing Home Inc, Chester, WV

Fox Nursing & Rehabilitation Center, Warrington, PA

Fox Run Manor, Findlay, OH

Fox Valley Nursing Center Inc, South Elgin, IL

Foxwood Springs Living Center, Raymore, MO

Frame House Manor, Indianapolis, IN

Frame Nursing Home Inc, Indianapolis, IN

Framingham Nursing Home, Framingham, MA

Jan Frances Care Center, Ada, OK

Frances Mahon Deaconess Nursing Home, Glasgow, MT

Frances Residence, Saint Paul, MN

Sarah Frances—Tally-Ho Manor, Boonton, NJ

Francis Convalescent Center, Fort Worth, TX

Francis Residence II, White Bear Lake, MN

Francis Scott Key Hospital Center/Mason F Lord Nursing Facility, Baltimore, MD

Franciscan Care Center Inc, Appleton, WI

Franciscan Convalescent Hospital, Merced, CA

Franciscan Health Care Center, Louisville, KY

Franciscan Nursing Home, Joliet, IL

Franciscan Villa, Broken Arrow, OK

Franciscan Villa, South Milwaukee, WI

Franida House Nursing Home, Brookline, MA

Frankenmuth Convalescent Center, Frankenmuth, MI

Frankfort Community Care Home Inc, Frankfort, KS

Frankfort Heights Manor, West Frankfort, IL

Frankfort Nursing Home, Frankfort, IN

Frankfort Terrace, Frankfort, IL

Franklin Care Center, Gladstone, OR

Franklin Care Center, Waynesburg, PA

Franklin Convalescent Center, Franklin Park, NJ

Franklin County Health Care Center, Winchester, TN

Franklin County Nursing Home, Preston, ID

Franklin County Nursing Home, Malone, NY

Franklin County Nursing Home, Chambersburg, PA

Franklin Court Nursing Center, Baltimore, MD

Franklin General Hospital, Hampton, IA

Franklin Grove Health Care Center, Franklin Grove, IL

Franklin Guest Home Inc, Winnsboro, LA

Franklin Health Care Center, Franklin, GA

Franklin Health Care Center, Franklin, TN

Franklin Healthcare Center, Franklin, MN

Franklin Healthcare Centre, Franklin, IN

Franklin House Healthcare, Franklin, MA

Franklin Manor, Frankfort, KY

Franklin Manor Convalescent Center, Southfield, MI

Franklin Manor Nursing Home, Franklin, TN

Franklin Nursing Center, Franklin, NE

Franklin Nursing Center of Sidney, Sidney, OH

Franklin Nursing Center of Vandalia, Vandalia, OH

Franklin Nursing Home, Franklin, IN

Franklin Nursing Home, Hampton, IA

Franklin Nursing Home, Franklin, LA

Franklin Nursing Home, Braintree, MA

Franklin Nursing Home, Greenfield, MA

Franklin Nursing Home, Flushing, NY

Franklin Nursing Home, Franklin, OH

Franklin Nursing Home, Franklin, TX

Franklin Park Nursing Home, Franklin Square, NY

Franklin Personal Care, Franklin, KY

Franklin Place East, Minneapolis, MN

Franklin Plaza, Cleveland, OH

Franklin United Methodist Home, Franklin, IN

Franklin Woods Health Care Center, Columbus, OH

Martha Franks Baptist Retirement Center, Laurens, SC

Frankston Nursing Center, Frankston, TX

Franvale Nursing Home, Braintree, MA

Fraser Intermediate Care Facility, San Diego, CA

Fraser Rest Home of Falmouth, North Falmouth, MA

Fraser Rest Home of Hyannis, Hyannis, MA

Fraser Rest Home of Sandwich, Sandwich, MA

Fraser Villa, Fraser, MI

Frasier Meadows Manor Health Care Center, Boulder, CO

Frazee Retirement Center, Frazee, MN

Frazier Nursing Home, Saint Louis, MO

Frederic Care Center Inc, Frederic, WI

Frederick Boulevard Group Home, Akron, OH

Frederick Health Care Center, Frederick, MD

Frederick Mennonite Home, Frederick, PA

Frederick Villa Nursing Center, Baltimore, MD

Fredericka Convalescent Hospital, Chula Vista, CA

Fredericksburg Nursing Home, Fredericksburg, TX

Fredericksburg Nursing Home, Fredericksburg, VA

Free State Crestwood Inc, Wills Point, TX

Freeburg Care Center, Freeburg, IL

Freedom Care Pavilion, Bradenton, FL

Freedom Crest Nursing Home, Falmouth, MA

Freedom Village Healthcare Center, El Toro, CA

Freelandville Community Home, Freelandville, IN

Freeman Convalescent Home Inc, Iron Mountain, MI

Freeman Nursing Home, Pepperell, MA

Freeman Nursing Home, Freeman, SD

Freeport Manor Nursing Center, Freeport, IL

Freeport Nursing Home, Freeport, ME

Freeport Terrace, Freeport, IL

Freeport Towne Square I, Freeport, ME

Freeport Towne Square II, Freeport, ME

Fremont Care Center Inc, Fremont, NE

Fremont Manor Nursing & Convalescent Home, Riverton, WY

Fremont Quality Care Nursing Center, Fremont, OH

John Douglas French Center for Alzheimer's Disease, Los Alamitos, CA

French Prairie Care Center, Woodburn, OR

Sarah Roberts French Home, San Antonio, TX

Frenchtown Convalescent Center, Monroe, MI

Frene Valley Geriatric & Rehabilitation Center, Hermann, MO
Frene Valley Health Center, Hermann, MO
Fresno Care & Guidance Center, Fresno, CA
Fresno Convalescent Hospital, Fresno, CA
Fresno Westview Convalescent Hospital, Pimole, CA
Frey Village, Middletown, PA
Frickell Family Care Home, Denver, CO
Fridley Convalescent Home, Fridley, MN
Friedler's Nursing Home, Baltimore, MD
Friedwald House, New City, NY
Friel Nursing Home Inc, Quincy, MA
Friel Nursing Home Inc, Wallaston, MA
Friend Manor, Friend, NE
Friendly Acres Inc, Newton, KS
Friendly Home Inc, Woonsocket, RI
Friendly Manor Nursing Home Company, Eufaula, OK
Friendly Nursing Home, Pitman, PA
Friendly Nursing Home Inc, Miamisburg, OH
Friendly Village, Rhinelander, WI
Friends Care Center, Yellow Springs, OH
Friends Fellowship Community Inc, Richmond, IN
Friends Hall at West Chester, West Chester, PA
Friends Home at Woodstown, Woodstown, NJ
Friends Homes Inc, Greensboro, NC
Friends House, Santa Rosa, CA
Friends Nursing Home Inc, Sandy Spring, MD
Friendship Care Center, Herrin, IL
Friendship Care Center, Marion, IL
Friendship Community, Lititz, PA
Friendship Haven, Chattanooga, TN
Friendship Haven I, Sherburn, MN
Friendship Haven II, Sherburn, MN
Friendship Haven Inc, Fort Dodge, IA
Friendship Health Center, Portland, OR
Friendship Healthcare Center, McVille, ND
Friendship Home, Audubon, IA
Friendship Home, Deadwood, SD
Friendship Homes, National City, CA
Friendship House, Willmar, MN
Friendship House Fellowship Home, Danville, KY
Friendship House Inc, Kalispell, MT
Friendship Manor, Rock Island, IL
Friendship Manor, Scottsville, KY
Friendship Manor Care Center, Grinnell, IA
Friendship Manor Convalescent Center, National City, CA
Friendship Manor Lakeside, Lakeside, CA
Friendship Manor Nursing Home, Nashville, IL
Friendship Manor Nursing Home, Pewee Valley, KY
Friendship Manor Nursing Home, Detroit, MI
Friendship Manor Nursing Home, Roanoke, VA
Friendship Nursing Home Inc, Cleveland, GA
Friendship Villa, Spalding, NE
Friendship Villa Care Center, Miles City, MT
Friendship Village, Waterloo, IA
Friendship Village, Kalamazoo, MI
Friendship Village, Bloomington, MN
Friendship Village, Dayton, OH
Friendship Village, Milwaukee, WI
Friendship Village Health Center, Columbus, OH
Friendship Village of Dublin Health Center, Dublin, OH
Friendship Village of South County, Saint Louis, MO
Friendship Village of South Hills, Pittsburgh, PA
Friendship Village of Tempe, Tempe, AZ
Friendship Village of West County, Chesterfield, MO
Friendship Village—Schaumburg, Schaumburg, IL
Friendsview Manor Infirmary, Newberg, OR
Friendswood Arms Convalescent Center, Friendswood, TX
Frigon Nursing Home Inc, Central Falls, RI
Front Steps, Shakopee, MN
Frontier Extended Care Facility, Longview, WA

Frontier Manor, Gainesville, TX
Frostburg Community Hospital Extended Care Facility, Frostburg, MD
Frostburg Village of Allegany County, Frostburg, MD
Fruitvale Care Convalescent Hospital, Oakland, CA
Fryeburg Health Care Center, Fryeburg, ME
Fuller House, Stoneham, MA
Fullerton Manor, Fullerton, NE
Fulton County Family Care Home, Wauseon, OH
Fulton County Infirmary, Gloversville, NY
Fulton County Medical Center, McConnellsburg, PA
Fulton County Nursing Center, Salem, AR
Fulton Manor Care Center, Fulton, MO
Fulton Medical Care Center, Perrinton, MI
Fulton Presbyterian Manor, Fulton, MO
Furgala Nursing Home, Lancaster, NY
G A F Lake Cook Terrace, Northbrook, IL
A G Gaston Home for Senior Citizens, Birmingham, AL
Gables, Rochester, MN
Gables Inc, West Hartford, CT
Gables Nursing Home, Madison, OH
Gade Nursing Home Inc, Greenville, OH
Gade Nursing Home Inc 1, Greenville, OH
Gadsden Health Care Center Inc, Gadsden, AL
Gadsden Nursing Home, Quincy, FL
Gafney Home for the Aged, Rochester, NH
Gaines Mill Place, Springfield, IL
Gainesville Convalescent Center, Gainesville, TX
Gainesville Health Care Center, Gainesville, GA
Gainesville Health Care Center Inc, Gainesville, MO
Gainesville Manor, Hopkinsville, KY
Gainesville Nursing Center, Gainesville, FL
Galaxy Manor Nursing Center, Cleveland, TX
Gale Home, Manchester, NH
Galena Manor, Galena, KS
Galena Park Home, Peoria, IL
Galena Park Nursing Home, Peoria Heights, IL
Galena Stauss Hospital & Nursing Care Facility, Galena, IL
Galesburg Nursing & Rehabilitation Center, Galesburg, IL
Galilean Center, Anadarko, OK
Caroline K Galland Home, Seattle, WA
Gallatin County Rest Home, Bozeman, MT
Gallatin Health Care Associates, Gallatin, TN
Gallatin Sunrise Center, Gallatin, MO
Gallipolis Development Center, Gallipolis, OH
Gallup Care Center, Gallup, NM
Gamma Road Lodge, Wellsville, MO
Garber Nursing Home, Garber, OK
Garden County Lewellen Nursing Home, Lewellen, NE
Garden Court Nursing Center Inc, Bossier City, LA
Garden Crest Convalescent Hospital, Los Angeles, CA
Garden Family Care Home, Maumee, OH
Garden Gate Manor, Cheektowaga, NY
Garden Grove Convalescent Hospital, Garden Grove, CA
Garden Manor Extended Care Center Inc, Middletown, OH
Garden Manor Nursing Home Inc, Lakewood, CO
Garden Nursing Home & Convalescent Hospital, Santa Cruz, CA
Garden of the Gods Care Center, Colorado Springs, CO
Garden Plaza Convalescent Hospital, Los Angeles, CA
Garden Pointe Care Center Inc, Black Jack, MO
Garden State Health Care Center, East Orange, NJ
Garden State Manor, Holmdel, NJ
Garden Terrace Healthcare Center, Vista, CA
Garden Terrace Manor, Spokane, WA

Garden Terrace Nursing Center, Douglasville, GA
Garden Terrace Nursing Center, Graham, TX
Garden Terrace Nursing Home, Chatham, NJ
Garden Valley Retirement Village, Garden City, KS
Garden View Care Center, Shenandoah, IA
Garden View Care Center, O'Fallon, MO
Garden View Home, Chicago, IL
Garden Villa Nursing Home, El Campo, TX
Gardena Convalescent Center, Gardena, CA
Gardendale Nursing Home, Gardendale, AL
Gardendale Nursing Home, Jacksonville, TX
Gardens Skilled Nursing Facility, Sacramento, CA
Gardenview Care Center, Hillsboro, OR
Gardenview Nursing Home, Cincinnati, OH
Gardiner Group Home, Gardiner, ME
Gardiner Nursing Home, Houlton, ME
Gardner Heights Inc, Shelton, CT
Gardner House Rest Home, Roxbury, MA
Gardner Manor Nursing Home, Gardner, MA
Gardner Nursing Home of Star City Inc, Star City, AR
Gardner's Grove Nursing Home, Swansea, MA
Garfield County Health Center Inc, Jordan, MT
Garfield County Hospital District, Pomeroy, WA
Garfield Geropsychiatric Hospital, Oakland, CA
Garfield Memorial Hospital, Panguitch, UT
Garfield Park Health Facility, Indianapolis, IN
Garland Convalescent Center, Hot Springs, AR
Garland Convalescent Center, Garland, TX
Garland Rest Home, Newton, MA
Garlock Memorial Convalescent Home Inc, Hagerstown, MD
Garnets Chateau, Jerseyville, IL
Garrard Convalescent Home, Covington, KY
Garrard County Home for Senior Citizens, Lancaster, KY
Garrard County Memorial Hospital—SNF, Lancaster, KY
Garrett Park Manor, Dallas, TX
Garrison Memorial Hospital—ICF, Garrison, ND
Garrison Nursing Center, Garrison, ND
Garrison Nursing Home Inc, Baltimore, MD
Garrison Nursing Home Inc, Garrison, TX
Garrison Valley Center Inc, Garrison, MD
Garvey Manor Nursing Home, Hollidaysburg, PA
Marcus Garvey Nursing Company Inc, Brooklyn, NY
Garwood Home, Champaign, IL
Gary Memorial Hospital, Breaux Bridge, LA
Gasconade Manor Nursing & Care Center, Owensville, MO
Gaslite Villa Convalescent Center Inc, Canal Fulton, OH
Gaspard's Nursing Care Center Inc, Port Arthur, TX
Gassville Nursing Center, Gassville, AR
Gaston Memorial Hospital Extended Care Service, Gastonia, NC
Gatesway Foundation Inc, Broken Arrow, OK
Gatesway Foundation Inc II, Broken Arrow, OK
Gateway Care Center, Portland, OR
Gateway Manor Inc, Lincoln, NE
Gateways to Better Living 1, Youngstown, OH
Gateways to Better Living 3, Youngstown, OH
Gateways to Better Living 4, Youngstown, OH
Gateways to Better Living 5, Youngstown, OH
Gateways to Better Living 9, Youngstown, OH
Gateways to Better Living Inc, Austintown, OH
Gateways to Better Living No 8, Boardman, OH
Gateways to Better Living 10, Youngstown, OH
Gateways to Better Living 16, Youngstown, OH
Gaulden Manor, Baltimore, OH
Virginia Gay Hospital Inc, Vinton, IA

Gaye Haven Intermediate Care Facility Inc, Las Vegas, NV

Gayhart's Nursing Home, Waverly, OH

Gayle Street Residential Center, Fort Morgan, CO

Gaylord Community Hospital & Nursing Home, Gaylord, MN

Gaymont Nursing Center, Norwalk, OH

Geary Community Nursing Home, Geary, OK

Geer Memorial Health Center, Canaan, CT

Gem Care Center, Miami Beach, FL

Gem State Homes Inc 1, Nampa, ID

Gem State Homes Inc 2, Meridian, ID

General Baptist Nursing Home, Mount Carmel, IL

General Baptist Nursing Home, Campbell, MO

General Baptist Nursing Home, Independence, MO

General Care Convalescent Center, Clarksville, TN

General Hospital, Lovington, NM

Genesee County Nursing Home, Batavia, NY

Genesee Hospital Extended Care Facility, Rochester, NY

Genesee Nursing Home, Utica, NY

Geneseo Good Samaritan, Geneseo, IL

Genesis, Columbus, OH

Genesis House, Genoa, IL

Geneva Care Center, Geneva, IL

Geneva General Hospital Nursing Home Company Inc & Progressive Care Unit, Geneva, NY

Geneva Health Care, Geneva, OH

Geneva Lake Manor, Lake Geneva, WI

Genoa Care Center, Genoa, OH

Gentle Care of Loogootee, Loogootee, IN

Gentry House, Arma, KS

George Good Samaritan Center, George, IA

John George Home, Jackson, MI

Georgetown Manor, Louisville, KY

Georgetown Nursing Home Inc, Georgetown, OH

Georgetown Sweetbriar Nursing Home Inc, Georgetown, TX

Georgia Grace Memorial Home Inc, Statesboro, GA

Georgia Manor Nursing Home, Amarillo, TX

Georgia Regional Development Learning Center, Decatur, GA

Georgia Retardation Center, Atlanta, GA

Georgia Retardation Center—Athens, Athens, GA

Georgia War Veterans Nursing Home, Augusta, GA

Georgian Bloomfield, Birmingham, MI

Georgian Court Nursing & Rehabilitation Center, San Diego, CA

Georgian Court Nursing Home, Tulsa, OK

Georgian Court Nursing Home of Buffalo Inc, Buffalo, NY

Georgian Gardens, Potosi, MO

Georgian Home, Evanston, IL

Georgian House, Tacoma, WA

Georgiana Nursing Facility, Georgiana, AL

Gerald Caring Center, Gerald, MO

Gerarda House, Bloomington, MN

Geras Nursing Home, Mount Pleasant, TX

Geri-Care Inc, Cleveland, OH

Geriatric Authority of Milford Nursing Home, Milford, MA

Geriatric Center—Mansfield Memorial Homes, Mansfield, OH

Geriatrics Nursing Center, Jonesboro, AR

Geriatrics Nursing Center Inc—Forrest City, Forrest City, AR

Geriatrics Nursing Center Inc—Heber Springs, Heber Springs, AR

Geriatrics Nursing Center of West Memphis, West Memphis, AR

German Masonic Home Corp, New Rochelle, NY

German Old Folks Home Inc, Lawrence, MA

Germantown Home, Philadelphia, PA

Germantown Hospital Skilled Nursing Facility, Philadelphia, PA

Gertha's Nursing Center Inc, Evansville, IN

Gethsemane Group Home, Virginia, MN

Gettysburg Lutheran Retirement Village, Gettysburg, PA

Gettysburg Village Green Nursing Center, Gettysburg, PA

Ghana Village Nursing Home, Oklahoma City, OK

Gibbs Boarding Home, Wilmington, DE

Gibbs Care Center, Steelville, MO

Gibbs-McRaven Sheltered Care Home, Jonesboro, IL

Gibson Community Hospital Annex, Gibson City, IL

Gibson Manor, Gibson City, IL

Gibson Nursing Center, Aspermont, TX

Gibson Rest & Convalescent Home, Gibson, GA

Gibsonburg Health Care Center, Gibsonburg, OH

Giddings Convalescent Center, Giddings, TX

Carrie Elligson Gietner Home Inc, Saint Louis, MO

Gig Harbor Group Home, Gig Harbor, WA

Gil Mor Manor, Morgan, MN

Gila County Care Center, Globe, AZ

Gila Regional Medical Center, Silver City, NM

Gilbert Old Peoples Home of Ypsilanti, Ypsilanti, MI

Giles Family Care Home, Commerce City, CO

Gill Odd Fellows Home, Ludlow, VT

Gillett Nursing Home, Gillett, WI

Gillette Nursing Home, Warren, OH

Gillette's The Country Place, Warren, OH

Gilman Nursing Center, Gilman, IL

Gilman Nursing Home, Gilman, WI

Gilmer Convalescent & Nursing Center, Gilmer, TX

Gilmer Nursing Home, Saint Augustine, FL

Gilmer Nursing Home, Ellijay, GA

Gilmore's White-Cliff Nursing Home, Greenville, PA

Ginger Cove, Annapolis, MD

Girdler House, Beverly, MA

Girouard St Jude Nursing Home, South Barre, VT

Glacier County Medical Center Nursing Hom, Cut Bank, MT

Glacier Hills, Ann Arbor, MI

Glad Day Nursing Center, Beaumont, TX

Glades Health Care Center, Pahokee, FL

Gladeview Health Care Center, Old Saybrook, CT

Gladstone Convalescent Care Facility, Gladstone, OR

Gladstone Nursing Home, Kansas City, MO

Gladwin Nursing Home, Gladwin, MI

Gladwin Pines Nursing Home, Gladwin, MI

Glanzman Colonial Nursing Center, Toledo, OH

Glasgow Health Care Facility, Glasgow, KY

Glasgow Nursing Home, Cambridge, MD

Glasgow State—ICF, Glasgow, KY

Glastonbury Health Care Center, Glastonbury, CT

Glen Arvin Personal Care Home, Lexington, KY

Glen Ayr Health Center, Lakewood, CO

Glen Bridge Nursing & Rehabilitation Center, Niles, IL

Glen Ellen Convalescent Hospital, Hayward, CA

Glen Field Health Care Center, Milwaukee, WI

Glen Halla Intermediate Care Facility, Henderson, NV

Glen Haven Home, Glenwood, IA

Glen Hazel Regional Center, Pittsburgh, PA

Glen Hill Convalescent Center, Danbury, CT

Glen Manor, Cincinnati, OH

Glen Oaks Convalescent Center, Shelbyville, TN

Glen Oaks Home, Shreveport, LA

Glen Oaks Nursing Home, New London, MN

Glen Oaks Nursing Home, Lucedale, MS

Glen Oaks Nursing Home Inc, Northbrook, IL

Glen Orchard Home, Cincinnati, OH

Glen Parke, Cincinnati, OH

Glen Retirement Village, Shreveport, LA

Glen Ridge Manor, Glendale, AZ

Glen Rose Nursing Home, Glen Rose, TX

Glen Terrace Convalescent Center, Norwalk, CA

Glen Valley Nursing Home, Glenwood Springs, CO

Glenburn Rest Haven Home Inc, Linton, IN

Glenburney Nursing Home, Natchez, MS

Glencoe Area Health Center, Glencoe, MN

Glencrest Nursing Rehabilitation Center Ltd, Chicago, IL

Glencroft Care Center, Glendale, AZ

Glendale Care Center, Glendale, AZ

Glendale Health Care Center Inc, Naugatuck, CT

Glendale Home, Mansfield, OH

Glendale Manor, Topeka, KS

Glendale Memorial Hospital & Health Center Skilled Nursing Facility, Glendale, CA

Glendale Nursing Home, Glendale, AZ

Glendale Nursing Home, Woburn, MA

Glendale Nursing Home, Scotia, NY

Glendale Nursing Home Inc, Wadley, GA

Glendeen Nursing Home, Billings, MT

Glendive Medical Center—Nursing Home, Glendive, MT

Glendora Nursing Home, Wooster, OH

Glengariff Health Care Center, Glen Cove, NY

Glenhaven Care Center, Glenwood City, WI

Glenkirk Circle, Mundelein, IL

Glenlora Nursing Home, Chester, NJ

Glenmont, Hilliard, OH

Glenmore Recovery Center, Crookston, MN

Glenn Haven Nursing Home, Dayton, OH

Glenn Ireland II Development Center, Tarrant, AL

Glenn View Manor, Mineral Ridge, OH

Glennon Place, Kansas City, MO

Glenoaks Convalescent Hospital, Glendale, CA

Glenpool Health Care Center, Glenpool, OK

Glenridge Center, Glendale, CA

Glenside Manor Haverford State Hospital LTC, Haverford, PA

Glenside Nursing Home, New Providence, NJ

Glenview Manor, Glasgow, KY

Glenview of Tyler Nursing Home Inc, Tyler, TX

Glenview Terrace Nursing Home, Glenview, IL

Glenvue Nursing Home, Glenville, GA

Glenward Health Care Center, Hamilton, OH

Glenwood Care, Salt Lake City, UT

Glenwood Care Center, Defiance, OH

Glenwood Christian Nursing Home, Lamont, MI

Glenwood Convalescent Center, Florence, AL

Glenwood Convalescent Home, Lowell, MA

Glenwood Convalescent Hospital, Oxnard, CA

Glenwood Estate, Independence, KS

Glenwood Hills Intermediate Care Facility, Raleigh, NC

Glenwood Manor, Decatur, GA

Glenwood Nursing Home Inc, Glenwood, AR

Glenwood Park United Methodist Home, Princeton, WV

Glenwood Regional Medical Center Skilled Nursing Facility, West Monroe, LA

Glenwood Retirement Home Inc, Glenwood, MN

Glenwood State Hospital & School, Glenwood, IA

Glenwood Terrace, Springfield, IL

Glenwood Terrace Ltd, Glenwood, IL

Glisan Care Center Inc, Portland, OR

Gloucester Manor, Sewell, NJ

Gloversville Extended Care & Nursing Home Co Inc, Gloversville, NY

Glynn Memorial Home, Haverhill, MA

Gnaden Huetten Nursing & Convalescent Center, Lehighton, PA

Go Ye Village Med-Center, Tahlequah, OK

Goddard House, A Retirement & Nursing Home, Boston, MA

Goddard House Home for Aged Men, Worcester, MA

Godfrey's Foothill Retreat, Brigham City, UT

Gogebic Medical Care Facility, Wakefield, MI

Gold City Convalescent Center Inc, Dahlonega, GA

Gold Country Health Center, Placerville, CA

Gold Crest Nursing Home, Cincinnati, OH

Gold Crest Retirement Center, Adams, NE

Gold Star Nursing Home, Danville, PA

Gold Star Nursing Home, Goldthwaite, TX

Golden Acres, Onaga, KS

Golden Acres Intermediate Care Facility, Iva, SC

Golden Acres Manor, Carrington, ND

Golden Acres Nursing Home, Leoti, KS

Golden Age, Roseville, MN

Golden Age, Tomahawk, WI

Golden Age Care Center, Centerville, IA

Golden Age Care Center, Oregon City, OR

Golden Age Care Center, Amarillo, TX

Golden Age Convalescent Hospital, Capitola, CA

Golden Age Guest Home, Albert Lea, MN

Golden Age Health Care, Daytona Beach, FL

Golden Age Home, Lockhart, TX

Golden Age Inc, Lexington, NC

Golden Age Lodge of Burlington, Burlington, KS

Golden Age Manor, Dublin, TX

Golden Age Manor, Amery, WI

Golden Age Manor—Holmes, Houston, TX

Golden Age Manor—Long Point, Houston, TX

Golden Age Manor—North Loop, Houston, TX

Golden Age Manor—Rookin, Houston, TX

Golden Age Nursing Center, Jena, LA

Golden Age Nursing Home, Marion, IN

Golden Age Nursing Home, Denham Springs, LA

Golden Age Nursing Home, Greenwood, MS

Golden Age Nursing Home, Stover, MO

Golden Age Nursing Home, Lubbock, TX

Golden Age Nursing Home District, Braymer, MO

Golden Age Nursing Home Inc, Cleburne, TX

Golden Age Nursing Home of Guthrie Inc, Guthrie, OK

Golden Age Retirement Home, Cincinnati, OH

Golden Charm Nursing Center, Liberty, TX

Golden Crest Nursing Center Inc, North Providence, RI

Golden Crest Nursing Home, Hibbing, MN

Golden Doors of Franklin Parish Inc, Winnsboro, LA

Golden Empire Convalescent Hospital, Grass Valley, CA

Golden Gate Health Care Center, Staten Island, NY

Golden Good Shepherd Home Inc, Golden, IL

Golden Haven Nursing Home, Toledo, OH

Golden Heights Health Care Center Inc, Bridgeport, CT

Golden Heights Living Center, Garnett, KS

Golden Heritage Care Center, Temple, TX

Golden Hill Health Care Center, San Diego, CA

Golden Hill Health Care Center, Milford, CT

Golden Hill Nursing Home Inc, New Castle, PA

Golden Keys Nursing Home, Neodesha, KS

Golden Manor Inc, Steele, ND

Golden Manor Jewish Home for the Aged, San Antonio, TX

Golden Manor Nursing Home, Crane, TX

Golden Mesa Nursing Home, Mesa, AZ

Golden Oaks Nursing Home, South Saint Paul, MN

Golden Oaks Nursing Home Inc, Laurel, MD

Golden Palms Retirement & Health Center, Harlingen, TX

Golden Plains Care Center, Big Spring, TX

Golden Plains Care Center, Canyon, TX

Golden Plains Care Center, Hereford, TX

Golden Plains Care Center, Post, TX

Golden Plains Health Care Center, Hutchinson, KS

Golden Rule Home Inc, Shawnee, OK

Golden Rule Nursing Center, Richmond, IN

Golden Slipper Club Uptown Home, Philadelphia, PA

Golden Springs Health Care Center, Anniston, AL

Golden State Colonial Convalescent Hospital, North Hollywood, CA

Golden State Habilitation Convalescent Center, Baldwin Park, CA

Golden State West Valley Convalescent Hospital, Canoga Park, CA

Golden Triangle Convalescent Center, Port Arthur, TX

Golden Triangle Nursing Center, Murrieta, CA

Golden West Convalescent Hospital, Hawthorne, CA

Golden West Nursing Home Inc, Fort Collins, CO

Golden West Skills Center, Goodland, KS

Golden Years, Harrisonville, MO

Golden Years Convalescent Center, Portsmouth, OH

Golden Years Haven, Decatur, TX

Golden Years Home, Walworth, WI

Golden Years Homestead Inc, Fort Wayne, IN

Golden Years Lodge, Mount Pleasant, TX

Golden Years Manor, Lonoke, AR

Golden Years Manor, Felton, DE

Golden Years Nursing Home, Falcon, NC

Golden Years Nursing Home, Hamilton, OH

Golden Years Rest Home, Lackey, KY

Golden Years Rest Home, Marlin, TX

Golden Years Retirement Center, Oxford, MS

Golden Years Retreat, Bridgeport, TX

Goldenrod Manor Care Center, Clarinda, IA

Goldenview Health Care Center, Meredith, NH

George J Goldman Memorial Home for the Aged, Niles, IL

Goldwater Memorial Hospital, New York, NY

Golfcrest Nursing Home, Hollywood, FL

Golfview Manor Nursing Home, Aliquippa, PA

Golfview Nursing Home, Saint Petersburg, FL

Goliad Manor Inc, Goliad, TX

Good Neighbor Home, Manchester, IA

Good Neighbors Inc, Bridgton, ME

Good Samaritan, Rugby, ND

Good Samaritan Care Center, Phoenix, AZ

Good Samaritan Cedar Lodge, Hot Springs Village, AR

Good Samaritan Center, Idaho Falls, ID

Good Samaritan Center, Algona, IA

Good Samaritan Center, Estherville, IA

Good Samaritan Center, Forest City, IA

Good Samaritan Center, Ottumwa, IA

Good Samaritan Center, Postville, IA

Good Samaritan Center, Atwood, KS

Good Samaritan Center, Dodge City, KS

Good Samaritan Center, Junction City, KS

Good Samaritan Center, Clearbrook, MN

Good Samaritan Center, East Grand Forks, MN

Good Samaritan Center, Jackson, MN

Good Samaritan Center, Pelican Rapids, MN

Good Samaritan Center, Warren, MN

Good Samaritan Center, Gibbon, NE

Good Samaritan Center, Nelson, NE

Good Samaritan Center, Syracuse, NE

Good Samaritan Center, Osnabrock, ND

Good Samaritan Center, Sioux Falls, SD

Good Samaritan Convalescent Center, Antioch, TN

Good Samaritan Country Home, Malta, MT

Good Samaritan Health Care Center, Yakima, WA

Good Samaritan Home, Colby, KS

Good Samaritan Home, Menominee, MI

Good Samaritan Home, Saint Louis, MO

Good Samaritan Home, Liverpool, PA

Good Samaritan Home Inc, Evansville, IN

Good Samaritan Home Inc, Oakland City, IN

Good Samaritan Home of Flanagan, Flanagan, IL

Good Samaritan Home of Quincy, Quincy, IL

Good Samaritan Hospital, Zanesville, OH

Good Samaritan Luther Manor, Sioux Falls, SD

Good Samaritan Nursing Home, Saint Petersburg, FL

Good Samaritan Nursing Home, East Peoria, IL

Good Samaritan Nursing Home, Knoxville, IL

Good Samaritan Nursing Home, Cole Camp, MO

Good Samaritan Nursing Home, Sayville, NY

Good Samaritan Nursing Home Company Inc, Delmar, NY

Good Samaritan Nursing Home Inc, Avon, OH

Good Samaritan Rehabilitation & Care Center, Stockton, CA

Good Samaritan Village, Moscow, ID

Good Samaritan Village, Saint Francis, KS

Good Samaritan Village, Winfield, KS

Good Samaritan Village, Pipestone, MN

Good Samaritan Village, Alliance, NE

Good Samaritan Village, Sioux Falls, SD

Good Samaritan Village—Perkins Pavilion, Hastings, NE

Good Samaritan Village—Villa Grace, Hastings, NE

Good Samaritans Nursing Home Inc, Franklinton, LA

Good Shepherd Home Long-Term Care Facility Inc, Allentown, PA

Good Shepard Lutheran Home of the West, Littleton, CO

Good Shepherd Village, Springfield, OH

Good Shepherd Convalescent Center, Lakeview Terrace, CA

Good Shepherd Convalescent Hospital, Santa Monica, CA

Good Shepherd Geriatric Center, Mason City, IA

Good Shepherd Health Care Facility, Auburn, ME

Good Shepherd Home, Watford City, ND

Good Shepherd Home, Fostoria, OH

Good Shepherd Home for the Aged, Ashland, OH

Good Shepherd Home Ltd, Seymour, WI

Good Shepherd Lutheran Home, Rushford, MN

Good Shepherd Lutheran Home, Sauk Rapids, MN

Good Shepherd Lutheran Home, Blair, NE

Good Shepherd Lutheran Home, Cornelius, OR

Good Shepherd Nursing Home, Versailles, MO

Good Shepherd Nursing Home, Wheeling, WV

Good Shepherd Nursing Home & Residential Care Facility, Lockwood, MO

Good Shepherd Retirement Center, Peoria, AZ

Good Shepherd Villa, Mesa, AZ

Goodin's Rest Home, Columbia, KY

Goodman Gardens Nursing Home Company Inc, Rochester, NY

Goodwater Nursing Home, Goodwater, AL

Goodwill Intermediate Care Home, Brunswick, GA

Goodwill Mennonite Home Inc, Grantsville, MD

Goodwill Nursing Home, Macon, GA

Goodwin House, Alexandria, VA

Goodwin's of Exeter, Exeter, NH

Gordon Good Samaritan Center, Gordon, NE

Gordon Health Care Inc, Calhoun, GA

Gordon Lane Convalescent Hospital, Fullerton, CA

Gordon Memorial Health Care Facility, Spencer, WV

Gorham House, Gorham, ME

Goshen County Memorial Nursing Home, Torrington, WY

Gospel Light Nursing Home, Kingston, OH

Gosport Nursing Home, Gosport, IN

Mary Goss Nursing Home Inc, Monroe, LA

Gottesfeld House, Denver, CO

Governor Bacon Health Center, Delaware City, DE

Governor Harris Homestead, Eaton, OH

Governor Winthrop Nursing Home, Winthrop, MA

Governor's House, Lewistown, MT
Governor's House Nursing Home, Huntington, MA
Governors Park Nursing & Rehabilitation Center, Barrington, IL
Gowanda Nursing Home, Gowanda, NY
Gower Convalescent Center Inc, Gower, MO
Gowrie Manor, Gowrie, IA
Grace Brethren Village, Englewood, OH
Grace Convalescent Center, Detroit, MI
Grace Home, Graceville, MN
Grace Lodge Health Care Unit, Lynchburg, VA
Grace Manor Care Center, Burlington, CO
Grace Manor Nursing Home, Cincinnati, OH
Grace Nursing Home, Clinton, LA
Grace Nursing Home Inc, Livingston, CA
Grace Plaza of Great Neck Inc, Great Neck, NY
Grace Presbyterian Village, Dallas, TX
Grace Village Health Care Facility, Winona Lake, IN
Graceland Manor, Lawson, MO
Gracelands Inc, Oxford, MS
Graceland's of Pontotoc, Pontotoc, MS
Gracell Terrace, Chicago, IL
Gracewood Developmental Center, Gracewood, GA
Gracewood Nursing Home, Gracewood, GA
Gracewood State School & Hospital, Gracewood, GA
Grafton County Nursing Home, Woodsville, NH
Grafton Oaks Nursing Center, Dayton, OH
Graham Street Community Residence, Florence, SC
Graham's Nursing Home Inc, Valencia, PA
Theron Grainger Nursing Home, Hughes Springs, TX
Gramercy Park Nursing Center, Miami, FL
Grampian Nursing Home, Boston, MA
Granada Convalescent Hospital, Eureka, CA
Granada de Santa Fe, Santa Fe, NM
Granada Hills Convalescent Hospital, Granada Hills, CA
Granada Nursing Center, Baltimore, MD
Granbury Care Center, Granbury, TX
Grancare Nursing Center, Fond Du Lac, WI
Grancare Nursing Center, Green Bay, WI
Grancell Village of the Jewish Homes for the Aging, Reseda, CA
Grand Avenue Convalescent Hospital, Long Beach, CA
Grand Avenue Rest Home, Minneapolis, MN
Grand Bay Convalescent Home, Grand Bay, AL
Grand Blanc Convalescent Center, Grand Blanc, MI
Grand Care Convalescent Hospital, Anaheim, CA
Grand Chariton Manor Inc, Brunswick, MO
Grand Haven Nursing Home, Cynthiana, KY
Grand Island Manor Nursing Home, Grand Island, NY
Grand Islander Health Care Center, Middletown, RI
Grand Junction Care Center, Grand Junction, CO
Grand Junction Regional Center, Grand Junction, CO
Grand Lake Manor, Grove, OK
Grand Manner Inc, Geneva, OH
Grand Manor Health Related Facility, Bronx, NY
Grand Oaks Healthcare Center, Boise, ID
Grand Park Convalescent Hospital, Los Angeles, CA
Grand Place, Lakewood, CO
Grand Place, Stratford, OK
Grand Saline Manor, Grand Saline, TX
Grand Terrace Convalescent Hospital, Colton, CA
Grand Traverse Medical Care Facility, Traverse City, MI
Grand Valley Hospital, Pryor, OK
Grand Valley Nursing Center, Grand Rapids, MI
Grand View Care Center Inc, Blair, WI

Grand View Hospital Skilled Nursing Facility, Sellersville, PA
Grand View Rest Home, Fitchburg, MA
Grandview Care Center, Dayton, IA
Grandview Care Center, Saint Peter, MN
Grandview Care Center, Roseburg, OR
Grandview Center Inc, Athens, GA
Grandview Christian Home, Cambridge, MN
Grandview Convalescent Center, Martinsville, IN
Grandview Health Care, Oil City, PA
Grandview Health Care Center, Jasper, GA
Grandview Health Care Center, Grenada, MS
Grandview Health Care Center, Dayton, OH
Grandview Health Homes Inc, Danville, PA
Grandview HealthCare Center, Oelwein, IA
Grandview Heights, Marshalltown, IA
Grandview Living Center, Martinsville, IN
Grandview Manor, Berthoud, CO
Grandview Manor, Campbell, NE
Grandview Manor Care Center, Grandview, MO
Grandview Manor Care Center, Junction City, OR
Grandview Manor Nursing Home, Camp Point, IL
Grandview Nursing Home, Grandview, TX
Grandview Nursing Home Inc, Cumberland, RI
Grandview Resident Home for Senior Citizens, Grand Rapids, MI
Grandvue Medical Care Facility, East Jordan, MI
Grange Nursing Home, Mascoutah, IL
Granger Manor, Granger, IA
Grangers Nursing Home, Northborough, MA
Grangeville Convalescent Inc, Grangeville, ID
Granite Care Home, Sauk Rapids, MN
Granite County Memorial Nursing Home, Philipsburg, MT
Granite Farms Estates Medical Facility, Wawa, PA
Grant County Nursing Home, Sheridan, AR
Grant County Nursing Home, Petersburg, WV
Grant Cuesta Convalescent Hospital, Mountain View, CA
Grant Manor Inc, Williamstown, KY
Grant Manor Nursing Center, Colfax, LA
Grant Park Care Center, Washington, DC
Grants Good Samaritan Center, Grants, NM
Grants Lake IC Home, Butler, KY
Grants Lake Rest Home, Butler, KY
Granville County Group Home, Oxford, NC
Grapeland Nursing Home, Grapeland, TX
Grasmere Resident Home Inc, Chicago, IL
Grass Valley Convalescent Hospital, Grass Valley, CA
Gravette Manor Nursing Home, Gravette, AR
Gravlin Square, Bradley, IL
Gravois Health Care Center, Saint Louis, MO
Gray Nursing Home, Gray, GA
Grays Harbor Convalescent Center, Aberdeen, WA
Grays Nursing Home Inc, Platteville, WI
Grayson Manor Nursing Home, Leitchfield, KY
Grayson Square Health Care Center Inc, San Antonio, TX
Graystone Home Inc, Franklin, TN
Graystone Manor Convalescent Center, Portland, OR
Graystone Manor Nursing Home 2, Houston, TX
Graysville Nursing Home, Graysville, TN
Great Barrington Healthcare Nursing Home, Great Barrington, MA
Great Bend Manor, Great Bend, KS
Great Hall-Riverbend Center for Mental Health, Tuscumbia, AL
Great Lakes Care Center, Detroit, MI
Great Oaks Center, Silver Spring, MD
Great Oaks Inc, Kansas City, MO
Great Oaks Nursing Home, Roswell, GA
Great River Care Center, McGregor, IA
Great Southwest Convalescent Center, Grand Prairie, TX
Great Trail Care Center, Minerva, OH

Greater Harlem Nursing Home Company Inc, New York, NY
Greater Laurel Nursing Home, Laurel, MD
Greeley Care Home, Greeley, NE
Greeley Healthcare Center, Stillwater, MN
Mary Greeley Medical Center, Ames, IA
Green Acres Adams County Home, Gettysburg, PA
Green Acres Care Center, Gooding, ID
Green Acres Care Center, South Sioux City, NE
Green Acres Convalescent Center, Baytown, TX
Green Acres Convalescent Center, Beaumont, TX
Green Acres Convalescent Center, Center, TX
Green Acres Convalescent Center, Huntsville, TX
Green Acres Convalescent Center, Vidor, TX
Green Acres Convalescent Center, Bridge City, TX
Green Acres Convalescent Center, Humble, TX
Green Acres Healthcare, Mayfield, KY
Green Acres Inc, Milledgeville, GA
Green Acres Lodge, Rosemead, CA
Green Acres Manor, Toms River, NJ
Green Acres Nursing Home, North Branch, MN
Green Acres Nursing Home, Washington Court House, OH
Green Acres Nursing Home, Emory, TX
Green Acres Nursing Home Inc, Kenton, OH
Green Acres Rehabilitation Nursing Center, Wyndmoor, PA
Green Briar Nursing Center, Miami, FL
Green Cove Springs Geriatric Center, Green Cove Springs, FL
Green Hill Manor, Greensburg, KY
Green-Hill Manor Inc, Fowler, IN
Green Hills Center, West Liberty, OH
Green Hills Health Center, Ames, IA
Green Home Inc, Wellsboro, PA
Green Lea Manor, Mabel, MN
Green Meadows Health Care Inc, Linn, MO
Green Meadows Nursing Center, Haysville, KS
Green Mountain Nursing Home, Colchester, VT
Green Oak Nursing Home, Brockton, MA
Green Pine Acres Nursing Home, Menahga, MN
Green Ridge Nursing Home, Scranton, PA
Green River Rest Home, Liberty, KY
Green River Terrace Nursing Home, Auburn, WA
Green Tree Ridge, Asheville, NC
Green Valley Care Center, Eugene, OR
Green Valley Convalescent Center, New Albany, IN
Green Valley Health Care Center, Carrollton, KY
Green Valley Health Care Center, Dickson, TN
Green View Nursing & Convalescent Center, Schuylkill Haven, PA
Green-Wood Health Care Center, Pleasantville, NJ
Greenacres Care Center, Gooding, ID
Greenbelt Nursing Center, Greenbelt, MD
Greenbough Nursing Center, Clarksdale, MS
Greenbrae Convalescent Hospital, Greenbrae, CA
Greenbriar Care Center, Howell, MI
Greenbriar Convalescent Center, Wheelersburg, OH
Greenbriar—East Nursing Center, Deptford, NJ
Greenbriar Manor, Carbondale, IL
Greenbriar Manor, Indianapolis, IN
Greenbriar Nursing & Convalescent Center, Woodbury, NJ
Greenbriar Nursing & Convalescent Home, Slidell, LA
Greenbriar Nursing Center, Bradenton, FL
Greenbriar Nursing Center of Hammonton, Hammonton, NJ
Greenbriar Nursing Home, Sterling, MI

Greenbriar Nursing Home, Carthage, NY
Greenbriar Terrace Healthcare, Nashua, NH
Greenbrier Manor, Lewisburg, WV
Greenbrier Nursing Center Inc, Champaign, IL
Greenbrier Nursing Home, Enid, OK
Greenbrook Manor, Monroe, MI
Greenbrook Manor, Greenwood, SC
Greenbrook Nursing Center, Saint Petersburg, FL
Greenbrook Nursing Home, Green Brook, NJ
Greenbush Community Hospital, Greenbush, MN
Greencastle Nursing Home, Greencastle, IN
Greencrest Manor Inc, Greenville, TX
Greencroft Nursing Center, Goshen, IN
Greendale Health Care Center, Sheboygan, WI
Greene Acres Manor, Greene, ME
Greene Acres Nursing Home Inc, Paragould, AR
Greene County Hospital—Extended Care Facility, Leakesville, MS
Greene County Hospital & Nursing Home, Eutaw, AL
Greene County Medical Center, Jefferson, IA
Greene Haven, Springfield, MO
Greene Oaks Health Center, Xenia, OH
Greene Point Health Care, Union Point, GA
Greenery Extended Care Center, Worcester, MA
Greenery Rehabilitation & Skilled Nursing Center, Boston, MA
Greenery Rehabilitation Center, Pacifica, CA
Greenery Rehabilitation Center, Durham, NC
Greenery Rehabilitation Center, Dallas, TX
Greenery Rehabilitation Center—Seattle, Seattle, WA
Greenewood Manor, Xenia, OH
Greenfield, Princeton, IL
Greenfield Convalescent Center, Bridgewater, NJ
Greenfield Manor, Greenfield, IA
Greenhaven Country Place, Sacramento, CA
Greenhill Farm, Kezar Falls, ME
Greenhill Nursing Home, DeQuincy, LA
Greenhill Residence, Biddeford, ME
Greenhurst Nursing Home, Charleston, AR
Greenlawn Avenue Group Home, Akron, OH
Greenlawn Nursing Home, Middleborough, MA
Greenlawn Nursing Home, Mentor, OH
Greenleaf, Moorestown, NJ
Greenleaf House Nursing Home, Salisbury, MA
Greenleaf House Nursing Home, Salisbury, PA
Greenleaf Nursing & Convalescent Center Inc, Doylestown, PA
Greenleaf Properties Inc, Newport, NH
Greenpark Care Center, Brooklyn, NY
Greenridge Nursing Care, Big Rapids, MI
Greens Geriatric Health Center Inc, Gary, IN
Green's Nursing Center, Kenedy, TX
Greensboro Health Care Center, Greensboro, NC
Greensboro Health Care Inc, Greensboro, AL
Greensboro Nursing Home, Greensboro, VT
Greensburg Home—Redstone Presbytery, Greensburg, PA
Greensburg Nursing & Convalescent Center, Greensburg, PA
Greensprings Manor Healthcare, South Bend, IN
Greensview Health Care Center, Bagley, MN
Greentree Health Care Center, Clintonville, WI
Greentree Health Center Inc, Houston, TX
Greentree Manor Convalescent Home, Waterford, CT
Greenvale Convalescent Hospital, San Pablo, CA
Greenview Health Center, Peshtigo, WI
Greenview Manor, Grand Rapids, MI
Greenview Manor, Waco, TX
Greenview Manor Nursing Home, Wakefield, MA
Greenville Care Center Inc, Greenville, MI

Greenville Convalescent Home Inc, Greenville, MS
Greenville Nursing Home, Greenville, AL
Greenville Nursing Home, Greenville, TX
Greenville Villa, Greenville, NC
Greenway Manor, Spring Green, WI
Greenwich Bay Manor, East Greenwich, RI
Greenwich Laurelton Nursing & Convalescent Home, Greenwich, CT
Greenwich Woods Health Care Center, Greenwich, CT
Greenwood Acres Nursing Home, Baltimore, MD
Greenwood Center, Sanford, ME
Greenwood Convalescent Center, Greenwood, IN
Greenwood Health Care Center, Greenwood, SC
Greenwood Health Center, Hartford, CT
Greenwood House Nursing Home Inc, Warwick, RI
Greenwood Manor Nursing Home, Jerseyville, IL
Greenwood Manor Nursing Home, Hamilton, OH
Greenwood Nursing Home, Wakefield, MA
Greenwood Oaks Rest Home, Warwick, RI
Greenwood Park Care Center Inc, Seattle, WA
Greenwood Residence East, Saint Paul, MN
Greenwood Residence West, Saint Louis Park, MN
Greenwood Village South, Greenwood, IN
Gregg Home for the Aged Inc, Kilgore, TX
Arnold Gregory Memorial Hospital Skilled Nursing Facility, Albion, NY
Gregory House, Topsham, ME
Gregston Nursing Home, Marlow, OK
Greycliff at Cape Ann Convalescent Center, Gloucester, MA
Greynolds Park Manor Inc, North Miami Beach, FL
Greynolds Park Manor Rehabilitation Center, North Miami Beach, FL
Greystone Healthcare Center, Blountville, TN
Greystone on the Greene Inc, Philadelphia, PA
Griffeth Nursing Home, Ashland, OH
Griffeth Nursing Home Inc, Lexington, OH
Griffin Home for the Aged, Corunna, MI
Griffin Nursing Center, Knoxville, IA
Maurice Griffith Manor, Casper, WY
Griggs County Nursing Home, Cooperstown, ND
Griswold Care Center Inc, Griswold, IA
Gronna Good Samaritan Center, Worcester, MA
Gross Convalescent Hospital, Lodi, CA
Grosse Pointe, Grosse Pointe Woods, MI
Grossmont Gardens Health Care Center, La Mesa, CA
Grosvenor Health Care Center, Bethesda, MD
Groton Regency Retirement & Nursing Center, Groton, CT
Groton Residential Care Facility, Groton, NY
Theresa Grotta Center, West Orange, NJ
Group Home I, Ellsworth, WI
Group Home III, Ellsworth, WI
Group Living Home, Spicer, MN
Grouse Valley Manor, Dexter, KS
Grove Health Care Center, Neptune, NJ
Grove Manor, Grove City, PA
Grove Manor Nursing Home, Honey Grove, TX
Grove Manor Nursing Home Inc, Waterbury, CT
Grove School Resident Center, Lake Forest, IL
Grovecrest Care Center of Clarkston, Clarkston, MI
Grovecrest Home for the Aged, Pontiac, MI
Grovemont Nursing & Rehabilitation, Winter Haven, FL
Groveton Nursing Home, Groveton, TX
Grundy Care Center, Grundy Center, IA
Grundy County Home, Morris, IL
Grundy County Memorial Hospital, Grundy Center, IA
Gruter Foundation Inc, Wooster, OH

Guardian Angel Health Care Center, Green Bay, WI
Guardian Angel Nursing Home Inc, Kansas City, MO
Guardian Care Inc, Orlando, FL
Guardian Care of Ahoskie, Ahoskie, NC
Guardian Care of Burgaw, Burgaw, NC
Guardian Care of Elizabeth City, Elizabeth City, NC
Guardian Care of Elkin, Elkin, NC
Guardian Care of Farmville, Farmville, NC
Guardian Care of Goldsboro, Goldsboro, NC
Guardian Care of Henderson, Henderson, NC
Guardian Care of Kenansville, Kenansville, NC
Guardian Care of Kinston, Kinston, NC
Guardian Care of Monroe, Monroe, NC
Guardian Care of New Bern, New Bern, NC
Guardian Care of Roanoke Rapids, Roanoke Rapids, NC
Guardian Care of Rocky Mt, Rocky Mount, NC
Guardian Care of Scotland Neck, Scotland Neck, NC
Guardian Care of Walnut Cove, Walnut Cove, NC
Guardian Care of Zebulon, Zebulon, NC
Guardian Rehabilitation Hospital Inc, Los Angeles, CA
Guest Care Center at Spring Lake, Shreveport, LA
Guest House of Nashville, Nashville, AR
Guest House of Slidell, Slidell, LA
Guest House, Rochester, MN
Guest House, Shreveport, LA
Guest Ranch Utopia, Sheridan, WY
Guggenheimer Nursing Home, Lynchburg, VA
Guidance Center Sanitarium, Anaheim, CA
Guild Hall, Saint Paul, MN
Guilderland Center Nursing Home Inc, Guilderland Center, NY
Guilford Convalesarium, Fayetteville, PA
Guilliams Family Home, West Lafayette, OH
Guinn Nursing Home 1, Jay, OK
Guinn Nursing Home 2, Jay, OK
Gulf Coast Center/Sunland, Fort Myers, FL
Gulf Coast Convalescent Center, Panama City, FL
Gulf Coast Nursing Home of Moss Point Inc, Moss Point, MS
Gulf Convalescent, Fort Walton, FL
Gulfport Convalescent Center, Gulfport, FL
Gull Harbour Apartments, Moorhead, MN
Gunnison Health Care Center, Gunnison, CO
Gunnison Valley Hospital, Gunnison, UT
Rosalind & Joseph Gurwin Jewish Geriatric Center of Long Island, Commack, NY
Guthrie Retirement & Care Center, Guthrie, OK
Guttenberg Care Center, Guttenberg, IA
Gwynedd Square Center for Nursing & Convalescent Care, Lansdale, PA
M & S Anderson Health Care Unit, Holdrege, NE
H & S Care Center, Tamms, IL
H E B Nursing Center, Bedford, TX
Harold S Haaland Home, Rugby, ND
Habersham Home, Demorest, GA
Ferrier Harris Home for Aged, Saint Louis, MO
Hacienda Care Center, Livermore, CA
Hacienda Care Center, Petaluma, CA
Hacienda Convalescent Hospital, Long Beach, CA
Hacienda Convalescent Hospital, Porterville, CA
Hacienda de la Mesa Convalescent Hospital, La Mesa, CA
Hacienda de los Angeles, Phoenix, AZ
Hacienda de Monterey, Palm Desert, CA
Hacienda de Salud, Espanola, NM
Hacienda de Salud, Raton, NM
Hacienda de Salud—Bloomfield, Bloomfield, NM
Hacienda de Salud—Silver City, Silver City, NM
Hacienda Health Care, Hanford, CA

Hacienda Home for Special Service, New Port Richey, FL
Hackett Hill Nursing Center, Manchester, NH
Haddonfield Presbyterian Home, Haddonfield, NJ
Hadley Manor, Detroit, MI
Hage House, Bloomington, IL
Henry Hagen Residence, Hastings, MN
Hahn Rest Home, Springfield, MA
Haida Manor, Hastings, PA
Haines City Health Care, Haines City, FL
Halcyon House, Washington, IA
Ha-le Aloha Convalescent Hospital, Ceres, CA
Hale Convalescent & Nursing Home Inc, Groton, MA
Hale Ho Aloha, Honolulu, HI
Hale House, Boston, MA
Hale Makua Kahului, Kahului, HI
Hale Makua—Wailuku, Wailuku, HI
Hale Malamalama, Honolulu, HI
Hale Nani Health Center, Honolulu, HI
Hale Omao Nursing Home, Lawai, HI
Hales Rest Home, Spanish Fork, UT
Haleyville Health Care Center, Haleyville, AL
Halifax Convalescent Center Ltd, Daytona, FL
Anthony Hall Nursing Home, Indianapolis, IN
Mattie C Hall Health Care Center, Aiken, SC
William T Hall Memorial Convalescent Home, Portsmouth, VA
Hallam Terrace, Rockford, IL
Hallandale Rehabilitation Center, Hallandale, FL
Hallmar, Mercy Medical Center, Cedar Rapids, IA
Hallmark Anderson Health Care Center, Houston, TX
Hallmark Care Center, Mount Vernon, IA
Hallmark Care Center, Sioux City, IA
Hallmark Care Center, Omaha, NE
Hallmark House, Pekin, IL
Hallmark Manor, Federal Way, WA
Hallmark Manor Nursing Home, Indianapolis, IN
Hallmark Nursing Center, Denver, CO
Hallmark Nursing Center—Anaheim, Anaheim, CA
Hallmark Nursing Center—Richmond, Richmond, CA
Hallmark Nursing Center—Simi Valley, Simi Valley, CA
Hallmark Nursing Center—Tustin, Santa Ana, CA
Hallmark Nursing Centre, Schenectady, NY
Hallmark Nursing Centre, Troy, NY
Hallmark Nursing Centre Inc, Glens Falls, NY
Hallmark Nursing Centre Inc, Minoa, NY
Hallmark Nursing Home, Warner Robins, GA
Hallmark Nursing Home of New Bedford, New Bedford, MA
Hallworth House, Providence, RI
Halstad Lutheran Memorial Home, Halstad, MN
Halsted Manor, Harvey, IL
Halsted Terrace Nursing Center, Chicago, IL
Haltom Convalescent Center, Fort Worth, TX
Hamburg Center, Hamburg, PA
Hamburg Center Annex, Wernersville, PA
Hamburg Health Care Center, Hamburg, NY
Hamden Health Care Facility, Hamden, CT
Hamilton Arms Nursing & Rehabilitation Center, Lancaster, PA
Hamilton County Eastern Star Home Inc, Cincinnati, OH
Hamilton County Nursing Home & Residential Care Unit, Chattanooga, TN
Hamilton County Rest Home, Syracuse, KS
Hamilton Grove, New Carlisle, IN
Hamilton Heights Health Center, Arcadia, IN
Hamilton Hill Crest Manor, Hamilton, MO
Hamilton House, Bozeman, MT
Hamilton House Health Care Facility, Columbus, GA
Hamilton Manor, Aurora, NE
Hamilton Manor Nursing Home, Rochester, NY
Hamilton Medical Center Hospital—Skilled Nursing Facility, Lafayette, LA
Hamilton Memorial Home, Two Rivers, WI

Hamilton Memorial Nursing Center, McLeansboro, IL
Hamilton Nursing Home, Detroit, MI
Hamilton Nursing Home, Beaumont, TX
Hamilton Nursing Home, Hamilton, TX
Hamilton Pavilion Healthcare, Norwich, CT
Hamilton Plaza Nursing Center, Passaic, NJ
Hamlet Manor, Chagrin Falls, OH
Hamlin Terrace Health Care Center, Buffalo, NY
Hammer Residence—Apartment & Annex, Wayzata, MN
Hammer Residence—Gleason Lake Residence, Wayzata, MN
Hammett House, Sterling, IL
Hammond Holiday Home, Larned, KS
Hammond House Convalescent Home, Worcester, MA
Hammond Nursing Home, Hammond, IN
Hammond Nursing Home, Hammond, LA
Hammond Rest Home, Fenton, MI
Hammond State School, Hammond, LA
Hammond-Whiting Convalescent Center, Whiting, IN
Hampden House Retirement Home, Springfield, MA
Hampshire County Long-Term Care Facility, Northampton, MA
Hampshire Manor Nursing Home, Easthampton, MA
Hampstead Nursing Home, Hampstead, TX
Hampton Care Center, Hampton, IA
Hampton Court, West Jefferson, OH
Hampton Drive, Colorado Springs, CO
Hampton Hills Nursing Home, Wilbraham, MA
Hampton House, Wilkes-Barre, PA
Hampton Manor, Bay City, MI
Hampton Nursing Care Inc, Alhambra, IL
Hampton Nursing Center Inc, Sumter, SC
Hampton Nursing Home, Hampton, AR
Hampton Plaza, Niles, IL
Hanceville Nursing Home, Hanceville, AL
Hancock County Nursing Home, Carthage, IL
Hancock County Rest Haven, Lewisport, KY
Hancock County Sheltered Care, Augusta, IL
Hancock Geriatric Treatment Center, Williamsburg, VA
Hancock Manor Nursing Home, Sneedville, TN
Hancock Park Convalescent Hospital & Rehabilitation Center, Los Angeles, CA
Handmaker Jewish Geriatric Center, Tucson, AZ
Hannan House, Detroit, MI
Hannum Memorial Rest Home Inc, Bradford, PA
Hanover General Hospital—Hillview, Hanover, PA
Hanover Hall, Hanover, PA
Hanover Hill Health Care Center, Manchester, NH
Hanover House Inc, Massillon, OH
Hanover House Nursing Home, Birmingham, AL
Hanover House Retirement Facility, Fall River, MA
Hanover Nursing Center, Hanover, IN
Hanover Terrace, Hanover, NH
Knud Hansen Memorial Hospital, Saint Thomas, VI
Hansford Manor, Spearman, TX
Hanson Court Convalescent Center, Springfield, VT
Hansons Boarding Home, Thief River Falls, MN
Happiness House Rest Home, North Easton, MA
Happy Acres Home, Ronan, MT
Happy Harbor Methodist Home, La Porte, TX
Happy Siesta Nursing Home, Remsen, IA
Gracelen Terrace Care Center, Portland, OR
Haralson County Nursing Home, Bremen, GA
Harbert Hills Academy Nursing Home, Savannah, TN
Harbor Beach Community Hospital, Harbor Beach, MI

Harbor Beach Convalescent Home, Fort Lauderdale, FL
Harbor Convalescent Hospital, Torrance, CA
Harbor Crest Home Inc, Fulton, IL
Harbor Health Care, Aberdeen, WA
Harbor Healthcare & Rehabilitation Center Inc, Lewes, DE
Harbor Hill Manor Rest Home, Lynn, MA
Harbor Hills, Santa Cruz, CA
Harbor Home, York Harbor, ME
Harbor Inn Nursing Home Inc, South Boston, MA
Harbor View Center, Long Beach, CA
Harbor View Health Care Center, Jersey City, NJ
Harbor View House, San Pedro, CA
Harbor View Manor, West Haven, CT
Harbors Health Facility, Douglas, MI
Harborview Health Care Center, Morehead City, NC
Harborview Manor—A Long-Term Care Facility, Dartmouth, MA
Harbour Manor Care Center of St John's, Noblesville, IN
Harbour's Edge, Delray Beach, FL
Hardee Manor Care Center, Wachula, FL
Hardin County Home, Kenton, OH
Hardin County Nursing Home, Savannah, TN
Hardin Home Nursing Home, Savannah, TN
Mary Harding Home, Owensboro, KY
Harding Nursing Home, Waterville, NY
Hardtner Medical Center, Olla, LA
Harford Gardens Convalescent Center Inc, Baltimore, MD
William L Hargrave Health Center, Davenport, FL
Harlan Appalachian Regional Hospital—ECF, Harlan, KY
Harlan Nursing Home, Harlan, KY
Harlee Manor, Springfield, PA
Harlem Rest Home, Harlem, MT
Harley Road Community Residence, Williston, SC
Harlingen Good Samaritan Center, Harlingen, TX
Harmon House, Mount Pleasant, PA
Harmony Community Hospital, Harmony, MN
Harmony Gardens Care Center, Seattle, WA
Harmony House, Brewster, WA
Harmony House Health Care Center, Waterloo, IA
Harmony House Nursing Home, Bend, OR
Harmony House Nursing Home Inc, Shreveport, LA
Harmony Nursing Home, Saint Paul, MN
Harold Group Home, Olathe, CO
Stiles M Harper Convalescent Center, Estill, SC
Harper's Home for the Aged, Edmonton, KY
Harpeth Terrace Convalescent Center, Franklin, TN
Harr-Wood Nursing Home, Oswego, NY
Harrah Nursing Center Inc, Harrah, OK
Harral's Nursing Home, Buhl, ID
Harris Health Center, East Providence, RI
Harrisburg Manor Inc, Harrisburg, IL
George L Harrison House Episcopal Hospital, Philadelphia, PA
Harrison House, Snow Hill, MD
Harrison House, Christiana, PA
Harrison House Inc, Cincinnati, OH
Harrison House of Delmar, Delmar, DE
Harrison House of Georgetown, Georgetown, DE
Harrison Intermediate Care Residence, Harrisonburg, VA
Harrison Memorial Hospital, Cynthiana, KY
Harrison Nursing Center, Harrison, AR
Harrisonburg Nursing Center, Harrisonburg, LA
Harrison's Sanitorium, Lexington, KY
Harrod Nursing Home, Centerburg, OH
Harrodsburg Health Care Manor, Harrodsburg, KY
Harrogate, Lakewood, NJ
Harston Hall Nursing & Convalescent Home Inc, Erdenheim, PA

Hart Care Center, Hartwell, GA
Hart County Personal Care Home, Munfordville, KY
Hart House, Peoria, IL
Nancy Hart Memorial Medical Center, Elberton, GA
John Edward Harter Nursing Center, Fairfax, SC
Hartford Care Center, Hartford, WI
Hartford City Community Care Center, Hartford City, IN
Hartford Manor, Hartford, KS
Hartington Nursing Center, Hartington, NE
Hartley Hall Inc, Pocomoke City, MD
Hartrick House, Peoria, IL
Hartshorn House Retirement Home, Taunton, MA
Hartsville Convalescent Center, Hartsville, TN
Hartville Health Care Center Inc, Hartville, OH
Hartville Meadows, Hartville, OH
Hartwyck at Cedar Brook, Plainfield, NJ
Hartwyck at Oak Tree, Edison, NJ
Hartwyck West Nursing Home, Cedar Grove, NJ
Harty Nursing Home, Knightsville, IN
Harvard Manor Nursing Home, Cambridge, MA
Harvard Nursing Home Inc, Worcester, MA
Harvard Rest Haven, Harvard, NE
Harvest Heights, Decatur, GA
Harvest Home Estates, Kansas City, MO
Harvest Manor Nursing Home, Denham Springs, LA
Harvey's Love & Care Inc, Six Mile, SC
Haskell Nursing Center, Haskell, TX
Haskell Shamrock Care Center, Haskell, OK
Haskins Nursing Home, Secane, PA
Hass Hillcrest Care Center, Hawarden, IA
Hastings Regional Center, Hastings, NE
Hatley Health Care Inc, Clanton, AL
Hattiesburg Convalescent Center, Hattiesburg, MS
Aase Haugen Homes Inc, Decorah, IA
Hautamaki Westgate Rest Haven, Ironwood, MI
Havana Healthcare Center, Havana, IL
Havasu Nursing Center, Lake Havasu, AZ
Haven Convalescent Home Inc, New Castle, PA
Haven Crest Inc, Monongahela, PA
Haven Hall Nursing Center, Brookhaven, MS
Haven Health Center, Red Wing, MN
Haven Heritage House Children's Center, Shelbyville, IN
Haven Hill Home, Brecksville, OH
Haven Hill Residential Home, Harrington, DE
Haven Home, Kenesaw, NE
Haven Homes Health Center, Hastings, MN
Haven Homes of Maple Plain, Maple Plain, MN
Haven House, Wahoo, NE
Haven in the Hills Inc, Bostic, NC
Haven Manor, Smyrna, DE
Haven Manor, Waco, TX
Haven Manor Nursing Home, Kansas City, MO
Haven Manor Nursing Home, Far Rockaway, NY
Haven Nursing Home, Baltimore, MD
Haven Nursing Home, Boston, MA
Haven Nursing Home, Mexia, TX
Haven of Our Lady of Peace, Pensacola, FL
Haven Park Nursing Center, Zeeland, MI
Havenwood Care Center Inc, Marysville, WA
Havenwood-Heritage Heights, Concord, NH
Havenwood Rest Home, New Bedford, MA
Haverford Nursing & Rehabilitation Center, Havertown, PA
Haverhill Care Center, West Palm Beach, FL
Haverhill Manor Nursing Home, Haverhill, MA
Hawaii Select Care Inc, Honolulu, HI
Hawkins Care Center, Hawkins, TX
Hazel Hawkins Convalescent Hospital, Hollister, CA
Jesse Frank Hawkins Nursing Home, Newberry, SC

Haws Memorial Nursing Home, Fulton, KY
E A Hawse Continuous Care Center, Baker, WV
Hawthorne, Reading, PA
Hawthorne Convalescent Center, Hawthorne, CA
Hawthorne House, Freeport, ME
Hawthorne House, Sedalia, MO
Hawthorne House, Missoula, MT
Hawthorne Manor, Spokane, WA
Hawthorne Nursing Center, Charlotte, NC
Haxtun Hospital District, Haxtun, CO
Hayden Manor Care Center, Scottsdale, AZ
Hayden's Personal Care Home, Lexington, KY
Hayes Care Home, Baltimore, MD
Hayes Convalescent Hospital, San Francisco, CA
Hayes Residence, Saint Paul, MN
Haym Salomon Home for the Aged, Brooklyn, NY
Hays Good Samaritan Center, Hays, KS
Hays House Nursing Home, Nowata, OK
Hayward Convalescent Hospital, Hayward, CA
Hayward Hills Convalescent Hospital, Hayward, CA
Hayward Nursing Home, Hayward, WI
Hazard Nursing Home, Hazard, KY
Hazelcrest Manor Nursing Home, Bloomfield, NJ
Hazelden Foundation, Center City, MN
Hazelden Pioneer House, Plymouth, MN
Hazelridge Road Residence, Roanoke, VA
Hazel's Rest Home, Watertown, SD
Hazelwood Intermediate Care Facility/Mental Retardation, Louisville, KY
Hazen Nursing Facility Inc, West Valley City, UT
Hazlet Manor Care Center, Hazlet, NJ
Hazleton Nursing & Geriatric Center, Hazelton, PA
HCA—Parkridge Medical Center Skilled Nursing Facility, Chattanooga, TN
HCE Glenn-Mor Home, Thomasville, GA
HDC Residential Center, Davenport, IA
Head Injury Recovery Center at Hillcrest, Milford, PA
Healdsburg Convalescent Hospital, Healdsburg, CA
Healdton Nursing Home, Healdton, OK
Healing Springs Intermediate Care Facility Inc, Blackville, SC
Health Care Center at Abbey Delray South, Delray Beach, FL
Health Care Center at Brandermill Woods, Midlothian, VA
Health Care Center at Washington, Sewell, NJ
Health Care Institute, Washington, DC
Health Care Manor, New Hampton, IA
Health Care of Brentwood, Lecanto, FL
Health Center, Alliance, OH
Health Center at Abbey Delray, Delray Beach, FL
Health Center at Oakwood Village, Springfield, OH
Health Center at the Forum—Pueblo Norte, Scottsdale, AZ
Health Center of the Forum at Brookside, Louisville, KY
Health Havens Nursing Center, East Providence, RI
Health Inn, Fayetteville, TN
Health Inn Nursing Home, Winchester, TN
Health One St Mary's, Winsted, MN
Health Regency Care Center, Andersonville, TN
Health Related Facility & Nursing Home Company of Rome Inc, Rome, NY
Healthaven Nursing Home, Akron, OH
The Healthcare Center, Elizabethtown, KY
Healthcare Center at the Forum, Overland Park, KS
Healthcare Center at the Remington Club, San Diego, CA
Healthcare of Hilton Head Inc, Hilton Head Island, SC
Healtheast Transitional Community Care—Bethesda, Saint Paul, MN
Healthhaven Nursing Center, Greensboro, NC

Healthsouth Regional Rehabilitation Center, Cutler Ridge, FL
Healthsouth Regional Rehabilitation Center, Miami, FL
HealthSouth Rehabilitation Center, Florence, SC
Healthsouth Rehabilitation Center of New Orleans, Harahan, LA
Healthwin Hospital, South Bend, IN
Heardmont Health Care Center, Elberton, GA
Heart of Georgia Nursing Home, Eastman, GA
Heart of Mercy T-4, Chicago, IL
Heart of Mercy T-7, Chicago, IL
Heart of the Valley Center, Corvallis, OR
Hearthside Care Center, Coos Bay, OR
Hearthside Haven Inc, Laurel, MS
Hearthside Homes, Tower, MN
Hearthstone, York, NE
Hearthstone, Seattle, WA
Hearthstone Manor, Medford, OR
Hearthstone Nursing Center, Saint John, KS
Hearthstone Nursing Home, Fort Worth, TX
Hearthstone of Mesa, Mesa, AZ
Hearthstone of Northern Nevada, Sparks, NV
Hearthstone of Sun City, Sun City, AZ
Hearthstone Resident Care Center, Stillwater, OK
Heartland—Beavercreek, Dayton, OH
Heartland Care Center—Belleville, Belleville, KS
Heartland Centre, Saint Joseph, MO
Heartland-Fairfield, Thornville, OH
Heartland Health Care Center—Canton, Canton, IL
Heartland Health Care Center—Henry, Henry, IL
Heartland Health Care Center—Paxton, Paxton, IL
Heartland Healthcare Center, Johnston City, IL
Heartland Healthcare Center, Elizabethtown, KY
Heartland—Holly Glen, Toledo, OH
Heartland Home, Park Rapids, MN
Heartland-Lansing Nursing Center, Bridgeport, OH
Heartland Manor Inc Nursing Center, Casey, IL
Heartland Manor—Wakeeney, Wakeeney, KS
Heartland of Beckley, Beckley, WV
Heartland of Bellefontaine, Bellefontaine, OH
Heartland of Bucyrus, Bucyrus, OH
Heartland of Cedar Springs, New Paris, OH
Heartland of Charleston, Charleston, WV
Heartland of Chillicothe, Chillicothe, OH
Heartland of Clarksburg, Clarksburg, WV
Heartland of Connersville, Connersville, IN
Heartland of Corpus Christi, Corpus Christi, TX
Heartland of Eaton, Eaton, OH
Heartland of Fulton, Fulton, MO
Heartland of Greenville, Greenville, OH
Heartland of Hillsboro, Hillsboro, OH
Heartland of Indian Lake, Indian Lake, OH
Heartland of Indian Lake Nursing Center, Lakeview, OH
Heartland of Indian Lake Rehabilitation Center, Lakeview, OH
Heartland of Jackson, Jackson, OH
Heartland of Kettering, Kettering, OH
Heartland of Keyser, Keyser, WV
Heartland of Liberty, Liberty, MO
Heartland of Marietta, Marietta, OH
Heartland of Martinsburg, Martinsburg, WV
Heartland of Marysville, Marysville, OH
Heartland of Mentor Nursing Center, Mentor, OH
Heartland of Milwaukee, Milwaukee, WI
Heartland of North East San Antonio, San Antonio, TX
Heartland of Oak Ridge, Miamisburg, OH
Heartland of Perrysburg, Perrysburg, OH
Heartland of Piqua, Piqua, OH
Heartland of Portsmouth, Portsmouth, OH
Heartland of Preston County, Kingwood, WV
Heartland of Rainelle, Rainelle, WV
Heartland of Riverview, South Point, OH

Heartland of St Petersburg, Saint Petersburg, FL

Heartland of Shawano, Shawano, WI

Heartland of Springfield, Springfield, OH

Heartland of Urbana, Urbana, OH

Heartland of Wauseon, Wauseon, OH

Heartland Rehabilitation Center, Wichita, KS

Heartland—Thurber Village, Columbus, OH

Heartland-Willow Lane Nursing Center, Butler, MO

Heartwood Avenue Living Center, Vallejo, CA

Heath Nursing & Convalescent Center, Newark, OH

Heather Hill, Willmar, MN

Heather Hill Inc, Chardon, OH

Heather Hill Nursing Home, New Port Richey, FL

Heather Manor, Des Moines, IA

Heather Manor Nursing Center, Hope, AR

Heatherbank, Columbia, PA

Heathergreen II Inc, Jamestown, OH

Heathergreene Inc, Xenia, OH

Heathwood Health Care Center Inc, Williamsville, NY

Heathwood Nursing & Retirement Home, Newton, MA

Heaton House, Montpelier, VT

Heavener Nursing Home, Heavener, OK

F Edward Hebert Hospital—SNF, New Orleans, LA

Hebert's Nursing Home Inc, Smithfield, RI

Hebrew Home for Aged Disabled, San Francisco, CA

Hebrew Home for the Aged at Riverdale, New York, NY

Hebrew Home for the Aged at Riverdale—Fairfield Division, Bronx, NY

Hebrew Home for the Aged at Riverdale Inc, Bronx, NY

Hebrew Home for the Aged—North Dade, North Miami Beach, FL

Hebrew Home for the Aged—North Dade, North Miami Beach, FL

Hebrew Home & Hospital, Hartford, CT

Hebrew Home of Greater Washington, Rockville, MD

Hebrew Hospital for the Chronic Sick, Bronx, NY

Heffner's Ivy Cottage Nursing Home, Waynesville, OH

Hefner Village Nursing Center, Oklahoma City, OK

Hegg Memorial Health Center, Rock Valley, IA

Heinzerling Developmental Center, Columbus, OH

Heinzerling Memorial Foundation, Columbus, OH

Helena Care Center, Helena, OK

Helena Nursing Home Co, Helena, MT

Helix View Healthcare Center, El Cajon, CA

Hellenic Nursing Home for the Aged, Canton, MA

Helmwood Care Home, Tribune, KS

Helping Hand Intermediate Care Facility, Summit, IL

Helton Health Center, Hamilton, OH

Hemet Convalescent Center, Hemet, CA

Hemphill Care Center, Hemphill, TX

Hempstead Park Nursing Home, Hempstead, NY

Henard-Keller Shelter Care, Dongola, IL

Henard Sheltered Care Home, Jonesboro, IL

Henderson Convalescent Hospital, Henderson, NV

Henderson Nursing Home Inc, Morgantown, IN

Henderson Nursing Home Inc, Morgantown, IN

Henderson Rest Home, Henderson, KY

Hendersonville Nursing Home Ltd, Hendersonville, TN

Hendersonville Retirement Center, Hendersonville, NC

Hendricks Community Hospital, Hendricks, MN

Hendricks County Home, Danville, IN

Hendrix Health Care Center, Double Springs, AL

Hendrix Street Group Home, Lexington, SC

Hennepin County Detox Center, Minneapolis, MN

Hennesey Nursing Center, Giddings, TX

Hennessey Care Center, Hennessey, OK

Henning Nursing Home, Henning, MN

Hennis Care Centre, Dover, OH

Henrico Health Care Center, Highland Springs, VA

Henrietta Care Center, Henrietta, TX

Henry County Memorial Hospital Long-Term Care Unit, Mount Pleasant, IA

Henry County Nursing Home, Abbeville, AL

Henry County Nursing Home, Paris, TN

Henry County Residential Home, Napoleon, OH

Hensley Nursing Home Inc, Sayre, OK

Nim Henson Geriatric Center, Jackson, KY

Heritage, San Francisco, CA

Heritage, Tacoma, WA

Heritage Acres, Cedar Rapids, IA

Heritage Acres, Hardin, MT

Heritage Care Center, Iowa Falls, IA

Heritage Care Center, Mason City, IA

Heritage Care Center, Fairbury, NE

Heritage Care Center, Shelby, OH

Heritage Center Inc—Conway, Conway, AR

Heritage Convalescent Center, Torrance, CA

Heritage Convalescent Center, Atlanta, GA

Heritage Convalescent Center, Paris, IL

Heritage Convalescent Center, Amarillo, TX

Heritage Convalescent Center, American Fork, UT

Heritage Convalescent Hospital, Sacramento, CA

Heritage Fifty-Three, Moline, IL

Heritage Forest Lane, Dallas, TX

Heritage Gardens Health Care Center, Loma Linda, CA

Heritage Hall, Lawrenceburg, KY

Heritage Hall, Dillwyn, VA

Heritage Hall Big Stone Gap, Big Stone Gap, VA

Heritage Hall—Charlottesville, Charlottesville, VA

Heritage Hall—Clintwood, Clintwood, VA

Heritage Hall East, Agawam, MA

Heritage Hall—Front Royal, Front Royal, VA

Heritage Hall Health Care, Blackstone, VA

Heritage Hall—King George, King George, VA

Heritage Hall Leesburg, Leesburg, VA

Heritage Hall Nassawadox, Nassawadox, VA

Heritage Hall North Nursing Home, Agawam, MA

Heritage Hall Nursing Center, Centralia, MO

Heritage Hall South Nursing Home, Agawam, MA

Heritage Hall Tazewell, Tazewell, VA

Heritage Hall West, Agawam, MA

Heritage Hall—Wise, Wise, VA

Heritage Haven Care Center, Schofield, WI

Heritage Health Care Center, Tuscaloosa, AL

Heritage Health Care Center, Globe, AZ

Heritage Health Care Center, Inverness, FL

Heritage Health Care Center, Tallahassee, FL

Heritage Health Care Center, Chanute, KS

Heritage Health Care Center, Gering, NE

Heritage Healthcare, West Lafayette, IN

Heritage Healthcare Center, Naples, FL

Heritage Healthcare Center, Naples, FL

Heritage Healthcare Center, Chicago, IL

Heritage Healthcare Center, Takoma Park, MD

Heritage Healthcare Center Venice, Venice, FL

Heritage Healthcare Centre, Zeeland, MI

Heritage Hearth, Missoula, MT

Heritage Hills, McAlester, OK

Heritage Hills Nursing Centre, Smithfield, RI

Heritage Home, Parsons, KS

Heritage Home, Plainview, TX

Heritage Home Care Center, Saint Elmo, IL

Heritage Home of Bancroft, Bancroft, IA

Heritage Home of Florence Inc, Florence, SC

Heritage House, Kankakee, IL

Heritage House, Atlantic, IA

Heritage House, Orange City, IA

Heritage House, Miami, FL

Heritage House, Wilkes-Barre, PA

Heritage House, Eagle Lake, TX

Heritage House, Rosebud, TX

Heritage House-Columbus Jewish Home for the Aged, Columbus, OH

Heritage House Convalescent Center, Martinsville, IN

Heritage House Convalescent Center, Shelbyville, IN

Heritage House Convalescent Center of Putnam County Inc, Greencastle, IN

Heritage House Nursing Home, Valdosta, GA

Heritage House Nursing Home, Winfield, KS

Heritage House Nursing Home, Danvers, MA

Heritage House of Champaign, Champaign, IL

Heritage House of Charleston, Charleston, IL

Heritage House of Greensburg, Greensburg, IN

Heritage House of New Castle, New Castle, IN

Heritage House of Richmond, Richmond, IN

Heritage House of Vandalia, Vandalia, IL

Heritage House Summerville, Augusta, GA

Heritage Inc, Bridgeport, WV

Heritage Inn, Saint Simons Island, GA

Heritage Inn—Barnesville, Barnesville, GA

Heritage Inn Nursing Home, Fairborn, OH

Heritage Inn of Hartwell, Hartwell, GA

Heritage Inn of Whigham, Whigham, GA

Heritage L T Health Care Center, Framingham, MA

Heritage Lakewood Health Care Center, Wichita, KS

Heritage Living Center, Saint Paul, NE

Heritage Manor, Bloomington, IL

Heritage Manor, Peru, IL

Heritage Manor, Streator, IL

Heritage Manor, Dubuque, IA

Heritage Manor, Findlay, OH

Heritage Manor, Bartlesville, OK

Heritage Manor, Canton, TX

Heritage Manor, Plano, TX

Heritage Manor, The Woodlands, TX

Heritage Manor, Elroy, WI

Heritage Manor, Rice Lake, WI

Heritage Manor, Rice Lake, WI

Heritage Manor Care Center, Newton, IA

Heritage Manor Care Center, Dayton, TX

Heritage Manor Care Center of Hondo, Hondo, TX

Heritage Manor—Corinth, Corinth, MS

Heritage Manor, Elgin, IL

Heritage Manor Health Care Center, Fort Wayne, IN

Heritage Manor Health Care Center, Chisholm, MN

Heritage Manor Health Care Center of Ligonier, Ligonier, IN

Heritage Manor Healthcare Center, Mayfield, KY

Heritage Manor Inc, Shelbyville, IN

Heritage Manor Inc, Winthrop, ME

Heritage Manor Inc, Devine, TX

Heritage Manor—Indianola, Indianola, MS

Heritage Manor, Jewish Home for Aged, Youngstown, OH

Heritage Manor Lafayette, Lafayette, LA

Heritage Manor Marrero, Marrero, LA

Heritage Manor New Iberia North, New Iberia, LA

Heritage Manor New Iberia South, New Iberia, LA

Heritage Manor No 2, Alexandria, LA

Heritage Manor—North, Fort Wayne, IN

Heritage Manor Nursing & Convalescent Home, Springfield, IL

Heritage Manor Nursing Center, Flint, MI

Heritage Manor Nursing Center, Minster, OH

Heritage Manor Nursing & Convalescent Home, Beardstown, IL

Heritage Manor Nursing & Convalescent Home, El Paso, IL

Heritage Manor Nursing & Convalescent Home, Mount Sterling, IL

Heritage Manor Nursing Home, Mendota, IL

Heritage Manor Nursing Home, Chattanooga, TN

Heritage Manor Nursing Home, Sherman, TX

Heritage Manor of Alexandria No 1, Alexandria, LA

Heritage Manor of Alexandria North, Alexandria, LA

Heritage Manor of Baton Rouge, Baton Rouge, LA

Heritage Manor of Bossier City, Bossier City, LA

Heritage Manor of Cleveland, Cleveland, MS

Heritage Manor of Clinton, Clinton, MS

Heritage Manor of Collegedale, Collegedale, TN

Heritage Manor of Collierville, Collierville, TN

Heritage Manor of Columbia, Columbia, MS

Heritage Manor of Columbia, Columbia, TN

Heritage Manor of Crowley, Crowley, LA

Heritage Manor of Elizabethton, Elizabethton, TN

Heritage Manor of Emporia, Emporia, KS

Heritage Manor of Ferriday, Ferriday, LA

Heritage Manor of Franklinton, Franklinton, LA

Heritage Manor of Gonzales, Gonzales, LA

Heritage Manor of Greenwood, Greenwood, MS

Heritage Manor of Grenada, Grenada, MS

Heritage Manor of Hammond, Hammond, LA

Heritage Manor of Hiawatha, Hiawatha, KS

Heritage Manor of Holly Springs, Holly Springs, MS

Heritage Manor of Houma, Houma, LA

Heritage Manor of Iowa Park, Iowa Park, TX

Heritage Manor of Kaplan, Kaplan, LA

Heritage Manor of Lawrence, Lawrence, KS

Heritage Manor of Mansfield, Mansfield, LA

Heritage Manor of Many No 1, Many, LA

Heritage Manor of Many No 2, Many, LA

Heritage Manor of Memphis, Memphis, TN

Heritage Manor of Monteagle, Monteagle, TN

Heritage Manor of Mountain Grove, Mountain Grove, MO

Heritage Manor of Normal, Normal, IL

Heritage Manor of Osawatomie, Osawatomie, KS

Heritage Manor of Red Boiling Springs, Red Boiling Springs, TN

Heritage Manor of Rogersville, Rogersville, TN

Heritage Manor of Springfield, Springfield, MO

Heritage Manor of Vivian, Vivian, LA

Heritage Manor of Westwood, Shreveport, LA

Heritage Manor of Yazoo City, Yazoo City, MS

Heritage Manor Rolling Fork, Rolling Fork, MS

Heritage Manor Shreveport, Shreveport, LA

Heritage Manor South, Shreveport, LA

Heritage Manor Thibodaux, Thibodaux, LA

Heritage Nursing & Convalescent Center, Mobile, AL

Heritage Nursing & Rehabilitation Center, North Miami Beach, FL

Heritage Nursing & Rehabilitation Center, North Miami Beach, FL

Heritage Nursing Center, Haynesville, LA

Heritage Nursing Center, Sheboygan, WI

Heritage Nursing Home, Quitman, TX

Heritage Nursing Home, Port Washington, WI

Heritage Nursing Home Inc, Muskogee, OK

Heritage Nursing Home Inc, Athens, PA

Heritage Nursing Home Inc, Goldthwaite, TX

Heritage Nursing Manor, Lamesa, TX

Heritage of Bel Air, Norfolk, NE

Heritage of Bridgeport, Bridgeport, NE

Heritage of Cimarron, Cimarron, KS

Heritage of Edina, Edina, MN

Heritage of Elmwood Nursing Home, Elmwood, WI

Heritage of Emerson, Emerson, NE

Heritage of Geneva, Geneva, NE

Heritage of Red Cloud, Red Cloud, NE

Heritage of St Louis Inc, Saint Louis, MO

Heritage of Stockton, Stockton, CA

Heritage of Wauneta, Wauneta, NE

Heritage Paradise, Paradise, CA

Heritage Park, Plano, TX

Heritage Park Care Center, Carbondale, CO

Heritage Park Care Center, Roy, UT

Heritage Park Manor, Littleton, CO

Heritage Park of Bradenton, Bradenton, FL

Heritage Place, Soldotna, AK

Heritage Place, Mesquite, TX

Heritage Regency Inc, Richmond, IN

Heritage Rehabilitation Center, Denver, CO

Heritage Residential Care Center, Devine, TX

Heritage Shadyside, Pittsburgh, PA

Heritage Sheltered Care Home, Hutsonville, IL

Heritage Square New Boston, New Boston, OH

Heritage Square Retirement Home, Dixon, IL

Heritage Summerville Inc, Augusta, GA

Heritage, Girard, KS

Heritage Towers, Doylestown, PA

Heritage Village Health Center, Gerry, NY

Heritage Village Nursing Home, Holdenville, OK

Heritage Village Nursing Home, Richardson, TX

Heritage Village of Eskridge, Eskridge, KS

Heritage Village of Rose Hill, Rose Hill, KS

Heritage Village of Wakefield, Wakefield, KS

David Herman Health Care Center, Minneapolis, MN

Herman Sanitarium, San Jose, CA

Hermann Park Manor, Houston, TX

Hermiston Good Samaritan, Hermiston, OR

Hermitage in Northern Virginia, Alexandria, VA

Hermitage Manor Nursing Home, Owensboro, KY

Hermitage Nursing Home, Worcester, MA

Hermitage Nursing Home, Elizabethton, TN

Hermitage on the Eastern Shore, Onancock, VA

Hermitage Park Regional Care Center, Hermitage, MO

Hermitage, Muskegon, MI

Heron Lake Municipal Hospital & Community Nursing Care, Heron Lake, MN

Herreid Good Samaritan Center, Herreid, SD

Herrick Manor, Tecumseh, MI

K W Hess Ohio Pythian Home of Springfield Ohio, Springfield, OH

Hessmer Nursing Home Inc, Hessmer, LA

Hester Memorial Nursing Home, Dayton, OH

Hetzel Care Center Inc, Bloomer, WI

Flora & Mary Hewitt Memorial Hospital Inc, Shelton, CT

Hewitt House of People Inc, Saint Paul, MN

Hewitt Manor Inc, Shinglehouse, PA

Heyde Health System Inc, Chippewa Falls, WI

Hi-Acres Manor Nursing Center, Jamestown, ND

Hi-Plains Nursing Home, Hale Center, TX

Hialeah Convalescent Home, Hialeah, FL

Hiawatha Adult Home, Rochester, MN

Hiawatha Childrens Home, Rochester, MN

Hiawatha Manor, Pipestone, MN

Hibbard Nursing Home, Dover-Foxcroft, ME

Hickman County Nursing Home, Centerville, TN

Hickory Creek Nursing Center Inc, Dayton, OH

Hickory Creek of Athens, The Plains, OH

Hickory Estates Incorporated, Sumner, IL

Hickory House Nursing Home, Honey Brook, PA

Hickory Lane Care Center, Buffalo, MO

Hickory Manor Nursing Home Inc, Bastrop, LA

Hickory Nursing Pavilion Inc, Hickory Hills, IL

Hicks Golden Years Nursing Home, Monticello, KY

Hicks Nursing Home, Fryeburg, ME

Hidden Acres Manor Inc, Mount Pleasant, TN

Hidden Hollow Care Center, Orem, UT

Hidden Valley Health Care, Oak Hill, WV

Higgins Learning Center, Morganfield, KY

Higginsville Habilitation Center, Higginsville, MO

High Hope Care Center, Sulphur, LA

High Island Creek Residence, Arlington, MN

High Plains Nursing Center, Clovis, NM

High Plains Retirement Village, Lakin, KS

High Point Care Center, High Point, NC

High Point Lodge Care Center, Clear Lake, MN

High Street Convalescent Hospital, Oakland, CA

High Street Rest Home, Fitchburg, MA

High Valley Lodge, Sunland, CA

High View Health Care Center Inc, Middletown, CT

Highgate Manor of Rensselaer, Troy, NY

Highland Acres Extend-A-Care Center, Winsted, CT

Highland Care Center, Jamaica, NY

Highland Care Center, Salt Lake City, UT

Highland Care Home, Abilene, KS

Highland Chateau Health Care Center, Saint Paul, MN

Highland Convalescent Center, Bellingham, WA

Highland Convalescent Hospital, Duarte, CA

Highland Farms Inc, Black Mountain, NC

Highland Hall Care Center, New Castle, PA

Highland Hall Manor, Essex, CT

Highland Health Facility—Mental Retardation Unit, Baltimore, MD

Highland Home, Jackson, MI

Highland Home for the Aged, Genoa City, WI

Highland House Nursing Center, Grants Pass, OR

Highland House of Fayetteville Inc, Fayetteville, NC

Highland Manor, Phoenix, AZ

Highland Manor, New Ulm, MN

Highland Manor, Portland, TN

Highland Manor Nursing Home, Exeter, PA

Highland Manor Nursing Home, Dublin, VA

Highland Manor Nursing Home Inc, Fall River, MA

Highland Manor Rest Home, Worcester, MA

Highland Nursing & Rehabilitation Center, Brackenridge, PA

Highland Nursing Center, Ponca City, OK

Highland Nursing Center, Wichita Falls, TX

Highland Nursing Home, Highland, IN

Highland Nursing Home, San Antonio, TX

Highland Nursing Home Inc, Massena, NY

Highland Park Care Center, Houston, TX

Highland Park Complex, Pueblo, CO

Highland Park Health Care Center Inc, Highwood, IL

Highland Park Manor, Clinton, OK

Highland Park Manor, Enid, OK

Highland Park Manor, Okmulgee, OK

Highland Pines Nursing Home, Longview, TX

Highland Pines Nursing Manor, Clearwater, FL

Highland Rest Home, Dorchester, MA

Highland Street, East Rochester, NH

Highland Terrace Nursing Center, Camas, WA

Highland View Nursing Home, Troy, OH

Highlands, Tacoma, WA

Highlands Convalescent Center Inc, Renton, WA

Highlands Homes, Princeton, KY

Highlands, L T C Center, Fitchburg, MA

Highline Care Center Inc, Seattle, WA

Highline Convalescent Center, East Wenatchee, WA

Highmore Healthcare Center, Highmore, SD

Highview Convalescent Hospital, Oakland, CA

Highview Manor, Madawaska, ME

Highview Retirement Home Association, Rockford, IL

Highview Terrace, Paris, IL

Hilaire Farm Nursing Home, Huntington, NY

Hildebrand Care Center, Canon City, CO

Hill Country Care Inc, Dripping Springs, TX

Hill Country Manor, Llano, TX

Hill Haven Nursing Home, Syracuse, NY

Hill Haven Nursing Home of Rochester County, Webster, NY

Keith Hill Nursing Home Inc, Grafton, MA

Hill Nursing Home, Idabel, OK
Hill Top, Lake Bluff, IL
Hill Top Home of Comfort Inc, Killdeer, ND
Hill Top House, Bucklin, KS
Hill Top House Nursing Home Inc, Dayton, OH
Hill Top Nursing Home, Boerne, TX
Hill View Health Care Facility, Portsmouth, OH
Hill View Manor, New Castle, PA
William Hill Manor Health Care Center, Easton, MD
Hillaire Care Center, Hillsboro, OR
Hillandale Health Care, Hamilton, OH
Hillbrook Nursing Home, Clancy, MT
Hillcreek Manor, Louisville, KY
Hillcrest Care Center, Boise, ID
Hillcrest Care Center, Bellevue, NE
Hillcrest Care Center, Laurel, NE
Hillcrest Care Center, Hettinger, ND
Hillcrest Care Center, Waterville, OH
Hillcrest Care Center, Sandy, UT
Hillcrest Central, Knoxville, TN
Hillcrest Convalescent Center, Detroit, MI
Hillcrest Convalescent Center, Pasco, WA
Hillcrest Convalescent Center Inc, Durham, NC
Hillcrest Convalescent Home Inc, Milwaukee, WI
Hillcrest Convalescent Hospital, Fresno, CA
Hillcrest Convalescent Hospital, Long Beach, CA
Hillcrest Estates, Liberty, IN
Hillcrest Haven Convalescent Center, Pocatello, ID
Hillcrest Health Care Center, Owensboro, KY
Hillcrest Health Care Center, Mankato, MN
Hillcrest Health Care Center, Rush City, MN
Hillcrest Health Care Center, Wayzata, MN
Hillcrest Health Center, Bozeman, MT
Hillcrest Health Center Inc, Magee, MS
Hillcrest Health Center Skilled Nursing Facility, Oklahoma City, OK
Hillcrest Healthcare Center, Jeffersonville, IN
Hillcrest Home, Harrison, AR
Hillcrest Home, Geneseo, IL
Hillcrest Home Inc, Sumner, IA
Hillcrest Manor, Fredonia, KS
Hillcrest Manor, Aberdeen, MS
Hillcrest Manor, Blackwell, OK
Hillcrest Manor, Luling, TX
Hillcrest Manor, Wylie, TX
Hillcrest Manor Nursing Center, Waco, TX
Hillcrest Manor Nursing Home, Charlotte, NC
Hillcrest Manor Nursing Home Inc, Winchester, VA
Hillcrest Manor Sanitarium, National City, CA
Hillcrest Manor Skilled Care Div, Sanford, ME
Hillcrest Manor—Sunnyside, Sunnyside, WA
Hillcrest Medical Center SNF, Tulsa, OK
Hillcrest North, Knoxville, TN
Hillcrest Nursing Center, Fredericktown, OH
Hillcrest Nursing Center, Moore, OK
Hillcrest Nursing Center, Grove City, PA
Hillcrest Nursing Centre, North Muskegon, MI
Hillcrest Nursing Home, Prescott, AR
Hillcrest Nursing Home, San Bernardino, CA
Hillcrest Nursing Home, Avon Park, FL
Hillcrest Nursing Home, Corbin, KY
Hillcrest Nursing Home, Scottsville, KY
Hillcrest Nursing Home, Fitchburg, MA
Hillcrest Nursing Home, Red Lake Falls, MN
Hillcrest Nursing Home, McCook, NE
Hillcrest Nursing Home, Oswego, NY
Hillcrest Nursing Home, Spring Valley, NY
Hillcrest Nursing Home, Peebles, OH
Hillcrest Nursing Home, Van Wert, OH
Hillcrest Nursing Home, Tishomingo, OK
Hillcrest Nursing Home, Hamilton, TX
Hillcrest Nursing Home, Grandview, WA
Hillcrest Nursing Home, Twin Lakes, WI
Hillcrest Nursing Home, West Allis, WI
Hillcrest Nursing & Retirement Home, Plainview, MN
Hillcrest Retirement Village Ltd, Round Lake Beach, IL

Hillcrest—South, Knoxville, TN
Hillcrest—West, Knoxville, TN
Hilldale Convalescent Center, La Mesa, CA
Hillebrand Nursing Center, Cheviot, OH
Hillhaven Alameda, Alameda, CA
Hillhaven—Brookvue Convalescent Hospital, San Pablo, CA
Hillhaven Care Center, Pasadena, CA
Hillhaven Care Center, San Luis Obispo, CA
Hillhaven Castro Valley, Castro Valley, CA
Hillhaven Convalescent Center, Mill Valley, CA
Hillhaven Convalescent Center, San Francisco, CA
Hillhaven Convalescent Center, Savannah, GA
Hillhaven Convalescent Center, Springfield, MO
Hillhaven Convalescent Center, Raleigh, NC
Hillhaven Convalescent Center, Akron, OH
Hillhaven Convalescent Center, Madison, TN
Hillhaven Convalescent Center, Memphis, TN
Hillhaven Convalescent Center, El Paso, TX
Hillhaven Convalescent Center, Salt Lake City, UT
Hillhaven Convalescent Center, Vancouver, WA
Hillhaven Convalescent Center—Bolivar, Bolivar, TN
Hillhaven Convalescent Center—Germantown, Cordova, TN
Hillhaven Convalescent Center—Modesto, Modesto, CA
Hillhaven Convalescent Center & Nursing Home—Birmingham, Birmingham, AL
Hillhaven Convalescent Center & Nursing Home—Mobile, Mobile, AL
Hillhaven Convalescent Center of Camden, Camden, TN
Hillhaven Convalescent Center of Chapel Hill, Chapel Hill, NC
Hillhaven Convalescent Center of Delray Beach, Delray Beach, FL
Hillhaven Convalescent Center of Huntingdon, Huntingdon, TN
Hillhaven Convalescent Center of Ripley, Ripley, TN
Hillhaven Convalescent Center—Sarasota1, Sarasota, FL
Hillhaven Convalescent Center—West Point, West Point, MS
Hillhaven Convalescent Hospital, Anaheim, CA
Hillhaven Convalescent Hospital, Burlingame, CA
Hillhaven Convalescent Hospital, Claremont, CA
Hillhaven Convalescent Hospital, Menlo Park, CA
Hillhaven Convalescent Hospital, Orange, CA
Hillhaven Convalescent Hospital, Woodland, CA
Hillhaven—Corpus Christi, Corpus Christi, TX
Hillhaven Extended Care, Santa Cruz, CA
Hillhaven Fair Oaks, Carmichael, CA
Hillhaven Hayward, Hayward, CA
Hillhaven Health Care, Monterey Park, CA
Hillhaven Health Care, Greenville, SC
Hillhaven Health Care, Jefferson City, TN
Hillhaven Health Care Center, Phoenix, AZ
Hillhaven Health Care Center of Raleigh, Memphis, TN
Hillhaven Health Care of Gastonia, Gastonia, NC
Hillhaven Healthcare, Yuma, AZ
Hillhaven Healthcare, Van Nuys, CA
Hillhaven Healthcare Center, Sanford, FL
Hillhaven Highland House, Highland, CA
Hillhaven LaSalle Nursing Center, Durham, NC
Hillhaven Lawton Convalescent Hospital, San Francisco, CA
Hillhaven/Maryville Convalescent Center, Maryville, TN
Hillhaven Nursing Center—East, Baton Rouge, LA
Hillhaven Nursing Center Inc, Adelphi, MD

Hillhaven Nursing Center—West, Baton Rouge, LA
Hillhaven Nursing Home, Vancouver, WA
Hillhaven—Oakland, Oakland, CA
Hillhaven of Alamance Inc, Graham, NC
Hillhaven of Highland Inc, Highland, IL
Hillhaven of Little Rock, Little Rock, AR
Hillhaven of Topeka, Topeka, KS
Hillhaven Orange Nursing Center, Durham, NC
Hillhaven Rehabilitation & Convalescent Center, Asheville, NC
Hillhaven Rehabilitation & Convalescent Center, Durham, NC
Hillhaven Rehabilitation & Convalescent Center, Wilmington, NC
Hillhaven Rehabilitation & Convalescent Center, Norfolk, VA
Hillhaven Rehabilitation Convalescent Center, Marietta, GA
Hillhaven Rose Manor Convalescent Center, Durham, NC
Hillhaven Roseville Convalescent Hospital, Roseville, CA
Hillhaven San Francisco, San Francisco, CA
Hillhaven San Leandro, San Leandro, CA
Hillhaven—Sherwood Convalescent Hospital, Sacramento, CA
Hillhaven Sunnybrook Convalescent Center, Raleigh, NC
Hillhaven Victorian, San Francisco, CA
Hillhaven Wichita, Wichita, KS
Hillhaven Willow Pass, Concord, CA
Hillhouse Convalescent Home, Bath, ME
Hills & Dales Child Development Center, Dubuque, IA
Hillsboro Community Nursing Home, Hillsboro, ND
Hillsboro Healthcare Center, Hillsboro, IL
Hillsboro House Nursing Home, Hillsborough, NH
Hillsboro Manor Nursing Home, El Dorado, AR
Hillsboro Nursing Home, Hillsboro, IL
Hillsborough County Nursing Home, Goffstown, NH
Hillsdale County Medical Care Facility, Hillsdale, MI
Hillsdale Manor Convalescent Hospital, San Mateo, CA
Hillside Acres, Willard, OH
Hillside Convalescent Center, Des Moines, IA
Hillside Convalescent Inc, Portland, OR
Hillside Haven Nursing Home, Rushville, IN
Hillside Health Care Center Inc, Milwaukee, WI
Hillside Healthcare, Jefferson City, MO
Hillside Heights Convalescent Center, Eugene, OR
Hillside House, Wilmington, DE
Hillside House Inc, Santa Barbara, CA
Hillside Living Center, Yorkville, IL
Hillside Lodge Nursing Home & Convalescent Center, Beeville, TX
Hillside Manor, Washington, IN
Hillside Manor, Glenwood, IA
Hillside Manor, Missoula, MT
Hillside Manor, McMinnville, OR
Hillside Manor, Kingsport, TN
Hillside Manor Convalescent Hospital, San Rafael, CA
Hillside Manor Health Related Facility, Jamaica Estates, NY
Hillside Manor Nursing Center, Gatesville, TX
Hillside Manor Nursing Home, Hartford, CT
Hillside Manor of San Marcos Inc, San Marcos, TX
Hillside Manor Retirement Home, Waterbury, CT
Hillside Nursing Home, South Portland, ME
Hillside Nursing Home, Deerfield, MA
Hillside Nursing Home, Cincinnati, OH
Hillside Nursing Home, Marion, OH
Hillside Rest Home, Amesbury, MA
Hillside Rest Home, Winchendon, MA
Hillside Terrace, Cobden, IL
Hillside Terrace, Ann Arbor, MI

Hillside Villa Care Center, Salt Lake City, UT
Hilltop Care Center, Cherokee, IA
Hilltop Care Center, Watkins, MN
Hilltop Care Center, Pine Brook, NJ
Hilltop Convalescent Center, Escondido, CA
Hilltop Convalescent Center, Charleston, IL
Hilltop Convalescent Hospital, Bakersfield, CA
Hilltop Haven, Gunter, TX
Hilltop Health Care Center, Hilltop, WV
Hilltop Home, Lyndon, KS
Hilltop Lodge, Owingsville, KY
Hilltop Lodge Inc Nursing Home, Beloit, KS
Hilltop Manor, Brookston, MN
Hilltop Manor Convalescent Hospital No 2, Auburn, CA
Hilltop Manor Inc, Cunningham, KS
Hilltop Manor Inc, Union, MS
Hilltop Nursing Center, Harrison, AR
Hilltop Nursing Center No 1, Pineville, LA
Hilltop Nursing Center No 2, Pineville, LA
Hilltop Nursing Home, Forsyth, GA
Hilltop Nursing Home, Kuttawa, KY
Hilltop Nursing Home, Cincinnati, OH
Hilltop Nursing Home, Portsmouth, OH
Hilltop Nursing Home, Parker, SD
Hilltop Nursing Home, Hilltop, WV
Hilltop Nursing Home & Community Clinic, Cripple Creek, CO
Hilltop Private Nursing Home, Middletown, NJ
Hilltop Rehabilitation Hospital, Grand Junction, CO
Hilltop Rest Home, Science Hill, KY
Hilltop Rest Home, Hardwick, MA
Hilltop Rest Home, Springfield, MA
Hilltop Retirement Home, Quinn, SD
Hilltop Village, Kerrville, TX
Hillview Care Center, Altoona, PA
Hillview Care Center Inc, Milwaukee, WI
Hillview Convalescent Hospital, Morgan Hill, CA
Hillview Health Care Center, Columbia, TN
Hillview Health Care Center, La Crosse, WI
Hillview Healthcare Center, Vienna, IL
Hillview Lodge Inc, Arnold, MO
Hillview Manor, Scottsville, KY
Hillview Manor, Goldthwaite, TX
Hillview Nursing Home, Cincinnati, OH
Hillview Nursing Home, Flushing, OH
Hillview Nursing Home, Dresden, TN
Hillview Nursing Home, Elizabethton, TN
Hillview Nursing Home Inc, Bastrop, LA
Hillview Nursing Home Inc, Mineola, TX
Hillview Retirement Center, Greenville, IL
Hilo Hospital, Hilo, HI
Hilton Convalescent Home, Ferndale, MI
Hilty Memorial Home, Pandora, OH
Hinds Residential Center, Jackson, MS
Hines Health Care Center, Jasper, TX
Hines Health Care Center, San Augustine, TX
Hines Nursing Home, Pineland, TX
Hinton Home Inc, Farmersville, TX
Grady H Hipp Nursing Center, Greenville, SC
Hiram W Davis Medical Center, Petersburg, VA
Caleb Hitchcock Health Center at Duncaster, Bloomfield, CT
Hitz Memorial Home, Alhambra, IL
Hobart Good Samaritan Center, Hobart, OK
Hobart Good Samaritan Home, Hobart, OK
Hobbs Health Care Center, Hobbs, NM
Hocking Valley Community Hospital, Logan, OH
Arthur B Hodges Center Inc, Charleston, WV
Bishop Joseph H Hodges Continuous Care Center, Wheeling, WV
Hodges Boulevard Cluster Homes, Jacksonville, FL
Hoemako Long-Term Care, Casa Grande, AZ
Hoffman Health Care Center, Hoffman, MN
Hoffman Home, Morris, MN
Charles V Hogan Regional Center & John T Berry Rehabilitation Center, Danvers, MA
Hoikka House Inc, Saint Paul, MN
Holbrook Nursing Home, Holbrook, MA
Holbrook Nursing Home Inc, Buckhannon, WV

Holden Manor Care Center, Holden, MO
Holden Nursing Home Inc, Holden, MA
Holdenville Nursing Home, Holdenville, OK
Holgate Quality Care Nursing Center, Holgate, OH
Holiday Care Center, Daytona Beach, FL
Holiday Care Center, Toms River, NJ
Holiday Heights Nursing Home, Norman, OK
Holiday Hills Retirement Center, Dallas, TX
Holiday Home of Evansville, Evansville, IN
Holiday House, Manchester, CT
Holiday House, Saint Albans, VT
Holiday House of Portsmouth, Portsmouth, VA
Holiday Lodge, Hamlin, TX
Holiday Lodge, Longview, TX
Holiday Manor, Princeton, IN
Holiday Manor Nuring Home, Scranton, PA
Holiday Manor Nursitarium, Canoga Park, CA
Holiday Nursing Center, Center, TX
Holiday Pines Manor, Woodville, TX
Holiday Resort Inc, Emporia, KS
Holiday Retirement Center, Sweetwater, TX
Holiday Retirement Home Inc, Manville, RI
Holladay Healthcare Center, Salt Lake City, UT
Holladay Park Medical Center Skilled Nursing Facility Unit, Portland, OR
Holladay Park Plaza, Portland, OR
Holland Home—Brown Home, Grand Rapids, MI
Holland Home for the Aged, South Holland, IL
Holland Home—Fulton Manor, Grand Rapids, MI
Holland Home—Raybrook Manor, Grand Rapids, MI
Holland Nursing Center North, Springdale, AR
Holland Nursing Center West Inc, Springdale, AR
Hollenbeck Home for Aged Convalescent Unit, Los Angeles, CA
Hollidaysburg Veterans Home, Hollidaysburg, PA
Hollingsworth House Nursing & Retirement, Braintree, MA
Hollis Park Manor Nursing Home, Hollis, NY
Holliston Manor Nursing Home, Holliston, MA
Holliswood Care Center Inc, Hollis, NY
Holly Care Center, Nampa, ID
Holly Center, Salisbury, MD
Holly Convalescent Center, Holly, MI
Holly Hall, Houston, TX
Holly Heights Nursing Home Inc, Denver, CO
Holly Hill, Anna, IL
Holly Hill Health Care Facility, Brazil, IN
Holly Hill House Nursing Home, Sulphur, LA
Holly Hill Intermediate Care Facility, Valdosta, GA
Holly Hill Manor Inc, Towson, MD
Holly Hill Nursing Home, New Castle, IN
Holly Hill Nursing Home, Newbury, OH
Holly Hills Care Center, Emmett, ID
Holly Manor Nursing Home, Mendham, NJ
Holly Manor Nursing Home, Farmville, VA
Holly Nursing Care Center, Holly, CO
Holly Point Manor, Orange Park, FL
Holly Terrace Nursing Home, North Ridgeville, OH
Holly Tree Convalescent Hospital, Hayward, CA
Hollycrest Home Inc, Snohomish, WA
Hollywell Health Care Center, Randolph, MA
Hollywood Hills Nursing Home, Hollywood, FL
Holmdel Nursing Home, Holmdel, NJ
Holmes Convalescent Center, Virginia Beach, VA
Holmes Lake Manor, Lincoln, NE
Holmes Regional Convalescent Home, Melbourne, FL
Holmes Regional Nursing Center, Melbourne, FL
Holmesdale Convalescent Center, Kansas City, MO

Holmgreen Health Care Center, Corpus Christi, TX
Holstein Good Samaritan Center, Holstein, IA
Amie Holt Care Center, Buffalo, WY
Holt Manor Inc, Rockford, IL
Holton Manor, Elkhorn, WI
Holy Family Health Center, Des Plaines, IL
Holy Family Home, Parma, OH
Holy Family Home, Philadelphia, PA
Holy Family Home for the Aged, Brooklyn, NY
Holy Family Manor Inc, Bethlehem, PA
Holy Family Residence, Scranton, PA
Holy Family Villa, Lemont, IL
Holy Spirit Retirement Home, Sioux City, IA
Holyoke Geriatric & Convalescent Center, Holyoke, MA
Holyoke Nursing Home, Holyoke, MA
Homage Manor Nursing Home, Pineville, LA
Home Association Inc, Tampa, FL
Home for Aged Blind, Yonkers, NY
Home for Aged People, Fall River, MA
Home for Aged Protestant Women, Pittsburgh, PA
Home for Aged Pythians, Greenville, TX
Home for Aged Women, Worcester, MA
Home for Aged Women—Minquadale, Wilmington, DE
Home for Jewish Parents, Oakland, CA
Home for the Aged of the Protestant Episcopal Church, Alhambra, CA
Home for the Aged, Saginaw, MI
Home for the Jewish Aged, Philadelphia, PA
Home of Angels, Ontario, CA
Home of Hope Inc, Vinita, OK
Home of the Innocents, Louisville, KY
Home of the Sages of Israel, New York, NY
Homecrest Foundation, Evanston, IL
Homedale Care Center, Homedale, ID
Homeland Center, Harrisburg, PA
Homestead I, Painesville, OH
Homestead II, Painesville, OH
Homestead Hall, Worcester, MA
Homestead Health Care Center, Lincoln, NE
Homestead Health Center, Stamford, CT
Homestead Health Center Inc, Wichita, KS
Homestead Inc, Kittery, ME
Homestead Manor Nursing Home, Stamps, AR
Homestead Manor Nursing Home, Homestead, FL
Homestead Nursing Center, Lexington, KY
Homestead Nursing Center of New Castle Inc, New Castle, KY
Homestead Nursing Home, Deer River, MN
Homestead Nursing Home, Tulsa, OK
Homestead Nursing & Rehabilitation Center, Willow Grove, PA
Homestead of Fair Oaks, Fair Oaks, CA
Homestead Rest Home, Phoenix, AZ
Homestead Rest Home, Leominster, MA
Homestead Rest Home, North Adams, MA
Homestead, Cheyenne, WY
Homestead Village Inc, Lancaster, PA
Hometown Nursing Home of Celina, Celina, OH
Hometown Nursing Home of Ottawa, Ottawa, OH
Hometown Nursing Home of Paulding, Paulding, OH
Homeview Center of Franklin, Franklin, IN
Homeward Bound, New Hope, MN
Homeward Bound Brooklyn Park, Brooklyn Park, MN
Homewood Convalescent Hospital Inc, San Jose, CA
Homewood Health Care Center, Glasgow, KY
Homewood Retirement Center, Martinsburg, PA
Homewood Retirement Center—Hanover, Hanover, PA
Hominy Nursing Home, Hominy, OK
Homme Home for the Aging, Wittenberg, WI
Honoka'a Hospital, Honoka'a, HI
Honorage Nursing Care, Florence, SC
Hood Memorial Hospital—Skilled Nursing Facility, Amite, LA
Hood River Care Center, Hood River, OR

Hooper Care Center, Hooper, NE
Hoopeston Regional Nursing Home, Hoopeston, IL
Hoosick Falls Health Center, Hoosick Falls, NY
Hoosier Christian Village, Brownstown, IN
Hoosier Hills Health Care Center, Bloomington, IN
Hoosier Village, Indianapolis, IN
Hoots Memorial Hospital, Yadkinville, NC
Hoover, Anderson, IN
Hooverwood, Indianapolis, IN
Hope Hall Convalescent Home Inc, Waterbury, CT
Hope House, Arcola, IL
Hope House Manor Inc, Springfield, OH
Hope Intermediate Residences Inc, Williamsport, PA
Hope Manor, Fresno, CA
Hope Manor, Joplin, MO
Hope Nursing Home, Lomira, WI
Hope Park Cottage, Anchorage, AK
Hope Residences, Waterville, MN
Hope School, Springfield, IL
Hopedale Garden Nursing Home, Hopedale, MA
Hopedale House, Hopedale, IL
Hopedale Nursing Home, Hopedale, IL
Hopehill Nursing Home, Greensburg, PA
Hopewell Convalescent Center, Hopewell, VA
Hopewell Health Care Center, Sumter, SC
Hopkins County Nursing Home, Sulphur Springs, TX
Hopkins Health Center, North Providence, RI
Hopkins House Nursing & Rehabilitation Center, Wyncote, PA
Hopkins Nursing Facility, Woodburn, KY
Hopkins Nursing Home Inc, Waltham, MA
Horizon Apartments, West Saint Paul, MN
Horizon Healthcare Nursing Center—Albuquerque, Albuquerque, NM
Horizon Healthcare Nursing Center—Santa Fe, Santa Fe, NM
Horizon Home II, Mankato, MN
Horizon House, Seattle, WA
Horizon House II, Fort Thomas, KY
Horizon Manor Nursing Center, Nocona, TX
Horizon Senior Care, Canonsburg, PA
Horizon South Living Center, Oglesby, IL
Horizon West Health Care, Minneapolis, MN
Horizons Health Care, Eckert, CO
Horizons of Tuscarawas & Carroll Counties Inc, Dover, OH
Horizons Unlimited, Rhinelander, WI
Horn Harbor Nursing Home Inc, Gloucester, VA
Horn Nursing Home Inc, Wooster, OH
Horne Home, Manzanola, CO
Hornell Nursing Home & HRF, Hornell, NY
Horry County Community Residence, Conway, SC
Hospice of the Central Coast, Monterey, CA
Hospice of the East San Gabriel Valley, West Covina, CA
Hospital Skilled Nursing Facility, Sidney, NY
Hospitality Care Center, Madison, GA
Hospitality Care Center 1, Sandusky, OH
Hospitality Care Center 2, Sandusky, OH
Hospitality Care Center of Albany, Albany, GA
Hospitality Care Center of Charlotte, Charlotte, NC
Hospitality Care Center of Hermitage Inc, Hermitage, PA
Hospitality Care Center of Macon, Macon, GA
Hospitality Care Center of Thomasville, Thomasville, GA
Hospitality Care Center Toledo, Toledo, OH
Hospitality Home East, Xenia, OH
Hospitality Home West, Xenia, OH
Hospitality House, Bedford, IN
Hospitality House, Massillon, OH
Hospitality House Inc, Bloomington, IN
Hospitality House Inc, Alice, TX
Hospitality House Nursing Home, Anderson, CA
Hospitality Manor, Kenosha, WI

Hospitality Nursing Home, Clyde, OH
Hot Springs Convalescent Inc, Hot Springs, MT
Hot Springs Nursing Home, Hot Springs, AR
Hotel Butler Residential Center, Butler, IN
Hotel Dieu Hospital Skilled Nursing Facility, New Orleans, LA
Hotel Reed Nursing Center, Bay Saint Louis, MS
Houghton County Medical Care Facility, Hancock, MI
Houghton Nursing Care Center Inc, Houghton, NY
Houlton Regional Hospital, Houlton, ME
Houlton Residential Center, Houlton, ME
Houma Health Care, Houma, LA
House of Care, Portland, OR
House of Loreto, Canton, OH
House of the Holy Comforter, Bronx, NY
Houston County Group Home, Caledonia, MN
Houston County—LaCrescent Home, LaCrescent, MN
Houston County Nursing Home, Crockett, TX
Houston Health Care Inc, Cloverdale, IN
Houston Health Care Inc—Crawfordsville, Crawfordsville, IN
Houston House, Houston, MO
Houston Village Inc, Indianapolis, IN
Hovenden Memorial Good Samaritan Center, Laurens, IA
Howard Good Samaritan Center, Howard, SD
Howard Lake Care Center, Howard Lake, MN
Petra Howard House, Saint Paul, MN
Howard Twilight Manor, Howard, KS
Howd Nursing Home, Moravia, NY
Howe Avenue Nursing Home Inc, New Rochelle, NY
Howell's Child Care Center Inc/Bear Creek, LaGrange, NC
Howell's Child Care Center Inc (Riverbend), New Bern, NC
Howell's Child Care Center—Walnut Creek, Goldsboro, NC
Hoyt Nursing Home, Saginaw, MI
Hubbard Hill Estates Inc, Elkhart, IN
Huber Restorium, Saint Petersburg, FL
L S Huckabay Memorial Hospital, Coushatta, LA
Sarah Bonwell Hudgins, Hampton, VA
Hudson Elms Inc, Hudson, OH
Hudson Health Care, Hudson, MA
Hudson Memorial Nursing Home, El Dorado, AR
Hudson Valley Nursing Center, Highland, NY
Hudson View Care & Rehabilitation Center, North Bergen, NJ
Hudson View Nursing Home Inc, Yonkers, NY
Hudsonville Christian Nursing Home, Hudsonville, MI
Hudspeth Center—Azalea Intermediate Care Facility, Whitfield, MS
Hudspeth Center—Rosewood Skilled Nursing, Whitfield, MS
Lillian M Hudspeth Nursing Home, Sonora, TX
Hueytown Nursing Home, Hueytown, AL
Hughes Convalescent Inc, West Hartford, CT
Rose Anna Hughes Presbyterian Home, Louisville, KY
Hughes Springs Nursing Home, Hughes Springs, TX
Hugo Golden Age Home, Hugo, OK
Hugo Manor Nursing Home, Hugo, OK
Human Development Center, Corpus Christi, TX
Human Resources Health Center, Miami, FL
Humana Hospital—Clinch Valley Long-Term Care Unit, Richlands, VA
Humana Hospital Marksville, Marksville, LA
Humana Hospital Oakdale, Oakdale, LA
Humana Hospital Springhill, Springhill, LA
Humana Hospital Ville Platte, Ville Platte, LA
Humana Hospital Winn Parish, Winnfield, LA
Humbert Lane Health Care Center, Washington, PA
Humble Skilled Care Facility, Humble, TX

Humboldt Care Center—North, Humboldt, IA
Humboldt Care Center—South, Humboldt, IA
Humboldt General Hospital, Winnemucca, NV
Humiston Haven, Pontiac, IL
Muriel Humphrey Residence Charlson, Eden Prairie, MN
Muriel Humphrey Residence Fraser, Eden Prairie, MN
Muriel Humphrey Residence Westby, Eden Prairie, MN
Humphreys County Memorial Hospital Intermediate Care Facility, Belzoni, MS
Humphreys County Nursing Home, Belzoni, MS
Humphreys County Nursing Home Inc, Waverly, TN
Hunt Community, Nashua, NH
Hunt Nursing & Retirement Home Inc, Danvers, MA
Hunt Street Personal Care Home, Jackson, MS
Hunter House, Peoria, IL
Hunterdon Convalescent Center Inc, Flemington, NJ
Hunterdon Hills Nursing Home, Glen Gardner, NJ
Huntersville Oaks Nursing Home, Huntersville, NC
Huntingburg Convalescent Center Inc, Huntingburg, IN
Huntingdon County Nursing Home, Huntingdon, PA
Huntington Beach Convalescent Hospital, Huntington Beach, CA
Huntington Convalescent Center, Newport News, VA
Huntington Drive Skilled Nursing Center, Arcadia, CA
Huntington Health Care & Retirement Center, Burgaw, NC
Huntington Park Care Center, Papillion, NE
Huntington Park Convalescent Center, Huntington Park, CA
Roger Huntington Nursing Center, Greer, SC
Huntington Square Convalarium, Daytona Beach, FL
Huntsville Manor, Huntsville, TN
Huntsville Nursing Home Inc, Huntsville, AL
Hurlbut Nursing Home, Rochester, NY
Ruth Wilson Hurley Manor, Coalgate, OK
Huron County Medical Care Facility, Bad Axe, MI
Huron Health Care Center, Huron, OH
Huron Nursing Home, Huron, SD
Huron Valley Nursing Care Facility, Ypsilanti, MI
Huron Woods Nursing Home, Kawkawlin, MI
Hurst Care Center, Hurst, TX
Hurstdale Rest Home, Springfield, MA
Hurwitz House, Baltimore, MD
Huston Nursing Home, Hamden, OH
Hutcheson Extended Care Unit, Fort Oglethorpe, GA
Hutchinson Good Samaritan Center, Hutchinson, KS
Hutchinson Heights, Hutchinson, KS
Hutton Nursing Center I, Salem, OH
Hutton Nursing Center II, Salem, OH
Hutton Nursing Center III, Salem, OH
Hutton Nursing Home, Kingston, NY
Hy-Lond Convalescent Hospital, Fresno, CA
Hy-Lond Convalescent Hospital, Merced, CA
Hy-Lond Convalescent Hospital, Modesto, CA
Hy-Lond Convalescent Hospital, Sacramento, CA
Hy-Lond Convalescent Hospital, Sunnyvale, CA
Hy-Lond Convalescent Hospital, Westminster, CA
Hy-Lond Home, Garden Grove, CA
Hy-Pana House Convalescent Hospital, Fresno, CA
Hy-Pana House Convalescent Hospital, Stockton, CA
Hyattsville Manor, Hyattsville, MD
Alice Hyde Nursing Home, Malone, NY
Hyde Park Convalescent Home, Boston, MA

Hyde Park Convalescent Hospital, Los Angeles, CA
Hyde Park Nursing Home, Kansas City, MO
Hyde Park Nursing Home, Staatsburg, NY
Hyland Convalescent Home, Iron Mountain, MI
Hyland Hills Care Center, Beaverton, OR
I O O F Home, Mason City, IA
I Street House, Salida, CO
Iberville Living Center, Plaquemine, LA
Idaho County Nursing Home, Grangeville, ID
Idaho Falls Care Center, Idaho Falls, ID
Idaho Falls Group Homes Inc, Idaho Falls, ID
Idaho Falls Group Homes Inc No 2, Ammon, ID
Idaho Falls Nursing Home, Scottsdale, AZ
Idaho Healthcare Center—Coeur d'Alene, Coeur d'Alene, ID
Idaho State School & Hospital, Nampa, ID
Idaho State Veterans Home—Boise, Boise, ID
Ideal Health Care Center, Ideal, GA
Ideal Nursing Home, Norton, OH
Ideal Rest Home Inc, Mobile, AL
Idle Acre Sanitarium & Convalescent Hospital, El Monte, CA
Idlehour Nursing Center Inc, Murfreesboro, AR
Idlewood Nursing Home, Saint Francisville, LA
Idylwood Acres Convalescent Hospital, Sunnyvale, CA
Iliff Care Center, Denver, CO
Iliff Nursing Home, Dunn Loring, VA
Illinois Knights Templar Home for Aged, Paxton, IL
Illinois Masonic Home, Sullivan, IL
Illinois Presbyterian Home, Springfield, IL
Immaculate Mary Home, Philadelphia, PA
Immanuel Lutheran Home, Kalispell, MT
Imperial Convalescent & Geriatric Center Inc, Chicago, IL
Imperial Convalescent Hospital, La Mirada, CA
Imperial Convalescent Hospital, Studio City, CA
Imperial Health Care Inc, Atlanta, GA
Imperial Health Center, Richmond, VA
Imperial Manor, Imperial, CA
Imperial Manor, Toledo, OH
Imperial Manor Convalescent Center, Madison, TN
Imperial Manor Nursing Home, Imperial, NE
Imperial Nursing Center of Elgin, Elgin, IL
Imperial Nursing Center of Hazel Crest, Hazel Crest, IL
Imperial Nursing Center of Joliet, Joliet, IL
Imperial Skilled Care Center, Warren, OH
Imperial Village Care Center, Lakeland, FL
Independence Care Center, Independence, IA
Independence Health Care Center, Independence, MO
Independence—Highland, Ravenna, OH
Independence House, Wheat Ridge, CO
Independence Manor, Meriden, CT
Independence Manor, Shawnee, OK
Independence Manor Care Center, Independence, MO
Independence—Meridian, Ravenna, OH
Independence Place, Herrin, IL
Independence Regional Health Center—Extended Care, Independence, MO
Independence—Vine, Kent, OH
Independence—Washington, Ravenna, OH
Indian Creek Convalescent Center, Corydon, IN
Indian Creek Nursing Center, Overland Park, KS
Indian Creek Nursing Center, New Castle, PA
Indian Haven Nursing Home, Indiana, PA
Indian Hills Care Center, Sioux City, IA
Indian Hills Manor, Ogallala, NE
Indian Hills Nursing Center, Council Bluffs, IA
Indian Hills Nursing Center, Euclid, OH
Indian Hills Nursing Home, Cameron, MO
Indian Hills Nursing Home Inc, Chillicothe, MO

Indian Meadows Nursing Center, Overland Park, KS
Indian River Estates Medical Facility, West Vero Beach, FL
Indian River Nursing Home & Health Related Facility Inc, Granville, NY
Indian River Village Care Center, Vero Beach, FL
Indian Trail Care Center Inc, Carey, OH
Indian Trails Mental Health Living Center, Topeka, KS
Indian Valley Hospital DP/SNF, Greenville, CA
Indian Village Health Center Inc, Fort Wayne, IN
Indiana Presbyterian Homes, Indiana, PA
Indiana Pythian Home, Lafayette, IN
Indiana Veterans Home, West Lafayette, IN
Indianapolis Retirement Home Inc, Indianapolis, IN
Indianola Good Samaritan Center—East, Indianola, IA
Indianola Good Samaritan Center—West, Indianola, IA
Indigo Manor, Daytona Beach, FL
Ingham County Medical Care Facility, Okemos, MI
Inglemoor Inc, Englewood, NJ
Inglemoor West Nursing Home, Livingston, NJ
Ingleside, Mount Horeb, WI
Ingleside Convalescent Center, Detroit, MI
Ingleside Nursing Home, Old Tappan, NJ
Inglewood Health Care Center, Inglewood, CA
Inglewood Manor Nursing Home, Jackson, MS
Inglis House, Philadelphia Home for Physically Disabled Persons, Philadelphia, PA
Charles M Ingram Sr Community Residence, Cheraw, SC
Ingram Manor Nursing Home, Pell City, AL
Inisfail Childrens Home, Faribault, MN
Inland Christian Home Inc, Ontario, CA
Inman Nursing Home, Inman, SC
Inn-Conneaut Health Center, Conneaut, OH
Inn-Madison Health Center, Madison, OH
Inner City Nursing Home Inc, Cleveland, OH
Inns of Evergreen—Central, Baltimore, MD
Inns of Evergreen—Northeast, Baltimore, MD
Inns of Evergreen—Northwest, Baltimore, MD
Inns of Evergreen—South, Baltimore, MD
Inns of Evergreen—West, Baltimore, MD
Innsbruck Healthcare Center, New Brighton, MN
Inter-City Christian Manor, Allen Park, MI
Intercommunity Sanitarium, Long Beach, CA
Interim Care—Metropolitan Hospital, Philadelphia, PA
Intermed of Batesville, Batesville, AR
International Falls Group Home, International Falls, MN
International Nursing Home, Danville, IL
Inver Grove Care Center, Inver Grove Heights, MN
Inverness Healthcare Center, Inverness, FL
Iola Hospital & Nursing Home, Iola, WI
Iona Glos Specialized Living Center, Addison, IL
Ionia Manor, Ionia, MI
Iosco County Medical Care Facility, Tawas City, MI
Iowa City Care Center, Iowa City, IA
Iowa Jewish Senior Life Center, Des Moines, IA
Iowa Lutheran Hospital, Des Moines, IA
Iowa Masonic Nursing Home, Bettendorf, IA
Iredell Memorial Hospital, Statesville, NC
Iris Haven Nursing & Convalescent Center, Chillicothe, TX
Iron County Medical Care Facility, Crystal Falls, MI
Iron County Rest Home, Parowan, UT
Iron River Nursing Home, Iron River, MI
Iroquois Resident Home, Watseka, IL
Irvine Health Care Center, Irvine, KY
William Irvine Home Trust, Wheatland, WY
Irving Care Center, Irving, TX
Irving Living Center, Irving, TX

Isabella County Medical Care Facility, Mount Pleasant, MI
Isabella Geriatric Center, New York, NY
Island Manor Nursing Center, Vashon Island, WA
Island Nursing Home, Honolulu, HI
Island Nursing Home, Deer Isle, ME
Island Nursing Home Inc, Deer Isle, ME
Island Terrace Nursing Home, Lakeville, MA
Island View Manor, Ketchikan, AK
Islands Convalescent Center Inc, Friday Harbor, WA
Issaquah Care Center, Issaquah, WA
Italy Convalescent Center, Italy, TX
Itasca Medical Center C&NC Unit, Grand Rapids, MN
Itasca Nursing Home, Grand Rapids, MN
Itasca Nursing Home, Itasca, TX
Ivinson Memorial Hospital, Laramie, WY
Ivorena Care Center, Eugene, OR
Ivy Hall Geriatric Center, Baltimore, MD
Ivy Hall Nursing Home Inc, Elizabethton, TN
Ivy House, Painesville, OH
Ivy Manor, Bountiful, UT
Ivy Nursing Center, Denver, CO
Ivy Ridge Care Center, Philadelphia, PA
J & C Residential Care Facility, Pueblo, CO
J Claude Fort Community Residence, Gaffney, SC
J S Tarwater Developmental Center, Wetumpka, AL
Jacaranda Manor, Saint Petersburg, FL
Jacinto City Healthcare Center, Jacinto City, TX
Jack Cline Nursing Home, Cook Springs, AL
Jackman Region Health Center, Jackman, ME
Jacksboro Nursing Center, Jacksboro, TX
Jackson Center Nursing Home, Milwaukee, WI
Jackson County Convalescent Center, Graceville, FL
Jackson County Hospital & Nursing Home, Scottsboro, AL
Jackson County Medical Care Facility, Jackson, MI
Jackson County Memorial Hospital, Altus, OK
Jackson County Nursing Home, Murphysboro, IL
Jackson County Nursing Home Inc, Holton, KS
Jackson County Personal Care Home, Pascagoula, MS
Jackson County Public Hospital, Maquoketa, IA
Jackson Friendly Home, Jackson, MI
Jackson Health Care Facility, Jackson, AL
Jackson Healthcare Center, Jackson, NJ
Jackson Heights Nursing Home, Miami, FL
Jackson Heights Nursing Home, Farmer City, IL
Jackson-Madison County General Hospital—Specialty Unit, Jackson, TN
Jackson Manor Inc, Jackson, TN
Jackson Manor Nursing Home, Jonesboro, LA
Jackson Manor Nursing Home, Jackson, MO
Jackson Manor Nursing Home Inc, Miami, FL
Jackson Municipal Nursing Home, Jackson, MN
Jackson Parish Hospital, Jonesboro, LA
Jackson Park Christian Home, Nashville, TN
Jackson Park Convalescent Center, Seymour, IN
Jackson Square Nursing Center, Chicago, IL
Jackson Square Nursing Center of East Fort Worth, Fort Worth, TX
Jackson Square Nursing Center of Texas Inc, Fort Worth, TX
Stonewall Jackson Hospital Long-Term Care Unit, Lexington, VA
Jacksonville Convalescent Center, Jacksonville, FL
Jacksonville Convalescent Center, Jacksonville, IL
Jacksonville Nursing Center, Jacksonville, AR
Jacksonville Terrace Ltd, Jacksonville, IL
Jacob's Dwelling, Coshocton, OH
Jacobsen Nursing Home, Seattle, WA

Jacobson Memorial Hospital Care Center, Elgin, ND
Jamaica Hospital Nursing Home Company Inc, Jamaica, NY
Jamaica Towers Nursing Home, Boston, MA
Ellen James Rest Home, Boston, MA
James G Johnston Memorial Nursing Home, Johnson City, NY
Larry James Home, Waseca, MN
James Manor Rest Home, Fitchburg, MA
Mary James Nursing Home, Montrose, MI
James River Convalescent Center, Newport News, VA
James Square Health & Rehabilitation Centre, Syracuse, NY
James Valley Nursing Home, Redfield, SD
Jamestown, Stillwater, MN
Jamestown Family Care Home, Jamestown, OH
Jamieson Nursing Home, Harrisville, MI
Janesville Health Care Center, Janesville, WI
Janesville Nursing Home, Janesville, MN
Janney House, Mont Clare, PA
January Care Home Inc, Evant, TX
Janus, Bloomington, MN
Japanese Retirement Home—Intermediate Care Facility, Los Angeles, CA
Jaquith Nursing Home—Adams Inn, Whitfield, MS
Jaquith Nursing Home—Washington Inn, Whitfield, MS
Jarvis Heights Nursing Center, Fort Worth, TX
Jasper Convalescent Center, Jasper, TX
Jasper County Care Facility, Newton, IA
Jasper County Nursing Home, Bay Springs, MS
Jasper Nursing Center Inc, Jasper, IN
Jaylene Manor Nursing Home, Saint Petersburg, FL
Jean Carol's Nursing Home Inc, Canton, OH
Jeanne Jugan Residence, Pawtucket, RI
Jean's Nursing Home Inc, College Station, AR
Jefferson Christian Nursing Home, Grand Rapids, MI
Jefferson City Manor Care Center, Jefferson City, MO
Jefferson Convalescent Home Inc, Pine Bluff, AR
Jefferson County Home, Birmingham, AL
Jefferson County Nursing Home, Dandridge, TN
Jefferson Davis County—Extended Care Facility, Prentiss, MS
Jefferson Davis Nursing Home, Jennings, LA
Jefferson Geriatric Center, Jefferson, OH
Jefferson Healthcare Center, Jefferson, LA
Jefferson Hills Manor Inc, Pittsburgh, PA
Jefferson House, Newington, CT
Jefferson House Care Center, Tacoma, WA
Jefferson Manor, Jefferson, IA
Jefferson Manor, Louisville, KY
Jefferson Manor, Brookville, PA
Jefferson Manor Nursing Center, Passaic, NJ
Jefferson Manor Nursing Home, Baton Rouge, LA
Jefferson Meadows Care Center, Baraboo, WI
Jefferson Nursing Center, Monticello, FL
Jefferson Nursing Center, Festus, MO
Jefferson Street Nursing Home, Saint Charles, MO
Jeffersonian Manor, Charles Town, WV
Jeffersonian Nursing Home, Mount Vernon, IL
Jeffersonville Nursing Home, Jeffersonville, IN
Jeffrey Place Nursing Center, Waco, TX
Elmira Jeffries Memorial Home Inc, Philadelphia, PA
Jenkins Hall, Richmond, IN
Jenkins Memorial Inc, Baltimore, MD
Jenkins Memorial Nursing Home, Wellston, OH
Jenkins Methodist Home, Watertown, SD
Jenkins Nursing Home Inc, Marion, SC
Jennings American Legion Hospital Skilled Nursing Facility, Jennings, LA

Eliza Jennings Home, Cleveland, OH
Jennings Guest House, Jennings, LA
Jennings Hall Inc, Garfield Heights, OH
Jennings Health Care Inc, Augusta, GA
Jennings Terrace, Aurora, IL
Chris Jensen Nursing Home, Duluth, MN
Jerome Home, New Britain, CT
Jerri's Benevolent Manor, Saint Louis, MO
Jerseyville Care Center, Jerseyville, IL
Jesmond Nursing Home, Nahant, MA
Jesup Manor Nursing Center, Jesup, GA
Jesup Rest-A-While Nursing Home, Jesup, GA
Jewish Center for Aged, Chesterfield, MO
Jewish Convalescent Center—Scotts Level, Baltimore, MD
Jewish Geriatric Center, Cherry Hill, NJ
Jewish Home, Atlanta, GA
Jewish Home & Hospital for Aged—Bronx Division, Bronx, NY
Jewish Home & Hospital for Aged—Manhattan Division, New York, NY
Jewish Home for Aged, Dayton, OH
Jewish Home for Aged—Prentis Manor, Southfield, MI
Jewish Home for the Aged, New Haven, CT
Jewish Home for the Aged, Portland, ME
Jewish Home for the Aged, Worcester, MA
Jewish Home for the Aged, Providence, RI
Jewish Home for the Aged, Houston, TX
Jewish Home for the Aged 2, Detroit, MI
Jewish Home for the Blind, Chicago, IL
Jewish Home for the Elderly of Fairfield County, Fairfield, CT
Jewish Home of Central New York, Syracuse, NY
Jewish Home of Eastern Pennsylvania, Scranton, PA
Jewish Home of Greater Harrisburg, Harrisburg, PA
Jewish Home of Rochester, Rochester, NY
Jewish Hospital Skilled Nursing Facility, Louisville, KY
Jewish Nursing Home of Western Massachusetts, Longmeadow, MA
Jewish Peoples Convalescent Home, Chicago, IL
Jewish Rehabilitation Center for Aged of the North Shore Inc, Swampscott, MA
JHMCB Center for Nursing & Rehabilitation Inc, Brooklyn, NY
Jo-Lin Health Center Inc, Ironton, OH
Jodoin Home, Chester, NH
Johanna Nursing Home, Salt Lake City, UT
Johanna Shores, Arden Hills, MN
Anna John Nursing Home, Oneida, WI
John Paul II Nursing Center, Kenedy, TX
John XXIII Home, Hermitage, PA
Amy Johnson Residence, Saint Paul, MN
C W Johnson Intermediate Care Facility, Inman, SC
Calvin D Johnson Nursing Home, Belleville, IL
Johnson Care Home, Memphis, TN
Clarence Johnson Care Center, Greensboro, NC
Johnson County Care Center, Warrensburg, MO
Johnson County Intermediate Care, Adrian, GA
Johnson County Nursing Center, Olathe, KS
Johnson County Residential Care Facility, Olathe, KS
Dale Johnson Center, Bellwood, IL
Johnson Health Center, Lakeland, FL
Johnson Home, Westminster, CO
Johnson House, Boulder, CO
J B Johnson Nursing Center, Washington, DC
Lyndon B Johnson Medical Nursing Center, Johnson City, TX
Johnson-Mathers Nursing Home, Carlisle, KY
Johnson Memorial Hospital & Home, Dawson, MN
Johnson Nursing Home, Troy, OH
Johnson Rehabilitation Nursing Home, Chicago, IL
Johnson Rest Home, Erskine, MN
Johnson Rest Home, Fosston, MN

Robert Wood Johnson Jr Health Care, Plainfield, NJ
Johnson's Health Care Center Inc, Harriman, TN
Johnsons Long Lake Home, Walker, MN
Johnson's Meadowlake Home Inc, Conway, AR
Johnson's Riverside Boarding Home Inc, Thief River Falls, MN
Johnston County Memorial Nursing Center Inc, Smithfield, NC
Johnston Nursing Home, Lancaster, OH
Johnstone Developmental Center, Wheatridge, CO
JoLene's Nursing Home Inc, Salisbury, NC
Joliet Terrace, Joliet, IL
Jolley Acres Nursing Home, Orangeburg, SC
Jolly Rest Home Inc, Pascoag, RI
Jones Convalescent Hospital, San Leandro, CA
Jones County Nursing Home, Ellisville, MS
Jones-Darr, Chillicothe, MO
Franke Tobey Jones Home, Tacoma, WA
Jones-Harrison Residence, Minneapolis, MN
Jones Health Center, Orange, TX
Jones Valley Nursing Home, Bessemer, AL
Jonesboro Human Development Center, Jonesboro, AR
Jonesborough Nursing Home, Jonesborough, TN
Jonesburg Caring Center Inc, Jonesburg, MO
Jonesville Rest Home, Jonesville, KY
Joplin Health Care Center, Joplin, MO
Joplin House, Joplin, MO
Jordan & Cole Residential Care Facility, Pueblo, CO
J J Jordan Geriatric Center, Louisa, KY
Ranken Jordan Home for Convalescent Crippled Children, Saint Louis, MO
Jordan Residential Services Inc, Pueblo, CO
Jordan's Nursing Home, Bridgman, MI
Jorgensen House, Minneapolis, MN
Maria Joseph Manor, Danville, PA
Josephine Sunset Home, Stanwood, WA
Josephson Nursing Home, Ironwood, MI
Journey House, Plymouth, MN
Helen Newberry Joy Hospital Annex, Newberry, MI
Joywells, Brownsville, KY
Judson Park, Cleveland Heights, OH
Judson Park Health Center, Des Moines, WA
Judson Village, Cincinnati, OH
Jeanne Jugan Center, Kansas City, MO
Jeanne Jugan Residence, Somerville, MA
Jeanne Jugan Residence, Bronx, NY
Julia Convalescent Hospital, Mountain View, CA
Julia's Valley Manor, Sioux City, IA
Julien Care Facility, Dubuque, IA
Juliette Manor, Berlin, WI
Junction City Nursing Home, Junction City, AR
Juneau Pioneers Home, Juneau, AK
Jupiter Care Center, Jupiter, FL
Jupiter Convalescence Pavilion, Jupiter, FL
Kabul Nursing Home Inc, Cabool, MO
Kachina Point Health Center, Sedona, AZ
Kade Nursing Home, Washington, PA
Kaderly Home, New Philadelphia, OH
Kadoka Nursing Home, Kadoka, SD
Kah Tai Care Center, Port Townsend, WA
Kahl Home for the Aged & Infirm, Davenport, IA
Kahlwood Hospitality Home, Hamilton, MT
Kahuku Hospital, Kahuku, HI
Kalkaska Memorial Health Center, Kalkaska, MI
Kanakuk Nursing Home, Duncan, OK
Kanawha Community Home, Kanawha, IA
John J Kane Allegheny County Home, Pittsburgh, PA
John J Kane Regional Center, McKeesport, PA
John J Kane Regional Center—Ross Township, Pittsburgh, PA
John J Kane Regional Center—Scott Township, Pittsburgh, PA
Kankakee Royale Inc, Kankakee, IL

Kankakee Terrace, Bourbonnais, IL
Kansas Christian Home Inc, Newton, KS
Kansas City Presbyterian Manor, Kansas City, KS
Kansas Masonic Home, Wichita, KS
Abrom Kaplan Memorial Hospital, Kaplan, LA
Kappes Nursing Home, West Allis, WI
Kare Centre, Biloxi, MS
Karen Acres Nursing Home, Des Moines, IA
A Sam Karesh Long-Term Care Center, Camden, SC
Karin's Kottage, Freeland, WA
Karlson Specialized Living Center, Springfield, IL
Karlstad Memorial Nursing Center, Karlstad, MN
Karmenta Health Care Center, Madison, WI
Karnes City Care Center, Karnes City, TX
Karrington Care Center, Portland, OR
Katahdin Nursing Home, Millinocket, ME
Kateri Residence, New York, NY
Katherine Convalescent Hospital, Salinas, CA
Kathleen's Residential Care, Emmetsburg, IA
Katie Jane Memorial Home, Saint Louis, MO
Katyville Healthcare Center, Katy, TX
Ka'u Hospital, Pahala, HI
Kauai Care Center, Waimea, HI
Kauai Veterans Memorial Hospital, Waimea, HI
Andrew Kaul Memorial Hospital—Extended Care Facility, Saint Marys, PA
Kaw Valley Manor, Bonner Springs, KS
Kaweah Manor Convalescent Hospital, Visalia, CA
Sena Kean Manor, Smethport, PA
Kearny Mesa Convalescent & Nursing Home, San Diego, CA
Kearsley—Christ Church Hospital, Philadelphia, PA
Keen Mountain House, Keen Mountain, VA
Keeneland Nursing Home, Weatherford, TX
George B Kegley Manor, Bastian, VA
Keiro Nursing Home, Los Angeles, CA
Keith Acres Nursing Home, Blytheville, AR
Keizer Retirement & Health Care Village, Keizer, OR
Keller Nursing Home, Spokane, WA
Kelliher Good Samaritan, Kelliher, MN
Bill Kelly House, Minneapolis, MN
Kelly's Retirement Home, Pierre, SD
Kelsey Memorial Hospital Inc, Lakeview, MI
Kemp Care Center, Kemp, TX
Kemper County Nursing Home, DeKalb, MS
Ken-Joy Convalescent Center, Hope, IN
Mary Kendall Ladies Home, Owensboro, KY
Kendallville Manor Healthcare Center, Kendallville, IN
Kendallville Nursing Home, Kendallville, IN
Kendallwood Trails Nursing Center Inc, Gladstone, MO
Kenesaw Nursing Home Inc, Baltimore, MD
Kenmare Community Hospital, Kenmare, ND
Kenmore Mercy Hospital Skilled Nursing Facility, Kenmore, NY
Kennebec Valley Medical Center Gardiner Division, Gardiner, ME
Kennebunk Nursing Home, Kennebunk, ME
Kennedale Nursing Home, Kennedale, TX
Kennedy Convalescent Hospital, Los Angeles, CA
Kennedy Living Center, Martinsville, IN
Kennelly House, Burnsville, MN
Kennett Health Care Center, Kennett, MO
Kenney Health Care, Ligonier, IN
Kenney Presbyterian Home, Seattle, WA
Kenniebrew Home, Harvey, IL
Kenoza Hillcrest Nursing Home, Haverhill, MA
Kenoza Manor Convalescent Center, Haverhill, MA
Kensington Gardens Nursing Center, Kensington, MD
Kensington I Group Home, Columbia, SC
Kensington II Group Home, Columbia, SC
Kensington Manor, Sarasota, FL
Kensington Manor, Dallas, TX
Kenson Nursing Home, Baltimore, MD

Kent Community Hospital Long-Term Care Unit, Grand Rapids, MI
Kent Convalescent Center, Smyrna, DE
Kent Convalescent Hospital, Pasadena, CA
Kent County Nursing Home, Jayton, TX
Kent Nursing Center, Fort Worth, TX
Kent Nursing Home, Holmes, NY
Kent Nursing Home Inc, Warwick, RI
Kent Quality Care, Kent, OH
Kentland Nursing Home, Kentland, IN
Kentmere, Wilmington, DE
Kenton Manor, Greeley, CO
Kentucky Rest Haven, Madisonville, KY
Kentwood, Augusta, GA
Kentwood Manor Nursing Home Inc, Kentwood, LA
Kenwood Healthcare Center Inc, Chicago, IL
Kenwood House, Richmond, KY
Kenwood Manor, Enid, OK
Kenwood Terrace Nursing Center Inc, Cincinnati, OH
Kenwood View Nursing Home, Salina, KS
Kenya Village Nursing Home, Duncan, OK
Kenyon Sunset Home, Kenyon, MN
Keokuk Area Hospital, Keokuk, IA
Keokuk Convalescent Center, Keokuk, IA
Kepler Home Inc, Elizabethtown, PA
Kepley House, Pittsfield, IL
Kermit Nursing Center, Kermit, TX
Kern Place, Grand Prairie, TX
Lillian Kerr Nursing Home, Phelps, WI
Kessler Home, Story, WY
Keswick Home for Incurables of Baltimore City, Baltimore, MD
Bertha D Garten Ketcham Memorial Center Inc, Odon, IN
Ketcham's Nursing Home, Crooksville, OH
Ketchikan Pioneers Home, Ketchikan, AK
Ketter Manor Inc, Falls City, NE
Kettering Convalescent Center, Kettering, OH
Kewanee Care Home, Kewanee, IL
Kewaunee Health Care Center, Kewaunee, WI
Key Circle Hospice Inc, Baltimore, MD
Key City Retirement Home, Sturgis, SD
Key Pine Village, Lecanto, FL
Key West Convalescent Center, Key West, FL
Keystone Healthcare Center, Indianapolis, IN
Keystone Nursing Care Center, Keystone, IA
Keystone Nursing Home, Leominster, MA
Keysville Convalescent & Nursing Center Inc, Keysville, GA
Kidwell Rest Home, Romney, WV
Kilbourn Care Center, Milwaukee, WI
Kilgore Nursing Center, Kilgore, TX
Killeen Nursing Center, Killeen, TX
Kimball County Manor, Kimball, NE
Kimberly Convalescent Hospital, Santa Maria, CA
Kimberly Hall Nursing Home—North, Windsor, CT
Kimberly Hall Nursing Home—South, Windsor, CT
Sage View Care Center, Rock Springs, WY
Kimberly Woods, Columbus, OH
Kimbrough Nursing Home, Springfield, MO
Kimes Convalescent Center, Athens, OH
Kimwell Health Care Center A Skilled Nursing Facility, Fall River, MA
Kin ON Nursing Home, Seattle, WA
Kinder Nursing Home, Kinder, LA
Kindlehope, Willmar, MN
King-Bruwaert House, Burr Ridge, IL
King City Convalescent Center, Tigard, OR
King City Manor, King City, MO
King David Care Center of Atlantic City, Atlantic City, NJ
King David Center at Palm Beach, West Palm Beach, FL
King Family Care Home, Arvada, CO
James C King Home, Evanston, IL
King James Care Center, Chatham, NJ
King James Care Center of Mercer, Hamilton Square, NJ
King James Care Center of Middletown, Navesink, NJ
King James Care Center of Somerset, Somerset, NJ
King Manor, Neptune, NJ

King Nursing Home, Houghton Lake, MI
King Road ICF, Chichester, NH
King Springs Village, Sayrna, GA
King Street Home Inc, Port Chester, NY
King Tree Center, Dayton, OH
King William Health Care Center, San Antonio, TX
Kingdom Nursing Home Association Inc, Fulton, MO
Kingman Health Care Center, Kingman, AZ
Kings Convalescent Center, Hanford, CA
Kings Daughters & Sons Home, Louisville, KY
King's Daughters & Sons Home, Wrentham, MA
King's Daughters & Sons Home, Memphis, TN
King's Daughters & Sons Home for Aged Men & Women, Ashland, KY
King's Daughters & Sons Nursing Home, Durant, OK
King's Daughters & Sons Rest Home Inc, Meridian, MS
King's Daughters Home, Mexico, MO
King's Guest Home Inc, Winnsboro, LA
Kings Harbor Care Center, Bronx, NY
Kings Harbor Manor Facility, Bronx, NY
King's Manor Methodist Home Inc, Hereford, TX
Kings Mountain Convalescent Center, Kings Mountain, NC
Kings Mountain Hospital—Skilled Nursing Facility, Kings Mountain, NC
King's Retirement Home, Bozeman, MT
Kings Terrace Nursing Home & Health Related Facility, Bronx, NY
Kings Vista Convalescent Hospital, Fowler, CA
Kingsbridge Heights Long-Term Home Health Care, Bronx, NY
Kingsbridge Heights Manor, Bronx, NY
Kingsbury Memorial Manor (NCHS), Lake Preston, SD
Kingsbury Rehabilitation & Retirement Centre, Lebanon, IN
Kingsdale Manor, Lumberton, NC
Kingsland Hills Care Center, Kingsland, TX
Kingsley Convalescent Hospital, Los Angeles, CA
Kingstree Community Residence, Kingstree, SC
Kingstree Nursing Facility Inc, Kingstree, SC
Kingsway Arms Nursing Center Inc, Schenectady, NY
Kinkora Pythian Home, Duncannon, PA
Kinney Nursing Home, Gouverneur, NY
Kinton Nursing Home Inc, Fuquay-Varina, NC
Kinzua Valley Health Care, Warren, PA
Kirby Pines Manor, Memphis, TN
Kirkhaven, Rochester, NY
Kirkland Convalescent Center, Kirkland, WA
Kirkland Convalescent Home Inc, Williston, SC
Kirksville Manor Care Center Skilled Nursing Facility, Kirksville, MO
Kirkwood by the River, Birmingham, AL
Kirkwood Manor, New Braunfels, TX
Kirkwood Nursing Home, Wakefield, MA
Kissimmee Good Samaritan Nursing Center, Kissimmee, FL
Kissimmee Health Care Center, Kissimmee, FL
Kit Carson Convalescent Hospital, Jackson, CA
Kith Haven, Flint, MI
Kitsap Peninsula House, Tacoma, WA
Kittson County Nursing Home, Hallock, MN
Kittson Memorial Hospital, Hallock, MN
Kiva at Sun Ridge, Surprise, AZ
Kiva House, Lexington, KY
Kivel Care Center, Phoenix, AZ
Kiwanis Manor Inc, East Troy, WI
KJ's TLC, Sheridan, WY
Klearview Manor, Fairfield, ME
Klima Kastle—Rock Home, Whitewood, SD
Klingerman Nursing Center, Orangeville, PA
Klondike Manor, Louisville, KY

Knapp Haven, Chetek, WI
Ada S McKinley Knight House, Chicago, IL
Knight's Nursing Home, Littlefield, TX
Knights Templar Clinic, Arlington, TX
Knolls West Convalescent Hospital, Victorville, CA
Knollview Manor, Muskegon, MI
Knollwood, Washington, DC
Knollwood Hall, Winston-Salem, NC
Knollwood Manor Inc, Millersville, MD
Knollwood Nursing Home, Worcester, MA
Knopp Nursing Home Inc 1, Fredericksburg, TX
Knopp Nursing & Retirement Home 2 Inc, Fredericksburg, TX
Knott County Nursing Home, Hindman, KY
Knott Nursing Home, Charles Town, WV
Knottsville Home, Philpot, KY
Joseph B Knowles Home for the Aged, Nashville, TN
Knowlton Manor Nursing Home, Upton, MA
Knox County Nursing Home, Knoxville, IL
Knox County Nursing Home, Edina, MO
Knox Estates, Kankakee, IL
John Knox Manor Inc II, Montgomery, AL
John Knox Village of Lubbock Inc, Lubbock, TX
John Knox Village Medical Center, Weslaco, TX
John Knox Village Care Center, Lee's Summit, MO
John Knox Village Medical Center, Pompano Beach, FL
John Knox Village Medical Center, Tampa, FL
John Knox Village of Central Florida Inc, Orange City, FL
Knoxville Convalescent Center, Knoxville, TN
Knoxville Health Care Center Inc, Knoxville, TN
Knutson Manor Nursing Center, El Dorado, KS
Kodiak Island Hospital, Kodiak, AK
Koep Group Home, Fergus Falls, MN
Kohala Hospital, Kapaau, HI
Kokomo Nursing Home—Greentree Manor, Kokomo, IN
Kona Hospital, Kealakekua, HI
Kooda Home, Morris, MN
Kosary Home, Oak Forest, IL
Kountze Nursing Center, Kountze, TX
KPHA/Narrows Drive, Tacoma, WA
Kramm Healthcare—Broadway, Milton, PA
Kramm Healthcare Center Inc, Milton, PA
Kramm Nursing Home Inc, Watsontown, PA
Kraus Home Inc, Chicago, IL
Kraus House, Milton, NH
Kraver Institute, North Miami Beach, FL
Kremmling Memorial Hospital, Kremmling, CO
Kristen Beth Nursing Home Inc, New Bedford, MA
Kristi Lee Manor Inc, Colorado City, TX
Kroegers House, Faribault, MN
Krypton House, Metropolis, IL
Kuakini Geriatric Care Inc, Honolulu, HI
Kula Hospital, Kula, HI
Kurthwood Manor Nursing Home, Leesville, LA
Milton & Hattie Kutz Home, Wilmington, DE
Kutztown Manor Inc, Kutztown, PA
K'Way Kare Nursing Home, Holland, TX
Kyakameena Sanitorium, Berkeley, CA
L D S Hospital Transitional Care Center, Salt Lake City, UT
L & M Cedar Manor Home, Baker, OR
La Belle Manor, La Belle, MO
La Belle's Rest Home, Shelburne Falls, MA
La Boure Care Center, Dallas, TX
La Canada Care Center, Tucson, AZ
La Casa Mental Health Center, Norwalk, CA
La Colina Healthcare, Tucson, AZ
La Dora Lodge Nursing Home, Bedford, TX
La Habra Convalescent Hospital, La Habra, CA
La Hacienda Nursing Home, Tucson, AZ
La Hacienda Nursing Home Inc, San Diego, TX

La Jolla Convalescent Hospital, La Jolla, CA
La Mesa Care Center, Yuma, AZ
La Moure Healthcare Manor, La Moure, ND
La Paz Geropsychiatric Center, Paramount, CA
La Porte Care Center, La Porte, TX
La Posada, Alamosa, CO
La Posada Convalescent Home, Miami, FL
La Residencia NC, Santa Fe, NM
La Rocca Nursing Home, Tuscaloosa, AL
La Salette Rehabilitation & Convalescent Hospital, Stockton, CA
La Salle Nursing Home Inc, Jena, LA
La Sierra Convalescent Hospital, Merced, CA
La Siesta Care Center, Hobbs, NM
La Verna Heights Retirement Center, Savannah, MO
La Verna Village Nursing Home Inc, Savannah, MO
La Vida Llena Retirement Center, Albuquerque, NM
LaBelle View Nursing Center, Steubenville, OH
Lacey Manor, Hanford, CA
Lacey Nursing & Rehabilitation Center, Forked River, NJ
Lackawanna County Health Care Center, Olyphant, PA
Lackey Convalescent Home, Forest, MS
Lackey Manor Nursing Home, Oklahoma City, OK
Lacoba Homes Inc, Monett, MO
Laconia Nursing Home, Bronx, NY
LaCrescent Healthcare Center, LaCrescent, MN
Ladera Health Care Center Inc, Albuquerque, NM
Ladies Grand Army of the Republic Home, Pittsburgh, PA
Lady of the Oaks Nursing Home, Lafayette, LA
Lady of the Sea General Hospital, Galliano, LA
Ladysmith Nursing Home, Ladysmith, WI
Lafayette Christian Nursing Center, Grand Rapids, MI
Lafayette Convalescent Home, Marblehead, MA
Lafayette Convalescent Hospital, Lafayette, CA
Lafayette Extended Care, Lafayette, AL
Lafayette General Medical Center Skilled Nursing Facility, Lafayette, LA
Lafayette Good Samaritan Center, Lafayette, MN
Lafayette Guest House—East, Lafayette, LA
Lafayette Guest House—West, Lafayette, LA
Lafayette Health Care Center, Philadelphia, PA
LaFayette Health Care Inc, LaFayette, GA
Lafayette Healthcare Center, Lafayette, IN
Lafayette Manor, Darlington, WI
Lafayette Manor Inc, Uniontown, PA
Lafayette Manor Nursing Home, Lexington, MO
LaFayette Nursing Home Inc, Lafayette, AL
Lafayette Nursing Home Inc, North Kingstown, RI
Lafayette Villa Health Care, Norfolk, VA
LaFollette Community Nursing Home, LaFollette, TN
Lafon Nursing Home of the Holy Family, New Orleans, LA
Lafon United Methodist Nursing Home, New Orleans, LA
Lafourche Home for the Aged & Infirm Inc, Thibodaux, LA
LaGrange Nursing Home, Lagrange, IN
Laguna Rainbow Nursing Center, New Laguna, NM
Morris Lahasky Nursing Home, Erath, LA
Lahey's Nursing Home, Duncan, OK
Lahser Hills Nursing Center, Southfield, MI
Lake Alfred Restorium, Lake Alfred, FL
Lake Andes Health Care Center, Lake Andes, SD
Lake Bluff Health Care Center, Lake Bluff, IL
Lake Charles Care Center, Lake Charles, LA

Lake City Health Care Center, Lake City, TN
Lake City Nursing Home, Lake City, MN
Lake City-Scranton Convalescent Center, Scranton, SC
Lake Country Manor, Marietta, OK
Lake Country Manor, Breckenridge, TX
Lake County Adult Residential Center, Mentor, OH
Lake County Child Development Center, Mentor, OH
Lake County Convalescent Home, Crown Point, IN
Lake County Rehabilitation Center Inc, East Chicago, IN
Lake Crest Villa, Evanston, IL
Lake Crystal Healthcare Center, Lake Crystal, MN
Lake District Hospital & Skilled Nursing Facility, Lakeview, OR
Lake Drive Nursing Home Inc, Baltimore, MD
Lake Drive Nursing Home Inc, Henryetta, OK
Lake Erie Institute of Rehabilitation, Erie, PA
Lake Eustis Care Center, Eustis, FL
Lake Forest Good Samaritan Village Health Care Center, Denton, TX
Lake Forest Nursing Center, El Toro, CA
Lake Haven Health Care Center Inc, Benton, KY
Lake Haven Manor, Duluth, MN
Lake Haven Nursing Home, Worthington, MN
Lake Highlands Retirement & Nursing Home, Clermont, FL
Lake Holiday Manor, Roselawn, IN
Lake Jackson Nursing Home, Lake Jackson, TX
Lake Lodge, Lake Worth, TX
Lake Mills Care Center, Lake Mills, IA
Lake Norden Care Center, Lake Norden, SD
Lake Owasso Residence, Shoreview, MN
Lake Park Care Center, Lake Park, IA
Lake Park Center, Waukegan, IL
Lake Park Nursing Care Center, Sylvania, OH
Lake Park Nursing & Retirement Center, Dallas, TX
Lake Park Retirement Residence, Oakland, CA
Lake Placid Health Care Center, Lake Placid, FL
Lake Region Lutheran Home, Devils Lake, ND
Lake Region Nursing Home, Fergus Falls, MN
Lake Ridge Health Care Center, Roseville, MN
Lake Shore Hospital Inc HRF, Irving, NY
Lake Shore Nursing Center, Cleveland, OH
Lake Shore Nursing Centre, Chicago, IL
Lake Shore Nursing Home Inc, Irving, NY
Lake Taylor Hospital—Long-Term Care Unit, Norfolk, VA
Lake Towers Health Center, Sun City Center, FL
Lake View, Arvada, CO
Lake View Care Center, Bigfork, MT
Lake View Community Nursing Home, Lawton, MI
Lake View Home, Monticello, IN
Lake Vue Gardens, Kirkland, WA
Lake Waccamaw Convalescent Center, Lake Waccamaw, NC
Lake Wales Convalescent Center, Lake Wales, FL
Lake Wales Hospital Extended Care Facility, Lake Wales, FL
Lake Worth Health Care Center, Lake Worth, FL
Lake Worth Nursing Home, Fort Worth, TX
Lake Worth Nursing Home, Lake Worth, TX
Lakecity Healthcare Center Nursing Home, Morrow, GA
Lakecrest Development Care Center, Orem, UT
Lakefront Health Care Center Incorporated, Chicago, IL
Lakehaven Nursing Home, Valdosta, GA
Lakeland Convalescent Center, Lakeland, FL
Lakeland Convalescent Center, Detroit, MI
Lakeland Health Care Center, Lakeland, FL

Lakeland Health Care Center, Jackson, MS
Lakeland Health Care Center, Haskell, NJ
Lakeland Healthcare Center, Effingham, IL
Lakeland Lodge Nursing Home, Heber Springs, AR
Lakeland Loving Care Center Inc, Milford, IN
Lakeland Manor Inc, Ardmore, OK
Lakeland Nursing Center, Angola, IN
Lakeland Nursing Home, Pineville, LA
Lakeland Nursing Home, Geneva, OH
Lakeland Nursing Home of Walworth County, Elkhorn, WI
Lakeland Villa Convalescent Center, Lakeland, GA
Lakeport Skilled Nursing Center Inc, Lakeport, CA
Lakeridge Village Health Care Center, Lakewood, CO
Lakeshore Convalescent, Oakland, CA
Lakeshore Heartland, Nashville, TN
Lakeshore Heights Nursing Center, Gainesville, GA
Lakeshore Inn Nursing Home, Waseca, MN
Lakeshore Lutheran Home, Duluth, MN
Lakeshore Nursing Home, Crescent City, FL
Lakeshore Nursing Home, Rochester, NY
Lakeshore Nursing Home & Retirement Center, Nashville, TN
Lakeshore Villas Health Care Center, Tampa, FL
Lakeside Boarding Home, Chicago, IL
Lakeside Care Center, Lubbock, TX
Lakeside Center, Ah Gwah Ching, MN
Lakeside Convalescent Center, Athens, TX
Lakeside Health Center, West Palm Beach, FL
Lakeside Health Center Inc, Michigan City, IN
Lakeside Lutheran Home, Emmetsburg, IA
Lakeside Medical Center, Pine City, MN
Lakeside Nursing Center, Lake City, AR
Lakeside Nursing Center, Dallas, PA
Lakeside Nursing Home Inc, Ithaca, NY
Lakeside Place, Highland Heights, KY
Lakeside Plantation, Naples, FL
Lakeside Residential Care Facility, East Hampton, CT
Lakeview Care Center, Glenwood, MN
Lakeview Childrens Home, Sauk Centre, MN
Lakeview Christian Home of the Southwest Inc, Carlsbad, NM
Lakeview Convalescent Center Inc, Wayne, NJ
Lakeview Health Care Center, Carmel, IN
Lakeview Health Care Center, Lamar, MO
Lakeview Health Center, Harrisville, RI
Lakeview Health Center, Pascoag, RI
Lakeview Health Center, West Salem, WI
Lakeview House Nursing Home, Haverhill, MA
Lakeview Living Center, Chicago, IL
Lakeview Lutheran Manor Nursing Home, Cadillac, MI
Lakeview Manor, Weyauwega, WI
Lakeview Manor Inc, Indianapolis, IN
Lakeview Manor Nursing Home, New Roads, LA
Lakeview Manor Nursing Home, Lakewood, NJ
Lakeview Memorial Hospital, Two Harbors, MN
Lakeview Methodist Health Care Center, Fairmont, MN
Lakeview Nursing & Geriatric Center Inc, Chicago, IL
Lakeview Nursing Center, Sanford, FL
Lakeview Nursing Center, Grand Island, NE
Lakeview Nursing Home, Birmingham, AL
Lakeview Nursing Home, Morgantown, KY
Lakeview Nursing Home Inc, Birmingham, AL
Lakeview Nursing Home Inc, Gridley, CA
Lakeview Nursing Home Inc, Farmerville, LA
Lakeview Rest Home, Newton, MA
Lakeview Rest Home, Firth, NE
Lakeview Skilled Nursing Home, Ellisville, MS
Lakeview Terrace Christian Retirement Community, Altoona, FL
Lakeview Terrace Medical Care Facility, Altoona, FL
Lakeview Village Inc, Lenexa, KS

Lakewood Care Center, Milwaukee, WI
Lakewood Convalescent Home, Hot Springs, AR
Lakewood Manor, Waterville, ME
Lakewood Manor Baptist Retirement Community Inc, Richmond, VA
Lakewood Manor North, Los Angeles, CA
Lakewood Manor Nursing Center, Hendersonville, NC
Lakewood Meridian Health Center, Lakewood, CO
Lakewood Nursing Home, Lakewood, CO
Lakewood Nursing Home, Plainfield, IL
Lakewood of Voorhees, Voorhees, NJ
Lakewood Park Health Center, Downey, CA
Lakewood Village, Fort Worth, TX
Lalla Convalescent Center, Austin, TX
Lamar Convalescent Center, Vernon, AL
Lamar County Hospital & Nursing Home, Vernon, AL
Jane Lamb Health Center, Clinton, IA
Lambs Inc, Libertyville, IL
Lamesa Nursing Center, Lamesa, TX
LaMoine Christian Nursing Home, Roseville, IL
Lamoni Manor, Lamoni, IA
Lamp, Brook Park, OH
Lamp Nursing Home, Lisbon, ME
Lampasas Manor, Lampasas, TX
Lanai Community Hospital, Lanai City, HI
Lancashire Hall, Lancaster, PA
Lancashire Nursing Home, Kilmarnock, VA
Lancaster Convalescent Hospital, Lancaster, CA
Lancaster County Care Center, Lancaster, SC
Lancaster Living Center, Lancaster, WI
Lancaster Manor, Lincoln, NE
Lancaster Nursing Home Inc, Lancaster, TX
Lancaster Residential Center, Lancaster, TX
Lancia Convalescent Center, Steubenville, OH
Lancia Country Club Manor, Steubenville, OH
Lancia Villa Royale Nursing Home, Steubenville, OH
Landis Homes Retirement Community, Lititz, PA
Landmark Learning Center—Facility I, Opa Locka, FL
Landmark Learning Center—Miami Facility II, Opa Locka, FL
Landmark Medical Center, Pomona, CA
Landsun Homes Inc, Carlsbad, NM
Lane House, Crawfordsville, IN
Lane Memorial Hospital Geriatric Unit, Zachary, LA
Lane's Nursing Home—Monette, Monette, AR
Lane's Rest Home Inc—Caraway, Caraway, AR
Lanessa Extended Care Facility, Webster, MA
Lanett Geriatric Center Inc, Lanett, AL
Langhorne Gardens Nursing Center, Langhorne, PA
Langton Place, Saint Paul, MN
George H Lanier Memorial Nursing Home, Valley, AL
Lanier North Nursing Home, Gainesville, GA
Lanier Nursing Home, Cumming, GA
Lanore's Nursing Home, Draper, UT
Lansdowne Rest Home, East Lansdowne, PA
Lanterman Developmental Center, Pomona, CA
Lantern Park Care Center, Coralville, IA
Lantern Park Manor, Colby, KS
Lapeer County Medical Care Facility, Lapeer, MI
LaPlata Nursing Home, LaPlata, MO
LaPorte United Methodist Home, LaPorte, PA
Larchwood Lodge Nursing Home Inc, Waltham, MA
Largo Manor Care, Largo, MD
Larimore Good Samaritan Center, Larimore, ND
Lark Ellen Towers Skilled Nursing Facility, West Covina, CA
Lark Manor Convalescent Hospital, Los Gatos, CA
Larksfield Place, Wichita, KS
Hattie Larlham Foundation, Mantua, OH
Larsen's Nursing Home, Lehi, UT

Las Cruces Nursing Center, Las Cruces, NM
Las Flores Convalescent Hospital, Gardena, CA
Las Flores Nursing Center, Mesa, AZ
Las Fuentes Care Center, Prescott, AZ
Las Palomas Health Care Center, Albuquerque, NM
Las Vegas Convalescent Center, Las Vegas, NV
Las Vegas Medical Center, Las Vegas, NM
Las Villas Del Norte Health Center, Escondido, CA
LaSalle Convalescent Home, Minneapolis, MN
LaSalle County Nursing Home, Ottawa, IL
LaSalle General Hospital, Jena, LA
LaSalle Nursing Home, Detroit, MI
Lasata, Cedarburg, WI
Lassen Community Skilled Nursing Facility, Susanville, CA
Latah Care Center Inc, Moscow, ID
Latah Center Inc, Spokane, WA
Latham Care Center, California, MO
Latham Estates, Lake Forest, IL
Latham Nursing Home, Anderson, SC
Latham Nursing Home, Salt Lake City, UT
Lathrop Health Facility Inc, Lathrop, MO
Rose Hawthorne Lathrop Home, Fall River, MA
Latimer Nursing Home, Wilburton, OK
Ozie LaTrece Home for the Aged, Detroit, MI
Latta Road Nursing Home, Rochester, NY
Latta Road Nursing Home A, Rochester, NY
Laub Pavilion of Cleveland Ohio, Cleveland, OH
Lauderdale Christian Nursing Home, Killen, AL
Lauderdale County Nursing Home, Ripley, TN
Laura Baker School, Northfield, MN
Laurel Avenue Rest Home Inc, Bridgeport, CT
Laurel Care Center, Laurel, MT
Laurel Convalescent Hospital, Fontana, CA
Laurel Creek Health Care Center, Manchester, KY
Laurel Crest Manor, Ebensburg, PA
Laurel Foster Home Inc, Coventry, RI
Laurel Glen Convalescent Hospital, Redwood City, CA
Laurel Health Center, Uniontown, PA
Laurel Heights Convalescent Hospital, San Francisco, CA
Laurel Heights Home for the Elderly, London, KY
Laurel Hill Health Care, Pickens, SC
Laurel Hill Nursing Center, Grants Pass, OR
Laurel Hill Nursing Home, Dunmore, PA
Laurel Lane, Clifton, CO
Laurel Living Center, Hamburg, PA
Laurel Living Center Inc, Manchester, CT
Laurel Manor Care Center, Colorado Springs, CO
Laurel Manor Health Care, New Tazewell, TN
Laurel Manor Nursing Home, Stroudsburg, PA
Laurel Park—A School for Effective Living, Pomona, CA
Laurelbrook Sanitarium, Dayton, TN
Laurelhurst Care Center, Portland, OR
Laurels, A Rehabilitation Center, Saint Petersburg, FL
Laurelton Center, Laurelton, PA
Laurelwood Health Care Center, Rock Island, IL
Laurelwood Health Care Center, Jackson, TN
Laurelwood Manor Nursing Home, Gaston, OR
Laurelwood Nursing Center, Elkton, MD
Laurens County Convalescent Center Inc, Dublin, GA
Laurens Health Care Center, Laurens, SC
Laurens State Community Residence, Aiken, SC
Laurie Ann Nursing Home, Newton Falls, OH
Laurie Nursing Home/Laurie Knolls, Laurie, MO
Lavilla Grande, Grand Junction, CO
LaVilla Nursing Center, Detroit, MI
Law-Den Nursing Home, Detroit, MI

Lawn View Nursing Home, Tishomingo, OK
Lawrence Convalescent Center, Portland, OR
Lawrence County Nursing Center Inc, Monticello, MS
Lawrence County Nursing Home, Mount Vernon, MO
Lawrence Hall Nursing Home, Walnut Ridge, AR
Lawrence Manor Nursing Home, Indianapolis, IN
Lawrence Manor Nursing Home, Lynn, MA
Lawrence Nursing Home Inc, Arverne, NY
Lawrence Place, Lincoln, IL
Lawrence Presbyterian Manor, Lawrence, KS
Lawrenceburg Health Care Center, Lawrenceburg, TN
Lawrenceburg Manor, Lawrenceburg, TN
Lawrenceville Nursing Home, Lawrenceville, NJ
Lawson Nursing Home Inc, Clairton, PA
Walter J Lawson Memorial Home for Children, Rockford, IL
Lawton Heights Nursing Center, Lawton, OK
Lawton Nursing Home, Fort Wayne, IN
Layton Home, Wilmington, DE
Le Havre Convalescent Hospital, Menlo Park, CA
Le Sueur Residence, Waterville, MN
Albert Lea Boarding Care Center, Albert Lea, MN
Lea County Good Samaritan Village, Hobbs, NM
Lea Manor Health Care Center, Norwalk, CT
Leader Health Care & Rehabilitation Center II, Norristown, PA
Leader Nursing & Rehabilitation—Allentown, Allentown, PA
Leader Nursing & Rehabilitation Center, Cherry Hill, NJ
Leader Nursing & Rehabilitation Center, West Deptford, NJ
Leader Nursing & Rehabilitation Center, Easton, PA
Leader Nursing & Rehabilitation Center, Harrisburg, PA
Leader Nursing & Rehabilitation Center, Sunbury, PA
Leader Nursing & Rehabilitation Center II—Bethlehem, Bethlehem, PA
Leader Nursing & Rehabilitation Center—Bethel Park, Bethel Park, PA
Leader Nursing & Rehabilitation Center—Camp Hill, Camp Hill, PA
Leader Nursing & Rehabilitation Center—Carlisle, Carlisle, PA
Leader Nursing & Rehabilitation Center—Dallastown, Dallastown, PA
Leader Nursing & Rehabilitation Center—East, Kingston, PA
Leader Nursing & Rehabilitation Center—Elizabethtown, Elizabethtown, PA
Leader Nursing & Rehabilitation Center—Green Tree, Pittsburgh, PA
Leader Nursing & Rehabilitation Center I, Norristown, PA
Leader Nursing & Rehabilitation Center I—Bethlehem, Bethlehem, PA
Leader Nursing & Rehabilitation Center—Jersey Shore, Jersey Shore, PA
Leader Nursing & Rehabilitation Center—Laureldale, Laureldale, PA
Leader Nursing & Rehabilitation Center—Lebanon, Lebanon, PA
Leader Nursing & Rehabilitation Center—North, Williamsport, PA
Leader Nursing & Rehabilitation Center—Pottstown, Pottstown, PA
Leader Nursing & Rehabilitation Center—Pottsville, Pottsville, PA
Leader Nursing & Rehabilitation Center—Sinking Spring, Sinking Spring, PA
Leader Nursing & Rehabilitation Center—South, Williamsport, PA
Leader Nursing & Rehabilitation Center—West, Kingston, PA
Leader Nursing & Rehabilitation Center—West Reading, West Reading, PA

Leader Nursing & Rehabilitation Center—Yeadon, Yeadon, PA
Leader Nursing & Rehabilitation—Pike Creek, Wilmington, DE
Leader Nursing & Rehabilitation Center—Chambersburg, Chambersburg, PA
Leader Nursing & Rehabilitation Center, Wilmington, DE
Leader Nursing & Rehabilitation Center, Madison, WI
Leahi Hospital, Honolulu, HI
Leake County Memorial Hospital & Skilled Nursing Facility, Carthage, MS
Leavenworth County Convalescent Infirmary, Leavenworth, KS
Lebanon Care Center, Lebanon, MO
Lebanon Country Manor, Lebanon, OH
Lebanon County Life Support, Lebanon, PA
Lebanon Health Care Center, Lebanon, OH
Lebanon Manor, Lebanon, IL
Lebanon Manor, Lebanon, MO
Lebanon Nursing Home, Lebanon, OH
Lebanon Valley Brethren Home, Palmyra, PA
Lebanon Valley Home, Annville, PA
Ledgecrest Convalescent Home, Kensington, CT
Ledges Manor, Boone, IA
Ledgeview Nursing Home, West Paris, ME
Ledgewood Manor Inc, North Windham, ME
Ledgewood Nursing Care Center, Beverly, MA
Ann Lee Home, Albany, NY
Lee Convalescent Center, Fort Myers, FL
Lee County Constant Care Inc, Beattyville, KY
Lee County Nursing Home, Dixon, IL
Linda Lee Rest Home, Worcester, MA
Lee Manor, Des Plaines, IL
Lee Manor Home for the Retired, Fairfax, VA
Lee Manor Nursing Home, Tupelo, MS
Marjorie P Lee Home for the Aged, Cincinnati, OH
Lee Rest Home, Waltham, MA
Sara Lee Nursing Home Inc, Doylestown, OH
Lee Street, Arvada, CO
Leelanau Memorial Hospital, Northport, MI
Lee's Rest Home, Newell, SD
Lee's Summit Nursing Center, Lee's Summit, MO
Leesburg Healthcare Center, Leesburg, FL
Leesburg Nursing Center, Leesburg, FL
Leesburg Sunrise Retirement Homes, Leesburg, VA
Leesville State School, Leesville, LA
Leeward Nursing Home, Waianae, HI
Leewood Manor Nursing Home Inc, Milan, MO
Leewood Nursing Home, Tucson, AZ
Leewood Nursing Home, Annandale, VA
LeFlore Nursing Home, Poteau, OK
Legacy Lodge Nursing Home, Russellville, AR
Leigh Lane Care Center, Greenfield, OH
Leigh Manor, Picher, OK
Leisure Arms Health Related Facility, Troy, NY
Leisure Arms Nursing Home, Houston, TX
Leisure Center, Caldwell, KS
Leisure Chateau Care Center, Lakewood, NJ
Leisure Hills Healthcare Center, Hibbing, MN
Leisure Hills Inc, Grand Rapids, MN
Leisure Homestead Association, Stafford, KS
Leisure Lodge, McGehee, AR
Leisure Lodge, Monticello, AR
Leisure Lodge, Anahuac, TX
Leisure Lodge, Carthage, TX
Leisure Lodge, Gilmer, TX
Leisure Lodge, Kaufman, TX
Leisure Lodge—Caldwell, Caldwell, TX
Leisure Lodge Centerville, Centerville, TX
Leisure Lodge—Cleburne, Cleburne, TX
Leisure Lodge—Coleman, Coleman, TX
Leisure Lodge—Hamilton, Hamilton, TX
Leisure Lodge—Hearne, Hearne, TX
Leisure Lodge—Henderson, Henderson, TX
Leisure Lodge Inc—Camden Bruce Street, Camden, AR
Leisure Lodge Inc—Camden Magnolia Road, Camden, AR
Leisure Lodge Inc—Crossett, Crossett, AR

Leisure Lodge Inc—DeWitt, De Witt, AR
Leisure Lodge Inc—Hamburg, Hamburg, AR
Leisure Lodge Inc—Lake Village, Lake Village, AR
Leisure Lodge Inc of Nashville, Nashville, AR
Leisure Lodge Inc—Searcy, Searcy, AR
Leisure Lodge Inc—West Memphis, West Memphis, AR
Leisure Lodge—Junction, Junction, TX
Leisure Lodge—Lampasas, Lampasas, TX
Leisure Lodge of Brady, Brady, TX
Leisure Lodge—Overton, Overton, TX
Leisure Lodge—Palacios, Palacios, TX
Leisure Lodge—Rosenberg, Rosenberg, TX
Leisure Lodge—Rusk, Rusk, TX
Leisure Lodge—Sulphur Springs, Sulphur Springs, TX
Leisure Lodge Texarkana, Texarkana, TX
Leisure Lodge—Weatherford, Weatherford, TX
Leisure Lodge—Wortham, Wortham, TX
Leisure Manor, Saint Petersburg, FL
Leisure Manor, Okmulgee, OK
Leisure Oaks Convalescent Center, Defiance, OH
Leisure Park Health Center, Lakewood, NJ
Leisure Village, Wayne, MI
Leisure Village Nursing Center, Tulsa, OK
Leisure Years Nursing Home, Owensboro, KY
Leithchfield Health Care Manor, Leitchfield, KY
Lelah G Wagner Nursing Home, Panama City, FL
Leland Home, Waltham, MA
Lely Palms of Naples Health Care Center, Naples, FL
Lemberg Home & Geriatric Institute Inc, Brooklyn, NY
Lemington Home for the Aged, Pittsburgh, PA
Lemon Grove Convalescent Center, Lemon Grove, CA
Lemon Park Community Residence, Barnwell, SC
Lena Continental Manor Nursing Home Inc, Lena, IL
Lena Crews Family Care Home, Denver, CO
Lenawee County Medical Care Facility, Adrian, MI
Lenbrook Square, Atlanta, GA
Lenevar Community Residence, Charleston, SC
Lennox Good Samaritan Center, Lennox, SD
Lenoir Health Care Center, Columbia, MO
Lenoir Memorial Hospital Inc, Kinston, NC
Lenox Care Center, Lenox, IA
Lenox Nursing Home Inc, Bradford, MA
Leon Care Center, Leon, IA
Leon Valley Lodge, Leon Valley, TX
Leonard Nursing Home, Leonard, TX
Leonardville Nursing Home, Leonardville, KS
Leroy Village Green Nursing Home & Health Related Facility Inc, Leroy, NY
Les Fontaines Retirement Community, New Orleans, LA
Letcher County Golden Years Rest Home, Jenkins, KY
Levelland Development Center, Levelland, TX
Levelland Nursing Home, Levelland, TX
Levindale Hebrew Geriatric Center & Hospital Inc, Baltimore, MD
Lewes Convalescent Center, Lewes, DE
Ann Lewis Rest Home Inc, Middleborough, MA
Lewis County Manor, Hohenwald, TN
Lewis County Nursing Home District, Canton, MO
Lewis County Residential Health Care Facility, Lowville, NY
Lewis Health Care Facilities Inc—Hyden Manor, Hyden, KY
Mary Lewis Convalescent Center/UAB, Birmingham, AL
Lewis Memorial Christian Village, Springfield, IL
Lewis Memorial Methodist Home, Franklin, KY
Lewisburg United Methodist Homes, Lewisburg, PA

Lewiston Care Center, Lewiston, ID
Lewiston Villa, Lewiston, MN
Lewisville Hotel for Senior Citizens, Lewisville, IN
Lexington Country Place, Lexington, KY
Lexington Court Care Center, Lexington, OH
Lexington Health Care Center, Lombard, IL
Lexington House, New Britain, CT
Lexington House, Lexington, IL
Lexington Manor Health Care, Lexington, KY
Lexington Manor Nursing Center, Lexington, TN
Lexington Nursing Home, Lexington, OK
Lexington West Inc—Batesburg Group Home, Batesburg, SC
Libbie Convalescent Center, Richmond, VA
Libby Care Center, Libby, MT
Liberal Good Samaritan Center, Liberal, KS
Liberty Care & Rehabilitation Center, Centralia, WA
Liberty Commons, Chatham, MA
Liberty County Nursing Home, Chester, MT
Liberty Hall Nursing Center, Colchester, CT
Liberty Hill Healthcare Center, Winfield, IL
Liberty House, Marion, IL
Liberty House Nursing Home, Jersey City, NJ
Liberty House Nursing Home, Thomasville, NC
Liberty House Nursing Home, Clifton Forge, VA
Liberty House Nursing Home, Harrisonburg, VA
Liberty House Nursing Home, Roanoke, VA
Liberty House Nursing Home, Waynesboro, VA
Liberty Intermediate Care—Bristol, Bristol, FL
Liberty Manor Inc, Midway, GA
Liberty Nursing & Rehabilitation Center, Allentown, PA
Liberty Pavilion Nursing Home, Danvers, MA
Libertyville Manor Extended Care Facility, Libertyville, IL
Lida Home Nursing Home, Minonk, IL
Lieberman Geriatric Health Centre, Skokie, IL
Life Care Center, Banner Elk, NC
Life Care Center Inc, Fitzgerald, GA
Life Care Center of Altamonte Springs, Altamonte Springs, FL
Life Care Center of Athens, Athens, TN
Life Care Center of Boise, Boise, ID
Life Care Center of Bountiful, Bountiful, UT
Life Care Center of Bruceton—Hollow Rock, Bruceton, TN
Life Care Center of Church Hill, Church Hill, TN
Life Care Center of Cleveland, Cleveland, TN
Life Care Center of Coos Bay, Coos Bay, OR
Life Care Center of Copper Basin, Ducktown, TN
Life Care Center of Crossville, Crossville, TN
Life Care Center of Donelson, Nashville, TN
Life Care Center of East Ridge, Chattanooga, TN
Life Care Center of Eldorado, Eldorado, IL
Life Care Center of Erwin, Erwin, TN
Life Care Center of Greeneville, Greeneville, TN
Life Care Center of Hilo, Hilo, HI
Life Care Center of Kennewick, Kennewick, WA
Life Care Center of LaCenter, LaCenter, KY
Life Care Center of Morehead, Morehead, KY
Life Care Center of Morgan County, Wartburg, TN
Life Care Center of Morristown, Morristown, TN
Life Care Center of New Market, New Market, VA
Life Care Center of North Glendale, Glendale, AZ
Life Care Center of Overland Park, Overland Park, KS
Life Care Center of Paducah, Paducah, KY
Life Care Center of Paradise Valley, Phoenix, AZ
Life Care Center of Punta Gorda, Punta Gorda, FL
Life Care Center of Richland, Richland, WA

Life Care Center of Ritzville, Ritzville, WA
Life Care Center of Scottsdale, Scottsdale, AZ
Life Care Center of Sierra Vista, Sierra Vista, AZ
Life Care Center of Tucson, Tucson, AZ
Life Care Center of Tullahoma, Tullahoma, TN
Life Care Center of Yuma, Yuma, AZ
Life Care of Anthony, Anthony, KS
Life Care of Cheyenne, Cheyenne, WY
Life Care of Enfield, Enfield, IL
Life Care—West, Greeneville, TN
Lifecare Center of Alton Inc, Alton, IL
Lifecare Center of Benton, Benton, IL
Lifecare Center of Jonesboro Inc, Jonesboro, IL
Lifecare Center of McLeansboro Inc, McLeansboro, IL
Lifecare Center of Pinckneyville, Pinckneyville, IL
Lifecare Manor, Medicine Lodge, KS
Lifecare of Greensburg, Greensburg, KS
Lifecare of Harper, Harper, KS
Lifecare of Kingman, Kingman, KS
Lifecare of Kiowa, Kiowa, KS
Lifecare of Pratt, Pratt, KS
Lifecare of Wellington, Wellington, KS
Lifecare Rehabilitation Center, Haviland, KS
Lifecare Training Center at Haven, Haven, KS
Lifecare Training Center of Medicine Lodge, Medicine Lodge, KS
Lighthouse Convalescent Home, Selma, AL
Lilac City Convalescent Center, Spokane, WA
Lilburn Health Care Center, Lilburn, GA
Lily Pond Nursing Home, Staten Island, NY
Lima Convalescent Home, Lima, OH
Lima Estates Medical Care Facility, Lima, PA
Lima Manor, Lima, OH
Limestone Health Facility, Athens, AL
Lincoln Avenue & Crawford's Home, Cincinnati, OH
Lincoln Care Center, Lincoln, CA
Lincoln Care Center, Detroit, MI
Lincoln Care Center, Carrollton, MO
Lincoln Care Center, Fayetteville, TN
Lincoln Community Hospital & Nursing Home, Hugo, CO
Lincoln Community Nursing Home, Lincoln, MO
Lincoln Continuous Care Center, Hamlin, WV
Lincoln Convalescent Center Inc, Baltimore, MD
Lincoln County Hospital Inc, Lincolnton, NC
Lincoln County Medical Center, Ruidoso, NM
Lincoln East Nursing Home, Wichita, KS
Lincoln Glen Skilled Nursing, San Jose, CA
Lincoln Haven Rest Home, Lincoln, MI
Lincoln Hill Manor Rest Home, Spencer, MA
Lincoln Hill Nursing Center, Quincy, IL
Lincoln Hills Nursing Home, Tell City, IN
Lincoln Hills of New Albany, New Albany, IN
Lincoln Home Inc, Belleville, IL
Lincoln House, Lincoln, IL
Lincoln Land Nursing Home, Lincoln, IL
Lincoln Lodge Nursing Center, Connersville, IN
Lincoln Lutheran Home, Racine, WI
Lincoln Manor Inc, Decatur, IL
Lincoln Manor Nursing Center, Connersville, IN
Lincoln Memorial Nursing Home, Goulds, FL
Lincoln Nursing Center, Jefferson City, MO
Lincoln Nursing Center, Lincolnton, NC
Lincoln Nursing Home, Worcester, MA
Lincoln Park Healthcare Inc, Monroe, LA
Lincoln Park Intermediate Care Center, Lincoln Park, NJ
Lincoln Park Nursing & Convalescent Home, Lincoln Park, NJ
Lincoln Park Terrace Inc, Chicago, IL
Lincoln Residential Center, Brookhaven, MS
Lincoln Rest Home, Lincoln, MA
Lincoln Village Convalescent Center, Racine, WI
Lincolnshire Health Care Center, Merrillville, IN

Linda-Mar Convalescent Hospital, Pacifica, CA
Linda Valley Convalescent Hospital, Loma Linda, CA
Linda Vista Care Center, Ashland, OR
Lindale Nursing Center, Lindale, TX
Lindberg Rest Home, Kerkhoven, MN
Lindbergh Health Care Center, Beaumont, TX
Linden Bay Care Center, Brooklyn, NY
Linden Grove Health Care Center, New Berlin, WI
Linden Grove of Waukesha, Waukesha, WI
Linden Hall, Kennett Square, PA
Linden Health Care Center, Dayton, OH
Linden Healthcare Center, Stillwater, MN
Linden Lodge Nursing Home, Brattleboro, VT
Linden Manor, North Platte, NE
Linden Nursing & Retirement Home, Rockland, MA
Lindenwood Health Care Center, Peoria, IL
Lindenwood Nursing Home Inc, Omaha, NE
Lindon Care & Training Center, Pleasant Grove, UT
Lineville Nursing Facility, Lineville, AL
Linn Care Center, Albany, OR
Linn Community Nursing Home Inc, Linn, KS
Linn Manor Care Center, Marion, IA
Linn Manor Nursing Home, Linn, MO
Linnea Residential Home, Chisago City, MN
Linton Nursing Home, Linton, IN
Linwood Convalescent Center, Linwood, NJ
Linwood Gardens Convalescent Center, Visalia, CA
Linwood Place, Victoria, TX
Lions Manor Nursing Home, Cumberland, MD
Lisner-Louise Home, Washington, DC
Litchfield Nursing Centre Inc, Litchfield, MI
Litchfield Terrace Ltd, Litchfield, IL
Litchfield Woods Health Care Center, Torrington, CT
Little Bird Nursing Home Inc, Weatherford, OK
Little Brook Nursing & Convalescent Center, Califon, NJ
Little Company of Mary Health Facility Inc, San Pierre, IN
Little Creek Sanitarium, Knoxville, TN
Little Egypt Manor, Harrisburg, IL
Little Falls Hospital, Little Falls, NY
Little Flower Haven, Earling, IA
Little Flower Manor, Darby, PA
Little Flower Manor—Diocese of Scranton, Wilkes-Barre, PA
Little Flower Nursing Home & HRF, East Islip, NY
Little Flower Nursing Home Inc, Saint Louis, MO
Little Forest Medical Center, Akron, OH
Little Forest Rehabilitation Center, Youngstown, OH
Little Friends Inc, Naperville, IL
Little Neck Nursing Home, Little Neck, NY
Little Nursing Home, Montclair, NJ
Little River Nursing Home, Ashdown, AR
Little Rock Nursing Center, Little Rock, AR
Little Sisters of the Poor, San Pedro, CA
Little Sisters of the Poor, Washington, DC
Little Sisters of the Poor, Chicago, IL
Little Sisters of the Poor, Saint Paul, MN
Little Sisters of the Poor, Saint Louis, MO
Little Sisters of the Poor, Oregon, OH
Little Sisters of the Poor—Home for the Aged, Cleveland, OH
Little Sisters of the Poor Home for the Aged, Pittsburgh, PA
Little Sisters of the Poor—St Joseph's Home for the Aged Health Care Unit, Richmond, VA
Littlefield Hospitality House, Littlefield, TX
Littlefork Municipal Hospital, Littlefork, MN
Littleton House, Littleton, MA
Littleton Manor Nursing Home, Littleton, CO
Live Oak, Shreveport, LA
Live Oak Care Center, Santa Cruz, CA
Live Oak Living Center—Greenridge Heights, Richmond, CA

Live Oak Medical Nursing Center, Blanco, TX
Livermore Manor Convalescent Hospital, Livermore, CA
Living Care Community, Yakima, WA
Living Center East, Cedar Rapids, IA
Living Center of Griffin, Griffin, GA
Living Center, Enid, OK
Living Center West, Cedar Rapids, IA
Living Challenge, Minneapolis, MN
Living Skills Center, Saint Paul, KS
Livingston Care Center, Howell, MI
Livingston Convalescent Center, Livingston, MT
Livingston Convalescent Center, Livingston, TX
Livingston County Health Related Facility—Skilled Nursing Facility, Mount Morris, NY
Livingston County Rest Home, Smithland, KY
Livingston County Skilled Nursing Facility, Geneseo, NY
Livingston Manor, Pontiac, IL
Livingston Manor Care Center, Chillicothe, MO
Livingston Nursing Home, Bessemer, AL
Livonia Nursing Center, Livonia, MI
Llanfair House, Wayne, NJ
Llanfair Terrace, Cincinnati, OH
Martha Lloyd School—Camelot ICF/MR, Troy, PA
Lo-Har Lodge Inc, El Cajon, CA
Loch Haven Lodge, Orlando, FL
Lock Haven Hospital, Lock Haven, PA
Lock Haven Hospital—Extended Care Facility, Lock Haven, PA
Lockerbie Healthcare Center, Indianapolis, IN
Lockney Care Center, Lockney, TX
Locust Grove Nursing Home, Hiram, TX
Locust Grove Nursing Home, Wills Point, TX
Locust Grove Retirement Village, Mifflin, PA
Locust Mountain Health Care Facility Inc, Shenandoah, PA
Locust Ridge Nursing Home Inc, Williamsburg, OH
Lodge Nursing Home, Navarre, OH
Lodge, Neptune, NJ
Lodi Good Samaritan Center, Lodi, WI
Loeb Center Montefiore Medical Center, Bronx, NY
Logan County Home, Bellefontaine, OH
Logan County Home for the Aged, Napoleon, ND
Logan County Nursing Center, Paris, AR
Logan Elm Health Care Center, Circleville, OH
Logan Health Care Center, Logan, OH
Logan Health Village, Logan, WV
Logan Healthcare Facility—Skilled Nursing Facility, Weymouth, MA
Logan Manor, Whiting, NJ
Logan Manor Nursing Home, Logan, KS
Logan Park Care Center, Logan, WV
Logan Square East Care Center, Philadelphia, PA
Logan Valley Manor, Lyons, NE
Logan Valley Nursing Center, Logan, UT
Loma Linda Health Care, Moberly, MO
Loma Linda Rest Home, Pine Bluff, AR
Ray Graham Lombard Community Living Facility, Lombard, IL
Lomita Care Center, Lomita, CA
Lompoc Hospital District Convalescent Care Center, Lompoc, CA
London House Convalescent Hospital, Santa Rosa, CA
London House Convalescent Hospital, Sonoma, CA
London Springs Care Center, Heber City, UT
Lone Pine Convalescent Hospital, Lone Pine, CA
Lone Pine Nursing Home Inc, New Bremen, OH
Lone Tree Convalescent Hospital, Antioch, CA
Lone Tree Health Care Center, Lone Tree, IA
Lone Tree Lodge, Meade, KS

Long Beach Grandell Company, Long Beach, NY
Long Beach Memorial Nursing Home Inc, Long Beach, NY
Long Home, Lancaster, PA
Long Island Nursing Home, Flushing, NY
Long Island Tides Nursing Home, Long Beach, NY
Long Lake Manor Inc, Port Orchard, WA
Long Lake Nursing Home, Long Lake, MN
Long Prairie Memorial Hospital & Home, Long Prairie, MN
Long-Term Care at Neponset—Ashmont Manor, Boston, MA
Long-Term Care at Neponset—Bostonian Nursing Care Center, Boston, MA
Long-Term Care at Neponset—Neponset Hall, Boston, MA
Long Term Care Facility, Danville, PA
Long Term Care Unit, Wernersville, PA
Longhouse Residence, Spencer, IA
Longleaf Nurse Care Center Inc, Ruston, LA
Longmeadow Care Center, Ravenna, OH
Longmeadow Nursing Home—Camden, Camden, AR
Longmeadow Nursing Home of Malvern, Malvern, PA
Longmeadow of Taunton A Skilled Nursing Facility, Taunton, MA
Longview Home, Missouri Valley, IA
Longview Nursing Center, Grandview, MO
Longview Nursing Home Inc, Manchester, MD
Longwood Health Care Center, Longwood, FL
Longwood Manor Sanitarium, Los Angeles, CA
Longwood Villa Geriatric Nursing Center, Boothwyn, PA
Longworth Manor, Felicity, OH
Longworth Villa, Charlestown, IN
Lonoke Nursing Home Inc, Lonoke, AR
Loogootee Nursing Center, Loogootee, IN
Loomis House Inc, Holyoke, MA
Lorain Manor Nursing Home, Lorain, OH
Loraine Nursing Home, Loraine, TX
Lorantffy Care Center Inc, Akron, OH
Lord Chamberlain Skilled Nursing Facility, Stratford, CT
Loretta Nursing Home, Shawneetown, IL
Loretto Geriatric Center, Syracuse, NY
Loretto Motherhouse Infirmary, Nerinx, KY
Lorien Nursing & Rehabilitation Center, Columbia, MD
Loring Hospital, Sac City, IA
Loris Hospital Extended Care Facility, Loris, SC
Lorraine Manor, Hartford, CT
Los Arcos Health Care Center, Flagstaff, AZ
Los Banos Convalescent Hospital, Los Banos, CA
Los Gatos Convalescent Hospital, Los Gatos, CA
Los Gatos Meadows Geriatric Hospital, Los Gatos, CA
Los Lunas Hospital & Training School, Los Lunas, NM
Los Palos Convalescent Hospital, San Pedro, CA
Lost Creek Care Center, Lima, OH
Lost Rivers Nursing Home, Arco, ID
Josina Lott Foundation Residential Center, Toledo, OH
Lou Del Nursing Home Inc, Forest Grove, OR
Loudon Healthcare Center, Loudon, TN
Loudon Valley Country Manor I & II, Purcellville, VA
Loudonville Nursing Home Inc, Loudonville, OH
Loudoun Long-Term Care Center, Leesburg, VA
Anthony Louis Treatment Center, Plymouth, MN
Louis Pasteur Care Center, San Antonio, TX
Louisa Health Care Center, Louisa, VA
Louisburg Nursing Home, Louisburg, NC
Louise Caroline Rehabilitation & Nursing Center, Saugus, MA

Louisiana Guest House of Baton Rouge, Baton Rouge, LA
Louisiana Living Center, Vallejo, CA
Louisiana Special Education Center, Alexandria, LA
Louisiana War Veterans Home, Jackson, LA
Louisville Care Center, Louisville, NE
Louisville Lutheran Home, Jeffersontown, KY
Louisville Protestant Althenheim, Louisville, KY
Lourdes Inc, Pontiac, MI
Lourdes-Noreen McKeen Residence for Geriatric Care Inc, West Palm Beach, FL
Lovato Residential Care Facility, La Junta, CO
Dorothy Love Retirement Community, Sidney, OH
Loveland Good Samaritan Village, Loveland, CO
Loveland Health Care, Loveland, OH
Lovelett Health Care Center, Auburn, ME
Lovely Hill Nursing Home, Pawling, NY
Lovely's Rest Home, North Middletown, KY
Lovin' Care Center, Kenton, OH
Lovingston Health Care Center, Lovingston, VA
Lovington Good Samaritan Center, Lovington, NM
Lowell Healthcare Center, Lowell, IN
Lowell Medical Care Center, Lowell, MI
Lower Umpqua Hospital, Reedsport, OR
Lowe's Nursing & Convalescent Home, Thonotosassa, FL
Lowman Home, White Rock, SC
LPN Geriatric Nursing Center, Newark, OH
LPN Health Care Facility, Newark, OH
Lu Ann Nursing Home, Nappanee, IN
Lu-Ken Manor, Ardmore, OK
Lubbock Health Care Center, Lubbock, TX
Lubbock Hospitality House, Lubbock, TX
Lucas County Children Services—Extended Care Unit, Maumee, OH
Lucas Nursing Center, Lucas, KS
Lucero Residential Care Facility, Las Animas, CO
Lufkin Nursing Center, Lufkin, TX
Luling Care Center, Luling, TX
Lums Pond Group Home, Bear, DE
Luther Acres, Lititz, PA
Luther Crest, Allentown, PA
Luther Haven, Detroit, MI
Luther Haven Nursing Home, Montevideo, MN
Luther Home, Grand Rapids, MI
Luther Home, Marinette, WI
Luther Home of Mercy, Williston, OH
Luther Manor, Dubuque, IA
Luther Manor, Milwaukee, WI
Luther Manor, Wauwatosa, WI
Luther Manor Nursing Home, Saginaw, MI
Luther Manor Retirement & Nursing Center, Hannibal, MO
Martin Luther—Holt Home, Holt, MI
Martin Luther Manor, Bloomington, MN
Martin Luther Memorial Home—South Haven, South Haven, MI
Martin Luther Memorial Home, South Lyon, MI
Martin Luther Nursing Home, Clinton, NY
Martin Luther—Saginaw Home, Saginaw, MI
Luther Memorial Home, Madelia, MN
Luther Memorial Home, Mayville, ND
Luther Park Health Center, Des Moines, IA
Luther Woods Convalescent Center, Hatboro, PA
Lutheran Altenheim Society of Missouri, Saint Louis, MO
Lutheran Care Center, Altamont, IL
Lutheran Center for the Aging, Smithtown, NY
Lutheran Community Home Inc, Seymour, IN
Lutheran Good Shepherd Home & Nursing Home, Concordia, MO
Lutheran Haven, Oviedo, FL
Lutheran Health Care Association, Saint Louis, MO
Lutheran Health Facility, Alhambra, CA

Lutheran Health Facility of Anaheim, Anaheim, CA
Lutheran Health Facility of Carlsbad, Carlsbad, CA
Lutheran Home, Peoria, IL
Lutheran Home, Muscatine, IA
Lutheran Home, Strawberry Point, IA
Lutheran Home, Frankenmuth, MI
Lutheran Home, Monroe, MI
Lutheran Home, Belle Plaine, MN
Lutheran Home, Cape Girardeau, MO
Lutheran Home, Omaha, NE
Lutheran Home, Napoleon, OH
Lutheran Home, Westlake, OH
Lutheran Home & Services for the Aged, Arlington Heights, IL
Lutheran Home at Kane, Kane, PA
Lutheran Home at Ocean View, Ocean View, NJ
Lutheran Home at Telford, Telford, PA
Lutheran Home at Topton, Topton, PA
Lutheran Home for the Aged, Vinton, IA
Lutheran Home for the Aged, Erie, PA
Lutheran Home for the Aging Inc, Wauwatosa, WI
Lutheran Home Inc, Herington, KS
Lutheran Home (LHHS), Eureka, SD
Lutheran Home of Brockton Inc, Brockton, MA
Lutheran Home of Middletown Inc, Middletown, CT
Lutheran Home of New Orleans, New Orleans, LA
Lutheran Home of Northwest Indiana Inc, Crown Point, IN
Lutheran Home of Southbury, Southbury, CT
Lutheran Home of the Good Shepherd, Havre, MT
Lutheran Home of the Good Shepherd, New Rockford, ND
Lutheran Home of West Texas, Lubbock, TX
Lutheran Home of Worcester Inc, Worcester, MA
Lutheran Home—Permian Basin, Midland, TX
Lutheran Homes Inc, Fort Wayne, IN
Lutheran Memorial Home, Sandusky, OH
Lutheran Memorial Nursing Home, Twin Valley, MN
Lutheran Memorial Retirement Center, Twin Valley, MN
Lutheran Nursing Homes Inc—Albemarle Unit, Albemarle, NC
Lutheran Nursing Homes Inc—Hickory Unit, Hickory, NC
Lutheran Nursing Homes Inc—Salisbury Unit, Salisbury, NC
Lutheran Old Folks Home, Toledo, OH
Lutheran Pioneer Home, Mallala, OR
Lutheran Retirement Home, Jamestown, NY
Lutheran Retirement Home Inc, Northwood, IA
Lutheran Retirement Home of Southern Minnesota, Truman, MN
Lutheran Senior Citizens Home Inc, Little Falls, MN
Lutheran Senior City Inc, Columbus, OH
Lutheran Sunset Home, Grafton, ND
Lutheran Welfare Concordia Home, Cabot, PA
Luverne Nursing Facility, Luverne, AL
Luverne Residential Facility, Luverne, MN
Lyden Nursing Home, Astoria, NY
Lydia Healthcare Center, Robbins, IL
Lydian Corporation, Orange, CT
Sophia Lyn Convalescent Hospital, Pasadena, CA
Lynchburg Nursing Home, Lynchburg, VA
Lyndon Lane Nursing Center, Louisville, KY
Lyngblomsten Care Center, Saint Paul, MN
Lynhurst Healthcare Center, Indianapolis, IN
Lynn Care Center, Front Royal, VA
Lynn Convalescent Home & Infirmary, Lynn, MA
Lynn Haven Nursing Home, Gray, GA
Lynn Home for Elderly Persons, Lynn, MA
Lynn Lodge Nursing Home, Longview, TX
Lynn Shore Rest Home, Lynn, MA

Lynn Shores Manor, Virginia Beach, VA
Lynnhaven Nursing Center Inc, Corpus Christi, TX
Lynnhurst Healthcare Center, Saint Paul, MN
Lynnwood Manor Health Care Center, Lynnwood, WA
Lynwood Care Center, Lynwood, CA
Lynwood Healthcare Center, Fridley, MN
Lynwood Manor, Adrian, MI
Lynwood Nursing Home Inc, Mobile, AL
Lyon Manor, Rock Rapids, IA
Mary Lyon Nursing Home, Hampden, MA
Lyons Convalescent Center, Lyons, IN
Lyons Good Samaritan Center, Lyons, KS
Lysock View Nursing Home, Montoursville, PA
Lytle Nursing Home Inc, Lytle, TX
Lytton Gardens Health Care Center, Palo Alto, CA
Linden Grove—Menomonee Falls, Menomonee Falls, WI
Mabank Nursing Home, Mabank, TX
Mabee Health Care Center, Midland, TX
Mac House, McPherson, KS
Macanell Nursing Home Inc, Center Point, IN
MacArthur Convalescent Hospital, Oakland, CA
Maccabee Gardens Extended Care, Saginaw, MI
MacKenzie Nursing Home Inc, Melrose, MA
Mackinac Straits Hospital Long-Term Care Unit, Saint Ignace, MI
Maclare Residence, South Saint Paul, MN
Maclen Rehabilitation Center, Lake Worth, FL
Macomb Nursing & Rehabilitation Center, Macomb, IL
Macon County Nursing Home District—Loch Haven, Macon, MO
Macon Health Care Center, Macon, GA
Macon Health Care Center, Macon, MO
MACtown Inc, Miami, FL
Madalawn Nursing Home, Brockton, MA
Madden Kimball Home, Kimball, MN
Madeira Nursing Inc, Madeira, OH
Madeleine Villa Convalescent Center, Marysville, WA
Madera Rehabilitation & Convalescent Center, Madera, CA
Madigan Estates, Houlton, ME
Madison, Montclair, NJ
Madison Convalescent Center, El Cajon, CA
Madison Convalescent Center, Madison, WI
Madison County Nursing Home, Edwardsville, IL
Madison County Nursing Home, Canton, MS
Madison County Nursing Home, Sheridan, MT
Madison County Nursing Home—Ennis, Ennis, MT
Madison County Sheltered Care Home, Edwardsville, IL
Madison Elms, London, OH
Madison Health Care, Madison, OH
Madison House, Morgantown, WV
Madison Lutheran Home, Madison, MN
Madison Manor, Madison, KS
Madison Manor, Richmond, KY
Madison Manor Nursing Center, Passaic, NJ
Madison Manor Nursing Center, Mars Hill, NC
Madison Manor Nursing Home, Madison, AL
Madison Manor Nursing Home, Hyattsville, MD
Madison Memorial Hospital, Fredericktown, MO
Madison Nursing Center, Madison, FL
Madison Nursing Home, Madison, IN
Madison Nursing Home, Cincinnati, OH
Madison Parish Home for the Aged, Tallulah, LA
Madison Village Nursing Home, Madison, OH
Madisonville Manor, Madisonville, KY
Madisonville Nursing Home No 1, Madisonville, TX
Madisonville Nursing Home No 2, Madisonville, TX

Madisonville Nursing Home No 3, Madisonville, TX
Madonna Centers, Lincoln, NE
Madonna Hall, Cleveland, OH
Madonna Home of Mercy Hospital of Watertown, Watertown, NY
Madonna Manor, Ludlow, KY
Madonna Manor, Villa Hills, KY
Madonna Manor Nursing Home, North Attleboro, MA
Madonna Nursing Center, Detroit, MI
Madonna Residence Inc, Brooklyn, NY
Madonna Towers Inc, Rochester, MN
Madrid Home for the Aging, Madrid, IA
Maehill Care Center, Farmington, MO
Maggie Johnson's Nursing Center, Austin, TX
Magic Star Nursing Home, Borger, TX
Magic Valley Manor, Wendell, ID
Magnolia Care Center, Wadsworth, OH
Magnolia Convalescent Hospital, Riverside, CA
Magnolia Gardens Convalescent, Granada Hills, CA
Magnolia Gardens Nursing Home, Lanham, MD
Magnolia Hall Inc, Chestertown, MD
Magnolia Haven Nursing Home, Tuskegee, AL
Magnolia Health Care, Seattle, WA
Magnolia Manor, Montgomery, AL
Magnolia Manor, Salem, OR
Magnolia Manor, Rock Hill, SC
Magnolia Manor, Jefferson, TX
Magnolia Manor Inc, Metropolis, IL
Magnolia Manor Intermediate Care Facility, Americus, GA
Magnolia Manor Methodist Nursing Care, Americus, GA
Magnolia Manor North, Rock Hill, SC
Magnolia Manor Nursing Center, Magnolia, AR
Magnolia Manor Nursing Home, Columbus, MS
Magnolia Manor Nursing Home Inc, Shreveport, LA
Magnolia Nursing Home, Jackson, MS
Magnolia Rest Home Inc, Fitchburg, MA
Magnolia Special Care Center, El Cajon, CA
Magnolia Wood Health Care Center, Watseka, IL
Magnolias Nursing & Convalescent Center, Pensacola, FL
Magoun Manor Nursing Home, Medford, MA
Mahaska Manor, Oskaloosa, IA
Samuel Mahelona Memorial Hospital, Kapa'a, HI
Mahnomen County & Village Hospital, Mahnomen, MN
Mahoning Valley Nursing & Rehabilitation Center, Lehighton, PA
Main Line Nursing & Rehabilitation Center, Paoli, PA
Maine Stay Nursing Home, Sanford, ME
Maine Veterans Home, Augusta, ME
Mainstream, Saint Paul, MN
Maison de Sante Inc, Ville Platte, LA
Maison Hospitaliere, New Orleans, LA
Maison Orleans II, New Orleans, LA
Maison Orleans Nursing Home, Arabi, LA
Maison Teche Nursing Center, Jeanerette, LA
Majestic Convalescent Hospital, Lynwood, CA
Majestic Pines Care Center, Hayward, CA
Majestic Towers Health Center, Saint Petersburg, FL
Mala Strana Health Care Center, New Prague, MN
Malden Home for Aged Persons, Malden, MA
Malden Nursing Center, Malden, MO
Malden Nursing Home, Boston, MA
Malden Nursing Home, Seattle, WA
Malheur Memorial Hospital, Nyssa, OR
Malin Health Care Center, Wytheville, VA
Mallard Bay, Cambridge, MD
Malta Home for the Aging, Granville, PA
Maluhia, Honolulu, HI
Malvern Nursing Home, Malvern, AR
Mammoth Nursing Home Inc, Manchester, NH

Manahawkin Convalescent Center, Manahawkin, NJ
Manatawny Manor Inc, Pottstown, PA
Manatee Convalescent Center Inc, Bradenton, FL
Manawa Community Nursing Center, Manawa, WI
Manchester House Nursing Convalescent Center, Media, PA
Manchester Manor Convalescent Hospital, Los Angeles, CA
Manchester Manor Inc, Manchester, CT
Manchester Manor Nursing Facility, Lakehurst, NJ
Manda Ann Convalescent Home Inc, Houston, TX
Mandan Villa, Mandan, ND
Mandarin Manor, Jacksonville, FL
Manden Nursing Home, South Portland, ME
Manderley Health Care Center, Osgood, IN
Mangum Nursing Center, Mangum, OK
Tom Mangum Home, Lancaster, SC
Manhattan Convalescent Center, Tampa, FL
Manhattan Health Care Center, Jackson, MS
Manhattan Manor Guest House, Harvey, LA
Manhattan Manor Nursing Home, Buffalo, NY
Manila Nursing Home, Manila, AR
Manilla Manor, Manilla, IA
Manistee County Medical Care Facility, Manistee, MI
Manistee Heights Care Center, Manistee, MI
Manitowoc Health Care Center, Manitowoc, WI
Mankato House Health Care Center, Mankato, MN
Mankato Lutheran Home, Mankato, MN
Manley's Manor Nursing Home Inc, Findlay, OH
Manly Care Center, Manly, IA
Mann Nursing Home, Westerville, OH
Manning Convalescent Home Inc, Portsmouth, VA
Manning Gardens Convalescent Hospital, Fresno, CA
Manning Plaza, Manning, IA
Manokin Manor, Princess Anne, MD
Manoogian Manor, Livonia, MI
Manor Care of Barley Kingston, York, PA
Manor Care of Barley North, York, PA
Manor Care of Columbia, Columbia, SC
Manor Care Convalescent Rehabilitation Center of Lynn, Lynnwood, WA
Manor Care Convalescent Rehabilitation Center of Spokane, Spokane, WA
Manor Care Division of Miller's Merry Manor, Wabash, IN
Manor Care Nursing & Rehabilitation Center, Arlington, VA
Manor Care Nursing Center, Tucson, AZ
Manor Care Nursing Center, Palm Desert, CA
Manor Care Nursing Center, Boca Raton, FL
Manor Care Nursing Center, Dubuque, IA
Manor Care Nursing Center, Overland Park, KS
Manor Care Nursing Center, Reno, NV
Manor Care Nursing Center, Barberton, OH
Manor Care Nursing Center, Canton, OH
Manor Care Nursing Center, North Olmsted, OH
Manor Care Nursing Center, Oregon, OH
Manor Care Nursing Center of Akron, Akron, OH
Manor Care Nursing Center of Northeast Heights, Albuquerque, NM
Manor Care Nursing Center of Fountain Valley, Fountain Valley, CA
Manor Care Nursing Center of Hemet, Hemet, CA
Manor Care Nursing Center of Mayfield Heights, Mayfield Heights, OH
Manor Care Nursing Center of Rocky River, Cleveland, OH
Manor Care Nursing Center of Wichita, Wichita, KS
Manor Care Nursing Home, Denver, CO
Manor Care Nursing Home, Cincinnati, OH

Manor Care of Boynton Beach, Boynton Beach, FL
Manor Care of Camino Vista, Albuquerque, NM
Manor Care of Charleston, Charleston, SC
Manor Care of Citrus Heights, Citrus Heights, CA
Manor Care of Dunedin, Dunedin, FL
Manor Care of Meadow Park, Tacoma, WA
Manor Care of Mountainside, Mountainside, NJ
Manor Care of Plantation, Plantation, FL
Manor Care of Ruxton, Towson, MD
Manor Care of Sarasota, Sarasota, FL
Manor Care of South Ogden, Ogden, UT
Manor Care of Towson, Towson, MD
Manor Care of Wheaton, Wheaton, MD
Manor Care of Woodside Nursing Center, Cincinnati, OH
Manor Care of Pinehurst, Pinehurst, NC
Manor Care Potomac, Potomac, MD
Manor Care Rehabilitation & Nursing Center, West Columbia, SC
Manor Care Rossville, Baltimore, MD
Manor Care Sandia Nursing Center, Albuquerque, NM
Manor Care Sharpview, Houston, TX
Manor Care South Nursing & Rehabilitation Center, York, PA
Manor Care Topeka, Topeka, KS
Manor Care of Webster, Webster, TX
Manor Care of Westerville Nursing Center, Westerville, OH
Manor Care Willoughby, Willoughby, OH
Manor Grove Inc, Kirkwood, MO
Manor Home, Geneva, OH
Manor Home for the Aged Inc, Erie, PA
Manor House at Riverview, Noblesville, IN
Manor House Care Center, Sigourney, IA
Manor House Inc, Youngstown, OH
Manor House of Carmel, Carmel, IN
Manor House of Dover, Dover, TN
Manor Inc, Pine City, MN
Manor Lodge Convalescent Hospital, Bakersfield, CA
Manor Nursing Home, Independence, KS
Manor Nursing Home, Morrisville, VT
Manor Nursing Home, Longview, WA
Manor Oak Skilled Nursing Facilities Inc, Cheektowaga, NY
Manor Oak Skilled Nursing Facilities Inc, Jamestown, NY
Manor Oak Skilled Nursing Facilities Inc, Warsaw, NY
Manor of Kansas City, Kansas City, KS
Manor of Topeka Inc, Topeka, KS
Manor Pines Convalescent Center, Fort Lauderdale, FL
Manor Retirement & Convalescent Center, Mexia, TX
Manor Square Convalescent Home, San Antonio, TX
Manors at Hobe Sound, Hobe Sound, FL
Mansfield Nursing Home, Mansfield, MO
Mansfield Nursing Home, Mansfield, TX
Mansion Health Care Center, Wellsville, OH
Mansion House Nursing Home, Spokane, WA
Mansion Nursing & Convalescent Home, Sunbury, PA
Mansion Nursing Home, Central Falls, RI
Mansion Rest Home, Malden, MA
Manson Good Samaritan, Manson, IA
Manzanita Manor, Payson, AZ
Manzano del Sol Good Samaritan Village, Albuquerque, NM
Maple Care Center, Maple Heights, OH
Maple Convalescent Hospital, Los Angeles, CA
Maple-Crest, Omaha, NE
Maple Crest Boone County Nursing Home, Belvidere, IL
Maple Crest Manor, Fayette, IA
Maple Farm Nursing Center, Akron, PA
Maple Grove Home, Tecumseh, NE
Maple Grove Intermediate Care Home, Sanger, CA
Maple Grove Lodge Inc, Louisiana, MO
Maple Hall Nursing Home, Worcester, MA

Maple Heights, Mapleton, IA
Maple Hill Nursing Home, Dallas, PA
Maple Hill Nursing Home, Selmer, TN
Maple Hill Nursing Home Ltd, Long Grove, IL
Maple Hill Rest Home, Springfield, MA
Maple Knoll Village, Cincinnati, OH
Maple Lane Health Care Facility, Shawano, WI
Maple Lane Nursing Home, Merchantville, NJ
Maple Lane Nursing Home, Barton, VT
Maple Lawn Health Center, Eureka, IL
Maple Lawn Lodge, Moberly, MO
Maple Lawn Manor, Hydro, OK
Maple Lawn Medical Care Facility, Coldwater, MI
Maple Lawn Nursing Home, Fulda, MN
Maple Lawn Nursing Home, Palmyra, MO
Maple Leaf Health Care Center, Manchester, NH
Maple Leaf Nursing Home, Manchester, NH
Maple Manor, Osage, IA
Maple Manor Christian Home Inc—Adult Division, Sellersburg, IN
Maple Manor Health Care Center, Greenville, KY
Maple Manor Health Care Center, New Richmond, WI
Maple Manor Nursing Center, Ontonagon, MI
Maple Manor Nursing Home, Aplington, IA
Maple Manor Nursing Home, Rochester, MN
Maple Manor Nursing Home, Langdon, ND
Maple Mountain Manor, Berlin, PA
Maple Nursing Home, Chesterland, OH
Maple Terrace Shelter Care Home, Chicago, IL
Maple Tree Inn Inc, Swanton, OH
Maple Valley, Ashley, MI
Maple Valley Nursing Home, Maple City, MI
Maple View Manor Inc, Rocky Hill, CT
Maple View Manor Nursing Home, Bainbridge, OH
Maple View Nursing Home, Washington, MA
Maple Wood Nursing Home, Bloomer, WI
Maplecrest Home, Bucyrus, OH
Maplecrest Living Center, Madison, ME
Maplecrest Nursing & Home for the Aged, Struthers, OH
Maplecrest Nursing Home, Sullivan, ME
Mapleleaf Healthcare Center, Mount Pleasant, IA
Maples Convalescent Home, Wrentham, MA
Maples Nursing & Retirement Center, Wrentham, MA
Maples Nursing Home, Bluefield, WV
Mapleside Manor, Amboy, IL
Mapleton Community Home, Mapleton, MN
Mapleton Health Care Facility Inc, Indianapolis, IN
Mapleview Care Center Inc, Louisville, OH
Mapleview Manor, Dayton, OH
Maplewood Care Center, Saint Paul, MN
Maplewood Care Center, Lincoln, NE
Maplewood Health Care Center, North Aurora, IL
Maplewood Health Care Center, Jackson, TN
Maplewood Manor, Terre Haute, IN
Maplewood Manor, Missoula, MT
Maplewood Manor Convalescent Center Inc, Philadelphia, PA
Maplewood Manor Inc, Keota, IA
Maplewood Manor Nursing Home, Amesbury, MA
Maplewood Maple Manor Care Center, Maplewood, MN
Maplewood Nursing Center, Reidsville, NC
Maplewood Nursing Center Inc, Marion, OH
Maplewood Nursing Home Inc, Webster, NY
Maplewood of Sauk Prairie, Sauk City, WI
Maquoketa Care Center, Maquoketa, IA
Mar-Ka Nursing Home, Mascoutah, IL
Mar Lima Inc—Diamondhead Extended Care Center 1, North Lima, OH
Mar-Saline Manor Care Center, Marshall, MO
Mar Vista Sanitarium, Los Angeles, CA
Maralie Convalescent Hospital, Cotati, CA
Maranatha Baptist Care Center, Brooklyn Center, MN

Maranatha Manor, Brookfield, MO
Maranatha Rest Home, Westminster, MA
Maranatha Village, Springfield, MO
Marathon Manor, Marathon, FL
Marbridge Villa, Manchaca, TX
Marceline Healthcare, Marceline, MO
Marcelle Home, Louisville, OH
Marco Polo Rest Home Inc, Boston, MA
Marcus Manor Convalescent Hospital, San Jose, CA
Samuel Marcus Nursing & Retirement Home, Weymouth, MA
Marengo Nursing Home, Linden, AL
Marett Boulevard Community Residence, Rock Hill, SC
Margaret Manor, Chicago, IL
Margaret Manor North Branch, Chicago, IL
Margaretville Memorial Hospital Nursing Home, Margaretville, NY
Margie Anna Nursing Home Inc, Lebanon, TN
Mari de Villa Retirement Center Inc, Manchester, MO
Maria Care, Red Bud, IL
Maria Home, Minneapolis, MN
Maria-Joseph Center, Dayton, OH
Maria Linden, Rockford, IL
Maria Manor Health Care, Saint Petersburg, FL
Marian Catholic Home, Milwaukee, WI
Marian Center for Adult Resident, Chicago, IL
Marian Extended Care Center, Santa Maria, CA
Marian Franciscan Home, Milwaukee, WI
Marian Hall, Flint, MI
Marian Home, Fort Dodge, IA
Marian Home, Sublimity, OR
Marian Home—Ursuline Sisters, Louisville, KY
Marian Manor, Boston, MA
Marian Manor Corporation, Pittsburgh, PA
Marian Manor Nursing Care Center, Riverview, MI
Marian Manor Nursing Home, Glen Ullin, ND
Marian Manor of Taunton, Taunton, MA
Marian Nursing Home, Radisson, WI
Marianna Convalescent Center, Marianna, FL
Marianwood Extended Healthcare Services, Issaquah, WA
Maries Manor Nursing Home, Vienna, MO
Marietta Convalescent Center, Marietta, OH
Marietta Health Care Center, Marietta, GA
Marietta Manor, Cleveland, OH
Marietta Place Nursing Home, Chillicothe, OH
Marigold Health Care Center, Galesburg, IL
Marin Convalescent & Rehabilitation Hospital, Tiburon, CA
Marina Care Center, Culver City, CA
Marina Convalescent Center, Alameda, CA
Marina View Manor Inc, Milwaukee, WI
Marinuka Manor, Galesville, WI
Mariola Nursing Center, Grants Pass, OR
Marion County Convalescent Center, Marion, SC
Marion County General Hospital & Nursing Home, Hamilton, AL
Marion County Healthcare Center, Indianapolis, IN
Marion County Home—Eastlawn Manor, Marion, OH
Marion County Nursing Home, Yellville, AR
Francis Marion Manor, Marion, VA
Marion Manor, Marion, KS
Marion Manor Nursing Home Inc, Marion, OH
Marion Memorial Nursing Home, Buena Vista, GA
Marion Nursing Home, Calhoun, LA
Marion Sunset Manor, Guin, AL
Mariposa Manor, Mariposa, CA
Stella Maris, Baltimore, MD
Maristhill Nursing Home, Waltham, MA
Mark Rest Center—CareServe, McConnelsville, OH

Mark Twain Convalescent Hospital, San Andreas, CA
Market Square Health Care Center, South Paris, ME
Markhill Manor Ltd, Sevierville, TN
Markle Health Care, Markle, IN
Marklund Children's Home, Bloomingdale, IL
Marks Nursing Home, Toledo, OH
Marks Sunset Manor, Olney, IL
Marlborough Health Care Center Inc, Marlborough, CT
Marlesta No 1, Findlay, OH
Marlesta No 2, Findlay, OH
Marlette Community Hospital Long-Term Care Unit, Marlette, MI
Marlin Manor, Jackson, MI
Marlinda Convalescent Hospital at Pasadena, Pasadena, CA
Marlinda-Imperial Convalescent Hospital, Pasadena, CA
Marlinda Nursing Home, Lynwood, CA
Marlora Manor Convalescent Hospital, Long Beach, CA
Marlow Manor, Marlow, OK
Marmaton Valley Home, Uniontown, KS
Marmet Health Care Center, Marmet, WV
Marquardt Memorial Manor Inc, Watertown, WI
Marquette County Medical Care Facility, Ishpeming, MI
Marquette Manor, Indianapolis, IN
Marquette Manor, Saint Louis, MO
Marrs Nursing Home, Mohegan Lake, NY
MARS—Ellsworth Home, Stow, OH
MARS—Lakeview Home, Stow, OH
MARS—Springfield Group Home, Akron, OH
Marshall County Care Facility, Marshalltown, IA
Marshall County Group Homes Inc, Argyle, MN
Marshall County Hospital & LTC, Benton, KY
Marshall County Nursing Center, Marysville, KS
Marshall Habilitation Center, Marshall, MO
Marshall Health Care Facility, Machias, ME
Marshall Home, Watertown, MA
Marshall Lane Manor, Derby, CT
Marshall Manor, Guntersville, AL
Marshall Manor, Marshall, MI
Marshall Manor, Britton, SD
Marshall Manor Nursing Home Inc, Marshall, TX
Mary Marshall Manor Inc, Marysville, KS
Marshall Nursing Center, Marshall, AR
Marshalltown Manor Care Center, Marshalltown, IA
Marshalltown Medical Surgical Center Skilled Nursing Facility, Marshalltown, IA
Marshfield Living Center, Marshfield, WI
Marshwood Nursing Care Center, Lewiston, ME
Martha & Mary Nursing Home, Poulsbo, WA
Martha Jefferson House Infirmary Health Care Unit, Charlottesville, VA
Marthas Vineyard Hospital—Skilled & Intermediate Care Facility, Oak Bluffs, MA
Martin dePorres Nursing Home Inc, Lake Charles, LA
Martin Family Care Home, Denver, CO
George A Martin Gerontology Center, Cincinnati, OH
Martin House, Burlington, CO
Martin Luther Homes Inc, Pontiac, IL
Martin Nursing Home, Boston, MA
Martin Street Group Home, Silverdale, WA
Martinez Convalescent Hospital, Martinez, CA
Martin's Rest Home, Cynthiana, KY
Martinsville Convalescent Center, Martinsville, VA
Marwood Manor Nursing Home, Port Huron, MI
Marwood Rest Home Inc, Philadelphia, PA
Mary Anna Nursing Home Inc, Wisner, LA
Mary Avenue Care Center, Lansing, MI
Mary Conrad Center, Anchorage, AK
Mary Elizabeth Nursing Center, Mystic, CT

Mary Ellen Convalescent Home Inc, Hellertown, PA
Mary Ellen Nursing Home, Somerville, MA
Mary Gran Nursing Center, Clinton, NC
Mary Health of the Sick, Newbury Park, CA
Mary Joseph Residence—Little Sisters of the Poor, New Orleans, LA
Mary-Jude Nursing Home, West Allis, WI
Mary-Land Rest Home, Medway, MA
Mary Louise Nursing Home, Cleveland, OH
Mary Queen & Mother Center, Saint Louis, MO
Marycrest Manor, Culver City, CA
Marycrest Manor, Livonia, MI
Maryetta's Rest Home, Carthage, MO
Maryfair Manor, Indianapolis, IN
Maryfield Nursing Home, High Point, NC
Maryhaven Inc, Glenview, IL
Maryhill Manor, Niagara, WI
Maryhouse Inc, Pierre, SD
Maryknoll Nursing Home Inc, Maryknoll, NY
Maryland Baptist Aged Home, Baltimore, MD
Maryland Gardens, Phoenix, AZ
Maryland Intensive Behavior Management Program, Baltimore, MD
Maryland Manor of Glen Burnie, Glen Burnie, MD
Maryland Masonic Homes, Cockeysville, MD
Marymount Manor, Eureka, MO
Marysville Care Center, Marysville, CA
Maryville Health Care Center, Maryville, MO
Maryville Nursing Home, Beaverton, OR
Marywood Convalescent Center, Wausau, WI
Mason Care Center, Mason, TX
Mason City Area Nursing Home, Mason City, IL
Mason Health Care Facility Inc, Warsaw, IN
Mason Terrace Rest Home, Brookline, MA
Masonic & Eastern Star Home of North Carolina Inc, Greensboro, NC
Masonic & Eastern Star Home of Oregon, Forest Grove, OR
Masonic Health Care Center Inc, Dousman, WI
Masonic Home, Union City, CA
Masonic Home, Wilmington, DE
Masonic Home, Charlton, MA
Masonic Home, Manchester, NII
Masonic Home & Health Facility, Utica, NY
Masonic Home & Hospital, Wallingford, CT
Masonic Home of Florida, Saint Petersburg, FL
Masonic Home of Missouri, Saint Louis, MO
Masonic Home of New Jersey, Burlington, NJ
Masonic Home of Pennsylvania, Lafayette Hill, PA
Masonic Home of Virginia—Health Care Unit, Richmond, VA
Masonic Home of Washington, Des Moines, WA
Masonic Homes, Elizabethtown, PA
Masonic Widows & Orphans Home, Louisville, KY
Massachusetts Hospital School Skilled Nursing Facility, Canton, MA
Mast Boarding Home, Greenwood, DE
Masters Health Care Center, Algood, TN
Matagorda House Nursing Home, Bay City, TX
Mater Dei Nursing Home, Newfield, NJ
Mather Home, Evanston, IL
Mather Nursing Center, Ishpeming, MI
Mathers Nursing Home, Greene, IA
Matney's Colonial Manor, South Sioux City, NE
Matney's Morningside Manor, Sioux City, IA
Matney's Westside Manor, Sioux City, IA
Mattapoisett Nursing Home, Mattapoisett, MA
Mattatuck Extended Care Inc, Waterbury, CT
Mattatuck Health Care Facility Inc, Waterbury, CT
Mattingly Health Care Center, Energy, IL
Mattoon Health Care Center, Mattoon, IL
Matulaitis Nursing Home, Putnam, CT
Maunalani Nursing Center, Honolulu, HI
Max-Uhl Nursing Home, Springfield, OH

Mayers Memorial Hospital DP/SNF, Fall River Mills, CA
Mayfair Manor Convalescent Center, Lexington, KY
Mayfair Nursing Home, Hempstead, NY
Mayfair Nursing Home, Tulsa, OK
Mayfair Village Nursing Care Center, Columbus, OH
Mayfield Care Center, Chicago, IL
Mayfield Manor, Mayfield, UT
Mayflower Gardens Convalescent Hospital, Lancaster, CA
Mayflower Home, Grinnell, IA
Mayflower House Nursing Home & Child Care Center, Plymouth, MA
Mayflower Nursing Home, Plymouth, IN
Maynard Rest Home, Pawtucket, RI
Mayo Memorial Nursing Home, Northfield, VT
Mayo Nursing & Convalescent Center, Philadelphia, PA
Sadie G Mays Memorial Nursing Home, Atlanta, GA
Maysville Extended Care Facility, Maysville, KY
Mayview Convalescent Center, Raleigh, NC
Mayview State Hospital, Bridgeville, PA
Mayview State Hospital—Long-Term Care Unit, Bridgeville, PA
Maywood Acres Healthcare, Oxnard, CA
Maywood Manor Inc, Kerens, TX
Mazotti Family Care Home, Denver, CO
MBW on Center, New Ulm, MN
Mc Allister Nursing Home Inc, Tinley Park, IL
McAlester Regional Hospital, McAlester, OK
McAllen Good Samaritan Center, McAllen, TX
McAllen Nursing Center, McAllen, TX
McAuley Center, Urbana, OH
McAuley House, Chicago, IL
McAuley Manor, Aurora, IL
McCall's Chapel School Inc, Ada, OK
McCallum Family Care Center, Denver, CO
Margaret McLaughlin McCarrick Care Center Inc, Somerset, NJ
Bishop McCarthy Residence, Vineland, NJ
McCarthy Nursing Home, Stoughton, WI
McCaskill Nursing Home, Maysville, OK
McCauley Cluster, Tallahassee, FL
Mary McClellan Skilled Nursing Facility, Cambridge, NY
McClure Convalescent Hospital, Oakland, CA
McComb Extended Care & Nursing Home, McComb, MS
McComb Retirement/Boarding Center, Douglas, WY
McComb Retirement/Boarding Center, Douglas, WY
McConaughey Guest Home, Cameron, WV
McCone County Nursing Home, Circle, MT
Nancy J McConnell Home, Lancaster, SC
McCormack Rest Home, Fairhaven, MA
McCovy Golden Age Home Inc, Denver, CO
McCrea Manor Nursing Center, Alliance, OH
McCready Comprehensive Care Unit, Crisfield, MD
McCrite Plaza Health Center, Topeka, KS
McCurdy Residential Center Inc, Evansville, IN
McCurtain Manor Nursing Center, Broken Bow, OK
McDonald County Nursing Center, Anderson, MO
McDonough Home, Pittsburgh, PA
McDowell Continuous Care Center, Gary, WV
McDowell Nursing Center, Nebo, NC
McDowell Skilled Nursing Facility, Greensburg, KY
McElrath Rest Home, Paducah, KY
McFadden Memorial Manor, Malden, MA
McFarlan Home, Flint, MI
McFarland House, Barre, VT
McGee Nursing Home, Teague, TX
McGills Nursing Home—South, Dayton, OH
McGirr Nursing Home, Bellows Falls, VT
McGowan Nursing Home, Methuen, MA
McGraw Nursing Home, Adena, OH

A M McGregor Home, East Cleveland, OH
McGuffey Health Care Center, Gadsden, AL
McGuire Memorial Home for Retired Children, New Brighton, PA
McIntosh Nursing Home Inc, McIntosh, MN
McIntosh Nursing Home Inc, Muskogee, OK
McKay-Dee Transitional Care Center, Ogden, UT
McKay Memorial, Soap Lake, WA
McKendree Village Inc, Hermitage, TN
McKenzie Manor Living Center, Springfield, OR
McKerley Harris Hill Nursing Home, Penacook, NH
McKerley Health Care Bedford—Ridgewood, Bedford, NH
McKerley Health Care Center, Keene, NH
McKerley Health Care Center, Rutland, VT
McKerley Health Care Center—Claremont, Claremont, NH
McKerley Health Care Center—Derry, Derry, NH
McKerley Health Care Center—Donald Street, Bedford, NH
McKerley Health Care Center—Franconia, Franconia, NH
McKerley Health Care Center—Laconia, Laconia, NH
McKerley Health Care Center—Lebanon, Lebanon, NH
McKerley Health Care Center—Morrisville Inc, Morrisville, VT
McKerley Nursing Home, Concord, NH
McKey Boarding Home, Wyarno, WY
McKinley Court, Decatur, IL
McKinley Life Care Centre, Canton, OH
McKinley Manor, Gallup, NM
McKinley Terrace, Decatur, IL
McKinney Intermediate Care Facility, Pickens, SC
McLarney Manor, Brookfield, MO
McLean Care Center, McLean, TX
McLean County General Hospital Inc, Calhoun, KY
McLean County Nursing Home, Normal, IL
McLean Home, Simsbury, CT
McLeod I, Bishopville, SC
McLeod II Group Home, Bishopville, SC
McLoud Nursing Center Inc, McLoud, OK
McMahon-Tomlinson Nursing Center, Lawton, OK
McMillan Home, Worthington, MN
McMinn Memorial Nursing Home, Etowah, TN
McMinnville Health Care Center, McMinnville, TN
McMurray Hills Manor, McMurray, PA
McNairy County Health Care Center, Selmer, TN
McRae Manor Inc, McRae, GA
McVane Memorial Nursing Home, Crivitz, WI
McVitty House Inc, Salem, VA
Mead Nursing Home, Meadville, PA
Belle Meade Home, Greenville, KY
Meadow Brook, Blackville, SC
Meadow Brook Manor of North Miami, North Miami, FL
Meadow Brook Medical Care Facility, Bellaire, MI
Meadow Creek Nursing Center, San Angelo, TX
Meadow Crest Inc, Bethel Park, PA
Meadow Glade Manor, Battle Ground, WA
Meadow Green Nursing Center, Waltham, MA
Meadow Haven Nursing Center, Rock Hill, SC
Meadow Lawn Nursing Center, Davenport, IA
Meadow Manor Inc, Taylorville, IL
Meadow Manor Nursing Home, Grand Meadow, MN
Meadow Park Care Center, Prescott, AZ
Meadow Park House, Rochester, MN
Meadow Park Nursing Home, Flushing, NY
Meadow View Convalescent Home, North Reading, MA
Meadow View Health Care Center, Salem, IN
Meadow View Manor, Grass Valley, CA

Meadow View Manor Nursing Home Inc, Sheboygan, WI
Meadow View Nursing Center, Joplin, MO
Meadow View Nursing Center, Williamstown, NJ
Meadow View Park, Garden Grove, CA
Meadow Wind Health Care Center Inc, Massillon, OH
Meadow Wood Nursing Home Inc, Georgetown, OH
Meadowbrook Acres, Charleston, WV
Meadowbrook Care Center, Holland, MI
Meadowbrook Care Center, Cincinnati, OH
Meadowbrook Care Center, Van Alstyne, TX
Meadowbrook Convalescent Hospital, Hemet, CA
Meadowbrook Convalescent Hospital, San Jose, CA
Meadowbrook Estates, McLeansboro, IL
Meadowbrook Health Care Center, Lexington, KY
Meadowbrook Living Center, Montgomery, OH
Meadowbrook Lodge, Magnolia, AR
Meadowbrook Manor, Los Angeles, CA
Meadowbrook Manor, Carlinville, IL
Meadowbrook Manor, Clemmons, NC
Meadowbrook Manor, Rapid City, SD
Meadowbrook Manor, Maynardville, TN
Meadowbrook Manor of Asheboro, Asheboro, NC
Meadowbrook Manor of Boca Cove, Boca Raton, FL
Meadowbrook Manor of Cherryville, Cherryville, NC
Meadowbrook Manor of Decatur, Decatur, TN
Meadowbrook Manor of Duplin, Warsaw, NC
Meadowbrook Manor of Flagler, Bunnell, FL
Meadowbrook Manor of Gastonia, Gastonia, NC
Meadowbrook Manor of Hartford, Fowler, OH
Meadowbrook Manor of Kingsport, Kingsport, TN
Meadowbrook Manor of LaBelle, LaBelle, FL
Meadowbrook Manor of LaFollette, LaFollette, TN
Meadowbrook Manor of Lenoir, Lenoir, NC
Meadowbrook Manor of Monticello, Monticello, FL
Meadowbrook Manor of Quincy, Quincy, FL
Meadowbrook Manor of Shelby, Shelby, NC
Meadowbrook Manor of Siler City, Siler City, NC
Meadowbrook Manor of Sparta, Morganton, NC
Meadowbrook Manor Rest Home, Worcester, MA
Meadowbrook Nursing & Convalescent Center, Seattle, WA
Meadowbrook Nursing Center, Pulaski, TN
Meadowbrook Nursing Home, Tucker, GA
Meadowbrook Nursing Home, Plattsburgh, NY
Meadowbrook Nursing Home, Shawsville, VA
Meadowcrest Living Center, Gretna, LA
Meadowgreen, Dallas, TX
Meadowhaven Health Care Center, Butler, IN
Meadowlands Rehabilitation Center, Canonsburg, PA
Meadowlane Healthcare Center, Benson, MN
Meadowlark Community Residence, Rock Hill, SC
Meadowlark Convalescent Hospital, San Diego, CA
Meadowlark Hills, Manhattan, KS
Meadowood, Grayville, IL
Meadowood, Bloomington, IN
Meadowood, Worcester, PA
Meadowood Nursing Home, Bessemer, AL
Meadowood Skilled Nursing Facility & Intermediate Care Facility, South Hadley, MA
Meadows, Rolling Meadows, IL
Meadows Convalescent Hospital, Atwater, CA
Meadows—East, Louisville, KY
Meadows Manor Inc, Terre Haute, IN
Meadows Manor North Inc, Terre Haute, IN

Meadows Manor South, Manchester, CT
Meadows Manor—West, Manchester, CT
Meadows Mennonite Home, Chenoa, IL
Meadows Nursing Center, Vidalia, GA
Meadows Nursing Center, Dallas, PA
Meadows Nursing Home, Fremont, MI
Meadows of Grayling, Grayling, MI
Meadows—South, Louisville, KY
Meadows, Cooperstown, NY
Meadowvale Care Center, Bluffton, IN
Meadowview Care Center, Emporia, KS
Meadowview Care Center, Kerrville, TX
Meadowview Lodge, Huntsville, AR
Meadowview Manor Health Care, Bridgeport, WV
Meadowview Nursing & Convalescent Center, Louisville, KY
Meadowview Nursing Home, Minden, LA
Meadowview Nursing Home, Lakeville, MA
Meadowview Nursing Home, Northfield, NJ
Meadowview Retirement Home, Mayfield, KY
Meadville Care Center, Meadville, PA
Meadville Hillside Home, Meadville, PA
Meadville Nursing Home, Meadville, MS
Mechanicsville Care Center, Mechanicsville, IA
Mecklenburg Autistic Group Homes Inc, Charlotte, NC
Med Inn & Parker Hill—SNF, Boston, MA
Med-Vale Nursing Home, Medfield, MA
Meda Nipple Convalescent Home, Thompsontown, PA
Medalion Health Center, Colorado Springs, CO
Medallion II Board & Lodge Home, Minneapolis, MN
Medallion Manor, Provo, UT
Medco Center of Bowling Green, Bowling Green, KY
Medco Center of Brandenburg, Brandenburg, KY
Medco Center of Campbellsville, Campbellsville, KY
Medco Center of Chandler, Chandler, IN
Medco Center of Clarksville, Clarksville, IN
Medco Center of Danville, Danville, IN
Medco Center of Elizabethtown, Elizabethtown, KY
Medco Center of Elkhart, Elkhart, IN
Medco Center of Evansville—North Inc, Evansville, IN
Medco Center of Fordsville, Fordsville, KY
Medco Center of Fort Wayne, Fort Wayne, IN
Medco Center of Franklin, Franklin, KY
Medco Center of French Lick, French Lick, IN
Medco Center of Hardinsburg, Hardinsburg, KY
Medco Center of Henderson, Henderson, KY
Medco Center of Morganfield, Morganfield, KY
Medco Center of Mt Vernon, Mount Vernon, IN
Medco Center of Newburgh, Newburgh, IN
Medco Center of Owensboro, Owensboro, KY
Medco Center of Paducah, Paducah, KY
Medco Center of Pembroke, Pembroke, KY
Medco Center of South Bend, South Bend, IN
Medco Center of Springfield, Springfield, KY
Medco Plaza of Fort Wayne, Fort Wayne, IN
Medco Springs of French Lick, French Lick, IN
Medford Convalescent & Nursing Center, Medford, NJ
Medford Leas, Medford, NJ
Medford Nursing Home, Medford, OK
Medi-Branch Nursing Center, Pocola, OK
Medi-Care Nursing Home, Cleveland, OH
Medi-Home of Arkoma, Arkoma, OK
Medi-Home of Prairie Grove, Prairie Grove, AR
Medi-Home of Rogers Inc, Rogers, AR
Medic-Ayers Nursing Center, Trenton, FL
Medic Home Health Center, Melbourne, FL
Medic-Home Health Center of Melbourne, Melbourne, FL
Medical Arts Center—Coastal Georgia, Brunswick, GA

Medical Arts Convalescent Hospital, Perris, CA
Medical Arts Health Facility, Columbus, GA
Medical Arts Health Facility, Lawrenceville, GA
Medical Arts Nursing Center Inc, Montrose, PA
Medical Care Center, Lynchburg, VA
Medical Center Beaver Pennsylvania—Long-Term Care Unit, Beaver, PA
Medical Center Convalescent Hospital, San Bernardino, CA
Medical Center Nursing Home, Clarendon, TX
Medical Center Nursing Home—DeGoesbriand Unit, Burlington, VT
Medical Center of Baton Rouge Skilled Nursing Facility, Baton Rouge, LA
Medical Hill Rehabilitation Center, Oakland, CA
Medical Park Convalescent Center, Decatur, AL
Medical Park Nursing Center, High Point, NC
Medical Park Nursing Center, Mount Olive, NC
Medical Plaza Nursing Center, Paris, TX
Medicalodge East of Arkansas City, Arkansas City, KS
Medicalodge East of Coffeyville, Coffeyville, KS
Medicalodge East of Kansas City, Kansas City, KS
Medicalodge Inc of Texarkana, Texarkana, AR
Medicalodge North of Arkansas City, Arkansas City, KS
Medicalodge North of Kansas City, Kansas City, KS
Medicalodge North of Pittsburg, Pittsburg, KS
Medicalodge of Atchison, Atchison, KS
Medicalodge of Butler, Butler, MO
Medicalodge of Clay Center, Clay Center, KS
Medicalodge of Columbus, Columbus, KS
Medicalodge of Dewey, Dewey, OK
Medicalodge of Douglass, Douglass, KS
Medicalodge of Eureka, Eureka, KS
Medicalodge of Fort Scott, Fort Scott, KS
Medicalodge of Goddard, Goddard, KS
Medicalodge of Halls Ferry, Saint Louis, MO
Medicalodge of Kinsley, Kinsley, KS
Medicalodge of Leavenworth, Leavenworth, KS
Medicalodge of Neosho, Neosho, MO
Medicalodge of Paola, Paola, KS
Medicalodge of Troy, Troy, MO
Medicalodge of Wichita, Wichita, KS
Medicalodge South of Kansas City, Kansas City, KS
Medicalodge South of Pittsburg, Pittsburg, KS
Medicalodge West of Coffeyville, Coffeyville, KS
Medicana Nursing Center, Lake Worth, FL
Medicare Pavilion Corporation, Waterbury, CT
Medicenter of Lakewood, Lakewood, NJ
Medicenter of Neptune, Neptune, NJ
Medicenter of Tampa, Tampa, FL
Medicenter—Virginia Beach, Virginia Beach, VA
Medicos Health Care Center, Detroit, MI
Medigroup Castle Park, Normandy, MO
Medigroup Heritage Park Inc, Rolla, MO
Medigroup North Village Park Inc, Moberly, MO
Medi-Home Inc—Fort Smith, Fort Smith, AR
Medilodge of Richmond, Richmond, MI
Medilodge of Romeo, Romeo, MI
Medilodge of Yale, Yale, MI
Medina Memorial Hospital Skilled Nursing Facility, Medina, NY
Medina Nursing Center Inc, Durand, IL
Mediplex of Beverly: A Long-Term Care Facility, Beverly, MA
Mediplex of Danbury, Danbury, CT
Mediplex of East Longmeadow, East Longmeadow, MA
Mediplex of Lexington—Long-Term Care Facility, Lexington, MA
Mediplex of Newington, Newington, CT

Mediplex of Newton—Long-Term Care Facility, Newton, MA
Mediplex of Wethersfield, Wethersfield, CT
Mediplex Rehabilitation—Camden, Camden, NJ
Medlantic Manor at Lamond—Riggs, Washington, DC
Medlantic Manor at Layhill, Silver Spring, MD
Medway Country Manor Nursing Home, Medway, MA
Meeker County Community Home, Litchfield, MN
Meharry-Hubbard Hospital, Nashville, TN
Meister Road Homes, Lorain, OH
Mel-Haven Convalescent Home, Corsicana, TX
Melber Rest Home, Melber, KY
Melchor Nursing Home, Baltimore, MD
Meline Manor Inc, Jacksonville, IL
Mellen Manor, Mellen, WI
Melody Manor Convalescent Center, Leakesville, MS
Melrose Care Center A Long-Term Care Facility, Melrose, MA
Melrose Hospital & Pine Villa, Melrose, MN
Melrose Manor Health Care Center, Louisville, KY
Melrose Nursing Center, Tyler, TX
Melville Rest Home, Boston, MA
Memorial Community Hospital—Long-Term Care Facility, Edgerton, WI
Memorial Conv Center, Belleville, IL
Memorial Convalescent Center, Adel, GA
Memorial Hall—Bristol Memorial Hospital, Bristol, VA
Memorial Heights Nursing Center, Idabel, OK
Memorial Home, Saint Louis, MO
Memorial Home for the Aged, Moundridge, KS
Memorial Hospital, Odessa, WA
Memorial Hospital at Easton, Easton, MD
Memorial Hospital Inc—SNF, Manchester, KY
Memorial Hospital Long-Term Care Unit, Owosso, MI
Memorial Hospital Medical Care Facility, Dodgeville, WI
Memorial Hospital of Danville Long-Term Care Unit, Danville, VA
Memorial Hospital Skilled Nursing Unit, Towanda, PA
Memorial Hospital Skilled Nursing Unit, Chattanooga, TN
Memorial Manor, Mondovi, WI
Memorial Manor Nursing Home, Bainbridge, GA
Memorial Masonic Home, Perry, IA
Memorial Medical Nursing Center, San Antonio, TX
Memorial Nursing Center, Frederick, OK
Memorial Nursing Home, Macon, GA
Memorial Nursing Home Long-Term Care Unit, Medford, WI
Memorial Nursing Home of Boscobel, Boscobel, WI
Memphis Convalescent Center, Memphis, TX
Memphis Health Care Center, Memphis, TN
Mena Manor, Mena, AR
Menard Convalescent Center, Petersburg, IL
Menard Manor, Menard, TX
Mendocino Skilled Nursing Facility, Ukiah, CA
Mendota Lutheran Home, Mendota, IL
Menlo Park Health Care Center, Portland, OR
Menno-Haven, Chambersburg, PA
Menno-Olivet Care Center, Menno, SD
Mennonite Friendship Manor Inc, South Hutchinson, KS
Mennonite Home, Albany, OR
Mennonite Home, Lancaster, PA
Mennonite Memorial Home, Bluffton, OH
Menomonee Falls Health Care Center, Menomonee Falls, WI
Menorah Home & Hospital for the Aged & Infirm, Brooklyn, NY
Menorah Manor, Saint Petersburg, FL
Menorah Nursing Home Inc, Brooklyn, NY

Menorah Park Center for the Aging, Beachwood, OH
Mentor Way Villa Nursing Home, Mentor, OH
Mequon Care Center, Mequon, WI
Merced Convalescent Hospital, Merced, CA
Merced Manor, Merced, CA
Mercer Convalescent Center, Trenton, NJ
Mercer County Geriatric Center, Trenton, NJ
Mercer County Living Center, Mercer, PA
Mercer County Nursing Home, Aledo, IL
Mercer Island Care Center, Mercer Island, WA
Mercerville Nursing Center, Mercerville, NJ
Mercy Bellbrook, Rochester Hills, MI
Mercy Care Center, Omaha, NE
Mercy Care Center, Roseburg, OR
Mercy Convalescent Center, Saint Louis, MO
Mercy Extended Care Facility, Vicksburg, MS
Mercy Health & Rehabilitation Center Nursing Home Company Inc, Auburn, NY
Mercy Health Care Center, Erie, PA
Mercy Health Care Center, Nanticoke, PA
Mercy Health Care Rehabilitation Center, Homewood, IL
Mercy Health Center Skilled Nursing Unit, Dubuque, IA
Mercy Healthcare Center, Tupper Lake, NY
Mercy Hospital, Bakersfield, CA
Mercy Hospital, Evergreen Park, IL
Mercy Hospital, Council Bluffs, IA
Mercy Hospital & Health Care Center, Moose Lake, MN
Mercy Hospital—Grayling, Grayling, MI
Mercy Hospital Health Related Facility, Watertown, NY
Mercy Hospital Medical Center, Des Moines, IA
Mercy Hospital Nursing Care Center, Johnstown, PA
Mercy Hospital Skilled Nursing Facility, New Orleans, LA
Mercy Hospital—Skilled Nursing Facility, Buffalo, NY
Mercy Manor, Oakland, CA
Mercy Medical, Daphne, AL
Mercy Medical Center Mt Shasta DP/SNF, Mount Shasta, CA
Mercy Medical Center of Durango Inc, Durango, CO
Mercy Nursing Home Inc, North Little Rock, AR
Mercy Nursing Home Inc, Houston, TX
Mercy Pavilion of Battle Creek, Battle Creek, MI
Mercy Rehabilitation & Care Center, San Diego, CA
Mercy Residential & Rehabilitation Center, Milwaukee, WI
Mercy Services for Aging—University Park, Muskegon, MI
Mercy Siena Woods, Dayton, OH
Mercycare, North Hornell, NY
Mercycare (Mercy Hospital of Sacramento DP/SNF), Sacramento, CA
Mercyknoll Inc, West Hartford, CT
Mere Point Nursing Home, Brunswick, ME
Meriden Nursing Home, Meriden, CT
Meridian Arms Living Center, Youngstown, OH
Meridian Care Center, Columbia, SC
Meridian Convalescent Home, Meridian, MS
Meridian Geriatric Center, Meridian, TX
Meridian Long Green, Baltimore, MD
Meridian Manor, Mounds, IL
Meridian Nursing & Rehabilitation Center, Silver Spring, MD
Meridian Nursing Center, Plantation, FL
Meridian Nursing Center, Meridian, MS
Meridian Nursing Center—Beeville, Beeville, TX
Meridian Nursing Center—Cardinal, South Bend, IN
Meridian Nursing Center—Caton Manor, Baltimore, MD
Meridian Nursing Center—Catonsville, Catonsville, MD

Meridian Nursing Center—Corsica Hills, Centreville, MD
Meridian Nursing Center—Cromwell, Baltimore, MD
Meridian Nursing Center—Dyer, Dyer, IN
Meridian Nursing Center—East Lake, Elkhart, IN
Meridian Nursing Center—Hamilton, Baltimore, MD
Meridian Nursing Center—Heritage, Baltimore, MD
Meridian Nursing Center—Homewood, Baltimore, MD
Meridian Nursing Center—Loch Raven, Baltimore, MD
Meridian Nursing Center—Mooresville, Mooresville, NC
Meridian Nursing Center—Multi-Medical, Towson, MD
Meridian Nursing Center—Perring Parkway, Baltimore, MD
Meridian Nursing Center—Randallstown, Randallstown, MD
Meridian Nursing Center—River Park, South Bend, IN
Meridian Nursing Center—St Augustine, Saint Augustine, FL
Meridian Nursing Center—Salisbury, Salisbury, NC
Meridian Nursing Center—Severna Park, Severna Park, MD
Meridian Nursing Center—The Pines, Easton, MD
Meridian Nursing Center—Voorhees, Voorhees, NJ
Meridian Nursing Center—Westfield, Westfield, NJ
Meridian Nursing Center—Millville, Millville, NJ
Meridian Nursing Center—Hammonds, Brooklyn Park, MD
Meridian Nursing Home, Indianapolis, IN
Meridian Nursing Home Inc, Comanche, OK
Meridian Nursing Center—LaPlata, LaPlata, MD
Merihil Health Care Center, Lewisburg, TN
Meriwether Memorial Hospital & Nursing Home, Warm Springs, GA
A Merkle C Knipprath Nursing Home, Clifton, IL
Merlin Health Retreat, Merlin, OR
Merrill Memorial Manor, Gardiner, ME
Merrillville Convalescent Center, Merrillville, IN
Merrimack County Nursing Home, Boscawen, NH
Merrimack River Valley House, Lowell, MA
Merrimack Valley Nursing & Rehabilitation Center, Amesbury, MA
Merriman House, North Conway, NH
Merritt House, Biwabik, MN
Merritt Manor Convalescent Hospital, Tulare, CA
Merritt Manor Nursing Home, Merritt Island, FL
Merritt Plaza Nursing Home, Marshall, TX
Merry Haven Health Care Center, Snohomish, WA
Merry Heart Nursing Home, Succasunna, NJ
Merry Manor Corp, Holton, KS
Merry Wood Lodge, Elmore, AL
Merrymount Manor Nursing Home, Quincy, MA
Merryville Nursing Center, Merryville, LA
Mertens House, Woodstock, VT
Mesa Christian Home, Mesa, AZ
Mesa Extended Care, Mesa, AZ
Mesa Lutheran Hospital, Mesa, AZ
Mesa Manor Nursing Center, Grand Junction, CO
Mesa Springs Health Care Center, Abilene, TX
Mesa Verde Convalescent Hospital, Costa Mesa, CA
Mesabi Home, Buhl, MN
Mesquite Tree Nursing Center, Mesquite, TX

Messenger House Care Center, Bainbridge Island, WA
Messiah Village, Mechanicsburg, PA
Metacom Manor Health Center, Bristol, RI
Metairie Health Care Center, Metairie, LA
Metcalfe County Nursing Home, Edmonton, KY
Meth-Wick Manor, Cedar Rapids, IA
Methodist Church Home for the Aged, Bronx, NY
Methodist Country House, Wilmington, DE
Methodist Health Center, Madison, WI
Methodist Home, Chicago, IL
Methodist Home for the Aging, Birmingham, AL
Methodist Home of DC, Washington, DC
Methodist Home of Enid Inc, Enid, OK
Methodist Home, Orangeburg, SC
Methodist Hospital Extended Care Facility, Saint Louis Park, MN
Methodist Hospital (SNF D/P Bruceville Terrace), Sacramento, CA
Methodist Hospitals of Memphis Skilled Care Facility, Memphis, TN
Methodist Manor, Storm Lake, IA
Methodist Manor Health Center, West Allis, WI
Methodist Manor House, Seaford, DE
Methodist Manor Inc, West Allis, WI
Methodist Nursing Home Inc, Fort Smith, AR
Methodist Nursing Home of Middle Tennessee, Winchester, TN
Methodist Retirement Homes Inc, Durham, NC
Methuen Nursing & Rehabilitation Center, Methuen, MA
Metro Care Center, Minneapolis, MN
Metroplex Care Center, Grand Prairie, TX
Metropolis Good Samaritan Home, Metropolis, IL
Metropolitan Jewish Geriatric Center, Brooklyn, NY
Metropolitan Nursing Center, Bridgeview, IL
Metter Nursing Home, Metter, GA
Metzenbaum Residence, Chesterland, OH
Metzmeier Nursing Home, Campbellsville, KY
Mexia Nursing Home, Mexia, TX
Mexico Manor Inc, Mexico, MO
Meyer Care Center, Higginsville, MO
Harry Meyering Center Inc, Mankato, MN
Meyersdale Manor, Meyersdale, PA
Mi Casa Nursing Center, Mesa, AZ
MI Nursing & Restorative Center, Lawrence, MA
Miami Beach Hebrew Home for the Aged, Miami Beach, FL
Miami Christel Manor Inc, Miamisburg, OH
Miami Haven, Cleves, OH
Miami Health Care Center, Troy, OH
Miami Jewish Home for the Aged at Douglas Gardens, Miami, FL
Miami Nursing Center, Miami, OK
Michael Manor, Gettysburg, PA
Michael Manor, Douglas, WY
Andrew Michaud Nursing Home, Fulton, NY
Michealsen Health Center, Batavia, IL
Michigan Christian Home, Grand Rapids, MI
Michigan City Health Care, Michigan City, IN
Michigan Masonic Home, Alma, MI
Michigan Shores, Manitowoc, WI
Mickel Nursing Home, Clarksville, AR
Micoll Residence, Hastings, MN
Mid-America Convalescent Centers Inc, Chicago, IL
Mid-America Nursing Center of Lincoln, Lincoln, KS
Mid-City Care Center, Memphis, TN
Mid-Maine Medical Center—Charles A Dean Memorial Hospital, Greenville, ME
Mid Nebraska Lutheran Home, Newman Grove, NE
Mid-South Christian Nursing Home, Memphis, TN
Mid State ICF/MR Broad, Altoona, PA
Mid State ICF/MR Inc, Altoona, PA
Mid State ICF/MR Inc, Altoona, PA
Mid-Wilshire Convalescent Hospital, Los Angeles, CA

Middle Georgia Nursing Home, Eastman, GA
Middle River Health Facility, Hawthorne, WI
Middlebelt-Hope Nursing Center, Westland, MI
Middlebelt Nursing Centre, Livonia, MI
Middleboro Rest Home, Middleborough, MA
Middlebury Convalescent Home Inc, Middlebury, CT
Middlebury Manor Nursing & Convalescent Home, Akron, OH
Middlesex Convalescent Center Inc, Middletown, CT
Middleton Village Nursing Home, Middleton, WI
Middletown Health Care Center, Middletown, OH
Middletown Healthcare Center Inc, Middletown, CT
Middletown Park Manor Health Facility, Middletown, NY
Midland Care Center, Nampa, ID
Midland Care Center Inc, Midland, TX
Midland Hospital Center, Midland, MI
Midland King's Daughter's Home, Midland, MI
Midland Manor, Tacoma, WA
Midland Villa, Falls City, NE
Midlands Center Infant Care Unit, Columbia, SC
Midtown Care Home, Somerset, KY
Midtown Manor, Salt Lake City, UT
Midtown Manor Nursing Home, Kansas City, MO
Midway Care Center Inc, Fosston, MN
Midway Care Center Inc, Portland, OR
Midway Hospital Skilled Nursing Facility, Saint Paul, MN
Midway Manor Convalescent Center, Kent, WA
Midway Manor Nursing Home Inc, Shreveport, LA
Midway Nursing Home, Maspeth, NY
Midwest Covenant Home, Stromsburg, NE
Midwest Nursing Center, Baxter Springs, KS
Midwestern Parkway Heritage Manor, Wichita Falls, TX
Mielke's Nursing Home, Toledo, OH
Mifflin Care Center, Mansfield, OH
Mifflin Healthcare Center, Shillington, PA
Milan Care Center Inc, Milan, MO
Milan Health Care Inc, Milan, TN
Milan Healthcare Center, Milan, IN
Milcrest Nursing Center, Marysville, OH
Milder Manor, Lincoln, NE
Milestone Inc, Rockford, IL
Milestone Inc—Elmwood East, Rockford, IL
Milestone Inc—Elmwood Heights, Rockford, IL
Miletree Health Care Center, Spencer, WV
Milford Health Care Center Inc, Milford, CT
Milford Manor, Milford, DE
Milford Manor, West Milford, NJ
Milford Manor Nursing Home, Baltimore, MD
Milford Manor Rest Home Inc, Milford, MA
Milford Nursing Center, Milford, IA
Milford Nursing Home, Milford, NH
Milford Valley Convalescent Home Inc, Milford, PA
Milford Valley Memorial Nursing Home, Milford, UT
Mill Haven Care Center, Millstadt, IL
Mill Hill Nursing Home, Worcester, MA
Mill Pond Rest Home, Ashland, MA
Mill Pond Rest Home, Hanover, MA
Mill Valley Care Center, Bellevue, IA
Millard Good Samaritan Center, Omaha, NE
Millbrae Serra Convalescent Hospital, Millbrae, CA
Millcreek Group Home, Wilmington, DE
Millcreek of Arkansas, Fordyce, AR
Millcroft, Newark, DE
Mille Lacs Hospital & Home, Onamia, MN
Miller Care Center Inc, Louisville, OH
Miller County Nursing Home, Tuscumbia, MO
Miller Memorial Community—Edward Pavilion/Caroline Hall, Meriden, CT

Miller Memorial Health Care Center, Andover, OH
Miller Memorial Nursing Home, Chappell, NE
Nathan Miller Center for Nursing Care Inc—White Plains Center Division, White Plains, NY
Nathan Miller Center for Nursing Care Inc—Nathan Miller Center Division, White Plains, NY
Miller Nursing Home, Colquitt, GA
Susan B Miller Nursing Homes Inc, Woodstock, VA
Miller's Merry Manor Inc, Garrett, IN
Miller's Merry Manor, Hope, IN
Miller's Merry Manor, Logansport, IN
Miller's Merry Manor, Middletown, IN
Miller's Merry Manor, New Carlisle, IN
Miller's Merry Manor, Sullivan, IN
Miller's Merry Manor, Tipton, IN
Miller's Merry Manor Community, Indianapolis, IN
Miller's Merry Manor Inc, Chesterfield, IN
Miller's Merry Manor Inc, Columbia City, IN
Miller's Merry Manor Inc, Culver, IN
Miller's Merry Manor Inc, Dunkirk, IN
Miller's Merry Manor Inc, Fort Wayne, IN
Miller's Merry Manor Inc, Hartford City, IN
Miller's Merry Manor Inc, Hobart, IN
Miller's Merry Manor Inc, Huntington, IN
Miller's Merry Manor Inc, Indianapolis, IN
Miller's Merry Manor Inc, Lagrange, IN
Miller's Merry Manor Inc, Mooresville, IN
Miller's Merry Manor Inc, Peru, IN
Miller's Merry Manor Inc, Plymouth, IN
Miller's Merry Manor Inc, Portage, IN
Miller's Merry Manor Inc, Rockport, IN
Miller's Merry Manor Inc, Syracuse, IN
Miller's Merry Manor Inc, Wabash, IN
Miller's Merry Manor Inc, Wakarusa, IN
Miller's Merry Manor Inc, Walkerton, IN
Miller's Merry Manor Inc, Warsaw, IN
Miller's Progressive Care, Riverside, CA
Millhouse, Trenton, NJ
Millie's Rest Home, Sutherland, IA
Mills Community Home, New York Mills, MN
Mills Manor, Meriden, CT
Mills Manor, Mayfield, KY
Millsboro Nursing Home, Millsboro, DE
Millville Health Center, Millville, PA
Millway Nursing Home, Milwaukee, WI
Milner Community Health Care Inc, Rossville, IN
Milton Health Care Facility A Skilled Nursing Facility, Milton, MA
Milton Home, South Bend, IN
John Milton Nursing Home, Kissimmee, FL
Miltonview Nursing Home, Boston, MA
Milwaukee Catholic Home, Milwaukee, WI
Milwaukee County Mental Health Complex Rehabilitation Center—Central, Wauwatosa, WI
Milwaukee County Mental Health Complex Rehabilitation Center—South, Wauwatosa, WI
Milwaukee County Mental Health Complex Rehabilitation Center—West, Wauwatosa, WI
Milwaukee Jewish Convalescent Center, Milwaukee, WI
Milwaukee Jewish Home, Milwaukee, WI
Milwaukee Protestant Bradford Terrace, Milwaukee, WI
Milwaukee Protestant Home Infirmary, Milwaukee, WI
Milwaukie Convalescent Center Inc, Milwaukie, OR
Mimbres Memorial Nursing Home, Deming, NM
Mimosa Manor, Keller, TX
Minami Keiro Nursing Home, Los Angeles, CA
Minden Medical Center Skilled Nursing Facility, Minden, LA
Miner Nursing Home, Parsons, KS
Miner Nursing & Residential Care Center, Miner, MO
Mineral County Nursing Home, Superior, MT

Mineral Point Living Center, Mineral Point, WI
Mineral Wells Care Center, Mineral Wells, TX
Miners Colfax Medical Center, Raton, NM
Minerva Convalescent Center Inc, Minerva, OH
Minerva Fisher Hall Group Home, Vienna, VA
Minerva Park Nursing Home, Columbus, OH
Mingo Health Care Center Inc, Williamson, WV
Minidoka Memorial Hospital & Extended Care Facility, Rupert, ID
Minneapolis Good Samaritan Center, Minneapolis, KS
Minneola Nursing Home, Minneola, KS
Minneota Manor, Minneota, MN
Minnequa Medicenter Inc, Pueblo, CO
Minnesota Jewish Group Home II—Tikvah, Saint Paul, MN
Minnesota Masonic Home Care Center, Minneapolis, MN
Minnesota Odd Fellows Home, Northfield, MN
Minnesota Supervised Living Facility, Saint Peter, MN
Minnesota Valley Memorial Hospital, Le Sueur, MN
Minnesota Veterans Home, Hastings, MN
Minnesota Veterans Home, Minneapolis, MN
Minnetonka Health Care Center Inc, Excelsior, MN
Minnewaska Lutheran Home, Starbuck, MN
Mira Costa Convalescent Hospital, Torrance, CA
Mira Vista Care Center, Mount Vernon, WA
Miracle Hill Nursing & Convalescent Home, Tallahassee, FL
Mirada Hills Rehabilitation & Convalescent Hospital, La Mirada, CA
Miramar Lodge Nursing Home, Pass Christian, MS
Misericordia Convalescent Home, York, PA
Misericordia Home, Chicago, IL
Mission Bay Convalescent Hospital, San Francisco, CA
Mission Boulevard Convalescent Hospital, Fremont, CA
Mission Care Detox Center, Plymouth, MN
Mission Convalescent Home, Jackson, TN
Mission Convalescent Hospital, San Gabriel, CA
Mission Farms Nursing Home, Plymouth, MN
Mission Lodge Sanitarium, San Gabriel, CA
Mission Manor Nursing Home, Mount Vernon, TX
Mission Skilled Nursing Facility, Santa Clara, CA
Mission Terrace Convalescent Hospital, Santa Barbara, CA
Mission Villa Convalescent Hospital, San Francisco, CA
Mississippi Children's Rehabilitation Center, Jackson, MS
Mississippi County Nursing Home, Blytheville, AR
Mississippi Extended Care of Greenville Inc, Greenville, MS
Missouri Slope Lutheran Care Center, Bismarck, ND
Missouri Valley Nursing Center, Pierre, SD
Mitchell Convalescent Center, Camilla, GA
Mitchell-Hollingworth Annex to Eliza Coffee Memorial Hospital, Florence, AL
Mitchell Manor, Mitchell, IN
Mitchell Manor Convalescent Home Inc, McAlester, OK
Mitchell Retirement Nursing Center, Mitchell, SD
Mitchell Village Care Center, Mitchellville, IA
Mitchell's Nursing Home Inc, Danville, AR
Mizpah Nursing Home Inc, Locust Hill, VA
MJG Nursing Home, Brooklyn, NY
Moberly Caring Center, Moberly, MO
Mobridge Care Center, Mobridge, SD
Mochel Manor, Kansas City, MO
Modern Acre Home, Fulton, MO

Modern Care Convalescent & Nursing Home, Jacksonville, IL
Moderncare West Seattle Inc, Seattle, WA
Modesto Convalescent Hospital, Modesto, CA
Mogck Home for Aged, Mitchell, SD
Mogck's Rest Home, Mitchell, SD
Mohawk Valley Nursing Home Inc, Ilion, NY
Mohun Hall Infirmary, Columbus, OH
Molalla Manor Care Center, Molalla, OR
Molena Intermediate Care Home, Molena, GA
Moline Nursing & Rehabilitation Center, Moline, IL
Molokai General Hospital, Kaunakakai, HI
Mom & Dad's Home & Health Care Center, Sioux Falls, SD
Momence Meadows Nursing Home, Momence, IL
Monadnock Christian Nursing Home, Jaffrey, NH
Monarch Care Center, Seattle, WA
Monarch Heights, Ortonville, MN
Monclova Care Center, Monclova, OH
Monmouth Convalescent Center, Long Branch, NJ
Monmouth Nursing Home, Monmouth, IL
Monroe City Manor Care Center, Monroe City, MO
Monroe Community Hospital, Rochester, NY
Monroe Convalescent Center, Monroe, MI
Monroe County Care Center, Woodsfield, OH
Monroe County Nursing Home, Waterloo, IL
Monroe County Rest Home, Aberdeen, MS
Monroe Health Care Facility, Tompkinsville, KY
Monroe Intermediate Care Facility, Monroe, GA
Monroe Manor, Paris, MO
Monroe Manor Nursing Center, Monroe, LA
Monroe Manor Nursing Home, Monroeville, AL
Monroe Manor Nursing Home, Monroe, WI
Monroe Pavilion Health Center Inc, Chicago, IL
Monroe Village Health Care Center, Jamesburg, NJ
Monrovia Convalescent Hospital, Duarte, CA
Monsignor Bojnowski Manor Inc, New Britain, CT
Monsignor Fitzpatrick Pavilion for Skilled Nursing Care, Jamaica, NY
Monson State Hospital, Palmer, MA
Montana Center for the Aged, Lewistown, MT
Montana Developmental Center, Boulder, MT
Montana State Hospital—ICF, Deer Lodge, MT
Montana Veterans Home, Columbia Falls, MT
Montana West Retirement Home Inc, Great Falls, MT
Montcalm Nursing Home, Montclair, NJ
Montclair Manor Convalescent Hospital, Montclair, CA
Montclair Nursing Center, Omaha, NE
Montclair Nursing Home, Montclair, NJ
Montclair Nursing Home, Glen Cove, NY
Monte Cassino Healthcare Center, Toluca, IL
Monte Vista Child Care Center, Montclair, CA
Monte Vista Grove, Pasadena, CA
Monte Vista Lodge, Lemon Grove, CA
Montebello Nursing Home, Hamilton, IL
Montebello on Academy, Albuquerque, NM
Montefiore Home, Cleveland Heights, OH
Montello Care Center, Montello, WI
Montello Manor, Lewiston, ME
Monterey Care Center, Rosemead, CA
Monterey Care Center, Wichita Falls, TX
Monterey Convalescent Hospital, Monterey, CA
Monterey Nursing Center, Scottsdale, AZ
Monterey Nursing Inn, Grove City, OH
Monterey Park Convalescent Hospital, Monterey Park, CA
Monterey Pines Skilled Nursing Facility, Monterey, CA
Montezuma Health Care Center, Montezuma, GA
Montgomery Care Center Inc, Cincinnati, OH

Montgomery Country Nursing Home, Mount Ida, AR
Montgomery County Geriatric & Rehabilitation Center, Royersford, PA
Montgomery County Infirmary, Amsterdam, NY
Montgomery County Nursing Home, Ashland City, TN
Montgomery General Elderly Care, Montgomery, WV
John L Montgomery Medical Home, Freehold, NJ
Montgomery Manor, Santa Rosa, CA
Montgomery Memorial Hospital—Skilled Nursing Facility, Troy, NC
Montgomery Nursing Home, Montgomery, NY
Montgomery Terrace, Nokomis, IL
Monticello Big Lake, Monticello, MN
Monticello Community Healthcare Center, Monticello, IN
Monticello Convalescent Center of Hinsdale, Hinsdale, IL
Monticello Hall, Kelso, WA
Monticello Manor Nursing Home, Fort Lauderdale, FL
Montowese Health Care Center, North Haven, CT
Montrose Bay Health Care Center, Fairhope, AL
Montrose Care Center, Houston, TX
Montrose Convalescent Hospital, Montrose, CA
Montrose Health Center, Montrose, IA
Montrose Nursing Home, Montrose, MI
Montvale Health Center, Maryville, TN
Montvista at Coronado, El Paso, TX
MontVue Nursing Home, Luray, VA
Monument Hill Nursing Center, La Grange, TX
Moody Care Center, Moody, TX
Moore & Pike County Nursing Home, Bowling Green, MO
E Dene Moore Memorial Home, Rifle, CO
Moore-Few Nursing Home, Nevada, MO
Sarah Moore Home Inc, Delaware, OH
Moorehaven Care Center, La Center, WA
Mooreland Golden Age Nursing Home, Mooreland, OK
Moores Haven Dungarvin VI, Shoreview, MN
Moore's Nursing Home, Pittsburg, TX
Moorhead Healthcare Center, Moorhead, MN
Moorings Health Center, Arlington Heights, IL
Moorings Park, Naples, FL
Charles P Moorman Home for Women, Louisville, KY
Moosa Memorial Hospital, Eunice, LA
Moose Lake Regional Treatment Center, Moose Lake, MN
Moosehaven Health Center, Orange Park, FL
Moraine Community Living Facility, Highland Park, IL
Moran Manor, Moran, KS
Moran Manor, Westernport, MD
Morans Home Inc, Bellwood, PA
Moravian Hall Square, Nazareth, PA
Moravian Home Inc, Winston-Salem, NC
Moravian Manor, Lititz, PA
Morehead Memorial Nursing Center, Eden, NC
Morehead Nursing Center, Morehead City, NC
Allen Morgan Nursing Center, Memphis, TN
Morgan County Appalachian Regional Hospital, West Liberty, KY
Morgan County Care Center, McConnelsville, OH
Edwin Morgan Center Scotland Memorial Hospital—SNF, Laurinburg, NC
Morgan Health Center, Johnston, RI
Morgan Manor Convalescent Center, Morgantown, WV
Morgan Memorial Home, Stockton, IL
Morning Star Manor, Fort Washakie, WY
Morning Star Nursing Home, Oklahoma City, OK
Morning Sun Care Center, Morning Sun, IA
Morning View Care Center, Centerburg, OH

Morning View Care Center, Danville, OH
Morning View Care Center, Marion, OH
Morning View Care Center 2, Fulton, OH
Morning View Care Center III, Sunbury, OH
Morningside Care Center, Ida Grove, IA
Morningside Care Center, Stoughton, WI
Morningside Center, Chillicothe, MO
Morningside Health Center, Sheboygan, WI
Morningside House Nursing Home Company, Bronx, NY
Morningside Manor, Alcester, SD
Morningside Manor, San Antonio, TX
Morningside Nursing Home, Norman, OK
Moroun Nursing Home, Detroit, MI
Morrell Memorial Convalescent Center Inc, Hartsville, SC
Morrilton Manor Inc, Morrilton, AR
Bishop Morris Care Center, Portland, OR
Morris Hills Multicare Center, Morristown, NJ
Morris Lincoln Nursing Home, Morris, IL
Morris Memorial Nursing & Convalescent Home, Milton, WV
Morris Nursing Home, Bethel, OH
Morris Park Nursing Home, Bronx, NY
Morris View, Morris Plains, NJ
Morrison Community Hospital Skilled Nursing Facility, Morrison, IL
Morrison Nursing Home, Whitefield, NH
Morrisons Cove Home, Martinsburg, PA
Morristown Healthcare, Morristown, IN
Morristown Rehabilitation Center, Morristown, NJ
Morro Bay Convalescent Center, Morro Bay, CA
Morrow County Extended Care Facility, Mount Gilead, OH
J Michael Morrow Memorial Nursing Home, Arnaudville, LA
Morrow Manor Inc, Chesterville, OH
Morrow Memorial Home for the Aged, Sparta, WI
Joseph L Morse Geriatric Center, West Palm Beach, FL
Morton Health Care Limited, Morton, IL
Morton Nursing Home, Morton, WA
Morton Terrace Ltd, Morton, IL
Val Morys Haven, Columbus, NE
Moscow Care Center, Moscow, ID
Moses-Ludington Nursing Home Company Inc, Ticonderoga, NY
Moses Taylor Hospital—Skilled Nursing Facility, Scranton, PA
Moshannon Heights, Philipsburg, PA
Mosholu Parkway Nursing Home, Bronx, NY
Moss Bluff Manor, Lake Charles, LA
Moss Oaks Health Care, Pooler, GA
Mosser Nursing Home, Trexlertown, PA
Mother Hull Home Inc, Kearney, NE
Mother Joseph Manor, Aberdeen, SD
Mother Margaret Hall, Mount Saint Joseph, OH
Mother of Good Counsel Home, Saint Louis, MO
Mother of Mercy Nursing Home, Albany, MN
Mother of Perpetual Help Home, Brownsville, TX
Mother Teresa Home, Cold Spring, MN
Mother Theresa Home, Lemont, IL
Mott Good Samaritan Nursing Center, Mott, ND
Margaret E Moul Home, York, PA
Moulton Health Care Center, Moulton, AL
Moultrie County Community Center, Lovington, IL
Moultrie Rest-A-While Nursing Home, Moultrie, GA
Mound View Health Care Center, Moundsville, WV
Moundridge Manor, Moundridge, KS
Mounds Park Residence, Saint Paul, MN
Moundville Nursing Facility, Moundville, AL
Mt Adams Care Center, Goldendale, WA
Mt Alverna Home Annex Inc, Parma, OH
Mt Alverna Home Inc, Parma, OH
Mt Ascutney Hospital & Health Center, Windsor, VT
Mt Ayr Health Care Center, Mount Ayr, IA

Mt Baker Care Inc, Bellingham, WA
Mt Carmel Care Center, Burlington, WI
Mt Carmel Health Care Center, Milwaukee, WI
Mt Carmel Home—Keens Memorial, Kearney, NE
Mt Carmel Nursing Center, Mount Carmel, PA
Mt Carmel Nursing Home, Manchester, NH
Mt Dora Healthcare Center, Mount Dora, FL
Mt Gilead Shelter Care Home, Carrollton, IL
Mt Greylock Extended Care Facility, Pittsfield, MA
Mt Healthy Christian Home, Cincinnati, OH
Mt Holly Center, Mount Holly, NJ
Mt Holly Nursing Home, Louisville, KY
Mt Hope Dunkard Brethren Church Home, Manheim, PA
Mt Hope Nursing Center, Mount Hope, KS
Mt Ida Rest Home, Newton, MA
Mt Joseph Inc, Concordia, KS
Mt Laurel Convalescent Center, Mount Laurel, NJ
Mt Lebanon Manor, Pittsburgh, PA
Mt Loretto Nursing Home, Amsterdam, NY
Mt Macrina Manor Nursing Home, Uniontown, PA
Mt Miguel Covenant Village, Spring Valley, CA
Mt Olivet Homes Inc, Minneapolis, MN
Mt Olivet Rolling Acres, Excelsior, MN
Mt Olivette Care Center, Carmichael, CA
Mt Olivette Meadows Convalescent Hospital, Sacramento, CA
Mt Orab Nursing Care Center, Mount Orab, OH
Mt Pleasant Convalescent Hospital, San Jose, CA
Mt Pleasant Home, Jamaica Plain, MA
Mt Pleasant Hospitality House, Mount Pleasant, TX
Mt Pleasant Manor, Matawan, NJ
Mt Pleasant Nursing Home, Cleveland, OH
Mt Pleasant Total Living Center, Mount Pleasant, MI
Mt Pleasant Village, Monroe, OH
Mt Ridge Health Care Center Inc, Franklin, NH
Mt Royal Towers, Birmingham, AL
Mt Royal Villa, North Royalton, OH
Mt Rubidoux Convalescent Hospital, Rubidoux, CA
Mt St Francis Health Center, Woonsocket, RI
Mt St Joseph, Lake Zurich, IL
Mt St Joseph, Euclid, OH
Mt St Joseph Nursing Home, Waterville, ME
Mt St Joseph Residence & Extended Care Center, Portland, OR
Mt St Mary's Long-Term Care Facility Inc, Niagara Falls, NY
Mt St Rita Health Center, Cumberland, RI
Mt St Vincent Home, Holyoke, MA
Mt St Vincent Nursing Center, Seattle, WA
Mt San Antonio Gardens, Pomona, CA
Mt Shelter Care Home, Vienna, IL
Mt Tabor Care Center, Portland, OR
Mt Trace Nursing Center, Sylva, NC
Mt Vernon Care Center, Baltimore, MD
Mt Vernon Care Center Inc, Mount Vernon, IL
Mt Vernon Manor, Fort Lauderdale, FL
Mt Vernon Nursing Center, Southfield, MI
Mt Vernon Nursing Center, Alexandria, VA
Mt Vernon Nursing Home, Mount Vernon, OH
Mt Vernon Park Care Center, Springfield, MO
Mt Washington Care Center, Cincinnati, OH
Mt Zion Geriatric Center, Indianapolis, IN
Mountain City Convalescent & Rehabilitation Center, Hazelton, PA
Mountain City Health Care, Mountain City, TN
Mountain Creek Manor, Chattanooga, TN
Mountain Home Good Samaritan Village, Mountain Home, AR
Mountain Home Nursing Center, Mountain Home, AR

Mountain Lake Good Samaritan Village, Mountain Lake, MN
Mountain Laurel Manor, Corbin, KY
Mountain Laurel Nursing Center, Clearfield, PA
Mountain Manor, Carmichael, CA
Mountain Manor Nursing Home, Pikeville, KY
Mountain Manor Nursing Home Inc, Fort Payne, AL
Mountain Manor of Prestonburg, Prestonsburg, KY
Mountain Meadows Nursing Center Inc, Monte Vista, CO
Mountain Park Convalescent Care Facility, Lake Oswego, OR
Mountain Rest Nursing Home, Scranton, PA
Mountain Shadow Health Care Center, Scottsdale, AZ
Mountain Shadows Health Care Center, Las Cruces, NM
Mountain Towers Healthcare, Cheyenne, WY
Mountain Valley Rest Home, Salyersville, KY
Mountain View Care Center, Colorado Springs, CO
Mountain View Care Center, Kimberly, ID
Mountain View Care Center, Bozeman, MT
Mt View Child Care Center Inc, Loma Linda, CA
Mountain View Convalescent Care Center, Oregon City, OR
Mountain View Convalescent Center, Clayton, GA
Mountain View Convalescent Hospital, Mountain View, CA
Mountain View Health Care Center, Elkhorn City, KY
Mt View Health Facility, Lockport, NY
Mountain View Healthcare, Windsor, CT
Mountain View Hospital, Payson, UT
Mountain View Hospital & Nursing Home, Madras, OR
Mountain View House, Aurora, CO
Mountain View Lodge Inc, Big Spring, TX
Mountain View Manor, Shamokin, PA
Mountain View Manor Good Samaritan, Eureka, MT
Mountain View Manor—Hillsdale, Hillsdale, PA
Mountain View Manor Nursing Center, Bryson City, NC
Mt View Nursing & Rehabilitation Center, Greensburg, PA
Mountain View Nursing Home, Montgomery, MA
Mountain View Nursing Home, Ossipee, NH
Mt View Nursing Home, Wausau, WI
Mountain View Nursing Home Inc, Aroda, VA
Mountain View Oregon, Klamath Falls, OR
Mountain View Personal Care & Retirement Home, Lewistown, MT
Mountain View Place, El Paso, TX
Mountain View Rest Home, Chattanooga, TN
Mountain View Sanitarium, Sylmar, CA
Mountain Vista Care Center, LaGrande, OR
Mountain Vista Health Park, Denton, NC
Mountain Vista Nursing Home, Wheat Ridge, CO
Mountainview Memorial Nursing Home, White Sulphur Springs, MT
Mountainview Nursing Home, Spartanburg, SC
Mountrail Bethel Home, Stanley, ND
Moyle Manor, Yucca Valley, CA
Moyle's Hi-Desert Convalescent Hospital, Yucca Valley, CA
Moyle's Sky Harbor Healthcare Center, Yucca Valley, CA
Mozark Health Resort, Camdenton, MO
Mud Pike Home, Celina, OH
F F Mueller Residential Center, Springfield, OH
C A Mues Memorial Good Samaritan Center, Arapahoe, NE
Muffett Nursing Home, Cornwell Heights, PA
Muhlenberg Community Hospital, Greenville, KY

Mul-Care Convalescent Hospital, Indio, CA
Mulberry Lutheran Home, Mulberry, IN
Mulberry Manor, Stephenville, TX
Mulberry Manor Inc, Anna, IL
Mulberry Park, Florence, SC
Mulder Health Care Facility, West Salem, WI
Muldrow Nursing Home, Muldrow, OK
Muleshoe Nursing Home, Muleshoe, TX
Mullen Home—Little Sisters of the Poor, Denver, CO
Mullican Nursing Home, Savoy, TX
Mullins Nursing Home, Waverly, OH
Mullis Manor II, Folkston, GA
Mullis Manor III, Hazlehurst, GA
Mullis Manor Inc, Homerville, GA
Muncie Health Care Center Inc, Muncie, IN
Muncy Valley Hospital—Skilled Nursing Facility, Muncy, PA
Munday Nursing Center, Munday, TX
Municipal Hospital & Granite Manor, Granite Falls, MN
Munster Med-Inn, Munster, IN
Murdoch Center, Butner, NC
Murdock Manor, Lafayette, IN
Murfreesboro Health Care Center, Murfreesboro, TN
Mary Murphy Nursing Home, Boston, MA
Murphy Medical Center, Murphy, NC
Murray-Calloway County Hospital Convalescent Division, Murray, KY
Murray Manor Convalescent Center, Murraysville, PA
Muscatine Care Center, Muscatine, IA
Muscatine General Hospital, Muscatine, IA
Muscle Shoals Nursing Home, Muscle Shoals, AL
Muscogee Manor, Columbus, GA
Muskego Nursing Home, Muskego, WI
Muskegon Correctional Facility, Muskegon, MI
Mustang Nursing Home, Mustang, OK
Myers Nursing & Convalescent Center, Kansas City, MO
Myers Nursing Home, Beardstown, IL
Myrtle Beach Manor, Myrtle Beach, SC
Myrtle Point Care Center, Myrtle Point, OR
Myrtles Health Care Facility, Columbia, MS
Mystic Manor Inc, Mystic, CT
Mystic Nursing & Rehabilitation Center, Fitchburg, MA
Nacogdoches Convalescent Center, Nacogdoches, TX
Naeve Parkview Nursing Home, Wells, MN
Nampa Care Center, Nampa, ID
Nancy Ann Convalescent Home, Foster, RI
Nansemond Convalescent Center Inc Health Care Unit, Suffolk, VA
Naomi Heights Nursing Home, Alexandria, LA
Napa Nursing Center, Napa, CA
Narraguagus Bay Health Care Facility, Milbridge, ME
Nashville Health Care Center, Nashville, TN
Nashville Manor, Nashville, TN
Nashville Metropolitan Bordeaux Hospital—Nursing Home, Nashville, TN
Nashville Nursing Home, Nashville, AR
Nassau Nursing Home, Oceanside, NY
Natatana Care Center, De Leon, TX
Natchitoches Manor, Natchitoches, LA
Natchitoches Parish Hospital—Long-Term Care Unit, Natchitoches, LA
National Health Care, Poway, CA
National Health Care Center, Fort Oglethorpe, GA
National Health Care Center of Fort Lauderdale, Fort Lauderdale, FL
National Health Care Center of Hendersonville, Hendersonville, TN
National Health Care Center of Sumter, Sumter, SC
National Healthcare Center, Hudson, FL
National Healthcare Center of Lawrenceburg, Lawrenceburg, TN
National Healthcare Center of Panama City, Panama City, FL
National Lutheran Home for the Aged, Rockville, MD

Nature Trail Home Inc, Mount Vernon, IL
Navarre Community Health Center, Navarre, OH
Nazareth Hall, El Paso, TX
Nazareth Home, Louisville, KY
Nazareth House, Fresno, CA
Nazareth House, Los Angeles, CA
Nazareth House, San Diego, CA
Nazareth House, San Rafael, CA
Nazareth House, Stoughton, WI
Nazareth Nursing Home & Health Related Facility, Buffalo, NY
Nazarethville, Des Plaines, IL
NCF Eastridge House, Beloit, WI
Neal Home, Logansport, IN
Nebraska City Manor, Nebraska City, NE
Nebraska Veterans Home, Grand Island, NE
Nebraska Veterans Home Annex, Norfolk, NE
Nederland Nursing Home, Nederland, TX
Needham/Hamilton House Convalescent Center, Needham, MA
Needham's Nursing Home Inc, Bellingham, WA
Negley Nursing & Rehabilitation Center, Pittsburgh, PA
Negro Old Folks Home Inc, LaGrange, GA
Nehalem Valley Care Center, Wheeler, OR
Neighborhood Convalescent Home Inc, Lincoln, RI
Neighbors, Byron, IL
Neighbors of Woodcraft Home, Gresham, OR
Neillsville Memorial Home, Neillsville, WI
Nekton Inc, Saint Paul, MN
Nekton on Frost, Maplewood, MN
Nekton on Goodrich, Saint Paul, MN
Nekton on Greysolon, Duluth, MN
Nekton on Hodgson Rd, Shoreview, MN
Nekton on Imperial Court, Stillwater, MN
Nekton on London Road, Duluth, MN
Nekton on Minnehaha Park, Minneapolis, MN
Nekton on Mississippi, Saint Paul, MN
Nekton on Queen, Minneapolis, MN
Nekton on Sextant, Little Canada, MN
Nekton on Springvale, Duluth, MN
Nekton on Stillwater Lane, Lake Elmo, MN
Nekton on Wallace, Duluth, MN
Nekton on Wheeler, Saint Paul, MN
Nekton on William, Edina, MN
Nekton on Wyoming, Saint Paul, MN
Neligh Nursing Center, Neligh, NE
Nella's Inc, Elkins, WV
Nelson Broadview Nursing Home, Parma, OH
Knute Nelson Memorial Home, Alexandria, MN
Nelson Manor, Newton, IA
Nelson Manor Nursing Home, Boston, MA
Nelson Nursing Home, Fairfield, IA
Nelson's Rest Home, Sturgis, SD
Nemaha County Good Samaritan Center, Auburn, NE
Nentwick Convalescent Home Inc, East Liverpool, OH
Neodesha Nursing Home, Neodesha, KS
Neosho Senior Center, Neosho, MO
Neponsit Health Care Center, Neponsit, NY
Nesbit Nursing Home, Seguin, TX
Nesconset Nursing Center, Nesconset, NY
Neshaminy Manor Home, Doylestown, PA
Neshoba County Nursing Home, Philadelphia, MS
George H Nettleton Home, Kansas City, MO
Sarah R Neuman Nursing Home, Mamaroneck, NY
Nevada Habilitation Center, Nevada, MO
Nevada Manor, Nevada, MO
Mayor Michael J Neville Manor, Cambridge, MA
Henry C Nevins Home Inc, Methuen, MA
New Albany Nursing Home, New Albany, IN
New Athens Home For the Aged, New Athens, IL
New Bedford Jewish Convalescent Home, New Bedford, MA

New Brighton Care Center, New Brighton, MN
New Brighton Manor Care Center, Staten Island, NY
New Castle Community Care Center, New Castle, IN
New Castle Healthcare Center, New Castle, IN
New Community Extended Care Facility, Newark, NJ
New Concord Nursing Center, New Concord, OH
New Connection Primary Treatment, Saint Paul, MN
New Dawn Convalescent Center, Furnace, OH
New Dawn Health Care & Retirement Center, Dover, OH
New Dawn Inc, Fulda, MN
New Dawson Springs Nursing Home, Dawson Springs, KY
New Detroit Nursing Center, Detroit, MI
New Directions, Saint Paul, MN
New Ellenton Geriatric Center Inc, New Ellenton, SC
New England Friends Home, Hingham, MA
New England Home for the Deaf, Danvers, MA
New England Rehabilitation Hospital, Woburn, MA
New England Rehabilitation Hospital of Portland, Portland, ME
New Fairview Health Care, New Haven, CT
New Florence Nursing Home Inc, New Florence, MO
New Forestville Health & Rehabilitation Center, Forestville, CT
New Foundations, Saint Paul, MN
New Frontier Personal Care & Retirement Center, Livingston, MT
New Glarus Home Inc, New Glarus, WI
New Glen Oaks Nursing Home, Glen Oaks, NY
New Gouverneur Hospital Skilled Nursing Facility, New York, NY
New Hampshire Centennial Home for the Aged, Concord, NH
New Hampshire Odd Fellows Home, Concord, NH
New Hampton Care Center, New Hampton, IA
New Haven Care Center, New Haven, MO
New Haven Nursing Center, New Haven, CT
New Haven Nursing Home, Odessa, MO
New Haven O'Rest Inc, Van Buren, AR
New Homestead, Guthrie Center, IA
New Horizon Health Care, Athens, GA
New Horizon Home, Konawa, OK
New Horizon Nursing Home, Springfield, OH
New Horizon Rehabilitation Center, Ocala, FL
New Horizons Care Center, Lovell, WY
New Horizons Developmental Center—Casa del Sol, Carrizozo, NM
New Horizons Developmental Center—Casa Linda, Carrizozo, NM
New Horizons of Pittsburg, Pittsburg, KS
New Horizons of Valley Center, Valley Center, KS
New Horizons of Winfield, Winfield, KS
New Jersey Firemen's Home, Boonton, NJ
New Jersey Home for Veterans at Paramus, Paramus, NJ
New Lakeview Convalescent Home, Cheshire, CT
New Life Treatment Center, Woodstock, MN
New Lincoln Hospital, Toledo, OR
New London Care Center, New London, IA
New London Convalescent Home, Waterford, CT
New Madrid Nursing Center, New Madrid, MO
New Mark Care Center, Kansas City, MO
New Martinsville Health Care Center, New Martinsville, WV

New Medico Rehabilitation & Skilled Nursing Center at Pioneer Valley, Northampton, MA
New Medico Rehabilitation & Skilled Nursing Center Lenox Hill, Lynn, MA
New Medico Rehabilitation & Skilled Nursing Care of Wisconsin, Waterford, WI
New Medico Rehabilitation & Skilled Nursing Center Forest Manor, Middleborough, MA
New Medico Rest & Skilled Nursing Center at Columbus, East Boston, MA
New Medico Rest & Skilled Nursing Center at Lewis Bay, Barnstable, MA
New Medico RSNC at Brook Wood, Holyoke, MA
New Medico Skilled Nursing Center—Christian Hill, Lowell, MA
New Mexico Veterans Center, Truth or Consequences, NM
New Milford Nursing Home, New Milford, CT
New Oaks Care Center, Des Moines, IA
New Orleans Home & Rehabilitation Center, New Orleans, LA
New Paltz Nursing Home, New Paltz, NY
New Perry Nursing Home, Perry, GA
New Pine Grove Villa Nursing Home, Millbury, MA
New Ralston House, Philadelphia, PA
New Richland Care Center, New Richland, MN
New Riviera Health Resort, Coral Gables, FL
New Rochelle Nursing Home, New Rochelle, NY
New Sans Souci Nursing Home, Yonkers, NY
New Seaera Convalescent Home, Long Beach, WA
New Sharon Care Center, New Sharon, IA
New Town Nursing Home, New Town, ND
New Ulm CRF I, New Ulm, MN
New Ulm CRF II, New Ulm, MN
New Underwood Good Samaritan Center, New Underwood, SD
New Vanderbilt Nursing Home, Staten Island, NY
New Visions Treatment Center, Minneapolis, MN
New Way Inc, Anna, IL
New York Congregational Home for the Aged, Brooklyn, NY
New York Manor Inc, Aurora, IL
New York State Veterans Home, Oxford, NY
Newark Health & Extended Care Facility, Newark, NJ
Newark Healthcare Centre, Newark, OH
Newark Manor Nursing Home, Newark, DE
Newark Manor Nursing Home, Newark, NY
Newark-Wayne Community Hospital Inc—Skilled Nursing Facility, Newark, NY
Newaygo Medical Care Facility, Fremont, MI
Newberg Care Home, Newberg, OR
Newberry Convalescent Center, Newberry, SC
Newberry Nursing Home, Kansas City, MO
Newburgh Health Care & Residential Center, Newburgh, IN
Newbury Port Society Home for Aged Women, Newburyport, MA
Newburyport Society Home for Aged Men, Newburyport, MA
Doctor Kate Newcomb Convalescent Center, Woodruff, WI
Newell Good Samaritan Center, Newell, IA
Newfane Health Facility, Newfane, NY
Newfield House Convalescent Home, Plymouth, MA
Newhall Nursing Home, Salem, MA
Newkirk Nursing Center Inc, Newkirk, OK
Newlight Baptist Nursing Home, Detroit, MI
Newman Memorial Hospital SNF, Shattuck, OK
Newmans Lakewood Nursing Home, Jackson, NJ
Newnan Healthcare Center, Newnan, GA

Newport News Baptist Retirement Community Health Care Unit, Newport News, VA

Newton & Wellesley Nursing Home, Wellesley, MA

Newton Convalescent Home, West Newton, MA

Newton County Nursing Home, Jasper, AR

Newton Manor Rest Home, Worcester, MA

Newton Nursing Home, Newton, NJ

Newton Presbyterian Manor, Newton, KS

Newton Rest Haven Inc, Newton, IL

Newtonhouse, Atlanta, GA

Niagara Falls Memorial Nursing Home Company Inc, Niagara Falls, NY

Niagara Frontier Nursing Home Company Inc, Getzville, NY

Niagara Geriatric Center, Niagara Falls, NY

Niagara Lutheran Home Inc, Buffalo, NY

Nicholas County Health Care Center, Richwood, WV

Nichols House Nursing Home, Fairhaven, MA

Nicholson's Nursing Home, Winthrop, ME

Nicol Home Inc, Glasco, KS

Nicole Manor, Burrillville, RI

Nicollet Health Care Center, Minneapolis, MN

Florence Nightingale Nursing Home, New York, NY

Nightingale Home, Statesboro, GA

Nightingale Home, Nashua, NH

Nightingale North Nursing Home, Sterling Heights, MI

Nightingale Nursing Home, Warren, MI

Nightingale Nursing Home, Waconia, MN

Nightingale West Nursing Home, Westland, MI

Nikkel Family Care Home, Denver, CO

Nile Health Care Center, Minneapolis, MN

Nims Rest Home, Natick, MA

Ninnescah Manor Inc, Clearwater, KS

Niobrara County Memorial Nursing Home, Lusk, WY

Nipple Convalescent Home, Liverpool, PA

Nishna Care Center, Malvern, IA

Nisqually Valley Care Center, McKenna, WA

Joseph T Nist Geriatric Nursing Home, Louisville, OH

Nixa Park Care Center, Nixa, MO

Bishop Noa Home, Escanaba, MI

Noble Building, Hartford, CT

Edward John Noble Hospital of Alexandria Bay, Alexandria Bay, NY

Noblesville Healthcare Center, Noblesville, IN

Noblesville Nursing Home, Noblesville, IN

Nocona Nursing Home, Nocona, TX

Nodaway Nursing Home Inc, Maryville, MO

Nokomis Golden Manor, Nokomis, IL

Nopeming Nursing Home, Nopeming, MN

Nora Springs Care Center, Nora Springs, IA

Norcliffe Rest Home, Brooklyn, CT

Norfolk Community Hospital, Norfolk, VA

Norfolk Nursing Center, Norfolk, NE

Norfolk Nursing Home, Stoughton, MA

Norhaven, Saint Paul, MN

Norlite Nursing Centers of Marquette, Marquette, MI

Norlock Manor, Rochester, NY

Normandy Farms Estates Nursing Care Facility, Blue Bell, PA

Normandy Farms Estates West, Lansdale, PA

Normandy House, Wilmette, IL

Normandy House Nursing Home, Melrose, MA

Normandy Nursing Center, Normandy, MO

Normandy Terrace Inc, San Antonio, TX

Normandy Terrace Inc—Northeast, San Antonio, TX

Norridge Nursing Centre Inc, Chicago, IL

Norristown State Hospital Long-Term Care Unit, Norristown, PA

Norse Home Inc, Seattle, WA

Norseland Nursing Home, Westby, WI

North Adams Home Inc, Mendon, IL

North Alabama Nursing Home, Russellville, AL

North American Healthcare Center, White Hall, IL

North Arkansas Life Care Center, Horseshoe Bend, AR

North Arundel Nursing & Convalescent Center, Glen Burnie, MD

North Bend Nursing Center, North Bend, WA

North Berwick Nursing Home, North Berwick, ME

North Carolina Cancer Institute—Skilled Nursing Facility, Lumberton, NC

North Carolina Special Care Center, Wilson, NC

North-Central Care, Spokane, WA

North Central Good Samaritan Center, Mohall, ND

North Central Health Care Facility, Wausau, WI

North Central Human Services, Forest City, IA

North Charleston Convalescent Center, Charleston, SC

North Claiborne Hospital, Haynesville, LA

North Country Nursing & Rehabilitation Center, Bemidji, MN

North Division Residential Center, Sterling, CO

North End Community Nursing Home, Boston, MA

North Fairfield Geriatric Center, Fairfield, CT

North Florida Special Care Center, Gainesville, FL

North Grand Care Center, Ames, IA

North Hardin Nursing & Convalescent Center, Radcliff, KY

North Horizon Health Care Center, Saint Petersburg, FL

North Jersey Nursing Center Restorative Care, Wayne, NJ

North Kickapoo, Lincoln, IL

North Las Vegas Care Center, North Las Vegas, NV

North Lincoln Village, Greensburg, IN

North Macon Health Care Facility, Macon, GA

North Manor Center, Youngstown, OH

North Mississippi Medical Center—Pontotoc Nursing Home, Pontotoc, MS

North Mississippi Nursing Home Inc—Baldwyn Nursing Facility, Baldwyn, MS

North Mississippi Retardation Center—Wood Lane ICF/MR, Oxford, MS

North Mississippi Retardation Center—Woodlea Skilled Nursing Home, Oxford, MS

North Monroe Healthcare, Monroe, LA

North Ottawa Care Center, Grand Haven, MI

North Panola Nursing Center, Sardis, MS

North Pennsylvania Convalescent Center, Lansdale, PA

North Place Nursing Center, Nacogdoches, TX

North Ridge Care Center, New Hope, MN

North Ridge Care Center, Manitowoc, WI

North River Nursing Home, Hanover, MA

North Rockford Convalescent Home, Rockford, IL

North Sabine Nursing Home Inc, Pleasant Hill, LA

North St Paul Care Center, North Saint Paul, MN

North Shore Center, Saint Petersburg, FL

North Shore Convalescent Home, Saugus, MA

North Shore Health Care Center, Milwaukee, WI

North Shore Manor Inc, Loveland, CO

North Shore Nursing Home, Miami, FL

North Shore Terrace, Waukegan, IL

North Shores Healthcare Center, Houston, TX

North Side Manor, North Providence, RI

North Side Nursing Home, Sapulpa, OK

North 16th Street Group Home, Arlington, VA

North Star Homes, Bemidji, MN

North Towne Manor, Topeka, KS

North Valley Hospital, Tonasket, WA

North Valley Hospital & Extended Care Center, Whitefish, MT

North Valley Nursing Home, Stevensville, MT

North Vernon Nursing Home, North Vernon, IN

North Walk Villa Convalescent Hospital, Norwalk, CA

North Willow Center, Indianapolis, IN

North Wood Good Samaritan Center, Jasper, IN

Northampton—Accomack Memorial Hospital, Nassawadox, VA

Northampton Manor Inc, Frederick, MD

Northampton Nursing Home Inc, Northampton, MA

Northaven Nursing Center, Dallas, TX

Northboro Rest Home, Northborough, MA

Northbridge Nursing Home, Northbridge, MA

Northbrook Manor Care Center, Cedar Rapids, IA

Northcoast Care Center, Pittsburgh, PA

Northcrest Living Centre, North Muskegon, MI

Northcrest Nursing Home, Napoleon, OH

Northcrest Retirement Community, Ames, IA

Northeast Care Center Inc—Alpha, North Royalton, OH

Northeast Health Care Center, Wichita, KS

Northeast Healthcare Center of Muncie, Muncie, IN

Northeast House Inc, Minneapolis, MN

Northeast Pediatric Care, Billerica, MA

Northeast Residence I, White Bear Lake, MN

Northeast Residence II, White Bear Lake, MN

Northern Cochise Community Hospital & Nursing Home, Willcox, AZ

Northern Dutchess Hospital, Rhinebeck, NY

Northern Itasca Health Care Center, Bigfork, MN

Northern Lights Community Residence, Thief River Falls, MN

Northern Lights Manor Nursing Home, Washburn, WI

Northern Metropolitan Residential Health Care Facility Inc, Monsey, NY

Northern Montana Long Term Care, Havre, MT

Northern Pines Good Samaritan Center, Blackduck, MN

Northern Surry Skilled Nursing Facility, Mount Airy, NC

Northern Virginia Training Center, Fairfax, VA

Northfield Hospital & HO Dilley Skilled Nursing Facility, Northfield, MN

Northfield Manor, West Orange, NJ

Northfield Manor Health Care Facility, Louisville, KY

Northfield Retirement Center, Northfield, MN

Northfield Villa Inc, Gering, NE

Northgate Care Center, Waukon, IA

Northgate Convalescent Hospital, San Rafael, CA

Northgate Manor, North Tonawanda, NY

Northgate Manor, San Antonio, TX

Northgate Park Nursing Home, Florissant, MO

Northgate Rehabilitation Center, Seattle, WA

Northgate Unit of Lakeview Christian Home of the Southwest Inc, Carlsbad, NM

Northhampton County Home—Gracedale, Nazareth, PA

Northhaven Health Care Center, Knoxville, TN

Northland Manor, Jackman, ME

Northland Nursing Center, Detroit, MI

Northland Terrace, Columbus, OH

Northline Manor, Houston, TX

Northome Nursing Home, Northome, MN

Northridge Residence, Ortonville, MN

Northshore Living Center, Slidell, LA

Northshore Manor, Bothell, WA

Northside Convalescent Center, Atlanta, GA

Northside Haven, Jackson, MS

Northside Manor Living Center, Mount Vernon, OH

Northside Nursing Home, Youngstown, OH

Northview, Pensacola, FL

Northview Development Center, Eastland, TX

Northview Nursing Home, Johnstown, OH

Northview Villa, Omaha, NE

Northview Village, Saint Louis, MO

Northway Convalescent Center, Birmingham, AL
Northway Healthcare Center, Houston, TX
Northwest Care Continuing Center, Detroit, MI
Northwest Community Continuing Care Center, Arlington Heights, IL
Northwest Continuum Care Center, Longview, WA
Northwest Health Care Center, Milwaukee, WI
Northwest Home for the Aged, Chicago, IL
Northwest Hospital Skilled Nursing Facility, Seattle, WA
Northwest Iowa Health Center, Sheldon, IA
Northwest Manor Health Care Center, Indianapolis, IN
Northwest Medical Center, Thief River Falls, MN
Northwest Mediplex, Austin, TX
Northwest Nursing & Convalescent Center, Baltimore, MD
Northwest Nursing Center, Oklahoma City, OK
Northwest Ohio Development Center, Toledo, OH
Northwest Regional Intermediate Care Home, Rome, GA
Northwood, Tacoma, WA
Northwood Convalescent Center, Lowell, MA
Northwood Deaconess Hospital & Home Association, Northwood, ND
Northwood Health Care Center, Marble Falls, TX
Northwood Hills Health Care Center, Humansville, MO
Northwood Manor Nursing Home, Carrollton, TX
Northwood Nursing Center, Philadelphia, PA
Northwood Nursing Home, South Bend, IN
Northwood Nursing Home, Manchester, NH
Northwoods Healthcare Center, Belvidere, IL
Nortonian Nursing Home, Rochester, NY
Norwalk Manor, Norwalk, IA
Norwalk Memorial Home, Norwalk, OH
Norway Convalescent Center, Norway, ME
Norwegian Christian Home & Health Center, Brooklyn, NY
Norwegian Old Peoples Home, Boston, MA
Norwell Knoll Nursing Home, Norwell, MA
Norwichtown Convalescent Home, Norwich, CT
Norwood Health Center, Marshfield, WI
Norwood Nursing Center, Huntington, IN
Norwood Nursing Home, Norwood, MA
Norwood Park Home, Chicago, IL
Norworth Convalescent Center, Worthington, OH
Notchcliff, Glen Arm, MD
Notre Dame Convalescent Home Inc, Norwalk, CT
Notre Dame Hills Living Center, Belleville, IL
Notre Dame Long-Term Care Center, Worcester, MA
Nottingham Manor, Dallas, TX
Nottingham Village, Northumberland, PA
Novato Convalescent Hospital, Novato, CA
Novi Care Center, Novi, MI
Nowata Nursing Home, Nowata, OK
Nu-Roc Nursing Home, Blackwell, WI
Nu-Roc Nursing Home, Laona, WI
NuCare Convalescent Center, Dyersburg, TN
NuCare Convalescent Center, Laurel, MS
NuCare Convalescent Center, Humboldt, TN
NuCare Convalescent Center, Lexington, TN
NuCare Convalescent Center Inc, Hot Springs, AR
Nugent Convalescent Home, Hermitage, PA
Nursecare of Atlanta, Atlanta, GA
Nursecare of Shreveport, Shreveport, LA
Nursing Care Center of Bristol, Bristol, CT
Nursing Center, Milledgeville, GA
Nursing Center of Canton, Canton, IL
Nursing Center of Greenwood Methodist Home, Greenwood, SC
Nursing Home of Arab, Arab, AL
Nursing Home of Boaz, Boaz, AL
Nursing Home of Tallassee Inc, Tallassee, AL

Nutmeg Pavilion Healthcare, New London, CT
Nuuanu Hale, Honolulu, HI
Nyack Manor Nursing Home, Valley Cottage, NY
Horace Nye Home, Elizabethtown, NY
Nye Regional Medical Center, Tonopah, NV
Nygaard Manor, Stoughton, WI
Nella's Nursing Home, Elkins, WV
O'Berry Center—Skilled Nursing Facility, Goldsboro, NC
Oahe Manor, Gettysburg, SD
Oahu Care Facility, Honolulu, HI
Oak Bluffs Nursing Center, Clearwater, FL
Oak Cove Health Center, Clearwater, FL
Oak Crest, De Kalb, IL
Oak Crest Care Center, Salem, OR
Oak Crest Inn, New Braunfels, TX
Oak Crest Manor Inc, North Scituate, RI
Oak Crest Nursing Home Inc, Tuscumbia, AL
Oak Crest Residence, Elgin, IL
Oak Dale Manor, Sand Springs, OK
Oak Glen Care Center, McMinnville, OR
Oak Glen Nursing Home, Coal Valley, IL
Oak Grove Community Residence, Laurens, SC
Oak Grove Health Care Center, Oak Grove, MO
Oak Grove Manor, Omaha, NE
Oak Grove Manor Inc, Idabel, OK
Oak Grove Nursing Center, Conway, AR
Oak Grove Nursing Home Inc, Deshler, OH
Oak Grove Nursing Home Inc, Groves, TX
Oak Grove Resident Treatment Center, Minneapolis, MN
Oak Grove Retirement Home, Duncan, MS
Oak Haven Nursing Home, Boston, MA
Oak Haven Nursing Home, Palestine, TX
Oak Haven Nursing Home Inc, Center Point, LA
Oak Hill Care Center, Farmington, MI
Oak Hill Home of Rest & Care Inc, Greensburg, PA
Oak Hill Intermediate Care Home, College Park, GA
Oak Hill Manor Nursing Home, Ithaca, NY
Oak Hill Nursing Center, Pawtucket, RI
Oak Hill Nursing Home, Middleborough, MA
Oak Hill Nursing Home Annex, Farmington, MI
Oak Hill Nursing Home Health Care Unit, Staunton, VA
Oak Hill Residence, Littleton, NH
Oak Hills Care Center, San Antonio, TX
Oak Hills Nursing Center, Lorain, OH
Oak Hills Nursing Home, Jones, OK
Oak Hollow Nursing Center, Middle Island, NY
Oak Island Skilled Nursing Center, Revere, MA
Oak Knoll Nursing Home, Ferguson, MO
Oak Lawn Convalescent Home, Oak Lawn, IL
Oak Lawn Manor, Eaton, OH
Oak Lea Nursing Home, Harrisonburg, VA
Oak Manor Extended Care Facility, Columbus, GA
Oak Manor Health Care Center, Decatur, IL
Oak Manor Nursing Center, Booneville, AR
Oak Manor Nursing Center, Flatonia, TX
Oak Manor Nursing Center Inc, Largo, FL
Oak Manor Nursing Home, Elkhart, IN
Oak Manor Nursing Home, Holyoke, MA
Oak Manor Nursing Home, Commerce, TX
Oak Manor Nursing Home, Gladewater, TX
Oak Manor Nursing Home, Linden, TX
Oak Manor Nursing Home, Nacogdoches, TX
Oak Manor Nursing Home, Texarkana, TX
Oak Meadow Nursing Center, Alexandria, VA
Oak Meadows Convalescent Center, Los Gatos, CA
Oak Meadows Learning Center, Auburn, IN
Oak Park, Saint Louis, MO
Oak Park Care Center, Lake Charles, LA
Oak Park Convalescent & Geriatric Center, Oak Park, IL
Oak Park Convalescent Hospital, Pleasant Hill, CA
Oak Park Health Care Inc, Bedford, OH

Oak Park Manor & Residential Care Facility, Kansas City, MO
Oak Park Nursing Center Inc, Grass Valley, CA
Oak Park Nursing Home Inc, Pine Bluff, AR
Oak Pavilion Nursing Center, Cincinnati, OH
Oak Pointe Manor, Sarasota, FL
Oak Ridge Acres, Hiawatha, KS
Oak Ridge Care Center, Franksville, WI
Oak Ridge Convalescent Center, Bloomfield, CT
Oak Ridge Convalescent Center, Richmond, IN
Oak Ridge Health Care, Oak Ridge, TN
Oak Ridge Homes, Aitkin, MN
Oak Ridge Manor, Durant, OK
Oak Ridge Manor Nursing Center, Wayne, NJ
Oak Ridge Manor Nursing Home, Kansas City, MO
Oak Ridge Nursing Home, El Dorado, AR
Oak Springs, Arlington, VA
Oak Springs of Warrenton, Warrenton, VA
Oak Terrace, Mount Vernon, IL
Oak Terrace Care Center, Davenport, IA
Oak Terrace Healthcare Center, Springfield, IL
Oak Terrace Nursing Home, Minnetonka, MN
Oak Tree Lodge, Gainesville, TX
Oak Valley Care Center, Oakdale, CA
Oak Valley Nursing Home, Macon, GA
Oak View Manor, Ozark, AL
Oak View Nursing Home, Summerville, GA
Oak Villa Health Care Center, Hillsboro, OR
Oak Village Care Center, Baldwin, MI
Oak Village Inc, Oaktown, IN
Oak Woods, Mer Rouge, LA
Oakbrook Convalescent Center, Summerville, SC
Oakbrook Healthcare Centre Inc, Oakbrook, IL
Oakbrook Manor of Thorp, Thorp, WI
Oakcliff Convalescent Home Inc, Waterbury, CT
Oakcrest Manor, Austin, TX
Oakcrest Manor & Skilled Nursing Unit—St Mary's Unit, Dyersville, IA
Oakdale Nursing Home, Judsonia, AR
Oakdale Nursing Home, West Boylston, MA
Oakes Manor Good Samaritan Center, Oakes, ND
Margaret Clark Oakfield Convalescent Center of Columbus, Columbus, OH
Oakhaven Inc, Darlington, SC
Oakhaven Manor, Warsaw, MO
Oakhaven Nursing Center, Richmond, KS
Oakhurst Convalescent Center, Elma, WA
Oakhurst Manor Nursing Center, Ocala, FL
Oakland Care Center, Royal Oak, MI
Oakland Care Center, Oakland, NJ
Oakland County Medical Care Facility, Pontiac, MI
Oakland Heights, Oakland, NE
Oakland Manor Nursing Home, Oakland, IA
Oakland Nursing Center, Hillsboro, OH
Oakland Park Nursing Home, Thief River Falls, MN
Oaklawn Health Care Center, Mankato, MN
Oakley House Care Center, Baton Rouge, LA
Oakley Manor, Oakley, KS
Oakmont East Nursing Center, Greenville, SC
Oakmont Manor, Flatwoods, KY
Oakmont North Nursing Center, Travelers Rest, SC
Oakmont Nursing Center, Oakmont, PA
Oakmont of Union, Union, SC
Oakmont West, Greenville, SC
Oaknoll Retirement Residence, Iowa City, IA
Oakridge Convalescent Home Inc, Hillside, IL
Oakridge Convalescent Hospital, Oakland, CA
Oakridge Gardens Nursing Center Inc, Menasha, WI
Oakridge Home, Wadena, MN
Oakridge Home, Westlake, OH
Oakridge Nursing Home, Wewoka, OK
Oakridge of Plattsburg, Plattsburg, MO
Oaks at Forsyth, Winston-Salem, NC
Oaks Convalescent Center, Lima, OH
Oaks Living Center, Orange, TX
Oaks Lodge Rest Home Inc, Fort Smith, AR

Oaks Nursing Home, Marshallville, GA
Oaks Nursing Home, Burnet, TX
Oaks Nursing & Rehabilitation Center, Wyncote, PA
Oaks Residential & Rehabilitation Center, Gainesville, FL
Oaks, Petaluma, CA
Oaks, Monroe, LA
Oakton Pavilion Inc, Des Plaines, IL
Oakview, Lebanon, PA
Oakview Care Center, Durand, WI
Oakview Convalescent Hospital, Glendora, CA
Oakview Convalescent Hospital, Tujunga, CA
Oakview Home, Conrad, IA
Oakview Home Intermediate Care, Waverly Hall, GA
Oakview Manor, Dayton, OH
Oakview Manor Health Care Center, Calvert City, KY
Oakview Manor Nursing Center, Hubbard, TX
Oakview Medical Care Facility, Ludington, MI
Oakview Nursing Home, Cincinnati, OH
Oakview Regional Care Center, Williston, FL
Oakville Health Care Center, Memphis, TN
Oakwood Care Center, Pasadena, CA
Oakwood Care Center, Clear Lake, IA
Oakwood Convalescent Home, Webster, MA
Oakwood Estate, Morton, IL
Oakwood Health Care Center, Kewanee, IL
Oakwood Health Care Center, New Castle, IN
Oakwood Health Care Center, Walterboro, SC
Oakwood Health Care Center, Lewisburg, TN
Oakwood Health Care Center Inc, Newport, RI
Oakwood Intermediate Care Facility, Somerset, KY
Oakwood Knoll Nursing Center Inc, Kernersville, NC
Oakwood Long Term Care Center, Boston, MA
Oakwood Lutheran—Hebron Hall, Madison, WI
Oakwood Manor, Kansas City, MO
Oakwood Manor, Bucyrus, OH
Oakwood Manor Nursing Home, Vidor, TX
Oakwood Nursing Center, Eustis, FL
Oakwood Nursing Home, Manchester, MA
Oakwood Park Su Casa, Tampa, FL
Oakwood Place, Texarkana, AR
Oakwood Residence Inc, Minneapolis, MN
Oakwood Terrace, Inc, Evanston, IL
Oakwood Villa, Altoona, WI
Oakwood Villa Care Center, Hutchinson, KS
Oakwood Village Nurse Care Center, Lafayette, LA
Oasis, Golden Valley, MN
Obion County Rest Home, Union City, TN
O'Brien Memorial Nursing Home, Masury, OH
O'Brien's Rest Home, Rapid City, SD
Ocala Geriatric Center Inc, Ocala, FL
Ocala Health Care Center, Ocala, FL
Ocean Convalescent Center, Lakewood, NJ
Ocean Park Nursing Home, Seaside, OR
Ocean Point Health Care Center, Somers Point, NJ
Ocean Promenade Health Related Facility, Rockaway Park, NY
Ocean Springs Nursing Center, Ocean Springs, MS
Ocean Trail Convalescent Home Inc, Southport, NC
Ocean View Convalescent Center, Long Beach, WA
Ocean-View Nursing Home, New Smyrna Beach, FL
Oceana County Medical Care Facility, Hart, MI
Oceanside Convalescent & Rehabilitation Center, Atlantic City, NJ
Oceanside Nursing Home, Tybee Island, GA
Oceanside Nursing Home, North Quincy, MA
Oceanview Care Center, Bandon, OR
Oceanview Convalescent Hospital, Santa Monica, CA
Oceanview Nursing Home, Lubec, ME

Oceanview Nursing Home, Far Rockaway, NY
Ochoco Nursing Home, Prineville, OR
Ochsner Foundation Hospital—Skilled Nursing Facility, Jefferson, LA
DCI—Thompson Avenue Group Home, West Saint Paul, MN
Oconee Community Residence No 1, Seneca, SC
Oconee Community Residence No 2, Seneca, SC
Oconee Health Care Center, Oconee, IL
Octavia Manor Inc, Colfax, IL
Odd Fellow & Rebekah Nursing Home, Ennis, TX
Odd Fellow & Rebekah Nursing Home Inc, Lockport, NY
Odd Fellow-Rebekah Home, Mattoon, IL
Odd Fellow & Rebekah Home, Jackson, MI
Odd Fellows Home, Greensburg, IN
Odd Fellows Home, Dell Rapids, SD
Odd Fellows Home Association Inc, Liberty, MO
Odd Fellows Home of California Infirmary, Saratoga, CA
Odd Fellows Home of Massachusetts, Worcester, MA
Odd Fellows Home of Ohio, Springfield, OH
Odd Fellows Home of Pennsylvania, Middletown, PA
Odd Fellows Rest Home, Checotah, OK
Odell Nursing Home, Concord, NC
Odin Care Center, Odin, IL
O'Donnell House, Chicago, IL
Oelwein Care Center, Oelwein, IA
Ogden Care Center North, Ogden, UT
Ogden Manor, Ogden, IA
OHCC—Meadow Park, Saint Helens, OR
Ohesson Manor, Lewistown, PA
Ohio District Council Nursing Home, Zanesville, OH
Ohio Eastern Star Home, Mount Vernon, OH
Ohio Extended Care Center, Lorain, OH
Ohio House, Cincinnati, OH
Ohio Masonic Home, Springfield, OH
Ohio Pythian Sisters Home of Medina, Medina, OH
Ohio Residential Services Inc—Elyria, Elyria, OH
Ohio Valley Health Care, Parkersburg, WV
Ohio Valley Manor Convalescent Center, Ripley, OH
Ojai Valley Community Hospital, Ojai, CA
Okeechobee Health Care Facility, Okeechobee, FL
Okemah Pioneer Nursing Home Inc, Okemah, OK
Oklahoma Christian Home, Edmond, OK
Oklahoma County Home, Oklahoma City, OK
Oklahoma Methodist Home for the Aged, Tulsa, OK
Okmulgee Terrace Nursing Home Inc, Okmulgee, OK
Olathe Good Samaritan Center, Olathe, KS
Olathe Nursing Home, Olathe, KS
Old Capital Inn Convalescent & Nursing Home, Louisville, GA
Old Colony Road Rest Home Inc, Norton, MA
Old Court Nursing Center, Randallstown, MD
Old Masons' Home of Kentucky, Shelbyville, KY
Old Orchard Manor, Skokie, IL
Old Peoples Home—City of Chicago, Chicago, IL
Olds Hall Good Samaritan Center, Daytona Beach, FL
Olds Manor, Grand Rapids, MI
Mary M Olin Clinic, Penny Farms, FL
Olive Ridge Care Center, Oroville, CA
Olive Vista, Pomona, CA
Paul Oliver Memorial Hospital, Frankfort, MI
Olivewood Convalescent Hospital, Colton, CA
Olivewood Health Care Center, Shelbyville, IL
Olivia Healthcare Center, Olivia, MN
Olmsted Manor Skilled Nursing Center, North Olmsted, OH
Olney Care Center, Olney, IL
Olney Nursing Center, Olney, TX

Olsen Manor Nursing Home, Amarillo, TX
Julia Olson Rest Home, Belle Fourche, SD
Olson Terrace, Rockford, IL
Olympia Convalescent Hospital, Los Angeles, CA
Olympia Manor, Olympia, WA
Olympic Health Care, Sequim, WA
Olympus Care Center, Salt Lake City, UT
Omaha Nursing Home Inc, Omaha, NE
Omega House, Charleston, IL
Omegon Residential, Minnetonka, MN
Ommert, Reisterstown, MD
Omni Manor, Youngstown, OH
Omro Care Center, Omro, WI
Onalaska Care Center, Onalaska, WI
One-Eighty Court Nursing Home, Keene, NH
One Sewall Street, Island Falls, ME
Oneida City Hospital—Extended Care Facility, Oneida, NY
Oneida County Nursing Home, Malad, ID
O'Neill Nursing Center, O'Neill, NE
Oneonta Manor Nursing Home, Oneonta, AL
Oneonta-Richmond Inc, Oneonta, NY
Oneota Riverview Care Facility, Decorah, IA
Ontario County Health Facility, Canandaigua, NY
Ontario Nursing Home, Ontario, CA
Ontonagon Memorial, Ontonagon, MI
Oosterman Melrose Rest Home, Melrose, MA
Oosterman's Rest Home, Wakefield, MA
Opelika Health Care, Opelika, AL
Opelousas General Hospital—Skilled Nursing Facility, Opelousas, LA
Opelousas Health Care, Opelousas, LA
Open Arms Nursing Home, Winchendon, MA
Open Door Community Living Facility, Sandwich, IL
OPP Nursing Facility, Opp, AL
Opportunity Foundation of Central Oregon, Redmond, OR
Opportunity Homes Inc, Lisbon, OH
Opportunity House Inc, Sycamore, IL
Opportunity Manor, Saint Cloud, MN
Opportunity Manor II, Saint Cloud, MN
Orange City Municipal Hospital, Orange City, IA
Orange County Home & Infirmary, Goshen, NY
Orange County Nursing Home & Home for Adults, Orange, VA
Orange Health Care Center, Orange, CT
Orange Park Care Center, Orange Park, FL
Orange Park Convalescent Hospital, Orange, CA
Orange Village Care Center, Masury, OH
Orange West Convalescent Hospital, Buena Park, CA
Orangeburg Convalescent Hospital, Modesto, CA
Orangeburg Nursing Home Inc, Orangeburg, SC
Orangegrove Rehabilitation Hospital, Garden Grove, CA
Orangetree Convalescent Hospital, Riverside, CA
Orangevale Convalescent Hospital, Orangevale, CA
Orangewood Health Facility—American Baptist Estates, Phoenix, AZ
Orchard Crest Care Center, Sandy, OR
Orchard Gables Convalescent Hospital, Hollywood, CA
Orchard Grove Extended Care Centre, Benton Harbor, MI
Orchard Hill, Madison, WI
Orchard Lake Resthaven, West Bloomfield, MI
Orchard Lane Nursing Facility, Baldwin City, KS
Orchard Manor, Grove City, PA
Orchard Manor Inc, Medina, NY
Orchard Manor—North, Lancaster, WI
Orchard Manor—South, Lancaster, WI
Orchard Park, Tacoma, WA
Orchard Park Health Care Center Inc, Orchard Park, NY
Orchard Park Living Center, Farmington, ME

Orchard Ridge Nursing Center, New Port Richey, FL
Orchard View Manor, East Providence, RI
Orchard Village Intermediate Care Facility, Skokie, IL
Orchards Villa Nursing Center, Lewiston, ID
Oregon Care Center, Oregon, MO
Oregon City Care Center Inc, Oregon City, OR
Oregon Health Care Center—Evergreen, Lincoln City, OR
Oregon Health Care Center—Highland, Klamath Falls, OR
Oregon Manor Ltd, Oregon, WI
Oregon-Washington Pythian Home, Vancouver, WA
Orford Road Residence, Lyme, NH
Orinda Rehabilitation & Convalescent Hospital, Orinda, CA
Orlando Care Center, Orlando, FL
Orlando Health Care Center, Orlando, FL
Orlando Lutheran Towers, Orlando, FL
Orlando Memorial Convalescent Center, Orlando, FL
Orleans Convalescent & Retirement Home, Orleans, MA
Orleans County Nursing Home, Albion, NY
Ormond Beach Health Care, Ormond Beach, FL
Ormond in the Pines, Ormond Beach, FL
Orofino Care Center, Orofino, ID
Orono Nursing Home Inc, Orono, ME
Orono Woodlands, Long Lake, MN
Oroville Community Convalescent Hospital, Oroville, CA
Orrington Group Home, Orrington, ME
Orthodox Jewish Home for the Aged, Cincinnati, OH
Ortonville Nursing Home, Lake Orion, MI
Orvilla Inc, Eagan, MN
Osage Beach Health Care Center, Osage Beach, MO
Osage Manor Inc, Osage City, KS
Osage Nursing Home, Nowata, OK
Osawatomie Rest Home, Osawatomie, KS
Osborn, Rye, NY
Osceola Good Samaritan Center, Osceola, NE
Osceola Inn, Clearwater, FL
Osceola Leisure Manor, Osceola, IA
Osceola Nursing Home, Osceola, AR
Osceola Nursing Home Inc, Ocilla, GA
Oshkosh Care Center, Oshkosh, WI
Osseo Area Municipal Hospital & Nursing Home, Osseo, WI
Osseo Health Care Center, Osseo, MN
Ossian Health Care, Ossian, IN
Ossian Senior Hospice, Ossian, IA
Ossipee Group Home, Center Ossipee, NH
Ostrander Care Center, Ostrander, MN
Oswego Hospital Extended Care Facility, Oswego, NY
Othello Convalescent Center, Othello, WA
Otsego County Memorial Hospital, Gaylord, MI
Ottawa Care Center, Ottawa, IL
Ottawa County Riverview Nursing Home, Oak Harbor, OH
Ottawa Retirement Village, Ottawa, KS
Otter Tail Lake Residence, Battle Lake, MN
Otter Tail Nursing Home, Battle Lake, MN
Otterbein Care Center, Otterbein, IN
Otterbein-Lebanon Home, Lebanon, OH
Ottumwa Manor, Ottumwa, IA
Ottumwa Regional Health Center, Ottumwa, IA
Ouachita Convalescent Center, Camden, AR
Our House of Minnesota Inc 1, Saint Paul, MN
Our House of Minnesota Inc 2, Saint Paul, MN
Our House, Farmington, ME
Our Island Home, Nantucket, MA
Our Lady of Angels Retirement Home, Joliet, IL
Our Lady of Compassion Care Center, Anchorage, AK
Our Lady of Fatima Villa, Saratoga, CA
Our Lady of Good Counsel, Saint Paul, MN

Our Lady of Hope Residence—Little Sisters of the Poor, Latham, NY
Our Lady of Lourdes Regional Medical Center—Skilled Nursing Facility, Lafayette, LA
Our Lady of Mercy Convalescent Home, Hubbell, MI
Our Lady of Mercy Home, Kansas City, MO
Our Lady of Perpetual Help, Atlanta, GA
Our Lady of Prompt Succor Nursing Home, Opelousas, LA
Our Lady of the Lake Regional Medical Center Skilled Nursing, Baton Rouge, LA
Our Lady of Victory, Bourbonnais, IL
Our Lady's Haven, Fairhaven, MA
Our Lady's Home, Oakland, CA
Our Lady's Residence, Pleasantville, NJ
Our Place, Murphysboro, IL
Outagamie County Health Center, Appleton, WI
Outreach Minneapolis—Stevens Group Home, Minneapolis, MN
Outreach Northeast Group Home, Minneapolis, MN
Outreach Plymouth Home East, Plymouth, MN
Outreach Plymouth Home West, Plymouth, MN
Overland Park Manor, Overland Park, KS
Overlin Boarding Home, Sheridan, WY
Overlook Castle Nursing Home, Millersburg, OH
Overlook House, Cleveland, OH
Overlook Medical Clinic, New Wilmington, PA
Overlook Nursing Home, Burrillville, RI
Overlook Park Health Care Center, Norwalk, CT
Overlook Villa Care Center, Bellville, OH
Overton County Nursing Home, Livingston, TN
Ovid Convalescent Manor, Ovid, MI
Owatonna Health Care Center, Owatonna, MN
Owen County Home, Spencer, IN
Ruth Owen Family Care Home, Commerce City, CO
Owens Home, Montgomery City, MO
Owensville Convalescent Center Inc, Owensville, IN
Owenton Manor Inc, Owenton, KY
Owsley County Health Care Center, Booneville, KY
Oxford Convalescent Home, Oxford, WI
Oxford Manor Nursing Home, Haverhill, MA
Oxford Manor Nursing Home, Oxford, PA
Oxford Nursing Home, Brooklyn, NY
Oxford View Nursing Center, Oxford, OH
Oxnard Manor Convalescent Hospital, Oxnard, CA
Ozanam Hall of Queens Nursing Home Inc, Bayside, NY
Ozark Care Centers Inc, Osage Beach, MO
Ozark Nursing & Care Center, Ozark, MO
Ozark Nursing Center, West Plains, MO
Ozark Nursing Facility, Ozark, AL
Ozark Nursing Home, Fredericktown, MO
Ozark Nursing Home Inc, Ozark, AR
Ozark Riverview Manor, Ozark, MO
Ozarks Methodist Manor, Marionville, MO
Pacific Care Center, Hoquiam, WA
Pacific Care Center Inc, Morro Bay, CA
Pacific Care Center Inc, Pacific, MO
Pacific Care Convalescent Hospital, Oakland, CA
Pacific Convalescent Center, Santa Monica, CA
Pacific Convalescent Hospital, Eureka, CA
Pacific Crest Rehabilitation Center & Specialty Care, Gresham, OR
Pacific Gardens Convalescent Hospital, Fresno, CA
Pacific Grove Convalescent Hospital, Pacific Grove, CA
Pacific Haven Convalescent Home, Garden Grove, CA
Pacific Park Convalescent Hospital, San Bernardino, CA

Pacific Regency—Arvin, Arvin, CA
Pacific Regency—Bakersfield, Bakersfield, CA
Pacific Regency—Lakeport, Lakeport, CA
Pacific Regency/Taft, Taft, CA
Padgett Nursing Home, Tampa, FL
Pageland Community Residence, Pageland, SC
Paintsville Health Care Center, Paintsville, KY
Paisley House, Youngstown, OH
Palatine Nursing Home, Palatine Bridge, NY
Palemon Gaskins Nursing Home, Ocilla, GA
Palestine Nursing Center, Palestine, TX
Palisade Manor, Garretson, SD
Palisade Nursing Home, Palisade, CO
Palisade Nursing Home, Guttenberg, NJ
Palisade Nursing Home Company Inc, Bronx, NY
Palm Bay Care Center, Palm Bay, FL
Palm Beach County Home & General Care Facility, West Palm Beach, FL
Palm Court Nursing & Rehabilitation Center, Fort Lauderdale, FL
Palm Crest East Nursing Home, Elyria, OH
Palm Crest Nursing Home, Elyria, OH
Palm Garden, Clearwater, FL
Palm Garden, Gainesville, FL
Palm Garden, Ocala, FL
Palm Garden, Orlando, FL
Palm Garden of Winter Haven, Winter Haven, FL
Palm Garden (Pensacola), Pensacola, FL
Palm Garden—Tampa, Tampa, FL
Palm Gardens Nursing Home, Brooklyn, NY
Palm Grove Convalescent Center, Garden Grove, CA
Palm Haven Convalescent Hospital, Manteca, CA
Palm Manor Nursing Home, Chelmsford, MA
Palm Shores Retirement Center, Saint Petersburg, FL
Palm Springs Healthcare, Palm Springs, CA
Palm Terrace Convalescent Center, Riverside, CA
Palm Terrace Healthcare Center, Laguna Hills, CA
Palm Tree Nursing Home, Brooklyn, NY
Palm Vista Care Center, Upland, CA
Palmcrest Medallion Convalescent, Long Beach, CA
Palmcrest North, Long Beach, CA
Palmer Home for the Aged, Palmer, MI
Palmer Home Inc, Dover, DE
Palmer House Healthcare Nursing Home, Palmer, MA
Judson Palmer Home, Findlay, OH
Palmer Pioneer Home, Palmer, AK
Palmetto Convalescent Center, Simpsonville, SC
Palmetto Extended Care Facility, Miami, FL
Palmetto Health Center, Hialeah, FL
Palms Convalescent Home, Miami, FL
Palms Health Care Center, Sebring, FL
Palmview Healthcare Center, Port Charlotte, FL
Palmwood Health Care Center, Piper City, IL
Palmyra Intermediate Care Center, Palmyra, TN
Palmyra Nursing Home, Albany, GA
Palmyra Nursing Home, Palmyra, PA
Palo Alto Nursing Center, Palo Alto, CA
Palo Duro Convalescent Home Inc, Claude, TX
Palo Pinto Nursing Center, Mineral Wells, TX
Palomar Convalescent Center, Escondido, CA
Palomares Care Center, Pomona, CA
Pam Group Home, Puyallup, WA
Pampa Nursing Center, Pampa, TX
Pamplico Highway Community Residence, Florence, SC
Pana Health Care Center, Pana, IL
Panama City Developmental Center, Panama City, FL
Panama City Nursing Center, Panama City, FL
Panola Nursing Home, Carthage, TX
Panorama, Bowling Green, KY
Panorama City Convalescent & Rehabilitation Center, Lacey, WA

Paoli Nursing Home, Paoli, IN
Papillion Manor Inc, Papillion, NE
Paquette Home Inc, Central Falls, RI
Paradise Convalescent Hospital, Paradise, CA
Paradise Hills Convalescent Center, San Diego, CA
Paradise Oaks Quality Care Nursing Center, Cloverdale, OH
Paradise Rehabilitation Convalescent, Los Angeles, CA
Paradise Valley Health Care Center, National City, CA
Paradise Valley Living Center, Belle Plaine, KS
Paradise Village, Medina, OH
Paragould Nursing Center, Paragould, AR
Paramount Chateau Convalescent Hospital, Paramount, CA
Paramount Convalescent Hospital, Paramount, CA
Paramus Health Care Center, Paramus, NJ
Parc Center Apartments, Saint Petersburg, FL
PARC Cottage, Saint Petersburg, FL
PARC Home, Bellwood, IL
PARC Residential Care Facility, Peoria, IL
Margaret R Pardee Memorial Hospital, Hendersonville, NC
Paris Healthcare Center, Paris, IL
Paris Manor Nursing Center, Paris, TN
Paris Nursing Home, Paris, TX
Paris Retirement Inn Inc, Paris, AR
Park Avenue Baptist Home, Denver, CO
Park Avenue Health Care Center, Bridgeport, CT
Park Avenue Health Care Home, Herrin, IL
Park Avenue Home, Faribault, MN
Park Avenue Nursing, Convalescent & Retirement Home, Arlington, MA
Barbara Park Convalescent Center, Middletown, OH
Park Boulevard, Muskogee, OK
Park Central Nursing Home, Port Arthur, TX
Park Centre Healthcare at La Posada, Green Valley, AZ
Park Dale Rest Home, Boston, MA
Park Forest Care Center, Portland, OR
Park Geriatric Village, Highland Park, MI
Park Haven Care Center, Smithton, IL
Park Haven Nursing Center Inc, Greenville, TX
Park Highlands, Athens, TX
Park Hill Manor Nursing Home, Rindge, NH
Park Hope Nursing Home, Rochester, NY
Park House Ltd, Chicago, IL
Park Imperial Convalescent Center, Lawndale, CA
Park Lake Health Care Center, Maitland, FL
Park Lake Village Care Center, New Port Richey, FL
Park Lane Manor Inc, Altus, OK
Park Lane Nursing Home, Evergreen Park, IL
Park Lane Nursing Home, Scott City, KS
Park Lawn Center, Worth, IL
Park Lawn Home, Manitowoc, WI
Park Manor, Denver, CO
Park Manor, Waterbury, CT
Park Manor, De Soto, TX
Park Manor, Park Falls, WI
Park Manor Care Center, Fort Dodge, IA
Park Manor Care Center, Muskegon Heights, MI
Park Manor Convalescent Center, Walla Walla, WA
Park Manor Health Care Center, Milwaukee, WI
Park Manor Nursing & Convalescent Home, Rawlins, WY
Park Manor Nursing Home, Liberty, IN
Park Manor Nursing Home, Baltimore, MD
Park Manor Nursing Home, Pepperell, MA
Park Manor Nursing Home, Bloomfield, NJ
Park Manor Nursing Home, Oklahoma City, OK
Park Marino Convalescent Center, Pasadena, CA
Park Marion Nursing Center, Brookline, MA
Park Merritt Intermediate Care, Oakland, CA

Park Nursing & Convalescent Center, Saint Louis Park, MN
Park Nursing Center Inc, Taylor, MI
Park Nursing Home, Rockaway Park, NY
Park Place Care Center Inc, Raytown, MO
Park Place Health Care Center, Great Falls, MT
Park Place Manor, Belton, TX
Park Place Nursing Center, Grand Island, NE
Park Place Nursing Center, Tyler, TX
Park Place Nursing Home, Palestine, TX
Park Plaza Healthcare Center, Saint Louis Park, MN
Park Plaza Inc, Detroit, MI
Park Plaza Nursing Center, Groesbeck, TX
Park Plaza Nursing Center Inc, San Angelo, TX
Park Plaza Nursing Home, Mart, TX
Park Plaza Nursing Home, Whitney, TX
Park Pleasant Inc, Philadelphia, PA
Park Point Manor, Duluth, MN
Park Rest Hardin County Health Center, Savannah, TN
Park Ridge Care Center Inc, Seattle, WA
Park Ridge Healthcare Center, Park Ridge, IL
Park Ridge Nursing Home, Rochester, NY
Park River Estates Care Center, Coon Rapids, MN
Park River Good Samaritan Center, Park River, ND
Park Rose Care Center, Tacoma, WA
Park Row Health Care Center, Corsicana, TX
Park Royal Medical, Longview, WA
Park Shore, Seattle, WA
Park Strathmoor, Rockford, IL
Park Street Group Home, Houlton, ME
Park Summit, Coral Springs, FL
Park Superior Healthcare, Newport Beach, CA
Park Terrace Convalescent Center, Tulsa, OK
Park Terrace Nursing & Rehabilitation Center, Worcester, MA
Park View Care Center, Sac City, IA
Park View Care Center Inc, Portland, OR
Park View Haven Nursing Home, Coleridge, NE
Park View Health Center, Winnebago, WI
Park View Home, Woodville, WI
Park View Home No 1, Sioux City, IA
Park View Manor, Aroma Park, IL
Park View Manor Inc, Canton, OH
Park View Nursing Center, San Jose, CA
Park View Nursing Center, Carney's Point, NJ
Park View Nursing Center, Edgerton, OH
Park View Nursing Home, Providence, RI
Park View Nursing Home, Bountiful, UT
Park View Nursing Home Inc, Massapequa, NY
Park Villa, Clyde, KS
Park Villa Convalescent Center, Tucson, AZ
Park Village Health Care Center, Dover, OH
Park Village Pines, Kalamazoo, MI
Park Vista Unit, Ohio Presbyterian Home, Youngstown, OH
Park West Care Center, Seattle, WA
Parkdale Care Center, Price, UT
Parkdale Manor, Maryville, MO
Parke County Nursing Home Inc, Rockville, IN
Francis E Parker Memorial Home, New Brunswick, NJ
Francis E Parker Memorial Home, Piscataway, NJ
Parker Jewish Geriatric Institute, New Hyde Park, NY
Sophia Huntington Parker Home, Medina, OH
Parkhill East Nursing Home, Locust Grove, OK
Parkhill Medical Complex, Chillicothe, IL
Parkhill North Nursing Home, Salina, OK
Parkhill South Nursing Home, Locust Grove, OK
Parkhurst Manor Ltd, Morristown, TN
Parkland Care Center, Tacoma, WA
Parkland Convalescent Hospital, San Leandro, CA
Parkland Health, Wentworth, WI
Parkland Manor, Prague, OK

Parkmont Care Center, Fremont, CA
Parkridge Manor, Des Moines, IA
Parkrose Nursing Home, Portland, OR
Parks Good Samaritan Village, Odessa, TX
Park's Memorial Home, Auburn, IL
Parkshore Manor Health Care Center, Brooklyn, NY
Parkside Care Center, Little Chute, WI
Parkside Gardens, Burbank, IL
Parkside Health Care Inc, Bainbridge Island, WA
Parkside Homes Inc, Hillsboro, KS
Parkside Lutheran Home, Lisbon, ND
Parkside Manor, Stuart, NE
Parkside Manor Convalescent Center, Wenatchee, WA
Parkside Meadows Inc, Saint Charles, MO
Parkside Nursing Care Center, Union Gap, WA
Parkside Rest Home, Peabody, MA
Parkside Special Care Center, El Cajon, CA
Parkside Towers, Saint Louis, MO
Parkston Nursing Center, Parkston, SD
Parkston Supervised Living Center, Parkston, SD
Parkview Acres Convalescent Center, Dillon, MT
Parkview Care Center, Fairfield, IA
Parkview Care Center, Osborne, KS
Parkview Care Center, Fremont, OH
Parkview Care Center, Bryant, SD
Parkview Care Center, Fort Worth, TX
Parkview Care Center Inc, Milwaukee, WI
Parkview Care Center Inc, Ripon, WI
Parkview Colonial Manor, O'Fallon, IL
Parkview Convalescent Care, Billings, MT
Parkview Convalescent Center, Wilmington, DE
Parkview Convalescent Center, Evansville, IN
Parkview Convalescent Center, Paducah, KY
Parkview Convalescent Center, Paris, TX
Parkview Convalescent Centre, Elwood, IN
Parkview Convalescent Hospital, Anaheim, CA
Parkview Convalescent Hospital, Hayward, CA
Parkview Convalescent Unit, Dyersburg, TN
Parkview Gardens Care Center, Waterloo, IA
Parkview Guest Care Center, Winnfield, LA
Parkview Haven, Francesville, IN
Parkview Haven Nursing Home, Deshler, NE
Parkview Health Center, Volga, SD
Parkview Healthcare Inc, Parkersburg, WV
Parkview Home, Freeport, IL
Parkview Home, Frankfort, IN
Parkview Home, Wayland, IA
Parkview Home, Belview, MN
Parkview Home, Hancock, MN
Parkview Home Inc, Dodge, NE
Parkview Julian Convalescent, Bakersfield, CA
Parkview Learning Center, Macksville, KS
Parkview Manor, Wellman, IA
Parkview Manor, Pikeville, KY
Parkview Manor, Dayton, OH
Parkview Manor, Walters, OK
Parkview Manor, Weimar, TX
Parkview Manor, Green Bay, WI
Parkview Manor Care Center, Woodward, IA
Parkview Manor Inc, Reinbeck, IA
Parkview Manor Nursing Home, Atlanta, GA
Parkview Manor Nursing Home, Indianapolis, IN
Parkview Manor Nursing Home, Ellsworth, MN
Parkview Manor Nursing Home—Blytheville, Blytheville, AR
Parkview Manor Nursing Home Inc, Denver, CO
Parkview Medical Recovery Center Inc, New Haven, CT
Parkview Nursing Center, Muncie, IN
Parkview Nursing Home, West Frankfort, IL
Parkview Nursing Home, Bloomfield, NJ
Parkview Nursing Home, Bronx, NY
Parkview Nursing Home, Waco, TX
Parkview Nursing Home—Fort Smith, Fort Smith, AR
Parkview Nursing Home Inc, Shawnee, OK

Parkview Real Convalescent Hospital, Bakersfield, CA
Parkview Terrace, Platteville, WI
Parkway Care Home, Edwardsville, KS
Parkway Center, Sterling, IL
Parkway Health Care Center, Wichita, KS
Parkway Manor, Fulton, KY
Parkway Manor Care Center, Lubbock, TX
Parkway Manor Health Care Center, Saint Paul, MN
Parkway Manor Health Center, East Orange, NJ
Parkway Manor Nursing Home, Everett, MA
Parkway Medical Center, Louisville, KY
Parkway North Care Center, Battle Ground, WA
Parkway Nursing Center, Snohomish, WA
Parkway Nursing Home, Pinellas Park, FL
Parkway Nursing Home, Hamilton, OH
Parkway Pavilion Healthcare, Enfield, CT
Parkway Rest Home Inc, Allentown, PA
Parkway Terrace Nursing Home, Wheaton, IL
Parkwell Health Care Center: A Skilled Nursing Facility, Boston, MA
Parkwood Development Center Intermediate Care Facility, Valdosta, GA
Parkwood Health Care Center, Chattanooga, TN
Parkwood Health Care Facility, Phenix City, AL
Parkwood Health Care Inc, Lebanon, IN
Parkwood Nursing Home, Columbus, OH
Parkwood Place, Lufkin, TX
Parma Care Center, Parma, OH
Parmiter Nursing Home, Malta, OH
Margaret S Parmly Residence, Chisago City, MN
Charles Parrish Memorial Nursing Center, Dunn, NC
Parrott Avenue Home, Portsmouth, NH
Parrott's Home, Lynn, IN
Parr's Rest Home, Louisville, KY
Parsons Good Samaritan Center, Parsons, KS
Parsons I Group Home, Summerville, SC
Parsons II Group Home, Summerville, SC
Parsons Presbyterian Manor, Parsons, KS
Partlow Developmental Center, Tuscaloosa, AL
Pasadena Care Center, Pasadena, TX
Pasadena Manor, Saint Petersburg, FL
Pasadena Manor, South Pasadena, FL
Pasco Nursing Center, Dade City, FL
Paseo Residential II, Blue Springs, MO
Paso Robles Convalescent Hospital, Paso Robles, CA
Passavant Retirement & Health Center, Zelienople, PA
Passport, Rhinelander, WI
Nancy Patch Retirement Home, Leominster, MA
Patchogue Nursing Center, Patchogue, NY
Patrician Inc, North Royalton, OH
A Holly Patterson Geriatric Center, Uniondale, NY
Patterson Gardens Convalescent Center, Santa Barbara, CA
Patterson Health Center Inc, Columbus, OH
Patterson's Pleasant View Personal Care Home, Shepherdsville, KY
Paul Victorious House, Charlottesville, VA
Paulding Memorial Medical Center Long Term Care Unit, Dallas, GA
Paul's Run, Philadelphia, PA
Pauls Valley State School, Pauls Valley, OK
Pavilion, Cincinnati, OH
Pavilion at Camargo Manor, Cincinnati, OH
Pavilion at Shell Point Village, Fort Myers, FL
Pavilion Care Center, Oakland, CA
Pavilion Health Care Center, Louisville, KY
Pavilion Healthcare Center of Valparaiso, Valparaiso, IN
Pavilion Nursing Home, McKinney, TX
Pawhuska Nursing Home, Pawhuska, OK
Pawnee Care Center, Pawnee, OK
Pawnee Manor, Pawnee City, NE
Pawtucket Institute for Health Services, Pawtucket, RI

Pawtuxet Village Nursing Home Inc, Warwick, RI
Payette Lakes Care Center, McCall, ID
Paynesville Community Hospital/Koronis Manor, Paynesville, MN
Paynesville Good Samaritan Home, Paynesville, MN
Payson Care Center, Payson, AZ
Peabody Glen Nursing Care Center, Peabody, MA
Peabody Home, Franklin, NH
Peabody Manor Inc, Appleton, WI
Peabody Memorial Nursing Home Inc, Peabody, KS
Peabody Retirement Community, North Manchester, IN
Peace Haven Association, Saint Louis, MO
Peace Memorial Home, Evergreen Park, IL
Peach Tree Place, Weatherford, TX
Peachbelt Nursing Home, Warner Robins, GA
Peachwood Inn, Rochester Hills, MI
Pearl River County Nursing Home, Poplarville, MS
Pearl Villa Convalescent Hospital, Pomona, CA
Pearlview Extended Care & Nursing Center, Brunswick, OH
Pearsall Manor, Pearsall, TX
Pebble Creek Nursing Center, El Paso, TX
Pecan Grove Nursing Center, Austin, TX
Pecan Grove Training Center, Alexandria, LA
Pecan Lane, Florence, SC
Pecan Manor 1, Milledgeville, GA
Pecan Manor 3, Milledgeville, GA
Pecan Manor Nursing Home, Statesboro, GA
Pecos Nursing & Rehabilitation Center, Chandler, AZ
Pecos Nursing Home, Pecos, TX
Pecos Valley Care Center, Fort Sumner, NM
Pedersen Nursing Home Inc, Seattle, WA
Pedone Nursing Center, Maple Heights, OH
Peirce Nursing Home, Alpena, MI
Pekin Manor, Pekin, IL
Pekrul Manor, Enid, OK
Peleske Group Home, Erhard, MN
Pelham House Nursing Home, Newton, MA
Pelham Parkway Nursing Home, Pelham, GA
Pelham Parkway Nursing Home, Bronx, NY
Pelican Lake Health Care Center, Ashby, MN
Pelican Valley Health Center, Pelican Rapids, MN
Pella Community Hospital, Pella, IA
Pellcare Corp, Winston-Salem, NC
Pellcare—Hickory, Hickory, NC
Pemberton Manor Inc, Greenwood, MS
Pembilier Nursing Center, Walhalla, ND
Pembina County Memorial Nursing Home, Cavalier, ND
Pembina Trail, Wadena, MN
Pembrook Nursing Center, Detroit, MI
Pemiscot Memorial Hospital Long-Term/Skilled Care Unit, Hayti, MO
Pend Oreille Pines, Newport, WA
Pender Care Centre, Pender, NE
Pender Memorial Hospital—Skilled Nursing Facility, Burgaw, NC
Pendleton Memorial Methodist Hospital—Skilled Nursing Facility, New Orleans, LA
Pendleton Nursing Home, Franklin, WV
Penfield Nursing Home, Penfield, NY
Penick Memorial Home, Southern Pines, NC
Peninsula General Nursing Home, Far Rockaway, NY
Peninsula Rehabilitation Center, Lomita, CA
Annie Penn Memorial Hospital—Skilled Nursing Facility, Reidsville, NC
Penn Lake House, Bloomington, MN
Penn Lutheran Village, Selinsgrove, PA
Penn Mar Therapeutic Center, El Monte, CA
Penn Yan Manor Nursing Home Inc, Penn Yan, NY
Pennhurst Modular Home Community, Spring City, PA
Pennknoll Village Nursing Home, Everett, PA
Pennsburg Manor, Pennsburg, PA
Pennswood Village, Newtown, PA
Pennsylvania Memorial Home, Brookville, PA

Pennsylvania Soldiers' & Sailors' Home, Erie, PA
Penny Pack Manor Nursing Home Inc, Philadelphia, PA
Pennyrile Home, Hopkinsville, KY
Penobscot Nursing Home, Penobscot, ME
Penobscot Valley Hospital, Lincoln, ME
Pensacola Health Care Facility, Pensacola, FL
People Inc—Dayton House, Saint Paul, MN
Peoples Child Care Residence, Saint Paul, MN
People's Nursing Care Center, Independence, IA
Peoria Healthcare Centre, Peoria Heights, IL
Peotone Bensenville Home, Peotone, IL
Pepin Manor Care Center, Pepin, WI
Perdue Medical Center, Miami, FL
Perham Memorial Hospital & Home, Perham, MN
B J Perino Nursing Home Inc, Pekin, IL
Perkins Convalescent Home, Philadelphia, PA
Perry Community Hospital & Nursing Home, Marion, AL
Perry County Nursing Center, Perryville, AR
Perry County Nursing Home, Perryville, MO
Perry County Nursing Home, Linden, TN
Perry Green Valley Nursing Center, Perry, OK
Perry Health Facility, Perry, FL
Perry Lutheran Home, Perry, IA
Perry Manor, Perry, IA
Perry Nursing Home, Perry, OK
Perry Ridge Nursing Home Inc, Perry, OH
Perry Village Nursing Home, New Bloomfield, PA
Pershing Convalescent Home Inc, Stickney, IL
Pershing Estates, Decatur, IL
Pershing General Hospital & Nursing Home, Lovelock, NV
Pershing Regional Health Center, Marceline, MO
Person County Memorial Hospital—SNF, Roxboro, NC
Perth Amboy Nursing Home, Perth Amboy, NJ
Peru Nursing Home, Peru, IN
Petersburg General Hospital, Petersburg, AK
Petersburg Healthcare Center, Petersburg, IN
Peterson Enterprises Inc—Ridgeway Home, Cincinnati, OH
Peterson Enterprises Inc—Springdale Home, Springdale, OH
Peterson Enterprises Inc—352 Waterside Home, Canal Fulton, OH
Peterson Nursing Home, Osage City, KS
P A Peterson Home for the Aging, Rockford, IL
Peterson Park Health Care Center, Chicago, IL
Peterson Ridge Home, Cincinnati, OH
Pettipaug Manor, Essex, CT
Pettit Childrens Home, Sauk Centre, MN
Pfeiffer's Community Home, West Valley City, UT
Pharr Nursing Home, Pharr, TX
Pheasant Wood Nursing Home, Peterborough, NH
Phelps Community Medical Center, Phelps, KY
Phenix City Nursing Home, Phenix City, AL
Philadelphia Nursing Home, Philadelphia, PA
Philadelphia Nursing Home, Philadelphia, PA
Philadelphia Protestant Home, Philadelphia, PA
Philip Nursing Home, Philip, SD
Phillips County Good Samaritan Retirement Center, Malta, MT
Phillips County Home, Phillipsburg, KS
Phillips Home, Fayette, MO
Phillips House Nursing Home, Natick, MA
Phillips Manor Nursing Home, Lynn, MA
Phillips Nursing Home, Provo, UT
Phoebe Home, Allentown, PA
Phoenix Jewish Care Center, Phoenix, AZ
Phoenix Mountain Nursing Center, Phoenix, AZ
Phoenix Residence Inc, Saint Paul, MN
Phoenix Residential Centers Inc, Broadview Heights, OH

Phoenixville Convalescent Manor, Phoenixville, PA
Physician's Hospital for Extended Care, Reno, NV
Physicians Nursing & Convalescent Center, Mount Pleasant, TX
Piatt County Nursing Home, Monticello, IL
Picayune Convalescent Center, Picayune, MS
Pickard Presbyterian Convalescent Center, Albuquerque, NM
Pickaway Manor Care Center, Circleville, OH
Pickens County Health Care Inc, Reform, AL
Pickens General Nursing Center, Jasper, GA
Pickering Manor Home, Newtown, PA
Pickerington Health Care Center, Pickerington, OH
Pickett County Nursing Home, Byrdstown, TN
Pickwick Manor Nursing Home, Iuka, MS
Piedmont Gardens Health Facility, Oakland, CA
Piedmont Geriatric Hospital, Burkeville, VA
Piedmont Hall, Milledgeville, GA
Piedmont Health Care Center—Health Care Unit, Charlottesville, VA
Piedmont Hospital Extended Care Unit, Atlanta, GA
Piedmont Hospital & Nursing Home, Piedmont, AL
Piedmont Nursing Center, Greenville, SC
Piedmont Residential Developmental Center, Concord, NC
Piedmont Retirement Center, Thomasville, NC
Pierce County Nursing Home, Blackshear, GA
Pierce Manor, Pierce, NE
Pierce Memorial Baptist Home Inc, Brooklyn, CT
Pierremont Heritage Manor, Shreveport, LA
Piety Corner Nursing Home, Waltham, MA
Piety Place, Ellsworth, WI
Pigeon Falls Nursing Home, Pigeon Falls, WI
Piggott Nursing Center, Piggott, AR
Pike Manor Health Care Center, Troy, AL
Pikes Peak Manor, Colorado Springs, CO
Pikesville Nursing & Convalescent Center, Pikesville, MD
Piketon Nursing Center, Piketon, OH
Pilgrim Haven Health Facility, Los Altos, CA
Pilgrim Manor, Cromwell, CT
Pilgrim Manor, Plymouth, MA
Pilgrim Manor, Grand Rapids, MI
Pilgrim Manor of Bossier City—North, Bossier City, LA
Pilgrim Manor of Bossier City—South, Bossier City, LA
Pilgrim Manor of Pineville, Pineville, LA
Pilgrim Manor Rehabilitation & Convalescent Center, Plymouth, IN
Pilgrim Place Health Services Center, Claremont, CA
Pilgrim Rehabilitation & Skilled Nursing Center, Peabody, MA
Pilgrim's Pride Nursing Home, Mashpee, MA
Pillars Health Care, Springfield, OH
Pillsbury Board & Care Home, Minneapolis, MN
Pilot House, Cairo, IL
Pinal County Nursing Center, Florence, AZ
Pinal General Hospital, Florence, AZ
Pinar Terrace Manor, Orlando, FL
Pine Acres, Dixon, IL
Pine Acres Care Center, De Kalb, IL
Pine Acres Nursing Home, Madison, NJ
Pine Bluff Nursing Home, Pine Bluff, AR
Pine Brook Care Center, Englishtown, NJ
Pine County Group Home, Sandstone, MN
Pine Crest Convalescent Hospital, Maywood, CA
Pine Crest Guest Home, Hazlehurst, MS
Pine Crest Haven, Paola, KS
Pine Crest Nursing Center, Morrow, OH
Pine Crest Nursing Home, Nacogdoches, TX
Pine Crest Nursing Home, Merrill, WI
Pine Grove Nursing Center, Center, TX
Pine Grove Rest Home, Marlborough, MA
Pine Haven Care Center Inc, Pine Island, MN

Pine Haven Christian Home, Sheboygan Falls, WI
Pine Haven Convalescent Center of Henderson Inc, Henderson, NC
Pine Haven Home, Philmont, NY
Pine Haven Nursing Home, Evansville, IN
Pine Haven Nursing Home, Lufkin, TX
Pine Haven Nursing Home Inc, Leesville, LA
Pine Hill Rest Home, Lynn, MA
Pine Hill Senior Citizens Home Inc, Quitman, LA
Pine Hurst Nursing & Convalescent Home, Ligonier, PA
Pine Kirk Nursing Home, Kirkersville, OH
Pine Knoll Convalescent Center, Taylor, MI
Pine Knoll Nursing Home, Carrollton, GA
Pine Knoll Nursing Home, Lexington, MA
Pine Knoll Nursing Home, Lyndonville, VT
Pine Lake ICMRF—Babcock Center, Columbia, SC
Pine Lake Nursing Home, Greenville, FL
Pine Lane Healthcare, Mountain Home, AR
Pine Lawn Manor Care Center, Sumner, IL
Pine Lodge Nursing Home, Warren, AR
Pine Lodge Nursing Home, Atlanta, TX
Pine Manor Health Care Center, Clintonville, WI
Pine Manor Nursing Home, Springfield, MA
Pine Manor Nursing Home Inc, Columbus, GA
Pine Oaks Nursing Center, Allegan, MI
Pine Oaks Nursing Center, Mexico, MO
Pine Point Nursing Care Center, West Scarborough, ME
Pine Rest Nursing Home, Northampton, MA
Pine Rest Nursing Home, Paramus, NJ
Pine Ridge Care Center, San Rafael, CA
Pine Ridge Health Care Inc, Greer, SC
Pine Ridge Home 1, Cloquet, MN
Pine Ridge Home 2, Cloquet, MN
Pine Ridge Home 3, Cloquet, MN
Pine Ridge Manor, Waupaca, WI
Pine Ridge Residence, Bagley, MN
Pine River Group Home, Pine River, MN
Pine Rock Farm, Warner, NH
Pine Run Medical Center, Doylestown, PA
Pine Shadow Retreat, Porter, TX
Pine Street Group Home, Bangor, ME
Pine Towers Convalescent Hospital, San Francisco, CA
Pine Tree Lodge Nursing Center, Longview, TX
Pine Tree Villa, Louisville, KY
Pine Valley Manor, Richland Center, WI
Pine Valley Nursing Center, Richfield, OH
Pine View Care Center, Saint Charles, IL
Pine View Continuous Care Center, Harrisville, WV
Pine View Good Samaritan Center, Valentine, NE
Pine View Health Care Center, Peshtigo, WI
Pine View Manor Inc, Stanberry, MO
Pine View Manor Inc, Wexford, PA
Pine View Nursing Home, Black River Falls, WI
Pinebrook Place Healthcare Center, Venice, FL
Pinecrest Care Center, Gallipolis, OH
Pinecrest Convalescent Home, North Miami, FL
Pinecrest Convalescent Home, Daingerfield, TX
Pinecrest Manor, Mount Morris, IL
Pinecrest Manor, Hopkinsville, KY
Pinecrest Manor Convalescent Home, Cle Elum, WA
Pinecrest Manor Nursing Home, Bernice, LA
Pinecrest Medical Care Facility, Powers, MI
Pinecrest Nursing Home, Humboldt, KS
Pinecrest State School, Pineville, LA
Pinedale Nursing Home, Newport, AR
Pinehill Nursing Center, Byromville, GA
Pinehope Nursing Home, Hope, AR
Pinehurst Convalescent Center, Pompano Beach, FL
Pinehurst Convalescent Center, Seattle, WA
Pinehurst Nursing Center, Pinehurst, NC
Pinehurst Nursing Home, Centerville, IN

Pinehurst Park Terrace, Seattle, WA
Pineland Center, Pownal, ME
Pineland Nursing Home, Lakewood, NJ
Piner's Nursing Home, Napa, CA
Pines at Davidson, Davidson, NC
Pines Convalescent Center, Williamsburg, VA
Pines Nursing & Convalescent Home, Dillon, SC
Pines Nursing Home, Miami, FL
Pines Village Care Center, North Fort Myers, FL
Pineview Health Care, Winfield, AL
Pineview Health Care Center Inc, Pineview, GA
Pineview Manor Extended Care Centre, Clinton, MD
Pineview Manor Inc, Beaver, OH
Pineview Nursing Home, Gurdon, AR
Pineview of Hillman, Hillman, MI
Pineview Residence, Saint Paul, MN
Pinewood Care Center, Coeur d'Alene, ID
Pinewood Convalescent Center, Spartanburg, SC
Pinewood Health Care Center, Monmouth, IL
Pinewood Manor Inc, Hawkinsville, GA
Pinewood Manor Nursing Home, Jasper, TX
Pinewood Nursing Home, Waldron, AR
Pinewood Terrace Nursing Center, Colville, WA
Piney Mountain Home, Fayetteville, PA
Pineywood Acres, Corrigan, TX
Pink-Bud Home for the Golden Years, Greenwood, AR
Pinnacle Care Center, Morganton, NC
Pinnacle Care Center, Wilmington, NC
Pinnacle Care Center Nursing & Rehabilitation, Huntington, WV
Pinnacle Care of Seneca, Seneca, SC
Pinnacle Nursing Home, Rochester, NY
Pioneer Care Center, Brigham City, UT
Pioneer Center Community Living Facility, McHenry, IL
Pioneer Estate, Chandler, OK
Pioneer Health Care Center, Rocky Ford, CO
Pioneer Health Center, Marceline, MO
Pioneer Home, Fort Collins, CO
Pioneer Home, Prairie Farm, WI
Pioneer Home Inc, Fergus Falls, MN
Pioneer House, Sacramento, CA
Pioneer Lodge, Coldwater, KS
Pioneer Manor, Hugoton, KS
Pioneer Manor, Frederick, OK
Pioneer Manor Board & Care, Gillette, WY
Pioneer Manor Nursing & Convalescent Home, Gillette, WY
Pioneer Manor Nursing Home, Hay Springs, NE
Pioneer Memorial Care Center, Erskine, MN
Pioneer Memorial Hospital—Heppner, Heppner, OR
Pioneer Memorial Nursing Home, Viborg, SD
Pioneer Nursing Home, Baudette, MN
Pioneer Nursing Home, Big Timber, MT
Pioneer Nursing Home Health District, Vale, OR
Pioneer Nursing Home Inc, Melbourne, AR
Pioneer Nursing Home of Hughes County Inc, Wetumka, OK
Pioneer Place Nursing Home, Irving, TX
Pioneer Ridge Healthcare, Ferndale, WA
Pioneer Trace Nursing Home, Flemingsburg, KY
Pioneer Valley Manor Rest Home, Greenfield, MA
Pioneer Village I, Topeka, KS
Pioneer Village II, Topeka, KS
Pioneer Village III, Topeka, KS
Pioneer Village IV, Topeka, KS
Piper Group Home, Fergus Falls, MN
Pipestone County Medical Center, Pipestone, MN
Piqua Manor, Piqua, OH
Pisgah Manor Health Care Center, Candler, NC
Pittsburg Care Center, Pittsburg, CA
Pittsburg Nursing Center, Pittsburg, TX
Pittsfield Convalescent Center, Pittsfield, ME
Pittsfield Nursing Center, Pittsfield, IL

Placerville Pines Convalescent Hospital, Placerville, CA
Placid Memorial Hospital Inc, Lake Placid, NY
Plains Convalescent Center, Plainview, TX
Plains Nursing Center, Plains, GA
Plainview Long-Term Care Facility, New Bedford, MA
Plainview Manor Inc, Plainview, NE
Plainville Health Care Center, Plainville, CT
Plainville Nursing Home, Plainville, MA
Plainwell Pines Nursing Centre, Plainwell, MI
Plano Nursing Home, Plano, TX
Plant City Health Care, Plant City, FL
Morton F Plant Rehabilitation & Nursing Center, Clearwater, FL
Plantation Care Center, Murray, UT
Plantation Care Center Inc, Salem, OR
Plantation Estates Medical Facility, Matthews, NC
Plantation Hills Nursing Home, Forsyth, MO
Plantation Key Convalescent Center, Tavernier, FL
Plantation Manor, McCalla, AL
Plantation Manor Inc, Atoka, OK
Plantation Nursing Home, Plantation, FL
Plantation Nursing Home, Brownwood, TX
Plaquemine Manor Nursing Home Inc, Plaquemine, LA
Plateau Valley Hospital District Nursing Home, Collbran, CO
Platte City Caring Center, Platte City, MO
Platte County Memorial Nursing Home, Wheatland, WY
Platte Nursing Home, Platte, SD
Plattsmouth Manor, Plattsmouth, NE
Plaza De Retiro Inc, Taos, NM
Plaza del Rio Care Center, Peoria, AZ
Plaza Health Care Center Inc, Westminster, CO
Plaza Manor—A Geriatric & Convalescent Center, Kansas City, MO
Plaza Nursing & Convalescent Center, Elizabeth, NJ
Plaza Nursing Center, Pascagoula, MS
Plaza Nursing Home Company Inc, Syracuse, NY
Pleasant Acres, Hull, IA
Pleasant Acres, New Lisbon, WI
Pleasant Acres Convalescent Hospital, Morgan Hill, CA
Pleasant Acres Nursing Home, Everett, WA
Pleasant Care Living Center, Pleasantville, IA
Pleasant Grove Health Care Center, Pleasant Grove, AL
Pleasant Hill Care Center, Saint Paul, MN
Pleasant Hill Convalescent Center, Piketon, OH
Pleasant Hill Health Facility, Fairfield, ME
Pleasant Hill Nursing Center, Pleasant Hill, IL
Pleasant Hill Nursing Home, Oregon, MO
Pleasant Hill Nursing Home, Wichita Falls, TX
Pleasant Hill Village, Girard, IL
Pleasant Hills Health Center, Jackson, MS
Pleasant Living Convalescent Center, Edgewater, MD
Pleasant Manor, Mount Pleasant, MI
Pleasant Manor Care Center, Mount Pleasant, IA
Pleasant Manor Inc, Faribault, MN
Pleasant Manor Nursing & Convalescent Center, Baltimore, MD
Pleasant Manor Nursing Home, Alexandria, LA
Pleasant Manor Nursing Home, Attleboro, MA
Pleasant Manor Nursing Home, Sapulpa, OK
Pleasant Manor Nursing Home, Rutland, VT
Pleasant Manor Nursing Home Inc, Ashdown, AR
Pleasant Manor Nursing Home, Waxahachie, TX
Pleasant Meadows Christian Village, Chrisman, IL
Pleasant Park Manor, Oskaloosa, IA
Pleasant Place Home for Care, Louisville, KY
Pleasant Rest Nursing Home, Collinsville, IL

Pleasant Street Rest Home Inc, Attleboro, MA
Pleasant Valley Health Care Center, Muskogee, OK
Pleasant Valley Hospital Extended Care, Camarillo, CA
Pleasant Valley Infirmary, Argyle, NY
Pleasant Valley Manor, Sedan, KS
Pleasant Valley Manor, Stroudsburg, PA
Pleasant Valley Manor Care Center, Liberty, MO
Pleasant Valley Nursing Center, Springdale, AR
Pleasant Valley Rehabilitation & Convalescent Hospital, Oxnard, CA
Pleasant Valley Rehabilitation & Convalescent Hospital, Oxnard, CA
Pleasant View, Whiting, IA
Pleasant View, Rock Port, MO
Pleasant View Convalescent Home, Northumberland, PA
Pleasant View Convalescent Hospital, Cupertino, CA
Pleasant View Good Samaritan, Corsica, SD
Pleasant View Good Samaritan Center, Saint James, MN
Pleasant View Health Care Center, Metter, GA
Pleasant View Health Care Center, Barberton, OH
Pleasant View Home, Morrison, IL
Pleasant View Home, Albert City, IA
Pleasant View Home, Inman, KS
Pleasant View Home Inc, Manheim, PA
Pleasant View Lodge, Indianapolis, IN
Pleasant View Luther Home, Ottawa, IL
Pleasant View Manor, Reedley, CA
Pleasant View Manor, Watertown, CT
Pleasant View Manor, Huntington, WV
Pleasant View Manor Inc, Pleasanton, KS
Pleasant View Nursing Home, Lisbon, OH
Pleasant View Nursing Home, Walla Walla, WA
Pleasant View Nursing Home, Monroe, WI
Pleasant View Nursing Home, Phillips, WI
Pleasant View Nursing Home of Mt Airy Inc, Mount Airy, MD
Pleasant View Rest Home, Harrisonville, MO
Pleasanton Convalescent Hospital, Pleasanton, CA
Pleasantview Care Center, Warrensburg, MO
Pleasantview Home, Kalona, IA
Pleasantview Manor, Stockbridge, MI
Pleasantview Nursing Home, Parma, OH
Plott Nursing Home, Ontario, CA
Plum City Care Center, Plum City, WI
Plum Grove Nursing Home, Palatine, IL
Plum Tree Convalescent Hospital, San Jose, CA
Plumblee Nursing Center, Plymouth, NC
Plymouth Court, Plymouth, MI
Plymouth Harbor Inc, Sarasota, FL
Plymouth House Health Care Center, Norristown, PA
Plymouth Inn, Plymouth, MI
Plymouth Manor Care Center, Le Mars, IA
Plymouth Manor Nursing Home, Milwaukee, WI
Plymouth Nursing Home, Plymouth, MA
Plymouth Place Inc, La Grange Park, IL
Plymouth Square, Stockton, CA
Plymouth Tower, Riverside, CA
Plymouth Village, Redlands, CA
Pocahontas Continuous Care Center, Marlinton, WV
Pocahontas Convalescent Center, Pocahontas, AR
Pocahontas Manor, Pocahontas, IA
Pocopson Home, West Chester, PA
Poet's Seat Nursing Home, Greenfield, MA
Pohai Nani Care Center, Kaneohe, HI
Point Loma Convalescent Hospital, San Diego, CA
Point Lookout Village Health Care Center, Point Lookout, MO
Point Pleasant Beach Nursing Home, Point Pleasant, NJ
Pointe Coupee General Hospital, New Roads, LA

Pointe Coupee Parish Nursing Home, New Roads, LA
Polish Army Veterans Home, Sterling Heights, MI
Polk City Manor, Polk City, IA
Polk County Nursing Home, Cedartown, GA
Berthold S Pollak Hospital, Jersey City, NJ
Polo Continental Manor, Polo, IL
Polyclinic Medical Center—Extended Care Facility, Harrisburg, PA
Pomeroy Care Center, Pomeroy, IA
Pomeroy Hill Nursing Home, Livermore Falls, ME
Pomona Valley Nursing Center, Pomona, CA
Pomperaug Woods, Southbury, CT
Ponca City Nursing Home, Ponca City, OK
Ponce de Leon Care Center, Saint Augustine, FL
Pond Meadow Healthcare Facility Nursing Home, Weymouth, MA
Pond Point Health Care Center Inc, Milford, CT
Pondera Medical Center—Extended & Long-Term Care, Conrad, MT
Ponderosa, Aurora, CO
Ponderosa Villa, Crawford, NE
Pontchartrain Guest House, Mandeville, LA
Pontiac Nursing Center, Pontiac, MI
Pontiac Nursing Home, Oswego, NY
Pope County Care Center Inc, Golconda, IL
Pope John Paul II Center for Health Care, Danbury, CT
Pope Nursing Home, Weymouth, MA
Poplar Community Hospital & Nursing Home, Poplar, MT
Poplar Grove Rest Home, Greenville, KY
Poplar Living Center, Casper, WY
Poplar Manor Nursing Home, Baltimore, MD
Poplar Valley Living Center, Loogootee, IN
Port Allen Care Center Inc, Port Allen, LA
Port Angeles Care Center, Port Angeles, WA
Port Charlotte Care Center, Port Charlotte, FL
Port Chester Nursing Home, Port Chester, NY
Port Jefferson Health Care Facility, Port Jefferson, NY
Port Orchard Care Center, Port Orchard, WA
Port Rehabilitation & Skilled Nursing Center, Newburyport, MA
Port Royal Community Residence, Port Royal, SC
Port St Lucie Convalescent Center, Port Saint Lucie, FL
Portage County Home, Stevens Point, WI
Portage County Nursing Home, Ravenna, OH
Portage Group Homes—Nichols, Portage, OH
Portage Group Homes—Restle, Portage, OH
Portage Group Homes—Werner, Portage, OH
Portage Valley Inc, Pemberville, OH
Portage View Hospital, Hancock, MI
Helen Porter Nursing Home, Middlebury, VT
Porter Hills Presbyterian Village, Grand Rapids, MI
Porterfield Geriatric Treatment Center, Marion, VA
Porter's Nursing Home, Saint George, UT
Porthaven Care Center, Portland, OR
Portland Adventist Convalescent Center, Portland, OR
Portland Community Care Center—East, Portland, IN
Portland Community Care Center—West, Portland, IN
Portland Convalescent Center Inc, Portland, CT
Portland Health Care Facility, Oklahoma City, OK
Posada Del Sol, Tucson, AZ
Poteau Nursing Home, Poteau, OK
Poteet Nursing Home, Poteet, TX
Potomac Center, Hagerstown, MD
Potomac Valley Nursing Center, Rockville, MD
Potsdam Nursing Home, Potsdam, NY
Julia Wilson Pound Health Care Center, Indiana, PA
Powder River Manor, Broadus, MT

Powell County Memorial Hospital Long-Term Care Unit, Deer Lodge, MT
Powell Nursing Home, Powell, WY
Powellhurst Nursing Home, Portland, OR
Powell's Convalescent Home, Hamilton, OH
Power County Nursing Home, American Falls, ID
Powhatan Nursing Home, Falls Church, VA
Poydras Home, New Orleans, LA
Poydras Manor Nursing Home, Saint Bernard, LA
Prairie Acres, Friona, TX
Prairie City Nursing Center, Prairie City, IL
Prairie Community Nursing Home, Terry, MT
Prairie Estates, Flora, IL
Prairie Estates, Elk Point, SD
Prairie Good Samaritan Center, Miller, SD
Prairie Haven Nursing Home, Kensington, KS
Prairie Health Care, Prairie du Chien, WI
Prairie Hills Home for Elderly, Belle Fourche, SD
Prairie Lakes Health Care Center—Nursing Home, Watertown, SD
Prairie Manor, Chicago Heights, IL
Prairie Manor, Blooming Prairie, MN
Prairie Manor Nursing Home, Pine Prairie, LA
Prairie Manor Rest Home, Sharon Springs, KS
Prairie Sunset Home, Pretty Prairie, KS
Prairie View Care Center, Limon, CO
Prairie View Care Center, Woonsocket, SD
Prairie View Home, Princeton, IL
Prairie View Home, Sanborn, IA
Prairie View Inc, Slayton, MN
Prairie View Manor, Clinton, OK
Prairie View Rest Home, Lewistown, MO
Prairie View Rest Home Inc, Warsaw, IN
Prairie Village Living Center, Washington, IN
Prairie Vista Care Center, Holyoke, CO
Prairieview Homes Inc, Underwood, ND
Prairieview Lutheran Home, Danforth, IL
Prather Methodist Memorial Home, Alameda, CA
Praxis Nursing Home, Easton, PA
Prayer Tower Rest Home, New Orleans, LA
Preakness Hospital, Paterson, NJ
Premont Nursing Home Inc, Premont, TX
Presbyterian Community Care Center, Ontario, OR
Presbyterian Denver Hospital, Denver, CO
Presbyterian Home, Evanston, IL
Presbyterian Home, Cambridge Springs, PA
Presbyterian Home at 58th Street, Philadelphia, PA
Presbyterian Home for Aged, Philadelphia, PA
Presbyterian Home for Central New York, New Hartford, NY
Presbyterian Home Inc, Quitman, GA
Presbyterian Home of DC, Washington, DC
Presbyterian Home of Hawfields Inc, Mebane, NC
Presbyterian Home of High Point, High Point, NC
Presbyterian Home of Moshannon Valley, Philipsburg, PA
Presbyterian Home of Redstone Presbytery, Johnstown, PA
Presbyterian Home of South Carolina—Clinton, Clinton, SC
Presbyterian Home of South Carolina—Florence, Florence, SC
Presbyterian Home of South Carolina—Summerville, Summerville, SC
Presbyterian Home—Oil City, Oil City, PA
Presbyterian Homes Johanna Shores, Saint Paul, MN
Presbyterian Homes of the Presbytery of Huntingdon, Hollidaysburg, PA
Presbyterian Lodge, Erie, PA
Presbyterian Manor, Wichita Falls, TX
Presbyterian Manor, Huntington, WV
Presbyterian Manor at Farmington, Farmington, MO
Presbyterian Manor at Rolla, Rolla, MO
Presbyterian Medical Center of Oakmont, Oakmont, PA
Presbyterian Medical Center of Washington Pennsylvania, Washington, PA

Presbyterian Nursing Center, Lakeland, FL
Presbyterian Village, Austell, GA
Presbyterian Village East, New Baltimore, MI
Presbyterian Village Health Care Center, Little Rock, AR
Presbyterian Village North Health Services, Dallas, TX
Presbyterian Village of Detroit, Detroit, MI
Presbyterian Village of Homer Inc, Homer, LA
Prescott Country View Nursing Home, Prescott, KS
Prescott House Nursing Home, North Andover, MA
Prescott Nursing Center, Prescott, AR
Prescott Samaritan Village, Prescott, AZ
Presentation Care Center—Rolette, Rolette, ND
Presentation Manor Nursing Home, Boston, MA
Presidential Convalescent Home Inc, Quincy, MA
Presidential Woods Health Care Center, Adelphi, MD
Presque Isle Nursing Home Inc, Presque Isle, ME
Preston Care Center, Preston, MN
Prevost Memorial Hospital, Donaldsonville, LA
Price Hill Nursing Home, Cincinnati, OH
Price Memorial, Eureka, MO
Pride Institute, Eden Prairie, MN
Primghar Care Center, Primghar, IA
Primrose Manor, Danville, IN
Primrose Place Health Care Center, Springfield, MO
Primus Mason Manor Rest Home, Springfield, MA
Prince of Peace Retirement Community, Sioux Falls, SD
Princeton Care Center Inc, Princeton, MO
Princeton Health Care Center, Princeton, WV
Princeton Health Care Manor, Princeton, KY
Princeton House Rest Home, Lowell, MA
Princeton Nursing Home, Princeton, NJ
Dr Paul Baker Pritchard Jr Community Residence, Greenwood, SC
Procare Development Center, Gaston, IN
John C Proctor Endowment Home, Peoria, IL
Professional Care Home, Hartford, KY
Professional Care Inc, Troy, IL
Professional Care Nursing Center, Dale, IN
Progress Valley II, Richfield, MN
Progressive Living Center, Lufkin, TX
Project Independence Ridgewood, Worthington, MN
Project New Hope 1-5, Alexandria, MN
Project New Hope 6, Alexandria, MN
Project New Hope 7, Alexandria, MN
Project New Hope—Starbuck, Starbuck, MN
Project Turnabout, Granite Falls, MN
Promenade Health Care Facility, Auburn, ME
Promenade Nursing Home, Rockaway Park, NY
Prophets Riverview Good Samaritan Center, Prophetstown, IL
Prospect Hill Home, Keene, NH
Prospect Hill Manor Nursing Home, Somerville, MA
Prospect Hill Nursing Home, Waltham, MA
Prospect Hill Rehabilitation Center, East Windsor, CT
Prospect Lake Health Care Center, Pueblo, CO
Prospect Manor, Cleveland, OH
Prospect Nursing Home, North Bennington, VT
Prospect Park Care Center, Prospect Park, PA
Prospect Park Nursing Home Inc, Brooklyn, NY
Prospect Park Skilled Nursing Facility, Estes Park, CO
Prosser Memorial Hospital, Prosser, WA
Protection Valley Manor, Protection, KS
Providence Center, Chicago, IL
Providence—Chehalis, Chehalis, WA
Providence Children's Nursing Center, Portland, OR

Providence Convalescent Residence, Charlotte, NC
Providence Health Care, Sparta, GA
Providence Health Care, Thomaston, GA
Providence Health Care, Warrenton, GA
Providence Health Care Center, Beaver Falls, PA
Providence Home, Jasper, IN
Providence House Nursing Home, Worcester, MA
Providence House Nursing Home of Milbury, Millbury, MA
Providence House Nursing Home of South Bridge, Southbridge, MA
Providence Medical Center Skilled Nursing Facility, Portland, OR
Providence Place Inc, Kansas City, KS
Providence Rest, Bronx, NY
Providence Retirement Home, New Albany, IN
Provident Nursing Home, Boston, MA
Provincial House—Adrian, Adrian, MI
Provincial House—Alpena, Alpena, MI
Provincial House—Battle Creek, Battle Creek, MI
Provincial House—Cass City, Cass City, MI
Provincial House—Hastings, Hastings, MI
Provincial House Kalamazoo, Kalamazoo, MI
Provincial House Marshall, Marshall, MI
Provincial House—Midland, Midland, MI
Provincial House of Portage, Kalamazoo, MI
Provincial House Sault Sainte Marie, Sault Sainte Marie, MI
Provincial House South, Lansing, MI
Provincial House—Traverse City, Traverse City, MI
Provincial House West, Lansing, MI
Provinical House—Tawas City, Tawas City, MI
Provo Care Center, Provo, UT
Pueblo Manor Nursing Home, Pueblo, CO
Pueblo Norte Nursing Center, Show Low, AZ
Puget Sound Healthcare Center, Olympia, WA
Pulaski Health Care Center, Winamac, IN
Pulaski Health Care Center, Pulaski, TN
Pulaski Health Care Center Health Care Unit, Pulaski, VA
Pulaski Nursing Home, Pulaski, GA
Pulley Care Center, South Point, OH
Pulley Nursing Home, South Point, OH
Pullman Convalescent Center, Pullman, WA
Purcell Center, Cincinnati, OH
Helen Purcell Home, Zanesville, OH
Purcell Nursing Home, Purcell, OK
Purple Hills Manor Inc, Bandera, TX
Puryear Nursing Home, Puryear, TN
Putnam Acres Care Center, Ottawa, OH
Putnam City Convalescent Center, Bethany, OK
Putnam County Care Center, Unionville, MO
Putnam Nursing Home, Palatka, FL
Puxico Nursing Center, Puxico, MO
PVA No 1 Inc—Overlook House, Cleveland Heights, OH
QC II Nursing Care Center of Patterson, Patterson, LA
Quabbin Valley Convalescent Center Inc, Athol, MA
Quaboag Nursing Home, West Brookfield, MA
Quachita Valley Nursing Center, Hot Springs, AR
Quail Ridge Living Center, West Siloam Springs, AR
Quaker Gardens, Stanton, CA
Quaker Heights Nursing Home, Waynesville, OH
Quaker Hill Manor, Baxter Springs, KS
Quaker Villa, Lubbock, TX
Quakertown Manor Convalescent & Rehabilitation Center, Quakertown, PA
Qualicare Nursing Home, Detroit, MI
Quality Care Health Center, Lebanon, TN
Quality Care Murray, Murray, UT
Quality Care Nursing Center, Hot Springs, AR
Quality Care of Waco, Waco, TX
Quality Convalescent Center, Fort Worth, TX
Quality Health Care Center, Urbandale, IA

Quality Health of Fernandina Beach, Fernandina Beach, FL
Quality Health of Orange County Inc, Winter Garden, FL
Quapaw Nursing Home, Quapaw, OK
Quarry Hill Treatment Program, Rochester, MN
Quarryville Presbyterian Home, Quarryville, PA
Queen Anne Care Center, Seattle, WA
Queen Anne Nursing Home Inc, Hingham, MA
Queen Care Center, Minneapolis, MN
Queen City Nursing Center, Meridian, MS
Queen City Nursing Home, Cincinnati, OH
Queen of Carmel Nursing Home, Morganville, NJ
Queen of Peace Residence, Queens Village, NY
Queens-Nassau Nursing Home, Far Rockaway, NY
Quiburi Mission Samaritan Center, Benson, AZ
Quiet Acres, Washington Court House, OH
Quiet Oaks Health Care, Crawford, GA
Quincy Nursing Home, Quincy, MA
Quinlan Home, Saint Paul, MN
Quinlan Manor, Sacramento, CA
Quinsippi LTC Facility Inc, Quincy, IL
Quinton Memorial Health Care Center, Dalton, GA
Quinton Nursing Home Inc, Quinton, OK
Quitman County Nursing Home, Marks, MS
Quincy United Methodist Home, Quincy, PA
Quyaana Care Center, Nome, AK
R G R Sanitarium, Los Angeles, CA
Raceland Health Care, Raceland, LA
Racine Residential Care, Racine, WI
Radford Community Hospital, Radford, VA
Radford Hills Convalescent Center, Abilene, TX
Rae-Ann Geneva, Geneva, OH
Rae Ann Nursing Center, Cleveland, OH
Rae-Ann Suburban, Westlake, OH
Rafael Convalescent Hospital, San Rafael, CA
Rafferty's Nursing Home, Clinton, OH
Rahway Geriatrics Center Inc, Rahway, NJ
Rainbow Beach Nursing Center Inc, Chicago, IL
Rainbow Health Care Center, Bristow, OK
Rainbow House, Manitowoc, WI
Rainbow Nursing Center, Bridgeton, NJ
Rainbow Nursing Home, Peabody, MA
Rainbow Residence, Owatonna, MN
Rainbow Springs Care Center, Mineral Point, MO
Rainier Vista Care Center, Puyallup, WA
Raintree Convalescent Hospital, Fresno, CA
Raintree Health Care Center, Evanston, IL
Raleigh Care Center, Portland, OR
Ralls Nursing Home, Ralls, TX
Ralston House, Philadelphia, PA
Ramapo Manor Nursing Center Inc, Suffern, NY
Ramona Manor Convalescent Hospital, Hemet, CA
Ramsbottom Center Inc, Bradford, PA
Ramsey Home, Des Moines, IA
Ramsey Nursing Home, Saint Paul, MN
Ranch Terrace, Sapulpa, OK
Rancho Bernardo Convalescent Hospital, Poway, CA
Rancho de Vida Convalescent Hospital, Los Angeles, CA
Rancho Encinitas, Encinitas, CA
Rancho Mirage Healthcare Center, Rancho Mirage, CA
Rancho Vista Health Center, Vista, CA
Ranchwood Lodge Home, Wilburton, OK
Ranchwood Nursing Center, Yukon, OK
Randol Mill Manor, Arlington, TX
Randolph County Nursing Home, Pocahontas, AR
Randolph County Nursing Home, Sparta, IL
Randolph Hills Nursing Home, Wheaton, MD
Randolph House, Vandalia, IL
Randolph House Nursing Home, Andover, MA

John Randolph Nursing Home Inc, Hopewell, VA
Randolph Nursing Home, Winchester, IN
Helen Raney Nursing Home Inc, Broken Arrow, OK
Range Center, Chisholm, MN
Range Center—Birchwood Home, Eveleth, MN
Range Center—Mapleview, Hibbing, MN
Range Center—Oakwood Home, Chisholm, MN
Range Center Westwind, Chisholm, MN
Ranger Park Inn, Santa Anna, TX
Rapid City Care Center, Rapid City, SD
Rapid City Nursing Center, Rapid City, SD
Rapids Nursing Home, Grand Rapids, OH
Rappahannock Westminster-Canterbury Inc, Irvington, VA
Raritan Health & Extended Care Center, Raritan, NJ
Rathfon Convalescent Home Inc, Selinsgrove, PA
Rathjen House, Albert Lea, MN
Ratliff Nursing Home, Cape Girardeau, MO
Ravenna Good Samaritan Center, Ravenna, NE
Ravenswood Village Nursing Home, Ravenswood, WV
Ravenwood Health Care Center, Waterloo, IA
Ravenwood Lutheran Village, Hagerstown, MD
Rawlings Nursing Home, Sandersville, GA
Rawlins House Inc, Pendleton, IN
Rayne-Branch Hospital, Rayne, LA
Rayne Guest Home Inc, Rayne, LA
Rayville Guest House, Rayville, LA
Reading Nursing Center, West Reading, PA
Reagan County Care Center, Big Lake, TX
John A Reagan Residence, Hartsville, SC
Reagan's Resident Care Facility, Somerville, MA
Rebecca Residence for Protestant Ladies, Pittsburgh, PA
Rebekah—Odd Fellow Care Home, Hutchinson, KS
Rebold Manor, Okmulgee, OK
Reconstruction Home Inc, Ithaca, NY
Recuperative Center, Roslindale, MA
Red Bank Convalescent Center, Red Bank, NJ
Red Bank Health Care Center Inc, Red Bank, TN
Red Bay Nursing Home, Red Bay, AL
Red Carpet Health Care Center, Cambridge, OH
Red Castle Home, Litchfield, MN
Red Haven Nursing Home Inc, Cincinnati, OH
Red Hills Rest Haven Corporation, Sumner, IL
Red Oak Good Samaritan Center, Red Oak, IA
Red Oaks Healthcare Center, Michigan City, IN
Red River Haven Nursing Home Inc, Bogata, TX
Red Rock Manor Inc, Hinton, OK
Red Rose Inn, Cassville, MO
Red Wing Group Home, Red Wing, MN
Red Wing Health Center, Red Wing, MN
Redbanks, Henderson, KY
Redbud Retreat Nursing Home, Naples, TX
Redeemer Residence Inc, Minneapolis, MN
Redford Geriatric Village, Detroit, MI
Redmond Health Care Center, Redmond, OR
Redstone Villa, Saint Albans, VT
Redwood Christian Convalescent Hospital, Napa, CA
Redwood Convalescent Hospital, Castro Valley, CA
Redwood Terrace, Escondido, CA
Redwoods, Mill Valley, CA
Reed City Hospital, Reed City, MI
John M Reed Nursing Home, Limestone, TN
Sarah A Reed Retirement Center, Erie, PA
Walter Reed Convalescent Center, Gloucester, VA
Reeders Memorial Home, Boonsboro, MD
Reedley Convalescent Hospital, Reedley, CA

Reedwood Extended Care Center, Portland, OR
Reelfoot Manor Nursing Home, Tiptonville, TN
Reentry House, Minneapolis, MN
Jack Rees Nursing & Rehabilitation Center, New Castle, PA
Reformed Presbyterian Home, Pittsburgh, PA
Refugio Manor, Refugio, TX
Regency, Springfield, IL
Regency Care Center, Norwalk, IA
Regency Care Center of Carthage, Carthage, MO
Regency Care Center of Monroe, Monroe, WA
Regency Care Center of Spokane, Spokane, WA
Regency Care Center of Webb City, Webb City, MO
Regency Care Walla Walla, Walla Walla, WA
Regency Hall Nursing Home Inc, Allison Park, PA
Regency Health Care Center, Lake Worth, FL
Regency Health Care Center, Eatonton, GA
Regency Health Care Center, DeSoto, KS
Regency Health Care Center, Eureka, KS
Regency Health Care Center, Florence, KS
Regency Health Care Center, Halstead, KS
Regency Health Care Center, Hoisington, KS
Regency Health Care Center, Olathe, KS
Regency Health Care Center, Wichita, KS
Regency Health Care Center, Yates Center, KS
Regency Health Care Center, Grafton, VA
Regency Health Care Center—Newport, Newport, TN
Regency Hills Convalescent Hospital, Pittsburg, CA
Regency House, Alexandria, LA
Regency House Convalescent Center, McAlester, OK
Regency Manor, Independence, KY
Regency Manor, Chelan, WA
Regency Manor Nursing Center, Temple, TX
Regency Nursing & Rehabilitation Treatment Center, Forestville, MD
Regency Nursing Center, Escondido, CA
Regency Nursing Centre, Niles, IL
Regency Oaks, Riverside, CA
Regency Oaks Skilled Nursing Care, Long Beach, CA
Regency Park Convalescent Center, Detroit, MI
Regency Park Manor Health Care Center, Tulsa, OK
Regency Place of Castleton, Indianapolis, IN
Regency Place of Dyer, Dyer, IN
Regency Place of Fort Wayne, Fort Wayne, IN
Regency Place of Greenfield, Greenfield, IN
Regency Place of Greenwood, Greenwood, IN
Regency Place of Lafayette, Lafayette, IN
Regency Place of South Bend, South Bend, IN
Regency South Care Center, Spokane, WA
Regency Terrace South, Milwaukee, WI
Regent Care Center, Hackensack, NJ
Regent Park Long-Term Care Center, Brockton, MA
Regents Park, Boca Raton, FL
Regents Park of Jacksonville, Jacksonville, FL
Regents Park of Sarasota, Sarasota, FL
Regina Community Nursing Center, Norristown, PA
Regina Community Nursing Center at 65th Street, Philadelphia, PA
Regina Continuing Care Center, Evansville, IN
Regina Memorial Complex, Hastings, MN
Region Park Hall, Faribault, MN
Regional Healthcare Inc, Newport, AR
Regional Memorial Hospital, Brunswick, ME
Rego Park Nursing Home, Flushing, NY
Rehabilitation Hospital at Heather Hill, Chardon, OH
Rehoboth McKinley Christian Hospital, Gallup, NM
Reisch Memorial Nursing Home, Carrollton, IL
REM Beltrami, Bemidji, MN
REM Bemidji, Bemidji, MN

REM Bloomington Inc, Bloomington, MN
REM—Buffalo Inc, Buffalo, MN
REM Canby A & B, Canby, MN
REM Fairmont A, Fairmont, MN
REM Fairmont B, Fairmont, MN
REM—Fernwood Inc, Saint Cloud, MN
REM—Grant Inc, Hoffman, MN
REM—Hoffman Inc, Hoffman, MN
REM Lyndale Inc, Minneapolis, MN
REM Madelia, Madelia, MN
REM Mankato—A, Mankato, MN
REM Mankato B, Mankato, MN
REM Mankato C, Mankato, MN
REM Marshall Inc A B C, Marshall, MN
REM Minnetonka, Minnetonka, MN
REM Montevideo Inc, Montevideo, MN
REM Nicollet, Minneapolis, MN
REM Osakis Inc, Osakis, MN
REM—Park Heights, Red Wing, MN
REM Pillsbury Inc, Minneapolis, MN
REM Pleasant, Minneapolis, MN
REM—Red Wing Inc, Red Wing, MN
REM Redwood Falls Inc A&B, Redwood
  Falls, MN
REM Rochester Northwest, Rochester, MN
REM Rochester Southeast, Rochester, MN
REM Roseau, Roseau, MN
REM St Cloud Inc, Saint Cloud, MN
REM—Sauk Centre Inc, Sauk Centre, MN
REM Southeast, Minneapolis, MN
REM Tyler, Tyler, MN
REM Waite Park Inc, Waite Park, MN
REM Willow Creek A, Rochester, MN
REM Willow Creek B, Rochester, MN
Ren-Villa Nursing Home, Renville, MN
Renaissance Care Center, Yakima, WA
Renaissance House, Chicago, IL
Renaissance Manor, Oak Park, IL
Renaissance Place—Humble, Humble, TX
Renaissance Place—Katy, Katy, TX
Rendezvous Medi-Home, McDermott, OH
Renfro Nursing Home, Waxahachie, TX
Rennes Health Center, De Pere, WI
Rennes Health Center—Peshtigo, Peshtigo, WI
Reno Convalescent Hospital, Modesto, CA
Reno Healthcare, Reno, NV
Renotta Nursing Home, Wray, CO
Renova Center for Special Services,
  Mechanicsburg, PA
Rensselaer Care Center, Rensselear, IN
Renton Terrace Nursing Center, Renton, WA
Republic Park Care Center, Republic, MO
Resa On Eden Prairie Rd, Minnetonka, MN
Reservoir Manor, Shelbyville, IL
Reservoir Nursing Home Inc, Waltham, MA
Residence I, Shoreview, MN
Residence III, Saint Paul, MN
Residence II, Shoreview, MN
Resident Care Nursing Home, Framingham,
  MA
Residential Alternatives I, Buffalo, MN
Residential Alternatives II, Brooklyn Center,
  MN
Residential Alternatives III, Brooklyn Park,
  MN
Residential Alternatives IV, Robbinsdale, MN
Residential Alternatives V, Buffalo, MN
Residential Alternatives VI, Cambridge, MN
Residential Alternatives VIII, Robbinsdale,
  MN
Residential Alternatives IX, Robbinsdale, MN
Residential Alternatives X, Maple Grove, MN
Residential Services of Northeast Minnesota I,
  Duluth, MN
Residential Services of Northeast Minnesota
  II, Duluth, MN
Residential Services of Northeast Minnesota
  Inc III, Duluth, MN
Resort Health Related Facility, Arverne, NY
Resort Lodge Inc, Mineral Wells, TX
Resort Nursing Home, Arverne, NY
Rest Awhile Nursing Home, Moultrie, GA
Rest Harbor Extended Care Center, Gresham,
  OR
Rest Haven Central Skilled Nursing Center,
  Palos Heights, IL
Rest Haven Convalescent & Rest Home,
  Sedalia, MO

Rest Haven Health Care Center, Verona, WI
Rest Haven Homes Inc, Grand Rapids, MI
Rest Haven Manor Inc, Albion, IL
Rest Haven Nursing Home, Bogalusa, LA
Rest Haven Nursing Home, Medford, MA
Rest Haven Nursing Home, Ripley, MS
Rest Haven Nursing Home, Fayetteville, NC
Rest Haven Nursing Home, McDermott, OH
Rest Haven Nursing Home, Cushing, OK
Rest Haven Nursing Home, Tulsa, OK
Rest Haven Nursing Home, Schuylkill Haven,
  PA
Rest Haven Nursing Home, El Paso, TX
Rest Haven Nursing Home Inc, Greenville,
  OH
Rest Haven Rest Home Inc, Williamstown,
  MA
Rest Haven South Skilled Nursing Center,
  South Holland, IL
Rest Haven West Skilled Nursing Facility,
  Downers Grove, IL
Rest Haven—York, York, PA
Restful Acres Care Center, Kenedy, TX
Restful Acres Inc, Waynesboro, MS
Resthave Home of Whiteside County,
  Morrison, IL
Resthaven, Independence, MO
Resthaven Corporation, Boston, MA
Resthaven Geriatric Center, Greenville, SC
Resthaven Health Care Center, Bremerton,
  WA
Resthaven Health Care Facility, Patten, ME
Resthaven Healthcare Center, Cando, ND
Resthaven Intermediate Care Home,
  Buchanan, GA
Resthaven Manor Nursing Center, Memphis,
  TN
Resthaven Nursing Center, Lake Charles, LA
Resthaven Nursing Home, Jonesport, ME
Resthaven Nursing Home, Barnstable, MA
Resthaven Nursing Home, Braintree, MA
Resthaven Patrons, Holland, MI
Restorative Care Center, Seattle, WA
Restview Nursing Home, Cincinnati, OH
Resurrection Catholic Nursing Home,
  Marbury, AL
Resurrection Nursing Pavilion, Park Ridge, IL
Resurrection Rest Home, Castleton-on-
  Hudson, NY
Retama Manor North—Pleasanton,
  Pleasanton, TX
Retama Manor Nursing Center, Alice, TX
Retama Manor Nursing Center, Edinburg, TX
Retama Manor Nursing Center, McAllen, TX
Retama Manor Nursing Center, Raymondville,
  TX
Retama Manor Nursing Center—Brownsville,
  Brownsville, TX
Retama Manor Nursing Center—Corpus
  Christi, Corpus Christi, TX
Retama Manor Nursing Center—Cuero,
  Cuero, TX
Retama Manor Nursing Center—Del Rio, Del
  Rio, TX
Retama Manor Nursing Center—East, Cuero,
  TX
Retama Manor Nursing Center—East, Laredo,
  TX
Retama Manor Nursing Center—Harlingen,
  Harlingen, TX
Retama Manor Nursing Center
  Inc—Jourdanton, Jourdanton, TX
Retama Manor Nursing Center—North, San
  Antonio, TX
Retama Manor Nursing Center—Rio Grande
  City, Rio Grande City, TX
Retama Manor Nursing Center—South,
  Laredo, TX
Retama Manor Nursing Center—South,
  Pleasanton, TX
Retama Manor Nursing Center—South, San
  Antonio, TX
Retama Manor Nursing Center—Weslaco,
  Weslaco, TX
Retama Manor Nursing Center—West, Cuero,
  TX
Retama Manor Nursing Center—West,
  Laredo, TX

Retama Manor Nursing Center—West, San
  Antonio, TX
Retama Manor Nursing Center—West,
  Victoria, TX
Retama Manor—Robstown, Robstown, TX
Retama Manor—South, Victoria, TX
Retirement & Nursing Center, Austin, TX
Retirement & Nursing Center—Corpus
  Christi, Corpus Christi, TX
Retirement Care Center of Hempstead,
  Hempstead, TX
Retirement Center, Baton Rouge, LA
Retirement Center of Wright County, Buffalo,
  MN
Retirement Ranch of Clovis, Clovis, NM
Retreat Nursing Home, Monticello, GA
Revere Home, Revere, MN
Revmont Nursing Home, West Union, OH
Rexburg Nursing Center, Rexburg, ID
Reynolds Nursing Home Inc, Adena, OH
R J Reynolds—Patrick County Memorial
  Hospital Inc, Stuart, VA
Rhea County Nursing Home, Dayton, TN
Rheem Valley Convalescent Hospital, Moraga,
  CA
Rheem Valley Convalescent Hospital, Rheem,
  CA
Rheems Guest & Nursing Home, Rheems, PA
A G Rhodes Home Inc, Atlanta, GA
Rib Lake Health Care Center, Rib Lake, WI
Julia Ribaudo Home, Lake Ariel, PA
Rice House, Chicago, IL
Rice Lake Convalescent Center, Rice Lake,
  WI
Rice Springs Care Home Inc, Haskell, TX
William B Rice Eventide Home, Quincy, MA
Riceville Community Rest Home, Riceville,
  IA
Rich Mountain Manor, Mena, AR
L Richardson Memorial Hospital—Skilled
  Nursing Facility, Greensboro, NC
Richardson Manor Care Center, Richardson,
  TX
Richardson Nursing Home, Norfolk, VA
Richboro Care Center, Richboro, PA
Richey Manor Nursing Home, New Port
  Richey, FL
Richfield Care Center, Richfield, UT
Richfield Nursing Center, Salem, VA
Richfield Outreach Group Home, Richfield,
  MN
Richland Convalescent Center Inc, Columbia,
  SC
Richland Hills Nursing Home, Fort Worth,
  TX
Richland Hills Nursing Home, Richland Hills,
  TX
Richland Homes, Sidney, MT
Richland Manor, Olney, IL
Richland Manor, Johnstown, PA
Richland Manor Nursing Home, Bluffton, OH
Richland Nursing Home, Delhi, LA
Richland Parish Hospital, Delhi, LA
Richland Parish Hospital, Rayville, LA
Richland State Community Residence, Aiken,
  SC
Richmond Home for Ladies Health Care Unit,
  Richmond, VA
Richmond Memorial Hospital, Rockingham,
  NC
Richmond Nursing Home, Richmond, VA
Richmond's Boarding Home, Jackson, MS
Richton Crossing Convalescent Center,
  Richton Park, IL
Riddle Memorial Hospital-Based Skilled
  Nursing Facility, Media, PA
Rideout Memorial Hospital D/P, Marysville,
  CA
Ridge Convalescent Center, Lake Wales, FL
Ridge Crest Care Center, Warren, OH
Ridge Crest Convalescent Center Inc,
  Feasterville, PA
Ridge Crest Nursing Center, Warrensburg,
  MO
Ridge Road Residence, Greenville, SC
Ridge Terrace, Freeport, IL
Ridge Terrace Health Care Center, Lantana,
  FL

Ridge View Manor Nursing Home, Buffalo, NY

Ridgecrest, Waco, TX

Ridgecrest Convalescent Center, Ridgeland, SC

Ridgecrest Manor, DeLand, FL

Ridgecrest Manor Nursing Home, Duffield, VA

Ridgecrest Nursing Home, West Monroe, LA

Ridgecrest Retirement Village, Davenport, IA

Ridgefield Care Center, Ridgefield, WA

Ridgeland Living Center, Palos Heights, IL

Ridgemont Terrace Inc, Port Orchard, WA

Ridgetop Haven Inc, Ridgetop, TN

Ridgeview Care Center, Oblong, IL

Ridgeview Health Care Center Inc, Jasper, AL

Ridgeview Lodge Nursing Center, DeQueen, AR

Ridgeview Manor, Kalamazoo, MI

Ridgeview Nursing, Malden, MO

Ridgeview Nursing & Convalescent Center, Wichita Falls, TX

Ridgeview Pavilion, Evanston, IL

Ridgeview Rest Home Inc, Cromwell, CT

Ridgeview Terrace Convalescent & Nursing Center, Rutledge, TN

Isabelle Ridgway Nursing Center, Columbus, OH

Ridgeway Manor, Owingsville, KY

Ridgeway Manor Inc, Catonsville, MD

Ridgewood, River Falls, WI

Ridgewood Care Center, Racine, WI

Ridgewood Care Center Inc, Ottumwa, IA

Ridgewood Court Nursing Home, Attleboro, MA

Ridgewood Health Care Center, Milan, TN

Ridgewood Health Care Center Inc, Jasper, AL

Ridgewood Health Care Facility Inc, Southington, CT

Ridgewood Home, Ridgewood, NJ

Ridgewood Manor, Dalton, GA

Ridgewood Manor Inc, Washington, NC

Ridgewood Manor Nursing Home, Fort Worth, TX

Ridgewood Nursing Center, Springfield, OH

Ridgewood Nursing Center Inc, Youngstown, OH

Ridgewood Place, Akron, OH

Ridgway Manor Nursing Center, Ridgway, IL

Rikard Nursing Homes—Keisler & Holstedt Bldgs, Lexington, SC

Rikard Nursing Homes—Rikard Convalescent Bldg, Lexington, SC

Riley Health Care Facility, Indianapolis, IN

Riley Nursing Home, Fresno, CA

Riley's Oak Hill Manor Inc North, North Little Rock, AR

Riley's Oak Hill Manor South, Little Rock, AR

Rimrock Villa Convalescent Hospital, Barstow, CA

Rinaldi Convalescent Hospital, Granada Hills, CA

Ring Nursing Home East, Springfield, MA

Ring Nursing Home—Ridgewood, Springfield, MA

Ring Nursing Home—South, Springfield, MA

Ringgold Nursing Care Center Inc, Ringgold, LA

Ringling Nursing Home, Ringling, OK

Rio Sol Nursing Home Inc, Mansura, LA

Rio Verde Healthcare Center, Cottonwood, AZ

Ripley Manor Nursing Home, Ripley, MS

Ripley Road Nursing Home Inc, Cohasset, MA

Ripon Area Residential Center, Ripon, WI

Rising Star Nursing Center, Rising Star, TX

Rising Sun Care Center, Rising Sun, IN

Rita's Rest Home, Mystic, CT

Rita's Rest Home, New Bedford, MA

Rittenhouse Care Center, Philadelphia, PA

Ritter Healthcare Center, Indianapolis, IN

River Bluff Convalescent Hospital, Riverbank, CA

River Bluffs of Cahokia, Cahokia, IL

River Falls Area Hospital Kinnic Long-Term Care, River Falls, WI

River Falls Care Center, River Falls, WI

River Forest Nursing Care Center, Three Rivers, MI

River Garden Hebrew Home for the Aged, Jacksonville, FL

River Glen Continuing Care Center, Southbury, CT

River Heights Nursing Home, Tampa, FL

River Heights Retirement Center Inc, Kansas City, MO

River Hills East Health Care Center, Milwaukee, WI

River Hills in Keokuk, Keokuk, IA

River Hills South Health Care Center, Milwaukee, WI

River Hills West Health Care Center, Pewaukee, WI

River Manor Health Related Facility, Brooklyn, NY

River Mede Manor, Binghamton, NY

River Oaks, Mount Carmel, IL

River Oaks, Steele, MO

River Oaks Care Center, Fort Worth, TX

River Oaks Care Center, Wichita Falls, TX

River Oaks Convalescent Center, Clarksdale, MS

River Oaks Convalescent Center, Columbus, TX

River Oaks Estates Nursing Center, Norman, OK

River Oaks Health Care Center, Lake City, MN

River Oaks Nursing Care Center Inc, San Angelo, TX

River Pines Living Center, Stevens Point, WI

River Terrace Healthcare Nursing Home, Lancaster, MA

River Valley Health Care Center, Wabasha, MN

River Valley Living Center, Madison, IN

River Valley Nursing Center Inc, Sacramento, CA

River Walk Manor, Salisbury, MD

River West Medical Center—Skilled Nursing Facility, Plaquemine, LA

River Willows Nursing Center, Abbeville, GA

Riverbend Convalescent Center, Natick, MA

Riverbend Nursing Home, Grand Blanc, MI

Riverbluff Nursing Home, Rockford, IL

Riverchase Health Care Center, Birmingham, AL

Rivercrest Long-Term Care Facility, Concord, MA

Riverdale Convalescent Center, Glendale, CA

Riverdale Gardens Nursing Home, West Springfield, MA

Riverdale Manor, Markesan, WI

Riverdale Manor, Muscoda, WI

Riverdale Nursing Home, Bronx, NY

Riverdell Health Care, Boonville, MO

Riverfront Manor Inc, Tiffin, OH

Riverfront Terrace, Paducah, KY

Rivergate Convalescent Center, Riverview, MI

Rivergate Terrace, Riverview, MI

Riverhead Nursing Home & Health Related Facility, Riverhead, NY

Riveridge Manor Inc, Niles, MI

Riverlands Health Care Center, Lutcher, LA

Rivermont Convalescent & Nursing Center, South Pittsburg, TN

Riverpark Convalescent Center, Spokane, WA

Riverpark Living Center, Eugene, OR

River's Edge Nursing & Rehabilitation Center, Philadelphia, PA

Rivershores Living Center, Marseilles, IL

Riverside Board & Care, McIntosh, MN

Riverside Care Center, Miami, FL

Riverside Convalescent Center, North Hollywood, CA

Riverside Convalescent Center—Hampton, Hampton, VA

Riverside Convalescent Center—Mathews, Mathews, VA

Riverside Convalescent Center—Saluda, Saluda, VA

Riverside Convalescent Center—West Point, West Point, VA

Riverside Convalescent Home, Toledo, OH

Riverside Convalescent Hospital, Chico, CA

Riverside Convalescent Hospital, Sacramento, CA

Riverside Convalescent-Smithfield—Health Care Unit, Smithfield, VA

Riverside Correctional Facility—Comprehensive Care Unit, Ionia, MI

Riverside Cottage Rest Home, Bakersfield, CA

Riverside Foundation, Lincolnshire, IL

Riverside Health Care Center, East Hartford, CT

Riverside Health Care Center, Missoula, MT

Riverside Health Care Center, Danville, VA

Riverside Healthcare, Calhoun, KY

Riverside Hospital Skilled Care, Reno, NV

Riverside Manor, Ames, IA

Riverside Manor, Battle Creek, MI

Riverside Manor, Piketon, OH

Riverside Manor, San Angelo, TX

Riverside Manor Nursing & Rehabilitation Center, Newcomerstown, OH

Riverside Medical Center, Franklinton, LA

Riverside Nursing Center, Milledgeville, GA

Riverside Nursing Center, McKeesport, PA

Riverside Nursing Center, Oconto, WI

Riverside Nursing Center of Covington, Covington, GA

Riverside Nursing Center of Thomaston, Thomaston, GA

Riverside Nursing Centre, Grand Haven, MI

Riverside Nursing Home, Waycross, GA

Riverside Nursing Home, Boston, MA

Riverside Nursing Home, Haverstraw, NY

Riverside Nursing Home, East Providence, RI

Riverside Nursing Home, Saint Albans, WV

Riverside Nursing Home Inc, Monroe, LA

Riverside Nursing Home Inc, Jenks, OK

Riverside of Macon, Macon, GA

Riverside Regional Convalescent Center, Newport News, VA

Riverside Rest Home, Dover, NH

Riverside Tappahannock Hospital, Tappahannock, VA

Riverside United Methodist Hospital's Extended Care Unit, Columbus, OH

Riverstreet Manor Nursing & Rehabilitation Center, Wilkes-Barre, PA

Riverton Heights Convalescent Home, Seattle, WA

Riverview Care Center, Fort Wayne, IN

Riverview Care Center, Des Moines, IA

Riverview Care Center, Bossier City, LA

Riverview Center for Jewish Seniors, Pittsburgh, PA

Riverview Center for Retirement Living, Spokane, WA

Riverview Convalescent Center, Silverton, OR

Riverview Estates Inc, Marquette, KS

Riverview Extended Care Residence, Red Bank, NJ

Riverview Health Center, Kaukauna, WI

Riverview Heights, Waverly, MO

Riverview Home, Cincinnati, OH

Riverview Home I, Brookston, MN

Riverview Homes, Ashland, KY

Riverview Manor, Wanamingo, MN

Riverview Manor, Flandreau, SD

Riverview Manor, Wisconsin Rapids, WI

Riverview Manor Inc, Morrilton, AR

Riverview Manor Inc, Oxford, KS

Riverview Manor Inc, Hannibal, MO

Riverview Manor Nursing Home, Marion, IN

Riverview Manor Nursing Home, Pleasant Valley, IA

Riverview Manor Nursing Home, Prestonsburg, KY

Riverview Manor Nursing Home, Sainte Genevieve, MO

Riverview Manor Nursing Home, Owego, NY

Riverview Nursing Center, Mokane, MO

Riverview Nursing Centre, Baltimore, MD

Riverview Nursing Home, Rome, GA

Riverview Nursing Home, Crookston, MN

Riverview Nursing Home, Steubenville, OH

Riverview Nursing Home, Vermilion, OH
Riverview Nursing Home Inc, Coventry, RI
Riverview Nursing Home Inc, Rich Creek, VA
Riverview Retirement Center, East Peoria, IL
Riverview Skilled Nursing Facility, Gonzales, LA
Riverview Terrace, Tomahawk, WI
Riverways Manor, Van Buren, MO
Riverwood Convalescent Home, Arkadelphia, AR
Riverwood Health Care Center, Biddeford, ME
Riverwood Inn, Puyallup, WA
Riviera Manor Inc, Chicago Heights, IL
Riviera Nursing & Convalescent Hospital, Pico Rivera, CA
RN Nursing & Convalescent Home Inc, El Paso, TX
Ro-Ker Nursing Home, Alliance, OH
Roanoke City Nursing Home, Roanoke, VA
Roanoke Manor Nursing Home, Kansas City, MO
Roanoke United Methodist Home, Roanoke, VA
Roanoke Valley Nursing Home, Rich Square, NC
Robbin House Convalescent Home, Quincy, MA
Robbinswood—An Assisted Living Centre, Grand Haven, MI
Roberta Nursing Home, Roberta, GA
Roberts Health Centre Inc, North Kingstown, RI
Roberts Memorial Nursing Home, Morton, TX
Roberts Nursing Home, Napa, CA
Robertson County Health Care, Springfield, TN
Robings Manor Nursing Home, Brighton, IL
Robinson Developmental Center, McKees Rocks, PA
Robinson Nursing Center, Robinson, TX
Robinson's Health Care Facility, Gardiner, ME
Robinswood School, Lake Charles, LA
Robinwood Care Center Inc, Toledo, OH
Robison Jewish Home, Portland, OR
Robison Nursing Home Inc, Dayton, WA
Rochelle Community Living Facility, Peoria, IL
Rochelle Health Care Center West, Rochelle, IL
Rochelle Healthcare East, Rochelle, IL
Rochester Friendly Home, Rochester, NY
Rochester Healthcare Center, Rochester, MN
Rochester Manor, Rochester, NH
Rochester Manor, Rochester, PA
Rochester Nursing Home, Rochester, IN
Rock County Health Care Center, Janesville, WI
Rock Creek Manor, Washington, DC
Rock Haven Nursing Center, Nacogdoches, TX
Rock Hill Convalescent Center Inc, Rock Hill, SC
Rock Island County Health Care Center, Rock Island, IL
Rock Rapids Health Centre, Rock Rapids, IA
Rock View Good Samaritan Center, Parshall, ND
Rockaway Care Center, Edgemere, NY
Rockcastle County Hospital, Mount Vernon, KY
Rockdale Nursing Home, Rockdale, TX
Rockford Health Care Center, Rockford, IL
Rockford Manor, Shively, KY
Rockhaven Sanitarium, Verdugo City, CA
Rockhill Mennonite Community, Sellersville, PA
Rockingham County Nursing Home, Epping, NH
Rockland Convalescent Center, Rockland, ME
Rockmart Intermediate Care Center, Rockmart, GA
Rockport Nursing Center, Rockport, TX
Rockridge at Laurel Park, Northampton, MA
Rockville Memorial Nursing Home, Rockville, CT

Rockville Nursing Center Inc, Rockville Centre, NY
Rockville Nursing Home Inc, Rockville, MD
Rockville Residence Manor, Rockville Centre, NY
Rockwall Nursing Care Center, Rockwall, TX
Rockwell Community Nursing Home, Rockwell, IA
Rockwood Health Care Center, Rockwood, TN
Rockwood Manor Infirmary, Spokane, WA
Rocky Bay Health Care Facility, Gig Harbor, WA
Rocky Knoll Health Care Facility, Plymouth, WI
Rocky Mountain Health Care Center, Denver, CO
Rockynol Retirement Community, Akron, OH
Rodger Rest Home, Boston, MA
Rofay Nursing Home, Bronx, NY
Rogers City Hospital Long-Term Care Unit, Rogers City, MI
Rogers Nursing Center, Rogers, AR
Rogue Valley Care Center, Medford, OR
Rogue Valley Manor, Medford, OR
Rohr Home, Bartow, FL
Rohrigs Nursing Home No 1, Uhrichsville, OH
Roland Park Place Inc, Baltimore, MD
Rolfe Care Center, Rolfe, IA
Rolla Community Hospital—SNF, Rolla, ND
Rolla Manor Care Center, Rolla, MO
Rolling Acres Care Center, North Lima, OH
Rolling Acres Nursing Home, Florence, AL
Rolling Acres Retirement Center Inc, Raleigh, MS
Rolling Fields Nursing Home Inc, Conneautville, PA
Rolling Green Village, Nevada, IA
Rolling Green Village, Greenville, SC
Rolling Hills, Starkville, MS
Rolling Hills, Sparta, WI
Rolling Hills Care Center Inc, Catoosa, OK
Rolling Hills Convalescent Center, Anderson, IN
Rolling Hills Health Care Center, New Albany, IN
Rolling Hills Health Center, Topeka, KS
Rolling Hills Hospital Skilled Nursing Facility, Elkins Park, PA
Rolling Hills Manor, Zion, IL
Rolling Hills Manor, Millmont, PA
Rolling Hills Nursing Center, Branson, MO
Rolling Meadows, Fond Du Lac, WI
Rolling Meadows Health Care Center, Wichita Falls, TX
Roma Memorial Nursing Home, Three Rivers, TX
Roman Eagle Memorial Home Inc, Danville, VA
Rome & Murphy Memorial Hospital Skilled Nursing Facility, Rome, NY
Rome-Parkway Inc, Rome, NY
Romeo Nursing Center, Romeo, MI
Ron Joy Nursing Home, Boardman, OH
Roncalli Health Center Inc, Bridgeport, CT
Roncalli Woodland Inc, Waterbury, CT
Kenneth J Roney Convalescent Home, Dearborn Heights, MI
Roo-Lan Healthcare Center, Lacey, WA
Rooks County Home, Plainville, KS
Roosevelt General Nursing Home, Portales, NM
Roosevelt Memorial Nursing Home, Culbertson, MT
Roosevelt Park Nursing Centre Inc, Muskegon, MI
Roosevelt Square, Murphysboro, IL
Roosevelt Square Nursing Home, Springfield, IL
Locustwood Health Care Center, Rockford, IL
Rosalie Nursing Home Inc, Wisner, LA
Rosary Hill Home, Justice, IL
Rosary Hill Home, Hawthorne, NY
Roscoe Community Nursing Home Company Inc, Roscoe, NY
Roscoe Nursing Center, Roscoe, TX
Rose Arbor Manor, Sterling, CO

Rose Care Center of Benton I, Benton, AR
Rose Care Center of Benton II, Benton, AR
Rose Care Center of Fort Smith, Fort Smith, AR
Rose Care Center of Jacksonville, Jacksonville, AR
Rose Care Center of Jonesboro, Jonesboro, AR
Rose Care Center of Little Rock, Little Rock, AR
Rose Care Center of Rogers, Rogers, AR
Rose Care Center of Stuttgart, Stuttgart, AR
Rose Care Center of Trumann, Trumann, AR
Rose City Nursing Home, Portland, OR
Rose Convalescent Hospital, Baldwin Park, CA
Rose Cottage Health Care Center, Central Falls, RI
Rose Garden Convalescent Center, Pasadena, CA
Rose Garden Nursing Home, Mount Vernon, OH
Rose Haven Health Care Center, Hugo, OK
Rose Haven ICF/MR & Skilled Nursing Facility, Thomasville, GA
Rose-Haven Ltd, Litchfield, CT
Rose Haven Nursing Center, Roseburg, OR
Rose Haven Nursing Home, Marengo, IA
Rose Haven of Kaufman Inc, Kaufman, TX
Rose Haven Retreat, Atlanta, TX
Rose Hill Care Center Inc, Commerce City, CO
Rose Hill Nursing Home, Berryville, VA
Rose Hill Personal Care Center, Terrell, TX
Rose House, Moline, IL
Rose Lane Health Center, Massillon, OH
Rose Lane Nursing Home, Loup City, NE
Rose Lawn Geriatric Center, Alliance, OH
Rose Lawn, West Lafayette, OH
Rose Manor, Waterbury, CT
Rose Manor Health Care, Birmingham, AL
Rose Manor Intermediate Care Facility, Lexington, KY
Rose Marian Hall, Chicago, IL
Rose-Mary, The Grasselli Rehabilitation & Education Center, Euclid, OH
Rose Mary's Home, Denver, CO
Rose Mountain Care Center, New Brunswick, NJ
Rose Nursing Home, Cleveland Heights, OH
Rose of Sharon Manor, Roseville, MN
Rose Park Convalescent & Rehabilitation Center, Cleveland, OH
Rose Skill Care Nursing Center of Jonesboro, Jonesboro, AR
Rose Terrace Lodge, Nicholasville, KY
Rose View Manor, Williamsport, PA
Rose Villa Care Center, Bellflower, CA
Rose Villa Health Care Inc, Milwaukie, OR
Rose Vista Home, Woodbine, IA
Rose Vista Nursing Center, Vancouver, WA
Rose Wood Rest Home Inc, Claymont, DE
Roseau Area Hospital, Roseau, MN
Rosebud Health Care Center, Forsyth, MT
Rosebud Nursing Home, Gregory, SD
Rosedale Manor, Saint Petersburg, FL
Rosedale Manor, Covington, KY
Rosedale Nursing Home, Silex, MO
Rosedale Rest Home, Owensboro, KY
Rosegate Care Center, Columbus, OH
Roselawn Manor, Lansing, MI
Roselawn Manor Nursing Home, Spencerville, OH
Roselawn Manor Rest Home, Worcester, MA
Roselawn Retirement Home, New Albany, MS
Rosemont Health Care Center, Orlando, FL
Rosemont Manor, Rosemont, PA
Rosemont Nursing Home, Mansfield, OH
Roseview Nursing Center Inc, Shreveport, LA
Roseville Convalescent Hospital, Roseville, CA
Roseville East, Milwaukee, WI
Roseville Manor, Milwaukee, WI
Roseville Nursing Home, Milwaukee, WI
Roseville of De Pere, De Pere, WI
Rosewood C Center Inc of Swansea, Swansea, IL
Rosewood Center, Owings Mills, MD

Rosewood Convalescent Center, Gwynn, VA
Rosewood Convalescent Hospital, Pleasant Hill, CA
Rosewood-Damen Nursing Home Inc, Chicago, IL
Rosewood Gardens, Rensselaer, NY
Rosewood Health Care Center, Grafton, WV
Rosewood Health Facility, Bakersfield, CA
Rosewood Manor, Muncie, IN
Rosewood Manor, Estherville, IA
Rosewood Manor, Galion, OH
Rosewood Manor, Memphis, TN
Rosewood Manor, Veradale, WA
Rosewood Manor Health Care Center, Bowling Green, KY
Rosewood Manor Living Center, Norman, OK
Rosewood Manor Nursing Center, Maple Shade, NJ
Rosewood Nursing Center Inc, Lake Charles, LA
Rosewood Nursing Home, Jacksonville, FL
Rosewood Nursing Home, West Allis, WI
Rosewood Rest Home, Fall River, MA
Rosewood Terrace, Salt Lake City, UT
Rosholt Nursing Home, Rosholt, SD
Roslyn Nursing & Rehabilitation Center, Roslyn, PA
Betsy Ross Health Related Facility, Rome, NY
Ross Manor, Dillsboro, IN
Ross Manor Nursing Home, Ridley Park, PA
Ross Nursing Home, East Liverpool, OH
Ross Nursing Home 1 Inc, Wagoner, OK
Ross Nursing Home 2 Inc, Wagoner, OK
Ross Nursing Home Inc, Brentwood, NY
Rosscare Convalescent Hospital, Capitola, CA
Rosscare Convalescent Hospital, Milpitas, CA
Rosscare Convalescent Hospital, Morgan Hill, CA
Rosscare Convalescent Hospital, Santa Maria, CA
Rosser Nursing Home, Roanoke, AL
Rossmoor Manor, Walnut Creek, CA
Rossville Convalescent Center, Rossville, GA
Rossville Valley Manor, Rossville, KS
Roswell Nursing Center, Roswell, NM
Rotan Nursing Center, Rotan, TX
Rotary Ann Home, Eagle Grove, IA
Roubal Nursing Home, Stephenson, MI
Roundup Memorial Nursing Home, Roundup, MT
Wayne Rounseville Memorial Convalescent Hospital, Oakland, CA
Rouse-Warren County Home, Youngsville, PA
Routt Memorial Hospital Extended Care Center, Steamboat Springs, CO
Rowan Court Nursing Home, Barre, VT
Rowland, Covina, CA
Roxboro Nursing Center, Roxboro, NC
Roxbury Home for Aged Women, Boston, MA
Royal Care of Cleveland Home for Aged, Cleveland, TN
Royal Care of Erin Inc, Erin, TN
Royal Care of Pigeon Forge, Pigeon Forge, TN
Royal Care Skilled Nursing Facility, Long Beach, CA
Royal Convalescent Hospital, Brawley, CA
Royal Elaine Intermediate Care Facility, LaGrange, GA
Royal Elm Inc, Elmwood Park, IL
Royal Fontana Nursing Center Inc, Urbana, IL
Royal Glades Convalescent Home, North Miami Beach, FL
Royal Home, El Cajon, CA
Royal Living Center, New Baden, IL
Royal Manor, Royal Palm Beach, FL
Royal Manor, Nicholasville, KY
Royal Manor Care Center, Missoula, MT
Royal Manor Convalescent Hospital Inc, Sacramento, CA
Royal Manor Inc, East Greenwich, RI
Royal Manor Inc, Warwick, RI
Royal Megansett Nursing Home, Falmouth, MA
Royal Neighbor Home, Davenport, IA
Royal Nursing Center, Highland Park, MI
Royal Nursing Home, Mesa, AZ

Royal Oak Nursing Resort, Dade City, FL
Royal Oaks, Madison, NJ
Royal Oaks Convalescent Hospital, Galt, CA
Royal Oaks Convalescent Hospital, Glendale, CA
Royal Oaks Life Care Facility, Sun City, AZ
Royal Palm Convalescent Center, Vero Beach, FL
Royal Terrace Care Center Inc, Olathe, KS
Royal Terrace Health Care Center, McHenry, IL
Royal Vista Care Center, Ellensburg, WA
Royal Willow Nursing Care Center, Wilmington, IL
Royale Convalescent Hospital, Santa Ana, CA
Royale Gardens Healthcare Facility, Grants Pass, OR
Royalview Manor, Broadview Heights, OH
Royalwood Care Center, Torrance, CA
Rubin's Brierwood Terrace Convalescent Hospital, Los Angeles, CA
Ruby Hill Nursing Home, Birmingham, AL
Ruby Mountains Manor, Elko, NV
Ruby's Rest Home, Middlesboro, KY
Rudnick Community Residence, Aiken, SC
Ruidoso Care Center, Ruidoso, NM
Ruleville Health Center, Ruleville, MS
Rulon House, Pocatello, ID
Rural Health Care Facility, Indianapolis, IN
Rush County Nursing Home, LaCrosse, KS
Rush Health Care Management Inc, Rushville, IN
Rush Memorial Hospital—Swing Bed Unit, Rushville, IN
Rushville Millers Merry Manor, Rushville, IN
Rusk County Nursing Home, Ladysmith, WI
Rusk Nursing Home Inc, Rusk, TX
Abbiejean Russell Care Center, Fort Pierce, FL
Abbiejean Russell Care Center, Fort Pierce, FL
Russell Convalescent Home, Russell, KY
Russell Nursing Home, Albany, OH
Russell Park Manor, Lewiston, ME
Russell Retirement, Charleston, MO
Richard B Russell Building (GWV), Milledgeville, GA
Russellville Health Care Manor, Russellville, KY
Russellville Nursing Center Inc, Russellville, AR
Rust-McGills Nursing Center, Dayton, OH
Rutherford County Convalescent Center, Rutherfordton, NC
Ruthven Community Care Center, Ruthven, IA
Rutland Heights Hospital—Skilled Nursing Facility, Rutland, MA
Rutland Nursing Home Co Inc, Brooklyn, NY
Rutledge Avenue Community Residence, Charleston, SC
Hannah M Rutledge Home for the Aged, Chippewa Falls, WI
Rutledge Manor Care Home Inc, Springfield, IL
Ryan Nursing Center, Amherst, VA
Ryan Nursing Home Inc, Ryan, OK
Rydal Park of Philadelphia Presbyterian Homes on the Fairway, Rydal, PA
Ryder Memorial Skilled Nursing Facility, Humacao, PR
Residential Alternatives VII, Big Lake, MN
S & R Foster Home, Cheyenne, WY
S & R Foster Home, Cheyenne, WY
Sabetha Manor, Sabetha, KS
Sabine Oaks Home, Beaumont, TX
Sable Care Center Inc, Aurora, CO
Sacramento Convalescent Hospital, Sacramento, CA
Sacred Heart Convalescent Hospital, Pasadena, CA
Sacred Heart Free Home for Incurable Cancer, Philadelphia, PA
Sacred Heart Home, Chicago, IL
Sacred Heart Home, Avilla, IN
Sacred Heart Home, Louisville, KY
Sacred Heart Home, Hyattsville, MD
Sacred Heart Home, Bronx, NY

Sacred Heart Home Inc, Plattsburgh, NY
Sacred Heart Hospice, Austin, MN
Sacred Heart Manor—Philadelphia, Philadelphia, PA
Sacred Heart Nursing Home, New Bedford, MA
Saddle Brook Convalescent Home, Saddle Brook, NJ
Safe Harbor, Owatonna, MN
Safehaven of Gwinnett, Lawrenceville, GA
Safford Care Center, Safford, AZ
Ellen Sagar Nursing Home, Union, SC
Sage Crossing, Spring Park, MN
Sage Healthcare Center, Midland, TX
Sager Nursing Home, Fair Haven, VT
Saginaw Community Hospital, Saginaw, MI
Saginaw Geriatric Home, Saginaw, MI
Sahara House, Princeton, MN
Sailors' Snug Harbor, Sea Level, NC
St Agnes Health Care Center, Chicago, IL
St Agnes Home, Kirkwood, MO
St Agnes Nursing Home, Breaux Bridge, LA
St Alexis Hospital Skilled Nursing Facility, Cleveland, OH
St Aloisius Medical Center, Harvey, ND
St Andre Health Care Facility, Biddeford, ME
St Andrew's Nursing Home, Bottineau, ND
St Andrews Estates Medical Center, Boca Raton, FL
St Andrews Hospital Gregory Wing, Boothbay Harbor, ME
St Andrew's Presbyterian Manor, Buffalo, NY
St Ann Home, Dover, NH
St Ann Skilled Nursing Center, Sandusky, OH
St Anna's Asylum, New Orleans, LA
St Anne Center, Rockford, IL
St Anne Convalescent Center, Detroit, MI
St Anne General Hospital—Skilled Nursing Facility, Raceland, LA
St Anne Home, Fort Wayne, IN
St Anne Home for the Elderly, Greensburg, PA
St Anne's Convalescent Hospital, Castro Valley, CA
St Annes Home, San Francisco, CA
St Anne's Home, Columbia, PA
St Anne's Home for the Elderly, Milwaukee, WI
St Annes Hospice, Winona, MN
St Anne's Mead Nursing Facility, Southfield, MI
St Ann's Convalescent Home, Arabi, LA
St Anns Healthcare Center Inc, Chester, IL
St Ann's Home, Oklahoma City, OK
St Ann's Nursing Home, Panhandle, TX
St Anns Residence, Minneapolis, MN
St Ann's Rest Home, Milwaukee, WI
St Ansgar Good Samaritan Center, Saint Ansgar, IA
St Anthony Center, Houston, TX
St Anthony Elder Center on Main, Minneapolis, MN
St Anthony Health Care, Lafayette, IN
St Anthony Health Center, Minneapolis, MN
St Anthony Health Center, Saint Anthony Village, MN
St Anthony Home, Crown Point, IN
St Anthony Nursing Center, Warren, MI
St Anthony Nursing Home, Carroll, IA
St Anthonys Continuing Care Center, Rock Island, IL
St Anthony's Medical Center—Rehabilitation Center, Saint Louis, MO
St Anthony's Nursing Home Inc, Metairie, LA
St Antoine Residence, North Smithfield, RI
St Augustine Geriatric Center, Saint Augustine, FL
St Augustine Home for the Aged, Indianapolis, IN
St Barbara's Memorial Nursing Home, Monongah, WV
St Barnabas Nursing Home, Gibsonia, PA
St Barnabas Nursing Home, Chattanooga, TN
St Benedict Home for Aged, Niles, IL
St Benedict Nursing Home, Farmington, MI
St Benedict Nursing Home, San Antonio, TX
St Benedict's Center, Saint Cloud, MN

St Benedict's Family Medical Center Inc, Jerome, ID
St Brendan Care Center, Spokane, WA
St Cabrini Hospital Skilled Nursing Facility, Seattle, WA
St Cabrini Nursing Home Inc, Dobbs Ferry, NY
St Camillus Health Center, Wauwatosa, WI
St Camillus Place, Little Falls, MN
St Camillus Residential Health Care Facility, Syracuse, NY
St Casimir Health Care Facility, Lewiston, ME
St Catherine Laboure Manor, Jacksonville, FL
St Catherine's Infirmary, Racine, WI
St Catherine's Residence & Nursing Center, North Bend, OR
St Charles Nursing Home, Newellton, LA
St Charles Care Center, Covington, KY
St Charles Health Care Center, New Orleans, LA
St Charles Health Care Center, Saint Charles, MO
St Charles Hospital, Luling, LA
St Charles Manor Nursing Center Inc, Luling, LA
St Christopher Convalescent Hospital, Hayward, CA
St Christopher Convalescent Hospital & Sanitarium, Signal Hill, CA
St Clair County Medical Centre, Goodells, MI
St Clair County Specialized Living Center, Belleville, IL
St Clair Health Care Center, Cook Springs, AL
St Clair Nursing Center, Saint Clair, MO
St Clare Convalescent Center, Detroit, MI
St Claire's Nursing Center, Sacramento, CA
St Clare Manor, Lockport, NY
St Clare Retirement Community, Cincinnati, OH
St Clare's Home for Aged, Newport, RI
St Cloud Health Care Center, Saint Cloud, FL
St Cloud Manor, Saint Cloud, MN
St Coletta School Alverno Cottage, Jefferson, WI
St Croix Care Center, Prescott, WI
St Croix Health Center, New Richmond, WI
St Croix Valley Good Samaritan Center, Saint Croix Falls, WI
St Dominic Nursing Home, Houston, TX
St Edna Convalescent Center, Santa Ana, CA
St Edward Home, Akron, OH
St Elizabeth Briarbank Home for the Aging, Bloomfield Hills, MI
St Elizabeth Care Center, Saint Elizabeth, MO
St Elizabeth Health Care Center, Baker, OR
St Elizabeth Health Center, East Hartford, CT
St Elizabeth Healthcare Center, Delphi, IN
St Elizabeth Home, Saint Cloud, MN
St Elizabeth Home, Providence, RI
St Elizabeth Hospital, Wabasha, MN
St Elizabeth Hospital Medical Center Skilled Nursing Unit, Lafayette, IN
St Elizabeth Nursing Home, Waco, TX
St Elizabeth Nursing Home, Brookfield, WI
St Elizabeth Toluca Lake Convalescent Hospital, North Hollywood, CA
St Elizabeth's Hospital/Skilled Nursing Unit, Chicago, IL
St Elizabeth's Nursing Home, Janesville, WI
St Erne Sanitarium, Inglewood, CA
St Francis Nursing Center—East, Pittsburgh, PA
St Frances Home, Fond Du Lac, WI
St Francis Continuing Care & Nursing Home Center, Burlington, IA
St Francis Convalescent Pavilion Inc, Daly City, CA
St Francis Country House, Darby, PA
St Francis Extended Care Center, Evanston, IL
St Francis Extended Care Inc, Hayward, CA
St Francis Extended Health Care, Bellingham, WA
St Francis Gardens, Albuquerque, NM
St Francis Heights Convalescent Hospital, Daly City, CA
St Francis Home, Worcester, MA

St Francis Home, Saginaw, MI
St Francis Home, Breckenridge, MN
St Francis Home, Waite Park, MN
St Francis Home, Laconia, NH
St Francis Home, Tiffin, OH
St Francis Home, La Crosse, WI
St Francis Home Inc, Superior, WI
St Francis Home of Williamsville, Williamsville, NY
St Francis Hospital, Honolulu, HI
St Francis Hospital Nursing Home, Memphis, TN
St Francis Hospital of New Castle Skilled Nursing Center, New Galilee, PA
St Francis Hospital SNF, Tulsa, OK
St Francis Manor, Grinnell, IA
St Francis Medical Center Skilled Nursing Care Unit, Monroe, LA
St Francis Nursing Center, Colorado Springs, CO
St Francis Nursing Home, San Antonio, TX
St Francis Nursing Home of Oberlin Inc, Oberlin, LA
St Francis Rehabilitation Hospital & Nursing Home, Green Springs, OH
St Francis Residence, Tampa, FL
St George Care Center, Saint George, UT
St George Health Care Center Inc, Saint George, SC
St George Nursing Home, Eden, NY
St Gerard's Nursing Home, Hankinson, ND
St Helena Parish Hospital, Greensburg, LA
St Helena Parish Nursing Home, Greensburg, LA
St Ignatius Nursing Home, Philadelphia, PA
St James House of Baytown, Baytown, TX
St James Manor, Crete, IL
St James Nursing Center, Saint James, MO
St James Nursing Home Skilled Facility, Saint James, NY
St James Parish Hospital, Lutcher, LA
St James Place Nursing Care Center, Baton Rouge, LA
St James Plaza Health Related Facility, Saint James, NY
St Jo Nursing Center, Saint Jo, TX
St Joan Antida Home, West Allis, WI
St John-Bon Secours Senior Community, Detroit, MI
St John Kronstadt Convalescent Center, Castro Valley, CA
St John Lutheran Care Center, Mars, PA
St John Lutheran Home, Springfield, MN
St John Medical Center, Tulsa, OK
St John Neumann Nursing Home, Philadelphia, PA
St John of God Nursing Hospital, Los Angeles, CA
St Johnland Nursing Home Inc, Kings Park, NY
St John's Center, Kearney, NE
St John's Center, Springfield, OH
St Johns County Senior Citizens Home, Saint Augustine, FL
St John's Episcopal Homes for the Aged & the Blind, Brooklyn, NY
St Johns Episcopal Hospital South Shore Division, Far Rockaway, NY
St John's Health Care Center, Lauderdale Lakes, FL
St John's Home for the Aged, Evansville, IN
St John's Home of Milwaukee, Milwaukee, WI
St John's Hospital Long-Term Care Unit, Jackson, WY
St Johns Lutheran Home, Albert Lea, MN
St John's Lutheran Home, Billings, MT
St John's Lutheran Home—Billings Heights, Billings, MT
St John's Mercy Skilled Nursing Center, Saint Louis, MO
St John's Mercy Villa, Springfield, MO
St John's Nursing Home, Covington, KY
St John's Nursing Home Inc, Lynchburg, VA
St John's Nursing Home Inc & Home for the Aging, Rochester, NY
St Johns Nursing Home of Lowell, Lowell, MA
St John's of Hays, Hays, KS

St John's Regional Medical Center, Oxnard, CA
St Johns Rest Home, Victoria, KS
St Johnsbury Convalescent Center, Saint Johnsbury, VT
St Joseph Care Center, Kansas City, KS
St Joseph Care Center, Spokane, WA
St Joseph Convalescent Center, Polson, MT
St Joseph Convalescent Center Inc, Saint Joseph, MO
St Joseph Convalescent Hospital Inc, Castro Valley, CA
St Joseph Gerontology Center, Alliance, NE
St Joseph Home, Brinkley, AR
St Joseph Home for the Aged, Freeport, IL
St Joseph Home for the Aged, Holland, PA
St Joseph Home of Chicago Inc, Chicago, IL
St Joseph Hospice, Louisville, OH
St Joseph Hospital, Aberdeen, WA
St Josephs Hospital Nursing Home of Yonkers New York Inc, Yonkers, NY
St Joseph Infant Home, Cincinnati, OH
St Joseph Life Enrichment Center Inc, Port Charlotte, FL
St Joseph Living Care Center, Mount Clemens, MI
St Joseph Manor, Florence, CO
St Joseph Manor, Brockton, MA
St Joseph Medical Center Pavilion, Burbank, CA
St Joseph Mercy Hospital, Centerville, IA
St Joseph Mercy Hospital, Clinton, IA
St Joseph Nursing & Health Care Center, Pittsburgh, PA
St Joseph Nursing Home, Lacon, IL
St Joseph Nursing Home, Upper Frenchville, ME
St Joseph Nursing Home, Hamtramck, MI
St Joseph Nursing Home, Arcadia, WI
St Joseph Nursing Home Company of Utica, Utica, NY
St Joseph of the Pines Inc, Southern Pines, NC
St Joseph Residence, New London, WI
St Joseph Villa, Omaha, NE
St Joseph Villa, Flourtown, PA
St Joseph Villa, Salt Lake City, UT
St Joseph West Mesa Hospital, Albuquerque, NM
St Joseph's Care Center, Phoenix, AZ
St Joseph's Care Center—Morningside, South Bend, IN
St Joseph's Care Center—Notre Dame, South Bend, IN
St Joseph's Care Center West, South Bend, IN
St Joseph's Care Center—Melrose, Mishawaka, IN
St Joseph's Convalescent Hospital, Ojai, CA
St Josephs Center, Scranton, PA
St Joseph's Hill Infirmary Inc, Eureka, MO
St Joseph's Home, Saint Charles, MO
St Josephs Home, Ogdensburg, NY
St Joseph's Home, Kenosha, WI
St Joseph's Home for Infirm & Aged, Monroe, LA
St Joseph's Home for the Aged, Jefferson City, MO
St Joseph's Home for the Aged, West Allis, WI
St Joseph's Home for the Elderly, Palatine, IL
St Joseph's Home of Peoria, Peoria, IL
St Joseph's Home of Springfield, Springfield, IL
St Josephs Home for the Aged, Detroit, MI
St Joseph's Hospital & Nursing Home of Del Norte Inc, Del Norte, CO
St Joseph's Hospital Restorative Care, Asheville, NC
St Josephs Hospital—Skilled Nursing Facility, Elmira, NY
St Joseph's Manor, Trumbull, CT
St Joseph's Manor, Portland, ME
St Joseph's Manor, Boston, MA
St Josephs Manor, Olean, NY
St Joseph's Manor, Meadowbrook, PA
St Joseph's Nursing Home, Catonsville, MD
St Joseph's Nursing Home, Norfolk, NE
St Joseph's Nursing Home, Hillsboro, WI

St Joseph's Nursing Home, La Crosse, WI
St Joseph's Residence, Enfield, CT
St Joseph's Residence, Dallas, TX
St Joseph's Villa Inc, David City, NE
St Jude Convalescent Center, Livonia, MI
St Jude Manor Nursing Home, Jacksonville, FL
St Jude Nursing Home, Milwaukee, WI
St Jude Skilled Nursing Facility, Kenner, LA
St Jude's Health Care Centre, Spokane, WA
St Lawrence Dimondale Center, Dimondale, MI
St Louis Altenheim, Saint Louis, MO
St Louis Good Shepherd Homes Inc, Saint Louis, MO
St Lucas Convalescent & Geriatric Center, Faribault, MN
St Luke Center, Cincinnati, OH
St Luke Community Nursing Home, Ronan, MT
St Luke Convalescent Center—Central, Columbus, OH
St Luke Convalescent Center—East, Columbus, OH
St Luke General Hospital, Arnaudville, LA
St Luke Hospital, Davenport, IA
St Luke Lutheran Home, Baltimore, MD
St Luke Lutheran Home, North Canton, OH
St Luke Manor, Fortuna, CA
St Luke Manor, Hazelton, PA
St Luke Manor of Batavia, Batavia, NY
St Luke Nursing Home Company Inc, Oswego, NY
St Luke Pavilion, Hazelton, PA
St Luke's Episcopal Church Home, Highland Park, MI
St Luke's Extended Care Center, Spokane, WA
St Lukes Extended Care Center & Nursing Centre, San Leandro, CA
St Luke's Good Samaritan Village, Kearney, NE
St Luke's Group Home, Bloomington, MN
St Luke's Home, Dickinson, ND
St Luke's Lutheran Home, Spencer, IA
St Lukes Lutheran Home, Blue Earth, MN
St Luke's Methodist Hospital, Cedar Rapids, IA
St Luke's Nursing Center, Carthage, MO
St Lukes Nursing Home, Birmingham, AL
St Lukes Presbyterian Nursing Center, Buffalo, NY
St Luke's Skilled Nursing Facility, Phoenix, AZ
St Margaret Hall, Cincinnati, OH
St Margaret's Daughters Nursing Home, New Orleans, LA
St Margarets House & Hospital for Babies, Albany, NY
St Mark Village Inc, Palm Harbor, FL
St Marks Lutheran Home, Austin, MN
St Martha Manor, Chicago, IL
St Martin Deporres Nursing Home, Detroit, MI
St Martin's-in-the-Pines, Birmingham, AL
St Martinville Nursing Home, Saint Martinville, LA
St Mary's Convalescent Center, Saint Mary's, GA
St Mary Guest Home, Morgan City, LA
St Mary Home, West Hartford, CT
St Mary Square Living Center Inc, Freeport, IL
St Mary's Home, Saint Paul, MN
St Mary's Home for the Aged Inc, Manitowoc, WI
St Marys Home of Erie, Erie, PA
St Mary's Hospital, Norton, VA
St Mary's Hospital for Children, Bayside, NY
St Mary's Hospital Skilled Nursing Facility, Enid, OK
St Mary's Infant Home Inc, Norfolk, VA
St Marys Manor, Saint Marys, KS
St Mary's Manor, Blue Springs, MO
St Mary's Manor, Niagara Falls, NY
St Mary's Manor, Lansdale, PA
St Mary's Memorial Home, Glendale, OH
St Mary's Nursing Center, Leonardtown, MD
St Marys Nursing Center, Detroit Lakes, MN

St Mary's Nursing Home, Saint Clair Shores, MI
St Marys Nursing Home, Milwaukee, WI
St Mary's Nursing Home, Sparta, WI
St Mary's Rehabilitation Center, Minneapolis, MN
St Mary's Residential Training School, Alexandria, LA
St Mary's Square Living Center, Galesburg, IL
Gateway Terrace, Irvington, IL
St Marys Villa Nursing Home, Pierz, MN
St Mary's Villa Nursing Home, Elmhurst, PA
St Matthew Lutheran Home, Park Ridge, IL
St Matthews Manor, Louisville, KY
St Michael Convalescent Hospital, Hayward, CA
St Michael's Evangelical Lutheran Home for the Aged, Fountain City, WI
St Michaels Hospital & Nursing Home, Sauk Centre, MN
St Michael's Nursing Home, Tyndall, SD
St Olaf Residence, Minneapolis, MN
St Ottos Care Center, Little Falls, MN
St Patricks Home for the Aged & Infirm, Bronx, NY
St Patricks Manor Inc, Framingham, MA
St Patrick's Residence, Joliet, IL
St Paul Baptist Church Home for the Aged, Indianapolis, IN
St Paul Health Center, Denver, CO
St Paul Hermitage, Beech Grove, IN
St Paul Home Inc, Kaukauna, WI
St Paul Homes, Greenville, PA
St Paul's Church Home Inc, Saint Paul, MN
St Paul's Health Care Center, San Diego, CA
St Pauls Home, Belleville, IL
St Pauls House/Grace Convalescent Home, Chicago, IL
St Paul's Retirement Community, South Bend, IN
St Paul's Towers, Oakland, CA
St Peter Community Hospital & Health Care Center, Saint Peter, MN
St Peter Regional Treatment Center, Saint Peter, MN
St Peter Villa Nursing Home, Memphis, TN
St Peters Manor Care Center, Saint Peters, MO
St Petersburg Cluster, Saint Petersburg, FL
St Raphaels Home for the Aged, Columbus, OH
St Regis Health Center, New Haven, CT
St Regis Nursing Home & Health Related Facility Inc, Massena, NY
St Richard's Villa Inc, Muenster, TX
St Rita's Home for the Aged Inc, Columbus, OH
St Rita's Nursing Home, Saint Bernard, LA
St Roses Home, New York, NY
St Simeon's Episcopal Home Inc, Tulsa, OK
St Sophia Geriatric Center, Florissant, MO
St Stephen Group Homes A & B, Bloomington, MN
St Teresa's Manor, Manchester, NH
St Teresas Nursing Home Inc, Middletown, NY
St Theresa Convalescent Hospital, Pico Rivera, CA
St Theresa Home, Cincinnati, OH
St Therese Convalescent Hospital Inc, Hayward, CA
St Therese Home, New Hope, MN
St Thomas Convalescent Center, Houston, TX
St Thomas More Hospital & Progressive Care Center, Canon City, CO
St Vincent Community Living Facility, Freeport, IL
St Vincent de Paul Nursing Home, Berlin, NH
St Vincent New Hope, Indianapolis, IN
St Vincent's Nursing Home, Montclair, NJ
St Vincent's Nursing Home, Bismarck, ND
St William's Home for the Aged, Milbank, SD
St Williams Nursing Home, Parkers Prairie, MN
Sainte Ann's Home—The Heritage, Rochester, NY
Sainte Ann's Nursing Home, Juneau, AK
Sainte Clara's Manor, Lincoln, IL

Salamanca Nursing Home Inc, Salamanca, NY
Thad E Saleeby Developmental Center, Hartsville, SC
Salem Care Center, Salem, MO
Salem Community Hospital, Salem, OH
Salem Convalescent Center, Salem, OH
Salem County Nursing & Convalescent Home, Salem, NJ
Salem Hills Nursing Care Center, Purdys, NY
Salem Lutheran Home, Elk Horn, IA
Salem Lutheran Home Skilled Nursing Facility, Oakland, CA
Salem Mennonite Home for Aged, Freeman, SD
Salem Nursing Home, Salem, KY
Salem Park Nursing Home, Cincinnati, OH
Salem Village, Joliet, IL
Salemhaven Inc, Salem, NH
Salerno Bay Manor, Port Salereno, FL
Salina Nursing Center, Salina, KS
Salina Presbyterian Manor, Salina, KS
Salinas Care Center, Salinas, CA
Saline Care Center, Harrisburg, IL
Saline County Rest Home Inc, Marshall, MO
Salisbury Nursing Home, Salisbury, MD
Salisbury Nursing Home, Worcester, MA
Salmi Boarding Home, Aurora, MN
Salmon Brook Convalescent Home, Glastonbury, CT
Salmon Valley Care Center, Salmon, ID
Salsbury Baptist Home, Charles City, IA
Salt River Nursing Home, Shelbina, MO
Saluda Nursing Center, Saluda, SC
Salvation Army Harbor Light, Minneapolis, MN
Salyersville Health Care Center, Salyersville, KY
Samaritan Bethany Home, Rochester, MN
Samaritan Care Center, Medina, OH
Samaritan Home, Topeka, KS
Samaritan Home, West Bend, WI
Samaritan-Keep Nursing Home Inc, Watertown, NY
Samaritan White Mountains Care Center, Springerville, AZ
Samarkand Health Center, Santa Barbara, CA
Sampson County Memorial Hospital—Skilled Nursing Facility, Clinton, NC
San Andreas Convalescent Hospital No 679, San Andreas, CA
San Augustine Nursing Center, San Augustine, TX
San Bruno Convalescent Hospital, San Bruno, CA
San Diego Convalescent Hospital, La Mesa, CA
San Diego Hebrew Home for the Aged, San Diego, CA
San Diego Intermediate Care Center, San Diego, CA
San Filippo Rest Home Inc, Malden, MA
San Francisco Community Convalescent Hospital, San Francisco, CA
San Gabriel Convalescent Center, Rosemead, CA
San Jacinto Heritage Manor, Deer Park, TX
San Joaquin Gardens Health Facility, Fresno, CA
San Jose Care & Guidance Center, San Jose, CA
San Jose Nursing Center, San Antonio, TX
San Juan Living Center, Montrose, CO
San Juan Manor, Farmington, NM
San Juan Nursing Home, Anacortes, WA
San Juan Nursing Home Inc, San Juan, TX
San Luis Care Center, Alamosa, CO
San Luis Convalescent Hospital, Newman, CA
San Luis Manor, Green Bay, WI
San Marco Convalescent Hospital, Walnut Creek, CA
San Marino Manor, San Gabriel, CA
San Mateo Convalescent Hospital, San Mateo, CA
San Pedro Manor, San Antonio, TX
San Pedro Peninsula Hospital Pavilion, San Pedro, CA
San Saba Nursing Home Inc, San Saba, TX

San Simeon by the Sound—Skilled Nursing Facility, Greenport, NY

San Tomas Convalescent Hospital, San Jose, CA

Sanborn Gratiot Memorial Home, Port Huron, MI

Sandalwood Convalescent Home, Oxford, MA

Sandalwood Healthcare Centre, Wheaton, IL

Sandburg Care Center Inc, Galesburg, IL

Sande Convalescent Home, Big Sandy, MT

Sanders Community Residence, Aiken, SC

Francis N Sanders Nursing Home Inc, Gloucester, VA

Sandhaven, Lamar, CO

Sandhaven Convalescent Center, Sandwich, IL

Sandhills Manor, Broken Bow, NE

Sandmont Gala Nursing Home, Trenton, GA

Sandpiper Bay Healthcare Center, Wichita, KS

Sandpiper Convalescent Center, Mount Pleasant, SC

Sandpoint Manor, Sandpoint, ID

Sandretto Hills Care Center, Prescott, AZ

Sands Point Nursing Home, Port Washington, NY

Sandstone Area Nursing Home, Sandstone, MN

Sandstone Heights, Little River, KS

Sandusky Nursing Home Inc, Sandusky, OH

Sandy Creek Nursing Home, Wayland, MI

Sandy Regional Convalescent & Rehabilitation, Sandy, UT

Sandy Ridge Care Center, Milton, FL

Sandy River Nursing Care Center, Farmington, ME

Sanfield Manor, Hartland, ME

Sanford Health Care Facility, Sanford, ME

Sanford Memorial Hospital, Farmington, MN

Sanger Convalescent Hospital, Sanger, CA

Sanilac Medical Care Facility, Sandusky, MI

Sannes Skogdalen, Soldiers Grove, WI

Sansbury Memorial Infirmary, Saint Catherine, KY

Santa Anita Convalescent Hospital, Temple City, CA

Santa Barbara Convalescent Hospital, Santa Barbara, CA

Santa Clarita Convalescent Hospital, Newhall, CA

Santa Clarita Convalescent Hospital, Santa Clarita, CA

Santa Fe Convalescent Hospital, Long Beach, CA

Santa Fe Trail Nursing Center, Burlingame, KS

Santa Maria El Mirador Calle Quedo, Alcalde, NM

Santa Maria El Mirador Group Home A, Alcalde, NM

Santa Maria El Mirador Group Home B, Alcalde, NM

Santa Maria El Mirador Group Home C, Alcalde, NM

Santa Maria El Mirador Sycamore, Alcalde, NM

Santa Maria El Mirador Vista del Sur, Alcalde, NM

Santa Marie Nursing Home, Green Bay, WI

Santa Monica Convalarium, Santa Monica, CA

Santa Monica Convalescent Center II, Santa Monica, CA

Santa Paula Health Care, Santa Paula, CA

Santa Rita Health Care Center, Green Valley, AZ

Santa Rita Health Care Center, Tucson, AZ

Santa Rosa Convalescent Center, Tucson, AZ

Santa Rosa Convalescent Center, Milton, FL

Santa Rosa Convalescent Hospital, Santa Rosa, CA

Santa Rosa Extended Care Facility, Guayamas, PR

Santa Ynez Valley Recovery Residence, Solvang, CA

Sapulpa Nursing Center Inc, Sapulpa, OK

Sarasota Nursing Pavilion, Sarasota, FL

Sarasota Welfare Home Inc, Sarasota, FL

Saratoga County Infirmary/Health Related Facility, Ballston Spa, NY

Saratoga Hospital Nursing Home, Saratoga Springs, NY

Saratoga of Evanston, Evanston, IL

Saratoga Place Subacute Hospital, Saratoga, CA

Sarcoxie Nursing Center, Sarcoxie, MO

Sargent Manor Health Care Center, Forman, ND

Sargent Nursing Center, Sargent, NE

Sartori Memorial Hospital, Cedar Falls, IA

Sauer Memorial Home, Winona, MN

Sauk County Health Care Center, Reedsburg, WI

Saunders County Care Center, Wahoo, NE

Saunders House, Lower Merion, PA

Savana Cay Manor, Port Saint Lucie, FL

Savannah Beach Nursing Home Inc, Tybee Island, GA

Savannah Convalescent Center, Savannah, GA

Savannah Square Retirement Community Nursing Home, Savannah, GA

Savoy Care Center Inc, Mamou, LA

Savoy Convalescent Home, New Bedford, MA

Savoy Medical Center Skilled Nursing Unit, Mamou, LA

Saxony Health Center, Saxonburg, PA

Saxton Riverside Care Center, Saint Joseph, MO

Saybrook Convalescent Hospital, Old Saybrook, CT

Saylor Lane Convalescent Hospital, Sacramento, CA

Sayre Christian Village Nursing Home, Lexington, KY

Sayre House Inc, Sayre, PA

Scalabrini Villa, North Kingstown, RI

Scallop Shell Nursing Home Inc, South Kingstown, RI

Scandia Village Retirement Center, Sister Bay, WI

Scandinavian Home for the Aged, Cranston, RI

Scenery Hill Manor Inc, Indiana, PA

Scenic Circle Care Center, Modesto, CA

Scenic City Manor, Iowa Falls, IA

Scenic Hills Care Center, Ferdinand, IN

Scenic Hills Nursing Center, Bidwell, OH

Scenic View Health Care Center, Baldwin, GA

Scenic View Nursing Home, Millersburg, OH

Frances Schervier Home & Hospital, New York, NY

Scheurer Hospital—Long-Term Care Unit, Pigeon, MI

Schleicher County Medical Center, Eldorado, TX

A W Schlesinger Geriatric Center Inc, Beaumont, TX

Schmitt Woodland Hills Inc, Richland Center, WI

Schnepp Health Care Center, Saint Louis, MI

Schofield Residence, Kenmore, NY

Schoolcraft Medical Care Facility, Manistique, MI

Schooner Estates—Seville Park Plaza, Auburn, ME

Schowalter Villa, Hesston, KS

Schroder Manor Retirement Community, Hamilton, OH

Samuel Schulman Institute, Brooklyn, NY

Samuel Schulman Institute for Nursing & Rehabilitation, Brooklyn, NY

Schulze Nursing Home, Dayton, OH

Schussler Rest Home, Worcester, MA

Schuyler County Nursing Home, Queen City, MO

Schuyler Hospital Skilled Nursing Facility, Montour Falls, NY

Schuyler Nursing Center, Schuyler, NE

Scioto Memorial Convalescent Center, Portsmouth, OH

Scioto Street Home, Urbana, OH

Scituate Ocean Manor Nursing Home, Scituate, MA

Scothwood Health Care Center, Bloomington, IL

Scotia Village, Laurinburg, NC

Scotland County Nursing Home, Memphis, MO

Scotland Good Samaritan Center, Scotland, SD

Scott County Nursing & Personal Care Home, Morton, MS

Scott County Nursing Center, Winchester, IL

Scott County Nursing Home, Oneida, TN

Elizabeth Scott Memorial Care Center, Maumee, OH

John Scott House Nursing & Rehabilitation Center, Braintree, MA

Scott Manor Nursing Home Inc, Indianapolis, IN

Mary Scott Nursing Center, Dayton, OH

Scott Nursing Home, Smyrna, DE

Scott Villa Living Center, Scottsburg, IN

Scottish Home, North Riverside, IL

Scottish Home, Riverside, IL

Scottish Rite Park, Des Moines, IA

Scott's Rest Home, Haverhill, MA

Scottsbluff Nursing Center, Scottsbluff, NE

Scottsboro Nursing Home, Scottsboro, AL

Scottsburg Nursing Home, Scottsburg, IN

Scottsdale Heritage Court, Scottsdale, AZ

Scottsdale Memorial Convalescent Plaza, Scottsdale, AZ

Scottsdale Memorial Skilled Nursing Facility, Scottsdale, AZ

Scottsdale Village Square, Scottsdale, AZ

Scribner Good Samaritan Center, Scribner, NE

Scripps Home, Altadena, CA

Scripps Memorial Hospital—Oceanview Convalescent Hospital, Encinitas, CA

Sea-Crest Health Care Center, Brooklyn, NY

Sea Level Hospital—SNF/ICF, Sea Level, NC

Sea Spray Group Home, Lewes, DE

Sea View Hospital & Home, Staten Island, NY

Sea View Nursing Home, Rowley, MA

Seabreeze Care Center, Texas City, TX

Seabrook of Hilton Inc, Hilton Head Island, SC

Seabury Center, Odessa, TX

Seacoast Health Center Inc, Hampton, NH

Seacrest Convalescent Hospital, San Pedro, CA

Seacrest Nursing & Retirement Center, West Haven, CT

Seacrest Village Nursing Home, Tuckerton, NJ

Seaford Retirement & Rehabilitation Center, Seaford, DE

Seagate Nursing Home, Toledo, OH

Seago Manor, Seagoville, TX

Seal Residential Care Home, Augusta, KS

Searles Group Home, Rockford, IL

Sears Manor, Brunswick, GA

Sears Memorial Methodist Center, Abilene, TX

Seaside Care Center, Fullerton, CA

Seaside Care Center, Portland, OR

Seaside Nursing & Retirement Home, Portland, ME

Seatoma Convalescent Center, Des Moines, WA

Seattle Keiro, Seattle, WA

Seattle Specialized Group Home, Seattle, WA

Seaview Convalescent Hospital, Eureka, CA

Sebasticook Valley Health Care Facility, Pittsfield, ME

Sebastopol Convalescent Hospital, Sebastopol, CA

Sebo Heritage Manor Nursing Home, Hobart, IN

Seborg Terrace, Rockford, IL

Sebring Care Center, Sebring, FL

Secessionville Community Residence, Charleston, SC

Second Midlands ICMRF, Columbia, SC

Second Shamrock Care Center, Kingfisher, OK

Secrest-Giffin Care Facility, Sandusky, OH

Sedgwick Convalescent Center, Sedgwick, KS

Sedgwick County Hospital & Nursing Home, Julesburg, CO

Seguin Convalescent Home, Seguin, TX

Seguin Services Home I, Berwyn, IL

Seguin Services Home III, Berwyn, IL

Seguin Services Home IV, Cicero, IL

Sehome Park Care Center, Bellingham, WA
Seidle Memorial Hospital, Mechanicsburg, PA
Seiling Nursing Center, Seiling, OK
Seitz Nursing Home, Dallastown, PA
Selah Convalescent Home Inc, Selah, WA
Selby Good Samaritan Center, Selby, SD
Self Nursing Home Inc, Hueytown, AL
Selfhelp Home for the Aged, Chicago, IL
Selinsgrove Center, Selinsgrove, PA
Sells Rest Home Inc, Matthews, MO
Selma Convalescent Hospital, Selma, CA
SEM Haven Health Care Center, Milford, OH
Seminary Manor, Galesburg, IL
Seminary Memorial Home, Red Wing, MN
Seminole Estates Nursing Center Inc, Seminole, OK
Seminole Manor, Donalsonville, GA
Seminole Nursing Center, Seminole, TX
Seminole Nursing Pavilion, Seminole, FL
Seminole Pioneer Nursing Home Inc, Seminole, OK
Seminole Villa Care Center, Springfield, OH
SEMO Care Center, Sikeston, MO
Senath Nursing Home, Senath, MO
Senatobia Convalescent Home, Senatobia, MS
Seneca Manor, West Seneca, NY
Seneca Nursing Home & HRF, Waterloo, NY
Senior Citizens Center, Coushatta, LA
Senior Citizens Home, Hosmer, SD
Senior Citizens—Merrill Residence, Kalamazoo, MI
Senior Citizens Nursing Home, Madisonville, KY
Senior Citizens Nursing Home, Broken Arrow, OK
Senior Citizens Nursing Home, Winters, TX
Senior Citizens Nursing Home, Spokane, WA
Senior Estates of Kansas City, Kansas City, MO
Senior Health Care Inc, Wilmington, OH
Senior Home, Montezuma, IA
Senior Home, Monticello, IA
Senior Manor Nursing Center Inc, Sparta, IL
Senior Village Nursing Home, Opelousas, LA
Senior Village Nursing Home, Blanchard, OK
Senior Village Nursing Home, Perryton, TX
Sentara—Hampton General Hospital, Hampton, VA
Sentara Nursing Center, Barco, NC
Sentara Nursing Center—Chesapeake, Chesapeake, VA
Sentara Nursing Center—Norfolk, Norfolk, VA
Sentara Nursing Center—Portsmouth, Portsmouth, VA
Sentry Care Simpsonville Inc, Simpsonville, SC
Sephardic Home for the Aged Inc, Brooklyn, NY
Sepulveda Convalescent Hospital Inc, Van Nuys, CA
Sequatchie Health Care Center, Dunlap, TN
Sequim Nursing Center, Sequim, WA
Sequoias, Portola Valley, CA
Sequoias San Francisco Convalescent Hospital, San Francisco, CA
Sequoyah East, Roland, OK
Sequoyah Manor, Sallisaw, OK
Lefa L Seran Skilled Nursing Facility, Hawthorne, NV
Serene Manor Medical Center, Knoxville, TN
Serenity Corner, Spearfish, SD
Serenity Haven Nursing Home, Garland, TX
Serenity Hill Nursing Home, Wrentham, MA
Serenity Rest Home, Merrimac, MA
Serrano Convalescent Hospital—North, Los Angeles, CA
Serrano Convalescent Hospital—South, Los Angeles, CA
Sessions Homestead, Livingston, MT
Seth Mann Home for the Aged II, Randolph, MA
Elizabeth Seton Residence, Wellesley, MA
Seton Hill Manor, Baltimore, MD
Seven Acres Jewish Geriatric Center, Houston, TX
Seven Eleven North High, Lake City, MN

Seven Hills Health Care Center, Lynchburg, VA
Seven Oaks Convalescent Care Center, Bonham, TX
Seven Oaks Nursing Home Inc, Olney, TX
1778 Prosperity Inc, Maplewood, MN
7th Street, Brighton, CO
Seventh Street Home, Faribault, MN
Seventh Ward General Hospital—Skilled Nursing Facility, Hammond, LA
Severin Intermediate Care Home, Benton, IL
Seville Nursing Center, Salem, MO
Therese K Sexton Home—North, North Mankato, MN
Therese K Sexton Home—South, North Mankato, MN
Seymour Care Center, Seymour, IA
Shabbona HealthCare Center, Shabbona, IL
Shadescrest Health Care Center, Jasper, AL
Shadow Hill Convalescent Hospital, Sunland, CA
Shadowbrook Convalescent Hospital, Oroville, CA
Shady Acres Convalescent Center, Douglas, GA
Shady Acres Health Care Center, Newton, TX
Shady Creek Health Care Facility, Greencastle, IN
Shady Grove Adventist Nursing Center, Rockville, MD
Shady Grove Rest Home, Kennesaw, GA
Shady Lake Nursing Home, Lake Providence, LA
Shady Lane Gloucester County Home, Clarksboro, NJ
Shady Lane Home Inc, Manitowoc, WI
Shady Lane Nursing Home, Wadena, MN
Shady Lawn, Savannah, MO
Shady Lawn East, Kenosha, WI
Shady Lawn Home, Cynthiana, KY
Shady Lawn Home, Dalton, OH
Shady Lawn Nursing Home, Cadiz, KY
Shady Lawn Nursing Home Inc, Vicksburg, MS
Shady Lawn Rest Home Inc, Hadley, MA
Shady Lawn West, Kenosha, WI
Shady Nook Care Center, Lawrenceburg, IN
Shady Oak Nursing Home Inc, Moulton, TX
Shady Oaks, Lake City, IA
Shady Oaks, Monroe, LA
Shady Oaks Health Care Center, Thayer, MO
Shady Oaks Manor 1, Abilene, TX
Shady Oaks Manor 2, Abilene, TX
Shady Oaks Nursing Center, Sherman, TX
Shady Rest Care Center, Cascade, IA
Shady Rest Care Center Inc, Pryor, OK
Shady Rest Nursing Home, Fort Myers, FL
Shady View Nursing Home, Oklahoma City, OK
Shadyside Care Center, Shadyside, OH
Shadyside Nursing & Rehabilitation Center, Pittsburgh, PA
Shadyside Nursing Home, Duncanville, TX
Shadyway Group Home, Wayzata, MN
Shaffer Plaza, Steubenville, OH
Shafter Convalescent Hospital, Shafter, CA
Shakamak Good Samaritan Center, Jasonville, IN
Shakopee Friendship Manor, Shakopee, MN
Shalem Rest, Massillon, OH
Shalimar Plaza Nursing Home, Salina, KS
Shalom Geriatric Center Inc, Kansas City, MO
Shalom Home, Saint Paul, MN
Shalom Nursing Home, Mount Vernon, NY
Shamrock Health Care, Dublin, GA
Shandin Hills Behavior Therapy Center, San Bernardino, CA
Shandin Hills Convalescent Hospital, San Bernardino, CA
Shane Hill Nursing Home Inc, Rockford, OH
Shangri-La Corporation, Salem, OR
Shangri-La Health Care Center, LaFontaine, IN
Shangri-La Rest Home Inc, Medina, OH
Shannon House, Chicago, IL
Shannondale Health Care & Retirement Center, Knoxville, TN

Shanoan Springs Residence Inc, Chickasha, OK
Share Medical Center, Alva, OK
Sharmar Nursing Center, Pueblo, CO
Sharon Care Center, Los Angeles, CA
Sharon Care Center Inc, Centralia, WA
Sharon General Hospital Long-Term Care Unit, Sharon, PA
Sharon Health Care Elms Inc, Peoria, IL
Sharon Health Care Oaks Inc, Peoria, IL
Sharon Health Care Pines Inc, Peoria, IL
Sharon Health Care Regency, Peoria, IL
Sharon Health Care Woods Inc, Peoria, IL
Sharon Heights Convalescent Hospital, Menlo Park, CA
Sharon Manor Nursing Home, Sharon, MA
Sharon Nursing Home, Olney, MD
Sharon Towers, Charlotte, NC
Sharon Village, Charlotte, NC
Sharonlane Inc, Shawnee, KS
Sharonview Nursing Home, South Vienna, OH
Sharp Knollwood, San Diego, CA
Sharp Nursing Home, Sidney, AR
Sharp's Personal Care Home, Falmouth, KY
Shasta Convalescent Hospital, Redding, CA
Shasta Home, Columbus, OH
Shaughnessy-Kaplan Rehabilitation Skilled Nursing Facility, Salem, MA
Edwin Shaw Hospital, Akron, OH
Hannah B G Shaw Home for the Aged Inc, Middleborough, MA
Shawn Manor Nursing Home, Ponca City, OK
Shawnee Care Center, Shawnee, OK
Shawnee Christian Nursing Center, Herrin, IL
Shawnee Colonial Estates Nursing Home Inc, Shawnee, OK
Shawnee House, Harrisburg, IL
Shawnee Manor, Lima, OH
Shawnee Shelter Care, Simpson, IL
Shawnee Springs Nursing Home, Winchester, VA
Shawnee Sunset Estates, Shawnee, OK
SHC Hastings House, Lodi, OH
SHC Lafayette Road Home, Medina, OH
Shea Convalescent Hospital, San Bernardino, CA
Shea Convalescent Hospital, Upland, CA
Shea Convalescent Hospital, Whittier, CA
Shearer Richardson Memorial Nursing Home, Okolona, MS
Sheboygan County Comprehensive Health Center, Sheboygan Falls, WI
Sheboygan Retirement Home & Beach Health Care Center Inc, Sheboygan, WI
Sheepscot Valley Health Center, Coopers Mills, ME
Sheepshead Nursing Home, Brooklyn, NY
Sheffield Care Center, Sheffield, IA
Sheffield Convalescent Hospital, San Francisco, CA
Shelby Convalescent Center, Shelby, NC
Shelby County Health Care Center, Memphis, TN
Shelby Manor Health Center, Shelbyville, KY
Shelby Memorial Home, Shelbyville, IL
Shelby Memorial Hospital Nursing Home, Shelbyville, IL
Sheldon Healthcare Inc, Sheldon, IL
Sheldonville Nursing Home, Wrentham, MA
Shell Rock Care Center, Shell Rock, IA
Sheltering Arms Nursing Home, Walnut Ridge, AR
Sheltering Oak, Island Lake, IL
Sheltering Pine Convalescent Hospital, Millbrae, CA
Shelton Group Home, Richville, MN
Shelton Lakes Residence & Health Care Center Inc, Shelton, CT
Shemwell Nursing Home, Providence, KY
Shenandoah County Memorial Hospital—Long-Term Care Unit, Woodstock, VA
Shenandoah Geriatric Treatment Center, Staunton, VA
Shenandoah Home Inc, Ranson, WV
Shenandoah Manor, Ronceverte, WV
Shenandoah Manor Nursing Center, Shenandoah, PA

Shenandoah Manor Nursing Home, Clifton Forge, VA
Shenandoah Valley Health Care Center, Buena Vista, VA
Shenango Presbyterian Home, New Wilmington, PA
Shepherd Hills Health Care, LaFayette, GA
Shepherd of the Hill, Kendallville, IN
Shepherd of the Valley Care Center, Casper, WY
Shepherd of the Valley Nursing Home, Niles, OH
Sheppard Health Care Inc, Ellenboro, WV
Doctor Philip Sher Jewish Home, Omaha, NE
Sheraton Convalescent Center, Sepulveda, CA
Sherbrooke Nursing Center, Grand Rapids, MI
Sheridan Care Center, Sheridan, OR
Sheridan Health Care Center, Zion, IL
Sheridan Health Care Center Inc, Sheridan, IN
Sheridan Manor Nursing Home Inc, Tonawanda, NY
Sheridan Memorial Nursing Home, Plentywood, MT
Sheridan Nursing Home, Kenosha, WI
Sheridan Special Care Center Inc, Sheridan, IN
Sheriden Woods Health Care Center, Bristol, CT
Sheriff Manor Nursing Home, Boston, MA
Sherman County Good Samaritan Center, Goodland, KS
Sherman Nursing Center, Sherman, TX
Sherman Oaks Care Center, Muskegon, MI
Sherman Oaks Convalescent Hospital, Sherman Oaks, CA
Sherrelwood Residential Care Facility, Denver, CO
Sherrill House Inc, Boston, MA
Sherwin Manor Nursing Center, Chicago, IL
Sherwood Care Center, Williams Bay, WI
Sherwood Convalescent Home, Indianapolis, IN
Sherwood Convalescent Hospital, Van Nuys, CA
Sherwood Health Care, Bryan, TX
Sherwood Health Care of Lubbock Inc, Lubbock, TX
Sherwood Manor Inc, Sequim, WA
Sherwood Manor Nursing Home, Tulsa, OK
Sherwood Oaks, Mars, PA
Sherwood Oaks Health Center, Fort Bragg, CA
Sherwood Park Nursing Home Inc, Salem, OR
Sherwood Terrace Nursing Center, Tacoma, WA
Shetley Nursing Home, Bell City, MO
Sheyenne Care Center, Valley City, ND
Shiawassee County Medical Care Facility, Corunna, MI
Shields Adult Care Home Inc, Pittsburg, KS
Shields Nursing Center, El Cerrito, CA
Shiloh Manor of Canton Inc, Canton, KS
Shingle Creek Option, Brooklyn Park, MN
Shipley Manor Health Center, Wilmington, DE
Shire—Dungarvin IV, Elk River, MN
John P Shirk Memorial Home, Faulkton, SD
Shirkey Leisure Acres, Richmond, MO
Shoals Nursing Home, Tuscumbia, AL
John H Shook Home for the Aged, Chambersburg, PA
Shore Acres Nursing & Convalescent Home, Saint Petersburg, FL
Shore Cliff Retirement Home, Gloucester, MA
Shore Haven Nursing Home, Grand Haven, MI
Shore Home West, Skokie, IL
Shore Homes East, Evanston, IL
Shore View Nursing Home, Brooklyn, NY
Shoreham Convalescent Center, Marietta, GA
Shoreham Terrace, Saint Joseph, MI
Shorehaven, Oconomowoc, WI
Shoreline Healthcare Center, Taft, TX
Shores Health Center, Bradenton, FL
Shorewood Heights Health Care Center, Shorewood, WI
Shoshone Living Center, Kellogg, ID

Shoshone Medical Center Extended Care Unit, Kellogg, ID
Shreveport Manor Guest Care, Shreveport, LA
Shrewsbury Lutheran Retirement Village, Shrewsbury, PA
Shrewsbury Manor Nursing Home, Shrewsbury, NJ
Shrewsbury Nursing Home Inc, Shrewsbury, MA
Shuffield Nursing Home Inc 1, Brady, TX
Shuffield Rest Home Inc No 2, Brady, TX
Shuksan Convalescent Center, Bellingham, WA
Shurtleff Manor Residential, Mount Carmel, IL
Sibley Care Center, Sibley, IA
Sidney Health Center, Sidney, IA
Sidney Nursing Center, Sidney, NE
Sidney Square Convalescent Center, Pittsburgh, PA
Siemers Board & Care, Montgomery, MN
Siemon Nursing Home Inc, Somerset, PA
Sierra Convalescent Center, Carson City, NV
Sierra Developmental Center, Sparks, NV
Sierra Health Care Center, Sparks, NV
Sierra Health Care Center, Truth or Consequences, NM
Sierra Health Care Convalescent Hospital, Davis, CA
Sierra Madre Skilled Nursing Facility, Sierra Madre, CA
Sierra Meadows Convalescent Hospital, Oakhurst, CA
Sierra Valley Community Hospital, Loyalton, CA
Sierra View Care Center, Baldwin Park, CA
Sierra View Convalescent Hospital, Fresno, CA
Sierra View Homes Inc, Reedley, CA
Sierra Vista, Highland, CA
Sierra Vista Care Center, Sierra Vista, AZ
Sierra Vista Care Center, Napa, CA
Sierra Vista Care Center, Oregon City, OR
Sierra Vista Nursing Home, Loveland, CO
Siesta Home of Pratt Inc, Pratt, KS
Siesta Park Retirement Home, Oskaloosa, IA
Sifly Street Community Residence, Orangeburg, SC
Sigourney Care Center, Sigourney, IA
Sikeston Convalescent Center, Sikeston, MO
Sikeston Health Care Inc, Sikeston, MO
Sikeston Nursing Center, Sikeston, MO
Silas Creek Manor, Winston-Salem, NC
Silent Night Nursing Home, Lancaster, TX
Silsbee Convalescent Center, Silsbee, TX
Silver Bell Nursing Home, Versailles, IN
Silver Bluff, Canton, NC
Silver Court Nursing Center Inc, Cherry Hill, NJ
Silver Creek Manor, Bristol, RI
Silver Creek Manor, San Antonio, TX
Silver Crest Manor Inc, Anadarko, OK
Silver Cross Home, Brookhaven, MS
Silver Gardens Care Center, Silverton, OR
Silver Haven Care Center, Burleson, TX
Silver Haven Nursing Home, Schenectady, NY
Silver Lake Nursing & Rehabilitation Center, Dover, DE
Silver Lake Nursing & Rehabilitation Center, Bristol, PA
Silver Lake Nursing Home, Staten Island, NY
Silver Leaves, Garland, TX
Silver Oak Health Center, Hutchinson, KS
Silver Oaks Nursing Center, New Castle, PA
Silver Ridge Village, Bullhead City, AZ
Silver Spring Convalescent Center, Milwaukee, WI
Silver Star Nursing Home, Ardmore, OK
Silver Threads Nursing Center, Houston, TX
Silver Wood Good Samaritan, Silverton, ID
Silverbrook Manor, Niles, MI
Silver Stream Nursing & Rehabilitation Center, Spring House, PA
Simater Memorial Home Inc, Minonk, IL
L O Simenstad Nursing Unit, Osceola, WI
L O Simenstad Nursing Care Unit, Hudson, WI
Simi Valley Adventist Hospital, Simi, CA

Simla Good Samaritan Center, Simla, CO
Simmons Loving Care Health Facility, Gary, IN
Simmon's Nursing Home Inc, Violet, LA
Simmons Nursing Home Inc, Billerica, MA
Simpson House Inc, Philadelphia, PA
Simpson Memorial Home, West Liberty, IA
Simpsons Foster Care, Aguilar, CO
Marion Sims Nursing Center, Lancaster, SC
Singing River Hospital System—Extended Care Facility, Pascagoula, MS
Singleton Health Care Center, Cleveland, OH
Sinton Manor, Sinton, TX
Sioux Care Center, Sioux Rapids, IA
Sioux Center Community Hospital, Sioux Center, IA
Sister James' Nursing Home, Yankton, SD
Sisters of Bon Secours Nursing Care Center, Saint Clair Shores, MI
Sisters of Charity Hospital Skilled Nursing Facility, Buffalo, NY
Sitka Pioneers Home, Sitka, AK
Charles T Sitrin Nursing Home Company Inc, New Hartford, NY
Siuslaw Care Center, Florence, OR
Sixth Street House, Rochester, MN
Skaalen Sunset Home, Stoughton, WI
Skagit Valley Convalescent Center Inc, Sedro Woolley, WA
Skiatook Nursing Home, Skiatook, OK
Skilled Nursing Facility at North Hill, Needham, MA
Skilled Nursing Facility of Flagstaff Medical Center, Flagstaff, AZ
Skilled Nursing Facility of St Tammany Parish Hospital, Covington, LA
Skokie Meadows Nursing Center No I, Skokie, IL
Skokie Meadows Nursing Center No II, Skokie, IL
Sky View Haven Nursing Home, Croton-on-Hudson, NY
Sky View Nursing Center, Hurley, WI
Sky Vue Terrace Nursing Center, Pittsburgh, PA
Skyland Care Center Inc, Sylva, NC
Skyline Adolescent Services, Los Angeles, CA
Skyline Convalescent, Salinas, CA
Skyline Convalescent Hospital, Los Angeles, CA
Skyline Convalescent Hospital, San Jose, CA
Skyline Healthcare, Pocatello, ID
Skyline Manor & Skyline Villa, Omaha, NE
Skyline Manor Nursing Home, Floyd, VA
Skyline Nursing Home, DeSoto, TX
Skyline Terrace Convalescent Home, Woodstock, VA
Skyline Terrace Nursing Center, Tulsa, OK
Skylyn Health Center, Spartanburg, SC
Skyview Convalescent Hospital Inc, Wallingford, CT
Skyview Living Center of Stamford, Stamford, TX
Skyview Living Center—San Antonio, San Antonio, TX
Skyview Nursing Center, Oklahoma City, OK
Skyview Nursing Home, Jacksonville, IL
Skyview Personal Care Home, Mayfield, KY
Slack Nursing Home, Gothenburg, NE
Slate Belt Nursing & Rehabilitation Center, Bangor, PA
Slaton Care Center, Slaton, TX
Slayton Manor, Slayton, MN
Sleepy Eye Care Center, Sleepy Eye, MN
Sleepy Hollow Manor Nursing Home, Annandale, VA
Sleigh Bell Residence, Youngstown, OH
Slovene Home for the Aged, Cleveland, OH
Smackover Nursing Home, Smackover, AR
Barbara P Smiley Living Center, Peoria, IL
Smith-Barr Manor, Louisiana, MO
Smith County Health Care Center, Carthage, TN
Eunice C Smith, Alton, IL
Gerrit Smith Infirmary, Eaton, NY
Smith Group Home, Frazee, MN
Helen Lewis Smith Pavilion, Fairbury, IL
Smith Home for Aged Women, Ashtabula, OH

Smith House Skilled Nursing Facility, Stamford, CT
Smith Medical Nursing Care Center, Sandersville, GA
Smith Nursing & Convalescent Home Inc, Mountain Top, PA
Smith Nursing Home Inc, Canton, OH
Smith Rest Home, Worcester, MA
Smith Square, Moline, IL
Stephen Smith Home for the Aged, Philadelphia, PA
Washington & Jane Smith Home, Chicago, IL
Ella Smither Geriatric Center, Huntsville, TX
Smith's Nursing Home, Wolfe City, TX
Smithview Manor Nursing Home, Lawson, MO
Smithville Convalescent Center, Smithville, MO
Smithville Western Care Center, Wooster, OH
Smyrna Nursing Center Inc, Smyrna, TN
Smyth County Community Hospital Inc—Long-Term Care Unit, Marion, VA
Snapper Creek Nursing Home Inc, Miami, FL
Snellville Nursing & Rehabilitation Center, Snellville, GA
Snow Valley Living Center, Lisle, IL
Edward Snyder Old People's Home, Reedsburg, WI
Snyder Memorial Health Care Center, Marienville, PA
Snyder Nursing Center, Snyder, TX
Snyder Nursing Home Inc, Salem, VA
Snyder Oaks Care Center, Snyder, TX
Snyder Village Health Center, Metamora, IL
Snyder's Vaughn-Haven Inc, Rushville, IL
Social Circle Intermediate Care Facility, Social Circle, GA
Society for Danish Old Peoples Home, Chicago, IL
Society for Handicapped Citizens of Medina County Inc, Wadsworth, OH
Socorro General Hospital, Socorro, NM
Socorro Good Samaritan Village, Socorro, NM
Sodonia's Home, Fulton, MO
Sogge Good Samaritan Center, Windom, MN
Soldiers & Sailors Memorial Hospital Health Related Facility, Penn Yan, NY
Soldiers' Home in Massachusetts, Chelsea, MA
Solheim Lutheran Home, Los Angeles, CA
Solomon Valley Manor, Stockton, KS
Solon Nursing Care Center, Solon, IA
Solstice—Brookhollow, Boise, ID
Solstice Inc—Shenandoah, Boise, ID
Solstice—Lakewood, Boise, ID
Sombrillo Intermediate Care Facility, Los Alamos, NM
Somers Manor Nursing Home Inc, Somers, NY
Somerset Community Hospital, Somerset, PA
Somerset Golden State Convalescent Hospital, West Sacramento, CA
Somerset House, Chicago, IL
Somerset Manor Inc, Bingham, ME
Somerset Nursing Home, Reading, MA
Somerset State Hospital—Mentally Retarded Unit, Somerset, PA
Somerset Valley Nursing Home, Bound Brook, NJ
Somerville Health Care Center, Somerville, TN
Somerville Home for the Aged, Somerville, MA
Sonogee Estates, Bar Harbor, ME
Sonoma Acres, Sonoma, CA
Sonora Convalescent Hospital Inc, Sonora, CA
Sorenson Convalescent Hospital, Whittier, CA
Souderton Mennonite Homes, Souderton, PA
Sound View Specialized Care Center, West Haven, CT
Sourdough Place, Valdez, AK
Souris Valley Care Center, Velva, ND
South Bay Child Care Center, Hawthorne, CA
South Bay Keiro Nursing Home, Gardena, CA
South Broadway Nursing Home Inc, New Philadelphia, OH
South Cameron Hospital, Cameron, LA

South Cape Nursing Home, Cape May Court House, NJ
Coastal Center—Department of Mental Retardation, Ladson, SC
South Carolina Episcopal Retirement Community, Columbia, SC
South Carolina Vocational Rehabilitation Comprehensive Center, West Columbia, SC
South Center Manor, Center City, MN
South County Convalescent Center, Arroyo Grande, CA
South County Nursing Centre, North Kingstown, RI
South Cove Manor, Boston, MA
South Dallas Nursing Home, Dallas, TX
South Davis Community Hospital Inc, Bountiful, UT
South 4th Street, Montrose, CO
South Fulton Hospital—Extended Care Facility, East Point, GA
South Gate Care Center, Saint Louis, MO
South Harper Street Community Residence, Laurens, SC
South Haven Manor Nursing Home, Montgomery, AL
South Haven Nursing Home Inc, Birmingham, AL
South Heritage Nursing Center, Saint Petersburg, FL
South Hills Convalescent Center, Canonsburg, PA
South Hills Health Care Center, Eugene, OR
South Hills Manor, Dimmitt, TX
South Lafourche Nursing Center, Cut Off, LA
South Lawn Shelter Care, Bunker Hill, IL
South Lyon Community Hospital, Yerington, NV
South Main Community Residence, Greenwood, SC
South Meadows Nursing Home, Diboll, TX
South Mississippi Retardation Center, Long Beach, MS
South Monaco Care Center, Denver, CO
South Morgan Health Care Center, Decatur, AL
South Mountain Manor Inc, Phoenix, AZ
South Mountain Restoration Center, South Mountain, PA
South Oaks Health Care Inc, McMinnville, TN
South Park Care Center, Kansas City, MO
South Park Development Center, Brownwood, TX
South Park Guest Care Center, Shreveport, LA
South Park Health Care Center, Oklahoma City, OK
South Park Inc, Pocatello, ID
South Park Manor, Corpus Christi, TX
South Pasadena Convalescent Hospital, South Pasadena, CA
South Peninsula Hospital, Homer, AK
South Place Nursing Center, Athens, TX
South Plains Nursing Center, Brownfield, TX
South Port Nursing Center, Port Charlotte, FL
South Portland Nursing Home Inc, South Portland, ME
South Roanoke Nursing Home Inc, Roanoke, VA
South Salem Care Center, Salem, OR
South Shore Convalescent Hospital, Alameda, CA
South Shore Health Care Center, South Shore, KY
South Shore Manor, Saint Francis, WI
South Shore Nursing Facility, Rockland, MA
South Shore Nursing Home Inc, Freeport, NY
South Side Manor Nursing Home, Pueblo, CO
South Street Health Care Center, Lafayette, IN
South Valley Health Center, West Jordan, UT
South Washington Street Nursing Home, Tiffin, OH
South Windsor Nursing Center, South Windsor, CT
Southampton Estates, Southampton, PA
Southampton Memorial Hospital—East Pavilion, Franklin, VA

Southampton Nursing Home Inc, Southampton, NY
Southaven Health Care Center, Southaven, MS
Southdade Catholic Nursing Home Inc, Miami, FL
Southdale Health Care Services Inc, Superior, WI
Southdown Care Center, Houma, LA
Southeast Arizona Medical Center, Douglas, AZ
Southeast Colorado Hospital & LTC, Springfield, CO
Southeast Nursing Center, San Antonio, TX
Southeastern Dakota Nursing Home, Vermillion, SD
Southeastern General Hospital Long-Term Care Facility, Lumberton, NC
Southeastern Nursing Home, Indianapolis, IN
Southeastern Virginia Training Center, Chesapeake, VA
Southern Baptist Hospital—Skilled Nursing Facility, New Orleans, LA
Southern Hills Nursing Center, Tulsa, OK
Southern Hospitality Living Center, Saint George, UT
Southern Manor Inc, Temple, TX
Southern Nursing Home, Fordyce, AR
Southern Oaks Health Care, Saint Cloud, FL
Southern Oaks Manor, Oklahoma City, OK
Southern Pines Nursing Center, New Port Richey, FL
Southern Pointe, Colbert, OK
Southern Virginia Mental Health Institute, Danville, VA
Southern Wake Short-Term Skilled Nursing Facility, Fuquay-Varina, NC
Southern Wisconsin Center for the Developmentally Disabled, Union Grove, WI
Southfield Care Center, Webster City, IA
Southfield Healthcare Center, Pasadena, TX
Southfield Rehabilitation Hospital, Southfield, MI
Southgate Health Care, Metropolis, IL
Southgate Health Care Center, Carneys Point, NJ
Southgate Nursing Center, Jefferson City, MO
Southgate Village Inc, Bessemer, AL
Southhaven Home, Robinson, IL
Southlake Care Center, Merrillville, IN
Southland Care Center, Fayette, MO
Southland Geriatric Center, Norwalk, CA
Southland Nursing Home, Marion, AL
Southland Villa Nursing Center, Temple, TX
Southminster, Charlotte, NC
Southpoint Manor, Miami Beach, FL
Southport Manor Convalescent Center, Southport, CT
Southridge Living Center, Biddeford, ME
Southridge Manor Care Home, Louisburg, KS
Southside Care Center, Minneapolis, MN
Southside Community Hospital, Farmville, VA
Southside Healthcare Center, Indianapolis, IN
Southside House, Rochester, MN
Southside Nursing Center Inc, Jacksonville, FL
Southside Regional Medical Center, Petersburg, VA
Southside Virginia Training Center, Petersburg, VA
Southview Acres Health Care Center, West Saint Paul, MN
Southview Manor Care Center, Cozad, NE
Southview Nursing Center, Tyler, TX
Southwest Care Centers Inc, San Antonio, TX
Southwest Convalescent Center, Hawthorne, CA
Southwest Extended Care Center, McComb, MS
Southwest Florida Retirement Center, Venice, FL
Southwest Health Care Center, Middleburg Heights, OH
Southwest Health Center Nursing Home, Cuba City, WI

Southwest Health Center Nursing Home, Platteville, WI
Southwest Homes, Little Rock, AR
Southwest Louisiana State School, Iota, LA
Southwest Manor, Worthington, MN
Southwest Mediplex, Austin, TX
Southwest Senior Care Inc, Las Vegas, NM
Southwestern Convalescent Manor, Oklahoma City, OK
Southwestern Developmental Center, Bainbridge, GA
Southwestern Medical Center Skilled Nursing Facility, Lawton, OK
Southwestern Nursing Home & Rehabilitation Center, Pittsburgh, PA
Southwestern Virginia Mental Health Institute, Marion, VA
Southwestern Virginia Training Center, Hillsville, VA
Southwood Convalescent Center Inc, Henderson, TX
Southwood Nursing Home, Elizabethton, TN
Southwood Nursing Home, Austin, TX
Sovereign Home, Chicago, IL
Rachel Sovereign Memorial Home, Bay City, MI
Sowder Nursing Home Inc, Brodhead, KY
Spalding Convalescent Center, Griffin, GA
Spang Crest Nursing Home, Lebanon, PA
Spanish Cove, Yukon, OK
Spanish Gardens Nursing Center, Dunedin, FL
Spanish Lake Nursing Center, Florissant, MO
Spanish Oaks Center, Vienna, IL
Spanish Peaks Mental Health Center, Pueblo, CO
Sparks Nursing Center, Central City, KY
Sparr Convalescent Hospital, Los Angeles, CA
Sparta Health Care Center, Sparta, GA
Sparta Health Care Center, Sparta, TN
Sparta Terrace, Sparta, IL
Spartanburg Community Residence Unit 1, Spartanburg, SC
Spartanburg Community Residence Unit 2, Spartanburg, SC
Spartanburg Convalescent Center Inc, Spartanburg, SC
Spear Convalescent Home, Markleysburg, PA
Gladys Spellman Nursing Center, Cheverly, MD
Spencer Health Care Center, Spencer, IN
Spencer Municipal Hospital, Spencer, IA
Spencer Nursing Home, Spencer, NC
Spencer Terrace, Norris City, IL
Spencer's Personal Care Home, Jackson, MS
Spiro Nursing Home, Spiro, OK
Theo Spivey Nursing Home, Gainesboro, TN
SPJST Rest Home 1, Taylor, TX
SPJST Rest Home 2, Needville, TX
Split Rock Nursing Home, Bronx, NY
Spokane Valley Good Samaritan, Greenacres, WA
W W Spradling Rest Home, Louisville, KY
Sprain Brook Manor Nursing Home, Scarsdale, NY
Sprawka Residential Care Facility, Sterling, CO
Spring Branch Healthcare Center, Houston, TX
Spring City Health Care Center, Spring City, TN
Spring Creek Health Care Center, Fort Collins, CO
Spring Creek Nursing Center, Huber Heights, OH
Spring Grove Care Center, Richmond, IN
Spring Hill Manor Convalescent Hospital, Grass Valley, CA
Spring Hill Manor Nursing Home, Mobile, AL
Spring Hill Nursing Center, Spring Hill, KS
Spring House Estates Medical Facility, Spring House, PA
Spring Lake Village, Santa Rosa, CA
Spring Meadows Extended Care Facility, Holland, OH
Spring Meadows Health Care Center, Clarksville, TN

Paul Spring Retirement Community, Alexandria, VA
Spring River Christian Village Inc, Joplin, MO
Spring Shadows Pines, Houston, TX
Spring Valley, Arvada, CO
Spring Valley Convalescent Home, Worcester, MA
Spring Valley Convalescent Hospital, Spring Valley, CA
Spring Valley Health Care Center, Jeffersonville, GA
Spring Valley Health Care Center, Spring Valley, WI
Spring Valley Health Care Center Inc, Elberton, GA
Spring Valley Nursing Center, Spring Valley, IL
Spring View Manor Inc, Conway Springs, KS
Spring View Nursing Home, Lebanon, KY
Springbrook Manor, Grand Rapids, MI
Springdale Convalescent Center, Atlanta, GA
Springdale Convalescent Center, Cartersville, GA
Springdale Village, Camden, SC
Springfield Comprehensive Care Center, Lindside, WV
Springfield Convalescent Center, Springfield, VT
Springfield Health Care Center, Springfield, MO
Springfield Health Care Center, Springfield, TN
Springfield Municipal Hospital, Springfield, MA
Springfield Residential Center, Springfield, MO
Springfield Terrace Ltd, Springfield, IL
Springhaven Nursing Care, Georgetown, KY
Springhill Manor, Battle Creek, MI
Springs Manor Care Center, Cambridge Springs, PA
Springs Road Living Center, Vallejo, CA
Springs Village Care Center, Colorado Springs, CO
Springside of Pittsfield Long-Term Care Facility, Pittsfield, MA
Springview Center, Springfield, OH
Springview Manor, Lima, OH
Springview Nursing Home, Freehold, NJ
Springville Nursing Center, Coushatta, LA
Springwood Nursing Center Ltd, Sarasota, FL
Spruce Manor Nursing Home, Springfield, MA
Spruce Residence, South Saint Paul, MN
Spruce Villa, Salem, OR
Spruce Woods Apartments, Bemidji, MN
Sprucewood Health Care Center, Macomb, IL
Spur Care Center, Spur, TX
Spurgeon Manor, Dallas Center, IA
Square Road Group Home, Saint Albans, ME
Stacyville Community Nursing Home, Stacyville, IA
Stadium Manor Nursing Home, Boston, MA
Stafholt Good Samaritan Center, Blaine, WA
Standing Stone Health Care Center, Monterey, TN
Standish Community Hospital, Standish, MI
Stanford Convalescent Center—Eighth Ave, Fort Worth, TX
Stanford Convalescent Center—Jennings, Fort Worth, TX
Stanford Convalescent Center—Pennsylvania, Fort Worth, TX
Stanford Court Nursing Center, Santee, CA
Stanford Court Nursing Center of La Mesa, La Mesa, CA
Stanford Court Nursing Center of Mission Hills, San Diego, CA
Stanford—Hemphill, Fort Worth, TX
Stanford House, Stanford, KY
Stanley Convalescent Hospital, Westminster, CA
Stanley Total Living Center Inc, Stanley, NC
Stanly Manor, Albemarle, NC
Stanmarie, Linden, MI
Stanton Care Center, Stanton, IA
Stanton Care Center, Stanton, TX
Stanton Hill Convalescent Hospital Inc, Castro Valley, CA

Stanton Nursing Center, Stanton, KY
Stanton Nursing Home, Stanton, NE
Stanton Pines Convalescent Home Inc, Hopkins, SC
Stapeley In Germantown, Philadelphia, PA
Star City Nursing Center, Star City, AR
Star Manor of Northville, Northville, MI
Star Nursing Home, Bethesda, OH
Star of David Convalescent Home, Boston, MA
Starcrest Home of Conyers, Conyers, GA
Starcrest of Lithonia, Lithonia, GA
Starcrest of McDonough, McDonough, GA
Molly Stark Hospital, Louisville, OH
Starkville Manor Nursing Home, Starkville, MS
Starmount Villa, Greensboro, NC
Starnes Nursing Home Inc, Harvey, IL
Starr Farm Nursing Center, Burlington, VT
Starr Nursing Home, Abilene, TX
State Center Manor, State Center, IA
State College Manor Ltd, State College, PA
State Convalescent Hospital, South Gate, CA
State Hospital South Geriatric—Intermediate Care Facility, Blackfoot, ID
Statesboro Nursing Home, Statesboro, GA
Statesman Nursing Center, Levittown, PA
Staunton Manor Nursing Home Inc, Staunton, VA
Steere House, Providence, RI
Steffen Group Home, Barrett, MN
Steigelman's Rest Home, Sheridan, WY
Stella Manor Nursing Center, Russellville, AR
Stella Maris, Cleveland, OH
Stenton Hall, Philadelphia, PA
Step by Step Inc, Carnegie, PA
Step by Step Inc, Wilkes-Barre, PA
Stephens House, Alamosa, CO
Stephenson Nursing Center, Freeport, IL
Stephenville Nursing Home Inc, Stephenville, TX
Stepping Stones Group Home, Milaca, MN
Sterling Care Center, Sterling, IL
Sterling County Nursing Home, Sterling City, TX
Sterling Home of Bridgeport, Bridgeport, CT
Sterling Manor Nursing Center, Maple Shade, NJ
Sterling Place, Baton Rouge, LA
Sterling Presbyterian Manor, Sterling, KS
Sterlington Hospital, Sterlington, LA
Stern Square, Sterling, IL
Stetson Manor Nursing Home, Norwell, MA
Steuben County Infirmary, Bath, NY
Stevencroft, Saint Paul, MN
Stevens Bennett, Haverhill, MA
Stevens Convalescent Center, Hallettsville, TX
Stevens House, Galesburg, IL
Stevens Nursing Home, Yoakum, TX
Stevens Square, Minneapolis, MN
Stewart Health Center, Raleigh, NC
Stewart Lodge, Madison, OH
Stewartville Nursing Home, Stewartville, MN
Stigler, Stigler, OK
Still Waters Community Elders Home, Calumet, MI
Stillmeadow Convalescent Center, Malvern, AR
Stillwater Convalescent Center, Columbus, MT
Stillwater Health Care, Bangor, ME
Stillwater Health Center, Dayton, OH
Stillwater Maple Manor Health Care Center, Stillwater, MN
Stillwater Nursing Home Inc, Stillwater, OK
Stillwater Residence, Stillwater, MN
Stillwater Rosewood Care Center, Stillwater, OK
Stilwell Nursing Home, Stilwell, OK
Ann Stock Center, Fort Lauderdale, FL
Stockdale Nursing Home, Stockdale, TX
Stocker Home for Women—Clara Baldwin Stocker, West Covina, CA
Stockley Center, Georgetown, DE
Stockton House, Flint, MI
Stockton Nursing Home Inc, Stockton, MO
Stokes-Reynolds Memorial Hospital—SNF, Danbury, NC

Stollwood Convalescent Hospital, Woodland, CA
Stone Acre Rest Home Inc, Springfield, MA
Stone Arch Health Care Center, Pittstown, NJ
Stone Manor Convalescent Center, Indianapolis, IN
Stone Road Nursing Center Inc, Kilgore, TX
Stonebrook Nursing Home, Austin, TX
Stonegate Nursing Center, Stonewall, OK
Stonegates, Greenville, DE
Stonehaven Convalescent Hospital Inc, Hayward, CA
Stonehedge-Chittenango Nursing Home, Chittenango, NY
Stonehedge Convalescent Center Inc, West Roxbury, MA
Stonehedge Nursing Home, Rome, NY
Stonehill Care Center, Dubuque, IA
Stonehill Manor Nursing Home, Easton, MA
Stonehouse Hill Nursing Home, Worcester, MA
C-K Stone's Manor Inc, Smethport, PA
Stoneybrook Healthcare Center, Houston, TX
Storla Sunset Center, Letcher, SD
Story County Hospital, Nevada, IA
Stouffer Terrace, Oregon, IL
Stovall Care Center, Denver, CO
Stow—Glen Health Care Center, Stow, OH
Stow Rest Home, Stow, MA
Strand-Kjorsvig Community Rest Home, Roslyn, SD
Strasburg Nursing Home, Strasburg, ND
Stratford Care Center, Stratford, IA
Stratford Hall Nursing Center, Richmond, VA
Stratford Nursing & Convalescent Center, Stratford, NJ
Stratford Nursing Center, Stratford, OK
Stratford Pines Nursing Home, Midland, MI
Stratton House, Townshend, VT
Myron Stratton Home, Colorado Springs, CO
Strawn Nursing Home Inc, Naches, WA
Stroh Resident Homes, Colorado Springs, CO
Strong Memorial Hospital Skilled Nursing Facility, Rochester, NY
Strong Nursing Home, Strong, ME
Stroud Health Care Center, Stroud, OK
Stroud Manor Inc, East Stroudsburg, PA
Stroud Memorial Nursing Home, Marietta, SC
Stroud Shamrock Care Center, Stroud, OK
Strum Nursing Home, Strum, WI
Stuart Convalescent Center, Stuart, FL
Stuart House, Centralia, MO
Studio City Convalescent Hospital, Studio City, CA
Sturges Convalescent Home, Mansfield, OH
Sturgis Community Health Care Center (Nursing Home) NCHS, Sturgis, SD
Sturgis Community Rest Home, Sturgis, KY
Stuttle Community Living Facility, Peoria, IL
Styrest Nursing Home, Carbondale, IL
Styrons Arrowhead Nursing Center, Jonesboro, GA
Su Casa Personal Care, Tucson, AZ
Sublette County Retirement Center, Pinedale, WY
Suburban Acres Nursing Center, Marshall, TX
Suburban Manor Convalescent & Nursing Home, Acton, MA
Suburban Pavilion Inc, North Randall, OH
Sudbury Pines Nursing Home, Sudbury, MA
Sugar Creek Convalescent Center, Greenfield, IN
Sugar Creek Rest Inc, Worthington, PA
Sugar Valley Home Inc, Mound City, KS
Sullivan Convalescent Center, Sullivan, IN
Sullivan County Home & Infirmary, Liberty, NY
Sullivan County Nursing Home, Claremont, NH
Sullivan Health Care Center, Sullivan, IL
Sullivan House, Ottawa, IL
Sullivan Living Center, Sullivan, IL
Sullivan Nursing Center, Sullivan, MO
Sullivan Park Health Care Center Inc, Endicott, NY
Sulphur Springs Nursing Home, Sulphur Springs, TX
Summer Hill Nursing Home, Old Bridge, NJ

Summer Meadows, Longview, TX
Summer Trace Retirement Communities, Carmel, IN
Summerfield Convalescent Hospital, Santa Rosa, CA
Summerfield Manor Nursing Home, Louisville, KY
Summerford Nursing Home Inc, Falkville, AL
Summerlin Lane Nursing Home, Bastrop, LA
Summers County Continuous Care Center, Hinton, WV
Summit Acres Nursing Home, Caldwell, OH
Summit Acres Nursing Home Inc—Home B, Caldwell, OH
Summit Convalescent Center, Summitville, IN
Summit Convalescent Home Inc, Jewett City, CT
Summit County Home, Tallmadge, OH
Summit Health Care Center, Wilkes-Barre, PA
Summit Home, Detroit Lakes, MN
Summit House, Fort Wayne, IN
Summit House I, Saint Louis Park, MN
Summit House II, Saint Louis Park, MN
Summit House Health Center, Bar Harbor, ME
Summit Manor, Columbia, KY
Summit Manor Health Care Center, Saint Paul, MN
Summit Medical Center Inc, Providence, RI
Summit Nursing & Convalescent Home Inc, Cincinnati, OH
Summit Nursing Home, Lakewood, NJ
Summit Nursing Home Inc, Catonsville, MD
Summit Park Hospital—Rockland County Infirmary, Pomona, NY
Summit Ridge Retirement Center, Harrah, OK
Sumner Home for the Aged, Akron, OH
Sumner Lodge, Sumner, WA
Sumter Nursing Home, York, AL
Sun Air Convalescent Hospital, Panorama City, CA
Sun City Convalescent Center, Sun City, CA
Sun Dial Manor, Bristol, SD
Sun Grove Care Center, Peoria, AZ
Sun Health Care Center, Sun City, AZ
Sun Mar Nursing Center, Anaheim, CA
Sun Mountain Nursing Center, Rome, GA
Sun Prairie Health Care Center, Sun Prairie, WI
Sun Terrace Health Care Center, Sun City Center, FL
Sun Valley Health Care Center, Harlingen, TX
Sun Valley Lodge, Sun City, AZ
Sun Valley Manor, Pleasant Hill, CA
Sun Valley Manor, Saginaw, MI
Sun Valley Nursing Center Inc, Alliance, OH
Sunair Home for Asthmatic Children, Van Nuys, CA
Sunbury Community Hospital—Skilled Nursing Unit, Sunbury, PA
Sunbury Nursing Home, Sunbury, OH
Suncoast Manor, Saint Petersburg, FL
Suncoast Manor Nursing Center, Bradenton, FL
Suncoast Nursing Home, Saint Petersburg, FL
Suncrest Nursing Center, Chillicothe, MO
Sundale, Morgantown, WV
Anna Sundermann Home, Seward, NE
Sundial Manors Nursing Home Inc, Aubrey, TX
Sunharbor Manor, Roslyn Heights, NY
Sunhaven Convalescent Hospital, Fullerton, CA
Sunland Center—Gainesville Facility I, Gainesville, FL
Sunland Center—Gainesville Facility II, Gainesville, FL
Sunland Center—Gainesville Facility III, Gainesville, FL
Sunland Center—Miami Facility III, Opa Locka, FL
Sunland—Marianna Facility II, Marianna, FL
Sunlawn Nursing Home, Hightstown, NJ
Sunny Acres, Calhoun, KY
Sunny Acres, Dekalb, TX
Sunny Acres Care Center, Sidney, OH

Sunny Acres Convalescent Hospital, Fairfield, CA
Sunny Acres Nursing Center Inc, Bad Axe, MI
Sunny Acres Nursing Home, Petersburg, IL
Sunny Acres Nursing Home, Chelmsford, MA
Sunny Acres Nursing Home, Williamsburg, MA
Sunny Acres Nursing Home, Bradford, OH
Sunny Acres Nursing Home Inc, Fork, SC
Sunny Acres Villa, Thornton, CO
Sunny Haven Convalescent Center, Sunnyside, WA
Sunny Hill, Denver, CO
Sunny Hill Care Center, Tama, IA
Sunny Hill Health Care Center, Madison, WI
Sunny Hill Nursing Home, Joliet, IL
Sunny Hills Convalescent Hospital, Fullerton, CA
Sunny Hills Nursing Center, Decatur, TX
Sunny Knoll Care Centre, Rockwell City, IA
Sunny Knoll Retirement Home Inc, Franklin, NH
Sunny Point Health Care Center, Smithville, TN
Sunny Ridge, Sheboygan, WI
Sunny Ridge Health Services Center, Nampa, ID
Sunny Shores Health Center, Saint Petersburg, FL
Sunny Vale Nursing Home, Wausau, WI
Sunny Vee Nursing Home Inc, Delaware, OH
Sunny View, Zanesville, OH
Sunny View Adult Care Home, Coffeyville, KS
Sunny View Care Center, Ankeny, IA
Sunny View Manor, Cupertino, CA
Sunny View Nursing Home, Warwick, RI
Sunny Villa Care Center, Upper Sandusky, OH
Sunny Vista Care Center, Portland, OR
Sunnybreeze Nursing Home Inc, Hamilton, OH
Sunnycrest Manor, Dubuque, IA
Sunnycrest Nursing Center, Dysart, IA
Sunnyfield Nursing Home, Cranbury, NJ
Sunnyland Villa, Springfield, OH
Sunnymere Inc, Aurora, IL
Sunnypines Convalescent Center, Rockledge, FL
Sunnyrest Health Care Facility Inc, Colorado Springs, CO
Sunnyside Care Center, Salem, OR
Sunnyside Center, Enid, OK
Sunnyside Convalescent Hospital, Fresno, CA
Sunnyside Farms Nursing & Convalescent Home, Manasquan, NJ
Sunnyside Nursing Center, Torrance, CA
Sunnyside Nursing Home, Sarasota, FL
Sunnyside Nursing Home, Lake Park, MN
Sunnyside Nursing Home, East Syracuse, NY
Sunnyside Presbyterian Home Health Care Unit, Harrisonburg, VA
Sunnyside Rest Home, Oxbridge, MA
Sunnyside Retirement Center 2, Taylor, TX
Sunnyslope Care Center, Ottumwa, IA
Sunnyslope Nursing Home, Bowerston, OH
Sunnyvale Convalescent Hospital, Sunnyvale, CA
Sunnyvale Manor, Dallas, TX
Sunnyview Convalescent Center, Los Angeles, CA
Sunnyview District Nursing Home of Grundy County, Trenton, MO
Sunnyview Home, Butler, PA
Sunnyview Village, Princeton, WI
Sunray East Convalescent Hospital, Los Angeles, CA
Sunrest Health Facilities Inc, Port Jefferson, NY
Sunrise Community—Miami, Goulds, FL
Sunrise Convalescent Center, San Antonio, TX
Sunrise Country Manor, Milford, NE
Sunrise Courts, Roselle, IL
Sunrise Group Home 1—Goulds, Goulds, FL
Sunrise Guest Home, Fredericksburg, IA
Sunrise Haven, Puyallup, WA
Sunrise Hill Care Center, Traer, IA

Sunrise Home, Two Harbors, MN
Sunrise Homes Inc, Lisbon, OH
Sunrise Manor, Fort Pierce, FL
Sunrise Manor, Sioux City, IA
Sunrise Manor & Convalescent Center Inc, Amelia, OH
Sunrise Manor Care Center, Fayetteville, AR
Sunrise Manor Nursing Home, Hodgenville, KY
Sunrise Manor Nursing Home, Somerset, KY
Sunrise Manor Nursing Home, Bay Shore, NY
Sunrise Manor of Virden Inc, Virden, IL
Sunrise Nursing Home for the Blind Inc, Milwaukee, WI
Sunrise Nursing Home Inc, Somerville, MA
Sunrise Nursing Home of Georgia Inc, Moultrie, GA
Sunrise Retirement Home of Arlington, Arlington, VA
Sunrise Terrace, Winfield, IA
Sunrise Terrace Retirement Home, Oakton, VA
Sunrise View Convalescent Center, Everett, WA
Sunset Boulevard Convalescent Hospital 1, Hayward, CA
Sunset Care Center, Jacksonville, TX
Sunset Care Corporation, Bowman, ND
Sunset Estates, Tecumseh, OK
Sunset Estates of El Reno Inc, El Reno, OK
Sunset Estates of Maud, Maud, OK
Sunset Estates of Watonga Inc, Watonga, OK
Sunset Haven, El Paso, TX
Sunset Haven Health Center, Cherry Valley, CA
Sunset Haven Nursing Home, Curtis, NE
Sunset Heights Nursing Home, Belle Glade, FL
Sunset Hill Home for Aged & Infirm, Lawrenceburg, KY
Sunset Home Inc, Maysville, MO
Sunset Home of the United Methodist Church, Quincy, IL
Sunset House, Toledo, OH
Sunset Knoll Inc, Aurelia, IA
Sunset Manor, Brush, CO
Sunset Manor, Woodstock, IL
Sunset Manor, Waverly, KS
Sunset Manor, Jenison, MI
Sunset Manor, Sault Sainte Marie, MI
Sunset Manor, Titusville, PA
Sunset Manor, Irene, SD
Sunset Manor, Dallas, TX
Sunset Manor Convalescent Hospital, El Monte, CA
Sunset Manor Inc, Frontenac, KS
Sunset Manor Nursing Home, Greencastle, IN
Sunset Manor of Canton, Canton, IL
Sunset Manor of Lexington, Lexington, OK
Sunset Nursing & Retirement Home of Union, Union, MO
Sunset Nursing Center, Concordia, KS
Sunset Nursing Center, Ironton, OH
Sunset Nursing Home, Park Rapids, MN
Sunset Nursing Home, Bowling Green, MO
Sunset Nursing Home, Cleveland, OH
Sunset Nursing Home Inc, Boonville, NY
Sunset Point Nursing Center, Clearwater, FL
Sunset Skilled Nursing & Rehabilitation Center, Eureka, CA
Sunset Terrace Convalescent Center, Coeur d'Alene, ID
Sunset Terrace Extended Care Facility, Coeur d'Alene, ID
Sunset Valley, Chamberlain, SD
Sunset View, Millersburg, OH
Sunset Villa Nursing Home, Roswell, NM
Sunset Village of the Ozarks, Waynesville, MO
Sunshine Children's Home, Maumee, OH
Sunshine Gardens, Spokane, WA
Sunshine Haven, Lordsburg, NM
Sunshine Health Care Center Inc, Commerce City, CO
Sunshine Manor I, Dexter, MO
Sunshine Manor Nursing Center, Carlinville, IL
Sunshine Meadow Care Center, Lincoln, IL
Sunshine Nursing Home, Stoneham, MA

Sunshine Nursing Home, New London, TX
Sunshine Place, Harmony, MN
Sunshine Rest Home, Pontotoc, MS
Sunshine Terrace Convalescent Hospital Inc, Los Angeles, CA
Sunshine Terrace Foundation, Logan, UT
Sunshine Villege Nursing Home, Pinellas Park, FL
Sunshine Vista, Seattle, WA
Sunwest Nursing Center, Sun City West, AZ
Sunwood Care Center, Redwood Falls, MN
Superior Care Home, Paducah, KY
Superior Good Samaritan Center, Superior, NE
Superior Health Haven, Munising, MI
Superior Shores Nursing Center, Munising, MI
Sur La Rue de Breen, Saint Paul, MN
Sur La Rue de Skillman, Maplewood, MN
Sur La Rue de Wheelock Ridge, Saint Paul, MN
Surf & Sand Health Center, Duluth, MN
Surfside Nursing Home, Far Rockaway, NY
Surry Community Nursing Center, Mount Airy, NC
Susanna Wesley Health Center Inc, Hialeah, FL
Susque View Home Inc, Lock Haven, PA
Susquehanna Center for Nursing & Rehabilitation, Harrisburg, PA
Susquehanna Lutheran Village, Millersburg, PA
Susquehanna Nursing Home & Health Related Facility, Johnson City, NY
Sussex County Homestead, Newton, NJ
Sutter Oaks Alzheimer Center—Sacramento, Sacramento, CA
Sutter Oaks Nursing Center—Arden, Sacramento, CA
Sutter Oaks Nursing Center—Carmichael, Carmichael, CA
Sutter Oaks Nursing Center—Midtown, Sacramento, CA
Sutton Community Home, Sutton, NE
Sutton House, Mount Vernon, IL
Sutton Place Convalescent Center, Lake Worth, FL
Suwannee Health Care Center, Live Oak, FL
Suwannee Valley Nursing Center, Jasper, FL
Swaim Health Center, Newville, PA
Clara Swain Manor, Ocean Grove, NJ
Swainsboro Nursing Home, Swainsboro, GA
Swampscotta Nursing Home, South Windham, ME
Swan Manor Inc, LaCygne, KS
Swanholm Nursing & Rehabilitation Center, Saint Petersburg, FL
L M Swanson Nursing Home, Gallatin, TN
Swanton Health Care & Retirement Center, Swanton, OH
Sweden Valley Manor, Coudersport, PA
Swedish Retirement Association, Evanston, IL
Sweeny House, Sweeny, TX
Sweet Brook Nursing Home Inc, Williamstown, MA
Sweet Memorial Nursing Home, Chinook, MT
Sweet Springs Caring Center, Sweet Springs, MO
Sweetbriar Development Center, West Columbia, TX
Sweetbriar Nursing Home, Bellville, TX
Sweetbriar Nursing Home, Brenham, TX
Sweetbriar Nursing Home, Columbus, TX
Sweetbriar Nursing Home, Taylor, TX
Sweetwater Nursing Center, Sweetwater, TX
Sweetwater Valley Convalescent & Nursing Home Inc, Sweetwater, TN
Swift County Home, Benson, MN
Swiss Home Health Related Facility, Mount Kisco, NY
Swiss Villa Living Center, Vevay, IN
Swiss Village Inc, Berne, IN
Swope Ridge Health Care Center, Kansas City, MO
Sycamore Creek Nursing Center, Coraopolis, PA
Sycamore Manor Health Center, Montoursville, PA

Sycamore Park Convalescent Hospital, Los Angeles, CA
Sycamore View Healthcare, Clinton, MO
Sycamore View Nursing Home, Memphis, TN
Sycamore Village Health Center, Kokomo, IN
Sydney House, Vicksburg, MS
Sykesville Eldercare Center, Sykesville, MD
Syl-View Health Care Center, Sylvania, GA
Sylacauga Health Care Center Inc, Sylacauga, AL
Sylcox Nursing Home & Health Related Facility, Newburgh, NY
Sylvan Manor Health Care Center, Silver Spring, MD
Sylvan Manor Inc, Bridgeport, CT
Sylvester Health Care Inc, Sylvester, GA
Sylvester Nursing Home, Muncie, IN
Syracuse Home Association, Baldwinsville, NY
Syverson Lutheran Home, Eau Claire, WI
T L C Convalescent Hospital, El Cajon, CA
Taber Street Nursing Home, New Bedford, MA
Tabitha Nursing Home, Lincoln, NE
Table Rock Health Care Center, Kimberling City, MO
Tabor Manor Care Center, Tabor, IA
Tabor Villa Inc, Portland, OR
Tacoma Lutheran Home & Retirement Community, Tacoma, WA
Tacoma Terrace Convalescent Center, Tacoma, WA
Taft Hospital & Convalescent Center, Sinton, TX
Tahlequah Nursing Home, Tahlequah, OK
Tahoe Forest Hospital D/P SNF, Truckee, CA
Tahoka Care Center, Tahoka, TX
Talihina Manor Nursing Home, Talihina, OK
Tall Oaks Fellowship House, Reston, VA
Talladega Nursing Home, Talladega, AL
Tallahassee Convalescent Home, Tallahassee, FL
Tallahassee Developmental Center, Tallahassee, FL
Tallahatchie General Hospital—Extended Care Facility, Charleston, MS
Tallpines Health Care Facility, Belfast, ME
Talmadge Park Health Care, East Haven, CT
Tamarac Convalescent Center, Tamarac, FL
Tamarack, Plymouth, NH
TAMC—Aroostook Health Center Division, Mars Hill, ME
Tammerlane Inc, Sterling, IL
Tampa Health Care Center, Tampa, FL
William & Sally Tandet Center for Continuing Care, Stamford, CT
Tanglewood Convalescent Center, Lake City, FL
Tanglewood Health Care Center, Ridgeway, SC
Tanner Chapel Manor Nursing Home, Phoenix, AZ
Tappahannock Manor Convalescent Center & Home for Adults Health Care Unit, Tappahannock, VA
Tara Gardens Personal Care Home, Iola, KS
Tara Health Care Center, Riverdale, GA
Tarpon Health Care Center, Tarpon Springs, FL
Tarpon Springs Convalescent Center, Tarpon Springs, FL
Tarrytown Hall Nursing Home, Tarrytown, NY
Tarzana Health Care Center, Tarzana, CA
Tasks Unlimited Training Center, Minneapolis, MN
Tates Creek Health Care Center, Lexington, KY
Tattnall Nursing Care, Reidsville, GA
Taunton Female Charity Association Inc, Raynham Center, MA
Taunton Nursing Home, Taunton, MA
Alice Byrd Tawes Nursing Home, Crisfield, MD
Tawes/Bland Bryant Nursing Center, Catonsville, MD
Taylor-Brown Memorial Hospital Nursing Home, Waterloo, NY

Taylor Care Center, Jacksonville, FL
Fannie E Taylor Home for the Aged, Jacksonville, FL
Taylor Home, Laconia, NH
Taylor Hospital, Bangor, ME
Taylor House, Springfield, IL
James S Taylor Memorial Home, Louisville, KY
Taylor Living Center for Seniors, Taylor, MI
Taylor Manor Nursing Home, Versailles, KY
Taylor Nursing Home, Taylor, AR
Taylor Nursing & Rehabilitation Center, Taylor, PA
Taylor Park Health Care & Rehabilitation Center, Rhinelander, WI
Taylor Run Group Home, Alexandria, VA
Ruth Taylor Geriatric & Rehabilitation Institute/Westchester County Medical Center, Hawthorne, NY
Taylor Total Living Center For the Developmentally Disabled, Taylor, MI
Taylorville Care Center Inc, Taylorville, IL
Teachers Homes Healthcare Center, Minneapolis, MN
Teague Nursing Home, Teague, TX
Teakwood Manor, Stamford, TX
Team Center, Saint Paul, MN
Teaneck Nursing Home, Teaneck, NJ
Teat Personal Care Home, Jackson, MS
Tecumseh Care Center, Tecumseh, NE
Tehema County Health Center, Red Bluff, CA
Tejas, Dallas, TX
Tekakwitha Nursing Home, Sisseton, SD
Tekamah Nursing Center, Tekamah, NE
Tekoa Care Center, Tekoa, WA
Tel Hai Nursing Center Inc, Honey Brook, PA
Temenos House Inc, Wheat Ridge, CO
Temple Care Center, Temple, TX
Temple City Convalescent Hospital, Temple City, CA
Haig S Temple Geriatric Center II, Bridgeville, PA
Julia Temple Center, Englewood, CO
Temple Manor Nursing Home, Temple, OK
Temple Park Convalescent Hospital, Los Angeles, CA
Tender Care Gaylord, Gaylord, MI
Tender Care Home, Gulfport, MS
Tensas Care Center, Newellton, LA
Teresa Rest Home Inc, East Haven, CT
Teresian House Nursing Home Company Inc, Albany, NY
Terrace at Westside, Cincinnati, OH
Terrace Garden Care Center, Garden City, KS
Terrace Gardens Health Care Center, Colorado Springs, CO
Terrace Gardens Nursing Center, Wichita, KS
Terrace Gardens Nursing Center, Oklahoma City, OK
Terrace Gardens Nursing Home, Midland, TX
Terrace Heights Care Center, Boulder, CO
Terrace Manor, Dell Rapids, SD
Terrace Manor Nursing Home Inc, Russellville, AL
Terrace Nursing Home Inc, Waukegan, IL
Terrace Park Convalescent Hospital, Tulare, CA
Terrace View, Lawrenceburg, IN
Terrace View Castle Nursing Home, Millersburg, OH
Terrace View Convalescent Center, Seattle, WA
Terrace Villa Care Center, Salt Lake City, UT
Terrace West Nursing Center, Midland, TX
Terraceview Living Center, Shell Lake, WI
Terracina Convalescent Hospital, Redlands, CA
Terre Haute Nursing Home, Terre Haute, IN
Terrebonne General Medical Center, Houma, LA
Terrell Care Center, Terrell, TX
Terrell Convalescent Center 1, Terrell, TX
Terrell Convalescent Center 2, Terrell, TX
Terreno Gardens Convalescent Center, Los Gatos, CA
Terry Haven Nursing Home, Mount Vernon, TX
Terwilliger Plaza Inc, Portland, OR

Teton Medical Center—Nursing Home, Choteau, MT
Teton Nursing Home, Choteau, MT
Texarkana Nursing Center, Texarkana, TX
Texas County Missouri Health Care Center Inc, Licking, MO
Texas Terrace Convalescent Center, Saint Louis Park, MN
Texhoma Christian Care Center, Wichita Falls, TX
Texoma Manor Inc, Kingston, OK
Becky Thatcher Nursing Home, Hannibal, MO
Roland Thatcher Nursing Home, Wareham, MA
Becker/Shoop Center, Racine, WI
Thelma Terrace, Wood River, IL
Theodore I Residence, West Saint Paul, MN
Therapeutic Community Residence, Lindstrom, MN
Thibodaux Hospital & Health Centers, Thibodaux, LA
Thirty-Nine Summer Nursing Home, Keene, NH
3030 Park Health Center, Bridgeport, CT
Thomas Care Centers Inc, Houston, TX
Thomas County Care Center, Colby, KS
Thomas Drive Community Residence, Florence, SC
Thomas House, Washington, DC
Thomas Nursing Center, Thomas, OK
Thomas Rest Haven, Coon Rapids, IA
Thomasville Health Care Center, Thomasville, GA
Thomasville Nursing Home, Thomasville, AL
Thompson Farm Group Home, Camden, DE
Geraldine L Thompson Medical Home, Allenwood, NJ
Thompson House, Brattleboro, VT
James R Thompson House, Decatur, IL
Thompson Nursing Home Inc, Canandaigua, NY
Thomson Manor Nursing Home Inc, Thomson, GA
Thornapple Manor, Hastings, MI
Thorne Crest Retirement Center, Albert Lea, MN
Thorne-Crest South, Albert Lea, MN
Thornton Heights Terrace Ltd, Chicago Heights, IL
Thornton Manor Nursing Home, Lansing, IA
Thornton Nursing Home, Northborough, MA
Thornwald Home, Carlisle, PA
Thorton Hall Health Care Unit, Norfolk, VA
Thousand Oaks Health Care Center, Thousand Oaks, CA
Three Fountains Inc, Medford, OR
301 Sylvan Way, Bremerton, WA
Three Oaks Intermediate Care Home, Macon, GA
Three Rivers Convalescent Center, Fort Wayne, IN
Three Rivers Convalescent Center, Cincinnati, OH
Three Rivers Health Care Center Inc, Painted Post, NY
Three Rivers Manor, Three Rivers, MI
Three Rivers Nursing Center, Marked Tree, AR
377 Main Street, Winona, MN
Three Sisters Healthcare Center, Indianapolis, IN
Three Springs Lodge Nursing Home Inc, Chester, IL
Three Thirty Five Ridgewood, Minneapolis, MN
Throckmorton Nursing Center, Throckmorton, TX
Thunderbird Health Care Center, Phoenix, AZ
Thunderbird House, Duluth, MN
Thurston Woods Village, Sturgis, MI
Tibbits Health Related Facility, White Plains, NY
Tidd Home, Woburn, MA
Tidings of Peace Nursing Center, Broken Arrow, OK
Tierra Pines Nursing Center, Largo, FL
Tierra Rose Care Center, Salem, OR
Tieszen Memorial Home, Marion, SD

Margaret Tietz Center for Nursing Care Inc, Jamaica, NY
Tiffany Heights, Mound City, MO
Tiffany Rest & Retirement Home, Rockland, MA
Tiffany Square Care Center, Grand Island, NE
Tiffany Square Convalescent Center, Saint Joseph, MO
Tiffany II Rest Home, Rockland, MA
Tiffin Developmental Center, Tiffin, OH
Tift Health Care Inc, Tifton, GA
Tifton Nursing Home, Tifton, GA
Tigard Care Center, Tigard, OR
Tilden Nursing Center, Tilden, NE
Tillamook Care Center, Tillamook, OR
Tillers, Oswego, IL
Tilton Terrace, Wilmington, DE
Timbercrest—Church of the Brethren Home Inc, North Manchester, IN
Timberlake Care Center, Kansas City, MO
Timberlane Drive Community Residence, Columbia, SC
Timberlane Manor, Edmond, OK
Timberlyn Heights Nursing Home, Great Barrington, MA
Timely Mission Nursing Home, Buffalo Center, IA
Timpanogos Care Center, Orem, UT
Tindles Personal Care Home, Cloverport, KY
Brent B Tinnin Manor, Ellington, MO
Tinton Falls Conva-Center, Tinton Falls, NJ
Tioga Community Nursing Home, Tioga, ND
Tioga General Hospital Health Related Facility, Waverly, NY
Tioga Manor Nursing Center, Tioga, LA
Tioga Nursing Home Inc, Waverly, NY
Tippecanoe Villa, West Lafayette, IN
Tipton Manor Inc, Tipton, MO
Tipton Nursing Home, Tipton, IN
Titonka Care Center, Titonka, IA
Titus Memorial Presbyterian Home, Sullivan, IL
Titusville Nursing & Convalescent Center, Titusville, FL
TLC 1 Woodburn Care Center, Woodburn, OR
TLC Home for the Elderly, Ocean Springs, MS
TLC Of Miles City Inc, Miles City, MT
Toccoa Nursing Center, Toccoa, GA
Tockwotton Home, Providence, RI
Sarah A Todd Memorial Home, Carlisle, PA
Todholm Care Center, Springville, UT
Toledo Mental Health Center, Toledo, OH
Tolstoy Foundation Nursing Home Company Inc, Valley Cottage, NY
Tomah Care Center, Tomah, WI
Tomorrows Hope Inc, Meridian, ID
Toms River Convalescent Center, Toms River, NJ
Tonganoxie Nursing Center, Tonganoxie, KS
Tooele Valley Nursing Home, Tooele, UT
Toole County Nursing Home, Shelby, MT
Toombs Nursing & Intermediate Care Home, Lyons, GA
Topanga Terrace Convalescent Center, Canoga Park, CA
Topeka Convalescent Center, Topeka, KS
Topeka Presbyterian Manor Inc, Topeka, KS
Topham's Tiny Tots Care Center, Orem, UT
Torrance, Torrance, CA
Torrance State Hospital—Long-Term Care Facility, Torrance, PA
Torrey Pines Care Center, Las Vegas, NV
Torrey Pines Convalescent Hospital, La Jolla, CA
Torrington Extend-A-Care Center, Torrington, CT
Torry Pines Home for the Aged, Detroit, MI
Total Life Care Center, Houston, TX
Toth's Rest Home, Barberton, OH
A Touch of Kindness, Basin, WY
Toulon Health Care Center, Washington, IL
Touro Infirmary, New Orleans, LA
Touro Shakespeare Home, New Orleans, LA
Toward Independence Inc, Xenia, OH
Tower Hill Nursing Home, Muskogee, OK
Tower Hill Rest Home, Fitchburg, MA

Tower Lodge Nursing Home, Wall, NJ
Tower Village Inc, Saint Louis, MO
Towers Nursing Home, Smithville, TX
Town & Country Convalescent Center, Tampa, FL
Town & Country Manor, Santa Ana, CA
Town & Country Manor Inc, Boerne, TX
Town & Country Nursing Center, Minden, LA
Town & Country Nursing Center Inc, Minden, LA
Town & Country Nursing Home, Lowell, MA
Town & Country Nursing Home, Midland, MI
Town Centre Health Care, Merrillville, IN
Town & Country Manor, Milwaukee, WI
Town Hall Estates, Breckenridge, TX
Town Hall Estates, Hillsboro, TX
Town Hall Estates, Keene, TX
Town Hall Estates, Rusk, TX
Town Hall Estates Health Care Facility, Whitney, TX
Town Hall Estates Nursing Center, Wauconda, IL
Town Hall Estates Windsor Inc, Windsor, OH
Town Manor Nursing Home, Lawrence, MA
Town of Vici Nursing Home, Vici, OK
Town Park Convalescent Center, Houston, TX
Towne Avenue Convalescent Hospital, Pomona, CA
Towne House Retirement Community, Fort Wayne, IN
Towne Oaks Nursing Center, Ruston, LA
Townhouse Convalescent, Fresno, CA
Towns County Nursing Home, Hiawassee, GA
Township Manor Nursing Center, Elkins Park, PA
Towson Convalescent Home Inc, Reisterstown, MD
Dulaney Towson Nursing & Convalescent Center, Towson, MD
Trace Haven Nursing Home, Natchez, MS
Tracy Convalescent Hospital, Tracy, CA
Tracy Nursing Home, Tracy, MN
Tradition House Healthcare, Joplin, MO
Hermina Traeye Memorial Nursing Home, Johns Island, SC
Tranquility Nursing Home, Randolph, VT
Transitional Care Unit at UVRMC, Provo, UT
Transitional Care Unit—Extended Care Facility, Denver, CO
Transitional Level of Care Center at Community General Hospital, Reading, PA
Transitional Living Center, Columbia, SC
Traverse County Nursing Home, Wheaton, MN
Traylor Nursing Home Inc, Roanoke, AL
Traymore, Dallas, TX
Treasure Isle Care Center, North Bay Village, FL
Treasure Isle Convalescent Home, Miami, FL
Treasure Valley Manor, Boise, ID
Treats Falls House, Orono, ME
Treemont Health Care Center, Houston, TX
Tremont Nursing Center, Tremont, PA
Tremont of Dallas, Dallas, TX
Trempealeau County Health Care Center, Whitehall, WI
Tressie's Nursing Home, Oberlin, OH
Treutlen County Nursing Home, Soperton, GA
Trevecca Health Care Center, Nashville, TN
Trevilla of Golden Valley, Golden Valley, MN
Trevilla of New Brighton, New Brighton, MN
Trevilla of Robbinsdale, Robbinsdale, MN
Treyton Oak Towers, Louisville, KY
Tri City Convalescent Center, Oceanside, CA
Tri-City Health Care Center, Portland, OR
Tri-County Convalescent Home, Adamsville, TN
Tri-County Extended Care Center, Fairfield, OH
Tri-County Manor Nursing Center, Horton, KS
Tri-County Nursing Home, Vandalia, MO
Tri-County Nursing Home Inc, Louisville, MS
Tri-County Nursing Home Inc, Richland, MO
Tri-County Retirement & Nursing Home, Hatton, ND

Tri-State Convalescent Center, Clarkston, WA
Tri State Manor Nursing Home, Lansing, IL
Triad Rehabilitation Center, Winston-Salem, NC
Triad United Methodist Home, Winston-Salem, NC
Tri-County Memorial Hospital—Nursing Home, Whitehall, WI
Trident Halfway House, Thief River Falls, MN
Trigg County Manor Personal Care Home, Cadiz, KY
Dan C Trigg Memorial Hospital, Tucumcari, NM
Trimble Nursing Center, Bedford, KY
Trimont Nursing Home, Trimont, MN
Trinidad State Nursing Home, Trinidad, CO
Trinity Court Nursing Home, Little Rock, AR
Trinity Haven, Jeannette, PA
Trinity Home, Dayton, OH
Trinity House, Sacramento, CA
Trinity Lutheran Home, Round Rock, TX
Trinity Lutheran Home, Shiner, TX
Trinity Lutheran Manor, Merriam, KS
Trinity Manor Adult Care Home, Dodge City, KS
Trinity Memorial Hospital, Trinity, TX
Trinity Nursing Home, Minot, ND
Trinity Park West, Livonia, MI
Trinity Terrace, Fort Worth, TX
Trinity Towers, Midland, TX
Tripoli Nursing Home, Tripoli, IA
Tripp Good Samaritan Center, Tripp, SD
Tripp Shelter Care Home, Cobden, IL
Troost Avenue Nursing Home, Shawnee, MO
Tropico Convalescent Hospital, Glendale, CA
Troy Hills House, Parsippany-Troy, NJ
Troy House Inc, Troy, MO
True Light Inc, Sandusky, OH
Trull Nursing Home, Biddeford, ME
Trulson House, Galesburg, IL
Harry S Truman Restorative Center, Saint Louis, MO
Truman Lake Manor, Lowry City, MO
Truman Manor Nursing Home, Sedalia, MO
Truman Medical Center East, Kansas City, MO
Trussville Health Care Center, Trussville, AL
Violet Tschetter Memorial Home, Huron, SD
Tucker House II, Philadelphia, PA
C M Tucker Jr Human Resources Center, Columbia, SC
Tucker Nursing Center, Tucker, GA
Tucson Medical Center Sub-Acute Unit, Tucson, AZ
Tudor House Nursing Home Corp, Jamaica Plain, MA
Tudor Oaks Health Center, Hales Corners, WI
Tudor Oaks Health Center, Muskego, WI
Tuell Nursing Home Inc, Melrose, MA
Tuff Memorial Home, Hills, MN
Tule Lake Manor, Tacoma, WA
Tulia Care Center, Tulia, TX
Tully Brook Rest Home, Athol, MA
Tulsa Christian Home Inc, Tulsa, OK
Tulsa Jewish Community Retirement & Health Care Center Inc, Tulsa, OK
Tulsa Nursing Center, Tulsa, OK
Tuolumne General Hospital SNF, Sonora, CA
Tupelo Manor Nursing Home, Tupelo, MS
Turlock Convalescent Hospital, Turlock, CA
Turner Geriatric Center, Galveston, TX
Isla Carroll Turner Health Care Center, Houston, TX
Turner Nursing Home, Childress, TX
Turtle Creek Health Care Center, Jacksonville, FL
Tuscola County Medical Care Facility, Caro, MI
Tuskegee Health Care Facility Inc, Tuskegee, AL
Tustin Manor, Tustin, CA
Tutor Nursing Home Inc, Temple, TX
Tuttle Nursing Center, Tuttle, OK
Twain Haven Nursing Home, Perry, MO
Mark Twain Manor, Bridgeton, MO
Tweeten Lutheran Health Care Center, Spring Grove, MN

24 Katahdin Street, Penobscot, ME
24 Rhode Island Street Nursing Home, Buffalo, NY
2020 Adolescent Receiving Center, Minneapolis, MN
Twilight Acres Inc, Wall Lake, IA
Twilight Acres Nursing Home Inc, Eugene, OR
Twilight Gardens Home Inc, Norwalk, OH
Twilight Haven, Fresno, CA
Twilight Home Inc, Corsicana, TX
Twilight Nursing Home Inc, Jeffersonville, IN
Twilight Nursing Home Inc, Bangs, TX
Twilight Personal Care Home, Woodburn, KY
Twin Birch Health Care Center, Spring Park, MN
Twin Cedar Nursing Home, Post, TX
Twin Cities Convalescent Center, Templeton, CA
Twin City Health Care Center Inc, Uhrichsville, OH
Twin City Linnea Home, Saint Paul, MN
Twin City Nursing Home, Gas City, IN
Twin City Nursing Home, Hartshorne, OK
Twin Falls Care Center, Twin Falls, ID
Twin Lakes Care Center, San Augustine, TX
Twin Lakes Center, Burlington, NC
Twin Lakes Nursing Home, Albany, KY
Twin-M Nursing Home, Canton, OH
Twin Maples Health Care Facility, Durham, CT
Twin Maples Nursing Home Inc, McArthur, OH
Twin Oaks, Mansfield, OH
Twin Oaks Care Center, Sweet Home, OR
Twin Oaks Community Living Facility, Pekin, IL
Twin Oaks Convalescent Center, Alma, GA
Twin Oaks Convalescent Center, Jacksonville, TX
Twin Oaks Convalescent Home, South Boston, VA
Twin Oaks Nursing & Convalescent Home, LaPlace, LA
Twin Oaks Nursing Home, Mobile, AL
Twin Oaks Nursing Home, Campbelltown, PA
Twin Oaks Retirement Center, Waco, TX
Twin Palms Care Center, Artesia, CA
Twin Pines Adult Care Center, Kirksville, MO
Twin Pines Care Center, Salt Lake City, UT
Twin Pines Health Care, Santa Paula, CA
Twin Pines Nursing Center, Lewisville, TX
Twin Pines Nursing Home, Victoria, TX
Twin Pines Retreat, Cuyahoga Falls, OH
Twin Rivers Care Center, Anoka, MN
Twin Rivers Medical Center, Arkadelphia, AR
Twin Rivers Nursing Care Center, Defiance, OH
Twin Towers, Cincinnati, OH
Twin Town Treatment Center, Saint Paul, MN
Twin View Nursing Home, Twin City, GA
Twin Willow Nursing Center, Salem, IL
Twinbrook Medical Center, Erie, PA
Twinbrook Nursing Home, Louisville, KY
Twinbrooke South, San Benito, TX
Twinbrooke South—McAllen, McAllen, TX
Twining Hall, Holland, PA
Two Fifty Two West Wabasha Street, Winona, MN
2201 East 10th Street Home, Pueblo, CO
Tylertown Extended Care Center, Tylertown, MS
Tyndall Good Samaritan Center, Tyndall, SD
Tyrone Medical Inn, Saint Petersburg, FL
Tyson Manor Health Facility, Montgomery, AL
Uihlein Mercy Center, Lake Placid, NY
Uinta Healthcare Center Inc, Evanston, WY
Uintah Care Center, Vernal, UT
Ukiah Convalescent Hospital, Ukiah, CA
Ulster County Infirmary & Annex, Kingston, NY
John Umstead Hospital—ICF, Butner, NC
Unicare Health Facility of Huntingburg, Huntingburg, IN
Unicoi County Nursing Home, Erwin, TN
Union City Christel Manor, Union City, OH

Union City Health Care Center, Union City, TN
Union City Manor Nursing Center, Union City, TN
Union County General Hospital, Clayton, NM
Union County Nursing Home, Blairsville, GA
Union County Skilled Nursing Home, Anna, IL
Union Forge Nursing Home, Lebanon, NJ
Union House Nursing Home Inc, Glover, VT
Union Manor, Marysville, OH
Union Memorial Extended Care, Baltimore, MD
Union Memorial Hospital—SNF/ICF, Monroe, NC
Union Mission Nursing Home Inc, Haverhill, MA
Union Printers Home & Hospital, Colorado Springs, CO
Union Square Nursing Center, Boston, MA
Unitarian Universalist House, Philadelphia, PA
United Cerebral Palsy Association Home of Cuyahoga County, Cleveland, OH
United Cerebral Palsy Residential Center, Seattle, WA
United Cerebral Palsy/Spastic Children's Foundation, Sylmar, CA
United Christian Church Home, Annville, PA
United Church Colony Homes Inc, Gasport, NY
United Convalescent of Post, Post, TX
United District Hospital & Home, Staples, MN
United Health Care Center, Big Spring, TX
United Hebrew Geriatric Center, New Rochelle, NY
United Helpers Canton Nursing Home Inc, Canton, NY
United Helpers Cedars Nursing Home Inc, Ogdensburg, NY
United Helpers Nursing Home Inc, Ogdensburg, NY
United Hospital, Port Chester, NY
United Hospital & Nursing Home, Saint Paul, MN
United Memorial, Greenville, MI
United Methodist Convalescent Homes of Connecticut Inc, Shelton, CT
United Methodist Health Care Center, Clinton, OK
United Methodist Health Care Center, East Providence, RI
United Methodist Health Center, Pittsburgh, PA
United Methodist Home, Topeka, KS
United Methodist Memorial Home, Warren, IN
United Methodist Village, Lawrenceville, IL
United Odd Fellow & Rebekah Home, Bronx, NY
United Pioneer Home, Luck, WI
United Presbyterian Home, Ackley, IA
United Presbyterian Home, Washington, IA
United Presbyterian Home at Syosset Inc, Woodbury, NY
United Presbyterian Home for Aged People, Pittsburgh, PA
United Retirement Center, Brookings, SD
United Zion Home Inc, Lititz, PA
Unity House, Worthington, MN
University Convalescent & Nursing Home, Livonia, MI
University Convalescent & Nursing Home Inc, Wheaton, MD
University Convalescent Center East Inc, Deland, FL
University Convalescent Center West, Deland, FL
University Health Care Center, Minneapolis, MN
University Health Care Center, Nashville, TN
University Heights Nursing Home, Albany, NY
University Hills Nursing Center, Bryan, TX
University Manor, Lubbock, TX
University Manor Health Care Center Inc, Cleveland, OH

University Nursing Care Center, Gainesville, FL
University Nursing Center, Upland, IN
University Nursing Center, Hamilton Square, NJ
University Nursing Center, McKinney, TX
University Nursing Home, Bronx, NY
University Nursing & Rehabilitation Center, Philadelphia, PA
University Park, Richmond, VA
University Park Care Center, Pueblo, CO
University Park Convalescent Center, Tampa, FL
University Park Heritage Manor, Wichita Falls, TX
University Park Nursing Center, Fort Wayne, IN
University Terrace Good Samaritan Village, Las Cruces, NM
University Towers Medical Pavilion, Kansas City, MO
University Village Inc, Tulsa, OK
Upjohn Community Nursing Home, Kalamazoo, MI
Upland Convalescent Hospital, Upland, CA
Uplands Home for Church Women, Baltimore, MD
Lifequest Nursing Center, Quakertown, PA
Upper Valley Rest Home, Spearfish, SD
Upton County Convalescent Center, McCamey, TX
Uptown Home for the Aged, Philadelphia, PA
Urbana Nursing Home, Urbana, IL
Utah State Training School, American Fork, UT
Utica Nursing Home, Utica, OH
Al Vadheim Memorial Hospital, Tyler, MN
Vahle Terrace, Jerseyville, IL
Vale Care Center, San Pablo, CA
Valencia Woods Nursing Center, Valencia, PA
Valerie Manor, Torrington, CT
Valhaven Nursing Center, Valley, NE
Valle Star Nursing Home, Alpine, TX
Valle Verde Health Facility, Santa Barbara, CA
Valle Vista Convalescent Hospital, Escondido, CA
Valle Vista Manor, Lewistown, MT
Vallejo Convalescent Hospital, Vallejo, CA
Valley Care & Guidance Center, Fresno, CA
Valley Care Center, Porterville, CA
Valley Care Center, Idaho Falls, ID
Valley Care Center, Okanogan, WA
Valley Care Nursing Home Inc, Sewickley, PA
Valley Convalescent Center, Fresno, CA
Valley Convalescent Hospital, Bakersfield, CA
Valley Convalescent Hospital, El Centro, CA
Valley Convalescent Hospital, San Bernardino, CA
Valley Convalescent Hospital, Watsonville, CA
Valley Crest Nursing Home, Wilkes-Barre, PA
Valley Fair Lodge, Colorado City, TX
Valley Falls Terrace, Spartanburg, SC
Valley Gardens Health Care Center, Stockton, CA
Valley Grande Manor, Weslaco, TX
Valley Grande Manor Inc, Brownsville, TX
Valley Group Home 1, Moorhead, MN
Valley Group Home 2, Karlstad, MN
Valley Haven Geriatric Center Inc, Wellsburg, WV
Valley Haven Nursing Home, Sanders, KY
Valley Health Care Center, Billings, MT
Valley Health Care Center, Chilhowie, VA
Valley Health Care Center, Renton, WA
Valley Health Care Center, Hayward, WI
Valley Health Care Center Inc, Valley Falls, KS
Valley Health Services Inc, Herkimer, NY
Valley Health Village, South Charleston, WV
Valley Hi Nursing Home, Woodstock, IL
Valley Home, Thief River Falls, MN
Valley Homes, Mount Vernon, WA
Valley Hospital, Palmer, AK
Valley House, Cincinnati, OH
Valley House Healthcare, Tucson, AZ
Valley Manor Care Center, Concord, CA
Valley Manor Care Center, Montrose, CO

Valley Manor Convalescent Hospital, North Hollywood, CA
Valley Manor Health Care Center, Denver, CO
Valley Manor Nursing Center, Coopersburg, PA
Valley Manor Nursing Home, New Philadelphia, OH
Valley Manor Nursing Home, Plymouth, WI
Valley Memorial Home—Almonte, Grand Forks, ND
Valley Memorial Home—Medical Park, Grand Forks, ND
Valley Mills Care Center, Valley Mills, TX
Valley Nursing Home, Westwood, NJ
Valley Nursing Home, Saint Marys, OH
Valley Oaks Health Care Center, Gridley, CA
Valley Palms Care Center, North Hollywood, CA
Valley Park Convalescent Center, Barbourville, KY
Valley Rehabilitation Center, Toppenish, WA
Valley Rest Home, Eden Valley, MN
Valley Rest Nursing Home, Totowa Boro, NJ
Valley Road Nursing Home, Salem, OH
Valley Skilled Nursing Facility, Sacramento, CA
Valley Terrace Nursing Center, Puyallup, WA
Valley View, Beaumont, CA
Valley View Care Center, Riverbank, CA
Valley View Care Center, Nebraska City, NE
Valley View Care Center, LaGrande, OR
Valley View Care Center, Anson, TX
Valley View Care Centre, North Platte, NE
Valley View Care Home, Lawrence, KS
Valley View Castle Nursing Home, Millersburg, OH
Valley View Estates Nursing Home, Hamilton, MT
Valley View Health Care, Rome, GA
Valley View Health Care Center, Canon City, CO
Valley View Health Care Center, Elkhart, IN
Valley View Health Care Center, Saratoga, WY
Valley View Health Care Facility, Marksville, LA
Valley View Home, Glasgow, MT
Valley View Home—Blair County, Altoona, PA
Valley View Manor, Craig, CO
Valley View Manor, Lamberton, MN
Valley View Manor, Frankfort, OH
Valley View Manor Inc, Frenchtown, NJ
Valley View Manor Nursing Home, Norwich, NY
Valley View Medical Center, Cedar City, UT
Valley View Nursing Center, Eldora, IA
Valley View Nursing Home, Lenox, MA
Valley View Nursing Home, Houston, MN
Valley View Nursing Home, Akron, OH
Valley View Nursing Home, Lancaster, OH
Valley View Nursing Home, Martins Ferry, OH
Valley View Nursing Home, Cheswick, PA
Valley View Nursing Home, Eastland, TX
Valley View Nursing Home, Granbury, TX
Valley View Nursing Home, Berkeley Springs, WV
Valley View Nursing Home Inc, Westfield, MA
Valley View Professional Care Center, Junction City, KS
Valley View Residential Care Home, Bayfield, CO
Valley View Retirement Community, Boise, ID
Valley View Retirement Community, Belleville, PA
Valley View Skilled Nursing Center, Ukiah, CA
Valley View Villa Nursing Home, Fort Morgan, CO
Valley View Village, Des Moines, IA
Valley Vista Care Center, Saint Maries, ID
Valley Vista Care Center, Junction City, KS
Valley Vista Care Center, The Dalles, OR

Valley Vista Good Samaritan Center, Wamego, KS
Valley Vue Care Center, Armstrong, IA
Valley West Convalescent Hospital, Williams, CA
Valley West Health Care Center, Eugene, OR
Valleyview Health Care Center, Jordan, MN
Vallhaven Care Center, Neenah, WI
Valliant Nursing Center Inc, Valliant, OK
Valor Aspen, Wayzata, MN
Valor Hemingway, Saint Paul, MN
Valor Kentucky, Minneapolis, MN
Valor Lexington, Circle Pines, MN
Valor Minnetonka, Minnetonka, MN
Valor Sunlen, Minneapolis, MN
Valor Vincent, Minneapolis, MN
Valvista Pavilion, Athens, TX
Van Allen Nursing Home, Little Falls, NY
Van Ark Care Center, Tucumcari, NM
Van Ayer Manor Nursing Center, Martin, TN
Van Buren Convalescent Center, Belleville, MI
Van Buren County Nursing Home, Clinton, AR
Van Buren Good Samaritan Center, Keosauqua, IA
Van Buren Nursing Center, Van Buren, AR
Van Dora Nursing Home, Foxborough, MA
Van Doren Nursing Home, Rego Park, NY
Van Duyn Home & Hospital, Syracuse, NY
Van Dyk Manor, Montclair, NJ
Van Dyk Nursing & Convalescent Home, Ridgewood, NJ
Van Dyke Convalescent Center, Effingham, IL
Van Hook School of Florida Inc, DeLeon Springs, FL
Van Nuys Health Care, Van Nuys, CA
Van Rensselaer Manor, Troy, NY
Van Wert Manor, Van Wert, OH
Vanceburg Health Care, Vanceburg, KY
Vanco Manor Nursing Center, Goodlettsville, TN
Vancrest, Van Wert, OH
Vanderklish Hall Nursing Home, Newton, MA
Vanguard Residential Services Inc I, Manning, SC
Vanguard Residential Services Inc II, Manning, SC
Vantage Convalescent Center, Phoenix, AZ
Vantage Convalescent Center, Little Rock, AR
Varnum Park Rest Home, Waltham, MA
Vassar Rest Home, Vassar, MI
Vegas Valley Convalescent Hospital, Las Vegas, NV
Venango Manor, Franklin, PA
Venice Nursing Pavilion—North, Venice, FL
Venice Nursing Pavilion—South, Venice, FL
Venoy Continued Care Center, Wayne, MI
Ventura Convalescent Hospital, Ventura, CA
Ventura Estates Health Manor, Newbury Park, CA
Venturan Convalescent Center, Ventura, CA
Venture Group Home, Minneapolis, MN
VerDelle Village Inc, Saint Albans, VT
Verdries Nursing Center, Kalamazoo, MI
Verdugo Valley Convalescent Hospital, Montrose, CA
Verdugo Vista Convalescent Hospital, La Crescenta, CA
Verland Foundation Inc, Sewickley, PA
Vermilion Health Care Center, Kaplan, LA
Vermilion Manor Nursing Home, Vermilion, OH
Vermillion Convalescent Center, Clinton, IN
Vermillion Manor Nursing Home, Danville, IL
Vermont Achievement Center, Rutland, VT
Vermont Knolls Convalescent Hospital, Los Angeles, CA
Vermont State Nursing Home, Waterbury, VT
Vernon Care Center, Vernon, TX
Vernon Convalescent Hospital, Los Angeles, CA
Vernon Green Nursing Home, Vernon, VT
Vernon Hall Inc, Cambridge, MA
Vernon Manor, Viroqua, WI
Vernon Manor Children's Home, Wabash, IN
Vernon Manor Health Care Facility, Vernon, CT

Vero Beach Care Center Inc, Vero Beach, FL
Verrazano Nursing Home, Staten Island, NY
Versailles Healthcare Center, Versailles, OH
Vespers Nursing Home, Wilkesboro, NC
Vestal Nursing Center, Vestal, NY
Veterans Memorial Hospital SNF/ICF Facility, Pomeroy, OH
VFW Parkway Nursing Home, Boston, MA
Via Health Care Center/The Hermitage Richmond Virginia United Methodist Homes Inc, Richmond, VA
Vian Nursing Home, Vian, OK
Vicksburg Convalescent Home, Vicksburg, MS
Vicksburg Trace Haven, Vicksburg, MS
Victoria Haven Nursing Facility, Norwood, MA
Victoria Health Care Center, Asheville, NC
Victoria Home for Retired Men & Women, Ossining, NY
Victoria Manor Nursing Center, North Cape May, NJ
Victoria Martin Nursing Home, Saint Petersburg, FL
Victoria Nursing Home, Portland, OR
Victoria Nursing & Rehabilitation Center, Victoria, TX
Victorian Heights Nursing Center, Manchester, CT
Victorian Manor, Taylorville, IL
Victorian Manor, Liberal, KS
Victorian Mansion Retirement Home, Attleboro, MA
Victorian Villa Nursing Home, Canton, ME
Victory Garden Nursing Home, Duncannon, PA
Victory Lake Nursing Center, Hyde Park, NY
Victory Lakes Convalescent Care Center, Lindenhurst, IL
Victory Memorial Hospital & Nursing Home, Stanley, WI
Victory Park Nursing Home, Norwood, OH
Victory Village of the Jewish Home for the Aging, Reseda, CA
Victory Way House, Hayden, CO
Vida Nueva Care Center, Amarillo, TX
Vienna Convalescent Hospital, Lodi, CA
View Heights Convalescent Hospital, Los Angeles, CA
View Park Convalescent Center, Los Angeles, CA
Viewcrest Convalescent Center, Tacoma, WA
Viewcrest Nursing Center, Duluth, MN
Vigo County Home, Terre Haute, IN
Viking Manor Nursing Home, Ulen, MN
Viking Nursing Facility Inc, Cape Elizabeth, ME
Villa, Green River, WY
Villa Camillus, Columbia Station, OH
Villa Campana Health Center, Tucson, AZ
Villa Care Center, Cleveland, OH
Villa Care Center, San Antonio, TX
Villa Cascade Care Center, Lebanon, OR
Villa Clement, West Allis, WI
Villa Convalescent Center, Daly City, CA
Villa Convalescent Center Inc, Troy, OH
Villa Convalescent Hospital, Riverside, CA
Villa Crest Inc, Manchester, NH
Villa De Marillac Nursing Home, Pittsburgh, PA
Villa del Sol, Marshalltown, IA
Villa Elena Convalescent Hospital, Norwalk, CA
Villa Elizabeth, Grand Rapids, MI
Villa Fairborn, Fairborn, OH
Villa Fairmont Mental Health Center, San Leandro, CA
Villa Feliciana Chronic Disease Hospital & Rehabilitation Center, Jackson, LA
Villa Gardens, Pasadena, CA
Villa Georgetown, Georgetown, OH
Villa Grandview, Grandview, MO
Villa Guadalupe, Gallup, NM
Villa Haven Nursing Center, Breckenridge, TX
Villa Health Care Center, Sherman, IL
Villa Health Care Center, Mora, MN
Villa Inn Nursing Center, Palestine, TX
Villa Loretto Nursing Home, Mount Calvary, WI

Villa Manor Care Center Inc, Porterville, CA
Villa Manor Nursing Home, Lakewood, CO
Villa Maria, Tucson, AZ
Villa Maria Care Center, Long Beach, CA
Villa Maria Care Center, Santa Maria, CA
Villa Maria Convalescent Home Inc, Plainfield, CT
Villa Maria Healthcare Center, Hurley, WI
Villa Maria Healthcare Ltd, Fargo, ND
Villa Maria Inc, Mulvane, KS
Villa Maria Nursing & Rehabilitation Center Inc, North Miami, FL
Villa Marie Skilled Nursing Facility, Jefferson City, MO
Villa Marin Retirement Residences, San Rafael, CA
Villa Mary Immaculate, Albany, NY
Villa North Nursing Home, Toledo, OH
Villa Northwest Convalescent Center, Houston, TX
Villa Nursing Center, Mount Pleasant, TX
Villa Oaks Convalescent Hospital, Pasadena, CA
Villa of Oswego, Oswego, KS
Villa of St Francis Nursing Home, Morris, MN
Villa Pines Living Center, Friendship, WI
Villa Pueblo Towers, Pueblo, CO
Villa Rancho Bernardo, San Diego, CA
Villa Rosa Nursing Home, Mitchellville, MD
Villa Royal Health Care Center, Medford, OR
Villa St Cyril—Home For Aged, Highland Park, IL
Villa St Joseph, Overland Park, KS
Villa St Michael Nursing & Retirement Center, Baltimore, MD
Villa St Vincent, Crookston, MN
Villa Santa Anna Home for the Aged Inc, Beachwood, OH
Villa Scalabrini, Northlake, IL
Villa Siena, Mountain View, CA
Villa Siesta Nursing Home, Van, TX
Villa Springfield, Springfield, OH
Villa Teresa, Harrisburg, PA
Villa Valencia, Laguna Hills, CA
Villa Vista Inc, Cromwell, MN
Villa West, Monclova, OH
Village, Cameron, MO
Village at Brandon, Brandon, FL
Village at Countryside, Safety Harbor, FL
Village at Vance Jackson, San Antonio, TX
Village at Westerville Nursing Center, Westerville, OH
Village Care, Galion, OH
Village Christian Parke, Zionsville, IN
Village Convalescent Center, Gresham, OR
Village Convalescent Center, McAllen, TX
Village Creek Manor Inc, Wynne, AR
Village East, Aurora, CO
Village Green Nursing Home, Phoenix, AZ
Village Healthcare Center, Houston, TX
Village House, Newport, RI
Village Inn Nursing Home, Dixon, IL
Village Manor, Hyde Park, MA
Village Manor, Lincoln, NE
Village Manor Health Care Inc, Plainfield, CT
Village Manor Nursing Home, Quitman, TX
Village North Health Center, Saint Louis, MO
Village Nursing Home, Sullivan, IN
Village Nursing Home, Hico, TX
Village Nursing Home Inc, Skokie, IL
Village Nursing Home Inc, New York, NY
Village on Canyon Creek, Temple, TX
Village on the Green, Longwood, FL
Village on the Heights, San Antonio, TX
Village Rest Home, Easton, MA
Village Rest Home, Leominster, MA
Village Rest Home of Brockton, Brockton, MA
Village Sheltered Care Home, Cobden, IL
Village Square Nursing Center, Orwell, OH
Village Villa Nursing Home, Nortonville, KS
Village Vista Skilled Nursing Facility, Lancaster, PA
Villas of Shannon Nursing Home, Shannon, IL
Ville de Sante, Omaha, NE
Villisca Good Samaritan Center, Villisca, IA
Vincennes Healthcare, Vincennes, IN

Vincentian Home for Chronically Ill, Pittsburgh, PA

Vindobona Nursing Home Inc, Braddock Heights, MD

Vinewood Nursing Home, Plainfield, IN

Vintage Faire Convalescent Hospital, Modesto, CA

Vintage Health Center, Denton, TX

Vintage Villa Nursing Center, Dexter, MO

VIP Manor, Wood River, IL

Virden Nursing Center, Virden, IL

Virgil Sanitarium & Convalescent Hospital, Los Angeles, CA

Virginia Baptist Hospital—Skilled Nursing Unit, Lynchburg, VA

Virginia Hall Nursing Home, Shreveport, LA

Virginia Home, Richmond, VA

Virginia Manor Convalescent Home Inc, Everett, WA

Virginia Regional Medical Center & Nursing Home, Virginia, MN

Virginia Synod Lutheran Home at Roanoke, Roanoke, VA

Virginia, Waukesha, WI

Virginian Health Care Unit, Fairfax, VA

Visalia Convalescent Hospital, Visalia, CA

Vista Continuing Care Center, Pasadena, TX

Vista Del Cerro Convalescent Center, El Cajon, CA

Vista Del Mar Care Center, Vista, CA

Vista Del Monte, Santa Barbara, CA

Vista Del Sol Care Center, Los Angeles, CA

Vista Gardens Nursing Home, Red Oak, IA

Vista Grande Nursing Home, Cortez, CO

Vista Grande Villa, Jackson, MI

Vista Hills Health Care Center, El Paso, TX

Vista Laguna Aftercare Facility Inc, Chicago, IL

Vista Manor, Titusville, FL

Vista Nursing Home Inc, Heavener, OK

Vista Pacifica Convalescent Home, Riverside, CA

Vista Pacificia Center, Riverside, CA

Vista Ray Convalescent Hospital, Lodi, CA

Vista Ray Convalescent Hospital 2, Lodi, CA

Vistavue Care Center, Kennewick, WA

Vivian's Nursing Home, Amarillo, TX

Volmer Nursing Home, North Vassalboro, ME

Volunteers of America ICF/MR No 20, Huntsville, AL

Henry & Jane Vonderlieth Living Center Inc, Mount Pulaski, IL

Marshall C Voss Health Care Facility, Harriman, TN

Wabash Christian Retirement Center, Carmi, IL

Wabash Healthcare Center, Wabash, IN

Wabasso Healthcare Center, Wabasso, MN

Wachusett Manor Nursing Home, Gardner, MA

Waconia Healthcare Center, Waconia, MN

Waddell Nursing Home, Galax, VA

Waddington Convalescent Home, Fayette City, PA

Wadesboro Nursing Home Inc, Wadesboro, NC

Wadsworth Glen Health Care Center, Middletown, CT

Wadsworth Health Care Center Inc, Wadsworth, OH

Wagner Good Samaritan Center, Wagner, SD

Wagner Heights Convalescent Hospital, Stockton, CA

Margaret Wagner House, Cleveland, OH

Wagnon Place Inc, Warren, AR

Wahiawa General Hospital, Wahiawa, HI

Wahpeton Health Care Center, Wahpeton, ND

Wahroonga Home, Columbus, OH

Waimano Training School & Hospital, Pearl City, HI

Waite Park Nursing Home Inc, Waite Park, MN

Wakefield Health Care Center, Wakefield, NE

Wakonda Heritage Manor, Wakonda, SD

Wakulla Manor, Crawfordville, FL

Walbridge Memorial Convalescent Wing, Meeker, CO

Walden House Healthcare Nursing Home, Concord, MA

Walden Oaks Health Care Center, San Antonio, TX

Waldon Health Care Center, Kenner, LA

Waldron Health Care Home Inc, Waldron, IN

Annie Walker Nursing Home, Mount Sterling, KY

Walker Care Center, Centralia, WA

Walker Convalescent Hospital Inc, Richmond, CA

Walker Methodist Health Center, Minneapolis, MN

Walker Nursing Home Inc, Virginia, IL

Walker Post Manor, Oxford, NE

Walker Road Group Home, Dover, DE

Walker's Veterans Home, Spearfish, SD

Lurleen B Wallace Developmental Center, Decatur, AL

Wallingford Convalescent Home Inc, Wallingford, CT

Wallingford Nursing & Rehabilitation Center, Wallingford, PA

Wallowa County Memorial Hospital, Enterprise, OR

Walnut Convalescent Hospital, Los Angeles, CA

Walnut Creek Convalescent Hospital Inc, Walnut Creek, CA

Walnut Creek Nursing Home, Oklahoma City, OK

Walnut Grove, Grandview, WA

Walnut Grove Village, Morris, IL

Walnut Hill Convalescent Center, Petersburg, VA

Walnut Hill Convalescent Home, New Britain, CT

Walnut Hills Convalescent Center Inc, Austin, TX

Walnut Hills Nursing Home Inc, Walnut Creek, OH

Walnut Hills Pavilion, Massillon, OH

Walnut Hills Rest Home, Walnut Creek, OH

Walnut Manor, Walnut, IL

Walnut Manor Care Center, Clarksburg, OH

Walnut Mountain Nursing Home, Liberty, NY

Walnut Place, Dallas, TX

Walnut Ridge Convalescent Center, Walnut Ridge, AR

Walnut Valley Manor, Augusta, KS

Walnut Whitney Convalescent Hospital, Carmichael, CA

Walsenburg Care Center Inc, Walsenburg, CO

Walsh Healthcare Center, Walsh, CO

Mary Manning Walsh Nursing Home Company Inc, New York, NY

Walsh Terrace, Galesburg, IL

Arnold Walter Nursing Home, Hazlet, NJ

Walton County Convalescent Center, DeFuniak Springs, FL

Walton County Hospital Convalescent Wing, Monroe, GA

Wanaque Convalescent Center, Haskell, NJ

Wannamaker Street Community Residence, Orangeburg, SC

Wapakoneta Manor, Wapakoneta, OH

Wapello Nursing Home, Wapello, IA

Ward Manor Inc, Tahlequah, OK

Ware Avenue Personal Care Home, East Point, GA

Ware Manor Nursing Home, Waycross, GA

Ware Memorial Care Center, Amarillo, TX

Wareheime Residential Care, Greeley, CO

Warm Beach Health Care Center, Stanwood, WA

Warm Springs State Hospital, Warm Springs, MT

Warminster Hospital-Based Skilled Nursing Facility, Warminster, PA

Warner Care Home 1, Cokato, MN

Warner Care Home 2, Cokato, MN

Warner Care Home 3, Cokato, MN

Warren Haven, Oxford, NJ

Warren Hills Personal Care & Nursing Facility, Warrenton, NC

Warren Manor, Warren, PA

Warren Manor Nursing Home, Selma, AL

Warren Medical Services, Warren, PA

Warren Park Nursing Home, Indianapolis, IN

Warren State Hospital Long-Term Care Facility, Warren, PA

Warrensburg Manor Care Center, Warrensburg, MO

Warrensville Center, Warrensville Heights, OH

Warroad Care Center, Warroad, MN

Warsaw Health Care Center, Warsaw, VA

Warsaw Nursing Home, Warsaw, IN

Wartburg Home of the Evangelical Lutheran Church, Mount Vernon, NY

Wartburg Lutheran Home for the Aging, Brooklyn, NY

Warwick Health Centre, Warwick, RI

Warwick Rest Home Inc, Warwick, RI

Wasatch Care Center, Ogden, UT

Wasatch County Hospital—Skilled Nursing Facility, Heber City, UT

Wasatch Villa Convalescent Nursing Home, Salt Lake City, UT

Washington Nursing Home, Cincinnati, OH

Booker T Washington Nursing Home, Shreveport, LA

Washington Care Center, Washington, IA

Washington Center for Aging Services, Washington, DC

Washington Christian Village, Washington, IL

Washington Convalescent Hospital, San Leandro, CA

Washington County Convalescent Center, Chipley, FL

Washington County Extended Care Facility, Sandersville, GA

Washington County Health Center, Washington, PA

Washington County Hospital Extended Care Facility, Hagerstown, MD

Washington County Infirmary & Nursing Home, Chatom, AL

Washington County Public Hospital & Nursing Home, Akron, CO

Washington Health Care Center—Riverside, Centralia, WA

Washington Healthcare Center—Aldercrest, Edmonds, WA

Washington Healthcare Center Gold Leaf, Ellensburg, WA

Washington Healthcare Center—Northcrest, Spokane, WA

Washington Healthcare Center—Unicrest, Spokane, WA

Washington Healthcare Center—Valley Crest, Spokane, WA

Washington Home, Washington, DC

Washington House, Alexandria, VA

Washington Manor, Kenosha, WI

Washington Manor Nursing & Rehabilitation Center, Hollywood, FL

Washington Manor Nursing Center, Dayton, OH

Washington Nursing & Convalescent, Los Angeles, CA

Washington Nursing Facility, Washington, DC

Washington Odd Fellows Home, Walla Walla, WA

Washington Rehabilitation Center Southcrest, Spokane, WA

Washington Square Nursing Center, Warren, OH

Washington Terrace Nursing Center, Ogden, UT

Washita Valley Nursing Center, Lindsay, OK

Washoe Care Center, Sparks, NV

Watauga Nursing Care Center, Boone, NC

Watch Hill Manor Ltd, Westerly, RI

Waterbury Convalescent Center Inc, Waterbury, CT

Waterbury Extended Care Facility Inc, Watertown, CT

Waterbury Nursing Center, Waterbury, CT

Waterford Commons, Toledo, OH

Waterford Convalescent Center, Hialeah Gardens, FL

Waterford Health & Rehabilitation Center, Waterford, CT

Waterford Health Center, Juno Beach, FL

Waterford Manor Rest Home, Wareham, MA

Waterfront Health Care Center, Buffalo, NY
Waterfront Terrace Inc, Chicago, IL
Waterman Convalescent Hospital, San Bernardino, CA
Waterman Heights Nursing Home Ltd, Smithfield, RI
Waters Edge, Alameda, CA
Watertown Convalarium, Watertown, CT
Waterview, Cedar Grove, NJ
Waterview Hills Nursing Center Inc, Purdys Station, NY
Waterview Nursing Care Center, Flushing, NY
Waterview Villa, East Providence, RI
Waterville Care Center, Waterville, MN
Waterville Convalescent Center, Waterville, ME
Watkins Home, Winona, MN
Manda Ann/Watkins Convalescent Home, Houston, TX
Watrous Nursing Home Inc, Madison, CT
Watseka Health Care Center, Watseka, IL
Layton W Watson Nursing Home, Gallaway, TN
Watson Nursing Home, Fort Worth, TX
Watsonville Care Center East, Watsonville, CA
Watsonville Care Center West, Watsonville, CA
Watts Home, Mansfield, OH
Waubay Rest Home, Waubay, SD
Waukegan Pavilion, Waukegan, IL
Waukon Good Samaritan Center, Waukon, IA
Waunakee Manor Health Care Center, Waunakee, WI
Wausa Nursing Center, Wausa, NE
Wausau Manor, Wausau, WI
Wautoma Care Center Inc, Wautoma, WI
Waveny Care Center, New Canaan, CT
Waverly Health Care Center, Waverly, VA
Waverly Heights, Gladwyne, PA
Way Fair Restorium, Fairfield, IL
Way Twelve Halfway House, Wayzata, MN
Wayland Health Center, Providence, RI
Anthony Wayne Living Center, Fort Wayne, IN
Wayne Care Centre, Wayne, NE
Wayne Care Nursing Home, Waynesboro, TN
Wayne Continuous Care Center, Wayne, WV
Wayne Convalescent Center, Wayne, MI
Wayne County Care Center, Wooster, OH
Wayne County Memorial Hospital Skilled Nursing Facility, Honesdale, PA
Wayne County Nursing Home, Waynesboro, TN
Wayne County Nursing Home & Health Related Facility, Lyons, NY
Wayne Haven Nursing Home, Wayne, NJ
Wayne Health Related Facility/Skilled Nursing Facility, Bronx, NY
Wayne Living Center for Seniors, Wayne, MI
Wayne Living Center Nursing Care, Wayne, MI
Wayne Manor Nursing Home, Boston, MA
Wayne Manor Rest Home, Wooster, OH
Wayne Nursing & Rehabilitation Center, Wayne, PA
Wayne Total Living Center For the Developmentally Disabled, Wayne, MI
Waynesburg Rest Home, Waynesburg, KY
Waynesville Nursing Center, Waynesville, MO
Waynoka Nursing Center, Waynoka, OK
Wayside Farm Inc, Peninsula, OH
Wayside Nursing Care Facility, Missoula, MT
Wayside Nursing Home Inc, Worcester, MA
WCTU Home for Women, Los Angeles, CA
We Care Home for the Aged, Sturgis, SD
We Care Nursing Facility, Arcola, IL
Weakley County Nursing Home, Dresden, TN
Weakleys Home for Adults No 1, Vienna, VA
Weakleys Home for Adults No 2, Vienna, VA
Weatherford Care Center 1, Weatherford, TX
Weatherford Care Center 2, Weatherford, TX
Weatherford Nursing Center, Weatherford, OK
Webber Nursing Center, Fort Worth, TX
Webco Manor, Marshfield, MO
Weber Health Care Center Inc, Wellington, OH

Webster at Rye, Rye, NH
Webster Continuous Care Center, Cowen, WV
Webster House Long Term Care Facility, Webster, MA
Webster Manor Long-Term Care Facility, Webster, MA
Webster's Rest Home, Terre Haute, IN
Wecare Health Facility, Columbus, OH
WECARE Nursing Center, Wildwood, FL
Wedgemere Convalescent Home, Taunton, MA
Wedgewood, Grand Island, NE
Wedgewood Health Care, Saint Petersburg, FL
Wedgewood Health Care, Inver Grove Heights, MN
Wedgewood Manor Healthcare Center, Clarksville, IN
Wedgewood Nursing Home, Great Neck, NY
Wedgewood Nursing Home, Spencerport, NY
Wedgewood Nursing Home, Fort Worth, TX
Wedgwood Rehabilitation Center, Seattle, WA
Wedow Private Home Care, Michigan City, IN
Weekes Rest Home Inc, Stoughton, MA
Weier Retirement Nursing Home, Belleville, IL
Weirton Geriatric Center, Weirton, WV
Weisbrod Memorial County Hospital & Nursing Home, Eads, CO
Weiser Care Center, Weiser, ID
Welbourne Hall, Watertown, WI
Welcome Home for the Blind, Grand Rapids, MI
Welcome Nursing Home, Franklin, IN
Welcome Nursing Home Inc, Oberlin, OH
Weld County Community Center Group Home, Greeley, CO
Weldwood Health Care Center, Golden Valley, MN
Wellesley, El Monte, CA
Wellesley Manor Nursing Home, Wellesley, MA
Wellington Care Center, Wellington, TX
Wellington Estates Inc—Hartford-Salem Manor, Wellington, OH
Wellington Hall Nursing Home, Hackensack, NJ
Wellington Manor, Tampa, FL
Wellington Manor, Wellington, OH
Wellington Manor Nursing Home, Arlington, MA
Wellington Plaza Therapy & Nursing Center, Chicago, IL
Wellman House Rest Home, Brookline, MA
Wells Nursing Home, Wells, TX
Wells Nursing Home Inc, Johnstown, NY
Wells Personal Care Home, Jackson, MS
W Frank Wells Nursing Home, MacClenny, FL
Wellspring Therapeutic Community, Minneapolis, MN
Wellsville Highland Inc, Wellsville, NY
Wellsville Manor Care Center, Wellsville, KS
Wellsville Manor Nursing Home, Wellsville, NY
Welsh General Hospital, Welsh, LA
Welsh Home for the Aged, Rocky River, OH
Welsh Nursing Facility, Welsh, LA
Wentworth Home for the Aged, Dover, NH
Mark H Wentworth Home, Portsmouth, NH
Wentzvill Park Care Center, Wentzville, MO
Clara Werner Dormitory, Watertown, WI
Wesbury United Methodist Community, Meadville, PA
Weskota Manor, Wessington Springs, SD
Wesley Acres, Des Moines, IA
Wesley Care Center, Des Moines, WA
Wesley Glen Inc, Columbus, OH
Wesley Hall Inc, Cincinnati, OH
Wesley Health Care Center Inc, Saratoga Springs, NY
Wesley Highland Manor, Memphis, TN
Wesley Highland Place, Memphis, TN
Wesley Homes—The Gardens, Des Moines, WA
Wesley Homes—Wesley Terrace, Des Moines, WA
Wesley Manor, Frankfort, IN

Wesley Manor Health Care Center, Kittanning, PA
Wesley Manor Methodist Home for the Aging, Dothan, AL
Wesley Manor Nursing Center & Retirement Community, Louisville, KY
Wesley Manor Retirement Village, Jacksonville, FL
Wesley Nursing Center—Asbury Care Center—Epworth Place, Charlotte, NC
Wesley-on-East Ltd, Rochester, NY
Wesley Pines, Lumberton, NC
Wesley Terrace Methodist Home for the Aging, Auburn, AL
Wesley Towers Inc, Hutchinson, KS
Wesley Village, Pittston, PA
Wesley Village U M C Health Care Center, Macomb, IL
Wesley Woods Health Center, Atlanta, GA
Wesleyan Arms Inc, High Point, NC
Wesleyan Health Care Center, Marion, IN
Wesleyan Health Care Center, Rapid City, SD
Wesleyan Health Care Center Inc, Denton, MD
Wesleyan Nursing Home, Georgetown, TX
Wesleyan Nursing Home Inc, Seward, AK
Wesleyan Nursing Home Inc, Charlotte, NC
Wessel's Nursing Home, Charlotte, NC
Wessex House of Gadsen, Gadsden, AL
Wessex House of Huntsville, Huntsville, AL
Wessex House of Kingsport, Kingsport, TN
Wessex of Jacksonville, Jacksonville, AL
West Acres Nursing Home, Brockton, MA
West Bay Manor, Warwick, RI
West Bay Nursing Center, Oldsmar, FL
West Bend Care Center, West Bend, IA
West Bloomfield Nursing & Convalescent Center, West Bloomfield, MI
West Caldwell Care Center, West Caldwell, NJ
West Care Home, Klamath Falls, OR
West Carroll Memorial Care Center, Oak Grove, LA
West Carroll Memorial Hospital, Oak Grove, LA
West Chester Arms Nursing & Rehabilitation Center, West Chester, PA
West Chicago Terrace, West Chicago, IL
West Coke County Hospital District Nursing Home, Robert Lee, TX
West County Care Center, Ballwin, MO
West End Health Care Center, Nashville, TN
West Gate Village Inc, Brewton, AL
West Hartford Manor, West Hartford, CT
West Haven Health Care, Bluffton, IN
West Haven Nursing Center, West Haven, CT
West Haven Nursing Home, Apollo, PA
West Hickory Haven, Milford, MI
West Hill Convalescent Home, Rocky Hill, CT
West Hills Convalescent Center, Portland, OR
West Hills Health Care Center, Coraopolis, PA
West Hills Lodge, Owatonna, MN
West Hills Nursing Home Inc, Cincinnati, OH
West Home, Detroit Lakes, MN
West Jordan Care Center, West Jordan, UT
West Kentucky Manor, Clinton, KY
West Lafayette Care Center, West Lafayette, OH
West Lake Lodge Nursing Home, Guilford, CT
West Lake Manor Health Care Center, Augusta, GA
West Lawrence Care Center, Far Rockaway, NY
West Liberty Health Care Center Inc, West Liberty, KY
West Linn Care Center Inc, West Linn, OR
West Los Angeles Pavilion, Los Angeles, CA
West Magic Care Center, Twin Falls, ID
West Main Nursing Home, Mascoutah, IL
West Melbourne Health Care Center, West Melbourne, FL
West Mesa Health Care Center, Albuquerque, NM
West Michigan Care Center, Allendale, MI
West Millard Care Center, Delta, UT
West Monroe Guest House Inc, West Monroe, LA

West Morgan Health Care, Decatur, AL
West Orange Manor, Winter Garden, FL
West Palm Beach Village Care Center, West Palm Beach, FL
West Park Long-Term Care Center, Cody, WY
West Park Villa Health Care Center, Cincinnati, OH
West Plains Health Care Center, West Plains, MO
West Point Care Center, West Point, IA
West Point Living Center, West Point, NE
West Rest Haven Inc, West, TX
West Ridge Manor, Knoxville, IA
West Rock Health Care, New Haven, CT
West Roxbury Manor Nursing Home, Boston, MA
West Salem Manor, West Salem, IL
Sam B West Health Care Center of Atherton Baptist Home, Alhambra, CA
West Side Care Center, Fort Worth, TX
West Side Health Care Center, Gary, IN
West Side Health Care Center, Cincinnati, OH
West Side House, Worcester, MA
West Side Rest Home, Ronan, MT
West Springfield Nursing Home, West Springfield, MA
West Suburban Shelter Care Center, Hinsdale, IL
West Texas Care Center, Midland, TX
West Torrance Care Center, Torrance, CA
West Trail Nursing Home, Plymouth, MI
West Union Good Samaritan Center, West Union, IA
West View Manor, Wooster, OH
West View Nursing Home, Murray, KY
West View Nursing Home Inc, West Warwick, RI
West Vue Home Inc, West Plains, MO
West Wind Care Center, Monahans, TX
West Winds Nursing Home, Union Lake, MI
Westbay Manor I, Westlake, OH
Westbay Manor II, Westlake, OH
Westborough Nursing Home, Westborough, MA
Westbrook Acres, Gladbrook, IA
Westbrook Good Samaritan Center, Westbrook, MN
Westbrook Heights Rest Home, West Brookfield, MA
Westbrook Manor, Kalamazoo, MI
Westbrook Manor Nursing Center, Parsons, KS
Westbury Nursing Home, Jenkinsburg, GA
Westbury Place, Houston, TX
Westchester Care Center, Tempe, AZ
Westchester House, Chesterfield, MO
Westcliff, Amarillo, TX
Westcott Care Center, Danielson, CT
Westerly Health Center, Westerly, RI
Westerly Nursing Home Inc, Westerly, RI
Western Avenue Residence, Waterville, ME
Western Carolina Center, Morganton, NC
Western Center, Canonsburg, PA
Western Convalescent Hospital, Los Angeles, CA
Western Hall County Good Samaritan Center, Wood River, NE
Western Hills Care Center Inc, Cincinnati, OH
Western Hills Health Care Center, Lakewood, CO
Western Hills Health Care Center, Lawton, OK
Western Hills Nursing Home, Comanche, TX
Western Hills Nursing Home, Fort Worth, TX
Western Home, Cedar Falls, IA
Western Manor, Ranger, TX
Western Manor Nursing Home, Billings, MT
Western Maryland Center, Hagerstown, MD
Western Medical Center—Bartlett, Santa Ana, CA
Western Nebraska Nursing Home, Mitchell, NE
Western Nebraska Veterans Home, Scottsbluff, NE
Western Neuro Care Center, Tustin, CA
Western Nursing Home, Buffalo, OK

Western Oaks Health Care Center, Bethany, OK
Western Pennsylvania Eastern Star Home, Pittsburgh, PA
Western Prairie Care Home, Ulysses, KS
Western Reserve Convalescent Home, Erie, PA
Western Reserve Convalescent Homes, Kirtland, OH
Western Reserve Extended Care, Kirtland, OH
Western Reserve Psychiatric Center, Northfield, OH
Western Restoration Center, Pittsburgh, PA
Western State Hospital, Staunton, VA
Western State Hospital Intermediate Care Facility, Hopkinsville, KY
Western Village, Green Bay, WI
Westfall Nursing Home, Bucyrus, OH
Westfield Health Care Center Inc, Westfield, NY
Westfield Manor Health Care Center Inc, Meriden, CT
Westfield Manor Nursing Home, Westfield, MA
Westfield Village, Westfield, IN
Westford Nursing Home, Westford, MA
Westgate Convalescent Center, San Jose, CA
Westgate Gardens Convalescent Center, Visalia, CA
Westgate Manor, Bangor, ME
Westgate Manor Convalescent Hospital, Madera, CA
Westgate Manor Nursing Home, Saint Louis, MI
Westgate Nursing Center, Rocky Mount, NC
Westgate Nursing Center of Tarboro, Tarboro, NC
Westgate Nursing Home, Rochester, NY
Westhaven Nursing Home, Hamilton, OH
Westhaven Nursing Home Inc, Stillwater, OK
Westhaven Personal Care Home, Jackson, MS
Westhills Village Health Care Facility, Rapid City, SD
Westhope Home, Westhope, ND
Westlake Convalescent Hospital, Los Angeles, CA
Westlake Nursing Center, Oklahoma City, OK
Westlake Pavilion, Franklin Park, IL
Westland Convalescent Center, Westland, MI
Westland Manor Nursing Home, Lakewood, CO
Westledge Nursing Home, Peekskill, NY
Westmere Convalescent Home, Albany, NY
Westminster Terrace—Rose Anna Hughes Campus, Louisville, KY
Westminster Canterbury House, Richmond, VA
Westminster-Canterbury of Hampton Roads Inc, Virginia Beach, VA
Westminster-Canterbury of Lynchburg Inc—Health Care Unit, Lynchburg, VA
Westminster-Canterbury of Winchester Inc, Winchester, VA
Westminster Gardens, Duarte, CA
Westminster Health Care Center, Austin, TX
Westminster Healthcare Center, Clarksville, IN
Westminster Manor, Dallas, TX
Westminster Oaks Health Center, Tallahassee, FL
Westminster-Thurber Retirement Community, Columbus, OH
Westminster Towers, Orlando, FL
Westminster Villa Nursing & Convalescent Center, Westminster, MD
Westminster Village, Allentown, PA
Westminster Village Health Center, Dover, DE
Westminster Village Inc, Scottsdale, AZ
Westminster Village Inc, Bloomington, IL
Westminster Village Inc, Ponca City, OK
Westminster Village Muncie Inc, Muncie, IN
Westminster Village North Inc, Indianapolis, IN
Westminster Village West Lafayette Inc, West Lafayette, IN
Westmont Care Center, Logan, IA
Westmont Convalescent Center, Westmont, IL

Westmoreland Health Center, Waukesha, WI
Westmoreland Manor, Greensburg, PA
Westmoreland Place, Chillicothe, OH
Westmount Health Facility, Queensbury, NY
Weston County Manor, Newcastle, WY
Weston Hadden Convalescent Center, Bennington, VT
Weston Manor Nursing & Retirement, Weston, MA
Westover Retirement Community, Hamilton, OH
Westpark Community Hospital—Skilled Nursing Facility, Hammond, LA
Westpark Healthcare Campus—Aristocrat West, Cleveland, OH
Westpark Village Retirement Center, Billings, MT
Westport Convalescent Center, Richmond, VA
Westridge Apartments, Canon City, CO
Westridge Health Care, Terre Haute, IN
Westridge Health Care Center Nursing Home, Marlborough, MA
Westridge Manor Inc, Nacogdoches, TX
Westridge Nursing Center, Lancaster, TX
Westshire Retirement & Healthcare Center, Cicero, IL
Westside Boarding Care Home, Waseca, MN
Westside Convalescent Center, Atlantic City, NJ
Westside Development Center, Corsicana, TX
Westside Health Care, Los Angeles, CA
Westside Health Care Inc, Greenville, SC
Westside Home Inc, Lexington, NE
Westside Village Health Center, Indianapolis, IN
Westview Acres Care Center, Leon, IA
Westview Care Center, Britt, IA
Westview Care Center, Indianola, IA
Westview Care Center, Seymour, TX
Westview Convalescent Center Inc, Attawaugan, CT
Westview Health Care Center Inc, Racine, WI
Westview Living Center, Guthrie, OK
Westview Manor, Derby, KS
Westview Manor, McGregor, TX
Westview Manor, Odessa, TX
Westview Manor Health Care Center, Bedford, IN
Westview Medical Care Home, Port Wentworth, GA
Westview Nursing Center, Peabody, KS
Westview Nursing Center, Herculaneum, MO
Westview Nursing Home, Indianapolis, IN
Westview Nursing Home, Scottdale, PA
Westview Nursing Home—IMD, Milwaukee, WI
Westview Rest Home, East Bridgewater, MA
Westville Nursing Home, Westville, OK
Westward Heights Nursing Home, Lander, WY
Westwinds Geriatric Center, Ellisville, MO
Westwood, Fremont, CA
Westwood Convalescent & Rest Home, Sioux City, IA
Westwood Convalescent Home Inc, Troup, TX
Westwood Hall Hebrew Home, Long Branch, NJ
Westwood Health Care Center, Saint Louis Park, MN
Westwood Health Care Center, Bluefield, VA
Westwood Healthcare Center, Fort Walton Beach, FL
Westwood Healthcare Center, Keene, NH
Westwood Hills Health Care Center Inc, Poplar Bluff, MO
Westwood Manor, Topeka, KS
Westwood Manor, Corpus Christi, TX
Westwood Manor Inc, Chicago, IL
Westwood Manor Nursing Center, Wilson, NC
Westwood Manor Nursing Home Inc, DeRidder, LA
Westwood Nursing Center, Detroit, MI
Westwood Nursing Center, Clinton, MO
Westwood Rehabilitation Medical Center, Boardman, OH
Westwood Transitional Care Unit—Richmond Memorial Hospital, Richmond, VA

Westy Community Care Home Inc, Westmoreland, KS
Wetherell Place, Effingham, IL
Wetumka Nursing Home Inc, Wetumka, OK
Wetumpka Nursing Facility, Wetumpka, AL
Wetzler Convalescent Home Inc, Blue Ball, PA
Wewoka Nursing Home Inc, Wewoka, OK
Wexford House Nursing Center, Wexford, PA
Weyauwega Health Care Center, Weyauwega, WI
Wharton Manor, Manhattan, KS
Wharton Manor, Wharton, TX
May Cravath Wharton Nursing Home, Pleasant Hill, TN
Wheat Ridge Regional Center, Wheat Ridge, CO
Wheat State Manor Inc, Whitewater, KS
Wheatland Hills Retirement Center Inc, Radford, VA
Wheatland Lodge, South Haven, KS
Wheatland Manor, Wheatland, IA
Wheatland Memorial Nursing Home, Harlowton, MT
Wheatland Nursing, Russell, KS
Wheatlands Health Care Center, Kingman, KS
Wheatridge Manor Nursing Home Inc, Denver, CO
Wheeler Care Center, Wheeler, TX
Wheeling Continuous Care Center, Wheeling, WV
Whetstone Convalescent Center, Columbus, OH
Whetstone Valley Nursing Home, Milbank, SD
Whidbey Island Manor Inc, Oak Harbor, WA
Whispering Pines, Valparaiso, IN
Whispering Pines Care Center, Starke, FL
Whispering Pines Care Center, Vancouver, WA
Whispering Pines Care Home, Pine Bluffs, WY
Whispering Pines Convalescent Center, New Port Richey, FL
Whispering Pines Good Samaritan Center, Pine River, MN
Whispering Pines Nursing Home, Plain Dealing, LA
Whispering Pines Nursing Home, Fayetteville, NC
Whispering Pines Nursing Home Inc, Winnsboro, TX
White Acres—Good Samaritan Retirement Village & Nursing Center, El Paso, TX
White Bear Lake Care Center, White Bear Lake, MN
White Billet Nursing Home, Hatboro, PA
White Birch Nursing Home, Paterson, NJ
White Bluff Manor, Savannah, GA
White Care Center Inc, White, SD
White Community Hospital, Aurora, MN
White County Nursing Home, Carmi, IL
White Cross Health Center, Lindsborg, KS
Dixie White House Nursing Home Inc, Pass Christian, MS
Eartha M M White Nursing Home, Jacksonville, FL
Elihu White Nursing & Rehabilitation Center, Braintree, MA
Griffin White Home, Haverhill, MA
White Haven Annex at Clark Summit, Clarks Summit, PA
White Haven Center, White Haven, PA
White Haven Center Annex—Allentown, Allentown, PA
White House Nursing Home, Orange, NJ
Mary E White Developmental Center, Columbia, SC
White Oak Convalescent Home, Canton, OH
White Oak Estates, Spartanburg, SC
White Oak Manor, Mio, MI
White Oak Terrace, Tryon, NC
White Oak Villa Nursing Home, Marshfield, MO
White Pine Care Center, Ely, NV
White Pines Living Center, Oregon, IL
White Plains Center for Nursing Care, White Plains, NY

White Plains Nursing Home, Bronx, NY
Reginald P White Intermediate & Skilled Care Facility, Meridian, MS
White Ridge Health Center, Lee's Summit, MO
White River Convalescent Home Inc, Calico Rock, AR
White River Health Care Center, White River, SD
White Sands of La Jolla, La Jolla, CA
White Settlement Nursing Center, Fort Worth, TX
White Settlement Nursing Center, White Settlement, TX
White Shell, Little Falls, MN
White Sulphur Springs Family Care Center, White Sulphur Springs, WV
Whitecliff Manor, Cleveland Heights, OH
Whitehall Boca Raton, Boca Raton, FL
Whitehall Convalescent & Nursing Home, Chicago, IL
Whitehall Convalescent Home, Saint Petersburg, FL
Whitehall Convalescent Home, Ann Arbor, MI
Whitehall Convalescent Home, Novi, MI
Whitehall Home, Novi, MI
Whitehall—Leader, Lancaster, PA
Whitehall Manor, Whitehall, MI
Whitehall Manor Nursing Home, Barnstable, MA
Whitehall North, Deerfield, IL
Whitehall Nursing Center Inc, Crockett, TX
Whitehall Pavilion Nursing Home, Barnstable, MA
Whitehaven Care Center, Memphis, TN
Whitehills Health Care Center, East Lansing, MI
Whitehouse Country Manor, Whitehouse, OH
Whitehouse Health Care Center, Roseville, MN
Whitesboro Nursing Home Inc, Whitesboro, TX
Whitesburg Manor Health Care Center, Huntsville, AL
Whitewater Healthcare Center, Saint Charles, MN
Whitewood Rehabilitation Center, Waterbury, CT
Whitfield Nursing Home Inc, Corinth, MS
Whitman Convalescent Center, Colfax, WA
Walt Whitman Convalescent Center, Philadelphia, PA
Whitmore Lake Convalescent Center, Whitmore Lake, MI
Whitney Center Medical Unit, Hamden, CT
Whitney Homestead Rest Home, Stow, MA
Irene Whitney Center for Recovery, Minneapolis, MN
Whitney Manor Convalescent Center Inc, Hamden, CT
Whitridge Nursing Wing RIGA Residence of Noble Horizons, Salisbury, CT
Whittaker Rest Home, Weymouth, MA
Whitten Center—Campus Units 1, 2, 4-7, 9, 10, Clinton, SC
Whitten Center—Circle II, Units 19-22, Clinton, SC
Whitten Center Med A, B, C, & D, Clinton, SC
Whitten Center—Suber Center Units A1, 2, B1, 2, Clinton, SC
Whitten Center—Webb, Units 26-29, Clinton, SC
Whoolery's Residential Care Facility, Colorado Springs, CO
Wibaux County Nursing Home, Wibaux, MT
Wichita Falls Convalescent Center, Wichita Falls, TX
Wichita Presbyterian Manor, Wichita, KS
Wickenburg Nursing Home, Wickenburg, AZ
Wickliffe Country Place, Wickliffe, OH
Wicomico Nursing Home, Salisbury, MD
Wide Horizons Care Center, Ogden, UT
Wide Horizons Inc, Wheat Ridge, CO
Wide View Rest Home, Paullina, IA
Widows Home of Dayton, Dayton, OH
Wiener Memorial Medical Center, Marshall, MN

Wiersma's Nursing Home, Allendale, NJ
Wightman Center for Nursing & Rehabilitation, Pittsburgh, PA
Wil Mar Nursing Home, Utica, MI
Wilber Nursing Home, Wilber, NE
Wilburton Nursing Home Inc, Wilburton, OK
Wilcox Health Care Center, Alma, MI
Wilcox Memorial Hospital, Lihue, HI
Wild Rose Manor, Wild Rose, WI
Wilder Health Care Center, Saint Paul, MN
Wilder Nursing Home, Dadeville, AL
Wilder Residence East, Saint Paul, MN
Wilder Residence West, Saint Paul, MN
Wildwood Health Care Center, Puyallup, WA
Wildwood Health Center, Madison, MO
Wildwood Intermediate Care Home, Talking Rock, GA
Wildwood Manor Inc, Gary, IN
Wildwood Manor Mount Inc, Gary, IN
Wiley Avenue Home, Barnesville, OH
Wileyvale Community Nursing Home, Houston, TX
Wilford Manor—Center for Independent Living, East Saint Louis, IL
Wilge Memorial Home, Mitchell, SD
Wilhelms Nursing Home, Sarasota, FL
Wilkes Health Care, Washington, GA
Helen Wilkes Residence, Lake Park, FL
Wilkin County Group Home, Breckenridge, MN
Will-O-Bell Inc, Bartlett, TX
Will-O-Lee Nursing Home 1, Oberlin, OH
Willamette Lutheran Home, Salem, OR
Willamette Nursing Home Inc, Portland, OR
Willamette View Convalescent Center, Milwaukie, OR
Willapa Harbor Care Center, Raymond, WA
Willard Quality Care Nursing Center, Willard, OH
William & Mary Nursing Center, Saint Petersburg, FL
William Penn Nursing Center, Lewistown, PA
Williams Care Manor, Omaha, NE
Williams County Hillside Nursing Home, Bryan, OH
Williams Health Care—Glenridge, Augusta, ME
Williams Health Care—Gray Birch, Augusta, ME
Williams Health Facility, Mitchell, IN
Williams Home, Hancock, MN
Williams Home for the Aged, Flint, MI
Williams Manor, Scottsburg, IN
Williamsbridge Manor, Bronx, NY
Williamsburg Care Center, Williamsburg, IA
Williamsburg Care Center, Farmington Hills, MI
Williamsburg Healthcare Inc, Crawfordsville, IN
Williamsburg Landing, Williamsburg, VA
Williamsburg Nursing Home, Williamsburg, KY
Williamsburg Retirement Inn, Little Rock, AR
Williamsport Home, Williamsport, PA
Williamsport Nursing Home, Williamsport, MD
Williamsville Suburban Nursing Home, Williamsville, NY
Williamsville View Manor, Williamsville, NY
Willimansett East Nursing Home, Chicopee, MA
Willimansett West Nursing Home, Chicopee, MA
Willis Convalescent Center, Willis, TX
Willis Nursing Center, Homestead, PA
Willmar Regional Treatment Center, Willmar, MN
Willoughby Nursing Home, Brooklyn, NY
Willow Bend Care Center, Mesquite, TX
Willow Brook Care Center, Denver, CO
Willow Brook Christian Home, Columbus, OH
Willow Care Center, Hannibal, MO
Willow Care Nursing Home & Willow West Apartments, Willow Springs, MO
Willow Dale Care Center, Battle Creek, IA
Willow Garden Care Center, Marion, IA

Willow Glen Convalescent Hospital Rest Care Center, San Jose, CA
Willow Haven, Tonkawa, OK
Willow Haven Nursing Home, Zanesville, OH
Willow Knoll Nursing Center, Middletown, OH
Willow Manor, Lansing, MI
Willow Manor Convalescent Center Inc, Vincennes, IN
Willow Manor Nursing Home, Lowell, MA
Willow Park Care Facility, Hudson, WI
Willow Park Health Care Center, Lawton, OK
Willow Point Nursing Home, Vestal, NY
Willow Rest Home, Waterbury, CT
Willow Ridge Inc, Amery, WI
Willow Ridge Living Center, Fort Wayne, IN
Willow Tree Care Center Inc, Gresham, OR
Willow Tree Convalescent Hospital Ltd, Oakland, CA
Willow Valley Lakes Manor Healthcare, Willow Street, PA
Willow Valley Manor, Lancaster, PA
Willow Wood Health Care, Rock Falls, IL
Willow Wood New Orleans Home for Jewish Aged, New Orleans, LA
Willowbrook Manor, Flint, MI
Willowbrook Manor Nursing Home, Longview, TX
Willowbrook Manor Rest Home, Millis, MA
Willowbrook Nursing Home, Lake Mills, WI
Willowcrest, South Milwaukee, WI
Willowdale Nursing Home, New Holstein, WI
Willowfield, Delavan, WI
Willowlake Convalescent Hospital, Long Beach, CA
Willowood Nursing & Retirement Facility, Great Barrington, MA
Willowood Nursing Home Inc, Brunswick, OH
Willowood Nursing Home of North Adams, North Adams, MA
Willowood Nursing Home of Williamstown, Williamstown, MA
Willows Nursing Home, Alexandria, IN
Willows, Parkersburg, WV
Willows Convalescent Center Central, Minneapolis, MN
Willows Convalescent Center South, Minneapolis, MN
Willows East Health Care Center, Minneapolis, MN
Willows Health Center, Rockford, IL
Willows Nursing Home, West Chester, OH
Willows Nursing Home, Sun Prairie, WI
Willows Rehabilitation Center, Valparaiso, IN
Willowview Convalescent Hospital, Willows, CA
Wilmington Extended Care Facility, Wilmington, OH
Wilmot Community Home, Wilmot, SD
Wilmot Nursing Home, Wilmot, AR
Wilshire Care Center, Los Angeles, CA
Wilshire Manor Nursing Home, Alexandria, LA
Wilshire Nursing Home, Oklahoma City, OK
Wilson Apartments, Saint Paul, MN
Herman M Wilson Health Care Center, Gaithersburg, MD
Wilson Hospital Skilled Nursing Facility, Johnson City, NY
Wilson Manor Convalescent Hospital, Spring Valley, CA
Wilson Nursing Center, Wilson, OK
Wilson Nursing Home, Wilson, KS
Wilson's Family Care Services, Brighton, CO
Wilton Meadows Health Care, Wilton, CT
Wilton Nursing Home, Wilton, IA
Winamac Nursing Home, Winamac, IN
Winchester House, Libertyville, IL
Winchester Living Center, San Jose, CA
Winchester Lodge, Alvin, TX
Winchester Manor Health Care Center, Winchester, KY
Winchester Mt Vernon House IV, Winchester, MA
Winchester Nursing Center Inc, Winchester, MA
Winchester Place I & II, Canal Winchester, OH

Winchester Terrace, Mansfield, OH
Wincrest Nursing Center, Chicago, IL
Wind Crest Nursing Center, Copperas Cove, TX
Windcrest at Regents Point, Irvine, CA
Windemere, West Bloomfield, MI
Winder Nursing Inc, Winder, GA
Windermere, Augusta, GA
Windham Hills Healthcare Center, Willimantic, CT
Windmill Nursing Pavilion LTD, South Holland, IL
Windom CRF, Windom, MN
Windsong Village Convalescent Center, Pearland, TX
Windsor, Richmond, VA
Windsor Care Center, Cedar Falls, IA
Windsor Care Center, Mount Sterling, KY
Windsor Estates Convalescent Center, Independence, MO
Windsor Estates Nursing Home, Salina, KS
Windsor Estates of Kokomo, Kokomo, IN
Windsor Hall Retirement Center, Windsor, CT
Windsor Health Care Center, Windsor, CO
Windsor House Convalescent Hospital, Vacaville, CA
Windsor Manor, Glendale, CA
Windsor Manor, Columbiana, OH
Windsor Manor Nursing & Rehabilitation Center, Palos Hills, IL
Windsor Medical Center Inc, North Canton, OH
Windsor Nursing Home, South Yarmouth, MA
Windsor Nursing Home, Youngstown, OH
Windsor Park Manor Medical Facility, Carol Stream, IL
Windsor Park Nursing Home, Queens Village, NY
Windsor Park Nursing Home Inc, Cincinnati, OH
Windsor Woods Convalescent Center, Hudson, FL
Windsor's Resthaven, Windsor, MO
Windybush Group Home, Wilmington, DE
Winebrenner Extended Care Facility, Findlay, OH
Winebrenner Haven, Findlay, OH
Winfield Rest Haven Inc, Winfield, KS
Winkel Personal Care Home, Laurel, MT
Winkler Nursing Home, L'Anse, MI
Winnebago Adolescent Treatment, Winnebago, MN
Winnebago Baptist Home, Winnebago, MN
Winner Nursing Home, Winner, SD
Winning Wheels Inc, Prophetstown, IL
Winnsboro Manor Nursing Center, Winnsboro, LA
Winnsboro Nursing Home, Winnsboro, TX
Winnwood Nursing Home Inc, Winnsboro, TX
Winona Manor Nursing Home, Winona, MS
Winslow Convalescent Center, Winslow, AZ
Winslow Convalescent Center, Bainbridge Island, WA
Winslow House, Marion, IA
Louise & John L Winslow Memorial Nursing Home, Tomball, TX
W R Winslow Memorial Home Inc, Elizabeth City, NC
Winston County Nursing Home, Louisville, MS
Winston Manor Convalescent & Nursing Home, Chicago, IL
Winston-Salem Convalescent Center, Winston-Salem, NC
Winter Gables Rest Home, Framingham, MA
Winter Garden Health Care Center, Winter Garden, FL
Winter Haven Nursing Home, Houston, TX
Winter Hill Rest Home, Worcester, MA
Winter Park Care Center, Winter Park, FL
Winter Park Towers, Winter Park, FL
Winterhouse, Zanesville, OH
Winterset Care Center—North, Winterset, IA
Winterset Care Center South, Winterset, IA

Wintersong Village of Delaware, Delaware, OH
Wintersong Village of Hayesville, Hayesville, OH
Wintersong Village of Knox, Knox, IN
Wintersong Village of Laurelville, Laurelville, OH
Wintersong Village of Washington Court House Inc, Washington Court House, OH
Winthrop Health Care Center, New Haven, CT
Winthrop Health Care Center, Winthrop, MN
Winthrop House Nursing Home, Medford, MA
Winthrop Manor Nursing Home, Rome, GA
Winthrop Road Rest Home, Brookline, MA
Wintonbury Continuing Care Center, Bloomfield, CT
Winyah Extended Care Center Inc, Georgetown, SC
Wiregrass Nursing Home, Geneva, AL
Wisconsin Avenue Nursing Home, Washington, DC
Wisconsin Lutheran Child & Family Service, Milwaukee, WI
Wisconsin Odd Fellow-Rebekah Nursing Home, Green Bay, WI
Wisconsin Veterans Home, King, WI
Wish-I-Ah Care Center Inc, Auberry, CA
Wishek Home for the Aged, Wishek, ND
Wishing Well Health Center, Fairmont, WV
Wishing Well Manor Inc, Fairmont, WV
Wisner Manor, Wisner, NE
Nathaniel Witherell, Greenwich, CT
Witmer House, Long Branch, NJ
Woburn Nursing Center Inc, Woburn, MA
Wolcott Hall Nursing Center Inc, Torrington, CT
Wolcott Rest Home, Wolcott, CT
Wolcott View Manor, Wolcott, CT
Wolf Memorial Good Samaritan Center, Albion, NE
Wolfe Nursing Home Inc, Scottdale, PA
Women's Aid Home, Manchester, NH
Wood-Acre Inc, Berkeley, MO
Wood Convalescent, Wichita Falls, TX
Wood Convalescent Center, Paducah, TX
Wood Convalescent Center of Quanah, Quanah, TX
Wood County Nursing Home, Bowling Green, OH
Wood Crest Nursing Center, Midwest City, OK
Wood Dale Health Care Center, Dalton, GA
Wood-Dale Home Inc, Redwood Falls, MN
Frank Wood Convalescent Home, Boston, MA
Wood Lake Group Home, Burlington, IA
Wood Lake Nursing Home, Clute, TX
Wood-Lawn Inc, Batesville, AR
Wood Manor Inc, Claremore, OK
Wood Memorial Nursing Center, Mineola, TX
Wood Mill Convalescent Home, Lawrence, MA
Wood Nursing & Convalescent Center, Waurika, OK
Wood Nursing & Convalescent Center, Vernon, TX
Wood Nursing Home, Mico, TX
Wood Presbyterian Home Inc, Sweetwater, TN
Wood River Convalescent Center, Shoshone, ID
Wood Village Manor, Troutdale, OR
Woodbine Nursing & Convalescent Center, Alexandria, VA
Woodbine, Oak Park, IL
Woodbridge Health Care Center, Evansville, IN
Woodbridge Nursing Center, Woodbridge, VA
Woodbridge Nursing Pavilion, Chicago, IL
Woodburn Personal Care Home, Woodburn, KY
Woodbury Health Care Center, Woodbury, MN
Woodbury Health Related Facility, Woodbury, NY
Woodbury Nursing Center Inc, Woodbury, TN
Woodbury Nursing Home, Woodbury, NY

Woodbury West Care Center, West Des Moines, IA
Woodcliff Lake Manor Nursing Home, Woodcliff Lake, NJ
Woodcreek Nursing Center, Tyler, TX
Woodcrest Center, New Milford, NJ
Woodcrest Nursing Home, Flushing, NY
Wooddale Health Centre, Sun City, AZ
Woodfield Manor Inc, Niles, MI
Woodford Memorial Hospital Intermediate Care Facility, Versailles, KY
Woodford of Ayer Nursing Home, Ayer, MA
Woodfords Group Home I, Portland, ME
Woodfords Group Home II, Portland, ME
Woodhaven Care Center, Ellinwood, KS
Woodhaven Care Center, Monroeville, PA
Woodhaven Manor, Demopolis, AL
Woodhaven Nursing Home, Port Jefferson Station, NY
Woodhaven Nursing Home, Sulphur Springs, TX
Woodhaven of Livonia, Livonia, MI
Woodhaven Village Inc, Montvale, VA
Woodland Acres/Cass County Home, Logansport, IN
Woodland Acres Health Care Center, Brainerd, MN
Woodland Acres Nursing Home Inc, Saint Clairsville, OH
Althea Woodland Nursing Home, Silver Spring, MD
Woodland Care Center, Reseda, CA
Woodland Care Center, Camden, NJ
Woodland Care Center, Lawton, OK
Woodland Convalescent Center, Woodland, WA
Woodland Convalescent Center Inc, North Smithfield, RI
Woodland Health Center, Topeka, KS
Woodland Health Center, Brookfield, WI
Woodland Hills Nursing Center, Allen, OK
Woodland Lafayette, Lafayette, CA
Woodland Manor, Springfield, MO
Woodland Manor, Columbus, OH
Woodland Manor Inc, Siloam Springs, AR
Woodland Manor Nursing Care, Arnold, MO
Woodland Manor Nursing Center, Attica, IN
Woodland Manor Nursing Home, Somerville, OH
Woodland Manor Nursing Home, Conroe, TX
Woodland Nursing Center, Mount Zion, IL
Woodland Nursing Home, Muncie, IN
Woodland Nursing Home Corp, New Rochelle, NY
Woodland Park Care Center, Salt Lake City, UT
Woodland Park Home, Tulsa, OK
Woodland Retirement Center, Orbisonia, PA
Woodland Retirement Home of Loudoun County, Lovettsville, VA
Woodland Skilled Nursing Facility, Woodland, CA
Woodland Springs Nursing Center, Waco, TX
Woodland Terrace Health Care Facility, Elizabethtown, KY
Woodland Terrace Residential Training Center, Montesano, WA
Woodland Village Health Care Center, Cullman, AL
Woodland Village Health Care Center, New Orleans, LA
Woodland Village Nursing Home Inc, Suring, WI
Woodlands Convalescent Center, Newburgh, IN
Woodlands Nursing Center, Tampa, FL
Woodlands Nursing Center, Athens, TX
Woodlands Skilled Nursing Center, Rutherfordton, NC
Woodlawn (First Allied), Skowhegan, ME
Woodlawn Group Home, Columbia, SC
Woodlawn Hills Care Center, San Antonio, TX
Woodlawn Manor Nursing Home, Everett, MA
Woodlawn Nursing Home, Wichita, KS
Woodlawn Nursing Home, Mansfield, OH

Woodley Manor Nursing Home Inc, Montgomery, AL
Woodmere Health Care Center, Plantsville, CT
Woodmere Health Care Center Inc, Woodmere, NY
Woodmere Health Related Facility, Woodmere, NY
Woodmont Nursing Home, Fredericksburg, VA
Woodmont of Ann Arbor, Ann Arbor, MI
Woodpecker Hill Nursing Home, Greene, RI
Woodrest Nursing Home, Walker, MN
Woodridge, Fairfield, OH
Woodridge Convalescent Center, Grapevine, TX
Woodridge House, Brockton, MA
Woodruff Convalescent Center, Bellflower, CA
Woodruff County Nursing Home, McCrory, AR
Woodruff Health Care, Woodruff, SC
Woods Haven Senior Citizens Home, Pollock, LA
Woods Memorial Convalescent Hospital, La Verne, CA
Woodside Convalescent Center, Rochester, MN
Woodside Lutheran Home, Green Bay, WI
Woodside Manor, South Chicago Heights, IL
Woodside Manor Nursing Home Inc, Rochester, NY
Woodside Nursing Center, Oklahoma City, OK
Woodside Village Care Center Ltd, Mount Gilead, OH
Woodspoint Nursing Home, Florence, KY
Woodstock-Kenosha Health Center, Kenosha, WI
Woodstock Residence, Woodstock, IL
Woodsview Nursing Center, Clyde, OH
Woodvale Dodge Center, Dodge Center, MN
Woodvale VI, Owatonna, MN
Woodvale III, Austin, MN
Woodvale V, Albert Lea, MN
Woodvale VII, Albert Lea, MN
Woodview, South Boston, VA
Woodview Healthcare Inc, Fort Wayne, IN
Woodview Home, Ardmore, OK
Woodview Residential Services—Wadena, Wadena, MN
Woodville Convalescent Center, Woodville, TX
Woodville State Hospital Long-Term Care, Carnegie, PA
Woodward House, Columbus, OH
Woodward Nursing Center, Woodward, OK
Woodward State Hospital & School, Woodward, IA
Wooldridge Place, Corpus Christi, TX
Woonsocket Health Centre, Woonsocket, RI
Wooster Nursing Home, Bowling Green, OH
Workmen's Circle Home, Media, PA
Workmen's Circle Home & Infirmary, Bronx, NY
Wornall Health Care Center, Kansas City, MO
Worth County Convalescent Center, Grant City, MO
Worthington Christian Village, Worthington, OH
Worthington Manor, Parkersburg, WV
Worthington Nursing & Convalescent Center, Worthington, OH
Worthington Regional Hospital, Worthington, MN
Wrangell General Hospital—LTC Facility, Wrangell, AK
Wren House, Duluth, MN
Wright Nursing Center, Lakewood, OH
Wright Nursing Home Inc, San Antonio, TX
Wright's Nursing Home, Largo, FL
Wrightsville Manor Nursing Home, Wrightsville, GA
Wunderley Nursing Home, Toledo, OH
Wurtland Health Care Center, Wurtland, KY
Wyandot County Home, Upper Sandusky, OH
Wyandot Manor, Upper Sandusky, OH
Wyant Woods Care Center, Akron, OH
Wyatt Manor Nursing Home, Jonesboro, LA

Wylie-Brunson Residence, Saint Matthews, SC
Wymore Good Samaritan Center, Wymore, NE
Wyncote Church Home, Wyncote, PA
Wyndcrest Nursing Home, Clinton, IA
Wynhoven Health Care Center, Marrero, LA
Wyoming Continuous Care Center, New Richmond, WV
Wyoming County Community Hospital Skilled Nursing Facility, Warsaw, NY
Wyoming Pioneer Home, Thermopolis, WY
Wyoming Retirement Center, Basin, WY
Wyoming Valley Health Care, Wilkes-Barre, PA
Wyomissing Lodge, Reading, PA
Wyotech Group Home, Riverton, WY
Wythe County Community Hospital, Wytheville, VA
Wythe House, Wytheville, VA
Will-O-Lee Nursing Home 2, Oberlin, OH
Xenia Family Care Home, Xenia, OH
Yadkin Nursing Care Center, Yadkinville, NC
Yakima Convalescent, Yakima, WA
Yale Manor Nursing Home, Dayton, OH
Yale Nursing Home, Yale, OK
Yalobusha County Nursing Home, Water Valley, MS
Yancey Nursing Center, Burnsville, NC
Yankton Care Center, Yankton, SD
Yaphank Infirmary, Yaphank, NY
Yaquina Care Center Inc, Newport, OR
Ye Olde House, Mont Clare, PA
Yell County Nursing Home, Ola, AR
Yellowstone Care Center, Idaho Falls, ID
Ygnacio Convalescent Hospital, Walnut Creek, CA
Yingst Nursing Home Inc, Quakertown, PA
Yoakum Memorial Nursing Home Inc, Yoakum, TX
Yolo General Hospital SNF D/P, Woodland, CA
York Convalescent Center, Elmhurst, IL
York Convalescent Center, Yorktown, VA
York County Hospital & Home, York, PA
York Hospital, York, ME
York Lutheran Home, York, PA
York Manor, Muskogee, OK
York Terrace, Pottsville, PA
Yorkdale Health Center Inc, Rockford, IL
Yorkshire Health Care Center, Columbus, OH
Yorkshire Manor, Minneapolis, MN
Yorktown Health Care Center Inc, Yorktown, IN
Yorktown Manor Home, Yorktown, TX
Bertha M Young Rest Home, Pittsfield, MA
C C Young Memorial Home—Young Health Center, Dallas, TX
Youngstown Developmental Center, Mineral Ridge, OH
Yuba City Care Center, Yuba City, CA
Yukon Convalescent Home, Yukon, OK
Yuma Life Care Center, Yuma, CO
Yuma Nursing Center, Yuma, AZ
YWCA Arnett Pritchett Foundation Home, Lexington, KY
Zachary Manor Nursing Home, Zachary, LA
Zartman Nursing Home, Franklin, OH
Zastrow Care Center Inc, Gilman, WI
Zeigler Collingwood Home, Toledo, OH
Zeigler Colonial Manor Inc, Zeigler, IL
Zendt Home, Richfield, PA
Zenith Apartments, Lakeville, MN
Zephyr Haven Nursing Home, Zephyrhills, FL
Zerbe Sisters Nursing Center Inc, Narvon, PA
Zimmerman Nursing Home, Reedsburg, WI
Zimmerman Nursing Home Inc, Carlisle, AR
Zion Grove Nursing Center, Shelby, MS
Zion Nursing Home Inc, Cincinnati, OH
Zion's Care Center, Salt Lake City, UT
Zions Health Care Complex, Hurricane, UT
Zohlman Nursing Home, Richlandtown, PA
Zumbrota Nursing Home, Zumbrota, MN

CORPORATE NURSING HOME HEADQUARTERS

ABCM Corp
PO Box 436
Hampton, IA 50441
(515) 456-5636

Adventist Health System—USA
PO Box 200188, 2221 E Lomar Blvd
Arlington, TX 76006-0188
(817) 649-8700

Advocare Inc
4343 Langley Ave
Pensacola, FL 32504
(904) 478-2049

Alden Management Services
4200 W Peterson, Ste 140
Chicago, IL 60646
(312) 286-3883

Alexian Brothers Health Systems
600 Alexian Way
Elk Grove Village, IL 60007
(708) 640-7550

Altercare Inc
7222 Day Ave SW
Navarre, OH 44662
(216) 767-3458

American Baptist Homes of the Midwest
11985 Technology Dr
Eden Prairie, MN 55344
(612) 941-3175

American Baptist Homes of the West
PO Box 6669, 400 Roland Way
Oakland, CA 94621
(415) 635-7600

American Health Care Centers
200 Smokerise
Wadsworth, OH 44281
(216) 336-6684

American Health Centers Inc
PO Box 10
Parsons, TN 38363
(901) 847-6343

American Medical Services Inc
1051 E Ogden Ave
Milwaukee, WI 53202
(414) 271-1300

Americare Corp
500 W Wilson Bridge, Ste 245
Worthington, OH 43085
(614) 431-3315

Amerigard
6245 N Inkster
Garden City, MI 48135
(313) 421-3300

Amity Care
4415 Highline Blvd, Ste 100
Oklahoma City, OK 73108
(405) 943-1144

Angell Group
PO Box 1670
Clemons, NC 27012
(919) 998-8445

ARA Living Centers
15415 Katy Fwy, Ste 800
Houston, TX 77094
(713) 578-4600

Arbor Health Care
PO Box 840, 1100 Shawnee Rd
Lima, OH 45802
(419) 227-3000

Arbor Living Centers of Florida Inc
2750 N 29th Ave, Ste 200 N
Hollywood, FL 33020
(305) 925-3908

Arvada Management
1390 Stuart St
Denver, CO 80204
(303) 825-8846

Associated Health Care Management Co
Inc
3800 Park East
Beachwood, OH 44122
(216) 831-6600

Atrium Living Centers Inc
938 Lafayette St
New Orleans, LA 70113
(504) 561-0413

Autumn Corp
PO Box 7728
Rocky Mount, NC 27804
(919) 443-6265

Baptist Home Assn
4700 Tabor St, Bldg 12
Wheatridge, CO 80033
(303) 424-5589

Beth Sholom Homes of Virginia
PO Box 29331
Richmond, VA 23229
(804) 750-2183

Bethesda Care Centers
1465 Kelly Johnson Blvd, Ste 200
Colorado Springs, CO 80920
(719) 548-0500

Beverly Enterprises
155 Central Shopping Ctr, Ste 3324
Portsmouth, AR 72913

Board of School Ministry
3881 Highland Ave
Saint Paul, MN 55110
(612) 426-5013

Bon Secours Health Systems
1505 Marriottsville Rd
Marriottsville, MD 21104
(301) 442-5511

Brian Center Management Corp
1331 4th St Dr NW
Hickory, NC 28603
(704) 322-3362

Britthaven Inc
PO Box 190, 4th St
Hookerton, NC 28538
(919) 747-3314

Buckeye Family & Nursing Home
573 Superior Ave
Dayton, OH 45407
(513) 278-7849

Buckner Baptist Benevolences
PO Box 271189
Dallas, TX 75227
(214) 328-3141

Cardinal Medical
9300 Shelbyville Rd
Louisville, KY 40222
(502) 425-3620

Care Centers of Michigan
23900 Orchard Lake Rd
Farmington Hills, MI 48024
(313) 471-3297

Care Enterprises
2742 Dow Ave
Tustin, CA 92680
(714) 544-4443

Caremet Inc
1630 S Countyfarm Rd
Warsaw, IN 46580
(219) 267-7211

Catholic Charities
525 Washington St
Buffalo, NY 14203
(716) 856-4494

Catholic Charities-Archdiocese of NY
1011 1st Ave
New York, NY 10022
(212) 371-1000

Central Park Lodges
1970 Landings Blvd, Ste 200
Sarasoata, FL 34231
(813) 921-7220

Chartham Management
850 Promontory Pl SE
Salem, OR 97302
(503) 585-0200

Christian Church Campuses
920 S 4th St
Louisville, KY 40203
(502) 583-6533

Christian Homes
200 N Postville
Lincoln, IL 62656
(217) 732-9651

Christian Missionary Alliance Foundation
15000 Shell Point Blvd
Fort Myers, FL 33908
(813) 466-1111

Cloverleaf Enterprises
8355 Rockville Rd
Indianapolis, IN 46234
(317) 271-8888

Collingswood Nursing Center
299 Hurley Ave
Rockville, MD 20850
(301) 762-8900

Columbia Corp
214 Overlook Ct, Ste 175
Brentwood, TN 37027
(615) 370-0180

Community Care Centers
2101 Enterprise Ave
Muncie, IN 47304
(317) 286-6035

Community Lifecare Enterprises
828 S 2nd St
Springfield, IL 62074
(217) 523-9368

Complete Care Inc
7025 W Hwy 22
Crestwood, KY 40014
(502) 241-4466

Comprehensive Health Care Associates Inc
1266 1st St, Ste 8
Sarasota, FL 34236
(813) 365-6194

Convalescent Services
200 Galleria Pkwy, Ste 1800
Atlanta, GA 30339
(404) 956-8999

Country Villa Service Corp
11266 Washington Pl
Culver City, CA 90230
(213) 390-8049

Courville Management
49 Derry Rd
Hudson, NH 03051
(603) 883-4422

Covenant Benevolent Inst
2725 W Foster
Chicago, IL 60625
(312) 878-8200

Crestwood Hospitals
4635 Georgetown Pl
Stockton, CA 95207
(209) 478-5291

Crown Investments Inc
710 Whetstone St
Monroeville, AL 36460
(205) 743-3609

CSJ Health Systems
3720 E Bayley
Wichita, KS 67218
(316) 689-4000

Diversicare Corp
105 Reynolds
Franklin, TN 37065
(615) 794-3313

Diversified Health Services
Plymouthwoods, 527 Plymouth Rd, Ste 415
Plymouth Meeting, PA 19462
(215) 825-5311

Ebenezer Society
2722 Park Ave
Minneapolis, MN 55407
(612) 879-2200

Eden Park Management
22 Holland Ave
Albany, NY 12209
(518) 436-4731

Eks Management
3322 W Peterson
Chicago, IL 60659
(312) 463-8672

Elder Care Services Inc
57 Summer St
Rowley, MA 01969
(508) 948-7383

EPI Corp
9707 Shelbyville Rd
Louisville, KY 40223
(502) 426-2242

Episcopal Homes Foundation
PO Box 1027
Lafayette, CA 94549
(415) 283-0680

EV Lutheran/Good Samaritan Society
PO Box 5038, 1000 West Ave N
Sioux Falls, SD 57117-5038
(605) 336-2998

Everhealth Foundation
8000 S Painter
Whittier, CA 90602
(213) 945-2861

First American Care Facility
5100 Eden Ave S, Ste 305
Edina, MN 55436
(612) 929-2122

First Atlantic Corp
222 Auburn St
Portland, ME 44103
(207) 797-0088

First Humanics Corp
12755 S Mur-Len, Ste B6
Olathe, KS 66062
(913) 782-4300

Forum Group Inc
8900 Keystone Crossing
Indianapolis, IN 46240
(317) 846-0700

Franciscan Sisters
1220 Main St
Lemont, IL 60439
(708) 257-7776

General Health Management, Inc
333 E River Dr
East Hartford, CT 06108
(203) 289-9300

Genesis Health Ventures
148 W State St, Ste 100
Kennett Square, PA 19348
(215) 444-6350

Georgia Baptist Medical Center
300 Parkway Blvd NE
Atlanta, GA 30312
(404) 653-4000

Geriatric and Medical Centers
5601 Chestnut
Philadelphia, PA 19139
(215) 476-2250

Golden State Health Centers Inc
13347 Ventura Blvd
Sherman Oaks, CA 91423
(818) 986-1550

Good Neighbor Services
2177 Youngman Ave, Ste 200
Saint Paul, MN 55116
(612) 698-6544

GraceCare Inc
140 W Germantown Pike, Ste 100
Plymouth Meeting, PA 19462
(215) 834-8006

Greenery Rehabilitation Group
400 Center St
Newton, MA 02158
(617) 244-4744

Guardian Foundation Inc
1900 Powell St, Ste 1000
Emeryville, CA 94608
(415) 596-4800

Hanover Healthcare
20251 Century Blvd
Germantown, MD 20874
(301) 540-0440

HBA Management Inc
5310 NW 33rd, Ste 211
Fort Lauderdale, FL 33309
(305) 731-3350

HCF Inc
2615 Fort Amanda Rd
Lima, OH 45804
(419) 999-2010

Health & Home Management Inc
7370 N Cicero
Lincolnwood, IL 60646
(708) 674-7370

Health Care Associates
90 Avon Meadow Ln
Avon, CT 06001
(203) 678-9755

Health Care Group
1060 8th, Ste 405
San Diego, CA 92101
(619) 234-4327

Health Care Management
1010 S Main St
Dayton, OH 45409
(513) 461-2707

Health Concepts Corp
303 Hurstbourne Ln
Louisville, KY 40222
(502) 425-0366

Health East
559 Capitol Blvd
Saint Paul, MN 55103
(612) 221-2520

Health Enterprises of America
1268 N River Rd
Warren, OH 44483

Health Systems
PO Box 1450
Corbin, KY 40701
(606) 528-9600

Heritage Enterprises
115 W Jefferson, Ste 401
Bloomington, IL 61702-3188
(309) 828-4361

Hillhaven Corp
1148 Broadway Plaza
Tacoma, WA 98401
(206) 575-4901

Holy Cross Health Systems
3606 E Jefferson Blvd
South Bend, IN 46615
(219) 233-8558

Homewood Retirement Centers/UCC
2750 Virginia Ave
Williamsport, MD 21795
(301) 582-1628

Horizon Healthcare Corp
6001 Indian School Rd NE, Ste 530
Albuquerque, NM 87110
(505) 881-4961

Houston Companies
PO Box 661
Crawfordsville, IN 47933
(317) 362-0905

HS Healthcare
1111 S Dunlap Rd
Savoy, IL 61874
(217) 398-5966

Integrated Health Services Inc
11019 McCormick Rd, Ste 400
Hunt Valley, MD 21031
(301) 584-7050

International Health Care Management
130 S 1st St
Ann Arbor, MI 48104
(313) 663-3130

JE Holland Associates
846 N Cleveland-Masillon Rd
Akron, OH 44313
(216) 666-4161

Lemire Enterprises
130 Silver St
Manchester, NH 03103
(603) 669-1810

Life Care Centers of Cleveland
PO Box 3480
Cleveland, TN 37311
(615) 476-3254

Life Care Centers of Kansas
Box 428
Medicine Lodge, KS 67104
(316) 886-3469

Life Care Services Corp
800 2nd Ave
Des Moines, IA 50309
(515) 245-7650

Lifelink Corporation
331 S York Rd
Bensenville, IL 60106
(708) 766-3570

LifeQuest
10th & Juniper Sts
Quakertown, PA 18951
(215) 536-1842

Lincoln Lutheran of Racine
3716 Douglas Ave
Racine, WI 53402
(414) 639-3174

Linden Grove Inc
13700 W National Ave
New Berlin, WI 53151
(414) 797-4600

Little Sisters of the Poor
110-39 Springfield Blvd
Queens Village, NY 11429
(718) 464-4920

LTC
1430 Larimer St, Ste 300
Denver, CO 80202
(303) 592-1227

Lucas Corp
126 Franklin Pl
South Bend, IN 46601
(219) 233-3400

Lutheran Health Systems
PO Box 6200, 1202 Westrac Dr
Fargo, ND 58106
(701) 293-9053

Lutheran Services for the Aging Inc
2304 S Main St
Salisbury, NC 28144
(704) 637-2870

Lutheran Social Ministries
189 S Broad St
Trenton, NJ 08601
(609) 393-3440

Manor Care Inc
10720 Columbia Pike
Silver Spring, MD 20901
(301) 593-9600

Martin Luther Homes Inc
PO Box 607, 804 S 12th
Beatrice, NE 68310
(402) 223-4066

Medical Facilities of America
2917 Penn Forest Blvd, Ste 300
Roanoke, VA 24018
(703) 989-3618

Medicalodges Inc
PO Box 509
Coffeyville, KS 67337
(316) 251-6700

Medicrest of California
4020 Sierra College Blvd, Ste 100
Rocklin, CA 95677
(916) 624-6238

Medilodge of Romeo
309 S Bailey
Romeo, MI 48065
(313) 752-2581

Mediplex Inc
2101 Washington St
Newton, MA 02162
(617) 969-6480

Mennonite Brethren Homes
856 S Reed Ave
Reedley, CA 93654
(209) 638-3615

Meridan Healthcare
515 Fairmont Ave
Towson, MD 21204
(301) 296-1000

Meritcare
1 PPG Pl, Ste 2260
Pittsburgh, PA 15222
(412) 391-4469

Methodist Homes for the Aging
1424 Montclair Rd
Birmingham, AL 35210
(205) 956-4150

Missionary Oblates of Mary Imm
267 E 8th St
Saint Paul, MN 55101
(612) 292-8622

Morning View Care Center
134 N Woods Blvd
Columbus, OH 43235
(614) 847-1070

Multicare Management
401 Hackensack Ave
Hackensack, NJ 07601
(201) 488-8818

National Benevolent Assn of the Christian
   Church (Disciples of Christ)
11780 Borman Dr, Ste 200
Saint Louis, MO 63146
(314) 993-9000

National Health Corp
PO Box 1398
Murfresboro, TN 37133
(615) 890-2020

National Healthcare Affiliates Inc
651 Delaware Ave
Buffalo, NY 14202
(716) 881-4425

National Healthcare Inc
1 Paces West, Ste 1500, 2727 Paces Ferry
   Rd NW
Atlanta, GA 30339
(404) 431-1500

National Heritage Corp
15770 N Dallas Pkwy, 5th Fl
Dallas, TX 75248
(214) 233-3900

New MediCo Associates
100 Federal St
Boston, MA 02110
(617) 426-4100

North Central Health Services Inc
930 10th St
Spearfish, SD 57783
(605) 642-4641

Northport Health Services
2707 Hwy 82 Bypass
Northport, AL 35476
(205) 333-0600

Northwestern Service Corp
181 Front St
Berea, OH 44017
(216) 243-4732

Oakwood Living Centers Inc
7297 Lee Hwy, Ste K
Falls Church, VA 22042
(703) 536-1900

Ohio Presbyterian Retirement Services
1001 Kingsmill Pkwy
Columbia, OH 43085
(614) 888-7800

OMG Corp
PO Box 460
Hookerton, NC 28538
(919) 749-5983

Omnilife Systems Inc
1207 N High St
Columbus, OH 43201
(614) 299-3100

Pacific Homes
21021 Ventura Blvd, Ste 400
Woodland Hills, CA 91364
(818) 594-0200

Parke Care Inc
11223 Cornell Park Dr, Ste 201
Cincinnati, OH 45242
(513) 489-4788

Pavilion Health Care Centers
432 E Jefferson
Louisville, KY 40202
(502) 583-2851

Peninsula United Methodist Homes
1013 Centre Rd, Ste 101
Wilmington, DE 19805
(302) 633-7864

Philadelphia Presbyterian Homes
PO Box 607
Villanova, PA 19085
(215) 527-6370

Pinnacle Care Corp
1919 Charlotte Ave, Ste 300
Nashville, TN 37203
(615) 327-0500

Pleasant Valley Health Services
3801 Las Pasas Rd, Ste 106
Camarillo, CA 93010
(805) 388-2705

Presbyterian Homes Inc
1217 Slate Hill Rd
Camp Hill, PA 17011-8012
(717) 737-9700

Presbyterian Homes of New Jersey
103 Carnegie Ctr, Ste 102
Princeton, NJ 08453
(609) 987-8900

Presbyterian Homes of Western New York
4455 Transit Rd
Williamsville, NY 14221
(716) 631-0120

Presbyterian Ministries
720 Seneca
Seattle, WA 98101
(206) 622-1300

Prestige Care Inc
6623 NE 82nd Ave
Portland, OR 97220
(503) 253-9650

Proviso Assn for Retarded Citizens
4100 Litt Dr
Hillside, IL 60162
(708) 547-3550

Quality Care Management
932 Baddour Pkwy
Lebanon, TN 37087
(615) 444-1836

Ray Graham Assn for the Handicapped
420 W Madison
Elmhurst, IL 60126
(708) 530-4554

Redwood Care Centers Inc
2885 Harris St
Eureka, CA 95501
(707) 443-1627

Renaissance Health Care
4718 Old Gettysburg Rd, Ste 111
Mechanicsburg, PA 17055
(717) 731-0300

Res-Care Health Services
100 Embassy Square Office Park, Ste 105
Louisville, KY 40299
(502) 491-3464

Retirement Housing Foundation Inc
401 E Ocean Blvd, Ste 300
Long Beach, CA 90802
(213) 437-4330

Rose Care Inc
7 Halstead Circle
Rogers, AR 72756
(501) 636-5716

Rotsell Baldwin and Associates Inc
2151 NE Coachman Rd
Clearwater, FL 34625
(815) 443-0443

Saint Francis Health Care Services
PO Box 1270, 1515 Dragoon Trail
Mishawaka, IN 46544-9270
(219) 256-3940

Samaritan Senior Services
1118 E Missouri, Ste B
Phoenix, AZ 85014
(602) 277-1992

School Sisters of St Francis
1501 S Layton Blvd
Milwaukee, WI 53215
(414) 384-4105

Senior Care Inc
2950 Breckenridge Ln, Ste 8
Louisville, KY 40220
(502) 456-2172

Shive Nursing Centers
1330 Medical Park Dr
Fort Wayne, IN 46825
(219) 482-3551

Signature Corp
2501 W Peterson
Chicago, IL 60659
(312) 784-0800

Soundcare Inc
1748 Jefferson Ave
Tacoma, WA 98402
(206) 383-5495

Southern California Presbyterian Homes
1111 N Brand Blvd, Ste 300
Glendale, CA 91202
(818) 247-0420

Southern Management Services
455 N Indian Rock Rd
Belleair Bluffs, FL 34640
(813) 585-6333

Springwood Associates
500 Iles Park Pl, Ste 104
Springfield, IL 62718
(217) 522-2001

Summit Health Ltd
2600 W Magnolia Blvd
Burbank, CA 91505
(213) 201-4000

Sunbelt Healthcare Centers Inc
500 Winderley Pl, Ste 115
Maitland, FL 32751-7206
(407) 660-2440

Sycamore Enterprises
9245 N Meridian St, Ste 224
Indianapolis, IN 46260
(317) 848-0977

Thro Company
PO Box 1236
Mankato, MN 56001
(507) 625-8741

Tiffany Care Centers
Box 208, 507 State St
Mound City, MO 64470
(816) 442-3128

Tressler-Lutheran Services Assn
2331 Market St
Camp Hill, PA 17011
(717) 692-4340

Trinity Living Centers
420 NW 5th St, Ste 4B
Evansville, IN 47708
(812) 421-8466

Truco Inc
4723 Taft St
Wichita Falls, TX 76308
(817) 692-8977

Tullock Management
PO Box 70
Advance, NC 27006
(919) 998-5001

Unicare
105 W Michigan
Milwaukee, WI 53203
(414) 271-9696

United Church Homes
320 W Maple St
Upper Sandusky, OH 43351
(419) 294-4941

Vantage Healthcare
PO Box 16
Evansville, IN 47701
(812) 425-8716

Vari-Care Inc
800 Medical Arts Bldg, 277 Alexander St
Rochester, NY 14607
(716) 325-6940

Vincentian Sisters of Charity
8200 McKnight Rd
Pittsburgh, PA 15237
(412) 364-3000

Volunteers of America Care Facilities
7530 Market Place Dr
Eden Prairie, MN 55344
(612) 941-0305

Waverly Group
PO Box 12000
Jackson, MS 39236
(601) 932-2984

Wesley Homes
1817 Clifton Rd NE
Atlanta, GA 30329
(404) 325-2988

Wesley Retirement Services Inc
3520 Grand Ave
Des Moines, IA 50309
(515) 271-6789

Western Health Care Corp
2465 Overland Rd, Ste 202
Boise, ID 83705
(208) 343-7013

White Oak Manor Inc
PO Box 3347
Spartanburg, SC 29304
(803) 582-7503

Wilshire Foundation Inc
9100 Wilshire Blvd, Ste 340
Beverly Hills, CA 90212
(213) 278-5240

Wis-Care Inc
PO Box 67
Walworth, WI 53184
(414) 275-9331